8/04

D0821075

Who's Who of American Women®

Who's Who of American Women®

2004~2005

121 Chanlon Road
New Providence, NJ 07974 U.S.A.
www.marquiswhoswho.com

Who'sWho of American Women®

Marquis Who's Who®

Chief Executive Officer	Gene M. McGovern	**Chairman**	Wilbur L. Ross, Jr.
Senior Managing Director	Fred Marks	**President**	James A. Finkelstein
Managing Director, Special Projects	Jon Gelberg		
Director, Editorial & Product Development	Robert Docherty		

Editorial

Managing Editors	Karen Chassie	
	Eileen Fanning	
Senior Editors	Alison McGowan	
	Danielle Netta	
	Francine Richardson	
Editors	Patricia Delli Santi	
	Laura Koserowski	
	Deanna Richmond	
	Sandy Sauchelli	
	Kate Spirito	

Editorial Services

Director	Debby Nowicki
Production Manager	Paul Zema
Production Editor	Daniel D. Crawford
Freelance Manager	Mary SanGiovanni
Editorial Services Assistant	Ann Chavis
Special Projects Supervisor	Sola Osofisan
Mail Processing Manager	Kara A. Seitz

Mail Processing Staff	Betty Gray
	Hattie Walker

Marketing

Director, Marketing & Creative Services	Michael Noerr
Creative Services Manager	Rose Butkiewicz
Production Manager	Jeanne Danzig
Marketing Specialist	Jill Tarbell

Research

Managing Editor	Kerry Nugent Morrison
Senior Research Editors	Maria L. Myers
	Jennifer Podolsky
Research Editors	Eric Amato
	Todd Kineavy
	Megan Ritson

Editorial Systems

Director	Jack Zimmerman
Technical Project Leader	Ben Loh
Composition Programmer	Tom Haggerty
Database Programmer	Latha Shankar

Published by Marquis Who's Who® LLC.

Copyright ©2004 by Marquis Who's Who® LLC. All rights reserved.

No part of this publication may be reproduced, stored in a retrieval system, or transmitted, in any form or by any means—including, but not limited to, electronic, mechanical, photocopying, recording, or otherwise—or used for any commercial purpose whatsoever without the prior written permission of the publisher and, if publisher deems necessary, execution of a formal license agreement with publisher.

For information, contact:
Marquis Who's Who®
121 Chanlon Road
New Providence, New Jersey 07974
1-908-673-1001
www.marquiswhoswho.com

WHO'S WHO OF AMERICAN WOMEN® is a registered trademark of Marquis Who's Who® LLC.

Library of Congress Catalog Card Number   50-58231
International Standard Book Number   0-8379-0430-7 (Classic Edition)
International Standard Serial Number   0083-9841

No payment is either solicited or accepted for the inclusion of entries in this publication. Marquis Who's Who has used its best efforts in collecting and preparing material for inclusion in this publication, but does not warrant that the information herein is complete or accurate, and does not assume, and hereby disclaims, any liability to any person for any loss or damage caused by errors or omissions in this publication, whether such errors or omissions result from negligence, accident, or any other cause.

Manufactured in the United States of America.

920.72
WHO
2004-05

Table of Contents

Preface

Marquis Who's Who is proud to present the 2004-2005 Edition of *Who's Who of American Women.* The 24th edition is the most comprehensive ever—with biographical profiles as diverse as Sandra Day O'Connor, the first woman Supreme Court justice, and 14-year-old golf phenomenon, Michelle Wie.

This edition presents a fascinating picture of the status of today's American women. In 1958, when Marquis Who's Who published the first edition of *Who's Who of American Women,* the vast majority of those who were included were volunteer workers involved in civic, religious, and club activities.

As you will see in the pages that follow, today's American women are involved in all areas of enterprise and endeavor. This 24th Edition of *Who's Who of American Women* features a host of CEOs, college presidents, entrepreneurs, technologists, government officials, doctors, lawyers, and key figures from practically every field. You will find over 32,000 listings in this edition. Each listing provides you with critical biographical information, including educational background, family history, work history, civic activity, memberships, honors and awards. In many cases hobbies and special interests are also listed.

Factors such as position, noteworthy accomplishments, visibility, and prominence in a field are all taken into account in making selections for the book. Final decisions concerning inclusion or exclusion are made following extensive discussion, evaluation, and deliberation.

Biographical information is gathered in a variety of manners. In most cases, we invite our biographees to submit their biographical details.

In many cases, though, the information is collected independently by our research and editorial staffs, which use a wide assortment of tools to gather complete, accurate, and up-to-date information.

To help you more effectively use this volume, we have provided several indexes, which give you the opportunity to reference our biographees by geographic location (state and city) and by professional title.

While the Marquis Who's Who editors exercise the utmost care in preparing each biographical sketch for publication, in a publication involving so many profiles, occasional errors may appear. Users of this publication are urged to notify the publisher of any issues so that adjustments can be made.

All of the profiles featured in *Who's Who of American Women* are available on *Who's Who on the Web* (www.marquiswhoswho.com) through a subscription. At the present time, subscribers to *Who's Who on the Web* have access to all of the names included in all of the Marquis Who's Who publications as well as many new biographies that will appear in upcoming publications.

We sincerely hope that this volume will be an indispensable reference tool for you. We are always looking for ways to better serve you and welcome your ideas for improvements. In addition, we continue to welcome your Marquis Who's Who nominations. *Who's Who of American Women* and all Marquis Who's Who publications pay tribute to those individuals who make significant contributions to our society. It is our honor and privilege to present their profiles to you.

Standards of Admission

The foremost consideration in selecting Biographees for *Who's Who of American Women* is the extent of an individual's reference interest. Such reference interest is judged on either of two factors: (1) the position of responsibility held, or (2) the level of achievement attained by the individual.

Admissions based on the factor of position include:

Members of the U.S. Congress

Federal judges

Governors of states covered by this volume

Premiers of Canadian provinces covered by this volume

State attorneys general

Judges of state and territorial courts of highest appellate jurisdiction

Mayors of major cities

Heads of major universities and colleges

Heads of leading philanthropic, educational, cultural, and scientific institutions and associations

Chief ecclesiastics of the principal religious denominations

Principal officers of national and international business

Admission for individual achievement is based on objective qualitative criteria. To be selected, a person must have attained conspicuous achievement.

Key Information

[1] **SCHAFFER, STACY LYNN,** [2] elementary school educator; [3] b. Skokie, Ill., Feb. 16, 1958; [4] d. Barry and Lorraine (Lebovitz) Lutz; [5] m. Bennett Shaffer, June 12, 1985; [6] children: Brandon, Bret, Alison. [7] Student U. Ill. Chgo, 1976-78; BE Nat. Louis U., 1980, MEd, 1984. [8] Cert. elem. tchr., Ill., learning disabilities. [9] Tchr. Edison Elem Sch., Skokie, 1980-81, primary tchr. learning disabilities, 1982—1987; ass't. supt. Learning Disabilities curriculum Skokie elementary schs., 1987—1998; supt., 1998—[10] tchr. remedial reading Madison Elem. Sch., Skokie, summers, 1980, 81, cons., lectr. in field. [11] Author: Beginning Reading Series for grades K-2, 1994; contbr. articles to profl. jours., mags., 2nd edit., 2001 [12] Vol. MADD, Am. Cancer Soc. [13] Capt. USAFR, 1985—2001; [14] Recipient Good Apple award. 1992. [15] Mem. NEA, Ill. Tchrs. Assn., Ill. Coun. Learning Disabilites (bd. dirs. 1989—), Internat. Reading Assn., Phi Beta Kappa. [16] Democrat. [17] Jewish. [18] Running, pottery. [19] Home: 1842 Willow Ln [20] Office: 22 Alexander Ave *

KEY

[1]	Name
[2]	Occupation
[3]	Vital statistics
[4]	Parents
[5]	Marriage
[6]	Children
[7]	Education
[8]	Professional certifications
[9]	Career
[10]	Career-related
[11]	Writings and creative works
[12]	Civic and political activities
[13]	Military
[14]	Awards and fellowships
[15]	Professional and association memberships, clubs and lodges
[16]	Political affiliation
[17]	Religion
[18]	Achievements information
[19]	Home address
[20]	Office address
[*]	Researched by Marquis Who's Who

Table of Abbreviations

The following abbreviations and symbols are frequently used in this book.

*An asterisk following a sketch indicates that it was researched by the Marquis Who's Who editorial staff and has not been verified by the Biographee.

A

A Associate (used with academic degrees only)

AA, A.A. Associate in Arts, Associate of Arts

AAAL American Academy of Arts and Letters

AAAS American Association for the Advancement of Science

AACD American Association for Counseling and Development

AACN American Association of Critical Care Nurses

AAHA American Academy of Health Administrators

AAHP American Association of Hospital Planners

AAHPERD American Alliance for Health, Physical Education, Recreation, and Dance

AAS Associate of Applied Science

AASL American Association of School Librarians

AASPA American Association of School Personnel Administrators

AAU Amateur Athletic Union

AAUP American Association of University Professors

AAUW American Association of University Women

AB, A.B. Arts, Bachelor of

AB Alberta

ABA American Bar Association

ABC American Broadcasting Company

AC Air Corps

acad. academy, academic

acct. accountant

acctg. accounting

ACDA Arms Control and Disarmament Agency

ACHA American College of Hospital Administrators

ACLS Advanced Cardiac Life Support

ACLU American Civil Liberties Union

ACOG American College of Ob-Gyn

ACP American College of Physicians

ACS American College of Surgeons

ADA American Dental Association

a.d.c. aide-de-camp

adj. adjunct, adjutant

adj. gen. adjutant general

adm. admiral

adminstr. administrator

adminstrn. administration

adminstrv. administrative

ADN Associate's Degree in Nursing

ADP Automatic Data Processing

adv. advocate, advisory

advt. advertising

AE, A.E. Agricultural Engineer

A.E. and P. Ambassador Extraordinary and Plenipotentiary

AEC Atomic Energy Commission

aero. aeronautical, aeronautic

aerodyn. aerodynamic

AFB Air Force Base

AFL-CIO American Federation of Labor and Congress of Industrial Organizations

AFTRA American Federation of TV and Radio Artists

AFSCME American Federation of State, County and Municipal Employees

agr. agriculture

agrl. agricultural

agt. agent

AGVA American Guild of Variety Artists

agy. agency

A&I Agricultural and Industrial

AIA American Institute of Architects

AIAA American Institute of Aeronautics and Astronautics

AIChE American Institute of Chemical Engineers

AICPA American Institute of Certified Public Accountants

AID Agency for International Development

AIDS Acquired Immune Deficiency Syndrome

AIEE American Institute of Electrical Engineers

AIM American Institute of Management

AIME American Institute of Mining, Metallurgy, and Petroleum Engineers

AK Alaska

AL Alabama

ALA American Library Association

Ala. Alabama

alt. alternate

Alta. Alberta

A&M Agricultural and Mechanical

AM, A.M. Arts, Master of

Am. American, America

AMA American Medical Association

amb. ambassador

A.M.E. African Methodist Episcopal

Amtrak National Railroad Passenger Corporation

AMVETS American Veterans of World War II, Korea, Vietnam

ANA American Nurses Association

anat. anatomical

ANCC American Nurses Credentialing Center

ann. annual

ANTA American National Theatre and Academy

anthrop. anthropological

AP Associated Press

APA American Psychological Association

APGA American Personnel Guidance Association

APHA American Public Health Association

APO Army Post Office

apptd. appointed

Apr. April

apt. apartment

AR Arkansas

ARC American Red Cross

arch. architect

archeol. archeological

archtl. architectural

Ariz. Arizona

Ark. Arkansas

ArtsD, ArtsD. Arts, Doctor of

arty. artillery

AS American Samoa

AS Associate in Science

ASCAP American Society of Composers, Authors and Publishers

ASCD Association for Supervision and Curriculum Development

ASCE American Society of Civil Engineers

ASHRAE American Society of Heating, Refrigeration, and Air Conditioning Engineers

ASME American Society of Mechanical Engineers

ASNSA American Society for Nursing Service Administrators

ASPA American Society for Public Administration

ASPCA American Society for the Prevention of Cruelty to Animals

assn. association

assoc. associate

asst. assistant

ASTD American Society for Training and Development

ASTM American Society for Testing and Materials

astron. astronomical

astrophys. astrophysical

ATLA Association of Trial Lawyers of America

ATSC Air Technical Service Command

AT&T American Telephone & Telegraph Company

atty. attorney

Aug. August

AUS Army of the United States

aux. auxiliary

Ave. Avenue

AVMA American Veterinary Medical Association

AZ Arizona

AWHONN Association of Women's Health Obstetric and Neonatal Nurses

B

B. Bachelor

b. born

BA, B.A. Bachelor of Arts

BAgr, B.Agr. Bachelor of Agriculture

Balt. Baltimore

Bapt. Baptist

BArch, B.Arch. Bachelor of Architecture

BAS, B.A.S. Bachelor of Agricultural Science

BBA, B.B.A. Bachelor of Business Administration

BBB Better Business Bureau

BBC British Broadcasting Corporation

BC, B.C. British Columbia

BCE, B.C.E. Bachelor of Civil Engineering

BChir, B.Chir. Bachelor of Surgery

BCL, B.C.L. Bachelor of Civil Law

BCLS Basic Cardiac Life Support

BCS, B.C.S. Bachelor of Commercial Science

BD, B.D. Bachelor of Divinity

bd. board

BE, B.E. Bachelor of Education

BEE, B.E.E. Bachelor of Electrical Engineering

BFA, B.F.A. Bachelor of Fine Arts

bibl. biblical

bibliog. bibliographical

biog. biographical

biol. biological

BJ, B.J. Bachelor of Journalism

Bklyn. Brooklyn

BL, B.L. Bachelor of Letters

bldg. building

BLS, B.L.S. Bachelor of Library Science

BLS Basic Life Support

Blvd. Boulevard

BMI Broadcast Music, Inc.

BMW Bavarian Motor Works (Bayerische Motoren Werke)

bn. battalion

B.&O.R.R. Baltimore & Ohio Railroad

bot. botanical

BPE, B.P.E. Bachelor of Physical Education

BPhil, B.Phil. Bachelor of Philosophy

br. branch

BRE, B.R.E. Bachelor of Religious Education

brig. gen. brigadier general

Brit. British, Brittanica

Bros. Brothers

BS, B.S. Bachelor of Science

BSA, B.S.A. Bachelor of Agricultural Science

BSBA Bachelor of Science in Business Administration

BSChemE Bachelor of Science in Chemical Engineering

BSD, B.S.D. Bachelor of Didactic Science

BSEE Bachelor of Science in Electrical Engineering

BSN Bachelor of Science in Nursing

BST, B.S.T. Bachelor of Sacred Theology

BTh, B.Th. Bachelor of Theology

bull. bulletin

bur. bureau

bus. business

B.W.I. British West Indies

C

CA California

CAA Civil Aeronautics Administration

CAB Civil Aeronautics Board

CAD-CAM Computer Aided Design–Computer Aided Model

Calif. California

C.Am. Central America

Can Canada, Canadian

CAP Civil Air Patrol

capt. captain

cardiol. cardiological

cardiovasc. cardiovascular

CARE Cooperative American Relief Everywhere

Cath. Catholic

cav. cavalry

CBC Canadian Broadcasting Company

CBI China, Burma, India Theatre of Operations

CBS Columbia Broadcasting Company

C.C. Community College

CCC Commodity Credit Corporation

CCNY City College of New York

CCRN Critical Care Registered Nurse

CCU Cardiac Care Unit

CD Civil Defense

CE, C.E. Corps of Engineers, Civil Engineer

CEN Certified Emergency Nurse

CENTO Central Treaty Organization

CEO chief executive officer

CERN European Organization of Nuclear Research

cert. certificate, certification, certified

CETA Comprehensive Employment Training Act

CFA Chartered Financial Analyst

CFL Canadian Football League

CFO chief financial officer

CFP Certified Financial Planner

ch. church

ChD, Ch.D. Doctor of Chemistry

chem. chemical

ChemE, Chem.E. Chemical Engineer

ChFC Chartered Financial Consultant

Chgo. Chicago

chirurg. chirurgical

chmn. chairman

chpt. chapter

CIA Central Intelligence Agency

Cin. Cincinnati

cir. circle, circuit

CLE Continuing Legal Education

Cleve. Cleveland

climatol. climatological

clin. clinical

clk. clerk

C.L.U. Chartered Life Underwriter

CM, C.M. Master in Surgery

CM Northern Mariana Islands

CMA Certified Medical Assistant

cmty. community

CNA Certified Nurse's Aide

CNOR Certified Nurse (Operating Room)

C.&N.W.Ry. Chicago & North Western Railway

CO Colorado

Co. Company

COF Catholic Order of Foresters

C. of C. Chamber of Commerce

col. colonel

coll. college

Colo. Colorado

com. committee

comd. commanded

comdg. commanding

comdr. commander

comdt. commandant

comm. communications

commd. commissioned

comml. commercial

commn. commission

commr. commissioner

compt. comptroller

condr. conductor

Conf. Conference

Congl. Congregational, Congressional

Conglist. Congregationalist

Conn. Connecticut

cons. consultant, consulting

consol. consolidated

constl. constitutional

constn. constitution

constrn. construction

contbd. contributed

contbg. contributing

contbn. contribution

contbr. contributor

contr. controller

Conv. Convention

COO chief operating officer

coop. cooperative

coord. coordinator

CORDS Civil Operations and Revolutionary Development Support

CORE Congress of Racial Equality

corp. corporation, corporate

corr. correspondent, corresponding, correspondence

C.&O.Ry. Chesapeake & Ohio Railway

coun. council

CPA Certified Public Accountant

CPCU Chartered Property and Casualty Underwriter

CPH, C.P.H. Certificate of Public Health

cpl. corporal

CPR Cardio-Pulmonary Resuscitation

C.P.Ry. Canadian Pacific Railway

CRT Cathode Ray Terminal

C.S. Christian Science

CSB, C.S.B. Bachelor of Christian Science

C.S.C. Civil Service Commission

CT Connecticut

ct. court

ctr. center

ctrl. central

CWS Chemical Warfare Service

C.Z. Canal Zone

D

D. Doctor

d. daughter

DAgr, D.Agr. Doctor of Agriculture

DAR Daughters of the American Revolution

dau. daughter

DAV Disabled American Veterans

DC, D.C. District of Columbia

DCL, D.C.L. Doctor of Civil Law

DCS, D.C.S. Doctor of Commercial Science

DD, D.D. Doctor of Divinity

DDS, D.D.S. Doctor of Dental Surgery

DE Delaware

Dec. December
dec. deceased
def. defense
Del. Delaware
del. delegate, delegation
Dem. Democrat, Democratic
DEng, D.Eng. Doctor of Engineering
denom. denomination, denominational
dep. deputy
dept. department
dermatol. dermatological
desc. descendant
devel. development, developmental
DFA, D.F.A. Doctor of Fine Arts
D.F.C. Distinguished Flying Cross
DHL, D.H.L. Doctor of Hebrew Literature
dir. director
dist. district
distbg. distributing
distbn. distribution
distbr. distributor
disting. distinguished
div. division, divinity, divorce
divsn. division
DLitt, D.Litt. Doctor of Literature
DMD, D.M.D. Doctor of Dental Medicine
DMS, D.M.S. Doctor of Medical Science
DO, D.O. Doctor of Osteopathy
docs. documents
DON Director of Nursing
DPH, D.P.H. Diploma in Public Health
DPhil, D.Phil. Doctor of Philosophy
D.R. Daughters of the Revolution
Dr. Drive, Doctor
DRE, D.R.E. Doctor of Religious Education
DrPH, Dr.P.H. Doctor of Public Health,
  Doctor of Public Hygiene
D.S.C. Distinguished Service Cross
DSc, D.Sc. Doctor of Science
DSChemE Doctor of Science in Chemical
  Engineering
D.S.M. Distinguished Service Medal
DST, D.S.T. Doctor of Sacred Theology
DTM, D.T.M. Doctor of Tropical Medicine
DVM, D.V.M. Doctor of Veterinary
  Medicine
DVS, D.V.S. Doctor of Veterinary Surgery

E

E, E. East
ea. eastern
E. and P. Extraordinary and Plenipotentiary
Eccles. Ecclesiastical
ecol. ecological
econ. economic
ECOSOC Economic and Social Council (of
  the UN)
ED, E.D. Doctor of Engineering
ed. educated
EdB, Ed.B. Bachelor of Education
EdD, Ed.D. Doctor of Education
edit. edition
editl. editorial
EdM, Ed.M. Master of Education
edn. education
ednl. educational
EDP Electronic Data Processing
EdS, Ed.S. Specialist in Education

EE, E.E. Electrical Engineer
E.E. and M.P. Envoy Extraordinary and
  Minister Plenipotentiary
EEC European Economic Community
EEG Electroencephalogram
EEO Equal Employment Opportunity
EEOC Equal Employment Opportunity
  Commission
E.Ger. German Democratic Republic
EKG Electrocardiogram
elec. electrical
electrochem. electrochemical
electrophys. electrophysical
elem. elementary
EM, E.M. Engineer of Mines
EMT Emergency Medical Technician
ency. encyclopedia
Eng. England
engr. engineer
engring. engineering
entomol. entomological
environ. environmental
EPA Environmental Protection Agency
epidemiol. epidemiological
Episc. Episcopalian
ERA Equal Rights Amendment
ERDA Energy Research and Development
  Administration
ESEA Elementary and Secondary Education
  Act
ESL English as Second Language
ESPN Entertainment and Sports
  Programming Network
ESSA Environmental Science Services
  Administration
ethnol. ethnological
ETO European Theatre of Operations
Evang. Evangelical
exam. examination, examining
Exch. Exchange
exec. executive
exhbn. exhibition
expdn. expedition
expn. exposition
expt. experiment
exptl. experimental
Expy. Expressway
Ext. Extension

F

F.A. Field Artillery
FAA Federal Aviation Administration
FAO Food and Agriculture Organization (of
  the UN)
FBA Federal Bar Association
FBI Federal Bureau of Investigation
FCA Farm Credit Administration
FCC Federal Communications Commission
FCDA Federal Civil Defense Administration
FDA Food and Drug Administration
FDIA Federal Deposit Insurance
  Administration
FDIC Federal Deposit Insurance Corporation
FE, F.E. Forest Engineer
FEA Federal Energy Administration
Feb. February
fed. federal
fedn. federation

FERC Federal Energy Regulatory
  Commission
fgn. foreign
FHA Federal Housing Administration
fin. financial, finance
FL Florida
Fl. Floor
Fla. Florida
FMC Federal Maritime Commission
FNP Family Nurse Practitioner
FOA Foreign Operations Administration
found. foundation
FPC Federal Power Commission
FPO Fleet Post Office
frat. fraternity
FRS Federal Reserve System
FSA Federal Security Agency
Ft. Fort
FTC Federal Trade Commission
Fwy. Freeway

G

G-1 (or other number) Division of General
  Staff
GA, Ga. Georgia
GAO General Accounting Office
gastroent. gastroenterological
GATE Gifted and Talented Educators
GATT General Agreement on Tariffs and
  Trade
GE General Electric Company
gen. general
geneal. genealogical
geod. geodetic
geog. geographic, geographical
geol. geological
geophys. geophysical
geriat. geriatrics
gerontol. gerontological
G.H.Q. General Headquarters
GM General Motors Corporation
GMAC General Motors Acceptance
  Corporation
G.N.Ry. Great Northern Railway
gov. governor
govt. government
govtl. governmental
GPO Government Printing Office
grad. graduate, graduated
GSA General Services Administration
Gt. Great
GTE General Telephone and
  Electric Company
GU Guam
gynecol. gynecological

H

HBO Home Box Office
hdqs. headquarters
HEW Department of Health, Education and
  Welfare
HHD, H.H.D. Doctor of Humanities
HHFA Housing and Home Finance Agency
HHS Department of Health and Human
  Services
HI Hawaii
hist. historical, historic

HM, H.M. Master of Humanities
HMO Health Maintenance Organization
homco. homeopathic
hon. honorary, honorable
Ho. of Dels. House of Delegates
Ho. of Reps. House of Representatives
hort. horticultural
hosp. hospital
H.S. High School
HUD Department of Housing and Urban Development
Hwy. Highway
hydrog. hydrographic

I

IA Iowa
IAEA International Atomic Energy Agency
IATSE International Alliance of Theatrical and Stage Employees and Moving Picture Operators of the United States and Canada
IBM International Business Machines Corporation
IBRD International Bank for Reconstruction and Development
ICA International Cooperation Administration
ICC Interstate Commerce Commission
ICCE International Council for Computers in Education
ICU Intensive Care Unit
ID Idaho
IEEE Institute of Electrical and Electronics Engineers
IFC International Finance Corporation
IGY International Geophysical Year
IL Illinois
Ill. Illinois
illus. illustrated
ILO International Labor Organization
IMF International Monetary Fund
IN Indiana
Inc. Incorporated
Ind. Indiana
ind. independent
Indpls. Indianapolis
indsl. industrial
inf. infantry
info. information
ins. insurance
insp. inspector
insp. gen. inspector general
inst. institute
instl. institutional
instn. institution
instr. instructor
instrn. instruction
instrnl. instructional
internat. international
intro. introduction
IRE Institute of Radio Engineers
IRS Internal Revenue Service
ITT International Telephone & Telegraph Corporation

J

JAG Judge Advocate General
JAGC Judge Advocate General Corps
Jan. January

Jaycees Junior Chamber of Commerce
JB, J.B. Jurum Baccalaureus
JCD, J.C.B. Juris Canoni Baccalaureus
JCD, J.C.D. Juris Canonici Doctor, Juris Civilis Doctor
JCL, J.C.L. Juris Canonici Licentiatus
JD, J.D. Juris Doctor
jg. junior grade
jour. journal
jr. junior
JSD, J.S.D. Juris Scientiae Doctor
JUD, J.U.D. Juris Utriusque Doctor
jud. judicial

K

Kans. Kansas
K.C. Knights of Columbus
K.P. Knights of Pythias
KS Kansas
K.T. Knight Templar
KY, Ky. Kentucky

L

LA, La. Louisiana
L.A. Los Angeles
lab. laboratory
L.Am. Latin America
lang. language
laryngol. laryngological
LB Labrador
LDS Latter Day Saints
LDS Church Church of Jesus Christ of Latter Day Saints
lectr. lecturer
legis. legislation, legislative
LHD, L.H.D. Doctor of Humane Letters
L.I. Long Island
libr. librarian, library
lic. licensed, license
L.I.R.R. Long Island Railroad
lit. literature
litig. litigation
LittB, Litt.B. Bachelor of Letters
LittD, Litt.D. Doctor of Letters
LLB, LL.B. Bachelor of Laws
LLD, L.L.D. Doctor of Laws
LLM, L.L.M. Master of Laws
Ln. Lane
L.&N.R.R. Louisville & Nashville Railroad
LPGA Ladies Professional Golf Association
LPN Licensed Practical Nurse
LS, L.S. Library Science (in degree)
lt. lieutenant
Ltd. Limited
Luth. Lutheran
LWV League of Women Voters

M

M. Master
m. married
MA, M.A. Master of Arts
MA Massachusetts
MADD Mothers Against Drunk Driving
mag. magazine
MAgr, M.Agr. Master of Agriculture
maj. major

Man. Manitoba
Mar. March
MArch, M.Arch. Master in Architecture
Mass. Massachusetts
math. mathematics, mathematical
MATS Military Air Transport Service
MB, M.B. Bachelor of Medicine
MB Manitoba
MBA, M.B.A. Master of Business Administration
MBS Mutual Broadcasting System
M.C. Medical Corps
MCE, M.C.E. Master of Civil Engineering
mcht. merchant
mcpl. municipal
MCS, M.C.S. Master of Commercial Science
MD, M.D. Doctor of Medicine
MD, Md. Maryland
MDiv Master of Divinity
MDip, M.Dip. Master in Diplomacy
mdse. merchandise
MDV, M.D.V. Doctor of Veterinary Medicine
ME, M.E. Mechanical Engineer
ME Maine
M.E.Ch. Methodist Episcopal Church
mech. mechanical
MEd., M.Ed. Master of Education
med. medical
MEE, M.E.E. Master of Electrical Engineering
mem. member
meml. memorial
merc. mercantile
met. metropolitan
metall. metallurgical
MetE, Met.E. Metallurgical Engineer
meteorol. meteorological
Meth. Methodist
Mex. Mexico
MF, M.F. Master of Forestry
MFA, M.F.A. Master of Fine Arts
mfg. manufacturing
mfr. manufacturer
mgmt. management
mgr. manager
MHA, M.H.A. Master of Hospital Administration
M.I. Military Intelligence
MI Michigan
Mich. Michigan
micros. microscopic, microscopical
mid. middle
mil. military
Milw. Milwaukee
Min. Minister
mineral. mineralogical
Minn. Minnesota
MIS Management Information Systems
Miss. Mississippi
MIT Massachusetts Institute of Technology
mktg. marketing
ML, M.L. Master of Laws
MLA Modern Language Association
M.L.D. Magister Legnum Diplomatic
MLitt, M.Litt. Master of Literature, Master of Letters
MLS, M.L.S. Master of Library Science

MME, M.M.E. Master of Mechanical Engineering
MN Minnesota
mng. managing
MO, Mo. Missouri
moblzn. mobilization
Mont. Montana
MP Northern Mariana Islands
M.P. Member of Parliament
MPA Master of Public Administration
MPE, M.P.E. Master of Physical Education
MPH, M.P.H. Master of Public Health
MPhil, M.Phil. Master of Philosophy
MPL, M.P.L. Master of Patent Law
Mpls. Minneapolis
MRE, M.R.E. Master of Religious Education
MRI Magnetic Resonance Imaging
MS, M.S. Master of Science
MS, Ms. Mississippi
MSc, M.Sc. Master of Science
MSChemE Master of Science in Chemical Engineering
MSEE Master of Science in Electrical Engineering
MSF, M.S.F. Master of Science of Forestry
MSN Master of Science in Nursing
MST, M.S.T. Master of Sacred Theology
MSW, M.S.W. Master of Social Work
MT Montana
Mt. Mount
MTO Mediterranean Theatre of Operation
MTV Music Television
mus. museum, musical
MusB, Mus.B. Bachelor of Music
MusD, Mus.D. Doctor of Music
MusM, Mus.M. Master of Music
mut. mutual
MVP Most Valuable Player
mycol. mycological

N

N. North
NAACOG Nurses Association of the American College of Obstetricians and Gynecologists
NAACP National Association for the Advancement of Colored People
NACA National Advisory Committee for Aeronautics
NACDL National Association of Criminal Defense Lawyers
NACU National Association of Colleges and Universities
NAD National Academy of Design
NAE National Academy of Engineering, National Association of Educators
NAESP National Association of Elementary School Principals
NAFE National Association of Female Executives
N.Am. North America
NAM National Association of Manufacturers
NAMH National Association for Mental Health
NAPA National Association of Performing Artists

NARAS National Academy of Recording Arts and Sciences
NAREB National Association of Real Estate Boards
NARS National Archives and Record Service
NAS National Academy of Sciences
NASA National Aeronautics and Space Administration
NASP National Association of School Psychologists
NASW National Association of Social Workers
nat. national
NATAS National Academy of Television Arts and Sciences
NATO North Atlantic Treaty Organization
NATOUSA North African Theatre of Operations, United States Army
nav. navigation
NB, N.B. New Brunswick
NBA National Basketball Association
NBC National Broadcasting Company
NC, N.C. North Carolina
NCAA National College Athletic Association
NCCJ National Conference of Christians and Jews
ND, N.D. North Dakota
NDEA National Defense Education Act
NE Nebraska
NE, N.E. Northeast
NEA National Education Association
Nebr. Nebraska
NEH National Endowment for Humanities
neurol. neurological
Nev. Nevada
NF Newfoundland
NFL National Football League
Nfld. Newfoundland
NG National Guard
NH, N.H. New Hampshire
NHL National Hockey League
NIH National Institutes of Health
NIMH National Institute of Mental Health
NJ, N.J. New Jersey
NLRB National Labor Relations Board
NM New Mexico
N.Mex. New Mexico
No. Northern
NOAA National Oceanographic and Atmospheric Administration
NORAD North America Air Defense
Nov. November
NOW National Organization for Women
N.P.Ry. Northern Pacific Railway
nr. near
NRA National Rifle Association
NRC National Research Council
NS, N.S. Nova Scotia
NSC National Security Council
NSF National Science Foundation
NSTA National Science Teachers Association
NSW New South Wales
N.T. New Testament
NT Northwest Territories
nuc. nuclear
numis. numismatic
NV Nevada

NW, N.W. Northwest
N.W.T. Northwest Territories
NY, N.Y. New York
N.Y.C. New York City
NYU New York University
N.Z. New Zealand

O

OAS Organization of American States
ob-gyn obstetrics-gynecology
obs. observatory
obstet. obstetrical
occupl. occupational
oceanog. oceanographic
Oct. October
OD, O.D. Doctor of Optometry
OECD Organization for Economic Cooperation and Development
OEEC Organization of European Economic Cooperation
OEO Office of Economic Opportunity
ofcl. official
OH Ohio
OK Oklahoma
Okla. Oklahoma
ON Ontario
Ont. Ontario
oper. operating
ophthal. ophthalmological
ops. operations
OR Oregon
orch. orchestra
Oreg. Oregon
orgn. organization
orgnl. organizational
ornithol. ornithological
orthop. orthopedic
OSHA Occupational Safety and Health Administration
OSRD Office of Scientific Research and Development
OSS Office of Strategic Services
osteo. osteopathic
otol. otological
otolaryn. otolaryngological

P

PA, Pa. Pennsylvania
P.A. Professional Association
paleontol. paleontological
path. pathological
PBS Public Broadcasting System
P.C. Professional Corporation
PE Prince Edward Island
pediat. pediatrics
P.E.I. Prince Edward Island
PEN Poets, Playwrights, Editors, Essayists and Novelists (international association)
penol. penological
P.E.O. women's organization (full name not disclosed)
pers. personnel
pfc. private first class
PGA Professional Golfers' Association of America
PHA Public Housing Administration
pharm. pharmaceutical

PharmD, Pharm.D. Doctor of Pharmacy
PharmM, Pharm.M. Master of Pharmacy
PhB, Ph.B. Bachelor of Philosophy
PhD, Ph.D. Doctor of Philosophy
PhDChemE Doctor of Science in Chemical
  Engineering
PhM, Ph.M. Master of Philosophy
Phila. Philadelphia
philharm. philharmonic
philol. philological
philos. philosophical
photog. photographic
phys. physical
physiol. physiological
Pitts. Pittsburgh
Pk. Park
Pky. Parkway
Pl. Place
P.&L.E.R.R. Pittsburgh & Lake Erie
  Railroad
Plz. Plaza
PNP Pediatric Nurse Practitioner
P.O. Post Office
PO Box Post Office Box
polit. political
poly. polytechnic, polytechnical
PQ Province of Quebec
PR, P.R. Puerto Rico
prep. preparatory
pres. president
Presbyn. Presbyterian
presdl. presidential
prin. principal
procs. proceedings
prod. produced (play production)
prodn. production
prodr. producer
prof. professor
profl. professional
prog. progressive
propr. proprietor
pros. atty. prosecuting attorney
pro tem. pro tempore
PSRO Professional Services Review
  Organization
psychiat. psychiatric
psychol. psychological
PTA Parent-Teachers Association
ptnr. partner
PTO Pacific Theatre of Operations, Parent
  Teacher Organization
pub. publisher, publishing, published
pub. public
publ. publication
pvt. private

Q

quar. quarterly
qm. quartermaster
Q.M.C. Quartermaster Corps
Que. Quebec

R

radiol. radiological
RAF Royal Air Force
RCA Radio Corporation of America
RCAF Royal Canadian Air Force

RD Rural Delivery
Rd. Road
R&D Research & Development
REA Rural Electrification Administration
rec. recording
ref. reformed
regt. regiment
regtl. regimental
rehab. rehabilitation
rels. relations
Rep. Republican
rep. representative
Res. Reserve
ret. retired
Rev. Reverend
rev. review, revised
RFC Reconstruction Finance Corporation
RFD Rural Free Delivery
rhinol. rhinological
RI, R.I. Rhode Island
RISD Rhode Island School of Design
Rlwy. Railway
Rm. Room
RN, R.N. Registered Nurse
roentgenol. roentgenological
ROTC Reserve Officers Training Corps
RR Rural Route
R.R. Railroad
rsch. research
rschr. researcher
Rt. Route

S

S. South
s. son
SAC Strategic Air Command
SAG Screen Actors Guild
SALT Strategic Arms Limitation Talks
S.Am. South America
san. sanitary
SAR Sons of the American Revolution
Sask. Saskatchewan
savs. savings
SB, S.B. Bachelor of Science
SBA Small Business Administration
SC, S.C. South Carolina
SCAP Supreme Command Allies Pacific
ScB, Sc.B. Bachelor of Science
SCD, S.C.D. Doctor of Commercial Science
ScD, Sc.D. Doctor of Science
sch. school
sci. science, scientific
SCLC Southern Christian Leadership
  Conference
SCV Sons of Confederate Veterans
SD, S.D. South Dakota
SE, S.E. Southeast
SEATO Southeast Asia Treaty Organization
SEC Securities and Exchange Commission
sec. secretary
sect. section
seismol. seismological
sem. seminary
Sept. September
s.g. senior grade
sgt. sergeant
SHAEF Supreme Headquarters Allied
  Expeditionary Forces

SHAPE Supreme Headquarters Allied
  Powers in Europe
S.I. Staten Island
S.J. Society of Jesus (Jesuit)
SJD Scientiae Juridicae Doctor
SK Saskatchewan
SM, S.M. Master of Science
SNP Society of Nursing Professionals
So. Southern
soc. society
sociol. sociological
S.P.Co. Southern Pacific Company
spkr. speaker
spl. special
splty. specialty
Sq. Square
S.R. Sons of the Revolution
sr. senior
S S Steamship
S S S Selective Service System
St. Saint, Street
sta. station
stats. statistics
statis. statistical
STB, S.T.B. Bachelor of Sacred Theology
stblzn. stabilization
STD, S.T.D. Doctor of Sacred Theology
std. standard
Ste. Suite
subs. subsidiary
SUNY State University of New York
supr. supervisor
supt. superintendent
surg. surgical
svc. service
SW, S.W. Southwest
sys. system

T

TAPPI Technical Association of the Pulp
  and Paper Industry
tb. tuberculosis
tchg. teaching
tchr. teacher
tech. technical, technology
technol. technological
tel. telephone
Tel. & Tel. Telephone & Telegraph
telecom. telecommunications
temp. temporary
Tenn. Tennessee
Ter. Territory
Ter. Terrace
TESOL Teachers of English to Speakers of
  Other Languages
Tex. Texas
ThD, Th.D. Doctor of Theology
theol. theological
ThM, Th.M. Master of Theology
TN Tennessee
tng. training
topog. topographical
trans. transaction, transferred
transl. translation, translated
transp. transportation
treas. treasurer
TT Trust Territory
TV television

TVA Tennessee Valley Authority
TWA Trans World Airlines
twp. township
TX Texas
typog. typographical

U

U. University
UAW United Auto Workers
UCLA University of California at Los Angeles
UDC United Daughters of the Confederacy
U.K. United Kingdom
UN United Nations
UNESCO United Nations Educational, Scientific and Cultural Organization
UNICEF United Nations International Children's Emergency Fund
univ. university
UNRRA United Nations Relief and Rehabilitation Administration
UPI United Press International
U.P.R.R. United Pacific Railroad
urol. urological
U.S. United States
U.S.A. United States of America
USAAF United States Army Air Force
USAF United States Air Force
USAFR United States Air Force Reserve
USAR United States Army Reserve
USCG United States Coast Guard
USCGR United States Coast Guard Reserve
USES United States Employment Service

USIA United States Information Agency
USMC United States Marine Corps
USMCR United States Marine Corps Reserve
USN United States Navy
USNG United States National Guard
USNR United States Naval Reserve
USO United Service Organizations
USPHS United States Public Health Service
USS United States Ship
USSR Union of the Soviet Socialist Republics
USTA United States Tennis Association
USV United States Volunteers
UT Utah

V

VA Veterans Administration
VA, Va. Virginia
vet. veteran, veterinary
VFW Veterans of Foreign Wars
VI, V.I. Virgin Islands
vice pres. vice president
vis. visiting
VISTA Volunteers in Service to America
VITA Volunteers in Technical Assistance
vocat. vocational
vol. volunteer, volume
v.p. vice president
vs. versus
VT, Vt. Vermont

W

W, W. West
WA Washington (state)

WAC Women's Army Corps
Wash. Washington (state)
WATS Wide Area Telecommunications Service
WAVES Women's Reserve, US Naval Reserve
WCTU Women's Christian Temperance Union
we. western
W. Ger. Germany, Federal Republic of
WHO World Health Organization
WI Wisconsin
W.I. West Indies
Wis. Wisconsin
WSB Wage Stabilization Board
WV West Virginia
W.Va. West Virginia
WWI World War I
WWII World War II
WY Wyoming
Wyo. Wyoming

X, Y

YK Yukon Territory
YMCA Young Men's Christian Association
YMHA Young Men's Hebrew Association
YM & YWHA Young Men's and Young Women's Hebrew Association
yr. year
YT, Y.T. Yukon Territory
YWCA Young Women's Christian Association

Z

zool. zoological

Alphabetical Practices

Names are arranged alphabetically according to the surnames, and under identical surnames according to the first given name. If both surname and first given name are identical, names are arranged alphabetically according to the second given name.

Surnames beginning with De, Des, Du, however capitalized or spaced, are recorded with the prefix preceding the surname and arranged alphabetically under the letter D.

Surnames beginning with Mac and Mc are arranged alphabetically under M.

Surnames beginning with Saint or St. appear after names that begin Sains, and are arranged according to the second part of the name, e.g. St. Clair before Saint Dennis.

Surnames beginning with Van, Von, or von are arranged alphabetically under the letter V.

Compound surnames are arranged according to the first member of the compound.

Many hyphenated Arabic names begin Al-, El-, or al-. These names are alphabetized according to each Biographee's designation of last name. Thus Al-Bahar, Neta may be listed either under Al- or under Bahar, depending on the preference of the listee.

Also, Arabic names have a variety of possible spellings when transposed to English. Spelling of these names is always based on the practice of the Biographee. Some Biographees use a Western form of word order, while others prefer the Arabic word sequence.

Similarly, Asian names may have no comma between family and given names, but some Biographees have chosen to add the comma. In each case, punctuation follows the preference of the Biographee.

Parentheses used in connection with a name indicate which part of the full name is usually deleted in common usage. Hence Chambers, E(lizabeth) Anne indicates that the usual form of the given name is E. Anne. In such a case, the parentheses are ignored in alphabetizing and the name would be arranged as Chambers, Elizabeth Anne. However, if the name is recorded Chambers, (Elizabeth) Anne, signifying that the entire name Elizabeth is not commonly used, the alphabetizing would be arranged as though the name were Chambers, Anne. If an entire middle or last name is enclosed in parentheses, that portion of the name is used in the alphabetical arrangement. Hence Chambers, Elizabeth (Anne) would be arranged as Chambers, Elizabeth Anne.

Where more than one spelling, word order, or name of an individual is frequently encountered, the sketch has been entered under the form preferred by the Biographee, with cross-references under alternate forms.

Who'sWho of American Women®

Biographies

AADLAND, KATHLEEN A. counselor, army intelligence officer; b. Britton, S.D. d. Inguald Martin and Mabel Laverne A.; widowed; 1 child, Mabel Ann. Aadland Wojcik. BS, S.D. State U., 1973; MS, No. State U., Aberdeen, S.C., 1976; postgrad., U. Ill., 1982-85. Cert. guidance and counseling, tchr. Pres. Aadland & Assocs. Inc., Maddock, N.D., 1992—. Bd. dirs. 21st Century Rehamesteading Bd., Jamestown, N.D. Roman Catholic. Office: AA Inc PO Box 100 Maddock ND 57480 E-mail: knehlich@brittansd.com.

AALL, PAMELA R. foundation administrator; BA, Harvard U.; MA in internat. affairs, Columbia U.; postgrad., London Sch. Economics. Acting dir. U. S. Inst. Peace, Washington; cons. Pres. Com. Arts/Humanities, Inst. Internat. Edn., Washington; mgr. internat. relations fellowship program Rockefeller Found. Co-editor: (book) Managing Global Chaos: Sources of and Responses to International Conflict. Office: US Inst Peace 1200 17th St NW Ste 200 Washington DC 20036-3011

AARON, BARBARA ROBINSON, real estate broker; b. Washington, Sept. 19, 1941; d. Tremain Fisher and Margaret Coe (Edgerton) Robinson; m. John Marshall Aaron III, June 27, 1964; children: Anne Kimbrough, Jennifer Coe. BA in Econs., Duke U., 1963. Cert. residential broker. Investment assoc. Old Colony Trust Co., Boston, 1963-64; ednl. tester Pa. State U., State Coll., 1964-65; real estates salesperson Trans Indies Realty & Investment, Guaynabo, P.R., 1973-75; real estate saleswoman Wellborn Real Estate, Reston, Va., 1975-76; real estates saleswoman Worthington & Vincent, Falmouth, Mass., 1977-80; real estates salesperson Chimney House Real Estate, Reston, 1976-77, 80-83, real estate mgr., 1983-95; real estate broker, asst. mgr. Coldwell Banker Stevens, Realtors, Reston, 1995—. Mem. Nat. Assn. Realtors, Realtors Brokerage Coun., Va. Assn. Realtors, No. Va. Assn. Realtors (std. forms com. 1989—, profl. stds. com., strategic planning com., bd. dirs.), Greater Reston C. of C. (bd. dirs. 1990-97, pres. 1992-93). Office: Realtors 11890 Sunrise Valley Dr Reston VA 20191-3302

AARON, CYNTHIA G. judge; b. Mpls., May 3, 1957; d. Allen Harold and Barbara Lois (Perlman) A.; m. Craig D. Higgs, May 15, 1993. Student, Brandeis U., 1975-77; BA with honors and distinction, Stanford U., 1979; JD cum laude, Harvard U., 1984. Bar: Calif. 1984, U.S. Dist. Ct. (so. dist.) Calif. 1984, U.S. Ct. Appeals (9th cir.) 1984, U.S. Dist. Ct. (no. dist.) Calif. 1986, U.S. Dist. Ct. (ctrl. dist.) Calif. 1988, U.S. Supreme Ct. 1991. Rsch. asst. to Prof. Alan Dershowitz Law Sch. Harvard U., 1982-83; trial atty. Fed. Defenders San Diego, Inc., 1984-88; ptnr. Aaron & Cortez, 1988-94; U.S. magistrate judge U.S. Dist. Ct. (so. dist.) Calif., San Diego, 1994—. Instr. Nat. Inst. for Trial [illegible] 1990—02; adj. prof. Calif. Western Sch. Law, San Diego, 1990—93; adj. prof. law sch. U. San Diego, [illegible] dirs. San Diego Vol. Lawyer Program, 2001—. Mem.: San Diego County Judges Assn. (bd. dirs., pres. 2001—02), Lawyers Club San Diego, City Club San Diego, Phi Beta Kappa. Office: US Dist Ct So Dist 940 Front St Ste 1185 San Diego CA 92101-8940

AARON, SHIRLEY MAE, tax consultant; b. Covington, La., Feb. 28, 1935; d. Morgan and Pearl (Jenkins) King; m. Richard L. King, Feb. 16, 1952 (div. Feb. 1965); children: Deborah, Richard, Roberta, Keely; m. Michael A. Aaron, Nov. 27, 1976 (dec. July 1987). Adminstrv. asst. South Central Bell, Covington, La., 1954-62; acct. Brown & Root, Inc., Houston, 1962-75; timekeeper Alyeska Pipeline Co., Fairbanks, Alaska, 1975-77; adminstrv. asst. Boeing Co., Seattle, 1979-93; pres. Aaron Enterprises, Seattle, 1977—; owner Gabriel's Dinner Club, La., 1993—. Contbr.: Who's Cooking What in America by Phyllis Hanes, 1993. Bd. dirs. Burien 146 Homeowners Assn., Seattle, 1979—, pres., 1980-83, 92. Mem. NAFE. Avocation: singing, art. Home: 131 Gerard St Mandeville LA 70448-5808

AARON-TAYLOR, SUSAN WENDY, sculptor, educator; b. Bklyn., July 11, 1947; d. Irving and Frances Estelle (Sidorofsky) Aaron; m. Harry William Taylor, June 27, 1971; 1 child, Jay Philip Aaron Taylor. BS, Wayne State U., 1969; MFA, Cranbrook Acad. Art, 1973. Tchr. h.s. art Groves H.S., Birmingham, Mich., 1969-71; prof. art Coll. Creative Studies, Detroit, 1973—; studio artist, sculptor Pleasant Ridge, Mich., 1969—. One person shows include Xochipilli Gallery, Birmingham, Mich., 1988, 92, 95, South Bend (Ind.) Regional Mus. Art, 1993, Cranbrook Acad. Art Mus., Bloomfield Hills, Mich., 1994, Muskegon (Mich.) Mus. Art, 1997, Xochipilli Gallery, Anderson Gallery, Pontiac, Mich., 1998, Detroit Contemporary, 2002, Downriver Coun. for the Arts, 2004, others; exhibited in group shows Inst. Culture, Zacateca City, Zacateca, Mex., 1989, Detroit Inst. Arts, 1995, Guadalupe Gallery, Santa Fe, N.Mex., 2002, Hand Artes Gallery, Truchas, N.Mex., 2004, others. Assn. Ind. Colls. Art grantee, 1981, 83. Mem. Am. Crafts Coun., Surface Design Assn. Avocations: jungian psychology, metaphysics, alchemy. Home: 51 Fairwood Blvd Pleasant Ridge MI 48069-1216 Office: Coll Creative Studies 201 E Kirby St Detroit MI 48202-4048

ABAKOUI, ROKI ANN, psychologist, consultant; b. Sault Ste. Marie, Mich., June 6, 1959; d. Freddie George Mounce and JoAnne Georgina Fleury. BA, Elmhurst Coll., 1982; MA, U. North Tex., 1995, PhD, 1998. Lic. clin. psychologist Ill., 1999. Air traffic contr. Denver Air Route Traffic Control Ctr., Longmont, Colo., 1982—88, Wash. Air Route Traffic Control Ctr., Leesburg, Va., 1988—90; profl. psychology intern So. Ill. U. Counseling Ctr., Carbondale, 1997—98, staff psychologist, 1998—. Pvt. cons., Carbondale, 1999—; presenter in field. Mem.: APA, Assn. for Size Diversity and Health. Progressive. Avocations: travel, gardening. Office: SIUC Counseling Center Mc4715 Carbondale IL 62901 E-mail: rokia@siu.edu.

ABARBANELL, GAYOLA HAVENS, financial planner; b. Chgo., Oct. 21, 1939; d. Leonard Milton and Lillian Love (Leviten) Havens; m. Burton J. Abarbanell, June 1, 1965 (div. 1972); children: Jeffrey J. Reddick, Dena Reddick Lamb. Student, UCLA, 1975; student, San Joaquin Coll. Law, 1976-77. CFP; cert. sr. advisor, registered fin. advisor; lic. real estate rep. Calif.; lic. life ins. broker, Calif., Wash., Nev., N.Y., Ill., S.C.; lic. securities broker; cert. fin. advisor; cert. long term care, health ins. and disability ins. Postal clk., Van Nuys, Calif., 1966-69; regional mgr. Niagara Cyclo Massage, Fresno, Calif., 1969-72; owner, mgr. AD Enterprises, Fresno, 1970-72; agt., field supr. Equitable of Iowa, Fresno, 1972-73; rep. Ciba Pharms., Fresno, 1973-75; owner, operator Creativity Unltd., Fresno, 1975-76; registered fin. advisor Univ. Securities Corp., L.A., 1976-83, Fin. Network Inv. Corp., Torrance, Calif., 1983-99, Nat. Planning corp., Santa Monica, Calif., 1999—. Lectr. seminars for civic orgns.; mem. adv. bd. Financial Network, Torrance, Calif., 1985-88. Co-author: Guidelines to Feminist Consciousness Raising, 1985. Mem. bus. adv. bd. of 2d careers. Recipient award Women in Ins., 1972. Mem. Bus. and Profl. Assn., L.A. Internat. Assn. Fin. Planners (bd. dirs. 1993-94), Inst. Cert. Fin. Planners, So. Calif. Socially Responsible Investment Profls., Fin. Planning Assn. (L.A. chpt. bd. dirs. 2001-02), ACLU, NOW (nat. consciousness raising coord. 1975-76), Gay Acad. Union, Nat. Gay Task Force, Culver City C. of C., Internat. Assn. Fin. Planners, Social Investment Forum, Rotary (founding mem. L.A. Westside Sunrise Club sgt. at arms 1990-91, community svc. chair 1991-94, v.p. 1992-93, found. chair 1993-94). Democrat. Jewish. Avocations: photography, ceramics, painting, design. Home: 57124 Mono Wind Way North Fork CA 93643-9797 Office: Nat Planning Corp Ste 103 5625 Green Valley Cir Culver City CA 90230-7120 Office Phone: 310-216-7767. E-mail: gay.abarbanell@natplan.com.

ABATE, CATHERINE M. former state senator; b. Margate, N.J., Dec. 8, 1947; d. Joseph and Carolyn (Fiore) A.; m. Ronald E. Kliegerman, Oct. 28, 1978; 1 child, Kyle. BA, Vassar Coll., 1969; JD, Boston U., 1972. Bar: N.Y. 1973, U.S. Dist. Ct. (so. dist.) N.Y. 1976. Staff atty. Legal Aid Soc., N.Y.C., 1972-74, 75-78, supervising atty., 1979-81, dir. tng., 1981-85; exec. dep. commr. N.Y. State Div. Human Rights, 1986-88; chairperson N.Y. Crime Victims Bd., 1988-90; commr. N.Y.C. Dept. Probation, N.Y., 1990-92, N.Y.C. Dept. Correction, N.Y., 1992-94; mem. N.Y. State Senate, Albany, 1995-98. Acting chmn. Gov.'s Task Force on Criminal Justice, N.Y., 1983; chmn. N.Y. State Platform on Criminal Justice, 1984; dist. leader Dem. Party, 1981-86; 1st vice chmn. county com. Dem. Party, N.Y. County; mem. judiciary com., chmn. criminal justice and pub. safety com., N.Y.C., 1982-86; mem. adminstrv. bd. Ams. for Dem. Action, N.Y.C., 1983—; bd. dirs. Village Nursing Home, 1987—. Mem. Bar Assn. City N.Y. (criminal cts. com. 1982-86), Congress Italian Ams. (adv. bd. 1984), Nat. Women's Polit. Caucus, Women in Criminal Justice, Nat. Assn. Crime Victims Compensation Bd. (bd. dirs. 1989—), Nat. Orgn. Italian-Am. Women (bd. dirs. 1986—). Roman Catholic. Avocation: tennis. Home: 303 Mercer St New York NY 10003-6706

ABBE, ELFRIEDE MARTHA, sculptor, graphic artist; b. Washington; d. Cleveland Jr. and Frieda (Dauer) A. Student, Art Inst. Chgo., 1937; B.F.A., Cornell U., 1940; postgrad., Syracuse U., 1947. Author and illustrator: books including The Plants of Virgil's Georgics, 1965; One-woman exhbns. include Carnegie-Mellon U., 1962, 69, Cornell U., 1963, Trinity Coll., Hartford, 1964, Arts Club of Washington, 1972, Cornell Club of N.Y., 1977, Copley Soc. Boston, 1978, Woods-Gerry Gallery, R.I. Sch. Design, 1983; represented in permanent collections Met. Mus. Art., Watson Library, Boston Mus. Fine Arts, Cin. Art Mus., Dumbarton Oaks, Washington, Houghton Library, Harvard U., Hunt Library, Carnegie-Mellon U., N.Y. Pub. Library, Rosenwald Collection Nat. Gallery, Kew Gardens Library, Royal Bot. Garden, Edinburgh, Nat. Library, Canberra, Australia; sculpture placed in Mann Library, Kroch Library and Morrison Hall, Cornell U., McGill U., N.Y. Bot. Gardens, Hunt Library, Pitts., Pres.'s Office, Keene (N.H.) State Coll., Herzog August Bibliothek, Wolfenbüttel, Fed. Republic Germany (bronze bust of founder), Abbe Mus., Bar Harbor, Maine (bronze bust of founder Dr. Robert Abbe). Recipient Gold medals Pen and Brush, N.Y.C., 1964, Margaret Sussman Meml. award 1987, Gold medals Nat. Arts [illegible] 1970, Gold medals Acad. Artists Assn., Springfield, Mass., 1976, Founders' Prize Pen and Brush, [illegible] award Salmagundi Club N.Y., 1978; Elliot Liskin award, 1979, Catherine Lorillard Wolfe Club award, 1993. Fellow Nat. Sculpture Soc. (Barrett-Colea prize 1984); mem. Nat. Soc. Mural Painters, Phi Kappa Phi.

ABBEY, LINDA ROWE, artist, educator; d. Robert Bradford and Elizabeth Spencer Rowe; m. Bruce James Abbey, Aug. 23, 1969; 1 child, Jason James. AA, Piedmont Coll., Charlottesville, Va., 1986; BA, Hanover Coll., Hanover, Ind., 1966. Cert. tchg. N.J., 1969, Va., 1975. Tchg. english as a fgn. lang. Peace Corps, Bizerte, Tunisia, 1966—68; tchg. english to italian navy officers Shenker Inst., Rome, Italy, Taranto, Italy, 1969—69; fourth grade tchr. Princeton Regional Sch., Princeton, NJ, 1969—72; title I tchr. Charlottesville City Sch., Charlottesville, Va., 1974—89; fifth grade tchr. St. Anne's Belfield Sch., Charlottesville, Va., 1989—90; artist self-employed, Syracuse, NY, 1990—. Watercolor tchr. to adults and children, Syracuse, NY, 1993—; watercolor tchr. Everson Mus. of Art, Syracuse, NY, 1997—2001; vol. artist McKinley Brighton Elem. Sch., Syracuse, NY, 1995—; judge of artwork for on my own time show Syracuse U., Syracuse, NY; founding mem. of pleiades A Group Of Six To Eight Artists Who Exhibit Together, Syracuse, NY, 1998—. One-woman shows include Watermark Gallery, Balt., Md., Fox & Fowle, Architects, N.Y.C., Straun Art Gallery, Jacksonville, Ill., prin. works include paintings of su chancellor's house (The Brochure received a bronze medal from the Coun. for Advancement and Support of Edn., 2001), On MY Own Gallery, Syracuse, N.Y., Onondaga Pk. featured twelve paintings in a Plexi frame to raise money for trees damaged in the 1998 Labor Day Storm, 1998—2000, exhibitions include AAUW Invitational Show, Skanaeateles, N.Y., Rene Foteuil Gallery, N.Y.C., Edith Barrett Fine Arts Gallery, Utica Coll., Utica, N.Y., Goodsight Gallery with Pleiades, Cazenovia, N.Y., Veerhoff Gallery, Washington, SUNY Ints. of Tech., Utica/Rome, N.Y., Lagerquist Gallery, Atlanta, Ga., Artifice Gallery, Syracuse, N.Y., Gallery 210 Juried Exhbn., Fine Details Gallery, Skaneateles, N.Y., Kirkland Art Ctr., Ctrl. N.Y. Juried Show, Clinton, N.Y., Adirondacks Nat. Exhbn. of Am. Watercolors, Old Forge, N.Y., Represented in permanent collections commd. paintings of su campus. Organizer of Art on the Porches, art show for over 50 artists in neighborhood, Syracuse, NY, 2001—03. Recipient Golden Rule Award, JC Penny and McKinley Brighton Sch., Syracuse, NY, 1997, Bronze medal Award, NY State Coun. for Advancement and Support of Edn., 2001, Best Watercolor, Delavan Award, Hon. Mention, 1992, 1994, 1996, Second Pl. Watercolor, Regional Art Show, 2000, 2002; grantee John DeFrancisco N.Y. Art and Cultural Grants, 2003. Mem.: Onondaga Art Guild (assoc.; pres. 1998—99, sec. 2000).

ABBINANTE, VITA, sales executive, administrator; b. Chgo., Nov. 5, 1948; d. Michael and Madeline Abbinante; divorced; children: Maria Theresa Gehard, Valerie Gehard, Leslie Gehard. Grad., Selan Beauty Sch., Chgo., 1976, Coll. of DuPage, 1971. Pres., owenr Gehard Enterprises, Elmhurst, Ill., 1992-96; mfrs. rep. Widdes Mktg., Northbrook, Ill., 1996-98; v.p. Metaltech Mfg., Jamestown, N.Y., 1998—. Bd. dirs., sec.-treas. MMAC, Jamestown, N., 1998—, Eisenhauer Group, Lake Bluff, Ill., 1996—, Buck Sci., Schiller Park, Ill., 1994-96. Author: (poems) Words of Praise, 1984, Hearts of Fire, 1985; contbr. poetry to Am. Poetry Anthology, Am. Poetry Assn., Eternal Echoes. Mem. NAFE, Jamestown Bus. and Profl. Women's Club. Roman Catholic. Avocations: reading, boating, creative writing, horseback riding. Home: 10116 W Cermak Rd Westchester IL 60154-4511

ABBOTT, ANN AUGUSTINE, social worker, educator; b. Green Bay, Wis., July 6, 1943; d. Walter A. and Ethel D. Augustine. BS in Psychology, St. Norbert Coll., W. DePere, Wis., 1965; MSS in Social Work, Bryn Mawr Coll., 1969, PhD (NIMH fellow), 1977, postgrad. in higher edn. adminstrn., 1978. Acad. tutor, counselor Devereux Schs., Devon, Pa., 1965-67; psychol. clin. coord. Pa. State U., University Park, 1969-71; social worker Tidewater Mental Health Clinic, Williamsburg, Va., 1971-72; adj. prof. Pa. State U., King of Prussia, 1973-75; vis. lectr. C.C. of Phila., 1975-76; asst. prof. dir. social work, cmty. psychology Widener U., Chester, Pa., 1976-81, project dir. Univ. Yr. for Action, 1976-81, project cons. Adult Competency Tng. Grant, 1976-81; with sch. social work Rutgers U., Camden, 1981—2001, assoc. prof., 1987—2001, assoc. dean, 1993—2001; prof., MSW program dir. grad. social work dept. West Chester U., Pa., 2001—. Faculty fellow NIAAA/NIDA/OSAP, 1990-93. Tennis coach Nat. Jr. Tennis League, Phila., 1974-76; budget rev. bd. United Way, vice-chair allocations com., 1979-86; trustee Ins. Trust, 1995-98, chair, 1996-98. Vocation Rehab. Tng. grantee, 1964. Fellow Am. Orthopsychiat. Assn., Coll. Physicians of Phila.; mem. NASW (nat. bd. mem. region IV 1988-91, del. assembly rep. 1979-89, pres. Pa. state chpt. 1987-89, nat. pres.-elect 1992-93, nat. pres. 1993-95), Coun. on Social Work Edn. (commn. on accreditation 1997-2000), Am. Group Psychotherapy Assn., Internat. Fed. Social Workers (v.p. for N.Am. 1994-96). Home: PO Box 637 Villanova PA 19085-0637 Office: Grad Social Work Dept West Chester U Reynolds Hall West Chester PA 19383 E-mail: aabbott@wcupa.edu.

ABBOTT, BARBARA LOUISE, artist, educator; b. San Francisco, Calif., Oct. 16, 1941; d. C. Paige and Mary Ellen Abbott; m. Edward Michael Seman, Nov. 21, 1964 (div. June 1980); children: Jill, Janet, Michael Paige. BFA, U. Utah, 1982; MFA, Ariz. State U., 1986. Prof. art Edinboro U. Pa., Edinboro, Pa., 1989—90, La. State U., Shreveport, La., 1990—96; prin., owner Abbott Art Studio, San Jose, Calif., 1996—. Prin. works include Quilt Kiosks, Shreveport, La., 1993, Great Blue Herons, Santa Cruz, Calif., 2000, Perro Feliz, San Jose, Calif., 2002, exhibitions include Award Winning Prints, Phila. Print Club, Phila., 1986, Marking Time: Making Space, South of Mkt. Cultural Ctr., San Francisco, 2001, book, Twice Descending, 1991. Fellow Fulbright-Hays fellowship, U.S. Govt., 1993. Home and Studio: 778 Crestview Drive San Jose CA 95117

ABBOTT, GINA, municipal government executive; b. Patuxent River, Md., Oct. 12, 1954; d. Ralph Orlando Pivero and Nancy Dinicola; m. Winthrop S. Abbott, Jr., Nov. 13, 1977 (dec. Aug. 1996). BSBA, U. Phoenix, 1989. Cert. profl. pub. buyer. From purchasing asst. to small order buyer Tex. Instruments, Colorado Springs, 1984-89; from buyer to procurement & contracts dir. El Paso County Govt., Colorado Springs, 1990—. Recipient cert. of achievement Fed. Emergency Mgmt. Assn. Mem. Nat. Inst. Govtl. Purchasing, Rocky Mtn. Govtl. Purchasing Assn. (v.p. 2001). Avocations: cooking, baking, traveling, watching sports. Office: El Paso County Govt 27 E Vermijo Ave Colorado Springs CO 80903-2208 Home: 14 Anita Rd Colorado Springs CO 80906-3110

ABBOTT, LINDA JOY, stained glass artisan, educator, photographer; b. Hempstead, NY, Oct. 10, 1943; d. Edward Morton Brandstatter and Evalyne Manchik; divorced 1971; children: David Edward Black, Adam Michael Black. AAS in Design, SUNY at FIT, N.Y.C., 1963; Cert. paralegal, Tarrant County C.C., Fort Worth, Tex., 1983; student, Disney Inst. Wildlife Photog., 2000, N.Y. Inst. Photography, 2001. Fashion designer Alyssa/Little Craft, N.Y.C., 1963-65; bus. owner Virgin Islands Diving Sch., St. Thomas, V.I., 1972-76; stained glass artisan Creative Glass, Salt Lake City, 1978-81, Linda Abbott Glass Art, Willow Park, Tex., 1981-86; founder, stained glass artisan, instr. Crystal Rainbow Glass Studio, Dania, Fla., 1986-99; stained glass [illegible] Glass Studio, 1999—; freelance photographer. Freelance calligrapher various cos., Covina, [illegible] artist, Lancaster, 1976—78; cons. various stained glass cos., 1989—; product cons. various stained glass equipment mfrs., 1994—; sem. instr. Internat. Art Glass Supplies Assn., 1994—, coord. seminars, chair, 1999; mem. steering com. Art Glass Am., Tampa, 1998; guest instr. MISC Studios nationwide, 1999—; webmaster Cert. Career Inst., Clearfield, Utah; instr. in field. Author: E-Magine This! Book One, 2002 co-author: (books) Hot & Wired, 1993, Some Things Fishy, 1993, Rainforest, 1994, Stargazing, 1995, Image is Everything, 1996; prodr. (video) Hot & Wired; contbr. articles to mags. in field. Recipient Best in Show award City Art Assn., 1978, Glass Expo, Salt Lake City, 1982. Mem. So. Fla. Ferret Club, Internat. Art Glass Suppliers Assn. (com. chair 1996—), Internat. Stained Glass Designers Assn. (pres. 1995-99), Art Glass Guild Artisans (dir. 1996—), Art Glass Am. (founder), Ednl. Consumer Conf. Jewish. Avocations: scuba diving, white water rafting, animal welfare causes, wildlife photography. Personal E-mail: lotus954@aol.com.

ABBOTT, REBECCA PHILLIPS, museum director, art consultant, photographer; b. Giessen, Germany, Jan. 10, 1950; d. Charles Leonard and Janet Alice (Praeger) Phillips. BA, Emory and Henry Coll., 1973; postgrad., Georgetown U., 1975, Am. U., 1982-88. Assoc. univ. registrar Am. U., Washington, 1977-81, assoc. dir. adminstrv. computing, 1981-84, dir. adminstrv. computing, 1984-88; dir. membership Nat. Mus. of Women in the Arts, Washington, 1988-89, dir., 1989-98; cons. in fine arts, 1998—. Fine arts photographer. Selected solo exhbns., Includes Anton Gallery, Public Places Private Views, 1992, The Wind, 1994, Canal Views, 1996, Burton Marinkovich Fine Art, Shadows at 18th and K, 1998; Selected group exhbns. includes The Annex Gallery, Metaphysical Landscapes,1989, Embassy of Japan: East Meets West, 1995, Nippon Gallery, Assimilations, 1997. Mem. Am. Assn. Mus., Mus. Art Table.

ABBOTT, REGINA A. neurodiagnostic technologist, consultant, business owner; b. Haverhill, Mass., Mar. 5, 1950; d. Frank A. and Ann (Drelick) A. Student, Pierce Bus. Sch., Boston, 1967-70, Seizure Unit Children's Hosp. Med. Ctr. Sch. EEG Tech., 1970-71. Registered electroneurodiagnostic technologist Advanced Fuller Sch. Massage Therapy, 2001, nat. cert. massage therapist Nat. Cert. Bd. Therapeutic Massage and Bodywork. Tech. dir. electrodiagnostic labs. Salem Hosp., 1972-76; lab. dir. clin. neurophysiology Tufts U. New Eng. Med. Ctr., Boston, 1976-78; clin. instr. EEG program Laboure Coll., Boston, 1977-81; adminstrv. dir. dept. Neurology Mt. Auburn Hosp., Cambridge, Mass., 1978-81; tech. dir. clin. neurophysiology Drs. Diagnostic Service, Virginia Beach, Va.; tech. dir. neurodiagnostic ctr. Portsmouth Psychiatric Ctr., 1981-87; founder, pres., owner Commonwealth Neurodiagnostic Services, Inc., 1986—, Hands on Health-Care, 2001—. Co-dir. continuing edn. program EEG Tech., Boston, 1977-78; mem. adv. com. sch. neurodiagnostic tech. Laboure Coll., 1977-81, Sch. EEG Tech. Children's Hosp. Med. Ctr., Boston, 1980-81; assoc. examiner Am. Bd. Registration of Electroencephalographic Technologists, 1977-83; mem. guest faculty Oxford Medilog Co.; cons. Nihon Kohden Am., 1981-83; cons., educator Teca Corp., Pleasantville, N.Y., 1981-87; allied health profl. staff mem. Virginia Beach Gen. Hosp., Humana Hosp. Bayside, Virginia Beach; clin. evaluator Calif. Coll. for Health Scis., 1995—. Contbr. articles to profl. jours. EIL scholar, Poland/USSR, 1970; recipient Internat. Woman of Yr. award in bus. and sci. Internat. Biographical Ctr., London, 1993-94, Woman of Yr. award Am. Biographical Inst., 1993. Mem.: NAFE, Am. Soc. Electro Neurodiagnostic Technologists, Am. Massage Therapy Assn. Avocations: running, art collecting, photography, reading, investing.

ABBOTT, VERNA RUTH, social studies educator; b. Shawnee, Okla., July 4, 1925; d. James Ivan and Gladys Beatrice (Bennett) Forston; m. Lowell Woodrow Abbott, June 25, 1946 (dec. June 1989); children: Carlin, Priscilla, Patricia. BS, East Tenn. State U., Johnson City, 1967. Cert. tchr. polit. sci., history and speech, Tenn. Broadcaster KGFF Radio, Shawnee, 1943-48, WNAD Radio, U. Okla., 1948-50; broadcaster women's TV show WJHL-TV, Johnson City, 1960; tchr., audio-visual coord. Dobyns-Bennett H.S., Kingsport, Tenn., 1966-93; mem. Bd. Edn., Kingsport City Schs., 1993—. Sponsor domestic exch. Dobyns-Bennett H.S., Kingsport, 1982-93. Author articles and essays. Liaison, Kingsport Bd. of Mayor and Aldermen,

1993-97; chmn. Kingsport Schs. Safety Coun., 1995—; mem. bd. distinction Tenn. Sch. Bds. Assn., 1999. Named Outstanding Sch. Bd. Mem., Tenn. Congress Parents and Tchrs., 1996-97. Mem. AAUW, DAR (program com. 1996), LWV, Ret. Tchrs. Assn. Baptist. Avocations: volunteering, speaking. Home: 4321 Stagecoach Rd Kingsport TN 37664-2137 Office: Kingsport City Schs 1701 E Center St Kingsport TN 37664-2608

ABDELLAH, FAYE GLENN, retired public health service executive; d. H. B. and Margaret (Glenn) Abdellah. BS in Tchg., Columbia U., 1945, MA in Tchg., 1947, EdD, 1955; LLD (hon.), Case Western Res. U., 1967, Rutgers U., 1973; DSc (hon.), U. Akron, 1978, Cath. U. Am., 1981, Monmouth Coll., 1982, Ea. Mich U., 1987, U. Bridgeport, 1987, Georgetown U., 1989; D in Pub. Svc. (hon.), Am. U., 1987; LHD, D in Pub. Svc., U. S.C., 1991; D in Mil. Nursing (hon.), USUHS, 2002. RN N.Y., D.C. Commd. officer USPHS, Rockville, Md., 1949, advanced through grades to rear adm., 1970, dep. surgeon gen., chief nurse officer, 1970—87, dep. surgeon gen., 1981—89, chief nursing edn. br., divsn. nursing, 1949—59, surgeon gen., 1989; chief rsch. grants br. Bur. Health Manpower Edn., NIH, HEW, Rockville, 1959—69; dir. Office Rsch. Tng. Nat. Ctr. for Health Svcs. R & D, Health Svcs. Mental Health Adminstrn., Rockville, 1969; acting dep. dir. Nat. Ctr. for Health Svcs. R & D, Rockville, 1971, Bur. Health Svcs. Rsch. and Evaluation, Health Resources Adminstrn., Rockville, 1973; dir. Office Long-Term Care, Office Asst. Sec. for Health, HEW, Rockville, 1973—80; exec. dir. Grad. Sch. Nursing Uniformed Svcs. U. Health Scis., Bethesda, Md., 1993—, founding dean, prof. emeritus, 2001—. Prof. nursing, Emily Smith chair U. S.C., Columbia, 1990—91; dean, prof. Grad. Sch. Nursing, Uniformed Svcs. U. Health Scis., 1993—2002, founding dean, prof. emerita, 1993—2002. Author: Effect of Nurse Staffing on Satisfactions with Nursing Care, 1959, Patient Centered Approaches to Nursing, 1960, Better Patient Care Through Nursing Research, 1965, 2d edit., 1979, 3d edit., 1986, Intensive Care, Concepts and Practices for Clinical Nurse Specialists, 1969, New Directions in Patient Centered Nursing, 1972, Preparing Nursing Research for the 21st Century, 1994; contbr. articles to profl. jours. Named to TC Nursing Hall of Fame, Columbia U., 1999, Nat. Women's Hall of Fame, 2000; recipient Mary Adelaide Nutting award, 1983, Oustanding Leadership award, U. Pa., 1987, 1999, Disting. Svc. award, 1973—89, Surgeon Gen.'s medal and medallion, 1989, Achievement award in aging, Allied-Signal, 1989, Gustav O. Lienhard award, Inst. Medicine NAS, 1992, Breaking Ground in Women's Health award, 2001, G.W. "Sonny" Montgomery award, Dept. Vets. Affairs, 2002. Fellow: Am. Acad. Nursing (charter, past v.p., pres.); mem.: AAAS, ANA (hon.), APA, Assn. Mil. Surgeons U.S., Douglas Soc., Phi Lambda Theta, Sigma Theta Tau (Disting. Rsch. Fellow award 1989). Home: 3713 Chanel Rd Annandale VA 22003-2024

ABDUL, PAULA (JULIE), singer, dancer, choreographer; b. L.A., June 19, 1963; d. Harry and Lorraine A.; m. Emilio Estevez, Apr. 29, 1992 (div. 1994); m. Brad Beckerman, 1996 (div. 1998). Student, Calif. State Univ., Northridge; studied tap, jazz with Joe Tramine, the Bella Lewitzky Co. Laker Girls cheerleader, choreographer L.A. Lakers basketball team; choreography for Jacksons singing group, Janet Jackson, ZZ Top, Arnold Schwarzenegger, Tom Hanks, The Tracey Ullman Show, others. Judge American Idol: The Search for a Superstar, 2002—. Albums: Forever Your Girl, 1988, Shut Up and Dance, 1990, Spellbound, 1991, Head Over Heels, 1995; TV films Touched By Evil, 1997, Amy Fuentes, The Waiting Game, 1998, Denise Walton, Mr. Rock 'n' Roll: The Alan Freed Story, 1999; choreographer films Private School, 1983, Dragnet, 1987, Can't Buy Me Love, 1987, The Running Man, 1987, Coming to America, 1988, Bull Durham, 1988, Action Jackson, 1988, Dance to Win, 1989, The Karate Kid Part III, 1989, She's Out of Control, 1989, The Doors, 1991, Jerry Maguire, 1996, American Beauty, 1999, Black Knight, 2001. Recipient Soul Train award, Am. Video Arts award choreographer of yr., Nat. Acad. Video Arts and Scis., 1987, Emmy award best choreography for the Tracy Ullman Show, 1988-89, MTV award best female video, best dance video, best choreography in a video, best editing in a video for hit Straight Up, 1989. Office: c/o Atlas Third Rail Mgmt 9169 Sunset Blvd Los Angeles CA 90069*

ABEL, ELIZABETH A. dermatologist; b. Hartford, Conn., Mar. 16, 1940; d. Frederick A. and Rose (Borovicka) Abel; m. Barton Lane; children: Barton Lane, Geoffrey Lane, Suzanne Lane. Student, Colby-Sawyer Coll., 1957-60; BS, Wash. Hosp. Ctr. Sch. Med. Tech., 1961, U. Md., 1965, MD cum laude, 1967. Diplomate Am. Bd. Dermatology. Intern San Francisco Gen. Hosp., 1967-68; resident in medicine, fellow in oncology U. Calif. Med. Ctr., San Francisco, 1968-69; resident in dermatology NYU Med. Ctr., 1969-72, chief resident, 1971-72, USPHS research trainee in immunology, 1972-73; dep. chief dept. dermatology USPHS Hosp., S.I., N.Y., 1973-74; instr. clin. dermatology Columbia U. Coll. Physicians and Surgeons, N.Y.C., 1974-75, Stanford (Calif.) U. Sch. Medicine, 1975-77, clin. asst. prof. dermatology, 1977-82, asst. prof. dermatology, 1982-90, clin. assoc. prof., 1990-96, clin. prof., 1996—. Asst. editor Jour. Am. Acad. Dermatology, 1993-98; mem. med. adv. bd. The Nat. Psoriasis Found., 1993-95. Contbr. articles to profl. sci. jours. Mellon Found. fellow, 1983, 87. Fellow Am. Acad. Dermatology; mem. N.Am. Clin. Dermatologic Soc., San Francisco Dermatologic Soc., Internat. Soc. Dermatology Surgery, Pacific Dermatologic Assn., Women's Dermatologic Soc., Noah Worcester Dermatologic Soc., Alpha Omega Alpha. Avocations: piano, golf, travel, reading. Office: 2660 Grant Rd Ste D Mountain View CA 94040-4315 Office Phone: 650-938-6244.

ABEL, MARY ELLEN KATHRYN, quality control executive, chemist; b. Cleve., Nov. 3, 1949; d. Arthur L. and Dorothy Virginia (DeLura) Jaklic; m. Burton E. Abel, June 22, 1990; stepchildren: Stephanie, Russell E., Christopher A., Darrell A.; 1 child, Matthew Anthony. AA with honors, Lakeland C.C., 1985; BS in Chemistry magna cum laude, Lake Erie Coll., Painesville, Ohio, 1991. Lab technician W.S. Tyler Inc., Cleve., 1969-71, C-E Tyler, Cleve., 1974-76; quality control mgr., environ. coord. Morton Salt, Painesville, 1977—. Treas. com. mem. Boy Scouts Am., 1988-90, sr. mem. explorer scouts marksmanship post, 1987-90, sec. local com., 1987-90; mem. Lake County Indsl. Cmty. Awareness Emergency Response Adv. Panel, 1987-90, 2000—; mem. citizens' rep. Lake County Solid Waste Policy Bd., 2000—. Mem. NAFE, AAUW, Am. Chem. Soc., Gold Wing Road Riders Assn. Republican. Roman Catholic. Avocations: traveling, photography, tutoring math. Home: 391 Manhattan Pkwy Painesville OH 44077-5024 Office: Morton Salt A Rohm and Haas Co PO Box 428 Grand River OH 44045-0428 E-mail: mabel@mortonsalt.com.

ABELES, KIM VICTORIA, artist; b. Richmond Heights, Mo., Aug. 28, 1952; d. Burton Noel Wright and Frances Elizabeth (Sander) Hoffman. BFA in Painting, Ohio U., 1974; MFA in Studio Art, U. Calif., Irvine, 1980. Free-lance artist, L.A., 1975—. Lectr. varius schs. and art ctrs., 1980—; vis. disting. artist Calif. State U., Fullerton, 1985-87; assoc. prof. Calif. State U., Northridge, 1998—. Author, illustrator Crafts, Cookery and 'Country Living, 1976, Kim Abeles, 1988, Kim Abeles: Encyclopedia Persona, 1993, author, photographer: Impressions, 1979, work featured in Artery, 1979, Pacific Poetry and Fiction Review, 1980, Fiction Internat., 1985, artist (one-woman shows) U. Calif., Irvine, 1979, 1980, Mcpl. Art Gallery, L.A., 1981, L.A. City Hall, 1982, Phyllis Kind Gallery, Chgo., 1983, Karl Bornstein Gallery, Santa Monica, Calif., 1983, 1985, 1987, (one-woman shows) Pepperdine U., Malibu, Calif., 1985, A.I.R. Gallery, N.Y.C., 1986, Chapman Coll., Orange, Calif., 1986, Mount St. Mary's Coll., L.A., 1987, Atlanta Pavilion, 1990, Calif. Mus. of Sci. and Industry, L.A., 1991, Laguna Art Mus. Satellite Gallery, Costa Mesa, Calif., 1991, Turner-Krull Gallery, L.A., 1992, Lawrence Miller Gallery, N.Y.C., 1992, Santa Monica Mus. Art (15 yr. survey), L.A., 1993, Nat. Mus. Fine Arts, Santiago, Chile, 1996, Mus. Modern Art, Rio de Janeiro, 1996, Cmplejo Cultural Recoleta, Buenos Aires, 1986, Centro Cutural Consolidado, Caracas, 1997, Cepa Gallery, Buffalo, 1998, A.R.T., Inc., N.Y.C., 1989, Contemporary Arts Ctr., Cin., 2000, Art Resources Transfer, N.Y.C., 2001, Intersection, San Francisco, 2001, Calif. Sci. Ctr., L.A., 2000—01, Coll. Environ. Design, Calif. Poly. U., Pomona, 2002, (commd.) Marriott Hotels, 1999, City of Pasadena, 1999, San Fernando Valley Constituent Svc. Ctr., 2001, Marvin Braude San Fernando Valley Constituent Svc. Ctr., 2001—03, City of Pasadena, 2002, (exhibitions) Mus. of Contemporary Art, L.A., L.A. County Mus. Art, Calif. African-Am. Mus., Allen Meml. Art Mus., Ohio, (group shows) Silpakorn U., Bangkok, 2002, co-author Surface tension Problematics of Site, 2003. Honored for Outstanding Student Rsch. & Creative Achievement U. Calif., 1979; recipient U.S. Steel award Exhbn. of the Associated Artists of pitts., 1977, Clean Air award Air Quality Mgmt. Dist., Calif., 1992; hand Hollow Found. fellow, 1984, Design Team fellow Panorama City Libr., Calif., 1992-93, J. Paul Getty Trust Fund for the Visual Arts fellow, 1994; Pollock-Krasner Found. grantee, 1990, Calif. Arts Coun. grantee, 1990, L.A. Cultural Affairs grantee, 1991, 95, 96, U.S. Info. Agy. grantee, 1995-97; commissioned by Panorama City Pub. Libr., L.A., 1993, Met. Transp. Authority, L.A., 1995, Dept. Transp., L.A., 2000; recipient Richard Neutra award for Profl. Excellence, 2001. E-mail: kimabeles@earthlink.net.

ABELL, ANNA ELLEN, primary school educator; b. Phila., Nov. 24, 1945; d. Elwood George Daeche and Anna Pauline Pflaumer; m. DeLeon Abell, Aug. 24, 1974; children: Sara Abigail, Beth Ann, Rebecca Nöel. B in Music Edn., Westminster Choir Coll., 1967; postgrad., Assn. Christian Sch. Internat., Piscataway Unified Sch. Dist. Educator Piscataway (N.J.) Sch. Dist., 1967—74; pvt. music tchr. Orange Coast Christian Sch., San Clemente, Calif., 1982—89, 6th grade tchr., 1989—90; jr. high tchr. Dana Point (Calif.) Christian Sch., Calif., 1991—94; 5th grade tchr. Capo Beach Calvary Sch., Dana Point, 1994—98, kindergarten tchr., 1998—. Distbr. JuicePlus/NSA, Dana Point, 2001—. Choral mem. Sanctuary Choir, San Clemente, Calif., 1990—; bell choir mem. Sounds of Bronze, San Clemente, Calif., 1992—. Mem.: Assn. Christian Schs. Internat. Republican. Presbyterian. Avocations: cooking, reading, health and nutrition.

ABELL, JAN MEISTERHEIM, architect; b. Chgo. d. Philip and Dolores (Krumdick) Meisterheim. BArch, Ohio U., 1969. Registered architect, N.Y., Fla. Architect apprentice Verster, Djikstra, Cannegieter, Amsterdam, The Netherlands, 1970-72, Stevens, Bertin, O'Connell, Rochester, N.Y., 1972-76; architect McElvy, Jennewein Stefany, Howard, Tampa, Fla., 1976-79; prin., owner Abell Garcia Partnership Architects, Tampa, 1980—. Adj. faculty mem. U. South Fla., Tampa, 1989-96; Beinecke Reeves disting. chair in Archtl. Preservation, U. Fla., 1995-97. Prin. works include Port Tampa City Libr. (Fla. Trust Outstanding Preservation Project award), B.C. Graham Elem. Sch. (Outstanding Preservation Project award), restoration of Sunrise Theatre, Ft. Pierce, Fla., restoration of St. Paul AME Ch. (Fla. Trust Outstanding Preservation Project award), Leiman Wilson House (Gt. Am. Home award Nat. Trust for Hist. Preservation, Outstanding Preservation Project award Hillsborough County Planning Commn.), Edson Keith Estate, Sarasota, Fla. (Fla. Preservation award), Founder's House, Koreshan State Hist. Park, Estero, Fla. (Outstanding award for Restoration, Fla. Trust for Hist. Preservation), master plan for Hist. Tampa Bay Hotel, Writers Studio (Hillsborough County Planning award 1995); exhbns. include Women in Arch., Washington, 1987, Fla./Caribbean Arch., San Juan, P.R. Recipient numerous awards for arch., 1979—, Women of Achievement award Bus. and Profl. Women's Assn., 1982, Fla. Trust award, 1995. Fellow AIA (juror Broward County chpt. Honor awards 1990, Nat. AIA Honor awards 1993, Nat. Com. on Design co-chmn. publs., Medal of Honor Fla. Cen. chpt. 1990), AIA Fla. Assn. (Comty. Svc. award 1979). Office: Abell Garcia Architects 2201 W Dekle Ave Tampa FL 33606-3118

ABELL, SARA NIGHTINGALE, music educator, musician; b. Toledo, Ohio, Apr. 28, 1952; d. Homer Scott and Alice (Walbolt) Nightingale; m. Ralph "Casey" Abell, May 10, 1986; children: Alison Margaret, Nathan Samuel. MusB, Bowling Green State U., 1974; MusM, Coll. Conservatory Music U. Cin., 1978, D in Music Edn., 1993. Elem. music tchr. Toledo Pub. Schs., 1974—76; music edn. tchg. asst. Coll.-Conservatory Music, U. Cin., 1976—78; elem. music tchr. Mt. Healthy Pub. Schs., Cin, 1979—84; tchr. pre-sch. music classes Musical Arts Ctr., Cin, 1980—82; music edn. tchg. asst. Coll.-Conservatory of Music U. Cin, 1983—86; pre-sch. music tchr. Little Lambs Children's Ctr., Columbus, Ohio, 1994—97; pre-sch. and elem. music tchr. Acad. Fine Arts, Highland Village, Tex., 1999—2002; dir. music Trinity Presbyterian Ch., Flower Mound, Tex., 2002—. Mem.: Tex. Music Educators Assn., Music Educators Nat. Conf., Sigma Alpha Iota (Denton Alumni chpt.), Ariel Club in Tex. Fedn. Women's Clubs.

ABELLA, MERCEDES, occupational therapist; b. Baracoa, Oriente, Cuba, Apr. 6, 1926; came to U.S., 1951; d. Anacleto and Bruniquilda (Oliveros) A.; m. George Michael Selizki, May 21, 1980. Diploma, Escuela del Hogar, Havana, 1949; cert. in occupational therapy, NYU, 1954, BS, 1959, MA, 1972. Staff occupational therapist FDR Rehab. Ctr., Havana, 1954-56, Queens (N.Y.) Gen. Hosp., 1957; sr. occupational therapist Rusk Inst. Rehab. Medicine, N.Y.C., 1958-59; supr. St. Mary's Hosp. for Children, Bayside, N.Y., 1960; cons. WHO, Madrid, Spain, 1961-64; supr., student coord. Rusk Inst. Rehab. Medicine, N.Y.C., 1964-67, asst. dir., 1976—. Cons. World Rehab. Fund, C.Am. and China, 1970-90; mem. Accreditation Coun. for Occupational Therapy Edn., 1994—. Recipient award of excellence New Eng. Ednl. Coun., Supr. of Yr. award N.Y. Ednl. Coun., ABREU award, 1995; Kellogg Found. fellow, 1951-54. Fellow Am. Occupational Therapy Assn. (vice chair career mobility 1982-87), N.Y. State Occupational Therapy Assn. (chair state conf. 1994). Baptist. Avocations: travel, reading, needlework/sewing. Office: Rusk Inst Rehab Medicine 400 E 34th St New York NY 10016-4998

ABELS, DEBBIE, publishing executive; married; 1 child. MusB, Duke U. Various positions Charlotte (N.C.) Observer, v.p. human resources. Cellist The Western Piedmont Symphony. Mem.: Internat. House (bd. dirs.). Office: Charlotte Observer 600 S Tryon St Charlotte NC 28202-1842*

ABERNATHY, DIXIE FRIEND, elementary school educator, principal; Sci. tchr. Southwest Jr. High Sch., Gastonia, NC; asst. principal Forest Heights Elementary; principal Belmont Middle Sch., 1998—2000, N. Belmont Elementary, Belmont, NC, 2000—. Named N.C. State Sci. Tchr. of Yr., 1993. Office: N Belmont Elementary 210 School St Belmont NC 28012

ABERNATHY, KATHLEEN Q. government agency administrator; b. Louisville, June 5, 1956; m. Charles Abernathy, June 30, 1984; 1 child, Julia 1 stepchild, Charles Jr. BS magna cum laude, Marquette U., Milw., 1982; JD, Cath. U. Am., Washington, 1984. Assoc. Kadison, Pfaelzer Woodard Quinn & Rossi, 1986—87, Thelen, Marrin, Johnson and Bridges, 1987—88; dir. fed. affairs COMSAT, 1988—90; spl. asst. to gen. counsel FCC, Washington, legal advisor to chmn. James H. Quello and Commr. Sherrie P. Marshall, 1992—93, commr., 2001—; v.p. fed. regulatory AirTouch Comm., Inc., 1993—98; v.p. regulatory affairs U.S. West, Inc.; ptnr. Wilkinson Barker Knauer, 1999—2000; v.p. pub. policy BroadBank Office Comm., Inc., 2000—01. Adj. prof. Georgetown U. Law Ctr., Washington, Cath. U. Am., Washington. Named one of Most Powerful Women in TV, Electronic Media mag.; recipient Forerunner Accolade, Women in Cable and Telecom., Milestone award, Cath. U. Am. Sch. Law. Mem.: Washington Bar Assn., Fed. Comm. Bar Assn. (past pres.). Office: Fed Comm Commn 445 12th St SW Washington DC 20554*

ABERNATHY, VICKI MARIE, retired nurse; b. L.A., Feb. 14, 1949; d. James David and Margaret Helen (Quider) Abernathy; m. Dirk Klaus Ernst Wiese, Aug. 15, 1968 (div. 1973); 1 child, Zoe Erde. Student, U. Calif., Riverside, 1966-67, L.A. City Coll., 1968-69; AA in Nursing, Riverside City Coll., 1971-74. RN, Calif.; cert. med.-surg. nurse. Staff nurse Riverside (Calif.) County Hosp., 1974, Oceanside (Calif.) Community Hosp., 1974-76; with Scripps Hosp., Encinitas, Calif., 1976—2001, ambulatory surgery unit and endoscopy coord., 1981-94, staff nurse short stay unit and endoscopy, 1994—2001, ret., 2001. Mem. Quali Bot. Gardens. Mem. San Diego Zool. Soc., San Elijo Lagoon Conservancy, Birch Aquarium at Scripps, Cardiff Edn Found., Quail Botanical Gardens. Democrat. Avocations: camping, fishing, travel, reading, grandchildren.

ABERNETHY, IRENE MARGARET, civic worker, retired county official; b. Ord, Nebr., Mar. 28, 1924; d. Glen Dayton and Margaret Lillian (Jones) Auble; m. Don R. Abernethy, Aug. 8, 1954 (dec. Nov. 1980); children: Jill Adele Abernethy Johnson, Ted Verne (dec.). BA cum laude, Hastings Coll., 1946; postgrad., U. Nebr., 1950-53. Tchr. Ord High Sch., 1946-50, Scottsbluff (Nebr.) High Sch., 1950-55, Grand Island (Nebr.) Sr. High Sch., 1961-62; mem. Hall County Bd. Suprs., Grand Island, 1979-98, chmn., 1984, 95; ret., 1998. Vice-chair Hall County Rep. Ctrl. Com., Grand Island, 1971-73; chair campaign Congresswoman Virginia Smith for Hall County, 1974-80; sr. v.p. Nebr. Rep. Founders Day, Lincoln, 1981; chair Gov.'s Juv. Justice Adv. Group, Lincoln, 1981-91; mem. Nebr. Commn. on Law Enforcement and Criminal Justice, Lincoln, 1970-91, Nebr. Commn. on Local Govt. Innovation and Restructuring, 1997-2000; bd. dirs. Head Start, 1979-2002, Hall County Leadership Tomorrow, 1990-94, Indsl. Found., 1991, College Park, 1991-98, Cmty. Help Ctr., 1991-96, Family Violence Coalition, 1993-2002, Midland Area Agy. on Aging, 1993-95; adv. com. Region III Mental Health Bd., quality rev. team, 1996-99; active Nat. Coalition State Juvenile Justice Adv. Groups, 1981-91, Partners in Cmty. Planning, 1994-97, Grand Island Area Edn. 2000, Grand Island Bd. Edn., 1998-2000; task force on needs Heartland United Way, Hall County Hist. Soc., 2003. Named Woman of Yr., Grand Island Independent, 1980, Bus. and Profl. Woman, Grand Island, 1980, Beta Sigma Phi, 1982, Alpha Delta Kappa, 1982, 2000, Nebr. chpt. NASW, 1983, Merit Mother of Nebr., 2002; recipient Svc. to Mankind award Sertoma, 1983-84, recognition award PTA, 1988, Outstanding Cmty. Svc. award Rotary, 1985, Cmty. Leadership award Ak-Sar-Ben, 1995, Outstanding Alumni award Hastings Coll., 1996, Hall County Rep. Hall of Fame award, 1997, Disting. Citizenship award Grand Island Elks, 1997, cert. of appreciation Grand Island-Hall County Dept. Health, 1998, A.L. Carlisle Child Advocacy award Coalition for Juvenile Justice, 2001; honoree Nebr. Commn. on Status of Women, 1998, 2000; recipient Spirit of Youth award Girls and Boys Town, 2000. Mem. LWV (local pres. 1962-64, state bd. dirs. 1965-69), AAUW (local pres. 1966-68, state bd. dirs. 1970-71), YWCA (local pres. 1974-75, Woman of Distinction award 1988), Nebr. Assn. County Ofcls. (pres. 1985, Pres.'s award for Disting. Leadership 1997, County Ofcl. of Yr. award 1998), Assn. Child Abuse Prevention, Grand Island Area C. of C. (bd. dirs. 1992-94, Disting. Svc. award 1999), Philanthropic Ednl. Orgn. (local pres. 1970-71), Rotary, Woodland Golf Club Ladies Assn. (champion 1961, 63, 64, local pres. 1963), Riverside Golf Club (champion 1969), Grand Island Woman's Club (past bd. dirs.), Pi Lambda Theta. Republican. Methodist. Avocations: travel, music, photography, golf, spectator sports. Home: 707 S Blaine St Grand Island NE 68803-6146

ABERNETHY, SHARRON GRAY, language educator; b. Tishomingo, Miss., Mar. 22, 1945; d. Dennis F. Gray (deceased) and Lyda Waddell Gray; m. Elliott Lee Abernethy, Jr.; children: Damon, Ryan (Deceased). BA, Secondary Edn., U. North Ala., Florence, 1966; MA in Latin and Am. Studies, U. Ala., Tuscaloosa, 1971, PhD, 1982, EdS, 1976; cert., U. Carlos III, Madrid, 2000. Cert. ESADE Barcelona, Spain, 1999. Spanish/Latin Am. history tchr. Deshler H.S., Tuscumbia, Ala., 1966—68; Spanish/English tchr. Eastwood Jr. H.S., Tuscaloosa, 1968—68; rsch. asst. U. Ala., Tuscaloosa, 1969—70, tchg. asst., 1970—73, Spanish instr., 1977, Spanish prof. (part-time) Huntsville, 1988—90, 1994—96, Spanish prof., 1996—, departmental internat. internship coord., 2001—; Spanish/Am. history tchr. Eastwood Jr. H.S., Tuscaloosa, 1973—76; Spanish prof. Miss. State U., Meridian, 1982—84; Spanish instr. Meridian H.S., 1982—85; owner Sir Speedy Printing franchise, Pittsburg, 1986—87, Huntsville, 1988—93; reviewer John Wiley & Sons, Inc., New York, NY, 2002—. Faculty advisor Phi Sigma Iota, Huntsville, 1997—; participant numerous confs./workshops on curricular and instrnl. improvement, 1999—. Vol. St. Jude's Children's Hosp., Memphis, 1977—78, Riley Hosp., Meridian, 1981—83; bd. dirs. Harris Home for Children, Huntsville, 1990—92; supporter/vol. Chi-Ho Home for Children, Huntsville, 1988—2001; mem./officer Huntsville West Kiwanis, Huntsville, 1988—94; chair Huntsville West Kiwanis/Chi-Ho Benefit Golf Tournament, Huntsville, 1990—93; leader Cub Scouts, Meridian, 1981—84; mem. Rep. Women, Huntsville, 1988—89; tchr., deacon, com. mem. adminstrn., stewardship, fin., hospitality, pastoral search coms., co-editor 1993 ch. history/dire First Presbyn. Ch., Huntsville, 1988—2002. Mem.: Naita (UAH liaison to North Ala. Internat. Trade Assn. 1999—, bd. dirs. 2003, 1999—), Exec. Women Internat. (VIP award 2001). Republican. Presbyterian. Avocations: piano, travel, golf, culinary arts.

ABERT, AMBER CHRISTINE, home remodeling contractor; b. East Alton, Ill., Sept. 15, 1969; d. Jerry Lee Abert and Bette Lee (Gause) Schenk. AS in Radio Broadcasting, Lewis & Clark C.C., Godfrey, Ill., 1990; B in Gen. Studies, S.E. Mo. State U., 1992. V.p. sales Jerry Abert Siding & Window Co., East Alton, Ill., 1990—. Mem. NAFE, Jr. League of Greater Alton (pub. rels. chair, 1994-96), Nat. Auctioneer Assn., Ill. State Auctioneer Assn., Gen. Federated Woman's Club (corr. sec. Dist. 22 2002-2004), Wood River Women's Club (pres. 2002—). Avocation: auctioneer. Office: Jerry Abert Siding & Window 631 Broadway East Alton IL 62024-1220 Address: 721 Halloran Ave Wood River IL 62095-1762

ABEY, KATHY MICHELE, district representative, congressional caseworker; d. George Melvin Abey and Catherine Harrison-Abey Windsor; children: Loren Michele Crutchley, Michael Jarrod Horney, Casey Wade Horney, William Ryan. Cert. paralegal, Chesapeake Coll., 1988. Cert. compensation claims specialist U.S. Dept. of Labor. Asst. mgr. Hardees/Imasco Foods, Inc, Stevensville, Md., 1984—87; legal asst. The Legal Aid Bur., Balt., 1988—95; hearings specialist Health Mgmt. Assocs., Balt., 1995—98; paralegal, legal asst. Conrad and Chirumbole, Gaithersburg, Md., 1998; hearings specialist Health Mgmt. Assocs./DEAP Program, Balt., 1998—2000; congl. caseworker, dist. rep. U.S. Ho. of Reps., Bel Air, Md., 2000—. Vol. Libr. of Congress Vets. History Project, Washington, 2002; sec. Eric Rada Vocat. Scholarship Fund, Queenstown, Md., 1981—82; vol. photographer Chicamicomico Life Saving Sta., Rodanthe, NC, 2000; mem. client cmty. adv. bd. Legal Aid Bur., Balt., 1983—84; bd. dirs. Boy Scouts of Am. Troop 278, Stevensville, Md., 1990—94; sec. Queen Anne's County H.S. Football Boosters, Centreville, Md., 1998—2000, Queen Anne's County H.S. Athletic Boosters, 2000—01; pres. Queen Anne's County H.S. Football Boosters, 2000—01; mem., client adv. Dorchester County AIDS Found., Cambridge, 1998—2000; bd. mem. Queen Anne's County Consumer Adv. Bd., Centreville, 1998—99. Named Fair Grand Champion in Photography, Queen Anne County, 2003. Republican. Methodist. Avocations: photography, reading, camping, music/theater, travel.

ABISH, CECILE, artist; b. N.Y.C. m. Walter Abish. B.F.A., Bklyn. Coll., 1953. Instr. art Queens Coll. Vis. artist U. Mass, Amherst, Cooper Union, Harvard U. Solo exhbns. include Newark Coll. Engring., 1968, Inst. Contemporary Art, Boston, 1974, U. Md., 1975, Alessandra Gallery, N.Y.C., 1977, Wright State U., Dayton, Ohio, 1978, Carpenter Ctr., Cambridge, Mass., 1979, Anderson Gallery, Va. Commonwealth U., Richmond, 1981, SUNY-Stony Brook, 1982, Ctr. for Creative Photography, Tucson, 1984, Books & Co., N.Y.C., 1996; group exhbns.: Detroit Inst. Art, 1969, Aldrich Mus. Art, 1971, 10 Bleecker St., N.Y.C., 1972, Lakeview Ctr. Arts, Peoria, Ill., 1972, Bykert Gallery, N.Y.C., 1971-74, Michael Walls Gallery, N.Y.C., 1975, Fine Arts Bldg. Gallery, N.Y.C., 1976, Mus. Modern Art, N.Y.C., 1976, Hudson River Mus., 1979, Atlanta Arts Festival, 1980, New Mus., N.Y.C., 1980, 81, Kuntsgebaude, Stuttgart, Fed. Republic

Germany, 1981, Long Beach (Calif.) Mus., 1983, Edith C. Blum Art Inst., Bard Coll., Annandale-on-Hudson, N.Y., 1984, Mus. Modern Kunst, Vienna, Austria, 1985, U. R.I., Kingston, 1985, Art Defense Galleries, Paris, 1993, Architektur Zentrum, Vienna, 1993, Artists Space, N.Y.C., 1994, Islip Art Mus., N.Y., 1995, P.S. 1 Contemporary Art Ctr., N.Y., 1999; numerous commns.; represented in permanent collections; published photo works: Firsthand, 1978, Chinese Crossing, 1986, 99: The New Meaning, 1990. Nat. Endowment Arts fellow, 1975, 77, 80; CAPS fellow, 1975. Mem. Coll. Art Assn. Office: Cooper Station PO Box 485 New York NY 10276-0485

ABLES-FLATT, JEAN ANN, commissioner; Cert. geneal. record specialist. Commr. Tex. Hist. Commn., Austin, 1999—. Vol. genealogist Terrell Pub. Libr.; chmn. Kaufman County Hist. Commn.; historic sites chmn. Terrell Heritage Soc.; historian, archivist, arts/drama coord. First United Meth. Ch. of Terrell; bd. dirs. Preservation Tex. Recipient Heritage Jubilee award, City of Terrell, award, Terrell C. of C. Office: PO Box 12276 Austin TX 78711-2276

ABLOW, ROZ KAROL (ROSELYN KAROL ABLOW), painter, curator; b. Allentown, Pa. BA, Bennington Coll., 1954; student, Boston U. Instr. Bunting Inst., 1988, Newton Arts Ctr., Mass., 1989-92, New Arts Ctr., Newton, Mass., 1993-95. Curator New Arts Ctr., Newton, Mass., 1994. Solo exhbns. at Amherst (Mass.) Coll., 1976, Impressions Gallery, Mass., 1979, Clark GAllery, Lincoln, Mass., 1984, Pine Manor Coll., Brookline, Mass., 1991, Miami U., Oxford, Ohio, 1995, Art Guild of Old Forge, N.Y., 2002; group shows include Smithsonian Traveling Exhbn., 1978-80, Fitchburg Art Mus., 1988, The Bunting Inst., Radcliffe Coll., 1988, David Brown Gallery, Provincetown, Mass., 1988, Pratt Graphic Ctr. Internat. Monotype Show, 1989, Gallery 30, Burlingame, Calif., 1993, New Art Ctr., Newton, Mass., 1994, others; represented in permanent collections Mobil Corp., Chemical Bank, N.Y., New Eng. Mutual Life Ins. Co., Boston, Conn. Gen. Life, Hartford, Sears, Roebuck & Co., Chgo., Broadway Crown Plaza Hotel, N.Y., The Pucker Gallery, Boston. Bunting Inst. fellow Radcliffe Coll., 1988; grantee Mass. Arts Lottery Coun., 1990-91. Address: Pucker Gallery Boston MA 02116

ABOLINS, RUTA, archivist; b. Seattle, Wash., Jan. 1, 1962; d. Otto Abolins and Dzidra Radzins Kunz. BFA in Film, U. Wis., Milw., 1986; MA in Popular Culture, Bowling Green State U., Ohio, 1989; MA in Libr. and Info. Studies, U. Wis., Madison, 1998. Media archivist, Wis. ctr. for film & theater rsch. U. of Wis., Madison, 1990—98; media archivist, Walter J. Brown media archives and Peabody awards collection U. of Ga., Athens, Ga., 1998—2000, dir. Walter J. Brown media archives and Peabody awards collection, 2000—. Founding mem. Athens Film Found. Mem.: Assn. of Moving Image Archivists (bd. mem. 1999—2003). Avocations: travel, hiking. Office: Main Library U Ga 325 South Jackson St Athens GA 30602-1641 Office Phone: 706-542-4757. E-mail: abolins@uga.edu.

ABOOD, DENISE MAROON, finance company executive; b. Cleve., Oct. 7, 1961; d. George David and Martha Ellen (Maroon) A. BA magna cum laude, Wittenberg U., 1983. CPA, Ohio. Sr. auditor, supr. Coopers & Lybrand, Cleve., 1983-87; sr. fin. analyst The Progressive Corp., Cleve., 1987-89, investment contr., 1989-94; treas. TIG Ins. Co., Dallas, 1994-95, v.p., CFO comml., 1995-96; sr. v.p., COO PW Fin. Solutions, Dallas, 1996—. Mem. AICPA, Dallas Soc., La Cima Club. Avocations: golf, weight training, music, art appreciation.

ABOUSSIE, MARILYN, retired state justice; b. Wichita Falls, Tex., June 9, 1948; m. John A. Hay, Jr., Dec. 9, 1973; 1 child, John A. III. BA, Midwestern U., 1969; JD, U. Tex., 1974. Bar: Tex. 1974. Assoc. Foreman, Dyess, Prewett, Rosenberg & Henderson, Houston, 1974-76; pvt. practice San Angelo, Tex., 1976-78; ptnr. Smith, Davis, Rose, Finley & Hofmann, San Angelo, Tex., 1978-83; judge 340th Dist. Ct., San Angelo, 1983-86; justice Tex. Ct. Appeals, Austin, 1986-98, chief justice, 1998—2004. Named Outstanding Juvenile Judge, Tex. Inst. on Children and Youth, 1986, Outstanding Alumnus, Midwestern State U., 1987. Mem. ABA, State Bar Assn. of Tex. Episcopalian. Office: Tex Ct Appeals Supreme Ct Bldg PO Box 12547 Austin TX 78711-2547

ABRAHAM, KAREN A. university administrator; b. Los Alamos, N.Mex., May 12, 1945; d. Lawrence T. and Wadette G. A. BS, U. N.Mex., 1967, MA, 1968, EdD, 1971; grad., Havard U., 1981. Asst. dean students U. N.Mex., Albuquerque, 1970-72, assoc. dean students, dir. student activities, 1972-87, dir. alumni rels., exec. dir. alumni assn., 1987—. Mem. faculty staff Alumni Rels. Summer Inst. Coun. for Advancement and Support of Edn., Williamstown, Mass., 1996-2000. Recipient fellowship Dept. Edn., 1967-70; Woman on the Move award YWCA Albuquerque, 1992, Student Svc. award U. N.Mex., 1991, Regent's Meritorious Svc. medal, 1982, Lobo award Mortar Bd., 1988. Mem. Am. Soc. Assn. Execs., Coun. Advancement and Support of Edn. (bd. trustees 1993-96), Coun. Alumni Assn. (exec. bd. trustees 1995-97). Presbyterian. Home: 815 Suzanne Ln SE Albuquerque NM 87123-4502 Office: U NMex Alumni Hodgin Hl # 111 Albuquerque NM 87131-0001

ABRAHAM, KATHARINE GAIL, economics educator; b. Dayton, Ohio, Aug. 28, 1954; d. William Hamilton and Roberta Taylor (Grannis) A.; m. Graham Neil Horkley, May 25, 1985; children: Ian Robert Horkley, Benjamin William Horkley. Student, Carleton Coll., 1972-74; BS, Iowa State U., 1976; PhD, Harvard U., 1982. Asst. prof. Sloan Sch. Mgmt. MIT, Cambridge, Mass., 1980-85; rsch. assoc. Brookings Inst., Washington, 1985-87; assoc. prof. econs. U. Md., College Park, 1987-91, prof. econs., 1991-97. Commnr. labor stats. U.S. Bur. Labor Stats., 1993—; rsch. assoc. Nat. Bur. Econ. Rsch., 1987-95. Author 2 books; assoc. editor Quar. Jour. Econs., 1985-92; bd. reviewers Indsl. Rels., 1984-93; contbr. articles to profl. jours. Named Outstanding Young Alumnus Iowa State U., 1988; recipient Disting. Achievement Citation award Iowa State U. Alumni Assn., 1999; grad. fellow NSF, 1977-80. Mem. Am. Econ. Assn., Indsl. Rels. Rsch. Assn., Com. on the Status Women in the Econs. Profession. Office: US Bur Labor Stats 2 Massachusetts Ave NE Washington DC 20212-0022

ABRAHAM, NOËL JEANETTE, social worker; d. J. D. and M. H. Abraham. BA, St. Mary's U. of Minn., 1992; MSW, Loyola U., 1994; Master's, Loyola U., Chgo., 2002. Cert. sch. social worker Ill., LCSW Ill. Internship Early Childhood Family Edn. Program, St. Mary's U. of Minn., Winona, 1991—92, House of the Good Shepherd, 1992—93; social worker Luth. Social Svcs. of Ill., Chgo., 1993—95, Children's Home and Aid Soc. of Ill., Chgo., 1994—2000, Uhlich Children's Home, Chgo., 2000—01; externship Mannheim Mid. Sch., Melrose Pk., Ill., 2001—02; part-time social worker Met. Family Svcs., Chgo., 2001—02, Roy Elem. Sch., Northlake, Ill., 2002; elem. and mid. sch. social worker Hillside (Ill.) Acad., 2002—. Pres. Loyola U. Chgo. Sch. of Social Work Alumni Bd. Dirs., 1997—99, sec., 1998—99. Mem.: Sch. Social Work Assn. of Am., Ill. Assn. of Social Workers, Nat. Assn. of Social Workers (Ill. Chpt.), Alpha Delta Omega. Democrat. Roman Catholic. Avocations: reading, exercise, music, gardening, walking. Office: Hillside Acad 431 N Hillside Ave Hillside IL 60646

ABRAHAMSON, SHIRLEY SCHLANGER, state supreme court chief justice; b. N.Y.C., Dec. 17, 1933; d. Leo and Ceil (Sauerteig) Schlanger; m. Seymour Abrahamson, Aug. 26, 1953; 1 son, Daniel Nathan. AB, NYU, 1953; JD, Ind. U., 1956; SJD, U. Wis., 1962. Bar: Ind. 1956, N.Y. 1961, Wis. 1962. Asst. dir. Legis. Drafting Research Fund, Columbia U. Law Sch., 1957-60; since practiced in Madison, Wis., 1962-76; mem. firm LaFollette, Sinykin, Anderson & Abrahamson, 1962-76; justice Supreme Ct. Wis., Madison, 1976-96, chief justice, 1996—; prof. U. Wis. Sch. Law, 1966-92; v.p. conf. Chief Justices, 2002—. Bd. visitors Ind. U. Sch. Law, 1972—02, U. Miami Sch. Law, 1982-97, U. Chgo. Law Sch., 1988-92, Brigham Young U., Sch. Law, 1986-88, Northwestern U. Law Sch., 1989-94; chmn. Wis. Rhodes Scholarship Com., 1992-95; chmn. nat. adv. com. on ct.-adjudicated and ct.-ordered health care George Washington U. Ctr. Health Policy, Washington, 1993-95; mem. DNA adv. bd. FBI, U.S. Dept. Justice, 1995-2001; bd. dirs. Inst. Jud. Adminstrn., Inc., NYU Sch. Law; chair Nat. Inst. Justice's Commn. Future DNA Evidence, 1997-2001. Editor: Constitutions of the United States (National and State) 2 vols, 1962. Mem. study group program of rsch., mental health and the law John D. and Catherine T. MacArthur Found., 1988-96; mem. coun. fund for rsch. on dispute resolution Ford Found., 1987-91; bd. dirs. Wis. Civil Liberties Union, 1968-72; mem. ct. reform adv. panel Internat. Human Rights Law Group Cambodia Project, 1995-97. Mem. ABA (coun., sect. legal edn. and admissions to bar 1976-86, mem. commn. on undergrad. edn. in law and the humanities 1978-79, standing com. on pub. edn. 1991-95, mem. commn. on access to justice/2000 1993—02, mem. adv. bd. Ctrl. and East European law initiative 1994-99, mem. consortium on legal svcs. and the public 1995-2001, vice-chair ABA Coalition for Justice 1997-2000), Wis. Bar Assn., Dane County Bar Assn., 7th Cir. Bar Assn., Nat. Assn. Women Judges, Am. Law Inst. (mem. coun. 1985—), Am. Philos. Soc., Am. Acad. Arts and Scis.*

ABRAHM, JANET LEE, hematologist, oncologist, palliative care specialist, educator; b. San Francisco, Mar. 14, 1949; d. Paul Milton and Helen Lesser Abrahm; m. David Rytman Slavitt, Apr. 16, 1978. Student, U. Calif., Berkeley, 1969; BA, U. Calif., San Francisco, 1970, MD, 1973. Diplomate in internal medicine, hematology and oncology Am. Bd. Internal Medicine; ciplomate Am. Bd. Hospice and Palliative Medicine. Intern and resident medicine Mass. Gen. Hosp., Boston, 1973-75, hematology fellow, 1975-76; chief resident medicine Moffitt Hosp. U. Calif., San Francisco, 1976-77; hematology/oncology fellow Hosp. U. Pa., Phila., 1977-80; postdoctoral fellow medicine U. Pa., Phila., 1977-78, postdoctoral trainee medicine, 1977-80, asst. prof. medicine, 1980-86, Hosp. U. Pa. and VA Med. Ctr., Phila., 1986-89, assoc. prof. medicine, 1989-2000; attending physician Hosp. U. Pa., Phila., 1980-93; from staff physician to faculty scholar Phila. VA Med. Ctr., 1982—97, faculty scholar Project Death in Am., 1997—2000; med. dir. Wissahickon Hospice UPHS, 1998-2000; assoc. prof. medicine and anesthesia Harvard Med. Sch., 2001—; attending physician Dana-Farber Cancer Inst., Brigham and Women's Hosp., Boston, 2001—. Prin. investigator Palliative Care Fellowship Grant, 1996-2001, 03—; mem. concensus panel on End-of-Life Care, ACP, 1997—; chmn. adv. com. Cancer Care VA Dist. 4, 1987-90; sec. subspecialty bd. hematology Am. Bd. Internal Medicine, 1987-92, sec. SEP subcom. hematology, 1993-95; mem. tech. adv. group Cancer Care Region 1, 1990-95; med. oncology cons. cancer pain consultation panel Ctr. for Continuing Edn. U. Pa. Sch. Nursing, 1990-2000; mem. quality of life and cancer edn. com. Pa. Cancer Adv. Bd., 1994-97; mem. human resources coun. of VHA VISN, 1996-97, councillor Region 1, AVOCOM, 1996-97, TAPC mem., 2000-02, Am. Acad. Hospice and Palliative Medicine, 1999-, ACP, 2000 , others; attending physician Brigham and Women's Hosp., Boston, 2001—; dir. pain and palliative care program Dana-Farber Career Inst., Boston, 2001—; adj. prof. medicine, U. Pa. Sch. Medicine, 2001-. Author: Clinical Care of the Terminal Patient, 1982, Pain Management in Hematology: Basic Principles and Practice, 1990, 1994, 1999, Pain Management in Kelley W. Textbook of Internal Medicine, 1996, 2000, Anemia, Pain Management in Geriatric Secrets, 1996, 2000, 2004, A Physician's Guide to Pain and Symptom Management in Cancer Patients, 2000; contbr. (booklets) Caring for the Terminally Ill Patient at Home-A Guide for Family Caregivers, 1986, Caring for the Cancer Patient at Home - A Guide for Patients and Families, 1986; reviewer New Eng. Jour. Medicine, JAMA, Cancer, Archives Internal Medicine, Annals Internal Medicine; contbr. numerous articles to profl. jours. Recipient Manual award Merck, 1973; Fife Medicine scholar, 1973. Fellow: ACP, Am. Acad. Hospice and Palliative Medicine (bd. dirs.); mem.: Am. Pain Soc., Am. Assn. Cancer Edn. (program com. 1993), Am. Soc. Clin. Oncology, Am. Soc. Clin. Hypnosis, Am. Soc. Hematology, Alpha Omega Alpha, Phi Beta Kappa. Home: 35 West St #5 Cambridge MA 02139 Office: Dana Farber Cancer Inst 44 Binney St Boston MA 02115 E-mail: jabrahm@partners.org.

ABRAMS, DONNA MARIE, art educator; d. Edward Charles and Mary Helen Smith; m. Jeffry Morris Abrams, Apr. 11, 1981; children: Dana Marie, Aaron Edward. BA, Douglass Coll., 1976. Cert. tchr. art N.J. Tchr. art Mt. St. Mary Acad., Watchung, NJ, 1976—. Owner Arts and Crafts by Donna, Gillette, NJ, 1976—. Series children's books on grieving, 1997—98. Named Best in Show in t-shirt design contets, Fabricland, 1990; recipient 4th Pl. award in ornament contest, Suburban News, 1988, Hon. Mention, 1989, 1990, 1st Pl. award, Treasure Island Ornament Contest, 2001. Mem.: Nat. Art Edn. Assn. Roman Catholic. Office: Mt St Mary Acad 1645 Rte 22 and Terrill Rd Watchung NJ 07069

ABRAMS, FAY PFAELZER, art gallery owner, educator; b. Phila., Pa., July 9, 1941; d. Morris Pfaelzer and Marjorie Helen Lesser; m. Jonathan Abrams, June 16, 1962; children: Wendy Paige, Melissa Sue. BA, Mills Coll., 1962; MA, U. N.Mex., 1974. Cert. Tchr. Calif. Tchr. San Francisco Pub. Sch., San Francisco, 1963—64, Boston Pub. Sch., Boston, 1964—67, Albuquerque Pub. Sch., Albuquerque, 1973—74; prin., owner Mariposa Gallery, Inc., Albuquerque, 1974—. Pres. Capitol Arts Found. Mem.: Albuquerque Art Bus. Assn. (bd. dir. 1999—), Albuquerque Conv. & Vis. Bureau. Democrat. Jewish. Office: Mariposa Gallery 3500 Central Ave SE Nob Hill Albuquerque NM 87106-1446 Office Phone: 505-268-6828.

ABRAMS, ROBERTA BUSKY, hospital administrator, nurse; b. Bklyn., Feb. 16, 1937; d. Albert H. and Gladys Busky; m. Robert L. Abrams, June 28, 1959 (div. 1977); children: Susan Abrams Federman, David B. BSN, U. Rochester, 1959; MA, Fairfield U., 1977. Asst. head nurse Jewish Hosp., Bklyn., 1959-60; instr. medicine/surgery Bklyn. Hosp., 1960-62, U. Rochester, N.Y., 1963-64; instr. ob-gyn Malden (Mass.) Hosp. Sch. Nursing, 1965-66; instr. prospective parents ARC, San Rafael, Calif., 1968-69; instr. ob-gyn SUNY, Farmingdale, 1970-71; instr. maternal/child health Stamford (Conn.) Hosp., 1971-75; clinician maternal/child health Lawrence Hosp., Bronxville, N.Y., 1975-78; asst. prof. nursing Ohio Wesleyan U., Delaware, 1981-84; dir. Elizabeth Blackwell Hosp. at Riverside Meth., Columbus, Ohio, 1978-86; dir. nursing Henry Ford Hosp., Detroit, 1986-87, assoc. adminstr. nursing, 1988-92. Sr. ptnr. Health Quad, Inc., 1997—; cons. maternal/child nursing currents Ross Labs., 1984-94; state coord. maternal/child health First Am. Home Care Co., 1994-95; dir. women's and children's health Arcadia Health Systems, 1995-96; lectr., cons. in field. Contbr. articles to profl. jours. Mem. LWV, Assn. for Women's Health, Obstetrics and Neonatal Nursing, Greater Detroit Orgn. Nurses Execs., Lamaze Internat., Sigma Theta Tau. Home and Office: 32478 Dunford St Farmington Hills MI 48334-2724

ABRAMS, RONI, business education educator, communications consultant, trainer; b. N.Y.C. d. William and Edith Lillian (Monkarsh) Abrams. BA, U. Miami, 1971. Mng. editor Corset, Bra and Lingerie Mag., N.Y.C., 1972-75; assoc. advt. dir. TV World Mag., N.Y.C., 1976-80; pres. Roni Abrams Assoc., Ltd., Bklyn., 1981—; founder The Ctr. for Networking, Bklyn., 1982—. Design and conduct tng. programs in field of perception, interpersonal comm., negotiations, mgmt., sales, orgnl. devel. and personal transformation; spkr. in field. Contbg. author: (textbook) Basic Sales Skills Business to Business, 1995; contbr. articles to profl. jours. Asst. to dir. Impact on Hunger, N.Y.C, 1980; coord. campaign com. to elect Paul Wrablica for state assembly, N.Y.C., 1988. Mem. Sales and Mktg. Execs. of Greater N.Y. (faculty). Avocations: theater, opera, travel. Home and Office: Roni Abrams Assocs Ltd 2820 Avenue J Brooklyn NY 11210-3736

ABRAMS, ROSALIE SILBER, retired state agency official; b. Balt., June 2, 1916; d. Isaac and Dora (Rodbell) Silber; 1 child, Elizabeth Joan. RN, Sinai Hosp.; postgrad., Columbia U.; BS, Johns Hopkins U., 1963, MA in Polit. Sci. Pub. health nurse USNR, 1945-46; bus. mgr. Sequoia Med. Group, Calif., 1946-47; asst. bus. mgr. Silber's Bakery, Balt., 1947-53; mem. Md. Ho. of Dels., 1967-70, Md. Senate, 1970-83, majority leader, 1978-82; chmn. Dem. Party of Md., 1978-83, chmn. fin. com., 1982-83; dir. Office on Aging, State of Md., 1983-95, ret., 1995. Chair World War II Meml. Commn., 1996-2000; commr. Balt. City Commn. on Aging, 1997—; host Outlook TV show, 1983-90; guest lectr., witness before congl. coms. Platform com. on nat. healthcare Dem. Nat., Com., 1979—; chmn. Md. Humane Practices Commn., 1978-83, mem., 1971-74; mem. New Coalition, 1979-83, State-Fed. Assembly Com. on Human Resources, 1977-83, Md. Comprehensive Health Planning Agy., 1972-75, Md. Commn. on Status of Women, 1968—, Am. Jewish Com. Chair Med. Supplies Com. for Needy and Elderly in Odessa, Ukraine; chair dept. human resources, dept. health and mental hygiene, transp., housing and cmty. devel., econ. and employment devel., Interagy. Com., 1984-95; bd. dirs. Sinai Hosp., Balt., 1973-2000, Balt. Jewish Coun., Cross Country Improvement Assn., 1969—,Fifth Dist. Reform Dems., 1967—; chmn. legis. com. Balt. Area Coun. on Alcoholism, 1973-75; mem. adv. bd. long term care project U. Mc., Balt., 1986; mem. Md. Adv. Com. for Adult and Cmty. Svcs., 1984; mem. nat. adv. bd. Pre-Retirement Edn. Planning, 1986—; mem. State Adv. Coun. on Nutrition, 1988—; spl. trustee Sheppard-Pratt Hosp., 1992-2000. With Nurse Corps USN, 1944-46. Recipient Louise Waterman Wise Cmty. Svc. award, 1969, award Am. Acad. Comprehensive Health Planning, 1971, Balt. News Am. award, Women of Distinction in Medicine, 1971, traffic safety award, Safety First Club of Md., 1971, ann London Scott Meml. award for legis. excellence, Md. chpt. NOW, 1975, Md. Nurses Assn., 1975, svc. award Balt. Area Coun. on Alcoholism, 1975, First Citizens award Md. Senate Pres., 1999, named to Md. Women's Hall of Fame, Md. Commn. for Women and Women Legislators of Md. Gen. Assembly, 1994, numerous others; 1st ann. Rosalie S. Abrams Firsts award awarded by Women Legislators of Md., 2004. Mem. AARP, Md. Order Women Legislators (pres. 1973-75), Nat. Conf. State Legislatures (human resources and urban affairs steering com. 1977-83), Nat. Legis. Conf. (human resources task force, intergovtl. rels. com. 1975-83), Md. Gerontol. Assn. (bd. dirs. 1984—), Nat. Fedn. Dem. Women, Am. Jewish Congress, Am. Soc. on Aging, Md. Gerontol. Assn. Home: North Oaks 725 Mt Wilson Ln Apt 729 Baltimore MD 21208

ABRAMS, ROZ, newscaster; married; 2 children. BS in Sociology, Western Mich. U.; MA in Speech, U. Mich. Anchor KRON-TV, San Francisco, CNN; anchor/reporter WXIA-TV, Atlanta; with WABC-TV, NYC, 1986—2003, weekend anchor, gen. assignment reporter, anchor Eyewitness News at 5 PM, host program Making It; co-anchor 5pm and 11pm news WCBS-TV, NYC, 2004—. Editl. adv. bd. Making Waves Am. Women in Radio and TV, 2003—. Co chair NY Reads Together. Recipient numerous awards including Centennial award for svc. and achievement in media Greater Harlem C. of C. Office: WABC-TV/ABC Inc Seven Lincoln Sq New York NY 10023-5998

ABRAMS, RUTH IDA, retired state supreme court justice; b. Boston, Dec. 26, 1930; d. Samuel and Matilda A. BA, Radcliffe Coll., 1953; LLB, Harvard U., 1956; hon. degree, Mt. Holyoke Coll., 1977, Suffolk U., 1977, New Eng. Sch. Law, 1978. Bar: Mass. 1957. Ptnr. Abrams Abrams & Abrams, Boston, 1957-60; asst. dist. atty. Middlesex County, Mass., 1961-69; asst. atty. gen. Mass., chief appellate sect. criminal div., 1969-71; spl. counsel Supreme Jud. Ct. Mass., 1971-72, assoc. justice 1977-2000; retired Supreme Jud. Ct., Boston, 2000; assoc. justice Superior Ct. Commonwealth of Mass., 1972-77. Mem. Gov.'s Commn. on Child Abuse, 1970-71, Mass. Law Revision Commn. Proposed Criminal Code for Mass., 1969-71; trustee Radcliffe Coll., from 1981 Editor: Handbook for Law Enforcement Officers, 1969-71. Recipient Radcliffe Coll. Achievement award, 1976, Radcliffe Grad. Soc. medal, 1977 Mem. ABA (com. on proposed fed. code from 1977), Mass. Bar Assn., Am. Law Inst., Am. Judicature Soc. (dir. 1978), Am. Judges Assn., Mass. Assn. Women Lawyers. Home: Supreme Jud Ct Mass 180 Beacon St Cambridge MA 02116

ABRAMS, STEPHANIE BASS, performing company executive; b. Chgo., Jan. 14, 1978; d. Stuart G. Abrams and Shirley Bass-Richardi; m. Scott D. McFarlin, Aug. 9, 2003. Student, U. Tex., 1996. Tchr. San Francisco Sch. Circus Arts, 1999—2001, San Francisco Conservatory Music, 2001—02, Acrosports, San Francisco, 2000—02; artistic dir. Head Over Heels/Splash Circus, Emeryville, Calif., 2002—04, Acrosports City Circus, Emeryville, Calif., 2004—. Cons. various circus troupes and individual performers, San Francisco, 2000; founder and dir. theatre co. Kinetic Theory Exptl., 2001—. Named Best of Fringe, San Francisco Fringe Festival, 2001; grantee, Chaney Found., 2002. Mem.: Theatre Bay Area, Theatre Comm. Group, Internat. Thespian Soc. Avocations: sewing, crafts, making costumes. Office Phone: 415-289-6808. E-mail: fluide@waxproductions.com.

ABRAMS-COLLENS, VIVIEN, artist; b. Cleve. BFA, Carnegie-Mellon U.; MFA, Instituto Allende, San Miguel de Allende, Mex. Art tchr, Biblioteca Publica, San Miguel de Allende, Mex., 1969, Cleve. Mus. Art, 1971-72; instr. drawing Cuyahoga C.C., Cleve., 1974; design instr. Manhattanville Coll., Purchase, N.Y., 1985-86. Artist-in-residence Bennington (Vt.) Coll., 1980; vis. artist in painting SUNY, Purchase, N.Y., 1983; lectr. in field. One-woman shows include Akron (Ohio) Art Inst., 1976, The New Gallery Contemporary Art, Cleve., 1977, 80, Luise Ross Gallery, N.Y.C., 1984, Coup de Grâce Gallery, N.Y.C., 1992, 100 Church Street, N.Y.C., 1992, Lisa Stern Gallery, Mountainville, N.Y., 1993, Lycian Ctr. Galleries, Sugarloaf, N.Y., 1994, Mus. Hudson Highlands, Cornwall-on-Hudson, N.Y., 1995; selected group exhbns. include Butler Inst. Am. Art, Ohio, 1976, 77, Cleve. Mus. Art, 1976, 77, 79, 81, 84 (1st Prize in Painting 1981), Akron Inst. Art, 1977, Harbourfront Gallery, Toronto, 1978, Marilyn Pearl Gallery, N.Y.C., 1978, 82, Phoenix Mus. Art, 1979, Soho Ctr. Visual Artists, N.Y.C., 1979, Washington Sq. East Galleries, N.Y.C., 1980, Little Rock (Ark.) Art Mus., 1982, Steven Rosenberg Gallery, N.Y.C., 1983, Ericson Gallery, N.Y.C., 1983, Sculpture Ctr., N.Y.C., 1983, A.I.R. Gallery, N.Y.C., 1983, Aldrich Mus. Contemporary Art, Ridgefield, Conn., 1984, 86, 92, Luise Ross Gallery, 1984, Mus. of the Hudson Highlands, 1985, City Gallery, N.Y.C., 1987, Squibb Gallery, Princeton, N.J., 1988, Cleve. Inst. Art, 1988, Mansfield Art Ctr., Ohio, 1989, OIA Salon, N.Y.C., 1991, Middletown Art Ctr., 1994 (Oil/Acrylic award 1994), Dietrich Contemporary Arts, N.Y.C., 1994, Cleve. Ctr. for Contemporary Art, 1994, Mansfield (Ohio) Art Ctr., 1995; permanent collections include Cleve. Found., Cleve. Art Assn., The Currier Gallery Art, Home Ins. Co., We. Electric, J.P. Morgan & Co., Continental Corp., Progressive Ins. Co., Nat. City Bank Cleve., Sohio, Walter & Samuels, Inc., Columbus Mus. Arts & Scis., Cleve. Mus. Art, Aldrich Mus. Contemporary Art; commns. include AT&T Longlines. Mem. fellows exec. com. MacDowell Colony, 1982-85. Cleve. Found. grantee, 1976, Athena Found. grantee, 1984; Hand Follow Found. fellow, 1983, fellow MacDowell Colony, Peterborough, N.H., 1979, 81, 85; recipient 1st prize Cleve. Mus. Art 62nd May Show, 1981, award Middletown Art Ctr., 1994; named to Shaker Heights H.S. Hall of Fame, 1994. Office: 196 Mountain Rd Cornwall On Hudson NY 12520-1803 also: Newburgh Art Gallery 394 Broadway Newburgh NY 12550-5304

ABRAMSON, JILL, newspaper publishing executive; AB in History and Lit., Harvard U., 1976. Stringer Time mag., 1974-76, Boston bur. mgr., reporter, 1976-77; with NBC News Election Unit, 1979-81; sr. writer Am. Lawyer, 1981-88; editor Legal Times, 1986-88; with New York Times, Washington, 1988—, Chernoff Silver, 1988-97; dep. bur. chief The Wall Street Jour., 1993-97; enterprise editor Washington bur. New York Times,

1997—2003, mng. editor, 2003—. Co-author: Where They Are Now: The Story of Women of Harvard Law 1974, 1976, Strange Justice, 1994. Office: NY Times 229 W 43rd St New York NY 10036

ABRAMSON, LESLIE HOPE, lawyer; b. Queens, N.Y., 1943; 1 child, Laine. Grad., Queens Coll.; JD, UCLA. Bar: Calif. 1970. Lawyer L.A. County Pub. Defender's Office, 1970—77; pvt. practice, 1977—. Co-author: (with Richard Flaste) The Defense is Ready: My Life in Crime, 1997. Recipient award for outstanding trial atty., Criminal Cts. Bar Assn., 1985. Mem.: Calif. Attys. for Criminal Justice (pres.). Office: Ste 940 4929 Wilshire Blvd Los Angeles CA 90010-3823*

ABRAMSON, PATTY, investment company executive; BA in polit. sci., Elmira Coll.; MA in journalism, Am. U. V.p. Hager, Sharp & Abramson; founder, pres. Abramson Comm.; founding ptnr., mng. dir. Women's Growth Capital Fund; co-founder WomenAngels.net. Del. White House Conf. on Small Bus.; bd. dirs. VIPdesk.com, Enfish Tech.; bd. adv. Patrick Microwave, iDolls. Mem. DC Commn. Women, DC Human Rights Commn.; Mayor's Overall Econ. Devel. Commn. Named Small Bus. Adv. Yr., Small Bus. Adminstrn., Businesswoman Yr., Women in Comm. Office: Women's Growth Capital Fund 1025 Thomas Jefferson St NW Ste 305 Washington DC 20007 Office Phone: 202-342-1431. Office Fax: 202-342-1203.*

ABRAMSON, SARA JANE, radiologist, educator; b. New Orleans, La., May 12, 1945; m. Walter Squire; children: Harrison, Russell, Zachary, Andrew. BA, Sarah Lawrence Coll., 1967; postgrad., Tulane U., 1967-69; MD, Mt. Sinai Sch. Medicine, 1971. Diplomate Am. Bd. Radiology, cert. added qualifications pediat. radiology. Intern in pediatrics Mt. Sinai Hosp., N.Y.C., 1971-72, resident in pediatrics, 1972-73; resident in radiology St. Luke's Children's Mercy Hosp., Kansas City, Mo., 1973-76; asst. prof. radiology U. Mo., 1976-79, Harvard U. Med. Sch., Cambridge, Mass., 1979-81; fellow in pediatric radiology Children's Hosp., Boston, 1979-81; asst. prof. radiology Columbia Coll. Physicians & Surgeons, N.Y.C., 1981-88, assoc. prof. radiology, 1988-93; assoc. attending radiologist Babies Hosp. Columbia Presbyn. Med. Ctr., N.Y.C., 1981-93, dep. dir. divsn. pediatric radiology, 1992-93; assoc. prof. radiology Cornell U. Med. Coll., N.Y.C., 1993-99, prof., 1999—; assoc. attending radiologist, assoc. mem. Sloan-Kettering Cancer Ctr., Meml. Hosp., N.Y.C., 1993-98, attending radiologist, mem., 1999—. Mem. radiology elective program Columbia U. Med. Sch., N.Y.C., 1981-93, radiology residency program reevaluation, 1984-93, program coord. affiliated hosps. teaching program, 1991-93, med. student advisor, 1991-93; mem. faculty coun. Columbia U., 1987-93; cons. in pediatric radiology Blythedale Children's Hosp., 1982—, Bet Israel Hosp., N.Y.C., 1983—, Harlem Hosp., N.Y.C., 1983—, N.Y. Foundling Hosp., 1988—, Lenox Hill Hosp., 1990—, Morristown Meml. Hosp., 1990—; lectr., presenter in field. Contbr. over 40 articles to profl. jours., chpts. to books. Named Radiology Tchr. of Yr., Columbia Coll. Physicians and Surgeons, 1992. Fellow Am. Coll. Radiology (del. N.Y. chpt. 1991—, alt. del. 1984-91, co-chair nominating com. 2000—); mem. AMA, Soc. for Pediat. Radiology (bd. dirs. 2000—), Radiology Soc. N.Am., European Soc. for Pediat. Radiology, Soc. Thoracic Radiology, Am. Assn. Ultrasound in Medicine, Am. Assn. Women in Radiology, N.Y. Roentgen Soc. (exec. com. 1999—, sec.-treas. 1991-94, v.p. 1996-97, pres.-elect 1997-98, pres. 1998-99, moderator, pediat. program chair spring conf. 1991), N.Y. State Radiological Soc. (chmn. residents sect. 1998—, treas. 2002—, guest lectr. spring conf. 1990-98), Nat. Children's Cancer Study Group, Caffey Soc., Neuhauser Soc., Kirkpatrick Soc. Office: Sloan-Kettering Cancer Ctr 1175 York Ave New York NY 10021-7169

ABREU, SUE HUDSON, physician, army officer, organizational and healthcare consultant; b. Indpls., May 24, 1956; d. M.B. Hudson and Wilma (Jones) Hudson Black. BS in Engring., Purdue U., 1978; MD, Uniformed Services U., 1982; grad., U.S. Army Command & Gen. Staff, 1988, Armed Forces Staff Coll., 1990. Commd. 2d lt. U.S. Army, 1978, advanced to col., 1999, ret., 2002; intern Walter Reed Army Med. Ctr., Washington, 1982-83, resident in diagnostic radiology, 1983-85, fellow in nuc. medicine, 1985-87, staff nuc. medicine physician, 1987-88; med. rsch. fellow Walter Reed Army Inst. Rsch., Washington, 1988-89; chief nuc. medicine svc. Womack Army Med. Ctr., Ft. Bragg, NC, 1990—96, chief dept. radiology, 1991-92, 96-98, med. dir. quality assurance, 1998-2001, asst. dep. commdr. clin. svcs., 2001—02; orgnl. and healthcare cons., 2002—. Nuc. medicine cons. to Army Surgeon Gen., 2000-2002; bd. dirs. Intersocietal Commn. for Accreditation Nuclear Medicine Labs., 2001-, sec. 2003. Named Outstanding Interdisciplinary engr., Purdue U. Tri-Svc., 2001; named to Hall of Fame, ROTC, 2004. Fellow Am. Coll. Nuclear Physicians (pres. 2001); mem. Am. Coll. Radiology, Soc. Nuc. Medicine, Soc. Women Engrs., Am. Soc. Nuclear Cardiology, European Assn. Nuc. Medicine, U.S. Parachute Assn., Mortar Bd., Tau Beta Pi, Omicron Delta Kappa, Phi Kappa Phi, Sigma Gamma Tau. Avocations: calligraphy, parachuting. Home: 613 Saddlebred Ln Raeford NC 28376-5535 Fax: 910-875-3886. E-mail: sueabreu@mindspring.com.

ABRIL, MARCIA (ELA I. CARDINAS), writer; b. Jesus Maria, Santander, Colombia, Mar. 21, 1928; came to U.S., 1985; d. Jorge Benjamin and Ana Isabel (Valenzuela) Tellez; m. Rafael A. Cardenas, Mar. 12, 1959; children: Willyam, Harold, Alix, Ela, Rafael, Katiana. BA in Edn. and Psychology, Normal Superior A. Narino, Malaga, Santander, 1950. Prodr. Continental Network Channel 14 TV, Miami, Fla., 1989. Participant/writer Mcpl. Matanzas en el Exilio, Miami, Fla., 1986. Author: Para ti Cartagena, 1982, Aguilas e Ilusiones, 1986, Insolito, 1990, 2d edit., 1995, Girasol y Yo, 1994, Viento y Sol, 1995; author/composer: Colombia Aqui Esta tu Gente, Miami, 1986. Vol. Empresa Promotora de Turismo, Cartagena, 1982-83; benefactor Biblioteca Nacional, Bogota, Colombia, 1982, U. Nacional de Colombia, Bogota, 1982; guest/participant Primer Encuentro de la Cultura Hispanoamericana, Bogota, 1983. Recipient Honorary award Municipio de Matanzas en el Exilio, Miami, 1986, Meritory award Eva Am. Prodns., 1995, Cert. of Recognition, U.S. Libr. of Congress, 1995. Roman Catholic. Avocations: writing, dance, swimming, reading. Office: 815 SW 8th St Miami FL 33130-3703

ABRIOLA, LINDA M. civil engineer, environmental engineer; BS in Civil Engring. with highest honors, Drexel U., 1976; MS in Civil Engring., Princeton U., 1979, MA in Civil Engring., 1980, PhD in Civil Engring., 1983. Project engr. Procter and Gamble Mfg. Co., S.I., NY, 1976—78; rsch. asst. dept. civil engring. Princeton U., NJ, 1979—83, postdoctoral rschr. dept. civil engring., 1983—84; vis. assoc. prof. dept. petroleum engring. U. Tex., Austin, 1991; vis. scientist dept. geotech. engring. Universitat Politecnica de Cataluna, Barcelona, 1992; asst. prof. dept. civil and environ. engring. U. Mich., Ann Arbor, 1984—90, assoc. prof. dept. civil and environ. engring., 1990—96, prof., dir. Environ. and Water Resources Engring. Program, 1996—2003; dean engring., prof. civil and environ. engring. Tufts U., 2003—. Mem. environ. engring. com. USEPA Sci. Adv. Bd., 1990—96; mem. com. on groundwater clean-up alternatives NRC, 1991—94, mem. water sci and tech. bd., 1994—97; mem. sci. adv. com. Western Region Hazardous Substance Rsch. Ctr., 1995—. Contbr. articles to profl. jours. Recipient Presdl. Young Investigator award, NSF, 1985, Faculty award for Women Scientists and Engrs., 1991, Outstanding Educator award, Assn. for Women Geoscientists, 1996; Vis. Scientist's grant, Spanish Ministry of Edn. and Sci., 1992, Disting. Darcy lectr., Nat. Groundwater Assn., 1996. Mem.: Am. Geophys. Union (hydrology divsn. 1992—94), Assn. Environ. Engring. Profs. (bd. dirs. 1990—92). Office: Dean Engring Tufts U Medford MA 02155

ABSHER, DONNA ATKINS, textile designer; b. Ft. Ord, Calif., July 25, 1956; d. James Edward and Mary Ward (Shearin) Atkins; m. Glen Alan Downs, Jan. 2, 1982 (div. Nov. 1990); m. Robert Blair Martin, June 29, 1991 (div. 1998); 1 child, Parker James Blair Martin; m. Ray Grubb Absher, Oct. 20, 2002. AAS in Fashion Design, SUNY, 1977; BS in Textile Tech., N.C. State U., 1978. Head designer Chatham Mills, Pittsboro, N.C., 1978-81; dept. mgr. JC Penney, Wilson, N.C., 1982-85; house mem.'s asst. N.C. Legislature, Raleigh, N.C., 1985-86; dir. product devel. Doblin Fabrics, Morganton, N.C., 1989-94; pres., CEO Martin Textiles, Ltd., Hickory, N.C., 1994—. Freelance designer, stylist Carolina Mills, Hickory, 1995-97; automotive textile designer, CMI Industries, Elkin, N.C., 1998-2000; design ops. mgr. Chatham-Borgstena Automotive Textiles, Mt. Airy, N.C., 2001—. Mem.: Overmountain Victory Trail Assn. Southern Baptist. Avocations: traveling, choral singing. E-mail: donnaaa@earthlink.net.

ABSHER, ROBIN DAWN, security firm executive, private investigator; b. Concord, N.C., Dec. 28, 1971; d. Judy Kay Tinch and David Eugene Absher, Wayne Tinch (Stepfather) and Margaret Amy Absher(Stepmother); life ptnr. C. L. Crawford, Sept. 25, 1998. Student, U. Nev., 1990—91, Detective Tng. Inst., Calif., 2002—03. Dir., ptnr. Ultraimaging Corp., Henderson, Nev., 1998—. Mem.: Nev. State Firefighters' Assn. Inc., Nat. Police & Trooper Assn., Nev. Fraternal Order of Police. Office: Ultraimaging Corp 848 Wintersweet Rd Henderson NV 89015 Personal E-mail: eyessoblu30@aol.com. E-mail: ultraimagingcorp@aol.com.

ABTS, GWYNETH HARTMANN, retired dietician; b. Union, Ill., Oct. 31, 1923; d. William John and Olga Anna (Krause) Hartmann; m. Rufus Heath Jr., Apr. 6, 1942 (div. Dec. 1945); m. Harold Henry Abts, Feb. 14, 1948; children: Leigh, Michael, Patricia. BS, U. Ill., 1945; postgrad., U. Oreg., 1945-46, U. Ill., Elgin, 1957, No. Ill. U., 1966, 74, 82, 87. Registered dietitian, Ill., Lic. Ill. Dietitian. Clin. dietitian St. Joseph Hosp., Elgin, 1947; asst. dietitian French Hosp., San Francisco, 1948-50, Elgin State Hosp., 1950-58; dietary cons. Ill. Youth Commn., Springfield, 1958-70; food adminstr. Ill. Dept. of Corrections, Springfield, 1970-85. Mem. Food and Nutrition Cou. on Govt. Commodities, Springfield, 1980-85; bd. dirs. Ill. Nutrition Assn., Urbana, 1983. Pres. PTO, Geneva, 1972. McHenry County Home Econ. scholar U. Ill., 1941-45. Mem. Am. Dietetic Assn. (citizens ambassador program to Australia and New Zealand and China), Fox Valley Home Economists, West Suburban Dietetic Assn., AAUW. Lutheran. Avocations: quilting, cooking, duplicate bridge. Home: Apt 107 975 N 5th Ave Saint Charles IL 60174-1284

ABUDULMAJID, IMAN See IMAN

ABUHL, JEANNE MARIE, sales professional; b. Des Moines, May 13, 1946; d. Albert James and Marjorie Jeanette (Larson) Abuhl. Student, Moody Bible Inst., 1966, local cmty. colls. Exec. sec. to v.p. Scripture Press Found., Glen Ellyn, Ill., 1967-73; asst. to nat. field dir. Youth for Christ/USA, Wheaton, Ill., 1973-75; office mgr. Youth for Christ Internat., Geneva, 1975-78; mgr. client svcs. McKay-Doerschuk & Co., Wheaton, 1983-84; realtor Baird & Warner, Wheaton, 1984—96, Realty Execs. Premiere, 1996—2001; project sales mgr. RAFaganel Builders, Batavia, Ill., 2001—; dir. adminstrv. svcs. Follett Coll. Stores, Elmhurst, Ill., 1978-83. Republican. Evangelical. Office: Rafaganel Builders 1387 Wind Energy Pass Batavia IL 60510 Home: 61 Chippewa Dr Oswego IL 60543-8926 E-mail: jmabuhl@juno.com.

ACAMPORA, PATRICIA L. state legislator; b. Waukegan, IL, Dec. 10, 1945; m. Alan Croce; children: Stacey, Christy. Student Suffolk Cmty. Coll., 1989, student Dowling Coll. Office mgr. Dr. Harvey Wolfe, 1980—83; exec. chief of staff NY State Assemblymember, 1983—90; asst. county exec. Suffolk County Exec. Robert Gaffney, 1990—93; assemblywoman dist. 1 N.Y. State Assembly, Albany, 1993—. Mem.: Am. Legis. Exchange Coun., East End Women's Network, League of Women Voters, Italian Am. Legislators. Office: 400 W Main St Ste 201 Riverhead NY 11901-2807 E-mail: acampop@assembly.state.ny.us.*

ACEVEDO, ELIZABETH MORRISON, special education educator; b. Kittanning, Pa., Apr. 22, 1938; d. Thomas L. and Ethel (Morrison) McKelvey; m. Ruben Acevedo, Oct. 11, 1963; children: Thomas B., Samantha Jo Acevedo-Fox, Holly Elizabeth. BA, Muskingum Coll., 1960; MS, Pepperdine U., 1980; postgrad., Claremont Grad. Sch., 1988-90, Azusa-Pacific U. Lifetime credentials in English and spl. edn., Calif., Pa.; credential in resource specialist, Calif.; cert. adminstr., Calif. Tchr. Armstrong Sch. Dist., Ford City, Pa., 1970-77, Glendora (Calif.) Unified Sch. Dist., 1979-80, resource specialist, 1980-97; adj. prof., field supervisor Grad. Sch. of Edn., Azusa-Pacific U., Azusa, Calif., 1997—. Cons. reading program The Acevedo Advantage, Glendora, 1986—. Contbr. articles to profl. jours. Bd. dirs. christian edn. Ch. Brethren, Glendora, 1989—. Grantee Claremont (Calif.) Grad. Sch., 1989. Mem. AAUW, ASCD, Calif. Assn. Resource Specialists, Pi Lambda Theta (membership com.). Democrat. Mem. Ch. Brethren. Avocations: reading, jogging, sewing, refinishing antique wood pieces. Home: 643 N Wabash Ave Glendora CA 91741-2116 E-mail: eacevedo@apu.edu.

ACEVEDO-RHODES, EILEEN, psychologist, educator; b. Md., Feb. 2, 1954; d. Fernando Acevedo and Ruth Rhodes; m. Carlos Santiago, Aug. 24, 1977; children: Natalia Santiago, Cristina Santiago. BA in Edn., U. Ctrl. Bayamon, 1985; student, U. Santiago, Spain, 1981; EdD, U. Interamericana, P.R., 1993. Pvt. practice, PR, 1981—; prof. edn. U. Ctrl., 1988; prof. social scis. U. P.R., 1999—. Cons. mental health emergency medicine Bayamen County, PR, 1995—; spkr. in field. Contbr. articles to profl. and ednl. jours. Mem.: APA, ACA, Phi Delta Kappa. Avocations: aerobics, fitness.

ACHTENBERG, ROBERTA, former federal official; b. L.A., July 20, 1950; d. Louis and Beatrice A.; 1 child. AB, U. Calif., Berkeley, 1972; postgrad., U. Calif., San Francisco, 1972-73; JD, U. Utah, 1975. Bar: Calif., U.S. Dist. Ct. (no. dist.) Calif., U.S. Ct. Appeals (9th cir.). Exec. dir. Nat. Ctr. Lesbian Rights, 1989-90; asst. sec. fair housing and equal opportunity HUD, Washington, 1993-95, Sr. Adv. to Sec., 1995—; sr. v.p. pub. policy dept. San Francisco C. of C., 1995—. Mem. County Bd. Suprs., City and County of San Francisco; bd. dirs. Bay Area Air Quality Mgmt. Dist., 1991-93; trustee, Calif. State U. Mem. Order of Coir, Phi Beta Kappa. Office: San Francisco C of C Pub Policy Dept 235 Montgomery St 12th Fl San Francisco CA 94104

ACHTERMAN, GAIL LOUISE, lawyer; b. Portland, Oreg., Aug. 1, 1949; AB in Econs. with distinction, Stanford U., 1971; MS in Natural Resource Policy and Mgmt., U. Mich., 1975, JD cum laude, 1974. Bar: Oreg. 1974, U.S. Dist. Ct. Oreg. 1978, U.S. Supreme Ct. 1978, U.S. Ct. Appeals (fed. and 10th cirs.). Atty.-advisor U.S. Dept. Interior, 1975-78; asst. for natural resources Gov. Neil Goldschmidt, 1987-91; mem. Stoel Rives LLP, Portland, 1978-2000; dir. Inst. for Natural Resources, Oreg. State U., Corvallis, 2003—. Exec. dir. Deschutes Resources Conservancy, 2000-2003; adj. prof. forest policy, Coll. Forestry, Oreg. State U., 1991—. Mem. Oreg. Water Resources Commn., 1981-85, Gov.'s Growth Task Force, 1998; mem. pres.'s bd. advisors Oreg. State U., 2000—03, Oreg. Transp. Commn., 2000—. Mem. N.W. Environment Watch, Oregon Garden, Am. Leadership Forum, Oreg. Women's Forum, Portland C. of C. (bd. dirs. 1996-99). Office: Oreg State U INR Dirs Office 210 Strand Ag Hall Corvallis OR 97331

ACKER, ANN, lawyer; b. Chgo., July 21, 1948; BA, St. Mary's Coll., 1970; JD, Loyola U., 1973. Bar: Ill. 1973. Partner Chapman and Cutler, Chgo. Mem.: Nat. Assoc. of Bond Lawyers, Chicago Bar Assoc., Amer. Bar Assoc. Office: Chapman and Cutler 111 W Monroe St Ste 1700 Chicago IL 60603-4006*

ACKER, ROSE L. elementary school educator; b. Washington, May 10, 1945; d. Samuel L. and Bessie L. Acker. BA, Howard U., 1970; MA, U. D.C., 1979; EdD, George Washington U., 1994. Coord., instr. U. D.C., Washington; dictaphone transcriber editor NEA of Sch. Adminstrs., Washington; with U.S. Office Personnel Mgmt., Washington; sec.-adminstrv. aide H. Vogel Law Firm; educator D.C. Pub. Schs., Washington; counselor Fairfax County Pub. Sch., Ft. Belvoir Elem. Sch., Va. Recipient Regional Supts. Cert. of Merit, Outstanding Tchr. of Yr. award. Mem. LWV, Internat. Reading Assn., Am. Assn. Counseling and Devel., Washington Tchrs. Assn., D.C. Alliance Sch. Educators, Nat. Coun. Negro Women (life), George Washington Alumni Assn. (past pres., del.), Delta Sigma Theta, Pi Lambda Theta, Chi Sigma Iota, Phi Delta Kappa (pres. for membership, Bessie Gabbard Disting. award Leadership 2002-2003). Home: 1301 Delaware Ave SW Apt 212N Washington DC 20024-3911

ACKER, VIRGINIA MARGARET, nursing educator; b. Madison, Wis., Aug. 11, 1946; d. Paul Peter and Lucille (Klein) A. Diploma in nursing, St. Mary's Med. Ctr., Madison, 1972; BSN, Incarnate Word Coll., San Antonio, 1976; MS in Health Professions, S.W. Tex. State U., 1980; postgrad., U. Tex., 1992-93. RN, Tex. Staff nurse St. Mary's Hosp., Milw., 1972-73, Kenosha (Wis.) Meml. Hosp., 1973-74, S.W. Tex. Meth. Hosp., San Antonio, 1974-75, Met. Gen. Hosp., San Antonio, 1975-76; instr. Bapt. Meml. Hosp. Sys. Sch. Nursing, San Antonio, 1976-83; DON, Meml. Hosp., Gonzales, Tex., 1983-84; instr., DON, Victoria Coll., Cuero, Tex., 1984-86; DON, Rocky Knoll Health Care Facility, Plymouth, Wis., 1986-87, Unicare Health Facilities, Milw., 1987-88; coord. nursing edn. St. Nicholas Hosp., Sheboygan, Wis., 1989-90; instr. U. Wis., Oshkosh, 1990-92, St. David's Hosp., Austin, Tex., 1992-95; coord. quality improvement Bailey Square Surgery Ctr., Austin, 1995-98; coord. regulation compliance South Austin Hosp., 1998—2003; program dir. Prevent Inc., 2003—. Roman Catholic. Avocations: cross-stitching, reading, camping, fishing. Home: 129 Copano Cove Rd Rockport TX 78382

ACKERLY, WENDY SAUNDERS, construction company executive; b. Chgo., July 23, 1960; d. Robert S. Jr. and Linda Ackerly. BS in Atmospheric Sci., U. Calif., Davis, 1982; postgrad., U. Nev., Reno, 1985. Programmer U. Calif, Davis, 1982-83; cons. software Tesco, Sacramento, 1983; software engr. Bently Nev. Corp., Minden, Nev., 1984-85; mgr. computer scis. Jensen Electric Co., Reno, 1985-86, software engr. Cameron Park, Calif., 1986-89; sr. engr. Aerojet, Sacramento, 1989-96, test ops. specialist, 1996-98; dir. design and devel. Kerry King Constrn., Inc., 1998—, sec.-treas., 1991—. Mem. Nat. Space Soc., Planetary Soc., U.S. Tennis Assn., Calif. Aggie Alumni Assn. Republican. Avocations: tennis, hiking, travel, piano. Office: PO Box 269 Rescue CA 95672-0269

ACKERMAN, ARLENE, school system administrator; BA in Elem. Edn., Harris Stowe Tchrs. Coll.; MA in Ednl. Adminstrn. an dpolicy, Washington U.; MA in Edn., EdD in Adminstrn., Planning and Social Policy, Harvard U. Supt. San Francisco Unified Sch. Dist., 1999—, Washington (D.C.) Pub. Schs., 1997—99. Bd. mem. WestEd Regional Edn. Lab., 2003—; mem. Bay Area Sch. Reform Collaboration; program advisor BROAD-Urban Supts. Acad. Trustee San Francisco Fine Arts; bd. govs. San Francisco Symphony; active San Francisco Workforce Investment Bd. Recipient Apple for the Tchr. award, Iota Lambda Sorority, Disting. Alumni award, Harris Stowe Tchrs. Coll.; McDonnell Douglas fellow. Mem.: ASCD, Presdl. Commn. on Hist. Black Colls. and Univs., Nat. Assn. Black Sch. Educators, Coun. of the Great City Schs., Am. Assn. Sch. Adminstrs., Phi Delta Kappa. Office: 555 Franklin St San Francisco CA 94102

ACKERMAN, ARLENE ALICE, accountant, business consultant, artist, writer; b. Omaha, Mar. 24, 1936; d. Walter Nelson and Mildred Eleanor (Krimlofski) A. BA in Social Sci. and Econs., San Francisco State U., 1962; MA in Polit. Sci., Purdue U., 1967; grad., U.S. Dept. Def. Info. Sch., 1973, U.S. Army Command-Gen. Staff Coll., 1977. CPA, Ind. Acct., adminstr. Peeples & MacDonald, CPAs, Sacramento, 1961-66; acct. chief acct.'s office Purdue U., West Lafayette, Ind., 1966-67; adj. gen. and info. officer, editor newspaper 123d Army Res. Command, Ind., 1972-75; mng. ptnr. Piano Showcase, Indpls., 1975-83; adminstr. Bennett Thrasher & Co. CPAs, Atlanta, 1983-86, Melvin Belli Law Offices, San Francisco, 1990; bus. cons. Ackerman & Assocs., Indpls., 1986-90; acctg. mgr., acting CFO Lera Dynalectric, San Francisco, 1991-94; CFO Nat. Home Bus. Assn., St. Helena, Calif., 1994-96; prin. Ackerman & Assocs., Fairfax, Calif., 1996-2000; fin. analyst Exodus Comm., Inc., Santa Clara, Calif., 2000—. Editor Mus. Indian Heritage Newsletter, Indpls., 1971-77; exhibited in group shows at Marin Agrl. Land Trust, San Rafael, Calif., 1993, Marin County Fair & Exposition, San Rafael, 1993, 96, Marin Soc. Artists, Ross, Calif., 1993, 94, Monterey Peninsula Mus. Art Christmas Miniature Show, 1993, Artisans Gallery, Mill Valley, Calif., 1993-95, Sonoma-Marin Fair, Petaluma, Calif., 1993-94, San Mateo (Calif.) County Fair, 1992-94, Sonoma County Fair, Santa Rosa, Calif., 1993-95; contbr. articles to Army profl. jours. Mem. Atlanta Feminist Women's Chorus. Officer U.S. Army, 1956-61, 67-71; col. USAR, ret., 1988. Mem. Soc. Children's Book Writers and Illustrators (assoc.), Marin Soc. Artist, San Francisco Early Music Soc., Nat. Assn. Miniature Enthusiasts. Avocations: classical piano, painting, drawing, writing children's stories, miniature artist. Home: 1506 E Rock Springs Rd Atlanta GA 30306 E-mail: ladycolonel@comcast.net.

ACKERMAN, FELICIA, philosophy educator, writer; b. Bklyn., June 23, 1947; d. Arthur and Zelda (Sondack) A. AB summa cum laude, Cornell U., 1968; PhD, U. Mich., 1976. Asst. prof. philosophy Brown U., Providence, 1974-79, assoc. prof., 1979-91, prof., 1991—. Vis. asst. prof. philosophy UCLA, 1976; vis. hon. lectr. logic and metaphysics U. St. Andrews, Scotland, 1983; sr. Fulbright lectr. Hebrew U., 1985. Contbr. articles and short stories to various mags. Recipient O. Henry award for short story pub. in Prize Stories, 1990; fellow Ctr. for Advanced Study in Behavioral Scis., NEH, 1988-89. Mem. ACLU, NAACP, Am. Philos. Assn., Amnesty Internat. Office: Brown U Dept Philosophy PO Box 1918 Providence RI 02912-1918 Business E-Mail: felicia_ackerman@brown.edu.

ACKERMAN, PAGE, retired librarian, educator; b. Evanston, Ill., June 30, 1912; d. John Bernard and Florence Page. BA, Agnes Scott Coll., Decatur, Ga., 1933; B.L.S., U. N.C., 1940. Cataloger Columbia Theol. Sem., 1942-43; post librarian U.S. Army, Aberdeen Proving Ground, Md., 1943-45; asst. librarian Union Theol. Sem., Richmond, Va., 1945-49; reference librarian UCLA, 1949-54, asst. univ. librarian, 1954-65, asso. univ. librarian, 1965-73, univ. librarian, 1973-77, prof. Sch. Info. and Library Sci., 1973-77, 82, 83; vis. prof. Sch. Librarianship, U. Calif., Berkeley, 1978, 80. Recipient award of distinction in libr. sci. UCLA Alumnae Assn., 1977, Disting. Career Citation, Assn. Coll. and Rsch. Librs., 1989. Mem. ALA, AAUW (Status of Women award 1973), Calif. Libr. Assn., Coun. on Libr. Resources (bd. dirs. 1975-90). Home: Royal Oaks Manor 1763 Royal Oaks Dr N Bradbury CA 91010 E-mail: page@ucla.edu.

ACKERMAN, VALERIE B. sports association executive; m. Charlie Rappaport; children: Emily, Sally. Grad., U. Va., 1981, UCLA Sch. Law, 1985. Assoc. Simpson, Thacher & Bartlett, N.Y.C.; staff atty. NBA, 1988, spl. asst. to commr., 1990-92, dir. bus. affairs, 1992—94, v.p. bus. affairs, 1994—96; pres. WNBA, 1996—. Bd. dirs. USA Basketball; exec. com. Naismith Meml. Basketball Hall of Fame. Trustee March of Dimes. Named to, GTE Acad. All-Am. Hall of Fame, 1999, Scholar Athlete Hall Fame, Inst. for Internat. Sport, 2003; recipient Disting. Alumna award, U. Va. Women's Ctr., 1997. Office: Olympic Tower 645 Fifth Ave New York NY 10022-5910 also: WNBA Enterprises LLC 450 Harmon Meadow Blvd Secaucus NJ 07094-3618*

ACKERSON, PATRICIA KATHLEEN FREIS, art educator, artist; b. Plainfield, N.J., Sept. 22, 1970; d. Peter Charles and Kathleen Claire Freis; m. Richard Stephen Ackerson, June 15, 1996. BFA in Illustration and Design, Marywood Coll., Scranton, Pa., 1993. Woodshop asst. K & S Marine Woodcraftsmen, Long Branch, NJ, 1988—90; designer / woodcrafter Long Br. Mfg. & Design, Long Branch, NJ, 1992—94; asst. tchr. Metuchen-Edison YMCA, Metuchen, NJ, 1995—98, substitute tchr., 1999—; art tchr. St. Francis Cathedral Sch., Metuchen, 1999—. Calligrapher, Edison, NJ, 1984—; custom-made craft designer, Edison, 1990—; freelance illustrator, Edison, 1990—; calligrapher NJ Polic Benevolent Assn. Contbr. program design St. Francis of Assisi Cathedral bull.; carbothello drawings/paintings, Barron Arts Ctr. Exhbn.; illustrator (calendar cover) St. Francis of Assisi Sch. calendar, calligrapher St. Francis of Assisi. Mem.: Nat. Mus. of Women in the Arts (hon.; mem. 2003—), Nat. Cath. Ednl. Assn. (assoc.; mem. 2003—). Roman Catholic. Avocations: reading, drawing, music, travel. Home: 61 Sixth St Edison NJ 08837 Office: St Francis Cathedral Sch 528 Main St Metuchen NJ 08840 Personal E-mail: pattifa@aol.com.

ACORD, LEA, dean; MS in Pediatric Nursing, PhD in Higher Edn. Adminstrn., U. Pitts. Asst. prof. Sch. of Nursing U. Pitts., 1972-81; exec. dir. Ill. Nurses Assn., 1981-88; dir., assoc. prof. Sch. of Nursing, U. Maine, 1988-95; dean, prof. Coll. of Nursing, Mont. State U., Bozeman. Contbr. articles to profl. publs. Recipient Peggy Musseh1 award for excellence Mont. Nurses Assn., 1997, Jean McLean Nursing Edn. award Maine State Nurses Assn., 1994, Hartford Gerontol. Curriculum award Assn. of Colls. of Nursing, 1998. Mem. Sigma Theta Tau (dean's task force). Office: Mont State U Bozeman Coll Nursing PO Box 173560 Bozeman MT 59717-3560

ACTON, ELIZABETH S, corporate financial executive; b. 1952; V.p. multinational banking group Continental Bank, Chgo.; exec. v.p. fin., CFO Ford Motor Credit Co., Dearborn, Mich.; v.p., treas. Ford Motor Co., Dearborn, Mich., 2000—02; exec. v.p., CFO Coamerica Inc., Detroit, 2002—. Office: Coamerica Tower at Detroit Ctr MC 3391 500 Woodward Ave Detroit MI 48226

ACTON, ELLEN HALL, minister, educator; b. Cin., Nov. 17, 1946; d. Charles Thomas and Mary Hall Pearson; m. John Raymond Acton, Mar. 29, 1970 (div. Feb. 10, 1978); 1 child, Ida Denise. MusB, U. Cin., 1968, MusM, 1974; MDiv, Princeton (N.J.) Theol. Sem., 1987; D of Ministry, San Francisco Theol. Sem., 1997. Ordained min. of word & sacrament Presbyn. Ch. (U.S.A.); cert. tchr. N.J., Ohio. Elem. tchr. Birmingham (Ala.) Pub. Schs., 1968—69; profl musician Birmingham Symphony Orch., 1968—70; instrumental music tchr. Cin. Pub. Schs., 1978—84, pastor Bethany Presbyn. Ch., Alliance, Ohio, 1987—98; assoc. pastor 1st United Presbyn. Ch., Alliance, 1998—2001; pastor Southfield (Mich.) Presbyn. Ch., 2001—. Chairperson Self-Devel. of People Com., New Philadelphia, Ohio, 1992—98; commr. Gen. Assembly, Presbyn. Ch. (U.S.A.), Albuquerque, 1996; area chairperson Com. on Ministry, Muskingum Valley Presbytery, New Philadelphia, 1999—2001; adj. prof. Mt. Union Coll., Alliance, 1998—2000. Contbr. 8 Sophia Sermons. Facilitator, organizer SWAN, Alliance, 1998—2001; mem., vol. Alliance Area Domestic Violence Shelter. Named a Woman of Faith, Muskingum Valley Presbytery, 1999. Mem.: Widows of Sophia, South Oakland NAACP, Leadership Oakland Alumni. Avocations: reading, travel, walking, movies, mythology. Office: Southfield Presbyn Ch 21575 W Ten Mile Rd Southfield MI 48075

ADA, ALMA FLOR, education educator, writer; b. Camagüey, Cuba, Jan. 3, 1938; came to U.S., 1970; d. Modesto Arturo Ada and Alma Lafuente; children: Rosalma, Alfonso, Miguel, Gabriel Zubizarreta. Diploma in Spanish studies, U. Complutence, Madrid, 1960, B of Humanities, U. Cath., Lima, Peru, 1963, PhD, 1965. Assoc. prof. Emory U., Atlanta, 1970-72; prof. Mercy Coll. Detroit, 1972-75; prof. Sch. Edn. U. San Francisco, 1976—. Author: The Gold Coin (Christopher award 1991), My Name is María Isabel, 1993, The Unicorn of the West, 1994, Dear Peter Rabbit, 1994, Where the Flametrees Bloom, 1995, Gathering the Sun, 1997, Under the Royal Palms, 1998 (Pura Belpré award 2000), The Lizard and the Sun, 1997, The Malachite Palace, 1998, Yours Truly, Goldilocks, 2002, Three Golden Oranges, 1999, Friend Frog, 2000, With Love, Little Red Hen, 2003, I Love Saturdays...y domingos, 2003, A pesar del amor, 2003, A Magical Encounter: Latino Children's Literature in the Classroom, 2003; co-author: Authors in the Classroom. A Transformative Education Experience, 2003. Recipient Ann. award L.A. Bilingual Dirs. Assn., 1993, Calif. State PTA Assn., Simon Weisenthal Mus. of Tolerance award, 1998, Gold medal Parenting Mag., 1998, Purá Belpré, 2000; Fulbright scholar, 1966-68. Mem. Internat. Bd. Books for Young People, Nat. Assn. for Bilingual Edn., Calif. Assn. for Bilingual Edn. Office: U San Francisco Ignatian Heights San Francisco CA 94117

ADAIR, ELEANOR REED, environmental biologist; b. Arlington, Mass., Nov. 28, 1926; d. Kenneth Clarke and Margaret (McVeigh) Reed; m. Robert Kemp Adair, June 21, 1952; children: Douglas, Margaret, James (dec.). BA, Mt. Holyoke Coll., 1948; MA, U. Wis., 1951, PhD, 1955. From rsch. asst. to lectr., sr. scientist Yale U., New Haven, 1960—. From asst. fellow to fellow John B. Pierce Lab., New Haven, 1966—96; sr. scientist Electromagnetic Radiation Effects, Air Force Rsch. Lab., Brooks AFB, Tex., 1996—2001, sr. scientist emeritus, 2001—; cons. sci. adv. bd. EPA, 1983—89. Editor: Microwaves & Thermoregulation, 1983; contbr. articles to jours. Bd. dirs. Am. Himalayan Found., 1990—. Fellow AAAS, APA, IEEE, Am. Inst. Med. and Biol. Engring., N.Y. Acad. Scis.; mem. Bioelectromagnetics Soc. Avocations: mountain trekking, gardening, buddhism. Home: 50 Deepwood Dr Hamden CT 06517

ADAM, PATRICIA ANN, legislative aide; b. Mobridge, S.D., May 22, 1936; d. George T. and Madge Mickelson; m. Thomas C. Adam, Aug. 28, 1959; children: Kathleen Bykowski, Paula Adam-Burchill, Karlton Adam, Sarah Adam Axtman. BA in Speech Pathology, U. S.D., 1958, MA in Speech Pathology, 1961. Dir. 1st Nat. Bank, Selby, S.D.; sec. S.D. State Senate. Bd. dirs. Cmty. 1st Bancshares. Bd. dirs. AAUW Nursery Sch., 1965—, YMCA, Children's Care Hosp. and Sch., Sioux Falls, S.D., U. S.D. Found., Vermillion, Oahe Found., S.D., Pierre Sch. Found.; pres. Pierre Sch. Bd., 1977-86; bd. dirs. Sch. Bd. Assn., pres.; mem. City of Pierre Pk. and Recreation Bd.; pres. bd. trustees S.D. State Hist. Soc. Office: State Capitol Pierre SD 57501

ADAMAK, M. JEANELLE, broadcast executive; b. Odessa, Tex., Aug. 18, 1952; d. E.W. and Jo Martin; m. Russell J. Adamak, July 19, 1973; children: Aaron, Ashley. BS in Mgmt./Telecom., Ind. Wesleyan U., 1995. Dir. devel. Odessa Coll., 1986-90; exec. v.p. WFYI TelePlex, Indpls., 1990—. Chair Exec. Women's Leadership Program, Indpls., 1994-96, Vol. Action Ctr. Com., Indpls., 1996—. Mem. Vol. Action Ctr., United Way, 1996-98; bd. dirs. YWCA, Indpls., 1995-99, Cmty. Svc. Coun.-United Way, Indpls., 1996—, Prevent Blindness, Ind., 1996-2000. Recipient Devel. award So. Ednl. Comm. Assn., 1988. Office: WFYI TelePlex 1401 N Meridian St Indianapolis IN 46202-2304 E-mail: jadamak@wfyi.org.

ADAMITIS, TINA THERESA, art educator, artist; b. Neptune, NJ, July 21, 1963; d. Anthony P. and Barbara Jean Ventura; m. John Matthew Adamitis, Aug. 17, 1985; children: Jessica Ann, John Anthony. BA, Georgian Ct. Coll., 1981—85, MA, 1999—2003. Elem. Sch. Tchr., Art Educator State of NJ. Dept. of Edn., Bd. of Examiners, 2001. Elem. sch. tchr. Howell Twp. Bd. of Edn., NJ, 2000—01, substitute tchr., 1996—2000, tchr. of art, 2001—. Art instr. Guild of Creative Art, Shrewsbury, NJ, 1997—99; profl. artist & commn. artist of ho. portraits Self Employed, Freehold, NJ, 1997—. Author: (curriculum guide) A.R.T. Art Research & Technology: A Cross Curricular Approach. Treas. Boy Scouts of Am., Monmouth Coun., Troop 13, Farmingdale, NJ, 2002—. Mem.: NJ. Art Educators Assn., Guild of Creative Art, Freehold Art Soc. (2nd v.p. 1999—2003). Roman Catholic. Avocations: bicycling, outdoors, music, art.

ADAMS, ALGALEE POOL, college dean, art educator; b. Columbia, Mo., Nov. 6, 1919; d. William I. and Anna Ethelene (Dunning) Pool; 1 dau., Judith Dean Adams. BS in Art and English, U. Mo., 1941, MA in Art, 1951; Ed.D. in Fine Arts and Art Edn, Pa. State U., 1960; postgrad. Inst. Adminstrv. Advancement, for Women, U. Mich.; postgrad., Inst. Ednl. Mgmt., Harvard U. Tchr. art Cuba (Mo.) High Sch., 1941-42, Hickman H.S., Columbia, 1942-43; art specialist elem. schs. St. Joseph, Mo., 1943-45; tchr. art St. Clair (Mo.) H.S., 1946-49; pub. sch. art supr. Webb City, Mo., 1949-51; instr. dept. of art St. Cloud (Minn.) State U., 1951-58, asst. prof., 1958-60, assoc. prof., 1960-63, prof., 1963-64, chmn. dept. art, 1959-64; prof. art edn. Mass. Coll. Art, Boston, 1964-77, also chmn. divsn. of edn., 1967-70, dir. tchr. placement, 1964-70, dir. grad. programs in edn., 1970-77; chmn. grad. coun., 1970-74; dean Firelands Coll. Bowling Green State U., Huron, Ohio, 1977-85; owner Adams Miniature Fiber Arts, Columbia, 1989. Liaison with bus. and industry; mem. gov.'s adv. commn. on edn. in arts, 1958, 67; assoc. dir. Project Renewal Mass. State Coll. System, 1974-76; art curriculum cons. to numerous pub. schs. in, Minn., 1951-64; art cons. to Minn. Ins. Info. Ctr., 1960-62; chmn. Eastern Arts Student Conf., N.Y.C., 1968; participant Internat. Conf., Notre Dame U., 1968; field reader HEW, 1966-70 Vol. tutor state literacy program; docent Detroit Inst. Arts; mem. Columbia Cultural Affairs Commn. Recipient Artisian Status award Internat. Guild Miniature Artisians, 1991, Fellow status award, 1995, Citation of Merit for Outstanding Achievement and Meritorius Svc. to Edn. Alumni Bd. U. Mo., 1997, Disting. Svc. award Mo. Western State Coll., 2001. Mem.: Zonta. Home: Columbia, Mo. Died Sept. 13, 2002.

ADAMS, ALICE, sculptor; b. N.Y.C., Nov. 16, 1930; d. Charles P. and Loretto G. (Tobin) A.; m. William D. Gordy, Feb. 7, 1969; 1 dau., Katherine Adams Gordy. Student, Adelphi Coll., 1948-50; BFA, Columbia U., 1953; postgrad. (French Govt. fellow), 1953-54; postgrad. Fulbright Travel grantee, L'Ecole Nat d'Art Decoratif, Aubusson, France, 1953-54. Lectr. Manhattanville Coll., Purchase, N.Y., 1960-79; instr. sculpture Sch. Visual Arts, 1980-87. One-woman shows include N.Y.C., 1972, 74, 75, Hal Bromm Gallery, N.Y.C., 1979, 80; exhibited in group shows at Whitney Mus. Am. Art, N.Y.C., 1971, 73, Indpls. Mus. Art, 1974, Nassau County Mus. Fine Arts, Roslyn, N.Y., 1977, Wave Hill, Riverdale, N.Y., 1979, Mus. Modern Art, N.Y.C., 1984, Lehman Coll. Art Gallery, N.Y.C., 2000-01; represented in permanent collections Weatherspoon Gallery U. N.C., Greensboro, U. Nebr., Everson Mus., Syracuse, N.Y., Haags Gemeternuseum, The Hague, Netherlands, Am. Craft Mus., N.Y.C., Edwin I. Ulrich Mus., Wichita, Kans.; pub. commissions include Bot. Garden, Toledo, Ohio, Design Team Seattle Transit Project, St. Louis Metro-Link Project, Midland Metro, Birmingham, Eng., Port Authority of N.Y. and N.J., Thomas Jefferson U., Phila., N.Y.C. Bd. Edn., State of Conn., Denver Internat. Airport, N.Y.C. Metro. Transp. Authority, U. Tex. San Antonio, Broward County, Fla., U. Del., Newark. Creative Artists Pub. Svc. grantee, 1973-74, 76-77, Nat. Endowment for Arts Artists grant, 1978-79, Richard Florsheim grant, 1999, Am. Acad. of Arts and Letters grant, 1984; Guggenheim fellow, 1981-82; Rockefeller Found. resident, Bellagio, Italy, 2002. Home: 3370 Fort Independence St Bronx NY 10463-4502

ADAMS, BARBARA, English language educator, poet, writer; b. N.Y.C., Mar. 23, 1932; d. David S. Block and Helen (Taxter) Block Tyler; m. Elwood Adams, June 6, 1952; (dec. 1993); children: Steven, Amy, Anne, Samuel. BS, SUNY, New Paltz, 1962, MA, 1970; PhD, NYU, 1981. Prof. English Pace U., N.Y.C., 1984-2000, dir. bus. comm., 1984-2001. Poet in residence Cape Cod Writers' Conf., 1988. Author: Double Solitaire, 1982, The Enemy Self: The Poetry & Criticism of Laura Riding, 1990, Hapax Legomena, 1990, Negative Capability, 1999 (1st Prize for Fiction), (book of poems) The Ordinary Living, 2004, (play) God's Lioness and the Crow: Sylvia Plath and Ted Hughes, 2000; contbr. poems, stories, articles to various mags. and jours. Recipient 1st prize for poetry NYU and Acad. Am. Poets, 1975, 1st prize for fiction Negative Capability contest, 1999; Penfield fellow NYU, 1977. Mem. PEN, Poetry Soc. Am., Poets and Writers. Home: 59 Coach Ln Newburgh NY 12550-3818

ADAMS, BEEJAY (MEREDITH ELISABETH JANE ADAMS), retired sales executive; b. Jefferson Barracks, Mo., June 9, 1920; d. Alden Humphrey and Louise Marion (Banta) Seabury; m. Merlin Francis Adams, July 10, 1948 (dec. 1977); children; S(tephen) Kent, Mark Francis. AB, Bradley U., 1942. Svc. editor Peoria (Ill.) Jour. Star, 1942-46; women's program dir. Sta. WEEK-AM, Peoria, 1946-47; on air personality Sta. KSD-AM, St. Louis, 1948; lectr. Sch. Assembly Svc., Chgo., 1948-49; pres. M.F. Adams, Inc., Quincy, Ill., 1977-85; commodities broker Quincy, 1985-87; pres. MarKent, Inc., Quincy, 1975-99; sec., treas. Miss. Belle Distbn. Co., Inc., Quincy, 1976—2003, v.p., treas., 1979—2003; ret., 2003. Active Quincy Svc. League, 1949-57, local polit. campaigns, co-chmn. local presdl. campaigns, 1952-77; founder, past pres. Quincy Jr. Theatre, 1953-78; charter mem. Quincy Cmty. Theatre; co-chmn. coll. fund drive Quincy Coll., 1988, chmn. 1989; asst. majority leader State Mary Lou Kent; campaign chair, legis aide to Mary Lou Kent. Recipient Ill. Women of Achievement award, Mayor of Quincy, 2000. Mem. Quincy C. of C., Sales and Mktg. Execs. Club, Quincy Art Club, Atlantis Study Club, Quincy Country Club, Phi Beta Phi. Anglican. Avocations: golf, reading, home repair, traveling, politics. Home: 2303 Jersey St Quincy IL 62301-4343

ADAMS, BELINDA JEANETTE SPAIN, nursing administrator; b. Rome, Ga., Dec. 05; d. Oscar Joe and Eleanor (Camacho) Spain. Diploma, Ga. Bapt. Hosp. Sch. Nursing, Atlanta, 1974; BS in Nursing, Med. Coll. Ga., Augusta, 1976; MS in Nursing, Ga. State U., Atlanta, 1980, PhD in Human Resource Devel., 1998. Cert. clin. specialist in med.-surg. nursing, intravenous nurse. Critical care flight nurse Critical Care Medflight, Inc., Atlanta, 1984-88; intravenous therapy coord. DeKalb Gen. Hosp., Atlanta, 1974-81; asst. prof. Mercer U., Atlanta, 1981-87; corp. dir. infusion/high tech. svcs. Kimberly Quality Care, Atlanta, 1988-92; cons. Profl. Learning Systems, 1992—; asst. prof. Clayton State Coll., Morrow, Ga., 1992-94, Ga. Bapt. Coll. Nursing, Atlanta, 1994-95. Clin. examiner Excelsior Coll., Albany, N.Y., 1995—. Mem. ANA, Infusion Nurses Soc. (rsch. com., entrepreneur com.), Ga. Nurses Assn., Sigma Theta Tau. Home and Office: 3433 N Moorings Way Coconut Grove FL 33133

ADAMS, BEVERLY JOSEPHINE, data processing specialist; b. Kansas City, Kans., Nov. 29, 1951; d. Cecil and Eula Laverne (Lynch) Brown; m. Theodore Lavern Adams, Sept. 20, 1969; children: Theodore Lavern Jr., Terry Levar, Traveon LeVar. AA in Data Processing, Kansas City Kans. Community Coll., 1980; BS in Mgmt. and Computers, Park Coll., Parkville, Mo., 1986; postgrad., Rockhurst Coll.; MA, Webster U., 1991. Sr. data processor AT&T, Kansas City, Mo., 1984-86, computer programmer, 1987—, profl. devel. and career devel. facilitator tng. orgn., 1991-96; v.p. ops. AT&T Alliance. Lectr. in field. Editor: (newspaper) Courier, 1969, (newsletter) Kansas City Link, 1987. Cons. Youth of Am., Kansas City, 1983; mem. Kansas City Chief's Football, 1968-72, Coalition Labor Union Women, Washington, 1984, AFL-CIO City Labor Coun., Kansas City, 1984; dir. ch. adult and youth choir, Kansas City, 1982—; Kans. state advisor Young Women's Christian Coun. Named one of Outstanding Young Women of Am., 1981-96, SCLC Achiever in Industry and Bus., 1997. Mem. NAFE, Alliance AT&T Employees (chairperson 1987, treas. 1988-89, regional dir., v.p. ops. 1998—), Profl. Women's Fedn., Young People's Willing workers, Nat. Alliance (nat. outstanding mem. award), Alpha Kappa Alpha (exec. bd., philacter, chairperson Debutante Ball), Gamma Mu Gamma (program chmn. 1985, exec. bd., pres.). Clubs: Wecomo (svcs. award 1983), Young Adults Action (bd. dirs., Leadership award 1980), YWCA (Kansas City). Republican. Pentecostal. Avocations: golf, sewing, singing. Home: 701 NE Lake Pointe Dr Lees Summit MO 64064-2135 Office: AT&T Comms 2121 E 63rd St Kansas City MO 64130-3493 E-mail: ttbadams@msn.com.

ADAMS, CAROL H. dean; d. Wilfred L. and Sadie Dean Hoskins; m. John W. Adams, Apr. 10, 1966; children: Craig J., Dina R. BA in Edn., Mich. State U., 1965; MS in Edn., CUNY, Queens, 1975. Tchr. K-6 N.Y.C. Bd. Edn., 1965—72; tech. cons. Green Leigh Assocs., N.Y.C., 1972—74; instr. tchr. edn. York Coll. CUNY, Jamaica, 1974—75; instr. SUNY Brockport, Rochester, 1975—77; prof. devel. edn. Monroe C.C., Rochester, 1977—91, acad. dean, 1991—. Cons. Greenleigh Assn., N.Y.C., 1972—74; cons. tchr. edn. Corning C.C., NY, 2003. Bd. dirs. YWCA, Rochester, 1989—; mem. steering com. AALDP United Way, Rochester, 1992—93; mem. adv. bd. youth/family project U. Rochester, 2000. Recipient Women's History award, Rochester City Sch. Dist., 1997, Chancellor's award for excellence, SUNY, 2000. Mem.: AAUW, Nat. Inst. Leadership Devel., Am. Assn. Women in Cmty. and Jr. Colls., Nat. Assn. Devel. Edn., The Links (v.p. 2002), Leaders League for Innovation, Phi Delta Kappa. Home: 106 Elmore Rd Rochester NY 14618 Office: Monroe Community Coll 1000 E Henrietta Rd Rochester NY 14623

ADAMS, CAROLYN LEE, poet, artist; b. Houston, Oct. 17, 1956; d. Samuel Thurman and Ivy Berdetta (Shunk) Bridgeman; m. Tommy Matt Davis, Dec. 7, 1982 (div. Jan. 1987); children: Evon Lee Davis, Steven Thomas Davis; m. Matthew Lee Adams, June 24, 2000. Grad. h.s., Houston. Floral designer Flowers, Inc., Houston, 1975—77; underwriting clk. Great So. Life Ins. Co., Houston, 1977—80; acctg. clk. Cahaba Constrn., Houston, 1980—85; sec., graphics specialist, and adminstrv. coord. Baylor Coll. Medicine, Houston, 1985—. Exhibitions include Baylor Coll. Medicine, 1991, 1992, Diverseworks Gallery, Houston, 1991, The Fountainhead Gallery, 1991, The Firehouse Gallery, 1992;, author numerous poems; co-editor: Curbside Rev., 2000—; contbr. articles to profl. jours. Mng. mem. Flying Dutchman Writers Troupe. Recipient 2d Pl. award for nat. poetry contest, The New Press Literary Quarterly, 1993, 2d Pl. award for poetry contest, Zuzu's Poetry Quarterly, 1994. Avocations: photography, stained glass, collage art, computer graphics, needlecrafts.

ADAMS, CHRISTINE BEATE LIEBER, psychiatrist, educator; b. Greensboro, N.C., June 20, 1949; d. Paul Lieber Adams and Marjorie Pinckney (Quackenbos) Ould; 1 child, Justin McKendree Adams-Tucker. Ed., Agnes Scott Coll., 1967-69; BA in English Lit. with honors, U. Fla., 1971, MD, 1976. Diplomate Am. Bd. Psychiatry and Neurology (examiner 1985), Am. Bd. Child Psychiatry (examiner 1984, 91), Nat. Bd. Med. Examiners. Resident in gen. psychiatry U. Louisville Sch. Medicine, 1976-78, fellow in child psychiatry, 1978-80, asst. clin. prof. dept. psychiatry and behavioral scis., 1981—, attending psychiatrist consultation-liaison svc., 1992, 93; pvt. practice, Louisville, 1980—. Med. advisor Social Security Adminstrn., HHS, Louisville, 1986—; child psychiatry cons. Seven Counties Svcs., Ky. Dept. Human Resources, 1989, 93; physician advisor Nat. Health Svcs., Louisville, 1993-2000, physician reviewer in child and adult psychiatry, 2000-01; physician advisor Magellan Behavioral Health Svcs., 2003—; physician reviewer Lifespring Mental Health Svcs., 2001-02; physician advisor Magllan Behavioral Health, Columbia, Md., 2003—; reviewer Am. Jour. Psychiatry, 1983—; cons. So. Ind. Mental Health and Guidance Ctr., Jeffersonville, 1981 83, U. Fla., 1982; presenter in field. Contbr. articles to med. jours., chpts. to books. Mem dirs. Gainesville (Fla.) Women's Health Ctr., 1973-75, Discover Louisville Orch., 1999-2001, mem. Jefferson County (Ky.) Juvenile Justice Commn. 1982-86. Recipient award Nat. Psychiat. Endowment Fund, 1980. Fellow Am. Acad. Child and Adolescent Psychiatry (com. on rights and legal matters 1984-92); mem. Am. Psychiat. Assn. (mem. com. family violence and child sexual abuse 1987-94), Am. Acad. Psychiatry and Law, Nat. Com. for Prevention Child Abuse, Ky. Psychiat. Assn., Ky. Acad. Child Psychiatry (sec.-treas. 1980-81, pres.-elect 1981 82, pres. 1982-83). E-mail: cbladams@bellsouth.net.

ADAMS, CHRISTINE HANSON, advertising executive; b. Hackensack, N.J., May 24, 1950; d. Kenwood Alwin and Doris (Rogers) Hanson; m. L. Ashby Adams III, June 1, 1974 (div. Aug. 1993); 1 child, Nathaniel Kaufman. BA, Lafayette Coll., 1972; MBA, Duke U., 1979. Med. sales rep. Hoffman-LaRoche, Nutley, N.J., 1972-75; sr. market rsch. analyst Burroughs Wellcome Co., Research Triangle Park, N.C., 1976-77, product planner, 1978; dir. market research Sterling Drug Inc., N.Y.C., 1979-81; group product mgr. Pfizer Inc., N.Y.C., 1981-83; account supr. Kallir Philips Ross Inc., N.Y.C., 1983, v.p., account group supr., 1984-86; v.p., account supr. Baxter Gurian and Mazzei Inc., Beverly Hills, Calif., 1987-89, account group v.p., 1990-91, sr. v.p. account group, supr., 1991-93, sr. v.p. mgmt. supr., 1994; sr. v.p. group acct. dir. Kallir Philips Ross Inc, N.Y., 1994-96; sr. v.p. mgmt. supr. Torre Lazur Comm., Parsippany, N.J., 1996-98; v.p., mgmt. supr. Integrated Comm. Corp., Lawrenceville, N.J., 1998-2000; sr. v.p. mgmt. supr. Nelson Comms., Inc., Princeton, N.J., 2001—. Cons. advt. Wellness Cmty., Santa Monica, Calif., 1988-92. Active membership com. St. Michael's Episcopal Ch., Studio City, Calif., 1987-93, altar guild, 1988-93, tchr. Sunday sch., 1990-91. Named Young Career Woman Bus. Profl. Women's Assn., Chapel Hill, N.C., 1978. Mem. Healthcare Mktg. and Comms. Coun., Healthcare Businesswomen's Assn. Republican. Avocations: fashion design, sewing, music, 19th-century English Literature. Home: 8 Villa Dr Princeton Junction NJ 08550-1241 Office: Integrated Comm Corp 989 Lenox Dr Ste 300 Lawrenceville NJ 08648-2315 E-mail: adamskaufman@home.com.

ADAMS, CINDY, journalist; b. N.Y.C., Apr. 24; d. Harry and Jessica (Sugar); m. Joey Adams, Feb. 14. News commentator Sta. WABC-TV, N.Y.C., 1967-70; interviewer NBC-TV, 1970-73; dir., asst. to pres. Miss Universe, Inc., N.Y.C., 1970-77, Good Morning Am., 1996—98; columnist N.Y. Post, N.Y.C., 1981—. Interviewer of celebrities for Fox-TV's "A Current Affair", 1986-91, Lifetime Cable, 1991—; commentator fashion show Bonds for Israel, N.Y., 1970-85; lectr. Keedick Lectr. Service, N.Y., 1970-80. Author: Sukarno of Indonesia, 1965, Lee Strasberg, 1980, Jolie Gabor, 1978, The Gift of Jazzy, 2003; contbr. articles to mags.; designer jewelry Cartier, N.Y. 1971. Avocation: traveling. Office: NY Post 1211 Avenue Of The Americas New York NY 10036-8790

ADAMS, CLARA I. academic administrator; BSc in Chemistry, Morgan State Coll., 1954; MSc in Chemistry, Iowa State Coll., 1957; PhD in Chemistry, U. Mass., 1970. Chemist Nat. Heart Inst. NIH, Bethesda, Md., 1957—59; asst. prof. chemistry Morgan State U., Balt., 1959—68, assoc. prof. chemistry, 1968—73, prof., chmn. chemistry dept., 1973—75, dean Sch. Grad. Studies, 1975—85, acting v.p. acad. affairs, 1985—86, v.p. acad. affairs, 1986—; tchg. fellow Smith Coll., Northampton, Mass., 1963—65. Mem. com. on minority grad. edn. Coun. Grad. Schs. in the U.S., regional rep. on bd. dirs., 1983—84, 1986—88; mem.-at-large exec. com. Northea. Assn. Grad. Schs., 1977—79, pres., 1979—81; mem. Accreditation Bd. Engring. and Tech. Mem. Md. State Legis./Univ. Coun. on Provision of Acad. Svcs. to Gen. Assembly, 1977—80; bd. dirs. Nat. Aquarium in Balt., 1977—82, v.p. bd. dirs., 1979—82. Named one of 100 Women Who Influence Balt., Balt. Mag., 1983; recipient Disting. Alumnus award, Morgan State U., 1976. Mem.: AAUP, AAAS, Mid. States Assn. Schs. and Colls., Commn. Higher Edn., Am. Assn. State Colls. and Univs., Am. Chem. Soc. Office: Morgan State U VP Acad Affairs 300 Truth Hall Baltimore MD 21251

ADAMS, CONSTANCE EWING, school psychologist, art therapist; b. Troy, N.Y., Oct. 15, 1946; d. Walter Duncan and Gabrielle Roberts (Solomon) Ewing; m. Robert Maurice Adams, Aug. 23, 1969; children: Karen Gayle, Louise Katherine, Robert Ewing. BA, Denison U., 1968; MA,

Ft. Hays (Kans.) State U., 1977; MS, Ea. Ky. U., 1988; EdD, U. Ky., 1999. Cert. art therapist, sch. psychologist, Ky. Counselor High Plains Comprehensive Cmty. Mental Health Ctr., Hays, 1970-72, art therapist, 1974-75; instr. Ft. Hays State U., 1974-79; sch. psychologist Madison County Schs., Richmond, Ky., 1987—2002, dir. psychol. svcs., 2002 . Presenter in field; mem. adv. bd. Richmond Youth Svcs. Ctr., 1994—; mem.-at-large Sch. Psychology Coun., Ky. Dept. Edn., Frankfort, 1993-98; chmn. adv. coun. Clark Moores Youth Svcs. Ctr., 2001—. Paintings exhibited in one-woman show, other invitational and juried exhbns., 1975-79. Mem. Kans. Gov.'s Commn. on Criminal Adminstrn., Hays, 1975; chair, pers. dir. Friendship Home, Youth Care, Inc., Kans., 1970-77; responder Ky. Cmty. Crisis Respnse Team, 1993-. Mem. LWV (pres., bd. dirs. Hays chpt. 1970-79, bd. dirs., bull. editor, 2d v.p. Madison County chpt. 1980—), Nat. Assn. Sch. Psychologists (cert., Govtl. and Profl. Rels. award 1996), Am. Art Therapy Assn. (registered), Ky. Assn. for Psychology in Schs. (exec. coun. 1990—, program chair 1990-91, legis. chair 1991—, Ky. Sch. Psychologist of Yr. 1991), Ky. Assn. Sch. Adminstrs. Home: 390 Adams Ln Richmond KY 40475-8763 Office: Madison County Schs 707 N 2nd St Richmond KY 40475-1259

ADAMS, DIANE LORETTA, physician; b. St. Louis, Nov. 3, 1948; m. William McKinley Adams; children: Kareem McKinley, Dawn Caron, Akeem Michael. BS, Howard U., 1969; MD, N.J. Med. Sch., 1976; MPH, Johns Hopkins U., 1980, resident in gen. preventive medicine, 1980. Resident in family practice Howard U. Hosp., Washington, 1976-79; chief med. officer USCG Shipyard, Curtis Bay, Md., 1980-83, Bur. Engraving and Printing, Washington, 1983-85; med. officer St. Elizabeth Hosp., Washington, 1985-86; rsch. analyst Office Asst. Sec. Health, Rockville, Md., 1987-90; chief minority health svcs. rsch. program Agy. Health Care Policy and Rsch., Rockville, 1990-93; congl. fellow office of Congressman Louis Stokes U.S. Ho. of Reps., Washington, 1990; sr. med. adv. Agy. Health Care Policy and Rsch., Rockville, 1993-99, Agy. Healthcare Rsch. and Quality, Dept. Health/Human Svcs., 1999-2000, cons., 2000—; clin. assoc. prof. dept. phys. therapy U. Md., 1993—2000; dir. health policy, rsch. and profl. med. affairs Nat. Med. Assn., 2001—02. Cons. rep. AIDS Task Force, 1987-93; lectr. intensive bioethics Georgetown U. Kennedy Inst. Ethics, 1991; sr. health policy fellow, Ga. Ctr. Advanced Telecommns. Tech. Editor: Health Issues for Women of Color: A Cultural Diversity Perspective, 1995. Named to, Md. Women's Hall of Fame, 1997, Black Coll. Alumni Hall of Fame in Medicine, 2001, Women of Achievement in Md. History, 2002; recipient Adminstrs. Outstanding Cmty. Svc. award, Agy. Health Care Policy and Rsch., 1996. Mem.: APHA, Am. Coll. Preventive Medicine, Alpha Kappa Alpha (mem. internat. program com. 1998—2002, Outstanding Comt. Svc. award 1981—85). Avocation: equitation. Home: 17032 Barn Ridge Dr Silver Spring MD 20906-1106

ADAMS, ELIZABETH HERRINGTON, banker; b. Tulsa, May 25, 1947; d. James Dillon and Helen (Allderdice) Herrington; m. Phillip Hollis Hackney, Mar. 5, 1977 (dec. Jan. 1990); m. Keith R. Adams, Sept. 4, 1993. Student, No. Ariz. U., 1965-67, 68-69. With Coldwater (Kans.) Nat. Bank, summers 1964-67, The Ariz. Bank, Phoenix, 1969, Flagstaff, 1970-71; asst. cashier The Wilmore (Kans.) State Bank, 1972—2001, The Coldwater Nat. Bank, 1974-83, cashier, ops. officer, 1984—; v.p. The Coldwater (Kans.) Nat. Bank, 1998—2002, sr. v.p., 2002—. Bd. dirs. The Coldwater Nat. Bank. Bd. dirs. Pioneer Lodge Nursing Home, Coldwater, 1984-89; mem. sch. site coun., 1993-94; life mem. Girl Scouts, chmn. Neighborhood Cookie Drive, 1991-95; bd. dirs., mem. strategic planning com. Wheatbelt Area Girl Scout Coun., 1994-96—; elder 1st Presbyn. Ch., Coldwater; Kans. Lung Assn. Vol. Spkrs. Bur., 1998—; mem. Ch. Session Bd., Coldwater, 1994-2000. Mem. Fin. Women Internat., Cmty. Bankers Assn. Kans. (membership com. 1991-94, INPAC com. 1992-93), Kans. Ind. Bankers (gen. svcs. com. 1986-87), PEO, Alpha Omicron Pi, Lake Coldwater Archtl. Rev. Bd. Republican. Avocation: music (pianist). Office: Coldwater Nat Bank PO Box 726 Coldwater KS 67029-0726

ADAMS, FRANCES GRANT, II, lawyer; b. Wheeling, W.Va., Nov. 30, 1955; d. Jack Richard and Frances Irene (Grant) A. BA, W.Va. U., 1976, JD, 1979; MA, Webster U., 1983. Bar: W.Va. 1979, U.S. Dist. Ct. (so. dist.) W.Va. 1979, U.S. Ct. Mil. Appeals 1979, U.S. Supreme Ct. 1988, D.C. 1989. Asst. staff judge advocate armament divsn. USAF, Eglin AFB, Fla., 1979-82, dep. staff judge advocate Keflavik, Iceland, 1982-83, staff judge advocate 71st Air Base Group Vance AFB, Okla., 1984-86, chief gen. torts sect. claims and tort litig. staff hdqrs. Washington, 1986-88, chief mgmt. and analysis br. claims and tort litig. divsn. Legal Svcs. Agy., 1988-92, sr. tort atty. tort claims and litig. divsn. Legal Svcs. Agy., 1992-97, chief internat. torts br., 1997—; atty. environ. law and litig. divsn., Legal Svcs. Agy. USAFR, USAF, Washington, 1992—99. Program chmn. Pentagon chpt. Fed. Bar Assn., 1989-90. Mem. DAR (chmn. procedures manual W.Va. chpt. 1989-92), Magna Carta Dames, Ancient and Honorable Arty. Co., Air Force Assn. (life), Ret. Officers Assn. (life). Avocations: photography, travel, farming, gardening.

ADAMS, GABRIELLE, biologist; b. Mateszalka, Hungary; BSc, McMaster U., 1963; PhD, Carleton U., 1968. From postdoctoral fellow to rsch. officer Nat. Rsch. Coun. Canada, 1967-71; rsch. assoc. biology dept. Carleton U., 1971-75; with rsch. jour.. Inst. Biol. Scis. Nat. Rsch. Coun. Can., 1975—93, dir. gen., 1993—. Office: Inst Biol Scis Bldg M54 1200 Montreal Rd Ottawa ON Canada K1A 0R6 E-mail: gabrielle.adams@nrc-cnrc.gc.ca.

ADAMS, INGRID G. federal government intelligence specialist; b. Washington, Oct. 11, 1959; d. Norbert Green and Marion Zeno Joseph; m. Keith Michael Adams, Mar. 1994 (div. Apr. 21, 1998); 1 child, Oliver ; children: Ashaunta, Diondra, Dana Tumblin. BA magna cum laude in Psychology, So. U., 1983. Case worker Office Family Security State of La., Hahnville, La., 1984—87, supr. eligibility worker Thibodaux, La., 1987—88; import specialist U.S. Customs Svc., New Orleans, 1989—98; intelligence specialist Dept. Homeland Security, New Orleans, 1998—. Ind. assoc. Pre Paid Legal Svcs., Ada, Okla., 2003—; spkr. Green's Consulting Co., St. Rose, La., 2003. Mem. com. Curtis Johnson Campaign, St. Rose, 1999, Dems. for Mary Landreu, St. Rose, 1999; bd. dir. Dem. Women Orgn., 1998—2001. Mem.: Positive Women/Men of New Orleans, St. Charles Hist. Found., So. U. Alumni Assn. (2d v.p. 2001—03). Democrat. Baptist. Avocations: writing, singing, dance, stamp collecting, reading. Home: 309 Turtle Creek Lane Saint Rose LA 70087 Office: Dept Homeland Security 423 Canal St Rm 242 New Orleans LA 70130

ADAMS, JANE MILLER, retired psychotherapist; b. Shreveport, La., June 10, 1922; d. Charles Frederick and Lucile Elizabeth (Day) Miller; m. James Franklin Adams, June 8, 1946. BA, La. State U., 1950, MSW, 1960. Bd. cert. social worker La.; bd. cert. diplomat. Am. Bd. of Examiners of Clin. Social Work, emeritus. Clin. social worker Ctrl. La. State Hosp., Pineville, 1957-62, Forest Glen Mental Health Outpatient Clinic, Pineville, 1962-64; med. social worker La. Pub. Health, Alexandria, 1964-67; adminstr., therapist Alexandria Outpatient Alcoholism Clinic, 1967-73; psychotherapist Episcopal Diocese La., Pineville, 1974-82, pvt. practice, Pineville, 1982-92. Cons. and spkr. in field. Pink lady vol. Huey P. Long Regional Hosp., Pineville, 1982-85; vol. to cons. Cmty. Mental Health Day Care Ctr., Alexandria, 1984-85; staff cons. Ctrl. La. Alcoholism Clinic, Alexandria, 1975-78; alcoholism cons. Forest Glen Mental Health Outpatient Clinic, 1975-78. Democrat. Episcopalian. Avocations: gardening, poetry. Home: 404 Hiawatha Trl Pineville LA 71360-4407

ADAMS, JEAN RUTH, retired entomologist, biomedical researcher; b. Edgewater Park, N.J., Aug. 17, 1928; d. Herbert Raymond and Gertrude Gladys (Budd) A. BS, Rutgers U., 1950, PhD (Trubeck fellow), 1962. Registered profl. entomologist. Lab. technician Rohm & Haas Co., Bristol, Pa., 1951-57; postdoctoral fellow U. Pa., Phila., 1961-62; rsch. entomologist USDA Agr. Rsch. Ctr., Beltville, Md., 1962-96, collaborator, 1996—, ret. Cons. insect pathology, electron microscopy. Mem. editl. bd. Jour. Invertebrate Pathology, 1986-89; editor: Atlas of Invertebrate Viruses, 1991, Insect Potpourri: Adventures in Entomology, 1992; contbr. articles to sci. jours. Mem. nominating com. D.C. Bapt. Conv., 1977—79; dir. Acteens, Mission Youth Orgn, D.C. Bapt. Conv., 1972—86, 1988—92, sec., 1993—97; Sunday sch. tchr. 1st Bapt. Ch., Hyatsville, Md., 1962—, chmn. Christian edn. bd., 1973—74, mem. nominating com., 1974—77, mem. bd. missions, 1977—80, ch. treas., 1973—74, mem. choir, 1979—, diaconate, 1980—86, 1998—2000, 2002—, vice chmn., 1981—82, chmn., 1982—91; trustee Bapt. Home, 1982—91, sec., 1985—91; trustee Sunday sch. bd. SBC, 1991—99; chmn. nominating com. D.C. Bapt. Conv., 2000—01. Mem. Am. Registered Profl. Entomologists (bd. dirs. Chesapeake chpt. 1989—, pres. 1991-93, sec.-treas. 1997—), Electron Microscopy Soc. Am. (chmn. sci. exhibits ann. meeting 1982), Entomol. Soc. Am., Am. Soc. for Cell. Biology, Soc. for Invertebrate Pathology (sec. 1982-84), Washington Soc. for Electron Microscopy (coun. 1976-83, sec.-treas. 1976-78, 80-82), Washington Entomol. Soc., Md. Entomol. Soc., Sigma Xi, Sigma Delta Epsilon. Home: 6004 41st Ave Hyattsville MD 20782-3058 Office: USDA Agr Rsch Ctr Bldg 011A W Insect Biocontrol Lab Rm 214 Beltsville MD 20705

ADAMS, JODY, chef, restaurant owner; m. Ken Rivard; children: Oliver Rivard, Roxanne Rivard. Student, Brown U. Apprentice, class asst. Nancy Verde Barr; chef Seasons restaurant, Boston, 1983—86; sous chef Hamersley's Bistro, Boston, 1986—90; exec. chef Michela's, Boston, 1990—94; ptnr., chef Rialto, Cambridge, 1994—; ptnr. Sapphire Restaurant Group, Cambridge, 1994—, blu, Boston, 2001, Noik, Cambridge, Mass., 2002. Named Best Chef, Boston Mag., 1997; named one of Five Rising Stars, Restaurant Hospitality, 1992, Am.'s Best Young Chef's to Keep Your Eye On, Esquire mag., 1992, Am.'s Ten Best new Chefs, Food and Wine mag., 1993; named to Fine Dining Hall of Fame, Nation's Restaurant News, 2000; recipient Perrier-Jouet Best Chef award N.E., James Beard Found., 1997. Office: Sapphire Restaurant Grp 20 Univ Rd Cambridge MA 02138

ADAMS, JOYCE M. academic administrator; b. Dickinson, Tex., Dec. 21; d. Clarence L. and Effie R. Adams. BS, Prairie View A&M U., 1965; MS, Tex. Woman's U., 1978, PhD, 1996. RN Tex. Staff nurse M.D. Anderson Hosp., Houston, 1967—73; instr., prof. San Jacinto Coll., Houston, 1973—94, dept. chmn., 1994—98, assoc. dean, 1998—2003, dean program devel. instl. effectiveness and health careers, 2003—. V.p. Bd. of Vocat. Nurse Examiners for State of Tex. Bd. dirs. Eastwood Health Clinic, Houston, 1999—2003, Benevolent Mission Internat., Houston, 1994—2003; chair health com.. Shalom Zone Mobile Health Ministries, Houston, 1998—. Grantee, Tex. Nurses Assn., 2000—02. Mem.: ANA, Tex. Nurses Assn., Sigma Theta Tau. Office: San Jacinto Coll 13735 Beamer Rd Houston TX 77048

ADAMS, JULIE KAREN, clinical psychologist; b. Portland, Oreg., Dec. 12, 1955; d. Allen Hays and Susanna Angelina (Meyers) A. B, Willamette U., 1977; M, Ctrl. Wash. U., 1982; cert. in bus. adminstrn., U. Wash., 1986; D, Pacific U., 1992; MS, Columbia U., 2000. Lic. clin. psychologist; cert. counselor, sch. psychologist, Wash. Sch. psychologist Highline Sch. Dist., Seattle, 1987-90; psychology intern Elmcrest Psychiat. Hosp., Portland, Conn., 1990, clinician, 1991; rsch. asst. Yale U., New Haven, Conn., 1991; clinician Advanced Clin. Svcs., Seattle, 1991-93; postdoctoral fellow U. Wash., Seattle, 1991-93; acad. counselor Johns Hopkins U., Balt., 1993; behavior intervention specialist Edmonds (Wash.) Sch. Dist., 1993-94, Marysville Sch. Dist., Marysville, Wash., 1994-99; instr. Seattle U., 1995-99. Guest spkr. in field to profl. assns., also Pacific U., U. Wash., U. Oreg., 1989—. Contbr. articles to profl. jours.; freelance writer: Psychology Today Mag.; contbr. (book chpt.) Women in Communication. Mem. tng. com., kids week com., nursing home com., pub. policy com. Jr. League of Seattle, 1988—; health care researcher Wash. State Legis., Olympia, 1993; campaigner Bush for Pres., Seattle, 1988, 92; rsch. asst. to state senator Oreg. State Legis., Salem, 1985; press page nat. conv. Rep. Nat. Com., Detroit, 1980; student grad. v.p., faculty rep. com. Pacific U. Sch. of Profl. Psychology, 1989-90. Mem. APA (health psychology com. student rep. 1992-93), Wash. Psychol. Assn., Soc. Profl. Journalists, Willamette U. Alumni Assn. (bd. dirs. 1983-88), Vols. for Outdoor Wash. (bd. dirs. 1986-87), City Club of Seattle (membership com. 1986-88), Jr. League Seattle, Psi Chi, Beta Alpha Gamma. Avocations: writing, skiing, american history, reading, traveling. Home: 10105 SW Melnore St Portland OR 97225-4354 E-mail: ja365@columbia.edu.

ADAMS, KAREN HOEVE, university administrator; b. Holland, Mich., Jan. 3, 1961; d. Erville Wayne and Nella Ruth (Heemstra) Hoeve; m. James Franklin Adams Jr., July 1, 1989; children: Lucas James, Matthew Wayne (twins). BA, Calvin Coll., 1983; MS in Edn., Ind. U., 1985, EdD, 1995. Asst. dir. student fin. assistance Bloomington Office Student Fin. Assistance, Ind. U., 1985-89; computing edn. trainer Ind. U. Computing Svcs., Bloomington, 1989-91, planning and comms. adminstr., 1991—97; chief staff Office V.P. for Info. Tech. and Rsch. Ind. U., 1997—. Bd. dirs. Bloomington Pops, 1993—. Home: 2301 E Arden Dr Bloomington IN 47401-6890 Office: Office of VP for Info Tech 601 East Kirkwood Ave Bloomington IN 47405

ADAMS, KAYE MABRY, periodical editor; Exec. editor So. Living, Birmingham, Ala. Co-author: The Ultimate Southern Living Cookbook, 1999. Office: So Living 2100 Lakeshore Dr Birmingham AL 35209-6721*

ADAMS, LAVONNE MARILYN BECK, critical care nurse, nursing educator; b. Bridgeport, Conn., Feb. 22, 1965; d. Adolf and Hazel B. (Henderson) Beck. ASN, Kettering Coll. Med. Arts, 1985; BSN, Wright State U., 1988; MSN, Andrews U., 1992, PhD, 2003. CCRN. Staff nurse Kettering (Ohio) Med. Ctr., 1985-89, resource staff nurse, 1989-95, instr. in nursing, 1989-92; asst. prof. nursing Kettering (Ohio) Coll. Med. Arts, 1992—99, Southwestern Adventist U., Keene, Tex., 1999—2003, assoc. prof., 2003—; PRN staff nurse Huguley Mem. Hosp., 2002—. Asst. leader kindergarten divsn. Seventh-day Adventist Ch., Kettering, 1987—93, Arlington Seventh Day Adventist Ch., 2001—03; mem. Southwestern Sem. Oratorio Chorus, 1999—. Mem.: Am. Assn. Critical Care Nurses, Nat. League Nursing, Pi Lambda Theta, Sigma Theta Tau, Phi Kappa Phi. Avocations: music, travel. Home: 7000 Welch Ct Fort Worth TX 76133-6726 Office: Southwestern Adventist Univ 100 W Magnolia Keene TX 76059

ADAMS, LILIANA OSSES, music performer, harpist; b. Poznan, Poland, May 16, 1939; came to U.S., 1978, naturalized, 1990; d. Sylwester and Helena (Koswenda) O.; m. Edmund Pietryk, Sept. 4, 1965 (div. Aug. 1970); m. Bruce Meredith Adams, Feb. 3, 1978. MA, Music Acad. Poznan, Poland, 1971. Prin. harpist Philharm. Orch. of Szczecin, Poland, 1964-72, Imperial Opera and Ballet Orch., Tehran, Iran, 1972-78; pvt. music tchr. Riyadh, Saudi Arabia, 1979-81; soloist Austrian Radio, 1981-86; solo harpist, pvt. tchr. harp and piano Antioch, Calif., 1986—. Music cons. Schs. and Librs., Calif., 1991—. Contbr. articles to profl. jours. Mem. Am. Fedn. of Musicians, Am. Harp Soc., Music Tchrs. Assn. Calif., Internat. Soc. of Harpers, U.K. Harp Assn., Internat. Harp Ctr. (Switzerland). Home: PO Box 233 Antioch CA 94509-0023 E-mail: harpliliana@comcast.net.

ADAMS, LORETTA, marketing executive; b. Panama; BS in Internat. Mktg., Am. U., 1962; postgrad. in Econs., U. Panama, Panama City, 1963-64. Mgmt. trainee Sears Roebuck & Co., Panama City, Panama, 1962-63, mgmt. pers., 1963-65; supr. internat. advertising projects Kenyon & Eckhardt Advertising, Inc., N.Y.C., 1965-68; asst. rsch. dir. divsn. L.Am. and Far E. Richardson-Vicks Internat., Mexico City and Wilton, Conn., 1968-69, rsch. dir. divsn. Mex. and L.Am., 1969-75, mem. top mgmt. strategic planning team, 1975-78; founder, pres. Mkt. Devel., Inc., San Diego, 1978—. Contbr. articles to profl. jours. Mem. Am. Mktg. Assn., European Soc. for Opinion & Market Rsch., Advt. Rsch. Found., Coun. Am. Survey Rsch. Orgns., Market Rsch. Assn. Office: Market Devel Inc 600 B St Ste 1600 San Diego CA 92101-4584

ADAMS, LORRAINE, reporter; BA in English, Princeton U., 1981; MA in English, Columbia U., 1982. With The Concord (N.H.) Monitor, 1983, 84, The Dallas Morning News, 1984-92, The Washington Post, 1992-93, projects reporter, 1993-99, justice dept. reporter, 1999—. Recipient Pulitzer Prize for investigative reporting, 1992. Office: Washington Post 1150 15th St NW Washington DC 20071-0002

ADAMS, MARGARET BERNICE, retired museum official; b. Toronto, Ont., Can., Apr. 29, 1936; arrived in U.S., 1948, naturalized, 1952; d. Robert Russell and Kathleen Olive (Buffin) A.; m. Alberto Enrique Sánchez-Quiñonez, Nov. 30, 1956 (div. 1960). AA, Monterey Peninsula Coll., 1969; BA, San Jose State U., 1971; MA, U. Utah, 1972. Curator ethnic arts Civic Art Gallery, San Jose, Calif., 1971; staff asst. Utah Mus. Fine Arts, Salt Lake City, 1972; lectr., curator Coll. Seven, U. Calif., Santa Cruz, 1972-74; part-time educator Cabrillo Coll., Aptos, Calif., 1973, Monterey Peninsula Coll., 1973-84; dir. U.S. Army Mus., Presidio of Monterey, 1974-83; chief. mus. br. Ft. Ord Mil. Complex, 1983-88. Guest curator Am. Indian arts Monterey Peninsula Mus. Art, 1975-88. Author: Indian Tribes of North America and Chronology of World Events in Prehistoric Pueblo Times, 1975, Historic Old Monterey, 1976; contbg. editor Indian Am., Writing on the Wall, WWII Patriotic Posters, 1987; contbr. articles to jours. Mem. Native Am. adv. panel AAAS, Washington, 1972-78; mem. rev. and adv. com. Project Media, Nat. Indian Edn. Assn., Mpls., 1973-78; working mem. Program for Tng. Am. Indian Counsellors in Alcoholism Counselling and Rehab. Programs, 1972-74; mem. hist. adv. com. Monterey County Bd. Suprs., 1987-89. Grad. fellow, dean's scholar U. Utah, 1972; dean's scholar Monterey Peninsula Coll., 1969, San Jose State U., 1971. Mem. Am. Anthrop. Assn., Am. Assn. Museums, Soc. Am. Archeology, Nat., Calif., Indian Edn. Assns. Home: PO Box 192 Cedar Ridge CA 95924-0192

ADAMS, MARTHA JEAN MORRIS, art educator, artist; d. Frank Elliott and Theodosia Ellen (Dever) Morris; m. John Hines Adams, Sr., Aug. 3, 1962; children: John Hines Jr., Jean Karole Adams Meares. BS in Edn., Elizabeth City State U., 1985. Art tchr. Hertford County Schs., Winton, NC, 1986—99, 2002—, Franklin County Schs., Louisburg, NC, 1999—2000, Vancer County Schs., Henderson, NC, 2000—02. Mem. county-wide sch. improvement com. Hertford County Schs., Winton, 1993—94; program enhancement chmn. Riverview Elem., Murfreesboro, NC, 1994—96; mem. exec. bd. Profl. Educators N.C., Raleigh, 1993—2003. Vol. Spl. Olympics Riverview Elem., Ahoskie, NC, 1992—96; participant N.C. Ctr. for Advancement Tchg., Cullowhee, 1996, 1999; Sunday sch. tchr. Grantee, N.C. Arts Coun., 1993—94, U.S. Govt., 1995—97. Mem.: Nat. Art Edn. Assn. Baptist. Avocations: reading, cooking. Home: 103 Springlake Dr Murfreesboro NC 27855 Office: Ahoskie Elem Sch 200 N Talmage Ave Ahoskie NC 27910

ADAMS, MARYLYN DEWEY, music educator; b. Elmira, N.Y., Nov. 22, 1939; d. Guy Hazlett Dewey and Jane Emlyn Laye; m. Wayne Leroy Adams (div.); 4 children. BS in Edn., SUNY, Fredonia, 1961. Cert. music edn. K-12, ESOL, gifted and talented, music K-12. Vocal music tchr. 7-12 Corning Northside Jr.-Sr. H.S., Corning, NY, 1961—62; music tchr. K-12 Morrisville-Eaton Cen. Sch., Morrisville, NY, 1962—63; substitute tchr., organist Pub. Sch. and Cmty. Ch., Morrisville, 1964—81; coop. ext., 4-H vol. Madison Co. 4-H and Coop. Ext., Morrisville, 1967—81; assoc. Adams Assocs., Morrisville, 1976—81; food svc. worker, drama participant Morrisville Ag & Tech Coll., 1978—81; savings and loan counselor 1st City Fed. S&L, Bradenton, Fla., 1981—84; vocal music tchr. King Mid. Sch., Bradenton, 1984—88; min. of music Ft. King Presbyn. Ch., Ocala, Fla., 1988—96; vocal music tchr. NMMS- Marion County Pub. Schs., Ocala, 1988—96; vocal/keyboard tchr. HMS-Marion County Pub. Schs., Ocala, 1996—. Contbr. mem. Statue of Liberty-Ellis Island Found., N.Y.C., 2000; mem., rschr. various co. hist. socs. N.Y. and Pa., 1996; marcher, adviser March of Dimes (Mothers' March), N.Y. and Fla., 1964; advocate, contbg. mem. Habitat for Humanity, Ocala, 1988; Leader, vol. Boy/Girl Scouts, 4-H-Coop Ext., Cornell Camp Bd., Morrisville, 1969—81; mem., performer Civic Theater/ Appleton Mus., Ocala, 1988; supporter Marion Cultural Alliance, Ocala, 2001; com. initiator, mem. ACE-Arts for Complete Edn., Ocala; vol. Dept Juvenile Justice, Ocala; founder, coord. HMS Intergenerational Arts Day, Ocala, 2000; mem. United Presbyn. Women, Morrisville and Ocala, 1962. Named Miss Congeniality of N.Y. State, Miss N.Y. State Contest, 1958, Participant - City to City Exch. to Siberia, Palatka Friendship Soc., 1992; recipient Vol. Cert., Dept of Juvenile Justice, 1998; grantee USIA Grant Chaperone to USSR, Marion Cty Pers. Dirs., 1990; scholar N.Y. State scholarship nursing and edn., N.Y. State U. Bd. of Regents, 1957, music scholar, Soc. for Preservation and Encouragement of Barbershop Quartet Singing in Am., 1957. Mem.: AAUW (past pres.), NEA, Fla. State Poets Assn., Fla. Edn. Assn., Am. Assn. Ret. Persons, State of Fla. Notaries (notary-public-at-large 1984—), Marion County Music Assn. (past pres. 1988), MENC and Fla. Vocal Assn., Marion Edn. Assn (com. vol. 1988), Optimist Club Ocala (sgt.-at-arms 2001—), Delta Psi Omega, Kappa Delta Pi, NY State Sch. Music Assn. Conservative. Presbyterian. Avocations: genealogy, music, stamps, travel. Office: Howard Mid Sch 1108 NW Martin Luther King Blvd Ocala FL 34475 Personal E-mail: MSA440@aol.com. Business E-Mail: adamsm1@marion.k12.fl.us.

ADAMS, NANCY R. nurse, retired military officer; b. Rochester, N.Y., Apr. 20, 1945; BSN, Cornell U.; MSN, Cath. U. Am.; grad., U.S. Army War Coll. Advanced through grades to maj. gen. U.S. Army, 1991; comdr. William Beaumont Army Med. Ctr., S.W. Regional Med. Command; chief Army Nurse Corps; asst. surgeon gen. for pers. and comdr. U.S. Army Ctr. for Health Promotion and Preventive Medicine; lead agt. TRICARE Region VII U.S. Army; chief nurse Frankfurt Army Regional Med. Ctr., 1987—89; staff asst. profl. affairs and quality assurance Office of Asst. Sec. of Def., asst. inspector gen., dir. intensive care nursing course; nursing cons. Army Surgeon Gen., 1989—91; commd. Nurse Corps U.S. Army, 1967—; commdg. gen. Tripler Army Med. Ctr., Hawaii, 1998—2002; sr. advisor to the dir. TRICARE Mgmt. Activity, 2002—. Decorated Legion of Merit, Meritorious Svc. medal, Def. Svc.medal. Fellow: Am. Acad. Nursing; mem.: ANA, Am. Orgn. of Nurse Execs., Assn. of Mil. Surgeons of the U.S., Sigma Theta Tau. Office: TRICARE Mgmt Activity 16401 E Centretech Pkwy Aurora CO 80011-9043

ADAMS, PHOEBE-LOU, journalist; b. Hartford, Conn., Dec. 18, 1918; d. Harold Irving and Alice (Burlingame) A. AB cum laude, Radcliffe Coll., 1939. Reporter Hartford Courant, 1942-45; with editorial staff Atlantic Monthly, Boston, 1945—. Author: A Rough Map of Greece, 1965. Office: The Atlantic 77 N Washington St Ste 500 Boston MA 02114-1916

ADAMS, ROSE ANN, nonprofit administrator; b. McHenry, Ill., Apr. 4, 1952; d. Clemens Jacob and Marguerite Elizabeth (Freund) A. BS in Edn., Ill. State U., 1974; MEd, U. Ark., 1979. Supt., exec. dir. Clinton County Children's Services, Wilmington, Ohio, 1979-81; dir. ednl. and adult svcs. Bost Human Devel. Svcs., Ft. Smith, Ark., 1981-87; adminstrv. officer Cen. Ark. Devel. Coun., Benton, 1987; adminstrv. officer, interim Head Start dir., dir. resource devel. Community Orgn. Poverty Elimination Pulaski, Lonoke Counties, Little Rock, 1987-93; exec. dir. So. Early Childhood Assn., 1993-94; sr. cons. Earl Moore and Assocs., Little Rock, 1994-2000, exec. v.p., 1999-2000; exec. dir. Ark. Cmty. Action Agys. Assn., Little Rock,

2000—. Coord. White House Conf. on Families, 1980; mem. Task Force Child Abuse; charter mem. Am. Lung Assn.; active Welfare adv. Bd., Clinton County, 1979—81; pres., v.p. Ark. Single Parent Scholarship Fund.; trustee Morris Found., Multiple Sclerosis Soc.; active Home Econs. Extension Svcs. Adv. Com., 1979—81; mem. adv. bd. U. Ark. Women's Ctr., 1979; chair Ark. Health Promotion Coalition; vice-chair Pulaski County Local Planning Group; chair Ark. Com. on Women's Concerns; mem. adv. com. Ark. Mentors; Ark. Hunger Coalition, 2001—. Named one of Outstanding Young Women of Am., 1982. Mem.: Am. Bus.Women's Assn. (Woman of Yr. Avant Garde chpt. 1992), U. Ark. (Little Rock) Alumni Assn. (bd. dirs., v.p. 1999—). Avocations: antique collection, sports, music. Home: Sonata Trl # 1 Little Rock AR 72205-1632 Office: Ark Cmty Action Agys Assn Ste 1020 300 S Spring St Little Rock AR 72201 E-mail: radams@acaaa.org.

ADAMS, RUTH-ANNE, chef; Grad., Culinary Inst. Am. Pastry chef Michela's, 1993; mem. staff The Blue Rm.; chef Rialto, 1994, sous chef, 1995—99; chef Red Clay, Casablanca, Cambridge, Mass. Office: Casablanca 40 Brattle St Cambridge MA 02138

ADAMS, SHARON BUTLER, minister, philosopher, researcher; b. Chgo., Ill., Oct. 30, 1949; d. Lionel Augustus and Clara Bernice Butler; m. Vernon McFadden Jr., June 13, 1968 (div. Oct. 1977); children: Vernon McFadden III, Aleceia Marie McFadden. Ordained min. African-Am. Universal Ministry. Engring. technician Servitron, Baton Rouge, 1976—78; instr. Coml. Bus. Coll, Baton Rouge, 1978—80; project mgr. Minority Engrs. La., Baton Rouge, 1980—86; cleric adminstr. Baton Rouge African-Am. Cath. Cong., 1997—98, cleric adminstr., So. Region, 1998—99; interim pastor Imani Temple, Baton Rouge, 1998—99; pastor Ch. of the Living God, Baton Rouge, 1999—2002. Advisor Kwanzaa celebration A-A Universal Apostolic Ministry, Baton Rouge, 1999—; dir. Females in Ministry, Baton Rouge, 1999—; spiritual adv. Jazz and Heritage Festival, New Orleans, 2001—; cons. NAACP, New Orleans, 2001; advisor La. Dept. of Environ. Quality, 1990. Author to newspapers and jours. Panelist New Orleans Jazz & Heritage Festival, 2002, Jazz Festival, 2003; bd. dirs. Cmty. Devel. Project, Baton Rouge, 1998, La. Dem. Project, Baton Rouge, 2000. Recipient Kwanazz Celebration award, Mayor & Metr. Coun. of Baton Rouge, 2001. Mem.: Internat. Black Environ. & Econ. Justice, Soc. Am. Music. Avocation: reading, sewing, singing and playing musical instruments. Office: Church of the Living God 623 Iberville St Baton Rouge LA 70802-4849 E-mail: asharon@bellsouth.net.

ADAMS, SUSAN LOIS, music educator; b. New Albany, Ind., July 27, 1946; d. Frank Mitchell, Sr. and Dorothy Stalker Adams. BA, Smith Coll., 1968; MS in Edn., Ind. U., 1970, postgrad., 1994. Cert. tchr. Ind. Tchr. Lafayette (Ind.) Sch. Corp., 1969—70, New Albany-Floyd County Consol. Sch. Corp., 1970—. Mem. editl. com. (hymnal) Chalice Hymnal, 1995; co-editor: (hymnal companion) Chalice Hymnal Worship Leaders' Companion, 1998. Elder Ctrl. Christina Ch., New Albany, 1996—98, Ctl. Christian Ch., New Albany, 2000—02. Recipient Honored Laywoman, Commn. Women-Ind. Region Christian Ch., 1998. Mem.: Ind. Music Educators, Music Educators Nat. Conf., Nat. Assn. Disciple Musicians (pres. 1988, chair workshop 1989, 2001). Mem. Christian Ch. (Disciples Of Christ). Avocations: travel, reading.

ADAMS, VALENCIA I. [illegible] executive; b. Atlanta; BBA, Ga. State U.; postgrad. in Mgmt., Columbia U., Emory [illegible] consumer svcs. BellSouth Corp., Atlanta, v.p., chief diversity officer, 2002—. Former mem. adv. coun. to pres. BellSouth Telecom. Inc.; mentor BellSouth Mentor Exch. Program; trustee Ga. Coun. on Econ. Edn.; bd. dirs. BellSouth Found., Prevent Child Abuse Ga., Possible Woman Found. Chairperson Met. Atlanta United Way Campaign, 1998. Named Woman of Yr., Women Looking Ahead News Mag., 2004; recipient Jr. Achievement Vol. award, Gov. Ga., Bus. Assoc. of Yr. award, Am. Bus. Women's Assn. Mem.: Atlanta C. of C. (life). Office: BellSouth Corp 1155 Peachtree St NE Atlanta GA 30309-3610 Office Phone: 404-249-2365.

ADAMS, VELMA M. assistant principal, consultant; b. Balt., Oct. 1, 1945; d. George and Anna Jones; m. Kenneth G. Adams, Jan. 5, 1946; 1 child, Mark. MusB in Edn., Howard U., 1968; MusM, Morgan State U., 1978; Profl. Cert. for Adminstrn. and Supervision, Queens Coll. Cert. bldg. and dist. adminstrn. N.Y., 1996. Choral and gen. music tchr. Balt. City Pub. Schs., 1968—80; vocal and gen. music tchr. Uniondale (N.Y.) Pub. Schs., 1980—99, asst. prin., 2000—; discipline supr. Lawrence Rd. Jr. High, Uniondale, 1999—2000. Recipient Jenkins PTA award, PTA of Turtle Hook Mid. Sch., 1998. Mem.: ASCD, The Mid. Sch. Adminstr., Curriculum Audit Mgmt. Ctrs., Inc. (assoc.), Nassau Music Educators Assn. (life; pres.). Democrat. Episcopalian. Achievements include development of peer mediation program. Avocations: avid reader, mediation consultant, curriculum auditor, rehearsal and show pianist, computer enthusiast. Home: 71 21 Sutton Place #2 Fresh Meadows NY 11365 Office: Turtle Hook Middle School 975 Jerusalem Ave Uniondale NY 11553 Office Phone: 516-918-1303. E-mail: velmaa1@hotmail.com.

ADAMS, VOLEEN, surgeon; b. Chgo., Apr. 13, 1950; d. John Richard and Patricia Seymour Adams. BS, U. of Notre Dame, 1971; MD, Johns Hopkins U., 1976. Intern St. Mary's Hosp., Baltimore, 1977—78, res., 1979—81, fellow, 1982—85; surgeon Meriks Med. Ctr., Springfield, Mass., 1986—. Mem.: AMA (pres. 1990—92). Avocations: beer brewing, gourmet cooking, reenacting. Office: Meriks Med Ctr 20 Wareham St Springfield MA 01108-1305

ADAMS-ALLEN, JUNE EVELYN, real estate broker; b. Houston, Feb. 14, 1956; d. S.G. and Martilla (Traylor) Adams; m. Larry Craig Strickland, June 19, 1982 (div. May 1984); m. Theodore Allen Jr., Aug. 16, 1985; 1 child, Jesselyn Evette Allen. BBA in Acctg., U. Houston, 1978. Lic. real estate broker, Tex. Receptionist State Rep. Craig Washington, Houston, 1976-80; revenue acct. Chevron U.S.A., Houston, 1980-85; acct. Gulf Interstate Engring. Co., Houston, 1978; auditor, acct. Dwight Staes CPA, Houston, 1979-80; broker, owner J.E.A. Unltd. Realty, Houston, 1987—; broker assoc. ERA Classic Properties, Spring, Tex., 1989-92. Apt. locator Tex. Apt. Locators, Houston, 1984-85; substitute tchr., Aldine Ind. Sch., Houston, 1988-93; real estate instr. George Leonard Real Estate Sch., Houston, 1995—; owner J.E.A. Unltd. Locators, Houston, 1994—, J.E.A. Unltd. Svcs., Houston, 1987—. Author: JEA Way-Apartment Locating and the Real Estate Transaction, 1994. Mem. Houston Assn. Realtors and Credit Union. Avocations: swimming, chess, bowling, camping, mathematics problem solving. Office: JEA Unltd Realty/Locators PO Box 230603 Houston TX 77223-0603

ADAMS-CAMPBELL, LUCILLE L. health facility administrator; Dir. Howard U. Cancer Ctr., Washington. Office: Howard U Cancer Ctr 2041 Georgia Ave NW Washington DC 20060-0001

ADAMSON, JANE NAN, retired elementary school educator; b. Amarillo, Tex., Feb. 5, 1931; d. Carl W. and Lydie O. (Martin) Ray (dec.); 1 child, Dave R. Student, Eastfield Coll., Amarillo Coll., Richland Coll. Univ. Dallas, U. North Tex.; BS, West Tex. A&M U., Canyon, 1953; MEd, Tex. A&M U., Commerce, 1975; diploma, Inst. Children's Lit., 1991; cert., Bur. Edn. and Rsch., 1995; PhD, Am. Coll. Metaphys. Theology, 2000. Cert. elem. tchr., Tex.; lic. real estate salesman. Tchr. Dallas Ind. Sch. Dist., ret. Avocations: music, traveling, decorating, writing, dog training.

ADAMSON, LYNDA G. literature educator, writer; b. Erwin, NC, Aug. 22, 1945; d. Norman E. and Irma Smith Gossett; m. Frank M. Adamson Jr., Dec. 18, 1971; children: Frank M. III, Gregory T. BA, U. NC, 1967, MA, 1968; PhD, U. Md., 1981. Prof. English Prince George's Coll., Largo, Md., 1969—2001, chair lit. dept., 1986—87, chair English dept., 1995—2001, prof. emerita, 2001—. Creator travel study program Prince George's Coll. Author: (reference work) Themes in the Modern American Novel, Recreating the Past: A Guide to American and World Historical Fiction for Children and Young Adults, A Reference Guide to Historical Fiction for Children and Young Adults, Notable Women in American History: A Guide to Biographies and Autobiographies, American Historical Fiction Novels for Adults and Young Adults, World Historical Fiction for Adults and Young Adults, Notable Women in World History: A Guide to Biographies and Autobiographies, Literature Connections to American History, K-6, Literature Connections to American History, 7-12, Literature Connections to World History, K-6, Literature Connections to World History, 7-12; contbr. articles to profl. jours. Editor dir. Woodmont Civic Assn., Arlington, Va.; vol. Arlington Ctrl. Libr.; choir Foundry United Meth. Ch., Washington, 1988—2003, com. mem., 1970—2003; sec., instr. Arlington Learning in Retirement Inst., 2002—. Recipient Faculty Excellence award, Faculty Senate at Prince George's Coll., 1995; grantee, NEH, 1989. Mem.: U.S. Bd. on Books for Young Adults, Internat. Rsch. in Children's Lit., Capitol Choices, Choral Arts Soc. Washington. Democrat. Methodist. Avocations: travel, music, miniatures, art. E-mail: ladamson@alumni.unc.edu.

ADAMSON, MARY ANNE, geographer, systems engineer; b. Berkeley, Calif., June 25, 1954; d. Arthur Frank and Frances Isobel Adamson; m. Richard John Harrington, Sept. 20, 1974. BA with highest honors, U. Calif., Berkeley, 1975, MA, 1976, postgrad., 1976-78. Cert. tchr. earth scis., Calif.; cert. cave rescue ops. and mgmt., Calif.; lic. EMT, Contra Costa (Calif.) County, 1983. Tchg. asst. dept. geography U. Calif., Berkeley, 1976; geographer, environ. and fgn. area analyst Lawrence Livermore (Calif.) Nat. Lab., 1978-83, cons., 1983-86; sys. engr. ESL, Sunnyvale, Calif., 1986-90; rsch. analyst, rsch. devel. and analysis Pacific Gas & Electric Co., San Francisco, 1990-93, asst. to gen. auditor internal audit dept., 1993—. Asst. editor Vulcan's Voice, 1982; contbr. articles to profl. jours. Staff mem. ARC/Am. Trauma Soc./Sierra Club Urgent Care and Mountain Medicine seminars, 1983-98. With USNR, 1983—, comdr., 1999—. Recipient Navy Achievement medal, 1992, Navy Commendation medal, 2003. Mem. Assn. Am. Geographers (life), Assn. Pacific Coast Geographers, Nat. Speleol. Soc. (geology, geography sects., sec., editor newsletter Diablo Grotto chpt. 1982-86), Toastmasters Internat. Club (adminstrv. v.p. Blue Monday Club 1991), Sierra Club (life), Nature Conservancy (life), U. Calif. Alumnae Assn., Phi Beta Kappa. Home: 4603 Lakewood St Pleasanton CA 94588-4342 Office: PG&E Corp Dept Internal Auditing 245 Market St San Francisco CA 94105-1702

ADAMS-PASSEY, SUELLEN S. retired elementary school educator; b. Cin. d. Raymond J. and Thelma P. (Munk)Sweany; m. Douglas Passey ; children; Amy, Jacqueline, James, Sarah, Kristina, Zoya. BS in Edn., Kent State U. Cert. elem. tchr., Wash. Tchr. 4th and 5th grades Chgo. Jr. Sch., Elgin, Ill.; gen. dir., program developer Courtyard Theatre, Edmonds, Wash.; tchr. 4th grade Edmonds (Wash.) Dist. 15; tchr. 4th, 5th and 6th grades combination class Martha Lake Elem. Sch., Lynnwood, Wash.; founder Suellen Adams Sch. of Hope for Orphans, Armenia, 2003. Bd. dirs. Pub. Edn. Fund for Dist. 15, 1985-87; pres. Seattle Storytellers Guild, 1985-88; bd. dirs. Seattle Folklore Soc. 1998-2004, founder and chair, concert com. 1988-2002, dir. Crackerbarrel Mornings, 1982-87, co-chair, student subsidy program, 1989-2000, Seattle Opera Guild.

ADATO, LINDA JOY, artist, educator; b. London, [illegible] and Renee (Katz) Falber; m. Albert Adato, June 26, 1966; 1 child, Vanessa. Student, Hornsey (Eng.) Coll. of Art, 1960-61; BA in Pictorial Arts, UCLA, 1966, MA in Art Edn., 1967. Adj. lectr. in art Manhattanville Coll., Purchase, NY, 1987—2000; printmaking tchr. Silvermine Sch. of Art, New Canaan, Conn., 1995—. Exhibitions include Achenbach Found. for Graphic Arts, Fine Arts Mus., San Francisco, 1987, Decordova Mus., Lincoln, Mass., 1990, Portland (Oreg.) Art Mus., 1994, Art Complex Mus., Duxbury, Mass., 1994, Newark Pub. Libr., 1994, Housatonic Mus. Art, Bridgeport, Conn., 1998, Old Print Shop, N.Y.C., 1998, 2002, De Cordova Mus., Lincoln, Mass., 1998-99; mem. travelling exhbn. Am. Print Alliance, 1998—, 5th Brit. Internat. Miniutre Print Exhbn., 2003-04. Recipient anonymous prize for prints NAD, 1990, Karlene Cusick Purchase award Print Club Albany, 1995; William Meyerowitz Meml. award Audubon Artists, 1996, Atlantic Papers award 1997; purchase award Internat. Miniature Print Exhibit, Conn. Graphic Arts Ctr., 1997, Alice Pauline Schafer Meml. purchase award Print Club, Albany, 1998, Gold medal of Honor Audubon Artists, 2000, Ralph Fabri medal of Merit Audubon Artists, 2002, Art Students League of N.Y. award, Audubon Artists, 2003. Mem. Soc. Am. Graphic Artists (treas. 1995-2002, purchase award 1985). Home: 20 Pratt St New Rochelle NY 10801-4314

ADATO, PERRY MILLER, documentary producer, director, writer; b. Yonkers, N.Y. d. Perry and Ida (Block) Miller; m. Neil M. Adato, Sept. 11, 1955; children: Laurie, Michelle. Student, Marshalov Sch. Drama, N.Y.C., New Sch. Social Rsch.; LHD (hon.), Ill. Wesleyan U., 1984. Film rsch. coord. CBS-TV Network, N.Y.C., 1959—64, prodr., 1964; assoc. prodr. NET, N.Y.C., 1964—68, prodr., dir., 1968—72, Sta. 13/WNET-TV (formerly NET), N.Y.C., 1972—92; writer Sta. 13/WNET-TV, N.Y.C., 1989, 1996—97, 1999—2001, prodr., dir., 1999—. Exec. prodr. Alvin H. Perlmutter Inc./Ind. Prodn. Fund, 1992-96; guest lectr. on film Harvard U., Columbia U., NYU, Yale U., U. Ill., others, 1970—; lectr. Fairfield (Conn.) U., 1974-75; film lectr. Smithsonian Assocs., Washington, 1997, 98, 99, 2001, 2003, Columbia (Md.) Festival of Arts, 1998, 99; mem. film award jury Am. Film Inst., Beverly Hills, Calif., 1974; judge film award Creative Artists Pub. Svc., N.Y.C., 1976; first chmn. UN Women in the Arts Film Com., 1976-77; pres. jury Montreal Internat. Festival Films on Art, 1990; mem. jury Pompidou Ctr., Paris Internat. Festival of Films on Art, 1994. Producer, dir.: (TV documentary films) Dylan Thomas: The World I Breathe, 1968 (Emmy award for outstanding achievement in cultural documentary 1968), Gertrude Stein: When This You See, Remember Me, 1970 (Montreal Festival Diplome d'Excellence 1970, Am. Film Festival Blue Ribbon award 1970, 2 Emmy nominations for outstanding direction and outstanding achievement in cultural documentary 1971), The Great Radio Comedians, 1972 (Am. Film Festival Red Ribbon award 1972), An Eames Celebration: Several Worlds of Charles and Ray Eames, 1973 (Chgo. Internat. Film Festival Silver Hugo award 1973, Am. Film Festival Red Ribbon award 1973), Mary Cassatt: Impressionist From Philadelphia, 1974 (Women in Communications Clarion award 1974), Georgia O'Keeffe, 1977 (Dirs. Guild Am. award for documentary achievement 1977-1st woman to receive any Dirs. Guild Am. award, NCCJ Christopher award 1978, Com. for Internat. Events Golden Eagle award 1978, Women in Communications Clarion award 1978, Alfred I. DuPont/Columbia U. citation 1978), Frankenthaler: Toward a New Climate, 1978 (Am. Film Festival Blue Ribbon award in fine arts 1979), Picasso: A Painter's Diary, 1980 (Dirs. Guild Am. award for directorial achievement in TV documentary 1980, Alfred I. DuPont/Columbia U. award for excellence in broadcast journalism 1980, Com. for Internat. Events Golden Eagle award 1980, Am. Film Festival Blue Ribbon award in fine arts 1980, Montreal Internat. Festival of Films on Art First prize for Best Biography of an Artist 1981), Carl Sandburg: Echoes and Silences, 1982 (Women in Communications Matrix award 1982, American Women in Radio and TV Pinnacle award for TV documentary 1982, Dirs. Guild Am. award for achievement in TV documentary 1983), Eugene O'Neill: A Glory of Ghosts, 1984-85, Broadcast, 1986 (Most Outstanding Achievement in TV Documentary award Dirs. Guild Am. 1986, Spl. Jury award San Francisco Film Festival 1985, Internat. Film and TV Festival of N.Y. Silver medal 1986); exec. producer (TV series) Women in Art, 1974-78, Art of the Western World, 1985-89; producer, dir., writer: A White Garment of Churches, 1989 (Clarion award 1990, Silver Plaque award Chgo. Internat. Film Festival 1990, Assn. Visual Comm. Silver Cindy award 1990); exec. prodr. rsch. and devel. 3 part series Asian Art, 1990-94; prodr., dir. Great Tales in Asian Art, 1994-96; writer Dream Journeys-Nature in East Asian Art, 1994-95; prodr. R & D Alfred Steiglitz, 1996-98, (working title) Writer, Alfred Steiglitz, 1996-98; prodr., dir., writer Alfred Steiglitz-The Eloquent Eye, 1999-2001, Georgia O'Keefe: A Life in Art, 2003. Comm. Internat. Events Golden Eagle award, 2002, Montreal Internat. Festival Films Art Selection, 2002; hon. bd. dirs. Weston-Westport (Conn.) Arts Coun., 1981-89. Poynter fellow Yale U., 1976; grantee NEA, 1977-78, 93, NEH, 1980, 83, 91, 93, 99; Calhoun Coll. assoc. fellow Yale U., 1993—; subject tribute, Montreal Internat. Art Film Festival, 1990; recipient Westport (Conn.) Arts Coun. Lifetime Achievement award in visual arts category, 1996; film retrospective Nat. Gallery Art, Washington, 1998, film festival award for biog. Houston World Fest, 2002, hon. award lifetime achievement Montreal Internat. Festival Films Art, 2002. Mem. Dirs. Guild Am., Writers Guild Am., N.Y. Women in Film and TV.

ADAWI, NADIA SHARON, energy cooperative executive; b. Princeton, NJ, Aug. 29, 1958; d. Ibrahim Hussein and Gerda (Obert) Adawi; m. Patrick John Loll, June 18, 1983. BSEE, U. Mo., 1980; MBA, Yale U., 1997. Electronics engr. FCC, Washington, 1980-81; cons. engr. Washington, 1981-89; asst. dir. advanced cellular tech. Ameritech Mobile Communications, Schaumburg, Ill., 1989-93; regional ops. mgr. Ericsson, Inc., Schaumburg, 1993-95; bus. ethics cons. Arthur Andersen, N.Y.C., 1997-99; dir. ops. The Energy Cooperative, Phila. Mem. Sustainable Bus. Network of Greater Phila.; fin. com. The Other Side. Named one of Phila. Bus. Jour. Women of Distinction, 2001. Mem.: NOW, Am. Solar Energy Soc. Avocations: music, literature. Home: 329 S 46th St Philadelphia PA 19143-1801 E-mail: nsadawi@aol.com.

ADAY, LUANN, social science educator; With U. Chgo.; prof. behavioral scis. Sch. Pub. Health U. Tex., Houston, 1986—. Author: At Risk in America: The Health and Health Care Needs of Vulnerable Populations in the United States; co-author: (with C.E. Begley, D. Lairson, C. Slater) Evaluating the Healthcare System: Effectivenss, Efficiency and Equity. Mem. NAS Inst. Medicine. Office: U Tex Houston Health Sci Ctr 1200 Hermann Pressler Dr Houston TX 77030-3900 E-mail: laday@utsph.uth.tmc.edu.

ADCOCK, BETTY-LEE, real estate company executive, real estate broker; b. Waldo, Kans., Nov. 19, 1921; d. Ralph Preston and Hazel (Pangburn) Beatty; m. Charles Warren Adcock, Feb. 17, 1945; 1 dau., Roberta Lee. B.S. in Journalism, Kans. State Coll., 1946; grad. Realtors Inst. Lic. real estate broker, Hawaii; cert. residential specialist, residential broker. Mem. pub. relations staff Boeing Airplane Co., Wichita, Kans., 1942-45; biographical staff AP, N.Y.C., 1945-46; real estate salesman and broker, Honolulu, 1972— ; prin. broker, pres., owner Adcock, Ltd., real estate mktg., Honolulu, 1983—. Recipient Girl Scout Award of Merit, Kitzingen, Germany, 1960, spl. award Am. Cancer Soc., Middlebury, Vt., 1956. Mem. Nat. Assn. Realtors. Hawaii Assn. Realtors, Honolulu Bd. Realtors, Honolulu Zool. Soc., Friends of Waikiki Aquarium, Nat. Trust for Historic Preservation, Honolulu Art Acad., Friends of Iolani Palace, Bishop Mus., Hawaii Hist. Soc., Hawaii Humane Soc., Hist. Hawaii Found., Chi Omega. Republican. Episcopalian. Home and Office: Adcock Ltd 2415 Alia Aina Pl Honolulu HI 96821-1001

ADCOCK, MURIEL W. special education educator; b. Chgo. BA, U. Calif. Sonoma State, Rohnert Park, 1979. Cert. spl. edn. tchr., Calif., [illegible] The Concordia Sch., Concord, Calif., 1980-85; tchr., cons. Tenderloin Community [illegible], 1985-86; adminstr. Assn. Montessori Internat.-USA, San Francisco, 1988, tchr., advisor, 1989—. Course asst. Montessori Spl. Edn. Inst., San Francisco, 1985-87, tchr. spl. edn., 1990, tchr. cons., 1991—, rschr. 1992—. U.S. mng. editor World Futures: The Jour. of Gen. Evolution, 2000—; contbr. articles to profl. jour. Sec. Internat. Forum World Affairs Coun., San Francisco, 1990-95, program chair, 1993-95, pres./founder Club of Budapest, U.S., 2000—. Mem. ASCD, Am. Orthopsychiat. Assn., Internat. Soc. Sys. Scientists, Internat. Sys. Inst., Assn. Montessori Internat., N.Am. Montessori Tchrs. Assn., Assn. Childhood Edn. Internat., Smithsonian Assocs., N.Y. Acad. Scis., Internat. Sys. Inst. Avocations: general evolutionary systems theory, sustainable development, educational systems design, ethical leadership. Office: 4040 Civic Center Dr Ste 200 San Rafael CA 94903

ADCOX, MARY SANDRA, dietician, consultant; b. Portsmouth, Ohio, Dec. 4, 1939; d. Philip Henry and Bertha Mae (Hansgen) Riddinger; m. Steve Jordan Jr., Dec. 5, 1962 (dec. May 1972); 1 child, Michael Philip; m. Henry Lonzo Adcox Jr., Sept. 30, 1972. BS in Food and Nutrition, U. Cin., 1961; MEd, Tex. State U., 1984. Registered dietitian Commn. on Dietetic Registration. Rsch. dietitian U.S. Army Inst. Surg. Rsch., Ft. Sam Houston, 1964-65; chief dietitian Luth. Gen. Hosp., San Antonio, 1966-67; dir. dietetics Santa Rosa Med. Ctr., San Antonio, 1967-72, San Antonio Cmty. Hosp., 1972-75; adult edn. instr. San Antonio Coll., 1973-84; food svc. supr. San Antonio Ind. Sch. Dist., 1975-96, ret., 1996. Sch. food svc. cons., San Antonio, 1996—. Author: Dietetic Assistant Program, 1983, Diet Manual: San Antonio Community Hospital, 1st edit., 1973, Diet Manual: Santa Rosa Medical Center, 4th edit., 1969. Past den. leader Boy Scouts Am. 1st lt. U.S. Army, 1962—64. Mem. Am. Dietetic Assn., San Antonio Dietetic Assn., U. Cin. Alumni Assn., Tex. State U. Alumni Assn., San Antonio Area Ret. Tchrs. Assn., Delta Zeta. Baptist. Avocations: piano, organ, herb gardening. Home: 5503 Oo-Loo-Te-Ka Dr San Antonio TX 78218-5041

ADCROFT, PATRICE GABRIELLA, former editor; b. Scranton, Pa., Apr. 15, 1954; d. Joseph Raymond and Patricia Ann (Ryan) Adcroft. BA In Mag. Journalism and Creative Writing, Syracuse U., 1976. Editor-in-chief Carbondale (Pa.) Miner Mid Valley Gazette, 1976—77; staff writer Good Housekeeping Mag., N.Y.C., 1978—80; mng. editor Family Media/Alive and Well, N.Y.C., 1980—81; freelance writer, editor N.Y.C., 1981—82; sr. editor CBS Mags. Family Weekly, N.Y.C., 1982—84, Omni Mag., N.Y.C., 1984—85, exec. editor, 1985—86, editor-in-chief, 1986—90; Editor-in-Chief Seventeen Magazine, 1998—2001. Vis. prof. Syracuse U., 1992—93. Editor-in-chief Omni Future Medical Almanac, 1987, NetGuide Mag., 1994—95, deputy editor InStyle Mag., 1995—98; author: (novels) Every Day Doughnuts; contbr. writer Arthur C. Clarke's 2019, 1986, Omni Book of Continuum, 1982. Bd. advisors SCI Ctr. for Advanced Studies in Mgmt. Wharton Sch., U. Pa. Roman Catholic.

ADDICOTT, BEVERLY JEANNE, retired elementary school educator; b. Youngstown, Ohio, Nov. 9, 1948; m. Gerald Leslie Addicott, Mar. 30, 1974; 1 child, Katherine Elizabeth. BS in Edn., Youngstown State U., 1971, cert. media specialist, 1978; cert. in ESL, 1995. Cert. tchr., Ohio, Fla. Tchr. Mathews Sch. Dist., Vienna, Ohio, 1972-75, media specialist, 1975-78, supr. media, 1978-79; media specialist Brevard County Schs., Melbourne, Fla., 1987-91, tchr., 1991—2000. Chef du jour Haven for Children, Melbourne, 1989-94; vol. Habitat for humanity, Melbourne, 1993, University Park PTO, Melbourne, 1989-2000. Mem. Melbourne Alumnae Panhellenic (chair fundraiser 1992), Jr. League of South Brevard (parent educator 1992-95). Avocations: cross-stitch, knitting, crocheting.

ADDIS, DEBORAH JANE, management consultant, editor; b. Rahway, NJ, Jan. 29, 1950; d. Emmanuel and Stella (Oles) Addis; m. James Eldin Reed, Apr. 14, 1983. BA, Bowling Green State U., 1972; MA in Orgn., Mgmt. and Pub. Policy, Lesley U., Cambridge, Mass., 1992. cons. House Judiciary Com., Washington, 1999-2000. Pub. info. officer Dept. Transp., State of Ohio, 1972-73; dir. pub. info. and edn. Dept. Commerce, State of Ohio, 1973-75; press sec. Atty. Gen., State of Ohio, 1975-77; dep. press sec. Office of Gov., Commonwealth of Mass., Boston, 1978-79; sr. account exec.

Miller Comms., Boston, 1979-80; v.p., prin. Addis & Reed Cons., Inc., Boston, 1981-91, pres., 1992—. Adj. faculty Lesley Coll. Grad. Sch., 1992-95; bd. dirs. Can. Inst. Internat. Affairs, Boston; cons. in field. Author monograph and numerous articles, congl. testimony; mng. editor The American Canada Watch, 1995—. Bd. govs. Women's City Club of Boston, 1982-85; mem. Ohio Task Force on Domestic Violence, Columbus, 1976; pres. Asbestos Victims Campaign, Boston, 1987-90. Mem. New Eng.-Can. Bus. Coun. (bd. dirs. 1994-98), Inst. Mgmt. Cons. (bd. dirs. New Eng. chpt. 1988-89), Mass. Audubon Soc., Harvard Club of Boston, Boston Atheneum. Democrat. Avocations: photography, herpetology (turtles), hiking, travel. Home: 25 Holly Ln Brookline MA 02467-2156 Office: Addis & Reed Cons Inc PO Box 85 Chestnut Hill MA 02467 E-mail: addis@addisreed.com.

ADDIS, KAY TUCKER, newspaper editor; AB in English, Coll. of William and Mary, 1970. Editor The Virginian-Pilot, Norfolk, 1996—. Office: The Virginian-Pilot 150 W Brambleton Ave Norfolk VA 23510-2075 also: Virginian Pilot P O Box 449 Norfolk VA 23501-0449

ADDISON, HELEN KATHERINE, marketing professional, art dealer; b. N.Y.C., June 4, 1954; d. Arthur Michael and Helen Irene (Ernst) Weber; m. Keith Robert Scott, Oct. 1, 1979 (div. Oct. 1986). BA, Syracuse U., 1973; MBA, Cornell U., 1978. Prin. Addison & Assocs. Advt. and Pub. Rels., Orleans, Mass., 1980—, Addison Art Gallery, Orleans, Mass., 1995—. Bd. corporators Seamens Bank, Provincetown, 1995—. Recipient Creative Excellence award Hotel Sales and Mktg. Assn., 1993-2003, South Shore Ad Club, 1990-93, Cape Cod Ad Club, 1989-92. Mem. Orleans C. of C. (v.p. 1992), Addison Art Gallery (pres.). Unitarian Universalist. Office: Addison & Assoc PO Box 2756 43 S Orleans Rd Orleans MA 02653-2422

ADDISON, LINDA LEUCHTER, lawyer, writer; b. Allentown, Pa., Nov. 25, 1951; d. Marcus and Sophie Theresa (Tisch) Leuchter; m. Max M. Addison, Sept. 10, 1977; 1 child, Alexandra Leuchter Addison. BA with honors, U. Tex., 1973, JD, 1976. Bar: Tex. 1976, U.S. Dist. Ct. (so. dist.) Tex. 1977, U.S. Dist. Ct. (no. dist.) Tex. 2000, U.S. Dist. Ct. (ea. dist.) Tex. 2003, U.S. Ct. Appeals (5th cir.) 1981, U.S. Ct. Appeals (fed. cir.) 2003, U.S. Supreme Ct. 2003. Assoc. Fulbright & Jaworski LLP, Houston, 1976—83, ptnr., 1984—, exec. com., tech. ptnr., 2002—. Expert on fed. and Tex. evidence. Author: Federal Civil Procedure and Evidence During Trial, 1997, Texas Evidence, 2003; contbr. chpt. to book; mng. editor Tex. Law Rev. 1975-76; contbr. articles to profl. jours. Trustee U. Tex. Law Sch. Found., 1994—; mem. fed. jud. evaluation com. of Sens. Hutchison and Cornyn, 1997-; exec. com. chancellor's coun., U. Tex. Sys., 1999-; bd. dirs. Holocaust Mus. Houston, 2001; mem. Commn. of 125, U. Tex., Austin, 2003—, vice chmn. task force of centennial commn., 1981-83. Named one of Am.'s Top 50 Women Litigators, Nat. Law Jour., 2001, Tex. Go To Litigators, Tex. Lawyer, 2002, Most Fascinating People in Houston, Friends of Tex. Med. Ctr. Libr., 2001, Hon. Barrister, U. Tex. Sch. Law bd. advocates, 2000, Outstanding Young Lawyer of Houston, 1984-85, Woman on the Move, Tex. Exec. Women, 2000, Woman to Watch, Jewish Women Internat., 2002; named one of Am. Bd. Trial Advs., 1986, One of Best Lawyers in Am., Woodard and White, 2003; named to Chambers and Ptnrs. USA, 2004. Fellow: Tex. Bar Found. (trustee 2003—), Houston Bar Found. (life), Am. Bar Found. (life); mem.: ABA, Am. Bd. Trial Advs., World Internat. Patent Orgn. (arbitration and mediation ctr. domain name panel 2002—), Am. Intellectual Property Law Assn., Am. Arbitration Assn. (internat. panel 1992—, panel of neutrals, large complex case panel), Tex. Law Rev. Ex-Editors Assn. (life), Houston Young Lawyers Assn. (chmn. cont. legal edn. com. 1977—78, bd. dirs. 1978—81, Outstanding Chmn. award), Tex. Young Lawyers Assn. (bd. dirs. 1981—83), Houston Bar Assn. (chmn. cont. legal edn. com. 1981—82, mem. jud. evalns. com. 1982—83, Pres.'s award for outstanding svc. 1982), State Bar Tex. (chmn. bar jour. com. 1988—90, adminstr. rules evidence com. 1988—90, chmn. bar jour. com. 1991—99), United Way, deTocqueville Soc., Anti-Defamation League (bd. dirs. S.W. Region 1992—94), Friar Soc., Omicron Delta Kappa. Office: Fulbright & Jaworski LLP 1301 McKinney St Ste 5100 Houston TX 77010-3095

ADEKSON, MARY OLUFUNMILAYO, therapist, counselor, educator; b. Ogbomoso, Nigeria; came to U.S., 1988; d. Gabriel and Deborah Williams; children: Adedayo, Babatunde. BA in English and Am. Lit., Brandeis U., 1975; MEd in Guidance and Counseling, Obafemi Awolowo U., Ile-Ife, Nigeria, 1987; PhD, Ohio U., 1997. English tchr. Ctrl. Sch. Bd., Ibadan, Nigeria, 1968-88; acting prin. Abe Tech. Coll., Ibadan, Nigeria, 1978; coord. guidance svcs. Min. Edn., Ile-Ife, 1984-88; part-time lectr. Obafemi Awolowo U., Ile-Ife, 1986-88; vice prin. Olubuse Meml. HS, Ile-Ife, 1987-88; grad. asst. Ohio U., Athens, 1988-91. Vol. contract worker, trainer Careline, Tri-County Mental Health Ctr., Athens, 1988-92; vol. My Sister's Place, Athens, 1989, Good Works Athens, 1989, Montgomery County Hotline, 1994; contract worker Tri County Activity Ctr., Athens, 1989-92, therapist II Woodland Ctr., Gallipolis, Ohio, 1991-92; part-time lectr. U. Md., 1993, coord. tutorial svc.; dir. Christian Book Ctr., Ile-Ife; vol., part-time counselor DWI program Prince George's County Health Dept., Hyattsville, Md.; counselor Potomac Healthcare Found. Mountain Manor Treatment Program; adj. prof. Bowie (Md.) State U. Counseling Program, 1997-98; asst. prof. St. Bonaventure U., 1998-2004, assoc. prof. 2004-; faculty adviser Chi Sigma Iota, Phi Rho chpt. Vol. Montgomery County Police Dept.; mem. Alcohol and Other Drug Abuse Adv. Coun., Montgomery County, Md.; mem. adv. com. Germantown (Md.) Libr.; mem. Gaithersburg (Md.) City Adv. Com.; chmn. bd. dirs. Faith Enterprises; bd. dirs. Faith Consultancy Group, Olean Cultural Dialogue Group. Recipient Gold medal West African Athletic Assn., 1965; Internat. Peace scholar P.E.O., 1990-91, Wien Internat. scholar Brandeis U., 1973-75. Mem. ACA, Am. Mental Health Counselors Assn. Network on Children and Teens (membership chair 1991-92, chair 1993-98), Am. Assn. Counseling and Devel. (award for internat. grad. students 1990), Counseling Assn. Nigeria (planning com. 1986), Oyo State Nigeria Assn. Guidance Counselors (chmn. Oranmiyan local govt. area 1986-88), Chi Sigma Iota (program coord. Ohio U. chpt. 1990, faculty advisor Phi Rho chpt.). Avocations: meeting people from around the world, jogging, walking, playing tennis, reading.

ADELMAN, IRMA GLICMAN, economics educator; b. Cernowitz, Rumania, Mar. 14, 1930; came to U.S., 1949, naturalized, 1955; d. Jacob Max and Raissa (Ettinger) Glicman; m. Frank L. Adelman, Aug. 16, 1950 (div. 1979); 1 son, Alexander. BS, U. Calif., Berkeley, 1950, MA, 1951, PhD, 1955. Teaching assoc. U. Calif., Berkeley, 1955-56, instr., 1956-57, lectr. with rank asst. prof., 1957-58; vis. asst. prof. Mills Coll., 1958-59; acting asst. prof. Stanford, 1959-61, asst. prof., 1961-62; assoc. prof. Johns Hopkins, Balt., 1962-65; prof. econs. Northwestern U., Evanston, Ill., 1966-72, U. Md., 1972-78; prof. econs. and agrl. econs. U. Calif. at Berkeley, 1979-94; prof. emeritus, 1994—. Cons. divsn. indsl. devel. UN, 1962-63, AID U.S. Dept. State, Washington, 1963-72, World Bank, 1968—, ILD, Geneva, 1973—. Author: Theories of Economic Growth and Development, 1961, (with A. Pepelasis and L. Mears), Economic Development: Analysis and Case Studies, 1961, (with Eric Thorbecke) The Theory and Design of Economic Development, 1966, (with C.T. Morris) Society, Politics and Economic Development— A Quantitative Approach, 1967, Practical Approaches to Development Planning-Korea's Second Five Year Plan, 1969, (with C.T. Morris) Economic Development and Social Equity in Developing Countries, 1973, (with Sherman Robinson) Planning for Income Distribution, 1977-78, (with C. T. Morris) Comparative Patterns of Economic Growth, 1850-1914, 1987, (J. Edward Taylor) Village Economies: Design, Estimation and Application of Village Wide Economic Models, 1996, Institutions and Development Strategies: Selected Essays of Irma Adelman Vol. I, 1994, Vol. II, 1994. Decorated Order of the Bronze Tower (Korea); fellow Ctr. Advanced Study Behavioral Scis., 1970-71; named Women's Hall Fame U. Calif., Berkeley, 1994. Fellow Am. Acad. Arts and Scis., Econometric Soc., Royal Soc. Encouragement Arts, Mfg. and Commerce (Berkeley citation 1996); mem. Am. Econ. Assn. (mem. exec. com., v.p. 1969-71). Office: Univ Calif Dept Agr & Natural Resources 207 Giannini Hall Spc 3310 Berkeley CA 94720-3310

ADELMAN, SUSAN HERSHBERG, surgeon; b. Rochester, N.Y., Oct. 8, 1941; m. Martin Adelman. BA in Geology, U. Mich.; MD, Wayne State U., 1967. Diplomate Am. Bd. Surgery, Am. Bd. Pediatric Surgery. Intern Henry Ford Hosp., Detroit, 1967-68, resident in surgery, 1968-72; resident in pediatric surgery Childrens Hosp., Detroit, 1972-74; clin. assoc. prof. surgery U. Mich.; med. dir. Coordinated Health Care Inc. Hosp. staff Riverview Hosp., Detroit, Children's Hosp., Detroit, Oakwood Hosp., Dearborn, Mich., Mott Children's Hosp.-U. Mich.; rep. AMA, White House Health Profls. Rev. Group, 1993. Editor Detroit Med. News, 1981—. Fellow ACS (mem. profl. liability com., Cert. of Spl. Competence in Pediatric Surgery); mem. AMA (del. 1991—, coun. on med. svcs., intracoun. taskforce on Medicaid, chair surg. caucus, pres. OSMAP, adv. com. women in medicine, consortium on study of the fedn. and health policy agenda), Am. Soc. of Gen. Surgeons (bd. dirs.), Mich. State Med. Soc. (1st woman pres.), Wayne County Med. Soc. (1st woman pres.). Office: AMA 515 N State St Chicago IL 60610-4325

ADELSMAN, JEAN (HARRIETTE ADELSMAN), newspaper editor; b. Indpls., Oct. 21, 1944; d. Joe and Beatrice Irene (Samuel) A. BS in Journalism, Northwestern U., 1966, MS in Journalism, 1967. Copy editor Chgo. Sun-Times, 1967-75, fin. news editor, 1975-77, entertainment editor, 1977-80, asst. mng. editor features, 1980-84; now mng. editor Daily Breeze, Torrance, Calif. Office: Daily Breeze 5215 Torrance Blvd Torrance CA 90503-4077

ADELSON, GLORIA ANN, financial executive; b. Savannah, Ga., Aug. 3, 1944; d. Lee Roy and Edith Thelma (Horovitz) Schraibman; m. Joseph Harvey Adelson, Mar. 19, 1967 (dec.). BA in Polit. Sci., U. Fla., 1965; MA in Bus., Webster U., 1991. Budget analyst U.S. Dept. Labor, Silver Spring, Md., 1967; mgmt. analyst U.S. Naval Supply Ctr., Charleston, S.C., 1967-69, budget analyst, 1969-70, head fin. mgmt. staff, 1970-73, head. ops. and maintenance br., 1973-75; mgmt. coord. officer So. Divsn. Naval Facilities Engring. Commd., Charleston, 1975-80, dir. budget br., 1980-85, dir. budget and programs divsn., 1985-88, dep. dir. programs and comptroller dept., 1988—. Fin. sec., treas. Synagogue Emanu-El, Charleston, 1982-88, program chmn., 2002-2004; pres. Sisterhood Emanu-El, Charleston, 1993-94, 95-96; active patron com. Am. Cancer Soc., Charleston, 1989, 91, 95, 97; mem. fed. sector com. United Way, Charleston, 1991; bd. dirs. so. br. Women's League for Conservative Judaism, 1996-98, v.p., 1998-2002, pres., 2002-2004, mem. Internat. bd. dirs., 2001—; mem. Trident Area Cmty. Excellence Comm. Team, 1995-99, examiner for quality awards, 1999; published fgn. interpreter's list S.C. World Trade Ctr, 1998, 99, 2001, 2002. Mem. Am. Soc. Mil. Comptrs. (chmn. coms. Charleston chpt. 1987—, v.p. Navy, 1990-91, pres., 1991-92), Charleston C. of C. (Leadership Charleston 1997-98), Arthritis Found., Arthritis Vol. Adv. Comm. (co-chair arthritis support group). Avocations: reading, fitness. Home: 4 Berwick Cir Charleston SC 29407-3414 Office: So Divsn Naval Facilities Engring Command 2155 Eagle Dr Charleston SC 29406-4804 Personal E-mail: happygaa@aol.com.

ADERHOLDT, TRACI EAVES, music educator; b. Rutherfordton, N.C., Mar. 3, 1964; d. Julian Bobby and Alice Faye (Waldrop) Eaves; m. James Lamar Aderholdt, June 17, 2000. B in Music Edn., U. N.C., 1986; M in Music Edn., Converse Coll., 1992. Drama tchr. Montgomery County Sch., Troy, NC, 1986—87; gen. music tchr. Shelby City Sch., Shelby, NC, 1987—2001, 2002—, Gaston County Sch., Gastonia, NC, 2001—02. Music dir. Greater Shelby Cmty. Theater, Shelby, 1988—95; pianist Cleve. County Choral Soc., Shelby, 1988—99, Eastside Bapt. Ch., Shelby, 1991—97, First Bapt. Ch., Kings Mt., NC, 1997—. Mem.: Am. Choral Dir. Assn. (SSA all-state coord. 1994—95), Music Educators Nat. Conf. Baptist. Avocations: antiques, painting, coin collecting, drawing. Home: 357 Beattie Rd Kings Mountain NC 28086

ADICKES, SANDRA ELAINE, English language educator, writer; b. N.Y.C., July 14, 1933; d. August Ernst and Edythe Louise (Oberschlake) A.; children: Delores, Lily, Cynthia. BA, Douglass Coll., 1954; MA, CUNY, 1964; PhD, NYU, 1977. Asst. registrar NYU, 1954-55; sec. McCann Erickson, J. Walter Thompson Cos., N.Y.C., 1955-60; English tchr. N.Y.C. Bd. Edn., 1960-70, 1980-88; instr. edn. N.Y.C. Tech. Coll., 1970-72; asst. prof. English S.I. C.C., N.Y.C., 1972-77; dir. project chance Bklyn. Coll., 1977-80; assoc. prof. to prof. English Winona (Minn.) State U., 1988-98, prof. emerita, 1998—. Cons. Antioch Coll. N.Y.C., 1970; guest tutor London U., 1979. Author: The Social Quest, 1991, Legends of Good Women, 1992, To Be Young Was Very Heaven, 1997; editor: By A Woman Writt, 1973; contbr. articles to profl. jours. Co-founder Tchrs'. Freedom Sch. Project, Miss., 1963-64, Tchrs'. Com. for Peace Vietnam, 1965-66. Named Woman of Yr. Nat. Assn. Negro Bus. Profl. Women, N.J., 1966. Mem. MLA, Midwest Modern Lang. Assn., Nat Coun. Tchrs. of English, Popular Culture Assn. Democrat. Home: 19 Davids Ct Dayton NJ 08810-1302 E-mail: s.adickes@att.net.

ADILETTA, DEBRA JEAN OLSON, business analyst consultant; b. Gloucester, Mass., Oct. 1, 1959; d. Melvin Porter Jr. and Ruth Margaret (Dahlmer) Olson; m. Mark Anthony Adiletta, Aug. 25, 1984; children: Christopher Michael, Nichole Brianna, Mark Andrew. BA, Coll. of Holy Cross, Worcester, Mass., 1981; MBA, U. Rochester, 1986. Systems analyst Eastman Kodak Co., Rochester, NY, 1981—85, infosystems specialist, 1985—86, personal computer area mgr., 1986—87, bus. analyst cons., 1987—90, info. sys. co-dir., 1990—92, bus. sys. specialist, 1992—2003. Seminar instr., Rochester, 1987. Fin. advisor Sts. Peter and Paul Ch., Rochester, 1985-86; div. chairperson United Way, Rochester, 1987. Mem. Assn. Systems Mgmt., Holy Cross Alumni Assn. (class agt. 1981—, sec. 1983-84, treas. 1984-88, v.p. 1988-90, pres. 1990-91, bd. dirs. 1992—). Avocations: snow and water skiing, horseback riding.

ADKERSON, DONYA LYNN, clinical counselor; b. Mattoon, Ill., Oct. 5, 1959; d. Edwin Dwayne and Sonya Jeanne (Abernathie) Adkerson; m. George Anthony Ferguson, May 20, 1990; children: Tiana Jo Berry, Thomas A.R. Ferguson. MA, So. Ill. U., Edwardsville, 1983. Outpatient dir. Children's Ctr. for Behavioral Devel., Centerville, Ill., 1983-90; pvt. practice psychotherapy Evaluation & Therapy Svc., Edwardsville, 1991-92; dir. Alternatives Counseling, Inc., 1993—; grant coord. Ill. Sex Offender Mgmt. Bd., 2003—. Cons. St. Louis City Juvenile Ct., 1991-94, Covenant Children's Home, 1991-93, U. Ill., 1997-2000. Co-author: Adult Sexual Offender Assessment Packet, 1994. Pres. Ill. Network for Mgmt. Abusive Secuality, 1991; clin. mem. Assn. Treatment of Sex Abusers, exec. bd., 1995—2000, chair orgn. and devel. com., 1996—2000; mem. ethics and stds. com., founding mem. Ill. Assn. Treatment Sex Abusers, 1996—2001, Madison County Child Protection Task Force, 1999—; mem. 3d Jud. Cir. Family Violence steering com., 1996—; mem. Adolescent Perpetrator Network, 1987—95; exec. bd. Arts League Players Theatre, Edwardsville, 1996—; former chmn. Metro-East Task Force on Sexual Offenders; mem. Madison County Child Protection task force, Am. Profl. Soc. on Abuse of Children, Ill. Sex Offender Mgmt. Bd. assessment and treatment subcoms. Mem. Ill. Counseling Assn., Ill. Mental Health Counselors Assn. Avocations: gardening, theater, water gardening. Office: Alternatives Counseling Ste 3 10 Cottonwood Rd Glen Carbon IL 62034-4326

ADKINS, JEANNE M. state agency administrator; b. North Platte, Nebr., May 2, 1949; BA, U. Nebr. Journalist; mem. Colo. Ho. of Reps., 1988—99, chairwoman judiciary com., vice-chairwoman legal svcs. com., mem. fin. com., regional air quality control coun., state edn. accountability commn.; dir. policy and planning Colo. Dept. Edn.; dir. Colo. Student Loan Program, 2002—. Founding sec. Douglas County Econ. Devel. Coun., bd. dirs., 1988. Fellow Vanderbilt U. Govt., Gates fellow JFK Sch. Govt. State/Local Program, Toll fellow. Mem. Am. Soc. Newspaper Editors, Soc. Profl. Journalists, Suburban Newspaper Assn. Republican. Baptist. Office: CSLP 999 18th St Ste 425 Denver CO 80202*

ADKINS, KATHY FORESTER, music educator; b. Chattanooga, Jan. 4, 1955; d. Clyde Douglas and Vonnie Gray Forester; m. Terry Amon Adkins, Mar. 18, 1978; children: Amonie, Kerry, Cole. MusB in Piano, Wesleyan Coll., 1976; MusM in Theory/Composition, Ea. Ky. U., 1980; EdD in Edn., U. Tenn., 2003. Cert. tchr. music edn. Tchr. elem. music Dade County Schs., Trenton, Ga., 1978—84; entertainer, musician The Forester Sisters, Trenton, 1984—96; tchr., choral dir. Catoosa County Schs., Ringgold, Ga., 1996—97, Dade County Schs., Trenton, 1997—. Recipient Grammy award nominations (3), 1984—96. Mem.: Ga. Music Educators Assn., Phi Kappa Phi. Avocations: gardening, quilting.

ADKINS, PATRICIA ANN, school system administrator, educator; b. Salisbury, Md., Jan. 26, 1972; d. Flora Ann Vickers; m. Hunter Todd Adkins, Jan. 26, 1995. BS in Spl. Edn. summa cum laude, U. Md. Ea. Shore, Princess Anne, Md., 1994; MA in Pub. Sch. Adminstrn. summa cum laude, Salisbury (Md.)U., 1998. Cert. tchr. Md., Sch. Adminstr. I, Sch. Adminstr. II. Spl. edn. tchr. J. M. Bennett HS, Salisbury, Md., 1994—99; asst. prin. Wicomico HS, Salisbury, 1999—. Keynote spkr. Md. Student Svc. Alliance, Towson, Md., 2001. Contbr. articles to profl. jours. Mem.: Learning Disabilities Assn. (Prin.'s scholarship - Pres. award 2001), Coun. Exceptional Children, Assn. Supervision and Curriculum Devel., Nat. Assn. of Secondary Sch. Prins. Office: Wicomico HS 201 Long Ave Salisbury MD 21804 E-mail: padkins@wcboe.org.

ADKINS, SANDRA KAY, music educator, church musician; d. Clyde Patrick Kumpf and Winifred Geraldine Kunpf; m. James Allen Adkins, Nov. 1, 1980; children: Christopher Allen, Jennifer Anne. BS in Music, Labanon Valley Coll., Annville, Pa., 1972; MEd in Music, Towson (Md.) U., 1979; MEd in counseling, Loyola Coll. in Md., Balt., 1989. Cert. APC Md. Tchr. Balt. County Pub. Schs., 1972—75, Howard County Pub. Schs., 1975—. Adjudicator, Md., 1999—. Mem. bd. Howard County Summer Theatre, 1989—95. Named Music Educator of Yr., Howard County Parents Sch. Music, 1997; recipient Tchg. Excellence award, Howard CC. Mem.: Am. Choral Dirs. Assn., Music Educators Nat. Assn., Delta Kappa Gamma (pres. 1994—96). Methodist. Avocations: reading, crossword puzzles, cross stitch. Home: 9394 Furrow Ave Ellicott City MD 21042

ADKINS, SUSAN, health services administrator; Grad., U. Kans. Dir. Menninger Ctr. Family Solutions, Topeka. Address: Menningers PO Box 809045 Houston TX 77280

ADKINS CAMPBELL, ANGELA DAWN, speech-language pathologist; b. Ashland, Ky., Apr. 30, 1973; d. Clarence Wayne Adkins and Betty Ruth Ison Adkins; m. Mark Daniel Campbell, Oct. 6, 2001. BS summa cum laude, Ea. Ky. U., 1995, MA, 1996; rank I in spl. edn., Morehead State U., 1997. Cert. cert. clin. competence Am. Speech-Lang. Assn. Speech pathologist Elliott County Bd. Edn., Sandy Hook, Ky., 1997—; speech-lang. pathologist Easter Seals/Geiger Speech and Hearing, Ashland, Ky., 1998—99. Adj. faculty, instr. Morehead (Ky.) State U., 1997—; cons. Lexington (Ky.) Area Tech., 2001—02; vice-chair Big East Coop. SLP Cadre, Ashland, Ky., 2001—02; sch.-based examiner Psychol. Corp., San Antonio, 2001—. Mem.: Ky. Speech Lang. Hearing Assn., Am. Speech Lang. Hearing Assn., Phi Kappa Phi. Baptist.

ADLER, CAROL ELLEN, publishing executive, writer; b. Rochester, N.Y., Dec. 5, 1938; d. Leonard Anthony Stalker and Helen Dorothy Hurvitz; children: Deborah, Naomi. Student, Brandeis U.; AB, U. Mich., 1961; MFA, Norwich U., 1991; postgrad., U. Rochester. Writer Montgomery, Searcy & Denney, Inc. Attys.-at-Law, West Palm Beach, Fla., 1986—87; instr. Creative Writing State of Fla. Correctional Instns., 1987—89; tchr. Creative Tchg. Svcs., Seminole and Juno Beach, Fla., 1991—92; prin., dir. pub. rels. VitaChek, 1992—98; pres., co-founder PenArt Prodns., Inc., 1998—2000; pres., founder Dandelion Books, LLC, Tempe, Ariz., 2000—. Instr. English Northwood U., West Palm Beach, 1987—88; poet-in-residence Palm Beach County Sch. Sys., West Palm Beach, 1988; assoc. Smart Svcs., Inc., Palm Beach, Fla., 1988—89; dir. spl. projects 21st Century TV Internat., West Palm Beach, 1995—97; dir. publs. TriNeuro-Genics Inc., 1996—98; v.p., dir. pub. rels. Mother Nature's Farms, Inc., 1999—2000; sr. v.p. Am. Wellness Assn., 1992—98. Home and Office: 5250 S Hardy Dr #3067 Tempe AZ 85283*

ADLER, LOUISE DECARL, judge; b. 1945; BA, Chatham Coll., Pitts.; JD, Loyola U., Chgo. Bar: Ill., 1970, Calif., 1972. Practicing atty., San Diego, 1972-84; standing trustee Bankruptcy Ct. So. Dist. Calif., San Diego, 1974-79, chief bankruptcy judge, 1996—2001. Mem. editorial bd. Calif. Bankruptcy Jour., 1991-92. Fellow Am. Coll. Bankruptcy; mem. San Diego County Bar Assn. (chair bus. law study sect. 1979, fed. ct. com. 1983-84), Lawyers Club of San Diego (bd. dirs. 1972-73, treas. 1972-75, sec. 1972-74, v.p. 1974-75), San Diego Bankruptcy Forum (bd. dirs. 1989-92), Nat. Conf. Bankruptcy Judges (bd. dirs. 1989-91, sec. 1992-93, v.p. 1993-94, pres. 1994-95). Office: US Bankruptcy Ct 325 W F St Rm 2 San Diego CA 92101-6017 Office Phone: 619-557-5661.

ADLER, MADELEINE WING, academic administrator; b. Ohio; d. George and Bette Wing; m. Frederick S. Lane; children: J. Peter Adler, Rand Lane, Cary Lane. BA in Polit. Sci., Northwestern U., 1962; MA in Polit. Sci., U. Wis., 1963, PhD in Polit. Sci., 1969. Asst. prof. polit. sci. Am. U., Washington, 1965-67; cons. Charles Nelson Assoc., N.Y.C., 1967-68; asst. prof. Queens Coll. CUNY, N.Y.C., 1969-74, assoc. prof. Queens Coll., 1974-86, assoc. dean, 1983-86; v.p. acad. affairs, prof. polit. sci. Framingham (Mass.) State Coll., 1986-92; pres. West Chester (Pa.) U., 1993—. Staff mem. Joint Com. Orgn. Congress, Washington, 1965-66; vis. asst. prof. Pa. State U., summers 1967-71; dir. profl. staff recruitment N.Y.C. Urban Acad., 1975-78; pres. Ctr. Applied Rsch. and Analysis Social Scis., Inc., 1976-86; mem. crosscutting rsch. panel, office rsch. and evaluation U.S. HEW, 1978-80; program coord. N.E. region Soc. Coll. and Univ. Planning, 1987-89; mem. exec. bd. Am. Coun. Edn./Nat. Identification Project, State of Mass., 1987-92, vice chair exec. bd., 1991—. Author: (with Harold Savitch) Decentralization at the Grassroots: Political Innovation in New York City and London, 1974; contbr. article to profl. jours. Mem. Comty. Bd. 14, Bklyn., 1978-81, Gov.'s Award Panel for Humanities, 1993—, Gov.'s Comty. Svc. Adv. Bd., 1994—, Chester County Comty. Found., 1994—; appointee Bklyn. Econ. Devel. Corp., 1982-86; bd. advisors Acad. Search Consultation Svcs., 1994—. Mem. Pa. Assn. Colls. and Univs. (com. acad. issues 1993—). Home: 100 E Rosedale Ave West Chester PA 19382-4927 Office: Office of Pres West Chester Univ Philips Meml Bldg West Chester PA 19383

ADLER, MARGOT SUSANNA, journalist, radio producer; b. Little Rock, Apr. 16, 1946; d. Kurt Alfred and Freyda (Nacque) A. BA, U. Calif., Berkeley, 1968; MS, Columbia U., 1970. Newscaster Sta. WBAI-FM, N.Y.C., 1968-71, host talk show, 1972-90; chief Washington bur. Pacifica News Svc. Network; corr., prodr. All Things Considered, Morning Edit., Nat. Pub. Radio, N.Y.C., 1978—, host Justice Talking, 1999—. Instr. radio comms. Goddard Coll., Plainfield, Vt., 1977; instr. religion and ecology Inst. for Social Ecology, Vt., 1986-93. Author: Drawing Down the Moon, 1979, Heretic's Heart, 1997; co-prodr., dir. (radio drama) War Day, 1985; contbr. articles to prof. jours. Nieman fellow Harvard U., 1982. Mem. Phi

Beta Kappa. Avocations: swimming, bird watching, science fiction. Home: 333 Central Park W New York NY 10025-7145 Office: Nat Pub Radio 801 2nd Ave Rm 701 New York NY 10017-4781 E-mail: madler@npr.org.

ADLER, NANCY ELINOR, psychologist, educator; BA, Wellesley Coll., 1968; MA, Harvard U., 1971, PhD, 1973. Asst. prof. psychology U. Calif., Santa Cruz, 1972-76, assoc. prof. psychology, 1976-77, assoc. prof. med. psychology dept. psychiatry and pediat. San Francisco, 1977-84, prof. med. psychology depts. psychiatry and pediat., 1984—, dir. health psychology program, 1988—, program dir. NIMH tng. program, 1991—, vice chair dept. psychiatry, 1994—; dir. Ctr. for Health and Cmty., 1998—. Vis. asst. rsch. psychologist Inst. Personality Assessment and Rsch., U. Calif., Berkeley, 1975; mem. peer rev. panel Ad Hoc Sci. Study Sects., Nat. Inst. Child Health and Human Devel., 1977—, Nat. Heart, Lung and Blood Inst., 1993; adv. com. for five-yr. plan Demographic and Social Scis. Br., Ctr. for Population RSch., Nat. Inst. Child Health and Human Devel., 1986-87, adv. com., 1991-2000; sr. rsch. scientist in psychology Yale U., New Haven. 1994-95; review com. Intramural Rsch. NIMH, 1997, sci. adv. bd. Ctr. Advancement Health, Washington, 1995-96, bd. trustees, 1996—; grant reviewer NSF, Social Scis. and Humanities Rsch. Coun. Can., Soc. Behavioral Medicine, March of Dimes, Ctrs. for Disease Control, Econ. and Social Rsch. Coun.; presenter in field. Author: (with others) Health Psychology-A Handbook: Theories, Applications, and Challenges of a Psychological Approach to the Health Car System, 1979, Preventing Preterm Birth: A Parent's Guide, 1988, SES & Health in Industrialized Nations, 1999; adv. bd. Ency. Mental Health, 1995—; assoc. editor Health Psychology, 1984-90, Women's Health: Research in Gender, Behavior and Policy, 1994-98; mem. editl. bd. Jour. Population and Environment, 1982-88, Health Psychology, 1994—; manuscript reviewer Jour. Personality and Social Psychology, Jour. Nervous and Mental Disease, Personality and Social Psychology Bull., Jour. Health and Social Behavior, Jour. Applied Social Psychology, Basic and Applied Social Psychology, Psychology Women Quarterly, The Western Jour. Medicine, Jour. Am. Med. Assn., Am. Jour. Pub. Health, many others; contbr. articles in field. Recipient Best Rsch. Paper award Soc. for Adolescent Medicine, 1984; NSF fellow, 1968-72, U. Calif. Regents Summer fellow, 1974; grantee in field. Fellow: Am. Psychol. Soc., APA (sec.-treas. divsn. 34 1975—78, pres. divsn. 34 1979—80, planning com. for nat. conf. on tng. in health psychology 1982—83, chairperson fellow com. divsn. 34 1982—86, participant Arden House conf. on edn. and tng. in health psychology 1983, chairperson nominations com. 1989—90, task force on promotion of population psychology 1992—97); mem.: Inst. of Medicine, Soc. for Rsch. on Adolescence, Assn. Med. Sch. Profs. Psychology, Soc. Advancement Social Psychology, Internat. Assn. Applied Psychology, Soc. Exptl. Social Psychology, Phi Beta Kappa, Sigma Xi. Office: U Ca Health Psychology Program 3333 California St San Francisco CA 94118-1981 E-mail: nadler@itsa.ucsF.edu.

ADLER, PEGGY ANN, writer, illustrator, consultant; b. N.Y.C., Feb. 10, 1942; d. Irving and Ruth Adler; children: Tenney Whedon Walsh, Avery Denison Walsh (Mrs. Adam I. Lapidus). Student, Bennington Coll., 1959—60, Columbia U., 1962. Illustrator, author children's books, 1958—; logistics and ticket sales and mgmt. the world premiere "Butch Cassidy and Sundance Kid", 1969; agt. Jan J. Agy., Inc., N.Y.C., 1981-82; freelance talent agent Cuzzins Mgmt., N.Y.C., 1982-83; personal mgmt. and pub. rels. cons. Madison, Conn., 1985-95. [illegible] Fredericksen, Pvt. Investigator, Conn. and N.Y., 1990—96; investigative rschr., writer, ill. cons., 1986—; asst. investigator Ho. of Reps. October Surprise Task Force, Washington, 1992; pvt. investigator; child care provider, 1998—. Author (illustrator): The Adler Book of Puzzles and Riddles, 1962, The 2nd Adler Book of Puzzles and Riddles, 1963, Metric Puzzles, 1977, Math Puzzles, 1978, Geography Puzzles, 1979; author: Hakim's Connection, 1988; co-author: Skull and Bones: The Skeleton in Bush's Closet?, 1988; contbr. illustrator numerous books including Hot and Cold, 1959, Numbers New and Old, 1960, Reading Fundamentals for Teen-Agers, 1973, Do a Zoomdo, 1975, Pet Care, 1974, Caring for Your Cat, 1974; graphic designer : various book covers, posters, and logos; pub. rels. Sweetie, Baby, Cookie, Honey (Freddie Gershon), 1986, rschr. Passion and Prejudice: A Family Memoir (Sallie Bingham), 1989, The Village Voice, 1991, 1992, numerous others; contbr. The President's Private Eye: The Journey of Detective Tony U, from N.Y.P.D. to the Nixon White Ho., 1990; cons., rschr.: Bush's Boys Club: Skull and Bones, 1990; cons. Spy Saga (Philip H. Melanson), 1990; contbr. Lies of Our Times; licensee/story cons. 60 Minutes, 1991; cons., rschr. : London Sunday Times, 1991; contbr. The Independent London, 1994, 1995; rsch. assoc. for Ron Rosenbaum, I Stole the Head of Prescott Bush! More Scary Skull and Bones Tales (N.Y. Observer), 2000, Inside Skull and Bones' Secret Initiation Ritual (N.Y. Observer), 2001. Founder Shoreline Youth Theatre, Inc., 1979, bd. dirs., 1979—81, mem. adv. bd., 1981—86; bd. dirs. Greens Condominium Assn. Branford, Conn., 1975—78, Arts Coun. Greater New Haven, 1971—73, Planned Parenthood Greater New Haven, 1972—73, Assassination Archives and Rsch. Ctr., Washington, 1990—96; v.p., bd. dirs. Pub. Info. Rsch., Washington, 1989; hon. mem. Forgotten Families; chmn. majority subcom. study com 10 Killingworth Turnpike bldg., mem. charter revision commn. Town of Clinton, 1997—98, author, charter revisions, legal notice and ballot questions, 1998, mem. design adv. bd., 2000—, chmn. design adv. bd., 2003—, mem. Clinton Landing study com., 2003—04, charter revision commn., 2003—04; vol. Clinton Pub. Schs.; mem. hist. dist. commn. Town of Clinton, 2001—, elected constable, 2001—. Mem.: Charter Revision Commn. (vice chmn. 2003—04), Conn. Soc. Genealogists Inc., Assn. Former Intelligence Officers (program coord. 1997—, bd. dirs. 1997—, pres. New Eng. chpt. 2001—03, Gen. Richard G. Stilwell Chmn.'s award 2001), Duck Island Yacht Club (membership com. 1997—2000, social com. 1997—2004, Duck Stop 1997—, Don Dyson Corinthian award 1998). Home and Office: 5 Liberty St Clinton CT 06413

ADLER, POSY (ROSLYN ADLER), artist, educator; b. Chgo., Ill., Feb. 6, 1916; d. Leon and Julia (Sonnenschein) Woolf; m. Leon Adler, Nov. 1, 1937 (dec.); children: Larry, Janet. BE, Nat. Coll. Edn., Evanston, Ill., 1975; MFA in Sculpture, Goddard Coll., Plainfield, Vt., 1975; studied with Roger Armstrong, Eliot O'Hara, Barbara Neijna, Robert Stoetzer. Art tchr. Miami (Fla.)-Dade Coll., Miami, Fla., 1964-84; sculpture tchr. Saddleback Coll., Mission Viejo, Calif., 1984—. Art tchr. Newport Harbor Mus., Irvine Fine Arts Ctr., Met. Art Ctr., Dade County C.C., New Sch. Fine Arts. Exhibited sculpture and watercolors in shows at Art Angles, Calif., Artist's Unlimited, Fla., Bacardi Art Gallery, Fla., Blunt Gallery, Ctr. for the Arts, Boca Raton, Fla., Design Ctr. South, Calif., Grove House Gallery, Fla., Jockey Club Art Gallery, Fla., U. Fla. Lowe Art Gallery, Fla., Met. Art Ctr., Fla., Mus. Science, Miami, Neiman Marcus Art Gallery, Rauchbach Galleries, Tolley Gallery, Turnberry Gallery; commissions include: Sherman Gardens, Calif., Sports Clinic, Laguna Hills, Calif., Temple Or Olom, Miami. Ind. state v.p. Mental Health Soc., Frankfort, 1954-55, bd. dirs., Miami, Fla., 1957-62; hospice vol., Laguna Hills, Calif., 1990-99; vol. Adult Day Care Ctr., Laguna Hills, 1999. Mem. Am. Crafts Coun., Orange Co. Fine Arts, Ceramic League Miami, Creative Arts Guild, Dana Point Coastal Arts Coun., Florida Craftsman, Laguna Arts Assn., Miami Cultural Arts Alliance, Nat. League Am. Penwomen, Nat. Mus. Women in the Arts, Niguel Art Assn., Sculptors of Fla., Women's Caucus for Art. Democrat. Jewish. Avocations: travel, sculpting, painting, craft work.

ADLIS, SUSAN ANNETTE, biostatistician; b. Mpls., Mar. 7, 1951; d. Paul and Miriam A. BA, Coll. St. Catherine, St. Paul, 1972; BS, U. Minn., Mpls., 1982, MS, 1987. Med. technologist U. Minn., Mpls., 1983-85, tchg. asst., 1985-87; epidemiologist Minn. Dept. Health, Mpls., 1987-88; rsch. asst. U. Minn., Mpls., 1988-90; rsch. analyst Abbott Northwestern Hosp., Mpls., 1990-92; biostatistician Park Nicollet Inst., Mpls., 1992—. Mem. protocol rev. com. Health Sys. Minn., Mpls., 1993-98. Contbr. articles to profl. jours. Mem. AAAS, APHA, Am. Statis. Assn., Am. Soc. Clin. Lab. Scis., N.Y. Acad. Scis. Achievements include research on health services and internal medicine. Office: Park Nicollet Inst 3800 Park Nicollet Blvd Minneapolis MN 55416-2527 E-mail: adliss@parknicollet.com.

ADOLPH, DIANE JOYCE, retired underwriter; b. L.A. d. Erwin Lorraine and Geraldine (Kimport) Winter; m. Donald Oscar Adolph, Feb. 18, 1954; children: Donna Pembrooke, Darra Lee Buesser, Denise Bierman. Cert. gen. ins., Ins. Inst. Am., 1983; AA, Moorpark (Calif.) Coll., 1987. Forms control clk. State Farm Ins. Co., Thousand Oaks, Calif., 1977-78, pricing control clk., 1979-81, underwriting asst., 1981-83, underwriter, 1983-89. Pres. Arts League, La Quinta, Calif., 1992-94; mem. publicity, pub. rels. com. Cmty. Concerts, La Quinta, 1992; bd. dirs., v.p. Arts Found., La Quinta, 1994—; chmn. Roundtable West's Books for the Bookless Project, Coachella Valley, 1994—; v.p. Viva Found. Hist. Soc., 1994—; mem. Friends of La Quinta Sr. Ctr., 1998—, Friends of La Quinta Libr., 1996—; bd. dirs. Harvest Our Wellness Found., 1999—. Recipient Vol. of Yr. award Arts League, 1992, Most Dedicated Vol. award Arts Found., 1999. Mem. La Quinta C. of C. (exec. amb. 1993-96, Citizen of Yr. 1994), Toastmasters (Toastmaster of Yr. 1988), Soroptomist Internat. (bd. dirs. 1998—). Republican. Avocations: reading, travel, exercise, cooking and entertaining, golf. Home: 55105 Riviera La Quinta CA 92253-4764

ADOLPH, KATHRYN ANN, passenger service employee; b. Hartington, Nebr., Dec. 20, 1945; d. Edmund Leonard and Elizabeth Claire Arens; m. Lester Leroy Adolph, Jan. 2, 1965 (div. July 1998); children: Leslie Marie, Edmund Glenn. BS in Adult and Occupation Edn., Kans. State U., 1981. Passenger svc. employee Trans World Airlines, Kans. City, Mo., 1978—2001, Am. Airlines, Kans. City, Mo., 2001—. Industry expert (TV appearance) CNN. Avocations: writing, photography.

ADOLPHSON, VANESSA, counseling administrator, educator, chemist; b. Bakersfield, Calif., Oct. 13, 1973; d. Juan A. and Elena L. Garza; m. David J. Adolphson, Apr. 28, 2001; children: Marissa E., Blake J. BS in Chemistry, Calif. State U. Bakersfield, 1996; MS in Sch. Counseling, U. La Verne, 2000, MEd in Ednl. Mgmt., 2003. Sch. counselor Winterstein Adult Ctr., Sacramento, 2000—; counselor Stanford Home For Children, Sacramento, 1998—2000. Evening sch. adminstr. Winterstein Adult Ctr., Sacramento, 2001—. Activist Foster Youth Forum, Sacramento, 1998—2000. Mem.: Phi Sigma Sigma (life; jud. bd. 1994—95). D-Conservative. Roman Catholic. Avocations: travel, tennis, painting. Office: Winterstein Adult Center 900 Morse Ave Sacramento CA 95864 Office Phone: 916-971-7414. Personal E-mail: vangarza@hotmail.com. E-mail: vadolphson@sanjuan.edu.

ADOMAITIS, ALYSSA DANA, design educator, consultant; b. Queens, N.Y., Mar. 12, 1972; d. Edmundas and Charlotte Adomaitis. Student, Parson's Sch. Design, 1991—95, Fashion Inst. Tech., 1993—94; BS, SUNY, Oneonta, N.Y., 1994; MBA, L.I. U., 1997; PhD, U. Minn., 2002. Visual merchandiser Saks Fifth Ave., N.Y.C., 1994—95; undergrad. academic advisor U. Minn., 1998—2000; personal care asst. At Home Ltd., 1999; personal asst. to chmn. bd. Mart Travel Group, 1999—2002; tchg. asst. U. Minn., 2000—02, rsch. asst., 2001, student curator, 2001; asst. prof. Calif. State Polytechnic U., Pomona, Calif., 2002—. Cons. Fred Segal, 2003—; presenter in field; mem. fundraising com. Calif. Polytechnic U., [illegible] scholars com., 2002—, mem. honors com., 2002—. Contbr. articles to profl. jours. Fellow Adminstrv. [illegible] 1998—2000; grantee Design, Housing, and Apparel Block grant, 2001; scholar, Minn. Assn. family and Consumer Scis., 2000. Mem.: Apparel Merchandising Mgmt. Assn. (co-chmn. 2002—), Assn. Image Cons., Am. Mktg. Assn., Internat. Textile & Apparel Assn. (mem. graduate edn. com. 2002—), The Fashion Group Internat., N.Y. Road Runners Club. Home: 13284 Cardinal Ridge Rd Unit E Chino Hills CA 91709 Office: Apparel Merchandising and Mgmt Calif State U 3801 West Temple Ave Pomona CA 91768

ADOUR, COLLEEN MCNULTY, art educator; b. Columbus, Ohio, Dec. 15, 1961; d. Helen Dooley and John Patrick McNulty. BFA in Studio Arts, cum laude, Syracuse U., 1980, postgrad. in MFA program in Studio Arts, 1980—84; grad. level ceramics summa cum laude, Alfred U., 1994; MFA in Art History, magna cum laude, SUNY, Binghamton, 2002. Daytime supr., art and music libr. Bartle Libr., SUNY, Binghamton, NY, 2000—02; coll. art tchr., lectr. Broome C.C., SUNY, Binghamton, NY, 2003—. Pub. info. mgr. Everson Mus. Art, Syracuse, NY, 1982—84. Notary pub. Dept. Of State, Divsn. Licensing Svcs., Albany, NY, 1998—2003; insp. of elections Broome County Bd. Of Elections, Binghamton, NY, 1998—2003. Mem.: Binghamton U. Medieval and Renaissance Group (assoc.; v.p., treas. 2000—01). Office: Broome Cmty Coll Cmty Edn PO Box 1017 Binghamton NY 13902

ADREON, BEATRICE MARIE RICE, pharmacist; b. Huntington, W.Va., July 23, 1929; d. Lloyd Emerson and Beatrice (Odell) Rice; student Mary Washington Coll., 1947-49; B.S. in Pharmacy, Med. Coll. Va., 1952; M.A. in Spl. Studies and Women's Studies, George Washington U., 1976; m. Harry Barnes Adreon, Jr., Dec. 27, 1952. Summer vol. worker pharmacies De Paul Hosp., Norfolk, Va., 1949, U.S. Marine Hosp., Norfolk, 1950; pharmacist Washington Clinic, 1954-71; counselor George Washington U., 1976-77, cons. gerontology health scis. dept., 1977— ; cons. medicine control traffic patterns nursing homes Cross & Adreon, Washington, 1962-87; founder, pres. Pharmacy Counseling Services, Inc., 1978—. Instr. advanced first aid ARC, 1952—, civil def. instr., 1952—; vol. Spanish Edn. Devel. Center, Washington, 1972; mem. Arlington (Va.) Community Services Bd., 1980-83; chmn. com. substance abuse. Recipient Arnold and Marie Schwartz award in pharmacy, 1980. Mem. Acad. Pharmacy Practice and Mgmt., Am. Pharm. Assn., Va. Pharm. Assn., Potomac Pharmacists Assn., Am. Inst. History of Pharmacy, Nat. Council Patient Info. and Edn. (task force pub. info.), Panhellenic Assn., Kappa Epsilon. Episcopalian (mem. bishop's com. neighborhood services 1967-69, chmn. services for aged div. 1967-69). Contbr. articles in field to profl. jours. Home: 4524 19th Rd N Arlington VA 22207-2352

ADRI, (ADRI STECKLING COEN), fashion designer; b. St. Joseph, Mo. Ed., Sch. Fine Arts, Washington U., St. Louis, Parson Sch. Design. With B.H. Wragge; owner, pres. Adri Studio, Ltd., N.Y.C., 1983—. Critic Parsons Sch. Design, 1982—; with Claire McCardell in 2-person showing, Innovative Contemporary Fashion, Smithsonian Instn., Washington, 1971. Two-woman show (with Claire McCardell) Smithsonian Instn., Washington, 1972. Recipient Coty award, 1982, Internat. Best Five award, Tokyo, 1986. Office: 143 W 20th St 11th Fl New York NY 10011-3630

ADRIANOPOLI, BARBARA CATHERINE, librarian; b. Fort Dodge, Iowa, Jan. 27, 1943; d. Daniel Joseph and Mary Dolores (Coleman) Hogan; m. Carl David Adrianopoli, June 28, 1969; children: Carlin, Laurie. BS, Mundeline Coll., 1966; MLS, Rosary Coll., 1975; student, Ozark Rsch. Inst., 1999-2000. Cert. in Pranic Healing and Dowsing Ozark Rsch. Inst. Dir. br. and extension svcs. Schaumburg Twp. (Ill.) Dist. Libr., 1979—. Mem. diversity com. N. Suburban/Suburban Libr. Sys., Wheeling, Ill., 1995—; mem. comm. Hoffman Estates History Mus., 2004. Columnist local newspaper, 1995—, Sr. Connection, 2000—; contbr. articles to profl. jours. Mem. com. Schaumburg Twp. Disabled, 1981-95; historian Village of Hoffman Estates, 1986-99; adv. com. Hoffman Estates Sister Cities, 1996-98, Hoffman Estates History Commn., 2004-; asst. coach St. Viator H.S., 1999-2003; mem. adv. bd. Cmty. Information Network, 1994—; organizer, mem. Northwest Corridor-St. Patrick's Day Parade com., 1986-2003; trainer A World of Difference Anti-Defamation League, 1994; mem. Com. For Choices For Success-Seminars For Young Women, 1996—; mem. Hoffman Estates Sr. and Disabled Commn., 2001; apptd. 8th Dist. State Dem. Com. Women, 2002. Recipient Hoffman Estates Citizen of Yr. award, VFW, 1995. Mem.: ALA, Dorothy Brown Clerk of Cook County Cts. Adv. on Womens Issues (co-chair 2002—), Ill. Libr. Assn. Democrat. Roman Catholic. Home: 1105 Kingsdale Rd Schaumburg IL 60194-2378 Office: Schaumburg Twp Pub Libr 130 S Rosedale Rd Schaumburg IL 60193

ADRIAZOLA, ANA, Spanish and Latin American culture educator; b. Arequipa, Peru, July 7, 1945; came to U.S., 1990; d. Jorge-Roberto and María Adriazola; m. Jose O. Rodriguez, Dec. 6, 1974; children: Ana María, Aurora-Luz. EdD, Nat. U. San Agustin, Arequipa, 1985, D History and Anthropology, 1989. Cert. prof. secondary history and social scis. Prin. pvt. schs. So. Peru Cooper Co., Tacna, 1972-76, coord. ednl. and technol., 1976-81; conservator, curator Museo San Agustin U., Arequipa, 1982-83; prof. Colls. Edn. and History U. Nat. San Agustin, 1984-89; prof. Spanish and culture U. N.C., Charlotte, 1991-92, Fla. Atlantic U., Boca Raton, 1994—. Advisor textiles Kontisuyo Archaeol. Program, Moquegua, Peru, 1984-89. Mem. NAFE, MLA, Sigma Delta (pres. 1994-95). Avocation: writing fiction and literary criticism. Home: 2250 NW 8th St Boca Raton FL 33486-1450

ADSIT, ROBIN VIVA, artist, educator; d. Theodore Brainard and Aunita Hazel Adsit; m. Charles Rodney Metts, Aug. 16, 1980; children: Zia Robin Adsit-Metts, Addison Rodney Adsit-Metts. BFA, San Francisco Art Inst., 1979; MA, San Francisco State U., 1986; MFA, Ohio State U., Columbus, 1991. Lectr. Ohio State U., Columbus, 1991—92, U. So. Maine, Portland, 1992—93; adj. faculty Shorter Coll., Rome, Ga., 1994—96; faculty gov.'s honor program Valdosta State U., Ga., 1995—95; lectr. Berry Coll., Rome, Ga., 1996—2000, Bucknell U., Lewisburg, Pa., 2001—02. Adjudicator Governor's Honors Program, Atlanta, 1997—98. Korean cultural center exhibition, Cultural Narratives, exhibition, the columbus museum of art, 81st Annual Columbus Art League Exhibition, exhibition, Overview, San Francisco Art Institute Annual, exhibition, southern exposure gallery, Beyond Power: A Celebration, An Exhibition of Art by Northern California Women, exhibition, LeGrange National XI: Paintings, Prints, Drawings, The Samek Art Gallery, Studio Arts Faculty, Bucknell University, exhibition, university of new haven, Silent Dialogues: A Group Show, national exhibition, Skin, Union Street Gallery, trienniel exhibition of contemporary art, CrossCurrents, Walter Anderson Museum of Art, exhibition, vanderbilt university, Exploring Family: Myth and Memory, Sarratt Gallery (Honorarium, 2000), exhibition, berry college, Robin Adsit and Jere Lykins, Moon Gallery, trienniel exhibition of contemporary art, CrossCurrents, The Walter Anderson Museum of Art, exhibition, Governor's Honor Faculty Exhibition. Recipient Outstanding Student award, Pacific NW Coll. of Art, 1976; grantee Sara Jane Pyne Materials Funds, Ohio State U., Dept. of Art, 1990 and 1991; Residency fellowship, The Hambidge Ctr., 1995, Travel grant, Ohio State U., Dept. of Art, 1990, Artist grant, Pollock-Krasner Found., Inc., 2003-2004. Mem.: Coll. Art Assn. (assoc.), Phi Kappa Phi (hon.), D-Liberal.

ADUJA, MELODIE WILLIAMS, state senator; b. Honolulu, Jan. 25, 1960; m. Lee Williams; children: William, Amber. BA, Hawaii Loa Coll., Kaneohe, 1981; ML, Golden Gate U. Sch. of Law, 1991, JD, 1987. Legis. aide State Rep. Alfred Lardizabal, 1982—83; dep. processing atty. Prosecutor's Office, Honolulu, 1987—91; atty. Law Office of Melodie R. Williams Aduja, 1992—; commr. Transport. Commn. City and County of Hawaii, 1999—2000; senator Hawaii State Senate, 2002—. Dir. Nat. Kidney Found. of Hawaii, 1997—98; bd. mem. Hina Mauka Recovery Ctr., 1998—2001; dir. [illegible] 2001; mem. Kahaluu Neighborhood Bd., 1999—2001; dir. Hawaii Filipino Lawyers Assn., 1993—94; mem. San Francisco Area Women Tax Lawyers, 1992—93. Mem.: Calif. State Bar. Democrat. Roman Catholic. Office: State Capital Rm 231 415 S Beretania St Honolulu HI 96813 E-mail: senaduja@Capitol.hawaii.gov., melodie@aduja.com.

AEHLERT, BARBARA JUNE, health services executive; b. San Antonio, June 17, 1956; d. Bobby Ray and Ronella Su (Light) Mahoney; m. Dean A. Aehlert, Sept. 6, 1980; children: Andrea, Sherri. AA in Nursing, Glendale (Ariz.) C.C., 1976; BS in Profl. Arts, St. Joseph's Coll., Windham, Maine, 1997. Cert. ACLS instr., affiliate faculty, BLS instr., Basic Trauma Life Support instr., emergency med. tng./paramedic instr., ATLS and PEPP course coord. Gen. mgr. Hosp. Ambulance Svc., Phoenix, 1982-83; critical care nurse Samaritan Health Svcs., Phoenix, 1978-80, coord. patient transp., 1980-82, mgr. clin. programs, 1983-92; dir. emergency med. svcs. edn. EMS Edn. and Rsch., 1992-97; pres. S.W. EMS Edn. Inc., Glendale, Ariz., 1997—. EMS coord., City of Mesa Fire Dept., 2001—. Author: ACLS Quick Review Study Guide, 2d edit., 2001, ACLS Quick Review Slide Set, 1994, ACLS Quick Review Study Cards, 2003, PALS Study Guide, 1994, ECGs Made Easy, 2d edit., 2001, ECGs Made Easy Lesson Plans, 1996, Mosby's Computerized Paramedic Test Generator, 1996, Aehlert's EMT Basic Study Guide, 1997, ECGs Made Easy Study Cards, 2003. Republican.

AELION, C. MARJORIE, adult education educator; BS summa cum laude, U. Mass., 1980; MSCE, MIT, 1983; PhD, U. N.C., 1988. Park ranger Nat. Park Svc., Cape Cod Nat. Seashore, South Wellfleet, Mass., 1976-78; biologist, resource assessment divsn. Nat. Marine Fisheries, Woods Hole, Mass., 1978-84; rsch. asst. MIT, Cambridge, Mass., 1981-83, U. Mass.-Amherst, Amherst, Peru, 1983-84, U. N.C., Chapel Hill, 1986-88, tchg. asst., 1987; hydrologist U.S. Geol. Survey, Water Resources Divsn., Columbia, S.C., 1988-91, faculty mem., 1991-97; asst. prof. dept. environ. health scis. U. S.C., Columbia, 1991-97, assoc. prof., 1997-2001, prof., 2001—. Presenter in field. Contbr. articles to profl. jours. Fulbright-Hayes scholar, 1980-81; Bd. Govs.' fellow U. N.C., 1984-86, Dissertation fellow, 1988, NSF fellow in engring., 1991-94; grantee U.S. EPA, 1991-93, Hazardous Waste Mgmt. Rsch. Fund, 1991-94, 99-2002, Nat. Geographic Soc., 1992, S.C. Dept. Health and Environ. Control and Hazardous Waste Mgmt. Rsch. Fund, 1991-94, U. S.C., 1993-94, NSF, 1993-00, 99—, Fulbright Scholar, 2002; grad. student travel grantee award U. N.C., 1988; Rsch. Fellowship, Internat. Agrl. Ctr., The Netherlands, 2002. Mem. Am. Chem. Soc., Am. Soc. Microbiology, Assn. for Women in Sci. (sec. S.C. chpt. 1996-97, pres. S.C. chpt. 1997-98), Soc. Women Engrs., Soc. Environ. Toxicology and Chemistry, Phi Kappa Phi, Delta Omega. Office: U SC Environ Health Scis Dept Columbia SC 29208-0001

AFFLECK, MARILYN, sociology educator; b. Logan, Utah, July 1, 1932; d. Clark B. and Velda (Bryson) A.; children: Michelle Alisa, Kimberly Kay, Lacey Dawn. BA, U. Okla., 1954; MA, Brigham Young U., 1957; PhD, UCLA, 1966. Instr., Central State Coll., Edmond, Okla., 1958-60; asst. prof. Fla. State U., Tallahassee, 1966-68; asst. prof. sociology U. Okla., Norman, 1968-70, asso. prof., 1971-90, interim dean Grad. Coll., 1978-79, asst. dean, 1976-82. Editor Free Inquiry in Creative Sociology Jour., 1984-90. Recipient AMOCO Good Teaching award U. Okla., 1974 Mem. Okla. Sociol. Assn. (pres. 1974-75), South Ctrl. Women's Studies Assn. (treas. 1979-83), Phi Beta Kappa. Democrat. Mem. Lds Ch. Home: 6395 Corky Dr NE Norman OK 73026-3135

AFFONSO, DYANNE D. dean; BSN, U. Hawaii, 1966; MN in Nursing, U. Wash., 1967; MA in Clin. Psychology, U. Ariz., 1980, PhD in Clin. Psychology, 1982. Asst. prof. sch. nursing U. Miss., 1967-68; OB staff nurse, night charge nurse Kinchloe AFB Hosp., Mich., 1968-70; instr. sch. nursing U. Hawaii, 1970-73; asst. prof. coll. nursing U. Ariz., 1974-77, assoc. prof. coll. nursing, 1978, coord. psychiatric mental health nursing coll. nursing, 1982-84, joint appointment in psychology dept. psychology, 1983; assoc. prof. sch. nursing U. Calif., San Francisco, 1984-87, prof. sch. nursing, 1988; prof., dean sch. nursing Emory U., Atlanta, 1993-98, assoc. prof. women's & children's divsn. sch. pub. health, 1993—. Prof. sch.

nursing Emory U., Atlanta, 1998—. Contbr. articles to profl. jours.; presenter in field. Mem. NAS (mem. inst. medicine 1994), NIH (mem. adv. coun. nat. inst. child health & human devel. 1979-83, mem. agenda com. nat. inst. child health & human devel. 1982, mem. scientific rev. com. nat. ctr. nursing rsch. 1986, mem. adv. coun. nat. ctr. nursing rsch. 1986-88, mem. steering com. rsch. patient outcomes nat. ctr. nursing rsch. 1991, sec.'s conf. 1993, charter mem. adcv. coun. office rsch. on women's health 1995). Office: Emory U Sch Nursing 531 Asbury Cir Atlanta GA 30322-0001

AFOAKU, OYIBO HELISITA, academic administrator; b. Abakaliki, May 6, 1961; came to U.S., 1986; d. Nweke Samuel and Akunkwo Obijele Victoria (Chidumeh) Akpu; m. Osita George, Aug. 30, 1986; children: MmaChukwu, NzubeChukwu, OnyinyeChukwu, AmalaChukwu. Edn. cert., Fed. Coll. Edn., Katsina, Nigeria, 1984; nat. svc. cert., Fed. Republic of Nigeria, Benin-City, 1985; BA in History, Wash. State U., 1990, tchg. cert., 1991; MA, U. No. Colo., 2001. Libr. technician II/clerical asst. II Holland & Owen Librs. Wash. State U., Pullman, 1987-92, office asst. II Western Jour. Black Studies, 1992-93; asminstrv. asst. III Marcus Garvey Ctr. for Black Edn. U. No. Colo., Greeley, 1994-97, asst. dir., 1997—, mem. adv. bd. dirs., 1994—, co-founder, coord. Ann. Africana Night, 1994—. Co-founder, coord. Weld World Festival; spkr., presenter, and workshop condr. at spl. events promoting diversity and multiculturalism. Mem. Marcus Garvey Ctr. Cmty. Friends Program; city commr. Greeley Human Rels. Commn. Mem. AAUW, Internat. Friends and Families, Women Internat. League for Peace and Freedom, Greeley Interfaith Assn., Greeley Human Rela. Commn. (city commr.) Avocations: cultural exchanges, academic and cultural programmings, reading, cooking, volunteer services. Office: Marcus Garvey Ctr for Black Cultural Edn 928 20th St David House Greeley CO 80639-0001 Home: 3308 Forrester S Bloomington IN 47401-7115 Fax: 970 351-2337. E-mail: oyibo.afoadku@unco.edu.

AFTEL, MANDY, perfumer; b. Detroit, Mar. 2, 1948; d. James Samuel Aftel and Ruth May Ellias; 1 child, Chloe. BA, U. Mich., 1969, MA, 1970. Psychotherapist for artists and writers, Berkeley, Calif., 1977—2000; perfumer Grandiflorum Perfumes, Berkeley, 1996—97, Aftelier Perfumes, Berkeley, 1997—. Author: Death of a Rolling Stone: The Brian Jones Story, 1982, When Talk Is Not Cheap, 1984, The Story of Your Life, 1995, Essence and Alchemy: A Book of Perfume, 2001 (Richard B. Solomon award, 01). Mem. adv. bd. creative writing program St. Mary's Coll., Moraga, Calif., 2001—. Mem.: Artisan Natural Performers Guild (founder). E-mail: mandy@aftelier.com.

AFTERMAN, JEAN, professional sports team executive; BA in History of Art, U. Calif., Berkeley, 1979; JD, U. San Francisco, 1991. Aide Don Nomura, 1994—99; pvt. practice, 1999—2001; asst. gen. mgr. N.Y. Yankees, Bronx, 2001—, v.p., 2003—. Office: NY Yankees Yankee Stadium E 161 St & River Ave Bronx NY 10451*

AFTOORA, PATRICIA JOAN, transportation executive; b. Cleve., Jan. 2, 1940; d. Joseph Patrick and Frances Dolores (Fabis) Hunady; m. Albert B. Aftoora, Feb. 17, 1989; 1 child, Christopher Hunady; stepchildren: Melissa, Matthew, Richard. Student, Fenn Coll., Cleve., 1957-59, UCLA, 1959-61, John Carroll U., Cleve., 1961-63. Various positions Chesapeake and Ohio Ry. Co., Balt. and Ohio R.R. Co., Cleve., 1962-73; asst. corp. sec. Chessie System, Inc., Cleve., 1973-79; dept. corp. sec. Chessie System Inc. and Affiliates, Cleve., 1979-80; corp. sec. Chesapeake and Ohio Ry. Co., Balt. and Ohio R.R. Co., Cleve., 1980-87, CSX Transp. Inc., Balt., 1986-87; asst. v.p., asst. corp. sec. CSX Corp., Richmond, Va., 1987-89, v.p., corp. sec., from 1989; now v.p., corp. sec. CSX Transp., Inc., Jacksonville, Fla. Mem. Am. Soc. Corp. Secs. Inc., Nat. Assn. Records Mgrs. and Adminstrs. Home: 1211 Creek View Way Ponte Vedra Beach FL 32082-2509 Office: CSX Transp Inc 500 Water St Jacksonville FL 32202-4423

AGAJANIAN, GILDA, pianist; b. Apr. 03; d. Oganes and Azatuhi (Tosunian) A. BA, U. So. Calif., 1973, Grad. Study, 1974-76; Diploma, Am. Coll. of Musicians, Austin, Tex., 1981, Artist Diploma, 1984. Russian educator, Calif., 1976-81; music educator Gilda Agajanian Piano Studio, La Habra Heights, Calif., 1987—; profl. classical pianist Calif., 1985—; entrepreneur, ptnr. Aggie's Restaurants, Calif., 1981-89. Mem. Westshore Musicians Club (pres. 1992-95), Music Tchrs. Nat. Assn., Calif. Assn. of Profl. Music Tchrs. (chmn. recitals 1992—), Dominant Club (sec. 1994-96), nat. Guild of Piano Tchrs., AAUW, Woman's Club of Hollywood. Avocations: Slavic langs. and lits., exotic birds, dogs, cats, horticulture. Office: Gilda Agajanian Piano Studio 2039 N Cypress St La Habra Heights CA 90631

AGARD, EMMA ESTORNEL, psychotherapist; b. Bronx, N.Y. BA, Queens Coll.; MSW, Fordham U., 1962; cert. in Psychoanalytic Psychotherapy, Tng. Inst. for Mental Health, 1979; cert. in Child and Adolescent Psychotherapy, Postgrad. Ctr. for Mental Health, 1982. Supr. social work Foster Care Div., N.Y.C., 1968-72; asst. dir. Henry St. Settlement Urban Family Ctr., N.Y.C., 1972-74; tng. analyst, sr. supr. Tng. Inst. for Mental Health, N.Y.C., 1974—; pvt. practice psychotherapist N.Y.C., 1974—. Lectr. social work Columbia U., N.Y.C., 1977-90; adj. asst. prof. NYU, 1978-80; field instr. N.Y.C. Housing Authority, 1974-80; dist. dir., cons. Am. Consultation Ctrs., Bklyn. and N.Y.C., 1985—, dir. Park Slope br.; field instr. Sch. Social Svc. Fordham U., 1985—. Mem. Albemarle-Kenmore Neighborhood Assn., Bklyn., 1974—99. Fellow N.Y. State Soc. Clin. Social Work Psychotherapists (pres. Bklyn. chpt. 1988-91); mem. Profl. Soc. Tng. Inst. for Mental Health (sec.), Nat. Assn. Social Workers (diplomate), Acad. Cert. Social Workers, Nat. Coalition 100 Black Women, Delta Sigma Theta. Avocations: oil painting, tennis, yoga, swimming. Address: 109 E 36th St New York NY 10016-3447

AGARD, NANCEY PATRICIA, nursing administrator, consultant; b. Amsterdam, N.Y., Mar. 3, 1955; d. Richard Edward and Jean Elizabeth (Sweet) Agard. Diploma, St. Mary's Hosp. Sch. Nursing, 1976; BS, SUNY, 1981; MS, Syracuse U., 1986. RN N.Y. Staff nurse St. Mary's Hosp., Amsterdam, 1976-77, St. Luke's Hosp., Utica, NY, 1980-81; tchg. and rsch. ctr. nurse SUNY Health Sci. Ctr., Syracuse, 1977-80, 1984-90, clin. edn. specialist, 1981-84, lectr., 1984-90, cons., 1986; assoc. dir. practice and govtl. affairs N.Y. State Nurses Assn., Latham, 1990—2000; cons., 2000—; quality specialist Albany (N.Y.) Med. Ctr., 2002—. Mem. immunization action plan com. N.Y. State Dept. Health, Albany, 1993—98, mem. medicaid managed care adv. com., 1993—96, mem. immunization coalition, 1994—99, mem. turning point initiative com., 1997—98, mem. adult immunization coalition, 1997—2000; mem. health family com. N.Y. State Fedn. Prevent Child Abuse, 1993—96; mem. workplace violence com. Healthcare Assn. N.Y. State, 1998—99, mem. latex allergy workgroup, 1998—2000; mem. regional activities & legis. com. N.Y. State Emergency Med. Svc. Coun., 1999—2003. Vol. Karen Burstein, Mary Eileen Callan, Aileen Gunther Campaigns, Albany, 1994—96. Rural Immunization grantee, Merck Vaccine Divsn., 1992—93. Mem.: LWV, AACN, ANA, Nat. Assn. Clin. Nurse Specialists, Emergency Nurses Assn. (liaison 1996—97), NY State Nurses Assn., Arts Ctr. of Capital Region, Sigma Theta Tau (media award 1993). Democrat. Avocations: piano, pets, plants, pottery.

AGEE, EVE, anthropologist; b. Fayetteville, Ark., Sept. 1, 1967; d. Jacob Claude and Martha Jeanne Agee; m. Scott Andrew Lozen, Oct. 13, 2001. BA, Coll. William and Mary, 1990; MA, U. Va., 1994, PhD, 1999. Women's health rschr. U. Benin, Lome, Togo, 1990—91; English tchr. Am. Cultural Ctr./U.S. Embassy, Lome, Togo, 1991; instr. U. Va., Charlottesville, 1993, dir. health care rsch., 1993—94, mem. faculty, 1998—99; White House appointee Clinton Adminstrn., Washington, 1999—2001; pres. Agee Cons., Washington, 2001—, Eve Agee Life Path Coaching, 2001—. Cons. Cmty. Preservation and Devel. Corp., Washington, 1999—2001; dir. 1st Nat. Early Childhood Summit, U.S. Dept. Edn., Washington, 2001. Author: Menopause: Path to Woman's Empowerment, 2002; contbr. articles to profl. jours. Group organizer Habitat for Humanity, Va., 1999. Grantee NSF, 1993. Mem.: Am. Anthropology Assn. Avocations: yoga, hiking, sculpting, poetry, art. Office: Agee Cons & Life Path Coaching 1234 19th St NW Ste 700 Washington DC 20036

AGEE, NELLE HULME, retired art history educator; b. Memphis, May 22, 1940; d. John Eulice and Nelle (Ray) Hulme; m. Bob R. Agee, June 7, 1958; children: Denise, Robyn. Student, Memphis State U., 1971—72; BA, Union U., Jackson, Tenn., 1978; postgrad., Seminole Okla. Col., 1982, Okla Bapt. U., 1984; MEd, Ctrl. State U., Edmond, Okla., 1989. Cert. tchr. art, history Ky., Tenn., Okla. Offices svcs. supr. So. Bapt. Theol. Sem., Louisville, 1961—64; kindergarten tchr. Shively Heights Bapt. Ch., Louisville, 1965—70; editl. asst. Little Publs., Memphis, 1973—75; tchr. art Humboldt HS, Tenn., 1978—82. Vis. artist-in schs. Tenn. Arts. Commn., Nashville, 1978, 81, 82; adj. prof. art history Seminole Col., Okla., 1985—86, 1989; asst. prof. art and edn. Okla. Bapt. U., 1989—98; spkr. art orgns, ch. groups; tchr. art workshops Humboldt City Sch. Sys.; tchr. Cultural Arts Day Camp, Jackson, Tenn., 1982. Exhibited in various shows. Nat. pres. ministers' wives conf. So. Bapt. Conv., 1988; vol. Mabee-Gerrer Mus., Shawnee; bd. dirs. Robert Dotson Foun., Mabee-Gerrer Mus., Family Resource Ctr., 1993—98; active vol. Salvation Army Aux., Shawnee. Recipient Disting. Classroom Tchr. award, Tenn. Edn. Assn., 1982. Mem.: Goals 2000, Alpha Delta Kappa, Delta Kappa Gamma. Republican. Baptist. Avocations: stained glass, pottery, travel. Home: 14 Woodmanor Pl Jackson TN 38305-1718

AGHDASHLOO, SHOHREH, actress; b. Tehran, Iran; m. Houshang Touzie, 1987; 1 child, Tara. Degree in Internat. Rels., 1984. Actor: (films) Shatranje bad, 1976, Gozaresh (The Report), 1977, Sootah Delaan, 1978, Guests of Hotel Astoria, 1989, Twenty Bucks, 1993, Maryam, 2000, Surviving Paradise, 2000, America So Beautiful, 2001, House of Sand and Fog, 2003 (best supporting actress award L.A. Film Critics Assn., 2003, best supporting actress award N.Y. Film Critics Cir., 2003, Ind. Spirit award for best supporting female, 2004, Acad. award nomination for best supporting actress, 2004).

AGNEW, JANET BURNETT, secondary school educator; b. Spartanburg, S.C., Aug. 29, 1936; d. James and Ruby Evelyne (Burnett) A.; 1 child, James Gilmour. BA, U. N.C., Greensboro, 1958; MA in Teaching, Converse Coll., Spartanburg, S.C., 1966; postgrad., Clemson (S.C.) U., 1970-72, U. S.C., Columbia, 1990—97. Cert. tchr., prin., math. supr., gen. sci. and physics. Tchr. gen. math. for Tech. and algebra I & II Greensboro Schs.-Aycock, 1958-60; tchr. coll. prep. math. Air Force Dependent H.S., Stevenville, Nfld., Can., 1960-61; tchr. gen. math. and algebra Roebuck H.S. Spartanburg Schs. #6, 1962; tchr. gen. phys. and sci. Campobello Sch. Spartanburg Schs. #1, 1962-63; tchr. math. and algebra Spartanburg Schs. #7, 1965-68, substitute tchr., 1975-76; tchr. gen. math. for techs. and algebra I & II Pacolet & Broome H.S., Spartanburg Sch. #3, 1976-98; corp. sec. Delagrave Co., Spartanburg, 1963-75; instr. math. Spartanburg Meth. Coll., 1968-75; ret., 1998. Cons., 1998—. Contbr. articles to profl. jours. Pres. Gen. Fedn. Women's Clubs-S.C., Columbia, 1978—80, chmn. trustees, 1985—87, 1988—91, 1991—97, 1999—2000, 2001—03, chmn. scholarship com., 1991—93, 1995—97; sec.-treas. so. region Gen. Fedn. Women's Clubs, 1990—92; v.p. so. region Gen. Fedn. Women's Clubs-S.C., 1992—94; pres. so. region Gen. Fedn. Women's Clubs, 1994—96. Recipient Svc. award Spartanburg March of Dimes, 1967, 68. Mem.: NEA-R (life), Gen. Fedn. Women's Clubs Jubilee Club (pres. 1996—2000, sec. 2000—02), Spartanburg County Retired Educators Assn. (sec. 2000—01, v.p. 2001—03, pres. 2003—), Piedmond Jr. Woman's Clubs (pres. 1974, 1976, Clubwoman of Yr. 1974, 1974, 1976), Spartanburg County Assn. Educators (rep. to del. assembly 1987—98, dist. dir. 1988—91, NEA rep. assembly 1989—97, v.p., pres. elect 1991—92, pres. 1992—93), Nat. Coun. Tchrs. Maths., S.C. Tchrs. Math. (life), S.C. Edn. Assn.-R (life; Rep. dist. dir. #3 1999—2001, chmn. by-laws and politics com. 1999—2001, del. assembly 1999—, v.p. 2001—02, pres. 2002—03, sec. 2004—), Spartanburg Coun. Federated Women's Clubs (pres. 1989—92, 2000—), Spartanburg Country Club Women's Golf Assn., Delta Kappa Gamma (chpt. v.p. 2000—02, pres. 2002—04). Democrat. Presbyterian. Avocations: crafts, travel. Home: 140 Burnett Dr Spartanburg SC 29302-3402 E-mail: janetag@yahoo.com.

AGONITO, ROSEMARY, publishing company executive; b. Syracuse, N.Y., Feb. 22, 1937; d. Mariangelo and Filomena (Albanese) Giambattista; m. Joseph Agonito, July 1, 1961; children: Giancarlo, Mae Lee. BA, LeMoyne Coll., 1959; MA, Niagara U., 1961; PhD, Syracuse U., 1975. Asst. instr. Syracuse (N.Y.) U., 1969-75; instr. Colgate U., Hamilton, N.Y., 1973-75; assoc. prof. Rochester (N.Y.) Inst. Tech., 1976-83; pres. New Futures Enterprises, Syracuse, 1983—. Author: History of Ideas on Women, 1977, Promoting Self Esteem in Young Women, 1988, No More "Nice Girl", 1993, Your Dream Mde Easy, 1999, Dirty Little Secrets: Sex in the Workplace, 2000. Mem. Mayor's Commn. Women, Syracuse, 1986-92; co-chair City-County Human Rights Commn., Syracuse, 1988-93; mem. N.Y. State Adv. Coun. Equal Opportunity for Women, Albany, N.Y., 1988-92; bd. dirs. Girls Inc. of Ctrl. N.Y., 1999-, Matilda Joslyn Gage Found., 2000-. Independent. Avocation: travel. Office Phone: 315-469-3902.

AGOSTI, DEBORAH ANN, state supreme court justice; BA cum laude, U. Toledo, 1973, JD, 1976. Bar: Nev., U.S. Supreme Ct. Dep. pub. defender Montgomery County, Ohio, 1977; sr. staff atty. Sr. Citizens Legal Assistance Program, Washoe County, 1977—79; dep. dist. atty., 1979—82; justice of the peace Reno Twp., Nev., 1982—85; dist. judge 2d Jud. Dist., Reno, 1985—99; justice Nev. Supreme Court, Carson City, 1999—, now chief justice. Trustee Nat. Jud. Coll., 2001—, Pretrial Svcs. Resource Ctr., 1999—; co-chmn. jury improvement commn. Supreme Ct. of Nev., 2001—; mem., dean's adv. bd. U. Toledo Coll. Law. Chmn. Task Force to Revitalize Interest in Attendance at Washoe County Bar Meetings, 2001—. Named Outstanding Young Woman for State of Nev., 1983, One of Am.'s 100 Young Women of Promise, Good Housekeeping mag., 1985, Reno's Outstanding Woman for 1986, One of Three Outstanding Young Nevadans, Reno Jaycees, 1986, Outstanding Women Lawyer, No. Nev. Women Lawyer's Assn., 1993, Judge of Yr., Nev. Dist. Judge's Assn., 1989, Woman of Achievement, Nev. Women's Fund, 1998, Woman of Distinction, Nat. Assn. Women Bus. Owners-So. Nev. Chpt., 2004, One of Nev.'s First One Hundred Women Attys. Master: Bruce Thompson Inn of Ct.; mem.: No. Nev. Women Lawyers Assn., Nat. Assn. Women Judges, Soroptimists Internat. of Truckee Meadows (life woman of Distinction 2001). Office: Supreme Ct Nev 201 S Carson St Carson City NV 89701-4702

AGRAIT, NILSA IVETTE, speech language pathologist; arrived in U.S., 1986; d. Jorge Geronimo and Maria E. (Castro) Agrait; m. Antonio Reyes, June 11, 1994; children: Amanda Liz Reyes-Agrait, Anthony Gabriel Reyes-Agrait, Jorge Geronimo, Maria E. Castro. AA, Palm Beach CC, 1990; BA, U. South Fla., Tampa, 1991, MS, 1997. Speech lang. pathologist asst. Tampa Gen. Rehab., Tampa, Fla., 1991—92; speech lang. therapist Pinellas County Sch., St. Petersburg, Fla., 1992—93, Hillsborough County Sch. Dist., Tampa, 1993—95; speech lang. pathologist Hillsborough County Sch. Dist, Tampa, 2000—, Menorah Manor, St. Petersburg, 1998, Pasco County Schools, Wesley Chapel, Fla., 1999—2000. Bd. dirs. Iglesia de Dios Pentecostal, Tampa, Fla., 1993—94. Test examiner (rsch. study) test of expressive lang., 1998, test of sematic skills- intermediate, 2003. Regional sec. Ambassadors of Christ Youth Assn., S.E. region U.S., 1987—91, regional pres., 1991—93. Recipient Dedication of the Sixth Regional Annual Youth Conv., Ambassadors of Christ Youth Assn., Miami, Fla., 1990. Avocations: reading, movies, home improvement projects. E-mail: nilsa.agrait@sdhc.k12.fl.us.

AGRANOV, SHARON DUKE, paralegal; b. Washington, D.C., Jan. 17, 1970; d. Alan and Judith Silverman Duke; m. Sean Joseph Agranov, Oct. 9, 1994; 1 child, Samantha. BA, Am. Univ., 1992. Cert.: George Washington Univ. (Paralegal cert.) 1993. Libr. asst. Groom & Nordberg, Washington, 1992—93; regulatory specialist Preston Gates Ellis & Rouvelas Meeds LLP, Washington, 1993—. Activities chair B'nai B'rith DC Metro Couples, Washington, 1997, pres., 1998. Recipient Chpt. Leadership award, Am. Univ. Alumni Assn., 1999. Mem.: Nat. Capital Area Paralegal Assn., Am. Univ. Alumni Assn. (sec. 2000—04). Office: Preston Gates Ellis& Rouvelas Meeds LLP 1735 New York Ave Washington DC 20006

AGRAWAL, AMITA, management consultant; b. Akron, Ohio, May 30, 1976; d. Ram Prasad and Saroj Agrawal. BS(hon.), St. Xavier's Coll., Bombay, India, 1997, U. Tex., Austin, 1999; MPH, U. Mich., 2001. Peer mentor U. Tex., Austin, 1998—99; project developer and analyst Health Systems Rsch., UIC Med. Sch., Rockford, Ill., 2000; bus. healthcare cons. ZS Assocs., Evanston, Ill., 2001—. Project developer, rschr. Am. Pub. Health Ann. Mtg., 2001. Editor: sales alignment software training manual. Project site mgr. Chgo. Cares, Chgo., 2003; publicity coord. Indian Cultural Assn., Austin, Tex., 1999. Mem.: Am. Coll. Healthcare Execs., Chgo. Archtl. Found. Hindu. Avocations: outdoor and water activities, choreographing, travel, reading. Home: 8313 E Via de las flores Scottsdale AZ 85258 Office: ZS Assocs 1800 Sherman Ave Evanston IL 60201 Personal E-mail: a_amita@hotmail.com. E-mail: amita_agrawal@yahoo.com.

AGRE, JOY ELAINE, music educator; b. Kans. City, Mo., Oct. 11, 1962; d. Carl Edward and Jean Elizabeth Zerweck; m. Gary Steven Agre, July 16, 1988; children: Stephanie Nicole, Jared Michael. MusB, U. of Mo., St. Louis, St. Louis, Mo., 1982—84, EdM, 1986—91. Cert. Teaching Mo., 1984. Music tchr. Normandy Sch. Dist., St. Louis, 1984—96, Hazelwood Sch. Dist., Hazelwood, Mo., 1996—; dir. of music St. Charles Christian Ch., St. Charles, Mo., 2001—. Author: (journal) Mo. Jour. of Rsch. in Music Edn. Girl scout leader Girl Scout Coun. of Greater St. Louis, St. Louis, 1998—2003; chair of worship and music com. St. Charles Christian Ch., St. Charles, Mo., 2001—02. Recipient Teacher of the Year award, 1995. Mem.: Music Educators Nat. Conf., NEA. Christian Ch. (Disciples Of Christ). Avocations: travel, reading, sewing, spending time with my family, computer literacy. Home: 83 Pineview Ridge Court St. Charles MO 63303 Office: Hazelwood School District 7350 Howdershell Road Hazelwood MO 63042 Personal E-mail: agregjsj@mindspring.com. E-mail: jagre@sun.hazelwood.k12.mo.us.

AGRICOLA, DIANNE G. secondary education educator, tutor; b. Portsmouth, Va. d. James H. and Vermelle E. (Pinnix) Griffin; m. William Edward Agricola, Apr. 19, 1975; 1 child, William Edward Jr. AA, Chowan Coll., 1974; BA in Journalism, U. S.C., 1982; BA in English, Christopher Newport U., 1988. Cert. English, journalism educator. Asst. acct. Va. Nat. Bank, Norfolk, 1970-75; mortgage loan assoc. Bank of Va., Richmond, 1976, VNB Mortgage Corp., Richmond, Va., 1975; legal sec. Wilmeth & DeLoach, Hartsville, S.C., 1976-80; reporter Tidewater News, Franklin, Va., 1984; subs. tchr. Franklin Schs., 1984-85, Southampton County Schs., Courtland, Va., 1985-86; summer sch. tchr. Franklin H.S., 1988; tchr. English and journalism Greensville County H.S., Emporia, Va., 1988-98; tchr. English Hunt-Mapp Mid. Sch., Portsmouth, Va., 1998-99, Hidden Valley H.S., Grants Pass, Oreg., 1999—. Mem. Oreg. Educators Assn., Journalism Educators Assn., Chowan Coll. Alumni Assn. (v.p. 1989-94, pres. 1995), Christopher Newport U. Edn. Found. Alumni Assn., Sigma Tau Delta, Alpha Epsilon Rho, Beta Sigma Phi. Methodist. Avocations: reading, bowling, swimming, home decorating and design, shopping. Office: Hidden Valley High Sch 3701 Willett Dr Grants Pass OR 97526 Home: 869 NE Tokay Hts Grants Pass OR 97526-3598

AGÜERO-TORRES, IRENE BEATRIZ, language educator; b. Barquisimeto, Venezuela, Jan. 30, 1958; d. David Agüero Segura and Ana P. Torres Puerta de Agüero; m. M. A. Morgan; 1 child, Chispa Maria. BS cum laude, Northeastern U., 1987; MA, U. Mass., 1996. Cert. tchr. Mass., 2000. Instr. Spanish Phillips Acad., Andover, Mass., 1987—88; lectr. Spanish U. Mass., Amherst, 1988—93, Amherst (Mass.) Coll., 1989—93, Coll. of Holy Cross, Worcester, Mass., 1993—94, Tuft U., Medford, Mass., 1995—96, U. Mass., Boston, 1996, Wheelock Coll., Boston, 1994—2000, Brandeis U., Waltham, Mass., 1997—99; tchr. Spanish Walsh Mid. Sch., Framingham, Mass., 2000—. Instr. Pine Tree Lang. Summer Camp, Inlet, NY, 1994. Northeastern U. Integrating Women Studies Bibliography grantee, 1986, Mass. Empowering Educators with Technology grantee, 2002. Mem.: Spanish Book Club (dir. 1999—). Avocations: reading, golf, tennis, music, cooking, photography. Office: Walsh Mid Sch 301 Brook St Framingham MA 01701

AGUILAR, GLADYS MARIA, counselor, educator; b. Mérida, Mexico, Mar. 16, 1965; came to the U.S., 1968; d. Francisco Javier and Gladys Maria (Salazar) Aguilar; children: Emmanuel, Daniel. BS cum laude, Loyola Marymount U., 1987; MS, Calif. State U., 1990. Cert. in pupil personnel svcs. Youth min. St. Francis of Assisi Parish, L.A., 1987-88; sch. counselor Concern Counseling Svcs., Fullerton, Calif., 1988-89; bilingual behavioral therapist Inst. for Applied Behavioral Analysis, L.A., 1988-89; sch. counselor, tchr. St. Lucy's Priory High Sch., Glendora, Calif., 1989-90; intern Cath. Psychol. Svcs. Cath. Charities of L.A., L.A., 1990-93; bilingual elem. sch. counselor L.A. Unified Sch. Dist., 1993-96; therapist Foothill Cmty. Mental Health Ctr., 1996-97; mental health cons. Plz. de la Raza Preschool Corp., 1996—; bilingual elem. sch. tchr. Ont.-Montclair Sch. Dist., 1997—2003, Azusa Unified Sch. Dist., 2003—. Marriage, family and child counseling intern Brown & Assocs., Whittier, Calif., 1989-93. Eucharistic min., lector St. Francis of Assisi Cath. Ch., 1986-92. Mem. Soc. Children Book Writers and Illustrators, Calif. Tchrs. Assn., Calif. Assn. Marriage and Family Therapists, Calif. Assn. Bilingual Educators, L.A. Sch. Counselors Assn., Psi Chi, Alpha Sigma Nu. Avocations: travel, folkloric dancing, reading. Home: 836 N Forest Hills Dr Covina CA 91724-3609 Office: 700 S Lark Ellen Ave Azusa CA 91702

AGUILAR, JULIA ELIZABETH, real estate company executive; b. Organal, Mex., Feb. 16, 1943; came to U.S., 1965; d. Felix and Leticia (Rodriguez) Vergara; m. Aaron Aguilar, Feb. 1, 1964; children: Juan Antonio, Elizabeth, Alex. Grad., San Fernando (Calif.) Adult Sch., 1980; Real Estate Assoc., Anthony Real Estate Sch., Sepulveda, Calif., 1985. Real estate assoc. ERA Rocking Horse Realty, San Fernando, 1986-98; owner Home Sweet Home Realty, San Fernando, 1998—. Author poetry, cooking recipes, song lyrics, 1996, Musical Poetry, 1997. Democrat. Roman Catholic. Avocations: writing, gardening, knitting, painting. Home: 626 Newton St San Fernando CA 91340-2107 Office: Home Sweet Home Realty 563 S Brand Blvd San Fernando CA 91340-4051

AGUILAR, JULIA SHELL, publishing executive; BS in Sociology and Psychology, MS in Social Work Adminstrn., Va. Commonwealth U. Dir. human resources Times-Advocate, Escondido, Calif., 1982—84; v.p. human resources L.A. Daily News, 1984—87; dir. human resources John P. Scripps Newspapers, 1987—90; pres., then pub. San Luis Obispo (Calif.) County Telegram-Tribune, 1990—98; dir. mgmt. devel. E.W. Scripps Co., Cin., 1998—2000; gen. mgr. Knoxville (Tenn.) News-Sentinel, 2000—. Office: Knoxville News-Sentinel 2332 News Sentinel Dr PO Box 59038 Knoxville TN 37950-9038*

AGUILAR, MIRIAM REBECCA, technology project manager; b. Torrance, Calif., Feb. 6, 1963; d. Samuel Conklin and Victoria Lizarraga Aguilar; children: Samantha Victoria Reed, Olivia Linda Reed. AA in Liberal Arts, L.A. Harbor Coll., 1984; BA in Anthropology Minor Art History, Colo. State U., 1998; M of Internat. Pub. Mgmt., Monterey Inst. of Internat. Studies, 2001. Cert. travel counselor Travel and Trade Career Inst. IT market analyst Kagan World Media, Carmel, Calif., 2000; tech. project mgr. CTB McGraw-Hill, Monterey, Calif., 2001—. Proposed design and devel. for creation of Internat. Lang. and Culture Meml. Mus. and Rsch. Ctr. World Trade Ctr. Author: (pub. project) Developing and Designing An Administrative Model for an International Language and Culture Museum and Research Center. Bd. dirs. internat. programs Internat. Lang. and Culture Found., Monterey, 1999. Mem.: Internat. Lang. and Culture Found. (life; bd. dirs. internat. programs 1999, treas. 2002). Avocations: reading, travel, gardening, research, yoga. Home: #17 930 Casanova Ave Monterey CA 93940 Personal E-mail: miriama0206@yahoo.com.

AGUILAR-BRYAN, LYDIA, medical educator, medical researcher; b. Mexico City, Feb. 25, 1951; m. Joseph Bryan; 1 child. MD, U. Nacional Autonoma de Mex., 1975; PhD in Population Studies, U. Tex., 1985. Rsch. assoc. Inst. Biomed. Rsch., U. Nacional Autonoma de Mex., Mexico City, 1985—86, Baylor Coll. of Medicine, Dept. of Medicine, Divsn. of Endocrinology, Houston, 1987—88, postdoctoral fellow, 1988—90, instr., 1990—91, asst. prof., 1991—; prof. M.D. Anderson Cancer Ctr. U. Tex. Contbr. articles to profl. jours. Recipient postdoctoral fellowship, Juvenile Diabetes Found., 1988—90. Mem.: AAAS, Endocrine Soc., Biophys. Soc., Am. Diabetes Assn. (Rsch. grantee 1995—). Office: U Tex MD Anderson Cancer Ctr 1515 Holcombe Blvd Houston TX 77030-4009

AGUILERA, CHRISTINA, vocalist; b. Dec. 18, 1980; Vocalist New Mickey Mouse Club, 1994-96; vocalist theme song for Disney animated film Mulan, 1998 (Golden Globe nominee for best original song in a motion picture); debut album Christina Aguilera (RCA), 1999 (Grammy award, Best New Artist, 2000), My Kind of Christmas, 2000, Mi Reflejo, 2000, Complete, 2002, Stripped, 2002 (Grammy award, Best Female Pop Vocal Performance for song "Beautiful", 2003); singles: What A Girl Wants, 1999, The Christmas Song, 1999, Genie in a Bottle, 1999; video: The Genie Gets Her Wish, 1999. Recipient ALMA award, best new artist, 1999. Office: 244 Madison Ave # 314 New York NY 10016-2817*

AGUILERA, DONNA CONANT, psychologist, researcher; b. Kinmundy, Ill. d. Charles E. and Daisy L. (Frost) Conant; m. George Limon Aguilera; children: Bruce Allen, Craig Steven. BS, UCLA, 1963, MS, 1965; PhD, U. So. Calif., 1974. Teaching asst. UCLA, 1965, grad. rsch. asst., 1965-66; prof. Calif. State U., L.A., 1966-81; cons. crisis intervention Didi Hirsch Community Mental Health Ctr., L.A., 1967-82. Mem. Def. Adv. Com. Women in the Services, 1978-82; originator, project dir. Project Link Lab. U. Author: (books) Crisis Intervention: Theory and Methodology, 1974, Crisis Intervention: Theory and Methodology, 9th edit., 2002, Review of Psychiatric Nursing, 1977, Review of Psychiatric Nursing, 7th edit., 1978, Crisis Intervention: Therapy for Psychological Emergencies, 1983, Clinical Depression. A Life Span Approach, 2003; contbr. articles to profl. jours. Docent Huntington Libr. San Marino, Calif. 1991-2000; mem., mgr. disaster mental health svcs. ARC. NIH fellow, 1972-75 Fellow Am. Acad. Nursing (sec. 1976-77, pres. 1977-79), Assn. Psychiat. Nurse Specialists, Internat. Acad. Eclectic Psychotherapists (pres. 1987-89); mem. Am. Nursing Assn., Faculty Women's Assn., Am. Psychol. Assn., Calif. Psychol. Assn., AAUP, Alpha Tau Delta, Sigma Theta Tau Office: Ste A175 31441 Santa Margarita Pkwy Rancho Santa Margarita CA 92688-1836 Fax: 949-766-9206. E-mail: DCA@cox.net.

AGUIRRE, LINDA, state senator; b. Flagstaff, Ariz., July 12, 1951; m. John Aguirre. BA, Ariz. State U., 1978, MA, 1986. Cert. elem. tchr., prin., Ariz. Dem. rep. dist. 23 Ariz. Ho. of Reps., 1983-98; Dem. senator dist. 23 Ariz. State Senate, 1998—. Mem. bd. dirs. Mountain Park Health Ctr., Legis. Svc. YMCA; pres. Nat. Hispanic Sch. Bd. Caucus; mem. fin. instns. and retirement, judiciary and rules coms. Ariz. State Senate, vice chair edn. com. County coord. ACE; coach recreational T-ball. Mem. Nat. Sch. Bd. Assn., Ariz. Sch. Bd. Assn. (legis. com.). Office: Ariz State Senate State Senate Rm 311 1700 W Washington Phoenix AZ 85007-2890 also: 1612 E Saint Ave Phoenix AZ 85040 Office Fax: 602-542-4511.

AGUIRRE, PAMELA ANN, manufacturing executive; b. Dearborn, Mich., Dec. 12, 1958; d. Hank Aguirre; 3 children. Doctorate (hon.), Lawrence Technol. U., 1998. CEO, chmn. bd. Mexican Industries, Detroit, 1994—. Bd. dirs. SBA, 1996; bd. dirs. Mich. Minority Bus. Devel. Coun., Hank Aguirre Cancer Awareness Found., The Children's Ctr. Recipient Hispanic Bus. Alliance award, 1996 Mem. Econ. Club of Detroit, (bd. dirs.), others. Office: Mexican Industries Aguirre Plaza 1801 Howard St Detroit MI 48216-1920 Fax: 313-963-6217.

AGUIRRE-BATTY, MERCEDES, Spanish and English language and literature educator; b. Cd Juarez, Mex., Dec. 20, 1952; came to U.S., 1957. d. Alejandro M. and Mercedes (Péon) Aguirre; m. Hugh K. Batty, Mar. 17, 1979; 1 child, Henry B. BA, U. Tex., El Paso, 1974, MA, 1977. Cert. online tchr., Calif. Instr. ESL Paso del Norte- Prep Sch., Cd Juarez, 1973-74; tchg. asst. ESL and English U. Tex., El Paso, 1974-77; instr. ESL English Lang. Svcs., Bridgeport, Conn., 1977-80; instr. Spanish and English, coord. modern lang. Sheridan (Wyo.) Coll., 1980—, pres. faculty senate, 1989-90; pres. faculty senate, chair dist. coun. No. Wyo. C.C. Dist., 1995-96. Planning com. No. Wyo. C.C. Dist., 1996-97; mem. advanced placement faculty Spanish cons. Coll. Bd. Ednl. Testing Svc., 1996-99; adj. prof. Spanish, U. Autonoma Cd Juarez, 1975; adj. prof. Spanish and English, Sacred Heart U., Fairfield, Conn., 1977-80; spkr. in field. Bd. dirs. Wyo. Coun. for the Humanities, 1988-92; translator county and dist. cts., Sheridan; vol. Wmen's Ctr.; translator Sheridan County Meml. Hosp.; del. Citizen Ambassador Program, People to People-India, 1996. NEH fellow, 1991-92; Wyo. State Dept. Edn. grant, 1991. Mem. MLA (del. assembly 1998-2000, 2004-), Wyo. Fgn. Lang. Tchrs. Assn. (pres. 1990-92), Am. Assn. Tchrs. Spanish and Portuguese (founder, 1st pres. Wyo. chpt. 1987-90), TESOL, Sigma Delta Mu (v.p. 1992-99, pres. 2000—), Sigma Delta Pi (Alpha Iota chpt. pres. 1974-75). Avocations: travel, reading, archeology, languages, geography. Office: Sheridan Coll NWCCD 3059 Coffeen Ave Sheridan WY 82801-9133

AHEARN, GERALDINE, medical/surgical nurse, writer, poet; b. Bklyn., Aug. 14, 1950; d. Louis Principessa and Patricia Donato; m. James J. Ahearn, Aug. 13, 1972 (div. June 4, 2001); children: Alicia Danielle, Katherine Ann. AA, Suffolk County CC, Selden, N.Y., 1971; diploma in nursing, Ctrl. Islip State Hosp. Sch. Nursing, 1974. LPN, N.Y., Ariz., RN N.Y., Ariz., cert. CCRN, Am. Heart Assn., EKG technician, Am. Heart Assn. RN Bayshore (N.Y.) Hosp., 1970—83, Farmingville (N.Y.) Clinic, 1986—87, Sachem Schs., Farmingville, 1988—93; freelance writer Mesa, Ariz., 1993—. Instr. CPR ARC, Coram, NY, 1986—90, instr. first aid, 1986—90, instr. CPR, Bohemia, NY, 1986—90. Author: (book) Inspirations, 2001, Words to Live By, 2001, Life's Poetic Journey, 2002, The Nurse in the Purse, Vol. 1, 2003; contbr. poetry to anthologies. Leader Girl Scouts U.S., Farmingville, 1988—91; catechist Farmingville Ch., 1985—87. Republican. Roman Catholic. Avocation: gardening. Home and Office: 3506 E Caballero St Mesa AZ 85213 E-mail: HrT4Angel@aol.com.

AHEARN, HOLLY ANDE, music educator; d. Hugh David and Edna Olive Ahearn. MusB in Vocal Music Edn., U. Mass., 1986; MusM in Voice Performance, U. Conn., 1996. Cert. secondary music tchr. grades 5-12 Mass. Music tchr. 7-9 Holyoke (Mass.) Pub. Schs., 1987—88; choral dir. 6-8 Danvers (Mass.) Pub. Schs., 1988—89; music tchr. K-6 Claremont (N.H.) Pub. Schs., 1989—90, Quabbin Regional Sch. Dist., Barre, Mass., 1992—93; choral dir., music tchr. 5-8 Lowell (Mass.) Pub. Schs., 1995—99; choral dir. 6-8 Burlington (Mass.) Pub. Schs., 1999—2000; choral dir., music tchr. K-8 Brookline (Mass.) Pub. Schs., 2000—. Adjudicator Mass. Music Educators' Assn., 1998—2003. Recipient Bd. Regents Honor scholarship, State of Mass., 1981—86, grad. assistantship, U. Conn., 1990—92, 1st pl. award profl. divsn., Conn. Chpt. Nat. Assn. Tchrs. Singing, 1996. Mem.: Am. Guild Mus. Artists, Music Educators Nat. Conf., Am. Choral Dirs.' Assn. Avocations: gardening, travel.

AHERN, MARY ANN, reporter; m. Thomas Ahern; 3 children. BA, John Carroll U., 1976; MEd, Northeastern Ill. U., 1979; M Journalism, Northwestern U., 1982. Tchr. 2 Chgo. area H.S., 1976—79; reporter, weekend anchor Sta. WEEK-TV, Peoria, Ill., 1982—85; polit. reporter Sta. WXIA-TV, Atlanta, 1985—89; gen. assignment reporter NBC 5, Chgo., 1989—. Office: NBC 454 N Columbus Dr Chicago IL 60611

AHL, SALLY WEBB, religious studies educator; b. New Rochelle, N.Y., Apr. 6, 1938; d. Gertrude Voland Moffett. BS, Cornell U., 1960; BA summa cum laude, Barrington Coll., 1969; PhD, Brandeis U., 1972, MA, 1973; MS in Edn., U. Kans., 1989, PhD in Edn., 1992. Cert. tchr. Mich. County ext. agt. home econ. Coop. Ext. Svc., Scottville, Mich., 1960—62; tchr. home econ. Ludington Pub. Sch., Ludington, Mich., 1962—66; prof. of bibl. studies Tarkio (Mo.) Coll., 1973—82; libr. asst., instr. Bibl. Hebrew U. Kans., Lawrence, Kans., 1989; pvt. instr. in Bibl. Hebrew; leader of colloquia Reading Scripture in Hebrew, 2003. Author: Classical Hebrew: A Handbook for the Analysis of Words, 2000. Ministerial asst. various ch., Mo., 1975—82. Recipient Am. Bible Soc. award, Barrington Coll., 1969; fellow Mary E. Hirschfield fellow, Brandeis U.; scholar, 1970—73. Home: 3323 Iowa Street no 337 Lawrence KS 66046-5218

AHLERS, LINDA L. retail executive; BA in Retailing, U. Wisc. Buyer, Target Stores Dayton Hudson Corp., 1977-83, divsn. mdse. mgr., Target Stores, 1983-85, dir. mdse. planning and control, 1985-88, v.p. mdse. planning and control, 1988, sr. v.p. Target Stores, 1988-95, exec. v.p. merchandising, dept. store divsn., 1995-96; pres., dept. store divsn. Dayton Hudson Corp. (now Marshall Field's), 1996—; bd. dirs. Dayton Hudson Corp., 1997—. Dir. Guthrie Theatre; mem. Com. of 200, Detroit Renaissance Bd., Minn. Women's Econ. Roundtable. Office: Target Corp 1000 Nicollet Mall Minneapolis MN 55403-2467*

AHLQUIST, JANET SUE, musician, music educator; b. Worland, Wyo. d. John Orrin Ahlquist and Thelma Evelyn Jorgensen; children: J. Kirk Roberts, Tracy Sandmann Roberts, Jon M. Roberts. MusB, Juilliard; artist diploma, Longy Sch. Music, 1985; M, Eastman Sch. Music, 1989, performer's cert., 1990. Accompanying asst. Eastman Sch. Music, Rochester, N.Y., 1988-90, tchng. asst., 1990; prof. music Casper (Wyo.) Coll., 1991-99. Dir. Humanities Festival 2000, Casper, 1999—, artistic. dir. Casper Chamber Music Soc., 1993-99; convention artist Music Tchrs. Nat. Assn., Casper, 1997. Performing artist (CDs): Soul of Russia, Piano Classics by Portuguese Masters, 1992. Faculty Senate mem. Casper Coll., 1992-94; mem. Women Studies, 1994-99, Coun. Fgn. Rels., 1996-99, Performing Arts Coalition, 1999. Recipient Gov.'s award Wyo. Arts Coun., gov., 1998, Performance prize French Piano Inst., 1997; Gulbenkian grant Gulbenkian Found., Am.-Portuguese Soc., 1987, Wyo. Arts Coun. grant 1992. Mem. Music Tchrs. Nat. Assn., Music Tchrs. Assn., Coll. Music Soc., Performing Arts Coalition, Cultural Affairs Com. Avocations: bicycling, skiing, hiking. Home: 110 Coldstream Dr Berwyn PA 19312-1108

AHLRICHS, NANCY SURRATT, marketing professional; b. Harrisburg, Pa., Oct. 13, 1952; d. Joe Free and Mary Alice (Norris) Surratt; m. Karl J. Ahlrichs, Sept. 10, 1983. BA in Anthropology, Purdue U., 1974, MS in Phys. Anthropology, 1976. Project specialist A.B. Dick Co., Chgo., 1978-81, sr. instructional designer, 1981-82; mgr. tng. and devel. Equitable Relocation Mgmt. Corp., Chgo. and Orlando, 1982-83; v.p. Todd Persons Communications, Inc., Orlando, 1984-87, Gary Bitner Pub. Rels., Orlando, 1987-89; v.p. client svcs. Right Assocs., San Diego, 1989-90, v.p. profl. svcs. Indpls., 1992-94; mktg. cons., entrepreneur Indpls., 1994—; sr. orgn. devel. cons. RCI, Indpls., 1995—; v.p. bus. devel. HR Dimensions, LLC, 1997—2008; dir. mktg. ONEX, Inc., 1998—99, dir. organizational evolution, 1999—2000; pres. EOC Strategies, LLC, 2001—. Bd. dirs. Interactive Info. Svcs., Cleve. Author: Competing for Talent, 2000, Manager of Choice, 2003; prodr.: (videotape) The Big Push, 1983; author/ghost writer: over 50 mag. and trade jour. articles; writer, prodr., dir. : (over 50 corp. videotapes); columnist: www.InsideIndianaBusiness.com. Major gifts chmn. Am. Heart Assn., San Diego, 1990-91. Recipient Pres.'s award Cen. Fla. Zool. Soc., 1988. Mem.: Kiwanis Indpls. (bd. dirs. 1995—2001, mktg. com., chmn. downtown program 1994—95, numerous other coms. 1994—95, named Kiwanian of Yr. 2001), Phi Kappa Phi. Democrat. Lutheran. Avocations: anthropology, psychology, reading, gardening, gourmet cooking. Office: 1075 Broad Ripple Ave Indianapolis IN 46220 E-mail: nancy@eocstrategies.com.

AHLSTEDT, LINDA FOXX, music educator; b. Ithaca, N.Y., Oct. 1, 1947; d. Kenneth Clair and Ruth Patience (Knowles) Foxx; m. Douglas Frederick Ahlstedt, Feb. 1, 1969; children: Charlotte, Kirsten, Björn Jonathan. MusB, SUNY, Fredonia, 1969; MEd, U. Md., 1971. Permanent cert. K-12 music N.Y. Composer: (children's musical) Orff to the Circus, 1987, Dancin' Dinosaurs, 1989, The Colorful Kingdom, 1990, The Unicorn, 1995; editor: The Orff Echo, 2001—02. Recipient N.Y. Music Educator award, Rochester Philharm. Orch., 1995. Mem.: Music Educators Nat. Assn., Greater Rochester Orff Assn. (pres. 1990—92), Am. Orff Schulwerk Assn. (life; bd. dirs. 1992—2001, pres. 1999—2001). Presbyterian. Avocations: skiing, reading, composing, travel. Home: 12 Knollwood Dr Pittsburgh PA 15215 Office: Penfield Ctrl Sch Dist 1750 Scribner Rd Penfield NY 14526 E-mail: dolin1@mindspring.com.

AHMAD, MIRZA MUZAFFAR, economic advisor; b. Qadian, India, Feb. 28, 1913; came to U.S., 1972; d. Mirza and Sarwar (Sultana) Bashir; m. Amatul Q. Ahmad, May 8, 1939; 1 child, Zahir Ahmad. BA, Gov. Coll., Lahore, India, 1933; BA with honors, London U., 1935; postgrad. law, Middle Temple, London, 1935; postgrad., Corpus Christie Coll., Oxford, London, 1938. Several govt. positions, India, 1939-47; additional chief sec. West Pakistan Province, 1959-62; sec. commerce Govt. of Pakistan, 1962, sec. fin., 1963-66, fed. minister, fin. minister planning commn., 1966—70, econ. adviser, fin. adviser to the pres., 1970-71, adviser for fgn. loans and consortium, 1971-72; exec. dir. bd. World Bank, 1972-74; dep. exec. sec., staff mem., con. Joint Ministerial Com. of Bd. Govs. World Bank and IMF, 1974-93. Mem. Pakistan del. to Commonwealth Prime Ministers' Conf., 1962, 64; negotiator with World Bank for Indus Basin Devel. Fund, 1964; leader Pakistan del. to 8th consortium meeting, Washington, 1966, Pakistan del. to meetings of Econ. Coun. of Indonesia-Pakistan Econ. and Cultural Cooperation, 1966-69, Pakistan del to ministerial meetings Colombo Plan Conf., Geneva, 1987, Pakistan del. to People's Republic of China, 1967; chmn. ministerial meetings 17th Colombo Plan Conf., 1966. Amir/pres. Ahmadiya Movement in Islam, Inc. Recipient Hilal Quaid Azam award, Sitari Pakistan award Pres. of Pakistan. Moslem. Home: 9920 New London Dr Potomac MD 20854-4845 Office: Ahmadiya Movement in Islam Baitur Rahman 15000 Good Hope Rd Silver Spring MD 20905-4120

AHMADIA, PHYLLIS, lawyer; b. Pittsburg, Calif., Mar. 27, 1949; d. Fred Alton Gatter and Irene Lillian Bohanan; m. Jamil S. Ahmadia; children: Sarah, Gabriella, Aron. BA, U. Calif., Santa Barbara, 1971; JD, U. Calif., San Francisco, 1977. Bar: Calif. 1977, Hawaii 1986. Ptnr. Bornstein & Gatter, Attys., Fairfax, Calif., 1977—79, Gatter & Wallace, San Rafael, Calif., 1979—82; coord. adminstrv. justice program HCC-UHH, Hilo, 1982—88; ptnr. Ahmadia & Lee Loy, Hilo, Hawaii, 1986—97, Ahmadia & Carey, Hilo, 1998—. Lectr. pre-law Golden Gate U., San Francisco, 1977—78. Mem.: ATLA. Republican. Avocations: doll collecting, quilting. Office: Ahmadia & Carey 1315 Kalanianaole Hilo HI 96720

AHMED, GAIL R. music educator; b. Martins Ferry, Ohio, Oct. 2, 1953; d. Edgar Milton and Margaret Elizabeth Horner; m. Bashir Gakhru Ahmed, Aug. 25, 1979; 1 child, Aisha. BA, West Liberty State Coll., 1975; MEd, U. Dayton, 1991. Cert. music profl. K-12. Music educator Edison Local Schs., Ironton, Ohio, 1975—77, Tipp City (Ohio) Schs., Tipp City, 1977—. Music dir. Tippecanoe Cmty. Band, Tipp City, 1979—; gen. music rep. Ohio Music Educator's Nat. Conf., Columbus, 1985—90; mem. gifted com. Tipp City Schs., 1999—2002; cons. curriculum devel. Dayton Islamic Sch., Beavercreek, 1997—98; dist. gen. music rep. Ohio Music Educator's Nat. Conf., Columbus, 1985—90; orchestral dir. Tippecanoe H.S. Mus., Tipp City; presenter Lesson Plans that Work TRIAD OMEA State Conv., 1995. Dir. United Meth. Church Bell Choir, Tipp City, 1985—87. Grantee Environ. Edn. grantee, Miami County Park Dist., 2001—02. Mem.: NGAC, Music Educator's Nat. Conf. (dist. gen. music rep. 1985—90, Ohio cbt. dist. II treas. 2002—, 25-Yr. mem. 2001), Friends of Libr. Avocations: travel, music, needlework, reading. Office: Tipp City Schs 90 S Tippecanoe D Tipp City OH 45371 Home: 535 Stonecress Dr Tipp City OH 45371-1216 Personal E-mail: grahmed@hotmail.com.

AHMOSE, NEFERTARI A. journalism educator; b. Kingston, Jamaica, Oct. 3, 1951; arrived in U.S., 75; d. Cecil Alexander Rose and Florence Rhodian Daley. Student, L.A. Valley Coll., 1975. Journalist Jamaica Daily News, 1974—80; pub. African Expression, Bronx, NY, 1982—91; politician Kemet-Kush, Ensley, Ala., 1985—2001; founder Afrikan U. in West, Bklyn., 1996—, Wafrakan Ins. Co., 2003—, Afrikan People Stock Exchange, 2003—. Leader Wafrakan Empress Afrikan Diasporan Nation. Author: Black Sovereign-The Black Alternative, 1992, Harmonization, Unification and Standardization in Afrikan Tribal Vernaculars into Kiafrakan Language-Dictionary and Grammar, 1996, Ki-Afrakan-English Excerxises, 1997, Ki-Afrakan Grammar, 1996, Ki-Afrakan Dictionary, 1996, Incorp. Afrakan Standard Language, 1994, Sex Education for Youngsters, 1994. Founder Afrikan Bank and Investment Trust, Merkutu Currency, Kemet-Kush (now Wafrakan Polit. Party), NY, 2000—. Mailing: PO Box 971 Bronx NY 10472

AHRENDTS, ANGELA, apparel executive; 3 children. Grad., Ball State U., 1981. Pres. Pringle of Scotland; with Warnaco, Inc., v.p. Valentino intimate apparel and Ungaro intimate apparel; v.p. sales Carmelo Pomodoro, pres.; v.p. merchandising Donna Karen Co., 1992, pres. Donna Karen Collection, 1992; v.p. gen. mdse. mgr. Henri Bendel; v.p. corp. merchandising and design Liz Claiborne, Inc., N.Y.C., 1998—2000, sr. v.p. corp. merchandising, group pres., 2000—02, exec. v.p., 2002—. Recipient Alumni Achievement award, Ball State U., 2003. Achievements include featured in Time Magazine Style and Design Women in Fashion Power List, 2004. Office: Liz Claiborne Inc 1441 Broadway New York NY 10018*

AHRENS, LYNN, lyricist; b. NY, Oct. 1, 1948; m. Neil Costa. BA in Comms., Syracuse U., 1970. Author book, lyricist: Once On This Island, 1995 (Olivier award best musical, Tony nominations for best book and score, NAACP award for best playwright), Lucky Stiff, 1988 (Helen Hayes award for best musical), lyricist: Once on this Island, 1990, My Favorite Year, 1993, Ragtime, 1996 (Grammy nomination, Tony award, 1998, Drama Desk award, 1998, Outer Critics Cir. award, 1998) Anastasia, 1997 (2 Acad. award nominations, 2 Golden Globe nominations), Bartok the Magnificent, 1999, With Voices Raised, 1999, Seussical, 2000, A Man of No Importance, 2002, co-author, lyricist: A Christmas Carol, 1994, Schoolhouse Rock, 1973—85 (Emmy award, 4 Emmy nominations), 1992—98. Mem.: AMPAS, NARAS, ASCAP, Dramatists Guild Coun. Office: c/o William Morris Attn Peter Franklin 1325 Avenue Of The Americas New York NY 10019-6026

AHRENS, PAMELA, state government administrator; b. Portland, Oreg., Nov. 15, 1945; m. Steve Ahrens; children: Melissa Ann, Elaine, Annette, Shannon. Grad., Ea. Wash. State U. Mem. Idaho Ho. of Reps., 1980-94; dir. Idaho State Dept. Adminstrn., Boise, 1995—; past owner equipment rental bus. Chmn. Statewide Safety and Loss Control Com. Named to Hall of Fame, Idaho Rep. Party. Mem. Nat. Assn. State Chief Adminstrs. (past pres.), Idaho Hosp. Assn. (dir. polit. activities), Idaho Rep. Women's Fedn. (nat. fedn. rep. v.p.), Idaho Info. Tech. Resource Mgmt. Coun. (chair), Lincoln Day Banquet Assn. (past pres.), Rotary (pres.). Republican. Presbyterian. Home: 5186 S Farmhouse Pl Boise ID 83716-9013 Office: State Idaho Dept Adminstrn PO Box 83720 Boise ID 83720-3720

AI, AMY LEE, medical educator; m. Danyi Dan Wang. MA, U. Mich., 1990, MSW, 1993, MS, 1994, PhD, 1996. Nat. Inst. Aging postdoctoral rsch. fellow U. Mich., Ann Arbor, 1996—98; rsch. fellow sect. cardiac surgery U. Mich. Health Sys., Ann Arbor, 1998—2003; asst. prof. rsch. human devel., gerontology, spirituality and mental health, psychopathology U. Wash., Seattle, 1999—2003; aff. rschr. integrative medicine U. Mich., 2003; assoc. prof. U. Wash., 2004—. Grantee, Nat. Inst. Aging/Nat. Ctrs. Complementary and Alt. Medicine NIH, 1999—2003, John Templeton Found., 2002—; Hartford scholar, John A. Hartford Found., 2002—. Mem.: APHA, APA, Gerontol. Soc. Am. Avocations: music, swimming, travel, meditation, movies. Office Phone: 206-221-7781.

AIELLO, KIMBERLY JEAN, surgical technologist; b. Batavia, N.Y., Feb. 4, 1957; d. Samuel C. and Mary E. Scime; m. Lawrence Joseph Aiello, Aug. 7, 1982; children: Amanda Catherine, Phillip Joseph. Cert. Surg. Tech., Niagara County C.C., Sanborn, N.Y., 1976. Surg. technologist DeGraff Meml. Hosp., North Tonawanda, NY, 1976—. Mem.: Assn. Surg. Technologists (cert.). Democrat. Roman Catholic. Avocations: reading, kickboxing, walking, sewing, cooking.

AIGEN, BETSY PAULA, psychotherapist; b. N.Y.C., Sept. 13, 1938; d. Abraham H. and Gertrude (Rosenblum) Wasserman; m. Ronald Aigen, Dec. 7, 1957 (div. Jan. 1979); m. Isadore Schumukler, June 20, 1982; children: Jennifer Loren, Samantha Devin. BA, New Sch. Social Research, 1971; MA, Columbia U., 1972; D of Psychology, Rutgers U., 1980. Group co-leader, asst. psychotherapist Inst. Rational Psychotherapy, N.Y.C., 1967-72; asst. course instr. Columbia U., N.Y.C., 1971-72; psychotherapist Mt. Carmel Guild, Englewood, N.J., 1980-82, SELF Edn. Learning and Feeling, N.Y.C., 1982—; founder, dir. Surrogate Mother Program, N.Y.C., 1985—. Cons. Police Chief Tng. Community Workshops Assn., N.Y.C., 1973-74, Richmond Fellowship Mental Health Halfway Houses, Eng. and U.S., 1970-75. Contbr. articles to profl. jours. Chmn. Tenants Com., N.Y.C., 1975-85; active Profl. Theatre, 1956-67. Mem. Nat. Orgn. Women, RESOLVE, Adoptive Parents Com., Am. Psychol. Assn., N.Y. St. Psychol. Assn., N.J. St. Psychol. Assn., N.Y. Assn. Feminist Therapists. (co-founder, charter), Am. Orgn. Surrogate Parenting Practitioners (founder, charter). Democrat. Jewish. Home: 220 W 93rd St Apt 1A New York NY 10025-7412 Office: Surrogate Mother Program Childbirth Cons Svcs 220 W 93rd St Apt 1A New York NY 10025-7412

AIGNER, EMILY BURKE, Christian lay minister; b. Henrico, Va., Oct. 28, 1920; d. William Lyne and Susie Emily (Willson) Burke; m. Louis Cottrell Aigner, Nov. 27, 1936; children: Lyne, Betty, D. Muriel (dec.), Willson, Norman, William, Randolph, Dorothy. Cert. in Bible, U. Richmond, 1969; postgrad., So. Bapt. Sem. Extension, Nashville, 1987, Va. Commonwealth U., 1981; diploma in Bible, Liberty Home Bible Inst., 1992, masterlife grad., 1994. Deacon Four Mile Creek Bapt. Ch., Richmond, Va., 1972—, trustee, 1991, dir. Woman's Missionary Union, 1986-

94, treas., 1984-89, dir. Sunday sch., 1969-78, 84-85, 1989-93. Spl. edn. tchr., 1993-99; acctg. tech., 1959-80. Prodr. Dial-A-Devotion for pub. by telephone, 1978-85. Solicitor ARC, Henrico County, 1947-49, induction ctr. vol., 1994-97; solicitor, United Givers' Fund, Henrico County, 1945-48; sec.-treas. soliciting funds Bible Edn. in Varina Sch., 1946-49; singer Bellwood Choir, Chesterfield County, Va., 1965-70; telephone counselor Richmond Contact, 1980-82; Am. Cancer Soc., Richmond, 1980-82; program chmn. Varina (Va.) Home Demonstration Club, 1950-53; worker Vol. Visitor Program Westport Convalescent Home, 1983—; vol. patient rep. Richmond Meml. Hosp., 1994-98, chaplain, 1996-97; jail min. Richmond City Jail, 1973—; lay minister to sr. adults Four Mile Creek Ch., 2002—. Named Woman of Yr., Henrico Farm Bur., 1996. Mem. UDC, Am. Assn. Christian Counselors, Gideons Internat. (sec. Va. aux. 1977-80, 82-84, new mem. plan rep. 1981, 85, 91, 94, zone leader 1988-91, state cabinet rep. 1989-90, pres. Richmond N.E. Camp 1976-78, sec.-treas. 1980-82, 93, scripture sec. 1973-75, 87-89, v.p., 1997-98, chmn. Va. state widows com. 1993-97, pres. Richmond East Camp, 2000-02), State Aux. (tng. leader, 2004), Henrico Farm Bur. (women's com. 1994—), Alpha Phi Sigma. Home: 9717 Varina Rd Richmond VA 23231-8428

AIKEN, ANN L. federal judge; b. Salem, Oreg., Dec. 29, 1959; m. James R. Klonoski; 5 children. MA in Polit. Sci., Rutgers U., New Brunswick, 1976; BS in Polit. Sci., U. Oreg., 1974, JD, 1979. Bar: Oreg. 1980, U.S. Dist. Ct. Oreg. 1981. Law clk. Pub. Defender Svcs., Inc., 1979-80, Office of Legal Counsel to Gov. of Oreg., 1979-80, Judge Edwin E. Allen; atty. Sahlstrom and Dugdale PC, 1980-82; chief clk. Oreg. Ho. of Reps., 1982-83; atty. Thorp, Dennett, Purdy, Golden and Jewett PC, 1983-88; judge Lane County Dist. Ct., Oreg., 1988-92, Lane County Circuit Ct., 1993-98, U.S. Dist. Ct., Eugene, Oreg., 1998—. Aaald staff Betty Roberts for U.S. Senate, 1974, Kulongoski for Gov., 1982; adminstv. asst. to Oreg. speaker pro tem Albert Densmore, 1974-75, Office of Rep. James Weaver, 1976; staff Weaver for Congress com., 1976, office clk., 1976-77; mem. adv. bd. Jr. League of Eugene; bd. visitors U. Oreg. Sch. of Law, 1997—; bd. dirs. Relief Nursery, 1989—, Roland K. Rodman Inn of Court (Eugene chap.), 1990—, Lane Co. Child Advocacy Ctr., 2000; mem Nat. Chldn's. Alliance, 1998—. Eagleton fellow, 1975-76, Health, Edn. and Welfare Pubs. Svc. Edn. fellow, 1975-76. Mem. Oreg. Circuit Ct. Judges' Assn., Oreg. Jud. Conf., Oreg. Women Lawyers Assn., Oreg. State Bar Assn., Am. Leadership Forum.

AIKEN, LINDA HARMAN, nurse, sociologist, educator; b. Roanoke, Va., July 29, 1943; d. William Jordan and Betty Philips (Warner) Harman; children: June Elizabeth, Alan James. BSN, U. Fla., 1964, M in Nursing, 1966; PhD in Sociology, U. Tex., 1973. Nurse Med. Ctr. U. Fla., Gainesville, 1964-65, instr. coll. nursing, 1966-67; instr. sch. of nursing U. Mo., Columbia, 1967-70, clin. nurse specialist sch. of nursing, 1967-70; program officer Robert Wood Johnson Found., Princeton, N.J., 1974-76, dir. rsch., 1976-79, asst. v.p., 1979-81, v.p., 1981-87; Claire M. Fagin Leadership prof. nursing, prof. sociology U. Pa., Phila., 1988—, dir. Ctr. for Health Svcs. and Policy Rsch., 1988—, rsch. assoc. population studies ctr. Mem. Sec. Health and Human Svcs. Commn. on Nursing, 1988, Pres. Clinton's Nat. Health Care Reform Task Force, 1993; commr. Physician Payment Rev. Commn. nat. adv. coun. U.S. Agy. for Health Care Care Policy and Rsch. Author: Health Policy and Nursing Practice, 1981, Nursing in the 1980s, 1982, Applications of Social Science to Clinical Medicine and Health Policy, 1986, Evaluation Studies Rev. Ann., 1985, Charting Nursing's Future, 1991, Hospital Restructuring in North America and Europe, 1997; contbr. articles to profl. jours. Mem. Adv. Council Social Security, 1982-83. Recipient Joint Secretarial commendation U.S. Dept. Health and Human Services and HUD, 1987; NIH Nurse Scientist fellow, 1970-73. Mem. ANA (Jessie M. Scott award 1984), Am. Acad. Arts and Scis., Assn. Health Svcs. Rsch. (Disting. Investigator), Inst. Medicine, Nat. Acad. Scis., Nat. Acad. Social Ins., Am. Acad. Nursing (pres. 1979-80), Am. Sociol. Assn. (chair med. sociology sect. 1983-84), Sociol. Rsch. Assn., Coun. Nurse Rschrs. (Nurse Scientist of Yr. 1991), Sigma Theta Tau, Phi Kappa Phi. Home: 2209 Lombard St Philadelphia PA 19146-1107 Office: U Pa 420 Service Dr Philadelphia PA 19104-4210

AIKENS, MARTHA BRUNETTE, national park service administrator; b. Jayess, Miss., Aug. 23, 1949; d. Walter and Elnora La Doris (Bridges) A.. BS in Social Sci., Alcorn State U., 1971; postgrad., George Williams Coll., 1974, Fla. Internat. U., 1977, George Washington U., 1979, Pa. State U., 1979, U. So. Calif., D.C. Ext., 1980. Social worker Pearl River County Devel. Corp., Picayune, Miss., 1971—72; environ. ednl. specialist Nat. Park Svc., Homestead, Fla., 1973—75, environ. ednl. coord., 1973—75, comm. specialist, 1976—78; park mgr. Bklyn., 1978—79, Dept. Interior's Mgmt. Program, 1979—80, St. Augustine, Fla., 1979—83, Washington, 1983—88. Instr., cons. Coll. African Wildlife Mgmt., Tanzania, 1980, Fed. Law Enforcement Tng. Ctr., Glynco, Ga., 1983—, Stephen T. Mather Employee Devel. Ctr., Harper's Ferry, W.Va., 1988—91; supt. Independence Nat. Hist. Pk., Phila., 1991—; chair Nat. Pk. Svc. Women's Conf., New Orleans, 1991. Author: tchrs. guides on Everglades Nat. Park, 1973—76, park brochure, 1977; contbr. chapters to books chpts. to books. Active Dept. Interior's Partnership in Edn. Commn., Washington, 1983—, Fed. Interagy Commn. on Edn., Washington, 1983—, Nat. Park Svc. Employee Rels. Task Force, Washington, 1983—, 21st Century Task Force, 1988—, Salt River Bay Nat. Hist. Pk. and Ecol. Preserve Adv. Commn., 1993—, Strategic Planning Task Force, Atlanta, 1981—83, S.E. Regional Equal Opportunity Commn., Atlanta, 1982—83; bd. trustees Walnut St. Theatre, Phila., 1993—; bd. dirs. Peopling of Phila., 1993—; mem. Leading by Example, 1992—. Recipient Star 104.5 Woman of Yr. award, 1993.

AIKMAN, ELFLORA ANNA, senior citizens center administrator; b. Marion, Ill., July 21, 1929; d. John Frederick and Elsa Flora (Weber) Kaeser; m. Samuel Vick Aikman, Dec. 24, 1949; children: Vicki Ann Aikman Hayes, Vance J., Valerie Sue Aikman Henshaw, Samuel Vick III. Student, So. Ill. U., 1949, John A. Logan Coll., 1970, 80, 87, cert. food handler, 1984. Numerous positions, 1947-67; sec. Color-Craft Products, Detroit, 1967-69; admitting clk. Marion Meml. Hosp., 1969-70, appointed to task force, 1989—; co-owner, office mgr., decorating cons. House of Color, Marion, 1970-79; sec., bookkeeper, receptionist Mitchell-Hughes Funeral Home, Marion, 1979-80; receptionist Meredith Funeral Home, Marion, 1980—94; exec. dir. Marion Sr. Citizens Ctr., 1981—99. Columnist Marion Daily Republican, 1984; columnist, contbr. Sr. World, 1987; producer program Sta. WGGH, 1989. Editor monthly newsletter The Yodler, 1984-99; co-designer, decorator Meredith Funeral Home; decorator Marion Meml. Hosp. Chapel, 1971, 77; columnist, contbr. newspaper Old Friends, 1989. Organist, jr. choir dir. St. Clair, Mo., 1958-63; organist, jr. choir organizer, sr. choir organizer Trinity Episcopal Ch., Mt. Vernon, Ill., 1964-67; choir mem. United Ch. Christ, Plymouth, Mich., 1967-69; organist Myers Funeral Home, Mt. Vernon, 1964-67; com. mem. Girl Scouts Am., Mt. Vernon, 1964-67, PTA, St. Clair, Mo., 1960-63; pack officer Boy Scouts Am., Mt. Vernon, 1964-67; home rm. mother, St. Clair, Mo., Mt. Vernon, 1958-67; chmn. Vols. to Arts, Mt. Vernon, Ill., 1966-67; library asst. Plymouth (Mich.) Mid. Sch., 1968-69; com. mem. Williamson County (Ill.) Sesquicentennial Celebration, 1989; mem. Marion Meml. Hosp. Aux., 1980—2002, Hearts Helping Heart, Marion, 1987—2002; asst. organist and choir mem., Sunday sch. tchr. Zion United Ch. of Christ, Marion, mem. numerous other ch. coms.; mem. So. Ill. Easter Seal Soc., 1987. Recipient Svc. Plaque Marion Recreation Dept. Bd., 1983, cert. award svc. to Chautauqua Ill. Humanities Coun., 1986, cert. of recognition for outstanding svc. to sr. citizens 1995-1999, cert. recognition Modern Woodmen Am., Camp 3600, 1998, Mayors Svc. award (city of Marion), 1996, cert. recognition AARP Tax Counsel Elder, cert. recognition IRS, plaque 40 yrs. svc. to music ministry Zion UCC, 1999. Mem. Marion C. of C. (com. 1988), Marion S.A.L.T. (charter mem.), TRIAD (charter mem., treas.), Beta Sigma Phi. Avocations: crocheting, sewing, reading, playing piano and organ, grandchildren. Home: 516 S Market St Marion IL 62959 Office: Marion Sr Citizens Ctr 507 W Main St Marion IL 62959-2437

AILLONI-CHARAS, MIRIAM CLARA, interior designer, consultant; b. Veere, The Netherlands, July 31, 1935; arrived in US, 1958; d. Maurits and Elzina (De Groot) Taytelbaum; m. Dan Ailloni-Charas, Oct. 8, 1957; children: Ethan Benjamin, Orrin, Adam. Degree in Interiors, Pratt Inst., 1962; BSc, SUNY, Albany, 1978. Interior designer S.J. Miller Assocs., N.Y.C., 1960-63; interior design cons. Rye Brook, NY, 1963—88, 1990—2003; exec. v.p. Contract 2000 Inc., Port Chester, NY, 1988-90; interior design cons. Scottsdale, Ariz., 2003—. Treas. Temple Guild, Congregation Emanu-El, Rye, N.Y., 1979-88, co-chmn., 1988-96, chair, 1996-97, trustee, 1986-92. Recipient Cert. of Merit, U.S. Jaycees, 1962, March of Dimes, 1989, 91. Mem.: Westchester C. of C. (Area Devel. Coun. 1988—90), Westchester Assn. Women Bus. Owners (bd. of dir. 1988—93), Allied Bd. Trade, Am. Soc. Interior Designers, Nat.Trust of Hist. Preservation. Home and Office: 30600 N Pima Rd #92 Scottsdale AZ 85262 E-mail: mailloni@cox.net.

AINSWORTH, JOAN HORSBURGH, university development director; b. Cleve., Dec. 30, 1942; d. Donald Francis and Elaine Mildred Horsburgh; m. Richard B. Ainsworth Jr., Oct. 30, 1965; children: Richard B. III, Alison. BA, Wells Coll., 1965; MBA, Case Western Res. U., 1986. Cert. fund raising exec. Social worker San Diego County (Calif.) Welfare Dept., 1966-68; social worker, vol. coord. Washtenaw County (Mich.) Juvenile Ct., Ann Arbor, 1968-70; adminstrv. asst. to pres. Med. Ventures, Ltd., Cleve., 1985-86; dir. Project MOVE, Office of Mayor City of Cleve., 1986-89; dir. devel. and pres.'s programs Case Western Res. U., Cleve., 1989-97, dir. spl. gifts and prin. projects, 1997-98, dir. devel. Coll. Arts and Scis., 1998-2001, asst. dean for devel. Coll. Arts and Scis., 2001—. Trustee, v.p. Children's Aid Soc., Cleve., 1989—, pres., 1997—; trustee, chair devel. Project: LEARN, Cleve., 1990-96; past trustee, cmty. vol. Jr. League Cleve., Inc., 1971—; mem. Vol. Ohio, 1987-96. Named Hon. Mayor City of Cleve., 1989. Mem.: Coun. for Advancement and Support of Edn., Nat. Assn. Fundraising Profls. (cert, chair publicity Greater Cleve. chpt. 1994—96). Avocations: flying, tennis, boating, travel. Home: 2023 Lyndway Rd Cleveland OH 44121-4265 Office: Case Western Res U 10900 Euclid Ave Cleveland OH 44106-1712 E-mail: joan.ainsworth@case.edu.

AITCHISON, ANNE CATHERINE, retired environmental activist; b. Pontiac, Mich., Dec. 27, 1939; d. Willard Francis and Elizabeth (Smith) Speer; m. Robert Terrington Aitchison, Aug. 10, 1963; children: Hannah, Guy, Will. MusB, U. Mich., 1963, MusM, 1965. Chair Naperville (Ill.) Area Recycling Ctr., 1980-89, exec. dir., 1989-93, Sun Shares, Durham, N.C., 1994-96; ret., 1996; cons. Rsch. Triangle Inst., Research Triangle Park, N.C., 1996—. Mem. Citizen's Solid Waste Adv. Com., Will County, Ill., 1989-90, Task Force on Solid Waste, Ill., 1989-90, Task Force on Degradable Plastic, Ill., 1990-91, Mayor's Adv. Com. on Plastic Recycling, Chgo., 1990, Chmn.'s Environ. Com., DuPage County, 1993; cons. cmty. recycling Rsch. Triangle Inst., Durham. Co-author: Resource Recycling, 1991, Environmental Policy for DuPage County, 1993. Founding mem. Naperville Chamber Winds, 1981—93; dir. DuPage Environ. Awareness Ctr., 1987—93; mem. Chmn.'s Environ. Commn., DuPage County, 1992—93, Durham County Solid Waste Adv. Bd., 1994—96; bd. dirs. Durham Symphony, 1994—2000, 2001—, mem. edn. outreach com., 1994—, pres., 2002—03; bd. dirs. Meals on Wheels, Durham, 1999—, pres. bd., 2001—02; bd. dirs., membership chmn. Friends of Durham Libr., 1999—2001. Named Individual Recycler of Yr. Keep Am. Beautiful, 1987, Outstanding Woman Leader YWCA, 1988. Mem. Ill. Recycling Assn. (co-pres. 1987-90, founding dir. 1980—, Pied Piper of Recycling 1989), Women in Waste, Ill. Environ. Coun. (bd. dirs. 1989-90), LWV (bd. dirs. Naperville chpt. 1977-93), Kiwanis (Disting. Svc. award 1987). Avocation: flute.

AITCHISON, BRIDGET MARY, theater educator, theater director; b. L.A., Feb. 27, 1969; d. James and Donna Jean Calcandis, Frederick Anthony Searles; children: Donna Grace, Heather Margaret. Student, U. N.H., 1986—88; BA with honors, U. NSW, 1991; D in Creative Arts, U. Wollongong, NSW, 2001. Head faculty of drama Wesley Inst., Sydney, Australia, 1998—. Dir., facilitator Using Drama to Help Street Kids, 1996. Dir., prodr., writer (touring theatrical prodn.) Back From Nowhere, 2000 (Arts Contbn. cert. NSW Mental Health Assn., 2001, Mental Health Matters award, 2001); actor: 36 commls., TV shows, stage appearances; dir., prodr., artistic dir. BookMark, 1999, A Dry and Thirsty Land, 2000, Sacrifice and Remembrance, 2001; dir., prodr.: Runaways, 1997 (Queen's Trust award for Young Australians, 1996); author: Transformational Drama: Theatre for Community and Social Change, 2002; co-author: Youth Arts and Social Change, 2002; contbr. articles to profl. jours.; prodr., dir. : Bach's Easter Cantata No. 4, 2002; J.B., 2002; Why the Cross?, 2003; Watch This Space!, 2003. Pres. Students Against Drunk Driving, Manchester, NH, 1984—86; orientation counselor U. N.H., Durham, 1986—88; arts/youth worker/activist Sydney, 1995—2001. Recipient Queens Trust award for Young Australians, 1996. Mem.: AFTRA, SAG, MEAA, Australian Coll. Edn., Cultural Studies Assn. Australia, Drama Australia, Edn. Drama Assn. NSW, Australasian Drama Studies Assn. Avocations: violin, folk art, drama, chess, snorkeling. E-mail: bri@butterfly-b.com.

AITCHISON, SUANN, elementary school educator; b. Paterson, N.J., Oct. 1, 1941; d. Archie Wilson and Isabell (Farrow) A. BA, William Paterson Coll., 1963, MEd, 1976; student, Fairleigh Dickinson U., 1991, St. Peter's Coll., 1996. Cert. elem. edn., reading tchr., elem. reading specialist. Tchr. 3d grade Fair Lawn (N.J.) Pub. Schs., 1963-64, 70-71, tchr. 2d grade, 1964-70, 71-87, tchr. reading, 1987-95, reading specialist, 1997—; tchr. reading and math. Fair Lawn (N.J.) Bd. Edn., 1996—; literacy specialist grades 6-8 Meml. and Thomas Jefferson Mid. Schs., Fair Lawn, 2003—. Adj. prof. William Paterson Coll., 1977; developer curriculum guides for remedial reading, 1989, lang. arts and reading for ESL children, 1989, lang. arts and reading for gifted children, 1989, libr. skills and lit. for neurologically impaired children, 1991; mem. Coun. Basic Edn., 1997; com. mem. Bergen County Celebrates Excellence and Pride in Our Pub. Schs., 1997. Active Observation and Evaluation Revision Com., 1995, Cerebral Palsy Ctr.; choir Ch. in Radburn, 1993—95; mem. Garretson Forge Found., 1993—95; assoc. Cerebral Palsy Ctr., 1993—95; mem. com. Bergen County Celebrates Excellence and Pride in Edn., 1997; mem. Coun. for Basic Edn., 1997, Borough Fair Lawn Family Aquatic Study Com., 1997—; dist. reading tchr. family literacy reading take home program grades 1-2 elem. schs., 1999—; mem. 1st class Fair Lawn Police Dept.'s Citizen's Police Acad. Course, 2002; reapptd. mem. adv. com. Ams. with Disability Act, 2002—; com. mem. Fair Lawn Rep. County Com., 1986—98, rec. sec., 1994; vol. Gov. Whitman primary and gen. election campaigns, 1992; mem. Fair Lawn mayor and coun. adv. com. Ams. With Disabilities Act, 1996. Mem. AAHPERD, ASCD (premium mem. 1995—), AAUW, N.J. Reading Assn. (North Jersey coun. 1987-95), Coun. Exceptional Children, N.J. ASCD, Math. Assn. Am., Nat. Coun. Tchrs. of English, Coun. Ednl. Diagnostic Svcs., Fair Lawn Rep. Club (trustee 1997), Fair Lawn Pride Com. Assn., Nat. Assn. Secondary Prins. Baptist. Avocations: singing, reading, restaurant dining, theater, concerts. Home: 38-56 Van Duren Ave Fair Lawn NJ 07410-5018 Office: Fair Lawn Bd Edn 37-01 Fair Lawn Ave Fair Lawn NJ 07410-4919

AITKEN, ANNE E. computer company executive; Mktg. & media Coca-cola Co., 1986-92; dir. advt. Burger King, Corp., 1992-95; dir. mktg. Blockbuster Entertainment, Inc., 1995-97; v.p. mktg. Expert Software, Inc., Coral Gables, Fla., 1997—. Office: Expert Software Inc 800 S Douglas Rd Coral Gables FL 33134-3157

AJA-HERRERA, MARIE, fashion designer, educator; b. Bedford, England, Mar. 19, 1955; d. Henry and Ariadne Swiejkowski; m. Manny Anjel Aja-Herrera, Oct. 24, 1981. BA in Fashion, U. Ctrl. England, 1977; MA in Fashion/Textiles, Lodz U./Krakow U., Poland, 1980; MA in Design Studies, Ctrl. St. Martins, England, 1995; postgrad. cert. in Edn., U. London, 1981. Head fashion dept. Southend Coll. Essex U., 1981—84; head womenswear design (Byblos) Ghirombelli/Pacanina Modas/Santini S.A., Barcelona, Milan, London, 1984—88; head womenswear design Jefferson Internat. PLC, Hong Kong, 1988—89; sales exec., design & edn. coord. Lectra Sys., 1989; chair fashion design, chair fashion merchandising Am. Coll. in London, 1989—92; design dir. CAD, knitwear, textiles Jacques Vert PLC, 1992—95; dean faculty of art and design Am. U. Dubai, United Arab Emirates, 1995—96; head of design Twins/NIKE Enterprise PLC, 1996—97; chair fashion design Savannah (Ga.) Coll. Art & Design, 1997—. Cons. Herrera UK Ltd., 1982-95. Fellow: Soc. Artists & Designers (lic.); mem.: Textile Inst., Polish Union Artists, The Fashion Group Internat., Clothing & Footwear Inst. Avocations: horse riding, skiing, collecting antiques, travel. Office: Savannah Coll Art & Design HR-Clinard Hall Drayton St Savannah GA 31401-5644 Office Phone: 912-525-6650. E-mail: mcajaher@scad.edu.

AJELLO, EDITH H. state legislator; b. Apr. 26, 1944; d. Kenneth Aaron and Rozella Christine (Ewoldt) Hanover; children: Linell, Aaron. BA, Bucknell U., 1966. Store mgr. V. George Rustigian Rugs, Inc., 1981-93, 94—; interim exec. dir. Vols. in Providence Schs., 1993; mem. R.I. Ho. of Reps., 1993—. Democrat. Home and Office: 29 Benefit St Providence RI 02904-2743 E-mail: rep-ajello@rilin.state.ri.us.

AJZENBERG-SELOVE, FAY, physicist, researcher; b. Berlin, Feb. 13, 1926; came to U.S., 1940, naturalized, 1946; d. Mojzesz A. and Olga (Naiditch) A.; m. Walter Selove, Dec. 18, 1955. BS in Engring., U. Mich., 1946; MS, U. Wis., 1949, PhD, 1952; DSc (hon.), Smith Coll., 1995, Mich. State U., 1997, Haverford Coll., 1999—. Rsch. fellow Calif. Inst. Tech., 1952, 54; lectr. Smith Coll., 1952-53; cons., fellow MIT, Cambridge, 1952-53; from asst. prof. to rsch. assoc. prof. Boston U., 1953-57; mem. faculty Haverford Coll., 1957-70, prof. physics, 1962-70, acting chmn. dept. physics, 1967-69; rsch. prof. U. Pa., Phila., 1970-73, prof. physics, 1973—, assoc. chmn., 1989-93. Vis. asst. prof. Columbia, summer 1955, Nat. U. Mexico, summer 1955; lectr. U. Pa., 1957; cons. in field, 1962-63; vis. assoc. Calif. Inst. Tech., 1973-74; Exec. sec. com. physics faculties in colls. Am. Inst. Physics, 1962-65, mem. adv. com. manpower, 1963-68, adv. com. vis. scientists program, 1963-67; commr. Commn. on Coll. Physics, 1968-71; exec. sec. ad hoc panel on nuclear data compilations NAS-NRC, 1971-75; mem. Commn. on Nuclear Physics, Internat. Union Pure and Applied Physics, 1972-78, chairperson. 1978-81; mem. U.S. del. low energy nuclear physics to USSR, AEC, 1966; mem. Distinguished Faculty Awards Commn. Commonwealth of Pa., 1976; mem. nuclear sci. adv. com. Dept Energy-NSF, 1977-80; mem. numerical data adv. bd., assembly math. and phys. scis. NRC, 1977-79; lectr. U. Minn., 1994 Author: A Matter of Choice, Memoirs of a Female Physicist, 1994; editor: Nuclear Spectroscopy, vol. A and B, 1960; bd. editors Phys. Rev. C., 1981-83. Mem. Bower awards com. Franklin Nat. Meml., 1993. Recipient Christian R. and Mary F. Lindback award for disting. teaching, 1991, Nicholson medal for humanitarian svc. Am. Phys. Soc., 1999, 1st Disting. Alumni fellow in Physics, U. Wis., 2001; Smith-Mundt fellow, 1955; Guggenheim fellow, 1965-66. Fellow AAAS (mem. governing coun. 1974-80, mem. com. on coun. affairs 1977, 78), Am. Phys. Soc. (chairperson divsn. nuclear physics 1973-74); mem. AAUP, NRC (mem. phys. scis. panel, associateship program 1988-91), Am. Inst. Physics (mem. com. on pub. edn. and info. 1980-83), Phi Beta Kappa, Sigma Xi (nat. lectr. 1973-74). Home: 118 Cherry Ln Wynnewood PA 19096-1209 Office: U Pa Philadelphia PA 19104-6396

AKER, SUZANNE DEVERSE, physical movement educator; b. Kansas City, Mo., Sept. 19, 1926; d. Earnest Hillborn and Clara Maude Scruggs; m. Meredith Eugene Aker, Jan. 28, 1960 (div. Feb. 1977); children: alan Morrow, Jan Ameen, John Bettis, Elizabeth Aker, Laura Greer. Student, Ballet Theater Sch., 1953; BA, Tulsa U., 1962. Cert. profl. dance tchr. Profl. dancer Burchmann Dancers, Hollywood, N.Y., 1944-45; tchr. Tulsa U., 1959-62; chmn. dept. dance Tex. Tech. U., Lubbock, 1962-69; founding artistic dir., choreographer, tchr. Ballett Lubbock, 1969-2000; phys. movement tchr. Covenant Health Sys., Lubbock, 2000—. Choreographer Tex. Tech. U., 1963-85, Lubbock Theater Ctr., 1965-76, Lubbock Christian U., 1981-90; choreographer, tchr. Wayland Bapt. U., Plainview, Tex., 1979-83. Assoc. Cmty. of Holy Spirit Episcopal Convent, 1985—. Nat. Endowment for Arts grantee, 1980; recipient Pathfinder's award Lubbock C. of C., 1987. Mem. Chi Omega (v.p. 1946), Alpha Psi Omega (hon.), Delta Psi Kappa (hon.). Avocations: icon painting, dance related artwork. Home: 5016 27th St Lubbock TX 79407

AKERS, MICHELLE ANNE, professional soccer player; b. Santa Clara, Calif., Feb. 1, 1966; BS in Liberal Studies and Health, U. Ctrl. Fla., 1989. Forward Tyreso Football Club, Sweden, 1990, 1992, 1994, Orlando (Fla.) Calibre Soccer Club, 1993, U.S. Women's Nat. Soccer Team, Chgo., 1985—. Author: Face to Face with Michelle Akers: Standing Fast; columnist: Soccer Jr. mag., 1995—, Sidekicks mag., 1994—, 1995—. Named All-Am., Ctrl. Fla. Athlete of Yr., 1988—89, MVP, CONCACAF Qualifying Championship, 1994, U.S. Soccer Female Athlete of Yr., 1990, 1991, ESPN Athlete of Yr., 1985; recipient Hermann Trophy, Golden Boot award, FIFA Women's World Championship, 1991, Silver Ball award, 1991, Gold medal, Atlanta Olympics, 1996. Mem.: Women's Sports Found. (adv. bd. 1992—), U.S. Soccer Fedn. (nat. bd. dirs. 1990—95), Soccer Outreach Internat. (founder 1998). Office: US Soccer Fedn US Soccer House 1801 S Prairie Ave Chicago IL 60616-1319

AKIBA, LORRAINE HIROKO, lawyer; b. Honolulu, Dec. 28, 1956; d. Lawrence H. and Florence K. (Iwasa) Katsuyama. BS with honors, U. Calif., Berkeley, 1977; JD, U. Calif., San Francisco, 1981. Bar: Hawaii 1981, U.S. Dist. Ct. Hawaii 1981, U.S. Ct. Appeals (9th cir.) 1981, U.S. Supreme Ct. 1986. Dir. State of Hawaii Dept. Labor and Indsl. Rels., 1995—2000; ptnr. Cades, Schutte, Fleming & Wright, Honolulu, 1981—94, McCorriston Miller Mukai and MacKinnon, Honolulu, 2000—. Lawyer rep. 9th Cir. Jud. Conf., 1991-94; mem., past treas. Hawaii Inst. for Continuing Legal Edn., Honolulu, 1987—. Chairperson attys. divsn. Aloha United Way, Honolulu, 1991, statewide chairperson, 1995; mem. State of Hawaii Environ. Coun., Honolulu, 1990-94, chair, 1992. Named one of Outstanding Young Women Am., 1985. Mem. ABA, Hawaii Bar Assn., Hawaii Women Lawyers Assn., Hawaii Women Lawyers Found. (pres. 1988-92), Phi Beta Kappa. Clubs: Honolulu. Office: McCorriston Miller Mukai MacKinnon LLP PO Box 2800 Honolulu HI 96803-2800 E-mail: LHA@m4law.com.

AKIL, HUDA, neuroscientist, educator, researcher; b. Damascus, Syria, May 19, 1945; came to U.S., 1968; d. Fakher and Widad (Al-Imam) A.; m. Stanley Jack Watson Jr., Dec. 21, 1972; children: Brendon Omar, Kathleen Tamara. BA, Am. U., Beirut, Lebanon, 1966, MA, 1968; PhD, UCLA, 1972. Postdoctoral fellow Stanford U., Palo Alto, Calif., 1974-78; from asst. prof. to prof. psychiatry and neuroscience U. Mich., Ann Arbor, 1979—. Mem. adv. bd. Neurex Corp., Menlo Park, Calif., 1986—, Neurobiol. Techs., Inc., 1994-97; sec. Internat. Narcotics Rsch. Conf., 1990-94. Editor: (jour.) Pain and Headache: Neurochemistry of Pain, 1990; contbr. articles over 300 articles to profl. jours., 1971—2001. Recipient Pacesetter award Nat. Inst. Drug Abuse, 1993, Pasarow award Pasarow Found., 1994, Bristol-Myers Squibb award, 1998, Edward Sachar award Columbia U., 1998; Rockefeller scholar, Beirut, 1963-66; Alfred P. Sloan fellow, Stanford, Calif., 1974-78; grantee Nat. Inst. Drug Abuse, Washington, 1978—, NIMH, Washington, 1980—, Markey Found., U. Mich., 1988-97. Fellow Am. Coll. Neuropsychopharmacology (pres. 1997-98), U. Mich. Soc. Fellows; mem. Inst. Medicine/NAS, Soc.for Neuroscience (pres. 2002-03). Achievements include first to produce physiological evidence for existence of naturally occurring opiate-like substances (endorphins) in brain; described phenomenon of stress-induced analgesia; described functions and regulation of endorphins in brain and pituitary gland; contributed to understanding of biological mechanisms of morphine tolerance and physical dependence; (with colleagues) cloned two main types of opiate receptors, described critical brain circuits relevant to stress and depression. Office: Mental Health Rsch Inst 205 Zina Pitcher Ann Arbor MI 48109-2214

AKIN, ANN FOSTER, special education educator; b. Danbury, Conn., Apr. 11, 1953; d. Thomas Joseph and Sarah Foster; m. Kent Brown Akin, Aug. 22, 1981; children: Hannah Kathleen, Nicholas Kent. BA in Psychology, Elem. Edn. and Edn. for Blind, Dominican Coll., 1976; EdM Edn. of Blind and Visually Impaired, Boston Coll., 1981. Cert. tchr. for blind and partially seeing, elem. edn. N.Y., 1977. Itinerant tchr. for blind and visually impaired Bd. Coop. Ednl. Svcs., Ashville, NY, 1977—. Coord. religious edn. St. Mary's Ch., Mayville, NY. Mem.: AAUW, Coun. for Exceptional Children, Assn. for the Edn. and Rehab. Blind and Visually Impaired, Mayville-Chautauqua Lions Club (pres. 2003—), Eta Nu (pres. 1989—90).

AKIN, DONNA RAE, retired elementary school educator; b. Hobart, Ind., Aug. 20, 1945; d. Raymond Paul and Doris Mildred Vasil; m. William Gerald Akin, Mar. 28, 1970; 1 child, Renee K. Akin Youssef. BS in Edn., Ind. State U., 1967; MS in Edn., Ind. U., 1970. Elem. educator Merrillville (Ind.) Cmty. Sch., 1967—2001; ret. Adv. bd. Merrillville Prime-Time, 1992—94; mem. state bd. Prime-Time Com., Ind., 1994. Editor: (sch. newspaper) Fieler Fun-Times, 1989—2000 (1st pl., 1992). Sec. Ind. Ballet Theatre, N.W., 2001—02; moderator debates League of Women Voters, Crown Point, Ind., 1998—2000, sec., 2000—01. Mem.: AAUW (pres. 1993—95, state nominating com. 1999—2000, 2000—02, named gift honoree 1997), Lake Lodge Eastern Star. Avocations: swimming, exercising. Home: 11556 Westwood Pl Crown Point IN 46307

AKINS, CINDY S. human resources professional; BS, U. Ill.; MS in Labor and Indsl. Rels., Loyola U., Chgo. Various supervisory positions pub. sector; mgr. human resources Zurich Life Ins., Schaumburg, Ill.; dir. human resources Morningstar Inc., Chgo., from 1996, v.p. human resources. Mem. Am. Compensation Assn. (cert. compensation profl.). Office: Morningstar Inc 225 W Wacker Dr Chicago IL 60606-1224 Fax: 312-696-6001.

ALAIMO, TERRY M. financial consultant; b. Orange, N.J., Dec. 3, 1955; d. Louis Joseph and Julia Clara (Carlin) Mazziotto; m. Salvatore Alaimo, June 5, 1972 (div. Mar. 1975); 1 child, Roxanne. Student, William Patterson Coll., 1974-78. Organizer 1199 Nat. Union Health and Human Svc., N.Y.C., 1984-88; organizing coord. Pub. Employers Fedn., N.Y.C., 1988-89; organizer 1199 Nat. Union N.Y.C., 1989-92, v.p., 1992-96; cons. S.I. (N.Y.) Amalgamated Transit Union, 1992-97, Svc. Employees Internat. Union, Washington, 1997, 1199 N.W., Seattle, 1997-99, fin. advisor Prudential Securities, 1999-2000, Montauk Securities, Paramus, N.J., 2000—. Coord. Dinkins for Mayor, S.I., 1990, 94, Albanese for Congress, S.I., 1992. Mem. Nat. Abortion Rights Action League. Democrat. Avocations: painting, writing, travel.

ALANDER, VIRGINIA NICKERSON, retired student assistance coordinator; b. Springfield, Ill., Aug. 16, 1931; d. Carl Lee Nickerson and Zola Audrey Mitchell; m. Robert Huntley Alander, June 16, 1956 (dec. Nov. 1966); children: Dirk, Erik, Link. BS, U. Wis., 1953; MS, Ill. State U., 1973. Tchr. Elmhurst (Ill.) Jr. High, 1953-55, Woodruff High Sch., Peoria, Ill., 1955-56; vol. tchr. Kikongo Mission, Leopoldville, Belgian Congo, 1956-58; tchr., student asst. coord. Joliet West High Sch., Joliet, Ill., 1965-95, dir. Tiger Paws dance team, 1969-93; ret., 1995. Contbr. articles on organizing teams and motivation. Vice-chairperson Joliet Twp. High Sch. Found., 1995-99. Named to Ill. Drill Team Assn. Hall of Fame, Let's Cheer Mag. Hall of Fame, U.S. Cheerleading Assn. Hall of Fame. Mem. Ill. Drill Team Assn. (pres.). Lutheran. Avocations: travel, antiques, theatre. Home: 23545 W Fern St Plainfield IL 60544-2323

ALANIZ, THEODORA VILLARREAL, elementary school educator; b. Mercedes, Tex., Feb. 16, 1951; d. Alejandro and Maria (Villarreal) A. BS in Elem. Edn., Pan Am. U., 1979; MEd, Tex. A&I U., 1984; cert. in counseling, U. Tex., 1992. Cert. vocat. counselor, Level I and II lic. chem. dependency counselor, South Tex. C.C. Asst. tchr. Mercedes Ind. Sch. Dist., 1973-78; tchr. Pharr (Tex.)-San-Juan-Alamo Ind. Sch. Dist., 1979-91, Edcouch-Elsa (Tex.) Ind. Sch. Dist., 1991-93; counselor Donna Ind. Sch. Dist., 1993—. Census rep. Diocese of Brownsville, 1974-75; choir mem. Sacred Heart Ch., Mercedes, Tex., 1974-78, 3rd grade tchr., 1975-78; rep. Cancer Soc., Mercedes, 1980-81, Assn. Tex. and Profl. Educators to Pharr and Elsa Ind. Sch. Dists. Scholar Title VII Bilingual/Bicultural, 1978-79. Roman Catholic. Avocations: physical fitness, pencil drawing, sight seeing. Address: RR 4 Box 161-c Mercedes TX 78570-9313

ALARCON, SYLVIA M. music educator; b. Laredo, Tex., July 1, 1949; d. Arturo Alarcon, Jr. and Gloria Dalrymple Alarcon. B of Music Edn., U. Tex., El Paso, 1971. Pvt. music tchr., Alamogordo, N.Mex., 1970—; band dir. Alamogordo Pub. Schs., Alamogordo, 1971—2001. Clarinetist/soloist U. of Tex. at El Paso, 1967—71; asst. band dir. Alamogordo H.S., 1971—2001; clarinetist with orch. Alamogordo Music Theater, 1980—90, Grace Meth. Orch., Alamogordo, 1990. Bass guitarist, singer Immaculate Conception Ch., 2001—; singer, Resurection Choir Grace Meth. Orch., 2003; coach for 21 and under Young Am. Bowling Assn., Alamogordo, 1975; coach for 14, 16, and 18 yr. old Girls Softball Assn., Alamogordo, 1991—94. Named Alamogordo Womens Bowler of Yr., 1998—99; named to Outstanding Young Woman of Am., 1982, N.Mex. Music Hall of Fame, N.Mex. Music Edn. Nat. Conf., 2001; recipient Alamogordo City Doubles Bowling champion, 1992, N.Mex. Large Group Contest winner, State of N.Mex., 1993, Alamogordo City Doubles Bowling champion, 1994, Alamogordo Womens Bowler of Yr., 1994—95, N.Mex. Large Group Contest winner, State of N.Mex., 1995, 1999, Alamogordo City Doubles Bowling champion, 2001. Mem.: N.Mex.-Alamogordo Assn. Classroom Tchrs., Music Educators Nat. Conf., Bus. and Profl. Women, Phi Beta Mu. Roman Catholic. Avocations: bowling, softball, repairing musical instruments.

ALARIE-ANDERSON, PEGGY SUE, physician assistant; b. Flint, Mich., Feb. 8, 1957; d. Albert Joseph Jr. and Elizabeth Anna (Eksten) A.; m. John L. McAttee III, Oct. 3, 1980 (div. Aug. 1987); m. Donn P. Anderson, Aug. 23, 1997. AAS, Mott C.C., 1983; BS, Mich. State U., 1988; MS, U. Detroit-Mercy, 1994. Physician asst. supr. emergency rm. Hurley Med. Ctr., Flint, Mich., 1996—. Fellow Am. Acad. Physician Assts., Mich. Acad. Physician Assts.; mem. Soc. Emergency Physician Assts., Am. Acad. Surg. Physician Assts., Sigma Theta Tau. Avocations: dance (ballet, ballroom, tap, jazz). Home: 5072 Scott Rd Mount Morris MI 48458-9724 Office: Hurley Med Ctr 1 Hurley Plz Flint MI 48503-5902

ALBA, BENNY, artist; b. Columbus, Ohio, 1949; Student, Kent State U., 1968-70; BA in Psychology, U. Mich., 1982. Artists in residence Mont. Artists Refuge, Basin, 2003. Artist-in-residence St. Charles Boy's Pres. Sch., Columbus, 1982-85, Mont. Artist Refuge, Basin, 2002; lectr. Columbus Cultural Arts Ctr., 1983-84, 93; presenter in field; panelist Calif. Inst. for Intergral Studies, San Francisco, 1995. One-woman shows include Columbus Cultural Arts Ctr., 1993, Apprentice Alliance, San Francisco, 1994, Las Vegas (Nev.) Mus., 1994, Artist TV Access, San Francisco, 1994, Western Wyo. Coll., Rock Springs, 1994, A Gallery in the Clock Tower, San Francisco, 1994, Ctr. for Psychol. Studies, Albany, Calif., 1994, Idyllwild (Calif.) Sch. Music and Art, 1995, Merced (Calif.) Coll. Art Gallery, 1997, North Country Mus. of Art, Park Rapids, Minn., 1997, Martinez (Calif.) City Hall, 1997, Martinez Arts and Culture Com., 1997, Office of Sup. Contra County Ct., Martinez, 1997, State Bd., Sacramento, Calif., 1997, Saginaw (Mich.) Art Mus., 1998, Met. Transp. Co., Oakland, Calif., 1998, Commonwealth Club, San Francisco, 1998, San Francisco State U. Club, 1998, Zen Ctr., San Francisco, 1998, Hastings Coll. Law, 1999, U. Oreg., Eugene, 1999, Oakland Higher Edn. Ctr., 1999, The Arts Ctr., Jamestown, N.D., 2000, North Valley Arts Coun., Grand Forks, N.D., 2000, Lake Region Heritage Ctr., Devils Lake, N.D., 2000, Bismarck (N.D.) Art and Galleries Assn., Valley Art Ctr., Clarkston, Wash., 2000, Pacific Grove Art Ctr., Calif., 2000, Rogue C.C., Grants Pass, Oreg., 2000, Sedona (Ariz.) Art Ctr., 2000, ARC Gallery, Chgo., 2000, Napa City County Libr., 2000, East Bay Mcpl. Utilities Dist., 2002, Birnbaum's Broadway Frame, Missoula, Mont., 2003, exhibited in group shows at throughout U.S.A., San Francisco, 1992, YWCA, Youngstown, Ohio, 1992, Mus. Without Walls, Bemis Pt., N.Y., 1993, Davis (Calif.) Art Ctr., 1993, Kunst für Begegnungen, Munich, 1993, Ednl. Testing Svc., Emeryville, Calif., 1993—94, Diablo (Calif.) Valley Coll. Gallery, 1994, N.Mex. Art League, Albuquerque, 1995, Nat. Congress Art & Design, Salt Lake City, 1995, Danville (Calif.) Fine Arts, 1995, Lillian Paley Ctr. Visual Arts, Oakland, 1995, Lamar U., Beaumont, Tex., 1996, John Jay Coll. of Criminal Justice, N.Y., 1996, Serra House, Stanford U., 1996, Fed. Bldgs. Window Project, Oakland, 1996, Civic & Cultural Ctr., Brea, Calif., 1997, Palm Springs (Calif.) Desert Mus., 1997, Am. Embassies Program, Rangoon, Burma, 1997, Downey (Calif.) Mus. Art, 1997, Am. Embassies Program, Lesotho, Africa, 1998, Nairobi, Africa, 2004, Bangladesh, 1999, Mus. Downtown L.A., 1998, Sun Gallery, Hayward, Calif., 1998, Hoyt Inst. Fine Arts, New Castle, Pa., 1998, Maude Kers Art Ctr., Eugene, 1998, Bolinas (Calif.) Mus., 1998, George Ohr Mus., Biloxi, 1998, Galesburg (Ill.) Civic Art Ctr., 1999, Coll. Notre Dame Md., Balt., 1999, Las Vegas Art Coun., 2000, Lincoln Ctr., Ft. Collins, Colo., 2000, Works Gallery, San Jose, Calif., 2000, Ohlone Coll., Freemont, Calif., 2000, Fredericksburg (Va.) Coll. Creative Arts, 2000, Gallery Rt. One, Pt. Reyes Ste, Calif., 2000, The Print Ctr., Phila., 2001, Palm Springs Desert Mus., 2001, Masur Mus. of Art, Monroe, La., 2001, Brownsville (Tex.) Art League, 2001, Period Gallery, Omaha, 2001, Art Assn. of Harrisburg, Pa., 2001, Fredericksburg CCA/Mary Washington Coll., Va., 2001, Palos Verdes Art Ctr., Rancho Palos Verdes, Calif., 2001, Viridian Artists Inc. Gallery, N.Y.C., 2001, South Cobb Arts Alliance, Mableton, Ga., 2001, Havre De Grace (Md.) Arts Commn., 2001, Steamboat Springs (Colo.) Arts Coun., 2001, ArtsBenecia, Calif., 2001, WomanMade Gallery, Chgo., 2001, Tex. Artists Mus., Port Arthur, 2001, MakeReady Press Gallery, Montclair, N.J., 2001, Impact Artists Gallery, Buffalo, 2001, others, Represented in permanent collections Nat. Mus. Women in Arts, Ark. Arts Ctr., Little Rock, U. Mich. Mus. Art, Kalamazoo Inst. Arts, Greenpeace, Ulli Wachter (Germany), Las Vegas Art Mus., Ctr. for Psychol. Studies, Albany, Calif., Birmingham (Ala.) Mus. Art, Portland (Oreg.) Art Mus., Tyler (Mich.) Mus. Art, Canajoharie Libr., N.Y., Mint Mus., Charlotte, N.C., others, exhibited in group shows at Mountain Art, Bernardville, NJ, 2002, Fredericksburg (Va.) for Creative Arts, 2002, Wenatchee (Va.) Valley Coll., 2002, Alice Arts Ctr., Oakland, Calif., 2002, Central Mo. State U., 2002, San Pablo (Calif.) City Arts Gallery, 2003, one-woman shows include [illegible] Palo Alto, Claif., 2003, U. Ala., Montgomery, Ala., 2003, Zerox Corp., Palo Alto, Calif., 2004, U. Ala., Montgomery, 2003, exhibited in group shows at Tex. Artists Mus., Port Arthur, Tex., 2002, Fredericksburg (Ba.) Ctr. for Creative Arts, 2002, Wenatchee (Wash.) Valley Coll., 2002, Alice Arts Ctr., Oakland, Calif., 2002, Ctrl. Mo. State U., Warrensburg, Mo., 2002, San Pablo (Calif.) City Gallery, 2003, U. Calif., Berkeley, Calif., 2003, Kellog G. Calif. State Polytec, Pomona, Calif., 2003, State Polytech. U., 2004, 2003, U. Mont., Butte, 2003, Nicolet Coll. Art Gallery, Rhinelander, Wis., 2003, Coos Art Mus., Coos Bay, Wash., 2003, Wenatchee Valley Coll., Wenatchee, Wash., 2003, 2002, Tex. Artists Mus., Port Arthur, Tex., 2002, Ctrl. Mo. State U., Warrensburg, Mo., 2002. Bd. dirs. No. Calif. Women's Caucus for Art, 1991, sec. 1991-92, phone liaison, 1991-93. Recipient Lenore Miles award North Platte Valley Art Gallery, 1991, Body of Work award Women Artists, A Celebration, 1990, Merit award San Francisco Women Artist Gallery, 1986, Dr. S. Mackoff award Palm Springs Desert Mus., 1997, Junor Adobe Gallery award, 2000, San Francisco (Calif.) Women Artists, 2001, Art Assn. Palo Alto, 2001, 03, Adobe Gallery, Castro Valley, Calif., 2003., 2d Pl. award Gallery '76, Wenatchee Valley Coll., Wash., 2003. Mem. Women's Caucus for Art (bd. dirs. No. Calif. 1991-94, sec. 1991-92), Calif. Soc. Printmakers (v.p. 1999, pres. 2004). Studio: 4219 M L King Jr Way Oakland CA 94609-2321 Office Phone: 510-547-4512.

ALBAGLI, LOUISE MARTHA, psychologist; b. Queens, N.Y., Jan. 15, 1954; d. Meyer Nathan and Leah (Bleier) Greenberg; m. Eli S. Albagli, July 31, 1977. BA in Psychology summa cum laude, CUNY, 1976; D of Clin. Psychology, Rutgers U., 1983. Cert. Reiki master. Clin. psychology intern Postgrad. Ctr. Mental Health, N.Y.C., 1980-81; staff psychologist Queens County Neuropsychiat. Inst., Jackson Heights, N.Y., 1981-83, Bklyn. Community Counseling Ctr., 1981-84; sr. clin. psychologist Richard Hall Community Mental Health Ctr., Bridgewater, N.J., 1984-86; pvt. practice Germantown, Md., 1985—2001; mem. adj. faculty Rutgers U., 1990-93; ret. Jin Shin Jyutsu practitioner, 1995—, self-help tchr., 1996—. Mem. Nat. Register Health Care Providers, Am. Psychol. Assn., N.J. Psychol. Assn. (com. inter-profl. rels.), Internat. Childbirth Edn. Assn., RESOLVE, Raritans, Phi Beta Kappa.

ALBAIN, KATHY S. oncologist; b. Monroe, Mich., June 4, 1952; d. James Jay and Elizabeth G. (Jakscy) A. BS in Chemistry summa cum laude, Wheaton Coll., 1974; MD, U. Mich., 1978. Diplomate Am. Bd. Internal Medicine, Am. Bd. Oncology. Instr. physical diagnosis U. Mich. Med. Sch., 1978; intern U. Ill. Med. Ctr., Chgo., 1978-79, resident in internal medicine, 1979-81, clin. instr. medicine, 1980-81; instr. in medicine U. Ill. Hosps. and Clinics, 1980-81; fellow dept. medicine sect. hematology/oncology U. Chgo. Med. Ctr./U. Chgo. Hosps. and Clinics, 1981-84; asst. prof. medicine Loyola U. Chgo. Strich Sch. Medicine, 1984-91, assoc. prof. medicine divsn. hematology/oncology, 1991—; attending physician Hines (Ill.) VA Hosp., 1984—, Loyola U. Chgo. Foster G. McGaw Hosp., 1984—. Co-investigator multidisciplinary lung cancer staging and rsch. group U. Chgo. and Michael Reese Hosp. Med. Ctrs., 1982-84; coord. ann. breast cancer screening program Sr. Ctr. LaGrange, Ill., 1985-91; mem. med. adv. bd. Y-Me Nat. Breast Cancer Orgn., 1987—; co-dir. Multidisciplinary Breast Care Ctr. Loyola U. Med. Ctr., 1991—, dir. Multidisciplinary Lung Cancer Evaluation Ctr., 1994—; mem. oncology med. adv. bd. Eli Lilly and Co., 1993—; co-investigator nat. surg. adjuvant breast and bowel project U. Chgo., 1982-84; mem. breast cancer com., breast cancer working group, lung cancer com., lung cancer working group S.W. Oncology Group, 1986—, mem. gynecol. cancer com. and working group, 1989—, sarcoma and brain coms., 1990—, chair com. on women's health, 1992—; mem. intergroup lung cancer working cadre Nat. Cancer Inst., 1993—, mem. breast cancer intergroup com. on correlative scis. Nat. Cancer Inst., 1995, mem. breast cancer intergroup chairs com., 1994—; clin. trials co-chair Sec. of HHS Nat. Breast Cancer Action Plan, 1993-94; mem. adv. panel State of Ill. Breast and Cervical Cancer Rsch. Fund, 1994—; charter mem. adv. com. on rsch. in women's health NIH, 1995—; mem. Early Breast Cancer Trialists' Collaborative Group, 1995—; mem. clin. trials working group Sec. of Health Nat. Breast Cancer Action Plan, 1995—; rschr., lectr., presenter in field. Reviewer jours. Cytometry, Breast Cancer Rsch. and Treatment, Cancer Rsch., Jour. Clin. Oncology, Cancer, Chest; contbr. articles to profl. publs. Mem. sr. choir Grace Luth. Ch., River Forest, Ill. Nat. Cancer Inst. fellowship tng. grantee, 1981-84, grantee Bristol-Myers, 1988-93, Squibb Mark Co., 1989, UpJohn Co., 1990, 92, Office Rsch. on Women's Health/Nat. Cancer Inst., 1992, 93-95, Nat. Cancer Inst., 1993—. Mem. ACP, Am. Assn. Cancer Rsch., Am. Fedn. Clin. Rsch., Am. Soc. Clin. Oncology, Internat. Assn. for Study of Lung Cancer, Christian Med. and Dental Soc. Home: 220 S Maple Ave Oak Park IL 60302-3031 Office: Loyola U Med Ctr Divsn Hematology/Oncology 2160 S 1st Ave Maywood IL 60153-3304

ALBANESE, CATHERINE, religious studies educator; PhD in Am. Religious History, U. Chgo. Prof. religious studies U. Calif., Santa Barbara, 1987—. Recipient John Simon Guggenheim Meml. fellowship, 2003, Presdl. Rsch. fellowship in the humanities, Office of U. Calif. Pres. Richard Atkinson. Office: U Calif Santa Barbara Religious Studies Dept 3001 HSSB Santa Barbara CA 93106

ALBANO, PAIGE LYNNE, small business owner; b. Paterson, N.J., June 9, 1968; d. Harry P. and Gloria June (Baldecchi) A. BA in Comm. with highest honors, Rutgers U., 1992. Nat. cert. massage therapist. Entertainer/cheerleader N.J. Nets Basketball, Seacacus, 1985-86; attractions host Walt Disney World Corp., Orlando, Fla., 1987; waitress Ramada Rennaisance, East Brunswick, N.J., 1989-90, Bay St. Restaurant, Edison, N.J., 1990-91; owner A&A Assocs., Bayville, N.J., 1991—, Bodyworks Holistic Therapy, Bayville, N.J., 1992—. Cons. Altieri Chiropractic Ctr., Bayville, 1991—; bus. developer A & A Assocs., Toms River, N.J., 1992—. Organizer Kids' Day America, 1997. Mem. No. Ocean Sml. Bus. Assn. (founding mem., Speaking award 1994), Golden Key, Alpha Sigma Lambda. Avocations: dance, exercising, reading, writing, travel. Office: 738 Atlantic City Blvd Bayville NJ 08721-2543

ALBARRACIN, DOLORES, psychologist, educator; d. Carlos and Marta R. Albarracín; m. Martin P. Repetto, June 1, 1962; children: Maria de los Angeles Repetto, Martin J. Repetto. PhD, U Ill., Champaign-Urbana, 1997. Asst. prof. Psychology Dept., U. Fla., Gainesville, Fla., 1997—; grad. asst. and fellow Psychology Dept., U. Ill., Champaign-Urbana, Ill., 1992—97. Author: (jour. article) Jour. of Personality and Social Psychology, Health Psychology, 2000, Jour. of Personality and Social Psychology, 2001, Psychol. Bull., 2001; : Personality and Social Psychology Bull., 2001, Advances in Exptl. Social Psychology, 2002, Health Psychology, 2003; editor: (book) Handbook of attitudes and attitude change, 2004. Recipient Scientist Devel. Award, NIMH, 1999-2003; grantee R 03 Rsch. Grant, 1997-1999, R 01 Rsch. Grant, NIH, 2001-2006. Mem.: Soc. of Intermerican Psychology (us rep. 2000—02), Am. Psychol. Soc., Soc. of Personality and Social Psychology, APA, Soc. of Exptl. Social Psychology. Home: 3629 SW 97th Way Gainesville FL 32608 Office: University Fla Psychology Dept Gainesville FL 32611 E-mail: dalbarra@ufl.edu.

ALBAUM, JEAN STIRLING, psychologist, educator; b. Beijing, Jan. 11, 1932; came to U.S., 1936; d. Richard Henry and Emma Bowyer (Lueders) Ritter; m. B. Taylor Stirling, Aug. 15, 1953 (div. 1965); 1 child, Christopher Taylor Stirling; m. Joseph H. Albaum; stepchildren: Thomas Gary, Lauren Jean. BA, Beloit (Wis.) Coll., 1953; MS, Danbury (Conn.) State U., 1964, U. La Verne, Calif., 1983; PhD, Claremont (Calif.) Grad. Sch., 1985. Lic. ednl. psychologist, Calif. Spl. edn. tchr. Charter Oak (Calif.) Sch. Dist., 1966-80, psychologist, coord. elem. counseling Claremont Sch. Dist., 1980—2002; pvt. practice in ednl. psychology Encino, Calif., 1987—2003. Clin. supr. marriage, family and child counselor interns Claremont Grad. Sch., 1984—2000; adj. prof. U. La Verne, 1988—; oral commr. Bd. Behavioral Sci. Examiners, Sacramento, 1989—2001. Contbr. articles to profl. jours. Hostess L.A. World Affairs Coun., 1980—; pres. Woodley Homeowner's Assn., Encino, 1986-89. Grantee Durfee Found., 1986, 92. Mem. Am. Psychol. Assn., Calif. Assn. Marriage, Family and Child Therapists, Calif. Assn. Lic. Ednl. Psychologists. Avocations: travel, international relations, history, sailing, skiing. Office: Edn Ctr 2080 N Mountain Ave Claremont CA 91711-2643

ALBEE, GLORIA, playwright; b. Brockton, Mass., Apr. 26, 1931; d. Earl Fredric and Rita Marie (Walls) Albee; m. Leonard Goodman, Jan. 13, 1961 (div.); 1 child, Anna Albee Goodman. Student, Boston U., 1948-49, U. Wash., 1972-74, Sarah Lawrence Coll., 1975-76, Hunter Coll., 1986-92. Playwright: Medea, 1975, Helen of Sparta, 1991; plays produced include Medea, Nothing Personal, The Yellow Wallpaper. Recipient John Golden Theatre award Hunter Coll., 1986, Mary M. Fay award in poetry Hunter Coll., 1990, Honorable Mention award Jane Chambers Playwriting Award, 1994; Rockefeller Bros. Found. grantee; Nat. Arts Club Lit. scholar, 1990. Mem. Dramatists Guild. Home: 110 W End Ave 14C New York NY 10023-6342 E-mail: GALBEE1707@aol.com.

ALBEE, LENORE K. management consultant; MBA, U. Mo., St. Louis, 1985. Ptnr. Ernst & Young, St. Louis, 1989—2000; mng. dir. BearingPoint, St. Louis, 2001—03; COO Fedora Inc., St. Louis, 2003—. Bd. dirs. Support Dogs Inc., St. Louis, 1993—95, Greater Mo. Leadership Challenge, St. Louis, 2003; pres. Historyonics Theatre Co., St. Louis, 1995—2002. Office: Fedora Inc 222 Parkhurst Ter Saint Louis MO 63119 E-mail: lenore.albee@mindspring.com.

ALBERGO, MARGARET, broadcast executive; Student, Suffolk C.C. Started as asst. to dir. programming Cablevision Sys. Corp., 1976; dir. ops. & adminstrn. Rainbow Programming Holdings, 1991, former v.p. corp develop.; sr. v.p. ops. Rainbow Programming Holdings (now known as Rainbow Media Holdings); sr. v.p. planning & performance, 1996—99; exec. v.p. planning & ops. Cablevision Sys. Corp., 1999—. Office: Cablevision Sys Corp 1111 Stewart Ave Bethpage NY 11714-3501

ALBERNATHY, KATHLEEN Q. federal agency administrator; married; 1 child. BS magna cum laude; JD, Cath. U. Am. Dir. fed. affairs Comsat World Systems Divsn.; v.p. fed. regulatory AirTouch Comm., Inc.; v.p. regulatory affairs U.S. West, Inc.; ptnr. Wilkinson Barker Knauer; v.p. pub. policy BroadBand Office Comm.; commr. FCC, Washington, 2001—. Adj. prof. Georgetown U. Law Ctr., Cath. U. Am. Columbus Sch. Law. Mem.: D.C. Bar Assn., Fed. Comm. Bar Assn. (past pres.). Office: FCC 445 12th St SW Washington DC 20554

ALBERS, DOLORES M. secondary school educator; b. Lander, Wyo., June 2, 1949; AA, Casper Coll., 1969; BS, U. No. Colo., 1972; postgrad., U. N.C., U. Wyo., Chadron State. Physical edn. instr. for grades K-12, 6th and 8th grade sci. tchr. Bent County Sch. Dist. 2, McClave, Colo., 1972-75; physical edn./health instr. Sweetwater County Sch. Dist. # 2, Green River, Wyo., 1972—. Mem. phys. edn. coun. Mid. and Secondary Schs., 1999—2003, chmn. phys. edn. coun., 2002—03. Mem., chmn. Green River Parks and Recreation Bd.; coord. Hoops for Heart; co-chmn. United Way Sweetwater County, 1999-2001. Named Tchr. of Yr., Ctrl. Dist., 1994—95, Nat. Assn. Sport and Phys. Edn., 1995. Mem. AAHPERD, AALR, ASCD/NFOIA, NEA, Wyo. Edn. Assn., Wyo. Assn. Health, Phys. Edn., Recreation and Dance (Tchr. of Yr. award 1994-95), Green River Edn. Assn., Nat. Assn. for Sport and Phys. Edn., Mid. and Secondary Sch. Phys. Edn. Coun. (chmn. 2002-03). Roman Catholic. Avocations: alpine skiing, backpacking, snowmachining, woodworking, crewel. Home: 1745 Massachusetts Ct Green River WY 82935-6229 Office: Green River HS 1615 Hitching Post Dr Green River WY 82935-5771

ALBERS, SHERYL KAY, state legislator; b. Sauk County, Wis., Sept. 9, 1954; d. Marcus J. and Norma Anderson Gumz; 1 child, Joel Albert. BA, Ripon Coll., 1976; postgrad., U. Wis. Mem. Wis. State Assembly, 1991—, mem. judiciary com., children and families com., chmn. property rights/land mgmt. com. Publicity chmn. Sauk County Rep. Party, 1978-80, vice chmn., 1980-82, chmn., 1982-83, mem. exec. com.; assembly Rep. Caucus Wis., 1987-91; mem. Local Emergency Planning Com. Juneau County; mem. Joint Com. on Fin., 1997&; mem. Savey Foun. Scholarship Com. Recipient Campbell award Sauk County Rep. Com., 1981, 90, Top 10 County award Wis. State Rep. Party, 1982, Pacesetter award Wis. Forage Coun., 1983, Bovay award Rep. Party Wis., 1990; named one of Outstanding Farmers Sauk County Farm Bur., 1982. Mem. Sauk County Farm Bur. (dir., treas. 1977-82), Sauk County Hist. Soc., Agrl. Bus. Coun. Wis., Kiwanis. Republican. E-mail: Rep.Albers@legis.state.wi.us.

ALBERT, ELIZABETH ANN SALISBURY, elementary school educator; b. Hornell, N.Y., Sept. 1, 1943; d. Matthew B. Salisbury and Elizabeth Harrington; 1 child, John E. Jacobs Jr. BAE, U. Fla., 1965. Mem.: NEA, Nat. Edn. Assn., Alpha Chi Omega. Democrat. Avocations: reading, genealogy. Home: 108 SW 10th Ct Boynton Beach FL 33426

ALBERT, ELIZABETH FRANZ (MRS. HENRY B. ALBERT), investor, artist, conservationist; b. Chgo., Nov. 9, 1923; d. Herbert George and Louise Anders Franz; m. Henry Burton Albert, Oct. 24, 1964 (dec. July 1980). Student, Chevy Chase Jr. Coll., 1942. Investor stock market, real estate. Breeder several champion Miniature Poodles. Exhibitions include portraits, still life (various painting awards); contbr. biology textbook; editor: biology textbook. Former mem. Landmarks Preservation Coun. Chgo. Mem.: Am. Farmland Trust, Nat. Trust Hist. Preservation, Cousteau Soc. (founding mem.), Natural Resources Def. Coun., Environ. Def. Fund (Osprey Soc.), Nat. Mus. Women in the Arts (charter mem.), Chgo. Symphony Orch. Soc., Art Inst. Chgo. (life). Republican. Episcopalian. Achievements include design of a house in college within the architectural field; conservationist who campaigned against the herbicide Dacthal which causes lymphoma and Parkinson's Disease and is used by lawn care companies, home owners, farmers, and golf course greens keepers. Avocations: music, renovating houses, antiques, gardening, reading. Home: 316 Courtland Ave Park Ridge IL 60068

ALBERT, KRISTEN ANN, music educator; b. Harrisburg, Pa., July 29, 1962; d. Charles Orth and Kathryn Johnson Froehlich; m. Douglas Lee Albert, Aug. 31, 2001. BS in Edn., Millersville U., 1983; EdM, Shippensburg U., 1989. Cert. instrnl. II Pa. Dept. Edn., 1983, specialist II Pa. Dept. Edn., 1989. Music specialist Warwick Sch. Dist., Lititz, Pa., 1984—84, Manheim Twp. Sch. Dist., Lancaster, Pa., 1984—89, guidance counselor, 1990—92, Hempfield Sch. Dist., Landisville, Pa., 1989—90; music specialist Lampeter (Pa.)-Strasburg Sch. Dist., 1992—2000; instr. music edn. West Chester (Pa.) U., 2001—01; asst. prof. music edn. West Chester U. Pa., 2001—. Co-dir. Children's Choir Lancaster, 2000—. Contbr. articles to profl. jours. Mem. Allegro: The Chamber Orch. Lancaster, 2001—04. ETeaching/eLearning grant, West Chester U., 2002, 2003. Mem.: ACDA, TI:ME (instr.), OAKE, Music Educators Nat. Conf. Lutheran. Avocations: golf, reading, computers. Office: West Chester Univ Pa Swope Hall West Chester PA 19383

ALBERT, SUSAN WITTIG, writer, English educator; b. Maywood, Ill., Jan. 2, 1940; d. John H. and A. Lucille (Franklin) Webber; m. William Albert, 1986; children by previous marriage: Robert, Robin, Michael. BA, U. Ill., 1967; PhD, U. Calif.-Berkeley, 1972. Instr. U. San Francisco, 1969-71; asst. prof. to assoc. prof. U. Tex., Austin, 1971-79; assoc. dean Grad. Sch., U. Tex., Austin, 1977-79; dean Sophie Newcomb Coll., New Orleans, 1979-81; dean of faculty. grad. dean S.W. Tex. State U., San Marcos, 1981-82, v.p. acad. affairs, 1982-86, prof. English, 1981-87. Founder Story Circle Network, Inc., 1997. Author: Work of Her Own, 1992, Writing From Life, 1996; author: (China Bayles novels) Thyme of Death, 1992; author: Witch's Bane, 1993, Hangman's Root, 1994, Rosemary Remembered, 1995, Rueful Death, 1996, Love Lies Bleeding, 1997, Chile Death, 1998, Lavender Lies, 1999, Mistletoe Man, 2000, Bloodroot, 2001, Indigo Dying, 2003, An Unthymely Death, 2003, A Dilly of a Death, 2004; author: (Robin Paige novels) Death at Bishop's Keep, 1994; author: Death at Gallows Green, 1995, Death at Daisy's Folly, 1997, Death at Devil's Bridge, 1998, Death at Rottingdean, 1999, Death at Whitechapel, 2000, Epsom Downs, 2001, Death at Dartmoor, 2002, Death at Glamis Castle, 2003, Death in Hyde Park, 2004; author: (Cottage Tales of Beatrix Potter novels) The Tale of Hill Top Farm; editor: With Courage and Common Sense: Memoirs from the Older Women's Legacy Circles, 2003; contbr. articles to profl. jours. Danforth grad. fellow, 1967-72 Home: PO Box 1616 Bertram TX 78605 E-mail: china@tstar.net.

ALBERTA, FRANCES RITA, principal; b. Hackensack, N.J., July 1, 1947; d. Frank James Ambrosino and Madeline Mary Aliano Ambrosino; m. Philip Charles Alberta, July 5, 1969; children: Philip Charles, Francis Gerard, Charles Michael. MS, Manhattan Coll., 2000. Cert. sch. adminstr., supr. N.Y. Tchr. St. Joseph Sch., East Rutherford, NJ, 1989—96, prin., 2000—. Named Outstanding Tchr. of Yr., Archdiocese of Newark, 1992. Mem.: NCEA, Nat. Assn. Elem. Sch. Prins., Nat. Coun. Tchrs. Math., Cath. Sch. Adminstrs. Assn. N.Y. State. Office: St Joseph Sch 20 Hackensack St East Rutherford NJ 07073 Personal E-mail: fralberta@comcast.net. E-mail: sjser@comcast.net.

ALBERTS, CELIA ANNE, lawyer; b. Denver, May 3, 1953; d. Robert Edward and Barbara Ellen Alberts. BA in French, U. Colo., 1975, JD, 1979; LLM in Taxation, U. Denver, 1984. Bar: Colo. 1979, U.S. Dist. Ct. Colo. 1979, U.S. Ct. Appeals (10th cir.) 1979. Assoc. Dietze, Davis & Porter, Boulder, Colo., 1979-82; sole practice Boulder, 1983-84; assoc. Loser, Davies, Magoon & Fitzgerald, Denver, 1984-87; adj. prof. law U. Denver, 1988; v.p., sr. counsel Merrill Lynch, Denver, 1989-96; sole practice Golden, Colo., 1997—. Mem. ABA, Colo. Bar Assn., Denver Bar Assn. (estate/probate divs.). Avocations: sports, crafts, reading, music. Home and Office: 237 Lamb Ln Golden CO 80401-9426

ALBIN, MELANIE ARLISSE, marriage and family therapist; b. Louisville, Ky., Feb. 24, 1957; d. Mori Irving and Verna Nadine Albin. M in Psychology, New Sch. for Social Rsch., N.Y., 1983; Specialist in Marriage and Family Therapy, Spalding U., Louisville, 1986. Lic. marriage and family therapist Ky., Ind. Dir. LifeSpring Mental Health Svcs., New Albany, Ind., 1984—99; marriage and family therapist Parkview Psychiat. Svcs., Louisville, 1999—, Louisville, 2001—. Author: Total Wellness-How to Live a Peaceful and Harmonious Life, 2002. Mem.: Am. Assn. for Marriage and Family Therapy (clin. mem., approved supr.). Avocations: Golden Retrievers, raising birds and fish, walking, reading. Home: 1911 Buttonwood Rd Louisville KY 40222 Office: Ctr for Integrative Health 105 N Lyndon Ln Louisville KY 40222

ALBINO, JUDITH ELAINE NEWSOM, university president; b. Jackson, Tenn. m. Salvatore Albino; children: Austin, Adrian. BJ, U. Tex., 1967, PhD, 1973. Mem. faculty sch. dental medicine SUNY, Buffalo, 1972-90, assoc. provost, 1984-87, dean sch. arch. and planning, 1987-89, dean grad. sch., 1989-90; v.p. acad. affairs and rsch, dean system grad. sch. U. Colo., Boulder, 1990-91, pres., 1991-95, pres. emerita, prof. psychiatry, 1995-97; pres. Calif. Sch. Profl. Psychology Alliant Internat. U., San Francisco, 1997—. Contbr. articles to profl. jours. Acad. Adminstrn. fellow Am. Coun. on Edn., 1983; grantee NIH. Fellow APA (treas., bd. dirs.); mem. Behavioral Scientists in Dental Rsch. (past pres.), Am. Assn. Dental Rsch. (bd. dirs.). Office: Calif Sch Profl Psychology Alliant Internat U Office Pres 2728 Hyde St Ste 100 San Francisco CA 94109-1251 Fax: 415-771-5908. E-mail: jalbino@alliant.edu.

ALBRECHT, KATHE HICKS, art historian, visual resources manager; b. Ann Arbor, Mich., Aug. 21, 1952; d. Richard Brian and Mafalda (Brasile) Hicks; m. Mark Jennings Albrecht, July 20, 1973; children: Nicole, Alexander, Olivia. BA in Art History, UCLA, 1975; MA in Art History, Am. U., 1989. Slide libr. asst. Am. U., Washington, 1986-88, visual resources curator, 1991—; pres.-elect Visual Resources Assn., 2003, pres., 2004—. Co-coord. Mus. Ednl. Site Licensing Project (Nat. Initiative Getty), 1994; presenter Southeastern Coll. Art Conf., Georgetown U., 1995, Richmond, Va., 1997, Norfolk, Va., 1999; mem. Conf. on Fair Use (Dept. of Commerce) VRA rep. to Digital Future Coalition, 1996—; mem. Nat. Initiative for a Networked Cultural Heritage, 1996-2003. Vol. Fairfax County Pub. Sch. Sys., 1980-2000; re-election com. Rep. Nat. Com., Washington, 1984; Rep. precinct worker Mason dist., 1980s. Grantee Getty Art History Info. Program, 1994-97; Am. U. (image processing, database devel.), 1995, 2003. Mem. Art Librs. Soc. N. Am., Coll. Art Assn., Am. Assn. Mus., Southeastern Coll. Art Conf., Visual Resources Assn. (pres. Mid-Atlantic region 1995-96, 2000-02, chair nat. membership com., 1995-97, chair intellectual property rights com. 1996-2000, pres. elect 2003—). Presbyterian. Avocation: antique and prints collecting. Office: Am Univ 4400 Massachusetts Ave NW Washington DC 20016-8001 E-mail: Kalbrec@american.edu.

ALBRESKI, MELODY LOUISE, emergency nurse practitioner; b. Raton, N.Mex., Mar. 15, 1961; d. Ray Richard Coombs and Mary Ellen Foster; m. Robert Gregory Albreski, Jr., July 16, 1983 (div. Jan. 1994); children: Brandon, Ross. Student, U. N.Mex., 1981—83; ADN, Trinidad (Colo.) State Jr. Coll., 1995. RN Colo., N.Mex., cert. legal nurse cons. Adminstrv. asst. Hasstech, Inc., San Diego, 1984—91; RN ICU Mt. San Rafael Hosp., Trinidad, 1995—97, 1998—; RN, mgr. Caring Unlimited Arme Health/Hospice, Raton, 1996—98; RN emergency room/neuro ICU Parkview Hosp., Pueblo, Colo., 1999—2000; v.p. Castellini & Albreski Assoc. Inc., Raton, 2002—. Del. lobbyist Indsl. Union Coun., Washington, 2003. Mem.: United Mine Workers Am. (N.Mex. state compac sec. 2002—04, compac chair 2002—04), Phi Theta Kappa. Democrat. Roman Catholic. Avocations: reading, travel.

ALBRIGHT, JULIA SZUR, artist; b. Nixon-Edesen, N.J., Feb. 14, 1915; d. Kalman and Mary Kovacs Szur; m. Wilbur Elliott Albright, Mar. 1, 1909 (dec.); children: Barbara Lee, Marye Lou. One-woman shows include U. Ariz., 1965, exhibited in group shows, Las Cruces, N.Mex., Tubac, Ariz., Tucson, El Paso. Home and Studio: 8044 Coley Davis Rd 6B Nashville TN 37221-2310

ALBRIGHT, MADELEINE KORBEL, former secretary of state; b. Prague, Czechoslovakia, May 15, 1937; d. Josef and Anna (Speeglova) Korbel; m. Joseph Medill Patterson Albright, June 11, 1959 (div. 1983); children: Anne Korbel, Alice Patterson, Katharine Medill. BA with honors in Polit. Sci., Wellesley Coll., 1959; student, John's Hopkins U.; MA, cert.Russian Inst., Columbia U., 1968, PhD, 1976. Washington coord. Maine for Muskie, 1975-76; chief legis. asst. to U.S. Senator Muskie, 1976-78; mem. staff NSC, 1978-81, White House, 1978-81; sr. fellow in Soviet and Eastern European Affairs Ctr. for Strategic and Internat. Studies, Ctr. for Strategic and Internat. Studies, 1981; fellow Woodrow Wilson Internat. Ctr. for Scholars, Washington, 1981-82; Research prof. internat. affairs, dir. women in fgn. service Sch. Fgn. Service Georgetown U., 1982-93; pres. Ctr. for Nat. Policy, 1985-93; fgn. policy coord. Mondale for Pres. campaign, 1984, to Geraldine A. Ferraro, 1984; vice chmn. Nat. Dem. Inst. for Internat. Affairs, Washington, 1984-93; perm. rep. of the U.S. UN, N.Y.C., 1993-97; Sec. U.S. Dept. of State, 1997-2001; founder The Albright Group, 2001—; chair Nat. Dem. Inst., Washington, 2001—; Michael and Virginia Mortara Endowed prof. in practice of diplomacy Georgetown Sch. Fgn. Svc.; Disting. scholar William Davidson Inst., U. Mich. Bus. Sch. Sr. fgn. policy advisor Dukakis for Pres. Campaign, 1988; mem. Pres.'s Cabinet, NSC; bd. dirs. N.Y. Stock Exchange. Author: Poland: The Role of the Press in Political Change, 1983, Madam Secretary: A Memoir, 2003; contbr. articles to profl. jours., chpts. to books. Bd. dirs. Beauvoir Sch., Washington, 1968-76, chmn., 1978-83; trustee Black Student Fund, 1969-78, 82-93, Dem. Forum, 1976-78, Williams Coll., 1978-82, Wellesley Coll., 1983-89; mem. exec. com. D.C. Citizens for Better Pub. Edn., 1975-76; bd. dirs. Washington Urban League, 1982-84, Atlantic Coun., 1984-93, Ctr. for Nat. Policy, 1985-93, Chatham House Fedn., 1986-88. Mem. Council Fgn. Relations, Am. Polit. Sci. Assn., Czechoslovak Soc. Arts and Scis. Am., Atlantic Council U.S. (dir.), Am. Assn. for Advancement Slavic Studies. Democrat.*

ALCON, SONJA L. retired medical social worker; b. Orange City, Iowa, Aug. 2, 1937; d. Albert Lee Gerard and Clarice Victoria (Brown) deBey; m. Richard J. Gebhardt, June 6, 1959; children: Russell, Cheryl, Kurt Gebhardt Ryan; m. George W. Ryan, Dec. 28, 1968; 1 child, Alanna (dec.); m. David E. Alcon, July 20, 1985. BA, Western Md. Coll./McDaniel Coll., 1959; MSW, U. Md., 1973. Caseworker Springfield State Hosp., Sykesville, Md., 1959-61; dir. social work dept. Hanover (Pa.) Gen. Hosp., 1966-96; ret., 1996. Part-time worker Matthews Hallmark Store, Hanover, 1997-99, 2002; part-time sales assoc. BONTON Dept. store, Hanover, 2003; field instr. Western Md. Coll., 1967-96, mem. social work adv. coun., 1979-81, 84-86; clin. assoc. prof. sch. social work and social planning U. Md., 1987-92; cons. Golden Age Nursing Home, Hanover, 1973-76, Carlisle (Pa.) Hosp., 1974-78, Hanover Vis. Nurse Assn., 1977-83, emergency svcs. Mental Health Clinic, 1972; chmn. profl. adv. com. Vis. Nurse Assn. Hanover and Spring Grove, Inc., 1986-89; ind. beauty cons. Mary Kay 1999-2000. Bd. dirs. Hospice of York, 1980-82, Hanover chpt. ARC, 1976-79, Adams-Hanover Mental Health, 1973-76; pres. Human Svcs. Orgn., 1980, v.p., 1985-86; mem. adv. coun. Hanover Hospice, 1982-85; treas. Hanover Cmty. Progress Com., 1976-80; mem. Adams-Hanover Sheltered Workshop Com., 1968-70; bd. dirs. Hanover Cmty. Players, 1974-77, sec., 1982; organizer local chpt. Make Today County and Preemie Parent Support Group, 1979; initiator, co-trustee Children's Cardiac Fund, 1979-92; mem. Hanover Oratorio Soc., 1964-85; adv. bd. United Cerebral Palsy South Ctrl. Pa., 1989-90; active YWCA, 1979-84, 96-98; co-organizer Adams-Hanover chpt. Compassionate Friends, 1983; mem. vestry All Saints Episcopal Ch., 1973-74, 76-79, 83-86, 97, vestry sec., 1975, diocesan del. Ctrl. Pa., 1978, 80-86, mem. altar guild, 1968-86, 92-93, treas. ch. women, 1979-83, ch. choir, soloist, 1975—; with Hanover Gen. Hosp. Aux., Harmony Ct. No 146 (consolidated with Dr. J.M. Hyson Meml. Ct. No. 106, 2003), Order Amaranth, Hanover Chpt. No. 378, Order of the Eastern Star, Samaria Shrine No. 43, Order of White Shrine Jerusalem; mem. adv. group Inst. Pastoral Care, 1976-77; mem. adv. coun. Parents Anonymous, 1976-79, 85-92; mem. bd. dirs. Episcopal Home at Shippensburg, 1979-85, Ea. Star Home at Warminster, Pa., 1987-89; mem. Queen Christina Found., Grand Court of Pa., 1995-98; adminstr. Hanover Gen. Hosp. Spl. Needs Fund, 1986-96; cmty. adv. com. Healthsouth Rehab. York, 1995-96; co-facilitator I Can Cope classes Am. Cancer Soc., 1989-92; active Cmty. Needs Coalition, 1990-96, South Ctrl. Pa. Coalition for Organ/Tissue Donation, 1994-98; mem. Case Mgmt. Network South Ctrl. Pa., 1994-96; vol. Hanover Gen. Hosp., Hanover Area Coun. Chs. Recipient York Daily Record Exceptional Citizen award, 1979, Spl. Recognition cert. Col. Richard Mcallister chpt. DAR, 1980; finalist YWCA Salute to Women, 1986, 87, Companion of the Temple award Grand Encampment, Knights Templar, 1999. Mem.: NASW, Acad. Cert. Social Workers, Pa. White Shrine Club (pres. 2002—03), Md. Alumni Assn. (bd. dirs. 1983), Samaria Shrine (worthy high 2000), Daus. of the Nile, Social Order of Beauceant (Westminster Assembly No. 245 1999, worthy pres. 1999, organizer, worthy pres. Elizabethtown Assembly No. 265 2000—01, supreme worthy pres. 2003—), Order of Amaranth Harmony Ct. No. 146 (royal patron 1988—89, royal matron 1995—96, grand historian 1998—99, royal matron 1999—2000, grand standard bearer 2001—02, royal patron 2001—02, grand rep. to Eng. 2002—03), Order of White Shrine of Jerusalem (life; Worthy High Priestess 1994—95, Watchman of Shepherds 1999—2000, Supreme Worthy Herald 1999—2000, Material Objective), Order Eastern Star (life; Worthy Matron 1985—86, Hanover chpt. worthy 1986). Home: 6308 Tamarind Dr Spring Grove PA 17362-8949

ALCORN, KAREN ZEFTING HOGAN, artist, art educator, journalist; b. Hartford, Conn., Sept. 29, 1949; d. Edward C. and Doris V. (Anderson) Zefting; m. Wendell R. Alcorn, Apr. 12, 1985. BS, Skidmore Coll., 1971; MFA, Boston U., 1976. Secondary art tchr. Scituate (Mass.) High Sch., 1971-73, Milton (Mass.) High Sch., 1973-79; engr. VEDA, Inc., Arlington, Va., 1979-80; analyst Info. Spectrum, Inc., Arlington, Va., 1980-82, Pacer Systems, Inc., Arlington, Va., 1982-84; dir. ops., mgr. tng. program Starmark Corp., Arlington, Va., 1984; sr. systems analyst VSE Corp., Arlington, Va., 1984-85; analyst, tech. writer Allen Corp., Las Vegas and Fallon, Nev., 1987-88; mem. faculty Western Nev. C.C., 1989, 97-2000; instr. Newport (R.I.) Art Mus., 1990-92; dir. North Tahoe (Calif.) Art Ctr. Dir. Artward Bound, 1994; instr. Sierra Nevada Coll., 1995-98; acting edn. dir., instr. Brewery Arts Ctr., 1996-97; dir. Art Gallery Western Nevada C.C., Carson City, 1999-2000; trustee Western Nev. C.C. Found., 2000-03; arts cons., Nev., 2004-. Exhibitions include Am. Artists Profl. League Grand. Nat., N.Y.C., 1995, 1998, 2003, Nev. Biennial, 1996, Catharine Lorillard Wolfe Art Club, N.Y.C., 1996, 2000, Nat. Oil and Acrylic Painters Soc., 1996, 1998, 2000, Nev. State Libr. and Archives, 1997, Salmagundi Club, N.Y.C., 1997, 1998, 2000, 2002, Allied Artists Am., N.Y.C., 1997, Butler Inst. Am. Art, Youngstown, Ohio, 2001, Audubon Artists Inc., 2001, Great Still Life Adventure II, 2002; columnist, writer: Artifacts Mag., 1998—2001. Finalist Artists' Mag., 1994; recipient Silver medal, Calif. Discovery Awards, 1994, Sarah Marshall and Ida Kaminski Meml. award, Salmagundi Club, 2000, Art Calendar Centerfold Contest award, 1999, Giffuni Pastel award; grantee Sierra Arts Found., 1996. Mem.: Nat. Oil and Acrylic Painters Soc. (signature mem.), Am. Artists Profl. League (Coun. Am. Artist Socs. Graphic award 1995, 1998, Giffuni Pastel award 2003, fellow 2004). Address: PO Box 8000 PMB 360 Mesquite NV 89024 E-mail: alcornart@att.net.

ALCOSSER, SANDRA BETH, English language educator, writer; b. Washington, Feb. 3, 1944; d. Karl Richard and Bernetta Elaine (Hutson) Weis; m. Philip Maechling, May 24, 1978. BA, Purdue U., 1972; MFA, U. Mont., 1982. Assoc. editor Mademoiselle Mag., N.Y.C., 1966-69; workshop dir. Lower East Side Svc. Ctr., N.Y.C., 1973-75; dir. Poets in the Park-Ctrl. Park, N.Y.C., 1975-77; solo artist Nat. Endowment for the Arts, various, 1977-85; tchg. asst. U. Mont., Missoula, 1980-82; instr. to asst. prof. English La. State U., Baton Rouge, 1982-87; assoc. prof. English San Diego State U., 1987-89, dir. creative writing program, 1988-91, 99—, prof. English, 1990—; faculty affiliate U. Mont., Missoula, 1995—, Richard Hugo writer in residence, 2000—. Vis. prof. Southern U., Baton Rouge, 1983; writer-in-residence Glacier Nat. Park, Mont., 1978, U. Mich., Ann Arbor, 1994. Author: Each Bone a Prayerpoetry, 1982, A Fish to Feed All Hunger, 1986, (Associated Writing Program award for Poetry), Sleeping Inside the Glacier, 1997, Except by Nature, 1998 (Nat. Poetry Series selection, James Laughlin award Acad. Am. Poets, William Stafford Poetry award Pacific N.W. Booksellers, Larry Levin award Va. Commonwealth U.); author: (with others) The Central Park Book, 1977, Ariadne's Thread: A Collection of Contemporary Women's Journals, 1982, Introspections: American Poets on One of their Own Poems, 1997; editor The Pushcart Prize Anthology, 1989-91; mem. editorial bd. Poetry International, 1996; contbr. poems to profl. jours. Poetry fellow Nat. Endowment for the Arts, Wash., 1985, 91, COMBO fellow San Diego Arts Council, 1987, Bread Leaf fellow Middlebury Coll., Vermont, 1992, Creative Arts fellow Mont. Arts Council, Helena, Mont., 1993-94. Mem. Poets and Writers, Associated Writing Programs. Avocations: animal rehab., environ. protection, hiking, cross-country skiing. Home: 5791 County Line Rd Florence MT 59833-6056 Office: San Diego State Dept English & Comparative Lit San Diego CA 92182 E-mail: alcosser@mail.sdsu.edu.

ALCOTT-JARDINE, SUSAN, artist, writer; b. LA, June 7, 1940; d. William Kenneth and Hazel Stella (Pearson) Allin; m. Neal J. Jardine, 1996; student LA Harbor Coll., 1958-59, El Camino Coll., 1959-61, Calif. State U., 1961-64, Writers Guild Am. West, Inc., 1970-74; postgrad. U. Calif., L, artist co-program U. Judaism, 2000-; divsn. Teaching asst., lab. technician Calif. State U., LA, 1963-64; with Musifon, Inc., LA, 1965-69; with Mickey Garrett & Assocs., Pub. Rels., LA, 1967-68; freelance reader Screen Gems TV, Burbank, Calif., 1972; corp. sec.-treas., adminstrv. asst., dir. Don Perry Enterprises, Inc., LA, 1969-80; free-lance bus. and pub. rels. writing svc. Susan Alcott's Scribe Svcs. Ltd., Sherman Oaks, Calif., 1981-88; pub. rels. adminstr., editor, feature writer the Spl. Friends of Kenny Rogers Kenny Rogers Prodns. Inc., LA, 1981-87; with music pub. and copyright dept. Cooper, Epstein & Hurewitz, Beverly Hills, Calif., 1988-90; with Sta. KRCA-TV, Burbank, Calif., 1990-94; with Fischbach, Perlstein, Lieberman & Yanny, LA, 1995-96; owner, fine artist ltd. edit. art prints Greendoor Edits., 1999-; actress theatres So. Calif.; actress films, TV, commls.; author numerous poems; contbr. articles to popular mags; pvt. and permanent art collections, U.S., Ctrl. Am.; editor: Patterns, 1982; lyricist Nobody's Child. Recipient Writers Guild Found. award, 1972, cert., 1974, Dorothy Daniels Hon. Writing award Nat. League of Am. PEN Women, 1994, 97; 1st place Fiction Nat. League Am. Pen Women-Simi Valley Br., 1988. Mem. ASCAP, PEN Am. West (Friend), Artist Co-Op7, Screen Actors Guild, Folk Art Soc. Am., Nat. Writers Union (steering com. 1998-2000). Office: PO Box 56839 Sherman Oaks CA 91413-1839 Office Phone: 818-906-9650. E-mail: susanajardine@greendooreditions.com.

ALDAHL, DEBORAH CAMPBELL, elementary school educator; b. Atlanta, Sept. 23, 1951; d. Ted Denson and Leoneard Myrtle Beshers; children: James, Rachel Aldahl Heine. Student, U. Barcelona, Spain, 1978—79; BA, U. Calif., Irvine, 1981; cert. in bilingual cross cultural, U. So. Calif., L.A., 1984. Adminstrv. asst. Agy. for Internat.l Devel., Washington, 1983; tchr. L.A. Sch. Dist., 1984—. Mem.: Calif. Tchrs. Assn., Computer-User Educators, United Tchrs. L.A. (chpt. chair 1987—98). Democrat. Universal Unitarian. Avocations: reading, travel, weightlifting, dance. Home: 1516 Malcolm Ave Los Angeles CA 90024 Office: Cheremoya Ave Elem Sch 6017 Franklin Ave Los Angeles CA 90068 E-mail: daldahl@earthlink.net.

ALDAVE, BARBARA BADER, law educator, lawyer; b. Tacoma, Dec. 28, 1938; d. Fred A. and Patricia W. (Burns) Bader; m. Rafael Aldave, Apr. 2, 1966; children: Anna Marie, Anthony John. BS, Stanford U., 1960; JD, U. Calif., Berkeley, 1966. Bar: Oreg. 1966, Tex. 1982. Assoc. law firm, Eugene, Oreg., 1967-70; asst. prof. U. Oreg., 1970-73, prof., 2000—; vis. prof. U. Calif., Berkeley, 1973-74; from vis. prof. to prof. U. Tex., Austin, 1974-89, co-holder James R. Dougherty chair for faculty excellence, 1981-82, Piper prof., 1982, Joe A. Worsham centennial prof., 1984-89, Liddell, Sapp, Zivley, Hill and LaBoon prof. banking fin. and comml. law, 1989; dean Sch. Law, prof. St. Mary's U., San Antonio, 1989-98, Ernest W. Clemens prof. corp. law, 1996-98; Loran L. Stewart prof. corp. law, dir., Ctr. for Law and Entrepreneurship U. Oreg. Sch. Law, 2000—. Vis. prof. Northeastern U., 1985-88, 98, Boston Coll. 1999-2000, Cornell U., 2002; ABA rep. to Coun. Inter-ABA, 1995-99; NAFTA chpt. 19 panelist, 1994-96. Pres. NETWORK, 1985-89; chair Gender Bias Task Force of Supreme Ct. Tex., 1991-94; bd. dirs. Tex. Alliance Children's Rights, Lawyer's Com. for Civil Rights Under Law of Tex., 1995-2000; nat. chair Gray Panthers, 1999-2003. Recipient Tchg. Excellence award U. Tex. Student Bar Assn., 1976, Appreciation awards Thurgood Marshall Legal Soc. of U. Tex., 1979, 81, 85, 87, Tchg. Excellence award Chicano Law Students Assn. of U. Tex., 1984, Hermine Tobolowsky award Women's Law Caucus of U. Tex., 1985, Ethics award Kugle, Stewart, Dent & Frederick, 1988, Leadership award Women's Law Assn. St. Mary's U., 1989, Ann. Inspirational award Women's Advocacy Project, 1989, Appreciation award San Antonio Black Lawyers Assn., 1990, Spl. Recognition award Nat. Conv. Nat. Lawyers

Guild, 1990, Spirit of the Am. Woman award J. C. Penney Co., 1992, Sarah T. Hughes award Women and the Law sect. State Bar Tex., 1994, Ann. Tchg. award Soc. Am. Law Tchrs., 1996, Legal Svcs. award Mexican-Am. Legal Def. and Ednl. Fund, 1996, Woman of Justice award NETWORK, 1997, Ann. Peacemaker award Camino a la Paz, 1997, Outstanding Profl. in the Cmty. award Dept. Pub. Justice, St. Mary's U., 1997, Charles Hamilton Houston award Black Allied Law Students Assn. St. Mary's U., 1998, Woman of Yr. award Tex. Women's Polit. Caucus, 1998, award Clin. Legal Edn. Assn., 1998, Lifetime Achievement award Jour. Law and Religion, 1998, Harriet Tubman award African-Am. Reflections, 2002. Mem.: ABA (com. on corp. laws, sect. banking and bus. law 1982—88), Inter-Am. Bar Assn., Tex.-Mex. Bar Assn., Stanford U. Alumni Assn., Order of Coif, Delta Theta Phi (Outstanding Law Prof award St. Mary's U. chpt. 1990, 1991), Omicron Delta Kappa, Iota Sigma Pi, Phi Delta Phi. Roman Catholic. Home: 86399 N Modesto Dr Eugene OR 97402-9031 Office: U Oreg Sch Law Eugene OR 97403-1221 Office Phone: 541-346-3985. Business E-Mail: aldave@law.uoregon.edu. E-mail: balaw98@aol.com.

ALDAY, MARTA PERDOMO, library technology consultant, media consultant, art dealer; b. Havana, Cuba, Mar. 24, 1945; d. Jose E. and Celia (Gutierrez) Perdomo; m. Gonzalo Alday, Nov. 23, 1963; children: Marta Elena, Gonzalo Luis, Juan Antonio, Carolina Maria. AA, U. Fla., 1964, BA cum laude, 1973; MLS, Fla. State U., 1980. Cert. media specialist, Fla. Media specialist Heritage Christian, Miami, Fla., 1982-83, Palmer Sch., Miami, 1983-91; libr. dir., media specialist Jones Coll., Miami, 1991-92, Belen Jesuit Prep. Sch., Miami, 1992—2001; co-founder Consortium for Online Tech. Resources Miami Dept. Schs., Pompano Beach, Fla., 2001—. Mem. adv. bd. dor libr. stds. Fla. Coun. Ind. Schs., Miami, 1990—; panel mem. Archdiocese of Miami Schs., 1992—. Author: Handbook of Philosophy and Procedures, 1990. Coord. youth activities Big Five Club, Miami, 1988; chmn. St. Mary Cath. Hispanic Club, Miami, 1994. Recipient Outstanding Svc. award St. Mary Cathedral, Miami, 1989. Mem. ALA, Am. Assn. Sch. Librs., Fla. Assn. Media Edn., Dade County Libr. Assn., Phi Kappa Phi. Democrat. Avocations: reading, volunteering.

ALDEA, PATRICIA, architect; b. Bucharest, Romania, Mar. 18, 1947; came to U.S., 1976; d. Dan Jasmin Negreanu and Sonia (Friedgant) Philip-Negreanu; m. Val O. Aldea, Feb. 17, 1971; 1 child, Donna-Dana. March, Ion Mincu, Bucharest, 1970. Registered architect, N.Y. Architect, project. mgr. The Landmark Preservation Inst., Bucharest, 1971-76; architect Edward Durell Stone Assn., N.Y.C., 1977-79; sr. assoc. architect, project mgr. Alan Lapidus P.C., N.Y.C., 1980-2001; assoc. project arch., mgr. HLW, N.Y.C., 2001—02; plan examiner DOB, N.Y.C., 2003—. Columnist Contemporanul art jour., 1969-73. Hist. landmarks study fellow Internationes Fed. Republic of Germany, 1974. Office: DOB 120-55 Queens Blvd Kew Gardens NY 11415

ALDERDICE, CYNTHIA LOU, artist; b. Des Moines, Mar. 16, 1932; d. Charles Lloyd and Marion Maxine (Hinn) Sandahl; m. Lee Edward Alderdice, Jan. 30, 1954; children: Cheryl Lynn, Kirk Bryan. BA, U. Tex., 1957. Pres. Am. Art Assocs., Inc., Bethesda, Md., 1966-92; v.p. Am. Art Make-A-Frame, Inc., Rockville, Md., 1972-97; pres. Am. Art Assocs, Inc., Annapolis, Md., 1997—. V.p., bd. dirs. Pyramid Atlantic, Inc., Riverdale, Md., 1994—; com. mem. Jewelry from Walters Art Gallery and Zucker Family Collection, 1987, Greek Gold from Beenaki Mus., 1991; com. mem. [illegible] Annapolis, Md., 1988. One-woman shows include: Touchstone Gallery, Washington, 1993, 95, 97, 99, 2002, [illegible] Contemporary Fine Art Gallery, Centreville, Md., 1995, U. Md., University College, Annapolis, 1996, Md. Fedn. of Art, Annapolis, 1997, Robert C. Williams Am. Museum of Papermaking, Atlanta, 1998, Richards Gallery, Westbrook Gallery, Robert Ferst Ctr. for the Arts, Atlanta, 1998, Air Gallery, Annapolis, 1998, Zaruba Gallery, Rockville, Md., 1999, Ellen Noel Art Museum, Odessa, Tex., 1999, Mill River Gallery, Ellicott City, Md., 1999, 2000, Towson (Md.) U., 2000, The Morris Mechanic Theater, Balt., Md., 2002, others; exhibited in group shows Mus. Contemporary Art, Chamalieres, France, 1991, Walters Art Gallery, Balt., 1991, Inst. of the Arts George Mason U., Fairfax, Va., 1995, Montpelier Cultural Arts Ctr., Laurel, Md., 1995, Tarrytown Gallery, Austin, Tex., 1995, Fairbanks Arts Assn., Alaska, 1997, Melvin Art Gallery, Lakeland, Fla., 1997, Towson State U., Md., 1997, Montgomery Coll., Rockville, Md., 1997, Corcoran Mus. Art, Washington, 1997, Fernbank Mus. of Natural History, Atlanta, 1997, 98, Ann Arundel C.C., Annapolis, Md., 1997, 98, Tallahassee Museum of Natural History, 1998, Fed. Res. Bd., Washington, 1998, Washington Arts Club, 1998, Ellen Noel Art Museum, TX, 1999, American Swedish History Museum, 2000, Hanoi Coll. of Fine Art, 2000, Am. Swedish Hist. Mus., Phila., Pa., 2000, Red River Valley Museum, 2001, The Art Gallery at U. Md., Coll. Pk., Md., 2001, Kirkpatric Galleries at Omniplex, Okla. City, Okla., 2001, Hand Workshop Art Ctr., Richmond, Va., 2002, Carla Massoni Gallery, Chestertown, Md., 2002, numerous others; permanent collections include Musee d'Art Contemporain of Chamalieres, France, Artist Book Collection Balt. Mus. Art, Md. Fedn. Art, Internat. Monetary Fund Collection, Washington, Freedie Mac's Collection Honoring Washington Artists, U. Md., The Jane Voorhees Silmmerli Art Mus., N.J., Robert C. Williams Am. Mus. Papermaking, Ga. Tech. Univ., U. Md., Fisher Coll. Bus. Ohio State U., Columbus Ohio, D.C. Commn. for the Arts and Humanities, Washington, D.C., others; author: Best of Printmaking. Recipient individual artist award Md. Arts Coun., 1992. Mem. Md. Fedn. Art (pres., bd. dirs. 1985-87), Md. Printmakers, So. Graphics Art Coun., Friends Cardinal Gallery (hon.), Friends of Dard Hunter. Avocations: tennis, swimming, reading, working on computer. Studio: Annapolis Bus Pk 2104 Renard Ct Annapolis MD 21401-6748

ALDERMAN, AMY JOY SPIGEL, elementary school educator; b. Boston, May 16, 1961; d. Gerald David and Rosalind Natalie (Kisloff) Spigel; m. Wesley Lee Alderman, June 22, 1988; children: Adam Michael, Sara Elizabeth. BA, U. Mass., 1983. Cert. tchr. Mass., Tex. Tchr. Daniel Webster Elem. Sch., Dallas, 1983—88, T. C. Wilemon Elem. Sch., Waxahachie, Tex., 1991—97, E. B. Wedgeworth Elem. Sch., Waxahachie, 1997—99, Turner Mid. Sch., Waxahachie, 2000—, lang. arts dept. chairperson, 2000—01. Mem.: Newspapers in Edn., Assn. Tex. Profl. Educators. Avocations: assertive discipline, accelerated reading, philosophies. Home: 4230 Black Champ Rd Midlothian TX 76065

ALDERMAN, MINNIS AMELIA, psychologist, educator, small business owner; b. Douglas, Ga., Oct. 14, 1928; d. Louis Cleveland Sr. and Minnis Amelia (Wooten) A. AB in Music, Speech and Drama, Ga. State Coll., Milledgeville, 1949; MA in Supervision/Counseling Psychology, Murray State U., 1960; postgrad., Columbia Pacific U., 1987—. Tchr. music Lake County Sch. Dist., Umatilla, Fla., 1949-50; instr. vocal/instrumental music, dir. band, orch., choral Fulton County Sch. Dist., Atlanta, 1950-54; instr. English, speech, debate, vocal and instrumental music Elko County Sch. Dist., Wells, Nev., 1954-59, dir. drama, band, choral and orchestra, 1954-59; tchr. English and social studies Christian County Sch. Dist., Hopkinsville, Ky., 1960; instr. psychology, counselor critic prof. Murray (Ky.) State U., 1961-63, U. Nev., Reno, 1963-67; owner Minisizer Exercising Salon, Ely, Nev., 1969-71, Knit Knook, Ely, 1969—, Minimimeo, Ely, 1969—, Gift Gamut, Ely, 1977—; prof. dept. fine arts Wassuk Coll., Ely, 1986-91, assoc. dean, 1986-87, dean, 1987-90; counselor White Pine County Sch. Dist., Ely, 1960-68; dir. Child and Family Ctr. Ely Indian Tribe, 1988-93. Supr. testing Ednl. Testing Svc., Princeton, N.J., 1960-68, Am. Coll. Testing Program, Iowa, 1960-68, U. Nev., Reno, 1960-68; chmn. bd. White Pine Sch. Dist. Employees Fed. Credit Union, Ely, 1961-69; psychologist mental hygiene div. Nev. Pers., Ely, 1969-75, dept. employment secrity, 1975-80; sec.-treas. bd. dirs. Gt. Basin Enterprises, Ely, 1969-71; speaker at confs.; rep. Ely/East Ely Bus. Coun., 1997—; mem. Econ. Devel. Bd., 1998—; prof. Great Basin C.C., 1999—. Author various news articles, feature stories, pamphlets, handbooks and grants in field. Pvt. instr. piano, violin, voice and organ, Ely, 1981—. Dir. Family Resource Ctr. (Great Basin Rural Nev. Youth Cabinet), 1996—; bd. dirs. band Sacred Heart Sch., Ely, 1982-99; mem. Gov.'s Mental Health State Commn., 1963-65, Ely Shoshone Tribal Youth Camp, 1991-92, Elys Shoshone Tribal Unity Conf., 1991-92, Tribal Parenting Skills Coord., 1991, White Pine C. of C., 2000-; bd. dirs. White Pine County Sch. Employees Fed. Credit Union, 1961-68,, pres., 1963-68; 2d v.p. White Pine Community Concert Assn., 1965-67, pres., 1967, 85—, treas., 1975-79, dr. chmn., 1981-85; chmn. of bd., 1984; bd. dirs. White Pine chpt. ARC, 1978-82; mem. Nev. Hwy. Safety Leaders Bd., 1979-82; mem. Gov.'s Commn. on Status Women, 1968-74, Gov.'s Nevada State Juvenile Justice Adv. Commn., 1992-94; mem. White Pine C. of C.; dir. White Pine Legisl. Coalition, 2002—; mem. White Pine Overall Econ. Devel. Plan Coun., 1992-99; sec.-treas. White Pine Rehab. Tng. Ctr. for Retarded Persons, 1973-75; mem. Gov.'s Commn. on Hwy. Safety, 1979-81, Gov's. Juvenile Justice Program; sec.-treas. White Pine County Juvenile Problems Cabinet, 1994—; dir. Ret. Sr. Vol. Program, 1973-74; vice chmn. Gt. Basin Health Coun., 1973-75, Home Extension adv. Bd., 1977-80; sec.-treas. Great Basin chpt. Nev. Employees Assn.; bd. dirs. United Way, 1970-76; vice chmn. White Pine Coun. on Alcoholism and Drug Abuse, 1975-76, chmn., 1976-77, White Pine County Bus. Coun., 1998—; dir. White Pine Coalation; grants author 3 yrs. Indian Child Welfare Act, State Hist. Preservation, Fair and Recreation Bd. Centennial Fine Arts Ctr.; originator Community Tng. Ctr. for Retarded People, 1972, Ret. Sr. Vol. Program, 1974, Nutrition Program for Sr. Citizens, 1974, Sr. Citizens Ctr., 1974, Home Repairs for Sr. Citizens, 1974, Sr. Citizens Crafters Assns., 1976, Inst. Current World Affairs, 1989, Victims of Crime, 1990-92, grants author Family Resource Ctr., 1995; bd. dirs. Family coalition, 1990-92, Sacred Heart Parochial Sch., 1982—, dir. band, 1982—; candidate for diaconal ministry, 1982-93; dir. White Pine Cmty. Chior, 1962— invited performer Branson Jubilee Nat. Ch. Chior Festival, Mo., Ely Meth. Ch. Choir, 1960-84; chior dir., organist Sacred Heart Ch., 1984—; Precinct reporter ABC News, 1966; speaker U.S. Atty. Gen. Conf. Bringing Nev. Together; bd. dirs. White Pine Juvenile Cabinet, 1993—, Ely/East Ely Bus. Coun., 1997—, Econ. Devel. Bd., 1998—. Named scholar, Nat. Trust for Hist. Preservation, 2000; recipient Recognition rose, Alpha Chi State Delta Kappa Gamma, 1994, Recognition Rose, 2002, Perserving America's Treasures in the 21st Century, 2001; grantee, Nat. Trust for Historic Preservation, L.A., 2000. Fellow Am. Coll. Musicians, Nat. Guild Piano Tchrs.; mem. NEA (life), UDC, DAR, Nat. Fedn. Ind. Bus. (dist. chair 1971-85, nat. guardian coun. 1985—, state guardian coun. 1987—), AAUW (pres. Wells br. 1957-58, pres. White Pine br. 1965-66, 86-87, 89-91, 93—, bd. dirs. 1965-87, rep. edn. 1965-67, implementation chair 1967-69, area advisor 1969-73, 89-91), Nat. Fedn. Bus. and Profl. Women (1st v.p. Ely chpt. 1965-66, pres. Ely chpt. 1966-68, 74-76, 85—, bd. dirs. Nev. chpt. 1966—, 1st v.p. Nev. Fedn. 1970-71, pres. Nev. chpt. 1972-73,nat. bd. dirs. 1972-73), White Pine County Mental Health Assn. (pres. 1960-63, 78—), Mensa (supr. testing 1965—), White Pine C. of C., Delta Kappa Gamma (br. pres. 1968-72, 94-99, state bd. 1967—, chpt. parliamentarian 1974-78, 99—, state 1st v.p. 1967-69, state pres. 1969-71, nat. bd. 1969-71, state parliamentarian 1971-73, 95—, chmn. state nominating com. 1995-97, chmn. bylaws com. 2003—, workshop presenter on aging 1995, presenter 1998-99), White Pine Knife and Fork Club (1st v.p. 1969-70, pres. 1970-71, bd. dirs. 1979—), Soc. Descs. of Knights of Most Noble Order of Garter, Nat. Soc. Magna Charta Dames. Office: PO Box 150457 Ely NV 89315-0457

ALDERMAN, SHIRLEY M., insurance agent; b. Woodlawn, Va., July 13, 1944; d. Raymond G. and Pearl M. [illegible] Alderman, June 6, 1964 (div.); children: Sheila G. Shupe, Melanie D. Stone. Student, Nat. Bus. Coll., Roanoke, Va., 1963. Lic. property, casualty, health, life agt. 1974. Sec., bookkeeper, agt. Hanks Ins., Galax, Va., 1965—80, owner, pres., 1980—. Pres. TiA Inc., Galax, 1998—. Sec.-treas. Woodlawn Pentecostal Holiness Ch., Va., 2000. Office Phone: 276-236-2297.

ALDERSON, GLORIA FRANCES DALE, rehabilitation specialist; b. Rainelle, W.Va., May 11, 1945; d. Orval Rupert and Juanita Rose (Nelson) Dale; m. Grayson Raines Alderson, June 3, 1964; children: John Grayson, James Leslie. ADN, U. Charleston; BS, W.Va. U. DON Charleston Area Med. Ctr., Charleston, 1977-84; head nurse Eye & Ear Clinic, Charleston, 1981-84; owner, operator ABZ Nursing, Kanawha County, W.Va., 1983-87; rehab. specialist W.Va., 1983—. Bd. dirs. Profl. and Social Com. on Nursing. Bd. dirs. Urban Politics Symposium, Charleston, 1978; election campaign mgr. Rep. Party, Charleston. Bd. Regents scholar, W.Va. U., 1974-77; named Woman of Yr., Am. Biographical Assn., 1996-97, Internat. Ambassadore with hn. title HE, Cambridge, Eng. and the Crown, 1998. Mem.: AAUW, Internat. Platform Assn., Internat. Soc. Poets (Nominee Poet of Yr. 1997), Am. Rehab. Profls., Am. Bd. Disability Analysts (life; cert., diplomate), Menniger Soc., Order Ea. Star. Avocations: painting, writing. Home and Office: 1089 Highland Dr Saint Albans WV 25177-3675

ALDERSON, JO BARTELS, writer, poet; b. Janesville, Wis., Sept. 21, 1930; d. Frederick Carl William and Rose Augusta Theresa (Griesbach) Bartels; m. James Michael Alderson, Sr., June 21, 1952; children: James Jr. (Mick), Kaye, Jaye, Ann, Erica. BA, Milton Coll., 1952. Part-time reporter Janesville Gazette, 1949—52; tchr. Oshkosh (Wis.) Area Schs., 1958—59, play dir., 1962—67; proofreader The Paper for Ctrl. Wis., Oshkosh, 1968—70; tchr. writing workshops Johnson Found., Racine, Wis., 1969—70; guide/publs. editor Paine Art Ctr. and Arboretum, Oshkosh, 1974—92; freelance writer, 1960—. Pres., editor, bd. mem. Wis. Fellowship Poets, 1960—; bd. mem. Coun. for Wis. Writers, Milw., 1962—78, pres., 1976—78; judge various state and nat. literary contests; judge H.S. forensic contests; treas., dir., actor, bd. mem. The Co. for Wis. Arts, Oshkosh, 1977—94. Author: (biography) The Man Mazzuchelli, 1974, Rain From a Clear Sky, 1991 (Nat. Fedn. Press Women award, 1993), (history book) Wisconsin's Early French Habitants, 1998 (Nat. Fedn. Press Women award, 1999), (poetry book) Owls, 1980, Owls Too and II, 1984, Tri-Owls, 1988 (1st place Nat. Fedn. Press Women, 1989), Rudd Owls (1st place Nat. Fedn. Press Women, 1996), From the Fairy Tales, 2003; editor: (anthology) Poems Out of Wisconsin III, 1967, (history book and catalogue) 30th Anniversary Book of Paine Art Center, 1981, (mag.) inner-mission, 1983—92; contbr. poetry, articles, essays and play revs. to publs. Dir., actor 4 cmty. theatre groups, Wis., 1953—95; founder, pres., bd. mem. The Grand Opera House Com., Oshkosh, 1965—80; mem. Oshkosh Found. Arts Com., 1997—98. Recipient 4th Pl., Nat. Legacies Contest, N.Y., 1994. Mem.: Coun. for Wis. Writers (newsletter editor), Wis. Regional Writers, Wis. Fellowship Poets (bd. mem. 1951—, newsletter editor), Nat. Fedn. Press Women, Wis. Press Women (treas. 2000—, newsletter editor). Avocations: travel, remodeling houses, art, sewing, exploring nature. Home: 1950 Georgia St Oshkosh WI 54902

ALDERSON, MARGARET NORTHROP, arts administrator, educator, artist; b. Washington, Nov. 28, 1936; d. Vernon D. and Margaret (Lloyd) Northrop; m. Donald Marr Alderson, Jr., June 4, 1955; children: Donald Marr III, Barbara Lynn Hennessy, Brian Keith, Graham Dean. Student, George Washington U., 1954-55; AA, Monterey Peninsula Jr. Coll., 1962. Staff, tchr. Galerie Jaclande, Springfield, Va., 1972-73; artist, tchr. Studio 7 Torpedo Factory Art Ctr., Alexandria, Va., 1974—, dir. ctr., 1979-85; tchr. Fairfax County Recreation, 1972-73, Art League Schs., Alexandria, 1978—92. Tchr. ann. Feb. Workshops Accapulco, Mex., 1985-2000, English painting workshop, 1989-91, 93, 95, 98, Santa Fe workshop, 1991-92, 95-96, 98, 2000, Italian Watercolor workshop, 1996-97, Provence France workshop, 1995, Day of Dead workshop, Mex., 2000, Andalusian workshop, 2000, Bali Painting workshop, 2000, Irish Painting Workshop, 2002; ptnr. Soho Hubris Art Gallery, N.Y., 1977-78; pres. Touchstone Gallery, Washington; cons. in field. One woman shows include Way Up Gallery, Livermore, Calif., 1971, Lynchburg (Va.) Coll., 1978, Farm House Gallery, Rehobeth, Del., 1979, Art League Gallery, Alexandria, 1980, 86, 93, Lyceum Mus., Alexandria, 1987, Alexandria Mus., 1987-88, William Ris Gallery, Stone Harbor, N.J., 1988, Touchstone Gallery, Washington, 1992, 94, 96, 98, 2000, 2002, 20th Century Gallery, Williamsburg, Va., 1996, Mus. Southwest, Midland, Tex., 1998; exhibited in group shows at Art League Gallery, Alexandria, 1972—, Lynchburg Coll., 1978, Montgomery (Ala.) Mus., 1980, Art Barn, 1989, Moscow-Washington Art Exch. Exhibit Internat., Moscow, 1990, Washington, 1991, Fernbank Mus. Natural History Mus., 1997-98, Bennet Gallery, Knoxville, Tenn., 1998; represented in permanent collections Texaco, Inc., Phillip Morse Collection, United Va. Bank, CSX Corp., Fannie Mae Corp., Acacia Fin. Group, Office U.S. Atty. Gen., Office Ins. Gen., EPA, Aerospace Corp., Texaco Corp.; traveling shows include Chrysler Mus. Biennial, 1988, Audubon Artists Nat. Show, 1989, Balt. Regional Watercolor Ann., 1989. Project supr. City Alexandria for Torpedo Factory Art Ctr., 1978-83; festival chmn. City Festival Cultural Arts, Livermore, Calif., 1971; bd. dirs. Cultural Alliance Greater Washington, 1982—, Torpedo Factory Art Ctr., 1978—; mem. Ptnrs. Liveable Places, 1979—, Catherine Llorilard Wolfe Art Soc.; pres. Touchstone Art Coop.; mem. Virginians for the Arts. Recipient Balt. watercolor regional ann. Md. Foun. award, 1989, Elgie and David Ject Kay award Audubon Artists ann., 1989, 1st pl. award in watercolor Arts League, 1975, 76, 77, 82, 84-85, numerous purchase awards, Jane Morton Norman award Ky. Nat. Watercolor Show, 1986, Adirondack Nat. Watercolor Show, 1987, 3d award Catherine Lorillard Show, N.Y.C., 1987, Albert Ehringer award, 1989, Holbein award Mid Atlantic Watercolor Regional show, 1992, Pruchase award d'Arches Paer Co., Knickerbocker Exhibit, Best in Show award Deland Mus. Art, 1993, Catherine Lovell award, 1993; nominated Woman of Yr. Alexandria C. of C., 1992, 93, Living Legend award City Alexandria Commn. Women, 1999. Mem. Fed. Nat. Mortgage Assn., Va. Watercolor Assn. (pres. 1982, 1st place award ann. exhibit 1980, 82, excellence award 1989, 94), Potomac Valley Watercolorists (pres. 1978), Torpedo Factory Artists Assn. (pres. 1977-78), Springfield Art Guild (pres. 1977), Artists Equity, Am. Coun. Arts., Am. Watercolor Soc., Am. Coun. Univ. & Community Arts Ctrs., Phila. Watercolor Club, Watercolor West, Soc. Layerists Multi-Media, Va. Watercolor Soc. Am. Profl. Artists' League, Am. Mgmt. Assn., Nat. Hist. Trust, Ga. Watercolor Soc., Miss. Watercolor Soc., La. Watercolor Soc., Ky. Watercolor Soc., Catherine Llorilard Wolfe Club. Republican. Home: 2204 Windsor Rd Alexandria VA 22307-1018 Studio: Torpedo Factory Art Ctr 105 N Union St # 7 Alexandria VA 22314-3217 E-mail: margalderson@worldnet.att.net.

ALDREDGE, THEONI VACHLIOTIS, costume designer; b. Athens, Greece, Aug. 22, 1932; d. Gen. Athanasios and Meropi (Gregoriades) Vachliotis; m. Thomas E. Aldredge, Dec. 10, 1953. Student, Am. Sch., Athens, 1949—53, Goodman Theatre, Chgo.; LHD, De Paul U., 1985. Mem. design staff Goodman Theatre, 1951-53; head designer N.Y. Shakespeare Festival, 1962—. Designer numerous Broadway and off Broadway shows, ballet, opera, TV spls.; films include Girl of the Night, You're a Big Boy Now, No Way to Treat a Lady, Uptight, Last Summer, I Never Sang for My Father, Promise at Dawn, The Great Gatsby (Brit. Motion Picture Acad. award 1976), Network, The Cheap Detective, The Fury, The Eyes of Laura Mars (Acad. Sci. Fiction Films award), The Champ, Semi-Tough, The Rose, Monsignor, Annie, Ghostbusters, Moonstruck, We're No Angels, Stanley and Iris, Other People's Money, Night and the City, Addams Family Values, Milk Money, Mrs. Winterbourne, The Mirror Has Two Faces, The First Wives Club; over 100 Broadway shows include A Chorus Line (Theatre World award 1976), Annie (Tony award 1977), Barnum (Tony award 1979), Dream Girls, Woman of the Year, Onward Victoria, La Cage Aux Folles (Tony award 1984), 42d Street, A Little Family Business, Merlin, Private Lives, The Corn Is Green, The Rink, Blithe Spirit, Chess, Gypsy (1989 revival), Oh, Kay, The Secret Garden, Nick and Nora, High Rollers, Putting It Together, Annie Warbucks, The Flowering Peach, School for Scandal, Taking Sides, The Three Sisters, St. Louis Woman, The Best Man, "EFX" MGM Grand, Follies 2001 Revival. Recipient Obie award for Disting. Svc. to Off-Broadway Theatre Village Voice, Maharam award for Peer Gynt, N.Y.C. Liberty medal, 1986, Career Achievement award Costume Designers Guild, 2000, DePaul U., 1999, TDF Irene Sharaff Lifetime Achievement award, 2002, numerous Drama Desk and Critic awards; inducted into Theatre Hall of Fame. Mem. United Scenic Artists, Costume Designers Guild, Acad. Motion Picture Arts Scis. (Oscar award Great Gatsby 1975).

ALDRICH, ANN, federal judge; b. Providence, June 28, 1927; d. Allie C. and Ethel M. (Carrier) A.; m. Chester Aldrich, 1960 (dec.); children: Martin, William; children by previous marriage: James, Allen; m. John H. McAllister III, 1986. BA cum laude, Columbia U., 1948; LLB cum laude, NYU, 1950, LLM, 1964, JSD, 1967. Bar: D.C. bar, N.Y. bar 1952, Conn. bar 1966, Ohio bar 1973, Supreme Ct. bar 1956. Research asst. to mem. faculty N.Y. U. Sch. Law; atty. IBRD, 1952; atty., rsch. asst. Samuel Nakasian, Esq., Washington, 1952-53; mem. gen. counsel's staff FCC, Washington, 1953-60; U.S. del. to Internat. Radio Conf., Geneva, 1959; practicing atty. Darien, Conn., 1961-68; asso. prof. law Cleve. State U., 1968-71, prof., 1971-80; judge U.S. Dist. Ct. (no. dist.) Ohio, Cleveland, 1980—. Bd. govs. Citizens' Communications Center, Inc., Washington; mem. litigation com.; guest lectr. Calif. Inst. Tech., Pasadena, summer 1971 Mem. Fed. Bar Assn., Nat. Assn. of Women Judges, Fed. Communications Bar Assn., Fed. Judge Assn. Episcopalian. Office: US District Court Ste 17B 801 W Superior Ave Cleveland OH 44113-1829

ALDRICH, PATRICIA ANNE RICHARDSON, retired magazine editor; b. St. Paul, Apr. 6, 1926; d. James Calvin and Anna Catherine (Eskra) Richardson; m. Edwin Chauncey Aldrich, July 31, 1948; 1 son, Mason Calvin. Student, Stout Inst., 1944-45; BS in Journalism; scholar, Northwestern U., 1948. Editor Child's World News, The Child's World, Inc., Chgo., 1952-57; assoc. editor Home Life mag. Advt. Div., Inc., Chgo., 1957-71, editor, 1971-90, ret., 1990; pres. Aldrich Enterprises, Inc., Chgo. Mem. steering com., publicity chmn. Evanston Urban League, 1961-64. Democrat.

ALDRIDGE, HELEN BELINDA OLIVER, primary school educator; b. Fayetteville, N.C., Dec. 9, 1954; d. Eliza Oliver Price; m. Theodore Dail Aldridge; children: Kevin, LaKisha, Javon. BS in Elem. Edn., Fayetteville State U., 1977, M in Elem. Edn., 1998. Cert. Nat. Bd. Profl. Tchg. Stds. 2000. 3d grade tchr. Laurinburg (N.C.) Primary Sch., 1977—78; tchg. asst. North Drive Elem. Sch., Goldsboro, NC, 1986—90; kindergarten tchr. Spring Creek Elem. Sch., Goldsboro, NC, 1990—. Mem.: N.C. Assn. Educators (Association Representative 1991—94). Office: Spring Creek Elem Sch 1050 St John Church Rd Goldsboro NC 27534-6909 Business E-Mail: helen.aldridge@wcps.org.

ALEMAN, MARTHANNE PAYNE, environmental planner, consultant; b. Houston, Dec. 3, 1938; d. Charles Franklin and Evelyn Inez (Dudley) Payne; m. Samuel Garza Alemán, July 5, 1968. BS in Landscape Arch. magna cum laude, Tex. A&M U., 1988; MS in Interdisciplinary Studies, Tex. Tech. U., 1989; PhD in Urban and Regional Sci., Tex. A&M U., 1995. Engrng. aide City of Austin, 1966-69, Bryant-Curington Engrs., Austin, 1969-72; entrepreneur Rio Verde Farm, San Benito, Tex., 1972-83; rsch. asst. Tex. Tech. U., Lubbock, 1988-91, Tex. A&M U., College Station, 1993-94; cons. Rio Verde Land & Investment Corp., Calvert, Tex., 1995—. Sec./treas., bd. dirs. Tex. Avocado Growers Assn., Weslaco, 1979-83. Author: Soil Salinity in the Texas Lower Rio Grande Valley: Cause for Concern, 1987, Export-Driven Development of Soil and Water Resources: Barrier to Sustainable Development and Inducement to Desertification, 1995. Mem. and active participant Robertson County Hist. Commn., Calvert, 1980-83. Smithsonian Instn. intern, Washington, 1987, Presdl. scholar U.S. Fed. Register, 1993; recipient Nat. Collegiate Archtl. and Design award, U.S. Achievement Acad., Lexington, Ky., 1989. Mem. Am.

Planning Assn., Soil and Water Conservation Soc. of Am. (vol. Heart of Tex. chpt., Waco, Tex.). Avocations: breeding, showing, and training collies. Office: Rio Verde Land and Investment Corp 201 E Browning Calvert TX 77837 Office Phone: 979-364-2631.

ALEMAN, SHEILA B. special education educator; b. Waverly, N.Y., May 8, 1956; d. Anthony J. and Mary K. (Wright) Niemira; m. Edwin A. Aleman, Oct. 7, 1978. BA, William Paterson Coll., Wayne, N.J., 1978, MEd, 1982, postgrad., 1992. Cert. tchr. of handicapped, supr., N.J. Tchr. of handicapped Paterson (N.J.) Pub. Schs., 1978—. Exec. prod. Paterson Edn. Assn. Cable Access, 1991—. Co-author: Special Education Report Card, 1985. Bd. dirs., mem. state com. Kids Voting-U.S.A., Paterson Edn. Found., 1995—. Named Tchr. of Yr., Gov.'s Tchr. Recognition Program, 1991-92. Mem. Paterson Edn. Assn. (exec. bd. 1991—, co-founder/co-chair spl. edn. com. 1993—). Democrat. Roman Catholic. Avocations: Japanese embroidery, reading. Home: 38 Henry Ter Lincoln Park NJ 07035-2007

ALENIKOFF, FRANCES, choreographer, performer, writer, dancer, artist; b. N.Y.C., Aug. 20, 1920; d. Clement Jack Lipman and Ruth (Alder) Taylor; m. Martin Freedman, 1956 (div. 1973); children: Francesca Rheannon. BA, Bklyn. Coll., 1940. Founding mem. Dance Theatre Workshop, N.Y., 1968—. Soloist and company at colls., univs., theaters, in festivals and community ctrs. in U.S. and abroad, 1959-93; soloist in films including Frekoba, 1969, Alenka, 1968, Episodes On The Edge, 1973, Shaping Things, 1978; soloist at Lincoln Ctr., 1985; choreographer for Zaide, 1956, L'Histoire Du Soldat, 1957, Josephine Baker Show On Broadway, 1964, Joan and the Devil, 1978; performer Dream Play, 1970, Oddfellows Players, 1991-95; participant in various art festival, 1966-86; dir. Eden's Expressway, 1975—; dance critic Dance News, 1970-82; staff writer Craft Horizons Mag., 1971-74; actress in Wheels Over Indian Trails, 1993, Witness, Blood Summer Rituals, 1994; dancer, choreographer St. Mark's Dancespace, 1996, 98, 2000, 03, 04, Frederick Loewe Theater, 1996, Dance Theatre Workshop, 1996, 97, Soho Arts Festival, 1996, 97, Judson Ch., N.Y.C., 1997, 2001, Downtown Arts Festival, 1998, 99, Dixon Place, Merce Cunningham Studio, 2000, Lifetime TV, 2000, Tribeca Performing Arts Ctr., 2000, Dixon Place, N.Y.C., 2001, 02, Judson Meml. Ch., 2001, Bruno Walter Auditorium Lincoln Ctr., 2003; contbr. articles to profl. jours. Recipient Grant N.Y. State Coun. on the Arts, 1972-80, NEA, 1973-74, N.Y. City Cultural Coun., 1978, Meet the Composer, 1980, N.J. State Coun. on the Arts, 1972, Cine Internat. Golden Eagle award, 1978; named Pick of Yr. for Best in Dance, Village Voice, 1997. Mem. Dancers Over Forty, Artists and Writers Alliance East Hampton. Home: 537 Broadway New York NY 10012-3930 Address: 68 Hog Creek Rd East Hampton NY 11937

ALES, BEVERLY GLORIA RUSHING, artist; b. Laplace, La. d. William Pinckney and Clementine Marie (Madere) Rushing; m. Warren Vincent Ales (dec. June 1991); children: Merrick Vance Patrick, Sheryl Ann (dec.), Lori Patrice. Student, La State U., U. New Orleans. Office mgr. Nat. Auto Assn., New Orleans; cosmetician Labiche's Inc., New Orleans; art gallery owner, mgr. Gallery Toulouse, New Orleans, Village D'Artiste, Metairie, La.; pvt. practice Metairie. Past pres. Metairie Art Guild, Le Petit Art Guild, New Orleans, New Orleans Art Assn.; art tchr. East Jefferson H.S., T.H. Harris Mid. Sch., Magnolia Spl. Sch. Author poetry. Active Rep. Nat. Com., Rep. Pres. Trus, East Jefferson Hosp. Aux.; bd. dirs. Rep. Women's Club in Jefferson Parish; bd. dirs., bd. parliamentarian Rep. Women of Jefferson Parish, 2000—, parliamentarian, 2000-2004; past pres. La Soc. De Femme, Metarie. Recipient Great Lady award East Jefferson Hosp. Aux., Legion of Merit award. Mem. Nat. Mus. Women in Arts (charter), Nat. Authors Registry, Internat. Soc. Poets (bd. dirs.), Heart Ambassadors (v.p.), Plimsol Club. Roman Catholic. Home: 1500 Melody Dr Metairie LA 70002-1924

ALESCHUS, JUSTINE LAWRENCE, retired real estate broker; b. New Brunswick, N.J., Aug. 13, 1925; d. Walter and Mildred Lawrence; m. John Aleschus, Jan. 23, 1949; children: Verdene Jan, Janine Kimberley, Joanna Lauren. Student, Rutgers U. Dept. sec. Am. Bapt. Home Mission Soc., N.Y.C., 1947-49; claims examiner Republic Ins. Co., Dallas, 1950-52; broker Damon Homes, L.I., 1960-72; pres. Justine Aleschus Real Estate, Smithtown, NY, 1975—2002; ret. Exclusive broker estate of Kenneth H. Leeds, L.I., N.Y., 1980-90. Past pres. Nassau-Suffolk Coun. of Hosp. Aux, 1981-82; hon. mem. aux. St. Catherine of Siena, Smithtown, N.Y., past pres., hosp. adv. bd.; past pres. L.I. Coalition for Sensible Growth, Inc.; past v.p. Suffolk County coun. Boy Scouts Am. Mem. Sky Island Club (gov.), S.C. Citizen Police Acad. (alumni). Republican. Lutheran. Address: 2261 The Woods Dr East Jacksonville FL 32246 E-mail: landauntjay@aol.com.

ALESSE, JUDITH, special education educator; b. N.Y.C., Apr. 16, 1953; d. Joseph and Rose Alesse. BA cum laude, Hofstra U., 1977; MS, Adelphi U., 1979. Cert. spl. edn. tchr. N.Y. Spl. edn. tchr. Malverne (N.Y.) Sch. dist., 1980—. V.p. Nassau Reading Coun., Nassau County, NY, 2001—. Office: HT Herber Mid Sch 75 Ocean Ave Malverne NY 11565

ALEX, JOANNE DEFILIPP, elementary school educator; m. Joseph Alex; children: Jessica, Joel, Julianna. BA in Art and Edn., Colby Coll., 1976; grad./cert., Montessori Methods, 1982; MEd, U. Maine, 2001. Tchr., kindergarten, Montessori schs., Various Cities, 1979-83; founder, tchr. Montessori Sch., Stillwater, Maine, 1983—; instr. U. Maine, 2003. AMS Montessori intern supr., Univ. student tchr. placements (supr. tchr.); presenter numerous workshops and confs.; trained facilitator of Systematic Tng. for Effective Parenting; instr. parenting courses; ednl. cons.; facilitator Project Learning Tree, Project Wild, Project Aquatic, Project Wet workshops; coord 1st Maine Tchrs. Forum, 1998. Co-author: I Wonder What's Out There? A Vision of the Universe for Primary Classrooms, 2002. Selected to attend Nat. Geographic Soc. Summer Inst., 1993, Nat. Geographic Soc. Alliance Leadership Acad., 1999; named State Coord. Maine, Nat. Geographic Soc. Action 2003!, Outstanding Environ. Educator of Yr. (nat.), Am. Tree Found., 1994, Tchr. of Yr., Maine Audubon Soc., 1995, Maine Tchr. of Yr., 1998; recipient award for outstanding contbns. to child-care in Maine, 1996; state finalist Presdl. Award for Excellence in Elem. Sci. Tchg. Mem. Am. Montessori Soc. (cert. tchr.), N. Am. Montessori Tchrs. Assn., Maine Montessori Assn. (treas.). Avocations: biking, hiking, wild flowers, children's books, children's resources. Office: Stillwater Montessori Sch 1024 Stillwater Ave Unit 1 Old Town ME 04468-5112 Office Phone: 207-827-2404. E-mail: jalex1@adelphia.net.

ALEX, PAULA ANN, foundation administrator; b. New Haven, May 1, 1945; d. Ralph P. and Louise A. (Pesanelli) A. Student, Conn. Coll., 1962-64; diploma, U. Paris, Sorbonne, 1966; BA, Am. U., 1967; cert. bus. mgmt., NYU, 1978. Exec. asst. Olin Corp., Stamford, 1968-72, Wheelabrator-Frye, N.Y.C., 1973-75; account exec. SSC & B: Lintas, N.Y.C., 1976-82; account supr. Lawrence Charles Free & Lawson, N.Y.C., 1982—84; v.p. Advt. Ednl. Found., N.Y.C., 1985-88, exec. v.p., 1989—, mng. dir., bd. dirs., 1992—. Mem. exec. com. Murray Hill Aux. Lenox Hill Hosp., N.Y.C. Mem. Am. Acad. Advt., Am. Advt. Fedn. Bd., Advt. Women N.Y. Avocations: southeast asian art, opera, riding. Office: Advt Ednl Found 220 E 42d St Ste 3300 New York NY 10017-5806 Office Phone: 212-986-8060. E-mail: pa@aef.com.

ALEXAKOS, FRANCES MARIE, counselor, business owner, psychology educator, researcher, producer, editor; b. Fitchburg, Massachusetts, Dec. 29, 1947; d. Samuel Rosario and Mary (Cucchiara) Sciabarrasi; m. Haritos Kyniacou Agadakos (dec. Feb. 1987); m. Demetrios P. Alexakos (dec. Dec. 1999); children: Katerina, Demetra, Artemis, Alexis. BA in Psychology, U. Mass., 1970; MA in Psychology, Assumption Coll., 1972; BA in Studio art, U. R.I., 1994; cert. in Humanities, Salve Regina U., 1996, PhD, 2003. Social worker, psychologist Mass.; cert. tchr., sch. counselor, R.I. Sr. med. social worker Roger William Hosp., Providence, 1972-78; prof. psychology Johnson & Wales U., Providence, 1991—96; dir. mktg. Oak Internat. Academies, Guadelahara, Mexico, 1996-97; sch. counselor Westerly Sch., 1998—2002; prof. psychology and sociology Dean Coll., RI, 2003—. Mem. vis. faculty summer ethics inst., Dartmouth Coll., 1998. Editor: Mediterranean bur. chief Slugfest lit. mag., 1997-2002; author: Medicine and Health Rhode Island Physicians' Attitudes Toward Genetic Testing and Breast Cancer, 1999. Active Zoning Bd. of Rev., Wakefield, RI, 2001—; trustee U. R.I. Found.; health com. R.I. Women's Commn., 2001—. Daus. of Penelope Scholar, 1994; NIH grantee, 1998; named Person of Yr., Wakefield C. of C., 1987, Leadership R.I. Award 1995. Mem. LWV (chair ednl. grants com.); Rotary (chmn. charitable gifts 2003); Golden Key Honor Soc. Greek Orthodox.

ALEXANDER, ALISON F. communication educator; b. Petersburg, W.Va., Oct. 21, 1949; d. Leason Robert and Ardella (Hevener) Alexander; m. James E. Owers, Feb. 6, 1946; children: Katharine, James. BA, Marshall U., Huntington, W.Va., 1971; MA, U. Ky., 1974; PhD, Ohio State U., 1979. Asst. prof. U. Mass., Amherst, 1979-85, assoc. prof. dept. communication, 1985—. Editor Jour. Broadcasting & Electronic Media; contbr. articles to profl. jours. Mem. Broadcast Edn. Assn., Speech Communication Assn. (div. officer 1983-89), Internat. Communication Assn., Eastern Communication Assn. (v.p.). Democrat. Office: Univ of Mass Dept Communication Amherst MA 01003

ALEXANDER, ANNA MARGARET, artist, writer, educator; b. Greenville, Tex., Jan. 26, 1913; d. Samuel Jefferson and Elizabeth (Smith) Fooshee; m. Joseph C. Jake Alexander, Feb. 12, 1936 (dec. 1988); children: Joanna, Ellen Alexander Stein, Mardi. BA, Rice U., 1933. Cert. tchr. Tchr., Klein, Tex., 1933-38; fashion artist, writer, adv. mgr. Smart Shop, Houston, 1938-43; fashion artist, writer Kreeger's, New Orleans, 1943-45, Everitt Buelow Ralph Rupley, 1953-68; owner Ideas Ink, 1950—54; art tchr. Spring Branch, Houston, 1968-74. Founder Historic Outdoor Art Gallery, New Braunfels, Tex. Vol. literacy program, ch., hist. socs., sr. citizen groups, children's mus., food bank; leader, camp counselor Girl Scouts U.S.A., Houston, 1956-60; pres. Girl's Booster Club, Houston, 1966-68; bd. dirs. St. Francis Episc. Day Sch., 1965-70; Sunday sch. tchr. St. Francis Ch., Houston, 1958-62; active PTA. Mem. Advt. Club Houston, Univ. Women Houston, DAR, Colonial Dames New Braunfels, Garden Club, Ret. Tchrs. Assn., C. of C. Vis. Bur. (downtown design rev. commn., 45 Yrs. as Vol. award 1983), others. Avocations: ecology, church activities, gardening, volunteerism, travel, family activities. Home: 909 Allen Ave New Braunfels TX 78130-4903

ALEXANDER, ANNE A. sales consultant; b. Bartlesville, Okla., Aug. 22, 1927; d. Francis Willard and Cloe Gray Alexander; children: Josiah A. Turner, Kathleen Jane Turner, Christopher R. Turner, Dennis T. Wallace, Jennifer J. Wallace. Degree in Visual Art Edn., U. Kans., 1975, MA, 1980. Cert. tchr., Kans., Mo. Artist Hallmark Cards, Kansas City, 1963-64; art tchr. North Kansas City (Mo.) Schs., 1975-88; sales cons. Transworld Sys. Inc., Mission, Kans., 1991—. Pvt. artist and art tchr., Kansas City. Restored historic statues Old St. Mary's Ch., Kansas City, 1992—; one-woman shows include Parkville (Mo.) Art Gallery, 1986, Mo. Artists Invitational, Riverfront, Jefferson City, Mo., 1985 (award), Art in the Woods, Corporate Woods, Overland Park, Kans., 1982 (Purchase award), River Bend Art Show, Atchison, Kans., 1980 (1st pl. award); exhbns. in group shows include Cottonstone Gallery, Jefferson City, Mo., 1979; represented in pvt. collections throughout the U.S. Vol. Greater Kansas City Cmty., 1968—; bd. mem. Share, Kansas City, 1978-79, SafeHaven, Clay, Platte and Ray Counties, 1978-94, WomenSpeak Steering Com., Kansas City, 1994—, Forward Kansas City, 1994—; commr. Met. Commn. on Status of Women, Kansas City, 1980-82, Kansas City Mo. Human Rels. Commn., 1982-90, Mayor's Key to the City Commn., Kansas City, 1993-95; participant Women's Leadership Inst.-Avila, Kansas City, 1984, Consensus City Planning, Kansas City, 1994; chair Tri-County Domestic Violence Bd., Platte, Clay and Ray Counties, 1990-94; active Sosland Series, Kansas City Pub. Libr., 1998—; bd. govs. Citizen's Assn., Kansas City, 1999; mem. Gladstone (Mo.) Planning Commn., 2000—. Mem. Sales Profls. Internat. (bd. mem. 1996—, Rookie of the Yr. 1997). Episcopalian. Avocations: reading, gardening, advocate for women's issues, dining with friends. Office: Transworld Sys Inc 5799 Broadmoor St Ste 312 Mission KS 66202 Office Phone: 913-677-0020.

ALEXANDER, BARBARA LEAH SHAPIRO, clinical social worker; b. St. Louis, May 6, 1943; d. Harold Albert and Dorothy Miriam (Leifer) Shapiro; m. Richard E. Alexander. B in Music Edn., Washington U., St. Louis, 1964; postgrad., U. Ill., 1964-66; MSW, Smith Coll., 1970; postgrad., Inst. Psychoanalysis, Chgo., 1971-73, grad., child therapy program, 1976-80; cert. therapist Sex Dysfunction Clinic, Loyola U., Chgo., 1975. Diplomate in Clin. Social Work. Rsch. asst., NIMH grantee Smith Coll., 1968-70; probation officer Juvenile Ct. Cook County, Chgo., 1966-68, 70; therapist Madden Mental Health Ctr., Hines, Ill., 1970-72; supr., therapist, field instr. U. Chgo., U. Ill. Grad. Schs. Social Work; therapist Pritzker Children's Hosp., Chgo., 1972-82; therapist, cons., also pvt. practice, 1973—; pres. On Good Authority, 1992—; intern Divorce Conciliation Svc., Circuit Ct. Cook County, 1976-77. Contbr. articles to profl. jours. Bd. dirs., Grant Park Concerts Soc.; sec. Art Resources in Teaching. Recipient Sterling Achievement award Mu Phi Epsilon, 1964. Mem. Nat. Fed. Soc. for Clin. Social Work (chmn. 20th ann. conf., exec. bd.), Ill. Soc. Clin. Social Work (pres. 1986-90, bd. dirs., chmn. svcs. to mems. com., dir. pvt. practitioners' referral service), Assn. Child Psychotherapists, Amateur Chamber Music Players Assn., Jewish Geneal. Soc., Smith Coll. Alumni Assn. (bd. dirs., v.p. 1992-94). Home and Office: 6 Horizon Ln Galena IL 61036-9258

ALEXANDER, BARBARA TOLL, financial consultant; b. Little Rock, Dec. 18, 1948; d. Lawrence Jesser and Geraldine Best (Proctor) Toll; m. Lawrence Allen Alexander, Jan. 25, 1969 (div. 1980); m. Thomas Beveridge Stiles, II, Mar. 7, 1981; stepchildren: Thomas B. Stiles III, Jonathan E. Stiles. BS, U. Ark., 1969, MS, 1970. Asst. v.p. Wachovia Bank & Trust Co., Winston-Salem, N.C., 1972-77; security analyst Investors Diversified Services, Mpls., 1977-78; 1st v.p. Smith Barney Inc., N.Y.C., 1978-84; mng. dir. Salomon Bros., N.Y.C., 1984-91, Dillon Read & Co., 1992-97, UBS Securities, 1997—99, sr. advisor, 1999—2004. Bd. dirs., chmn. audit com. Centex Corp.; bd. dirs., chmn. audit com. Harrah's Entertainment, Inc.; bd. dirs., mem. audit com. Burlington Resources; former chmn. policy adv. bd. Joint Ctr. for Housing Studies of Harvard U.; exec. fellow Harvard U.; mem. nat. adv. bd., bd. dirs. HomeAid Am.; chmn. audit com., mem. exec. com. Habitat for Humanity Internat. Presbyterian.

ALEXANDER, CHRISTINE E. manufacturing executive; b. Norfolk, Va., Dec. 25, 1953; d. Earl and Smiley Thompson; children: Richard L. Hart Jr., Christopher Scott Hart. Student, Tidewater C.C., Virgina Beach, Va., 1994—96. Account exec. WNOR Radio Sta., Norfolk, 1970—72; realtor Bill Jones Realty, Hilton Head Island, SC, 1972—78; pub. rels. dir. Phoenix Inferno, Miami, Fla., 1978—80; account exec. WGH Radio Sta., Norfolk, Va., 1980—86; CEO and pres. Wrecker Wholesalers Inc., Chesapeake, Va., 1987—97, Coastal Art, Inc., Norfolk, 1998—. Chmn. Bus. Adv. Coun., Washington, 2003. Episcopalian. Avocations: tennis, art, swimming. Office: Coastal Art Inc 1170 E Olney Rd Norfolk VA 23504

ALEXANDER, CONSTANCE JOY (CONNIE ALEXANDER), stone sculptor; b. Hillsboro, Ohio, Oct. 13, 1939; d. Laurence Adair and Martha Ellen (Hill-Overman) Lucas; m. Anfred Agee Alexander, June 6, 1959; children: Troy Arthur, Andrea Ellen. Grad., Cin. Art Acad., 1961, postgrad., 1962, Atlanta Coll. of Art, 1977. Represented by Miller Gallery Cin., also various galleries in Ga. and Fla. Exhibited in group exhibitions at Southeastern Artists Ga. Jubilee Festival (1st in sculpture award 1974), Southeastern Arts & Crafts Festival, Macon (Ga.) Colisuem, 1977 (1st in sculpture), World's Fair, Knoxville, Tenn., 1982, David Schaeffer Gallery, Alpharetta, Ga., 1988-93, Ga. Marble Festival, Jasper, 1989 (1st place award), Ariel Gallery, Soho, N.Y., 1989 (award of excellence), 90, 45th Ann. Pen & Brush Sculpture Exhbn., Soho, N.Y., 1991 (Excalibur Bronze Sculpture Foundry award), Ariel Gallery, Soho, 1989-91, Tim Verstegen's The Dutch Framer Gallery, Canton, Ga., 1989-93, Artistic Frames & Gallery, Jasper, Ga., 1991-93, Trinity Gallery, 1994-2003, Atlanta, 1994, Gallery 300, Atlanta, 1994; represented in permanent collections Cin. Pub. Libr., Ga. Inst. Tech., Atlanta, Hartsfield Internat. Airport, North Dekalb Coll., Coca-Cola Internat. Hdqrs., State Art Collection Ga. Sculpture. Recipient Artfest award Habitat for Humanity, 1998. Soc. Friends. Avocations: cross country rock collecting, photography, poetry, home restoration. Office: Trinity Gallery 315 E Paces Ferry Rd NE Atlanta GA 30305-2307 Home: 351 Cherokee St Canton GA 30114 E-mail: trinitygallery@mindspring.com.

ALEXANDER, DOLORES ANNE, retired journalist, advocate; b. Newark, Aug. 10, 1931; d. Dominick DeCarlo and Cecelia Irene Osekavage; m. Aaron J. Alexander, Mar. 1, 1957 (div. May 1, 1961). BA, CCNY, 1961. Stringer N.Y. Times, N.Y.C., 1959—60; reporter Newark Evening News, 1961—64, Newsday, Garden City, NY, 1964—69; exec. dir. Nat. NOW, N.Y.C., 1969—70; co-owner Mother Courage Restaurant, N.Y.C., 1971—77; copy editor Time Inc., N.Y.C., 1974—94; co-founder, spokeswoman Women Against Pornography, N.Y.C., 1979—83; freelance writer nat. women's mags., N.Y.C. Spkr. on feminist issues numerous colls. nationwide, 1970—94; organizer 1st Congress to Unite Women. Co-founder NOW, N.Y.C., 1966; del. Nat. Women's Conf., Houston, 1977; Pres. Carter appointee Nat. Adv. Com. for Women, Washington, 1978—79; officer North Fork Women for Women Fund, Greenport, NY, 1996—2002. Finalist, Catherine L. O'Brian award, 1967, Wonder Woman award, 1983. Mem.: Vet. Feminists Am. (medal of honor 1996, Feminist Authors award 2002). Achievements include pioneering work as leader of second wave women's movement. Avocations: gardening, sailing, bicycling, travel. Home: 965 Mill Creek Dr Southold NY 11971-2624 Personal E-mail: dalexa@optonline.net.

ALEXANDER, EDNA M. DEVEAUX, elementary school educator; d. Richard and Eva (Musgrove) DeVeaux. BBA, Fla. A & M U., 1943; BS in Elem. Edn., Fla. A&M U., 1948; MS in Supervision and Adminstrn., U. Pa., 1954; cert., U. Madrid, 1961; postgrad., Dade Jr. Coll., U. Miami. Sec. Dunbar Elem. Sch., 1943-46, tchr., 194-55, Orchard Villa Elem., 1959-66; prin. A. L. Lewis Elem. Sch., 1955-57; reading specialist North Cen. Dist., 1966-69; tchr. L. C. Evans Elem. Sch., 1969-71. First black woman newscaster in Miami, Sta. WBAY, 1948. V.p. Fla. Coun. on Human Rels. Dade County, Coun. for Internat. Visitors Greater Miami; vice chmn. Cmty. Action Agy. Dade County; chmn. Dade County Minimum Housing Appeals Bd.; active Vol. Unltd. Project Nat. Coun. Negro Women; sponsor Am. Jr. Red Cross, Girl Scouts U.S.; trustee Fla. Internat. U. Found., 1974—79; mem. Jacksonville Symphony Assn. Guild Bd., Salvation Army Women's Aux., Jacksonville U. Friends of Libr. Bd.; past pres. Episcopal Churchwomen of Christ Ch., Miami; bd. dirs. YWCA. Named to Miami Centennial Women's Hall of Fame, 1996. Mem. AAUW (life, Edna M. DeVeaux Alexander fellowship named in her honor Miami br., del. seminar 1977), NEA (life), LWV, Fla. Edn. Assn., Classroom Tchrs. Assn., Dade County Edn. Assn. (chmn. pub. rels. com.), Dade County Reading Assn., Assn. for Childhood Edn., Internat. Reading Tchr. Assn., U. Pa. Alumni Assn., Alpha Kappa Alpha. Avocations: composing lyrics and music, gardening, travel, golf, photography. Home: 805 Blue Gill Rd Jacksonville FL 32218-3660

ALEXANDER, ICIE M. communications executive; b. Knoxville, Tenn., Apr. 10, 1933; d. Jasper J. and Gracie L. (Taylor) Casey; m. William C. Alexander, July 14, 1954 (dec. 1982); 1 child, Billie Jean. Diploma in Supr., Ohio State Extension Studies, 1972. Instr. printing Columbus (Ohio) State Inst., 1967—70; supr. Dept. Printing Columbus (Ohio) Devel. Ctr., 1970—89; loan officer Columbus (Ohio) State Sch. Fed. Credit Union, 1982—89; sec. Labor Union Columbus (Ohio) Devel. Ctr., 1983—86; pres. Internat. Tng. in Comm., Columbus, 2002—03. Treas. Corban Comm. Rsch. Coun., Columbus, 2001—03. Performer: (play) Black to the Truth, 2000. Mentor Cassady Elem. sch., Columbus, 2000—02, Granville T. Woods Sch., Columbus, 2003—; vol. receptionist Corban Commons Sr. Cmty., 2004—. Mem.: Mt. Calvery Bapt. Dist. Assn. (gen. sec. 2001, Dedicated Svc. award 2002), East Columbus (Ohio) Civic Assn., East Columbus (Ohio) Dem. Club (chmn. fundraising 1995—2003), Cmty. Svc. Club. Democrat. Baptist.

ALEXANDER, JANE, actress, former federal agency administrator, producer, author, theater educator; b. Boston, Oct. 28, 1939; d. Thomas Bartlett and Ruth (Pearson) Quigley; m. Robert Alexander, July 23, 1962 (div. 1969); 1 child, Jason; m. Edwin Sherin, Mar. 29, 1975. Student, Sarah Lawrence Coll., 1957-59, U. Edinburgh, 1959-60; LHD, Wilson Coll., 1984; DFA (hon.), The Julliard Sch., 1994, N.C. Sch. Arts, 1994; PhD (hon.), U. Pa., 1995; DFA (hon.), The New Sch. Social Rsch., 1996; PhD (hon.), Duke U., 1996; LHD (hon.), The Coll. of Santa Fe, 1997; PhD, Sarah Lawrence Coll., 1998; DFA (hon.), Smith Coll., 1999, Pa. State U., 2000. Ind. TV, film and theatrical actress, 1962—; chmn. Nat. Endowment for Arts, Washington, 1993-97. Guest artist in residence Okla. Arts Inst., 1982, tchr. adult theatre workshop, 1984, 91, tchr. master class, 1990, Francis Eppes prof. Fla. Stat Univ., 2002—; bd. trustees Wildlife Conservation Soc., 1997—, Am. Bird Conservancy, 1995-98, The MacDowell Colony, 1997—, Arts Internat., 2000—. Author: (with Greta Jacobs) The Bluefish Cookbook, 5 edits., 1979-95, ; translator: (with Sam Engelstad) The Master Builder (Henrik Ibsen), 1978; Command Performance, An Actress in the Theater of Politics, 2000; appeared in prodns.: Charles Playhouse Boston, 1964-65, Arena Stage, Washington, 1965-68, 70—, Am. Shakespeare Festival; plays include Major Barbara, Mourning Becomes Electra, Merry Wives of Windsor, Stratford, Conn., summers 1971-72; Broadway prodns. include The Great White Hope, 1968-69 (Tony award 1969, Drama Desk award, Theatre World award), 6 Rms Riv Vu, 1972-73 (Tony nomination), Find Your Way Home, 1974 (Tony nomination), Hamlet, 1975, The Heiress, 1976, First Monday in October, 1978 (Tony nomination), Goodbye Fidel, 1980, Monday After the Miracle, 1982, Night of the Iguana, 1988, Shadowlands, 1990-91, The Visit, 1992 (Tony nomination), The Sisters Rosensweig, 1993 (Drama Desk award 1992-93, Tony award nomination, Obie award 1993), Honour (Tony nomination), 1998; also appeared in plays The Time of Your Life, Present Laughter, 1975, The Master Builder, 1977, Losing Time, 1980, Antony and Cleopatra, 1981, Hedda Gabler, 1981, Old Times, 1984, Approaching Zanzibar, 1989, Mystery of the Rose Bouquet, 1989, The Cherry Orchard, 2000, Mourning Becomes Electra, 2002, Rose and Walsh, 2003, Ghosts, 2003; appeared in films The Great White Hope, 1970 (Acad. award nomination), A Gunfight, 1970, The New Centurions, 1972, All the President's Men, 1976 (Acad. award nomination), The Betsy, 1978, Kramer vs. Kramer, 1979 (Acad. award nomination), Brubaker, 1980, Night Crossing, 1981, Testament, 1983 (Acad. award nomination), City Heat, 1984, Sweet Country, 1986, Square Dance, 1987, Glory, 1989, The Cider House Rules, 1999, Sunshine State, 2001, The Ring, 2002, Carry Me Home, 2003; appeared in TV films Welcome Home Johnny Bristol, 1971, Miracle on 34th Street, 1973, Death Be Not Proud, 1974, This Was the West That Was, 1974, Eleanor and Franklin, 1976 (Emmy nomination), Eleanor and Franklin: The White House Years, 1977 (Emmy nomination, TV Critics Circle award), Lovey, 1977, A Question of Love, 1978, Playing for Time, 1980 (Emmy award 1980), Calamity Jane: The Diary of a Frontier Woman, 1981, Dear Liar, 1981, Kennedy's Children, 1981, In the Custody of Strangers, 1982, When She Says No, 1983, Mountainview, 1989, Daughter of the Streets, 1990, A Marriage: Georgia O'Keeffe and Alfred Stieglitz, 1991; appeared in TV spls. A Circle of Children, 1977, Blood and Orchids, 1986, Calamity Jane,

1984 (Emmy nomination), Malice in Wonderland, 1985 (Emmy nomination), In Love and War, 1987, Open Admissions, 1988, A Friendship in Vienna, 1988, Stay the Night, 1992, The Jenifer Estess Story, 2001; appeared in TV series: Law and Order Spl. Victims Unit, 2000, (Emmy nomination); Intimate Portrait, Lifetime TV Biography, 1998. Recipient Achievement in Dramatic Arts award St. Botolph Club, 1979, Israel Cultural award, 1982, Western Heritage Wrangler award, 1985, Helen Caldicott Leadership award, 1984, Living Legacy award Women's Internat. Ctr., San Diego, 1988, Environ. Leadership award Eco-Expo, 1991, Muse award N.Y. Women in Film, 1993, Torch of Hope award, 1992, Lectureship award NIH, 1994, Houseman award The Acting Co., 1994, medal UCLA, 1994, Outer Critics Circle award Disting. Voice in Theatre, 1994, Helen Hayes award Am. Express Tribute, 1994, Women of Achievement award Anti-Defamation League, 1994, Margo Jones award, 1995, Mass. Soc. award, 1995, N.Am. Mont Blanc de la Culture award, 1995, Common Wealth award, 1995, Creative Coalition: Christopher Reeve First Amendment award, 1998, Outstanding Leadership for Advancement in Arts, People for Am. Way, 1998, Lifetime Achievement award Americans for Arts and U.S. Conf. Mayors, 1999, Harry S. Truman award for pub. svc., Independence, Md., 1999; Woman of Achievement Award, San Antonio, Tex., 2000, Director's Guild of Am. award, 2002; named to Theatre Hall of Fame, 1993. Mem. AFTRA, SAG, Actors Equity Assn., Acad. Motion Picture Arts and Scis., Acad. Arts and Scis., Actors Fund. Office: William Morris Agy c/o Samuel Liff 1325 Avenue of Americas New York NY 10019

ALEXANDER, JENNIFER LYNN, marketing professional; d. Steven Charles and Diane Marie Alexander. BS, U. Wis., LaCrosse, 2000; MBA, Concordia U., 2003. Mktg. coord. Western Products, Milw., 2000—02; account exec. Promotional Svcs. Group, New Berlin, Wis., 2002—. Mem.: Am. Mktg. Assn. (v.p. fin. and ops. 1999—2000). Home: 8365 Watertown Plank Rd Milwaukee WI 53213

ALEXANDER, JOYCE MARY, illustrator; b. Pepin, Wis., Mar. 31, 1927; d. Colonel and Martha (Varnum) Yochem; m. Don Tocher, June 27, 1955 (div. 1962); m. Dorsey Potter Alexander, Nov. 1, 1963. Student, Coll. Arts and Crafts, 1946, Acad. of Art, 1961-62. Co-founder, owner Turtle's Quill Scriptorium Publishers, Berkeley, Calif., 1963—. Author: Thaddeus, 1972, Happy Bird Day, 1980; illustrator numerous books including: Soil and Plant Analysis, A Practical Guide for the Home Gardener, 1963, CAlifornia Farm and Ranch Law, 1967, Chinatown, A Legend of Old Cannery Row, 1968, The Sea: Excerpts from Herman Melville, 1969, Of Mice, 1966, David: Psalm Twenty-Four, 1970, Shakespeare: Selected Sonnets, 1974, The Blue-Jay Yarn, 1975, Psalm One Hundred Four, 1978, Messiah: Choruses from Handel's Messiah, 1985, A Flurry of Angels, Angels in Literature, 1986, Eleven Poems by Emily Dickinson, A Packet of Rhymes, 1989, Psalm Eight (A Nature Psalm), 1991, Poems, Emily Dickenson, 1992, Comfort Me With Apples-Excerpts From Literature Involving Food, 1993, Father William, 1994, Alice by Lewis Carroll, Excerpts from Alice in Wonderland, 1999; work represented in permanent collections Hunt Botan. Libr. at Carnegie-Mellon U. Republican. Office: Turtle's Quill Scriptorium PO Box 643 Mendocino CA 95460-0643

ALEXANDER, JUDITH ELAINE, psychologist; b. Worcester, Mass., Nov. 30, 1948; d. Frank E. and Winnona V. (Tracy) A.; divorced; children: Kimberly, Jenniferlyn. BS, Worcester State Coll., 1981; MA, Assumption Coll., Worcester 1989; cert. Antioch New Eng. Keene, N.H., 1991. Lic. psychologist. Dir. mental health Indian Health Svc., Ft. Thompson, S.D., 1992-95; cons. self employed, 1995—; psychologist VAMC, Dublin, Ga., 2001—. Adj. faculty Mt. Wachusett C.C., Gardner, Mass., 1996—, Western New Eng. Coll., 1996—. Contbr. articles to profl. jours. Mem. APA, NEA, Nat. Assn. Forensic Counselors, Mass. Tchrs. Assn. Home: PO Box 338 Crownpoint NM 87313-0338

ALEXANDER, LYNN See MARGULIS, LYNN

ALEXANDER, MARIAN G. elementary school educator; b. Cleveland, Nov. 7, 1915; BA, U. Mich., 1936; M Edn., Toledo U., 1954. Tchr. Bd. of Edn. Toledo, Ohio, 1956—84, ret., 1984—. Home: 541 S Saint Asaph St Alexandria VA 22314-4116

ALEXANDER, MARIANNE ELLIS, academic administrator; b. Washington, D.C., June 3, 1940; d. James Garfield and Marian Bissell Ellis; m. Duane F. Alexander; children: Keith, Kristin. BA, Pa. State U., 1962; MA, U. Md., 1964, PhD, 1972. Rsch. staff Md. Constnl. Conv., Annapolis, 1967—68; legis. analyst senate fin. com. Md. Gen. Assembly, Annapolis, 1975—76, staff dir. women's legis. caucus, 1976—78; asst. prof. polit. sci. Goucher Coll., Balt., 1978—84; coord. Pub. Leadership Edn. Network Goucher Coll., Washington, 1984—86, exec. dir., 1986—97, pres., 1997—2003, pres. emeritus, 2003—, bd. dir. Pres., CEO Ellis Alexander Enterprises, 2003—. Contbg. author: Notable Maryland Women, 1977. Chair Women Administrs. in Higher Edn., Washington, 1993—95; mem. nat. bd. Girl Scouts USA, N.Y.C., 1993—2002; founding pres. Pa. State Profl. Women's Network, Washington, 1997—2000; chmn. Hist. St. Mary's City Commn., 1987—89, bd. dir., 1997—2003, Girl Guiding and Scouting World Found., 2000—03. Mem.: Pa. State Alumni Assn. (pres. 2003—). Avocations: music, hiking, gardening. Home: 4713 Manor Ln Ellicott City MD 21042 Office: Pub Leadership Edn Network #900 1001 Connecticut Ave NW Washington DC 20036 Office Phone: 202-872-1585. Personal E-mail: marianne-alexander@yahoo.com.

ALEXANDER, MARJORIE ANNE, artist, art consultant; b. Chgo., Apr. 16, 1928; d. Alexander and Nancy Rebecca (Cordrey) Roberts; m. Harold Harman Alexander, June 13, 1948; children: Jeffrey C., Cassandra J., Peter B., Timothy C., Patrick J. Student, Wilson Jr. Coll., 1945-47; MFA in Painting, U. Ill., 1968, MA in Art Edn., 1972. cert. tchr. K-12: Ill., Minn. Graphic artist Barry Martin Studio, Rumson, N.J., 1963-65; instr. painting, drawing U. YMCA, Champaign, Ill., 1968-72; teaching asst. U. Ill., Urbana, 1968-72, rsch. assoc., 1972-76; instr. art Champaign High Sch., 1973-75, Urbana High Sch., 1976-80, Concordia Acad., St. Paul, Minn., 1982-84, U. Minn., Mpls., 1984-87, design, housing and apparel artist in residence St. Paul, 1984-88; craft cons. and educator tech. asstance program USAID, OAS, U. Minn., Kingtson, Jamaica, 1986—. Design cons. J.A.M. Corp., Mpls., 1988—; tech. cons. OAS, Kingston, 1990-91, Blandin Found. grantee, Minn., 1989—; rsch. and product devel. agrl. unilization rsch. inst., 1992-95; tech. cons. Zabbaleen Paper Project, Assn. for the Protection of the Environment, Cairo, 1993—, St. Lucia Paper project Weyerhauser Found., 1994—, paper project YMCA, Jamaica, W.I., 1997—; co-curator Paper Trivia and Treasure exhibit Goldstein Mus. Design/U. Minn., St. Paul, 2000. Works have appeared in more than 35 solo shows, 1960—, more than 75 invitational shows nationally and internationally, 1985—; work chosen for inclusion from 1996 Internat. Calendar Papierfabak Schufelen Lenningen, Germany; work chosen for poster paper exhibit Leopold-Hoesch Mus., Doren, Germany, 1999; traveling exhibit, Bavaria, Germany, Geneva; work chosen for exhibit Mus. Santa Maria Della Scala, Siena, Italy, 2003, Augsburg Coll. Mpls., 2003, Hist. Mus. Jeongju, South Korea, 2004; represented in permanent collection Imadate, Fukui, Japan, U. Ill., Weisman Art Mus., U. Minn., So. Cross U., NSW, Australia, Montclair (N.J.) Art Mus., Am. U. Cairo, other univs. and colls. and coll. collections; co-author (book): Selected Papers, 1994, Handcrafted paper and Paper Products Made from Indigenous Plant Fibers, 1997; contbr. articles to profl. jours, columns to newspaper. Vestry mem. St. John's Episcopal Ch., Champaign, 1975-78, St. Matthew's Episcopal Ch., St. Paul, 1989—. Recipient Celebrity award, Minn. State Fair, 1984, book First award, 1986, Honorable mention, 3d On/Off Paper Nat., Wis., 1984, 1st prize cmty. fine art exhibit, St. Paul, Minn., 2002, 2003; grantee, Blandin Found., U. Minn., 1989—90, OAS, 1990—91, Agrl. Utilization Rsch. Inst., 1992—95, Weyerhauser Found., 1997, Minn. Arts Bd., 1999. Mem.: Internat. Assn. Hand Papermakers and

Paper Artists (pres. 2003—), Nat. League Am. Penwomen (state v.p. 1994—96, Minn. art chair 2002—), Friends of Dard Hunter Paper Mus. (com. chair 1990—95). Episcopalian. Avocations: swimming, cooking, theatre, travel.

ALEXANDER, MARTHA SUE, retired librarian; b. Washington, June 8, 1945; d. Lyle Thomas and Helen (Goodwin) Alexander; m. David Henry Bowman, June 11, 1965 (div. 1982); 1 child, Elaine BA, U. Md., 1967; MS in Library Sci., Cath. U. Am., 1969. Librarian U. Md., College Park, 1969-72, head acquisitions, 1973-75; asst. univ. librarian George Washington U., Washington, 1975-78, assoc. univ. librarian, 1978-82; univ. librarian U. Louisville, 1983-90; dir. libraries U. Mo., Columbia, 1990—2002; ret., 2002. Chmn. bd. dirs. SOLINET (Southeastern Library Network), 1987-88. Coord. U. Louisville United Way, 1987; bd. dirs. Mo. Libr. Network Corp., 1990-2002; coord. United Way campaign U. Mo., 2002. Mem. ALA (chmn. poster sessions 1983-85, co-chmn. nat. conf. in Cin. 1989), Am. Assn. Higher Edn., Athletic Assn. U. Louisville (vice chmn., bd. dirs. 1989-90), D.C. Library Assn. (pres. 1981-82), Women Acad. Libr. Dirs. Exch. Network. Episcopalian. Home: 100 Mumford Dr Columbia MO 65203-0226

ALEXANDER, MICHELE YERMACK, private school educator; b. Pitts., Sept. 16, 1947; d. Michael and Bernadette (Vogel) Yermack; m. Michael Allen Alexander, Aug. 14, 1971; children: Alexia Michele, Aaron Michael, Adam Michael. BS in Biology, George Mason U., 1969; MA in Sci. Edn., Ohio State U., 1975, postgrad., 1975-79. Cert. sci. tchr., Va., Ohio, Pa. 8th grade sci. tchr. Fred M. Lynn Mid. Sch., Woodbridge, Va., 1969-71; 7th grade sci. tchr. Orange (Va.) Intermediate Sch., 1971-72; sci.-biology tchr. Groveport (Ohio) Madison H.S., 1972-77; biology tchr. Sewickley (Pa.) Acad., 1980-87; substitute tchr. Corpus Christi Sch., Wilmington, Del., 1991-92, full-time sci. tchr., sci. coord., 1993—. Quality monitor Stream Watch of Del., Hockessin, 1989—; state co-dir. Del. Sci. Olympiad, 2002—; bd. dirs.; mem. com. to write Wilmington Diocesan Sci. Curriculum Guidelines, 1995-96. Editor: Energy Activities for the Classroom, 1976. Mem. Sewickley Watershed Assn., 1980-87; nature guide Sewickley Nature Guides, 1980-87; bd. dirs. Conservation Consultants, Sewickley, 1980-87; sec. Bon Ayre Civic Assn., Hockessin, 1981-88, treas., 1988-89; co-leader Girl Scouts U.S., Wilmington, 1989-90; mem. St. Mary of the Assumption Parish Coun., Hockessin, 1990-93. Mem. Nat. Sci. Tchrs.' Assn., Corpus Christi Home and Sch. Assn. (bd. dirs., v.p. 1989-91, pres.-elect 1991-92, pres. 1992-93), Del. Tchrs. Sci., Del. Adv. Coun. Sci. and Environ. Edn., Del. Nature Soc., Phi Delta Kappa. Roman Catholic. Avocations: ballet, baseball, photography, reading. Home: 803 Ciderbrook Rd Hockessin DE 19707-1325

ALEXANDER, MICHELLE LYNN, music educator; b. Stevens Point, Wis., July 24, 1974; d. James Allen and Margaret Louise Barden; m. James Duane Alexander, Jr., June 13, 1998; 1 child, Hunter James. MusB, U. Wis., Stevens Point, 1997; MEd, U. Wis., LaCrosse, 2004. Band and choral dir. Mondovi H.S., Wis., 1997—. Mem.: Music Educators Nat. Conf. Roman Catholic. Home: 303 Spring St Eau Claire WI 54703 Office: Mondovi High School 337 N Jackson St Mondovi WI 54755 Personal E-mail: jmhalex@hotmail.com. Business E-Mail: malexander@mondovi.k12.wi.us.

ALEXANDER, MYRNA B. psychologist, counselor; b. Phila., Apr. 14, 1949; BA, U. Md., 1971, MA, 1972, AGS, 1973; EdD, George Washington U., 1981; BS, Am. Holistic Coll. Nutrition, 1995; postgrad., various training insts. Cert. clin. mental health counselor; nationally cert. counselor; cert. employee assistance profl.; cert. and lic. marriage and family therapist; lic. profl. counselor, Va., Washington. Rehab. counselor Learning Disability Ctr., Clinton, Md., 1973; program dir., vocat. rehab. counselor Walden Res., Kensington, Md., 1974; sr. crisis intervention therapist Emergency Psychiat. Svc., Md., 1974-79; employee assistance program administr., counselor U.S. Dept. Energy, Washington, 1980-81; counseling dir. Profl. Counseling Svcs., Arlington, Va., 1973—; regional mgr. counseling AT&T, Oakton, Va., 1984-96; pvt. practice psychotherapy/cons., 1973—. Asst. prof. U. Md., 1976, George Washington U., Washington, 1992, 94, 96; vis. prof. George Mason U., Va., 1990; employee assistance profl. cons. Contbr. articles to profl. jours; guest spkr. pub. radio and pub. TV. Outstanding Cmty. Effort award Cmty. Leaders and Noteworthy Ams., 1979-80. Mem. Employee Assistance Profl. Assn (pres.), Am. Counselors Assn., Assn. of Employee Assistance Program Profls. (pres. 1994-95). Avocations: exercise, nutrition, holistic health, personal development. Home and Office: 3850 9th Rd S Arlington VA 22204-4169

ALEXANDER, NANCY A. information technology manager, consultant; b. Kansas City, Kans., Mar. 31, 1957; d. Carl Glenn and Norma Louise Hanks; m. Steven Dale Alexander, May 20, 1981; 1 child, Anne Louise. AS in Computer Info. Systems, Kansas City (Kans.) C.C., 1989; BS in Computer Info. Systems, Friends U., Wichita, Kans., 1999, MS in Mgmt. Info. Systems, 2001. Sec., a/c schedule control Trans World Airlines, Inc., Kansas City, Mo., 1976—79, coord. scheduling and planning group, 1979—80, planner, facilities and equipment engring., 1980—81, master planner, facility and equipment programs, 1981—82, mgr., facility and equipment programs, 1982—83; office mgr. Steven D. Alexander, Chtd., Overland Park, Kans., 1983—. Faculty adv. bd. Kansas City (Kans.) C.C., 1988—90; cons. Profl. Support, Inc., Shawnee, Kans., 1983—. Software developer Legal Billing and Analysis System, 1989; author: Think of Your Future, 1992. Troop leader Girl Scouts Am., Shawnee, 1988—92; county coun. rep., project leader 4-H, Olathe, Kans., 1994—97, judge, 1995—97; youth group leader Master's Cmty. Ch., Kansas City, Kans., 1999—2001. Avocations: travel, racquetball, swimming, painting.

ALEXANDER, S. ALLAN, magistrate judge; b. Greenville, Miss., Aug. 25, 1951; BA, William Woods Coll., 1973; JD, U. Miss., Oxford, 1978. Bar: Miss. 1978. Law clk. to chief judge U.S. Dist. Ct., Greenville, 1978-80; assoc. Holcomb, Dunbar, Connell, Merkel, Tollison & Khayat, Oxford, 1980-82; ptnr. Tollison and Alexander, Oxford, 1982-90, Tollison Austin and Twiford, Oxford, 1990-94; magistrate judge U.S. Dist. Ct. N. Miss., Oxford, Miss., 1994-. Adj. prof. sch. law U. Miss., Oxford, 1989-90, 97; sec. young lawyers sect. Miss. Bar, 1988-89; chair Miss. Bar Com. on Cts. in 21st Century 1990-93; mem. Continuing Legal Edn. Commn., 1989-92. Editor-in-Chief Miss. Law Jour., 1977. Bd. dirs. Domestic Violence Project, Oxford, 1983-86, United Way, Lafayette County, Miss., 1986-87. Mem. ABA, Miss. Bar Assn., Am. Inns of Ct., Fed. Bar Assn., Miss. Bar Found.

ALEXANDER, SUE, writer; b. 1933; Student, Drake U., 1950—52, Northwestern U., 1952—53. Writer. Author: Small Plays for You and a Friend, 1973, Nadir of the Streets, 1975, Peacocks Are Very Special, 1976, Witch, Goblin and Sometimes Ghost, 1976, Small Plays for Special Days, 1977, Marc the Magnificent, 1978, More Witch, Goblin and Ghost Stories, 1978, Seymour the Prince, 1979, Finding Your First Job, 1980, Whatever Happened to Uncle Albert? and Other Puzzling Plays, 1980, Witch, Goblin and Ghost in the Haunted Woods, 1981, Witch, Goblin and Ghost's Book of Things to Do, 1982, Nadua the Willful, 1983, Dear Phoebe, 1984, World Famous Muriel, 1984, Witch, Goblin and Ghost Are Back, 1985, World Famous Muriel and the Scary Dragon, 1985, Lila on the Landing, 1987, There's More-Much More, 1987, America's Own Holidays, 1988, World Famous Muriel and the Magic Mystery, 1990, Who Goes Out on Halloween?, 1990, Sara's City, 1995, What's Wrong Now, Millicent?, 1996, One Time, Mama, 1999, Behold the Trees, 2001. Home and Office: 6846 Mclaren Ave Canoga Park CA 91307-2525

ALEXANDER, VERA, dean, marine science educator; b. Budapest, Hungary, Oct. 26, 1932; came to U.S., 1950; d. Paul and Irene Alexander; div.; children: Graham Alexander Dugdale, Elizabeth Alexander. BA in Zoology, U. Wis., 1955, MS in Zoology, 1962; PhD in Marine Sci., U. Alaska, 1965; LLD, Hokkaido U., Japan, 1999. From asst. prof. to assoc. prof. marine sci. U. Alaska, Fairbanks, 1965-74, prof., 1974—, dean Coll. Environ. Scis., 1977-78, 80-81, dir. Inst. Marine Sci., 1979-93, acting dean Sch. Fisheries and Ocean Scis., 1987-89, dean, 1989—. Mem. adv. com. to ocean scis. divsn. NSF, 1980-84, chmn. adv. com., 1983-84; mem. com. to evaluate outer continental shelf environ. assessment program Minerals Mgmt. Svc., Bd. Environ. Sci. and Tech. NRC, 1987-91, mem. com. on geophys. and environ. Data, 1993-98; mem. adv. com. Office Health and Environ. Rsch., U.S. Dept. Energy, Washington, 1987-90; vice chmn. Arctic Ocean Scis. Bd., 1988-89; commr. U.S. Marine Mammal Commn., 1995—; U.S. del. North Pacific Marine Sci. Orgn., 1991-2002, vice-chmn., 1999-2002, chmn., 2002—; bd. govs. Western Regional Aquaculture Ctr., 1989—; mem. sci. adv bd. NOAA, 1998—; bd. govs. consortium for oceanographic rsch. and edn.; mem. ocean rsch. adv. panel Nat. Oceans Leadership Coun., 1998-2002; mem. internat. steering com. Census of Marine Life, 1999—; mem. Pres.'s Panel on Ocean Exloration, 2000; pres. Arctic Rsch. Consortium U.S., 2003-. Editor: Marine Biological Systems of the Far North (W.L. Rey), 1989. Sec. Fairbanks Light Opera Theatre Bd., 1987-88; chair Rhodes Scholar Selection Com., Alaska, 1986-95; pres. Arctic Rsch. Consortium U.S., 2003—. Research grantee U. Alaska. Fellow AAAS, Arctic Inst. N.Am., Explorers Club (sec., treas. Alaska/Yukon chpt. 1987-89, 91-99, pres. 1990-91); mem. Am. Soc. Limnology and Oceanography, Am. Geophys. Union, Oceanography Soc., Am. Fisheries Soc., Nature Conservancy of Alaska (bd. dirs.), Rotary (pres. 1999-2000). Avocations: classical piano, horsemanship. Home: 3875 Geist Rd Ste E Fairbanks AK 99709 Office: U Alaska PO Box 707220 Fairbanks AK 99775 E-mail: veraialex@aol.com., vera@sfos.uaf.edu.

ALEXANDRE, KRISTIN KUHNS, public relations executive, writer; b. Dayton, Ohio, July 15, 1948; d. James Edward and Faith (Colgan) Kuhns; m. DeWitt Loomis Alexandre, 1988; children: James Andrew, Cynthia Lenox Banks. BA, Sweet Briar, 1968. Editor C.I.T. Finance Corp., N.Y.C., 1970-73; newscaster Channel 5 News, N.Y.C., 1973-74, Channel 13 News, N.Y.C., 1974-75; editor Champion Internat., N.Y.C., 1975-76; copy editor House Beautiful, N.Y.C., 1975-76; pub. rels. officer Economic Devel. Adminstrn. Puerto Rico, N.Y.C., 1976-80; pres. Kristin Alexandre Pub. Rels., N.Y.C., 1980—. Bd. dirs. Kuhns Investment Corp., Dayton; pres. Robert Kuhns, Inc., Dayton. Bd. trustees Friends Clarence Dillo Libr. Mem. New York Jr. League. Home: PO Box 367 Far Hills NJ 07931-0367

ALEXIS, GERALDINE M. lawyer; b. N.Y.C., Nov. 3, 1948; d. William J. and Margaret Daly; m. Marcus Alexis, June 15, 1969; children: Marcus L., Hilary I., Sean C. BA, U. Rochester, 1971; MBA, JD, Northwestern U., 1976. Bar: Ill. 1976, Calif. 2001, U.S. Dist. Ct. (no. dist.): Calif 1976, Ill, 1976, U.S. Trial Bar: 1985, U.S. Ct. Appeals (7th cir.): 1986, U.S. Ct. Appeals (5th cir.). 1996, bar: (U.S. Ct. Appeals (9th cir.)) 2002. Law clk. to Hon. John F. Grady, justice U.S. Dist. Ct., Ill., Chgo., 1976-77; assoc. Sidley & Austin, Chgo., 1977-79, 81-83, ptnr., 1983-2000; advisor U.S. Dept. Justice Office Legal Counsel, Washington, 1979-81; ptnr. McCutchen, Doyle, Brown & Enersen (now Bingham McCutchen LLP), San Francisco, 2001—. Mem.: ABA (co-chair fin. mkts. and instns. com. antitrust sect.), Bar Assn. San Francisco (chair antitrust and trade regulation sect.). Democrat. Office: Bingham McCutchen LLP 3 Embarcadero Ctr San Francisco CA 94111

ALEXIS, SHIRLEY DAVIDSON, secondary school educator; b. Cleve., Jan. 16, 1947; d. Prinston Luther and Ruth Lee Davidson; m. Clive Emanuel Alexis, June 28, 1986. BA in English, Ohio U., 1969; MA in Performing Arts, Am. U., 1977. Tchr. Cleve. Pub. Schs., 1969—75; grad. instr. Am. U., Washington, 1976—77; tchr. Arlington (Va.) Pub. Schs., 1977—78, Montgomery County (Md.) Pub. Schs., 1978—79, 1982—; tour guide, instr. Tourmobile Sightseeing Co., Washington, 1977—82; tchr. instr. Montgomery County (Md.) Pub. Schs., 1998—. Mem.: NAACP, Nat. Coun. Tchrs. English. Home: 9213 Turtle Dove Ln Gaithersburg MD 20879 Office: Montgomery County Pub Schs 850 Hungerford Dr Rockville MD 20879

ALF, MARTHA JOANNE, artist; b. Berkeley, Calif., Aug. 13, 1930; d. Foster Wise and Julia Vivian (Kane) Powell; m. Edward Franklin Alf, Mar. l7, 1951; 1 child, Richard Franklin. BA with distinction, San Diego State U., 1953, MA in Painting, 1963, jr. coll. teaching credential, 1969; MFA in Pictorial Arts, UCLA, 1970. Rsch. asst. Health and Welfare Dept., Seattle, 1956; tchg. asst. in drawing, instr. design San Diego State U., 1963; instr. drawing L.A. Valley Coll., 1970-73, El Camino Coll., Hawthorne, Calif., 1971; instr. drawing and painting L.A. Harbor Coll., Wilmington, Calif., 1971-75; instr. art UCLA Extension, 1971-79. Instr. contemporary art Brand Library Art Ctr., Glendale, Calif., 1973; vis. artist Calif. State Coll., Bakersfield, 1980; freelance art critic Artweek, Oakland, Calif., 1974-77; guest curator Lang Art Gallery, Scripps Coll., Claremont, Calif., 1974. Retrospective exhbn. Fellows Contemporary Art, L.A. Mcpl. Art Gallery, San Francisco Art Inst., 1984; represented in permanent collections L.A. County Mus. Art, Chem. Bank N.Y., Ga. Mus. Art., Israel Mus. Art, Jerusalem, L.A. County Mus. Art, McCrory Corp., N.Y., Metromedic, Inc., L.A., N.Y., San Diego Mus. Art, San Jose Mus., Santa Barbara Mus. Art, Southland Corp., Dallas, Spencer Mus. Art U. Kans., Lawrence, Met. Mus. Art., N.Y., Phoenix Art Mus., Fresno Art Mus., Grand Rapids Art Mus., Orange County Mus. Art, Newport Beach, Calif., Palm Springs Desert Mus., Laguna Art Mus., U. Calif. Santa Barbara Art Gallery, Eli Broad Collection, Santa Monica, U. Va. Bayley Art Mus., Charlottesville; one-woman shows include John Berggruen Gallery, San Francisco, 1977, Forth Worth Art Mus., 1988, Susan Caldwell Gallery, N.Y., 1980, Dorothy Rosenthal Gallery, Chgo., 1982, Eloise Pickard Smith Gallery Cowell Coll. U. Calif., Santa Cruz, 1983, Newspace Gallery, L.A., 1976-85, 90-2000, 03, Henry Gardiner Gallery, Palm Beach, 1986, Tortue Gallery, Santa Monica, 1988, Jan Baum Gallery, L.A., 1988, Trabia Gallery, N.Y., 1990, 871 Fine Arts, San Francisco, 1991, Art Inst. of So. Calif., Laguna Beach, Calif., 1991, Fresno Art Mus., 1992, Mt. San Antonio Coll., Walnut, Calif., 1993; exhibited in group shows at San Diego Mus. of Art, 1964, 67-68, 70-71, 77-78, 83, Whitney Mus. Contemporary Art Biennial, 1975, Newport Harbor Art Mus., 1975, Marion Koogler McNay Art Inst., San Antonio, 1976, Long Beach Mus. Art, 1972, 82, 86, Am. Acad. Arts and Letters, N.Y., 1985, 96, Henry Art Gallery U. Wash., Seattle, 1985, L.A. County Mus. of Art, 1979 (Kay Neilson award 1997), 82, Womens Mus., Washington, 1994, Bakersfield Mus. Art, 1999, Santa Barbara Mus. Art, 2001, Calif. State U., L.A., 2001, Laguna Beach Art Mus., 2001, San Jose Mus. Art, 2003-2004, Pasadena Mus. Calif. Art, 2004, Contemporary Arts Ctr., New Orleans, 2004, Norton Mus. Art, West Palm Beach, Fla., 2004, Hudson River Mus., Yonkers, N.Y., 2004. Nat. Endowment for Arts grantee, 1979, 89; recipient Richard Florsheim Art Fund award, 1996, Calif. Heritage Mus. print commn., 1998. Avocations: body building, walking, reading, keeping journal, bird study and videos. Home: 103 Brooks Ave Venice CA 90291-3254 Office Phone: 310-396-3031. E-mail: alf1@earthlink.net.

ALFANO, ELAINE, state representative; b. Washington, Feb. 24, 1952; m. Salvatore c. Alfano; two children. BA, Goddard Coll., 1974. Justice of peace, 1992-96; mem. Vt. Ho. of Reps., 1997—. Asst. to pres. Woodbury Coll. Bd. dirs. Vt. Children's Forum. Jewish. Home: PO Box 93 East Calais VT 05650-0093

ALFORD, ALANA FLOYD, art educator; b. Louisville, Sept. 13, 1974; d. Larry and Joanna Slider; m. Jason Shane Alford; 1 child, Gabriel. BA, We. Ky. U., 1996; MA, Spalding U., 2000. Tchr. Valley H.S., Louisville, 1996—99, Manual H.S., Louisville, 1999—. Mem.: AAUW, Ky. Art Edn. Assn. Office: duPont Manual HS 120 W Lee St Louisville KY 40208

ALFORD, CONSTANCE KEITH, recreational facility executive, artist; b. Louisville, Mar. 27, 1943; d. Jack Edwin Rogers and Constance Kennedy Moehlman; m. Prentiss Keith Alford, Sept. 4, 1965; children: Claiborne Kennedy, McKenna Caswell. AB, Randolph-Macon Woman's Coll., 1965; MA, U. Miss., Oxford, 1967, MFA, 1972. Art tchr. Clay County H.S., Green Cove Springs, Fla., 1965-66; art instr. U. Miss., Oxford, 1967-72, asst. prof. art, 1972-73; asst./assoc. prof. art Alcorn State U., Lorman, Miss., 1975-96; summer crafts counselor Camp Monterey, Tenn., 1984-95, camp dir., 1996—. Lectr. art Elizabeth Gaskell Coll., Manchester, Eng., 1972-73; bd. mem. Miss. Cultural Crossroads, Port Gibson, Miss., 1978-82, dir., cons. summer art for children, 1983-84; commn. panelist Miss. Arts Commn., Jackson, 1988; dir. Port Gibson Main St. Bd., 1991-98. Exhibited at La. World Fair Exposition, New Orleans, 1984; invitationals include Appalachian State U.-Catherine U. Smith Gallery, Boone, N.C., 1988; one-woman shows include N.E. La. U. Gallery, Monroe, 1993, MGCCC Gallery, Gautier, Miss., 2001; group shows include JCC Gallery, Ellisville, Miss., 1999, Bi-State Exhibit, Meridian, Miss., 1999, Miss. Art Colony Travelling Exhibit, 1984—, revolving art program, Miss. Gov.'s Mansion, 1989-90, others. Guest spkr. Alumnae Career Day, Randolph-Macon Woman's Coll., Lynchburg, Va., 1974; mem. Port Gibson Preservation Commn., 1992-98, chmn., 1994-98; mem. Claiborne County Preservation Commn., Port Gibson, 1992-98, v.p., 1996-98; participant, hostess Countryside Inst., Port Gibson, 1996. Recipient purchase award Peat Marwick, Jackson, 1987; Fulbright-Hays Tchr. Exch., Manchester, Eng., 1972-73. Mem. Miss. Art Colony (v.p. 1999—, bd. mem., 1st pl. 1984, Fontaine award Best in Workshop 1985, Marie Hull 1st place 1986, Top Purchase prize 1998, 1st place 1998, 2nd place 1999). Episcopalian. Avocation: collecting art. Home: 1208 Church St Port Gibson MS 39150-2610 E-mail: cm4keith@aol.com.

ALFORD, FRANCES HOLLIDAY, artist, retired elementary school educator; b. Houston, Tex., Oct. 1, 1945; d. Samuel and Nancy Hayes Holliday; m. John R. Alford Jr., Oct. 25, 1996. MEd, U. of Ariz., 1970—72. Cert. Tchr. Tex., 1980. Tchr. Tex. Pub. Schools, 1989—94. Vol. U.S. Peace Corps, 1979—80; trustee The Congl. Ch. of Austin, Austin, Tex.; chair, director's cir., fund raising com. Nat. Peace Corps Assn., Washington, 2001—03; pres. Friends of Korea, Washington. Mem.: AAUW (assoc.), Coun. for Exceptional Children, Austin Area Textile Artists (assoc.), 1812 Club (assoc.). Non-Partisan. Protestant/ Congregational. Avocations: travel, art quilting, philanthrophy. Home: 8100 Hickory Creek Dr Austin TX 78735 Personal E-mail: francesholliday@aol.com.

ALFORD, JOAN FRANZ, entrepreneur; b. St. Louis, Sept. 16, 1940; d. Henry Reisch and Florence Mary (Shaughnessy) Franz; m. Charles Hebert Alford, Dec. 28, 1978; stepchildren: Terry, David, Paul. BS, St. Louis U., 1962; postgrad., Consortium of State U., Calif., 1975-77; MBA, Pepperdine U., 1987; postgrad., Fielding Inst., 1988-90. Head user svcs. Lawrence Berkeley (Calif.) Lab., 1977-78, head software support and devel., Computer Ctr., 1978-82, dep. head, 1980-81; regional site analyst mgr. Cray Rsch., Inc., Pleasanton, Calif., 1982-83; owner, pres. Innovative Leadership, Oakland, Calif., 1983-91; realtor, assoc. Mason-McDuffie Real Estate, Inc., Oakland, Calif., 1991-96, Coldwell Banker, Oakland, Calif., 1996—. Treas. Oakland Multiple Listing Svc., 1994, pres., 1997; bd. dirs. East Bay Regional Data, Inc. Contbr. articles to profl. jours. Bd. dirs., sec., Vol. Ctrs. of Alameda County, 1985, chair nom. com., 1990-91, pres. bd. dirs., 1991—; campaign mem. Marge Gibson for County Supr., Oakland, 1984; mem. Oakland Piedmont Rep. Orgn., Alameda County Apt. Owners Assn., 1982. Mem. Assn. Computing Machinery, Spl. Interest Group on Computer Pers. Rsch. (past chmn.), Nat. Assn. Realtors, Calif. Assn. Realtors (bus. and tech. com. 1997, 2002, bd. dirs. 1997-2003, profl. awards com. 2002, membership com. 2003), Oakland Assn. Realtors (co-chair computer user com. 1992-93, chair 1993-94, bd. dirs. 1995—, chair bus. and tech. 1996, pres. 1998, co-chmn. profl. stds. com. 2001-2004, Realtor of Yr. award 1998), Internat. Platform Assn., Small Owners for Fair Treatment, San Francisco Opera Guild, Claremont Pool and Tennis Club, Lakeview Club. Republican. Avocations: swimming, skiing, opera, horseback riding, gardening. Home: 2605 Beaconsfield Pl Piedmont CA 94611-2501 Office: Coldwell Banker 6137 La Salle Ave Oakland CA 94611-2801 E-mail: realtor@joanalford.com.

ALFORD, PAULA N. federal agency administrator; b. Monterey, Calif., Nov. 18, 1952; d. Paul and Thelma Nuschke; m. James K. Alford; 1 child, Karen Louise. BA, Scripps Coll., 1974; MPA, George Washington U., 1978. Fed. rels. assoc. Adv. Commn. Intergovernmental Rels., 1979-81; dir. fed. legislation and regulations Nat. Assn. Towns and Twps., 1982-86; cons. hazardous materials transp. and environ. issues, 1986-88; dir. external affairs Monitored Retrievable Storage Rev. Commn., 1988-89, Nuclear Waste Tech. Rev. Bd., Arlington, Va. Author various publs. in field. Mem. Pi Alpha Alpha. Office: Nuclear Waste Tech Review Bd 2300 Clarendon Blvd Ste 1300 Arlington VA 22201-3351

ALFORD, RENEE MARIE, speech pathology/audiology services professional, educator; d. James, Jr. and Claudia Mae Alford, Aloysius (Stepfather) and Emily Patricia Chisley(Stepmother). BS in Speech and Lang. Pathology, U. DC, 1986, MS in Speech and Lang. Pathology, 1993. Cert. speech-lang. pathology Va., lic. speech/lang. disorders PreK-12 Va.; cert. early/primary edn. PreK-3 Va., devel. reading assessment Fairfax County Pub. Schs. Tchr. Fairfax County Pub. Schs., Alexandria, Va., 1990—, speech and lang. pathologist, 1990—2000, Chesapeake Ctr., Inc., Springfield, Va., 1998. Presenter mentoring program Fairfax County Pub. Schs., Alexandria, 2001—; presenter troops tchrs. program Old Dominion U., Ft. Belvior, Va., 2002—. Clinic team coord. Mid-Atlantic Pom and Dance Assn. Named Outstanding Young Women of Am., 1988; scholar, U. DC, 1982, 1983; Dept. of Edn. Minority Tng. grantee, 1988—90. Mem.: Am. Speech-Lang. Hearing Assn. (life cert. clin. competence in speech-lang. pathology), Nat. Allied Health Honor Soc., Delta Sigma Theta (life scholar 1984), Phi Delta Kappa (life). Avocations: dance team coach, pom pon coach.

ALFREY, LYDIA JEAN, musician educator; b. Kingsport, Tenn., July 16, 1954; d. Milburn Flay and Betty Jo (Sensabaugh) Brooks; m. Charles Leonard Alfrey, Oct. 2, 1987; children: Benjamin Daniel, Tyler Nathaniel, Ryan Daniel. BA, Anderson (Ind.) U., 1977. Music tchr. Huntington Sch., Ferriday, La., 1978-80; elem. tchr. Warner Christian Acad., Daytona Beach, Fla., 1982-83; pvt. instr. Eustis, Fla., 1993—; prin. pianist First Bapt. Ch., Eustis, 1994—98, Mt. Dora, 2003—. Adjudicator piano competitions Lake County Music Tchrs., Eustis, 1994-97; dir., coord. Summer Music Camps, Eustis, 1994, 95, 97; pianist jazz orch.; guest artist numerous recitals. Mem.: Music Tchrs. Nat. Assn. (publicity chairperson, Fla. chpt. rec. sec. 1994—2001), Nat. Guild Piano Tchrs., Delta Omicron, Kappa Delta Pi, Pi Kappa Lambda. Baptist. Avocations: floral arranging, interior designing, oil painting. Home: 1375 Old Mount Dora Rd Eustis FL 32726-7949

ALGAZI, NANCY, health facility administrator; b. La Havana, Cuba, Jan. 26, 1940; d. Arturo Fernandez and Esther Novo; m. Isaac Algazi, Apr. 17, 1958; 1 child, Arturo J. Gonzalez. MA, U. Havana, 1961, Doctorate in Psychology, 1963. Owner Dollar Realty, Miami, Fla., 1967—82; owner and pres. Velox Internat., Miami, 1983—92; office mgr. CAC Med. Ctrs., Miami, 1991—2001. Talk show host WRHC-Radio Sta., 1990. Mem. adv. coun. United Way Dade and Monroe Counties, Miami, 1983—89; vol. Lions Indsl. Home for the Blind, Miami, 1982—84; mem. adv. coun. Area Agy. on Aging, Miami, 1983—89. Recipient First Pl. Media award, Am. Cancer Soc., 1990. Home: 900 NE 195 St Ste 212 Miami FL 33179 E-mail: I.Algazi@bellsouth.net.

ALI AHMAD, SUSAN VAUGHAN, music educator; b. Chamblee, Ga., Nov. 9, 1963; d. James Donald Vaughan and Sally Janeille Garrett; m. Haissam Ali Ahmad, Aug. 31, 1984; 1 child, Ryan. BMus in Edn., Shorter Coll., Rome, Ga., 1985. Cert. tchr. Ga., 1989. Min. of music Clear Springs Bapt. Ch., Alpharetta, Ga., 1985—; music specialist Fulton County Bd. of Edn., Atlanta, 1989—; sch. arts chair Fulton County Schs., 1997—. Elem. music adv. bd. Fulton County Bd. of Edn., Atlanta, 1990—; music com. Atlanta Olympic Com., Atlanta, 1995; music curriculum advisor McMillan/McGraw/Hill Pub., Atlanta, 1998; music educators leadership inst. advisor Ga. State U., Atlanta, 1998—. Bible tchr. Clear Springs Bapt. Ch., Alpharetta, Ga., 1986—2003; associational music dir. Roswell Bapt. Conv., Roswell, Ga., 1998—2000. Recipient Tchr. of the Yr. award, Coca Cola, 1992—93. Mem.: Music Educators Leadership Inst., Ga. Music Educators Assn. Baptist. Home: 705 Brookstone Ct Alpharetta GA 30004 Office: Lake Windward Elem Sch 11770 East Fox Ct Alpharetta GA 30005 Personal E-mail: ahmad@fulton.k12.ga.us.

ALIBRIO-CURRAN, FRANCES J. retired music educator; b. New Britain, Conn., Jan. 16, 1954; d. Joseph and Frances Elizabeth Alibrio; m. Joseph Patrick Curran, July 17, 1993; stepchildren: Joseph Patrick Curran Jr., Shawn Allen Curran. BS, U. Conn., 1976; MusM, U. Mass., Lowell, 1988. Cert. tchg. Dept. Edn., Mass. Asst. music instr. New Britain Sch. Dist., 1972; arts & crafts supr. Lafayette Newbrite Neighborhood Action Corp., New Britain, 1973; lunch coord. Human Resources Agy., New Britain, 1976; theatre arts program instr. Waterford Country Sch., Conn., 1976; gen. music tchr. Suffield (Conn.) Bd. Edn., 1976—77; orch. dir., vocal music tchr. Northborough-Southborough (Mass.) Pub. Sch., 1977—2003; ret., 2003. Musician: Thayer Conservatory Orch., 1977—79, Belmount Symphony Orch., 1980—82, G. Marlboro Symphony Orch., 1990—91, Parkway Concert Orch., 1991—2003. Mem.: Music Educator's Nat. Conf., Mass. Sch. Orch. Assn. (sec. exec. bd. 1990—93), Mass. Music Educators Assn. (exec. bd. 1987—89, ctrl. dist. rep. 1987—89). Episcopalian. Avocations: bicycling, skiing, swimming, canoeing, hiking. Home: 73 Highbank Rd Franklin MA 02038-2573 E-mail: josephcurran@juno.com.

ALICEA, YVETTE, special education educator; b. Bronx, Aug. 27, 1962; d. Gregorio and Lucia Alicea; m. Leontitsis Eleftherios, Sept. 19, 1997. BA in Modern Langs., U. P.R., 1987; MS in Spl. Edn., CUNY, 1995. Cert. tchr. N.Y. Tchr. English José de Choudens, Arroyo, PR, 1983—84; tchr., asst. prin. St. Patrick's Bilingual Sch., Guayama, 1987—91; tchr. bilingual spl. edn. P.S. 26, N.Y.C. Bd. Edn., 1991—95; tchr. English Betsis Lang. Sch., Athens, Greece, 1996—99; tchr. spl. edn. P.S./M.S. 306, N.Y.C. Bd. Edn., 1999—2000, P.S. 46, N.Y. C. Bd. Edn., 2000—. Recipient Appreciation plaque, Parents Assn. of P.S. 26, Bronx, 1995. Avocations: reading, literature, movies. Home: 163 Timberwood Trail Chelsea AL 35043

ALIGA, OLIVIA R. music teacher, choral director; b. Manila, Philippines, Sept. 8, 1951; d. Fernando Bellapaz Rocha and Thelma Reyes Rocha; m. Norman Asis Aliga, Apr. 24, 1976; children: Norman Vincent, Ferdinand Alphonse, Chester. AM in Music, Pilar Coll., Zamboanga City, Philippines; B of Music, U. Philippines, 1974, postgrad., Vandercook Coll. Music, Chgo. Cert. in Kindermusik. Mem. faculty Vallejo (Calif.) Conservatory of Music, 1982-83; music tchr. New Life Christian Sch., Middleton, Wis., 1983-86; choral dir. Lombard (Ill.) Chorale, 1986—. Music dir. Winfield Cmty. United Meth. Ch., 1988—, trustee, 1995—; bd. dirs. U. Philippines Club Am., Chgo., 1996—, music dir., 1999; music dir., vocal coach U. of the East Med. Chorale, Chgo., 1990-95. Pianist, performed to benefit Marklund Found., Chgo., 1997, and the U. Philippines Club Am., Chgo., 1991. Named to Filipino Am. Chicago Hall of Fame, 1999. Mem. Ill. Music Assn., Ill. State Music Tchrs. Assn., Ill. Philippine Med. Soc. Aux., Philippine Med. Assn. Chgo. Aux., U. PHilippines Club Am. (pres. 2003). Methodist. Avocations: raising orchids, flower arrangements, collecting stamps and coins.

ALINDER, MARY STREET, writer, lecturer; b. Bowling Green, Ohio, Sept. 23, 1946; d. Scott Winfield and McDonna Matlock (Sitterle) Street; m. James Gilbert Alinder, Dec. 17, 1965; children: Jasmine, Jesse, Zachary. Student, U. Mich., 1964-65, U. N.Mex., 1966-68; BA, U. Nebr., 1976. Mgr. The Weston Gallery, Carmel, Calif., 1978-79; chief asst. Ansel Adams, Carmel, 1979-84; exec. editor, bus. mgr. The Ansel Adams Pub. Rights Trust, Carmel, 1984-87; freelance writer, lectr., curator, Gualala, Calif., 1989—; ptnr. The Alinder Gallery, Gualala, 1990—2003; selector and writer biographies Focal Press Ency., 3d edit., 1993. Curator Ansel Adams Centenial Celebration, 2002, Ansel Adams: 80th Birthday Retrospective, Friends of Photography, Carmel, Acad. Sci., San Francisco, Denver Mus. Natural History, Ansel Adams and the West, Calif. State Capitol, Sacto., 2001; co-curator One With Beauty, M.H. deYoung Meml. Mus., 1987, Ansel Adams: American Artist, The Ansel Adams Ctr., San Francisco; lectr. Nat. Gallery Art, Barbican Ctr., M.H. deYoung Meml. Mus., Stanford U., L.A. County Mus., U. Mich.; vis. artist and lectr. Nebr. Art Assn., 1997; Wallace Stegner meml. lectr. Peninsula Open Space Inst., Mountainview, Calif., 1998, Assn. Internat. Photographic Art Dealers, N.Y.C., 1999, Cin. Art Mus., 2000, Eiteljorg Mus., Indpls., 2001; mem. faculty Stanford U., Spring 2000. Author: Picturing Yosemite (Places), 1990, The Limits of Reality: Ansel Adams and Group f/64 (Seeing Straight), 1992, Ansel Adams, A Biography (Henry Holt), 1996, Mabel Dodge Luhan, 1997 (ViewCamera), Ansel Adams: Milestone, 2002, Group f/64, (with others) the Scribner Encyclopedia of American Lives, 1998; co-author: Ansel Adams: An Autobiography, 1985; co-editor: Ansel Adams: Letters and Images, 1988; columnist Coast and Valley Mag., 1993-98, Ansel Adams: Political Landscape; columnist biz travel.com, 1996-98; political landscape (Civilization), 1999; contbr. articles to jours. and popular mags. E-mail: alinders@mcn.org.

ALKON, ELLEN SKILLEN, physician; b. L.A., Apr. 10, 1936; d. Emil Bogen and Jane (Skillen) Rost; m. Paul Kent Alkon, Aug. 30, 1957; children: Katherine Ellen, Cynthia Jane, Margaret Elaine. BA, Stanford U., 1955; MD, U. Chgo., 1961; MPH, U. Calif., Berkeley, 1968. Diplomate Nat. Bd. Med. Examiners, Am. Bd. Pediat., Am. Bd. Preventive Medicine in Pub. Health. Chief sch. health Anne Arundel County Health Dept., Annapolis, Md., 1970-71; practice medicine specializing in pediat. Mpls. Health Dept., 1971-73, dir. MCH, 1973-75, commr. health, 1975-80; chief preventive and pub. health Coastal Region of Los Angeles County Dept. Health Svcs., 1980-81; chief pub. health West Area Los Angeles County Dept. Health Svcs., 1981-85; acting med. dir. pub. health Los Angeles County Dept. Health, 1986-87, med. dir. pub. health, 1987-93; med. dir. Coastal Cluster Health Ctrs. L.A. County Dept. Pub. Health Svcs., 1993-96, CEO, 1996-98, med. dir., 1998-2000; dir. Pub. Health Edn. in Medicine, 2000—. Adj. prof. UCLA Sch. Pub. Health, 1981—; adminstr. vis. nurses svc., Mpls., 1975-80. Fellow Am. Coll. Preventive Medicine, Am. Acad. Pediat.; mem. So. Calif. Pub. Health Assn. (pres. 1985-86, 2004-), Minn. Pub. Health Assn. (pres. 1978-79), Am. Pub. Health Assn., Calif. Conf. Local Health Officers (pres. 1990-91), Calif. Ctr. for Pub. Health Advocacy (pres. 2002-03), Delta Omega. Office: Los Angeles County DHS 241 N Figueroa St Rm 143 Los Angeles CA 90012 E-mail: ealkon@ladhs.org.

ALLAMON, KAREN HENN, minister; b. Jackson, Mich., Aug. 1, 1958; d. Richard Leonard and Lujean Lirones Henn; m. Randall M. Allamon, Nov. 26, 1983; children: Matthew B., Lucas A. BFA, Webster U., 1992; MDiv, Princeton Theol. Sem., 1994—96, post grad, 2002—. Crisis Counselor Life Crisis Services - St. Louis, 1992. Pastor Barre Ctr. Presbyn. Ch., Albion, NY, 1996—; interim spiritual care coord. Hospice of Orleans County, Albion, NY, 1998—99; critical incident stress debriefer COVA, Albion, NY, 1998—2001; instr., worship, sacraments, preaching Presbytery of Genesee Valley, Rochester, NY, 2001—04. Presbyn. worship coord. Presbyn. of Genessee Valley, Rochester, NY, 2001—. Cmty. leadership participant Albion Sch. Sys., NY, 1996; mem. Ministirial Alliance, Albion, NY, 1996—; Legacy of Love endowment com. ARC of Orleans County, Albion, NY, 2003. Recipient One of the Fastest Growing Congregations in the US: US Congl. Study, Eli Lilly Found., 2002, Excellence in Evangelism, Synod of the NE, Presbyn. Ch. (USA), 1998—99, Preaching prize, Princeton Theol. Sem., 1996, Bibl. Theology; Hebrew, Eden Theol. Sem., 1994; Synod Mission Partnership Grant: Leadership Devel., Synod of the NE, 2003. Mem.: Albion Area Ministerium (vice pres. 2003, treas. 2002). Achievements include development of family systems leadership group for pastors. Office: Barre Center Presbyterian Church 4706 Oak Orchard Albion NY 14411 Office Phone: 585-589-9639. E-mail: karen.allamon@ptsem.edu.

ALLAMONG, BETTY D. academic administrator; b. Morgantown, W.Va., Apr. 8, 1935; d. Lonnie R. and Jessie R. (Hoffman) Davis; m. Joseph K. Allamong, Sept. 12, 1954; 1 child, John Bradley. BS, W.Va. U., 1961, MA, 1964, PhD, 1971; student, Inst. for Ednl. Mgmt. Harvard U., 1984. Instr. biology Morgantown High Sch., W.Va., 1961-67; instr. edn. W.Va. U., Morgantown, 1965-67, instr. biology, 1967-72; asst. to full prof. biology Ball State U., Muncie, Ind., 1972-87, assoc. dean, scis. and humanities, 1981-86, dean, scis. and humanities, 1986-87; provost and v.p. acad. affairs Bloomsburg U., Pa., 1987-92. Mem. Ind. Corp. for Sci. & Tech., 1983-87. Co-author: Energy for Life, 1976; author numerous lab. manuals; contbr. articles to profl.jours. Recipient Women of Achievement edn. award Women in Comms. Inc., Muncie, 1981. Fellow Ind. Acad. Sci. Home: 253 Pixler Hill Rd Morgantown WV 26508-9541

ALLAN, JANET D. dean; BSN, Skidmore Coll., 1964; MS in Cmty. Health Nursing, U. Calif.-San Francisco, 1968; PhD in Med. Anthropology. Cert. adult nurse practitioner ANA. Former dean Health Sci. Ctr. U. Tex., San Antonio; dean Univ. of Maryland Sch. of Nursing, Baltimore, Md., 2001—. Recipient 2001 Distinguished Researcher Award. Office: Univ Maryland Sch Nursing 655 West Lombard St Baltimore MD 21201-1579

ALLARDICE, SUSAN M. manufacturing executive; b. Harrisburg, Pa., Nov. 12, 1949; d. Richard E. Bryson and Jacqueline L. Bryson-Kapp; m. John M. Allardice, Aug. 15, 1981; children: Shawn P. Lyter, Benjamin H. Miller, Theodore W. Miller, John M., Scott B., Julie A. Ray. Student, Juniata Coll., Huntington, Pa., 1967—69. CFO Releasomers, Inc., Bradford Woods, Pa., 1982—. Actor: (theatre) Comtra Theatre, CLO (Best Actress, Best Dir. Theatre Asso. of PA, 1988); dir.: (community arts organization) Cranberry Area Council for the Arts. Dir. Cranberry Area Coun. for Arts; vol. Allegheny County Ct. Apptd. Spl. Advocates, Pittsburgh, Pa., 2002—03. Recipient Vol. in Arts award, WQED, 1990. Mem.: Money Bags Investment Club (chief finanacial ptnr. 1998—2003). Avocations: travel, reading, bicycling, cooking, gardening. Home: 508 Delmar Rd Bradfordwoods PA 15015 Office: Releasomers Inc P O Box 82 Bradfordwoods PA 15015 Personal E-mail: bryson@zoominternet.net.

ALLBRIGHT, KARAN ELIZABETH, psychologist, consultant; b. Oklahoma City, Jan. 28, 1948; d. Jack Gahnal and Irma Lolene (Keesee) Allbright. BA, Oklahoma City U., 1970, MAT, 1972; PhD, U. So. Miss., 1981. Cert. sch. psychologist, psychometrist; lic. psychologist, Okla., Ark. Psychol. technician Donald J. Bertoch, PhD, Okla. City, 1973-76; asst. adminstr. Parents' Assistance Ctr., Okla. City, 1976-77; psychology intern Burwell Psycho-ednl. Ctr., Carrollton, Ga., 1980-81; staff psychologist Griffin Area Psychoednl. Ctr., Ga., 1981-85; clinic dir. Sequoyah County Guidance Clinic, Sallisaw, Okla., 1985-88; psychologist Baker Psychiat. Clinic, Ft. Smith, Ark., 1988-90; cons. Harbor View Mercy Hosp., 1988-90, Integris Bethany Med. Ctr., 1992-99; pvt. practice Okla. City, 1990—, Mercy Health Ctr., 1996—. Cons. Family Alliance (parents Anonymous) Sequoyah County, 1985-88; lectr. various orgns.; bd. dir. workshops. Mem. Task Force to Prevent Child Abuse, Fayette County, Ga., 1984-85, Task Force on Family Violence, Spalding County, Ga., 1983-85; assoc. bd. dir. Lyric Theatre. Named to Outstanding Young Women in Am., 1980. Mem. APA, Southeastern Psychol. Assn., Nat. Assn. Sch. Psychologists (cert. sch. psychologist), Okla. Psychol. Assn. Nat. Register Health Svc. Providers in Psychology, Okla. City Orchestra League, Psi Chi, Delta Zeta (chpt. dir. 1970-72). Democrat. Presbyterian. Home: 3941 NW 44th St Oklahoma City OK 73112-2517 Office: Northwest Mental Health Assocs 3832 N Meridian Ave Oklahoma City OK 73112-2849

ALLEGRA, ANTONIA, editor, writer; b. San Francisco, Feb. 21, 1946; d. Carlo Louis and Antonette Delfina (Laiolo) Lastreto; m. John H. Griffin, Aug. 14, 1965 (div. Feb. 1983); children: John, Deanna, Paul; m. Donn L. Black, Apr. 14, 1996. Student, Harvard U., 1969-71, Santa Clara U., 1963-65; Culinary Degree, Ecole de Cuisine Gaston, LeNotre, Paris, 1978, Le Cordon Bleu, Paris, 1981. Food editor San Diego (Calif.) Tribune, 1982-88; dir. culinary programs Beringer Winery, St. Helena, Calif., 1988-91; co-host Wine Valley Radio, St. Helena, 1995—; dir. Symposium for Profl. Food Writers, 1989—; dir. adminstrn. and comm. liaison Culinary Inst. of Am., St. Helena, 1991-95; pres. Internat. Assn. of Culinary Profls., Louisville, 1997; editor-in-chief Appellation Mag., Napa, Calif., 1992-96. Lectr./cooking demonstrator Seabourn/Radisson Cruises, 1975-93; judge various food competitions; panelist various food/wine confs.; speaker in field; writing coach, career coach. Author: (book) Napa Valley: The Ultimate Winery Guide, 1993; contbr. articles to profl. jours.; author introductions to books in field. Recipient award for Best New Regional Mag. (Appellation), Western Pub. Assn., L.A., 1994; named Woman of Distinction in the Culinary Professions, U. Calif. San Diego Cancer Ctr., 1987. Mem. Internat. Assn. of Culinary Profls. (v.p. 1996-97, pres. 1997-98), Internat. Women's Forum West, Assn. of Food Journalists (v.p. 1987), Napa Valley Culinary Alliance (pres. 1988-89), San Francisco Profl. Food Soc. (bd. dirs. 1989-90), Les Dames d'Escoffier Internat. (pres. San Francisco chpt. 1992), Napa Valley Wine Libr. Assn., Sonoma County Culinary Guild, Women for WineSense, Internat. Women's Forum, Sigma Delta Chi, others. Avocation: cooking. Office: Antonia Allegra & Assocs PO Box 663 Saint Helena CA 94574-0663

ALLEN, ALICE, communications and marketing executive; b. N.Y.C., May 31, 1943; d. C. Edmonds and Helen (McCreery) A.; 1 child, Helen. Student, Conn. Coll., 1961. Pres. Alice Allen, Inc., N.Y.C., 1970-83; sr. v.p. Robert Marston, N.Y.C., 1983-84, Cunningham & Walsh, N.Y.C., 1984-86, Carl Byoir (acquired by Hill & Knowlton), N.Y.C., 1986; sr. v.p., dir. comms. and corp. mktg. Hill & Knowlton, N.Y.C., 1986-88; pres., owner Allen Comms. Group, Inc., N.Y.C., 1988-95, Alice Allen Comms, 1995—. Bd. dirs. Family Dymanics, N.Y.C., 1976-78, Veritas, 1980-85; v.p. Jr. League, N.Y.C., 1975-76; mem. adv. bd. Enterprise Found., 1992-2001. Mem. Pub. Rels. Soc. Am., Pub. Publicity Assn. (pres. 1969-71), Women's Media Group, Comm. Network. Office: Alice Allen Comms 320 E 72nd St New York NY 10021-4769

ALLEN, BARBARA, state legislator; Atty.; mem. Kans. Ho. of Reps. from 21st dist., 1987-2000, Kans. Senate from 8th dist., Topeka, 2001—. Mem. appropriations com., fiscal oversight com., social svcs. budget com., chairperson tourism com. Kans. Ho. of Reps. Republican. Office: Kansas Senate State Capitol Topeka KS 66612 Home: 7427 Walmer St Overland Park KS 66204-2056 Home Fax: 913 384 5400; Office Fax: 913 498 8488. E-mail: allen@house.state.ks.us.

ALLEN, BARBARA KIRKMAN, politcal organization administrator; b. Asheville, N.C., July 23, 1931; d. Walter Alfred and Georgia Esmerald (Lewallen) Kirkman; m. Luke C. Allen, Jr., Sept. 9, 1949; 1 child, Michael Kirkman. With, Carolina Power and Light Co., Raleigh, N.C., 1950-96, mgr. adminstrv. svcs., 1979. Bd. dirs. N.C. Women's Forum; bd. deacons New Hope Bapt. Ch., Raleigh; mem. J.J. Singers; mem. adv. bd. Wake County coun. Girl Scouts U.S.; mem. adv. council Women in Econ. Devel; chairperson Acad. Women, YWCA; bd. dirs. N.C. Cmty. Colls., Wake County Coll. Aging; bd. assocs. Meredith Coll.; bd. dirs. N.C. State U. Humanities Found.; mem. exec. bd. N.C. Equity Inc.; Dem. chmn., N.C.,

1998—. Mem. N.C. Symphony Soc., Greater Raleigh C. of C. (mem. Mayor's com. of '85), Women of Raleigh (trustee). Office: NC Democratic Party 220 Hillsborough St Raleigh NC 27603-1724

ALLEN, BEATRICE, music educator, pianist; b. N.Y.C., June 30, 1917; d. Samuel and Rose (Krell) Hyman; m. Eugene Murray Allen, Jan. 23, 1937; children: Marlene Allen Galzin, Julian Lewis. Student, NYU, 1933—36; diploma (scholar), Inst. Musical Arts, N.Y.C., 1939, postgrad. (scholar), 1939—40; diploma (fellow, letter commendation), Juilliard Grad. Sch., N.Y.C., 1943; BA magna cum laude, Cedar Crest Coll., 1980. Mem. faculty prep. div. Juilliard Sch. Music, N.Y.C., 1957—69, Moravian Coll., 1967—68, Northampton County Area CC, 1968—70, Manhattan Sch. Music, N.Y.C., 1969—89. Mem. founding faculty Cmty. Music Sch., Allentown, Pa., 1982—; artist-in-residence, condr. Tchrs. Workshop, Antioch Coll., Yellow Springs, Ohio, 1966; Bach lectr., recitals various univs.; concert appearances Town Hall, N.Y.C., Chautauqua, NY, others. Named Winner, NJ Artists contest, 1936. Mem.: Pa. Music Tchrs. Assn., Music Tchrs. Nat. Assn. (program chmn. Lehigh Valley chpt. 1981—82). Address: 580 Morningstar Lane Bethlehem PA 18018-3752

ALLEN, BELLE, management consulting firm executive, communications executive; b. Chgo. d. Isaac and Clara (Friedman) Allen., U. Chgo. Cert. conf. mgr. Internat. Inst. Conf. Planning and Mgmt., 1989. Report, spl. correspondent The Leader Newspapers, Chgo., Washington, 1960-64; cons., v.p., treas., dir. William Karp Cons. Co. Inc., Chgo., 1961-79, chmn. bd., pres., treas., 1979—; pres. Belle Allen Comms., Chgo., 1961—; nat. corr. CCA Press, 1990—. Apptd. pub. mem., com. on judicial evaluation Chgo. Bar Assn., 1998—; v.p., treas., bd. dirs. Cultural Arts Survey Inc., Chgo., 1965-79; cons., bd. dirs. Am. Diversified Rsch. Corp., Chgo., 1967-70; v.p., sec., bd. dirs. Mgmt. Performance Systems Inc., 1976-77; cons. City Club Chgo., 1962-65, Ill. Commn. on Tech. Progress, 1965-67; hearing mem. Ill. Gov.'s Grievance Panel for State Employees, 1979—; hearing mem. grievance panel Ill. Dept. Transp., 1985—; mem. adv. governing bd. Ill. Coalition on Employment of Women, 1980-88; spl. program advisor President's Project Partnership, 1980-88; mem. consumer adv. coun. FRS, 1979-82; reporter CCA Press, 1990—; panel mem. Free Press vs. Fair Trial Nat. Ctr. Freedom of Info. Studies Loyola U. Law Sch., 1993, mem. planning com. Freedom of Info. awards, 1993; conf. chair The Swedish Inst. Press Ethics: How to Handle, 1993. Editor: Operations Research and the Management of Mental Health Systems, 1968; contbr. articles to profl. jours. Mem. campaign staff Adlai E. Stevenson II, 1952, 56, John F. Kennedy, 1960; founding mem. women's bd. United Cerebral Palsy Assn., Chgo., 1954, bd. dirs., 1954-58; pres. Dem. Fedn. Ill., 1958-61; pres. conf. staff Eleanor Roosevelt, 1960; mem. Welfare Pub. Rels. Forum, 1960-61; bd. dirs., mem. exec. com., chmn. pub. rels. com. Regional Ballet Ensemble, Chgo., 1961-63; bd. dirs. Soc. Chgo. Strings, 1963-64; mem. Ind. Dem. Coalition, 1968-69; bd. dirs. Citizens for Polit. Change, 1969; campaign mgr. aldermanic election 42d ward Chgo. City Coun., 1969; mem. selection com. Robert Aragon Scholarship, 1991; mem. planning com. mem. Hutchins Era reunion U. Chgo., 1995, 2000. Recipient Outstanding Svc. award United Cerebral Palsy Assn., Chgo., 1954, 55, Chgo. Lighthouse for Blind, 1986, Spl. Comms. award The White House, 1961, cert. of appreciation Ill. Dept. Human Rights, 1985, Internat. Assn. Ofcl. Human Rights Agys., 1985; selected as reference source Am. Bicentennial Rsch. Inst. Libr. Human Resources, 1973; named Hon. Citizen, City of Alexandria, Va., 1985; [illegible] nat. exhibit for Faces of Chicago, 1990. Mem. AAAS, NOW, AAAU, Affirmative Action Assn. (bd. dirs. 1981-85, chmn. mem. and programs com. 1981-85, pres. 1983—), Fashion Group (bd. dirs. 1981-83, chmn. Restrospective View of an Hist. Decade 1960 70, editor The Bull. 1981), Indsl. Rels. Rsch. Assn. (bd. dirs., chmn. pers. placement com. 1960-61), Sarah Siddons Soc., Soc. Pers. Adminstrs., Women's Equity Action League, Nat. Assn. Inter-Group Rels. Ofcls. (nat. conf. program 1959), Publicity Club Chgo. (chmn. inter-city rels. com. 1960-61, Disting. Svc. award 1968), Ill. C. of C. (cmty. rels. com., alt. mem. labor rels. com. 1971-74), Chgo. C. of C. and Industry (merit employment com. 1961-63), Internat. Press Club Chgo. (charter 1992—, bd. dirs. 1992—), Chgo. Press Club (chmn. women's activities 1969-71), U. Chgo. Club of Met. Chgo. (program com. 1993—, chair summer quarter programs 1994), Soc. Profl. Journalists (Chgo. Headline Club 1992—, regional conf. planning com. 1993, co-chair Peter Lisagor awards 1993, program com. 1992—), Assn. Women Journalists, Nat. Trust for Historic Preservation. Office: 111 E Chestnut St Ste 29J Chicago IL 60611

ALLEN, BETTY (MRS. RITTEN EDWARD LEE III), mezzo-soprano; b. Campbell, Ohio, Mar. 17, 1930; d. James Corr and Dora Catherine (Mitchell) A.; m. Ritten Edward Lee, III, Oct. 17, 1953; children: Anthony Edward, Juliana Catherine. Student, Wilberforce U., 1944-46; certificate, Hartford Sch. Music, 1953; pupil voice, Sarah Peck More, Zinka Milanov, Paul Ulanowsky, Carolina Segrera Holden; LHD (hon.), Wittenberg U., 1971; MusD (hon.), Union Coll., 1981; DFA (hon.), Adelphi U., 1990, Bklyn. Coll., 1991; LittD (hon.), Clark U., 1993; MusD (hon.), New Sch. Social Rsch., 1994. Faculty Phila. Mus. Acad., 1979, Manhattan Sch. Music, 1971, N.C. Sch. Arts, 1978-87; now faculty Harlem Sch. Arts. Tchr. master classes Inst. Teatro Colon, 1985-86, Curtis Inst. Music, 1987—; exec. dir. Harlem Sch. Arts, 1979, now pres.; vis. faculty Sibelius Akademie, Helsinki, Finland, 1976; mem. adv. bd. music panel Amherst Coll.; mem. music panel N.Y. State Council of the Arts, Dept. State Office Cultural Presentations, Nat. Endowment Arts.; bd. dirs. Arts Alliance, Karl Weigl Found., Diller-Quaile Sch. Music, U.S. Com. for UNICEF, Manhattan Sch. Music, Theatre Devel. Fund, Children's Storefront; mem. adv. bd. Bloomingdale House of Music; bd. vis. artists Boston U.; bd. dirs., mem. exec. com. Carnegie Hall, Nat. Found. for Advancement in the Arts; bd. dirs. Chamber Music Soc. of Lincoln Ctr., N.Y.C. Housing Authority Orch., Independent Sch. Orch., N.Y.C. Opera CO., Joy in Singing, Arts & Bus. Coun.; mem. Mayor's adv. comm. Cultural Affairs. Appeared as soloist: Leonard Bernstein's Jeremiah Symphony, Tanglewood, 1951, Virgil Thomson's Four Saints in Three Acts, N.Y.C. and Paris, 1952, N.Y.C. Light Opera Co., 1954; recitalist, also soloist with major symphonies on tours including ANTA-State Dept. tours, Europe, N. Africa, Caribbean, Can., U.S., S.Am., Far East, 1954-, S.Am. tour, 1968, Bellas Artes Opera, Mexico City, 1970; recital debut, Town Hall, N.Y.C., 1958, ofcl. debuts, London, Berlin, 1958, formal opera debut, Teatro Colon, Buenos Aires, Argentina, 1964; U.S. opera debut San Francisco Opera, 1966; N.Y.C. opera debut, 1973, Mini-Met. debut, 1973; Broadway debut in Treemonisha, 1975; opened new civic theaters in San Jose, Calif., and Regina, Sask., Can., concert hall, Lyndon Baines Johnson Library, Austin, Tex., 1971; artist-in-residence, Phila. Opera Co.; appeared with Caramoor Music Festival, summer 1965, 71, Cin. May Festival, 1972, Santa Fe Opera, 1972, 75, Canadian Opera Co., Winnipeg, Man., 1972, 77, Washington Opera Co., 1971, Tanglewood Festival, 1951, 52, 53, 67, 74, Oslo, The Hague, Montreal, Kansas City, Houston and Santa Fe operas, 1975, Saratoga Festival, 1975, Casals Festival, 1967, 68, 69, 76, Helsinki Festival, 1976, Marlboro Festival, 1967-74, numerous radio and TV performances, U.S., Can., Mex., Eng., Germany, Scandinavia; rec. artist, London, Vox, Capitol, Odeon-Pathe, Decca, Deutsche Grammophon, Columbia Records, RCA Victor records; represented U.S. in Cultural Olympics, Mexico City, 1968. Recipient Marian Anderson award, 1953-54, Nat. Music League Mgmt. award, 1953, 52 St Am. Festival Duke Ellington Meml. award, 1989, Bowery award Bowery Bank, 1989, Harlem Sch. of the Arts award Harlem Sch. and Isaac Stern, 1990, Womans Day Celebration award St. Thomas Episcopal Ch., 1990, St. Thomas Ch. award St. Thomas Catholic Ch., 1990, Men's Day Celebration award St. Paul's Ch., 1990, Martell House of Segram award Avery Fisher Hall, 1990; named Best Singer of Season Critics' Circle, Argentina and Chile, 1959, Best Singer of Season Critics' Circle, Uruguay, 1961; Martha Baird Rockefeller Aid to Music grantee, 1953, 58; John Hay Whitney fellow, 1953-54; Ford Found. concert soloist grantee, 1963-64 Mem. NAACP, Urban League, Hartford Mus. Club (life), Am. Guild Mus. Artists, Actors Equity, AFTRA, Silvermine Guild Artists, Jeunesses Musicales, Gioventu Musicale, Student Sangverein Trondheim, Unitarian-Universalist Women's Fedn., Nat. Negro Musicians Assn. (life), Concert Artists Guild, Met. Opera Guild, Amherst Glee Club (hon. life), Union Coll. Glee Club (hon. life), Met. Mus. Art, Mus. Modern Art, Am. Mus. Natural History, Century Assn., Sigma Alpha Iota (hon.) Unitarian-Universalist. Clubs: Cosmopolitan, Second. Office: Harlem Sch of Arts 645 Saint Nicholas Ave New York NY 10030-1098

ALLEN, BRENDA KAY, elementary school educator; b. Poplar Bluff, Mo., Dec. 11, 1957; d. Harold Alan and Earline Smith Robertson; m. Thomas Franklin Allen, Dec. 31, 1978; children: Joshua Sutherland, Silas Wright, Emily Harper. B Music Edn., Murray State U., 1983; MA, S.E. Mo. State U., 2000. Cert. tchr. Mo. Tchr. Poplar Bluff Sch. Dist., 1986—. Dir. R-1 Schs. Safe Schs. Healthy Students, Poplar Bluff, Mo., 2002—. Mem.: Mo. Music Educators Assn., Nat. Assn. Music Edn., Mo. State Tchrs. Assn. Avocations: sailing, scuba diving, aviation. Office: Poplar Bluff 5th and 6th Grade Ctr 3209 Oak Grove Rd Poplar Bluff MO 63901

ALLEN, CAROL MARIE, radiologic technologist; b. Alma, Ark., Nov. 4, 1941; d. Rhuel Teal and Blake Marie (Hickey) Edwards; m. Richard William Varney, Oct. 4, 1965 (dec. Mar. 1978); 1 stepchild, Mary Beth Varney ; m. Michael Thomas Allen, Dec. 24, 1979; stepchildren: Richard Lawrence, Peter Michael, Nicola Susan. 2 yr. cert., Sparks Regional Med. Ctr.-Sch. Radiology, 1961. Cert. Am. Registry Radiologic Technologists, State Conn. Registry Radiologic Technologists, clin. densitometry Mass. Staff technologist Sparks Regional Med. Ctr., Ft. Smith, Ark., 1961—62, La Puente (Calif.) Hosp., 1962—64; asst. chief technologist La Harbor (Calif.) Hosp., 1964—67; traffic contr. Lawrence and Meml. Hosp., Pequot Treatment Ctr., New London, Conn., 1967—; clin. densitometry technologist L&M Pequot Treatment Ctr., 1998—2003, traffic controller, 2003—. Contbr. Critical Thinking Developing Skills in Radiography, 1999. Vol. ARC, Conn. Mem.: Am. Soc. for Radiologic Technologists, Internat. Soc. for Clin. Densitometry. Democrat. Avocations: gardening, antiques, reading. Home: 11 Route 165 Preston CT 06365-8414 Office: Lawrence & Meml Hosp 365 Montauk Ave New London CT 06320 also: Pequot Emergency Treatment Ctr 52 Hazelnut Hill Rd Groton CT 06340

ALLEN, CHARITY E. music educator; d. Delmer L. and Ramona P. Allen. MusB in Edn., Ctrl. State U., Edmond, Okla., 1982, MusM in Edn., 1991. Educator Guthrie Pub. Schs., Okla., 1982—90, Edmond Pub. Schs., 1990—. Grantee, Edmond Ednl. Endowment, 2002—03. Mem.: Edmond Assn. Classroom Tchrs., Okla. Educators Assn., Nat. Educators Assn., Music Educators Nat. Conf., Okla. Music Educators Assn., Okla. Choral Dirs. Assn., Am. Choral Directors Assn., Ctrl. Okla. Choral Dirs. Assn. (assoc.). Conservative.

ALLEN, CHARLOTTE, secondary school educator; BS in Edn., Athens State Coll. Tchr. sci. East Lawrence High Sch., Trinity, Ala., 1988—. Coach cheerleading; camp dir. Nat. Cheerleading Assn. Named Outstanding Sci. Tchr., 1992. Mem. Nat. Assn. Geology Tchrs. Avocations: church activities, hiking.

ALLEN, CYNTHIA LEA, nurse; b. Syracuse, NY, Sept. 13, 1956; d. Robert Bayette and Betty Ruth [illegible] SUNY, Morrisville, 1978. Staff RN University Hosp., Syracuse, NY, 1978—82, Egleston Children's Hosp., Atlanta, 1982—84, Tulane Med. Ctr., New Orleans, 1985—, Davis Med. Ctr., Sacramento, 1985—, St. Vincent Hosp., Erie, Pa., 1986, Dallas Children's Hosp., Tex., 1986, Kapiolani Hosp. for Women and Children, Honolulu, 1987—88, staff and transport nurse, 1989—90; transport nurse pediatric ICU SUNY Upstate Med. U., Syracuse, NY, 1990—.

ALLEN, DANIELLE, political scientist, educator; BA, Princeton U., 1993; MA, Harvard U., 1998, PhD, 2001; MPhil, U. Cambridge, 1994, PhD, 1997. Assoc. prof. dept. politics and com. on social thought and dept. classical langs. and lits. U. Chgo., 1997—. Author: (book) The World of Prometheus: The Politics of Punishing in Democratic Athens, 2000. Fellow, NSF, 1997, Frank Inst. for Humanities fellow, U. Chgo., 1999. Office: U Chgo Dept Classics 1010 East 59 th St Chicago IL 60637

ALLEN, DAWN, secondary school educator, writer; b. Kans. City, Kans., Jan. 31, 1957; d. Dallas I. and Nona F. Davis; m. John Allen; children: Patrick, Barrett. BS in Edn., Pitts. State U., 1980. Cert. Tchr. Kans., 1980. Homeless instr. JCC, Overland Pk., Kans., 1994—96; English tchr. Indian Trail Jr. H.S., Olathe, Kans., 1995—2000, Chisholm Trail Jr. H.S., Olathe, 2000—. Recipient Homeless Instr. Tchr. of the Yr. award, Safe Home, 1997. Mem.: Nat. Coun. of Tchr. of English, Olathe Edn. Assn. (bldg. rep., exec. bd.), Kans. Edn. Assn., Delta Kappa Gamma. Office: Chisholm Trail Junior High 16700 W 159th Olathe KS 66062 Business E-Mail: dallencst@mail.olathe.k12.ks.us.

ALLEN, DEBBIE, actress, choreographer, dancer, television director; b. Houston, Jan. 16, 1950; d. Vivian Ayers; m. Win Wilford (div.); m. Norm Nixon; 2 children: Vivian, Norman, Jr. BA, Howard U. Appeared in Broadway musicals including Purlie, 1972, West Side Story (revival), Guys and Dolls, Raisin, Aint Misbehavin, Sweet Charity, 1986 (revival, Tony Award); appeared in (play) Sweet Charity, Los Angeles, 1985, choreographer Broadway prodn. Carrie, 1988; (TV spl.) Dancing in the Wings, 1985, (TV series) Fame, 1982-87 (3 Emmys for choreography), In the House, 1995; dir. TV series A Different World, 1988-92; dir. episodes TV series Family Ties; dir., producer films including The Fish That Saved Pittsburgh, 1979, Fame, 1980, Ragtime, 1981, JoJo Dancer, Your Life is Calling, 1986, Mona Must Die, 1994, Blank Check, 1994, Out-of-Sync, 1995, Everything's Jake, 1999, (TV movie) C Bear and Jamal (voice), 1996; star, dir., prod., co-writer, choreographer The Debbie Allen Special, ABC-TV, 1988; dir., choreographer Polly (mus. version Disney's Pollyanna), 1989; dir., appeared in CBS Stompin' at the Savoy, 1992; rec. album Special Look, MCA Records, 1989; dir. pilot and 1st episode NBC series The Fresh Prince of Bel Air, 1990; dir., choreographer NBC-Disney movie Polly II, 1990; choreographer of 63d Acad. Awards, 1991, 64th Acad. Awards, 1992, 65th Acad. Awards, 1993, 66th Acad. Awards, 1994; dir. (TV) Cool Women, 2000. Mem. exec. com. dean's adv. bd. UCLA Sch. Theatre, Film and TV, 1993. Office: William Morris Agency 151 S El Camino Dr Beverly Hills CA 90212-2775

ALLEN, DIANE BETZENDAHL, state legislator; b. Newark, Mar. 8, 1948; arrived in U.S., 1970; BA in Philosophy, Bucknell U., 1970. Pres. VidComm, Inc.; mem. N.J. Gen. Assembly, Trenton, 1996-98, N.J. Senate, Dist. 7, Trenton, 1998—; Rep. Conf. leader, 2003; mem. Senate transp. com., 2003; mem. health, sr. svcs. com., 2003. Majority whip N.J. State Senate, 1998—, vice chair environ. com., vice chair transp. com., women's issues, children and family svcs. com. Del. to Rep. Nat. Conv., 1996; bd. dirs. N.J. State Aquarium, Foster Care Consortium N.J., Family Svcs. of Burlington County, Youth Work Found., Moorestown Vis. Nurses Assn., United Way; mem. Com. to End Homelessness. Republican. Address: NJ State Senate PO Box 098 Trenton NJ 08624-0098 E-mail: SenAllen@njleg.org.

ALLEN, DIXIE J. state representative; b. 1935; married; 3 children. BSBA, Ctrl. Ohio State U.; postgrad., Nat. U., L.A.; DHL (hon.), Ctrl. Ohio State U. Civilian employee USAF; state rep. dist. 39 Ohio Ho. of Reps., Columbus, 1998—, ranking minority mem. banking, pensions and securities com., mem. fin. and appropriations, and homeland security engring. and archtl. design coms., mem. human svcs. subcom. Adv. bd. Women in Leadership; personnel adv. bd. Daybreak; adv. bd. Coll. Arts and Scis., Ctrl. State U. Mem.: NAACP, SCLC, Miami Valley Mil. Affairs Assn., Delta Sigma Theta. Office: 77 S High St 10th fl Columbus OH 43215-6111

ALLEN, DOROTHEA, secondary school educator; b. Rockaway, NJ, Apr. 30, 1919; d. Harrison Engleman and Caroline (Tierney) Allen. AB, Montclair U., 1941, MA, 1949. Cert. secondary, sci., math. tchr., counselor, supr., prin. N.J. Tchr. sci. and math. Denville (N.J.) Jr. High Sch., 1942-46; tchr. sci. Boonton (N.J.) High Sch., 1946-94, supr. sci. dept., 1978-94. Lab. technician Drew Chem. Corp., Boonton, 1942—47; tech. asst. Bell Telecom. Lab., Whippany, NJ, 1956; rsch. scientist Warner Lambert Rsch. Inst., Morris Plains, NJ, 1959—62; tchr. sci. enrichment Boonton Summer Sch., 1963—85; curriculum developer Morris County Vocat.-Tech. Sch., Denville, 1987; project evaluator Mid. States Assn., 1973, 79; facilitator Ptnrs. in Edn. Program; promoter Media Ctr. Open House; cons., reviewer Am. Biol. Tchr. Mag., 1975—; com. mem. Sch. Articulation Program Boonton Schs., 1991—94; media ctr. spkr Meet the Author; sponsor Student Showcase of Excellence in Sci., 1990—94; faculty sponsor, mentor h.s. students, 1966—94; mentor Alt. Rt. Program Tchrs. N.J. Organizer Am. Dental Health Clinic, Boonton, 1968—72; presenter, spkr. in field. Author: Research Projects for High School Biology, 1971, Biology Teacher's Desk Book, 1979, Science Activities for Every Month of the School Year, 1981, Science Demonstrations for Elementary Classrooms, 1988, Hands-on Science, 1991; contbr. articles to profl. jours., including Am. Biology Tchr. Mem. career com. N.J. divsn. Theobald Smith Soc., 1975—76, mentoring program, 1992—; fundraiser Am. Hemophilia Found., Rockaway, NJ, 1985—, Am. Heart Assn., 1995—, Muscular Dystrophy Found., 1995—, Nat. Children's Cancer Soc., 1996—; mothers march vol. March of Dimes, 1990—; cons. Cmty. Mid. Sch. Planning Com., Boonton, 1988—90; bd. advisors ABI Rsch., 1995—. Named Outstanding Biology Tchr., Nat. Assn. Biology Tchrs., 1972, Outstanding Sci. Tchr., Rsch. Assn. N.Am., 1980, Woman of the Yr., 1993—98; named to Sci. Edn. Hall of Fame, 1994—98, Boonton H.S. Wall of Fame, 1996, 1997, 1998; recipient Disting. Citizen's award, Town of Rockaway, 1984, Gov.'s and Edn. award, N.J. Dept. Edn., 1984, Morris County Tchr. of the Yr. award, 1990, Presdl. award, NSF, 1984, Cert. of Honor, State of N.J., 1985, World Lifetime Achievement award, 1994, Internat. Order of Merit, 1994, Spotlight award, Boonton Bd. Edn., 1980—86, Tchr. of Yr., 1984, 1990, Women's Inner Cir. of Achievement award, 1995. Mem.: NSTA, ASCD, NEA, NEA Ret., Morris Area Sci. Alliance, N.J. Dept. Edn. Exec. Acad., N.J. Dept. Edn. Exec. Acad., N.J. Alliance for Math. and Sci., N.J. Prins. And Suprs. Assn., N.J. Edn. Assn., Assn. Presdl. Award Winners in Sci. Tchg., Nat. Assn. Secondary Sch. Prins., Morris County Ret. Educators Assn. Avocations: reading, propagating plants, collecting gold coins. Home: 115 Jackson Ave Rockaway NJ 07866-3039

ALLEN, ELIZABETH MARESCA, marketing and telecommunications executive; b. Red Bank, N.J., Jan. 4, 1958; d. Paul William Michael and Roberta Gertrude (Abbes) Maresca; m. David D. Allen; 1 child, Brandon D. Student, Brookdale Community Coll., 1976 77; A Bus. Adminstrn., Tidewater C.C., 1988; BA in Bus. Mgmt., Va. Wesleyan Coll., 1997. Systems analyst Methods Research Corp., Farmingdale, N.J., 1977-79; divsn. mgr. Abacus Comm. L.P., Va. Beach, Va., 1979—2003, dir. telecomm., dir. client svcs.; divsn. sales mgr. AmeriComm Direct Mktg., Chesapeake, 2003—. V.p. Charlestowne Civic League, Virginia Beach, 1983—84, Plantation Lakes Homeowners Assn., Chesapeake, Va., 1992—; advisor Commonwealth Coll., Norfolk, 1984—91; commr. S. Norfolk Revitalization Commn., 1999—2001; del. Va. Rep. Conv., 1993—; mem. gov.'s coun. Rep. Nat. Com., 1997, bd. dirs. [illegible] Norfolk, Va., 1996—00. Mem.: Williamsburg Area C. of C. (exhibit chmn. 1987), Hampton Roads C. of C. (com. chmn. 1985, 1989), Women's Network Hampton Roads (publicity chmn. 1988—91, chmn. publicity for Job Fair 1989). Republican. Roman Catholic. Avocations: tennis, Civil War history, collecting antiques, gardening. Office: AmeriComm Direct Mktg 804 Greenbriar Ln Chesapeake VA 23320

ALLEN, FRANCES MICHAEL, publisher; b. Charlotte, N.C., Apr. 7, 1939; d. Thomas Wilcox and Lola Frances (Horne) A.; m. Joseph Taylor Lisenbee, Feb. 24, 1955 (div. 1957); 1 child, Leslie Autice., Abilene (Tex.) Christian Coll., 1954-56, Chico (Calif.) State U., 1957-59. Art dir. B&E Publs., L.A., 1963-65, editor, 1969-70; art dir. Tiburon Corp., Chgo., 1970-75; founder, editor Boxers, Internat., L.A., 1970-76; editor The Hound's Tale, 1974, Saints, Incorp., 1974-76; founder, editor Setters, Incorp., Costa Mesa, Calif., 1975-85; founder, owner Michael Enterprises, Midway City, Calif., 1976—; editor Am. Cocker Rev., Midway City, 1980-81; editor, pub. Am. Cocker Mag., 1981-99; editor, co-pub. Sporting Life, 1991; editor, pub. The Royal Spaniels, 1995—. Author: The American Cocker Book, 1989; editor, pub. The Royal Spaniels, 1995— (Dogs Writer's Assn. awards 1995, 96, 99); illustrator: The First Five Years, 1970, The Aftercare of the Ear, 1975, The Shenn Simplicity Collection, 1976, The Miniature Pinscher, 1967; prin. works include mag. and book covers for USA, most widely published show dog artist world wide, past 30 yrs. Recipient Dog World Award Top Producer, 5 times, 1966-88, 10-time winner and nominee Dog Writers Assn. Am., winner best breed publ. World Congress Pet Publs., Ukraine, 1995, winner Kirk Paper Co. award of excellence. Mem. Dog Writers Assn. Am. Republican. Mem. Ch. of Christ. Avocations: dog breeding, ballooning, photography, art. Home and Office: 14531 Jefferson St Midway City CA 92655-1030 Office Phone: 714-893-0053. E-mail: baliwck@socal.rr.com.

ALLEN, GLORIA ANN, realtor; b. Paterson, N.J., May 1, 1940; d. Victor and Anna (Nagorny) Borovoy; m. Byron Paul Allen, July 7, 1964 (div. Jan. 1986); children: Andreya Monica, Sarah Patricia. Student, Cir. in Sq. Acting Sch., N.Y.C., 1963-64; MA, Johns Hopkins U., 1962; MBA, Golden Gate U., 1986. Lic. real estate broker, Calif. Tchr. Elem. Sch., East Rutherford, N.J., 1963; social worker Bur. Child Welfare City of N.Y., 1964-68; social worker Dept. Social Svcs. City and County San Francisco, 1968-78; property mgr. San Francisco, 1981-91; broker assoc. Ritchie and Ritchie, San Francisco, 1992, Evans Pacific Realtor, San Francisco, 1993-94, Frank Howard Allen Realtors, San Francisco, 1994-97, Fred Sands City Properties, San Francisco, 1997-2001, Caldwell Banker, San Francisco, 2001—. Fin. com. mem. St. Mary's Cathedral, San Francisco, 1993—. Mem. Nat. Assn. Realtors, Nat. Network Comml. Real Estate Women (chief fin. officer 1987-89, co-chair facilities Nat. Conv. 1993), San Francisco Assn. Realtors. Democrat. Office: Coldwell Banker 1801 Lombard St San Francisco CA 94123 E-mail: gloria@sirius.com.

ALLEN, JANICE FAYE CLEMENT, nursing administrator; b. Norfolk, Nebr., Aug. 19, 1946; d. Allen Edward and Hilda Bernice (Stange) Reeves; m. Roger Allen Clement, Oct. 6, 1968 (dec. July 1974); m. August H. Allen, Sept. 17, 1988. RN, Meth. Sch. Nursing, Omaha, 1967; BSN magna cum laude, Creighton U., 1978; MSN, U. Nebr., 1981. Cert. in nursing adminstrn., infection control. With Meth. Hosp., 1967-68, 72-83, asst. head nurse, 1974-77, staff devel. nurse, 1977-81, dir. staff adminstrv. svcs., 1981-83; pub. health nurse Wichita-Sedgwick County Health Dept., Wichita, Kans., 1970-72; dir. nursing Meth. Med. Ctr., St. Joseph, Mo., 1983-84; v.p. nursing and profl. svcs. Broadlawns Med. Ctr., Des Moines, 1984-93; dir. staff mgmt./infection control Ea. N.Mex. Med. Ctr., Roswell, 1993-2000; infection control practitioner Carl T. Hayden VA Med. Ctr., Phoenix, 2000—; faculty mem. U. Phoenix, 2002. Adj. clin. faculty nursing Drake U. Nursing, Des Moines, 1986-93, adv. bd., 1984-93, Ctrl. Campus Practical Nursing, 1984-93; mem. adv. bd. Des Moines Area C.C. Dist., 1987—, Des Moines Area C.C. Nursing Bd., 1987-93, Grandview Coll., 1988-93; bd. dirs. Vis. Nurse Svcs., 1988-93; assoc. Am. Coll. Healthcare Execs., Dept. of Veteran Affairs VISN 18 Leadership Devel. Inst. Graduate, 2003. Mem.: ANA, Nat. Assn. for Healthcare Quality, Nurses Orgn. Vet. Affairs, N.Mex. Orgn. Nurse Execs., Assn. Infection Control and Epidemi-

SIMMS LIBRARY
ALBUQUERQUE ACADEMY

ology, Iowa Orgn. Nurse Execs. (treas. 1987, sec. 1989, pres.-elect 1993), Iowa League for Nursing (treas. 1987—89, pres. 1989), Colloquium Nursing Leaders Ctrl. Iowa, Ctrl. Iowa Nursing Leadership Conf. (pres. 1985), N.Mex. Nurses Assn., Am. Orgn. Nurse Execs. (bd. dirs. 1995), Altrusa of Roswell, Sigma Theta Tau (pres. Zeta Chi chpt. 1990—92). Home: 20278 N 104 Ave Peoria AZ 85382 Office: Carl T Hayden VA Med Ctr 650 E Indian Sch Rd Phoenix AZ 85012 Office Phone: 602-277-5551. Business E-Mail: jan.allen@med.va.gov.

ALLEN, JOAN, actress; b. Rochelle, Ill., Aug. 20, 1956; Student, Ea. Ill. U., No. Ill. U. Founding mem. Steppenwolf Theatre Co., Chgo.; theater appearances include (debut) And A Nightingale Sang, N.Y.C. (Clarence Derwent award, Drama Desk award, Outer Critics Circle award 1984), Steppenwolf Theatre Co., also Hartford, 1983, The Marriage of Bette and Boo, N.Y. Shakespeare Festival, 1986, Burn This! (Tony awrd for Best Actress 1988) Mark Taper Forum, L.A., also N.Y.C., 1987, The Heidi Chronicles, N.Y.C., 1988, 89; film appearances include Compromising Positions, 1985, Peggy Sue Got Married, 1986, Manhunter, 1986, Tucker: The Man and His Dream, 1988, In Country, 1989, Ethan Frome, 1993, Searching for Bobbie Fischer, 1993, Josh and S.A.M., 1993, Nixon, 1995 (Acad. award nominee for best supporting actress 1996), Mad Love, 1995, The Crucible, 1996, Ice Storm, 1997, Face/Off, 1997, Pleasantville, 1998, Veronica Guerin, 1999, All the Rage, 1999, When the Sky Falls, 2000, The Contender, 2000, Off the Map, 2003; TV appearances include miniseries Evergreen, 1985, All My Sons, 1986, Am. Playhouse, PBS, 1987, Robert Frost, Voices and Visions, PBS, 1988, TV film The Room Upstairs, 1987, Without Warning: The James Brady Story, 1991, Say Goodnight, Gracie, PBS, The Mists of Avalon, 2001. Office: ICM care Brian Mann 8942 Wilshire Blvd Beverly Hills CA 90211-1934

ALLEN, JOYCE SMITH, librarian; b. Englewood, N.J., Aug. 1, 1939; d. Harold Willard and Mary Elizabeth Smith; m. Jim Frank Allen, Mar. 1974 (div. 1982); 1 child, Shani Jamilla. BA, Howard U., 1961; MLS, Atlanta U., 1966; cert. in advanced studies, U. Ill., 1974. Reference librarian Howard U., Washington, 1966-73; mgr. libr. Meth. Hosp. Ind., Indpls., 1974-94; libr., dir. distance learning Aenon Bible Coll., Indpls., 1994—; libr. Rowland Design Inc., 1995—2001. Instr. Ind. Vocat. Tech. Coll., 1979, 85, Med. Library Assn., 1982-95, Martin Ctr. Coll., Indpls., 1983-84. Author career materials. Vol. Indpls. Police Dept. Libr., 1977, Children's Mus., Indpls., 1987—88, Children;'s Bureau, 2001—, Black Expo, 1995—, Minority Health Fair, 1995—. Recipient Minority Bus. and Profl. Achiever award Ctr. for Leadership Devel., Indpls., 1981, Central Ind. Area Libr. Svcs. Authority cert. of Excellence, 1990. Mem. ALA, Internat. Tng. In Comm., Ch. and Synagogue Libr. Assn. (pres. 1992-93, 95-96), Med. Libr. Assn., Coun. on Libr. Technicians, Spl. Librs. Assn., Indpls. Interdenominational Ch. Users' Assn. Democrat. Avocations: travel, reading, needlepoint, bicycling. Home: 3815 N Bolton Ave Indianapolis IN 46226-4826 Office: Aenon Bible Coll 3919 Meadows Dr Indianapolis IN 46205-3113 E-mail: jsaallen@hotmail.com.

ALLEN, JULIE O'DONNELL, lawyer; BA, Stanford U., 1980; JD, U. Iowa, 1983. Bar: Iowa 1983, Ill. 1985, U.S. Dist. Ct. (no. dist.) Ill., U.S. Ct. Appeals (8th and 7th cirs.). Jud. clk. to Chief Judge Donald P. Lay, U.S. Ct. Appeals for 8th Circuit, 1983-84; assoc. Sidley & Austin, Chgo., 1985—, ptnr. Contbr. articles to law publs. Office: Sidley & Austin 1 S First National Plz Chicago IL 60603-2000 Fax: 323-853-7036. E-mail: jallen@sidley.com.

ALLEN, KAREN ALFSTAD, information technology executive; b. Wichita, Kans., Nov. 21, 1942; d. Harold Daniel and Myrtle (Creach) Keefer; m. Richard Allen, Dec. 16, 1962 (dec. 1994). AS, Oreg. Inst. of Tech., L.A., 1964; AA, Pasadena City, 1973; BS, Calif. State U., Pasadena City, 1974. Administra. asst. Transamerica, Los Angeles, 1974-75; v.p. Calif. Fed., Los Angeles, 1975-86; mgmt. cons. PriceWaterhouseCoopers, Los Angeles, 1986-90; mgr. large accounts J.D. Edwards, Denver, 1990-92; sr. v.p. Insecon Computer Sys., Encino, Calif., 1992—93; sr. project dir. MCI Systemhouse, Cerritos, Calif., 1995-98; delivery mgr. EDS, Cerritos, 1998-2000; chief info. officer Exult, Irvine, Calif., 2000—. Vol. Youth Motivation Task Force, L.A., 1982—86, Huntington Libr., Big Wheel Soc., Children's Hosp. of Orange County, L.A.; bd. dirs. Polit. Action Com. Calif. Fed., L.A., 1984—86, Arcadia Arts Coun., 1993—2002. Recipient Honors Calif. State U., Los Angeles, 1974. Mem. Nat. Trust for Historic Preservation, Internat. Facility Mgmt., So. Calif. Emergency Assn., NAFE, NOW, U. Club L.A. Democrat. Home: 5161 Via Marcos Yorba Linda CA 93887 Office: Exult 4 Park Pl Irvine CA 92614 E-mail: karen.allen@exult.net.

ALLEN, LEATRICE DELORICE, psychologist; b. Chgo., July 15, 1948; d. Burt and Mildred Floy (Taylor) Hawkins; m. Allen Jr. Moore, July 30, 1965 (div. Oct. 1975); children: Chandra, Valarie, Allen; m. Armstead Allen, May 11, 1978 (div. May 1987). AA in Bus. Edn., Olive Harvey Coll., Chgo., 1975; BA in Psychology, Chgo. State U., 1977; M in Clin. Psychology, Roosevelt U., 1980; MS in Health Care Adminstrn., Coll. St. Francis, Joliet, Ill., 1993. Lic. clin. profl. counselor. Clk. U.S. Post Office, Chgo., 1967—72; clin. therapist Bobby Wright Mental Health Ctr., Chgo., 1979—80, Cmty. Mental Health Coun., Chgo., 1980—83, assoc. dir., 1983—. Cons. Edgewater Mental Health, Chgo., 1984—, Project Price, Chgo., 1980—83; victim svcs. coord. Cmty. Mental Health Coun., Chgo., 1986—87; mgr. youth family svcs. Mile Sq. Health Ctr., Chgo., 1987—88; coord. Evang. Health Sys., Oakbrook, Ill., 1988—93; adminstr. Human Enrichment Devel. Assn., Hazel Crest, Ill., 1993—96; dir. Ada S. McKinley, Chgo., 1996—. Fellow, Menninger Found., 1985; scholar, Chgo. State U., 1976, Roosevelt U., 1978. Mem.: Chgo. Coun. Fgn. Rels., Chgo. Sexual Assault Svcs. Network (vice-chair, bd. dirs.), Soc. Traumatic Stress Studies (treatment innovations task force), Ill. Coalition Against Sexual Assault (del. 1985—), Nat. Orgn. for Victim Assistance, Am. Profl. Soc. on Abuse of Children. Avocations: aerobics, reading, theater, dining, making and collecting dolls. Office Phone: 773-884-5412. Business E-Mail: lallen@adasmckinley.org.

ALLEN, LINDA LEE, administrative assistant; b. Bowden, Ga., Apr. 20, 1940; d. Paul Hughen and Jessie Estelle (Huddleston) Lee; m. James Harrell Mosley, June 8, 1958 (div. Nov. 1968); children: Cynthia L. Mosley-Mizushima, Suzanne R. Mosley Goldston; m. Calvin Theodore Allen, Mar. 1, 1987. Exec. Sec. Cert., Massey Draughons Jr. Coll., Atlanta, 1960. Cert. Profl. Sec. Profl. Secs. Internat. Inst. for Cert. Legal sec. Am. Soc. of Composers, Authors & Pubs., Atlanta, 1964-69, Valley Forge Corp., Atlanta, 1969-74, Met. Life Ins. Co., Atlanta, 1982-84; adminstrv. asst. WANG Labs., Inc., Dayton, Ohio & Montgomery, Ala., 1984-86, Ala. Dept. Indsl. Rels., Montgomery, 1989-92, Ala. Office of Water Resources, Montgomery, 1992—. Com. chair Exec. of Yr. in State Govt., Montgomery, 1994-95, 97-98; mem. planning com. Profl. Devel. Conf. for State Secs. and Office Profls., Montgomery, 1995-96, Ann. Seminar for State Secs., Montgomery, 1992-94. Mem. profl. staff recruitment com. Macedonia Bapt. Ch., Union Springs, Ala., 1994-98, mem. ann. 4th of July and homecoming celebration com., 1995, 97, vol. shut-in outreach sr. program, 1996-98. Sec. of Yr. in State Govt., State Capital Chpt., Profl. Secs., Internat., Montgomery, 1995 (chpt. pres. 2000-2001). Mem. Am. Water Resources Assn., Tri-Rivers Waterway Devel. Assn., Ala. Rural Water Assn., Am. Soc. Notaries. Avocations: genealogy, fishing, needlework, reading. Office: Ala Office of Water Resources 401 Adams Ave Ste 434 Montgomery AL 36104-4325

ALLEN, LINDA S. editor, writer; d. Jim J. and Barbara J. Holland; children: Amy L. Cason, Mandy S. Devich, Jeremy S., Ethan M. BS in Journalism/News Editl., U. Colo., Boulder, 1992. Electronics technician AT&T, Denver, 1973—83, master prodn. scheduling specialist, 1983—89; intern reporter Longmont Times-Call, Longmont, Colo., 1991—92; rschr. The NY Times-Rocky Mountain Bur., Denver, 1992—94; staff reporter The Stuart News, Fla., 1994—97; pub. info. officer Big Bros. Big Sisters of Martin County, Stuart, Fla., 1997—99; editor/writer LRP Publs., Palm Beach Gardens, Fla., 1999—. Author: (non-fiction) You Don't Know Jack. The Tale of a Father Once Removed, WaveMaker. Victim advisor Thornton/Northglenn Police Depts., Colo., 1989—94. Mem.: Fla. Press Assn. (assoc.). Liberal. Christian. Avocations: wilderness hiking/backpacking, downhill skiing, travel. Personal E-mail: lindaallen@comcast.net.

ALLEN, LOIS ARLENE HEIGHT (MRS. JAMES PIERPONT ALLEN), musician; b. Kenton, Ohio, Sept. 2, 1932; d. Robert Harold and Frances (Sims) Height; m. James Pierpont Allen, June 14, 1953; children: Daniel Pierpont, Carole Elizabeth. BS, Ohio State U., 1954, MA, 1958. Tchr. jr. and sr. high music Upper Arlington H.S., Columbus, Ohio, 1954-56; h.s. music supr. Westerville, Ohio, 1956-57; tchr. music Ohio State U. Sch., 1957-59; pvt. tchr. music Columbus, 1960—. Exec. dir. Battelle Scholars Program Trust Fund, 1983-86; ch. organist, choir dir. Mountview Bapt. Ch., Upper Arlington, Ohio, 1960-77, moderator, 1996-97; ednl. radio interviewer WOSU, 1970, 71, 72. Mem. Project Hope, Ctrl. Ohio, 1967-73; mem. sustaining bd. Maryhaven House for Alcoholic Women, 1969-73, 1st v.p.; mem. women's bd. Columbus Symphony, 1965-79, 91—, bd. trustees edn. com., 1992-2004, co-chair edn. com. women's assn., 1992-2004, charter mem. trustee's cir., 2000, bd. dir., chmn. youth coun., 1965-68, pres.-elect women's assn., 1973, chmn. edn. com., 1991—, pres., 1974-76; pres. vol. coun. Am. Symphony Orch. League, 1987-89; organist, choir master The Ch. of St. Edwards, 1990-92; chmn. juried art competition Cen. Ohio Arts Festival, 1969, 70, chmn. fine and applied arts, 1971, gen. chmn. of festival, 1972; area chmn. United Appeals Franklin County, 1966-68, Heart dr., 1968-85; pres. Ohio State U. Sch. Friends Sch. Music, 1977-78; trustee Columbus Symphony Orch., 1973-81, Opera/Columbus, 1981-85; v.p. women's guild Opera/Columbus, 1986-94, pres., 1987-88; mem. vol. coun. Am. Symphony Orch. League, 1981—, v.p., 1983-84, mem. exec. com., 1986-88, mem. artistic affairs com., 1987-89, pres., 1987-88; organist, choir dir. North Congregational Ch., 1979-85; area leader Rep. Party, 1966-68; mem. Mayor's Award Coun. Com., 1981-84; active Connexions, Columbus Literacy Coun.; bd. dir., pres. Ohio Theatre Shop, 1995-96, publicity dir. 1996--; bd. dir., pres. Women's Bd. Columbus Mus. Art, 1991—; organist Glen Echo Presbyn. Ch., 2002--. Recipient Columbus Symphony Advocate award, 2002. Mem. Am. Guild Organists, Choristers Guild Am., Fedn. Am. Bapt. Musicians, Ctr. Sci. and Industry, Ohio State Hist. Soc., Ohio Orgn. Orchs. (treas. 1976-79, sec. 1979-82), Nat. Trust U.S.A., Mountview Bapt. Ch. (moderator 1996—), Rotary Club (Women of Yr. Upper Arlington Ohio 1995), Order Ea. Star, White Shrine of Jerusalem, Ohio State U. Alumnae of Franklin County Club (pres. 1962-64, 71-72), Tau Beta Sigma, Delta Omicron, Kappa Delta (Cen. Ohio Woman of Yr. 1970). Home: 3355 Somerford Rd Columbus OH 43221-1436 E-mail: jallen6@columbus.rr.com.

ALLEN, LOLA, insurance agent; b. Oakland, CA, Nov. 19, 1964; d. George William and Carol Annette (Goss) Davis. AA in bus., Laney Coll., 1996. Lic. insurance agent/notary pub., Calif. Comm. operator U.S. Army, 1985-90; tech. records U.S. Dept. HUD, San Francisco, 1990-92; account mgr. asst. Gallagher Heffernan Ins., San Francisco, 1992-94; account mgr. small bus. Calif. Insurance & Assocs., San Francisco, 1994-96; inside sales rep. Sweet & Baker Ins., San Francisco; special accounts mgr. Tanner Insurance Brokers, Pleasanton, Calif., 1997-99; account mgr. Crist, Fritschi & Paterson, Oakland, Calif., 1999—. COO, Aging Specialist & Assocs., Oakland, 1998—, Tri-Valley Ins. Profls. Editor: (newsletter) Tri-Valley Tribune, 1998-99. Vol. Safe Grad Nite, U.S. Army, 1988, S.F. Aids Found., San Francisco, 1996—. With U.S. Army, 1985-90. Mem. Tri-Valley Insurance Profls. (pres. 1999—, mem. Yr. 1998-99), Nat. Notary Assn. Avocations: reading, writing, cmty. work, sr. citizens. Office: Ins Personnel Svc 595 Market St #2520 San Francisco CA 94105-2802

ALLEN, LOUISE, writer, educator; b. Alliance, Ohio, Sept. 21, 1910; d. Earl Wayne and Ella Celesta (Goodall) Allerton; m. Benjamin Yukl, June 27, 1936; children: Katherine Anne Yukl Johnston, Kenneth Allen, Richard Lee, Margaret Louise Yukl Border. Student, Cleve. Coll. Western Res. U., 1963, Lakeland C.C., 1981-84. Co-founder Sch. Writing, Cleve., 1961-62; founder, dir. Allen Writers' Agy., Wickliffe, Ohio, 1963-84; editorial assoc. criticism service Writer's Digest mag., 1967-69; instr. Cuyahoga C.C., 1965-81, Lakeland C.C., Mentor, Ohio, 1973-81, Scottsdale C.C., 1984-88; writer. Author: (poems) Confetti, 1987; contbr. articles to mags.; composer (hymn) The Foot of the Cross. Mem. AAUW, Mensa, Assn. Mundial de Mujures Periodistas y Escritoras, Women in Communications, Nat. League Am. Pen Women, DAR, Shore Writers Club (founder), Euclid Three Arts Club, Women's City Club (Cleve.). Republican. Congregationalist. Deceased. Home: Chandler, Ariz. Died July 18, 2001.

ALLEN, MARILYN MYERS POOL, theater director, video producer; b. Fresno, Calif., Nov. 2, 1934; d. Laurence B. and Asa (Griggs) Myers; m. Joseph Harold Pool, Dec. 28, 1955; children: Pamela Elizabeth, Victoria Anne, Catherine Marcia; m. Neal R. Allen, Apr. 1982. BA, Stanford U., 1955, postgrad., 1955-56, U. Tex., 1957-60, West Tex. State U., summer 1962, 63, Odessa Coll., 1987-88. Free-lance radio and TV actress; adj. prof. theatre Midland Coll., 1997—98; dir. Globe Theater, Odessa, 1998, 2002; asst. mng. dir. Amarillo Little Theatre, 1964—66, mng. dir., 1966—68, Horseshoe Players, touring profl. theater, 1969—73; actress multi-media prodn. Palo Duro Canyon, 1971; dir. touring children's theatre, 1978—79; guest actress in Medea at Amarillo Coll., 1981; guest reciter Amarillo Symphony, 1972, Midland-Odessa Symphony, 1984. Pres. Tex. Non-Profit Theatres, 1972-74, 75-77, bd. dirs., 1988-91; 1st v.p. High Plains Ctr. for Performing Arts, 1969-73; adv. mem. dept. fine arts Amarillo Coll., 1980-82; adv. mem. Tex. Constnl. Revision Commn., 1973-75; mem. adv. coun. U. Tex. Coll. Fine Arts, 1969-72; cmty. adv. com. for women Amarillo Coll., 1975-79; conv. program com. Am. Theatre Assn., 1978, program participant, 1978-80, bd. dirs., 1980-83; bd. dirs. Amarillo Found. Health and Sci. Edn., 1976-82, program v.p., 1979-81; bd. dirs. Domestic Violence Coun., 1979-82, March of Dimes, 1979-81, Tex. Panhandle Heritage Found., 1964-82, Friends of Fine Arts, West Tex. State U. (now West Tex. A&M U.), 1980-82, Amarillo Pub. Libr., 1980-82, Amarillo Symphony, 1981-82; publicity chmn. Midland Cmty. Theatre, 1984-87, bd. govs., 1986-92, sec., 1987-88, v.p., 1988-92; bd. dirs. Globe of the Great S.W., Odessa, 1998—, v.p. media, 2000-02, v.p. vols., 2002-; mem. Mus. of S.W., Midland Arts Assembly; bd. dirs. Midland County Rep. Women, Ways and Means Ch., 1991, 1st v.p., 1992, publicity chair, 1994; mem. Midland County Redistricting com., 1991; cultural exch. del. from Midland, Tex., to Dong Ying, China, 1993; Tex. UIL one act play adjudicator, 1974-99; mem. Diocesan Comm. Com., N.W. Tex., co-chmn. Companion Diocese Com., Spain, 2003—. Recipient cert. of appreciation Woman of Yr., Amarillo Bus. and Profl. Women's Club, 1966, Best Actress award for Hedda Gabler role Amarillo Little Theatre, 1965, Best Dir. award for Rashomon, 1967, 1st Pl. award for video spl. Tex. Press Conf., 1988, 1st Pl. award for news Tex. Press Conf., 1989, Disting. Svc. award Tex. Non-Profit Theatres, 1992; named Amarillo Woman of Yr., Beta Sigma Phi, 1980, Broadcaster of the Yr., Rocky Mountain Press Conf., 1988, Hamhock of Yr., Midland Cmty. Theatre, 1992, Outstanding Svc. award Midland Arts Assembly, 1992; Travel fellow AAUW, 1973, 78. Fellow Am. Assn. Cmty. Theatre (dir. 1969-72, 82-84, v.p. planning and devel. 1985-87, co-chair AACT/Fest '95), Internat. Amateur Theatre Assn. 23d World Congress (del. Monaco 1997); mem. USTA (sr. women's team sect. winner 1993, 94), S.W. Theatre Conf. (dir. 1973-76, 82-84, exec. com. 1982-84, Disting. Svc. award 1985), Tex. Theatre Coun. (dir. 1974-78, exec. com., pres. 1975-76), AAUW (br. pres. 1973-75, state chmn. cultural interests 1975-77, 86-88, state program v.p. 1977-79, state bd. dirs. 1984-88, program v.p. Midland 1988-89), Episc. Ch. Women (program v.p. Midland 1988-89, outreach chair 1996, program v.p., pres.-elect 1997-98, pres. 1999-2000), DAR (chpt. chaplain 1971-75, historian 1975-77), C. of C. (finc arts coun.), U.S. Tennis Assn. (sr. mixed doubles sect. winner 1999), U.S. Judo Assn., Symphony Guild, Amarillo Art Assn., Midland Symphony Guild (arrangements chmn. 1983-84), Act IX, Amarillo Law Wives Club (pres. 1976-77), Hamhocks (v.p. 1985-86).

ALLEN, MARYON PITTMAN, former senator, journalist, lecturer, interior and clothing designer; b. Meridian, Miss., Nov. 30, 1925; d. John D. and Tellie (Chism) Pittman; m. Joshua Sanford Mullins, Jr., Oct. 17, 1946 (div. Jan. 1959); children: Joshua Sanford III, John Pittman, Maryon Foster; m. James Browning Allen, Aug. 7, 1964 (dec. June 1978). Student, U. Ala., 1944—47, Internat. Inst. Interior Design, 1970. Office mgr. for Dr. Alston Callahan, Birmingham, Ala., 1959-60; bus. mgr. psychiat. clinic U. Ala. Med. Center, Birmingham, 1960-61; life underwriter Protective Life Ins. Co., Birmingham, 1961-62; women's editor Sun Newspapers, Birmingham, 1962-64; v.p., ptnr. Pittman family cos., J.D. Pittman Partnership Co., J.D. Pittman Tractor Co., Emerald Valley Corp., Mountain Lake Farms, Inc., Birmingham; mem. U.S. Senate (succeeding late husband James B. Allen), 1978; dir. pub. rels. and advt. C.G. Sloan & Co. Auction House, Washington, 1981; feature writer Birmingham News, 1964; writer syndicated column Reflections of a News Hen, Washington, 1969-78; feature writer, columnist Maryon Allen's Washington, Washington Post, 1979-81; columnist McCall's Needlework Mag., 1993—. Owner The Maryon Allen Co. Cliff House (Restoration/Design), Birmingham. Contbg. editor: So. Accents Mag., 1976—78. Mem. Ladies of U.S. Senate unit ARC, Former Mems. of Congress, Ala. Hist. Commn., Blair House Fine Arts Commn.; charter mem. Birmingham Com. of 100 for Women; mem. steering com. Ala. Gov.'s Mansion; trustee Children's Fresh Air Farm; trustee, deacon, elder Ind. Presbyn. Ch., Birmingham; Dem. Presdl. elector, Ala., 1968. Recipient 1st place award for best original column Ala. Press Assn., 1962, 63, also various press state and nat. awards for typography, fashion writing, food pages, also several awards during Senate service; sponsor, U.S. Navy Nuclear submarine, U.S.S. Birmingham, S.S.N. 695, launched Newport News, Va., 1977, commissioned 1978. Mem. Nat. Press Club, 1925 F Street Club, 91st Congress Club, Congl. Club, Birmingham Country Club. Home and Office: Cliff House 3215 Cliff Rd S Birmingham AL 35205-1405 E-mail: maryonallenco@aol.com.

ALLEN, MAUREEN JANET, music educator; d. Michael E. and Maxine B. Reilly; 1 child, Ryan C. MusM, Hartt Sch. Music, 1995. Music tchr. Williamsville East H.S., East Amherst, NY, 1991—; choir dir. St. Amelia Roman Cath. Ch., Tonawanda, NY, 2001—. Mem.: Erie County Music Educator's Assn. (bd. mem. 1997—2001). Office: Williamsville East High School 151 Paradise Rd East Amherst NY 14051 E-mail: mallen@williamsvillek12.org.

ALLEN, NANCY JANETTE, school librarian; b. Wichita Falls, Tex., Mar. 20, 1972; d. Marvin and Janet Koenig; m. Wade Scott Allen, July 22, 1995; children: Grace, William, Emma. B, Tex. Luth. U., 1994. Cert. tchr. Tex., 1995, learning resources Tex., 2002. Tchr. Angleton (Tex.) Mid. Sch. West, 1998—2002, libr., 2002—. Mem.: Delta Kappa Gamma. Office: Angleton Intermediate School 1800 N Downing Angleton TX 77515 Personal E-mail: nancya7@msn.com.

ALLEN, NANCY JEAN, adult education educator; b. Dover, N.J., Oct. 11, 1952; d. James Carrell and Jean (Schmidt) Dalrymple; m. William Timothy Allen, Mar. 12, 1983. BS, West Ga. Coll., 1975, MEd, 1976. Cert. tchr. Fla. Tchr. adult handicap Westside Tech., Winter Garden, Fla., 1984—93, workforce edn. coord., 1993—96; tchr. adult basic edn. Winter Park (Fla.) Tech., 1996—, chairperson adult handicapped dept. Rep. supt. adv. coun. Winter Park Tech., 1996—97, peer, coach, 2002—, mem. safety com.; trainer Orange County Pub. Schs., Orlando, Fla., 1999—2000; chairperson Dept. Adult Gen. Edn., Winter Park, 2002—. Chairperson Relay for Life Am. Cancer Soc., Winter Park, 1999—2000; mem. leadership team West Orange Consortium, Winter Garden, 1996. Finalist Tecaherrific, Walt Disney World, 1992. Mem.: Coun. Occupl. Edn. (chairperson orgn. and structure com.), Adult and Cmty. Educators Fla., Orange County Adult and Cmty. Edn. Assn., Orange County Vocat. Assn., Fla. Literacy Coalition, Adult and Cmty. Educators Fla., Assn. Work Force Edn. (bd. dirs. 2001—, Educator of the Yr. 1999—2000). Republican. Presbyterian. Avocations: golf, walking, gardening, swimming. Home: 268 Carriage Hill Dr Casselberry FL 32707 Office: Winter Park Tech Orange County Schs 901 Webster Ave Winter Park FL 32789 Business E-Mail: allenn@ocps.k12.fl.us.

ALLEN, NATALIE, cable news anchor; Postgrad., Memphis State U.; B in Radio, T.V. and film, U. So. Miss. News anchor, reporter Sta. WREG-TV, Memphis, 1985-88, Sta. WFTV-TV, Orlando, Fla., 1988-92; co-anchor CNN Today, News Stand, Atlanta, 1992—. Recipient Emmy award for Spot News Reporting, 1989, Edward R. Murrow award, 1990. Office: CNN Cable News Network 1 CNN Ctr NW Atlanta GA 30303-2762

ALLEN, NORMA ANN, librarian, educator; b. Balt., Jan. 22, 1951; d. James Crawley and Thelma Agusta (Keaton) Ghee; children: Lamont Ricardo Ghee, Alissa S. Allen, Avery O. Allen. BA in Adminstrn. Mgmt., Sojourner Douglass Coll., Balt., 1987; MS in Instrnl. Tech., Towson State U., 1999. Instr. data processing PSI Inst., Balt., 1987-88; acquisition technician Social Security Adminstrn., Balt., 1987-89, reference librarian, 1989-91, acquisitions librarian, 1991—; librarian United Bapt. Membership Conv., Balt., 2002—. Instrnl. developer Computer Asst. Instrn., Towson U., 1995—; bus. computer tech. instr. Balt. City C.C., 2000—; freelance floral designer/arranger, freelance instr. basic writing skills and computer literacy; instr. bus. computer tech. Balt. City C.C., 2000—. Sec., bd. dirs. New Image Child Care Facility, Balt., 1992, chmn. bd. dirs., 2001-02; instr. active reading literacy program Enoch Pratt Libr., Balt., 1992; instr. United Missionary Bapt. Conv., 1997, libr., 2003. Multicultural scholar Towson U., 1995-96. Mem. ALA, Spl. Librs. Assn., Horizon User Group. Office: Social Security Adminstrn 6401 Security Blvd Rm 571 Baltimore MD 21235-0001 E-mail: norma.allen@ssa.gov.

ALLEN, PATRICIA J. library director; b. McLean County, Ky., Nov. 10, 1941; d. Richard Louis and Helen (Hancock) Jones; m. Jerry M. Mize, Mar. 19, 1960 (div. 1978); children: Martin P., Elizabeth M. Atherton; m. Lawrence A. Allen, Nov. 24, 1983 (div. 1985). Student, Murray (Ky.) State U., 1959-60; BA, Ky. Wesleyan Coll., 1962; MA, Western Ky. U., 1974; MLS, U. Ky., 1982; postgrad., U. N.C., 1983-84. Libr. pub. elem. schs., Daviess County, Ky., 1963-70; media specialist pub. elem., mid. and high schs. McLean County, Ky., 1970-78; head pub. svcs., assoc. prof. libr. sci. Ky. Wesleyan Coll., Owensboro, 1978-83; asst. dir. Evansville (Ind.) Vanderburgh County Pub. Libr., 1985-89; dir. Carmel (Ind.) Clay Pub. Libr., 1989-91, Sanibel (Fla.) Pub. Libr., 1991—. Mem. adj. faculty Western Ky. U., Bowling Green, 1977-78, Ind. U., Bloomington, 1988; workshop presenter Nursing Home Activities Dirs. Assn., Owensboro, Ky., 1981; cons. Ky. Dept. Librs. and Archives, Frankfort, 1982, Purchase (Ky.) Regional Libr. Sys., Murray, 1983, Henderson (Ky.) C.C. Libr., 1988. Editor: Emergency Handbook, 1987, Circulation Policies and Procedures, 1988, Sanibel Public Library Building Program Statement, 1992; contbr. article to profl. jours. Pres. Ret. Sr. Vol. Program Adv. Coun., Evansville, 1986-88; bd. dirs. Evansville Goodwill Industries, 1987-89. Named Outstanding Citizen of the Yr., Sanibel-Captiva Islands C. of C., 1995; Caroline M. Hewins scholar U. Ky., 1982, Margaret Ellen Kalp scholar U. N.C., 1983-84; hon. Ky. Col., 1981. Mem. ALA, Ky. Libr. Assn., Fla. Libr. Assn. (Transformer award 1996), Pub. Libr. Assn., Libr. Adminstrs. and Mgrs. Assn., S.W. Fla. Libr. Network (bd. dirs. 1997—, pres. 1999-2001), Zonta (bd. dirs. 1999-2001), Beta Phi Mu. Democrat. Baptist. Avocations: travel, walking, swimming, needlework, reading. Office: Sanibel Pub Libr 770 Dunlop Rd Sanibel FL 33957-4016 E-mail: pallen@sanlib.org.

ALLEN, ROBERTA, fiction and nonfiction writer, conceptual artist, photographer; b. N.Y.C., Oct. 6, 1945; d. Sol and Jeanette (Waldner) A. Student, Inst. Bellas Artes, Mex., 1971. Lectr. Corcoran Sch. Art, Washington, 1975, Kutztown State Coll., 1979, C.W. Post Coll., 1979. Instr. creative writing Parsons Sch. Design, N.Y.C., 1986; instr. The Writer's Voice, 1992—97, The New Sch., 1993—, Dept. Continuing Edn., NYU, 1993—99; Tennessee Williams fellow, writer-in-residence U. of the South, Sewanee, Tenn., 1998; adj. asst. prof. Columbia U. Sch. of the Arts, 1998—99, Eugene Lang. Coll., 2000. Author: Partially Trapped Lines, 1975, Pointless Arrows, 1976, Pointless Acts, 1977, Everything in The World There Is To Know Is Known By Somebody, But Not By the Same Knower, 1981, Amazon Dream, 1993; author: (fiction) The Daughter, 1992, The Dreaming Girl, 2000, The Traveling Woman, 1986, Certain People, 1997; author: (writing guide) Fast Fiction, 1997, The Playful Way to Serious Writing, 2002, (Personal Growth) The Playful Way to Knowing Yourself, 2003; one-woman shows include Galerie 845, Amsterdam, Netherlands, 1967, John Weber Gallery, N.Y.C., 1974—75, 1977, 1979, Inst. for Art and Urban Resources, 1977, 1980, Galerie Maier-Hahn, Dusseldorf, Germany, 1977, MTL Galerie, Brussels, 1978, C.W. Post Coll., Glenvale, N.Y., 1978, Galerie Walter Storms, Munich, 1981, Kunstforum, Stadt. Galerie in Lenbachhaus, 1981, Galeria Primo Piano, Rome, 1981, Perth Inst. Contemporary Arts, 1989, Art Resources Transfer, Inc., 2001, SUNY, Binghamton, 2001. Fellow McDowell Colony, 1971—72; grantee LINE, 1985.

ALLEN, SUZANNE, financial planning executive, insurance agent, writer; b. Santa Monica, Calif, May 31, 1963; d. Raymond A. and Ethel Allen; m. Steve Milstein Roth, Dec. 27, 1992, (div. 2000). BA, U. Calif., Santa Cruz, 1986; MA in Edn., Calif. State U., L.A., 1990; postgrad., Art Ctr. Sch. Design, 1994—. Cert. tchr., Calif.; lic. real estate agt., Calif. Interviewer LA Times Newspaper, 1986-88; educator LA Unified Sch. Dist., 1987-90, Burbank Unified Sch. Dist., Calif., 1990-94, 1994—2000; ptnr. fin. svc. Roth & Assoc./NY Life, LA, 1993-2000; educator Pasadena Unified Sch. Dist., 2001—02; ptnr. fin. svc. Pacific Life Ins. Co.; v.p. Jarvis & Mandell LLC Estate Planning Svc., Mass. Mut. Ins. Co., 2001—; agt. Mass. Mut. Ins., Beverly Hills, Calif. Ptnr. Retirement Educators Fin. Svc.; agt.-cons. Frasier Fin. Group, 2001—02. Model, actor :, 1998—; author: End of Days, 2001—; author: (pen name Quinn Allen) I Will Serve You All My Days, Black Dahlia, Alone, 2002, I Miss Him, 2003, (poem) Waiting for Godot, 2003, The Pasadena Porch, 2004, I'm Sad You Went Away, 2004, DNA Destiny, 2004, Disclaimer, 2004. Mem. PTA, United Tchr. Pasadena, Civil War Trust; vol. SPCA/Humane Soc., 1999—; mem. Nat. Trust Hist. Preservation, Honor Roll mem.; bd. mem. Bungalow Heaven Neighborhood Assn.; hon. mem. Top Bus. Rep. Party for Sen. Tom Delany. Recipient 4 Silver Cups, Internat. Poet of Merit, 6 Bronze medal, Internat. Poets Soc., Silver Outstanding Achievement in Poetry Trophy, 2003, 3 silver trophies for outstanding achievement in poetry, 2003, Piece of the Roof award, N.Y. Life Ins. Co. for Roth & Assocs., 1994, Nat. Leadership award, Nat. Rep. Congl. Com., 2003. Mem.: NEA, Libr. of Congress, Nat. Soc. for Hist. Preservation, Burbank Tchrs. Union, Internat. High IQ Soc., Abraham Lincoln Assn., Internat. Soc. Poets (hon.). Avocations: painting, illustrating, writing, weight training, old house renovation. Office: Jarvis & Mandell LLC 1875 Century Park E # 1550 Los Angeles CA 90067 also: Michael's Agy Mass Mut Beverly Hills Office 1875 Century Park E # 1550 Los Angeles CA 90067

ALLEN, THERESA OHOTNICKY, neurobiologist, consultant; b. Torrington, Conn., Apr. 27, 1948; d. Frank Richard and Helen Theresa (Drozdenko) Ohotnicky; m. Thomas Atherton Allen, Aug. 12, 1972; children: Melanie Atherton, Abigail Baldwin. BA, U. Conn., 1970; MS, Villanova U., 1975; PhD, Duke U., 1978; cert. in bus. adminstrn., U. Pa., 1983. Realtor. Rsch. assoc. U. Pa., Phila., 1981-83; sci. dir. Drexel U., Phila., 1983-84; cons. on neurobiology to sci.-oriented cos., 1984—. Contbr. articles to profl. jours., also chpts. to books. Bd. dirs. Gladwyne (Pa.) Libr. League, 1986—, Athena Inst. for Women's Wellness, Haverford, Pa., 1989-93; trustee Gladwyne Libr., 1988—, pres., 1991-93; com. chmn. Jr. League Phila., 1989-90. Fellow Inst. Neurol. Scis., U. Pa., 1978-80, NIH, 1980-81. Mem.: Phila. Country Club, Humane Soc., Phila. Skating Club, Phi Beta Kappa. Episcopalian. Avocations: skiing, gardening, antiques. Home: 1433 Waverly Rd Gladwyne PA 19035-1224

ALLEN, VICKY, sales and marketing professional; b. Springfield, Pa., May 27, 1957; d. James Joseph and Ann Marie (Cifone) Cattafesta; m. James Francis DeLeone, Aug. 11, 1979 (div. 1982); m. Dennis Ronald Allen, June 30, 1990; children: Amber, Austen. BBA in Computer Sci., Temple U., 1979. Quality assurance Burroughs Corp., Downingtown, Pa., 1977, software QA, 1978, systems analyst, 1979-81; program analyst Crocker Internal Systems, San Jose, Calif., 1981-83; sr. systems analyst Avantek, Inc., Santa Clara, Calif., 1983-84; product mktg. program specialist Micro Focus, Palo Alto, Calif., 1984-96; OEM sales account mgr. Netscape Comms. Corp., Mountain View, Calif., 1996-99; mgr. Nortel Networks Strategic Relationships, 1999—2002; inside sales Polycom, Milpitas, Calif., 2002—03; sales mktg. specialist Steel Eye Tech., Mountain View, Calif., 2003—. Programmer cons. Fin. Group, Palo Alto, 1985-86. Active Sierra Club. Mem. Phi Sigma Sigma (sec. 1978-79). Democrat. Roman Catholic. Avocations: music, hiking, biking, race walking. Office: Steel Eye Tech 2660 Marine Way #200 Mountain View CA 94043 E-mail: squirlr1@yahoo.com.

ALLEN, VICTORIA TAYLOR, archivist; b. N.Y.C., June 22, 1942; d. Robert Grayson and Margaret (Seckel) Taylor; m. Ernest G. Allen, Dec. 28, 1985 (dec. Apr. 1989). BA in French, Mary Washington Coll./U. Va., 1964; MAT in English, Manhattanville Coll., 1979. Tchr. of French, Chatham Hall, Chatham, Va., 1965-73, Masters Sch., Dobbs Ferry, N.Y., 1973-79; tchr. English, Convent of the Sacred Heart, N.Y.C., 1979-86; archivist The Convent of the Sacred Heart, Greenwich, Conn., 1995—. Mem. adv. bd. Barat House, Manhattanville Coll., Purchase, N.Y., 1994—; mem. adv. bd. Open Door Health Ctr., Ossining, N.Y., 1986-90. Author; (booklet) Traditions and Customs of Sacred Heart Education, 1998. Roman Catholic. Avocations: photography, travel, cooking, gardening.

ALLEN, YVONNE, principal; Elem. sch. tchr.; vocat.-tech. instr.; adj. prof. Lambrith U.; prin. Whiteville (Tenn.) Elem. Sch. Recipient Nat. Educator award, Milken Family Found., 1996. Mem.: West Tenn. Assn. Elem. Schs. (past pres.), Nat. Assn. Elem. Sch. Prins., Nat. Bd. for Profl. Tchg. Stds. (bd. mem., past pres.). Office: Whiteville Elem Sch Hwy 100 Box 659 Whiteville TN 38075

ALLER, MARGO FRIEDEL, astronomer; b. Springfield, Ill., Aug. 27, 1938; d. Jules and Claire (Cornick) Friedel; m. Hugh Duncan Aller, Aug. 17, 1964; 1 child, Monique Christine. BA, Vassar Coll., 1960; postgrad., Harvard U., 1961-62; MS, U. Mich., 1964, PhD, 1969. Mathematician programmer Smithsonian Astrophys. Obs., Cambridge, Mass., 1960-62; rsch. assoc. U. Mich., Ann Arbor, 1970-76, assoc. rsch. scientist, 1976-85, rsch. scientist, 1985—. Mem. users' com. Nat. Radio Astronomy Observatory, 1984-86. Mem. Internat. Union of Radio Sci., Am. Astron. Soc., Internat. Astron. Union, Sigma Xi. Avocation: skiing. Office: U Mich Dept Astronomy 817 Dennison Bldg Ann Arbor MI 48109-1090 E-mail: mfa@umich.edu.

ALLEY, KIRSTIE, actress; b. Wichita, Kans., Jan. 12, 1951; children: William True, Lillie. Student, U. Kans., Kans. State U. Actress: (stage prodns.) Cat on a Hot Tin Roof, Answers; (feature films) Star Trek II: The Wrath of Khan, 1982, Blind Date, 1984, Champions, 1984, Runaway, 1984, Summer School, 1987, Shoot to Kill, 1988, Look Who's Talking, 1989, Daddy's Home, 1989, One More Chance, 1990, Madhouse, 1990, Sibling Rivalry, 1990, Look Who's Talking Too, 1990, Look Who's Talking Now, 1993, Village of the Damned, 1995, It Takes Two, 1995, Sticks and Stones, 1996, Nevada, 1996, For Richer of Poorer, 1997 (People's Choice award 1997), Deconstructing Harry, 1997 (People's Choice award 1997), Toothless, 1997, Drop Dead Gorgeous, 1999, The Mao Game, 1999, Back by Midnight, 2002; (TV mini-series) North and South Book I, 1985, North and South, Book II, 1986, The Last Don, 1997, The Last Don Part II, 1998 (Emmy nomination), Blonde, 2001, Salem Witch Trials, 2002; (TV movies) Sins of the Past, 1984, A Bunny's Tale, 1984, The Prince of Bel Air, 1985, Stark: Mirror Image, 1986, Infidelity, 1987, David's Mother, 1994 (Emmy award, Lead Actress - Special, 1994), Radiant City, 1996, Profoundly Normal, 2003, Family Sins, 2004; (TV series) Masquerade, 1984-85, Cheers, 1987-1993 (Emmy award as Outstanding Lead Actress in a Comedy Series 1991); prodr., actress Veronica's Closet, 1997-2000; tv appearances include The Match Game, The Love Boat, The Hitchhiker, The Roseanne Show; co-prodr.: Nevada, 1997. Spokesperson for Narcanon Drug Rehab.; founder Ch. of Scientology, Mission of Wichita. Recipient People's Choice award, 1998.*

ALLISON, ADRIENNE AMELIA, not-for-profit developer; b. Toronto, Ont., Can., Nov. 2, 1940; d. Harold Whitfield and Emmeline Amelia (Banister) Hedley; m. Stephen Vyvyan Allison, Jan. 2, 1960 (div. 1984); children: Mark Hedley, Myles Stephen, Alexander Andrew; m. Armin U. Kuder, Aug. 26, 1989 (div. 2002). BA, George Washington U., 1978; MA, Georgetown U., 1980; MPA, Harvard U., 1986. Social sci. analyst AID, Washington, 1980-85, project mgr., 1986-89, presdl. com. on HIV epidemic, 1987-88; program dir. Centre for Devel. and Population Activities, 1988-91; v.p. Centre for Devel. and Population Activities, 1991-98; dir. maternal and neonatal health program Johns Hopkins Program in Reproductive Health, Balt., 1998—2001; internat. cons., 2001—. Adj. prof. George Washington U. Sch. Pub. Health, Johns Hopkins U. Sch. Hygiene and Pub. Health. Co-author: Vegetable Gardening in Bangladesh, 1975. Chair peace commn. Episcopal Diocese of Washington, 2002—; mem. vestry St. Albans Parish, Washington, 1984—. Mem.: APHA, Cosmos Club. Home: 8011 Glendale Rd Chevy Chase MD 20815-5902 Personal E-mail: adrienneaallison@aol.com.

ALLISON, ANNE MARIE, retired librarian; b. Oak Park, Ill., Oct. 3, 1931; d. Gerald Patrick and Anna Evelyn (Beam) Myers; m. James Dixon Alison, Aug. 28, 1954; children: Mark, Mary, Clare, Ruth, Edward. BA in French, St. Mary of the Woods Coll., 1951; postgrad., U. Fribourg, 1952-53; MLS, Rosary Coll., 1968. Asst. libr. Triton Coll., River Grove, Ill., 1967-68; asst. libr. tech. svcs. Moraine Valley Community Coll., Palos Hills, Ill., 1968-69; dir. learning resources, head libr. Coll. Lake County, Grayslake, Ill., 1969-71; asst. head catalog dept. Kent (Ohio) State U. Librs., 1971-73, head processing dept., 1973-79, asst. dir. libr. svcs., 1979-81; acting dir. Fla. Atlantic U. Libr., Boca Raton, 1980-81; asst. dir., head tech. svcs. Wayne State U. Librs., Detroit, 1981-83; dir. librs. U. Cen. Fla., Orlando, 1983-97, ret., 1997. Past chair, bd. dirs. Fla. Extension Libr., Tampa; bd. dirs. Ctr. for Libr. Automation, Gainesville, Fla., Cen. Fla. Holocaust Meml. Resource Ctr., Orlando; adj. prof. Libr. and Info. Sci., U. S. Fla., Tampa. Editor: OCLC: A National Library Network, 1979; contbr. articles to profl. jours. Arbitrator alternative dispute resolution program Better Bus. Bur. Cen. Fla., Maitland, 1985—; active Friends Winter Park Pub. Libr., Friends of Orlando Pub. Libr. Recognized for Outstanding Leadership in Edn. Cen. Fla. Ednl. Consortium for Women, 1990. Mem. ALA (chair profl. ethics com.), Fla. Libr. Assn., Fla. Assn. Coll. and Rsch. Librs. (pres. bd. dirs.). Avocations: fruit farming, collecting china. Office: U Cen Fla PO Box 25000 Orlando FL 32816-0001

ALLISON, CARRIE FRANCES, English language educator; b. Kansas City, Mo., Aug. 27, 1979; d. Suzanne Eileen Lattimer; m. Donald James Rolling, June 28, 2003. BA in English, BS in Edn., N.W. Mo. State U., Maryville, 2001. English tchr. Raytown (Mo.) H.S., 2001—. Author: (chapbook of poetry) Pointing Toward Home. Mem.: Nat. Coun. Tchrs. of English. Avocations: owning a basset hound, writing, reading.

ALLISON, JOAN KELLY, music educator, pianist; b. Denison, Iowa, Jan. 25, 1935; d. Ivan Martin and Esther Cecelia (Newborg) K.; m. Guy Hendrick Allison, July 25, 1954 (div. Apr. 1973); children: David, Dana, Douglas, Diane. MusB, St. Louis Inst. of Music, 1955; MusM, So. Meth. U., 1976. Korrepetitor Corpus Christi (Tex.) Symphony, 1963-85; staff pianist Am. Inst. Mus. Studies, Graz, Austria, 1974-89; prof. Del Mar Coll., Corpus Christi, 1976—2002. Adj. prof. Del Mar Coll., 1959-75, Corpus Christi State U., 1978-93, Tex. A&M U., Corpus Christi, 1993—; program dir. Corpus Christi Chamber Music Soc., 1986—; piano chmn. Corpus Christi Young Artists' Competition, 1987—; chmn. Del Mar Coll. Student Programs Com., 1986-88, 91-92, 94-95, 2001-02; chmn. radio com., S.Tex. Pub. Broadcasting Svc., Corpus Christi, 1987-88; asst. mus. dir. Little Theater, Corpus Christi, 1970-74; judge, Houston Symphony Auditions, 1988, S.C. Young Artist Competition, Columbia, 1990; freelance accompanist, 1955—, adjudicator, 1960—; v.p. united fac., Del Mar Coll., 1986-88; pianist with Del Mar Trio, 1965-95, Young Audiences, Inc., 1975-83; recital tours in U.S., Mex., Austria, 1954-88. Piano soloist, St. Louis Symphony, 1956, 57, Bach Festival Orch., St. Louis, 1955, Corpus Christi Symphony; recipient Artist Presentation award, Artist Presentation Soc., St. Louis, 1956; contbr. articles to profl. jours., including Internat. Piano Quar. Co-chmn. Mayor's Com. on Recycling, Corpus Christi, 1989-91; bd. dirs. Corpus Christi Symphony; adv. bd. Corpus Christi Concert Ballet; mem. steering com. cultural devel. plan City of Corpus Christi, 1995-96. Recipient Women in Careers award YWCA, 1985. Mem. Music Tchrs. Nat. Assn., Tex. Music Tchrs. Assn., Corpus Christi Music Tchrs. Assn., Liszt Soc. (contbr. to jour.). Avocations: foreign travel, water-skiing, hiking, acting in community theatre. Home: 4709 Curtis Clark Dr Corpus Christi TX 78411-4801 E-mail: Jallison@the-i.net.

ALLISON, MERITA ANN, state legislator; Mem. S.C. Ho. of Reps., 1993—; spl. program coord. Springs Indust-Lyman Complex. Republican. Home: 209 Spartanburg Hwy Lyman SC 29365-1844 Office: SC House of Reps State House Columbia SC 29211

ALLISON, PAMELA SUE, special education administrator; b. St. Louis, May 1, 1954; d. James W. and Ruth E. Wetton; m. Scott D. Mirly, June 7, 1975 (div. Mar. 1992); children; Anna E., Lara B.; m. Willis D. Allison, Jnov. 8, 1992. BS in Edn., S.E. Mo. State U., Cape Girardeau, 1975, MA in Edn., 1980; EdS, S.W. Mo. State U., Springfield, 1987. Cert. supt., spl. edn. dir., prin., elem. tchr., Mo. Elem. and spl. edn. tchr. Strain-Japan R-16 Sch., Sullivan, Mo., 1976-79; elem. tchr. St. Clair (Mo.) Sch., 1979-81; elem. prin. Strain-Japan, 1981-84, Pierce City (Mo.) Sch., 1984-89, Washington (Mo.) Sch. Dist., 1987-92; spl. edn. tchr., adminstr. Spl. Svcs. Coop., Hillsboro, Mo., 1992-95; dir. spl. svcs. Grandview Sch. Dist., Hillsboro, 1995—. Adj. prof. S.W. Bapt. U., Bolivar, Mo., 1997; dir. elem./spl. edn. Mo. Leadership Acad., Jefferson City, Mo., 1989—. Contbr. articles to profl. publs.; designer curriculum in field. Chair Grandview Cmty. 2000 Com., Hillsboro, 1996—; bd. dirs. Wyman Ctr., Inc., Eureka, Mo., 1990-92; master assessor Mo. Leadership Acad., Jefferson City, 1995—; in-svc. presenter Coop. Sch. Dists., St. Louis, 1997. Mem. Mo. Spl. Edn. Adminstrn., Mineral Area Local Adminstrn. Spl. Edn., Mo. Women's Network (del., chair 1992-93, award), Kiwanis (v.p. 1991-92, Mo. membership chmn. 1991-92, Kiwanian of Yr. 1991, Mo. del. 1991-92, Mo-Ark to internat. convs. 1989-92). Democrat. Lutheran. Avocations: swing dance, canoeing, travel, reading. Office: Apt B103 1208 Florida Rd Durango CO 81301-4441

ALLMAN, MARGARET ANN LOWRANCE, counseling administrator; b. Carmel, Calif., June 2, 1938; d. Edward Walton and Rhoda Elizabeth (Patton) Lowrance; m. Jackie Howard Hamilton, Dec. 21, 1959 (div. May 1976); children: John Scott Hamilton, David Lee Hamilton, Dennis Lynn Hamilton; m. Jack Fredrick Allman, Dec. 22, 1977; stepchildren: John Frederick, James Paul, Jeffrey Lee. AA, Christian Coll., 1958; BA in Spanish, U. Mo., 1960, MEd, 1971, EdD, 1994. Tchr. Spanish Neosho (Mo.) HS, 1961-62, asst. prin., 1974-77; florist Wallflower Shop and Greenhouse, Joplin, Mo., 1962-69; dean girls Joplin Sr. HS, 1967-69; florist, bookkeeper Mueller's Garden Ctr., Columbia, Mo., 1969-71; instr. edn., asst. dean of students Columbia Coll., 1971-74; dir. guidance Am. Cmty. Sch., Buenos Aires, 1978-81; tchr. Spanish, psychology Ava (Mo.) HS, 1982-84; tchr. Spanish, social studies McDonald County HS, Anderson, Mo., 1984-88; counselor, acad. advisor Mo. So. State U., Joplin, 1988—2003. Cons. Mo. So. State Univ., 1990—; mem. internat. task force Mo. So. State Coll., 1994—96; mem. adv. bd. Adult Basic Edn., Joplin, 1992—; presenter Ctr. Applications Psychol. Type Internat. Conf., 1996. Named to Outstanding Young Women Am., 1972; recipient William D. Phillips Music award, 1st Christian Ch., Columbia, 1956. Mem.: Southwest Mo. Sch. Counselor Assn. (sec. 1994—97, v.p. 1992—94, 1999—2001, mem. governing bd., chmn. publs. and rsch. com. 1997—99), Mo. Sch. Counselor Assn., Phi Theta Kappa, Sigma Delta Pi, Phi Sigma Iota (romance lang., pres. 1959—60), Delta Eta Chi, Sigma Phi Gamma, Kappa Delta Pi. Avocations: music, photographer, sketch artist, needlecrafts, jewelry crafts. Home: 1214 Circle Dr Neosho MO 64850-1301

ALLMAN, MARGO HUTZ, sculptor, painter; b. N.Y.C., Feb. 23, 1933; d. Werner H. and Avis (Newcomb) Hutz; m. William B. Allman, Feb. 19, 1954; children: Avis Louise, David Drue. Student, Smith Coll., 1950-51, Moore Coll. Art, 1952-55, Hans Hofmann Sch. Art, 1953, U. Del., 1967-70. Artist-in-residence Canakkale Seramik, Canada, Turkey, 1995. One-woman shows include Wallingford (Pa.) Art Ctr., 1964, Windham Coll., 1974, Bloomsburg State Coll., 1976—77, Moore Coll. Art and Design, 1979, Marian Locks Gallery, Phila., 1984, McKinney Gallery West Chester U., Pa., 1994, Gomez Gallery, Balt., 2002, exhibited in group shows at Phila. Art Alliance, 1954, Del. Art Mus., Wilmington, 1958, 1965, 1967, 1993, 2000, Print Club, Phila., 1959, U. Del., 1977, Del. State Arts Coun., Wilmington, 1981, C. Grimaldis Gallery, Balt., 1983, Art in Form Gallery, Karlsruhe, Germany, 1984, Contemporary Women Artists Phila., 1986—87, Del. Ctr. Contemporary Arts, Wilmington, 1995, 2002, Long Beach Island Found. Arts and Scis., Loveladies, N.J., 1995, Cecil County Arts Coun., Elkton, Md., 1998—99, Chester County Art Assn., West Chester, 1999—2001, 2003, Regional Ctr. Women Arts, 2001, 2003, Moore Galleries Kimmel Ctr. Performing Arts, Phila., 2004, Represented in permanent collections Del. Mus., Phila. Mus., Tidewater Pub. Co., Centerville, Md., Hercules, Inc., Wilmington, Connolly Bove Lodge & Hutz LLP. Bd. dirs. Robert Small Dance Co., N.Y.C., 1979—80. Recipient Mildred Boericke prize, Print Club, 1958, Landscape prize, Wilmington Trust Bank, 1969, Disting. Alumnae award, Moore Coll. Art Design, 1998. Mem.: Phila. Mus. Art, Nat. Mus. Women Arts (charter), Del. Art Mus., Del. Ctr. Contemporary Arts, Moore Coll. Art and Design Alumnae Assn. Home: 202 State Rd West Grove PA 19390-8906

ALLMAND, LINDA F(AITH), retired library director; b. Port Arthur, Tex., Jan. 31, 1937; d. Clifton James and Jewel Etoile (Smith) Allmand. BA, North Tex. State U., 1960; MA, U. Denver, 1962. Clerical asst. Gates Meml. Libr., 1953-55; libr. asst. Houston Pub. Libr., 1955-58; children's libr. Denver Pub. Libr., 1960-63; children's coord. Anaheim (Calif.) Pub. Libr., 1963-65; br. mgr. Dallas Pub. Libr, 1965-71, chief br. svcs., 1971-81; dir. Ft. Worth Pub. Libr., 1981-98; instr. North Tex. State U., Denton, 1967—. Instr. Dallas County C.C., 1981; bldg. [illegible] Dallas Pub. Libr., 1974-80, Hurst Pub. Libr., 1977-78, Jacksonville (Tex.) Pub. Libr., 1976-79, Carrollton Pub. Libr., 1979-81, Haltom (Tex.) City Pub. Libr., 1984, Iowa Park (Tex.) Pub. Libr., 1985, S.W. Regional Libr., Ft. Worth, 1987. Author: 1981-2000, Ft. Worth Public Library-Facilities and Long-Range Planning Study, 1982; contbr. chpts. to books, articles to profl. jours. Bd. dirs. City of Dallas Credit Union, 1973-81, Sr. Citizen's Ctrs., Inc., 1982; com. chmn. Goals for Dallas, 1967-69; mem. Forum Ft. Worth, 1983; mem. Edn. Info. Task Force, Downtown Fort Worth, Inc., 1992-93; mem. women's health adv. bd. Harris Meth. Hosp., 1999-2004. Pilot Club of Port Arthur scholar, 1954, Libr. Binding Inst. scholar, 1958; recipient Disting. Alumnus award North Tex. State U., 1983, U. North Tex., 1998, Leadership Ft. Worth, 1982-83; named Tarrant County Newsmaker of Yr., 1984, Outstanding Leader Ft. Worth Star Telegram, 1989, Outstanding Woman of Yr. Mayor's Commn. on Status of Women, 1989. Mem. ALA, AAUP, AAUW (Tarrant County pres.-elect 1998, pres. 1999), Tex. Libr. Assn. (pres. pub. libr. divsn. 1980-81, chmn. planning com. 1982-84, pres.-elect 1985-86, pres. 1986-87, Libr. of Yr. award 1985, North Tex. Pub. Adminstr. of Yr. award 1990), Tarrant Regional Librs. Assn., Am. Mgmt. Assn., Dallas County Librs. Assn. (pres. 1968-69), Downtown Ft. Worth Rotary Club (mem. edn. info. task force 1992-93), Freedom to Read Found., Ft. Worth C. of C. (bd. dirs. 1993-95), Sister Cities, Inc., Ft. Worth Pub. Libr. Found. Home: 701 Timberview Ct N Fort Worth TX 76112-1715

ALLOCCA, ANTOINETTE, computer company executive; m. Mark Greenspan; children: Simone, Judy, Joey, Olivia. Grad., Hofstra U., 1978. Sales position, N.Y.C., 1980-88; sole salesperson Essential Data Corp., pres. Office: Essential Data Corp 45 Church St Stamford CT 06906-1711 Fax: 203-352-2809.

ALLRED, GLORIA RACHEL, lawyer; b. Phila., July 3, 1941; d. Morris and Stella Bloom; m. William Allred (div. Oct. 1987); 1 child, Lisa. BA, U. Pa., 1963; MA, NYU, 1966; JD, Loyola U., L.A., 1974; JD (hon.), U. West Los Angeles, 1981. Bar: Calif. 1975, U.S. Dist. Ct. (cen. dist.) Calif. 1975, U.S. Ct. Appeals (9th cir.) 1976, U.S. Supreme Ct. 1979. Ptnr. Allred, Maroko, Goldberg & Ribakoff (now Allred, Maroko & Goldberg), L.A., 1976—. Contbr. articles to profl. jours. Pres. Women's Equal Rights Legal Def. and Edn. Fund, L.A., 1978—, Women's Movement Inc., L.A. Recipient Commendation award L.A. Bd. Suprs., 1986, Mayor of L.A., 1986, Pub. Svc. award Nat. Assn. Fed. Investigators, 1986, Vol. Action award Pres. of U.S., 1986. Mem. ABA, Calif. Bar Assn., Nat. Assn. Women Lawyers, Calif. Women Lawyers Assn., Women Lawyers L.A. Assn., Friars (Beverly Hills, Calif.), Magic Castle Club (Hollywood, Calif.) Office: Allred Maroko & Goldberg 6300 Wilshire Blvd Ste 1500 Los Angeles CA 90048-5217

ALLSTON, CHARITA CAPERS, music educator; d. Lloyd Sterling and Viretta Thomas Bond; children: Paul Capers Jr., Wayne Capers. AS in Music Edn., Essex County Coll.; BS in Voice, William Paterson Univ. Cert. tchg. cert. State of N.J. K-12. Acctg. tech. U.S. Postal Svc., Newark, 1973—91; choral instr. Orange Bd. of Edn., Orange, NJ, 1991—93, Elizabeth (N.J.) Bd. of Edn., 1993—99, Newark (N.J.) Newark Bd. of Edn., 1999—. Choir mem. R.P. Means Gospel Choir, 1975—99, M.A. Zimmerman Youth Choir, 1975—79, M.D. Birt AME Choir, 1977—92, Polyphonics Com. Ens., 1975—90; choir dir. Henry Tucker Male Chorus, 1977—84, rainbow Children's Choir, 1989—91, Chancellor Choir, 1989—91, St. Matthews Children's Choir, 1988—92, Angels of Zion Youth Choir, 1993—95, Allston/Shepard Gospel Music Works, 1991—2003, Park Ave. Christian Ch. Inspirational Choir and Crusaders For Christ, 1993—. Contbr. vocals and piano for record album by Buddy Terry; cinematographer: (organ and vocals for nat. television) Dr. Albert Lewis Gospel Hour - Gospel Explosion; contbr. organ and vocals for nat. television Bobby Jones Gospel Show: Black History Month Mass Concert, over 100 concerts and major events, US. Tennis Opening, 2002, in Going Home Celebration (Funeral) Lionel Hampton, 2002, Jubilation Choir N.J. Performing Arts, 2000, 02, Ray Charles Celebrates Christmas with the Voices of Jubilation, 2002. Recipient Charita C. Allston Resolution, City of Newark N.J., 1997, R.P. Means Adult Gospel Choir, 1997, Charita C. Allston Resolution for N.J. Performing Arts, City of Newark, N.J., 2003.

ALMES, JUNE, retired education educator, librarian; b. Pitts., Feb. 14, 1934; d. Donald John Rowbottom and Marie Catherine (Linz) Douglas; widowed; children: Lawrence John, Douglas Alan. BS in Edn., Ind. U. of Pa., 1955; MLS, U. Pitts., 1969. Tchr. Shippensburg (Pa.) Area High Sch., 1964-68; assoc. prof. Lock Haven (Pa.) U., 1971-94; ret., 1990. Instr. Changsha U. Electric Power, Hunan, China, 1989-90, 95. Trustee Ross Pub. Libr., Lock Haven, 1975-80, community story programs, 1973-86; tutor Clinton City Literacy Found., Lock Haven, 1979; pres. Ea. Clinton Co. Democratic Women's Club, 2003—. Mem. Am. Assn. Sch. Librs., Pa. Assn. Sch. Librs., ACLU, Phi Kappa Phi, Phi Delta Kappa. Democrat. Avocations: playing bridge, reading, travel, literacy. Home: 228 East Hillside Dr Lock Haven PA 17745-1733 E-mail: jalmes@lhup.edu.

ALMÉSTICA, JOHANNA LYNNETTE, mental health counselor, administrator; b. Ponce, P.R., Aug. 4, 1970; arrived in U.S., 1988; d. Joaquin Alméstica and Margarita Bracero. BA in Psychology, U. Mass. Boston, 1993; MS in Counseling Psychology, Our Lady of Lake U., 1999. Counselor, case mgr. supr. Acute Treatment Ctr. Dimock Cmty. Health Ctr., Roxbury, Mass., 2000—. Mem.: APA. Roman Catholic. Avocation: reading. Office: Dimock Cmty Health Ctr Acute Treatment Ctr 41 Dimock St Roxbury MA 02119*

ALMORE-RANDLE, ALLIE LOUISE, special education educator; b. Jackson, Miss, Apr. 20; d. Thomas Carl and Theressa Ruth (Garrett) Almore; m. Olton Charles Randle, Sr., Aug. 3, 1974. BA, Tougaloo (Miss.) Coll., 1951; MS in Edn., U. So. Calif., L.A., 1971; EdD, Nova Southeastern U., 1997. Recreation leader Pasadena Dept. Recreation, Calif., 1954-56; demonstration tchr. Pasadena Unified Sch., 1956-63; cons. spl. edn. Temple City Sch. Dist., Calif., 1967; supr. tchr. edn. U. Calif., Riverside, 1971; tchr. spl. edn. Pasadena Unified Sch. Dist., 1955-70, dept. chair spl. edn. Pasadena H.S., 1972-98, also adminstrv. asst. Pasadena HS, 1993-98, surrogate parent, 2001—; ind. rep. Am. Comm. Network, Inc., 1997—; surrogate parent Pasadena Unified Sch., Pasadena, Calif., 2001. Supr. Evelyn Frieden Ctr., U. So. Calif., LA, 1970; mem. Coun. Exceptional Children, 1993—; ednl. cons. Shelby Renee Ednl. Ctr., Gardena, Calif., 2000—. Organizer Northwest Project, Camp Fire Girls, Pasadena, 1963; leader Big Sister Program, YWCA, Pasadena, 1966; organizer, dir. March on The Boys' Club, the Portrait of a Boy, 1966; organized Dr. Allie's Book Mobile Project, 2002; pub. souvenir jours. Women's Missionary Soc., AME Ch., State of Wash. to Mo.; mem. NAACP, Ch. Women United, Afro-Am. Quilters LA, established Dr. Allie Louise Almore-Randle Scholarship Award, Pasadena HS, 1998; co-established Theressa Garrett Almore Music Scholarship award Jackson State U., Jackson, Miss., 1989; founding mem. Cmty. Women of San Gabriel Valley, 1998, Women of Pasadena, 2002. Recipient Cert. of Merit, Pasadena City Coll., 1963, Outstanding Achievement award Nat. Coun. Negro Women, Pasadena, 1965, Earnest Thompson Seton award Campfire Girls, Pasadena, 1968, Spl. Recognition, Outstanding Community Svc. award The Tuesday Morning Club, 1967, Dedicated Svc. award AME Ch., 1983, Educator of Excellence award Rotary Club of Pasadena, 1993, Edn. award Altadena NAACP, 1994; named Tchr. of Yr., Pasadena Masonic Bodies, 1967, Woman of the Yr. for Community Svc. and Edn., Zeta Phi Beta, 1992, Commendation, City of Pasadena; grad. fellow U. So. Calif., LA, 1970, recognition Uniformly Excellent Work and Exceptional Commitment and Dedication to Altadena/Pasadena Communities, Pasadena African Amer. Sch. Administr., 1998, Cert. Achievment in Educational Leadership, First AME Ch., 1998, Fran Cook Salute Great Inspiring Educator Award, United Tchr. of Pasadena, 1998, Named Outstanding Educator, Nat. Sorority Phi Delta Kappa, 1998. Mem. NAACP (life; bd. mem., chmn. ch. workers com. 1955-63, Fight for Freedom award West Coast region 1957, NAACP Edn. award Altadena, Calif. chpt. 1994), ASCD, Calif. Tchrs. Assn., Calif. African Am. Geneal. Soc., Nat. Coun. Negro Women, African Pan Am. Doctoral Scholars, L.A. World Affairs Coun., Phi Delta Gamma (hospitality chair 1971—), U. So. Calif. Alumni Assn. (life), Tougaloo Coll. Nat. Alumni Assn. (life), Phi Delta Kappa, Alpha Kappa Alpha (life, membership com.), Phi Delta Phi (founder, organizer 1961), Phi Delta Kappa, Phi GAmma Sigma. Democrat. Mem. Ame Ch. Avocations: wedding director, photography, gardening, family history. Home: 1710 La Cresta Dr Pasadena CA 91103-1261 Fax: 626-797-5549. E-mail: akainger@acninc.net.

ALOFF, MINDY, writer; b. Phila., Dec. 20, 1947; d. Jacob and Selma (Album) A.; m. Martin Steven Cohen, June 16, 1968 (div. June 2000); 1 child, Ariel Nikiya. AB in English, Vassar Coll., 1969; MA in English, SUNY, Buffalo, 1972. Asst. prof. English U. Portland, Oreg., 1973-75; editor Encore Mag. of the Arts, Portland, 1977-80, Vassar Quar., Poughkeepsie, N.Y., 1980-88; dance critic New Republic, Bklyn., 1993—2001; cons. The George Balanchine Found., 2000—. Coord. Portland Poetry Festival, 1974—75; adj. assoc. prof. Barnard Coll., 2000—, asst. prof. practice, 2002—03. Author: (poems) Night Lights, 1979; author essays and revs. theatrical dancing and lit. for N.Y. Times Weekend, Book Rev. and Arts & Leisure, New Republic mag., Nation mag., Threepenny Rev., Dance mag., New Yorker mag., ann. Ency. Britannica, others. Recipient Whiting Writers award Mrs. Giles Whiting Found., N.Y.C., 1987; Woodrow Wilson Found. fellow, 1969, Woodburn fellow SUNY-Buffalo, 1972, Am. Dance Festival Dance Critics Inst. fellow, New London, Conn., 1977, John Simon Guggenheim Meml. Found. fellow, 1990. Mem. PEN Am. Ctr., Nat. Book Critics Circle (bd. dirs. 1988-91), Phi Beta Kappa.

ALOISI, CAROL ANN, marketing executive; b. Plainfield, N.J., Nov. 29, 1953; d. Edward Charles and Evelyn Helen (Nowhark) Schaffernoth; m. Michael Francis Aloisi, Jan. 20, 1979. BA, Rutgers the State U., 1978; MBA, Rutgers the State U., Newark, 1991. Mgr. employment Bamberger's/Macy's, Newark, 1975-78; pers. adminstr. John Wiley & Sons., N.Y.C., 1978-79, corp. pers. mgr., 1979-81; mgr. pers. adminstrn. Ortho Diagnostic Sys., Inc., Raritan, N.J., 1981-82, mgr. employee rels., 1982-83, dir. employee rels., 1984-85, nat. account exec., 1985-87, product mgr., 1987-89, dir. mktg., 1989-92; gen. mgr. Ortho Diagnostic Systems Inc., Raritan, 1992-93; pres. Career Mgmt. Cons., Inc., Belle Mead, N.J., 1994—. Recipient Tribute to Women in Industry award YWCA/TWIN of Cen. N.J., 1987. Mem. Tribute to Women in Industry, Internat. Assn. Career Mgmt. Profls. Avocations: tennis, birdwatchiing, biking. Office: Career Mgmt Cons Inc 40 Catskill Ct Belle Mead NJ 08502-4527

ALONZO, LORETTA J. real estate broker; d. Eugene and Felina Hicks; m. Peter N. Alonzo, Dec. 18, 1971; children: Stacy, Darren. B in Real Estate, Morton Coll., 1983. Real estate salesperson Dennis Realty, Berwyn, Ill., 1976—78, Pechous Realty, Berwyn, 1978—83; real estate broker Century 21 RBI, North Riverside, Ill., 1983—96, Century 21 Alonzo, LaGrange Park, Ill., 1996—. Pres. West Towns Bd. Realtors, Cicero, Ill., 1989—91; dist. v.p. Ill. Assn. Realtors, Springfield, 1992; real estate instr., 1992—; exec. dir. Multiple Listing Svc., Lisle, Ill., 1999—. Named Woman of Yr., Mex.-Am. Bus. and Profl. Women's Club, Chgo., 1987, Realtor of Yr., West Towns Bd. Realtors, 1987, 1991, 1995, 2000. Avocations: golf, fishing. Office: Century 21 Alonzo & Assocs 1011 E 31st St La Grange Park IL 60526 E-mail: C21LJA@aol.com.

ALPERN, LINDA LEE WEVODAU, health agency administrator; b. Harrisburg, Pa., July 16, 1949; d. William Irvin Wevodau and Maretia Christine (Mills) Staley; m. Neil Stephen Alpern, Apr. 12, 1985; 1 child, Philip Wevodau. BS in Edn., Shippensburg (Pa.) U., 1971. Unit program coord. Pa. Div. Am. Cancer Soc., Harrisburg, 1973-75, unit exec. dir., 1975-76, div. svc. dir., 1976-81, div. med. affairs dir. Hershey, 1981-83; div. crusade dir. Md. Div. Am. Cancer Soc., Balt., 1983-87, div. v.p. for field ops., 1988, div. dep., exec. v.p. ops., 1988-95, divsn. chief oper. officer, 1995-96; sr. v.p. field ops. Mid-Atlantic divsn. Am. Cancer Soc., Balt., 1997—. Bd. dirs., sec. Cmty. Assn.; treas., v.p., pres. PTA; trustee Balt. Hebrew-Congregation Day Sch., 2000-03; bd. electors Balt. Hebrew Congregation, nominating com., 2001-03—. Democrat. Methodist. Avocations: photography, gardening, reading. Home: 4108 Colonial Rd Baltimore MD 21208-6042

ALPERS, DENISE KAY ANDERSON, music educator; b. Mpls., July 11, 1969; d. Carl Frederick and Kathrine Ann Anderson; m. John Charles Alpers, July 27, 2002. MusB, Concordia Coll., 1991; MusM, U. S.D., 2000. Tchr. orch. Jamestown (N.D.) Schs., 1991—92, Sioux Falls (S.D.) Schs., 1993—. Dir. youth orch. Sioux Empire Youth Symphonies, Sioux Falls, 1999—; musician First Luth. Ch., Sioux Falls, 1993—; mem. curriculum com. Sioux Falls Pub. Schs., 2001—02. Mem.: NEA, Am. String Tchrs. Assn. Avocations: reading, walking, bicycling, composing, arranging music.

ALPERS, SVETLANA LEONTIEF, art educator; b. Cambridge, Mass., Feb. 10, 1936; d. Wassily W. Leontief and Estelle Marks Leontief; m. Paul Joel Alpers, Jan. 31, 1958 (div.); children: Benjamin, Nicholas. BA, Radcliffe Coll., 1957; PhD, Harvard U., 1965. From instr. to assoc. prof. U. Calif., Berkeley, 1962—75, prof. art history, 1975—94; vis. rsch. prof. dept. fine arts NYU, N.Y.C., 1999—. Adv. bd. Women's Caucus for Art, 1974—77; co-chair Representations, 1983—93; adv. bd. History of the Human Scis.; mem. U.S. Nat. Com. on History of Art, 1975—90; rep. of the visual arts Renaissance Soc. Am., 1976—79; mem. mus. and hist. orgns. panel NEH; cons. Nat. Pub. Radio, 1976—80; publs. com. J. Paul Getty Trust, 1984—87, mem. sr. fellowships com., 1987—90; mem. bd. of advisors Ctr. Advanced Studies in Visual Arts, 1989—93; adv. bd. Sci. in Context, —; visitor Ecoles des Hautes Etudes en Sciences Sociales, Paris, 1991. Author: (book) The Decoration of the Torre de la Parada, 1971, The Art of Describing, 1983 (Eugene M. Kayden award, 1983), Rembrandt's Enterprise, 1988 (Charles Rufus Morey award), Tiepolo and the Pictorial Intelligence (written with Michael Baxandall), 1994, The Making of Rubens, 1995. Fellow Woodrow Wilson fellow, 1957—58, AAUW, 1961—62, Guggenheim fellow, 1972—73, Ctr. Advanced Studies in Behavioral Scis., 1975—76, ACLS fellow, 1978—79, Vis. fellow, Netherlands Inst. Advanced Study, 1979, Fellow, Wissenschaftskolleg zu Berlin, 1992—93; scholar Vis. scholar, Getty Ctr. for History of Art and Humanities, 1987—88. Fellow: AAAS; mem.: Phi Beta Kappa.

ALPERT, ANN SHARON, retired insurance claims examiner; b. Indpls., Feb. 24, 1938; d. Oscar and Adele Alpert. BS in Edn., Ind. U., 1959. Tchr. Indpls. Pub. Schs., 1959-60; libr. George Fry & Assocs., Chgo., 1960-62, DeLeuw, Cather & Co., Chgo., 1962-65, Arthur Young & Co., CPAs, Chgo., 1965-74; statis. asst. Sargent & Lundy, Chgo., 1974-81, computer liaison agt., 1981-83, tech. editor, 1983-87; sales assoc. Jewelmaster, Inc., Chgo., 1987-88; claims processor Benefit Trust Life Ins. Co., 1988-90; claims examiner Ft. Dearborn Life Ins. Co., 1990-91, sr. disability claims examiner, 1991—; ret. Fellow: Life Mgmt. Inst. (assoc.).

ALPERT, DEIRDRE WHITTLETON (DEDE ALPERT), state legislator; b. N.Y.C., Oct. 6, 1945; d. Harry Mark and Dorothy (Lehn) Whittleton; m. Michael Edward Alpert, Jan. 1, 1964; children: Lehn, Kristin, Alison. Student, Pomona Coll., 1963-65; LLD (hon.), Western Am. U., 1994. Mem. from 78th dist. Calif. State Assembly, Sacramento, 1990-96; mem. from 39th dist. Calif. Senate, Sacramento, 1997—. Chair Women Legislators' Caucus, Sacramento, 1993, Assembly Edn. Com., 1995, Senate Revenue and Taxation Com., 1997-98, Senate Edn. Com., 1999-2000, Senate Appropriations Com., 2001—, Joint. Com. to Develop a Master Plan, 1999—; active Calif. Tourism Commn., Sacramento, 1990—, Calif. Libr. Allocations Bd., Sacramento, 1993—; mem. com. Natural Resources, Revenue and Taxation, Agr. and Water, Edn., select com. on Calif.'s Wine Industry, Econ. Devel.; chair Genetics and Pub. Policy, Family, Child and Youth Devel. Coll. and U. Admissions and Outreach, Juvenile Justice; vice chair Joint Com. on Fisheries and Aquaculture, Pacific Fisheries Legis. Task Force, Pacific States Marine Fisheries Commn. Author: Mammography Quality Assurance Act 1992, Assembly Bill 114 of 1993, Workplace Violence Safety Act, 1994, Battered Women's Protection Act, 1994, ABC, 1995, California Assessment Academic Achievement Act, 1995. Spl. advocate Voices for Children, San Diego, 1982-90; mem. bd. Solana Beach (Calif.) Sch. Bd., 1983-90, also pres.; pres. Beach and County Guild United Cerebral Palsy, San Diego, 1986. Recipient Beach and County Guild legis. award Calif. Regional Occupation Program, 1991-92, Am. Acad. Pediats., 1991-92, San Diego Psychol. Assn., 1993-94, Commitment to Children award Calif. Assn. for Edn. of Young Children, 1991-92, Legis. Commendation award Nat. Assn. for Yr.-Round Edn., 1991-92, State Commn. on Status of Women, 1993-94, Friend of Public Edn. award Calif. Sch. Bds. Assn., 1997-98, Legis. Champion award Calif. Union Safety Employees, Unsung Hero award Youth Law Ctr., 1995-96, Champion for Children award Voices for Children, 1995-96; named Friend of Yr., Children's PKU Network, 1991-92, Woman of Yr., Nat. Women's Polit. Caucus San Diego, 1991-92, Orgn. for Rehab. through Tng., 1993-94, High Tech Legislator of Yr., Am. Electronics Assn., 1991-2001, Calif. Sch.-Age Consortium, 1993-94, Women of Distinction, Soropimists Internat. of La Jolla, 1993-94, Assemblymember of Yr., Calif. Assn. Edn. Young Children, 1993-94, Calif. Tourism Hall of Fame, 1997—, Legis. of Yr., Calif. State U. Alumni Coun., 1999, Legis. of Yr., Calif. Women for Agriculture, 1999, Honored Patriot, U.S. Selective Svc. Sys., 1999, Legis. of Yr., Profl. Engrs. Calif. Govt., 1997, Outstanding Senator of Yr., Calif. Sch. Bd. Assn., 1998, Legis. of Yr., Am. Elec. Assn., 1995-96, Legis. of Yr., Calif. League Mid. Schs., 1995, Outstanding Legis. of Yr., Nat. Women's Polit. Caucus, S.D. chpt., 1995-96, Outstanding Assenbly Mem. of Yr., Calif. Sch. Bds. Assn., 1994; Recognition for Outstanding Legis. Efforts, Paw PAC, 1997. Mem. Calif. Elected Women's Assn. for Edn. and Rsch. (pres. 1995-96). Democrat. Avocations: golf, reading. Office: State Capitol Bldg Rm 5050 Senate District 39 Sacramento CA 95814 also: 1557 Columbia St San Diego CA 92101-2934 E-mail: dede.alpert@sen.ca.gov.

ALSAPIEDI, CONSUELO VERONICA, psychoanalytic psychotherapist, consultant; b. N.Y.C., Nov. 9, 1927; d. Vernon Joseph Karram and Constance Agatha Taylor; m. John Romeo Alsapiedi, May 12, 1951; children: John Rino, Sharon Anne. BA, Seton Hill Coll., 1949; MSW, Fordham U., 1972; D Social Work, Psychoanalytic Inst. for Clin.Social Workers, N.Y.C., 1985. Lic. and cert. social worker, N.Y.; cert. alcoholism counselor, substance abuse counselor; bd. cert. diplomate. Case aide II, Cath. Charities, Bklyn., 1949-51, clin. social worker, 1963-70, clin. social worker rep. in Family Ct., 1965-70; inpatient and outpatient psychiat. social worker Office Mental Health, Queens Village, N.Y., 1972-95; pvt. practice psychoanalytic psychotherapy, N.Y.C., 1975—, Forest Hills, N.Y., 1989—. Ednl. lectr.; condr. workshops; psychotherapist staff outpatient psychotherapy svcs. A Family Ctr., Rosedale, NY, 1999—2002; psychotherapist-children ages 5 to adults, all ages. Vol. Nat. Mental Health Assn., Albany, N.Y., 1994. Mem. N.Y. State Soc. for Clin. Social Work Psychotherapy (diplomate 1979—, sec.-rec. sec. 1985-99, membership chmn. 1989-90, pres. Queens chpt. 1986-88, rec. sec. 1992-99), Brain Injury Assn., Menninger Soc. Roman Catholic. Avocations: piano, music, ballet and stage performances, art appreciation. Office: 71-36 110th St Ste 1K Forest Hills NY 11375-4838 Office Phone: 718-268-0734.

ALSIP, CHERYL ANN, small business owner; b. Jersey City, Aug. 1, 1957; m. Manuel Edward Alsip, May 23, 1992 (dec. Oct., 1992); 1 child, Jeremy Tyler. Student, Bergen C.C., Paramus, N.J., 1979-82, Broward C.C., Coconut Creek, Fla., 1983-84; AS in Electronic Engring., NEC-Bauder, Ft. Lauderdale, Fla., 1988; AS in Acctg., Internat. Corr. Sch., Scranton, Pa., 1997. Various clerical positions, N.Y.C. and N.J., 1979-81; pers. mgr. Universal Merchandising, Inc., Clifton, N.J., 1981-82; store mgr. Travelers Transp. Inc. doing business as The Gift Shop, Deerfield Beach, Fla., 1983; gen. mgr. Travelers Transp. Inc. doing business as Budget Rent-A-Car, Pompano Beach, Fla., 1982-84; various office and technical positions Fla., 1985-91; ind. contractor Mary Kay, Pompano Beach, Fla., 1991-92; customer svc. rep. Taleigh, Inc., Boca Raton, Fla., 1992; tech. writer, technician various Fla. Cos., 1992-93; owner, operator CALA Distinctive Enterprises, Salcha, Alaska, 1992—2003; freelance writer, English editor Alaska, 1999-2000; desktop pub., editor CALA Distinctive Enterprises, 1992—2003; owner, operator CHAMA Enterprises, 2004—. Commr. Boy Scouts of Am., 1992—; mem. Comty. Emergency Response Team, Pompano Beach, Fla., 1997-98—; vol. Aux. Police Dept., Pompano Beach, 1997-98; mem. CAP, 1996-2000; bd. dirs. Golden Valley Elec. Assn., Fairbanks, 2000-03; bd. dirs., mem., sec. Sacha Cmty. Coun., 2002-03. With U.S. Army, 1975-78. Mem. Internat. Soc. Cert. Electronic Technicians, Navy League of the U.S. Republican. Roman Catholic. Avocations: camping, handcrafts, reading. Home and Office: PO Box 140097 Salcha AK 99714-0097 E-mail: camalsip@alaska.net.

ALSOP, MARIN, conductor; d. LaMar and Ruth A. Student, Yale Univ., Julliard Sch. Debut with Symphony Space, N.Y.C., 1984; founder, artistic dir. Concordia Chamber Orchestra, N.Y.C., 1984—; asst. condr. Richmond Symphony, Va., 1987; music dir. Eugene Symphony Orchestra, Oreg., 1989—96, Long Island Philharmonic, 1989—96, Colorado Symphony Orchestra, Denver, 1993—; principal guest condr. City of London Sinfonia, 1999—; principal condr. Bournemouth Symphony Orchestra, England, 2003—. Guest condr. San Francisco Symphony Orchestra, Boston Pops, Los Angeles Philharmonic Orchestra, 1991, City Ballet Orchestra, 1992; dir. Cabrillo Music Festival, Calif., 1991—; concertmaster Northeastern Pennsylvania Philharmonic, Scranton; founder, mem. String Fever (swing band), 1980—. Recipient Koussevitzky Conducting prize Tanglewood Music Festival, 1988. Office: Colo Symphony Orch Boettcher Concert Hall 821 17th St Ste 700 Denver CO 80202-3000

ALSUP, JANET MARIE, language educator; b. St. Louis, Mo., July 20, 1967; d. Henry G. and Jeanette M. Alsup. PhD, U. Mo. Columbia, 2000. Tchr. Secondary English Mo., 1989. Tchr. H.S. English South Callaway R2 H.S., Mokane, Mo., 1990—96; asst. prof. English Purdue U., West Lafayette, Ind. Author: But Will It Work with Real Students?; contbr. articles to profl. jours. Fellow Ctr. for Undergraduate Instrnl. Excellence, Purdue U. Sch. of Liberal Arts, 2003. Mem.: Internat. Reading Assn., Nat. Coun. Tchrs. English. Achievements include research in Conducted And Published Results Of Qualitative, Empirical Research Projects About The Teaching Of First-Year College Composition And The Development Of Teacher Professional Identity. Home: 622 Ferry Street Apt #4 Lafayette IN 47901 Office: Purdue University English Dept 500 Oval Drive West Lafayette IN 47907 E-mail: jalsup@sla.purdue.edu.

ALT, BETTY L. sociology educator; b. Walsenburg, Colo., Nov. 12, 1931; d. Cecil R. and Mary M. (Giordano) Sowers; m. William E. Alt, June 19, 1960; 1 child, Eden Jeanette Alt Murrie. BA, Colo. Coll., 1960; MA, NE Mo. State U., 1968. Instr. sociology Indian Hills Community Coll., Centerville, Iowa, 1965-70; dept. chmn. Middlesex Community Coll., Bedford, Mass., 1971-75; instr. sociology Auburn U., Montgomery, 1975-76; div. chmn. Tidewater Community Coll., Virginia Beach, Va., 1976-80; program coord. Pikes Peak Community Coll., Woomera, Australia, 1980-83; instr. sociology Hawaii Pacific Coll., Honolulu, 1983-86, U. Md., Okinawa, Japan, 1987-88, Christopher Newport Coll., Newport News, Va., 1988-89, U. Colo., Colorado Springs, 1989-96, U. So. Colo., Pueblo, 1992—. Co-author: (nonfiction) Uncle Sam's Brides, 1990, Campfollowing: A History of the Military Wife, 1991, Weeping Violins: The Gypsy Tragedy in Europe, 1996, Slaughter in Cell House 3, 1997, Wicked Women, 2000, Black Soldiers-White Wars, 2002, Keeper of the Keys, 2003, Fleecing Grandma and Grandpa, 2004. Mem. League Women Voters. Mem. AAUW, Pen Women, N.E. Mo. State U. Alumni Assn. (bd. dirs. 1993-97). Home: 2460 N Interstate 25 Pueblo CO 81008-9614 Office: Colo State U - Pueblo 2200 Bonforte Blvd Pueblo CO 81001-4901

ALTEKRUSE, JOAN MORRISSEY, retired preventive medicine educator; b. Cohoes, N.Y., Nov. 15, 1928; d. William T. Dee and Agnes Kay (Fitzgerald) Morrissey; m. Ernest B. Altekruse, Dec. 17, 1950; children—Philip, Clifford, Lisa, Janice, Charles, Sean, Lowell, Patrick, E. Caitlin. AB, Vassar Coll., N.Y., 1949; MD, Stanford U., Calif., 1960; MPH, Harvard U., Cambridge, 1965; DPH, U. Calif., Berkeley, 1973; MPS, Loyola U., New Orleans, 1999. Cons., program dir. Calif. State Health Dept., 1966-69; mem. faculty U. Heidelberg, Germany, 1970-72; med. dir. regional office Fla. State Health Dept., 1972-75; prof., dir. health adminstrn. Sch. Pub. Health, U. S.C., Columbia, 1975-77; prof. preventive medicine Univ. S.C. Sch. of Medicine, Columbia, 1975-94, chmn. dept., 1979-89, disting. prof. emerita, 1994—. Fellow, assoc. dir. Irish Peace Inst., U. Limerick, Ireland, 1990; vis. scholar Ctr. for Rsch. in Disease Prevention, Stanford U., 1992; women in medicine liaison officer Assn. Am. Med. Colls., 1980-94; mem. editl. bd. Aspen Publs. Mem. editorial bd. Family and Community Health Jour., Jour. Community Health; editorial adv. bd. VA Practitioner. Sr. docent chair, vol. bd. mem. Hunter Mus. Am. Art, Chattanooga; activist in social justice, peace and health advocacy orgns. Lt. USMC, 1949—51, sr. surgeon USPHS, 1960—64, capt. USPHS. Recipient Adminstrn. award Women in Higher Edn., 1989, Achievement award S.C. Commn. on Women, 1990, Ann. award, 1991, Life Achievement award Emma Willard Sch., 1996; WHO travel fellow, Eng., 1974; grantee NIH, NCI, Ctr. for Disease Control, pvt. founds; recipient Alumni award of merit Harvard Sch. Pub. Health, 1997. Fellow: APHA (mem. emerita), Assn. Tchrs. Preventive Medicine (pres. 1986, Spl. Recognition award 1995), Am. Coll. Preventive Medicine; mem.: Nat. Bd. Med. Examiners (comprehensive test com. 1986—92), Am. Heart Assn. (SC affiliate pres. 1986, agenda planning com. 1987—89, women and minorities leadership com. 1989—92, Lifetime Achievement award 1992), Am. Bd. Med. Specialties, Am. Bd. Preventive Medicine (trustee 1983—92), Emma Willard Sch. Alumni Assn. (bd. dirs. 2003—), Am. Womens Med. Assn., Harvard Sch. Pub. Health Alumni Assn. (pres. 1999—2001, leadership coun. 2003—), Harvard Alumni Assn. (bd. dirs. 2001—03). Democrat. Roman Catholic. Office: 730 Germantown Cir Apt 918 Chattanooga TN 37412-1859

ALTENHOFEN, JANE ELLEN, federal agency administrator, auditor; b. Seneca, Kans., Sept. 4, 1952; d. Justin Leo and Marva Mae (Sextro) A.; m. John Dean Arnette, Sept. 12, 1975 (div. Mar. 1978). BBA cum laude, Wichita (Kans.) State U., 1973; MPA, Am. U., 1982; cert., Inst. Internal Auditors, 1986. Cert. internal auditor, cert. fraud examiner, cert. govt. fin. mgr. Auditor U.S. Gen. Acctg. Office, Kansas City, Kans., 1974-76, Honolulu, 1976-80, Washington, 1980-84, Fed. Emergency Mgmt. Agy., Washington, 1984-89; insp. gen. U.S. Internat. Trade Commn., Washington, 1989-99, Nat. Labor Rels. Bd., Washington, 1999—. Mem. Adopt a Grandparent Program, Wichita, 1973; vol. reading course work to blind students, Wichita, 1973; vol. Vis. Nurse Assn., Washington, 1986—; host, traveler, Wash. area rep. SERVAS, 1987—; commr. Adv. Neighborhood Commn., Washington, 1986-89; troop leader Girl Scouts U.S., Washington, 1983-85; foster home Washington Humane Soc., 1994—. Mem. Inst. Internal Auditors, Nat. Intergovtl. Audit Forum, Assn. Govt. Accounts, Nat. Assn. Cert. Fraud Examiners, Phi Kappa Phi, Pi Alpha Pi. Home: 507 2nd St SE Washington DC 20003-1928 Office: Nat Labor Rels Bd 1099 14th St NW Rm 9820 Washington DC 20570-0001

ALTER, ELEANOR BREITEL, lawyer; b. N.Y.C., Nov. 10, 1938; d. Charles David and Jeanne (Hollander) Breitel; children: Richard B. Zabel, David B. Zabel. BA with honors, U. Mich., 1960; postgrad., Harvard U., 1960-61; LLB, Columbia U., 1964. Bar: N.Y. 1965. Atty., office of gen. counsel, ins. dept. State of N.Y., 1964-66; assoc. Miller & Carlson, N.Y.C., 1966-68, Marshall, Bratter, Greene, Allison & Tucker, N.Y.C., 1968-74, mem. firm, 1974-82, Rosenman & Colin, 1982-97, Kasowitz, Benson, Torres & Friedman, N.Y.C., 1997—. Fellow U. Chgo. Law Sch., 1988; adj.

prof. law NYU Sch. Law, 1983-87; vis. prof. law U. Chgo., 1990-91, 93; lectr. in field. Editorial bd.: N.Y. Law Jour. Contbr. articles to profl. jours. Trustee Lawyers' Fund for Client Protection of the State of N.Y., 1983—, chmn., 1985—; bd. visitors U. Chgo. Law Sch., 1984-87. Mem. Am. Law Inst., Am. Coll. Family Trial Lawyers, N.Y. State Bar Assn., Assn. of Bar of City of N.Y. (libr. com. 1978-80, com. on matrimonial law 1977-81, 87-88, 2002—, judiciary com. 1981-84, 94, 95, 96, exec. com. 1988-92), Am. Acad. Matrimonial Lawyers, Internat. Acad. Matrimonial Lawyers. Office: Kasowitz Benson Et Al 1633 Broadway New York NY 10019 Office Phone: 212-506-1760.

ALTER, MARIA POSPISCHIL, language educator; b. Vienna; came to U.S., 1947; d. Karl and Ludmilla (Von Adamovic) Pospischil; divorced; children: Assunta, Sylvia, Nora. BA, U. Okla., 1948, MA, 1950; PhD, U. Md., 1961. Instr., asst. prof. Howard U., Washington, 1955-66; asst. prof. Case Western U., Cleve., 1966-70; acad. cons. Am. Assn. Tchrs. German, Phila., 1970-73; prof. Villanova (Pa.) U., 1974—. Author: The Role of the Physicians in Schnitzler's and Corossa's Work, 1961, A Modern Case for German, 1971. Mem. Assn. German, Modern Lang. Assn. Home: 830 Montgomery Ave Bryn Mawr PA 19010-3343 Office: Villanova U Lancaster Pike Villanova PA 19085

ALTER, SHIRLEY JACOBS, jewelry store owner; b. Beaumont, Tex., June 23, 1929; d. Morris Louis and Helen (Dow) Jacobs; m. Nelson Tobias Alter, June 12, 1949; children: Dennis, Keith, Brian, Wendy. Student, U. Tex., Austin, 1950. Owner Alter's Gem Jewelry Co., Beaumont, 1950—. Pres. Nat. Coun. Jewish Women, Beaumont, 1965, 66, Sisterhood of Temple Emanuel, Beaumont, 1967, 68, Buckner Bapt. Benevolence Aux., Beaumont, 1970-72; bd. dirs. Temple Emanuel, pres. elect, 1994-96, pres. 1996-98; active Beaumont Music Commn., 1990; founder Beaumont Reach to Recovery, 1973; active BMW Drive for the Cure of breast cancer, 1997. Named Hero, Susan Komen Found., 1997. Democrat. Office: Alters Gem Jewelry 3155 Dowlen Beaumont TX 77706

ALTERSITZ, JANET KINAHAN, principal; b. Orange, N.J., May 19, 1951; d. Patrick Joseph and Ida (Ciamillo) K.; 1 child, Jacob. AA, County Coll. Morris, 1971; BA, Glassboro State Coll., 1973; MEd, Ariz. State U., 1980. Educator Washington (N.J.) Twp. Mid. Sch., 1974-77, Deer Valley Sch. Dist., Phoenix, 1977-82; asst. prin. Desert Sky Mid. Sch., Glendale, Ariz., 1983-86, prin., 1986—. Cons. and presenter in field. Mem. ASCD, NAASP (mid. level rep. 1993—), Nat. Mid. Sch. Assn., Western Regional Mid. Level. Assn. (program chmn. 1992), Ariz. Sch. Adminstrs. (sec., treas. 1989-90, pres. 1990-91), Cen. Ariz. Mid. Level. Assn. (bd. dirs. 1989—, exec. dir. 1994—), P.O.K. Democrat. Roman Catholic. Home: 4642 W Villa Rita Dr Glendale AZ 85308-1520 Office: Desert Sky Mid Sch 5130 W Grovers Ave Glendale AZ 85308-1300 E-mail: jaltersitz@ds.dvusd.org.

ALTFEST, KAREN CAPLAN, diversified financial services company executive, director; b. Mont., Que., Can. d. Philip and Betty (Gamer) Caplan; m. Lewis Jay Altfest; children: Ellen Wendy, Andrew Gamer. Tchr.'s diploma, McGill U.; BA cum laude, Hunter Coll., 1970, MA, 1972; PhD, CUNY, 1979. CFP, N.Y. V.p. L. J. Altfest & Co., Inc., N.Y.C., 1985—; dir. fin. planning program New Sch. Univ., N.Y.C., 1989—. Dir. CFP program Pace U., White Plains, N.Y., 1988-90. Author Robert Owen, 1978, Keeping Clients for Life, 2001; co-author: Lew Altfest Answers Almost All Your Questions about Money, 1992; contbr. articles to fin. jours. Founding chmn. Yorkville Common Pantry, N.Y.C., 1980-84; v.p. P.S. 6 PTA, N.Y.C., 1991-92; bd. dirs. Temple Shaaray Tefila, 1993—. Named Planner of Month, Mut. Funds Mag., 2000; named one of 200 Best Fin. Planners in U.S., Worth Mag., 1996, 1997, 1998, Best Fin. Advisors, Med. Econs. Mag., 1998, 100 Top Advisors, Mut. Funds Mgrs., 2002, Best 100 Planners, Mut. Funds Mag., 2002, Top Wealth Mgrs (firm), Bloomberg, 2003; recipient Cmty. Svc. award, Temple Shaaray Tefila, 1985; profile on cover, Fin. Planning Mag., 2001. Mem.: Women's Econ. Round Table, Fin. Women's Assn., Nat. Assn. Personal Fin. Advisors (chair N.E.-Mid Atlantic Conf. 1995, bd. dirs. N.E. region 1996—2003, v.p. 1997—99, pres. N.E.-Mid Atlantic region 1999—2001, chmn. 2001—03, Achievement cert. N.E. Region 1995, award for outstanding svc. to NE region 2001, 2003), Fin. Planning Assn. (bd. dirs. N.Y. chpt. 1994—99, bd. dirs. 2000—, dir. for pub. rels., Dedicated Svc. cert. 1998, 1999, 2000, 2001, 2002, 2003), Assn. for Women's Econ. Devel., Assn. for Can. Studies in U.S., Nat. Assn. Women Bus. Owners (chmn. FOCUS 1993—95, bd. dirs.), CUNY PhD Alumni Assn. (v.p. 1982—84), Phi Alpha Theta. Achievements include featured on cover of Fin. Planning Mag., 2001. Office: LJ Altfest & Co Inc 116 John St Rm 1120 New York NY 10038-3305 E-mail: karen@altfest.com.

ALTMAN, ADELE ROSENHAIN, radiologist; b. Tel Aviv, June 4, 1924; came to U.S., 1933, naturalized, 1939; d. Bruno and Salla (Silberzweig) Rosenhain; m. Emmett Altman, Sept. 3, 1944; children: Brian R., Alan L., Karen D. Diplomate Am. Bd. Radiology. Intern Queens Gen. Hosp., N.Y.C., 1949-51; resident Hosp. for Joint Diseases, N.Y.C., 1951-52, Roosevelt Hosp., N.Y.C., 1955-57; clin. instr. radiology Downstate Med. Ctr., SUNY, Bklyn., 1957-61; asst. prof. radiology N.Y. Med. Coll., N.Y.C., 1961-65, assoc. prof., 1965-68; assoc. prof. radiology U. Okla. Health Sci. Ctr., Oklahoma City, 1968-78; assoc. prof. dept. radiology U. N.Mex. Sch. Medicine, Albuquerque, 1978-85. Author: Radiology of the Respiratory System: A Basic Review, 1978; contbr. articles to profl. jours. Fellow Am. Coll. Angiology, N.Y. Acad. Medicine; mem. Am. Coll. Radiologist, Am. Roentgen Ray Soc., Assn. Univ. Radiologists, Radiol. Soc. N.Am., B'nai B'rith Anti-Defamation League (bd. dirs. N.Mex. state bd.), Hadassah Club.

ALTMAN, EDITH G. sculptor; b. Altenberg, Germany, May 23, 1931; arrived in U.S., 1939; BA, Wayne State U., 1949; student, Marygrove Coll., 1956-57. Instr. visual arts and printing project U. Omaha, 1984; asst. prof. painting, grad. advisor U. Chgo., 1984-85; vis. asst. prof. painting Sch. Art Inst. Chgo., 1985-86. Lectr. painting U. Ill., Columbia Coll., Oakton CC. Chgo. One-woman shows include NAME Gallery, 1987, Spertus Mus. Gallery Contemporary Art, 1988, Rockford Art Mus., 1989, State of Ill. Mus. Gallery, Chgo., 1992, Loyola U. Fine Arts Gallery, 1993, Peace Mus., Chgo., 1993, Mitchell Mus., Ill., 1995, Minn. Mus. Am. Art, 1995, Lindeau Mus., Altenburg, Germany, 2001, Frauen Mus., Bonn, Germany, 2001, Contextual Cultural U. Chgo., 2001, Natl. Museum of Szczecin, Poland, 2002-. Hyde Park Art Ctr., 2002. others; exhibited in group shows Art Inst. Chgo., 1975, 79, 81, 85, Mus. Contemporary Art, Chgo., 1976, 81, 83, 97, Acad. Kunst, Berlin, 1987, Barbicon Ctr., London, 1990, Knoxville Mus. Art, Tenn., 1998, N.J. State Mus., 1999, Okla. City Art Mus., 1999, Decordova Mus., 2000; represented in permanent collections Standard Oil Co., Mus. Contemporary Art, Chgo., 1997, State of Ill., Yale U. Mus., Holocaust Mus., Peace Mus., Gallery 312, Chgo., 2003; contbr. articles to profl. jours., newspapers. Named Art Matters fellow, 1994; Individual Artist fellow, Ill. Arts Coun., 1984, 1994, Internat. grantee, 2003, Individual Artist Fellow grantee, NEA, 1990—91. Mem. Chgo. Artist Coalition (founding mem., mem. com. artists rights, 1988). Address: 811 W 16th St Chicago IL 60608-2222

ALTMAN, MIMI ANGSTER, business owner; b. Chgo., Jan. 13, 1935; d. Herbert Charles and Marian Agnes (McGrath) Angster; m. Robert S. Altman, Jan. 31, 1970; 1 dau., Marian Catherine. Mus.B., DePauw U., 1957. Lic. real estate broker, Ill.; cert. piano tuner. Owner, mgr. secretarial service, Joliet, Ill., 1966-67; legal sec. various firms, Waukegan, Ill.; adminstrv. asst. to pres. Lake Forest Sch. Mgmt., Ill., 1982-84; owner, operator Exec. Mgmt. Co., Bannockburn, Ill., 1982—; owner Village Sec., Deerfield, Ill. Exec. dir. United Way of Highland Park/Highwood, Inc., 1986-88, Northbrook Leisure Found., 1986-88. Mem. Am. Bus. Women's Assn., Nat. Assn. Secretarial Svcs., Nat. Assn. Resume Svcs. Deerfield/Lincolnshire Ill. Rotary Club (pres. 1992-93), Mu Phi Epsilon (pres. North Shore chpt., internat. exec. sec.-treas. 1982—, exec. dir.

1983—), Kappa Kappa Gamma. Republican. Presbyterian. Lodges: Women of Rotary Found. Inc. (pres.), Zonta Internat. (local and dist. officer). Avocation: travel. Home: Deerfield, Ill. Died 2003.

ALTMANN, JEANNE, zoologist, educator; b. N.Y.C., Mar. 18, 1940; BA Math., U. Alta., Can., 1962; MAT, Emory U., 1970; PhD, U. Chgo., 1979. Rsch. assoc., co-investigator U. Alta., Canada, 1963-65, Yerkes Regional Primate Rsch. Ctr., Atlanta, 1965-67, 69-70; rsch. assoc. dept. biology U. Chgo., 1970-85, assoc. prof. dept. ecology and evolution, 1985-89, prof., dept. ecology & evolution, 1989—98; rsch. curator, assoc. curator primates Chgo. Zool. Soc., 1985—; prof., dept. ecology & evolutionary biology Princeton U., NJ, 1998—, faculty assoc., Office of Population Rsch., 1999—. Hon. lectr. dept. zoology U. Nairobi, Africa, 1989-90; vis. prof. evolutionary biology U. Chgo., 1991—; bd. sci. dirs. Karisoke Rsch. Ctr., Rwanda, 1980-82, 86-89, acting chairperson, 1980; mem. biosocial perspectives on parent behavior and off-spring devel. com. Social Sci. Rsch. Coun., 1984-91; mem. adv. coun. dept. ecology and evolutionary biology Princeton (N.J.) U., 1991—; mem. rev. com. dept. zool. rsch. Nat. Zool. Park, Smithsonian Inst., Washington, 1992; mem. com. Internat. Ethol. Congress, 1992—; mem. vis. com. dept. anatomy and biol. anthropology Duke U., Durham, N.C., 1993; reviewer manuscripts various jours. Author: (with S. Altmann) Baboon Ecology: African Field Research, 1970, Baboon Mothers and Infants, 1980; editor: Animal Behaviour, 1978-82; consulting editor: Am. Jour. Primatology, 1981—; mem. editorial panel: Monographs in Primatology, 1982-90; mem. editorial bd. Bioscience, 1983-88, ISI Reviews in Animal Science, 1988, Human Nature, 1989-92, Internat. Jour. Primatology, 1990—, Am. Naturalist, 1991—; contbr. articles to profl. jours. Fellow Ctr. Advanced Study in Behavioral Scis., 1990-91. Fellow Animal Behavior Soc. (mem. exec. com 1978-82, 84-87, mem, nominating com. 1987-89, pres. 1985-86), Animal Behavior Soc.; mem. NSF (mem. sci. adv. panel psychobiology program 1983-86, mem. adv. panel for vis. professorships for women 1987, 88, mem. adv. panel conservation and restoration biology 1990, mem. task force behavioral, biol. and social scis. Looking Toward the 21st Century 1990-91, mem. adv. coun. directorate for social, behavioral and econ. scis. 1992—), Internat. Primatol. Soc. (v.p. conservation, mem. exec. coun.). Home: 54 Hardy Dr Princeton NJ 08540-1211*

ALTOMARA, RITA ECKE, library director, writer; b. Englewood, N.J., June 27, 1950; d. Russell and Rita (Walsh) Ecke; m. Gary John Altomara, Dec. 14, 1969; 1 child, Ginevra Marie. BA, Barnard Coll., 1972; MS, Columbia U., 1975. Jr. libr. Ft. Lee (N.J.) Pub. Libr., 1974-77, sr. libr., 1977-80, prin. libr., 1980-82, asst. dir., 1982-84, dir., 1984—. Coord. Women's Info and Referral Svc., Ft. Lee, 1975—. Author: Hollywood on the Palisades, 1983. Mem. exec. bd. Ft. Lee Hist Soc., 1982—; liaison Bergen County Office Hist. and Cultural Affairs, Hackensack, NJ, 1978—. Mem.: ALA, N.J. Libr. Assn. Roman Catholic. Home: 121 Engle St Cresskill NJ 07626-2246 Office: Ft Lee Pub Library 320 Main St Fort Lee NJ 07024-4706 Office Phone: 201-592-3628.

ALTOMARE, ERICA VON SCHEVEN, psychologist; b. Trenton, N.J., Jan. 11, 1950; d. Eric Kurt and Lorraine (Seabridge) Von Scheven; m. Joseph E. Altomare, Aug. 14, 1971; children: Mikal Melissa, Damon Joseph, Reice Eric. RN, Helene Fuld Sch. Nursing, 1970; BSN, Clarion U., 1986; MA in Clin. Psychology, Edinboro U., 1988; PhD in Counseling Psychology, U. Pitts., 1999—. RN, psych. clin. specialist in child and adolescent psychiatry and mental health nursing, cognitive behavioral therapist. Staff nurse N.Y. Hosp., N.Y.C., 1970-71; instr. Northeastern Hosp., Phila., 1971-74; Venango County Vocat. Tech. Sch., Oil City, Pa., 1974-81; psychology intern Meadville (Pa.) Mental Health Clinic, 1988-89; rsch. asst. Cleft Palate Clinic, Erie, Pa., 1987-89; psychotherapist, psychologist PSY Svcs., Titusville, Pa., 1989—96, asst. prof. psychology, 2001—. Instr. U. Pitts., 1989—2000, rsch. asst. Pitt Mother and Child Project, 1997—99; psychology intern U. Buffalo Counseling Ctr., 2000—01; presenter, counselor Ctrs. N.Y. Conf., 2001. Bd. dirs. Forest/Warren (Pa.) Mental Health Svcs., 1975-78, Forest/Warren Children Svcs., 1975-78, Tionesta (Pa.) Area Health Svcs., Inc., 1976-78, Western Pa. Behavioral Health Network, 1994—; producer Miss Crawford County Scholarship Pageant, Meadville, 1986-89; workshop presenter Titusville Area Hosp., 1989-91. Mem. APA (assoc.), Learning Disabilities Assn. (adv. bd. 1993-2000), Pa. Psychol. Assn., N.W. Pa. Psychol. Assn., Pa. Soc. Behavioral Medicine and Biofeedback, Alliance Mentally Ill of Pa., Soc. Rsch. in Children (writer, rsch. presenter 2003), Am. Cleft Palate Assn. (writer, rsch. presenter 1994). Democrat. Avocations: travel, downhill skiing, racquetball, horseback riding. Home: 700 Rockwood Dr Titusville PA 16354-1244 Office: Univ Pitts Bradhurst Sci Ctr Titusville PA 16354 Office Phone: 814-827-4430. E-mail: altomar@pitt.edu.

ALTON, ANN LESLIE, judge, lawyer, educator; b. Pipestone, Minn., Sept. 10, 1945; d. Howard Robert, Jr. and Camilla Ann (DeMong) A.; m Gerald Russell Freeman Sr.; children: Brady Michael Alton Freeman, Matthew Alton Freeman (dec.). BA, Smith Coll., 1967; JD, U. Minn., 1970; postgrad., Nat. Jud. Coll., U. Nev., 1989. Bar: Minn. 1970, U.S. Dist. Ct. Minn. 1972, U.S. Supreme Ct. 1981. Apptd. gen. jurisdiction state trial ct. judge civil and criminal jurisdiction Dist. Ct., 4th Jud. Dist., Hennepin County, Minn., 1989—, elected, 1990, 2002—, mem. exec. com., 1995—98, chair psychol. svcs. com., 1996, vice chair adminstrv. com., 1989-94, asst. county atty. Mpls., 1970-89, felony prosecutor, criminal divsn., 1970-75, acting chief citizen protection divsn., 1975-76, chief citizen protection/econ. crime divsn., 1976-79, chief econ. crime unit, 1979-85, sr. atty. civil divsn. handling labor and employment law, 1989-89, mem. civil com., 1989—, presiding judge probate/mental health div., 1995-98, mem. exec. com., 1995-98, chair psychol. svcs. to ct. com., 1997-2000, 2002. Adj. prof. law Hamline U. Law Sch., St. Paul, 1973-77, 2004—; adj. prof. U. Minn. Law Sch., 1978-82; lectr. in field, 1970—; sr. faculty Minn. Advocacy Inst., Minn. CLE, 1988—; mem. faculty Nat. Inst. Trial Advocacy, U. Notre Dame Law Sch., 1989—, asst. team leader North Ctrl. Regional Jury Trial Advocacy Course, 1991—; sr. critiquing judge Jud. Trial Skills Tng. Program Minn. Supreme Ct. Continuing Edn. Program for State Cts., 1993—; mem. faculty intensive trial advocacy program Widener U. Sch. of Law, Wilmington, Del., 1993-96; bd. dirs. Pan-O-Gold Realty Co., 1986-89, Alton Realty Co., 1986-89, Alton Found., 1999—. Author articles, pamphlet, manual. Vice-chmn. bd. dirs. Minn. Program on Victims of Sexual Assault, 1974-76; bd. dirs. Physician's Health Plan (now Allina), Health Maintenance Organization, 1976-80, exec. com., 1977-80; mem. legal drug abuse subcom. Gov. Minn. Adv. Com. Drug Abuse, 1972-74; bd. visitors U. Minn. Law Sch., 1979-85; mem. child abuse project coordinating com. Hennepin County Med. Soc., 1982-83, chmn. corp., labor, ins. subcom., 1982; commr. corrections task force sex offenders, 1999-2001. Recipient Honorable Mention Roscoe Pound award for Excellence in Tchg. Trial Advocacy, Roscoe Pound Inst., Washington, 2000. Mem. ABA (jud. adminstrn. divsn.), Minn. Bar Assn. (criminal law, labor and employment law, civil litigation sects.), Hennepin County Bar Assn. (ethics com. 1973-76, criminal law com. 1973—, vice chmn. 1979-80, 83-84, unauthorized practice law com. 1977-78, individual rights and responsibilities com. 1977-78, labor and employment law com. 1985—, civil litigation com. 1985—), Minn. Dist. Judges Assn. (benefits com. 1991—, mem. program and edn. com. 1993—, mem. worker compensation risk mgmt. com. 1995-97), U. Minn. Law Sch. Alumni Assn. (bd. dirs. 1979-85), Nat. Women Judges, Douglas K. Amdahl Inn of Ct. (master, exec. bd. 2002—). Achievements include first to establish first 24 hour citizen complaint for economic crime in U.S.; include first to establish first woman prosecuting felony jury trials for Hennepin County; changing state-wide systems for sexual assault and child abuse victims and for battered women. Office: 1251-C Hennepin County Govt Ctr 300 S 6th St Minneapolis MN 55487 E-mail: ann.alton@courts.state.mn.us.

ALTSCHUL, B J, public relations counselor; b. Jan. 28, 1948; d. Lemuel and Sylva (Behr). Student, Goucher Coll., 1965-67; BA, U. South Fla., 1970; MA, U. Md., 1995. Reporter St. Petersburg (Fla.) Times, 1973—74; dir. pub. rels. Valkyrie Press, Inc. St. Petersburg, 1974—77; founding editor Bay Life, Clearwater, Fla., 1977—79, Tampa Bay Monthly, Clearwater, 1977—79; mng. editor Fla. Tourist News, Tampa and Orlando, 1981; founder Capital Comms. of Tampa, 1981; owner, prin. b j Altschul & Assocs. (formerly Capital Comms. of Tampa), 1985—. Mgr. editl. and info. svcs. Va. Pt. Authority, Norfolk, 1985-88; dir. pub. rels. Va. Dept. Agr. and Consumer Svcs., Richmond, 1988-93; adj. faculty Old Dominion U., Norfolk, 1986-88, U. Richmond, 1990, 94, Washington Ctr. for Internships, 1995-96; mgr. pub. rels. U. Md. Biotech. Inst., 1997-99; lectr. dept. comm. U. Md., 1999-2001; asst. prof. Am. U., 2001—. Author: Cracker Cookin' & Other Favorites, 1984; contbg. author: Virginia: A Commonwealth Comes of Age, 1988. Bd. dirs. Pinellas County Big Bros.-Big Sisters, 1980-82, Fla. Folklore Soc., 1984-85. Mem. Fla. Motion Picture and TV Assn. (treas. 1976-78), Hampton Rds. C. of C. (comm. pub. rels. Internat. Azalea Festival 1986, chmn. publs. 1987), Va. Conf. on World Trade (chmn. pub. rels. com.), Downtown Norfolk Devel. Corp. (chmn. urban living com.), Pub. Rels. Soc. Am. (chmn. Mid.-Atlantic Dist. 1988, chmn. govt. sect. 1989, bd. dirs., chmn. accreditation, chmn. Univ. Rels. Nat. Capital chpt., 2002-), Va. State Agy. Pub. Affairs Assn. (pres. 1990), Internat. Assn. Bus. Communicators (v.p. mem. svcs. Richmond chpt. 1996), Nat. Assn. Sci. Writers, D.C. Sci. Writers Assn. (bd. dirs. 2004—), Forum Agr. and Consumer Topics (founder, chmn. 1992). Avocations: piano, Irish set dancing, sailing, classical, folk, and jazz music. Office: B J Altschul & Assocs 14100 Beechvue Ln Silver Spring MD 20906 Personal E-mail: sunrises111@hotmail.com.

ALTSCHUL, SERENA, newscaster; b. N.Y.C. Anchor/reporter Channel One News (formerly Whittle Comm.); contbr. Choose or Lose '96 campaign MTV Networks, corr. MTV News, host True Life documentary series, host, co-prodr. True Life: Fatal Dose, host, co-prodr. True Life: I'm a Hacker, host True Life: Unfiltered, host with Kurt Loder pre- and post-Video Music Awards, host with Kurt Loder and Carson Daly Grammy Awards spl. Participant roundtable panels Newseum, Washington, MTV Networks. Prodr.: (documentaries) The Last Party; featured N.Y. Times, Washington Post, appeared CNN. Office: MTV Networks 1515 Broadway New York NY 10036

ALTSCHULER, MARJORIE, advertising executive; V.p., rsch. and account mgmt. dir. Foote, Cone & Belding, N.Y.C.; v.p., strategic planner, new bus. developer J. Walter Thompson Co., N.Y.C., 1990-94; sr. v.p., new bus. dir. McCann-Erickson Worldwide, N.Y.C., 1994-97, exec. v.p., new bus. dir., 1997—. Office: 750 3d Ave New York NY 10017

ALTSCHULER, RUTH PHYLLIS, realtor, secondary school educator; d. Morris and Sarah Dina Gass; m. Bruce Robert Altschuler, Oct. 27, 1974; children: Joan, Wendy, Cheryl. AA, Nassau County, 1972; BS in English, Towson U., 1998. Cert. tchr. English grades 5-12 Md., lic. realtor Md. Pres. Cognitive Photonics, Ft. Meade, Md., 1989—90; dir. sales and mktg. Cobalt Rsch., Columbia, Md., 1997—99, CEO, 2001—03; tchr. English Prince George County Pub. Sch. Sys., Md., 1999; instr. English writing Howard C.C., Columbia, 2000; tchr. English Balt. City Pub. Sch. Sys., 2001. Realtor Long and Foster Realtors, Columbia, 2002—. Stop smoking facilitator Am. Cancer Soc., San Antonio, 1979—80; troop leader Girl Scouts Am., Ft. Meade, Md., 1991; precinct chmn. Rep. Party Bexar County, San Antonio, 1976—92, Cat USAF 1970—74. Named Outstanding Young Woman Am., Jaycees, 1981. Mem. NEA, Acad. Am. Poets, Phi English Teachers Golden Key. Jewish. Avocations: writing, sailing, singing, sewing, cooking. Office: Cobalt Rsch LLC PO Box 458 Simpsonville MD 21150-0458

ALTURA, BELLA T. physiologist, educator; b. Solingen, Germany; came to U.S., 1948; d. Sol and Rosa (Brandstetter) Tabak; m. Burton M. Altura, Dec. 27, 1961; 1 child, Rachel Allison. BA, Hunter Coll., 1953, MA, 1962; PhD, CUNY, 1968. Instr. exptl. anesthesiology Albert Einstein Coll. Medicine, Bronx, 1970-74; asst. prof. physiology SUNY Health Sci Ctr., Bklyn., 1974-82, assoc. prof. physiology, 1982-97, rsch. prof. physiology, 1997—, rsch. prof. pharmacology, 1998—. Vis. prof. Beijing Coll. of Traditional Chinese Medicine, 1988, Jiangxi (China) Med. Coll., 1988, Tokyo U. Med. Sch., 1993, U. Brussels Esramé Hosp., 1995, Humboldt U.-Charité Hosp., 1995, Kagoshima U., Japan, 1995, U. Birmingham, England, 1996, Self Med. Def. Coll. Japan, 1996, Nat. Def. Med. Sch., Japan, 1996, Albert Szent Gyorgi Med. U., Szeged, Hungary, 1997; mem. Nat. Coun. on Magnesium and Cardiovascular Disease, 1991—; cons. NOVA Biomedical, 1989—; Niche pharm. cons. Protina GmbH, Munich, 1992—96, Otsuka Pharm. Co., Japan, 1995—97, Roberts Pharm. Co., 1999—2000; co-prin. investigator NIH, Nat. Heart, Lung and Blood Inst., NIMH, Nat. Inst. on Alcoholism and Alcohol Abuse. Contbr. over 700 articles to profl. jours. Fellowship NASA, 1966-67, CUNY, 1968; co-recipient Gold-Silver medal French Nat. Acad. Medicine, 1984, Silver medal Mayor of Paris, 1984, Seelig award for lifetime rsch. on magnesium, Am. Coll. Nutrition, 2002, Outstanding Inventor of Yr., SUNY, 2002. Mem. Am. Physiol. Soc., Am. Soc. Pharmacology and Exptl. Therapeutics, Am. Soc. for Magnesium Rsch. (founder, treas. 1984—), Hungarian Soc. Electrochemistry (hon. co-pres. 1995-96), Nat. Heart, Lung and Blood Inst., Nat. Inst. on Alcohol Abuse and Alcoholism, Phi Beta Kappa, Sigma Xi. Achievements include first measurement ionized magnesium with ion selective electrode in blood, serum and plasma in health and disease states; demonstration that substances of abuse can cause cerebrovasospasm and stroke. Office: SUNY Health Sci Ctr Box 31 450 Clarkson Ave Brooklyn NY 11203-2205 Office Phone: 718-270-2205. E-mail: baltura@downstate.edu.

ALUMBAUGH, JOANN MCCALLA, magazine editor; b. Ann Arbor, Mich., Sept. 16, 1952; d. William Samuel and Jean Arliss (Guy) McCalla; m. Lyle Ray Alumbaugh, Apr. 27, 1974; children: Brent William, Brandon Jess, Brooke Louise. BA, Ea. Mich. U., 1974. Cert. tchr. Mich. Assoc. editor Chester White Swine Record Assn., Rochester, Ind., 1974-77; prodn. editor United Duroc Swine Registry, Peoria, Ill., 1977-79; dir. pres. Nat. Assn. Swine Records, Macomb, Ill., 1979-82; free-lance writer, artist Ill. and Nat. Specific Pathogen Free Assn., Ind. producers, Good Hope, Emden, Ill., 1982-85; editor The Hog Producer Farm Progress Publs., Urbandale, Iowa, 1985-99; exec. editor Nebr. Farmer, Kans. Farmer, Mo. Ruralist, We. Beef Prodr., Beef Prodr., Farm & Fireside, 1999—2003; dir. comms. Farms.Com, 2003—. Family Living Program, Farm Progress Show, 1985—, Master Farm Homemaker Program, 1989-99; mem. U.S. Agrl. Export Devel. Coun., Washington, 1979-82; apptd. mem. Blue Ribbon Com. on Agr., 1980-81. Contbr. numerous articles to profl. jours. Precinct chmn. Rep. Party, Linden, Iowa, 1988; mem. Keep Improving Dist. Schs., Panora, Iowa, 1990-91; v.p. Sunday sch. com. Sunset Circle, United Meth. Ch., Linden, 1990-91; pres. PTA, Panorama Schs., Panora, 1993-94; coach Odyssey of Mind Program World Competition, 1994—. Mem. Iowa Master Farm Homemakers, Guthrie County Prok Prodrs., McDonough County and Ill. Porkettes (county pres. 1978—79, Bellringer award 1979), Nat. Pork Prodrs. Coun., Iowa Pork Prodrs. Assn. (legis. com. 1990—95, hon. master pork prodr.), U.S. Animal Health Assn., Am. Agrl. Editors Assn. (chmn. dist. svc. com. 1991, master writer 1997, pres.-elect 1998, pres. 1999, chmn. adv. coun. 1999—2002, co-chmn. comm. clinic, comm. clinic, trustee 2002—), World of Difference award 1995, Oscar in Agr. 1999), Internat. Platform Assn. Avocations: reading, painting, flower gardening. Home: 2644 Amarillo Ave Linden IA 50146-8029 Office: PigChamp Aspen Business Park 426 S 17th Ames IA 50010

ALVARADO, LINDA G. construction executive; Doctorate (hon.), Dowling Coll. Pres., CEO Alvarado Constrn., Inc., Denver, 1976—. Owner Colorado Rockies franchise; corp. dir. 3M, Pepsi Bottling Group, Pitney

Bowes and Lennox Industries. Chmn. bd. dirs. Denver Hispanic C. of C.; commrs. White House Initiative for Hispanic Excellence in Edn. Named Revlon Bus. Woman of Yr., 1996, Bus. Woman of Yr., U.S. Hispanic C. of C., 1996, 100 Most Influential Hispanics in Am., Hispanic Bus. Mag., others; recipient Nat. Minority Supplier Devel. Coun. Leadership award, 1996, Sara Lee Corp. Frontrunner award, 2001, Horatio Alger award, others, inducted into Nat. Women's Hall of Fame, Colo. Women's Hall of Fame. Office: Alvarado Construction 1266 Santa Fe Dr Denver CO 80204-3546

ALVARADO, SANDRA JACQUELINE, television director; b. Santiago, Chile, July 18, 1964; d. Abraham S. and Fresia C. (Gomez) A.; children: Jordan Alexander Korcowicz, Brandon Michael Korcowicz. AA cum laude, Valley Coll., 1983; BA, Calif. State U., Northridge, 1986. Fl. dir. Univision Network, L.A., 1987-88; casting coord. Ralph Edwards/Stu Billet Prodns., L.A., 1988-89; with several prodn. cos., L.A., 1989-90; dir. Sta. KWHY-TV, L.A., 1990-93, prodr., 1993-94; assoc. dir., dir. Sta. KMEX-TV, L.A., 1994—2001; co-founder Aces TV, Studio City, Calif., 2001—. Recipient Golden Mic, Radio/TV News Assn., 1998, Emmy award, 2000. Mem. Nat. Assn. Broadcast Employees & Technicians/Comms. Workers of Am., Screen Actors Guild, AFTRA. Avocations: working out, tennis, rollerblading, dance, singing. Office: Aces TV 12400 Ventura Blvd #188 Studio City CA 90045

ALVAREZ, AIDA, former federal agency administrator; b. Aguadilla, P.R., July 22, 1949; BA cum laude, Harvard U., 1971; LLD (hon.), Iona Coll., 1985. News reporter, anchor Metromedia TV, N.Y.C.; reporter N.Y. Post, N.Y.C.; mem. N.Y.C. Charter Revision Commn.; v.p. N.Y.C. Health and Hosps. Corp., 1984—85; investment banker 1st Boston Corp., N.Y.C., San Francisco, 1986-93; dir. Office Fed. Housing Enterprise Oversight, Washington, 1993-97; adminstr. Small Bus. Adminstrn., 1997-2001. Mem. bd. dirs. PacifiCare Health Systems Inc., 2003-, Former mem. bd. dirs. Nat. Hispanic Leadership Agenda, N.Y. Cmty. Trust, Nat. civic League; former chmn. bd. Mcpl. Assistance Corp./Victim Svcs. Agy., N.Y.C.; N.Y. State chmn. Gore Presdl. Campaign, 1988; nat. co-chmn. women's com. Clinton Presdl. Campaign, 1992; mem. President's Econ. Transition Team, 1992. Recipient Front Page award, award for excellence AP. 1982, Emmy nomination for reporting guerrilla activities in El Salvador. Democrat.*

ALVAREZ, CHRISTINA, counselor; b. Albany, N.Y., Dec. 23, 1977; d. Angel Noel and Linda Geraldine Alvarez. BA, U. Albany, 1999, MSW, 2003. Program aide unit dir. Schenectady (N.Y.) Boys and Girls Clubs, 1997—99; cmty. support specialist Wildwood Day Svcs., Albany, 1999—. Intern Centrocivico Hispanoamericano, Inc., Albany, 2002—. Tchr., missionary Calvary Tabernacle, Schenectady, 1999—2003. Recipient Tulip Ct. Mem., City of Albany, 2000. Republican. Avocations: travel, music. Home: Apt 2 73 Winthrop Ave Albany NY 12208 Personal E-mail: calvarez@workmail.com.

ALVAREZ, JULIA, writer; b. NYC, 1950; Attended, Conn. Coll., Bread Loaf Sch. English, Middelbury Coll.; BA summa cum laude, Middlebury Coll., 1971; MFA, Syracuse U., 1975. Poet-in-the-schools, Ky., 1975—78, 1975—78, 1975—78; prof. creative writing and English Phillips Andover Acad., Mass., 1979—81, U. Vt., 1981—83, U. Ill., 1985—88; prof. English Middlebury Coll., 1988—. Jenny McKean Moore vis. writer George Wash. U., 1984. Author: (novels) How the Garcia Girls Lost Their Accents, 1991 (selected as notable book Am. Libr. Assn., 1992), In the Time of Butterflies, 1994, The Other Side, 1995, YO!, 1997, Something to Declare, 1998, In the Name of Salomé, 2000, The Secret Footprints, 2000, How Tia Lola Came to Stay, 2001, A Cafecito Story, 2001, Before We Were Free, 2002, (poetry) The Woman I Kept to Myself, Homecoming: New and Collected Poems. Recipient Benjamin T. Marshall Poetry Prize, Conn. Coll., 1968, 1969, prize, Acad. Am. Poetry, 1974, poetry award, La Reina Press, 1982, Third Woman Press award, first prize in narrative, 1986, award for younger writers, Gen. Elec. Found., 1986, syndicated fiction prize for "Snow" grant from Ingram Merrill Found., PEN, 1990, Josephine Miles award, PEN Oakland, 1991; grantee, Nat. Endowment Arts, 1987—88; creative writing fellow, Syracuse U., 1974—75, Robert Frost Poetry fellowship, Bread Loaf Writers' Conf., 1986, Kenan grant, Phillips Andover Acad., 1980, exhbn. grant, Vt. Arts Coun., 1984—85. Office: Susan Berghol Literary Svcs 17 W 10th St 5B New York NY 10011 Office Phone: 212-387-0545. Office Fax: 212-387-0546.*

ALVAREZ, OFELIA AMPARO, medical educator; b. Havana, Cuba, Mar. 29, 1958; BS, U. Puerto Rico, 1978, MD, 1982. Diplomate Nat. Bd. Med. Examiners, Am. Bd. Pediat., Sub-bd. Pediatric Hematology-Oncology. Pediatric residency Univ. Children's Hosp., San Juan, P.R., 1982-85; fellow pediatric hematology, oncology Children's Hosp. L.A., 1985-88; asst. prof. pediat. Loma Linda (Calif.) U., 1988-95, assoc. prof., 1995-2000; assoc. prof. clin. pediats. Univ. Miami, 2001—. Med. advisor Candlelighters, Inland Empire, 1988-2000. Contbr. articles to profl. jours. Bd. mem., med. advisor Make-A-Wish Found., Inland Empire, 1994-95. Clin. oncology fellow Am. Cancer Soc., 1985-86; pediatric rsch. fund Loma Linda U., 1993-95. Fellow: Am. Acad. Pediat.; mem.: AAUW, Histiocyte Soc., Am. Soc. Hematology, Am. Soc. Pediatric Hematology/Oncology, Am. Soc. Clin. Oncology, Beta Beta Beta. Roman Catholic. Office: Univ Miami Divsn Pediats Hematology Oncology Dept Pediats PO Box 016960 Miami FL 33101 E-mail: oalvarez2@med.miami.edu.

ALVARIÑO DE LEIRA, ANGELES (ANGELES ALVARIÑO), biologist, oceanographer; b. El Ferrol, Spain, Oct. 3, 1916; came to U.S., 1958, naturalized, 1966; d. Antonio Alvariño-Grimaldos and Carmen Gonzalez Diaz-Saavedra; m. Eugenio Leira-Manso, Mar. 16, 1940; 1 child, Angeles. BS Letters and Humanities summa cum laude, U. Santiago de Compostela, Spain, 1933; M in Natural Scis., U. Madrid (now U. Complutense), 1941, Doctorate cert., 1951; DSc summa cum laude, U Madrid (now U. Complutense), 1967. Cert. biologist-oceanographer, 1952, Spanish Inst. Oceanography. Prof. biology Coll. El Ferrol, Spain, 1941-48; fishery rsch. biologist dept. Sea Fisheries Spain, 1948-52; histologist Superior Coun. Sci. Rsch., 1948-52; biologist, oceanographer Spanish Inst. Oceanography, 1950-57; biologist Scripps Inst. Oceanography-U. Calif. San Diego, LaJolla, 1958—69; fishery rsch. biologist Nat. Marine Fisheries Svc. S.W. Fisheries Sci. Ctr., NOAA, U.S. Dept. Commerce, La Jolla, 1970-87; emeritus scientist Nat. Marine Fisheries Svc. S.W. Fisheries Ctr., NOAA, U.S. Dept. Commerce, La Jolla, 1987—; assoc. prof. U. Nat. Autonomous Mexico, 1976, San Diego State U., 1979-82; rsch. assoc. U. San Diego, 1982—, assoc. prof., 1982—. Vis. prof. Poly. Tech. Mexico, 1982—, U. Parana, Brazil, 1982. Author: Spain and the First Scientific Oceanic Expedition (1789-1794) Malaspina and Bustamante with the Corvettes "Descubierta" and "Atrevida", 2000, 2d deluxe edit., 2003; contbr. over 100 articles to profl. jours., chpts. in books; discovered 22 new species and the indicator species for various oceanic currents, ocean dynamics, and the study of the biotic environment of fish spawning grounds, study of plankton predators and the impact in fisheries, bunch of plankton populations carried by ships into exotic oceanic areas and throughout interoceanic canals, studies on Chaetognatha and Siphonophora in all world oceans and of Hydromedusae in the Atlantic, Pacific and Indian oceans; studies on the reproductive processes in Chaetognatha, others. Brit. Coun. fellow, 1953-54, Fulbright fellow, 1956-57; NSF grantee, 1961-69, U.S. Office Navy grantee, 1958-69, Calif. Coop. Oceanic Fishery Investigations grantee, 1958-69, UNESCO grantee, 1979; recipient Great Silver Medal of Galicia, Spain, presented by King Juan Carlos and Queen Sofia of Spain, 1993. Fellow Am. Inst. Fishery Rsch. Biologists, Natural History Assn.; mem. Am. Assn. Rschrs. on Marine Scis. Achievements include discovery of biotic differences in the habitat of various fishes; sci. work on the fauna represented in about 100 color plates from specimens of plankton, fishes, turtles, birds. It includes a total of near 200 species collected along the South Atlantic and Pacific (up to Alaska, western Pacific Islands, the Philippines, Australia and back to Spain), during oceanic sci. expedition of 1789-1794 with specific identification, description, behavior and distribution; scientist in British, U.S., Mexican and Spanish research vessels in cruisers and expeditions in the Atlantic and Pacific Oceans. Home: 7535 Cabrillo Ave La Jolla CA 92037-5206 Office: Nat Marine Fisheries Svc SW Fisheries Sci Ctr PO Box 271 La Jolla CA 92038-0271

ALVARO, MAUREEN TERESA, music educator; b. Plattsburgh, N.Y., May 23, 1976; d. Donald Charles and JoAnn Elizabeth McCoy; m. Anthony Joseph Alvaro, Aug. 19, 2000; 1 child, Laura Rose. Bachelor of Music, Ithaca Coll., 1997, Master of Music, 2001. Cert. music tchr. permanent N.Y. Music tchr. St. Daniel's Sch., Syracuse, NY, 1998—2001; pvt. music tchr. Camillus, NY, 1998—; music tchr. St. Patrick's Sch., Syracuse, 1998—. The Band Bus, Syracuse, NY, 1999—2001, Marcellus Ctrl. Sch.s., NY, 2001—. Flutist St. Joseph's Ch. Folk Group, Camillus, 1990—, Ctrl. N.Y. Music Educators Wind Ensemble, Syracuse, 1999—. Mem.: Ctrl. N.Y. Flute Assn. (mem. flute choir 1998—, v.p. 2000—), N.Y. State Sch. Music Assn., Music Educators Nat. Conf. Roman Catholic. Avocation: painting. Home: 101 West Way Camillus NY 13031

ALVILLAR-SPEAKE, THERESA, federal agency administrator; Grad., Calif. State U.; MBA, Golden Gate U. Asst. dir. program devel. minority bus. devel. agy. Dept. Commerce, 1991—93; mgr. small bus. and disabled vet. bus. enterprise programs State Calif. Dept. Transp.; exec. dir. Calif. Employment Devel. Dept., 1994—97, asst. dir. bus. rels., 1997—2000; dir. minority econ. impact Dept. Energy, Washington, 2001—. Founder NEDA San Joaquin Valley. Office: Dept Energy Econ Impact and Diversity 1000 Independence Ave SW Washington DC 20585-0001

ALVING, BARBARA, federal agency administrator; BS with highest distinction, Purdue U.; MD cum laude, Georgetown U., 1972. Joined dept. hematology and vascular biology Walter Reed Army Inst. Rsch., 1980, chief dept. hematology and vascular biology; dir. hematology/med. oncology sect. Washington Hosp. Ctr., 1997—99; rsch. investigator Divsn. Blood and Blood ProductsFDA Bur. Biologics; leader divsn. blood diseases and resources Nat. Heart, Lung and Blood Inst. NIH, Bethesda, Md., 1999—2001, dep. dir. Nat. Heart, Lung and Blood Inst., 2001—03, acting dir. Nat. Heart, Lung and Blood Inst., 2003—. Editor 3 books; contbr. articles to profl. jours. Achievements include patents in field. Office: Nat Heart Lung and Blood Inst Bldg 31 31 Center Dr MSC 2486 Bethesda MD 20892-2846

ALWARD, RUTH ROSENDALL, nursing consultant; d. Henry Rosendall and Freda Jonkman; m. Samuel Alward, Jan. 17, 1976. RN, Butterworth Hosp. Sch. Nursing, Grand Rapids, Mich.; BSN summa cum laude, Hunter Coll./CUNY, N.Y., 1980; MA Tchrs. Coll., Columbia U., 1982, EdM, 1983, EdD, 1986. Sr. clin. nurse Wadsworth VA Hosp., L.A., 1966-68; exec. dir. nursing Care Corp, Grand Rapids, Mich., 1968-71; nursing cons. Humana Inc., Louisville, 1972-76; asst. prof., dir. nursing adminstrn. grad. prog. Hunter Coll., CUNY, N.Y.C., 1986-90; pres. Nurse Exec. Assocs., Inc., Washington, 1990—; series editor Delmar Pubs. Inc., Albany, 1993-96. Co-author: The Nurse's Shift Work Handbook, 1993, The Nurse's Guide to Marketing, 1991; contbr. articles to profl. jours.; mem. editorial adv. bd. Jour. of Nursing Adminstrn. Bd. dirs., past pres. James Lenox House Assn.; bd. dirs. IONA Sr. Svcs. Mem. Va Nurses Assn. (mem. fin. com.), Nat. League Nursing (treas. D.C. chpt.), Am. Orgn. Nurse Execs., Sigma Theta Tau. Home and Office: 2011 N St NW Washington DC 20036-2301

AMADIO, BARI ANN, metal fabrication executive, former nurse; b. Phila., Mar. 26, 1949; d. Fred Deutscher and Celena (Lusky) Garber; m. Peter Colby Amadio, June 24, 1973; children: P. Grant, Jamie Blair. BA in Psychology, U. Miami, 1970; diploma in Nursing, Thomas Jefferson U., 1973, Johnston-Willis Sch. Nursing, 1974; BS in Nursing, Northeastern U., 1977; MS in Nursing, Boston U., 1978; JD, Quinnipiac Sch. Law, 1983. Faculty Johnston-Willis Sch. Nursing, Richmond, Va., 1974-75; staff, charge nurse Mass. Gen. Hosp., Boston, 1975-78; faculty New Eng. Deaconess, Boston, 1978-80, Lankenau Hosp. Sch. of Nursing, Phila., 1980-81; pres. Original Metals, Inc., Phila., 1985—, also bd. dirs. Owner Silver Carousel Antiques, Rochester, Minn. Treas. Women's Assn. Minn. Orch., Rochester, 1986-87, pres., 1987-89, life advisor, 1989—, editor newsnotes, 1985-87; mayor's coms. All Am. City Award Com., Rochester, 1984-88; bd. dirs. Rochester Civic League, 1988-94, pres.-elect, 1990-91, pres., 1991-92, Rochester Civic Theatre, 2003—; pres. Rochester Friends of Mpls. Inst. Arts, 1989-90, Folwell PTA, 1990-91; state liaison Gateway, 1990-91; bd. dirs. Rochester Civic Theatre, 1993-99, 2003--, v.p., 1994-95, pres., 1995-96; Minn. site coord. Pew Charitable Trust's Project 540, 2002—. Recipient Joe Saidy award Rochester Civic Theatre, 1999, Mayor's Artistic and Cultural Achievement medal of honor, 2003. Mem.: NAFE, Nat. Assn. Food Equipment Mfrs., Zumbro Valley Med. Soc. Aux. (Rochester, fin. chmn. 1986—90, treas. 1988—90), Am. Soc. Law and Medicine, Rotary Club Rochester, Friends of Mayowood, Order of the Eastern Star (trustee), Sigma Theta Tau, Phi Alpha Delta. Avocations: fencing, painting, writing poetry, piano, squash.

AMADO, HONEY KESSLER, lawyer; b. Bklyn., July 20, 1949; d. Bernard and Mildred Kessler; m. Ralph Albert Amado, Oct. 24, 1976; children: Jessica Reina, Micah Solomon, Gabrielle Beth. BA in Polit. Sci., Calif. State Coll., Long Beach, 1971; JD, Western State U., Fullerton, Calif., 1976. Bar: Calif. 1977, U.S. Dist. Ct. (ctrl. dist.) Calif. 1981, U.S. Ct. Appeals (9th cir.) 1981, U.S. Supreme Ct. 1994. Assoc. Law Offices of Jack M. Lasky, Beverly Hills, Calif., 1977-78; pvt. practice Beverly Hills, Calif., 1978—. Mem. family law exec. com. Calif. State Bar, 1987-91; lectr. in field. Contbr. articles to profl. jours.; mem. editl. bd. L.A. Lawyer mag., 1996—, articles coord., 1999-2000, chair, 2000-01. Mem. Com. Concerned Lawyers for Soviet Jewry, 1979-90; nat. v.p. Jewish Nat. Fund, 1995-97, 2002—; bd. dirs. Jewish Nat. Fund L.A., 1990-98, 2002—, Women's Alliance Israel; mem. pres.'s coun. Am. Jewish Com., 2002—; sec. L.A. region, bd. dirs., 1991-94, Am. Jewish Congress, Jewish Feminist Ctr., 1992-99, co-chair steering com., 1994-96; mem. Commn. on Soviet Jewry of Jewish Fedn. Coun. Greater L.A., 1977-83, chmn., 1979-81, commn. on edn., 1982-83, cmty. rels. com., 1979-83; mem. pres.'s coun. Am. Jewish Com., L.A., 2003—, bd. dirs., 2002—; co-chair European affairs subcom. Internat. Rels. Com. L.A. Region, 2003—. Mem. Calif. Women Lawyers (bd. govs. 1988-90, 1st v.p. 1989-90, jud. evaluations co-chair 1988-90), San Fernando Valley Bar Assn. (family law mediators and arbitrators planel 1983-94, judge pro-tem panel 1987-94), Beverly Hills Bar Assn. (family law mediators panel 1985-94), L.A. County Bar Assn. (family law sect., appellate cts. com. 1987—, chmn. subcom. to examine reorgn. Calif. Supreme Ct. 1990-94, judge pro tem panel 1985-95, appellate jud. evaluations com. 1989—, dist. 2 settlement program 1996—), Calif. State Bar, Calif. Ct. Appeal. Democrat. Jewish. Office: 261 S Wetherly Dr Beverly Hills CA 90211-2515 Office Phone: 310-550-8214.

AMADOR, ANNE, architect, composer; b. Racine, Wis., Apr. 29, 1958; d. Anthony s. and Marian A. Methenitis; m. Germán Amador, Jr., Aug. 20, 1983; children: Cristián Mateo, Isabel Celeste. BA, Rice U., 1980, MusB, 1995; MArch, U. Houston, 1983. Registererd arch., Tex.; registered interior designer, Tex. Intern arch. Sobel/Roth Archs., Houston, 1980-83, Ceria & Coupel, Houston, 1983-84; project arch. 3/D Internat., Houston, 1984-89, 91-93; interior arch. Gensler & Assocs., London, 1991; artistic dir. Chimney Rock Studios, Houston, 1993—. Vis. student St. Hilda's Coll., Oxford (Eng.) U., 1989-90. Composer (choral music) Satires of Circumstance, 1991 (Soc.for the Promotion of New Music award 1991), (choral) Whither Thou Goest, 1995, (choral/instrumental) Processional-St. Philip, 2000. Bd. dirs. St. Philip Child's Day In Presch., Houston, 1995—; deacon St. Philip Presbyn. Ch., Houston, 1999-01. Mem. Tanglewood Garden Club (com. mem.), Rice U. Bus. and Profl. Women (program chair 1995-96), Rice Design Alliance, The Shepherd Soc. Avocations: piano, running. Home: 1022 Chimney Rock Rd Houston TX 77056-2001 E-mail: anamador@msn.com.

AMADOR, MIRANDA BARBARA, artist; b. London, Sept. 4, 1957; came to U.S., 1960; d. Stefan I. and Barbara (Kownacka) Ulankiewicz; m. Luis Valentine Amador, June 14, 1980 (div. 1987). AD in Fine Art, Am. Acad. Art, Chgo., 1978; AD in Comml. Art, Am. Acad. Art, 1978; BFA, Sch. Art Inst. Chgo., 1983. Med. illusrator, graphic artist Qually & Co., Chgo., 1980-82; art dir. Playboy Erotic Fantasies Videos Playboy Mag., Chgo., 1981-83; creative dir. Santa Monica (Calif.) Propellor, 1984-85; art dir., prodn. designer L.A., 1985—. Judge Cable Ace Awards in art direction, 1994-95. Illustrator (book) Brain Tumors in the Young, 1981-82; art dir. CA Lottery for Spanish Channel, 1996, CLIO award; co-editor, cons. History of Neurosciences, L.A. Mem. AFI, Art Inst. Chgo. (life.). Avocations: photography, writing, drawing, sports, travel. Home and Office: 9312 1/2 W Olympic Blvd Beverly Hills CA 90212-4510

AMAKI, AMALIA, curator; b. Atlanta; d. Norman Vance and Mary Lee (Hill) Peek. BA in Journalism, Ga. State U., 1971; BA in Photography, U. N.Mex., 1980; MA in Modern Art and European Art, Emory U., Atlanta, 1992, PhD in Am. Art, 1994. Asst. prof., instr. art history Morehouse Coll., Atlanta, 1985—87; asst. prof. art history Spelman Coll., Atlanta, 1987—98, 1999—2000, North Ga. Coll. and State U., Dahlonega, 1998—99; asst. prof., curator Paul R. Jones Collection U. Del., Newark, 2000—. Commn. art work Miller Brewing Co., Milw., 1991, Seagrims Gin, N.Y.C., 1995, Coca Cola Co., Atlanta, 1996, Hartsfield Internat. Airport, Atlanta, 1996, Atlanta, 99, Absolut Vodka, N.Y.C., 2002. Chair pub. art program Fulton CountyArts Coun., Atlanta, 1993—96. Recipient Individual Artist award, Ga. Coun. for Arts, 1994, Women in the Arts award, Sec. of State of Ga., 1995, Individual Artist award, Nat. Endowment for Arts, 1995. Mem.: Emory U. Alumni Bd. of Govs. (bd. mem.), Mus. of Contemporary Art (Ga.) (bd. mem.), Coll. Art Assn. Avocations: gardening, reading, walking, travel, tennis.

AMANCIO, RUTH CARSON, safety engineer; b. Honolulu, Nov. 13, 1956; d. Caliupe Carson and Julia (Donios) Amancio; m. Rodney Mitsuo Kaneshiro, June 8, 1980 (div. June 1992); children: Alane Kapeka Kaneshiro, Jolie Mikala Kaneshiro. AS, U. Hawaii, 2001. Cert. health safety profl., AHERA asbestos project designer, bldg. insp., contractor/supr., supr. constrn.; OSHA 500 trainer 2003. Sales supr. Affirmed Med. Svc., Honolulu, 1982-96; safety adminstr. Albert C. Kobayashi Inc., Waipahu, Hawaii, 1996—; safety mgr., cons. OSHCON Inc., Honolulu, 1998—99; staff St. Francis Med. Ctr., Honolulu, 1999—2001, Integrated Svcs. Inc., Honolulu, 2001—03; with Oshcon Inc., Honolulu, 2002—03, Metcalf Constrn. Co., Inc., Honolulu, 2003—. Trainer ARC, Honolulu, 1994—96; rec. sec. Non-Traditional Employment Task Force, 1996—. Mem.: Gen. Contractors Assn., Am. Soc. Safety Engrs. (scholar 1992—95), Vets. Safety (scholar 1996), Phi Theta Kappa (2d v.p. 1992—96). Avocations: sewing, music, dance, aerobic weight training, reading.

AMARA, LUCINE, opera and concert singer; b. Hartford, Conn., Mar. 1, 1925; d. George and Adrine (Kazanjian) Armaganian; married, Jan. 7, 1961 (div. June 1964). Student, Music Acad. of West, 1947, U. So. Calif., 1949-50. Artistic dir. N.J. Assn. Verismo Opera, Ft. Lee. Tchr. master classes, U.S., Mex., Can. Appeared at Hollywood Bowl, 1948, soloist, San Francisco Symphony, 1949-50; career includes over 1000 operatic performances; with Met. Opera, N.Y.C., from 1950, sang 800 performances, 9 new prodns., 5 opening nights, 57 radio broadcasts, 4 telecasts including appeared on Met. Opera: In Performance, 1982, 83, 84, 85, 86, 87, 88, 90, 91; recorded Pagliacci, 1951, 60; singer with New Orleans, Hartford, Pitts., Central City operas, 1952-54, appeared Glyndebourne Opera, 1954, 55, 57, 58, Edinburgh Festival, 1954, singer, Aida, Terme Di Caracalla, Rome, 1954, also Stockholm Opera, N.Y. Philharm., St. Louis Civic Light Opera, 1955-56; has appeared in leading or title roles in several operas including: Tosca, Aida, Amelia in Un Ballo in Maschera, Turandot, Riverside Opera Assn., 1986, others; appeared with St. Petersburg (Fla.) Opera, Venezuela Philharm. Orch., 1988, 93; opera and concert tour, USSR, 1965, 91, Manila, 1968, Paris, Mex., 1966, Hong Kong and China, 1983, Yugoslavia, 1988; rec. artist, Columbia, RCA, Victor, Angel records, Met. Opera Record Club; albums include: Beethoven's Symphony No. 9, Leoncavallo's, I Pagliacci, Puccini's La Bohème, Verdi Requiem. Recipient 1st prize Atwater-Kent Radio Auditions, 1948; inducted to Acad. Vocal Arts Hall Fame, 1989. Office: PO Box 3024 Fort Lee NJ 07024-9024 E-mail: lamara@nyc.rr.com.

AMATO, DEBORAH DOUGLASS, aerospace engineer; b. Mo. d. Clyde and Wilma Douglass; m. Michael Amato, 1996. BS, MIT, 1994; MS, U. Md., 1998. Programmer Orbital Scis. Corp., Va., 1993; aerospace engr. NASA-Goddard Space Flight Ctr., Greenbelt, Md., 1993—. Mem. AIAA. Avocations: music, swimming. Office: NASA Goddard Space Flight Ctr Greenbelt MD 20771-0001

AMATO, ISABELLA ANTONIA, real estate executive; b. Noto, Italy, July 17, 1942; d. Raimondo and Giuseppa (Pinna) Sesta; m. Vincent Amato; children: Alice, Claudine. Acctg. diploma, Inst. Tech. and Commerce, 1962. Cert. Comml. Investment Mgr., Comml. Investment Inst., Specialist Real Estate Securities, Real Estate Securities and Syndication Inst. V.p., dir. Thomas F. Seay & Assocs., Chgo., 1977-81; treas. Seay & Thomas Inc., Chgo., 1979-81; CFO Group One Investments, Chgo., 1981—; exec. v.p., registered prin. First Group Securities, Ltd., Chgo., 1983-95, pres., 1995—. Vol. translator Altrusa Lang. Bank, Chgo., 1980-86; v.p. Jr. Woman Club, Elk Grove Village, Ill., 1977; chairperson Atty. Exec. Forum, Chgo., 1985. Mem. Nat. Assn. Securities Dealers (prin.), Nat. Assn. Realtors, Chgo. Real Estate Bd., Real Estate Fin. Forum, Altrusa Profl. Woman (treas. Chgo. club 1984-85), YWCA Circle of Friends. Office: Group One Investments 77 W Washington St Ste 1005 Chicago IL 60602-2805

AMATO, ROSALIE, secondary school educator; b. Racalmuto, Agrigento, Sicily, June 3, 1920; came to U.S., 1923; d. Nicolo and Francesca (Macaluso) A. BS, Buffalo State U., 1964, MEd, 1968. Office supr. Wm. Hengerer Co. (Sibley's), Buffalo, N.Y., 1941-51; installation personnel Remington Rand, Dayton, Ohio, 1951-53; office supr., acctg. City of Buffalo, 1953-61; home econs. tchr. Buffalo Bd. Edn., 1964-70, supr. home econs. federally funded projects, 1971—. Vol. Civil Def., State of N.Y., 1953-58 (Cert. Pub. Service, 1958). Mem. Am. Home Econs. Assn. (area coord. 1973-75), Kappa Delta (treas. 1962-63), Phi Epsilon Omicron (pres. 1968-70). Roman Catholic. Avocations: art, design, concerts, opera, bowling. Home: 327 Colvin Ave Buffalo NY 14216-2338

AMAYA-THETFORD, PATRICIA, elementary school educator; b. Orange, Calif., Feb. 25, 1965; d. Guillermo Jimenez and Maria Angelina (Avalos) Mojarro; m. Elias Amaya, Oct. 22, 1988 (dec. Oct. 1993); children: Eliana Ashley, Hunter C.; m. Gary S. Thetford, June, 1999. BA in Spanish, U. Calif., Irvine, 1987; MS in Instrnl. Leadership Curr. & Instrn, Nat. U., 1998. Cert. elem. tchr., bilingual, cert. bilingual competence, Calif., 1989. Biliterate instrnl. asst. Franklin Elem. Sch., Santa Ana, Calif., 1986-89, bilingual tchr., 1989-91, Alcott Elem. Sch., Pomona, Calif., 1991-97, bilingual resource tchr., 1997—. Mem. ASCD, NEA, Calif. Tchrs. Assn., U. Calif.-Irvine Alumnae Assn., Calif. Assn. Bilingual Edn. Avocations: travel, reading, writing, collecting children's literature books. Home: 7415 Jola Drive Riverside CA 92506 Office: Alcott Elem Sch 1600 S Towne Ave Pomona CA 91766-5367

AMBADY, NALINI, social psychologist, educator, researcher; b. Calcutta, India; came to U.S., 1983; d. Shanker and Viji Ambady; m. Raj Marphatia, June 8, 1988; children: Maya Mallika, Leena Anupama. PhD, Harvard U., 1991. Asst. prof. Holy Cross Coll., Worcester, Mass., 1993-94, Harvard U., Cambridge, Mass., 1994-99, Ruth and John Hazel assoc. prof. social sci., 1999—2004; prof., social psychology Tufts U., Medford, Mass., 2004—. Recipient, Behavioral Sci. Rsch. prize AAAS, 1993, Presdl. Early Career award U.S. Govt., 1998, Excellence in Mentoring Award, Harvard U., 2000. Office: Tufts U The Psychology Bldg 490 Boston Ave Medford MA 02155

AMBERS, ANN, bishop, educator; b. Brusly, La., Feb. 26, 1948; d. Fannie Mae Jones and Eddie Elmore, Sr., Oliver Jones, Jr. (Stepfather); m. Jackie Roy Ambers, Sept. 3, 1994; m. Lester Moore Jackson, Feb. 11, 1967 (dec. May 24, 1987); children: Gregory, Felita, Lindsey. B, Golden State Sch. Theology, 1989; M, Bell Grove Theol. Sem., 1993, DD (hon.), 1998. Cert. Ordination New St. Paul Missionary Bapt. Ch., 1988, Missionary Lic.-Exec. Sec. Nat. Bapt. Women Min. Conv., 1988. Substitute tchr. Iberia Parish Sch. Bd., New Iberia, La., 1998—; assoc. min. New St. Paul Missionary Bapt. Ch., Oakland, Calif., 1987—93; acctg. clk. Iberia Parish Sheriff's Dept., New Iberia, 1998—2000; pastor True Vine Full Gospel Ch., Oakland, 1990—93, Port Allen, La., 1993—; exec. sec. J. Bryant Aids Found., Oakland, 1991—93; exec. dir. True Vine Ministries, Oakland, 1988—93. Nat. pres. Nat. Bapt. Women Min. Conv., New Iberia, 2003; assoc. min. Union Bapt. Ch., Brusly, La., 1999—2003; state mission pres. La. Freewill Bapt. Assn., Baton Rouge, 1999—2003; nat. amb. #1 Nat. Bapt. Women Min. Conv., Berkeley, Calif., 1990—2003. Recipient Cert. Of Award, Nat. Bapt. Women Min. Conv., 1989, Cert. Of Honor, Alpha Tron Task Force, 1990, Alphatron Christian Task Force, 1990, Disting. Achievement Award, Greater Resurrection Bapt. Ch., 1996, Disting. Svc. award, J. Bryant Aids Found., 1991, Disting. Achievement Award, New St. Paul Missionary Bapt. Ch., 1988, Disting. Achievement, One True Vine Outreach Ministries, 1997. Home: PO Box 14313 New Iberia LA 70562-4313 Office: One True Vine Outreach Ministries 731 Field Street New Iberia LA 70560 Personal E-mail: drapambers@hotmail.com. E-mail: revambers@yahoo.com.

AMBORN, PAULINE GALL, music educator; b. Racine, Wis., July 23, 1967; d. Robert Gilbert and Janet Gall; m. Mark Owen Amborn, June 4, 1994. BA, Carthage Coll., Kenosha, Wis., 1989; M of Music Edn., U. Wis., Whitewater, 2000. Choral music tchr. Kenosha Unified Sch. Dist., 1989—; ad-hoc tchr. fine arts dept. Carthage Coll., Kenosha, 1995—. Choral music dir. Kenosha Youth Choir - Kenosha Symphony, 1998—2000; vocal music dir. Kenosha Youth Performing Arts Co., 1999—2001. Actor: (mus. theater performances) A Grand Night for Singing, You're a Good Man, Charlie Brown, Joseph and the Amazing Technicolor Dreamcoat, Smoke on the Mountain. Vol., mem. Racine Theatre Guild, 1994—2003, v.p., 1997—2002. Mem.: Music Educators' Nat. Conf., Am. Choral Dirs.' Assn. (mid.-level state chair for stds. and repertoire com. 1998—2002). Office: Tremper H S Choral Music Dept 8560 26th Ave Kenosha WI 53143 E-mail: pamborn@kusd.edu.

AMBROSE, ADELE D. communications executive; B in Journalism, U. Pitts. Joined Western Electric, 1978; sr. mgmt. positions pub. rels. AT&T Wireless Svcs., Inc., 1991—99, v.p. pub. rels., 1999—2001, exec. v.p. pub. rels. and investor comm., 2001—. Mem.: Arthur W. Page Soc. Office: [illegible] Bldg 1 7277 164th Ave NE Redmond WA 98052

AMBROSE, DONETTA W. federal judge; b. New Kensington, Pa., Nov. 5, 1945; m. J. Raymond Ambrose Jr., Aug. 19, 1972., one child. BA, Duquesne U., 1963-67, JD cum laude, 1967-70. Law clerk to Hon. Louis L. Manderino Commonwealth Ct. Pa., 1970-71, Supreme Ct. Pa., 1972; asst. atty. gen. Pa. Dept. Justice, 1972-74; pvt. practice atty. Ambrose & Ambrose, Kensington, Pa., 1974-81; asst. dist. atty. Westmoreland County, Pa., 1977-81; judge Ct. Common Pleas Westmoreland County, 1982-93, U.S. Dist. Ct. (we. dist.) Pa., Pitts., 1994—. Resident advisor Duquesne U., 1967-70. Scholar Pa. Conf. State Trial Judges, 1992, State Justice Inst., 1993. Mem. ABA, Nat. Assn. Women Judges, Am. Judicature Soc., Pa. Bar Assn., Women's Bar Assn. Western Pa., Pa. Conf. State Trial Judges (sec. 1992-93), Westmoreland County Bar Assn., Italian Sons and Daus. Am., William Penn Fraternal Assn., New Kensington Women's Club, Delta Kappa Gamma. Office: 911 US Courthouse Office 700 Grant St Rm 620 Pittsburgh PA 15219-1906

AMBROSE, JUDITH ANN, designer; b. San Jose, Calif., Oct. 22, 1940; d. Howard Linse and Beula May (Russell) Shannon; m. James Paul Ambrose, Apr. 17, 1965; children: Sheryl Ann Beckey, James Paul Jr. BS, Salem Coll., Winston-Salem, N.C., 1962; postgrad., Purdue U., 1963-64. Lic. home econ tchr Fla, NC. Home econs. tchr. Broward County, Ft. Lauderdale, Fla., 1962-67; owner Decorative Accents, Ft. Lauderdale, 1984-99; wedding coord. Christ Ch. United Meth., Ft. Lauderdale, 1990—. Home econs. curriculum dir. Broward County Schs., Ft. Lauderdale, Fla., 1965—66. Pres Parent Tchr Fellowship Westminster Acad, 1982—83; mem resource group Children's Diagnostic and Treatment Ctr, Fla., 1997—2003; bd. dirs. Children's Diagnostic and Treatment Ctr., Ft. Lauderdale, 2001—, sec. bd. dirs., 2003—; founder Friends of Jack & Jill Nursery, Ft Lauderdale; organizer shoe fund for children in community Christ Methodist Ch, 1992—; mem. Pres's Coun. Ft. Lauderdale, 1989; founder Sunflower Cir. of Friends for COTC, 2004—; bd. dirs. Jack & Jill Nursery Sch, Ft Lauderdale, 1974—2000; mem. Beaux Arts, 1986—90. Recipient Outstanding Community Serv Award, Jr League of Ft Lauderdale, 1989, Golden Rule Award, J C Penney, Ft Lauderdale, 1995, Heart of the Cmty. Vol. of Yr. award, Children's Diagnostic and Treatment Ctr., Broward, Fla., 2002. Mem.: AAUW, Charity Guild (chmn. fall function 1992, publicity chmn. 1993—96, chmn. fall function 1997, pres. 1998—99, bd dirs 2001—04, rep to Kids in Distress), Coral Ridge Jr Women's Club (hon.; past pres, Clubwoman of the Yr 1975—76). Republican. Methodist. Avocations: growing orchids, volunteer work. Home: 4720 NE 25th Ave Fort Lauderdale FL 33308-4811

AMBROSE, LAUREN, actress; b. New Haven, Conn., Nov. 16, 1978; d. Frank and Annie Ambrose; m. Sam Handel, 2001. Attended, Conn. Ednl. Ctr. Arts, Yale U., Tanglewood Inst., Boston U. Actor(guest appearances): (TV series) Law & Order, 1992—98, Party of Five, 1999, Saving Graces, 1999, Six Feet Under, 2001— (Emmy nom. Supporting Actress Drama, 2003); (plays, off-Broadway) Soulful Scream of a Chosen Son, 1992; (films) In & Out, 1997, Can't Hardly Wait, 1998, Summertime's Calling Me, 1998, Psycho Beach Party, 2000, Swimming, 2000. Office: c/o United Talent Agency 9560 Wilshire Blvd Ste 500 Beverly Hills CA 90212*

AMBRUS, CLARA MARIA, physician; b. Rome, Dec. 28, 1924; came to U.S., 1949, naturalized, 1955; d. Anthony and Charlotte (Schneider) Bayer; m. Julian Lawrence Ambrus, Feb. 17, 1945; children: Madeline Ambrus Lillie, Peter, Julian, Linda Ambrus-Broenniman, Steven, Katherine Ambrus-Cheney, Charles. Student, U. Budapest (Hungary), 1943-47; MD, U. Zurich, Switzerland, 1949; postgrad., U. Paris, 1949; PhD, Jefferson Med. Coll., 1955. Diplomate: Am. Bd. Clin. Chemists. Research asst. Inst. Histology, Embryology and Biology U. Budapest, 1943-45; demonstrator in pharmacology U. Budapest Med. Sch., 1946-47; asst. dept. pharmacology U. Zurich Med. Sch., 1947-49; asst. dept. therapeutic chemistry and virology Inst. Pasteur, Paris, 1949; asst. prof. pharmacology Phila. Coll. Pharmacy and Sci., 1950-52, assoc. prof., 1952-55; research assoc. Roswell Park Meml. Inst., Buffalo, 1955-58, sr. cancer research scientist, 1958-64, assoc. scientist, 1964-69, prin. cancer research scientist, 1969-85; prof. pharmacology State U. N.Y., Buffalo Med. and Grad. Schs., 1955[00bf], assoc. prof. pediatrics, 1955-76, prof. pediatrics, 1976, research prof. ob-gyn, 1983[00bf]; chmn., founder, chief of R&D Hemex Inc., 1984—. Contbr. articles to med. and sci. jours. Trustee Nichols Sch., Buffalo, Community Music Sch. Decorated lady comdr. Equestrian Order of the Holy Sepulchre of Jerusalem; named Outstanding Woman of Western N.Y., Cmty. Adv. Coun., SUNY, Buffalo, 1980, Med. Woman of Yr., Buffalo Gen. Hosp., 2000; recipient award for excellence in clin. care, D'Youville Coll., 2004, George F. Koepf, MD award, Hauptman-Woodward Med. Rsch. Inst., Buffalo, 1997. Fellow: ACP, Internat. Soc. Hematology; mem.: Hungarian Acad. Sci. (fgn. mem.), Am. Med. Women's Assn., Buffalo Acad. Medicine, Am. Soc. Hematology, Am. Physiol. Soc., Am. Fedn. Clin. Rsch., Am. Soc. Cancer Rsch., Am. Soc. Pharmacology and Exptl. Therapeutics, Saturn Club, Clarksburg Country Club, Garrett Club, Sigma Xi. Home: 143 Windsor Ave Buffalo NY 14209-1020 also: West Hill Farm Boston NY 14025 Office: Buffalo Gen Hosp 100 High St Buffalo NY 14203-1154 E-mail: jlambrus@netscape.net.

AMEND, KATE, film editor, educator; b. San Francisco, June 27, 1947; d. Carroll Conrad and Mary Florence (Saller) A. BA, U. Calif., Berkeley, 1969; MA, Calif. State U., San Francisco, 1973. Instr. humanities City Coll. San Francisco, 1973-78; instr. humanities and women's studies Diablo Valley Coll., Pleasant Hill, Calif., 1973-78; adminstr. Through the Flower Corp., Santa Monica, Calif., 1978-81; rschr., adminstr. Judy Chicago's Dinner Party, Santa Monica, Calif., 1978-81; film editor L.A., 1982—. Adj. prof. Sch. Cinema & Tv U. So. Calif., L.A., 1992—. Film editor Metamorphosis: Man Into Woman, 1989, Legends, 1990, Asylum, 1992, Skinheads, USA, 1993, Spread The Word, 1994, Arrested Development: In The House, 1995, The Long Way Home, 1997 (Academy award 1997), Tobacco Blues, 1997, Some Nudity Required, 1998, Into the Arms of Strangers, 2001 (Academy award 2001, ACE award 2001), Pandemic: Facing AIDS, 2002, Beah: A Black Woman Speaks, 2003. Mem. Internat. Documentary Assn., Am. Cinema Editors, Am. Motion Picture Acad. Democrat. Avocations: gardening, tennis, cooking, jazz.

AMENDT, MARILYN JOAN, personnel director; b. Marshalltown, Iowa, June 21, 1928; d. Floyd Wilford and Helen Mary (Scheid) Peterson; m. Virgil E. Amendt, Sept. 4, 1949 (div. Aug. 1971); children: Gregory F., Scott R., Brad A. AA, Stephens Coll., Columbia, Mo., 1948; postgrad., U. Mich., 1978, U. Wis., Superior, 1980-83. Cert. personnel mgr. Office mgr. S&O Products, Inc., Marshalltown, Iowa, 1961-71; life underwriter Lincoln Liberty Life Ins. Co., Marshalltown, Iowa, 1971-72; retail store mgr. Amy's Fashions, Marshalltown, Iowa, 1972-74, Maurices, Inc., Marshalltown, Iowa, 1974-76, corp. personnel dir. Duluth, Minn., 1976-84; sr. v.p., dir. human resources Ohrbach's, Inc., N.Y.C., 1984-87; dir. personnel adminstrn. AMCENA Corp., N.Y.C., 1987—91; pres., owner Success Strategies, Des Moines, 1992—. Lectr. U. Wis, Superior, 1981-82, U. Minn., Duluth, 1981-82. Founder, pres., bd. dirs. Mid-Iowa Sheltered Workshop, Marshalltown, 1968-76; mem. Hostess com. Duluth (Minn.) Day Luncheon, 1983; keynote speaker Am. Bus. Women's Day, Mpls. and Duluth, 1984, 85, 86, 90; bd. pres. Young Women's Resource Ctr., 1994-95, bd. dirs., Des Moines, 1992—. Mem. Am. Bus. Women's Assn. (dist. v.p. 1982, nat. v.p. 1983, nat. pres. 1984, woman of the yr. 1978). Avocations: speaking, traveling, sports, reading. Home: 2233 Country Club Blvd Des Moines IA 50325-8602

AMENTA, JOYCE ANN, United Nations executive; b. Washington, Oct. 26, 1943; d. Kenneth John and Hildegard (Klinge) McCallister; m. Howard Richard Schmidt, Aug. 9, 1986. BA in Sociology with honors, George Washington U., 1967; MPA, Am. U., 1987. Cert. pvt. pilot; cert. in data processing. Computer programmer U.S. Dept. Commerce, Suitland, Md., 1967-74; tech. rep. Information, Inc., [illegible] 1974-77; sr. analyst com. rules and adminstrn. U.S. Senate, Washington, 1977-80; dir. computer ctr. U.S. Dept. Transp., Washington, 1981-90; dir. info. resources mgmt. Nuc. Regulatory Commn., Washington, 1987-90; dir. sci. and tech. info. IAEA, Vienna, Austria, 1990-96; dir. info. tech. svcs. UN, N.Y.C., 1996—. Pres. Women's Forum, Vienna, 1992-95. Recipient Excellence in Adminstrn. award U.S. Govt., 1989. Mem. Am. Nuc. Soc. (chmn. Austria local sect. 1994-95), Toastmasters Internat. Office: UN Info Tech Svcs Divsn S1912B New York NY 10017

AMER, TAHANI R. aerospace engineer; b. Egypt; arrived in U.S., 1983; AS, BS, MS in Engring. Aerospace engr. Langley Rsch. Ctr. NASA, Hampton, Va., 1994—. Moslem. Avocation: Avocation: physical fitness. Office: NASA Langley Rsch Ctr Mail Stop 236 Bldg 1230 Rm 217 Hampton VA 23681-2199

AMERIAN, MARY LEE, physician; b. Burbank, Calif., May 15, 1956; d. Sam and Alice Anterasian; m. Roger Amerian, Aug. 11, 1979; children: Nicole, Danielle. BA, UCLA, 1979, MD, 1983. Pvt. practice, Santa Monica, Calif., 1987—; intern in internal medicine UCLA Sch. Medicine, 1983—84, resident in dermatology, 1984—87. Reipient Sandoz award Sandoa Pharm., 1983. Fellow Am. Acad. Dermatology, Am. Soc. Dermatol. Surgery; mem. Calif. Med. Assn., L.A. Med. Assn. Avocation: the arts. Office: 2336 Santa Monica Blvd Ste 209 Santa Monica CA 90404-2067

AMERO, JANE ADAMS, state senator; b. Rumford, Maine, Aug. 6, 1941; d. William Anthony and Evangeline Jean (McInnis) Adams; m. Gerald M. Amero, Sept. 4, 1961; children: Scott Martin, Brett Douglas, Melanie Jane. BA, Cornell U., 1963. Tchr. South Portland (Maine) Sch. Dist., 1965-67; mem. Cape Elizabeth (Maine) Sch. Bd., 1975-81, Maine Bd. Edn., Augusta, 1987-92, chair, 1989-92; mem. dist. 30 Maine Senate, Augusta, 1992—, mem. edn. com. & reappt. com., 1992-94. Asst. majority leader, chair legis. coun., state and local govt. com., 1994-96, Maine Senate, minority leader, 1997—, legis. coun., 1996—; mem. Maine Coalition for Excellence in Edn., 1990—, Commn. to Evaluate Tech. Coll. System, Augusta, 1990-91, 3 sch. funding task forces, Augusta, 1987-88, 90-91. Coun. mem. Town of Cape Elizabeth, 1983-92, chair, 1987; mem., pres. Catherine Morrill Day Nursery, Portland, 1981-87; mem. Commn. on Restructuring State Govt., Augusta, 1991; corporator Maine Med. Ctr., Portland, 1989—; active Vol. Lawyers Project, Portland, 1984-90; mem. Ptnrs. for Progress in Portland Leadership Initiative, 1990-94; bd. dirs. Portland Regional Opportunity Program, 1997—, Vis. Nurses Assn./Hospice, 1993—, Ronald McDonald House, Portland, 1995—. Recipient Svc. Above Self award Rotary Clubs, Cape Elizabeth, South Portland, 1991; named Regional Citizen of Yr. in Greater Portland Area, Greater Portland Coun. Govts., 1993, Art Adv. of the Yr. Maine Art Edn. Assn., 1998. Mem. Nat. Assn. State Bds. of Edn. (mem. nat. study com. on parent and cmty. invilvement in schs. 1989, Disting. Svc. award 1993), LWV (Emily Farley award Portland chpt. 1989), Phi Beta Kappa, Phi Kappa Phi. Republican. Avocations: golf, swimming, political campaigns, reading, family activities. Home: 444 Old Ocean House Rd Cape Elizabeth ME 04107-2625 Office: Maine State Senate 3 State House Sta Augusta ME 04333-0003

AMES, LOIS WINSLOW SISSON, social worker, educator, writer; b. Boston, Jan. 21, 1931; d. Winslow Chase and Lois (Barton) Sisson; m. Robert Webb Ames, Dec. 15, 1956 (div. Aug. 1969); children: Elisabeth Harriett Winslow Ames, Adam Barton. AB, Smith Coll., 1952; AM in Psychiat. Social Work, U. Chgo., 1958. LCSW Mass., cert. social worker Acad. Cert. Social Workers, bd. cert. diplomate Nat. Registry Health Care Providers in Clin. Social Work, bd. cert. diplomate clin. social work Am. Bd. Examiners Clin. Social Work. Caseworker children's divsn. City of Chgo. Pub. Welfare Dept., 1953—56; intern Family Svc. Salvation Army, Chgo., 1956—57, Ill. Neuropsychiat. Inst., Chgo., 1957—58; child care worker Inst. for Juvenile Rsch., William Healy Residential Treatment Ctr., Chgo., 1957; psychiat. social worker Lake County Mental Health Clinic, Gary, Ind., 1958—59; pvt. clin. practice, 1958—; counselor Hyde Park Unitarian Cooperative Nursery Sch., Chgo., 1964—68; lower and middle sch. counselor U. Chgo. Lab. Schs., 1966—69; lectr. Northeastern U., Boston, 1969—77, asst. prof. Coll. Criminal Justice, 1970—77, coord. social welfare and social work practice curriculum, 1970—77, asst. dir. The Weekend Coll., 1969—70, dir. The Weekend Coll., 1970—72; lectr. psychiatry dept. psychiatry Harvard Med. Sch., Cambridge (Mass.) Hosp., 1982—; asst. editor Women's Page Tucson Daily Citizen, 1952—53. Dir. The Cmty. Svc. Practicum, Boston, 1972—77; vis. lectr. Sch. Social Work Smith Coll., Northampton, Mass., 1975; mem. adv. com. career edn. Lincoln Sudbury Regional H.S., 1975—77; mem. adv. bd. Mass. Correctional Instn., Concord, Mass., 1977—82; cons. in field; lectr. psychiatry Harvard Med. Sch., Cambridge Hosp., Mass., 1982—. Editor (with L. Gray Sexton): Anne Sexton: A Self Portrait in Letters, 1977; mem. editl. bd.: Suicide and Life Threatening Behavior; contbr. chapters to books;, author poems and essays. Bd. mem. adv. bd. Franklin Pierce Coll., NH, 1982—85. Recipient Adminstrn. Alumni citation, U. Chgo., Sch. Social Svcs., 1974, Affirmative Action cert appreciation, Northeastern U., 1976; rsch. fellow, State Ill. Mental Health Grant, 1956—57, Nat. Inst. Mental Health Grant, 1957—58, Ella Lyman Cabot Trust Grant, 1966, Ill. Arts Coun., 1967, U. Chgo. Lab. Schs., 1967. Mem.: NASW (registered social worker, diplomate in clin. social work), New Eng. Poetry Club (bd. mem. 1987—92). Home: 285 Marlborough Rd Sudbury MA 01776

AMEY, RAE, project management and development consultant; b. Shreveport, La., Sept. 26, 1947; d. Bruce Harold and Genevieve (Amey) Gentry; m. John E. Scarborough, Dec. 18, 1971 (div. Nov. 1979). Student, La. State U., 1968-70, U. Houston, 1972-74; BA in Liberal Arts, Antioch U., 1985; grad., U. So. Calif., 1987-89. Freelance photographer, Calif., 1973—; adminstrn. coord. Y.E.S. Inc., Sta. KCET-TV, L.A., 1980-83; freelance ednl. TV writer, cons. L.A., 1983-84; asst. to pres. prodn. So. Calif. Consortium, Cypress, 1984, project mgr., dir. devel., project dir. The Human Condition, 1985-87; v.p. devel. and outreach The Calif. Channel, L.A., 1990-92, project dir., 1991, 92; pres. Video Nexus, L.A., 1987—; owner Rae Amey Enterprises, L.A., 1999-2000; pres. Rae Amey Enterprises, Inc., 2000—. Editor TV guide book, 1985; photography exhbns. include: Contemporary Art Mus., Houston, 1973, Galveston (Tex.) Arts Ctr., 1975, Cameravision Gallery, L.A.,1980, Aloft, Pasadena, 1989. Co-founder Harbor Arts Alliance; mem., bd. dirs. African Am. Arts Coun.; founder, chair, bd. dirs. CIVICS: a video project for cmty. edn. and conversation, 1993—; advisor Congress on Racial Equality; sr. advisor Civil Soc., bd. mem. Hollywood Chpt., ACLU, 2003-2004. Ellen Torgesson Shaw scholar Annenberg Sch. Communications, U. So. Calif., 1989. Mem. Women in Communications (bd. dirs., v.p. campus svcs. 1987-88, exec. v.p. 1988-89, bd. dirs. scholarship and edn. fund L.A. chpt.). Democrat. Home and Office: 255 S Grand Ave Apt 1914 Los Angeles CA 90012-3096

AMEZCUA, ESTHER HERNANDEZ, elementary school educator; b. Guadalajara, Jalisco, Mexico, Nov. 9, 1949; came to the U.S., 1961; d. Rodolfo (stepfather) and Guillermina (Hernandez) Sanchez; m. Juan Elizondo Amezcua, June 23, 1973; children: Juanguillermo Gabriel, Jaime Jose Vicente. BA, U. Calif., Davis, 1972. Life tchg. credential, Calif.; multicultural and bilingual credential. With Sacramento City Unified Sch., 1973—; intermediate tchr. William Land Elem., 1973-81, 83-93, primary tchr., 1981-83, 2002—; intermediate tchr., head tchr. Oak Ridge Elem., 1993-97, Caroline Wenzel Elem., 1997—2002. Head tchr. William Land Sch., Sacramento, 1976-83, 89-93, Oak Ridge Elem., Sacramento, 1993-94, mentor tchr. Sacramento Unified Sch. Dist., 1991-93. Vol. Short Term Emergency Assistance Ctr., Davis, Calif., 1990—; dance instr. ballet folklorico, Sacramento, 1990—; vol. tutor, Sacramento, 1993—. Named Educator of Yr. Yolo County, Mexican-Am. Concilio of Woodland, 1997. Mem. Hispanic Educators Sacramento, Calif. Tchrs. Assn., Sacramento City Tchrs. Assn. Democrat. Roman Catholic. Avocations: reading, crocheting, sightseeing, dance, [illegible] Home: 2207 Monte Vista Pl Davis CA 95616-4932 Office: William Land Sch 2120 12th St Sacramento CA 95818 E-mail: amezcua20@yahoo.com.

AMGOTT, MADELINE, television producer, media consultant; b. N.Y.C., Aug. 31, 1921; d. Samuel and Rose (Kanter) Barotz; m. David Karr, Sept. 5, 1942 (div. 1956); children: Andrew, Katharine Karr-Kaitin; m. Milton Amgott, Dec. 15, 1962; 1 child, Seth; 1 stepchild, Margo. BA cum laude, Bklyn. Coll., 1952. Feature coordinator CBS News, N.Y.C. Prodr. WNBC-TV Not for Women Only, CBS News 60 Minutes, Morning Show, 30 Minutes, Bill Moyers' Constitution Hours, Phil Donahue spl. documentary The Human Animal, Good Housekeeping A Better Way, Today Show, CNBC Home and Family Hour, Real Story, Hans Hofman, Artist/Teacher, Teacher/Artist, PBS, 2003; cons. Times Mirror, N.Y.C., King Features Entertainment, TBM; bd. dirs. Am. Jour. Nursing Pub. Co., N.Y.C. Co-author: Teenage Gangs, 1957. Mem. West Pride, W. 86th St. Tenants Assn.; co-founder 168 W 68th St Tenants Assn.; mem. N.Y.C. Bicentennial Commn., 1987-89. Recipient Emmy Nat. Acad. TV Arts, 1981, 82, 83; Ohio State award, 1976. 78; Peabody award, 1976; Matrix award, 1976, award Greater Miami Film Festival, Internat. Film Festival of N.Y., others. Mem. Women's Forum, Women in Communications, Inc. Avocations: gardening, tennis, bicycling.

AMIDON, BARBARA STONE, forensic specialist, psychologist; b. Worcester, Mass., Jan. 17, 1949; m. Marc C. Amidon, Oct. 9, 1972; children: Mary Louise, Philip Stone. BA, Lake Erie Coll., 1971; MA, Assumption Coll., 1974; PhD, Boston (Mass.) Coll., 1995. Lic. psychologist Mass., cert. forensic psychologist Mass. Social worker Big Bros./Big Sisters, Hyannis, Mass., 1978—81; hotel keeper Lighthouse Inn, West Dennis, Mass., 1978—; restaurant owner Carriage Trade, South Harwich, Mass., 1978—85, Bishop's Ter., West Harwich, Mass., 1984—97; psychology intern Cape Cod (Mass.) Human Svcs., Hyannis, 1990—95; forensic psychologist Justice Resource Inst., Boston, 1995—2003; cons. Juvenile Cts., 2003—. Mem. Legis. Working Com. Changes in Juvenile Justice, Boston; mentor Com. Juvenile Ct. Clinic Credentialing, Worcester, Mass., 1999—; corporator Cape Cod 5 Cents Savings Bank, South Yarmouth, Mass., 1987—; adj. prof. Cape Cod C.C., 2003—; mem. psychol. assessment team Cape Cod Hosp., 2003—. Mem. Dennis (Mass.) Housing Authority, 1975—85. Mem.: Dennis (Mass.) C. of C., Harwich Dennis (Mass.) Rotary Club (pres. 2000—01, Paul Harris fellow 1998). Home: PO Box 128 West Dennis MA 02670 Office Phone: 508-737-5749.

AMISANO, BERNADETTE PARKER, artist; b. Flint, Mich., June 30, 1954; d. Wayne L. and Doloris J. (Anderson) Parker; m. James A. Moses, June 1, 1973 (div. 1984); m. Albert D. Amisano, May 21, 1994. AA, San Jacinto Coll., 1979; BA magna cum laude, Elmira Coll., 1993. Intern Nat. Portrait Gallery Smithsonian Inst., Washington, 1993. Exhibited paintings at numerous shows including Shows at the George, Waters, West End and Arnot Art Mus., 1993-95. Vol. Arnot Art Mus., Elmira, N.Y., 1992, Rockwell Art Mus., Corning, N.Y., 1993-96. Mem.: Arts of So. Tier Finger Lakes, Women You Want to Know. Republican. Avocations: gourmet cooking, travel, gardening, music. Home: Apt 2606 1370 S Ocean Blvd Pompano Beach FL 33062-7140

AMM, SOPHIA JADWIGA, artist, educator; b. Czestochowa, Poland, June 13, 1932; arrived in Can., 1948,arrived in U.S., 1987; d. Romuald Witold and Jadwiga Wactawa (Kotowska) Sulatycki; m. Bruce Campbell Amm, Aug. 5, 1961; children: Alicia, Alexander, Christopher, Bruce Jr., Gregory. Diploma in nursing, Ont. Hosp., 1953; cert. in pub. health nursing, U. Toronto, Ont., Can., 1960; BFA with honors, York U., 1980; MFA, Norwich U., 2000. RN. Pvt. duty nurse Allied Registry, Toronto, 1954-56; asst. head nurse Reddy Meml. Hosp., Montreal, Canada, 1957-59; pub. health nurse Dist. of Sudbury, Canada, 1960-62; pvt. duty nurse Gen. Hosp., Millinocket, Maine, 1962-66; counselor to new immigrants Ont. Welcome House, Toronto, 1982; vis. nurse St. Elizabeth Vis. Nurses Assn., Toronto, 1983-87; artist, tchr. YMCA, Appleton, Wis., 1994. Art rental and sales Art Gallery Hamilton, 1985—2003; condr. art workshops Very Spl. Arts Wis. festivals, 1989, 90, 92; artist resident Studios Midwest, Civic Art Ctr., Galesburg, Ill., 2003. One-woman shows include Bergstrom Mahler Mus.,

Neenah, Wis., 1991, Alfonse Gallery, Milw., 2001, exhibited in group shows at Harbourfront Exhbn. Gallery, Toronto, IDA Gallery, York U., 1980—81, 1986, Calumet Coll., York U., 1981, 1984, Simpson's Art Gallery, Toronto, 1984, Art Gallery Hamilton, Can., 1985—86, 2001, Pastel Soc. Can., Ottawa, 1985, Carnegie Gallery, Dundas, Can., 1986, Gallery 68, Burlington, Can., 1986, Del Bello Gallery, Toronto, 1986—93, Neville Pub. Mus., Green Bay, Wis., 1987—89, 1992, 1994—97, Consilium Pl., Scarborough, Can., 1987, 1989, 1992—93, Charles A. Wustum Mus. Fine Arts, Racine, Wis., 1990—91, 1994, Gallery Ten, Rockford, Ill., 1992 (3d pl. award, 1992), 1994—95, New Vision Gallery, Marshfield, Wis., 1992, 2001, U. Wis. Gallery, Madison, 1992, 1994, Butler Inst. Am. Art, Youngstown, Ohio, 1993, Lakeland Coll., Wis., 1994, Alverno Coll., Milw., 1994, 1997, Ariz. State U., 1995, Bergstrom Mahler Mus., 1995—96 (1st pl. award, 1995, 3d pl. award, 1996, 1997), Appleton Art Ctr., 1995, 1996, 2002, 2003, 2004, Ctr. Visual Arts, Wausau, Wis., 1996, Marian Coll. Art, Fond du Lac, Wis., 1996, Anderson Art Ctr., Kenosha, Wis., 1997, Stage Gallery, Merrick, N.Y., 1997, 1998, Norwich U. Vt. Coll. Gallery, Montpelier, 1998—2000, T. W. Wood Gallery, 2000, Hendrickson Art Ctr., Waupaca, Wis. (Hon. Mention, 2000, 2002), West Bend Gallery, 2000, Art Quest Nat. Juried Exhbn., Ft. Smith, 2001, N.E. Exposure, Priebe Gallery Exhbn. (Jurors award, 2001), Fulton St. Gallery, Troy, N.Y., 2002, Paine Art Ctr., Oshkosh, Wis., 2002, 2003, Galesburg (Ill.) Civic Art Ctr., 2003, Hothouse Ctr., Chgo., 2003, St. Norbert's Coll., De Pere, Wis., 2003, Midwest Studios, Galesburg, Ill., 2003. Vol. art tchr. children with disabilities, Appleton, 1988—89, disabled srs. Colony Oaks Nursing Home, Appleton, 1988—91. Recipient award of Excellence, North York (Can.) Arts Coun., 1982, 1986, Best in Show, Etobicoke (Can.) Arts Coun., 1982, 1987; Project grantee, Very Spl. Arts Wis., 1989. Mem.: Wis. Painters and Sculptors, Appleton Art Ctr., Nat. Mus. Women Arts. Roman Catholic. Avocations: golf, gardening. Home: 1109 N Briarcliff Dr Appleton WI 54915-2848

AMODEO-SMARGON, CHRISTINE JOANNE, adult education educator, real estate rehabilitator; b. Albany, N.Y., Apr. 26, 1973; d. Charles John Jr. and Suomi Erin Amodeo; m. Adam Joshua Smargon, Sept. 23, 2000. AA in Liberal Arts, Sage Jr. Coll. of Albany, 1993; BS in Elem. Edn., Coll. of St. Rose, Albany, 1997. Cert. pre-K through 6th provisional tchr. N.Y. State Dept. of Edn. Resdl. habilitation provider Cath. Charities Disabilities Svcs., Latham, NY, 1996—; Americorps mem. Schenectady (N.Y.) Bridge Builders, 1997—98; adult edn. tchr. Schenectady City Sch. Dist., 1998—2001, City Sch. Dist. of Albany, 2001—. Cons. Nat. Assn. Magnet Schs., Washington, 2000—01; computing cons. SMJ Consulting and Design, Albany, 2003—. Mem. Colonie (N.Y.) Jaycees, 1996—2000; choir mem. St. Margaret Mary's Ch. / Angel Cake Players, Albany, 1986—93; v.p. So. Saratoga County Jaycees, Clifton Park, NY, 2001—03; bd. mem. Singles Outreach Svcs., Colonie, 1998—99. Recipient Mungenast award (Family of Yr.), N.Y. State Jaycees, 2003. Mem.: Colonie Jaycees (dir. 1997—98, Jaycee of Yr. 1998), So. Saratoga County Jaycees (membership svcs. v.p. 2003—, individual devel. v.p. 2002—03, Individual Devel. V.p. of the Quarter 2003), Phi Delta Kappa (webmaster 2000—03, webmaster Epsilon Omicron chpt. 1996—, Svc. award 1999). Democrat. Roman Catholic. Home: 6 Adirondack St Albany NY 12203-2702 Office: Adult Learning Ctr 27 Western Ave Albany NY 12203 Personal E-mail: chrissysmargon@yahoo.com. E-mail: csmargon@albany.k12.ny.us.

AMON, ANGELIKA, medical researcher; b. Austria, 1967; arrived in U.S., 1994; BA, U. Vienna, PhD, 1993. Postdoctoral fellow Whitehead Inst. Biomedical Rsch., fellow; mem. faculty Ctr. Cancer Rsch. MIT, Cambridge, Mass., 1999—. Assoc. prof. biology MIT; investigator Howard Hughes Med. Inst., Chevy Chase, Md. Recipient Alan T. Waterman award, NSF, 2003, Presdl. Early Career award; fellow Helen Hay Whitney fellowship; Whitehead fellow. Office: Ctr Cancer Research 40 Ames St E17-110 Cambridge MA 02139*

AMON, CAROL BAGLEY, federal judge; b. 1946; BS, Coll. William and Mary, 1968; JD, U. Va., 1971. Bar: Va. 1971, D.C. 1972, N.Y. 1980. Staff atty. Communications Satellite Corp., Washington, 1971-73; trial atty. U.S. Dept. Justice, Washington, 1973-74; asst. U.S. atty. Ea. Dist. N.Y., 1974-86, U.S. magistrate, 1986-90, dist. ct. judge, 1990—. Recipient John Marshall award U.S. Dept. Justice, 1983. Mem. Assn. Bar of City of N.Y., Va. State Bar Assn., D.C. Bar Assn. (chair codes of conduct com. of jud. conf. 1998-2001). Office: US District Court 225 Cadman Plz E Brooklyn NY 11201-1818

AMOS, BETTY GILES, restaurant company executive, accountant; b. Lebanon, Mo., July 18, 1941; d. Clarence Edgar and Clara Mae (Gann) Giles; m. E.L. Amos, Sept. 18, 1959 (div. Oct. 1965); 1 child, Jeffrey Lee; m. Thomas R. Righetti, Jan. 2, 1983. BBA magna cum laude, U. Miami, Coral Gables, Fla., 1973, MBA, 1976; D of Bus. Adminstrn. honoris causa, Johnson & Wales U., 1990. CPA, Fla. Sec. City of Lebanon, 1959-63; dept. head Empire Gas Co., Lebanon, 1963-68; fin. analyst asst. Biscayne Assocs., Ltd., Miami, Fla., 1968-73; investment mgr. Universal Restaurants Inc., Miami, 1973-77; pvt. practice acct., investment mgr. Miami, 1977-83; pres. The Abkey Cos., Miami, 1983—. Founder Mega Bank, Miami, 1983-94; mem. adv. com. Fuddruckers, Inc., Boston, 1986-2002. Trustee Miami Project, 1986-89, United Fund of Dade County, 1992—; pres. Humane Soc. Greater Miami, 1994-2000, bd. dirs., 1993-2000; mem. pres. coun. U. Miami, 1994—, mem. founder's soc., 1994—, bd. trustees, 1997—; mem. presdl. search com. U. Miami, 2000—; dir. Wings Over Miami Aviation Mus., treas., 2002-03, pres., 2004—; bd. dirs. IVAX Corp., 2003—; mem. audit com. Miami-Dade County Sch. Bd., 2004—. Recipient Philip J. Romano Founders award, 1988. Mem. AICPA, Fla. Inst. CPAs, Am. Women's Soc. CPAs, Coconut Grove C. of C. (trustee 1988-2001), Nat. Assn. Women Bus. Owners (Outstanding Woman Bus. award 1993), U. Miami Alumni Assn. (nat. pres. 1999-2001), Iron Arrow, Internat. Women's Forum, Women of Tomorrow (Orange Bowl com. 2002-), Women's Exec. Leadership. Republican. Roman Catholic. Avocations: snow skiing, water skiing, scuba diving, tennis. Home: 13724 SW 92nd Ct Miami FL 33176-6858 Office: The Abkey Cos 3444 48 Main Hwy 3d Floor PO Box 330927 Miami FL 33233-0927 Office Phone: 305-442-4284.

AMOS, HELEN, hospital administrator; b. Mobile, Ala. BA, Mt. St. Agnes Coll., 1962; MS, U. Notre Dame, 1968; DHL (hon.), Coll. Misericordia, 1987, Coll. Notre Dame Md., 1999. Joined Sisters of Mercy. Provincial adminstr. Sisters of Mercy Province Balt.; pres. Sisters of Mercy of the Union; pres., CEO Mercy Med. Ctr., 1992—99; exec. chair Mercy Health Svcs. Bd. Trustees, 1999—. Bd. dirs. Mercy Ridge, St. Joseph Health Sys., Downtown Mgmt. Dist. Authority, Balt., The Greater Balt. Com., United Way Ctrl. Md., Md. Hosp. Assn., Loyola Coll. Md., St. Mary's Seminary, Balt., Archdiocesan Bd. Fin. Adminstrn., Balt. Office: Mercy Health Svcs Mercy Med Ctr 301 St Paul Pl Baltimore MD 21202

AMOS, LINDA K. academic administrator; b. Findlay, Ohio, Sept. 7, 1940; d. Blond G. and Dorotha (Brinkman) A. BS, Ohio State U., 1962, MS, 1964; EdD, Boston U., 1977. Asst. dean of baccalaureate affairs Boston U. Coll. Nursing, 1971-74, dean, prof., 1975-80, U. Utah Coll. Nursing, Salt Lake City, 1980—2000; assoc. v.p. for health scis. U. Utah, Salt Lake City, 1998—. Cons. Social Sci. Rsch. Inst., Boston; chmn. Commn. on Collegiate Nursing Edn., 1998-2000; bd. dirs. Univ. Health Network. Contbr. articles to profl. jours. Chmn. Presdl. Commn. on Status of Women, U. Utah, 1995—99; bd. dirs. Utah Heart Assn.; trustee U. Utah Hosp. Served as cons. with USPHS. Named for Outstanding Contbns. to the Nursing Profession, Utah Citizen's League for Nursing, 1989; recipient VA Chief Nurse award for promoting unity between edn. and practice, Distng. Woman prize Salt Lake Jr. Assistance League, 2004. Fellow Am. Acad. Nursing (governing coun. 1986-90, selection com. 1995—98); mem. ANA, Am. Assn. Colls. of Nursing (pres. 1984-86), Nat. Adv. Coun. on Nurse Tng., Utah Women's Forum, Internat. Women's Forum, Salt Lake City Rotary, Sigma Theta Tau (internat. nominating com. 1995-97, Mary Tolle Wright award for excellence in leadership 1991).

AMOS, THERESA ANN, marketing professional; BA in Comm., U. Colo., Colorado Springs, 1985. Cert. sailing. Mktg. mgr. Subway Devel. Corp. San Diego, 1990—94; dir. bus. devel. and account supr. Janis Brown and Assocs., San Diego, 1996—99; dir. corp. mktg. Boxlot, San Diego, 1999—2001; dir. Marcom Bidland Sys., San Diego, 2001; v.p. bus. devel. and mktg. Computer Market Rsch., San Diego, 2001—02; v.p. comm. techs. The Dakota Group, San Diego; v.p. mktg. comm. Path Network Techs., San Diego, 2001—02; dir. comm. strategies Four Sq., San Diego, 2002—. Mem. adv. bd. Cmty. Options, San Diego, 2003; mem. adv. bd. cord blood options Stem Cell Consortium, Calif., 2003. Vol. Am.'s Cup, San Diego, 1992, Am. Diabetes Assn., San Diego, 1994. Mem.: Nat. Home Builders Assn., Bldg. Industry Assn., Biocom. Avocations: sailing, running, bodybuilding, writing, dance. Home: 13066 Signature Pt Dr #64 San Diego CA 92130 Office: Four Square 5205 Kearny Villa Way San Diego CA 92123

AMOS-MANDELA, TIYE UHURA, systems analyst, researcher; b. Phila., Pa., Mar. 2, 1960; d. Benjamin Wilbur and Louise Johnson; children: Ayele Tumi, Mawusi Jelani. BA, Crown Coll., St. Bonifacious, Minn., 1983; MBA, Regis U., Denver, Colo., 2002. Feature editor Christian Tribune, Chgo., 1984—86; sr. programmer Market Facts, Oak Pk., Ill., 1986—87, Transmark Inc., Chgo., 1987—90; sr. programmer analyst Am. Hosp. Assn., Chgo., 1990—98; tech. specialist Cyborg Systems, Chgo., 1998—99; sr. bus. analyst Heller Fin., A GE Capital Co., Chgo., 1999—2002. Cons., 2002—. Author: I Toot My Own Horn. Team mem. Kairos Prision Ministry, Fla., 2003—03; ch. adminstr. Christ Cmty. Ch., Church, Ill., 1986—2003; mem. Living Hope Cmty. Ch., 2003—. Mem.: Black Data Processing Associates (assoc.; pub. rels. com. 1990—2001). Avocations: technology, creative writing, researching biblical/african history, swimming, camping. Office Phone: 773-820-2423. Personal E-mail: tiyeu@msn.com. E-mail: tiyeam@sbcglobal.net.

AMPOLA, MARY G. pediatrician, geneticist; b. Syracuse, N.Y., Nov. 2, 1934; d. Mariangelo and Filomena (Albanese) Giambattista; m. Vincent G. Ampola, Aug. 7, 1966; children: Leanna, David. BA cum laude, Syracuse U., 1956; MD, SUNY, Syracuse, 1960. Diplomate Am. Bd. Pediatrics. Intern George Washington Univ. Hosp., Washington, 1960-61; pediatric resident Children's Nat. Med. Ctr., Washington, 1961-63, chief resident in pediatrics, 1963-64; genetics fellow Children's Hosp. Med. Ctr., Boston, 1964-66; metabolic diseases fellow Mass. Gen. Hosp., Boston, 1966-67; cytogeneticist New Eng. Med. Ctr., Boston, 1967-69, dir. pediatric amino acid lab., 1969—, pediatrician, 1969—, acting chief clin. genetics divsn. dept. pediatrics, 1989-96, chief divsn. metabolism, dept. pediatrics, 1996—; from asst. to assoc. prof. pediatrics New Eng. Med. Ctr./Tufts U. Sch. Medicine, Boston, 1967-92, prof., 1992—. Chmn. PL-1 selection com. dept. pediat. New Eng. Med. Ctr., 1975—, chmn. residency com., 1981—87, mem. curriculum com., 1981—84, mem. hosp. quality assurance com., 1982—92, mem. residency com., 1987—98, bd. dirs. Ctr. Children Spl. Needs, 1987—2003; chmn. evaluation and promotions com. Tufts U. Sch. Medicine, 1998—. Editor: Early Detection and Management of Inborn Errors, 1976; author: Metabolic Diseases in Pediatric Practice, 1982; contbr. chpts. to books and articles to profl. jours. Named Alumna of Yr., SUNY Coll. Medicine, 1980. Fellow Am. Acad. Pediatrics (sect. genetics); mem. Am. Soc. Human Genetics, New Eng. Pediatric Soc. (sec.-treas. 1993—), Soc. Inherited Metabolic Disorders, Soc. Study Inborn Errors Metabolism, Phi Beta Kappa. Republican. Office: New Eng Med Ctr 750 Washington St Boston MA 02111-1526 E-mail: mampola@tufts-nemc.org.

AMRON, CORY M. lawyer; b. NYC; BA, U. Rochester, 1974; JD, Harvard U., 1977. Ptnr. Vorys, Sater, Seymour and Pease, LLP. Mem.: Commercial Real Estate Women Fellows of the Am. Bar Found. (state chair 2001—), Women's Bar Assn. DC (tres. 1982—83, mem., bd. dirs. 1994—97, Woman Lawyer Yr. 2004), Am. Bar Assn. (mem., Task Force Law Schools and Profession: Narrowing the Gap 1988—92, chair, Commn. Women Profession 1991—94, mem., Commn. Domestic Violence 1998—2002), Bar Assn. DC (chair, Young Lawyers Sect. 1983—84, mem., bd. dirs. 1985—87, mem., Out of Box Com., Sect. Legal Edn. 2001—), DC Bar (editor, DC Practical Manual 1985—87, chair, Commerical Real Estate Com. 1986—89, mem., Steering Com., Real Estate Housing and Land Use Sect. 1989—94, mem., Reproductive Cancer Task Force 1994—96). Office: Vorys Sater Seymour and Pease LLP 11th Fl 1828 L St NW Washington DC 20036-5109*

AMSLER, JANA, chef; Grad., CHIC; student, Las Belles Artes, Elmhurst, Ill. Pastry, soup and salad chef Salbute, Hinsdale, Ill., 1997—. Office: Salbute 20 E 1st St Hinsdale IL 60521

AMSTADT, NANCY HOLLIS, retired language educator; b. Chgo., Ill., Mar. 1, 1932; d. James George and Agnes Green Hollis; m. Ervin Carl Amstadt, Dec. 27, 1952; children: Elaine, Joan, Steven, Carolyn. BA, De Paul U., 1952; MA, San Diego State U., 1966. English & history tchr. Sweetwater H.S. Dist., Chula Vista, Calif., 1957—59; tchr., counselor Santa Clara City Schs., Santa Clara, Calif., 1959—63; secondary English tchr. San Diego City Schs., San Diego, 1966—91; English instr. San Diego C.C., San Diego, 1993—95; ret., 1995. Chmn. dept. English Kearny H.S., San Diego, 1985—91. Exhibitions include San Diego Art Inst., 1984—2003. Mem. U.N. Gender Equity, San Diego, 2001—04; docent art gallery U. Calif., San Diego, 1998—2004; program dir. San Diego Mus. Art, San Diego, 1968—2003. Democrat. Avocations: tennis, women refugees, art history, classical music, Chinese exercise. Home: 1097 Alexandria Drive San Diego CA 92107

AMSTER, LINDA EVELYN, newspaper executive, consultant; b. N.Y.C., May 21, 1938; d. Abraham and Belle Shirley (Levine) Meyerson; m. Robert L. Amster, Feb. 18, 1961 (dec. Feb. 1974). BA, U. Mich., 1960; M.L.S., Columbia U., 1968. Tchr. English Stamford High Sch., Conn., 1961-63; research librarian The Detroit News, 1965-67, The N.Y. Times, N.Y.C., 1967-69, supr. news research, 1969-74, news research mgr., 1974—. Bd. dirs. Council for Career Planning, N.Y.C., 1982— Editor: The New York Times Passover Cookbook, 1999, Kill Duck Before Serving, 2002, The New York Times Jewish Cookbook, 2003; contbr. articles to books, N.Y. Times and other publs. Mem. adv. com. N.Y.C. 100 Greater N.Y. Centennial Celebration. Mem. Spl. libraries Assn. Clubs: Coffee House. Home: 336 Central Park W New York NY 10025-7111 Office: The NY Times 229 W 43rd St New York NY 10036-3959

AMSTUTZ, MARGARET, academic administrator; b. Knoxville, Tenn., May 22, 1967; d. Jerome David Amstutz, Margaret Jane Amstutz. MA Eng., Am. Lit., Wash. U., 1992. Publications dir. Mo. Humanities Coun., St. Louis, 1995—95, program dir., 1997—97; asst. to the pres. U. of Ga., Athens, 1997—. Bd. dirs. Center Coll. Alumni, Danville, 1996—2000. Mem.: Ga. Assn. of Women in Higher Edn., Phi Beta Kappa. Office: U Ga Office of the President Athens GA 30602

AMUNDSON, BEVERLY CARDEN, artist; b. Kansas City, Kans., Dec. 31, 1937; d. Linton Franklin and Arlene Rose Carden; m. Jerry Warren Amundson; children: Sherry Camargo, Cynthia Harmison, Eric. Student, Kansas City (Mo.) Art Inst., 1955—58; studied with, Robert Byerley, Harry Fredman, Daniel Greene, Burton Silverman, Albert Handell and Anita Louise West. Freelance illustrator, designer, Kansas City, Mo., 1958—64; founding ptnr., dir. Amundson & Assoc. Art Studio, DBA The Amundson Group, Kansas City, Mo., 1964—2003, AGI Inc., Kansas City, Kans., 1994—, Taipei, 1994—, Hong Kong, 1994—, AGI Packaging Svs. Ltd., Kansas City, Kans., 1999—, Hong Kong, 1999—. Lectr., cons. in field; pvt. lessons and workshops, Merriam, Kans. One-woman shows include, Shawnee Mission, Kans., Kansas City Artists Coalition, Mo., 2001, work exhibited in shows and galleries nationwide. Com. worker Rep. Party, Merriam. Recipient numerous awards; scholar, Kansas City Art Inst., 1955—58. Mem.: Conn. Pastel Soc., Degas Pastel Soc., Chgo. Artists Coalition, Kansas City Artist Coalition, Am. Soc. Classical Realism, Portrait Soc. Am. (signature), Mid-Am. Pastel Soc. (signature), Nat. Pastel Soc. Am. (signature). Covenant Ch. Avocations: travel, textile weaving. Studio: 9903 West 70th Terrace Merriam KS 66203 Office: AGI Inc AGI Packaging Svcs Home Offices 1100 Cambridge Circle Drive Kansas City KS 66103

AMUNDSON, JOY A. pharmaceutical and health products executive; V.p. corp. hosp. mktg. Abbott Labs., Abbott Park, Ill., 1993-94, v.p. Abbott HealthSys., 1994-95, sr. v.p. chem. and agrl. products, 1995-98, sr. v.p. Ross Products, 1998—; corp. officer, 1990. Office: Abbott Labs 100 Abbott Park Rd Abbott Park IL 60064-6400

AN, SAMANTHA HAE JUNG, executive recruiter, social worker; b. Je Judo, Korea, Mar. 10, 1973; d. Dong Chul and Young Hwa An. BA, Rutgers U., 1996; MSW, U. Md., Balt., 2000. Human svc. worker Monmouth Med. Ctr., Children's Crisis Intervention Svc. Unit, Long Branch, NJ, 1996—97; office asst. Md. Aids Profl. Edn. Ctr., Baltimore, Md., 1997—97; social work intern WPNPC, The Family Support & Career Ctr., Balt., 1998—99; adminstrv. specialist intern Md. State Dept. Human Resources, Balt., 1998—99; recreation attendant U. Md. Athletic Ctr., Balt., 1998—2000; program mgr., grad. intern Employee Assistance Program HUD, Washington, 1999—2000; lead staffing specialist Sony Electronics, Inc., Park Ridge, NJ, 2000—. Ordained elder Bethany Presbyn. Ch., Bloomfield, NJ, 2003. Avocations: travel, volleyball, running, reading, photography. Home: 170 Van Winkle St # 1 East Rutherford NJ 07073 Office: Sony Electronics Inc 1 Sony Dr Park Ridge NJ 07656-8003 Personal E-mail: sanmsw@yahoo.com. E-mail: samantha.an@am.sony.com.

ANANG, AMMA CECILIA, dance company administrator; MFA in Dance, Mills Coll. Co-founder, mgr, costume designer, dancer, make-up artist Ocheami Dance Co., Seattle. Office: PO Box 31635 Seattle WA 98103-1635

ANANIA, ANDREA, insurance company executive; Grad., Queens Coll.; MBA, U. Pa. Various positions Unisys Corp.; sr. v.p., divsn. sys. info. officer Cigna Corp., 1995—98, chief info. officer, 1998—2001, exec. v.p., chief info. officer, 2001—. Office: Cigna Corp 1 Liberty Pl Philadelphia PA 19192-1550

ANANIASHVILI, NINA, ballerina; b. Tbilisi, Republic of Georgia; Student, Choreographic Sch. of Georgia; grad., Bolshoi Ballet Sch., 1981. Ballerina Bolshoi Ballet, 1981—. Guest artist Am. Ballet Theatre, N.Y.C.; performed with Kirov Ballet, N.Y.C. Ballet, Royal Ballet, The Royal Danish Ballet, Royal Swedish Balltet, others. Roles include La Bayadere (Nikiya), Don Quixote (Kitri), Giselle, The Golden Age (Rita), Mlada, Raymonda, Romeo and Juliet, Swan Lake (Odette-Odile), The Dying Swan, A Dream of the Rose, Balanchine's Apollo, Raymonda Variations, Symphony in C, The Prince of the Pagodas, The Nutcraker. Recipient Gold medal Varna Competition, 1980, 5th Moscow Competition, 1985, Grand prix 4th Moscow Competition 1981, 3rd Jackson Competition, 1986, Outstanding Achievements in Fine Arts award Russia State, 1992, STate prize Georgia, 1993. Office: Am Ballet Theatre 890 Broadway New York NY 10003-1211

ANASTOLE, DOROTHY JEAN, retired electronics company executive; b. Akron, Ohio, Mar. 26, 1932; d. Helen (Sagedy) Dice; children: Kally, Dennis, Christopher. Student, De Anza Jr. Coll., Cupertino, Calif., 1969. Various secretarial positions in mfg., 1969-75; office mgr. Sci. Devices Co., Mountain View, Calif., 1975-76; exec. adminstrv. sec. corp. office Cezar Industries, Palo Alto, Calif., 1976-77; office and pers. mgr. AM Bruning Co., Mountain View, 1977-81; dir. employee rels. Consol. Micrographics, Mountain View, 1981-83; pers. mgmt. cons., 1983-84; mgr. adminstrn./employee rels. Mitsubishi Electronics Am., Inc., Sunnyvale, Calif., 1984-89, sr. mgr., 1989-91, corp.-nat. v.p., 1991-96, ret., 1996. Nat. adv. Field Philanthropy, 1992-96. Bd. dirs. Agnew State Hosp., San Jose, Calif., 1966-72, div. chmn. program mentally retarded, 1966-72, staff tutor, 1966-72; bd. dirs. Project Hired, Sunnyvale, 1991-93; bd. advisors The Senior Staff, 1994-96. Recipient Svc. award Agnew State Hosp., 1972.

ANAWALT, PATRICIA RIEFF, anthropologist, researcher; b. Ripon, Calif., Mar. 10, 1924; d. Edmund Lee and Anita Esto (Capps) Rieff; m. Richard Lee Anawalt, June 8, 1945; children: David, Katherine Anawalt Arnoldi, Harmon Fred. BA in Anthropology, UCLA, 1957, MA in Anthropology, 1971, PhD in Anthropology, 1975. Cons. curator costumes and textiles Mus. Cultural History UCLA, 1975-90, dir. Ctr. for Study Regional Dress, Fowler Mus. Cultural History, 1990—; trustee S.W. Mus., L.A., 1978-92; rsch. assoc. The San Diego Mus. Man, 1980—, UCLA Inst. Archaeology, 1994—. Trustee Archaeol. Inst. Am., U.S., Can., 1983-95, 98—; traveling lectr., 1975-86, 1994-2000, Pres.'s Lectureship, 1993-94, Charles E. Norton lectureship, 1996-97; cons. Nat. Geog. Soc., 1980-82, Denver Mus. Natural History, 1992-93; apptd. by U.S. Pres. to Cultural Property Adv. Com., Washington, 1984-93; fieldwork Guatemala, 1961, 70, 72, Spain, 1975, Sierra Norte de Puebla, Mex., 1983, 85, 88, 89, 91. Author: Indian Clothing Before Cortés: Mesoamerican Costumes from the Codices, 1981, paperback edit., 1990; co-author: The Codex Mendoza, 4 vols., 1992 (winner Archaeol. Inst. Am. 1994 James Wiseman Book award), The Essential Codex Mendoza, 1996; mem. editl. bd. Ancient Mesoamerica; contbr. articles to profl. jours. Adv. com Textile Mus., Washington, 1983-87. Grantee NEH, 1990, 96, J. Paul Getty Found. 1990, Nat. Geog. Soc., 1983, 85, 88, 89, 91, Ahmanson Found., 1996; Guggenheim fellow, 1988. Fellow Am. Anthrop. Assn.; mem. Centre Internat. D'Etude Des Textiles Anciens, Am. Ethnol. Soc., Soc. Am. Archaeology, Soc. Women Geographers (Outstanding Achievement award 1993), Textile Soc. Am. (bd. dirs. 1992-96, co-coord. 1994 biennial symposium). Avocations: ballet, reading, hiking. Office: Fowler Mus Cultural History Ctr Study Of Regional Dress Los Angeles CA 90095-0001 E-mail: panawalt@arts.ucla.edu.

ANCHIE, TOBY LEVINE, health facility administrator; b. New Haven, Conn., Jan. 21, 1944; d. Solomon and Mary (Karlins) Levine; m. Alonzo C. Moreland III; children from previous marriage: Michael D., Robert P. BSN, U. of Conn., 1966; MA in Edn. magna cum laude, Nor. Ariz. U., 1984. RN Ariz., Conn., Ga. Coord. spl. projects, nurse coord., adult day hosp. Barrow Neurol. Inst. of St. Joseph's Hosp. and Med. Ctr., Phoenix, 1984-87, mgr., 1985-92, mgr. adminstrv. and support svcs., neuroscis., 1992-94, mgr. rsch. adminstrn., 1994-97, dir. rsch. adminstrn., 1997-2000, exec. dir. R&D, 2000—. Cons.; presenter in field; faculty mem. U. Phoenix; adv. bd. mem. Myasthenia Gravis Assn.; adv. coun. mem. Office Disability Prevention Ariz. Dept. Health Svcs., strategic planning com. mem. Contbr. articles to profl. jours., chpts. in books. Mem.: NAFE, Ariz. Assn. Neurosci. Nurses, Assn. Clin. Rsch. Coords. (Ariz. chpt.), Soc. Rsch. Adminstrs., World Fedn. Splty. Nursing Orgn. (chair membership com. 1993—95), Am. Bd. Neurosci. Nursing (treas, 1995—96), Assn. Clin. Rsch. Profls. (continuing edn. com.), Am. Assn. Neurosci. Nurses (nominating com. 2003—04, bd. dirs., pres.). Home: 3112 S Los Feliz Dr Tempe AZ 85282-2854 Office Phone: 602-406-3178. E-mail: tanchie@chw.edu.

ANCKER-JOHNSON, BETSY, physicist, engineer, retired automotive company executive; b. St. Louis, Apr. 29, 1927; d. Clinton James and Fern (Lalan) Ancker; m. Harold Hunt Johnson, Mar. 15, 1958; children: Ruth P. Johnson, David H. Johnson, Paul A. Johnson (dec.), Marti H. Johnson. BA in Physics with high honors (Pendleton scholar), Wellesley Coll., 1949; PhD in Exptl. Physics magna cum laude, U. Tuebingen, Germany, 1953; D.Sc. (hon.), Poly. Inst. N.Y., 1979, Trinity Coll., 1981, U. So. Calif., 1984, Alverno Coll., 1984; LL.D. (hon.), Bates Coll., 1980. Instr., jr. research physicist U. Calif., Berkeley, 1953-54; physicist Sylvania Microwave Physics Lab., 1956-58; mem. tech. staff RCA Labs., 1958-61; rsch. specialist Boeing Co., 1961-70, exec., 1970-73; asst. sec. U.S. Dept. Commerce for Sci. and Tech., 1973-77; dir. phys. rsch. Argonne Nat. Lab., Ill., 1977-79; v.p. for environ. activities GM, Warren, Mich., 1979-92; 9. Affiliate prof. elec. engring. U. Wash., 1961-73; mem. Energy Rsch. Adv. Bd., 1983-87, adv. com. on inertial confinement fusion Dept. Energy, 1992-94, US Safety Rev. Panel NSF, 1987-88; cons. Inland Steel Inc., 1991-96; adv. com. Rowan Sch. Engring., 1993-96; Regents vis. prof. U. Calif., Berkeley, 1988-89. Author of 70 sci. papers; patentee in field. Mem. staff Inter-Varsity Christian Fellowship, 1954-56; mem. vis. com. elec. and computer divsn. MIT, U.S. Dept. Def. Sci. Bd.; mem. adv. bd. Stanford U. Sch. Engring., Fla. State U., Fla. A&M U., Congl. Caucus for Sci. and Tech.; trustee Wellesley Coll., 1971-77; chair bd. dirs. World Environ. Ctr., 1988-93, dir., 1988-99; founding trustee Johnson Scholarship Found., 1991-2001; founding dir. Work Place Influence, 1997—, dir. Enterprise Devel. Internat., 1992—; mem. faculty adv. coun. U. Tex. Sch. Engring., 1998—; bd. dirs. Tex. Environ. Forum, 2000-01. AAUW fellow, 1950-51; Horton Hollowell fellow, 1951-52; NSF grantee, 1967-72; recipient Chmn's. award Am. Assn. Engring. Socs., 1986. award of honor Licensing Execs. Soc. Fellow AAAS, IEEE, Am. Phys. Soc. (councillor-at-large 1973-76); mem. NRC (bd. engring. edn. 1991-95, com. on women in sci. and engring. 1990-96, office sci. and engring. pers. adv. com. 1993-96), Nat. Acad. Engring. (councillor 1995-2001), Air Pollution Control Assn., Soc. Automotive Engrs. (bd. dirs. 1979-81), Phi Beta Kappa, Sigma Xi.

ANCRUM, CHERYL DENISE, dentist; b. Bklyn., Sept. 28, 1958; d. Ida Jackson. BA in Psychology, Harvard U., 1980; DDS, Columbia U., 1986, MPH, 1989. Dentist. Credit analyst Hartford (Conn.) Nat. Bank, 1980-81; statis. coding instr., analyst Aetna Ins. Co., Hartford, 1981-82; dental asst. Gouverneur Hosp., N.Y.C., 1983; clk. typist Columbia Presbyn. Med. Ctr., N.Y.C., 1984-86; gen. practice resident Beth Israel Med. Ctr., N.Y.C., 1986-87; dental attending Montefiore Med. Ctr., Bronx, 1987-89; rsch. assoc., dentist North Ctrl. Bronx Hosp., 1989-90; dental dir. Manhattan Men's House of Detention, N.Y.C., 1989-97; pvt. practice, 1998—. Dental extern North Ctrl. Bronx. Hosp., 1985-86. Vol. St. John Episc. Hosp., Bklyn., 1974-75, Mt. Auburn Hosp., Cambridge, 1978, Harlem Hosp., N.Y.C., 1987-88; health adv. Harvard U., Cambridge, 1977-80; active Sutton for Mayor Campaign, Bklyn., 1977; mem. Girl Scouts U.S., Bklyn., 1969-75, Operation PUSH, Hartford, 1981-82, Hartford Black Women Network, 1980-82, Kuumba Singers, Harvard U., 1977-78, New Temple Singers, Cambridge, 1978-80; mem. tape commn. Bridge St. A.M.E. Ch., Bklyn., 1987-88; fin. sec. Flower Guild, Allen A.M.E. Church, Queens, 1994-97; bd. dirs. F.I.S.H. of Uniondale, 1991-96. A Better Chance scholar, 1973-76, Am. Fund for Dental Health scholar, 1982-84, Clark Found. scholar, 1983-86, selected profl. fellow AAUW, 1985-86; recipient Letter of Commendation, Columbia U., 1983, Applewhite award, 1986, William Bailey Dunning award, 1986, Lester R. Cain Pathology prize, 1986; named to Outstanding [illegible], 1999; Mem. ADA, Nat. Dental Assn. (rec. sec. 1998-2000), FDI World Dental Fedn., NY State Dental Soc., Acad. Gen. Dentistry, Am. Assn. Pub. Health Dentistry, Am. Profl. Practice Assn., Order Ea. Star (Elizabeth Moore chpt. sec. 1995-96), Delta Sigma Theta (Nassau alumnae chpt. journalist, 1992-96, 2d v.p., 1995-96). Democrat. Mem. African Methodist Episcopal Ch. Avocations: creative arts, writing, reading, music, skating. Office: 230 Hilton Ave Ste 203 Hempstead NY 11550-8116 Office Phone: 516-483-8375. E-mail: cherlyancrumdds@verizon.net.

ANDEREGG, KAREN KLOK, business executive; b. Council Bluffs, Iowa; d. George J. and Hazel E. Klok; m. George F. Anderegg Jr., Aug. 27, 1970 (div. Dec. 1993); m. William Drake Rutherford, Jan. 2, 1994. BA, Stanford U., 1963. Copywriter Vogue mag., N.Y.C., 1963-72; copy editor Mademoiselle mag., N.Y.C., 1972-77, mng. editor, 1977-80; assoc. editor Vogue Mag., N.Y.C., 1980-85; editor-in-chief Elle mag, N.Y.C., 1985-87; pres. Clinique USA, 1987-92; bus. cons. Portland, Oreg., 1993—. Bd. dirs. Oreg. Dental Svcs. Health Plans, Ethicspoint; bus. adv. bd. mem. Portland State U. Bd. dirs. Oreg. Hist. Soc. Mem.: Cosmetic Exec. Women.

ANDERS, ALLISON, film director, screenwriter; b. Ashland, Ky., Nov. 16, 1954; Co.-dir. (film) Border Radio, 1982 (Best First Film award UCLA); writer, dir. (feature films) Gas, Food, Lodging, 1992 (Best New Dir. award N.Y. Film Critics Circle 1992), Mi Vida Loca, 1994, Four Rooms (segment "The Missing Ingredient"), 1995, Things Behind the Sun, 2001; dir.: Grace of My Heart, 1996, (TV episode) Sex and the City; prodr. Lover Girl, 1998; co-dir., co-writer Sugar Town, 1999. Recipient Samuel Goldwyn 1st prize, 1986; Nicholl fellow, 1986, MacArthur fellow, 1995. Office: UTA 9560 Wilshire Blvd 5th Fl Beverly Hills CA 90212-2401

ANDERS, KATHRYN, artist, educator; b. Calif., 1944; m. Elliot Anders; 1 child, Robert Anderson. BA in Econs., U. La Verne, Calif., 1966; MA in Edn., Calif. State U., Dominguez Hills, 1975; MA in Adminstrn., Calif. State U., Northridge, 2003. Tchr. secondary English, Cachbasas, Calif., 1971—; mentor tchr. journalism Palos Verdes, Calif., 1971—; master tchr. video prodn. Auburn, Calif., 1971—. Presenter in field. Author: (book of poetry) Ordinary Things, 2000; exhibitions include Garden of the World, 2003, Thousand Oaks Cmty. Ctr., 2002—03, Doyon Gallery, Camarillo, Calif., 2002—03. Mem.: ASCD, Conf. of Living Free/English (chair 2001—04), Calif. Assn. Tchrs. English, Nat. Coun. Tchrs. English.

ANDERSEN, FRANCES ELIZABETH GOLD, religious leadership educator; b. Hot Springs, Ark., Feb. 11, 1916; d. Benjamin Knox and Pearl Scott (Smith) Gold; m. Robert Thomas Andersen, June 27, 1942; children: Nancy Ruth (Mrs. Bernd Neumann), Robert Thomas. BA, UCLA, 1936, sec. teaching credential, 1937. Tchr. math. L.A. City Schs., 1937-42, 46-48; faculty Ariz. State Coll., Tempe, 1943-45; mem. nat. bd. missions United Meth. Ch., 1940-44; dir. Christian edn. 1st Presbyn. Ch., Phoenix, 1943-45, Trinity Meth. ch., L.A., 1953-55, 1st Bapt. Ch., Lakewood, Calif., 1955-57, Grace Bapt. Ch., Riverside, 1958-83, chmn. nursery sch. bd., 1969-83; mem. nat. bd. Bible sch. and youth Bapt. Gen. Conf., 1966-71; coord. leadership tng. insts. Greater L.A. Sunday Sch. Assn., 1956-80; exec. dir. San Bernardino-Riverside Sunday Sch. Assn., 1959—; prin. Riverside Christian Sch., 1985-87, bd. dirs., 1985—. Mem. Christian edn. bd. S.W. Bapt. Conf., 1956-59, 63-66, 72-75, 80-83; bd. dirs. GLASS, 1956—; dir. Women's guild, Calif. Bapt. Coll., Riverside, 1983-96. Author: How to Organize Area Leadership Training Institutes, 1964. Pres. Univ. Jr. H.S., PTA, Riverside, 1963-64, Poly. H.S., PTA, 1965-67; life mem. PTA; judge Nat. Sunday Sch. Tchrs. Awards, 1993-2003. Named Grace Bapt. Mother of Yr., 1981, People Who Make a Difference Press-Enterprise, 1984, One of Outstanding Women of Riverside, Calif. Bapt. Coll., 1985. Mem. Sons of Norway, Alpha Delta Chi (nat. pres. 1950-51, exec. sec. 1952-54), Pi Mu Epsilon. Avocations: travel, entertaining, music. Home: 1787 Prince Albert Dr Riverside CA 92507-5852

ANDERSEN, MARGO K. federal agency administrator; BA, Gettysburg Coll.; M in Mgmt., George Washington U. Program mgr. for arts programs Nat. Endowment for the Arts, Am. Correctional Assn.; dir. Office Fin. Mgmt. and Performance Measurement, Office Innovation and Improvement U.S. Dept. Edn., Washington. Office: US Dept Edn IES Rm 500F 555 New Jersey Ave NW Washington DC 20208

ANDERSEN, SUSAN HACKES, early childhood educator; b. Mt. Vernon, N.Y., Apr. 20, 1927; d. John R. and Ruth Edna (Misch) Hackes; m. Birger G. Andersen, Aug. 29, 1959; children: Jon, Kristi. BS magna cum laude, U. Wis., 1949; MA, Hunter Coll., 1954. Tchg. credential, N.Y.; life diploma, Calif. Profl. modern dancer various cos., N.Y.C., 1949-54; presch. tchr., dir. Walt Whitman Sch.-Peter Pan Nursery Sch., N.Y.C., 1951-55; kindergarten tchr. various schs., Calif., 1955-59; child care ctr. dir. Atonement Presch., San Diego, 1971-80, various schs., Calif., 1983-84, Little Beginnings Child Devel. Ctr., Arlington, Va., 1985-92; early childhood educator various schs., Conn., 1993—. Cons. M/A-Com. Linkabit, San Diego, 1982-83. Co-founder Arlington (Va.) Dirs. Assn., 1986; child adv., activist Worthy Wage Campaign, Washington, 1992—; bd. mem. East Lyme (Conn.) Pub. Trust Found., 1994—; mem. Vision 2000: People Dedicated to Cmty. Svcs., East Lyme, 1994—; vol. Garde Arts Ctr., New London, Conn., 1993—. Mem. Nat. Mus. for Women in the Arts (charter), Children's Mus. of S.E. Conn. (charter mem.), Nat. Assn. for the Edn. Young Children, Southeast Assn. Young Children (sec. 1992—), Mashantucket Pequot Mus. and Rsch. Ctr., Phi Kappa Phi, Pi Lambda Theta. Democrat. Unitarian Universalist. Avocations: travel, theater, dance, music, writing. Home: 17 Stone Cliff Dr Niantic CT 06357-1513

ANDERSEN, SUSAN MARIE, political scientist, educator, researcher, clinician, policy advisor; b. Santa Monica, California, June 6, 1955; BA in psychology(hon.), U. Calif., Santa Cruz, 1977; PhD in psychology, Stanford U., 1981. Lic. psychologist Calif., N.Y. Asst. prof. psychology Univ. Calif., Santa Barbara, 1981-87; assoc. prof. NYU, N.Y.C., 1987-94, prof., 1994—, dir. grad. studies in psychology, 1993—97, 2000—02. Cons. Edn. Commn. of the States; Grantmaker Forum for Cmty. and Nat. Svc., Common Cents N.Y.; grants panel, social and group processes rev. panel NIMH, 1992-94, 96, Integrative Grad. Edn. and Rsch. Tng. rev. panel NSF, 2003; other panels. Assoc. editor Jour. Social and Clin. Psychology, 1987-92; Social Cognition, 1993; Jour. Personality and Social Psychology: Attitudes and Social Cognition, 1994-95; Psychol. Rev., 1998-2000; mem. editl. bd. Jour. Personality and Social Psychology, 1990-93, 2000-01, Nouvelle Revue de Psychologie Sociale, 2002—; ad hoc reviewer Jour. Comm. Rsch., Jour. Exptl. Psychology: Learning, Memory & Cognition, Jour. Exptl. Social Psychology, Jour. Personality, Jour. Rsch. in Personality, Motivation and Emotion, Personality and Social Psychology Bull., Psychol. Sci., NSF, Australian Social Sci. Rsch. Coun., Social Sci. and Human Rsch. Coun. of Can., Brit. Jour. Clin. Psychology, Brit. Jour. Social Psychology, Jour. Abnormal Psychology; contbr. numerous articles to profl. jour. Chair svc. learning task force White House Congl. Conf. on Character Bldg.; mem. rsch. and evaluation com. Character Edn. Partnership; mem. rsch. adv. bd. Kellogg Found. Nat. Initiative on Cmty. Svc. in Edn.; Learning in Deed; mem. edn. policy task force Inst. for Comm. Policy Studies, George Washington U.; mem. Russell Sage Found.'s Social Identity Consortium. Recipient Golden Dozen Award N.Y.Univ., 1993; Harold J. Plous Award UCSB, 1985; NIMH grantee, 1985-86, 92-98; sr. fellow Inst. for Comm. Policy Studies, George Washington U. Fellow: APA, Soc. Personality and Social Psychology (mem. exec. com.), Am. Psychol. Soc.; mem.: Soc. Psychol. Study of Social Issues, Soc. Advancement of Socio Econ., Soc. Exptl. Social Psychology, Internat. Soc. Self and Identity. Office: Dept Psychology NY Univ 6 Washington Pl 4th Fl New York NY 10003-6603 E-mail: andersen@psych.nyu.edu.

ANDERSON, ADA, retired cattle rancher, retired court reporter; b. Springdale, Ark., Jan. 1, 1916; d. James Reuben and Eva Francis (Gash) Smiths; m. Tyrell Clay [illegible] Grad. h.s., Ramona, Okla. Sec., bookkeeper, clk. Budd Post & Hardwood Co., Fayetteville, Ark., 1935-45; ofcl. ct. reporter State of Ark. 13th Chancery Cir. Ct., Fayetteville, 1946-81; raising beef cattle Elkins, Ark., 1993—2002. Recipient Cert. of Appreciation, State Jud. Coun. Ark., 1978. Mem. Am. Legion Women's Aux. Democrat. Mem. Ch. of Christ. Avocations: travel, bowling, reading, writing, horse races. Home: 2905 Hwy 16 Elkins AR 72727-9600

ANDERSON, ALLAMAY EUDORIS, health educator, home economist; b. N.Y.C., July 18, 1933; d. John Samuel and Charlotte Jane (Harrigan) Richardson; m. Edgar Leopold Anderson, Jr., Apr. 14, 1967 (div. Apr. 14, 1963); 1 child, David Lancelot; m. Diane Kay Swartz, July 19, 2003. B.A., Queens Coll., CUNY, 1975; profl. mgmt. cert. Adelphi U., 1978; M.S. in Edn., Fordham U., 1984. Mem. staff sch. food svc. dietitian Bd. Edn., N.Y.C., 1968-88; tchr. home and career skills Louis Armstrong Mid. Sch., 1988; spl. edn. tchr. Manhattan H.S., N.Y.C., 1989-95, coord AIDS resource, 1995, ret. 1995; profl. devel. cons., N.Y.C., 1978—; ptnr. Masiba Bldg. Corp., Corona, N.Y., 1975-82; adj. lectr. home econs. Queens Coll., 1987; owner AEA Devel. Svc., 1987-97; mem. exec. bd. SEDAA, Fordham U., 1997-2004. Devel. coord. League for Better Cmty. Life, Inc., 1977; treas. exec. bd., 1970-76; officer N.Y.C. Cmty. Devel. Agy., 1980-83; mem. Kwanzaa Adv. Com. (P.R.) Urban Coalition, 1983, L.I. # 28 Episcopal Cursillo, 1991; vestry mem. youth ministries Grace Episcopal Ch., 1982-85, vestry mem., 1996-99; mem. NAACP (local Women's History Month honoree); asst. presiding ptnr. Dynamic Investors Club, 1996—; Bridges chairperson Srs. of Dorie Miller, 2003. Recipient Elmcor Cmty. Svc. award Elmcor Youth and Adult Activities, Inc., 1989, Alumni Achievement award Fordham U. Sch. Edn., 2000, Cmty. Svc. award N.Y. State United Tchrs., 2001. Mem. Nat. Soc. Fund Raising Execs., Assn. Fundraising Profls., Nat. Assn. Investment Clubs, Langston Hughes Libr. Action Com. (bd. dirs. 1987—, treas. 1989, Kwanza chair 1994-97), Queens Coll. Home Econs. Alumni Assn. (v.p., chmn. bylaws com. 1982), United Fedn. Tchrs. (Ret. Tchrs. chpt.), Negro Bus. and Profl. Women's Clubs (Profl. award 1998), hi Delta Kappa.

ANDERSON, AMY LEE, realtor; b. Tampa, Fla., July 24, 1950; d. Ernest William and Gloria June (Terrell) Denham; m. Arnold Albin Anderson Jr., Dec. 21, 1986; children: Melissa Lee, Nancy Marie. BA, U. Tampa, 1971. Lic. realtor Nat. Bd. Realtors. Sys. analyst Nat. CSS, Tampa, 1971-79; field analyst Digital Equipment Corp., Meriden, Conn., 1979-84; dir. nat. accounts Canaan Computer Corp., Stratford, Conn., 1984—92; realtor Prudential Carolinas Realty, Raleigh, N.C., 1992-95, Block & Assocs., Raleigh, 1995—97, Prudential Carolinas Realty, Raleigh, NC, 1997—2000, Midway Airlines, Raleigh, NC, 2001, Keller Williams Realty, Raleigh, NC, 2002—. Exec. staff Canaan Computer Corp., Stratford, 1987-92. Editor (manual) Corporate Policies, 1986; co-author: Start at the Top, 1989. Treas. PTA, Basking Ridge, N.J., 1989; advisor Tarheel Challenge Acad., Clinton, N.C., 1995; participant Paws Walk for Cancer, Raleigh, 1995. Mem. Data Processing Mgmt. Assn. (publicity com. 1978-92), Capital City Club (membership com. 1993—). Republican. Episcopalian. Avocations: needlework, reading, landscaping, upholstering.

ANDERSON, ANITA A. secondary school educator; b. Winston-Salem, N.C., Sept. 13, 1938; d. Birden Dixon and Lovie Josephine McCoy; m. Clarence B. Crumpton (dec.); children: Clarence B., Victoria E.; m. William Webb (dec.); 1 child, William R.; m. William Wallace Parker, Sept. 8, 1992 (dec. June 1998); m. William G. Anderson, Mar. 27, 1999. BS in English and Social Studies, U. Detroit-Mercy, 1973; MEd, Marygrove Coll., Detroit, 1974, cert. secondary adminstrn., 1994; computerized office cert., Acock Computerized Ctr., Athens, Ga., 1986; postgrad., Oakland U., Rochester, Mich., 1996—. Tchr., dept. head Western H.S., Las Vegas, Nev., 1974-76; tchr. reading, dir. learning ctr. Ecorse (Mich.) H.S., 1976=81; tchr., coord. reading Winston-Salem-Forsyth County Schs., 1981-87; tchr. math. Holt (Ala.) H.S., 1987-88; tchr. algebra and sci. Pontiac (Mich.) Pub. Schs., 1988—, self-esteem, self-awareness and peer rels. grant writr, 1989—. Self-esteem facilitator, substance abuse specialist Washington Mid. Sch., Pontiac, 1991—. Author: (tng. manual) Surving Societal Stressors, 1990. Bd. dirs. Fedn. Youth Svcs., Detroit, 1991—. Recipient Tech. of Yr. award N.C. Bd. Edn., 1994; grantee 1st of Am. Bank, Inc., 1994-95. Mem. AAUW, Internat. Reading Assn., Am. Bus. Women Assn., NAACP (life, bd. dirs. Detroit 1990—), Lions (bd. dirs. Detroit 1992—, sec.-editor 1993-95, Melvin Jones fellow 1997), Order Ea. Star (worthy matron 1996—), Daus. of Isis (dir. team I 1996-97), Gamma Phi Delta (life, internat. Greek queen 1979). Avocations: horticulture, travel, reading, drama, surfing the internet. Office: Washington Middle Sch 701 Menominee Rd Pontiac MI 48341-1544

ANDERSON, BARBARA ANN, property manager; b. Springfield, Ill., July 16, 1940; d. Robert F. and Maurine (Ehringer) Engel; m. William J. Tewksbury, July 13, 1963 (div. Apr. 1978); children: Allison L. Heiduk, Maurine McAdams; m. Norman K. Anderson, July 1, 1978; children: Amy Lynn Mayfield, Barry. BA, U. Ariz., 1962. Cert. elem. tchr., Calif. Tchr. Jefferson Sch. Dist., Santa Clara, Calif., 1962-63; tchr. dist. 102 LaGrange (Ill.) Sch. Dist., 1963-66; dir. Family Svc. Agy., George AFB, Calif., 1967-69; pres. Old Danish Food Farm, Inc., Solvang, Calif., 1979—; property mgr. Solvang, 1990—. Dir. Direct Link for Disabled, Solvang, 1994-96; nat. treas. Nat. Charity League, L.A., 1986-90; asst. treas. Vis. Nurse Assn., Santa Barbara, 1989-91; v.p. Jr. League Santa Barbara, 1977-78; regional dir. Assistance League, Santa Barbara, 1989-91; dir. Santa Ynez Valley-Cottage Hosp. Aux., 1992-96; mem. Episc. Ch. Women, pres., 1996-97; v.p. Santa Ynez Valley Cottage Hosp. Aux., 1998-99, bd. dirs. Solvang Theaterfest, 1999—, pres. 2002-04 Named one of Outstanding Young Women of Am., 1971; Paul Harris fellow Rotary Internat. Mem. Confiere Chaime Rotisseurs, Santa Barbara Alumnae Assn., Kappa Kappa Gamma (advisor house bd. Epsilon Psi chpt. 1982-94, pres., v.p., sec., treas., advisor 1972-95). Republican. Avocations: gardening, travel, skiing, golf, choir singing. Home: 281 Oster Sted Solvang CA 93463-2957

ANDERSON, BARBARA MCCOMAS, lawyer; b. Ft. Belvoir, Va., Dec. 18, 1950; d. Ben C. Jr. and Elsa A. McComas; m. Roy Ryden Anderson Jr., Dec. 11, 1982; 1 child, Ryden McComas Anderson. BA, Trinity U., San Antonio, 1972; JD, U. Tex., 1978. Bar: Tex. 1978; cert. in estate planning and probate Tex. Bd. Legal Specialization. From assoc. to ptnr. Locke Purnell Rain Harrell, Dallas, 1978-97; of counsel Locke Liddell & Sapp, LLP, Dallas, 1997—; pvt. practice Dallas, 1997—. Fellow: Coll. of State Bar of Tex., Tex. Bar. Found., Am. Coll. Trusts and Estates Counsel; mem.: Tex. Acad. Probate and Trust Lawyers (charter), Dallas Bar Assn., Tex. Bar Assn. (chair real estate, probate and trust law sect. 2003—). Avocations: reading mysteries, gardening. Office: PO Box 181147 Dallas TX 75218-8147

ANDERSON, BEVERLY JACQUES, academic administrator; b. New Orleans, Sept. 10, 1943; d. Alvin Joseph and Dorothy Ann (Angelety) Jacques; m. Ronald Lee Anderson, Sept. 6, 1967; children: Montina Jacquel, Monique Janee, Montez Jacques. BS cum laude, Dillard U., 1965; MS, Howard U., 1967; PhD, Cath. U. Am., 1978. Instr. math. Howard U., Washington, 1967-69; from instr. to prof. U. D.C., Washington, 1969-91, dean coll. arts & scis., 1994-97, provost, v.p. for acad. affairs, 1997—2000; sr. consortium rsch. fellow office of the chancellor for edn. and profl. devel. U.S. Dept. Def., 2000—. Instr. math. upward bound program, summer Dillard U., Howard U., Coll. V.I.; dir. minority affairs NRC, Washington, 1988—92; dir. instl. self-study U. D.C., 1992—94; bd. dirs. Prince Georges C.C., chmn.; presenter in field. Columnist Prince Georges News, 1991-95; contbr. articles to profl. jours. Chair adv. com. FDA, Washington, 1989—94; bd. dirs. Greater S.E. Healthcare Sys. Found., Washington, 1994—, Ft. Washington Hosp., 1988—, chair, 1994—98, 2000—; bd. dirs. YMCA Metro Washington, 1992—95. Named Outstanding Alumni, Howard U., 1997, recipient [illegible] Faculty award, 1988, Outstanding Cmty. Svc. award, Washington View Mag., 1990, Citation Assn. Women in Math., 1991, Cmty. Svc. award, Greater S.E. Healthcare Sys., 1993, Faculty Rsch. award, Nat. Assn. Equal Opportunity in Higher Edn., 1993, Stewardship award, United Negro Coll. Fund, 1996; grantee, Office Naval Rsch., NASA, Office Post Secondary Edn., Nat. Security Agy., Office Minority Health U.S. Dept. Health and Human Svcs. Mem. Pi Mu Epsilon, Beta Kappa Chi, Phi Delta Kappa. Democrat. Roman Catholic. Avocation: travel. Home: 705 Muirfield Cir Fort Washington MD 20744-7021 Office: Univ DC 4200 Connecticut Ave NW Washington DC 20008-1175

ANDERSON, CAROLE ANN, nursing educator, academic administrator; b. Chgo., Feb. 21, 1938; d. Robert and Marian (Harrity) Irving; m. Clark Anderson, Feb. 14, 1973; 1 child, Julie. Diploma, St. Francis Hosp., 1958; BS, U. Colo., 1962, MS, 1963, PhD, 1977. Group psychotherapist Dept. Vocat. Rehab., Denver, 1963-72; psychotherapist Prof. Psychiatry and Guidance Clinic, Denver, 1970-71; asst. prof., chmn. nursing sch. U. Colo., Denver, 1971-75; therapist, coordinator The Genessee Mental Health, Rochester, N.Y., 1977-78; assoc. dean U. Rochester, N.Y., 1978-86; dean, prof. Coll. Nursing Ohio State U., Columbus, 1986-2001, prof., 2001—, vice provost acad. adminstrn., 2001—. Lectr. nursing sch. U. Colo., Denver, 1970-71; prin. investigator biomed. rsch. support grant, 1986-93, clin. rsch. facilitation grant, 1981-82; program dir. profl. nurse traineeship, 1978-86, advanced nurse tng. grant, 1982-85. Author: (with others) Women as Victims, 1986, Violence Toward Women, 1982, Substance Abuse of Women, 1982; editor Nursing Outlook, 1993—. Pres., bd. dirs. Health Assn., Rochester, 1984-86; mem. north sub area council Finger Lakes Health Systems Agy., 1983-86, longrange planning com., 1981-82; mem. Columbus Bd. Health; dir. Netcare Mental Health Ctr. Am. Acad. Nursing fellow. Mem. ANA, Ohio Nurses Assn., Am. Assn. Colls. Nursing (bd. dirs. 1992-94, pres.-elect 1994-96, pres. 1996-98), Sigma Theta Tau. Home: 406 W 6th Ave Columbus OH 43201-3137 Office: The OH State U Office Acad Affairs 203 Bricker Hall 190 N Oval Mall Columbus OH 43210-1358 E-mail: anderson.32@osu.edu.

ANDERSON, CATHERINE M. consulting company executive; b. N.Y.C., Feb. 28, 1937; d. Edward Charles and Elizabeth (O'Shea) McElligott; m. Robert Brown Anderson, June 22, 1963; children: Mark Robert, Jennifer Elizabeth. BA, Rutgers U., 1959, MA, 1960. Staff asst. to pres. Chatham Coll., Pitts., 1960-61; instr. urban studies ctr. Rutgers U., New Brunswick, N.J., 1961-63; prin. urban renewal coord. City of Cleve., Cleve., 1963-64; regional admisions counselor Am. Inst. Fgn. Study, Pitts., 1964-74; chief planner, mgr. emergency ops. ctr. Allegheny County Govt., Pitts., 1975-79; dir. accreditation svcs. Energy Cons., Inc., Pitts., 1981-83; pub. involvement cons. Pitts., 1983—. Contbr. articles to profl. jours. Committeewoman Mt. Lebanon (Pa.) Mcpl. Dem. Com., 1970-85; active United Way Allegheny County, Pitts., mem. rev. com., 1980—, chmn. rev. com., 1986-89; bd. dirs. Mt. Lebanon Nature Conservancy, v.p., 1985-88, pres., 1988-92; bd. dirs. Conservation Cons. Inc., v.p., 1983-92, pres., 1992-95; bd. dirs. Pitts. chpt. Women's Transp. Seminar, v.p., 1992-94, pres. 1994-95; bd. dirs. Exec. Women's Coun. Greater Pitts., v.p., 1986-88; bd. dirs. Carnegie-Mellon U. Art Gallery, 1986-89, USC Citizens for Land Stewardship, 1997-99. Recipient Robert L. Wells award Mt. Lebanon Nature Conservancy, 1991, Outstanding Svc. award Exec. Women's Coun., 1988; Eagleton Inst. Politics grad. fellow Rutgers U., 1960. Mem.: Women's Press Club Pitts., Women's Transp. Seminar (v.p. 1992—94, pres. 1994—95, nat. bd. dirs.), Exec. Women's Coun. (charter, v.p. 1987—88, Outstanding Svc. award 1988), Am. Soc. Hwy. Engrs. (sr.; bd. dirs. Pitts. chpt. 1998—, Pres.'s award Pitts. sect. 2001). Home and Office: 2061 Outlook Dr Upper Saint Clair PA 15241-2223 E-mail: kabob@adelphia.net.

ANDERSON, CHERINE E. television and film production manager, special events planner, marketing executive; b. Kingston, Jamaica, Mar. 21; d. Percival and Joyce A. (Brown) A. BS, Fordham U., 1986. Community rels. assoc. N.Y.C. Pks. and Recreation Dept., 1986; employee activities coord. The Rockefeller Group, N.Y.C., 1986-87, employment interviewer, 1987-88; licensing coord. DC Comics-a Div. of Time-Warner, N.Y.C., 1988-90; employee rels. coord. ARC, N.Y.C., 1990; freelance spl. events planner N.Y.C., 1990—; auditor N.Y.C. Bd. Edn., 1991-94; affiliate mktg. mgr. Nickelodeon, Nick at Nite MTV Networks, 1996—; mktg. mgr. brand/franchise, movie and affiliate mktg. Nickelodeon. Prodn. mgr. Bklyn. Shakespeare Co., 1991—; assoc. producer Sports Desk Program-WNYE-FM, Bklyn., 1989-91; prodn. mgr. for film The Best Kept Secret, 1992; mng. dir. (13 week TV series) African Theatre and Drama Prodn., 1993; line producer and asst. dir. for film Angel Walk Prodn., 1993; v.p. ops. and prodn. mgr. In Stitches Entertainment, 1994—. Contbr. articles to profl. jours. Bd. dirs. N.Y. Dist. Circle K - An Internat. Collegiate Svc. Orgn., N.Y.C., 1983-87; vol. mem. Vol. Svcs. for Children, 1986—. Named Disting. Sec. L.P. Merridew Award Circle K Internat., 1987, Outstanding Dist. Bd. Mem., 1987. Mem.: N.Y. Women in Film and TV, Nat. Assn. Minorities in Comm. (v.p. 2002, pres. 2003), Am. Mgmt. Assn. (cert. 1988, mgmt. cert. 1990). Democrat. Avocations: racquetball, theatre, reading, travel, writing.

ANDERSON, CHRISTINE MARLENE, software engineer; b. Washington, D.C., Nov. 19, 1947; 2 children. BS in Math., U. Md., 1969. Mathematician Naval Oceanographic Office, Suitland, Md., 1969-71; sr. analyst, fgn. tech. divsn. Planning Rsch. Corp., Ohio, 1971-72; computer scientist USAF Avionics Lab., Wright-Patterson Air Force Base, Dayton, Ohio, 1971-74; sr. analyst USAF C3 Ctr., Cheyenne Mountain, Colorado Springs, Colo., 1974-76; chief computer tech. section USAF Wright Lab./Armament Directorate, Eglin Air Force Base, Fla., 1982-92; ADA 9X project mgr. Office Sec. Defense, 1987-94; chief software tech. br. Phillips Lab., Kirtland Air Force Base, N.Mex., 1992-93, chief, space soperations and simulation divsn.oftware rsch. ctr., 1993-96, dir. space and missiles tech. directorate, 1996; mem. sr. exec. svcs., dir. space vehicles directorate Phillips Lab., Kirtland Air Force Base, Air Force Rsch. Lab., N.Mex., 1996—. Co-chmn. on Ada computer programming lang. Am. Nat. Standards Inst., 1989—; editor Ada standard Internat. Standards Orgn., 1991—. Co-author: Aerospace Software Engineering, 1991; contbr. articles to profl. jours. Recipient Engr. of the Year USAF Armament Lab., 1989, Software Engring. award Am. Inst. Aeronautics, 1991, Program Mgr. of the Year award USAF Armament Lab., 1992, Sec. of Defense medal for Meritorious Civilian Svc., 1996. Fellow AIAA (chair software systems tech. com. 1987-89, bd. dirs. 1989—, Aerospace Software Engring. award 1991). Office: Air Force Rsch Lab AFRL/VS Aberdeen Ave SE Kirtland Afb NM 87117-0001

ANDERSON, CLAIRE W. gifted and talented educator; b. Albuquerque, May 22, 1930; d. Wentworth Henry and Clara Lea (Magruder) Corley; m. William James Young (div.); children: Gayle L. Mirkin, D. Young, Sherry B. Butler; m. Wallace L. Anderson. Student in Engring., U. Miss., 1946; BA, Rice U., 1951, postgrad., 1993; MEd, U. Houston, 1962, postgrad., 1963, Carnegie Mellon U., Tex. A&M, 1992. Cert. elem. and secondary tchr., early childhood, exceptional children tchr., Tex. Tchr. Golfcrest Elem. Shc., Houston, 1959-60, Montrose, Poe Elem. Sch., Houston, 1960-62, St. Mark's Private Sch., Houston, 1962-63; substitute teaching Spring Branch Ind. Sch. Dist., Houston, 1965-68; tchr. Meml. Hall, Houston, 1968-73; instr. English, math. Internat. Hispanic U., Houston, 1971-74; tchr. Dogan Elem. Sch., Houston, 1971-74, Lanier Mid. Sch., Houston, 1974-79, High Sch. Health Profl., Houston, 1979-90, Clifton Mid. Sch., Houston, 1990-91, Jesse H. Jones Sr. High Sch., Houston, 1992—. Adj. tutoring David Livingston and Assoc., Houston, 1960-65; instr. Internat. Hispanic U., Houston, 1971-74, Houston C.C., 1984—. Internat. Ednl. Comm. Ctr., High Point, N.C., 1990, Houston C.C. Sys., 1991; invited judge Kiev, Ukraine Math. and Sci. Competitions, 1989; facilitator Tex. Coun. of Women Sch. Execs. Summer Conf., 1994—; active The Rice/HISD Sch. Writing Project; acad. sponsor secondary edn. svc. and sci. clubs. Pres. bd. dirs. Women for Justice, 1990-94; active Houston Photography Ctr., Mus. Fine Arts, Houston Health Objectives 2000, Children's Mus.; coord. study and enrichment tutoring program, 1994. Recipient Tex. award for Excellence in Tchg. and Outstanding Svc. to the Cmty., 1994; scholar Precalculus Design Team, Dow Jones scholar Pa. State, Advance Placement scholar Tex. A&M, Woodrow Wilson; grantee NSF, Impact II. Mem. IEEE, Nat. Coun. Tchrs. Math., Nat. Coun. Tchrs. English, Am. Acoustic Soc., Assn. Calculating Machinery, Assn. for Early Childhood Edn. (internat. chairperson), Tex. Assn. Edn. Tech., Tex. Computers Educators Assn., N.Y. Acad. Sci., Internat. Coun. Computers in Edn., Phi Delta Kappa. Office: 7414 Saint Lo Rd Houston TX 77033-2732

ANDERSON, DARLEEN SHIRCLIFFE, hospital system administrator; b. Boston, Dec. 19, 1951; d. Albert Craycroft and Doreen Agnes (Newberg) Shircliffe; m. Billy Gray Anderson, June 9, 1973; children: Brandon, Brittany. Diploma in nursing, N.C. Bapt. Hosp., 1973; BSN, Old Dominion U., 1982; MS in Advanced Adult Nursing and Adminstrn., Hampton U., 1985. RN, Va.; cert. nursing adminstr. Staff nurse intensive and neuro ICU N.C. Bapt. Hosp., Winston-Salem, 1973-74, staff and charge nurse, 1974-76; staff nurse ICU Bapt. Meml. Hosp., Memphis, 1974; clin. coord. neuro ICU Sentara Norfolk (Va.) Gen. Hosp., 1977-79, quality assurance coord., 1979, critical care staff devel. coord., 1979-84, trauma program dir., 1984-89, adminstrv. advisor burn trauma ICU, 1988-89, DON, 1989-91, v.p., 1992—. Site reviewer Trauma Ctr. Designation, Va., 1983-91, EMS Designs Co., Calif., 1986; expert witness reviewer legal firms, Hampton Roads, Va., 1987-91 Mem. ACA, ANA (tri level 1983—), Am. Trauma Soc., Am. Orgn. Nurse Execs., Am. Assn. Neuro Sci. Nurses (treas. 1978, pres. 1980), Sigma Theta Tau. Baptist. Home: 1224 Heathcliff Dr Virginia Beach VA 23464-5848 Office: Sentara Leigh Hosp 830 Kempsville Rd Norfolk VA 23502-3920

ANDERSON, DENICE ANNA, editor; b. Detroit, Nov. 11, 1947; d. Carl Magnus and Geraldine Elizabeth (Willer) A. BA in Journalism, Mich. State U., 1970. Copy editor/reporter The State News, East Lansing, Mich., 1965-70; reporter/copy editor/photographer The Tecumseh (Mich.) Herald, 1966-68, 99—; copy editor/entertainment editor The State Jour., Lansing, Mich., 1970-76; freelance writer State Jour./Lansing Mag., 1977-79; freelance corr. Collier's Year Book, N.Y.C., 1977-79; copy editor, proofreader Booz, Allen & Hamilton, N.Y.C., 1980-81, Rogers & Wells, N.Y.C., 1981-83, Advanced Therapeutics Comm., N.Y.C., 1983-84; freelance editor, N.Y.C., Santa Fe, Clinton, Mich., 1984—. Contbr. articles to profl. jours. Bd. dirs., sec. March of Dimes, Lansing, 1972-76; vol./writer Polio Info. Ctr., N.Y.C., 1984-88; vol. Vol. Involvement Svcs., Santa Fe, N.M., 1989. Mem. Editorial Freelancers Assn. Lutheran. Home: 210 E Church St Clinton MI 49236 Office Phone: 517-456-4990.

ANDERSON, DENISE W. publishing executive, musician; b. Idaho Falls, Idaho, July 11, 1958; d. Lyle L. Ward, Ruby Haymore; m. Daniel J. Anderson; children: Grace, Dorothy, Camille, Teresa, Eliza, Rachel, Daniel, Jr. AA in Arts and Scis., Ricks Coll., 1978; BA in Univ. Studies, Valley City State U., 2001; student in Sch. Psychology, Minot State U., 2004—. Piano tchr. Anderson Music Studio, Ray, ND, 1983—2003, music performer, composer, recorder, 1983—2003; newspaper columnist The Teller, Milnor, ND, 1998—2000, Ransom County Gazette, Lisbon, ND, 1998—2000; ind. writer, tchr. Anderson Pub. Co., Ray, ND, 1998—2000; ind. bus. owner and operator Anderson Enterprises, Ray, 1998—. Parent educator The Parenting Coalition, Williston, ND, 1995—95; substitute tchr. Ray Pub. Sch., 2001—02. Columnist: The Voice of Experience, 2002; prodr.: The Voice of Experience Web-site, 2001—. Vol. leader Williston Basin Food Co-op, 1983—87; mem., chmn. Piano Festival Thursday Musical Br., Nat. Fedn. Music Clubs, Williston, 1993—97; choir founder, dir. Gwinner Cmty. Choir, Gwinner, ND, 1998—98; foster parent Williams County Social Svcs., Williston, ND, 1994—96; tchr., lay leader LDS Ch., 1976—, dir. pub. affairs, 1998—2000; mem., officer Piano Tchrs. Assn., Williston, 1983—87. Mem.: Nat. Cmty. Educators Assn., Am. Mother's Inc., Ray Lions Club (mem. cmty. devel. com. 2001—02). Mem. Lds Ch. Avocations: creating with multi-media, music, writing, organization. Home: PO Box 325 Ray ND 58849 Office: Anderson Enterprises PO Box 344 Minot ND 58701-0344 Personal E-mail: denisewa@nccray.com. Business E-Mail: denise@thevoiceofexperience.net.

ANDERSON, DORIS EHLINGER, lawyer; b. Houston; d. Joseph Otto and Cornelia Louise (Pagel) Ehlinger; m. Wiley Anderson, Jr. (dec.); children: Wiley Newton III, Joe E. BA, Rice U., 1946; permanent high sch. tchr. cert., U. Houston, 1948; JD, U. Tex., 1950; MLS in Museology, U. Okla., 1985. Bar: Tex. 1950, U.S. Supreme Ct. Assoc. Ehlinger & Anderson, Houston, 1950-52, ptnr., 1965—; assoc. Price, Guinn, Wheat & Veltmann, Houston, 1952-55, Wheat, Dyche & Thornton, Houston, 1955-65; life mem. Rice Assocs., Houston, 1984—. Hist. lectr., Harvard Negotiation Seminar, 1992 Edn. for Ministry, U of South, 1999. Editor: Houston City of Destiny, 1980; contbr. articles to hist. pubs. and to Bayou Bend. Parliamentarian Harris County Flood Control Task Force, Houston, 1975-2003; dir. Houston Bapt. Mus Am. Architecture and Decorative Arts, 1980-90, curator costume, 1980; apptd. ambassador Inst. Texan Culture U. Tex, San Antonio; past pres. gen. San Jacinto Descendants; docent Bayou Bend Mus. Fine Arts, Houston. Recipient best interpretive exhibit award Tex. Hist. Commn., 1983, Outstanding Woman of Yr. award YWCA, Houston, 1983; named adm. Tex. Navy, 1980. Mem. ABA, UDC (pres. Jefferson Davis chpt.), Assn. Women Attys. Houston, Houston Bar Assn., Daus. Republic Tex. (parliamentarian gen.), Am. Mus. Soc., Harris County Heritage Soc., Kappa Beta Pi (pres. Lamda alumni). Episcopalian. Home: 5556 Cranbrook Rd Houston TX 77056-1600 Office: Ehlinger & Anderson 5556 Sturbridge Dr Houston TX 77056-1623

ANDERSON, DOROTHY FISHER, social worker, psychotherapist; b. Funchal, Madeira, May 31, 1924; d. Lewis Mann Anker and Edna (Gilbert) Fisher (adoptive father David Henry Fisher); m. Theodore W. Anderson, July 8, 1950; children: Robert Lewis, Janet Anderson Yang, Jeanne Elizabeth. BA, Queens Coll., 1945; AM, U. Chgo., 1947. Diplomate Am. Bd. Examiners in Clin. Social Work; lic. clin. social worker, Calif.; registered cert. social worker, N.Y. Intern Cook County (Ill.) Bur. Pub. Welfare, Chgo., 1945-46, Ill. Neuropsychiat. Inst., Chgo., 1946; clin. caseworker, Neurol. Inst. Presbyn. Hosp., N.Y.C., 1947; therapist, Mental Hygiene Clinic VA, N.Y.C., 1947-50; therapist, Child Guidance Clinic Pub. Elem. Sch. 42, N.Y.C., 1950-53; social worker, counselor Cedarhurst (N.Y.) Family Service Agy., 1954-55; psychotherapist, counselor Family Service of the Midpeninsula, Palo Alto, Calif., 1971-73, 79-86, George Hexter, M.D., Inc., 1972-83; clin. social worker Tavistock Clinic, London, 1974-75, El Camino Hosp., Mountain View, Calif., 1979; pvt. practice clin. social work, 1978-92; ret., 1992. Cons. Human Resource Services, Sunnyvale, Calif., 1981-86. Hannah G. Solomon scholar U. Chgo., 1945-46; Commonwealth fellow U. Chgo., 1946-47. Fellow Soc. Clin. Social Work (Continuing Edn. Recognition award 1980-83); mem. Nat. Assn. Social Workers (diplomate in clin. social work). Avocations: sculpture, tennis, travel, drawing, pastels.

ANDERSON, ELIZABETH ANN, special education educator; d. Ed Rembert Bonner II and Stella Maureen Bonner; children: Monty Ed Fields, Randy Howell Fields, Micheal Marc Fields, Mary Elizabeth Hanson, Loretta Elaine Irwin, Jenifer Maureen Poma. EdB summa Cum Laude, Ea. N.Mex., 1971, M, 1974; postgrad., Calif. State U., Domiguez Hills, 1992. Cert. tchg. elementary, learning diabled, pupil pers. Calif. Dept. Edn. Tchr. spl. edn. Del Amo Psychiat. Hosp., Torrance, Calif.; sch. counselor Sierra Mid. Sch., Roswell; tchr. spl. edn. Roswell Schs., Lake Elsinore (Calif.) United Sch. Dist., 1993—. Named Walmart Tchr. of Yr., Butterfield Tchr. of Yr. Mem.: N.Mex Sch. Counselors (assoc.; v.p.pres. mid. sch. 1985—86), Phi Kappa Phi (assoc.). Personal E-mail: aander3810@aol.com.

ANDERSON, ELLEN RUTH, state legislator; b. Gary, Ind., Nov. 25, 1959; d. John Ernest Anderson and Marion Jane (Reeves) Martin; m. Andrew J. Dawkins. BA in History, Carleton Coll., 1982; JD, U. Minn., 1986. Bar: Minn., 1987, U.S. Dist. Ct. Minn. 1988. Jud. law clk. Minn. Ct. Appeals, St. Paul, 1987-88; atty. Hennepin County Pub. Defender, Mpls., 1988-91; staff atty. Minn. Edn. Assn., St. Paul, 1991-92; mem. Minn. Senate from 66th dist., St. Paul, 1993—. Democrat. Office: State of Minn G-24 Capitol 75 Constitution Ave Saint Paul MN 55155-1601

ANDERSON, EVELYN LOUISE, elementary teacher; b. Abilene, Tex., Apr. 10, 1943; d. Dexter W. and Hattie M. Armstrong; m. E. Wade Anderson, Dec. 22, 1962; children: Cynthia Gail, Tresa Lynet. BA magna cum laude, Sul Ross State Coll., 1985. Kindergarten tchr. Socorro Ind. Sch. Dist., El Paso, Tex., 1985-86; tchr. kindergarten through 3d grade, resource rm. Ft. Stockton Ind. Sch. Dist., 1986-90; tchr. kindergarten Lydia Rippy Elem. Sch., Aztec, N.Mex., 1990—. Organizer Children's Libr., Ft. Stockton (Tex.) Pub. Libr., 1980-84, pre-school tchr. First Bapt. Ch., Ft. Stockton, Tex., 1979-84. Nominee Disney Tchr. awrd, 2000. Mem. Coun. Exceptional Children, Kappa Delta Pi. Democrat. Avocations: writing, reading, travel, oil painting, crocheting. Home: 1709 Winter Ct Farmington NM 87401-2086

ANDERSON, FRANCILE MARY, secondary school educator; b. Poland, Ind., Nov. 10, 1926; d. Matthew Henry and Emma Alvina (Dettinger) Worthman; m. Robert Charles Anderson, Aug. 23, 1953; children: Sally Quick, Sue Wilkinson, Robert Charles, Russell. BA, U. Mich., 1948. Tchr. Pontiac (Mich.) Sch. Dist., 1948-54. Co-organizer Mich. Law Related Edn. Conf., Lansing, 1978; mem. exec. bd. North Ctrl. Assn. Commn. on Schs., Tempe, Ariz., 1996-99. Trustee North Oakland Med. Ctrs., Pontiac, 1994—; campaign chair United Way of Oakland County, 1995. Recipient Disting. Svc. award Mich. Assn. Secondary Sch. Prins., 1987; named to Mich. Edn. Hall of Fame, 1990. Mem. Oakland County Hosp. Assn. (pres.), Oakland County Bar Law Libr. Found., North Ctrl. Assn. Mich., North Oakland Med. Ctrs. Found. (pres.), Delta Kappa Gamma. Republican. Presbyterian. Home: 2570 Silverside Dr Waterford MI 48328-1760 E-mail: franan@coast.net.

ANDERSON, GEORGIA GRIFFIN, educational designer; d. A. C. Griffin, Sr. and Georgia T. Griffin; m. Tracey L. Anderson, May 14, 1987. BS, U. Tenn., 1984. Libr. clerk U. Tenn., Chattanooga, 1986—89; merchandise mgr. JoAnn Fabrics, Dallas, 1989—98; design cons. Fabric Factory, Dallas, 1998—99, Hancock Fabrics, Arlington, Tex., 1999; textbook supr. Tarrant County Coll. SE, Arlington, 2001—. Hon. chair Bus. Adv. Coun., Tex., 2003. With USAF, 1973—76. Mem.: Nat. Assn. Female Execs., Phi Theta Kappa. Avocations: reading, singing, piano.

ANDERSON, GERALDINE LOUISE, medical researcher; b. Mpls., July 7, 1941; d. George M. and Viola Julie-Mary (Abel) Havrilla; m. Henry Clifford Anderson, May 21, 1966; children: Bruce Henry, Julie Lynne. BS, U. Minn., 1963. Med. technologist Swedish Hosp., Mpls., 1963-68; hematology supr. lab. Glenwood Hills Hosp., Golden Valley, Minn., 1968-70; assoc. scientist pediats. U. Minn. Hosps., Mpls., 1970-74; instr. health occupations, med. lab. asst. Suburban Hennepin County Area Vocat. Tech. Ctr., Brooklyn Park, Minn., 1974-81, 92-95, St. Paul Tech. Vocat. Inst., Brooklyn Park, 1978-81; rsch. med. technologist Miller Hosp., St. Paul, 1975-78; rsch. assoc. Children's and United Hosps., St. Paul, 1979-88; sr. lab. analyst Cascade Med. Inc., Eden Prairie, Minn., 1989-90; lab. mgr. VAMC, Mpls., 1990; tech. support scientist INCSTAR Corp., Stillwater, Minn., 1990-94; mem. network staff Clin. Design Group, Chgo., 1992-98; regulatory affairs product analysis coord. Medtronic Neurol., Mpls., 1995; quality assurance documentation coord. Lectec Corp., Minnetonka, Minn., 1995; clin. rsch. monitor Eli Lilly Rsch. Labs., Indpls., 1995-98; sr. clin. rsch. assoc. Covance, Inc., Princeton, N.J., 1998-99. Sr. clin. rsch. assoc. Parexel Internat., Inc., Chgo., 1999—2000, Med. Tech. Rsch. Assn./AAI Internat., Boston, 2000—01; regional clin. assoc. Wyeth, Collegeville, Pa., 2001—02; mem. health occupations adv. com. Hennepin Tech. Ctrs., 1975—90, chairperson, 1978—79; mem. hematology slide cdn. rev. bd. Am. Soc. Hematology, 1977—96; mem. flow cytometry and clin. chemistry quality controll subcoms. Nat. Com. for Clin. Lab. Stds., 1988—92; cons. FCM Specialists, 1989—99, 2002—, Clin. Design Group, 1992—98; mem. rev. bd. Clin. Lab. Sci., 1990—91, The Learning Laboratorian Series, 1991; contbr., presenter in Svc. Rev. in Clin. Lab. Sci., audio taped study program for ASMT, 1992. Contbr. articles to profl. jours. Charter orgns. rep. Viking Coun. troop 534 Boy Scouts Am., 1988—90; resource person lab. careers Robbinsdale (Minn.) Sch. Dist., 1970—79; active Women Scientists Spkrs. Bur., 1989—92, Helping Hands, 2002—, Med. Lab. Tech. Polit. Action Com., 1978—99; observer UN 4th World Conf. on Women, Beijing, 1995; del. Crest View Home Assn., 1981—; sci. and math. subcom. Minn. High Tech. Coun., 1983—88; bd. dirs. Big Pine Lake Property Owners, 1996—. Recipient Svc. awards and honors, Omicron Sigma. Mem.: NAFE (Twin Cities Network), AAUW, AAAS, Grad. Women in Sci., Inc., Great Lakes Internat. Flow Cytometry Assn. (charter mem. 1992), Internat. Soc. Analytical Cytology, Am. Soc. Hematology, Minn. Med. Tech. Alumni, Assn. Clin. Rsch. Profls., World Future Soc., Assn. Women in Sci., Twin Cities Hosp. Assn. (spkrs. bur. 1968—70), Am. Soc. Clin. Lab. Sci. (del. to ann. meetings 1972—, chmn. hematology sci. assembly 1977—79, nomination com. 1979—81, bd. dirs. 1986—88), Soc. Clin. Rsch. Assocs., Am. Soc. Profl. and Exec. Women, Minn. Soc. Med. Tech. (sec. 1969—71), Minn. Emerging Med. Orgns., Nat. Assn. Women Cons., Inc., Soc. Tech. Comm., Soc. Clin. Rsch. Assocs., Assn. Clin. Rsch. Profls., Women in Comm., Inc., Am. Med. Writers Assn., Alpha Mu Tau, Sigma Delta Epsilon (corr. sec. XI chpt. 1980—82, pres. 1982—84, nat. membership com. 1990—92, nat. nominations chair 1991—92, nat. v.p. 1992—93, nat. pres.-elect 1993—94, nat. pres. 1994—95, bd. dirs. 1996—2001, chmn. bd. dirs. 2000—01). E-mail: gerrlou@comcast.net.

ANDERSON, GILLIAN, actress; b. Chgo., Aug. 9, 1968; d. Edward and Rosemary A.; m. Errol Clyde Klotz, Jan. 1, 1994; 1 child, Piper. BFA, DePaul U., 1990; grad., Goodman Theatre Sch., Chgo. Appeared on TV as Dana Scully in X-Files, 1993-2002 (Emmy award for Outstanding Lead Actress in a Drama Series, 1997, Golden Globe award for Best Actress in a Drama Series, 1997); stage appearance in Absent Friends, Manhattan Theatre Club, 1991 (Theatre World award 1991), The Philanthropist, Along Wharf Theater, 1992, The Vagina Monologues, 1999, 2000, What the Night is For, 2002-03, The Sweetest Swing in Baseball, 2004; appeared in films Three at Once, 1986, A Matter of Choice, 1988, The Turning, 1992, X-Files the Movie, 1998, The Mighty, 1998, Playing By Heart, 1998, Hellcab, 1998, Princess Mononoke, 1999, The House of Mirth, 2000 (British Independent Film award for Best Actress, 2000); TV guest appearances in Class of '96, 1993, Reboot, 1995, The Simpsons, 1997, Frasier, 1999, Harsh Realm, 1999. Office: William Morris Agy 151 S El Camino Dr Beverly Hills CA 90212-2775

ANDERSON, GLENDA, special education educator, sales executive, financial planner; d. Ross and Janice Richardson; m. David Anderson, July 22, 1995; children: Jacob Glover, Nicholas Glover. BS, Met. State Coll., Denver, 1972; MA, Ft. Hays (Kans.) State U., 1982. Cert. life, health, home and car ins. agt. Primerica; spl. edn. K-12, elem. edn. Colo., securities rep. Primerica. Spl. edn. tchr. Denver Pub. Schs., 1984—; beauty cons. Avon, Denver, 1985—; fin. planning and ins. rep Primerica Fin. Planning, Denver, 1994—; e-business owner, web master www.BuyFromHome.org, Aurora, Colo., 2000—; children's books rep. Usborne Books, Aurora, 2003—. Mentor, master mentor Denver Pub. Schs., 1999—. Avocations: travel, home building, handicrafts. E-mail: glendaga@hotmail.com.

ANDERSON, GLORIA LONG, chemistry educator; b. Altheimer, Ark., Nov. 5, 1938; d. Charley and Elsie Lee (Foggie) L.; 1 child, Gerald Leavell. BS, Ark. Agr. Mech. & Normal Coll., 1958; MS, Atlanta U., 1961; PhD, U. Chgo., 1968. Instr. S.C. State Coll., Orangeburg, 1961-62, Morehouse Coll., Altanta, 1962-64; teaching and rsch. asst. U. Chgo., 1964-68; assoc. prof., chmn. Morris Brown Coll., Atlanta, 1968-73, Callaway prof., chmn., 1973-84, acad. dean, 1984-89, United Negro Coll. Fund disting. scholar, 1989-90, Callaway prof. chemistry, 1990—, interim pres., 1992-93, Fuller E. Callaway prof. chemistry, 1993-99, 99—, dean sci. and tech., 1995-97, interim pres., 1998-99, Fuller E. Callaway prof. chemistry, 1999—. Contbr. articles to profl. jours. Bd. dirs. Corp. for Pub. Broadcasting, Washington, 1972-79, vice chmn. 1977-79; Pub. Broadcasting Atlanta, 1980—; mem. Pub. Telecommunications Task Force, Atlanta, 1980. Postdoctoral rsch. fellow NSF, 1969, faculty industry fellow, 1981, faculty rsch. fellow Southeastern Ctr. for Elec. Engring. Edn., 1984. Fellow Am. Inst. Chemists (cert. profl. chemist); mem. Nat. Sci. Tchrs. Assn., Am. Chem. Soc., Sigma Xi. Baptist. Home: 560 Lynn Valley Rd SW Atlanta GA 30311-2331 Office: Morris Brown Coll Dept Chemistry 643 ML King Jr Dr NW Atlanta GA 30314-4140

ANDERSON, GWYN C. computer company executive, computer consultant; b. LaCrosse, Wis., Aug. 8, 1966; d. Robert Bernard and Alice Helaine Anderson. Owner Enhanced Ideas, LaCrosse, 1996—; e-commerce webmaster www.enhancedideas.com. Avocations: rollerskating, camping, horseback riding, swimming, science fiction. Office: Enhanced Ideas PO Box 3602 La Crosse WI 54602-3602 Office Phone: 608-788-6156. E-mail: enhancedideas@earthlink.net.

ANDERSON, HOLLY GEIS, women's health facility administrator, commentator, educator; b. Waukesha, Wis., Oct. 23, 1946; d. Henry H. and Hulda S. Geis; m. Richard Kent Anderson, June 6, 1969. BA, Azusa Pacific U., 1970. CEO Oak Tree Antiques, San Gabriel, Calif., 1975-82; pres., founder, CEO Premenstrual Syndrome Med. Clinic, Arcadia, Calif., 1982—, Breast Healthcare Ctr., 1986-89, Hormonal Treatment Ctrs., Inc., Arcadia, 1992-94; with Thyroid Ctr., 2001—. Lectr. radio and TV shows, L.A.; on-air radio personality Women's Clinic with Holly Anderson, 1990—. Author: What Every Woman Needs to Know About PMS (audio cassette), 1987, The PMS Treatment Program (video cassette), 1989, PMS Talk (audio cassette), 1989. Mem. NAFE, The Dalton Soc., Am. Hist. Soc. of Germans from Russia. Republican. Avocations: writing, genealogy, travel, hiking, boating. Office: PMS Treatment Clinic 150 N Santa Anita Ave Ste 755 Arcadia CA 91006-3148 Office Phone: 626-447-0679. Personal E-mail: hra3@earthlink.net.

ANDERSON, ILSE JANELL, clinical geneticist; b. Elmhurst, Ill., May 3, 1959; d. Lowell Leonard and Avis Janell Anderson; m. Nicholas Thomas Potter, June 24, 1989; children: Nils Andrew, Anders Matthew. BS in Biology, Lehigh U., 1981; MD, N.Y. Med. Coll., 1985. Diplomate Nat. Bd. Med. Examiners, Am. Bd. Pediatrics, Am. Bd. Med. Genetics. Resident pediatrics U. Conn., Farmington, 1985-88, fellow human genetics, 1988-91; clin. geneticist Med. Ctr. U. Tenn., Knoxville, 1991—. Mem. Phi Beta Kappa. Office: Univ Tenn Med Ctr 1930 Alcoa Hwy Ste 435 Knoxville TN 37920-1520

ANDERSON, JALA, newscaster; married. Reporter NBC 17, Raleigh, NC. Bd. dirs. Big Bros./Big Sisters, Durham and Orange Counties, Northwest Ohio. Recipient Regional award for excellence in journalism, Nat. Assn. Black Journalists, 1994, scholarship, Scripps-Howard Found., 1992, 2d pl. award for Best Enterprise Reporting, AP, 1998, 1st pl. Best Enterprise Reporting, 1999. Mem.: W.Va. Assn. Black Journalists (founder), N.W. Ohio Black Media Assn. (pres.). Office: NBC 17 Studios 1205 Front St Raleigh NC 27609

ANDERSON, JANE ELLSWORTH, retired secondary school educator; b. Chillicothe, Ohio, Mar. 30, 1943; d. Henry Branch and Beatrice Clara (Trainer) Ellsworth: m. George Leonard Anderson, Jr., Sept. 9, 1964; children: Doug, Jeff, Michele. BS in Edn., Ohio State U., 1983, MS in Edn., 1994. Cert. tchr. grades 7-12, Ohio. Long distance operator Ohio Bell Telephone Co., Dayton, 1962-64; real estate agt. Donna Vaughn Realtors, Dayton, 1965-67; sales rep., mgr. Tupperware Dayton Party Sales, 1972-74; tchr. Westerville (Ohio) City Schs., 1984—2003; ret. Advisor Westerville H.S. Yearbook, Golden Warrior, 1986 (1st pl. award), 1987 (1st pl. award). Various positions Englewood Hills Elem. Sch. PTA, Englewood, Ohio, 1971—76; phone counselor Bridge Counseling Ctr., Columbus, 1980—81; mem. Dem. Congl. Campaign Com., Dem. Senators Campaign Com.; youth dir. Unity Ch., Columbus, Ohio, 1978—80. Mem.: Natural Resources, St. Labre Indian Sch., Am. Indian Youth, St. Joseph's Indian Sch., Nat. Parks Conservation, Habitat for Humanity, Eastern Paralyzed Veterans, Emily's List, So. Poverty Law Ctr., U.S. Holocaust Meml. Mus. Avocations: writing, reading, biking, photography.

ANDERSON, JANE LOUISE, association executive; d. Charles Keith and Dorothea Celeste (Prouty) A.; m. Paul Ellsworth Bennett, May 1, 1970 (div. March 1972); m. Ernest Rowell Jackson, Dec. 28, 1998. BA, U. Mich., Ann Arbor, Mich., 1971, MA, 1975. Certified Association Executive (CAE) Am. Soc. of Assn. Executives/DC, 2003. Editor Univ. Mich. Internat. Ctr., Ann Arbor, Mich., 1973—74; program assoc. U. Mich. Office of Student Svcs., Ann Arbor, Mich., 1974—76; resource devel. cons. Luth. Resources Commn., Washington, 1977—80, sr. resource devel. officer, 1981—84, asst. dir., 1985—90; exec. dir. Fulbright Assn., Washington, 1990—. Treas. Coalition for Am. Leadership Abroad, Washington, 1997—, dir., 1995—; CEO adv. coun. mem. Greater Wash. Soc. of Assn. Exec., Washington, 2000—; strategic planning adv. coun. mem. Am. Soc. of Assn. Exec., Washington, 1996—97. Contbr. articles pub. to profl. jour. Vol. trainer The Support Ctr., Washington, 1983—93; dir. NY Ave. Found., Washington, 1986—90. Mem.: Greater Wash. Soc. of Assn. Exec., Am. Soc. of Assn. Exec., Phi Beta Kappa. Avocations: travel, reading, cooking, drawing. Office: Fulbright Assn 666 11th St NW St 525 Washington DC 20001 E-mail: jane.anderson@fulbright.org.

ANDERSON, JEAN R. women's health physician; b. 1953; MD, Vanderbilt U. Intern and resident in obstetrics and gynecology Vanderbilt U.; attending physician Met. Nashville Gen. Hosp., 1983—86; assoc. prof. dept. population and family health sci. Johns Hopkins Sch. Pub. Health, Balt., assoc. prof. gynecology and obstetrics; founding dir. Johns Hopkins HIV Women's Health Program, Balt., 1987—; faculty Johns Hopkins U., Balt., 1987—. Cons. to Brazilian Ministry of Health, 1998. Author, editor: The Manual for the Clinical Care of Women with HIV, 2001; contbr. articles to profl. jour. Recipient CIBA award for cmty. svc., Vanderbilt U. Sch. Medicine, 1977. Fellow: Am. Coll. Obstetricians and Gynecologists; mem.: Am. Acad. HIV Medicine. Office: Johns Hoplins Divsn Gynecologic Specialties Harvey 319 600 N Wolfe St Baltimore MD 21287*

ANDERSON, JEWELLE LUCILLE, musician, educator; b. Alexandria, La., Jan. 4, 1932; d. William Andrew and Ethel Dee (Hall) Anderson. Student, Springfield Coll., 1981-82; MusB, Boston U., 1984; postgrad., Harvard U., 1995-96. Cert. tchr. music and social studies Mass. Soloist Ch of the Redeemer Episcopal Ch., Chestnut Hill, Mass., 1964-69, St. James Episcopal Ch., Cambridge, Mass., 1970-75; kindergarten tchr. and music dir. Trinity Episcopal Ch., Boston, [illegible] Hire, Boston, 1986; music dir. Days in the Arts summer program Boston Symphony Orch., Tanglewood, Mass., summer 1991, 92; chorale dir. Boston Orch. Chorale, 1996-97; tchr. scholar Harvard Grad. Sch. of Edn., 1998-99. Founder Jewelle Anderson Found., Inc., Boston, 1996. Vol. ARC, Boston, 1994—; bd. dirs. Mattapan Cmty. Health Ctr., Boston, 1990—92; founder, pres. Dr. William and Ethel Hall Anderson Scholarship, 1989—. Recipient Am. Music award, Nat. Fedn. Music, 1970, Spl. Individual award, 1969, Outstanding Contbn. to Humanity award, Alexandria Civic Improvement Coun., 1967, Outstanding Achievement award, Boston Tchrs. Union, 2000, Cope Plaque for Outstanding Achievement, 2000, Action for Boston Cmty. Devel. award, 2003. Mem.: AAUW, Black Educators Alliance of Mass., Amnesty Internat., Women Svc. Club (head youth group 1989—, 1st v.p. 2002), Alpha Kappa Alpha. Democrat. Baptist. Avocations: walking, boating. Office: PO Box 124 Boston MA 02117-0124

ANDERSON, JOAN BALYEAT, religion educator, minister; b. Cin., Apr. 14, 1926; d. Hal Donal and Myrtle (Skinner) Hukill Balyeat; m. Jerry William Anderson, Jr., Sept. 13, 1947: children: Katheleen, Diane. AA, Stephens Coll., 1946. Ordained Christian minister, Ohio, 1988. Christian ch. bible tchr., Cin., 1944—; Christian counselor, advisor, 1964—; founder, pres., dir., ruling elder, and pastor Loving God "Complete Bible" Christian Ministries and First Ch., Cin., 1988—. Christian Bible tchr., preacher, pastor daily and Sunday radio throughout the east and midwest, 1988—. Mem. Am. Conservative Cause, 1998—2001, Capitol His. Soc., 2000—; legacy leader supporter George Washington's Mt. Vernon, 2001—; coord., collector Heart Fund, T.B., 1948—90; civic assn. officer, rep. edn. com. to all Madeira Schs., 1960—62; co-founder, officer Grassroots, Inc., Cin., 1962—65; mem. Cin. Art Mus., 1972—, Cin. Zoo, 1974—, Colonial Williamsburg Found., 1979—, Nat. Right to Life, 1980—, MADD, 1985—, Heritage Found., 1996—, Am. Conservative Union, 1998, Ronald Reagan Presdl. Found., 1998—, Parents TV Coun., 1998—2001, Am. Policy Ctr., 1998—2001, U.S. Justice Found., 1998—, Nat. Right to Work Legal Def. Found., 1998—, Nat. Security Ctr., 1998—, U.S. Intelligence Ctr., 1998—, Jud. Watch, 1999—, Young Ams. Found., 2000—; supporter The Liberty Com., 2001—; lifelong activist for preservation of U.S. Constn. and Bill of Rights; mem. U.S. Rep. Senatorial Adv. Com., Washington and Cin., 1987—88; mem. Rep. Senatorial Commn., Washington & Cin., 1996—2000; mem. Am. Prayer Network, 1998—. Mem. Blue Book of Cin. Avocation: touring america by car. Home: 7208 Sycamorehill Ln Cincinnati OH 45243-2101 Office: Loving God Complete Bible Christian Mins/1st Ch PO Box 43404 Cincinnati OH 45243-2101

ANDERSON, JOLENE SLOVER, small business owner, publishing executive, consultant; b. Tulare, Calif. James P. Sr., and Helen B. (Walters) Slover; m. Douglas R. Anderson, June 14, 1975; 1 child, Sabrina Jo. Student, Victor Valley Coll., Riverside C.C. Model Connor Sch. Modeling, Fresno, Calif., 1955-65; actress M. Kosloff Studios, Hollywood, Calif., 1965; nat. sales mgr. Armed Services Publs., 1966-68; pres., dir. Sullivan Publs., Inc., Riverside, Calif., 1970-82; pres., chief exec. officer Heritage House Publs., Riverside, 1983-84; pres. Jolene S. Anderson Pub. Cons., Inc., Riverside, 1987—. Bd. dirs. Riverside County Econ. Devel. Coun. Co-comdr. March AFB, Inland Empire Tourists and Conv.; mem. YWCA, City of Riverside Cultural Heritage Bd., Yr. 2000 Com., 1988, Riverside County Philharm. Bd., Temecula-Murrieta Econ. Devel. Corp.; mem. 101 Things to Do in Riverside com., Jurupa C. of C. Named Woman of Achievement YWCA, 1989, Humanitarian of Yr. Rotary, 1990 Mem. Riverside Downtown Assn., Sun City/Menifee Valley C. of C., Greater Riverside C. of C., Temecula Valley C. of C. (tourism com.), Carson Valley C. of C., Murrieta C. of C., Soroptimists (Riverside chpt., Athena award 1989). Office: PO Box 800 Riverside CA 92502-0800

ANDERSON, JOYCE LORRAINE, nurse; b. Newman Grove, Nebr., May 16, 1930; d. Fredrick Carl Stone and Hulda Caroline Nordgren; children: Bonita Lynne Peters, Richard Eugene. Student, Ctrl. C.C., Central City, Nebr., 1950. Rural tchrs. cert., cert. staff mem. Rural sch. tchr. Dist. 47 Platte County, St. Edward, Nebr., 1947—48, Dist. 40 Platte County, Lindsay, Nebr., 1948—51; nurse aid Hosp., Newman Grove, 1973—76; nurse aid, cert. staff mem. Newman Grove Mid Nebr. Luth. Home, 1977—2001. Active Newman Grove Civic Improvement Club, 1985—2001; vol. sing along leader Mid. Nebr. Luth. Home, Newman Grove, 1978—; life mem. Looking Glass United Meth. Ch., Newman Grove, 1930—; active United Meth. Women, 1950—; ch. pianist Looking Glass United Meth. Ch., Newman Grove, 1950—. Home: 53777 829 Rd Newman Grove NE 68758

ANDERSON, JOYCE ANN, lawyer; b. Keene, N.H., Mar. 10, 1950; d. Russell Roland and Theresa Marie (Beauregard) Wilder; m. Joseph Martin Anderson, May 5, 1984 (dec.). Student, Bryn Mawr Coll., 1967—69; BA magna cum laude, Yale Coll., 1971; JD, Cornell U., 1974; MLL in Taxation, Boston U., 1977. Bar: N.H., N.Mex., Mass., Ohio. Atty. Bell & Kennedy, Keene, NH, 1974—76, Smith Connor & Wilder, Nashua, 1976—90, Yarbro & Assocs., Las Cruces, N.Mex., 1992—93, pvt. practice, 1993; analyst Chase Manahttan Mortgage, Columbus, 1993—96; atty. pvt. practice, Brookline, NH, 1996—97, Smith-Weiss, Shepard & Durmer, Nashua, 1997—98, Kenneth C. Downes & Assocs., Albuquerque, 2002, Holt & Babington, Las Cruces, 2003—; CEO, treas. Tumut Gadara Corp., Las Cruces, 1998—2003. Home: 337 Day Dreamer Dr Las Cruces NM 88005 Office Phone: 505-524-8812. Business E-Mail: joyce@tumut.com.

ANDERSON, JUDITH ANN, artist, writer; b. Cin., Ohio, May 14, 1940; d. Clair Henry Stagge, Jean (Akeman) Stagge; m. Rondal Ambrose Anderson, June 13, 1959 (dec.); children: Andrew, Christopher, Lynn. Celebrity tutor Am. Diabete's Auction Gala, Cin., 2002; tchr. Cin. Women's Club; tchr. workshops in field, 1997—2003. Contbr. articles to profl. jours.; prin. works include Cin. (Ohio) Music Hall, 2003. Contbg. artist Wellness Cmty., 2003. Mem.: Ky. Watercolor Soc., Cin. Art Club, Ohio Watercolor Soc., Tex. Watercolor Soc., Northwest Watercolor Soc., Nat. Watercolor Soc. Avocation: interior design. Home: 3644 Langhorst Ct Cincinnati OH 45236

ANDERSON, JUDITH HELENA, English language educator; b. Worcester, Mass., Apr. 21, 1940; d. Oscar William and Beatrice Marguerite (Beaudry) A.; m. E. Talbot Donaldson, May 18, 1971 (dec. Apr. 1987). AB magna cum laude, Radcliffe Coll., 1961; MA, Yale U., 1962, PhD, 1965. Instr. English Cornell U., Ithaca, N.Y., 1964-66, asst. prof. English, 1966-72; vis. lectr. Coll. Seminar Program, Yale U., New Haven, 1973; vis. asst. prof. English U. Mich., Ann Arbor, 1973-74; assoc. prof. Ind. U., Bloomington, 1974-79, prof., 1979—, Chancellor's prof., 1999—, dir. grad. studies, 1986-90, 93, mem. governing bd. univ. Inst. for Advanced Study, 1983-85, 86-88. Morris W. Croll lectr. Gettysburg Coll., 1988, Kathleen Williams lectr., 1989, 95; dir. Folger Inst. Seminar, 1991. Author: The Growth of a Personal Voice, 1976, Biographical Truth, 1984, Words that Matter, 1996; editor: (with Elizabeth D. Kirk) Piers Plowman, 1990, (with Donald Cheney and David A. Richardson) Spenser's Life and the Subject of Biography, 1996; mem. editl. bd. Spenser Ency., 1979-90, Duquesne Studies in Lang. and Lit., 1976—, Spenser Studies, 1986—; mem. adv. bd. Textbase of Women Writers, Brown U., 1989-2000; contbr. articles on Renaissance lit. to profl. jours. Woodrow Wilson fellow, 1961-62, 63-64, NEH summer fellow and sr. rsch. fellow, 1979, 81-82, Dulin fellow Folger Libr., 1991; Huntington Libr. rsch. grantee, 1978, 97, NEH fellow, 1985-86, Mayers Found. fellow, 1990-91, Nat. Humanities Ctr. fellow, 1995-96, Newberry-NEH fellow, 2002-03; recipient Outstanding Scholar award Office of Women's Affairs Ind. U., 1996. Mem. MLA (mem. exec. com. Renaissance divsn. 1973-78, 86-90, del. to assembly 1991-93, publs. com. 1999-2002), AAUP, Spenser Soc. (pres. 1980, 88), Renaissance Soc. Am. (rep. for English to coun. 1991-93), [illegible] 2004—), Shakespeare Assn., Chaucer Soc., Phi Beta Kappa. Home: 2525 E 8th St Bloomington IN 47408-4214 Office: Ind U Dept English Bloomington IN 47405 Office Phone: 812-855-8224.

ANDERSON, KAREN MILDRED, music educator; b. Chgo., July 30, 1944; d. Kenneth Axel and Mildred Anneta Anderson. BA, Trinity Internat. U., Deerfield, Ill., 1966; MusM, No. Ill. U., 1972. Editor, arranger J.C. Deagan, Inc., Chgo., 1964—68; tchr. Marquardt Dist. # 15, Glendale Heights, Ill., 1966—95, Rockford (Ill.) Christian Sch., 1995—. Accompanist Glenbard No. H.S., Carol Stream, Ill., 1968—94; accompnaist, singer Pedagogues, Delta Kappa Gamma, Dupage County, Ill., 1975—85; tchr. music and drama camp Cedar Lake (Ind.) Christian Conf. Ctr., 1985—96; singer Jack Schrader Singers, Wheaton, 1980—92. Organist Wheaton (Ill.) E.F. Ch., 1971—95, 1st Evang. Free Ch. Rockford, 1995—. Named Alumna of Yr., Trinity Internat. U., 2000. Mem.: Music Educators Nat. Conf., Delta Kappa Gamma. Republican. Evangelical. Avocations: reading, embroidery, travel. Office: Rockford Christian Sch 220 Hemlock Rockford IL 61107 Office Phone: 815-391-8006.

ANDERSON, KATHRYN D. surgeon; b. Ashton-Under-Lyne, Lancashire, Eng., Mar. 14, 1939; came to U.S., 1961; m. French Anderson, June 24, 1961. BA, Cambridge (Eng.) U., 1961, MA, 1964; MD, Harvard U., 1964. Diplomate Am. Bd. Surgery with cert. in spl. competence in pediat. surgery. Intern in pediat. Children's Hosp., Boston, 1964-65; resident in surgery Georgetown U. Hosp., Washington, 1965-69, chief resident in surgery, 1969-70, attending surgeon, 1972-74; chief resident in pediat. surgery Children's Hosp., Washington, 1970-72, sr. attending surgeon, 1974-92, surgeon-in-chief L.A., 1992—; vice chmn. surgery George Washington U., Washington, 1984-92. Prof. surgery U. So. Calif. Fellow: ACS (sec. 1992—2001, first v.p. 2001—02), Royal Coll. Surgeons (Eng.); mem.: Soc. Univ. Surgeons, Am. Surg. Assn., Am. Pediat. Surg. Assn. (sec. 1988—91, pres. 1999—2000), Am. Acad. Pediat. (sec. surg. sect. 1982—85, chmn. 1985—86). Avocations: opera, yoga. Office: Childrens Hosp 4650 W Sunset Blvd Los Angeles CA 90027-6062

ANDERSON, KERRII B. food service executive; b. 1957; BS, Elon Coll., 1978; MBA, Duke U., 1987. CPA. With Peat, Marwick, Mitchell & Co., Greensboro, N.C., 1978-84, RJ Reynolds Corp., Winston-Salem, N.C., 1984-85, Key Co., Greensboro, N.C., 1985-87; sr. v.p., CFO, chmn. bd. M/I Schottenstein Homes Inc., Columbus, 1987—2000; exec. v.p., CFO Wendy's Internat., Dublin, Ohio, 2000—, also bd. dirs. Bd. dirs. The Lancaster Colony Corp., M/I Schottenstein Homes, Inc. Mem. fin. com. The Columbus Found.; bd. mem. Grant-Riverside Hosp.; mem. dean's adv. com. Fisher Coll. Bus., Ohio State U. Office: Wendys Internat Inc One Dave Thomas Blvd Dublin OH 43017*

ANDERSON, KRISTIE, construction company executive; b. Ringgold, Georgia, May 18, 1977; d. James Morris and Deborah Sue A. Student, Dalton State Coll. Sec., office mgr. Anderson Construction & Home Bldg., Rossville, Georgia, 1993-99; owner Kristie M. Anderson Home Bldg., Rossville, 1995—. Mem. Home Builder Assn. Republican. Avocations: art, reading. Home: 237 Meadowview Ln Ringgold GA 30736-2657 Office: Kristi M Anderson Home Bldg 140 Anderson Ln Rossville GA 30741-4682

ANDERSON, KRISTINE JO, librarian; b. Aug. 1, 1945; d. Elvin Cornelius and Hilda Ellen A. MLS, U. Oreg., 1969; PhD in Comparative Lit., SUNY, Binghamton, 1983. Libr. Northeastern U., Boston, 1971-78; indexer MLA, N.Y.C., 1984-86; libr. N.Y.C. Pub. Libr., 1986-88; bibliographer for English and theatre Purdue U., W. Lafayette, Ind., 1988—. Contbr. articles to profl. jours. Mem. ALA, Soc. Utopian Studies, MLA Office: Humanities Soc Sci Edn Library Purdue U Stewart Ctr West Lafayette IN 47906 E-mail: kanderso@purdue.edu.

ANDERSON, LAURIE MONNES, state representative; b. Coronado, Calif., Dec. 31, 1945; 2 children. BA, Willamette U., 1968; MA, U. Colo., 1972; BSN, Radford U., 1982. Rsch. biologist, 1972—78; pub. health nurse, 1982—; supr. pub. health nurse, 1991—; mem. Oreg. Ho. of Reps., 2000—. Mem. budget com. Gresham-Barlow Sch. Dist., 1991—; mem. Healthy Start of Clackamas County, 1994—; mem. adv. coun. Oreg. Child Abuse Assessment. Mem.: Oreg. Sch. Bd. Assn. (dir. 1996—). Democrat. Office: 900 Court St North East H-390 Salem OR 97301

ANDERSON, LINDA JEAN, critical care nurse, psychiatric nurse practitioner; b. Louisville, Ky., Mar. 28, 1956; d. James Phillip and Ellabelle Jean (Crowder) Anderson; children: Bradley, Vanessa, Frances, Joseph; m. Donald W. Goodman. BSN, U. Louisville, 1989, MSN, 2000. ARNP, Ky., Ind. Staff nurse Audubon Regional Med. Ctr., Louisville, 1989-90; nurse clinician Vis. Nurses Assn. Louisville, 1990-95; staff nurse Southwest Hosp., Louisville, 1990-2000; rsch. coord. electrophysiology-cardiology U. Louisville, 1993-94; staff nurse Ctr. for Behavioral Health Bapt. East Hosp., 1996-2000; psychiat. clin. coord. U. Louisville Healthcare Univ. Hosp., 2000—02; pvt. practice Rose Island Counseling & Cons., Prospect, Ky., 2002—, Pk. View Psychiat. Svc., Jeffersonville, Ind., 2002—. Mem. alumni bd. govs. U. Louisville Sch. Nursing, 1988-97. Mem. Am. Psychiat. Nurses Assn., Sigma Theta Tau. Avocations: watercolor painting, charcoal & pencil sketching, poetry, flute. Home: PO Box 21694 Louisville KY 40221

ANDERSON, LYNN (RENE ANDERSON), singer; b. Grand Forks, N.D., Sept. 26, 1947; d. Casey and Liz Anderson; m. Glenn Sutton (div.); 1 child, Lisa; m. Harold Stream III (div.); children: Gray, Melissa. Singer, rec. artist, 1966—; appeared on Lynn Anderson Spls. Appearances on Lawrence Welk Show, 1967-70, Grand Old Opry, 1967, Ed Sullivan Show, Bob Hope Spls., Starsky and Hutch, (NBC Movie of the Week); TV guest appearances L. Frank Baum's The Marvelous Land of Oz, 1981, Country Gold, 1982, Law and Order, 1991, XXX's and OOO's, 1994, Babylon 5, 1994; rec. artist: (songs) I Never Promised You a Rose Garden, Cry, Listen to a Country Song, Your're My Man, Top of the World, Rocky Top, (albums) Encore, Under the Boardwalk, Greatest Hits, Rose Garden, What She Does Best, 1988, (duet with Gary Morris) You're Welcome to Tonight, 1983, What She Does Best, 1988, Country Spotlight, 1991, (with Emmylou Harris and Marty Stuart) Cowboys' Sweetheart, 1992; discs include Latest and Greatest, 1998, Anthology: The Columbia Years, 1999, Anthology: The Chart Years, 1999, Live at Billy Bob's Texas, 2000. Recipient Grammy award; named Female Artist of the Decade by Record World, 1971, Best Female Vocalist, CMA Awards, Most Promising, Best Female Vocalist, Acad. Country Music Awards, Best Country Performance-Female, People's Choice awards. Office: Buddy Lee Attractions 38 Music Sq E Nashville TN 37203-4304

ANDERSON, MABEL M. state legislator; b. Fall River, Mass., Mar. 25, 1924; m. George Anderson. BS, Mass. State Coll., Bridgewater, 1946; postgrad., Brown U., 1960. Instr. English, Pawtucket, R.I.; mem. R.I. Ho. of Reps., Providence, 1983—. Spkr. pro tem R.I. Ho. of Reps., mem. agrl. lands preservation commn. Trustee Pawtucket Pub. Libr., 1962-73. Recipient Corning award for Cmty. Svc., 1966. Mem. Pawtucket Women's Club (past pres.), Gen. Fed. Women's Clubs, Quality Hill Neighborhood Assn Democrat. Home: 26 South St Pawtucket RI 02860-4314 Office: RI Senate State Capitol Providence RI 02903

ANDERSON, MARY ANN GRASSO, theater association executive; b. Rome, N.Y., Nov. 3, 1952; d. Vincent and Rose Mary (Pupa) Grasso; m. J. Wayne Anderson, Feb. 14, 2004. BA in Art History, U. Calif., Riverside, 1973; MLS, U. Oreg., 1974. Dir. Warner Rsch. Collection, Burbank, Calif., 1975-84; mgr. CBS TV/Docudrama, Hollywood, Calif., 1984-88; v.p., exec. dir. Nat. Assn. Theatre Owners, North Hollywood, Calif., 1988—; CEO, R/C Theatres. Instr. theatre arts UCLA, 1980-85, Am. Film Inst., L.A., 1983-88. Screen credits: [illegible] Silent Lovers, A Bunnies Tale, [illegible] commr. Burbank Heritage Commn. Recipient Friend award, Tripod Sch., 1999, Stace award, Dolby, 2002, Intersoc. Ken Mason award, 2004. Mem.: Found. of the Motion Picture Pioneers, Acad. Motion Picture Arts and Scis., Retinitis Pigmentosa Internat. (The Vision award 1996), Bus. and Profl. Women's Assn. (Woman of Achievement award 1983), Phi Beta Kappa. Democrat. Avocations: traditional music and dance, environmental activities, tennis, yoga. Office: Nat Assn Theatre Owners 750 1st St NE Ste 1130 Washington DC 20002

ANDERSON, MARY ELIZABETH, protection services official; b. Flint, Mich., Sept. 12, 1949; d. Buford Herbert and Florence Mary (DuPrey) A. AB, U. Mich. Flint, 1976. Lic. social worker, Mich. From residence dir. to cmty. affairs dir. YWCA Greater Flint, 1977-84; dep., sgt. Genesee County Sheriff Dept., Flint, 1984-96, lt., 1996—. Mem. Criminal Justice Women of Mich. (award 1995), Planned Parenthood USA, So. Poverty Law Ctr., Hope United Meth. Ch., U. Mich. Alumni Assn. Home: 3926 Arlene Ave Flint MI 48532-5263 Office: Genesee County Sheriff Dept 1002 S Saginaw St Flint MI 48502-1410 E-mail: manderson91@comcast.net.

ANDERSON, MARY JANE, public library consultant; b. Des Moines, Jan. 23, 1935; d. William Kenneth and Margaret Louise (Snider) McPherson; m. Charles Robert Anderson, Oct. 21, 1965 (div. Oct. 24, 1989); 1 child, Mary Margaret. BA in Edn., U. Fla., 1957; MLS, Fla. State U., 1963. Elem. sch. librarian Dade County Schs., Miami, Fla., 1957-61; children's/young adult librarian Santa Fe Regional Library, Gainesville, Fla., 1961-63; br. librarian Jacksonville (Fla.) Pub. Library, 1963-64, chief of children's services, 1964-66, head of circulation, 1966-67; pub. library cons. Fla. State Library, Tallahassee, 1967-70; dir. tech. processing St. Mary's Coll. of Md., St. Mary's City, 1970-72; coordinator children's services Balt. County Pub. Library, Towson, Md., 1972-73; exec. dir. young adult services div. ALA, Chgo., 1973-75, exec. dir. assn. for library service to children, 1973-82; pres. Answers Unltd., Inc., Deerfield, Ill., 1982-92; dir. Wilmington (Ill.) Pub. Libr., 1993-97; dir. media svcs. Newark (Ill.) County Sch. Dist., 1997-98; dir. Maud P. Palenske Pub. Libr., St. Joseph, Mich., 1998-2000; coord. Sr. Net Learning Ctr., Ariea IV Agy. Aging, St. Joseph, 2000—03; libr. cons., 2000—. Instr. and cons. in field; part-time faculty No. Ill. U., 1985-86, Nat. Coll. Edn., Evanston, Ill., 1989; head youth svcs. Waukegan (Ill.) Pub. Libr., 1988-93; mem. exec. com. U.S. sect. Internat. Bd. on Books for Young People, 1973-82; mem. adv. bd. Reading Rainbow, TV series, 1981-84; mem. sch. bd. Avoca Sch. Dist. 37, 1985-87; mem. ALSC Newbery Medal Com., 1991. Editor: Top of the News, 1971-73, Fla. State Library Newsletter, 1967-70, Nor'Easter (North Suburban Library System Newsletter), 1984-88; contbr. articles to profl. jours. Bd. dirs. Child Devel. Assocs. Consortium, 1975—83, Coalition for Children and Youth, 1978—80; mem. City of Wilmington Downtown Redevel. Commn., 1996—98; with Episcopal Diocese Chgo. Diocesan Coun., 1988—94, standing com., 1994—97, dep. to gen. conv., 1997; mem. Bishop's search com., 1997—98; province V rep., 1998—99; mem. vestry St. Thomas' Episcopal Ch., Morris, Ill., 1996—98; with Episcopal Diocese West, Mich.; mem. Diocesan cons. team, 1999—, alt. dep. to gen. conv., 2003—; deanery rep. St. Paul's Episc. Ch., St. Joseph, Mich., 2000—01, lay eucharistic min., 1999—, mem. vestry, 2003—. Mem. ALA (coun. 1992-2000, com. on orgn. 1999-01), Rotary (sec.-treas. 1994-96, pres. 1996-97), Wilmington C. of C. (bd. dirs. 1996-97, sec. 1997), Caxton Club (Chgo.), Beta Phi Mu, Sigma Kappa. Episcopalian.

ANDERSON, MARY JANE, music educator; b. St. Louis, Oct. 9, 1954; d. William Edward and Katherine Ruth Anderson. Student, The Juilliard Sch., 1967—72; BFA in Piano Performance, Stephens Coll., 1976; MM in Piano Performance, So. Ill. U., Edwardsville, 1991. Piano faculty St. Louis Conservatory and Schs. for the Arts, St. Louis, 1977—81, So. Ill. U., Edwardsville, 1984—; pvt. piano instr. St. Louis, 1975—. Adjudicator state and local piano competitions, Mo. and Ill.; soloist St. Louis Symphony, St. Louis Philharmonic; recitalist, orchestral soloist numerous performances throughout Midwest U.S., Pa, NY. Recipient 1st pl. Profl. Debut Recital, Artist Presentation Soc., 1975, 1st pl. Dimitri Mitropoulos Nat. Piano Competition, Stephens Coll., 1972, scholarship winner, Dimitri Mitropoulos Piano Competition; scholar Piano scholarship, Am. Acad. Arts in

Europe, 1975. Mem.: St. Louis Area Music Tchrs. Assn. (pres. 2002—), Mo. Music Tchrs. Assn., Music Tchrs. Nat. Assn. Avocations: reading, fishing, crossword puzzles. Office: So Ill U Edwardsville Music Dept PO Box 1771 Edwardsville IL 62026-1771 Office Phone: 618-650-2022. Business E-Mail: manders@siue.edu.

ANDERSON, MIKKI MELINDA, massage therapist, small business owner; b. Vallejo, Calif., Feb. 17, 1949; d. John Sinclair and Margaret (Beam) Abbott; m. Michael Conroy, 1967 (div. 1971); m. Michael Anderson. Student, Western Wash. State U.; AA, Green River C.C., Auburn, Wash.; student, Holistic Hands Massage Clinic, Laguna Hills, Calif., Utah Myotherapy Inst., Salt Lake City. Lic. massage therapist; Holistic health practitioner. Owner Stressbusters Massage Co., Laguna Hills, Calif., 1982—. Mem. Nat. Emergency Response team, Calif., 1997. Mem. Internat. Massage Assn., Nat. Assn. Pregnancy Massage Therapists (officer). Republican. Avocations: travel, cooking, exercise, interior design. Home: 6 Windhaven Pl Aliso Viejo CA 92656-3303 Office: Ste D 26548 Moulton Pkwy Laguna Hills CA 92653-6200

ANDERSON, MONICA LUFFMAN, school librarian, educator, real estate broker; b. Ramsgate, Kent, U.K., Sept. 28, 1914; arrived in U.S., 1952; d. Percy Victor Luffman and Rosalind Dismorr; m. Howard Richmond Anderson, Dec. 22, 1951 (dec.); children: Monica Jane, James Stewart. BA in English with honors, London U., 1936; MS in Libr. Sci., Simmons Coll., 1968; EdM in Ednl. Media, Boston U., 1970. Evacuation officer London Borough of Acton, 1940—41; dir. Coun. for Edn. in World Citizenship, London, 1941—47; from asst. to head of sect. with diplomatic status UNESCO, Paris, 1947—50; H.S. libr. Holliston, Mass., 1968—70; coord. libr. svcs. Lincoln-Sudbury (Mass.) Regional H.S., 1970—81; real estate broker Coldwell Banker Residential Brokerage, Wayland, Mass., 1982—. Author brochures. Troop leader Girl Scouts Am., Weston, Mass., 1963—65; tutor in English Laotian Refugees, Weston, Mass., 1981—82, Literacy Unltd., Framingham, Mass., 1998—. Democrat. Avocations: gardening, reading, Boston Annual Walk for Hunger. Home: 2214 Heatherwood at Kings Way Yarmouth Port MA 02675 Office: Coldwell Banker Resdl Brokerage 311 Boston Post Rd Wayland MA 01778

ANDERSON, NANCI LOUISE, computer analyst; b. Lynchburg, Va., Sept. 21, 1944; d. Ashby Littleton and Louise Elvin (Kirby) Marsh; 1 child, Toni Lynn Nelson. AAS in Computer Sci., Ctrl. Tex. Coll., 1983, AAS in Microcomputer Tech., 1985, BA Computer Programming, 2001. Real estate salesperson Blake Isley Real Estate, Lynchburg, Va., 1974; sec. U.S. Army, Germany, 1975-80; office mgr. Am. Solar Energy Soc., Killeen, Tex., 1981-82; programmer BDM, West Fort Hood, Tex., 1982-87; analyst, programmer PRC, Inc., West Fort Hood, Tex., 1987—96; sys. mgr. Maden Tech Consulting, 1996—. Mem. Clipper User's Group. Avocations: reading, swimming, horseback riding, walking. Home: 1202 Royal Crest Dr Killeen TX 76549-1071 Office: Maden Tech Cons USA OTC Network Ops Ctr Fort Hood TX 76544

ANDERSON, NANCY KEECH, music educator; b. Canton, NY, Mar. 19, 1945; d. Harold and Dorothy Wilson Keech; m. Jack Kirk Anderson; children: Roy, Cheryl, Serena, Keil. BA cum laude, Kalamazoo Coll., 1967; MS, U. Ill., Champaign, 1968. Cert. K-12 music tchg. and supervision Ill., Early Childhood Music Gordon Inst. for Music Learning, Level One Orff Assn. of Am. Tchr. Champaign (Ill.) Pub. Schs., 1968—72; faculty Anderson (Ind.) U., Anderson, 1978—89; tchr., k-5 music Cahokia (Ill.) Pub. Schs.; music and movement tchr. So. Ill. U., Suzuki String Devel. Program, Edwardsville; ctr. dir. and tchr. Music Together of Metro East, Edwardsville; dir. Masterworks Childrens Chorus, Belleville, Ill., 2000—. Clinician StarNet, Chgo. Pub. Schs.; ch. organist and choir dir. Zion Luth. Ch., Huron, Ohio, 1972—77, United Meth. Ch., Carlinville, Ill., 1989—91; choir dir. First Bapt. Ch., Edwardsville, Ill., 1991—2000; guest lectr. So. Ill. U., Edwardsville, Ill., Millikin U., Decatur, Ill.; clinician Riverview Gardens Early Childhood Ctr., St. Louis, St. Louis C.C., St. Louis, Brain Devel. Clinic, Children's Home and Aid Soc., Granite City, Ill., Ill. Resource Ctr., Des Plaines, Ill. Contbr. articles to profl. music jours. Recipient Golden Apple award, St. Clair County, Ill., 1995. Mem.: Ind.Elem. Music Educators Assn. (pres. 1987—89), Suzuki Assn. Ams. (clinician, nat. conf., Mpls. 2002), Music Educators Nat. Conf., Am. Choral Dirs. Assn., Gordon Inst. for Music Learning, Pi Kappa Lambda, Mu Phi Epsilon, Phi Beta Kappa. Home: 16 Dogwood Ln Glen Carbon IL 62034 Personal E-mail: mcc@apci.net.

ANDERSON, NORMA V. state legislator; b. Elyria, Ohio, July 6, 1932; Student, Denver U., Jones Real Estate Coll. Owner, operator KBJ Stables; office mgr. Capitol Solar; supr. Time, Inc.; mem. Colo. Ho. of Reps., Dist. 30, 1986-98; house majority leader; mem. Colo. Senate, Dist. 22, Denver, 1998—; senate majority leader, chair bus. affairs and labor com., mem. edn. com.; mem. legis. audit com., mem. local govt. com. Mem. State Adv. Coun. on Labor Dept., State Compensation Bd., Regional Transp. Dist. Bd. Vice-chair Health Environ. Welfare Insts.; bd. dirs. Foothills Found.; mem. budget com. R-1 Sch. Dist. Mem. Nat. Conf. State Legislatures (energy and transp. com. chair), West Chamber (bd. mem.), Am. Cancer Soc., Edn. 2000, Bear Creek Jr. Sports Assn. Republican. Office: State Capitol 200 E Colfax Ave Ste 263 Denver CO 80203-1716 E-mail: norma.anderson.senate@state.co.us.

ANDERSON, PAMELA, actress; b. Ladysmith, Can., July 1, 1967; d. Barry and Carol Anderson; m. Tommy Lee, 1995 (div. 1998); children: Brandon Thomas Lee, Dylan Jagger Lee. Syndicated columnist Jane, 2002—, Marie Claire, 2002—, Can. Elle, 2002—; launched clothing line "The Pamela Collection", 2003—. Actor: (TV series) Home Improvement, 1991—93, Baywatch, 1992—97; actor, exec. prodr.: (TV series) V.I.P., 1998; actor(voice): Stripperella, 2003—, : (TV films) Baywatch: River of No Return, 1992, Come Die with Me: A Mickey Spillane Mike Hammer Mystery, 1994, Baywatch: Forbidden Paradise, 1995, Naked Souls, 1996, Baywatch: Hawaiian Wedding, 2003, (guest appearances): (TV series) Charles in Charge, 1990, Married...with Children, 1990, 1991, Top of the Heap, 1991, Days of Our Lives, 1992, The Nanny, 1997, Home Improvement, 1997, Just Shoot Me, 2001, Less Than Perfect, 2002, (guest appearances, voice) Futurama, 1999, : (films) Snapdragon, 1993, Raw Justice, 1994, Naked Souls, 1995, Barb Wire, 1996, Scary Movie 3, 2003, (music videos for) Aerosmith, Lit, Cinderella, Vince Neil, Bree Sharp, Methods of Mayhem, Jaz-Z, Kid Rock. Activist PETA; participant Nat. Conf. Viral Hepatitis, Can. Liver Found.; founder Pamela Anderson Found.; grand marshall S.O.S. ride Am. Liver Found., 2002. Recipient Linda McCartney award for animal rights, 1999. Achievements include has appeared a record twelve times on the cover of Playboy. Office: William Morris Agy 151 El Camino Dr Beverly Hills CA 90212*

ANDERSON, PATRICIA SUE, writer; b. San Springs, Okla., July 14, 1940; d. John Monroe and Annabelle A. BA in Psychology, Okla. State U., 1963. Co-owner, CEO River's West Prodns. CEO River's Bend Literary Agy., Cleveland, Okla., 1984-99. Author: Organizational Handbook, 1985, Campaign Organization, 1990, Getting Women to Participate, 1991; (screenplays) Nightmares Do Come True, Desert Conspiracy, Mriqtrishna; (novels) A Cold Wind in August, Surviving Toxic Parents. Democrat. Methodist. Home and Office: RR 1 Box 272 Cleveland OK 74020-9723 E-mail: pande86245@aol.com.

ANDERSON, PEGGY REES, accountant; b. Casper, Wyo., Sept. 8, 1958; d. John William and Pauline Marie (Harris) Rees; m. Steven R. Anderson, May 26, 1984 (div. Sept. 1990). BS in Acctg. with honors, U. Wyo., 1980. CPA. Audit staff to sr. Price Waterhouse, Denver, 1980-84; asst. contr. to contr. Am. Investments, Denver, 1984-88; cons. ADI Residential, Denver, 1988-89; contr., treas. Plante Properties, Inc., Denver, 1989-92; acctg. mgr. Woodward-Clyde Group, Inc., Denver, 1992-96; internat. fin. mgr. USWest, Inc., Denver, 1996-98, Media One Group, Denver, 1998—2000; internat. fin. cons. Orica Inc., Denver, 2001—02; internat. acctg. coord. Newmont Mining Corp., Denver, 2003—04; assoc. mgr. Great-West Healthcare, Denver, 2004— Diving scholar U. Wyo., 1976-78. Mem. Colo. Soc. CPAs. Roman Catholic. Avocations: skiing, swimming, aerobics, needlepoint, golf.

ANDERSON, RACHAEL KELLER, retired library administrator; b. N.Y.C., Jan. 15, 1938; d. Harry and Sarah Keller; m. Howard D. Goldwyn; children: Rebecca Anderson, Michael Goldwyn, Bryan Goldwyn, David Goldwyn. AB, Barnard Coll., 1959; MS, Columbia U., 1960. Librarian CCNY, 1960-62; librarian Mt. Sinai Med. Ctr., N.Y.C., 1964-73, dir. library, 1973-79; dir. Health Scis Libr. Columbia U., N.Y.C., 1979-91, acting v.p., univ. libr., 1982; dir. Ariz. Health Scis. Libr., U. Ariz., Tucson, 1991-2001; assoc. dir. Ariz. Telemedicine Program, 1996—2001; ret., 2001. Bd. dirs. Med. Libr. Ctr. of N.Y., N.Y.C., 1983-91; mem. biomed. libr. rev. com. Nat. Libr. Medicine, Bethesda, Md., 1984-88, chmn., 1987-88; mem. bd. regents Nat. Libr. Medicine, 1990-94, chmn., 1993-94; pres. Ariz. Health Info. Network, 1995. Contbr. articles to profl. jours. Mem. Med. Libr. Assn. (pres.-elect 1996-97, pres. 1997-98, bd. dirs. 1983-86, 98-99), Assn. Acad. Health Scis. Libr. Dirs. (bd. dirs. 1983-86, 90-93, pres. 1991-92). E-mail: rachaela@ahsl.arizona.edu.

ANDERSON, RACHEL LYN, behavior researcher; b. Sacramento, Calif., Apr. 9, 1955; d. Melvin and Regina (Viteri) A.; m. Ralph Everett Dodson, Oct. 19, 1985 (div. July 1990). BA, Calif. State U., Sacramento, 1988. Drug treatment counselor The Effort, Sacramento, 1980-88, Sierra Family Svcs., Roseville, Calif., 1988-89; staff rsch. assoc. U. Calif., Davis, 1989—. Project developer The Lindesmith Ctr. Eastern Europe. Contbr. chpt. to book. Mem. bd. dirs. Harm Reducation Svcs., Sacramento, 1993-2000, Mending, 1994-96; adminstr. Sacramento Area Needle Exchg., 1993—; County Pub. Health adv. bd., 1996-2002. Democrat. Avocations: gardening, theater, reading, travel, listening to music. Home: 8015 Freeport Blvd Sacramento CA 95832-9702 Office: U Calif Davis 4150 V St # 500 Sacramento CA 95817-2214

ANDERSON, ROBERTA JOAN See MITCHELL, JONI

ANDERSON, ROBIN MARIE, secondary school educator; b. Blue Island, Ill., Apr. 18, 1965; d. Donald Albert Anderson and Rosemary (Campbell) King. BA in English, No. Ill. U., DeKalb, 1988; MEd, U. North Tex., Denton, 1997. Cert. tchr. secondary edn., English, reading, Tex.; cert. libr., Tex. Tchr. English North Garland (Tex.) H.S., 1990-92, Lakeview Centennial H.S., Garland, 1992-93; tchr. reading Nimitz H.S., Irving, Tex., 1993-99; 8th grade reading tchr. Bowman Middle Sch., Plano, Tex., 1999—2002; libr. media specialist Ford Middle Sch., Allen, Tex., 2002—. Attendance policy violators com., student vol. svc. hour com. Nimitz H.S.; prin.'s coun. Bowman Mid. Sch., Allen, Tex., safety coun. Chmn. adv. bd. Irving C.A.R.E.S., 1995; sponsor Cultural Awareness Soc., Irving, 1995-96, Jr. Historians, Irving, 1994—; co-sponsor Bowman Raiders Are Great (BRAG); mem. Safety Coun., Bowman; mem. Bowman Reads Com. Recipient High Spirited Citizen award Irving Conv. and Visitors Bur., 1996. Mem. ASCD, Internat. Reading Assn., Assn. Tex. Profl. Educators, Tex. Assn. for Improvement of Reading (conf. spkr. 1995). Republican. Avocations: reading, music, environmental issues, aerobics, movies. Office: Ford Middle Sch 630 Park Pl Allen TX 75002

ANDERSON, ROSE L. DYESS, elementary school educator, poet; b. Laurel, Miss., Dec. 24, 1941; d. James Lamar and Mildred Josephine (Moore) Dyess; m. Rushel Talmadge Anderson, May 13, 1965; 1 child, Joel Alan. BE, William Carey Coll., Hattiesburg, Miss., 1964; grad., Univ. So. Miss., Hattiesburg, Miss. Elem. tchr. Natchez-Adams Pub. Sch., Natchez, Miss., 1968—. Author: (poetry) Lifes Fleeting Days, 1996, The Winds of Change Keep on Blowing, 1997. Facilitator numerous workshops and conf. within dist., Miss. Early Childhood Conf, Summer Math and Sci. Conf., Miss. Univ. for Women; mentor tchr. for numerous student tchrs. Alcorn State Univ., Univ. So. Miss. Nominee Disney Tchr of the Yr., 1995; recipient Golden Apple award, Covington Rd. Ch. of Christ, Miss., 1996, Tchr. of the Yr., Frazier Primary Sch., Miss., 2002. Mem.: Miss. Edn. Assn., Nat. Libr. of Poetry, Alpha Delta Kappa (chaplin, treas., historian). Republican. Ch. Of Christ. Achievements include design of and edited a children's activity page for a religious newspaper, The Magnolia Messenger; movtivantional spkr. for ch. ladies day activites. Avocations: writing, painting, interior decorating, gardening, travel. Home: 505 Lindberg Ave Natchez MS 39120 Office: Frazier Primary Sch 1445 George F West Blvd Natchez MS 39120

ANDERSON, ROSE MARIE, insurance agent; b. Leonville, La., Aug. 10, 1945; d. Napoleon Badeaux and Marie Leonie Rivette; m. Earl William Anderson, Oct. 9, 1965; children: William Christopher, Charles Terrence. AS in Bus. adminstrn., T.H. Harris Tech. Coll., Opelousas, La., 1965. Claims clk. Dwight W. Andrus Ins. Agy., Lafayette, La., 1968-72; personal lines customer svc. rep. Trinity Universal Ins. Co., Lafayette, 1972-75; comml. lines underwriter CAR Ins. Agy., Alexandria, La., 1989-90; comml. lines CSR Jim Thomasee Ins. Agy., Alexandria, 1990-93; comml. underwriter B&S Underwriters, Inc., Alexandria, 1993-99. Bd. dirs. Horse Helping the Handicapped, Pineville, La., 1989-94. Mem. Nat. Assn. Ins. Women, Ctrl. La. Claims Assn., Lions (sec. Alexandria 1997-98, pres. 1989-99, zone chmn., Lion of Yr. award 1997). Home: 99 Ragan Dr Alexandria LA 71303-2264

ANDERSON, ROSLYN, newscaster; Grad., So. U., 1986. With WVSB-TV (not WLOV), West Point, Miss.; weather anchor, reporter WROK-TV, Meridian, WLBT, Jackson, 1993—. Recipient Weekend Weathercast award, Miss. Associated Press, 1996. Mem.: Delta Sigma Theta. Methodist. Office: WLBT 715 S Jefferson Jackson MS 39201

ANDERSON, RUTH ILENE MONIER, music educator; b. Peoria, Ill., Oct. 15, 1953; d. Ralph Leland and Ilene Ellen (Steffens) Monier; m. Craig Michael Anderson, July 14, 1979; children: Christopher, Bjorn. BA, St. Olaf Coll., 1975. Cert. coach Mankato State U., 1975. Tchr. music Lowpoint-Washburn Unit Dist., Washburn, Ill., 1975—76, Barron Area Schs., Wis., 1976—. Owner restaurant County Seat, Barron, 2003—; mem. resiliency com. Barron Area Schs., 1998—, mem. core planning team-vision com., strategic planning com., 2002—; cons. Local theaters Wis., 2002—; dir. music Am. Legion and Aux., Green Bay, Wis., 2003. Composer (musical): Mary's Story, 1988, Norsk Jul, 1994, Who Snuffed Vinny, 2001; composer: (play) To Have and To Hold, 2000. Mem.: Barron Federated Music Club (past pres.), Northwest United Educators, Wis. Music Educators Assn., Barron C. of C. (promotion chmn. 1995—), Phi Delta Kappa. Lutheran. Avocations: reading, hiking, travel, skiing. Home: 1461 16th St Barron WI 54812*

ANDERSON, RUTH LUCILLE, interior designer, educator, artist, librarian, archivist; b. Cyprus Hills, N.Y. d. Arthur Albert and Marie Rose (Weston) Buehler; m. Gunnar Bohlin Anderson; children: Anna Kristine Kornblatt, Deborah Val. Grad., N.Y. Sch. Applied Design Women; Cert., N.Y. Sch. Interior Design; BA, Adelphi U., 1979, MA, 1981; postgrad., NYU, Nat. Acad. Sch. Fine Arts, 1987. Cert. pub. libr. N.Y., pub. libr. profl. cert. SUNY Edn. Dept., 2001, archives, qualified interior designer Nat. Coun. Interior Design Qualification. Fabric cons. F. Schumacher & Co., N.Y.C., 1954-60; sr. interior designer W&J Sloane, N.Y.C., 1960-83; adj. assoc. prof. Nassau C.C., 1979—, Adelphi U., 1980; instr. Hofstra U., 1990—; asst. to rsch. libr. Cradle Aviation, Mitchel Air Field, 1998—; libr. Planting Fields Libr., Oyster Bay, NY. Mem. faculty Parson (New Sch.), 1980-81; lectr. in field. Paintings and sculptures exhibited at W&J Sloane, Cold Springs Harbor, Oyster Bay Cove, Adelphi U. and 75 Varick St., N.Y.C., Garden City and Cold Spring Harbor Gallery, 1993, Planting Fields, Oyster Bay, N.Y., 2003. Mem. Nat. Trust Historic Preservation. Recipient Spl. participation award Open Door Program, N.Y.C.; named Partner in Edn. N.Y.C. Pub. Schs., 1991-92. Mem. Am. Soc. Interior Designers (profl. mem. 1976), Early Flyers.

ANDERSON, RUTH T. retired air traffic controller; b. Bartow, Fla., July 2, 1935; d. John Benjamin Thompson and Susan Ettie Scott; m. Malcolm Edward Jack Anderson; m. Perry Brannon, Jr. (div. Oct. 29, 1973); children: Glenda Brannon Parrish, Ronald Allen Brannon. AA Computer Acctg. Technology, SE Coll. of Tech., Mobile, Ala., 1992. Air traffic control specialist FAA, Dothan, Ala., Gulfport, Miss., Mobile, Ala., 1972—89, EEO investigator FAA, Atlanta, 1985—89. Methodist. Avocation: reading, writing, sewing and crafting, fishing. Home: 1983 Powell Tr Abbeville AL 36310

ANDERSON, RUTH YARNNELLE, real estate professional, educator; b. Celina, Ohio, Sept. 30, 1922; d. Dennis Sidney and Grace Yarnnelle (Reed) Springer; m. Orviel Willard Fallang, Sept. 2, 1944 (dec. 1970); children: Dennis Joseph, David James, Michelle Yarnnelle, Jennifer Leigh Fallang Bell; m. Nels Edvard Anderson Sr., June 15, 1972 (dec.). BS, Miami U., Oxford, Ohio, 1950; MEd, Ohio State U., 1954. Cert. tchr., Ohio; lic. realtor, Ohio. Tchr. Franklin County Schs., Columbus, Ohio, 1951-55, Kettering (Ohio) City Schs., 1955-60; real estate professional Crestmark Realtors, Dayton, 1977—. Sec., treas. Luth. JOY Group, Oakwood, Ohio, 1989—; pres. Ohio Vet. Med. Assn. Aux., 1969-70. With USN, 1942-45. Named Honorary Ky. Col. Commonwealth of Ky., 1985. Mem. AAUW, Nat. Soc. Hist. Preservation, Nat. Assn. Realtors, Ohio Assn. Realtors, Dayton Area Bd. Realtors, Ohio Hist. Soc., Rails to Trails Conservancy, Order Amaranth (conductress 1990, royal matron 1993-94), Order Ea. Star, Dayton Woman's Club, Dayton Horse Show Assn. (sec. 1983-88, bd. dirs. 1983—, chmn. advt. 1981—). Republican. Avocations: photography, travel, bowling, bicycling, reading. Home: 939 Brittany Hills Dr Dayton OH 45459-1520 Office: Crestmark Realtors 310 Dellwood Ave Dayton OH 45419-3523

ANDERSON, SALLY MIDGETTE, social services administrator, linguist; b. N.Y.C., Jan. 9, 1938; d. William Raymond and Charlotte Noyes Driver; m. Willard Franklin Midgette, May 27, 1961 (dec. Apr. 1978); children: Anne Leland, Alexander Dameron; m. Donald Bernard Anderson, Mar. 15, 1980. BA, Vassar Coll., 1960; MA in Tchg., Reed Coll., 1968; PhD, U. N.Mex., 1987. Pers. interviewer Harvard U., Cambridge, 1960-61; tchr., adminstr. St. Ann's Sch., Bklyn., 1975-80; rschr. U. N.Mex., Albuquerque, 1988-98; youth worker The Unity Ctr. for Teens, Roswell, N.Mex., 1995-2000, Boys' and Girls' Club, 2000—01. Adj. prof. U. N.Mex., 1988-98. Author: The Navajo Progressive in Discourse, 1995; editor: Athabaskan Language Studies, 1996; asst. Analytical Lexicon of Navajo, 1992. Bd. dirs. REACH 2000, Roswell, 1992-99, Boys'/Girls' Club, Roswell, Assurance Home, Roswell, 1998-2001; mem. vestry St. Andrew's Episc. Ch., 1999-2002; mem. N.Mex. Arts Commn., 2003. Recipient Excellence in the Humanities award N.Mex. Endowment for the Humanities, 1997, Svc. to Mankind award Roswell Sertoma Club, 1999, Ea. N.Mex. West Tex. Dist., 1999, Greater Rocky Mountain Region, 1999. Democrat. Episcopal. Avocation: choral singing. Home: 3600 La Joya Rd Roswell NM 88201-9108 Office: Anderson Offices 409 E College Blvd Roswell NM 88201-7524

ANDERSON, SARA, special education educator; b. Peoria, Ill., July 8, 1975; d. Royce William and Katherine Ann Farmer; m. David William Anderson, June 5, 1998; 1 child, Reece William. Elem. Edn., U. No. Iowa, Cedar Falls, 1998; postgrad., Drake U., Des Moines, Iowa. Cert. elementary educator K-6, mild/moderate mental disabilities K-6, mildly disabled K-6. Special class tchr. Johnston Cmty. Schs., Johnston, Iowa, 1999—. Philanthropy chairwoman Gamma Phi Beta, Cedar Falls, Iowa, 1996. Mem.: Johnston Edn. Assn., Nat. Edn. Assn., Iowa State Edn. Assn., Kappa Delta Pi. Lutheran. Avocations: singing in a Christian band, reading, listening to music. Office: Horizon Elem 5905 NW 100th St Johnston IA 50131 Home: 8824 Highland Oaks Dr Johnston IA 50131-2229

ANDERSON, SONDRA C. music educator; b. Miami, Fla., Apr. 15, 1961; d. Lowell and Cynthia M. Crawford; m. Grover Frank Carter, Jr., July 28, 1984 (div. June 1998); children: Sarah Carter, Joshua Carter; m. DuWayne Richard Anderson, June 10, 2000. MusB, U. Ga., Athens, 1983; M in Early Childhood Edn., Piedmont Coll., Demorest, Ga., 2001. Activities dir. Westminster Terrace, Louisville, 1984—87; pvt. voice and piano tchr. Livingston, Tenn., 1987—90, Winder, Ga., 1990—96; elem. music tchr. Barrow County Schs., Winder, Ga., 1996—; church pianist First Bapt. Ch., Winder, Ga., 1992—. Dir. Youth Praise Team, First Bapt. Ch., Winder, Ga., 2002—. Mem.: Ga. Assn. Educators, Ga. Music Educators Assn., Music Tchrs. Nat. Assn. Baptist. Avocations: reading, sewing, swimming, aerobics, gardening. Home: 564 Miles Patrick Rd Winder GA 30680 Office: Statham Elem Sch 1970 Broad St Statham GA 30666

ANDERSON, STACEY ANN, school psychologist; b. Crestline, Ohio, Mar. 4, 1964; d. James Edward Anderson, Sr. and Mary Jane (Vangeloff) Anderson. Postgrad., Walden U., 2004; MA in Psychology, U. W.Va. (now Marshall University), 1990; BS in Edn., Ashland Coll. (now Ashland U.), 1985. Cert. sch. psychologist Ariz., W.Va. Tchr. jr. h.s. sci. Crestview Local Schs., Ashland, Ohio, 1986—88; tutor Human Resource Bur., Mansfield, Ohio, 1987—88; substitute tchr. Kanawha & Jackson County Schs., Charleston, W.Va., 1988—90; counselor Sexual Assault Unit Family Svcs. Kanawha Valley, Charleston, W.Va., 1990; sch. psychologist Kanawha County Schs., Charleston, W.Va., 1990—91; sch. psychologist Yuma County Accommodation Sch. Dist. #99, Yuma, Ariz., 1995—2002; sch. psychologist Yuma Sch. Dist. 1, Yuma, Ariz., 1991—2002. Supr. interns Yuma Sch. Dist. 1, Yuma, 1994—2002. Mem. edn. com. Gila Mountain United Meth. Ch., Yuma, 2000—02; Bd. dirs. Learning Pad Presch., Yuma, 2000—02. Mem.: APA, Am. Psychol. Assn. Grad. Students, Nat. Assn. Sch. Psychologists, Psi Chi. Methodist. Avocations: travel, shopping, cars, biking, collecting. Office: Yuma Sch Dist 1 450 Sixth St Yuma AZ 85364

ANDERSON, SUSAN ELAINE MOSSHAMER, educational consultant, organization consultant, musician, mezzo soprano; b. Detroit, Mar. 29, 1946; d. Edgar Lee and Reta (McDonough) Mosshamer; m. Thomas Scott Anderson Jr., Nov. 1, 1975; children: Elizabeth Erin, Kirk William. MusB with honors, Mich. State U., 1967; MEd with high honors, Wayne State U., 1982. Profl. singer (mezzo), pianist and organist, 1968—; sch. choral music dir. grades 7-12, 1968-77; instrnl. designer, orgnl. devel. cons. Myers-Briggs Adminstr., Ednl. Rschr., 1982—; pres. Orgl. Strategies Ltd., Bloomfield Hills, Mich., 1995—2002. Collaborating author: The Challenge of Living, 1983, Death and Dying, 1996; award-winning tng. programs for Ill. Dept. Employment Security and Ford Motor Co. Vol. Roeper Sch., Bloomfield Hills, 1988-95, Cranbrook Schs., Bloomfield Hills, 1993-2002. Mem. ASCD, Problem-Based Learning Network, Assn. Psychol. Type, Mortar Board, Phi Kappa Phi. Avocations: skiing, reading, music. Home and Office: 1825 Reis Ct Rochester Hills MI 48309

ANDERSON, SUSAN STUEBING, business equipment company executive; b. Cin., Nov. 7, 1951; d. Edward Norman and Ruth Marcella Stuebing; m. Randall Anderson, 1988. BA, Western Ky. U., 1973, MA, 1975. Legis. aide U.S. Ho. of Reps., 1975-80; legis. cons. Harvard U., 1981; spl. asst. Nat. Telecommunications and Info. Adminstrn.-U.S. Dept. Commerce, Washington, 1981, dept. asst. sec., 1982-85, acting asst. sec. for communications and info., 1983; dir. Computer and Bus. Equipment Mfrs. Assn., Washington, 1985-86; mgr. govt. affairs Xerox Corp., Washington, 1987-92; mgr. investor svcs. Office of the Corp. Sec., Stamford, Conn., 1992—. Presbyterian. Office: Xerox Corp 800 Long Ridge Rd Stamford CT 06902-1288

ANDERSON, TESS, information technology manager, education educator; b. Port Arthur, Tex., Mar. 4, 1971; d. Charles Emmett and Carliss Darlene Beard; m. Scott Edward Anderson, Apr. 9, 1994; children: Hayden Judge, Avery Camille. BA English, Lamar U., Beaumont, Tex., 1993, MA English, 2000. Cert. Tech. Writer Lamar U., 1993. Adj. instr. english Lamar U., Beaumont, Tex., 2001—03; adj. instr. Angelina Coll., Lufkin, Tex., 2001—; ops. mgr. DynaSource, Inc., Beaumont, Tex., 2003—. Web developer St. Charles Cath. Ch., Nederland, Tex., 2000—. Contbr. articles to profl. jour. Educator St. Charles Cath. Ch., Nederland, Tex., 2001-03. Mem.: Soc. for Tech. Comm. Roman Cath. Avocations: reading, writing, exercising, scrapbooks, travel. Home: 617 Hardy Ave Nederland TX 77627

ANDERSON, THERESA A. retail executive; With First Union Nat. Bank, Lowe's Co. Inc., Wilkesboro, NC, 1986—, mgr.divsnl. merchandising, 1996—98, v.p. merchandising, 1998—99, v.p. store support, 1999—2000, sr. v.p. ops. and merchandising support, 2000—01, sr. v.p. merchandising sales and svc., 2001—. Office: Lowes Co Inc 1605 Curtis Bridge Rd Wilkesboro NC 28697*

ANDERSON, URSULA M. pediatrician; b. Cheshire, England, 1929; MB BS, Liverpool (Eng.) U., 1953, diploma in pub. health, 1956; diploma in psychol. medicine, London U., 1958; diploma in child health, Royal Coll. Physicians, London. Diplomate Am. Bd. Pediats. Intern and resident Liverpool United Tchg. Hosps., 1953—57; fellow dept. pediatrics Yale U., New Haven, 1960—63; assoc. prof. pediats. SUNY, Buffalo; dir. maternal and child health Buffalo/Erie County; med. dir. interagy. programs for children, regional med. cons. U.S. Dept. Health, Edn. and Welfare; chief divsn. cmty. pediats., assoc. prof. pediats U. Toronto, Canada; disting. prof., rsch. prof. Forest Inst. Profl. Psychology. Cons. divsn-rsch. WHO, Geneva; cons. Nat. Perinatal Assn., National and Regional Head Start Programs; chmn. N.Y. State Task Force on Health Manpower, Albany, NY; mem. pediat. delegation to USSR People to People. Author: Reading Instruction, Dimensions and Issues, 1968, Weeds and Seedlings, 1991, The Psalms of Children, Their Songs and Laments, 1997, Immunology of the Soul, The Paradigm for the Future, 2000, Taking Out the Violence, 2003; contbr. numerous articles to profl. jours. Recipient Merit of Excellence award, UN Open U.; grantee numerous grants for rsch. edn. and svc., U.S. and Can. Fellow: Am. Acad. Pediats.; mem.: Royal Coll. Surgeons. Mailing: 8275 Crumb Hill Rd East Otto NY 14729-9748

ANDERSON, VICKI, retired librarian; b Hazleton, Pa., June 17, 1928; d. Steven and Edith Potochney; m. Richard Anderson. BA, San Diego State Coll., 1961; MLS, U. Calif., Berkeley, 1962; postgrad., U. Pa., 1985—86. Libr. San Diego City Pub. Libr., 1962—64, San Diego City Schs., 1965—90; ret., 1991. Mem. Calif. State Coun. Edn., San Francisco, 1968—71, San Diego Citizen Adv. Com., 1978; spkr. San Diego City Coll., 1965; instr. Grossmont (Calif.) Coll., 1975—80, San Diego State Coll., 1981. Author: Fiction Sequels For readers to to16, 1989, 2d edit., 1998, Fiction Index for Readers 10 to 16, 1992, Cultures Outside the United States in Fiction, 1994, Latina/o Literature Themes & Issues in Fiction, 1998, Immigrants in the United States in Fiction, 1994, Native Americans in Fiction, 1994, Crime Novel: Its History and Context in Children's Literature in Production, 2003. Chmn. Public Employees Coord. Coun., San Diego, 1978—79; mem. N. Mt. Village Planning Com.; committeeman Willow Precinct Dem. Party, Phoenix, 1995; state com. mem. Dem. Party State Com., Phoenix, 1995; active Legislative Dist. 18, Phoenix, 1994; mem exec. com. Maricopa County Dem. Party, 2002; chmn. Legis. Dist. 6, 2002; pres. Kensington-Talmadge Cmty. Assn., San Diego, 1976—78. Grantee, Dakota State Coll., 1970. Mem.: AAUW (v.p. fin.), Moon Hills Cmty. Group (chmn.), Ariz. Silver Haired Legislators (elected del.). Democrat. Avocations: reading, sewing, weaving. Home: 12833 N Fifteenth Ave Phoenix AZ 85029 Personal E-mail: valjest@aol.com.

ANDERSON, VICKI SUSAN, legislative staff member, travel consultant; b. Seattle, Jan. 11, 1961; d. Vergil and VickiAnn Davis; m. Todd V. Anderson, Mar. 13, 1982 (div. May 1990); children: David V. Davis, Brandun C. Anderson. Grad., Northside H.S., Houston Voc. Ctr., Warner Robins, Ga., 1979. Computer operator The Boeing Co., Seattle, 1987; clerk, typist Wash. Dept. Licensing, Olympia, Wash., 1987-90; adminstrv. support Ho. of Reps., Olympia, Wash., 1987-90, supr., 1990—. Organizer food drive Farmers Market, Olympia. Mem. Am. Soc. Legis. Clks. and Secs. (site selection com., tech. and innovation com.). Southern Baptist. Avocations: charity fundraising, travel, family. Office: Ho of Reps PO Box 40600 Olympia WA 98504-0600 Home: 7447 Blockhouse Ln SW Rochester WA 98579-9272 E-mail: Anderson_VI@leg.wa.gov.

ANDERSON, ZINA-DIANE, real estate company executive; b. East Orange, N.J., Jan. 14, 1964; d. Sylvester Sr. Anderson and Barbara Ann (Anderson) Atlantic. Student, Essex County Coll., 1988. Counselor for homeless parents and children Isaiah House Shelter, East Orange, 1992-94; real estate adminstr. Anderson & Co., East Orange, 1994—. Advocate Mental Health Assn., East Orange, 1992—. Candidate for county com., dist. #9 third ward Dem. Party, East Orange, 1996. Mem. NAFE (assoc.), Am. Mus. Natural History (assoc.), Smithsonian (assoc.). Baptist. Avocations: reading, writing, classical music. Office: Anderson & Co 111 Madonna Pl East Orange NJ 07018-2413

ANDERSON-SPIVY, ALEXANDRA, writer, editor; b. Boston, Mass, May 14, 1942; d. Henry and Marion Ruth (Thompson) Fuller; m. Samuel O.J. Spivy; children: Lafcadio, Genevieve, Oscar. BA, Sarah Lawrence Coll., 1961. Art editor Paris Rev., 1972-76, Village Voice, NYC, 1973-76; features assoc. Vogue mag., NYC, 1976-78; sr. editor Portfolio mag., NYC, 1979-83; editor-in-chief Arts and Antiques mag., NYC, 1983-85; exec. editor Am. Photographer, NYC, 1985-87; arts editor Smart mag., NYC, 1988-90; contbg. arts editor Esquire mag., NYC, 1990-94; NY editor The Argonaut, 1992-96; reviews editor The Art Jour., 1995-2000; editor-in-chief The Craftsman on CD-ROM, 1996—; projects editor Interactive Bur., 1996-99; editl. dir. Circle.com, 1999-2001. Chair bd. dir. Franklin Furnace; bd. gov. Colby Coll. Art Mus.; profl. fellow Morgan Libr. Author: Anderson and Archer's SoHo: The Essential Guide to Art and Life in Lower Manhattan, 1979, Living With Art, 1988, Portraits of Olga, 1992, Keith Haring, Last Works, 1995, Gardens of Earthly Delight: The Art of Robert Kushner, 1997, Foliage: Photographs by Harold Feinstein, 2001; mem. adv. bd. Rev. Mag., 1998-2000. V.p., Mus. Modern Art, Contemporary Arts Coun.; pres., Bd. of Dir., Exhibitions Internat., 2000-. Recipient Art Critics' award NEA, 1978; Travel grant Japan Found., 1976. Mem. Internat. Art Critics' Assn. (pres. Am. chpt. 1994-98).

ANDERSSON, HELEN DEMITROUS, artist; b. Kotzebue, Alaska, Sept. 9, 1958; d. Thomas Wade Sr. and Rose (Koonook) Sours; children: Jason Ray, Gwendolyn Joyce Field. Student, U. Fairbanks, 1980, U. Hilo, Hawaii, 1981. Exhibited works in Anchorage Mus. History and Arts Show, Stephan Fine Arts, 1984. Recipient 1st pl. Alaska Silver Anniversary Juried Arts Show. Avocations: painting, drawings, carvings, sewing, beadwork.

ANDERT, DARLENE (DARLENE ANDERT-SCHMIDT), management consultant; BA in Bus. Mgmt. and Comms., Alverno Coll., Milw., 1983; MSA in Adminstrn., Ctrl. Mich. U., 1993; EdD, George Washington U., 2003. Cert. fin. mgr. Merrill Lynch Donald T. Regan Sch. Adv. Fin. Mgmt., 1987; cert. mgmt. cons. Inst. Mgmt. Cons., 1994., cert. county ct. mediator

Fla. Supreme Ct., 2003. Pres., owner Dance in Exercise, Inc., Milw., 1980-85; pres. Andert Governance Corp. (formerly Concepts in Mgmt., Inc.), Cape Coral, Fla., 1989—. Mem. bd. arbitrators NASD Regulation Inc., 2000. Author: Diversity at Work, 1995. Trustee Lee County Electric Coop., Inc., 1994—; past pres. Healthy Start Coalition of S.W. Fla., inc. Mem.: ASTD, Nat. Assn. Bus. Women, Inst. Mgmt. Cons. Office: PO Box 100235 Cape Coral FL 33910

ANDLETON, SUZANNE SPURLOCK, art educator; b. Washington, Oct. 17, 1952; d. Harry Lee and Virgie G. Spurlock; m. Richard Floyd Andleton, Oct. 10, 1981; children: Lydia Janice, Julia Leigh. BA, Va. Tech U., 1974; MEd in Art, George Mason U., 1982. Tchr. art elem. and mid. sch. Prince William County, Va., 1974—86; tchr. art mid. and h.s. Virginia Beach City Pub. Schs., Va., 1986—. Workshop presenter Consortium Interactive Instrn., Va., 1994. One-woman shows include, McLean, Va., 1979, exhibitions include The Undertaking, Occoquan, Va., 1978—80, Manassas, Va., 1978—80, 1983, Woodbridge, Va., 1980. Art advisor Habitat for Humanity, Va., 1992. Mem.: Nat. Art Edn. Assn., Sigma Lambda Sigma. Avocations: painting, gardening, quilting.

ANDORA, SUZANNE E. communications company executive; b. Passaic, N.J., Sept. 27, 1964; d. Anthony D. and Colleen A.; m. Richard E. Barron. BA, William Smith Coll., 1986; MBA, Yonsei U., Seoul, 1991. Staff asst. oversight and investigations subcom. U.S. Ho. of Reps. Energy and Commerce Com., Washington, 1986-88; mgr. internat. client svcs. Inter-Gram Pub. Rels., Seoul, 1991; account exec., sr. account exec. Edelman Pub. Rels., N.Y.C., 1992-93, account supr., sr. account supr., 1993-95, v.p., 1995—. Mem. Women in Comm., Am. C. of C. (Seoul), Korea Soc. (steering com. young profls. adv. coun. N.Y.C., 1995-97). Avocations: korean language, skiing, hiking, camping, very active in korea society. Home: 49 Alan Ave Glen Rock NJ 07452-2403 Office: Edelman Pub Rels 1500 Broadway Ste 504 New York NY 10036-4048

ANDRADE, CAROLYN L. foreign language educator; MA in Linguistics, MEd in Elem. Edn., Ohio U. Tchr. Instituto Guatemalteco-Americano, Am. Sch. Guatemala; sec. pub. sch. Dept. Técnico Pedagogico, Morelia, Mex.; spanish tchr. Cin. Public Schs., 1983. Recipient Florence Steiner Leadership in Foreign Lang. Edn. K-12 award, 1992; grantee Foreign Lang. Asst. Act, Sister Cities Internat. U.S.-USSR Youth Exchange Program. Mem. Ohio Foreign Lang. Assn., Nat. Network for Early Lang. Learning.

ANDRADE, EDNA, artist, art educator; b. Portsmouth, Va. d. Thomas Judson and Ruth (Porter) Wright; m. C. Preston Andrade, Jr., July 12, 1941 (div. 1960). BFA, Pa. Acad. Fine Arts/U. Pa., 1937. Supr. art elem. schs., Norfolk, Va., 1938-39; instr. drawing and painting Newcomb Art Sch., Tulane U., 1939-41; lectr. U. N.Mex., 1971; prof. Phila. Coll. Art, 1959-72, 73-82, prof. emeritus, 1982—; prof. art Temple U., 1972-73. Adj. prof. art Ariz. State U., 1986—, critic Pa. Acad. Fine Arts, 1988—89. Artist, designer, OSS, 1942-44, free-lance designer, Washington, 1944-46, free-lance painter, designer, muralist, Phila. and N.Y.C., 1946—, artist-in-residence, Hartford Sch. Art and Tamarind Inst., 1971, U. Sask., Can., 1977, U. Zulia, Maracaibo, Venezuela, 1980, Ariz. State U., Tempe, 1981, 83, Fabric Workshop, Phila., 1984, Hollins Coll., Va., 1985; vis. artist, Skidmore Coll., 1973, 74, one-woman shows E. Hampton Gallery, N.Y.C., Peale Galleries Pa. Acad, Rutgers U. U, Hartford,Marian Locks Gallery, 1989, 1971,74, 77, 83, 1989, Phila., Hollins Coll., 1986; internat. shows Acad. Fine Arts, 1993, Locks Gallery, Phila., 1993-94, 97, 99, 2002-04, Inst. Contemporary Art, Phila., 2003; group shows include AAAL, In This Acad., Pa. Acad. Fine Arts, Phila., William Penn Meml. Mus., Harrisburg, Three Centuries Am. Art, Phila. Collects Art Since 1940, Phila. Mus. Art, Bklyn. Mus., Ft Worth Art Ctr., Des Moines Art Ctr., Philbrook Art Ctr., Tulsa, Contemporary Phila. Artists, 1990, Phila. Mus. Art, Artists Choose Artists, Inst. of Contemporary Art, Phila., 1991, Klein Gallery, Univ. City Sci. Ctr., Phila., 1998, Phila. Mus. Art, 2000, others; represented in permanent collections, Phila. Mus. Art, Pa. Acad. Fine Arts, Print Club, Balt. Mus. Art, Addison Gallery Am. Art, McNay Art Inst., San Antonio, Montclair (N.J.) Art Mus., Nat. Collection Fine Arts, Library of Congress, USIA, Albright-Knox Art Gallery, Buffalo, Tamarind Collection, U. N.Mex. Mus., Woodmere Art Mus., Phila., Yale Art Gallery, Mus. Fine Arts, Houston, Dallas Mus. Fine Arts, Am. Tel. & Tel. Co., Bell of Pa., Phila., Fed. Res. Bank, Phila., Price-Waterhouse, Phila., Edwin A. Ulrich Mus. Wichita State U., Pepsi-Cola, Leeway Found., Phila., Please Touch Mus., Phila., Va. Mus. Fine Arts, Richmond. Mem. Mayor's Cultural Adv. Council, Phila., 1984-85. Recipient 1st and 2d Cresson European Traveling scholarships Pa. Acad., 1936, 37, Eyre medal Phila. Water Color Club, 1968, Mary Smith prize Pa. Acad. Fine Arts, 1968, Childe Hassam Meml. purchases AAAL, 1967, 68, Hazlett Meml. award in arts, 1980, Honor award Women's Caucus for Art, 1983, Hunt award visual arts Phila. Women's Way, 1984, Roland Gallimore Meml. award Interior Design Coun., Phila. Mayor's Arts and Culture award, 1991, Founders award Samuel S. Fleisher Art Meml., 1993, Disting. Daughter Pa. award, 2002., Mem. Fellowship of Pa. Acad. Fine Arts, Coll. Art Assn. (Disting. Tchr. of Art award 1996).

ANDRADE, MANUELA PESTANA, art educator; b. Funchal, Portugal, Oct. 10, 1937; d. Silvestre and Eulalia (Vieira Da Luz) Pestana; m. Manuel Cristao, Jan. 11, 1956 (dec. May 1970); 1 child, Maria Pestana Goldstein; m. Pedro Manuel Rapazote (div. Feb. 1977); 1 child, Antonio Pedro; m. Virgil Sousa Andrade, July 15, 1986. BA, U. Porto, Portugal, 1978, 82, MA, 1980, 84. Tchr. Externato liceal de Moncao, Portugal, 1971-74, Ministry Edn., Portugal, 1971-87; dept. head Prep. Sch. Ermezinde, Portugal, 1981-82, 83-84, master tchr., 1984-85, 86; tchr. Portuguese United Edn. Sch., 1987—, ednl. dir., 1988—. Author of poems; one-woman shows include Ctr. Internat. D'Art Contemporain, Paris, 1984, Funchal, Madeira, Portugal, 1984, Fall River (Mass.) Art Assn., 1988, Heritage Park, Fall River, 1988, Pilgrim Soc., Plymouth, Mass., 1989, Portuguese Am. Fedn. 25th Anniversary Festival, Bristol, R.I., 1990, Bentley Coll., Waltham, Mass., 1992, Portuguese Am. Women's Assn., Providence, 1998, Newport (R.I.) Art Mus., 1999; represented in permanent collections Nat. Kunsan U., South Korea, Portuguese-Am. Bus. Assn., Portuguese-Am. Fedn., Nat. Soc. Fine Arts, Nat. Trust Historic Preservation, Casa da Madeira Norte, Portuguese Tchrs. Assn., Fall River Assn., Home: 27 Alfred St Fall River MA 02721-2620

ANDRAKE, NANCY CAROLYN, secondary school educator; b. Elmira, N.Y., Jan. 12, 1944; d. Stephen Francis Andrake and Theresa Ida Skoreski; m. Edward J. Jeziorski Jr., July 4, 1970 (div. Feb. 1984); children: Jennifer Granger, Carolyn Jeziorski, Edward Jeziorski, Patrick Jeziorski. BA cum laude, Coll. Misericordia, Dallas, 1965; MA, Fla. State U., 1967; postgrad., SUNY Stonybrook, Elmira Coll., SUNY Cortland, U. Del. Latin/English tchr. Hammondsport (N.Y.) Sch. Dist., 1966—70; Latin/Greek/English tchr. Horseheads (N.Y.) Sch. Dist., 1970—; English/study skills tchr. Elmira (N.Y.) Summer Sch., 1984—. Sales assoc. Kaufmann's Dept. Store, Horseheads, 1995—; cons. Latin Regents Exam N.Y. State Dept. Edn., Albany, 1985—. Leader Girl Scouts Am., Hammondsport, 1965—70, Elmira, 1980—90; mem., pres. St. Casimir's Parish Coun., Elmira, 1984—90. Fellow Rockefeller Found., Am. Sch. Athens, 1989; grantee NEH, 1982; scholar Corning Sister Cities, to teach in Poland, 1999. Mem.: Nat. Jr. Classical League, N.Y. State Jr. Classical League (co-chair 1986—96), Classical Assn. Empire State (bd. dirs. 1986—96), Am. Fedn. Tchrs., N.Y. State United Tchrs., Horseheads Tchrs. Assn. (rep. 1985—90, 2002—), Lambda Iota Tau, Sigma Phi Sigma, Kappa Gamma Pi. Roman Catholic. Avocations: European travel, reading, music, taking students on trips. Home: 51 Ashland Ave Elmira NY 14903 Office: Horseheads High Sch 401 Fletcher St Horseheads NY 14845

ANDRAU, MAYA HEDDA, physical therapist; b. Digboi, Assam, India, Apr. 15, 1936; came to U.S., 1946; d. William Henry and Klara Irén Judit (Sima) Andrau; married, Sept. 1971 (div. July 1989); children: Francis Meher Traver, Darwin Meher Traver. BS in Phys. Therapy, Columbia U., 1958; MA in Social Anthropology, NYU, 1966. Lamaze cert. childbirth educator; lic. and registered phys. therapist. Phys. therapist Beekman-Downtown Hosp., N.Y.C., 1959-60; physiotherapist Stamford (Conn.) Hosp., 1963-64, Benedictine Hosp., Kingston, N.Y., 1966-69; pvt. practice in phys. therapy and lamaze Woodstock, NY, 1968-71; chief phys. therapist No. Duchess Hosp., Rhinebeck, NY, 1970-71; phys. therapist Waccamaw Pub. Health Dist., S.C. Dept. Health, Myrtle Beach, 1982-84; pain clinic specialist Pain Therapy Ctr. of Columbia (S.C.), Richland Meml. Hosp., 1986-87; phys. therapist Comprehensive Med. Rehab. Ctr., Conway, SC, 1988-92; phys. therapist, instr. conditioning program Pawleys Island (S.C.) Wellness Inst., 1993; phys. therapist Total Care, Inc., N. Myrtle Beach, S.C., 1993-97. Instr. phys. conditioning and therapeutic exercise courses, 1980—97; instr. conditioning program Health Focus Brief for TV, 1990; pvt. phys. therapist and instr. Conditioning-Wellness Program UNCA (Coll. for Srs.), Asheville, NC, 1998, Asheville-Buncombe Tech. C.C., Asheville, 1999, Blue Ridge C.C., Flat Rock, NC, 1999—2000, Elderhostel, Montreat, NC, 1999, 2001, 03, Crescent View Retirement Cmty., Arden, NC, 2001. Mem. Meher Spiritual Ctr., Inc., Alpha Kappa Delta. Follower of Avatar Meher Baba. Avocations: gardening, reading, walking, handwork, singing.

ANDRÉ, JOY LARAE, elementary school educator, adult education educator, language educator; b. L.A., Apr. 29, 1936; d. Wilmont H. and Loree B. Fugate; m. William Albert André, June 25, 1960 (div. Dec. 1974); children: Scott, Brent. BA in Music and Edn., Pepperdine U., 1957, postgrad., 1958—75. Life tchg. credential Calif., cert. lang. devel. specialist Calif. Tchr. elem. and adult edn. L.A. Unified Sch. Dist., 1957—93; tchr. adult edn. Saddleback Valley Unified Sch. Dist., Mission Viejo, Calif., 1993—. Mentor tchr. selection com. L.A. Unified Sch. Dist., 1984, bilingual coord., 1985—91, master tchr., 1987—88, ESL coord., 1990—91. Recipient Govt. Studies Program award, Close Up Found., 1998; scholar, Pepperdine U., 1980; Coe fellow. Mem.: AAUW, United Tchrs. L.A., Calif. Ret. Tchrs. Assn., Orange County Natural History Assn., L.A. Conservancy, Laguna Niguel Women's Club (participant/vol. sec. 2002—03). Republican. Presbyterian. Avocations: photography, scrapbooks, collecting Indian art and miniature decorative boxes, reading, travel. Home: 9 Killini Laguna Niguel CA 92677

ANDREAE, CHRISTINE EWING, writer; b. Stamford, Conn., July 13, 1942; d. William and Mary (Challinor) Ewing; m. Frederick Shedd Andreae, Aug. 19, 1967; children: Morgan MacKenzie, Timothy Ewing. BA, Manhattanville Coll., 1964; MAT, Yale U., 1967. Author: Seances and Spiritualists, 1974, Trail of Murder, 1992, Grizzly, 1994, A Small Target, 1996, One Woman's Death, 1996, Smoke Eaters, 2000, When Evening Comes, 2000. Bd. dirs. Blue Ridge Hospice, 1989-95, vol., 1990—. Recipient Founder's award Blue Ridge Hospice, 1994, Lit. award Shenandoah Arts Coun., 1996. Mem. Mystery Writers Am., Sisters in Crime, Internat. Assn. Crime Writers, Women Writing the West.

ANDREAS, CAROL, sociologist, educator; b. Newton, kans., Nov. 10, 1933; d. Willis Everett and Hulda Suzanne (Penner) Rich; m. Carl Andreas, May 1951 (div. Aug 1971); children: Joel, Ronald, Peter. BA, Bethel Coll., 1953; MA, U. Minn., 1954; PhD, Wayne State U., 1964. Lectr. U. Mich., 1967-68; asst. prof. Oakland U., Mich., 1968-71; instr. Oakland C.C., Calif., 1971-72, Hope Inst. U. Colo., Denver 1978-81, prof. sociology U. No. Colo., Greeley, 1988-94, prof. emeritus sociology, 1991—. Vis. prof. Colorado Coll., summer 1972, U. Nacional del Centro del Peru, 1974, U. Oreg., 1986; adj. assoc. prof. U. Colo., Colorado Springs, 1981-84; vis. assoc. prof. Ea. Washington U., 1985; Disting. prof. Simon Fraser U., Vancouver, B.C., Can., summer 1989. Author: Sex and Caste in America, 1971, Nothing Is As It Should Be, 1976, When Women Rebel, 1985, Meatpackers and Beef Barons, 1994. Activist Anti-War Movement, Vietnam and U.S. Women's Movements, U.S. and L.Am., Farmworkers' Unions, Labor and Civil Rights. Mem. Union of Radical Sociologists (founder, jour. The Insurgent Sociologist). Avocations: writing poetry, journalism, art, music, hiking. Home: 131 S Sherwood St Fort Collins CO 80521-2616

ANDREASEN, NANCY COOVER, psychiatrist, educator, neuroscientist; d. John A. Sr. and Pauline G. Coover; children: Robin, Susan. BA summa cum laude, U. Nebr., 1958, PhD, 1963; MA, Radcliffe Coll., 1959; MD, U. Iowa, 1970. Instr. English Nebr. Wesleyan Coll., 1960-61, U. Nebr., Lincoln, 1962-63; asst. prof. English U. Iowa, Iowa City, 1963-66, resident, 1970-73, asst. prof. psychiatry, 1973-77, assoc. prof., 1977-81, prof. psychiatry, 1981-92, Andrew H. Woods prof. psychiatry, 1992-97, Andrew H. Woods chair psychiatry, 1997—. Dir. Mental Health Clin. Rsch. Ctr. 1987—, The MIND Inst., Albuquerque, 2002-; sr. cons. Northwick Pk. Hosp., London, 1983; acad. visitor Maudsley Hosp., London, 1986; adj. prof psychiatry U. N.Mex., Albuquerque. Author: The Broken Brain, 1984, Introductory Psychiatry Testbook, 1991; editor: Can Schizophrenia be Localized to the Brain?, 1986, Brain Imaging: Applications in Psychiatry, 1988, Brave New Brain: Conquering Mental Illness in the Era of the Genome, 2001; Am. Jour. Psychiat., 1988—, dep. editor, 1989—93, editor-in-chief, 1993—; contbr. articles to profl. jours. Recipient Rhonda and Bernard Sarnat award NAS, 1999, C. Charles Burlingame award, 1999, Arthur P. Noyes award in schizophrenia, 1999, Lieber prize Nat. Alliance for Rsch. on Schizophrenia and Depression, 2000, Pres.'s Nat. Medal Sci., 2000, Interbrew Baillet-Latour Health Prize, 2000; Woodrow Wilson fellow, 1958-59, Fulbright fellow Oxford U., London, 1959-60. Fellow Royal Coll. Physicians Surgeons Can. (hon.), Am. Psychiat. Assn. (Adolf Meyer award 1999), Am. Coll. Neuropharmacologists, Royal Coll. Medicine; mem. Am. Acad. Arts and Scis., Am. Psychopathol. Assn. (pres. 1989-90), Inst. Medicine of NAS (coun. 1996—). Office: U Iowa Hosps and Clinics 200 Hawkins Dr Iowa City IA 52242-1057

ANDREASON, (SHARON) LEE, sculptor; b. Lebanon, Oreg., Mar. 20, 1937; d. LeRoy and Galdys Edwina (Wells) A.; m. Raymond Locke Eller, Aug. 30, 1957 (div. 1981); 1 child, Jordan Lee; m. Stoddard Pintard Johnston, Dec. 21, 1985 (div. 1998). Performing artist Screen Extras Guild, Hollywood, Calif., 1962-70; profl. artist, Carmel, Calif., 1981—, Jimena de la Frontera, Spain, 1998—. One-woman shows include Pacific Grove Art Ctr., 1984, Zantman Art Gallery, Carmel, 1989, Highlands Sculpture Gallery, Carmel, 1991, 92, 93, Galeria Brisamar, Marbella, Spain, 1993, Smith Cosby Gallery, Carmel, 1995, Silver Light Gallery, Carmel, 1996, 97, 98, 99, 2000, 2001, Marin-Price Galleries, 1997, Linnemann Gallery, Chgo., 1998, Galerie de Sculpture, Paris, 1999, Amsteleen Gallery, Amsterdam, 2000, Galeria Harpe, Marbella, Spain, 2000, Galeria Las Palomas, Gaucin, Spain, 2000; group exhbns. include Monterey County (Calif.) Mus. Art, 1984, Gallery Mack, Seattle, 1993, Am. Acad. Equine Art, Ky. Horse Park, Lexington, 1993, 94, 95, Galeria Serie, Madrid, 1993, Galeries Krieseler, Madrid, 1994-95, Galeria Brisamar, Marbella, 1995, Galeria Sculpture, Paris, 1995, 96, 98, 99, Signature Gallery, Del Mar, Calif., 1995, Signature Gallery, San Diego, 1995, Galeria Iris Ryman, Marbella, Spain, 1996, Nova Galeria De Arte, Malaga, Spain, 1996-99, 2000-04, Ky. Derby Mus., Louisville, 1996, 97-99, Sammer Gallery, Puerto Banus, Spain, 2001, 2002, 2003, Baltasar Gallery, Sante Fe, 1999, 2000, Horizon Gallery, Sante Fe, 2000-04, David Lee Gallery, Scottsdale, Ariz., Cody Gallery, Los Olivos, Calif., 2003-04; juried show Nat. Sculpture Soc., N.Y.C., 2004; most of her works are produced in bronze and sold for pvt. and pub. collections; represented in collections internationally. Founder Horse Power Internat., Inc., 1989-97, Horse Power Sanctuaries, Inc., Horse Power Protection Projects, Inc., 1991-97; authored horse protection legislation Sacramento, 1993-94. Recipient Gwendolyn May award for outstanding achievement for individual humane contbn. Monterey County SPCA,

Monterey, Calif., 1994, recipient, Legion of St. Frances Awd., Internatl. Generic Horse Assn./Horse Aid, lifelong beneficience awd., 1999. Mem. Conv. on the Welfare and Protection of Animals in Transit (N.Am. Free Trade Agreement animal legis. group), Internat. Sculpture Ctr., Nat. Sculpture Soc. Avocations: sailing, horse riding and related activitics, ancient art and civilizations.

ANDREATTA, SUSAN L. anthropologist; b. Syracuse, N.Y., Feb. 3, 1961; d. Antonio Geno and Ellen Jean Andreatta; m. Timothy David Johnston, June 27, 1998. B, U. Del., 1984; M, Iowa State U., 1986; PhD, Mich. State U., 1994. Asst. prof. U. N.C., Greensboro, 1996—2003, dir. Project Green Leaf, 2001—, assoc. prof., 2003—. Co-author: (book) Language and Community Building: The Migrant Farmworker Experience in North Carolina, 2001; contbr. articles to profl. jours. Planning com. U.S. Nat. Com. World Food Day, Washington, 2001—02; liaison Student Action with Farmworkers, Durham, NC, 1997—2002. Mem.: Carolina Farm Stewardship Assn. (sec. 1997—2000), Am. Anthropology Assn. (culture and agr. treas. 2001—03), Soc. Applied Anthropology (bd. dirs. 2001—).

ANDREEVA, TATIANA, art gallery owner; b. St. Petersburg, Russia, Dec. 4, 1954; arrived in US, 1994; d. Neal and Lydia; 1 child, Nikita Lukichev. BA in Journalism, ST. Petersburg U.; MA in Art Bus., U. Manchester. V.p. St. Petersburg Radio, 1992—94; gen. mgr. Magic Radio, Classical Radio, St. Petersburg, 1992—94; pres. Andreeva Fine Art Portraits, Santa Fe, 1994—. Office: Andreeva Fine Art Portraits 217 W San Francisco Santa Fe NM 87501

ANDREINI, ELIZABETH B. stockbroker, elementary education educator; b. Pitts., Aug. 7, 1949; d. Louis Ernest and Alice (McCoy) Braun; m. Alan John Andreini, Apr. 20, 1975 (div. July 1981); 1 chld, Alan John. AA, Centenary Coll. for Women, Hackettstown, N.J., 1969; student, U. Fla., 1969; BS, Youngstown (Ohio) State U., 1972. Cert. tchr., Calif.; registered rep. N.Y. Stock Exch. Asst. youth dir. YWCA, Portland, Maine, 1972-74; Oppenheimer & Co., N.Y.C., 1974-76; Paine Webber Jackson & Curtis, N.Y.C., 1976-77; Oppenheimer & Co., San Francisco, 1982-84; aide Reed Sch., Tiburon, Calif., 1985-87; K-1 tchr. Bright Beginnings Sch., Corte Madera, Calif., 1991-92; registered rep. Charles Schwab, Corte Madera, 1993—. Dir. Metrin Skincare bd. dirs. Pixley Arms Homeowners. Mem. task force New Corte Madera Recreation Ctr., 1995; mem. neighborhood emergency relief team Corte Madera Fire Dept., 1995. Mem. DAR, Mt. Tam Racquet Club, San Francisco Jr. League. Republican. Christian Scientist. Avocations: swimming, dance, running, golf, skiing. Office: Charles Schwab Corp 403 Corte Madera Town Ctr Corte Madera CA 94925-1215 Home: 825 Ketch Dr Apt 301 Naples FL 34103-4183

ANDREOLI, KATHLEEN GAINOR, nurse, educator, dean; b. Albany, N.Y., Sept. 22, 1935; d. John Edward and Edmunda Elizabeth (Ringlemann) Gainor; children: Paula Kathleen, Thomas Anthony, Karen Marie. BSN, Georgetown U., 1957; MSN, Vanderbilt U., 1959; DSN, U. Ala., Birmingham, 1979. Staff nurse Albany Hosp. Med. Ctr., 1957; instr. St. Thomas Hosp. Sch. Nursing, Nashville, 1958—59, Georgetown U. Sch. Nursing, 1959—60, Duke U. Sch. Nursing, 1960—61, Bon Secours Hosp. Sch. Nursing, Balt., 1962—64; ednl. coordinator, physician asst. program, instr. coronary care unit nursing inservice edn. Duke U. Med. Ctr., Durham, NC, 1965—70; ednl. dir. physician asst. program dept. medicine U. Ala. Med. Ctr., Birmingham, 1970—75, clin. assoc. prof. cardiovasc. nursing Sch. Nursing, 1970—77, asst. prof. nursing dept. medicine, 1971, assoc. prof., 1972—, assoc. prof. nursing Sch. Pub. and Allied Health, 1973—; assoc. dir. Family Nurse Practitioner Program, 1976, assoc. prof. cmty. health nursing Grad. Program, 1977—79, assoc. prof. dept. pub. health, 1978—79; prof. nursing, spl. asst. to pres. for ednl. affairs U. Tex. Health Sci. Ctr., Houston, 1979—82, acting dean Sch. Allied Health Scis., 1981, v.p. for ednl. svcs., interdisciplinary edn., internat. programs, 1983—87; v.p. nursing affairs Rush-Presbyn.-St. Lukes's Med. Ctr., Chgo., 1987—; dean Rush U. Coll. Nursing, 1987—. Mem. nat. adv. nursing coun. VHA, 1992; cons. in field. Author, editor, with others: Comprehensive Cardiac Care, 1983; editor: Heart and Lung, Jour. of Total Care, 1971; contbr. articles to profl. jours. Active Internat. Nursing Coalition for Mass Casualty Edn., 2002—; mem. adv. bd. Robert Wood Johnson Clin. Nurse Sch. Program; mem. vis. com. Vanderbilt U. Sch. Nursing; mem. Leadership Ill., 1991; mem. nat. nursing asdv. com. Voluntary Hosp. Am., 1991; mem. governing coun. Inst. for Hosp. Clin. Nursing Edn., Am. Hosp. Assn., 1993; bd. dirs. Ill. League for Nursing, 1994, Lyrie Opera Chgo. Guild; adv. bd. Hospice Ptnrs. Recipient Founder's award, N.C. Heart Assn., 1970, Disting. Alumni award, Vanderbilt U. Sch. Nursing, 1985, Leadership Tex. award, 1985, Disting. Alumni award, U. Ala. Sch. Nursing, 1991. Fellow: Am. Acad. Nursing; mem.: ACNA, ANA, Internat. Nursing Coalition for Mass Casualty Edn., Inst. Medicine of Chgo., Nat. Nursing Adv. Coun. Hosps. Am., Am. Heart Assn. Coun. Cardiovasc. Nursing, Coun. Family Nurse Practitioners and Clinicians, Ala. Heart Assn., Nat. League Nursing, Inst. Medicine of NAS, Am. Assn. Colls. Nursing, Rotary One Club Chgo., Phi Kappa Phi, Alpha Eta, Sigma Theta Tau (Dreher Outstanding Dean award 2003). Roman Catholic. Home: 1212 N Lake Shore Dr Chicago IL 60610-2402 Office: Rush Presbyn-St Luke's Med Ctr 600 S Paulina St Ste 1080 Chicago IL 60612-3806 Business E-Mail: Kathleen_G_Andreoli@rush.edu.

ANDREUCCI-BUDNEY, DEBORAH ANN, artist; b. Parsippany, N.J., Mar. 29, 1955; d. Nicholas and Florence (Bevacqua) Andreucci; life ptnr. Robert H. Budney, Dec. 10, 1998; children: Nicholas Anagelo Budney, Sarah Jean Budney, Hailey Christine Budney. Grad., DuCret Sch. of the Arts, North Plainfield, N.J., 1979, Centenary Coll., Hackettstown N.J., 1986. Graphic artist numerous clients, including Warner Brothers, AT&T, Pfizer, Hoffman La Roche, Warner Lambert Pharmaceutical, Beneficial Management Corporation, Johnson & Johnson, Park Davis, Ciba Giga, Sandoz (Novartis). Series of carousel paintings, Carousel News and Trader Mag., cover illustration, Morris County booklet, N.J. Bicentennial booklet, exhibitions include Carousels.com, N.J. Craftsman's Show, 1976, one-woman shows include Joyland Books U.K., 2003. Mem.: Morris County Art Assn. (assoc.), NJWBOA (assoc.), NJSBA (assoc.), CFIDS Assn. (life), Morris County C. of C. (assoc.). Roman Catholic. Home and Studio: Pro-Graphix Fine and Graphic Arts 355 Lake Shore Dr Lake Hiawatha NJ 07034 E-mail: deborah.budney@verizon.net.

ANDREW, DOLORES MOLCAN, art educator, artist; b. Corning, N.Y., July 11, 1928; d. Ferdinand Joseph and Evelyn May (Marnin) Molcan; m. R. Hugh Andrew, June 12, 1954; children: Julia, Douglas, Catherine. BFA in Painting, Syracuse U., 1951; postgrad., Towson State U., 1975-77; MFA in Art Edn., Md. Inst., 1982. Cert. tchr. embroidery, mixed media. Adult edn. tchr. Columbia (Md.) Assoc., 1971-72, Essex C.C., Balt., 1976-80, from asst. to assoc. prof. art, 1980—98; tchr. Rehoboth Art League, Rehoboth Beach, Del., 1985—, Goucher Coll., Towson, Md., 1990-95; supr. paintings & photography Md. State Fair, Timonium, 1987—. Judge, lectr. in field. Author: Italian Renaissance Textiles, 1986, Medieval Tapestry Designs, 1992, American Sampler Designs, 1996; designer copyrights for crewel designs; exhbns. include Gibson Island, Md., 1993, 98, Garrett C.C., McHenry, Md., 1994, others; contbr. illustrations to Balt. Sun, 1988—. Nat. dir. judging certification Nat. Acad. Needlearts, 1988-94, nat. pres., 1990-94. Em. NLAPW (pres. Carroll br. 1976-78, Md. state pres. 1992-94), Artists Equity Assn. (corr. sec. Md. chpt. 1987-92, recording sec. 1987-92), Md. Pastel Soc. (charter, pres. 1985-87), Embroiderers Guild Am. (charter). Democrat. Episcopalian. Avocations: reading, swimming, baking, canoeing.

ANDREW, JANE HAYES, non-profit organization executive; b. Phila., Jan. 1, 1947; d. David Powell and Vivian Muriel (Seager) Hayes; m. Brian David Andrew, June 14, 1977; 1 child, Kevin Hayes. AB, Barnard Coll., 1968; grad., Harvard Arts Adminstrn. Inst., 1972; MBA, U. Wash., 1994. Mgr. theater Minor Latham Playhouse, Barnard Coll., N.Y.C., 1970-74; co. mgr. Houston Ballet, 1974-77, Ballet West, Salt Lake City, 1978-83; gen. mgr. Pacific N.W. Ballet, Seattle, 1983-87. Organizer non-profit consortium nat. ballet cos. and nat. presenting orgns., 1987; pres., exec. dir. Ballet/America, 1988-91; ind. cons. arts mgmt., 1991-94; dir. Found. for Internat. Understanding Through Students, 1993-97; panelist NEA Dance Program Presentors, 1987-88, 88-89, 89-90, Seattle Arts Commn. dance grants, 1989, 90; cons. Ariz. Arts Commn., Phoenix, 1985-86; com. mem. 25th Anniversary of World's Fair, Seattle, 1986-87; panelist NEA Local Programs, 1987; vol. Interlace H.S., 1997. Editor (directory) Philadelphia Cultural Orgns., 1977. Bd. dirs. Good Shepherd Adv. Bd., Seattle, 1985-87. Recipient Dorothy D. Spivack award Barnard Coll., 1972. Mem. Dance/USA (chmn. mgrs. coun. 1986). Home and Office: 7706 146th Ave NE Redmond WA 98052-4105

ANDREWS, BETTY BAUSERMAN, retired secondary school educator, property manager; b. Luray, Va, Dec. 29, 1935; d. Raymond Edgar Bauserman and Elizabeth Elaine Houser; m. George Norman Andrews, July 26, 1964 (dec. Apr. 1996). BS, Madison Coll., 1958; postgrad., U. Va., 1964-68, George Mason U., 1969—. Cert. coll. profl. cert., Va. Classroom tchr. Clarke County HS, Berryville, Va., 1958-64, Loudoun Valley HS, Purcellville, Va., 1964-68; proofreader Missles and Rockets mag., Washington, 1964, Loudoun County HS, Leesburg, Va., 1968-69; head libr. media specialist Broad Run HS, Ashburn, Va., 1969-2000. Cons., libr. reorganizer Logetronics Corp., Springfield, Va., 1974; mem. sch. improvement team Broad Run HS, Ashburn, 1996-2000. Adv. bd. Sterling (Va.) Pub. Libr., 1998—. Mem. NEA, James Madison U. Alumni Assn., Va. Edn. Assn. (life), Loudoun Edn. Assn. (life), Loudoun Educators Media Assn. (life), Nat. Soc. DAR, Sparlandria Investment Club, Am. Assn. Univ. Women (AAUW), Alpha Gamma Delta. Democrat. Methodist. Avocations: antique collecting, gardening, investing, sailing, reading. Home: 821 Golden Arrow St Great Falls VA 22066-2517 E-mail: striperrtripes@aol.com.

ANDREWS, DONNA L. professional golfer; b. Lynchburg, VA, Apr. 12, 1967; d. James Barclay and Helen Louise (Munsey) Andrews. BBA, U. N.C., 1989. Qualified golfer LPGA Tour, Fla., 1990; winner Ping-Cellular One Golf Tounament, Portland, Oreg., 1993, Ping-Welch's Golf Tournament, Tucson, Ariz., 1994, Dinah Shore Major Golf Tournament, Palm Springs, Calif., 1994, Longs Drugs Challenge, Lincoln, CA, 1998. Office: LPGA 100 International Golf Dr Daytona Beach FL 32124-1092

ANDREWS, GAYLEN, measurable response public relations expert; Pres. Blitz Media-Direct, Middle Island, NY. Office: Blitz Media-Direct Communications Bldg PO Box 102 Middle Island NY 11953-0102

ANDREWS, JANE SILVEY, musician; b. Marshall, Tex., May 15, 1953; d. James Harold and Mary Louise Silvey; m. Robert Franklin Andrews, Nov. 22, 1980; children: Zane, Byron, Banning. BME, Centenary Coll. La., 1975; MM, S.W. Baptist Theological Sem., 1979, DMA, 1986. Prof. piano/theory So. Baptist Coll., Walnut Ridge, Ark., 1979-82; adj. prof. piano S.W. Baptist Theol. Sem., Ft. Worth, 1987—; staff accompanist Arlington Choral Soc., 1986—; keyboardist Tex. Wind Symphony, 2001—; pvt. piano tchr. Ft. Worth, 1986—; organist Overton Park United Meth. Ch., Ft. Worth, 1997—. Mem. Ft. Worth Piano Tchrs. Forum (pres. 1994-96), Ft. Worth Music Tchrs. Assn., Creative Motion Alliance (sec.) Baptist. Home: 7512 Meadow Creek Dr Fort Worth TX 76123-1002

ANDREWS, JANICE D. elementary school educator; b. Metropolis, Ill., Mar. 15, 1947; d. Leo Charles and Frieda Lavene (Lamb) Downey; m. Jerry D. Andrews, Jan. 8, 1972; 1 child, Jennifer Denise. BS, U. Tampa, 1969; MA, U. South Fla., 1977. Cert. elem. tchr., Fla. Tchr. Pinellas County Sch. Bd., St. Petersburgh, Fla., Hillsborogh County Sch. Bd., Tampa, Fla. Mem. NEA, Fla. Teaching Profession, Hillsborough Classroom Tchrs. Assn., Kappa Delta Pi, Phi Delta Kappa.

ANDREWS, JEAN, artist; b. Kingsville, Tex., Dec. 23, 1923; d. Herbert and Katharine Andrews; divorced; children: Robert Fleming Wasson Jr., Jean Andrews Wasson (dec.). BS in Home Economics, U. Tex., 1944; MS in Edn., Tex. A & I Univ., 1966; PhD in Fine Arts, U. North Tex., 1976. Cert. home economist. Artist, writer, Austin, Tex. Vis. scholar dept. integrative biology U. Tex., Austin, adv. coun. Coll. Natural Sci., 1983-, past mem. exec. com., 1986-97, chmn. botany dept. vis. com., 1985-1993; presenter to seminars and confs. in field. Author: Sea Shells of the Texas Coast, 1971, Shells and Shores of Texas, 1977, Texas Shells: A Field Guide, 1981, Peppers: The Domesticated Capsicums, 1984, rev. edit., 1995, The Texas Bluebonnet, 1985, rev. edit., 1993, An American Wildflower: Florilegium, 1992, Texas Monthly Field Guide to Shells of the Texas Coast, 1992, Red Hot Peppers, 1993, Texas Monthly Field Guide to the Shells of the Florida Coast, 1994, The Peppers Lady's Pocket Pepper Primer, 1998, The Pepper Trail, 2000; also articles; one-woman shows include RGK Found. Gallery, Austin, 1993; numerous others. Nat. adv. bd. Leadership Am., 1988-95; trustee Laguna Gloria Art Mus., 1985-91, Nat. Wildflower Rsch. Ctr., 1987-94, adv. coun. 1995—; past trustee Art Mus. of S. Tex.; past bd. dirs. Planned Parenthood; mem. Austin Symphony Soc., Friends of Huntington Gallery/Univ. Tex., others. Recipient Disting. Alumna award U.North Tex., 1991, Hall of Honor award U. Tex. Coll. Natural Sci., 1991, Disting. Alumna award U. Tex. Austin, 1997; endowments include Jean Andrews vis. professorship in human nutrition, and vis. professorship in tropical and econ. botany, endowed scholar Tex. Found. for Women's Resources, U. Tex.; endowed scholar in art U. North Tex., others; named Tex. Inst. Letters. Mem. DAR, Am. Malacol. Union, Tex. Pepper Found. (life), Tex. State Tchrs. Assn. (life), U. Tex. Alumni Assn. (life), U. North Tex. Alumni Assn. (life), Colonial Dames of 17th Century, Nat. Soc. Ams. of Royal Descent, Nat. Soc. Colonial Dames in Am., Nat. Soc. Magna Charta Dames, Daus. of Cin., Huguenot Soc., Order of Descendants of Ancient Planters, Daus. of the Confederacy, Descendents of Ancient Planters, Jamestowne Soc., Descendants of Colonial Govs. E-mail: thepepperlady@aol.com.

ANDREWS, DAME JULIE (JULIA ELIZABETH WELLS), actress, singer; b. Walton-on-Thames, Eng., Oct. 1, 1935; d. Edward C. and Barbara Wells; m. Tony Walton, May 10, 1959 (div.); 1 child, Emma Walton ; m. Blake Edwards, 1969; adopted children: Amy Edwards, Joanna Edwards stepchildren: Jennifer Edwards, Geoffrey Edwards. studied with pvt. tutors, studied voice with Mme. Stiles-Allen. Debut as singer, Hippodrome, London, 1947; appeared in pantomime Cinderella, London, 1953; appearances include (Broadway prodns.) The Boy Friend, NYC, 1954, My Fair Lady, 1956-60 (NY Drama Critics award 1956), Camelot, 1960-62, Putting It Together, 1993, Victor/Victoria, 1995 (Tony award nominee Best Actress in a Musical); films include Mary Poppins, 1964 (Acad. award for Best Actress 1964), The Americanization of Emily, 1964, Torn Curtain, 1966, The Sound of Music, 1966, Hawaii, 1966, Thoroughly Modern Millie, 1967, Star!, 1968, Darling Lili, 1970, The Tamarind Seed, 1973, 1979, Little Miss Marker, 1980, S.O.B, 1981, Victor/Victoria, 1982, The Man Who Loved Women, 1983, That's Life!, 1986, Duet For One, 1986, A Fine Romance, 1992, Relative Values, 2000, The Princess Diaries, 2001, Unconditional Love, 2002; TV debut in High Tor, 1956; star TV series The Julie Andrews Hour, 1972-73 (Emmy award for Best Variety Series), Julie, 1992; also spls.; TV movies include Our Sons, 1991, One Special Night, 1999, Eloise at the Plaza, 2003; author: (as Julie Edwards): Mandy, 1971, The Last of the Really Great Whangdoodles, 1974; recs.: The King and I, 1992. Named World Film Favorite (female), 1967; named to 100 Great Britons, 2002; recipient Golden Globe award, Hollywood Fgn. Press Assn., 1964, 1965, Lifetime Achievement award, Kennedy Ctr., 2001. Achievements include knighted by Queen Elizabeth, 1999.*

ANDREWS, LAUREEN E. foundation administrator; b. Seneca Falls, N.Y., July 28, 1954; d. Lawrence J. and Anita A.; m. Craig T. Scherer, Oct. 4, 1983; children: Casey Alena, Lindsey Adele. BA, George Washington U., 1976; MA in Law and Diplomacy, Fletcher Sch. Law and Diplomacy, Mass., 1978. Lobbyist, editor League of Women Votersof the U.S.A., Washington, 1978-80; dir. internat. rels. League of Women Voters Edn. Fund, Washington, 1980-85; dep. dir. def. budget project Ctr. Budget & Policy Priorities, Washington, 1985—; dep. dir. Ctr. for Stategic & Budgetary Assessments, Washington. Editor: (legis. newsletter) Report from the Hill, 1978-80. Mem. Phi Beta Kappa. Office: Ctr for Strategic & Budgetary Assessments 1730 Rhode Island Ave NW Washington DC 20036-3101

ANDREWS, MELINDA WILSON, human development researcher; b. N.Y.C., Aug. 12, 1956; d. William Maurice and Natalie Maxine (Amos) Wilson; m. James Robert Andrews, Dec. 3, 1977; children: Christopher Wilson Andrews, William James Andrews. BBA in Mgmt./Mktg., Abilene (Tex.) Christian U., 1977; MS in Human Devel., U. Tex., Dallas, 1988, postgrad., 1994—. Logics adminstr. Texas Instruments, Dallas, 1977-79, contract adminstr., 1979-81, 82-83; grocery mgr., co-asst. store dir. Tom Thumb, Dallas, 1981-82; teaching asst. U. Tex. at Dallas, Richardson, Tex., 1988-91, rsch. asst., 1991—. Dir. creative presch. coop., Richardson, 2000-02; dir. Waterview Christian Presch., 2002—; validator NAEYC, 2002—; presenter in field. Contbr. articles to profl. jours. Mem. Richardson Symphony Orch., 1977-79, Canyon Creek Elem. PTA, 5th v.p., 1994-95, libr. rep., 1992-94; treas. exec. bd. Creative Presch. Coop., 1998-99, sec. ex. bd. 1999-2000, dir., 2000-02; Cub Scout leader, com. chmn., Pack 1001, 2002—; asst. dir. English as second lang. sch. Waterview Ch. of Christ. Mem. Soc. for Rsch. in Child Devel. (co-author paper-poster session 1991, 93 confs.), Southwest Soc. for Rsch. in Child Devel., Psi Chi. Mem. Ch. of Christ. Avocations: music, animals, carpentry. Home and Office: 1089 Edith Circle Richardson TX 75080-2331 E-mail: melindaandrews@worldnet.att.net.

ANDREWS, MINERVA WILSON, retired lawyer; b. Rock Hill, S.C., Feb. 1, 1925; d. York Lowry and Minnie de Foix (Long) Wilson; m. Robert Taylor Andrews, Apr. 15, 1950; children: Susan Allison (Mrs. Robert N. Wiles), Stuart Davidson. AB, U. S.C., 1945; LLB, U. Va., 1948. Bar: Va. 1948. Trial atty. antitrust divsn. U.S. Dept. Justice, Washington, 1949—55; assoc. atty. Bauknight, Prichard, McCandlish & Williams, Fairfax, Va., 1963—72, Boothe, Prichard & Dudley, 1972—80; ptnr. Boothe, Prichard & Dudley, and McGuire, Woods, et al. (merged), McLean, Va., 1980—91; ret., 1992. Author: Carolina-Virginia Recollections, 1999, A Carolina-Virginia Genealogy, vol. 2, 2000. Pres. Nat. Soc. Arts & Letters, 1994—96; bd. dir. Mclean Citizen Assn., 1968—2000, Fairfax/Falls Church United Way, Vienna, Va., 1988—2001; life elder Lewinsville Presby. Church, McLean, 1980—. Named Citizen of the Yr. Fairfax County Fedn. Citizen Assn. and Washington Post, 1997. Mem.: Nat. Soc. Arts and Letters (pres. Wash. chpt. 1973—74), Fairfax Bar Assn. (past chmn. real estate com.), Va. Bar Assn. (chmn. real property com. 1980—82, William B. Spong Jr. Professionalism award 2001), Va. State Bar (past chmn. real property sect.). Republican. Office: Court Square Bldg 310 4th St NE Ste 300 Charlottesville VA 22902-1288

ANDREWS, ROSALIND, probation officer; b. N.Y.C., June 19, 1943; m. Arthur J. Andrews, Feb. 23, 1979. BA, CUNY, 1965; MA, Cath. U. Am., 1972. Tchr. Long Island City (N.Y.) H.S., 1967-70; probation officer U.S. Probation Office, Washington, 1972-78, supervising probation officer, 1978-83; probation programs specialist Adminstrv. Office U.S. Cts., Washington, 1983-85; chief U.S. probation officer U.S. Dist. Ct. for Ea. Dist. Tenn., Knoxville, 1985—. Contbg. author: The Right To Remain Silent: The Probation Officer's Moral Dilimma, 1979. Vol. tchr. Queens Coll., CUNY, Prince Edward County, N.Y., 1963; bd. dirs. Sexual Assault Crisis Ctr., Heska Amuna Synagogue; mem. East Tenn. Task Force for Victims' Rights; founding mem. Chiefs' Adv. Coun. Mem. Phi Beta Kappa. Jewish. Avocations: foreign travel, eating good food. Office: US Dist Ct for Ea Dist Tenn PO Box 991 Knoxville TN 37901-0991

ANDREWS, SALLY MAY, healthcare administrator; b. Westfield, Mass., Feb. 29, 1956; d. Roger N. and Dorothy M. (Goodhind) A. Student, U. Conn., 1974-76; BA, Simmons Coll., Boston, 1978; MBA, Boston U., 1986. Payroll clk. Children's Hosp., Boston, 1978-79, asst. payroll supr., 1979-81, staff analyst dept. medicine, 1981-83, asst. adminstr. dept. medicine, 1983-86, adminstr. dept. medicine, 1986-97, vice chair adminstrn. and strategic planning dept. medicine, 1998-01; exec. dir. divsn. for rsch. and edn. in complementary and integrative med. therapies Harvard Med. Sch., Boston, 2002—. Mem. bd. overseers Lasell Coll., Newton, Mass., 1993-2001, trustee, 2001—. Mem. Am. Mgmt. Assn., Adminstrs. of Internal Medicine, Assn. Adminstrs. in Acad. Pediatrics (pres. 1996-97). Congregationalist. Office: Osher Inst Harvard Med Sch Landmark Ctr Ste 22A 401 Park Dr Boston MA 02215

ANDREWS, SALLY S. lawyer; BA, Duke U.; MAT, Harvard U.; MA, U. N.C.; JD, U. Tex., 1984. Bar: Tex., U.S. Tax Ct., U.S. Dist. Ct. Tex., U.S. Ct. Appeals (5th Cir.), U.S. Supreme Ct., 2003. With Rockefeller Bros. Fund; faculty assoc. Duke U. Med. Ctr., Tex. Med. Ctr. Sch. Pub. Health; pvt. practice Houston. Case ed.: journal Texas International Law Jour., 1983—84; author: (book) Elder Law Handbook Houston Bar, 2001. Advisory mem. tech. adv. com., Greater Houston YMCA, mem. endowment devel. com.; vol. Peace Corps, Ethiopia, mem. U.S. govt. selection and tng. staff. Recipient, 1996 Women on The Move Award, Houston Chronicle. Mem.: Houston Bar (bd. mem. Houston Lawyer Referral Svcs. 2003—), State Bar Tex. (4-C Grievance Comm. 1991—95, chair 1994—95), Houston Estate Fin. Forum (fellow 1990—), Houston Bus. and Estate Coun. (fellow 2002—), Tex. Acad. Probate & Trust Lawyers (fellow 1996—), Coll. State Bar Tex. (fellow 2000—), Houston Bar Found, asst. gov, Christian Legal Soc., Tex. Exec. Women, Rotary (pres. Galleria area club 1995—96, asst. gov. 1996—98), Phi Beta Kappa. Office: 2 Bering Pk 800 Bering Dr Ste 200 Houston TX 77057-2130

ANDREWS, THEODORA ANNE, retired librarian, educator; b. Carroll County, Ind., Oct. 14, 1921; d. Harry Floyd and Margaret Grace (Walter) Ulrey; m. Robert William Andrews, July 18, 1940 (div. 1935); 1 child, Martin Harry. BS with distinction, Purdue U., 1953; MS, U.Ill., 1955. Asst. reference libr. Purdue U., West Lafayette, Ind., 1955-56, pharmacy libr., 1956-79, instr. libr. sci., 1956-60, asst. prof., 1960-65, assoc. prof., 1965-71, prof., 1971-79, 91-92, prof. libr. sci., pharmacy, nursing and health sis. libr., 1979-90, spl. bibliographer, 1991-92, prof. emeritus libr. sci., 1992—. Del. Ind. Gov.'s Conf. Librs. and Info. Svcs., 1978. Author: A Bibliography of the Socioeconomic Aspects of Medicine, 1975, A Bibliography of Drug Abuse Including Alcohol and Tobacco, 1977, A Bibliography of Drug Abuse, Supplement, 1977-80, 1981, Bibliography on Herbs, Herbal Remedies and Natural Foods, 1982, Substance Abuse Materials for School Libraries, An Annotated Bibliography, 1985, Guide to the Literature of Pharmacy and the Pharmaceutical Sciences, 1986; sect. editor Advances in Alcohol and Substance Abuse, 1981-92; contbr. articles to profl. jours. Mem. Purdue Women's Caucus, 1973—, v.p., 1975-76, pres., 1976-77; m. Internat. Women's Yr. Regional Planning Com., 1977. Grad. fellow U. Ill., 1954-55. Mem. ALA, AAUP, Spl. Libr. Assn. (John H. Moriarty award Ind. chpt. 1972), Med. Libr. Assn., Am. Assn. Colls. Pharmacy, Kappa Delta Pi, Delta Rho Kappa. Baptist. Office: Purdue U Sch Pharmacy West Lafayette IN 47907

ANDREYCHUK, RAYNELL, Canadian senator; b. Saskatoon, SK, Canada, Aug. 14, 1944; BA, U. Sask., 1966, BLL, 1967; LLD honoris causa (hon.), U. Regina, 1993. Senator The Senate of Can., Ottawa, Canada, 1993—. Office: 575-F Centre Block The Senate of Canada Ottawa ON Canada K1A 0A4

ANDRIAN-CECIU, ROXANNE R. engineer, program manager; b. Bucarest, Romania, Dec. 2, 1960; came to the U.S., 1998; d. Alexandru and Adina Andrian; m. Aurel Mike Ceciu, Sept. 14, 1985; children: Sebastian, Stefan. Engring. diploma, Poly. Inst., Bucarest, 1984; MS, U. Paul Sabatier, Toulouse, France, 1992; PhD, U. Montreal, Can., 1999. Registered profl. engr., Can. Engr.; supr. Machine Tool Enterprise, Bucarest, 1984-86; design engr. Machine Tool Inst., Bucarest, 1986-90; program coord. G. Soros Found. for An Open Soc., Bucarest, 1990-91; rsch./tchg. asst. U. Montreal, 1993-97; mfg. engr. Bombardier-Canadair, Montreal, 1998; design engr. GE, Erie, Pa., 1998-99; bus. analyst Six Sigma Black Belt, GE, Erie, 1999—. Cons. owner R. Andrian-Cons., Montreal, 1996-98. Mem. ASME (assoc., chmn. Erie chpt. 1999—), Soc. Mfg. Engrs., Soc. Automotive Engrs. (affiliate), Soc. Women Engrs. (sect. rep. Erie chpt. 1999—). Achievements include inventor of device for the tool-holders clamping, unlocking and rotation, tool magazine, device for tool transport. Office: GE 2901 E Lake Rd Erie PA 16531-0001 E-mail: roxanne.andrian@trans.ge.com.

ANDRZEJEWSKI, PAT See BENATAR, PAT

ANDUJAR, NORMA BURGOS, former state official; b. Chgo., Oct. 29, 1954; children: Roberto, Norman. BA in Econs. cum laude, U. P.R., 1976, MPA, 1982. Cert. mgr. of housing. Pres., exec. dir. Codevisa, Inc., 1986-90; cons. Dept. Transp. and Pub. Works, 1990; cons. Strategic Planning project P.R. Planning Bd., P.R. 2005, 1990-92; pres., assoc. mem. P.R. Planning Bd., 1993-98; sec. of state P.R., 1998-99. Chmn. bd. Old San Juan Corp. Recipient Spl. Recognition award Govt. of P.R., 1994, Exemplary Pub. Servant award, 1994, others. Mem. Am. Planning Soc., P.R. Planning Soc., Soc. for Internat. Devel., U. P.R. Alumni (pub. adminstrn. chpt.), Internat. Downtown Assn., P.R. C. of c. (transp. adminstrn. com.), U.S. Tennis Assn., P.R. Tennis Assn., P.R. Economists Assn. Mem. New Progressive Party. Roman Catholic. Office: Sec of State PO Box 3271 San Juan PR 00902-3271

ANGARAN, SALLY JEAN, school system administrator; d. Julius Kanner and Celia Flam; m. James M. Angaran; children: Jenny Takeda, Jeremy. Student, U. Calif., 1965—69. Prin. Territorial Sch., Eugene, Oreg., 1975—80; coord. Albany (Oreg.)Edn., 1980—90; with Dayton (Oreg.) Sch. Dist., Dayton. Home: 4103 S Sunray Salem OR 97302 Office: Dayton Sch Dist 801 Ferry St Dayton OR 97114

ANGARD, NANCY TELLIS, medical/surgical nurse; b. N.Y.C., May 17, 1952; d. Albert and Rose Tellis. AS in Nursing, Hillsborough C.C., Tampa, Fla., 1992; BA, Graceland U., Lamoni, Iowa, 1997. RN Fla., cert. ambulatory women's health, NCC. Contr. F.A. Components, Inc., Elmhurst, NY, 1982—85; program mgr.Advanced Reproductive Techs. Program, Univ. Cmty. Hosp., Tampa, Fla., 1992—. Fla. sect. chair Assn. Women's Health, Obstetric & Neonatal Nurses. Contbr. articles to profl. jours. Recipient Leadership and Profl. Devel. award, Wyeth Ayerst, 1999. Mem.: [illegible] Thivor, 1937 Bayonridge St Wesley Chapel FL 33543 Other ABC Program Univ Cmty Hosp 3100 E Fletcher Ave Tampa FL 33513 Personal E-mail: nanangard@aol.com.

ANGELES, CARMEN M. pathologist; arrived in U.S., 1967; children: Maria Angela, Joseph Patrick, Carmichael. MD, U. Santo Tomas, Manila, 1965. Diplomate Am. Bd. Pathology. Asst. lab. dir. Brunswick Hosp. Ctr., Amityville, NY, 1982—93; dir. pathology and lab. svcs., 1993—; dir. lab. Kyto-Meridien Diagnostics, Woodbury, NY, 1990—99; staff pathologist Dianon Sys., Woodbury, 1990—2003, Labcorp, Uniondale, NY, 2003—. Mem.: Nassau-Suffolk Soc. Pathologists. Office: Brunswick Hosp Ctr 366 Broadway Amityville NY 11701

ANGELL, ELLEN, interior designer; b. Centralia, Mo., Mar. 16, 1927; d. Robert Loren and Margaret Amanda Jane (Smith) A. Cert., N.Y. Sch. Design, 1946. Interior designer Denver Dry Goods, 1946-49; cons. home furnishings Barker Bros., Los Angeles, 1950-52; interior designer Joske's, Houston, 1952-55, Showroom Finer Furniture, Corpus Christi, Tex., 1955-66, Braslau's, Corpus Christi, 1966-70, Browning Bros., Corpus Christi, 1970—. Lectr. in field. Author: The Layman's Handbook of Interior Design, 1972. Fellow Am. Soc. Interior Designers (long range planning nat. com. 1987-89, nat. bd. dirs. 1984-86, regional v.p., Medalist award 1984, Commendation for Outstanding Service 1986); mem. Am. Inst. Interior Designers (sec., chmn., bd. dirs. Tex. chpt. 1959-75, Outstanding Interior Designer 1974). Democrat. Avocations: meditation, writing. Home. 346 Southern St Corpus Christi TX 78404-1853 Office: Browning Bros 2001 S Staples St Corpus Christi TX 78404-3000

ANGELL, LOIS LOUISE, writer, comedienne, poet; b. Riceville, Iowa; d. Kenneth Edwin and Marie E. (Dynes) A.; 1 child, Jim Barrett. Student, Am. U., 1959-60, G.U. U. Alberta, 1978. Staff dir. Justice Rehnquist U.S. Supreme Ct., 1971-80; pub. rels. dir. Better Comm. Found., Silver Spring, Md., 1984; free lance writer and performer Arlington, Va. Talk and news show guest. Performer at comedy and supper clubs, radio and TV. Recipient Spl. Achievement award U.S Dept. Justice, 1971, Outstanding Svc. to the Arts in Comm. award Capital Hill Arts Workshop, 1984. Mem. NAFE, Washington Ind. Writers, The Capitol Hill Club, Internat. Platform Assn., Capitol Hill Poetry Group (founder), Nat. Conf. Rsch. on Women, Nat. Capitol Spkrs. Assn., Washington Conv. and Visitors Assn., World Affairs Coun., The Cato Inst. Episcopalian. Home: The Georgetown 2512 Q St NW #314 Washington DC 20007

ANGELL, MARCIA, pathologist, editor-in-chief; b. Knoxville, Tenn., Apr. 20, 1939; BS, James Madison U., 1960; MD, Boston U., 1967. Resident in internal medicine Mt. Auburn Hosp., resident in pathology; resident in internal medicine Univ. Hosp.; resident in pathology New Eng. Deaconess Hosp.; with New Eng. Jour. Medicine, Boston, 1979—, exec. editor, 1988, interim editor-in-chief, 1999—. Lectr. Harvard U. Author: Science on Trial: The Clash of Medical Evidence and the Law in the Breast Implant Case; co-author: Basic Pathology. Named One of 25 Most Influential Ams. Time Mag., 1997. Mem. ACP, Inst. Medicine, Assn. Am. Physicians, Mass. Med. Soc. Office: New Eng Jour Medicine 10 Shattuck St Boston MA 02115-6011

ANGELL, M(ARY) FAITH, federal magistrate judge; b. Buffalo, May 7, 1938; d. San S. and Marie B. (Caboni) A.; m. Kenneth F. Carobus, Oct. 27, 1973; children: Andrew M. Carobus, Alexander F. Carobus. AB, Mt. Holyoke Coll.; MSS, Bryn Mawr Coll.; JD, Temple U. Bar: Pa. 1971, U.S. Dist. Ct. (ea. dist) Pa. 1971, U.S. Ct. Appeals (3rd cir.) Pa. 1974, U.S. Supreme Ct. 1979; Acad. Cert. Social Workers. Dir. social work, vol. svcs. Wills Eye Hosp., Phila., 1961-64, 65-69; dir. soc. work dept. juvenile divsn. Defender Assoc., Phila., 1969-71; asst. atty. City of Phila., 1971-72; asst. atty. gen. Commonwealth of Pa., Phila., 1972-74, deputy atty. gen., 1974-78; regional counsel ICC, Phila., 1978-80, regional dir., 1980-88; adminstrv. law judge Social Security Adminstrn., Phila., 1988-90; U.S. magistrate judge U.S. Dist. Ct. (ea. dist.) Pa., Phila., 1990—. Adj. prof. Temple U. Law Sch., Phila., 1976-94, clin. instr., 1973-76; co-chmn. Commn. on Gender, 3d Cir. Task Force on Equal Treatment in Cts., 1994—99; mem. com. on racial and gender bias in the justice sys. Supreme Ct. of Pa., 2000-02. Federal trustee Defender Assn. Phila., 1985-90; bd. dirs. Child Welfare Adv. Bd., Phila., 1984-90, Federal Cts. 200 Adv. Bd.,

---

Phila., 1987-88, Phila. Woman's Network, 1986-88. Recipient Sr. Exec. Svc. award U.S. Govt., 1980. Mem. NASW, FBA (chair exec. com., pres. 1990-92, recognition 1992), Nat. Assn. Women Judges, Fed. Magistrate Judges Assn. (dist. dir. 1994-98), Phila. Bar Assn. (chmn. com. 1976-77), Temple Am. Inn of Cts. (master 1993-98), Third Circuit Task Force on Equal Treatment in the Courts (co-chair Commn. on Gender 1994-97), Temple Law Alumni Exec. Bd. (Women's Law Caucus Honoree 1996). Office: US District Court 601 Market St 3030 US Courthouse Philadelphia PA 19106

ANGELO, E. JOANNE, child, adolescent and adult psychiatrist; b. Boston, Feb. 11, 1936; d. Gaspar and Eda (Polcari) A. AB, Mt. Holyoke Coll., 1957; MD, Tufts U., 1961. Diplomate Am. Bd. Psychiatry and Neurology. Pvt. practice, Boston, 1969—; med. dir. Canarsie Mental Health Ctr., Bklyn., 1967—69; staff psychiatrist Cmty. Mental Health Svc. Ctr., Boston, 1969—73; psychiat. dir. Laboure Ctr., South Boston, Mass., 1974—78. Cons. Chandler Sch. for Women, Boston, 1971-72, Kennedy Meml. Hosp., Boston, 1971-74, St. Margaret's Hosp., Boston, 1976-83, North Suffolk Health Ctr., Boston, 1978-79; mem. staff St. Elizabeth's Hosp., Boston, Good Samaritan Hospice Boston. Mem. editl. bd. (Jour.) Nat. Cath. Bioethics Quar. Mem. Pontifical Acad. for Life (corr.). Office: 403 Commonwealth Ave Boston MA 02215-2326

ANGELO, LARIAN, economist; b. N.Y.C., Oct. 9, 1953; d. Lawrence and Jeanette Angelo. BA, Bklyn. Coll., 1975; PhD, New Sch. for Social Rsch., 1990. Rsch. dir. United Elec. Radio Workers, Pitts., 1986-90; chief economist N.Y. City Coun./Fin., N.Y.C., 1990-94, spl. advisor, 1994-99, dep. dir., 1999-2001, dir. coun. fin. divsn., 2002—; cons. on urban issues City of Amsterdam, The Netherlands, 2000—. Lectr. John Jay Coll., N.Y.C., 1991-95, Queens Coll., N.Y.C., 1996-99; cons. urban issues City of Amsterdam, 2000. Contbr. articles to profl. jours. Chmn. bd. Pub. Access TV Sta., N.Y.C., 1999. Mem. Gay and Lesbian Ind. Dems. Democrat. Roman Catholic. Avocations: fencing, opera, reading club. Office: NY City Coun Fin Divsn 250 Broadway New York NY 10007-2516 E-mail: finangel@council.nyc.ny.us.

ANGELOU, MAYA (MARGUERITE JOHNSON), writer, playwright, actress, activist; b. St. Louis, Missouri, Apr. 4, 1928; d. Bailey and Vivian (Baxter) Johnson; 1 son, Guy Johnson. Studied dance with Pearl Primus, N.Y.C.; degrees (hon.), Smith Coll., 1975, Mills Coll., 1975, Lawrence U., 1976, Portland State U., 1973, Occidental Coll., 1979, Atlanta U., 1980, U. Ark., 1980, U. Minn., 1980, Austin Coll., 1980, Wheaton Coll., 1981, Kean Coll., 1982, Spelman Coll., 1983, Boston Coll., 1983, Winston-Salem U, 1984, U. Brunesis, 1984, Howard U., 1985, Tufts U., 1985, Va. Commonwealth U., 1985, Northeastern U., 1992, Academy of Southern Arts & Letters, 1993, Drown U., 1994, U Durham, UK, 1995, Hope Coll., 2001, Columbia U., 2003, Eastern Conn. U., 2003. Taught modern dance The Rome Opera House and Hambina Theatre, Tel Aviv; writer-in-residence U. Kans., Lawrence, 1970; disting. vis. prof. Wake Forest U., 1974, Wichita State U., 1974, Calif. State U., Sacramento, 1974, apptd. mem. Am. Revolution Bicentennial Council by Pres. Ford, 1975-76; 1st Reynolds prof. Am. Studies, Wake Forest U. since 1981, a lifetime appointment. Author: I Know Why the Caged Bird Sings, 1970, Just Give Me A Cool Drink of Water 'Fore I Die (nominated for Pulitzer Prize), 1971, Georgia, Georgia, 1972, Gather Together in My Name, 1974, Oh Pray My Wings are Gonna Fit Me Well, 1975, Singin' and Swingin' and Gettin' Merry Like Christmas, 1976, And Still I Rise, 1978, The Heart of a Woman, 1981, Shaker, Why Don't You Sing?, 1983, All God's Children Need Traveling Shoes, 1986, Now Sheba Sings the Song, 1987, I Shall Not Be Moved, 1990, On the Pulse of Morning: The Inaugural Poem, 1993, Lessons in Living, 1993, Wouldn't Take Nothing for My Journey Now, 1993, My Painted House, My Friendly Chicken, and Me, 1994, The Complete Collected Poems of Maya Angelou, 1994, Phenomenal Women: Four Poems for Women, 1995, A Brave and Startling Truth, 1995, From a Black Women to a Black Man, 1996, Kofi and His Magic, 1996, Extravagant Spirits, 1997, Making Magic in the World, 1998, Even the Stars Look Lonesome, 1997, A Song Flung Up To Heaven, 2002; (plays) Cabaret for Freedom, 1960, The Least of These, 1966, Gettin' Up Stayed On My Mind, 1967, Ajax, 1974, Moon On a Rainbow Shawl, 1988; (screenplays) Georgia, Georgia, 1972, All Day Long, 1974; appeared on TV in The Richard Pryor Special, guest appearances Sister, Sisters, 1982, Touched By An Angel, 1995, Moesha, 1999, Runaway, 2000; author/prodr. Three Way Choice, Afro-American in the Arts (Golden Eagle award); wrote and presented Trying to Make it Home, 1988; writer for Oprah Winfrey's Harpo Prodns.; poetry writer for film Poetic Justice, 1993; appeared in plays: Porgy and Bess, 1954-55 (Europe), 1957 (U.S.), Calypso, 1957, The Blacks, 1960, Mother Courage, 1964, Medea, Look Away, 1973, Ajax, 1974, And Still I Rise, 1976, Moon on a Rainbow Shawl, 1988; appeared in films: (TV miniseries) Roots, 1977 (Emmy Nom. best sup. actress), (features) Poetic Justice, 1993, How to Make an American Quilt, 1995; dir. films: Down in the Delta, 1998; spoken word albums include The Poetry of Maya Angelou, 1969, Women in Business, 1981, Been Found, 1996; contbd. articles, short stories, poems to Black Scholar, Chgo. Daily News, Cosmopolitan, Harper's Bazaar, Life Mag., Redbook, Sunday N.Y. Times, Mademoiselle Mag., Essence, Ebony Mag., Calif. Living Mag, Ghanaian Times. Apptd. by Dr. Martin Luther King Jr. No. Coord. Southern Christian Leadership Conf., 1959-60, apptd. by Pres. Ford to Bicentennial Commn., by Pres. Carter to Nat. Commn. on Observance of Internat. Women's Yr., ambassador, Unicef Internat., 1996. Chubb fellowship award Yale U., 1970, named Woman of Yr. in Comm., 1976; Ladies Home Jour. Top 100 Most Influential Women, 1983, The Matrix award, 1983, The North Carolina Award in Lit., 1987, Woman of the Yr. Essence Mag., 1992, Disting. Woman of N.C., 1992, Horatio Alger award, 1992, Grammy award best spoken word or non-traditional album, 1994 (for recording of "On the Pulse of the Morning"), Grammy award best spoken or non-traditional album, 1994 (for recording of "Phenomenal Woman"), NAACP Image Award for Outstanding Literary Work for "Even the Stars Look Lonesome", 1997, National Medal of Art, 2000. Mem. AFTRA, Dirs. Guild Am., Equity, Harlem Writers Guild, Am. Film Inst. (trustee), Women's Prison Assn., Horatio Alger Assn. Dist. Americans, Nat. Soc. Prevention of Cruelty to Children (Maya Angelou Ctr. opened 1992), W.E.B. duBois Found., Nat. Soc. Collegiate Scholars, Nat. Soc. High School Scholars. Office: c/o Dave La Camera Lordly and Dame Inc 51 Church St Boston MA 02116-5417*

ANGIER, NATALIE MARIE, science journalist; b. N.Y.C., Feb. 16, 1958; d. Keith and Adele Bernice (Rosenhal) A.; m. Richard Steven Weiss, July 27, 1991. Student, U. Mich., 1974-76; BA, Barnard Coll., 1978. Staff writer Discover Mag., N.Y.C., 1980-83, Time Mag., N.Y.C., 1984-86; editor Savvy Mag., N.Y.C., 1983-84; journalism educator NYU, N.Y.C., 1987-89; became reporter N.Y. Times, N.Y.C., 1990, now science correspondent Washington. Author: Natural Obsessions, 1988, The Beauty of the Beastly, 1995. Recipient Pulitzer Prize for beat reporting, 1991, Journalism award GM Inl. Bd., 1991, Lewis Thomas award Marine Biol. Labs., 1990, Journalism award AAAS, 1992, Disting. Alumna award Barnard Coll., 1993. Mem. Nat. Assn. Sci. Writers. Avocation: weightlifting. Office: NY Times Washington Bureau 1627 I St NW Fl 7 Washington DC 20006-4007

ANGRIST, GEORGENE LEITER, social studies educator; b. Mpls., Dec. 28, 1951; d. George Otto and Josephine Gertrude Leiter; m. James Ford Angrist, Oct. 18, 1975. BS, U. Minn., Mpls., 1973, MEd, 1982. Social studies educator Spring Valley H.S., Minn., 1973—74; social studies tchg. asst. U. Minn., Mpls., 1981—82; social studies educator Coon Rapids H.S., Minn., 1974—. Student tchg. supr. Coon Rapids H.S., Minn., 1985—, mem. bldg. leadership team, 1990, mentor program, 1992—. Mem., freedom writer Amnesty Internat., Mpls., 1989—. Mem.: Anoka Hennepin Edn. Minn. (union rep. 1997—, Outstanding Tchr. award 1999). Office: Coon Rapids HS 2340 Northdale Blvd Coon Rapids MN 55433

ANGSTADT, FRANCES VIRGINIA, language arts and theatre arts educator; b. Dover, Del., Oct. 11, 1953; d. T. Richard Sr. and Frances Virginia (Kohout) A. BA, Del. State U., 1976; MFA, Cath. U. Am., 1982; postgrad. in PhD program, Tex. U. Tech. Lighting designer, assoc. dir. écarté dance Theatre, Dover, 1981-93; alternative tchr. Lake Forest H.S., Felton, Del., 1982-87; English tchr. Dover H.S., 1987-89; lang. arts and theater tchr. Ctrl. Mid. Sch., Dover, 1989—2003; lighting designer Harrisburg (Pa.) Ballet, 1991-93. Lighting designer, artistic advisor Act I Players, Dover, 1983-93, lighting designer Balt. Shakespeare Festival, 1994, Kimberly Mackin Dance Co., Balt., Axis Theatre, 1996-99, Women's Project at Theatre Project, Balt., 1997-2000; adj. faculty Del. State U., Dover, 1985-89, Wilmington Coll., Dover, 1996-2001; tech. advisor 2d St. Players, Milford, Del., 1994-2001; dance leadership Visual and Performing Arts Commn., Dover, 1994-2000; English devel. com. state (testing) assessment team Dover Dept. of Edn., 1997-2000, ESL assessment team, 2000-2001, intern visual and performing arts, 2002-2003. Mem. Vietnam Vets. Meml. Com., Dover, 1985-87; sec. mem. Dover Arts Coun., 1983-93, tech. advisor, 1988-94; sec. Capital Educators Assn., Dover, 1993-2001; tech. advisor City of Dover First Night, 1997-2001; mem. Balt. Theatre Alliance. All Am. Youth Honor Band scholar, 1972, Del. State U. scholar, Dover, 1974-76; Chancellor's guaranteed fellow 2001—; apptd. to adjudicator Del. Theatre Assn., 1986. Mem. ACLU, AAUW, HRC, NGLTF, Nat. Coun. Tchrs. English, U.S. Inst. Tech. Theatre, Assn. Theatre Higher Edn., Theatre Communications Group, S.W. Theatre Assn. Avocations: swimming, biking, voice, visual art, dance lighting. Address: 3011 25th St Lubbock TX 79410

ANGUIANO, LUPE, advocate; b. La Junta, Colo., June 12, 1929; d. Jose and Rosario (Gonzalez) A. Student, Ventural (Calif.) Jr. Coll., 1948, Victory Noll Jr. Coll., Huntington, Ind., 1949-52, Marymount Coll., Palos Verdes, Calif., 1958-59, Calif. State U., L.A., 1965-67; MA, Antioch-Putney, Yellow Springs, Ohio, 1978. S.W. regional dir. NAACP Legal Def. and Ednl. Fund, L.A., 1965-69; civil rights specialist HEW, Washington, 1969-73; S.W. regional dir. Nat. Coun. Cath. Bishops, Region X, San Antonio, 1973-77; pres. Nat. Women's Employment and Edn. Inc., L.A., 1979-91; cons. Cisco Sys. Inc., 1998-99; pres., cons. Lupe Anguiano & Assocs., 1981—; dir. devel. La Jolla Inst., Van Nuys, Calif., West Valley Alliance; fund devel. dir. Girl Scouts of the San Fernando Valley, Chatsworth, Calif.; rep. Primerica, Valencia, Calif. Cons. Tex. Dept. Human Resources, Dept. Labor, Women's Bur., U.S. Office Pers. Mgmt., USCG, Washington, 1990-92; tech. cons. Cisco Sys. Inc.; developer regional networking acad., Oxnard Coll.; part-time faculty mem. Ventura (Calif.) Coll.; proposal reader U.S. Office Edn., Women's Equity Act; mem. Tex. Adv. Coun. on Tec.-Vocat. Edn., Calif. del. White House Conf. on Status of Women, 1967; founding mem. policy coun. Nat. Women's Polit. Caucus, 1971—; Tex. and nat. del. Intrnat. Women's Yr., 1976-77; chmn. Nat. Women's Polit. Caucus Welfare Reform Task Force, 1977; co-developer Cisco Networking Acad. in Ventura County high schs. Author (with others): U.S. Bilingual Edn. Act, 1967, Tex. AFDC Employment and Edn. Act, 1977; manuals for Women's Employment and Edn. Model program. Co-chmn. Nat. Peace Acad. Campaign, 1977 81; founder, bd. dirs Nat. Chicana Found. Inc., 1971-78; bd. dirs. Calif. Coun. Children and Youth, 1967, Rio Grande Fedn. Chicano Health Ctrs., S.W. rural states, 1974-76, Women's Lobby, Washington, 1974-77, Rural Am. Women, Washington, 1978—, Small Bus. Coun. Greater San Antonio; mem. Pres.'s Coun. on Pvt. Sector Initiatives, 1983. Recipient Cmty. award Coalition Mex.-Am. Orgns., 1967, Outstanding Svc. award Washington, 1968, Thanksgiving award Boys' Club, 1976, Outstanding Svc. award Tex. Women's Polit. Caucus, 1977, Mex. Am. Legal Defense award, 1980, Vista award for Exceptional Svc. to coal and poverty, 1980, Headliner award San Antonio Women in Comm., 1978, Woman of Yr. award Tex. Women's Polit. Caucus, 1978, Pres.'s Vol. Action award 1983, Leadership award Nat. Network Hispanic women, 1989; named Outstanding Woman of Yr., L.A. County, 1972, Woman of the 80's, Ms. Mag.,, 1980, Nat. Pres.'s award Nat. Image Inc., 1981, Wonder Woman Found. award, 1982, Pres.'s Vol. Action award, 1983, Act. of Yr., San Antonio SBA, 1984; selected one of Am.'s 100 Most Important Women, Ladies Home Jour., 1988, 89; featured in CBS TV series An American Portrait, 1985, Leadership award Nat. Network Hispanic Women, 1989. Mem. Nat. Assn. Female Execs., Pres.'s Assn., Am. Mgmt. Assn. Republican. Roman Catholic. Office: Primerica 25060 Stanford Ave Valencia CA 91355-3411 Home: 1031 Kumquat Pl Oxnard CA 93036-1533 Office Phone: 805-983-8517. Office Fax: 805-983-8519. E-mail: languian@gte.net.

ANISIMOVA, TANYA, cellist, educator; b. Brozny, USSR, Feb. 15, 1966; came to U.S., 1990; d. Mikhail Alekseevich Anisimov and Zoya Marsanovna Islamova; m. Alexander Sergeevich Anufriev, Aug. 24, 1999. Diploma cum laude, Moscow State Conservatory, 1989; artist diploma, Boston U., 1992; M Musical Arts, Yale U., 1995. Cellist Moscow Conservatory String Quartet, 1987-89. Tchr. cello and chamber music; artistic dir. Mousetrap Concert Series, Washington Grove, Md., 1999; resident Ctr. for Creative Arts, 1995, 96, 99. Composed, recorded CD Music from Mt. San Angelo, 1995. Recipient 1st prize Concertino Prague Internat. Competition, 1981, All-USSR String Quartets Competition, 1987, Laureate 1st Dmitri Shostakovich Chamber Music Competition, St. Petersburg, Russia, 1987, Min-On Internat. Chamber Music Competition, Tokyo, 1989; Meet a Composer Found. grantee, 1999. Mem. Nat. Music Tchrs. Assn., Kindler Cello Club. Avocations: painting, mushroom picking. Home: PO Box 752 Washington Grove MD 20880-0752

ANISTON, JENNIFER, actress; b. Sherman Oaks, Calif., Feb. 11, 1969; d. John and Nancy Aniston; m. Brad Pitt, July 29, 2000. Attended, Fiorello La Guardia School of Music, Art & Performing Arts, N.Y.C. Actor: (TV series) Ferris Bueller, 1990, Molloy, 1990, The Edge, 1992, Muddling Through, 1994, Friends, 1994—2004 (Emmy award best actress, 2002, Golden Globe award best actress, 2003, People's Choice award favorite female television performer, 2001, 2002, 2003, 2004), (guest appearances) Herman's Head, 1992—93, Quantum Leap, 1992, Burke's Law, 1994, : (TV films) Camp Cucamonga, 1990, Sunday Funnies, 1993; (films) Leprechaun, 1993, She's the One, 1996, Dream for an Insomniac, 1996, Til There Was You, 1997, Picture Perfect, 1997, The Thin Pink Line, 1998, The Object of My Affection, 1998, The Iron Giant (voice), 1999, Office Space, 1999, Rock Star, 2001, The Good Girl, 2002, Bruce Almighty, 2003, Along Came Polly, 2004; (plays) For Dear Life, Dancing on Checkers' Grave, (music videos) I'll Be There For You, 1995, Walls, 1996, I Want To Be In Love, 2001. Office: PMK/HBH 8500 Wilshire Blvd Ste 700 Beverly Hills CA 90211*

ANKENEY, JEAN B. state legislator; b. Foochow, Peoples Republic of China, Mar. 29, 1922; 3 children. BA, Hiram Coll., 1944; MA, Case Western Res. U. Mem., Chittenden County Vt. Senate, Montpelier, 1993—. V.p. Chittenden County Solid Waste Bd.; mem. adv. bd. Adelphia Cable Pub. Access TV. Recipient Susan B. Anthony award YWCA, 1990. Mem. Common Cause. Address: 245 Saint George Ln Williston VT 05495-9307

ANN-MARGRET, (ANN-MARGRET OLSSON), actress, performer; b. Stockholm, Apr. 28, 1941; came to U.S., naturalized, 1949; d. Gustav and Anna Olsson; m. Roger Smith, 1967. Student, Northwestern U. Performer radio shows, band tours; appeared with: George Burns, Las Vegas, 1961; headliner numerous appearances, Las Vegas, 1961—; made NYC debut Radio City Music Hall, 1991; actress numerous films including Pocketful of Miracles, 1961, State Fair, 1961, Bye Bye Birdie, 1962, Viva Las Vegas, 1963, The Pleasure Seekers, 1964, Kitten With a Whip, 1964, Bus Riley's Back in Town, 1964, Once A Thief, 1965, Cincinnati Kid, 1965, Stagecoach, 1966, Made in Paris, 1966, The Swinger, 1966, Murderers' Row, 1967, The Tiger and the Pussycat, 1967, R.P.M., 1970, C.C. & Company, 1971, Carnal Knowledge, 1971, Train Robbers, 1972, Outside Man, 1972,

Tommy, 1975, Joseph Andrews, 1976, The Last Remake of Beau Geste, 1977, Magic, 1978, The Cheap Detective, 1978, Lookin' To Get Out, 1978, The Villain, 1979, Middle-Age Crazy, 1980, The Return of the Soldier, 1982, I Ought To Be in Pictures, 1982, Twice in a Lifetime, 1985, 52-Pick-up, 1987, A Tiger's Tale, 1988, A New Life, 1988, Something More, Newsies, 1992, Grumpy Old Men, 1993, Grumpier Old Men, 1995, Seduced by Madness, 1996, The Limey, 1999, Any Given Sunday, 1999, The Last Producer, 2000, Interstate 60, 2002; several TV spls., 1975-76; TV films Who Will Love My Children, 1983, A Streetcar Named Desire, 1984, Our Sons, 1991, Nobody's Children, 1994, Seduced by Madness: The Diane Borchardt Story, 1996, Blue Rodeo, 1996, Life of the Party: The Pamela Harriman Story, 1998, Happy Face, 1999, The 10th Kingdom, 2000, Perfect Murder, Perfect Town, 2000, A Woman's a Helluva Thing, 2001; mini-series The Two Mrs. Grenvilles, 1987, Alex Haley's Queen, 1993, Scarlett, 1994, Blonde, 2001; TV series Four Corners, 1998; author: (with Todd Gold) Ann-Margret: My Story, 1994. Recipient 2 Acad. award nominations, 4 Emmy nominations, 5 Golden Globes. Office: William Morris Agy 151 S El Camino Dr Beverly Hills CA 90212-2775*

ANNS, ARLENE EISERMAN, publishing company executive; b. Pearl River, N.Y. d. Frederick Joel and Anna (Behnke) Eiserman. Student, Fairleigh Dickinson U., 1946-48; BS, Utah State U., 1950; postgrad., Traphagen Sch. Design, 1957, NYU, 1958, Hunter Coll., 1959-60. Rsch. and promotion asst. Archtl. Record, N.Y.C., 1952-56; asst. rsch. dir. Esquire Mag., N.Y.C., 1956-62; rsch. mgr. Am. Machinist publ. McGraw-Hill, Inc., N.Y.C., 1962-67, mktg. svc. mgr., 1967-69, 69-71, sales mgr., 1976-77, dir. mktg., 1977-78; v.p. mktg. svcs. Morgan Grampian, Inc., N.Y.C., 1971-72; mktg. dir. Family Health and Diversion mag., 1972-74; dist. sales mgr. Postgrad. Medicine, 1974-76; advt. sales mgr. Contempory Ob/Gyn, 1976-78, dir. profl. devel., 1978-80; pub. graduating engr., dir. mktg. Aviation Week Group, 1980-90; pub. World Aviation Directory; dir. comms. Aviation Week Group, 1990-92; v.p. Phase, Ltd., 1993—. Mem. Am. Mktg. Assn., Pharm. Advt. Club, Advt. Women N.Y., Advt. Club N.Y., Sales Exec. Club, Employment Mgmt. Assn., Am. Soc. Pers. Adminstrs., Nat. Orgn. Disability (bd. dirs.), Internat. Platform Assn., Coll. Placement Coun., U. Va. Libr. Assoc. Bd., Svc. Corps Ret. Execs. (chair), Wings Club, Dir. Assn., Pi Sigma Alpha. Home: Barnahill Farm 6653 Celt Rd Stanardsville VA 22973-3638

ANROMAN, GILDA MARIE, college program director, lecturer, educator; b. New Haven, Conn., July 19, 1959; d. Owen Francis Anroman and Edera (Vagnini) Felice. BA, Trinity Coll., Washington, 1983; M in Applied Anthropology, U. Md., 1994, grad. cert. in historic preservation, 1997, postgrad., 1994—. Cert. yoga instr. Clin. technologist Nat. Health Lab., Vienna, Va., 1983-85; dept. mgr., clin. technologist Anmed/Biosafe Inc., Rockville, Md., 1985-92; rsch. asst. U. Md., College Pk., 1992-94, instr. dept. anthropology, 1994-97, acad. advisor, 1996-99, asst. dir. College Park Scholars College Park, 1999—2000, asst. dir. undergrad. programs R.H. Smith Sch. Bus., 2000—03; program dir. Cath. U. of Am., Columbus Sch. Law, Washington, 2003—. Lectr. U. Md., 2003—. Rep. College Pk. Historic Dist. Commn., 1994-95. Scholar State of Conn., Hartford, 1977, Senatorial scholar, State of Md., Annpolis, 1995-99, Del. scholar, Annapolis, 1998-99; recipient Margaret Cook award for historic preservation Prince George's County, Md., 1997. Mem. AAUW, Am. Anthropol. Assn., Am. Hist. Assn., Am. Soc. Environ. History, Am. Studies Assn., Inst. of Early Am. History/Culture, Orgn. Am. Historians, Soc. for Hist. Archaeology, Nat. Trust for Historic Preservation, Nat. Coun. on Pub. History, Assn. for the History Medicine. Home: 34-D Ridge Rd Greenbelt MD 20770 Office: Cath Univ Am Columbus Sch Law Washington DC 20064 Business E-Mail: ganroman@eng.umd.edu.

ANSELMI, ELVIRA, psychologist, researcher; d. Pasquale and Maria Arpino; m. Gregory D. Anselmi, Aug. 12, 1984; 1 child, Eustace J. PhD, Fairleigh Dickinson U., Teaneck, N.J., 1998. Lic. psychologist N.J. Clin. coord. traumatic brain injury model system Kessler Med. Rehab. Rsch. and Edn. Corp., West Orange, NJ, 1999—; psychologist, neuropsychologist in pvt. practice Verona, NJ, 2001—. Mem.: N.J. Assn. Cognitive Therapists, N.J. Psychol. Assn., APA. Achievements include research in the efficacy of psychological therapies in brain injury. Avocations: gardening, portrait drawing. Home: 100 Highland Ave Montclair NJ 07042-1912 Office: 25 Grove Ave Montclair NJ 07044 Office Phone: 973-233-0441.

ANSORGE, IONA MARIE, retired real estate agent, musician, educator; b. Nov. 3, 1927; d. Edgar B. and Marie Louise (Bleeke) Bohn; m. Edwin James Ansorge, Sept. 13, 1949; children: Richard, Michelle. BA, Valparaiso U., 1949; cert. teaching, Drake U., 1964; MA, U. Iowa, 1976. Min. of music Our Savior Luth. Ch., Des Moines, 1949-63; tchr. Johnston (Iowa) High Sch., 1964-75; instr. Iowa Meth. Sch. Nursing, Des Moines, 1978-87; owner, pres. Bed and Breakfast in Iowa, Ltd., 1982-86; realtor Better Homes and Gardens First Realty, Des Moines, 1986-92. Pres. Des Moines Jaycee-ettes; spearheaded drive Des Moines Zoo; founder Messiah Luth. Ch., Des Moines, 1978; started Iowa Bed and Breakfast Industry, 1982; owner, pres. Bed and Breakfast in Iowa, Ltd.; mem. First Luth. Ch.; permanent sec. Class of 1949, Valparaiso U. Mem. LWV, AAUW, Am. Choral Dirs. Assn., Des Moines Bd. Realtors, Women's Coun. Realtors, Realtor's Million Dollar Club, Jaycee-ettes (pres. Des Moines chpt. 1957-58), Valparaiso U. Guild (charter mem. Des Moines chpt.), Mortar Bd. Lutheran. Avocations: playing piano and organ, tennis, bridge, reading. Home: 8345 Twinberry Pt Colorado Springs CO 80920-5394

ANTAL, ANN SLAUGHTER, adult education educator; d. Frank Rives and Ann Lovelace (Gorsuch) Slaughter; m. Michael Jerry Antal, Jr., June 8, 1972; children: Dickinson James, Rachel Caroline. BA, Mt. Holyoke Coll., 1971; MA, Tufts U., 1973; tchr. certification, U. Hawaii, 1991. Freelance translator, 1974—83; instr., trainer Berlitz, Honolulu, 1983—85; ESL instr. McKinley Cmty. Sch. for Adults, Honolulu, 1985—2003, ESL instr., coord. No Child Left Behind, 2003—. Mem. sch. adv. coun. McKinley Cmty. Sch. for Adults, Honolulu, 2000—. Mem.: Hawaii TESOL, Hawaii Assn. Lang. Tchrs. Avocations: walking, hiking, travel, cooking, reading. Office: McKinley Cmty Sch for Adults Ste 216 634 Pensacola St Honolulu HI 96814

ANTALEK, EILEEN ELIZABETH, educational consultant; b. Burtonwood, Eng., Jan. 16, 1957; d. Henry and Sarah Louise O'Connor; m. Michael Antalek, Feb. 16, 1980; children: Peter, Sarah. BA, Framingham State Coll., 1991; M in English, Clark U., 1994, EdD, 2004. House maintenance, Grafton, Mass., 1989-90; tutor Framingham (Mass.) State Coll., 1990-91, Clark U., Worcester, 1991-93, asst. dir. spl. needs, 1993-94, tchg. asst., 1994-95; asst. dir. Educational Directions, Westborough, Mass., 1995—. Cable access prodr. Grafton Cable Network, 1986—88. Publicity dir. North Grafton United Meth. Ch., 1986—88, Sunday sch. tchr., 1989—95, Sunday sch. supt., 1992—95, chair bd. edn., 1988—92, chair pastor parish rels., 1999—, chair space needs com., 2000—. Scholar Resident, Clark U., 1991—96, Nat. Merit, 1975, 1976, David O. Wilson, Anderson Coll., 1976. Mem.: Consortium for Learning Disabilities, Phi Eta Sigma. Avocations: textile art, motorcycling, painting, music, hiking. Office: Educational Directions 57 E Main St Ste 224 Westborough MA 01581 Fax: 508-870-1505.

ANTHONY, JOAN CATON, administrative judge; b. South Bend, Ind., July 28, 1939; d. Joseph Robert and Margaret Catherine (McMeel) Caton; m. Robert Armstrong Anthony, Jan. 3, 1980; 1 child, Peter. BA, Marquette U., 1961; MA, Northwestern U., 1963; JD, Catholic U. Am., 1979. Bar: D.C. 1980, Va. 1982. Instr. English Marquette U., Milw., 1963-65, George Washington U., Washington, 1965-69, asst. prof., 1969-70; spl. asst. student affairs HEW, Washington, 1970-72; dir. Office Student and Youth Affairs U.S. Office Edn., Washington, 1972-74, legis. specialist, 1974-78; chief mgmt. ops. br. Fed. Wildlife Permit Office U.S. Fish and Wildlife Svc., Washington, 1978-81; assoc. Cate and Goodbread, Washington, 1981—85; atty., advisor office legis. counsel U.S. Dept. Interior, 1991-95; staff atty. Interior Bd. Land Appeals, 1995—2003; adminstrv. judge Def. Office of Hearings and Appeals, U.S. Dept. Def., 2003—. Mem. U.S. del. to 2d meeting Conf. Parties to Conv. on Internat. Trade in Endangered Species of Wild Fauna and Flora, San Jose, Costa Rica, 1979. Contbr. lit. revs., essays and articles on univ.-cmty. rels., western settlement and internat. negotiations to various publs. Pres. Franklin Forest Frolickers, 1985—86; den leader Cub Scouts, mem. com. Boy Scouts Am., 1990—2000; parent vol. Fairfax County Pub. Schs., 1987—2001; treas. Greater McLean Rep. Women's Club, 1987—88; bd. dirs. McLean Citizens Assn., 1982—83, Fairfax County Humane Soc., 1983. Recipient Spl. Achievement award U.S. Fish and Wildlife Svc., 1981. Mem. D.C. Bar, Va. Bar, DAR (Freedom Hill chpt.). Roman Catholic. Home: 2011 Lorraine Ave Mc Lean VA 22101-5331

ANTHONY, KATHRYN HARRIET, architecture educator; b. NYC, Sept. 11, 1955; d. Harry Antoniades and Anne (Skoufis) Anthony; m. Barry Daniel Riccio, May 24, 1980 (dec. Jan. 2001). AB in Psychology, U. Calif., Berkeley, 1976, PhD in Architecture, 1981. Rsch. promotion Kaplan/McLaughlin/Diaz Architects and Planners, San Francisco, 1980-81; vis. lectr. U. Calif., Berkeley, Calif., 1980-81, 82-83, San Francisco State U., Calif., 1981; assoc. prof. Calif. State Poly. U., Pomona, Calif., 1981-84; asst. prof. U. Ill., Urbana-Champaign, Ill., 1984-89, assoc. prof., 1989-96, chair bldg. rsch. coun., 1994-97, prof. architecture, 1996—, chair design faculty, 2002—. Guest lectr. numerous orgns., coll. and univ.; mem. numerous comm. Coll. of Fine and Applied Arts, Sch. Architecture, Housing Rsch. and Devel. Program, Dept. Landscape Architecture. Author: Design Juries on Trial: The Renaissance of the Design Studio, 1991, Designing for Diversity: Gender, Race, and Ethnicity in the Architectural Profession, 2001, Running for Our Lives: An Odyssey with Cancer, 2004; co-editor Jour. Archtl. Edn. 47:1, 1993; mem. editl. bd. Jour. Archtl. and Planning Rsch., 1989-92, Jour. Archtl. Edn., 1990-95, Environ. and Behavior Jour., 1991—; reviewer Landscape Jour., 1990; contbr. articles to profl. jours; co-designer, co-prodr. (exhibit) Shattering the Glass Ceiling: The Role of Gender and Race in the Archtl. Profession, Nat. Conv. AIA, 1996. Recipient Collaborative Achievement award AIA, 2003; Creative Achievement award Assn. Collegiate Sch. Architecture, 1992; grant US Army C.E.R.L., 1993, grant U. Ill., 1984, 87, 92, 93, 95, 96, grant Graham Found., 1989-91, 93-96, grant Decatur Housing Authority, 1988, grant Upgrade Cos., Peoria, Ill., 1987, grant Nat. Endowment for Arts, 1986-87, grant LA County Cmty. Devel. Commn., 1984, grant Calif. State U. and Coll., 1982, 83, summer grant U. Calif., Berkeley, 1980; fellow Acad. Leadership Program Com. Instnl. Coop., 1996-97. Mem. Environ. Design Rsch. Assn. (bd. dir. 1989-92, treas. 1990-92, co-editor Coming of Age: Proceedings of 21st Ann. Conf. 1990), Chgo. Women in Architecture. Home: 309 W Pennsylvania Ave Urbana IL 61801-4918 Office: U Ill Sch Architecture 611 Taft Dr Champaign IL 61820-6922 E-mail: kanthony@uiuc.edu.

ANTHONY, MICHELE, entertainment executive; Ptnr. Manatt, Phelps, Rothenberg & Phillips; sr. v.p. Sony Music, N.Y.C., 1990, exec. v.p., 1993-94, Sony Music Entertainment, N.Y.C., 1994—. Recipient Norma Zarky Entertainment Law award. Mem. State Bar Calif., Beverly Hills Bar Assn., L.A. County Bar Assn. Office: Sony Music Entertainment 550 Madison Ave New York NY 10022-3211

ANTHONY, NAKIA LACQUERS, healthcare educator; b. Memphis, Tenn., Dec. 16, 1974; d. Joselyn Ann Boatwright; m. Ellis O Anthony, Jan. 31, 1973; 1 child, Gavriel Baruch-Ellis. Master's Credits, Miss. Valley State U., Itta Bena, Miss., 2001—03. Respite care coord. Mercy Home Healthcare, Memphis, Tenn., 1999—; ednl. facilitator Dorsey-Ford Inst., Memphis, Tenn., 1998. Author: (children's literature) Meditations for God's Heritage. Pres. Bus. and Profl. Women's League, Memphis, 2003. Grantee, Tenn. Humanities Coun., 2001. Church Of God In Christ. Avocations: reading, motivational speaking. Home: PO Box 341621 Memphis TN 38184 Office: Strong Tower Faith Ministry 2500 Mount Moriah Suite H232 Memphis TN 38115 Personal E-mail: mercyhomehealth@excite.com. E-mail: strongtower@excite.com.

ANTHONY, SHEILA FOSTER, government official; b. Hope, Ark., Nov. 8, 1940; m. Beryl F. Anthony; children: Alison, Lauren. BA, U. Ark., 1962; JD, Am. U., 1984. Bar: Ark. 1985, D.C. 1985, U.S. Ct. Appeals (D.C. cir.) 1987, U.S. Supreme Ct. 1992. Tchr. Ark. Pub. Schs., 1962-63, 74-76; with Dow, Lohnes & Albertson, Washington, 1985-93; asst. atty. gen. Dept. of Justice, Washington, 1993-95; commr. FTC, Washington, 1997—. Del. Dem. Nat. Conv., 1980; justice of the peace Union County, Ark., 1969; trustee South Ark. U., 1971-75. Democrat. Office: FTC 600 Pennsylvania Ave NW Washington DC 20580-0001

ANTHONY, SUSAN, secondary school educator; Tchr. secondary geography Anchorage Sch. Dist. Recipient Disting. Tchr. K-12 award Nat. Coun. for Geog. Edn., 1992. Office: Anchorage Sch District PO Box 196614 Anchorage AK 99519-6614

ANTHONY, SYLVIA, social welfare organization executive; b. Boston, Oct. 5, 1929; d. Charles and Josephine (Guastaferro) Caccamesi; children: Lyn Newbury, Edward Charles Souza Jr., Dean Souza. Student, Northeastern U., Boston, 1968-69, Lee Inst., 1966, 86-87. Lic. real estate broker, Mass. Founder, pres. Life for the Little Ones, Inc., Everett, Mass., 1987-94, Sylvia's Haven, Everett, 1994—2004, Devens, Mass., 1997—. Recipient Arthur L. Whitaker award Am. Bapt. Ch. of Mass., 1992, Recognition award Commonwealth of Mass. State Senate, Ho. of Reps., Gov. of Mass., 1997, 99, Mass. Gov.'s Hwy Safety Bur., 1998, Mayor Dean J. Mazzarella City of Leominster, 1999, named Hometown Hero WBZ TV, Boston, 2001; Daily Point of Light award Points of Light Found., 2002, Amb. for Peace award The Interreligious and Internat. Fedn. for World Peace, 2002; Commendation from Pres. George Bush, 2002. Address: PO Box 1166 Groton MA 01450

ANTHONY, VIRGINIA QUINN BAUSCH, medical association executive; b. Odessa, Tex., June 9, 1945; d. William Francis and Florence Elizabeth (Decker) Quinn; m. E. James Anthony; 1 child, Justin. BA, Mt. Holyoke Coll., 1967. Exec. dir. Am. Acad. Child and Adolescent Psychiatry, Washington, 1973—. Recipient Spl. Presdl. citation Am. Psychiat. Assn., 1995, Exec. Achievement award AMA, 1999. Mem. Am. Soc. Assn. Execs. Office: Am Acad Child & Adolescent Psychiatry 3615 Wisconsin Ave NW Washington DC 20016-3007

ANTHONY, WILMA TYLINDA, customer representative; b. Friars Point, Miss., July 11, 1954; d. John Thomas and Ellen (Ward) A. BS in Edn., Langston U., 1979; postgrad. in Interdisciplinary Studies, U. Oreg. Salesperson, Meier & Frank, Eugene, Oreg., 1976-78; vault teller 1st Interstate Bank, Portland, Oreg., 1979-80; mapping analyst Portland Gen. Electric Co., from 1980 -1997, sales assoc., Nike, 1998-99, Beaverton, cashier, Nike, 2000-, Telethon div. chief Mt. Hood Council Campfire, Inc., Gladstone, Oreg., 1982—; profl. model, 1987—; loaned exec. Columbia-Willamette United Way, 1982, in-house campaigner, Portland Gen. Electric Co., 1981. Active Nat. Fedn. Rep. Women, Portland; sec. Multnomah Young Reps., 1986; elected com. person Precinct 7, Washington County, 1986, re-elected, 1988; mem. planning adv. bd. City of Tualatin; vol. State Games of Oreg., 1987-88; line mem. Marshall for All Join Hands, 1986; sec. Washington Young Republicans, 1988. Recipient Leadership in Community Svcs. award Portland Gen. Electric, 1986; Honorable Mention Vol. of Yr. award Portland Gen. Electric, 1986, ACE award, 2002, Cmty. Involvement award, 1984. Mem. Toastmasters (v.p. 1984, Competence cert. 1984), U.S. Women Open Golf Tournament (chartered mem.), Kappa Delta Pi. Baptist. Office: Portland Gen Electric Co 121 SW Salmon St Portland OR 97204-2977

ANTHONY-PEREZ, BOBBIE COTTON MURPHY, psychology educator, researcher; b. Macon, Ga., Nov. 15, 1923; d. Solomon Richard and Maude Alice (Lockett) Cotton; m. William Anthony, Aug. 22, 1959 (dec.); 1 child, Freida; m. Andrew Silviano Perez, June 20, 1979. BS, DePaul U., 1953, MS, 1954, MA, 1975; MS, U. Ill., 1959; PhD, U. Chgo., 1967. Tchr. Chgo. Pub. Schs., 1954-68; math. coord. U. Chgo., 1965; prof. Chgo. State U., 1968-95, coord. Black Studies Program, 1982-83, 90-94; with psychol. svcs. Chgo. Pub. Schs., 1971-72; rsch. coord. Urban Affairs Inst. Howard U., Washington, 1978; coord. higher edn., careers counseling, campus ministry Ingleside Whitfield Parish, 1978-84, comm. chmn., 1991-92, 95. Contbr. numerous articles to profl. jours., chpts. to books. V.p. Cmty. Affairs Chatham Bus. Assn., 1981-85, asst. sec., 1985-86, sec., 1986-87, directory com., 1987, 88; bus. rels. chmn. Chatham Avalon Pk. Cmty. Coun., 1984—, newsletter editor, 1993—; bd. dirs. United Meth. Found. at U. Chgo., 1980-84, Cmty. Mental Health Coun. Inc., 1979-83; pub. edn. chairperson Chatham Avalon unit Am. Cancer Soc., 1977-88, 90-97, pub. info. chairperson, 1988-94; pres. Aux. Chgo. chpt. Tuskegee Airmen, Inc., 1994-95, rec. sec., 1998-99, parliamentarian, 1991-95, newsletter feature writer, 1999—. NSF fellow, 1957, 58, 59; recipient numerous awards religious, civic and ednl. instns. and assns. Mem. APA, Internat. Assn. Applied Psychology, Internat. Assn. Cross-Cultural Psychology, Internat. Assn. Ednl. and Vocat. Guidance, Assn. Black Psychologists (elder 1995—, pres. Chgo. chpt. 1995-96, past pres.), Chgo. Psychol. Assn., Nat. Coun. Tchrs. Math., Am. Ednl. Rsch. Assn., Midwest Ednl. Rsch. Assn., Am. Soc. Clin. Hypnosis, Midwestern Psychol. Assn., Chgo. Soc. Clin. Hypnosis. Methodist. Office: Chgo State U Dept Psychology 9501 S King Dr Chicago IL 60628-1501

ANTICH-CARR, ROSE ANN, state legislator; b. Apr. 11, 1938; married John Carr; 1 son, Marc Antich. Grad., Hammond Bus. Coll.; postgrad., Ind. U. N.W. Radio and TV personality, lectr. positive mental attitude and stress control, astrologist; mem. Ind. Senate from 4th dist., 1991—, asst. caucus chair, 1996—. Mem. town coun., 1983-87. Democrat. Roman Catholic. Home: 5401 Lincoln St Merrillville IN 46410-1926 Office: Ind State House 200 W Washington St Indianapolis IN 46204-2728 E-mail: roseann@urisp.com.

ANTMAN, KAREN, oncologist; b. N.J., July 26, 1948; MD, Columbia U. Coll. Physicians and Surgeons, 1974. Diplomate Am. Bd. Internal Medicine, Am. Bd.. Med. Oncology. Intern Columbia Presbyn. Med. Ctr., N.Y.C., 1974—75, resident, 1975—77; fellow Dana Farber Cancer Inst., Boston, 1977—79; chief med. oncology Columbia U., N.Y.C.; attending physician N.Y. Presbyn. Hosp., 1993—; dir. Herbert Irving Cancer Ctr.; Wu prof. of medicine and prof. pharmacology Columbia U., N.Y.C., 1993—. Office: Columbia Univ Coll Physicians and Surgeons Divsn Med Oncology MHB 6NK 435 177 Ft Washington Ave New York NY 10032

ANTOINE, JANET ANNE, social worker; b. Chgo., Nov. 1, 1945; d. Karl Frederick Abrath and Aniela Domitilda Chappas; m. Lawrence Verne Antoine Sr., Sept. 4, 1964 (dec.); children: Lawrence V. Jr., Dennis Patrick. BA, Loyola U., Chgo., 1969; MPS, Western Ky. U., 1977; MS in Social Work, U. Louisville, 1981. Social worker Cabinet for Human Resources, Brandenburg, Ky., 1977-79, Louisville, 1979-81, Cath. Charities, Louisville, 1981-82, dir. maternity svcs., 1982-84; social worker Cabinet for Human Resources, Louisville, 1984-86, Dept. of Vet. Affairs, U.S. Govt., Louisville, 1986—. Site supr. Sr. Companion program, Louisville, 1987—. Cmty. vol. Army Com Svc., Ft. Knox and Ft. Gordon, 1968-77, 2d St. Neighborhood Assn., 1979-96, Old Louisville Neighborhood Assn., 1982-92. Recipient VA Sec. Hand & Heart award, 1998-99. Mem. NASW, AAUW, NOW. Roman Catholic. Avocations: needlepoint, gardening, reading, painting, tennis. Home: 1840 Fleming Rd Louisville KY 40205-2420 Office: VA Med Ctr Louisville 800 Zorn Ave Louisville KY 40206-1433 E-mail: Antoine.Janet@Louisville.Va.Gov.

ANTON, BARBARA, writer; b. Pocono Pines, Pa., Apr. 3, 1926; d. Walter B. and Emma Agnes (Hess) Miller; m. Albert Anton, June 23, 1949. Grad. Gemologist, Gemol. Inst. of Am., 1964. Fashion and design editor Nat. Jeweler Mag., N.Y.C., 1956-58; freelance writer novels/plays, 1956—; staff writer Writer's Guidelines and News Mag.; instr. sr. divsn. U. South Fla., 2000—. Writing instr. Sr. Acad./Elderhostel U. South Fla., 1999—. Contbr. articles to numerous nat. mags. including Cosmopolitan, Family Circle, Bride's Mag., Saturday Evening Post, Thera Lit. Mag.:, author plays, (novels) Egrets to the Flames (Top Ten/Fla. Writers Festival, 1995), short stories, 13 plays produced off-Broadway, 1995—2003. Recipient First Prize Humor, Manatee Writers Contest, 2000—01, 1st prize, Father's Hall of Fame Contest, 2000—01, over 100 awards for various writings, 14 awards, Fla. Studio Theatre Shorts Contest. Mem. Dramatists Guild.

ANTON, CHERYL L. sales executive; b. Toledo, Ohio, Nov. 3, 1953; d. Ralph Herbert Snyder and Coletta Marie Piekut Nickerson; 1 child, John Daniel. Student, U. Toledo, 1972-80. With Kroger Co., Toledo, 1972-80; dept. supr. merchandising, sales dir. Growth Unltd., Toledo, 1979-80; owner CJ's Bar, Toledo, 1980-82; sales rep. Armour Food Co., Orlando, Fla., 1983-85; dist. sales mgr. Jones Dairy Farm, 1985-87; regional sales mgr. Southland Corp., 1987-92; Southeast regional sales mgr. McLane Co., Orlando, 1995-97; mid-south regional sales mgr. Ty, Inc., 1999—. Mem. NAFE (network dir. 1979—), Nat. Assn. for Women. Democrat. Address: PO Box 3118 Bella Vista AR 72715-0118

ANTONACCI, LORI (LORETTA MARIE ANTONACCI), marketing executive, consultant; b. Riverton, Ill., Mar. 31, 1947; d. Antonio and Gena Marie A. BA, Bradley U., 1969. Broadcast copywriter Sta. WIRL-TV, Peoria, Ill., 1969; comms. specialist Walgreen Co., Chgo., 1970-72; creative supr. Nat. Assn. Realtors, Chgo., 1973-74; creative dir., prodr. Steve Sohmer, Inc., N.Y.C., 1975-79; promotion specialist Ziff-Davis Publs., 1979-80; promotion mgr. Psychology Today, 1980-81; mktg. svcs. dir. DIS Consulting, N.Y.C., 1982-84; promotion dir. Crain's N.Y. Bus., N.Y.C., 1984-85; pres. Antonacci & Assocs., 1985-99, mktg. dir., chief exec. group, 2000—. Advisor, instr. Gallatin Sch. NYU, 1986—. Co-founder, bd. dirs. Artists Talk on Art, Inc., 1974—; Artists Comm. Fed. Credit Union, 1986-89, N.Y. Women's Agenda, 1992, bd. dirs. 1992—, v.p. events 1993-95; bd. dirs. Women's City Club, N.Y.C., 1994—, v.p. devel. 1994-95; bd. dirs. Ctr. for Advancement of Youth, Family & Cmty. Svcs. 1997—. Recipient Golden Eagle award CINE, 1976; award U.S. Indsl. Film Festival, 1977; CEBA award, 1979; Bronze medal Internat. Film and TV Festival N.Y., 1979, Am. Graphic Design awards 1996-97. Mem. Advt. Women N.Y. (profl. devel. com. 1983-85, program com. 1986-90, chmn. speakers bur. 1988-90, chmn. pub. policy com. 1991-95, industry issues 1998—), Women in comm., Am. Women in Radio and TV. Address: 15 E 10th St New York NY 10003-5930

ANTONELLI, ANGELA MARIA, federal agency administrator; b. Aug. 4, 1963; BA, Cornell U., 1985; MPA, Princeton U., 1988. Asst. br. chief White House Office of Mgmt. and Budget, 1989-93; cons. Lewin-VHI, Inc,., Vienna, Va., 1993-95; dir. Roe Inst. for Econ. Policy Studies Heritage Found., 1995—; chief financial off. U.S. Dept. H.U.D., Washington, 2001—. Office: US Dept HUD Financial Off 451 7th St SW Washington DC 20410-9000 E-mail: angela.antonelli@heritage.org.

ANTONIUK, VERDA JOANNE, secondary school educator; b. Moline, Ill., Sept. 10, 1936; d. Joe Oscar and Verda Mathilde (Oakberg) Butts; m. Vladimir Antoniuk, Sept. 1, 1972; children: Daniel Sean, Stephen Dwight. Diploma in missions, Moody Bible Inst., 1957; BS in Edn., Ea. Ill. U., 1960; MA in Internat. Rels., Calif. State U. Stanlslaus, Turlock, 1981, cert. in ESL, 1989. Cert. tchr., ESL tchr., bilingual, crosscultural, lang. and acad. devel. cert., Calif. Tchr. Wheatridge (Colo.) H.S., 1960-61, Modesto (Calif.) City Schs., 1971-73, Modesto Jr. Coll., 1979-80, 84-89, Turlock Christian H.S., 1980-83, Turlock H.S., 1989—; part-time faculty edn. dept. Chapman U., 1995; missionary Oversease Missionary Fellowship, Littleton, Colo., 1961-69. Tchr. Turlock Adult Sch., 1969-79, 84-89, program dir. ESL, 1976-79, amnesty coord., 1986-89; cons. Britannica-ARC Project, Oakland, Calif. and Boston, 1993-94; ednl. cons. Valley Fresh, Turlock, 1987-88. Translator multi-media U.S. Constitution, Britannica, 1993; cons. to book on amnesty, 1987; contbt. to book Intervarsity Christian Fellowship, 1965. Sunday sch. supt. Evang. Free Ch., Turlock, 1979-82; cons. Spanish work Turlock Covenant Ch., 1990—; mem. Malaysian Youth Coun., Kuala Lumpur, 1967-68. Mem. Calif. Tchrs. English to Spkrs. of Other Langs., Nat. Assn. Bilingual Educators, Tchrs. of English to Spkrs. of Other Langs. Republican. Avocations: reading, macintosh computers, writing, collecting stamps and coins. Home: 553 South Ave Turlock CA 95380-5606

ANTOUN, ANNETTE AGNES, newspaper editor, publisher; b. Franklin, Pa., Mar. 7, 1927; d. Adrien Uriel and Charlotte Mary (McMullen) Adelman; m. Frederic George Antoun, July 19, 1947 (dec.); children: Frederic G., Gregory S., Lawrence J., Mark J. (dec.), Laureace A., Scott J., Jonathan M., Lisa A. Student, Allegheny Coll., Meadville, Pa. Founder, editor-pub. Paxton Herald, Harrisburg, Pa., 1960—; founder, owner Graphic Svcs., advt. and graphics, Harrisburg, 1972—; owner Comms. Sys. Design, 1978—; pres. Susquehanna Valley Assocs., Inc., 1978—. Co-editor French Creek Patriot, cmty. newspaper, Cochranton, Pa., 1972. Mem. comms. com. Tri-County United Fund, 1973, mem. com. children's svcs., 1975-79; bd. dirs. Pa. Am. Lung Assn., 1973-98, treas., 1976, sec., 1979-80, v.p., 1980-81, treas., 1996-98; counselor to bd. Am. Lung Assn., 1989-90; bd. dirs. Harris Commn., 1975-79, Cath. Social Svc. Harrisburg, 1972-76; mem. extension planning com. YMCA, 1975-79; mem. bd. govs. Camp Curtin YMCA, 1980-85; mem. exec. bd. Lower Paxton Coalition Cmty. Groups, 1973-93; mem. comms. bd. Cath. Diocese Harrisburg, 1971-80; co-chmn. Dauphin County Ethics Com., 1979-81; chmn. bldg. com. Juvenile Detention Home, 1976-80; chmn. fund raising com. Greater Harrisburg Arts Coun., 1977-79; mem. Dauphin County bd. com. children and youth, 1982-85; vice chmn. Dauphin County Election Voting Machine Com., 1982—; mem. Tri-County Solid Waste Mgmt. Com., 1983-87; bd. dirs. Salvation Army Rehab. Svcs., 1992—, Capitol Pavilion Rehab., 1992—; mem. exec. com. spl. events United Negro Coll. Fund, 1993-98; spl. events chmn. Ctrl. Pa. UNCF, 1993-94, bd. dirs. H. John Heinz Ctr., 1994—; vice chmn. Millenium commn. City of Harrisburg, 1999—. Recipient Advocate award Paxton Area Jaycees, 1969, 73, citation Am. Legion Pa., 1971, 74, CAP, 1972, medallion Am. Legion Pa., 1972; award Am. Cancer Soc., 1969-89, March of Dimes award, 1969-89, AARP award, 1988, MADD award Hist. Preservation award, All Am. City Participation award, Nat. award Am. Lung Assn., 1992, Am. Legion REgional award, 1994, Pioneer award John Heinz Ctr., 1996, Cmty. Svc. award VFW, 1996, award for historic rehab. City Harrisburg, 1992, Cit of Harrisburg award, 1998, Gettysburg Monument Preservation award, 1998; numerous others. Mem. Am. Lung Assn. Pa. (treas. 1995-98), Internat. Platform Assn. Home: 4910 Earl Dr Harrisburg PA 17112-2125 Office: 101 Lincoln St Harrisburg PA 17112-2543

APELBAUM, PHYLLIS L. delivery messenger service executive; b. Chgo., July 3, 1940; d. Harry Kelmanson and Evelyn Reiner Cohen; 1 child, Mark Apelbaum. Instr. Am. United Cab Co., Chgo., 1957-65; gen. mgr. City Bonded Messenger Svc., Chgo., 1960-74; founder, pres. Arrow Messenger Svc., Inc., Chgo., 1974—. 1st chair Affirmative Action Adv. Bd. of Chgo., 1991-92; chair Variety Club Children's Carnival, Chgo., 1990-94; mem. bicycle com. City of Chgo., 1992-95, parking task force, 1993-95; gov. Ill. Coun. on Econ. Edn., Chgo., 1995—; mem. Lakefront SRO Adv. Bd., Chgo., 1989-94; mem. Chgo. Police bd., 1995—. Recipient Small Bus. Innovative Mgmt. award Bank of Am., 1994; named Entrepreneur of the Yr., Ernst & Young, 1992, Nat. Small Bus. Person of the Yr., Small Bus. Assn., 1990; named to Entrepreneurship Hall of Fame, U. Ill., Chgo., 1993. Mem. Messenger Courier Assn. of Am. (bd. dirs. 1989—), Messenger Svc. Assn. Ill. (co-founder, pres.), Nat. Assn. Women Bus. Owners, The Chgo. Network, Execs. Club of Chgo. Office: Arrow Messenger Svc Inc 1322 W Walton St Chicago IL 60622-5340*

APEL-BRUEGGEMAN, MYRNA L. entrepreneur; b. Cleve., July 19, 1942; d. Melvin Arthur and Merle Ruth (Hoffman) Rehlender; children: Timothy, Kristen, Michelle, Kim; m. Earl L. Brueggeman, May 7, 1994. BS in Edn., Kent State U., 1965, M. in Edn. Counseling, 1987. Cert. tchr., Ohio; lic. minister, Ohio. Owner, mgr. real estate investments, Kent, Ohio; owner, founder IHS Counseling Ctr., Ravenna, Ohio; owner, mgr., founder IHS Home Sweet Home, Ravenna, Ohio; owner IHS Bookstore; co-owner Chapel on the Lakes. Owner Stow Estates, LLC, Southington Estates, LLC, Orchard Estates, Orchard Plaza, LLC. Mem. NAFE, Ohio Manufactured Housing Assn. (bd. dirs., pres. We. Res. chpt.), Internat. Soc. Profl. Hypnotists, Sigma Epsilon, Chi Sigma Iota.

APODACA, CLARA R. federal official; b. Las Cruces, N.Mex., Sept. 24, 1934; d. A.D. and Sally H. Melendres; children: Cindy Sherman, Carolyn Folkman, Jerry, Jeff, Judy, Bellamy. Degree in elem. edn., N.Mex. State U., 1955. Mgr. family bus., 1964-74; First Lady N.Mex., 1975-79; owner, mgr. Apodaca Co., Santa Fe, 1979-83; sales dir. City of Santa Fe, 1983-85; dir. office cultural affairs State N.Mex., Santa Fe, 1985-87; dep. Dukakis for Pres., Boston, 1988; gen. asst. to chmn. Dem. Nat. Com., Washington, 1989-93; sr. advisor, asst. sec. Dept. Treasury, Washington, 1993-97; dir. protocol Overseas Pvt. Investment Corp., Washington, 1997—. Bd. dirs. N.Mex. State U. Found., Washington Performing Arts Soc., 1993-98, Hispanics in Philanthropy, Calif., 1998—, Nat. Hispanic Cultural Ctr., D.C. Commn. on Arts and Humanities, White House Commn. on Save Am. Treas.; chmn. Jeff Apodaca Fund. Roman Catholic. Home: 6223 Utah Ave NW Washington DC 20015-2431 Office: 101 Constitution Ave NW Washington DC 20001

APONTE, ELSIE, conservationist; b. Chgo., May 1, 1958; d. Antonio Aponte and Soledad Florenciani. BA in Sociology, Pontifical Cath. U., Ponce, P.R., 1981; postgrad., Ponce Sch. Of Medicine, 1999—2003. Credit and billing dept. staff Damas Hosp., Ponce, 1981—86; dir. Conservation Trust of P.R., Ponce, 1987—. Dir. Damas Hosp. Coop., Ponce, PR, 1986. Mem.: Woman Art Mus. Achievements include design of scientific plot in a natural reserve.

APPEL, GLORIA, advertising executive; Exec. v.p. Grey Advt. Inc. (now Grey Global Group), N.Y.C., 1990—. Office: Grey Advt Inc 777 3rd Ave New York NY 10017-1401

APPEL, LIBBY, theater director; m. Paul Robert Appel (div.); children: Irwin, Susan. BA, U. Mich.; MA, Northwestern U. Artistic dir. Ind. Repertory Theatre, 1992—96, Oreg. Shakespeare Festival, Ashland, Oreg., 1996—. Dean, artistic dir. Sch. Theatre Calif. Arts Inst., Calencia, Calif.; head acting program Calif. State U., Long Beach, Calif.; tchr. acting Goodman Theatre, Chgo.; assoc. dir. Calif. Shakespearan Festival, Visalia, Calif.; freelance dir. in field. Author: Mask Characterization: An Acting Process; co-author: (plays) Shakespeare's Women, Shakespeare's Lovers; prodr.: (films) Inter/Face: The Actor and The Mask. Office: Oregon Shakespeare Festival PO Box 158 Ashland OR 97520*

APPEL, MARSHA CEIL, association executive; b. N.Y.C., Dec. 3, 1953; d. Albert and Stella Joy (Glaser) A.; m. Mark D. Marcellus, Sept. 10, 1978; children: Sam, Jill. BA, SUNY, Albany, 1974; MSLS, Syracuse U., 1975. Info. specialist Am. Assn. Advt. Agys., N.Y.C., 1976-79, mgr. member info. svc., 1979-89, v.p., 1989-97, sr. v.p., 1997—. Author: Illustration Index IV, 1980, Illustration Index V, 1984, Illustration Index VI, 1988, Illustration Index VII, 1993, Illustration Index VIII, 1998; editor What's New in Advertising and Marketing, 1978-80; mem. adv. bd., contbr. Ency. Advt., 2002; contbr. Super Searchers on Madison Avenue, 2003. Mem. Spl. Librs. Assn. (chmn. advt. and mktg. div. 1982-83). Office: Am Assn Advt Agys 405 Lexington Ave New York NY 10174-0002

APPEL, NINA SCHICK, law educator, dean, academic administrator; b. Feb. 17, 1936; d. Leo and Nora Schick; m. Alfred Appel Jr.; children: Karen Oshman, Richard. Student, Cornell U.; JD, Columbia U., 1959. Instr. Columbia Law Sch., 1959-60; adminstr. Stanford U., mem. faculty, prof. law, 1973—, assoc. dean, 1976-83; dean Sch. Law Loyola U., 1983—. Mem. Am. Bar Found., Ill. Bar Found., Chgo. Bar Found., Chgo. Legal Club, Chgo. Network. Jewish. Office: Loyola U Sch Law 1 E Pearson St Chicago IL 60611-2055

APPELBAUM, ANN HARRIET, lawyer; b. Decatur, Ill., 1948; d. Irving and Cecelia (Hecht) A.; m. Neal Borovitz, July 4, 1982; children: Abby, Jeremy. BA, Barnard Coll., 1970; JD, Boston U., 1973. Bar: N.Y. 1974, U.S. Dist. Ct. (so. dist.) N.Y. 1975, U.S. Ct. Appeals (2nd cir.) 1975, U.S. Supreme Ct. 1978. Assoc. Hart & Hume, N.Y.C., 1974-76, Warshaw, Burstein, N.Y.C., 1976-80; counsel Jewish Theol. Sem. & Jewish Mus., N.Y.C., 1980—. Mem. Nat. Assn. Coll. and Univ. Attys. Office: The Jewish Theological Seminary 3080 Broadway New York NY 10027-4650

APPELL, LOUISE SOPHIA, consulting company executive; b. Northampton, Mass., Sept. 22, 1930; d. Romeo Edward and Phyllis Teresa (Szynal) Fortier; m. Melville Joseph Appell, July 26, 1953 (div. 1975); children: Melissande Foglio, David Maxcim; m. Clifford Harding Querolo, June 1, 1991 (dec. 1992). BA, Smith Coll., 1951; MA, U. Ky., 1966, PhD, 1972. Instr. U. Ky., 1966-68; dir. spl. edn. grad. program Catholic U. Am., Washington, 1969-76; assoc. dir. nat. com. Arts for the Handicapped, Washington, 1976-80; owner, pres. Louise Appell Cons. Svcs., Washington, 1980-82; assoc. Macro Systems, Inc., Silver Spring, Md., 1982-84, dir. edn. product devel., 1984-85, dir. ednl. product devel., 1985—, v.p., 1985—, ret., 1996. E-mail: lsapell@patriot.net.

APPERSON, JEAN, psychologist; b. Durham, N.C., June 8, 1934; d. James Harry and Dorothy Elizabeth (Johnson) Apperson; m. Calvin Adams Pope, Mar. 23, 1956 (div. 1967); 1 child, Richard Allan. BA, U. S. Fla., 1966; MA, Mich. State U., 1970, PhD, 1973. Cert. in psychoanalysis Mich. Psychoanalytic Coun., 1990. Teaching asst. Mich. State U., E. Lansing, 1968-69; psychiatric technician St. Lawrence Community Mental Health Ctr., Lansing, Mich., 1968-69, psychology intern, 1969-71, Mich. State U. Counseling Ctr., 1971-73; clin. psychologist U. Mich. Counseling Ctr., Ann Arbor, 1973-81; pvt. practice psychology and psychoanalysis Ann Arbor, 1974—. Mem., chmn. Mich. Bd. Psychology, Lansing, 1984-91. Contbr. articles to profl. jours.; cons. editor Am. Psychol. Assn. Catalog of Selected Documents, 1975-80. USPHS grantee, 1969-70; NIMH grantee, 1970-71. Fellow Mich. Psychol. Assn. (chmn. women's issues com. 1981-83); mem. APA (com. on sci. and profl. ethics and conduct 1977-80), Mich. Soc. Psychoanalytic Psychology (treas. [illegible]), Mich. Psychoanalytic Coun. (tchg. and supervising analyst, mem. at large 1991-93, tng. com. 1992-2001, pres. 1995-97, v.p. for edn. and tng. 1998-2001), Assn. for Advancement of Psychology, Am. Women in Psychology, Mich. Women Psychologists. Democrat. Unitarian Universalist. Avocations: french language and culture, gardening, nature study, music. Home: 7224 Chelsea Manchester Rd Manchester MI 48158-9443 Office: Ste 23E 555 E William St Ann Arbor MI 48104-2428 E-mail: jeanatapp@aol.com.

APPLE, DAINA DRAVNIEKS, government agency official; b. Kuldiga, Latvia, July 6, 1944; came to U.S., 1951; d. Albins Dravnieks and Alina A. (Bergs) Zelmenis; divorced; 1 child, Almira Moronne; m. Martin A. Apple, Sept. 2, 1986. BSc, U. Calif., Berkeley, 1977, MA, 1980. Economist Pacific S.W. Rsch. U.S. Forest Svc., Berkeley, 1976-85, mgr. regional land use appeals San Francisco, 1986-88, program analysis officer, engring., 1988-90, asst. regulatory officer, 1990-95, strategic planner nat. forest sys. resources program, 1995-98, policy analyst, 1998—2002; adminstr. workplace rels. Pacific Southwest Region, Vallejo, Calif., 2002—03, staff asst. to dep. chief programs and legislation, 2004—. Author: Public Involvement in the Forest Service-Methodologies, 1977, Public Involvement, Selected Abstracts for Natural Resource Managers, 1979, The Management of Policy and Direction in the Forest Service, 1982, An Analysis of the Forest Service Human Resource Management Program, 1984, Organization Design-Abstracts for Natural Resources Users, 1986, Social and Legal Forces Changing the Management of National Forests, 1996, Water and the Forest Service, 2000, The Forest Service as a Learning Organization, 2000, Evolution of U.S. Water Policy, 2001; contbg. editor Jour. Women in Natural Resources, 1987—. Fellow Soc. Am. Foresters (chair Nat. Capital Soc. 2000), Phi Beta Kappa Soc.; mem. AAAS, ESA, N.Y. Acad. Sci., Washington (D.C.) Acad. Scis., Am. Water Resources Assn., Am. Forestry Assn., m. Latvian Assn. (bd. dirs. 1995-97), Phi Beta Kappa Assocs. (nat. sec. 1985-88, pres. No. Calif. 1982-84), Commonwealth Club of Calif., Exch. Club of Capitol Hill, Sigma Xi. Avocations: organization and political theory, ballroom dancing, tennis, film. Office: USDA Forest Svc PL&C, 5 NW 1400 Independence Ave SW Washington DC 20250-1103 Office Phone: 202-205-1422. E-mail: dapple@fs.fed.us.

APPLE, JACKI (JACQUELINE B. APPLE), artist, writer, educator; b. N.Y.C. Student, Syracuse U.; BFA, Parsons Sch. Design. Curator exhbns. and performance Franklin Furnace, N.Y.C., 1977-80; prodr., host Sta. KPFK-FM, North Hollywood, Calif., 1982-95; mem. sr. faculty Art Ctr. Coll. Design, Pasadena, Calif., 1983—. Mem. faculty adv. com. Art Ctr. Coll. Design, Pasadena, 1993, Faculty Coun. rep., 2000[00bf]; vis. faculty UCSD, LaJolla, 1995-99. Contbg. writer: L.A. Weekly, 1983-89; contbg. editor: Artweek, 1983-90, High Performance Mag., 1984-95; performance works include The Garden Planet Revisited, 1982, The Amazon, the Mekong, the Missouri and the Nile, 1985, Palisade, 1987, Fluctuations of the Field, 1989, (with J. Adler) A Stone's Throw..., 2000, Kokoro No Mai, 2003; writer, performer, dir., prodr.: (record) The Mexican Tapes, 1979-80, (performance/installation/audio work) Voices in the Dark, 1989-97, (radio art work) Swan Lake, 1989; artist, prodr.: (installations and audio work) The Culture of Disappearance, # 1-5, 1991-95; author, designer: (book, installation) Trunk Pieces, 1975-78, (cd) Thank You for Flying American, 1995, Ghost Dances/On the Event Horizon 1996; six part radio art series Redefining Democracy in America Parts, 1991-92; (site specific installation) Zeitghosts: Angels in the Architecture, 1996, Sanctuary, 1996, Hidden Desires, 1998, A Stone's Throw...The Last Witnesses, 2001, Kokoro No Mai, 2002; (photowork) ghost.dance series 1995—, Aviary of the Lost # 3, 2004, (photo/audio performance) You Don't Need a Weatherman, 1999; pub. art projects Aliso-Pico Cmty. Ctr., 1997-2000, Venice Oakwood Cmty. Ctr., 2000-03, Martin Luther King Rehab Ctr., 2000-03, Queen Anne Cmty. Ctr., L.A., 2001-, Little Tokyo Br., L.A. Pub. Libr., 2002-; author: Doing it Right in L.A., 1990; prodr. EarJam Music Festival, 2000, 01, 02, 04. Recipient Vesta award Media Arts Women's Bldg., 1990, Faculty Enrichment grant Art Ctr. Coll. Design, 2001; NEA visual artists fellow, 1979, 81; InterArts program grantee NEA, 1984-85, 91-92; Calif. Arts Coun. Visual Arts/New Genres fellowship, 1996; grantee Durfee Foundation, 2003. Mem. Internat. Art Critics Assn., Nat. Writers Union, Coll. Art Assn., Am. Composers Forum. Home: 3532 Jasmine Ave Los Angeles CA 90034-4947 E-mail: jaworks@sprintmail.com.

APPLE, KATHY, medical association administrator; MSc. RN. Nurse various, 1975—92; assoc. dir. nursing practice Nev. State Bd. Nursing, 1992—96, exec. dir., 1996—2001, Nat. Coun. State Bds. Nursing, Chgo., 2001—. Dir.-at-large Nat. Coun. State Bd. Nursing, 1999—2001, bd. dir., mem. multistate regulation task force, APRN coord. task force, task force to study feasibility of core competency exam for nurse practioners. Office: Nat Council State Bds Nursing 676 North St Clair St Ste 550 Chicago IL 60611-2921

APPLEBAUM, ANNE, journalist, writer; b. Washington, D.C., 1964; m. Radek Sikorski; children: Alexander, Tadeusz. Grad, Yale U., 1986. Correspondent The Independent, London, 1988—90; journalist Economist, London, 1988—92; fgn. editor Spectator Mag., London, 1993—94, deputy editor, 1994—; columnist The Daily Telegraph, London, 1994—; columnist, mem. editl. bd. Wash. Post, 2002—. Author: (book) Between East and West: Across the Borderlands of Europe, 1995, Gulag, A History, 2004 (Nat. Book award nominee, 2003, Pulitzer Prize for general nonfiction, 2004), several writings have appeared in The Wall St. Jour., the Fin. Times, The Internat. Herald Tribune, Fgn. Affairs, Boston Globe, The Ind., The Guardian, Commentaire, Suddeutsche Zeitung, Newsweek, The New Criterion, others. Recipient Charles Douglas Home Meml. Trust award, 1992; Marshall Scholar, London Sch. Economics, St. Antony's Coll., Oxford. Office: Washington Post 1150 15th St NW Washington DC 20071*

APPLEBY, JOYCE OLDHAM, historian, educator; b. Omaha, Apr. 9, 1929; d. Junius G. and Edith (Cash) Oldham; children: Ann Lansburgh Caylor, Mark Lansburgh, Frank Bell Appleby. BA, Stanford U., 1950; MA, U. Calif., Santa Barbara, 1959; PhD, Claremont Grad. Sch., 1966. With Mademoiselle mag., 1950-52; asst. prof. history San Diego State U., 1967-70, asso. prof., 1970-73; prof. history, asso. dean Coll. Arts and Letters, 1973-75, prof., 1976-81. Vis. asso. prof. U. Calif., Irvine, 1975-76; vis. prof. UCLA, 1978-79, prof. history, 1981—; vis. fellow St. Catherine's Coll., U. Oxford, 1983; Harmsworth prof. Am. History, U. Oxford, 1990-91; Bd. fellows Claremont Grad. Sch. and U. Center, 1970-73 Author: Economic Thought and Ideology in Seventeenth-Century England, 1978, Capitalism and a New Social Order, 1983, Liberalism and Republicanism in the Historical Imagination, 1992; co-author: Telling the Truth about History, 1994; co-editor: Knowledge and Postmodernism in Historical Perspective, Inheriting the Revolution, 2000; mem. bd. editors Democracy, 1980-83, William and Mary Quar., 1980-83, 18th Century Studies, 1982-87, Ency. Am. Polit. History, Am. Hist. Rev., 1988—, Jour. Interdisciplinary History, 1989—, The Papers of Thomas Jefferson, 1988—, The Adams Papers, 1990—; contbr. articles to profl. jours.; mem. adv. bd. Am. Nat. Biography. Mem. Am. Acad. Arts and Scis., Am. Philos. Soc., Smithsonian Inst. (coun.), Am. Hist. Assn. (pres.), Orgn. Am. Historians (pres.), Inst. Early Am. History and Culture (coun. 1980-86, chmn. 1983-89). Home: 615 Westholme Ave Los Angeles CA 90024-3209 Office: UCLA Dept History Los Angeles CA 90024

APPLEBY, PENNY E. secondary school educator; b. Chgo., Sept. 29, 1947; d. George Edward and Audrey Margaret (Anderle) Ligler; m. William D. Harrison, Dec. 29, 1973 (div. Mar. 1986); 1 child, Kristin R. Harrison ; m. Donald T. Appleby, Aug. 1, 1987; children: Paul A. Harrison, Stephen M. Harrison, Jennifer Appleby Ward. B of Music Edn. in Voice, Stetson U., 1973, MEd in Literacy, 1983. Cert. tchr. N.Y., Maine. Music tchr. K-6 Woodward Ave. Elem., Deland, Fla., 1973—83, 1985—86, Golden Hill Elem., 1983—85; reading specialist 7-12 SS. Seward Inst., 1983—85; reading specialist 7-12 Auburn (Maine) Sch. Dept., 1986—; choir dir. High St. Congl. Ch., Auburn, 2000—. Drama dir. Edward Little H.S., Auburn, 1987—; vice pres. Cmty. Little Theatre, Auburn, 1998—2000, dir. plays, 1988—. Pond rep. Turner Watershed Com. Town of Turner, Maine, 2003; choir mem. High St. Congl. Ch., Auburn, 1988—. Mem.: NEA, Assn. Prins. and Curriculum, Delta Kappa Gamma (music chair 1987—2001). Republican. Congregational. Avocations: costume designer, sewing, reading, acting, singing. Office: Edward Little HS Auburn ME 04210

APPLEFIELD, SANDRA, small business owner; b. N.Y.C., Aug. 13, 1931; d. Saul and Estelle Cohen; m. Lawrence Applefield, Feb. 13, 1955; children: Janet Dee, Debbi Lee, Dean Scott, Glenn Andrew. BS, NYU, 1952; Masters Degree, Queens Coll., 1952. Tchr. H.S., N.Y.C., 1953—62; pvt. bus. owner Port Richey, Fla., 1976—. Commr. Pasco County Mosquito Control Dist., Odessa, Fla., 1996—; bd. mem. Jewish Cmty. Ctr./Home Congregation Bethtefillah, Port Richey, 1999—. Mem.: AAUW, Pride in Port Richey (founder), Citizen's Assn. Port Richey, Fla. Mosquito Control Assn. (corr. sec. 2000—03). Democrat. Jewish. Avocations: travel, reading, antiques, fitness, flea markets. Home: 5033 Waterside Dr Port Richey FL 34668 Office: Am Mail Specialists 8001 Apple-Six Dr Port Richey FL 34668

APPLEGATE, CHRISTINA, actress; b. L.A., Calif., Nov. 25, 1971; d. Nancy Priddy; m. Johnathon Schaech, Oct. 20, 2001. Film appearances include: Jaws of Satan, 1980, Streets, 1990, Don't Tell Mom the Babysitter's Dead, 1991, Across the Moon, 1994, Vibrations, 1995, Wild Bill, 1995, Mars Attacks!, 1996, Nowhere, 1997, Claudine's Return, 1998, The Big Hit, 1998, Mafia!, 1998; TV appearances include: (series) Days of Our Lives, 1974, Washingtoon, 1985, Heart of the City, 1986, Married...With Children, 1987-97, All My Life, 1998, Jesse, 1998-2000, Friends, 2002, (TV movies) Grace Kelly, 1983, Dance 'til Dawn, 1988, (spls.) Rate the '80's Awards, 1989, MTV's 1989 Ann. Emmy Awards, 1989, Time Warner Presents the Earth Day Special, 1990, The 4th Ann. Am. Comedy Awards, 1990, The 43d Ann. Primetime Emmy Awards Presentation, 1991, (episodes) Father Murphy, 1981, Quincy, 1983, Charles in Charge, 1984, 84, All Is Forgiven, 1986, Leave It to Beaver, 1986, Amazing Stories, 1986, Silver Spoons, 1986, Family Ties, 1987, 21 Jump St., 1988, Animal Crack-Ups, 1988, Hour Magazine, 1988, Win, Lose, or Draw, 1988, The Pat Sajak Show, 1989, Live with Regis and Kathy Lee, 1989, The Arsenio Hall Show, 1989, A View From the Top, 2003; film appearances include Just Visiting, 2001, The Sweetest Thing, 2002.

APPLEYARD, DIANE PAIGE, human service administrator; b. Sept. 23, 1947; BA, Birmingham-So. Coll., 1969; MA in English, Vanderbilt U., 1973. Asst. editor Meth. Pub. Co., 1971-73; secondary sch. tchr. Escambia County, Fla., 1973-78; tchr. Dept. Def., Germany, 1973-78; dir. John Appleyard Agy., Inc., 1984—, v.p., 1989—; pres. Healthcare R&D Inst., Inc., Pensacola, Fla. Bd. dirs. U.S. Girls Scout Coun., W. Fla., v.p., 1988-95; bd. dirs. N.W. Fla. Rehab. Found., 1989-95, Pensacola Jr. Coll. Found., 1990—, Pensacola Jr. Coll., 1993—; trustee Nat. Com. Quality Health Care, 1995—, mem. exec. com., 1995—. Office: Healthcare R&D Inst Inc 4400 Bayou Blvd Pensacola FL 32503-2673 Fax: 850-494-0289.

APSELOFF, MARILYN FAIN, English educator; b. Attleboro, Mass. d. Arthur A. and Eva (Lubchansky) Fain; m. Stanford S. Apseloff, Nov. 21, 1956; children: Roy, Stan and Glen (twins), Lynn Susan. Student, Bryn Mawr Coll., 1952-54; BA, U. Cin., 1956, MA, 1957. From instr. to prof. English Kent (Ohio) State U., 1968—2003; ret., 2003. Adv. bd. mem. Parents' Choice, Waban, Mass., 1978—. Author: They Wrote for Children Too, 1989, Elizabeth George Speare, 1991; co-author: Nonsense Literature for Children, 1989 (award 1990); rev. editor Children's Literature Assn. Quarterly, 1984-87. Grad. fellow U. Cin., 1956-57. Mem. MLA (session chair 1977, 78), Children's Literature Assn. (pres. 1979-80, dir. Harvard conf. 1978). Avocations: bridge, swimming. Office: Kent State Univ English Dept Kent OH 44242-0001

APSON, JANE R. public health educator; b. N.Y.C., Feb. 17, 1946; d. Philip and Anna Rahl; m. Bernard Apson, Oct. 21, 1968. BA in Math., Skidmore Coll., 1967; MS in Pub. Health, Johns Hopkins U., 1978; PhD in

Human Devel., U. Md., 1990. Cert. health edn. specialist Nat. Commn. for Health Edn. Credentialing, Inc. Computer programmer GE Co., Schenectady, N.Y., 1967-68; rsch. assoc. Sch. Hygiene Johns Hopkins U., Balt., 1975-79; pub. health educator Worcester County Health Dept., Snow Hill, Md., 1979—; assoc. prof. Salisbury (Md.) State U., 1995—2001. Adj. faculty mem. Wor-Wic Tech. C.C., Berlin, Md., 1985, 82, 88. Cmty. vol. John F. Kennedy Inst., Balt., 1975, cmty. organizer, v.p., pres. Logan Village Improvement Assn., Balt., 1973-79; cmty. organizer, v.p. Greater Dundalk (Md.) Cmty. Coun., 1975-79; mem. AIDS curriculum com. Worcester County Bd. Edn., Snow Hill, 1989-95; bd. dirs. Jerusalem Day Care Ctr., Snow Hill, 1994-98; officer, bd. dirs. Worcester Chorale, Berlin and Ocean City, Md., 1995-2002; bd. dir. Ea. Shore Area Health Edn. Ctr., 1997-2003. Recipient Gov.'s award for risk mgmt., 1996; N.Y. State Regents scholar, 1963-67. Mem. APHA, Soc. Pub. Health Edn., Nat. Headache Found. Avocations: gourmet cooking, knitting, sewing, elderhosteling. Office: Worcester County Health 6040 Public Landing Rd PO Box 249 Snow Hill MD 21863-0249 Fax: (410) 632-0906.

APTAKER, JANET MARCIA, social worker; b. Washington, Nov. 21, 1953; d. Edward and Louise Aptaker. Cert. social worker N.Y.; master practitioner neurolinguistic programming Brief Therapy Inst. Sr. social work clinician Ctr. Urban Cmty. Svcs., N.Y.C., 1999—2001; support services supr. Flemister Ho., N.Y.C., 2001—. Co-clin. dir. Identity Ho., N.Y.C., 1999—. Sculpture, Va. Artists Show, Va. Mus., Richmond. Bd. mem. Miami (Fla.) Design Preservation League, 1987—99, Miami Beach Cmty. Devel. Corp., 1987—90, South Beach New Dems., Miami Beach, 1988—90. Recipient cert. appreciation, Miami Design Preservation League, 1998. Avocations: jazz, travel, dance, bicycling, swimming. Personal E-mail: jma212@hotmail.com.

APTER, EMILY, language educator; BA in History and Lit., Harvard U., 1977; PhD in Comparative Lit., Princeton U., 1983. Prof. French NYU, N.Y.C. Recipient Guggenheim fellowship, 2003, Mellon fellowship, Rockefeller fellowship, ACLS fellowship, NEH fellowship, Coll. Art Assn. fellowship. Office: 19 University Pl 634 New York NY 10003

AQUADRO, JEANA LAUREN, graphic designer, educator; b. Key West, Fla., June 10, 1957; d. Charles Frasure and Geraldine Ferguson (Norton) A.; m. John A. Crawford. B Environ. Design magna cum laude, N.C. State U., 1979; MFA, Yale U., 1984. Graphic designer various projects for Cooper-Hewitt Nat. Mus. Design, Whitney Mus. Am. Art, Shearson Lehman Bros., Citicorp Investment Bank, Abbeville Press, UNICEF, others, N.Y.C., 1984-91; asst. dir. graphic design dept. Mus. Modern Art, 1988-89; design cons. Solomon R. Guggenheim Mus., 1989-91; prof. Savannah Coll., Savannah, Ga., 1991—2001; graphic design cons., 2001—. Bd. dirs. Wilderness S.E. Recipient The Am. Fedn. of Arts award of Excellence, 1988, Fed. design achievement award Nat. Endowment for Arts, 1992, Presidential award for design excellence Fed. Govt., 1994. Avocations: aquatic sports, travel, gardening. Studio: 3 Pinewood Ave Savannah GA 31406

ARAGONÉS-ENDA, LILLIAN ESTELLA, elementary school educator; b. N.Y.C., June 8, 1954; d. Aragonés-Panis Fernando and Santa (Colon) Oyola; m. Robert Alan Enda, July 28, 1990; children: Damian Marcel Brown, Jeremy Isaiah. AA, Cumberland County Coll., 1974; BA in Elem. Edn., Glassboro State Coll., 1988; postgrad., Seton Hall U., 1995—. Resource lab. asst. Migrant/Bilingual Curriculum Resource, Vineland, N.J., 1981-82; bilingual/ESL tchr. Vineland Pub. Schs., 1983-87; bilingual tchr. Millville (N.J.) Pub. Schs., 1989-90; elem. tchr. Hillside (N.J.) Pub. Schs., 1990-97, Holocaust/tolerance presenter, 1997—. Outreach worker Casa Prac, Inc., Vineland, 1983-86; adult ESL instr. Cumberland County Coll., Vineland, 1986-87; adult ESL tchr. Atlantic City (N.J.) Casinos, 1986-87; reading tchr. Spark Summer Program, Vineland, 1989; dir. women's seminar N.J. Coun. of Humanities, Trenton, 1997. Editor: Lessons From the Holocaust: Lesson Designs for Grades K-12, 1997. Participant ednl. seminar N.J. Holocaust Commn., Trenton, 1997; founding tchr. A.P. Morris Sr. Citizen Exch. Program, Hillside, 1996-97, A.P. Morris Homeless Collection Drive, Hillside, 1995-97; active pub. rels. Puerto Rican Festival N.J., Vineland, 1985-87. Recipient Axelrod award Anti-Defamation League, 1997, Technology in the Classroom award AT&T, 1995; grantee N.J. Coun. for Humanities, 1996. Mem. Puerto Rican Festival N.J. (pub. rels. com. 1985-87), ASCD. Avocations: art, writing, reading, storytelling. Office: AP Morris Sch 143 Coe Ave Hillside NJ 07205-2830

ARAI, MIZUHO, social sciences educator; b. Chiba, Japan, July 10, 1969; d. Mitsue and Masami Arai; m. Michael S. Shairs, Mar. 15, 2003. PhD, Boston U., 2002. Adj. faculty U. Mass., Boston, 2000—; rsch. fellow Boston U., 2002—; tchr. cross-cultural psychology, social psychology, rsch. methods women, culture and identity. Achievements include Cross-cultural research on career development of women and integration of work and family roles. Cross-cultural research on family violence. Office: U Mass 100 Morrissey Blvd Boston MA 02125-3393 E-mail: mizuho.arai@umb.edu.

ARAMBEL, PHYLLIS ANN, elementary school educator; b. Hays, Kans., Aug. 12, 1952; d. Melvin Joseph and Barbara Ann (Bennett) Eichman; m. Joseph John Arambel, Apr. 7, 1984; children: Jeremy Sage, Spenser Miles, Alexander Joseph. BEd, U. No. Colo., 1974; postgrad. Cert. elem. tchr., Colo., Wyo. Primary tchr. Queensland (Australia) Dept. Edn., 1974-76; 1st grade tchr. Gertrude Burns Elem. Sch., Newcastle, Wyo., 1976-77; western U.S. ednl. cons. Rand McNally, San Francisco, 1977-78; K-2 Mountain Sch. tchr. Poudre R-1 Dist., Ft. Collins, Colo., 1978-79; constrn. supr. CAR-MEL, Inc., Pierre, S.D., 1979-80; 3rd grade tchr. Sweetwater County Sch. Dist. #1, Rock Springs, Wyo., 1980-87; ret., 1987; 3d grade tchr. Holy Spirit Cath. Sch., 2003—. Pres./founder The Children's Discovery Found., Rock Springs, 1991—, sec., 1991-93, fundraising chairperson, 1991—, pres., 1996—, exec. dir. Discovery Station, 1997—; pres./founder Westridge Sch. PTO, Rock Springs, 1996-97; founder Westridge Hist. Soc., 1998-2002; coord. Sch. Boxtops for Edn., 1996-2002. Tiger Cub Group coach Boys Scouts Am., Rock Springs, 1996-97; soccer team parent, 1992-97, asst. registration commr., 1996-99, newsletter editor and pub., 1996—, coach, 1997—; wolf den leader Cub Scouts, Rock Springs, 1997-98, bear leader, 1998-99, webelos leader, 1999-2001, 2003-; founder, chair Cmty. Carnival, 2003; sec. bd. dirs. Competitive Soccer League, 2003; level D soccer coach, Wyo., 1996—, competitive soccer coach, 2003—. Mem. Overland Sch. Hist. Soc. (founder 2000—), Girl Scouts U.S. (life), Phi Sigma Iota (life). Avocations: travel, gardening, photography, camping, scrapbooking. Home: 904 Bonners Way Rock Springs WY 82901-4362 E-mail: jarambel@wyoming.com.

ARANDA, SANDRA LOUISE, speech pathology/audiology services professional; b. San Jose, Calif., Oct. 7, 1970; d. Peter Mora and Jerry Louise Aranda. BA in Speech-Lang. Pathology, San Jose State U., 1994, MA in Edn. Speech Pathology and Audiology, 1996; cert. in early childhood edn. infants and preschoolers with disabilities, 1996. Speech-lang. pathologist George Mayne Elem. Sch., Santa Clara, 1996—97, Mariano Castro Elem. Sch., Mountain View, 1996—97, Santa Clara Sch. Dist., 1997—98, Mountain View Sch. Dist., 1998—2000, Oak Grove Sch. Dist., San Jose, 2000—. Mem. support staff com. Santa Teresa Elem. Sch., 2000—. Mem.: AAUW, Calif. Speech Hearing Assn. (adv. bd. com. dist. 4 2001—02, Outstanding Achievement award 2003), Santa Clara Speech Hearing Assn. (co-social chair 1997—98, rec. sec. 1999—2000, v.p. 2000—01, pres. 2001—02, past pres. 2002—03), Am. Speech Hearing Assn. Roman Catholic. Avocations: reading, painting, cardio circuit training, animals. Home: PO Box 667 Morgan Hill CA 95038 E-mail: cccslplic@aol.com.

ARBEITER, JOAN, artist, educator; b. N.Y.C., May 8, 1937; d. David and Winifred Arden (Lembke) Berman; m. Jay David Arbeiter, June 15, 1958 (div. May 1990); children: Lisa B., Gail Arbeiter Goldstein. BA, CUNY, 1959; MFA, Pratt Inst., 1981. Lic. art tchr. N.Y., N.J. Tchr. N.Y.C. Sch. Sys. Bd. Edn., 1959-63; dir. Joan Arbeiter Studio Sch., Metuchen, NJ, 1976-90; instr. art, coord., founder [illegible] Sch. Art, Plainfield, NJ, 1978—, instr. color and design, 1978—, instr. art history, 1981—, instr. art appreciation, 1983—; workshop instr. N.J. Teen Arts Festival, 1998—. Juror various art orgns., NJ, 1981—; cons. Ednl. Testing Svc., Princeton, NJ, 1988; curator travelling art exhibit Age As a Work of Art, Plainfield, Boston, N.Y.C., 1985—86, Lives and Works, N.Y.C., 2000; artist-in-residence Sch. Arts, NJ, 1995—2001; presenter paper, slides Coll. Art Assn. Conf., San Antonio, 1995, N.Y.C., 2003; presenter, moderator Nat. Mus. Women in Arts, Wash., 1997, Artists Talk on Art, N.Y.C., 2000; bd. dirs. Women's Studio Ctr. One-woman shows include Ceres Gallery, N.Y.C., 1985, 1987, 1989, 1993, 1997, 2000, Columbia U., 1986, Stony Brook-Millstone Watershead Assn. Gallery, Pennington, N.J., 1991, Wagner Coll., S.I., N.Y., 1992, Douglas Coll. Ctr., New Brunswick, N.J., 1992, 1996, Union County Coll., Cranford, N.J., 1999, exhibited in group shows at Ramapo Coll., Mahwah, 1980, Brookdale Coll., Lincroft, N.J., 1980, Westbeth Gallery, N.Y.C., 1980, Ceres Gallery, 1983—, N.Y. Feminist Art Inst., N.Y.C., 1985—88, Soho 20 Gallery, 1990, 1998, Noyes Mus., Oceanville, N.J., 1995, 1998, Krasdale Corp. Gallery, Bronx, N.Y., 1995, Monmouth Mus., Lincroft, 1996, Kingsbourgh CC, Bklyn., 1999, Kunstler Forum, Bonn, Germany, 1999, EPA, Washington, 2001—02, Represented in permanent collections Noyes Mus., Oceanville, Fairmount Chem., Newark, CSR Group Archs. and Builders-Leon Cohen, Nutley, N.J., JFK Med. Ctr., Edison, N.J., Muhlenberg Regional Med. Ctr., Plainfield, 1st Presbyn. Ch., Metuchen, N.J., MS Found., N.Y.C., pvt. collections; co-author: (book) Lives and Works: Talks with Women Artists, vol. 2, 1999. Recipient 1st pl. mixed media, Westfield Art Assn., 1978, 1st pl. all media award, Metuchen Cultural Arts Commn. Art Exhbn., 1988, Best in Show award, Artists League Ctrl. N.J., 1989, AIA award, Hunterdon Arts Ctr. N.J., 1996, People's Choice award, Watchung Arts Ctr., N.J., 1998, Excellence award, Manhattan Arts Mag., 2000; grantee, Vt. Studio Colony, 1987. Mem.: Varo Registry, Art Table, Women's Caucus Art, Coll. Art Assn., Women's Studio Ctr. (N.Y.C.) (hon.; bd. dirs.), Alpha Beta Kappa. Studio: 41 Victory Ct Metuchen NJ 08840-1430

ARBUTINA, PETRA, advertising executive; Sr. v.p., media dir. Ketchum Advt. (now Egann St. James Advt.), Pitts., 1995—. Office: Egann St James Advt 6 Ppg Pl Fl 13 Pittsburgh PA 15222-5425

ARCA, PATRICIA GENEVIEVE, retired mental health nurse; b. Oakland, Calif., May 30, 1938; d. David and Dorothy Rose (Medina) A. B, Providence Coll. of Nursing, Oakland, 1960; M in Psychology, John F. Kennedy U., Orinda, Calif., 1979. RN, Calif. Staff nurse Eden Hosp., Castro Valley, Calif., 1960-62; psychiat. nurse VA, Menlo Pk., Calif., 1962-63; pub. health nurse Dominican Mission, Ocosingo, Chiapas, Mex., 1963-65; staff nurse ob. Gorgas Hosp., Panama Canal Zone, 1966-67; adminstr. Na Balom Cultural Ctr., Chiapas, Mex., 1968-72; dir. nursing svcs. Emanuel Hosp., Turlock, Calif., 1972-74; cmty. mental health nurse County of San Mateo, Calif., 1974-80; dir. residential care Phoenix Programs, Concord, Calif., 1980-82; clin. mental health nurse case mgr. City and County of San Francisco, 1983—2002, ret., 2002. Bd. del. Svc. Internat. Employee Union, San Francisco, 1983—; del. East Bay Ctrl. Labor Coun. Mem.: Calif. Alliance of Ret. Am. (captian), Ret. Employees of City and County of San Francisco (SEIU delegate to East Bay Reg. Conference), Alliance Ret. Ams., Congress for Calif. Srs. (trustee). Avocations: photography, travel, kayaking. Home: 792 Videll St San Lorenzo CA 94580-1143 E-mail: patarca@earthlink.net.

ARCENEAUX, JANICE HARMON, director; b. Lafayette, La., Nov. 10, 1952; d. Shirley and Adeline Jessie Harmon; m. Larry Jules Arceneaux, June 8, 1974; children: Terrence Jovan, Lakeah Jeanise. BS in Biochemistry, So. U., Baton Rouge, 1974; MS in Organic Chemistry, U. Houston, 1976; MS in Ednl. Mgmt., U. Houston-Clear Lake, 1995. Cert. tchr. chemistry, phys. sci. Tex., K-12 ednl. adminstr. Tex. Sr. rsch. chemist Dow Chem. Co., Freeport, Tex., 1976—81; chem. lab. tech. instr. Houston Ind. Sch. Dist., 1981—93, magnet programs sci. specialist, 1993—95, dist. secondary sci. specialist, 1995—98, mgr. sci. K-12, 1998—. Mem. Nat. Com. Sci. Edn. Standards and Assessment, 1994—96; mem. coord. coun. for edn. NAS, 1990—95; cons. McKenzye Group, Houston, Washington, 1994—2002; adv. bd. Bus. Bodies Child Devel. Ctr., Houston, 1983—. Contbr. articles to profl. jours. Assoc./mem. Jack and Jill of Am., Houston, 1990—; membership/voter turnout dr. Clear Creek Ind. Sch. Dist., Houston, 1990—98. Named Tchr. of the Yr., Nat. Orgn. Black Chemists, 1990; recipient Outstanding Young Educator award, Houston Area Jr. C. of C., 1984, Award for Tchg. Excellence, U. Houston Dept. Chemistry, 1976. Mem.: Nat. Orgn. for Profl. Advancement of Chemists and Chem. Engrs., Nat. Sci. Tchrs. Assn., Phi Kappa Phi, Delta Kappa Gamma (fin. chmn.). Achievements include research in synthesis of new compounds that showed pharmacological activity in treating epilepsy; development of of flame retardant polyurethane foam systems. Avocations: reading, writing. Home: 11623 Sagevale Ln Houston TX 77089 Office: Houston Ind Sch Dist 3830 Richmond Ave Houston TX 77027

ARCENEAUX, PAMELA DAVIS, librarian; b. Panama City, Fla., Jan. 17, 1954; d. Willie Parker Davis Jr. and Amanda Elizabeth (Brown) Davis; m. Paul Lindsey Arceneaux, Aug. 14, 1976. BA History, West Ga. Coll., 1976; MLS, La. State Univ., 1977. Libr. tech. asst. La. State Libr., Baton Rouge, 1978; young people's libr. La. State U., 1978—81; ref. libr. The Historic New Orleans Collection, 1981—. Mem.: La. Libr. Assn. (Foote award com. 1992—94, subject specialist sec. 1998—2000, Foote award com. 2000, Lucy B Foote award 1999). Avocations: acting, singing, reading, knitting, roses. Office: Historic New Orleans Collection Williams Rsch Ctr 410 Chartres St New Orleans LA 70130

ARCHABAL, NINA M(ARCHETTI), historical society director; b. Long Branch, N.J., Apr. 11, 1940; d. John William and Santina Matilda (Giuffre) Marchetti; m. John William Archabal, Aug. 8, 1964; 1 child, John Fidel. BA in Music History cum laude, Radcliffe Coll., 1962; MAT in Music History, Harvard U., 1963; PhD in Music History, U. Minn., 1979. Asst. dir. humanities art mus. U. Minn., Mpls., 1975-77; asst. supr. edn. divsn. Minn. Hist. Soc., St. Paul, 1977-78, dep. dir. for program mgmt., 1978-86, acting dir., 1986-87, dir., 1987—. Bd. dirs. U.S. nat. com. Internat. Coun. Mus. Trustee, bd. dirs. Am. Folklife Ctr., Libr. of Congress, 1989-98; bd. dirs. N.W. Area Found., 1989-98, St. Paul Acad. and Summit Sch., 1993—; v.p. Friends of St. Paul Pub. Libr., 1983-93; bd. regents St. John's U., Collegeville, Minn., 1997—; overseer Harvard Coll., Cambridge, Mass., 1997—. NDEA fellow U. Minn., 1969-72, U. Minn. grad. fellow, 1974-75; recipient Nat. Humanities medal The White House, 1997. Mem. Am. Assn. State and Local History (sec. 1986-88), Am. Assn. Mus. (v.p. 1991-94, chair bd. dirs. 1994-96). Office: Minn Hist Soc 345 Kellogg Blvd W Saint Paul MN 55102-1906

ARCHAMBAULT, JOALLYN, museum administrator, anthropologist; b. Claremore, Okla., Feb. 13, 1942; BA, U. Calif., Berkeley, 1970, MA, 1974, PhD, 1984. Dir. Am. Indian Program Nat. Mus. Natural History, Washington, 1986—; lectr. in Native Am. studies U. Calif., Berkeley, 1976—79, chair ethnic studies dept. Coll. of Arts and Crafts; rsch. assoc. Ctr. for the Study of Race, Crime and Social Policy, Cornell U., Ithaca, NY, 1980—82; asst. prof. anthropology U. Wis., Milw., 1983—86. Vis. faculty Oglala Lakota Coll., Pine Ridge, SD, Calif. State U., Hayward, U. N.Mex., Navajo C.C., Tsaile, N.Mex., Mills Coll., Oakland, Calif., Johns Hopkins U., Balt.; lectr. in field. Contbr. contbr. articles to profl. jours., chpts. to books; curator (exhbn.) Plains Indian Arts: Change and Continuity, 1987, 100 Years of Plains Indian Painting, 1989, Indian Basketry and Their Makers, 1990, Seminole!, 1990. Fellow Doctoral fellow, Ford Found., 1970—75. Mem.: Plains Anthropol. Soc., Studies in Am. Indian Lit., Soc. for Applied Anthropology, Native Am. Art Studies Assn., Coun. for Mus. Anthropology, Anthropol. Soc. of Washington, Am. Ethnol. Soc., Am. Anthropol. Assn. (mem. commn. on Native Am. reburial). Office: National Museum of Natural History 10th St and Constitution Ave NW Washington DC 20560

ARCHEY, MARY FRANCES ELAINE (ONOFARO), academic administrator, educator; b. Elkins, W Va, Sept. 15, 1947; d. Ross and Carmela Gallo Onofaro; m. Rick Archey. BA in Social Sci. Edn., U. Pitts., 1968; MEd in Social Sci. Edn., Indiana U. of Pa., 1969; EdD in Higher Edn. Adminstrn. and Counseling, WVa. U., 1981; Profl. Cert. in Human Resource Devel., Pa. State U., 1996. Cert. nat. counselor 1984. Asst. prof. sociology West Liberty State Coll., Wheeling, W.Va., 1969—72; dean of students W. Va. Northern C.C., Wheeling, W.Va., 1972—85; asst. dean instrn. C.C. Allegheny County South Campus, West Mifflin, Pa., 1986—96; dean bus. and acctg. C.C. of Allegheny County, Pitts., 1996—99; dean arts and sci. C.C. of Allegheny County-South Campus, West Mifflin, Pa., 1999—, Adj. instr. bus., 1988. Adj. instr. bus. C.C. of Allegheny County-South Campus, West Mifflin, Pa., 1988—. Ctrl. Pa. regl. dir. U. Pitts. Alumni Assn., 2001—; past pres., current chair nominations com. U. Pitts. Alumnae Coun., 1998—; vol food packager Greater Pitts. Food Bank, Duquesne, 1995—; vol. tester, interviewer Greater Pitts. Literacy Coun., 1987—96. Fellow: The Ed. Policy and Leadership Ctr. (fellow 2002—03); mem.: ASTD, AAUW, Am. Coll. Personnel Assn., Am. Assn. Higher Edn. (life), Am. Counseling Assn., St. Elizabeth's Women's Club, Phi Delta Gamma (v.p. 2000—), Beta Sigma Phi (svc. chairperson 1987—, Order of the Rose 1994), Delta Kappa Gamma-Alpha Phi Chpt. (past pres. 1996—, newsletter editor 1996—). Democrat. Roman Catholic. Avocations: reading, gardening. Home: 333 Old Clairton Rd Pittsburgh PA 15236 Office: CC of Allegheny -South Campus 1750 Clairton Rd West Mifflin PA 15122 Personal E-mail: marchey@ccac.edu.

ARCHIBALD, BRIGITTE EDITH, language educator; b. Kaiserslautern, Germany, Aug. 22, 1942; arrived in U.S., 1947; d. Ludwig and Alma (Schaefer) Zapp; m. John Duncan Archibald, Aug. 29, 1970; children: David Andrew, Elisabeth Anna. BA in Modern Lang., Kings Coll., 1964; MA in German, U. Mainz, Germany, 1966; PhD in Germanic Lang. & Lit., U. Tenn., 1975. Head libr. Thelma Dingus B. Libr., Wallace, NC, 1972—73; asst. prof. fgn. lang. NC A&T State U., Greensboro, 1976—82, assoc. prof. fgn. lang., 1982—95, prof. fgn. lang., 1995—. Oral proficiency assessor N.C. Dept. Pub. Instruction, 1994; presenter, cons. in field. Contbr. articles to profl. jours., local newspapers. Vol. neighbor to neighbor campaign Easter Seal Soc., 1992—94; vol. tchr. 4th grade German Caldwell Elem., 1984; judge Guilford County Elections, 1995—; vis. com. to McLeansville prison Trinity Ch., 1992—, mission com., 1990—, personnel com., 1992—97, Sunday sch. tchr., 1999—. Home: 1 Bayberry Ct Greensboro NC 27455 Office Phone: 336-288-7420.

ARCHIBALD, CLAUDIA JANE, parapsychologist, counselor, consultant; b. Atlanta, Nov. 14, 1939; d. Claud Bernard and Doris Evelyn (Linch) A. B in Psychology, Georgia State U., 1962; BTh., Emory U., 1964; DD, Stanton Coll., 1969. Pvt. practice psycho-spiritual counselor, Atlanta, 1960-98; ret., 1998; minister Nat. Spiritualist Assn., Atlanta, 1969-72; parapsychologist Ctr. for Life, Atlanta, 1985-86, Inst. of Metaphysical Inquiry, Atlanta, 1980—, also bd. dirs., founder, 1980—. Motivational spkr., 1996—. Author: (book) Quantitative Symbolism, 1980, short stories; dir. Phoenix Dance Unltd., 1984-90; choregrapher (dance) Phoenix Rising, 1985. Vol. Aid Atlanta, 1987-89. Recipient City Grant award Bur. Cultural Affairs, Atlanta, 1985, 86. Mem. Am. Psychical Rsch. Assn., Soc. Metaphysicians (corr. Eng. chpt.), Am. Assn. Parapsychology, Nat. Assn. Alcoholism and Drug Abuse Counselors, Ga. Addiction Counselors' Assn., N.Am. Ballet Assn., Nat. Leather Assn., Echoes of the People, Native Am. Orgn., Sun Dancer, Regional Soc. Victorian Preservation (founder, dir. 1990—). Avocations: writing, painting. Home: 464 E Hightower Trl Social Circle GA 30025-3022

ARCHULATA, MARGIE BACA, city clerk; b. Albuquerque, May 18, 1948; City clk. Office of Mayor, Albuquerque, 2001—. Office: Office of City Clk/Govt Bld 1 Civic Plz NW Rm 11110 Albuquerque NM 87102-2167

ARCHULETA, NANCY E. engineering executive; b. Las Cruces, N.M. CEO Mevatec Corp., Huntsville, Ala. Past chairwoman bd. dirs. Latin Am. Mgmt. Assn.; bd. dirs. Pepsi Co. Office: Mevatec Corp 1525 Perimeter Pkwy NW Ste 500 Huntsville AL 35806-3558

ARCHULETA, RANDI LISA, psychologist; b. L.A., Sept. 13, 1966; d. Robert Gurevitch and Susan Bea Westheimer; m. Anthony Gordon Archuleta, May 13, 1995; 1 child, Anthony Jade. BA, Pitzer Coll., 1988; PhD, Calif. Sch. Profl. Psychology, 1993. Lic. clin. psychologist. Staff psychologist Monsour Counseling Ctr., Claremont, Calif., 1994-99; prof. psychology U. N.Mex., Taos, 2002—. Co-dir., founder Claremont Colls. Coalition on Disordered Eating (CODE), 1996-99, trainer oral licensure, 1997-99, peer edn. leader, 1999. Sponsor Eating Disorder Awareness Week, 1997, 98. Mem. APA. Office: 124 N Las Palmas Ave Los Angeles CA 90004-1048

ARDELT, MONIKA, sociologist, educator; b. Wiesbaden, Germany, Apr. 29, 1960; arrived in U.S., 1988; d. Manfred Ardelt, Waltraud Ardelt; m. Dietmar H. Kaul, Sept. 1, 1990; children: Michelle Kaul-Ardelt, Gabriel Kaul-Ardelt. Diplom in sociology, Johann Wolfgang Goethe U., Frankfurt/Main, Germany, 1987; PhD, U. N.C., 1994. Assoc. prof. sociology U. Fla., 1994—. Contbr. articles to profl. jours. Fellow Brookdale Nat. fellow, Brookdale Found., 1999. Mem.: Gerontol. Soc. Am. Office: Univ Fla PO Box 117330 Gainesville FL 32611-7330 Office Phone: 352-392-0251 247. Business E-mail: ardelt@soc.ufl.edu.

ARDEN, SHERRY W. publishing company executive; b. N.Y.C., Oct. 18, 1930; d. Abraham and Rose (Bellak) Waretnick; m. Hal Marc Arden (div. 1974); children: Doren, Cathy; m. George Bellak, Oct. 20, 1979. Student, Columbia U. Publicity dir. Coward-McCann, N.Y.C., 1965-67; producer Allan Foshko Assoc., ABC-TV, N.Y.C., 1967-68; sr. v.p., pub. William Morrow & Co., N.Y.C., 1968-85, pres., pub., 1985-89; owner Sherry W. Arden Lit. Agy., 1990—. Mem. Assn. Am. Pubs. (dir.) Clubs: Pubs. Lunch.

ARDISANA, BETH, communications company executive; BS in Math./Computer Sci., U. Tex.; MBA, U. Detroit; M in Mech. Engring., U. Mich. Various mgmt. positions in vehicle design/devel., product planning and mktg. Ford Motor Co.; prin. owner ASG Renaissance, Detroit. Active Pres.'s Task Force for Implementation of Alternative Fuel Vehicles; bd. dirs. Heidelberg Project. Mem. Nat. Assn. Women Bus. Owners (named top 25 women bus. owners of distinction in Mich. by Detroit chpt. 1996, 97), Nat. Tech. Svc. Assn., Mich. Minority Bus. Devel. Coun., Mich. Hispanic C. of C. (bd. dirs.). Office: ASG Renaissance Fairlane Plaza N 290 Town Center Dr Ste 624 Dearborn MI 48126-2754 Fax: 248-358-4499.

ARDISON, LINDA G. author, writing educator; b. Ft. Smith, Ark., Apr. 11, 1940; d. Bill Eugene and Mildred M. (Fry) Tanner; m. Gary Winship Ardison, June 10, 1962; children: Amy Roberts Wotman, Elizabeth Winship Senft, Matthew Tanner. AA, Stephens Coll., 1960; student, Middlebury Coll., 1960-61; postgrad., Bread Loaf Sch. of English, 1960; BA, U. Ark., 1962. Adminstrv. asst. Wachovia Nat. Bank, Winston-Salem, N.C., 1962-63; English tchr. Wiley Jr. High Sch., Winston-Salem, 1963-64; writing instr. York Coll. of Pa., 1984—. Vis. poet York Country Day Sch., 1986, instr. poetry workshop, 1993. Author: Essential Love: Poems About Mothers and Fathers, Daughters and Sons, 2000, (short story in anthology) Voices from the Couch, 2001; editor Standard lit. mag., 1959-60; asst. editor

Keystone News, 1980-82; contbr. articles, poems, plays, short stories to jours. Bd. dirs. York County Med. Soc. Aux., York, 1978-80; mem. Jr. League of York, 1974-75; adult educator Living Word Cmty. Ch., York, 1980-90; bd. dirs. Human Life Svcs., York, 1989-93. Recipient 3d place for fiction in annual coll. contest The Atlantic Monthly, 1960, First place fiction award New Millenium Writings, 1998; Bread Loaf scholar The Atlantic Monthly, 1960; Pa. Arts Coun. fellowship grantee, 1990-91. Mem. York County Med. Soc. Alliance, Pa. Med. Soc. Alliance, Med. Soc. Alliance. Republican. Avocations: reading, literary research. Home: 260 School St York PA 17402-9543 Office: York Coll of Pa Country Club Rd York PA 17405 E-mail: lardison@ycp.edu.

AREEN, JUDITH CAROL, law educator, dean; b. Chgo., Aug. 2, 1944; d. Gordon Eric and Pauline Jeanette (Payberg) A.; m. Richard M. Cooper, Feb. 17, 1979; children: Benjamin Eric (dec.), Jonathan Gordon. AB, Cornell U., 1966; JD, Yale U., 1969. Bar: Mass. 1970, D.C. 1972. Program planner for higher edn. Mayor's Office City of N.Y., 1969-70; dir. edn. voucher study Ctr. for Study Pub. Policy, Cambridge, Mass., 1970-72; mem. faculty Georgetown U., Washington, 1972—, assoc. prof. law, 1972-76, prof., 1976—, prof. cmty. and family medicine, 1980-89, assoc. dean Law Ctr., 1984-87; dean, exec. v.p. for law affairs Georgetown U, Washington, 1989—. Gen. counsel, project coord. Office Mgmt. and Budget, Washington, 1977—80; spl. counsel White House Task Force on Regulatory Reform, Washington, 1978—80; cons. NIH, 1984, NRC, 1985; bd. dirs. Kroll, Inc. Author: Youth Service Agencies, 1977, Cases and Materials on Family Law, 4th edit., 1999, Law, Science and Medicine, 1984, 2d edit., 1996. Mem. Def. Adv. Com. Women In Svcs., Washington, 1979-82; trustee Cornell Univ., 1997-2001. Woodrow Wilson Internat. Ctr. for Scholars fellow, 1988-89, Kennedy Inst. Ethics Sr. Rsch. fellow, Washington, 1982—. Mem. ABA, D.C. Bar Assn., Am. Law Inst. E-mail: areen@law.georgetown.edu.

ARELLA, ANN MARIETTA, music educator, vocalist; b. Montclair, N.J., Jan. 29, 1951; d. Peter John and Evelyn Elizabeth (De Carlo) Arella; m. William John Wallace, Feb. 9, 1974 (dissolved May 1983); children: Ryan Wallace, Shannon Wallace. MusB, Ind. U., Bloomington, 1973; student, Manhattan Sch. Music, N.Y., 1975; grad. cert., William Patterson U., N., 1983; MA, New Jersey City Univ., N.J., 1991; postgrad., Shenanaoah Univ., Va., 2002—. Tchr. remedial reading & math Indep. Child Study Teams, Jersey City, 1983—86; tchr. choral music Lodi (N.J.) Bd. of Edn., 1986; singer Sacred Heart Ch., Suttern, NY, 1990—95, pianist, 1990—95; ch. music dir. Immaculate Conception, Mahwah, NJ, 1995—99; pvt. piano & voice tchr. Mahwah, NJ, 1998—2002. Ch. musician, 1974—99. Singer: Ridgewood Gilbert & Sullivan Opera Co., 1985—89; singer: (operatic soloist) Opera Festival di Roma, 2000; performer: Teotro Verdi, 1999. Fellow, Shenandoah Conservatory of Music, 2001. Mem.: NEA, Lodi Edn. Assn. (chmn. 1989—93, membership com. 1989—93, adj. rep. 1987—). Republican. Roman Catholic. Avocations: golf, weight training, decorating. Home: 1211 Sycamore Ln Mahwah NJ 07430 Office: Lodi Bd Edn S Main & Hunter Sts Lodi NJ 07644 E-mail: arella201@aol.com.

ARENA, KELLI, news correspondent; b. Bklyn., N.Y., Dec. 17, 1963; d. Melvin Mullins and Mary Ann (Scafa) Tracy. BFA, NYU, 1985. Prodr. various shows CNN, N.Y.C., 1985-89, prodr. spl. reports, 1988-89, line prodr., 1988-90, supervising prodr., 1990-92, exec. prodr. London, 1992, news editor N.Y.C., 1992-93, reporter, anchor, 1993—. Youth dir. St. George's Ch., N.Y.C., 1989-93. Recipient Peabody award U. Ga., 1987, Cable Ace award, 1987, Gold award Houston Internat. Film Festival, 1987, Nat. Headliner award Atlantic City Press Club, 2002, Emmy award for Sept. 11th coverage, CNN, 2002; named Topten Fin. Journalist Jour. Fin. Reporting, 1989-92; named Best Corr. N.Y. Festivals, 2002. Mem. Soc. Am. Bus. Editors and Writers, Internat. Womens Media Found. Office: CNN 820 1st St NE Washington DC 20002-4243 E-mail: kelli.arena@turner.com.

ARENAL, JULIE (MRS. BARRY PRIMUS), choreographer; Tchr. Herbert Berghof Studio; asst. on tng. program Lincoln Center Repertory Theatre. Dancer with cos. of Anna Sokolow, Sophie Maslow, John Butler, Jack Cole, Jose Limon; choreographer: Marat/Sade for, Theatre Co. of Boston, Harvard U. Loeb Theatre, Municipal Theatre, Atlanta, Hair, on Broadway (Most Original Choreographer of Year award Sat. Rev. 1968), also London; dir., choreographer Hair, Stockholm (Best Dir.-Choreographer of Year award 1969); choreographer, dir. Isabel's a Jezebel; choreographer: Indians on Broadway, Fiesta for Ballet Hispanico, 1972, 20008 1/2, Boccaccio, 1975, A Private Circus, 1975, Free to Be You and Me, 1976, The Referee, 1976, El Arbito, 1978; choreographer for San Francisco Ballet, Nat. Ballet de Cuba, (film) King of the Gypsies, Great Expectations, Fur. Friends, 1980, Mistress, 1991, Once Upon a Time in America, Houston Grand Opera Co., Porgy and Bess, 1995, Great Expectations, 1997; dir., choreographer (stage) Funny Girl, Tokyo, 1979-80; dir. N.Y. Express Hip Hop Dance Co., commd. by Spoleto Festival of the Two Worlds, N.C. and Italy; toured 7 cities in People's Republic of China. N.E.A. grantee for A Puerto Rican Soap Opera, Ballet Hispanico, 1973, Oreg. Shakespeare Festival, 1997, Porgy and Bess City Opera, N.Y.C. Opera, 2000, Am. Family PBS TV Series, 2002.

ARENS, CHRISTINE M. pianist, educator, composer; b. Queens, N.Y., May 31, 1968; d. Hans and Claire M. Arens. BMusic, Belmont U., Nashville, 1989, M Music Edn., 1990. Profl. pianist self employed, Lake Wales, Fla., 1991—; owner Music by Christine, Lake Wales, 1992—; tchr. of piano self employed, Nashville and Lake Wales, 1989—; owner Chrisnote Pub., Lake Wales, 1999—. Pianist Marriott Hotels, Orlando, Fla., 1995—. Rec. artist, composer CD, With Quiet Intensity, 1999; author: (piano instrn. books) Bridge to Technique, 1997, Roundabout Etudes, 1997, The Adult's Music Odyssey at the Keyboard, 1996. Mem. Music Tchrs. Nat. Assn., Fla. State Music Tchrs. Assn., Ridge Music Tchrs. Assn. (sec. 1999—), Sigma Alpha Iota. Office: Music by Christine PO Box 7484 Winter Haven FL 33883-7484 E-mail: chrisnote2@aol.com.

ARETZ, BARBARA JANE, reading specialist, educator; b. Long Beach, Calif., Dec. 28, 1943; d. Raymond John and Violet Dorothy (Wurn) A. BA, U. San Diego, 1965; Cert. Elem. Tchr., Immaculate Heart Coll., 1968; MEd in Reading, Loyola U., 1975; postgrad. in Christian Spirituality, Creighton U., 1980-85. Cert. ESL tchr., reading specialist, lang. arts content specialist, alpha phonics tchr., lang. therapist. Tchr. 4th grade St. Laurence Sch., Amarillo, Tex., 1978-79; tchr. 6th grade, prin. St. Mary's Sch., Odessa, Tex., 1979-81; tchr. 6th grade Lamesa (Tex.) Mid. Sch., 1981-83; prin. St. Mary's Sch., 1983-85; tchr. reading Midland (Tex.) Ind. Sch. Dist., 1985—. Team leader Midland Ind. Sch. Dist., 1997—, mem. Reading Club, San Jacinto Jr. H.S., 1997—. Recipient grant Diocese of Amarillo, 1981, Linda Laird Meml. award Acad. Lang. Therapy, 1993. Mem. Internat. Reading Assn., Tex. Classroom Tchr. Assn., Midland Reading Assn. (sec. 1986). Roman Catholic. Avocations: house remodeling, gardening, animal lover, miniature house building.

ARFSTEN, BETTY-JANE, nurse; b. N.Y.C., Sept. 28, 1946; d. William Paul and Jennie (Reyes) Brock; m. Oluf D. Arfsten, June 1, 1973 (dec.). BSN, Adelphi U., 1985; grad., Eastern Sch., 1966. RN, N.Y. Nurse clinician Meml. Sloan Kettering, N.Y.C., 1985-86; charge nurse Booth Meml. Med. Ctr., Flushing, N.Y., 1986-89; nurse coord. IVF Australia, Mineola, N.Y., 1990-93; occupl. health nurse Johnson Controls Inc., Tampa, Fla., 1994-99; triage nurse CIGNA Healthcare, Tampa, Fla., 2000—. After hours triage nurse CIGNA Health Care, Tampa, 2000—. Mem. AACN, NAACOG, Am. Assn. Occupl. Health Nurses, ADA, Am. Hosp. Assn., Am. Assn. Diabetes Educators, Am. Fertility Soc., Oncology Nurses Soc. Home: 18821 Tournament Trl Tampa FL 33647-2459

ARGENZIANO, NANCY, state legislator; b. Bklyn., Jan. 1, 1955; 1 child, Joseph Hall. Student in pre-vet. medicine, Broward C.C. Lic. real esate agt. Mem. Fla. Ho. of Reps., Tallahassee, 1996—, now chmn. elder affairs and long term care com., mem. tourism com., mem. property & probate com. Mem. utilities and comm. com., elder affairs and long term care com., responsibility com.; real estate investor; owner stained glass bus. Bd. dirs. DeRosa Civic Assn., 1994-95, Withlacoochee Basin Initiative, 1995—. Republican. Roman Catholic. Office: State Capitol Rm 1201 Tallahassee FL 32399-1300

ARGERS, HELEN, novelist, playwright; b. Valisburg, N.J. BA; graduate studies, Europe. Writer advt. copy. Workshop lectr. 6th Ann. Metro. Writers Conf. Seton Hall U., South Orange, N.J., 1996; lectr. hist. sociol. view of Am., 1876 N.J. Hist. Soc., 1998. Author: A Lady of Independence, 1982, Noblesse Oblige, 1994, (play) The Home Visit, 1986 (Winner Nat. One-Act-Play Competition 1986, Weisbrod award 1987), A Scandalous Lady, 1991, A Captain's Lady, 1991, An Unlikely Lady, 1992, The Gilded Lily, 1998, (short story) The Ozymandias Bush (Nelson Algren award finalist 1990), Repossession (Writer's Digest Short Story Competition award); author (under pseudonym Helen Archery) The Age of Elegance, 1992, The Season of Loving, 1992, Lady Adventuress, 1994, Duel of Hearts, 1994; humor columnist Worrall Newspapers, 2003-04; classical and popular reviewer Arts and Entertainment for some 20 newspapers. Recipient Resolution of Honor, State of N.J., 1994, 97. Mem. Nat. Hist. Soc., Jane Austen Soc. N. Am., N.J. State Opera Guild.

ARGIROKASTRITIS, DIANE MARIE, media specialist; b. Detroit; d. John T. and Frances Anne Wojcik; m. Konstantinos Argirokastritis, June 21, 1980; children: Christina, Antonio, Caroline. BS in Bus. Edn., Ea. Mich. U., Ypsilanti; M in Libr. Info. Sci., Wayne State U., 2001. Proofreader UN FAO, Rome, 1976—79; lectr. Ionio U., Corfu, Greece; ref. libr. Lenox Twp. Libr., Lenox Twp., Mich., 1997—2000; libr. media splst. Seminole Elem. Sch., Mt. Clemens, Mich., 2000—03, Jefferson Middle Sch., Pontiac, Mich., 2003—. Home: 4835 Shelbyshire Shelby Township MI 48316

ARGRETT, LORETTA COLLINS, assistant attorney general, educator; b. Carlisle, Miss., Oct. 7, 1937; d. Joseph Daniel and Katie Marie (Jones) C.; m. James H. Argrett Jr., Mar. 28, 1959 (div.); children: Lisa Argrett Ahmad, Brian E.; m. Vantile E. Whitfield, May 29, 1993. BS cum laude, Howard U., 1958; student, Technische Hochschule, Zurich, Switzerland, 1958; postgrad., Howard U., 1966-67, George Washington U., 1968; JD, Harvard U., 1976. Bar: D.C. Ct. Appeals 1976, U.S. Dist. Ct. D.C. 1977, U.S. Ct. Appeals D.C. 1977, U.S. Tax Ct. 1977. Chemist NIH, 1958-59, 59-61; tchr. Duval County Bd. Instrn., Fla., 1961-62; chemist Hazleton Labs., Reston, Va., 1965-66, FDA, 1966-68; chemist, supr. lab. Walter Reed Army Inst. of Rsch., 1968-73; summer assoc. Mahoney, Hadlow, Chambers & Adams, Jacksonville, Fla., summer 1975, Arent, Fox, Kintner, Plotkin & Kahn, Washington, summer 1975, assoc., 1976-78, Stroock & Stroock & Lavan, Washington, 1978-79; legis. atty. Joint Com. on Taxation U.S. Congress, 1979-81; ptnr. Wald, Harkrader & Ross, Washington, 1981-86; pvt. practice Washington, 1986; assoc. prof., then prof. Sch. Law, Howard U., Washington, 1986—; Asst. Atty. Gen. in Tax Div. U.S. Dept. of Justice. Sec. bd. meetings Opportunity Funding Corp., 1984-93; adj. prof. Georgetown Law Ctr., Washington Coll. Law, 1986-88, Am. U., 1988; mem. vis. com. Harvard Law Sch., 1987-93; apptd. mem. adv. com. grad. tax program U. Balt. Law Sch., 1986—; mem. spl. com. on gender D.C. Cir. Task Force on Gender, Race and Ethnic Bias, 1992-95. Contbr. articles to profl. jours. Bd. trustees Free the Children Trust; bd. dirs. Jubilee Enterprise of Greater Washington, Inc.; adv. bd. Jubilee Support Alliance; mem. NAACP, Pub. Defender Svc. of D.C. Lucy Moten fellow, 1958. Fellow Am. Bar Found.; mem. ABA (sect. on taxation, chair task force capital cost recovery 1985, vice chair com. women and minorities 1993-95, lobbyist), Nat. Bar Assn., Washington Bar Assn., D.C. Bar Assn. (mem. atty. client arbitration bd. 1984-90, legal ethics com. 1993—), Harvard Law Sch. Alumni Assn., Sigma Xi (assoc.), Beta Kappa Chi. Office: Howard U Law Sch 2900 Van Ness St NW Washington DC 20008-1106

ARGUEDAS, CRISTINA C. lawyer; b. 1953; BA, U. N.H.; JD, Rutgers U., 1979. Bar: Calif. 1979. Dep. fed. defender U.S. Dist. Ct. (no. dist.) Calif.; ptnr. Cooper, Arguedas & Cassman, Emeryville, Calif. Lawyer rep. U.S. Ct. Appeals (9th cir.) Jud. Conf. Named one of 50 Top Lawyers Nat. Law Jour., 1998. Mem. Calif. Attys. for Criminal Justice (past pres.). Office: Cooper Arguedas & Cassman 5900 Hollis St Ste N Emeryville CA 94608-2008

ARGUELLO, BARBARA ANN, nursing assistant; b. Hotchkiss, Colo., Feb. 20, 1950; d. Lloyd Arguello and Gloria Mabel (Trujillo) Henderson. Desktop publishing studies, Stratford Career Inst., Washington, 2002. Cert. nursing asst., Mo. Nurses aide Birch Ave. Manor, Greeley, Colo., 1970—72, Orangeview, Anaheim, Calif., 1973—75; injection mold oper. Inca Plastics, Santa Ana, Calif., 1976—78; nurses aide Bonnell, Greeley, 1981—89; pvt. duty nurse Gericare, Joplin, Mo., 1990; sewing machine oper. Nat. Mills, Webb City, Mo., 1991; nursing asst. Spring River Christian Village, Joplin, 1992—. Republican. Pentecostal. Avocations: collecting miniatures, linguistics, writing children's stories and poems, drawing, computer programming. Home: 626 S Walker Webb City MO 64870-2753 Office: Spring River Christian Village 201 S Northpark Ln Joplin MO 64801

ARGYROPOULOS, URSULA, food service executive; b. Aachen, Germany; Student, Internat. Sch. Confectionary Arts. Chef., instr. Newbury Coll., Brookline, Mass., 1985—97; chef, owner, instr. Ursula Art of the Cake, Boston, 1997—. Named Saccone award, Les Dames d'Escottier. Office: Art of the Cake 11 Grovenor Rd Boston MA 02130

ARHOLEKAS, IRENE, secondary school educator; b. Johannesburg, Oct. 3, 1971; arrived in US, 1977; B in Lit. and Creative Writing, CUNY, 1991; M in British and Am. Lit., SUNY, Stonybrook, 1992. Lectr. composition U. Md., Heidelberg, Germany, 1993—94; tchr. English Inst. N.Am. Studies, Barcelona, 1994—97; tcrh. Benjamin N. Cardozo H.S., Bayside, NY, 1998—2003; owner Archos Comm., Astoria, NY, 2000—. Adj. lectr. ESL & English Nassau C.C., Garden City, NY, 2001—. Author: Being a Greek-American Girl, 2003; columnist: Nat. Herald, 2001, pub.: ezine greekamericangirl.com, 2003. Mem.: Hellenic Am. Educators Assn., Elpides, Phi Beta Kappa. Avocations: travel, theater, opera. Office: Archos Comm 3811 Ditmars Blvd Astoria NY 11105

ARIAS-HASKINS, GLORIA, state representative; b. Bogota, Colombia, July 11, 1956; d. Salomon and Betty Bardon Arias; m. Terry E. Haskins, June 3, 1978 (dec.); children: David, Brian, Hayden, Harlan. Student, CUNY, Bob Jones U. Mem. SC Ho. of Reps., 2001—. Pub. rels. com. Jr. League, 1993—94; spokeswoman Cancer Soc.; bd. dirs. Legal Aux. Greater Greenville, 1987—94, Carolina Hope Christian Adoption Agy. Republican. Office: State Capitol 326 D Blatt Bldg Columbia SC 29211

ARIENS, KARLA RAE, library director; b. Tremonton, Utah, July 3, 1966; d. Paul Elias and Lorna May Adams; m. Thaddeus William Ariens, Mar. 17, 1988; children: Talia Louise, Tori May, Terese Claire. BS in Elem. Edn., Utah State U., 1988. Tchr. asst. Children's Home, Logan, Utah, 1988-89; music specialist Hilltop Sch., Logan, Utah, 1988-89; chpt. I aide Adams Elem. Sch., Logan, Utah, 1989-90; gifted/talented specialist Cache County Sch. Dist., Logan, Utah, 1989-90; libr. dir. Brookville (Ind.) Town-Twp. Libr., 1991—2002. Sec. Franklin County Cmty. Network Com., Brookville, 1995. Mem. Lds Ch. Avocations: music, cooking, reading, piano, singing.

ARIFI, FATANA BAKTASH, artist, educator; arrived in U.S., 2000; d. Mohammed Arif and Bibishreen Arifi. Diploma in art(hon.), Women Orgn. of Afghanistan, 1983; diploma in painting (hon.), Nat. Assn. Artists, Afghanistan, 1985; MFA, Kabul (Afghanistan) U., 1987. Art instr. Kabul (Afghanistan) U., 1989—92; freelance artist, designer Afghan Internat. Orgn., 1994—99; dir. Maimanagi Fine Arts Ctr., Peshawar, Pakistan, 1995—99; art instr. Inst. of Fine Arts, Peshawar, 1996; founder, editor Art and Culture Jour., Peshawar, 1997—99; art instr. Hunarkada Acad. Visual and Performance Arts, Peshawar, 1998; sr. cert. framer Michael's Art and Crafts, Alexandria, Va., 2001—. Mem. selection com. Afghan Artistic Competitions, Peshawar, Pakistan. Author: (book) Drawing and Painting, 1988, Painting and it's Status in Afghanistan, 1998, Drawing Technical Metodes, 1999; illustrator (children's story books), 1995—99; dir.: (mag.) The Afghan Musaic, 1999. Recipient award, Artist Festival, Japan, 1981, Nat. Painting award, Ministry of Culture, Afghanistan, 1983, 1985, 1987, award, Women Orgn., Afghanistan, 1983, Army Mus., Afghanistan, 1986, Nat. Assn. Artists of Afghanistan, 1986, Youth Orgn. Afghanistan, 1985. Achievements include development of new style in painting named Handasism. Avocations: writing, poetry, cooking, music.

ARING, MONIKA KOSMAHL, education economist, consultant, researcher; b. Gablonz, Germany, Mar. 14, 1945; d. Heinrich G. and Gisela Ilse (Zelder) Kosmahl; m. Roomet Joost Aring, June 19, 1965 (dec.); children: Antje, Emily. BA, Bklyn. Coll., 1972; MPA, Harvard U., 1989. Dir. Pro Portsmouth Inc., Portsmouth, N.H., 1976-80; cons. Monika Aring Assocs., Portsmouth, 1980-88; v.p. pub. rels. Internt. Hotels, Portsmouth, 1980-82; v.p. mktg. Am. Leadership Forum, Denver, 1989-91; dir. Inst. for Edn. and Employment, Edn. Devel. Ctr. Inc., Newton, Mass., 1991-96, dir. CTr. for Workforce Devel., 1996—; exec. dir. Ctr. Edn. and Tng. Employment Ohio State U., Columbus, Ohio, 2002—03; sr. policy analyst workforce and econ. develop. RTI Internat., Wash., DC, 2003—. Project dir. Options for a New Downtown, Portsmouth, 1976-78, N.H. Blue Ribbon Commn. on Edn. and Employment, 1986-88; advisor Edn. Commn. of U.S., 1999—; mem. UNESCO Forum on Lifelong Learning, 1999; tech. advisor U.S Dept. Edn., 1995; keynote spkr. Asian Pacific Econ. Commn., 1999. Author: Global Best Practice in Workforce Development, 1996, also other studies. Social entrepreneur/cons. N.H. Coun. for Humanities, 1977, Somersworth (N.H.) Children's Festival, 1980, Asia Devel. Bank, 1999, U.S. AID, Peru, India, Africa, 1997. Recipient Mayor's award City of Portsmouth, 1978, Leadership award C. of C., 1980; guest of German Parliament, Bonn, 1993. Mem. Knowledge Navigators Found. Avocations: outdoor sports, music, designing, foreign languages (german, russian, french, spanish). Home: Apt 26 350 9th St SE Washington DC 20003-2168 Home Fax: 202-543-2332. E-mail: monikakaring@yahoo.com., maring@rti.org.

ARIOSA, CORAZON ENCILA, accountant; b. Manila, Feb. 2, 1946; arrived in U.S., 1982; d. Feliculo V. Encila and Monica A. Manuel; m. Amerigo S. Ariosa, June 20, 1969 (dec. Oct. 1977); children: Gloria E., Glover M., Lourdes E. AA in Commerce, Philippine Coll. Commerce, Manila, 1965, BS in Acctg., 1968. Sec., document examiner Philippine Nat Bank, Manila, 1970—82; staff assoc., svc. rep. Pacific Bell, San Francisco, 1982—2002; svc. rep. San Francisco (Calif.) Chronicle, 2003—. Inst. agt. Primerica, San Leandro, Calif., 1999—. Pres. Filipino Cmty. Oakland, Calif., 1995—96, Filipino Women's Club, Alameda, Calif., 1996—98. Mem.: Bay Area Woman's Club (pres. 1998—2000). Roman Catholic. Avocation: travel.

ARIZAGA, LAVORA SPRADLIN, retired lawyer; b. Garvin County, Okla., Apr. 29, 1927; d. Gervase Eugene and Donah Lavorah (Eddings) Spradlin; m. Francisco DePaula Arizaga, Aug. 10, 1946; children: F.D. III, Lavora Cristina Arizaga Ewan, Rebecca Maria Arizaga Armour, Nicolas Antonio. BA, U. Okla., 1952; JD, U. Houston, 1979. Bar: Tex. 1979. Sole practitioner, Houston, 1979-92. Pres. United Meth. Women, St. Luke's United Meth. Ch., Midland, 1996-98; chmn. Affirmative Action Adv. Bd., City of Houston, 1984-86. Mem. AAUW, LWV (pres. Beaumont, Tex. 1960-61, v.p. Tex. 1983-85, pres. Houston 1985-87, Midland, Tex. 1997-99). Home: 1809 Kensington Ln Midland TX 79705-1706 E-mail: larizaga@aol.com.

ARKHIPOVA, IRINA R. biologist; b. Moscow, Aug. 14, 1960; arrived in U.S., 1991; d. Robert G. Arkhipov and Natalia B. Livanova; m. Sergei V. Pokrovski, Mar. 7, 1981; 1 child, Andrew Pokrovski. BS/MS, Moscow State U., 1983; PhD, Inst. Molecular Biology, Moscow, 1986. Rsch. scientist Inst. Molecular Biology, Moscow, 1986—90; postdoctoral fellow U. Edinburgh, Scotland, 1990—91, Harvard U., Cambridge, Mass., 1991—94, rsch. assoc., 1994—2000, staff scientist, 2000—. Author: Drosophila Retrotransposons, 1995; contbr. articles to profl. jours. Fellow, The Wellcome Trust, London, 1990—91; grantee rsch. planning grant, NSF, 1996—97. Mem.: Genetics Soc. Am. Home: 65 Virginia Rd Waltham MA 02453 Office: Harvard Univ Dept Molecular Cellular Biology 7 Divinity Ave Cambridge MA 02138

ARKING, LUCILLE MUSSER, nurse, epidemiologist; b. Centre County, Pa., Jan. 26, 1936; d. Boyd Albert and Marion Anna (Merryman) Musser; m. Robert Arking, May 8, 1959; children: Henry David, Jonathan Jacob. RN, Episcopal Sch. Nursing, 1958; BSN, U. Pa., 1968; MSN, Wayne State U., 1986, postgrad., 1991—96. Psychiat. rsch. nurse Boston City Hosp., 1958; hosp. supr. Phila. Psychiat. Ctr., 1959-61; pub. health nurse Cmty. Nursing Svc., Phila., 1961-64; DON Green Acres Nursing Ctr., Phila., 1966-67; head nurse U. Va., Charlottesville, 1967-68; asst. DON U. Ky., Lexington, 1968-70; asst. dir. nursing edn. Rio Hondo Hosp., Downey, Calif., 1973-75; DON Bellwood Hosp., Bellflower, Calif., 1974-75; nurse epidemiologist Henry Ford Hosp., Detroit, 1975-84, dir. hosp. epidemiology, 1984-89, sr. clin. epidemiologist, 1990-94; v.p. clin. svcs. Great Lakes Rehab. Hosp., Southfield, Mich., 1994-96; adminstr. Cadillac Nursing Ctr., Detroit, 1997-99; exec. dir. St. Anthony Nursing Care Ctr., Warren, Mich., 1999—2001; with office of internat. affairs Pusan (South Korea) Nat. U., 2001; with St. James Nursing Ctr., Detroit, 2002—03, Arking Cons. Assocs., 2003—. Lectr. drug abuse Fountain Valley, Calif., 1970-75; instr. Santa Ana Coll., 1971-73. Contbr. articles to profl. jours. Co-founder Parents and Friends Learning Disabilities Orgn., 1968-70; dean leader Cub Scouts, Fountain Valley, 1968-75; bd. dirs. Wellness Networks, Detroit, 1982-86; mem. Mich. Gov. AIDS Task Force, 1985-86, Mich. Med. Soc. AIDS Task Force, 1986. Women's Club of Centre County scholar, 1954-58; grantee Cmty. Nursing Svc. Ednl., 1963-64; USPHS nursing trainee, 1965. Mem. APHA (mem. epidemiology sect. 1975-99), ANA, Mich. Nurses's Assn. (AIDS task force 1987-89, HIV adv. com. 1989-90), Assn. Practitioners Infection Control, Sci. Rsch. Soc., Assn. Women in Sci., Sigma Xi. Home: 4705 Stoddard Dr Troy MI 48085-3504 Office Phone: 248-689-5286. Personal E-mail: brkac@aol.com.

ARKKELIN, CORA RINK, realtor; b. Custer City, Pa., Jan. 21, 1928; d. Frederick Henry Rink and Esther Harriet Rink-Reed; m. Wallace G. Arkkelin, Mar. 17, 1944 (dec. Apr. 1999); children: Wallace Jr. (dec.), Linda, Harold, Gerald, Daniel. Student, Kent State U., Lake Erie Coll. Machine operator Chanpion Hardware, Geneva, Ohio, 1950-57; office mgr., ins. agt. Miller Realty Ins., Geneva, Ohio, 1958-62; realtor, broker Miller Realty Co., Inc., Geneva, Ohio, 1962-88, Ara REalty, Geneva, Ohio, 1988-91, Coldwell Banker Hunter Realty, Geneva, Ohio, 1991—. Owner auto salvage yard; raced at Speedway 7, Conneaut, Ohio, 1970—94, Sharon Speedway, Hartford, Ohio, 1994—; racing at Painesville Speedway. Race car driver Powder Puff Derby, 1949-64, Men's Racing Divsn. Painesville Speedway, 1958—. Mem. Nat. Bd. Realtors, Ashtabula County Bd. Realtors (sec.-treas., Realtor of Yr. 1988), Tri County Racing Assn.

(sec.-treas. 1963-64), Geneva Kiwanis. Avocation: auto racing. Home: 5434 W Maple Rd Geneva OH 44041-8127 Office: Coldwell Banker Hunter Realty 385 S Broadway Geneva OH 44041-1808 E-mail: hurricanecora50@yahoo.com.

ARLEN, JENNIFER HALL, law educator; b. Berkeley, Calif., Jan. 7, 1959; d. Michael John and Ann (Warner) A.; m. Robert Lee Hotz, May 21, 1988; children: Michael Arlen Hotz, Robert Arlen Hotz. BA, Harvard U., 1982; JD, NYU, 1986, PhD in Econ., 1992. Bar: NY 1987, US Ct. Appeals (11th cir.) 1987. Summer clk. US Dist. Ct. (ea. dist.), Bklyn., 1984; summer assoc. Davis Polk & Wardwell, NYC, 1985; law clk. US Cir. Judge, 11th cir., Savannah, Ga., 1986-87; asst. prof. law Emory U., Atlanta, 1987-91, assoc. prof. law, 1991-93; prof. law U. So. Calif., LA, 1994—2002, Ivadelle and Theodore Johnson prof. law and bus., 1997—2002; prof. law NYU, 2002—03, Norma Z. Paige prof. Law, 2003—. Vis. prof. law U. So. Calif., 1993; dir. U. So. Calif. Ctr. Law, Econs. Orgn., 2000—02; vis. prof. law Calif. Inst. Tech., 2001, Yale U., 2001—02; mem. acad. bd. NYU Ctr. Law, Bus., 2003—. Olin fellow U. Calif. Sch. Law, Berkeley, 1991. Mem. ABA, Am. Assn. Law Schs. (chair remedies sect. 1994, chair elect 1993, mem. exec. com. 1990-91, 95, chair torts sect. 1995, chair-elect 1994, treas. 1991, sec. 1992-93, exec. com. bus. assns. sect. 1995-96, 2000—, chair law and econ., sect. 1996, chair-elect law and econs. sect. 1995, chair 1996), Am. Law and Econ. Assn. (bd. dirs. 1991-93, program com. 1999), Am. Econ. Assn., Order of Coif, Am. Law Inst. Democrat. Office: NYU Law Sch 40 Washington Square S New York NY 10012

ARLINGHAUS, SANDRA JUDITH LACH, mathematical geographer, educator; b. Elmira, N.Y., Apr. 18, 1943; d. Donald Frederick and Alma Elizabeth (Satorius) Lach; m. William Charles Arlinghaus, Sept. 3, 1966; 1 child, William Edward. AB in Math., Vassar Coll., 1964; postgrad., U. Chgo., 1964-66, U. Toronto, 1966-67, Wayne State U., 1968-70, MA in Geography, 1976; PhD in Geography, U. Mich., 1977. Vis. instr. math. U. Ill., Chgo., 1966; vis. asst. prof. geography Ohio State U., Columbus, 1977-78, lectr. math., 1978-79, Loyola U., Chgo., 1979-81, asst. prof. math., 1981-82; lectr. math. and geography U. Mich., Dearborn and Ann Arbor, 1982-83; founding dir. Inst. Math. Geography, Ann Arbor, 1985—; pres. Arlinghaus Enterprises, Ann Arbor, 1998—. Guest lectr. U. Chgo., 1979, 87, 2000-01, U. Calif., 1979, Syracuse U., 1991, U. No. Iowa, 1991; guest lectr. U. Mich., Ann Arbor, 1983, 90-93, adj. prof. math. geography, population-environ. dynamics Sch. Natural Resources and Environ., 1994—, adj. prof. Coll. Architecture and Urban Planning, 1997, 2001—; cons. Transp. Rsch. Inst., Coll. Architecture, 1985-86, Coll. Edn., 1992, Cmty. Sys. Found., 1993—; prodr. Ann Arbor Cmty. Access TV, 1988-90; dir. spatial analysis divsn. Cmty. Systems Found., 1996—, dir. fellowship tng. divsn., 1996—; co-founder Arlinghaus Enterprises, 1997, pres. 2000-02, mgr., 2003—. Author: Down the Mail Tubes: The Pressured Postal Era, 1853-1984, Essays on Mathematical Geography, 1986, Essays on Mathematical Geography-II, 1987, An Atlas of Steiner Networks, 1989, Essays on Mathematical Georgraphy-III, 1991; co-author: Population-Environment Dynamics, Sectors in Transition, 1992 and later editions through 1998, Mathematical Geography and Global Art, 1986, Environmental Effects on Bus Durability, 1990, Fractals in Geography, 1993, Graph Theory and Geography: An Interactive View, Ebook 2002, Wiley; founder, editor, co-author Solstice, 1990—, Image Interactive Atlases, Image Game Series, Image Discussion Papers, Internat. Soc. Spatial Scis., 1995—; author, editor-in-chief Practical Handbook of Curve Fitting, 1994; co-author, editor-in-chief Practical Handbook of Digital Mapping: Terms and Concepts, 1994; editor-in-chief Practical Handbook of Spatial Stats., 1995; editor internat. monograph series; reviewer Mathematical Reviews, 1992—; contbr. articles, book reviews to profl. jours. in field of geography, psychology, math., biology, history, philately. Mem. City of Ann Arbor Planning Commn., 1995-2003, sec., 1997-2002, chair, 2002-2003, vice-chmn., 2003; mem. City of Ann Arbor Environ. Commn., 2000-03; bd. dirs., chmn. Bromley Homeowners Assn., Ann Arbor, 1989-93, pres., 1990-93, 95-96; mem. ordinance revisions com. City of Ann Arbor, 1996-2003, mem. master planning com., 2002-03; bd. dirs. World Jr. Bridge Championships, Ann Arbor, 1990-91, Dolfins Inc., 1993-96; artist Math. Awareness Week, Lawrence Tech. U., 1988; trustee Cmty. Sys. Found., 1995-2001; co-vice chair citizens adv. com. NE Ann Arbor master plan revision, 1999-2000; adv. bd. City of Ann Arbor Police Dept. Neighborhood Watch, 2001—; mem. exec. com. Comty. Sys. Found., 2003—, sec. bd. trustees, 2003— Recipient Cmty. Svc. award, City of Ann Arbor, 1999, Pres.'s Vol. Svc. award, Pres. Bush's Coun. Svc. and Civic Participation, 2003—. Fellow Am. Geog. Soc. (rep. search com. for curator of collection in Golda Meir Libr. U. Wis.-Milw. Libr. 1993-94); mem. AAAS, Am. Math. Soc., Math. Assn. Am., Assn. Am. Geographers, Internat. Soc. Spatial Scis. (founder), N.Y. Acad. Scis., Engring. Soc. Detroit, Regional Sci. Assn. Achievements include discovery of exact fractal characterization of the geometry of central place theory and its electronic interpretation; alignment of earth marking sculptures to solstices and equinoxes in Minnesota, Washington, Alaska, New Brunswick, Canada, and USSR; creator of one of world's first refereed electronic journals; creator of applications of chaos theory in geography and population environment dynamics, maps for major international projects for Syria and Pakistan. Office: U Mich Sch Natural Resources Ann Arbor MI 48109

ARMACOST, MARY JANE, healthcare company executive; BA, Denison U. Bd. dirs. Mills-Peninsula Hosps., chmn. bd. dirs.; mem. governing bd. Sutter Health Inc., Sacramento, 1996—, chmn. bd. dirs., 1997—. Trustee Denison U., Ohio, 1981—; San Francisco Zool. Soc., 1985—. Office: Sutter Health Inc 2200 River Plaza Dr Sacramento CA 95833-4134

ARMACOST, MARY-LINDA SORBER MERRIAM, former academic administrator, consultant; b. Jeannette, Pa., May 31, 1943; d. Everett Sylvester Calvin and Madeleine (Case) Sorber; m. E. William Merriam, Dec. 13, 1969 (div. 1975); m. Peter H. Armacost, July 10, 1993. Student, Grove City Coll., 1961-63; BA, Pa. State U., 1963-65, MA, 1965-67, PhD, 1967-70; HHD (hon.), Carroll Coll., 1991; LLD (hon.), Wilson Coll., 1994. Rsch. assoc. Pa. State U., University Park, 1970-72; asst. prof. speech Emerson Coll., Boston, 1972-79, dir. continuing edn., 1974-77, spl. asst. to pres., 1977-78, v.p. adminstrn., 1978-79; asst. to pres. Boston U., 1979-81; pres. Wilson Coll., Chambersburg, Pa., 1981-91, Moore Coll. Art and Design, Phila., 1991-93; sr. fellow Office of Women in Higher Edn. Am. Coun. on Edn., 1994—; interim pres. Moore Coll. Art and Design, Phila., 1998-99; pres. emerita, 2000. Adj. prof. U. Pa. Grad. Sch. Edn., 2003; cons. Govt. Edn. and Secondary Edn. Act Title III, Alameda County, Calif., 1968. Bd. govs. New Eng. chpt. NATAS, 1980-81; bd. dirs. Sta. WITF, Inc., Harrisburg, Pa., 1982-91, chmn. bd., 1988-91; bd. dirs. Chambersburg Hosp., 1984-89, vice chmn. bd., 1987-89; bd. dirs. Elderhostel, 1997-2002; vice-chmn., 2000-2002; trustee Monmouth U., N.J., 1994-99, Sta. WHYY-FM-TV, Phila., 1992-93, Boston Zool. Soc., 1980-81, Arts Boston, 1979-81, Scotland Sch. Vets. Children, Pa., 1984-90, Randolph-Macon Woman's Coll., Lynchburg, Va., 2001-02; bd. dirs. Fla. Orch., 1993-97, co-chair edn. com., 1995-97, mem. exec. com., 1995-97; mem. exec. com. Found. for Ind. Colls., 1989-91, WEDU-TV, 1998-2002, chair planning com., mem. exec. com., bd. dirs., 1998-2002; pres. Chambersburg Area Coun. Arts, 1988-90; chmn. higher edn. com. Gen. Assembly Presbyn. Ch., 1987-90; elder Falling Spring Presbyn. Ch., 1988-90; fellow Am. Coun. Edn., 1977-78, commn. on govtl. rels., 1985-89, commn. on women, 1992-93; mem. exec. com. Pa. Assn. Colls. and Univs., 1984-90, mem. exec. com. Assn. Presbyn. Colls. and Univs., 1983-88, pres., 1986-87; mem. edn. adv. com. John S. & James L. Knight Found., 1998-2000; mem. Presbyn. Edn. Bd., exec. com., Pakistan 2003—. Recipient Disting. Alumna award Pa. State U., 1984, Disting. Dau. of Pa., 1986, Athena award Chambersburg C. of C., 1988, Outstanding Alumnae award Sch. Dist. Jeannette, 1991. Mem.: Phi Kappa Phi. E-mail: mlsma@cs.com.

ARMAN GELENBE, DENIZ, concert pianist; b. Ankara, Turkey, Oct. 8, 1944; came to U.S., 1962; d. Abdul Kerim and Ayse Mediha (Raif) A.; m. Erol Gelenbe, June 8, 1968; 1 child, Pamir Emre. Student, Eastman Sch. Music, 1962-64; MusB, Juilliard, 1967, MusM, 1968; postgrad., U. Mich., 1970-71. Founder, artistic dir., prof. piano Paris U., 1979-90; founder, artistic dir. Arman Ensemble, N.C., 1991—, Arman Ensemble, Arman Trio, Paris, 1994—. Dir. summer music program, Normandy, France, 1999—; vis. assoc. prof. piano U. Ctrl. Fla., Orlando, 1998—2003, artist in residence, assoc. prof. piano, 2001—03; sr. lectr., keyboard coord. for collaborative performance Trinity Coll. Music, London, 2003—. Musician (recitals): Carnegie Weill Hall, Salle Gaveau, Nat. Gallery Art, Tonhalle, Wigmore Hall, Concerts de Midi; musician: (soloist) Ensemble Orchestral Paris, New Japan Philharm., Ankara Presdl. Symphony Orch., Presdl. Symphony Orch., N.C. Symphony; musician: (CD) with Haydn Quartet, 1994, 2000, Arman Ensemble, 1996, Arman Trio, 2000. Emerging Artist grantee, Durham, N.C., 1984. Mem. Chamber Music Am., Coll. Music Soc. Avocations: painting, reading, walking. Home: Flat 67 Campbell Ct 1-7 Queens Gate Gardens London SW7 4PD England Office: Trinity Coll Music KIng Charles Ct Old Royal Naval Coll, Greenwich London SE10 9JF England E-mail: arman@dur.mindspring.com.

ARMANI, AIDA MARY, small business executive; b. Amman, Jordan, Apr. 13, 1952; came to U.S., 1956; d. Raji Naiem and Wardeh Elias (Kazanjian) Kawar; m. Steven Earl McBride, Apr. 7, 1973 (div. July 1983); children: Nathaniel Joseph, Aaron Keith. Beauty lic., Martin Anthony Beauty Sch., 1970; cert. in hypnotherapy, Sidona Inst. Hypnotherapy, 1995; cert. imagery therapist, Internat. Inst. Visualization, 1996. Stylist/colorist Jean-Madeline, Phila., 1970-74; colorist Hair Impulse, Media, Pa., 1975-80; colorist/stylist Talent, Bryn Mawr, 1980-83; colorist Salon 600, Bryn Mawr, Pa., 1983-86, James & Co., Wayne, Pa., 1986-87; colorist, cons., head dept., artistic dir. Raya-Haig Salon, Bala Cynwyd, Pa., 1987—; entrepreneur, owner Aida, Inc., West Chester, Pa., 1995—; animal imagery therapist, 2000—. Mem. artistic team Goldwell of Pa., 1995-96, educator, 1990-96; pvt. practice dream interpreter, hypnotherapy counselor, West Chester, Pa., 1995—. Inventor hair styling devices; appeared in opera Acad. of Music., Pa., 1996. Sunday sch. tchr. Ch. of the Savior, Wayne, Pa., 1981-86, leader divorced/singles group, 1987-92; mem. Internat. Inst. Visualization & Rsch., 1995-96. Mem. Internat. Beauty Soc., Art & Fashion, Intercoiffure Internat., Hair Color Exch. Avocations: needlepoint, dance, teaching sunday school, interior decorating. Home: 226 Chestnut St Newtown Square PA 19073-3306 Office: Raya-Haig Beauty Ctr 401 E City Line Ave Bala Cynwyd PA 19004-1122 also: Aida Armani Color Group 914 Lancaster Ave Bryn Mawr PA 19010

ARMATRADING, JOAN, singer, songwriter; b. St. Kitts, West Indian Islands, Dec. 9, 1950; BA with honors, MBE, U. London, 2001; DLitt, U. Liverpool, 2000; Mus D, Birmingham U., 2002. Albums include Whatever's for Us, 1972, Back to the Night, 1974, Joan Armatrading, 1976, Show Some Emotion, 1977, To the Limit, 1978, Steppin' Out, 1979, Me Myself I, 1980, How Cruel, 1980, Walk Under Ladders, 1981, The Key, 1983, Track Record, 1983, Secret Secrets, 1985, Sleight of Hand, 1986, The Shouting Stage, 1988, Hearts & Flowers, 1990, The Very Best Of, 1991, Square The Circle, What's Inside, 1994, Lullabies, 1998, The Messenger, A Tribute Song to Nelson Mandela, 2000; CD: Lover's Speak, 2003 Named Hon. fellow, Northampton U., 2003. Fax: 0181 992 6593. E-mail: enquiries@joanarmatrading.com

ARMEN, MARGARET MEIS, lawyer; b. Dayton, Ohio, Oct. 12, 1947; d. Joseph John and Florence Catherine (Ryan) Meis. BA, Carlow Coll., 1969; JD, Cleveland State U., 1978. Bar: Ohio 1978, Washington, DC 1980. Tchr. Pitts. City Sch., 1969—70, Archdiocese of Washington, DC, 1970—73; pers. adminstr. Stouffer Foods Corp., Cleve., 1973—75, Hospitality Motor Inns, Inc., Cleve., 1976—78; atty. adv. US Gen. Acctg. Office, Washington, 1978—, sr. atty., 1986—. Dir. Am. Assn. for Budget and Program Analysis, Washington, 1986—93, pres., 1993—94; dir. Pub. Fin. Pub., Inc., Washington, 1990—2002, pres., 2003—. Exec. editor: Cleve. State U. Law Rev., 1972—78; contbr. articles to profl. jours. Mem.: Exec. Women in Govt. (v.p. 2002—03), Internat. Alliance for Women (sec. 2004). Office: US Gen Acctg Office 441 G Street, NW Washington DC 20548 E-mail: armenm@gao.gov.

ARMENDARIZ, ALMA DELIA, small business owner, researcher; b. Kansas City, Mo., Nov. 2, 1970; d. David Armendariz and Elena Leon Frankoviglia. Student, Washburn U., 1989-90, Fla. Keys C.C., 1993, Coll. of the Ozarks, 1990, Palm Beach C.C., 1998. Cert. capt. USCG. Rschr., first mate The Wild Dolphin Project, Grand Bahama Banks, The Bahamas, 1992; mem. search and recovery team Marine Mammal Stranding Network, Key West, Fla., 1992-94; rschr., first mate DolphinWatch, Key West, 1991-94; surveyor Grand Strand Bottlenose Dolphin Surveys, Myrtle Beach, S.C., 1995-96; mem. adv. bd., adminstr. Save-A-Pet of Fla., Palm Beach, 1998-2000; owner, operator, pres. DolphinWatch, Key West, Fla., 2000—. Intern Ekotecture Internat. Environ. Architecture and Cmty. Planning, Palm Beach, 1991-93. Mem. Harbour Br. Oceanographic Inst., Fla. Keys Wild Dlphin Alliance; Dolphin Project. Mem. World Wildlife Found., Women in the Arts, Surfrider Found., Ctr. for MarineConservation, Internat. Campaign for Tibet, Reef Relief, Harbour Br. Ocean. Inst., The Dolphin Project. Avocations: surfing, free diving, triathlon, travel. Home: 1200 Varela St Key West FL 33040-3314

ARMENTROUT, KERI JANELLE, minister, educator; b. Ft. Worth, Mar. 27, 1979; d. Billy J. and Janelle K. Johnson; m. Karl Armentrout. BA in English Lit., Tex. A&M U., 2001; postgrad., Dallas Theol. Sem., 2001. Piano tchr., College Station, Tex., 1998—2001; min. Campus Crusade for Christ, 2001—. Mem. choir Campus Crusade for Christ, Ft. Collins, Colo., 2001. Mem.: Prestonwood Baptist Ch., Brazos Valley Music Tchrs. Assn., Tex. Music Tchrs. Assn., Music Tchrs. Nat. Assn., Tex. A&M Century Singers. Republican. Baptist. Avocations: singing, dance, sewing.

ARMFIELD, DIANA MAXWELL, artist, educator; b. Ringwood, Eng., June 11, 1920; d. Joseph Harold Armfield and Gertrude Mary Uttley; m. Bernard Dunstan, 1949; 3 children. Student, Slade Sch. Art, Ctrl. Sch. Arts and Crafts, London. Tchr. Byam Shaw Sch. Art, 1959-89. Artist-in-residence, Perth, Australia, 1985, Jackson, Wyo., 1989. One-woman shows include Browse & Darby, London, 1979-2000, 03, Royal Acad. Friends Rm. Gallery, 1995, Royal Cambrian Acad., 2001, Albany Gall, Cardiff, 2001, Albany Gallery, Cardiff, 2002, also in U.S., Australia, Netherlands; author: (books) Mitchell Beazley Pocket Guide to Painting in Oils, Mitchell Beazley Pocket Guide to Drawing, The Art of Diana Armfield (Julian Halsby); represented in pub. collections at Yale Ctr. for Brit. Art, Govt. Eng., Faringdon, Mercury Asset Mgmt., Lancaster City, Victoria and Albert Mus. Textiles. Commr. HRH Prince of Wales, Reuters, Contemporary Art Soc. Wales, Natural Trust. Mem. Royal Acad. Art, New English Art Club (hon.), Royal W. of Eng. Acad., Royal Cambrian Acad. (hon. ret.), Pastel Soc. (hon.), Royal Watercolor Soc. Avocations: music, gardening. Address: 10 High Park Rd Kew Richmond Surrey TW9 4BH England

ARMISTEAD, KATHERINE KELLY (MRS. THOMAS B. ARMISTEAD III), interior designer, travel consultant, civic worker; b. Apr. 14, 1926; d. Joseph Anthony and Katherine Arnold (Manning) Kelly; m. Thomas Boyd Armistead III, Nov. 29, 1952. Grad., Finch Jr. Coll., 1946. Cert. travel cons. Editor news Sta. WOR, N.Y.C., 1946—51; with Dumont TV, 1951—52; editor Social Svc. Rev., L.A., 1956—57; interior designer L.A., 1963—; travel cons. Gilner Internat. Travels, Beverly Hills, Calif., 1980—. Mem. editl. bd. Previews Mag., 1984—87. Pres. Jrs. Social Svc., L.A., 1962—64; nat. chpt. chmn. Assoc. Alumnae of Sacred Heart, 1960—66; pres. Las Floristas, 1967—68; coord. Jr. Mannequin Assisteens, Assistance League So. Calif., 1971—72; pres. docent coun. L.A. County Mus. Art, 1976—77, pres. decorative arts coun., 1977—80, chmn. Am. Antiques Conf., 1979—81, mem. costume coun., mem. past pres.' coun., 1981—, mem. capital gifts campaign com.; pres. L.A. Orphanage Guild, L.A., Calif., 1969—70, bd. dirs., 1970—. Recipient Eve award, Assistance League So. Calif. Mem.: Inst. Cert. Travel Agts., Am. Soc. Travel Agts., Lady Grand Cross Equestrian Order of the Holy Sepulchre of Jerusalem, Bel Air Garden Club, Birnam Wood Golf Club. Republican. Roman Catholic.

ARMITAGE, KAROLE, dancer; b. Madison, Wis., Mar. 3, 1954; Studied, N.C. Sch. of the Arts, with Bill Evans, U. Utah, 1971-72. Dancer Geneva (Switzerland) Opera Ballet, 1973-75, Merce Cunningham Dance Co., 1976-81; choreographer, artistic dir. The Armitage Ballet (formerly Armitage Dance Co.), N.Y.C., 1981—90; dir. MaggioDanza di Firenze, Florence, Italy, 1995—98; assoc. choreographer Centre Chorégraphique Nationale-Ballet de Lorraine, Nancy, France; dir. Venice Biennale of Contemporary Dance, 2004. Choreographer of ballets including: Ne, 1978, Do We Could 1979, Veritige, 1980, Drastic-Classicism, 1981, It Happened at Club Bombay Cinema, 1981, Slaughter on MacDougal Street, 1981, Paradise, version 1, 1981, The Last Gone Dance, 1983, Paradise, version 2, 1983, A Real Gone Dance, 1983, (with Rosella Hightower) The Nutcracker, 1983, Tasmanian Devil, 1984, GV-10, 1984, The Water Duets, 1985, The Mollino Room, 1985, The Elizabethan Phrasing of the Late Albert Ayler, 1986, The Tarnished Angels, 1987, Les Stances a Sophie, 1987, Duck Dances, 1988, Kammerdisco, 1988, GoGo Ballerina, 1988, Contempt, 1989, Forty Guns, 1990, Dancing Zappa, 1990, Jack and Betty, 1990, The Marmot Quickstep, 1991, Renegade Dance Wave, 1991, Overboard, 1991, Segunda Piel, 1992, Happy Birthday Rossini, 1992, Hucksters of the Soul, 1993, I Had A Dream. 1993, Hovering at the Edge of Chaos, 1994, Tattoo and Tutu, 1994, The Dog Is Us, 1994, The Return of Rasputin, 1994, Apollo e Dafne, 1997, Time Is the Echo of an Axe Within a Wood, 2004; (dance for TV) Parafango, 1983, Ex-Romance, 1984; (arts program) The South Bank Show, 1985; (feature films) Without You, I'm Nothing, 1989, Chain of Desire, 1991, Search and Destroy, 1994; (videoclips) Love School for the Dyvinals, 1990, Vogue for Madonna, 1991, In The Closet for Michael Jackson, 1992; (world tours) Milli Vanilli, 1990, Madonna's Blonde Ambition, 1991, The Dyvinals, 1991; (videoclips for feature film) Kuffs, 1990; writer, dir., choreographer (feature film) Hall of Mirrors, 1992. Guggenheim fellow, 1986. Office: Armitage Found 9 N Moore St Ste 4 New York NY 10013-2414

ARMITAGE, SHELLEY SUE, American studies educator; b. Ft. Worth, June 17, 1947; d. Robert Allen and Dorothy Mae (Dunn) A. BA, Tex. Tech. U., 1969, MA, 1971; PhD, U. N.Mex., 1983. Asst. prof. English Tarrant County Jr. Coll., Ft. Worth, 1971-78; lectr. Am. lit. Skidmore Coll., Colo. Inst., Adirondacks, 1977, 78; assoc. prof. Am. lit. West Tex. State U., Canyon, 1983-89; prof. Am. studies U. Hawaii, Honolulu, 1990-96; prof. cultural studies U. Memphis, 1993; chair women's studies U. Tex., El Paso, 1996-2001, Roderick Chair, 1995. Sr. Fulbright U., Nova Lisboa, Portugal, 1990; disting. Fulbright chair of lit. U. Warsaw, 2000; Fulbright sr. specialist U. Lodz, Poland, 2002; Fulbright Orszagh chair, Hungary, 2004. Author: John Held Jr., 1987 (N.Y. Times Notable Book), Kewpies and Beyond: Rose O'Neill, 1994 (Eudora Welty prize.U. Press Miss., 94), Women's Work: Cultural Essays, 1995, The Journals of Peggy Pond Church, 2001 (Border Books prize), Reading Into Photography, 1981. Cons. Oldham County Hist. Commn., Vega, Tex.; referee Praxis, El Paso; exec. dir. N.Mex. NEH, Albuquerque, 1985. Recipient Women Artists and Writers award Rockefeller found., 1985, Internat. Women's Studies award Ford Found., 1997, award NEH, 1999, U. Oreg., 1974, U. N.Mex., 1979, Emily Toth Prize Pop Culture Assn., Am. Studies Assn.; Women's Studies Confs., Costa Rica, Warsaw, Cuba, 2000-01, Nature and Society NEH U. Ill., 1999. Mem. Am. Studies Assn., We. History Assn., MLA, Soc. Photographic Educators. Methodist. Avocations: naturalist, photographer, documentary film consulting, organic farming. Home: PO Box 524 Vega TX 79092 Office: U Tex English Dept 500 W University Ave El Paso TX 79968

ARMS, ANNELI (ANNA ELIZABETH ARMS), artist, educator; b. NYC, May 23, 1935; d. William Emil and Elizabeth Maria (Bodanzky) Muschenheim; m. John M. Arms, Sept. 1, 1956; 1 child, Thomas C. BA, U. Mich., 1958. Represented in permanent collections US State Dept., NY Pub. Libr., Libr. of Congress, N.Y. Hist. Soc. Recipient Nora Mirmont award Heckscher Mus., 1984, Guild Hall Sculpture award, 1987; scholar Art Students League N.Y., 1958. Mem. Nat. Drawing Assn., Fedn. Modern Painters and Sculptors (bd. dirs. 1988-, v.p. 1996—), Manhattan Graphics Ctr. (bd. dirs. 1995—, exhbn. chmn. 2002-), Artists Alliance East Hampton (exhbns. com. 1988—), Artists Equity N.Y. Avocations: opera, movies, swimming, museums, reading. Studio: 113 Greene St New York NY 10012-3823

ARMS, KAREN G. social sciences educator; b. Anita, Iowa, Oct. 5, 1934; d. Edwin Lamar Gardner and Dorothy Dee Phelps; children: Deborah Lynn, Denise Lauree. BS, N.W. Mo. State U., 1957; MS, U. Akron, 1972; PhD, Kent State U., 1974. Cert. Family Life Educator Nat. Coun. on Family Rels., 1998. From mem. faculty sch. of family & consumer studies to dir. Kent State U., Kent, Ohio, 1974—84, dir. sch. of family & consumer studies, 1984—89; assoc. prof. U. Conn., Stamford, Conn., 1989—. Fellow Am. Coun. Edn., Washington, 1986—87; chmn. Human Svc. Planning Coun., Stamford, 1998—; mem. Nat. Coun. on Family Rels., 1973—, Groves Internat. Conf. on Marriage & Family, 1975—. Contbr. columns in newspapers Parent Advocate, 1998, statistical database The State of Stamford Report, 2001. Vol. Exec. Internat. Svc. Corp., Beirut, 1999; bd. dir. United Way, Stamford, 1992—, Stamford Symphony Orch., Stamford, 1992—2001. Recipient Partnership in Edn. award, Urban League of S.W. Conn., 1995; scholar Seminar Abroad scholarship, Fulbright-Hays, Egypt, 2002. Avocations: tennis, golf, grandchildren, property development, volunteering. Office: Univ of Conn Stamford One University Place Stamford CT 06901 E-mail: armsk@stamford.uconn.edu.

ARMSTRONG, ALEXANDRA, financial advisor; b. Washington, Sept. 26, 1939; d. Rhoda Elizabeth (Forbes) Armstrong; m. Jerry J. McCoy, 1994. BA in History, Newton (Mass.) Coll. Sacred Heart, 1960. Cert. fin. planner, 1977. Exec. sec. Ferris & Co., Washington, 1961—66, registered rep., 1966—77; sr. v.p. Julia Walsh & Sons, Washington, 1977—83; pres. Alexandra Armstrong Advisors Inc., Washington, 1983—91; chmn. Armstrong, Welch & MacIntyre Inc., Washington, 1991—2000, Armstrong, MacIntyre & Severns, Inc., Washington, 2001—. Bd. experts Boardroom Reports, 1987—. Author: On Your Own: A Widow's Passage To Emotional and Financial Wellbeing, 1993, 3d edit., 2000. Mem. Washington Jr. League, 1961—; vice chmn. Nat. Coun. Friends of Kennedy Ctr., Washington, 1987-91; pres. Nat. Capital coun. Boy Scouts Am., 1999-2000, chmn., 2000-01; mem. bd. visitors Sch. Bus. Georgetown U., 1988-91; v.p. programs Internat. Women's Forum, 1991-93, v.p. membership 1997-99, dir. IWF leadership found., 2001-; bd. dirs. Reading is Fundamental, 1993—, treas. 2000-2003; chmn. Found. Fin. Planning, 1999-2000, bd. dirs., 1997-2003. Named Bus. Woman of Yr. Washington Bus. and Profl. Women's Club, 1978; recipient award of excellence for commerce Boston Coll. Alumni Assn., 1985, Woman Who Makes a Difference award Internat. Women's Forum, 1992, Silver Beaver award Boy Scouts Am., 1991, Loren Dutton award, Internat. Assn. Registered Fin. Cons., 2003, Beta Gamma Sigma chpt. honoree Georgetown U., 1992. Mem. Internat. Assn. for Fin. Planning (bd. dirs. 1980-87, chmn. emeritus, pres. 1986-87), Nat. Assn. Investment Clubs (columnist monthly mag. 1978—, Disting. Svc. award 1993), Nat. Assn. Securities Dealers (bus. conduct com. dist. 10 1986-89, vice chmn. 1988-89), Nat. Assn. Women Bus. Owners (pres. Capital Area chpt. 1980-81), D.C. Estate Planning Coun., Nat. Capital Area Coun., Econ. Club (Washington), Cosmos Club (Washington), Econ. Club, (N.Y.C.), Fin. Planning Assn. (Lifetime Achievement award 2001), Nat. Capital Area Coun., Nat. Capital Gift Planning Coun. D.C., Republican. Roman Catholic. Home: 3560 Winfield Ln NW Washington DC 20007-2368 Office: 1155 Connecticut Ave NW Ste 250 Washington DC 20036-4314 Office Phone: 202-887-8135. E-mail: aarmstrong@amsindc.com.

ARMSTRONG, ANNE LEGENDRE (MRS. TOBIN ARMSTRONG), retired ambassador; b. New Orleans, Dec. 27, 1927; d. Armant and Olive (Martindale) Legendre; m. Tobin Armstrong, Apr. 12, 1950; children: John Barclay, Katharine, Sarita A. Hixon, Tobin and James L. (twins). BA in English, Vassar Coll., 1949. Co-chmn. Rep. Nat. Com., 1971-73; counsellor to U.S. Pres., 1973-74; U.S. amb. to Gt. Britain and No. Ireland London, 1976-77; chmn. adv. bd. Ctr. for Strategic and Internat. Studies (formerly affiliated with Georgetown U.), 1981-87, chmn. bd. trustees, 1987-99, chmn. exec. com., 1999—; chmn. Pres.'s Fgn. Intelligence Adv. Bd., 1981-90; dir. Promontory Interfinancial Network, LLC. Commn. on Integrated Long Term Strategy, 1987; adv. coun. GM Corp., 1998. Bd. regents Smithsonian Instn., 1978-94, emeritus, 1994; bd. overseers Hoover Instn., 1978-97; co-chmn. Reagan-Bush Campaign, 1980; bd. regents Tex. A&M U., 1997-2003; U.S. Commn. on Nat. Security/21st Century, 1999-2001; mem. Gov.'s Coun. Sci. and Biotech. Devel., Gov.'s Task Force on Homeland Security. Recipient Gold Medal award for disting. svc. to humanity Nat. Inst. Social Scis., 1977, Rep. Woman of Yr. award, 1979, Texan of Yr. award, 1981, Presdl. Medal of Freedom award, 1987, Golden Plate award Am. Acad. Achievement, 1989; named to Tex. Women's Hall of Fame, 1986. Mem. English-Speaking Union (chmn. 1978-80), Coun. Fgn. Rels., Am. Assocs. of Royal Acad. Trust (trustee 1985—, vice-chmn. 1996), Alfalfa Club, Capitol Hill Club, Phi Beta Kappa. Republican.

ARMSTRONG, CAROL SUE, music educator; b. Olympia, Wash., Mar. 28, 1944; d. James H. and Virginia Ellen Davis; m. A. Wendell Armstrong, June 9, 0968; children: Jeremy, Wendy (Armstrong) Vega. MusB edn., Washburn U., Topeka, Kans., 1962—66. Music tchr. USD 441, Wetmore, Kans., 1966—2003. Tchr. Kans. Music Edn. Assn., 1966—, Music Edn. Nat. Conf., 1966—. Recipient Tchr. of the Yr., ATA/ Salina, Kans., 1988, ATA/ Topeka, Kans., 1992, Nominated Disney Tchr. of the Yr., Topeka, Kans., 2000, 1st Pl. Trophy for Show Choir (3 times), All Am. Music Festival/ Orlando, Fla. Republican. Achievements include Won many superior ratings with music groups; performed 35 musicals in my 37 yrs. of teaching. Avocations: piano, ceramics, camping, grandchildren. Home: PO Box 158 Wetmore KS 66550

ARMSTRONG, DENISE GRACE, medical association administrator; Diploma, Briarcliffe Coll., L.I., N.Y., 1974; AAS in Mktg. magna cum laude, Nassau C.C., 2000. Staff asst. Klar, Klar & Tifford, law office, East Meadow, L.I., N.Y., 1974-76, Nassau Acad. Medicine and Nassau County Med. Soc., Garden City, L.I., N.Y., 1976-80; adminstr. Suffolk County Dental Soc., Hauppauge, L.I., N.Y., 1980 87, exec. dir Hauppauge, N.Y., 1988-89; dir. mktg. Med. Soc. of State of N.Y., 1989—. Mem. NAFE, Am. Soc. Assn. Execs., Am. Assn. Med. Soc. Execs., Mktg. Rsch. Assn., Phi Theta Kappa. Office: 420 Lakeville Rd New Hyde Park NY 11042-1121

ARMSTRONG, DIANA ROSE, financial consultant; b. Alvada, Ohio, June 2, 1944; d. J. Joseph and Priscilla Rose Saltzman; m. Philip Bruce Armstrong; children: David Shannon, Laura Ann, Lisa Kay. BS in Edn., Bowling Green Sttae U., 1966, MS in Guidance and Counseling, 1969. CFP. Fin. planner Smith Barney, Morristown, N.J., 1994, sr. v.p. pres.'s coun., 1995—. Mem. AAUW. Republican. Avocations: reading, investing, cooking. Office: Smith Barney 10 Madison Ave Lbby 1 Morristown NJ 07960-7312 Home: 4 Trails End Ct Warren NJ 07059-6775

ARMSTRONG, ELIZABETH NEILSON, curator; b. Winchester, Mass., June 30, 1952; d. Douglas Byron and Ruth Mary (Publow) A.; m. Daniel Alexander Boone, Mar. 1, 1985; children: Olivia Armstrong Boone, Phoebe Elizabeth Boone. BA, Hampshire Coll., 1974; MA, U. Calif., Berkeley, 1982. Grants adminstr. NEH, Washington, 1976-79; rsch. asst. San Francisco Mus. Modern Art, 1979-81; cons. Lowie Mus. Anthropology, Berkeley, 1981-82; Nat. Endowment for Arts curatorial intern Walker Art Ctr., Mpls., 1982-83, asst. curator, 1983-86, assoc. curator, 1986-89, curator, 1989-96; sr. curator Mus. Contemporary Art, San Diego, 1996—. Mem. adv. bd. Capp Street Project, San Francisco, 1987; guest curator Ctr. for Book Arts, N.Y.C., 1989; panelist NEA, Washington, 1988, 89, Pew Charitable Trust, 1994; cons., reviewer Nat. Gallery Art, Washington, 1990. Author: First Impressions, 1989; author, editor: Tyler Graphics: The Extended Image, 1987, Jasper Johns: Printed Symbols, 1990, In the Spirit of Fluxus, 1993. Mem. adv. com. Minn. Percent for Art Program, St. Paul, 1987; bd. dirs. Artpaper, Mpls., 1989-93. Recipient govt. merit award for outstanding performance NEH, 1979; humanities grad. rsch. grantee U. Calif., 1981; fellow for mus. profls. Nat. Endowment for Arts, 1989. Mem. Print Coun. Am., Minn. Ctr. for Book Arts. Avocations: snorkeling, tennis, skiing. Office: San Diego Mus Contemporary Art 700 Prospect St La Jolla CA 92037-4228

ARMSTRONG, KAREN LEE, special education educator; b. Schenectady, N.Y., Dec. 6, 1941; d. William James and Rita Mae (Peabody) Safford; m. John Edward Armstrong, July 14, 1962; 1 child, Lori Ellen. BA in English, SUNY, Albany, 1963, MS in Spl. Edn., 1986. Tchr. English Ballston Lake High Sch., Burnt Hills, N.Y., 1963-66; tchr. spl. edn. Oak Hill Sch., Scotia, N.Y., 1975-88, Schenectady City Schs., 1988—; mem. policy bd. Ctr. Profl. Edn., 2001—. Mem. curriculum coun., lead tng. sessions Schenectady Schs., 1988—; mem. Shared Decision Making Team, 1994—, spl. edn. del. to China, U.S. del. to South Africa, 1995; lectr. in field of behavior mgmt. V.p. bd. edn. Oak Hill Sch., mem. bd. edn., 2001—. Mem. Coun. for Exceptional Children, Coun. for Children with Behavioral Disorders., Amnesty Internat. (founding Schenectady br.), Adirondack Mountain Club. Sufi. Avocations: hiking, camping, gardening. E-mail: armstrongk@schenectady.k12.ny.us.

ARMSTRONG, LEONA MAY BOTTRELL, retired counselor, educator; b. Rochester, Ill., Aug. 14, 1930; d. Vernon Sampson Bottrell and Leonia Ruth (Meeks) Cooper; m. Bryce Glenn Armstrong, June 11, 1950 (div. 1975); children: Steven Lee, Rebecca Sue, Paul Bryce, (twins) Kevin John and Brian Mark. BS, U. Indpls., 1952; MS, U. Wis., 1967. Tchr., Dayton, Ohio, 1952-55; sch. counselor Oshkosh, Verona, West Allis, Wis., 1967-88; pvt. practice as counselor, astrologer, tchr. Milw., 1988-95; ret., 1995. Reiki master Reiki Healers Internat., 1992; guest spkr. in area of parapsychology and metaphysics U. Minn., U. Wis., Milw., other schs., 1980—; spkr. World Peace Program, Milw., 1987. Ecumenical spkr. United Ch. Women, 1966. Named Outstanding Sr. Woman, Philalethea Lit. Soc., 1952, one of Outstanding Personalities in Midwest, AAUW and Profs. at U. Wis.-Oshkosh, 1968. Mem. Nat. Coun. for Geocosmic Rsch. Home and Office: 4514 67th St Kenosha WI 53142-1602 E-mail: leonaarmstrong@acronet.net.

ARMSTRONG, MARIE CYNTHIA, music educator; b. Balt., Mar. 3, 1957; d. James Lee and Edna Lucille (dec.) Franklin; m. Michael Warren Hill, Oct. 15, 1985 (div.); children: Antonia D., Lakesheia D.; 1 child, Glennis. BS in Music, Morgan State U., Balt., 1986. Minister of music St. Paul Bapt. Ch., Balt., 1987—99; tchr. Leith Walk Elem. Sch., Balt., 1995—; minister of music Timothy Bapt. Ch., Balt., 2000—; organist St. Paul Comty. Ch., Balt., 2001—. Mem.: Hampton U. Choir Dirs. and Organists Guild, Nat. Assn. Music Educators, ASCD, Zeta Phi Beta Sorority (2d Anti-Basilus). Office: Leith Walk Elem Sch 1235 Sherwood Ave Baltimore MD 21239 E-mail: reerun2@aol.com.

ARMSTRONG, MARY M. insurance company executive; Various positions Safeco Corp., Seattle, 1973-94, v.p., chief info. officer, 1994—. Office: SAFECO Corp SAFECO Plaza Seattle WA 98185

ARMSTRONG, SAUNDRA BROWN, federal judge; b. Oakland, Calif., Mar. 23, 1947; d. Coolidge Logan and Pauline Marquette Brown; m. George Walter Armstrong, Apr. 18, 1982 BA, Calif. State U.-Fresno, 1969; JD magna cum laude, U. San Francisco, 1977. Bar: Calif. 1977, U.S. Supreme Ct. 1984. Policewoman Oakland Police Dept., 1970-77; prosecutor, dep. dist. atty. Alameda County Dist. Atty., Oakland, 1978-79, 80-82; staff atty. Calif. Legis. Assembly Com. on Criminal Justice, Sacramento, 1979-80; trial atty. Dept. Justice, Washington, 1982-83; vice chmn. U.S. Consumer Product Safety Commn., Washington, 1984-86; commr. U.S. Parole Commn., Washington, 1986-89; judge Alameda Superior Ct., 1989-91, U.S. Dist. Ct. (no. dist.) Calif., San Francisco, 1991—. Recipient commendation Calif. Assembly, 1980 Mem. Nat. Bar Assn., ABA, Calif. Bar Assn., Charles Houston Bar Assn., Black C. of C., Phi Alpha Delta Republican. Baptist. Office: US Dist Ct N Calif 1301 Clay St Rm 390C Oakland CA 94612-5217

ARMSTRONG SQUALL, PAULA ESTELLE, executive secretary; b. N.Y.C., Apr. 12, 1946; d. John Calvin and Irene (Shomo) A.; 1 child, Tonia Patricia Armstrong Fripp. Equivalency diploma, Malcolm King Coll., N.Y., 1988. Sec. Police Athletic League, N.Y.C., 1980-84, Harlem World Disco, N.Y.C., 1985-89, Nat. Black Theatre, N.Y.C., 1990-93, Manhattan Psychiat. Ctr., N.Y.C., 1994-95, Westside Bulletin Issues in Mental Health, 1996-97. Disc jockey (as Lady Pea). Avocations: art, poetry, ping pong/table tennis, music disc jockey, crochet.

ARNDT, CARMEN GLORIA, secondary school educator; b. N.Y.C., Mar. 29, 1942; d. Charles Joseph and Pura María (Rios) A. BA in Spanish, Pace U., 1968; MA in Spanish, NYU, 1970; profl. diploma, Fordham U., 1975. Lic. asst. prin., prin. Simultaneous translator UN, N.Y.C., 1968; instr. Marymount Manhattan Coll., N.Y.C., 1968-70; tchr. Bd. Edn., N.Y.C., 1970—, dir. Bilingual Comprehensive H.S., 1975-78; chmn. sch. based mgmt./shared decision com. L.D. Brandeis H.S., N.Y.C., 1990—, asst. prin., 1984, interim acting asst. prin., 1994, coord. coop. tech./trades, 1993-96, ESL and fgn. lang. dept., 1994-96, bilingual grade advisor, 1998; ret. Chmn. restructuring com. Bd. Edn., N.Y.C., 1990—; bd. dirs. 1st N.Y.C. Comprehensive Bilingual Program, 1975-79; mem. adj. faculty Fordham U., N.Y.C., 1972-75, CCNY, 1985—; coord. ESL and fgn. lang. dept. Author: Conversational Spanish, 1975, Native Language Art K-8, 1975; contbr. articles to profl. jours.; featured in Dominicanos en New York (book). Electioneer, Dem. Party, N.Y.C. Mem. P.R. Edn. Assn. (chairperson-mentor 1988, del.), United Fedn. Tchr. (del. 1985-88), State Assn. Bilingual Edn., Am. Assn. Tchrs. of Spanish and Portuguese, Assn. Suprs. Curriculum Devel., Phi Beta Kappa. Roman Catholic. Avocations: crochet, reading, walking, writing. Home: Apt 3G 50 W 97th St New York NY 10025-6005

ARNDT, DIANNE JOY, artist, photographer; b. Springfield, Mass., Dec. 20, 1939; d. Samuel Vincent and Carrie Lillian Annino; m. Joseph Vincent Bower, June 16, 1979 (dec.); 1 child by previous marriage, Christabelle Nita Arndt. Student, Art Students League, 1965-71; BFA with honors in Painting, Pratt Inst., 1974; postgrad., Columbia U., 1979-86; MFA, Hunter Coll., 1981. Photojournalist. Photo cons. to mags. and bus., N.Y.C., 1978—; artist, filmmaker, 1962—. One-woman shows include Modernage, N.Y., 1992, 96, 99-2000, 2002, others; group shows include Islip Art Mus., L.I., N.Y., 1999, White Walls Conceptual Art Jour., Chgo., 2000, numerous others; exhbns. include Am. Cultural Ctr., U.S., New Delhi and Bombay, 1987, Bathurst Arms Installation, Eng., 1987, Camden Arts, London, 1987, Nat. Inst. Archtl. Edn., 1988, Phillip Morris Traveling Photo Exhibit, 1988, Centennial Libr. Gallery, Isca Graphics, Edmonton, Alta., Can., 1988, Nat. Inst. Archtl. Edn., 1988, N.Y. Sci. & Tech. Gallery, N.Y., USSR, 1989, Mercer Gallery, 1989, Circolo Pickwick, Alessandria, Italy, 1989, Balt. Mus. Industry, 1992, Aaron Davis Hall, 1992, N.Y. City Coll., Alijira Gallery, Newark, 1994, UN, 1994, Phila. Art Alliance, Phila., 1995, Columbia U., 1995, Severoceske Mus., Liberec, Bohemia, 1996, Naproskovo Mus., Prague, 1996, Modern Age, N.Y.C., 1996, Lever House, N.Y.C., 1996, St. Marks/Bowery, N.Y.C., 1997, Eighth Floor Gallery, N.Y.C., 1997, Velan Gallery, Torino, Italy, 1998, Islip Art Mus., 1998, 99, Bound for Glory, N.Y., 1999-2000, In Frame, Chgo., 2000, St. Francis Coll., 2001; represented in permanent collections Archives Can. Postal Mus., Ottawa, Jean Brown Archives, Mass., Franklin Furnace, N.Y., Nat. Inst. Design and Lalit Kala Akademi, Ne WDelhi, Printed Masser, N.Y., Tate Gallery, London; films include Mullenium, N.Y., 1985, A.I.R., N.Y., 1978, Women's Interart Ctr., N.Y., 1976, Artists Space, N.Y., 1975. Mem. Am. Soc. Media Photographers, Am. Soc. Picture Profls., Artists Talk on Art (bd. dirs.), Profl. Women Photographers, Working Press Nation.

ARNDT, JANET S. state legislator; b. Providence, May 23, 1947; m. Kenneth G. Arndt; 4 children. AB, Gordon Coll., 1968; MEd, Boston U., 1970; student, U. Mass., 1998—, CAGS, 2002; EdD, U. Mass. Amherst, 2003; cert., Advanced Grad. Study. Specialist, counselor Early Childhood, 1987—; N.H. state rep. Dist. 27, Rockingham, 1992—2002; mem. children, youth and juvenile justice com. N.H. Ho. of Reps., mem. const. and statutory rev. com.; chmn. election law com., 1997—2002. Asst. prof. Gordon Coll., 1995, N.H. Tech. Coll., 1997—2001, adj. prof., 2001—, chair early childhood, elem. and spl. edn. dept., 2002—. Mem. Friends of the Libr. of Windham, chmn., 1991-92; active Girl Scouts Am., publicity chairperson; scholarship chmn. Nat. Order of Women Legislators; exec. bd. Rockingham County; events chairperson Nesmith Libr.; mem. edn. task force ALEC, mem. ch. early childhood task force; mem. nat. coun. of state legislators Coun. of State Govt.; chair Rockingham County Register of Deeds, 1996-02; mem. early childhood mental health coun., 2003-; mem. bd. N.H. Kids Coll., 2003. Recipient M. Carter award for Outstanding Libr. Svc., 1995; named Leader of Yr. Windham Girl Scouts, 1995. Mem. N.H. Order Women Legislators, Gordon Coll. Alumni Coun. Address: NH House of Reps 8 Crestwood Rd Windham NH 03087-1429 Office Phone: 978-867-4814. E-mail: jarndt@gordon.edu.

ARNDT, JOAN MARIE, media specialist, educator; b. Stillwater, Minn., Sept. 7, 1945; d. Harriet Joan (Richert) A. BA, Coll. of St. Catherine, St. Paul, 1967; MA, U. Minn., 1970, degree in media specialty, 1973. Cert. librarian, elem. educator. Libr. media specialist Roseville Area Sch., Minn., 1967—. Prof. grad. and continuing studies dept. Hamline U., St. Paul, 1981—; guest lectr. U. Wis., Eau Claire, 1985, Coll. St. Thomas, St. Paul, Upper Mississippi Media Conf., 1988; book reviewer U. Minn., Mpls., 1988—, Five Owls, Mpls., 1988—; workshop cons. Columbia Hts. Sch., Mpls., Osseo Pub. Sch. Mem. ALA, NEA, Am. Assn. Sch. Libr., Minn. Edn. Media Orgn., Minn. Reading Assn., Minn. Edn. Assn., Friends of Ramsey County Libr. Kerlan Collection. Lutheran. Avocations: walking, reading, travel. Home: 5730 Donegal Dr Shoreview MN 55126-3701 Office: Cen Park Media Ctr 535 County Road B2 W Roseville MN 55113-3519

ARNDT, REBECCA DEWEY, music educator; b. Denver, Mar. 27, 1977; d. Steven John and Colleen Yvonne Dewey; m. Robert Phillip Arndt, July 19, 2003. MusB in Edn., Adrian Coll., Mich., 2000. Cert. tchr. Mich. Tchr. Waterford Schs., Mich., 2000—. Chorus mem. Grace Episcopal Ch., Lapeer, Mich., 2000. Mem.: Alpa Sigma Alpha (life; ritual chair 1997—99). Home: 7085 Hickory St Flushing MI 48433 Personal E-mail: dewey524@yahoo.com.

ARNEZ, NANCY LEVI, educational leadership educator; b. Balt., July 6, 1928; d. Milton Emerson Levi and Ida Barbour (Rusk) Levi Washington. AB, Morgan State Coll., 1949; MA, Columbia U., 1954, EdD, 1958. Tchr. English Druid Jr. H.S., Balt., 1949-52, Houston Jr. H.S., Balt., 1952-57; asst. to admissions officer Tchrs. Coll., Columbia U., N.Y.C., 1957-58, grad. asst., 1957; head dept. English Cherry Hill Jr. H.S., Balt., 1958-62; assoc. prof., dir. student teaching Morgan State Coll., Balt., 1962-66; co-founder Cultural Linguistic Early Childhood Follow Through Approach; prof., asst. dir./dir. Ctr. for Inner City Studies, Northeastern Ill. U., Chgo., 1966-74; prof., assoc. dean, acting dean Sch. Edn. Howard U., Washington, 1974-80, chmn. dept. ednl. leadership, 1980-86, prof., 1980-93, prof. emeriti, 1993—. Author: Partners in Urban Education: Teaching the Inner City Child, 1973, The Struggle for Equality of Educational Opportunity, 1975, Administrative Issues in the Implementation of the Response to Educational Needs Project, 1979, The Besieged School Superintendent, 1981, School Based Administrator Training, 1982; mem. editorial bd.: Phi Delta Kappan, 1975-80, Jour. Negro Edn., 1975-80, Black Child Jour., 1980— ; contbr. articles to profl. jours. State treas., mem. exec. com. Md. State council UN Children's Fund, 1965; founder Operation Champ, Balt, 1965; mem. adv. bd. Better Boys Found., Chgo., 1966-74, Mus. African-Am. History, 1969; state chmn. Right to Read, Washington, 1973-80; treas. Com. to Elect Douglass Moore to City Council, 1982. African Am. Inst. grantee, 1974; Spencer Found. grantee, 1976; AAUW grantee, 1977. Mem. Am. Assn. Sch. Adminstrs. (editorial bd. 1982), Assn. for Study of Afro-Am. Life and History, African Am. Heritage Assn., African Am. Writers Guild, Nat. Alliance Black Sch. Educators, D.C. Alliance Black Sch. Educators (pres. 1986-88), Phi Delta Kappa. Presbyterian. Home: 3122 Cherry Rd NE Washington DC 20018-1612

ARNOLD, BARBARA EILEEN, state legislator; b. North Adams, Mass., Aug. 3, 1924; d. Lester Flemming and Sarah (Van Hagen) Smith; m. William E. Arnold, Dec. 5, 1946; children: Wynn, Jefffrey, Gayle, Christopher. BA in Psychology, U. Mass.; postgrad., Keene State Coll. Spl. edn. tchr. Easter Seal Rehab. Ctr., Manchester, NH, 1967-74; state legislator NH, 1982-95; Rep. floor leader Ho. of Reps., 1989-95; mem. N.H. Coun. Vocat. Tech. Edn., 1986-95, State and Fed. Rels. Commn.; chmn. Manchester Rep. Del.; vice chmn. Ways and Means, 1992—95. Sec. N.E. State Coun. Vocat. Edn.; adv. bd. edn. N.H. Dept. Corrections; mem. adv. coun. adult rehab. Easter Seal Soc., NH, 1990—; state adv. com. Vocat. Child Care Programs, 1993—95; mem. com. for children, families, social svcs. Nat. Conf. of State Legislatures; bd. registration City of Manchester, 1999—; Manchester chmn. Dole for Pres. campaign, 1995, Gov. Judd Gregg for U.S. Senate, 1992; chair Manchester Rep. Com., 1993—95, George W. Bush for Pres., Manchester, 1999; chmn. Manchester Rep. Com., 1992—95; chmn. Manchester Senator John E. Sununu Campaign, 2002; past mem. vestry, registered lay leader, mem. diocesan commn., del. gen. conv. Episcopal Ch.; bd. dirs. ARC, 1975—96, chmn. bd. dirs., 1977—80. Mem. Nat. Order Women Legislators, Nat. Fedn. Rep. Women, Greater Manchester Federated Rep. Women's Club, N.H. Kappa Kappa Gamma Alumni Assn. (pres. 1990-91). Address: 374 Pickering St Manchester NH 03104-2744

ARNOLD, JANET NINA, health care consultant; b. Poughkeepsie, N.Y., Apr. 23, 1933; d. Paul Dudley and Pauline Katherine (Board) Bartram; m. Robert William Arnold, Dec. 19, 1954; children: Paul Dudley, Janet Elizabeth. AB cum laude, Vassar Coll., 1955; postgrad. Sch. Med. Tech., Albany Med. Coll., 1955-56; MS in Microbiology cum laude, Vassar Coll., 1963; MHSM, Webster Coll., 1981. Rsch. asst., med. technologist H. Aird Boswell, M.D., Troy, NY, 1956-59; tchg. supr., adminstrv. cons. Vassar Bros. Hosp., Poughkeepsie, 1959-69; adv. to med. lab., lectr. med. mycology Vassar Coll., Poughkeepsie, 1961-66; asst. adminstr., lab. mgr. Boulder (Colo.) Meml. Hosp., 1975-80; cons. hosp. planning Mercy Med. Ctr., Denver, 1981-82; clin. lab. dir./adminstr. Humana, Denver, 1982-85, cons. health care mgmt., 1982-85, MRI, 1985—. Ptnr., 1988; cons. health care mgmt. Humana, Inc., 1982-96, Columbia/HCA Health Sys., 1992-96; pres. Arnold and Assocs., 1988—; ptnr. InterExec (divsn. MRI), 1994—; acad./adminstrv. cons. U. Guam, Vassar Coll., Boulder Cmty. Hosp., Humana Int., 1990-97, others; adj. faculty Vassar Coll.; sec., bd. dirs. Summer Fest Youth Union, 1977-79, pres., 1979-82; teaching fellow Vassar Coll., 1961-63, unrestricted fund chmn., 1989-96, co-chair major gifts, 2002—. Assoc. editor Am. Jour. Med. Tech., 1980-88; contbr. articles to profl. jours. Contbr. NMC, 1988-92. NSF rsch. fellow, 1960-62. Mem. Am. Acad. Microbiology, Soc. for Gen. Microbiology, Am. Soc. Med. Technologists, Colo. Pub. Health Assn., Soc. Women Environ. Profls., Med. Mycological Soc. of the Ams. Republican. Episcopalian. Home: 4195 Chippewa Dr Boulder CO 80303-3610 Office Phone: 303-543-7965. E-mail: r-j-arnold-assoc@att.net.

ARNOLD, JEAN ANN, health science facility administrator; b. Coronado, Calif., Nov. 17, 1948; d. Scott Crittenden Daubin and Barbara Jean (Spooner) Annowada; m. Lonnie Lea Arnold, July 14, 1973; children: Danielle Louise and Casey Jean (twins). Student, Santa Barbara City Coll., Calif., 1966-67, U. Wyo., Laramie, 1968-69; BS in Allied Health Scis./Health Svcs. Adminstrn., Weber State U., 1995. Registered Technol., LIc. Technol., Calif., Wash. Staff technol. x-ray Mt. Auburn Hosp., Cambridge, Mass., 1971-72, Victor Valley Hosp., Victorville, Calif., 1972-74, Fairfield Hosp., Calif., 1974-76; chief technol. Oakridge Med. Group, Roseville, Calif., 1976-78; staff technol. radiation therapy U. Cancer Ctr., U. Hosp., Seattle, 1979-84; staff technol. Providence Med. Ctr., Seattle, 1984; relief technol. UCSD Med. Ctr., San Diego, 1984-85; staff technol. Scripps Meml. Hosp., La Jolla, Calif., 1984-87, dir. radiation oncology, 1987—95; mgr. radiation oncology Deaconess Med. Ctr., Spokane, 1995—98, St. Alphonsus Regional Med. Ctr., Boise, Idaho, 1999—. Clin. coord., instr. San Diego Radiation Therapy Tech. Edn. Program. Producer Video, Occpl. Radiation Safety 1988. Mem. Soc. for Radiation Oncology Adminstrs., Calif. Soc. Radiologic Technologists, Am. Soc. Radiologic Technologists, Am. Registry Radiologic Technologists (job analysis adv. com., radiation therapy exam. com., item writer Therapy Tech.). Republican. Baptist.

ARNOLD, JEANNE ELOISE, anthropologist, educator; b. Cleve., 1955; d. Lawrence Fred and Marybelle Eloise Arnold. BA, U. Mich., 1976; MA, U. Calif., Santa Barbara, 1979, PhD, 1983. Prof. anthropology U. No. Iowa, Cedar Falls, 1984-88, UCLA, 1988—, assoc. dir. Inst. Archaeology, 1988-99. Vis. instr. anthropology Rice U., Houston, 1981; vis. prof. anthropology Oreg. State U., Corvallis, 1983-84; sr. archaeologist Infotec Rsch., Inc., Sonora, Calif., 1986-87; cons. in field. Author 4 books; contbr. more than 45 articles and revs. to profl. jours. and over 25 chpts. to books. Rsch. grantee NSF, 1988-91, 95-99, 98—; Rsch. and Ednl. grantee UCLA and Santa Barbara, 1977—. Mem. Soc. Am. Archaeology, Soc. Calif. Archaeology, Cotsen Inst. Archaeology (mem. editorial bd. 1988—), Sigma Xi, Phi Beta Kappa. Avocations: photography, cinema, collecting ethnographic arts. Office: UCLA Dept Anthropology Box 951553 Haines Hall Los Angeles CA 90095-1553

ARNOLD, MARGARET MORELOCK, music specialist, educator, performer; b. Craig AFB, Ala., May 12, 1959; d. William Daniel Morelock and Margaret Haynie Morelock Stapleton; m. Barry Raynor Arnold, Aug. 15, 1984. B of Music Edn., U. Montevallo, 1981; MEd in Music, U. South Ala., 1996. Cert. tchr. Fla., Ala. Tchr. music Staley Mid. Sch., Americus, Ga., 1981-82, Eastview Elem. Sch., Americus, Ga., 1982-84; tchr. music/mass prep. St. Thomas More Schs., Pensacola, Fla., 1984-85; tchr. music W.H. Rhodes Elem., Milton, Fla., 1985—; realtor Century 21, Richardson, Fla. Pvt. voice instr., Americus, 1981-84, Milton, 1989—; guest condr. Santa Rosa All-County Chorus, Milton, 1989, 95, Santa Rosa Celebrates the Arts, 1986—. Asst. dir.: arts festivals, 1993—; singer (soprano, soloist): Gulf Coast Chorale, Singfest, Inc., The Choral Soc. Pensacola; dir.: (band) Change of Command, 2003. Dir. elem. chorus performing for Santa Rosa Convalescent Ctr., Milton, 1985—, Whiting Field, 2003, Live at the Capital, Tallahassee, 1986, Santa Rosa Celebrates the Arts, 1986-, Ptnrs. in Edn.-K-Mart and City of Milton and WEAR-TV, 1990—. Recipient Young Artist Competition S.E. Regional award Nat. Assn. Tchrs. of Singing, S.E. region, 1993; winner State of Ala. Young Artist competition, 1993; Computer Software grant Santa Rosa Ednl. Found., 1994. Mem. NEA, Music Tchrs. Nat. Assn., Nat. Assn. Realtors, Fla. Assn. Realtors, Santa Rosa Profl. Educators, Music Educators Nat. Conf., Pensacola (Fla.) Music Tchrs. Assn., Delta Kappa Gamma (music chair 1988-94), Kappa Delta Pi,

Phi Kappa Phi. Presbyterian. Avocations: walking, gardening, volunteer for nursing home. Home: 5820 Kirkland Dr Milton FL 32570-8251 Office: WH Rhodes Elem 5563 Byrom St Milton FL 32570-3822 Business E-Mail: arnoldm@santarosa.k12.fl.us.

ARNOLD, NANCY KAY, writer; b. Kalamazoo, Mich., May 9, 1951; d. Byron Lyle and Ada (Doorlag) Arnold; m. Louis Scott Hubert, May 5, 1989 (div. Jan. 29, 2002). BFA in Painting, Western Mich. U., 1983, postgrad., 1985-86. Writer Advanced Systems & Designs, Inc., Farmington Hills, Mich., 1987—89; pres., owner TechWrite, Kalamazoo, 1989—2002; writer Northrop Grumman IT, 2002—. Writer Northrop Grumman IT, 2002—. Author: (poetry) Tetragonal Pyramids, 1982; exhibited in group shows, Kalamazoo, 1983, Western Mich. U., 1982, 85. Mem. AAUW, NAFE, Kalamazoo County C. of C., Humane Farming Assn. Am. People for Ethical Treatment of Animals. Libertarian. Avocations: bicycling, skiing, reading, piano, singing, guitar, mandolin. Office: PO Box 481 Oshtemo MI 49077-0481 Office Phone: 269-375-7690. E-mail: nancya@net-link.net.

ARNOLD, RUTH SOUTHGATE, librarian; b. Cin., Oct. 2, 1950; d. Roger Frederick Arnold and Harriet Hendershot Wolf Arnold; m. Louis Dolive; children: Caroline Elizabeth Dolive, William Arnold Dolive. BA, Eckerd Coll., 1972; MSLS, Simmons Coll., 1977. Cert. libr. Va. Info. specialist Warner-Eddison Assocs., Inc., Cambridge, Mass., 1977—79; asst. dir. Augusta County Libr., Fishersville, Va., 1979—81; tech. svcs. libr. Staunton (Va.) Pub. Libr., 1987—91, dir., 1991—. Mem. ednl. com. Woodrow Wilson Birthplace, Staunton, 1998—2002; v.p. Staunton (Va.) Downtown Devel. Assn., 2003—, bd. mem., 2001—04. Named Woman of the Yr., Staunton Bus. & Profl. Women's Orgn., 1997; fellow Paul Harris, Rotary, 1995. Mem.: ALA, Va. Pub. Libr. Dirs. Assn. (sec., regional rep. 1997—2002), Va. Libr. Assn. (2d v.p. 2000—01), Staunton Rotary Club (pres. 1998—99). Presbyterian. Avocations: choral singing, contra dancing. Office: Staunton Pub Libr 1 Churchville Ave Staunton VA 24401 Office Phone: (540) 332-3902. Office Fax: (540) 332-3906. Business E-Mail: arnoldrs@ci.staunton.va.us.

ARNOLD, SANDRA RUTH KOUNS, photographer; b. Cleburne, Tex., Jan. 20, 1941; d. Wyatt Allen and Ethel Louise (Gandillon) Kouns; m. William Patrick Arnold, Feb. 27, 1960; children: Allyson Arnold House, Lynn Ann Workman. Student, Hill Coll., Cleburne, Tex., 1975, 78-79, 95, Richland Coll., Dallas, 1986, 94, Sam Houston State U., 1996, 97, 2001; profl. cert., Tex. Sch. Profl. Photography. Lic. realtor Tex., cert. photographer Profl. Photographers Assn., Nat. Profl. Photographers Assn. Decorator, owner Baileys Home Improvements, Cleburne, 1971-77; realtor Red Carpet and Holliday Assocs., Cleburne, 1979-98; pub./patient rels. Meml. Hosp., Cleburne, 1982-86; mktg./patient rels. staff, asst. coord. Walls Regional Hosp., Cleburne, 1986; mktg. mgr. Harris Meth. Health System, Ft. Worth, 1986-88; mktg./physician recruiting dir. Kimbro Med. Ctr., Cleburne, 1988-92; profl. photographer, 1996—; antique shop owner My Favorite Things, 1995-98. Owner, v.p. A&A Plastic Co., 1969-98; vocalist weddings, theaters, and chs., Cleburne, 1959—. Contbr. articles to profl. jours. Established Area Alzheimer Support Group, Cleburne, 1984, Cleburne Women's Tennis League; coord., cons. Adopt-A-Sch./Cleburne Schs., 1984—; mem., actress Carnegie Theater; active Johnson County Hist. Commn., PTA; vol. Johnson County Meml. Hosp., 1972—96; ARC; established crime watch neighborhood program, 1998; vol. mus. entertainment for hosp. patient; active St. Mark Meth. Ch., Cleburne. Named one of Outstanding Women of S.W., 1979. Mem.: Cleburne C. of C., Heritage Assembly (charter), Women's Forum, Beta Sigma Phi (pres., Woman of Yr. 1963, 1981). Avocations: music, genealogy, travel, antiques, yoga, music, genealogy, travel, antiques. Home and Office: PO Box 63 Cleburne TX 76033-0063

ARNOLD, SUSAN E. consumer products company executive; b. Pitts. BA, U. Pa., 1976; MBA, U. Pitts., 1980. Joined Procter and Gamble, Cin., 1980, dir. cosmetics and fragrances, v.p. P&G Fabric Care, v.p. global personal beauty care and global feminine care, 1999—2000, pres. global personal beauty care and global feminine care, 2000—02, pres. personal beauty and feminine care, 2002—, also bd. dirs. Bd. mem. Reflect.com, Cin. Zoo, Goodyear Tire & Rubber Co. Named Top Marketer and One of the 21 to Watch in the 21st Century, Advt. Age, Career Woman of Achievement, YWCA, 2000; named one of Fortune mags. 50 Most Powerful Women in Bus., 2002; recipient Best Boss award, Cosmetic Exec. Women, 2003. Office: Procter & Gamble Plaza Cincinnati OH 45202*

ARNOLD, WINNIE JO, retired mental health nurse, nursing administrator; b. Cromwell, Okla., May 21, 1929; d. Robb Henry and Luella (Odom) Boatman; widowed; children: Linda, Cherie. BSEd, Okla. U., 1962; ADN, Amarillo Coll., 1974; BSN, St. Joseph's Coll., 1977. RN, Tex. Charge nurse Northwest Tex. Hosp., Amarillo; staff nurse, team leader High Plains Bapt. Hosp., Amarillo; adminstr. Healthcare Svcs., Amarillo; dir. nurses Tex. Dept. Corrections, Amarillo, 1989-97. Vol. ARC. Recipient Vol. award ARC, 1989, Pilot Club, 1989. Mem. Am. Kidney Found., Women's Bus. Assn. (Bus. Woman of Yr. 1989). Home: 216 Ramada Trl Amarillo TX 79108-1128 E-mail: wjatexan@msn.com.

ARNOLD-CHAPMAN, INGRID M, writer; b. Wuerzburg, Germany, Apr. 21, 1949; children: Grant D. Chapman, Melanie A. Chapman. Degree Banking & Fin., Kauefmaennische Berufsschule, Wuerzburg, Germany, 1968. Cert. Silver Master grad. Comml. real estate broker, Tulsa, Okla., 1976—2002. Fundraiser Tulsa U. for the Gifted, 1995—2000. Mem.: Bus. and Profl. Women's Club. Christian. Avocation: poetry, romance novel writing. Home: PO Box 150176 Tulsa OK 74115-0176 Personal E-mail: honorstudent012@yahoo.com.

ARNOLD-JONES, JANICE E. state representative; b. Ft. Bragg, N.C., Mar. 20, 1952; m. John L. Jones; children: Robert, Mary Ellen. BA in Speech Communication, U. N.Mex., 1974. Inside sales GESCO, Albuquerque and Honolulu, 1974—78; acct. exec. KGU Radio, Honolulu, 1978—79, Athens Banner Herald-Daily News/WRFC Radio, 1980—81, Peters Prodns., 1981—82; v.p. Lightning Corp., 1982—87, Parallax, Inc., 1998—; state rep. dist. 24 N.Mex. Ho. of Reps., Santa Fe, 2002—. Mem.: Area Coach Adm. Am. Youth Soccer Orgn., Sandia H.S. Area Neighborhood Assn. Republican. Office: State Capitol Room 412C Santa Fe NM 87503

ARNOLD-OLSON, HELEN B. nonprofit consultant; b. Cedar Rapids, Iowa, Sept. 22, 1948; d. Duane Arnold Sr. and Henrietta Dows; m. Edward R. Krieger Jr., May 23, 1970 (div. Aug. 1974); m. Reuben I. Olson, July 2, 1982; 1 child, Andrew R. Olson. B in Music cum laude, Cornell Coll., 1970. Office mgr. Irving R. Zimmerman Co., Chgo., 1973-75; loan officer comml. and residential Banco Mortgage Co., Chgo., 1975-77, 79-82; asst. v.p., mgr., mortgage lending Olympic Savings & Loan Assn., Berwyn, Ill., 1977-79; underwriter, cons. Fed. Housing Adminstrn., Chgo., 1976-83; co-owner, pres. and exec. chef Hawkeye Nut Co., Cedar Rapids, 1983-87; pres. Dows Farms, Inc., Cedar Rapids, 1987-96; dir. devel. YWCA of Cedar Rapids and Linn County, 1996—2000; pres. Green Light, LLC, Arnold-Olson Assocs., Hel's Kitchen, 2000—; nonprofit cons. Bd. dirs. The Dows Cos., Cedar Rapids, Cedar Rapids Airport Commn. Bd. dirs., co-chair capital campaign endorsement The History Ctr., Cedar Rapids, 1996—; v.p., bd. dirs. Friends of the Zoo, Cedar Rapids, 1997—; bd. dirs. Kingston Hill Home for Aged Women, Cedar Rapids, 1998—. Recipient Leadership for Five Seasons award Cedar Rapids Area C. of C., 1996. Mem. AAUW, Assn. Fund Raising Profls., Iowa Women's Found., Variety Club of Iowa (bd. dirs., past chair, Sunshine award 1999), Rotary. Presbyterian. Avocations: cooking, traveling. Home: 3840 Bever Ave SE Cedar Rapids IA 52403-4366 Office: Arnold-Olson Assocs 3840 Bever Ave SE Cedar Rapids IA 52403 E-mail: HBAO48@aol.com.

ARNOLD-ROGERS, JUDY, education educator, language educator, coach; b. Knoxville, Tenn., Sept. 15, 1949; d. James Elisha and Grace (Harrison) Arnold; m. Talbot Wentworth Rogers, Oct. 26, 1984; children: Jesse, Sarah. BA in English, Carson Newman Coll., 1970; MA in English, U. Tenn., 1972, EdD in Curriculum and Instrn., 1978, postdoct., 1985—. Cert. tchr. English grades 9-12 Tenn., supr. and adminstr. Tenn. Tchr English, tennis coach Bearden Sr. High Sch., Knoxville, 1972—86; asst. prof. English Roane State C.C., Rockwood, Tenn., 1986—90; assoc. prof. edn. Tenn. Wesleyan Coll., Athens, Tenn., 1990—93, ednl. coord., women's tennis coach, 1990—91, 1992, chair edn. dept., 1991—93; prof. grad. edn. Lincoln Meml. U., Harrogate, Tenn., 1993—. Presenter in field. Contbr. articles to profl. jours. Mem.: NEA (del. rep. assembly, del. assemblies), AAUW (corr. sec. local br. 1999—2001, 2002—, br. pres. 2003—, chair membership, mem. ednl. equity com., 1st v.p. program chair Knoxville br., endowment winner leadership contributions), Tenn. Assn. Colls. Tchr. Educators, Tenn. Edn. Assn. (newsletter editor 1992, chair human rels. 1992—94, mem. higher edn. bd. dirs., PreK-Grad. bd. dirs.), Nat. Coun. Higher Edn., Nat. Coun. Tchrs. English (newsletter editor Assembly on Expanded Perspectives in Learning, mem. exec. bd.), Delta Kappa Gamma (pres 1996—98, Alpha Tau chpt., chair profl. dept.). Avocations: tennis, writing, music.

ARNONE, MARY GRACE, radiologic technologist; b. Bronx, N.Y., Dec. 28, 1961; d. Anthony Rocco and Mary Helen (Doring) A. AA, Acad. Health Sci., U.S. Army, 1982. Lic. radiologist NY, mammographer NY. Radiology technologist, 1982—, Our Lady of Mercy Hosp., Bronx, NY, 1988—. With U.S. Army, 1982-86. Democrat. Lutheran.

ARNOT-HEANEY, SUSAN EILEEN, not-for-profit fundraiser; b. East Orange, N.J., Aug. 10, 1957; d. Robert B. and Mae (Cockcroft) A.; m. Kevin Barry Heaney, Mar. 28, 1992. BA, Coll. William and Mary, 1979; postgrad., Cambridge U., 1977; cert., NYU, 1979. Promotion asst. Viking Press/Penguin Books, N.Y.C., 1979-82; mgr. promotion Rizzoli Internat. Publs., N.Y.C., 1982-83; mgr. advt. promotion USA Today, N.Y.C., 1983-85; promotion dir. 50 Plus mag., N.Y.C., 1985-88, In Fashion mag., N.Y.C., 1988-89; mktg. svcs. mgr. TAXI mag., N.Y.C., 1989-90; dir.. pub. rels. and spl. events Elizabeth Arden, N.Y.C., 1990-97; dir. global pub. rels. Avon Products, N.Y.C., 1997—2002; dir. Avon Breast Cancer Crusade, 2000—. Career adv. Coll. William and Mary, 1980—; bd. dirs. Cosmetic Exec. Women Found., 1999—. Writer/editor quar.: (newsletter) 50 Plus Market Update, 1985-88. Vol. cook, fundraiser Cathedral Soup Kitchen, St. John the Divine, 1983-85; vol. Women in Need Image Workshops, 1990-94; mem. nat. leadership com. Save the Children Fedn., 1993-97; steering com. Dress for Success, N.Y., 1998—. Recipient Best of N.Y. Addy award for advt., 1986. Mem. Cosmetic, Toiletries and Fragrance Assn. (chair pub. rels. com., ex officio bd. dirs. 1994-96), Cosmetic Exec. Women (bd. dirs., philanthropy com.), Women in Comms. Inc. (chpt. publicity com. 1985-86, fin. com. 1986-87, spl. events com. 1986-87), NOW, Fashion Group Internat., William and Mary Alumni Soc. (chpt. pres. 1986-90, exec. bd. 1983-86, 90-92), AAUW (chpt. corr. sec. 1983-86, chair com. on women's work 1984-86), Mcpl. Art Soc. Methodist. Avocations: travel, music, theater, reading, art collecting, film. Home: 230 W 107th St Apt 2C New York NY 10025-3041

ARNOW, PAT, freelance writer, editor, photographer; b. Chgo., Jan. 31, 1949; d. Robert D. and Edna L. Arnow; m. Steven L. Giles, Nov. 25, 1978. BA, Marshall U., 1981. Pub. info. officer Woodland Ctr., Gallipolis, Ohio, 1979-84; editor Now & Then Mag., East Tenn. State U., Ctr. for Appalachian Studies and Svcs., Johnson City, 1986-94, So. Exposure Mag., Inst. for So. Studies, Durham, NC, 1994-96, culture In These Times, Chgo., 1997—98; rsch. editor Reader's Digest, Pleasantville, NY, 2000—02. Chair Independent Press Assn., 1996—98, chair pubs. com. Appalachian Consortium Press, Boone, N.C., 1990-91. Mng. editor Jour. of Appalachian Studies Assn., 1990-94; co-playwright Cancell'd Destiny, 1990; contbr. articles to profl. jours. Home: 572 Grand St Apt 1902 New York NY 10002

ARNTZ, BARBARA C. elementary school educator; b. Mauston, Wis., Aug. 30, 1932; d. Edwin and Oranda Ruth Lenore Kuska; m. Robert L. Arntz, Sept. 11, 1954 (dec. Dec. 1990). BE, Wis. State U., 1965. Cert. tchr. Wis. Tchr. Cherry Br. Sch., Woodford, Wis., 1951—52, Utica (Wis.) Grade Sch., 1952—53, Wayne Ctr. Sch., South Wayne, Wis., 1952—55, Brick Ch. Sch., Walworth, Wis., 1955—57, Walworth Grade Sch., Walworth, Wis., 1958—67, Westside Sch., Sun Prairie, Wis., 1967—90. Cons., presenter in field. Author: A Guide to Journal Writing, 1983, Student Guide to Olbrich Gardens, 1992. Vol. Ret. Sr. Vol. Program, Madison, Wis., 1994—; election ofcl. City Clk. Office, Madison, Wis., 1992—. Recipient Svc. award, State of Wis. DPI, 1990, Math Edn. award, Wis. Math. Coun., 1990. Mem.: Wis. State Hist. Soc. (docent 1998—). Avocations: painting, crocheting, poetry, sewing.

ARON, EVE GLICKA SERENSON, personal care industry executive; b. NYC, Sept. 5, 1937; d. Max and Edith (Gitelson) Serenson; m. Joel Edward Aron, Dec. 13, 1964; children: Jennifer, Joshua, Eric. BS, CCNY, 1958; MS, Yeshiva U., 1960; MBA with honors, Iona Coll., 1985. Med. technician Albert Einstein Coll. Medicine, Bronx, NY, 1959-60; chemist Strasenburgh labs., Belleville, NJ, 1961-63, Roche Labs., Nutley, 1963-67; sr. chemist Pantene Labs. div. Roche, 1967-69; mgr. R&D Combe Inc., White Plains, NY, 1978-85, assoc. dir. R&D, 1985-95, dir. tech., 1995—2002; tech. cons. to personal care industry Ft. Myers, Fla., 2002—. Dir. website Vagisil Women's Health Ctr., 2000-02. Contbr. articles to profl. jours. Tutor Literacy Vols. of Am.; resident dir., bd. dirs. Sevilla Condo Assn.; bd. dirs. Residents Alliance for a Quality Lifestyle. Mem.: NOW, Soc. Cosmetic Chemists (sec. Conn. chpt. 1989—90, chair 1992, chpt. advisor 1993, hospitality/membership chair 1994—96, program com. co-chair 1997, employment chair 1999—2002), Am. Chem. Soc. (legis. action network). Avocations: golf, tennis, walking, swimming. Home and Office: 10504 Sevilla Dr Apt 201 Fort Myers FL 33913 E-mail: ejaron@earthlink.net.

ARONSON, ESTHER LEAH, retired foundation administrator, psychotherapist; b. Bklyn., Sept. 8, 1941; d. Nathan and Nellie (Borack) Aronson; m. Joel Allen Bernstein, Sept. 8, 1967 (div. Jan. 1978). BA, Bklyn. Coll., 1965; MA, New Sch. for Social Rsch., N.Y.C., 1982; MSW, NYU, 1984, PhD, 1996. LCSW. Resource cons. N.Y.C. Human Resources Adminstrn., 1965-82; counselor Fordham-Tremont Cmty. Mental Health Ctr., Bronx, 1982-83, South Beach Psychiat. Ctr., Bklyn., 1983-84; social worker Alfred Adler Clinic, N.Y.C., 1984-85; pvt. practice clin. social work psychotherapist N.Y.C., 1986—; program developer Emanu-El Midtown YM-YWHA, N.Y.C., 1987-88, dir. ret. adult divsn., 1988—2001. Lectr. Am. Mus. Natural History, N.Y.C., 1978. Contbr. articles to profl. jours. Mem.: NAFE, Soc. for Pub. Health Edn., N.Y. State Soc. Clin. Social Work Psychotherapists, Inc., Am. Orthopsychiat. Assn., Inc., Kappa Delta Pi, Phi Delta Kappa. Avocation: collecting Middle Eastern and East Indian art. Home: 2 Fifth Ave Apt 31 New York NY 10011

ARONSON, LUANN MARIE, actress; b. Ithaca, N.Y., Nov. 18, 1964; d. Arthur Lawrence and Marilyn Ann (Lundeen) A. MusB, Ithaca Coll., 1986; MusM, Southern Meth. U., Dallas, 1988 Appeared as Guenevere in the Nat. Tour of Camelot, 1991; originated the role of Betty Schaefer in the workshop prodn. of Sunset Boulevard at Andrew Lloyd Webber's Sydmonton Festival, London, 1992; features soloist in the Music of Andrew Lloyd Webber, Radio City Music Hall, N.Y.C., 1992; as Maria in the Far East Tour of the Sound of Music, 1992; as Christine Daaé on Broadway in Phantom of the Opera, N.Y.C., 1992-94; as Christine Daaé in the Internat. Tour of The Phantom of the Opera, 1995; as Marian Paroo in The Music Man, 1997, 2000; as Laurie in Oklahoma!, 1997, 2000; as Sharon in Master Class, 1999, as Aldonza in Man of La Mancha, 1999; participant Encores Series City Ctr., 1998. Recipient Outstanding Young Alumni award Ithaca Coll. Alumni Assn., 1994; Blossom Music Festival scholar, 1988, Tanglewood Summer Music Festival scholar, 1986. Mem. Actor's Equity Assn.

ARONSON, MARGARET RUPP, school psychologist; b. Lewistown, Pa., Dec. 12, 1921; d. Frederick Augustine and Claire S. (Schellenberg) Rupp; m. Martin Jerome Aronson, Oct. 31, 1948; children: Eris L. Aronson Renczenski, Frederick Rupp, Scott Charles. BA, Pa. State U., 1942, MS, 1943; JD, St. John's U., 1986. Nat. cert. sch. psychologist. Clin. psychologist Inst. Pa. Hosp., Phila., 1943-48, Georgetown Hosp., Washington, 1948-50; ind. cons. Patchogue (N.Y.) Pub. Schs., 1986-96, Luth. Ministries, Queens and Nassau County, N.Y., 1996—. Editor Winter Olympics Pindar Press, 1980-82. Mem. Met. Golf Assn., Phi Beta Kappa, Phi Kappa Phi, Psi Chi. Avocation: golf. Home: Windsor Gate, Great Neck NY 11020

ARONSON, VIRGINIA L. L. lawyer; b. Bremerton, Wash., June 4, 1947; m. Simon Aronson. BA, U. Chgo., 1969, MA, 1973, JD, 1975. Bar: Ill. 1975. Ptnr. Sidley Austin Brown & Wood, Chgo. Staff mem. U. Chgo. Law Review, 1974—75; mem. exec. & mgmt. com. Sidley Austin Brown & Wood. Contbr. articles to profl. jours. Mem. adv. bd. U. Chgo. Law Review; mem. leadership coun. Chgo. Pub. Edn. Fun.; mem. bd. dirs. Chgo. Ctrl. Area Com. Mem. Am. Coll. Real Estate Lawyers, Chgo. Mortgage Attys. Assn., Chgo. Fin. Exch., The Chgo. Network. Office: Sidley Austin Brown & Wood Bank One Plz 10 South Dearborn St Chicago IL 60603

AROVA, SONIA, artistic director, ballet educator; b. Sofia, Bulgaria, June 20, 1928; came to U.S., 1954; d. Albert and Rene (Melamedoff) Errio; m. Thor Sutowski, Mar. 11, 1965; 1 child, Arlane. Grad., Fine Arts Sch., Paris, 1940, Fine Arts Sch., Eng., 1944. Ballerina Internat. Ballet, London, 1944-47, Rambert Ballet, London, 1947-50, Festival Ballet, London, 1950-54, Am. Ballet Theater, N.Y.C., 1954-58, Ballet deChamps-Elysees, Paris, 1958-60, Ballet Russe, 1960-62, Royal Ballet, London, 1962-63; artistic dir. Nat. Ballet, Oslo, 1964-70, Hamburg (Germany) Ballet, 1970-71; co-dir. San Diego Ballet, 1971-75; dir. State of Ala. Ballet, 81-96, Ballet South, Birmingham, 1981-86; artistic advisor Calif. Ballet, San Diego, 1996—. Instr. Sch. Fine Arts, 1975-96; guest tchr. Australian Ballet, 1993, 94, Bayerische Staatsballet, Munich, Germany, 1994. Recipient World Championship of Dance award Ballet Jury, Paris, 1939; decorated knight of First Order, King Olav of Norway, 1971. Office: Calif Ballet 8276 Ronson Rd San Diego CA 92111-2015

ARP, ARLENE, pre-school educator; b. Detroit, Mich., Sept. 30, 1951; life ptnr. Gwen Spratt; 1 child, Ila Arp-Spratt. BA in Religious Studies(hon.), Ind. U., 1993; cert. in Primary Edn., Montessori Tchr. Coll. Montessori Primary Education Teaching Certificate Montessori Tchr. Coll. NW, 1988. Primary montessori tchr. Nat. Ctr. for Montessori Edn., Seattle, 1987—92; early childhood tchr. Austin Ind. Sch. Dist., Tex., 1992—94, DeKalb County Sch. Dist., Atlanta, 1994—99, Pvt. Tutor, Atlanta, 1999—. Recipient Recognition for earning a Early Childhood.Generalist Nat. Bd. Certification for Profl. Tchg. Standards, DeKalb County Bd. of Edn., 1996. Mem.: Internat. Honor Soc. and Profl. Assn. in Edn. (hon.).

ARPINO, DENISE MARIE, minister; b. San Diego, Nov. 6, 1958; m. Jeffery A. Arpino, May 25, 1991; children: Isaiah Charles, Sarah Elizabeth. BA in Religion, Augustana Coll., Rock Is., Ill., 1982; MDiv, Lutheran Theological Seminary, Gettysburg, Pa., 1987. Pastor Sidman - Elton Parish, Sidman and Elton, Pa., 1987—90, Trinity Luth. Ch., Sidman, Pa., 1990—95, assoc. pastor Altoona, Pa., 1995—97; pastor Simpson -Temple United Parish, Altoona, Pa., 1997—. Asst. to the Bishop, youth ministries Allegheny Synod of ELCA, Altoona, Pa., 1990—92; dean Altoona Area Conf. of the Allegheny Synod, Altoona, Pa., 1996, 6th Ward Ministries, Altoona, Pa., 1997—; worship chairperson Allegheny Synod Assembly, Altoona, Pa., 2001. Bd mem. Family Svc. of Blair County, Altoona, Pa., 2001—; Q -Site Coun. Baker Elem. Sch., Altoona, Pa., 2001—. Recipient Ecumenism award, Ecumenical Conf., 2003. Office: Simpson - Temple United Parish 2212 6th Ave Altoona PA 16602-2236

ARP LOTTER, DONNA, venture capitalist, investor; b. Henrietta, Tex., Dec. 17, 1950; d. T.S. Jr. and Coy Lee (Howard) Grimsley; m. Bruce D. Lotter, Feb. 18, 1984; children: Brandon, Collin. BS, Midwestern State U., 1975, MS in Counseling, 1979. Sales rep. Burroughs-Wellcome Co., Fort Worth, Tex., 1978-79; sales mgr. Procter & Gamble Co., Dallas, 1979-84; pres. Arp-Lotter Investments, Colleyville, Tex., 1984—; mayor City of Colleyville, Tex., 1999—. Prin. DBL Investments, Inc.; sec., officer KCB Corp., Inc.; bd. dirs. Landmark Bank. Mem. adv. bd.: Philanthropy in Tex. mag. Chmn., trustee Baylor Hosp., Grapevine, Tex., 1998; bd. dirs. Am. Cancer Soc., North Tex. Commn., Am. Heart Assn., BRIT, 2003, Tarrant Co. Coll. Found.; adv. bd. Tex. Bank, 2002; bd. govs. N.E. Arts Coun.; city councilperson, City of Colleyville, 1996-98, mayor (pro tem.). 1997-98, mayor, 1999—; mem. exec. com. Ft. Worth Opera Assn.; bd. dirs. Casa Manana Teatro; officer Mayor's Coun. Tarrant County; bd. regents Midwestern State U. Named Alumnus of Yr., Midwestern State U., 1995, Colleyville Citizen of Yr., 2002; Hardin scholar, 1975; recipient Legacy of Women award Am. Heart Assn., 1995, Vol. of Yr. award, Colleyville, 1996, State of Tex. Local Leader award, 1998; voted Most Influential Female of Tarrant County, Tex., 1997, 98, 99, 2000, Woman of Influence award Tarrant County Women's Ctr., 2001, U.S. Inspiring Woman award Gen. Mills Corp., 2001, Disting. Woman award Northwood U., 2003. Mem. Bus. Profl. Womens Club, Nat. Assn. Women Bus. Owners, Colleyville C. of C. (pres. 1995). Republican. Baptist.

ARQUIT, NORA HARRIS, retired music educator, writer; b. Brushton, N.Y., June 30, 1923; d. Samuel Elton George and Esther Cecelia (Gillen) Harris; m. Gordon James Arquit, Nov. 12, 1948; children: Christine Elaine Arquit, Kevin James Arquit, Candace Susan Arquit-Martel. BS in Music Edn., Ithaca Coll., 1945, MS, 1962; postgrad., St. Lawrence U., 1946-47, 74, Cornell U., 1970-71, N.Y. State Coll., Potsdam, 1973. Cert. aerospace edn. with techicians rating. Music dir., band dir., tchr. N.Y. and N.J. State Schs., 1945—80. Guest conductor U.S. Air Force Band, Washington, Dutch and Am. band students, Schiedam, Holland, opening Am.-Can. Seaway, Massena, N.Y., 1975; U.S. Navy Band, Washington, various massed bands in U.S.A., Canada, Europe; dir. bands Worlds Fair, 1964, 65; 1st woman guest conductor Tri-State Honors Band Phillips U., Enid, Okla.; dir., coord. St. Lawrence County ann. H.S. Band Day, 1973-2002; past supvr. coll. student practice tchrs., N.Y.; mem. Mid-States Commn. Secondary Schs. and Colls. Evaluations. Author: Before My Own Time and Since, 1978, From Hamlet to Cold Harbor, 1989, Our Lyon Line, 1993, The History of the New York State, Society of the National Society of the Daughters of the American Colonists, 1994. Past adjudicator h.s. and coll. band contests; past dir., coord. ann. St. Lawrence County Band Day; past capt. aux. USAF Civil Air Patrol; past John Philip Sousa bd. dirs. rep. to Hall of Fame enshrinement of Sousa. Named Dist. Band Master Am., First Chair Am.; recipient Letter of Commendation for People to People Diplomacy for work with student band groups, Embassy at the Hague, Europe, honored for 39 yrs. of svc. on Band Day, St. Lawrence County, 2002. Mem.: AAUW (past divsn. meeting rep.), Women Band Dirs. Nat. Assn. (past nat. pres., Silver Baton), N.Y. State Ret. Tchrs. Assn., N.Am. Band Dirs. Coordinating Coun. (pres. 1978, past nat. v.p.), Am. School Band Dirs. Assn. (emeritus mem. 1980, N.Y. state chmn. 2003—, past chmn. internat. band com., past nat. and state ofcr., honored nat. covention 2003), Internat. Assn. U. Women, Colonial Daughters of the XVIIC (chpt. councillor 1988-91, past. mem. coms.), Soverign Colonial Soc., Soc. New England Women, De Schilpen Soc. (Holland), Kings County Hist. Soc. Nova Scotia, Daughters of Union Vets., N.Y. Ct. Assts. of Nat. Soc. Women Descendents of Ancient and Honorable Artillery Co. (past state officer, corr. sec., com. chmn.), Denison Soc., Daughters Am. Colonists (N.Y. state regent 1991—94, hon. state regent, life 1994), Soc. Colonial Dames of Seventeenth Century (past state officer, past state pres, registrar), Colonial Daughters Seventeenth Century

(Atlantic Coast chmn. 2000—, nat. com. chmn. 2000—, past pres.), Daus. Colonial Wars, DAR (life; hon. regent Cayuga chpt., past state com. chmn., genealogical chmn.), Soc. Magna Charta Dames and Barons, Plantagenet Soc., Colonial Order of The Crown (Charlemagne), Soc. Sons and Daus. of the Pilgrims, Soc. U.S. Daughters 1812 (past pres., past Onondaga chpt. pres., past state ofcr.), Soc. Daughters of Founders & Patriots of Am. (past pres., past state pres., registrar), Soc. Sons and Daughters of Colonial Wars, Soc. New England Women, De Schilpen Mus. Soc. Netherlands, Daughters of Am. Colonists (nat. com chmn. 1994—97, atlantic sect.chmn genealogy 2003—), Summit N.J. Club (past mem. spl. panel), Nat. Fedn. Music Club (past mem. editl.com.), State Officers Club DAR, Ithaca Music Club (past pres.), Delta Omicron. Avocations: writing, photography, research. Home: 130 Christopher Cir Ithaca NY 14850-1702

ARRIEU-KING, CYNTHIA M. echocardiographer, poet, educator; b. Kingston, N.Y. d. Henry and Danielle Rosine Arrieu King. BA in French, BA in English, U. Louisville, 1995; MFA in Poetry, U. Pitts., 1999. Tchg. asst. U. Pitts.; part-time instr. U. Louisville, vis. asst. prof. creative writing, 1999—99; echocardiographer Bapt. Hosp. East, Louisville, 2001—. Author poetry; contbr. poetry to publs. Mem. Grief and Condolences Com., Louisville, 2003—03. Scholar Artistic Achievement award, Spalding U., 1991; Trustees scholar, U. Louisville, 1991—96, Tchg. Assistantship, U. Pitts., 1996—99. Independent.

ARRINGTON, CAROLYN RUTH, education consultant; b. May 20, 1942; d. Robert Ray and Grace Dotson; m. Wayne Vernon Arrington; children: Kevin Ray, Kemp Gray, Korey shay, Wayne, Kimberly. AA, Ohio Valley Coll., 1962; BA, Fairmont State Coll., 1964; MA, W.Va. U., 1966, EdD, 1994. Cert. pub. sch. adminstr., 1993. Tchr. Greenbrier Bd. Edn., Lewisburg, W.Va., 1964-68; supr. Mason County Bd. Edn., Point Pleasant, W.Va., 1968-70; media specialist Kanawha County Bd. Edn., Charleston, W.Va., 1970-71; asst. dir., dir., asst. divsn. chief W.Va. Dept. Edn., Charleston, 1971-89, asst. state supt. schs., 1989-98; v.p. Arrington Assocs., Inc., 1998—. Edn. and bus. cons.; inspirational motivational spkr. Author numerous poems and children's stories; developer workshop materials. Bd. dirs. YWCA, Charleston, 1988-91. Recipient medal of merit Edn. Ohio Valley Coll.; SEA fellow U.S. Dept. Edn., 1984. Mem. Assn. Ednl. Comm. and Tech. (pres. 1979-80, Edgar Dale award 1975, Spl. Svc. award 1982), Wva. Ednl. Media Assn. (pres. 1975-76). Office: Arrington Assocs Inc Charleston WV

ARRINGTON, HARRIET ANN HORNE, historian, biographer, researcher, writer; b. Salt Lake City, June 22, 1924; d. Lyman Merrill and Myrtle (Swainston) Horne; m. Frederick C. Sorensen, Dec. 22, 1943 (div. Dec. 1954); children: Annette S. Rogers, Frederick Christian, Heidi S. Swinton; m. Gordon B. Moody, July 26, 1958 (div. Aug. 1963); 1 child, Stephen Horne; m. Leonard James Arrington, Nov. 19, 1983. BS in Edn., U. Utah, 1957. Cert. tchr., Utah, Ga. Supr. surg. secs. Latter-day Saints Hosp., Salt Lake City, 1954-58; tchr. Salt Lake City Schs., 1957-58, Glynn County Schs., Brunswick, Ga., 1958-59, 60—; from med. sec. to office mgr. Dr. Horne, Salt Lake City, 1962-83; tchr. Carden Sch., Salt Lake City, 1973-74, women's history rschr., biographer. Mem. Utah Women's Legis. Coun.; co-establisher, bd. dirs. Arrington Archives, Utah State U.; spkr. hist. and women's confs. Author: (essays) Heritage of Faith, 1988, Worth Their Salt, 1997, Nearly Everything Imaginable: The Everyday Life of Utah's Mormon Pioneers, 1999; contbg. author (biographies) Encyclopedia of Women in American History, 1999, Pioneer Women of Faith and Fortitude, 1999, Encyclopedia of Utah History, 1999, Turn of the Century Lineage Profiles, DAR, 1996. Dist. chmn. Utah Rep. Com., 1972-76; mem. art com. Salt Lake City Bd. Edn.; chmn. art exhibit Senator Orrin Hatch's ann. Utah Women's Conf., 1987; past pres. L.D.S. Women's Relief Soc., Twin Falls, cultural refinement and/or spiritual living tchr., Alaska, Ga., Utah, Idaho; chmn. Utah Women Artists' Exhbns., AAUW, Utah divsn., 1986-87, Springville Mus. of Art. Nominated Pres. Ronald Reagan's Vol. Action award Utah Women Artists' Exhbn., 1987; recipient resolution of appreciation Utah Arts Coun., 1989, Friends of the Humanities award Utah State U., 1995. Mem.: NSDAR (nat. vice chmn. Women in Am. History 2000—04), DAR (regent 1998—2000, Utah State DAR bd. historian 2000—02, Princess Timpanogos Utah Chpt., 1st vice-regent Princess Timpanogos, dir.), AAUW (Utah state cultural refinement chmn., cert. of appreciation 1988), Old Main Soc. Utah State U., Cannon-Hinckley History & Dinner Club, Classics Club (v.p. 2003—), Xi Alpha (past pres. alumni chpt.), Chi Omega. Avocations: art, writing, gourmet cooking, needlepoint. Home and Office: 2236 S 2200 E Salt Lake City UT 84109-1135 Personal E-mail: harrietarrington@aol.com.

ARRINGTON, REBECCA CAROL, occupational health nurse; b. Longmont, Colo., Apr. 14, 1948; d. Theodore Victor Anderson and Lucinda Beth Panabaker; m. Charles Arthur Keeran, Aug. 2, 1968 (div. 1973); m. C. R. Arrington, Oct. 30, 1982. RN, St. Mark's Sch. Nursing, Salt Lake City, 1970; BS in Profl. Arts, St. Joseph's Coll., Standish, Maine, 1993. RN Okla. Recovery rm. nurse McArthur Pk. Med. Ctr., Irving, Tex., 1976-77; claims analyst Blue Cross/Blue Shield, Dallas, 1977-78, 78-79; staff RN Parkland Meml. Hosp., Dallas, 1978; occupl. health nurse City of Tulsa, 1979—, wellness coord., 1984—, mgr. occupl. health, 1997. Ind. assoc. Mannatech, 1998; privacy officer Health Ins. Portability & Acctg. Act, 2003. Mem.: ANA, Tulsa Area Assn. Occupl. Health Nurses (mem. nominating com. 1988—90, treas. 1990—93, pres. 1993—94), Okla. Nurses Assn., Am. Assn. Occupl. Health Nurses. Republican. Baptist. Avocations: sewing, crafts, fishing, camping. Office: City of Tulsa 1145 S Utica Ave Ste 453 Tulsa OK 74104-4041 Office Phone: 918-596-7083. E-mail: ambrosia@familynet.net., barrington@ci.tulsa.ok.us., stepstohealth@cimtel.net.

ARRIOLA-NICKELL, GAIL EMILY, development executive; b. Austin, Tex., June 19, 1958; d. Manuel I. and Delia Arriola; m. James A. Nickell, Mar. 23, 1996. AA in Interior Design, Fashion Inst. Design, 1982; BA in Art History, Calif. State U., L.A., 1995; MA, Pacifica Grad. Inst., 1998, PhD in Mythological Studies, 2003. Mgr. Stereomedia, Inc., Burbank, Calif., 1992—93; co-editor Calif. State U., L.A., 1995—96; dep. dir. develop. Dayle McIntosh Ctr., Anaheim, Calif., 1995—2001; dir. develop. visual arts Orange County Children's Therapeutic Arts, Santa Ana, Calif., 2001—. Author poetry. Mem. Orange County United Way Hispanic, 2000—, Develop. Multi-Ethnic Leadership Inst., Orange County, 2000—, Very Spl. Arts Orange County, 2002—; participant Orange County Supr. Ct. Com. Initiatives Conf., 1999, Housing & Comty. Develop. Steering Com., 1999—2000; participant humans rels. com. future Humans Rels. Conf., 2000. Avocations: sailing, poetry. Office: Orange County Children's Therapeutic Arts Ctr 280 N Broadway Santa Ana CA 92701

ARROTT, PATRICIA GRAHAM, artist, art instructor; b. Pitts., July 27, 1931; d. George Patterson and Helen (Gilleland) Graham; m. Anthony Schuyler Arrott, June 6, 1953; children: Anthony Patterson, Helen Graham, Matthew Ramsey, Elizabeth. BFA in Painting and Design, Carnegie-Mellon Univ., 1954; postgrad., Nat. Acad. Design, N.Y.C., 1985-87, Art Students League, 1980-91. Cert. tchr. art, Pa. Instr. children's ceramics Handcraft House, Vancouver, B.C., Can., 1970-72; courtroom artist Vancouver, B.C., Can., 1972-73; pvt. portrait artist Vancouver, N.Y.C., 1975—; instr. Art Students League, N.Y.C., 1993-99. Group shows include Nat. Acad. Design Ann. Exhbn., 1990, 92, 94, Cork Gallery, Lincoln Ctr., N.Y.C., 1991, Pen & Brush Club, N.Y.C., 1988-98, Silver Point Etc. traveling exhbn., 1992-93; represented by Eleanor Ettinger Gallery, N.Y.C., 1997—. Recipient Helen M. Loggie Prize, 1990, and cert. of merit, 1994, Nat. Acad. Design; recipient Emily Nicholas Hatch award Pen & Brush Club, 1989-91, Elizabeth Morse Genius award, 1988, 90, 93, 95, others. Mem. Art Student's League (life; mem. bd. 1989-92, women's v.p. 1991-92), Am. Fine Arts Soc. (mem. bd. 1991-92), Mayflower Soc. (life), Kappa Kappa Gamma (life). United Presbyterian.

ARROWSMITH, NANCY, journalist; b. Oxford, Eng., Nov. 19, 1950; arrived in U.S., 1950; d. William Ayres and Jean Reiser Arrowsmith; 1 child, Anna Eleonore. Student, U. Calif., Santa Cruz, 1967—69, U. Vienna, Austria, 1977—79. Translator from German and Italian, Bisbee, Ariz., 1972—; lectr. on gardening and environ. issues, 1985—; founder, dir. Noah's Ark, Schiltern, Austria, 1989—97, Kraut & Rueben, Organic Gardening Mag., Munich, 1984—89; faculty dept. fgn. lang. U. Ariz., 2003—. Advisor Seedsavers Exchange, Decorah, Iowa, 1994—; garden advisor Lower Austrian Govt., St. Poelten, 1990—96. Author: A Field Guide to the Little People, 1997, Die Welt der Naturgeister, 1994, Das Grosse Buch der Naturgeister, 2002, Chemical Free Spot Removal, 1986, Household Tips for Kitchen, House and Laundry, 1985, List of Austrian Vegetable Varieties, 1994, History of our Family, 2002; editor: Kraut & Rüben, 1984—89; translator: Seed to Seed, 1995, Agrobiodiversität und Pflanzengenetische Ressourcen, 2001. Recipient 2d place Journalism Conservation award, Lower Austrian Govt., 1989, Ford Conservation award, Ford Conservation Found., 1991, Cultural Award for conservation for life work, Lower Austrian Govt., 1996. Home: PO Box 1707 Bisbee AZ 85603

ARROYO, CARMEN ELSIE, state legislator; b. Corozal, P.R., Jan. 2, 1933; d. Jose Dolores and Maria Francisca Rosado Archillas; m. Pablo Arroyo, 1955 (div.); children: Pablo, Zaida, Jose Garcia, Maria Arroyo Aguirre, Iris, Nilda (dec.), David, Rolando, Yvette Colon; m. Hector Ramierz, 1985. AA, Hostos C.C.; BA, Coll. New Rochelle. Assemblywoman N.Y. State Assembly, Albany, 1994—. Mem. aging, children's and families coms., alcoholism and drug abuse, edn. coms. N.Y. State Assembly, women's caucus, Puerto Rican Hispanic task force, Black and Puerto Rican caucus. Mem. adv. bd. Lincoln Hosp, 1973—, Comty. Sch. Bd. # 7, 1975—; exec. dir. South Bronx Comty. Corp., 1977—. Recipient Outstanding Svc. award Am. Hispanic Educators, 1977—, Svc. award Comty. Sch. Dist. 7, 1980, 84, Office Continuing Edn. award, Disting. Svc. award, 1992, Recognition award Bronx County Dem. Comty., 1983, Svc. award South Bronx Comty. Corp., 1984, Puerto Rican Charities award, 1987; Named Woman of Yr., United Orgn. of Bronx, 1977. Democrat. Office: Legis Office Bldg NY State Assembly Rm 734 Albany NY 12248-0001

ARSENAULT, SAMANTHA, Olympic athlete; b. Salem, Mass., Oct. 11, 1981; d. Edward and Jeanne Arsenault. Student, U. Ga. Swimmer U. Mich., 2000—01. Recipient Gold medal 4 x 200-meter freestyle (team) Sydney Olympics, 2000; 2d pl. 200-meter freestyle U.S. spring nats., 1999, 3d pl. 100-meter and 200-meter freestyle U.S. summer nats., 1999; first internat. title win, 200m free, World Cup Paris, 2000 Office: USA Swimming 1 Olympic Plz Colorado Springs CO 80909-5746

ARTERBERRY, PATRICIA, elementary school educator; b. Huntingburg, Ind., Apr. 11, 1947; d. Otis T. Barnett and Fanny Delores Wessell; m. Ronnie G. Arterberry, Oct. 15, 1994; 1 child, Eric Alan. BS, U. Evansville (Ind.), 1970, MA, 1973. Tchr. grade 3 Tell City (Ind.) Troy Twp. Schs., tchr. primary grades. Active Boy Scouts Am.; mem. United Meth. Ch. Recipient Dist. award of Merit, Boy Scouts Am. Mem. NEA, Ind. Tchrs. Assn., TCTTCTA, Delta Kappa Gamma. Home: 9575 Sweetwater Rd Tell City IN 47586-9707

ARTERTON, JANET BOND, federal judge; b. Philadelphia, Feb. 8, 1944; m. F. Christopher Arterton; two children. BA, Mt. Holyoke Coll., 1966; JD, Northeastern U., 1977. Law clk. to Hon. Herbert J. Stern U.S. Dist. Ct. N.J., 1977-78; ptnr. Garrison & Arterton, 1978-95; judge U.S. Dist. Ct. Conn., New Haven, 1995—. Fellow Am. Bar Found., Conn. Bar Found.; mem. ATLA, Nat. Employment Lawyers Assn., Conn. Employment Lawyers Assn., Conn. State Trial Lawyers Assn. (bd. govs. 1990-95), Conn. Bar Assn. (mem. adv. com. state ct. rules 1992, mem. fed. jud. selection com. 1991-93, mem. exec. com. women and the law sect. 1990-93, chairperson fed. practice sect. 1993-95. Office: US Dist Ct Conn 141 Church St New Haven CT 06510-2030

ARTHUR, BEATRICE, actress; b. N.Y.C., May 13, 1926; d. Philip and Rebecca Frankel; m. Gene Saks, May 28, 1950 (div.); 2 sons. Student, Blackstone Coll., also Franklin Inst. Sci. and Arts; student acting with, Erwin Piscator, Dramatic Workshop, New Sch. Social Research. Theatrical appearances include: Lysistrata, 1947, Dog Beneath the Skin, 1947, Gas, 1947, Yerma, 1947, No Exit, 1948, The Taming of the Shrew, 1948, Six Characters in Search of An Author, 1948, The Owl and the Pussycat, 1948, Le Bourgeois Gentilhomme, 1949, Yes Is for a Very Young Man, 1949, Creditors, 1949, Heartbreak House, 1949, Three Penny Opera, 1954, 55, Shoestring Revue, 1955, Seventh Heaven, 1955, The Ziegfeld Follies, 1956, What's The Rush?, summer 1956, Mistress of the Inn, 1957, Nature's Way, 1957, Ulysses in Nightown, 1958, Chic, 1959, Gay Divorcee, 1960, A Matter of Position, 1962, Mame, 1966 (Tony award best supporting mus. actress), Fiddler on the Roof, 1964, Bermuda Avenue Triangle, 1996, For Better or Worse, 1996; one woman shows, ...And Then There's Bea, San Francisco,2001, An Evening With Bea Arthur, L.A., 2001, Bea Arthur on Broadway: Just Between Friends, 2002; stock appearances with Fiddler on the Roof, Circle Theatre, Atlantic City, summer 1951, State Fair Music Hall, Dallas, 1953, Music Circus, Lambertville, N.J., 1953, resident commedienne, Tamiment (Pa.) Theatre, 1953; numerous TV and nightclub appearances, 1948-; motion picture appearances That Kind of Woman, 1959; Lovers and Other Strangers, 1970, Mame, 1974, History of the World Part I, 1981, Stranger Things, 1995; TV movie: My First Love, 1988; TV appearances include All in the Family, 1971, leading role in TV series Maude, 1972-78 (Emmy award for Best Actress in a Comedy Series 1977), The Golden Girls, 1985-92 (Emmy award for Best Actress in a Comedy Series 1988), The Beatrice Arthur Spl., TV series 30 Years of TV Comedy's Greatest Hits; TV guest appearance: Malcolm in the Middle, 2000. Mem. Artists Equity Assn., SAG, AFTRA.*

ARTING, PATRICIA DEE, special education educator; b. Aurora, Colo., June 12, 1955; d. Virginia Mae and Marion Leroy Bowman; m. George Michael Arting, May 24, 1980; children: Ian Paul, Aaron Leigh. B in edn., U. of Hawaii at Manoa, 1993—96. Spl. Edn.and Elem. Edn. State Of Nev., 2003. Spl. ed tchr. Monaluа Intermediate Sch., Honolulu, 1996—97, Lompoc Valley Mid. Sch., Lompoc, Calif., 1997—2000, Cashman Mid. Sch., Las Vegas, 2000—01, Sedway Mid. Sch., North Las Vegas, 2001—. Sch., Las Vegas, 2000—01, Sedway Mid. Sch., North Las Vegas, 2001—03. Vol. buddy Spl. Olympics, Vandenberg AFB, Calif., 1997—2000. Nominee Disney Am. Tchr. award, 2000; recipient Spl. Recognition for Supporting Students Learning, NE Region/ Clark County Sch. Dist., 2002—03. Mem.: Assoc. For Curriculum and Devel., Coun. for Exceptional Children (assoc.). Avocations: herpetology, swimming.

ARTL, KAREN ANN, business owner, author; b. Bainbridge, N.Y., July 4, 1950; d. Douglas Robert and Beverly Florence (Schofell) Moore; m. Robert Edward Gurney, June 15, 1969 (div. June 1981); children: Douglas Albert Gurney, Rebecca Susan Gurney; m. Jeffrey Joseph Artl, Nov. 8, 1986; 1 child, Grace Beverly. BA in Edn., SUNY Coll. at Oneonta, 1972; MA in Reading and Edn., Cleve. State U., 1981. Tchr. reading Independence (Ohio) Mid. Sch., 1979-81; sr. editor Am. Greetings Corp., Cleve., 1981-87; mem. adj. faculty Lorain Community Coll., Cleve., 1987-89; creative dir. Gibson Greetings, Inc., Cin., 1994-97; owner Cresta Creative, 1999—. Owner, pres. WordsWorth Studio, Inc.; conf. speaker, trainer, cons. Social Expression Industry. Author: You Can Write Greeting Cards, 1999, M. Washington, etc., 1991, (children's book) I'm Me and You're Not, 1991, How Noah Knew What to Do!, 1998, The Baby King, 1999, Babies of the Bible, 1999, The Animal Babies Easter, Ten Ways to Please God; inspirational plaque line for Christian market; editor CR Gibson/Gift Books, 1993, Gibson Greetings, 1993. Vol. Am. Cancer Soc., Cleve., 1991. Mem. AAUW, NAFE, Greeting Card Assn., Greeting Card Creative Network, Soc. Children's Book Writers. Lutheran. Avocations: writing inspirational materials, activities to combat illiteracy. Home and Office: Cresta Creative 1005 Skyway Blvd Colorado Springs CO 80906-1748

ARTZ, CHERIE B. lawyer; b. Cin., Jan. 3, 1949; d. Joseph Meyer and Esther Epstein Fish; m. William Edward Artz, May 15, 1976; children: Rachel, Lindsey. BS, U. Cin., 1969; MA, George Washington U., 1973, JD with honors, 1985. Bar: Va. 1985, U.S. Ct. Appeals (fed. cir.) 1986, D.C. 1987, U.S. Supreme Ct. 1989, U.S. Ct. Appeals (4th cir.) 1990, U.S. Ct. Appeals (5th cir.) 1991, U.S. Ct. Appeals (6th cir.) 1992, Md. 1995. Tchr. Cin. Pub. Schs., 1969-71, Piscataway (N.J.) Pub. Schs., 1971-72; social worker Arlington (Va.) Juvenile Ct., 1973-82; law clk. U.S. Ct. Appeals Fed. Cir., Washington, 1985-86; lawyer Schnader Harrison Segal & Lewis, LLP, Washington, 1986—, ptnr., 1994—2001; v.p., gen. counsel Resource Cons., Inc., 2001—. Mem. George Washington U. Law Rev., 1984. Bd. dirs. Temple Rodef Shalom, Falls Church, Va., 1991—, pres., 1996-98; bd. dirs. Union Am. Hebrew Congregations, 2001—, Mid Atlantic Coun., Washington, 1998—; bd. overseers N.Y. Sch. Hebrew Union Coll., N.Y.C., 1999—; Fellow Am. Bar Found., 2001—. Home: 964 Saigon Rd Mc Lean VA 22102-2119 Office: Resource Cons Inc Ste 800 2650 Park Tower Dr Vienna VA 22180

ARTZ, ETHEL ANGELA CLEAVENGER, elementary education educator, consultant; b. Fort Belknap, Mont., Nov. 14, 1958; d. Kenneth James and Eliza Stanley C.; m. Jerome Daniel Artz, Aug. 15, 1998; 1 child, Reesa Eliza. BS in Elem. Edn., U. Mont., Billings, 1983; postgrad., U. Calif., Davis, 1996-98. Cert. pharmacy technician; cert. in conflict resolution and comm.; cert. in elem. edn. Aupair L.I. Governess, South Hampton, 1983; ednl. instr. Stockton (Calif.) Christian, 1983-86; ESL instr. Eikaiwa Gakuin Japanese Sch., Fukuoka, Japan, 1989-90, Cultural Homestay Internat., Granite Bay, Calif., 1990-91; ednl. field studies dir. Ednl. Tour Co., San Francisco, 1991-97; youth tng. specialist Indian Dispute Resolution Svcs., Sacramento, 1997-99; positive youth devel. character edn. specialist Sacramento City Unified Sch. Dist., 1999—. Participant Youth Travel Abroad work program, New Zealand, Australia, Europe, 1988; mem. Indian Edn., Havre, Mont., 1989—96; trainer, jr. dispute resolution svcs. cons. Indian Dispute Resolution Svcs., Inc. ; with Sacramento County Office Edn., U.S. Dept. Housing and Urban Devel., Am. Indian Edn., Nat. Conf. Peacemaking and Conflict Resolution, George Mason U., Seminole Tribe Fla. Housing Dept. Home: 3912 Loreto Way Sacramento CA 95821 Office: Sacramento City Unified 520 Capitol Mall Fl 6 Sacramento CA 95814-4701

ARUTT, CHERYL, clinical and forensic psychologist, educator; b. Fort Knox, KY, May 13, 1966, DA Women's Studies summa cum laude, UCLA, 1993; MA Clin. Psych., Calif. Sch. Prof. Psych., Los Angeles, 1995, PsyD, 1997. Lic. psychologist, Calif. Psychol. asst. Barbara Cort Counter, PhD, Beverly Hills, CA, 1995-99, forensic psychologist, 1999—; adj. asst. prof. Calif. Sch. Prof. Psychology, Los Angeles, 1999—; pvt. practice clin. psychologist Beverly Hills, CA, 1999—. Author: Healing Together: A Program for Couples, 1997 (named outstanding doctoral project CSPP, Los Angeles); Counselor, trainer, adv. Los Angeles Commn. on Assaults Against Women, 1991-97. Recipient George Heller Meml. Scholarship Am. Fedn. TV and Radio Artists, 1991, John Dales Memorial Scholarship, SAG, Los Angeles, 1992. Mem. APA, Phi Beta Kappa. Office: 9735 Wilshire Blvd Ste 208 Beverly Hills CA 90212 E-mail: Dr_Arutt@hotmail.com.

ARUTYUNYAN, EMMA, radio broadcaster; b. Yerevan, Armenia, Aug. 14, 1946; arrived in U.S., 1988; d. Hambartsum and Vartanush (Babayan) A.; m. Sako Mkrtchyan, Feb. 17, 1971; 1 child, Aram. MS, State U. Yerevan, 1969. Radioastrophysicist, rsch. scientist Byurakan Astrophys. Observatory, Armenia, 1969-78; mem. physics faculty Polytech Inst. Yerevan, Armenia, 1978-87; internat. radio-broadcaster Voice of Am., Washington, 1992—2003; news editor Horizon TV, L.A., 2003—. Contbr. sci. articles to profl. jours. Recipient award Ctrl. Com. Dosaaf USSR, Moscow, 1967, Pres. Ctrl. Com. Dosaaf USSR, 1967. Mem. Smithsonian Instn. (nat. assoc.), Nat. Geog., Am. Mus. Natural History.

ARVIN, ANN MARGARET, microbiology and immunology educator, researcher; Degree, Brown U.; M in Philosophy, Brandeis U.; MD, U. Pa., 1972. Resident U. Calif. San Francisco Med. Ctr., 1975; fellow Stanford (Calif.) Hosp. and Clinics, 1978; mem. faculty Stanford U. Sch. Medicine, 1978—, Lucille Packard Prof. Pediat., prof. microbiology and immunology, assoc. dean rsch., 2001—. Co-chair rsch. team investigating possible uses of flu virus in bio-terrorism Stanford U., 2003—. Trustee Am. Herpes Found.; mem. exec. com. VZV Rsch. Found. Recipient E. Mead Johnson award for rsch. in pediat., 1992. Mem.: Inst. Medicine. Office: Stanford U Sch Medicine 300 Pasteur Dr Rm G312 Stanford CA 94305 Business E-Mail: aarvin@stanford.edu.*

ARVIO, SARAH, poet; b. Phila., Apr. 3, 1954; d. Raymond Paavo Arvio and Cynthia Mallory. MFA in Poetry, Columbia U. Sch. Arts, 1983. Author: Visits from the Seventh, 2002 (2003-2004 Winner Rome Prize in Literature Am. Acad. Arts and Letters); translator: (poems) Ships Afire, 1988, Daimon, 1992, (documentary film) Azul, 1988; contbr. poems to numerous mags. including The New Yorker, Yale Review, Massachusetts Review, Paris Review; anthologized: Best American Poetry (Scribner), 1998, KGB Bar Book of Poems (Morrow). Recipient B.F. Connors prize, Paris Review, 1997, Frederich Bock prize, 2000, Prix de Nome, 2003. Home and Office: 314 E 9th St # 1 New York NY 10003-7918

ARVISAIS, KARI LYNN, marriage and family therapist; b. Hayward, Calif., July 25, 1967; d. Edward A. and Carolyn J. (Edgar) A. BA in Psychology, U. Mass., 1989; postgrad., UNLV, 1991, 93-94; MS in Counseling Psychology, St. John's U., 1993. Lic. marriage and family therapist. Marriage and family therapist Charter Behaviorial Health, Las Vegas, 1994-95; marriage and family therapist, drug and alcohol counselor Cmty. Counseling, Las Vegas, 1995-97; marriage and family therapist HBI, Las Vegas, 1997; pvt. practice Las Vegas, 1995—. Hot-line counselor Suicide Prevention, Las Vegas, 1992; vol. homeless shelter Market Ministries, New Bedford, Mass., 1989-90. Mem. Am. Assn. of Marriage and Family Therapists, Nev. Assn. of Marriage and Family Therapy (clin. mem.), Am. Orthopsychiat. Assn. (clin. mem.). Avocations: animal lover, reading, movies, music, computers. Home: Po Box 672 Golden CO 80402-0672

ARYSTANBEKOVA, AKMARAL KHAIDAROVNA, diplomat; b. Alma-Ata, Kazakhstan, May 12, 1948; came to U.S., 1991; d. Khaidar Arystanbekov and Sharbanu Bekmanovna Nurmuhamedova. BA in Chemistry, Kazakh State U., Alma-Ata, 1971, PhD in Chemistry, 1975. Mem. faculty Kazakh State U., Alma-Ata, 1975-78; chief dept., sec. Ctrl. Com. Kazakh Komsomol, Alma-Ata, 1978-83; dpe. chmn. Kazakh Friendship Soc., Alma-Ata, 1983-84, chmn., 1984-89; min. fgn. affairs Ministry Fgn. Affairs, Alma-Ata, 1989-91; permanent rep., amb. Permanent Mission of Republic of Kazakhstan to UN, N.Y.C., 1992—99. Mem. Supreme Coun. Kazakh SSR, Alma-Ata, 1985-90, Presidium of Supreme Coun. Kazakh SSR, Alma-Ata, 1987-90. Recipient awards Supreme Coun. USSR, Moscow, 1970, 81. Avocations: classical music (opera), playing the piano. Home and Office: Permanent Mission of Kazakhstan to UN 866 U N Plz Rm 586 New York NY 10017-1822

ARZBERGER, MARSHA, state senator; b. St. Joseph, Mo. m. Gus Arzberger; 2 children; 2 step-children. BS in Edn. with honors, N.W. Mo. State U.; MPA with distinction, postgrad. in Polit. Sci., Ariz. State U. Cert. tchr., Okla., Ariz.; registered med. lab. technologist; lic. pilot. Tchr. Okla. Sch. Bus. and Tech., Tulsa; substitute tchr. Willcox (Ariz.) H.S., dean Draughon's Bus. Coll., Kansas City, Mo.; ptnr. ranch; owner mgr. apt. complexes, asst. for spl. projects Ariz. Bd. Regents; Dem. senator dist. 8 Ariz. State Senate. Author novel; contbr. articles to profl. jours. Mem. cmty. com. Willcox Schs.; pilot Civil Air Patrol, group comdr. S.E. Ariz., search pilot, Search and Rescue Mission comdr.; campaign mgr. Senator Gus Arzberger; organizer Town Halls in Dist. 8 for 3 state legislators; precinct committeeperson; del. State Dem. Caucus; mem. Cochise Coll. Found. Bd., Farm Bur., Cattle Growers, Friends of Libr., Sulphur Springs Hist. Soc., Cochise County Dems., LWV, Cowbelles. Recipient State Comdr.'s commendation Civil Air Patrol. Mem. AAUW, AARP, Bus. and Profl. Women, Western Writers Assn., Aircraft Owners and Pilots Assn. Office: Ariz State Senate State Capitol Rm 313 1700 W Washington Phoenix AZ 85007 E-mail: marzberg@azleg.state.az.us.

ARZOUMANIAN, LINDA LEE, early childhood educator; b. Madison, Wis., Apr. 29, 1942; d. James Arthur Luck and Rosemary M. (Peacock) Engstrom; children: Stephan, Aaron. BS, Stout State U., Menomonie, Wis., 1964; MEd, Ohio U., Athens, 1969; EdD, Nova U., 1994. Cert. tchr. vocat., secondary, cmty. coll., Ariz. Residence hall asst. Ohio U., Athens, 1965-67; quality control supr. Advalloy, Inc., Palo Alto, Calif., 1967; tchr. adult edn. Eau Claire (Wis.) Pub. Sch., 1964-65; patient svc. dietitian Camden Clark Meml. Hosp., Parkersburg, W.Va., 1970; adminstr. pre-sch. Fishkill (N.Y.) Meth. Nursery Sch., 1976-84; substitute tchr. Tucson Unified Sch. Dist., 1987; tchr. pre-sch. Tanque Verde Luth. Presch., Tucson, 1988-89; cons., early childhood ednl. curriculum specialist Tucson Unified Sch. Dist., 1988-93; instr. Ctrl. Ariz. Coll., 1990-98, Prescott Coll., 1991-92; dist. moderator Sch. Cmty. Partnership Coun., Tucson, 1988-90; dir. child and family svcs. in prevention, early intervention and treatment in sys. managed care CODAC Behavioral Health Svcs., Tucson, 1990-99, dir. mgmt. info. sys., 1999, dir. cmty. svcs., 1999-2000; supt. of schs. Pima County, 2000—. Mem. supts. adv. cabinet Tucson Unified Sch. Dist., 1988-89, mem. curriculum and instrn. coun., 1989-90, spl. edn. pre-sch. adv. com., 1989-91, info. tech. bond rev. com., 1989—, sex edn. curriculum adv. com., core curriculum com., 1988-90, 2000 com., 1988-89, and various others; nat. child devel. assoc. adv./field adv., nat. child devel. assoc. rep. Nat. Assn. for Edn. of Young Children; grantswriter Comstock Found.; validator early childhood programs for Nat. Acad. Early Childhood Programs; appt. Ariz. State Bd. Edn., 2002. Mem. Dutchess County Child Devel. Com., Poughkeepsie, N.Y., 1979-81; advancement chmn. troop 1968 Boy Scouts Am., Tucson, 1986, com. person troop 194, 1986-89; mem. joint com. on site based decision making Tucson Unified Sch. Dist./Tucson Edn. Assn., 1989-98; life mem. Ariz. PTA; mem. Early Childhood Edn. Coun. Consortium; mem. mgmt. com. Healthy Families of Pima County; commr. Met. Edn. Commn.; mem. Pima County Youth Coun., Greater Tucson Strategic Planning for Econ. Devel. Mem.: AAUW, Ariz. Sch. Bds. Assn., Am. Assn. Edn. Svc. Agys. (Fed. Relations Repr. (Ariz.)), Tucson Assn. Edn. Young Children (past pres.), Nat. Assn. Edn. Young Children, Tucson Rep. Women, Pima County Supt. and Governing Bd. Collaborative, Tucson Hispanic C. of C., Tucson Met. C. of C., So. Ariz. Forums on Children and Families, Cath. Cmty. Svc. (bd. dirs.). Avocations: basketmaking, quilting, hiking, gardening, cooking. Home: 8230 E Ridgebrook Dr Tucson AZ 85750-2442 Office: 3100 N 1st Ave Tucson AZ 85719-2513 : 130 W Congress Tucson AZ 85701

ASAAD, KOLLEEN JOYCE, special education educator; b. West Union, Iowa, July 13, 1941; d. Leonard Henry and Catherine Adelade (Bishop) Anfinson; children: Todd, Robin, Tara, Jason. BA in Elem. Edn., Upper Iowa U., 1961; MA in Spl. Edn. and Adminstrn., U. Cin., 1973. Elem. tchr. Fredericksburg (Iowa) Elem. Sch., 1961-62, Tyler Sch., Cedar Rapids, Iowa, 1962-64, Oasis Sch., 29 Palms, Calif., 1964-69, Longfellow Sch., Waterloo, Iowa, 1969-70; spl. edn. tchr. Fairview Sch., Cin., 1970-77; learning disabilities tchr. Lincoln Sch., Portsmouth, Ohio, 1977-78; dir. spl. edn. Vermilion Assn. for Spl. Edn., Danville, Ill., 1978-94; dir. edn. Swann Spl. Care Ctr., Champaign, Ill., 1994-97, ret., 1997. Mem. Govtl. Rels. Com., Ill. Coun. for Exceptional Children, Jacksonville, Ill., 1992. Bd. mem. Crosspoints, Danville, Catlin Music Boosters, pres. Named Best Adminstr., Regional Supt. of Schs., 1991. Mem. Coun. for Exceptional Children, Coun. for Adminstrs. of Spl. Edn., Ill. Adminstrs. of Spl. Edn., Assn. for Persons with Severe Handicaps, Exec. Club. Lutheran. Avocations: reading, art. Home: 122 Mapleleaf Dr Catlin IL 61817-9646

ASAKAWA, TAKAKO, dancer, dance teacher, director, choreographer; b. Toyko, Feb. 23, 1939; came to U.S., 1962; d. Kamenosuke and Chiaki Asakawa. Student, Tokyo schs., 1962-91. Prin. dancer Martha Graham Dance Co., N.Y.C., 1962-76, 81—; dancer Alvin Ailey, 1968-69, Pearl Lang, 1967, Lar Lubovitch, 1974-80. Guest tchr. at numerous schs. and univs. throughout world, including Moscow Culture Exch. Program, Martha Graham Sch., Juilliard Sch.; co.-founder Asakawalker Dance Co.; dir. Paris Opera Ballet Co., Am. Ballet Theater, Het Nationale Ballet in Amsterdam and various univs. throughout world. Performed all major roles in GRaham reperatory throughout world, including Paris Opera House, Covent Garden; Broadway and TV performances include Eliza in The King and I, Bell Tel. Hour. Named Legendary Woman of Am., St. Vincent's Hosp. Mem. Am. Guild Musical Artists Home and Office: 20 W 64th St Apt 29-E/F New York NY 10023-7180

ASANBE, COMFORT BOLA, psychologist, educator; d. David Atte and Martha Abon Odeyemi; m. Joseph Adebola Asanbe, Feb. 27, 1982 (dec. Aug. 19, 1996); children: Olaniran Omoniyi, Opeyemi Ajike. BA, U. Ilorin, Nigeria, 1983; MA in Edn., Austin Peay State U., 1989; PhD, Tenn. State U., Nashville, 1996. Lic. psychologist/health svcs. provider Tenn. Bd. of Examiners in Psychology, 2003. Tchr. Ilorin Grammar Sch., Ilorin, Nigeria, 1980—83; instr. Austin Peay State U., Clarksville, Tenn., 1997—2001; psychologist Metro-Davidson County Sch. Sys., Nashville, 2001—02; asst. prof. Tenn. Technol. U., Cookeville, Tenn., 2002—. Psychology intern U. Tenn. Med. Ctr., Memphis, 2000—01; presenter in field. Workshop presenter Stephen's Ctr. for Child Abuse Prevention, Livingston, Tenn., 2003; exec. mem. Children Internat. Edn. Coun. (CIEC) Program, Clarksville, Tenn., 1992—98. Faculty Rsch. grantee, Tenn. Technol. U., 2004. Mem.: APA, Tenn. Psychol. Assn., Southeastern Psychol. Assn., Phi Kappa Phi, Psi Chi. Avocations: travel, cooking, sewing. Office: Tenn Technol U 1000 N Dixie Ave Cookeville TN 38505-001 Office Phone: 931-372-3217. Home Fax: 931-372-3400.

ASARCH, ELAINE, interior designer, anthropologist; b. Des Moines, Nov. 4, 1944; d. Morris and Rose (Sherman) Feintech; m. Richard Asarch, Aug. 17, 1965; children: Deborah, Chad, Jonathan, Adam, David. BA, U. Iowa, 1966; postgrad., U. Colo., 1992—. Tchr. spl. edn. Univ. Hosp. Schs., Iowa City, 1966-69; tchr. Raleigh Hill Elem. Sch., Portland, Oreg., 1969; learning therapist Psychol. & Guidance Ctr., Devner, 1974; interior designer Sipple/Asarch Design, Denver, 1981-83, Elaine Asarch Design Assocs., Englewood, Colo., 1983—. Dir., prodr. documentary on domestic violence; contbr. articles, photographs to Better Homes and Garden, 1980. Mktg. chmn. Jr. League of Denver, 1985-87; mem. com. Rose Found., Denver, 1990—; Pres., chmn. women's campaign Allied Jewish Fedn. of Denver, 1990-93; chmn. cmty. rels. com., 1994-96; mem. steering com. Harvard Womens Studies in Religion, 1994-99; founder Cmty. Help and Abuse Info. Agy. Recipient Ann. award, Yeshiva Toras Chaim, Denver, 1994, Tree of Life award, Herzl Day Sch., Denver, 1997, Golda Meir award, Allied Jewish Fedn. Colo., 2001. Mem. Am. Soc. Interior Designers (cert.). Achievements include research in relationship between environment and healing with relationship to medical practices. Home: 1000 E Tufts Ave Englewood CO 80110-5931

ASATO, SUSAN PEARCE, business executive, educator; b. Dallas, Dec. 29, 1949; d. Joe Camp and Sue (Dickey) Pearce; m. Morris T. Asato, Apr. 1, 1973. Student, U. Internat., Saltillo, Mex., 1968; BE, U. Tex., 1973; MBA, Calif. State U., San Bernardino, 1981. Tchr. Austin (Tex.) Ind. Sch. Dist., 1972-73; rsch. assoc. U. Tex., Austin, 1973-77; dir. Tairyu (Japan) English Ctr., 1977-78; purchasing agt. U. Calif., Riverside, 1978-83; gen. mgr. corp. purchasing ABC-TV, Hollywood, Calif., 1983-90; dir. purchasing and material mgmt. Mira Costa Coll., Oceanside, Calif., 1990—. Instr., lectr. U. Calif., Riverside, 1981-83. Bd. dirs. Santa Margarita YCMA, 1996—, Theatre Found., 1993—. Mem. Nat. Assn. Purchasing Mgrs., Nat. Assn. Ednl. Buyers, Nat. Contract Mgmt. Assn., Calif. Assn. Sch. Bus. Ofcls., Calif. Assn. Pub. Purchasing Ofcls., Oceanside Rotary Internat. (bd. dirs., Paul Harris fellow 1998). Episcopalian. Home: Mira Costa Coll 1 Barnard Dr Oceanside CA 92056-3820

ASCH, SUSAN MCCLELLAN, pediatrician; b. Cleve., Dec. 31, 1945; d. William Alton and Alice Lonore (Heide) McClellan; m. Marc Asch, Sept. 10, 1966; children: Marc William, Sarah Susan, Rebecca Janney. AB, Oberlin (Ohio) Coll., 1967; MA, Mich. State U., 1968, PhD, 1975; MD, Case Western Res., 1977. Diplomate Nat. Bd. Med. Examiners, Am. Bd. Pediatrics, Am. Bd. Emergency Pediatrics. Instr. sociology Mich. State U., East Lansing, 1971-73; resident in pediatrics Children's Nat. Med. Ctr., Washington, 1977-80, chief resident in ambulatory and emergency pediatrics, 1979-80; asst. to dir. Office for Med. Applications of Rsch. NIH, Bethesda, 1980-81; pvt. practice in pediatrics Millinocket (Maine) Regional Hosp., 1981-84; assoc. dir. emergency Akron (Ohio) Children's Hosp., 1984-87; asst. prof. pediatrics Northeastern Ohio U. Coll. Medicine, 1984-87; dir. emergency St. Paul Children's Hosp., 1987-91; asst. prof. pediatrics U. Minn., 1987-93, clin. asst. prof., 1993—; pvt. practice pediatrics Stillwater, Minn., 1992—; sec. Lakeview Meml. Hosp., 1999—2001, vice chief of staff, 2001—03, chief of staff, 2003—. Nat. faculty PALS Am. Heart Assn., Mpls., Dallas, 1987-94; mem. task force, sub-bd. emergency pediatrics Am. Bd. Pediatrics, 1987-93. Assoc. editor Pediatric Emergency Medicine, 1992, contbr., 1992, 96. State bd. dirs., nat. and affiliate faculty PALS Minn. affiliate Am. Heart Assn., 1988—; chmn. SIDS task force, Minn. Dept. Maternal and Child Health, St. Paul, 1990-92. Mem. Am. Acad. Pediatrics (nat. faculty advanced pediatric life support 1989—, exec. com. sect. on emergency pediatrics 1988-90, chair Minn. emergency pediatric com. 1989-91, nat. svc. commendation 1991), Minn. Med. Assn. (emergency svcs. com. 1990, ho. of dels. 1994), Alpha Omega Alpha. Democrat. Mem. Soc. Of Friends. Avocations: travel, quarter horses. Home: 34 N Oaks Rd North Oaks MN 55127-6325 Office: Stillwater Med Group 921 Greeley St S Stillwater MN 55082-5935 Office Phone: 651-439-1234. E-mail: Susan@asch.org.

ASCHENBRENER, CAROL ANN, pathologist, educator; b. Dubuque, Iowa, Dec. 22, 1944; d. Lester Bernard and Marian Barbara (Wiehl) Kemp; m. Thomas D. Aschenbrener, June 10, 1968 (div. Oct. 1972); 1 child, Erin Jean. BA, Clarke Coll., 1966; MS in Anatomy, U. Iowa, 1968; MD, U. N.C., 1971. Diplomate Am. Bd. Pathology. Intern in pathology U. Iowa Hosps., 1971-72, resident in anatomic pathology, neuropathology, 1972-74; instr. pathology Coll. Medicine U. Iowa, Iowa City, 1974, asst. prof., 1974-79, assoc. prof., 1979-87, prof., 1987—, assoc. dean, 1983-88, sr. assoc. dean, 1988-90, exec. assoc. dean, 1990—. Bd. dirs. 1st Nat. Bank, Iowa City. Contbr. articles to profl. jours., chpts. to med. texts. Bd. dirs. alumni bd. Clarke Coll., Dubuque, 1983-87. Nat. Merit scholar, 1962-66; Am. Cancer Soc. fellow, 1972-73. Fellow Coll. Am. Pathologists, Am. Assn. Neuropathologists; mem. AMA (sect. del.), Assn. Am. Med. Colls. (chmn. student affairs nat. com. 1987-89), Iowa Med Soc. (sec., treas. bd. trustees 1985—), Liaison Com. on Med. Edn., Nat. Bd. of Med. Examiners, Nat. Cancer Inst. (edn. adv. com.), Alpha Omega Alpha. Democrat. Roman Catholic. Avocations: reading, travel, gardening, hot air ballooning. Home: 1603 16th St NW Apt 5 Washington DC 20009-3036

ASCHER, NANCY LOUISE, surgeon; b. Detroit, Mar. 15, 1949; d. Meyer S. and Beckie (Berger) A.; m. John. P. Roberts, Dec. 10, 1992; children: Becky, John. AB, U. Mich., 1970, MD, 1974; PhD, U. Minn., 1985. Instr. surgery U. Minn., Mpls., 1982-85, staff surgeon, dir. liver transplant, 1982-87, assoc. prof., 1987; prof. surgery U. Calif., San Francisco, 1988—, chief transplant svc., 1989—, prof., vice chmn., 1993—99, chmn., dept. surg., 1999—. Presenter in field. Contbr. articles to profl. jours. Schering scholar, 1979; recipient Koret Israel prize, 1993. Fellow Am. Coll. Surgeons (surg. forum com.); mem. AMA, AAAS, Am. Assn. Immunologists, Am. Soc. Transplant Surgeons (publs. and programs com., edn. com., chair edn. com., councilor-at-large, sec., pres 2001-2002), Am. Surg. Assn., Calif. Med. Assn., Minn. Surg. Soc. (scholar 1982), Mpls. Surg. Soc., San Francisco Med. Soc., Internat. Transplantation Soc. (sec. local orgn. com.), Soc. U. Surgeons, Soc. Clin. Surgery, Surg. Biology Club, Acad. Medicine Task Force, Pacific Coast Surg. Soc., Live Transplant Soc., Inst. Medicine, Phi Beta Kappa, Phi Kappa Phi, others. Office: U Calif Box 0780 505 Parnassus Ave San Francisco CA 94122-2722

ASCHHEIM, EVE MICHELE, artist, educator; b. NYC, Aug. 30, 1958; d. Emil and Lydie Aschheim. BA, U. Calif., Berkeley, 1983; MFA, U. Calif., Davis, 1987. Asst. prof. Occidental Coll., L.A., 1990, Sarah Lawrence Coll., Bronxville, N.Y., 1994-97. Vis. critic Md. Inst. Coll. Art, Balt., 1998-2000; lectr. Princeton (N.J.) U., 1991, 93, 98, 2000, sr. lectr., 2001—, dir. visual arts program, 2003—. One-woman shows include Stefan Stux Gallery, 1997, Galerie Rainer Borgemeister, Berlin, 1999, 2001, Galleri Magnus Åklundh, Lund, Sweden, 1999, Galerie Benden and Klimczak, Cologne, Germany, 1999, U. Mass. Gallery, Amherst, 2003, Larry Becker Contemporary Art, Phila., 2004, Eve Ashem Guy Corriero, Patrick Verelst Gallery, Antwerp, 2004; group exhbns. include Sackler Mus., Cambridge, Mass., 1997, Kunstmuseum Winterthur, Switzerland, 1998, Akademie der Künste, Berlin, 1998, Fonds régional d'art contemporain de Picardie and Museé de Picardie Amiens, 1997, Parrish Mus., L.I., N.Y., 1999, Stark Gallery, N.Y.C., 1999, U. Calif., San Diego, 1999, Landesgalerie Oberosterreich, Linz, Austria, 1999, Pratt Gallery, N.Y.C., 1999, So. Meth. U., 2000, N.Y. Studio Sch., 2000, Hunter Coll. Leubsdorf Gallery, N.Y.C., 2000, Maier Mus., Lynchburg, Va., 2000, Tucson Art Mus., 2000, Mus. Contemporary Art, Miami, 2001, D.A.A.D. Galerie, Berlin, U. Art Mus. Calif. State U., Long Beach, 2001, Colby Coll., 2002, N.Y. Hist. Soc., 2002, O.S.P. Gallery, Boston, 2002, Black and White Gallery, Bklyn., 2003, U. Mass., Amherst, 2003, Bill Maynes Gallery, N.Y.C., 2003, 179th Ann. Invitational Nat. Acad. Design, N.Y.C., Ins Lichtgemct, Kunst Mus. Bonn, Germany; represented in permanent collections at Fogg Mus., Nat. Gallery, Washington, N.Y. Hist. Soc., Hamburger Bahnhof, Berlin, M.O.C.A., Miami, Yale U. Art Gallery, Kunstmus., Bonn; artist (catalog) Eve Aschheim Paintings and Drawings, 1999, Eve Aschheim Drawings, 2003. Recipient Rosenthal award AAAL, 1997; fellow NEA, 1989, Pollock-Krasner Found., 1990, 2001, NY Found. for Arts, 1991; grantee Elizabeth Found., 1997. Mem. Am. Abstract Artists. E-mail: easchh@aol.com.

ASCONE, TERESA PALMER, artist, educator; b. Cortland, N.Y., Nov. 1, 1945; d. Lawrence Henry and Bernice Rosella (Holcomb) Palmer; m. Michael Wayne Ascone, Oct. 15, 1965; 1 child, Michael Palmer. Student, Alaska Meth. U., Alaska Pacific U., U. Alaska. Painter/tchr. Alaska Pacific U., Anchorage, 1989-91, U. Alaska, 1992; pvt. tchr. watercolor Anchorage, 1992—; owner Alaskan Portfolio, 1981—; tchr. U. Alaska, Anchorage, 1992—, dir. Ultimate Watercolor Acad., 1998-2001. Juried shows include Alaska State Fair, 1979-80, Fur Rendezvous Juried Show, 1979, 80, All Alaska Juried Show, 1981, 84, 85, 90, Alaska Watercolor Soc. juried show, 1981, 83, 85, 86, 87, 88, 89, 90, 91, April in Paris juried exhibit at Capt. Cook Hotel, 1982, 83, 84, 87, Featured Artist, 1986, Watercolor Fairbanks, 1989, Women Artist of West 1st Ann. Internat. Show, 1990; one women shows include Anchorage Mcpl. Librs., 1980, 82, NBA Heritage Libr., 1986, Alaska Pacific U., 1989, Chitose City Hall, Chitose, Hokkaido, Japan, 1990; represented in permanent collection Alaska Pacific U., Raymond P. Atwood Collection, Lincoln, Nebr.; cover artist Arctic Horizons Mag., 1986, Alaska Horizons Mag., 1986, U. Alaska Anchorage Summer Sessions Catalog, 1997; subject of TV spl., 1988; developer, patentee original design, manufacture & mktg. The Ultimate Palette, 1993; author: We're All Artists: Watercolor for Everyone, 1994, Painting Pleasure: Adventures in Watercolor, 1999; editor, publisher Hot Press Mag., 1994; illustrator: Things in the Sky, 1995; contbr. articles to profl. publs. Mcpl. commr. Anchorage Sister Cities Commn., 1991-93. Recipient Vol. of Yr. Caverly Sr. Ctr., 1986, various art show awards to date; works chosen as ofcl. gifts to cities of Inchon, Korea and Magadan, Russia and Whitby, Eng. from city of Anchorage. Mem. Alaska Watercolor Soc. (v.p. 1983),Athena Soc. Avocations: writing, reading, skating, dance.

ASH, DOROTHY MATTHEWS, civic worker; b. Dresden, Germany, Nov. 10, 1918; came to U.S., 1924; d. Kurt Horst and Ana Matthesius; m. Harry A. Ash, Apr. 13, 1941 (dec. June 1981); children: Fredrick Curtis, Dorothea Ash Linklater. Dancer, 1933-40; treas. Inheritance Abstractors Inc., Chgo., 1949-70; reporter Miami (Fla.) Sun Post, 1983; reporter, columnist Social Mag., Miami, 1984—. Chmn. Miss Universe Pageant, 1983-85; cruise chmn. Miami U., 1984, mem. Pres.'s Club, 1983. Pres. Big Bros. and Big Sisters, 1982-83; founding mem. World Sch. of Arts, 1985—; founding Notable Douglas Gardens 1988: Pres.'s Club U. of Miami, 1989; founding and bd. mem. Cancer Link Rsch., 1990; mem. Bd. Animal Welfare; active Project: Newborn, Am. Cancer Soc., March of Dimes, chmn. quest for the best, 1988-92, winner celebrity gourmet gala, 1988, leading lady 1998; active Children's Resource, Erase Diabetes, founding and bd. mem. 1990, Cerebral Palsy Found., Theatre Arts League, Linda Ray Infant Ctr., Miami City Ballet, Am. Ballet; bd. dirs. Greater Miami Opera, 1975—, Leading Ladies, Inc. 1997; pub. rels. vol. Miami Heart Inst., 1988—; com. mem. Miami Beach (Fla.) Beautification Program, 1984; mem. bd. Miami Mayor's Ad Hoc Com., 1984; mem. com. Challenger Seven Meml., 1988; active Cousteau Soc.; numerous others. Named Woman of Yr., Big Bros. and Big Sisters, Miami, 1981, Best Dressed, Am. Cancer Soc., 1981, Outstanding Humanitarian and Civic Leader, Mayor City of Miami, 1985, Woman of the Yr., Project: New Born, 1985, Miss Charity, Biscayne Bay Hosp., 1986, Queen of Hearts, Miami Children's Hosp., 1988, Leading Lady, March of Dimes, 1998; recipient Shining Star award Bon Secours Hosp., 1993, Patron Recognition award Mia Heart Rsch. Inst., 1993, Goddess of Love award Villa Maria Hosp., 1995, Shining Angel, 2000, Star of the Century award Miami Heart Rsch. Inst., 2000, Miracle Maker award Big Bros./Big Sisters, 2001, Salute to Dorothy Ash, Mia Heart Inst., 2002, Hero of the Heart award Mia Heart Inst., 2003, Animal Welfare honoree Mia Heart Inst., 2003. Mem. Miami Internat. Press Club. Avocations: reading, writing, painting. Home: 10245 Collins Ave Bal Harbour FL 33154-1407 Home (Summer): 330 W Diversey Pky Apt 2209 Chicago IL 60657-6231

ASH, JENNIFER GERTRUDE, writer, editor; b. Jan. 16, 1963; d. Clarke and Agnes Ash; m. D.A. Joseph Rudick, Apr. 7, 1990; children: Clark Albert, Amelia, Eleanor. BA, Kenyon Coll., 1985; postgrad., New Sch. Social Rsch. Assoc. editor Women's Wear Daily, 1986-87; editor Town and Country, N.Y.C., 1992—95, writer, 1995—. Author: Private Palm Beach, 1992, The Expectant Father: Facts, Tips, and Advice for Dads-to-Be, 1995, revised edit., 2001. Fellow Frick Collection. Democrat. Roman Catholic. Home: 520 E 76th St New York NY 10021-3161*

ASHANTI, See DOUGLAS, ASHANTI

ASHBURN, SUE LAWSON FISHER, geriatrics nurse; b. Livingston, Tenn., Aug. 24, 1955; d. Deward R. and Helen R. (Fikes) Dailey; m. Larry F. Lawson, Oct. 18, 1972 (div. Dec. 1985); 1 child, Jonathan Curtis; m. Bill R. Fisher, July 7, 1986 (div. Dec. 1993); m. Larry C. Ashburn, Oct. 31, 1996. ADN, N.Y. Regents U., 1992. Staff vis. nurse Superior Home Health, Livingston, Tenn., 1991-92; team leader Quality Home Health, Livingston, Tenn., 1992-93; supr. nursing Century Home Health, Cookeville, Tenn., 1993-94, home tech. health care RN supervising team leader, 1994-95; dir. nurses and patient svcs. Elk Valley Home Health, 1995-97; with psychiat. program McFarland Splty. Hosp., 1997—; with psychiat. unit Columbia Smith County Hosp., 1997—; psychiat. nurse Vets. Alvin C. York Hosp., 1998—; house supr. Overton Nursing Home, 1996—. Mem. adv. bd. Clay County Ambulance, Celina, Tenn., 1994. Mem. Nat. League Nurses, Lions. Democrat. Avocations: gofling, swimming, horse-back riding, reading, clay ceramics. Home: 5021 Bapt Ridge Rd Hilham TN 38568

ASHCRAFT, NANCY OLSON, mining engineer; b. Charleston, W.Va., Nov. 8, 1959; d. Robert Edward and Jean Wadsworth Olson; m. Randy Ashcraft, Nov. 28, 1987; children: Kelly, Anna. BS in Mining Engring., Pa. State U., 1982. Cert. OSHA hazard tng. Lab. tech. R&P Coal Co., 1980; with Iselin Prep. Co., Homer City, Pa., 1981; chemist Sohio-Aft, Bridgeport, NJ, 1984; mining engr., chemist S.E. Coal Co., Isom, Ky., 1984—89; sr. lab. technician York Corp., Elyria, Ohio, 1996—97, asst. engr., 1997—99, engr., 1999—2000; staff engr. Carrier Corp., Indpls., 2001—. Internat. com. for sound and vibration York Corp., 2001—. Musician Christ the King Ch., North Olmsted, Ohio, 1994—2001, former editor; asst. diving coach Heritage Christian Sch., Indpls., 2002. Named Outstanding Young Woman of Am., 1984. Home: 4591 Abbey Dr Carmel IN 46033 Office Phone: 317-243-0851.

ASHDOWN, MARIE MATRANGA (MRS. CECIL SPANTON ASHDOWN JR.), writer, educator, lecturer, cultural organization administrator; b. Mobile, Ala. d. Dominic and Ave (Mallon) Matranga; m. Cecil Spanton Ashdown Jr., Feb. 8, 1958; children: Cecil Spanton III, Charles Coster; children by previous marriage: John Stephen Gartman, Vivian Marie Gartman. Degree, Maryville Coll. Sacred Heart, Springhill Coll. Feature artist, women's program dir. daily program Sta. WALA, WALA-TV, Mobile; v.p., dir. Met. Opera Guild, N.Y.C., opera instr. in-svc. program, 1970-80, Marymont Coll., N.Y.C., 1979-85; exec. dir. Musicians Emergency Fund, Inc., N.Y.C., 1985—. Internat. adv. coun. Van Cliburn Found., 1998—; cons. No. Ill. U. Coll. Visual and Performing Arts, 1985—; lectr. in field. Author: Opera Collectables, 1979, contbr. articles to profl. jours. Recipient Extraordinary Svc. award March of Dimes, Medal of Appreciation award Harvard Bus. Sch. Club NYC, Cert. Appreciation, Kiwanis Internat., Arts Excellence award NJ State Opera, Cipario award, Albanese-Puccini award Lincoln Ctr., 2002. Mem. AAUW, Nat. Inst. Social Scis., Com. for U.S.-China Rels. Avocations: collecting art, antique ceramics and porcelains, bookbinding. Home: 25 Sutton Pl S New York NY 10022-2456 Office: Musicians Emergency Fund Inc PO Box 1256 New York NY 10150-1256

ASHE, KATHY RAE, special education educator; b. Bismarck, N.D., Oct. 24, 1950; d. Raymond Charles and Virginia Ann (Mason) Lynch; m. Barth Eugene Olson, Aug. 11, 1973; 1 child, William Raymond; m. Fredrick A. Ashe, Aug. 5, 1994. BS, U. N.D., 1972, MS in Spl. Edn., 1987. Cert. elem. tchr. with spl. edn. credential, N.D. Instr. Grafton State Sch., N.D., 1972-74; tchr. spl. edn. Grand Forks Sch. Dist., N.D., 1974—. Bd. dirs. Agassiz Enterprises; mem. RAD com. Valley Jr. High; mem. transition governing bd., Region IV. Mem. spl. needs recreation program Grand Forks Park Bd., 1973—76; mem. Spl. Olympics Area Mgmt. Team, 1984—90; mem. region IV Low Incident Behavior Grant Com.; co-chair, vol. coord. Greater Grand Forks Soccer Club Tournament, 2000, 2001; bldg. rep. Grand Forks Edn. Assn., 2000—04; bd. dirs. Assn. Retarded Citizens, Devel. Homes, Inc.,

N.D. Sch. Blind Found., pres., 1997—. Named N.D. Tchr. of Yr., Coun. Chief State Sch. Officers, 1981. Mem. AAUW (pres. 1998-2000), Delta Kappa Gamma (sec. 1984-86, pres. 1990-94), Alpha Phi (alumni pres. 1984-86, 90-91, alumni treas. 1995—), Phi Delta Kappa. Republican. Roman Catholic. Avocations: sporting events, civic work, cross stitch, bowling, golf. Home: 3208 Walnut St Grand Forks ND 58201-7665 E-mail: ashekathy@hotmail.com.

ASHER, KATHLEEN MAY, communications educator; b. Vassar, Mich., Aug. 19, 1932; d. Thomas Henry and Jessie (Smith) Pierce; m. Donald William Asher, July 17, 1957; children: David Kevin, Diane Kerri. BS, Ctrl. Mich. U., 1956, MA, 1967. Cert. fundraiser Williamsburg Devel. Inst., cert. QTM trainer. Tchr. speech and theater Standish (Mich.) Pub. Schs., 1956-58, Vassar (Mich.) Pub. Schs., 1959-67; prof. speech, adminstr. Mott C.C., Flint, Mich., 1967-89; assoc. prof. speech Palm Beach C.C., Lake Worth, Fla., 1990—2001, fundraiser, 1991-95, 2003—, faculty polit. action chairperson, 1996-97, faculty emeritus, 2001, pres. elect, 2004. Cons. in speech, Flint, Mich., 1973—89; cons. quality total mgmt.; cons. in comms. and mgmt., Lake Worth, Fla., 2001—. Pres. Homeowner Assn., Lake Worth, 1993—95, 2003—, legal chair, 2003; mem. Vassar Zoning Bd.; officer City Coun.; chair Tuscola County Dem Com., 1975—85; del., whip Dem. Conv. and Rules Com., 1976; del. Fla. Dem. Conv., 1999. Mem. United Faculty Palm Beach C.C. (chpt. pres.), Fla. Tchg. Profession, NEA, Nat. Collegiate Hons. Coun. (collegiate 1991-95), Mich. Women's Studies Assn. (pres. 1974-75), C.C. Humanities Assn., Phi Theta Kappa (leadership prof.). Presbyterian. Avocations: percussion, reading, golf, bowling, biking. Home: 4713 Rainbow Dr Lake Worth FL 33463-3610 Office: Palm Beach CC 4200 Congress Ave Lake Worth FL 33461-4705 E-mail: profashl@directvinternet.com.

ASHHURST, ANNA WAYNE, foreign language educator; b. Phila., Jan. 5, 1933; d. Astley Paston Cooper and Anne Pauline (Campbell) Ashhurst; m. Ronald G. Gerber, July 22, 1978. AB, Vassar Coll., 1954; MA, Middlebury Coll., 1956; PhD, U. Pitts., 1967. English tchr. Internat. Inst. Spain, Madrid, 1954-56; asst. prof. Juniata Coll., Huntingdon, Pa., 1961-63; asst. prof. Spanish dept. Franklin and Marshall Coll., Lancaster, Pa., 1968-74, acting chmn. Spanish dept., 1972, convenor, fgn. lang. council, 1972-74; assoc. prof. dept. modern fgn. langs. U. Mo., St. Louis, 1974-78. Author: La Literatura Hispano-Americana en la Crítica Española, 1980. Mem. Welcome Wagon of Lancaster, Pa., 1968-70, 71-74 Fulbright-Hays grantee, Colombia, S.Am., summer 1963; Ford Humanities fellow, summer 1970; Mellon fellow, 1970-71 Mem. AAUW (pres. Ferguson-Florissant br. 1989-91, 95-98, chmn. St. Louis area interbranch coun. 1992-94, chair environ. task force Mo. 1992-95, local arrangements chair for Mo. state conv. 1997, Woman of Distiction award 1998), Internat. Inst. in Spain, Instituto Internacional de Literatura Iberoamericana, Am. Assn. Tchrs. Spanish and Portuguese. Home: 2105 Barcelona Dr Florissant MO 63033-2805

ASHKIN, ROBERTA ELLEN, lawyer; b. N.Y.C., July 1, 1953; d. Sidney and Beverly Ashkin. BA magna cum laude, Hofstra U., 1975; JD, St. John's U., N.Y.C., 1978. Bar: N.Y., 1979, U.S. Dist. Ct. (ea. and so. dists.), 1980, U.S. Dist. Ct. (no. and we. dists.) 2001. Program dir. Sta. WVHC-FM, N.Y.C., 1974-75; assoc. editor Matthew Bender, N.Y.C., 1975-79; assoc. Morris & Duffy, N.Y.C., 1979-81, Lipsig, Sullivan & Liapakis, N.Y.C., 1981-84, Julien & Schlesinger, P.C., N.Y.C., 1984-89; adminstrv. law judge N.Y.C. Dept. [illegible] & Glaser, P.C., N.Y.C., 1991-96, Baron & Budd, P.C., N.Y.C., 1996—2002; pvt. practice, 2002—. Chmn. bd. Actor's Classical Troupe, 1987-89; bd. dirs. Daytop Village Found., 2002-03; sr. dir. women's policy Gephardt for Pres. 2004 Campaign. Mem.: ATLA, Trial Lawyers for Pub. Justice (bd. dirs.), N.Y. Trial Lawyers Assn. (dep. treas. 2001, sec. 2002, 2003, bd. dirs., sec. 2003), N.Y. State Bar Assn., Phi Beta Kappa.

ASHLEIGH, CAROLINE, art and antiques appraiser; BA, Worcester (Mass.) Coll., 1973; cert. in appraisal studies, NYU, 1994. Profl. lectr. on connoisseurship; appraiser Home and Garden TV; edn. dept. staff Cranbrook Art Mus., Bloomfield Hills, 1997—; columnist Detroit Monthly Mag., 1988—; edn. dept. staff Detroit Inst. Art, 1988—; regional rep. William Doyle Auctioneers, N.Y.C., 1997—2000; columnist Detroit Legal News, 1998—. Appraiser Chubbs Antique Roadshow, WGBH-TV, Boston, 1996—; cons. Southeby's; lectr. in field. Columnist: Antiques Roadshow Insider, Mich. Bar Jour., Detroit Monthly, 1995—96, Hour Detroit mag.; subject of feature presentations N.Y. Times, Art and Antiques, Detroit Free Press, Antique Trader Mag., others. Mem. Appraisers Assn. Am. (bd. cert.; Midwest regional rep.), Detroit Inst. Arts, Cranbrook Art Mus. Home: 800 E Lincoln St Birmingham MI 48009-1784

ASHLEY, ELIZABETH, actress; b. Ocala, Fla., Aug. 30, 1941; d. Arthur Kingman and Lucille (Ayer) Cole; m. George Peppard (div.); 1 son, Christian Moore; m. James Michael McCarthy. Student ballet with, Tatiana Semenova; student, La. State U., 1957-58; grad., Neighborhood Playhouse, N.Y.C., 1961. Apptd. Pres.'s council 1st Nat. Council on the Arts, 1965-69; dir. Am. Film Inst., 1968-72 Appeared on Broadway in The Highest Tree, 1961, Take Her, She's Mine, 1962, Barefoot in the Park, 1963; motion pictures include The Carpet Baggers, 1963, Ship of Fools, 1964, The Third Day, 1965, Marriage of a Young Stockbroker, 1971, Paperback Hero, 1974, Golden Needles, 1974, Rancho Deluxe, 1975, 92 in the Shade, 1976, The Great Scout and Cathouse Thursday, 1976, Coma, 1978, Windows, 1980, Paternity, 1981, Lookin' to Get Out, 1982, Split Image, 1982, Dragnet, 1987, Dangerous Curves, 1987, A Man of Passion, 1988, Vampire's Kiss, 1989, Mallrats, 1995, Sleeping Together, 1997, Happiness, 1998, Just the Ticket, 1999; TV work includes (series) Evening Shade, CBS, 1990-94; TV movies include When Michael Calls, 1972, Second Chance, 1972, The Heist, 1972, Your Money or Your Wife, 1972, One of My Wives is Missing, 1976, The War Between the Tates, 1977, A Fire in the Sky, 1978, Svengali, 1983, Stage Coach, 1986, He's Fired, She's Hired, 1984, Warm Hearts, Cold Feet, 1987, The Two Mrs. Grenvilles, 1987, Orleans (series), The Rope, Blue Bayou, 1990, Reason for Living: The Jill Ireland Story, 1991, In the Best Interest of the Children, 1992, (mini series) The Buccaneers, 1995; stage appearances include The Enchanted, Washington, 1973, The Skin of Our Teeth, Washington, Broadway, 1975, Cat on a Hot Tin Roof, Stratford, Conn. and Broadway, 1974, Agnes of God; author: Postcards from the Road, 1978; TV guest appearances include Murder, She Wrote, Law & Order, The Larry Sanders Show, B.L. Stryker, Women ot the House, Burke's Law, others. Recipient Antoinette Perry award, 1962 Mem. Actors Equity, Screen Actors Guild, AFTRA. Office: Writers and Artists Agy 19 W 44th St Ste 1000 New York NY 10036-6095

ASHLEY, ELLA JANE (ELLA JANE RADER), medical technologist; b. Dewitt, Ark., Mar. 6, 1941; d. Clayton Ervin and Emma Mae (Coleman) Funderburk; m. Albert Ashley, Sept. 27, 1957 (div. Nov. 1962); 1 child, Cynthia Gayle. Student, Westark Community Coll. Cert. clin. lab. technologist, clin. lab. scientist. Lab. asst. U. Ark. Med. Ctr., Little Rock, 1966-67; lab. technician II, rschr. in lithium carbonate Ark. State Hosp., Little Rock, 1967-68; staff technologist Cooper Clinic, Ft. Smith, Ark., 1969-71; asst. chief technologist Lab. of Am. (Labcorp), Ft. Smith, 1972—, ops. mgr., 1997—2003; ret. Lab. of America (Labcorp), 2003. Mem. profl. adv. panel Med. Lab. Observer, 1976—. Research in lithium carbonate. Mem.: Am. Soc. Med. Tech. Methodist. Avocations: travel, theater, concerts, painting. Home: 1310 S Houston St Fort Smith AR 72901-7271

ASHLEY, KATHLEEN LABONIS, music educator; d. Edward Francis and Modesta Bubnis Labonis; m. Richard Raymond Ashley, Nov. 24, 1984; children: Christopher, Lisa. MusB, Immaculata Coll., Pa., 1979; MusM in Edn., Temple U., Phila., 1984. Cert. instrnl. II Pa. Secondary tchr. St. Basil Acad., Jenkintown, Pa., 1979—88; elem. tchr. St. Martin of Tours Dept. of Performing Arts, Phila., 1980—82; pre-sch. tchr. The Curiosity Shoppe, Doylestown, Pa., 1990—96; elem. tchr. Our Lady of Mt. Carmel, Doylestown, Pa., 1995—2000, St. Jude Sch., Chalfont, Pa., 1997—. Performing arts camp tchr. Brown Bag Arts Festival, Doylestown, Pa., 1991—96; ch. musician, performer St. Jude, Chalfont, Pa., 1997—. Composer: (songs) St. Jude School Song, 1997; arranger: instrumental music, 1979—; co-author: Pre-sch. and Elem. Sch. shows, 1990—2003. Steering com. for mid. states evaluation St. Basil Acad., Jenkintown, Pa., 1985; tchr. St. Jude Sch., Chalfont, Pa., 1994—. Scholar, Immaculata U., 1975—79. Mem.: Pa. Music Educators Assn., Nat. Cath. Educators Assn., Music Educators Nat. Conf. Avocations: drawing, painting, gardening, writing. Office: St Jude Sch 323 W Butler Ave Chalfont PA 18914

ASHLEY, LOIS A. retired university reference librarian; b. Detroit, Aug. 1, 1942; d. S. Elbert and Gertrude B. Hobson; m. Melvin Allen Ashley, June 27, 1964 (dec. Nov. 1996); children: Scott E., Paul D., Craig R. AA, William Tyndale Coll., Farmington Hills, Mich., 1989, BA in Humanities, 1991; MS in LS, Wayne State U., 1993. Spl. corr. Mich. Blue Shield, Detroit, 1963-68; reservation agt. United Airlines, Dearborn, Mich., 1968-70; asst. Office of Records and Registration William Tyndale Coll., 1989-91; grad. rsch. asst. Wayne State U., Detroit, 1992-93; reference libr. U. Detroit Mercy, 1993-99; adj. Oakland C.C., 2000—. Organist Gracious Savior Luth. Ch., 2000—; mem. Friends of the Detroit Pub. Libr.; founding chair ret. mem. roundtable Mich. Libr. Assn., 2001. Recipient scholarships. Mem. ALA (Black Caucus), AAUW, Assn. Coll. and Rsch. Librs., Mich. Libr. Assn., Nat. Coun. Negro Women, Founders Soc. Detroit Inst. Arts, Women of the Evang. Luth. Ch. in Am., Beta Phi Mu, Delta Epsilon Chi. Mem. Evang. Luth. Ch. in Am. Home: 19934 Mark Twain St Detroit MI 48235-1607

ASHLEY, LYNN, social sciences educator, consultant; b. Rock Island, Ill., Nov. 18, 1920; d. Francis Ford and Cleo Marguerite (Monahan) Haynes; m. Edward Messenger Ashley, Aug. 16, 1946; children: Edward Jr., Ann Rice, Rebecca Pocisk, William. BS in Social Psychology, Union Inst., Cin., 1978; MEd., U. Cin., 1979, EdD, 1985. Clk. Lumberman's Mutual Casualty Co., Chgo., 1940-41; account asst. Quaker Oats Co., Chgo., 1941-43; riveter Douglas Aircraft Co., Chgo., 1943-44; organizer, dir. Forest Park Youth Ctr., Forest Park, Ohio, 1967-73; staffing coord. Presbytery of Cin., 1973-78; grad. teaching asst. U. Cin., 1978-84; pres. Nat. Corrective Tng. Inst., Cin., 1979—. Cons., trainer Hamilton County Probation Dept., Warren County Juvenile Ct., 1987—, Allen County Juvenile Ct., Worth Ctr., Allen County, field rep.; adj. faculty Union Inst., 1986—, mem. undergrad. studies bd., mem. doctoral dissertation com. Spkr., adv. women vets. to schs. and orgns.; mem. Cin.-Harare, Zimbabwe Sister Cities Assn., 1989—, Ohio Gov.'s Adv. Com. on Women Vets., 1993—99; with Women in Mil. Svc. for Am. Councilwoman City of Forest Park, 1981—85, organizer cmty. rels. coun., 1983. With WAC, 1944—46. Recipient in Recognition award Forest Park City Coun., 1985, In Appreciation award Union Inst., 1987, Recognition award AMVETS, U. Cin., 1993, award Commonwealth of Ky., 1989; inducted into Ohio Vets. Hall of Fame, 1999. Mem. Am. Corrections Assn., Nat. Assn. Corrective Tng. Affiliates (pres. 1987), Women's Army Corp Vet. Assn. (selected rep. to dedication of Dole Inst. of Politics), Assn. Family and Conciliation Cts., Am. Probation and Parole Assn. Avocations: photography, foreign travel, computers, camping, fishing. Office: Nat Corrective Tng Inst 811 Hanson Dr Cincinnati OH 45240-1921 Office Phone: 513-825-9206.

ASHLEY, [illegible], [illegible] school educator; b. Schenectady, N.Y., Feb. 16, 1917; d. Richard J. and Margaret [illegible]; m. John Edward Ashley, Aug. 20, 1940 (dec.); children: Richard M.(dec.), John E. Jr., Willard Bishop. BA cum laude, SUNY, Albany, 1955, MA, 1958, cert. in French, Goucher Coll., 1959. Tchr. Burnt Hills-Ballston Lake H.S., Burnt Hills, NY, 1956, Roger B. Taney Jr. High Sch., Camp Springs, Md., Oxon Hill (Md.) Sr. H.S. Contbr. commentaries Kerrville Times. Sec. AAUW, Kerrville, Tex., 1976—80, pres., 1980—82; chmn., patron Kerrville Performing Arts Soc., 1980—2001; active Point Theatre, Schreiner U. Recipient Lifetime Achievement award, Hill Country Arts Found., 2003. Mem.: LWV, Animal Welfare Soc. Kerr County, Hill Country Arts Found. Unitarian Universalist. Home: 8 Chaparral Dr Kerrville TX 78028

ASHLEY, MARY J. media specialist; b. Murphy, NC, July 9, 1948; d. Forrest Bernard and Alice Evangeline Johnson; children: Stephanie R., Phillip J. BS in edn., Western Carolina U., 1970, MA in edn., 1979; EdS in lib. sci., Appalachian State U., 1989. Cert. tchr. NC, 1970, media coord. NC, 1989. Tchr. Cumberland County BOE, Fayetteville, NC, Roberson County BOE, Lumberton, NC, Clay County BOE, Hayesville, NC, St. Joseph (Md.) City Sch., Fainn County BOE, Blue Ridge, Ga., Cherokee County BOE, Murphy, NC, media coord., 1985—. Author: Learn NC Website, 2002. Chaplain Ranger Grange, Murphy, 2000—02. Mem.: NC Assn. Sch. Lib. (sec. 1995—2002), Alpha Iota, Delta Kappa Gamma (pres. 2002—04). Baptist. Avocations: reading, sewing, crafts, travel. Office: Hiwassee Dam Elem Mid Sch 336 Blue Eagle Cl Murphy NC 28906

ASHLEY, RENEE, writer, creative writing educator, consultant; b. Palo Alto, Calif., Aug. 10, 1949; BA in English with honors, BA in French, BA in World and Comparative Lit., San Francisco State U., 1979, MA, 1981. Instr. creative writing West Milford (N.J.) Cmty. Sch., 1983-85; instr. creative writing, cons. artist residencies Rockland Ctr. for Arts, West Nyack, NY, 1985—; mem. MFA in Creative Writing faculty Fairleigh Dickinson U., 2001—. Author: Salt, 1991 (Brittingham prize in Poetry 1991), The Various Reasons of Light, 1998, The Revisionist's Dream, 2001, Someplace Like This, 2003; contbr. to anthologies including Touching Fire: Erotic Writings by Women, 1989, What's a Nice Girl Like You?, 1992, Breaking Up Is Hard to Do, 1994, Dog Music, 1996, (textbook) Writing Poems, 1995; contbr. to American Voice, Antioch Rev., Harvard Rev., Kenyon Rev., Poetry. Fellow N.J. State Coun. Arts, 1985, 89, 94, 2003, Yaddo, Saratoga Springs, N.Y., 1990, McDowell Colony, Peterborogh, N.H., 1993-94, NEA, 1997-98; grantee Poets and Writers, Inc., 1986, N.Y. State Coun. Arts, 1986; recipient Washington prize in poetry Word Works, Inc., 1986, Lit. Excellence award, Kenyon Review, 1990, 92, Pushcart prize, 2000. Mem. MLA, Acad. Am. Poets, Poetry Soc. Am. (Ruth Lake Meml. award 1987, Robert H. Winner award 1989). Office: University of Wisconsin Press 1930 Monroe St #3rd Fl Madison WI 53711-2059 E-mail: reneea@verizion.net.

ASHLEY, SHARON ANITA, pediatric anesthesiologist; b. Goulds, Fla., Dec. 28, 1948; d. John H. Ashley and Johnnie Mae (Everett) Ashley-Mitchell; m. Clifford K. Sessions, Sept. 1977 (div. 1985); children: Cecili, Nicole, Erika. BA, Lincoln U., 1970; postgrad., Pomona Coll., 1971; MD, Hahnemann Med. Sch., Phila., 1976; M in Pub. Health, UCLA, 2000; M in bus. admin., Claremont Grad. U., 2003. Diplomate Am. Bd. Pain Mgmt., Am. Bd. Anesthesiologists. Intern pediatrics Martin Luther King Hosp., L.A., 1976-77, resident pediatrics, 1977-78, resident anesthesiology, 1978-81, mem. staff, 1981—; assoc. dean grad. med. edn. Charles Drew U. Medicine and Sci., 2002—. Named Outstanding Tchr. of Yr., King Drew Med. Ctr., Dept. Anesthesia, 1989, Outstanding Faculty of Yr., 1991. Mem. Am. Soc. Anesthesiologists, Calif. Med. Assn., L.A. County Med. Soc., Soc. Regional Anesthesia, Soc. Pediatric Anesthesia. Democrat. Baptist. Avocations: reading, crocheting, sailing. Office: Martin Luther King Hosp 12021 Wilmington Ave Los Angeles CA 90059-3099 Home: 5646 Alix Ct Torrance CA 90503-1876

ASHLEY-IVERSON, MARY E. retired librarian; b. L.A., Oct. 30, 1947; d. Curtis Lee Gosey and Allie Mae Sheppard-Gosey; m. Billy G. Ashley Sr., Nov. 14, 1965 (dec. Apr. 17, 1995); children: Billy G. Ashley Jr., Dexter Arnett(dec.) ; m. Willis Iverson Sr., July 6, 1997. Grad., Centennial H.S., Compton, Calif., 1965. Libr. asst. Crenshaw H.S., L.A., 1982—84; libr. clk. Stuttgart (Ark.) Pub. Libr., 1992—99; ret., 1999. Chmn. Records Preservation Com., Stuttgart-DeWitt, 2000—; rec. sec. Stuttgart Civic League, Stuttgart, 1988—91; mem. Wall of Tolerance Nat. Com. for Tolerance, 2001; bd. dirs. There Is Hope, Humphrey, Ark., 1995—, Resource Ctr. Aging, Stuttgart, 2000—. Recipient Dedicated Cmty. Svc. award, Modern Woodman Am., 1993. Mem.: NAACP. Democrat. Baptist. Avocations: coins, antiques, crystal. Home: 301 W Taft Stuttgart AR 72160-2600

ASHTON, BETSY FINLEY, broadcast journalist, author, lecturer; b. Wilkes-Barre, Pa., May 13, 1944; d. Charles Leonard Hancock Jones and Margaretta Betty (Hart) Jones Layton; m. Arthur Benner Ashton, Nov. 5, 1966 (div. 1972); m. Robert Clarke Freed, May 18, 1974 (div. 1981); m. Jacob B. Underhill III, Oct. 17, 1987. BA, Am. U., 1966; postgrad., Corcoran Sch. Art, 1968; postgrad. in fine arts, Am. U., 1969-71; student in painting, Corcoran Sch. Art, 1968. Tchr. art Fairfax County (Va.) Pub. Schs., 1967-70; reporter, anchor Sta. WWDC, Washington, 1972-73, Sta. WMAL-AM-FM, Washington, 1973-75; corr. Sta. WTTG-TV, Washington, 1975-76, Sta. WJLA-TV, Washington, 1976-82; consumer corr. CBS News and Sta. WCBS-TV, N.Y.C., 1982-86; sr. corr. Today's Bus., 1986-87; personal fin. contbr. CBS Morning Program, 1987, Lifetime Cable TV, 1988—; anchor FNN Money Talk, 1989; exec. editor Great Giving, 2000—. Bd. dirs. Lowell E. Mellett Fund for a Free and Responsible Press, Washington, 1979-82; courtroom artist numerous trials, Washington, 1978-81. Reporter TV news report Caffeine, 1981 (AAUW award 1982); reporter spot news 6 P.M. News, 1979 (Emmy award); author: Betsy Ashton's Guide to Living on Your Own, 1988. Concert master of ceremonies Beethoven Soc., Washington, 1979-82. Recipient Laurel award Columbia Journalism Rev., 1984, Outstanding Alumna award Am. U., 1985, Outstanding Media award Am. U., 1986, Best Consumer Journalism citation Nat. Press Club, 1983. Mem. AFTRA, NATAS, Author's Guild, Newswomen's Club N.Y., Soc. Profl. Journalists (pres. N.Y. chpt. 1994, 2000, Washington chpt. 1980-81, bd. dirs. N.Y. chpt. 1989—, co-chair 2004 nat. conv.), Friends of Thirteen (bd. dirs. 1995—), Sigma Delta Chi Found. (bd. dirs. 1996—), Alpha Chi Omega (v.p. chpt. 1964-66). Avocations: painting, drawing, golf.

ASHTON, DORE, writer, educator; b. Newark; d. Ralph N. and Sylvia (Ashton) Shapiro; m. Adja Yunkers, July 8, 1952 (dec. 1983); children—Alexandra Louise, Marina Svietlana; m. Matti Megged, 1985. BA, U. Wis., 1949; MA, Harvard U., 1950; PhD honoris causa, Moore Coll., 1975, Hamline U., 1982; attended, Minn. Coll. of Art, 2002. Asso. editor Art Digest, 1951-54, asso. critic N.Y. Times, 1955-60; lectr. Pratt Inst., 1962-63; head humanities dept. (Sch. Visual Arts), 1965-68; prof. Cooper Union, 1968—. Art critic, lectr., dir. exhbns. in arts; mem. adv. bd. John Simon Guggenheim Found, Dedalus Found. Author: Abstract Art Before Columbus, 1957, Poets and the Past, 1959, Philip Guston, 1960, The Unknown Shore, 1962, Rauschenberg's Dante, 1964, Modern American Sculpture, 1968, Richard Lindner, 1969, A Reading of Modern Art, 1970, Pol Bury, 1971; Cultural Guide for New York, 1972; Picasso on Art, 1972, The New York School: A Cultural Reckoning, 1973, A Joseph Cornell Album, 1974, Yes, But, A Critical Biography of Philip Guston, 1976, A Fable of Modern Art, 1980, American Art Since 1945, 1982, About Rothko, 1983, Jacobo Borges, 1984, 20th Century Artists on Art, 1985, Out of the Whirlwind, 1987, Fragonard in the Universe of Painting, 1988, Terence La Noue, 1992, Noguchi East and West, 1992, Ursula van Rydingsvard, 1995, The Delicate Thread: Teshigahara's Life in Art, 1997, À Rebours: La Rebellión Informalista, 1999, The Black Rainbow: The Work of Fernando de Szyszlo, 2003, The Walls of the Heart: The Work of David Rankin, 2001, William Tucker, 2001; also monographs; co-author: (with Denise Browne [illegible], 1981); co-editor: Redon, Moreau, Bresdin, 1961; N.Y. contbg. editor Studio Internat, 1961-74, Opus Internat, 1968-74, XXième Siècle, 1955-70; assoc. editor Arts, 1974-92; contbr. to: Vision and Value series (Gyorgy Kepes), 1966, The New Art Anthology (Gregory Battcock), 1966. Adv. bd. Guggenheim Found. Recipient Mather award for art criticism Coll. Art Assn., 1963, Art Criticism prize St. Louis Art Mus., 1988; Guggenheim fellow, 1964; Graham fellow, 1963; Ford Found. fellow, 1960; Nat. Endowment for Humanities grantee, 1980 Mem. Internat. Assn. Art Critics, Phi Beta Kappa. Home: 217 E 11th St New York NY 10003-7302 Office: Cooper Union Advancement Sci and Art 41 Cooper Sq New York NY 10003-7136

ASHWELL, RACHEL, entrepreneur, interior designer; b. Eng. children: Lily, Jake. Founder Shabby Chic by Rachel Ashwell Label, L.A., 1989—. Author: Shabby Chic, 1996, Rachel Ashwell's Shabby Chic Treasure Hunting and Decorating Guide, 1998, The Shabby Chic Home, 2000, The Shabby Chic Gift of Giving, 2001. Office: Rachel Ashwell Shabby Chic 6330 Arizona Cir Los Angeles CA 90045*

ASHWORTH, JULIE, elementary school educator; Tchr. Hawthorne Elem. Sch., Sioux Falls, S.D., 1990—. Participant Internat. Space Camp, Huntsville, Ala., 1993; S.D. tchr. participant Goals 2000 Forum, U.S. Dept. Edn., Washington, 1993; mem. S.D. Gov.'s Adv. Coun. on Cert. for Tchrs., 1994—; mem. exceptional needs standards com. Nat. Bd. for Profl. Tchg. Stds., Washington, 1994—; initiator, organizer S.D. Tchrs. Forum, 1994. Named S.D. Tchr. of Yr., Sioux Falls Sch. Dist., 1992, S.D. Elem. Tchr. of Yr., 1993. Home: 2015 Pendar Ln Sioux Falls SD 57105-3022 Office: Hawthorne Elem Sch 601 N Spring Ave Sioux Falls SD 57104-2721

ASKEW, PENNY SUE, choreographer, artistic director, ballet instructor; b. Fairview, Okla., Oct. 8, 1967; d. Donald Lee and Susan Lea (Johnson) A. BS in Psychology, Southwestern Okla. U., 1989, MS in Applied Psychology, 1996; MFA in Dance, U. Iowa, 2001. Ballet tchr. Western Okla. Ballet Acad., Clinton, 1986-88, owner, dir., 1988—; artistic dir. Western Okla. Ballet Theatre, Clinton, 1988—. Grad. asst. U. Iowa., 1999-2001 Choreographer: (musical theater) Oklahoma!, 1990, Kiss Me Kate, 1992, Quilters, 1993, Nunsense, 1993, Annie Get Your Gun, 1993, Guys and Dolls, 1994, Nunsense II, 1995, over 80 dance works. Named Outstanding Choreographer, RDA Nat. Craft of Choreography Con 1996, 98. Mem. Regional Dance Am./S.W. (sec. 1991—), Clinton Art in the Park Com. 1990-99, 2002, Kiwanis (bd. dirs. Clinton club 1996-97,2002-2003). Democrat. Avocations: reading, attending arts events. Office: Western Okla Ballet Theatre PO Box 1593 Clinton OK 73601-1593 E-mail: penask@earthlink.net.

ASKEY, THELMA J. federal agency administrator; b. Lakehurst, N.J. BA, Tenn. Tech. U., 1970; postgrad., George Washington U., Am. U. Press asst. Rep. John Duncan, 1972-74; editor Nat. Rsch. Coun. Marine Bd., 1974-76; asst. minority trade counsel Ho. Com. Ways and Means, 1976-79, minority trade counsel, 1979-94; staff dir. subcommitttee trade Ho. Com. on Ways and Means, 1995-98; commr. U.S. Internat. Trade Commn., Washington, 1998—2000; dir. U.S. Trade and Devel. Agy., Arlington, Va., 2001—. Office: US Trade and Devel Agy Office Dir 1000 Wilson Blvd Ste 1600 Arlington VA 22209-3901

ASKINS, JARI, lawyer, department chairman, state representative; b. Duncan, Okla., Apr. 27, 1953; d. Ollie M. and Jarita Askins. BA in Journalism, U. Okla., 1975, JD, 1980. Bar: Okla. V.p. closing office Stephens County Abstract Co., Duncan, Okla.; spl. dist. judge Stephens County, Okla., 1982—90; chmn. Okla. Pardon and Parole Bd., Okla. City, 1991—92; dep. gen. counsel Gov.'s Office, 1992—94; rep. Ho. of Reps., State of Okla., Okla. City, 1995—. Dep. majority fl. leader Okla. Ho. Reps., Okla. City, 2001—; mem. Okla. Judicial Conf., Okla. City. Mem Leadership Okla.; bd. trustees Cottey Jr. Coll., Nevada, Mo. Named to Okla. Woman's Hall of Fame, 2001. Mem.: ABA, Duncan C. of C. (Woman of Yr. 1995), Stephen's County Bar Assn., Okla. Bar Assn., Lions Club. Democrat. Office: 2300 N Lincoln Blvd Rm 301B Oklahoma City OK 73105 Home and Office: PO Box 391 Duncan OK 73534 E-mail: askinsja@lsb.state.ok.us.

ASKINS, NANCY ELLEN PAULSEN, training and organizational development professional; b. St. Paul, Nov. 2, 1948; d. Charles A. and Stasia (Sawicki) Paulsen; m. Arthur J. Askins, Apr. 28, 1979. BS in Home Econs., U. Cin., 1970, BS in Edn., 1971, MEd, 1972; postgrad., SUNY-Buffalo, 1974-76, Temple U., 1976, Walden U., 1988-92; student, Inst. Fin. Edn., 1982-85, cert. in mgmt., Am. Mgmt. Assn./Monmouth Coll., 1984. Cert. gaming supr. Edn. Inst. Am. Hotel and Motel Assn., cert. strategic planning facilitator; cert. quality mgr. Asst. aquatic supr. Cin. Recreation Commn., 1969-72; student affairs adminstr. U. Cin., 1970-72; mem. faculty student affairs adminstrn. Tex. Luth. Coll., 1972-73; mem. faculty, student affairs adminstr. SUNY-Geneseo, 1974-76; student affairs adminstr. Temple U., 1976-78; tchr. drug awareness coord. Adams Sch. Harlandale Sch. Dist., San Antonio, 1973-74; career life ins. agt., fin. planning cons. Phoenix Mut. Life Ins. Co., Phila., 1978-81; registered rep., securities agt. Phoenix Equity Planning Corp., Phila., 1980-81; owner Paulsen-Askins Fin. Svcs., Somers Point, N.J., 1980-81; mem. women's task force Phoenix Cos., 1980-81; tng. svcs. coord. Collective Fed. Savs. & Loan Assn., Egg Harbor City, N.J., 1981-82, asst. v.p., tng. dir., 1982-84; tng. mgr. Shore Meml. Hosp., Somers Point, N.J., 1984-86, wellness instr., 1984-89, dir. ednl. devel., 1986-89; dir edn. svcs. Holy Cross Hosp., Ft. Lauderdale, Fla., 1990-91, dir. cmty. and vol. svcs., 1991-94, part-time instr. wellness program, 1991-94; v.p. tng. and assoc. devel. Grand Casino, Biloxi, 1994-96; tng. svcs. coord. Gulf Coast Bus. Svcs., Gulfport, Miss., 1996-98; quality mgr. Hollywood Casino Resort/Tunica, Robinsonville, Miss., 1998—. Adj. prof. bus. and social scis. Atlantic C.C. Coll., Mays Landing, N.J., 1986-89; facilitator Assertiveness Tng. Group, Interpersonal Comms. Group, orgnl. and leadership devel. seminars and cons.; owner, exec. corp. cons. Askins Tng. and Cons., 1981—; mem. bd. examiners Malcolm Baldridge Nat. Quality Award, 2001, Pres.'s Quality Award, 2000, Tenn. Quality Award, 2000, Miss. Quality Award, 1999, 2000; instr. Inst. Fin. Edn., 1982-85, Ednl. Inst., Am. Hotel ad Motel Assn., 1999—; workshop presenter and spkr. in field; items writer Cert. Quality Improvement Assoc. Agy. chmn. United Way Campaign, Phila., 1979, 80; bd. dirs. South Jersey Regional Theater, 1983-86, chmn., 1983-84; active ann. Muscular Dystrophy Telethon, Phila.; active Girl Scouts U.S., 1956-74, 84—; mem. Parish coun., parish enrichment com., 1984-88, cantor St. Joseph Roman Cath. Ch., Somers Point, 1979-89; mem., lector Christ the King Cath. Ch., Southaven, Miss., 1998—; chmn. com. Women's Club St. Luke's Cath. Ch., Coconut Creek, Fla., 1992-94, parish coun., 1993-94; bd. dirs. Holly Shores Coun. Girl Scouts U.S., 1984-85; host fgn. exch. students Am. Scandinavian Student Exch. Program, 1985-87; mem. Somers Point Bd. Edn., 1986; mem. Libr. Adv. Bd. City of Margate, Fla., 1991-94, fundraising chmn., vice chmn., chmn. Recipient Brotherhood-Sisterhood Achievers award NCCJ, 1985, Rising Star award, 1997, Gold Dir. award, 1998 Carlson Learning Co., Minn.; named Biloxi Career Woman Bus. Profl. Women/Lighthouse of Biloxi, 1995, Women of Achievement Woman of Yr. Bus. Profl. Women Clarksdale, Coahoma County, Miss., 1999. Mem. N. Miss. chap. Am. Hotel & Motel Assn. (charter pres. 1999), Bus. and Profl. Women Robinsonville, Miss. (charter pres. 1999-2000), Bus. and Profl. Women Clarksdale (legis. com. chair, 1998-2000), Bus. and Profl. Women Lighthouse of Biloxi, Miss. (v.p. membership, newsletter ed., young careerist chair, chair 1997 Nat. Bus. Women's Week, selected Biloxi Career Woman, 1995, Bus. and Profl. Women Miss. (state 2d v.p., state membership chair, 1996-97, state legis. chair, 1999-20000, Greater Camden Assn. Life Underwriters (chmn. Life Ins. Week for South Jersey 1978-79, bd. dir. 1979-81, pub. rels. chmn. 1979-81, chmn. state edn. 1981), Am. Soc. for Quality (features editor Competitive Advantage quality divsn. 2000—), Am. Soc. Tng. and Devel. (treas. S. Jersey chpt., nat. dir. savs. and lending industry group 1983-84, hosps. and healthcare industry group 1984-86, nat. conf. speaker 1984-94, sec. Greater Broward/Ft. Lauderdale chpt, 1991, pres.-elect 1992, pres. 1993, nat. dir.-elect 1990-91, dir. 1991-92, Interfaith Trainers Cons. Network), Am. Hosp. Assn., Am. Soc. Health Edn. and Tng., Am. Mgmt. Assn., Fla. Soc. Healthcare Edn. and Tng., Greater Mainland C. of C. (v.p., treas., membership coord. 1979-89, Pres. award 1983), U. Cin. Alumni of Greater Phila. Area (pres. 1980-89), Greater Ft. Lauderdale C. of C. (diplomat 1992-93, edn. com. 1993-94), Alliance/The Women's Network (bd. dir. 1983-84), Rotary Internat., Rotary of Gulfport, MS, Rotary of Robinsonville, MS (sect. 1999, newsletter ed. 1998-99, pres.-elect 1999-2000, pres. 2000-2001), Rotary Dist. 6800 (chairperson, long range planning com. 1999-2001, mem. group study exch. com. 1999-2000, youth study exch. com. 1999-2000, chmn. matching grants com. 2001-2002). Democrat. Home: PO Box 445 915 Onondaga St Lewiston NY 14092 E-mail: quality4u@earthlink.net., nancyaskins@hwcc-tunica.com.

ASKOV, EUNICE MAY, adult education educator; b. St. Louis, Nov. 20, 1940; d. David Hull and Marjorie Jane (Gutgsell) Nicholson; m. Warren Hopkins Askov, Jan. 22, 1967; children: David, Karen. BA in English, Denison U., 1962; MA in English, U. Wis., 1966, PhD in Curriculum and Instrn., 1969. English and reading tchr. Rich Twp. High Sch., Park Forest, Ill., 1962-64; reading svc. reading specialist U. Wis., Madison, 1965-66, project asst. Wis. R & D Ctr. for Cognitive Learning, 1966-67, rsch. assoc., 1969-72, lectr. dept. curriculum and instrn., 1968-69; coord. adult basic edn. programs U. Wis. Extension, 1966-67; remedial reading specialist Lincoln Jr. High Sch., Madison, 1966; adult basic edn. tchr. Madison Vocat., Tech. and Adult Schs., 1967-68; asst. prof. elem. edn. Minn. State U., Bemidji, 1972-74; assoc. prof. Pa. State U., University Park, 1974-79, prof. edn., 1980—2001, disting. prof., 2001—. Presenter seminars on adult edn., Germany, 1986, 93; cons., speaker in field; mem. editorial bd. Jour. Ednl. Rsch., Adult Edn. Quarterly, Adult Basic Edn., Am. Reading Forum Yearbook; mem. steering com. Adult Literacy and Tech.; mem. panel nat. work group on cancer and literacy Nat. Cancer Inst.; organizer, coord. Pa. State Coalition for Adult Literacy; mem. adv. coun. Nat. Coalition for Literacy. Contbr. articles to profl. publs. Fulbright sr. scholar, 1983; Literacy Leader fellow Nat. Inst. for Literacy, 1994-95; recipient Alumni Achievement award U. Wis.-Madison Sch. of Edn., 1994, Career Achievement award Pa. State Coll. Edn.; Disting. fellow Flinders U. Inst. Internat. Edn., Australia, 1998. Mem. Am. Assn. Adult and Continuing Edn. (chair, mem. various coms., bd. dirs.),Commn. Profs. of Adult Edn., Am. Edn. Rsch. Assn., Am. Reading Forum, Internat. Reading Assn. (chair, mem. various coms.), Keystone State Reading Assn., Mid-State Literacy Coun. (bd. dirs., pers. com., long range planning com.), Mid-State Reading Coun. (pres.), Pa. Assn. Adult and Continuing Edn., Phi Beta Kappa, Phi Delta Kappa. Democrat. Methodist. Avocations: travel, aerobics, hiking, reading. Office: Pa State U Inst for Study Adult Lit 200 Rackley Bldg University Park PA 16802-3202 E-mail: ena1@psu.edu.

ASMAR, KATHLEEN, educational association administrator; b. Chgo., Dec. 30, 1952; d. Thomas Francis and Janice Elizabeth (Garrison) Martin; m. Mitchell Michael Asmar, Oct. 15, 1977; children: Michael, Elizabeth, Eric, John Philip. BA in Psychology, U. Houston, 1975; BS in Special Edn., U. So. Miss., 1996. Elem. educator Immaculate Conception Sch., Laurel, Miss., 1996—. Mem. NEA, Coun. Exceptional Children. Roman Catholic. Office: Immaculate Conception Sch 835 W 6th St Laurel MS 39440-3436

ASPENWALL, KATHRYN DEBLASIS, music educator; b. Wheeling, W.Va., Sept. 2, 1948; d. Josephine and James DeBlasis; m. James David Aspenwall, July 11, 1971; children: James David, Johanna Kathryn Caplan. MusB, U. of Cin., 1971; MusM, Duquesne U., 1979; postgrad., W. Va. U. Permanent Tchg. Cert. W.Va., 1984. Music tchr. Buckeye Local Schools, Rayland, Ohio, 1970—75; adj. instr. in flute Muskingum Coll., New Concord, Ohio, 1976—78; music tchr. Ohio County Schools, Wheeling, W.Va., 1981—2003; adj. instr. of flute West Liberty State Coll., West Liberty, W.Va., 1999—. Presenter WV Ctr. for Profl. Develop., Charleston, W.Va., 1995—; mentor Ohio County Schools, Wheeling, W.Va., 1990—2002; flutist Wheeling Symphony Orch., Wheeling, W.Va., 1970—91; co-owner The Gardens at Sunnyside, Mt. Pleasant, Ohio; keynote spkr. WV Symposium on Mentoring. Musician performer. Treas. Seceder Cemetery, Mt. Pleasant, Ohio, 1989—2003; choir dir., pianist, elder First Presbyn. Ch., Mt. Pleasant, Ohio, 1970—2003; officer - publicity Hist. Soc. of Mt. Pleasant, Mt. Pleasant, Ohio, 1995—2003. Presbyterian. Avocations: gardening, travel, painting. Home: PO Box 366 24 Union St Mount Pleasant OH 43939 E-mail: kaspenwa@1st.net.

ASPENWIND, LINDA EILEEN, social worker; b. Waterbury, Conn., Mar. 29, 1956; d. Dante Joseph and Elaine Lavorgna; m. Richard Allen Aspenwind, July 2, 1999; 1 stepchild, Ryan Suazo. BA in Theater and Creative Writing, Antioch Coll., 1976; MA in Humanities, SUNY, Buffalo, 1979; MA in Counseling Psychology, Antioch New Eng. Grad. Sch., Keene, N.H., 1991. Guide, educator, translator NYSE, N.Y.C., 1981—85, corp. liaison, 1985—89; psychotherapist Monadnock Family Svcs., Keene, 1989—95; children's case mgr. Taos (N.Mex.) Colfax Mental Health, 1995—96; dir. Indian Child Welfare Act Program Taos Pueblo, 1996—. Asst. mgr. Aspenwind Native Arts, Taos Pueblo, 1998—; natural farmer, gardner Aspenwind Farm, Taos Pueblo, 1999—. Contbr. poems to lit. jours.; dir., co-author (theater piece) Disarmament 101, Antioch New Eng., 1989—91. Mem. child protection team Taos Pueblo, 1996—, mem. cmty. alcohol forum, 1998—; co-founder Shakespeare's Sisters Women's Theater Co., SUNY, Buffalo, 1977—79. Mem.: Taos Econ. Devel. Corp. (participant food sector class 2000), Taos Native Plant Soc. Avocations: cooking, yoga, hiking, cross-country skiing, animals. Home: Taos Pueblo PO Box 497 Taos NM 87571 Office: Taos Pueblo CMS PO Box 1846 Taos NM 87571 E-mail: swallow@taosnet.com., swallow@newmex.com.

ASSAEL, ALYCE, artist; b. N.Y.C., Dec. 12, 1938; d. Joseph and Betty (Abrams) Friedman; m. Henry Assael, Aug. 19, 1961; children: Shaun, Brenda. Grad., Parsons Sch. Design, 1960; BS, NYU, 1960, M in Am. Folk Art, 1985. Window designer Henri Bendel, N.Y.C., 1960; interior store designer Macy's, N.Y.C., 1960-62; interior showroom designer Glenn of Mich., N.Y.C., 1962-63; illustrator for fashion catalogs and promotion pieces, N.Y.C., 1962-63; fine artist paintings and photographs, N.Y.C., 1964-70. Exhibited works in solo shows U. Pa., Phila., 1975, Ann Harper Gallery, Amagansett, N.Y., 1995; group shows at Louise Himmelfarb Gallery, Southampton,. N.Y., 1980, M.J. Green Gallery, Bridgehampton, N.Y., 1980, Guild Hall Mus., East Hampton, N.Y., 1997, 98, 99, 2001, The Creative Merge Gallery, Southampton, N.Y., 2003, Stoa Gallery, Forest Hills, N.Y., 2004; curator, catalog author Singular Visions show. Mem. Guild Hall Mus., Mus. Modern Art, Mus. Am. Folk Art, Queens Mus., Mus. of Women in the Arts. Avocations: photography, theatre, film.

ASSIE-LUMUMBA, N'DRI T. Africana studies educator; b. Potossou, Ivory Coast, 1952; d. Kouassi and Yaha (Kokora) Assie. Studnet, U. Abidjan, Ivory Coast, 1970-71; BA, U. Lyon, France, 1972; MA, U. Lyon, 1975; postgrad., U. Laval, Que., Can., 1976; PhD, U. Chgo., 1982. Rchr. U. Abidjan, 1975-76; postdoctoral fellow U. Houston, 1982-83; tchr., adminstr. U. Benin, CIRSSED, Lome, Togo, 1983-88; vis. Bard Coll., Annandale, N.Y., 1989, Vassar Coll., Poughkeepsie, N.Y., 1989-90; resident fellow Internat. Inst. for Ednl. Planning, Paris, 1990; dep. dir. Pan African Studies and Rsch. Ctr., Abidjan, 1996—; prof. Africana studies Cornell U., Ithaca, N.Y., 1991—. Cons. UNESCO, Paris, 1989, 94, UN Devel. Program, N.Y.C., 1997, 99, Forum for African Women, Nairobi, Kenya, 1997, Rockefeller Found., N.Y.C., 1999. Author: Les Africaine dans la politique, 1996; editor Jour. Comparative Edn., 1998—. Ford Found. fellow, 1991; Fulbright sr. rsch. felow, 1991-92; Rockefeller Found. grantee, 1996-97. Mem. AAUW, Assn. African Women for R&D (exec. com.), Comparative and Internat. Edn. Soc., Coun. for Devel. of Social Sci. Rsch. in Africa, Cornell Inst. for Social and Econ. Rsch., Pi Lambda Theta. Avocations: music (jazz, modern, african and classical), physical exercise, modern african dance, reading. Office: Cornell U Africana Studies 310 Triphammer Rd Ithaca NY 14850-2519

ASSINK, NELLIE GRACE, agricultural executive; b. Yakima, Wash., July 5, 1920; d. Martin Gilde and Grace Byl; m. George H. Assink, July 9, 1943 (dec. Nov. 1982); children: Macile Assink Zais, Jon Martin. BA, tchr.'s diploma in music and piano, Whitman Coll./Conserv. Music, 1942; postgrad., U. Wash. and Cen. Coll., 1944, 59. Gen. cert., Wash.; cert. supr. music. English tchr., libr. Mabton (Wash.) H.S., 1943-45; libr. Wide Hollow Sch., Yakima, 1948-49; English tchr., libr. Lower Naches (Wash.) Sch., 1960-80; pres. Assink Acres, Inc., Naches, 1982—. Ch. organist Meml. Bible Ch., Yakima, 1946-82; chmn. Christian Edn. Bd., 1981-82; bd. dirs., sec. Yakima County Farm Bur., 1985-99; libr. Meml. Bible Ch., Yakima, 1960—. Mem. Naches Union Irrigation Dist. (sec. 1993—), Yakima County Farm Bur. (past sec. 1997), Lower Naches Women's Club (pres. 1984-86, 2000-02), Yakima Music Club, Ch. Librs.-N.W. (past pres.). Republican. Avocations: genealogy, photography, classical piano. Home: 681 N Gleed Rd Naches WA 98937 Office: Assink Acres Inc 681 N Gleed Rd Naches WA 98937

ASTER, RUTH MARIE RHYDDERCH, business owner; b. Cleve., Aug. 15, 1939; d. Roy William and Ruth Marie (Teckmeyer) Rhydderch; m. Ferdinand Aster, Nov. 23, 1963; children: Anneliese Ruth Aster Wilt, Christian Josef Roy. Student, Cooper Sch. Art, 1956-57; BS, Kent State U., 1962. Art tchr. North Olmsted (Ohio) Jr. and Sr. H.S., 1962; art dept. chmn. Andrews Sch. for Girls, Willoughby, Ohio, 1963-64; co-owner, treas. Aster Cabinet Shop, Chesterland, Ohio, 1963—; co-owner, v.p., treas. Ferdl Aster Ski Sch., Chesterland, 1964—; owner, v.p., sec., treas. Ferdl Aster Ski Shop, Chesterland, 1972—; owner, v.p., advt. designer, fashion buyer, tour advisor Ferdl Aster Sport Ctr., Chesterland, 1985—. Chmn. region IV U.S. Ski Assn., Colorado Springs, Colo., 1980—84, Alpine ofcl., 1983—88; ski racing coach U.S. Ski Coaches Assn., Park City, Utah, 1980—89; ski racing coach, Alpine ofcl. Fedn. Internat. Ski, Bern, Switzerland, alpine ofcl.; adv. bd. First County Bank, Chesterland, 1992—2000; adv. coun. U.S. Postal Svc., Chesterland, 1993—2000; v.p., bd. mem. in charge zoning space Lake Cardinal Timbering Corp., 2002—. Exhibited paintings and photographs to various shows, 1963—. Creator blind ski program Cleve. Sight Ctr., 1969; trustee Chesterland (Ohio) Hist. Found., 1985—, past pres., past v.p., past treas.; past chair, vice chair Chester Twp. Zoning Commr., 1987—; life friend Geauga West Libr., 1989—, bd. dirs., historian; dir. history ARC, Cleve., amb., 1999—; bd. dirs. Geauga County Libr. Found., 1998—; bd. dirs., mrm. mktg. com. Geauga County Coun. for Arts and Culture, 2002—. Mem.: North Ea. Ohio Ski Retailers Assn. (bd. dirs. 1987—), Kent State U. Alumni Pvt. Sector Bus. Alliance, Chesterland C. of C. (past pres., v.p., treas., trustee 1985—, sec. to exec. bd. 2001—, Bus. Person of Yr. 1993), Internat. Platform Assn., Cmty. Improvement Corp. Geauga County (re-orgn. com., nominating com., trustee 1990—), Kent State U. Alumni Assn. (life), Chester Study Club (past v.p., pres. 1997—2003), Gamma Delta, Alpha Psi Omega, Chi Omega. Lutheran. Avocations: reading, hiking, hunting, collecting classic autos and historic homes. Office: Ferdl Aster Ski Shop 8330 Mayfield Rd Chesterland OH 44026-2520 Office Phone: 440-729-9472. E-mail: fasterskier@prodigy.net.

ASTMAN, BARBARA ANN, artist, educator; b. Rochester, N.Y., July 12, 1950; d. George William and Bertha Dinah (Meisel) A.; m. Noel Robert Harding, Feb. 23, 1977 (div. 1983); m. Joseph Anthony Baker, Aug. 29, 1984; children: Amy Astman Baker, Laura Astman Baker. A degree, RIT, 1970; grad., Ont. Coll. Art, Toronto, 1973. Prof photography dept. Ont. Coll. Art and Design (formerly Ont. Coll. Art), Toronto, 1975—; faculty York U., Toronto, 1978-80, 86. Lectr. in field. Solo exhbns. include Baldwin St. Gallery Photography, Toronto, 1973, Ryerson Photo Gallery, Toronto, 1974, Nat. Film Bd. Can., Ottawa, 1975, S.A.W. Gallery Inc., 1976, The Sable-Castelli Gallery Ltd., Toronto, 1977, 79-84, 86, 88, 90, The Jean Marie Antone Gallery, Annapolis, Md., 1979, Whitewater Gallery, North Bay, Ont., Bruce Art Gallery, Canton, N.Y., 1980, The Mendel Art Gallery, Saskatoon, Sask., 1981, The So. Alberta Art Gallery, Edmonton, Alta., 1981, The Art Gallery Peterborough, Ont., 1982, Galerie du Musee, Musee du Quebec, 1986, Ctr. d'Animation et de Diffusion de la Photographie, Quebec, 1986, Thunder Bay Art Gallery, Ont., 1992, The Robert McLaughlin Gallery, Oshawa, Ont., 1993, McIntosh Gallery, London, Ont., 1994, Gallery Stratford, Stratford, Ont., 1994, Art Gallery of Hamilton, 1995;, The Edmonton Art Gallery, Edmonton, Alberta, The Kamloops Art Gallery, Kamloops, B.C., 1996—, Jane Corkin Gallery, 1997, 99, 2001, 2003; group exhbns. include Lamkin Camerawork Gallery, San Francisco, 1975, Art Gallery Ont., Toronto, 1975, 80, 84, 93, Rochester (N.Y.) Meml. Art Gallery, Montreal Mus. Fine Arts, 1975, Harbourfront Art Gallery, Toronto, 1977, 80, The Sable-Castelli Gallery Ltd., 77, 81, Anna Leonowens Gallery, Halifax, N.S., 1977, London (Ont.) Regional Art Gallery, 1978, 83, Edmonton (Ont.) Art Gallery, 1978, The Winnipeg Art Gallery, 1979, Everson Mus., Syracuse, N.Y., 1979, Galerie Luca Polazzoli, Milan, 1979, H.F. Johnson Mus. Art, Ithaca, N.Y., 1979, George Eastman House, Rochester, N.Y., 1979, The Hamilton (Ont.) Art Gallery, La Galerie Powerhouse, Montreal, 1981, YYZ Gallery Toronto, 1982, Forum des Halles, Paris, 1985, Graves Art Gallery, Sheffield, U.K., 1985, San Diego Art Ctr., 1986, Hallwalls Gallery, Buffalo, 1986, La Galerie des Arts Lavalin, Montreal, 1988, Pro Mus. Contemporary Art, Finland, 1988, The Kamloops (B.C.) Art Gallery, 1989, The Koffler Gallery, Toronto, 1990, Art Gallery of Peterborough, Ont., 1992, Art Gallery of Hamilton, Ont., 1993, So. Alta. Art Gallery, Lethbridge, 1994; Art Gallery Hamilton, Gallerie Arts Tech., Montreal, Basel Art Fair, Switzerland, 1998-2003, Basel Art, Miami, 2002-03, Chgo. Art Fair, 1999, Nat. Gallery Can., Ottawa, Ont., 2000, Can. Mus. Contemporary Art, North York, Ont., 2000, Can. Mus. Contemporary Photography, Ottawa, 2000, 2001, Nat. Gallery Can., Ottawa, Art Gallery Hamilton, Ont., 2001, Kitchener-Waterloo Art Gallery, Ont., 2001, Art Basel, 2002, Basel Chgo. Art Fair, 2002, Toronto Photgraphers Workshop, 2002, Confedn. Art Ctr. Art Gallery, Prince Edward Island, 2003, Art Gallery of Bishop's U., Que., 2003; public collections include Agnes Etherington Art Ctr., Kingston, Ont., Art Gallery Hamilton, Art Gallery Ont., Toronto, Bibliotheque Nationale, Paris, The Gallery/Stratford, The Nickle Arts Mus., Calgary, Alta., The Robert McLaughlin Gallery, Oshawa, The Winnipeg Art Gallery, Victoria and Albert Mus., London; also involved with other pub. art projects. Coord. Colour Xerox Artists' Program, Visual Arts Ont., Toronto, 1977-83; bd. dirs. Art Gallery at Harbourfront, Toronto, 1983-85; apptd. mem. City of Toronto Pub. Art Commn., 1986-89; mem. curatorial team WaterWorks Exhbn., Toronto, 1988; chmn. Toronto Arts Awards, Visual Arts Jury, 1988; bd. dirs. Arts Found. of Greater Toronto, 1989-92. Mem.: Royal Can. Acad. Arts. Office: 23 Alcina Ave Toronto ON Canada M6G 2E7 Address: Jane Corkin Gallery 179 John St Toronto ON Canada M5T 1X4

ASTOR, BROOKE, foundation administrator, philanthropist, writer; b. Portsmouth, N.H. d. John Henry and Mabel (Howard) Russell; m. Vincent Astor. LLD (hon.), Columbia U., 1971, Brown U., 1980; LHD (hon.), Fordham U., 1980, NYU, 1986; PhD in Biomed. Sci. (honoris causa), Rockefeller U., 1986. Pres., trustee Astor Home for Children; trustee Hist. Hudson Valley, Marconi Internat. Fellowship; trustee and hon. chmn., mem. devel. com., mem. exec. com. N.Y. Pub. Libr., N.Y.C.; life trustee, mem. conservation com. N.Y. Zool. Soc.; trustee emeritus, mem. coun. of fellows Pierpont Morgan Libr. Trustee emeritus, chmn. vis. com. dept. Asian art, mem. acquisitions com., exec. com. ex officio Met. Mus. Art, N.Y.C.; life trustee Rockefeller U. Author: Patchwork Child, 1962, rev. edit., 1993, The Bluebird Is at Home, 1965, Footprints, 1980, The Last Blossom on the Plum Tree, 1986; feature editor: House and Garden, 1946-56, cons. editor, 1956-93. Mem. N.Y. State Pk. Commn., 1967-69. Decorated dame Venerable Order of St. John of Jerusalem; recipient Anniversary medal Astor, Lenox and Tilden Founds. of N.Y. Pub. Libr., 1961, award Sisters of Good Shepherd and Children of Madonna Heights Sch. for Girls, 1963, Client Award cert. N.Y. State Assn. Architects, 1964, award Pk. Assn. N.Y.C. Inc., 1965, Honor award HUD, 1966, cert. of appreciation City of N.Y., 1967, Albert S. Bard Merit award City Club N.Y., 1967, Award of Honor, Women's Aux. N.Y. chpt. AIA, 1968, Rector's award St. Phillip's Ch., 1968, Michael Friedsam medal Archtl. League N.Y., 1968, award Brotherhood-In-Action, Inc., 1968, Outstanding Contbn. award Am. Soc. Landscape Architects, 1968, Spirit of Achievement award Albert Einstein Coll. Medicine, Yeshiva U., 1969, Good Samaritan award P. Ballentine & Sons, 1969, Good Samaritan award Prospect Block Civic Assn., 1969, Disting. Svc. award N.Y. region Rotary, 1970, YWCA honor, 1970, Housing award N.Y. Met. chpt. Nat. Assn. Housing and Redevel. Officials, 1971, $24 award Mus. City of N.Y., award N.Y. Pub. Libr., 1972, Albert Gallatin medal NYU, 1972, spl. citation AIA, 1973, Medal of Merit award Lotos Club, 1973, commendation Neighborhood Com. for the Asphalt Green, 1975, commendation ARCS Found., 1976, Pres.'s medal Mcpl. Art Soc. N.Y., 1976, Gold Medal award N.Y. Zool. Soc., 1978, Elizabeth Seton Humanitarian award N.Y. Foundling Hosp., 1978, Little Apple award Met. Mus. Art, Little Apple award Morgan Library, Little Apple award N.Y. Public Library, Little Apple award N.Y. Zool. Soc., Little Apple award Rockefeller U., Little Apple award South St. Seaport and Sta. WNET-TV/Channel 13, 1978, New Yorker for N.Y. award Citizens Com. for N.Y.C., 1980, 1st Myer Myers Cultural award City of N.Y., award Citizens Housing and Planning Coun., 1980, Bishop's Cross, Diocese of N.Y., 1980, Forsythia award Bklyn. Bot. Garden, 1981, award Pks. Coun., 1981, Woman of Conscience award Appeal of Conscience Found., 1981, commendation Lower Manhattan Cultural Coun., 1984, Disting. New Yorkers award Bowery Savs. Bank, 1984, Gov.'s Arts award State of N.Y., 1985, Am. Acad. and Inst. Arts and Letters award, 1986, Marconi Internat. Fellowship Coun. award, 1986, landmark plaque and medallion N.Y. Landmarks Preservation Found., 1987, Gold medal St. Nicholas Soc., N.Y.C., 1987, Fashion Industry award Coun. of Fashion Designers Am., 1988, Presdl. Citizen's medal Pres. Reagan, 1988, Nat. Medal of Arts, Nat. Endowment for the Arts, 1988, World Monuments Fund The Hadrian award, 1991, annual humanitarian award ARC of Greater N.Y., 1993, Eleanor Roosevelt medallion City of N.Y., 1993, 8th Annual Town & Country Most Generous American award, The Hearst Corp. and Hearst Mags., 1993, The Mayor's award of Honor and Culture, City of N.Y., 1993, 10th Annual Humanitarian award N.Y., 1993, Richard Rodgers award for Disting. Svc., Profl. Children's Sch., 1994, Scroll of Honor, N.Y. coun. Navy League of U.S., 1994; Brooke Astor Day proclaimed by Mayor of N.Y.C., March 5, 1992. Fellow Am. Acad. Arts and Scis.; mem. Mcpl. Art Soc. N.Y., Pilgrims U.S., Venerable Order St. John of Jerusalem (dame), The Century Assn., Colony Club, Knickerbocker Club, N.Y. Yacht Club, Sleepy Hollow Country Club.

ATAMIAN, SUSAN, nurse; b. Cambridge, Mass., Sept. 14, 1950; d. Raymond H. and Alice (Chakerian) A. BA, Simmons Coll., 1972, MS, 1995. RN, Mass.; cert. infection control. Staff nurse Mass. Gen. Hosp., Boston, 1972-74, pvt. duty nurse, 1975-76, staff nurse, 1976-77, Kimberly Nurses, Orange, Calif., 1982; rsch. study nurse Mass. Gen. Hosp., Boston, 1977-80, instr. nursing, 1982-84, sr. rsch. study nurse, 1984-87, dir. clin. rsch. nurse group, 1985-90, infection control nurse, 1988-90, infection control nurse clinician, 1990-92, coord., clin. rsch., vascular surg. div., 1992-99, individual assignments/spl. projects staff, 1999—2001, infection control practitioner, 2001—03, data quality nurse decision support unit, 2003—. Cons. nutrition and liver diseases, McGaw Labs., Santa Ana, Calif., 1980-81; chmn. faculty devel. libr. com. Shepard Gill Sch., Boston, 1983-84; mem. rsch. nurses forum, Mass. Gen. Hosp., 1992—. Class agt. 1972 Simmons Coll., 1972, 86-97, mem. com. alumnae fund, 1987-89, reunion com., 1990-2002, com. on classes, 1991-92, class of 1972 reunion fund chair, 1991-92, chmn. class of 1972 reunion fund 1996-97, v.p. Class of 1972, 1997--, mem. travel and edn. com., 2002—. Mem.: ANA, Coun. Armenian Am. Nurses (v.p. 2002—03, pres. 2003—), Assn. for Practitioners in Infection Control and Epidemiology, Rsch. Nurses Forum Mass. Gen. Hosp., Mass. Nurses Assn., Soc. for Vascular Nursing, Am. Nurses Found. Century Club, Simmons Coll. Alumnae Assn. (edn. and travel com. 2002—), Simmons Club Boston (bd. dirs. 1988—90, v.p. 1990—92, co-chmn. boutique 1992—94, mem. nominating com. 1994—95), Sigma Theta Tau, Simmons Coll. Nursing Honor Soc. Mem. Armenian Apostolic Ch. Avocations: travel, reading, knitting. E-mail: satamian@partners.org.

ATCHESON, SUE HART, business educator; b. Dubuque, Iowa, Apr. 12; d. Oscar Raymond and Anna (Cook) Hart; m. Walter Clark Atcheson (div.); children: Christine A. Hischar, Moffet Zoe, Claye Williams. BBA, Mich. State U.; MBA, Calif. State Poly. U., Pomona, 1973. Cert. tchr. and adminstr. Instr. Mt. San Antonio Coll., Walnut, Calif., 1968-90. Bd. dirs. faculty assn. Mt. San Antonio Coll., mem. acad. senate, originator vol. income tax assistance; spkr. in field; lectr. in bus. mgmt. Calif. State Poly. U., Pomona, 1973—75; cons., trainer Joint Venture between Mt. San Antonio Coll. and County of Los Angeles Dept. Pub. Social Svcs., summer, 2001. Author: Fractions and Equations on Your Own, 1975. Charter mem. Internat. Commn. on Monetary and Econ. Reform; panelist infrastructure funding reform, Freeport, Ill., 1989. Mem. Cmty. Concert Assn. Inland Empire (bd. dirs.), Scripps Coll. Fine Arts Found., Recyclers Club (pres. 1996).

ATCHINSON, JUDY FITZNER, composer; b. Schenectady, N.Y., Sept. 28, 1941; d. Eugene Adolf and Wanda (Nowicki) F.; m. Robert Alan Atchinson, May 15, 1971 (May 1978); m. Brian Michael O'Neil, May 11, 1990; children: Dawn Elizabeth, Beth Robin. B.Mus., Hartt Coll. Music, Hartford, Conn., 1964, MFA, 1970. Mem. faculty, cons. for new course on creative collaboration U. of the Arts, Phila., 1989. Adj. faculty Union Coll., Schenectady, 1979-86, Russell Sage Coll., Troy, N.Y., 1979-86; artist-in-residence Hudson Valley C.C., Troy, 1980-93, Barnard Coll., N.Y.C., 1995—, Skidmore Coll., Saratoga, N.Y.; guest artist Temple U., Phila., 1991, New Paltz (N.Y.) Coll., N.Y. State Theater Program, Albany, N.Y., 1981-89, N.Y. State Dance Mus., Saratoga, N.Y., 1992-95, Carlisle Project, Carlisle, Pa., 1992-95; artistic dir. Am. Composers Forum, Albany, 1986—. Composer: Electronic Music for Peter Pucci & Co., 1995, violin and cello piece, 1990, 2 pcs. for Barnard Coll., 1995, Diary, electronic and vocal piece/Smithsonian Mus., 1988, WomanSong/cello pieces, 1990, others; commns. Yale U. Clean WaterFestival, 1998, Graham Ensemble, N.Y.C., 1998. Bd. dirs. Saratoga City Ballet, Simons Rock Dance Festival, Poughkeepsie, N.Y., internat. Assn. Dance Musicians; founder, dir. Quest-Inner City Arts Found., Schenectady, 1993-96, 97, Dance Plus Dance Festival, Saratoga, 1990-96; advisor Law Order Justice, Schenectady, 1993-96; bd. dirs. Schenectady 2000, 1995-96. N.Y. Found. for Arts grantee, 1992-94, Meet the Composer grantee, 1980-96, Lila Wallace Reader's Digest grantee, 1993. Democrat. Avocations: gardening, reading physics, dogs, travel, thrift shop shopping. Home: 1131 Van Antwerp Rd Schenectady NY 12309-5925

ATCITTY, FANNIE L. elementary school educator, education educator; b. Shiprock, NM, Dec. 4, 1952; d. John and Betty Martin Lowe; m. Eugene Ronald Atcitty, Apr. 22, 1972 (dec. May 10, 2000); children: Antoinette, Ronald. BEd, Ea. N.Mex. U., 1978; M in Curriculum and Instrn., Doane Coll., 1997; M in Ednl. Leadership, Doane Coll., 2002. Elem. tchr. Central Consolidated Sch. Dist. 22, Shiprock, N.Mex., 1979—. Adj. instr. early childhood edn. program N.Mex. Highland U., Las Vegas, 1997—2002; adj. instr. edn. and tchr. prep. program Diné Coll., Shiprock, N.Mex., 1997—2002; profl. standards commn. mem. N.Mex. State Dept. Edn., Santa Fe, 2000—, tchr. assessment rev. panel, 1993—99, nat. com. for accreditation of tchr. edn. 1997—. Contbr. poetry to lit. publs. Edn. chairperson Shiprock (N.Mex.) Cmty. Planning Commn. 1994-99; mem. San Juan County Dem. Party, Farmington, 1998—2001, chairperson Cmty. Land Planning Bd., N.Mex., 1995—98; U.S Presdl. elector N.Mex., 1996. Recipient Golden Apple Found. award, Golden Apple Found. N.Mex., 2001. Mem.: Internat. Reading Assn., Am. Assn. Sch. Adminstrs , Las Amigas Women's Club. Democrat. Avocations: reading, walker, community events, gardening. Home: PO Box 3320 Shiprock NM 87420 Office: Mesa Elementary Sch PO Box 1803 Shiprock NM 87420

ATHANSON, MARY CATHERYNE, school system administrator; Area III supt. Pinellas County Sch. Dist., Gulfport, Fla., 1998—. Office: Pinellas County Sch Dist Office Area III 1001 51st S St Gulfport FL 33707-3638

ATHERTON, FLORA CAMERON, civic worker, former foundation executive; b. Waco, Tex.; d. William Waldo and Helen Emelyn (Miller) Cameron; m. Holt Atherton; children-- Ike Simpson Iampmann, III, Megan Cameron Kampmann. Dir., mem. exec. com. Certain-Teed Corp., 1971-78; exec. com. San Antonio World's Fair, 1968; mem. Pres.'s Mission to Latin Am., 1969; U.S. del. Inter-Am. Commn. Women, 1969-72; mem. citizens stamp adv. commn. U.S. Postal Service, 1969-71; cons. Bur. Inter-Am. Affairs, Dept. State, 1972-75; vice chmn. exec. com. Tex. Republican Party, 1968-69; del. Rep. Nat. Conv., 1960, 64, alt. del., 1968, sec. platform com., 1960; mem. Rep. Nat. Fin. Com., 1965—, pres., chmn. 1976-78; past pres. KAMKO Found.; trustee Trinity U., San Antonio, 1965—, chmn., 1976-78; trustee Sweet Briar Coll., 1969-78; mem. Pres.'s Commn. German-Am. Tricentennial, 1983-84; bd. dirs. San Antonio Art Inst., 1984—, mem. nat. council Met. Opera. Mem. Junior League, Colonial Dames Am. Home: 315 Westover Rd San Antonio TX 78209-5653 Office: 5701 Broadway St Ste 106 San Antonio TX 78209-5722

ATHIAS, LORI R. real estate broker; d. Selbert Athias and Inez Viner. Lic. real estate broker, lic. real estate salesperson, Prosource, St. Paul; cert. paralegal, Paralegal Inst. Paralegal, Mpls., 1991—94; real estate salesperson Eric Heard & Assocs., St. Paul, 1997—2002; real estate broker Global Realty, Robbinsdale, Minn., 2002—.

ATKINS, CANDI, management consultant, small business owner; b. Chgo., Aug. 19, 1946; d. Norman R. and Catherine Kay (Coughlin) Wolfe; children: James N., Amanda Kate. Assoc. in Edn., Thornton C.C., 1968. Chief exec. officer Candi Atkins & Assocs., Phoenix, 1992-95, Largo, Fla., 1995-97, Henderson, Nev., 1997—. Faculty Diablo Valley Community Coll., Pleasant Hill, Calif., 1982-85; nat. trainer HUD Occupancy Issues, 1984—. Author: Shopping for Big Wonderful Me, 1988, Management Forms for HUD Assisted Housing, 1991. Candi Atkins Day named in her honor Mayor of San Francisco, 1984; named to hon. Order Ky. Col. Mem. NAFE, Inst. Real Estate Mgmt. (exec. com. San Francisco chpt. 1980-84, instr. 1981-91, accredited resident mgr., cert. property mgr., Accredited Resident Mgmt. of Yr. 1980). Avocations: sailing, travel. Home: 243 Water Bridge Ct Henderson NV 89012-2283 E-mail: Caandi@aol.com.

ATKINS, CORY, state legislator, writer; BS in Political Sci. (magna cum), U. Mass. State rep. Mass. House, 1999—. Mem. Concord Town Com. Mem. League of Women Voters, Concord Mus., Belknap House. Democrat. Office: Rm 26 State House Boston MA 02133

ATKINS, JEANNINE CATHERINE, writer; b. Montclair, N.J., July 14, 1953; d. David Pierre and Marjorie Atkins. BA, U. Mass., 1980; MA, U. N.H., 1982. Author: Aani and The Tree Huggers, 1995, Mary Anning and The Sea Dragon, 1999, Becoming Little Women, 2001, Wings and Rockets: The Story of Women in Air and Space, 2003.

ATKINS, VICKI ALVINDA, realtor; b. South Bend, Ind., Nov. 16, 1945; d. Alvin Lee Atkins and Mildred Josephine Taylor-Atkins; children: Marvin L., Becky L. Student, Ind. U., South Bend, 1977—80. Property mgmt. various cos., Atlanta; realtor Remax Greater Atlanta, 2001—. Bd. sec. Learn To Grow, Inc., Atlanta. Realtor: Nat. Assn. Realtors, Atlanta Bd. Realtors (Mktg. Specialist of Yr. award 1999). Avocations: golf, travel. Home: 2431 Weatherstone Cir SE Conyers GA 30094 Office: Remax Greater Atlanta 1585 Holcomb Bridge Rd Roswell GA 30076 E-mail: vickiatkins@bellsouth.net.

ATKINSON, ALANNA BETH, music educator; b. Mobile, Ala., July 4, 1952; d. John Walter and Mildred Dalton Atkinson. BS in Music Edn., U. South Ala., 1974. Pvt. piano tchr., Mobile, 1973—; piano tchr. Indian Springs Elem. Sch., Mobile, 1975—2003, Morningside Elem. Sch., Mobile, 1987—2001, Kate Shepard Elem. Sch., 2003—, St. Mark Meth. Sch., 2003—. Organist Our Savior Luth., Mobile, 1973, Kingswood United Meth., Mobile, 1974—83, Forest Hill United Meth., Mobile, 1984—2002; vol. music leader Bible sch. Fulton Heights Meth., Mobile, 1998—; organist Westminster Presbyn., Mobile, 2002—; clarinetist Mobile Pops Band, 1995—; soprano Springhill Consort, 1992—97, Gloria Dei Chorale, 1999—2002; dulcimer player ch., cmty. and nursing home programs, Mobile, 1996—; tenor recorder West Minister Consort; mem. So. Ala. Presbyn. Cursillo, 2004, U. So. Ala. Guitar Ensemble, 2004. Recipient United Meth. Women Mission Pin, Kingswood Meth., 1983, Forest Hill Meth., 1985. Mem.: Mobile Music Tchrs. Assn. (2d v.p. 1978, 1982, treas. 1988—89, honors recital and social coms.), Am. Organist Guild (bd. dirs. 1984, 1990). Democrat. Presbyterian. Avocations: sewing, cats. Home: 1500 S Shan Dr Mobile AL 36693 Office Phone: 251-471-5451. E-mail: bethatkinson@mobis.com.

ATKINSON, BARBARA F. dean, medical educator, academic administrator; b. Mpls., Oct. 19, 1942; MD, Jefferson Med. Coll., Thomas Jefferson Univ., 1974. Diplomate Am. Bd. Anatomic and Clin. Pathology, Am. Bd. Cytopathology. Intern Hosp. U. Pa., Phila., 1974—75, resident in pathology, 1975—78; mem. faculty U. Kans., Kansas City; dir. resident program U. Kans. Med. Ctr., Kansas City. Assoc. scientist Wistar Inst. Anatomy and Biology, 1983—87; mem. staff dept. pathology Hosp. of U. Pa., 1978—87, dir. cytopathology, 1978—87, med. program dir. Sch. Cytotech., 1978—86; chmn. dept. pathology and lab. medicine Med. Coll. Pa., 1987—94; dir. Delaware Valley Regional Lab. Svcs., Med. Coll. Hosps. and St. Christopher's Hosp. for Children, 1991—96; chmn. dept. pathology and lab. medicine Med. Coll. Pa. and Hahnemann U., 1994—96; trustee Am. Bd. Pathology, 1992—95, pres., 1998—. Mem. editl. bd. Lab. Investigation, 1988—94, Modern Pathology, 1990—94, Human Pathology, 1992—94, manuscript reviewer Cancer, Diagnostic Cytopathology, Modern Pathology, 1988—94, abstract rev. bd. U.S. and Can. Acad. Pathology, 1989—92, rev. panel Am. Soc. Clin. Pathology Abstract, 1991—96; contbr. articles to profl. jours., chapters to books. Bd. dirs., treas. Laennec Soc. Phila., 1979—81; bd. dirs. Thyroid Soc. Phila., 1982—84; exec. com., bd. dirs. Med. Coll. Pa., 1994—96; bd. trustees Hahnemann U., 1994—96. Recipient Golden Apple Tchg. award for excellent sci. tchg., 1994; grantee, NIH, 1985—88, Takeda-Abbott R&D, 1989—94, NIA, 1991—94. Fellow: ASIM, Coll. Am. Pathologists; mem.: NAS (mem. Inst. Medicine), U.S. and Can. Acad. Pathology, Am. Soc. Clin. Pathology (Janet M. Glasgow Meml. scholarship 1974), Am. Soc. Cytopathology Office: U Kans Med Ctr 3901 Rainbow Blvd Kansas City KS 66160 Office Phone: 913-588-5268. E-mail: batkinson@kumc.edu.

ATKINSON, CHRISTINE ANNE, curator; b. Kansas City, Kans., May 26, 1965; d. John Patterson and Andrea Janet (Gresser) A. BA in Humanities, U. Colo., 1987. Lobby supr. Dept. of Visitor Svcs., Mus. of Modern Art, N.Y.C., 1988-89; pub. programs asst. Dept. of Edn., Mus. of Modern Art, N.Y.C., 1989-90; artist, educator Minn , 1994—; comic book artist asst. DC Comics/Peter Gross, 1992—; comic book artist instr. Minn. Mus. of Am. Art, Mpls., 1995-97; curatorial dir., visual curator No Name Exhbns, Mpls., 1999—2001; mem. adv. com. edn. publs. and programs Walker Art Ctr., 2003—. Tour guide Walker Art Ctr., Mpls. 1997—. com. teen arts coun., 1996-2002; adv. panel Mpls. Arts Commn., 1994-97; co-dir. Kulture Klub at Project Off Streets, 1996—. Neighborhood arts program Mpls. Arts Commn., 1994. Mem. Phi Beta Kappa. Home: 515 W 28th St # 2 Minneapolis MN 55408-2247 Office: No Name Exhbns PO Box 581696 Minneapolis MN 55458-1696

ATKINSON, HOLLY GAIL, physician, journalist, business executive, author, lecturer, human rights activist; b. Detroit, Oct. 20, 1952; d. John S. and Patricia Atkinson; m. Galen Jay Guengerich, Nov. 18, 2000. BA in Biology magna cum laude, Colgate U., 1974; MD, U. Rochester, 1978; MS in Journalism, Columbia U., 1981. Diplomate Nat. Med. Bds. Intern in internal medicine Strong Meml. Hosp., Rochester, N.Y., 1978-79; rschr. Walter Cronkite's Universe show CBS News, N.Y.C., 1981-82; med. reporter CBS Morning News, N.Y.C., 1982-83; on-air co-host Bodywatch health show PBS, 1983-88; contbg. editor and health columnist New Woman mag., 1983-88; on-air corr., med. editor, sr. v.p. programming/med. affairs Lifetime Med. TV, 1985-93; assoc. editor Journal Watch, 1986-90; med. corr. Today Show NBC News, N.Y.C., 1991-94; editor HealthNews, 1994—; exec. v.p. Reuters Health, N.Y.C., 1994-98, pres., CEO, 1998-2000; CEO New Media Health Answers Inc., 2000; pres. allHealth.com (iVillage health), 2000—. Lectr. Dept. Pub. Health Cornell U. Med. Coll., 1997 . Author: Women and Fatigue, 1986. Vol. nat. and local level Am. Heart Assn., 1984-91, bd. dirs., chmn. nat. comms. com. Am. Heart Assn., 1987-91; bd. dirs. Phys. Human Rights, 1994— (pres. 2002-), NOW Legal Def. and Edn. Fund, 1996—, Soc. Advancement Women's Health Rsch., 1997-99, Am. Lyme Disease Found. 1997-98. Recipient Young Achievers award Nat. Coun. Women, 1986, Achievement award Soc. Advancement Women's Health Rsch., 1995. Mem. Phi Beta Kappa. Office: iVillage.com 212 5th Ave 6th Fl New York NY 10010*

ATLAS, LIANE WIENER, writer; b. NYC; d. Louis and Frances (Ferne) Wiener; m. Martin Atlas, Mar. 5, 1944 (dec. Mar. 1997); children: Stephen Terry, Jeffrey L. AB, Vassar Coll., 1943; postgrad., Johns Hopkins U., 1953-55. Cert. fin. planner. Fgn. affairs officer Dept. State, Washington, 1962-68; sr. economist U.S. Commerce Dept., Washington, 1968-75, U.S. Treasury Dept., Washington, 1975-79, Riggs Nat. Bank, Washington, 1980-82; v.p. Fintapes Inc., Washington, 1984-87 pres., 1987-95; freelance writer Washington, 1995—. Mem. U.S. delegation UN Econ. Orgns., N.Y.C., Geneva, 1963, 64, 68, 79. Author: Middle East Financial Institutions, 1977, (audio cassettes) What Every Wife Should Know, 1986, rev., 1992, Financial Planning for Divorce, rev. edit. 1992; freelance writer Changing Times and other mags., 1982-87. Treas. Entertaining People/Washington Home, 1986—90, Smithsonian Craft Show, 1993—95, Smithsonian Women's Coms., 1996—97; mem. Kennedy Ctr. Circs. Bd., 1999—; info. specialist Nat. Gallery Art, 2004—. Fellow in econs. Johns Hopkins U., Balt., 1954-55; recipient Cert. of Appreciation U.S. Treasury Dept., Washington, 1977. Mem.: Washington Ind. Writers, Inst. CFPs, Smithsonian Women's Com., Vassar Club of Washington. Avocations: print collecting, travel, tennis. Home: 2254 48th St NW Washington DC 20007-1035

ATLAS, NANCY FRIEDMAN, judge; b. N.Y.C., May 20, 1949; BS, Tufts U., 1971; JD, NYU, 1974. Bar: N.Y. 1975, U.S. Dist. Ct. (so. and ea. dists.) N.Y. 1975, U.S. Ct. Appeals (2nd cir.) 1975, U.S. Dist. Ct. (so. dist.) Tex. 1982, U.S. Ct. Appeals (5th cir.) 1982, U.S. Dist. Ct. (no. dist.) Tex. 1989. Law clk. to Hon. Dudley B. Bonsal U.S Dist Ct. (so. dist.) N.Y., 1974-76; assoc. Webster & Sheffield, 1977-78; asst. U.S. atty. So. Dist. N.Y., 1979-82; shareholder Sheinfeld, Maley & Kay, P.C., Houston, 1982-95, also bd. dirs.; judge U.S. Dist. Ct. Tex., Houston, 1995—. Lectr. numerous programs CLE. Mng. editor NYU Ann. Survey Am. Law, 1973-74; contbr. numerous articles to profl. jours. Chair Tex. Higher Edn. coord. Bd., 1992-95; mem. Tex. Coun. Workforce and Econ. Competitiveness, 1993-95. Fellow: ABA Found., Houston Bar Assn., State Bar Tex.; mem.: FBA, ABA (co-divsn. dir. litigation sect. 1996—98, co-chair ADR com. 1994—95, mem. coun. 1998—2001, bus. and litigation joint task force on bankruptcy practice 1994—98), Am. Law Inst., Houston Bar Found. (trustee), Phi Beta Kappa. Office: US Courthouse 515 Rusk St 9015 Houston TX 77002-2605

ATLEE, DEBBIE GAYLE, sales consultant, medical educator; b. Oklahoma City, Jan. 8, 1955; d. Harold Phillip and Ella Ruth (Birks) A. BS in Nursing, U. Okla., 1977. RN, Okla.; cert. diabetes educator. Team leader ob-gyn Bapt. Med. Ctr. of Okla., Oklahoma City, 1977-80, asst. clin. supr. urology, 1980-81, nursing educator, diabetes educator, 1981-84; sales specialist Boehringer Mannheim Diagnostics, Inc., Indpls., 1984-99; diabetes educator Dept. Endocrinology U. Okla. Coll. Medicine, 1999-2000; bus. sales mgr. NovoNordisk Pharms., Inc., Princeton, NJ, 2000—02; diabetes case mgr. Ediba Diabetes Ctr. Excellence Integris Bapt. Med. Ctr., Okla. City, 2002—. Mem. regional piloting adv. group Nat. Diabetes Adv. Bd., Oklahoma City, 1984-85. Named Outstanding Bus. Woman, Bus. and Profl. Women, Capitol Hill chpt., 1981, Salesperson of Yr. 1987; recipient Outstanding Sales Achievement award, 1985, 87, 90, 91. Mem. Am. Diabetes Assn. (exec. bd. Met. chpt. 1985—, pres. 1987), Am. Assn. Diabetes Educators, Western Okla. Diabetes Educators (pres. 1984, Outstanding Svc. and Dedication award 1984, chpt. svc. award 1985, chpt. edn. award 1984), Nat. Bd. Cert. Diabetes Educator, U.S. Power Squadron (bd. dirs. Oklahoma City 1984, 87), U. Okla. Alumni Assn. (life). Republican. Roman Catholic. Avocations: sailing, photography, gardening, music. Home: 6213 Riviera Dr Oklahoma City OK 73112-7359 E-mail: debbie_atlee@integris_health.com.

ATTEE, JOYCE VALERIE JUNGCLAS, artist; b. Cin., Apr. 4, 1926; d. LeRoy Francis and Clara Marie (Becker) Jungclas; m. William Robert Attee III, Oct. 25, 1952; children: Robin Wilson, Wendy Ann. BA, Rollins Coll., 1948; postgrad., U. Cin., 1952, 54, Art Acad. Cin., 1962-64, Edgecliff Coll., 1967. One-man shows include Loring Andrews Rattermann Gallery, 1964, Town Club, 1966, 69, 72, 75, 78, 81, 82, 83, 84, 90, 98, Jr. League Office, 1975, Court Gallery, 1969, Bissingers', 1970, 76, Cin. Nature Ctr., 1974, 78, Cin. Country Day Sch., 1974; group shows include Town Club Cin. 1984, Bissinger's, 1984, Cin. Art Mus., 1962, Zoo Arts Festival, 1961, 62, 66, Town Club Cin., 1973-75, 77-79, 80-84, 85, Palm Beach (Fla.) Galleries, 1974, Showcase of Arts, 1976, Ursuline Cir., 1976, Court Galleries, 1977, Indian Hill Artists, 1957-76, 82, 83, 2002, 2003, Indian Hill; regional and local shows Nat. League Am. Pen Women, 1977, 78, also nat. biennial art exhibit, 1970, Nat. Bicentennial Show, Washington, 1976, James H. Barker Gallery, Palm Beach, Fla., 1979, 80, 81, 82, Nantucket, 1982, Cin. Women's Club Show, 1979, Cin. Nature Ctr., 1983, Kimberton (Pa.) Gallery, 1988-89, Town Club, 1995, Indian Hill, 1996; author: Elbey Jay, 1964. Recipient 1st prize in still life or flowers Cin. Womans Art Club, 1965, 69; Marjorie Ewell Meml. award, 1975. Mem. Women's Art Club Cin. (past. v.p.), Jr. League Cin., Jr. League Garden Circle (pres. 1974-75, spkr. on flower paintings 1990), Univ. Club, Indian Hills Club, Cin. Woman's Club. Episcopalian. Home: 8050 Indian Hill Rd Cincinnati OH 45243-3908

ATTKISSON, SHARYL T. newscaster, correspondent, writer; b. St. Petersburg, Fla. d. Robert F. Thompson and Judith Jon (Starr) Crist; m. James H. Attkisson, Feb. 18, 1984; 1 child, Sarah Judith Starr Attkisson. BS in Broadcast Journalism, U. Fla., 1982. Reporter, prodr. Sta. WTVX-TV, Ft. Pierce, Fla., 1982-85; reporter Sta. WBNS-TV, Columbus, Ohio, 1985-86, Sta. WTVT-TV, Tampa, Fla., 1986-90; anchor, corr. Cable News Network, Atlanta, 1990-93, CBS News, N.Y.C., 1993-94, CBS News Washington, 1995—. Mem. adv. bd. Coll. Journalism, U. Fla., Gainesville, 1994-97, chmn. telecom. adv. bd., 1996-97; host Healthweek series PBS, 1997—. Author: Unreliable Sources, 1993, (booklet) So...You Want an Agent?, 1997. Recipient 1st place TV Reporting Communicator's award Fla. Aeribus Inst., 1983, 1st place award Mature Media Nat. Awards, 1993, 1st place feature story Nat. Headliner Awards, 1983, 1st place investigative honor, 1997, 1st place pub. affairs award Nat. Assn. Black Journalists, 1994, Silver Medal award Mature Media, 1998, Alumni of Distinction Honor award U. Fla. Journalism Coll., 1999; 1st female journalist to fly on a B-52 combat mission from Fairford Royal AFB to Yugoslavia, 1999. Avocations: writing, gardening. Office: CBS News Washington 2020 M St NW Washington DC 20036-3368

ATTOLE, MARY BERTHA, writer; b. Lafayette, La., Dec. 12, 1958; d. Antoine and Elia Guillory Attole. Student, So. U., Baton Rouge, La., 1976—80. Tchr.'s aide Glendale Elem., Eunice, La., 1980—82; mem. staff Fred's Dept. Store, Eunice, 1983—85, John's IGA Grocery Store, Eunice, 1985—88. Author: My Brother's Keeper, 2001. Vol. So. Poverty Law Ctr.'s Civil Rights Meml. Visitors Ctr. Wall of Tolerance, St. Matilda Cth. Ch., Eunice, 1991—. Mem.: Alpha Mu Gamma. Democrat. Roman Catholic. Avocations: reading, genealogy, comedy, classic television, pets. Home: 310 N Martin Luther King Dr Eunice LA 70535

ATWATER, PHYLLIS Y. municipal administrator; b. Memphis, Nov. 4, 1947; d. Jeff D. and Thelda E. A.; m. John R. Ernst, Dec. 28, 1972. BA, Vassar Coll., 1968; MA, Boston U., 1970; postgrad., New Sch. Soc. Rsch., N.Y.C., 1974-82. Lectr. math. Tufts U., Medford, Mass., 1970-72; instr. math. higher edn. program Boston Model Cities Adminstrn., 1970-74, coord. program, 1971; instr. econs. SUNY, Old Westbury, 1977-82; dep. dir. adminstrn. and fin. Divsn. Solid Waste Mgmt., Commonwealth of Mass., 1984-88; pres. and chief operating officer Recoverable Resources/R2B2, Inc., Bronx, NY, 1989-91; dir. divsn. solid waste N.Y. State Dept. Environ. Conservation, 1992-93, regional dir., 1993-95; pvt. practice computer svcs. cons., 1995-99; assoc. commr. for info. tech. and adminstrn. N.Y.C. Dept. Employment, 2002—03; assoc. commr. N.Y.C. Dept. Small Bus. Svcs., 2003—. Assoc. Recycling Adv. Coun., EPA, Washington, 1990-93; vice chair Manhattan Solid Waste Adv. Bd., N.Y.C., 1991-92. Mem. founding bd. advisors N.Y. Feminist Art Inst., N.Y.C., 1979—81; bd. advisors The Labor Inst., N.Y.C., 1985—97, West Harlem Environ. Action Inc., N.Y.C., 1996—99; founder, pres., bd. dirs. Inst. for Labor and the Cmty., N.Y.C., 1997—; sec. bd. dirs. O.R.E., Inc., N.Y.C., 1998—; bd. dirs. Scenic Hudson, Inc., Poughkeepsie, NY, 2001—. Ford Found. fellow Nat. Fellowship Fund, 1975-78, Danforth Found., 1980-82.

ATWATER, TANYA MARIA, marine geophysicist, educator; b. Los Angeles, Aug. 27, 1942; d. Eugene and Elizabeth Ruth (Ransom) A.; 1 child, Alyosha Molnar. Student, MIT, 1960-63; BA, U. Calif., Berkeley, 1965; PhD, Scripps Inst. Oceanography, 1972. Vis. earthquake researcher U. Chile, 1966; research assoc. Stanford U., 1970-71; asst. prof. Scripps Inst. Oceanography, 1972-73; U.S.-USSR Acad. Scis. exchange scientist, 1973; asst. prof. MIT, 1974-79, assoc. prof., 1979-80, research assoc., 1980-81; prof. dept. geoscis. U. Calif., Santa Barbara, 1980—. Chairperson ocean margin drilling Ocean Crust Planning Adv. Com.; mem. pub. adv. com. on law of sea U.S. Dept. State, 1979-83; mem. tectonics panel Ocean Drilling Project, 1990-93; Sigma Xi lectr., 1975-76. Sci. cons.: Planet Earth: Continents in Collision (R. Miller), 1983; contbr. articles to profl. jours. Sloan fellow, 1975-77; recipient Newcomb Cleveland prize AAAS, 1980; named Scientist of Yr. World Book Ency., 1980. Fellow Am. Geophys. Union (fellows com. 1980-81, 94-95, Ewing award subcom. 1980., McElwane award subcom. 1994), Geol. Soc. Am. (Penrose Conf. com. 1978-80); mem. AAAS, Assn. Women in Sci, Am. Geol. Inst., Nat. Acad. Scis., Phi Beta Kappa, Eta Kappa Nu. Office: U Calif Dept Geoscis Santa Barbara CA 93106

ATWELL, CONSTANCE WOODRUFF, health services executive, researcher; b. Jan. 27, 1942; AB with high honors in psychology, Mount Holyoke Coll., 1963; MA, UCLA, 1965, PhD, 1968. Asst. prof. psychology Pitzer Coll., Claremont (Calif.) Grad. Sch., 1967-72, assoc. prof. psychology, 1972-77, prof. psychology, 1977-78; grants assoc. div. of rsch. grants NIH, Bethesda, Md., 1978-79; chief, Office of Clin. Applications of Vision Rsch. Nat. Eye Inst., NIH, Bethesda, 1979-81, asst. chief, Strabismus, Amblyopia and Visual Processing Br., 1980-81, chief, Strabismus, Amblyopia and Visual Processing Br., 1981-92, dep. assoc. dir. Extramural and

Collaborative Programs, 1988-92; assoc. dir. for extramural rsch. Nat. Inst. Neurol. Disorders and Stroke, Bethesda, 1992—, acting dep. dir., 1997-98. Rsch. proposal reviewer for the Nat. Found. March of Dimes, Nat. Inst. of Disability and Rehab. Rsch., Nat. Soc. to Prevent Blindness, U.S. Dept. Edn., NIH office of Program Planning and Evaluation, co-chair adv. com. women's health issues; mem. exec. com. Fed. Demonstration Partnership; mem. various adv. [illegible] tech. coms. and rsch. projects, co-chair improving peer rev. reinvention com. Contbr. articles to profl. publs. Reader for Recording for the Blind, 1973-78; trustee Claremont Collegiate Sch., 1975-77; chmn. guidance adv. com. Cabin John Jr. High Sch., 1980-81, exec. com., 1980—, pres. parent tchrs. assn., 1981-82; mem. exec. com. Winston Churchill High Sch. PTA, 1982-85. Recipient Nat. Merit scholarship, 1959-63; named Sara Williston scholar, Mary Lyon scholar. Mem. AAAS, Soc. for Neurosci., Assn for Women in Sci., Phi Beta Kappa, Sigma Xi. Office: Ninds Ste 3309 6001 Executive Blvd Bethesda MD 20892-9531 E-mail: ca23c@nih.gov.

ATWOOD, CAROL ANN, healthcare executive; b. Artesia, N.Mex., Sept. 26, 1945; BS in Phys. Therapy, U. Okla., 1967; MA in Healthcare Adminstrn., George Washington U., 1976. Staff phys. therapist St. Anthony Hosp., Oklahoma City, 1967-70; dir. rehab. svcs. U. Ky., Lexington, 1970-74; adminstrv. resident Thomas Jefferson U. Hosp., Phila., 1975-76; adminstr. Kaider-Permanente, Cleve. Med. Ctr., 1976-81; sr. assoc. adminstr. Cedars-Sinai Med. Ctr., L.A., 1981-91; sr. v.p. corp. svcs. Meth. Hosps. Dallas, 1991—93. Bd. dirs. The Wellness Cmty.-Foothills. Fellow Am. Coll. Healthcare Execs.; mem. Am. Phys. Therapy Assn., Healthcare Adminstrs. Assn. Northeast Ohio, Am. Heart Assoc., NW Harris County Div. Healthcare Execs. So. Calif., Hosp. Coun. So. Calif., Women in Health Adminstrn., Dallas Ft. Worth Hosp. Coun., C. of C., Rotary, Phi Beta Kappa. Avocations: skiing, aerobics, movies, theater. Office: Cypress Fairbanks Med Ctr Houston TX 77065

ATWOOD, COLLEEN, costume designer; Films include: Firstborn, 1984, (TV movie) Out of the Darkness, 1985, Bring on the Night, 1985, Manhunter, 1986, Critical Condition, 1987, Someone to Watch Over Me, 1987, The Pick-Up Artist, 1987, Torch Song Trilogy, 1988, Married to the Mob, 1988, Fresh Horses, 1988, For Keeps, 1988, Hider in the House, 1989, The Handmaid's Tale, 1989, Joe Versus the Volcano, 1990, Edward Scissorhands, 1990, Silence of the Lambs, 1991, Rush, 1991, Lorenzo's Oil, 1992, Love Field, 1992, Philadelphia, 1993, Born Yesterday, 1993, Cabin Boy, 1994, Wyatt Earp, 1994, Ed Wood, 1994, Little Women, 1994 (Acad. award nominee for best costume design 1994), Mars Attack's, That Thing You Do, 1994, Chicago, 2002 (Best Costume Design Academy award, 2003). Office: IATSE 13949 Ventura Blvd Ste 309 Sherman Oaks CA 91423-3570

ATWOOD, DONNA ELAINE, retired financial manager; b. Sewickley, Pa., Apr. 17, 1933; d. Donovan E. and Hazel Marie (Rush) Oelschlager; m. G. Richard Atwood, Oct. 22, 1955; children: Stephen Parker Atwood, Elaine Alden Atwood Henderson. BS in Commerce and Fin., Grove City Coll., 1955. Acctg. clk. 1st Nat. Bank, Coraopolis, Pa., 1949; asst. libr. Coraopolis Pub. Library, 1949—51; acctg. asst. Aluminum Co. of Am., Pitts., 1951—55; sec. to dean Grad. Sch. Indsl. Adminstrn. Carnegie Mellon U., Pitts., 1955—56; fin. sec., acct. Third Presbyn. Ch., Pitts., 1956—65; fin. mgr., acct. Dominical Sisters of the Sick Poor, Ossining, NY, 1972—92; ret. Mother advisor Internat. Order Rainbow for Girls N.Y., 1980—83, state chmn., 1985—, mem. state adv. bd., 1987—, gen. chmn. Grand Assembly com., 1987—93; sec. Internat. Order for Rainbow Girls N.Y., 1997—; pubs. chmn. Ossining Woman's Club, 1965—69, pres., 1969—71, house mgr., 1971—72; yearbook chmn. AAUW, Chappaqua, NY, 1964; sec. Internat. Order Rainbow for Girls N.Y., NY, 1997—; gen. chmn. grand assembly Internat. Order Rainbow for Girls, NY, 1987—93; treas. trustees Pleasantville United Meth. Ch., 1980—83, mem. pastor parish rels. com., 1989—91, sec. United Meth. Women, 1993—96, auditor, 1988—, mem. choir, 1980—. Mem.: DAR (chpt. libr. 1957, state page 1957—68), Women Descs. of Ancient and Honorable Arty. Co., Huguenot Soc., Daus. Am. Colonists (state page 1957—76, chpt. sec. 1961—64, nat. page 1968—79, state chmn. Golden Acorns and Pages 1970—73, nat. chmn. Golden Acorns and Pages 1973—79, state rec. sec. 1976—79, state chmn. pages 2000—03, state marshal 2003—), Colonial Dames XVII Century, Order Ea. Star (past matron 1962—63, grand Esther 1991, past matron 1996, chmn. com. 1997, trustee 1997—2002). Home: 21 Redwood Ln Briarcliff Manor NY 10510 E-mail: GRAtwood@aol.com.

ATWOOD, HOLLYE STOLZ, lawyer; b. St. Louis, Dec. 25, 1945; d. Robert George and Elise (Sauselle) Stolz; m. Frederick Howard Atwood III, Aug. 12, 1978; children: Katherine Stolz, Jonathan Robert. BA, Washington U., St. Louis, 1968; JD, Washington U., 1973. Bar: Mo. 1973. Jr. ptnr. Bryan Cave, St. Louis, 1973-82, ptnr., 1983—2001, mem. exec. com., 1995-2000, of counsel, 2002—. Bd. dirs. St. Louis coun. Girl Scouts U.S., 1976-86; trustee John Burroughs Sch., St. Louis, 1983-86. Mem. ABA, Met. St. Louis Bar Assn., Washington U. Law Sch. Alumni Assn. (pres. 1983-84). Clubs: Noonday (St. Louis) (bd. govs. 1983-86). Office: Bryan Cave One Metropolitan Sq 211 N Broadway Saint Louis MO 63102-2733 E-mail: hsatwood@bryancave.com.

ATWOOD, JOYCE CHARLENE, curriculum and instruction administrator, consultant; b. Chillicothe, Ohio, Apr. 29, 1943; d. Pearl and Blanche (Martindill) Workman. BS in Edn., Ohio U., 1965, MEd, 1969; postgrad., Ohio State U., 1976-88, Ashland U., 1992-97. Cert. tchr., supr., adminstr. 4th-6th grade tchr. Chillicothe (Ohio) City Schs., 1965-73, K-3d grade reading tchr., 1973-86, tchr. leader reading recovery, 1986-88, asst. prin. mid. sch., 1988-89, adminstrv. asst., 1989—, asst. supt. for curriculum and instrn., 1993—. Cons. study skills for mgmt. in industry Pickaway-Ross Joint Vocat. Sch., Chillicothe, 1984-88; mem. Child Care Adv. Bd., Portsmouth (Ohio), 1993— Sec., v.p. Big Bros. and Sisters, Ross County, 1989-93; mem. Walnut St. Ch. Staff Parish, Chillicothe, 1991-94, 99—; coord. Area Artist Series, Ross County, 1989—; edn. chairperson Ross County Area Labor Mgmt., 1990—; mem. Interagy. Childcare Vocat. Choir; bd. dirs. YMCA, 2002—. Named to Ross County Women's Hall of Fame, Ross County C. of C., 1993; recipient North Ctrl. Accredition award, 2002; George Washington U. Partnership award, 2002. Mem. ASCD (Ohio Creative Staff Devel. award 1997), Internat. Reading Assn., Nat. Assn. Edn. Young Children, Buckeye Assn. Sch. Adminstrs., Ohio Assn. for Curriculum Devel. (Staff Devel. Creative award 1997), Bus. and Profl. Women Assn., Altrusa, Kiwanis, Phi Delta Kappa. Methodist. Avocations: reading, gardening. Home: 10 Overlook Dr Chillicothe OH 45601-1925 E-mail: jatwood@mail.gsn.k12.oh.us.

ATWOOD, MARGARET ELEANOR, writer; b. Ottawa, Ont., Can., Nov. 18, 1939; d. Carl Edmund and Margaret Dorothy (Killam) A. BA, U. Toronto, 1961; AM, Radcliffe Coll., 1962; postgrad., Harvard U., 1962-63, 65-67; LittD (hon.), Trent U., 1973, Concordia U., 1980, Smith Coll., Northampton, Mass., 1982, U. Toronto, 1983, U. Waterloo, 1985, U. Guelph, 1985, Mt. Holyoke Coll., 1985, Victoria Coll., 1987, Univ. de Montréal, 1991, McMaster U., 1996; LLD (hon.), Queen's U., 1974. Lectr. in English U. B.C., 1964-65, Sir George Williams U., 1967-68, U. Alta., 1969-70; asst. prof. English York U., Toronto, 1971-72; writer-in-residence U. Toronto, 1972-73, U. Ala., Tuscaloosa, 1985. Berg Chair NYU, 1986; writer-in-residence Macquarie U., Australia, 1987, Trinity U., San Antonio, 1989. Author: (poetry) Double Persephone, 1961, The Circle Game, 1967, The Animals in That Country, 1968, The Journals of Susanna Moodie, 1970, Procedures for Underground, 1970, Power Politics, 1973, Poems for Voices, 1970, You Are Happy, 1975, Selected Poems, 1976 (Am. edit. 1978), Selected Poems, 1966-84, 1990, Margaret Atwood Poems, 1965-75, 1991, Two-Headed Poems, 1978, True Stories, 1981, Interlunar, 1984, Selected Poems II: Poems Selected and New, 1976-1986, 1986, Morning in the Burned House, 1995; (novels) The Edible Woman, 1969 (Am. edit. 1970), Surfacing, 1972, (Am. edit. 1973), Lady Oracle, 1976, Life Before Man, 1979, Bodily Harm, 1981, The Handmaid's Tale, 1985, Cat's Eye, 1988 (City Toronto Book award 1989, Coles Book of the Yr 1989, Can. Booksellers Assn. Author of the Yr., 1989, Book of the Yr. award Found. for Advancement of Can. Letters, Periodical Marketers Can., 1989, Torgi Talking Book award 1989), The Robber Bride, 1993 (award for Fiction Can. Authors Assn., 1993, Trillium award for Excellence in Ont. Writing 1993, Regional Commonwealth Lit. award), Alias Grace, 1996 (Giller Prize 1996, Medal of Honor for Literature, Nat. Arts Club 1997), The Blind Assassin, 2000 (The Booker Prize 2000, nominee for Internat. IMPAC Dublin Literary award, Dashiell Hammett Prize, Internat. Assn. of Crime Writers, 2001), Oryx and Crake, 2003 (Booker prize shortlist, 2003); (short stories) Dancing Girls, 1977, Bluebeard's Egg, 1983, Murder in the Dark, 1983, Wilderness Tips, 1991 (Trillium award 1992, Book of the Yr. award Periodical Marketers of Can., 1992), Good Bones, 1992; (juvenile) Up in the Tree, 1978, Anna'a Pet, 1980, For the Birds, 1990, Princess Prunella & the Purple Peanut, 1995; (non-fiction) Survival: A Thematic Guide to Canadian Literature, 1972, Second Words: Selected Critical Prose, 1982, Strange Things: The Malevolent North in Canadian Literature, 1995, Negotiating with the Dead, 2002. Recipient E.J. Pratt medal, 1961, Pres.'s medal U. Western Ont., 1965, YWCA Women of Distinction award, Gov. Gen.'s award, 1966, 1st pl. Centennial Commn. Poetry Competition, 1967, Union Poetry prize Chicago, 1969, Bess Hoskins prize of Poetry Chicago, 1974, City of Toronto Book award, 1977, Can. Booksellers Assn. award, 1977, award for short fiction Periodical Distbr. Can., 1977, St. Lawrence award for Fiction, 1978, Radcliffe Grad. medal, 1980, Molson award, 1981, Internat. Writer's prize Welsh Arts Council, 1982, Book of Yr. award Periodical Distbrs. of Can. and Found. for Advancement Can. Letters, 1983, Los Angeles Times Fiction award, 1986, Gov. Gen.'s Lit. award, 1986, Ida Nudel Humanitarian award, 1986, Toronto Arts award, 1986, Arthur C. Clarke award for Best Sci. Fiction, 1987, shortlisted for Ritz Hemingway prize, Paris, 1987, Commonwealth Lit. Prize regional award, 1987, 94, Silver medal for Best Article of Yr. Council for Advancement and Support of Edn., 1987, Nat. Mag. award 1st prize, 1988, Sunday Times award for literary excellence, YWCA Women of Distinction award 1988, Centennial medal Harvard U., 1990, John Hughes prize Welsh Devel. Bd., 1992, Commemorative medal 125th Anniversary of Can. Confedn., 1992, Trillium award for excellence in Ont. writing, 1995; Guggenheim fellow, 1981; decorated companion Order of Can., 1981, Order of Ont., 1990; named Woman of Yr. Ms. Mag., 1986, Humanist of Yr., 1987, Chevalier de l'Ordre des Arts et des Lettres, 1994. Fellow Royal Soc. of Can., Am. Acad. Arts and Scis. (fgn. hon. lit. mem. 1988). Address: care Oxford U Press 70 Wynford Dr Don Mills ON Canada M3C 1J9 Office: c/o Random House 299 Park Ave New York NY 10171-0002

ATWOOD, MARY SANFORD, writer; b. Mt. Pleasant, Mich., Jan. 27, 1935; d. Burton Jay and Lillian Belle (Sampson) Sanford; B.S., U. Miami, 1957; m. John C. Atwood, III, Mar. 23, 1957. Author: A Taste of India, 1969. Mem. San Francisco/N. Peninsula Opera Action, Suicide Prevention and Crisis Center, DeYoung Art Mus., Internat. Hospitality Center, Peninsula Symphony, San Francisco Art Mus., Mills Hosp. Assos. Mem. AAUW. Republican. Club: St. Francis Yacht. Office: 40 Knightwood Ln Hillsborough CA 94010-6132 E-mail: jazperkhat@mindspring.com.

ATZEFF, EFRODITA, fraternal organization administrator; b. Visheni, Kostur, Macedonia, Feb. 12, 1912; came to U.S., 1916; d. Atanas Thomas and Helena (Pandorff) Lebamoff; m. Peter George Atzeff, Oct. 27, 1935 (dec. Sept. 1982); 1 child, Doris Ellen Reynolds. Student, Internat. Bus. Coll., 1931, Ind. U., 1937, 38, 39, 40, Butler U., 1937. Sec. cen. com. Macedonian Patriotic Orgn. of U.S., Can., Australia, Brazil, and Belgium, Ft. Wayne, Ind., 1989-96. Mem. Macedonian Patriotic Orgn. of U.S., Can., Australia, Belgium and Brazil (pres., sec., treas. Kostur chpt. 1934—), Ft. Wayne Philharm. Soc., Ft. Wayne Mus. Art. Avocations: stamp collector, memorabilia. Home: PO Box 11026 Fort Wayne IN 46855-1026

AUBERTIN, MADELINE KATHERINE, retired nursing educator, medical/surgical nurse, mental health services professional; b. Detroit, May 16, 1930; Grad., Providence Hosp. Sch. Nursing; BS in Nursing Edn., Mercy Coll., 1951; MEd, Wayne State Coll., 1995. RN, Mich. Staff nurse Vets. Hosp., Dearborn, Mich., 1951-58; staff nurse, nursing educator St. John's Hosp., St. Louis, 1960-64; staff nurse U. Mich., Ann Arbor, 1965-66; instr., staff nurse Harper Hosp., Detroit; insvc. dir., nursing instr. Holy Cross Hosp., Detroit, 1966-68; insvc. instr., dir. Grace Hosp., Detroit, 1968-72; nursing instr. Wayne County Community Coll., Detroit, 1972-96; ret., 1996. Mem. ARC, Detroit, 1962-92, Am. Heart Assn., Southfield, Mich., 1962-92, Assn. for Learning Disabilities, Farmington, Mich., 1972-92, Nat. League of Nursing, Detroit, 1962-92. Democrat. Roman Catholic. Avocations: singing, church choir, sewing, reading. Home: 9576 Winston Redford MI 48239-1660 E-mail: Madge246@aol.com.

AUBIN, BARBARA JEAN, artist; b. Chgo., Jan. 12, 1928; d. Philip Theodore and Dorothy May (Chapman) A. BA, Carleton Coll., 1949; B Art Edn., Sch. Art Inst. Chgo., 1954, M Art Edn., 1955. Lectr. Centre D'Art & Haitian Am. Inst., Port-Au-Prince, Haiti, 1958-60; asst. prof. Sch. Art Inst. Chgo., 1960-67, Loyola U., Chgo., 1968-71; lectr. Calumet Coll., Hammond, Ind., 1971-75; prof. art Chgo. State U., 1971-91; ret., 1991. Vis. prof., artist Wayne State U., Detroit, Mich., 1965; vis. artist St. Louis C.C., Forest Park, Mo., 1980-81, U. Wis., Green Bay, 1981; co-curator Art for the Next Millennium Kimo Theatre Gallery, Albuquerque, 1997; spkr. and exhibiting artist, Womens's Caucus For Art Regional Conf./Exhibition, 1999. One-woman shows include Countryside Arts Ctr., Arlington Heights, Ill., 1954, 87, Avant Arts Gallery, Chgo., 1954, Riccardo's Restaurant and Gallery, Chgo., 1956, Evanston (Ill.) Twp. H.S., 1958, Centre d'Art, Port-au-Prince, Haiti, 1960, Chgo. Pub. Libr., 1960, Chgo. Acad. Fine Arts, 1965, Oxbow Summer Sch. Fine Arts, 1965, Lewis Towers Gallery, Loyola U., Chgo., 1970, Chgo. State U., 1971, 74, 85, North River Cmty. Gallery, Northeastern Ill. U., Chgo., 1974, Ill. Arts Coun., Chgo., Crossroads-Jr. Mus., Art Inst. Chgo., 1976, Fairweather Hardin Gallery, Chgo., 1978, 80, 85, 90, U. Wis., 1981, Illini Union Gallery, U. Ill., Urbana, 1986, Artemisia Gallery, Chgo., Katerina's, Chgo., 2002; exhibited in group shows at Art Inst. Chgo., 1960, 78, 80, 85, 89, Vanderpoel Art Assn., Beverly Art Ctr., Chgo., 1992, Ancient Echoes, Chgo., 1992, Renaissance Ct., Chgo. Cultural Ctr., 1993, 2001, 2002, Artemisia Gallery, Chgo., 1994, Art Place Gallery, Chgo, 1994, Chgo. State U., 1994, Chgo. Women's Caucus for Art, 1994, 98, 2000, Eastern Ill. U., Charleston, 1991, 1993-2001, ARC Gallery, Chgo., 1995, 97, 2004, N.Mex. Art League, Albuquerque, 1996, Mirage Gallery, Albuquerque, Barrington Arts Coun., 1997, Meridian Ctr., Washington, 1997, Chgo. Women's Caucus for Art No. Ill. U., 1998, Springfield Art Mus., Mo., 1999, (Patron Purchase award), Beacon St. Gallery, Chgo., 1999, DeKalb (Ill.) Area Women's Ctr., 1999, Mini-Millennium Women's Caucus For Art Nat. Gallery, 2000, Eastern Ill. U., Charleston, Ill., 2000-01, Chgo. Cultural Ctr., 2001-02; represented in permanent collections at Art Inst. Chgo., Ill. State Mus., Ball State Mus., Calumet Coll., Hammond, Ind., Shimer Coll., Waukegon, Ill., Kemper Group Collection, Long Grove, Ill., State of Ill. Bldg., Chgo., Seyfarth, Shaw, Fairweather & Geraldson, Washington, Ernst & Ernst, Chgo., Foote, Cone & Belding, Chgo., U.S. League of Savs. and Loans, Chgo., Northside Industries, Chgo., Keck, Cushman, Mahin & Cate, Chgo., Gould, Inc., Rolling Meadows, Ill., First Nat. Bank Chgo., Internat. Mineral and Chem., Skokie, Ill.; reporter Women Artists News, 1977, 80, 83-86. V.p. Midwest region Womens Caucus for Art, Chgo., 1982-88; founding mem. local chpt. Chgo. Women's Caucus for Art, 1973, bd. dirs., 2002, 2003, 2004; bd. dirs. Chgo. Artists' Coalition, 1992-94. Recipient George D. Brown Fgn. Travel fellow Sch. Art Inst. Chgo., 1955-56; Art grant Fulbright fellow, 1958-60, Huntington Hartford Fedn. grant, 1963, Project Completion grant Ill. Arts Coun., 1978-79, Chgo. Cultural Ctr., 2002, CAAPS grant, 2002. Mem. Arts Club Chgo., Chgo. Artists' Coalition, Chgo. Womens Caucus for Art. Home: The Hallmark 2960 N Lake Shore Dr #405 Chicago IL 60657-5645 E-mail: dittofcline@aol.com.

AUCHTER, NORMA HOLMES, musician, music educator; b. Rochester, N.Y., Jan. 3, 1922; d. Robert Edgar and Ruby (Lyon) Holmes; m. Ervin Frank Auchter, June 4, 1955; children: Robert Holmes Auchter, Ceci Ann Albecker, Allan Neil Auchter. BMus with distinction, U. Rochester, 1942, MMus Theory, 1944, DMus Arts Performance and Lit., 1977; studied with Carl Friedberg, N.Y.C., 1950-54. Instr. U. Conn., Storrs, 1943-45, U. Tex., Austin, 1945-46; faculty Eastman Sch. Music, Rochester, 1946-50; piano instr. Middlebury (Vt.) Coll., 1956-61; lectr., accompanist, mus. dir. St. Michael's Coll., Winnoski, Vt., 1967-72; assoc. prof. Tex. Tech. U., Lubbock, 1972-75; piano instr. SUNY, Geneseo, 1976-78; piano/theory prof. U. N.C., Pembroke, 1978-79; pvt. piano tchr. Houston, 1979—; mem. faculty Houston C.C. NW, 2003—. Adj. instr. Houston Cmty. Coll., 2003, piano instr. U. Vt., Burlington, 1960-72; co-owner Auchters House of Music, Burlington, 1956-72; debut recital, Town Hall, N.Y.C., 1952; concert tours U.S., Can., 1950-57; entertainer, lectr. adjudicator, workshops, master classes, TV sch., U.S., Can., 1950—; performing mem. Tuesday Mus. Club, Houston, 1980—. Collaborating artist with Paul Alvarez violin concerts; books and recordings for Mel Bay Pub. including Cabaret Treasures for Violin and Piano, 1995, Salon Gems for Violin and Piano, 1997. Mu Phi Epsilon Postgrad. grant, 1974. Mem. Nat. Guild of Piano Tchrs. (adjudicator), Music Tchrs. Nat. Assn. Home: 2828 Hayes Road #2815 Houston TX 77082 E-mail: nauchter@juno.com.

AUERBACH, ANITA L. clinical psychologist; b. Flushing, N.Y., Dec. 23, 1946; d. Ben and Gussie (Zuckerman) Weiss; m. Steven Miles Auerbach, May 25, 1969. BA cum laude, SUNY, Buffalo, 1968, MA, 1970; PhD (N.Y. State Regents fellow 1970-72), George Washington U., 1977. Diplomate Am. Bd. Med. Psychotherapists, Internat. Acad. Behavioral Medicine. Chief rsch. Youth Crime Control Project D.C. Dept. Corrections, 1970-74; intern clin. psychology No. Va. Tng. Ctr., Fairfax, 1974-75, staff psychologist, then chief psychol. svcs., 1975-79; pvt. practice clin. psychology Commonwealth Psychol. Assocs. PLC, McLean, Va., 1979—; founder,dir. Commonwealth Psychol. Assocs., 1979—, pres., 1979—; asst. clin. prof. psychology George Washington U. Lectr. Washington Tech. Inst., 1972-74, George Mason U., 1978—82; asst. clin. prof. psychology George Washington U., 2003—; cons. in field. Contbr. articles to profl. jours. Mem. adv. bd. World Children's Choir, 2000—02; mem. family edn. project Joseph P. Kennedy Jr. Found., 1977—79; mem. regional appeals bd. No. Va. Pub. Sch. Sys., 1977—79; mem. adv. bd. Value Options Behavioral Health, 2001—. Recipient N.Y. State Scholar Incentive award, 1969. Mem. APA, Am. Soc. Clin. Hypnosis (approved cons.), Va. Acad. Clin. Psychologists, Va. Psychol. Assn., No. Va. Soc. Clin. Psychologists, Washington Soc. Study Clin. Hypnosis, Psi Chi, Alpha Lambda Delta. Office: 1479 Chain Bridge Rd Mc Lean VA 22101-5730

AUERBACH, KATHRYN ANN, architecture and preservation educator, consultant; b. Doylestown, Pa., Aug. 21, 1954; d. John Joseph and Elizabeth Rose Auerbach; m. John Michael Pivarnik, May 25, 1991 (dec. Nov. 6, 2000); 1 child, Anika Theresa Pivarnik. BA in History, Coll. William & Mary, 1976. Asst. commr. Va. Rsch. Ctr. for Archaeology, Williamsburg, 1976—77; dir. historic programs Bucks County Conservancy, Doylestown, Pa., 1977—86; cons. historic preservation Kathryn Ann Auerbach, Erwinna, Pa., 1986—; instr. historic preservation Bucks County C.C., Newton, Pa., 1991—. Mem. hist. preservation adv. bd. Bucks County C.C., Newtown, Pa., 1990—. Bd. dirs. Tinicum Conservancy, Erwinna, Pa., 1992—2002. Recipient 3d Place C.A. Peterson prize, Hist. Am. Bldgs. Survey, Washington, 2003. Mem.: Kappa Alpha Theta, Sigma Pi Kappa. Roman Catholic. Avocation: gardening. Home: PO Box 39 Erwinna PA 18920

AUERBACHER, MARY JANE, church organist; b. Alhambra, Calif., Sept. 21, 1922; d. Alvah Jasper McConnel and Mamie Estelle Ruhe; children: Alice, Eleanore, Julia. BA, U. Redlands, 1944, MusB, 1947. Tchr. 1st grade Migratory Camp, Indio, Calif., 1944—45; founder Valley Pre. Sch. (accredited CAIS, WASC), Redlands, Calif., 1958; tchr. music Valley Prep. Sch., Redlands, 1960—76; organist, choir dir. several chs., San Bernadino, 1976—. Dean Am. Guild Organists, Redlands, 1980; pres. Spinet, 1986. Author: Devotions, 1995. Bd. dirs. Valley Prep. Sch., 1976—2001; pres. Am. Bapt. Women, Redlands, 1981—83, 1990—92. Named Gifr Honor, AAUW, Redlands, 1984, Woman of Yr., City of Redlands, 1986; recipient Grail award, Knights of Round Table, 1988. Mem.: Redlands Cmty. Music Assn. Baptist. Avocations: birdwatching, hiking, reading. Home: 121 Sierra Vista Dr Redlands CA 92373 Office: Christ the King Luth Ch 1505 Ford St Redlands CA 92373

AUERBACK, SANDRA JEAN, social worker; b. San Francisco, Feb. 21, 1946; d. Alfred and Molly Loy (Friedman) Auerback. BA, U. Calif., Berkeley, 1967; MSW, Hunter Sch. Social Work, 1972. LCSW. Clin. social worker Jewish Family Services, Bklyn., 1972-73, clin. social worker Hackensack, N.J., 1973-78; pvt. practice psychotherapy San Francisco, 1978—; dir. intake adult day care Jewish Home for the Aged, San Francisco, 1979-91. Mem.: NASW (bd. dirs. Bay Area Referral Svc. 1983—87, chmn. referral svc. 1984—87, state practice com. 1987—91, rep. to Calif. Coun. Psychiatry, Psychology, Social Work and Nursing 1987—95, chmn. 1989, regional treas. 1989—91, v.p. cmty. svcs. 1991—93, chmn. 1993, chair Calif. polit. action com. 1993—95, v.p. profl. stds. com. 2000—02, cert.), Mental Health Assn. San Francisco (trustee 1987—95). Home: 1100 Gough St Apt 8C San Francisco CA 94109-6638 Office: 450 Sutter St San Francisco CA 94108-4206

AUGER, KIMBERLY ANN, elementary school educator; b. Everett, Mass., July 3, 1970; d. Robert Charles and Patricia Ann (Cahill) Auger. B, Salem State Coll., 1992; EdM, Cambridge Coll., 2002. Tchr. Everett (Mass.) Pub. Sch., 1992—. Mem.: Mass. Tchrs. Assn. (bd. dirs. 2003—). Democrat. Roman Catholic. Avocations: bowling, skiing, travel. Home: 40 Woodward St Everett MA 02149 Office: Parlin Sch 587 Broadway Everett MA 02149

AUGHENBAUGH, DEBORAH ANN, mayor, retired elementary school educator; b. Bklyn., Oct. 15, 1922; d. James R. and Alice Lillian (Walsh) Donecho; m. William Irving Hopwood, Mar. 31, 1946 (dec. July 1966); 1 child, William James; m. Kenneth Merle Aughenbaugh, Oct. 20, 1973 (dec. Sept. 1997). BS, Towson (Md.) State Coll., 1952; MS, Shippensburg (Pa.) U., 1967. Cert. elem. tchr., guidance counselor, Md. Tchr. Balt. City Pub. Schs., 1952-54, St. John's Cath. Ch., Frederick, Md., 1960-63, Frederick County Bd. Edn., Frederick, 1963-84; mem. city coun. City of Burkittsville, Md., 1971-74, 80-83, mayor, 1986-95; ret., 1995. Mem. Gov.'s Policy Com. on Edn., 1994-95, Frederick County Bd. Edn., 1995-2002, v.p., 2000-01; mem. Md. Assn. Bds. of Edn. legis. com., 1995-97, 98-99. Chmn. Burkittsville Planning and Zoning Commn., 1969-79; mem. Frederick Recycling Com., 1989-91; mem. Frederick Solid Waste Adv. Bd., 1991-93; mem. Frederick County Bd. of Edn., 1995-2002, v.p., 2000-01; mem. Frederick County Park and Recreation Com.; mem. legis. com. Md. Assn. Bd. Edn., Nat. Bd. Edn., 1998—; mem. Frederick County Future Growth and Sch. Schedule Adv. Com. Mem. Frederick County Ret. Sch. Personnel (pres.-elect), Md. Mcpl. League (pres. Frederick County chpt. 1992, state legis. com. 1985-95, chair 1992-93, bd. dirs. 1985-95), Nat. League Cities (human devel. com. 1991-95), Frederick County Public Sch. Employees (pres. elect 2002-03, pres. 2003-04). Democrat. Avocations: reading, travel, crocheting. Home: PO Box 408 Burkittsville MD 21718-0408

AUGUR, MARILYN HUSSMAN, distribution executive; b. Texarkana, Ark., Aug. 23, 1938; d. Walter E. and Betty (Palmer) H.; m. James M. Augur, Dec. 29, 1962; children: Margaret M. Hancock, Elizabeth H. Taylor, Ann Louise Hardaway. BA, U. N.C., 1960; MBA, So. Meth. U., 1989. Pres. North Tex. Mountain Valley Water, Dallas, 1989—. Bd. dirs. Camden News Pub. Co., Little Rock. Trustee Hussman Found., Little Rock, 1991—, U. Tex. Southwestern Med. Found., 1993—, Nat. Jewish Hosp., 1993—2000, Marilyn Augur Family Found., Dallas, 1991—; bd. dirs. Baylor Health Sys. Found., 1992—, chmn., 1995; bd. dirs. Tate Lectr. Series, 1994—2000; mem. adv. bd., Salvation Army, 1996-, chmn. William Booth Soc., 1999-2000; mem. Tex. Bus. Hall Fame, 1992—98, exec. com., 1994—95; mem. Dallas Citizens Coun., 1994—; bd. dirs. Dallas County C.C. Dist. Found., 1995—; bd. mem. Dallas Helps, 1995—99, Charter 100, 1998—, Baylor Oral Health Found. Bd., 1998—2001; mem. exec. bd. So. Meth. U. Dedman Law Sch. & Cox. Bus. Sch., 1998—; bd. dirs. Children's Health Care Sys. Found., 1998—. Mem. Dallas Country Club, Crescent Club, Dallas Women's Club, Beta Gamma Sigma. Episcopalian. Avocations: travel, skiing, trekking. Office: North Tex Mountain Valley Water 3131 Turtle Creek Blvd Ste 1000 Dallas TX 75219-5439

AUGUST-DEWILDE, KATHERINE, banker; b. Bridgeport, Conn., Feb. 13, 1948; d. Edward G. and Benita Ruth (Miller) Burstein; m. David deWilde, Dec. 30, 1984; children: Nicholas Alexander, Lucas Barrymere. AB, Goucher Coll., 1969; MBA, Stanford U., 1975. Cons. McKinsey & Co., San Francisco, 1975-78; dir. fin. Itel Corp., San Francisco, 1978-79; sr. v.p., CFO PMI Group, San Francisco, 1979-85, pres., CFO, 1988-91; CEO, pres. First Republic Thrift & Loan of San Diego, 1988-96; exec. v.p. First Republic Bank, San Francisco, 1987—, sr. v.p., chief fin. officer, 1985-87, COO, 1996—. Mem. policy adv. bd. Ctr. for Real Estate and Urban Econs., U. Calif., Berkeley, 1987—2000; bd. dirs. First Republic Bank, Trainer, Wortham & Co., Inc. Bd. dirs. San Francisco Zool. Soc., 1993-2001, vice-chair, 1995-2000; trustee Carnegie Found., 1999-2004, Town Sch. for Boys, San Francisco, 1999—2004; mem. adv. coun. Stanford U. Grad. Sch. Bus., 2003—; trustee Mills Coll., 2004—. Mem. Women's Forum (bd. dirs.), Bankers Club, Belvedere Tennis Club, Villa Taverna. Home: 2650 Green St San Francisco CA 94123-4607 Office: First Republic Bank 111 Pine St San Francisco CA 94111-5602

AUGUSTINE, CYNTHIA H. lawyer; BA, Sarah Lawerence Coll., 1979; JD, Rutgers Law Sch., 1982. Bar: N.J., N.Y. Lawyer Pitney, Hardin, Kipp & Szuch, 1982, Times Co., 1986-93; ptnr., employment law Sabin, Bermant & Gould LLP, 1993—; sr. v.p., human resources New York Times Co., N.Y.C., 1998—. Bd. dirs. Urban Pathways. Mem. ABA. Office: The New York Times Co 1120 Aves Americas 8th fl New York NY 10036

AUGUSTINE, JEAN MAGDALENE, Canadian government official, member of parliament; b. St. George, Grenada, Sept. 9, 1937. BA, U. Toronto, Ont.; MEd, LLD (hon.), U. Toronto. Elem. sch. prin. Met. Toronto Separate Sch. Bd.; chair bd. dirs. Met. Toronto Housing Authority; mem. Can. Parliament for Etobicoke Lakeshore, 1993—; parliamentary sec. to the Prime Min. of Can. Govt. of Can., 1993—96, min. state (multiculturalism) and (status of women), 2002—. Vice chair ministerial task force on social security reform; mem. former chair standing com. on fgn. affairs and internat. trade, standing com. on citizenship and immigration; vice chair standing com. on human resources devel, mem. standing com. on human rights and status of persons with disabilities Ho. of Commons. Bd. dirs. Harbourfront, Cath. Children's Aid Soc., Can. Adv. Coun. on Status of [illegible] Metro Action Com. on Pub. Violence Against Women and Children Etobicoke Social Devel. Coun.; mem. Toronto Mayor's Task Force on Drugs, Metro Toronto Drug Abuse Prevention Task Force, Toronto Crime Inquiry, 1991; former chair women's caucus Nat. Liberal Caucus, Ont. Caucus Comm. Com., Social Policy Sub-Com. on Housing. Recipient Vol. award and pin Govt. Ont., Caribana Achievement award, Bob Marley award, Kay Livingstone award, Women of Distinction award YWCA, Women on the Move award Toronto Sun, Can. Black Achievement award 1994. Mem. Can. Assn. for Parliamentarians on Population and Devel. (founder, chair), Nat. Sugar Caucus (chair, sec. state multiculturalism status of women, 2002). Office: Ho of Commons 433 W Block Ottawa ON Canada K1A 0A6

AUGUSTINE, KATHY MARIE, state controller, state legislator, secondary education educator; b. L.A., May 29, 1956; d. Philip Blase and Katherine Alice (Thompson) A.; 1 child, Dallas; m. Chaz Higgs, Sept. 12, 2003. AB, Occidental Coll., 1977; MPA, Calif. State U., Long Beach, 1983. Flight attendant Continental Airlines, Houston, 1978-83; crew scheduler Delta Airlines, L.A., 1983-88; tchr. Diocese of Reno/Las Vegas, 1990-96; mem. Nev. Assembly, 1992-94, Nev. Senate, 1994-98. Mem. Nev. State Bd. Fin. Mem. Rep. Women's Club, Las Vegas, Nev., 1992—; former coun. of State Govts. West, chair elec. restructuring. Recipient Achievement award Bank of Am., Calif., 1974, Achievement Medallion Am. Legion, 1974, Congressional Internship grantee, Washington, 1975, Disting. Alumni award Calif. State U. Long Beach, 1997, Cmty. Appreciation award Frontier Girl Scout Coun., 1996, Svc. Excellence award Rep. Legis. of Yr., 1998; named Italian Am. of Yr., Augustus Soc. of So. Nev., 2003. Mem.: AAUW, Dept. Transp. Exec. Br. Audit Com. (bd. dirs.), Nat. Assn. State Auditors, Comptrollers and Treasurers, Jr. League of Las Vegas. Republican. Roman Catholic. Home: 1400 Maria Elena Dr Las Vegas NV 89104-1846 Office Phone: 775-684-5750. E-mail: kaugust@govmail.state.nv.us.

AUGUSTINE, ROSEMARY, vocational counselor, writer; b. Millville, N.J., Sept. 2, 1950; d. Ernest and Rose (O'Brien) A. Adminstrv. Cert., Peirce Coll., Phila., 1969. Exec. sec. Wheaton Industries, Millville, N.J., 1969-71; sec. Sports Conf. USAF, Ramstein, Germany, 1973; vocat. rehab. sec. Leesburg (N.J.) State Prison, 1974-75; adminstrv. asst. 20th Century Fox Film Corp., L.A., 1976-79; asst. to CFO Minoco So. Corp., L.A., 1980-82; divsn. adminstrv. mgr. Integrated Resources, Denver, 1982-86; mgr. investor rels. Intercap Monitoring, Denver, 1987-90; writer, publisher, owner Blue Spruce Publ. Co., Denver, 1991—; career coach, author pvt. practice, Denver, 1990—. Trainer Career Transition Ctrs., Colo., 1994—; founder www.careeradvice.com., 1996—. Author: Facing Changes in Employment, 1995, How to Live and Work Your Passion (and still earn a living), 2000, (newsletter) Career StrateGems, 1991—. Assoc. mem. Colo. Women's Leadership Coalition, Denver, 1995—; weekly facilitator Career Connection Network, Denver, 1996—. Recipient 1st pl. writing and design Small Bus. Rev., Denver, 1993. Mem. Denver Bus. Women's Network (bd. dirs., newsletter editor, 1995-96), Colo. Ind. Publs. Assn. (bd. dirs., pub. rels. 1995-96), Internet C. of C., Am. Soc. Tng. and Devel. Avocations: walking, hiking, biking, fishing. Office: Blue Spruce Pub Co Inc PO Box 24938 Denver CO 80224-0938

AUGUSTSON, EDITH, mental health clinician; b. Atlantic City, N.J., Dec. 3, 1975; d. Beth Augustson-Andt; 1 child, Nyasia. BA, Oswego (N.Y.) State U., 1997; MA, Towson (Md.) State U., 2001. Pub. rels. coord. for Office of Diversity Resources Towson State U., Balt., 1999—2000; substitute sch. psychologist Balt. City Pub. Sch. Sys., 2000—01; clinician Sch. Based Mental Health Program U. Md., 2001—. Creator, developer girls mentoring program Beautiful Mindz inc., Balt., 2003—; clin. in-svc. adv. bd. mem. U. Md. and Balt. Mental Health Systems, 2003—; coord. summer mental health inst. partnership for homeless children U. Md., Balt., 2003—. Recipient acad. recognition, United Fedn. Tchrs., 1993, Gov.'s Citation award, N.Y. State, 1993, Md. State Dels. award, Del. Nancy Hubers, 1999—2001, Womens Ctr. award, Towson State U. Women's Ctr., 2000; Senatorial scholar, Md. State Senators Office, 1999—2001. Mem.: APA (assoc.), Psi Chi (life), Alpha Kappa Alpha (life; various offices 1994—97). Avocation: walking. Office: U Md SMHP 680 W Lexington St Baltimore MD 21201

AUKOFER, CLARE ELIZABETH, newspaper editor; b. Milw., June 1, 1949; d. Herbert Anselm and Wanda Mary (Kaminski) A. BFA, U. Wis., Milw., 1972. Assoc. dir. comm. Ford's Theatre, Washington, 1973-74; assoc. editor Am. Rifleman mag., Washington, 1974-77; sr. comm. specialist GE, Rockville, Md., 1977-81, program mgr. comm. and edn. Charlottesville, Va., 1981-83; editor HELIX, dir. comm. U. Va. Health Scis. Ctr., Charlottesville, 1984-96; comms. cons., book editor U. Va. Ctr. for Study of Mind and Human Interaction, Charlottesville, 1996-98; pubs. dir. Cooper Ctr. Pub. Svc. U. Va., 1998-99; comms. dir. Prevent Cancer Found., Bristol, Va., 1999-2000; editor Special Sections Charlottesville Daily Progress, Va., 2000—. Adv. bd., adj. faculty U. Va. Continuing Edn. Pub. Program, 1994-96; theatre critic Charlottesville Daily Progress, 1981—. Chmn. arts com. 1st Night Va., Charlottesville, 1989-91; del. Charlottesville Dem. Caucus, 1991-99; mem. Charlottesville Dem. Com., 1998—; participant Leadership Charlottesville, 1992; vol. reading tutor Book Buddies. Inducted into Company of Good Cheer Pearson Internat. Can. Peacekeeping Ctr., N.S., 1998. Mem. Va. Assn. for Printing, Publs. and Pub. Rels. Profls. (pres. 1990-92, pres. emeritus 1992—). Avocations: theatre, gardening, reading, ailurophile, equestrian activities. E-mail: caukofer@dailyprogress.com.

AUKON-SHOAFF, LARISA, art educator, artist; arrived in US, 1996; d. Vladimir Aukon and Galina Gricino; m. Carl Mark Shoaff, June 11, 2001. MA in Art Edn., Latvian State Acad. of Arts, Riga, Latvia, 1990. Art tchr. Secondary Sch. # 44, Riga, Latvia, 1987—94; portrait drawing instr. Coconino C.C., Flagstaff, Ariz., 2002—; art tchr. Creationship, art for kids, Flagstaff, 2002—03. Artist in residence De Miguel Elem. Sch., Flagstaff, 2001—02, Flagstaff (Ariz.) Mid. Sch., 2002—02, Kindsey Cmty. Sch., Flagstaff, 2003, Killipp Elem. Sch., Flagstaff, 2003. One-woman shows include No. Ariz. U. Old Main Gallery, 2002—03. Avocations: reading, hiking, travel, gardening, pets. Personal E-mail: carlarashoaff@juno.com.

AULICINO, CHRISTINE WILKINSON, education educator; b. Paterson, N.J., July 24, 1944; d. Kenneth Lawrence Wilkinson and Heloise Litchfield Weber; children: Claire, Matthew. BA, Smith Coll., 1966; MA, Tchrs. Coll., Columbia Univ., N.Y., 1987. Cert. tchg. N.Y. Book designer Alfred A. Knopf, N.Y., 1970—75, self employed, N.Y., 1975—82; ednl. adminstrn. Cathedral Sch., N.Y., 1982—85; tchr. Riverdale County Sch., N.Y., 1986—91; sch. adminstr. Albany Acad. for Girls, NY, 1991—96, Laurel Sch., Cleve., 1996—. Adj. instr. Ursuline Coll., Cleve., 2001—. Author: Book of Hopes and Dreams, 1999. Office: Laurel Sch 1 Lyman Cir Shaker Heights OH 44122

AUMACK, SHIRLEY JEAN, financial planner, tax preparer; b. Newark, May 17, 1949; d. Herbert O. and Edythe V. (England) Marlatt; m. Kenneth J. Aumack, Oct. 25, 1969; children: Douglas, Steven. BA in Econs., Wilson Coll., 1971. Cert. fin. planner, enrolled agt., retirement counselor; registered investment advisor; registered rep., investment exec., accredited tax advisor Fin. Network. Account exec. N.J. Bell Telephone, Scotch Plains, N.J., 1972-76; ptnr., ind. contr. Personal Mgmt. and Planning Inc., Matawan, N.J., 1982-90, pvt. practice fin. planner tax and fin. aspects of divorce Fair Haven, 1990—; mng. supr. Employee Fin. Edn. Divsn. Fin. Network Investment Corp., 1998—. Instr. fin. planning Monmouth County Park Sys., Lincroft, NJ, 1991, Rutgers U., 1993—94, Rumson Cmty. Edn., 1995. Pres. Performing Arts Soc., Rumson Fair-Haven Regional High Sch., 1992-94. Mem.: Fin. Planning Assn., Accreditation Coun. for Accountancy and Taxation (tax advisor), Nat. Assn. Enrolled Agts., Inst. Cert. Fin. Planners, Internat. Assn. for Fin. Planning (seminar spkr. 1990). also: 2 Ethel Rd Bldg [illegible] 07730-1663

AUMILLER, WENDY L. utilities executive; BS, MBA, Miami U. CPA. Tchr. acctg. Miami U.; with Coopers and Lybrand; various positions in treasury strategic planning Cincinnati Gas & Electric Co., 1980—, asst. treas., gen. mgr. strategic planning, acting treas.; treas. Cinergy Corp., Cincinnati, 2002—. Office: Cinergy Corp 139 E 4th St Cincinnati OH 45202*

AUNE, DEBRA BJURQUIST, lawyer; b. Rochester, Minn., June 13, 1956; d. Alton Herbert and Violet Lucille (Dutcher) Bjurquist; m. Gary ReMine, June 6, 1981 (div. June 1993); children: Jessica Bjurquist ReMine, Melissa Bjurquist ReMine; m. David Aune, Jan. 1, 1995. BA, Augsburg Coll., 1978; JD, Hamline U., 1981. Bar: Minn. 1981. Assoc. Hvistendahl & Moersch, Northfield, Minn., 1981-82; adjuster Federated Ins. Cos., Owatonna, 1982-84; advanced life markets advisor Federated Life Ins. Co., Owatonna, 1984-87; mktg. svcs. advisor Federated Ins. Cos., Owatonna, 1987-89, 2d v.p., corp. legal counsel, 1989-92, v.p. gen. counsel, 1992-95, 1st v.p., gen. counsel, 1996-99; ind. cons., 1999—. Mem. Hamline Law Rev., 1979-80. Pres. Owatonna Ins. Women, 1983-84; charter commr. City of Owatonna, 1992—. Mem. ABA, Minn. State Bar Assn., 5th Dist. Bar Assn., Steele County Bar Assn. (sec. 1986-87, v.p. 1987-88, pres. 1988-89), Assn. Life Ins. Counsel, Alliance Am. Insurers (legal com. 1989—). Lutheran. Office: Federated Ins Cos 121 E Park Sq Owatonna MN 55060-3046

AUNIO, IRENE M. artist; b. Finland; m. Ernesto Saasto, Dec. 9 (dec. June 2000); children: Laurel Esken, Ernest, Robert. Student, Arts Students League, N.Y.C., Bklyn. Mus. Tchr. art Adult Edn. Prokect, Bklyn.; tchr. painting Elder hostal Program, Conn.; artist-in-residence Johnson Studies Ctr., Vt., 2001—. One-woman shows include Pen and Brush Club, N.Y., Bklyn. Mus., Panoras Gallery, Stony Brook Mus. Art, The Gallery Machias, Maine, Grist Mill Gallery, Chester, Vt., Jeanne Taylor Gallery, N.Y., Miriam Pearlman Gallery, Chgo., Belanthi Gallery, Bklyn., Brookhaven Gallery, Farmingdale, N.Y., Represented in permanent collections Evansville Mus. Fine Arts, Ind., Reading Mus. Fine Art, Pa., Norfolk Mus. Fine Art, Va., Va. State Coll., Seton Hall U., N.J., Art Students N.Y., The Nat. Bank Detroit, Ill., Std. Fed. Savings, Detroit, Detrout Edison, Ill., Macky Bell, Detroit, St. Joseph Mercy Hosp., Quaker Oats Co., Chgo., Dag Hammarskjord Plaza, N.Y., Pub. Svc. Elec. & Gas, N.J., Katz Comm., N.Y., Am. Hosp. Supply Corp., Chgo., Oakland Cmty. Hosp. Recipient Ranger Fund Purchase prize, Evansville Mus. Mem.: Nat. Assn. Women Artists, Allied Artists Am., Nat. League Am. Pen Women, Am. Watercolor Soc. Avocations: painting, swimming, dance.

AUR, MARINA V. choir conductor, music educator; b. Narva, Estonia, Russia, Jan. 4, 1963; came to the U.S., 1995; d. Victor Ivanovich and Zoja Dmitrievna Nikitin; m. Oleg Alfivich Aur, Oct. 14, 1988 (div. Feb. 1999). BA in Music, Coll. Music, Smolensk, Russia, 1982. Nat. cert. tchr. music in piano. Tchr. theory Sch. of Music, Narva, 1983-92; choir condr. Soc. of Finns, Narva, 1990-95, Day Star Christian Acad., Moses Lake, Wash., 1995—, Moses Lake Christian Sch., 1998—; pvt. piano tchr. Moses Lake, 1995—. Ch. pianist Ch. in Moses Lake, 1995—. Mem. Music Tchr. Nat. Assn. (audition chair Moses Lake chpt. 1999). Avocations: sewing, knitting, drawing, gardening, hiking. also: PO Box 1572 Moses Lake WA 98837-0245

AURELIO, KRISTEN JOAN, school psychologist; b. Perth Amboy, N.J., Oct. 31, 1971; d. Boniface P. and Concetta C. (Ricciardi) A. AA, Middlesex County Coll., 1991; BA, Seton Hall U., 1993; MA, Kean Coll., 1997; PsyM, Rutgers U., 2000, PsyD, 2003. Cert. sch. psychologist. Office and customer svc. supr. U.S. Census Bur., New Brunswick, N.J., 1990; asst. mgr. The Country's Best Yogurt, Edison, N.J., 1989-91; corp. trainer and bartender Chili's Grill and Bar, Edison, 1991-98; substitute tchr. Edison Twp. Bd. Edn., 1994-95. Grad. asst. Kean Coll., Union, N.J., 1995-97; camp advisor, Anytown, N.J., 1998. Active Boston to N.Y. AIDS Ride 2 N.Y. Cmty. Health Project, 1996, Susan G. Komen Breast Cancer Walkathon, 1993-2003. Mem. Am. Psychol. Assn., Nat. Assn. Sch. Psychologists, Psychology Club (grad. rep. 1995-97), Sch. Psychology Student Assn., N.J. Assn. Sch. Psychologists (student affiliate), N.J. Psychol. Assn., Phi Kappa Phi, Kappa Delta Pi, Psi Chi. Avocations: running, skiing, bicycling, weightlifting, aerobics.

AURORI, MICHELE DAWN, music educator; b. Bethpage, N.Y., Apr. 18, 1978; d. R.F. and N.L. Aurori. MusB magna cum laude, Ithaca (N.Y.) Coll., 2000; MusM summa cum laude, James Madison U., 2003. Tchr. Hanover County Pub. Schs., Ashland, Va., 2000—01, Westport (Conn.) Schs., 2003—. Tchg. asst. James Madison U., Harrisonburg, Va., 2001—03. Mem.: Am. String Tchrs. Assn., Pi Kappa Lambda.

AUSENBAUM, HELEN EVELYN, social worker, psychologist; b. Chgo., May 16, 1911; d. Herbert Noel and Mayme Eva A. AB, U. Calif., Berkeley, 1938, MSW, 1956. Social worker Alameda Welfare Commn., Oakland, Calif., 1939-42; exec. dir. ARC, Richmond, Calif., 1943-51; tchr. fifth grade Castro Elem. Sch., El Cerrito, Calif., 1951-53; guidance cons. Oakland Pub. Schs., 1953-76; founder, dir. Orinda Counseling Ctr., 1959-95; program dir. Support Svcs., Walnut Creek, Calif., 1978-84. Chair Rossmoor Com. for Common Concern, 1994-96, Mental Health Task Force Contra Costa County, 1978-84; mem. Contra Costa County Adv. Coun. on Aging, 1984-97. Mem. chair nominating com. Rossmoor Dem. Club, 1996; mem. and co-chair Mental Health Profls. of Rossmoor. Mem. NASW, Rotary. Democrat. Presbyterian. Avocations: stamps, freighter travel, reading. Home: 1936 Tice Valley Blvd Walnut Creek CA 94595-2203

AUST, ELIZABETH ANN (BETTY), artist; b. LA, June 11, 1921; d. Grange Sard and Margaret Ann (Salinas) Thatcher; m. Harold Ted Aust, Jr., Oct. 17, 1942 (dec. Oct. 2000); children: Janith L. Gandy, Bradley T. Student, UCLA, 1939—42. Exhibited in group shows at Ann. Statewide Art Show, Santa Rosa, Calif., 1976—88, Sonoma (Calif.) County Fair, 1976—85, Occidental (Calif.) Art Gallery, 1977—83, Spring Art Festival Charles Schultz Ice Arena, Santa Rosa, 1983, Ann. Apple Blossom Festival, Sebastopol, Calif., 1986—89, various galleries, 1980—89, paintings commisioned by, Larkfield (Calif.) Exch. Bank, 1986, Healdsburg (Calif.) Exch. Bank, 1987. Mem.: Artists Roundtable, Santa Rosa Art Guild, Nat. League Am. Pen Women.

AUSTER, ELLEN, finance company executive; BS, Wharton Sch. Bus., U. Pa., 1980; JD, George Washington U., 1983; masters in taxation law, NYU, 1983. With Deloitte & Touche LLP, 1984—, ptnr., 1996—; office leader Deloitte & Touche Long Island Office, 2003—. Ptnr. in charge of women's initiative for tri-state region Deloitte & Touche LLP; spkr. on women's issues. Named to, YWCA Acad. of Women Achievers, 1999. Mem.: Finl. Women's Assn. N.Y. Office: Deloitte & Touche LLP 2 Jericho Plz Jericho NY 11753-1683

AUSTER, NANCY EILEEN ROSS, economics educator; b. N.Y.C., Aug. 19, 1926; d. Norman L. and Edith Cornelia (Jacobson) Ross; m. Donald Auster, Aug. 18, 1946; children: Carol J., Ellen R. AB, Barnard Coll., 1948; MBA, Ind. U., 1954. Rsch. assoc. The Conf. Bd., N.Y.C., 1948-51; editor publs. Bur. Bus. Rsch. Ind. U., Bloomington, 1954-56; lectr. St. Lawrence U., Canton, N.Y., 1962-66; from asst. prof. to prof. Canton Coll. Tech., SUNY, 1966-82, disting. svc. prof. econs., 1982-91, disting. svc. prof. econs. emeritus, 1991—. Pres. univ. faculty senate SUNY, 1973 75; mem. chancellor's adv. com. disting. tchg. prof. SUNY, 1983-86, chair, 1986-87. Author: (with Donald Auster) Men Who Enter Nursing: A Sociological Analysis, [illegible] Lawrence County CETA, Canton, 1977 [illegible] Recipient Professions Excellence award N.Y. State/United Univ. Professions, 1991; USPHS grantee, 1966-70. Unitarian-Universalist. Avocations: running, skiing, birding, quilting. Home: 21 Craig Dr Canton NY 13617-1211

AUSTIN, ANN SHEREE, lawyer; b. Tyler, Tex., Aug. 25, 1960; d. George Patrick and Mary Jean (Brookshire) A. BA cum laude, U. Houston, 1983; JD, South Tex. Coll., 1987. Bar: Tex. 1987, U.S. Dist. Ct. (no. dist.) Tex. 1988, U.S. Ct. Appeals (5th cir.) 1989, U.S. Dist. Ct. (we. dist.) Tex. 1990, U.S. Ct. Appeals (D.C. cir.) 1992, U.S. Supreme Ct. 1992, U.S. Dist. Ct. (ea. dist.) Tex. 1993. With First City Ops. Ctr., Houston, 1980-85; law clk. Lipstet, Singer, Hirsch & Wagner, Houston, 1985-86, Pizzitola, Hinton & Sussman, Houston, 1986-87; briefing atty. Hon. Hal M. Lattimore Ct. Appeals, 2d Jud. Dist., Ft. Worth, 1987-88; assoc. Cantey & Hanger, Ft. Worth and Dallas, 1988-93, Smith, Ralston & Russell, Dallas, 1993-94, Russell, Austin & Henschel, Dallas, 1994-95; pvt. practice Arlington, 1995-96; prin. Landau, Omahana & Kopka, Ltd., Dallas, 1996-97; asst. city atty. City of Dallas, 1997—2002; atty. Law Offices of W. Blake Hyde, 2002—. Tchr. Project Outreach State Bar of Tex., 1992. Author: Personnel Rules, Park & Recreation Department, City Dallas, 2000; co-author Annual Meeting of Invited Attorneys, Construction Law, 1992; chpt. editor: Cases and Materials on Civil Procedure, 1987. Mem. Ft. Worth Hist. Preservation Soc., com. mem., 1992; fundraiser Prevention of Child Abuse in Am., 1988—, Women's Haven. Mem. Tex. Young Lawyers Assn. (jud. rev. com. 1990, women in the profession com., profl. ethics and grievance awareness com. 1992-94), Dallas Bar Assn. (jud. com. 1992-94, ethics com. 1999-01, cmty. involvement com., employment law sect. CLE com. 1999-2000), Dallas Assn. Young Lawyers, Dallas Women's Bar Assn., Ft. Worth Tarrant County Young Lawyers Assn. (treas. 1989-90, dir. 1989, co-chair Teen Ctr., co-chair Adopt-A-Sch. program, tchr. Constl. Rights, 5th grade class, chair CLE program), Tarrant County Women's Bar Assn., Am. Inns. of Ct., Garland Walker Inn; vol. Texas Mock Trial Competition. Methodist. Avocations: walking, reading, sky diving. Office: Law Offices of W Blake Hyde Ste 490/LB11 1301 E Collins Blvd Richardson TX 75081

AUSTIN, BERIT SYNNOVE, small business owner, central services specialist; b. Oslo, July 22, 1938; came to U.S., 1957; d. Johan Andreas and Astrid (Bjerke) Irgens; m. William Paul Austin, Dec. 22, 1961 (div. 1978); children: Lisa Christine, Paul Erik, Ivar Jon; m. Berit Synnove Funnemark, Feb. 20, 2000. AA, Saddleback Coll., 1984, AS, 1988. Accounts payable clk. Dynatech Corp., Santa Ana, Calif., 1976-78; accounts payable acct., jr. buyer/Kardex Brunswick Corp., Costa Mesa, Calif., 1978-81; fin. clk. Fluor Corp., Irvine, Calif., 1981-84; warehouse asst. Saddleback Coll., Mission Viejo, Calif., 1984—, instr. Norwegian lang. Owner, cons. Home Prescription, Lake Elsinore, Calif., Mission Viejo, 1984—. Mem. Sierra Country Club, Sons of Norway Fraternal Internat. Soc. (historian 1972, publicity dir. 1973, asst. soc. dir. 1974, social dir. 1992, cultural dir. 1994, pres. 1996). Republican. Lutheran. Avocations: gardening, bicycling, cross-country skiing, travel. Home and Office: Home Prescription PO Box 4013 Mission Viejo CA 92690-4013 E-mail: baustin7@yahoo.com.

AUSTIN, CAROLINE GERMAINE, small business owner; b. San Juan, PR, Jan. 19, 1965; d. Roberto Antonio and Theresa Austin; 1 child, Manuel Raphael. AA in Data Processing, AA in Bus. Mgmt., Coll. of the V.I., St. Thomas, US V.I., 1988; BA in Bus. Adminstrn., U. of the V.I., St. Thomas, US V.I., 1988. Receptionist/sec. Pivar Real Estate, St. Croix, U.S. V.I., 1987—88; asst. store mgr. Benetton, St. Thomas, U.S. V.I., 1989; office mgr. VI 7 Inc. (7 Eleven), St. Thomas, U.S. V.I., 1989; bookkeeper Yem Honda Hyundai Auto Svc., Oakland, Calif., 1993—2000; asst. legal sec. Iver A. Stridiron, Esq., St. Thomas, U.S. V.I., 1986; asst. account analyst Delta Dental Ins. Co., San Francisco, 1994—96; publs. coord. Childcare Health Program, Berkeley, Calif., 2003—; clerical specialist Bank of Am., Oakland, Calif., 1994; adminstrv. analyst/specialist CA Child Care Health Program/Childcare Health Program, Oakland, Calif., 1997—2001; bus. owner By The Stars, Oakland, Calif., 2002—. Lighting/ asst. sound dir., usher, office asst. Island Ctr. for the Performing Arts, St. Croix, Virgin Islands, 1987—89; office mgr. cons., sales rep. Tradewinds At Morningstar, St. Croix, 1988; office asst. cons. The Club St. Croix, St. Croix, Virgin

Islands, 1988—88; info. systems mgmt. cons. La Vida Yacht Charters, St. Thomas, Virgin Islands, 1984—84; computer resources asst. FROSTCO, St. Thomas, 1983. Composer (singer, producer): (music album) With Love, Caroline, (music video) Believe; author: (short stories compilation) Cafe Amore; singer: (music album) Roll It/Back to Back, Untitled. Election com. mem. The Party to Elect Iver A. Stridiron to the Senate, St. Thomas, 1981, The Party to Re-Elect Iver A. Stridiron to the Senate, St. Thomas, [illegible]. Recipient cert. achievement, CA Child Care Health Program, 1999, 2001. Mem.: NAFE, Caribbean Assn. of Women Entrepreneurs, Inst. of Noetic Scis. Avocations: travel, reading, studying east/west spiritual philosophies & mythologies, forensic pathology case studies, home improvement and decor. Office: By The Stars 693 39th St # 5 Oakland CA 94609 E-mail: info@bythestars.org.

AUSTIN, DIANA SUE, elementary school educator; b. Seminole, Okla., Dec. 23, 1956; d. James David McQuerry and Patricia Gail McQuerry-Coker; m. Kenneth Dale Austin, June 18, 1977; children: Jessica Austin Rubicam, Lindsay. BME magna cum laude, Okla. Bapt. U., Shawnee, Okla. Cert. tchg. Okla. Bd. Edn. Tchr. Sapulpa Sch., Okla., 1979—80; choral dir. Henryetta Sch., Okla., 1980—81; tchr. Okemah Sch., Okla., 1981—83, Hilldale Sch., Muskogee, Okla., 1983—85; choral dir. Cleveland Sch., Okla., 1986—90; tchr. Jenks Sch., Okla., 1990—98; choral dir. Bartlesville Sch., Okla., 1999—2003. Pianist Immanuel Bapt. Ch., Shawnee, Okla., 1975—79, Bartlesville Southern Ch., Okla., 1999—2003. Asst. dir. youth choir, Bartlesville, Okla., 1998—2003. Mem.: Okla. Educators Assn., Music Educators Nat. Conf., Am. Choral Dir. Assn. Bapt. Avocations: family, shopping, church activities. Home: 1022 Drexal Pl Duncan OK 73533

AUSTIN, ELIZABETH RUTH, retired elementary school educator; b. Glendale, Calif., June 28, 1928; d. Lloyd Lewis Austin and Mary Elizabeth Berryman. BA, Scripps Coll., 1950; postgrad., Occidental Coll., 1950—51, UCLA, 1959, U. S.C., 1961, Orange State Coll., 1964, U. Calif., Santa Barbara, 1975. Admitting office clk. Hosp. Good Samaritan, L.A., 1976—93; elem. tchr. Alhambra, Calif., 1951—55, L.A., 1957—62, Newport Beach, Calif., 1962—65, San Marino, Calif., 1974—76; ret. Home: 1428 S Marengo Ave Alhambra CA 91803

AUSTIN, GAYLA ROLSTON, music educator, musician; b. LaFollette, Tenn., Oct. 25, 1961; d. Jimmy Willard and Mary Emily Rolston; m. Scott Edward Austin, July 21, 1990; children: Taylor Reid, Parker Heath. BA, Tenn. Temple U., 1983; MusM, U. Tenn., 1985. Cert. tchr. Ga. Asst. prof. Tenn. Temple U., Chattanooga, 1984—91; with Cadek Conservatory of Music U. Tenn., Chattanooga, 1991—99; music tchr. Boynton Elem. Sch., Ringgold, Ga., 1999—. Pianist Ctrl. Bapt. Ch., Hixson, Tenn., 1991—. Dir.: (musical theater prodn.) Fiddler on the Roof, 1987, The Sound of Music, 1989, Camelot, 1990, Annie, Jr., 2001, The Music Man, Jr., 2003. Baptist. Home: 6096 Heritage Ridge Dr Hixson TN 37343 Office: Boynton Elementary School 3938 Boynton Dr Ringgold GA 30736 E-mail: gaustin.boy@catoosa.k12.ga.us.

AUSTIN, JEANNETTE HOLLAND, genealogist, writer; b. Atlanta, July 28, 1936; d. Laurel Benjamin Holland and Marguerite Elizabeth Evans; m. Jerry Franklin Austin, May 13, 1977 (dec. Mar. 1993); 1 child, Christopher Lewis (dec.) ; 1 child from previous marriage, Suzanne Teri Stucki. Legal sec. Smith, Field, Doremus & Ringel, Atlanta, 1954—63; profl. genealogist Atlanta, 1964—; owner www.genealoty-books.com, www.georgiapioneers.com. With Family History Ctr. Ch. LDS, Jonesboro, Ga., 1988—99. Author: The Georgians, 1984, Holland 1000-1988, 1988, Abstracts of Georgia Wills, DeKalb County Probate Records, etc. Recipient cert., Atlanta Ga. Temple, 2001. Republican. Mem. Lds Ch. Avocations: drawing, singing, oil painting, drama, biking. Home: 3010 Sherwood Dr Saint Simons Island GA 31520 Personal E-mail: jha@georgiapioneers.com.

AUSTIN, JOAN D. personal care industry executive; V.p., treas. A-dec Inc., Newberg, Oreg., 1963—; pres. Austin Industries, Newberg. Chmn. bd. Drug and Alcohol Treatment Ctr. at Springbrook N.W., Newberg. Mem. Internat. Women's Forum, Found. for Women's Resources Office: A-dec Inc 2601 Crestview Dr Newberg OR 97132-9529

AUSTIN, JOAN KESSNER, mental health nurse; b. Tell City, Ind., Sept. 24, 1944; d. Edward E. and Dorothy A. (Ziegelgraber) Kessner; m. David Ross Austin, Dec. 18, 1965; 1 child, Janet Lynn. Diploma, Deaconess Hosp., Evansville, Ind., 1965; BS in Nursing, Tex. Woman's U., 1975; MS in Nursing, Ind. U., 1978, DNS, 1981. Clin. instr. Tex. Woman's U., Denton, Tex.; prof. Ind U., Indpls. Contbr. articles to profl. jours. Grantee Nat. Inst. Neurol. Disorders and Stroke. Fellow Am. Acad. Nursing; mem. Epilepsy Found. Am. (profl. adv. bd. 1987-95), Inst. Medicine. Home: 3040 N Ramble Rd W Bloomington IN 47408-1052

AUSTIN, JUDY ESSARY, scriptwriter; b. Jackson, Tenn., Apr. 7, 1948; d. Hershel Dee and Elizabeth Sue (Rhodes) Essary; m. James Michael Austin, July 4, 1965; children: James Allan Austin, Julia Ann Austin Barr. AS, DeKalb Coll., 1988; BA in Communications and Journalism, Mercer U., 1989. Retail mgr. Bankers Note, Atlanta, 1980-84, Le Chocolat Elegant, Atlanta, 1984-85; student asst. student affairs DeKalb Coll., Dunwoody, Ga., 1987-88; asst. art dir. Sportime, Atlanta, 1990-92; writer, prodr. CAMA, Atlanta, 1993-94; freelance scriptwriter Atlanta, 1994—. Bd. dirs. Second Wind Orgn., Dekalb Coll., Dunwoody, 1987-88. Scholar Am. Bus. Womens Assn., 1987. Mem. Women in Communications, NAFE, Phi Kappa Phi. Avocations: photography, reading, flying, fishing, writing. Home: 3133 Raymond Dr Atlanta GA 30340-1826 E-mail: jaustin@bigzoo.net.

AUSTIN, KAREN, retail executive; b. Delphos, Ohio; BS in Computer Sci., Tri-State U. Various positions Kmart Corp., 1984—2002, sr. v.p., chief info. officer, 2002—. Office: Kmart Corp 3100 W Big Beaver Rd Troy MI 48084

AUSTIN, LINDA S. psychiatrist; b. 1951; m. Marshall Austin (div.); children: Stephanie, Matt. At, Stanford U.; BA, Duke U., 1973; MD, Duke U. Sch. of Medicine, 1976. Resident in psychiatry Duke U.; clin. instr. psychiatry Georgetown U., Washington; pvt. practice Chevy Chase, Md.; staff Med. U. S.C., 1986—89, asst. prof. psychiatry, 1989—99, assoc. dean pub. edn., 1996, prof. psychiatry, 1999—2000; staff Ea. Maine Med. Ctr. Heritage Psychiat. Assn., Bangor, Maine, 2000—. Dir. Obsessive-Compulsive Disorder program Med. U. S.C., 1989, mem. Hurricane Hugo response team, 89; featured in Depression: The Storm Within Am. Psychiat. Soc., 1990; host What's on Your Mind Nat. Pub. Radio, 1990—; TV appearances. Author: (books) What's Holding You Back? Eight Critical Choices for Women's Success, 1999, Heart of the Matter: How to Find Love. How to Make it Work., 2003; editor: Responding to Disaster: A Mental Health Clinician's Guide, 1989. Fellow child psychiatry, Georgetown U. Address: Heritage Psychiatric Assn Ste 403 15 Columbia St Bangor ME 04401*

AUSTIN, LOLA HOUSTON, psychologist; b. San Antonio, Dec. 27, 1939; d. Albert and Sarah Leola Houston; m. Craig L. Austin, July 4, 1972; children: Madie Grabda, Polly Toro, Julia Austin-Young, Carrie Austin-Bingamond. BA in Edn., North Tex. State U., 1966; MA in Edn., U. Incarnate Word, 1973; PhD in Clin. Psychology, Fielding Inst., 1987; postgrad. study in neuropsychol. evaluation, Santa Barbara, Calif., 2000. Elem. sch. tchr. Edgewood Ind. Sch. Dist., San Antonio Ind. Sch. Dist., Northside Ind. Sch. Dist., San Antonio, 1960—75; reading specialist Northside Ind. Sch. Dist., San Antonio, 1971—76; owner, dir. D & R Reading Clinic, San Antonio, 1976; psychologist San Antonio, 1997; neuropsychol. evaluator, 2000. Cons. Psychol. Corp., San Antonio, PAR; evaluator Child Protective Svcs., San Antonio. Co-chmn. fair King William Hist. Orgn., San Antonio, co-chair food booths. Mem.: APA, Nat. Acad. Neuropsychology, Delta Kappa Gamma (charter mem. Iota Beta chpt.). Office: D & R Reading Clinic Ste 103 503 E Ramsey San Antonio TX 78216

AUSTIN, PATRICIA DAVIS, academic administrator; b. Lynn, Mass., Oct. 7, 1943; d. Lorne C. and Margaret M. (Baker) Davis; m. Robert E. Kelley; children: Campbell, Taylor Emily, Loren. BA, Tufts U., 1965; MEd, Salem (Mass.) Coll., 1971; cert. advanced study, Harvard U., 1977. Editorial asst. Saturday Rev., N.Y.C., 1965-67; grant writer Malden (Mass.) Pub. Schs., 1977-85; cons. Austin Assocs., Wenham, Mass., 1985-91; project dir. North Shore C.C., Danvers, Mass., 1991-93; project leader The Network, Andover, Mass., 1993-95; pres., publ. Wright Stuff Press Ariz., Phoenix, 1996—2003; dir. found. and grants Phila. U., 2003—, adminstr. u., 2004—. Mem. edn. policies com. Tufts U., Medford, Mass., 1978-82; cons. R.I. Dept. Edn., Providence, 1994-95, Frank Lloyd Wright Found., Scottsdale, Ariz., 1997; mem. faculty Ariz. State U., 1998-99; cons. devel. Freedoms Found., Valley Forge, Pa., 1999—. Author: (children's books) Cher Locke: The Case of the Missing Cockatiels, 1996, Cher Locke: The Dragon's Tale, 1997. Bd. dirs. Ariz. Ctr. for the Book, 1998-99. Avocations: children, piano. Office: Phila U Sch House Ln and Henry Ave Philadelphia PA 19144

AUSTIN, REBECCA LYNNE, anthropologist, consultant; b. Takoma Park, Md., June 25, 1958; d. Eduardo and Pearl Austin. BA, Ft. Lewis Coll., 1980; MA, No. Ariz. U., 1989; PhD, U. of Ga., 2003. Anthropologist Impact Assessment, Kodiak Island and Anchorage, Alaska, 1990; supervisory anthropologist Navajo Nation Hist. Preservation Dept., Window Rock, Ariz., 1992—94; grad. tchg. asst. U. of Ga., Athens, Ga., 1994—97, instr. anthropology, 1999; environ. cons. Durango, Colo., 2002—; vis. instr. anthropolgy Fort Lewis Coll., Durango, Colo., 2003—04. Sci. adv. team Environ. Legal Assistance Ctr., Puerto Princesa City, Palawan, Philippines, 1998—. Rschr., designer (exhibitions) Tribes in Transition, 1989, 1990. Outreach worker S.W. Colo. Mental Health Ctr., Durango, Colo., 1981—85. Fellow, U. of Ga. Grad. Sch., 1999—2000; grantee Fulbright-Hayes grant, Fulbright and Philippine-American Ednl. Found., 1997—98; scholar, S.E. Asian Summer Studies Inst., 1996. Fellow: Am. Anthrop. Assn. (mem. anthropology and the environ. sect.); mem.: Soc. Applied Anthropology, Phi Kappa Phi. Avocations: hiking, mountain biking, cooking, furniture building, travel. Home: 1660 West 3rd Ave Durango CO 81301 Office: 2100 Lee Hwy 418 Arlington VA 22201

AUSTIN, SANDRA IKENBERRY, nursing educator, consultant; b. Lexington, Va., Dec. 22, 1941; d. William Peters and June Virginia (Blackwell) Ikenberry; m. Joseph M. Austin, Apr. 10, 1965; children: Joseph M. Jr., Susan C., Christopher M. BSN, U. Va., 1963; MSN, U. Calif., L.A., 1967; EdD, U. Mass., 1997. RN, Mass. Pub. health nurse Dept. Health, Waynesboro, Va., 1963-64; instr. U. Va., Charlottesville, 1964-65; staff nurse Santa Monica (Calif.) Hosp., 1965-66; faculty nursing Boston U., 1968-69, Quinsigamond C.C., Worcester, Mass., 1969-70, Fitchburg (Mass.) State Coll., 1973-96; assoc. prof. nursing Framingham (Mass.) State Coll., 1997—; project dir., sr. health edn. cons. HealthCo Consulting Inc., Shrewsbury, Mass., 1996—. Mem. Shrewsbury Town Meeting, 1992—95; chair steering com. Framingham State Coll. Nursing Honor Soc., 1998, faculty counselor/advisor, 1999, pres., 1999—2002. HBO and Co. Nurse scholar, 1995. Mem.: Assn. Critical Care Nurses, Nat. League Nursing (awards com. 1999—2001), Assn. Women's Health, Obstet. and Neonatal Nurses, Am. Ednl. Rsch. ASsn., Sigma Theta Tau (Epsilon Beta edn. chair 1993—95, Rho Phi chpt. pres. 2002—, rsch. grant 1996), Pi Lambda Theta. Republican. Congregationalist. Avocations: computer multimedia production, reading, walking. Home: 100 Harrington Farms Way Shrewsbury MA 01545-4081 Office: Framingham State Coll Nursing Dept Framingham MA 01701

AUSTIN, SANDRA J. small business owner; b. Clarkburg, W.Va., May 1, 1956; d. Mary Paden Austin Ford; adopted children: Michael Renwick, Reginald Renwick. Grad., Va. Learning Inst. Sch. of Massage, Falls Church, Va., 2000. Police cadet Met. Police D.C., Washington, 1974—77, police officer, 1977—91, drivers tng. instr., 1990—91, police detective, 1991—2000; ret.; massage therapist, owner Sanctus, Burke and Dumfries, Va., 2001—. Instr. percussion Boys and Girls Club, Washington, 1980—82; percussionist Met. Police D.C. Choir, 1980—82; founder Blue Angels Female Flag Football Team, 1996; percussionist gospel choir Howard U., 1974—77. Named Police Officer of Yr., Kiwanis, 1989, Policewoman of Yr., Women's Aux. Club, 1989, Uniformed Narcotic Officer of Yr., Coun. of God, 1989. Mem.: FOP (union rep. 1987—93). Avocations: softball, basketball, football, writing, crafts. Office: Sanctus Day Spa/Massage 9554 Old Keene Mill Rd #F Burke VA 22015

AUSTIN, TERRI JO, state representative; b. Elwood, Ind., May 17, 1955; m. Michael Austin; 2 children. B in Elem. Edn., B in Elem. Edn., M in Spl. Edn., Ball State U.; degree in Ednl. Adminstrn. and Supervision, Butler U. Classroom tchr., dist. administr. Anderson Cmty. Sch. Corp., 1983—; nat. cons. U.S. Dept. Edn.; dir. Madison County Cmty. Alliances to Promote Edn.; state rep. dist. 36 Ind. Ho. of Reps., Indpls., 2002—, vice chair, commerce and econ. devel. com., mem. ways and means, pub. policy, ethics and vets. affairs, and tech. R & D coms. Candidate Ind. Ho. of Reps., 2000; mem. alumni bd. Ball State Tchrs. Coll. Mem.: United Way of Madison County, AAUW, LWV, Anderson Area C. of C., Anderson Rotary Club. Democrat. Episcopalian. Office: Ind Ho of Reps 200 W Washington St Indianapolis IN 46204-2786

AUSTIN-HILL, SUZANNE S. mathematician, educator; d. Parker Joseph Smith, Jr. and Honore Beatrix Alexander. BA, George Wash. U., 1975; MS, Nova Southeastern U., 1982; PhD, U. Miami, 1992. Cert. secondary math. edn. Fla., 1980. Math. tchr. Fairfax (Va.) County Pub. Schs., 1975—78, Freeport (N.Y.) Pub. Schs., 1978—80, Miami-Dade (Fla.) County Pub. Schs., 1980—82; prof., math. Miami-Dade Coll., 1982—. Project dir., prin. investigator NSF, Arlington, Va., 1996—99, cons., 1999—2000, Eisenhower Profl. Devel. Project, Detroit, 2000—01. Author: (textbook) Algebra From a Different Executive Council Angle; contbr. articles to profl. jours. Co-chair The Whole Word Christian Acad., Miami, 2001. Named Best Educator, Miami Today, 1998; recipient Tchg. Excellence award, The Nat. Inst. for Staff and Orgnl. Devel., 1998. Mem.: Benjamin Banneker Assn., Inc. (sec. 1998—2000), Nat. Coun. Tchrs. Math. (panel mem. math. tchg. mid. sch. 1998—2000, 2004—, panel mem. ednl. materials com. 2000—03). Baptist. Avocations: reading, writing, travel, movies. Office: Miami Dade Coll 11011 SW 104 St Miami FL 33176 E-mail: saustin@mdc.edu.

AUSTIN-STEPHENS, ANN-MARIE, retail executive; b. Sept. 13; Various marketing positions Proctor and Gamble Co.; dir. tech. and brand mktg. Frito-Lay Co., 1996—99; v.p. strategic planning Circuit City, 1999—2000, sr. v.p., 2000—. Mem.: Black Career Women's Execucircle. Office: Circuit City 9950 Mayland Dr Richmond VA 23233-1464*

AUSTIN-THORN, CYNTHIA KAY, religious organization administrator, poet; b. Dallas, Feb. 24; d. Kenneth and Anita E. Fujii; m. George Austin, Dec. 20, 1978 (dec. July 1990); 1 child, Christopher; m. Kenneth Thorn, July 3, 1994 (dec. Aug. 1999). AAS, El Centro Coll., Dallas, 1987. Sr. accounts payable clk. Plymouth/Poco Shops, N.Y.C.; mgr. Funky Things, Huntington Beach, Calif.; with select inventory mgmt. office Joske's Dept. Store, Dallas; sec., receptionist George E. Austin Piano Tech., Dallas; owner, writer, design creator Son of Dust Creations, Dallas; active The Road to Damascus Ministries, Dallas. Contbg. poet: (anthologies) A Muse to Follow, 1996 (Editor's Choice award 1996), A Tapestry of Thoughts, 1996 (Editor's Choice award 1996), (cassettes) The Sound of Poetry, 1996, 97 (named 1 of 10 best poets 1996, 97), Searching for Soft Voices, 1997. Mem. choir 1st Family Ch., Dallas, 1996-97, 99, 2000, 2002. Recipient cert. of achievement 1st Family Ch., 1996. Republican. Avocations: creative writing, song writing, singing in church plays, [illegible] ministering to others. Home and Office: Apt B 10410 Lone Tree Ln Dallas TX 75218-3008

AUTH, JUDITH, library director; BA in English Lit., U. Calif., Riverside, 1968, grad. advanced mgmt. program, 1990; MLS, UCLA, 1971. Children's libr. Marcy br. Riverside City & County Pub. Libr., 1971-73, ctrl. libr. children's rm., 1973-75, coord. children's svcs., 1975-80, area br. supr., 1980-85, head ctrl. libr., 1985-87, acting head tech. svcs., 1987-88, asst. libr. dir., 1988-91, libr. dir., 1991—. Asst. to city mgr. in charge of entrepreneurial mgmt. program City of Riverside, 1988-91. Mem. ALA, Am. Soc. Pub. Adminstrn., Calif. Libr. Assn. (leadership inst. task force 1992-93, mem. assembly 1994), Calif. County Librs. Assn. (sec. 1992-94), So. Calif. Coun. Lit. for Children and Young People (bd. dirs. 1975-90). Office: Riverside City & County Libr 3581 Mission Inn Ave Riverside CA 92501-3306

AUTOLITANO, ASTRID, consumer products executive; b. Havana, Cuba, Aug. 25, 1938; came to U.S., 1966; d. Manuel and Efigenia (Giquel) Rodriguez; m. Dominick Autolitano, July 23, 1977; children: Astrid Martinez, Manuel Martinez. Student, U. Havana, 1962-64, El Camino Coll., Torrance, Calif., 1968-71, UCLA, Westwood, 1973-75, Columbia U., 1983. Multi-lingual sec. Mattel Toys, Hawthorne, Calif., 1966-69, coord. internat. sales, 1969-73, mgr. Pan Am. sales, 1973-78, dir. export sales and licensees, 1978-83, v.p. Latin Am., 1983-89, sr. v.p. Latin Am. El Segundo, Calif., 1989-95, exec. v.p. Latin Am., 1995-96, exec. v.p. Ams., 1996, pres. internat., 1996—.

AUTRY, CAROLYN, artist, art history educator; b. Dubuque, Iowa, Dec. 12, 1940; d. William Tilden and Vela (Laseman) A.; m. Peter Elloian, May 27, 1966; 1 dau., Cybele Justine. BA, U. Iowa, 1963, MFA, 1965. Instr. art, art history Baldwin-Wallace Coll., Berea, Ohio, 1965-66; adj. assoc. prof. art history dept. art Ctr. for Visual Arts U. Toledo, 1966-2001. Artist-in-residence Sch. Arts in France, Lacoste, 1984, 87, adj. instr. in printmaking, 1987. Exhbns. include San Francisco Mus. Art, 1973, Oakland Mus., 1975, Santa Barbara Mus., 1975, U. Mo., 1975, Ljubljana Internat. Biennial, 1975, 81, 87, Internationale Grafik Biennale, Frechen, W. Ger., 1976, Biella, Italy, 1976, Genoa, Italy, 1976, Leverkusen, Fed. Republic Germany, 1977, Phila. Mus. Art, 1980, 97, Visual Arts Ctr., Anchorage, Alaska, 1980, U. Louisville, 1981, U. Dallas, 1981, Grunwald Ctr. Graphic Arts, UCLA, 1981, Ohio State U., 1982, Belle Arts & Graphic Inc., Nyack, N.Y., 1982, Mus. Arts and Sci., Macon, Ga., 1983, U. Tenn., Knoxville, 1983, Pratt Graphics Ctr., NYC, 1983, Calif. State Coll. San Bernardino, 1983, Am. Embassy Cultural Ctr., Belgrade, Yugoslavia, 1983, Taipei Fine Arts Mus., 1983, 85, 87, 89, 91, 95, Museo Arte Contemporaneo, Ibiza, Spain, 1984, Drake U., 1985, Fla. State U., 1985, Irvine (Calif.) Fine Arts Ctr., 1986, Inter-graphic Internat., East Berlin, 1984, 87, Met. Mus. Art Ctr., Coral Gables, Fla., 1987, Fifth Internat. Graphic Exhbn., Catania, Italy, 1988, Korean Cultural Svc. Gallery, L.A., Walker Hill Gallery, Seoul, Korea, and Korean Embassy Cultural Ctr., Paris, 1989, Barbican Art Centre, London, Salford (Gt. Britain) Mus., Mead Gallery, U. Warwick, Coventry, Gt. Britain, Brighton and Poly. Gallery, Brighton, Gt. Britain, 1989, Internat. Exhbn. Prints, Kanagawa, Japan, 1989, 90, 95, 97, Gallery Fine Arts Ctr. Seoul, 1989, Nat. Exhbn. Prints, Ringling Sch. Art and Design, Sarasota, Fla., 1990, Internat. Impact Art Festival, Kyoto City Mus., Japan, 1990, 91, 92, 93, 94, Ohio Drawing and Printmaking Invitational, Upper Arlington, 1991, Fondation Mona Bismarck, Paris, 1991, Fine Arts Assn. Gallery, Hanoi, Republic of Vietnam, 1991, Prints Internat., 1992, Silvermine Guild Arts Ctr., New Caanan, Conn., 1993, Taejon (Korea) Expo Graphic Art, 1993, Soc. Am. Graphic Artists 65th Nat., N.Y.C., 1993, Architecture in Contemporary Print Making, Boston Archtl. Ctr., 1994, Am. Inst. Architecture, Washington, 1994, U. N.H., 1995, Midwest Select, South Bend Regional Mus. of Art, Ind., 1994, Triton Mus., Santa Clara, Calif., 1995, Mansfield (Ohio) Art Ctr., 1995, 20th Harper Nat. Exhbn., Macomb, Ill., 1996, Hunterdon Art Ctr., Clinton, N.J., 1996, Soc. Am. Graphic Artists 66th Nat. Print Exhbn., Hanover, N.J., 1997, Internat. Print Triennial, Cracow, Poland, 1997, Fla. Printmakers 9th Ann. Nat. Print Exhbn., Jacksonville, 1997, 11th Ann. Nat. Print Exhbn., 2000, Institut Franco-Américain, Rennes, France, 1997, Prized Impressions, Internat. Exhbn. of Prints, Phila. Mus. of Art, 1997, Nat. Print Exhbn., Calif. State Univ. Chico, 1997, 22d nat. Print Biennal Silvermine Guild Arts Ctr., Conn., 1998, Counterpoint Exhbn. Hill Country Arts Found., Tex., 1998, 99, 2000, Printmakers 98, Pittsburgh Ctr. for the Arts, Penn., 1998, U. Hawaii, Hilo, 2000, 13th Ann. McNeese Nat. Works on Paper Exhbn., McNeese State U., Lake Charles, La., Baton Rouge (La.) Gallery, 2000, Printwork 2K, 2000, The 7th Ann. Nat. Juried Exhbn., Barrett Art Ctr., Poughkeepsie, N.Y.C., 2000, 1st Biennial Nat. Print Competition, No. Ariz. U., Flagstaff, 2002, Internat. Print exhbn. invitational, Minsk, Belarus, 2002, Soc. Am. Graphic Artists 69th Nat. Exhbn. Arts Student League, NY, 2002, Interior/Exterior Landscapes, U. Wyo., Laramie and U. Dallas, Irving, Tex., 2002, 23d Nat. Print Exhbn., Art Link Contemporary Art Gallery, Ft. Wayne, Ind., 2003, L.S. Printmakers Soc. Juried Membership Exhbn., Browd Libr. Art Galleries, Glendale, Calif., 2003, Boston Printmakers Juried N.Am. Print Exhbn., 1971-81, 86-87, 2003, Soc. Am. Graphic Artists, Susan Teller Gallery, N.Y.C., 2004, Calif. State U., Chico, 2004, Works Gallery, San Jose, 2004, Fort Wayne, Ind., 2004, others; represented in permanent collections Libr. of Congress, Phila. Mus. Art, Worcester Art Mus., Mount Holyoke Coll., U. Colo., Bradley U., Calif. State U., San Diego, Ga. State U., U. S.D., U. N.D., U. Louisville, St. Lawrence U., U. Dallas, Hunterdon Art Ctr., Clinton, N.J., Fitchburg (Mass.) Mus., Duxbury (Mass.) Art Complex, Elvehjem Mus. Art U. Wis.-Madison, Inst. per la Cultura E L'Arte, Catania, Italy, Lakeview Mus. Arts and Scis., Peoria, Ill., Nat. Mus. Fine Arts, Hanoi. Recipient Boston Printmakers N.Am. Print Exhbn. award 1971, 79, 80, 81, 87, Pennell award Libr. Congress, 1971, 75, Phila. Print Club awards, 1972, 75, 79, Wesleyan Coll. Internat. award of merit, 1980, Anne Steele Marsh award Hunterdon Art Ctr., Clinton, N.J., 1991, Bradley U. Nat. award, 1991, Friends of the Janet Turner Gallery Nat. Exhbn. award Chico State U., Calif., 1995, Exhbn. award 16th Nat. Print Exhbn., Artlink, 1996, Exhbn. award 17th Nat. Print Exhbn., 1997, Counterpoint, 2000, Nat. Exhbn. award The Hill Country Arts Found., 2000; Ford Found. grantee, 1961-63, Ohio Arts Coun. grantee, 1979, 90, Yale-Norfolk Summer Sch. Art and Music scholar, 1962. Mem. Boston Printmakers (Louis Black award 1971), L.A. Printmakers Soc., Soc. Am. Graphic Artists (Jo Miller award 1985, Phillip Monteith award 1986), Calif. Soc. Printmakers, Coll. Art Assn. Am., The Print Club of Albany, N.Y. (Ledyard Logswell, Jr. Meml. prize 1995), Phi Beta Kappa. Address: 26114 W River Rd Perrysburg OH 43551-9128

AUTRY, DAVIDA MARIE, minister; b. Fortsmith, Ark., Nov. 16, 1964; d. David A. Corbin and Janet M. Winters; m. John Lester Autry, Apr. 23, 1994; 1 child, Mary Elizabeth ; 1 child, Emily Grace. BA, Univ. Ozarks, Clarksville, Ark., 1987; MDiv, Vanderbuilt Sch. Divinty, Nashville, Tenn., 1992. Elder United Meth. Ch. Pastor United Meth. Ch., Decatur, Ark., 1992—94, assoc. pastor Conway, Ark., 1994—2000, pastor Eureka Springs, Ark., 2000—03, assoc. pastor Ft. Smith, Ark., 2003—. Bd. mem. Conway Women's Shelter, Ark., 1996—99, Ark. Conf. Bd. Ministry, Little Rock, 2002—; various positions, bd. Ark. Annual Conf. of United Meth. Ch. Mem.: Am. Cancer Soc. (bd.). Meth. Achievements include have helped organize various out reach ministries such as food, emergency assistance; worked with elderly to obtain needed help in home repairs; have organized summer activities for underprivileged children. Avocations: reading, cooking, walking, family. Home: 3224 Edinburgh Dr Fort Smith AR 72908 Office: Wesly United Meth Ch 2200 Phoenix Ave Fort Smith AR 72901

AUTRY, LOLA MAE, music educator; d. William Marion Lineberry and Alice May Anderson-Lineberry; m. Ewart Arthur Autry, Feb. 21, 1941 (dec. Sept. 1981); children: Jerry Duane, Ewart Ronald, James Arthur, Lanny Lemuel, Martha Lynn Autry Crawford. BS, U. Memphis, 1939. Profl. photographer Self-employed, Hickory Flat, Miss., 1963—, tchr. piano, organ, voice, stringed instruments, art, 1939—, author, journalist, 1947—, lectr., 1982—, artist, 1987—, musician, 1932—. Vol. missionary related to ch. and writing careers, 1982—; dir. choirs Pine Grove Bapt. Ch., Hickory Flat, 1982—2000. Author (with E.A. Autry): (novel) The Turtle and the Oak (1st Pl. Fiction award Miss. Media Profls., 1992); author: (non-fiction) 52 Devotions with Original Songs for Primary Children; author: (with E.A. Autry) (non-fiction.) Bible Puppet Plays, (non-fiction) Don't Look Back Mama; oil painting, Little Girl with Yellow Daisy (First Pl. award Tupelo Women's Club and N.E. Miss. Art Assn., 2001); contbr. articles to The So. Advocate, Garden Design Mag., Seek Mag. Pres. Friends of Libr., Ashland, Miss., 1970; nat. and internat. missions vol. So. Bapt. Conv., Richmond, Va., 1981; mem. Benton Country Libraries, Ashland, Miss., 1959—60; vol.-tchg. and entertaining with music and slide programs, Bible study Nursing Homes, Ripley and Ashland, Miss., 1981—. Named one of 4 Top Photographers in the State, Miss. Inst. Arts and Letters, 1992; recipient Statewide Ageless Hero Award in field of Creativity award, Miss. Blue Cross and Blue Shield, 2003, several writing awards. Mem.: Christian Writers Guild, Nat. Fedn. Press Women.

AUXER, CATHY JOAN, elementary school educator; b. Chambersburg, Pa., May 16, 1951; d. Pat and Joan Irene Wedo; m. Jeffrey Lynn Auxer, Aug. 21, 1971 (dec. Aug. 23, 1996); 1 child, Jeffrey Lynn Auxer Jr. BS in Edn., Shippensburg State U., 1974; MEd, Shippensburg U., 1978. Cert. tchr. Pa., Md. 1st grade tchr. Mooreland Elem. Sch., Carlisle, Pa., 1975—2000, Worcester Prep. Sch., Berlin, Md., 2000—. Cons. Apple Learning Interchange, Berlin, 2001—. Co-author: (pamphlet) Whole Language, 1981; author: (lessons online) Computer Learning Found., 2000—01. Recipient 2d pl. award for lesson plan, Computer Learning Found. Tchrs., 2001. Mem.: Internat. Reading Assn., Eastern Shore Reading Coun. Home: 18 Carriage Ln Berlin MD 21811 E-mail: occookiemd@aol.com.

AUYONG, JAN, biologist; b. Honolulu, May 20, 1951; d. Clarence Kwai Fong and Janet Kam Yee (Lum) Auyong; m. Richard Holt Titgen. BA in Psychology, BS in Biol. Scis., U. Hawaii, 1974; MA in Biol. Scis., U. Calif., Santa Barbara, 1981; PhD Resources Devel., Tex. A&M U., 1983. Grad. rsch. asst. U. Calif., Santa Barbara, 1975-76; prin. investigator Marine Rev. Com., Solana Beach, Calif., 1976-78; grad. rsch. asst. Tex. A&M U., College Station, 1979-79, 81-83; policy analyst Dept. of Interior, Washington, 1980; specialist Sea Grant Ext. Svc., Honolulu, 1983-89, asst. dir., 1985-89; dep. dir. Nat. Coastal Resources R&D Inst., Newport, Oreg., 1989-92; prin. Mar Res Assocs., South Beach, Oreg., 1992-97; asst. dir. programs Oreg. Sea Grant, Corvallis, 1995—. Faculty Marine Resource Mgmt. Program Oreg. State U., Corvallis, 1992. Contbr. articles to profl. jours., chpts. to books. Vice pres. Lincoln County ARC, Newport, Oreg., 1992-95; advisor Ocean Recreation Coun. of Hawaii, 1985-89; chmn. organizing com. Congress on Coastal/Marine Tourism, 1989-91, 94-96, 97—. Recipient award Marine Option Program, Honolulu, 1989. Mem. Marine Tech. Soc. (recreation and tourism chair 1996—), Hawaii Assn. Women in Edn. [illegible] The Coastal Soc., Human Dimensions in Wildlife, PACON Internat. (Svc. award 1996).

AVAKIAN, ARLENE VOSKI, women's studies educator; b. N.Y.C., Apr. 4, 1939; d. Vaghinak and Berjouhe (Tutuian) A.; single; children: Neal Christopher Ryan, Leah Ryan. BS in Art History, Columbia U., 1961; MA in Social History, U. Mass., 1975, EdD, 1985. Exec. dir. female studies program Cornell U., Ithaca, N.Y., 1970-71; staff asst. women's studies U. Mass., Amherst, 1975-86, lectr. women's studies, 1986-93, assoc. prof. women's studies, 1993—2001, prof., dir., 2001—. Staff assoc. black studies, women's studies, faculty devel. project U. Mass./Smith Coll., Amherst, 1981-83; mem. faculty Sch. Social Work Smith Coll., Northampton, Mass., 1990-93. Author: Lion Woman's Legacy: An Armenian American Memoir, 1992; editor: Through the Kitchen Window: Women Explore the Intimate Meanings of Food and Cooking, 1997, paperback edit., 1998; co-editor: Afro-American Women and the Vote, 1997. Pres. Amherst (Mass.) Based Organization to Develop Equitable Shelter, 1989—; bd. dirs. Civil Liberties Union of We. Mass., Northampton, Mass., 1990—, Zoryan Inst. for Contemporary Documentation and Rsch., Cambridge, Mass., 1995-96; exec. bd. Project SAVE photographic archive of Armenian people, 1990-95. Scholar Rites and Reason program Brown U., Providence, 1982-84; recipient Commonwealth award for Outstanding Svc., State of Mass., Boston, 1985, David Burres award Civil Liberties Union of We. Mass., Northampton, 1993. Mem. Armenian Femisists (founding mem.). Avocations: cooking, gardening. Home: 333 Strong St Amherst MA 01002-1802 Office: U Mass Women's Studies 208 Bartlett Amherst MA 01003

AVEDON, MARCIA J. pharmaceutical executive; BA in Psychology summa cum laude, U. N.C., 1983; M in Indsl. and Orgnl. Psychology, George Washington U., 1987, PhD in Indsl. and Orgnl. Psychology with distinction, 1989. Intern U.S. Army Civilian Ctr., 1984; assoc. cons., sr. cons., cons. Booz-Allen & Hamilton, Inc., 1985—90; program mgr. Anheuser-Busch Cos., Inc., 1990—92, sr. cons., 1992—93, mgr. corp. succession planning, 1993—94, dir. mgmt. and orgn. devel. Campbell Taggart Inc., 1994—95; dir. orgn. and leadership devel. Honeywell Internat., 1995—97, v.p. human resources and comms. Performance Polymers, 1997—2000, v.p. human resources and comms. Performance Polymers and Chems., 2000—01, v.p. corp. human resources, 2001—02; v.p. talent mgmt. and orgn. effectiveness Merck & Co., Inc., Whitehouse Station, NJ, 2002, sr. v.p. human resources, 2003—. Bd. dirs. Jersey Battered Women's Svcs., 2000—; mem. adv. bd. Masters in Human Resources U. S.C., 1998—; corp. sponsor Cornell Ctr. for Advanced Human Resource Studies, 2001—. Mem.: Soc. for Human Resources Mgmt., Soc. for Indsl. and Orgnl. Psychology. Office: Merck & Co Inc PO Box 100 1 Merck Dr Whitehouse Station NJ 08889-0100

AVENI, BEVERLY A. executive aide; b. Stamford, Conn., Sept. 2, 1959; d. Lucille F. (Ferretti) A. BA in Polit. Sci., U. Conn., 1981. Legal asst. Cummings and Lockwood, Stamford, 1981-86; family law paralegal Piazza, Melmed and Ackerly, P.C., Stamford, 1986-88; litigation paralegal Abate and Fox, Stamford, 1988-95; exec. aide to mayor City of Stamford, 1995—. Pres. Conn. Assn. Paralegals, 1989-91; mem. seminar faculty, co-author seminar skills book for paralegal Conn. Discovery Skills, 1995. Vol. counselor Rape and Sexual Abuse Crisis Ctr., Stamford, 1983-87; dist. rep. Dem. City Com., Stamford, 1992-96, sec., 1994-96; local coord. Sen. Christopher Dodd's 1992 Reelection Campaign, 1994-96; mem. congl. dist. adv. coun. Conn. Permanent Commn. on Status of Women, 1996; mem. commn. City of Stamford's XV Charter Revision Commn., 1994-95; mem. Mayor's cabinet; Mayor's rep. on various civic coms. and bds.; bd. dirs. Women's Bus. Devel. Ctr., 1999—. Avocation: fitness. Office: City of Stamford 888 Washington Blvd Stamford CT 06901-2902 Home: # B 71 Dora St Stamford CT 06902-5414 Office Phone: 203-977-4150.

AVENT, SHARON L. HOFFMAN, manufacturing company executive; b. St. Paul, Feb. 7, 1946; d. Ebba and Harold Hoffman; m. Terry Avent; 2 children. Student, Hamline U., St. Paul. With Smead Mfg. Co., Hastings, Minn., 1965—, pres., CEO, 1998—; acquired The Atlanta Group (now Smead-Europe), Hoogezand, Netherlands, 1998—. Bd. dirs. Hastings Public Sch. Found. Named Minn. World Trader of the Year, World Trade Week, Inc., 2002; recipient Spirit of Life honoree, City of Hope, 2003. Office: Smead Mfg Co 600 Smead Blvd Hastings MN 55033-2219*

AVERILL, ELLEN CORBETT, secondary education science educator, administrator; b. Milledgeville, Ga. d. Felton Conrad and Vivian Iris (Brookins) Corbett; m. George Edmund Averill, July 31, 1971; 1 child, John Conrad. BS, U. Ga., 1966, MS, 1971; teaching cert., Columbus Coll., 1979, EdS, 1994. Grad. teaching asst. U. Ga., Athens, 1966-68; tchr. sci. Decatur (Ga.) City Schs., 1971-72; tchr. sci., chair dept. Kendrick High Sch., Columbus, Ga., 1980—. Rsch. asst. Caretta Rsch. Project, Savannah (Ga.) Sci. Mus., 1985, NEWMAST, Kennedy Space Ctr., 1986; rsch. assoc. Inhalation Toxicology Rsch. Inst., Albuquerque, summer, 1990; instr. sci. Gov.'s Honor Program Valdosta State Coll., summer, 1991, Woodrow Wilson Biotechnology Inst., Princeton, N.J., 1993. Contbr. articles to newspapers, jours.; inventor The Wrap-All, 1992. Mem. Nat. Sci. Tchrs. Assn. (program com., regional conf. 1993), Nat. Assn. Biology Tchrs. (Outstanding Biology Tchr. 1990-91), Ga. Sci. Tchrs. Assn. (dist. VI rep. 1988-90, secondary rep. 1990-91, pres.-elect 1991-92, pres. 1992-93, conf. coord. ann. conf. 1992, Dist. VI Sci. Tchr. of Yr. 1995), Coalition for Excellence in Sci. Edn. (orgnl. com. 1992-93), Ga. Sci. Tchrs. Edn. Found. (chair 1994-98), Valley Area Sch. Tchrs. (charter, pres.-elect 1996-97, pres. 1997-98), Muscogee Area Literacy Assn. (treas. 1992-93), Phi Delta Kappa (PDK Tchr. of Yr. 1992, v.p. 2002-), Delta Kappa Gamma Edn. Soc. Unitarian-Universalist. Avocations: procelain art, gardening, amateur radio operator. Home: 126 Waterway Dr Cataula GA 31804-4407 Office: Kendrick High Sch 6015 Georgetown Dr Columbus GA 31907-4698 E-mail: eaverill@ldl.net.

AVERSA, DOLORES SEJDA, educational administrator; b. Phila., Mar. 26, 1932; d. Martin Benjamin and Mary Elizabeth (Esposito) Sejda; m. Zefferino A. Aversa Jr., May 3, 1958; children: Dolores Elizabeth, Jeffrey Martin, Linda Maria. BA, Chestnut Hill Coll., 1953. Owner Personal Rep. & Pub. Rels., Phila., 1965-68; ednl. cons. Franklin Sch. Sci. and Arts, Phila., 1968-72; pres., owner, dir. Martin Sch. Bus., Inc., Phila., 1972—. File reader, cons. for ct. reporting and travel tng. Southwestern Pub. Co., 1990; mem. ednl. planning com. Ravenhill Acad., Phila., 1975-76. Active Phila. Mus. ARt, Phila. Drama Guild; mem. Met. Opera Guild, 2002, 8th Ward Rep. Exec. Com. Mem.: Lower Bucks County C. of C., Am. Soc. Travel Agts. (sch. divsn., nat. educators com., sec. Del. chpt., edn. chmn., PAC chmn. 1997—), Hist. Soc. Pa., World Affairs Coun. Phila., Phila. Hist. Soc., Pa. Sch. Counselors Assn., Am. Bus. Law Assn., Pa. Bus. Edn. Assn., Nat. Bus. Edn. Assn., Andrea Doria Survivor Assn., Chestnut Hill Coll. Alumnae Assn. (sec. class '53), Phila. Orch., Am.-Italy Soc., Met. Opera Guild, Stone Harbor Golf Club. Roman Catholic. Home: 2111 Locust St Philadelphia PA 19103-4802 Office: 2417 Welsh Rd Philadelphia PA 19114-2213 E-mail: msb-aversa@erols.com.

AVERY, BYLLYE YVONNE, health association administrator; BA in Psychology, Talladega Coll., 1959; MEd in Spl. Edn., U. Fla., 1969; LHD (hon.), Thomas Jefferson U., 1990, SUNY, Binghamton, 1990, Bowdoin Coll., 1993; LLD (hon.), Bates Coll., 1995. Occupl. and recreational therapy aide N.E. Fla. State Hosp., 1959-65; resource tchr. for emotionally disturbed Richard L. Brown Elem. Sch., Jacksonville, Fla., 1966-68; learning disabilities resource tchr. Waldo (Fla.) Cmty. Sch., 1969-70; head tchr. children's mental health unit U. Fla., Gainesville, 1970-76, instr. dept. psychiatry, 1970-76; co-founder, dir. edn. Gainesville, 1976-78; co-founder, [illegible] 1978-80; dir. CETA Santa Fe C.C., Gainesville, 1980-82; exec. dir., founder Nat. Black Women's Health Project, Atlanta, 1982-90, founding pres., 1990-97, Washington, 1997—. Vis. fellow dept. health and social behavior Sch. Pub. Health Harvard U., 1991-93; cons. in field. Contbr. articles to profl. publs.; prodr. films: It's Up To Us (PBS documentary), 1985, On Becoming A Woman: Mothers and Daughters Talking Together, 1987. Bd. dirs. Nat Women's Health Network, 1976-81, New World Found., 1986-91, W.K. Kellogg Internat. Friendship Program, 1989-94, Boston Women's Health Book Collective, 1990-92, Global Fund for Women, 1989—, Internat. Women's Health Coalition, 1989—; bd. visitors Tucker Found. Dartmouth Coll., 1990—; mem. women's cancer adv. bd. Dana Farber Cancer Ctr., Boston; mem. adv. com. on rsch. on women's health Office Rsch. on Women's Health, NIH, Bethesda, Md. Recipient Outstanding Woman of Color award Nat. Inst. Women of Color, 1987, NOW, 1987, Svc. award Religious Coalition for Abortion Rights, 1988, Outstanding Svc. to Women and Children award Children's Def. Fund, 1988, award for cmty. svc. in sci., health and tech. award Essence mag., 1989, John D. and Catherine T. MacArthur Found. Fellowship award, 1989, Women of Achievement award YWCA, Atlanta, 1990, Orthro Woman of 21st Century award Orthro Pharm., 1991, Cmty. Svc. award Spelman Coll., 1991, Trends Setters award Nat. Health Coun., 1993, Woman of Achievement award Ms. Found., 1993, Grassroots Realist award Ga. Legis. Black Caucus, 1994, Gustav O. Lienhard award Inst. of Medicine, 1994, Dorothy I. Height Lifetime Achievement award, 1995, Pres.' citation Am. Pub. Health Assn., 1995. Office: Nat Black Women's Health Project 600 Pennsylvania Ave SE Ste 310 Washington DC 20003-6300

AVERY, CAROLYN ELIZABETH, artist; b. Hartford, CT, Mar. 7, 1937; d. Russell Eugene and Frances Atwood Avery; m. Robert Franklin Mills, Oct. 11, 1975; stepchildren: Michelle Mills Garcia, Steven Robert; m. Clifton Messenger, Dec. 30, 1955 (dec. Feb. 1966); children: Stephen Lee, JoAnne Messenger Henderson, Gregory Clifton. One-woman shows include Springfield Libr. and Mus. Complex, Mass., Jasper Rand Mus., Westfield, Mass., Cottage Place Gallery, Ridgewood, N.J., exhibitions include Shore Rd. Gallery, Maine, Berkshire Art Gallery, Mass., Min. Theater of Chester Gallery, Mass., Woodwind Gallery, Maine, others, Green River Gallery, Millerton, N.Y., juried nat. group show: George Walter Vincent Smith Mus. Office Phone: 413-569-0384.

AVERY, MARY ELLEN, pediatrician, educator; b. Camden, N.J., May 6, 1927; d. William Clarence and Mary (Miller) Avery. AB, Wheaton Coll., Norton, Mass., 1948, DSc (hon.), 1974; MD, Johns Hopkins U., 1952; DSc (hon.), Trinity Coll., 1976, U. Mich., 1975, Med. Coll. Pa., 1976, Albany Med. Coll., 1977, Med. Coll. Wis., 1978, Radcliffe Coll., 1978; MA (hon.), Harvard U., 1974; LHD (hon.), Emmanuel Coll., 1979, Northeastern U., 1981, Russell Sage Coll., 1983, Meml. U., Newfoundland, 1993; DHL, Johns Hopkins U., 1999; LLD, Queen's U., Kingston, Ont., 2000. Intern Johns Hopkins Hosp., 1953—54, resident, 1954—57; rsch. fellow in pediat. Boston, 1957—59, Balt., 1959—69; assoc. prof. pediat. Johns Hopkins U., 1964—69; prof., chmn. dept. pediat. McGill U. Med. Sch., 1969—74; Thomas Morgan Rotch prof. pediat. Harvard U. Med. Sch., Boston, 1974—97, prof. emerita, 1997—; physician-in-chief Montreal Children's Hosp., 1969—74, Children's Hosp. Med. Ctr., Boston, 1974—85. Mem. Med. Rsch. Coun. Can.; mem. study sect. NIH, 1968—71, 1984—88. Author: The Lung and Its Disorders in the Newborn Infant, 4th edit., 1981; author: (with A. Schaffer) Avery's Diseases of the Newborn, 7th edit., 1998; author: (with H.W. Taeusch and R. Ballard) ; author: (with G. Litwack) Born Early, 1984; author, editor: (with L. First) Pediatric Medicine, 1988, 2d edit., 1994, also articles:, mem. edit. bd.: Pediatrics, 1965—71, Am. Rev. Respitory Diseases, 1969—73, Am. Jour. Physiology, 1967—73, Jour. Pediatrics, 1974—84, Medicine, 1985, Johns Hopkins Med. Jour., 1978—82, Clin. and Investigative Critical Care Medicine, 1990—96, New Eng. Jour. Medicine, 1990—95. Trustee Wheaton (Mass.) Coll., 1965—85, Radcliffe Coll., Johns Hopkins U., 1982—88. Recipient Mead Johnson award in pediatric rsch., 1968, Trudeau medal, Am. Thoracic Soc., 1984, Nat. Medal of Sci., NSF, 1991, Marta Philipson award, Karolinska Inst., Stockholm, 1998; Markle scholar in med. scis., 1961—66. Fellow: NAS (mem. coun. 1997—), AAAS (dir. 1989, pres. 2002—), Royal Coll. Physicians of Edinburgh, Am. Acad. Arts and Scis., Am. Acad. Pediat., Internat. Pediatric Assn. (standing com. 1986—89); mem.: Am. Pediatric Soc. (pres. 1990), Royal Coll. Pediat. and Child Health (hon.), Inst. Medicine (coun. 1987, Walsh McDermott award 2000), Soc. Pediatric Rsch. (pres. 1972—73), Am. Physiol. Soc., Can. Pediatric Soc., Alpha Omega Alpha, Phi Beta Kappa. Address: 300 Longwood Ave Boston MA 02115-5724 Office: Children's Hosp 300 Longwood Ave # HU432 Boston MA 02115-5737 Office Phone: 617-355-8330. Business E-Mail: nary.avery@tch.harvard.edu.

AVERY, MAURINE ANN, health record administrator; b. St. Paul, Aug. 19, 1929; d. Myron Rosenow and Myrtle Charlotte (Bladholm) Grant; m. Eugene Vernon Avery, June 29, 1951; children: Susan, Cathlin, James, William, Anne. BA, U. Minn., 1951; BA cum laude, Coll. St. Scholastica, 1976, MLS, 2004. Registered record adminstr. Health info. system analyst St. Louis Park Med. Ctr., Mpls., 1976-81; med. data specialist Found. for Health Care Evaluation, Mpls., 1981; instr. Seattle U., 1984-85; health record adminstr. Fircrest Sch., Seattle, 1986-88; med. records coord. Group Health, Inc., Mpls., 1988-91; health record cons. Good Samaritan of Minn., St. Paul, 1992-94; retired. Co-author: Medical Records in Ambulatory Care, 1984; contbr. articles to profl. publs. Mem. Am. Health Info. Mgmt. Assn. (Lit. award 1984), Zeta Tau Alpha. Mem. United Ch. of Christ. Avocations: writing, physical fitness. Home: 9505 Woodbridge Rd Bloomington MN 55438-1667

AVERY, SUSAN KATHRYN, electrical engineering educator, research administrator; b. Detroit, Jan. 5, 1950; d. Theodore Peter and Alice Jane (Greene) Rykala; m. James Paul Avery, Aug. 12, 1972; 1 child, Christopher Scott. BS in Physics, Mich. State U., 1972; MS in Physics, U. Ill., 1974, PhD in Atmospheric Sci., 1978. Asst. prof. elec. engring. U. Ill., Urbana, 1978-83; fellow CIRES U. Colo., Boulder, 1982—, assoc. prof. elec. engring., 1985-92, assoc. dean rsch. and grad. edn. Coll. Engring., 1989-92, prof. elec. engring., 1992—, dir. CIRES, 1994—; sec. USNC/URSI NRC, 1994—. Adv. com. chair Elec. and Communications Div. NSF, Washington, 1991-93, adv. panel atmospheric scis. program, 1985-88, steering com. CEDAR program, 1986-87, adv. com. engring. directorate, 1991-93, vis. professorship, 1982-83; working group ionosphere, thermosphere, mesosphere NASA, Washington, 1991—; mem.-at-large USNC/URSI NRC, Washington, 1991-93, com. on solar-terrestrial rsch., 1987-90; trustee Univ. Corp. for Atmospheric Rsch., 1991—, vice chair bd. trustees, 1993, sci. programs evaluation com., 1989-91; working group on tides in mesosphere and lower thermosphere Internat. Commn. Meteorology of Upper Atmosphere, 1981-86; mesosphere-lower thermosphere network steering com. Internat. STEP Program, 1989—, equatorial mid. atmosphere dynamics steering com., 1990—. Contbr. articles to Radio Sci., Adv. Space Rsch., Jour. Atmosphere Terrestrial Physics, Jour. Geophys. Rsch., others. Recipient Faculty Award for Women, NSF, 1991, Outstanding Publ. award NCAR, 1990; faculty fellow U. Colo., 1994; vis. fellow Coop. Inst. for Rsch. in Environ. Scis., 1982-83. Fellow Am. Meteorological Soc. (com. on mid. atmosphere 1990—); mem. IEEE, Am. Geophys. Union (com. edn. and human resources 1988-92), Am. Soc. Engring. Edn., Sigma Xi. Achievements include research on the dynamics of the mesosphere, stratosphere and troposphere with emphasis on unifying observational analyses and theoretical studies, on wave dynamics including the coupling of the atmosphere/ocean and interactions between large-scale and small-scale motions, on the use of ground-based doppler radar techniques for observing the clear-air atmosphere and use of new signal processing algorithms for radar data analysis. Office: U Colo Cires Cb 216 Boulder CO 80309-0001

AVESON, MARTHA CARALYN, pharmaceutical company executive; m. Russell Edward Aveson, Sept. 19, 1981. AS, Essex County Coll., 1974; BA, Rutgers U., 1976; MA, Montclair State U., 1983. Lab. technician Airwick Products, Teterboro, N.J., 1977-79; chemist SmithKlineBeecham, Parsippany, N.J., 1979-84; chemist II Shulton Toiletries, Inc., Clifton, N.J., 1984, Church and Dwight, Inc., Princeton, N.J., 1985-86; rsch. scientist Whitehall-Robins, Inc., Hammonton, N.J., 1986-92; sr. rsch. scientist/sr. clin. supplies assoc. Bayer Corp., Morristown, N.J., 1992-99. Patentee in field. Mem. Internat. Soc. Pharm. Engrs., Am. Chem. Soc. Avocations: snow skiing, hiking. Home: 5193 E Baseline Rd Belgrade MT 59714 E-mail: MTAveson@aol.com.

AVILA, LIDIA D. school administrator; b. Phoenix; d. Pete A. and Elvira (Duarte) A. B.A. in Edn., M.A. in Edn., 1968; Ed.D., Ariz. State U., 1981. Cert. elem. tchr., counselor, adminstr. Successively tchr., counselor, coordinator, Wilson Sch. Dist., Phoenix, 1958-73, prin., 1973-75; adult edn. tchr., Tempe, Ariz., 1966-68; fed. project reader cons., Phoenix, 1968-72; prin. Glendale Elem. Sch. Dist. (Ariz.), 1976—88; prin. Tucson, 1988-91, Phoenix, 1991—; textbook cons. Active Robert A Taft Inst. Govt., 1981; del. Inter-Club Council Women's Orgn. Greater Phoenix area; bd. dirs. YWCA, 1968-70; mem. steering com. 1st US-China Ednl. Conf, Beijing, 1997; mem. Ariz. Women's Town Hall, 1996; del. IFUWA Conf., Yokohama, Japan. Baylor U. Leadership/Mgmt. Inst. grantee 1980; NDEA grantee, UCLA Inst. Linguistics, Manila, Philippines, 1968. Mem. AAUW (state pres., mem. edn. found. panel), Am. Bus. Women's Assn. (Woman of Yr. 1982), Assn. Supervision and Curriculum Devel., Nat. Assn. Elem. Sch. Prins. (participant nat. fellows program), Delta Kappa Gamma, Phi Delta Kappa, Alpha Delta (pres., Golden Gift award). Office: 5810 N 49th Ave Glendale AZ 85301

AVILES, ALICE ALERS, psychologist; b. N.Y.C; d. Jose Oscar and Pauline (Irizarry) Alers; m. Jose A. Aviles, Aug. 13, 1954 (div. Oct. 1981); children: Jeffrey (dec.), Brian, Gregory; m. Clifford M. Goldman, June 29, 1997. BS magna cum laude, SUNY, Oswego, 1955; MA, Queens Coll., 1978; PhD, Yeshiva U., 1984; postdoctoral diploma in psychoanalysis and psychotherapy, Adelphi U., 1991. Lic. psychologist, N.Y. Tchr. elem. schs., Spring Valley, N.Y., 1955, Erlangen (Fed. Republic Germany) Am. Sch., 1955-56, Uniondale, N.Y., 1956, Freeport, N.Y., 1957-58, Island Park, N.Y., 1973-75; psychology clk. Fifth Ave. Ctr. for Counseling and Psychotherapy, N.Y.C., 1978-80; psychology intern St. Vincent's Hosp. and Med. Ctr., N.Y.C., 1980-81; psychologist Kingsboro Psychiat. Ctr., Bklyn., 1981-84; psychologist to assoc. psychologist South Beach Psychiat. Ctr., Bklyn., 1984-86; pvt. practice Valley Stream, N.Y., 1985—. From staff psychologist to sr. psychologist Luth. Med. Ctr., Bklyn., 1986-95; cons. Beach Terrace Care Ctr., Long Beach, N.Y., 1995-97; mem. adv. com. Hispanic Counseling Ctr. of Family Svc. Assn. of Nassau County, Hempstead, N.Y., 1978-80; cons. Nassau County Extended Care Ctr., Hempstead, 1997-99, Resort Nursing Home, Far Rockaway, N.Y., 1998-2000, Woodmere (N.Y.) Rehab. and Health Care Ctr., 1999-2000. Ford found. grad. fellow, 1978-81. Mem. APA, N.Y. State Psychol. Assn., Nassau County Psychol. Assn. (mem. pvt. practice com. 1992-93), Adelphi Soc. Psychoanalysis and Psychotherapy. Office: 10 Valley Ln E North Woodmere NY 11581-3629 Office Phone: 516-791-8326.

AVRAHAM, REGINA, retired secondary school educator; b. Ludenscheid, Germany, Aug. 15, 1935; Came to U.S., 1937. d. Joseph and Feiga (Press) Artman; m. Josef Esa Abraham, Mar. 12, 1962; children: Randi Beth, Jesse Richard. BS, City Coll., N.Y.C., 1955. Elem. tchr. N.Y. Bd. Edn., 1955-63, tchr., 1963-91; sci. cons., prin. writer N.Y.C. Bd. Edn. Sci. Curriculum, 1996—. Sci. and health magnet tchr. Bd. Edn., N.Y., 1987-91; presenter and cons. in field. Author: Our Founding Sisters, 1976, Readings in Life Science, 1986, Readings in Physical Science, 1986, The Downside of Drugs, 1988, Substance Abuse Treatment and Prevention, 1988, The Circulation System, 1989, The Digestive System, 1989, The Reproductive System, 1989; prin. writer Sci.-Lit. Connection, N.Y.C. Bd. Edn., 1996, contbg. writer, cons. A Study in Role Models, 1997, The Multiple Intelligences, 1998; contbg. editor: Celebrating the Century, 1999, Reading and Writing Connections, 2000, Celebrating Diversity, 2001; project coord., contbg. writer, editor, cons. Promoting Excellence through Best Practices,

2002. Woodrow Wilson fellow, 1989; named Tchr. of Yr., Bklyn. Sch. Bd., 1987. Mem. United Fed. Tchrs. Democratic. Avocations: theatre, opera, crossword puzzles, cats, N.Y. Mets. Home: 2218 Avenue P Brooklyn NY 11229-1508

AVRAM, HENRIETTE DAVIDSON, librarian, government official; b. N.Y.C., Oct. 7, 1919; d. Joseph and Rhea (Olsho) Davidson; m. Herbert Mois Avram, Aug. 23, 1941; children: Lloyd, Marcie, Jay. Student, Hunter Coll., N.Y.C., George Washington U.; ScD (hon.), So. Ill. U., 1977; DLitt (hon.), Rochester Inst. Tech., 1991; DSc (hon.), U. Ill., 1993. Systems analyst, methods analyst, programmer Nat. Security Agy., 1952-59; systems analyst Am. Rsch. Bur., 1959-61, Datatrol Corp., 1961-65; supervisory info. systems specialist Libr. of Congress, Washington, 1965-67, asst. coord. info. systems, 1967-70, chief MARC Devel. Office, 1970-76, dir. Network Devel. Office, 1976-80, dir. processing systems, network and automation planning, 1980-83, asst. libr. for processing svcs., 1983-89, assoc. libr. Collection Svcs., 1989-92; ret. Libr. Congress, 1992; chmn. network adv. com. Libr. of Congress, Washington, 1981-92, chmn. emerita network adv. com., 1992—. Chair subcom. 2 sectional com. Z39 Am. Nat. Standards Inst., 1966-80, RECON Working Task F, 1968-73, Internat. Rels. Round Table, 1986-87, subcom. 4 working group 1 on character sets Internat. Orgn. for Standardization, 1971-80; lectr. sch. of info. and libr. sci. Cath. U. Am., Washington, 1973-80, com. mem. strategies for 80's, 1980-81; bd. visitors libr. and learning resources com., 1980; mem. internat. standards coord. com. Info. Sys. Standards Bd., 1983-86; del. to U.S. nat. com. UNESCO/Gen. Info. Program, 1983; chair internat. rels. com. Nat. Info. Standards Orgn., 1983-92. Bd. editors: Jour. Library Automation, 1970-72; contbr. articles to profl. jours. Recipient Superior Svc. award Libr. of Congress, 1968, Margaret Mann citation, 1971, Fed. Woman's award, 1974, Achievement award ALA/Libr. Info. Tech. Assn., 1980, Meritorious Svc. award ANSI, 1992, Disting. Exec. Svc. award Fed. Govt., 1990; co-recipient Rsch. Libr. of Yr. award Assn. Coll. and Rsch. Libr. Acad., 1979. Fellow Internat. Fedn. Libr. Assns. and Instns. (chair working group on content designators 1972-77, chair profl. bd. 1979-81, mem. program mgmt. com. 1983-90, mem. exec. bd. 1983-87, 1st v.p. 1985-87); mem. ALA (bd. dirs., past pres. info sci. and automation div., John Ames Humphrey Forest Press award 1990, Melvil Dewey award 1981, Lippincott award 1988, Hon. Membership award 1997), Am. Soc. Info. Sci. (spl. interest group on libr. automation and networks 1965), Spl. Librs. Assn. (Recognition award 1990), Assn. Libr. and Info. Sci. Edn. (Libr. of Congress disting. svc. award 1992), Assn. Bibliog. Agys. Gt. Britain, Australia, Can. and U.S. (del. 1977—). Home: 44041 Fieldstone Way California MD 20619-2097 E-mail: havram@erols.com.

AVRECH, GLORIA MAY, psychotherapist; b. San Jose, Calif., Oct. 17, 1944; d. Benjamin and Lillian (Yudelowitz) A.; m. William Woodruff. BA, U. Calif., Berkeley, 1966; MSW, U. Md., 1969; PhD, Inst. Clin. Social Work, Calif., 1987. Bd. cert. social worker; cert. Jungian analyst. Sch. social worker Balt. City Pub. Schs., 1969-70; psychiatric social worker Calif. Dept. Social Welfare Cmty. Svcs. Br., L.A., 1970-72; clin. social worker Pasadena (Calif.) Child Guidance Clinic, 1972-82; pvt. practice psychotherapist Pasadena, 1976—. Field instr. U. So. Calif. Sch. Social Work, L.A., 1978-82. Contbr. book and movie revs., Jour. Psychological Perspectives, 1989-2003. VISTA fellow, Balt., 1967-68, Children's Bur. fellow, Balt., 1968-69. Mem. NASW, Soc. Clin. Social Work, Assn. Humanistic Psychology, Assn. Transpersonal Psychology, Analytical Psychology Club. Democrat. Avocations: shamanism, film, cats, cultural events. Office: 130 S Euclid Ave Ste 6 Pasadena CA 91101-2472

AVRETT, ROZ (ROSALIND CASE), writer, advertising creative director; b. Upper Montclair, N.J., Apr. 19, 1933; d. William Lyon and Doris Edna (Clift) Case; m. William Thomas Reynolds, Feb. 20, 1960 (div. 1968); 1 child, Gerald William Thomas; m. John Glenn Avrett, Dec. 31, 1972. BA in Creative Writing, Chatham Coll., 1951-55. Copy trainee Young & Rubicam, Inc., N.Y.C., 1955-56; copy writer Hicks & Greist, Inc., N.Y.C., 1958-61; sr. copy writer Dancer-Fitzgerald-Sample, N.Y.C., 1961-63; creative supr. The Marschalk Co., N.Y.C., 1963-68; assoc. creative dir. BBDO Internat., N.Y.C., 1968-78; author N.Y.C., 1978—. Advt. lectr. Sch. of Visual Arts, 1970, 71. Author: My Turn, 1983, 72nd and Rodeo, 1983; author short stories. Patron Met. Opera. Recipient Leadership award Am. Biog. Inst., Raleigh, N.C. Mem. PEN, Author's Guild, People for Ethical Treatment of Animals, Met. Opera Club, River Club. Republican. Episcopalian. Avocations: animal rights, opera.

AXELROD, JEAN KOLB, writer; b. Phila., Pa., July 13, 1928; d. Frazer Westmoreland Kolb and Florence MacKay; m. Frank Barton Exelrod, Oct. 6, 1966. BA, Univ. Pa., 1949. Freelance med. writer, travel writer various, Phila., 1980—; med. ad writer Lewis & Gilman, Phila. Author: Double Frill - History of Phila. Gen. Hosp. Nursing Sch., Honolulu Hawaiian Islands; contbr. articles to profl. med. and nursing jours., on travel to profl. jours. Election judge Election Official, Phila., 1994—. Mem.: Acad. of Vocal Arts, Germantown Cricket Club. Avocations: golf, tennis, travel. Home: 1918 Naudain St Philadelphia PA 19146

AXELROD, LEAH JOY, tour company executive; b. Milw., Sept. 7, 1929; d. Harry J. and Helen Janet (Ackerman) Mandelker; m. Leslie Robert Axelrod, Mar. 10, 1951; children: David Jay, Craig Lewis, Harry Besser, Garrick Paul, Bradley Neal, Nell Anne. BS, U. Wis., 1951. Creative drama specialist Highland Park (Ill.) Parks and Recreation Dept., 1962-82; program specialist Pub. Libr., Highland Park, 1972-82; ednl. cons. Bd. Jewish Edn., Chgo., 1973-80; children's edn. specialist Jewish Cmty. Ctr., Chgo., 1975-82; tour cons. My Kind of Town Tours, Highland Park, 1975-79, pres., 1979—. Co-owner Tours at the Mart, 1992-95. Editor: Highland Park: All American City, 1976; co-author: Highland Park By Foot or By Frame, 1980, Highland Park: American Suburb, 1982; co-editor: Adventures in Highland Park, 2001. Founding mem., v.p. Highland Park Hist. Soc., pres., 1987—94, past pres., 1994—; bd. dirs. Ill. State Hist. Soc., 1989—, exec. bd. dirs., 1999—; founder, bd. dirs. Chgo. Jewish Hist. Soc., 1975—; founder Team Ill., 1999, bd. mem., 1999—, sec., 2001—03; exec. com., adv. bd. Apple Tree Theatre Co., assoc. bd. pres., 2001—03; active Highland Park Hist. Preservation Commn.; pres. B'nai Torah Sisterhood, 1982—84; Bd. dirs. Midwest Zionist Youth Commn.; bd. dirs. Highland Park Hist. Soc., 1996—, Friends Jens Jensen, 1995—99. Mem. Nat. Assn. Women Bus. Owners, Am. Theatre Assn., Ill. Theatre Assn. (dir. creative dramatics 1977-79), Hadassah Club (Highland Park chpt.), Chgo. Area Women's History Conf. Bd., Coun. for Ill. History. Home: 2100 Linden Ave Highland Park IL 60035-2516 E-mail: tourtime@worldnet.att.net.

AXLEY, DIXIE L. insurance company executive; B in Social Welfare, Ill. Wesleyan U. Chartered property casualty underwriter. Pers. devel. specialist State Farm Mutual Automobile Ins. Co., Bloomington, Ill., 1987-88, supt., 1988-91, dir. mgmt. planning and info., 1991-93, mgr. pub. affairs, 1993-94, asst. divsn. mgr., 1994-95, asst. dir.- pub. affairs, then dir.- pub. affairs, 1995-96, asst. v.p.- pub. affairs, 1996-97, v.p. pub. affairs, 1997—. Office: State Farm Ins Cos Pub Affairs Dept 1 State Farm Plz Bloomington IL 61710-0001

AXTHELM, NANCY, advertising executive; V.p./prodn. group head Grey Worldwide (formerly Grey Advt. Inc.), sr. v.p., dep. dir. broadcast prodn., 1990—92, sr. v.p., dir. broadcast prodn., 1992—93, exec. v.p., dir. broadcast prodn., 1993—. Office: Grey Worldwide 777 3rd Ave Fl 10 New York NY 10017-1302*

AYDELOTTE, MYRTLE KITCHELL, retired nursing administrator; b. Van Meter, Iowa, May 31, 1917; d. John J. and Larava Josephine (Gutshall) Kitchell; m. William O. Aydelotte, June 22, 1956; children: Marie Elizabeth, Jeannette Farley. BS, U. Minn., 1939, MA, 1947, PhD, 1955; postgrad., Columbia U. Tchrs. Coll., 1948. Head nurse Charles T. Miller Hosp., St. Paul, 1939—41; surg. tchg. St. Mary's Hosp. Sch. Nursing, Mpls., 1941—42; instr. U. Minn., 1945—49; dir., dean State U. Iowa Coll. Nursing, 1949—57, prof., 1957—62; assoc. chief nurse VA Hosp. Rsch. for Nursing, Iowa City, 1963—64, chief nursing rsch., 1964—65; prof. U. Iowa Coll. Nursing, 1964—76, 1982—88; exec. dir. Am. Nurses Assn., 1977—81; ret., 1988. Dir. nursing U. Iowa Hosps. and Clinics, 1968—76; mem. sci. adv. bd. Ctr. Health Rsch. Wayne State U., 1972—76, Inst. Medicine, 1973—; cons. U. Minn., 1970, 82, 90, U. Rochester, 1971, U. Mich., 1970, 73, U. Colo., 1970—71, U. Hawaii, 1972—73, Ariz. State U., 1972, U. Nebr., 1972—73. Contbr. articles to profl. jours.; mem. editl. bd.: Nursing Forum, 1969—72, Jour. Nursing Adminstrn., 1971. Mem., v.p. Iowa City Libr. Bd., 1961—67; mem. Johnson County Bd. Health, 1967—70; mem. adv. com. family living courses Iowa City Bd. Edn., 1970—72. Served with Nurse Corps. U.S. Army, 1942—46. Mem.: Am. Acad. Nursing, Inst. Medicine, Am. Nurses Assn., Sigma Theta Tau (rsch. com. 1968—72). Home: 1570 East Ave Apt 106 Rochester NY 14610

AYDT, MARY I. secondary school educator; b. Lake Forest, Ill., Oct. 10, 1944; d. Stanley Adam Wrona and Sophie Steplyk; m. James C. Aydt, June 29, 1968; children: Michael, Stephen, Peter. BS in Edn., No. Ill. U., 1966; MA in Edn., St. Xavier U., Chgo., 1997. H.s. math. tchr. Mundelein (Ill.) Unit Dist., 1967—68, Sch. Dist. U-46, Elgin, Ill., 1968—74, 1985—; math. tchr. local CC, Elgin, 1980—87; ESL tchr. local YWCA, Elgin, 1980—87. Sponsor Nat. Honor Soc. Sch. Dist. U-46, Elgin, coach geometry in math competition. Worker, local soup kitchen, Elgin, 1996—. Mem.: AAUW (corr. sec. 1998—), NEA, Elgin Tchr. Assn., Ill. Edn. Assn., Kappa Delta Pi. Roman Catholic. Avocations: sports, travel, needlecrafts. Home: 1500 Easy St Elgin IL 60123 Office: Elgin High Sch 1200 Maroon Dr Elgin IL 60120

AYER, CLAIRE D. state representative, women's health nurse; b. Charlotte, Vt., Sept. 21, 1948; m. Alan Ayer; 3 children. RN, Jeanne Mance Sch. Nursing, 1969; BA cum laude in Environ. Studies, Middlebury Coll., 1992. Ob-gyn nurse; senator State of Vt., 2003—. Founding mem. Middlebury River Watershed Ptnr. Bd. dirs. Otter Creek Natural Resources Conservation Dist., 1992—; vol. Weybridge Sch.; mem. Middlebury Ara Land Trust, Weybridge Conservation Commn., Lake Champlain Sea Grant Com.; advisor U. Vt. Est. Natural Resources Bd. Office: 504 Thompson Hill Rd Weybridge VT 05753

AYERS, BETTY LOU, missionary, pastor; b. Tulsa, Okla., Sept. 4, 1945; d. Elijah Ayers and Jeweldean Hopkins Ayers. BS, Southwestern Assemblies of God U., 1967. Lic. preacher Okla. Dist. Coun. Assemblies of God, nat. apptd. home missionary to the Native Ams. Gen. Coun. Assemblies of God, ministerial cert. ordination Gen. Coun. Assemblies of God. With Teen Challenge, Phoenix, 1967—69; youth and children's pastor Indian Assembly of God, Winter Haven, Calif., 1969—70; active Sacaton (Ariz.) Assembly of God, 1970—71, Co-op Assembly of God, Laveen, Ariz., 1970—71; youth and children's pastor Maricopa (Ariz.) Indian Assembly of God, 1971—73; asst. pastor Grace All Tribes Assembly of God, Casa Grande, Ariz., 1976—77, pastor, 1977—83; apptd. home missionary evangelist Native Am. Children, 1983—85; pastor Stanfield (Ariz.) Indian Assembly of God, 1985—95, Cache (Okla.) All Tribes Assembly of God, 1996—. Republican. Avocation: playing cow bells. Office: Cache All Tribes Assembly of God PO Box 366 Cache OK 73527

AYERS, CAROLE ANNETTE, social studies educator; b. Winston-Salem, N.C., Dec. 8, 1946; d. Henry Leroy and Roxie Ann (Bullin) Ayers. BA, U.N.C.G., 1968; MA, Appalachian State U., 1975; PhD, U.N.C.G., 1993. Cert. history and social studies tchr. N.C., 1968, curriculum specialist N.C., 1993, early adolescence socials tudies-history 1999. Tchr. Surry County Schs., Mount Airy, NC, 1968—2003. Adj. prof. Surry Cmty. Coll., Dobson, NC, 1990—2003; bd. dirs. N.C. Coun. Social Studies, Greensboro, 2000—03; cons. Nat. Bd. Profl. Tchg. Stds., San Antonio, 2000—03. Contbr. articles to profl. jours. Chairperson bd. dirs. Charles Stone Libr., Pilot Mountain, NC, 2000—03; bd. dirs. Surry County Hist. Soc., Mount Airy, NC, 2001—03. Mem.: NEA, Surry County Asssn. Educators, N.C. Assn. Educators. Democrat. Methodist. Avocations: reading, genealogy, travel, decorating. Home: 161 Old Pinnacle Hotel Rd Pinnacle NC 27043 E-mail: a10301121@yahoo.com.

AYERS, JANET, technical college president; b. Bremen, Ga., Apr. 6, 1956; d. Etna Bentley; children: Jesset, Cole. BS in Edn., U. West Ga., Carrollton, 1977, MEd, 1981, EdS, 1986. Instr. Paulding County H.S., Dallas, Ga., 1977-78, Carroll Tech. Inst., 1977-81, chair bus. edn. divsn., 1981-88, v.p. student svcs., 1988-93, v.p. instructional and econ. devel., 1993-95, pres., 1995—. Bd. dirs. Ga. Edn. Advisement Coun., Carrollton. Mem. AAUW, West. Ga. LWV (pres. 1998-99), Ga. Assn. Supervision and Curriculum, Ga. Tech. Inst. Pres. Assn. (pres.), C. of C. of Carroll, Haralson, Douglas and Coweta Counties (bd. dirs.). Office: West Ctrl Tech Coll 176 Murphjy Campus Blvd Bremen GA 30110 E-mail: jayers@westcentral.org.

AYERS, JANICE R. social service administrator; b. Idaho Falls, Idaho, Jan. 23, 1930; 1 child, Thomas. MBA, U. So. Calif., 1952, MA, 1953. Gen. mgr. Tamasha Town and Pvt. Country Club, Anaheim, Calif.; asst. to dir. gen. svcs. Disneyland, Anaheim; state dir. Mental Retardation Assn., Las Vegas, Nev.; exec. dir., chief exec. officer 13-County Retired Sr. Vol. Program, Carson City, Nev. Cons. in field. Contbr. ariticles to profl. jours. Mem. Pub. Rels. Soc. Am., Nat. Assn. RSVP Dirs., Women in radio and TV, AAUW, Optimist Club, Las Vegas Club. Home: 1624 Karin Dr Carson City NV 89706-2626

AYERS, KATHERINE STONE, artist, chiropractor; d. Joseph Williams and Caroline Stone Ayers; m. Terry Kaye Hovey, Aug. 23, 1969 (div. 1988). BA, Vassar Coll., N.Y., 1958; B of Profl. Arts, Art Ctr. Sch., L.A., 1965; D of Chiropractice, Cleve. Chiropractic Coll., L.A., 1968; MA, Undenwood Coll., 1980. Chiropractic asst. various orgns., LA, 1966—68; med. sec. Dr. Weston, MD, LA, 1968—69; chiropractor Hovey Chiropractic Office, Canyon Country, Calif., 1969—80; somatic psychology artist Creative Processes, Big Island, Hawaii, 1980—94, artist Maui, Hawaii, 1999—. Tchr. Applied Kiniesology, LA and San Francisco, 1970, Bodynamics Integration, Vancouver, Canada, 1993—94. Author: (book chpt.) Handbook for Treatment of Attachment-Trauma Problems in Children. Mem.: Am. Assn. Univ. Women, Am. Assn. Ret. Persons. Avocations: swimming, gardening. Office: Creative Processes 23 Ehu Rd Makawao HI 96760

AYERS, KATHY VENITA MOORE, librarian; b. Amherst, Tex., Jan. 15, 1946; d. Charles Edward and Jean (Willman) Moore; children: Suzanne Flanary, Charles Flanary. BA, U. Ill., 1972, MLS, 1974. Cert. profl. libr., N.Mex.; cert. tchr., N.Mex. Dir. children's libr. Hayner Pub. Libr., Alton, Ill., 1974-76; dir. Ruidoso (N.Mex.) Pub. Libr., 1978-80; libr. media specialist Horgan Libr., N.Mex. Mil. Inst., Roswell, 1985-93; libr. N.Mex. Sch. Visually Handicapped, Alamogordo, 1993—. Workshop presenter Lewis & Clark Regional Libr. Systems, Ill., 1975; outreach programer Hayner Pub. Libr., 1974-76; del. Pre-White Ho. Conf., State of N.Mex., 1991. Contbr. articles to newspapers and profl. jours. Bd. dirs. Alton Symphony, 1975; mem. Altrusa, Ruidoso, 1979-84, Friend of Roswell Pub. Libr.; sec. Ruidoso Summer Festival, 1979; bd. dirs. Supts. Adv. Bd., Roswell, N.Mex., 1987-89; pres. Friends of Libr., Ruidoso, 1980-83, Parent Advocacy for Gifted Edn., 1990-92; v.p. Sunset PTA; bd. dirs. N.Mex. Libr. Found., 1992—; mem. State Task Force on Sch. Librs., 1999. Recipient Svc. award, Altrusa, 1979, Sunset PTA, 1989. Mem. N.Mex. Libr. Assn. (libr. devel. com., ednl. tech. roundtable vice chair 1991, chair elect 1992, co-chair state conv. local arrangements 1990-91, 2d v.p. 1993-94, 1st v.p. 1994-95, pres. 1995-96, Libr. Leadership award 2001), N.Mex. Acad. and Rsch. Librs. (vice chair 1992, pres. 1993), N.Mex. Taskforce for Sch. Librs., Kiwanis (bd. dirs. 1990-92). Avocations: travel, stained glass, music, hiking. Office: White Mountain Intermediate 201 White Mountain Dr Ruidoso NM 88345

AYLESWORTH, JULIE ANN, writer, personal care professional; b. Cin., Apr. 11, 1953; d. Robert Dean and Evelyn Jane (Francis) A. BA in Drama with honors, Vassar Coll., Poughkeepsie, N.Y., 1975. Adminstrv. asst. Gruber Realty Co., Cin., 1986-87, Gruber Design & Mktg., Cin., 1987-89. Radio broadcaster Radio Reading Svcs., Cin., 1980-81; job counselor Joy Ctr., Cin., 1980-81; consumer activist Marlowe House, Cin., 1984-86; dramatic coach Marlowe House, Cin., 1984-86; mem. Nightwriters, Highland Heights, Ky., 1986-88. Actress play Man of La Mancha, 1969; writer, dir. one-woman show Artist of the Woman as A Young Portrait, 1974; author: Quiet Times and Quotations, Vols. 1-16, 1979-84, Power Times, Vols. 1-25, 1984-89, Luna, Lazarus and Love, 1983, Of Her Own Free Will: A Schizoprhenic Succeeds, 1990; songwriter Color me Country, 2001, Land That I Love, 2002, Ain't No Place Like Cincinnati, 2001, There is a Light, 2002; contbr. articles to profl. jour. Telephone vol. Telecare, Cin., 1990; sch. crossing guard Cin. Police, 1978-80. Recipient Recognition award Joy Ctr., Cin., 1981, Merit award Radio Reading Svcs., Cin., 1981, Golden Poet awards World of Poetry, Editors Choice Award, Internat., Soc. of Poets, 1990-2002, Mem. Willing, Enabled Consumers are Needed (pres. 1984-86), Jesus' Art House (founder, owner 1986—). Republican. Avocations: cello, horticulture, zoological, reading, investing. Home and Office: 1673 Cedar Ave #409 Cincinnati OH 45224

AYLWARD, MARCIA EILEEN, artist, educator; b. Kansas City, Mo., Jan. 27, 1956; d. Charles Livingston and Rosemary Anita (Hughes) Aylward; m. John Davis Carroll, Oct. 9, 1993. BFA, Kansas City Art Inst., 1988; MFA, Parsons Sch. Design, 1991. Art instr. Kansas City Art Inst., Maplewood Woods C.C., Kansas City, Mo., Kansas City Acad.; asst. prof. Avila U., 1996—. Exhibitions include Cambridge Art Assn., 1999 (Nat. Prize show, 1999), 2000 (Nat. Prize show, 2000), Thornhill Gallery, 2001, Framing Girl Gallery, 2001. Home: 6010 Oak St Kansas City MO 64113-2217

AYRES, JANICE RUTH, social services administrator; b. Idaho Falls, Idaho, Jan. 23, 1930; d. Low Ray and Frances Mae (Salem) Mason; m. Thomas Woodrow Ayres, Nov. 27, 1953 (dec. 1966); 1 child, Thomas Woodrow Jr. (dec.). MBA, U. So. Calif., 1952, M in Mass Comms., 1953. Asst. mktg. dir. Disneyland, Inc., Anaheim, Calif., 1954-59; gen. mgr. Tamasha Town & Country Club, Anaheim, Calif., 1959-65; dir. mktg. Am. Heart Assn., Santa Ana, Calif., 1966-69; state exec. dir. Nev. Assn. Mental Health, Las Vegas, 1969-71; exec. dir. Clark Co. Easter Seal Treatment Ctr., Las Vegas, 1971-73; mktg. dir., fin devel. officer So. Nev. Drug Abuse Coun., Las Vegas, 1973-74; exec. dir. Nev. Assn. Retarded Citizens, Las Vegas, 1974-75; assoc., cons. Don Luke & Assocs., Phoenix, 1976-77; program dir. Inter-Tribal Coun. Nev., Reno, 1977-79; exec. dir. Ret. Sr. Vol. Program, Carson City, Nev., 1979—. Chair sr. citizen summit State of Nev., 1996; apptd. Nev. Commn. Aging Gov. Guinn, 2001; presenter in field. Bd. suprs., Carson City, Nev., 1992—; commr. Carson City Parks and Recreation, 1993—; obligation bond com., legis. chair Carson City; bd. dirs. Nev. Dept. Transp., 1993; active No. Corp. for Nat. and Cmty. Svc. by Gov., 1994, V&TRR Commn., 1993, chair, 1995; vice-chair, chair pub. rels. com., bd. dirs. Hist. V&TRR Bd.; chair PR Cmty./V&RR Commn. Nev. Home Health Assn.; appointed liaison Carson City Sr. Citizens Bd., 1995; chair summit Rural Nev. Sr. Citizens, Carson City; pres. No. Nev. R.R. Found., 1996—; chair Tri-Co-R.R. Commn., 1995, Gov.'s Nev. Commn. for Corp. in Nat. and Comty. Svc., 1997—, pres., 1998, Carson City Pub. Transp. Commn., 1998—; Carson City Commn. for Clean Groundwater Act, 1998—; chairperson Celebrate Svc. Conf. Americore, 2000; appointed by Gov. of Nev. Commn. on Aging, 2001—; appointed by Nev. Gov. new Nev. Commn. to Restructure the Historic V&T R.R., 2002—; mem. Nev. Commn. on Aging, 2001—; apptd. rep. of gov. to Nev. Commn. Recruitment V&T RR, 2002. Named Woman of Distinction, Soroptimist Club, 1988, Oustanding Dir. of Excellence, Gov. State of Nev., 1989, Outstanding Nev. Women's Role Model, Nev. A.G., 1996, Woman of Distinction, Carson Valley Optimist, 2002, Nev.'s Outstanding Older Worker for Experience-Works, 2002, Oldest CEO in Nev., 2002, Outstanding Nev. Pvt. Citizen, Nev. Gov. Guinn, Nev., 2003, Outstanding Dir., Vol. Action Ctr., J.C. Penney Co., invitee to White Ho. for outstanding contbns. to Am.; recipient Gold award, Western Fairs Assn., 2000, Woman of Distinction award, Soroptimist, 2003, Carson City Optimist, 2003, Nat. Optimist Conv., Reno, Nev., 2003, Outstanding Contbn. to Success of Women in Bus., Carson Valley Sorpotimists. Mem.: AAUW, Nat. Assn. Ret. and Sr. Vol. Dirs., Inc. (pres. 2003, nat. pres. 2003—), Internat. Assn. Bus. Commentators, No. Nev. Railroad Found. (pres. 1996—), Am. Soc. Assn. Execs., Nev. Assn. Transit Svcs. (bd. dirs., legis. chmn.), Nev. Fair and Rodeo Assn. (pres.), Nat. Soc. Fund Raising Execs., Women in Radio and TV, Pub. Rels. Soc. Am. (chpt. pres.), Internat. Platform Assn., Am. Mktg. Assn. (bd. dirs. 1999—), Am. Mgmt. Assn. (bd. dirs.), Nat. Women's Polit. Caucus, Nev. Women's Polit. Caucus. Home: 1762 Montelena Ct Carson City NV 89703-8376 Office: Ret Sr Vol Program 501 E Caroline St Carson City NV 89701-4054

AYRES, JUDITH ELIZABETH, federal agency administrator; b. Akron, Ohio, Sept. 3, 1944; d. William Hanes and Mary Helen (Coventry) A.; m. John Woolfolk Burke, III, June 17, 1978; 1 child, Elizabeth Coventry Ayres. BA, Miami U., Oxford, Ohio, 1966; postgrad., Internat. Christian U., Mitaka, Japan, 1968; MPA, Harvard U., 1980. With U.S. Dept. Interior, 1972-78, communication-legis liaison person, 1974-78; cons. San Francisco, 1978-82; regional adminstr. EPA, San Francisco, 1983-88; prin. William D. Ruckelshaus Assocs., San Francisco, 1988-89, The Environ. Group, San Francisco, 1989—; asst. adminr. int. affairs EPA, Washington, 2001—. Lectr., speaker in field. Contbr. articles to numerous publs. Del. Republican. Nat. Conv., 1988; bd. dirs. Women's Leadership Fund, Kennedy Sch. Govt., Harvard U.; mem. bd. Conservationists for Bush; co-chmn. Bush for Pres., Marin County, Calif., 1988, Calif. Conservationists for Bush, 1988. Mem. Women's Forum West, Harvard Club, Lambda Alpha. Republican. Avocations: music, natural history, skiing, sculling. Office: EPA Int Affairs 1200 Pennsylvania Ave NW MC 2610R Washington DC 20460

AYRES, MARY ELLEN, government official; b. Spokane, Wash., June 23, 1924; d. Frank H. and Marion (Kellogg) A. Student, U. Wash., 1942-43; BA, Stanford U., 1946; postgrad., Am. U., 1960. With Henry von Morpurgo, Advt., 1946-47; reporter Wenatchee Daily World, Wash., 1947-50, Washington Post, 1951-52; with U.S. Fgn. Service, Dept. State, 1950-51; mem. editorial staff Changing Times, 1952-61; editor Family Guide, Kiplinger Washington Editors, 1958-61, Bur. Labor Stats., Manpower Adminstrn., U.S. Dept. Labor, 1962-67; pub. info. specialist Bur. Indian Affairs, U.S. Dept. Interior, 1967-75; writer-editor Bur. Labor Stats., 1975—. Tchr. newsletter class Dept. Agriculture Grad. Sch., 1975-89, editing style and technique class, 1987-89; past treas. Govt. Info. Orgn. Mem. publicity com. Nat. Capitol YWCA, 1982-83; dir. Wenatchee High Sch. Scholarship Found., 1988-95. Mem. Nat. Assn. Govt. Communicators (founding treas., dir. 1975-80, 89-91, chmn. Blue Pencil Contest 1987, nat. capital chpt. treas. 1989), Nat. Press Club (Washington), Washington Athletic Club (Seattle), Am. News Women's Club, Am. Econ. Assn., Stanford U. Alumnae Assn., Kappa Kappa Gamma. Episcopalian. Home: 2400 Virginia Ave NW Apt C802 Washington DC 20037-2657 Office: Bur Labor Stats 2 Massachusetts Ave NE Washington DC 20212-0022 Fax: (202) 691-7890. Office Phone: 202-691-5856. E-mail: ayres_m@bls.gov.

AYRES, MARY JO, professional speaker, writer, composer; b. Aberdeen, Miss., Jan. 27, 1953; d. Walter Stephen and Sarah Louise (Pearson) Peugh; m. William Stanley Ayres, June 28, 1975; children: Elizabeth, Will. BS,

Miss. State U., Starkville, 1974; MEd, Delta State U., 1993. Tchr. Greenville (Miss.) Pub. Schs., 1974-75, Leland (Miss.) Acad., 1975-77, Leland United Meth. Child Devel. Ctr., Leland, 1984-91, chmn. bd. dirs., 1993—; profl. speaker Natural Learning, Leland, 1987—. Author: Happy Teaching and Natural Learning, 1992, Natural Learning from A-Z, 1997; prodr. cassette and CD 32 Natural Learning Songs from A-Z (Parent's Choice award), More Natural Learning Songs from A-Z (Parent's Choice award), Natural Learning Fun Songs (Parent's Choice award), Ms. Magnolia Puppet; contbr. articles to profl. jours. Mem. Assn. for Childhood Edn. Internat., Miss. Early Childhood Assn., So. Assn. for Children Under Six, So. Early Childhood Assn., Miss. Reading Assn., Internat. Reading Assn. Avocation: tennis.

AZAD, SUSAN S. lawyer; BS, Oreg. State U., 1984; JD, UCLA, 1989. Bar: Calif. 1989. With Latham & Watkins, L.A., 1989—, ptnr., 1997—. Mem. assocs. com. Latham & Watkins, L.A., 1992—94, fin. com., 1995—97, ethics com. Mem.: ABA, L.A. County Bar Assn. (litigation sect., jud. election evaluations com., Calif. state bar ct. rules com.), Women Lawyers Assn. L.A., Calif. Women Lawyers. Office: Latham and Watkins LLP 633 W Fifth St Ste 4000 Los Angeles CA 90071 Office Phone: 213-485-1234.

AZARIAN, MARY, illustrator; b. Washington, D.C., Dec. 8, 1940; d. L. G. and Eleanor Schneider; m. Tomas Azarian, July 24, 1962; 3 children. BA, Smith Coll., 1963. Elementary sch. teacher, Walden, Vt., 1963—67; freelance printmaker and illustrator, 1967—; founder Farmhouse Press, 1969—. One-woman shows include Lyndon State Coll., U. Conn., Chandler Gallery, Northfield, Vt., Beaver Coll. in the Schlesinger Libr., Radcliffe Inst. Advanced Study, Harvard U., Brown U., Lyman Allyn Art Gallery, Conn., Brattleboro Mus., Vt., Helen Day Art Ctr., Snowflake Bentley, 1999 (Caldecott award, 1999), The Wild Flavor, 1973, The Art of Living and Other Stories, 1981, The Caprilands Kitchen Book, 1981, The Magic Dulcimer, 1983, The Man Who Lived Alone, 1984, The Wildman: A Short Fable, 1985, Country Kitchens Remembered, 1986, Stubbornness, 1986, Talk Less and Say More, 1986, Gridley Firing, 1987, Caring for Your Own Dead, 1987, As Sweet as Apple Cider, 1988, Sea Gifts, 1989, Not By Bread Alone, 1990, Salty Wisdom, 1990, Barley Break, 1992, Where the Deer Were, 1994, A Symphony for the Sheep, 1996, Barn Cat: A Counting Book, 1998, Faraway Summer, 1998, The Four Seasons of Mary Azarian, 2000, Visits with the Amish, 2000, The Race of the Birkebeiners: A True Story, 2001, When the Moon Is Full, 2001, Louisa May and Mr. Thoreau's Flute, 2002, From Dawn till Dusk, 2002, A Christmas Like Helen's, 2004; author, illustrator: Farmer's Alphabet, 1981, From Barley to Beer: A Traditional English Ballad, 1982 (Parent's Choice award for illustration, 1983), A Gardener's Alphabet, 2000.*

AZARPAY, GUITTY, education educator; b. Teheran, Iran, Oct. 28, 1939; came to U.S., 1953, d. Rahim and Shekar (Dowlatshahi) A.; m. Ralph Werner Alexander, Dec. 18, 1963 (dec. 1998); 1 child, Vesa Alexander. PhD, U. Calif., Berkeley, 1964. Prof. U. Calif., Berkeley, 1963-94, U. Calif. Grad. Sch., Berkeley, 1994—. Author: Urartian Art & Artifacts, 1969, Sogdian Painting, 1981, Sasanian Sealstone: an Electronic Cataloging Project,2002; mem. editl. bd. Enclopaedia Iranica, 1994—. Mem. ABA, Am. Oriental Soc., Bulletin Asia Inst. Home: PO Box 908 Mill Valley CA 94942-0908 Office: Univ Calif Near Ea Studies Berkeley CA 94720-0001

AZELTON, REBECCA JOY, music educator; b. Jacksonville, Fla., Aug. 20, 1978; d. Melvin Vincent and Marlene Rogers James; m. Paul Brendan Azelton, Aug. 20, 1978. B, Southeastern Coll., 2000. Cert. music tchr. K-12 Fla., 2000. Gen. music tchr. Mike Moses Intermediate Sch., Nacogdoches, Tex., 2000—01; vocal/gen. music dir. Horace Mann Sch., Beverly Hills, Calif., 2001—03; choral dir. Landmark Mid. Sch., Jacksonville, Fla., 2003—.

AZICRI, NICOLETTE MALY, art educator, artist; b. Erie, Pa., Dec. 10, 1950; d. Nicholas and Sophie Agnes (Maciulewicz) Maly; m. Max Azicri, Apr. 14, 1973; children: David, Danielle (twins). BS in Edn., Edinboro U., 1971, BFA in Ceramics, 1985, MA in Painting and Ceramics, 1988; MA in Counseling, Gannon U., 1976. Cert. elem. edn., spl. edn., elem. counseling. Tchr. spl. edn. and grades K-12 Sch. Dist. of City of Erie, 1972-95. Faculty Pa. State, Erie, Behrend, 1996. Exhibited in group shows at Three Rivers Art Festival, Pitts., 1990, 93, 95 (award), 2002, Westmoreland C.C., Youngwood, Pa., 1990, 93, 95, 97, 99, Carnegie Art Mus., Pitts., 1993, Am. Facism Nat. Exhbn., Artsquad Contemporary Gallery, Easton, Pa., 1993, Art Assn. Harrisburg, Pa., 1994, 98, Resurgam Nat. Exhbn., Resurgam Gallery, Balt., 1994, Nat. Art League's Art Exhbn., Douglaston-N.Y.C., 1994, Mari Galleries, N.Y.C., 1994, Nicolet Coll. Gallery, Rhineland, Wis., 1995 (award), Antiquarium Gallery, Omaha, 1995-96, Coastal Ctr. for the Arts, St. Simon Island, Ga., 1994, 96 (award), 98, Art Ctr. of No. N.J., New Milford, 1995, Greater Midwest Internat. Ctrl. Mo. State U. Art Ctr. Gallery, 1995 (award), An Art Place Inc. Gallery, Chgo., 1995, Impact Women's Gallery, Buffalo, 1996, State of Arts Gallery, Itchaca, N.Y., 1996, Navarro Coun. Arts, 1998 (award), Hoyt Inst. Fine Arts, 1997 (award), Dayspring Dance and Workshop Arts Ctr., L.I., N.Y., 1997, Warehouse Living Arts Ctr., Corsicana, Tex., 1997 (award), Swann Gallery, Detroit, 1997, The Art Network Gallery, Ldnenhurst, N.Y., 1997, Tonowandas (N.Y.) Coun. on the Arts, 1997, Galex 37 Nat. Juried Exhibition Galesburg (Ill.) Civic Arts Ctr., 2003, 9th Annual Nat. Juried Show Prallville Mills, Artsbridge Gallery, Lamberstville, N.J., 2003, The Artful Women Nat. Juried Exhibition Binney & Smith Gallery, Bethlehem, Pa., 2003. Vol. Gertrude Barber Ctr., Erie, 1970, Hospitality House for Women, Erie, 1973-76, Spl. Olympics, Erie, 1973-76, 1st Night Erie Com., 1991-97, AAUW Holly Trail, Erie, 1994-96. Mem. AAUW, Erie Art Mus., Meadville Coun. of the Arts, Chautuaqua Art Assn., Nothwest Pa. Artists Assn. Avocations: biking, reading, cooking. Home: 4000 Ridgewood Dr Erie PA 16506-4062 Office Phone: 814-835-3780. E-mail: nickieazicki@msn.com.

AZRIELANT, AYA, jewelry manufacturing executive; b. Israel; Came to U.S. 1981. m. Ofer Azrielant; 3 children. BA in Fine Arts and Lit., Haifa U.; postgrad. in film-making, London. Designer, owner Aya Azrielant, N.Y.C. Avocation: collector of modern art. Office: Andin International Inc 609 Greenwich St New York NY 10014-3683 Fax: 212-886-6006.

AZZARONE, CAROL ANN, marketing executive; b. Jersey City, Aug. 1, 1946; d. Paul Buglione and Catherine (DellaFave) LiCalsi; m. Dominick L. Azzarone, May 13, 1967 (div. 1989); children: Anthony Paul, Kathryn Ann. AA, Bergen C.C., 1982; BA, Ramapo Coll., 1984. Editl. asst. McGraw-Hill, Inc., N.Y.C., 1964-69; real estate agt. Auburn Realty, Inc., Bergenfield, N.J., 1975-80, Weichert Realty, Morris Plains, N.J., 1975—; pub. rels. coord. Ridgefield (N.J.) Bd. Edn., 1982-84; mktg. dir. Spa Lady Corp., Fairfax, Va., 1984-86, Newson Fitness, Morristown, N.J., 1986-88; creative dir. Publ. Corp., Morristown, 1988-90; advt. dir. Ronton Advt., Union, N.J., 1990-98; mktg. v.p. Dynamic Tech. Group, Inc., Parsippany, N.J., 1998—. Adv. bd. N.J. Tech. Coun., 2001—03; cons. in field; spkr. in field. Editor (newsletters) Ridgefield Sch. News, 1982-84, Cliffside Park Sch. News, 1984-85, The Grapevine, 1985-86. Mem. advt. bd. N.J. Tech. Coun. N.J. Bell scholar N.J. Bell Corp., 1980, Bergen Community Coll. Alumni scholar 1981. Mem. NOW, NAFE (First Place award of excellence 1996, Jersey award), Advt./Pub. Rels. Assn., NJ Advt. Club, Phi Theta Kappa. Democrat. Roman Catholic. Avocations: cross country skiing, horseback riding, biking, reading. Office: Dynamic Tech Group Inc 1055 Parsippany Blvd Parsippany NJ 07054-1230

AZZI, JENNIFER L. professional basketball player; b. Oak Ridge, Tenn., Aug. 31, 1968; d. James and Donna Azzi. Diploma, Stanford U., 1990. Basketball player Arvika Basket, Sweden, 1995—96, Viterbo, Italy, Or-

chies, France, San Jose Lasers, 1996—99, Salt Lake City Starzz, 1999—2002, San Antonio Stars, 2003—. Mem. Nat. Women's Basketball Team. Named Al-Pac 10 1st team, 1988, 1989, 1990, MVP, NCAA Final Four, 1990, NCAA West Region, 1990, Naismith Nat. Player Yr., 1990; recipient gold medal, Goodwill Games, 1994, World Championship Qualifying team, 1993, U.S. Olympic Festival West Team, 1987, 2 gold medals, World Championship and Goodwill Games, 1990, bronze medal, Pan Am. Games, 1991, World Championship team, 1994, Wade Trophy, 1990, Kodak All-Am. 1st team, 1989, 1990, gold medal, U.S. Olympic Team, 1996. Office: San Antonio Silver Stars One SBC Ctr San Antonio TX 78219

BAARS, ELLA JANE, art educator; b. Paris, Tenn., Apr. 19, 1952; d. Elroy Vinson Griffin and Mattie Lou Futrell; m. Glenn George Baars, Aug. 14, 1971; children: Heather Rose, Amy Elizabeth. BA in Art, Maryville U. 1976; degree in elem. edn., Bethel U., 1994; M in Art Edn., Valdosta State U., 2002. Nat. bd. cert. in art, cert. tchr. K-8 classroom, 9-12 math, preK-12 art Ga. Art instr. Henry County H.S., Paris, 1977-83; ednl. tng. specialist State of Tenn., Jackson, 1983—85; store owner Fashion Gallery, Paris, 1985—89; bus. mgr. Microtech, Paris, 1991—94; tchr. mid. grades Marion County Schs., Whitwell, Tenn., 1994—95; adult learning dir. Sequatchie County Schs., Dunlap, Tenn., 1995—96; art instr. Coffee County Schs., Douglas, Ga., 1996—. Cons., facilitator Tchr. Ctr., Kennesaw, Ga., 2001—; regional rep. Allstate Festival of Art and Design, 2002—; participant onlist profl. list Tchr. Leader Network, SC, 2003. Exhibitions include Ga. Art Edn. Assn., 1999, 2000, Wiregrass Exhibit, 2002, S.E. Ga. Regional Exhibit, 2002. Dir. Youth Art Camp, Douglas Pks. and Recreation, 1997—2002; mem. Page, Ga., 1999—; bd. dirs. Coffee Alliance for Arts, Douglas, 2000—. Mem.: Profl. Assn. Ga. Educators (facilitator 1999—), Wiregrass Art Assn. (orgnl. bd. 2002—), Ga. Art Edn. Assn. (state bd. mem. 2001—, Youth Art Month 2002), Pi Lambda Theta. Baptist. Avocations: drawing, painting, crafts, camping, water sports. Office: Coffee H S 159 Trojan Way Douglas GA 31533 E-mail: jbaars@coffeek12.ga.us.

BAAS, JACQUELYNN, museum consultant, art historian; b. Grand Rapids, Mich., Feb. 14, 1948; BA in History of Art, Mich. State U.; PhD in History of Art, U. Mich. Registrar U. Mich. Mus. Art, Ann Arbor, 1974-78, asst. dir., 1978-82; editor Bull. Museums of Art and Archaeology, U. Mich., 1976-82; chief curator Hood Mus. Art, Dartmouth Coll., Hanover, N.H., 1982-84, dir., 1985-89, U. Calif. Berkeley Art Mus. and Pacific Film Archive, Calif., 1989-99, emeritus dir., 1999—; program dir. Awake: Art and Buddhism, 1999—. Cons. in field; organizer exhbns.; ind. art historian, program dir. Awake: Art & Buddhism in Am. Contbr. articles and essays to jours. and books. Mem. Coll. Art Assn. Am. Address: PO Box 162 The Sea Ranch CA 95497-0162 Office Phone: 510-406-4455.

BAASAN, RAGCHAA, diplomat; b. Ulaanbaatar, Mongolia, Nov. 19, 1943; d. Tumer and Demberel (Tsendsuren) Ragchaa; m. Jamsran Gendendaram, Sept. 1967; children: Enhbat, Enhtsetseg, Enhtuvshin. Diploma, Moscow Inst. Fgn. Langs. Asst. officer Ministry of External Rels., Ulaanbaatar, 1967-69; diplomat Mongolian Embassy in India, New Delhi, 1969-74; attache Ministry of External Rels./Asian Dept., Ulaanbaatar, 1974-78, 2d sec., 1981-83, Mongolian Embassy, Kabul, Afghanistan, 1978-81, Embassy Mongolia, New Delhi, 1983-88; 1st sec., counsellor Ministry External Rels., Ulaanbaatar, 1988-97; 1st sec., polit. Embassy Mongolia, Washington, 1997—. Decorated Polar Star Order (Mongolia); recipient Honor of Svc. award Govt. of Mongolia, 1991/ Buddhist. Avocations: reading, analysing, knitting, cooking. Home: XI Region SA Apt 18 Chinggis Ave 4 Ulaanbaatar 49 Mongolia Office: Embassy of Mongolia Washington DC 20007-3712 E-mail: Baasan@aol.com.

BABA, MARIETTA LYNN, business anthropologist, university administrator, b. Flint, Mich., Nov. 9, 1949; d. David and Lillian (Joseph) Baba; m. David Smokler, Feb. 14, 1977 (div. 1982); 1 child, Alexia Nicole Baba Smokler. BA with highest distinction, Wayne State U., 1971, MA in Anthropology, 1973, PhD in Phys. Anthropology, 1975; MBA, Mich. State U., 1994. Asst. prof. sci. and tech. Wayne State U., Detroit, 1975-80, assoc. prof. anthropology, 1980-88, prof., 1988—, spl. asst. to pres., 1980-82, econ. devel. officer, 1982-83, asst. provost, 1983-85, assoc. provost, 1985-89, dir. internat. programs, interim assoc. dean Grad. Sch., 1988-89, assoc. dean Grad. Sch., 1989-90, acting chair dept. anthropology, 1990-92, chair dept. anthropology, 1996-2001; dean, prof. anthropology Mich. State U. Coll. Social Sci., East Lansing, 2001—. Program dir. transformations to quality orgns., dir. social, behav., and econ. scis. NSF, 1994—96; evolution rschr. Wayne State U., 1975—82; cons. GM Rsch. Labs., 1980—92, Electronic Data Sys., 1990—93, McKinsey Global Inst., 1991; rsch. contractor GM/EDS, 1990—94; lectr. nat. and internat. symposia, profl. confs. Adv. for editor orgnl. anthropology: American Anthropologist, 1990-93; issued letters patent for method to map joint ventures and maps produced thereby; contbr. numerous papers and abstracts to tech. jours.; patentee in field. Mem. State Rsch. Fund Feasibility Rev. Panel, 1982—84; mem. adv. panel on tech. innovation and U.S. trade U.S. Congl. Office Tech. Assessment, 1990—91, mem. panel on electronic enterprise, 1993—94; active Leadership Detroit Class IV, 1982—83; dir. Mich. Tech. Coun. (S.E. divsn.), 1984—85. With USAF, 1992—94. Job Partnership Tng. Act grantee, 1981-90, NSF grantee, 1982, 84-85, 99-01. Fellow Am. Anthrop. Assn. (bd. dirs. 1986-88, exec. com. 1986-88, del. to Internat. Union Anthrop. and Ethnol. Sci. 1990-94, chair global comm. anthropology 1993-98), Nat. Assn. Practice Anthropology (pres. 1986-88), Soc. Applied Anthropology, Phi Beta Kappa, Sigma Xi (Morton Fried award 1991), Beta Gamma Sigma.

BABB, FLORENCE EVELYN, anthropologist, educator; b. Goshen, N.Y., Feb. 21, 1951; d. Roland Walker Babb, Marjorie (Knapp) Babb; 1 child, Daniel. BA in Anthropology and French, Tufts U., 1973; MA in Anthropology, SUNY Buffalo, 1976, PhD in Anthropology, 1981. Vis. asst. prof. anthropology Colgate U., Hamilton, NY, 1979—82; asst. prof., prof. anthropology, women's studies U. Iowa, Iowa City, 1982—, prof., chair Anthropology dept., 2001—03. Resident Bellagio Inc., 2003. Author: Between Field and Cooking Pot: The Political Economy of Market Women in Peru, 1998, After Revolution: Mapping Gender and Cultural Politics in Neoliberal Nicaragua, 2001. Recipient Fulbright award, 1990-91, Wenner-Gren award Rockefeller Found., 1992. Mem. Am. Anthropol. Assn., L.Am. Studies Assn., Assn. for Feminist Anthropology. Office: Univ Iowa Anthropology Dept 114 MacBride Hall Iowa City IA 52242-1322 Office Phone: 319-335-0522.

BABBY, ELLEN REISMAN, education administrator; b. Montreal, Que., Can., Oct. 21, 1950; came to U.S., 1973; d. Mark Reisman and Rose Gutwillig (Reisman); m. Lon Scott Babby, June 17, 1973; children: Kenneth Robert, Heather Lynn. Student, McGill U., 1968-70; BA, Beaver Coll., 1972; MA, Lehigh U., 1973, Yale U., 1976, M.Phil., 1977, PhD, 1980. Tchr. elem. schs. to coll. levels; instr. resident assoc. program Smithsonian Instn., Washington, 1980-82; exec. dir. Assn. for Can. Studies in U.S., Washington, 1982-92; with Nat. Fgn. Lang. Ctr. Johns Hopkins U., Washington, 1992-94; sr. dir. planning and devel. Nat. Assn. Fgn. Student Affairs Assn. Internat. Educators, Washington, 1995—99; v.p. Am. Coun. On Edn., Washington, 1999—. Author: Play of Language and Spectacle: A Structural Reading of Selected Texts by Gabrielle Roy, 1986. Contbr. articles on Quebec lit. to profl. jours. Mem. Assn. for Can. Studies in U.S., Am. Soc. Assn. Execs., Nat. Soc. Fund Raising Execs., Yale Alumni (del. 1989-92). Office: Am Coun On Edn One Dupont Cir #800 Washington DC 20036 E-mail: ellen@babby.com.

BABCOCK, BARBARA ALLEN, law educator, lawyer; b. Washington, July 6, 1938; d. Henry Allen and Doris Lenore (Moses) Babcock; m. Thomas C. Grey, Aug. 19, 1979. BA, U. Pa., 1960; LLB, Yale U., 1963; LLD (hon.), U. San Diego, 1983, U Puget Sound, 1988. Bar: Md. 1963, DC 1964. Law clk. US Ct. Appeals, DC, 1963; assoc. Edward Bennett Williams, 1964—66; staff atty. Legal Aid Agy., Washington, 1966—68; dir. Pub. Defender Svc. (formerly Legal Aid Agy.), 1968—72; asst. atty. gen. US Dept. Justice, 1977—79; assoc. prof. Stanford U., 1972—77, prof., 1977—, Ernest W. McFarland Prof. Law, 1986—97, Judge John Crown Prof. of Law, 1997—. Author (with others): Sex Discrimination and The Law: History, Theory and Practice, 1996; co-author (with Massaro): Civil Procedure: Problems and Cases, 2001; contbr. articles profl. jour. Recipient John Bingham Hurlbut Award for Excellence in Tchg., Stanford U., 1981, 1986, 1998, Margaret Brent Women Lawyers of Achievement Award, ABA, 1999. Democrat. Office: Stanford U Sch Law Stanford CA 94305

BABCOCK, CATHERINE EVANS, artist, educator; b. Rydal, Pa., Feb. 23, 1924; d. William Wayne and Marion (Waters) Babcock; m. Douglas Paul Torre, May 28, 1977; 2 stepchildren. Diploma, Sarah Lawrence Coll., 1942; BFA, Temple U., 1944, MFA, 1948. Tchr. Rudolf Steiner Sch., 1949; tchr. jr. high sch. Stratford, Conn., 1959-63; tchr. elem. art Locust Valley Primary and Elem. Sch., 1963-68; instr. Darien Cmty. Ctr., 1975-81; art tchr. Rowayton Arts Ctr., Conn., 1979—, also bd. mem. Rec. sec. Portrait painter; artist to Sea Svc. (USCG and USN); equestrian artist Fairfield Hunt Club Show's Benefit Horse Show, 1993; watercolor tchr. Darien Cmty. Assn., 1993-94. Illustrator: Atheneum, 1968 (libr. award), Cutaneous Cryosurgery (Douglas Torre), 1978, rev., 1979; translator: Undertow (Finn Havrevold), 1968; painter, mural for Babcock Surg. Wards, Temple U. Hosp., Phila., 1944; designer display Cryosurgery of Skin Cancer, Dallas, 1979 (Gold award); author: Biography in American References, 1989, (poem) Vikings Habitat, The National Library of Poetry, River of Dreams, 1994, Poetic Voices of America, 1995, Best Pastels, 1996, Chips and Chirps of Verses, 1998, Theatre of the Mind; exhbns. include internat. miniature shows Fine Arts Club, Washington, 1984, New Canaan Soc. for the Arts, 1988, 93, Grand Nat. Salmagundi Club, St. Petersburg Mus., Fla., Degas Pastel Soc., New Orleans, 1990-95, Mus. of Art, New Orleans, 1990, (portrait of husband) NY Hosp., Amb. Ernst Jaakson Mus. in Tallin, Estonia, 2001, Portrait of Sr. Ambassador of UN painted in 1997, kept in his NYC office, is now in mus. in ESTONIA, 2001; Cert. of Excellence from Miniature fSpc. (MSPG) of Washinton DC for portrait of a firefighter, 2002; author of poems. Recipient award including 10 USCG awards, Am. Acad. Dermatology Art Shows, 2 award, Rowayton Arts Ctr., 1993—94, Best Poems award, Nat. Libr. Poetry, 1996, Amherst Soc. award, Sparrowgrass Soc. award, cert. appreciation, USCG, 1971—82, Naval Sta. of N.Y., 1981, 1st prize, Rowayton Art Ctr., 2000, USCG award, Alexander Hamilton Custom House, 2000, Mdal of Honror, IBC Internat. Pro. Ctr., Cambridge, Eng., 2004. Mem. Internat. Soc. Poets (lifetime, Merit award 1997, medal 1997, Silver cup 2003, 2d Silver cup 2003), Met. Portrait Inst., Conn. Pastel Soc., Pastel Soc. Am. (cert. of merit), USCG Art Program (ofcl. artist), COGAP artist, 1999, London Diplomatic Acad., 2001. Congregationalist. Home and Office: 122 Rowayton Ave Norwalk CT 06853-1409

BABCOCK, HOPE SMITH, counselor, educator, program designer; b. Attleboro, Mass., July 3, 1941; d. Ezra Sheldon and Virginia (Fernandez) Smith; m. Robert C. Miner, June 20, 1959 (div. Oct. 1973); children: Eric, Robert, Jonathan, William, Garret; m. John A. Bucciarelli Jr., June 20, 1975 (dec. Aug. 1981); m. Richard B. Babcock, Nov. 8, 1997. AA, Brevard C.C., Cocoa, Fla.; BA, U. Ctrl. Fla., Orlando; MA, MHC, Webster U., Merritt Island, Fla. Cert. clin. hypnotherapist, pvt practice forensic hypnotist; lic. real estate agt. Fla.; domestic violence intervention specialist. Coord. suicide prevention jr./sr. high schs. Mental Health Assn., Rockledge, Fla., 1995-96; internat. hypnosis intervention arbitrator, instr. Juvenile Justice Ct. Alternatives, 1986-91; program designer, specialist, counselor, tchr. life skills Dept. Corrections-Probation/Parole Svcs., Cocoa, 1990—; counselor, tchr. Brevard County Jail, Sharpes, Fla., 1993-96; coord. parents, children, divorce Brevard County Ct. Sys., 1995-98; substance abuse counselor, life skills tchr. Alco-Rest Rehab. Ctr., Cocoa, 1997-2001. Cons., advisor Probationers Ednl. Growth Program, Cocoa, 1995—2001; bd. dirs. Turning Point Rehab. Ctr., 1996—98; domestic violence interventions svcs. facilitator Family Counseling Ctr., Rockledge, 2001. Program designer, implementer, arbitrator Juvenile Alternative Svcs. Program, 1985-91, Brevard County Mentoring Program, Merritt Island, 1999, Cmty. Crisis Response Team, 2002. Named J.C. Penney's Cmty. Vol. of Yr., 1993; recipient numerous awards of recognition. Avocations: real estate investing, international travel, interior crafts and decorating. Home: 4560 Horse Shoe Bnd Merritt Island FL 32953-7900

BABCOCK, JANICE BEATRICE, healthcare coordinator; b. Milw., June 2, 1942; d. Delbert Martin and Constance Josephine (Dworschack) B. BS in Med. Tech., Marquette U., 1964; MA in Healthcare Mgmt. and Supervision, Cen. Mich. U., 1975. Registered med. technologist and microbiologist, clin. lab. scientist, epidemiologist; cert. bioanalytical lab. mgr. Intern St. Luke's Hosp., Milw., 1963-64; microbiologist St. Michael's Hosp., Milw., 1964-65; supr. clin. lab. svc. VA Regional Office, Milw., 1965-66; hosp. epidemiologist VA Ctr., Milw., 1966-74, supr. anaerobic microbiology and rsch. lab., 1974-78, adminstrv. officer, chief med. tech., 1978-83, quality assurance coord., 1983-86, asst. to chief of staff profl. svcs., 1986-92; coord. constrn. vet. affairs outpatient clinic VHA Med. Ctr., Milw., 1992-94; coord. Coop. Adminstrv. Support Unit (CASU) VHA Nat. Ctr. for Cost Containment, Milw., 1993-94; health sys. specialist managed care/primary care VHA Managed Care, Milw., 1994—. Lectr. Marquette U., 1966-86, U. Wis., 1966-86, Med. Coll. Wis., 1966-86. Contbr. numerous articles to profl. jours. Rec. sec. Wis. Svc. League, 1989-92, corr. sec., 1991. Recipient Wood VA Fed. Woman's award, 1975, Profl. Achievement award Lab. World award, 1981, Disting. Alumni award Cen. Mich. U., 1986. Fellow Royal Soc. Health, Am. Acad. Med. Adminstrs. (Wis. state Dir. of the Yr. award 1989, Diplomate 1989, mem. editorial bd. Exec. jour. 1987—, editor 1994, regional dir. 1992—, mem. fed. exec. coun. 1994—); mem. Internat. Acad. Healthcare Mgmt., Internat. Soc. of Tech. Assessment in Health Care, Am. Soc. Microbiology, Am. Coll. Healthcare Execs., Am. Soc. Med. Tech. (Nat. Sci. Creativity award 1974, Nat. Microbiology Sci. Achievement award 1978, Mem. of the Yr. award 1979, Profl. Achievement Lectureship award 1981, French Lectureship award 1983), Assn. for Health Svcs. Rsch., Assn. Marquette U. Women (bd. dirs. 1987-93, v.p., sec.), Assn. Mil. Surgeons U.S. (lifetime), Nat. Assn. Med. Staff Svcs. (mem. editorial bd. Overview Jour. 1990-93), Wis. Assn. Med. Staff Svcs., Wis. Hosp. Assn. Fed. Execs. Assn. (Milw. 1983—), Alpha Mu Tau (pres. 1984-85), Alpha Delta Theta, Sigma Iota Epsilon, Alpha Delta Pi (Alumni Honor award 1979). Home: 6839 Blanchard St Milwaukee WI 53213-2853 Office: VHA Med Ctr 5000 W National Ave Milwaukee WI 53295-0001

BABCOCK, M. SANDRA, administrative assistant, writer; b. N.Y.C., June 23, 1954; d. James Albert Beebe, Sr. and Annah Elizabeth Scandell; m. William Clayton Babcock, Sr., Oct. 8, 1971; children: Monica Sandi, William Clayton Jr. Cert. in legal adminstr. asst., Merritt Davis Bus. Coll., Eugene, Oreg., 1982. Legal adminstrv. asst. Delay, Curran, Thompson, Pontarolo et al, Spokane, Wash., 1988—. Contbr. articles to newspapers; author: (short stories) Confronting the Evil, 1999 (First place award Preservation Found., Inc., 1999), Private Monty, The Truth Within Lies, 2000. Exec. sec. Greyhound Pets Am., Ariz., 1995—98; vol. Walk in the Wild Zoo, Spokane, 1990—98; officer, spkr., adoption rep. Greyhound Pets Am., Spokane, 1990—98. Democrat. Roman Catholic. Avocations: fly fishing, travel, golf, bicycling, hiking. Office: Delay Curran Thompson Pontarolo et al 601 W Main Ste 1212 Spokane WA 99201 Office Phone: 509-455-9500. Personal E-mail: sandi20@msn.com.

BABCOCK, MARGUERITE LOCKWOOD, addictions treatment therapist, educator, writer; b. Jacksonville, Fla., Jan. 1, 1944; d. Allen Seaman and Emilie (Lockwood) B. BA in Art History, Am. U., 1965; M Counselor Edn., U. Pitts., 1982. Lic. profl. counselor, Pa.; cert. addictions counselor Pa., nat. cert. counselor, master's addiction counselor (nat.). Addictions therapist South Hills Health Sys., Pitts., 1978-81; addiction therapist, clin. supr., clin. dir. Alternatives- Turtle Creek Mental Health/Mental Retardation/D&A Ctr., Pitts., 1981-86; addictions therapist, coord. Ligonier Valley Treatment Ctr., Stahlstown, Pa., 1986—88; addictions clin. supr., unit dir. Ctr. for Substance Abuse Mon-Yough, McKeesport, Pa., 1988-96; quality assurance Mon-Yough, McKeesport, 1996 [illegible] clin. supr. [illegible] House, Pitts., 1997-2000; co-founder, addictions cons. consortium Outcomes Builders, 2000—. Adj. instr. in addictions courses Seton Hill Coll., Greensburg, Pa., 1989-91, C.C. Allegheny County, West Mifflin, Pa., 1989-91, Pa. State U., McKeesport, 1993-97; pvt. trainer, writer, Acme, Pa., 1985—; ind. info. profl. in addictions, 2003—. Co-author, co-editor: Challenging Codependency: Feminist Critiques, 1995; mem. editl. bd. Jour. Tchg. in Addictions, 2000—; contbr. articles to profl. jours. Fellow Andrew Mellon Found., 1966-68, NSF, 1967. Mem.: Alpha Lambda Delta, Phi Kappa Phi. Avocation: website designer. Home and Office: 3533 Rt 130 Acme PA 15610-9712 E-mail: allele@lhtc.net.

BABER, YONGSOOK KIM, musician; b. Suwon, Korea (South), Sept. 15, 1959; d. Hyungkyu Kim and Imgyo Kim GEONG; m. Leonard William Barber, May 14, 1988; 1 child, Sarah Kim Barber. MusB, Dongduck Women's U., Seoul, South Korea, 1983; master music performance, Shenandoah U., Winchester, Virginia, 1988. Piano accompanist Frederick County Pub. Schools, Winchester, Va., 1988—95; piano tchr. Shenandoah U. Arts Acad., Winchester, Va., 1991—; piano accompanist Frederick County Pub. Schools, Winchester, Va., 2001—. Avocation: playing handbells. E-mail: YBaber@visuallink.com.

BABIAK, HEATHER, nurse, food service executive; b. Hinsdale, Ill., Mar. 29, 1973; d. Paul Louis and Darlene B. BS, U. Ill., 1995. RN, Ill., WA. Spl. edn. nurse Lyons (Ill.) # 103; nurse Westmont (Ill.) High Sch.; co-owner Williamsburg Group dba Fairview Creamery, Westmont. Mem. Am. U. Women Assn. (Read-a-thon, participant Career Day 1999), Am. Bus. Women Assn. (Read-a-thon), Ill. RN Assn., Ill Caucus for Adolescent Health (chmn. Willowbrook), Westmont C. of C., Sigma Theta Delta, Golden Key Soc., Alpha Lambda Delta, Phi Eta Sigma, Alpha Xi Delta. Avocations: piano, photography, swimming, aerobics, recycling. Home: 1017 Williamsburg St Westmont IL 60559-1043 E-mail: hbabiakl@aol.com.

BABITZKE, THERESA ANGELINE, health facility administrator; b. Madison, Ill., Dec. 19, 1925; d. Victor Joseph and Angela (Ziolkowski) Sobolewski; m. Douglas Christ Babitzke, May 2, 1953; children: Charlotte, Mary Ann, Rose Marie, Helen. Student, Quincy Coll., 1943; diploma, St. John's Sch. Nursing Edn., Springfield, Ill., 1949; student, U. Ill., Chgo., 1970; BA, St. Francis Coll., 1973; MA in Geronology summa cum laude, Sangamon State U., 1982. Co-founder, admin. dir. Mayslake Village, Oakbrook, Ill., 1962, St. Paschal's Infirmary, Oakbrook, 1962; night supr. Godair Home, Hinsdale, Ill., 1958-72; DON King Bruwaert House, Hinsdale, 1973-76; head nurse Mt. Sinai Hosp., Chgo., 1976-82; DON Rosary Hill Home, Justice, Ill., 1989—. Election judge Rep. Com. DuPage County, 1953-98, 2003; mem. adv. bd. Gower Grade Sch., 1973-76; mem. adv. com. Burr Ridge Marriot Brighton Gardens Assisted Living, 1996—. Named Ill. Nurse of Yr. of the Midwest, 1981, Catholic Woman of Yr. 1962, St. Mary's Ch., Joliet, Ill. Mem. Downers Grove and Suburban Nurses Club (pres. Downers Grove chpt.), U. of Ill. Gerontology, Forty and Eight, Premier Nurse Ill., Am. Legion Aux., Sigma Phi Omega (Eta chpt. U. Ill.). Roman Catholic. Avocations: travel, bicycling, doll collecting, reading.

BABROWSKI, CLAIRE HARBECK, fast food chain executive; b. Ottawa, Ill., July 25, 1957; d. John Clayton Harbeck and Corrine Ann (Lavender) French; m. David Lee Babrowski, July 3, 1982. Student, U. Ill., 1975-77; MBA, U. N.C., 1995. Dental asst., Ottawa, 1975-76; crew person McDonald's Corp., Ottawa, 1974-76, mem. restaurant mgmt. Champaign, Ill., 1976-80, ops. and tng. cons. St. Louis, 1980-84, ops. mgr., 1984-86, dir. nat. ops. Oak Brook, Ill., 1986-88, dir. ops. Phila., 1988-89, sr. regional mgr. Raleigh, NC, 1989—92, regional v.p., 1992—95, corp. v.p. ops., 1995—97, sr. v.p. ops., 1997—98, exec. v.p. U.S. Restaurant Sys., 1998—99, exec. v.p. Worldwide Restaurant Sys., 1999—2001, pres. McDonald's Asia/Pacific/the Middle East and Africa, 2001—03, chief restaurant ops. officer, 2003—. Chmn. N.C. Ronald McDonald's Children's Charities, Raleigh, 1989-95; relationship ptnr. Donatos Pizza, Pret A Manger, Chipotle Mexican Grill, chmn. bd. dirs. Author: (manual) Training Consultants Development Program, 1987. Mem. N.C. Restaurant Assn. (bd. dirs. 1992-95). Republican. Roman Catholic. Avocations: tennis, gardening. Office: McDonald's Corp One Kroc Dr Oak Brook IL 60523

BACA, JUDITH F. art educator; Founder, artistic dir. Social and Pub. Art Resource Ctr., Venice, Calif., 1976—; prof. fine arts UCLA, 1980—, prof. art for world arts and cultures, 1996—, vice chair Cesar Chavez Ctr., 1996—. Mural, The Great Wall of Los Angeles, Durango Mural Project: La Memoria De Nuestra Tierra, 15 Digital Tile Murals on the Venice Boardwalk, 2001, La Memoria de Nuestra Tierra: Colorado, La Memoria de Nuestra Tierra: California, Danzas Indigenas, World Wall: A Vision of the Future Without Fear, Represented in permanent collections Nat. Mus. Am. Art, Smithsonian, Wadsworth Antheneum, Hartford, Conn. Fellow, John Simon Guggenheim Meml. Found., 2003. Office: UCLA Bunche Hall 7349 Mailcode 155903 Los Angeles CA 90095-1559

BACA, STACEY, newscaster; married. BA in Broadcast News, U. Colo., Boulder, 1991. Staff writer Brighton Std.-Blade, Colo., 1991—92, Denver Post, 1992—96; anchor weekend am news WTKR-TV, Norfolk, Va., 1996—98, KNSD-TV, San Diego, 1999—2002, reporter, 1999—2002; co-anchor Sunday Morning News and reporter WLS-TV, Chgo., 2002—. Mem.: Nat. Assn. of Hispanic Journalists. Office: WLS-TV 190 N State St Chicago IL 60601

BACALL, LAUREN, actress; b. N.Y.C., Sept. 16, 1924; m. Humphrey Bogart, May 21, 1945 (dec. 1957); children: Stephen, Leslie; m. Jason Robards, July, 1961 (div.); 1 son, Sam. Student pub. schs., Am. Acad. Dramatic Art. Actress in Broadway plays Franklin Street, 1942, Goodbye Charlie, 1959; motion picture actress, 1944—, film appearances include To Have and Have Not, 1945, Confidential Agent, 1945, The Big Sleep, 1946, Dark Passage, 1947, Key Largo, 1948, Young Man With a Horn, 1949, Bright Leaf, 1950, How To Marry a Millionaire, 1953, Woman's World, 1954, The Cobweb, 1955, Blood Alley, 1955, Written on the Wind, 1956, Designing Woman, 1957, The Gift of Love, 1958, Flame Over India, 1959, Shock Treatment, 1964, Sex and the Single Girl, 1965, Harper, 1966, Murder on the Orient Express, 1974, The Shootist, 1976, Health, 1980, The Fan, 1981, Tree of Hands, 1987, Appointment With Death, 1987, Mr. North, 1988, Misery, 1990, A Star for Two, 1991, All I Want for Christmas, 1991, Ready to Wear (Prêt-à-Porter), 1994, My Fellow Americans, 1996, The Mirror Has Two Faces, 1996 (Golden Globe award, 1997, SAG award, 1997), The Line King: Al Hirschfield, 1996, Le Jour et la Nuit, 1997, Diamonds, 1999, Dogville, 2003, The Limit, 2003; appeared in Broadway play Cactus Flower, 1966-68, Applause, 1969-71 (Sarah Siddons award 1975); also road co., 1971-72, London co., 1972-73 (Tony award for best actress in a musical 1970); Broadway play Woman of the Year, 1981 (Tony award for best actress in a musical 1981, Sarah Siddons award 1983), Sweet Bird of Youth, 1983 (London, 1985, Australia, 1986, L.A., 1987; TV spl. The Paris Collections, 1968, Applause, 1973, A Commercial Break (Happy Endings), 1975; TV movies: Perfect Gentlemen, 1978, Dinner at Eight, 1989, The Portrait, 1992, A Foreign Field, 1993, From the Mixed Up Files of Mrs. Basil E. Frankweiler, 1995; author: Lauren Bacall By Myself, 1978, Lauren Bacall Now, 1994. Recipient Am. Acad. Dramatic Arts award for achievement, 1963, Standard award London Evening, 1973, Nat. Book award, 1979; decorated comdr. Order of Arts and Letters (France), 1995. Office: care Johnnie Planco William Morris Agy 1325 Avenue Of The Americas New York NY 10019-6026*

BACARELLA, FLAVIA, artist, educator; b. Bklyn. d. Salvatore John and [illegible] BFA, New Sch. for Social Rsch., N.Y.C., 1973; MFA, Bklyn. Coll./CUNY, 1983; student, N.Y. Studio Sch., 1980. Asst. prof. Herbert H. Lehman Coll., Bronx, 1995—. Grantee N.Y. Found. Arts, 1986. Mem. Coll. Art Assn. Office: Herbert H Lehman Coll Bedford Park Blvd W Bronx NY 10468

BACCUS, R. EILEEN TURNER, academic administrator; b. Oxford, N.C., Aug. 8, 1944; d. Nathaniel Benjamin and Gloria Constance (Davis) Turner; B.A., Fisk U., 1964; M.B.A., U. Conn., 1975, Ph.D., 1978; 1 son, Christopher Lloyd. Programmer, systems analyst IBM, N.Y., Mo., 1964-66; substitute tchr., Lakenheath AFB, Eng., 1967-69; asst. dir. fin. aid U. Conn., Storrs, 1970-74, asst. to dean Sch. Edn., 1974-77, dir. personnel services div., 1977-81; adminstr. treasury ops. Aetna Life & Casualty Co., Hartford, Conn., 1981-82, ops. mgr. discretionary asset mgmt., 1982-86; pres. Thames Valley State Tech. Coll., Norwich, Conn., 1986-92; pres. Northwestern Conn. Community Tech. Coll., Winsted, 1992—; cons. Ford Found., 1976, Tchr. Corps, 1977, Meriden (Conn.) Schs., 1979— ; dir. Conn. Savs. & Loan Assn. Mem. planning com. Conn. Legis. Black Caucus, 1980; mem. mgmt. team Ujima, Inc., Hartford, 1978-80; co-chmn. bd. Hartford Scholarship Found., 1971-75; treas. bd. Community Council Capitol Region, 1982-86; mem. community adv. bd. Jr. League Hartford, Inc., 1982— . Mem. Am. Ednl. Research Assn., Internat. Platform Assn., Links, Inc., Rotary Internat., Phi Delta Kappa, Pi Lambda Theta, Delta Sigma Theta. Democrat. Episcopalian. Home: 87 Woodland Ave Bloomfield CT 06002-1806 Office: Park Place E Winsted CT 06098-1798

BACH, CYNTHIA, educational program director, writer; b. Oct. 28; BA in Art Edn., UCLA, 1955; MPA, U. So. Calif., 1978; LDS, Calif. Luth., 1993. Cert. gen. elem., spl. secondary art, and gen. jr. h.s. tchr. Staff asst. L.A. Unified Sch. Dist., 1976; rainbow tchr., gifted coord. Trinity Elem. Sch., L.A., 1978-81; field worker/in-svc. for parents and staff educator Hubbard Elem. Sch., Sylmar, Calif., 1981-90; student observer Liggett Elem. Sch., Panorama City, Calif., 1990-92; tng. tchr. Calif. State U. (Northridge)-Vena Sch., Arleta, Calif., 1992-93; pres. Comprehensive Learning Systems. Rsch. bd. advisors Am. Biograph. Inst., Inc. Author: Alternatives to Retail Marketing for Seniors (Bur. of Consumer Affairs); creator: (game) Mighty is the Word. Lectr. Sr. Citizens Bur. Consumer Affairs, City Hall; past pres. local PTA; del. Children's Def. Fund Conf., 1998; sch. bd. dirs. St. Martin-in-the-Fields Parish Sch.; mem. coun. bd. Amnesty Internat.; sponsor Christian Found. for Children and Aging; mem. Mus. of Tolerance, Alliance for Tolerance; co-founder scholarship fund for women ministers; ofcl. hostess rep. for vis. diplomats through the World Affairs Coun. City of Los Angeles; lay eucharistic min., 1998. Named 79 State Evaluation Mar Team-outstanding educator, Phi Alpha Alpha, Nat. Acad. Hon. Soc. Pub. Affairs Adminstrn., Order of Internat. Fellows Edn., on Wall of Tolerance, Montgomery, Ala., Internat. Woman of Yr., 2003; recipient Spl. Recognition award, 21st Century Award for Achievement, Pres.'s Award of Merit as outstanding citizen in field of edn.; scholar, Nat. Art, Chouinard Art Inst. Mem. NAFE, AAUW, 1st Century Soc. UCLA, Nat. Mus. Women in Arts (assoc.), Phi Alpha Alpha. Avocations: reading, theology, old movies, writing, gardening. Home: 5140 White Oak Ave Apt 214 Encino CA 91316-2435

BACH, MICHELE, education educator; b. Puyallup, Wa., Aug. 25, 1947; BA, U. Md.; MS, U. Utah, Kans. State U. Math. prof. Kansas City (Kans.) C.C., 1986—. Office: Kansas City Kans Cmty Coll 7250 State Ave Kansas City KS 66112 Office Phone: 913-288-7160.

BACHAND, ALICE JEANNE, school library media specialist; b. Sayre, Pa., Sept. 21, 1957; d. Charles Edward and Donna Jeanne (Osborne) Merrick; m. James Joseph Bachand, July 17, 1982; children: Janelle Alison, Jodi Nicole. Student, Paul Valéry U., Montpellier, France, 1977-78; BA, Wartburg Coll., 1979; MLS, Emporia State U., 1985. French tchr. Dunlap (Iowa) H.S., 1979, Clifton-Clyde H.S., Clyde, Kans., 1980-85; sch. libr. media specialist Hillcrest H.S., Cuba, Kans., 1984-86, Linn (Kans.) H.S., 1986-92, Clay Center (Kans.) Cmty. Middle Sch., 1992—. V.p. WELCA, Concordia, Kans., 1989-91; sec. of edn., ALCW, Concordia, 1982-84; brownie helper Girl Scouts of Am., Clyde, 1995-96; ch. librarian, Concordia Lutheran Ch., 1984—. Mem. NEA (Kans. chpt. pres. 1991-92), DAR, Kans. Reading Assn., Kans. Assn. Sch. Librarians (nominating com. 1992), Thunderbird Reading Coun. Lutheran. Avocations: reading, sewing, crafts. Home: 1626 N 270 Rd Clyde KS 66938 Office: Clay Ctr Cmty Middle School 935 Prospect St Clay Center KS 67432-1849

BACHELDER, CHERYL ANNE, marketing professional; b. Columbus, Ohio, May 4, 1956; d. Max Edwin and Margaret Anne Stanton; m. Christopher Frank Bachelder, June 13, 1981; 2 children. BS, Ind. U., 1977, MBA, 1978. Asst. product mgr. Procter & Gamble Co., Cin., 1978-81; product mgr. The Gillette Co., Boston, 1981-84; sr. product mgr. R.J.R. Nabisco, Planters Life Savers Co., Parsippany, N.J., 1984, group product mgr., 1985-87; dir. mktg. Winston-Salem, N.C., 1987; v.p. mktg. R.J.R. Nabisco, Planters Life Savers Co., Winston-Salem, N.C., 1988-91; v.p., gen. mgr. Life Savers Div., Nabisco Foods Group, 1991-92; pres. Bachelder & Assoc., 1992-95; v.p. mktg. and product devel. Domino's Pizza Inc., Ann Arbor, MI, 1995—. Named one of 100 best and brightest women in advt. Advt. Age mag., Chgo., 1988; featured in Fortune Mag. People to Watch column, 1990. Office: Domino's Pizza Inc 30 Frank Lloyd Wright Dr Ann Arbor MI 48105-9759

BACHER, JUDITH ST. GEORGE, executive search consultant; b. New Rochelle, N.Y., July 14, 1946; d. Thomas A. and Rose-Marie (Martocci) Baiocchi; m. Albert Bacher, Jan. 2, 1972; 1 son, Alexander Michael. BS, Georgetown U., 1968; MLS, Columbia U., 1971. Rschr. Time mag., N.Y.C., 1968-71; librarian Mus. Modern Art, N.Y.C., 1971-72; cons. Informaco Inc., N.Y.C., 1972-74, Booz-Allen & Hamilton, N.Y.C., 1974-79; prin. Nordeman Grimm/MBA Resources, N.Y.C., 1979-96, Spencer Stuart, 1996—. Mem. White House Adv. Com. on Pers., Exec. Office of Pres., 1979-81. Mem. Assn. of Exec. Search Cons. (N.E. region chair 1994—), Internat. Assn. Corp. and Profl. Recruiters (bd. dirs. 1996-97), Phi Beta Kappa. Office: Spencer Stuart 277 Park Ave Fl 29 New York NY 10172-2998 Home: Apt 2921 500 E 77th St New York NY 10162-0009

BACHMAN, CAROL CHRISTINE, trust company executive; b. Buffalo, Jan. 20, 1959; d. Christian George and Joan Marie (Fincel) B. Student, Grad. Inst. Internat. Study, 1979-80; AB, Smith Coll., 1981; grad., New Eng. Sch. Banking, 1987. Trust asst. BayBank Middlesex, Burlington, Mass., 1984-85, sr. trust asst., 1985-87, trust adminstr., 1987, trust officer, 1987-88; estate settlement specialist Bank of Boston, 1988-90, system cons., 1990, mgr. adminstrv. support svcs., asst. v.p., 1990-96; sr. sys. analyst Fleet Boston, Dedham, Mass., 1996-2000; asst. v.p. Webster Fin. Advisors, Waterbury, Conn., 2001—02; cons., 2002—. Office: Webster Fin Advisors Webster Plz Waterbury CT 06702 E-mail: ccbachm@yahoo.com.

BACHMAN, SISTER JANICE, healthcare executive, religious order administrator; b. Coshocton, Ohio, Oct. 25, 1945; d. Edward Michael and Kathryn Elizabeth (Norris) B. Student, Ohio Dominican Coll., 1963-67; BS in Pharmacy, Ohio State U., 1971; MBA in Mgmt., Xavier U., 1976; MA in Christian Spirituality, Creighton U., 1989. Joined Dominican Sisters, 1963. Staff pharmacist St. George Hosp., Cin., 1971-73, dir. pharmacy svcs., 1973-76; instr. pharmacology and related courses Coll. Mt. St. Joseph, Cin., 1973-74; instr. pharmacology Sch. Nursing Bethesda Hosp., Cin., 1975; adminstrv. resident St. Joseph Hosp., Mt. Clemens, Mich., 1976-77, adminstrv. asst., 1977-78, asst. adminstr., 1978-79; corp. dir. religious programs St. Francis-St. George Hosp., Inc., Cin., 1979-80, asst. v.p. hosp. support svcs., 1980-82, v.p. therapeutic and diagnostic svcs., 1983-89; dir. exec. affairs Benedictine Health Sys., Inc., Duluth, Minn., 1989-90, vicaress Dominican Sisters St. Mary of the Springs, Columbus, Ohio, 1990-96. Editor: Guidelines for Developing an IV Admixture, 1976. Trustee Ohio Dominican Coll., 1980-96, mem. devel. com., 1984-94, physical facilities com., 1994-96; mem. radiologic tech. adv. bd. Xavier U., Cin., 1983-89; mem. MLT adv. bd. Coll. Mt. St. Joseph, 1983-85; trustee Program for Medically Underserved dba Health Moms and Babes, 1986-91, co-founder, chair, 1986-89; bd. dirs. Franciscan Health Sys. Cin., 1990-92; chmn. bd. dirs. Nazareth Towers, Columbus, 1990-94; bd. dirs. Dominican Acad., N.Y.C., 1990-95; trustee St. Mary of the Springs Montessori Sch., Columbus, 1990-95; trustee Milford (Ohio) Spiritual Ctr., 1993-99, vice chair, 1993-94, chair, 1994-98; mem. fin. com. Dominican Leadership Conf., 1994-96; bd. dirs. Westwood Civic Assn., Cin., 1979-86, past sec., past 1st v.p., past pres.; mem. steering com. Cong. Neighborhood Groups, Cin., treas., 1981-84; mem. planning divsn. bd. Cmty. Chest and Coun., Cin., 1981-88, chair single parent task force study, 1983-85; mem. rev. bd. City of Cin. Commercial/Indsl. Revolving Loan Fund, 1982-84; bd. dirs. Cin. Area Chpt. ARC, 1982-89, chair nursing and health com., 1983-87, bd. exec. com., 1987-89; bd. dirs. SW Ohio Residences, Cin., 1983-89, vice chair, 1984-87, chair, 1987-89; trustee Providence Fund, Franciscan Sisters of Stella, Niagara, N.Y., 1996—, C.G. Jung Assn. Ctrl. Ohio, co-chair program com., 1996-99; trustee Las Casas (Ministry to Cheyenne and Arapaho Native Ams.), Canton, Okla., 1996-2003, treas., 1997—2002. Recipient Cmty. Leadership award United Appeal and Cmty. Chest, 1985, 9th Ann. Living Faith award Columbus Met. Area Ch. Coun., 2000. Fellow Am. Coll. Healthcare Execs.; mem. Spiritual Dirs. Internat. Avocations: swimming, cross-country skiing, biking. Office: St Mary of the Springs 2320 Airport Dr Columbus OH 43219-2098 E-mail: janbachman@aol.com.

BACHMANN, GLORIA ANN, obstetrician, gynecologist, educator; b. Newark, N.J., Nov. 4, 1949; d. Paul Bachmann and Rose Detrolio; 1 child, Michael. BA, Rutgers U., 1970, MMS, 1972; MD, U. Pa., 1974. Diplomate Am. Bd. Ob-Gyn., Am. Bd. Med. Examiners. Resident in ob-gyn. Hosp. of the U. of Pa., 1974-78; instr. U. Medicine & Dentistry N.J./Robert Wood Johnson Med. Sch., New Brunswick, N.J., 1978-81; asst. prof. Robert Wood Johnson U. Hosp., New Brunswick, N.J., 1981-86, assoc. prof., 1986-92, prof., 1992—. Chief ob-gyn. Robert Wood Johnson U. Hosp., 1992—; dir. Women's Health Inst. Editl. bd. Maturitas, 1989—, Med. Crossfire, 1998, Managing Menopause, 1998—, Jour. of Reproductive Medicine, 1999—, Med. Aspects of Human Sexuality, 1989-92, OBG Mgmt., 1994—, Menopaul Mgmt., 1991-93, Obstetric Gynecology, 1990-94; contbr. chpts. to books and articles to profl. jours. Dir. Women's Wellness and Health Care Connection, New Brunswick, N.J., 1998—. Recipient Recognition award March of Dimes, 1982, 83, Planned Parenthood, 1987, 88, Award for Women's Health Edn. YMCA, 1984, Judge Advocate Gen. award Tri-State Metro, 1984, Lifetime Achievement award Middlesex County Commn. on the Status of Women, 1995, Women of Achievement award Del, Valley Girl Scouts, 1996. Fellow Am. Coll. Ob-Gyn. (Issue of the Yr. award 1988); mem. Am. Fertility Soc., Internat. Menopause Soc., Am. Med. Women's Assn. (Gender Equity Recognition 1994), N.J. Obs.-Gyn. Soc., N.Am. Menopause Soc., Acad. of Medicine of N.J., Phi Beta Kappa. Office: Robert Wood Johnson Med Sch Women's Health Inst 125 Paterson St Rm 2104 New Brunswick NJ 08901-1962 E-mail: gloria.bachmann@umdnj.edu.

BACHMANN, MICHELE, state legislator; m. Marcus Bachmann; 5 children. JD, Coburn Law; LLM, Coll. William and Mary. Mem. Minn. State Senate, 2000—, mem. capital investment com., edn. com., taxes com., E-12 edn. budget divsn. com., jobs, housing and cmty. devel. com., property tax budget divsn. com. Republican. Home: 1801 Johnson Dr Stillwater MN 55082 Office: 125 State Office Bldg 100 Constitution Ave Saint Paul MN 55155-1206 E-mail: sen.michele.bachmann@senate.leg.state.mn.us.

BACHNER, BARBARA LAVERDIERE, artist; b. Waterville, Maine, Sept. 14, 1934; d. Thaddeus Eugene and Bernadette Arthemise (Vashon) LaVerdiere; m. Robert Lawrence Bachner, Mar. 22, 1959; 1 child, Suzanne Jouvé. BA in Fine Arts magna cum laude, NYU, 1968; student, Nat. Acad. Sch. Design, 1975-78, Art Students League, 1977-80, 82-84; MFA in Studio Art, Johnson State Coll., 1999. Lectr. Ulster County Art Assn., 1992, Woodstock Sch. Art, 1994, tchr., 1999—2000; co-curator Belmont Towbin Mus., Woodstock Artists Assn., 2002—; panelist Women on Men, Denise Bibro, 2000; juror in field. One-woman shows include Kleinert Arts Ctr., Woodstock, NY, 1992, exhibited in group shows at Pastel Soc. Am., NYC, 1978, 1980, one-woman shows include TAI Gallery, 1994, 1998, Fletcher Gallery, Woodstock, 1995, Pen and Brush, NYC, 1995, Woodstock Artist Assn., 1997, Pen and Brush, NYC, 1999, Julian Scott Meml. Gallery, Johnson State Coll., Johnson, Vt., 1999, exhibited in group shows at Five Towns Juried Show, Woodmere, N.Y., 1983, Nat. Arts Club, NYC, 1984, Woodstock Artists Assn., 1989—, Artists of Ulster County, Kingston, NY, 1989, Pen & Brush, NYC, 1990—, Springfield (Mo.) Art Mus., 1990, U. Tex., Tyler, 1991, A.I.R. Gallery, NYC, 1992, SUNY, New Paltz, 1992, Gallery Korea, NYC, 1993, CUNY, Bayside, 1994, Barrett House, Poughkeepsie, N.Y., 1994, Woodstock Sch. Art, 1994—, Nat. Arts Club, NYC, 1995, Krasdale Corp. Galleries, White Plains, N.Y., 1995—96, Nat. Assn. Women Artists, 1996, Harper Collins, NYC, 1996, SUNY, New Paltz, 1996, The Art Studio, Bearsville, NY, 1997, Woodstock Artists Assn., 1997, Cork Gallery, Lincoln Ctr., NYC, 1998, NY State Mus., Albany, 1998, Dist. Coun. 37, NYC, 1999; author: Behind Closed Eyes, 1999; Exhibited in group shows at Orensanz Found., NYC, 1999, Nat. Assn. Women Artists, 1999—2001, Schoharie County Art Assn., Cobbleskill, N.Y., 1999, Interfaith Ctr., NYC, 1999, Biennale Internat. Dell'Arte Contemporanea, Florence, Italy, 1999, LA Printmaking Soc., No. Hollywood, Calif., 1999—2001, Elements 2000 Ernest Rubenstein Gallery, NYC, 2000, Florence New York Orensanz Found., 2000, It's About Time Barrett Art Ctr., Poughkeepsie, N.Y., 2000, Utopia/Dystopia Kleinert Art Ctr./Byrdciffe, Woodstock, NY, 2000, Nat. Assn. of Women Artists, Balt., 2000, Attleboro Mus., Mass., 2000, Denise Bibro Fine Art, NYC, 2000, About Shoes Studio, D'Ars, Milan, 2001, Grounds for Sculpture, Hamilton NJ, 2001, one-woman shows include Studio Dars, Milan, Italy, 2001, exhibited in group shows at Lankershim Arts Ctr., N. Hollywood, Calif., 2001, Purdue U. Galleries, West Lafayette, Ind., 2001, Roessler Gallery, Ravensburg, Germany, 2002, Represented in permanent collections Texaco Corp., Houston, Printmaking Workshop, NYC, Kaatsbaan Internat. Dance Ctr., Tivoli, NY, Four Seasons Hotel Corp., Las Vegas, Nev., Nat. Assn. Women Artists, numerous pvt. collections, one-woman shows include Gallery @49, NYC, 2002, exhibited in group shows at A.I.R. Gallery, 2002; subject of articles: ; Exhibited in group shows at Denise Bibro Fine Art, NYC, 2002, one-woman shows include Lab. Inst. Merchandisisng, 2003, TAI Gallery, 2003, Internat. Works on Paper/William Whipple Art Gallery, SW State Univ./Marshall, Minn., 2003, Tai Gallery, 2003, exhibited in group shows at Denise Bibro Fine Art, 2002, Monique Goldstrom, NYC, 2003. Mem.: Monique Goldstrom, Ulster Arts Alliance, Woodstock Artists Assn. (exhbn. com. 1991—94, svc. in the arts dir., dir. 1992—95, trustee 1995—2002, exhbn. com. 1998—2002, Dan Gottschalk award 1991, Breth-Borkmann award 1995), Pen & Brush (co-chair graphics divsn. 1994—98, Solo Show award 1993, 1996), NY Artists Equity Assn., Coll. Art Assn., Women's Caucus Art, Nat. Assn. Women Artists (rec. sec. 1999—2000, Medal of Honor 1998, Elizabeth Stanton Blake meml. award 1998), Art Students League (life Concours award 1978, 1981, 1984, Merit scholar 1979, 1983). Avocations: music, theater, travel. Home: 25 Sutton Pl S Apt 19N New York NY 10022-2455 E-mail: blbachner@earthlink.net.

BACHRACH, EVE ELIZABETH, lawyer; b. Oakland, Calif., July 4, 1951; d. Howard Lloyd and Shirley B. AB cum laude, Boston U., 1972; JD with honors, George Washington U., 1976. Bar: D.C. 1976, U.S. Dist. Ct. D.C. 1976, U.S. Ct. Appeals (D.C. cir.) 1976. Assoc. Stein, Mitchell & Mezines, Washington, 1976-79; assoc. gen. counsel Cosmetic, Toiletry, and Fragrance Assn., Washington, 1979-85; v.p., assoc. gen. counsel, corp. sec., 1985-95; v.p., deputy gen. counsel, corp. sec. Consumer Healthcare Products Assn., Washington, 1995-98, sr. v.p., gen. counsel, sec., 1998—. Guest lectr. Am. U., Washington, 1986—, George Washington Nat. Law Ctr., Washington, 1986—, Cath. U. Law Sch., 1988— Contbr. articles to profl. jours. Vol. lawyer Legal Counsel for the Elderly, Washington, 1978—. Mem.: ABA (food and drug com., antitrust sect., adminstrv. law sect.), Food Drug Law Inst. (chmn. writing awards com. 1982—88, vice chmn. 1987—89, chmn. 1990, adv. bd. 1998—2002, bd. dirs. 2002—, bd. dirs., editl. adv. bd. Update Mag. 2002—, editl. adv. bd. Food Drug Law Jour.), Fed. Bar Assn. (chmn. food and drug com. 1986—90), D.C. Bar Assn. Avocation: classical pianist. Office: Consumer Healthcare Products Assn 1150 Connecticut Ave NW Washington DC 20036-4104

BACHRACH, NANCY, advertising executive; b. Providence, Jan. 29, 1948; d. David and Maida Horovitz. BA magna cum laude, Conn. Coll. for Women, 1969; MA with honors, Brandeis U., 1973, PhD, 1975. Assoc. dir. Grey France, Paris, 1980—84; sr. v.p., account mgmt. Grey Advt., N.Y.C., 1985—91, exec. v.p., 1992—2001, chief mktg. officer, 2001—. Author: The Irrefutability of Skepticism, 1975. Named one of 100 Best and Brightest Women, Advt. Age, 1988; named to Acad. Women Achievers, 1992. Office: Grey Advt Inc 777 3rd Ave New York NY 10017-1401

BACKER, GRACIA YANCEY, state legislator; b. Jefferson City, Mo., Jan. 25, 1950; m. F. Mike Backer; 1 child, Justin. Student, S.W. Mo. State Coll. Mem. from dist. 20 Mo. Ho. of Reps., 1983—2000; majority floor leader, 1996-98; dep. chief of staff Gov. Roger Wilson, Mo., 2000; dir. divsn. employment security Mo. Dept. Labor, 2001—. Active NAACP. Democrat. Baptist. Home: 2885 State Road Tt New Bloomfield MO 65063-1643 Office: Divsn Employment Security Dept Labor 421 E Dunklin St PO Box 59 Jefferson City MO 65104-0059

BACKHAUS, PATRICIA DAWN, musician, educator; b. Milw., July 16, 1959; d. Ralph Robert Backhaus and Mary Jane Ramsburg. BA, Carroll Coll., 1981; MusM, U. Minn., 1983, MusD, 1986. Head Dept. Music Wis. Luth. Coll., Milw., 1983—2002; freelance musician, 1985—. Devel. v.p. Soli Deo Gloria Inst. for Arts, Inc., Waukesha, Wis., 2002—; mem. adv. bd. Milw. (Wis.) Pub. Schs. Music Task Force, 2000—01. Author: Creative Practice, 1985. Bd. dirs. Waukesha (Wis.) County Hist. Soc., 1998—99. Recipient Willard Griswald award, Waukesha County Hist. Soc., 1999. Mem.: Nat. Band Assn., Women Band Dirs. Internat. (pres. 2001—03, Silver Baton award 2002), Sigma Alpha Iota. Evang. Luth. Avocations: travel, cooking. Home: 2501 Madison St Waukesha WI 53188

BACKLAR, PATRICIA, education educator; Sr. scholar Oregon Health Scis. U.; rsch. assoc. prof. biotheics dept. philosophy Portland State U., adj. asst. prof. dept. psychiatry, asst. dir. ctr. ethics in health care. Mem. Nat. Bioethics Adv. Commn., 1996—; civil commitment task force Oreg. Atty. Gen.; ethics com. Oreg. State Hosp. Author: The Family Face of Schizophrenia, 1994; contbr. articles to profl. jours.

BACKOWSKI-DAWSON, THERESE MARIE, editor; b. Cleve., May 10, 1949; d. Henry Joseph and Therese Eleanor (Nicoll) Backowski; m. Alex Villena (div. 1974); m. Blase S. Amadio (div. 1986); children: Elizabeth Angelique, Charles Aaron, Angelo Benjamin, Margaret Eleanor, Jessica MariRose; m. Terry W. Dawson, June 28, 2003. Diploma, Erasmus Hall. Lic. vet. technician Ohio State Vet. Bd. Vet. technician Animal Med. Clinic, Dublin, Ohio, 1974-78; acct. Credit Bur. Svcs., Mansfield, Ohio, 1980-82; pres. Park Ave. Pets Inc., Mansfield, 1982—2002. Grooming judge Groom Expo West, Burbank, Calif., 1992; tchr. dog obedience Madison H.S. Adult Edn., Mansfield, 1984-94; animal trainer for film Shawshank Redemption, Castle Rock Pictures, 1994; freelance writer; spkr. in field; featured instr. documentary "Death Row Dogs". Editor Off Lead Mag.; featured instr. : (TV documentary) Death Row Dogs; Animal Planet's Cell Dogs. Mem. bd. advisors Madison Adult Edn. Divorced Homemakers to Work Program, 1985-91, Richland County 4-H, Mansfield, 1991-97; mem. block grant com. HUD, Mansfield, 1982-85, chmn., 1984-85; pres. Poplar St. Neighborhood Assn., Mansfield; leader Heritage Trail coun. Girl Scouts U.S., Mansfield, 1981-85. Named Employer of Yr. Mansfield City Schs., 1987-88, Dwar's Maxwell medal, 1999, 2000, 2001, 2002. Mem. NAFE, Nat. Dog Groomers Assn., Dog Writers Assn. Am., Richland County Kennel Club, Internat. Judges Assn. (grooming judge). Republican. Roman Catholic. Avocations: horseback riding, fishing, reading, swimming, golf, running. E-mail: offlead1@aol.com.

BACKSTEDT, ROSEANNE JOAN, artist; b. San Francisco, Dec. 15, 1941; d. Anthony and Tillie LaRocca; m. Lawrence Henry Backstedt, Aug. 9, 1964; 1 child, Simone Rose. Student, San Francisco Art Inst., 1960-64, U. Oreg., 1966-68, Aesthetic Realism Found., 1976—. Mem. Ceres Gallery, N.Y.C., 1991—. One-woman shows include Sullivan County Mus., Hurleyville, N.Y., 1972, Hansen Gallery, N.Y.C., 1973-77, The Viewing Rm., N.Y.C., 1978, Noho Gallery, N.Y.C., 1987, Ceres Gallery, N.Y.C., 1991—; group shows include Elysian Art Gallery, San Francisco, 1962-64, Portland Art Mus., 1969, Terrain Gallery, N.Y.C., 1979-85, 2000, Ligoa Duncan Gallery, N.Y.C., 1980, Krasdale Food Corp., Bronx, 1989, 91, 94, Z Gallery, N.Y.C., 1991, 92, World Trade Ctr., N.Y.C., 1991, Triplex Gallery, N.Y.C., 1992, Snug Harbor Cultural Ctr., S.I., N.Y., 1992, Lincoln Ctr., N.Y.C., 1994, Cedco Calendars, 1994-97, JCB Internat. Co., N.Y.C., 1996, Univ. Luth Ch., Harvard Square, Mass., 1996, Mills Pond Ho., St. James, N.Y., 1997, Artemisia Gallery, Chgo., 1997, Künstlerforum, Bonn, 1998, Orange County C.C., Middletown, N.Y., 1998, Soho 20 Gallery, N.Y.C., 1999, Kingsborough C.C., Bklyn., 1999, Caelum Gallery, N.Y.C., 2000-03, SUNY at Buffalo, 2000; presenter ART TALK, Aesthetic Realism Found., N.Y.C., 1998-01. Office: Ceres Gallery 547 W 27th St 2d Floor New York NY 10001

BACKUS, JAN, state legislator; b. Norristown, Pa., July 30, 1947; m. Stephen S. Blodgett; three children, three step-children. Student, U. Vt., U. Adelaide, South Australia, Kilkenny Tech. Coll. Mem. Vt. State Senate, 1989-94, 96-; Dem. nominee U.S. Senate, 1994. Home: PO Box 35 168 North St Winooski VT 05404-1308 Office: Vt State Senate State Capitol Montpelier VT 05602

BACON, A. SMOKI, television host; b. Brookline, Mass., Jan. 29, 1928; d. Alfred Leon and Ruth Dorothy (Burns) Ginepra; m. Edwin Conant Bacon, May 11, 1957 (dec. July 1974); children: Brooks Conant, Hilary Conant; m. Richard Francis Concannon, Oct. 13, 1979. Student, Art Inst. Boston, 1947; grad., Jackson Von Ladau Sch. Design, Boston, 1951. Pub. rels. cons., Boston, 1968—; pres. Bacon-Concannon Assocs., Boston, 1979-95; dir. craftsmobiles Summerthing Program, Boston, 1968-73; dir. exhibits Citifair, Boston, 1974; dir. Victorian exhibits Bicentennial Boston 200, 1975, dir. spl. events, 1976; cons. spl. events Inst. Contemporary Art, 1977-78, Boston Tea Party Ship, 1978-79; fundraiser Mass. Assn. Mental Health, 1979; dir. promotions Met. Ctr., 1979; coord. grand finale celebration Boston Jubilee 350, 1979-80; coord. Elliot Norton Awards, 1983; pub. rels. Dyansen Gallery, Boston, 1987-88, French Speaking League, 1987; cons. spl. events Jordan Marsh, 1987; fundraiser, pub. rels. Boston Philharmonic, 1988; coord. 30th anniversary celebration Charles Playhouse, 1988; fundraiser Elliot Norton Awards, 1989; coord. benefit New Eng. Premiere of film Glory Afro-Am. Mus., 1990; pub. rels. cons. Boston Chamber Music Soc., 1990; pub. rels. Paul Sorota Gallery of Fine Arts, 1990-91; fundraising cons. Internat. Inst., 1991; pub. rels., fundraiser Brookline H.S. Sesquicentennial Celebration, 1992-93; co-host radio show Celebrity Time, 1980—; co-host TV show On the Town. Guest lectr. Boston U. Sch. Pub. Rels., 1979, ARC, 1987, Radcliffe Coll. 4'O'Clock Forums, 1989, publicity club Boston, ARC, YMCA, Boston U. Sch. Pub. Rels., Mass Polit. Women's Conf., Women's Italian Club, Brookline Rotary, Harvard Coll. Rotary Club; contbg. editor Design Times Mag. Social calendar editor Boston Tab Newspaper, 1987-90; contbg. editor Design Times Mag.; columnist BeaconHill News. Candidate Dem. State Rep., Mass., 1980; Bastille Day chmn. French Libr. Boston, 1994—; local adv. com. Nat. Trust for Historic Preservation; bd. dirs. Boston Lit. Hour; host parents com. Harvard Coll.; bd. dirs. Mugar Libr., Spl. Collections, 1994—; vis. com. Mus. Fine Arts, Eqyptian Dept., 1994—; bd. trustees Boston Arts Festival, 1960-63; bd. dirs., treas. Samaritans, Boston, 1974-84; art auction chairperson WGBH-Pub. Radio-TV, Boston, 1969-70; bd. dirs. Urban League Ea. Mass., Boston, 1975-85, Elders Living at Home Program, Boston City Hosp. Kids Fund ; former mem. numerous civic coms. Recipient Woman of Great Achievement award Cambridge Young Women's Assn., 1991, appreciation award The Samaritans, 1991, Leadership award Friends of the Pub. Garden, 1975; named One of Boston's 100 Female Leaders, Boston Mag., 1980, One of the Boston Area Schs. Notable Grad. List, 1994, Appreciation award Samaritans, 1991, Honors on 70th birthday Gov. Argeo Paul Cellucci, Pres. of Senate Thomas Birmingham, Spkr. Ho. of Reps. Thomas Finnerman and Mayor of Boston Thomas Menino, 1998; Guest of Honor, Womens' City Club Ann. Dinner Dance, 1979; honored Those Who Help Keep Boston's Non-Profit Agencies Alive Horizons for Youth, 1972, Charitable and Civic Endeavors Boston Italian Women's Club, 1995; named to Women of Great Achievement, Cambridge Young Wome's Assn., 1991; donated personal ofcl. documents Women's Time Capsule Schlesinger Libr. Radcliffe Coll., 1981. Mem. AAUW, Harvard Club Boston, Women's City Club. Democrat. Avocation: artistics graphics. Home: 94 Beacon St Ste 1 Boston MA 02108-3329 Office: Bacon Concannon Assocs 94 Beacon St Boston MA 02108-3329 Fax: (617) 523-1998. E-mail: SmokBacon@aol.com.

BACON, BETTY J. NICHOLS, preschool educator and administrator; b. Erie, Pa., June 22, 1938; d. Andrew Jackson and Betty VanBuren (Crawford) Nichols; m. Robert Sargent Bacon, June 8, 1968; 1 child, Julie Sargent BA, U. Colo., 1962, MA, 1967; postgrad., Miami U., Oxford, Ohio. Cert. secondary tchr., Mass., secondary and elem. tchr., Ohio. High sch. tchr. Rogers Hall, Lowell, Mass., 1963-66; elem. tchr. Broomfield (Colo.) Sch. Dist., 1967-68, Sacred Heart Sch., Boulder, Colo., 1968-71, Talawanda Sch. Dist., Oxford, 1971-75, 81-82; tchr., adminstr. City of Oxford Preschool, 1982—. Leader workshops Butler County Tchrs. Assn., Hamilton, Ohio, 1972, 74, 85; v.p. Oxford Assn. Educationally Gifted, 1983-85. Neighborhood dir., troop leader Girls Scouts U.S., Oxford, 1982-91 (Key award 1988); mem. Butler County Mental Health Bd., Hamilton, 1985-87; chmn. membership drive McCullough-Hyde Hosp., Oxford, 1989; asst. coach Talawanda Girls Tennis Team, Oxford, 1994—. Named Oxford Citizen of the Yr., City Coun. Com., 1987. Mem. Ohio Tchrs. Assn., Butler County Assn. Edn. Young Children (Outstanding Child Profl. 1994), Alpha Omicron Pi. Republican. Lutheran. Avocations: tennis, reading, crafts, skiing. Home: 1011 S Valentia St Unit 34 Denver CO 80231-6814

BACON, CAROLINE SHARFMAN, investor relations consultant; b. Ann Arbor, Mich., Aug. 27, 1942; d. Mahlon Samuel and Mary Patricia (Potter) Sharp; m. William Lee Sharfman, Sept. 5, 1964 (div. 1985); m. James Edmund Bacon, Nov. 4, 1989. BA with distinction, U. Mich., 1964; MBA, Columbia U., 1975. Assoc. Goldman, Sachs & Co., N.Y.C., 1975-80, v.p., 1980-83, Goldman Sachs Money Markets Inc., N.Y.C., 1983-90; sr. cons. investor rels. Burson-Marsteller, 1991; mng. dir. Johnnie D. Johnson & Co. Investor Rels., N.Y.C., 1992-95. Investor rels. cons. Mem. Phi Beta Kappa, Phi Sigma Iota, Beta Gamma Sigma. Episcopalian.

BACON, CHANTAL, retail executive; b. Conn. Ptnr. (with Betsey Johnson) Betsey Johnson Label, N.Y.C., 1978—, now 24 stores nationwide, also London, also worldwide distbn. in Can., Europe and Japan. Office: Betsey Johnson's 248 Columbus Ave New York NY 10023-3331 also: Betsey Johnson's 138 Wooster St New York NY 10012-3180

BACON, JENNIFER GILLE, lawyer; b. Kansas City, Kansas, Dec. 26, 1949; BA with honors, U. Kansas, 1971, JD, 1976; MA, Ohio State U., 1973. Bar: Mo. Ptnr. Shughart, Thompson & Kilroy, Kansas City, Mo. Contbr. articles to profl. jours. Mem. ABA, Mo. Bar (pres.), Kansas City Metro. Bar Assn., Lawyers Assn. Kansas City. Office: Shughart Thompson & Kilroy 12 Wyandotte Plz 120 W 12th St Ste 1600 Kansas City MO 64105-1924

BACON, JERI ANN, music educator; b. Phoenix, July 23, 1954; d. James Weldon and Jo Ann Hale; m. Francis Farquhar Bacon, Nov. 30, 1986; 1 child, Patricia Louise. MusB, Ariz. State U., 1977. Cert. music tchr. N.J., 2000, classroom tchr. N.J., 2002. Music tchr. Burlington Twp. (N.J.) Pub. Sch., 1999—2000, Tabernacle (N.J.) Pub. Schs., 2000—01, Bridgeton (N.J.) Pub. Schs., 2002; clcm. tchr., tutor Huntington Learning Ctr., Cherry Hill, NJ, 2002—; kindergarten tchr. Marlton (NJ) Christian Acad., 2003. Orch. dir. Cherry Hill (N.J.) Bapt. Ch., 1999—2003. Mem. Parent's T.V. Coun., LA, 2002—03. Mem.: Music Educators Nat. Conf., N.J. Music Educators Assn. Republican. Avocations: music, cross stitch. E-mail: immuzikal@aol.com.

BACON, LISE, Canadian senator; b. Valleyfield, Canada, Aug. 25, 1934; Student, Coll. Marie de l'Incarnation, Academie Saint Louis de Gonzague, Institut Albert Thomas. Mgr. dept. Prudential Ins. Co. of Am., 1951—71; judge Can. citizenship ct., 1977—79; v.p. Can. Life and Health Ins. Assn. Inc., Quebec, 1979—81; mem. Nat. Assembly, Ottawa, Canada, 1981—94; senator The Senate of Can., Ottawa, 1994—. Bd. dirs. Theatre du Rideau Vert, Montreal, Oxfam Quebec. Recipient Ordre du merite belgo-hispanique, Ordre de Saint Hubert, Dame Comdr. Merit, Sovereign Mil. Hospitaller Order of St. John of Jerusale, Rhodes and Malta. Office: 269-I Centre Block The Senate of Canada Ottawa ON Canada K1A 0A4

BACON, LYDIA LEACH, human resources professional; b. Harrisburg, Pa., Nov. 9, 1948; d. Charles Franklin and Lorna Elizabeth (Rissinger) Leach; 1 child, Melahn Lyle; m. John Wallace Bacon, June 6, 2000. BS, Pa. State U., 1970. Flight attendant Pan-Am. World Airways, Miami, Fla., 1970-73, supr. in-flight services, 1974-80, relocation staff assoc., 1980-81, employee services staff assoc., 1981-82, affirmative action mgr., 1982-85, dir. system-wide EEO and affirmative action, 1986-87, dir. labor relations, 1987-92; dir. spl. projects The Beacon Coun., Miami, 1992-93; employee rels. rep. Am. Airlines, Miami, 1993-96, sr. human rels. rep., 1996-97, sr. human rels. specialist, 1997-98, counsel, 1998-99, counsel internat. employee rels., 2000—01, counsel arbitration unit, 2002—. Cons. Alert Security Systems, N.Y.C., 1987, Solar Reactor Techs., Miami, 1986-95; mem. Orgnl. Resource Counselors Equal Opportunity Group, 1981-86, Office Fed. Contracts Compliance Program Corp. Liaison, 1986-88; bd. dirs. Pan-Am. Mgmt. Club, 1983, 86, v.p., 1984, 87. Active Dade County Employ the Handicapped Com., 1981-85; mem. Pvt. Industry Council, 1985-86. Mem. Air Transport Assn. (human resources com.), Internat. Explorers Soc., Soc. for Human Resources Mgmt., Delta Gamma (social chmn.), Omicron Nu, Phi Kappa Phi. Republican. Avocations: hot air ballooning, golf, reading, skiing, boating. Office: Am Airlines 999 Ponce De Leon Blvd Coral Gables FL 33134-3000 E-mail: lydia.bacon@aa.com.

BACON, SYLVIA, judge, law educator; b. Watertown, S.D., July 9, 1931; d. Julius Franklin and Anne Rae (Hyde) B. AB, Vassar Coll., Poughkeepsie, N.Y., 1952; cert., London Sch. Econs., 1953; LLB, Harvard U. Law Sch., 1956; LLM, Georgetown Law Ctr., Washington, 1959. Bar: D.C. 1956, U.S. Supreme Ct. 1963. Law clk. to fed. judge, 1956-57; asst. U.S. Atty., 1957-65; assoc. dir. Pres. Commn. on Crime in D.C., 1965-67; trial atty. spl. projects U.S. Dept. Justice, 1967-69; exec. asst. U.S. atty. Washington, 1969-70; judge D.C. Superior Ct., Washington, 1970-92; judge-in-residence Columbus Sch. Law Cath. U. Am., Washington, 1993-95, lectr., 1995—2002, disting. lectr., 2002—; adjudicator Office of Compliance, U.S. Legis. Br., Washington, 1996—. Adj. prof. Georgetown Law Ctr., 1960-70, 72-74; mem. faculty Nat. Inst. Trial Advocacy, 1991—; bd. dirs. Nat. Ctr. State Cts., 1975-79, Nat. Coll. Criminal Def., 1978-86; mem. faculty Nat. Jud. Coll., 1974-79, bd. dirs., 1980-87; lectr. Am. Acad. Jud. Edn., 1972-82. Bd. dirs. Nat Home Libr. Found., 1968-70. Fellow ABA (bd. dirs. 1988-91); mem. AAUW, Bar Assn. D.C. (bd. dirs. 1965-67), D.C. Women's Bar Assn., Am. Inns of Ct., Exec. Women in Govt., Bus. and Profl. Women's Assn., Nat. Assn. Women Judges, Supreme Ct. Hist. Soc., Phi Beta Kappa Home: 2500 Q St NW Washington DC 20007-4373 Office: Cath U Am Columbus Sch Law 3600 McCormack Dr NE Washington DC 20064-0001

BADAU, KAREN SNYDER, psychologist, researcher; d. Charles Walter and Sandra (Frazer) Snyder; m. Ioan Cristian Badau, Sept. 2, 2000. PhD, Fordham U., 1999; MA, St John's U., 1991; BA, Manhattanville Coll., 1984. Professional Licensure, Psychology N.Y., 2000, La., 2002. Clin. instr. N.Y. Med. Coll., Valhalla, 1997—; psychologist asst. Westchester Med. Ctr., Valhalla, 1999—2001, psychologist, 2001—03, Mid-Hudson Forensic Psychiat. Ctr., New Hampton, NY, 2003—. Rsch. cons. St. Christopher-Jennie Clarkson Social Svcs., Dobbs Ferry, NY, 2000—01; psychologist, cons. Huntington Sch., Ferriday, La., 2002. Author: (chpt.) Adolescent Play Therapy; author: (under maiden name, K. Snyder) (treatment manual) Anger Management for Adolescents; author: (chpt.) Students Writing Across the Disciplines, (tchrs. manual) Beneath the Mask: Theories of Personality. Vol. mental health profl. ARC, White Plains, NY, 1999; vol. psychologist Families with Soldiers at War, Ferriday, La., 2003. Scholar Donald T. Brown Scholarship Award, Group Psychotherapy Found., 1998. Mem.: APA, Am. Group Psychotherapy Assn. Lutheran. Achievements include research in Developed and manualized the first 4-session Anger Mangement treatment for adolescents, and found significant treatment effects via a well-controlled research design. Avocations: hiking, international travel, languages, drawing, painting. Home: Bon Aire Park 14 Sussex Ct Suffern NY 10901 Personal E-mail: ksbadau@hotmail.com.

BADDERS, REBECCA SUSANNE, military officer, educator, writer; b. Knoxville, Tenn., Jan. 6, 1962; d. John Albert and Tamara Elizabeth Badders. BA in Edn., U. Fla., 1984; MA in Edn., U. South Fla., Tampa and St. Petersburg, 1997; MSM in Bus., Troy State U., 2002. Cert. profl. tchr., Fla. Commd. ensign USN, 1984, advanced through grades to lt. comdr., 1995; oceanographic watch officer Naval Facility Brawdy, Wales, 1984-86; oceanographic officer anti-submarine warfare Comdr. Undersea Surveillance, Norfolk, Va., 1986-90; dept. head Readiness Tng. Facility, Dam Neck, Va., 1990-93; tchr. Pinellas County Schs., Largo, Fla., 1994-97; commanding officer Naval Weapon Sta. res. det., Charleston, S.C., 1995-97; exec. officer Naval Res. Ctr., Kearny, N.J., 1997-99, Earle, N.J., 1999-2000, Naval Res. Profl. Devel. Ctr., New Orleans, 2000—03; commanding officer Naval Res. Ctr., Columbia, SC, 2003—. Faculty rep. Pinellas County Tchrs. Assn., Largo, 1994-97. Author: Maddy and the Peek-A-Boo Moon, 1995. V.p., bd. dirs. Pilot Club Internat., Mid-Pinellas, Fla., 1993-99. Recipient Navy Achievement medal, 1990, 93, 96, Navy Commendation medal, 2000, Meritorious Svc. medal, 2003. Mem.: Naval Res. Assn., Res. Officers Assn., Navy League of U.S., Coun. for Exceptional Children, U. Fla. Alumni Assn., U. South Fla. Alumni Assn., Troy StateAlumni Assn., LHS Alumni Assn., Internat. Order of Rainbow (worthy advisor, pres. 1975-82), Scabbard and Blade, Kappa Delta Pi. Republican. Episcopalian. Avocations: travel, computers, reading, gourmet cooking, arts. Home: 2620 Lee Rd Columbia SC 29207-5401 E-mail: rbadders@aol.com.

BADDOUR, ANNE BRIDGE, pilot; b. Royal Oak, Mich. d. William George and Esther Rose (Pfiester) Bridge; m. Raymond F. Baddour, Sept. 25, 1954; children: Cynthia Anne, Frederick Raymond, Jean Bridge. Student, Detroit Bus. Sch., 1948-50; BA, Pine Manor Coll. Stewardess Eastern Airlines, Boston, 1952-54; instr. aero. Powers Sch., Boston, 1958; co-pilot, flight attendant Raytheon Co., Bedford, Mass., 1958-63; flight dispatcher, ferry Pilot Comerford Flight Sch., Bedford, 1974-76; adminstrv. asst., ferry pilot Jenney Beachcraft, Bedford, 1976; mgr., pilot Balt. Airways, Inc., Bedford, 1976-77; rsch. test pilot Lincoln Lab. Flight Test Facility MIT, Lexington, 1977-97. Aviation cons., corp. pilot Energy Resources, Inc., Cambridge, Mass., 1974-84; holder World Class speed records for single-engine aircraft; Boston to Goose Bay, Labrador, 1985, Boston to Reykjavik, Iceland, 1985, Portland, Maine to Goose Bay, 1985, Portland to Reykjavik, 1985, Goose Bay to Reykjavik, 1985; records for twin-engine aircraft: Sept Isles to Goose Bay, 1988, Mont Joll to Goose Bay, 1988, Presque Isle to Goose Bay, 1988, Millinocket to Goose Bay, 1988, Bedford to Goose Bay, 1988, Goose Bay to Narssassrag, Greenland, 1988, Narssassrag to Klevelevic, Iceland, 1988, Narssassrag to Reykjavik, 1988, Bedford to Narssassrag, 1988, Millinochet to Narssassrag, 1988, Presque Isle to Narssassrag, 1988, Bedford to St. John, 1991, Bedford to Charlottetown, 1991, Charlottetown to Kennebunk, 1991, Charlottetown to Portsmouth, 1991, Muncton to Bedford, 1991, St. John to Kennebunk, 1991, St. John to Bedford, 1991, World Class Speed Records Single-Engine Aircraft, 1991, Bedford, Mass. to Sydney, Nova Scotia, Bedford, Mass. to Sydney, Nova Scotia to Beford, Mass., Portsmouth, New Hampshire to Sydney Nova Scotia to Portsmouth, Brunswick to Sydney Nova Scotia to Brunswick. Mem. campaign coun. Mus. Transp., Boston; mem. coun. assocs. French Libr. in Boston; commr. Commonwealth of Mass., Mass. Aero. Commn., 1979—83; trustee bd. adminstrn. Amelia Earhart Birthplace Mus., 1992—93; trustee Daniel Webster Coll., Nashua, NH, 1995—; v.p., trustee Friends of the Libr. Spl. Collections Boston U., 1997—; trustee Viscaya Mus., 2002—; bd. dirs. Smithsonian Nat. Air & Space Mus., 1998—, Cambridge Opera, 1977—79. Winner trophy Phila. Transcontinental Air Race, 1954, New Eng. Air Race, 1957, Clifford B. Harmon trophy Internat. Aviatrix, 1988; recipient Spl. Recognition award FAA, 1990; honoree Internat. Aviation Forest of Friendship, Atchison, Kans., 1991; named Pilot of the Year, New Eng. sect. Internat. Women Pilots Orgn./The Ninety-Nines, Inc., 1992. Mem.: DAR, Friends of Switzerland, Soc. Exptl. Test Pilots, U.S. Sea Plane Pilots Assn., Nat. Pilots Assn., Assn. Women Transcontinental Air Race, Bostonian Soc., Aircraft Owners Pilots Assn., Nat. Aero. Assn., Fedn. Aeronautique Internat., Ninety-Nines (New Eng. Safety trophy 1986), Fairchild Tropical Garden Club, Harvard Travellers Club, Boston Women's Travel Club, Chilton Club, Belmont Hill Club, Aero Club New Eng. (v.p. 1978—80, dir. 1978—2002). Home: PO Box 274 123 Old Town Rd Hancock NH 03449

BADEL, JULIE, lawyer; b. Chgo., Sept. 14, 1946; d. Charles and Saima (Hrykas) Badel. Student, Knox Coll., 1963—65; BA, Columbia Coll., Chgo., 1967; JD, DePaul U., 1977. Bar: Ill. 1977, U.S. Dist. Ct. (no. dist.) Ill. 1977, U.S. Dist. Ct. (ea. dist.) Mich. 1989, U.S. Dist. Ct. (no. dist.) Ind. 2002, U.S. Ct. Appeals (7th and D.C. cirs.) 1981, U.S. Supreme Ct. 1985. Hearings referee State of Ill., Chgo., 1974-78; assoc. Cohn, Lambert, Ryan & Schneider, Chgo., 1978-80, McDermott, Will & Emery, Chgo., 1980-84, ptnr., 1985-2001, Epstein, Becker & Green, PC, Chgo., 2001—. Legal counsel, mem. adv. bd. Health Evaluation Referral Svc. Chgo., 1980-89; bd. dirs. Alternatives, Inc., Chgo. chpt. Asthma and Allergy Found., 1993-94, Glenwood Sch. Author: Hospital Restructuring: Employment Law Pitfalls, 1985; editor DePaul U. Law Rev., 1976-77. Mem. ABA, Chgo. Bar Assn., Labor & Employment Alliance for Women, Columbia Coll. Alumni Assn. (1st v.p., bd. dirs. 1981-86), Pi Gamma Mu. Office: Epstein Becker & Green 150 N Michigan Ave Ste 420 Chicago IL 60601-7553 Office Phone: 312-499-1418.

BADEN, JOAN H. retired language educator; b. Kingston, N.Y., Dec. 31, 1926; d. Douglas Roy Alverson and Petronella Agnetta Bach; children: Barbara Fagan, Bruce. BA, SUNY, Albany, 1947, MA, 1948. Cert. tchr. N.Y. Tchr. Cornwall (N.Y.) H.S., 1947—51; instr. English SUNY, Albany, 1951—55, ret., 1955. Lectr. in field. Mem. arboretum adv. com. Town of Webster, NY, 1991—; docent Meml. Art Mus., Rochester, NY, 1981—2001. Named to Women's Hall of Fame, Webster, 1999. Mem.: Meml. Art Gallery, Am. Rose Soc. (judge horticulture design, Silver Honor medal 1999, Outstanding Judge 1996), Federated Garden Clubs (regional dir., past. pres.), Nat. Garden Club (regional dir. 1997—99, judge horticulture design, gardening cons., landscape design cons.). Presbyterian. Avocations: reading, travel, gardening. Home: 205 Curtice Pk Webster NY 14580

BADER, KATHLEEN M. chemicals executive; B in Liberal Arts, Notre Dame; MBA, U. Calif., Berkeley. With Dow Chem. Co., Chgo., 1973—, pres. bus. group styrenics and engineered products Zurich, Switzerland, 2000—. Adv. coun. US Homeland Security, 2002—; dean's coun. Harvard Sch. Govt. Named One of 50 Most Powerful Women in Internat. Bus., Fortune Mag., 2001—03. Office: Dow Chem Co 47 Bldg Midland MI 48667*

BADER, ROCHELLE LINDA (SHELLEY BADER), educational administrator; BA in Speech Arts, BA in Edn., Hofstra U., 1970; MLS, U. Md., 1973; EdD, George Washington U., 1993. Mgmt. intern Office Civil Pers., Dept. of the Army, Pentagon, Washington, 1971; circulation libr. George Washington U. Med. Libr., Washington, 1971-73; head reference libr. Himmelfarb Health Scis. Libr./George Washington U. Med. Ctr., Washington, 1973-75, head Audio Visual Study Ctr., 1975-78, chief Access and Facilities Svcs. Divsn., 1978-79, chief Reader Svcs. Divsn., 1979-80, assoc. dir., 1980, dir., 1980-90; dir. ednl. resources George Washington U. Med. Ctr., Washington, 1990—, assoc. v.p. ednl. resources, 1998—. Audio visual cons. Regional Med. Libr. Program, D.C. Metro area, 1977-79; mem. nat. adv. com. U. Iowa, 1984-85; mem. Med. Ctr. Faculty Senate Com. on Health Scis. Programs, George Washington U., Washington, 1989, chmn. Health Scis. Programs Ednl. Evaluation Com., 1993—, many other coms.; adv. com. Found. for Health Svcs. Rsch., 1992-93; presenter in field. Consulting editor: Biomedical Comms., 1983-84; mem. editorial rev. bd.: The Jour. of Biocommunication, 1988-92, Annual Statistics of Medical School Libraries in the United States and Canada, 12th, 13th and 14th edits., 1989-93; contbr. articles to profl. jours. Grantee Coun. on Libr. Resource, 1989-90, Nat. Libr. Medicine, 1991, NSF, 1993-94; recipient Disting. Svc. award Health Scis. Comms. Assn., 1986. Mem. Am. Med. Informatics Assn. (exec. com. edn. workshop group 1991—, MLA rep. to adv. coun. 1992—), Assn. Am. Med. Colls. (group on med. edn., coun. on acad. scos. 1991—), Assn. Acad. Health Scis. Libr. Dirs. (pres. 1986-87, chmn. fin. com. 1987-88), Assn. Biomedical Comms. Dirs. (membership com. 1989-91, program com. 1991), Health Scis. Comms. Assn. (coord. interactive media festival 1990-91, chmn. awards com. 1992, pres. 1984-85), Med. Libr. Assn. (bd. dirs. 1995—), Beta Phi Mu. Home: 12225 Seline Way Potomac MD 20854-2872 Office: George Washington U Med Ctr 2300 I St NW Washington DC 20037-2336

BADERINWA, SADE, newscaster; Grad., U. Md., College Park. Prodn. asst. This Week with David Brinkley, ABC News, Nightline, ABC News, World News Tonight, ABC News, NewsOne, ABC News; reporter WSLS, Roanoke, Va.; anchor morning and noon news WBAL-TV 11, Balt.; co-anchor Eyewitness News at 5pm, WABC 7, NY, 2003—; reporter Eyewitness News at 11pm, WABC 7, NY, 2003—. Worked with Boys and Girls Clubs. Achievements include testified before Balt. State Legis. and helped enact child eye safety laws. Office: 7 Lincoln Sq New York NY 10023*

BADGER, SANDRA RAE, health and physical education educator; b. Pueblo, Colo., Nov. 2, 1946; d. William Harvey and Iva Alberta (Belveal) Allenbach; m. Graeme B. Badger, Oct. 9, 1972; 1 child, Jack Edward. BA in Phys. Edn., U. So. Colo., Pueblo, 1969; MA in Arts and Humanities, Colo. Coll., 1979; postgrad., Adams State U., Alamosa, Colo., 1980-91. Cert. tchr., secondary endorsement in health and phys. edn., Colo. Head women's swimming coach Mitchell High Sch., Doherty High Sch., Colorado Springs, Colo., 1969-90; head dept. health edn. Doherty High Sch., 1979-2000; asst. coach cross country and track, men and women, indoor and outdoor track men and women U. Colo., 1996—. Trainer student asst. program CARE, Colorado Springs, 1983—; trainer drug edn. U.S. Swim Olympic Tng. Ctr., Colorado Springs, 1988-89; coach in track and field, Colorado Springs, 1989, 91; cons. Assocs. in Recovery Therapy, 1989—; asst. instr. scuba diving, 1999; dir. Colo. Health, Fitness and Coaching Conf., 1999—, Colo. Springs Health, Safety and Fitness Conf., 2001-04; speaker in field. Author, editor: Student Assistant Training Manual, 1983-95. Bd. dirs. ARC, Colo. Springs, 1990-96, sec., 1991-92, mem. health and safety com., 1990-95; reviewer ARC/Olympic Com. Sports Safety Tng. Manual Handbook Textbooks, update, 2004; mem. comprehensive health adv. com. Dept. Edn., State of Colo., Denver, 1991. Recipient Svc. award ARC, 1985, Coach of Yr. award Gazette Telegraph, 1979, 84, CARE award State of Colo., 1988, others; Gamesfield grantee, 1985; Nat. Coun. on Alcoholism grantee, 1990; nominated Readers' Digest Tchr. of Yr., 1998-99. Mem. NEA, Colorado Springs Edn. Assn. Avocations: scuba diving, running, travel. Office: U Colo 1420 Austin Bluffs PO Box 7150 Colorado Springs CO 80933-7150

BADHAM, JULIA AILEEN, artist; b. San Francisco, July 23, 1945; d. Thomas Floyd and Aileen Mary (Koeber) Laughlin; m. Dean Tussey Hallo, Nov. 22, 1985 (div. Apr. 1992); m. John MacDonald Badham, July 11, 1992. Student, Calif. State U., Northridge, L.A. Pierce Coll., Woodland Hills, Otis Art Inst., L.A., UCLA. Art dir., set decorator Pytka, Venice, Calif., 1984-90, Angel City Prodns., Hollywood, Calif., 1990-94; set decorator Warner Bros., Burbank, Calif., 1992, Disney, Glendale, Calif., 1993, Paramount Pictures, Hollywood, Calif., 1995. Art dir., set decorator over 200 TV commls., 1984-94; set decorator Point of No Return movie, 1992, Another Stakeout, 1993, Nick of Time, 1995. Mem. Set Decorators Soc. Am., Internat. Alliance of Theatrical and Stage Employees. Avocations: painting, sculpting. Office: c/o Elkins and Elkins 16830 Ventura Blvd Ste 300 Encino CA 91436-1715

BADITOI, BARBARA ELLEN, information scientist, educator; b. Detroit, Mich., Apr. 14, 1947; d. George and Mary Baditoi; 1 child, Brenden Alexander Moore. MEd, Pa. State U., 1972; EdD, Va. Poly. Inst. and State U., 2004. Postgrad. Profl. Lic. Commonwealth of Va., 2002. Tchr. Fairfax County Pub. Sch., Va., 1973—80, 1986—97; adminstr. Fairfax County Pub. Schools, 1997—2002. Adj. prof. Old Dominion U., Norfolk, Va., 2001—; acad. instr. Fairfax County Pub. Schools, 1999—. Author: (education workbook) Behavior Evaluation, Plan of Action and Instructional Plan: A Workbook Method for Assessing and Changing Student Behavior (Safety and Security Grant, 2000), (directory) The Aware Traveler's Directory, 1986 (Impact II Instrnl. Inquiry Rsch. Grant, 1993, Sallie Mae Tchg. With Tech. Grant, 1998). Newsletter editor Phi Delta Kappa, Fairfax, 2003—, Fairfax Assn. of Elem. Sch. Principals, 2001—02. Mem.: AAUW, ASCD (assoc.), Phi Delta Kappa Internat. (assoc.). Achievements include Mentor Teacher Trainer. Home: 5152 Linette Annandale VA 22003

BADU, ERYKAH, singer; b. Dallas, Feb. 26, 1972; 1 child. Student, Dallas Sch. Arts. Singer, songwriter: single On and On, 1997 (Grammy award for best female vocal performance, 1998), Baduizm, 1997 (Grammy award for best R&B album, 1997), Live!, 1997, Mama's Gun, 2000, Worldwide Underground, 2003; actor: (films) Cider House Rules, 1999, Blues Brothers, 2000. Recipient Favorite New Soul/R&B Artist award, Am. Music Awards, 1998, Grammy award for Best Rap Performance by a duo or group for You Got Me, 1999. Office: Motown Records 6th Fl 1755 Broadway New York NY 10019-3743*

BAE, SUE HYUN, psychologist, educator; b. Seoul, Kyung-Gee, Republic of Korea, [illegible]; d. Jung Hoo Bae and Jeeyoung Kim. BA, U. Calif., Berkeley, 1991; MEd, MA, Columbia U., 1994; PhD, U. Chgo., 2001. Psychotherapist Cancer Treatment Ctr. of Am., Gurnee, Ill., 1998—99; clin. adminstr. Heartland Alliance, Chgo., 1999—2001; asst. prof. Ill. Sch. Profl. Psychology Chgo., Argosy U., 2001—. Adj. faculty Ill. Inst. Art, Chgo., 2001; diversity tng. cons. Anixter Ctr., Chgo., 2003. Author: (book) The Psychotherapist's Perspective, 2003; contbr. articles to profl. jours. Recipient Faculty Rsch. award, Ill. Sch. Profl. Psychology, 2001. Mem.: APA, Soc. for Psychotherapy Rsch. Achievements include research in international psychology; cross-cultural studies, cross-cultural/multicultural psychotherapy; diversity training and teaching. Avocations: travel, golf, music. Office: Argosy U Ill Sch Profl Psychology 20 S Clark St Chicago IL 60603 Office Phone: 312-279-3944.

BAECKLER, VIRGINIA VAN WYNEN, librarian, writer; b. Englewood, N.J., June 18, 1942; d. Kenneth Gregg and Esther Grace (Thompson) Van Wynen; m. William W. Baeckler, Apr. 9, 1971; children— Gregg William, Sarah Angela. B.A., Cornell U., 1964, M.A., 1967; postgrad. Moscow State U. (USSR), 1967-69; M.L.S., Rutgers U., 1972. Head Slavic acquisitions Princeton U. Library, 1969-71; head Mercer County Library, Ewing, N.J., 1972-75; dir. Sources, Hopewell, N.J., 1975—; dir. Plainsboro (N.J.) Pub. Libr., 1991— . Author: Go, Pep and Pop!, 1976, PR for Pennies, 1978, Sparkle!, 1980, Storytime Science, 1986. Vol., tchr. YWCA of Princeton, N.J., 1979— . Mem. Nat. Sci. Tchrs. Assn., Alliance for Arts and Edu.,ALA, Ednl. Media Assn. (lobbyist). Democrat. Home: 26 Hart Ave Hopewell NJ 08525-1425

BAEHRE, EDNA VICTORIA, college president; b. Dreisen, Germany, Mar. 15, 1949; BA, Paedagogische Hochschule, Heidelberg, Germany, 1971; MA, SUNY, Buffalo, 1973, PhD, 1977. Pres. Harrisburg (Pa.) Area C.C., 1998—. Office: 1 Harrisburg Area CC Dr Harrisburg PA 17110-2999

BAER, KAREN FAUST, music educator, musician; b. Bklyn., Mar. 4, 1950; d. Morris Faust and Lillian Rosenberg; m. Paul Robert Baer, Aug. 27, 1972; children: Adam, Seth. MusB, Juilliard Sch., 1971, MS, 1972; postgrad., Westminster Coll., 1984—86. Cert. music tchr. NY. Asst. prof. SUNY, Purchase, 1972—74; vocal music dir. Rockville Centre (NY) Schs., 1974—77, 1980—; profl. pianist, accompanist NY, Cin., Boston, Phila., Italy, 1980—, Baer-Nelson Duo, Profl. Piano Duo, Julliard Sch., Hofstra U., Kingsborough Coll., Heckscher Mus., L.I. Librs., 1994—. Presenter confs. in field; lectr., performer N.Y.C. schs.; mem. Auburn Collegium Chamber Music Group, 1984—86; accompanist Nassau Area All State Mixed Chorus, 1990—, NYSSMA All-State Conf. Concerts, 1994—2000. Performer: WQXR Radio, 1966—68, 2000, WNYC Radio, 6467, 1999; debut : Am. Symphony Orch., Carnegie Hall, 1968; internat. debut : Todi Music Festival, 1969; performer (chamber music recitals): Tanglewood Music Ctr., 1971. Bd. dirs. Met. Youth Orch., Manhasset, NY, 1997—2000. Fellow, Tanglewood Music Ctr., 1971, Juilliard Sch., 1972; grantee, Rockville Centre Edn. Found., 1996; scholar, Todi Music Festival, Italy, 1969. Mem.: United Fedn. Tchrs., Piano Tchrs. Build, Music Educators Nat. Conf., Nat. Music Educators Assn., NYSSMA. Jewish. Avocations: gardening, quilting. Home: 2755 Bellmore Ave Bellmore NY 11710 E-mail: kfbaer@hotmail.com.

BAER, MARIA RENÉE, hematologist, researcher; b. N.Y.C., Jan. 6, 1952; d. George Bernard and Evelyn Joan (Mandl) Schless; m. Alan Nathaniel Baer, June 4, 1978; children: Tamara, Nicholas. BA, Harvard U., 1973; MD, Johns Hopkins U., 1979. Chief leukemia sect., prof. Roswell Park Cancer Inst., SUNY, Buffalo, assoc. prof. dept. pharmacology and therapeutics. Contbr. articles to profl. jours. Recipient Nat. Rsch. Svc. award, Divsn. Hematology Vanderbilt U., Nashville, 1984-86. Fellow ACP; mem. Am. Soc. Hematology, Am. Assn. Cancer Rsch., Am. Soc. Clin. Oncology, Cancer and Leukemia Group B, Divsn. Hematology Vanderbilt U., Nashville, 1982-84. Office: Roswell Park Cancer Inst Elm And Carlton St Buffalo NY 14263-0001 E-mail: maria.baer@roswellpark.org.

BAER, SUSAN M. airport executive; married; 1 child. BA in urban studies and anthropology, Barnard Coll.; MBA, NYU. Mgmt. analyst Port Authority of NY and NJ, mgr. pub. svcs. divsn. Tunnels, Bridges and Terminals Dept., mgr. Lincoln Tunnel, 1985—86, mgr. Port Authority Bus Terminal Manhattan, 1986—88, gen. mgr. Aviation Customer and Mktg. Svcs., 1988—94, gen. mgr. LaGuardia Airport, 1994-98, gen. mgr. Newark Internat. Airport, 1998—. Office: Newark Int & Teterboro Airports Conrad Rd, Bldg 1 Newark NJ 07114

BAERMANN, DONNA LEE ROTH, real estate property executive, retired insurance analyst; b. Carroll, Iowa, Apr. 28, 1939; d. Omer H. and Mae Lavina (Larson) Real; m. Edwin Ralph Baermann, Jr., July 8, 1961 (dec. Aug. 1997); children: Beth, Bryan, Cynthia. BS, Mt. Mercy Coll., Ames, 1973; student, Iowa State U.-Ames, 1957-61. Cert. profl. ins. woman; fellow Life Mgmt. Inst. ins. agt. Luthern Mut. Ins. Co., Cedar Rapids, Iowa, 1973; home economist Iowa-Ill. Gas & Electric Co., Cedar Rapids, Iowa, 1973-77; supr. premium collection Life Investors Ins. Co. (now Aegon USA), Cedar Rapids, Iowa, 1978-83, methods and procedures analyst, 1987-94; pres., CEO Baermann Apts. Inc., 1992-94, owner, pres., 1992—. Mem. telecom. study group com. 1982-83, mem. productivity task force, 1984-94, TAB cert. facilitator, 2001—. Vol. Mercy Med. Ctr., Cedar Rapids, Iowa, 2002—; apptd. by Mayor and City Coun. Housing Bd. Appeals, Cedar Rapids, 2003. Mem. Internat. Platform Assn., Citizens Com. for Person with Disabilities, Nat. Assn. Ins. Women, Nat. Mgmt. Assn. (bd. dirs. Cedar Rapids chpt.), DAR, Knights of Malta (named Damsel of Ancient Order of St. John, N.Y.C.), Chi Omega. Republican. Presbyterian. Home: 361 Willshire Ct NE Cedar Rapids IA 52402-6922 E-mail: dlrbaer@worldnet.att.net.

BAER-RIEDHART, JENNY, aeronautical engineer; b. San Bernardino, Calif. BS in Aero. Engring., Calif. Polytechnic State U., San Luis Obispo, 1974; MS in Human Resources Mgmt., U. Redlands, 1983. From aero. engr. to program mgr. ERAST Program NASA, Edwards AFB, Calif., 1983—2000, dep. chief Pub. Affairs Commercialization and Edn., 2000—. Office: NASA Dryden Flight Rsch Ctr PO Box 273 Edwards AFB CA 93523*

BAERWALD, SUSAN GRAD, television broadcasting company executive producer; b. Long Branch, N.J., June 18, 1944; d. Bernard John and Marian Grad; m. Paul Baerwald, July 1, 1969; children: Joshua, Samuel. Degre des Arts and Lettres, Sorbonne, Paris, 1965; BA, Sarah Lawrence Coll., 1966. Script analyst United Artists, L.A., 1978-80; v.p. devel. Gordon/Eisner Prodns., L.A., 1980-81; mgr. mini-series and novels for TV, NBC, Burbank, Calif., 1981-82, dir. mini-series and novels for TV, 1982, v.p. mini-series and novels for TV, 1982-89; exec. producer NBC Prodns., 1989-95, Savoy Pictures TV, 1995-96, Citadel Entertainment, 1996-97; sr. lectr. Am. Film Inst., 1999. Producer (TV movies) Blind Faith, 1990, One Spl. Victory, 1991, Cruel Doubt, 1992, A Time to Heal, 1994, Inflammable, 1995 (TV miniseries) Lucky/Chances, 1990. Bd. dirs. The Paper Bag Players, N.Y.C., 1974—, Women in Film Found., 2000, Non-Profit Alliance W.O.M.E.N., Inc., 1998; vol. L.A. Children's Mus., 1978-80; mem. awards com. Scott Newman Found., 1982-84; bd. dirs. L.A. Goal, 1996—. Recipient Vol. Incentive award NBC, 1983. Mem. ATAS (bd. govs. 1993-97, nat. awards chmn. 1997-98), Am. Film Inst., Hollywood Radio and TV Soc.

BAEZ, JOAN CHANDOS, folk singer; b. S.I., N.Y., Jan. 9, 1941; d. Albert V. and Joan (Bridge) B.; m. David Victor Harris, Mar. 1968 (div. 1973); 1 son, Gabriel Earl. Appeared in coffeehouses, Gate of Horn, Chgo., 1958, Ballad Room, Club 47, 1958-68, Newport (R.I.) Folk Festival, 1959-69, 85, 87, 90, 92, 93, 95, extended tours to colls. and concert halls, 1960s, appeared Town Hall and Carnegie Hall, 1962, 67, 68, U.S. tours, 1970—, concert tours in Japan, 1966, 82, Europe, 1970-73, 80, 83-84, 87-90, 93—, Australia, 1985; rec. artist for Vanguard Records, 1960-72, A&M, 1973-76, Portrait Records, 1977-80, Gold Castle Records, 1986-89, Virgin Records, 1990-93, Grapevine Label Records (UK), 1995-97, Guardian Records, 1995-97, European record albums, 1981, 83, award 8 gold albums, 1 gold single; albums include Gone From Danger, 1997, Rare, Live & Classic (box set), 1993, Dark Chords on a Big Guitar, 2003; author: Joan Baez Songbook, 1964, (biography) Daybreak, 1968, (with David Harris) Coming Out, 1971, And a Voice to Sing With, 1987, (songbook) An Then I Wrote, 1979. Extensive TV appearances and speaking tours U.S. and Can. for anti-militarism, 1967-68; visit to Dem. Republic of Vietnam, 1972, visit to war torn Bosnia-Herzegovina, 1993; founder, v.p. Inst. for Study Nonviolence (now Resource Ctr. for Nonviolence, Santa Cruz, Calif.), Palo Alto, Calif., 1965; mem. nat. adv. coun. Amnesty Internat., 1974-92; founder, pres. Humanitas/Internat. Human Rights Com., 1979-92; condr. fact-finding mission to refugee camps, S.E. Asia, Oct. 1979; began refusing payment of war taxes, 1964; arrested for civil disobedience opposing draft, Oct., Dec., 1967. Office: Diamonds & Rust Prodns PO Box 1026 Menlo Park CA 94026-1026 Office Phone: 650-328-0266.

BAEZ, JOANNE MARIE, school psychologist; b. Chgo., June 4, 1962; d. Rafael Marino and Maria Ana (Lopez) B. BA, Bradley U., Peoria, Ill., 1984; MS, Northwestern State U., Natchitoches, La., 1991; PsyD, Ctrl. Mich. U., 1997. Sch. psychologist Milw. Pub. Schs., 1992—. Mem. Hispanic women's adv. coun. Alverno Coll., Milw., 1992—. Mem. Hispanic Women's Adv. Coun., Alverno Coll., Milw., 1992—. Mem. Nat. Assn. Sch. Psychologists, 1986—, Psychologists Assn. of Milw. Pub. Schs. (sec. 1996—). Roman Catholic. Home: 3720A S 88th St Milwaukee WI 53228-1736 Office: Milw Pub Schs Div Spl Svcs Ctr Psychol Svcs 6620 W Capitol Dr Milwaukee WI 53216-2040

BAEZA FLORES, VIRGINIA, audit specialist; b. El Paso, Tex., Dec. 29, 1968; d. Ramon and Maria Asuncion (Beltran) B. Attended, U. Tex., El Paso, 1987-89; BBA, U. Tex., San Antonio, 1991. Acctg. intern U. S. Acctg. Assn., San Antonio, 1991; acct. Acctg. Reporting Consolidation Ctr., San Antonio, 1992-93, Valero Energy Corp., San Antonio, 1993—. Vol. programs rev. com. United Way. Mem. Am. Soc. of Women Accts., Inst. Internal Auditors. Democrat. Roman Catholic. Avocations: aerobics, reading, home improvement. Home: 2818 Redland Crk San Antonio TX 78259-3551 Office: 7990 1H-10 W 6000 North Loop 1604 West San Antonio TX 78249-1112

BAGGARLY, CLAIRE JOHNSON, music educator, department chairman; d. Loys Almon Johnson and Helen St. John Mooney; m. Nathaniel Perry Baggarly, June 7, 1969; 1 child, Mark Edward. AA, U. Fla., 1969; BA, Fla. Tech. U., 1973; EdM, U. Ctrl. Fla., 1979. Cert. tchr. Fla. Music educator Brevard County Sch. Sys., Fla., 1973—94; assoc. prof. music Brevard C.C., Cocoa, Fla., 1988—, dept. chair fine arts/phys. edn., 2001—. Mem.: Fla. Music Educators Assn., Music Educators Nat. Conf. Office: Brevard Cmty Coll 1519 Clearlake Rd Cocoa FL 32922

BAGGOTT, BRENDA JANE LAMB, elementary school educator; b. Augusta, Ga., Nov. 10, 1948; d. Morgan Barrett Jr. and Ollie Virginia (Toole) Lamb; m. John Carl Baggott, July 8, 1967 (div. Jan. 1998); children: Carla Baggott Walczak, John Carl Jr. Student, Truett McConnel Jr. Coll., 1966-67; BS in spl. Edn., Augusta Coll., 1974; postgrad., Southeastern La. U., 1976-77, U. New Orleans, 1977-78, U. Ctrl. Fla., 1987, 97—; MEd, Nova Southeastern U., 1997. Cert. spl. edn. tchr. in varying exceptionalities and mental handicaps, elem. tchr. ESOL, coaching for Spl. Olympics, Fla. Spl. Olympics tchr. Copeland Elem. Sch., Augusta, Ga., 1973-74; spl. edn. tchr. Percy Julian Spl. Sch., Marrero, La., 1974-78; Spl. edn. resource tchr. Rosemary Mid. Sch., Andrews, S.C., 1978; spl. edn. tchr. Bynum Elem. Sch., Gerogetown, S.C., 1979, Ridgewood Park Elem. Sch., Orlando, Fla., 1979-97; reading recovery tchr. Rock Lake Elem. Sch., Orlando, 1997—2002, corrective reading tchr., 2003—; lab tchr. Read 180, 2002—. Curriculum coord. Percy Julian Spl. Sch., 1975-77; mem. state tchr. mentally handicapped exam validation team Inst. for Instnl. Rsch. and Practice, Fla. Dept. Edn., Tampa, 1990—. Coord. Orange County Spl. Olympics, Orlando, 1984-85, coach, 1974—. Mem. Coun. for Exceptional Children, Internat. Reading Assn., Orange County Reading Coun., Reading Recovery Coun. N.Am., Fla. Reading Assn. Democrat. Baptist. Avocations: directing children's choirs, coaching special olympics. Office: Rock Lake Elem Sch 408 N Tampa Ave Orlando FL 32805-1296

BAGINSKI, MAUREEN A. federal agency administrator; BA in Russian and Spanish, MA in Slavic lang., SUNY, Albany; at, Moriz Torez Fgn. Lang. Inst., Moscow. Russian lang. instr. Nat. Security Agy./Ctrl. Security Svc., 1979, sr. ops. officer, nat. ops. ctr., signals intelligence nat. intelligence officer Russia, exec. asst. to the dir., dep. chief global access program, chief, directorate of ops., consumer products and svcs., asst. dep. dir. tech. and sys., chief, officer of the dir., dir. signals intelligence, 2001—03; exec. asst. dir. office of intelligence FBI, Washington, 2003—. Recipient Sustained Exec. Leadership award, Dir. Ctrl. Intelligence. Office: Fed Bur Investigation J Edgar Hoover Bldg 935 Penn Ave NW Washington DC 20535-0001*

BAGLEY, CONSTANCE ELIZABETH, law educator, lawyer; b. Tucson, Dec. 18, 1952; d. Robert Porter Smith and Joanne Snow-Willstadter. AB in Polit. Sci. with distinction, with honors, Stanford U., 1974; JD magna cum laude, Harvard U., 1977. Bar: Calif. 1978, N.Y. 1978. Tchg. fellow Harvard U., 1975-77; assoc. Webster & Sheffield, N.Y.C., 1977-78, Heller, Ehrman, White & McAuliffe, San Francisco, 1978-79, McCutchen, Doyle, Brown & Enersen, San Francisco, 1979-84, ptnr., 1984-90; lectr. bus. law Stanford (Calif.) U., 1988-90, lectr. mgmt., 1990-91, lectr. law and mgmt., 1991-95, sr. lectr. law and mgmt., 1995-2000, GSB Trust faculty fellow, 1997-98, lectr. Stanford Exec. Program; lectr. Stanford Mktg. Mgmt. Exec. Program; sr. lectr. bus. adminstrn. Harvard Bus. Sch., Boston, 1999-2000, assoc. prof., 2000—. Bd. dirs. Alegre Enterprises, Inc., Latina Publ. LLC, 1995-2000; corp. practice series adv. bd. Bur. Nat. Affairs, 1984—; faculty adv. bd. Stanford Jour. Law, Bus. and Fin., 1994—; lectr., planning com. Calif. Continuing Edn. Bar, L.A., San Francisco, 1983, 85-87; lectr. So. Area Conf., Silverado, 1988, Young Pres. Orgn. Internat. U. for Pres., Hong Kong, 1988; mem. faculty Youg. Pres. Orgn. Internat. U. for Pres., Praque, Czech Republic, 2002. Author: Mergers, Acquisitions and Tender Offers, 1983, Managers and the Legal Environment: Strategies for the 21st Century, 1991, 4th edit., 2002; co-author: Negotiated Acquisitions, 1992, Cutting Edge Cases in the Legal Environment of Business, 1993, 2d edit. 1998, Proxy Contests and Corporate Control: Strategic Considerations, 1997, Proxy Contests and Corporate Control: Conducting the Proxy Campaign, 1997, The Entrepreneur's Guide to Business Law, 1998, 2d edit., 2003; contbg. editor: Calif. Bus. Law Reporter, 1984-95; mem. editl. bd. Jour. Internet Law, 1997-99, 2001—; staff editor Am. Bus. Law Jour., 2000-. Vestry mem. Trinity Episcopal Ch., San Francisco, 1984-85; vol. Moffit Hosp. U. Calif., San Francisco, 1983-84; bd. dirs. Youth and Family Assistance, Redwood City, Calif., 1996-99. Mem. ABA, Acad. Mgmt., Acad. Legal Studies in Bus., Harvard Faculty Club, Cap and Gown Soc., Phi Beta Kappa. Republican. Office: Harvard Bus Sch Soldiers Field Boston MA 02163-1317 Business E-Mail: cbagley@hbs.edu.

BAGLEY, EDYTHE SCOTT, theater educator; b. Marion, Ala. d. Obie and Bernice (McMurry) Scott; m. Arthur Moten Bagley, June 5, 1954; 1 child, Arturo Scott. BEd, Ohio State U., 1949; MA in English, Columbia U.,

1954; MFA in Theater Arts, Boston U., 1965. Instr. Elizabeth City (N.C.) State Coll., 1953-56; asst. prof. Albany (Ga.) State Coll., 1956-57, A&T U., Greensboro, N.C., 1957-58, Norfolk (Va.) State Coll., 1963-65; assoc. prof. theater Cheyney (Pa.) U., 1971—, chair dept. theater arts. Cons. in black theater Mich. State U., East Lansing, 1969-71. Dir. coll. prodns., 1968-71. Spl. asst. to Coretta Scott King. Mem. NAACP, AAUW, NAFE, Nat. Coun. Negro Women, Theater Assn. Pa., The Links Inc. (chair com. on arts 1972-80), Womens Internat. League for Peace and Freedom, Nat. Assn. Dramatic and Speech Arts, Nat. Assn. Schs. of Theater, The Pa. Martin Luther King Jr. Assn. for Nonviolence (bd. dirs.), The Martin Luther King Jr. Ctr. for Nonviolent Social Change (bd. dirs.). Achievements include being featured in the book Sisters. Home: 2 Derry Dr Cheyney PA 19319 Office: Cheyney U Cheyney PA 19319

BAGWELL, MARSHA LYNN, actor, educator; d. Marshall Eckert and Dorothy Joines Bagwell. BA in Sociology, Ga. State U., 1970; postgrad., Manhattan Sch. Music, 1971; MFA in Acting, U. Ariz., 1995. Faculty musical theatre and acting Am. Musical and Dramatic Acad., N.Y.C., 1996—98; asst. prof., head acting and musical theatre divsn. U. Ariz. Sch. Theatre Arts, Tucson, 1998—. Actor: (Broadway plays) Desert Song, 1973, Chicago, 1975—77, Pirates of Penzance, 1985, Stratford Festival, 1990—92, (nat. tours) The Music Man, A Funny Thing Happened on the Way to the Forum, A Little Night Music; (TV series) Show Boat, Spenser: For Hire, One Life to Live, Guiding Light, (others). Named Best Supporting Actress for role of Katisha in Mikado, New Eng. Drama Critics, 2000; recipient Mac award, Ariz. Daily Star, 2002. Mem.: AFTRA, SAG, Am. Tchrs. Higher Edn., Voice and Speech Tchrs. Assn., Nat. Assn. Tchrs. Singing, Actors Equity Assn. Democrat. Office: Univ Ariz Sch Theatre Arts PO Box 210003 Tucson AZ 85721 Office Phone: 520-621-7008.

BAHNER, SUE (FLORENCE SUZANNA BAHNER), radio broadcasting executive; d. William and Florence (Quinlivan) McElwee; m. David S. Bahner; children: Suzanna Elizabeth, Caryl Aileen. Grad., Columbia Bus. Coll., 1950. Various exec. sec. positions, 1954-74; office mgr. Sta. WYRD, Syracuse, N.Y., 1974, gen. mgr., 1974-80, Sta. WWWG-AM, Rochester, N.Y., 1980-93, WDCW, Syracuse, 1993-98; pres. The Cornerstone Group, 1986—90, Crossway Cons., 1997—. Bd. dirs. Rescue Mission, Syracuse; active Eastern Hills Bible Ch. Mem. Greater Syracuse Assn. Evangelicals (treas. 1993-97), N.Y. State Assn. Evangelicals (sec. 1998—), Nat. Religious Broadcasters (pres. ea. chpt. 1984-98, bd. dirs. 1983—, 2d v.p. 1998-2000, mem. exec. com. 1992—). Office: Natl Religious Broadcasters 7839 Ashton Ave Manassas VA 20109-2883

BAHR, CARMAN BLOEDOW, internist; b. Middletown, Ohio, Mar. 24, 1931; d. Edwin Louis and Berneice Mae (Bacon) Bloedow; m. Walter Julien Bahr, Aug. 28, 1968 (dec. Sept. 1971). BA cum laude, Miami U., Oxford, Ohio, 1952; MD, Ohio State U., 1956; MS, U. Okla., 1996. Cert. diabetes educator, 1986, 92. Intern St. Luke's Hosp., Chgo., 1956-57; resident U. Okla. Health Sci. Ctr., 1957-60; assoc. prof. medicine Okla. Health Sci. Ctr., 1971-93, prof. emeritus, 1993. Fellow: ACP (Joslin 50 Yr. medal 2001); mem.: AMA (Physician's Recognition award 1976, 1979, 1982, 1985, 1988, 1991, 1994, 1998), Okla. Med. Assn., Am. Med. Women's Assn., Western Okla. Diabetes Educators, Am. Assn. Diabetes Educators, Am. Diabetes Assn. (chpt. pres. 1989, Robert Endress award 1985), Phi Beta Kappa. Home: [illegible] Oklahoma City OK 73111-6729 Office: VA Med Ctr 921 NE 13th St Oklahoma City OK 73104-[illegible] Personal E-mail: cbb2@cox.net.

BAHR, CHRISTINE MARIE, special education educator; b. Rolla, Mo., July 4, 1958; m. Michael Welton Bahr, June 16, 1984. BA, Fontbonne Coll., 1980; MS, So. Ill. U., 1984; PhD, Ind. U., 1988. Project coord. Vanderbilt U., Nashville, 1986-88; assoc. prof. Western Mich. U., Kalamazoo, 1988—. Mem. Coun. for Exceptional Children, Am. Ednl. Rsch. Assn.

BAHR, JANE MARIE, writer, retired English educator; BS in English, U. Wis., River Falls, 1971; MST in English, U. Wis., Whitewater, 1978. English tchr. Whitewater (Wis.) H.S., 1973-82, Eau Claire (Wis.) Meml. H.S., 1985, Glenwood City H.S., summers 1990-91; freelance writer Wis. Regional Writers' Assn., 1985—, Wis. Fellowship of Poets, 1981—, Wis. Arts Bd. Grant, 1998. Author poems in numerous publs. including Wis. Poets' Calendars, Poetry Out of Wis. V, Free Verse, Poetry Motel, Wallpaper Broadside Series, Poesy and Sweet Pea Press, among others. WRWA Soar scholar Sch. of Arts, U. Wis., Madison, 1999.

BAHR, LAUREN S. publishing company executive; b. New Brunswick, N.J., July 3, 1944; d. Simon A. and Rosalind J. Bahr. Student, U. Grenoble, France, 1964; BA (Branstrom scholar); MA, U. Mich., 1966. Asst. editor New Horizons Pubs., Inc., Chgo., 1967, Scholastic Mags., Inc., N.Y.C., 1968-71; supervising editor Houghton Mifflin Co., Boston, 1971; product devel. editor Appleton-Century-Crofts, N.Y.C., 1972-74; sponsoring editor McGraw-Hill, Inc., N.Y.C., 1974-75; editor Today's Sec. mag., 1975-77; sr. editor Media Systems Corp., N.Y.C., 1978; sr. editor coll. dept. CBS Coll. Pub., N.Y.C., 1978-82, mktg. mgr. fgn. langs., dir. mktg. adminstrn., 1982-83; from dir. devel. coll. divsn. to pub. cons. Harper & Row, N.Y.C., 1983-91; v.p., editl. dir. Atlas Edits., Inc., N.Y.C., 1991-98; dir. publs. Bank St. Coll. Edn., N.Y.C., 1999—2000; mng. editor Inkwell Pub., N.Y.C., 2000—02; editl. dir. 4 Lakes Colorgraphics, 2002—. Democrat. Jewish. Home: 444 E 82nd St New York NY 10028-5903

BAHRET, MARY ELLEN, lobbyist; BA in Polit. Sci. and Urban Studies, U. Pitts., 1994. Adminstrv. asst., recruiting asst. McKinsey and Co., Inc., 1993-95; exec. asst. J. Michael Eakin for Superior Ct. Judge Campaign, 1995; adminstrv. & policy asst. strategic planning/congl. affairs Rep. Nat. Com., 1995-96, coord. congl. comm. Office Congl. Affairs, 1996; asst. to the chief of staff Office of Senator Larry E. Craig, Washington, 1997, dep. press sec., 1997-98, legis. asst., 1997-99; mgr. Senate legis. affairs Nat. Fedn. Ind. Bus., Washington, 1999—2001; prin. OBC Group, Washington, 2001—.

BAIER, LUCINDA, corporate financial executive; BS in acctg., MS in acctg., Ill. State U. Self employed, 1984—87; experienced tax staff Arthur Andersen, 1987—89, experienced tax sr., 1989—90, tax mgr., 1990—93; corp. dir., taxes Gen. Dynamics, 1993—97; tax dir. ICI Americas, 1997, v.p. taxation, 1998, v.p. fin., 1998—99; sr. v.p. fin., tax and treas. US Office Products, 1999, sr. v.p. merchandising, 1999—2000; v.p., taxes Sears, Roebuck and Co., 2000—01, v.p. fin. credit services and fin. products, 2001—03, sr. v.p., gen. mgr., credit and fin. products, 2003—. Mem.: Executives Club of Chgo. Office: Sears Roebuck and Co 3333 Beverly Rd Hoffman Estates IL 60179

BAIER, SUSAN LOVEJOY, music educator; b. Canandaigua, N.Y., Jan. 30, 1953; m. Michael Francis Baier, July 17, 1976; children: Michael Franklin, Kimberly Lovejoy. MusB magna cum laude, Grove City Coll., 1975; EdM, Converse Coll., 1994. Cert. tchr. S.C. String tchr. Akron (Ohio) Pub. Schs., 1975—76; Suzuki violin tchr. Jewish Cmty. Ctr., Pitts., 1976—78, Carnegie Mellon U. Pre-Coll., Pitts., 1976—78; string tchr. Spartanburg (S.C.) County Dist. 7, 1979—94, Spartanburg (S.C.) County Dist. 6, 1994—2002, dist. orch. coord., 2002—. Violinst Greater Spartanburg Philharm., 1995—; mem. string quintet, violin soloist Nazareth Presbyn. Ch., Moore, SC, 1995—. Named Outstanding Tchr., Tchg. Music mag., 2000. Mem.: S.C. Music Educators Assn. (orch. divsn., festival chmn., all-state chmn., treas., pres.-elect, pres.), Am. String Tchrs. with Nat. Sch. Orch. Assn., Music Educators Nat. Conf. Office: Dorman HS 1050 Cavalier Way Roebuck SC 29376

BAIGIS, JUDITH ANN, nursing educator, academic administrator; b. Washington, Pa., July 26, 1941; d. Andrew J. and Mary Margaret (Mitchell) Baigis; m. Robert Wachbroit, June 26, 1989. Diploma, Geisinger Hosp. Sch. Nursing, Danville, Pa., 1962; BS, NYU, 1968, PhD, 1979. RN, Md., D.C. Instr. nursing NYU, N.Y.C., 1970-73, CUNY Lehman Coll., Bronx, N.Y., 1973-79; dir. community health nursing program U. Pa. Sch. Nursing, Phila., 1979-87; dir. long-term care Johns Hopkins U. Sch. Nursing, Balt., 1987-92; assoc. dean for rsch. Georgetown U. Sch. Nursing, Washington, 1992—, interim dean, 1998-99, prof., 1992—. Contbr. articles to nursing jours. Nat. Inst. Nursing Rsch. grantee, 1988-96. Mem. ANA, APHA, Am. Acad. Nursing, Assn. Community Health Nursing Educators. Office: Georgetown U Sch Nursing Box 571107 3700 Reservoir Rd NW Washington DC 20007-2111

BAIK-HAN, WON H. pediatrician, educator, consultant; b. Seoul, Jong Ro Gu, Republic of Korea, July 22, 1956; arrived in U.S., 1983; d. Hong In Baik and Ok Hee Chang; m. Muyol Han, Nov. 15, 1986; children: Jeffrey J. Han, Steven J. Han. MD, Ewha Woman's U., Seoul, 1981. Diplomate Am. Bd. Pediat. Intern Soon Chun Hyang U. Hosp., Seoul, Republic of Korea, 1981—82, resident in pediat., 1982—83; pediat. externship St. Elizabeth Hosp. Ctr., Youngstown, Ohio, 1983—84; vol. pediat. physician Flushing (N.Y.) Hosp. Med. Ctr., 1984—86, resident in pediat., 1986—89; fellow in allergy and clin. immunology St. Luke's/Roosevelt Hosp. Ctr., N.Y.C., 1989—91; clin. fellow in allergy & immunology and medicine Columbia U., N.Y.C., 1989—91; dir. pediat. allergy and immunology Flushing (N.Y.) Hosp. Med. Ctr., 1991—, dir. pediat. allergy and asthma clinic, 1991—, consulting physician medicine and pediat., 1991—, com. mem. pharmacy therapeutic com., 1999—. Dir. pediat. allergy Wyckoff Heights Med. Ctr., Bklyn., 1995—99; consulting physician pediat., allergy and immunology N.Y. Hosp. Queens, Flushing, 1997—2000; dir. pediat. allergy clinic Jamaica (N.Y.) Hosp. Med. Ctr., 2000—; asst. prof. pediat. Albert Einstein Coll. Medicine, Bronx, 1994—96, asst. clin. prof. pediat., 1999—; clin. asst. prof. pediat. Cornell U. Med. Coll., N.Y.C., 1997—99; regional spkr. allergy immunology Schering Plough Pharm. Co., NJ, 2001—. Author (with D.M. Rubin): Pediatric Emergency Medicine-Self Assessment and Review, 1994; author: (with A. Stock) Allergic & Immunologic Disease: Pediatric Emergency Medicine-Self Assessment and Review, 2nd edit., 1998. Consulting physician The Korean Am. Nail Assn. N.Y., Inc., Flushing, 1998—, The Korean Sr. Citizen Ctr., Corona, NY, 1999—. Recipient Presentation award for allergy and asthma, Soon Chun Hyang U. Hosp., Seoul, 1992, Physicians Recognition award, AMA, 1999—, Contbn. award for Korean Health Fair, Korean-Am. Nail Assn. N.Y., Inc., Flushing, 1999. Fellow: Am. Acad. Pediat.; mem.: Coalition for Asian Am. Children and Families (com. mem.), N.Y. Allergy, Asthma and Immunology Soc., Am. Acad. Allergy, Asthma and Immunology (Travel Grand award for rsch. project 1991), Hunter Coll. H.S. Korean-Am. Parents Assn. (pres. 2002—). Avocations: drawing and painting, playing pingpong and tennis, singing, collecting coins, stamps and collectibles, collecting antiques. Office: 1st Fl 143-20 Sanford Ave Flushing NY 11355 Office Phone: 718-460-3943.

BAIK-KROMALIC, SUE S. metallurgical engineer; b. Korea; m. Joseph. BS in Metall. Engring., Ohio State U. Project engr. Cummins Engine Co., Columbus, Ind; engring. staff, materials testing and devel. engr. Honda Am. Mfg., Inc., East Liberty, Ohio; trainer problem solving Honda Am., Inc., East Liberty, Ohio, new model project engr., leader tech. devel.; prodn. planning ops. and control; engring. coord. mfg. ops., cost & manpower [illegible] and control, asst. mgr. bus. mgmt. sys., staff engr. prodn. control. Guest spkr. Ohio State U., Columbus. Chmn. Opera Columbus Ball, 2003. Mem. ASM Internat. (Columbus chpt. awards chmn., chpt. devel. task force, sec., task force, membership devel. com., treas., chpt. coun., chair, vice-chair membership devel. com., chair membership devel. com., bd. trustees edn. found.). Roman Catholic. Avocation: golf. Office: Honda of Am Mfg Inc Honda Ops Office 24000 Honda Pkwy Marysville OH 43040-9251

BAILAR, BARBARA ANN, statistician, researcher; b. Monroe, Mich., Nov. 24, 1935; d. Malcolm Laurie and Clara Florence (Parent) Dezendorf; m. John Francis Powell (div. 1966); 1 child, Pamela; m. John Christian Bailar; 1 child, Melissa. BA, SUNY, 1956; MS, Va. Poly. Inst., 1965; PhD, Am. U., 1972. With Bur. of Census, Washington, 1958-88, chief Ctr. Rsch. Measurement Methods, 1973-79, assoc. dir. for statis. standards and methodology, 1979-88; exec. dir. Am. Statis. Assn., Alexandria, Va., 1988-95; sr. v.p. for survey rsch. Nat. Opinion Rsch. Ctr., Chgo., 1995—2001. Instr. George Washington U., 1984-85; head dept. math. and stats. USDA Grad. Sch., Washington, 1972-87. Contbr. articles, book chpts. to profl. publs. Pres. bd. dirs. Harbour Sq. Coop., Washington, 1988-89. Recipient Silver medal U.S. Dept. Commerce, 1980. Fellow Am. Statis. Assn. (pres. 1987); mem. AAAS (chair sect. stats. 1984-85), Internat. Assn. Survey Statisticians (pres. 1989-91), Internat. Statis. Inst. (Pres.'s invited speaker 1983, v.p. 1993-95), Cosmos Club. E-mail: bbailar@health.bsd.uchicago.edu.

BAILEY, CARLA LYNN, nursing administrator; b. Balt., June 4, 1957; d. Carlton L. and Helen P. (Wales) B. BSN, U. Md., Balt., 1979; MS in Health Sci., Towson (Md.) State U., 1987; PhD in Healthcare Mgmt., Century Brentwick U., 2000. Nurse clinician I, charge nurse, clin. nurse U. Md. Med. Systems, Balt., 1981—87; maternal transport coord. U. Md. Med. Systems Hosp., Balt., 1979—96; rsch. nurse Tokos Med. Corp., Balt., 1988—91; perinatal care coord. U. Md. Med. Systems/Hosp., 1993—99; perinatal programs dir. Md. Inst. Emergency Med. Svcs. Sys., 1999—. Mem. assoc. faculty U. Md. Sch. Nursing, 1993-95; mem. fetal and infant mortality rev. bd. Healthy Start; mem. State Commn. on Infant Mortality Prevention. Mem. Assn. Women's Health, Obstetric and Neonatal Nurses, Md. Nurse's Assn., Nat. Perinatal Assn., Md. Perinatal Assn. (bd. dirs., pres.).

BAILEY, CLAUDIA JEAN, retired professor, librarian, artist; b. Akron, Ohio, July 2, 1936; d. Lloyd Carl Lowe and Vergie P. Hively; m. Richard E. Bailey; children: Laurel Lynn Bailey-Wallace, Robert E. BA, Asbury Coll., 1960; MAL.S., U. Mich., 1966; MA, Ohio State U., 1970; BFA, U. R.I., 1992. Ref. libr. Columbus Pub. Libr., Columbus, Ohio, 1966—68; head journalism, acting head social work libr. Ohio State U., Columbus, Ohio, 1969—70; head fine arts libr. Bridgeport Pub. Libr., Bridgeport, Conn., 1970—72; head providence campus libr. CC of R.I., Providence, 1972—76, head Lincoln campus libr. Lincoln, RI, 1976—82, coord. ref./collection devel., 1982—87, ref. libr. Warwick, RI, 1987—97. Cosponsored libr. concerts and art exhibits Bridgeport Pub. Libr., Bridgeport, Conn., 1971—72; chairperson, faculty sabbatical com. CC of R.I., Warwick, RI, 1979—80. Author: A Guide To Reference And Bibliography For Theatre Research, 1971, A Guide To Reference And Bibliography For Theatre Research., 2d edit., 1983. Scholar Grad. Libr. Sci., State Of Ohio, 1965-66, Scholar Grad., London Theatre Libraries, 1968. Mem.: AEA, Westbrook Fine Arts Assn., George Chelena Chorale. Liberal. Avocations: art collages, drawing, painting, singing, opera, theater. Home: 19483 N 90th Ln Peoria AZ 85382-8560

BAILEY, DARLYNE, social worker, educator; b. N.Y.C., July 21, 1952; d. Arthur and Iris B. AB in Pyschology and Secondary Edn., Lafayette Coll., 1974; MSc in Pychiatric Social Work, Columbia U., N.Y.C., 1976; PhD Orgn. Behavior, Case Western Reserve U., 1988. Lic. ind. social worker, Ohio. Coord. specialized treatment Essex County Guidance Ctr., East Orange, N.J., 1976-82; dir. emergency access svcs. Cmty. Mental Health Orgn., Englewood, N.J., 1980-83; field instr. NYU Sch. Social Work, 1981-82; instr. Weatherhead Sch. Mgmt., Case Western Reserve U., Cleve., 1986-87; asst. prof. Mandel Sch. Applied Social Sci., Case Western Reserve U., Cleve., 1988-94, dean and assoc. prof., 1994-99, dean and prof., 1998—2001; dean and v.p. acad. affairs Tchrs. Coll., Columbia U., N.Y.C., 2002—, acting pres., 2003. Cons. to numerous profl. groups; orgnl. devel. specialist Mid-Atlantic Regional Med. Edn. Ctr. VA, Brecksville, Ohio, 1985-88, Shaker Heights (Ohio) Sch. Dist., 1988-90, Cuyahoga Plan, Cleve., 1989-90; trainer 9-to-5 Nat. Assn. Working Women, Cleve., Family Children and Adult Svcs., Columbus, 1988, Exec. Tng. Inst., 1988-90, The Free Med. Clinic of Greater Cleve., Cuyhoga County Dept. Human Svcs., Sr. and Adult Svcs., Luth. Chaplaincy Svc., Cleve., 1993, KPMG Peat Marwick project, Chgo., 1990-91, Ghana Assn. Pvt. Vol. Orgns. in Devel., Accra, 1992-94, Old Stone Ch. Project, Cleve., 1994, Cleve. Rape Crisis Ctr. Project, 1995 Co-author: (book) Strategic Alliances Among Health and Human Services Organizations: From Affiliations to Consolidations, 2000, Managing Human Resources in the Human Services, 2001; contbr. articles to profl. jours., chapters to books and book reviews. Mem. exec. com. bd. trustees Heights Youth Ctr., Inc., Cleveland Heights, Ohio, 1983-95; mem. Human Resources Devel. Com., Neighborhood Ctrs. Assn., Cleve., chair mgmt. and governance task force, 1988-90; bd. trustees Neighborhood Ctrs., Cleve., 1991-94, Tiffin U., 1992-95, Fedn. for Cmty. Planning, Cleve., 1995, Nat. Coun., Cleve., 1995; mem. book rev. com. NASW Press, Washington, 1992-95; cons. editor Social Work, 1996; mem. philantropy and volunteerism adv. com. Kellogg Found., Battle Creek, Mich., 1992; chairwoman Mandel Ctr. Nonprofit Orgn. Named Nat. Group XIII fellow, W.K. Kellogg Nat. Leadership Program; recipient George Washington Kidd award, Lafayette Coll., Easton, Pa., 1994, Crain's Cleveland Bus. Women Influence award, 1997; fellow, Salzburg Seminar, Austria, 1997. Fellow: Nat. Assn. Social Workers, Am. Othopysciatric Assn.; mem.: Coun. Social Work Edn. (bd. dirs.), Nat. Bd. Organizational Behavior Tchg. Soc. (past co-chair), Leadership Cleveland Class. Office: Tchrs Coll Columbia U 525 W 120th St New York NY 10027

BAILEY, DOROTHY JEAN, secondary school educator, consultant; b. Clarksdale, Miss., Jan. 24, 1948; d. A.D. and Nancy (Morbley) Bailey; 1 child, Miko Dawn Montgomery. AA Sociology, Compton Coll., 1969; BA Sociology, Cal State Univ. Long Beach, 1972; MA Pub. Adminstrn., Pepperdine Univ., 1977; MS Sch. Counseling, Univ. La Verne, 2001. Lic. real estate Calif., 1988, pupil personnel svcs. credential Calif., 2002. Social sci. analyst Libr. of Congress/Congressional Rsch. Svc., Washington, 1979—86; realtor Century 21 Sparrow, Long Beach, Calif., 1988—92; program coord. Martin Luther King Jr./Charles R. Drew Univ. of Medicine and Sci., L.A., Calif., 1989—90; case mgr./ early intervention network coord. Cal State Univ. Long Beach Found., Calif., 1992—94; cons. So. Calif. Alcohol & Drug Programs, Inc., Downey, Calif., 1994, Miller Children's Hosp. of Long Beach, Calif., 1994—95; program coord. Minority AIDS Program, L.A., Calif., 1995—97; tchr. advisor L.A. Unfied Sch. Dist/Harbor Occupl. Ctr., San Pedro, Calif., 1999—2001, tchr., 1997—. Mem.: Women Educators, Calif. Coun. for Adult Edn. (sec. 1999—2002, pres. 2002—03, State Excellence in Tchg. 2003). Avocations: collecting seashells, mentoring, reading, walking, art. Office: LA Unified Sch Dist/Harbor Occpul Ctr 740 N Pacific Ave San Pedro CA 90731

BAILEY, EXINE MARGARET ANDERSON, soprano, educator; b. Cottonwood, Minn., Jan. 4, 1922; d. Joseph Leonard and Exine Pearl (Robertson) Anderson; m. Arthur Albert Bailey, May 5, 1956. BS, U. Minn., 1944; MA, Columbia U., 1945; profl. diploma, 1951. Instr. Columbia U., 1947-51; faculty U. Oreg., Eugene, 1951—, prof. voice, 1966-87, coordinator voice instrn., 1969-87, prof. emeritus, 1987—; faculty dir. Salzburg, Austria, summer 1968, summer 1976. Vis. prof., head vocal instrn. Columbia U., summers 1952-59; condr. master classes for singers, developer summer program study for h.s. solo singers, U. Oreg. Sch. Music, 1988—, mem. planning com. 1998-99 MTNA Nat. Convention. Profl. singer, N.Y.C.; appearances with NBC, ABC symphonies; solo artist appearing with Portland and Eugene (Oreg.) Symphonies, other groups in Wash., Calif., Mont., Idaho, also in concert; contbr. articles, book revs. to various mags. Del. fine arts program to Ea. Europe, People to People Internat. Mission to Russia for 1990. Recipient Young Artist award N.Y.C. Singing Tchrs., 1945, Music Fedn. Club (N.Y.C.) hon. award, 1951; Kathryn Long scholar Met. Opera, 1945 Mem. Nat. Assn. Tchrs. Singing (lt. gov. 1968-72), Oreg. Music Tchrs. Assn (pres. 1974-76), Music Tchrs. Nat. Assn. (nat. voice chmn. high sch. activities 1970-74, nat. chmn. voice 1973-75, 81-85, NW chmn. collegiate activities and artists competition 1978-80, editorial com. Am. Music Tchr. jour. 1987-89), AAUP, Internat. Platform Assn., Kappa Delta Pi, Sigma Alpha Iota, Pi Kappa Lambda. Home: 17 Westbrook Way Eugene OR 97405-2074 Office: U Oreg Sch Music Eugene OR 97403

BAILEY, HELEN MCSHANE, historian; b. Gardner, Kans., Oct. 17, 1916; d. Harry Cramer and Maude Ethel (Kramer) McShane; m. James Edwin Bailey, Feb. 23, 1946; children: James Edwin, Barbara Ann Bailey Crawford. BA, Bethany Nazarene Coll., 1938. Adminstrv. asst. Office Chief of Staff, U.S. Army, Washington, 1941-48; historian U.S. Army ofcl. history of World War II, U.S. Army, Washington, 1948-58; research asst. George C. Marshall Research Found., Washington, 1958-59; historian Orgn. Joint Chiefs of Staff, Dept. Def., Pentagon, Washington, 1968-87; cons., 1987—. Mem. Am. Hist. Assn., Soc. Historians of Am. Fgn. Relations, World War Two Studies Assn., Soc. History in the Fed. Govt. Republican. Lutheran. Home: 9451 Lee Hwy Apt 415 Fairfax VA 22031-1812

BAILEY, JANET DEE, publishing company executive; b. Newark, Aug. 23, 1946; d. Richard and Mary Louise (Dee) Shapiro; m. John Frederick Bailey, May 9, 1971; children: Jason David, Juliana Dee. BA, U. Del., 1968; MBA, Pace U., 1981. Prodn. editor Prentice-Hall, Inc., Englewood Cliffs, N.J., 1968-70; dir. publs. Spl. Libraries Assn., N.Y.C., 1970-76; dir. mktg. services Knowledge Industry Publs., White Plains, N.Y., 1978-81, v.p., 1984-85; dir. inventory and contracts Macmillan Book Clubs, N.Y.C., 1981-84; group pub. Elsevier Sci. Pub. Co., N.Y.C., 1985-95, v.p. global mktg., 1996-99; v.p. STM books John Wiley & Sons, 1999—. Mem. Assn. Am. Publishers (chmn. jours. com., PSP exec. coun.), Soc. for Scholarly Publishing. Office: John Wiley & Sons Inc 605 Third Ave New York NY 10158

BAILEY, JOY Y. art educator; d. Nolan L. and Nancy L. Henry; m. Wayne O. Bailey, Jan. 12, 1980; children: Joshua N., Beau D. B of History, B of Secondary Edn., William Jewell Coll., 1988; M in Art Edn., N.W. Mo. State U., 1995. Cert. tchr. Dept. Elem. and Secondary Edn., 1988, Nat. Bd. Edn., 2003. Art educator Lathrop Schools, Mo., 1988—94, Smithville RII Schools, 1994—. Chair dist. art dept. Smithville RII Schools, 1996—, tchr. adv. com., 1998—, mentor new teachers, 1995—2001. Chair Smithville Arts Coun., 1996—99, mem., 1994, First Christian Ch., 1985. Recipient Excellence Edn. award. Mem.: Cmty. Teacher's Assn., Mo. State Teacher's Assn., Nat. Art Edn. Assn., Mo. Art Edn. Assn. Christian. Avocations: art, pottery.

BAILEY, JUDITH IRENE, university official, consultant; b. Winston-Salem, N.C., Aug. 24, 1946; d. William Edward Hege Jr. and Julia (Hedrick) Hege; m. Brendon Stinson Bailey, Jr, June 8, 1968. BA, Coker Coll., 1968; MEd, Va. Tech., 1973, EdD, 1976; postgrad., Harvard U., 1994,, 1994—95. Tchr. Chariho Regional H.S., Wood River Junction, RI, 1969—70, Prince William County Pub. Schs., Woodbridge, Va., 1968—72; asst. prin. Osbourn H.S., Manassas, Va., 1973; secondary sch. coord. Stafford (Va.) County Schs., 1973—74; middle sch. coord. Stafford County Schs., 1975—76; human rels. coord. Coop. Extension Svc. U. Md., College Park, 1976—79; dep. dir. Coop. Extension Svc. U. D.C., Washington, 1980-88; asst. v.p., dir. Coop. Extension U. Maine, Orono, 1988—92, interim v.p. for rsch. and pub. svc., 1992—93, v.p. rsch. and pub. svc., 1993—95, v.p. acad. affairs, provost, 1995—97; pres. No. Mich. U., Marquette, 1997—2003, Western Mich. U., Kalamazoo, 2003—. Adj. prof. George Mason U., Fairfax, Va., 1978; grad. student adv. U. Md., 1979—80;

spkr. and cons. in field; trustee Bronson Healthcare Group, Kalamazoo, 2003—; mem. steering com. Mich. Tri-Tech. Corridor, 2003—; mem. governing bd. Bioscis. Rsch. and Commercialization Ctr., 2003—; pres. Western Mich. U. Rsch. Found. Co-author: Contingency Planning for a Unitary School System; contbr. articles to profl. jours. Co-v.chmn. Lake Superior Cmty. Partnership, 1997—2003, bd. trustees Marquette (Mich.) Gen. Health Sys., 1998—2003; active Mich. Humanities Coun., 1999—2002, sec., treas., 2002—; mem. adv. bd. Huntington Bank, 2003—; apptd. by gov. to Mich. Quarter Commn., 2004; mem. Am. Coun. Edn. Commn. on Women, 2004; bd. dirs. Pine Tree State 4-H Found., 1988—97, Maine Toxicology Inst., 1992—95, Bangor (Maine) Symphony Orch, 1991—97, Shorebank, 1997—2003, Gilmore Keyboard Festival, 2003—. Recipient Disting. Alumni Achievement award, Coker Coll., 1998, Northwoods Woman Educator of Yr. award, 1999, Case V Chief Exec. Leadership award, 2002; fellow Susan Coker Watson fellow, 1967. Mem.: AAUW, Grand Rapids Econ. Club, Econ. Club Marquette County (bd. dirs. 1997—2003), Rotary (Paul Harris fellow 2004), Epsilon Sigma Phi (sec. Mu chpt. 1987, v.p. 1988, State Disting. Svc. award), Phi Kappa Phi, Phi Delta Kappa. Republican. Avocations: cooking, hiking. Home: 1201 Short Rd Kalamazoo MI 49008 Office: Western Mich U Office of the President 1903 W MIchigan Kalamazoo MI 49008-5202 E-mail: judi.bailey@wmich.edu.

BAILEY, JUDY LONG, outreach and education specialist, social worker; d. John H. and Sibyl K. Long; m. Charles A. Bailey, Jan. 1, 2001. BA, West Ga. U., Carrollton, 1969. Social caseworker Coweta Dept. of Family Svcs., Newnan, Ga., 1971—72, Lexington (SC) Dept. of Family Svcs., 1972—74; social work supr. Prince William Dept. Social Svcs., Manassas, Va., 1974—76; program specialist U.S. Dept. Agr., Washington, 1976—80; program analyst U.S. EPA, Washington, 1980—. Vol. Animal Welfare League of Arlington, Va., 1979—97, Fairfax County Pk. Authority, Alexandria, Va., 1990—2000. Mem.: Best Friends Animal Soc., Nature Conservancy. Avocations: gardening, animal welfare, reading. Home: 5004 Grimm Drive Alexandria VA 22304 Office: US EPA 4502T 1200 Pennsylvania Ave NW Washington DC 20460

BAILEY, LINDA KAREN, special education educator; b. Winthrop, Mass., Mar. 12, 1951; d. Wilbert Gould Bailey and Barbara Louise DeMott; 1 child, Shawnna Lee Clark. BA in English Lit., Southeastern Mass. U., North Dartmoutn, 1973; postgrad., Northeastern U., Boston, 1974—75, U. of Maine, 1984—2003. Cert. tchr. Maine, 2001. Autism cons. tchr. Auburn Sch. Dept., Maine, 1999—; family support worker SFW II KidsPeace New Eng., Lewiston, Maine, 2000—. Case mgmt. svcs. staff Auburn Sch. Dept., Auburn, Maine, 1999—, advisor ednl. technicians, 1999—, supervisor ABA summer sch., 2003—. Editor (contributing poet & co-editor): (poetry review) Northcoast Poetry Rev.; contbr. anthology Anthology of Poets No End to Fall River. Vol. Theater at Monmouth, Maine, 1994—2003, Spl. Family Weekend, Camden, Maine, 1984—2003. Mem.: Autism Soc. of Maine (assoc.; bd. of directors 2002—03). American Independent. Na. Avocations: writing, swimming, flute playing, reading. Home: PO Box 526 Monmouth ME 04259 Office: Auburn School Department 12 High St Auburn ME 04210 Personal E-mail: lsnog@aol.com. E-mail: lbailey@auburnschl.edu.me.

BAILEY, MARY KATHERINE, sculptor, writer; b. N.Y.C., Jan. 1, 1960; d. John Turner and Katherine (Gerwig) B.; m. Toby Stephen Welles. BA with honors, Brown U., 1982; MFA in Writing, Vt. Coll., 1999. Adj. prof. sculpture, Fairfield U., 1993-95; bd. dirs. Silvermine Guild Art Ctr., New Canaan, Conn., 1991-99. One person exhbns. include Art Place Gallery, Southport, Conn., 1987, Silvermine Guild Art Ctr., New Canaan, Conn., 1988, Anne Jaffe Gallery, Miami, 1989, Sound Shore Gallery, Stamford, Conn., 1991, Cast Iron Gallery, N.Y.C., 1992, Sacred Heart U., Fairfield, Conn., 1992, Housatonic Mus. Art, Bridgeport, Conn., 1993, Fairfield U., 1993.; in permanent collecions New Sch. Social Rsch., Housatonic Mus. Art, Zurich Reinsurance Ctr.; prodr., dir., writer: (video) The Surgery, 1994; prodr., dir., editor (video) The Culture of Food, 1998; contbr. short stories to Crescent Rev., Literal Latte, The New Renaissance, Bellingham Rev. Grantee New Eng. Found. Arts, 1993, Conn. Film and Video Competition Conn. Commn. on Arts and CPTV, 1995; recipient new voice fiction award The Writer's Voice, N.Y.C., 1997. Mem. Sculptors Guild, Silvermine Guild Art Ctr. Home: 240 Poverty Hollow Rd Redding CT 06896-2117

BAILEY, RITA MARIA, investment advisor, psychologist; b. Frankfurt, Germany; d. Ludwig and Gertrude (Cierniak) Fleischmann; m. William W. Bailey, Feb. 17, 1974; children: Anne Christine, Cynthia Patricia. BS in Psychology, Austin Peay U., 1975, MA in Psychology, 1977, postgrad., 1977-79. Cert. counselor, Tenn. Editor U.S. Army Spl. Warfare Inst., Ft. Bragg, N.C., 1967-74, edn. officer, 1979-82, Augsburg (Germany) Cmty. Ctr., 1982-85; pvt. practice counseling Leavenworth, Kans., 1985-90; pvt. practice investments, 1990—. Sr. investment advisor pvt. orgns., Washington, 1991—. Author: Extroversion and Introversion, 1978, Special Warfare Training Plan, 1981; author, editor tng. manual Foreign Small Arms, 1982. Dir. Energy Conservation Campaign, Clarksville, 1976; founder, dir. Women's Support Ctr., Leavenworth, 1986. Mem. Nat. Assn. Investors, Alpha Mu Gamma. Roman Catholic. Avocations: long distance swimming, gardening, German poetry.

BAILEY, STEPHANIE B.C. city health department administrator; BS, Clark U., Worchester, Mass.; MS in health svcs. adminstrn., Coll. of St. Francis; MD, Meharry Med. Coll., Nashville. Dir., health Metro Pub. Health Dept. of Nashville/Davidson Co., 1995—. Bd. dirs. Centerstone Cmty. Health Ctrs. Inc., 2002—. Mem. Nat. Adv. Com. on Rural Health, Nat. Adv. Com. for Elimination of Tuberculosis, Nat. Adv. Com. to CDC Dir. Recipient Excellence in Pub. Health award, ASTHO, 1999. Mem.: Nat. Assn. of County and City Health Officials (bd. mem.). Office: Metro Pub Health Dept 311 23rd Ave N Nashville TN 37203

BAILEY, SUE, federal agency administrator, osteopath; 1 child, Lee Bailey Hults. BA, U. Md., 1973; DO, Phila. Coll. Osteo. Medicine, 1977. Intern George Washington U. Hosp., Washington, 1978-81; resident Johns Hopkins U. Hosp., Balt., 1981-83; med. dir. in-patient program Washington Hosp. Ctr., 1983-85; v.p. Medlantic Healthcare Group, 1986-88; med. dir. Chevy Chase (Md.) Assocs. Inc., 1988-93; dep. asst. sec. def. for health affairs Dept. Def., Washington, 1994-95, asst. sec. for health affairs, 1998—. Mem. clin. faculty Georgetown U. Med. Sch., Washington, 1985-94. Lt. comdr. USNR. Office: Dept Def Office Health Affairs Room 3E346 1200 Defense Pentagon Rm 3e346 Washington DC 20301-1200

BAILEY, VICKY A. federal agency administrator; b. Indpls. BS, Purdue U.; postgrad., Ind. U., Indpls. Promotions dir. Glass Container divsn. Owens-Ill., Inc., Alton; asst. admissions officer Ind. U. Sch. Medicine; commr. Fed. Energy Regulatory Commn., 1993—2000; pres. PSI Energy, Inc., Ind., 2000—01; asst. secy. int. affairs and domestic policy U.S. Dept. Energy, Washington, 2001—. Rep. to bd. trustees N.AM. Electric Reliability Coun.; mem. exec. com. Gt. Lakes conv. Mid-Am. Regulatory Commrs. Conf.; mem. Keystone Ctr. Energy Bd.; mem. Harvard Electricity Policy Group. Mem. Ind. Coun. for Econ. Edn.; active Boys and Girls Club of Indpls.; past pres. Indpls. Pub. Schs. Edn. Found., Ind. Humanities Coun., Nat. Coalition of 100 Black Women. Recipient Ind. Sagamore of the Wabash award. Mem. Nat. Assn. Regulatory Utility Commrs. (exec. and electricity coms.). Republican. Office: US Dept Energy Policy & Int Affairs 1000 Independence Ave SW Washington DC 20585-0001

BAILEY, ZELDA CHAPMAN, hydrologist; b. Memphis, Aug. 2, 1949; d. John Franklin and Pearl Elizabeth (Skeens) Chapman; m. Charles Millard Bailey, June 3, 1972 (div. Dec. 1983); m. Patrick Tucci, Mar. 23, 1985; 1 child, Cara Nicole. BA in Geology, Ind. U., 1977. Cert. geologist, Ind.; cert. ground water profl., Nat. Water Well Assn.; registered profl. geologist, Tenn. Histologist, electron microscopist Ind. U. Med. Ctr., Indpls., 1967-76; hydrologic technician U.S. Geol. Survey, Indpls., 1977-79, hydrologist, 1979-84, Nashville, 1984-89, asst. dist. chief San Juan, PR, 1989-92, assoc. dist. chief Lakewood, Colo., acting dist. chief for Colo. and Wyo.; interim dir. Nat. Cave and Karst Rsch. Inst. Nat. Park Svc., 2001—03; dir. Boulder Labs Nat. Inst. Standards and Technologies, 2003—. Contbr. numerous articles to profl. jours. Mem. Am. Geophys. Union, Am. Assn. for Women in Sci., Internat. Assn. Hydrogeologists, Assn. Women Geoscientists. Avocations: photography, silver jewelry fabrication, needlework, gardening. Office: US Geol Survey WRD Bldg 53 MS 415 Denver Fed Ctr Lakewood CO 80225

BAILEY-MERSHON, GLENDA MARIAH, historian, educator, retired writer; b. Anderson, S.C., Mar. 8, 1949; d. Woodrow Wilson Bailey and Easter Ioa Covil; m. Edward Joseph Mershon, July 23, 1978; 1 child, Ansel Edward ; m. John Patrick Malone, Sept. 22, 1967 (div. Feb. 11, 1971); 1 child, John Walden Malone. BA, Knox Coll., 1974; MA, Governors State U., 1976. Rsch. assoc. Governors State U., U. Park, Ill., 1976—80; staff dir. Pk. Forest (Ill.) Hist. Project, 1980—82; planning rsch. assoc. Prairie State Coll., Chgo. Heights, Ill., 1983—85; asst. dir. pub. policy analysis program U. of Ill. at Chgo., Chgo., 1986—89, mem., women's studies tchg. collective, 1989—93; prin., owner Prairie Moon Books, Arlington Heights, Ill., 1993—99; pub. and editor Wild Dove Studio and Press, Palatine, Ill., 1993—2000; freelance writer and editor, 2000—. Mem. writing coop. Jane's Stories Press Found., Mount Prospect, Ill., 2000—; grantwriter and adv. bd. mem. 40th ACCORD Fla. Humanities Coun. Project, St. Augustine, Ill., 2003—; mem. adult adv. bd. Sisterspeak, Girl Scouts Ill. Crossroads Coun., Vernon Hills, Ill., 1998—2000. Author: (poetry) Shaconage/Blue Smoke, Birdtalk:Poems by Glenda Bailey-Mershon, (study guide) History of the American Women's Movement: A Study Guide with Essays; editor: (anthology) Jane's Stories II: An Anthology by Midwestern Women, Jane's Stories: An Anthology of Work by Midwestern Women, (nonfiction) The Activist's Campaign Notebook; author: Citizen's Guide to Zoning, Population Data for the Lao and Hmong: Park Forest, Illlinois. Established Ill. NOW archives U. of Ill. at Springfield, Springfield, Ill., 1999—2000; commr. Cable TV Commn., Park Forest, Ill., 1978—80; chmn. Com. for Non-partisan Local Govt., Park Forest, Ind., 1982—84; founding bd. mem. Pk. Forest Women's Conf., Park Forest, 1981—84. Named Outstanding Young Woman of Am., 1978; recipient Merit award, Ill. Hist. Soc., 1985. Mem.: NOW (mng. editor Ill. NOW Times 1991—94, bd. mem. legal and edn. fund 1997—2001, chmn. polit. action com. 1996—99, pres. Ill. 1994—97, pres. N.W. suburban chpt. 1992—94, v.p. Ill. 1986—87, pres. south suburban chpt. 1984—86, chmn. south suburban chpt. 1982—84, named Pioneering Ill. Woman 1999, Pres.'s award for leadership 1998), Unitarian-Universalists of St. Augustine, Phi Beta Kappa. Office: Jane's Stories Press Foundation PO Box 687 Mount Prospect IL 60056

BAILEY-STEIN, DEENA TAMARA, health care administrator; b. Haifa, Israel, June 13, 1947; came to U.S., 1960; d. Fred Ephraim and Devora (Glaser) Mansbacher; m. Wayne W. Bailey, Apr. 4, 1970 (div. 1977); 1 child, Devora Elyse; m. Randy Stein, Mar. 19, 1999. BS in Health Sci., U. Redlands, 1989; MHA, U. So. Calif., 1995. Mgr. dept. surgery Cedars-Sinai Med. Ctr., L.A., 1980-87, mgr. cardiovasc. intervention ctr., 1988-93; dir. Cardiology Mgmt. Svcs., 1993-94; adminstrv. resident UniHealth, Burbank, Calif., 1994-95; adminstrv. dir. UniHealth-Arroyo Seco Med. Group/Mgmt. Svcs., 1995—96; v.p., COO UniMed-Arroyo Seco Med. Group/Mgmt. Svcs., 1996—2000; dir. health svcs. Searchwest, Inc., L.A., 2001—02; v.p. bus. devel. JR Assocs., L.A., 2002—. Mem. Health Care Execs. So. Calif. (membership chair 2003—), Women in Health Adminstrn. (pres. 1993), Am. Coll. Cardiovasc. Adminstrs. (regional dir. 1990-92), U. So. Calif. Health Svcs. Adminstrs. Alumni Assn. (pres. 1996-97, v.p., chmn. mentoring program 1999-2001). Democrat. Jewish. Avocation: photography. Business E-Mail: deena@1jra.com.

BAILLOS, MARIANNE TKACH, secondary school educator; b. Cleve., Aug. 8, 1938; d. Michael Tkach and Mary Bugosh; children: Paul Michael, Peter Emanuel, Philip Andrew. BS, Mich. State U., 1960. Cert. tchr., Mich., Iowa, Va. Tchr. Singer Sewing Machine Co., Cleve., 1954; English tchr. Greece, 1960-61; tchr. Baldwin (Mich.) Pub. Schs., 1961-62, Waverly Pub. Schs., Lansing, Mich., 1962-67; mgr. real estate property Mason City, Iowa, 1978-88; area dir. Am. Cancer Soc., Mason City, 1987-89; tchr. Orange H.S., Orange County Schs., Orange, Va., 1991-92, Bassett H.S., Henry County Schs., Bassett, Va., 1992-95, Lancaster H.S., Lancaster County, Va., 1995-97, Dublin Mid. Sch., Pulaski County Schs., Pulaski, Va., 1997—. Pres. AAUW, Mason City, 1980-82; del. conf. Beijing, China, 2002. Mem.: AAUW (v.p. programs 1999—2001). Eastern Orthodox.

BAILYN, LOTTE, psychology and management educator; b. Vienna, July 17, 1930; came to U.S., 1937; d. Paul Felix Lazarsfeld and Marie (Jahoda) Albu; m. Bernard Bailyn, June 18, 1952; children: Charles, John. BA in Math. with high honors, Swarthmore Coll., 1951; MA in Social Psychology, Harvard U., 1953, PhD in Social Psychology, 1956; PhD (hon.), U. Piraeus, Greece, 2000. Rsch. assoc. Grad. Sch. Edn., Harvard U., Cambridge, Mass., 1956-57, rsch. assoc. dept. social rels., 1958-64, lectr., 1963-67; instr. dept. econs. and social sci. MIT, Cambridge, 1957-58, rsch. assoc. Sloan Sch. Mgmt., 1969-70, lectr., 1970-71, from sr. lectr. to prof., 1971-91, T Wilson prof. mgmt., 1991—, chair MIT faculty, 1997-99; acad. visitor Imperial Coll. Sci., Tech. and Medicine, London, 1991, 1995, 2000; disting. vis. prof. Radcliffe Coll., 1995-97. Trustee Cambridge Savs. Bank, 1975-98; mem. adv. coun. Suffolk U. Mgmt. Sch., Boston, 1983-86; mem. sr. coun. Leadership Devel. Inst., Rutgers U., 1986-89; panel mem. NAS, NRC, Washington, 1988-90; mem. task force in career devel. and maintenance IEEE, Washington, 1982-90; vis. scholar Imperial Coll. Sci. and Tech., London, 1982, New Hall, Cambridge (Eng.) U., 1986-87; scholar-in-residence Rockefeller Found. Study and Conf. Ctr., Bellagio, Italy, 1983; vis. fellow U. Auckland, N.Z., 1984. Author: Mass Media and Children, 1959, Living with Technology, 1980, Breaking the Mold: Women, Men, and Time in the New Corporate World, 1993; co-author: Working with Careers, 1984, Relinking Life and Work: Toward a Better Future, 1996, Beyond Work-Family Balance: Advancing Gender Equity and Workplace Performance, 2002; mem. editl. bd. Jour. Engring. and Tech. Mgmt., Cmty., Work and Family; contbr. chpts. to books and articles to profl. jours. Trustee Radcliffe Coll., 1974-79, Cambridge Fin. Group, Inc., 1998—; bd. dirs. Families and Work Inst., 1995—, Cambridge Savings Bank, 1998—. Recipient Grad. Soc. medal Radcliffe Coll., 1998, Everett Cherrington Hughes award for careers scholarship Acad. of Mgmt., 2003. Fellow APA; mem. Acad. Mgmt., Am. Sociol. Assn. Home: 170 Clifton St Belmont MA 02478-2604 Office: MIT Sloan Sch Mgmt 50 Memorial Dr Cambridge MA 02142-1347

BAIMA, JULIE MARTIN, special education educator; b. Lincolnton, N.C., July 26, 1969; d. Thomas Luther Martin and Grace Turbyfill Caudle; m. Charles Joseph Baima, Nov. 21, 1992; children: Madison Lyndsey, Ronald Thomas. BS, Ga. Coll., 1991, EdM, 1996; specialist in edn., Ga. Coll. and State U., 2000. Cert. early childhood edn. tchr., specific learning disabilities tchr., mental retardation specialist. Spl. edn. tchr. Washington County Bd. Edn., Sandersville, Ga., 1992—93, Bibb County Bd. Edn., Macon, Ga., 1993—2002, Monroe County Bd. Edn., Forsyth, Ga., 2002—. Mem.: NEA, Ga. Edn. Assn., Macon Jr. Woman's Club (1st v.p. 2000—02, pres. 2002—). Republican. Episcopalian. Avocations: walking, reading, scrapbooks. Home: 230 Northridge Dr Macon GA 31220

BAIMAN, GAIL, real estate broker; b. Bklyn., June 4, 1938; d. Joseph and Anita (Devon) Yalow; children: Steven, Susan, Barbara. Student, Bklyn. Coll., 1955-57. Lic. real estate broker, N.Y., Pa., Fla.; hypnotherapist, stress mgmt. cons.; firewalk instr. Pers.-pub. rels. dir. I.M.C., Inc., N.Y.C., 1970-72; pres., broker Gayle Baiman Assocs., Inc., N.Y.C., 1972-74; v.p., broker Tuit Mktg. Corp., Mt. Pocono, Pa., 1974-83; pres., broker Timeshare Sales, Inc., St. Petersburg/Orlando, Fla., 1983-98, founder, CEO Universal Rembrance U, Inc., 1998—. Author: Vacation Timesharing, A Real Estate, 1992. Mem. Am. Resort Developers Assn., Better Bus. Arbitration Assn., Internat. Resale Brokers Assn. (co-founder), Chmns. League, Better Bus. Bur. Arbitrators. E-mail: gbaiman@aol.com.

BAIN, LINDA L. academic administrator; BS in Phys. Edn. summa cum laude, Ill. State U., 1962, MS in Phys. Edn., 1968; PhD in Phys. Edn. and Learning Theory, U. Wis., 1974. Instr. Lowell Elem. Sch., Wheaton, Ill., 1962-64, East Peoria (Ill.) H.S., 1964-68, U. Mich., Ann Arbor, 1968-69; asst. prof. U. Ill., Chgo., 1969-75, U. Houston, 1975-78, assoc. prof., 1978-83, prof., 1983-88, chmn. dept. health, phys. edn. and recreation, 1980-82, assoc. dean rsch. Coll. Edn., 1982-88; prof. Calif. State U., Northridge, 1988-95, dean Sch. Comm., Health and Human Svcs., 1988-95, interim provost, v.p. academic affairs, 2003—; prof. San Jose (Calif.) State U., 1995—2000, provost, v.p. academic affairs, 1995—2000. Alderson lectr. U. Tex., 1982; Amy Morris Homans lectr. Nat. Assn. Phys. Edn. in Higher Edn., 1989; Ethel Martus Lawther lectr. U. N.C., Greensboro, 1992; Scholar lectr. Ill. State U., 1993; presenter in field. Co-author: Transition to Teaching: A Guide for the Beginning Teacher, 1983, The Curriculum Process in Physical Education, 1985, 2d edit., 1995; reviewer Rsch. Quar. for Exercise and Sport, 1977-95, Jour. Phys. Edn., Recreation and Dance, 1976-88; mem. editl. adv. bd. Youth and Soc., 1984-95, Jour. Phys. Edn., Recreation and Dance, 1984-87; editl. bd. Jour. Tchg. in Phys. Edn., 1985-95, Quest, 1991-94; book rev. editor Rsch. Quar. for Exercise and Sport, 1991-94; contbr. articles to profl. jours., chpts. to books. Bd. dirs. Am. Cancer Soc., San Fernando Valley, Calif., 1993-95; mem. health project policy bd. Calif. Phys. Edn., 1994-95; mem. met. bd. YMCA of Santa Clara Valley, 1998—; bd. dirs. Met. San Jose Collaborative for Acad. Excellence, 1998—; mem. hon. com. No. Exposure: New Art from Japan, San Jose Inst. Contemporary Art, 1999. Marie L. Carns fellow, 1972-73, Fellow AAHPERD, 1980, Am. Leadership Forum Silicon Valley, 1999; recipient Rsch. award So. Assn. Phys. Edn. of Coll. Women, 1983, Honor award AAHPERD, 1990, Jose Maria Cagigal Scholar lectr. Assn. Internat. Ecoles Superieures d'Edn. Physique, 1990, Disting. Adminstrn. award Nat. Assn. Phys. Edn. in Higher Edn., 1993, Alumni Achievement award Ill. State U., 1995, U. Wis. Sch. Edn., 1997, Tribute to Women in Industry award YWCA, Santa Clara Valley, 1999. Fellow Am. Acad. Kinesiology and Phys. Edn. Office: San Jose State U 1 Washington Sq San Jose CA 95192-0001

BAIN, MARISSA, social worker; b. Providence, Sept. 30, 1977; d. Bruce Alan and Laurie Eleanor Bain. BA, U. R.I., 1999; MSW, R.I. Coll., 2000. Cert. cmty. support prof. R.I. Social worker NRI Cmty. Svcs., Woonsocket, 1999—, program mgr., 2000—03. Vol. adv. Sexual Assault and Trauma Resource Ctr., Providence, 1997—99. Mem.: NASW, NOW (R.I. chpt.), Planned Parenthood Fedn. Am. Democrat. Home: 10 Josephine St Apt 207 North Providence RI 02904-5513

BAINBRIDGE, DONA BARDELLI, marketing professional; b. Irvington, NJ, Feb. 27, 1953; d. Alfred Bainbridge and Dona Ellen (Self) Bardelli; m. Harry M. Bainbridge, May 23, 1981 (dec.); 1 child, Harry Michael. Cert. de Langue, Sorbonne U., Paris, 1974; BA, U. Ky., 1975; MA in Internat. Studies, Am. U., 1978; MSc in Econs. and Social Planning in Devel. Countries, London Sch. Econs. Rsch. assoc. Woodrow Wilson Internat. Ctr. for Vis. Scholars, Washington, 1976-77, World Bank, Washington, 1977-79; legis. asst. to Congressman Marc Lincoln Marks Washington, 1979-80; itnernat. trade analyst Internat. Trade Adminstrn. U.S. Dept. Commerce, Washington, 1980-82; internat. mgmt. cons. Coopers and Lybrand, 1982-86; v.p. Bankers Trust Co. Internat. Pvt. Banking, 1986-88; sr. mktg. dir. internat. svcs. BDO Seidman, N.Y.C., 1988-90; founder, pres. D.H. Bainbriedge Assocs., 1990—. Chair nat. membership Am. Friends of London Sch. Econs., 1981-83, nat. bd. dirs., 1982-84, 94-96; chmn. mem. com.; mem. mktg. com., bd. dirs., vice chair Camp Sloane YMCA, Lakeville, Conn., 2000; chair Washington Com. Women's Studies in Religion program Div. Sch. Harvard U., 1996-98; trustee, co-chair capital campaign The Washington Episcopal Sch., Bethesda, Md., 1996-98; trustee The Town Hill Sch., Lakeville, Conn., 1999, N.W. Ctr. for Family Svcs., Lakeville, 2002; mem. adv. bd., chmn. White Plains Salvation Army, 1992-93; mem. bd. trustees Northwest Ctr. for Family Svcs., Lakeville, 2002. Mem. Soc. Internat. Devel. (D.C. chpt.), Bus. and Profl. Women's Clubs Am. (acad. scholar 1971), Nat. Press Club, Fin. Women's Assn. N.Y., Kiwanis. Democrat. Lutheran.

BAINBRIDGE, SUSAN W. elementary school educator; d. Frederick F and LaNoma Bainbridge; m. Lee Winder; children: Marissa Winder, Zachary Winder. BA in Art, St. Andrews Presbyn. Coll., N.C., 1976. Owner Art Start, San Diego, 1988—. Exhibitions include Visual Alchemy. Art mentor San Diego and Poway schs., San Diego, 1988—96. Recipient Purchase award, ALM Studio, 1999. Mem.: Rancho Bernardo Art Assn., San Diego Watercolor Soc., Ramona Art Guild, Arts Partnership, Artist's Way (founding), Phi Theta Kappa. Personal E-mail: susan@artstart1.com.

BAINS, LESLIE ELIZABETH, banker; b. Glen Ridge, N.J., July 28, 1943; d. Pliny Otto and Dorothy Ethel (Keeley) Tawney; m. Harrison Mackellar Bains Jr.; Harrison III, Tawney Elizabeth. BA, Am. U., 1965. Asst. treas. Citicorp, N.Y.C., 1965-73; v.p. Mfrs. Hanover, N.Y.C., 1973-80; v.p., divsn. exec. Chase Manhattan Bank, N.Y.C., 1980-86, v.p., group exec., 1986-87, sr. v.p. group exec., 1987-91; mng. dir. Global Pvt. Banking Group Citibank, N.Y.C., 1991-93; exec. v.p. Republic Nat. Bank, N.Y.C., 1993-2000; sr. exec. v.p. HSBC Bank USA, N.Y.C., 2000—, mem. sr. mgmt. com. Bd. dirs., chair fin. com. Interplast, 1991. Chmn. Ednl. Cable Consortium, Summit, NJ, 1987—91; bd. dirs., chair fin. com. Interplast Found.; bd. dirs. Junior Achievement of N.Y.; mem. exec. com., bd. dirs., chair devel. com. Roundabout Theater; bd. trustees Am. U., 1994—, vice chair bd. trustees, 2001—; bd. dirs. Jr. Achievement, N.Y.C., 1996—, chair investment com.; bd. visitors Terry Sanford Inst. Pub. Policy Duke U., Duke U. Med. Sch. Named Achiever of Yr. YWCA, 1985, One of Top 100 Women in Corp. Am., Bus. Month., 1989. Fellow Fgn. Policy Assn; mem. Am. Bankers Assn. (bd. dirs. pvt. banking coun.), Fin. Women Internat. (vice chmn. Edn. Found. 1980-81, treas. 1981-83, v.p. 1983-84, pres. 1984-85), Fin. Women's Assn., Women and Founds., Coun. Fgn. Rels., The Econ. Club of N.Y. Office: HSBC Bank USA 452 5th Ave New York NY 10018-2706*

BAINTON, DOROTHY FORD, pathology educator, researcher; b. Magnolia, Miss., June 18, 1933; d. Aubrey Ratcliff and Leta (Brumfield) Ford; m. Cedric R. Bainton, Nov. 28, 1959; children: Roland J., Bruce G., James H. BS, Millsaps Coll., 1955; MD, Tulane U. Sch. of Medicine, 1958; MS, U. Calif., San Francisco, 1966. Postdoctoral rsch. fellow U. Calif., San Francisco, 1963-66, postdoctoral rsch. pathologist, 1966-69, asst. prof. pathology, 1969-75, assoc. prof., 1975-81, prof. pathology, 1981—, chair pathology, 1987-94, vice chancellor acad. affairs, 1994—. Mem. Inst. of Medicine, NAS, 1990—. NIH grant, 1978-98. Fellow AAAS, Am. Acad. Arts & Scis.; mem. FASEB (bd. dirs.), Am. Soc. for Cell Biology, Am. Soc. Hematology, Am. Soc. Histochemists and Cytochemists, Am. Assn. of Pathologists. Democrat. Mem. Soc. Of Friends. Office: Office of Acad Affairs U Calif San Francisco Med Scis Bldg Rm 115 San Francisco CA 94143-0001 E-mail: baintond@chanoff.ucsf.edu.

BAIR, SHEILA COLLEEN, federal agency administrator; b. Wichita, Kans., Apr. 3, 1954; d. Albert E. and Clara F. (Brenneman) B.; m. Scott Cooper; 1 child, Preston Carlos. BA in Philosophy, U. Kans., 1975, JD, 1978. Bar: Kans. 1979. Teaching fellow Sch. Law, U. Ark., Fayetteville,

1978-79; atty.-advisor HEW, Kansas City, Mo., 1979-81; legal and policy advisor Office of Senator Bob Dole, Washington, 1981-86; of counsel Kutak, Rock & Campbell, Washington, 1986-87; dir. rsch. Bob Dole for Pres., Kans., 1987-88; legis. counsel N.Y. Stock Exch., Washington, 1988-91; commr. Commodity Futures Trading Commn., Washington, 1991—, acting chmn., 1993; Asst Secy Financial Inst Dept Treasury, Washington, 2001—. Candidate U.S. Ho. of Reps. from 5th Kans. dist., 1990; mem. bd. govs. Sch. Law, U. Kans., 1990-93; bd. dirs. Women's Campaign Fund, 1991—. Mem. ABA. Democrat. Office: US Dept Treasury Financial Insts 1500 Pennsylvania Ave NW Washington DC 20220

BAIR, SUSANNE PAULETTE, university foundation administrator; b. Rochester, Ind., Nov. 21, 1958; d. Richard Paul and M. Jeanette (Schluntz) B. BS, Ind. State U., 1981, MS, 1985; D of Phys. Edn., Ind. U., 1991. Athletic dir. Attica (Ind.) H.S., 1982-88; assoc. athletic dir. N.E. Mo. State U., Kirksville, 1991-93; dir. devel. and external affairs Sch. Health, Phys. Edn., Recreation, Ind. U., Bloomington, 1993—. Mem. alumni bd. Sch. Health, Phys. Edn., Recreation, Ind. U., Bloomington, 1993—. Trustee Ind. U., Bloomington, 1989-91; bd. dirs. Luth. Campus Ministry, Bloomington, 1995—. Mem. Rotary. Avocations: reading, woodworking, gardening. Office: Ind U Found PO Box 500 1500 N State Rd 46 Bypass Bloomington IN 47402-0500 Home: 1300 N Russell Rd Bloomington IN 47408-9792

BAIRD, LAUREL COHEN, clinical nurse; b. Chgo., Dec. 1, 1943; d. Carl Eugene and Joan Adele (Arenz) Patterson; m. Sidney Henry Cohen, June 29, 1968 (div. Nov. 1981); children: Elizabeth Ann Cohen, David Arthur Patterson, Douglas Edward, Deborah Sue; m. Frederick Joseph Foti, Jan. 19, 1985 (div. June 1994) m. Jack W. Baird (Nov. 10, 2001). Diploma in nursing, Swedish Covenant, 1967; BS, Moody Bible Inst., 1976. RN, N.J., Md. Staff nurse Overlook Hosp., Summit, N.J., 1980-82; pub. health nurse Patient Care Svc., West Orange, N.J., 1982-83; hospice nurse The Hospice, Inc., Montclair, N.J., 1984-92; fin. svc. rep. Primerica Fin. Svcs., Duluth, Ga., 1985-89; coord. home care Vis. Nurse Assn. Essex Valley, East Orange, N.J., 1993-96; Medicare case mgr. Aetna US Healthcare Cmty. Outreach, Fairfield, NJ, 1996-99; on-site nurse Johns Hopkins Cmty. Physicians, 1999—2001, Sun Plus Home Care, Pleasant Hill, Calif., 2001; hospice nurse care mgr. Sutter VNA and Hospice, Pleasant Hill, 2002—. State coord. La Leche League, N.J., 1976-78; hospice vol. The Hospice, Inc., 1992-98; mem. MADD, Rep. Presdl. Task Force, 1989. Lt. (j.g.) USNR, 1967-69. Mem. Adoptees Liberty Movement Assn. (spokesman 1977-83), DAR. Republican. Presbyterian. Avocations: orchid culture, gardening, marathoning, speed walking, piano. Home: 303 Eastgate Lane Martinez CA 94553- E-mail: lolly1331@aol.com.

BAIRD, LOURDES G. federal judge; b. 1935; BA with highest honors, UCLA, 1973, JD with honors, 1976. Asst. U.S. atty. U.S. Dist. Ct. (ctrl dist.) Calif., L.A., 1977-83; ptnr. Baird & Quadros, 1983-84, Baird, Munger & Myers, 1984-86; judge East L.A. Mcpl. Ct., 1986-87; adj. prof. law Loyola U., L.A., 1986-90; judge L.A. Mcpl. Ct., 1987-88, L.A. Superior Ct., 1988-90; U.S. atty. ctrl. dist. Calif., 1990-92; U.S. atty. U.S. Dist. Ct. (ctrl. dist.) Calif., L.A., 1990-92, judge, 1992—. Faculty civil RICO program Practicing Law Inst., San Francisco, 1984-85, western regional program Nat. Inst. Trial Advocacy, Berkeley, Calif., 1987-88; adj. prof. trial advocacy Loyola U., L.A., 1987-90. Recipient Silver Achievement award for the professions YWCA, 1994; named Woman of Promise, Hispanic Womens' Coun., 1991, Alumnus of Yr., UCLA Sch. Law, 1991. Mem. [illegible] Calif. Women Lawyers, Hispanic Nat. Bar Assn., UCLA Sch. Law alumni Assn. (pres. 1984). Office: US Dist Ct Ctrl Dist Calif Edward R Roybal Bldg 255 E Temple St Ste 770 Los Angeles CA 90012-3334

BAIRD, PATRICIA ANN, physician, educator; b. Rochdale, Eng. came to Can., 1955; d. Harold and Winifred (Cainen) Holt; m. Robert Merrifield Baird, Feb. 22, 1964; children— Jennifer Ellen, Brian Merrifield, Bruce Andrew BSc with gen. honors in biol. sci., McGill U., 1959, MD, CM, 1963; DSc (hon.), McMaster U., 1991; D Univ. (hon.), U. Ottawa, 1991; LLD (hon.), Wilfrid Laurier U., 2000. Intern Royal Victoria Hosp., Montreal, Que., Can., 1963-64; resident, fellow in pediat. Vancouver Gen. Hosp., B.C., Can., 1964-67; instr. pediat. U. B.C., Vancouver, 1968-72, from asst. prof. to prof., 1972-94, Univ. Killam Disting. prof., 1994—; head dept. med. genetics Grace Hosp., Vancouver, 1981-89, Children's Hosp., Vancouver, 1981-89, Health Scis. Centre Hosp., 1986-89. Med. cons. B.C. Health Surveillance Registry, 1977-90; chmn. genetics grants com. Med. Rsch. Coun., Ottawa, Ont., Can., 1982-87, mem. coun., 1987-90; mem. Nat. Adv. Bd. on Sci. and Tech. to Fed. Govt., 1987-91; mem. genetic predisposition study steering com. Sci. Coun. Can., 1987-90; chair Royal Commn. on New Reproductive Technologies, 1989-93; co-chair Nat. Forum Sci. and Tech. Couns., 1991; v.p. Can. Inst. for Advanced Rsch., 1991-2002, vice chmn. bd., 2002--; bd. dirs. Biomed. Rsch. Centre, 1986-89; bd. govs. U. B.C., 1984-90; temporary cons. WHO, 1999, 2000, 01, mem. human genetics ELSI planning group, 2000-02, mem. expert adv. panel on human genetics, 2002--. Contbr. articles to med. jours. Bd. govs. U. B.C., 1984-90. Decorated officer Order of Can., 2000, Order of B.C., 1992; recipient Commemorative medal for Confedn. of Can., 1992, Queen's Golden Jubilee medal, 2002. Fellow RCP Can., Royal Soc. Can., Can. Coll. Med. Geneticists (v.p. 1984-86); mem. Am. Soc. Human Genetics (chair nominating com. 1987-89), B.C. Med. Assn., Can. Med. Assn., Genetics Soc. Can., Genetic Epidemiology (adv. bd. 1991-94), Internat. Fedn. of Gyn. and Obs. (mem. ethics com. 1997-99). Avocations: skiing, cycling, music. Office: U BC Dept Med Genetics Vancouver BC Canada V6T 1Z3 Business E-Mail: pbaird@interchange.ubc.ca.

BAIRD, PENNY DRUE, interior designer; b. N.Y.C., July 19, 1951; d. Philip Robert and Terri Baird; m. Fred Deutsch, Dec. 31, 1991; children: Alexander Baird Deutsch, Benjamin Baird Deutsch, Philip Baird Deutsch; 1 child, Adam Baird Alpert. BA, U. Rochester, 1973; PsychD, Yeshiva U., 1991; attended, NY School of Interior Design. Pres. Dessins LLC, N.Y.C., 1982—. Archtl. Digest, 1997, 1998, 2000. Pres. City Meals on Wheels, N.Y.C., 1985—90; mem. women's com. N.Y. Hosp., N.Y.C., 1994—; mem. women's bd. Albert Einstein Coll. Medicine, N.Y.C., 1990—. Mem.: Phi Beta Kappa. Office: Dessins LLC 787 Madison Ave New York NY 10021*

BAIRD, ZOË, foundation president, lawyer; b. Bklyn., June 20, 1952; d. Ralph Louis and Naomi (Allen) B.; m. Paul Gewirtz, June 8, 1986; 2 children. AB, U. Calif., Berkeley, 1974, JD, 1977. Bar: Washington, 1979, Calif. 1977, Conn. 1989. Law clk. Hon. Albert Wollenberg, San Francisco, 1977-78; atty., advisor Office Legal Counsel U.S. Dept. Justice, Washington, 1979-80; assoc. counsel to Pres., The White House, Washington, 1980-81; assoc., then ptnr. O'Melveny & Myers, Washington, 1981-86; counsellor, staff exec. GE, Fairfield, Conn., 1986-90; v.p., gen. counsel Aetna Life & Casualty, Hartford, 1990-93, sr. v.p., gen. counsel, 1993-96; pres. Markle Found., N.Y.C., 1998—. Bd. dirs. Chubb Corp. Bd. dirs. James A. Baker III Inst. for Pub. Policy, Lawyers for Children Am., Brookings Inst., Save the Children. Mem. Am. Law Inst., Coun. on Fgn. Rels. Office: Markle Found 10 Rockefeller Plaza 16th Fl New York NY 10020-1903 E-mail: info@markle.org.*

BAIRSTOW, FRANCES KANEVSKY, arbitrator, mediator, educator; b. Racine, Wis., Feb. 19, 1920; d. William and Minnie (DuBow) Kanevsky; m. Irving P. Kaufman, Nov. 14, 1942 (div. 1949); m. David Steele Bairstow, Dec. 17, 1954; children: Dale Owen, David Anthony. Student, U. Wis., 1937-42; BS, U. Louisville, 1949; student, Oxford U., England, 1953-54; postgrad., McGill U., Montreal, Que., Can., 1958-59. Rsch. economist U.S. Senate Labor-Mgmt. Subcom., Washington, 1950-51; labor edn. specialist U. P.R., San Juan, 1951-52; chief wage data unit WSB, Washington, 1952-53; labor rsch. economist Can. Pacific Ry. Co., Montreal, Canada, 1956-58; asst. dir. indsl. rels. ctr. McGill U., 1960-66, assoc. dir., 1966-71, dir., 1971-85, lectr., indsl. rels. dept. econs., 1960-72, from asst. prof. to assoc. prof. faculty mgmt., 1972—83, prof., 1983-85; lectr. Stetson Law Sch., Fla.; spl. master Fla. Pub. Employees Rels. Commn., 1985-97. Cons. Nat. Film Bd. Can., 1965—69; arbitrator Que. Consultative Coun. Panel Arbitrators, 1968—83, Ministry Labour and Manpower, 1971—83, United Air Lines and Assn. Flight Attendants, 1990—95, Am. Airlines and Transport Workers Union, 1997—98, State U. Sys. Fla., 1990—2003, FDA, 1996—98, Social Security Adminstrn., 1996—2003, Am. Airlines, 1997—, Tampa Gen. Hosp., 1996—, Cargo Internat. Airlines, 2001, Govt. of Fla. and Fla. State Police, 2002—, Bell South and Comm. Workers Am., 2003—, USAF at Warner Robins and AFGE, 2003—; mediator Can. Pub. Svc. Staff Rels. Bd., 1973—85, So. Bell Tel., 1985—, AT&T and Comm. Workers Am., 1986—; cons. on collective bargaining arbitration OECD, Paris, 1979. Contbg. columnist: Montreal Star, 1971—85. Chmn. Nat. Inquiry Commn. Wider-Based Collective Bargaining, 1978; dep. commr. essential svcs. Province of Que., 1976—81. Fulbright fellow, 1953—54. Mem.: Ctrl. Fla. Indsl. Rels. Rsch. Assn. (pres. 1999), Nat. Acad. Arbitrators (bd. govs. 1977—80, program chmn. 1982—83, v.p. 1986—88, nat. coord. 1987—90), Indsl. Rels. Rsch. Assn. Am. (mem. exec. bd. 1965—68, chmn. nominating com. 1977), Can. Indsl. Rels. Rsch. Inst. (mem. exec. bd. 1965—68). Home and Office: 1430 Gulf Blvd Apt 507 Clearwater FL 33767-2856

BAJCSY, RUZENA, computer engineer; MSEE, Slovak Tech. U., 1957, PhD, 1967; PhD in Artificial Intelligence, Stanford U., 1972. Asst. prof. dept. computer and info. sci. U. Pa., 1972—77, assoc. prof., 1977—84, prof., 1984—, chmn. dept. computer and info. sci., 1985—90, head GRASP Lab.; asst. dir. Directorate for Computer and Info. Sci. and Engring. NSF; prof., dir. Ctr. for Info. Tech. Rsch. in the Interest of Society, U. Calif., Berkeley, 2003—. Mem. rev. bd. computer sci. dept. Stanford U., 1997. Contbr. articles to profl. publs. Fellow: AAAI, IEEE; mem.: NAE, Computer Rsch. Assn. Women, Nat. Inst. Medicine. Office: Ctr for Info Tech Rsch in Interest of Society 284 Herast Meml Mining Bldg MC 1764 Berkeley CA 94720-1800 Business E-Mail: bajcsy@eecs.berkeley.edu.

BAJOIE, DIANA E. state legislator; b. July 8, 1948; Former mem. La. State Ho. Reps. from 91st dist.; mem. La. State Senate, 1991—. Alt. del. Dem. Nat. Party Conf., 1978. Office: La State Senate State Capitol PO Box 15168 New Orleans LA 70175-5168

BAJWA, SHAZIA, sociologist; b. Karachi, Sindh, Pakistan, Aug. 2, 1974; arrived in U.S., 1987; d. Manzur Ahmed and Shamsa Bajwa; m. Babur Ahmed, Aug. 3, 1997. cert. in women studies, BA in Sociology cum laude, postgrad., Fla. Atlantic U., 2000—. Spkr. in field. Mem.: NOW, Am. Sociol. Assn., Alpha Kappa Delta, Golden Key. Home: 888 E 96th St Apt 2-I Brooklyn NY 11236

BAKAKOS, DIANA, middle school educator; b. N.Y.C., Apr. 2, 1952; d. Michael and Catherine (Itsines) Constant; m. Constantine Bakakos, Nov. 24, 1974; children: Chris Fotis, Vikki. BA with honors, Coll. of S.I., 1973, MS in Edn., 1976; PhD in Psychology, Neotarian Coll. of Philosophy, 1979; MS in Computer Edn., L.I. U., 1987. Tchr. I.S. 391 Bd. of Edn., Bklyn., 1978—. Instr. adult edn. Bklyn. Coll., 1988; adj. prof. Fordham U., Bronx, 1990; tchr. asst. Peer Intervention Program, N.Y.C., 1995; instr. grad. credits QUIPP N.Y.C. Pub. Schs., Bklyn., 1990. Civilian vol. N.Y.C. Police Dept., Bklyn., 1978; mem. Pellina Brotherhood Assn., Bklyn., 1970—, [illegible] Assn. of Can. and N.Am., Bklyn., 1978—, Hellenic Am. Edn. Assn., N.Y.C., 1982. Recipient Tchr. of Yr. Arista, 1988, N.Y. Alliance award, 1990, Wall of Tolerance hon., 2002, UFT Del., 2003. Mem. Doctorate Assn. of N.Y. Educators, United Fedn. of Tchrs. (chpt. mem.-at-large), Epsilon Delta Chi. Democrat. Greek Orthodox. Avocations: travel, swimming, dance, art, word games. Home: 8620 21st Ave Brooklyn NY 11214-4004

BAKEMAN, JOANNE, alcohol/drug abuse services professional, educator; b. Syracuse, N.Y., June 24, 1945; d. Willard Oliver Bakeman and Mary Elizabeth Hallinan; m. Ronald Anthony Cocciole, Sept. 4, 1965 (div. June 1987); children: Claire Cocciole, Christa Cocciole, Carrie Cocciole. BA in History and Govt., Rosary Hill Coll. (now Daemen Coll.), 1966; AAS in Nursing, Onondaga C.C., Syracuse, N.Y., 1973; MS in Health Edn., SUNY, Cortland, 1978; credential in alcohol/substance abuse counseling, Syracuse U., 1990. RN N.Y., CASAC, N.Y. Social studies tchr. Syracuse City Sch. Dist., 1968—73; RN Crouse Hosp., Syracuse, 1973—80, substance abuse therapist, 1988—91; dir. Ctr. for Holistic Living, Syracuse, 1980—87; pvt. practice substance abuse therapist Syracuse, Pulaski, Fulton, NY, 1987—; alcohol/drug abuse prevention edn. program tchr./counselor Marcellus N.E. Sys. Minoa Schs., 1987—88, 1991—94; job coach for substance abusers JOBS Plus!, Syracuse, 1994—. Chair admission and incidents bd. Transitional Living Svcs., Syracuse, 1995—; bd. dirs. Jericho Rehab. Cmty., Syracuse. Columnist: Mind/Body Connection, 1989—92; editor: Ctr. for Holistic Living Newsletter, 1982—87. Dist. com. woman Onondaga County Dem. Com., Town of Cicero, 1969—80. Mem.: Pulaski Hist. Assn., Town Onondaga Hist. Assn., N.Y. State Fedn. Alcohol Counselors, Nat. Assn. Drug/Alchol Counselors. Avocations: singing, dance, camping, hiking, travel. Home: 202 E Patricia North Syracuse NY 13212

BAKER, ALDEN, artist; b. Manhattan, N.Y., Jan. 10, 1928; d. Samuel Burtis Baker and Grace Whalley Higgins; m. Robert Oppenheim, Aug. 21, 1963 (dec. June 1986); 1 child, Jessica Oppenheim. Cert., Berkeley Secretarial Sch., 1948; student, Cape Sch. Art, summer 1957-63, Art Students League, N.Y.C., 1965-66. Reporter, ch. and sch. editor Montclair (N.J.) Times, 1951-53; publicity dir. Newark Mus., 1953-56; editor, pub. rels. dir. Assn. Jr. Leagues Am., N.Y.C., 1956-64. Pastel demonstrator, Xian, China, 1997. Exhbns. include Manhattan's Lincoln Ctr., LEver House, Salmagundi Club, Pen and Brush Club, Nat. Arts Club, Allied Artists Am., Catherine Lorillard Wolfe Art Club, Pastel Soc. Am., Hudson Valley Art Assn., The Queens, Bergen and Hammond Mus., Copley Gallery, Boston; curator: The Best of Pastel II, 1999; featured in Am. Artist Mag., 1995. Mem. Pastel Soc. Am. (bd. dirs. 1994-2000, signature, critiques chmn., bd. dirs., Mr. and Mrs. Andrew Giffuni award 1999), Pen and Brush, Inc. (chmn. pastel sect. 1997-2000, solo exhbn. award), Hudson Valley Art Assn., Am. Artist Profl. League (various awards), Art Ctr. N.J. (pres., newsletter editor, exhbn. chair), Salmagundi Club (Dianne Bernhard Gold medal 2000) Unitarian Universalist. Home: 100 Stone Hill Rd Apt P12 Springfield NJ 07081-2154

BAKER, ANITA, singer; b. Toledo, Jan. 26, 1958; m. Walter Bridgeforth, Jr., Dec. 24, 1988; 1 child, Walter Baker Bridgeforth. Mem. funk band Chapter 8, 1978-80; receptionist Quin & Budajh, Detroit, 1980-82; ind. singer, songwriter, 1982—. Rec. artist: (with Chapter 8) I Just Wanna Be Your Girl, 1980, (solo albums) The Songstress, 1983, Rapture, 1986 (Grammy award for best rhythm and blues vocal performance 1987), Giving You the Best That I Got, 1988 (Grammy awards for best rhythm and blues song, 1988, best rhythm and blues performance, female, single, 1988, best album, 1989), Compositions, 1990 (Grammy award for best rhythm and blues performance, 1990), Rhythm of Love, 1994 (Grammy award nominee for best album 1995, best female vocal 1995, best song 1995); songs include No More Tears, Angel, Caught Up in the Rapture, Sweet Love (Grammy award best rhythm and blues song 1987), Same Ol' Love, You Bring Me Joy, Been So Long, No One in the World. Recipient Grammy award gospel, soul, best performance, duo, group, choir or chorus, 1987, NAACP Image award, best female vocalist and best album of yr. Office: Atlantic Records # 900 9229 W Sunset Blvd # 900 West Hollywood CA 90069-3402 also: 8216 Tivoli Cove Dr Las Vegas NV 89128-7446

BAKER, ANN LONG, language educator; b. Shelbyville, Ind., Sept. 2, 1954; d. Martin Meredith Cherry and Lois Jayne Slaton; m. Scott Elliott Baker, Aug. 23, 1975; children: Kyle Martin, Holly Alison. BA with distinction in Spanish Edn., Purdue U., 1976; MA Edn., U. Evansville, 1982. Lectr. in Spanish U. Evansville, Ind., 1984—2000, asst. prof. in Spanish, 2000—, chair Dept. Fgn. Langs., 2003—. Interpreter Pan Am. Games, Indpls., 1987. Active Castle H.S. PTO, Castle H.S. Band Boosters Orgn. Mem.: Ind. Fgn. Lang. Tchrs. Assn., Soc. Hispanic Am. (past pres., treas.), Am. Coun. Tchg. of Fgn. Langs., Am. Assn. Tchrs. of Spanish and Portuguese, Kappa Delta Pi, Alpha Lambda Delta, Phi Sigma Iota, Sigma Delta Pi, Phi Beta Kappa, Phi Kappa Phi. Home: 7277 Nottingham Dr Newburgh IN 47630 Office: U Evansville 1800 Lincoln Ave Evansville IN 47722 Office Phone: 812-479-2196. Business E-Mail: ab39@evansville.edu.

BAKER, BETTY LOUISE, retired secondary school educator; b. Chgo., Oct. 17, 1937; d. Russell James and Lucille Juanita (Timmons) B. BE, Chgo. State U., 1961, MA, 1964; PhD, Northwestern U., 1971. Cert. tchr. secondary and elem. grades 3-8 math., Ill. Tchr. math. Harper H.S., Chgo., 1961-70, Hubbard H.S., Chgo., 1970-94, also chmn. dept.; ret., 1994. Part-time instr. Moraine Valley C.C., 1982-83, 84-86, 94—; reader AP calculus exams. Ednl. Testing Svc. Contbr. articles to profl. jours. Cultural arts chmn. Hubbard Parents-Tchrs.-Students Assn., 1974-76, 1st v.p., program chmn., 1977-79, 82-84, pres. 1979-81; organist Hope Luth Ch., 1964-95, accompanist S.W. Luth. Chorus, 1987—; organist and choir dir. Faith Luth. Ch., Oak Lawn, 1995—. Univ. fellow, 1969-70. Mem. Nat. Coun. Tchrs. Math., Ill. Coun. Tchrs. Math., Chgo. Tchrs. Union, Nat. Coun. Parents and Tchrs. (life), Sch. Sci. and Math. Assn., Am. Guild of Organists, Luth. Collegiate Assn., Walther League Hiking Club, Met. Math. Club Chgo., Kappa Mu Epsilon, Rho Sigma Tau, Mu Alpha Theta (sponsors), Kappa Delta Pi, Pi Lambda Theta, Phi Delta Kappa. Home: 6330 Pine Ridge Dr Apt 1D Tinley Park IL 60477-4928 E-mail: bakermus@aol.com.

BAKER, BRIDGET DOWNEY, publishing executive; b. Eugene, Oreg., Sept. 14, 1955; d. Edwin Moody and Patricia Baker; m. Guy Dominique Wood, June 30, 1977 (div. Oct. 1981); m. Raymond Keith Kincaid, June 27, 1987; 1 child, Jacob Kincaid 1 stepchild, Benjamin Kincaid. BA in English, French and Theatre, Lewis and Clark Coll., 1977; MA in Journalism, U. Oreg., 1985. Circulation dist. supr. The Register-Guard, Eugene, 1978-80, pub. relations coordinator, 1980-83, promotion dir., 1983-86, mktg. dir., 1986-88; corp. pub. rels. dir., 1989—. Bd. dirs. Guard Pub. Co., Lane Met. Partnership. Bd. dirs. Art Found. Western Oreg., 1995—, chmn., 1997—99; pres. Baker Family Found., 1998—; bd. dirs. Wilani Coun. Camp Fire, 1982—88, pres. bd. dirs., 1986—88; bd. dirs. Lane County United Way, 1982—88, cmty. info. com. chairperson, 1982—84, chair planning com., 1987—88; bd. dirs. Eugene Opera, 1988—91, pres. bd. dirs., 1990—91; bd. dirs. Lane CC Found., 1995—97. Named Woman of the Yr., Lane County Coun. Orgns., 1994; recipient 1st pl. advt. award, Editor and Pub. Mag., 1984, 1st pl. TV promotion, 1st pl. newspaper rsch. award, 1988, Best Mktg. Idea/Campaign award, Oreg. Newspaper Pub. Assn., 1984, 1985. Mem.: Pub. Rels. Soc. Am. (pres. greater Oreg. chpt. 1995—96, Spotlight award 1986), Internat. Mktg. Assn. (bd. dirs. western region 1986—88, internat. bd. dirs. 1995—2001, 1st pl. Best in the West awards 1983—91), U. Oreg. Alumni Assn. (bd. dirs. 1990—93), Eugene C. of C. (bd. dirs. 1989—92), Eugene Yacht Club, Downtown Athletic Club, Town Club (bd. dirs. 1995—97), Zonta Internat. (pres. Eugene Club 1994—96, area dir. 1997—98, lt. gov. Dist. 8 1998—2000, gov. 2000—02, internat. pub. rels. chair 2002—, Woman of the Yr. 2002). Republican. Avocations: sailing, folk dance, outdoor activities, piano. Office: Guard Pub Co PO Box 10188 Eugene OR 97440-2188

BAKER, BRINDA ELIZABETH GARRISON, infectious disease nurse; b. Groveland, Ga., May 9, 1946; d. Archie and Nora Lee (Haynes) Garrison; m. Jerome Baker, Feb. 1970 (div. 1972); children: Katrina Lenyse Adams, Kelbert Lenard Adams. Student, Savannah (Ga.) State Coll., 1964-68; LPN, Savannah Tech. Sch., 1968; ADN, Armstrong State Coll., 1984, BSN, 1990; postgrad., Armstrong Atlantic State U. RN, Ga.; cert. provider BLS, Am. Heart Assn. LPN Candler Gen. Hosp., Savannah, 1968-72, staff nurse Cross Country Traveling Corps, 1990; LPN Ga. Regional Hosp., Savannah, 1972-74, sr. staff nurse, 1989-92; LPN St. Joseph Hosp., Savannah, 1974-84, staff nurse, 1984-90; sr. nurse, clinic supr. Chatham County Health Ctr., Savannah, 1992-95, clinic supr., 1995—. Part-time clin. instr. Armstrong State Coll., Savannah, 1991—. Mem. ANA, Ga. Nurses Assn., Assn. Nurses in AIDS Care. Democrat. Roman Catholic. Avocations: bowling, reading, gardening, music, sports. Home: 1307 E 71st St Savannah GA 31404-5735 Office: Chatham County Health Dept 2 Wheeler St Savannah GA 31405

BAKER, CARLENE POFF, real estate agent, reporter; b. Blytheville, Ark., Sept. 29, 1934; d. Carl Allen and Albie Elizabeth (Ryan) Poff; m. William T. Baker, July 7, 1956 (dec. Oct. 11, 1992); 1 child, Lisa Kay. Student, Miss. County C.C., 2003—. Legal sec. Reid & Roy, Attys., Blytheville, 1951—60; co-owner Baker Printing, Blytheville, 1961—82; real estate sales assoc. Logan Real Estate, Blytheville, 1982—; hearing reporter Social Security Adminstrn. Office Hearings and Appeals, Little Rock, 1982—. Author: Papa, 1979, The Quiet Man, 1991, Albie's Story, 2002; contbr. articles to mags., columns in newspapers. Mem.: Ark. Realtors Assn., Nat. Realtors Assn., Miss. County Writers Guild (pres. 1981—). Republican. Baptist. Avocations: writing, travel, music. Home: PO Box 945 Blytheville AR 72316 Office: 520 Chickasawba Blytheville AR 72315 Office Phone: 870-762-2033.

BAKER, CLAUDIA MULLER, reading specialist; b. Queens, NY, Nov. 27, 1968; d. Rudolph Andrew and Janet Beatrice Muller; m. Rossie V. Baker, Jr., Aug. 10, 2002. BA, SUNY, Potsdam, N.Y., 1990; MEd, Old Dominion U., 1994; EdS, George Wash. U., 2003. Tchr. Portsmouth (Va.) Pub. Schs., 1991—2001; tchr., reading specialist Va. Beach City Pub. Schs., 2001—. Mem. writing com. Va. Bech Secondary Reading Curriculum, 2003—04. Girls soccer coach Independence Mid. Sch., Va. Beach, 2002—, sch. planning coun., 2002—03. Nominee Tchr. of Yr., Independence Mid. Sch., 2002—03. Mem.: Assoc. Curriculum and Devel. Avocations: swimming, bicycling, crafts. Home: 4653 Paul Revere Rd Virginia Beach VA 23455 Office: Ind Middle Sch 1370 Dunston Ln Virginia Beach VA 23455 Office Phone: 757-460-7500. Personal E-mail: cloib@msn.com. Business E-Mail: clbaker@vbcps.k12.va.us.

BAKER, CORNELIA DRAVES, artist; b. Woodbury, N.J., Mar. 2, 1929; d. Carl Zeno and Cornelia (Powell) Draves.; m. Philip Douglas Baker, July 16, 1955; children: Brinton, Todd, Claudia, Samuel. Student, Ohio Wesleyan U., 1947-50, Goethe U., Frankfurt, Germany, 1950-52. Travel dir. Am. Youth Hostels, Inc., N.Y.C., 1953-57. Artist Cornelia Gallery, Kumamoto, Japan, 1990—; gallery dir. Presbyn. Ch., Franklin Lakes, N.J., 1988-97, Marcella Geltman Gallery, New Milford, N.J., 1993-96; bd. dirs. Bergen Mus. Art and Sci., N.J., 1996-2000, corr. sec., mem. exec. com., 1999-2000. One-woman shows include Ramapo Coll., 1986, Shimada Mus., Kumamoto, 1990, Sekaikan Gallery, Tokyo, 1990, Am. Ctr., Fukuoka, 1990, Bergen Mus. Art and Sci., 1993, L'Atelier Inc. Gallery, 1994, N.Y. Theol. Sem., N.Y.C., 1996, The Gallery, Franklin Lakes, 1997, 2003, Office Congressman S.R. Rothman, Hackensack, N.J., 1997, Lee Hecht Harrison, Paramus, N.J., 1998, Willows Cafe, Ramsey, N.J., 2000; represented in permanent collections Bergen Mus. Art and Sci., Paramus, Beekley Internat. Skiing Fine Art and Graphics. Chair social problems com. Borough of Franklin Lakes Coun., 1973-76. Recipient Best of Show award Ringwood Manor Assn. of the Arts, 1987, Bergen Mus. Art and Sci., 1989, Emeriti award for excellence N.J. Ctr. for Visual Arts, 1989, Excellence cert. Internat. Art Competition, 1988, Women Making History in Arts award Bergen County, N.J., 1993, Crabbie award Art Calendar, 1994, Gold prize

RISO Edn. Found., Japan, 1997, Artist Showcase award Manhattan Art Internat., 2000, merit award Salute to Women in Arts. 2000. Mem. Nat. Assn. Women Artists (printmaking jury chmn. 1992-94), Salute to Women in the Arts (pres. 1988-90), Mastodon Artists Soc. (life), Altrusa Club of Bergen County, N.J. Republican. Presbyterian. Avocations: skiing, traveling, tennis. Home: 293 Green Ridge Rd Franklin Lakes NJ 07417 2011 E-mail: cdbaker@optonline.net.

BAKER, CYNTHIA JOAN, elementary education educator, historic site interpreter; b. Des Moines, Feb. 18, 1957; d. Lane Estil and Joan Arlene (Evenson) Goad; divorced; children: Wayne, Rachel, Nicholas. AA, Des Moines C.C., 1993; BA in Edn., Grandview Coll., Des Moines, 1996. Cert. elem. tchr., Iowa.. Mem. social svc. parent involvement prog. Head Start, Knoxville, Iowa, 1982-90, Knoxville (Iowa) Cmty. Sch., 1996; hist. interpreter Living History Farms, Urbandale, Iowa, 1994—; substitute tchr. various schs., Urbandale, Iowa, 1997—2001; kindergarten tchr. SE Warren Sch., 2001—. Asst. leader Boy Scouts Am., Knoxville, Iowa, 1990-93; tchr., youth leader Pleasantville (Iowa) Bapt. Ch., 1993-97; mem. Candle of the Lord Ladies Group, 1994—, pres. 1996-97; dir. Vacation Bible Sch. Knoxville Christian Ch. Named to dean's list Grandview Coll., Des Moines, 1995, 96, 97; Eleanore J. Grube scholar Grandview Coll., 1995. Baptist. Avocations: reading, sewing, crafts. Home: 314 E Jefferson St Knoxville IA 50138-2238

BAKER, DIANE LOUISE, financial professional; b. Wheeling, W.Va., Mar. 7, 1960; d. William Frederick and Louise Ann Blazier; m. Daniel Joseph Baker, June 13, 1981. AA, Cert. Applied Sci., W.Va. No., 1981. Cert. series 7, 63, 65 Securities and Exch. Commn., life, health and variable annuity agt. Fla., notary pub. Assoc. Bank of Palm Beach, Fla., 1983—87; registered asst. Dean Witter, West Palm Beach, Fla., 1987—91, Smith Barney, West Palm Beach, 1991—93, First Union, Palm Beach, 1993; asst. to dist. sales mgr. Merrill Lynch, Palm Beach, 1993—97, sr. assoc. Delray Beach, Fla., 1997—. Liaison amateur radio svc. ARC, West Palm Beach, 1991—92; advanced class amateur radio operator, 1991—. Mem.: Awana Club Internat. (sec.), Phi Theta Kappa. Republican. Baptist. Office Phone: 561-276-1684.

BAKER, DIANE R.H. dermatologist; b. Toledo, Nov. 17, 1945; BS, Ohio State U., 1967, MD cum laude, 1971. Diplomate Am. Bd. Dermatology. Intern U. Wis. Hosp., Madison, 1971-72, resident in dermatology, 1972-74, Oreg. Health Sci. Ctr., Portland, 1974-76; pvt. practce, Portland, 1976—. Clin. prof. dermatology Oreg. Health Sci. U., 1986—; mem. med. staff Meridian Park Hosp., Tualatin, Oreg., 1981—; dir. Am. Bd. Dermatology, 1995—, v.p., 2001. Mem.: AMA (del. 1995—), Oreg. Dermatol. Soc., Am. Dermatol. Assn. (v.p. 2001), Am. Acad. Dermatology (v.p. 1990), Alpha Omega Alpha. Office: 1706 NW Glisan St Ste 2 Portland OR 97209-2225*

BAKER, DINA GUSTIN, artist; b. Phila., Nov. 07; d. Albert Isadore Kevles and Rose Schwartz; m. John Calvin Gustin (dec. July 4, 1964); m. William Baker, Jan. 5, 1968. Student, Phila. Coll. Fine Arts, 1940, Barnes Found, 1942—46, Templer Tyler Sch. Fine Arts, 1943, Art Students League, 1945, Hayter Atelier 17, N.Y.C., 1945. One-woman shows include Roko Gallery, N.Y.C., 1963, Angeleski Gallery, 1965, Regensburg (Germany) Mus., 1974, Amerika House, Munich, 1974, Hamburg, Germany, 1974, Ingber Gallery, N.Y.C., 1976, 1978, 1980, 1982, Brigham Young U., Provo, Utah, 1983, Utah State U., Logan, 1983, Gracie Lawrence Gallery, Delray Beach, Fla., 1999, 2000, Ora Sorensen Gallery, Delray Beach, 2000—02, Represented in permanent collections Bergen Mus. Arts and Scis., Paramus, N.J., Rutgers U., Nelson Hall, Piscataway, N.J., NYU, N.Y.C., Gannet Found., Columbia U., Boca Raton (Fla.) Mus., exhibited in group shows at Guild Hall, East Hampton, N.Y., 1954, Art USA, N.Y.C., 1955, Acad Fine Arts, Phila., 1963, Nat. Acad. Design, N.Y.C., 1968, Lehigh U., Bethlehem, Pa., 1977, Montclair (N.J.) Art Mus., 1978, Parrish Mus., Southampton, N.Y., 1981, Ingber Gallery, N.Y.C., 1984, Bergen Mus. Arts and Scis., Paramus, N.J., 1984, Adlena Adlung Gallery, N.Y.C., 1991, Rutgers U., 1996, Gracie Lawrence Gallery, 1996, 1999, 2000, Ora Sorensen Gallery, 2000. Scholar, Phila. Coll. Fine Arts, 1940, Art Students League, 1945, Barnes Found., 1942—45. Mem.: Women in the Arts. Home: Bay Hill estates 11820 Blackwoods Ln West Palm Beach FL 33412

BAKER, ELIZABETH CALHOUN, magazine editor; b. Boston; d. John Calhoun and Elizabeth Marshall Evans B. BA cum laude, Bryn Mawr Coll.; MA, Radcliffe Coll. Fulbright scholar Inst. d'Art et d'Archeologie and Ecole du Louvre, Paris; Instr. art history Boston U., Wheaton Coll., Norton, Mass.; assoc. editor Art News, N.Y.C., 1963-65, mng. editor, 1965-73; editor Art in Am. mag., N.Y.C., 1973—. Instr. art history Sch. Visual Arts, N.Y.C., 1968-74; freelance art criticism. Recipient Lifetime Achievement award Coll. Art Assn., 1992; Nat. Endowment for Arts grantee, 1972 Office: Art in America Brant Publications 575 Broadway Fl 5 New York NY 10012-3230

BAKER, ELLEN SHULMAN, astronaut, physician; b. Fayetteville, N.C., Apr. 27, 1953; d. Melvin Shulman; m. Kenneth J. Baker; 2 daughters. BA in Geology, SUNY, Buffalo; MD, Cornell U., 1978; MS in Public Health, U. Tex., 1994. Diplomate Am. Bd. Internal Medicine. Resident U. Tex. Health Sci. Ctr., San Antonio; med. officer NASA Lyndon B. Johnson Space Ctr., Houston, 1981-84, astronaut candidate, 1984-85, astronaut, 1985—, mission specialist Shuttle Orbiter Atlantis Flight STS-34, 1989; mission specialist Shuttle Columbia flight, 1992; lead astronaut for med. issues; astronaut rep. Edn. Working Group at Johnson Space Ctr. Address: NASA Johnson Space Ctr Astronaut Ofc Houston TX 77058*

BAKER, FAITH MERO, retired elementary education educator; b. Pitts., May 9, 1941; d. Vincent G. and Georgetta (Rothwell) Mero; m. Gerald A. Baker, Dec. 22, 1968; children: Jeremy D., Kara L. BA, Carlow Coll., Pitts., 1963; MEd, U. Pitts., 1965, postgrad., 1966-68. Cert. elem. and spl. edn. tchr., Pa. Tchr. sci. Pitts. Pub. Schs., 1963-64, tchr. spl. edn., 1968-87, tchr., primary sci. specialist, 1987-98; ret. Leader instrnl. team Fulton Acad., Pitts., 1988—; facilitator, tchr. Project Wild and project Aquatic Wild, Project Learning Tree, Pitts., 1988—; mem. leadership team Fulton Acad. for New Am. Schs.-area Sch. to Career. Leader Girl Scouts U.S.A., Monroeville, Pa., 1979-86; mem. Supts. Roundtable Gateway Schs., Monroeville, Pa., 1987-89. Mem.: AAUW (chair scholarship com Monroeville br. 1996—), Pa. Bus. and Profl. Women's Assn. (mem. polit. action com., pres. Monroeville 1987—88, bd. dirs. dist.3 1991—, mem. polit. action com., pres. Monroeville 1992—93), Pitts. Fedn. Tchrs. (bldg. steward 1968—98), U. Pitts. Alumni Assn. (asst. v.p. 1987—88, sec. 1989—91, alumnae coun. recording sec. 1998—2000), Delta Kappa Gamma, Alpha Delta Kappa (treas. 1992—99), Phi Delta Gamma (pres. 1982—84, regional coord. 1984—86, sec. Kappa chpt. 1986—90, nat. v.p. 1992—94, nat. pres. 1994—96, nat. treas. 1998—2000, chpt. 2d v.p. 1999—2000, 1st v.p. 2000—02, pres. 2002—). Democrat. Roman Catholic. Avocations: sewing, gourmet cooking, writing, short stories and poetry. Home: 102 Penn Lear Dr Monroeville PA 15146-4734 E-mail: fayze@adelphia.net.

BAKER, GLORIA MARIE, visual artist, art educator; b. Petersburg, Ind. m. James Daniel Baker; children: David, Christopher. Pvt. practice, Evansville, Ind., 1976—. Artist (painting) Aztec Village, 1994 (Grumbacher Gold Medallion and The Excellence Gold award, 1994), The Dedicated, 1991 (Brown and Williamson Tobacco Corp. award, 1991, Dr. Martin Hydrus award Ga. Watercolor Soc., 03), The Domes, 1997 (2d pl.), Ascent to the Cathedral, 1998 (St. Cuthbert's Mill award, 1998, Grumbacner Bronze award), Double Ascent, 1999 (Winsor & Newton award, Document Framing Svc. award, 1999, 1st pl. Evansville Art Guild, Peabody Coal Co. award), Past, Present & Future, 1997, The Ascent (Houston B. Adams award, Evansville Mus. Arts & Sci.), Cathedral of Light, 2000 (2d pl., Dir.'s Choice award, 2000), The Dedicated, 1993, (included in books) Best of Watercolor, Best of Watercolor 2, Landscape Inspirations, The Complete Best of Watercolor, Vol.s 1 & 2, Chgo. Art Rev., 4th edit., Evansville Mus. of Arts and Sci. GiftShop, 2003; solo exhbn., Mus. Arts and Sci., Evansville, Ind., 2003. Chmn. Celia Sprue Assn., Evansville, 1995—2003. Mem.: Niagara Frontier Watercolor Soc., Watercolor Soc. Ala. (signature mem.), Ga. Watercolor Soc. (winner Nat. Exhibit 2003, Dr. Martin Hydrus award 2003), Pa. Watercolor Soc., Ky. Watercolor Soc., Petroleum Wives Club (v.p. 2003). Avocations: golf, gardening, reading, ballroom dancing. Home: 2711 Knob Hill Dr Evansville IN 47711 Office Phone: 812-476-5744.

BAKER, GWENDOLYN CALVERT, United Nations official; b. Ann Arbor, Mich., Dec. 31, 1931; m. James Baker; children: JoAnn, Claudia, James Jr. BA, U. Mich., 1964, MA, 1968, PhD, 1972. Tchr. Ann Arbor Pub. Schs., 1964-69; lectr. U. Mich., 1969-70, instr., 1970-72, assoc. prof., 1972-76, dir. affirmative action programs, 1976-78; chief minorities and women's programs Nat. Inst. Edn., Washington, 1978-84; v.p., dean, graduate and children's programs Bank St. Coll. Edn., N.Y.C., 1981-84; nat. exec. dir. YWCA of USA, N.Y.C., 1984-93; pres., CEO U.S. Com. for UNICEF, N.Y.C., 1993—2002; pres. Calvert Baker & Assocs. Inc.

BAKER, HELEN DOYLE PEIL, realtor, contractor; b. Los Angeles, June 26, 1943; d. James Cyril and Jacqueline (White) Doyle; m. Gary Edward Peil, Aug. 5, 1967 (dec. May 6, 1969); children: Andrea Christine, Kevin Doyle; m. Nathaniel W. Baker, Jr., Jan. 1, 1971 (div. July 23, 1983). AA, Santa Monica Coll., 1963; postgrad., U. Wash., 1963-64. Licensed real estate agent; cert. domestic violence counselor. Sales, mgmt. trainee Saks Fifth Ave., Beverly Hills, Calif., 1958-63; flight attendant Am. Airlines, Los Angeles, 1964-67; realtor, assoc. Stapleton Assocs., Honolulu, 1978-80; realtor Dolman Assocs. Inc., Kailua, Hawaii, 1980-87; loan rep. Honolulu Mortgage Co., Kailua, 1986-87; pres., owner, realtor Helen Baker Properties, Inc., Honolulu, 1987-93; v.p. Internat. Property Investment, Inc., Honolulu, 1993-94; owner Property Investment Internat., 1994—; loan officer Western Pacific Mortgage, Inc., 1999—2003; ind. contractor The Lender, LLC, 2003. Pres. Global Listing Svc. Hawaii Inc., 1990-96. Dir. Kailua Community Coun., 1987-91; pres., v.p., sec. Aikahi Community Assn., Kailua, 1980-85; vol. Am. Cancer Soc., Heart Assn. Schs., Kailua, 1971-86; adv. spouse abuse shelter, 1995-98. Mem. C. of C., Windward Spouse Abuse Coalition, Rotary. Avocations: tennis, fitness workout, reading, travel, music. Office: Property Investment Internat PO Box 37066 Honolulu HI 96837-0066 E-mail: propinvst@hawaii.rr.com.

BAKER, JANE E. secondary school educator; b. Birmingham, Ala., Sept. 13, 1956; d. John R. and Betty (Cockrell) B. BS, Auburn U., 1978; MA, U. Montevello, 1991. Tchr. Minor Jr. High Sch., Edgewater Jr. High Sch., Birmingham; instr. spl. studies U. Ala., Birmingham; tchr. Warrior (Ala.) Middle Sch.; second mile tchr. Jefco Bd. Edn., Birmingham, 1990; tchr. Bottenfield Jr. High Sch.; asst. prin. Shades Valley high Sch./Jefferson County Internat. Baccalaureate Sch.; prin. Minor Jr. High Sch., Gresham Mid. Sch., Shades Valley High Sch. Mem. Am. Heart Assn., Middle Sch. Study, Am. Cancer Soc., Nat. Mid. Sch. Assn., Nat. Assn. Secondary Sch. Prins., Ala. Assn. Secondary Sch. Prins.

BAKER, JEAN HARVEY, history educator; b. Balt., Feb. 9, 1933; d. F. Barton and Rose (Lindsay) Hopkins Harvey; m. R. Robinson Baker, Sept. 12, 1953; children— Susan Dixon, Robinson Scott, Robert W., Jean Harvey. AB, Goucher Coll., Towson, Md., 1961; MA, Johns Hopkins U., Balt., 1965, PhD, 1971. Lectr., instr. history Notre Dame Coll., Balt., 1967-69; instr. history Goucher Coll., Balt., 1969, asst. prof. history, 1969-75, assoc. prof. history, 1975-78, prof. history, 1979-82, Elizabeth Todd prof. history, 1981—. Author: The Politics of Continuity, 1973, Ambivalent Americans, 1976, Affairs of Party, 1983, Maryland: A History, Mary Todd Lincoln: A Biography, 1986, The Stevensons: A Family Biography, 1995; co-author: Civil War and Reconstruction, 2002; editor: Md. Hist. Mag., 1979, Votes for Women: The Suffrage Battle Revisited, 2001. Am. Coun. Learned Socs. fellow, 1976, NEH fellow, 1982, Newberry Libr. fellow, 1991, Rockefeller Ctr. fellow, 1998; recipient Faculty Teaching prize Goucher Coll., 1979, Willie Lee Rose prize in Southern history, 1989. Mem. Orgn. Am. Historians, Am. Hist. Assn., Berkshire Conf. Women Historians, Phi Beta Kappa. Democrat. Home: 8717 Mcdonogh Rd Baltimore MD 21208-1021 Office: Goucher Coll History Dept Towson MD 21204 Office Phone: 410-337-6267. E-mail: jbaker@goucher.edu.

BAKER, JOYCE MILDRED, medical/surgical nurse, volunteer; b. Racine, Wis., Oct. 19, 1927; d. Roy Ross Kelly and Ruth Alice Guy Kelly; children: James, Thomas, William, Donald, Frank(dec.). RN, Mt. Sinai Hosp., Chgo., 1948. RN Wis., cert. CPR, recovery rm. specialist, pediat., geriatrics, Wis. Pediat. RN St. Luke's Hosp., Racine, 1948—54; recovery rm. RN St. Mary's Hosp., Racine, 1955—62; supr. RN Lincoln Luth., Racine, 1962—73; charge RN Ridgewood Healthcare, Racine, 1973—94; acute care nurse So. Wis. Ctr., Racine, 1973—94. Vol. ARC, 1994—2000, Luth. High Thrift Shop, Racine, 1998—2003, Baby Books for New Mothers, St. Luke's Hosp., Racine, 2000—03, Cristo-Rey Downtown Food Pantry, Racine, 2002—03, Racine Emergency Shelter Task Force, Christmas Lights at the Zoo, United Way, 2004; vol. tutor San Juan Diego Sch., 2004; vol., mem. Olympia Brown Unitarian Ch., Racine, 1995—2003; bd. mem. Cerebral Palsy, 2002—03. Mem.: Kiwanis (pres. 2001—03). Avocations: writing, cooking, baking. Home: Apt 406 3608 Douglas Ave Racine WI 53402

BAKER, JUDITH ANN, retired computer technician; b. Junction City, Kansas, Mar. 2, 1947; d. David Daniel and Mildred Elaine Bates; m. Jimmy Ray Baker, Oct. 8, 1972; 1 child, Jimmy Ray Jr. Attended, East Ctrl. U., 1994—98; post grad., Tulsa C.C., 1999—. Cert. travel and tourism Draughon Coll., 1988. ADA support group leader; newsletter editor Multiple Sclerosis Assn. of Am., Tulsa, Okla., 1995—. Mem.: Ada Writing Club. Avocations: writing, painting, crafts, decorating. Home: 1011 Pruitt Rd Ada OK 74820 Personal E-mail: smiles2u@compworldnet.com. Business E-Mail: colorofms@wmconnect.com.

BAKER, KATHERINE RAMOS, music educator, conductor; d. Mary and Russell Baker. BA, Pacific Christian Coll., Fullerton, Calif., 1976; MusM in Choral Conducting, Calif. State U., Fullerton, 1985; EdD in Music Edn., U. Ill., Urbana, 1992. Cert. music tchr. Calif. Music tchr. Bonita Unified Sch. Dist., San Dimas, Calif., 1979—84; doctoral grad. asst. U. Ill., Urbana, 1984—87; dir. of choral activities and assoc. prof. of music Lewis-Clark State Coll., Lewiston, Idaho, 1994—2001; assoc. prof. of music and dir., grad. studies in music Calif. State U., Northridge, 2001—. Conductor (performance) Hildegard Chamber Singers/6th Annual International Women Composers Conference, co-facilitator and conductor/performer (retreat, monastery of st. gertrude, id) Growing Strong with Hildegard of Bingen, conductor/performer Celebrate the 900th Birthday of Hildegard of Bingen; author: (article) Idaho Music Notes; conductor (performance) CSU Northridge Women's Chorale at CMEA, keynote speaker (presentation) Assessment and the Standards-SCVA, participant (lcsc title iii technology grant), North Idaho College/Lewis-Clark State College Cooperative Technology Grant, induction sub-committee member, csun Carnegie Initiative, Teachers for a New Era, conductor (performance) Benedictinus 2000, conductor participant Innsbruck International Choral Festival 2000, honor choir conductor Idaho Music Educators, District II, Southeast Washington Music Educators Association; author: (multimedia software) Mozart's Requiem (TimeSketch Series, Electronic Courseware Systems), Bach's Magnificat and Vivaldi's Gloria (TimeSketch Series, Electronic Courseware Systems); college professor (teaching, lewis-clark state college) (Excellence in Tchg., Sch. of Arts and Sciences, 1996), master teacher (teaching) (Master Tchr., CSU Fullerton, 1982). Oblate Monastery of St. Gertrude, Cottonwood, Idaho. Mem.: MENC, ACDA/SCVA, Phi Delta Kappa. Roman Catholic. Avocation: travel. Office: CSU Northridge Music Dept 18111 Nordhoff St Northridge CA 91330-8314 Personal E-mail: drkrbaker@aol.com. E-mail: katherine.r.baker@csun.edu.

BAKER, KATHY WHITTON, actress; b. Midland, Tex., June 8, 1950; Appearances include (theatre) Fool for Love, 1983 (Obie award 1983, Theatre World award 1984), Desire Under the Elms, 1984, Aunt Dan and Lemon, 1986, (films) The Right Stuff, 1983, Street Smart, 1987 (Nat. Soc. Film Critics Best Supporting Actress award 1987), Permanent Record, 1988, A Killing Affair, 1988, Clean and Sober, 1988, Jacknife, 1989, Dad, 1989, Mr. Frost, 1989, Edward Scissorhands, 1990, Article 99, 1992, Jennifer 8, 1992, Mad Dog and Glory, 1993, To Gillian on Her 37th Birthday, 1996, Inventing the Abbotts, 1997, The Cider House Rules, 1999, Things You Can Tell Just By Looking at Her, 2000, The Glass House, 2001, Ten Tiny Love Stories, 2001, Assassination Tango, 2002, Cold Mountain, 2003 (TV movies) Nobody's Child, 1986, The Image, 1990, One Special Victory, 1991, Weapons of Mass Distraction, 1997, Oklahoma City: A Survivor's Story, 1998, Lush Life, 1993, Not in This Town, 1997, ATF, 1998, A Season of Miracles, 1999, Sanctuary, 2001, Door to Door, 2002, Too Young to Be a Dad, 2002 (TV series) Picket Fences, 1992-1996 (Emmy award Outstanding Lead Actress in a Drama Series, 1993, 1995, Golden Globe award, Best Actress in a TV Drama Series, 1994), Boston Public, 2001-2002, Murphy's Dozen, 2003. Office: ICM rep Corey Weissman 8942 Wilshire Blvd Beverly Hills CA 90211-1934

BAKER, KRISTI ANN, music educator, composer; b. Topeka, Dec. 10, 1957; d. J. Roland and Lila Ann (Kern) Williams; m. Charles Burton Baker; children: Barbara Lynn, Elizabeth Catherine. BS, Kans. State U., 1979, MusM, 1984. Cert. k-12 music tchr. Kans., 1979. Pvt. piano instr., Topeka, 1972—75; grad. tchg. asst. Kans. State U. Dept. Music, Manhattan, 1979—81; band and choral dir. Wakefield (Kans.) Pub. Schs., 1981—84; elem. music tchr. Ware Elem. Sch., Ft. Riley, Kans., 1984—88; choral dir. Junction City (Kans.) Middle Sch., 1988—2003, Abilene (Kans.) H.S., 2003—. Private piano/voice instr., Junction City and Abilene, Kans., 1981—; ch. organist, choir master various chs., Manhattan, Junction City, Abilene, Kans., 1988—; mem. commn. on music/liturgy Episcopal Diocese of Kans., 2001—. Composer: (sacred choral work) A Song for Advent, 1988, The Magic of Your Dreams, 2000. Named Winner youth talent auditions, Topeka Symphony Orch., 1974; recipient Superior Plus ratings, Nat. Piano Tchrs. Guild, 1968—75. Mem.: Music Educators' Nat. Conf., Kans. Music Educators Assn. (chair north ctrl. dist. middle level honor choir program 1995—96, 2002—03, chair Kans. state middle level honor choir program 2004—), Music Tchrs. Nat. Assn., Music Tchrs. Nat. Assn., Am. Choral Dirs. Assn., Order of the Eastern Star, Job's Daughters of Kans. (Grand Dir. Music 2000, guardian sec. Bethel #7 2000—). Republican. Episcopalian. Achievements include Piano or voice coach for several students who received state recognition and scholarships; five tours of Europe as pianist, singer and choral dir. Avocations: needlepoint, sewing, water sports. Home: 704 N Cedar Abilene KS 67410-2340 Office: Junction City Middle Sch 300 W 9th Junction City KS 66441-2304 Office Phone: 785-263-1260 119. E-mail: kbaker@oz-online.net.

BAKER, LESLIEGH, bank officer, lawyer; b. El Paso, Tex., June 10, 1960; d. Gilbert and Ferne Schrier. BA, U. Calif., Irvine, 1983; JD, Western State U., 1990. Bar: Calif. 1990. Intern, law clk. Legal Aid Soc. Orange County, Santa Ana, Calif., 1989-90; assoc. Konapalsky & Baker, Newport Beach, Calif., 1990-92, Law Offices of Richard L. Grant, Tustin, Calif., 1992-94; pvt. practice Costa Mesa, Calif., 1994-97; v.p. Bank of Yorba Linda, a divsn. of BYL Bank Group, Mission Viejo, Calif., 1997—. Mem. Dedicated Animal Welfare Group, Mission Viejo, 1999; vol. Pediat. Cancer Rsch. Found., Orange, 1995, 96. Mem. State Bar Calif., Fin. Women Internat. Avocations: boating, fishing, camping, crafts.

BAKER, LUCINDA, writer; b. Atlanta, Ill., July 10, 1916; d. Hazle Howard and Adah Rebecca (Mason) B.; m. Willard Alan Greiner, June 27, 1946. Student, Ariz. State Coll., 1934-38. Author: Place of Devils, 1976, Walk the Night Unseen, 1977, Memoirs of First Baroness, 1978, The Painted Lady, 1998; contbr. short stories to mags. Mem. Author's Guild, Mystery Writers Am., Romance Writers Am.

BAKER, LYNNE RUDDER, philosophy educator; b. Atlanta, Feb. 14, 1944; d. James Maclin and Virginia (Bennett) Rudder; m. Thomas B. Baker III, Feb. 1, 1969. BA, Vanderbilt U., 1966, MA, 1971, PhD, 1972; student, Johns Hopkins U., 1967-68. Asst. prof. philosophy Mary Baldwin Coll., Staunton, Va., 1972-76, Middlebury (Vt.) Coll., 1976-79, assoc. prof., 1979-84, prof., 1984-94, acting dean arts and humanities, 1982, chairperson humanities divsn., 1982-85, acting chairperson philosophy, 1986-87; prof. U. Mass., Amherst, 1989—, dir. philosophy grad. program, 1994—. Mem. panel to select summer seminars NEH, Washington, 1982, mem. panel to select fellows, 1989—90; Gifford lectr. U. Glasgow, Scotland, 2001. Author: Saving Belief: A Critique of Physicalism, 1988, Explaining Attitudes: A Practical Approach to the Mind, 1995, Persons and Bodies: A Constitution View, 2000; contbr. scholarly articles to profl. jours. Trustee Vanderbilt U., Nashville, 1969-70, mem. alumni bd. dirs., 1985-89. Mellon fellow, 1974, NEH fellow, 1983-84, Nat. Humanities Ctr. fellow, 1982-83, Woodrow Wilson Internat. Ctr. for Scholars fellow, 1988-89. Mem. Am. Philos. Assn. (program com. 1983, exec. com. 1992-95), Soc. for Philosophy and Psychology, Soc. Christian Philosophers (exec. com. 1992-95), Soc. Women in Philosophy, Phi Beta Kappa. Democrat. Episcopalian. Office: U Mass Dept Philosophy Amherst MA 01003

BAKER, MARGARET MOORE-FRITZ, retired school librarian, retired humanities educator; b. Washington, May 26, 1934; d. James Fritz; m. Claud Henry Baker, Jr., Sept. 8, 1956; children: Peter Fritz, Elizabeth Blair Baker Naime. BA, BEd, U. Colo., 1956. Cert. tchr. 1956. Libr. U. Colo., Boulder, 1956—57; tchr. grades 3,4,5 Superior Sch., Boulder County, Colo., 1957—59; book rev. Glencoe Wordsmithing, Baldwin City, 1993—. Book rev.: review books for radio, press, internet Baldwin Bookworm, Kansas Bookworm, 1994. Mem. Bladwin C. of C.; voter edn., newsletter, v.p. League of Women Voters, Grand Forks, ND, 1963—66, active environ. portfolio Salt Lake County, Utah, 1966—72, organizer, v.p. Manassas, Va., 1972—78, mem. pub. rels. newsletter edn. Lawrence-Douglas County, Kans., 1978—; libr. Oread Friends Meeting, Lawrence, Kans., 1995—. Mem.: Sister in Crime, Collie Club of Am., Older Women's League. Mem. Soc. Of Friends. Avocations: reading, needlework, bagpipe, dogs. Home and Office: Glencoe Wordsmithing 1009 N 600 Rd Baldwin City KS 66006-7205 E-mail: glencoe@knetconnect.

BAKER, MARIA LUISE, retired secondary school educator; b. Bad Reichenhall, Germany, Oct. 18, 1947; came to U.S., 1948; d. William and Maria Eleanore (Bauer) McStay; m. Clyde Norman Baker, July 29, 1969 (div. Jan. 1975). BA in Spl. Edn., Social Studies, U. No. Colo., 1969. Cert. tchr. secondary social studies/spl. edn. K-12. Tchr. spl. edn. Adams City H.S., Commerce City, Colo., 1969-76, 79-89, tchr. social studies, 1989—; tchr. spl. edn. Adams City Mid. Sch., Commerce City, 1976-79, mentor coord., 2002—03. Performance assistance team, mem. mentor program Adams County Sch. Dist. #14, 1990—; presenter insvcs. in field. Mem. Denver Mus. of Natural History, Denver Art Mus. Recipient Disting. Tchr. award/Colo., 1991-92, A-Plus Tchr. - Channel 4 (NBC), 1994; Title II mini-grantee, Title I grantee. Mem.: Am. Fedn. Tchrs. (v.p. 1979—82, pres. 1993—2001), Nat. Coun. for the Social Studies, Colo. Hist. Soc., Colo. Wildlife Fedn. Avocations: gardening, needlework. Office: Adams City High School 4625 E 68th Ave Commerce City CO 80022-2381 Business E-Mail: mbaker@acsd14.k12.co.us.

BAKER, MARY ANN, program manager; b. Coffeyville, Kans., Aug. 8, 1957; d. Earl D. and Lois L. (Benning) B. BS, St. Edward's U., Austin, Tex., 1979, MBA, 1994. Cert. project mgr. Software engr. Boeing Computer Svcs., Wichita, Kans., 1979-81, Martin Marietta, Denver, 1981-84, Tracor Aerospace, Austin, 1984-89; software project mgr. Wayne, Austin, 1989-93, Tracor Aerospace, Austin, 1992—2000; dir. programs BAE Systems, Austin, 2000—. Sec. Hidden Valley Water Coop., Austin, 1994-98. Recipient Cert. of Leadership, Univ. YWCA, Austin, 1987-88; named to Outstanding Young Women of Am., 1988. Mem. LWV, Soc. Women Engrs. (sec. 1994-98), Assn. Old Crows, Delta Mu Delta, Kappa Gamma Pi. Roman Catholic. Avocations: bicycle riding, water skiing, volleyball. Office: BAE Systems 6500 Tracer Ln Austin TX 78725-2000

BAKER, MARY EVELYN, retired librarian; b. Columbus, Ohio, May 8, 1912; d. Abram Jackson and Martha Maria (Dailey) Shoemaker; m. Richard Heinley Baker, Sept. 18, 1937 (dec.); children: Richard Shoemaker, David Guy. BA, Ohio State U., 1934; BS in Libr. Sci., Western Res. U., Cleve., 1935. Mem. staff State U., Columbus, 1935-37, 38-44, 1955-74, part-time libr., 1955-66, adminstrv. asst. to the dir., 1958, serial cataloger, 1958-67, asst. reviser, sr. cataloger, 1967-68, head serial div. catalog dept., 1968-71, head catalog dept., 1971-74. Libr. com. First Congl. Ch., Columbus, 1941-97, libr. co-chmn., 1962-65, 74-75, libr. chmn., 1976-97; past mem. ALA, sec. serials sect., resources and tech. div., 1970-73. Den mother Boy Scouts Am., Columbus, 1953-58; libr. co-chmn. Friendship Village, Dublin, Ohio, 1981-97, chmn., 1997—, pres. Mem. Ohioana Libr. Assn. (past chmn. various coms., life mem.), PEO (telephone chmn. chpt. V 1987—), DAR (past pres.), Ohio State Univ. Women's Club (past pres.), Agrl. Circle (past pres.), Franklin Co-Ret. Tchrs. Assn. (life mem.), Ohio Ret. Tchrs. Assn. (life mem.), Ohio State Alumni Assn. (life mem.), Polar Bear Alumni Assn. (founding mem.), Columbus North H.S. (life), Alumni Assn. Univ. Sch. (life), Ohio State U. Retirees Assn. (life, bridge chmn. 1984—), Women's Assn. (pres. 2003-2004), Ohio State U. Friends of the Librs., Ohio Hist. Soc., Worthington Hist. Soc. (life), Columbus Hist. Soc. (life), Ch. Women United of Columbus and Franklin County, Columbus Mus. Art, Columbus Zoo, Gypsies Travel Club, Motts Mil. Mus. (charter), Phi Mu (various offices including pres. active and alumni chpts.). Republican. Home: 6000 Riverside Dr Apt 233A Dublin OH 43017-1494

BAKER, MICHELE DAWN LITZ, management consultant; b. Omaha, Nebr., Sept. 18, 1961; d. William Eugene and Brenda Kerigan-Ann (Nugent) Litz; m. William Edward Baker, Mar. 28, 1985; stepchildren: Layla Marie Baker, Kristopher Michael Baker. BA Bus. Mgmt., Fla. Internat. U., 1991; MBA, St. Leo U., 2001. Cert. emergency mgr. Nat. Coordinating Coun. on Emergency Mgmt. Gen. office mgr. Rays Flt. Sch., Miami, Fla., 1977-78; asst. mgr. Sunland Movie Theatre, Miami, 1979-82; flt. attendant Chalks Internat. Airlines, Miami, 1982-83, emergency mgmt. coord. Metro-Dade Emergency Mgmt., Miami, 1983-93; emergency mgmt. dir. Pasco County Govt., New Port Richey, Fla., 1993—. Sec./treas. Gov.'s Hurricane Conf., Inc., 1996—. Class v.p. Leadership Pasco, 1997; class bd. dirs. Leadership Tampa Bay, Fla., 2002. Recipient cert. of appreciation for patriotic civilian svc. U.S. Dept. of Army, Miami, 1992, Humanitarian award, 1992. Mem. Nat. Coord. Coun. on Emergency Mgmt., Am. Soc. of Profl. Emergency Planners, Fla. Emergency Preparedness Assn. (v.p., pres.), ARC (state svc. coun.). Ind. Roman Catholic. Avocations: singing in church, friends, reading, exercise, computers. Home: 12829 Walnut Tree Ln Hudson FL 34669-2867 Office: Pasco County Emergency Mgmt 8744

BAKER, NANCY KASSEBAUM (NANCY KASSEBAUM), former senator, foundation official; b. Topeka, July 29, 1932; d. Alfred M. and Theo Landon, children: John Philip, Linda Josephine, Richard Landon, William Alfred; m. Howard Baker, 1996. BA in Polit. Sci, U. Kans., 1954; MA in Diplomatic History, U. Mich., 1956. Mem. Maize (Kans.) Sch. Bd., 1972-75; mem. Washington staff Sen. James B. Pearson of Kans., 1975-76; mem. U.S. Senate from Kans., 1979-96, mem. fgn. relations com., labor and human resources com., Indian Affairs com.; mem. com. fgn. rels., subcom. African affairs, 1980-96; mem. subcom. arts, edn. Arts & Humanities; mem. com. banking, housing & urban affairs, subcom. internat. fin. & monetary policy; former chmn. bd. trustees Robert Wood Johnson Found.; former co-chair the Presdl. Appointee Initiative Adv. Bd., Brookings Inst., Washington; commr. Commn. for Africa, England, 2004—. Mem. Kans. Press Women's Assn., Women's Assn. Instnl. Logopedics. Republican. Episcopalian.

BAKER, NANNETTE A. lawyer, city official; b. Tuscaloosa, Ala., Oct. 3, 1957; BS, U. Tenn., 1978; JD, St. Louis U., 1994. Bar: Mo., Ill. TV journalist, St. Louis, Memphis, Knoxville; law clk. to Odell Horton U.S. Dist. Judge, Memphis, 1994-95; with firm Lashley & Baer, P.C., 1995-96; assoc. firm Schlichter, Bogard & Denton, St. Louis, 1996-99; chair Bd. Election Commrs. for City of St. Louis, 1997-99; judge State of Mo. (22d jud. cir.), 1999—. Bd. dirs. St. Patrick's Ctr., Nat. Mus. Transport, Coll. for Living; mem. adv. bd. SSM Rehab. Inst. Mem. ABA, ATLA, Mo. Trial Lawyer Orgn., Ill. Trial Lawyer Orgn., Nat. Bar Assn., Mound City Bar Assn. Office: 100 S 4th St Ste 900 Saint Louis MO 63102-1823

BAKER, PAMELA, lawyer; b. Detroit, Apr. 6, 1951; d. William D. and Lois (Tukey) Baker; m. Jay R. Franke, June 10, 1972; children: Baker Eugene, Alexandra Britell. AB, Smith Coll., 1972; JD, U. Wis. Madison, 1976. Bar: Ill. 1976, Wis. 1976. Ptnr. Sonnenschein, Nath & Rosenthal, Chgo. Contbr. articles to profl. jour. Fellow Am. Coll. Employee Benefits Counsel (charter); Am. Bar Found.; mem. ABA (mem. employee benefits com. 1984—, chair-elect 1998-99, chair 1999-2000, mem. plan mergers and acquisitions com. 1985— mem. fed. regulation of securities com. 1989—, chair 1989-95), Ill. State Bar Assn. (sec. employee benefits sect. coun. 1989-90, vice chair 1990-91, chair 1991-92), Chgo. Bar Assn. (employee benefits com. 1978—, sec. 1984-85, vice chair 1985-86, chair 1987-88, fed. taxation com. 1980—, exec. coun. 1982-85). Office: Sonnenschein Nath & Rosenthal Sears Tower 233 S Wacker Dr Ste 8000 Chicago IL 60606-6491

BAKER, PATRICIA, health foundation administrator; BS, Wayne State U.; MS, U. Wis. Exec. dir. Planned Parenthood Conn.; dir. Conn. govt. program Oxford Health Plans; exec. dir. The Women's Ctr., Waukesha, Wis., 1978-85; nat. program dir. March of Dimes Birth Defects Found., until 1999; exec. dir. Conn. Health Found., Farmington, 1999—. Assoc. editor the Planned Parenthood Wis., 1985-87. Office: Conn Health Found 30 Batterson Park Rd Farmington CT 06032-2502

BAKER, PATRICIA ANN, publishing executive; b. Englewood, N.J., Apr. 3, 1939; BA, St. Mary's Coll. 1961. Prodn. designer Little, Brown Pubs., 1961-63; mktg. & promotion dir. Sunset Books, 1963-68; design & prodn. mgr. Hoover Instn. Press, Stanford, Calif., 1981-89, exec. editor, 1989—. Office: Hoover Instn Press Stanford U Stanford CA 94305-6010

BAKER, ROSALYN HESTER, state senator; b. El Campo, Tex., Sept. 20, 1946; BA, Southwest Tex. State U., 1968; grad., U. Southwestern La., 1969. Lobbyist, asst. dir. Govt. Rels. Nat. Edn. Assn., Washington, 1969-80; owner, retail sporting goods store Maui, Hawaii, 1980-87; legis. aide to Hon. Karen Honita Hawaii Ho. of Reps., Honolulu, 1987, mem., 1989-93, house majority leader, 1993. state senator Hawaii, 1993-98, majority leader, 1995-96; dir. office econ. devel. County of Maui, Hawaii, 1999—2002, chair health com., 2003—. Co-chair ways and means com., 1998; co-chair rules com. Hawaii State Dem. Conv., 1990, chair health com. 2003, resolutions com. 1994; mem. consumer protection and housing com. Del.-at-large Dem. Nat. Conv., 1984, 92, 96; mem. exec. com. Maui County Dem. Com. 1986-88; mem. Workforce Investment Bd., Lahaina Town Action Com.;

former vice chmn. Maui Svc. Area Bd. om Mental Health and Substance Abuse; former unit pres. Am. Cancer Soc., bd. dirs., Hawaii-Pacific; bd. dirs. Maui Econ. Devel. Bd. Mem.: Am. Cancer Soc., Maalaea Cmty. Assn., Kihei Cmty. Assn., West Maui Taxpayers Assn. Democrat. Home: PO Box 10394 Lahaina HI 96761-0394 Office: State Capitol Rm 220 Honolulu HI 96813 E-mail: senbaker@capitol.hawaii.gov.

BAKER, SANDRA KAY, music educator; b. Columbia, Mo., June 22, 1950; d. Oliver James and Shirley Mae (Barrett) House; m. John Lynn Baker, May 19, 1973 (div. Jan. 1989); 1 child, Jessica Lynn ; m. Philip Dale Bouchard, Sept. 18, 1993. BS in Music Edn., U. Mo., 1972; Master of Music in Performance, U. So. Ill., 1979. Life tchg. cert. instrumental music Mo., cert. facilitator and trainer in brain-based learning. Prof. violinist Am. Fedn. Musicians, 1975—; pvt. music tchr. St. Louis, 1975—81; music tchr. elem. orch. Parkway Sch. Dist., Chesterfield, Mo., 1978—81, 1986—; Suzuki violin tchr. St. Louis Conservatory and Schs. for the Arts, 1981—90. Presenter in field; orch. chmn. dist., fine arts and curriculum couns. Co-author (editor): dist. frameworks, curriculum guide, assessment. Bldg. campaign chair United Way Greater St. Louis, Arts and Edn. Coun. St. Louis. Mem.: ASCD, Suzuki Assn. Ams. (charter mem., coord. 2004 nat. conf.), Am. String Tchrs. Assn., Music Educators Nat. Conf. Avocations: reading, gardening, writing. Office: Parkway Sch Dist 455 N Woods Mill Rd Chesterfield MO 63017 Office Phone: 314-415-6400.

BAKER, SARA ANN KONTOFF, environmental artist, art educator; b. Boston, Oct. 2, 1933; d. Julian and Rose (Kutnick) Kontoff; m. Elliot Baker, June 13, 1954; children: Andrea, Melanie, Jonathan. BA in English Lit., Boston U., 1954; MS in Visual Studies, MIT, 1986. Tchr. English, social studies high sch., Havre de Grace, Pt. Perry, Md., 1954-55; dir. recreation & art therapy Washingtonian Hosp., Jamaica Plain, Mass., 1968-69; founder, co-dir. Ctr. for Creative Living & Tuftonboro (N.H.) Playhouse, 1970-75; lectr. art Wellesley (Mass.) Jr. High Sch., 1973; asst. prof. art history Art Inst. Boston, 1984, 85—; sr. lectr. art Northeastern U., Boston, 1986—. Lectr. art history Mt. Ida Coll., Newton, Mass. & Boston Archtl. Ctr., 1988, '89; cons. in field. One-woman shows include Painting, Galleria Sistina D'ArTe, Rome, Italy, 1978, Environ. Art, Gallery 355, Boston, 1981, Commn. for Neon Installation, Children's Mus., Boston, 1992, Matrix Gallery, Provincetown, 1993, Dean's Gallery, Sloan Sch., MIT, Cambridge, Mass., 1995, Villa delle Palme, Italy; exhibited in shows at Art Inst. Boston, Kyoto, Japan, 1973, Holographic Mus. N.Y., Attleboro (Mass.) Mus., 1985, 93, Newport (R.I.) Art Mus., 1986, Courtland Jessup Gallery, Provincetown, 1990, Boston Soc. Architects, 1996, Artists' Gallery, Wickford, R.I., 1997-98, Northeastern U., 1997, Fed. Res. Bank, 1997. Apptd. by mayor to Planning & Advisory Com., Kenmore-Fenway, Boston, 1988; co-chair Kenmore Residents Assn., Boston, 1988—. Recipient Press.'s prize in sculpture Cambridge (Mass.) Art Assn., 1972; finalist Westland Av. Sculpture competition. Mem. AAUP, Am. Assn. Coll. Profs., Boston Visual Artists Union (fair practice com. 1973-85), Women Artists Boston (co-chair 1974-75), Boston Soc. Architecture (art & architecture com. 1988-96), Coll. Art Assn., Art Inst. Boston (vice pres. art). Avocations: music, travel, photography. Studio: Boston Ctr for Arts 551 Tremont St Boston MA 02116-6338

BAKER, SHIRLEY KISTLER, university administrator; b. Lehighton, Pa., Mar. 16, 1943; d. Harvey Daniel and Miriam Grace (Osenbach) Kistler; m. Richard Christopher Baker, Oct. 22, 1966; children: Nicholas Christopher, India Jane. BA, Muhlenberg Coll., 1965; MA, MALS, U. Chgo., 1971, 1971,70; gerontology specialist. Franklin Inst., 1971-76; assoc. libr. Johns Hopkins U., Balt., 1976-82; assoc. dir. librs. MIT, Cambridge, 1982-89; dean univ. librs. Washington U., St. Louis, 1989-95, vice chancellor for info. tech., dean univ. librs., 1995—. Contbr. articles to profl. jours. Mem. ALA, Nat. Info. Standards Orgn (bd. dirs. 1990-94), Assn. Rsch. Librs. (bd. dirs. 1996-2002, pres. 2000-01), Coalition for Networked Info. (steering com. 1999—), Mo. Libr. Network Corp. (bd. dirs 1990-2000). Democrat. Avocations: reading, travel. Home: 6130 Alexander Dr Saint Louis MO 63105-2223 Office: Washington U Campus Box 1061 1 Brookings Dr Saint Louis MO 63130-4899 E-mail: baker@wustl.edu.

BAKER, SUSAN MARIE VICTORIA, writer, artist, musician; b. Phila., Pa., Aug. 30, 1961; d. John Joseph and Dorothy Phyllis Erdlen. BA in Liberal Arts/Comm., Rowan U., 1983; postgrad., U. of Arts, Phila. Ordained priestess. Published author, visual and performing artist. Art critic and healing artist. Author 3 books; songwriter (performed and published under name Chelsea Mann); art editor Avant mag., 1981; contbr. poetry to various publs.; composer numerous songs. Active animal rights and environ. activities; mem. Newport Cultural Arts Alliance, Sedona Arts Ctr. and Ascension Group. Recipient awards for poetry, creative writing.

BAKER, SUSAN P. public health educator; b. Atlanta, May 31, 1930; d. Charles Laban and Susan (Lowell) Pardee; m. Timothy Danforth Baker, June 23, 1951; children— Timothy D., David C., Susan L. AB, Cornell U., Ithaca, N.Y., 1951; M.P.H., Johns Hopkins U., Balt., 1968; ScD (hon.), U. N.C., 1998. Rsch. assoc. Office of Chief Med. Examiner, Balt., 1968-81; rsch. assoc. Sch. Hygiene and Pub. Health, Johns Hopkins U., Balt., 1968-71, asst. prof., 1971-74, assoc. prof., 1974-83, prof. health policy and mgmt., 1983—; assoc. chmn. dept. health policy and mgmt., 1997-99, joint appointment in environ. health scis., 1975—, joint appointment in pediatrics, 1989—; dir. Injury Prevention Ctr., 1987-88, co-dir., 1988—94, acting head div. pub. health, 1989-90, joint appointment emergency medicine Sch. Medicine, 1991—. Vis. prof. U. Minn. Sch. Pub. Health, 1975-87; chmn. nat. rev. panel for nat. accident sampling sys. Dept. Transp., Washington 1976-81; vice chmn. com. on trauma rsch. Nat. Rsch. Coun., Washington 1984-85; mem. adv. com. on injury control CDC, 1989-95; mem. Armed Forces Epidemiol. Bd., 1996-2000; commr. West Latir Ditch Assn., N.Mex., 1990—; vis. lectr. in injury prevention Harvard Sch. Pub. Health, 1984-87; John T. Law meml. lectr. U. Calgary, Alta., 1984; expert panel Age 60 rule FAA, 1991-93; cons. and lectr. in field. Author: (monograph) Fatally Injured Drivers, 1970 (Prince Bernhard medal 1974), The Injury Fact Book, 1984, 2d edit., 1992, Saving Children: A Guide to Injury Prevention, 1991, Injury Prevention: An International Perspective, 1998; contbr. articles to books and articles to profl. jours. Recipient Charles A. Dana award for pioneering achievements in health, 1989, Johns Hopkins U. Disting. Alumnus award, 1996, Am. Public Health Assn. Excellence award, 1999. Fellow Am. Assn. Automotive Medicine (bd. dirs. 1971-76, pres. 1974-75, award of merit 1985, Abe Mirkin Svc. award 2002), Aerospace Med. Assn. (editl. bd. 1994-97); mem. APHA (governing coun. 1975-77, jour. bd. 1983-87, award for excellence 1999), Am. Trauma Soc. (bd. dirs., Disting. Achievement award 1981, Stone lectr. 1985), Am. Assn. for Surgery of Trauma (hon., Fitts oration award 1996), Phi Beta Kappa, Delta Omega. Office: Johns Hopkins U Sch Hygiene & Pub Health 624 N Broadway Baltimore MD 21205-1900 Office Phone: 410-955-2078.

BAKER, VICTORIA JEAN, anthropology educator; b. Austin, Tex., Aug. 20, 1945; d. Leonidas and Virginia Capps Baker; 1 child, Maurits Vlek. PhD, U. Leiden, The Netherlands, 1988. Lectr. Am. Internat. Sch. of The Hague, Netherlands, 1967—83; rschr. Leiden Inst. Devel. Studies and Consultancy Svcs. (LIDESCO), Leiden, 1986—87. Lectr. U. Leiden, Netherlands, 1986; prof. anthropology Eckerd Coll., St. Petersburg, 1988—2002. Author: (book) A Sinhalese Village in Sri Lanka: Coping with Uncertainty, 1998, The Blackboard in the Jungle: Education in Disadvantaged Rural Areas, 1988. Recipient Robert A. Staub Disting. Tchr. award, Eckerd Coll., 1997; grantee Rotary Internat. tchg. grantee, 2001Rotary International, 2001; scholar Freeman Found. Student-Faculty grantee, 1998. Mem.: Fulbright Association (scholar 2000—01), Sigma Xi, Omicron Delta Kappa, Phi Beta Kappa. Avocation: travel. Home: 1244 Murok Way S Saint Petersburg FL 33705 Office: Eckerd Coll 4200 54th Ave S Saint Petersburg FL 33711 Business E-mail: bakervj@eckerd.edu.

BAKER-BOWENS, HELEN L. administrative assistant, genealogy researcher; b. Bronx, N.Y., Mar. 7, 1948; d. Kenneth L. and Ruth Jane (Watson) Baker; children: Clinton, George, Alphonso, Belynda, Marc. BA, St. Peter's Coll., Jersey City, 1984. Adie to city councilman Cit of Jersey City, 1982-84, exec. asst. to coun. pres., 1984-87; shelter mgr. Spouse Abuse Shelter, Clearwater, Fla., 1987-89; ch. sec. Lighthouse Bapt. Ch., Jersey City, 1979—85, Mt. Olive AME Ch., Clearwater, Fla., 1996—. Vice chair bd. Corp. of Employment and Tng., Jersey City, 1983-87. Author: (genealogy) Mt. Olive AME State Historical Designation, 1999, Nat. Designation, 2000. Mem. N.J. State Dem. Com., 1984. Recipient Mary McLeod Bethune award Women's Coalition, Jersey City, 1985. Mem. African Meth. Episcopal Ch. Avocations: genealogy, reading, fishing. Office: Mt Olive AME Ch 600 Jones St Clearwater FL 33755-4136

BAKER KNOLL, CATHERINE, lieutenant governor; b. Pitts. d. Nicholas James and Theresa Mary (May) Baker; m. Charles A. Knoll Sr. (dec.); children: Charles A. Jr., Mina B., Albert B., Kim Eric. BS in Edn. Duquesne U., 1952, MS in Edn. 1973. Dir. western Pa. region Safety Adminstrn. Dept. Transp., Pitts., 1971-79; exec. dir. community svc. Dept. of Adminstrn., Allegheny County, Pa., 1980-88; treas. Pa. Treasury Dept. Harrisburg, 1988—. Owner, operator pvt. bus. firm, Pitts., 1952-70. Mem. Pa. Dem. State Com., Pa. Fedn. Dem. Women, YMCA Bd., Pitts., Harrisburg, Duquesne U. Alumni Bd., Mom's House, Zontas Inc. Bd. Mem. Nat. Assn. State Treas., Women Execs. in State Gov., Coun. State Gov. (exec. com. ea. region). Roman Catholic. Office: Governor Office 225 Main Capitol Bldg Harrisburg PA 17120

BAKES, EMMA, astrophysicist; b. Eng., 1968; PhD in Astrophysics, London U.; student, Newcastle U. Rsch. asst. Princeton U.; asst. prof. Vassar Coll., 1995; astrophysicist NASA, Ames, Calif. Grantee numerous rsch. grants. Avocations: Kung Fu, running, weight lifting. Office: NASA Ames Rsch Ctr Bldg 245 Rm 233A Moffett Field CA 94035

BAKKE, HOLLY, bank commission official; BA, Drew U., 1973; grad. fellow, Inst. Court Mgmt. of Nat. Ctr. St. Courts, 1978; JD, Seton Hall U., 1982. Spcl. dep. commr. ins. litigation practices NJ Dept. Ins.; exec. dir. NJ Surplus Lines Ins. Guaranty Fund, 1989—2002, NJ Property-Liability Ins. Guaranty Assn., 1989—2002, NJ Med. Malpractice Reinsurance Assn., 1989—2002; commr. NJ Dept. Banking and Ins., 2002—. Mem.: NJ State Bar Assn. (chair Alternative Dispute Resolution Comm., Judicial Admin. Comm.). Office: PO Box 325 Trenton NJ 08625

BAKKE, LUANNE KAYE, music educator; b. Rochester, Ind., Apr. 3, 1937; d. Lyman Dean and Anna Lorraine (Bull) Burkett; m. Ronald Roark (div. 1981); m. Jacques Roland Bakke, Feb. 24, 1988; 1 child, Kathleen Anne. BA, Calif. St. U., Northridge, 1977; MusM, Calif. State U., Fullerton, 1981. Instr. Calif. State U., Fullerton, 1979—81, City Coll. Chgo., Karlsruhe, Germany, 1985—86, Gadsden City Coll., Gadsden, Ala., 1986—87; pvt. practice piano & voice Lander, Wyo., 1995—, Music dir. Wood'N Ship Prodn., L.A., Calif., 1978 80; prodr. & dir. Off the Track Singers, L.A., 1975—77. Contbr. The Anniston Star Newspaper, 1982—91; composer: (plays) The Adventure of Doraleen, 1981. Pres. Pomona Valley Music Tchrs. Assn., 1969; music dir. Anniston Cmty. Theater, Anniston, Ala., 1987—89; cmty. choir dir. Harmonic Jam, Granite Falls, Minn., 1992—95; creator Performing Arts in Miniature, 1997—. Recipient Frank Jones award for leadership in the arts, City of Anniston, 1986. Mem.: Music Tchrs. Nat. Assn., Pi Kappa Lambda. Republican. Avocations: scuba diving, hiking, care of animals. Home: 1244 Murok Way [illegible] E-mail: jbakke@wyoming.com.

BAKKEN, JILL, Olympic athlete; b. Portland, Oreg., Jan. 25, 1977; Mem. U.S. Women's Bobsled Team, Lake Placid, NY, 1994—. Mem. Armed Forces World Class Athlete Program. With U.S. Army Nat. Guard. Finalist Sportswoman of Yr., Women's Sports Found., 1998; nominee Nat. Dial award, 1995; recipient Gold medal, Internat. Push Competition, Gotha, Germany, 1997, 1st pl., U.S. Sliding Sport Championships, Park City, 2000, Gold medal, 2002 Olympic Games, Salt Lake City, U.S. Olympic Spirit award, 2002. Address: US Bobsled and Skeleton Fedn PO Box 828 421 Military Rd Lake Placid NY 12946-0828

BALABAN, VIVIAN, librarian, elementary school educator; b. Mount Vernon, N.Y., July 23, 1933; d. William and Claire Eisenberg Balaban. BS in Edn., CCNY, 1955; MS in Libr. Svc., Columbia U., 1960. Cert. elem. sch. tchr. grades K-6 N.Y., 1955, libr. N.Y., 1960. 2nd grade elem. sch. tchr. Brentwood (N.Y.) Pub. Schs., 1955—56; libr. trainee N.Y. Pub. Libr., N.Y.C., 1957—59, Mount Vernon (N.Y.) Pub. Libr., 1960—61; reference libr. CUNY Hunter Coll. Libr., N.Y.C., 1961—95. Vol. Headstart Day Care-Ednl. Alliance, N.Y.C., 1995—2003. Mem.: Chelsea For Peace. Democrat. Jewish. Avocations: travel, movies, theater, music, reading. Home: 365 W 28th St #16E New York NY 10001

BALABAN-PERRY, ELEANOR, retired advertising executive; b. Chgo., Sept. 2, 1914; d. Abraham and Anna (Gorindar) Balaban; m. Paul Noble Sutton, Mar. 1935 (div. 1940); m. Charles Edson Rose, June 1940 (div. 1960); m. William Perry Feb. 16, 1967 (dec. Sept. 1979); 1 child, Sydney Rose. BA, U. Wis. 1935; postgrad., U. Chgo., 1943, Loyola U. Chgo., 1991-92, Columbia Coll., 1990. Founder, CEO Elron, Chgo., 1949-61; mktg. exec. Roth Bros., Chgo., 1962-67; advt. dir. Carsons, Chgo., 1971-82; retired, 1982. Curriculum chair Inst. for Learning in Retirement, 1993, coord., presenter, 1993-95. Mem. editl. bd. Inst. for Learning in Retirement Jour., 1993-96; editor: Renaissance Court Anthology 1-2-3, 1994-96, Keeping Our Heads On Straight, Original Writing in the Golden Years, 1996; author numerous poems and short stories; presenter Loyola-Mundelein, Emeritus Connection, 1997-98; contbr. anthology, America's Favorite Poem, Norton, 1999. Citizens com. People for Am. Way, Washington, 1988. Recipient Honor award Cook County (Ill.) Sheriff, 1995, Ill. Cert. Lifetime Achievement award, Women History, 1995.

BALANDRAN, STELLA VARONA, interpreter, lyricist, composer, writer; b. NYC, May 16, 1932; d. Rafael Patricio Garcia and Stella Ginorio; m. Ricardo Balandran; m. Emilio Varona; children: Charles Varona, Henry Varona, Emil Varona. Student, Middlesex C.C, Middletown, Conn., 1966—68, New Haven U., 1970—72, U. Davis, 1990—92; cert. paralegal, Napa Valley Coll., 1993. Cert. mediator Conflict Resolution and Rsch. Inst. Interpreter/Transls. (Conn.) Police Dept. Ct., 1961—72; elderly specialist City of Meriden, 1972—74; mgr. Am. Cancer Soc., Vallejo, Calif., 1982—87; paralegal Solano County Legal Assistance, Vallejo, 1987—94; dir. Spanish Translations Lake County, Umatilla, Fla., 1997—; interpreter LanguageLine, Monterey, Calif., 2000—02. Composer: (Album) De Amantes A Extraños, 1987 (Album) Dare to Dream, 1991; author: (poetry) Am. Poetry Assn., World of Poetry, Nat. Libr. Poetry. Poems. Friends of the Libr., Umatilla, 1999—2000; bd. mem. Commn. on Aging, Meriden, 1972—74, Bd. Supers. Affirmative Action Com., Solano County, Calif., 1992—93; pres. P.R. Rep. Club, Meriden, 1964—67; del. Dem. State Conv., Orlando. Named Disting. Poet, 1996; named to. Internat. Poetry Hall of Fame, 1996; recipient various awards, San Francisco Festival de la Cancion, 1986, 1987, 1988, 1989, 1990, 1992, 1998. Mem.: ASCAP, NARAS, Am. Soc. Composers, Authors, Pubs., Latin Assn. Rec. Arts and Scis. Roman Catholic. Avocation: volunteer English as Second Language Teacher. Office: Spanish Translations of Lake County 95 S Trowell Ave Umatilla FL 32784 Personal E-mail: EstelaBMus@CS.Com. Business E-Mail: EstelaBMus@CS.Com.

BALASKI, BELINDA L. actress, educator; d. Lester Anthony Balaski and Norma Jean Jahn; 1 adopted child, Sharisse M. Bray. Actress, owner, tchr., creator BB's Kids Acting Sch., LA, 1986—. Author: (plays) The T-Files,

1999; star The Howling, Are You My Mother, Bobby Jo and the Outlaws, The Runaway, others. Recipient Best Supporting Actress, LA Drama Critics Cir., 1972, Robbie award for Best Supporting Actress, 1973, Robbie award for Best Actress, 1974. Office: BB's Kids Acting Sch PO Box 461011 Los Angeles CA 90046 Office Phone: 323-650-5437.

BALAS-WHITFIELD, SUSAN, artist; b. New Jersey, U.S.A. m. Marshall Whitfield. B.A., Rutgers U., Newark, 1964, N.Y. U., N.Y., 1961—64, Douglass Coll., New Brunswick, 1960—61. Tchr. WM. R. Satz. Sch., Holmdel, NJ, 1976—89; artist, 1976—. Author: (novels) Into The Triangle, A Teacher's Trot, 1989. Pres. Ranch Property Owners Assoc., Durango, Colo., 2000—03. Recipient Full Signature Mem., Pastel Society of Am., 2001, Artist of the Yr., Durango Co. Chamber of Commerce. Mem.: Pastel Soc. of Am., Salmagundi Club. Avocations: motorcycling, skiing, running, hiking. Home: 308 CottonWood Creek Rd Durango CO 81301 Office Phone: 970-259-0774.

BALAZ, BEVERLY ANN, publishing executive; b. Danbury, Conn., Dec. 15, 1949; d. William Charles and Loretta (Bielaczyc) B. BS in Edn., Western Conn. State U., 1972. Exec. sec., jr. copywriter Grolier Enterprises, Inc., Danbury, 1973-75; tchr. English and reading Brookfield Jr. HS, Conn., 1975-76; trainee advt. and sales promotion Grolier Ednl. Corp., Danbury, Conn., 1977-78, coord. advt. and sales promotion, 1978-79, mgr. advt. and sales promotion prodn., 1979-81, mgr. advt. and sales promotion, 1981-83, mgr. mktg. adminstrn., 1983-88, dir. direct mktg., 1988-90, v.p. mktg., 1991-95; pres. Facts on File Pub., NYC, 1996-97, William Charles & Assocs., Danbury, Conn., 1997-98; pub. Macmillan Libr. Reference USA, NYC, 1998-99; v.p., gen. mgr. Raintree Steck-Vaugher Pub., NYC, 2000-01; v.p. mktg. World Book, Inc., Chgo., 2001—02; v.p. sales and mktg. Charter Oaklending Group, LLC, Fairfield, Conn., 2002—. Vol. Danbury chpt. Am. Heart Assn.; bd. dirs. Arrowood Condominium Assn., 1989; officer exec. com., 1st v.p., dir. spl. events Keynotes, The Charles Ives Ctr. for the Arts. Mem. Direct Mktg. Assn., Women's Direct Response Group, Direct Mktg. Club N.Y.C. Democrat. Roman Catholic. Avocations: skiing, racquetball, boating. Home: 20 E Pembroke Rd Unit 73 Danbury CT 06811-3705 Office: Macmillan Libr Reference USA 1633 Broadway New York NY 10019-6708

BALBACH, RUTH T. elementary school educator; b. Perth Amboy, N.J., Oct. 15, 1947; d. John and Frances Ragula; m. Gordon J. Balbach, Apr. 30, 1977. BA, Georgian Ct. Coll., Lakewood, N.J., 1969, MA, 1978. Cert. tchg. N.J. Elem. educator Lakewood Bd. of Edn., 1969—. Named Tchr. of Yr., Lakewood Tchrs., 1998. Mem.: NEA, Ocean County Reading Coun., Lakewood Edn. Assn., Ocean County Edn. Assn., N.J. Edn. Assn., Alpha Delta Kappa (v.p. 1979—82). Avocations: travel, reading, art and science. Office: Lakewood Bd Edn 655 Princeton Ave Lakewood NJ 08701 Personal E-mail: ruth@balbach.org. Business E-Mail: ruth@balbach.org.

BALBAUGH, ETHEL L. insurance agent; b. San Antonio, Nov. 11, 1956; d. Gilbert S. Lemons and Josephine V. Lemons-Alley; m. Gary R. Balbaugh, Oct. 15, 1977; children: Robert, Sarah. Grad. H.S., San Antonio. Office mgr. Allstate Ins., San Antonio, 1993—99; ins. agt. Prudential Ins. Co., San Antonio, 1999—2002; property and casualty agt. AAA, San Antonio, 2002—. Active Women at the Well, San Antonio, 2001. Mem.: United Meth. Women. Avocations: church activities, walking, cooking. Home: 12726 Via Perfecto San Antonio TX 78233 Office: AAA Tex 13415 San Pedro San Antonio TX 78216

BALCH, NELDA CAROLINE KURTZ, humanities educator; b. Kelley's Island, Ohio, July 13, 1916; d. Robert John and Lydia Amelia (Schnittker) K.; m. Donald Arthur Balch, Aug. 8, 1948 (dec. 1969). BA, Albion (Mich.) Coll., 1937; MA, U. Minn., 1938; student, Yale U., 1941, Northwestern U., 1946, U. Mich., Mich. State U., U. Oregon. Asst. prof. Simpson Coll., Indianola, Iowa, 1939-43, West Liberty (W.Va.) State Coll., 1946, Linfield Coll., McMinnville, Oreg., 1946-52; prof., chair Kalamazoo (Mich.) Coll., 1954-81, prof. non-traditional classes, 1981-85, dir., reader Faculty Readers, 1960-92, dir., reader Noontime Tales, 1985—, emeritus prof., 1981—. Author: The Kalamazoo College Festival Playhouse; contbr. articles to Notable Women in American Theatre, 1989; dir., playwright Noel Coward, 1989, Camille and Rodin, Gertrude Stein, Paula M. Becker, Mabeland; actress; featured in Emancipated Spirits, 1983. Founder, mng. dir. Festival Playhouse, Kalamazoo, 1964-81; active Friends of Art Ctr., Venice, Fla., 1990—, Kalamazoo Arts Coun., 1987-94; Aero Club dir. ARC, Eng. and France, 1943-45; dir. Readers' Theatre, Venice Pub. Libr., 1996—, ann. readers benefit program, 1995—. Recipient Cmty. Arts. Medal, Kalamazoo Arts Coun., 1985; tchg. fellow U. Minn., 1938-39; Nelda K. Balch Playhouse dedicated in her honor, 1981. Mem. Am. Assn. Univ. Women (former v.p.), Kalamazoo Art Inst., Phi Beta Kappa. Democrat. Methodist. Avocations: painting, walking, swimming, writing, volunteerism. Home: 1780 B Lake Pl Venice FL 34293-1942

BALCOMB, MARY NELSON, design studio owner; b. Mich., Apr. 29, 1928; d. Andrew and Selma (Martin) Nelson; m. Robert S. Balcomb, July 3, 1948; children: Stuart V., Amis. AA, Am. Acad. Art, 1948; BFA cum laude, U. N.Mex., 1968; MFA, U. Wash., 1971. Advt. mgr. Broome Furniture Co., Albuquerque, 1949-55; designer Custom Interiors, Albuquerque, 1956-66; art tchr. Sandia Girls' Sch., Albuquerque, 1966-68; co-owner Woolcot, Inc., Bellevue, Wash., 1975-80; owner Balcomb Design Studio, Silverdale, Wash., 1981—. Author: Nicolai Fechin, Russian-American Artist, 1975 (Rounce and Coffin award), Les Perhacs, Sculptor, 1975, William F. Reese, American Artist, 1984 (Rounce and Coffin award), Robin-Robin/A Journal, 1995, Sergei Bongart, Russian-American Artist, 2002; contbr. articles to periodic jours. Creator Children's Art Ctr. Found., Seattle, 1972, bd. dirs., 1972-80. Recipient Painting award Frye Art Mus., 1994, Honorarium Prix de West Nat. Cowboy Hall of Fame and We. Heritage Mus., 1995. Mem. Author's Guild, Phi Kappa Phi, Lambda Rho. Home: PO Box 1922 Silverdale WA 98383-1922

BALDASSANO, CORINNE LESLIE, radio executive; b. N.Y.C., May 16, 1950; d. Nicholas and Olga Baldassano. BA cum laude, Queens Coll., CUNY, 1970; MA in Theatre, Hunter Coll., CUNY, 1975; MBA in Fin., NYU, 1986. Program dir., ops. mgr. Sta. KAUM-FM, Houston, 1977-79; dir. programming Sta. WSAI-FM, Cin., 1979-81, ABC Contemporary and FM Radio Networks, N.Y.C., 1981-84; regional mgr. affiliate rels. United Stas. Radio Networks, N.Y.C., 1985-87; dir. ABC Entertainment Radio Networks, 1987-90; v.p. programming ABC Radio Networks, 1990-94, Unistar Radio Networks, L.A., 1994, SW Networks, N.Y.C., 1994-95, sr. v.p. programming, 1995; gen. mgr. radio divsn. AP, 1997-99; v.p. broadcast programming SOUNDSBIG.COM, 1999—. Guest lectr. Wharton Sch. Bus., Phila., 1983, St. John's U., N.Y.C., 1983-84; bd. dirs. Country Radio Broadcasters, Inc., Nashville, 1990—, chmn. agenda com., 1990. Alumni mem. Govs. Com. Scholastic Achievement, N.Y.C., 1984-85. Named among 20 Most Influential Women in Radio, Radio Ink Mag., 1999. Mem. NYU Bus. Forum (bd. dirs. 1988-91, v.p., treas. 1990-91), Internat. Radio and TV Soc. (planning com., faculty/industry seminar 1986, 87, chmn. Summer Fellowship Program 1988), Nat. Music Found. (N.Y. bd. 1992-93, 94-96). Democrat. Roman Catholic. Avocations: travel, theatre, dance, running, music. Office: Soundsbig dot com 695 Atlantic Ave Boston MA 02111-2623

BALDRIDGE, JANE L. graphic artist, fine artist; b. Stevens Point, Wis., Feb. 23, 1959; d. Ralph Bayard and Elizabeth (McIntosh) Baldridge; m. Mark Harrington Brown, Oct. 11, 1978 (div. 1982); 1 child, Jason David Cook. Student, Calif. Inst. Arts, Valencia, 1977-78, Alfred Glassel Sch. Art, Houston, 1978-81. Artist, Tex., Calif., Mich., N.C., 1972—; owner The Village Gallery, Brooklyn, Mich.; salesperson, framer Fidler's Gallery, Wilmington, N.C.; asst. pub. Cape Fear Real Estate Directory, Wrightsville Beach, N.C.; owner, designer Artspeaks, Wilmington. Curator Arts Coun. Lower Cape Fear, Wilmington; tchr., lectr. in schs., Wilmington; advt. agy. cons. Exhibited in shows at Art Gallery Originals, Winston-Salem, N.C., Sea Pines Gallery, Hilton Head, S.C., Feast of the Pirates Art Show, Wilmington, N.C., St. John Mus., Wilmington, N.C., New Elements Gallery, Wilmington, New Eng. Art Inst., Boston, Women's Ctr. 10th Ann. Art Show, Chapel Hill, N.C., Piney Woods Art Festival, Wilmington, Fayetteville (N.C.) Mus. Art, Arts Festival, Dalton, Ga., Creative Resource Gallery, Wilmington, Art Mus., Mytrle Beach, S.C., Lincoln Ctr., N.Y.C., World Festival Paper, Kranj, Slovenia, numerous others; represented in collections at Merrill Lynch, Dean Witter Reynolds Inc., Landmark Homes, Inc., others. Mem. troop com. Boy Scouts Am., treas., 1998—. Recipinet Gold medal for Adams Cup (sailing, 1976, Gold medal for Art, Scholastic awards, 1974, Pres.'s award Calif. Inst. of the Arts, 1978, numerous awards for art; regional artist grantee, 1994, 2000. Mem. St. Louise Cameron Mus. Art, N.C. Coastal Fedn., Citizens Protecting Resources. Office: Artspeaks 8947 Shipwatch Dr Wilmington NC 28412-3537 E-mail: dolphinae@earthlink.net.

BALDRIDGE, KIM, science educator; BS in math., Minot State U., ND, 1982; MA in math., ND State U., 1985, PhD in theoretical chemistry, 1988. Joined San Diego Supercomputer Ctr., 1989, dir. integrative computational scis., 2002—; adj. prof. chemistry U. Calif., San Diego, 1997—. Hon. guest prof. U. Basel. Recipient award, Fulbright Found., 1997, Agnes Fay Morgan rsch. award, Iota Sigma Pi, 2000. Fellow: AAAS, Am. Phys. Soc. Office: San Diego Super Computer Ctr Dept Chemistry 9500 Gilman Dr La Jolla CA 92093-0505

BALDRIGE, LETITIA, writer, management training consultant; b. Miami Beach, Fla. d. Howard Malcolm and Regina (Connell) B.; m. Robert Hollensteiner; children: Clare, Malcolm. BA, Vassar Coll., 1946; postgrad., U. Geneva, 1946-48; DHL (hon.), Creighton U., 1979, Mt. St. Mary's Coll., 1980, Bryant Coll., 1987, Kenyon Coll., 1990. Personal-social sec. to amb. Am. Embassy, Paris, 1948-51; intelligence officer Washington, 1951-53; asst. to amb. Am. Embassy, Rome, 1953-56; dir. pub. rels. Tiffany & Co., 1956-60; social sec. The White House, 1961-63; pres. Letitia Baldrige Enterprises, Chgo., 1964-69; dir. consumer affairs Burlington Industries, 1969-71; pres. Letitia Baldrige Enterprises, Inc., Washington, 1972—. Author: Roman Candle, 1956, Tiffany Table Settings, 1958, Of Diamonds and Diplomats, 1968, Home, 1972, Juggling, 1976, Amy Vanderbilt's Complete Book of Etiquette, 1978, Amy Vanderbilt's Everyday Etiquette, 1979, Entertainers, 1981, Letitia Baldrige's Complete Guide to Executive Manners, 1985, Letitia Baldrige's Complete Guide to a Great Social Life, 1987, Complete Guide to the New Manners for the '90s, 1990, New Complete Guide to Executive Manners, 1993, (novel) Public Affairs Private Relations, 1990, More Than Manners! Raising Today's Kids to Have Kind Manners and Good Hearts, 1997, In the Kennedy Style, 1998, Legendary Brides, 2000, A Lady, First, 2001, New Manners fr New Times, 2003. Mem. adv. bd. Woodrow Wilson House, Washington, Reading Is Fundamental, Malcolm Baldrige Nat. Quality Awards, Woodrow Wilson Nat. Fellowship Found. Republican. E-mail: lbaldrige@aol.com.

BALDWIN, BONNIE, physician; b. Dallas, Dec. 18, 1954; d. Eugene and Mary Ellen Jericho; m. Robert Talbot Baldwin, May 28, 1985; children: Robert, Ryan. AB, Duke U., 1977; MD, Baylor Coll. Medicine, 1985. Gen. surgery resident U. Tex.-Houston, 1985-88; plastic surgery resident Baylor Coll. Medicine, Houston, 1988-91; asst. prof. M.D. Anderson Cancer Ctr., Houston, 1991-97; physician pvt. practice, Houston, 1997—. Med. advisor Reach for Recovery, Houston, 1999, cons. M.D. Anderson, 1998—. Contbr. articles to profl. jours. Named to Best Doctors in Am., 1998, Best Scientific Exhibit Am. Soc. Aesthetic Plastic Surgery, 1997. Fellow ACS; mem. Am. Soc. Plastic Surgery, Soc. Surg. Oncology. Office: Cons in Plastic Surgery 7737 Southwest Fwy Ste 201 Houston TX 77074-1865

BALDWIN, DOROTHY LEILA, secondary school educator; b. Irvington, N.J., Feb. 28, 1948; d. Daniel Thomas and Lillian Frances (Wainright) B. BA, Kean Coll., Union, N.J., 1969, MA in Edn. and Humanities, 1971; EdD in Adminstrn. and Supervision, Seton Hall U., 1987, cert. reading specialist, 1979, cert. bus. adminstr., 1985. Tchr., reading coord. St. Paul Apostle Sch. Irvington, 1969-74; tchr. Summit (N.J.) Jr. High Sch., 1975-79; social studies coord. K-9, chmn. dept. 7-9 Summit Pub. schs., 1979-87; social studies supr. Livingston (N.J.) Pub. Schs., 1987; prin. Point Road Sch, Little Silver, N.J., 1987-89; dir. gifted edn. K-12 Clifton, N.J., 1989-90; prin. Sch. Two, Clifton, N.J., 1989-90, Deerfield Sch., Mountainside, 1990-92, Eisenhower Sch., Bridgewater-Raritan, NJ, 1992—2003; prof. Fairleigh Dickinson U., Teaneck, NJ, 2003—. Adj. prof. Montclair (N.J.) U., Passaic County C.C., Morris County C.C.; tchr. adult and cmty. schs.; workshop coord.; cons. in field. Author books; contbr. articles to profl. jours. PTA scholar, 1965. Mem. ASCD, Nat. Assn. Elem. Sch. Prins., Nat. Coun. Social Studies, Am. Assn. Sch. Adminstrs., N.J. Assn. Elem. Sch. Prins., N.J. Prins. Ctr., Somerset County Assn. Elem. Sch. Prins., Phi Delta Kappa, Kappa Delta Pi. Home: 737 River Rd Chatham NJ 07928-1136 Office: Fairleigh Dickinson U 1000 River Rd Teaneck NJ 07666 Office Phone: 201-692-2863. Business E-Mail: dbaldwin@fdu.edu.

BALDWIN, IRENE S. corporate executive, real estate investor; b. Dodge City, Kans., Sept. 8, 1939; d. Albert A. McMichael and Eleanor L. (Johnson) McMichael McGrath; m. Miles Edward Baldwin, June 30, 1961. BS, Friends U., 1961. Dress designer, Wichita, 1959-61; social worker Sedgwick County, Kans., 1963-65; owner motel chain Kans., 1965—; comml. and agrl. real estate investor, 1971—. Owner motel chain, Kans., 1965—; comml. and agrl. real estate investor, 1971—; corp. sec.-treas. Baldwin, Inc., Kans., 1970—, fin. advisor, 1970—; pvt. practice fin. cons., Colby, Kans., 1975—; founder, advisor Charitable Found., Kans., 1980—; fundraiser various charitable orgns., 1982—; pvt. placement of homeless animals, Kans. and Nebr., 1965—; helped develop 1st artificial front leg for canines, 1985. Contbr. articles to profl. jours.; author: (short stories) My Pal Chopper, 2002. Fundraiser various charitable orgns., 1982—; pvt. placement of homeless animals, Kans. and Nebr., 1965—. Avocations: horseback riding, hiking, travel, sewing, drawing. Address: 2320 S Range Ave Colby KS 67701-9056

BALDWIN, JANICE MURPHY, lawyer; b. Bridgeport, Conn., July 16, 1926; d. William Henry and Josephine Gertrude (McKenna) Murphy; m. Robert Edward Baldwin, July 31, 1954; children: Jean Baldwin Grossman, Robert William, Richard Edward, Nancy Baldwin Kitsos. AB, U. Conn., 1948; MA, Mt. Holyoke Coll., 1950; postgrad., U. Manchester, Eng., 1950-51; MA, Tufts U., 1952; JD, U. Wis., 1971. Bar: Wis. 1971, U.S. Dist. Ct. (we. dist.) Wis. 1971. Staff atty. legis. coun. State of Wis., Madison, 1971-74, sr. staff atty., 1975-94; pvt. practice Madison, 1994—. Atty. adviser HUD, Washington, 1974—75, Washington, 1978—79. Fulbright fellow, 1950-51. Mem. AAUW, NOW, LWV (sec. 1996-99, v.p., 1999-2001, bd. dirs. Dane County 1996-2003, exec. com. 1997-2003, nominating com. 2002-), U.S. and Wis. Women's Polit. Caucus, Legal Assn. for Women (chmn. Marygold Meili award com. 1997-99), Wis. Bar Assn. (pres. govt. lawyers divsn. 1985-87, bd. govs. 1985-89, treas. 1987-89, participation of women in bar com. 1987-98, professionalism com. 1990-97, bd. bar examiners rev. 1990-94, law-related edn. com. 1992-95, govt. lawyers divsn. 1981—), Dane County Bar Assn. (legis. com. 1980-81, long range planning com. 1990-97, law for the pub. com. 1993-94), Wis. Women's Network, U. Wis. Univ. League, Older Women's League, Fulbright Assn. Home and Office: 125 Nautilus Dr Madison WI 53705-4329

BALDWIN, MARIE HUNSUCKER, retired secondary school educator; b. Dallas, Dec. 22, 1923; d. Clyde Augustus and Charlotte (Moore) Hunsucker; m. Brewster Baldwin, Aug. 20, 1946 (dec. July 1992); children: Jean Baldwin McLevedge, David, Stephen, Christopher. BS in Edn., Tex. Tech. U., 1944; MFA in Writing, Norwich U., 1988. Tchr. Pub. Sch., Corpus Christi, Tex., 1944-45, Presbyn. Day Sch., Corpus Christi, 1945-46, Pub. Sch., Moriah, N.Y., 1964-66; field dir. Vt. Girl Scout Coun., Burlington, 1966-78; ret. Vice chair Vt. State Dem. Com., Montpelier, 1976-80; apptd. mem. Gov.'s Adult Edn. Coun., 1983-89; founder, pres. Vt. Caths. for Free Choice, 1989—; elected Justice of the Peace, Middlebury, Vt., 1989—. Mem. ACLU (bd. 1984-90), AAUW, LWV (founder, pres. 1952-56), Cath. Daus. Am., Bus. and Profl. Women. Avocations: creative writing, walking, reading.

BALDWIN, PATRICIA ANN, lawyer; b. Detroit, May 3, 1955; d. Frank Thomas and Margaret Elyne (Velghe) Matthews; m. Jeffrey Kenton Baldwin, Aug. 23, 1975; children: Matthew, Katherine, Timothy, Philip. BA summa cum laude, Ball State U., 1976; JD, Ind. U., 1979. Bar: Ind. 1979, U.S. Dist. Ct. (so. dist.) Ind. 1979. Ptnr. Baldwin & Baldwin, Danville, Ind., 1979-94; dep. pros. atty. Hendricks County, Danville, 1980-90, pros. atty., 1995—; dep. pros. atty. Boone County, Ind., 1990-94. Sec.-treas., dir. T.F.W., Inc., Danville, 1983—90. Active Girl Scouts U.S., 1964—2000; cub scout leader Boy Scouts Am., 1986—99, badge counselor; mem. Hendricks County Rep. Women, 1976—, pres., 2001—03; mem. parish coun. Mary Queen of Peace Cath. Ch., 1976—80, 1981—83; bd. dirs. Cath. Social Svcs., Archdiocese of Indpls., sec. bd. dirs., 1986—; bd. dirs. Cummins Mental Health Ctr., 1982—86. Mem.: Hendricks County Bar Assn., Ind. Pros. Attys. Assn., Nat. Dist. Attys. Assn., Danville Conservation Club. Office: One Courthouse Sq #105 Danville IN 46122

BALDWIN, TAMMY, congresswoman; b. Madison, Wis., Feb. 11, 1962; AB in math./polit. sci., Smith Coll., 1984; JD, U. Wis., Madison, 1989. Pvt. practice as atty., 1989-92; Dane County supr. Board of Supervisors, 1986-1994; mem. 78th dist. Wis. State Assembly, 1993-99; mem. U.S. Congress from 2d Wis. dist., Washington, 1999—; mem. budget com., judiciary com. Mem. NOW, ACLU, Wis. State Bar Assn., Internat. Network Lesbian and Gay Ofcls., Nat. Women's Polit. Caucus. Democrat. Office: 1022 Longworth Ho Office Bldg Washington DC 20515 also: 10 E Doty St Ste 405 Madison WI 53703-5103*

BALDWIN ANDERSON, JANET E. researcher; d. Lucien Elmo and Agatha Elaine Baldwin; m. Donald Byron Spangler, Aug. 23, 1969 (div. Oct. 6, 1980); 1 child, Lorin Alane Spangler Young ; m. Richard Dean Anderson, Sept. 17, 1995. BA, U. Fla., 1968, EdM, 1973; PhD, U. Md., 1986. Chief test devel. and adminstrn. Md. State Dept. Edn., Balt., 1985—87; dir. rsch. GED testing svc. Am. Coun. Edn., Washington, 1987—98; prin. rsch. analyst, mgr. assessment program Edn. Stats. Svcs. Inst., Am. Insts. Rsch., Washington, 1998—. Mem.: APA, Internat. Coach Fedn., Am. Ednl. Rsch. Assn. (chair spl. interest group on adult edn. and adult literacy 1994—98), Nat. Coun. Measurement in Edn. (chair profl. practices com. 2000—03, editl. bd. Ednl. Measurement: Issues and Practices 2001—03), Kappa Delta Pi, Phi Lambda Theta, Phi Kappa Phi. Achievements include development of program of research about adult learners in the U.S. and in Canada who take the Tests of General Educational Development; direction of program of research and development in support of large-scale educational assessments of youth and of literacy proficiencies of adults in the U.S. Avocations: writing, reading, yoga, hiking, drawing. Office: Am Insts Rsch-ESSI 1990 K St NW Washington DC 20006

BALES, VIRGINIA SHANKLE, health administrator; BA in Chemistry, Emory U., Atlanta, 1971, MPH, 1977. Dep. dir. Nat. Ctr. Chronic Disease Prevention and Health Promotion Ctrs. for Disease Control and Prevention, 1988—98, dep. dir. program mgmt., 1998—2002, dir. adult and cmty. health divsn. Nat. Ctr. for Chronic Disease Prevention and Health Promotion, 2002—. Office: CDC DHHS Mailstop D14 1600 Clifton Rd NE Atlanta GA 30329-4018

BALICK, HELEN SHAFFER, retired judge; b. Bloomsburg, Pa. d. Walter W. and Clarissa K. (Bennett) Shaffer; m. Bernard Balick, June 29, 1967. JD, Dickinson Sch. Law, 1966, LLD (hon.), 1997. Bar: Pa. 1967, Del. 1969. Probate adminstr. Girard Trust Bank, Phila., 1966-68; pvt. practice law Wilmington, Del., 1969-74; staff atty. Legal Aid Soc. Del., Wilmington, 1969-71; master Family Ct. Del., New Castle County, 1971-74; bankruptcy judge, U.S. magistrate Dist. Del., Wilmington, 1974-80, bankruptcy judge, 1974-94, chief judge, 1994-98; ret., 1998. Guest lectr. Dickinson Sch. Law, 1981-87; lectr. Dickinson Forum, 1982. Pres. bd. trustees Cmty. Legal Aid Soc., Inc., 1972—74; trustee Dickinson Sch. Law, 1985—2000; mem. Citizens Adv. Com., Wilmington, 1973—74, Wilmington Bd. Edn., 1974; bd. dirs. Kutz Home, 1999—2001, Jewish Hist. Soc., 1999—; active U. Del. Libr. Assocs., 1998—, sec., 2000—, v.p., 2001—02; bd. govs. The Dickinson Sch. Law, Pa. State U., 2000—. Recipient Women's Leadership award Del. State Bar Assn., 1997; named to Hall of Fame of Del. Women, 1994. Mem.: AAUW, Dickinson Sch. Law Gen. Alumni Assn. (exec. bd. 1977—80, 1987—2000, v.p. 1981—84, pres. 1984—87, Outstanding Alumni award 1991, Career Achievement award 1998), Turnaround Mgmt. Assn. (bd. dirs. 1995—97), Wilmington Women in Bus. (bd. dirs. 1980—83), Del. Alliance Profl. Women (Trailblazer award 1984), Del. Bar Assn., Am. Bankruptcy Inst., Am. Coll. Bankruptcy, Am. Judges Assn., Nat. Conf. Bankruptcy Judges (bd. govs. 1986), Fed. Bar Assn. Home: 2319 W 17th St Wilmington DE 19806-1330

BALINT, ANNETTE, church administrator; b. Scranton, Pa., July 26, 1948; d. Gerard Salvatore Casciano and Caroline Linda Sanzero; m. Michael Stephen Balint, Apr. 12, 1969. Student, Lacka Jr. Coll., Scranton. Supr. Bell Tel., Scranton, 1966—72; office mgr. Angelica Healthcare, Scranton, 1972—85; coord. Villa St. Joseph Diocese of Scranton, 1985—. Coord. Villa St. Joseph, Dunmore, Pa., 1971—2003. Contbr. articles to local newspapers. Vol. Am. Cancer Soc., 2000—03, Meml. Sloan Kettering, 2000—03; active Altar and Rosary Soc., Scranton, 1966—. Recipient Appreciation award, Am. Cancer Soc., 2003, Attitude award, NRCI, 2003. Mem.: Dem. Women, Cath. Women's Club (bd. mem. 1982—). Home: 124 N St Cabrini Ave Scranton PA 18504 Office: Villa St Joseph 1600 Green Ridge Scranton PA 18504

BALIS, JENNIFER LYNN, retired academic administrator, computer technology educator; b. Hamlin, W.Va., Nov. 23, 1946; 1 child, Theodore Berndt. AA, Del Mar Coll., 1987; BA, U. Tex., 1989; BS, So. Ill. U., 1992. Peer counselor U. Tex., Edinburg, 1989-90; tchr. Mission (Tex.) Ind. Sch. Dist., 1990; instr. San Diego Job Corps, 1992-95; instr. computer tech. Kaskaskia Coll., Centralia, Ill., 1997—2002. Coord. Kaskaskia Coll. Vandalia Ctr., Vandalia, 1999-2001. Chmn., sec. Mulberry Grove Zoning Bd. Appeals, 1999—2002; vol. advocate S.A.F.E., 2003—; coord. Arthritis Support Group, Salem Township Hosp.; comp. tutor for sr. citizens, 2002—; vol. Salem Twp. Hosp., 2003—; instr. Tai Chi for Wellness to Healthy Living, 2003; com. mem. Alma Cmty. Ctr. With USNR, 1984—. Mem. Psi Chi (pres. 1989-90). Republican. Roman Catholic. Avocations: natural healing, folk medicine, mineral collector, archery.

BALKOWIEC, AGNIESZKA ZOFIA, science educator, researcher; b. Sokolow Podlaski, Poland, Sept. 30, 1968; d. Anna and Jerzy Michal Balkowiec. MD, Med. U. Warsaw, Poland, 1993, PhD, 1995. Instr. physiology Med. U. Warsaw, 1993—95, asst. prof., 1995—99; rsch. assoc. Case Western Res. U., Cleve., 1997—2001, instr. neuroscis., 2001—02; asst. prof. Oreg. Health & Sci. U., Portland, 2002—. Contbr. articles to profl. jours.; ad hoc reviewer Neuroscience. Recipient Sci. award, Polish Min. Health and Social Welfare, 1994, 1996, Prime Min. of Poland, 1996; rsch. fellow, Found. Polish Sci., 1995, Scientist Devel. grantee, Am. Heart Assn., 2002—. Mem.: Am. Heart Assn. (basic cardiovas. scis. coun. 2002, grantee 2002—), Soc. Neurosci. Achievements include discovery of the role of activity of nerve cells in regulation of growth factors; invention of setup for immunodetection of growth factors released from neurons following electrical stimulation. Avocations: travel, gourmet cooking, classical music. Office: Oregon Health & Sci U 611 SW Campus Dr Portland OR 97239 E-mail: balkowie@ohsu.edu.

BALL, AMY CATHERINE, education program manager; b. Abingdon, Va., Aug. 24, 1975; d. Willis and Darlene Crabtree Ball. BA in Sci., Va. Tech. U., 1996; M, Hollins U., 1998. Sales mktg. Farm Success, Abingdon, 1996—98, Kirklands, Roanoke, Va., 1998; mktg. dir. CFC Inc., Culpeper, Va., 1999—2000; educator The Crisis Ctr., Bristol, Va., 2000—02; edn. program dir. Washington County Schs., Abingdon, 2002—. Mem. adv. bd. CAUSE, Emory, Va., 2000—, Teen Dating Violence Coalition, Charlottesville, Va., 2001—02. Chmn. Bristol Coalition, 2002. Va. Exposition grantee, 1994. Mem.: Internat. Boer Goat Assoc., Va. Forage Coun., Am. Angus Assn. Democrat. Home: 26912 Denton Valley Rd Abingdon VA 24211 Office: Damascus Neighborhood Academy 21308 Monroe Rd Abingdon VA 24236

BALL, ARNETHA, education educator; BA in Edn., U. Mich., 1971, MA in Speech Pathology, 1972; PhD in Lang., Literacy and Culture, Stanford U., 1991. Ethnic studies resource specialist, speech pathologist, classroom tchr. Richmond (Calif.) Unified Sch. Dist., 1972—73; adminstrv. dir., classroom tchr. Children's Creative Workshop, Richmond, 1974—80; classroom tchr. Aurora (Ill.) Elem. Sch., 1984—86; speech pathologist Audiology Assocs. of Dayton, Ohio, 1986—87; external program evaluator L.A. Unified Sch. Dist., 1991—92; postdoctoral fellow U. Mich., 1991—92, asst. prof. edn., 1992—98, assoc. prof. edn., coord. literacy, lang. and culture program, 1998—99; assoc. prof. edn. Stanford (Calif.) U., 1999—. Mem. exec. com. Conf. on Coll. Composition and Comm., 1996—; mem. Standing Com. on Rsch., 1995. Contbr. articles to profl. jours.; mem. editl. bd.: Urban Education, 1996—, Assessing WRiting, 1995. Mem.: Nat. Coun. Tchrs. of English Found. (trustee 1996—), Am. Ednl. Rsch. Assn. (chair divsn. G nominating com. 1998—). Achievements include research in linking sociocultural and linguistic theory with educational practices; linguistic resources; linguistic practices among culturally and linguistically diverse populations. Office: Stanford U Sch Edn 485 Lasuen Mall Stanford CA 94305-309

BALL, BETTY JEWEL, retired social worker, consultant; b. Sherman, Tex., Aug. 9, 1933; d. Emmett Jesse and Ethel Viola (Chesnut) B. BS, Okla. Bapt. U., 1954; M.Religious Edn., Carver Sch., 1958; MSW, Smith Coll., 1964. Cert. and lic. clin. social workers, Ill. Psychiat. social worker Inst. for Juvenile Rsch., Chgo., 1964-66; dir. child devel. ctr. Infant Welfare Soc. Chgo., 1966-71; dir. day hosp. for children Madden Mental Health Ctr., Chgo., 1971-78; child and adolescent coord. Ill. Dept. Mental Health, Chgo., 1978-83; pvt. practice social work cons. Hoffman Estates, Ill., 1983-93. Home and Office: 1225 Via Rafael San Marcos CA 92069-7102

BALL, DEBORAH LOEWENBERG, education educator; BA, Mich. State U., 1976, MA, 1982, postgrad., 1981—83, PhD, 1988. Arthur F. Thurnau prof. U. Mich. Sch. Edn., Ann Arbor, 2000—. Lead author Stds. for Tchg. sect. Profl. Stds. for Tchg. Math., Nat. Coun. Tchrs. Math., 1989—91; mem. adv. bd. Investigations in Number, Data, Space, 1991—96; mem. Commn. on Behavioral and Social Sci. Edn. Nat. Rsch. Coun., [illegible] math. learning study, 1999—2000; chair math. study panel RAND Project: Improving the Quality of Educational Research and Devel., 1999—2000; mem. commn. on undergrad. experience U. Mich., 2000—01; co-chair tchr. edn. study Internat. Commn. on Math. Instrn., 2002—; bd. trustees Math. Scis. Rsch. Inst. U. Calif., Berkeley, 2003—. Contbr. articles to profl. jours.; mem. editl. bd.: Am. Ednl. Rsch. Jour., 1999—, Jour. Ednl. Rsch., 1990—93, Elem. Sch. Jour., 1991—. Recipient Raymond B. Cattell Early Career award for programmatic rsch., Am. Ednl. Rsch. Assn., 1997, Award for outstanding Scholarship on Tchr. Edn., Assn. Colls. and Schs. of Edn. in State Univs. and Land Grant Colls. and Affiliated Pvt. Univs., 1990. Office: U Mich 4119 Sch Edn Bldg 610 E University Ann Arbor MI 48109-1259

BALL, JUDY KAY, minister; b. Lima, Ohio, Sept. 28, 1944; d. Elvin Burke and Selma Elaine (Plummer) Feister; m. Carl James Seaman, June 7, 1961 (div. June 20, 1966); children: James Wade, Reese, Jerry Lee, Kristal Lynn; m. Anthony Ervin Ball, May 16, 1992. H.S. Grad., Lima, Ohio, 1961. Ordained minister Pentecostal Ch., 1978. Asst. cook Wapak Manor, Wapakoneta, Ohio, 1978—81; mealsite tech. PSA Agency on Aging, Lima, 1081—1984; pastor Shekinah Temple, St. Mary's, Ohio, 1982—. Sales assoc. Fashion Bug, St. Mary's, Ohio, 1998—; adv. bd. sec. Otterbein Homes, St. Mary's, Ohio, 1999—; pres. St. Mary's Ministerial Assn., 1999—; cmty. coord. Nat. Day of Prayer, Auglaize County, Ohio, 1999—. Host TV show Ask the Pastor WTLW TV, Lima, Ohio, 1999—, presenter on tapes Dial a Devotion, Fellowship of Chs., St. Mary's, Ohio, 1998—. Coord free meals Loaves and Fishes, Wapakoneta, Ohio, 2000—. Republican. Pentecostal. Home: 139 Windsor Dr Saint Marys OH 45885 Office: Shekinah Temple 519 Greenville Rd Saint Marys OH 45885 Office Phone: 419-394-7063.

BALL, MARCIA, vocalist; b. Orange, Tex., Mar. 20, 1949; m. Gordon Fowler. Student, La. State U., 1967. Mem. band Freda and the Firedogs, Austin, Tex., 1972-74; founder, mem. band Marcia Ball Band (formerly Marcia and the Misery Bros.), 1975. Performer (solo recording) I Want to Be a Cowboy's Sweetheart, 1975, (album) Circuit Queen, 1978, Soulful Dress, 1983, Hot Tamale Baby, 1986, Gatorhythms, 1989, Dreams Come True, 1991, Blue House, 1994, Let My Play with Your Poodle, 1997, Sing It!, 1998 (Grammy nominee for best contemporary blues album), Presumed Innocent, 2001, So Many Rivers, 2003; appeared at New Orleans Jazz and Heritage Festival, 1978-99. Recipient W.C. Handy award, 1998.

BALL, MARION JOKL, academic administrator; b. South Africa; d. Ernst and Erica Jokl. Student, Northwestern U., 1957-58; BA in Math. with distinction, U. Ky., 1961, MA in Math., 1965; EdD, Temple U., 1978. Math tchr. Bryan Station High Sch., Lexington, Ky., 1961-62; programmer, instr. dept. behavioral sci., and computer sci. U. Ky. Med. Ctr., Lexington, 1965-68; asst. dir., med. computer activity, asst. prof. Temple U., Phila., 1968-72; dir. computer systems and mgmt. group, assoc. prof. Temple U. Health Scis. Ctr., Phila., 1972-85; dir. acad. computing U. Md., Baltimore, 1985-87, assoc. v.p. info. resources, prof., 1985-91; v.p. Info. Svcs. U. Maryland, 1991—; adj. prof. sch. nursing Johns Hopkins U., Baltimore; v.p. clin. solutions divsn. Healthlink Inc., Houston, 2001—. Bd. dirs. Intellimed, CliniCom, Inc., 1986-88; panel mem. Nat. Libr. Medicine, 1985-86, 1988—; adv. bd. Systems Dimensions Ltd., 1974-75, Nat. Assn. Hosp. Admitting Mgrs., 1983-85, Sperry Corp., 1984—, MEAD Co., 1985, Office Tech. Assessment, 1987, Educom Consulting Group, 1988-89; chmn. Am. Med. Informatics Assn. Transition Task Force on Membership, 1989; chmn. Am. Med. Informatics Assn. internat. affairs com.; U.S. rep. MEDINFO, 1983—, MEDINFO scientific program com., 1989—; rsch. devel. com. Am. Med. Record Assn., 1978-83; mem. tech. subcom. com. on improving patient records, Inst. Medicine, co chair, 1989-91; cons. in field. Author: Selecting a Computer System for the Clinical Laboratory, 1971, What is AComputer?, 1972, How to Select a Computerized Hospital Information System, 1973; author: (with S Charp) Be a Computer Literate!, 1978, author: (with K. Hannah)Using Computers in Nursing (nursing book yr. award 1985), 1984; author: (with others) Healthcare Information Management Systems: A Practical Guide, 1990, New Hospital Information Systems, 1988, Nursing Informatics: Where Caring and Technology Meet, 1988, Cancer Informatics: Essential Technologies for Clinical Trials, 2002. Fellow NSF, Phila. Coll. Physicians. Mem. Am. Med. Informatics Assn. (Morris F. Collen Award, 2002), Am. Assn. for Med. Systems and Informatics, Am. Hosp. Assn., Am. Med. Records Assn., Internat. Med. Informatics Assn. (pres. 1992—), Assn. for Computing Machinery, Healthcare Information and Mgmt. Systems Soc. (bd. dirs. 1989-92), Montessori Soc., Network of Women in Computer Tech., Phila. Coll. Physicians, Inst. Medicine (tech. subcom. and bd. dirs. on improving the patient record 1989—, Mortarboard Sr. Woman's Honor Soc., Delta Phi Alpha, Kappa Delta Pi, Phi Mu Eplison; fellow Am. Coll. Med. Informatics, 1984-. Home: Roland Pk N 5706 Coley Ct Baltimore MD 21210-1344 Office: U of Md Info Svcs 100 N Greene St Baltimore MD 21201-1563

BALL, MILLIE (MILDRED PORTEOUS BALL), editor, journalist; b. New Orleans, Nov. 15, 1945; d. Harold Curtis and Mildred (Porteous) B.; m. Keith Cooper Marshall, Oct. 17, 1981. BA, Fla. State U., 1967. Editor young people's page The Times-Picayune, New Orleans, 1967-71, city desk reporter, 1971-79, staff writer Dixie Mag., 1979-82, staff writer living sect., 1982-89, travel editor, 1990—. Author: (with others) Fodor's New Orleans, 1990, Gault Millau New Orleans, 1991. Recipient various writing awards AP, La. Press Assn., Press Club New Orleans, Odyssey House, 1970-90, Lowell Thomas award Soc. Am. Travel Writers Found., 1992, Bronze Travel Journalist of Yr. award, 1994, Silver-Best Self-Illustrated Story award, 1994, Best Fgn. Story in Newspaper award, 1992, Best Newspaper Travel Sect., 1994, 95. Mem. Chi Omega. Presbyterian. Home: 530 Chartres St New Orleans LA 70130-2110 Office: The Times-Picayune 3800 Howard Ave New Orleans LA 70125-1429

BALL, PATRICIA ANN, physician; b. Lockport, N.Y., Mar. 30, 1941; d. John Joseph and Katherine Elizabeth (Hoffmaster) Ball; m. Robert E. Lee, May 18, 1973; children: Heather Lee, Samantha Lee. BS, U. Mich., 1963; MD, Wayne State U., 1969. Diplomate Am. Bd. Internal Medicine, Am. Bd. Hematology, Am. bd. Med. Oncology. Intern, resident Detroit Gen. Hosp., 1969-71; resident Jackson Meml. Hosp., Miami, Fla., 1971-72; fellow Henry Ford Hosp., Detroit, 1972-74; staff physician VA Hosp., Allen Park, Mich., 1974-77; pvt. practice in hematology and oncology Bloomfield Hills, Mich., 1977—. Faculty dept. medicine Wayne State U. Sch. Medicine, Detroit, 1974—. Mem.: AMA, ACP, Mich. Soc. Hematology and Oncology, Oakland County Med. Soc., Mich. Med. Soc., Detroit Inst. Arts, Founders Soc., Alpha Omega Alpha. Avocations: photography, skiing. Office: 44038 Woodward Ave Ste 101 Bloomfield Hills MI 48302-5036 E-mail: pball@dmc.org.

BALLANFANT, KATHLEEN GAMBER, newspaper executive, public relations company executive; b. Horton, Kans., July 11, 1945; d. Ralph Hayes and Audrey Lavon (Heryford) G.; children: Andrea, Benjamin. BA, Trinity U., 1967; postgrad. NYU, 1976, Am. Mgmt. Inst., 1977, Belhaven Coll., 1985. Pub. info. dir. Tex. Dept. Community Affairs, Austin, 1972-74; pub. affairs mgr. Cameron Iron Works, Houston, 1975-77, Assoc. Builders and Contractors, Houston, 1982-84; pres. Ballanfant & Assoc., Houston, 1977-82, 84—; pres. Village Life Inc., 1985—; pres., chief exec. officer Village Life Publs.; owner Village Life newspaper, Southwest News newspaper, Houston Observer/Times newspaper, Village Life Printing & Typesetting, South Post Oak newspaper; mem. adv. council on Construction Edn., Tex. So. U., Houston, 1984—; mem. task force on ednl. excellence Houston Ind. Sch. Dist., 1983—; mem. devel. bd. Inter First Fannin Bank, 1986-88; bd. dirs. Bellaire Hosp., Westbury-Southwest Assn., Westland YMCA. Author: Something Special-You, 1972, Prevailing Wage History in Houston, 1983, editor newspaper Bellaire Texan, [illegible] 1971. Vice pres. West Univ. Republic Women's Club, Houston, 1984—; fgn. vis. chmn. Internat. Inst. Edn., Houston, 1980—; docent Houston Zoo, 1982; bd. dirs. Westland YMCA. Named Tex. Woman of Achievement Tex. Womans Hosp., 1986; recipient Apollo IX Medal of Honor Gov. Preston Smith, 1970, Child Abuse Prevention award Gov. Dolph Briscoe, 1974, Tex. Community Newspaper Assn. (pres. 1988-89, bd. dirs. 1987-96). Mem. Bellaire C. of C. (bd. dirs. 1987-90, sec., treas. 1988), Inland Press Assn. (bd. dirs. 2001, weekly com. chmn. 2001-), Rotary. Republican. Presbyterian. Avocations: traveling, racquetball, reading. Office: Village Life Inc 5160 Spruce St Bellaire TX 77401-3309 E-mail: vlswnews@aol.com.

BALLANTINE, MORLEY COWLES (MRS. ARTHUR ATWOOD BALLANTINE), editor; b. Des Moines, May 21, 1925; d. John and Elizabeth (Bates) Cowles; m. Arthur Atwood Ballantine, July 26, 1947 (dec. 1975); children— Richard, Elizabeth Ballantine Leavitt, William, Helen Ballantine Healy. AB, Ft. Lewis Coll., 1975; LHD (hon.), Simpson Coll., Indianola, Iowa, 1980, U. Denver, 2002. Pub. Durango (Colo.) Herald, 1952-83, editor, pub., 1975-83, editor, chmn. bd., 1983—; dir. 1st Nat. Bank, Durango, 1976—2002, Des Moines Register & Tribune, 1977-85, Cowles Media Co., 1982-86. Mem. Colo. Land Use Commn., 1975-81, Supreme Ct. Nominating Commn., 1984-90; mem. Colo. Forum, 1985—; trustee Choate/Rosemary Hall, Wallingford, Conn., 1973-81, Simpson Coll., Indianola, Iowa, 1981 2002, U. Denver, 1984-2002, Fountain Valley Sch., Colorado Springs, 1976-89, trustee emerita, 1993—; mem. exec. com. Ft. Lewis Coll. Found., 1991—. Recipient 1st place for editl. writing Nat. Fedn. Press Women, 1955, Outstanding Alumna award Rosemary Hall, Greenwich, Conn., 1969, Outstanding Journalism award U. Colo. Sch. Journalism, 1967, Disting. Svc. award Ft. Lewis Coll., Durango, 1970, Athena award Female Cmty. Leader, 1997; named to Colo. Cmty. Journalism Hall of Fame, 1987, Colo. Bus. Hall of Fame, 2002; named Citizen of Yr., Durango Area Chamber Resort Assn., 1990, Colo. Philanthropist of Yr. Colo. Assn. Found./Assn. Fundraising Profls., 2000, Bonfils-Stanton Found. award, 2002. Mem. Nat. Soc. Colonial Dames, Colo. Press Assn. (bd. dirs. 1978-79), Colo. AP Assn. (chmn. 1966-67), Federated Women's Club Durango, Mill Reef Club (Antigua, W.I.) (bd. govs. 1985-91). Episcopalian. Address: care Durango Herald PO Drawer A Durango CO 81302

BALLANTYNE, CHRISTIE MITCHELL, medical educator; b. Houston, Sept. 13, 1955; m. Yasmine Attie, June 21, 1980; children: Maria Leyla, Christina, Katina. BA magna cum laude, U. Tex., 1977; postgrad., NYU, Madrid, Spain, 1977; MD cum laude, Baylor Coll. Medicine, 1982. Diplomate Am. Bd. Internal Medicine, Am. Bd. Internal Medicine subspecialty Cardiovascular Disease; cert. ACLS instr. Resident in internal medicine U. Tex. Southwestern Med. Sch., Dallas, 1982-85; fellowship in cardiology Baylor Coll. Medicine, Houston, 1985-87, instr. sect. atherosclerosis and cardiology dept. medicine, 1988-89, asst. prof. atherosclerosis & cardiology dept. medicine, 1989-95, assoc. prof. dept. medicine, 1996-2000, assoc. chief and clin. dir. sect. atherosclerosis, 1997, dir. lipid and atherosclerosis lab., 1999—, prof. dept. medicine, 2000—; dir., Ctr. for Cardiovasc. Disease Prevention Meth. DeBakey Heart Ctr., 2000—. Attending Ben Taub Gen. Hosp. Cardiac Catherterization Lab., Houston, 1988—, Lipid Metabolism and Atherosclerosis Clinic, The Meth. Hosp., Houston, 1988—, Ben Taub Coronary Care Unit, Houston, 1989—; faculty mem. Am. Heart Assn./Squibb Tng. Ctr. for Clin. Mgmt. of Lipid Disorders, Baylor Coll. Medicine, 1990; co-investigator Lipoprotein and Coronary Atherosclerosis Study, 1990; sci. grant rev. com. Am. Heart Assn. Tex. Affiliate, 1991-96; pharmacy and therapeutics com. The Meth. Hosp., 1992-95. Editor: lipidsonline.org; editor: (assoc.) Circulation, Jour. Cardiovasc. Risk; contbr. chapters to books, articles to profl. jours. Recipient Mosby scholarship award, Grant-in-Aid awards Am. Heart Assn. Tex. Affiliate, 1989, 91, Sanofi-Winthrop Grant-in-Aid award, 1994, Established Investigator award, 1996, Clin. Investigator award Nat. Heart Lung and Blood Inst., NIH, 1990, Caroline Wiess Law award in Molecular Medicine, 1992; named fellow Am. Heart Assn./Bugher Found. Ctr. for Molecular Biology in the Cardiovascular Sys., 1987-89. Fellow ACP, Am. Coll. Cardiology (sec. Tex. chpt. 1997-98, gov. 2001), Coun. on Clin. Cardiology Am. Heart Assn., Coun. on Arteriosclerosis; mem. Am. Fedn. Clin. Rsch. (sch. rep. for Baylor 1992), Am. Soc. Clin. Investigation, Tex. Med. Assn., Harris County Med. Soc., Houston Cardiology Soc. (pres. 1996), Am. Heart Assn. (pres. Houston chpt. 1999), Phi Kappa Phi, Phi Beta Kappa, Alpha Omega Alpha. Office: Baylor Coll Medicine Sect Atherosclerosis 6565 Fannin St # A601 Houston TX 77030-2704 E-mail: cmb@bcm.tmc.edu.

BALLANTYNE, MAREE ANNE CANINE, artist; b. Sydney, NSW, Australia, Oct. 22, 1945; came to U.S., 1946; d. Charles Venice and Yvonne Mavis (McSpeerin) Canine; m. Kent McFarlane Ballantyne, Apr. 22, 1967; children: Christopher Kent, Joel Sokson. AA, Del Mar Coll., 1966; BA in English, U. Tex., 1971; postgrad., U. South Ala., 1974, U. Houston, 1981, Sonoma State U., 1982, 84, 85. Exhibited paintings in Mass., Tex., Ala.; creator logo for Gulf Coast Area Childbirth Edn. Assn., 1972, logo for Calif. Health Resources, 1985; contbr. articles to profl. jours. Charter mem. Gulf Coast Area Childbirth Edn. Assn., Mobile, Ala., 1971-76; mem. Mus. Guild, Corpus Christi, 1978-80, Art Mus., Mobile, 1972-76, Nat. Trust for Hist. Preservation, 1977-80. Recipient Cert. Appreciation, USCG, 1993, Letter of Appreciation USCG, 1993. Mem. Nat. Mus. Women in Arts (charter). Avocations: reading about poet and artist william blake, women artists and literature, raising tropical plants, creating hand-painted greeting cards. Home: 1920 SW 56th Ave Plantation FL 33317-5938

BALLARD, BARBARA W. state legislator; m. Albert L. Ballard. B in Music Edn., Webster Coll., 1967; MS, Kans. State U., 1976, PhD, 1980. Rep. dist. 44 State of Kansas, 1993—; adminstr., dir. U. Kans., 1980—, asst. vice-chancellor, 1998—. Democrat. Home: 1532 Alvamar Dr Lawrence KS 66047-1605

BALLARD, CAROLINE SUSAN, music educator; b. Norfolk, Va., Oct. 17, 1960; d. Alvah Bell Hyslop, Jr. and Carolyn Elizabeth Hyslop; m. Randall Keith Ballard, Apr. 16, 1984; children: Jason Randall, Joshua Keith. BS in Secondary Edn., Old Dominion U., 1984. Cert. tchr. music edn. K-12 Va. Dir. bands Hamburg (Iowa) Comty. Schs, 1987—93; clarinet instr. Olympia (Wash.) Youth Symphonies, 1994—99; pvt. clarinet instr. Olympia, 1994—99; dir. bands Dinwiddie (Va.) County Pub. Schs., 2000—. Clarinetist Olympia Chamber Orch., 1996—98, N.W. Wind Symphony, Olympia, 1995—99, Tidewater Winds, Norfolk, Va., 1993—94. Clarinetist: CD Faust, 1997. Mem.: Va. Educators Assn., Va. Mid. Sch. Tchrs. Assn., Music Educators Nat. Conf., Va. Band and Orch. Dirs. Assn. Avocations: walking, reading, working with musical youth organizations. Office: Dinwiddie Mid Sch 12318 Boydton Plank Rd Dinwiddie VA 23841-2454

BALLARD, LAURA CLAY, small business owner; b. Biloxi, Miss., June 29, 1951; d. Elbert Homer Jr. and Jacqueline May (Giblin) Clay; m. Steven Anthony Register (div. Apr. 1982); 1 child, Steven Scott ; m. Frank James Butscher, Aug. 20, 1982 (div. Nov. 2000); m. Raymond Michael Ballard, Oct. 7, 2001. AS in Bus. Adminstrn., Jefferson State Jr. Coll., 1986; BS Social and Behavioral Sci. cum laude, U. Ala., 1987. Teletype operator Blue Cross Blue Shield, Columbus, Ga., 1971-72, asst. supr. data control, 1972-77; mgr. data processing So. Foods, Inc., Columbus, 1977-80, Zurn Industries, Birmingham, Ala., 1980-85; pres. Maid for All Seasons, Inc., Birmingham, 1989-92; owner Visual Studio, Trussville, Ala., 1993-97; realtor Century 21, Birmingham, 1997-99, Century 21 and Realty South, Trussville, 1997-99; customer rels. mgr. Jay Toyota, 2000—02; dir. customer rels. The Maids, Birmingham, 2002; adminstr. customer rels. L. Kianoff & Assocs., Birmingham, 2002—. Avocations: gardening, walking, photography, personal computing, birder. Home: 7365 Lake In The Woods Rd Trussville AL 35173-1749 E-mail: radiantredrunr@yahoo.com.

BALLARD, LINDA CHRISTINE, financial aid director; b. Houston, Aug. 19, 1959; d. Roosevelt Larue Sr. and Helen Ruth B.; 1 child, Alexandria Nickole Ballard-Demming. BBA, U. Houston, 1982. Data control supr. U. Houston, 1982-85, data entry supr., 1985-87, fin. aid. counselor, 1987-92, U. St. Thomas, Houston, 1992-93, dir. fin. aid, 1993—2000; dir. fin. aid and vet. affairs U. Houston at Clear Lake, Tex., 2000—01; dir. fin. aid Tex. So. U., Houston, 2001—. Chair sexual harassment com. U. Houston, 1991-93; mem. staff devel. com. U. St. Thomas, 1993-96, mem. data mgrs. com., 1995-97, 99, mem. scholar com., 1994-99, mem. enrollment mgmt. com., 1998-2000; mem. early awareness com. Tex. Assn. Fin. Aid Adminstrn., 2000—; presenter in field. Dir. youth dept. Greater True Vine Ch. Mem. Nat. Assn. Fin. Aid Adminstrs., Tex. Assn. Fin. Aid Adminstrs. (early awareness com. 2000—), Nat. Coalition Builders Inst. (train the trainer). Avocations: high school awareness programs, travel, financial aid compliance issues, workshops in field. Home: 5358 Linden Chase Houston TX 77066-3911 Office: Texas Southern University 3100 Cleburne Houston TX 77004

BALLARD, MARION SCATTERGOOD, software development professional; b. Montclair, N.J., Dec. 19, 1939; d. Alfred G. and Helen F. (Galey) Scattergood; m. Frederic L. Ballard Jr., Dec. 20, 1974; children: William, Robert; 1 stepchild, Anne A. Ballard. BA, Smith Coll., 1961; MA, U. Pa., 1963; MBA, American Univ., 1990. Lectr. Temple U., Phila.; mathematician UNIVAC, Blue Bell, Pa.; v.p. FINPAC Corp., Narberth, Pa.; pres. DataPlus, Inc, Washington. Former chmn. bd. Sandy Spring Friends Sch., Washington Area Women's Found.; former sec. bd. Sidwell Friends Sch.; bd. dirs. Levine Sch. Music. Mem. Nat. Assn. Women Bus. Owners, Phi Beta Kappa, Sigma Xi. E-mail: marionballard@comcast.net.

BALLARD, MARY MELINDA, financial communications and marketing/advertising executive, consumer advocate; b. Sikeston, Mo., Apr. 21, 1958; d. Claude M. and Mary (Birnbach) B.; m. Emil Pena, Jan. 1, 1989 (div. July 1990); m. Ronald C. Allison, Oct. 1994; 1 child, Reese Colton Allison. BA, Monmouth U., 1976; MBA, NYU, 1980; postgrad., Columbia U. V.p. corp. comm. United Brands Co., N.Y.C., 1976-79; v.p. mktg. Oscar de la Renta Ltd., 1979-81; pres., CEO Ficom Internat., Inc., N.Y.C., 1981—89; exec. v.p. Ruder Finn Inc., N.Y.C., 1989—; dir., CEO MBP Interests Inc., 1989—; ptnr. Affinity Ins. Advisors, 2003—, Kamero Ptnrs., 1994—; pres. Policyholders of Am., 2002—; officer, dir. Tex. Interlock Corp., 1995-96; exec. v.p., CFO Millenium Tech. Transfer, Inc., 1996—; officer dir. Capital Bank, 1997—. Bd. dirs. Reese Colton Enterprises, Inc., Millenium Tech. Transfer, Inc., Nat. Coun. Real Estate Investment Fiduciaries; pres. Policyholders of Am., 2002—; mem. adv. bd. Tex. Tech U., 2002—; cons., ins. adviser. Contbr. articles to profl. jours. Trustee Ballard Family Found., Children's Aid Soc.; exec. mem. Tex. Dem. Roundtable, 1994—. Recipient CLIO Ann. Report award Fin. World, 1984, 86. Mem. Internat. Assn. Bus. Communicators (Golden Quill 1984), Pub. Investor Relsa. Inst. Methodist. Avocations: collecting art, thoroughbred race horses, ranching. Home and Office: 15 Orange St Charleston SC 29401 Office Phone: 888-648-8823. E-mail: mballardal@aol.com.

BALLARD, ROBERTA A. pediatrics educator; AB in Chemistry, Earlham Coll., 1061; MD, U. Chgo., 1965. Diplomate Am. Bd. Pediat., Am. Bd. Neonatal Medicine, Am. Bd. Neonatal and Perinatal Medicine (chmn. 1992-95). Intern, then resident in pediat. U. Chgo. Hosps., 1965-67; resident in pediat. Stanford (Calif.) U., 1967-68; fellow in neonatology George Washington U. Hosp., Washington, 1968-69; fellow Cardiovasc. Rsch. Inst., 1970-72; acting dir. newborn svcs., instr. pediat. George Washington U. Hosp., Washington, 1969-70; dir. newborn svcs. Mt. Zion Med. Ctr.-U. Calif., San Francisco, 1972-90, chief dept. pediat., 1975-90, asst. clin. prof. pediat., 1973-75, adj. asst. prof., 1975-87, adj. assoc. prof., 1985-88, prof., 1988-91; chief div. neonatology dept. pediat. Children's Hosp. Phila., 1991—; dir. neonatology and newborn svcs. Hosp. of U. Pa., Phila., 1994—; prof. pediat.-ob-gyn., dir. neonatology fellowship progrram U. Pa. Sch. Medicine, 1991—. Mem. panel for consensus devel. infantile apnea and home monitoring NIH, 1986-87; mem. adv. bd. neonatal network Nat. Inst. Child Health and Human Devel., 1991—. Editor: Pediatric Care of the ICN Graduate, 1988, (with W. Taeusch) Schaffer and Avery's Diseases of the Newborn, 6th edit., 1991, 7th edit., 1998; reviewer Pediat.,

Jour. Pediat., Jour. Perinatology, Pediat. Pulmonology, Pediat. Rsch., New Eng. Jour. Medicine, Am. Jour. Ob-gyn., Archives Pediat. and Adolescent Medicine; mem. editl. bd. Contemporary Pediat.; contbr. articles to profl. jours. Grantee, NIH, 1993—. Mem. Am. Acad. Pediat., Soc. for Pediat. Rsch., Am. Pediatric Soc. Achievements include research on prevention and treatment of respiratory diseases in the newborn, antenatal steroids, chronic lung disease, inhaled nitric oxide to prevent chronic lung disease. Office: Childrens Hosp Phila Divsn Neonatology 34th and Civic Ctr Blvd Philadelphia PA 19104-4399 E-mail: ballard@email.chop.edu.

BALLARD, SUSAN DOYON, library director; d. Alfred O. and Mary M. Doyon; m. Roger P. Ballard, June 28, 1985. BA in English Lit., U. NH, 1974; MS in Libr. and Info. Sci., Simmons Coll., 1975. Media Supervisor Dept. of Edn., NH, 1978, Computer Technology Educator Dept. of Edn., NH, 2000. Dist. libr. Londonderry (NH) Sch. Dist., 1975—78, media coord., 1978—85, dir., libr. and media svcs., 1985—95, dir., libr. media and tech. svcs., 1995—; instr. Fitchburg (Mass.) State Coll., 1984, Plymouth (NH) State Coll., 1989; adj. faculty Rivier Coll., Nashua, NH, 2003—. Editor: (book) The Count on Reading Handbook. Named to Hall of Fame, Londonderry H.S., 1987; recipient NH Excellence in Edn. award for Ednl. Media, NH Dept. of Edn., 1994, Commitment to Excellence in Edn., Greater Manchester Chamber of Commerce, 2001. Mem.: ASCD, NH Ednl. Media Assn. (pres. 1992—93, Outstanding Svc. award 1994, Pres.'s award 1997), NH. Libr. Assn., New Eng. Ednl. Media Assn. (pres. 1994—95), Internat. Soc. for Tech. in Edn., Assn. for Ednl. Comm. and Tech., Am. Assn. of Sch. Librarians (sec. 1993—96, Nat. Sch. Libr. Media Program of Yr. 2000), NH Soc. for Tech. in Edn., Gamma Delta Epsilon, Alpha Xi Delta. Office: Londonderry Sch Dist 268 Mammoth Rd Londonderry NH 03053 Office Phone: 603-432-6920 ext. 108.

BALLARD, TINA ROWANN, music educator; d. Roger Rowan and Agusta Ann (Idol) Ballard. BS in Edn. cum laude, Western Carolina U., 1993; MusM, U. N.C., Greensboro, 1999. Lic. tchg. N.C. Camp counselor, counselor-in-tng. dir. Keyawwee Program Ctr., Sophia, NC, 1987, 1991—97; tchr. Pub. Schs. Robeson County, Lumberton, NC, 1995—98; band dir. Guilford County Schs., Gibsonville, NC, 2000—. Mem. sch. leadership team Ea. Guilford Mid. Sch., Gibsonville, 2000—. Bd. mem., participant Robeson Little Theater, Lumberton, NC, 1995—98; active Cape Fear Band, Fayetteville, NC, 1996—98, Greensboro (N.C.) Concert Band, 2000—; trainer, facilitator Girl Scouts Am., Tarheel Triad Coun., Colfax, NC, 1998—, event/trip organizer, 1998—, com. mem., 2000—, camp dir., 2000, 2002, 2003; mem. ch. coun. Cententary United Meth., Greensboro, 2002—. Mem.: Ctrl. Dist. Bandmasters Assn., N.C. Music Educators Assn., Music Educators Nat. Conf. Avocations: hiking, camping.

BALLARIAN, ANNA NEVARTE, retired art educator; b. Rochester, NY, Aug. 15, 1910; d. Aram M. and Adelina (Essayan) B. Design Diploma, Rochester Athenaeum (now RIT), 1930; BS in Art Edn., NYU, 1935; MA in Fine Arts, Alfred U., 1941; MA in Fine Art, Columbia U., 1949; postgrad., Alfred U. Art supr. and tchr. Rochester Pub. Schs.; art and craft prof. Columbia U., N.Y.C., 1946-47; artist, tchr. in residence Art Ctr., Cannon Beach, Oreg., 1967-68; asst. prof. U. Idaho, 1948; vis. prof. U. B.C., Can., 1964, Calif. State U., Hayward, 1970; prof. art, dir. SUNY, Plattsburgh, 1948-57; prof. art Calif. State U., San Jose, 1957-77; adv. for artist residency program Villa Montalvo, Saratoga, Calif., 1977-99. Author book on fabric collage; contbr. articles to mags.; exhibited works at N.Y. Craft Mus., 1973, San Francisco Mus. Art, Rochester Meml. Art Gallery, and in pvt. shows. Mem. Nat. League Am. Pen Women Inc. (dir. fine arts), Phi Kappa Phi, Delta Kppa Gamma (treas.). Christian. Avocations: painting, crafts, calligraphy, piano music, sports (skiing, tennis, hiking). Home: 1666 Gaton Dr #Cy23 San Jose CA 95125-4511

BALLESTEROS, PAULA MITCHELL, nurse; b. Jonesport, Maine, Oct. 18, 1950; d. Paul Frederick and Janice Madeline (Beal) Mitchell; m. Ernesto Gascon Ballesteros, Apr. 4, 1981; children: Christopher, Jonathan. BS in Profl. Arts, St. Joseph's Coll., 1984; BSN, Husson/Ea. Me. Med. Ctr. Baccalaureate Sch. Nursing, 1994; MBA, Husson Coll., 2004. Cert. Nursing Administrn. Patient care mgr. Ea. Me. Med. Ctr., Bangor, 1974—, bd. trustees, 1993-95. Chairperson adv. bd. Ea. Maine Tech. Coll., Bangor, Me., 1993-94; pres. Me. Coun. Nurse Mgrs., 1991-93, Ea. Me. Med. Ctr. auxiliary, Bangor, Me., 1993-95. Contbr. articles to profl. jours. Mem. St. Joseph Hosp. Auxiliary. Mem. Am. Orgn. Nurse Execs., Penobscot Med. Soc. Auxiliary, Me. Assn. Hosp. Auxiliaries (pres. 1994—). Democrat. Protestant. Avocations: skiing, tennis, reading. Home: 78 Packard Dr Bangor ME 04401-2531 Office: Ea Maine Med Ctr 489 State St Bangor ME 04401-6616 Office Phone: 207-973-7371. E-mail: pballesteros@emh.org.

BALLEW, KATHY I. controller; b. Sterling, Colo., Mar. 31, 1958; d. Arthur LeRoy Nelson and Dixie Irene Mann; m. Mark Ballew, Dec. 12, 1975 (div. Sept. 23, 1999); children: Mark Douglas, Amanda Jo. Diploma, Burns (Oreg.) Union H.S. Revenue audit Red Lion Casino, Elko, Nev., 1988, accounts payable, 1988, accounts receivable, 1988—89, office mgr., 1990—95, contr. Winnemucca Properties, 1995—99, contr. McClaskey Properties, 1999—. Avocations: fishing, camping, crafts, grandchildren. Home: 1910 Ruby View Dr Elko NV 89801

BALLIF-SPANVILL, BONNIE, psychologist, educator; BS with honors, Brigham Young U., 1962, PhD with distinction, 1966. Asst. rschr. R&D Ctr. U. Hawaii, Honolulu, 1966—68; with Fordham U. Grad. Sch. at Lincoln Ctr., N.Y.C., 1968—93, dir. Ctr. for Applied Motivation Rsch., 1975—84, coord. ednl. psychology and rsch. programs, 1979—83, 1985—87, chair divsn. psychology and edn. svcs., 1987—90; prof. psychology Brigham Young U., Provo, Utah, 1994—, dir. Women's Rsch. Inst., 1994—, mem. various univ. coms., 1994—. Cons. U.S. Govt., 1965—72, The Delphi Rsch. Group, N.Y.C., 1976—89; presenter in field. Contbr. articles to profl. jours. Recipient Bene Merenti award, 1988. Fellow: APA, Am. Psychol. Soc.; mem.: AAUW, Consortium on Peace, Rsch., Edn. and Devel., Nat. Women's Studies Assn., Assn. for Women in Devel., Internat. Peace Rsch. Assn., Phi Kappa Phi. Office: Brigham Young Univ 337SWKT Provo UT 84602

BALLINGER, CAROLYN ANN, nursing educator; d. John Leslie Webster and Florence Lurene Ice; m. Graham Edgar Markland, May 20, 1968 (div. May 1976); 1 child, Steven G. Markland ; m. Bobby J. Ballinger, May 15, 1976 (div. June 2000); 1 adopted child, Steven Joseph 1 child, Debra Lynn. ADN, No. Ky. U., 1976, BSN, 1988, A in Indsl. Edn., 1992, MSN, 1997. Charge nurse Bapt. Convalescent Ctr., Newport, Ky., 1976—79, St. Luke Hosp., Florence and Ft. Thomas, Ky., 1979—88; assoc. prof. Gateway Comty. and Tech. Coll., Edgewood, Ky., 1988—; field rep. Am. Nursing Care, Florence, Ky., 1992—, Interim Health Care, Edgewood, Ky., 2003—. Presenter in field. Named Ky. col., State of Ky., 1992, 2004; Rsch. scholar in Oxford, Eng., Ky. Cmty. and Tech . Coll. Sys., 2003. Mem.: Ky. Nurses Assn., Sigma Theta Tau (mem. Rho Theta chpt., Tchr.'s Leadership grad. 2004). Avocations: travel, walking, reading. Home: 133 W Dilcrest Cir Florence KY 41042 Office: Gateway Comty and Tech Coll 790 Thomas More Pkwy Edgewood KY 41017 E-mail: carolyn.ballinger@kctcs.edu.

BALLMAN, PATRICIA KLING, lawyer; b. Cin., May 1, 1946; d. John Joseph and Margaret Elizabeth (Stacy) Kling; children: Andrew J., Cara E. BS with honors, St. Louis U., 1967; JD with honors, Marquette U., 1977. Bar: Wisc. 1977, U.S. Dist. Ct. (ea. and we. dist Wisc.) 1980, U.S. Ct. Appeals (7th Cir.) 1983, U.S. Ct. Appeals (8th Cir.) 1986, U.S. Supreme Ct., 1986. Ptnr. Quarles & Brady, Milw., 1977—. Mem. fin. divsn., chair pers. subcom. United Way, Shorewood Bd. of Rev. Mem. ABA, Am. Acad. Matrimonial Lawyers (pres. Wis. chpt. 2002-04), Wis. Bar Assn. (pres. 2002-03), Milw. Bar Assn. (pre. 1995-95). Office: Quarles & Brady 411 E Wisconsin Ave #2040 Milwaukee WI 53202-4461

BALLONE, EILEEN MARIE, music educator, musician, organist; b. Hackensack, N.J., May 6, 1946; d. Frank Albert and Marie Lillian (Mancini) Caiazzo; m. Henry Frederick Ballone, May 4, 1968; children: Brian James, Marie Elena. BA in Elem. Edn., Caldwell Coll., 1986; MS in Elem. Edn., Marywood Coll., 1992; student, Fairleigh Dickinson U., 1965—66, Bergen C.C., Paramus, N.J., 1981. Liturgically cert. musician Archdiocese Newark; cert. elem. edn. tchr., nursery sch. tchr. N.J. Pvt. organ tchr., 1963—; with N.J. Bell Tel. Co., 1967—68, Am. Book-Stratford Press, INc., Saddle Brook, NJ, 1968—70; music tchr. Sacred Heart Sch., Rochelle Park, NJ, 1979—84, Annunciation Sch., Paramus, NJ, 1981—83, St. Anne's Sch., Fair Lawn, NJ, 1983—85, St. Philip the Apostle Sch., Saddle Brook, 1984—86; music tchr. grades K-8 St. Francis Assisi Elem. Sch., Ridgefield Park, NJ, 1986—; music tchr., chair music dept. Paramus Cath. Girls Regional H.S., 1986—90; music tchr. grades K-8 St. Leo's Elem. Sch., Elmwood Park, NJ, 1990—91, St. Philip the Apostle Elem. Sch., Saddle Brook, 1999—2000. Organist, choir dir. St. Michael's Ch., Palisades Park, NJ, 1967—77; asst. organist St. Margaret Cortona Ch., Little Ferry, NJ, 1978—84, St. Philip the Apostle Ch., Saddle Brook, 1978—84, head organist, 1984—86; dir. music, organist, choir dir. Our Lady Queen of Peace Ch., Maywood, NJ, 1987—99; dir., organist children's choir St. Francis Assisi Ch., Ridgefield Park, 1999—2003, dir. children's bell choir, 2000, dir., organist, choir dir., Hackensack, NJ, 1999—2002; dir. music, organist, choir dir. St. Margaret Cortona Roman Cath. Ch., Little Ferry, 2002—. Den mother Cub Scouts Pack 222 St. Philip the Apostle Parish, Saddle Brook; com. mem. Brownie Troop 772 St. Philip the Apostle Parish, Saddle Brook; v.p. St. Philip the Apostle Home-Sch. Assn., Saddle Brook, 1977—79, pres., 1979—83. Mem.: Am. Fedn. Musicians, Nat. Assn. Pastoral Musicians (pres. music edn. divsn. 2004—, chpt. mem., dirs. music ministry divsn.), Choristers Guild, N.J. Music Edn. Assn., Music Educators Nat. Conf., Nat. Cath. Edn. Assn. Roman Catholic. Home: 23 Rochelle Pkwy Saddle Brook NJ 07663-4616 Office Phone: 201-641-9159.

BALLOU, CLAUDIA ARCENEAUX, artist; b. Baton Rouge, Sept. 26, 1945; d. Claude Joseph and Barbara (Robin) Arceneaux; m. Teague Jackson, Dec., 1972 (div. 1974); m. Jack Wayne Ballou, Dec. 23, 1986. Student, U. Paris and Acad. Julian, 1965; grad., John McCrady Art Sch., New Orleans, 1966; postgrad., Temple U., 1977-78. Cert. ct. reporter. Tchr. fine art Shoeburyness (Eng.) H.S., 1967; graphic designer Kennesaw Press, Atlanta, 1968-77; graphics liaison Du Pont Co., Wilmington, Del., 1979-86; prodn. scheduler, with pub. rels. dept. Gregory & Assocs., Wilmington, 1987-88; v.p. graphic svcs. Peyton & Assocs., Inc., Wilmington, 1988-94; co-founder Chase Comms., Wilmington, 1994—; with Winterthur Mus., 2001—. Artist-in-residence Del. Arts Commn., Wilmington, 1993, 94. Mem. coun. Del. Art Mus., Wilmington, 1990-. Mem. Preservation Del., Nature Printing Soc.

BALL-SARET, JAYNE ADAMS, small business owner; b. East St. Louis, Ill., Apr. 10, 1956; d. H. Jay and Faye M. (Adams) Ball; m. Mitchell I. Saret. BA, Ea. Ill. U., 1977, MA, 1983. Interior designer Carter's Furniture, Charleston, Ill., 1977-85; from customer svc. advisor to dir. client svc. Consol. Comm., Mattoon, Charleston, Ill., 1985—; owner, designer Grand Ball Costumes, Charleston, 1985—. Pres., dir. Charleston Cmty. Theatre, 1983—85. Mem.: Phi Alpha Eta. Republican. Avocations: singing, directing, acting, sewing. Office: Grand Ball Costumes 609 6th St Charleston IL 61920-2018 Office Phone: 217-345-2617.

BALLWEG, SALLYANNE K. finance company executive; m. Brian Ballweg; 1 child, Mark. With met. divsn. mgmt. trainee Mfrs. Hanover Trust, 1978, mgr. corp. lending portfolios Met. & N.Am. divns.n, v.p., 1983, group exec. N.Am. divsn., 1986, credit exec. media group, 1990; team leader mid. mkt. banking group JP Morgan Chase, 1991—. Mem. bus. adv. bd. Merrill Lynch Ctr. for Study of Internat. Finl. Svcs. & Mkts.; adj. prof. fin. Hofstra U. Bd. dirs. YMCA, Long Island. Recipient Alumni Achievement award, Hofstra U., 1999. Mem.: Nat. Assn. Mothers' Ctr. (former. bd. dirs., corp. resource develop. com.), Frank G. Zarb Sch. Bus Alumni Assn. Hofstra U. (co-pres.), Exec. Women Golf Assn. Office: JP Morgan Chase 100 Duffy Ave Hicksville NY 11801

BALMASEDA, LIZ, columnist; b. Puerto Padre, Cuba, Jan. 17, 1959; AA, Miami-Dade (Fla.) C.C., 1979; BS Comm., Fla. Internat. U., 1981. Intern Miami Herald, Fla., 1980, with Spanish lang. publ., 1981, gen. assignment reporter, feature writer, 1987, with Sunday Mag. tropic, 1990, columnist, 1991—; ctrl. Am. bur. chief Newsweek, El Salvador, 1985; freelance columnist NBC News, Honduras. Appeared on NBC Today Show, Oprah show. Recipient 2d place Ernie Pyle award Scripps Howard Found, 1984, 3d place feature writing Fla. Soc. Newspaper Editors, 1st prize Guillermo Martinez-Marquez contest Nat. Assn. Hispanic Journalists., 1989, Pulitzer Prize for commentary, 1993, 1st prize commentary Fla. Soc. Newspaper editors. Office: The Miami Herald One Herald Plaza Miami FL 33132

BALOG, RITA JEAN, retired librarian; b. Ashtabula, Ohio, Sept. 24, 1930; d. Frederick Carroll and Marguerite Ethel (White) Grady; m. Richard Francis Balog, Oct. 16, 1949 (dec. Feb. 1988); children: Rebecca Kay, Richard Francis Jr., Ronald Frank, Robert Henry; m. Charles R. Haapala, Oct. 24, 1999. AA, Kent State U., 1977, BA in Gen. Studies, 1978, MLS, 1980. Clk., typist Harbor Pub. Libr., Ashtabula, 1973-75, children's libr., 1975-80; libr., dir. Harbor-Topky Meml. Libr., Ashtabula, 1980-97; ret., 1997. Vol. libr. Thomas Jefferson Elem. Sch., Harbor Spl. Sch., Ashtabula, 1972-75. Sec., mem. Ashtabula Archtl. Restoration and Rev. Bd., 1975-95; vol. leader Lake River coun. Girl Scouts U.S., Niles, 1958-73, mem. nominating com., 1989-91, bd. dirs., 1991-95, child camp dir.; trustee Coun. Ashtabula County Librs., chair, 1994-96. Mem. ALA, AAUW, Ohio Libr. Assn., N.E. Ohio Libr. Assn. (regional adv. bd. 1984-86), Coun. Ashtabula County Librs. (pres. 1985-86), Ashtabula Area Mus. and Hist. Soc. (trustee 1992-98), Zonta (pres. 1987-89). Democrat. Avocations: collecting rocks, wild flowers, swimming, needlecraft.

BALOGH, ANNE MARCELINE, personnel consultant; b. New Haven, Conn., Aug. 25, 1932; d. Mario and Rose Marie (Onofrio) Iannotti; m. Dominic Vincent Balogh, June 6, 1955 (dec. Aug. 1996); children: Rosanne, Dominic Jr., Christopher, Stephanie. AS, Quinnipiac Coll., 1952. Cert. personnel cons. Mgr. Fuller Brush Co., Conn., 1971-75; co-owner Baloghs Restaurant, Hamden, Conn., 1975-80; with Rita Personnel, Hamden, Conn., 1980-91, Cheney Assocs., Hamden, Conn., 1991—. Mem. bus. adv. bd. Easter Seals, New Haven; mem. divsn. I athletic exec. bd. Quinnipiac U. Mem. Human Resource Assn. Greater New Haven, Quinnipiac Coll. Alumni Assn. (nat. alumni bd. govs.). Republican. Roman Catholic. Avocations: travel, art, volunteerism. Home: 731 Still Hill Rd Hamden CT 06518-1104 Office: Cheney Divsn Headway Tech Resources 2321Whitney Ave Hamden CT 06518-2340

BALOGH, MARY, writer; b. 1944; English tchr. Kipling HS, Saskatchewan, Canada, 1967—82, Windthorst HS, Saskatchewan, 1982—88, prin., 1982—88. Author: numerous books including most recently, A Masked Deception, 1985, The Trysting Place, 1986, Secrets of the Heart, 1988, A Gift of Daisies, 1989, A Promise of Spring, 1990, Devil's Web, 1990, Snow Angel, 1991, Christmas Beau, 1991, A Christmas Promise, 1992, Courting Julia, 1993, Tempting Harriet, 1994, Lord Carew's Bride, 1995, The Temporary Wife, 1997, The Last Waltz, 1998, One Night for Love, 1999, More Than a Mistress, 2000, No Man's Mistress, 2001, A Summer to Remember, 2002, Slightly Married, 2003, Slightly Wicked, 2003, Slightly Scandalous, 2003, Slightly Tempted, 2004, Slightly Sinful, 2004, Slightly Dangerous, 2004. Home: Box 571 Kipling SK Canada S0G 2SO Office: c/o Random House 1745 Broadway New York NY 10019

BALSAM, MARION [illegible], pediatrician, retired naval officer; b. N.Y.C., Oct. 9, 1940; d. Emanuel and Dorothy Balsam; children: Ross Garret, Joclyn Page, Clifford Scott, Marissa Hale. BA, Cornell U., 1962; MD, NYU, 1966. Diplomate Am. Bd. Pediatrics. Chief Crippled Children's Svcs. Guam Dept. Pub. Health, 1971—74; joined USN, 1975, advanced through grades to Rear Adm., 1998; staff pediatrician Naval Hosp., Camp Pendleton, Oceanside, Calif., 1975—81; head inpatient pediats. Nat. Naval Med. Ctr., Bethesda, Md., 1981—85, dept. chair, 1985—89, dep. comdr., 1991—93; med. dir., chief of staff Naval Hosp., San Diego, 1989—91, comdr. Pensacola, Fla., 1993—95; fleet med. officer Naval Forces Europe, London, 1995—98; comdr. Naval Med. Ctr., Portsmouth, Va., 1998—2000; lead agt. Tricare, Mid-Atlantic Region, 1998—2000; dir. rsch. partnerships Nat. Children's Study, NICHD/NIH, 2003—. Fellow: Am. Acad. Pediatrics (mem. task force on terrorism and children, former mem. com. on pediat workforce, chmn. subcom. on women in pediats.). Avocations: photography, music, piano. E-mail: balsamm@nih.gov.

BALSAMELLO, MELISSA (MARLEY), elementary school educator; b. Red Bank, N.J., Aug. 5, 1975; d. Lucille (Perillo) M. BA in Psychology Douglass Coll., Rutgers U., 1997, EdM in Spl. Edn., 1998, postgrad., 1998—2001. Cert. early childhood edn., elem. edn., spl. edn., supr., psychology, dance/vocat. arts. Religious edn. tchr. St. Leo and Great, Lincroft, N.J., 1991-93; respite care provider, counselor ARC of Somerset, Manville, N.J., 1995; group leader, tchr. Happy Campers Ecology Camp, New Brunswick, 1996; tchg. asst., subsitute tchr. Douglass Child Study Ctr., New Brunswick, 1996-98; tchg. asst., field worker Douglass Devel. Disability Ctr., New Brunswick, 1995-96; store mgr. Pyramid Books, Highland Park, N.J., 1997-98; tchr., camp group leader Douglass Girl's Camp, New Brunswick, 1997-98; adminstrv. asst. to pres. United Bolt & Besel, 1998; tchr. 1st grade Franklin Park Sch., Somerset, NJ, 1998—2002, dance ensemble advisor, choreographer, 2000—02; 1st grade tchr. Woodrow Wilson Sch., Westfield, NJ, 2002—. Mem. selection com. Douglass Alumni Soc., 1995-97; program facilitator Coll. Orientation and Recruitment Svcs., 1995-96; house chairwoman Coll. Residence Life, 1995-98; mentor Douglass Coll. Emerging Leaders Program, 1995-98; divsn. leader, specialist Daisy Recreation, East Brunswick, 1997-99; counselor Friday Night Live, East Brunswick, 1999-2000; divsn. leader/specialist Daisy Recreation Ctr., East Brunswick, 1997-98; honors rev., tutor 2-8th, Edison, N.J., 1999-2003. Pres. Am. Assn. Mental Retardation, Rutgers chpt., 1995-96; vol., asst. coach N.J. Spl. Olympics, 1996-97. Recipient Presdl. Cmty. Svc. award, Ocean Twp., Washington, 1992, scholarship North Monmouth AAUW, 1996-97. Mem. ASCD, N.J. Edn. Assn., Am. Ednl. Rsch. Assn., Franklin Twp. Edn. Assn., Am. Assn. Mental Retardation (pres. chpt. 1995-97), N.J. Assn. Edn. Young Children, Rutgers U. Student Edn. Assn., Chi Sigma (pres. 1995). Avocations: crocheting, dance, drama, writing, art. Home: 24 Briar Cir Green Brook NJ 08812

BALSER, RUTH B. state legislator, psychologist; AB, U. Rochester, 1969; PhD, New York U., 1980. State rep. Mass. House, 1999—. Alderman City of Newton, 1988—95. Mem.: Mass. Psychol. Assn., Appalachian Mountain Club, Jewish Cmty. Relations Coun., Mass. Women's Political Caucus. Democrat. Office: Rm 134 State House Boston MA 02133 Office Fax: 617-722-2400. E-mail: rep.ruthbalser@hou.state.ma.us.

BALTER, BERNICE, religious organization administrator; Exec. dir. Women's League for Conservative Judaism, N.Y.C., 1978. Nat. adv. bd. MAZON. Office: 48 E 74th St New York NY 10021-2735

BALTER, FRANCES SUNSTEIN, civic worker; b. Pitts. d. Elias and Gertrude Susntein; m. James Stone Balter, May 15, 1948; children: Katherine (Mrs. Ross Anthony) (dec.), Julia Frances, Constance Cantor, Daniel Elias. Student, Sarah Lawrence Coll., 1939-41, New Sch. Social Rsch., 1941-43; cert. Inst. Arts Adminstrn., Harvard U., 1973. Adminstrv. asst., assoc. prodr. Ednl. TV Sta. WQED-TV, Pitts., 1963-67; prodr., mng. dir. Freedom Readers, 1964-67; co-founder, incorporator, sec. bd. dirs. Pitts. Coun. Arts, 1967-70; cultural cons. Mayor's Office Dir. Office Cultural Affairs, Pitts., 1968. Initiator Three Rivers Arts Festival 1960; co-dir. Ohio and Miss. River Valley Art Festival, 1961-62; mem. Pa. Coun. Arts, 1972-78; co-founder Pioneer Crafts Coun., Mill Run, Pa., 1972; exec. dir. Poetry on the Buses, 1974—. Bd. dirs. Coun. for Arts MIT, 1985-93, Palm Beach Festival, 1987-89. Named Woman of Yr. Art Post-Gazette, 1969. Mem. Nat. Soc. Arts and Letters.

BALTIMORE, LINDA OWLETT, psychologist, educator; b. Middlebury Center, Pa., Apr. 13, 1937; d. John Quentin and Kathleen Alice (Davis) Owlett; children: Kelliey K., Kristina M., Kevin V.(dec.). BS, Pa. State U., 1970; MA, Marywood U., Scranton, Pa., 1975; PhD, UCLA, 1991. Rsch. and tchg. asst. Pa. State U., University Park, 1968—70, asst. prof., instr. Wilkes-Barre, 1970—79; adminstr., coord. KNBC and ARC, Calif., 1980—82; ednl. cons. Higher Edn. and Bus., Calif., 1982—88; sr. rsch. and tchg. assoc. UCLA, 1988—92; ret., 1999; assoc., asst. prof. SUNY, Alfred, NY, 1992—99. Sales mgr., watchmaker jewelry industry, Pa. and N.Y., 1957—66; presenter and spkr. in field. Contbr. articles to profl. jours.; editor: CCFL Jour. for Coll. Consortium of Finger Lakes, 1994—95. Dist. trainer Am. Cancer Soc., Wilkes-Barre, 1970—79; trainer, supr. Interfaith Caregiving, Hornell, NY, 1996—99. Recipient Outstanding Svc. award, KNBC TV, 1982. Mem.: Pi Lambda Theta. Avocations: interior decorating, reading, arts, travel.

BALTIMORE, PAMELA A. GRAYSON, social worker, consultant; b. Camden, N.J., Aug. 16, 1961; d. Edward Daniel III and Janice Diane Grayson; m. Roderick Taylor Baltimore, Sept. 23, 1989; 1 child, Sebastian. B in Social Work, Rutgers U., 1987, M in Social Work, 1992. Lic. clin. social worker, N.J.; N.J. state cert. sch. social worker. Juvenile investigator State of N.J. Office of Pub. Defender, Camden, 1982-87; residential counselor Steinenger Ctr., Camden, 1989-90; family svc. specialist III State of N.J. Divsn. Youth and Family Svc., Camden, 1988-92; program supr., therapist Family Counseling Svc., Camden, 1992-99; cons. Pennsauken, N.J., 1999—. Pres. Rutgers U. EOF Adv. Bd., Camden, 1999—; deaconness Rock Ch. Family Worship Ctr., Phila., 1996—; mem. PTA, Roosevelt Sch., Pennsauken, 1998—. Mem. NASW, Delta Sigma Theta. Democrat. Avocations: reading, music, arts and crafts, cooking. Office: PO Box 2742 Camden NJ 08101-2742 E-mail: pgblcsw@aol.com.

BALTZ, MARY MELISSA, lawyer; b. July 5, 1952; d. Ellis Floyd and Helen Lawrence White; m. Richard J. Baltz, May 26, 1974 (div. May 2003); 1 child, Christopher. BA, St. Lawrence U., 1974; JD, George Washington U., 1979. Bar: N.Y. 1979, Fla. 1980, Miss. 2003. Assoc. Phillips Lytle Hitchcock Blame & Huber, Buffalo, 1979—80; staff atty. Dept. Vets. Affairs, Buffalo, 1980—87, Augusta, Maine, 1988—90; pvt. rschr./writer Brandon, Miss., 1995—2002, Fayetteville, NC, 1995—2002; staff atty. Butler, Snow, O'Mara, Stevens & Cannada, Jackson, Miss., 2003—. V.p. Women Lawyers Western N.Y., Buffalo, 1981—82. Pres. PTA, Fayetteville, 1999—2000. Mem.: Order Coif, Phi Beta Kappa. Roman Catholic. Avocations: quilting, reading, sewing, photography, baking. Office: Butler Snow OMara Stevens and Cannada Ste 1700 210 E Capitol St Jackson MS 39047

BALTZ, PATRICIA ANN (PANN BALTZ), elementary school educator; b. Dallas, June 20, 1949; d. Richard Parks and Ruth Eileen (Hartschuh) Langford; m. William Monroe Baltz, Sept. 6, 1969; 1 child: Kenneth Chandler. Student, U. Redlands, 1967-68; BA in English Lit. cum laude, UCLA, 1971. Cert. tchr. K-8, Calif. Tchr. 4th grade Arcadia (Calif.) Unified

Sch. Dist., 1972-74, 92—, substitute tchr., 1983-85, tchr. 3dr grade, 1985-87, tchr. 6th grade, 1987-90, tchr. 4th and 5th grade multiage, 1990—. Sci. mentor tchr. Arcadia Unified Sch. Dist., 1991-94; mentor Tech. Ctr. Silicon Valley, San Jose, Calif., 1991. Tchr. rep. PTA, Arcadia, 1980-93; mem. choir, children's sermon team, elder Arcadia Presbyn. Ch., 1980-93; chaperone, vol. Pasadena (Calif.) Youth Symphony Orch., 1988-90; vol. Am. Heart Assn., 1990-92. Recipient Outstanding Gen. Elem. Tchr. award, Outstanding Tchr. of the Yr. award Disney's Am. Tchr. Awards, 1993, Calif. Tchr. of Yr. award Calif. State Dept. Edn., 1993, Georgie award Girl Scouts of Am., 1993, The Self Esteem Task Force award L.A. County Task Force to Promote Self-Esteem & Personal & Social Responsibility, 1993, Profl. Achievement award UCLA Alumni Assn.; apptd. to Nat. Edn. Rsch. Policies & Priorities Bd., U.S. Sec. Edn. Richard Riley; Pann Baltz Mission Possible Scholar named in her honor. Mem. NEA, Nat. Sci. Tchrs. Assn., Calif. Tchr. Assn., Arcadia Tchrs. Assn. Avocations: reading, singing, calligraphy, book-making, computers. Home: 1215 S 3rd Ave Arcadia CA 91006-4205 Office: Arcadia Unified Sch Dist Camino Grove Elem Sch 700 Camino Grove Ave Arcadia CA 91006-4438

BALTZLEY, PATRICIA CREEL, secondary mathematics educator; b. Ft. Benning, Ga., Dec. 14, 1952; d. Buckner Miller and Mary Madeleine (O'Neill) Creel; m. Kevin Gerard Robinson, Nov. 15, 1975 (div. Dec. 21, 1981); children: Kevin G. Jr., Timothy Eugene; m. Jeffrey Lynn Baltzley, July 23, 1988 (dec. Dec. 1996). Student, St. Joseph's Coll., 1971-72; BA in Math., Coll. Notre Dame, 1975; MS in Math., Shippensburg State U., 1986. Cert. advanced profl., Md.; cert. in adminstn. and supervision. Acct. trainee Md. Nat. Bank, Balt., 1975-76; math. tchr. Notre Dame Preparatory Sch., Towson, Md., 1976-78, Carroll County Bd. Edn., Westminster, Md., 1978-91; math. program developer Ctr. for Social Orgn. of Schs. Johns Hopkins U., Balt., 1991—95; K-12 math. specialist Baltimore County Pub. Schs., 1995—98, 6-12 math. supr., 1998—. Adj. prof. Coll. Notre Dame, Balt., 1992--, Johns Hopkins U., 1995-97, Western Md. Coll., 1997--, Loyola Coll., 2000--; cons. Ctr. for Social Orgn., Johns Hopkins U., Learning Inst.; ind. cons. in field. Pres. Seton Ctr., Emmitsburg, Md., 1982-86; vol. Seton Shrine Ctr., Emmitsburg, 1986—. Recipient Presdl. Award for Excellence in Teaching Math. NSF, 1989; named Md. Math. Educator of Yr., 1977. Mem. ASCD, NEA, Md. Coun. Tchrs. Math. (pres. 1991-93), Nat. Coun. Tchrs. Math., Coun. Presdl. Awardees in Math., Md. Coun. Suprs. Math. (pres., 2000—), Coun. Adminstrs. and Suprs. in Edn. Democrat. Roman Catholic. Avocations: reading, basketball, walking. Home: 830 Glendale Rd York PA 17403-4130 Office: Baltiore County Pub Schs 6901 Charles St Towson MD 21204

BAMBERGER, PHYLIS SKLOOT, judge; b. N.Y.C., May 2, 1939; d. George Joseph and Martha (Wechselblatt) S.; m. Michael A. Bamberger, Dec. 19, 1965; children: Kenneth, Richard. BA, Bklyn. Coll., 1960; LLB, NYU, 1963. Bar: N.Y. 1963, U.S. Supreme Ct. 1967, U.S. Ct. Appeals (2d cir.) 1965, U.S. Dist. Ct. (so. dist.) N.Y. 1966, U.S. Dist. Ct. (ea. dist.) N.Y. 1979. Assoc. Legal Aid Soc., N.Y.C., 1963-67; assoc.-in-charge criminal appeals Bur. Legal Aid Soc., N.Y.C., 1967-72; atty.-in-charge, fed. def. svcs. unit/appeal Legal Aid Soc., N.Y.C., 1972-88; judge N.Y. State Ct. Claims designated to sit in the N.Y. State Supreme Ct., Bronx County, 1988—. Mem. N.Y. State Chief Judge's Jury Project, 1993-94; mem. com. on alts. to incarceration Office of Ct. Adminstrn., 1994-96, mem. criminal law and procedure adv. com., 1994-98, co-chair 1998-; mem. N.Y. State Chief Judge's Commn. on the Jury, 2003-, Jury Project, Office of Ct. Adminstrn., 2002. Author Criminal Appeals Handbook, 1984; editor, contbr. Practice Under the Federal Sentencing Guidelines, 1988, 90, 93, 2000 (also supplements); author, compiler Recent Developments in State Constitutional Law, 1985; contbr. numerous articles to publs. Mem. ABA, N.Y. State Bar assn. (co-chair presdl. com. on problems in criminal justice sys. 1986-88, mem. com. on the future of the profession), Assn. of Bar of City of N.Y. (chair com. on provision of legal svcs. to persons of moderate means 1995-98, 21st century com. 1992-95, chair com on probation 1993-94), Phi Beta Kappa. Office: Bronx County Courthouse 851 Grand Concourse Bronx NY 10451-2937

BAN, MARGO A. elementary school educator; d. Kent Carnahan; m. Stephen Ban; children: Hayley, Hannah, Marisa. MAT, NLU, Wheeling, IL, 2001. Cert. tchr. elem. edn. Ill., 2002. Auditor Deloitte & Touche, Chgo., 1989—94; fin. analyst Tenneco Packaging (now Pactiv), Lake Forest, Ill., 1994—97; fin. mgr. Ameritech, Hoffman Estates, Ill., 1997—2000; elem. tchr. Cary Dist. 26, Cary, Ill., 2002—.

BANAS, C(HRISTINE) LESLIE, lawyer; b. Swindon, Wiltshire, Eng., Oct. 29, 1951; arrived in U.S., 1957; d. Stanley M. and Helena Ann (Boryn) Banas; m. Dale J. Buras, May 1, 1976; children: Eric Buras, Andrea Buras. BA magna cum laude, U. Detroit, 1973; JD cum laude, Wayne State U., 1975. Bar: Mich. 1976, U.S. Supreme Ct. 1980. Atty. Hyman & Rice, Southfield, Mich., 1976-77, Hyman, Gurwin, Nachman, Friedman & Winkelman, Southfield, 1977-82, ptnr., 1982-87, Honigman Miller Schwartz and Cohn LLP, Detroit, 1987—. Contbr. articles to profl. jours. Chmn. bd. Women's Leadership Forum. Mem.: ABA, Fed. Bar Assn., State Bar Mich. (bd. dirs. real property law sect. coun., coun. treas.), Detroit Athletic Club, Women's Econ. Club (past pres.). Roman Catholic. Avocations: gardening, photography, skiing. Office: Honigman Miller Schwartz and Cohn LLP 32270 Telegraph Rd Ste 225 Bingham Farms MI 48025-2457 Office Phone: 248-566-8406. E-mail: lbanas@honigman.com.

BANAS, SUZANNE, middle school educator; b. Miami, Fla., Mar. 28, 1959; d. Frank and Norma (Eliscu) B. BA in Sci., U. Miami, 1981, MS, 1986; PhD, Union Inst., 1994. Cert. tchr. sci. gifted LD & EH, Fla.; Nat. Bd. Cert. Tchr. early adolescence generalist Nat. Bd. Profl. Tchg. Stds. Lead tchr. Dade County Pub. Schs., Miami, 1988—; curriculum writer Gender Equity Network, Miami, 1993—97, Arise Found., Miami, 1995—97; tchr., chairperson dept. sci., team leader Cutler Ridge Mid. Sch., Miami, 1990—; adj. prof. Fla. Internat. U., Miami, 1996—. Advisor Acad. for Instrnl. Leadership, Miami, 1994-96, Annenberg Challenge Grant, Miami, 1995-96; cons. Urban Sys. Initiative, 1995-98; Internet tchr. trainer/mentor, 1998—. Recipient Fla. Explores! award Fla. State U./TDRA, 1993, Tchr. of Yr. award Cutler Ridge Mid. Sch., 1996, Sharing success award dept. of environ. edn., 2000. Mem. Miami Dade County Sci. Tchrs. Assn. (pres. 1994—), Fla. Assn. Sci. Tchrs. (bd. dirs. 1998—), Nat. Sci. Tchrs. Assn. Office: Richmond Heights Mid Sch Sci Zoo Magnet 15015 SW103 Ave Miami FL 33176

BANASZYNSKI, CAROL JEAN, secondary school educator; b. Hawkins, Wis., Jan. 3, 1951; BS in Biology, U. Wis., LaCrosse, 1973; MS in Profl. Devel., U. Wis., Whitewater, 1987. Tchr. Deerfield Cmty. Schs., 1973—. Coach Youth T-ball/softball; co-chairperson Adopt-A-Highway; group leader 4-H Club; counselor Boy Scout Environtl. Merit Badge program Recipient Wis. H.S. Tchr. of Yr., 1997-98, Wis. Tchr. of Yr. 1998, Award of Excellence Wis. Assn. of Sch. Bds., 1997, Wis. Dept. of Instrn., 1997, Wis. Edn. Assn. Coun., 1997, Wis. Legis. Citation for Tchg. Excellence, 1997-98; named Educator of Yr. Nat. H.S. Assn., 1998, Outstanding Tchr. Radioshack/Tandy, 1999; Kohl fellowship, 1997, Monsanto fellowship, 2000. Mem. Nat. Biology Tchrs. Assn., Nat. Sci. Tchrs. Assn., Nat. Parks and Conservation Assn., Wis. Secondary Sci. Tchrs. (state conf. presenter), Wis. Elem. Sci. Tchrs., BioNet, DEA (scholarship com. chairperson), Wis. Edn. Assn. Coun., Dane County Talented and Gifted Coords. Assn. (vision com., dist. math meet coord.), Wis. Ctr. for Academically Talented Youth.

BANCEL, MARILYN, fund raising management consultant; b. Glen Ridge, N.J., June 15, 1947; d. Paul and Joan Marie (Spangler) B.; m. Rik Myslewski, Nov. 20, 1983; children: Carolyn, Roxanne. BA in English with distinction, Ind. U., 1969. Cert. fund raising exec. Ptnr. The Sultan's Shirt Tail, Gemlik, Turkey, 1969-72; prodn. mgr. High Country Co., San Francisco, 1973-74; exec. dir. East Bay Performance, Inc., 1976—79; pub. Bay Arts Rev., Berkeley, Calif., 1976-79; dir. devel. Oakland (Calif.) Symphony Orch., 1979-81; assoc. dir. devel. Exploratorium, San Francisco, 1981-86, dir. devel., 1986-91; prin. Fund Devel. Counsel, San Francisco, 1991-93; v.p. The Oram Group, Inc., San Francisco, 1993—. Co-chmn. capital campaign com. Synergy Sch., San Francisco, 1995-2000; adj. prof. U. San Francisco, 1993—. Author: Preparing Your Capital Campaign, 2000. Mem. adv. bd. Mus. City of San Francisco, 1995—, San Francisco Bot. Gardens, 1998-99. Fellow U. Strasberg, France, 1968. Mem. Assn. Fund-raising Profls. (bd. Golden Gate chpt. 1996-98, chmn. National Philanthropy Day, 2000, Outstanding Fundraising Exec. award 2002), Am. Assn. Fund Raising Counsel, Devel. Execs. Roundtable, Phi Beta Kappa. Democrat. Avocation: gardening. Office: The Oram Group Inc 275 Madison Ave New York NY 10016

BANCILA, EDITA, pathologist, educator; b. Romania; MD, U. Cluj, Romania, 1975. Diplomate Anatomic and Clin. Pathology Am. Bd. Pathology, 1982, Dermatopathology Am. Bd. Dermatology, 1984. Resident Pathology Robert Wood Johnson Med. U., New Brunswick, NJ, 1976—80; fellow Dermatopathology U. Pa. Hosp., Phila., 1980—81; physciain, dept. Pathology and Lab. Medicine Robert Wood Johnson Univ. Med. Group, New Brunswick, NJ, 1987—. Assoc. prof. Pathology Robert Wood Johnson Univ. Hosp., New Brunswick, NJ, 1987—. Office: Robt Wood Johnson Univ Hosp 1 Robert Wood Johnson Pl New Brunswick NJ 08903-2061

BANCROFT, ANN E. polar explorer; b. Mendota Heights, Minn., 1955; d. Dick and Debbie Bancroft Former tchr., coach, wilderness instr., St. Paul, Minn. Mem. Steger Internat. Polar Expedition, 1986 (first woman to reach the North Pole by dogsled); leader Am. Women's Antarctic Expedition, 1993 (first women's team to reach the South Pole on skis); mem. The Bancroft Arnesen Expdn. (first all women's crossing of Antarctica), 2000; founder (with Liv Anderson) yourexpedition internat. motivation co. Subject (corp. video) Vision of Teams, 1998, (documentary) Poles Apart, 1999; featured in Remarkable Women of the 20th Century, 1998. Founder Ann Bancroft Found; spokesperson Learning Disabilities Assn., Wilderness Inquiry (co-chair capital campaign), Girl Scouts U.S.A; bd. dirs. Youth Frontiers; judge Nuclear-Free awards, Nat. Women's Hall of Fame inductions. Named Ms. Mag. Woman of Yr., 1987 Glamour Mag. Woman of Yr., 2001; inductee Girls and Women in Sport Hall of Fame, 1992, Nat. Women's Hall of Fame, 1995; recipient Women First award YWCA, 1993; first woman in world to travel across the ice to North and South poles; (with Liv Anderson) first women in history to sail and ski across Antartica's landmass. Mem.: Melpomene Inst. and Medica (adv. bd.). Office: yourexpedition 119 N 4th St Ste 406 Minneapolis MN 55401-1790 Fax: 612-333-1325. E-mail: susan@yourexpedition.com.*

BANCROFT, ANNE (MRS. MEL BROOKS), actress, scriptwriter, television director; b. Bronx, NY, Sept. 17, 1931; d. Michael and Mildred (DiNapoli) Italiano; m. Mel Brooks, 1964; 1 son. Broadway stage appearances include Two for the Seesaw, 1957 (Tony award 1957), The Miracle Worker, 1959-60 (Tony award 1960), The Little Foxes, 1967-68, Devils, 1977, A Cry of Players, 1968-69, Golda, 1977-78, Duet for One, 1981, The Occupant, 2002; stage appearances include Mystery of the Rose Bouquet, 1989; motion pictures include Treasure of the Golden Condor, 1952, Don't Bother to Knock, 1952, Tonight We Sing, 1953, The Kid from Left Field, 1953, Demetrius and the Gladiators, 1954, Gorilla at Large, 1954, The Raid, 1954, A Life in the Balance, 1954, The Brass Ring, 1954, Naked Street, 1955, New York Confidential, 1955, The Last Frontier, 1955, Girl in the Black Stockings, 1957, Restless Breed, 1957, The Pumpkin Eater, 1964, Seven Women, 1966, Slender Thread, 1966, The Graduate, 1967 (Golden Globe for best actress, 1968), Young Winston, 1972, The Prisoner of 2nd Avenue, 1975, The Hindenburg, 1975, Lipstick, 1976, Silent Movie, 1976, The Turning Point, 1977, Fatso, 1979, The Elephant Man, 1980, To Be or Not to Be, 1983, Garbo Talks, 1984, Agnes of God, 1985, 'Night, Mother, 1986, 84 Charing Cross Road (Brit. Acad. award 1987), Torch Song Trilogy, 1988, Bert Rigby You're a Fool, 1989, Honeymoon in Vegas, 1992, Love Potion #9, 1992, Point of No Return, 1993, Mr. Jones, 1993, Malice, 1993, How to Make an American Quilt, 1995, Home for the Holidays, 1995, Dracula, Dead and Loving It, 1995, GI Jane, 1997, Critical Care, 1997, Great Expectations, 1998, Antz, 1998, Mark Twain's America in 3D, 1998, Up at the Villa, 1999, Deep in My Heart, 1999, Keeping the Faith, 2000, Heartbreakers, 2001; TV appearances include Kraft Music Hall, Jesus of Nazareth, 1977, Marco Polo, 1982, Broadway Bound, 1992, Mrs. Cage, PBS, 1992, Oldest Living Confederate Widow Tells All, 1994, The Homecoming, 1996, Sunchasers, 1997, AFI's 100 years ... 100 Movies, 1998, Deep in My Heart, 1999 (Emmy for best supporting actress, 1999), Haven, 2001, The Roman Spring of Mrs. Stone, 2003; dir., writer, star: (TV spl.) Annie The Woman in the Life of Men, 1970 (Emmy award 1970). Recipient Acad. award for performance in The Miracle Worker, 1962, Best Actress award Cannes Internat. Film Festival for performance in Pumpkin Eater, 1964, inducted into Theater Hall of Fame, 1992, Lifetime Achievement in Comedy award Am. Comedy Awards, 1996. Address: c/o The Culver Studios 9336 Washington Blvd Culver City CA 90232-2628 Office: ICM 8942 Wilshire Blvd Beverly Hills CA 90211*

BANCROFT, MARGARET ARMSTRONG, lawyer; b. Mpls., May 9, 1938; d. Wallace David and Mary Elizabeth (Garland) Armstrong; m. Alexander Clerihew Bancroft, Mar. 14, 1964; 1 child, Elizabeth Armstrong. BA magna cum laude, Radcliffe Coll.-Harvard U., 1960; JD cum laude, NYU, 1969. Bar: N.Y. 1971. Reporter Mpls. Star and Tribune, 1960-61, UPI, N.Y., N.J., 1961-66; ptnr. Law Firm of Dechert LLP. Adj. prof. law NYU Sch. Law. Bd. dirs., exec. com. Vis. Nurse Svc. NY; chair. Vis. Nurse Svc. NY Home Care, Inc. Mem. ABA (bus. law sect.), N.Y. State Bar Assn. (securities regulation com.), Assn Bar City N.Y. (com. on investment mngmt. regulation), Am. Law Inst. Office: Law Firm of Dechert LLP 30 Rockefeller Plz Fl 22 New York NY 10112-2200 Office Phone: 212-698-3590. E-mail: margaret.bancroft@dechert.com.

BANDEKA, FAUN ANN, elementary school educator; b. Price, Utah, Aug. 19, 1947; d. Harold Burdean and Verena A. (Anderson) Nielson; m. Daryl G. Bandeka, Oct. 19, 1974; children: Trisha Lynn, Philip Aaron. BS, U. Utah, 1973. 2nd grade tchr. Gallup-McKinnley County Sch., Gallup, N.Mex., 1973-74; tchr. third and first grades Gallup-McKinnley County Schs., 1975-77; third grade tchr. San Juan County Schs., Monticello, Utah, 1974-75; tchr. first and second grade Granite Sch. Dist., Salt Lake City, 1987—. Nat. dir. Pledge of Allegiance Centennial, Salt Lake City, 1991-92, Utah state dir., 1991-92; dir. Cmty./Sch. Centennial Celebration, Salt Lake City, 1995-96. Author: (textbook) Preparing Children for School, 1985, Utah: A Centennial Portrait, 1995; composer musical selections. Sec. Kearns Town Coun., Kearns, Utah, 1997-99; mem. Kearns Coalition, Kearns, 1997—; vol. editor/creator: Kearns Chronicle, 1998—; chairperson Miss Kearns Teen Scholarship Pageant, 1997-99. Recipient New Constellation award, Nat. Flag. Found., Washington, 1992, Tchr.'s medal of honor, Freedoms Foun. at Valley Forge, 1993, Centennial Book place, Utah State Archives, Salt Lake City, 1996, Unsung Hero award, Valley View Meml. Estates/West Valley City, 1999, Excel Outstanding Educator finalist, Granite Sch. Dist., 2000, Fulbright Meml. Fund Master Tchr., 2001, Internat. Soc. Poets award, 2002; grantee Fulbright Tchrs. grant, Internat. Inst. Edn. and Japanese/U.S. Edn. Commn., Japanese Govt., 1997. Mem. Salt Lake Composers Guild, NEA, Fulbright Meml. Fund (alumni), Internat. Poets Soc. Republican. Mem. Lds Ch. Avocations: reading, hiking, writing, scrap books. Office: Hillside Elem Sch 4283 South 6000 West West Valley City UT 84128 E-mail: faun_daryl@networld.com., faun.bandeka@granite.k12.ut.us.

BANDES, SUSAN JANE, museum director, educator; b. N.Y.C., Oct. 18, 1951; d. Ralph and Bessie (Gordon) B. BA, NYU, 1971; MA, Bryn Mawr Coll., 1973, PhD, 1978; postgrad., Mus. Mgmt. Inst., Berkeley, Calif., 1990. Asst. prof. Sweet Briar (Va.) Coll., 1978-83; project dir. Am. Assn. Mus., Washington, 1983-84; program officer J. Paul Getty Trust Grant Program, L.A., 1984-86; prof., dir. Kresge Art Mus. Mich. State U., East Lansing, 1986—. Author, editor: Caring for Collections, 1984, Affordable Dreams: The Goetsch-Winckler House and Frank Lloyd Wright, 1991; author: Abraham Rattner, The Tampa Museum of Art Collection, 1997, Pursuits and Pleasures: Baroque Paintings from the Detroit Institute of Arts, 2003; editor: The Prints of John S. de Martelly, 1903-1979; author, curator: Pursuits and Pleasures: Baroque Painting from the Detroit Institute of Arts, 2003. Recipient award Am. Philos. Soc., 1981, publ. award AIA, 1990; Samuel H. Kress fellow, 1972-73, 75-76, Whiting fellow, 1976-77; Fulbright-Hayes grant, 1974-75. Mem. Nat. Inst. for Conservation (treas. 1986-90), Mich. Alliance for Conservation (treas. 1994-95, sec. 1996-97, treas. 1997-98, pres. 1998-2000), Mich. Mus. Assn. (bd. dirs. 1987-92), Mich. Coun. for Humanities (coun. 1988-92), Midwest Art History Soc. (bd. dirs. 1997-2000). Avocation: collecting oriental rugs. Office: Mich State U Kresge Art Mus East Lansing MI 48824 Office Phone: 517-353-9834. E-mail: bandes@msu.edu.

BANDO, PATRICIA ALICE, director; b. Detroit, Apr. 4, 1953; d. Hiro Walter and Fumi Patricia (Takemoto) B. BS in Dietetics, Mich. State U., 1975; MA in Food Svc. Adminstrn., NYU, 1985. Registered dietitian. Dietetic intern The N.Y. Hosp., N.Y.C., 1975-76, clin. dietitian, sr. dietitian/adminstrv., 1981-86; food and beverage mgr. Trump Palace Hotel, Atlantic City, N.J., 1986; gen. mgr., dining dept. Cornell U., Ithaca, N.Y., 1986-89, asst. dir., dining dept., 1989-92, dir., dining dept., 1992-95, Boston Coll., Chestnut Hill, Mass., 1995—. Fundraiser One to One Mentoring, Boston, 1998. Mem. ADA, Mass. Dietetic Assn., Nat. Assn. of Coll. and Univ. Food svcs. (conf. edn. chair 1996-97), N.Y. So. Tier Dietetic Assn. (treas. 1992-95), Soc. of Foodsvc. Mgmt., Nat. Restaurant Assn., Mass. Restaurant Assn. (bd. dirs. 2003—, Employer Choice award 2003), New Seabury Country Club, Omicron Nu. Episcopalian. Avocations: golf, oil painting, watercolor, gourmet cooking. Home: 14 Holly Way Framingham MA 01701-4857 Office: Boston Coll Dining Svcs 66 Commonwealth Ave Chestnut Hill MA 02467-3843

BANE, MARY JO, political science educator; b. Princeville, Ill., Feb. 24, 1942; d. Fred W. and Helen (Callery) B.; m. Kenneth Winston, May 31, 1975. BS in Internat. Rels., Georgetown U., 1963; MAT, Harvard U., 1966, DEd, 1972. Tchr. English U.S. Peace Corps, Liberia, 1963-65; tchr. social studies Arlington (Mass.) Pub. Schs., 1966-67; tchr. English and social studies Brookline (Mass.) Pub. Schs., 1968-71; rsch. assoc. Ctr. Ednl. Policy Rsch. and Huron Inst. Harvard U., Cambridge, Mass., 1971-72, project co-dir. Ctr. Study of Pub. Policy, 1972-75, assoc. prof. edn., lectr. in sociology, 1977-80, assoc. prof. pub. policy, 1981-86, dir. Malcolm Wiener Ctr. for Social Policy, 1987-92, prof. pub. policy, 1986-90; Malcolm Wiener Prof. of Social Policy Kennedy Sch. of Govt., Harvard U., Cambridge, Mass., 1990-92; lectr. in Sociology U. Mass., Boston, 1972-75; assoc. dir. Ctr. Rsch. on Women, asst. prof. edn., lectr. in sociology Wellesley (Mass.) Coll., 1975-77; dep. asst. sec. for program planning and budget analyst Office Planning and Budget U.S. Dept. Edn., Washington, 1980-81; exec. dep. commr. N.Y. State Dept. Social Svcs., 1984-86, commr., 1992-93; asst. sec. Adminstrn. for Children and Families Dept. Health and Human Svcs., Washington, 1993-96; Prof. Pub. Policy Harvard U., Cambridge, Mass., 1997—; Ida Beam vis. prof. U. Iowa, 1980; chair bd. overseers panel study income dynamics Inst. Rsch. U. Mich., 1982-86, regents lectr. U. Calif., Berkeley, 1987; mem. adv. com. urban poverty NAS, 1986-90, chair com. child devel. rsch. and pub. policy, 1987-90; mem. pres. adv. coun. Columbia U. Tchrs. Coll., N.Y.C., 1988-92; mem. grants adv. coun. Smith Richardson Found., 1989-92; bd. dirs. Manpower Demonstration Rsch. Coun., 1989-92, 97—; active William T. Grant Found. Commn. on Work, Family and Citizenship, 1987-88. Author: (with others) Inequality: A Reassessment of the Effects of Family and Schooling in America, 1972, Here to Stay: American Families in the Twentieth Century, 1974, Japanese translation, 1981, (with George Masnick) The Nation's Families 1960-90, 1980; editor: (with Donald Levine) The Inequality Controversy, 1975, (with Manuel Carballo) The State and the Poor in the 1980s, 1984, (with Kenneth I. Winston) Gender and Public Policy: Cases and Comments, 1993, (with David Ellwood) Welfare Realities: From Rhetoric to Reform, 1994; contbr. articles to profl. jours. Fellow Nat. Acad. Pub. Adminstrn.; mem. Am. Sociol. Assn., Population Assn. Am., Assn. Pub. Policy Analysis and Mgmt. Office: Harvard Univ Kennedy Sch Govt 79 John F Kennedy St Cambridge MA 02138-5801

BANEY, LORI A. education educator; b. Burke, S.D., Dec. 2, 1962; d. George E. and Lois L. Baney. AAS in Vet. Tech., Colby (Kans.) C.C., 1983; AAS in Histology, Presentation Coll., 1987; BS in Human Resources, Friends U., 1994. Histology technician St. Luke's Hosp., Aberdeen, SD, 1986—87; history/serology technician S.D. State U. Diagnostic Lab., Brookings, 1987—89; instr. Colby C.C., 1989—. Mem.: AAUW, Kans. Vet. Technicians Assn. (pres., NAVTA liaison 1989—), Nat. Vet. Technicians Assn.

BANFIELD, ASHLEIGH DENNISTOUN, news correspondent; b. Winnipeg, Canada, Dec. 29, 1967; BA in Polit. Studies, French, Queens U., Ontario. News anchor KDFW FOX 4, Dallas; assoc. prodr. ABC World News Tonight; weekend evening news anchor CFRN, Edmonton; photgrapher, rschr., reporter CJBN, Kenora, Canada, 1988, CKY sta.-evening news, Winnipeg, 1989—92; prodr. CICT-TV, Canada, 1992—93, evening news anchor, 1993—95; co-anchored Newsfront, 2001; anchor, corr. MSNBC, 2000—; anchor A Region in Conflict, CNN, 2001—02, Ashleigh Banfield: On Location, 2002. Recipient Best News Anchor Emmy, award, Tex. Associated Press, awards, IRIS, 1994. Office: NBC News 30 Rockefeller Plz New York NY 10112

BANFIELD, JILLIAN, mineralogist, geomicrobiologist, educator; b. Armidale, NSW, Australia, Aug. 18, 1959; BSc, Australian Nat. U., Canberra City, 1981, MSc; MA, PhD, Johns Hopkins U., 1990. Assoc. prof. geology and geophysics U. Wis., Madison, 1995-99, affiliate faculty mem. dept. chemistry, 1998—, prof., 1999—. Prof. Mineral. Inst. U. Tokyo, 1996-98; vis. rsch. fellow ANU, 1998-2000. Recipient Geol. Soc. of Australia prize 1979, W.B. Clark prize in geology, 1979, Ampol prize, 1980, Dept. Energy's award for outstanding rsch., 1995, D.A. Brown medal Australin Nat. U., 1999; Mineralogical Soc. of Am. grantee, 1989; Owen Fellowship award, 1986-89, Eby fellow, 1986-90, Gilman Tuition fellow, 1986-90, H.I. Romnes Faculty fellow, 1998, John D. and Catherine T. MacArthur Found. fellow, 1999—, John Simon Guggenheim Found. fellow, 2000; Australian Nat. U. MSc scholar, 1983-84, Fulbright scholar, 1986, JFOL scholar Ariz. State U., 1988; Gast lectr. Geochem. Soc., 2000; NSF Earth Sci. Wk. lectr., 2000. Fellow Mineralogical Soc. Am. (Disting. lectr. 1994-95, mem. coun. 1996, award 1997); mem. Clay Minerals Soc. (mem. coun, Marion L. and Christie M. Jackson Mid-Career Clay Scientist award 2000). Office: U Wis Dept Geology and Geophysics 1215 W Dayton St Dept And Madison WI 53706-1600

BANFIELD, MARIAN D. federal agency administrator; BA in math, Transylvania U.; grad. classes in edn., U. Va, U. Colo., U. No. Colo., Grad. Sch. US Dept Agr. Mgmt. analyst US Dept Edn., Off. Under Sec. of Edn., Planning and Evaluation Svc., Wash., 2002—, US Dept Edn., Off. Intergovernmental and Interagency Affairs, 1997—2002; edn. program spec. US Dept Edn., Off. Vocat. and Adult Edn., 1993—97; project mgr. A.S.K. Assoc., Lawrence, Kans., 1988—90; math. instr. various jr. and sr. HS under contract with A.S. K. Assoc. Office: US Dept Edn 400 Maryland Ave SW Rm 6W223 Washington DC 20202 E-mail: marian.banfield@ed.gov.

BANFILL, SALLY ANNE, painter; b. Tacoma, Feb. 20, 1956; d. Arthur Charles and June Laverne Banfill; m. Nels Jonathan Royer. BFA, U. Hawaii, 1984. One-woman shows include Resource Ctr., Seattle, 1991, Wonderful World Art, 1992, Fenix Underground, 1993, Summer Song Gallery, 1996, Imogen Cunningham Gallery, 1997, Straylight Gallery, Missoula, Mont., 1997, Bastoky Gallery, Seattle, 1997, Parlour Rm., 1998, Madrona Automatic, 1999, Artists' Edge, Bremerton, Wash., 1999, 2003, Foster White Gallery, Kirkland, Wash., 2001, Smith Tower, Seattle, 2003, exhibited in group shows at Bastoky Gallery, 1996, Arts' Edge, 1998, Ctr. on Contemporary Art, 2001. With USN, 1974—78. Mem.: Soc. for Comml. Archeology. Roman Catholic. Avocation: photography. Personal E-mail: banfill@banfill.com.

BANGERT, LINDA S. aeronautical engineer; BS in Aero. Engring, MS in Aero. Engring. Aero. rsch. engr. Langley Rsch. Ctr. NASA, Hampton, Va. Avocation: Avocations: flying, reading mysteries and science fiction. Office: NASA Langley Rsch Ctr Mail Stop 254 Bldg 1244 Rm 103 Hampton VA 23681-2199 E-mail: L.S. Bangert@larc.nasa.gov.*

BANGS, MARY CONSTANCE (C BANGS), artist, curator; b. Elmira, N.Y., Oct. 19, 1946; d. Orval Ernest Bangs and Mary Isabelle Engle; m. Victor Louis Zeringo, June 29, 1969 (div. June 1978); m. Gregory Lee Matloff, Aug. 8, 1986. BFA, Phila. Coll. of Art, 1970; MFA, Pratt Inst., 1975. Curator discoveries Dept. of Parks and Recreation, City of New York, 1980—90, Elders Share the Arts, Bklyn., 1991—96; instr. SUNY, Empire State Corp. Coll., Bklyn., 1993—2003; with spl. projects Art Resource Transfer, Inc., N.Y.C., 2000—01. Instr. Tchrs. Coll., Columbia U., N.Y.C., 1985; adv. bd. Space Activity Soc., Internat. Astron. Fedn., Paris, 1995—2003; curator Messages From Earth, N.Y.C., 2000—; artist cons. Marshall Space Flight Ctr., Huntsville, Ala., 2001, NASA faculty fellow, 2002—05; curator Discoveris Elders Share the Arts, Bklyn., 1991—96. Curator (exhibitions) Discoveries: Exhbns. of the City's Underknown Older Artists, 1980—90; holographic space billboards, 2001, Represented in permanent collections Chrysler Mus., Norfolk, Va., Mint Mus., Charlotte, N.C., Pratt Inst., Bklyn., Accademia dei Fisiocritici, Siena, Italy, Pantcra Contrade Mus., Dipartimento di Fisica, Universita Degli Studi do Siena, Italy, Pace U., Civic Ctr. Campus, N.Y.C., Annabel Taylor Hall, Cornell U., Ithaca, N.Y., one-woman shows include Tompkins County Ctr. for Culture and Performing Arts, Ithaca, 1979, Pace U. Art Gallery, 1985, Ten Brooks Gallery, 1991, Belanthi Gallery, 1992, Accademia dei Fisiocritici, Siena, 1994, Art Resources Transfer, Inc., 1997, Audart, N.Y.C., 1998, Art Resources Transfers, Inc., 1999, 2001, exhibited in group shows at Pratt Manhattan Ctr., 1974, Pratt Phoenix Ctr., 1976, 1977, Staten Islands Annual Juried Exhbn., 1976, 1977, Islip Town Art Gallery, N.Y., 1979, Mint Mus., N.C., 1980, Chrysler Mus., 1950—80, Galeria San Juan, P.R., 1981, Cayman Gallery, 1983, Whitney Counterweight WC4, 10,000, 1983, Reynold Kerr Gallery, 1984, Cologne, Germany, 1985, S.R. Rage Gallery, N.Y.C., 1986, Helio Gallery, 1989, Sun Valley Arts Ctr., Idaho, 1990, Second Internat. Symposium on Electronic Art, Groningen, Holland, 1990, Z Gallery, N.Y.C., 1991, Dallas Mus. Beaux Arts Auction, various locations, 1992, Dallas, Tex., 1993, 1993, Tribeca 148, N.Y.C., 1994, Emerging Collector, 1994, 1995, Art Proper, 1994, 46th IAF Congress, Norway, 1995, CHRION, Ithaca, N.Y., 1996, Bklyn. Borough Hall., 1996, Deep Space, 1996, Pat Hern Gallery, N.Y.C., 1997, La Galeria, Quito, Eucador, 1998, Rotunda Gallery, Bklyn., 1998, Church, N.Y.C., 1999, Las Vegas Mus. of Art, 2002, Taipei Gallery, N.Y.C., 2001, 2002, Gallery 718, Bklyn., N.Y., 2003, Forms of Divinity, Brave Destiny, Williamsburg Hist. Ctr., 2003, P.M.S., 2004. Recipient Pub. award, United Press, 1981; grantee to create message plague, NASA, 2001; scholar Jerome Found., Bob Blackton Printmaking Workshop, N.Y.C., 1982. Mem.: Artist's Equity (bd. adv. 1996—98). Home: 417 Greene Ave Brooklyn NY 11216 Address: 210 11th Ave Rm 403 New York NY 10001-1210

BANK, BARBARA J. sociology educator; b. Chgo., Dec. 13, 1939; d. Julius Charles and Anna Catherine (Damm) Bank; m. Bruce Jesse Biddle, June 19, 1976. BS in Edn., Ill. State U., Normal, 1961; MA, U. Iowa, 1968, PhD in Sociology, 1974. Tchr. Rich Twp. H.S., Park Forest, Ill., 1961-63; from instr. to prof. emerita U. Mo., Columbia, 1969—, dir. grad. studies dept. sociology, 1978-82, chair dept. sociology, 1981-84. Vis. fellow Australian Nat. U., Canberra, 1984-85, 88, 93. Author: Contradictions in Women's Education, 2003; co-editor: Gender, Equity, and Schooling: Policy and Practice, 1997; assoc. editor Social Psychology of Edn., 1994-2000; contbr. articles to profl. jours.; presenter in field. Recipient Purple Chalk Tchg. award Coll. Arts and Scis., U. Mo., 1998; Fulbright sr. scholar, 1985; William T. Kemper fellow Excellence in Teaching, 2000. Mem. profl. orgns. Avocations: travel, reading. Home: 924 Yale Columbia MO 65203-1874 Office: U Mo Dept Sociology Columbia MO 65211-0001 E-mail: bankb@missouri.edu.

BANKO, RUTH CAROLINE, retired library director; b. Phillipsburg, N.J., Mar. 28, 1931; d. Arthur William and Virginia Miller (Wilson) Osborn; m. Marvin Kenneth Banko (dec.); children: David, Sallie, Susan, Joseph, Elisabeth. Cert. libr. tech. asst., Northampton AreaC.C. Salesman Stanley Home Products, 1958-95; dir. Riegelsville (Pa.) Pub. Libr., 1974-97. Social ambudsman County Agy. on Aging, Doylestown, Pa.; asst. dir. Pearl Buck Found., Dublin, Pa.; mem. Riegelsville Fire Aux., 1992—; councilman, Planning Commn., Riegelsville Borough Coun., 1972-89; mem. States Legis. Com., 1972-88; mayor Borough of Riegelsville, 1990-97; disaster chmn., blood chmn., bd. mem. ARC, Doylestown, 1966-86; pres. jr. high and area coun. PTA, Easton, 1966-74; pres. Boro Coun., 1980-81; v.p., trustee Riegelsville Pub. Libr. Recipient award for svc. ARC, Doylestown, Bucks County Libr. Dist., Life Membership award PTA, 1972, Mem. Pa. Boroughs Assn. (legis. com. 1972-97), Pa. Mayors Assn., Easton Area Coun. PTAs (life). Democrat. Lutheran. Home: 449 Easton Rd Riegelsville PA 18077-0223

BANKOS, JEAN, educational association administrator, educator; History tchr. Lafayette-Winona Mid. Sch.; pres. Va. Edn. Assn., Richmond, 2000—. Bldg. rep. Lafayette-Winona Mid. Sch.; mem. legis. com., negotiations team, lobby team, scholarship com., bd. dirs. Norfolk City Pub. Sch. Mem.: Va. Edn. Assn. (econ. benefits com., legis. com., bd. dirs., exec. and budget com.), Chesapeake Edn. Bay Assn. (sec., chair UniServ Coun.), Edn. Assn. Norfolk (pres. 1989—91). Office: Va Edn Assn 116 S Third St Richmond VA 23219

BANKS, DEIRDRE MARGARET, retired church organization administrator; b. Melbourne, Australia, May 9, 1934; came to U.S., 1975; d. Haldane Stuart and Vera Avice (Fisher) B. MA, Simpson Coll., 1980. Missionary nurse Leprosy Mission, Kathmandu, Nepal, 1960-69; dean of women Melbourne Bible Inst., 1970-75; asst. to dir. Bible Study Fellowship, Oakland, Calif., 1975-79; dir. adult ministries First Covenant Ch., Oakland, 1980-87, assoc. pastor for adults, St. Paul, 1987-89; exec. dir. Covenant Women Ministries, Chgo., 1989-99. Spkr. at women's retreats in U.S. and Australia. Chairperson ch. edn. bd. Pacific S.W. Conf. Evang. Ch., 1985-87, Gilead Group, Oakland, 1985-87; bd. dirs., chairperson Gilead Group Housing for Abused and Homeless Women and Children; bd. chmn. Barnabas Project for Abused and Homeless Women and Children, 1990-93; mem. bd. world mission Evang. Covenant Ch., 1986-89; bd. Covenant Enabling Residences Inc. for Developmentally Disabled Adults, pres., 1996-98; pastor Mission Covenant Ch., Orange, Mass., 2000--. Mem. Evangel. Covenant Ch.

BANKS, DIANE P. art educator, artist; b. Bklyn., Dec. 18, 1942; d. Raymond August Trauth and Lucille Rita Bucklo; children: Matthew Moss, Sarah Moss. BFA, Syracuse U., 1981, MFA, 1984. Adj. prof. Syracuse U., NY, 1984—86; vis. asst. prof. Rochester Inst. Tech., NY, 1985—86, New World Sch. of the Arts, Miami, 1988—89; adj. prof. Fla. Atlantic U., Boca Raton, 1989—94, Broward C.C., Davie, Fla., 1989—94; asst. prof. East Carolina U., Greenville, NC, 1994—98, Western Oreg. U., Monmouth, 1998—99; asst. prof., dir. core foundations Iowa State U., Ames, 1999—2000; asst. prof., coord. foundations U. Ctrl. Fla., Orlando, 2000—03, James Madison U., Harrisonburg, Va., 2003—; MacDowell resident MacDowell Colony, Peterborough, NH, 1981; resident Va. Ctr. for the Creative Arts, Sweet Briar, 1982, Yaddo, Saratoga Springs, NY, 1984, The Dorland Mtn. Colony, Temecula, Calif., 1984; workshop on bldg. sculptural vessels Fla. Craftsman, Inc., St. Petersburg, 2000; workshop on found materials/sculptural vessels Arrowmont, 2001; resident Syracuse (N.Y.) U., 2002, 03; workshop on profl. practices Cazenovia Coll., NY, 2003; workshop on non-traditional baskets Syracuse U., 2003, 04. Sculpture installation, The Everson Mus. Art, Syracuse, N.Y., 1981, Lee Hansley Gallery, Raleigh, N.C., 1997, one-woman shows include Syracuse Stage Gallery, 1980, Intimate Vessels, Tex. Woman's U., Denton, 2003, exhibitions include Ann. Basketry Invitational, Gallery Materia, Scottsdale, Ariz., 2003, inventions and constructions, New Baskets, Fla. Craftsman Gallery, St. Petersburg, 2000, prin. works include inventions and constructions New Baskets, Soc. for Arts and Crafts, Boston, 2000, New Baskets, Wustum Mus., Racine, Wis., 2000, New Baskets, Sch. of Art, East Carolina U., Greenville, N.C., 2001, New Baskets, Ky. Art & Craft Gallery, Louisville, 2001, exhibitions include The Am. Ann. Works on Paper Exhbn., Zaner Gallery, Rochester, N.Y., 1983, Jeffery Fuller Fine Art, Phila., 1983, Rutgers Nat. 83184, Stedman Art Gallery, Rutgers U., Camden, N.J., 1984, Cazenovia Coll., Chapman Gallery, Cazenovia, N.Y., 1984, The Faculty Show, Lowe Art Gallery, Syracuse, U., 1984, Prints, Drawings, Photographs: 47th Ann. Exhbns. Artists of Ctrl. N.Y., Munson-Williams-Proctor Inst., Utica, N.Y., 1984, The Syracuse Bicentennial 1984, The Everson Mus., 1984—85, Mt. San Angelo's Artists: touring exhbn. of works from collection of The Va. Ctr. for the Creative Arts, 1984—85, Hartwick Coll., Oneonta, N.Y., 1986, Gallery 10, Wash., D.C., 1987, Suspended in Space, Paint Creek Ctr. For The Arts, Rochester, Mich., 1987, exhibitions include sculpture All Fla. Show, Zack-Schuster Gallery, Miami, 1989, 38th Ann. All Fla. Show, Boca Raton Mus. Art, Fla., 1989, exhibitions include painting Spirit/Matter, Fla. Women's Caucus for Art, Tampa, Fla., 1989, exhibitions include Twenty Third Ann. Competition for N.C. Artists, Fayetteville Mus. Art, 1995, Craft Am. '95, Silvermine Gallery, New Canaan, Conn., 1995, Explorations: Shades of Difference, WCA-CT, Univ. Bridgeport, Conn., 1995, Crafts Nat. 29, Zoller, Penn State U., U. College Pk., Pa., 1995 (monetary award, 1995), The Wichita Nat., The Wichita Ctr. For The Arts, Kans., 1995, The Halpert Biennial, Appalachian State U., Boone, N.C., 1995, All Mixed Up. Associated Artists of Winston-Salem, N.C., 1995, Wearable Expressions: The Personal Art, Palos Verdes Art Ctr., Beckstrand Gallery, Calif., 1995, Collage: Diverse Fragments, Lee Hansley Gallery, Raleigh, N.C., 1995, Through Women's Eyes, The Women's Ctr., Chapel Hill, N.C., 1996, The Un-Portrait, Galleria Mesa, Ariz., 1996, Painting in-Gen., Associated Artists of Winston-Salem, N.C., 1996, Craft Forms '96, Wayne Art Ctr., Pa., 1997, Mixed Media Exhbn., Slidell Cultural Ctr., La., 1997, Southeastern Spectrum, Associated Artists of Winston-Salem, N.C., 1997, Aerial View, Pittsburg State U., Kans., 1997, 7th Ann. Nat. Juried Exhbn., 1708 Gallery, Richmond, Va., 1997, 20″ Ann. Vahki Exhbn., Galeria Mesa, Ariz., 1998, La Petite V, Alder Gallery, Eugene, Oreg., 1997, Feminie n women collectively: womankind, 621 Gallery, Tallahassee, Fla., 1998, 12″ Ann. Women in the Visual Arts 1998 Internat. Competition, Erector Sq. Gallery, New Haven, Conn., 1998, 10″ Ann. Nat. Art Competition Exhbn., U. Art Gallery, Truman State U., Kirksville, Mo., 1998, The Human Figure/Five Views, Campbell Hall Gallery, Western Oreg. U., Monmouth, Oreg., 1999, Arrowmont Nat. '99, Sandra J. Blain Gallery, Arrowmont Sch. Arts and Crafts, Gatlinburg, Tenn., 1999, Social Fiber: Unraveling the Messages, The Soc. Arts and Crafts, Boston, 1999, Craftforms '99, Wayne Art Ctr., Pa., 2000, exhibitions include (two person show) Diane Banks Recent Sculpture, Corvallis Art Ctr., Oreg., 1999, exhibitions include Arrowmont Nat. Summer Invitational, Gatlinburg, Tenn., 2001, Snyderman Gallery, Phila., exhbn. at SOFA, N.Y.C. Armory, 2001, Once Upon a Time: Artists Examine Fairy Tales, Legends and Myth, Wustum Mus. Fine Arts, Racine, Wis., 2001, Snyderman Gallery, Phila., exhbn. at SOFA, Chgo. Navy Pier, 2001, New Forms in Fiber, Trends and Traditions, Mobilia Gallery, Cambridge, Mass., 2001, Contemporary Fiber, Ark. Art Ctr., Little Rock, 2002, The Art of Contemporary Basketry, Gallery Materia, Scottsdale, Ariz., 2002, Fiber Survey 2002, Snyderman Gallery, Phila., 2002, Contemporary Baskets 2002, Del Mano Gallery, L.A., 2002, Am. Basketry, Ohio Craft Mus., Columbus, 2002, In Excess, Fla. Craftsman Gallery, St. Petersburg, 2002, Ignagural Show, A Little More Red (Internet Gallery), 2002, Snyderman Gallery, exhbn. at SOFA, Chgo. Navy Pier, 2002, Contemporary Basket Invitational, The Am. Art Co., Tacoma, Wash., 2003, Artists and the Cultivated Landscape, Wustum Mus. Fine Art, Racine, Wis., 2003, Snyderman Gallery, exhbn. at SOFA, N.Y.C., 2003, Made In The USA Contemporary Crafts, Peoria Art Guild, Ill., 2003, Represented in permanent collections Appalachian State U., Boone, N.C., Va. Ctr. For The Creative Arts, Sweet Briar, Va., Mint Mus., Charlotte, N.C., Renwick Gallery of the Nat. Mus. Am. Art, Smithsonian Inst., Wash., D.C., Ark. Art Ctr., Little Rock, Wustum Mus. Art, Racine, Wis., publication, Nouvel Objet, 2001. Recipient The Jean and Louis Dreyfus/MacDowell Fellow award, 1981, Nat. Endowment For The Arts Permanent Archive, The Smithsonian, Wash., D.C., 1997; grantee grad. fellowship, Syracuse U., 1982—83, 1983—84, Visual Artists fellowship for sculpture, Nat. Endowment for the Arts, 1984—85; Residency grant to install sculpture, Artpark, Niagara Falls, N.Y., 1985. Avocation: swimming. Home: 4001 Pirkey Ln Harrisonburg VA 22801 Office: James Madison Univ Sch Art & Art History MSC 7101 Studio Ctr Rm 212 Harrisonburg VA 22807

BANKS, DONNA JO, food products executive; b. Ft. McClellan, Ala., Sept. 6, 1956; d. Walter Dow and Joanne (Phelps) Cox; m. Bobby Dennis Banks, Dec. 27, 1983; children: Cynthia Marie, Elizabeth Anne, Sarah Diane. BS, U. Tenn., 1979, MS, 1980; PhD, Mich. State U., 1984. Assoc. statistician Kellogg Co., Battle Creek, Mich., 1983-84, mgr. product evaluation and stats., 1984-87, dir. cereal product devel., 1987-91, v.p. rsch. and devel., 1991-97, sr. v.p. rsch. and devel., 1997—99, sr. v.p. global innvoation, 1999—2000, sr. v.p. rsch., quality and tech., 2000—. Bd. mem. Mich. Life Scis. Corridor. Bd. mem. Mich. State U. Found. Named Disting. Alumni, Mich. State U. Coll. Agr. and Natural Resources, 2000; named to Acad. Women Achievers, YWCA N.Y.C., 1998. Mem.: Product Devel. Mgmt. Assn., Am. Assn. Cereal Chemists, Internat. Food Techs., Am. Statis. Assn., Sigma Xi. Democrat. Baptist. Avocations: racquetball, tennis, needlework, sewing. Home: 2027 Birch Bluff Dr Okemos MI 48864-5965 Office: 2 Hamblin Ave E Battle Creek MI 49017-3547

BANKS, MATTIE MARY, nurse; b. Nacogdoches, Tex., July 31, 1940; d. Lorena (Ross) Simpson; children: Dedra Gordon, Tyrus Lindsey. AA, L.A. Southwest Coll., 1981. Nurse attendent L.A. County/U So. Calif. Med. Ctr., 1964—, staff nurse pulmonary svc., 1982-85, staff nurse computerized imaging, 1985-89, staff nurse vascular intervention ste., 1989-97. Mem. Am. Radiology Nurses Assn., NAt. Black Nurse Assn. (v.p. 1997—), L.A. Southwest Coll. Nurse Alumni Assn. (v.p. 1996—), Black Women Network. Democrat. Avocations: playing cards, plays, community activities, football, travel. Home: 609 W 103rd St Los Angeles CA 90044-4539

BANKS, RELA, sculptor; b. Yaroslav, Poland, Oct. 8, 1933; came to U.S., 1947; d. Jacob and Frieda (Weintraub) Heuberg; m. Stanley Frederic Banks, Aug. 9, 1953; children: Andrew Howard, J. Monica, Gary Mitchell. Student, Mus. Modern Art, 1957, Art Students League, N.Y.C. and Woodstock, N.Y., 1958-61, Summit (N.J.) Art Ctr., 1966-75. Chmn. nat. juried exhibit Summit Art Ctr., 1976, mem. adminstrv. com., 1977-79, chmn. standing com. spl. events, trustee; mem. exec. com. Phoenix Gallery, N.Y.C., 1983; chmn. membership com. Stone Sculpture Soc. N.Y., 1980-82. One-woman shows include Robins Art Gallery, South Orange, N.J., 1973, Montclair (N.J.) Coll., 1974, Caldwell (N.J.) Coll., 1974, 83, Summit Art Ctr., 1976, Newark Acad., Livingston, N.J., 1976, Douglas Coll., New Brunswick, N.J., 1978, First Women's Bank, N.Y.C., 1979, Phoenix Gallery, 1979, 81, 83, Morris Mus. Arts and Scis., Morristown, N.J., 1983, Ann Leonard Gallery, Woodstock, 1983, NECCA Mus., Bklyn., Conn., 1985, Schiller-Wapner Galleries, N.Y.C., 1985, 87, Ann Norton Sculpture Galleries, West Palm Beach, Fla., 1987, David Gary Ltd, Millburn, N.J., 1988; exhibited in group shows at Phoenix Gallery, 1979, 83, Morris Mus. Art, 1979, 83, Invitational Woodstock Artists Assn., 1980, 84, Eilaine Benson Gallery, Bridgehampton, N.Y., 1980, Searles Art Ctr., Great Barrington, Mass., 1980, Nabisco Art Gallery, 1981, Summit Art Ctr., 1981, First Womens Bank, 1981, Fairleigh Dickinson U., Madison, N.J., 1983, NYU Grad. Sch. Bus., 1983, AT&T Gallery, Basking Ridge, N.J., 1984, Shering Plough Gallery, N.J., 1984, New Orleans Mus. Art, 1986, Gallery Contemporary Art at U. Colorado Springs, Colo., 1986, Schiller-Wapner Galleries, 1986, Lever House, N.Y.C., 1986, Aldrich Mus. Contemporary Art, Ridgefield, Conn., 1986, Okla. Art Ctr., Oklahoma City, 1987, "After Henry Moore", Emily Lowe Mus., Hofstra U., Hempstead, N.Y., 1988, group exhibition, Poland; represented in permanent collections New Orleans Mus. Art, Everson Mus., Syracuse, N.Y., Morris Mus. Sci. and Art, Okla. Art Ctr., Vassar Coll. Gallery, Poughkeepsie, N.Y., Millburn (N.J.) Pub. Library, Minn. Mus. Art, Mpls., Woodstock Hist. Soc., Fordham U., Lincoln Ctr., N.Y.C., Aldrich Mus. Contemporary Art, Warsaw Mus., Poland, various pvt. and corp. collections. Mem. Woodstock Artists Assn. Office: Rela Banks Studio 272 Yerry Hill Rd Woodstock NY 12498

BANKS, SUSAN REBECCA, music educator; b. Croatan, N.C., Dec. 13, 1957; d. Calvin Barclift and Marjorie Kathleen Banks. Assocs. in Fine Arts, Coll. of the Albemarle, 1978; BS in Music Edn., Atlantic Christian Coll., 1981. Cert. level I, II, III and masters class Orff Shulwerk Approach. Music tchr. JC Sawyer Elem., Elizabeth City, NC, 1981—92, Weeksville Elem., Elizabeth City, 1981—90; pvt. instructor, 1984—92; music tchr. P.W. Moore Elem., Elizabeth City, 1990—92, AB Combs Elem., Raleigh, NC, 1992—2003, River Dell Elem., 2003—. Pianist, organist Zebulon (N.C.) Meth., 1995—2000; music tchr. summer camp Combs Elem., Raleigh, 2001. Named Adult Musician of Yr., Elizabeth City, NC, 1989. Mem.: NEA, N.C. Assn. Edn., Music Educators Nat. Conf., Alpha Delta Kappa (corr. sec., sec., chaplain), Alpha Theta Kappa. Avocations: bicycling, reading. Home: 511 Southwick Ave Clayton NC 27520

BANKS, TYRA, model, actress; b. LA, Dec. 4, 1973; Founder Tyra Banks Scholarship, 1992, T-Zone summer camp for girls, 2000; lectr. at UCLA, Johns Hopkins, Georgetown U., others. Appeared on covers of Elle, Essence, Sports Illustrated, GQ Mag., Cosmopolitan, Shape, Harper's Bazaar, Esquire, Arena, Vogue, Victoria's Secret Catalog (contract with mag.). Featured in comml. for McDonald's, Nike, Pepsi, Nat. Milk Processor Promotion bd. Actor: (films) Higher Learning, 1995, A Woman Like That, 1997, Love Stinks, 1999, Love & Basketball, 2000, Coyote Ugly, 2000, Halloween: Resurrection, 2002, (voice) Eight Crazy Nights, 2002, Larceny, 2004; (TV films) Inferno, 1992, The Apartment Complex, 1999, Life-Size, 2000; (TV series) Fresh Prince of Bel-Air, 1993-94; (guest appearances) (TV series) include New York Undercover, Mad TV, The Oprah Winfrey Show, Just Shoot Me. Creator, writer, prodr., host, judge (TV series) America's Next Top Model, 2003. Achievements include being the first African American Woman on the cover of Sports Illustrated Swimsuit Issue. Office: IMG Models 304 Park Ave S Ph N New York NY 10010-5339

BANKS, VIRGINIA ANNE (GINGER BANKS), association administrator; b. Dallas, Mar. 19, 1949; d. James Houston and Mary Virginia (Bussey) B. B of Journalism, U. Tex., 1971. Traveling cons. Alpha Omicron Pi Fraternity, Indpls., 1971-73, adminstrv. asst. Nashville, 1973-74; pub. info. officer Tex. Dept. of Community Affairs, Austin, 1974-76; asst. dir. of comm. State Bar of Tex., Austin, 1976-78, assoc. editor Tex. Bar Jour., 1977-79, mng. editor Tex. Bar Jour, 1979-91, comm. dir., 1991-99, dir. pub. svcs. divsn., 1992-99, dir. info. tech. divsn., 1999-2000, dir. mem. svcs. divsn., 2000-01; spkr. Campuspeak, Inc., 2003—. Internat. rush chmn. Alpha Omicron Pi, Nashville, 1976-77, internat. v.p. ops., 1977-81, internat. pres., 1981-85, v.p. fund., 1985-90, mem. fraternity devel. com., 1985-89, pres. Pi Kappa Corp., 1991-95, mem. Austin Alumnae chpt., 1973—, alumnae adv. com. network specialist, 1996-98, del. nat. panhellenic Conf., 1987-93, chmn. Perry award com., 1992-98, mem. rituals, traditions and jewelry com., 1998—, chair rituals, traditions and jewelry com., 1998—; com. to devel. relationship statement, Nat. Panhellenic Conf., 1983, del., 1987-93, area advisor coll. Panhellenics com., 1985-88, chmn. liaison com., 1987-88, mem. Project Future collegiate concerns com., 1987-89, field cons. seminar com., 1987, chmn., 1988, resolutions com., 1988, chmn. pub. rels. com., 1991-93, mem. ednl. devel. com., 1991-93. Editor Alpha Omicron Pi Centennial History Book, 1995-97; contbr. articles to mags. Bd. dirs. Lone Star Girl Scout Coun., Austin, 1973-75, Nat. Interfraternity Found., 1986-89, M.L. Roller scholarship com., 1988-89, nominations com., 1988-89; mem. Humane Soc. Austin, 1981—; chmn. mag. adv. com. Ex-Students Assn., U. Tex., Austin, 1989-95; active Tarrytown United Meth. Ch. Recipient presdl. citation State Bar of Tex., 1981, 90, 94, presdl. citation Alpha Omicron Pi, 1988, 97. Mem. Am. Soc. Assn. Execs., Assn. Fraternity Advisors, Internat. Assn. Bus. Communicators, Nat. Assn. Bar Execs. (mem. pub. svcs. activities com. 1995-98, vice-chair pub. svc. activities com. 1996-97, chair pub. svcs. activities com. 1997-98, chair awards com. 1995-96, pub. rels. and comms. sect. 1991—, mem. sect.'s comms. audit com. 1994-95, chair sect.'s comms. audit com. 1995-98, mem. sect.'s coun., 1997-2000, sect.'s program com. 1995-98, co-chair sect.'s program com. 1996-98, sect.'s sec. 1998-2000, chair leadership award com. 2002, recipient, Wally Richter Leadership award, 2001), Women in Comms., PEO Sisterhood (chpt. R recording sec. 2002--), Alpha Omicron Pi (Austin alumnae chpt., Rose award 1991, Adele K. Hinton award 1997). Avocations: gardening, sailing, cooking. Home: 3108 W Terrace Dr Austin TX 78757-4332

BANKSON, MARJORY ZOET, former religious association administrator; m. Peter Bankson. BA in Govt. and Econs., Radcliffe Coll., 1961; M in Am. History, U. Alaska, 1961; postgrad., Va. Episcopal Sem., 1985; LLD, Va. Theol. Sem., 1999. H.S. history and English tchr.; counselor Dartmouth Coll., 1969-70; profl. potter, 1970-80; pres. Faith at Work, Falls Church, Va., 1985-2001. Editor, contbr. Faith@Work mag.; has written for Living Pulpit, Response, The Seminary Journal. Author: Braided Streams: Esther and a Woman's Way of Growing, Seasons of Friendship: Naomi and Ruth as a Pattern, This Is My Body: Creativity, Clay, and Change, The Call of the Soul: Six Stages of Spiritual Development, 1999 (videos) The Potter and Clay, With Tongues of Fire: Five Women from the Book of Acts. Mem. Ch. of the Savior, 1976—, Seekers Ch., Washington, DC, preacher, teacher Sch. Christian Living. Office: 106-B East Broad St Falls Church VA 22046-4501 E-mail: faithatwork@aol.com.

BANNICK, JANICE CAROL, automotive dealerships executive; b. Clinton, Iowa, Oct. 12, 1938; d. Claus John and Irma Jeanne (Switzer) Greve; m. Robert T. Gallagher, May 21, 1958 (div. Apr. 1967); children: Angela Jeanne, Carol Ellen; m. Mearl G. Bannick, June 24, 1967 (dec. Aug. 1991). Student, Old Dominion Coll., Norfolk, Va., 1956-58, U. Wis., Milw., 1980-83, U. Tex., Arlington, 1983-86, Bradley U., 1992-94. Contr. Kimberly Chrysler-Plymouth, Inc., Davenport, Iowa, 1974-79; cons. Davenport and Milw., 1979-80; contr. Stark Oldsmobile, Inc., Menomonee Falls, Wis., 1980-83; bus. mgr., field rep. Motors Holding divsn. Gen. Motors Corp., Detroit, 1986-89; contr., CFO S&K Chevrolet Pontiac and Oldsmobile, Peoria, Ill., 1989-96; automotive cons. Peoria and Springfield, Ill., 1996-97; contr., dealer acctg. Gen. Acceptance Corp., Bloomington, Ind., 1997-98; CFO Anthony Pontiac, Gurnee, Ill., 1998-2000, Lou Bachrodt Automall & Bachrodt Pontiac, Rockford, Ill., 2000-01; team sales rep. Internat. Teamworks Inc., Vacaville, Calif., 2001—; contr. Magourik Chevrolet-Olds, Inc.,

Dodge City, Kans., 2001—02; cons. MSXI, Ford Motor Co. Dealer Devel., Detroit, 2003—. Bd. dirs., treas. St. Marks Luth. Ch., Chillicothe, Ill., 1994-96, Peoria Art Gild, 1995-96. Republican. Avocations: watercolor painting, reading, running, walking, antique refinishing, gourmet cooking, golf. Home: 6318 N Ripley St Davenport IA 52806-2126 E-mail: bannick777@aol.com.

BANNING, DONNA ROSE, retired art educator; b. Belle Fourche, SD, July 2, 1934; d. Anzley Meltiah and Rose Helen (Kapsa) Walker; m. Robert Orval Banning (dec.); children: Bruce, Connie, Bernie, Callie. AA, Fullerton (Calif.) Coll., 1967; BA, Calif. State U., Fullerton, 1969; MA, Calif. State U., Long Beach, 1976. Cert. tchr. Calif., tchr. art K-12 Calif., state adminstr. K-12 Calif. Instr. visual arts El Modena HS, Orange, Calif., 1970—2003; dist. dept. chair fine arts Orange (Calif.) Unified Sch. Dist., 1974—78, 1982—92; crafts instr. Rancho Santiago Coll., Santa Ana, Calif., 1971—75, ceramics instr., 1974—92; visual arts instr. Calif. State U., Long Beach, 1977—78, 2004; ret., 2003. Instr. art edn. Chapman Coll., Orange; cons. Calif. sch. dists., Orange County, 1991—2003; mem. Calif. State Framework and Criteria Com., 1994—2002, Legis. Action Com. Arts Edn., 1991—2002; presenter in field. Contbr. . Named Tchr. of Yr., Calif. Gifted and Talented Assn., 1998, Disneyland Creativity Tchr. of Yr., Disneyland, 1998. Mem.: Orange County Arts Adminstrs. (Secondary Arts Tchr. of Yr. 2002), So. Calif. Ceramic Design Assn., Calif. Art Edn. Assn. (past pres., Tchr. of Yr. 2000), Nat. Art Edn. Assn. (v.p. 2004—, Pacific Region Tchr. of Yr. 2001), Calif. Alliance Arts Edn. Avocations: painting, pottery. Home: 2391 N Waterberry St Orange CA 92865-2851

BANNON, NANCY, performing arts educator; Grad., Juilliard Sch. Cert. yoga tchr. Instr. dance SUNY, Purchase, 2002—; dancer Doug Varone and Dancers, 1993—2000, Tere O'Connor Dance, 2000—02. Instr. dance Rutgers U. Recipient Bessie award, 2002. Office: SUNY Performing Arts Ctr MPO Box 140 Purchase NY 10577

BANSE, AMY L. communications executive, lawyer; married; 4 children. BA, Harvard U., Cambridge, Mass., 1982; JD, Temple U., Phila., 1987. Atty. for acquisitions Comcast, Phila., 1991—97, v.p., head of programming investment dept., 1997—. Office: Comcast 1500 Market St Philadelphia PA 19102

BANSKY-DONOVAN, BONITA A. social worker; b. Johnstown, Pa., Aug. 6, 1960; d. Francis W. and Margaret Bansky; m. J. Kelly Donovan, July 27, 1985; 1 child, Shane Michael. BS, Pa. State U., 1982; MSW, Marywood U., Pa., 1995. LCSW Pa., cert. social worker N.Y.; mediator. Dir. allocations and adminstrn. United Way of Broome County, Binghamton, NY, 1985—92; program coord. Cornell Coop. Ext., Binghamton, NY, 1994—95; clin. social worker Family and Children's Soc., Binghamton, NY, 1995—2002; pvt. practice clin. social worker Vestal, NY, 1998—; asst. dir. Crime Victims Assistance Ctr., Binghamton, NY, 2002—. Field adv. com., cons. assoc. Binghamton (N.Y.) U., 2003—. Bd. mem. Hoyt Found., Binghamton, NY, 2003. Mem.: Am. Counseling Assn., Nat. Assn. Social Workers. Avocations: assemblage artist, making jewelry, reading. Home: 108 Murray St Binghamton NY 13905 E-mail: bonnie.donovan18@verizon.net.

BANTA, VIVIAN L. insurance company executive; b. Lebanon; arrived in US, 1968; m. Robert Field; 1 child, Brandon. B in psychology, U. of Pacific, [illegible] Corp., 1987—97, sr. v.p. global securities svcs., 1991—93, exec. v.p. global securities svcs., 1993—95, exec. v.p. global investor svcs. (Chase Manhattan Corp. merged with Chemical Banking Corp.), 1995—97; sr. v.p., chief adminstrv. officer individual fin. svcs. Prudential Fin., 1998—2000, exec. v.p., CEO US Consumer Group, 2000—02, vice chmn. ins., 2002—. Named one of the 50 Most Powerful Women in Bus., Fortune, 2001, 2002, 2003. Office: Prudential Fin Inc 751 Broad St Newark NJ 07102-3777

BANTEL, LINDA MAE, former museum curator, consultant; b. King City, Calif., May 30, 1943; d. Clifford Burnett and Helen Vernelle (Mallicotte) Bantel; m. David Hollenberg, June 15, 1980; 1 child, Matthew Bantel Hollenberg. MA, NYU, 1973. Rsch. cons. N.Y. Hist. Soc., N.Y.C., 1975—76; guest co-curator Art Mus. of South Tex., Corpus Christi, 1977—79; rsch. assoc. Met. Mus. Art, N.Y.C., 1978—80; curator, dir. Mus. Pa. Acad. Fine Arts, Phila., 1980—95. Co-author (with James Thomas Flexner): The Face of Liberty: Founders of the U.S., 1975; author (with Marcus Burke): Spain and New Spain: Mexican Colonial Arts in Their European Context, 1979; author: The Alice M. Kaplan Collection, 1980, William Rush, American Sculptor, 1982; contbr. American Paintings in the Metropolitan Museum of Art Vol. II: A Catalogue of Works by Artists Born Between 1816-1845, 1985, Raphaelle Peale Still Lifes, 1988, contbr. (with others) Searching Out the Best, 1988, contbr. to Antiques mag., 1989; editor (with Jacolyn A. Mott): American Sculpture in the Museum of American Art of the Pennsylvania Academy of the Fine Arts, 1997. Mem.: Am. Assn. Mus., Coll. Art Assn. Home: 703 W Phil Ellena St Philadelphia PA 19119-3513 E-mail: lindabantel@aol.com.

BANUELOS, BETTY LOU, rehabilitation nurse; b. Vandergrift, Pa., Nov. 28, 1930; d. Archibald and Bella Irene (George) McKinney; m. Raul, Nov. 1, 1986; children: Patrice, Michael. Diploma, U. Pitts., 1951; cert., Loma Linda U., 1960. RN, Calif.; cert. chem. dependency nurse, addictions treatment specialist; ordained to ministry Ch. of God. Cons. occupl. health svc. Bd. Registered Nurses, 1984—. Lectr., cons. in field. Recipient Scholarship U. Pitts. Mem. Dirs. of Nursing, Calif. Assn. Nurses in Substance Abuse. Home and Office: 15 Oak Spring Ln Laguna Hills CA 92656-2980 Office Phone: 949-831-1767. E-mail: BettyB8@hotmail.com.

BAQUERO, LYNDA, newscaster, reporter; b. N.Y.C. BA in Broadcast Journalism, NYU. Various positions WCBS-TV, N.Y.C., 1977—92; reporter, news anchor NY1 News, N.Y.C., 1992—95; gen. assignment reporter WNBC-TV, N.Y.C., 1995—98, co-anchor weekend edits. News-Channel 4 at 6 and 11pm, 1998—2003, co-anchor weekday edits. News-Channel 4 at 6 and 11pm, 2003—. Reporter Centennial Olympic Games, Atlanta, summer 1996, Hurrican Hortense, P.R., Hurricane Georges, P.R., Haiti and Dominican Republic. Recipient Emmy award for religious programming, 1998. Office: WNBC 30 Rockefeller Plz New York NY 10112*

BARAB, PATSY LEE, nutritionist, consultant, realtor; b. Indpls., Sept. 24, 1934; 1 child, Gergory; m. John D. Barab Jr., Apr. 8, 1995. BS, Mich. State U., 1956, MA, 1970. Asst. prof. Med. Coll. Ga., Augusta, 1972-82; nutrition cons., 1982—. Assoc. Meybohm Realty, Inc., Augusta, 1987—. Docent Morris Mus. Art, 1992—; mem.. program com. Gertrude Herbert Art Inst., 1992—94; mem. program com. Imperial Theater, bd. dirs., 2001—03. Mem.: CRS, GRI, Nutritionists in Nursing Edn. (nat. chmn. 1983—84), Nutrition Today Soc. (charter), Soc. Nutrition Edn., Ga. Dietetic Assn., Am. Dietetic Assn., Million Dollar Club (life), Pi Beta Phi (arrowmont chmn. Augusta Alumnae CLub 1992—), Omicron Nu. Home: 3051 Walton Way Augusta GA 30909-3471

BARABASH, CLAIRE, lawyer, special education administrator, psychologist; b. N.Y.C., Oct. 22, 1940; d. Maurice Isaac and Sarah (Libowsky) B. BA, Bklyn. Coll., 1960; MS, CUNY, 1962; PhD, NYU, 1979; JD, Bklyn. Law Sch., 1994. Bar: N.J. 1994, N.Y. 1995, Ala. 2000; Diplomate Am. Coll. Forensic Examiners; lic. psychologist, sch. psychologist; cert. sch. dist. adminstr. Psychology intern Bklyn. Coll. Edn. Clinic, 1962-63; sch. psychologist Yonkers (N.Y.) Bd. Edn., 1963-65, N.Y.C. Bd. Edn., 1965-78, regional coord., 1978-82, dept. asst. supt., 1982-95, asst. supt. for clin. svcs., 1991-92; pvt. practice Margaretville, NY, 1996—; forensic cons., 1999—. Adj. assoc. prof. NYU, 1979-80, L.I. U., Bklyn., 1988-93. Named Outstanding Spl. Educator of Yr. Orthodox Jewish Tchrs., 1990, Brian E. Tomlinson award for disting. contbns. in psychology, 1991. Mem. APA, ABA, N.Y. State Bar Assn., N.Y.C. Assn. Sch. Psychologists (pres. 1979-80), Adminstrv. Women in Edn. (Woman of Yr. 1989, chair mentoring com. 1989-90), Acad. for Pub. Edn. Home: 101 Clark St Brooklyn NY 11201-2746

BARAD, JILL ELIKANN, family products company executive; b. N.Y.C., May 23, 1951; d. Lawrence Stanley and Corinne Elikann; m. Thomas Kenneth Barad, Jan. 28, 1979; children: Alexander David, Justin Harris. BA English and Psychology, Queens Coll., 1973. Asst. prod. mgr. mktg. Coty Cosmetics, N.Y.C., 1976-77, prod. mgr. mktg., 1977; account exec. Wells Rich Greene Advt. Agy., L.A., 1978-79; product mgr. mktg. Mattel Toys, Inc., L.A., 1981-82, dir. mktg., 1982-83, v.p. mktg., 1983-85, sr. v.p. mktg., 1985-86, sr. v.p. product devel., 1986, exec. v.p. product design and devel., exec. v.p. mktg. and worldwide product devel., 1988-89; pres. girls and activity toys div. Mattel Toys, Inc. (name now Mattel, Inc.), L.A., 1989-90; pres. Mattel USA, 1990-92; pres., COO Mattel, Inc., 1992-97, pres., CEO, 1997, chmn., CEO, 1997-2000. Trustee emeritus Queens Coll. Found.; chair exec. adv. bd. Children Affected by AIDS Found.; mem. bd. advisors The For All Kids Found., Inc.; vice chmn., bd. govs. Town Hall of Los Angeles. Exec. bd. Med. Scis. UCLA,

BARADZI, AMELIA, stained glass artist, restorationist; b. Bay Shore, NY, Mar. 26, 1947; d. Stephen A. and Frances (De Palma) B. BA, La. Technol. U., 1970. Cert. K-6 tchr., La. Tchr. St. John's Elem. Sch., Central Islip, N.Y., 1971-72; pres. Stained Glass Creations Ltd., Bay Shore, 1972-91; sec.-treas. Baradzi Glass Inc., Bay Shore, 1991-92; owner, mgr. Amelia Baradzi Studio, Bay Shore, 1993—, L.I. Stained Glass Restoration and Conservation Studio, Bay Shore, 1995—, Stained Glass Restoration Co., Bay Shore, 1998—. Designer, mfr., commissions art glass Poinsettia, 1985-87, Story of Creation, 1987, Peacock, 1989; designer, mfg. leaded glass Edwardian flowercases and sconces, 1994. Mem. Bus. Improvement Dist., Bay Shore, 1994-95. Roman Catholic. Avocations: fishing, gardening, painting, reading. Home: 50 Bay Ave Bay Shore NY 11706-8753 Office: Amelia Baradzi Studio 50 Bay Ave Bay Shore NY 11706-8753

BARAK, EVE IDA, science administrator; d. Henry Barak and Lotte Seligmann; m. Eugene Abraham Davidson, Mar. 18, 1990; m. David Elwood Briles, May 10, 1970 (div. 1982). AB magna cum laude, Brown U., 1965—68; PhD, Rockefeller U., 1968—74. Postdoctoral rschr. Wash. U., St. Louis, Mo., 1974—78; asst. prof. U. of Ala. in Birmingham, Birmingham, Ala., 1979—82; rsch. asst. prof. M.D. Anderson Tumor Inst., U. of Tex., Houston, Tex., 1983—86; sci. adminstr. NSF, Arlington, Va. Adv. editor Internat. Rev. of Cytology (Academic Press), San Diego. Contbr. articles to profl. jours. Mem.: Soc. for Glycobiology, Am. Soc. for Cell Biology. Office: National Science Foundation 4201 Wilson Boulevard Arlington VA 22230 Office Phone: 703-292-7113. E-mail: ebarak@nsf.gov.

BARAN, CHRISTINE, systems analyst; b. Rochester, N.Y., Apr. 21, 1958; d. Wolodymyr and Olha (Zyrak) B. AS, Rochester Inst. Tech., 1978, BS, 1980. Computer programmer Infodata Sys., Rochester, N.Y., 1980-83; sys. analyst Acumenics, Bethesda, Md., 1983-85; staff cons. Martin Marietta, Greenbelt, Md., 1985-88; sys. analyst, computer specialist Smithsonian Inst., Washington, 1988—. Cons. USAID, Washington, 1983-90 Recipient [illegible] Scientific Talent, Eastman Kodak Co., 1975—80. Mem. NAFE, LWV. Republican. Mem. Ukrainian Catholic. Home: 8607 Chase Glen Cir Fairfax Station VA 22039-3308 Office: Smithsonian Instn Comptr Office 955 Lenfant Plz SW Washington DC 20024-2119

BARANAUCKAS, CARLA MAY, journalist; b. Niagara Falls, N.Y., Aug 9, 1955; d. Charles Francis and Molly Ann (Mullen) B. Student, Allegheny Coll., 1973-75; BA cum laude, St. Olaf Coll., Northfield, Minn., 1977; postgrad., U. N.D., 1982-83; Grad. Sch. of Journalism, Columbia U., 1999. News asst. Mpls. Tribune, 1977-78; reporter Pampa (Tex.) News, 1978; reporter, copy editor Texarkana (Tex.) Gazette, 1978-79, Edwardsville (Ill.) Intelligencer, 1979-81; copy editor Grand Forks (N.D.) Herald, 1981-84, St. Louis Post-Dispatch, 1984-88; sports copy editor The N.Y. Times, 1988-92, met. copy editor, 1992-94; nat. copy editor, 1994-95; dep. nat. copy chief, 1995-99. Adj. faculty Columbia U. Grad. Sch. Journalism, 1995—. Vis. editor: The N.Y. Times on the Web, 1999, regional arts editor, 1999—. Participant Coro Found. Women in Leadership, St. Louis, 1987-88, Leadership N.Y., 1997-98; mem. Jr. League of N.Y., 1988—. Recipient English-Speaking Union grant for Internat. Conf. Oxford U., 1993. Mem. NAFE, AAUW, Am. Copy Editors Soc. (treas. 1997—), Nat. Acad. TV Arts and Scis., Nat. Press Club, Internat. Platform Assn., Soc. Profl. Journalists, Assn. for Women in Sports Media (v.p. 1991-92), Investigative Reporters and Editors, Women in Comm., Women in Leadership Alumnae, Coro Alumni, Coro Assocs., English-Speaking Union. Roman Catholic. Home: PO Box 5145 Weehawken NJ 07086-7804 Office: The NY Times 229 W 43rd St New York NY 10036-3959

BARANOVA, ELENA, professional basketball player; b. Russia, Jan. 28, 1972; arrived in U.S., 1997; Ctr., Israel, 1992—94, CKSK, Russia, 1994—97; ctr. Utah Starzz WNBA, 1997—99, ctr. Miami Sol, 1999, ctr. NY Liberty, 2003—. Recipient Gold medal, European Championship, Soviet Nat. Team, 1991, Barcelona Olympics, 1992, Bronze medal, European Championship, 1995. Avocations: shopping, housekeeping, electric piano. Office: Cleveland Rockers Gund Arena 1 Center Ct Cleveland OH 44115-4001

BARANOVICH, DIANA LEA, music educator; b. New Orleans, Nov. 1, 1961; d. Walter Horace and Margaret (Rothman) B.; m. Robert Charles Shoup, June 12, 1982; children: Nadia Lea, Raymond Christopher., Tammy Tran MusB, Loyola U., 1983, MEd, 1986; Dalcroze cert., Carnegie-Mellon U., 1993; postgrad., U. Houston, 1990-93. Cert. tchr. music, dance, drama, English, h.s. counselor, Tex. Tchr. music St. Tammany Schs., Slidell, La., 1983-84, Lynn Oaks Sch., Braithwaite, La., 1984-86; choir dir. Fort Bend Pub. Sch., Houston, 1990-93; tchr., cons. music and dance New Orleans, 1996—. Prof. music edn. Normal U. Beijing, China, 1995-97; cons., trainer tchrs. music and dance Kinderland Learning Ctr., Singapore, 1996—; vol. tchr. dance, movement and Chinese studies Alice Harte Elem. Sch., New Orleans, 1996-99; pvt. tchr. piano and movement, 1996—; tchr. tap dancing and choreography New Orleans Dance Acad., 1997-99; fine arts coord. Malaysian Ministry Edn., Kuala Lumpur, 2002—. Contbr. articles to profl. jours. Sponsor St. Joseph's Indian Sch., Childreach, Food for the Poor. Mem. Music Tchrs. Nat. Assn., Music for People, Dalcroze Soc. Am. (patron). Avocations: theater, ethnic dancing, creative writing, composing children's music, piano. Home: 2531 Binz St Houston TX 77004-7565

BARANSKI, CHRISTINE, actress; b. Buffalo, N.Y., May 2, 1952; d. Lucien and Virginia (Mazerowski) B.; m. Matthew Cowles, Oct. 15, 1983. BA, Juilliard Sch., 1974. Actor: (plays) include 'Tis a Pity She's a Whore, The Real Thing (Antoinette Perry award 1984), Cat on a Hot Tin Roof, She Stoops to Conquer, Angel City, Blithe Spirit, Coming Attractions, The Undefeated Rumba Champ, Otherwise Engaged, A Midsummer Night's Dream (Obie award 1983), Rumors (Antoinette Perry award 1989), Nick and Nora, 1991, Lips Together Teeth Apart, 1992; (films) Soup for One, 1982, Lovesick, 1983, Crackers, 1984, 9 1/2 Weeks, 1986, Legal Eagles, 1986, The Pick-up Artist, 1987, Reversal of Fortune, 1990, The Night We Never Met, 1993, Life with Mikey, 1993, Addams Family Values, 1993, The War, 1994, The Ref, 1994, Getting In, 1994, New Jersey Drive, 1995, Jeffrey, 1995, The Birdcage, 1996, The Odd Couple II, 1998, Bulworth, 1998, Cruel Inventions, 1999, Bowfinger, 1999, How the Grinch Stole Christmas, 2000, The Guru, 2002, Chicago, 2002, Marci X, 2003, Welcome to Mooseport, 2004; (TV series) Another World, 1983, All My Children, 1984, Cybill, 1995-98 (Emmy award for best supporting actress in a comedy series, 1995, Am. Comedy Award for funniest supporting female performer in a TV series, 1996), Happy Family, 2003; (TV films) Playing for Time, 1980, A Midsummer Night's Dream, 1982, Big Shots in America, 1985, The House of Blue Leaves, 1987, To Dance with the White Dog, 1993, Eloise at the Plaza, 2003, Eloise at Christmastime, 2003. Actor, exec. prodr.: (TV series) Welcome to New York, 2000-01.

BARANSKI, JOAN SULLIVAN, publisher; b. Andover, Mass., Apr. 6, 1933; d. Joseph Charles and Ruth G. (McCormack) Sullivan; m. Kenneth E. Baranski, Apr. 20, 1970. BS, U. Mass., Lowell, 1955. Tchr. Andover Public Schs., 1955-61; assoc. editor sci. and reading sch. dept. Holt, Rinehart and Winston, N.Y.C., 1961-65; promotion coord. sch. dept. Harcourt Brace Jovanovich, N.Y.C., 1965-74, mgr. div. verifiability and testing, 1974-75; editor-in-chief Teacher mag., Macmillan Co., Stamford, Conn., 1975-81; editor-in-chief sch. dept. Harper & Row Pubs., N.Y.C., 1981-84; v.p., editor-in-chief Globe Book Co., Simon and Schuster Edn. Group, 1984-88; pub. Joint Coun. Econ. Edn., N.Y.C., 1989-92; pub. Econs. Am., Nat. Coun. on Econ. Edn., N.Y.C., 1992-98; writer, editor, 1999—. Home and Office: 250 E 87th St New York NY 10128-3116 Office Phone: 212-369-6394.

BARAZZONE, ESTHER LYNN, academic administrator, educator; b. Charleston, W.Va., Mar. 7, 1946; d. Vincent and Alma Gladys (Wilson) B.; m. Jay Reise, Aug. 25, 1977 (div. 2004); children: Matthew, Nicholas. BA, New Coll., 1967; MA, Columbia U., 1969, PhD, 1982; cert. bus. adminstrn., U. Pa., 1981; D (hon.), Doshisha Women's Coll., 1999, Seoul Women's U., 2000. Mem. faculty Hamilton and Kirkland Coll., Clinton, NY, 1974-81; assoc. dir. corp. and found. rels. U. Pa., Phila., 1982-83; assoc. provost, dir. corp. and found. rels. Swarthmore (Pa.) Coll., 1983-87; v.p., acad. affairs, dean Phila. Coll. Textiles, 1987-92; pres. Chatham Coll., Pitts., 1992—. Bd. dirs. Dollar Bank. Author: (with others) To Beijing and Beyond, 1998; contbr. author: Succes Stories' Presidential Essays, 2000. Bd. dirs. Benedum Found., 2003, Coun. Internat. Exchange of Scholars, Coun. Presidents, The Carnegie, Pitts., 1993, Hist. Soc. Western Pa., 1993, World Affairs Coun., Pitts., 1994, Allegheny Conf., 1998, Duquesne Club, 2001; mem. adv. bd. Pitts. Symphony Orch., 1993. Grantee Am. Coun. Edn.-Nat. Identification Program Forum, 1992, YWCA, 1996; fellow Columbia U., 1968-72; Fulbright scholar Fulbright Internat. Scholar Exch., 1967-68; named Woman of Yr. Edn., Vectors of Pitts., 1999, Disting. Daughter of Pa., 2001; recipient Susan B. Anthony award, 1999, Pres.' medal Fatima Jinnah Women's U., Pakistan, 2001. Mem. Internat. Women's Forum (founding mem.), Coun. Ind. Colls. (bd. dirs., exec. com.), Duquesne Club, Longue Vue Club, Pitts. Golf Club. Office: Chatham Coll Woodland Rd Pittsburgh PA 15232 E-mail: barazzone@chatham.edu.

BARBA, ROBERTA ASHBURN, retired social worker, writer; b. Morgantown, W.Va., June 23, 1931; d. Robert Russell and Mary Belle (Rogers) Ashburn; m. Harry C. Barba, Jan. 28, 1956 (div. June 1963); 1 child, Gregory Robert; m. Robert Franklin Church, May 10, 1972. BSSW, W.Va. U., 1953; postgrad., U. Conn., Hartford, 1953-54; MSSW, NYU, 1957. Diplomate in Am. Bd. Examiners; lic. N.Y., W.Va. Pvt. practice, W.Va., 1968—; evaluator P.A.C.E., Star City, W.Va., 1973-74; social worker Family Svc. Assn., Morgantown, W.Va., 1974-75, 85-87; human resources asst., social worker Sundale Rest Home, Morgantown, 1977-79; cons., residential svcs. specialist Coordinating Coun. for Ind. Living, Morgan-[illegible] provider W.Va. Dept. Welfare, Human Svcs., Morgantown, 1980-87; social worker maternity svcs. Monongalia County Health Dept., Morgantown, 1985-87; social worker Hospice of Preston County, Kingwood, W.Va., 1988-89; shelter worker, field work instr. Bartlett House W.Va. Sch. Social Work, Morgantown, 1986-90; case mgr. Region VI Area Agy. on Aging, Fairmont, W.Va., 1990-92; case mgr. geriatric program W.Va. U., Morgantown, 1992-95; ret., 1995. Author: (with others) Working with Terminally Ill, 1990, (short fiction) Kids Know, 1992, Walk West on Bleecker Street, 1999; freedom writer Amnesty Internat., 1987—. Grantee George Davis Bivens Found., 1953-54. Mem. NASW (charter mem., cert. diplomate), ACLU, NOW, Acad. Cert. Social Workers, W.Va. Human Resources Assn., Phi Beta Kappa. Avocations: gardening, reading, dogs, cats, travel. Home: 429 Fairmont Rd Morgantown WV 26501-4244

BARBAREE, DOROTHY A. secondary school educator, antique dealer; b. Barnesville, Ga., Aug. 18, 1933; d. James Reginald and Annie Laurie (Butler) Askin; m. James Arthur Barbaree, Aug. 30, 1953 (div. Jan. 1999); children: Anne Shelley Barbaree Taylor, James Arthur., Jr. BS in Edn., U. Ga., 1954. Tchr. Griffin-Spalding County H.S., Griffin, Ga., 1955-57; libr. Regional Libr., Waycross, Ga., 1961; antiques dealer Cellar Door Antiques, Rock Hill, S.C., 1982—. Mem. societal concerns com. United Meth. Ch.; area coord. Equal Rights Coalition, S.C., 1978; mem. Ga. Status of Women Commn., 1969; chmn. March of Dimes, 1965, area coord. State of Ga., 1967; pres. Newcomers club, 1966, Jr. Women's Club, 1966, local chpt. LWV, 1973; with Waycross (Ga.) Svc. League, 1959—. Recipient State of Ga. Good Citizen award Ga. Fedn. Women's Clubs, 1966; named to Outstanding Young Women of Am., 1964, Personalities of the South, 1971. Mem. AAUW (state chair pub. policy 1977, Named Scholarship award 1994), LWV. Avocations: taking college classes, volunteering in congressman's office, tutor ing. Home: 3008 Harlinsdale Dr Rock Hill SC 29732-0214

BARBE, BETTY CATHERINE, marketing professional, retired financial analyst; b. Chgo., Dec. 24, 1930; d. Norbert Lambert and Helen Weishaar; m. Edward William, Aug. 8, 1953; children: Leonard Walter, Roger Andrew. Student, U. Toledo, 1970, 85. Acct. Gorr Printing, Allstate Ins., Muntz TV, Chgo., 1947-53; hostess Welcome Wagon Internat., Maumee, Ohio, 1965-70; v.p. sec., cost acctg. Craftmaster, Toledo, 1970-72; sec., estimator Grinnell Fire Protection, Toledo, 1972-73; exec. sec., payroll Crow, Inc. Aviation, 1973-77; asst. city clk., payroll City of Perrysburg, 1977-83, tax adminstr., 1983-98, ret., 1998; mktg. exec. Melaleuca, Inc. The Wellness Co., 2003—. Sec., vice chair Ohio Women's Policy and Rsch. Commn.; mem. adv. coun. Ohio Bicentennial Commn.; reading coach Evening St. Sch., Park Elem. Sch., Bluffsview Elem. Sch., 2001; active Big Sisters of Toledo, 1979, YWCA; vol. New Albany LPGA Golf Classic, Jamie Farr LPGA Golf Classic, Worthington Rep. Women's Club, 1999, Ptnrs. for Citizenship and Character. Paul Harris fellow Dublin-Worthington Rotary, Rookie Rotarian of Yr., 1999-00; honoree Maumee Valley coun. Girl Scouts U.S., 1990; named Woman of Yr., Bus. and Profl. Women Black Swamp Region II. Mem. Internat. Inst., Nat. Notary Assn., Nat. Fedn. Bds. and Profl. Women, Key to the Sea Bus. and Profl. Womens Orgn. (pres. 1982-84), Maumee Bus. and Profl. Women (pres. 1995-97), Maumee Valley Toastmasters (pres. 1989—, area gov.), Toledo Opera Soc. Assn., Two Toledos (sec., 1st v.p.), Christ Child Soc., Maumee C. of C. (sec.), Samagama Club, Zonta II (treas.), Maumee Valley Historical Soc., Rotary (sec. Dublin-Worthington chpt.). Republican. Roman Catholic. Avocations: football, reading, sewing, crafts, travel. Home: 55 Highland Ter Worthington OH 43085-2627 Office: Melaleuca Inc Wellness Co 3910 So Yellowstone Hwy Idaho Falls ID 83402-6003 E-mail: kellyfoz@aol.com.

BARBEAU, SANDRA ALENE, daycare administrator; b. Belleville, Ill., June 17, 1950; d. Henry Bernard and Lucille Marie Wuebbels; m. Dennis William Barbeau, Dec. 28, 1974; children: Sean Jeffrey, Ryan Eric. BS, U. South Fla., Tampa, 1978. Lic. clin. lab. technologist Fla., 1978; practical nurse, Fla., 1970. LPN St. Elizabeth Hosp., Belleville, Ill., 1972—73; med. lab. technologist Mease Hosp., Dunedin, Fla., 1978—80; early childhood tchr. Light of Christ Early Childhood Ctr., Clearwater, Fla., 1987—94; early childhood ctr. dir. Little Nazareth Early Childhood Ctr., Clearwater, Fla., 1994—. Roman Catholic. Avocations: reading, walking. Office: Little Nazareth Early Childhood Ctr 820 Jasmine Way Clearwater FL 33756

BARBER, BONNIE LEE, psychologist, educator; b. Santa Monica, Calif., June 6, 1962; d. Albert Barber and Mary Lee Sparling; m. David Butler. BA in Psychology, UCLA, 1983; PhD in Psychology, U. Mich., 1990. Asst. prof. Pa. State U., State College, 1990—95; assoc. prof. U. Ariz., Tucson, 1995—2003, prof., 2003—. Grantee, NSF, Spencer Found., William T. Grant Found., 1992—2003. Mem.: APS, APA, NCFR, SRCD, SRA. [illegible] Avocations: scuba diving, travel, photography. Office: Univ Ariz PO Box 210033 Tucson AZ 85721 E-mail: blbarber@ag.arizona.edu.

BARBER, ELAINE T. See FUDA, SIRI NARAYAN K.K.

BARBER, JOAN MARIE, artist; b. Portland, Oreg., Mar. 11, 1941; d. Wesley John and Borghild (Hovde) Wachtman; m. Willson Benn Barber, Dec. 31, 1965; children: Katherine Rose, Olive Mae. Student, Portland Mus. Art Sch., 1959-63. Exhibitions include Hoorn-Ashby Gallery, N.Y.C., Nantucket, Mass., 1996—, Ute Stebich Gallery, Lenox, Mass., 1996—, Erlich Gallery, Marblehead, Mass., 2002, one-woman shows include Hanna Gallery, Stockbridge, Mass., 1993, 1994, 1995, Ute Stebich Gallery, 1997, 1998, 2001, 2003, Deloney-Newkirk Gallery, Santa Fe, N. Mex., 1999, 2000, 2001, exhibited in group shows, Oreg., Calif., Va., Wash. D.C., N.J., Mass., 1964—. Democrat.

BARBER, MARSHA, business company executive; b. Peoria, Ill., Dec. 7, 1946; d. Jack R. and Dorothy M. Hursey; m. Thomas L. Barber, June 15, 1968; 1 child, Brett A. BS, So. Ill. U., Carbondale, 1968; postgrad., So. Ill. U., Edwardsville. Pres. Plus 1 Exec. Suites, Columbus. Instr. elem. edn., Alton, Ill.; regional coun. rep. Ill. Edn. Assn.; mem. So. Ill. U. Edn. Adv. Coun.; mem. Columbus Bd. Realtors; mem. Real Estate Buyers Agt. Coun. Mem. Women's Bus. Bd., Columbus, Ohio. Mem. NEA, Columbus Area C. of C. (small bus. adv. coun., exec. com., chair N.W. Area Bus. Coun.), Sports Car Club Am., Nat. Assn. Realtors, Ohio Assn. Realtors, Nat. Assn. Women Bus. Owners, Nat. Assn. Watch and Clock Collectors, Exec. Suite Assn., Dublin C. of C., So. Ill. U. Alumni Assn.

BARBER-FREEMAN, PAMELA TELIA, mathematician, educator, researcher; d. Lewis Eugene and Lucille Evans Barber; children: Leonardo Eugene Freeman, Lance Esonn Freeman, Lucyll Elizabeth Freeman. PhD, U. of Okla., Norman, 1993. Math tchr. Millwood Pub. Schools, Okla. City, 1972—85; counselor/dir. Rose State Coll., Midwest City, Okla., 1985—88; assoc. prof. Miss. State U., 1993—2000, Prairie View A&M U., Tex., 2000—. Editor: (jour.) Jour. of Rsch. Assn. of Minority Professors; contbr. articles to profl. jours. Del. Dem. Party, Okla., 1985, chairperson precinct 240, precinct chair, 1984—88, chairperson for ho. dist. 101, del. Okla. City, 1985; tchr. and facilitator Brookhollow Bapt. Ch., Houston, 2001—03, disciple Ch. Without Walls, 2001—03. Nominee HL Bd. of Trustees Black History Month Program, Miss. State U., 1996—97; named Oustanding African Am. Faculty, Miss. State U. African Am. Student Body, 1998; named to Order of Endowed Scholars, Miss. State U., 1997; recipient Tchr. Edn. Equity Project Ctr. for Advanced Study in Edn., CUNY - NSF, 1994; fellow Acad. of Excellence, Tex. A&M U., Tex. A&M U. Sys. Regents' Initiative, 2004; grantee Office of Rsch., Miss. State U., 1994, Miss. Insts. of Higher Learning, 1996—99, Miss. State U., 1997, Prairie View A&M BioMedical and Behavorial Scis. Rsch. Program, 2003. Fellow: Tex. A&M U. Sys. Acad. for Educator Devel. (assoc.). Achievements include research in MATH-PLACE resource ctr. funded through Dwight D. Eisenhower grant; tchr. networking, tng. and design (TR3); African Am. parental support (BAIT); multicultural evaluation (MERGES). Avocations: pencil art, piano. Office: Assoc Prof PO Box 4349 Prairie View TX 77446 Personal E-mail: pamela_freeman@pvamu.edu. E-mail: pamela_freeman@pvamu.edu.

BARBERIE, JILLIAN, newscaster, meteorologist; b. Ontario, Can., Sept. 26, 1966; m. Bret Barberie (div.). BA in broadcast journalism, Mohawk Coll. of Applied Arts & Tech. Weathercaster The Weather Network, Canada, 1990—92, WSVN, Miami, 1992—93, KTTV Fox 11 10 O'clock news, Los Angeles, 1993—95; co-anchor, weathercaster Morning News and Good Day LA, KTTV Fox 11, 1995—. Newscaster NFL on Fox, 2000—. Actress : (TV series) V.I.P., 1999—2002; guest apperances Clueless, 1996; Live! with Regis and Kathy Lee, 2000; Fastlane, 2002. Office: KTTV Fox 11 1999 S Bundy Dr Los Angeles CA 90025-5235*

BARBETTA, MARIA ANN, health information management consultant; b. Bristol, Pa., Mar. 20, 1956; d. Eugene and Anna Barbetta. AA, Bucks County C.C., 1976; BS, Coll. Allied Health Professions, Temple U., 1978. Dir. med. records Cumberland Regional Health Plan, Vineland, NJ, 1978; dir. health info. mgmt. St. Mary Hosp., Langhorne, Pa., 1978-2000; dir. staffing solutions Sourcecorp Healthserve, Trevose, Pa., 2000—03, asst. v.p., 2003—. Cons. med. records St. Joseph's Home for Aged, Holland, Pa., 1983-94; spkr., cons. The Longaberger Co., Newark, Ohio. Mem. adv. bd. Bucks County C.C. Bus. Sch., Newtown, Pa.; 1st v.p. Women's Guild St. Mary Med. Ctr., Langhorne, 2002-04. Mem.: Southeastern Pa. Health Info. Mgmt. Assn. (chmn. membership com. 1987—88, membership com. 1988—89, chmn. program and edn. 1989—90, sec. 1992—93, pres.-elect 1996—97, pres. 1997—98), RTAS Med. Record Users Group (co-chair 1993—94, 1994—95), Pa. Health Info. Mgmt. Assn. (edn. com. 1985—87, project mgr. strategic plan 1987—89, sec. 1990—91, edn. com. 1991—92, 1991—92, chairperson credentials com. 1999—2000, program chair 2001—02, chairperson creditials comm. 2001—02, chairperson arrangements com 2003—), Am. Health Info. Mgmt. Assn. (contbg. author jour. 1992, 1993, co-author practice brief 2003), Nat. Med. Records Imaging Users Group (sec. 1992—93, chair 1994—95, past chair 1995—98), Am. Mgmt. Assn. Avocations: reading, travel. Home: 4707 Grandview Ave Bensalem PA 19020-1011 Office: Trevose Corp Ctr 4622 Street Rd Trevose PA 19053 E-mail: mbarbetta@recordex.com.

BARBEY, ADÉLAÏDE, publisher; b. Vallorcine, France, Aug. 21, 1948; 1 child, Alice Gissinger-Barbey. Attachée de direction Inst. Etudes Politiques, Paris, 1971-74; chargée de mission French Ministry Culture, Paris, 1974-79; exec. editor Hatier, Paris, 1979-82; pub. Hachette Littérature Générale, Paris, 1982-95, mng. dir. TF1 Édits., 1996; cons. World Book, NYC, 2002—.

BARBIERI-LIGHTNER, PATRICIA, state representative; b. Kansas City, Mo., Dec. 15, 1957; m. David L. Lightner; 1 child. BA in Personal Adminstrn. and Art History, U. Kans., 1981; JD, Western State U., 1984. Enforcement atty. FAA, 1989—92; mem. Kans. Ho. of Reps., 1999—. Mem.: Kans. City Met. Bar Assn., Wycliff Homes Assn. (sec., treas.). Republican. Roman Catholic. Office: 175-W State Capitol 300 SW 10th Ave Topeka KS 66612

BARBO, DOROTHY MARIE, obstetrician, gynecologist, educator; b. River Falls, Wis., May 28, 1932; d. George William and Marie Lillian (Stelsel) B. BA, Asbury Coll., 1954, DSc (hon.), 1981; MD, U. Wis., 1958. Diplomate Am. Bd. Ob-Gyn. Resident Luth. Hosp. Milw., 1958-62; instr. Sch. Medicine Marquette U., Milw., 1962-66, asst. prof., 1966-67; assoc. prof. Christian Med. Coll. Punjab U., Ludhiana, India, 1968-72; assoc. prof. Med. Coll. Pa., Phila., 1972-87, prof., 1988-91, U. N.Mex., Albuquerque, 1991-99, prof. emerita, 1999—; med. dir. Women's Health Ctr., Albuquerque, 1991-99. Acting dept. chair Christian Med. Coll., Punjab U., 1970; dir. Ctr. for Mature Woman Med. Coll. Pa., 1983-91; examiner Am. Bd. Ob-Gyn, 1984-97; bd. dirs. Ludhiana Christian Med. Coll., N.Y.C., Svc. Master Co. Ltd., Downers Grove, Ill., 1982-91; bd. trustees Asbury Coll., 1996—, vice chair bd. trustees, chair acad. com. Co-author: Care of Post Menopausal Patient, 1985; editor: Medical Clinics of N.A., vol. 71, 1987; assoc. editor, contbg. author: Textbook of Women's Health, 1998; contbr. chpt. to book. Student chpt. sponsor Christian Med. and Dental Soc., Phila., 1973-93, trustee, 1991-95, pres., chair bd. trustees, 1997-99, chair com. for continuing med. and dental edn.; tchr., elder Leverington Presbyn. Ch., Phila., 1988-91; interviewer Readers Digest Internat. fellowships, Brunswick, Ga., 1982—; bd. dirs. Phila. chpt. Am. Cancer Soc., 1980-86, vol., 1984. Named sr. clin. trainee USPHS, HEW, 1963-65, one of Best Woman [illegible] ACOG, Am. Fertility Soc.; mem. Obstet. Soc. Phila. (pres. 1989-90), Phila. Colposcopy Soc. (pres. 1982-84), Philadelphia County Med. Soc. (com. chmn. 1989-90), Alpha Omega Alpha. Avocations: gardening, travel, collecting antiques.

BARBOSA, RHONA, music educator; BEd, U. of Hawaii at Manoa, 1997. Cert. tchr. Hawaii, 2002. Dir. of bands and orch. McKinley H.S., Honolulu, 1997; assoc. music dir. Aiea H.S., Hawaii, 1997—98, Moanalua H.S., Honolulu, 1998—. Com. chairperson Ctrl. Dist. Band Festival, Ctrl. Oahu Dist., 2001—03. Mem.: Oahu Band Dirs. Assn. (com. chairperson 1999—2001), Hawaii Music Educators Assn., Am. Choral Dirs. Assn., Music Educators Nat. Conf., Hawaii State Tchrs. Assn. Office: Moanalua High Sch 2825 Ala Ilima St Honolulu HI 96818

BARBOSA, SHAMEKA BROWN, copywriter; b. Far Rockaway, N.Y., Oct. 4, 1975; d. Jimmy Royce and Willene Brown; m. Michael Barbosa, Nov. 2, 2002. BA, Syracuse U., 1996; MS, Va. Commonwealth U., 1999. Jr. copywriter Newbridge Comm., N.Y.C., 1996—97; v.p./sr. copywriter Foote, Cone & Belding, N.Y.C., 1999—. Recipient Silver EFFIE award, N.Y. Am. Mktg. Assn., 2002, Gold World medal, N.Y. Festivals, 2002; Roaring 20s-Spl. Report, Advt. Age, 2003. Mem.: Adv. Women N.Y., African Ams. in Advt. (bd. dirs., co-chair corp. membership 2002—03), Am. Assn. Advt. Agys. (bd. dirs. Multicultural Advt. Intern Program Alumni Assn. 2002—03), Advt. Club of N.Y., One Line Club. Office: Foote Cone & Belding 100 W 33d St New York NY 10001

BARBOUR, CELIA, editor; With Bride mag., Martha Stewart Living, N.Y.C., assoc. editor, baby/weddings editor; editor Hallmark Mag. Time Inc. Custom Pub., 2003—. Office: 20 W 43d St 25th Fl New York NY 10036-7400

BARBOUR, CHARLENE, management firm executive; b. Smithfield, N.C., Aug. 23, 1949; d. Charles Ray and Charlotte June (Langdon) B.; m. Phil Barbour, Apr. 14, 1968; 1 child, Phillip Shaun. AA in Bus., Hardbarger Jr. Coll., 1968. Adminstrv. asst. N.C. Dept. Human Resources, Raleigh, 1970-80; account exec. Olson Mgmt. Group, Raleigh, 1980-86; pres., CEO Mgmt. Concepts, Inc., Garner, N.C., 1986—. Founder, ptnr. Wall St. Mortgage Corp., 1996. Pres. Garner chpt. ABWA, 2001—02; chmn. adv. bd. North State Bank Garner, 2000—03. Mem. Assn. Execs. N.C. (CEO conf. chmn. 1992-93, program com. 1992-93, trade show com. 1992-93), Garner C. of C. (comm. chmn. 1989, bd. dirs. 1995-98, vice chmn. membership and comm. 1989-92, chair pub. rels. 1996-97, vice chairwoman 1997-98, chairwoman 1998-99), Buena Vista Hospitality Group (coun. advisors 1992), Nat. Assn. of RV Parks and Campgrounds (mem. 2020 vision com. 1999-00, Exec. Dir. of Yr. award 1994), Campground Assn. Mgmt. Profls. (founder), Cardinal Club (founder), Rotary (founding mem. Garner Mid-day club 2000). Democrat. Baptist. Avocations: boating, golf, water activities. Home: 2320 Amelia Rd Clayton NC 27520-8307 Office: Mgmt Concepts Inc 605 Poole Dr Garner NC 27529-2597 Office Phone: 919-971-4626. E-mail: cbarbour@mgmt4u.com.

BARBOUR, CLAUDE MARIE, minister, educator; b. Brussels, Oct. 2, 1935; came to U.S., 1969; Diploma d'État d'Infirmières, École d'Infirmières, Paris, 1956; diploma d'Études Religieuses, Faculté Libre de Théolog, Paris, 1958; MST, N.Y. Theol. Sem., 1970; DST, Garrett Evang. Theol. Sem., 1973. Ordained to ministry Presbyn. Ch., 1974. Youth counselor Young Women's Christian Assn., Geneva, 1959-61, Edinburgh, 1965-67; missionary Paris Evang. Missionary Soc., So. Africa, 1962-64; deaconess Ch. of Scotland, Edinburgh, 1967-69; from asst. to assoc. pastor First United Presbyn. Ch., Gary, Ind., 1974-80; from asst. to assoc. prof. Cath. Theol. Union, Chgo., 1976-86, prof., 1986—, McCormick Theol. Sem., Chgo., 1990-96. Founder, dir. Shalom Ministries and Community, Chgo., 1975—; parish assoc. First Presbyn. Ch., Evanston, Ill., 1983—. World Coun. Chs. scholar, Geneva, 1969, United Presbyn. Ch. Commn. on Ecumenical Mission and Rels., N.Y., 1972; recipient Laskey award United Meth. Ch. Womens Div. the Bd. Global Ministries, N.Y., 1972, Civic award Ind. Women's Coun., 1976, Challenge of Peace award Chgo. Ctr. for Peace Studies, 1991, Martin P. Wolf O.F.M. award Justice, Peace and Integrity of Creation Coun. of the English-Speaking Conf. of the Order of Friars Minor, 1996. Mem. AAUW, Internat. Assn. for Mission Studies, Nat. Assn. Presbyn. Clergywomen, Am. Soc. Missiology, Assn. Prof. Mission, Midwest Fellowship Prof. Mission, Assn. Presbyn. in Cross-Cultural Mission. Home: 1649 E 50th St Apt 21A Chicago IL 60615-6110 Office: Catholic Theological Union 5401 S Cornell Ave Chicago IL 60615-5664 E-mail: barbour@ctu.edu.

BARCA, KATHLEEN, marketing executive; b. Burbank, Calif., July 26, 1946; d. Frank Allan and Blanch Irene (Griffith) Barnes; m. Gerald Albino Barca, Dec. 8, 1967 (dec. May 1993); children: Patrick Gerald, Stacia Kathleen. Student, Pierce Coll., 1964; B in Bus., Hancock Coll., 1984. Teller Security Pacific Bank, Pasadena, Calif., 1968-69, Bank Am., Santa Maria, Calif., 1972-74; operator Gen. Tel. Co., Santa Maria, 1974-83, supr. operator, 1983-84; account exec. Radio Sta. KRQK/KLLB, Lompoc, Calif., 1984-85; owner Advt. Unlimited, Orcutt, Calif., 1986-88; regional mgr. A.L. Williams Mktg. Co., Los Alamos, Calif., 1988-89; supr. Matol Botanical Internat., 1989-91; account exec. Santa Maria Times, 1989-95; owner a-garagesale.com, 2000—03, Network Mgmt., 2003—. Author numerous local TV and radio commercials, print advt. Activist Citizens Against Dumps in Residential Environments, Polit. Action Com., Orcutt and Santa Maria; chmn. Community Action Com., Santa Maria, Workshop EPA, Calif. Div., Dept. Health Svcs. State of Calif.; vice coord. Toughlove, Santa Maria, 1988-89; parent coord., mem. steering com. ASAP and Friends, 1988-89; mem. Sloco Access, 1997-99; mem. Friends San Luis Obispo Bot. Gardens, 1997-99; v.p. Seneca Hosp. Aux., 1998-2000; active Fire Svcs., 1998-2000. Mem. NAFE, Womens Network-Santa Maria, Ctrl. Coast Ad (recipient numerous awards), Santa Maria C. of C. (amb. representing Santa Maria Times 1990-94, asst. chief amb. 1993-94), Chester Piecemakers Quilt Club, Lake Almaner Womens Club. Democrat. Avocations: raising exotic birds, writing childrens books.

BARCLAY, KATHLEEN S. automotive executive; b. Milw. B in Bus., Mich. State U., 1978; MBA, MIT, 1991. With GM, Detroit, 1978—81; retail mgr. Southland Corp., Reno, Chgo.; human resource compensation mgr. Allen-Bradley Co., Milw.; with GM, Warren, Mich., 1985—, dir. compensation, 1992, dir. human resources vehicle sales svc., 1995, gen. dir. human resources mgmt. N.Am. ops., 1996—98, v.p. global human resources, 1998—. Bd. govs. MIT; adv. coun. human resources mgmt. Conf. Bd.; alumni bd. dirs. Mich. State U.; bd. dirs. Mich. Virtual U. Bd., Mich. Merit Award Bd. Sloan fellow, MIT, 1991. Fellow: Nat. Acad. Human Resources (bd. dirs.); mem.: Detroit Women's Econ. Club. Office: GM Corp 300 Renaissance Ctr Detroit MI 48265*

BARCLAY, MARTHA JANE, science educator, research scientist; b. Warren County, Ill., July 5, 1948; d. George Leonard and Edna Virginia Ault; children: Brad children: Austin. BS, U. Ill., 1970; MS, Ind. U., 1972; PhD, U. Tenn., 1979. Registered dietitian. Asst. prof. U. Iowa, Iowa City, 1979—86; prof. Western Ill. U., Macomb, 1986—2004. Rschr. Coun. Food and Agrl. Rsch., Champaign/Urbana, 1997—2003, McDonough County Extension Coun. Treas. McDonough County Teen Ct. Bd., Macomb, 2000—02. Named Hospitality Educator of Yr., Illinois Hotel and Lodging Assn., 2001-2002. Mem.: Ill. Assn. Family and Consumer Scis., Am. Assn. Family and Consumer Scis., Ill. Dietetic Assn., Am. Dietetic Assn., Midwest CHRIE (pres. 1990—91), Internat. CHRIE. Office: Western Ill U 1 University Cir Macomb IL 61455 Business E-Mail: MJ-Barclay@wiu.edu.

BARCUS, MARY EVELYN, primary school educator; b. Peru, Ind., Apr. 3, 1938; d. Arthur Gibson and Mildred (Neher) Shull; m. Robert Gene Barcus, Aug. 9, 1959; children: Jennifer Sue, Debra Lynn. BS, Manchester Coll., 1960; MA, Ball State U., 1964. Kindergarten tchr. Miami Elem. Sch., Wabash, Ind., 1960-64; elem. tchr. Crooked Creek Sch., Indpls., 1964-72; preschool tchr. Second Presbyn. Preschool, Indpls., 1980-85, Speedway Coop., Indpls., 1985-86; tchr. asst. St. Monica Cath. Sch., Indpls., 1990; preschool tchr., fun club tchr. Arthur Jordan YMCA, Indpls.; preschool tchr. Indpls. (Ind.) Children's Mus., 1979—. Docent sch. tours Children's Mus., Indpls., 1987—; interpreter at Indpls. children's mus.; facilitator Systematic Tng. Effective Parenting, Indpls. Writer: (children's songs) Piggback Songs for Infants and Toddlers, 1985, Piggyback Songs in Praise of God, 1986; editor elem. sch. newspaper; producer (with others) weekly show for cable TV. Profl. vol., libr. helper in local sch. systems; office helper North Cen. High Sch.; served on PTOs in various capacities; mem. Crossroads Guild, Parents Day Out of St. Luke's Meth. Ch., past mem. ch. bd., Two's Tchr. Early Childhood Ctr.; Sun. sch./vacation ch. sch. tchr.; bd. dirs. Manchester Coll. Parents Assn. Mem. AAUW (charter, sec.), NEA (life), Ind. Assn. Edn. Young Children (state conf. com.), Pi Lambda Theta. Democrat. Mem. Church of Brethren. Home: 2230 Brewster Rd Indianapolis IN 46260-1521

BARCUS, NANCY B. fine arts educator, writer; b. Cleve., Nov. 9, 1937; d. Paul and Doris (Garvin) Bidwell; m. James E. Barcus, May 28, 1961; children: Heidi Anne, J. Hans, Jeff Thomas. AB, U. Ky., 1961; MA in English Lit., SUNY, Geneseo, 1970; postgrad., Temple U. Cert. tchr., Tex., Ky. Tchr. Suzuki method violin Waco (Tex.) Ind. Sch. Dist., fine arts specialist at magnet sch.; past asst. dir. pub. rels., writer Baylor U., Waco; asst. prof. English and writing Houghton (N.Y.) Coll.; co-dir. Ctrl. Tex. Writing Project. Spkr. at workshops and seminars; script writer for media presentations; mag. editor and writer. Author ten books, including The Family Takes a Child, Central Texas Souvenirs; columnist The Wacoan; also feature articles, poems, brochures, newsletters. Named Outstanding Educator, Danforth Found. Assn. Mem.: Suzuki Assn. Am., Nat. Coun. Tchrs. English, Ctrl. Tex. Watercolor Soc., Nat. Writing Project, Phi Beta Kappa.

BARD, ELLEN MARIE, state legislator, former small business owner, small business owner; b. Mpls., Jan. 11, 1949; d. James Donald and Elaine (Frank) B.; m. Robert George Stiratelli, 1973; 1 child, Allison. BA, Pomona Coll., 1971; MS, Boston U., 1972, MIT, 1980. Rsch. analyst Mass. Parole Bd., Boston, 1972-78; dir. market rsch. Bay Banks, Inc., Boston, 1978-79; rsch. assoc. Internat. Coal Refining Co., 1980-82; owner, founder Techlink Corp., Jenkintown, Pa., 1982—; mem. Pa. Ho. of Reps., Harrisburg, 1994—. Twp. commr., Abington, Pa., 1990-94; bd. dirs. Montgomery County Lands Trust, 1993—; founder, bd. dirs. Earth Right, 1990—; founder Abington Trails Adv. Com., 1995—; mem. coun. of pres.'s assocs. Manor Jr. Coll., 1995—; mem. adv. bd. Abington Coll., Pa. State U., 1998—. Named Legislator of Yr., Pa. Tax Collectors Assn., 1996, Policymaker Yr., Penn Future, 2002, Regulator Yr., Pa. Ortho. Soc., 2002; recipient Cmty. Svc. award Willow Grove C. of C., 1996, Friend of Edn. award Abington Sch. Dist. Republican. Office: 1175 Old York Rd Abington PA 19001-3815 also: PO Box 202020 Harrisburg PA 17120-2020

BARD, MARJORIE, social welfare administrator; b. Balt. d. Harry B. and Eleanore M. Friedgood. BA, UCLA, 1956, MA, 1958, MA, 1982—83, PhD, 1988. Tchr. L.A. Sch. Dist., 1957—60; instr. Coll. Balt. County, 1971—78, UCLA, 1983—84; mgmt. crisis cons. L.A., 1985—; folklorist, oral historian, dir., pres. Women Organized Against Homelessness, 1985—. Workshop leader Gov.'s Conf. on Crime Victims, 1985; domestic violence victim adv., L.A., 1985—95; advisor W. L.A. Vets. Hosp., 1990—95; cons. in field; presenter in field. Author: Shadow Women: Homeless Women's Survival Stories, 1990, Organizational and Community Responses to Domestic Abuse and Homelessness, 1994; contbr. articles to publs., web pages; author: (e-book) Undetectable Homeless Women, 2003. Recipient Giraffe award, The Giraffe Found., 1995, Helping Vets. Step Out of Homelessness award, W. L.A. Vets. Hosp., 1994. Mem.: Authors Guild, Women in Film, Internat. Documentary Assn. Avocations: goldsmithing, sculpting, welding, carousel preservation, beachcombing. E-mail: islandr@goeaston.net.

BARDACH, JOAN LUCILE, clinical psychologist; b. Albany, N.Y., Oct. 3, 1919; d. Monroe Lederer and Lucile May (Lowenberg) B. BA, Cornell U., 1940; AM in Psychology, NYU, 1951; PhD in Clin. Psychology, 1957; cert. in psychoanalysis and psychotherapy, NYU, 1970. Supr. clin. psychologist NYU Rusk Inst. Rehab. Medicine, 1959-61; asst. chief and acting chief psychologist Rusk Inst. Rehab. Medicine, 1962-65, dir. psychol. services, 1965-82; research psychologist, mem. faculty N.Y. Med. Coll., 1961-62, clin. prof. rehab. medicine (psychology), 1976—; supr. postdoctoral program psychoanalysis and psychotherapy NYU, 1978—; pvt. practice clin. psychology and psychoanalysis N.Y.C., 1957—. Non-govtl. orgn. rep. to UN Internat. Ctr. Sociol., Penal and Penitentiary Rsch. and Studies, Messina, Italy, 1985—; prin. investigator NIMH, 1976-81; mem. adv. bd. Coalition Sexuality and Disability, Planned Parenthood, 1983-89; cons. in field. Contbr. articles to profl. jours., chpt. to books. Recipient 3 awards for ednl. film, Choices: In Sexuality With Physical Disability, Internat. Film Festivals, Pioneer award for Sexual Attitude Reassessment Workshops The Coalition on Sexuality and Disability, 1989; NIMH fellow Inst. Sex Rsch., U. Ind., 1976. Fellow Am. Orthopsychiat. Assn.; mem. APA, Am. Congress Rehab. Medicine, Sex Info. and Edn. Council U.S., Nat. Register Health Service Providers in Psychology, Eastern Psychol. Assn., N.Y. State Psychol. Assn. Home and Office: 50 E 10th St New York NY 10003-6223 Office Phone: 212-673-2436.

BARDEEN-HENSCHEL, ANN, anesthesiology educator; b. Milw., Sept. 17, 1921; d. Charles Russell Bardeen and Ruth Hames; widowed; children: Kira, Ingrid, Rhonda (dec.). BS in Med. Sci., U. Wis., 1942, MD, 1945. Diplomate in anesthesiology, London, Am. Bd. Anesthesiologists. Instr. anesthesiology U. Wis. Med. Sch., Madison, 1953-54; instr. anesthesia U. Sask., Saskatoon, Can., 1954-60; from asst. prof. to assoc. prof. Med. Coll. Wis., Milw., 1960-68; assoc. clin. prof. Froedtert Meml. Luth. Hosp., Milw., 1978—98; ret. Chair inst. rsch. com. Med. Coll. Wis., Milw., 1971-78, mem. tranfusion com., 1969—. Fellow Royal Coll. Physicians and Surgeons Can. (cert.), Faculty Anesthesia Royal Coll. Surgery London; mem. AAUW (name grantee), Am. Med. Women's Assn. (Civic Svc. award), Alpha Omega Alpha. Avocations: bird watching, travel.

BARDEN, JANICE KINDLER, personnel company executive; b. Cleve. d. Norman Allen and Bessie G. (Black) Kindler; m. Hal Barden, Nov. 12, 1944 (dec. Jan. 1985) 1 child, Sheryl Andrea Barden Coholan BBA, Miami U., Oxford, Ohio, 1947; M in Indsl. Psychology, Kent State U., 1948. Asst. dir. admissions Fairleigh Dickinson U., Teaneck, N.J., 1950-53; gen. mgr. Pilots Employment Assocs., Teterboro, N.J., 1953-71; founder, chmn. Aviation Pers. Internat., New Orleans, 1971—. Commr. jury U.S. Dist. Ct. (ea. dist.) La., New Orleans, 1965—; lectr. in field. Chmn. History of Aviation Collection U. Tex., Dallas, 1980—; served on Pres. Com. Rehab. Vietnam POW Pilots; mem. FAA's Blue Ribbon Panel. Recipient Disting. Alumnus award Kent State U., 1986, Cuyahoga Falls H.S., 1988, Doswell award Nat. Bus. Aircraft Assn., 1994. Mem. AAUW, Nat. Bus. Aircraft Assn. (chmn. conf. 1975, 85, 87, 90, 94, 2000, 2001, Am. Spirit award 2000), Flight Safety Found. (chmn. corp. seminar), Profl. Aircraft Maint. Assn., Bus. and Profl. Women's Club, Kent State Alumni Assn. (bd. dirs.

1976-82), Women in Aviation, Order of Rainbow (grand coord. 1973-84), Psi Chi. Republican. Episcopalian. Office: Aviation Pers Internat PO Box 6846 New Orleans LA 70174-6846 Office Phone: 504-392-3456. E-mail: jkbarden@apiaviation.com.

BARDIN, MARY BETH, telecommunications company executive; m. Keith Bardin; 3 children. B in Journalism, Ohio U., 1977. Reporter AP; with pub. rels. Fidelity Investments, Dallas; joined GTE, Stamford, Conn., 1988, mgr. customer comms., dir. employee comms., asst. v.p. internal comms., v.p. pub. affairs GTE telephone ops., 1994-97, v.p. pub. affairs nat. ops., 1997, sr. v.p. pub. affairs and comms., 1998—2000; (GTE and Bell Atlantic merged to form Verizon Comm., 2000); exec. v.p. pub affairs and comm. Verizon Comm. Inc., N.Y.C., 2000—. Adv. Bd. Coll. Comm. Ohio U. Office: Verizon Comm Inc 1095 Ave of the Americas New York NY 10036

BARDWICK, JUDITH MARCIA, management consultant; b. N.Y.C., Jan. 16, 1933; d. Abraham and Ethel (Krinsky) Hardis; m. John Bardwick, III, Dec. 18, 1954 (div.); children: Jennifer, Peter, Deborah; m. Allen Armstrong, Feb. 10, 1984. BS, Purdue U., 1954; MS, Cornell U., 1955; PhD, U. Mich., 1964. Lectr. U. Mich., Ann Arbor, 1964-67, asst. prof. psychology, 1967-71, assoc. prof., 1971-75, prof., 1975-83, assoc. dean, 1977-83; clin. prof. psychiatry U. Calif., San Diego, 1984—; pres. In Transition, Inc. (name changed to Judith M. Bardwick, PhD, Inc., 1991), La Jolla, Calif., 1983—. Mem. population rsch. study group NIH, 1971—75. Co-author: (book) Feminine Personality and Conflict, 1970; author: Psychology of Women, 1971, In Transition, 1979, The Plateauing Trap, 1986, Danger in the Comfort Zone, 1991, In Praise of Good Business, 1998, Seeking the Calm in the Storm, 2002; mem. editl. bd. Women's Studies, 1973—, Psychology Women Quar., 1975—; contbr. articles to profl. jours. Mem. social sci. adv. com. Planned Parenthood Am., 1973. Fellow: APA; mem.: Am. Psychosomatic Soc., N.Y. Acad. Scis., Midwest Psychol. Assn., Phi Beta Kappa. Home and Office: 1389 Caminito Halago La Jolla CA 92037-7165 Office Phone: 858-456-1443. E-mail: jmbwick@san.rr.com.

BARDYGUINE, PATRICIA WILDE, ballerina, ballet theatre executive; b. Ottawa, Ont., Can., July 16, 1928; came to U.S., 1943; d. John Herbert and Eileen Lucy (Simpson) White; m. George Bardyguine, Dec. 14, 1953; children: Anya, Youri. Student, Profl. Children's Sch., N.Y.C. Dancer Am. Concert Ballet, N.Y.C., 1943-44, Marquis De Queras Ballet Internat., N.Y.C., 1944-45, Ballet Russe De Monte Carlo, tours nationwide, 1945-49; guest artist Roland Petit Ballet De Paris, 1949; prin. ballerina Met. Ballet, touring throughout Europe, 1950, N.Y.C. Ballet, 1950-65; dir. Harkness House, N.Y.C., 1965-67; ballet mistress Am. Ballet Theater, N.Y.C., 1969-82; ret. artistic dir. Pitts. Ballet Theatre, 1997—, advisor, tchr., 1997—. Dir. Am. Ballet Theater Sch., 1979-82; dance panelist Nat. Endowment for Arts, N.Y. State Coun. for the Arts; judge Lausanne Internat. Competition; guest tchr., coach N.Y.C. Ballet, Joffrey Ballet, Dance Theater of Harlem, The Royal Ballet of Stockholm, Internat. Summer Seminar, Cologne, Germany, Heinz Bosl Found., Munich, St. Moritz, Japan, Australia, Republic of Korea. Soloist six European tours, also tour of Orient; numerous TV appearances; commd. by N.Y. Philharm. to choreograph ballets Festival, 1964, At the Ball, 1965, Viennese Evening, 1966, Petite Suite, 1967. Adminstr. scholar fund Sch. A. Ballet Group; mem. Nat. Bd. Regional Ballet; Fulbright panelist. Recipient YWCA award for Leadership in Arts and Letters, 1990, Cultural award for Extraordinary Contbns. to Cultural Life in Region, Pitts. Ctr. for Arts, 1997, Cultural [illegible] climate of the region Pitts. Ctr. for Arts, 1997; named Pitts. Woman of Yr. in Arts and Music, 1994. Mem. Am. Guild Mus. Artists, AFTRA, Dance/USA (bd. dirs.). Office: Pitts Ballet Theatre 2900 Liberty Ave Pittsburgh PA 15201-1511

BARFIELD, CYNTHIA K. social worker, psychotherapist; d. Carl B. and Colleen B. Anderson; m. Carl M. Barfield. BA in Sociology, Bethany Coll., 1970; MSW, U. Kans., 1981. Lic. clin. specialist. Social worker Social and Rehab. Svc., Olathe and Kansas City, Kans., 1972—83, Completed Adoption Home Studies, Kansas City, 1983—85; psychotherapist Ozanam Residential Treatment Ctr., Kansas City, Mo., 1985—90; day treatment coord. The Children's Pl., Kansas City, Mo., 1990—92; cons. Ozanam Behavior Intervention Support Team, Kansas City, Mo., 1992—98; coord. emotionally disturbed/supr. Lee's Summit (Mo.) R-7 Sch. Dist., 1998—. Cons. clin. supr. Ozanam, Kansas City, Mo., 1998—; pvt. practice psychotherapy, Kansas City. Author: How to Cool It, 1996, What to do When Kids Say No, 1999. Vol. Mo. Repertory Theater, Kansas City, Mo., 2002—; diaconate bd. Prairie Bapt. Ch., Prairie Village, Kans., 2003—. Grantee, Kans. Dept. Social and Rehab. Svcs., 1979—81, Lee's Summit R-7 Schs., 1999. Mem.: ACSW, NASW. Democrat. Avocations: reading, movies, cooking, travel, walking. Office: Lees Summit R-7 Sch Dist 600 Miller St Lees Summit MO 64063

BARFOOT, JOAN, writer; b. Owen Sound, Can., May 17, 1946; BA, U. We. Ont. Reporter Windsor Star, 1967-69; feature and news writer Mirror Publs., Toronto, Can., 1969-73, Toronto Sunday Sun, 1973-75; with London Free Press, 1976-79, 80-94. Can. del. First Internat. Feminist Book Fair and Festival, U.K., 1983; judge Gov.-Gen.'s award for English Lang. Can. Fiction, 1995, Trillium Lit. award, 1996. Author: Abra, 1978, Dancing in the Dark, 1982, Duet for Three, 1985, Family News, 1989, Plain Jane, 1992, Charlotte and Claudia Keeping in Touch, 1994, Some Things About Flying, 1997, Getting Over Edgar, 1999, Critical Injuries, 2001. Recipient First Novel award Books in Can., 1978, Marian Engel award, 1992. Mem. Writer's Union of Can., PEN Can. Address: 286 Cheapside St London ON Canada N6A 2A2

BARGAGLIOTTI, LILLIAN ANTOINETTE, nursing dean; b. Millington, Tenn., Dec. 29, 1949; d. Benard Wood and Georgeanne (Lowe) McIllwain; m. Ronald M. Prentice, Apr. 24, 1970 (div. 1975); m. bill L. Bargagliotti, July 8, 1978; 1 child, William Benard. RN, Tacoma Gen. Hosp., 1971; BSN, U. Tenn., 1976; MS, U. Calif., San Francisco, 1978; D in Nursing Sci., U. Calif., 1984. Staff nurse Tacoma (Wash.) Gen. Hosp., 1971, St. Joseph's Hosp., Tacoma, 1971-75, City of Memphis Hosp., 1975-76; instr. N.W. Miss. Jr. Coll., Senatobia, 1976-78; inservice coord. Eden Hosp., Castro Valley, Calif., 1978-79; instr. Ohlone Coll., Fremont, Calif., 1979-84; assoc. prof. nursing San Francisco State U., 1984-85; assoc. dean, prof. nursing U. San Francisco, 1985-89, interim dean, prof. nursing, 1989-91; assoc. DON Davies Med. Ctr., 1992; dean, prof. nursing Loewenberg Sch. Nursing, U. Memphis, 1992—. Clin. evaluator SUNY Western Performance Assessment Ctr., Long Beach and Palo Alto, Calif., 1982-85; program evaluator Collegiate Commn. for Nursing Edn. Contbr. articles to profl. jours. Capt. USAR, 1976-78. Mem. ANA, Tenn. Nurses Assn., Assn. Oper. Rm. Nurses (mem. jour. editl. bd. 1987-90), Nat. League for Nursing (program evaluator, pres.-elect 2003—), Tenn. Assn. Deans/Dirs. Nursing (pres. 1997-99, 99-2001), Sigma Theta Tau. Republican. Mem. Ch. of Christ. Home: 7423 Wood Rail Cv Memphis TN 38119-9007 Office: U Memphis 102 Newport Hall Memphis TN 38152-3740

BARGEN, NANCY LEE, music educator; b. Superior, Nebr., Feb. 15, 1942; d. Nels and Marie Hansen Sorensen; m. Gary L. Bargen, Aug. 4, 1963; children: Christine, Jed, Kimberly, Michael. BME, U. Nebr., 1963. Cert. Level I Nat. Orff Assn., 1990, Level II Nat. Orff Assn., 1991. Music tchr. k-12 Alvo-Eagle Pub. Sch., Eagle, Nebr., 1963—66; music tchr. k-6 Tri County Schs., Dewitt, Nebr., 1966—67; music tchr. k-4 Buhler Dist. 313, Hutchinson, Kans., 1981—86; music tchr. k-6 Lincoln Pub. Schs., Lincoln, Nebr., 1986—. Mem. state bd. Kans. Am. Orff-Schulwerk Assn., 1983—86. Choir dir. Am. Luth. Ch., Fairbury, Nebr., 1970—78, Emanuel Luth. Ch., Hutchinson, Kans., 1978—86, Christ Luth. Ch., Lincoln, 1987—. Lutheran. Avocations: reading, sports, music, bridge, bible study. Home: 7516 Sherman Lincoln NE 68506

BARGER, CATHY LYNN, music educator; b. Grand Junction, Colo., Dec. 30, 1954; d. Floyd Dee and Lila Fern Broughton; m. Stephen Jerome Barger, June 10, 1988; children: Zachariah Daniel, Aaron Joseph. BS in Elem. Edn., Bob Jones U., 1977, MEd in Music Edn., 1985. Cert. tchr. elem. edn. S.C., 1977, Idaho, 1978, Colo., 1980, tchr. elem. edn., k-12 music Assn. Christian Schs. Internat., 2000, tchr. elem. edn. Colo., 2001, tchr. k-12 music Colo., 2001. Prin., owner Cathy's Music Studio, Grand Junction, 1977—81; tchr. Twin Falls (Idaho) Christian Acad., 1977—81; writer Bob Jones U. Press, Greenville, SC, 1985—86; tchr. Pear Pk. Bapt. Sch., Grand Junction, Colo., 1987—88; prin., owner Cathy's Music Studio, 1987—2000; tchr. music Bookcliff Christian Sch., Grand Junction, 1996—2001, Chatfield Elem. Sch., Grand Junction, 2001—02; tchr. orch. and choir East Mid. Sch., Grand Junction, 2002—03. Bookkeeper Barger Trucking and Excavating, Grand Junction, Colo., 1988—2003, Fruita, Colo., 1988—2003; choral dir. Calvary Bible Ch., Grand Junction, Grand Mesa Bapt. Ch., Grand Junction. Author: Music for Christian Schools, 1987; singer: Western Colo. Chorale, 2003—. Mem.: Music Educators Nat. Conf., Bob Jones U. Alumni Assn. Republican. Avocations: cross stitch, stamping, calligraphy, reading, singing. Home: 1856 L Rd Fruita CO 81521 Office: Mesa County Valley Sch Dist 2115 Grand Ave Grand Junction CO 81501

BARGMANN, CORNELIA I. neuroscientist, science educator; b. Va. B in biochemistry, U. Ga., 1981; PhD, MIT, 1987. Postdoctoral rschr. MIT; named asst. prof. U. Calif., San Francisco, 1991, investigator Howard Hughes Med. Inst., 1995—, prof., 1998—, vice chair dept. anatomy, 1999—. Recipient Lucille P. Markey award, Takasago prize, W. Alden Spencer award, Charles Judson Herrick award, 2000; Searle scholar, 1992. Mem.: NAS, AAAS. Office: UCSF Dept Anatomy 513 Parnassus Ave PO Box 0452 San Francisco CA 94143-0452

BARIL, NANCY ANN, gerontological nurse practitioner, consultant; b. Paterson, N.J., May 10, 1952; d. Kenneth Gerald and Jeanette Elenore (Girodet) Keiser; m. Joel Mark Baril, Apr. 15, 1984; children: Jason Kenneth, Jennifer Jean. AA, Gulf Coast C.C., 1976; BSN, Fla. State U., 1978; MSN, UCLA, 1983. Registered pub. health nurse, Calif.; ANA cert. gerontol. nurse practitioner. Charge nurse, nurse preceptor Cedar Sinai Med. Ctr., L.A., 1979-83; nurse Nursing Svcs. Inc., Sherman Oaks, Calif., 1980-83; nurse practitioner Santa Monica (Calif.) Peer Counseling Ctr., 1983; nurse cons., gerontol. nurse practitioner Summit Health Ltd., Burbank, Calif., 1983-85; nurse cons. Geriatric Assocs., Granada Hills, Calif., 1983-85; nurse cons., gerontol. nurse practitioner ARA Living Ctrs., Glendale, Calif., 1986-87; DON, gerontol. nurse practitioner Astoria Convalescent Hosp. Sign of the Dove, Sylmar, Calif., 1988-91; gerontol. nurse practitioner Balboa Plz. Med. Group, 1991-98, Absolute Health Care, Mission Hills, Calif., 1998-2000, Ctr. Sr. Health, Akron, Ohio, 2000—01, Health Strata, Nashville, 2001—03, Dr. Martin Freimer, East Stroudsburg, Pa., 2003—. Mem. PTA, Granada Hills, 1985. Mem. ANA, Calif. Coalition Nurse Practitioners, Calif. Nursing Assn., Gerontol. Soc., Sigma Theta Tau (rec. sec. 1983-85). Democrat. Episcopalian. Home: 560 Fawn Lake Forest Hawley PA 18428 Office: 35 Stokes Ave East Stroudsburg PA 18301 Office Phone: 570-424-6763. E-mail: nannynp@aol.com.

BARK, MARTHA W. state legislator; BA in Econs., DePauw U. Mayor City of Medford, N.J., 1981-895; mem. N.J. Assembly, 1995-97, N.J. Senate, Dist. 8, Trenton, 1998—, dep. minority leader, 2004—. Mem. econ. growth com. N.J. State Senate, chair agr. and tourism com., cmty. and urban affairs com. Mem. Medford Sch. Bd., 1975-78, mem. Medford Twp. Com., 1980-87; mem. Burlington County Freeholder, 1984—. Republican. Office: NJ State Senate Dist Office 3000 Midlantic Dr Ste 103 Mount Laurel NJ 08054-1513 Address: NJ State Senate PO Box 098 Trenton NJ 08624-0098 E-mail: SenBark@njleg.state.nj.us.

BARKEMEIJER DE WIT, JEANNE SANDRA, graphic artist, illustrator, writer, multimedia consultant; b. Santa Ana, Calif., July 6, 1955; d. Hendrik Pieter and Nelly Maria Barkemeijer de Wit; m. Johnne J. Johnson, Sept. 6, 1996. Student, Am. Coll. Paramed. Arts Scis., Santa Ana, 1977-78, Computer Learning Ctr., Anaheim, Calif., 1985-86, Regional Occupational Program, Buena Park, Calif., 1986, Cen. Counties Regional Occupational Program, Santa Ana, 1986-87, 90-94, Rancho Santiago Coll., 1990-94. Cert. respiratory therapy tech. Freelance artist, writer, photographer, Santa Ana, 1972—; respiratory therapist Good Samaritan Hosp., Anaheim, 1978-79, Tustin (Calif.) Community Hosp., 1979-81, United Western Med. Ctrs., Santa Ana, Anaheim, 1981-86; office mgr., dir. spl. accounts D-Link Systems, Inc., Irvine, Calif., 1986-90; graphic artist, illustrator, contbg. writer West 17th mag., Santa Ana, 1990-94, also editor-in-chief, 1991; art dir. John Henry Found., Garden Grove, Calif., 1996—2000; bookkeeper and office mgr. Progeny Properties, Anaheim, Calif., 2002—. Graphic artist Santa Ana Unified Schs., 1974. Exhibited in group shows including Torrana Art League, 1970-72, Buzza Gibson Gallery, 1970, various galleries in Japan, Amsterdam, and N.Y., 1970, Very Spl. Arts Gallery, 1999-2002; illustrator: Sexual Positions for Chronic Lung and Cardiac Patients, 1984; author, designer numerous storyboard diskettes, 1988—; illustrations exhibited, The Very Special Arts Gallery, 1999-2002; contbg. photographer Smashing Books!, 2000; recs. include (CD's) Fragments, Dance With Me; webmaster for numerous sites. Vol. lab. technician Health Fair Expo 1992; vol. therapist Cancer Assn. Great Am. Smoke-Out, Costa Mesa, 1979-86, Lung Assn. Scamp Camp for Asthmatic Children, Santa Ana, 1986; vol. artist Heart Assn., L.A., 1986; vocalist, guitarist Easter Seal Telethon Orange County, 1978. Recipient Cert. Thanks Heart Assn., 1985, Cert. Appreciation Health Fair Expo Nat. Health Laboratories, 1992, Columbia medalist Front Page Graphics, 1990, Pacemaker award, 1991, 2d Pl. for layout and design, 2nd Pl., 1993, 1st, 2d and 4th pl., 3d Hon. Mention award JACC State Competition for mag. illustration, 1992. Democrat. Avocations: music, volunteering, theater arts. Home: 1551 W Chateau Ave Anaheim CA 92802-1315

BARKER, BARBARA, real estate professional; b. Pulaski, Tenn., July 18, 1938; d. Dan and Anna (Butler) Ingram; m. Emmet Barker, Nov. 25, 1960; children: Melanie, Lynn, Harvey, Dan. BS, U. Tenn., 1960. Home economist Knoxville (Tenn.) Utilities Bd.; tchr. Arlington High Sch., Arlington Heights, Ill.; pres. Barbara Barker and Assocs., Brownsville, Tenn., Deerfield (Ill.) Ptnrs.; also owner, mgr. Re/Max Deerfield, Coldwell Banker, Deerfield, Ill. Exec. bd., treas. Arden Shore Sch.; Wome's Bd. Union League Club. Mem. Nat. Assn. Realtors, Ill. Assn. Realtors, Women's Coun. Realtors (pres. 1993-94, exec. bd., North Shore Mem. of Yr. 1997), North Shore Bd. Realtors, Tenn. Home Econs. Assn. (v.p.). Home: 839 N Dearborn St Apt C Chicago IL 60610-3373

BARKER, BARBARA ANN, ophthalmologist; b. Paterson, N.J., Nov. 10, 1943; d. Earle Louis and Dorothy Louise (Williamson) Barker; m. Joel Ira Papernik, July 28, 1972; children: Deborah Papernik, Ilana Papernik. BA magna cum laude, Conn. Coll., 1965; BS, Yale U., 1967; MA, Rutgers Med. Sch., 1974; MD, Mt. Sinai Sch. Medicine, 1976. Diplomate Am. Bd. Ophthalmology. Intern Beth Israel Med. Ctr., 1977; resident Mt. Sinai Sch. Medicine/Beth Israel Med. Ctr., 1980, fellow in glaucoma, 1980-81, fellow cornea, refractive surgery, 1981-82; pvt. practice medicine specializing in ophthalmology, N.Y.C., 1983—. Rsch. technician The Rockefeller U., N.Y.C., 1965—66; tchr. Riverdale Country Sch., N.Y.C., 1967—68; rsch. asst. Sloan Kettering Inst., N.Y.C., 1969—72; asst. clin. prof. Mt. Sinai Sch. Medicine, N.Y.C., 1982—; mem. staff N.Y. Eye and Ear Hosp., Beth Israel/St. Luke's/Roosevelt Hosp. Recipient Resident Best Paper award, Beth Israel Med. Ctr., 1989, Honor award, Am. Acad. Ophthalmology, 1955; grantee Beth Israel Rsch. grant, 1983, NSF, 1966. Fellow: ACS, N.Y. Acad. Medicine; mem.: AMA, N.Y. County Med. Assn., Women's Med. Soc. NYC, Am. Med. Women's Assn., Phi Beta Kappa. Home and Office: 11 E 86th St New York NY 10028-0501 E-mail: bbarkermd@aol.com.

BARKER, CELESTE ARLETTE, computer scientist; b. Redding, Calif., Apr. 19, 1947; d. Edwin Walter Squires and Rachel (Kinkead) Layton; m. Julius Jeep Chernak, Sept. 13, 1970, (div. 1980); children: Sean Matthew, Bret Allen; m. Jackson Lynn Barker, Oct. 8, 1988. BA in Art, San Francisco State U., 1970; AA in Engring. Tech., Coll. Marin, 1980; MBA in Mgmt., Golden Gate U., 1988. Cert. netware engr. Art tchr. San Rafael (Calif.) Schs., 1971-75; owner, photographer Julius Chernak Photography, Novato, Calif., 1970-76; draftsman Donald Foster Drafting, San Rafael, 1975-76; surveyor Parks Dept. State Calif., Inverness, 1976; electric draftsman Pacific Gas & Electric, San Rafael, 1976-78, electric engring. estimator, 1978-79, mktg. rep. Santa Rosa, 1980-85, valuation analyst San Francisco, 1985-86, budget analyst, 1986-88, budget system project mgr., 1988-89, fin. asset mgr. Vallejo, Calif., 1989-90; ops. mgr. San Francisco Mus. Modern Art, 1990-91; cons. CB Cons., Atlanta, 1991-93; computer local area network mgr. Ga. Inst. Tech., Atlanta, 1993-94; systems integrator Bank South, Atlanta, 1994-95; mgmt. info. sys. mgr. Dinwiddie Constr., San Francisco, 1995-96; process/project mgr. Sybase, Inc., Emeryville, Calif., 1996-98; Wintel delivery mgr. Fair-Isaac Cos., San Rafael, Calif., 1998—2000; dir. support Kabira Techs., San Rafael, Calif., 2000—01; dir. tech. support PC Guardian, San Rafael, Calif., 2002—. Dir. Mariner Green Townhomes Assn., treas. 1987-88. Mem. Sierra Club. Avocations: photography, painting, backpacking. Home: 29 Woodside Way San Rafael CA 94901-1439 Office Phone: 415-259-3165. E-mail: cbarker@pcguardian.com.

BARKER, GLORIA S. government and community affairs professional; b. Greensboro, N.C., Mar. 8, 1938; d. George Frederick and Emma Lenoir (Oliphant) Shaw; m. Rodney Dinsmore Steele, Jr., Dec. 21, 1958 (Nov. 30, 1974); children: Laura Kimberlea Steele Young, Michael Shawn, Karen Elizabeth; m. Jeter Olive Barker, Jr., June 25, 1991. Student, Guilford Coll., 1956-57, N.C. State U., 1984-86. Engring. sec. J.E. Sirrine, Raleigh, N.C., 1975-76; legal sec., paralegal Thorp & Anderson, Raleigh, N.C., 1976-78, Kalyvas & Assocs., Myrtle Beach, S.C., 1978-80; paralegal Golden Corral Corp., Raleigh, S.C., 1981-89, adminstr. labor and employment law, 1989-93, dir. govt. and cmty. affairs, 1994-97, dir. corp. rels., 1997—. Commr. Gov.'s Commn. on Workforce Preparedness, Raleigh, N.C., 1995—; mem. State Govt. Affairs Coun.; mem. Gov.'s Work First Bus. Coun., 1998—. Mem. N.C. Restaurant Assn. (dir. 1994—), Nat. Restaurant Assn. (mem. com. chair 1993—), Assn. Execs. N.C., N.C. Free, Adult Student Orgn. N.C. State U. (pres. 1985-86). Republican. Methodist. Avocations: gardening, painting, sewing, camping. Office: Golden Corral Corp PO Box 29502 5151 Glenwood Ave Raleigh NC 27626

BARKER, HILDA JEAN, retired library director; b. New Hill, N.C., Aug. 12, 1938; d. John Hollie and Vila Belle (Melton) Barker; children: Rheth Alexander Fish, Hollie Ann Fish. BS, East Carolina U., 1960; MS in Edn., N.C. Agrl. and Tech. U., 1979; MLS, U. N.C., Greensboro, 1990. Cert. librarian, N.C. Bus. tchr. Contentnea H.S., Kinston, N.C., 1960-61; math. tchr. Great Bridge (Va.) Jr. H.S., 1961-62; spl. edn. tchr. Craddock Jr. H.S., Portsmouth, Va., 1962-63; sec. Dan River Mills, Danville, Va., 1963-64; bus. tchr. Bartlett Yancey H.S., Yanceyville, N.C., 1964-67, Rockingham C.C., Wentworth, N.C., 1967-72; dir. vols. Annie Penn Meml. Hosp., Reidsville, N.C., 1973-78; librarian Caswell County Schs., Yanceyville, 1978-87; bibliographer Elem. Sch. Libr. Collection, Greensboro, 1987-89; reference librarian Franklin County Libr., Louisburg, N.C., 1991, libr. dir., 1991-2001. Contbr. video revs. to Libr. Jour. Treas. Franklin County Partnership for Children, Louisburg, 1994—2001; vol. program com. Friends of Pittsboro Libr., [illegible] E-mail: hildajeanbarker@aol.com.

BARKER, SARAH EVANS, judge; b. Mishawaka, Ind., June 10, 1943; d. James McCall and Sarah (Yarbrough) Evans; m. Kenneth R. Barker, Nov. 25, 1972; 3 children. BS, Ind. U., 1965, LLD (hon.), 1999; JD, Am. U., 1969; LLD (hon.), U. Indpls., 1984; D in Pub. Svc. (hon.), Butler U., 1987; LLD (hon.), Marian Coll., 1991; LHD, U. Evansville, 1993; LLD (hon.), Wabash Coll., 1999, Hanover Coll., 2001; D of Civil Law (hon.), 2003. Bar: Ind. 1969, U.S. Dist. Ct. (so. dist.) Ind., 1969, U.S. Ct. Appeals (7th cir.) 1973, U.S. Supreme Ct., 1978. Legal asst. to senator U.S. Senate, 1969-71; spl. counsel to minority, govt. ops. com. permanent investigations subcom., 1971-72; dir. rsch. scheduling and advance Senator Percy Re-election Campaign, 1972; asst. U.S. atty. So. Dist. Ind., 1972-76, 1st asst. U.S. atty., 1976-77, U.S. atty., 1981-84; judge U.S. Dist. Ct. (so. dist.) Ind., 1984—, chief judge, 1994—2000. Assoc., then ptnr. Bose, McKinney & Evans, Indpls., 1977-81; mem. long range planning com. Jud. Conf. U.S., 1991-96, exec. com., 1989-91, standing com. fed. rules of practice and procedure, 1987-91, dist. judge rep., 1988-91; mem. jud. coun. 7th cir. Ct. Appeals, 1988-2000, jud. fellows commn. U.S. Supreme Ct., 1993-98; jud. adv. com., sentencing commn., 1995-97, bd. advisors, Ind. U., Purdue U., Indpls., 1989—; mem. pres.'s cabinet Ind. U., 1995—; bd. visitors Ind. U. Sch. of Law, Bloomington, 1984—; bd. dirs. Clarian Health Ptnrs., 1996—, Christian Theol. Sem., 1999-2001; bd. dirs. Einstein Inst. for Sci., Health and the Cts., 2001— Recipient Peck award Wabash Coll., 1989, Touchstone award Girls Club of Greater Indpls., 1989, Leach Centennial 1st Woman award Valparaiso Law Sch., 1993, Most Influential Women award Indpls. Bus. Jour., 1996, Paul Buchanan award of excellence Indpls. Bar Found., 1998, Thomas J. Hennessy award Ind. U., 1995, Disting. Citizen fellow Ind. U., 1999-2001; named Ind. Woman of Yr., Women in Comm., 1986, Ind. Univ. Disting. Alumni, 1996, Disting. Citizen fellow Ind. U., 1999-2001, Singing Hoosiers Disting. Alumni award Ind. U., 2000, Man for All Seasons award St. Thomas More Soc., 2000. Mem. ABA, Ind. Bar Assn., Indpls. Bar Assn. (Antoinette Dakin Leach award 1993), Fed. Judges Assn. (exec. com., bd. dirs. 2001—), Com. on Budget (judicial conf. 2001-), Einstein Inst. Sci., Health and Cts. (bd. dirs. 2001-), U.S. Judicial Conf. (spl. redaction rev. panel 2000-), Christian Theol. Sem. (bd. trustees 1999-), Lawyers Club, Kiwanis. Republican. Methodist. Office: US Dist Ct 210 US Courthouse 46 E Ohio St Indianapolis IN 46204-1903

BARKER, SYLVIA MARGARET, nurse; b. Glens Falls, N.Y., Sept. 11, 1914; d. Victor Howell and Julia Helen (Lansing) B. Student, Green Mountain Coll., 1933; diploma, Mt. Sinai Hosp. Sch. Nursing, 1936; BS, Columbia U., 1947, MA, 1951. RN, N.Y. Staff nurse Mt. Sinai Hosp., N.Y.C., 1936-37, gynecology head nurse, 1937-40, nursing arts asst. instr., 1940-41, nursing of children instr., 1941-45, nursing arts instr.-in-charge, 1945-48; instr. in charge nursing arts Michael Reese Hosp., Chgo., 1948-50; nursing of children supr. Mt. Sinai Hosp., N.Y.C., 1951-66, asst. dir. insvc. edn., 1966-72, assoc. dir. nursing, 1972-77, acting dir. nursing, assoc. dir. nursing, 1972, assoc. dir. nursing affairs, 1977-86, cons. nursing adminstrn., 1986-94. Hon. clin. assoc. faculty CUNY, 1984-87, 89-91; presenter SUNY, Downstate, 1982, N.Y. State Nurses Assn., 1982, Mt. Sinai Hosp., N.Y.C., 1983, 91, 92, United Hosp. Fund and Office of Profl. Discipline, N.Y.C., 1983, Cornell Med. Ctr., 1984, CCNY, 1984-91, Charleston W.Va. Eye, Ear, Nose and Throat Clinic, 1986, Hunter-Bellevue Sch. Nursing, 1987-91. Author: SMB-A Memoir, 2001, SMB-A Memoir Vol. 2 "As I Was Saying", 2003; co-author: The Sinai Nurse; contbr. articles to profl. jours. Bd. dirs. Nurses House, 1991—95, 2001—, sec., 1995—97, pres., 1997—2001. Recipient Alumni Achievement award Nursing Edn. Alumni Assn. Tchrs. Coll., 1994, Leadership in Profl. and Allied Orgns. Achievement award, 1999; writings and papers in Archives of Found. N.Y. State Nurses Assn., 1993; Guggenheim scholar Mt. Sinai Hosp. Sch. Nursing, 1936. Mem.: ANA (Coun. Nursing Adminstrn. Membership award 1998, Disting. Membership award 1998), N.Y. Counties RNs Assn. (bd. dirs. 1983—85, chair bylaws com. dist. 13 1983—91, exec. dir. 1993—94, search com., Recognition 50 Yr. Membership award 1989, Jane Delano Disting. Svc. award 1982), N.Y. State Nurses Assn. (bylaws com. 1982—85, nominating com. 1995, Nursing Svc. Adminstrn. award 1984, Recognition 50 Yr. Membership award 1986, Hon. Recognition award 1992), So. N.Y. League for Nursing, Nat. League for Nursing, Alumni Assn. of Mt. Sinai Hosp. Sch.

Nursing (bd. dirs. 1981—84, pres. 1987—91, treas. 1991—95, sec. 1995—2002, bd. dirs. 2002—), Sigma Theta Tau. Avocations: ballet, philharmonic orchestra, reading, writing, collecting owls. Home and Office: 788 Columbus Ave Apt 6K New York NY 10025-5942

BARKER, VIRGINIA LEE, nursing educator; [illegible] Nursing, 1952, BS, 1955, MS, 1961, EdD, 1969. Dean sch. nursing, prof. Alfred (N.Y.) U., 1969-78; prof., dean nursing U. Louisville, 1978-81; dean Mary Black Sch. Nursing, prof. U. S.C., Spartanburg, 1981-90; dean profl. studies, prof. nursing SUNY, Plattsburg, 1990-98, prof. nursing Plattsburgh, 1990—. Cons. nursing program NY Regents Coll., 1972—91; dir. federally funded telenursing project rural upstate NY, 1993—98; dir. project to develop virtual reality simulations edn. physicians, nurses, allied health pers. SUNY, Plattsburgh, 1995—. Contbr. articles to profl. jours., papers nat. and internat. confs. Mem. ARC. Grantee Disting. Practitioner, N.Y. State Nurses Assn. Mem.: AAUW, ANA, Internat. Coun. of Nurses, S.C. Deans and Dirs. Nursing Fedn. (chair), Am. Assn. Higher Edn., S.C. League Nursing, Nat. League Nurses (com. mem.), N.Y. Nurses Assn. (pres.), Ind. U. Sch. Nursing Alumni Assn. (pres.), Kappa Delta Pi, Phi Kappa Phi, Sigma Theta Tau. E-mail: virginia.barker@plattsburgh.edu.

BARKETT, ROSEMARY, circuit judge; b. Ciudad Victoria, Tamaulipas, Mex., Aug. 29, 1939; arrived in U.S., 1946, naturalized, 1958; BS summa cum laude, Spring Hill Coll., 1967; JD, U. Fla., 1970; LLD (hon.), Stetson U., St. Petersburg, Fla., 1987; LHD (hon.), Fla. Internat. U., Miami, 1987; LLD (hon.), John Marshall Law Sch., Chgo., 1990; LHD (hon.), U. So. Fla., Tampa, 1990; DCL (hon.), Spring Hill Coll., Mobile, Ala., 1990; LLD (hon.), Rollins Coll., Orlando, Fla., 1992, Nova U., Ft. Lauderdale, Fla., 1992. Bar: Fla., U.S. Dist. Ct. (so. dist.) Fla., U.S. Ct. Appeals (5th cir.), U.S. Supreme Ct. Pvt. practice, West Palm Beach, Fla., 1971—79; judge 15th Jud. Cir. Ct., Palm Beach County, Fla., 1979—82, administrative judge civil divsn., 1982—83, chief judge, 1983—84; appellate judge 4th Dist. Ct. Appeal, West Palm Beach, Fla., 1984—85; justice Supreme Ct. Fla., Tallahassee, 1985—92, chief justice, 1992—94; cir. judge U.S. Ct. Appeals (11th cir.), Miami, 1994—. Bd. dirs. Lawyers for Children, U.S. Assn. Constl. Law; faculty U. Nev., Reno, Nat. Jud. Coll., Fla. Jud. Coll., Appellate Judges Seminar, Inst. Jud. Adminstrn., NYU; lectr. in field; vis. com. Miami U. Law Sch.; bd. visitors St. Thomas U. Mem. editl. bd.: The Florida Judges Manual. Named Women of Distinction, Crohn's & Colitis Found., 1997; named to Fla. Women's Hall of Fame, 1986, Miami Centennial Hall of Fame, 1996; recipient Woman of Achievement award, Palm Beach County Commn. on Status of Women, 1985, Hannah G. Solomon award, Nat. Coun. Jewish Women, 1991, Lifetime Achievement award, Latin Bus. Profl. Women, 1992, Breaking the Glass Ceiling award, Fla. Fedn. Bus. Profl. Women's Clubs, Inc., 1993, Disting. Jurist award, Miss. State U., 1995, Margaret Brent Women Lawyers of Achievement award, ABA Commn. Women in Profession, 1996, Harriette Glasner Freedom award, ACLU, 1999. Mem.: ABA (Minority Justice Honoree 1992), Dade Marine Inst., Fed. Judges Assn., Am. Law Inst., Assn. Trial Lawyers Am. (Achievement award 1986), Acad. Fla. Trial Lawyers (Achievement award 1988, Rosemary Barkett award named in her honor 1992), Palm Beach Marine Inst., Nat. Assn. Women Judges (Honoree of Year 1999), Fla. Assn. Women Lawyers (Judge Mattie Belle Davis award 1991, Rosemary Barkett Outstanding Achievement award named in her honor 1999), Am. Acad. Matrimonial Lawyers (award 1984), Palm Beach County Bar Assn., Fla. Bar Assn. Office: US Ct of Appeals (11th cir) Fla 99 NE 4th St Rm 1223 Miami FL 33132-2140

BARKIN, ELAINE RADOFF, composer; b. N.Y.C., Dec. 15, 1932; m. George J. Barkin, Nov. 28, 1957; 3 children. BA in Music, Queens Coll., 1954, MFA in Composition, 1956; PhD in Composition and Theory, Brandeis U., 1971; Cert. in Composition and Piano, Berlin Hochschule Musik, 1957; studied with Karol Rathaus, Irving Fine, Boris Blacher, Arthur Berger. Lectr. in music Queens Coll., 1964-70, Sarah Lawrence, 1969-70; from asst. to assoc. prof. music theory U. Mich., 1970-74; from asst. prof. to prof. composition and theory U. Calif., L.A., 1974-97. Vis. asst. prof. Princeton (N.J.) U., 1974; lectr. in field. Asst. to co-editor: Perspectives of New Music, 1963-85; composer String Quartet, 1969, Sound Play for violin, 1974, String Trio, 1976, Plein Chant, alto flute, 1977, Ebb Tide, 2 vibraphones, 1977, ...the Supple Suitor...for soprano and five players, 1978, (chamber mini opera) De Amore, 1980, Impromptu for violin, cello, piano, 1981, (theatre piece) Media Speak, 1981, At the Piano, piano, 1982, For String Quartet, 1982, Quilt Piece graphic score for 7 instruments, 1984, On The Way To Becoming for 4-track Tape Collage, 1985, Demeter and Persephone for violin, tape, chamber ensemble, dancers, 1986, 3 Rhapsodies, flutes and clarinet, 1986, Encore for Javanese Gamelan Ensemble, 1986, Out of the Air for Basset Horn and Tape, 188, To Whom It May Concern 4 track tape collage, reader and 4 players, 1989, Legong Dreams, oboe, 1990, Gamélange for harp and mixed gamelan band, 1992, Five Tape Collages, Open Space CD #3, 1993, "for my friends' pleasure," soprano and harp, 1994, numerous improvised group and duo sessions on tape; produced cassette and video: New Music in Bali, 1994; "touching all bases" for electronic bass, electronic percussion, and Balinese gamelan, 1996, e: an anthology (music, texts and graphics) 1975-95, "poem" for wind ensemble, 1999, (Chamber Music and Improvisations) Open Space, 2000, CD # 12, Song for Sarah for Violin, 2001, Ballade for Violoncello, 2002, Tambellan, 2004. Recipient Fulbright award, 1957, awards NEA, 1975, 79, awards Rockefeller Found., 1980, Meet the Composer award, 1994. Home: 12533 Killion St Valley Village CA 91607-1533

BARKLEY, BRENNA C. music educator; b. Thousand Oaks, Calif., Oct. 6, 1978; d. Brian Evan and Marilyn Elizabeth Barkley. MusB in Piano Performance, U. Kans., 2001. Pvt. piano tchr., Overland Park, Kans., 1993—; sales rep. Disney Catalogue, Overland Park, 1999; temp. worker Bossler-Hix, Overland Park, 2000; piano instr. Make Music, Lawrence, Kans., 2001, Meyer Music, Overland Park, 2001, tchr., 2001—03. Accompanist U. Kans., Lawrence, 1997—2001, Blue Valley Schs., Overland Park, 2001. Scholar piano scholar, U. Kans., 1997. Mem.: Sigma Alpha Iota (alumnae mem., sgt.-at-arms 1999—2001). Presbyterian. Avocations: singing, flute, skiing, reading. Home: 9814 W 124 Terr Overland Park KS 66213

BARKO, HELEN MARIE, music educator; d. Carl Frank and Helen Basch; m. Paul Andrew Barko, June 28, 1974; children: Emily Helen, Stephanie Margaret, David Paul. BA, Ursuline Coll., 1971; MEd, Bowling Green State U., 1998. Cert. K-12 spl. edn. tchr. Ohio. Vocal/instrumental tchr. Nazareth Acad., Parma Heights, Ohio, 1971—74; vocal music dir. Libertyville (Ill.) HS, 1975—76; music tchr. St. Louise de Marillac HS, Northfield, Ill., 1976—79; music therapy tchr. Lucas County Bd. Mental Retardation and Devel. Disabilities, Toledo, 1980—85; elem. music tchr. St. Richard Sch., Swanton, Ohio, 1989—91; elem. music specialist, student character dir., music dir. Toledo Pub. Schs., 1991—. Mem. Shaker Heights Symphony, Pepper Pike, Ohio, 1969—74, Toledo Symphony Chorale, 1980—91. Den mother Cub Scouts, Swanton, Ohio, 1988—90; asst. troop leader Boy Scouts, Swanton, Ohio, 1990—93; mem. Swanton HS Band Boosters, 1996—; dir. St. Richard Folk Group, Swanton, 1986—99; cantor St. Caspar Ch., Wauseon, Ohio, 1999—2002, dir. choir, 2001—03. Named State Lady of the Yr., KC Ohio State Coun., 2002—03. Mem.: Ohio Music Educators Assn., Music Educators Nat. Conf. Roman Catholic. Avocations: hiking, bicycling, gardening, quilting, embroidery. Home: 2124 County Rd E Swanton OH 43558

BARLIS, BETTYE MONTGOMERY, medical center administrator, elementary school educator; b. Jackson, Miss., Aug. 5, 1940; d. William Franklin and Minnie Love (Greer) Montgomery; m. Jerry Donald Moore, Jan. 29, 1959; children: Jerry Donald Jr., David Montgomery, Elizabeth Ann Singleton; m. Arthur A. Barlis, Sept. 9, 1985. BS, Miss. Coll., 1960. Cert. elem. tchr., Miss. Elem. tchr. Jackson (Miss.) Pub. Schs., 1962-63; adminstr., v.p. Barlis Cataract & Eye Care Ctr., Dunedin, Fla., 1987—. Mem. NAFE, AAUW. Republican. Avocation: tennis. Home: 2080 Muirfield Way Oldsmar FL 34677-1937 Office: Barlis Cataract Eyecare Ctr 601 Main St Dunedin FL 34698-5848

BARLOCK, IDA BELLE, county board of elections clerk; b. Somerton, Ohio, May 26, 1933; d. Herman Ensley and Luella Mae (Albus) Carruthers; m. William O. Elwood, Sr., Jan. 9, 1949; 1 child, William O.; m. James B. Barlock, Sr., Feb. 12, 1966 (dec. May 1997). Grad. h.s., Tuscarawas, Ohio; student cosmetology, Canton, Ohio, 1957; computer student, Kent State U., New Phila., 1992. Owner Beaté A Go Go, 1960-90; clk. Tuscarawas County Bd. Elections, Ohio, 1994—. Color cons. Framisi Color, 1990-93, Ohio Dem. Party. Pres. NOW, Tuscarawas County, Ohio, (dem. activist 25 yrs.), 1980-89; exec. v.p. Tuscarawas County Dems., 1984—; sec., treas. Ohio Fedn. Dem. Women, Columbus, 1990—; county coord. Tuscarawas, Alice Robie Resnick for Ohio Supreme Ct.; vol. for many charities: Cancer, Heart, United Way, March of Dimes, and others. Named Outstanding Woman of Yr. Tuscarawas County Dems., New Phila., 1984, Woman of Yr., Tuscarawas County Young Dems., 1990; recipient spl. achievement award Ohio Federated Democrat Women, Columbus, 1994. Mem. Eagles, Moose. Democrat. Lutheran. Avocations: skiing, flower arranging, crafts, bowling, bridge. Home: 504 Hance Ave NW New Philadelphia OH 44663-1614 Office: Tuscarawas County Bd Elects PO Box 69 New Philadelphia OH 44663-0069

BARLOW, ANNE LOUISE, pediatrician, medical research administrator; b. Skipton-in-Craven, Eng., Jan. 28, 1925; came to U.S., 1951, naturalized, 1954; m. Howard Cadwell, May 19, 1951; children: Barbara Anne, John James Stewart; m. Alastair Ramsay, Dec. 19, 1969. MB BS, London (Royal Free Hosp.) Sch. Medicine for Women, U. London, 1948; diploma in child health, Royal Colls. Eng., 1950; MPH with honors, Yale U., 1952. House physician North Lonsdale Hosp., Barrow-in-Furness, Lancashire, Eng., 1948-49; house surgeon Royal Infirmary (Glasgow), Scotland, 1949; resident to profl. unit of child health Royal Hosp. for Sick Children, Glasgow, 1949-50; jr. hosp. med. officer Knightswood Infectious Diseases Hosp., Glasgow, 1950; Rotary Found. Internat. fellow U. Toronto Med. Sch., Ont., Can., 1950-51; research asst. Yale U. Sch. Pub. Health, New Haven, 1952-53; clinic physician in cancer prevention Arlington, Va., part-time 1953-54; resident, staff physician William H. Maybury Tb Sanatorium, Northville, Mich., 1954-56; research dir. Detroit Feeding Study with the Detroit City Health Dept., 1954-56; research asst., instr. sch. health U. Pitts. Grad. Sch. Pub. Health, 1957-62; pvt. practice medicine specializing in pediatrics Pitts., 1959-62; mem. courtesy staff St. Margaret Hosp., Pitts., 1959-62; research assoc. Tice Lab for Tb research, Cook County Hosp., Chgo., Ill., 1962; med. writer product info. Abbott Labs., North Chicago, Ill., 1963-66, med. specialist antibiotic medicine, 1966-68; mgr. clin. devel. pharm. products div. Abbott Lab., North Chicago, Ill., 1968-71, asst. med. dir., 1971-72, mgr. parenteral nutrition hosp. products div., 1972-73, med. dir., 1973-80, v.p. med. affairs hosp. products div., 1980-84; pres. Albamed, Inc., 1985—; asst. clin. prof. Med.Coll. Pa., 1988. Cons. maternal, child and sch. health, dir. well baby clinic Lake County (Ill.) Health Dept., 1963-76; pres. Tb Sanatorium Bd. Lake County Health Dept., Ill., 1976-79; dir., pres. Lake County Bd. Health, 1979-82; health officer Village of North Barrington, Ill., 1964-67; physician-adviser Head Start Lake County Community Action Project, 1970-84; chmn. profl. adv. com. Lake County Health Dept., 1972-84; preceptor Pediatric Nurse Assoc. Program; chmn. bd. Sutton Place Behavioral Health Inc., 2000—. Contbr. articles on maternal and infant care, pediatrics and nutrition; patentee high calorie solution of low molecular weight glucose polymer mixtures useful for intravenouse adminstrn. Bd. dirs. Heart Assn. of Lake County, 1979-84, chmn. nutrition com. 1980-82, v.p. 1982-83, pres., 1983-84; mem. sch. bd. Grant Twp. Cmty. H.S. (Ill. Dist. 124), 1973-79; sec. to governing bd. Spl. Edn. Dist. of Lake County, 1977-79; assoc. Nat. Coll. Edn., Evanston, Ill., 1976-84; chmn. Am. Women's Hosp. Svc., 1986-95; vol. Guardian ad Litem, 1989—. Recipient Charlotte Danstrom award for excellence Women in Mgmt., 1984, award of merit for outstanding contns. to pub. health Ill. Pub. Health Assn., 1975; recipient award of merit for outstanding community service to Lake County Community Action Project, 1976, award for outstanding and dedicated service as pres Lake County TB Sanatorium Bd., 1979, TWIN award YWCA, 1983. Mem. AAAS, NOW, LWV, AMA (chair sr. physician gov. com. 1996—), Am. Med. Women's Assn. (councilor for orgn. and mgmt. 1977-79, treas. 1980, 1st v.p. 1981, pres. 1983, chair found. 1992-95, Elizabeth Blackwell medal 1992), Fla. Med. Assn. (vice chair Internat. Med. Grad. sect. 1998—), Med. Women's Internat. Assn. (v.p. N. Am. 1993-95), Pan-Am. Med. Women's Alliance (pres. 2000), Nassau County Med. Soc. (pres. 2002-03). Home and Office: 20 S 19th St Fernandina Beach FL 32034-2767 E-mail: czardaska@aol.com.

BARLOW, BARBARA ANN, surgeon; b. Lancaster, Pa., June 20, 1938; d. William Barlow and Esther Stoll Barlow Lowry; m. Andre Zmurek. BA in psychology, Vassar Coll.; MA in psychology, Columbia U.; MD, Albert Einstein Coll. Medicine, 1967. Diplomte Am. Bd. Surgery. Intern Bronx (N.Y.) Mcpl. Hosp., 1967-68, resident in surgery, 1968-73; resident in pediatric surgery Columbia-Presbyn. Med.-Babies Hosp., N.Y.C., 1973-75; chief pediatric surgery Harlem Hosp., N.Y.C., 1975—2000, chief of surgery, 2000—; prof. surgery and epidemiology Columbia U. and Mailman Sch. Pub. Health, N.Y.C.; founder, exec. dir. Injury Free Coalition for Kids, 1988—. Recipient Safe Cmty. Award, US Dept. Transp., 1996, David E. Rogers award, Assn. Am. Med. Colleges, 2001, Disting. Career Award, Injury Ctrl. and Health Svcs. Sect., APHA, 2001, Pub. Svc. Award, Alfred P. Sloan Found., 2003. Mem. ACS, Am. Acad. Pediatrics (Injury and Poison Prevention Fellow Achievement Award, 1997), Am. Assn. for Surgery of Trauma, Am. Pediatric Surg. Assn., N.Y. Surgery Soc. Achievements include Featured in the Nat. Libr. Medicine exhibit "Changing the Face of Medicine" honoring women physicians, 2003. Office: Columbia U Mailman Sch Pub Health 722 W 168th St Rm 1709 New York NY 10032

BARLOW, CARROLEE, physician, scientist, educator; b. Page, Ariz., Sept. 24, 1963; d. Eslie and Carrol (Burham) B.; m. Kleanthis Gabriel Xanthopoulos, June 10, 1989. BA, U. Utah, 1985, MD, 1989; PhD, The Karolinska Inst., Stockholm, 1995. Diplomate Am. Bd. Endocrinology, Am. Bd. Internal Medicine. Study rsch. fellow Sch. Medicine U. Utah, Salt Lake City, 1986-89, The Rockefeller U., N.Y.C., 1988; resident N.Y. Hosp.-Cornell Med. Ctr.-U. Utah Med. Ctr., N.Y.C. and Salt Lake City, 1989-91; clin. assoc. NIH, Bethesda, Md., 1995-98; asst. prof. The Salk Inst., San Diego, 1998—. Presenter in field. Contbr. numerous articles to profl. jours. Recipient Caine scholarship U. Utah, 1988-89, Olga A. Logan scholarship, 1986-89, scholarship Nat. Panhellenic Assn., 1984-85, U. Utah Women's Club, 1982-83. Mem. Am. Women's Med. Assn. (Outstanding Women in Medicine award 1989), Alpha Omega Alpha, Phi Beta Kappa. Avocations: skiing, rollerblading, gardening. Office: The Salk Inst Genetics Lab 10010 N Torrey Pines Rd La Jolla CA 92037-1099

BARLOW, JEAN, art educator, painter; b. L.A., Dec. 13, 1940; d. Sydney R. and Rose (Ballen) Barlow; m. Gordon M. Nunes, Sept. 21, 1973 (dec. Dec. 1991). BA cum laude, UCLA, 1963, MA, 1965, MFA, 1968. Tchg. assoc. UCLA, 1964-68; instr. Univ. Adult Sch., L.A., 1966-70; lectr. Calif. State U., Long beach, 1967-69; instr. Beverly Hills (Calif.) Adult Edn., 1969, East L.A. Jr. Coll., 1969-70; lectr. UCLA, 1986, instr. ext. divsn., 1969-96; instr. Santa Monica (Calif.) City Coll., 1969—. Mentor program mem. Santa Monica City Coll., 1989-90; pvt. art tchr., L.A., 1970-96; cons. in field. One woman shows include Jenet Gallery, L.A., 1965, Santa Monica City Coll., 1974; new works on view at home, invitation only, 2001—03; exhibited in group shows at So. Calif., 1965, Orlando Gallery, L.A., 1967, 68, Santa Monica City Coll., 1974, 78, 80, 87, 88, 91, 94, 95, Living Room Gallery, 1997, Bergemot Station T2, 1999, Brentwood Park Group Art Exhibit; invitational pastel drawing Scripps Coll., So. Calif., 1965. Avocations: drawing and painting, photography, home landscape and decoration, creative cooking, writing.

BARLOW, LINDA, social services administrator, trainer; b. Jamaica, N.Y. d. Philip and Shirley (Simon) Kass; m. Steven Barlow, Aug. 20, 1972; children: Andrew, Gregory, Russell. BA, U. Bridgeport, 1969; MA, Boston U., 1970; profl. diploma, Fordham U., 1974. Cert. rehab. counselor. Counselor Manpower Devel. Tng. Program, Williamsburg, N.Y., 1970-75; vocat. rehab. counselor Elmhurst (N.Y.) Hosp., 1975-77; asst. dir. career planning & placement Stevens Inst. Tech., Hoboken, N.J., 1977-78; divsn. dir. EAC, Inc., Hempstead, N.Y., 1978—; cons., trainer NDRI, N.Y.C., 1983-94. Adv. mem. Hofstra U. Rehab. Counseling Program, NYU Rehab. Counseling Program; cons., trainer Nat. Assn. on Drug Abuse Problems; social worker saturday program Stoplift, 1996—. Author: (tng. manuals) Vocational Rehab in the Treatment Setting, 1990, Vocational Testing, 1990; contbr. articles to profl. jours. Vol. Queens Spl. Olympics, Make-A-Wish Found.; mem. Utopia Estate Civic Assn. Mem. Assn. Vocat. Rehab. Advocacy for Substance Abuse (Svc. award), Mental Health Assn., L.I. Coalition Full Employment. Office: 50 Clinton St Hempstead NY 11550-4281

BARLOW, NADINE GAIL, planetary geoscientist; b. La Jolla, Calif., Nov. 9, 1958; d. Nathan Dale and Marcella Isabel (Menken) B. BS, U. Ariz., 1980, PhD, 1987. Instr., planetarium lectr. Palomar Coll., San Marcos, Calif., 1982; grad. rsch. asst. U. Ariz., Tucson, 1982-87; postdoctoral fellow Lunar and Planetary Inst., Houston, 1987-89; NRC assoc. NASA/Johnson Space Ctr., Houston, 1989-91, vis. scientist, 1991-92, support scientist exploration programs office, 1992; vis. scientist Lunar and Planetary Inst., Houston, 1992-95; assoc. prof. U. Houston, Clear Lake, 1991-95; pres. Minerva Rsch. Enterprises, 1995-99; asst. prof. astronomy, dir. Robinson Obs. U. Ctrl. Fla., Orlando, 1996—2002; asst. prof. dept. physics and astronomy No. Ariz. U., Flagstaff, 2002—. Co-dir. intern program Lunar and Planetary Inst., 1988-89. Editor (slide set) A Guide to Martian Impact Craters, 1988; assoc. editor Encyclopedia of Earth Sciences, 1996; contbr. articles to profl. jours. Named among Outstanding Women and Ethnic Minorities Engaged in Sci. and Engring., Lawrence Livermore Nat. Lab., 1991, Alumna of Yr., Palomar Coll., 2003. Mem. AAUW (pres. Clear Lake chpt. 1991-93, program v.p. 1993-95, v.p. interbr. coun. 1990-91, chmn. Tex. task force on women and girls in sci. and math. 1991-92, dir. state pub. policy 1991-94, Tex. Woman of Yr. 1992, mem. pub. policy com. 1994-95, chmn. steering com. Tex. edln. equity 1994-95), Am. Astron. Soc. (pres. officer divsn. planetary scis. 1993-99, status of women in astronomy com. 1987-90, 1995-98, exec. com. divsn. for planetary scis. 1999-02), Meteoritical Soc., Am. Geophys. Union, Geol. Soc. Am. (planetary geology divsn. nominating com. 1996-97). Achievements include research and compilation of primary data source on 42,283 impact craters on Mars; identification of possible source craters for Martian meteorites. Office: No Arizona Univ Dept Physics and Astronomy NAU Box 6010 Flagstaff AZ 86011-6010

BARMORE, HEATHER A, music educator, vocalist; b. Plainview, NY, May 12, 1978; d. Bruce W and Sharon J Barmore. MusB, Ithaca Coll., 1996—2000; MA in Music Edn., Eastman Sch. Music, U. Rochester, 2004. Cert. Teacher NY State Edn. Dept., 2000. Instrumental music tchr. Greece Ctrl. Schools, Rochester, NY, 2002—, Hilton Ctrl. Schools, Hilton, NY, 2000—02. Vocalist Nik Entertainment Co., Rochester, NY, 2000—; substitute choir dir. First Congl. United Ch. of Christ, Fairport, NY, 2001—; pvt. music instr., Rochester, NY, 2000—; ind. cons. Partylite Gifts, Inc., 2004—. Ch. mem. and chancel choir mem. First Congl. United Ch. of Christ, Fairport, NY, 1992—. Wegmans Scholarship, Wegmans Food Markets, Rochester, NY, 1996—2000, 2000—03. Mem.: Internat. Double Reed Soc., Music Educators Nat. Conf. R-Consevative. United Ch. Of Christ.

BARNAO, LAURA, management assistant; b. Bklyn., Nov. 11, 1970; d. Frank Anthony and Mary Ann Barnao. B in Music Edn., B n Music, Stetson U., 1993; MusM, New Eng. Conservatory Music, 1995. Sr. asst. Goldman Sachs & Co., N.Y.C., 1997—. Singer: (Operas) Ctrl. City (Colo.) Opera, 1997, Dicapo Opera Theatre, 1998—2000. Mem. youth adv. bd. St. James Ch., N.Y.C., 2000—02; Stephen min. Stephen Ministry, N.Y.C., 2001—. Mem.: Hellgate Roadrunners Club, Omicron Delta Kappa, Phi Beta Kappa, Sigma Alpha Iota. Episcopalian. Avocations: running, reading, hiking, cooking, crafts. Office: Goldman Sachs & Co 85 Broad St New York NY 10004

BARNARD, CYNTHIA MARIE, art educator, artist; b. Torrance, Calif., Apr. 13, 1947; d. George Steve and Helen Joan Vico; m. John William Barnard, July 13, 1975; children: Nicolas, Sasha. BFA, U. So. Calif., 1969; MFA, Calif. State U., 1977. Cert. tchr. Prin., owner The Paper Moon, Hermosa Beach, Calif., 1977—83; realtor Redondo Beach, Calif., 1980—; gen. contractor Barnard and Barnard Constrn., Hermosa Beach, 1983—; tchr. Torrance (Calif.) Unified Sch. Dist., 1970—79. Adv. yearbook North HS, Torrance, 1991—, chmn. Dept. Visual and Performing Arts, 1997—; bd. dir. Sandpipers Philanthropic Orgn., Hermosa Beach. Grantee Pegasus grant, Exxon Mobil, 1999—2001, Claymation grant, Torrance (Calif.) Edn. Found., 2000, Edison (Calif.) Claymation/Animation grant, 2000. Fellow: Torrance (Calif.) Tchr. Assn., Calif. Tchrs. Assn. Eastern Orthodox. Avocations: ceramics, glass fusion, white-water rafting, camping, travel. Home: PO Box 505 Hermosa Beach CA 90254 Office: North High School 3620 W 182nd St Torrance CA 90504

BARNARD, JANET KINZY, music educator, elementary school educator; d. Robert Fredrick and Betty Spurrier Kinzy; m. James Curtis Barnard, Dec. 28, 1977; children: Julie Christina, Jamie Suzanne. MusB, Ea. N.Mex U., 1976, MEd, 1982. Registered music therapist Nat. Assn. of Music Therapy, 1977, lic. music tchr. N.Mex, 1980. Kindergarten tchr., band dir. St. Francis Cath. Sch., Gallup, N.Mex., 1979—80; music tchr. Lincoln-Jackson Elem. Sch., Clovis, N.Mex., 1980—81, James Bickley Elem. Sch., Clovis, 1981—2001; music tchr., curriculum integration specialist Lincoln-Jackson Arts Acad., Clovis, 2001—. Mentor Clovis (N.Mex.0 Mcpl. Schs., 2000—; clinician Hobbs (N.Mex.) Pub. Schools, 1998, Lovington (N.Mex.) Pub. Schs., 1998; tchr. music edn. Ea. N.Mex. U., Portales, N.Mex., 1999—; clinician IRA Conf., 2001. Dir.: (children's opera) Dragontale, 2003, (composer, choreographer) (children's musical) Musicians of the Sun, 2002; musician: Dulce Trio. Mem. Cmty. Band, Clovis, N.Mex., 1980—99; munchkin music tchr. Clovis (N.Mex.) C.C., 1999—2001. Named Tchr. Yr., Walmart, 2001. Mem.: Tex. Music Educators Assn., Am. Orff-Schulwerk Assn., N.Mex Music Educators Nat. Conf. (v.p. of gen. music 1993—95, facilitator and clinician 1999—, John Batcheller award for Excellence in Tchg. Elem. Music 1991), Philanthropic and Ednl. Orgn. Avocations: sewing, swimming, gardening, travel. Office: Lincoln-Jackson Arts Academy 206 Alphon Clovis NM 88101 Personal E-mail: all4js@plateautel.net. E-mail: jbarnard@clovis-schools.org.

BARNARD, KATHRYN ELAINE, nursing educator, researcher; b. Omaha, Apr. 16, 1938; d. Paul and Elsa Elizabeth (Anderson) B. BS in Nursing, U. Nebr., Omaha, 1960; MS in Nursing, Boston U., 1962; PhD, U. Wash., Seattle, 1972; DSc (hon.), U. Nebr., 1990. Acting instr. U. Nebr., Omaha, 1960-61, U. Wash., Seattle, 1963-65, asst. prof., 1965-69, prof. nursing, 1972—, assoc. dean, 1987-92, founding dir. Ctr. on Infant Mental Health and Devel., 2001—, Charles and Gerda Spence Endowed Prof. in Nursing, 2002—. Bd. dirs. Nat. Ctr. for Clin. Infant Programs, Washington, 1980- Chmn. rsch. com. Bur. of Community Health Svcs., MCH, 1987-89. Recipient Lucille Petry award Nat. League for Nursing, 1968, Martha Mae Eliot award Am. Assn. Pub. Health, 1983, Professorship award U. Wash., 1985 Fellow Am. Acad. Nursing (bd. dirs. 1980-82); mem. Inst. Medicine (Gustav O. Leinhard Award, 2002); mem. Am. Nurses Assn. (chmn. com.

1980-82, Jessie Scott award 1982, Nurse of Yr. award 1984), Soc. Research in Child Devel. (bd. dirs. 1981-87), Sigma Theta Tau (founders award in research 1987, Episteme Award, 2003). Democrat. Presbyterian. Home: 11508 Durland Ave NE Seattle WA 98125-5904 Office: University of Washington Family & Child Nursing Box 357920 Seattle WA 98195-7920

BARNARD, LINDA S. marriage and family therapist; b. Marion, Ind., Oct. 11, 1949; d. William Hershal Barnard Jr. and Maxine Barnard. BS, Huntington Coll., 1973; MA, Ball State U., 1977; PhD, So. Ill. U., 1979. Cert. marriage and family therapist Calif., expert traumatic stress Am. Acad. Traumatic Stress Bd. Asst. prof. U. So. Maine, Garkam, Maine, 1979—81; pvt. practice Barnard & Assocs., Sacramento, 1981—. Bd. dirs. Vols. Action Assistance, Sacramento; mem. trainer & steering com. Crisis Intervention Response Network, Sacramento. With U.S. Army, 1974—77. Mem.: Intevention Soc. Traumatic Stress Studies, Anxiety Disorders Assn. Am., Am. Assn. Experts in Traumatic Stress, Am. Assn. Marriage & Family Therapists. Avocations: woodworking, music, camping, golf, reading. Office: Barnard & Assocs 418 Alhambra Blvd Sacramento CA 95816 E-mail: lsbtraumadoc@compuserve.com.

BARNARD, PATRICIA A. human resources specialist; b. Dayton, Ohio, Mar. 24, 1949; BS in Sci., Elem. Edn. and English, U. Dayton, 1971; MS in Human Resources Adminstrn. and Orgnl. Effectiveness, Ctrl. Mich. U., 1996. With audit dept. Fla. Power and Light, Miami, Fla., 1972; fin. analyst, pers. adminstrn., asst. to CEO Mead Corp., Dayton, 1972—82, and 401(k) ops., 1982—85, mgr. coll. recruiting and rels., exempt ops. supr., retirement plans and 401(k), 1985—87; dir. compensation, benefits, staffing and EEO Zellerbach, Dayton, 1987—94; dir. spl. projects Georgia-Pacific Corp., Atlanta, 1994, dir. human resources, comm. papers, 1994—95, group dir. human resources, paper, 1995—97, group dir. human resources, paper and chemicals, 1997—98, v.p. compensation and benefits, 1998—99, sr. v.p. human resources, 1999—2001, exec. v.p. human resources, 2001—. Mem., mentor Ga. 100; mem. HR Leadership Forum, HR Roundtable, Ga. State U.; bd. dirs. Metro Atlanta Recovery Residences, Inc., Big Bros. and Big Sisters, N.W. Ga. Girl Scout Coun., Inc., Leukemia and Lymphoma Soc., Salvation Army. Mem.: Soc. for Human Resources Mgmt. (chmn. bd. Atlanta chpt.), Exec. Mgmt. Assn. Office: Georgia Pacific Corp 133 Peachtree St NE Atlanta GA 30303*

BARNARD, SYLVIA EVANS, classicist, educator; b. Greenfield, Mass., Dec. 11, 1937; d. Francis Edward and Clara Crosier Barnard; 1 child, Siobhan Reagan. BA, McGill U., 1959; BA, MA, Cambridge U., 1962; PhD, Yale U., 1966. Instr. classics Le Moyne Coll., Syracuse, NY, 1965—66; asst. prof. classics Kenyon Coll., Gambier, Ohio, 1966—67; assoc. prof. classics U. Albany, NY, 1967—. Vis. lectr. U. New Brunswick, Fredericton, 1966. Contbr. articles to profl. jours. Recipient Rsch. award, Am. Philos. Soc., 1979; Fulbright scholar, Cyprus, 2003. Mem.: Archaeol. Inst. Am. (past v.p. local chpt.), UN Assn. (bd. mem., past. pres. local chpt.) Green Party. Episcopalian. Avocation: writing. Home: 84 Willett St Albany NY 12210 Office: Univ Albany Dept English 1400 Washington Ave Albany NY 12222 Office Phone: 518-442-4046.

BARNDT, FAITH ANN, elementary school educator; b. Quakertown, Pa., Apr. 29, 1951; d. Walter Elmer and Lucy Trout Rieker Barndt. B in Religious Edn., Crown Coll.; LPN, North Tech. Edn., Riviera Beach, Fla. LPN Palm Beach Med. Group, West Palm Beach, Fla., 1969—70; John F. Kennedy Hosp., Atlantis, Fla., 1971—73, Waterview Nursing Home, Mound, Minn., 1978—81; elem. edn. tchr. Palmetto Elem. Sch., West Palm Beach, 1984—; LPN Hospitality Ho. Nursing Home, Bloomington, Ind., 1994. Mem. sch. adv. coun., innovation instrn. team, student coun. advisor Palmetto Elem. Sch., West Palm Beach, 1992—2002. Contbr. poetry to Poetry.com; dir., prodr. children's plays. Nominee Tchr. of Yr., Palm Beach County, 1991, 1992. Mem.: Internat. Reading Coun., Palm Beach Reading Assn., Fla. Reading Assn. Home: 1819 16th Ave N Lake Worth FL 33460 Office: Palmetto Elem Sch 5801 Parker Ave West Palm Beach FL 33405 E-mail: brndtck@aol.com.

BARNES, ADRIENNE, public information officer; b. Balt., June 17, 1962; d. Glen McKoy and Carolyn B. Dunn. BA, U. Md., 1985. Asst. mayor's rep. Mayor's Office, Balt., 1988-90, mayor's rep., 1990-93; HUB dir. Housing and Cmty. Devel., Balt., 1993-95; asst. chief info. svc. Dept. Pub. Works, Balt., 1995-97, chief cmty. affairs, 1997—. Active Big Sisters Club, Balt., 1989—, 43/44 Dem. Club, Balt., 1989—; chair Environ. Control Bd., Balt., 1998—. Mem. Nat. Orgn. Black Pub. Adminstrs. Avocations: reading, traveling, working with youths. Home: 2822 Rosalie Ave Baltimore MD 21234-7613 Office: Dept Pub Works 200 Holliday St Baltimore MD 21202-3618 also: Pub Works Dept 600 Abel Wolman Mcpl Bldg Baltimore MD 21202

BARNES, BETTY JEAN, educational administrator; b. Aug. 11, 1948; BS, Miss. State U., Starkville, 1971, MEd, 1978; postgrad., U. Miss., Oxford, 1987. Tchr. Burnsville (Miss.) Sch., 1972-84; dir. exceptional children Tishomingo County Schs., Iuka, Miss., 1984—. Vol. Am. Cancer Soc., 8 yrs., Tishomingo Manor Nursing Home, 9 yrs. Mem.: Miss. Profl. Educators, Coun. Adminstrs. in Spl. Edn., Miss. Spl. Edn. Coop, Delta Kappa Gamma. Office: Tishomingo County Schs 1620 Paul Edmondson Dr Iuka MS 38852-1212

BARNES, BRENDA C. food and apparel executive; m. Randall C. Barnes; 3 children. B in econ., Augustana Coll.; MBA, Loyola U. With PepsiCo, 1975—98, v.p. mktg. Frito-Lay, bus. mgr. Wilson Spring Sporting Goods; pres. Pepsi-Cola S., 1992; COO Pepsi-Cola N. Am., 1993—96, pres., CEO, 1996—98; interim pres. Starwood Hotels, 1999—2000; pres., COO Sara Lee Corp., 2004—. Adj. prof. Kellogg Grad. Sch. Mgmt.; guest lectr. N. Central Coll., 2002; bd. mem. Avon Products Inc., NY Times Co., Sears Roebuck & Co., Staples Inc.; dir. Lucas Film, LTD. Chair bd. trustees Augustana Coll. Office: Sara Lee Corp 3 First Nat Plz Chicago IL 60602 Office Phone: 312-726-2600.*

BARNES, CYNTHIA LOU, retired gifted and talented educator; b. Yale, Okla., Jan. 14, 1934; d. Ira and Billie (Reed) Canfield; m. Edward M. Barnes, Jr., June 1, 1954; children: Edis, Barbara, Warren, Adrienne. BS, U. Tulsa, 1970; MS, Okla. State U., 1981. Substitute tchr. Tulsa Pub. Schs., 1970-73, kindergarten tchr., 1981-94, gifted edn. tchr., 1994-97, cons. Guide for Tchg. Gifted in the Regular Classroom, 1996, substitute tchr., 1997—2002, 2nd semester gifted edn. tchr. Carver Mid. Sch., 1998; pre-sch. tchr. Meml. Drive Meth., Tulsa, 1976-81; ret., 1997. Curriculum coord. Barnard Elem. Sch., Tulsa, 1992—97, site-base co-chmn., 1992—93; bd. dirs. Gt. Expectations Educators, Inc., Tulsa; cons. kindergarten guide Tulsa Pub. Schs., 1985; presenter Elem. Educators Conf., 1994, 97. Author: (curriculum guide) Special Connections, 1996. Confirmation class coord. 1st Meth. Ch., Broken Arrow, Okla., 1999—2002, Collinsville (Okla.) Story Hour Reader, 2001—02. Grantee, Tulsa Edn. Fund, 1994, 1996. Mem.: Okla. Assn. Gifted, Creative, Talented, Tulsa Classroom Tchrs. Math. (conf. presider 1994), Tulsa County Reading Coun. Home: 7824 E 22nd Pl Tulsa OK 74129-2416

BARNES, JANET LYNN, artist; b. Balt., Mar. 9, 1959; d. Edwin Lee and Mary Magdeline B.. BA in Visual and Performing Arts, U. Md., 1979. Prin., owner Crop Cir. Ceilings, Balt. Author: Brunch with Beethoven, 2002; one-woman shows include City Hall, Balt., 1998, John Hopkins Space Telescope, 1998, book cover, Poe's Last Supper, 1998. Hon. bus. chmn. adv. coun. Nat. Rep. Congl. Com., 2003. Recipient Nat. Leadership award, Nat. Rep. Congl. Com., 2003. Mem.: Nat. and World Wildlife, Artists Equity NY, Md. Hist. Soc., Nat. Trust Hist. Preservation, Wash. Soc. Jungian Psychology, Md. Hang Glider Assn., Catherine Lorillard Wolfe Art Club, Salmagundi Club, Delta Pi Alpha. Republican. Avocations: hang-gliding, reading, writing, house renovation, African grey parrot. Home: 236 S Castle St Baltimore MD 21231

BARNES, JHANE ELIZABETH, fashion design company executive, designer; b. Balt., Mar. 4, 1954; d. Richard Amos and Muriel Florence (Chase) B.; m. Howard Ralph Feinberg, Dec. 12, 1981 (div.); m. 2d, Katsuhiko Kawasaki, Feb. 12, 1988. A.S., Fashion Inst. Tech., 1975. Pres., designer Jhane Barnes for ME, N.Y.C., 1976-78; pres., designer, owner Jhane Barnes Inc., N.Y.C., 1978—; owner Jhane Barnes Textiles, LLC, 1998—. Recipient Coty award Menswear Am. Fashion Critics, 1980, 1984, Contract Textile award Am. Soc. Interior Designers, 1983, 84, Product Design awards Inst. Bus. Designers and Contract Mag., 1983-86, 94, Outstanding Am. Menswear Designer award Woolmark, 1990, Dalmore, 1990, Good Design award 1997, 98, 99, Best of Neo Con award. I.D. 40, 1996, 97, 98, 99, 2000; named Most Promising Designer Cutty Sark, 1980, Outstanding Designer, 1982, Outstanding Menswear Designer, Coun. of Fashion Designers Am., 1982, Design Resources Coun., 1989, 94, Designer of Yr., Neckwear Assn. Am., 1997. Office: Jhane Barnes Inc 119 W 40th St Fl 20 New York NY 10018-2500 Fax: 212-575-2506.

BARNES, JO ANNE, investment advisor; b. Berwyn, Ill., Feb. 1, 1947; d. Robert Marshall and Margaret Hickman Barnes; children: Katherine Dorothy Schock, Alice Margaret Schock. BA in English, U. Minn., 1969; MAT in English, Northwestern U., 1972. Cert. fin. planner. Tchr., adviser New Trier H.S., Winnetka, Ill., 1972-75; editl. proofreader Arthur Andersen & Co., St. Charles, Ill., 1980-82; registered rep., v.p. investments Howe Barnes Investments, Chgo., 1983-91; exec. v.p., dir. mktg. Podesta & Co., Chgo., 1992; pres., chief investment officer Barnes Alliance, Inc., Chgo., 1993-96; portfolio mgr. Vestor Capital Corp., Chgo., 1997; sr. investment mgr. Vanguard Group, Valley Forge, Pa., 1997—. Host, prodr., writer (TV show) On Your Side, 1985-86; co-author, editor Investor's Workshop, 1994-96. Chmn. Planning Commn., Hampshire, Ill., 1978-80; dir. Builders Skills, Niles, Ill., 1988-90; pres., trustee Salem United Meth. Ch., Barrington, Ill., 1991-93; dir., treas. Women's Opportunity Fund, Oakbrook, Ill., 1995-98. Mem.: Religious Soc. of Friends (Pa.), Nature Conservancy, Audubon Soc. Avocations: poetry, hiking, biking, writing. Home: 2025 Greens Way Cir Collegeville PA 19426

BARNES, JUDITH ANN, real estate executive; b. Milw., Mar. 10, 1949; d. Einar and Eleanor Svea (Russell) B.; divorced; children: Krista Svea, Erik Leif. BA, Gustavus Adolphus Coll., 1970; grad., Wis. Sch. Real Estate, Milw., 1979; postgrad., Carroll Coll., 1980, U. Wis., 1978-80, 92. Tchr. Oak Grove Mid. Sch., Bloomington, Minn., 1970-71, Mukwonago (Wis.) H.S., 1971-72; sales mgr. Lincoln Park Homes, West Allis, Wis., 1972-73, v.p., 1973-74, pres., 1974-97, Palm Coast, Fla., 1997-2000; assoc. Coldwell Banker Comml. (Nicholson-Williams), 2000—01; with Hammock Dunes Real Estate Co., 2001—. Chmn. Mfrd. Housing Subdivision S.E. Wisc., Madison, 1978-80, sec. Southeastern Wis. Housing, Milw., 1981-82, treas., 1982-84. Bd. dirs. Waukesha YMCA, 1985-87, v.p. 1987-89; bd. dirs. YMCA Heritage Found., 1994-97; bd. dirs. Waukesha County United Way, 1984-87; coun. pres. Stetson U., 1996-2000; mem. alumni bd. Gustavus Adulphus Coll., St. Peter, Minn., 1974-80; trustee The Cooper Inst., Naples, Fla., 1987-93, mem. adv. bd., 1993—. Recipient Dedicated Svc. award Wis. Mfrd. Housing, 1975-84, 88, Vol. of Yr. award Univ. Lake Sch., 1995. Mem. Wis. Mfrd. Housing Assn. (bd. dirs. 1975-80), Ind. Bus. Assn. Wis. (trustee U. Lake 1991-96), [illegible], Milw. Women's Dist. Golf Assn. (bd. dirs. 1993, v.p. 1994, pres. 1995-96), Vasa Lodge, Hammock Dunes Country Club (adv. bd.). Republican. Lutheran. Avocations: golf, photography. Home: 3 Anastasia Ct Palm Coast FL 32137-2273 Office Phone: 386-446-6319. E-mail: jbhd@bellsouth.net.

BARNES, KAREN KAY, lawyer; b. June 22, 1950; d. Walter William and Vashti (Greenlee) Sessler; m. James Alan Barnes, Feb. 12, 1972; children: Timothy Matthew, Christopher Michael. BA, Valparaiso U., 1971; JD, DePaul U., 1978, LLM in Taxation, 1980. Bar: Ill. 1978, U.S. Dist. Ct. (no. dist.) Ill. 1978. Ptnr. McDermott, Will & Emory, Chgo., 1978-88; prin. William M. Mercer, Inc. and predecessor firm, Chgo., 1989-93; staff dir. legal dept. McDonald's Corp., Oak Brook, Ill., 1993-95, home office dir. legal dept., 1995-97, regulatory practice group leader and mng. counsel, 1998—. Instr. John Marshall Grad. Sch. Law, Chgo., 1986-87; mem. adv. bd. John Marshall Sch. Law, 1996—; bd. dirs. Flutes Unlimited; mem. adv. bd. dirs. Plan Sponsor Mag., 2000—. Contbr. case note to DePaul Law Rev., 1976, note and comment editor DePaul Law Rev., 1976-77, editor Taxation For Lawyers, 1986-88. Mem. Am. Coll. Employee Benefit Attys., Chgo. Bar Assn. (chair employee benefits com. 1991-92, co-chair symphony orch. 1999-2001), Midwest Pension Conf. (name chged to Midwest Benefits Coun.), WEB (pres. Chgo. chpt. 1986-88, v.p. nat. bd. 1988, pres. 1989-90, mem. adv. bd. 2001—), Profit Sharing Coun. Am. (legal and legis. com. 1994—, bd. dirs. 1997—, 2d vice chair 1997-98, 1st vice chair 1998-2000, chair 2000-02). Lutheran. Home: 586 Crescent Blvd # 402 Glen Ellyn IL 60137 Office: McDonald's Corp 2915 Jorie Blvd Oak Brook IL 60523 E-mail: karen.barnes@mcd.com.

BARNES, KAY, mayor; BS in Secondary Edn., U. Kans.; MS in Secondary Edn. and Pub. Adminstrn., U. Mo., Kansas City. Staff mem. Westport area Cross-Lines Coop. Coun.; pres. Kay Waldo, Inc., human resources devel. co., Kansas City, Mo.; mayor City of Kansas City, Mo., 1999—. Condr. over 400 pub. seminars Nat. Seminars, Inc.; cons., keynote spkr. 14 reginal confs. through U.S., Am. Bus. Women's Assn.; former co-host, prodr. cable TV show Let's Talk; former instr. U. Mo., Kansas City, U. Kans., Ctrl. Mich. U. Author: About Time! A Woman's Guide to Time Management. Co-founder Ctrl. Exch.; vol. Cross-Lines Coop. Coun.; a founder women's resource svc. U. Mo., Kansas City; developer multicultural women's speaking panels through western U.S.; mem. Jackson County (Mo.) Legislature, from 1974; mem. Kansas City City Coun., from 1979; chmn. Tax Increment Financing Commn., 1993-97; pres. bd. dirs. Women's Employment Network; mem. or dir. numerous other orgns., including Women's Found. Greater Kansas City, Greater Kansas City Sports Commn.; mem. chancellor's adv. bd. of Women's Ctr., U. Mo., Kansas City. Named One of 7 Outstanding Women in Kansas City, 1977. Mem. Greater Kansas City C. of C. (com.). Office: Mayor's Office City Hall 29th Fl 414 E 12th St Ste 2902 Kansas City MO 64106-2778*

BARNES, MAGGIE LUE SHIFFLETT (MRS. LAWRENCE BARNES), nurse; b. Redmond, Tex., Mar. 29, 1931; d. Howard Eldridge and Sadie Adilene (Dunlap) Shifflett; m. T.C. Fagan, Jan. 1950 (Dec. Feb. 1952); 1 child, Lawayne; m. Lawrence Barnes, Sept. 2, 1960. Student, Cogdell Sch. Nursing, 1959-60, Western Tex. Coll., 1972-76; postgrad., Meth. Hosp. Sch. Nursing, Lubbock, Tex., 1975; BSN, West Tex. State U., 1977; cert. legal nurse cons., Kaplan Coll., 2001. RN Tex., cert. gerontol. nurse. Floor nurse D.M. Cogdell Meml. Hosp., Snyder, Tex., 1960-64, medication nurse, 1964-76, asst. evening supr., 1976-78, charge nurse, after 1978, evening nursing supr., 1980; nursing supr. for 5 counties West Ctrl. Home Health Agy., Snyder, 1980-83; emergency rm. evening supr. Mitchell County Hosp., 1983-89; dir. nurses Snyder Oak Care Ctr., 1989-91, Mountain View Lodge, Big Spring, Tex., 1991-92, Med. Arts Hosp. Home Health, Lamesa, 1992—93, Metplex Home Health Svcs., Snyder, 1993-94, ret., 1994; weekend RN Snyder Oaks Care Ctr. Part time nurse 1994—, CNA Sch. instr.; leader Bible study, 1997—; vol. Helping Children Read Sch., Bible study at nursing homes; regional coord. home health svcs. Beverly Enterprises, 1983; legal nurse cons. Grad. Kaplan Coll., Boca Raton, Fla., 2001. Den mother Cub Scouts, Boy Scouts Am., Holliday, Tex., 1960-61; mem. PTA, Snyder, 1960-69; adviser Sr. Citizens Assn.; mem Tri-Region Health Sys. Agy., 1979—; mem. adv. bd. Scurry County Diabetes Assn., 1982—; mem. vol. reading program; ch. sec.-treas. Apostolic Faith Ch., 1956-58 Mem.: DAR, Emergency Dept. Nursing Assn., Vocat. Nurses Assn. Tex. (bd. dirs. 1963—65, divsn. pres. 1967—69), Rock and Roll Quilting Club (coord.). Avocation: bible study with nursing home residents. Home: 249 County Rd 349-B Snyder TX 79549

BARNES, MARGARET ANDERSON, business consultant; b. Johnston County, N.C. m. Benjamin Barnes, Dec. 26, 1959. BS, N.C. Ctrl. U., 1958; MA, U. Md., 1975; PhD, Columbia Pacific U., 1986. Lic. ins. agt., Md.; ordained Christian min. and elder in World Evangelism, 1992. Math. tchr. Tarboro (N.C.) Sch. Sys., 1959-61; math. statistician Bur. of Census, Suitland, Md., 1962-67, 69-70, Govt. of D.C., 1967-68; cons. NIH, Bethesda, Md., 1970-72; chief of data stds. Nat. Insts. of Health, Bethesda, Md., 1972-73; with exec. clearance office HEW, Rockville, Md., 1973-77; founder, pres. MABarnes Cons. Assoc., Lanham, Md., 1978-95. Commr. State of Md. Accident Fund, Balt., 1979-89; mem. adv. bd. Universal Bank, Lanham, 1980-83, Interstate Gen. Corp., St. Charles, Md., 1981-83; founder Christian Ministries, 1983—, Christ Centered Ministries Esprit, 1995—, Mleecole Pub., 1997—; profiled for First Record: "Women of Achievement in Prince George's County History", 1994. Chairwoman Glenwood Park Civic Assn., Lanham, 1967-80. Democrat. Avocations: piano, sewing, reading, song, prose and poetry writing, artistic designing. Home: PO Box 586 Lanham Seabrook MD 20703-0586 Office: Christ Centered Ministries Esprit PO Box 802 Lanham Seabrook MD 20703-0802

BARNES, MARYLOU RIDDLEBERGER, retired academic administrator, educator; b. Bridgewater, Va., Feb. 27, 1930; d. Hensel Dorsey Riddleberger and Ruby Elizabeth Heltzel; children: Tenley Elizabeth, Rachel Patricia. BS, Madison Coll., 1952; MS, Med. Coll. Va., 1957; MA, James Madison U., 1968; EdD, W. Va. U., 1975; DSc (hon.), U. Indpls., 1993. From staff phys. therapist to dir. clin. edn. Woodrow Wilson Rehab. Ctr., Fishersville, Va., 1958-64, dir clin. edn., 1964-67; chief phys. therapy Rockingham Meml. Hosp., Harrisonburg, Va., 1958-59; prof., dir., chair dept. phys. therapy W. Va. U., Morgantown, W. Va., 1968-79; from prof., chair dept. phys. therapy to prof. emeritus Ga. State U., Atlanta, 1979-95, ret., 1995, prof. emeritus, 1995—. Adv. bd. Perry Inst., Strafford, Pa., 1993-95; co-chair program com. Joint Am.-Can. Phys. Therapy Annual Conf. Author: Patient at Home, 1972, Neurophysiological Basis of Physical Therapy Care, vol. I, 1973, vol. II, 1977, Physical Therapy, 1989, Motor Control and Motor Learning in Rehabilitation, 1993; contbr. articles to profl. jours. Vol. Centennial Olympic Games, Atlanta, 1996, Goodwill Industries Book Ctr., Atlanta, 1999. Mem. Am. Phys. Therapy Assn. (nat. survey pool for accreditation of schs. 1974-95, pres. neurology sect. 1985-87, task force on profl. devel. 1994, chair continuing edn. bd. 1994-95, Mary McMillan Lectr. award 1992, Catherine Worthingham fellow 1994, leadership in edn. award 1995, svc. to neurology sect. award 1998, Lucy Blair Svc. award 1988). Presbyterian. Avocations: amateur archaeologist, travel, reading, tree climbers of am. Home: 133 Santolina Park Peachtree City GA 30269-3245 E-mail: mloubarnes@mindspring.com.

BARNES, PATIENCE PLUMMER, writer, editor; b. Mt. Vernon, N.Y., Sept. 28, 1932; d. Charles Sumner and Elinor Agnes (Keaney) Plummer; m. James John Barnes, July 9, 1955; children: Jennifer Chase Barnes Wilson, Geoffrey Prescott. BA, Smith Coll., 1954. With J. Walter Thompson Co., N.Y.C., 1950-55; freelance writer, editor, 1955—. Rsch. assoc. wabash Coll., 1988—. Author: (with J.J. Barnes) Hitler's Mein Kampf in Britain and America, 1930-39, 1980, James Vincent Murphy, Translator and Interpreter of Fascist Europe, 1880-1946, 1987, Private and Confidential: Letters from British Ministers in Washington to Their Foreign Secretaries in London, 1845-67, 1993, (with JJ Barnes) Nazi Refugee Turned Gestapo Spy: The Life of Hans Wesemann. 1895-1971, 2001, (with JJ Barnes) The American Civil War through British Eyes: Dispatches from British Diplomats, Vol. I, 2003: editor: Free Trade in Books; A Study of the London Book Trade Since 1800, 1964 (J.J. Barnes), Authors, Publishers and Politicians: The Quest for an Anglo-American Copyright Agreement, 1815-54, 1974 (J.J. Barnes); contbr. articles to profl. jours. Active Meals on Wheels, 1964—; jr. choir dir. St. John's Episcopal Ch., Crawfordsville, 1965-71; bd. dirs. Sugar Creek Swim Club, 1971-72, 72-, LWV, Montgomery County, 1981—, Crawfordsville unit Indpls. Symphony Orch., 1985-88, Mecklenburgh Festival Opera, London, 1985; del. Dem. State Conv., Indpls., 1988; mem. Feminist Theory Reading Group, Wabash Coll., 1993-2002. Avocations: sports, music, reading and creative writing, gourmet cooking, collecting antique and art glass. Home: 7 Locust Hl Crawfordsville IN 47933-3347 E-mail: barnesp@wabash.edu.

BARNES, PATRICIA ANN, art educator; b. San Antonio, Sept. 26, 1942; d. John Homer and Dorothy Bernice (Foster) Sanders; m. Henry Franklin Snodgrass, Oct. 31, 1960 (div. 1966); children: William Franklin, George Huston II, John Charles Joseph; m. Joseph LeRoy Barnes Jr., Aug. 18, 1969; children: Shana Lynn, Janna Lee, Joseph Leroy III. AAS, Bee County Coll., 1986; BFA, Corpus Christi State U., 1988; MA, Tex. A&M U., 1990. Art tchr. J.T.P.A. Summer Youth Program, Beeville, Tex., 1990; adj. art tchr. St. Philips Coll., San Antonio, 1991-93; art tchr. Runge (Tex.) Ind. Sch. Dist., 1993-96; art tchr., chmn. fine arts Skidmore (Tex.)-Tynan Ind. Sch. Dist., 1996—2001, chmn. fine arts, 2000—01; ret., 2001. Owner Patty's Pyrographics, Three Rivers, Tex., 1995—; Upward Bound art tchr. Coastal Bend Coll., Beeville, Tex., 1999; rep. Polyform Products, 1999—, Jacquard Products, 2001—; polymer clay instr. Michaels Arts and Crafts; tchr. JoAnn's, 2001—. Contr. art in book: Transfering Designs., 2002. Mem.: Victoria Polymer Clay Guild (founding), San Antonio Polymer Clay Guild (founding mem., parliamentarian), South Tex. Polymer Clay Guild (pres. 1999—, charter, founder), Coastal Bend Art Edn. Assn., Tex. Art Edn. Assn. (presenter convs. 1997—99, Region 5 rep. 2000—01), Nat. Polymer Clay Guild, Nat. Art Edn. Assn., Skidmore-Tynan Nat. Art Honor Soc. (sponsor 2001—), Skidmore-Tynan Fine Arts Booster Club (founder 2000—01, sponsor). Avocations: glass fusing, polymer clay art, reading, fishing, sewing. Home: RR 1 Box 497 Three Rivers TX 78071-9711 E-mail: pbarnes@the-i.net.

BARNES, SHARON D. academic advisor, music educator; b. Roanoke, Va., Apr. 16, 1958; d. Kermit Wayne and Doris Grisso Dudley; m. Kenneth Lane Barnes, June 16, 1978; 1 child, Derrick Cameron. BA cum laude, Hollins Coll., 1979, MA in Liberal Studies, 1985. Classical music dir. WVTF-FM Radio, Roanoke, Va., 1978-81; piano and voice instr. Roanoke Music Ctr., 1979-80; ind. piano and voice instr. Roanoke, 1979-92; piano instr. The Bandroom, Roanoke, 1980-91; acad. advisor Mary Baldwin Coll., Roanoke, 1997—. Choir dir. Westhampton Christian Ch., Roanoke, 1981-84; adj. faculty Mary Baldwin Coll., Staunton, Va., 1986—, Va. We. C.C., Roanoke, 1991-98; mem. web course in a box com. Mary Baldwin Coll., 1999—; instr. online course Introduction to Listening, 1999; presenter in field. Vocal soloist area chs., Roanoke, 1975-99; youth choir dir., accompanist Westhampton Christian Ch., Roanoke, 1997-99; PTA mem. Back Creek Elem., Roanoke, 1996-99; com. mem. Bd. Edn. Westhampton Christian, Roanoke, 1999—. Presser scholar Hollins (Va.) Coll., 1978. Mem. Internat. Alliance Women in Music, Music Tchrs. Nat. Assn., Va. Music Tchrs. Assn., Roanoke Valley Soc. for Prevention of Cruelty to Animals, Nat. Wildlife Assn., Phi Theta Kappa. Avocations: hiking, swimming, reading. Home: 6423 Ran Lynn Dr Roanoke VA 24018-5403 Office: Mary Baldwin Coll/Roanoke Ctr 108 N Jefferson St Ste 816 Roanoke VA 24016-1922 E-mail: sbarnes@mbc.edu.

BARNES, SHIRLEY MOORE, retired psychiatric social worker, genealogist; b. Bedminster, N.J., Jan. 13, 1931; d. George and Marian (Van Nuys) Moore; m. William E. Barnes, Sept. 13, 1952; children: John Leighton, Ellen Leigh, Kimberley Jean. Student, Tucson Coll., 1948-50; BA, Rutgers U., 1952; MSW, U. Pa., 1954. Lic. clin. social worker, Vt. Caseworker Children's Aid Soc., Phila., 1952-55; psychiat. social worker

West Jersey Hosp. and Psychiat. Clinic, Camden, N.J., 1960-61, VA Hosp., Brockton, Mass., 1972, Mental Health Svcs. Vt., Springfield, 1973-77, adminstr., coord. aftercare and rehab., 1977-82, psychiat. social worker, supr., 1982-96, developer psycho-rehab. for retarded and mentally ill Proctorsville, 1980-82, founder Beekman House, 1979; ret., 1996. Author: Thomas Edward Currin, Sr., Margaret Jane Cubbon, 1993, The Kindred Venturers, 1994, (with G. Moore) A Special Union, 1998The Lineage and History of the Four Van Nuys Sisters, 2002, The History & Lineage of Alexander Baird and His Descendants in Somerset County, N.J., 2002; contbr. articles to various publs. Bd. dirs. J.F. Tatum Sch. PTA, Haddonfield, N.J., 1966-68, High Rock Sch. PTA, Needham, Mass., 1971-72. Recipient 1d place for best all around work in art dept. N.J. Federated Women's Clubs, 1966. Mem. NASW, Acad. Cert. Social Workers, Nat. Geneal. Soc., New Eng. Hist. and Geneal. Soc. Avocations: genealogy, art, embroidery. Home: 13 Blossom Dr Billerica MA 01821-3114

BARNES, SUSAN LEWIS, lawyer; b. Palo Alto, Calif., June 11, 1943; d. Prof. and Mrs. L.J. Lewis; m. Sanford C. Barnes; 1 child, Jason Bullard Barnes. BS, Stanford U., 1965; JD, U. Wash., 1968. Law clk. Ariz. Ct. Appeals, Tucson, 1968-71, U.S. Atty.'s Office, Seattle, 1971-96, 1st asst. U.S. atty., 1994-96, interim U.S. Atty., 1993, 1st asst. U.S. Atty., 1991-93, chief civil divsn., 1982-91; ptnr. McKay Chadwell PLLC, Seattle, 1996—. Pres. Fed. Bar WDWN, 1995; lawyer's rep. 9th cir. Office: McKay Chadwell PLLC 701 5th Ave Ste 7201 Seattle WA 98104-7042

BARNES-KEMPTON, ISABEL JANET, microbiology educator, college dean; b. Union City, N.J., Sept. 22, 1936; d. Carl Robert and Isabel Sarah (Cappelletti) B.; m. John D. Bowman, June 15, 1978 (dec. Nov. 1986); m. Arnold J. Kempton, Feb. 5, 2000. BS, Pa. State U., 1958; MS, Cornell U., 1960; PhD, Hahnemann Med. Coll., 1969; postgrad., Inst. Ednl. Mgmt. Harvard U., 1991. Asst. prof. microbiology Hershey Med. Ctr., Pa. State U., 1968-73; asst. prof., then assoc. prof. Sangamon State U., Springfield, Ill., 1973-76; assoc. prof. med. tech. U. Wis., Madison, 1976-85; interim dean Sch. Allied Health Professions, 1981-84; prof. med. tech. Ferris State U., Big Rapids, Mich., 1985-2000; dean Coll. Allied Health Scis., 1985-2000, acting v.p. Acad. Affairs, 1992-93. Mem. Mich. Bd. Podiatric Medicine and Surgery, 1995—2002. Bd. dirs. Mecosta County Gen. Hosp., 1988-99, sec. 1991-94, pres., 1996-97, v.p. 1997-99, Alliance for Health, 1993-2002, Mich. Hemophilia Found., 1989-95, 97—, sec. 1991-94; active Mecosta Health Svcs., 1998-2002, Mecosta County Cmty. Found., 1999—; coord. St. Andrews Manna Food Pantry, 2002—; mem. Tamarack Dist. Libr. Bd., 2003—; pres. bd. Tamarack Dist. Libr., 2003—. Fellow Assn. of Schs. of Allied Health Professions (bd. dirs. 1989-91); mem. Coll. Health Deans (pres. 1988-90).

BARNETT, AMY DUBOIS, editor-in-chief; BA, Brown U.; MFA, Columbia U. Mng. editor Fashion Almanac Mag., 1996—98; editor-in-chief Edition Inside NY, 1999; mng. editor Fashion Planet Website; columnist, features editor Total NY Website; editor Essence Mag., 1999—2000; editor-in-chief Honey Mag., 2000—03; editor Teen People, 2003—. Office: Teen People/Time Inc 1271 Ave of the Americas New York NY 10020-1393

BARNETT, DOROTHY PRINCE, retired dean; b. Charlotte, N.C., Aug. 18, 1931; d. Abraham Hamilton and Susan (Peacock) Prince; m. Isaac Barnett, Dec. 27, 1977. AB, Oberlin Coll., 1953; MA, Syracuse U., 1954; EdD, Ind. U., 1962. Instr. Alcorn Coll., Lorman, Miss., summer 1954, So. U., Baton Rouge, 1954-55; asst. prof. N.C. Agrl. and Tech. State U., Greensboro, 1955-62, prof., 1962-94, chairperson dept. edn., 1966-77, chairperson dept. secondary edn. and curriculum, 1977-89, asst. dean, dir. tchr. edn. Sch. Edn., 1983-90, dean Sch. Edn., 1991-94, ret., 1994. Educator, reader U.S. Dept. Edn., Washington, 1968-94; mem. multicultural com. Met. project Am. Assn. Colls. for Tchr. Edn., Washington, 1990-92; cons. initiative conf. Phelps State Consortium, N.Y.C., 1971-73, Norfolk State U., Washington, 1981-89; reader Corp. for Pub. Broadcast, Washington, 1982; mem. bd. examiners Nat. Coun. for Accreditation of Tchr. Edn.; presenter state, nat. and local tchr. edn. confs., 1970-94; bd. dirs. Holmes Group. Contbr. articles to ednl. publs. Bd. dirs. Charlotte Hawkins Brown Hist. Found., Sedalia, N.C., Holmes Group, 1991-94. Recipient Honored Alumnus award Sch. Edn. Syracuse (N.Y.) U., 1992; John Hay Whitney Found. fellow, N.Y., 1961-62; Ellis L. Phillips Found. intern, N.Y., 1964-65. Mem. Phi Delta Kappa, Pi Lambda Theta, Kappa Delta Pi. Democrat. Presbyterian. Avocations: reading, music, walking, bridge. Home: 4702 Royalshire Rd Greensboro NC 27406-8705

BARNETT, MARILYN, advertising agency executive; b. Detroit; d. Henry and Kate (Boesky) Schiff; children: Rhona, Ken. BA, Wayne State U. Founder, part-owner, pres. Mars Advt. Co., Southfield, Mich. Bd. dirs. Mich. Strategic Fund; apptd. to Mich. bi-lateral trade team with Germany. Named Outstanding Retail Woman of Yr., Outstanding Retail Mktg. Exec., bd. dirs. Oakland U., Entrepreneur of Yr., Oakland Exec. of Yr.; named to Mich.'s Top 25 Women Bus. Owner's List. Mem. AFTRA (dir.), SAG, Exec. Women Am., Am. Women in Radio & TV (Top Agy. Mgmt. award, Outstanding Woman of Yr.), Internat. Women Forum, Com. of 200, Women's Econ. Club (Ad Woman of Yr.), Adcraft. Office: MARS Advt 23777 Southfield Rd Southfield MI 48075-3435 also: MARS Advt Co 6671 W Sunset Blvd Ste 1591 Los Angeles CA 90028-7170

BARNETT, MARTHA WALTERS, lawyer; b. Dade City, Fla., June 1, 1947; d. William Haywood and Helen (Hancock) Walters; m. Richard Rawls Barnett, Jan. 4, 1969; children: Richard Rawls, Sarah Walters. BA cum laude, Tulane U., 1969; JD cum laude, U. Fla., 1973. Bar: Fla. 1973, U.S. Dist. Ct. (mid. and so. dists.) Fla. 1973, U.S. Ct. Appeals (3d, 4th and 11th cirs.) 1975, DC 1989. Assoc. Holland & Knight LLP, Tallahassee, 1973—78, ptnr., 1979—. Bd. dirs., v.p. Fla. Lawyers Prepaid Legal Svc. Corp., 1978—80, pres., 1980—82, legis. com., 1983—84, mem. commn. on access to justice, 1984—86, exec. coun. tax sect., 1987—88, exec. coun. pub. interest. sect., 1989—91; active Fla. Commn. Ethics, 1984—87, chairperson, 1986—87, Fla. Taxation and Budget Reform Commn., 1989—; legal adv. bd. Martindale-Hubbell, 1990—; chair Ho. of Dels., 1994—96. Mem. Fla. Coun. Econ. Edn., Fla. Edn. Found.; bd. dirs. Lawyers Com. Civil Rights Under Law. Fellow: Am. Bar Found. (life); mem.: ABA (exec. coun. sect. on individual rights and responsibility 1974—86, bd. govs. 1986—89, task force on minorities in profession 1984—86, commn. on women in profession 1987—90, long range planning com. 1988—91, chair bd. govs. fin. com. 1988—89, bd. editors ABA Jour. 1990—94, exec. coun. sect. legal edn. and admission to bar 1990—94, chair commn. on pub. understanding about the law 1990—93, pres.-elect 1999—2000, pres. 2000—01, others), Tallahassee Bar Assn., Fla. Bar Assn. (exec. coun. pub. interest law sect. 1989—91), Am. Law Inst., Nat. Inst. Dispute Resolution (sec.-treas. 1988—94, bd. dirs. 1988—94, Gov. appt. Fla. Constitution revision Commn. 1997—98). Office: Holland & Knight LLP PO Drawer 810 Tallahassee FL 32302-0810

BARNETT, MARY LORENE, real estate manager; b. Saline County, Mo., Nov. 29, 1927; d. Grover Cleveland Renno and Emma Zue Rennison; m. Eugene Earl Boone, Aug. 24, 1946 (div. Aug. 1961); 1 child, Priscilla Sue Boone; m. Charles Owen Barnett, Nov. 11, 1961; 1 child, Robert E. BA in Psychology magna cum laude, Washburn U., 1979. Asst. contr. 1st State Savs., Sedalia, Mo., 1960-61; bookkeeper New Empire Ins., Sedalia, 1961-63; office mgr. Klassic Mfg., Sedalia, 1963-66; real estate mgr. Topeka, Kans., 1970—. Author: Charles Renno Family Record, 1996, Charles Renno Family, 1997. Bd. dirs. Shawnee County Coun. on Aging, Topeka. Recipient cert. of appreciation Bd. of County Commrs., Topeka, 1995. Mem. DAR, AAUW, LWV, Topeka Women's Club (1st v.p.), Ea. Star, Phi Kappa Phi, Psi Chi. Republican. Avocations: genealogy, poetry. Home: 3819 SW Lincolnshire Rd Topeka KS 66610-1360

BARNETT, MARY LOUISE, elementary school educator; b. Exeter, Calif., May 1, 1941; d. Raymond Edgar Noble and Nena Lavere (Huckaby) Hope; m. Gary Allen Barnett, Aug. 9, 1969; children: Alice Marie, Virginia Lynn. BA, U. of Pacific, 1963; postgrad., U. Mont., 1979-82, U. Idaho, 1984—. Cert. life elem. tchr., Calif.; standard elem. credential, Idaho; elem. tchr., Mont. Tchr. Colegio Americano de Torrean, Torreon, Coahuila, Mexico, 1962-63, Summer Sch. Primary Grades South San Francisco, 1963-66, Visalia (Calif.) Unified Sch. Dist., 1966-69, Sch. Dist. # 1, Missoula, Mont., 1969-73, Fort Shaw-Simms Sch. Dist., Fort Shaw, Mont., 1976-83, Sch. Dist. #25, Pocatello, Idaho, 1983-93, Greenacres Elem., Pocatello, 1993-94; tchr. 2d grade Bonneville Elem., Pocatello, 1994-95; tchr. Windsong Presch., Missoula, Mont., 1995-98, Headstart of Missoula, 1998-99; dir. Mary's Munchkins Presch., Missoula, 1999—. Beauty cons. Mary Kay. Foster mom Ednl. Found. Fgn. Students, Pocatello, Idaho, 1986-89; vol. Am. Heart Assn., Am. Cancer Soc., Pocatello, 1986-88, Bannock March of Dimes, Pocatello, 1988, Pocatello Laubach Lit. Tutoring, 1989; state v.p. membership, del. to P.W. Australian Mission Study; vice moderator Kendall Presbyn. Women, moderator, 1991—; moderator Kendall P.W. 1990-92; dean, treas. Presbyn. Ch., 1997—. Recipient scholarship Mont. Delta Kappa Gamma Edn. Soc., Great Falls, Mont., 1976, Great Falls AAUW, 1980, Great Falls Scottish Rite, 1981, Five Valleys Reading Assn., Missoula, Mont., 1982. Mem. AAUW (v.p. 2002—, mem. com. Idaho divsn. 1990-92, book chair 1995—, pres. Missoula chpt. 1998—), ASCD, NEA, Nat. Coun. Tchrs. English, Internat. Reading Assn., Assn. Childhood Edn. Internat., Laubach Literacy Tutors (sec. 1993—), Bus. and Profl. Women Pocatello (sec. 1993—, contact advisor Missoula After 5 1999—, mem. exec. bd. state professional and career devel.), Mortar Bd., Alpha Lambda Delta, Delta Kappa Gamma (state fellowship chmn., corr. sec. Pocatello chpt. 1986-88, 2d v.p. 1994-96, chmn. Western expansion, 200-03), Moose (musician 1981-82), Order Eastern Star (musician 1984-85), Gamma Phi Beta (sec. Laubach Tutors 1993-95), Delta Kappa Gamma (2d v.p. Phi chpt. 1996—, pres. 2000-02, 2002—). Democrat. Presbyn. Avocations: music, aquacise, aerobics, crafts, cross stitch. Home: 103 E Crestline Dr Missoula MT 59803-2412 Office: Clark Fork School 2525 Rattlesnake Drive Missoula MT 59803-2412 E-mail: Gabmarybarnett@aol.com.

BARNETT, MEGAN A. lawyer; b. Columbus, Ohio, Feb. 21, 1971; BA, U. Va., 1993; JD, Yale Law Sch., 1997. Bar: S.C. Bar 1998, D.C. Bar 1999. Analyst Solomon Bros., N.Y., 1993—94; law clerk Hon. R. Lanier Anderson, 11th Cir. Ct. Appeals, Macon, Ga., 1997—98; assoc. Gibson, Dunn & Crutcher, Washington, 1998—2002; dean admissions Yale Law Sch., New Haven, 2002—. Editor: Yale Law Jour., 1995—97. Office: Yale Law Sch 127 Wall St New Haven CT 06511

BARNETT, PEGGY G. music educator; b. Dallas, Sept. 15, 1935; d. Garnald Morris and Thelma Christean (Turner) Gregory; m. John Curtis Jones, Aug. 24, 1957 (div. June 1980); children: Lewis Gregory, Michael Wayne, Scott Carlton, Cynthia Luanne; m. Edward Ralph Burnett, Aug. 31, 2002. BS in Home Econs., Baylor U., 1956; MS in Housing and Interior Design, Okla. State U., 1957; student, Rykyu Classical Acad., Okinawa, Japan, 1964-68, Hampton (Va.) Inst., 1968-70. Nat. cert. tchr. music; cert. profl. master. Pvt. practice piano tchr., 1964—2002; founder, dir., piano thcr., music theory tchr. Music Arts Conservatory, Albuquerque, 1984—2002; ret., 2002. Mem. piano faculty Summer Piano Camp at Mary Hardin-Baylor U., Belton, Tex., summers 1980, 86. Performed two-piano and duet music, 1980-85; performed with ptnr. in master classes for well-known duettists. Choir dir., pianist and organist various chs., Okinawa, 1964-68, Hampton, Va., 1969-72, Las Vegas, Nev., 1972-74; talent judge Miss Teen Pageant, Albuquerque, 1993-96. Mem. Profl. Music Tchrs. N.Mex. (state membership chair 1982-83, adjudicator 1975—Tchr. of Yr. 1998), Music Tchrs. Nat. Assn., Nat. Guild Piano Tchrs., Tex. Music Tchrs. Assn., Abilene Music Tchrs. Assn. Avocations: downhill skiing, hiking, gardening.

BARNETT, SUE, nurse; b. Waukegan, Ill., Apr. 8, 1956; d. Jackie Laverne and Catherine Mary (LaMarche) B. AAS in Nursing, Elgin (Ill.) C.C., 1977. RN, Ill.; ANCC cert. in psychiat. and mental health nurse. Home health nurse Adv. Health Care, Oak Brook, Ill., 1977-97; staff nurse Fox Valley Nursing Home, South Elgin, Ill., 1978-79, Elgin Mental Health Ctr., 1979—. Music min., vol. St. John Neumann Ch., St. Charles, Ill., 1977—; vol. Labarus House Shelter, St. Charles, 1997—. Mem. Ill. Nurses Assn. (local unit sec. 1981-84, local unit grievance rep. 1984-96, local unit vice chair 1984-94, conv. rep. 1990-92). Roman Catholic. Avocations: reading, singing, volunteer work. Home: 561 South Dr South Elgin IL 60177-2529 Office: Elgin Mental Health Ctr-Gahagan Unit 750 S State St Elgin IL 60123-7692

BARNETT, VIVIAN ENDICOTT, curator; b. Putnam, Conn., July 8, 1944; d. George and Vivian (Wood) Endicott; m. Peter Herbert Barnett, July 1, 1967; children: Sarah, Alexander. AB magna cum laude, Vassar Coll., 1965; MA, NYU, 1971; postgrad., CUNY, 1979-81. Research asst. Solomon R. Guggenheim Mus., N.Y.C., 1973-77, curatorial assoc., 1978-79, assoc. curator, 1980-81, rsch. curator, 1981-82, curator, 1982-91; dir. Roethel Benjamin Archive at Guggenheim Mus., N.Y.C., 1991—. Author: (book) The Guggenheim Museum: Justin K. Thannhauser Collection, 1978, The Guggenheim Museum Collection 1900-1980, Kandinsky at the Guggenheim, 1983, 100 Works by Modern Masters from the Guggenheim Museum, 1984, Kandinsky and Sweden, 1989, Kandinsky in Major Collections in the West, 1989, Kandinsky Watercolours: Catalogue Raisonnè, vol I 1900-1921, 1992, Kandinsky Watercolours: Catalogue Raisonnè, vol II 1922-1944, 1994, Kleine Freuden, 1992, Das bunte Leben: Kandinsky in Lenbachhaus, 1995, The Blue Four: Feininger, Jawlensky, Kandinsky, Klee in the New World, 1997, Exiles and Emigre's, 1997, The Blue Four Collection at the Norton Simon Museum, 2002; contbg. author: Kandinsky in Paris: 1934-44, 1985, Exiles and Emigres: 1933-1945, 1997, The Joy of Color: The Merzbacher Collection, 1998, Mies in America, 2001, Die Bruche in Dresden, 2001. Fellow John Simon Guggenheim, 1990, Inst. Advanced Study, Princeton, 2003—04. Mem.: Coll. Art Assn. Am., Internat. Coun. Museums, Soc. Kandinsky (sec. 1992—2001). Office: Solomon R Guggenheim Mus 1071 5th Ave New York NY 10128-0112 E-mail: vbarnett@att.net.

BARNETTE, KIM BAILEY, counseling administrator; b. Homer, La., Dec. 13, 1961; d. Drew Bailey and Virginia G. Furlow; m. Roger D. Barnette, Nov. 20, 1991; 1 child, Taren Dusty. BS in Math. Sci., La. Tech. U., 1983, MA in Counseling, 1991, postgrad., 2001. Tchr. Minden (La.) HS, 1983—91; fin. aid off. Claiborne Vocat. Tech, Homer, La., 1991—97; asst. dean NW Tech. Coll., Minden, 1997—2002; dean of workforce devel. La. Cmty. Tech. Coll., Shreveport, La., 2002—03; state edn. specialist La. Dept. Pub. Safety Corrections, Baton Rouge, 2003—. Adj. prof. Centenary Coll., Shreveport, 2001—; state ACA auditor La. Dept of Pub. Safety, Baton Rouge, 1999—; notary State of La., 1992—. Author: Scholarships for Me, 1994. Edn. task force chair Claiborne Economic Devel., Homer, 2001—03; SPRE comm. La. Gov's Off., Baton Rouge, 1993—95; La. Work Ready Commn. La. Dept. Edn., 2003. Recipient TOYA, Jaycees, 1997. Mem.: Correctional Edn. Assoc. Methodist. Office: La Dept Pub Safety and Corrections 504 Mayflower Baton Rouge LA 70804 E-mail: kbarnett@oyd01.corrections.state.la.us.

BARNETT-STEWART, BARBARA ANNE, library catalog technician, writer; b. Delran, N.J., Nov. 19, 1975; d. Robert Arthur and Susan Marie Barnett; m. Robert Edward Stewart, Oct. 25, 2003. BA, U. of Md., 1999. Orch. mgmt. asst. Phila. Orch., 1999; devel. assoc. Opera Co. of Phila., 2000—02; libr. catalog technician Curtis Inst. of Music, Phila., 2003—. Freelance writer, database cons. Opera Co. of Phila., 2002—03. Contbr. articles and short stories to publs. Mem.: Sigma Alpha Iota (life; pres. Gamma Epsilon chpt. 1997—98, Sword of Honor 1999, Scholarship award 1999, Coll. Honor award 1998). Unitarian Universalist. Office: Curtis Inst Music 1726 Locust St Philadelphia PA 19103 Personal E-mail: babarnett@earthlink.net. E-mail: barbara.barnett@curtis.edu.

BARNEY, CAROL ROSS, architect; b. Chgo., Apr. 12, 1949; d. Chester Albert and Dorothy Valeria (Dusiewicz) Ross; m. Alan Fredrick Barney, Mar. 22, 1970; children: Ross Fredrick, Adam Shafer, John Ross. BArch, U. Ill., 1971. Registered architect, Ill. Assoc. architect Holabird & Root, Chgo., 1972-79; prin. architect Orput Assoc., Inc., Wilmette, Ill., 1979-81; prin. architect, pres. Ross Barney & Jankowski, Inc., Chgo., 1981—, also bd. dirs. Studio prof. Ill. Inst. Tech., Chgo., 1993-94; asst. prof. U. Ill., Chgo., 1976-78. Prin. works include Cesar Chavez Elem. Sch., Chgo., Glendale Heights (Ill.) Post Office, Little Village Acad. Pub. Sch., Fed. Campus, Oklahoma City. Plan commr. Village of Wilmette, 1986-88, mem. Econ. Devel. Commn., 1988-90, chmn. Appearance Rev. Commn., 1990-2000; trustee Children's Home and Aid Soc. Ill., Chgo., 1986—; mem. adv. bd. Small Bus. Ctr. for Women, Chgo., 1985—. Recipient Fed. Design Achievement award, 1992, Firm award AIA Chgo., 1995; Francis J. Plym travelling fellow, 1983. Fellow AIA (bd. dirs. Chgo. chpt. 1978-80, v.p. 1981-82, Disting. Svc. award Chgo. chpt. 1978, Ill. Coun. 1978, Honor award 1991, 94, 99, 2002); mem. Nat. Coun. Archtl. Registration Bds. (cert.), Chgo. Women in Architecture (founding pres. 1978-79), Chgo. Network, Cliff Dwellers Club (bd. dirs. 1995). Home: 601 Linden Ave Wilmette IL 60091-2819 Office: Ross Barney & Jankowski Inc 10 Hubbard St Chicago IL 60610 E-mail: crossbarney@rbjarchitects.com.

BARNEY, CHRISTINE J. artist; b. Bath, NY, Sept. 9, 1952; d. Willis H. and Elsa P. (Heney) Barney. BA, Goddard Coll., 1975; MA, NYU, 1988. Proprietor, designer, craftsperson Laurel Mountain Glass, Bosswell, Pa., 1975-83; tchg./tech. asst. Alfred (N.Y.) U., 1983-85; freelance designer Seguso Arte Vetro, Murano, Venice, Italy, 1985-87. Artist-in-residence Golden Glass Studio and Sch., Cin., 1991—92; guest artist Artpark, Lewiston, NY, 1992, Lewiston, 94; vis. artist Ohio State U., 1992, Tyler Sch. Art, Phila., 1993; lectr. in field. One-woman shows include Kavesh Gallery, Sun Valley, Kethun, Idaho, 1991, Christy/Taylor Gallery, Boca Raton, Fla., 1990—92, Vespermann Gallery, Atlanta, 1994, Portia Gallery, Chgo., 1997, 1997, Glass Gallery, Bethesda, Md., 2000, Art Elements Gallery, Milw., 2001, exhibited in group shows at Traver-Sutton Gallery, Seattle, 1982, So. Alleghenies Mus. Art, Loretto, Pa., 1983, Querini Stampaglia Gallery, Venice, 1984, U. di Architettura de Venezia, 1985, 80 Washington Sq. East Galleries, N.Y.C., 1988, Spaso Ho., Am. Embassy, Moscow, 1988—89, Grohe Gallery, Boston, 1989, 1995, Newark Mus., 1989, Sotheby's, N.Y.C., 1990, N.J. Ctr. Visual Arts, 1990, Morris Mus., Morristown, N.J., 1991, 1997, Mus. Am. Glass, Millville, N.J., 1993, Gallery at Wheaton Village, Millville, 1994, S. Shore Art Ctr., Cohasset, Mass., 1996, Holsten Gallery, Stockbridge, Mass., 1999—2001, Morgan Glass Gallery, Pitts., 2001, Yates County Arts Ctr., NY, 2002, Oxford Gallery, Rochester, 2002, Eleven Eleven Sculpture Space, Washington, 2003, Represented in permanent collections Corning Mus. Glass, Mus. Am. Glass, Millville, Tropicana Products, Inc., Bradenton, Fla., Centeon Pharm., King of Prussia, Pa.; contbr. articles to profl. jours. Creator Arts in Achievement awards Middlesex County Cultural and Heritage Commn., 1990—94; creator Artpark award, 1993. Recipient Carnegie Inst. prize, 1981; Creative Glass Ctr. Am. fellow, 1988, 1996, N.J. State Coun. Arts fellow, 1989—90. Avocation: dance. Home: 432 Monmouth St Jersey City NJ 07302-2326

BARNEY, LINDA SUSAN, manufacturing specialist; b. Latrobe, Pa., Mar. 31, 1948; d. William Kramer and Kathryn (Voytilla) B. BS in Edn., Ind. U. of Pa., 1970; BBA, Tampa (Fla.) Coll., 1983; MBA, Fla. Met. U., Tampa, 1996. Tchr. Greater Latrobe (Pa.) Sch. Dist., 1970-81; from staff acct. to acctg. supr. Systems and Simulation, Tampa, Fla., 1986-89; project acct. Olin Ordnance, St. Petersburg, Fla., 1989-96; mfg. specialist BIC Spl. Mkts. Divsn., Clearwater, Fla., 1997-98; cost acctg. mgr. HIT Promotional Products, Largo, Fla., 1998—. Recipient Small Bus. award, 1993. Mem. NAFE, AAUW, Internat. Platform Assn., Women's Inner Cir. of Achievement, Am. Biographical Inst. (dep. gov.). Democrat. Lutheran. Avocations: travel, golf, hiking, studies. Home: 3735 Darlington Rd Holiday FL 34691-3438

BARNHART, JO ANNE B. federal agency administrator; b. Memphis, Aug. 26, 1950; d. Nelson Alexander and Betty Jane (Fitzpatrick) Bryant; m. David Lee Ross, Feb. 14, 1976 (div. June 1983); m. David Ray Barnhart, May 24, 1986. Student, U. Tenn., 1968—70; BA, U. Del., 1975. Space and time buyer DeMartin-Marona & Assocs., Wilmington, Del., 1970—73; adminstrv. asst. Mental Health Assn., Wilmington, 1973—75; dir. SERVE nutrition program Wilmington Sr. Ctr., 1975—77; legis. asst. to Sen. William V. Roth, Jr., Washington, 1977—81; dep. assoc. commr. Office Family Assistance, HHS, Washington, 1981—83, assoc. commr., 1983—86; rep. staff dir. U.S. Senate Govt. Affairs Com., 1987—90; asst. sec. family support HHS, Washington, 1990—91, asst. sec. for children and families, 1991—92; staff U.S. Sen. William V. Roth, 1993—; comnr. Social Security Admin., Baltimore, Md., 2001—. Mem. adv. bd. on welfare indicators U.S. Dept. HHS, 1996—. Campaign mgr. U. S. Sen. William V. Roth, 1988, 1994; polit. dir. Nat. Rep. Senatorial Com., 1995—97, polit. and pub. policy cons., 1997—2001; mem. Social Security adv. bd., 1997—2001; commr. Social Security, 2001—. Republican. Methodist. Office: Social Security Admin Office of Commr Altmeyer Bldg 6401 Security Blvd Baltimore MD 21235-6401 Office Phone: 202-358-6000.

BARNHART, NIKKI LYNN CLARK, elementary school educator; b. Terre Haute, Ind., Mar. 14, 1940; d. Wilbur Ellis and Margaret Jane (Cork) Clark; m. James Walter Barnhart; children: Tracey Lynn, Kelly Jean, Darby Jane, Holly Anne. BEd, Shippensburg U., 1961, MEd, 1964; cert. reading specialist, Western Md. U., 1979; EdD, U. Md., 1984. Cert. elem. tchr., English tchr., guidance counselor, Pa.; cert. Reading Recovery. Tchr. Chambersburg (Pa.) Schs., 1961-62, Spring Grove (Pa.) Area Schs., 1963-66, Hanover (Pa.) Pub. Schs., 1967-2000. Presenter profl. conf. and convs. Author: Hanover through History, 1976. Mem. Hanover Borough Coun., 1993—; consistory mem. Emmanuel Ch., Hanover, 1984-92. Chpt. I parent mini-grantee Pa. Dept. Edn., 1996; recipient Outstanding Elem. Educator award Phi Delta Theta, 1999. Mem. Internat. Reading Assn. (exemplary program award for bldg. 1997), South Ctrl. Reading Coun. (various offices, Celebrate Literacy award 1996), Delta Kappa Gamma (Eta chpt., Alpha Alpha State Golden Anniversary award 1980, Alpha Alpha State Founder's award 1982). Republican. Mem. United Ch. of Christ. Avocations: reading, cooking. Office: Clearview Sch 100 W Clearview Rd Hanover PA 17331-1615

BARNHILL, WENDY RENEE, music educator; b. Waycross, Ga., July 28, 1973; d. Jack Wade Barnhill and Julia Ann Jacobs, Ray Ellis Jacobs (Stepfather). MusB in Edn., Valdosta State U., 1995. Band dir. Risley Mid. Sch., Brunswick, Ga., 1995—; asst. band dir. Glynn Acad., Brunswick, Ga., 1999—. Mem.: Women Band Dirs. Internat., Music Educators Nat. Conf., Ga. Music Educators Assn., Tau Beta Sigma, Sigma Alpha Iota. Personal E-mail: wbarnhill@hotmail.com.

BARNICK, HELEN, retired judicial clerk; b. Max, ND, Mar. 24, 1925; d. John K. and Stacy (Kankovsky) B. BS in Music cum laude, Minot State Coll., 1954; postgrad., Am. Conservatory of Music, Chgo., 1975-76. With Epton, Bohling & Druth, Chgo., 1968-69; sec. Wildman, Harrold, Allen & Dixon, Chgo., 1969-75; part-time assignments for temporary agy. Chgo., 1975-77; sec. Friedman & Koven, Chgo., 1977-78; with Lawrence, Lawrence, Kamin & Saunders, Chgo., 1978-81; sec. Hinshaw, Culbertson et al., Chgo., 1982; cert. to magistrate judge U.S. Dist. Ct. (we. dist.) Wis., Madison, 1985-91; dep. clk., case adminstr. U.S. Bankruptcy Ct. (we. dist.)

Wis., Madison, 1992-94; ret., 1994. Chancel choir 1st Bapt. Ch., Mpls., Fourth Presbyn. Ch., Chgo., Covenant Presbyn. Ch., Madison; choir, dir. sr. high choir Moody Ch., Chgo.; dir. chancel choir 1st Bapt. Ch., Minot, ND; bd. dirs., sec.-treas. Peppertree at Tamarack Owners Assn., Inc., Wisconsin Dells, Wis.; mem. Festival Choir, Madison. Mem. Christian Bus. and Profl. Women (chmn.). Bus. and Profl. Women Assn., Madison Symphony Orch. League, Madison Civics Club, Sigma Sigma Sigma. Home: 7364 Old Sauk Rd Madison WI 53717-1213

BARNUM, BARBARA STEVENS, writer, retired nursing educator; b. Johnstown, Pa., Sept. 2, 1937; d. William C. and Freda Inzes (Claycomb) Burkett; m. H. James Barnum (dec.); children: Lauren, Elizabeth, Catherine, Anne (dec.), Shauna, Sallee, David. AA in Nursing, St. Petersburg Jr. Coll., 1958; BPh, Northwestern U., 1967; MA, DePaul U., 1971; PhD, U. Chgo., 1976. RN, Ill., N.Y. dir. nursing svcs. Augustana Hosp. and Health Care Ctr., Chgo., 1970-71; dir. staff edn. U. Chgo. Hosps. and Clinics, 1971-73; prof. U. Ill., Chgo., 1973-79; dir. div. health svcs., sci. and edn. Columbia U. Tchrs. Coll., N.Y.C., 1979-87; editor Nursing & Health Care Nat. League for Nursing, N.Y.C., 1989-91; editor div. nursing Columbia-Presbyn. Med. Ctr., Columbia U., N.Y.C., 1991-95; prof. Sch. Nursing Columbia U., N.Y.C., 1995-98; ret., 1998. Chmn. bd. Barnum & Souza, N.Y.C., 1989-92; civilian cons. to surgeon gen. USAF, 1980-87. Author: Nursing Theory, Analysis, Application and Evaluation, 4th edit., 1994, Writing for Publication: A Primer for Nurses, 1995; author: (with K. Kerfoot) The Nurse as Executive, 4th edit., 1995; author: Spirituality and Nursing: From Traditional to New Age, 1996, 2d edit., 2003, Teaching Nursing in the Era of Managed Care, 1999, The New Healers: Minds and Hands in Complementary Medicine, 2002, (fiction) The Haunting of Lisa Tilden, 1999; editor: Nursing Leadership Forum, 1994—98. Mem. governing bd. Nurses House, 1979-86, Nat. Health Coun., 1981-90, others. Fellow Am. Acad. Nursing (governing bd. 1982-84); mem. Sigma Theta Tau (Founders' award 1979). Home: 80 Park Ave Apt 15G New York NY 10016-2547

BARNUM, MARY ANN MOOK, information management manager; b. Arlington, Va., Apr. 3, 1946; d. Conrad Payne and Barbara Heer (Held) Mook; m. William Douglas Barnum, Aug. 10, 1968. BS in Math., Radford U., 1967. Cert. tchr., Va., N.J., N.Mex. Math. tchr. Prince William County Schs., Woodbridge, Va., 1967-68; mathematician RCA Svc. Co., Andros Island, Bahamas, 1968-70; math. tchr. Cinnaminson (N.J.) Schs., 1970-73, Alamogordo (N.Mex.) Sch. System, 1973-74; data svcs. supr. A.M. Best Co., Oldwick, N.J., 1975-78; assoc. mgr. AT&T Communications, Piscataway, N.J., 1978-86; mgr. AT&T Info. Mgmt. Svcs., Piscataway, N.J., 1986-90, AT&T Bus. Comm. Svcs., Somerset, N.J., 1990-91; mem. tech. staff AT&T Network Systems, Berkeley Heights, N.J., 1991-95, Lucent Techs., Warren, N.J., 1995-96, mgr. AT&T, Morristown, NJ, 1996—98; retired. Sec. Cherry Hill (N.J.) Jaycettes, 1972-73; trustee Friends of Clarence Dillon Libr., Bedminster, N.J., sec., 1989-90, pres., 1990-92, mem., 1986-2000; mem. Far Hills Environ. Commn., 1990-92, chmn., 1992-94; mem. Far Hills Planning Bd., 1994-2000, Wildewood Women's Club, 2000-, Computer Group, 2001-, Wildewood Garden Club, 2000-; mem. Symphony League, Columbia, SC, 2001-. Mem. IEEE, Assn. Computing Machinery, Am. Soc. Quality Control, DAR, Descendants of Washington's Army at Valley Forge (capt. of the guard 1988-90, dep. adjutant gen. 1990-92, adjutant gen. 1992-96), Soc. Descs. of the Mayflower, Kappa Delta Pi. Presbyterian. Home: PO Box 23329 Columbia SC 14714

BAROLINI, HELEN, writer, translator, educator; b. Syracuse, N.Y., Nov. 18, 1925; m. Antonio Barolini, Nov. 8, 1950 (dec.); children: Teodolinda, Susanna, Nicoletta. AB magna cum laude, Syracuse U., 1947; MLS, Columbia U., 1959. Lectr. Pace U., Pleasantville, N.Y., 1990—. Lectr., Padua, Italy, Westchester CC, Valhalla, NY, 1988; writer-in-residence Quarry Farm, Elmira Coll., 1989; resident scholar Rockefeller Found.'s Bellagio Study Ctr., Lake Como, Italy, 1991; vis. artist Am. Acad. Rome, 2001. Author: Umbertina, 1979, 1999, The Dream Book, 1985, 2000, Love in the Middle Ages, 1986, Festa, 1988, 2002, Aldus and His Dream Book, 1991, Chiaroscuro, 1999, More Italian Hours, and Other Stories, 2001, Rome Burning, 2000; co-author: Literary Olympian II, Short Story International 32, Love Stories by New Women; contbr. stories to jours.; scholar-cons., advisor . (films) Tarantella. Recipient MELUS 2000 Lifetime Achievement award, Soc. for Study of Multi-Ethnic Lit. of U.S., 2000, Susan Koppelman award, Am. Culture Assn., 1987, Am. Book award, 1986, Marina-Velca Journalism prize, Italy, 1970, Sons of Italy Lit. Award, 2003; fellow, MacDowell Colony, 1974; grantee, Nat. Endowment for Arts, 1976. Mem.: Hudson Valley River Writers Assn., Authors Guild, PEN Am. Ctr., Phi Beta Kappa. Home and Office: 86 Maple Ave Hastings On Hudson NY 10706 E-mail: helenbarolini@juno.com.

BAROLINI, TEODOLINDA, literary critic; b. Syracuse, N.Y., Dec. 19, 1951; d. Antonio and Helen (Mollica) B.; m. Douglas Gardner Caverly, June 21, 1980 (dec. Nov. 1993); 1 child: William Douglas; m. James J. Valentini, Feb. 10, 2001. BA, Sarah Lawrence Coll., 1972; MA, Columbia U., 1973, PhD, 1978. Asst. prof. Italian U. Calif., Berkeley, 1978-83; assoc. prof. Italian NYU, 1983-89; prof., 1989-92; chmn. dept. Italian Columbia U., N.Y.C., 2002—2004, Lorenzo Da Ponte prof. Italian, 1999—. Author: Dante's Poets, 1984 (Howard R. Marraro prize MLA 1986, John Nicholas Brown prize Medieval Acad. Am. 1988, transl. into Italian as Il miglior fabbro 1993), The Undivine Comedy, 1992, transl. into Italian as La Commedia senza Dio, 2003; editor (with H.W. Storey) Dante for the New Millennium, 2003; contbr. articles to profl. jours. AAUW fellow, 1977, ACLS fellow, 1981, NEH fellow, 1986, Guggenheim fellow, 1998. Fellow Medieval Acad. Am., Am. Acad. Arts and Scis., Am. Philos. Soc.; mem. MLA, Dante Soc. Am. (v.p. 1983-86, 91-94, 95-97, pres. 1997-2003), Renaissance Soc. Am. Office: Columbia U Dept Italian 510 Hamilton Hall New York NY 10027

BARON, JENNIFER LYNNE, museum education director; b. Neptune, N.J., July 26, 1969; d. Joseph Michael Baron and Merrell Lee Schweers. BA in Art History and English Lit. cum laude, Mount Holyoke Coll., 1992; postgrad., York (Eng.) U., 1990. Mus. tchg. intern Bklyn. Mus. Art, 1991—92, edn. intern, 1992—93, mus. educator, 1993—2000; curatorial asst. Mount Holyoke Coll. Art Mus., South Hadley, Mass., 1991—92; edn. dir. Mattress Factory Mus., Pitts., 2001—. Disc jockey WMHC, South Hadley, Mass., 1990—92; acad. advisor Mount Holyoke Coll., South Hadley, 1990—92; edn. coord. Dahesh Mus. Art, N.Y.C., 1998—2001; art edn. cons., N.Y.C., 1998—2001; part-time edn. cons., N.Y.C., 1998—2001; mem. mktg. com. Mattress Factory Mus. Pitts., 2001—, mem. strategic planning com., 2001—; founder, owner Fresh Popcorn Prodns., 2004. Editor: Arsis Lit. and Creative Arts Jour., 1991—92; author, editor: Family Guide to James Turrell: Into the Light, 2002, contbg. writer: Mus. Mag., 1999—2001, songwriter, performer: albums The Ladybug Transistor, 1999, Albemarle Sound and Argyle Heir, 2001; editor: The Pittsburgh Signs Project, 2004. Mem. band New Alcindors, Pitts., 2002—; cmty. ptnr. Sprout Fund Pub. Art Program, Pitts., 2003; campaign vol. Nader/Laduke, Bklyn., 2000. Mem.: Western Pa. Mus. Coun., Pitts. Resources Mus. Edn., Nat. Art Edn. Assn., Future Tenant Gallery (mem. adv. bd. 2003—), Taburitza Assn. Am., Mount Holyoke Coll. Alumnae Assn., Ground Zero Action Network, Mount Holyoke Coll. Club Pitts. (admissions rep. 2003). Democrat. Avocations: music, photography, travel, swimming, reading.

BARON, SHERI, advertising agency executive; b. Bklyn., Sept. 3, 1955; d. Irwin Murray Glaser and Rosalind (Mendelson) Krasik; m. Peter T. Colonel, Sept. 20, 1981 (dec.); m. Alan R. Baron, Dec. 14, 1996. BA in Psychology, SUNY, Cortland, 1977. Account exec. Ted Bates Co., N.Y.C., 1978-80, SSC&B Advt. (name now Lowe), N.Y.C., 1980-82, v.p. acct. supr., 1983-84, sr. v.p. mgmt. supr., 1984-88, exec. v.p., 1988-94, bd. dirs.,

1990-94; pres. Gotham Inc., 1994—. Named to Am. Advt. Fedn. Hall of Achievement, 1993, 40 Under 40 List, Crain's N.Y. bus., 1994. Mem. Advt. Women N.Y., Cosmetic Exec. Women, Fashion Group Internat. Home: 11 W 20th St New York NY 10011-3704 Office: Gotham Inc 100 5th Ave Fl 16 New York NY 10011-6996 Business E-Mail: sherib@gothaminc.com.

BARONE, ANGELA MARIA, artist, researcher; b. Concesio, Brescia, Italy, June 29, 1957; arrived in U.S., 1983; d. Giuseppe and Adelmina (D'Ercole) Barone. Laurea cum laude in geol. scis., U. Bologna, Italy, 1981; PhD in Marine Geology, Columbia U., 1989; cert. in profl. photography, N.Y. Inst. Photography, 1992; cert. in fine art painting and drawing, N. Light Art Sch., Cin., 1993. Collaborative asst. Marine Geology Inst., Bologna, 1981-83, Inst. Geology and Paleontology, Florence, Italy, 1982-83, Sta. de Geodynamique, Villefranche, France, 1982; grad. rsch. asst. Lamont-Doherty Geol. Obs., Palisades, N.Y., 1983-89, postdoctoral rsch. asst., 1989; postgrad. rschr. Scripps Instn. of Oceanography, La Jolla, Calif., 1990-92; artist San Diego, 1993—. Contbr. articles to profl. jours. Mem.: Am. Geophys. Union (co-pres. meeting session 1990), Nat. Mus. Women Arts (assoc.). Home: 7540 Charmant Dr Apt 1222 San Diego CA 92122-5044

BARONE, KERRI LYNN, music educator; b. Landstuhl, Germany, Feb. 14, 1980; d. Joseph Leonard and Linda Ellen Barone. B, Ithaca (N.Y.) Coll., 2002. Cert. K-12 music edn. N.Y., 2002, Md., 2002. Tchr., string instrumental music Charles County Pub. Sch., Indian Head, Md., 2002—03, Fairfax County Pub. Schs., Fairfax County, Va., 2003—. Co-condr. Charles County Elem. All-County Orch., Charles County, Md., 2003; adminstrv. intern Brookhaven (N.Y.) Youth and Arts Orgn., 2001. Contbr. articles to profl. jours. Mem.: Am. String Teachers Assn., Music Educators Nat. Conf. Independent. Avocations: double bass, Italian.

BARONE, ROSE MARIE PACE, writer, retired educator, entertainer; b. Buffalo, Apr. 26, 1920; d. Dominic and Jennie (Zagara) Pace; m. John Barone, Aug. 23, 1947 BA, U. Buffalo, 1943; MS, U. So. Cal., 1950; cert. advanced study, Fairfield (Conn.) U., 1963. Tchr. Angola (N.Y.) High Sch., 1943-46, Puente (Calif.) High Sch., 1946-47, Jefferson High Sch., Lafayette, Ind., 1947-50; dir. Warren Inst., Bridgeport, Conn., 1951-53; instr. U. Bridgeport, 1953-54; tchr. bus. subjects Bassick H.S., Bridgeport, 1954-74, Harding H.S., Bridgeport, 1974-80; instr. Fairfield U., Conn., 1969; freelance writer, 1980—. Chair State Poetry Festival, 1987. Founder Pet Rescue; chmn. comty. affairs com. Area Coun. Cath. Women, 1988-90, sec., 1990-91, chmn. family affairs com., 1991, v.p., 1992-93; chmn. comty. affairs Ch. Women United, 1992—, state area chmn., 1995-97, sec., 2003, state UN chair, 1997—. Pace-Barone Minority yearly scholarship Fairfield U., Auerbach Found. scholar, 1956; recipient Playwriting prize Conn. Federated Women's Clubs, 1955, 1st prize for poetry, 1985, Short Story award Federated Women Conn., 1987, 88, 90, Citizen award Bridgeport Dental Assn., 1982, State/Town Hero award, 1986, Anniversary medal and marble statuette Fairfield U., Cnty. Care Successful Aging award, 1992, Salute to Women award YWCA, 1993, Woman of Substance award, 1994, State Commission Arts award, 2000, RSVP award, 2001. Mem. NEA, AAUW (treas. 1957-58, named gift grant 1989, cultural and poetry chair 1992—, rec. sec. 1992-93, internat. rels. 1993-94, v.p. program 1995-97, contest chair 1995—, Conf. of Women award 1997, Fairfield Citizen, Vol. Extraordinaire, 2001), Am. Assn. Ret. People (v.p. 1987-88, pres. 1988-89, 94-95, instr. 85 Alive, cmty. affairs chair 1990—), Owl (sec. 1987-89, pres. 1989-90), Nat. League Am. PEN Women (Bridgeport historian 1966-84, state historian 1985—, treas. bd. 1988-90, auth. book 1994-95, hist. of arts 1988-95, br. membership chair 1990, Nat. Historian award 1976, 88), Fairfield Area Poets (founder, pres. 1960—, editor 5 vols. Conn. poets), UN Assn. USA (pres. Bridgeport 1964-66, 68-70, v.p. 1988—, chmn. area UN Days 1960—, pres. Conn. 1971—, state chmn. UNICEF to 1984, area UNICEF Ctr. 1984—, state historian 1984—, chair Internat. Kite Fly), Conn. Bus. Tchrs., Bridgeport Edn. Assn. (sec. 1966-68), VFW (aux. 1989—), Am. Legion (aux. contest chair 1989—, historian 1993-95, Aux. Nat. Cmty. Svc. award 1993), Fairfield Arts Coun., Fairfield Philatelic Soc. (sec. 1977-78, founder advisor Philatelic Jrs. 1972-80), Fairfield U. Women's Club (founder, pres. 1950, 74—, v.p. 1973-74), Southport Women's Club (garden dept. sec. 1981-85, chmn. 1985-87), John & Rose Marie Barone Resource Ctr. St. Vincent's Coll., Pi Omega Pi. Home: 1283 Round Hill Rd Fairfield CT 06430-7329

BARON-MALKIN, PHYLLIS, artist, art educator; b. Newark, Apr. 15, 1927; d. Jack and Sadie Green; m. Milton Malkin (div.); m. Murray Baron; children: Kim, Robin, Jacki, Dara. Student, Culinary Sch. N.Y., 1947, Nat. Acad. Design, N.Y.C., 1971—76, Sch. Interior Design, Miami, Fla., 1978. Prin., owner Dade County Taxi, 1961—78, Jewelers, Ft. Lauderdale, Fla. Exhibited in group shows at Internat. Fine Arts Exhibit, Calif., Nat. Acad. Design, Newark Pub. Libr., Lever House, N.Y., Bernardsville State Show, Salmagundi Club, Nat. Arts Club, Miniature Show N.J., Catherine Larriland Wolfe Club, N.Y., Coun. Jewish Women, Teaneck, N.J., Greenwich Village, N.J. State Show, East Orange, Audonbon Show, Newark Mus., Jersey City Mus., one-woman shows include South Orange Gallery, N.J., Originique Gallery, Korby Gallery, Bloomfield Gallery, Delaney Gallery, Ft. Lauderdale, Tattum Gallery. Apptd. Broward County Art Coun.; mem. arts counsel Broward County, 1974. With USAF, 1945—46. Mem.: Nat. Pastel Soc. (selected to form organization). Democrat. Home: 7042 Golf Pointe Cir Tamarac FL 33321

BARR, ANN HELEN, director; d. John Roger and Hester Ann (Davis) Barr. B in Music Edn., Coll. Wooster, 1964; MA in Music Edn., UCLA, 1972. Tchr. music Huber Heights (Ohio) Schs., 1964—67; reconciliation specialist Merrill Lynch Pierce, Fenner & Smith, LA, 1968—72; tchr. Dayton (Ohio) Pub. Sch., 1978—98; flight dir. Challenger Learning Ctr., Dayton, 1998—2000, lead flight dir., 2000—. Hunger fund chair Westminster Presbyn. Ch., Dayton, 1984—. Kettering Found. grantee, 1983, Electronic Data Sys. grantee, 1999. Mem.: Civil Air Patrol, White Shrine of Jerusalem (worthy high priestess 1984). Avocations: gardening, travel, quilting, bridge, softball. Office: Challenger Learning Ctr 1401 Leo St Dayton OH 45404 Office Phone: 937-547-6196.

BARR, EMILY L. television station executive; BA in Film Studies, Carleton Coll., 1980; MBA in Mktg., George Washington U., 1986. News editor KSTP-TV, St. Paul, Minn., 1980-81, news promotion specialist 1981-82; writer, prodr. WJLA-TV, Washington, 1983-85; advtg. & promotion mgr. KHOU-TV, Houston, 1985-87, dir. creative svcs., 1987-88; dir. broadcast ops. WMAR-TV, Balt., 1988-93, acting gen. mgr., 1993, asst. gen. mgr., 1993-94; pres., gen. mgr. Sta. WTVD, Raleigh, N.C., 1994-97, Sta. WLS-TV, Chgo., 1997—. Grad. leadership program Greater Balt. Com., 1990; active NAPTE, 1988—, BPME, 1983-93, CBS Promotion Caucus, 1987-88. Vol. Mus. Broadcast Comms.; bd. dirs. United Cerebral Palsy-Chgo., Children's Meml. Hosp. Found.; commr. Chgo. State St. Commn. Recipient Dante award Joint Civic com. for Italian Americans, 1998. Mem. Ill. Broadcast Assn., Chgo./Midwest TV Acad., Chgo. C. of C. (bd. dirs.), Chgo. Cen. Area Com. (bd. dirs.). Office: 190 N State St Chicago IL 60601-3302

BARR, LOIS I. personnel administrator; b. Olympia, Wash., Feb. 8, 1949; d. Jacob Hatfield Barr and Irene Tourangeau; m. Steven Gottlieb Huber, May 1, 1966 (div. July 1976); children: Heidi Irene Pettenger, Hyrum H. Huber. BA, Pacific Western U., 1980, MBA, 1981, Stanford U., 1981. Newspaper statistics reporter Fairfield (Calif.) Daily Republic, 1972-73; pers. adminstr. Intel Corp., Livermore, Calif., 1978-81; massage therapist 4 Doctors, Aurora, Colo., 1984-85; jewelry buyer CVJ, Minden, Nev., 1992; vol. coord. Sierra Recovery, Gardnerville, Nev., 1993-95; grant writer URS Ch., Carson City, Nev., 1999—; vol. tchr. AARP Guardianship, Carson City, 1999—. Author: Caregiving and Guardianship for Seniors in Nevada, 2001;

author numerous poems. Vol., v.p. Nev. Network Against Domestic Violence, Reno; bd. dirs. Sunflower Ministry. Named Poet of Yr., Nat. Libr. Congress, Washington, 1989. Mem. Humane Soc. Democrat. Avocations: writing poetry, movie critic. Home and Office: PO Box 691 5LT Ca South Lake Tahoe CA 96156

BARR, MARLENE JOY, volunteer; b. Grosse Pointe Farms, Mich., Feb. 25, 1935; d. Max John and Viola Christina (Funke) Bielenberg; m. John Monte Barr, Dec. 17, 1954; children: John Monte Jr., Karl Alexander, Elizabeth Marie Letter. Student, Mex. City Coll., 1955; BA, Mich. State U., 1956; MA, Ea. Mich. U., 1959. Cert. elem. tchr. Tchr. A.G. Erickson Sch., Ypsilanti, Mich., 1956-66; chair 5th grade tchrs., sec. curriculum coun. Ypsilanti Pub. Schs., 1961-66; receptionist Barr, Anhut, and Assoc., P.C., Ann Arbor, Mich., 1989-95; vol. Thrift Shop Assn. of Ypsilanti, 1969—; block coord. Ypsilanti Recycling, 1990—. Mem. Fletcher Sch. Adv. Coun., 1980—81; v.p. Thrift Shop Assn., Ypsilanti, 1979—81, pres., 1981—83, 2002, scheduling chmn., 1993—96, chmn. nominating com., 1998, 1999; asst. leader Girl Scouts U.S., 1978—81; sec. troop 290 Boy Scouts Am., 1989—95, treas., 2000—; rm. mother Fletcher Elem. Sch., Ypsilanti, 1982—83; mem. chancel choir Emmanuel Luth. Ch., 1980—96, 1998—, youth coord., 1983—89, sec. youth standing com., 1983—89, ch. coun., 1986—90, sec. endowment com., 1995—96, chmn. ch. nominating com., 1999—2000; bd. dirs. Ypsilanti Cmty. Choir, 1984—; mem. High/Scope Ednl. Rsch. Fedn. Endowment Bd., 1993—96. Mem.: AAUW (life; chmn. gourmet arts study group 1968—), Ann Arbor Power Squadron of U.S. Power Squadron, Geneal. Soc. Wash. County, Law Wives of Washtenaw County (editor 1970—72), P.E.O. (chaplain 1991—93, chpt. pres. 1997—99, chmn. program com. 2000—01, treas. 2001—03, chmn. program com. 2004—), Depot Town Assn., Ypsilanti Hist. Soc. (life), Marquette County Hist. Soc. (life), Friends of the Ypsilanti Dist. Libr., Ann Arbor Bike Touring Soc. (co-chair One Hell of a Ride 1995), Chandler Birthday Club (treas. 1990), Ladies Lit. Club (corr. sec. 1976—78, sec. bd. trustees 1982—86, v.p. 1986—90, pres. 1990—92, treas. bd. trustees 1992—97), Ann Arbor Women's City Club (life; chmn. ways and means com. 1995—97, chmn. Home Tour 1996, 1997, asst. membership chmn. 1998—99, chmn. membership com. 1999—2002, nominating com. 1999—2002, chmn. Home Tour 2001), Alpha Delta Kappa (pres. Beta Zeta chpt. 1965—68, pres. Area X Pres. Coun. Mich. chpt. 1966—68, historian 1986—88, chmn. ways and means com. 1999—96, co-historian 2002—04), Lutheran. Avocations: skiing (7th in 50-59 age group Mich. divsn. NASTAR 1993), biking, hiking, boating, guiding youth ski trips.

BARR, M.E. See BIGELOW, MARGARET ELIZABETH BARR

BARR, ROSEANNE See ROSEANNE

BARRACLOUGH, MARY JANE, music educator; b. Oklahoma City, Dec. 20, 1949; d. Jesse Clarence and Nettie Mae (Wallace) Beal; m. Carl Stanley Barraclough, June 22, 1974; children: James Wallace, Charles Stanley. B in Music Edn., U. Mo., Kansas City, 1973. Vocal music instr. Ponca City (Okla.) Pub. Schs., 1973—. Den leader, instr. Boy Scouts Am., 1990—2003; mem., soloist Civic Chorus, Ponca City, 1980—95; soloist, musical dir. Ponca Playhouse Theater Prodns., 1984—95; vocal soloist local groups and chs.; bd. mem. Cmty. Concert Assn., Ponca City, Okla., 1980. Recipient Young Career award, Bus. and Profl. Women, 1976—77. Mem.: NEA, Music Educators Nat. Conf., Okla. Edn. Assn., Am. Guild Organists and Choir Dirs. (dean), Kappa Kappa Iota (local pres., state music chmn.). Baptist. Avocations: needlework, reading, music, travel. Home: 3000 Canterbury Ave Ponca City OK 74604

BARRAGÁN, CELIA SILGUERO, elementary school educator; b. Corcoran, Calif., Feb. 4, 1955; d. Frutoso Silguero and Olinda Gonzalez S.; m. Mario Barragán Jr., Nov. 12, 1977; children: Maricela Aimé, Mario Armando. BS, S.W. Tex. State U., 1976, MA, 1977. 3rd grade tchr. Crockett Elem. Sch., San Marcos, Tex., 1977—78, Bowie Elem. Sch., San Marcos, 1978—84; 5th grade tchr. Travis Elem. Sch., San Marcos, 1984—94, Hernandez Intermediate Sch., San Marcos, 1994—99; asst. prin., bilingual coord. Bonham Elem. Sch., San Marcos, 1985—86, title I reading tchr., trainer, cons., 1995—99; coord., trainer AVID Miller Jr. H.S., San Marcos, Tex., 1999—2000; ESL/Dyslexia tchr. Miller Jr. High, 2000—01; ESL/dyslexia tchr. Goodnight Jr. H.S., 2001—. Winter High ability program tchr. S.W. Tex. State U.; project math trainer, migrant tchr., Princeville, Ill.; cons., nat. trainer Lang. Cir. Project Read, Minn. Recipient Latino award for cmty. recognition S.W. Tex. State U. Mem. Internat. Reading Assn., Tex. Reading Assn., Tex. State Tchrs. Assn., Tex. Assn. Bilingual Edn., Tex. Classroom Tchrs. Assn., San Marcos (Tex.) Assn. Bilingual Edn., Tchr. of Yr. 1990-91, 94—, pres. 1995—, Bilingual Tchr. of Yr. 1991, Travis Elem. Tchr. of Yr. 1993, Hernandez Intermediate Tchr. of Yr. 1995, Secondary Tchr. of Yr. 1995), Orton Dyslexia Soc., Nat. Coun. Tchrs. Math., Tex. Assn. Bilingual Educators, Ill. Migrant Edn. Assn., Tex. Assn. Gifted and Talented, N.J. Writing Project, Assn. Comprehensive Edn. in Tex. Roman Catholic. Home: 1763 Loma Verde Dr New Braunfels TX 78130-1297 Office: Goodnight Jr H S 1805 Peter Garza Dr San Marcos TX 78666-5062 Business E-Mail: celia.barragan@san-marcos.isd.tenet.edu.

BARRANGER, MILLY SLATER, theater educator, writer; b. Birmingham, Ala., Feb. 12, 1937; d. C. C. Slater and Mildred (Hilliard) Hinson; m. G. K. Barranger, 1961 (div. 1984); 1 child, Heather Dalton Barranger Case. BA, U. Montevallo, 1958; MA, Tulane U., 1959, PhD, 1964. Lectr. La. State U., New Orleans, 1964-69; asst. to assoc. prof. Tulane U., New Orleans, 1969-82, chmn. dept. theatre, 1971-82, Alumni disting. prof., 1997—2003, Alumni disting. prof. emerita, 2003—; prof. U. N.C., Chapel Hill, 1982—2003, chmn. dramatic art, 1982-99; producing dir. PlayMakers Repertory Co., Chapel Hill, 1982-99. Pres. Am. Theatre Assn., 1978-79; disting. vis. assoc. prof. U. Tulsa, 1981; vis. young prof. in humanities U. Tenn., Knoxville, 1981-82; scholar-in-residence Yale Sch. Drama, New Haven, Conn., 1982. Author: Theatre: A Way of Seeing, 1980, 1986, 1991, 1995, 2001, Theatre: Past and Present, 1984, rev. edit., 2001, Understanding Plays, 1990, 1994, 2003, Jessica Tandy, 1991, Margaret Webster, 1994, Margaret Webster: A Life in the Theater, 2004; co-editor: Generations: An Introduction to Drama, 1971, Notable Women in American Theatre, 1989; contbr. articles to profl. jours. Trustee The Paul Green Found., 1982—. Recipient New Orleans Bicentennial award for achievement in the arts, 1976, award for profl. achievement S.W. Theatre Conf., 1978, Pres.'s award U. Montevallo, 1979. Mem. Coll. of Fellows of the Am. Theatre (bd. dirs. 1998-2001); Nat. Theatre Conf. (pres. 1991-93), League Profl. Theatre Women N.Y. Avocations: film, travel.

BARRAS, JONETTA ROSE, writer; b. New Orleans, Oct. 22, 1950; d. John Asemore and Lovetta Norma Barras; children: Umoja S. Turner, Afrika M.A. Abney. BA in Comms., Trinity Coll., 1994. Cmty. organizer various locations, 1969—78; program mgr. Arts D.C., 1978—80; cons. to various orgns. and govt. agys., 1980—85; regional editor The Am. Vision Mag., 1984—89; nat. editor The Washington Afro-American, 1984—88; asst. mng. editor Washington View Mag., 1989—91; writer The Harambee, A Young People's Newspaper, 1991—94; sr. reporter met. desk Washington Times newspaper, 1994—96; writer The Washington City Paper, 1996—98, Capital Style Mag., 1999—2000; columnist Washington Times, 1996—2000; contbg. editor Washington City Paper, 2000—01; freelance columnist 2001, 2001—; radio talk show host Sta. WPFW-FM, 2001—. Guest expert Iyanla Show, 2001; guest analyst Evening Exchange., Howard U. TV, 2001; keynote spkr. various venues; guest lectr. Duke U., 2001; founder, past pres. The Inst. for Preservation and Study of African Am. Writing, Inc., 1978. Author: (books) Whatever Happened to Daddy's Little Girl: The Impact of Fatherlessness on African-American Women, 2000, The Last of the Black Emperors: The Hollow Comeback of Marion Barry in the New Age of Black Leaders, 1998; contbr. collection of essays and stories The Men We Cherish, 1997, anthology of essays and commentary An Ear to the Ground: Presenting Writers from 2 Coasts, 1997; author: (poetry collection) The Corner Is No Place for Hiding, 1996; contbr. poetry collection Sisterfire: Black Womanist Fiction and Poetry, 1994, poetry collection In Search of Color Everywhere: A Collection of African-American Poetry, 1994; author: (poetry collection) Dawn Collection of Original Poetry, 1976; contbr. to numerous anthologies, newspapers, and mags. Named one of Top 50 Most Influential Journalists in Washington, Washingtonian Mag., 2001; recipient Cmty. Svc. award, Covenant House Washington, 1997, Award for Excellence in Journalism, Soc. Profl. Journalists; fellow Nat. Multicultural Children's Lit. Writing Inst. fellow, U. Wis., Madison, 1991. Address: PO Box 21477 Washington DC 20009

BARRATT, CYNTHIA LOUISE, pharmaceutical company executive; b. El Paso, Tex., Feb. 13, 1953; d. John Edward and Louise Joy (Lacy) B.; m. Nat G. Adkins, Jr., Oct. 5, 1980. BJ, U. Tex., 1975. Buyer Joske's of Tex., San Antonio, 1975-80, Craigs of Tex., Houston, 1981-83; v.p. sales ops. Akorn, Inc., Abita Springs, La., 1980-86; CEO, chmn. bd. dirs. NGLC Corp., Richmond, Tex., 1983—; pres., CEO, bd. dirs. CynaCon/Ocusoft, Richmond, 1986—. Mem. NAFE, Rosenberg/Richmond C. of C., DAR, Ft. Bend County Mus. Assn. Avocations: golf, snorkeling, skiing. Office: OcuSoft Inc PO Box 429 Richmond TX 77406-0429 E-mail: cbarratt@ocusoft.com.

BARREDO, RITA M. auditor; b. Torrington, Conn., June 24, 1953; d. Avelino and Josephine (DiNoia) B. BA, U. Conn., 1975; BS, Post Coll., 1981; MS in Acctg., U. Hartford, 1984, MBA, 1990. CPA, Conn.; cert. info. sys. auditor, cert. internal auditor; cert. mgmt. acct.; cert. govt. auditing profl.; diplomate Am. Bd. Forensic Accts., Am. Bd. Forensic Examiners. Timekeeper Timex Corp., Waterbury, Conn., 1976-85; auditor Def. Contract Audit Agy., Lowell, Mass., 1985—. Mem. AICPA, Am. Coll. Forensic Examiners, Am. Womens Soc. CPAs, Conn. Soc. CPA (continuing profl. edn. com. 1989-95, 97— social and recreation com. 1996-97), Inst. Mgmt. Accts. (sec. Waterbury chpt. 1994—), Inst. Internal Auditors, Info. Sys. Audit and Control Assn. Home: 130 Dawes Ave Torrington CT 06790-3627 Office: Def Contract Audit Agy 400 Main St East Hartford CT 06108-0968 Personal E-mail: rbarredo01@snet.net.

BARRERA, ELVIRA PUIG, counselor, therapist, educator; b. Alice, Tex., Dec. 11, 1943; d. Carlos Rogers and Delia Rebecca (Puig) B.; 1 child, Dennis Lee Jr. BA, Incarnate Word Coll., 1971; M of Counseling and Guidance, St. Mary's U., San Antonio, 1978; specialist degree in marriage and family therapy, St. Mary's U., 1989. Lic. profl. counselor; lic. marriage & family therapist; lic. chem. dependency counselor. Tchr. Edgewood Ind. Sch. Dist., San Antonio, 1965-74, Dallas Ind. Sch. Dist., 1971-72, Northside Ind. Sch. Dist., San Antonio, 1974; ednl. cons. Region 20-Edn. Service Ctr., San Antonio, 1974-79; career edn. coordinator San Antonio Ind. Sch. Dist., 1979-84, counselor, 1984-91; family coord. C.A.T.C.H. Project, U. Tex. Health Sci. Ctr., Houston and Austin, 1991-94; counselor Austin Ind. Sch. Dist., 1994-97, dist. transition counselor, 1997-98; vice prin. San Antonio Ind. Sch. Dist., 1998—. Cons. SBA, 1981, U.S. Office Edn., Washington, 1981-82, Tex. Edn. Agy., Austin, 1979-80; cons., writer San Antonio Ind. Sch. Dist. and Tex. Edn. Agy., 1985; cons. to various edn. publs. Chairperson career awareness exploring div. Boy Scouts Am., 1982-87. Named Disting. Alumna, Incarnate Word Coll., 1983; recipient Spurgeon award Boy Scouts Am., 1985, Merit award, 1986, Growth award, 1986, Internat. Profl. and Bus. Women's Hall of Fame, 1995. Mem. Am. Assn. Marriage and Family Therapy, San Antonio Hash House Harriers (treas. 1990-91), San Antonio Assn. Women Admistrs. Counselors, Incarnate Word Coll. Alumni Assn. (mem. adv. bd. 1990—), St. Mary's U. Alumni Assn. (v.p. Austin alumni chpt. 2003—), The Harp and Shamrock Soc. of Tex., Delta Kappa Gamma (2d v.p. 1982-84, 1st v.p. 1986-88), Chi Sigma Iota. Roman Catholic. Avocation: running. Home: 907 Aurora Cir Austin TX 78757-3415 Office: San Antonio Ind Sch Dist 515 Willow San Antonio TX 78202-1255

BARRETT, BARBARA MCCONNELL, ranch owner, community leader, lawyer; b. Indiana County, Pa., Dec. 26, 1950; d. Robert Harvey and Betty (Dornheim) McC.; m. Craig R. Barrett, Jan. 19, 1985. BS, Ariz. State U., 1972, MPA, 1975, JD, 1978, LHD (hon.), 2000. Bar: Ariz. 1978, U.S. Dist. Ct. Ariz. 1979, U.S. Supreme Ct. Ariz. 1979. Atty. The Dial Corp., Phoenix, 1976-80; assoc. gen. counsel, asst. sec. Southwest Forest Industries, Inc., Phoenix, 1980-82; vice chmn. CAB, Washington, 1982-83, mem., 1983-84, vice chmn., 1984-85; ptnr. Evans, Kitchel & Jenckes, P.C., Phoenix, 1985-88, 1989; dep. adminstr. FAA, Washington, 1988-89; pvt. practice internat. bus. and aviation law Paradise Valley, Ariz., 1989—; pres., CEO American Mngmt. Assn., N.Y.C., 1997-98, Triple Creek Ranch, Mont., 1993—; fellow Inst. Politics, Kennedy Sch. Harvard U., 1999. Chmn. bd. dirs. Valley Bank Ariz., 1997-2003; chmn. nominating com. The Lovelace Inst., 1996-2003, U.S.-Afghan Women's Coun., 2003—, mem. U.S. Adv. Commn. Pub. Diplomacy, 2003—, past mem. Adv. Com. on Women in the Services, nominated as Sec. USAF, 2004; treas. Asia-Pacific Econ. Cooperation Edn. Found., 1995-99; mem. exec. com., vice chairperson career opportunities subcom. U.S. Dept. Def., 1989-93; mem. adv. com. Gov.'s Regional Airport, Pres.'s Adv. Com. on Trade Negotiations; mem. Adminstrv. Coun. U.S., 1982-85; chmn. U.S. Sec. of Commerce Export Leaders Conf., 1988, Transp. Cluster Gov.'s Strategic Partnership for Econ. Devel., 1992-94; mem. Ariz. Disease Control Rsch. Commn., 1993-95; v.p. East Valley Partnership, 1992-94; v.p. Internat. Women's Forum, 1991-99, pres., 1999—2001, mem. coun. fgn. rels., 1992—; mem. Phoenix Coun. Fgn. Rels., 1979—; mem. steering com. Thunderbird Internat. Symposium, 1992—; mem. global dispute resolution Global Ctr. Dispute Resolution, 1999—; mem. adv. bd. China Mist Tea Co., 1998-99, Harvard Leadership Bd., 1999-2002; bd. dirs. numerous orgns. Chmn. Ariz. Dist. Export Coun., 1985-91, Ronald W. Reagan Scholarship Program, 1987-90, Airshow Can. Symposium, 1989, 91; chmn. World Trade Ctr. Ariz., 1992-94, chmn. emerita; bd. dirs. Nat. Air and Space Mus. Smithsonian Inst., 1988-89, Palms Clinic and Hosp. Corp., 1985—2000, Goldwater Inst., 1991—2002; trustee, devel. com., chairperson Thunderbird Am. Grad. Sch. Internat. Mgmt., Glendale, Ariz., Embry-Riddle Aeronaut. U., Prescott, Ariz., Daytona Beach, Fla., 1989-96; pres. World Affairs Ariz., 1987-88; vice chmn. Kid's Voting USA, 1989-94; trustee Lovelace Inst., 1995-99; bd. dirs., chairperson nominating com. Ctrl. Ariz. chpt. ARC, 1993-99; mem. Gov.'s Task Force Canamex Corridor, 1998—2001; pres. bd. Maricopa Colls. Found., 1997-98; sr. adv. com. Inst. Politics, Harvard, 1999—; vice regent, trustee George Washington's Fredericksburg Found., 1999—; mem. numerous bd. dirs. Named Woman of Yr., Ariz. State U., 1971, named to Hall of Fame, Coll. Pub. Programs, 1989, Coll. Liberal Arts, 1995; recipient Disting. Achievement award Ariz. State U., 1987, Coll. Bus., 1994, Woman Who Made a Difference award Internat. Women's Forum, 1988, Dick Cheney citation U.S. Sec. of Def., 1992, FAA Adminstr.'s award, 1989, Woman of the Yr. Network of Women in Hospitality, 1998, Horatio Alger award, 1999, Beta Gamma Nationwide Achievement award, 2000, Girl Scouts Today and Tomorrow award, 2000, Homeroom Hero award Teach for Am., 2002, Disting. Women's award Northwood U., 2002, Medal of Hon. DAR, 2003; named to Internat. Forest Friendship Hall of Fame, 2003; named one of 100 Women Who Made A Difference in Aviation, 2003; Dubois scholar, 1977. Mem. Am. Mgmt. Assn. (truste, chmn. exec. com., pres. N.Y.C. 1997-98, Lifetime Achievement award, 2002), Nat. Assn. Corp. Dirs. (faculty 1999, bd. dirs. 2000-02), Ariz. State U. Law Soc. (bd. govs. 1991-94), Ariz. State U. Found. (bd. dirs., program chair 1996—), Ariz. Women in Internat. Trade (bd. dirs., exec. com. 1989-94), Phoenix C. of C. (bd. dirs. 1989-95), Reagan Alumni Assn., Nat. Policy Forum, Econ. Club of Phoenix (past pres. 1990—).

BARRETT, BEATRICE HELENE, psychologist; b. Cin., Dec. 8, 1928; d. Oscar Slack and Helen (Kaiper) B.; m. Harold Sheffield Van Buren, Oct. 6, 1966 (div. Oct. 1985). BA, U. Ariz., 1950; MA, U. Ky., 1952; PhD, Purdue U., 1957. Grad. tchg. asst. in psychology U. Ky., Lexington, 1950-52; psychology asst. Longview State Hosp., Cin., 1951, staff psychologist, 1950, staff psychologist Children's Outpatient and Cons. Svcs. Ind. U. Med. Ctr., Indpls., 1954-57, chief psychologist, 1957-59; instr. psychology Ind. U. Med. Sch., Indpls., 1956-60; rsch. assoc. dept. psychiatry Ind. U. Med. Ctr., Indpls., 1959-60; pvt. practice clin. psychology Indpls., 1957-60; research fellow in psychology Sch. of Medicine Harvard U., Boston, 1960-62; lectr. in spl. edn. Grad. Sch. Edn., Boston U., 1962-63; dir. psychol. rsch. Walter E. Fernald State Sch., Belmont, Mass., 1962-69, dir. behavior prosthesis lab., 1963-92; chief psychologist, 1969-92; assoc. psychologist Eunice Kennedy Shriver Ctr. for Mental Retardation, Inc., Waltham, Mass., 1982-98. Instr. Mass. Psychol. Ctr., 1972; lectr. in spl. edn. Lesley Coll. Grad. Sch., 1974-76; adj. assoc. prof. Northeastern U., 1983-92; psychology cons. Carter Meml. Hosp., Indpls., 1959-60; mem. exec. com. Boston Behavior Therapy Interest Group, 1973-74; mem. human studies com. Eunice Kennedy Shriver Ctr., 1980-98. Cons. editor, mem. adv. bds. various profl. jours.; contbr. numerous articles to profl. jours. Mem. Ind. Gov.'s Youth Coun., 1959-61; mem. spl. adv. com. on mental retardation Ind. Dept. Pub. Instrn., 1959-61; mem. task force Mass. Mental Retardation Planning Project, 1965-66; mem. adv. bd. Cambridge Ctr. for Behavioral Studies, 1981-87, 93-2000, trustee, 1987-93, 94-2000, sr. fellow, 2001—, chair devel. com., 1987-89, mem. subcom. on planned giving, 1992-95, chmn. nominating com., 1992-93, mem., 1993-98, exec. com., 1993, 94-99, mem. subcom. on acad. and sci. programs, 1992-97, mem. editl. bd., 1998-99; treas. B.F. Skinner Found., 1996-2003, bd. dirs., 1997—; mem. com. on dance edn. Spl. Commn. on Performing Arts, 1976-77; mem. art acquisition com. DeCordova Mus., 1978-80, mem. contemporary arts coun., 1985-87; trustee Boston Repertory Ballet, 1977-79, Boston Ballet Co., 1970-76, sec. bd., 1974-75, exec. com., 1974-76. Grantee Nat. Assn. for Retarded Citizens, 1963, NIHM, 1963-76; recipient Lifetime Contbn. to frequency based rsch. and ednl. tech., Standard Celeration Soc. award, 1997. Fellow APA, Mass. Psychol. Assn. (Ezra Saul Psychol. Svc. award 1979), Behavior Therapy and Rsch. Soc. (charter clin.); mem. Assn. for Mentally Ill Children (human rights com. 1979-81), Eunice Kenndey Shriver Ctr. (mem. human studies comm. 1980-98), Am. Acad. on Mental Retardation (v.p. 1969-74, at-large exec. com. 1975-77), Am. Psychol. Assn., Am. Psychol. Soc., Ea. Psychol. Assn., Assn. Behavior Analysis (jour. adv. bd. 1983-87, chair task force on right to effective edn. 1986-91, presdl. adv. group on edn. and pub. policy 1994-95), Stage Harbor Yacht Club (Chatham, Mass., race com. 1984-86), Sigma Xi, Phi Kappa Phi. Home and Office: RFD 5 Box 236A Winter St Lincoln MA 01773

BARRETT, CATHERINE L. state representative; b. Cin., June 14, 1941; married; 3 children. BA in Bus. Adminstrn., Union Inst., Cin.; grad., Ctr. Policy Alternatives Flemming Fellows Inst.; fellow, Coun. State Govts. Bowhay Inst. Legis. Leadership Devel. Former mayor, Forest Park, Ohio; state rep. dist. 32 Ohio Ho. of Reps., Columbus, 1998—, ranking minority mem., human svcs. subcom., mem. fin. and appropriations, health, and ins. coms. Past councilwoman Forest Park City Coun. Recipient Ohio Hunger Heroine award, Ohio Assn. 2d Harvest; Harvard JFK Sch. Govt. Sr. Execs. in State and Local Govt. fellow, Eleanor Roosevelt Global Leadership Inst. fellow. Mem.: LWV, Negro Women Coun., Ohio, Ky. and Ind. Regional Coun. Govts., Forest Park Bus. Assn., Cin. Woman's Polit. Caucus, Cin. C. of C., Forest Park Women's Club, Delta Sigma Theta. Democrat. Office: 77 S High St 10th fl Columbus OH 63215-6111

BARRETT, COLLEEN CROTTY, airline executive; b. Bellows Falls, Vt., Sept. 14, 1944; d. Richard Crotty and Barbara (Hennessey) Blanchard; 1 child, Patrick Allen Barrett. A.A. with highest honors, Becker Jr. Coll., 1964. Legal sec. Oppenheimer Rosenberg Kelleher & Wheatley, San Antonio, 1968-72, adminstrv. asst., paralegal, 1972-78; corp. sec. Southwest Airlines, Dallas, 1978-1990, exec. asst. to pres. and chmn., 1980-85, v.p. adminstrn., corp. sec., 1985-90, exec. v.p. customs, 1990-2001, pres., COO, 2001—. Bd. dirs. J.C. Penney Co., 2004—. Mem. Leadership Tex. Democrat. Roman Catholic. Office: SW Airlines Co PO Box 36611 Dallas TX 75235-1611

BARRETT, CYNTHIA TOWNSEND, neonatologist; b. Santa Barbara, Calif., Sept. 8, 1937; d. George Barker and Elizabeth Louise (Magee) B. AB, Vassar Coll., 1958; MD, Harvard U., 1962. Diplomate. Am. Bd. Pediats. Intern, resident in pediats., pediat. chief resident U. Wash., 1962-66, fellow in physiology & biophysics, 1966-67; fellow in fetal cardiovascular physiology U. Calif., San Francisco, 1967-70; chief divsn. neonatology, assoc. prof. pediats. UCLA Sch. Medicine, 1970—. Mem. Internat. Newborn Intensive Care Soc., European Soc. Perinatal Rsch., Western Soc. Pediat. Rsch., Am. Thoracic Soc., Soc. Pediat. Rsch., Perinatal Rsch. Soc. Republican. Episcopalian. Home: 6778 Shearwater Ln Malibu CA 90265-4144 Office: UCLA Sch Medicine Dept Pediats Rm 12-467 Los Angeles CA 90095-0001 E-mail: cbarrett@mednet.ucla.edu.

BARRETT, ELIZABETH ANN MANHART, nursing educator, psychotherapist, consultant; b. Hume, Ill., July 11, 1934; d. Francis J. and Grace C. (Manhart) Fridy; children: Joseph B., Jeffrey F., Paula G. Brown, Pamela M. Temple, Scott D. BSN summa cum laude, U. Evansville, 1970, MA, 1973, MSN, 1976; grad., Gestalt Assocs. Psychotherapy, 1982; PhD in Nursing, NYU, 1983; grad., Am. Inst. for Mental Imagery, 1995. From instr. to asst. prof. nursing U. Evansville, Ind., 1970-76; staff nurse Welborn Bapt. Hosp., Evansville, 1975-76, Bellevue Psychiat. Hosp., N.Y.C., 1976-79; clin. tchr. CUNY, 1977-82; asst. prof. Adelphi U., 1979-80; group practice Nurse Healers, 1979-82; pvt. practice psychotherapy, 1980—. Nurse rschr. Mt. Sinai Med. Ctr., N.Y.C., 1982-86, asst. dir. nursing, 1983-86; assoc. prof. Hunter Coll., N.Y.C., 1986-89, prof., 1994-2001, prof. emerita, 2001—, dir. grad. studies, 1989-92, coord. Ctr. for Nursing Rsch., 1993-2001; cons. Internat. Soc. Univ. Nurses; co-chair adv. com. Martha E. Rogers Ctr. for Study of Nursing Svc., 1994-96; sec., treas. Am. Inst. for Mental Imagery, 2002—; com. mem. Regional Health Planning Coun., Evansville, 1974-77. Mem. editl. bd. Alt. Therapies in Health and Medicine, 1995—. Recipient Disting. Nursing Alumnus award NYU, 1994, Disting. Nurse Rschr. award Found. N.Y. State Nurses Assn., 1995. Fellow Am. Acad. Nursing; mem. ANA (cert. psychiat.-mental health), NOW, Nat. League Nursing, Ea. Nursing Rsch. Assn. (charter), Ea. Nursing Rsch. Soc., Soc. Rogerian Scholars (co-founder, 1st pres. 1988-90), Phi Kappa Phi, Sigma Theta Tau (Upsilon chpt. pres. 1986-88), Alpha Tau Delta, Sigma Xi. Home: 415 E 85th St Apt 9E New York NY 10028-6358 Office: 16 E 96th St Ste 1 A New York NY 10128

BARRETT, JANE HAYES, lawyer; b. Dayton, Ohio, Dec. 13, 1947; d. Walter J. and Jane H. Barrett BA, Calif. State U.-Long Beach, 1969; JD, U. So. Calif., 1972. Bar: Calif. 1972, U.S. Dist. Ct. (cen. dist.) Calif. 1972, U.S. Ct. Appeals (9th cir.) 1982, U.S. Supreme Ct. Assoc. Lawler, Felix & Hall, L.A., 1972—84; ptnr. Arter & Hadden, L.A., 1984—94; mng. ptnr. Preston, Gates & Ellis, L.A., 1994—2002; ptnr. Piper Rudnick, L.A., 2002—. Lectr. bus. law Calif. State U., 1973-75. Mem. adv. bd. Harriet Buhai Legal Aid Ctr., 1991-96, mem. bd. pub. counsel, 1996-98; pres. Pilgrim Parents Orgn. 1990-91; chmn. fin. Our Mother Good Counsel Sch.; bd. regents Loyola, H.S., 2000—. Named Outstanding Grad. Calif. State U., Long Beach, 1988, Outstanding Alumnae Polit. Sci., 1993, So. Calif. Super Lawyer, L.A. Mag., 2003. Fellow Am. Bar Found.; mem. ABA (bd. govs. 1980-84, chmn. young lawyers divsn. 1980-81, com. on delivery of legal svcs. 1985-89, exec. coun. legal edn. and admissions sects. 1985-89, fin. sec. torts and ins. practice 1982-83, adv. mem. fed. judiciary com. 9th circuit rep. 2000—03, v.p. 1997—, Am. Bar Endowment 1999, bd. dirs. 1990—, sec. 1993-95, v.p. 1998-99, pres., 1999-2000, bd. fellows young lawyers divsn. 1992—, del 9th cir. jud. conf., atty. del. U.S. Dist. Ct. ctrl. dist. Calif. Atty. Conf. 2002—), 9th Cir. Atty. Conf. (del. 2003), Calif. State Bar (com. adminstrn. of justice, editl. bd. Calif. Lawyers 1981-84), Legion Lex (bd. dirs. 1990-93), Los Feliz Homeowners Assn. (bd. dirs.). Democrat. Office: Piper Rudnick 1999 Ave of the Stars Los Angeles CA 90067 E-mail: jane.barrett@piperrudnick.com

BARRETT, JANET TIDD, academic administrator; b. Crystal City, Mo., Nov. 29, 1939; d. Lewis Samuel and Mamie Lou (Hulvey) Tidd; m. David Clark Barrett, June 3, 1961; children: Barbara, Pam. Diploma in nursing, St. Lukes Hosp. Sch. Nursing, 1960; BSN with honors, Washington U., St. Louis, 1964, MSN, 1979; PhD, St. Louis U., 1987. Assoc. prof. Maryville Coll., St. Louis, 1979-89; acad. dean Barnes Coll., St. Louis, 1989-91; dir. BSN program Deaconess Coll. Nursing, St. Louis, 1991-2000, acad. dean, 2000—02; nursing cons., 2002—. Contbn. author to Beare and Meyers: Principles of Medical-Surgical Nursing. St. Lukes Hosp. scholar; recipient Sister Agnita Claire Day Rsch. award St. Louis U. Mem.: Mo. League Nursing, Nat. League Nursing, St. Luke's Alumni Assn., Phi Delta Kappa, Pi Lambda Theta, Sigma Theta Tau. E-mail: barretjan@hotmail.com., jtbarrett02@charter.net.

BARRETT, JESSICA (DONNA ANN NIPERT), psychotherapist; b. Paterson, N.J., July 25, 1952; d. Donald Alfred and Gloria Emma (Lustica) Nipert; m. John David Barrett, Sept. 9, 1977 (div. June 1982); 1 child, Ashley Elizabeth. BA, UCLA, 1975; MA, Azusa Pacific U., 1981. Lic. marriage, family, child therapist; cert. hypnosis profl. With employee relations Engrs. and Architects Exec. Assn., L.A., 1975-79; practicing psychotherapy Toluca Lake and Burbank, Calif., 1983—; instr., supr. Phillips Grad. Inst., Encino, Calif., 1986-2000; psychotherapist Pasadena (Calif.) Outpatient Eating Disorders Program, 1987-88. Cons. Texaco Employee Assistance Program, Studio City, 1985—86, NBC Employee Assistance Program, Burbank, 1986—87, Burbank, 1993—; spl. therapist United Behavioral Health, Managed Health Networks, Cigna Behavioral Health, 1989—, Value Options Provider, 1986—, Health Mgmt. Resource Svcs., 1985—99; assessment and referral liaison Nat. Resource Cons., San Diego, 1983—93, Employee Support Sys. Corp., Orange, Calif., 1985—, Health and Human Resource Ctr., 1984—92, Blue Cross Preferred Provider and EAP Network, 1995—, U.S. Behavioral Health, 1998—. Mem. Employee Assistance Profls. Assn. (bd. dirs. 1983-86), Am. Assn. Marriage and Family Therapists (clin. 1983—), Phillips Grad. Inst. Alumni Assn. (sec.-treas. 1987-88, v.p. programs 1988-89), Eye Movement Desensitization Reprocessing Internat. Assn. (charter). Avocations: theater, improvisational comedy, piano, literature, travel. E-mail: ncrrgbl1@yahoo.com.

BARRETT, KRISTA E. psychotherapist, educator; b. Chgo., July 19, 1967; d. Jack Arthur and Barbara Ann Barrett. BA in Psychology cum laude, U. Tex., Austin, 1988; MSW, Columbia U., 1991. LCSW N. Mex., 1996. Family and group therapist Ctr. for Family Counseling, Oakland, Calif., 1991—93; program therapist Heights Hosp., Albuquerque, 1993—95; program coord. children's unit Meml. Hosp., Albuquerque, 1995—98; pre-sch. social worker Albuquerque Pub. Schs., 1998—2003. Field instr. Highlands U. N. Mex., Albuquerque, 1995; psychotherapist, pvt. practice, Albuquerque, 1997—. Named Nat. Merit Scholar, 1998. Mem.: Harwood Art Ctr., Sand Tray Tng. Inst. N. Mex., Nat. Assn. Social Workers, N. Mex. Assn. for Play Therapy (charter bd. mem., treas. 2000—), Nat. Assn. for Play Therapy, Psi Chi. Avocations: printmaking, tai chi, yoga, Jungian analysis, music. Office Phone: 505-888-1121.

BARRETT, LENORE HARDY, state legislator, mining and investment consultant; b. Newkirk, Okla., June 16, 1934; d. Floyd Jack and Minnie Bell (O'Dell) Hardy; m. Robert Michael Barrett, 1964; 1 child, Michael Hardy. BS, Okla. Bapt. U., 1956. State legislator Ho. of Reps., Boise, Idaho, 1993—. Active Idaho Farm Bureau Political Action Com., 1990-92; dir. Salmon River Electric Coop., Inc., Challis; police commr. Challis City Coun., 1984-89; mem. Assn. Idaho Cities Legis. Com., 2 yrs.; state committeewoman Custer County Rep. Ctrl. Com., Challis, 1982—. Mem. Nat. Inholder's Assn., Idaho Rep. Party, Ctrl. Idaho Mining Assn. (sec.), Custer County Farm Bureau, Grassroots for Multiple Use, Blue Ribbon Coalition, Order of Eastern Star (Grand Organist award Grand Chpt. Idaho 1985-86). Baptist. Avocations: music, painting, reading. Home: PO Box 347 143 W Pleasant Challis ID 83226 Office: Idaho Ho of Reps State Captiol Boise ID 83720-0001

BARRETT, LIDA KITTRELL, mathematics educator; b. Houston, May 21, 1927; d. Pleasant Williams and Maidel (Baker) Kittrell; m. John Herbert Barrett, June 2, 1950 (dec. Jan. 1969); children: John Kittrell, Maidel Horn, Mary Louise. BA, Rice U., 1946; MA, U. Tex., Austin, 1949; PhD, U. Pa., 1954. Instr. math. U. Conn., Waterbury, 1955-56; vis. appointment U. Wis., Madison, 1959-60; lectr. U. Utah, Salt Lake City, 1956-61; assoc. prof. U. Tenn., Knoxville, 1961-70, prof., 1970-80, head math. dept., 1973-80; assoc. provost No. Ill. U., DeKalb, 1980-87; dean, arts and scis. Miss. State U., Mississippi State, 1987-91; sr. assoc. Edn. and Human Resources Directorate NSF, Washington, 1991-95; prof. math. U.S. Mil. Acad., West Point, N.Y., 1995-98; adj. prof. U. Tenn., 1998—2001. Ind. math. cons., Knoxville, Tenn., 1964-80, 98—. Contbr. articles on topology, applied math. and math. edn. to profl. jours. Mem. Math. Assn. Am. (pres. 1989, 90), Am. Math. Soc., Soc. Indsl. and Applied Math., Nat. Coun. Tchrs. Math., Am. Assn. Higher Edn., Phi Kappa Phi, Sigma Xi. Episcopalian. E-mail: lida-k-barrett@att.net.

BARRETT, LINDA, insurance company executive; b. Cleve., May 29, 1962; d. Raymond Robert and Maryann Krause; m. Mark D. Hattman, June 7, 1986 (div. Feb. 1994); m. Charles W. Barrett, Oct. 19, 1996. Grad. high sch., Lakewood, Ohio. Personal lines customer svc. rep. Eckley Ins. Agy., Cleve., 1980-86, 89-92, World Wide Svcs., Cleve., 1986-87, Hoffman Ins. Agy., Berea, Ohio, 1987-89, Brooks & Stafford Agy., Cleve., 1992-95; comml. claims account Fedeli Group, Independence, Ohio, 1995-96; team leader for personal lines, account mgr. Ins. Ptnrs. Agy., Lakewood, Ohio, 1996—. Mem. ladies guild St. Christopher Ch., Rocky River, Ohio, 1998, 99, Aux. Guild Am. Legion, Rocky River, 1999. Mem. Ins. Women Internat. (v.p. 1999—, sec. 1999—, award 1991), Cath. Knights Ohio. Avocations: quilting, gardening, sewing, cooking. Home: 15529 Munn Rd Cleveland OH 44111-2061 Office: Ins Ptnrs Agy 1495 Warren Rd Lakewood OH 44107-3931

BARRETT, LINDA L. real estate consultant; b. Hudson, Mich., Aug. 16, 1948; d. David John and Georgia Elizabeth (Spengler) B.; m. Carl Gugino; 1 dau., Toni. Student, U. Mich., 1970-73. Cert. residential brokerage mgr. Sales mgr. Collins Real Estate, Hudson, Mich., 1973-79; owner, broker Homeland Real Estate, Lake Leann, Mich., 1979-82; mgr. broker Mid-Mich. Real Estate, Jackson, Mich., 1982-85; exec. v.p. Michael Saunders & Co., Sarasota, Fla., 1986-95, cons., 1995—. Mem. adv. bd. Sotheby's Internat. Mem. Econ. Devel. Coun., Com. of 100. Mem. AAUW, NAFE, Internat. Real Estate Fedn., Nat. Mktg. Inst., Nat. Assn. Realtors, Fla. Assn. Realtors, Sarasota C. of C., Global Travel Internat. Network, 2000 Notable Am. Women, Econ. Devel. Coun., CRB, Holistic Options, Profl.'s Network Investment Orgn., Field Club, The Oaks, Longboat Key Club. Avocations: gardening, golfing, yoga, travel, writing.

BARRETT, LORA MCNEECE, art educator, artist; BA, Elms Coll., 1972; MEd, U. Mass., 1987, EdD, 1993. Lic. profl. tchr. Mass. Art tchr. Holyoke (Mass.) Pub. Schs., 1972—84, tchr. support team, 1984—89, dir. parent involvement, 1989—91, arts resource tchr., 1991—, art dept. head, 1996—. Asst. prof. U. Mass., Amherst, 1996—. Contbr. book Flower Teachers: Stories for a New Generation, 2002. Named Mass. Visual Arts

Educator of the Yr., Mass. Alliance for Arts in Edn., 2001. Mem.: NEA, Mass. Art Edn. Assn. (Mass. Mid. Sch. Art Tchr. of the Yr. 2002), Mass. Tchrs. Assn., Nat. Art Edn. Assn., Pastel Painters Soc. Cape Cod. Democrat. Avocation: pastel and oil painting.

BARRETT, NANCY SMITH, university administrator; b. Balt., Sept. 12, 1942; d. James Brady and Katherine (Pollard) Smith; children: Clark, Christopher. BA, Goucher Coll., 1963; MA, Harvard U., 1965, PhD, PhD, Harvard U., 1968. Dep. asst. dir. Congl. Budget Office, Washington, 1975-76; sr. staff Council of Econ. Advisors, Washington, 1977; prin. research assoc. The Urban Inst., Washington, 1977-79; dep. asst. sec. U.S. Dept. Labor, Washington, 1979-81; instr. Am. U., Washington, 1966-67, asst. prof. econs., 1967-70, assoc. prof., 1970-74, prof., 1974-89; dean Coll. of Bus. Adminstrn. Fairleigh Dickinson U., Teaneck, N.J., 1989-91; provost, v.p. acad. affairs Western Mich. U., Kalamazoo, 1991-96, U. Ala., Tuscaloosa, 1996—2003, Wayne State U., Detroit, 2003—. Author: Theory of Macroeconomic Policy, 1972, 2d rev. edit., 1975, Theory of Microeconomic Policy, 1974, (with G. Gerardi and T. Hart) Prices and Wages in U.S., 1974; contbr. articles on econs. to profl. jours. Woodrow Wilson fellow, 1963-64; Fulbright scholar, 1973. Mem. Am. Econs. Assn., Phi Beta Kappa. Office: Wayne State Univ 4092 Faculty Adminstrn Bldg Detroit MI 48202 Home: 2033 Shorepointe Grosse Pointe Woods MI 48236 E-mail: nancy.barrett@wayne.edu.

BARRETT, PAULETTE SINGER, public relations executive; b. Paris, Dec. 20, 1937; came to U.S., 1947; d. Andrew M. and Agatha (Kinsbrunner) Singer; m. Laurence I. Barrett, Mar. 9, 1957 (div. 1983); children: Paul Meyer, David Allen, Adam Singer. BA, NYU, 1957; MS in Journalism, Columbia U., 1958. News dir. Yardney Electric Corp., N.Y.C., 1958-61; freelance writer newspapers and pub. relations orgns., N.Y.C. and Washington, 1961-73; assoc. dir. pub. info. Columbia U., N.Y.C., 1973-77; from account exec. to v.p., then sr. v.p. Edelman Pub. Rels. Worldwide, N.Y.C., 1977-80, sr. v.p. and gen. mgr., 1980, exec. v.p., gen. mgr., 1986-88, exec. v.p., dir. corp. affairs div., 1988-89; exec. v.p. Rowland Co., N.Y.C., 1980-82; exec. dir. communications UJA-Fedn./N.Y., N.Y.C., 1982-86; sr. v.p., mng. dir. Hill and Knowlton, Chgo., 1989-90; pres. Barrett Comm., Chgo. and N.Y.C., 1990—. Established The Barrett Workshops, tng. svcs., 1999—; comm. counsel The Barrett Group, 2002—. Pres. Found. of Women Execs. in Pub. Rels., 2003—. E-mail: paulettebarrett@earthlink.net.

BARRETT, TINA, professional golfer; b. Balt., Md., June 5, 1966; d. Barbara Smith; m. Dan Friedman, Nov. 27, 1993. BA cum laude, Longwood Coll., 1988. Winner Eastern Amateur, 1987, Md. State Amateur, 1988; golfer Ladies Pro Golf Assn., 1988—. Avocations: Balt. Orioles and Pheonix Suns fan. Office: c/o LPGA 100 International Golf Dr Ste B Daytona Beach FL 32124-1082

BARRETT-CONNOR, ELIZABETH LOUISE, epidemiologist, educator; b. Evanston, Ill., Apr. 8, 1935; m. James D. Connor; 3 children. BA in Zoology, Mt. Holyoke Coll., 1956; MD, Cornell U., 1960; DCMT in clin. medicine of tropics, London Sch. Hygiene and Tropical Medicine, 1965; DSc (hon.), Mt. Holyoke Coll., 1985; PhD (hon.), U. Utrecht, The Netherlands, 1996, U. Bergen, Norway, 1996, U. Helsinki, Finland, 2000. Diplomate Am. Bd. Internal Medicine, [illegible] Fla., 1965, Calif., 1970, cert. advanced epidemiology U. Minn., 1967, genetics Johns Hopkins U., 1968. Intern Parkland Meml. Hosp., Dallas, 1960—61, resident, 1961—63; resident infectious disease Jackson Meml. Hosp., Miami, Fla., 1963—64; instr. medicine U. Miami, Fla., 1965 68, asst. prof. medicine, 1968-70; asst. prof. community and family medicine U. Calif., San Diego, 1970-74, assoc. prof. community and family medicine, 1974-81, prof. community and family medicine, 1981—, acting chair dept. community and family medicine, 1981-82, chmn. dept. family and preventative medicine, 1982-97. Mem. hosp. infection control com. VA Med. Ctr., San Diego, 1971-81; Kelly West Meml. lectr. Am. Diabetes Assn., Indpls. 1987; vis. prof.Royal Soc. Medicine, London, 1989; John Rankin lectr. U. Wis., 1989; Don McLeod Meml. lectr., Halifax, N.S., Can., 1990; Elizabeth Blackwell lectr., Rochester, Minn., 1991; Lila Wallace vis. prof. N.Y. Hosp.-Cornell Med. Ctr., N.Y.C., 1992; Donald P. Shiley vis. lectr. Scripps Clinic and Rsch. Found., La Jolla, Calif., 1993; Leonard M. Schuman lectr. U. Mich., 1993; disting. vis. U. Western Australia, 1997; disting. lectr. geriatrics Duke U. Med. Ctr., Durham, N.C., 1998; Heath Clark lectr.,London, 1989, Pickering lectr., Cambridge, England, 2000. Contbr. articles to profl. jours. Recipient Frederick Murgatroyd prize, 1965, Kaiser award for excellence in tchg., 1982, Dr. of Yr. award San Diego Health Care Assn., 1987, merit award Nat. Inst. Aging, 1987, Making a Difference for Women's Health award Soroptimists, La Jolla, 9195, clin. svc. award Soc. for Advancement Women's Health Rsch., 1997, health award NIH, 1999, Stokes award Am. Soc. Preventative Cardiology, 2003; grantee NIH 1970—. Master: ACP (pubs. com. 1988—90, James D. Bruce Meml. award 1994); fellow: Am. Coll. Preventive Medicine (Katharine Boucot Sturgis lectr. 1986), Royal Soc. Medicine, Am. Coll. Nutrition, Am. Coll. Epidemiology (hon.), Royal Soc. Health, Am. Heart Assn. (chmn. budget com. coun. on epidemiology 1987—88, chmn. coun. on epidemiology 1989, Ancel Keys lectr. 1995, Elizabeth Barrett-Connor rsch. award 1995, Merit award 1998); mem.: APHA (chmn. epidemiology sect. 1989—90, Wade Hampton Frost lectr. 1993), Am. Soc. Preventive Medicine, N.Y. Acad. Scis., Internat. Bone and Mineral Soc., Am. Geriat. Soc., Am. Diabetes Assn., Western Assn. Physicians, Calif. Acad. of Preventative Medicine, Assn. Practitioners in Infection Control, Am. Soc. Tropical Medicine and Hygiene (emeritus), Internat. Epidemiol. Assn., Infectious Disease Soc. Am., Am. Fedn. Clin. Rsch., Am. Venereal Disease Assn. (v.p. 1977—78), Soc. Epidemiol. Rsch. (pres. 1983, Cassell Meml. lectr. 1997), Inst. Medicine, Assn. Tchrs. Preventive Medicine (bd. dir. 1987—99, Outstanding Educator award 1992), Sigma Xi, Phi Beta Kappa. Office: U Calif San Diego Family and Preventive Medicine 9500 Gilman Dr # Mc0607 La Jolla CA 92093-0607

BARRETTE, LINDA JONES, dean; b. Johnson City, Tenn., Mar. 30, 1946; d. Horace Easterly Jones and Una Mae Scott; m. Pierre Philip Barrette, Aug. 20, 1977. BS, East Tenn. State U., 1967; MSLS, Cath. U. Am., 1977; PhD, So. Ill. U., 1992. Cert. distance learning adminstr. profl., VTEL ESA installation, operation and svc. Libr. Park Rd. Elem. Sch., Charlotte, N.C., 1967-69; hed libr. Williamsburg Jr. High, Arlington, Va., 1969-77; libr. Harrisonburg (Va.) Jr. High, 1977-78; dean for learning resources John A. Logan Coll., Carterville, Ill., 1981—2002; pres. Learning, Tech. and Librs., Inc., Carbondale, Ill., 1982-91; sec.-treas. IPDN, Inc., St. Louis, 2000—02. Trainer-cons. So. Ill. Collegiate Common Market, Herrin, Ill., 1998-2000, mem. tech. adv. bd., 1998—; mem. adv. bd. Ill. State Libr., Springfield, 1998-2000, Ill. Digital Acad. Libr., Champaign, 1999—. Author: (software program) CARDPREP: Microcomputer Catalog Card, Label, Proofsheet and List Writer, 1985. Del. Ill. Regional White Ho. Conf. on Libr. and Info. Svcs., Carterville, 1990; bd. trustees Grace United Meth. Ch., 2002—. Recipient Outstanding Regional Leadership award Chair Acad., 1999, Excellence award John A. Logan Coll. Ctr. for Excellence in Tchg., Learning and Leadership, 2000. Fellow Postdoctoral Acad. Higher Edn.; mem. A Consortium of Midwest Colls. and Univs. (pres. 1999-2000), Am. Libr. Assn., So. Ill. Learning Resource Consortium (sec. 2000-01), Ill. Coun. C.C. Adminstrs. (sec. 1993-94, bd. dirs. 1993-96, pres. 1994-95), Ill. Libr. Assn., Rotary (pres. Carbondale-Breakfast chpt. 1992-93, award of merit 1996, Paul Harris fellow 1988, 99), Carbondale C. of C. (bd. dirs. 2001, chair online com. 1998), Phi Kappa Phi, Phi Kappa Delta. Methodist. Avocations: golf, swimming, crafts. Home: 662 Lake Shore Dr Murphysboro IL 62966-5222 E-mail: ljb@onemain.com.

BARRICK, DONNA MATZ, music educator; b. Seoul, Korea, Jan. 6, 1975; arrived in U.S., 1975; d. Donald Carl and Marilee Margaret Matz. BS in Music Edn., Bob Jones U., Greenville, S.C., 1996; M.Elem.Edn., Converse Coll., Spartanburg, S.C., 1997. Cert. tchr. in elem., spl. edn., learning disabilities, music edn., piano and early childhood S.C. Music tchr. Lake Forest Elem. Sch., Greenville, SC, 1996—98, Houston Elem. Sch., Spartanburg, SC, 1998—. Pianist Grace Bapt. Ch., Landrum, SC, 1993—; mem. Spartanburg Youth Theatre Adv. Bd., 2000—. Mem.: S.C. Music Educators Assn., Music Educators Nat. Conf. Office: Houston Elem Sch 1475 Skylyn Dr Spartanburg SC 29307

BARRICK, MARLA CARYN, music educator; b. Henderson, Tex., Dec. 1, 1966; d. Jerry Don and Toni Peterson Hale; m. Stephen Carl Barrick, Dec. 23, 1989; children: Christopher Weldon, Kaitlyn Nicole. EdM, U. of Tex., Austin, Tex., 1993—96; MusB edn., Baylor U., Waco, Tex., 1987—90; AA, Kilgore Jr. Coll., Kilgore, Tex., 1985—87. Cert. All-Level Music Edn. Tex., 1990, All Level Special Edn. Tex., Elem. Comprehensive Educ. Tex., ED/Autism Endorsement Tex. Music educ. specialist Temple ISD, Temple, Tex., 1990—94; music edn. specialist Copperas Cove ISD, Copperas Cove, Tex., 1994—2003, target reading tchr., 2003—. Children's choir dir. First Bapt. Ch., Copperas Cove, Tex., 1999—. Contbr. clinician Time Mgmt. for Music Educators/Tex. Music Educators Assn. Com. chair First Bapt. Ch., Copperas Cove, Tex., 2001—03. Recipient Semi-Finalist, Excellence in Tchg., HEB, 2003, Tchr. of the Week, Toyota, 2003, Excellence in Tchg., Killeen Daily Herald, Tchr. of the Month, Applebees. Mem.: Growing Minds Club, Assn. of Tex. Prof. Educators (campus rep. 1994—2003), Music Educators Nat. Conf., Tex. Music Educators Assn. Home: 2501 Dennis St Copperas Cove TX 76522 Office: CR Clements Intermediate School PO Box 580 Copperas Cove TX 76522 Personal E-mail: barrick@vvm.com. E-mail: marla@ccisd.com.

BARRIE, JULIE ANNE, lawyer; b. Washington, Nov. 24, 1969; d. Robert Wesley and Paula Brodie Barrie. BA, U. Rochester, 1987—91; JD, Georgetown U. Law Ctr., 1991—94. Atty. Patton Boggs, L.L.P., Washington, 1994—98, Koteen & Naftalin, L.L.P., Washington, 1998—99; spl. counsel FCC, Mass Media Bur., Washington, 1999—2001; dep. chief Strategic Analysis and Negotiations Divsn. FCC, Washington, 2001—. Mem.: Am. Women in Radio and TV (bd. mem., chair govt. rel. 1998—99), Fed. Comm. Bar Assn. Avocations: travel, politics. Home: 4000 Cathedral Ave NW #135B Washington DC 20016 Office: FCC IB 445 12th St SW Washington DC 20554 Business E-Mail: julie.barrie@fcc.gov.

BARRINGER, JOAN MARIE, counselor, educator, artist, writer; b. Washington, Sept. 30, 1955; d. John Thomas and Maria Reginia Barringer. BA in Latin Am. Studies, George Mason U., 1981; grad. in Creating and Selling Short Stories, Inst. Childrens Lit., 1995; MA in Edn. and Counsel ing, George Mason U., 1999. Translator and receptionist Brazilian Emb., Washington, 1975—83; dir. and founder day care Rainbow City Army-Navy Country Club, Arlington, Va., 1983—87; visitors svcs. Nat. Gallery Art, Washington, 1991—94; workshop and leadership conf. asst. Women's Ctr., Vienna, Va., 1996—2000; career counselor Dept. Rehab. Svcs., Alexandria, Va., 1998—99, Ind. Art. Bus. Studio of Nat. Arts, 2002—. Author: (book of poems) Metronome, 1979; co-author: Great Contemporary Poetry, 1978; designer CD cover, singer Gift of Love; Fairfax (Va.) Jour., 1992, Montgomery (Va.) Jour., 1992, Viena Art Soc., 2004, exhibitions include Graffiti Gallery, 2002, Greenbelt Cmty. Ctr., 2003, Joanne Ross Gallery, 2007, [illegible] 2001, [illegible] Unity Ch. Mem.: Assn. Rsch. and Enlightenment (wayshower 2001—), Women's Caucus for Art (editor, lay out designer, writer, photographer newsletter 1999—), Sigma Pi Alpha. Avocations: genealogy, travel, interior decorating, yoga, photography, Oceanography. Home: 11107 Hampton Rd Fairfax Station VA 22039

BARRIO, SOLEDAD, dancer; b. Madrid; m. Martin Santangelo; children: Gabriela Goldin Garcia, Stella Goldin Garcia. Founder mem., dancer Noche Flamenca, N.Y.C. Recipient Bessie award, 2001. Office: Noche Flamenca 168 W 86th St New York NY 10024 E-mail: marting@arrakis.es.

BARRISH, CAROL LAMPERT, psychologist; b. N.Y.C., Oct. 6, 1945; d. J. William and Sally (Bobrick) Lampert; m. Michael Louis Barrish, June 30, 1974; children: Jordan Seth, Jessica Lynne. BA, Queens Coll., 1967; MA, Columbia U., 1972; PhD, NYU, 1993. Licensed psychologist; cert. learning disabilities cons.; lic., cert. spl. edn. tchr.; cert. reading specialist; cert. tchr. Tchr., team leader elem. sch. Englewood (N.J.) Bd. Edn., 1969-72, reading cons., 1973-74; curriculum coord. Adams Town House, N.Y.C., 1974-75; ednl., learning disabilities cons. N.Y.C., 1974—; reading/learning disabilities specialist, 1975—; clin. psychology intern Risk Inst., NYU Hosp., N.Y.C., 1990-91; psychologist com. for spl. edn. N.Y.C. Bd. Edn., 1992—; spkr. for tchr. trainer groups, project coord. dist. 4, lecturer, 1998—. Pvt. clin. practice for cognitive psychology, sch., N.Y.C. Author: (with others) Assessment of Social Skills Problems with Learning Disabled Adolescents, 1993. Mem. APA, N.Y. State Psychol. Assn., Orton Dyslexia Soc., Children and Adults with Attention Deficit Disorder, Nat. Assn. Sch. Psychologists, Kappa Delta Pi. Avocations: tennis, skiing. Office: 305 E 86th St Apt 4G West New York NY 10028-4702

BARRITT, EVELYN RUTH BERRYMAN, nurse, educator, dean; b. Detroit, Sept. 4, 1929; d. George C. and Ruby (Mathews) Berryman; m. Ward LeRoy Barritt, Oct. 28, 1951; 1 dau., Kelli Jo. AA, Graceland Coll., 1949; diploma, Independence (Mo.) Sanitarium and Hosp. Sch. Nursing, 1952; BSN., Ohio State U., 1956, MA, 1962, PhD, 1971. Asst. instr. nursing Atlantic City Hosp., 1952-53; staff nurse Shore Meml. Hosp., Somers Point, N.J., 1953-54, Ohio State U. Hosp., Columbus, 1954-55; instr. White Cross Hosp., Columbus, 1955-57; asso. dir. nursing service Riverside Meth. Hosp., Columbus, 1957-64; asst. exec. dir. Ohio Nurses Assn., Columbus, 1964-65; dean Capital U. Sch. Nursing, Columbus, 1965-72, Coll. Nursing, U. Iowa, Iowa City, 1972-79, prof. nursing, 1972-80; prof. Sch. Nursing U. Miami, Fla., 1980—, dean, 1980-85. Bd. dirs. Health Coun. South Fla., 1988—, pres., 1990-92; bd. dirs. So. Fla. Perinatal Network, Inc., 1980-89, pres., 1984-86; mem. Fla. Bd. Ind. and Pvt. Colls. and Univs., 1980; co-chmn. Dade County Indigent Care Task Force, 1991-93. Author: Florence Nightingale: Her Wit and Wisdom, 1975; author, editor: Thoughts on CareGiving, 1998; contbr. articles to profl. jours. Mem. Am. Nurses Assn., Ohio Nurses Assn. (pres. dist. 1966-68), Iowa Nurses Assn., Fla. Nurses Assn., Graceland Univ. Alumni Assn., Am. Assn. Higher Edn., Am. Assn. Colls. Nursing (pres. 1976-78), Independence Hosp. Sch. Nursing Alumnae Assn. Home: 416 Park Blvd N Venice FL 34285-1332

BARRON, BRIGID, education educator; BS in Psychology, U. Calif., Santa Cruz, 1984; MA in Psychology, Vanderbilt U., 1989, PhD in Clin. Developmental Psychology, 1992. Intern in child clin. psychology U. Wash., 1991—92; instr. Peabody Coll., Vanderbilt U., 1992—93; sr. rsch. assoc. Learning Tech. Ctr., Vanderbilt U., 1992—95; asst. prof. edn. Stanford (Calif.) U., 1996—. Mem. adv. bd. tech. task force SPEAK-UP! Leadership Program for Girls; cons. Plugged-In Tech. Access Ctr., Comty. Kids Children's Program. Office: Stanford U Sch Edn 485 Lasuen Mall Stanford CA 94305-3096

BARRON, CATE, editor; m. Bob Vucic; 1 child, Alex ; children from previous marriage: Matthew, Michael, Sarah. Grad., Georgetown U. News dir. WMRF radio sta., Lewistown, Pa.; reporter, sect. editor The Sentinel, Lewistown; asst. city editor Lebanon edit. The Patriot-News, Harrisburg, Pa., 1985, assignment editor, Sunday editor, features editor, 1991—2003, mng. editor news content, 2003—. Tchr. journalism Pa. State U., Harrisburg; spkr. in field. Mem.: Pa. Soc. Newspaper Editors (v.p.). Office: Patriot-News 812 Market St PO Box 2265 Harrisburg PA 17105*

BARRON, MYRA HYMOVICH, lawyer; b. July 5, 1938; d. Leo and Lillian Estelle (Berman) Hymovich; m. Jerome Aure Barron, June 18, 1961; children: Jonathan Nathaniel, David Jeremiah, Jennifer Leah. AB cum laude, Smith Coll., 1959; student, L'Institut des Hautes Etudes, Geneva, 1957—58; MA, Johns Hopkins U., 1961; JD, Georgetown U., 1970. Bar: Va. 70, DC 72, NY. Instr. econs. U. ND, Grand Forks, 1962—64; econ. rsch. asst. U. N.Mex., Albuquerque, 1964—65; legal aid staff atty. Fairfax County, Va., 1971—72, asst. county atty., 1974—81; assoc. Melvin & Melvin, Syracuse, NY, 1973; counsel Fairfax County Redevel. and Housing Authority, Fairfax, Va., 1981—88; ptnr. Sprenger & Lang (formerly Weissbrodt, Swiss & Mc Grew, 1989—98, Weinberg & Jacobs, Rockville, Md., 1998—2000, of counsel, 2001—. Dep. gen. counsel Housing and Devel. Law Inst., 1988—94, of counsel, 1994—2000. Editor: Jour. Affordable Housing and Cmty. Devel. Law, ABA, 1993—99; contbr. articles to housing jours.; mem.: Georgetown Law Jour., 1967—68. Recipient Samuel Bowles award, Smith Coll., 1959. Mem.: LWV (local chmn. nat. events 1962—64), ABA (mem. governing com. 1994—99, co-chmn. profit practice group 2000—03, mem. forum on affordable housing and cmty. devel. law). Home: 3231 Ellicott St NW Washington DC 20008-2061 Office: Weinberg & Jacobs LLP 11300 Rockville Pike Ste 1200 Rockville MD 20852

BARRON, PEGGY PENNISI, management consultant; b. Chgo., Jan. 27, 1958; d. Louis Legendre and Jane Harriet (Peters) Pennisi; m. Stan Barron, May 3, 1986; children: Brian Alexander, Christine Deanna. BS with honors, U. Ill., Chgo., 1979. Data processing mgr. Oasis Aviation, Inc., L.A., 1980-87; pres. Millennium Enterprises, L.A., Calif., 1987—. Author: Broken Bloodlines, 1997, The Big Daddy, 1999. Mem. NAFE, Phi Beta Kappa, Phi Kappa Phi. Avocations: scuba diving, sky diving, cooking and travel. E-mail: peggybarron@comcast.net.

BARRON, ROS, artist; b. Boston, July 4, 1933; d. Louis and Ida (Titel) Myers; m. Harris Barron, Apr. 19, 1953; children: Matt Lewis, Nina Rebecca. B.F.A., Mass. Coll. Art, 1954. Fellow Bunting Inst., Harvard U., 1966-68; co-dir. Zone Visual Theater Co., 1970; assoc. prof. art U. Mass.-Harbor Campus, Boston, 1974—. Vis. artist U. Colo., Boulder, 1983; presenter Arts at the Bunting, 1997. Producer numerous video performance tapes.; one-woman shows include North Hall Gallery, Mass. Coll. Art, Boston, 1988, Watson Gallery, Wheaton Coll., Norton, Mass., 1989, Harbor Gallery U. Mass., Boston, 1990, Mobius, Boston, 1993, Brick Bottom Gallery, Boston, 1996; exhbns. include Whitney Mus. Am. Art, 1967-68, Helen Shlien Gallery, Boston, 1979, 82, Mus. Modern Art, N.Y.C., 1980, 84, Le Nouveau Musee, Lyon, France, 1979, Montevideo Gallery, Amsterdam, Holland, 1979, World Wide Video Festival, Kijkhuis, Holland, 1984, Hirschhorn Mus., Washington, 1984, North Hall Gallery; travelling group exhbns. include Project Rembrandt Biennial, 1991-92, Women's Caucus for Art, 1992; represented in permanent collections Mus. Fine Arts, Boston, Harvard U., Smith Coll. Collection, Worcester Art Mus., Addison Gallery Am. Art., Inst. Contemporary Art, Boston, Samuel P. Harn Mus. Art, U. Fla., Gainesville, Mus. of Modern Art, N.Y.C., Mus. Modern Art, N.Y.C.; performance Art: (with Harris Barron) Mr. & Mrs. Zone: Art Life Art, Mobius Theatre, Boston, 1987, Performance Art: (with Harris Barron) Mr. & Mrs. Zone Again, Mobius Theatre, Boston, 1997, Eartheart and other video works, Mobius Theatre, Boston, 1999, Eagle Air, The Life and Work of Harris Barron, 2001. Bd. dirs. Boston Performance Artists. Recipient Design award HUD, 1968; N.Y. Found. for Arts grantee, 1972; Guggenheim Found. grantee, 1972; Nat. Endowment Arts grantee, 1975; Rockefeller Found. grantee, 1978-80; Mass. Council Arts grantee, 1981-82, 83 Address: 30 Webster Pl Brookline MA 02445-[illegible]

BARRON, STEPHANIE, curator; AB, Barnard Coll., Columbia U., 1972; student, Harvard Inst. Arts Adminstrn., 1973; MA, Columbia U., 1974; postgrad., CUNY, 1975-76. Intern, curatorial asst. Solomon R. Guggenheim Mus., 1971-72; Nat. Endowment Arts intern in edn. Toledo Mus. Art, 1973-74; exhbn. coord. Jewish Mus., N.Y.C., 1975-76; assoc. curator modern art L.A. County Mus. Art, 1976-80, curator Twentieth Century art, 1980-94, coord. curatorial affairs, 1993-96, sr. curator Twentieth Century art, 1995—, v.p. edn. and pub. programs, 1996—2003; chief curator Modern and Contemporary Art, 2002—. Lectr., panelist in field. Contbr. articles to profl. jours. Mem. art adv. panel IRS, 1996—; advisor U.S. Holocaust Mus., 1996—; trustee Scripps Coll., 1996—; mem. steering com. Villa Aurora, 1994—. Decorated comdr.'s cross Fed. Republic of Germany, Order of Merit (Germany); recipient George L. Wittenborn award ARLIS, 1991, award for best Am. exhbn. of yr. Assn. Internat. Critics Art, 1991, 97, Theo Wormland Kunstpreis, 1992, George L. Wittenborn award, 1992, Alfred H. Barr Jr. award Coll. Art Assn., 1992, E.L. Kirchner prize, Switzerland, 1997, First Pl. award Am. Assn. Art Mus., 1998, Hon. Mention, ARLIS, 1998; named Woman of Yr., Bus. and Profl. Women of UJA, Jewish Fedn., 1991, Friends of Tel Hashomer, 1991; Nat. Endowment of Arts fellow, 1986-87; John J. McCloy fellow in art, 1981. Fellow Am. Acad. Arts and Scis.; mem. Am. Assn. Mus., Internat. Mus. Modern Art (internat. com. mus.), Internat. Coun. Mus., Internat. Com. for Mus. and Collections of Modern Art, Art Table. Office: LA County Mus Art 5905 Wilshire Blvd Los Angeles CA 90036-4597 E-mail: sbarron@lacma.org.

BARRON, THEODORA S. retired music educator; b. San Mateo, Calif., Dec. 16, 1941; d. Everts W. and Dorothea M. Sundblad; m. Rodney L. Barron, Aug. 14, 1971; children: Michael E., David W., Heather L. MA, U. Calif. Santa Barbara, 1966, BA, 1963; AA, Coll. San Mateo, 1961. Educator Cert. Dept. of Def. Dep. Schs., 1999, Gen. Secondary Life Diploma State Bd. of Edn., Calif., 1971, Spl. Secondary Life Diploma in Phys. Edn. State Bd. of Edn., Calif., 1971. Tchr. La Cumbre Jr. H.S., Santa Barbara, 1964—68, Spangdahlem Elem./Jr. H.S., Germany, 1968—70, Kubasaki H.S., Chatan-san, Japan, 1970—73, Stuttgart Elem./Jr. H.S., Germany, 1986—91, Ludwigsburg Elem. Sch., Germany, 1991—92, Kaiserslautern Mid. Sch., Germany, 1992—2001. Camp counselor Girl Scouts, San Mateo, Calif., 1960; dir. day camp San Mateo Recreation Dept., 1961—68; choir dir. - adults and children Robinson Barracks Chapel, Stuttgart, 1986—92; choir dir. - children Ramstein Chapel, Ramstein, Rheinland-Pfalz, Germany, 1993—96; choir dir. Vogelweh Chapel, Kaiserslautern, Rheinland-Pfalz; adv. bd. Messengers Youth Choir, Ramstein, 1993—94; choir dir.-children's Vogelweh Chapel, Kaiserslautern, 1993—2001; ski instr. Holiday Hill, Calif., 1968. Leader La Leche League, Kadena AFB, Japan, 1976—84. Recipient Svc. to Youth award, Boy Scouts of Am., 1985, Transatlantic Coun. Patch, 1986, Dist. Award of Merit, 1987, God and Svc. Recognition award, 1989. Mem.: Dillon Cmty. Ch. Choir, Summit Cmty. Band (clarinet player), Kappa Delta Pi. Congregational. Achievements include Directed 43 children's musicals with moral lessons - school and church. Avocations: downhill skiing, music, reading, travel. Home: PO Box 2699 Dillon CO 80435 Personal E-mail: rodbarron@earthlink.net.

BARROS, LYDIA, elementary school educator; d. Francisco and Maria Barros; m. Manuel A. Mendes, Jr., July 19, 2003. MA in Ednl. Tech., N.J. City U., Jersey City, 2003. 2d grade tchr. Carteret Elem. Sch., Bloomfield, NJ, 1996—2003, 6th grade tchr., 2003—. Roman Catholic. Avocations: travel, tennis, exercising, spending time with family. Home: 90 Schuyler Ave Kearny NJ 07032 Office: Carteret Sch 158 Grove St Bloomfield NJ 07003

BARRY, ANNE M. public health officer; BA in Occupl. Therapy, Coll. St. Catherine; JD, William Mitchell Coll. Law; MPH, U. Minn. Dep. commr. health Minn. Dept. Health, Mpls., commr. health, 1995—99; dep. fin. commr. Minn., 1999—; acting commr. fin., 2002. Office: Dept Fin 400 Centennial Bldg 658 Cedar St Saint Paul MN 55155

BARRY, CAROLYN MCNAMARA, psychologist, educator; d. James J. and Constance C. McNamara; m. Daniel J. Barry, June 2, 2001. BS in

Psychology, summa cum laude, Ursinus Coll., Collegeville, Pa., 1996; PhD in Human Devel., U. Md., 2001. Supr. grad student tchr. mentoring program Human Devel. Dept, U. Md., College Park, 2000—01; asst. prof. psychology Loyola Coll., Balt., 2001—. Contbr. articles to profl. psychology jours. Recipient Gold award, Girl Scouts Am., 1992. Mem.: Am. Psychol. Soc., Coun. on Undergraduate Rsch. (councilor psychology divsn. 2002—), Soc. [illegible] Rsch. in Child Devel., Psi Chi, Kappa Delta Pi, Phi Beta Kappa. Roman Catholic. Avocations: piano, piccolo, flute.

BARRY, DIANE DOLORES (DIANE BRANKS), podiatrist; b. Cornwall, Ont., Can., Apr. 3, 1958; d. George Henry and Dolores Angeline (Latulippe) Barry; m. Paul Lloyd Branks, Sept. 19, 1987; children: Katherine Ann Branks, Andrew Joseph Branks, Annemarie Elizabeth Branks. BS, U. San Diego, 1980; B in Med. Sci., Calif. Coll. Podiatric Medicine, 1983, D in Podiatric Medicine, 1985. Lab technician Scripps Rsch. Inst., La Jolla, Calif., 1980, Salk Inst., La Jolla, 1981, Quidel Labs., La Jolla, 1982; dry waller Barry Drywall, San Diego, 1985; med. office mgr. Bay Harbor Podiatry Group, Harbor City, Calif., 1985; podiatry resident VA West L.A., 1986; podiatrist Bay Harbor Podiatry Group, 1987-88, Southeast Med. Ctr., Huntington Park, Calif., 1987-88, Kaiser Permanente, Fontana, Calif., 1988-97, Baldwin Park, Calif., 1997—. NIH grantee, 1997. Fellow Am. Coll. Foot and Ankle Surgeons, Am. Coll. Foot and Ankle Orthops.; mem. Am. Podiatric Med. Soc., Am. Diabetic Assn., Calif. Podiatric Med. Soc. (alt. 1994, 96, del. 1995), So. Calif. HMO Podiatric Med. Soc. (founder, pres. 1989-91, 97-98, v.p. 1999—). Republican. Roman Catholic. Office: Kaiser Permanente Med Ctr 1011 Baldwin Park Blvd Baldwin Park CA 91706-5806

BARRY, JANET CECILIA, retired elementary school educator; b. Jersey City, N.J., May 12, 1944; d. John Aloysius and Mary Elizabeth (Hart) B. BA, William Paterson U., 1966; MA, Georgian Ct. Coll., 1978. Tchr. Paterson (N.J.) Pub. Sch. No. 12, 1966-68, Walnut St. Elem. Sch., Toms River, N.J., 1968-88; supr. instrn. Cedar Grove Elem. Sch., Toms River, N.J., 1988-90, North Dover Elem. Sch., 1990-94, Hooper Ave. Elem. Sch., 1994-95; ret., 1995. Supr. instruction Toms River Regional Schs. Mem. Aviation Space Edn. Found. Recipient N.J. Gov.'s Excellence in Teaching award, 1987. Mem. NEA, ASCD, Nat. Coun. Tchrs. English, Nat. Sci. Tchrs. Assn., N.J. Edn. Assn., Ocean County Edn. Assn., Toms River Edn. Assn., N.J. Reading Assn., N.J. ASCD, Internat. Reading Assn., Ocean County Reading Coun. (rec. sec., 1st v.p., pres.), Georgian Ct. Coll. Grad Sch. Alumni Assn., William Paterson U. Alumni Assn., N.J. Prins. and Suprs. Assn., Challenger Ctr. Space Edn. Educator's Network, Coun. Elem. Sci. Internat., Delta Kappa Gamma (chmn. programs ednl. svcs., comms., Zeta chpt.).

BARRY, JOYCE ALICE, dietician, consultant; b. Chgo., Apr. 27, 1932; d. Walter Stephen and Ethel Myrtle (Paetow) B. Student, Iowa State Coll., 1950—52, Loyola U., 1952—58; BS, Mundelein Coll., 1955; postgrad., Simmons Coll., 1963—64, U. Ga., 1979, Calif. We. U., 1980. Registered dietitian. Prodn. supr. Marshall Field & Co., Chgo., 1955-59; dir. food svcs. Women's Ednl. and Indsl. Union, Boston, 1959-62, Wellesley Pub. Schs., Mass., 1962-70; regional dietitian Canteen Corp., Chgo., 1970-83; gen. mgr. bus. devel. Plantation-Sysco, Orlando, Fla., 1983-87; dir. product devel., corp. quality assurance, procurement Marriott Internat. Hdqrs., Washington, 1987-95; owner food svc. cons. svc., 1995—. Cons. Stokes Food Svcs., Newton, Mass., 1960-70; vis. lectr. Affiliate Produce for Better Health Found. Mem.: AAUW, Nat. Hist. Trust, Sch. Nutrition Svcs., Cons. Dieticians in Healthcare Facilities, Am. Dietetics Assn. (career adv. cons.), Food and Culinary Profls., Dietitians in Bus. and Comm., Smithsonian Instn. (assoc.), Washington Opera Guild, Met. Opera Guild. Republican. Roman Catholic. Home and Office: 1009 Pearce Dr Apt 102 Clearwater FL 33764-1107

BARRY, MARYANNE TRUMP, federal judge; b. N.Y.C., Apr. 5, 1937; d. Fred C. and Mary Trump; m. John J. Barry, Dec. 26, 1982; 1 child, David W. Desmond. BA, Mt. Holyoke Coll., 1958; MA, Columbia U., 1962; JD, Hofstra U., 1974, LLD (hon.), Seton Hall U.; LLD (hon.), Caldwell Coll.; LLD (hon.), Kean Coll. Bar: NJ. 1974, N.Y. 1975, U.S. Ct. Appeals (3d cir.), U.S. Supreme Ct. Asst. U.S. Atty., 1974-75; dep. chief appeals div., 1976-77; chief appeals div., 1977-82; exec. asst. U.S. Atty., 1981-82; 1st asst., 1981-83; judge U.S. Dist. Ct., N.J., 1983-99, U.S. Ct. Appeals (3d cir.), Newark, 1999—. Chmn. Com. on Criminal Law Jud. Conf. of U.S., 1994-96. Fellow Am. Bar Found.; mem. ABA, N.J. Bar Assn., Am. Judicature Soc. (bd. dirs.), Assn. Fed. Bar State of N.Y. (pres. 1982-83). Office: US Ct Appeals PO & Courthouse Bldg Rm 333 PO Box 999 Newark NJ 07101-0999*

BARRY, MILDRED CASTILLE, artist; b. Sunset, La., Feb. 23, 1924; d. Joseph Hippomene and Beatrice Victoria (Tinney) Castille; m. Francis Xavier Barry, Aug. 16, 1947; children: Christopher, Kevin, Maureen, Robin, Shane, Kim. BA in Edn., Sam Houston U., 1958. Cert. tchr., Tex. Tchr. Sacred Heart Elem., Conroe, Tex., 1959-67, Conroe Sam Houston Elem., 1967-68, Houston Ind. Sch. Dist. Elem., 1968-69. Tchr., stuent of Ernest Gaines, author-in-residence U. So. La., Lafayette, 1985-87, instr. memoir writing classes, 1995-96. Exhibited in group shows Opelonsas, La., 1973 (1st pl.). With WAC, 1944-45. Mem. Writers Guild. Roman Catholic. Avocations: reading, writing, painting, sewing, traveling. Home: 309 Beverly Dr Lafayette LA 70503-3109

BARRY, MIRANDA ROBBINS, internet and television producer, writer, educator; b. NYC, Jan. 18, 1951; d. Philip Semple and Patricia Allen (White) B. AB, Stanford U., 1972; postgrad., Columbia Law Sch., N.Y.C., 1978-79, Bank St. Coll. Edn., 2003—. Prodn. rsch. coord. The Best of Families/CTW, N.Y.C., 1975-77; freelance story analyst CBS Inc., N.Y.C., 1976-81; asst. mgr. spl. programs devel. Sta. WNET 13, N.Y.C., 1977-78; exec. coord. Nat. TV Theatre, N.Y.C., 1981-82; story editor Am. Playhouse, N.Y.C., 1982-83, dir. program devel., 1983-87, exec. story cons., 1987; dir. internat. prodn. McNeil/Allyn Films, London, 1987-88; sr. prodr. (TV series) Ghostwriter CTW, 1990, supervising prodr., 1991-94; tchg. fellow N.Y.C. Bd. Edn., 2002—; dir. Mirror Repertory Co., Arts in Edn., 2003—. Instr. TV writing New Sch. Social Rsch., N.Y.C., 1982-83; instr. screen writing Womens Interart Ctr., N.Y.C., 1981-83; adj. assoc. prof. Columbia U. Sch. Film, 1986-87, prof., 1988, 94-96; writer One Life to Live, ABC-TV, N.Y.C., 1994-95; co-dir., organizer TV Theater Workshop Sta. KTCA, Mpls., 1983; creator TV series Mom and Dad/Embassy-NBC, 1983; v.p., lic. support Zing Sys. LP, Denver, 1995; cons. feature film Children's TV Workshop, 1996—; exec. in charge of devel. JP Kids, 1996-97, v.p. creative affairs, 1997-99, sr. v.p. creative affairs, 2000-03; exec. dir. Loire Valley Internat. Theatre Festival, 2003—. Author: Time for Kids Readers, 2003; (play) Friends and Relations, 1981, (TV adaptation) A World to Care For, (TV series) MedSchool, 1980, (TV miniseries) Sara and Gerald, 1988, Who is Max Mouse?, 1993; co-author: Quincy Script Blood Ties, 1980, Basil, 1990; (screenplay) Pinkerton's Angel, 1989; scriptwriting resource person Sundance Inst., 1984-86; story editor Eugene O'Neill Nat. Playwright's Conf., 1984—; co-exec. prodr. (TV series) Green Wilma, 1997; exec. prodr. Yahooligans, 1999—; project dir. Going Global, KQED and World Affairs Coun., 1999-2000; dir. Romeo and Juliet, Mirror Repertory Co., 2003. Rape victim counselor St. Luke's Hosp., N.Y.C., 1979-81; mem. alumnae bull. com. Miss Porter's Sch., 1979-84, vol. Children's Aid Soc.; exec. dir. Loire Valley Internat. Youth Theatre Festival, Pontlevoy, France, 2003-. McKnight grantee Playwright's Ctr., Mpls., 1983. Mem. Writers Guild Am-East, Dramatists Guild, N.Y. Women in Film (sec., bd. dirs. 1984-85, 90-91). E-mail: mirandabarry@earthlink.net.

BARRY, NANCY MARIE, bank executive; b. Kansas City, Kans., Aug. 2, 1949; d. John Joseph and Lorna Marie Barry. BA in Econs., Stanford U., 1971; MBA, Harvard U., 1975. Divsn. chief pub. sector mgmt. World Bank, Washington, 1986-87, divsn. chief indsl. devel., 1987-90; pres. Women's World Banking, N.Y.C., 1990—. Founding mem. World Bank Consultative Group to Assist the Poorest-Policy Advisory Group, Washington; adv. com. Harvard Social Enterprise, Mass. Mem. Harvard Club. Office: Women's World Banking 8 W 40th St Fl 9 New York NY 10018-3993 Office Fax: 212 768 8510. E-mail: [illegible]

BARRY, SANDRA, school system administrator; Degree, Neb.-Wesleyan U., Calif. State U., Fullerton. Educator and adminstr. Buena Pk. Sch. Dist., 1968—97; supt. Anaheim (Calif.) City Sch. Dist., 2000—. Office: Anaheim City Sch Dist 10015 East St Anaheim CA 92805*

BARRYMORE, DREW, actress; b. L.A., Feb. 22, 1975; d. John and Jaid Barrymore; m. Jeremy Thomas, 1994 (div. 1994); m. Tom Green, 2001 (div. 2002). Appearances include (films) Altered States, 1980, E.T.: The Extra-Terrestrial, 1982, Irreconcilable Differences, 1984, Firestarter, 1984, Cat's Eye, 1985, Poison Ivy, 1992, Bad Girls, 1994, Boys on the Side, 1995, Batman Forever, 1995, Mad Love, 1995, Wishful Thinking, 1996, Scream, 1996, Like a Lady, 1996, Everyone Says I Love You, 1996, All She Wanted, 1997, Best Men, 1997, Never Been Kissed, 1998 (also prodr.), Home Fries, 1998, The Wedding Singer, 1998, Ever After: A Cinderella Story, 1998, Never Been Kissed (also exec. prodr.), 1999, Olive, the Other Reindeer, 1999 (voice & exec. prodr.), Titan A.E., 2000 (voice), Charlie's Angels, 2000 (also prodr.), Donnie Darko (also exec. prodr.), 2001, Riding in Cars With Boys, 2001, Confessions of a Dangerous Mind, 2002, Charlie's Angels: Full Throttle (also prodr.), 2003, Duplex, 2003 (also prodr.), 50 First Dates, 2004; (TV episodes) Amazing Stories, 1985, Con Sawyer and Hucklemary Finn, 1985, 2000 Malibu Road, 1992; (host) Hansel and Gretel, 1986; (TV movies) Suddenly Love, 1978, Bogie, 1980, The Screaming Woman, 1986, Babes in Toyland, 1986, Conspiracy of Love, 1987, Beyond Control: The Amy Fisher Story, 1993; (TV spls.) Screen Actors Guild 50th Anniversary, 1984, Night of 100 Stars II, 1985, Happy Birthday, Hollywood, 1987, Disney's 30th Anniversary, 1987. Recipient Star, Hollywood's Walk of Fame, 2004.*

BARSHEFSKY, CHARLENE, lawyer, former diplomat; b. Aug. 11, 1950; BA with honors, U. Wis., 1972; JD, Catholic U., 1975. Ptnr. Steptoe & Johnson, Washington, 1975-93; dep. U.S. trade rep. Exec. Office of the Pres. of the U.S., Washington, 1993-96, U.S. trade rep., 1996—2001; pub. policy scholar Woodrow Wilson Internat. Ctr., Washington, 2001; sr. internat. ptnr. Wilmer, Cutler, & Pickering, Washington, 2001—. Mem.: bd. dirs., Intel Corp., 2004-. Office: Wilmer Cutler & Pickering 2445 M St Washington DC 20037-1420

BART, POLLY TURNER, real estate developer; b. Peterborough, N.H., Feb. 28, 1944; 1 child, Greta Rose Bart. BAcl, Radcliffe Coll., 1965; PhD in City Planning, U. Calif., Berkeley, 1979. Contbr. President's Nat. Urban Policy Report to Congress, Washington, 1980; asst. prof. U. Md., College Park, 1981-84; real estate salesperson Coldwell Banker Comml. Real Estate Services, Balt., 1984-87; pres. Investment Properties Brokerage, Inc., Balt., 1988-98, Greenbuilders, Inc., 1998—. Mem. historic preservation adv. coun. Goucher Coll. Fellow Danforth Found., 1975-79, Ford Found., 1981. Mem. Comml. Real Estate Women (co-founder). Home and Office: 4033 Osborne Rd Reisterstown MD 21136

BART, SUSAN T. lawyer; b. 1961; BA, Grinnell Coll., 1982; JD, U. Mich., 1985. Bar: Ill. 1985, U.S. Ct. Appeals (7th cir.) 1985. Law clk. to Hon. Richard D. Cudahy, Fed. Ct. Appeals (7th cir.), 1985—86; with Hopkins & Sutter, 1986—94, ptnr., 1992—94, Sidley Austin Brown & Wood (formerly Sidley & Austin), 1994—. Articles editor U. Mich. Law Review, Ann Arbor, 1984-85. Co-author: Illinois Estate Planning: Forms and Commentary, 1997 (Outstanding Achievement award Assn. for Continuing Legal Edn. (1998), rev., 2002. Mem. Chgo. Estate Planning Coun.; mem. bd. dirs., exec. com. Ill. Inst. Continuing Legal Edn. chair Cfgo. Bar Assn. Probable Practice Com. Div. I; mem. Chgo. Estate Planning Coun., Women's Bar Assn. of Ill., Phi Beta Kappa, Order of the Coif. Avocations: classics, literature, feminist theory and jurisprudence. Office: Sidley Austin Brown and Wood Bank One Plz 10 S Dearborn St Chicago IL 60603*

BARTEET, BARBARA BOYTER, retired social worker; b. Vivian, La., Oct. 19, 1935; d. Boyce Oliver and Agnes Pauline Boyter; m. James Bernard Barteet; children: Lindsey, Lezlie, Tracy, Jeffrey. AA, Yuba Jr. Coll., Marysville, Calif., 1968; BA, La. State U., Baton Rouge, 1971, MSN in Libr. Sci., 1972, MSN in Social Work, 1984; student music, Ann Arundel C.C., Md., 1996—. LCSW Calif., 1988, Md., 1995. Social Worker La. State Penitentiary, Angola, 1984—86; social worker Jerry Pettis VA Meml. Hosp., Loma Linda, Calif., 1986—89, U.S. Army, Germany, 1989—94. Civilian Ambassador United States, Beijeng, Nanking, Shanghai, China, 1996, India, Nepal, New Delhi, Agra, Jaipur, Katmandu, 1997. Mem.: AAUW, Nat. Assn. Gold Star Wives. Presbyterian. Avocations: reading, piano, singing, travel. Home: 514 West Ct Glen Burnie MD 21061-4778 Personal E-mail: barbarabarteet@aol.com.

BARTEL, TERESA J. art educator; b. Frankfurt, Germany, Mar. 30, 1956; d. Vern Gustave and Joan Ruth Johnson; m. Ron E. Bartel, May 29, 1982; children: Chip E., Amy Lynn. B Art Edn., U. Wis., Oshkosh, 1979. Art tchr. Luxemburg Casco (Wis.) Schs., 1979—. Art St. vol. Northeastern Wis. Arts Coun., Green Bay, Wis.; marathon vol. Cellcom, Green Bay; Heritage Hill vol. Wis. State Hist. Park, Green Bay. Mem.: Preble Music Parents (co-pres. 1998—2000), Wis. Art Edn. Assn., Nat. Art Edn. Assn. Avocations: tennis, photography, travel, hiking. Home: 1743 London Rd Green Bay WI 54311 Office: LC High Sch 619 Church Ave Casco WI 54205 Business E-Mail: tbartel@luxcasco.k12.wi.us.

BARTELL, ANGELA GINA BALDI, judge; b. Milw., Jan. 25, 1946; d. John Batiste and Marie Alma (Rank) Baldi; m. Jeffrey Bruce Bartell, Aug. 31, 1968; children: Jessica Marie, Carey Laurel, Chad Gerald, Dana Joyce, Nicholas John. BA, U. Wis., 1969, JD, 1971. Bar: Wis. 1972, U.S. Dist. Ct. (we. dist.) Wis. 1972. Intern Wis. Dept. Justice, Madison, 1970; law clk. to Hon. James E. Doyle U.S. Dist. Ct. (we. dist.) Wis., Madison, 1971-72; assoc., then ptnr. LaFollette Sinykin Law Firm, Madison, 1973-78; county judge Dane County Ct., Madison, 1978-79; chief judge Wis. Fifth Jud. Dist., 1982-88; cir. judge Dane County Cir. Ct., Madison, 1979—. Mem. Professionalism Commn., Madison, 1990-93; mem. Legal Edn. Commn., 1994-95; mem. adv. bd. Scan Child Abuse Prevention Project, Madison, 1988-90; assoc. dean Wis. Jud. Coll., 1999—. Jud. editor Wisconsin Judician Benchbooks, 3 vols., 1980-92 (Supreme Ct. award 1992), Wisconsin Jury Handbook, 1983; contbr.: State Bar Civil Forms Manual, 1992-99, Wisconsin Jury Instructions-Criminal, 1992-2002. Pres. Young Lawyers divsn. Wis. State Bar, Madison, 1974; bd. dirs. Dane County United Way, 1995-2001, chair bd., 2000-01; chair United Way Allocation Com.; planner, presenter Leadership Madison Forum, 1994. Fellow Am. Bar Found.; mem. Am. Law Inst., Nat. Assn. Women Judges, Rotary Club Madison (pres. 2002-2003), Phi Beta Kappa. Office: Dane County Cir Ct 210 Martin Luther King Jr Blvd Madison WI 53709-0002

BARTELLI, ALICE HILL, librarian, secondary education educator; b. Greenfield, Ill., Dec. 26, 1951; d. Byron Mitchell Hill Jr. and Mary (Valentine) Downard; m. Stephen Rhoades, Aug. 13, 1973. BA, Pitts. State U., Kansas, 1974; MLS, U. Hawaii, Honolulu, 1975. Cert. tchr. Ill. Librarian Libr. For the Blind & Physically Handicapped, Honolulu, 1975-76, Office of Library Svcs., Honolulu, 1976-77; audiovisual librarian Hawaii State Library, Honolulu, 1977-79, children's librarian, 1979-85; library cons. City Council, Greenfield, Ill., 1987-94; 1990substitute tchr. Greene County Sch. Dists., Ill., 1990—98; owner/operator Bartelli's Trading Post, Inc., Greenfield, Ill., 1998—. Coord. photography contest Com. for Hawaii, Nat. Library Week, Honolulu, 1982; story teller Honolulu Zoo, 1983, Bishop Mus., Honolulu, 1984, Greenfield Pub. Library, Ill., 1986—. Author: (guide book) Greene County Days, 1994, (profl. jour.) Illinois Libraries, 1991; compiler: (guide book) Greene County Days, 1995, (directory) A Directory of 16MM Film [illegible] broadcaster Hawaii Pub. TV, Honolulu, 1982-84; historian Civic Hist. Display Commn., Greenfield, 1986; building cons. Greenfield Pub. Library, 1987-94. Avocations: drawing, painting, genealogy, photography, horse-back riding.

BARTELS, BETTY JANE, nurse; b. Cin., Mar. 7, 1925; d. William Charles and Irene Agnes (McLean) Roth; m. Donald Arthur Bartels Sr., 1946; children: Donald A. Jr., Virginia, Frederick, Bernadette. Nursing diploma RN, Good Samaritan Hosp., 1946; postgrad., Barry Coll., 1966—70. Mem. U.S. Nurse Cadet Corps, 1943—46; nursing staff Hines Vets. Hosp., Chgo., 1945—46; RN Sun Ray Health Resort, Miami, Fla., 1949-51; vol. libr. St. James Cath. Sch., Miami, 1966-70; RN North Shore Med. Ctr., Miami, 1970-72; charge RN Villa Maria Rehab. Ctr., Miami, 1972-76; pvt. duty RN Miami, 1976-80; staff RN North Shore Med. Ctr., Miami, 1979-91. Author: Amotrophic Lateral Sclerosis: Helping the Patient with Lou Gehrigs Disease, 1979, RN Mag., 1979. Vol. Bon Secours Hosp./Villa Marla Nursing Ctr., 1990—. Mem. Third Order of St. Dominic (pres., moderator 1974-80, 92-2000, 02). Democrat. Roman Catholic. Avocations: do-it-yourself projects, fishing.

BARTELS, JEAN ELLEN, nursing educator; b. Two Rivers, Wis., July 15, 1949; m. Terry D. Bartels, Aug. 14, 1971; children: Justin Dean, Ashlee Jill. Diploma, Columbia Hosp. Sch. Nursing, 1970; BSN with honors, Alverno Coll., 1981; MSN, Marquette U., 1983; PhD in Nursing, U. Wis., 1990. Staff nurse ICU Columbia Hosp., Milw., 1970-76; prof. nursing Alverno Coll., Milw., 1983-99, dean nursing, 1990-99; chair Sch. Nursing Ga. So. U., Statesboro, 1999—. Asst. edn. editor Jour. Profl. Nursing; contbr. articles to profl. jours. Mem. ANA, AACN (pres.), Internat. Soc. for Sci. Study Subjectivity, Midwest Nursing Rsch. Soc., Am. Assn. Collegiate Schs. Nursing, Am. Ednl. Rsch. Assn., Am. Assn. Higher Edn., Sigma Theta Tau, Phi Kappa Phi. Home: 912 Brittany Ln Statesboro GA 30461-4499 Office: Ga So U PO Box 8158 Statesboro GA 30460-1000 E-mail: jbartels@GeorgiaSouthern.edu.

BARTELSTONE, RONA SUE, gerontologist; b. Bklyn, Jan. 10, 1951; d. Herbert and Hazel (Mittman) Canarick; m. Alan Joel Markowitz. BS in Social Welfare, SUNY, Buffalo, 1972; MSW, Ind. U., 1974. Lic. clin. social worker Fla., diplomate in social work, cert. care mgr., advanced social work case mgr. Social worker YM-YWHA of Greater Ny, NY, 1974-75; dist. supr. NYC Housing Authority, Bklyn., 1975-77; field instr. Barry U. Sch. Social Work, 1980-81; project dir. United Family & Children's Svc., 1977-81; faculty Miami Dade Cmty. Coll., 1981-82; adult educator Sch. Bd. Dade County, 1981-82; med. social worker Mederi Home Health Agy., 1979-82; mem. adj. faculty Nova U., 1986-88; pvt. practice Rona Bartelstone Assocs., Inc., Ft. Lauderdale, Fla., 1981—; team leader curriculum devel., cert. in geriatric care mgmt. U. Fla., 2002. Adj. faculty Fla. Internat. U. S.E. Ctr. on Aging, 1996; conf. co-chair, Vancouver, BC, Canada, 2001; co-chair Internat. Care Mgmt. Conf., 2003; adv. bd. Caregivers Marketplace, 2003; coalition ptnr. And Thou Shalt Honor Care Mgmt. Conf., 2003; cons. and trainer in field. Contbr. articles to various mags., chapters to books. Mem. funding panel Area Agy. on Aging, Miami, 1985—89; active Friends of the Family Counseling Svcs., Miami, 1983—88; adv. bd., chair internship subcom. Lynn U., 1993—97; exec. bd. Fla. Geriatric Care Mgrs., 1993—2000, pres.-elect, 1998—2000; chair tng. com., exec. v.p. Alzheimer's Assn., Miami, 1994—97, bd. dirs., 1999, v.p., 1999—2002; co-chair Nat. Acad. Cert. Care Mgrs., 1994—97, v.p., 1997—; trustee Fla. Coun. on Aging, 1996—2002; team leader curriculum devel. U. Fla. Dept. Continuing Edn.; bd. dirs. Jewish Vocat. Svcs., Miami, 1985—92. Recipient Dade County Citizen of the Yr. award, 1982, NASW Social Worker of the Yr. award, 1982-83, Trail Blazer award, 1984, Up & Comers award in health care Price Waterhouse and So. Fla. Bus. Jour., 1990. Mem.: NICLC, NASW (treas. 1987—89), Internat. Care Mgmt. Conf. (co-chair 2003), Fla. Coun. on Aging (trustee 1996—2002), Fla. Geriatric Care Mgr. Assn. (exec. bd. 1993—2000, pres.-elect 1998—2000, Broward County care mgmt. licensing com. 2001—), Nat. Acad. Cert. Care Mgr. (co-chmn. 1994—97, v.p. 1997—2001), Assn. Profl. Geriatric Care Mgrs. (pres. 1988—94, chmn. credential com. 1993—), Nat. Coun. on Aging, Am. Soc. on Aging (bd. dirs. 2003—06), Gerontology Soc. Am., Caregivers Market Place (adv. bd. 2003—04). Democrat. Jewish. Home: 5342 SW 33rd Way Fort Lauderdale FL 33312-5574 Office: 2699 Stirling Rd Ste C304 Fort Lauderdale FL 33312-6592 E-mail: rbartelstone@Rbacaremanagement.com.

BARTENSTEIN, JEULI, federal agency administrator; b. Chgo., Dec. 27, 1950; d. Eugene and Sylvia (Myers) B.; m. Michael William Carleton, Mar. 23, 1991. BA with highest honors, U. Ill., 1972; postgrad., U. Calif., Berkeley, 1973-75; MPA, SUNY, Albany, 1980. Aide to maj. leader N.Y. State Assembly, Albany, 1979-80; budget examiner U.S. Dept. Health and Human Svcs., Washington, 1980-85; program analyst solid waste USEPA, Washington, 1985-89, program mgr. environ. edn., 1989-90, dep. dir. EPA Inst., 1990-97, sr. policy analyst, 1998—; dep. dir. The Center Peace Corps, Washington, 1997-98. Internat. trainer USEPA, USAID, UN, Argentina, Hungary, India, Slovakia, Mex., 1993—; mgmt. cons. Creative Cons., Washington, 1996—; seminar leader Fed. Women's Program, Albany, 1980; owner, designer greeting card co. Hat Chat, 1988-91. Author: poem; contbr. article to profl. jour. Pres., v.p., fin. chair, mem. com. chair bd. dirs. Reading Is Fundamental, No. Va., 1987—; mentor, advisor The Women's Ctr., Vienna, pub. spkr., 1990—; tutor DC Pub. Schs., 1980-87. Recipient Leadership in Info Tech. Tng. award Industry Adv. Coun., 1997, Hammer award for reinvention Vice Pres. Gore, 1996. Mem. Am. Soc. Pub. Adminstrn., NOW, Nat. Women's Mus., Presdl. Mgmt. Alumni Group. Avocations: bowling, travel, basketry, charitable fundraising, needlework.

BARTH, FRANCES, artist; b. N.Y.C., July 31, 1946; d. Frank and Helen Barth. BFA, Hunter Coll., 1968, MA, 1970. Instr. Princeton U., 1975-79, Sarah Lawrence Coll., Bronxville, N.Y., 1979-85; prof. Yale U., 1986—. One-woman shows include, N.Y.C., 1974—, Jan Cicero Gallery, Chgo., 1981, 1985, U. Mass. Amherst, 1994, E.M. Donahue Gallery, N.Y.C., 1994, 1997, 2000, Millersville Coll., Pa., 1995, Marcia Wood Gallery, Atlanta, 1998, 2001, 2002, Moravian Coll., Pa., 1999, Donahue Sosinski, N.Y.C., 2000, exhibited in group shows at Moore Coll. Art, 1970, Whitney Mus. Am. Art, N.Y.C., 1972—73, Houston Mus. Contemporary Art, 1972, Corcoran Gallery Art, Washington, Bard Coll., Annandale-on-Hudson, N.Y.C., 1973, Trenton State Coll., 1974, Princeton U. Art Mus., 1975, High Mus. Art, Atlanta, 1976, Bennington Coll., 1976, San Francisco Art Inst., 1978, U. Pa., 1978, MIT, 1978, Jan Cicero, CHI, 1995, Moravia Coll., Pa., 1999, William Patterson Coll., Wayne, N.J., 1979, NYU, 1979, Va. Commonwealth U., Richmond, 1980, Sarah Lawrence Coll., 1981, Mus. Modern Art, 1981, Cleve. Mus. Art, 1983, Indpls. Mus., 1984, 1985, Princeton U., 1985, Hunter Coll., 1986, Yale U., 1987, Bennington Coll., 1991, Am. Acad. Arts and Letters, 1988, Met. Mus. Art, 1990, Andre Emmerich Gallery, 1991, La Viglie, Nimes, France, 1995, Charles Cowles Gallery, N.Y.C., 1996, Am. Acad. Arts and Letters, 1999, 2004, Tucson Mus. Art, 2003, Represented in permanent collections New 20th Century Wing, Met. Mus. Art, N.Y.C., Mus. Modern Art, Akron Art Inst., Albright-Knox Gallery, Am. Can Co., Greenwich, Conn., Amerada Hess Corp., N.Y.C., Chase Manhattan Bank, Cornell U., IBM Corp., N.Y.C., Mobil Oil Corp., Prudential Inst. Co., N.J., Whitney Mus. Am. Art, Lehman Bros., N.Y.C. and Chgo., Isham, Lincoln & Beale, Chgo., Security Pacific Nat. Bank, L.A., Swiss Bank Corp., N.Y.C., Cameron Iron Works, Houston, Mus. Modern Art, N.Y.C., Paul Haim Found., Paris, Humana, Inc., Louisville, Coudert Bros., N.Y.C., Dallas Mus. Art, Tucson (Ariz.) Art Mus.

Grantee Creative Artists Pub. Svc., 1973, NEA, 1974, 82, N.J. State Coun. on Arts, 1987, Adolph and Esther Gottlieb Ind. Support, 1993; John Guggenheim fellow, 1977; recipient Joan Mitchell Found. award, 1995.

BARTHLE, AUDREY JEAN, medical technician, educator; d. John Joseph and Mary Ann Catherine Fischer; m. Dana Joseph Barthle; children: Samuel, Sarah, Jessica. AS in Diagnostic Med. Sonography, Hillsborough C.C., 1988. Cert. Am. Registry Diagnostic Med. Sonographers Abdomen, 1988, ob-gyn. diagnostic med. sonographers Am. Registry Diagnostic Med. Sonographers, 1989, registered vascular technologist 1997, lic. basic X-ray 1993, cert. HIV 1987, basic life support 1986. Supr. sonography Holiday (Fla.) Diagnostic Clinic, 1988—89; sonographer South Bay Hosp., Sun City Center, Fla., 1989—98; clin. instr. Ultrasound Diagnostic Sch., Tampa, Fla., 1990—91; sonographer Watson Clinic LLP, Lakeland, Fla., 1991—97; pool sonographer East Pasco, Zephyrhills, Fla., 1992—95, Dade City Hosp., Dade City, Fla., 1993—95; vascular lab technologist Clearwater Cmty. Hosp., Clearwater, Fla., 1993—99; ultrasound supr. Northside Hosp. & Heart Inst., Saint Petersburg, Fla., 1999—, Fla. Ctr. Gastroenterology, Largo, 2003—. Sabbath Sch. kindergarten leader Seventh-day Adventist Ch., Brandon, Fla., 1989—94, ch. women's choir, 1991—93, Kindergarten Sabbath sch. leader New Port Richey, Fla., 1998—99, children's minstry dir. St. Petersburg, Fla., 1999—2001, bd. mem., 1999—2001, Sabbath sch. coun. mem., 1999—2002, vacation Bible sch. tchr., 1999—, dir. vol. screening com., 1999—, sch. bd. mem., 1999—, primary Sabbath sch. leader, 2000—02, ch. choir, 2001, home and sch. asst., 2001—02, jr. Sabbath sch. asst., praise singer, 2002—, children's ministry asst., 2002—, deaconess, 1998—99, adventurer tchr., 2003—. Mem.: Gulf Coast Autism Soc., Suncoast Echo Soc., Soc. Diagnostic Med. Sonography, Florida West Coast Ultrasound Soc. (treas. 1998—2001). Seventh Day Adventist. Avocations: Bible study, nature photography, writing. Office: Northside Hosp & Heart Inst 6000 49th St N Saint Petersburg FL 33709

BARTHOLET, ELIZABETH, law educator; b. N.Y.C., Sept. 9, 1940; d. Paul and Elizabeth (Ives) B.; divorced; children: Derek DuBois, Christopher, Michael. BA in English, Radcliffe Coll., 1962; LLB, Harvard U., 1965. Bar: Mass., U.S. Supreme Ct. Staff atty. legal def. fund NAACP, N.Y.C., 1968-72; counsel VERA Inst. of Justice, N.Y.C., 1972-73; pres., dir. Legal Action Ctr., N.Y.C., 1973-77; asst. prof. law Harvard U., Cambridge, Mass., 1977-83, prof. law, 1983—. Bd. dirs. Legal Action Ctr., N.Y.C. Author: Family Bonds: Adoption and the Politics of Parenting, 1993; contbr. articles to profl. jours. Mem. overseers com. to visit Harvard Law Sch., 1971-77; bd. overseers Harvard U., 1973-77, Civil Rights Rev. Authority U.S. Dept. Edn., 1979-81; mem. ethics adv. coms. Brigham and Women's Hosp., 1990—, Boston Fertility and Gynecology Assn., 1991—; bd. dirs. Legal Action Ctr., 1977—. Mem. Assn. Bar City of N.Y. (exec. com. 1973-77), Am. Arbitration Assn. (labor and comml. panels), Soc. Am. Law Tchrs. (bd. govs. 1977-88), Fed. Mediation and Conciliation Svc. Roster Arbitrators, Harvard Club. Democrat. Office: Harvard U Sch Law 1575 Massachusetts Ave Cambridge MA 02138-2801

BARTHOLOMEW, SHIRLEY KATHLEEN, municipal official; b. Marysville, Wash., Jan. 26, 1924; d. Clarence E. and Mary (Hall) B. Grad. high sch., Marysville, 1943. Sec. Everett (Wash.) Broadcasting Corp. Inc., 1960-77, 1st Pacific Broadcasting, Everett, 1977-80. News dir. Sta. KRKO, Everett, 1943-80. Mem. coun. COunty of Snohomish, Everett, 1980-89, chmn., 1987-90; mem. Marysville City Coun., 1994-2001. Named to Edward R. Morrow Broadcast Hall of Fame, 1980; recipient Mng. Editors Citation AP, 1958-73. Republican. Avocations: opera, symphony. Office: City of Marysville 4822 Grove St Marysville WA 98270-4456

BARTHWELL, ANDREA G. federal agency administrator; Grad., Wesleyan U.; med. degree, U. Mich. Dep. dir. for demand reduction Office Nat. Drug Control Policy Exec. Office of Pres., Washington, 2001—; exec. v.p. Human Resources Devel. Group; pres. Encounter Med. Group; pres., CEO BRASS Found., Chgo. Mem. nat. adv. bd. Ctr. for Substance Abuse Treatment; mem. drug abuse adv. com. FDA; mem. AIDS com. Ill. Dept. Alcoholism and Substance Abuse; mem. Nat. Black Alcoholism and Addictions Coun. Mem.: Am. Methadone Treatment Assn., Soc. Addiction Medicine (pres. bd. dirs.). Office: Exec Office of Pres Office of Nat Drug Control Policy 750 17th St NW Washington DC 20503

BARTIZAL, DENISE, psychologist; b. Naperville, Ill., Oct. 14, 1963; d. H. J. and Dolores Underwood Bartizal; m. Jeff Ellis, Oct. 5, 2002. BA, Tulane U., 1984; MS, NOVA Southeastern U., 1993; PsyD, Caribbean Ctr. Advanced Studies, 1998. Nat. bd. cert. behavior analyst. Mental health technician NOVA Geriatric Inst., Lauderhill, Fla., 1992—93; behavior analyst Dept. Children and Families, Ft. Lauderdale, Fla., 1993—97; psychologist intern Fed. Correctional Instn., Petersburg, Va., 1997—98; sr. psychologist Ctrl. State Hosp., Petersburg, 1998—2001, Southside Va. Tng. Ctr., Petersburg, 2000—01; dir. dept. psychology Catawba State Hosp., Va., 2001—. Spkr. in field. Mem.: APA, Aerobics and Fitness Assn. Am., Assn. Behavior Analysis. Republican. Episcopalian. Avocations: travel, classic fiction, fitness. Office: Catawba State Hosp PO Box 200 Catawba VA 24070

BARTLESON, AMY AILEEN, psychotherapist; b. Park Ridge, Ill., Sept. 28, 1968; d. Warner H. and Mary Lou B. MA, St. Mary's U., Mpls., 1993; postgrad., Walden U. Psychotherapist St. Joseph's Home for Children, Mpls., 1994-96, Luth. Social Svcs., Washburn, Wis., 1996, Behavioral Health Svcs., Ashland, Wis., 1996-99; rsch. coord. Ind. U., Bloomington, 1999—; assessment counselor BHC Meadows Hosp., Bloomington, 2000—. Mem. Soc. Of Friends. Avocations: hiking, reading, volunteer activities. Home: 506 Ballantine Rd Bloomington IN 47401-5018

BARTLETT, CHERYL ANN, public health service administrator; b. Norwich, Conn., June 28, 1954; d. William Jr. and Frances (Fredette) B.; m. Rogers Washburn Cabot Jr., June 5, 1982 (div. July 1995); m. Bruce Templin Miller, Sept. 10, 1995. ASN, Quinnipiac Coll., 1979; student healthcare adminstrn., Stonehill Coll. Cert. Infection Control, dialysis nursing, HIV/AIDS nursing. Nursing supr. Nantucket (Mass.) Cottage Hosp., 1981-95, dir. nursing, 1995, dir. clin. svcs., 1995-97; public health officer Public Health Assocs. of Nantucket, Southeastern, Mass., 1989—; exec. dir. Nantucket AIDS Network, 1989—. Spkr. in field. Bd. dirs. Nantucket Housing Authority Properties Inc., Nantucket, 1997—; apptd. pres. Cmty. Action Com., Cape Cod and Islands, 1993—; selectman Town of Nantucket, 1993-96, county commr., 1993-96, chmn. Nantucket Bd. Health, 1992-94; mem. Coun. for Health and Human Svcs., 1990-93, chmn., 96—, chmn., 1998-99; pres. bd. dirs. Family and Children's Svc. Recipient Cmty. Recognition award AIDS Action Com. of Mass., 1996, Outstanding Cmty. Health Program, U.S. Dept. of Health and Human Svcs., 1993, Outstanding Citizens award Nantucket Rotary Club, 1992, Recognition for Dedication and Commitment for the Care of AIDS Patients, Mass. State Senate, 1991, Mass. House of Reps., 1991. Mem. ANA, Assn. of Nurses in AIDS Care (govt. rels. com. 1997, chmn. govt. rels. com. 1999), Assn. of Infection Control Practitioners (nominating com. 1991-92, bd. dirs.), Mass. Nurses Assn., Alpha Sigma Lambda. Avocations: reading, gourmet cooking, 3rd world travel, public health volunteer work. Home: PO Box 1248 Nantucket MA 02554-1248 Office: Nantucket AIDS Network 35 Old South Rd Nantucket MA 02554-2895 E-mail: cbartlett@nanet.org.

BARTLETT, DEDE THOMPSON, non-profit executive; m. James Wesley Bartlett; children: Katherine Morgan, John Eriksen. BA, Vassar Coll.; MA, NYU. V.p., corp. sec. Philip Morris Cos. Inc., 1991-94, v.p. corp. affairs programs, 1995—2002; comms. cons., 2002—; now pres. Women's Forum of N.Y. Chair adv. bd. Nat. Domestic Violence Hotline; bd. dirs. Domestic Violence Crisis Ctr., Corp. Alliance to Edn Ptnr. Violence; pres. Women's Forum N.Y. Recipient honors, YWCA, N.Y.C., Nat. Ctr. for Victims of Crime, Plays for Living, Nat. Coun. Jewish Women, Ctr. Against Domestic Violence, Lifetime TV. Mem.: Vassar Club (Fairfield County, Conn.). Home: 643 Oenoke Ridge New Canaan CT 06840

BARTLETT, DIANE SUE, counselor; b. Laconia, N.H., Dec. 6, 1947; d. Fred Elmer and Dorothy Pearl (Wakefield) Davis; m. Josiah Henry Bartlett, Aug. 23, 1980; 1 stepchild, Juliet ; 1 child from previous marriage, Fred Louis Hacker. AA, Plymouth State Coll., 1982, MEd, 1988; B in Gen. Studies summa cum laude, U. N.H., 1984. Lic. clin. mental health counselor. Mental health counselor, Ossipee, NH, 1995—; police comm. specialist Divsn. Motor Vehicles, Concord, NH, 1970-76, br. office mgr., 1976-83, coord. motor vehicle registrations, 1983-84; tax collector City of Dover, NH, 1984; intern Lakes Region Mental Health Divsn., Laconia, NH, 1985; counselor Latchkey Pastoral Counseling, Laconia, 1984-87; family therapist Children's Best Interest, Laconia, 1988—. Mental health counselor Carroll County Mental Health Svcs., Wolfeboro, NH, 1988—95; participant N.H. Ann. Conf. Status and Role Women, Concord, 1985—87. Mem. Moultonboro (N.H.) Sch. Feasibility Study Commn., 1978, Carroll County Domestic Violence Coun., 1997—, Friends of Families Carroll County, 1995—; mem. adminstrv. bd. dirs., chmn. pastor-parish rels. com. United Meth. Ch., Moultonboro, 1983—94, mem. adminstrv. bd. dirs. N.H. ann. conf., 1986—88. Grantee, N.H. Charitable Found., 1985. Mem.: ACA, Am. Mental Health Counselors Assn. Avocations: skiing, swimming, reading, writing. Home: PO Box 14 Moultonborough NH 03254-0014 Office: Mountainside Bus Ctr 127 Route 28 Ossipee NH 03864-7300

BARTLETT, JANET SANFORD (JANET WALZ), school nurse; b. Bryn Mawr, Pa., Aug. 13, 1930; d. Edward Joseph Walz and Anna Downing (Little) Walz Tomlin; m. Joseph Richard Bartlett, May 6, 1952 (div. April 1972); children: Cheryl, Elaine, Karen, Lee, Patrick, Michael. Diploma nursing, Meml. Mission Sch. Nursing, 1953; EMT-I cert., El Paso C.C., 1983. RN, N.C., Tex. Office nurse William F. Hillier, M.D., Asheville, N.C., 1953-55; school nurse Ysleta Ind. Sch. Dist., El Paso, 1973-93. Author: (manual) Sch. Nurse Manual, 1979, Volunteer's Handbook, 1979, (cookbook) Bartlett Heritage Cookbook; editor: (newsletter) Nurses Notes Newsletter, 1983-88; co-creator, copyright, D.K. Buster, 1989. Mem. El Paso Health Issues Forum, 1985—88; co-chair El Paso Oral Health Commn., 1987—; life mem. PTA; pres. El Paso coun., bd. dirs. Campfire Girls, Inc., 1971—74, leader Blue Birds, Camp Fire guardian; active Boy Scouts Am., Girl Scouts Am.; com. chair El Paso chpt. Am. Cancer Soc.; co-chair Ysleta Sch. Dist. Employee Wellness, 1989—90, compiler manual; sec. Unite El Paso Birth Packet Com., 1993—96, chmn., 1996—; founder, chmn. Health Connection, 1996—; apptd. oral health svcs. adv. com. Tex. Bd. Health, 1995—2003, vice chmn., 1999—2001; mentor Sageland Elem. Sch., 1994—97; mem. vestry St. Alban's Anglo Cath. Ch., 1996—99, sr. warden, 1997—99. Recipient Outstanding Staff Support award Ysleta Vol. Svcs., 1988-89, Stand Up for El Paso award KDBC TV, 1991, REACH award YWCA/El Paso Healthcare System, 1992, Pub. Health Partnership award El Paso City-County Health and Environ. Dist., 1998, Older El Pasoans Hall of Fame award Mayor's Adv. Bd. on Aging, 1999, Access award ADA Coun. on Access, Prevention and Interprofl. Rels., 2003, E. Bud Tarrson Access to Oral Health Care award ADA Found., 2003; named Woman of Yr. El Paso Parks and Recreation, 1995; named to Ysleta Ret. Sch. Employees Assn. Hall of Fame, 2000, El Paso Women's Hall of Fame, El Paso Women's Commn., 2002. Mem. Nat. Assn. Sch. Nurses, Tex. Assn. Sch. Nurses (Pres.'s award 1990, Tex. Sch. Nurse of Yr. 1991), Tex. Assn. Sch. Nurses Region 19 (v.p. 1982, 83, Sch. Nurse of Yr. 1990), Ysleta Sch. Nurses Assn. (pres. 1988, Sch. Nurse of Yr. 1991, [illegible] award 1995), Assistance League of El Paso (yearbook chmn. 1994, 95, Sch. Bell. com. 1994—). Avocations: swimming, knitting, cooking, children, traveling. Home: 10249 Bayo Ave El Paso TX 79925-4347

BARTLETT, KATHARINE TIFFANY, law educator; b. New Haven, Feb. 16, 1947; d. Edgar Parmelee and Elizabeth (Clark) B.; m. Christopher H. Schroeder, Aug. 13, 1975; children: Emily, Ted, Elizabeth. BA, Wheaton Coll., 1968; MA, Harvard U., 1969; JD, U. Calif., Berkeley, 1975. Bar: Calif. 1975, N.C. 1980, U.S. Dist. Ct. (no. dist.) Calif. 1975, U.S. Dist. Ct. (mid. dist.) N.C. Law clk. to presiding justice Calif. Supreme Ct., San Francisco, 1975-76; atty. Legal Aid Soc. of Alameda County, Oakland, Calif., 1976-79; A. Kenneth Pye prof. of law Duke U., Durham, NC, 1979—; dean, 2000—. Vis. prof. UCLA, 1985-86, Boston U., 1990. Grad. prize fellow Harvard U., 1968-69, fellow Nat. Humanities Ctr., 1992-93. Mem. Am. Law Inst., Soc. Am. Law Tchrs., N.C. Women Attys., Am. Law Inst. (reporter for principles of family dissolution), Phi Beta Kappa. Democrat. Office: Duke Univ Law Sch Sci Dr and Towerview Rd Box 90362 Durham NC 27708-0362

BARTLETT, NORMA THYRA, retired administrative assistant; b. Raymond, S.D., June 7, 1922; d. Wilhelm Emil and Olga Sophie (Mailand) Claussen; m. Fred Otis Metcalf, Mar. 29, 1941 (dec. Apr. 1963); children: Linda E. Lepak, Barry Otis (dec. Feb. 2000); m. Francis Grindal Bartlett, Dec. 27, 1963. BA, U. Wash., 1969; Diploma, Inst. of Children's Lit., 1997. Cert. profl. sec. Office mgr. Fed. Old Line Ins. Co., Everett, Wash., 1949-55; supr. office svc. Scott Paper Co., Everett, Wash., 1958-63; tchr. bus. edn. Canyon Park Jr. H.S., Seattle, 1969, Bellevue (Wash.) C.C., 1969; exec. asst. Peoples Bank, Starkville, Miss., 1970-76; prin. Satellite Steno Svc., Starkville, Miss., 1976-77; office mgr. Donald Wiley & Assocs., Sydney, Australia, 1977-80. Bd. dirs. United Cmty. Fund Snohomish County, Everett, Wash., 1961-62; pres. Scott Paper Co. Fellowship Fund, Everett, 1961. Hon. life mem. United Luth. Ch. Women, Everett, Wash., 1958—; organizer, charter pres. Starkville Bus. and Profl. Women, 1972-74; pres. Welcome Wagon Club, Ocean Springs, Miss., 1982-83; tutor Jackson County Literacy, Ocean Springs, 1985-88; organizer Discourse, Ocean Springs, 1985-86. Norma T. Bartlett scholarship named in her honor Starkville Area Bus. and Profl. Women, 1978. Mem.: AAUW (Gig Harbor br. media rep. 1997—99), Intertel, Mensa (local sec. 1989—91, editor newsletter 1987—89), U. Wash. Alumni Assn. Democrat. Lutheran. Avocations: needlework, reading, writing, travel. Home: 1305 N Highlands Pkwy Apt C1 Tacoma WA 98406-2171 E-mail: fgbart@comcast.net.

BARTLETT, SHERIE, printing company executive; m. Tom Bartlett. CEO, pres. Data Source, Kansas City, Mo. Office: Data Source Inc 1400 Universal Ave Kansas City MO 64120-2140 Fax: 816-483-3284. E-mail: info@data-source.com.

BARTLETT, SHIRLEY ANNE, accountant; b. Gladwin, Mich., Mar. 28, 1933; d. Dewey J. and Ruth Elizabeth (Wright) Frye; m. Charles Duane Bartlett, Aug. 16, 1952 (div. Sept. 1982); children: Jeanne, Michelle, John, Yvonne. Student, Mich. State U., 1952-53, Rutgers U., 1972-74. Auditor State of Mich., Lansing, 1951-66; cost acct. Templar Co., South River, N.J., 1968-75; staff acct. Franco Mfg. Co., Metuchen, N.J., 1975-78; controller Thomas Creative Apparel, New London, Ohio, 1978-80; mgr. gen. acctg. Ideal Electric Co., Mansfield, Ohio, 1980-85; staff acct. Logangate Homes, Inc., Girard, Ohio, 1985-88; pvt. practice acctg. Youngstown, 1985—; acct. Universal Devel. Enterprises, Liberty Twp., Ohio, 1987-88. V.p. Lang Industries, Inc., Youngstown, 1984-93. Author: (play) Our Bicentennial-A Celebration, 1976. Mem. various orchs., Mich., Va., Ohio, soloist, Mich., Va.; mem. Human Rels. Commn., Franklin Township, 1971-77, Friends of Am. Art; treas. Heritage Found., New Brunswick, N.J., 1973-74, New London Proceeds Corp., 1979-83; commr. Huron Park Commn., Ohio, 1979-83; elected Dem. com. mem., N.J., Ohio, 1970-82; vol. IRS for small bus., 1988-94; mem. planning com. Youngstown State U. Tax Insts., 1990-95, presenter, 1990098; bd. dirs., treas. Discovery Place, Inc., 1991-95; mem. planning com. for Children's Miracle Network Telethon, Tod's Children's Hosp., Youngstown, 1985-2001. Mem.: NOW (treas. Youngstown chpt. 1986—93), NAFE, Am. Soc. Notaries, Am. Soc. Women Accts. (bd. dirs. 1986—88, v.p. 1988—89, pres. 1989—91, scholarship com. 1991—2001, chair chpt. devel. 1995—96, bd. dirs. 1996—2001, bd. dirs. 1996—, chair program com. 1997—2001), Chataqua Lit. and Sci. Cir., Youngstown Opera Guild, Internat. Platform Assn., Women's Jour. Network, Nat. Women's Polit. Caucus, Bus. and Profl. Women (v.p. 1980—2001), Citizen's League Greater Youngstown, Friends of Am. Art, Sci. Cir. Club (pres. 1979—), Chataqua Literary Club, Franklin JFK Club (treas. 1970—72, v.p. 1973—78), Investment Club (pres. 1997—99, treas. 1999—2001). Democrat. Unitarian Universalist. Avocations: music, knitting, needlecrafts. Home and Office: Bartlett Acctg Svcs 278 Melrose Ave Youngstown OH 44512-2355

BARTLETT, SUE, retired state legislator; b. Billings, Mont., July 4, 1947; m. Gene Fenderson. BA, Wash. U., St. Louis. Clk., recorder Lewis and Clark County, 1983-91; asst. sec. Mont. Senate, 1991-92, mem. from dist. 27, 1992—. Mem., Child Care Partherships, Bd. of Dirs., Mont. Women's Lobby, Montana NARAL. Democrat. Home: 416 N Beattie St Helena MT 59601-3701

BARTLETT, SUSAN J. state legislator; b. Fall River, Mass., Dec. 18, 1946; m. William A. Bartlett. BA, U. Vt., 1968; postgrad., Johnson State Coll. Mem., Lamoille County Vt. Senate, Montpelier, 1993—; small bus. owner. Address: PO Box 123 Hyde Park VT 05655-0123

BARTLEY, JACQUELINE PRIOR, public relations executive, journalist; b. Augusta, Ga., Mar. 10, 1947; d. Jim Henry Neal Prior and Sarah Cathleen Hennemeire; m. Benny Douglas Bartley, Sept. 11, 1970; 1 child, Heather Diana. BA in Journalism, U. S.C., 1969. Copy editor The Augusta Chronicle, 1972—79, news corr., 1979—85; publicity dir. Beech Island (S.C.) Hist. Soc., 1990—. Editor, contbg. writer: (newsletter) Four Centuries & More, 1995—. Pres. Beech Island Hist. Soc., 1995—; bd. dirs. Region III S.C. Heritage Corridor, Aiken, SC, 2001—. Recipient Vol. award, Beech Island Hist. Soc., 2001. Mem.: Aiken County Hist. Soc., Archaeol. Soc. S.C. (Vol. award 2001). Avocations: cross country skiing, snorkeling, biking. Office: Beech Island Hist Soc 144 Old Jackson Hwy Beech Island SC 29842

BARTLING, PHYLLIS MCGINNESS, oil company executive; b. Chillicothe, Ohio, Jan. 3, 1927; d. Francis A. McGinness and Gladys A. (Henkelman) Bane; m. Theodore Charles Bartling; children: Pamela, Theodore, Eric C. Student, Ohio State U., 1944-47. Bookkeeper, Bartling & Assocs., Bartling Oil Co., Houston 1974-80; sec.-treas., dir. both cos., 1980— . Co-chmn. ticket sales Tulsa Opera, 1956-61; bd. dirs. Tex. Speech and Hearing Ctr., Houston, 1967-70. Republican. Episcopalian. Avocations: gardening, bicycling, cooking, golf. Home and Office: 11 Inwood Oaks Dr Houston TX 77024 6803

BARTMESS, MICHELE, public relations specialist; b. Oakland, Calif., Apr. 1, 1945; d. Jacob LeRoy and Thressa Lewis Bartmess. BA, Brigham Young U., 1967; M, Westminster Coll., 1998. Editl. asst. LDS Ch., Salt Lake City, 1967—71; reporter Green Sheet Newspapers, Murray, 1972—83; publicist Salt Lake Repertory Theatre, Salt Lake City, 1984; mng. editor Green Sheet Newspapers, 1985—93; pub. rels. specialist Granite Sch. Dist., Salt Lake City, 1984—. Mem. adv. bd. Murray City Arts, 1983—85; bd. dirs. Miss Utah Scholar Pagent, Salt Lake City, 1998—2002. Mem.: Utah Press Assn., Nat. Press Assn. Office: Granite Sch Dist 340 E 3545 S Salt Lake City UT 84107 [illegible] E-mail: jamtab4@aol.com.

BARTNOFF, JUDITH, judge; b. Boston, Apr. 14, 1949; d. Shepard and Irene F. (Tennenbaum) B.; m. Eugene F. Sofer, Sept. 10, 1978; 1 child, Nelson Bartnoff Sofer. BA magna cum laude, Radcliffe Coll., 1971; JD (Harlan Fiske Stone scholar), Columbia U., 1974; LLM, Georgetown U., 1975. Bar: D.C. 1975, U.S. Dist. Ct. D.C. 1975, U.S. Ct. Appeals (D.C. cir.) 1980, U.S. Ct. Appeals (fed. cir.) 1985, U.S. Ct. Appeals (11th cir.) 1988, U.S. Ct. Appeals (3d cir.) 1989, U.S. Claims Ct. 1991. Fellow Inst. Pub. Interest Representation, Georgetown Law Ctr., Washington, 1974-75; staff atty. Coun. Pub. Interest Law, Washington, 1975-77; spl. asst. to asst. atty. gen. criminal divsn. Dept. Justice, Washington, 1977-78, assoc. dep. atty. gen., 1978-80; spl. asst. U.S. atty. Office of U.S. Atty., Washington, 1980-81, asst. U.S. atty., 1982-85; assoc. firm Patton, Boggs & Blow, 1985-87, ptnr., 1988-94, assoc. ind. counsel, 1993-94; assoc. judge Superior Ct. of D.C., Washington, 1994—. Mediator U.S. Dist. Ct. D.C., 1991-94; mem. com. on pro se litig. U.S Dist. Ct., 1991-94. Mem. D.C. Bar Task Force on Children at Risk, 1997—98, D.C. Child Support Guidelines Commn., 2003—. Fellow Am. Bar Found.; mem. Nat. Assn. Women Judges, D.C. Bar, Women's Bar Assn. Office: 500 Indiana Ave NW Washington DC 20001-2131 E-mail: bartnofj@dcsc.gov.

BARTO, DEBORAH ANN, physician; b. West Chester, Pa., July 27, 1948; d. Charles Guy and Jeannette Victoria (Golder) B. BA, Oberlin Coll., 1970; MD, Hahnemann U., 1974; Reiki III, N.W. Sch. Healing, 2003. Cert. Reiki master. Intern, resident Kaiser Permanente Hosp., San Francisco, 1974-77; dir. med. oncology Evergreen Hosp., Kirkland, Wash., 1980-85, head oncology quality assurance, 1992-94; med. dir. Cmty. Home Health Care Hospice, Seattle, 1981-84. Mem. hosp. ethics com. Evergreen Hosp., 1995-98, mem. integrative care com., 1996-2001. Mem. Evergreen Women's Physicians, Reiki III. Democrat. Buddhist. Avocation: horseback riding. Office: Evergreen Profl Plz 12911 120th Ave NE Ste E60 Kirkland WA 98034-3047

BARTO, SUSAN CAROL, writer; b. Bklyn., June 21, 1941; d. William O. and Eda (Birra) Forcellon; m. Harry W. Barto, Mar. 11, 1960; 1 child, William M. Cert., Katherine Gibbs, 1960; student, Union Coll., 1979-82. Sec. dean of students Montclair (N.J.) State Coll., 1960; sec. Presbyn. Synod of N.J., East Orange, N.J., 1961-62; exec. sec. Union County Rep. Com., Westfield, N.J., 1971-79; legis. aide State Senator James Vreeland-Morris County, N.J., 1977-79. Author of short stories. County com. woman Union County Rep. Com., Westfield, 1970-82; active New Providence (N.J.) Libr. Bd., 1979-86. Recipient plaque of appreciation New Providence (N.J.) Libr. Bd., 1986. Mem. Friends of the Hunterdon Mus. of Art (pres. 1996-99). Presbyterian. Home and Office: 1 Fisher Ct Lebanon NJ 08833-2107

BARTOL, KATHERINE AURELIA, music educator, mezzo soprano; b. Indpls., Dec. 6, 1959; d. Clarence Joseph and Sophia Martha Bartol; life ptnr. Gary Richard Beveridge, Dec. 23, 1994; children: Christa Lisette, Heather Katherine. BS in Music Edn., West Chester U., Pa., 1981, MusM, 1989; postgrad. studies, U.Minn., Ind. U. of Pa., Pa. State U. Cert. Level II instr. in Music Pa., Kodály II, OrffI, Peer Coaching. Private piano and voices instr., Selinsgrove, Pa., 1981—89; dir. show choir Susquehanna U., Selinsgrove, Pa., 1988—89; music instr., chorus dir. Selinsgrove Elem. Schs., 1981—83, Selinsgrove Middle Sch, 1983—97; dir. choral music, dept. chair Selinsgrove H.S., 1997—. Profl. singer Studio, Dance and Rock Bands, in New York and Pa., 1981—; cooperating tchr. Susquehanna U., 1985—, Pa. State U., 1995—. Performer: World Premiere John Rutter's Mass of the Children, 2003; singer: Nat. Anthem at Pa. State Edn. Assn. Ho. Dels meeting, 1989; contbr. articles to profl jours. and chpts. to tchr. guide. Vol. performer Area Nursing Homes, Snyder and Northumberland Counties, Pa. Mem.: NEA, Pa. Middle Sch. Assn. (Exemplary Choral Performance 1994), Am. Choral Dirs. Assn., Kodaly Educators Ea. Pa., Pa. State Edn. Assn., Pa. Music Educators Assn. (Exemplary Choral Performance 1993), Music Educators Nat. Conf. Avocations: skiing, snorkeling, bicycling, painting, travel. Home: 940 Strawbridge Rd Northumberland PA 17857 Office: Selinsgrove Area HS 500 N Broad St 17870

BARTOLACCI, PAULETTE MARIE, middle school educator, aerobics instructor; b. Phillipsburg, Pa., Aug. 19, 1969; d. Anthony Thomas and Pauline Virginia (Leh) B. BS in Elem. Edn., St. Joseph U., Phila., 1991; MS in Bilingual, Bicultural Studies, Lehigh U., 1997. 6th grade tchr. Our Lady of Prepetual Help, Bethlehem, Pa., 1992-93; 1-4th grade lang. arts tchr. for ESOL children Allentown (Pa.) Sch. Dist., 1993-97, interim asst. to dir. instrl. support svcs., 1998, 6th grade lang. arts tchr., 1997—, insvc. steering com. mem. Fellow Pa. State Nat. Writing Project, Fogelsville, Pa., 1993—, outreach mem., 1995—; cheerleading coach S. Mountain Middle Sch., Allentown, 1998-99, mem. leadership team for stds.-based edn., support tchr. for student tchrs., peer mentor for peer edn., also mem. sch. coun. Grantee Nat. Writing Project, Pa. State U., 1995-99. Mem. ASCD, Pa. Edn. Assn., Allentown Edn. Assn., Nat. Coun. Tchrs. of English, Aerobics and Fitness Assn. Am. (cert., instr. summer 1998) Republican. Roman Catholic. Avocations: aerobics, singing, jazz dancing, guitar. Home: 4139 Waterford Dr Center Valley PA 18034-8690

BARTOLETTI, GINA P. assistant principal, art educator; b. Wilkes-Barre, Pa., Sept. 1, 1961; d. Anthony Joseph and Angelica Elizabeth Izzo Bartoletti. BS in Art Edn., Kutztown U., 1984; MS in Sch. Leadership, Marywood U., 1996. Cert. K-12 art, prin.-adminstrv. K-12. Tchr. art Wilkes-Barre Area Sch. Dist., Pa., 1984—99, asst. prin., 1999—. Asst. coach softball Dallas Sch. Dist., 1984—89; head coach softball Wilkes-Barre Area Sch. Dist., 1989—94. Mem.: ASCD, Act 93 Adminstrs. Assn. (sec. 2001—), Pa. Assn. Elem. and Secondary Sch. Prins., Nat. Assn. Elem. and Secondary Sch. Prins. Avocations: softball, golf, yoga, meditation, gardening.

BARTOLI, CECILIA, soprano; b. Italy, 1967; d. Pietro Angelo and Silvana B. Attended, Academia de Santa Cecilia. Recording artist Decca/London, 1986—. Stage debut, Verona, 1987; appearances include La Scala, Met. Opera, Opéra Bastille, Carnegie Hall, Berlin, Nantes, Warsaw, Naples, Zürich, Orch. Hall, Chgo.; albums: include Rossini Recital, 1990, Mozart Arias, 1991, Rossini Heroines, 1992, Arie Antiche, 1992, The Impatient Lover: Italian Songs by Beethoven, Schubert, Mozart, Haydn, 1993 (Grammy award for best classical vocal performance, 1994), Mozart Portraits, 1995, An Italian Songbook, 1997 (Grammy award for best classical vocal performance, 1997), Vivaldi album, 1999 (Grammy award for best classical vocal performance, 2000), Gluck Italian Arias, 2001 (Grammy award for best classical vocal performance, 2001), The Salieri Album, 2003. Named Musical America's Vocalist of Yr., 1993. Office: c/o Edgar Vincent 157 W 57th St Ste 502 New York NY 10019-2210

BARTOLI, JILL SUNDAY, reading and language arts researcher and educator; b. Carlisle, May 17, 1945; d. Harvey Preston and Helen Elizabeth (Hershey) Sunday; m. James Carl Bartoli, June 26, 1971; children: David Carl, Daniel Joseph, Stephen Mario, Catherine Elizabeth, Patrick Preston. BA in English and Speech, U. Ky., 1966, MA in English, 1967; MEd in Reading, Shippensburg U., 1977; PhD in Lang. Arts and Family Literacy, U. Pa., 1986. Cert. supr. comm., cert. reading specialist, Pa. Tchr. English and speech Cumberland Valley H.S., Mechanicsburg, Pa., 1969-73; lectr. English Pa. State U., York, 1968-69; rsch. assoc. U. Pa., Phila., 1988-89, lectr., 1987-89; assoc. prof. Elizabethtown (Pa.) Coll., 1990—. Coll.-sch. partnership dir. Elizabethtown and Steelton Sch. Dist., 1989—, rsch. grant dir., writer, 1992—, partnership with Harrisburg Sch. Dist., 2002—. Author: Unequal Opportunity, 1995, Celebrating City Teachers, 2001; co-author: Reading/Learning Disability, 1988; contbr. articles to profl. jours.; rschr. on successful inner-city schs. Organizer, mem. Social Justice Coalition, Carlisle, Pa., 1990—; mem. cmty. svc. com. Elizabethtown Coll., 1992—. Mem. NAACP, Nat. Coun. Tchrs. of English (mem. nominating com. 1980-92, presenter), Nat. Assn. for Edn. of Young Children, Am. Ednl. Rsch. Assn. (session chairperson 1985-96), Internat. Reading Assn., Kappa Delta Pi (counselor 1992—), Phi Delta Kappa. Home: 316 Garland Dr Carlisle PA 17013-4229 Office: Elizabethtown Coll 1 Alpha Dr Elizabethtown PA 17022-2298 Office Phone: 717-361-1379. E-mail: bartoljs@etown.edu.

BARTOLO, DONNA MARIE, nursing administrator; b. Springfield, Ill., Mar. 21, 1941; d. Elmer Ralph Bartolomucci and Zoe (Rose) Cavatorta. Diploma in nursing, St. John's Sch. Nursing, Springfield, Ill., 1962; BS, Milliken U., 1976; MA, Sangamon State U., 1978. Pediatric nurse Springfield Clin., 1962—64, physician's asst., 1972—74; gynecol. nurse Watson Clin., Lakeland, Fla., 1964—66; cons. state sch. nurses Office of Edn. State of Ill., Springfield, 1974—78; assoc. dir. operating rm. svcs. Cedars-Sinai Med. Ctr., L.A., 1978—82, co-dir. div. nursing, 1981—82; surg. nurse Emory U. Hosp., Atlanta, 1966—70, asst. dir. nursing, surg. svcs., 1982—94; v.p. Clinical Oper., Heart Care Plus, Inc., 1999—2001; dir. surg. svcs., dir. nursing Emory U. Hosp., Atlanta, 1994—97, dir. nursing for surg. scis., 1998—2000; nurse surveyor Joint Commn. of Accreditation of Health Care Orgns., 2000—01; v.p. clin. ops. TeleHealth Home Monitoring Co., Atlanta, 2001—; v.p. nursing St. Mary's Hosp., Athens, Ga., 2001—02, nurse adminstr. cons. Cenetalin, Ill., 2002—. Adj. prof. Nell Hodgson Woodruff Sch. Nursing Emory U. Mem. editorial bd. Perioperative Nursing Quarterly; contbr. articles to nursing jours. Mem. Org. Nurse Execs., Ga. Assn. Nurse Exec. (pres. elect, pres. 1992), Assn. Operating Rm. Nurses, Sigma Theta Tau (sec. 1990—). Home: 1424 So Douglas Springfield IL 62704

BARTOLOTTI, VIRGINIA L. retired principal; b. Bklyn., Oct. 10, 1942; d. Emanuel A. and Rose (Campagna) Bartolotti. BS, Bklyn. Coll., 1964; MA, NYU, 1967; MS, Bklyn. Coll., 1975; PhD, NYU, 1987. Tchr. math. N.Y.C. Bd. Edn., 1964—78, math. coord., 1978—88, prin., 1988—99, hearing officer, 1999—2001.

BARTON, ALICE, physician, educator; b. West Long Branch, N.J., Sept. 29, 1953; d. David Knox and Ruth B. Barton; children: Lara, Seth, Peter. BA, Harvard U., 1975; MD, N.Y. Med. Coll., 1992. Diplomate Am. Bd. Internal Medicine. Tchr. art history Westover Sch., Middlebury, Conn., 1975-78; gen. surgery intern N.Y. Med. Coll., N.Y.C., 1992-93, resident in neurol. surgery, 1993-95; resident in internal medicine Stamford (Conn.) Hosp., 1995-97; attending physician ER Horton Hosp., Middletown, N.Y., 1997-98; attending physician HIV Ctr. St. Luke's-Roosevelt Hosp., N.Y.C., 1998-99; attending physician, asst. prof. medicine Ctr. Spl. Studies Cornell U. Med. Sch., N.Y.C., 1999—. Contbr. essays, articles to profl. jours. Recipient Janet M. Glasgow Meml. Achievement award, Am. Med. Women's Assn., Samuel Spiegel, MD Meml. award, N.Y. Med. Coll., 1992. Mem.: Phi Beta Kappa, Alpha Omega Alpha. Office: Cornell Chelsea Ctr Spl Studies 119 W 24th St New York NY 10011-1913 Home: 3 Hidden St Providence RI 02906-1418

BARTON, ANN ELIZABETH, retired corporate financial executive; b. Long Lake, Mich., Sept. 8, 1923; d. John and Inez Mabel (Morse) Seaton; m. H. Kenneth Barton, Apr. 3, 1948; children: Michael, John, Nancy. Student, Adrian Coll., 1943, Citrus Coll., 1967, Mt.San Antonio Coll., 1969—71, Golden Gate U., 1976, Coll. Fin. Planning, 1980—82. CFP. Tax cons., real estate broker, Claremont, Calif., 1967—72, Newport Beach, Calif., 1972—74; v.p., officer Putney, Barton, Assocs., Inc., Walnut Creek, Calif., 1975—94; ret., 1997. Bd. dirs. Fin. Svc. Corp. Mem.: Inst. CFP, Nat. Assn. Enrolled Agts., Calif. Soc. Enrolled Agts., Internat. Assn. Fin. Planners (registered investment advisor).

BARTON, BABETTE B. lawyer, educator; b. Los Angeles, Apr. 30, 1930; d. Milton Vernon and Ruth (Schreiber) Barancik; children: Jeffrey B. Barton, David R. Barton, Baird R. Barton. BS, U. Calif., Berkeley, 1951, LLB, 1954. Bar: Calif., U.S. Dist. Ct., U.S. Ct. Appeals 1955. Law clk. to Hon. Phil S. Gibson Calif. Supreme Ct., San Francisco, 1954-55; lectr., acting prof. U. Calif. Sch. Law, Berkeley, 1961-72, prof., 1972-99, prof. emeritus, 1999—; Adrian A. Kragen chair U. Calif., Berkeley. Cons. Calif. Inter Agy. Task Force on Electronic Funds Transfers, 1978-79, Dept. Treasury, 1963; adv. com. Calif. Bd. Legal Specialization, 1980-83. Contbr. chpts. to books in field. Adv. com. Alameda County Dir. Welfare, 1970 73; bd. dirs. Family Service Berkeley, 1967-74, Univ. Students' Coop. Assn., 1966-74. Recipient Citation award Boalt Hall Alumni Assn., 1997. Fellow Am. Law Inst., Am. Bar Found.; mem. ABA (taxation sect. chmn. tchg. tax. com. 1994-96, real property probate and trust sect. coun. 1977-79), Calif. State Bar (chmn. taxation sect. 1976-77, Joanne M. Garvey award taxation sect. 1997), Western Regional Bar Assn. (chmn. 1978-79), Am. Coll. Tax Counsel, San Francisco Tax Club, San Francisco Estate Planning Coun., Berkeley Tennis Club (bd. dirs. 1988-90, pres. 1990-91). Home: 16 Saint James Dr Piedmont CA 94611-3533 Office: U Calif Berkeley Sch Law 691 Simon Boalt Hl Berkeley CA 94720-0001

BARTON, BETTY LOUISE, school system administrator; b. Shawnee Mission, Kans., Jan. 12, 1931; d. David and Dora Elizabeth (Grother) Schulteis; m. William Clayton Barton, Aug. 11, 1951; children: Linda Ann, Sharon Elaine. BA, Washburn U., 1951; MS in Curriculum and Instrn., Kans. U., 1976, EdD, 1983. Cert. ednl. adminstrn., curriculum and instrn., Kans. Classroom tchr. Topeka Pub. Schs., 1951-52; music tchr. Shawnee Mission Schs., 1959-62, classroom tchr., 1962-65, 69-72, asst. prin., 1976-83, prin., 1983—96; elem. adminstr. DeSoto (Kans.) Schs., 2001—. Bd. dirs. Headstart, Shawnee Mission, 1991—. Child Abuse Coalition, Shawnee Mission, 1984-94, Parents as Tchrs., Shawnee Mission, 1989-93, Srs. Serving Schs., Shawnee Mission. Bd. dirs. Multidisciplinary Team, Johnson County, Kans., 1992-94; mem. early childhood adv. com. Johnson County C.C., 1988-93. Named Adminstr. of Yr., Shawnee Mission Schs., 1996; recipient award for outstanding dissertation, Internat. Reading Assn., 1984. Mem. ASCD, Shawnee Mission Adminstrs. Assn. (pres., Adminstr. of Yr. 1990), Phi Delta Kappa. Lutheran. Avocations: music, writing, gardening, reading. Home: 9301 High Dr Leawood KS 66206-1918 Office: Cherokee Elem Sch 8714 Antioch Rd Shawnee Mission KS 66212-3698

BARTON, ELIZABETH SPINDLER, psychologist, fiber artist; b. York, Eng., Apr. 27, 1943; came to the U.S., 1976; d. George Richard and Norah (Richardson) Spindler; m. John Laing Barton, Dec. 28, 1966; children: Alexandra Clare, Felicity Jane. BA, Hull (U.K.) U., 1965; MSc, Leeds (U.K.) U., 1967, PhD, 1975. Lic. psychologist, Ga. Clin. psychologist Claypenny Hosp., Easingwold, U.K., 1962-65, St. James Hosp., Leeds, U.K., 1965-66, Scalebor Park Hosp., Burley in Wharfedale, U.K., 1966-67, Kans. Neurol. Inst., Topeka, Kans., 1968-69, Meanwood Park Hosp., Leeds, 1969-76, St. Louis Devel. Disability Treatment Ctr., St. Louis, 1977-79; asst. prof. S.E. Mo. State U., Cape Girardeau, 1979-86; clin. psychologist U. Ga., Athens, 1987—. Solo shows include Brenau Coll., Gainesville, Ga., 1997, Callanwolde Ctr., Atlanta, 1998, Art Sch. Gallery, U. Ga., 1999, Tate Gallery, 2000, Atlanta Fin. Ctr., 2000, Lyndon Konse Art Ctr., 2001, Oconee Art Ctr., 2002, Guinnet Cultural Ctr., 2003; exhibited works in shows at Lyndon House Art Show, Athens, 1986, 87, 88, 93, 94, 95, Quilt Nat. 1995, San Diego Art Mus., 1996, Mobile (Ala.) Mus. Art, 1996, Halsey Gallery, Charleston, S.C., others; individual artist commn. Hartsfield Internat. Airport, 1995-96; contbr. articles to profl. jours. Individual Artist grantee State of Ga., 1994; Individual Artist grantee SAF/NEA, 1995. Office: Uga Athens GA 30602-0002

BARTON, JANICE SWEENY, chemistry educator; b. Trenton, N.J., Mar. 22, 1939; d. Laurence U. and Lillian Mae (Fletcher) S.; m. Keith M. Barton, Dec. 20, 1967. BS, Butler U., 1962; PhD, Fla. State U., 1970. Postdoctoral fellow Johns Hopkins U., Balt., 1970-72; asst. prof. chemistry East Tex. State U., Commerce, 1972-78, Tex. Woman's U., Denton, 1978-81; assoc. prof. Washburn U., Topeka, 1982-88, prof., 1988—, chair chemistry dept., 1992—. Mem. undergrad. faculty enhancement panel NSF, Washington, 1990; mem. NSF instr. lab. improvement panel, 1992, 96, 99; mem. NSF-AIRE site visit team, 2000; WUKBRIN (NIH grant) coord., 2001—. Contbr. articles to profl. jours. Active Household Hazardous Waste Collection, Topeka, 1991, Solid Waste Task Force, Shawnee County, Kans., 1990; mem. vol. com. YWCA, Topeka, 1984-87; bd. dir. Helping Hand Humane Soc., 2002—; grant coord. Kans. Biomedical Rsch Infrastructure Network, 2002—. Rsch. grantee Petroleum Rsch. Fund, Topeka, 1984-86, NIH, Topeka, 1985-88; instrument grantee NSF, Topeka, 1986, 95. Mem. Am. Chem. Soc. (sec. Dallas-Ft. Worth sect. 1981-82), Kans. Acad. Sci. (pres.-elect 1991, pres. 1992, treas. 1995—), Biophys. Soc., Sigma Xi (pres. TWU club 1980-81), Iota Sigma Pi (mem.-at-large coord. 1987-93). Home: 3401 SW Oak Pky Topeka KS 66614-3218 Office: Washburn U Dept Chemistry Topeka KS 66621 E-mail: janice.barton@washburn.edu.

BARTON, JEAN MARIE, psychologist, educator; b. Pitts., Mar. 24, 1945; d. Joseph Paul and Jean Marie (Anderson) Adamchic; m. Robert L. Barton, Jr., Aug. 14, 1965; children: Robert Joseph, Katherine Anne. BS summa cum laude, U. Pitts., 1965; MEd, Boston U., 1969; CAGS, Cath. U. Am., 1985, PhD in Ednl. Psychology, 1988. Cert. sch. psychologist, Md., nationally cert. sch. psychologist. Tchr./curriculum Wellesley (Mass.) pub. schs., 1965-69; lectr. U. R.I./R.I. Coll., Providence, 1969-72; curriculum specialist/tchr. St. Jane DeChantal Sch., Bethesda, Md., 1977-83, computer prog. dir., 1982-84; psychology assoc. Long Assocs., Bethesda, 1988—; psychol. cons. gifted unit Montgomery County Pub. Schs., Rockville, Md., 1985-99; sch. psychologist various schs. Archdiocese of Washington (Md.), 1987—; adj. mem. faculty Cath. U. Am., Washington, 1989—. Mem. evaluation team Cath. Schs. Studies, 1987-92; dir. Profl. Devel. Inst., Cath. U. Am., 1985-86; mem. adv. com., chairperson identification com. Jacob Javits Grant, Montgomery County Pub. Schs., 1989-92, project coord. Jacob Javitz grant, 1992-95, supt. adv. com. on Edn. of Gifted, 1992-96, on Spl. Edn.; assoc. dir. Ctr. for Advancement Cath. Edn. at Cath. U. Am., 1998—; mem. adv. com. on gifted edn. Md. State Dept. Edn., 1999-2000. Contbr. articles to profl. jours. U. Pitts. scholar, 1962-65. Mem. APA, ASCD, NASP, Am. Ednl. Rsch. Assn., Md. Sch. Psychologists Assn., Nat. Assn. for Gifted Children, Pi Lambda Theta. Home: 5008 Benton Ave Bethesda MD 20814-2804 Office: Cath U of America O'Boyle Hall Washington DC 20064-0001 E-mail: docjeanbarton@cs.com.

BARTON, NOREEN DUFFY, secondary school educator; b. Phila., June 7, 1926; d. John Joseph and Mary Josephine (McDonough) Brett; m. Thomas Francis Duffy, Feb. 22, 1960 (div. June 1971); children: Thomas B., John F., Joseph D.; m. Patrick Joseph Barton, Nov. 11, 1995. BA, Montclair (N.J.) State Coll., 1948; MEd, U. Va., 1966. Cert. secondary math., bus. and acctg. tchr., N.J. Tchr. math. and bus. Egg Harbor (N.J.) City High Sch., 1948-55, coach girls basketball, 1948-51; instr. math. North Adams (Mass.) Coll., 1964-65, Frostburg (Md.) State Coll., 1969-70; tchr. math. So. Regional High Sch., Manahawkin, N.J., 1964-65, 75—, chmn. dept., 1958-60; chess coach, 1979—. Tchr. confrat. Christian doctrine Star of Sea Sch., Atlantic City, 1958-60, Holy Spirit High Sch., Absecon, N.J., 1975-86; tchr., prin. Assumption Sch., Ponoma, N.J., 1971-75. Scholar NSF, 1959-60. Mem. NEA, Nat. Coun. Tchrs. Math., N.J. Math. Assn., N.J. Edn. Assn., So. Regional Tchrs. Assn. (assoc. rep. 1988—). Roman Catholic. Avocations: chess, watching baseball, basketball and football. Home: 739 Bayview Dr Absecon NJ 08201-1208 Office: So Regional High Sch RR 9 Manahawkin NJ 08050

BARTON-COLLINGS, NELDA ANN, political activist, newspaper, bank and nursing home executive; b. Providence, Ky., May 12, 1929; m. Harold Bryan Barton, May 11, 1951 (dec. Nov. 1977); children: William Grant (dec.), Barbara Lynn, Harold Bryan, Stephen Lambert, Suzanne; m. Jack C. Collings, Mar. 28, 1992 (dec. Feb. 2000). Student, Western Ky. U., 1947-49; grad., Norton Meml. Infirmary Sch. Med. Tech., 1950; student, Cumberland Coll., 1978, LLD (hon.), 1991. Lic. nursing home adminstr.; registered med. technician. Pres. Barton & Assocs. Inc., Corbin, Ky., 1977—2002; past pres., now chmn. Hazard Nursing Home Inc., Ky., 1977—2002, Health Sys. Inc., Corbin, Ky., 1978—2002, Corbin Nursing Home Inc., 1978—2002, Williamsburg Nursing Home, Inc., 1978—2002; pres. Key Distbg. Inc., 1980—, pres., chmn. bd., 1981-97; past pres., now chmn. The Whitley Whiz Inc., Williamsburg, 1983—2002; chmn. bd. dirs., now dir. Tri-County Nat. Bank, 1985-97, bd. dirs., now chmn. Harlan Nursing Home, Inc., 1986—2002; chmn. bd. dirs. Knott Co. Nursing Home, Inc., 1986; pres. Tri-County Bancorp, Inc., 1987—2002; chmn. bd. Instl. Pharmacy, Corbin, Ky., 1990—2002; past pres., now chmn. bd. Wolfe County Health Care Ctr., 1990—2002. Mem. exec. com. Corbin Deposit Bank, 1982-84; bd. dirs. Greensburg (Ky.) Deposit Bank, Williamsburg (Ky.) Nat. Bank, Campbellsville Nat. Bank, McCreary Nat. Bank, Tri County Nat. Bank, Somerset Nat. Bank, Laurel Nat. Bank; chmn., organizer, dir. Green County Bancorp Inc., 1987—2002; organizer, dir. Laurel Nat. Bank, 1996—2002; mem. nat. adv. com. SBA, 1990-92; active Nat. Policy Forum, 1994—96. Mem. Fedn. Coun. on Aging, 1982-87; bd. dirs. Leadership Ky., 1984-88, adv. com., 1987—92; bd. dirs. Cumberland Coll. Found., 1995, mem. devel. bd., 1981—; v.p. Southeastern Ky. Rehab. Com., 1981-93; mem. Fair Housing Task Force, Corbin, 1981-84, Ky. Mansions Preservation Found. Inc., Corbin Comty. Devel. Com., 1970-83; cub scout den mother, 1965-67; pres. Corbin Cen. Elem PTA, 1963-65; vice chmn. 9th dist. PTA, 1958-59; Rep. nat. committeewoman for Ky., 1968-96, sec., 1993-96; vice-chmn. Rep. Nat. Com., 1984-93; sec.-treas. Nat. Rep. Inst. Internat. Affairs, 1984-86; active numerous other polit. orgns. Recipient Ky. Woman of Achievement award Ky. Bus. and Profl. Women, 1983, Recognition award Joint Rep. Leadership, U.S. Congress, Dwight David Eisenhower award, 1970, John Sherman Cooper Disting. Svc. award Ky. Young Reps. Fedn., 1987, Outstanding Layperson award Ky. Med. Assn., 1992, Nelda Barton Comty. Svc. award Ky. Assn. Health Care Facilities, 1992, 5th Dist. Rep. Party Recognition award, 1996, Tribute to Nelda Barton-Collings Rep. Party of Ky. and 5th Dist. Lincoln Club, 1997, Disting. Recognition award Ky. State Senate, 2002, Nelda Barton Collings Rep. internship award established by Rep. Party of Ky., 1997, Jefferson Co. Ky. Office for Women Hall of Fame, 1999, Ky. State Senate Cert. for Outstanding Women in Bus. and Leadership, 1999; named Ky. Col., 1968, Ky. Rep. Woman of Yr., Ky. Fedn. Rep. Women, 1969; named to 5th Dist. Lincoln Club Hall of Fame, 1996; Nelda Barton Day proclaimed by Mayor of Corbin, 1973; Western Ky. U. Acad. scholar, 1947-49. Mem. Am. Coll. Nursing Home Adminstrs., Ky. Assn. Health Care Facilities (legis. com. 1980-97, Ira O. Wallace award 2002), Ky. Assn. Nursing Home Adminstrs. (bd. dirs., polit. action com. 1979—), Ky. Med. Aux. (chmn. health edn. com. 1975-77), Ky. Commn. on Women, Women's Aux. So. Med. Assn. (Ky. counselor), Whitley County Med. Aux. (pres. 1959-60), Aux. Ky. Med. Assn., Ky. Mothers Assn. (parliamentarian 1970—, hon. Mother of Ky. award 1983), Ky. C. of C. (bd. dirs. 1983—, v.p. Region 5 1985—, 1st vice chmn. 1989, chmn. 1990-91). Avocations: fishing, oil painting. Home: 1311 7th Street Rd Corbin KY 40701-2207

BARTOSHUK, LINDA J. otolaryngologist, educator; BA in Psychology, Carleton Coll., 1960; MS in Psychology, Brown U., 1963, PhD in Psychology, 1965; DSc (hon.), Carleton Coll., 2001. Pre-doctoral fellow PHS, 1960—64, NSF, 1960—64; lectr. Brown U., 1966—68; affiliate asst. prof. Clark U., 1966—69; rsch. psychologist Natick Labs, 1966—70; asst. John B. Pierce Found., 1970—73, assoc., 1974—85, fellow, 1985—89; asst. prof. dept. epidemiology and pub. health Yale U., 1971—76, assoc. prof. depts. epidemiology and pub. health and psychology, 1976—85, prof. depts. epidemiology and pub. health and psychology, 1985—88, prof. sect. otolaryngology dept. surgery and prof. dept. psychology, 1989—. Chair Gordon Conf. on Chem. Senses, 1978; mem. various coms. NIH, NRC. Editor: Chem. Senses, 1982—84; cons. editor: Perception and Psychophysics, 1972—86, Sensory Processes, 1976—79; contbr. articles to profl. jours. Recipient Pepper Neuroscience Investigator award, 1984—92, Manheimer award, Monell Chem. Senses Inst., 1990, Kreshover award, Nat. Inst. Dental Rsch., 1990, Disting. Contbn. award, New Eng. Psychol. Assn., 2000. Fellow: AAAS; mem.: APA (mem. at large exec. com. div. 6 1984—87, mem. NSF working group for com. on rsch. support 1985—87, program chair div. 6 1987, pres. div. 6 1988—89, pres. elect div. 1 2001, fellow div. 6 comparative and physiol. psychology, Neal Miller Lectr. 2000), NAS, Am. Assn. Dental Schs. (mem. women's affairs adv. com.), Soc. Exptl. Psychologists, Soc. for Study of Ingestive Behavior (bd. govs. 1987—89, 2000—03), Psychonomic Soc. (mem. publ. com. 1987—92), Ea. Psychol. Assn. (mem. program com. 1983—86, bd. govs. 1987—90, pres. 1990—91), Assn. Chemoreception Scis. (exec. chair 1980—81, Award for Outstanding Achievement in chem. senses 1998), Am. Psychol. Soc. (bd. dirs. 2001—03), Phi Beta Kappa, Sigma Xi. Office: Dept Surgery Yale U Sch Medicine PO Box 208041 New Haven CT 06520-8041

BARTOW, BARBARA JENÉ, university program administrator; b. Buffalo, June 26, 1950; d. Nicholas Michael Bojack and Lillian Lenore Bennett; m. Michael Hartzell Bartow; children: Barbara Simmons, Edward Michael Hagen. AA in Journalism, Miami Dade Jr. Coll., 1970; M. in Non-fiction Writing, USAF Air U., 1975, M. Adminstrn. Auto. mechanic Amoco, Miami, Fla., 1969-70; cargo dispatcher McKinley Transport Worldwide, Ont., Can., 1970-72; office adminstr. Modernage Furniture, Miami, 1972-74. Social svc. rep. Vets. Adminstrn. and DAV and Am. Legion, 1976—; commdr. DAV and Am. Legion, 1985-86; deputy chief of staff DAV, 1986. Contbr. poetry to World of Poetry, Internat. Soc. Poets, Internat. Libr. of Poetry, Libr. of Congress, 1990—. Active crisis intervention CASA, Fla., 1984-86; foster parent DCFS, Ill.; Dem. polit. activist, Ill., Fla., N.Y., Pa., 1976—. Sgt USAF, 1974-80. Recipient citation of merit DAV, Fla., 1985. Roman Catholic. Avocations: writing, social work, wheelchair racing. Home: 1515 Lantern Ln Joliet IL 60433-2910

BARTOW, DIANE GRACE, marketing and sales executive; b. Maspeth, N.Y., Apr. 20, 1948; d. Alfred Otto and Charlotte Florence (Bronnenkant) Bruggeman; m. Eugene A. Bartow, aug. 29, 1992; children: Jason, Trudi. AAS, Queensborough C.C., 1967; BS, Nova Southeastern U., 1979. Jr. acct. Exxon, N.Y.C., 1967-69; acct. BRM Assocs., N.Y.C., 1969, Texaco, N.Y.C., 1969-74; supr. Eutectic, Flushing, N.Y., 1974-76; regional industry dir. Am. Express, N.Y.C., 1976-83; v.p. Eastern Exclusives, Boston, 1983-85; pres. The Mktg. Dept., 1985-86; sr. v.p., gen. mgr. Rogers Merchandising Inc., 1986-92; exec. v.p., COO Bartow Ins. Agy., Inc., 1992—. Seminars Marketing to Win. Author tng. manual, travel newsletter, 1982, Ins. Update, 1992. Trustee, v.p. Murray Hill Neighborhood Assn., 1982, pres., 1997, 98, 99, 00, 01, 02, 03, 04; trustee 7 E 35th Corp., 1983; chmn. judging Promotion and Advt. awards, 1990, awards chair, 2001-02. Mem. Nat. Assn. Advt. and Promotional Allowances (judging chair 1996-00), Am. Soc. Travel Agts. (tour rels. com. 1983), Am. Hotel and Motel Mgmt. Assn., Am. Film Assn., Am. Mgmt. Assn., Life Underwriters, Sigma Mu Omega (pres. Bayside (N.Y.) 1966-67). Home: 7 E 35th St New York NY 10016-3810

BARTOW, NICOLE A. secondary school educator; b. Lincoln, Nebr., Feb. 2, 1970; d. Douglas William and Judith Dian Bartow. BA English Lit., George Mason U., 1991; JD, Santa Clara U., 1994; MEd, Marymount U., 1998. Bar: Calif. 1994; cert. secondary social studies tchr. 1997. Law clk. Joyce Kitchens, Atlanta, 1994; tchr. social studies Loudoun County Pub. Schs., Sterling, Va., 1997—. Editor: Santa Clara Law Rev., 1993—94. Mem. ACLU, Va., 2002—. Mem.: Loudoun Edn. Assn., Calif. Bar Assn. Avocations: travel, reading, football. Office: Park View High Sch 400 W Laurel Ave Sterling VA 20164

BARTUSKA, ANN, government official, biologist; b. Phila. BS in Biology, Wilkes Coll., 1975; MS in Botany, Ohio U.; PhD in Biology, W.Va. U. Program mgr. nat. acid precipitation assessment program N.C. State U., Raleigh; asst. dir. Southeastern Forest Expt. Sta., Forest Svc., USDA, Asheville, N.C., acting dir. ecosys. mgmt. Washington, spl. asst. chief, liaison to Nat. Biol. Survey, dir. forest health protection state and pvt. forestry orgn., dir. forest mgmt., 1998—2001, dep. chief rsch. and devel., 2004—; exec. dir. Invasive Species Initiative The Nature Conservancy, Va.,

2001—04. Mem. Ecol. Soc. Am. (v.p. for pub. affairs). Office: USDA Forest Svc Auditors Bldg 201 14th St SW Washington DC 20250-0001 Fax: 202-205-1045. E-mail: fm.wo@fs.fed.us.

BARTZ, CAROL, software company executive; b. Alma, Wis., Aug. 29, 1948; m. William Marr; 1 child. BS in Computer Sci. with honors, U. Wis., 1971; DSc (hon.), Worcester Poly. Inst.; LittD (hon.), William Woods U. With sales mgmt. dept. 3M Corp., Digital Equipment Corp., 1976-83; mgr. customer mktg. Sun Microsys., 1983-84, v.p. mktg., 1984-87, v.p. customer svc., 1987-90, v.p. worldwide field ops., exec. officer, 1990-92; chmn. bd., CEO Autodesk, Inc., San Rafael, Calif., 1992—. Pres. Sun Fed., from 1987; bd. dirs. AirTouch Comm., Bea Sys., Cadence Design Sys., Cisco Sys., Inc.; mem. President's Export Coun., 1994, President's Coun. Advisors on Sci. and Tech.; adv. coun. bus. sch. Stanford U. Bd. dirs. U. Wis. Sch. Bus., Nat. Breast Cancer Rsch. Found., Found. for Nat. Medals Sci. and Tech.; mem. adv. coun. Stanford U. Bus. Sch.; mem. Com. of 200; adv. for women's health issues; former mem. Ark. of Gov.'s Econ. Summit, Little Rock. Recipient Donald C. Burnham Mfg. Mgmt. award Soc. Mfg. Engrs., 1994. Mem. Calif. C. of C. (bd. dirs.). Avocations: gardening, tennis. Office: Autodesk Inc 111 Mcinnis Pkwy San Rafael CA 94903-2700

BARTZ, JUDITH ANDERSON, nurse; b. Bay City, Mich., July 28, 1954; d. Clifford Roy and Alice May (Mead) Anderson. AAS, Delta Coll., 1975; ADN, Coll. Lake County, 1980; BSN, U. Mich., 1995; cert. in Healthcare Ethics, Rush U., 2002; MSN, U. Phoenix, 2003. RN, Mich., 2003; cert. gerontol. nurse ANCC. Dir. rehab. Carestoel of McHenry, Ill., 1980-81; staff nurse Haven Park Nursing Ctr., Zeeland, Mich., 1982-87; staff nurse Pocono Med. Ctr., Stroudsberg, Pa., 1987-89, Bronson Meth. Hosp., Kalamazoo, 1989-95; charge nurse Bronson Vicksburg (Mich.) Hosp., 1995—. Item writer for cert. exam Assn. Rehab. Nurses, Skokie, Ill., 1984, book reviewer, 1987-93. Mem. domestic violence task force Bronson Meth. Hosp., Kalamazoo, 1993-94. Mem. ACCN (mem. abstract rev. panel, 1996-2002, module rev. panel, 2002—, ethics adv. panel, 2002), ARN, APIC, Sigma Theta Tau. Avocations: needlework, skiing, computers, reading. Home: 110 Lanark Ct Kalamazoo MI 49006-4357

BARZDA, SUSAN MARIE, special education educator, art educator; d. John Anthony and Verona Jewel (Brickner) Barzda. MusB, Heidelberg Coll., 1974; postgrad., Muskingum Coll., 2003—. Lic. tchr. music k-12 Ohio Dept. Edn., 1974, Qualified Mental Retardation Professional (QMRP) Ohio Dept. of Mental Retardation, Devel. Disability, 1980. Instr. instrumental and vocal music Rolling Hills Local Sch. Dist., Byesville, Ohio, 1974—76; tchr. music, supr. Cambridge Devel. Ctr., 1976—87; dir. high sch. band, tchr. music appreciation Bishop Rosecrans Cath. High Sch., Zanesville, 1981—85; adminstrv. asst. II Cambridge Devel. Ctr., 1987—93, 1989—93, qualified mental retardation profl., 1993—. Dir., instr. majorettes, drill team, and fife and drum corps Rolling Hills Local Sch. Dist., Byesville, Ohio, 1974—76, instr. Meadowbrook unit Guernsey county bicentennial fife and drum corps, 1975—76; dir. YMCA Y-ettes Baton Twirling Corps, 1978—81; coord. Spl. Olympics Cambridge Devel. Ctr., 1981—84, mem. devel. centers mini-team improve quality of svcs. individuals with mental retardation, 1977—79, mem. Ohio's mini-teams devel. centers, 1977—79, adult basic edn. grant coord., 1986—90. Play selection com. chair Cambridge Performing Arts Ctr., 1986—2003; sec. Cambridge City Band, 1980—81, Zanesville Meml. Concert Band, Zanesville, 2002—03; S.E.Ohio regional rep. Ohio Cmty. Theatre Assn., Columbus, 1999—2002, bd. mem. at large, 2003— [illegible] Greco Concert Band, Dover, 2002—03; tenor saxophone player Dick Simcox Big Band, Cambridge, 1981—85; clarinetist Southeastern Ohio Symphony, New Concord, 1982—84; mem., pit orch. mem., actress, dancer, choreographer, prodr., dir., musical dir., Cambridge Performing Arts Centre, 1977—2003; clarinettist Zanesville Meml. Concert Band, 1982—2003, Coshocton Cmty. Band, 2002—03. Recipient Jean Lisle Meml. award, Alliance Music Study Club, 1970, Dick Beal Outstanding Regional Rep. award, Ohio Cmty. Theatre Assn., 2002; scholar, Quota Club Alliance, Ohio, 1970; Rhodes-King scholar, Heidelberg Coll., 1970—71. Mem.: Philalethean Women's Soc. Alumni (life). Independent. Avocations: clarinet, acting, genealogy, travel. Office: Cambridge Developmental Ctr 66737 Old 21 Rd Cambridge OH 43725 Personal E-mail: subar@cambridgeoh.com.

BARZILAY, JUDITH MORGENSTERN, federal judge; b. Russell, Kans., Jan. 3, 1944; d. Arthur and Hilda Morgenstern; m. Sal (Doron) Barzilay, Aug. 19, 1973; children: Ilan, Michael. Bachelors, Wichita State U., 1965; MLS, Rutgers U., 1971, JD, 1981. Bar: N.J. 1981. Tchr. English Wichita (Kans.) H.S., 1965-67; editor Carter Wallace Pharms., Cranbury, N.J., 1967-68; tchr. English Hamilton Sch., Hamilton Twp., N.J., 1968-69; ref. libr. Suffolk County Coll., Selden, N.J., 1971-74, Somerset Coll., Somerville, N.J., 1975-76, East Brunswick (N.J.) Libr., 1977-78; law clk. Hon. Robert Tarleton, N.J. Superior Ct., Jersey City, 1982-83; atty. Williams, Caliri, Miller & Otley, Wayne, N.J., 1982-83, Dept. of Justice, N.Y.C., 1983-86, Siegel, Mandell & Davidson, N.Y.C., 1986-88; sr. atty., v.p. import and export, govt. affairs Sony Electronics, Park Ridge, N.J., 1988-95, 96-98; judge U.S. Ct. Internat. Trade, N.Y.C., 1998—. Mem. Treasury Sec.'s Com. on Comml. Ops. of U.S. Customs Svc., Washington, 1996-98. Bd. trustees Ramapo Coll., Mahwah, N.J., 1996-98. Recipient Tribute to Women and Industry award YWCA of Bergen County, N.J., 1993, Disting. Alumna award Wichita State U., 1996. Mem. Am. Assn. Exporters and Importers (exec. bd. dirs. 1992-98). Jewish. Office: US Ct Internat Trade One Federal Plz New York NY 10278 Fax: 212-264-5487.*

BASA, ENIKÖ MOLNAR, librarian; b. Huszt, Hungary, Sept. 7, 1939; came to the U.S., 1950; d. Julius Valentine and Terézia (Fejér) Molnár; m. Péter Basa, Nov. 19, 1966. BA, Trinity Coll., 1962; MA, U. N.C., 1965, PhD, 1972. Instr. U. Md., College Park, 1965-69; asst. prof. Dunbarton Coll., Washington, 1970-72; lectr. Am. U., Washington, 1972-75, Hood Coll., Frederick, Md., 1975-76; editor, serials cataloger Libr. of Congress, Washington, 1977—. Mem. symposium Libr. Congress, 1996. Author: Sandor Petöfi, 1980; editor: Twayne World Authors, 1974—, Hungarian Literature, 1993; translator: (play) Screenplay from Örkény, 1983; assoc. editor The Comparatist, 1976-82, editorial bd., 1992—; jour. rev. editor: Hungarian Studies Newsletter, 1975-82; guest editor: Rev. Nat. Lits., 1992; contbr. chpts. to books and articles and book revs. to profl. jours. Recipient Gold medal Pres. of Republic of Hungary, 1997; Kluge Staff fellow Libr. of Congress, 2002-03. Mem. MLA (Hungarian sect. chair 1980, 90), So. Comparative Lit. Assn. (founding v.p. 1977-79, 89—, sec.-treas. 1985-89, pres. 1992-94), Am. Hungarian Educators Assn. (pres. 1974-80, 88-92, exec. dir. 1980—), Internat. Assn. Hungarian Studies, Libr. Congress Profl. Assn. (v.p. 1991, pres. 1996). Avocations: reading, travel, needlework. Home: 4515 Willard Ave Apt 2210 Chevy Chase MD 20815-3685 Office: Serial Record Libr Congress Washington DC 20540-4160 E-mail: ebas@loc.gov.

BASCH, REVA, information services company executive; b. Chgo., Aug. 1, 1947; d. Victor Hugo and Hertha (Levi) B.; m. Jerrald C. Shifman, Apr. 17, 1982. BA in English Lit. summa cum laude, U. Pa., 1969; MLS, U. Calif., Berkeley, 1971. Head libr. Cogswell Coll., San Francisco, 1971-72; tech. info. specialist Gilbert Assocs. Inc., Reading, Pa., 1973-79; tech. libr. NuTech, San Jose, Calif., 1980-81; rsch. assoc. Info. on Demand, Berkeley, Calif., 1981-82, asst. dir. rsch., 1982-83, dir. rsch., 1983-86, v.p., dir. rsch., 1985-86; software designer Mead Data Ctrl., Personal Computer Sys. Group, Menlo Park, Calif., 1986-88; pres. Aubergine Info. Svcs., The Sea Ranch, Calif., 1986—. Author: Secrets of the Super Searchers, 1993, Electronic Information Delivery: Ensuring Quality and Value, 1995, Secrets of the Super Net Searchers, 1996, Researching Online for Dummies, 1998, 2d edit., 2000; columnist Online mag., CyberSkeptic's Guide to Internet Rsch.; contbr. articles to profl. jours. Recipient award for best paper UMI/Data Courier, 1990, Online Champion award Dun & Bradstreet. Mem. Assn. of Ind. Info. Profl.(pres.1991-92), Spl. Librs. Assn., Assn. Info. and Dissemination Ctrs., So. Calif. Online Users Group. Avocations: online communications, reading, travel, cooking.

BASCOM, RUTH F. retired mayor; b. Ames, Iowa, Feb. 4, 1926; d. Frederick Charles and Doris Hays Fenton; m. John U. Bascom, June 14, 1950; children: Lucinda, Rebecca, Ellen, Thomas, Paul, Mary. BS, Kans. State U., Manhattan, 1946; MA, Cornell U., 1949. Tchr. Dickinson County Cmty. H.S., Kans., 1946-48, Nat. Coll. Edn., Chgo., 1949-51. Co-chair Cascadia High Speed Rail, 1995-98. Chair City and State Bicycle Com., 1971-83; mem., chair Met. Park Bd., Eugene, 1972-82; past bd. pres. Youth Symphony, 1962-68; city councilor City of Eugene, Oreg., 1984-92, coun. v.p., pres., 1988-90, mayor, 1993-97; v.p., pres. LWV, Eugene, 1967-69; chair, Oreg. Passenger Rail Com., 2000—; state bd. 1000 Friends of Oreg., 1999—. Recipient Gold Leaf award Internat. Soc. Arboriculture, 1993; dedicated Ruth Bascom Riverbank Trail Sys., 2003. Democrat. Congregationalist. Avocations: music, tree farm, bicycling. Home: 2114 University St Eugene OR 97403-1542 E-mail: jbascomr@pacinfo.com.

BASH, DANIELLE RENEE, quality control engineer; b. Coshocton, Ohio, Aug. 30, 1976; d. David M. and Karen O. (Gilbert) Bash. BSBA in Bus. Mgmt., Tri-State U., Angola, Ind., 1998. Quality assoc. Foley Pattern Co., Inc., Auburn, Ind., 1994—98; corrective action coord. Magnequench Internat., Inc., Anderson, Ind., 1998—2002, quality engr., magnet divsn., 2000—02; small bus. devel. vol. Peace Corps, Morocco, 2002—03; quality engr. Nishikawa Std. Co., Topeka, Ind., 2003—. Discovery vol. Sci. Ctrl., Ft. Wayne, Ind., 1996—98; asst. lead/trainer DeKalb County 4-H Dog Club, Auburn, Ind., 1994—98; one-to-one match vol. Big Bros./Big Sisters N.E. Ind., Ft. Wayne, 1996—99, Big Bros./Big Sisters Madison County, Anderson, 1999—2002; mem. vol. support network Peace Corps, Fez, 2003. Home: 1000 Allison Blvd Auburn IN 46706 Personal E-mail: danielle_bash@scubadiving.com.

BASHORE, IRENE SARAS, art association administrator; b. San Jose, Calif. d. John and Eva (Lionudakis) Saras; m. Vincent Bashore (div.); 1 child, Juliet Ann. BA, Pepperdine U., 1950; MA in Theatre Arts, Calif. State U., Fullerton, 1977. Founder, exec. dir. Inst. for Dramatic Rsch., Fullerton, Calif., 1967—.

BASILE, SHEILA, secondary education educator, consultant; b. Hendersonville, N.C., Sept. 6, 1952; d. John Leroy and Mildred Irene (Burrell) Brevard; m. Anthony John Basile, June 7, 1951; children: Laurel, Cheryl, Anthony John. BA, Western Carolina U., Cullowhee, N.C., 1975; MA, Columbia U., 1979. Cert. in English and reading edn. K-12, N.Y. Cons. self employed, New Rochelle, 1981—. Cons. leadership assessment and feedback Ctr. for Creative Leadership, Greensboro, N.C., 1995-97; mgmt. tng cons. Nestle, Pitney Bowes, HBO, 1990-95. Recipient Chmn.'s awrd Nynex-Bell Atlantic, White Plains, N.Y., 1993, Corp. Quality award, 1993. Mem. Internat. Assn. Career Mgmt. Profls., Nat. Coun. Tchrs. English, N.Y. State English Coun., Orphan Train Heritage Soc. Am., Hauppauge Indsl. Assn., Advancement for Commerce, Industry & Tech., Inc., Rotary Club (mem. event steering com. 1999), Orienta Beach Club (Mamaroneck, N.Y.; mem. entertainment com. 1999). Avocations: running, special community [illegible] planning, writing, public speaking. Office: Lee Hecht Harrison 225 Broadhollow Rd Melville NY 11747 E-mail: teddybell@aol.com.

BASINGER, KAREN LYNN, renal dietitian; b. Mechanicsville, Md., July 4, 1955; d. Leonard Marcus and Mary Jane (Harding) Brookbank; m. Joseph Andrew Basinger, Nov. 17, 1984; 1 child, James Marcus. BS, U. Md., 1977; MS, Hood Coll., 1987. Lic. nutritionist. Libr technician Bowie (Md.) State Coll., 1973-79; instr. St. Mary's County Adult Edn., Leonardtown, Md., 1979-80; home economist Zamoiski Co., Balt., 1977-83; nutritionist/WIC coord. South County Health Plan, Prince Frederick, Md., 1979-80; nutritionist Walter Reed Army Med. Ctr., Washington, 1980-82; renal dietitian Mid Atlantic/BMA, Camp Springs, Md., 1982-87, Kidney Care Ctr., Landover, Md., 1987-99; instr. dietary intern program Andrews AFB, 1988-91; renal dietitian Silver Spring (Md.) Artificial Kindey Ctr., 1998—; outpatient dietitian Holy Cross Hosp., Silver Spring, 1999-2000; renal dietitian DaVita-Wheaton, Md., 1999—. Cons. Leisure World, 2002-; lectr. in field. Profl. adv. bd. Nat. Kidney Found./NCA, 1989-94; chair coun. on renal nutrition Nat. Kidney Found., 1993-94, program chair, 1990-92. Recipient Spl. Recognition Nat. Kidney Found./NCA, 1990, 92, Recognized Renal Dietitian/NCA, 1991, 94. Mem.: Washington Met. Coun. on Renal Nutrition (chair 1986—94, nutrition symposium chair 1989, chair 1986—94, 2001—02), Am. Dietetic Assn. (legis. chair renal practice group 2003—), Md. Home Econs. Assn. (bylaws chair 1982—94), Am. Home Econs. Assn., Am. Nutritionists Assn., U. Md. Aumni Assn. Democrat. Lutheran. Avocation: cross-stitch.

BASINGER, KIM, actress; b. Athens, Ga., Dec. 8, 1953; d. Don Basinger; m. Ron Britton, 1980 (div. Feb. 1990); m. Alec Baldwin, August 19, 1993 (div. 2002), 1 child. Student, Neighborhood Playhouse, N.Y.C. Model Eileen Ford Agy., N.Y.C., 1972-77; ind. actress, 1977—. (feature films) Hard Country, 1981, Mother Lode, 1982, Never Say Never Again, 1983, The Man Who Loved Women, 1983, The Natural, 1984, Fool for Love, 1985, 9 1/2 Weeks, 1986, No Mercy, 1986, Blind Date, 1987, Nadine, 1987, My Stepmother Is an Alien, 1988, Batman, 1989, The Marrying Man, 1991, Final Analysis, 1992, Cool World, 1992, The Real McCoy, 1993, Wayne's World 2, 1993, The Getaway, 1994, Ready to Wear (Prêt-à-Porter), 1994, L.A. Confidential (Golden Globe award for best supporting actress, 1998) (Academy Award for best supporting actress, 1998), 1997, I Dreamed of Africa, 2000, Bless the Child, 2000, 8 Mile, 2002, People I Know, 2002; (TV series) Dog and Cat, 1977; TV films include Katie-Portrait of a Centerfold, 1978, The Ghost of Flight 401, 1978, Killjoy, 1981; (TV miniseries) From Here to Eternity, 1980; (TV appearances) Gemini Man, 1976, Charlie's Angels, 1976, The Six Million Dollar Man, 1977, McMillan and Wife, 1977, Vega$, 1978, The Simpsons (voice only), 1998, 2002. Office: c/o Ron Meyer CAA 11288 Ventura Blvd #414 Studio City CA 91604*

BASKETT, CHRISTINA ST. CLAIR, fund raising executive; b. Cheyenne, Wyo., Feb. 17, 1960; d. William Warren and Christina Addison (Dann) St. Clair; m. Douglas Helm Baskett, Sept. 5, 1987; children: David Anderson, Robert William. BA, Wellesley Coll., 1982; MBA, MA, So. Methodist U., 1987. Cert. fund raising exec.. From asst. to dir. bldg. ops. to asst. dir. fin. aid New England Conservatory, Boston, 1982-85; asst. dir. devel. Dallas Symphony Assn., 1987-89; from dir. devel. to chief advancement officer Dallas Mus. Natural History, 1989—96, chief advancement officer, 1996—. Active Jr. League Dallas, 1995-2000; sec. bd. dirs. Wellesley Coll. Club, 1992-99; bd. dirs., chair fundraising com. First Presbyn. Day Sch., Dallas, 1994; singer Dallas Symphony Chorus, 1986-91. Mem. Nat. Soc. Fund Raising Execs. (treas., bd. dirs. 1995-97, v.p. adminstrn. 1998—), Assn. Fundraising Profls. (pres. 2000-02). Republican. Office: 4141 Spring Ave Addison TX 75201

BASKIN, MAUREEN LOUISE, special education educator; b. Wynnewood, Pa., Mar. 28, 1978; d. Paul William and Louise (O'Malley) Illian; m. Edward Alan Baskin, July 12, 2003. BS magna cum laude, Gwynedd-Mercy Coll., 2000; M in Elem. Edn., Widener U., 2003. Cert. spl. edn. elem. tchr. Pa. Spl. edn. tchr. Grace Park Sch., Swarthmore, Pa., 2000—. Mem.: NEA, Pa. State Edn. Assn. Avocations: photography, crafts, interior decorating, reading, movies. Office: Grace Park Sch 7th Ave Swarthmore PA 19081

BASKINS, ANN O. lawyer, computer company executive; b. Red Bluff, Calif., Aug. 5, 1955; AB, Stanford U., 1977; JD, UCLA, 1980. Bar: Calif. 1980. Assoc. Crosby, Heafey, Roach & May, 1980—81; v.p., gen. counsel, sec. Hewlett-Packard Co., Palo Alto, Calif., 1981—. Mem.: ABA, State Bar Calif., Assn. Gen. Counsel, Am. Soc. Corp. Secs., Am. Corp. Counsel Assn. Office: Hewlett Packard Co Mail Stop 1069 3000 Hanover St Palo Alto CA 94304

BASQUIN, MARY SMYTH (KIT BASQUIN), museum administrator; b. NYC, July 3, 1941; d. Joseph Percy and Virginia Sandford (Gibbs) Smyth; m. Maurice Hanson Basquin, Feb. 4, 1967 (div. Feb. 1984); children: Susan, Peter Lee, William. BA, Goucher Coll., Balt., 1963; MA, Ind. U., 1970. Asst. dir. pub. rels. Indpls. Mus. Art, 1971-72; dir. Washignton Gallery, Frankfort, Ind., 1972-79, Indpls., 1977-79, Kit Basquin Gallery, Milw., 1981-83; curator edn. Haggerty Mus. Marquette U., Milw., 1988-95; dir. outreach Milw. Wis. Humanities Coun., 1995-98; curator Marvin Lowe Retrospective, Ind. U. Art Mus., 1998; mktg. William Doyle Galleries, NYC, 1999, exhbn. mgr., 2000; rsch. assoc. Bklyn. Mus. Art, 2000; asst. print study rm. Met. Mus. Art, NYC, 2000—. Instr. art history Concordia U., Mequon, Wis., 1991, instr. Marquette U., Gaza, 1996; pres. contemporary art soc. Milw. Art Mus., 1986-87, prints and drawings subcom., 1991-99, pres. Print Forum, 1996-97; mem. program com. Midwest Mus. conf., Milw., 1992. Wis. editor: New Art Examiner, 1980—81; mem. St. Barts Singers, 1999—; contbr. articles to profl. jours. Trustee Ten Chimneys Found., Genesee Depot, Wis., 1997-99; mem. adv. bd. Ten Chimneys Found., 2000-01. Mem. Univ. Club NY, Univ. Club Milw. Episcopalian. Avocations: singing, fashion, theater, swimming. Home: 1675 York Ave Apt 19A New York NY 10128-6756

BASS, BETSY DAVES, ophthalmic assistant, artist; b. San Angelo, Tex., Oct. 22, 1954; d. James Albert and Elizabeth A. (Alf) Daves. BS in Edn., Tex. Tech. U., 1977; MS in Human Devel., U. Tex., Dallas, 1991. Certified Tchr., Tex. Tchr. Preschool Deaf, Odessa, Tex., 1977-78; sales assoc. Laura Ashley, Plano, Tex., 1988-93; ophthalmic asst. Craig Smith M.D., Dallas, Tex., 1994—. Author: (with others) The First Snow, 1973; exhibited in group shows at Dallas City Hall, 1993, 97, Dallas Visual Arts Ctr., 1996-98, Plaza of the Americas, 1995, State Fair Tex., 1997, Bath House, Dallas, 1998 and others. Vol. Medical City Hosp., Dallas, 1993—, Herrin House, Dallas, 1993—; adv. bd. Herrin House, Dallas, 1991—. Recipient Honorable Mention for sculpture Girls in Dresses, 1993. Mem. Tex. Sculpture Assn., Dallas Visual Art Ctr., Sigma Alpha Eta. Avocation: art.

BASS, EVELYN ELIZABETH, elementary school educator; b. Magnolia, Ark., Sept. 28, 1948; d. Marvin and Catherine (Grissom) Scott; m. Burlin Lee Hughes, July 17, 1971 (div. Aug. 1984); children: Tionna Latrice, Lee Otis Williams Jr.; m. John W. Bass Sr., July 23, 2000. BA, Ark. Bapt. Coll., 1971; MS in Edn., Ouachita Bapt. Coll., Arkadelphia, Ark., 1988; degree, U. Little Rock, 2000—02. Tchr. Pulaski County Spl. Sch. Dist., Little Rock, 1971-97; exec. dir. Lenea's Children's Cottage, Little Rock, 1997—; advisor Choice Care Inc., Little Rock, 1998—, owner, pres. Evelyn's Tutoring Svc., Little Rock, 1998—; presch. tchr. Graceland Kids' Educare Ctr., 2000—. Child devel. assoc. instr., advisor Grace Holiness Christian Acad., 1999—, also head instr., prin. 2004—; cons. in field. Author, composer: (poetry and songs) The Printed Word, 1993; (CDs) The Printed Word, 2003, Never Say Never, 2003; author: The Printed Word/Woman of God, 1995. Traffic judge Willard Proctor, Jr. Campaign, 1996, cir. ct. judge, 2000. Democrat. Apostolic. Avocations: singing, songwriting, writing fiction. Home: 2918 Dorset Dr Little Rock AR 72204 Office: [illegible] Jenkins Scott Adminstr 7601 Scott Hamilton Dr Little Rock AR 72209-3167

BASS, JANIS, musician; d. Milton Wolf and Hester Mayer; m. Alan R. Bass, Aug. 18, 1966; 1 child, Elisa C. BA, Antioch U., 1956; studied with, Lennie Tristano, 1959—60; postgrad., Yale U., 1962—64; studied with, Nadia Boulanger; masterclasses with Artur Rubenstein and Clifford Curzon, Am. Conservatory of Music at Fontainbleau, 1965. Registered concert salon performer Mich. Popular music performer Wright-Patterson AFB Officers' Club, Dayton, Ohio, 1951—56, Paul's Cafe, Dayton, 1951—56, Associated Booking Corp., Chgo., 1951—56; pianist, vocal music tchr. N.Y.C. Pub. Sch. Sys., 1956—60; pvt. piano tchr. Southfield, Mich., 1970—80; concert salon performer Janis Bass Concert Salon/Salon de Concert, Bloomfield Hills, Mich., Paris, 1980—. Avocations: politics, tai chi, French. Office: Janis Bass Concert Salon PO Box 31 Bloomfield Hills MI 48303-9998 E-mail: jbcs_jbsc@fastmail.fm.

BASS, KIMBERLEIGH ANNE, real estate company executive, risk management consultant; d. Sheldon A. Bass and Janeen L. Dobbins; life ptnr. Cheryl A. Turner. V.p. Marsh, Inc., Tampa, Fla., 1987—99; pres. Get Real Holding Corp., St. Petersburg, Fla., 1999—. Risk mgmt. cons. The Elements, St. Petersburg, 1999—. Mem. DIFFA, Dallas, 1992—96. Mem.: Nat. Assn. Ins. Women (assoc.). Democrat. Avocations: travel, theater, music, museums, sailing. Office: Get Real Holding Corp PO Box 16836 Saint Petersburg FL 33733 Personal E-mail: kabelement@aol.com. E-mail: gctrealcorp@aol.com.

BASS, LYNDA D. retired medical/surgical nurse, nursing educator; b. Suffolk, Va. d. H.M. and Katie Lea Bass. BSN, N.C. Agrl. and Tech. State U., Greensboro, 1968; MS in Nursing, Cath. U. Am., 1974; Gen. Surgery Clin. Specialist, George Washington U. Hosp., Washington. Cert. BCLS instr., CPR instr.-trainer. Med. surg. nurse Walter Reed Army Hosp., Washington; clin. instr. Suburban Hosp., Bethesda, Md.; edn./tng. quality assurance coord. Howard U. Hosp., Washington; clin. educator Providence Hosp., Washington; edn. specialist Vets. Affairs Md. Healthcare Sys., Balt. Coord. clin. staff devel. Mount Vernon Hosp., Alexandria, Va. Capt. USAR, 1967—71, Vietnam. Mem. Nat. Nursing Staff Devel. Assn., Vietnam Vets. Am., Chi Eta Phi.

BASS, RUTH MARY HASKINS, journalist; b. Springfield, Mass., July 18, 1934; d. Ralph Warner and Hilda Marie (Allen) Haskins; m. Milton R. Bass, May 27, 1960; children: Michael Jon, Elissa Allen, Amy Brunell. AB in English, Bates Coll., 1955; MS in Journalism, Columbia U., 1956. Police and ct. reporter The Berkshire Eagle, Pittsfield, Mass., 1956-61; freelance writer, editor Berkshire Week mag., Pittsfield, Mass., 1963-68; editor Berkshire Sampler, Pittsfield, Mass., 1977-87; assoc. sunday editor Berkshire Eagle, Pittsfield, Mass., 1987-90; Sunday editor Pittsfield, Mass., 1990-96; columnist Berkshire Eagle, Pittsfield, 1996—. Freelance travel writer, 1996—. Author: (book series) Herbal Sweets, Herbal Salads, Herbal Bread, Herbal Soups, Tomatoes Love Herbs, Peppers Love Herbs, Onions Love Herbs, Mushrooms Love Herbs, 1996; co-author: Teen Career Guide, 1962; editor The Paper, 1997-2002. Selectman Town of Richmond, 1972-77, mem. fin. com., 1990—, chmn., 1993—; mem. bd. health, 1972-90; leader Girl Scouts US, Richmond, 1982—. Recipient Best Column in New Eng. award UPI, 1988, Charles and Mary Kusik Citizenship award, Richmond, 1994. Avocations: tennis, gardening, photography, bird watching, needlework.

BASSETT, ANGELA, actress; b. N.Y.C., Aug. 16, 1958; m. Courtney Vance, 1997. BA in African-Am. Studies, Yale U., 1980; MFA, Yale Sch. of Drama, 1983. Appeared in (plays) Colored People's Time, 1982, The Mystery Plays, 1984-85, The Painful Adventures of Pericles, Prince of Tyre, 1986-87, Joe Turner's Come and Gone, 1986-87, (Broadway) Ma Rainey's Black Bottom, (Broadway) Joe Turner's Come and Gone, 1988, King Henry IV Part I, 1987; (TV movies) Line of Fire: The Morris Dees Story, 1991, The Jacksons: An American Dream, 1992, A Century of Women, 1994, Ruby's Bucket of Blood, 2001 (also producer), The Rosa Parks Story, 2002 (also exec. producer); guest appearances (TV Series) The Cosby

Show, 1985, 1988, Spenser: For Hire, 1985, A Man Called Hawk, 1989, Tour of Duty, 1989, 227, 1989, thirtysomething, 1989, Alien Nation, 1990, The Flash, 1991, Nightmare Café, 1992, The Bernie Mac Show, 2003; (films) F/X, 1986, Kindergarten Cop, 1990, Boyz N the Hood, 1991, City of Hope, 1991, Innocent Blood, 1992, Malcolm X, 1992, Passion Fish, 1992, What's Love Got to Do with It, 1993 (Acad. award nominee for best actress 1993, Golden Globe award best actress in a musical or comedy 1994), Strange Days, 1995, Panther, 1995, Waiting to Exhale, 1995, A Vampire in Brooklyn, 1995, Contact, 1997, How Stella Got Her Groove Back, 1998, Wings Against the Wind, 1999, Cosm, 1999, 50 Violins, 1999, Music of the Heart, 1999, Supernova, 2000, Whispers: An Elephant's Tale, 2000 (voice), Boesman and Lena, 2000, The Score, 2001, Sunshine State, 2002, Masked and Anonymous, 2003; exec. prodr. Our America, 2002. Office: care Doug Chapin Mgmt # 430 9465 Wilshire Blvd Beverly Hills CA 90212 also: Creative Artists Agy Wilshire Blvd Beverly Hills CA 90212-2613*

BASSETT, CAROL ANN, journalism educator, writer; b. Langley AFB, Va., Mar. 2, 1953; d. William Brainard and Genevieve (Rivaldo) B. BA summa cum laude in Humanities, Ariz. State U., 1977; MA in Journalism, U. Ariz., 1982. Ptnr. Desert West News, Tucson, 1985-90; freelance writer Tucson, 1980-95; freelance writer for mags. Missoula, Mont., 1995-98; mem. faculty Sch. Journalism U. Mont., Missoula, 1996-98; mem. faculty Sch. Journalism and Comm. U. Oreg., Eugene, 1998—. Author: A Gathering of Stones: Journeys to the Edges of a Changing World, 2002 (finalist Oreg. Book award 2003), Essays in American Nature Writing, 2000, American Nature Writing, 2001; editor Tucson Weekly, 1989-90; contbr. numerous articles to nat. and internat. mags. including N.Y. Times. Recipient 2d Place Gen. Reporting award Ariz. Press Club, 1987, Gold medal for best environ. documentary Houston Internat. Film Festival, 1990, 1st Place Gen. Reporting award Ariz. Press Club, 1992, Silver Medal for Energy Issues documentary, Houston Internat. Film Festival, 1992; co-recipient Alfred I. duPont Columbia award, 1984-85, First Place award Investigative Reporting, 1986, 1st Place Polit. Reporting, 1989, First Amendment Journalism award, 1986; grantee Fund for Investigative Journalism, 1985, 87, Corp. for Pub. Broadcasting, 1988, Oxfam Am., 1991. Address: Sch Journalism Univ Oreg Eugene OR 97403

BASSETT, DEBRA LYN, lawyer, educator; b. Pleasanton, Calif., Oct. 28, 1956; d. James Arthur and Shirley Ann (Russell) Bassett. BA, U. Vt., 1977; MS, San Diego State U., 1982; JD, U. Calif., Davis, 1987. Bar: Calif. 1987, DC 1990, U.S. Dist. Ct. (no. and ea. dists.) Calif. 1988, U.S. Ct. Appeals (9th cir.) 1988, U.S. Supreme Ct. 1991. Guidance counselor Addison Cen. Supr. Union, Middlebury, Vt., 1982-83, Milton (Vt.) Elem. Sch., 1983-84; assoc. Morrison & Foerster, San Francisco, 1986; jud. clk. U.S. Ct. Appeals (9th cir.), Phoenix, 1987-88; assoc. Morrison & Foerster, San Francisco and Walnut Creek, Calif., 1988-92; sr. atty. Calif. Ct. Appeal (3d appellate dist.), Sacramento, 1992-99; assoc. prof. Mich. State U., East Lansing, 2002—. Tutor civil procedure, rsch. asst. U. Calif., Davis, 1985—87, instr., 1995—2002, lectr., 1997—2002; adj. prof. McGeorge Sch. Law, 1998—99, dir. legal process, 1999—2000, vis. prof., 2000—01. Editor: U. Calif. Law Rev., 1985—86; sr. articles editor:, 1986—87. Mem. Steiner Chorale, 2002—. Mem.: ABA (vice chmn. ethics com. young lawyers divsn. 1989—91, exec. com. labor and employment law com. 1989—90), AAUW, APA (assoc.), Scribes. Democrat. Avocations: music, tennis, travel, hiking. Home: 915 Snyder Rd East Lansing MI 48823 Office: Mich State U DCL Coll Law 417 Law Coll Bldg East Lansing MI 48824 E-mail: debbie.bassett@law.msu.edu.

BASSETT, ELIZABETH EWING (LIBBY BASSETT), writer, editor; b. Cleve., July 22, 1937; d. Ben and Eileen Grace (Ewing) B.; m. Robert Richter, Feb. 20, 1994. AA, Bradford Jr. Coll., Mass., 1957. Girl Friday Time-Life, animated film cos., others, 1957-63; asst. producer, stage mgr. N.Y. State Pavilion at N.Y. World's Fair, 1963-64; writer, reporter, editor AP, N.Y.C., 1965-72; free-lance corr. AP, Newsweek, Voice of America, UNICEF, ABC Radio, Africa, 1972-74; resident corr. ABC News, Cairo, 1974-77; dir. publs. and comm. World Environment Ctr., N.Y.C., 1978-85; cons. writer, editor, editorial designer Women's Environ. and Devel. Orgn., 1989—98, UN orgns. and others, 1985—; co-organizer Project on Religion and Human Rights, 1994-95. Guest lectr. Am. U. Cairo, Rutgers U., Columbia U., L.I. U., Hunter Coll., CUNY; press officer Global Survival Conf., Oxford, Eng., 1988; press coord. Global Forum on Environ. and Devel., Moscow, 1990, Parliamentary Earth Summit, Rio de Janeiro, 1992; info. officer Internat. Green Cross/Global Forum, Kyoto, Japan, 1993; comm. coord. World Women's Congress for Healthy Planet, Miami, 1991; press. coord. WEDO Web, NGO Forum on Women, China, 1995. Author: The Growth of Environment in the World Bank, World Environment Center, 1982, UNEP N.Am. News, 1986-91, Shared Vision, 1988-92, The Global Forum Decade, 1995, Earth and Faith: A Book of Reflection for Action, 2000, also others; editor, deisgner: Women in African Economies--From Burning Sun to Boardroom, 2000, Liberian Women Peacemakers, 2004; assoc. editor, designer: The Bella Abzug Reader, 2003; editor, designer: Liberian Women Peacemakers, 2004. Mem. Soc. Profl. Journalists, Soc. Environ. Journalists.

BASSETT, HENRIETTA ELIZABETH, music educator; BA, Baylor U., 1952. Piano tchr., 1968—. Instrumentalist various Bapt. chs., 1945—; adminstr., dir. Beth Basset Music Camp Acad., 1948—; chmn. bd. dirs. Joy Springs Encampment, Inc., 1982. Composer: piano solos, Christmas cantata, solo and ensemble pieces. Dir. various plays and musical dramas; Sunday sch. tchr. Mem.: Am. Coll. of Musicians, Mesquite-Area Music Tchrs. Assn., Music Tchrs. Assn., The Baylor Alumni Assn., Keyboard Tchrs. Assn. Internat. Inc., Internat. Guild Tchrs. Piano. Avocations: collecting bells, gardening, cooking. : 645 E Tripp Rd Sunnyvale TX 75182-9633

BASSETT, TINA, communications executive; b. Detroit; m. Leland Kinsey Bassett; children: Joshua, Robert. Student, U. Mich., 1974, 76-78, 81, Wayne State U., 1979-80. Advt. dir. Greenfield's Restaurant, Mich. and Ohio, 1972-73; dir. advt. and pub. rels. Kresco, Inc., Detroit, 1973-74; pub's. rep. The Detroiter mag., 1974-75; pub. rels. dir. Detroit Bicentennial Commn., 1975-77; prin. Leland K. Bassett & Assocs., Detroit, 1976-86; intermediate job devel. specialist Detroit Coun. of the Arts, 1977; project dir. Detroit image campaign dept. pub. info. City of Detroit, 1975, spl. events dir., 1978, dep. dir. dept. pub. info., 1978-83, dir. dept. pub. info., 1983-86; pres., prin. Bassett & Bassett, Inc., Detroit, 1986—. Publicity chmn. Under the Stars IV, V, VI, VII, VIII, IX and X, Benefit Balls, Detroit Inst. of Arts Founders Soc., 1983-88, Detroit Inst. of Arts Founders Centennial Ball, 1985, publicity chmn. Mich. Opera Theater, Opera Ball, 1987; program lectr. Wayne County Close-Up Program, 1984; mem. ctrl. planning com. Am. Assn. Mus.; mem. Founders Soc., Detroit Inst. Arts, 1988—; mem., publicity chair Grand Prix Ball, 1989; co-chair, prodr. Mus. Hall Ctr. for Performing Arts; bd. dirs. arts coun. Detroit Inst. Arts, 1996, bd. dirs. cinema arts coun., 1996—; bd. dirs. Weizman Inst. Sci., 1996-97. Named Outstanding Woman in Agy. Top Mgmt., Detroit chpt. Am. Women in Radio and TV, 1989, one of Most Powerful Women in Mich., CORP Mag., 2002. Mem. AIA (hon., pub. dir. 1990-91, Richard Upjohn fellowship 1991), Detroit Hist. Soc., Internat. Women's Forum, Music Hall Assn., Pub. Rels. Soc. Am. (Advt. Woman of Yr. 1989), Woman's Advt. Club Detroit, Cinematic Arts Coun., DIA (bd. dirs. 1996-99). Home: 30751 Cedar Creek Dr Farmington Hills MI 48336-4989 Address: Bassett & Bassett 1502 Randolph St Ste 200 Detroit MI 48226-2295 Office Phone: 313-965-3010.

BASSEY, IDARA E. lawyer, educator; b. Bonn, Germany, May 7, 1969; arrived in U.S., 1969; d. Ephraim N. and Patricia M. Bassey. BA, Washington U., St. Louis, Mo., 1991; JD, U. Ga., Athens, 1994, LLM, 1996; D of Metaphysical Counseling, U. Metaphysics, Studio City, Calif., 2003. Bar: Ga. 1997. Jud. clerk Fulton County Superior Ct., Atlanta, 1992; tchg. asst. U. Ga. Sch. Law, Athens, 1993; rsch. asst. Dean Rusk Ctr. for Internat. and Comparative Law, Athens, Ga., 1993—94; sr. rsch. assoc. in African affairs Southern Ctr. for Internat. Studies, Atlanta, 1995—96; legal advisor AFRICARE, Washington, 1997—98; contract atty. Washington, 1999—2001; adj. prof. law Am. InterContinental U., Hoffman Estates, Ill., 2003—. Contbr. articles to various lit. jours. and anthologies. Fellow, Ford Found. in Pub. Internat. Law, 1994. Avocations: reading, travel, interacting with other cultures, writing non-fiction.

BASSIWA, LIZAMARIE, medical technologist; b. New Orleans, Nov. 8, 1965; d. Armando Bunag and Concha Alqueza Bassiwa. BS in Med. Tech., U. Md., 1988. Libr. asst. Albin O. Kuhn Libr. and Gallery, Catonsville, Md., 1985-86; customer svc. rep. Army & Air Forch Exch. Svc., Andrews AFB, Md., 1986; med. technologist Prince George's Hosp. Ctr., Cheverly, Md., 1988-89, Georgetown Univ. Hosp., Washington, 1989-90, Walter Reed Army Med. Ctr., Washington, 1990—; R&D team leader Walter Reed, 2002—. Asst. dir.: The Acceptance of Sherry Goldstein, 1998; stage mgr.: (play) Liga, 1997. Mem. nominating com. Outstanding Young Women of Am., 1997. Recipient Outstanding Performance as Med. Technologist award Dept. of Army—Walter Reed, 1993, 94, 95, 96, 97, Letter of Appreciation, Dept. of Army/Dept. of Navy, 1999, Commdr.'s award for civilian svc. Dept. of Army, 2002. Mem. Am. Soc. Clin. Pathologists (assoc., cert. microbiology technologist), Am. Soc. Microbiology. Avocations: volleyball, dance, cooking, crafts. Office: Walter Reed Army Med Ctr 16th St NW Washington DC 20307-0001

BASSLER, BONNIE, molecular biologist; BS, U. Calif., Davis, 1984; PhD, Johns Hopkins U., 1990. Rsch. scientist Agouron Inst., La Jolla, Calif., 1993—94; faculty dept. molecular biology Princeton U., 1994—96, faculty environ. inst., 1996—. Contbr. articles to profl. jours. Fellow Rsch. fellow, Agouron Inst., 1990—93, MacArthur Found. fellow, 2002. Achievements include research in quorum sensing. Office: Princeton U 329 Lewis Thomas Lab Princeton NJ 08544

BASSUK, ELLEN LINDA, psychiatrist; b. N.Y.C., Feb. 8, 1945; d. Irving and Molly (Pakarow) B.; children: Daniel, Sarah. BA, Brandeis U., 1964; MD, Tufts U., 1968; Dr.P.S. (hon.), Northeastern U., 1993. Diplomate Am. Bd. Psychiatry. Intern Mt. Auburn Hosp., Cambridge, Mass., 1968-69; resident psychiatry Univ. Hosp., Boston, 1969-70, Boston State Hosp., Boston, 1970-71, Beth Israel Hosp., Boston, 1971-73, dir. psychiat. emergency svcs., 1974-82; fellow Bunting Inst., Cambridge, Mass., 1982-84; assoc. prof. psychiatry Harvard Med. Sch., Boston, 1983—. Founder, pres. Nat. Ctr. on Family Homelessness, Newton, Mass., 1988—; mem. Com. on Health Care of Homeless Persons Inst. of Medicine, Washington, 1986-88. Editor: The Practitioners Guide to Psychoactive Drugs, 1977, 83, 91, 97; editor-in-chief Am. Jour. Orthopsychiatry, 1994-98; contbr. numerous articles to profl. jours. Fellow Am. Psychiat. Assn.; mem. Mass. Psychiat. Soc. Home: 20 Randolph Rd Chestnut Hill MA 02467-2338 Office: Nat Ctr on Family Homelessness 181 Wells Ave Newton MA 02459-3332 E-mail: ellen.bassuk@familyhomelessness.org.

BAST, KAROLYN (KAY) ANNE, dance educator, choreographer; b. Tulsa, Mar. 12, 1940; d. Lowell R. and Dorothy J. Butterfield; m. A. Daniel Bast, Aug. 17, 1963; children: Terri Lynn, Robin Kay, Steven Christopher. AA, Citrus Jr. Coll., Azusa-Glendora, Calif., 1970; BS, Calif. Polytech. U., Pomona, 1972, MS, 1981. Dance dir. The Show Stoppers, Chino, Calif., 1978-87; Europe dance dir. The Dance Masters, Alta Loma, Calif., 1992—. Dir. internat. dance tours; founder Internat. Performing Arts Competition, Anaheim, Calif., 1985-89. Author: Tap: The Dance of Sound, 1982. Mem. cultural planning com. Chino, Calif., 1982—, city parade dir., 1980-82; pres. Assistance League of Pomona Valley, 1991-92. Recipient numerous dance title awards. Republican. Lutheran. Avocations: needlepoint, crafts, interior decorating, travel. Home: PO Box 1594 Upland CA 91785-1594

BASTERRECHEA, IVETTE, research analyst; b. Hoboken, N.J., May 25, 1970; d. Zoila and Antonio Basterrechea; m. Keith Norvel Jones, May 3, 1999; children: Anabelle Jones, Eliza Jones. BA, Barnard Coll., N.Y.C., 1992; JD, Georgetown U., Washington, 1996. Bar: Conn. 1999. Commr. Adv. Neighborhood Commn., Washington, 2000—02; legal rsch. analyst InfoEdge Tech., Inc., Arlington, Va., 2001—. Sec. Hyde Parent-Tchr. Assn., Washington, 2003—. Mem. Ward 6 Dems., Washington, 1999. Liberal. Roman Catholic. Avocations: knitting, crochet. Home: 1610 D St NE Washington DC 20002 Office: InfoEdge Tech Inc 1101 Wilson Blvd Ste 1450 Arlington VA 22209

BASTIANICH, LIDIA MATTICCHIO, chef, food service executive; b. Italy, 1947; Owner Buonavia Restaurant, Forest Hills, NY, 1972—81, Villa Secondo, Fresh Meadows, NY, 1979—81, Felidia Restaurant, NY, 1981—; co-owner Becco Restaurant, NY, 1993—, Lidia's Restaurant, Kansas City, Mo., 1998—; founder, pres. Esperienze Italiane Travel, 1996—. Founder, owner Lidia's Flavors of Italy, 1988—; host, chef Lidia's Italian Table, 1998—2001, Lidia's Italian Am. Kitchen, 2001—. Author: (montly syndicated column) on Italian food, (cookbooks) La Cucina di Lidia, 1990, Lidia's Italian Table, 1998, Lidia's Italian American Kitchen, 2001. Established Lidia Matticchio Bastianich Found., 1999. Office: Felidia Restaurant 243 E 58th St New York NY 10022*

BASTIEN, JANE SMISOR, music educator; b. Hutchinson, Kans., Jan. 15, 1936; d. Herbert D. and Gladys I. (Haston) Smisor; m. James W. Bastien; children: Lisa Bastien Hanss, Lori Bastien Vickers. AA, Stephens Coll., 1955; BA, Barnard Coll., 1957; MA, Columbia U., 1958. Asst. prof. Tulane U., New Orleans, 1958-75; pvt. piano tchr., La Jolla, Calif., 1975—. Author/composer: Bastien Piano Books/Ednl. Piano Books for Children and Adults. Recipient Alumnae award Stephens Coll., 1960. Mem. Nat. Assn. Music Tchrs. (Lifetime Achievement award 1999), Music Tchrs. Assn. of Calif. (State Tchg. award 1996). Republican. Presbyterian. Avocations: gardening, collecting antiques. Home: 2431 Vallecitos Ct La Jolla CA 92037-3146 E-mail: jsbastien@aol.com.

BASTRENTA, BRIGITTE ELISABETH, school administrator; b. Moutiers, Savoie, France, Jan. 7, 1952; came to U.S., 1979; d. Marcel Rinaldo and Jeanne Eulalie (Chaville) B.; m. Rudolph Andrew Walter, Dec. 27, 1979; children: Laurie Nicole Walter, Julian Thomas Walter. BA, U. Paul Valéry, Montpellier, France, 1973, MA, 1974. Tchr. French Marin Acad., San Rafael, Calif., 1980-83, Arrowsmith Acad., Berkeley, Calif., 1989-96, dir. admission and devel., 1996—. Tchr. French Diablo Valley Coll., Pleasant Hill, Calif., 1990-95; mem. WASC Accreditation Commn., 1998—. Editor (newsletter) Arrowsmith in Action, 1999—. Co-pres. East Bay French-Am. Sch. PTA, Berkeley, 1991-93; mem. Natural Resources Def. Coun. Mem. Amnesty Internat., Doctors Without Borders, So. Poverty Law Ctr., The Carter Ctr. Democrat. Avocations: swimming, skiing, hiking, travel, cooking. Home: 333 Scottsdale Rd Pleasant Hill CA 94523 Office: Arrowsmith Acad 2300 Bancroft Way Berkeley CA 94704

BATCHELDER, ALICE M. federal judge; b. Aug. 15, 1944; m. William G. Batchelder III; children: William G. IV, Elisabeth. BA, Ohio Wesleyan U., 1964; JD, Akron U., 1971; LLM, U. Va., 1988. Tchr. Plain Local Sch. Dist., Franklin County, Ohio, 1965-66, Jones Jr. High Sch., 1966-67, Buckeye High Sch., Medina County, 1967-68; assoc. Williams & Batchelder, Medina, Ohio, 1971-83; judge U.S. Bankruptcy Ct., Ohio, 1983-85, U.S. Dist. Ct. (no. dist.) Ohio, Cleve., 1985-91, U.S. Ct. of Appeals (6th cir.), Cleveland, 1991—. Mem. ABA, Fed. Judge's Assn., Fed. Bar Assn., Medina County Bar Assn. Office: US Ct of Appeals (6th cir) 143 W Liberty St Medina OH 44256-2215

BATCHELDER, ANNE STUART, retired publishing executive, political organization worker; b. Lake Forest, Ill., Jan. 11, 1920; d. Robert Douglas and Harriet (McClure) Stuart; m. Clifton Brooks Batchelder, May 26, 1945; children: Edward, Anne Stuart, Mary Clifton, Lucia Brooks Student Lake Forest Coll., 1941-43. Clubmobile driver ARC, Eng., Belgium, France, Holland and Germany, 1943-45; pub., editor Douglas County Gazette, 1970-75, 79-90. Bd. dirs. Firstier Bank Omaha; dir., treas. U.S. Checkbook Com. Mem. Rep. Ctrl. Com. Nebr., 1955-62, 70-83, vice chmn. Ctrl. Com., 1959-64, chmn., 1975-79, mem. fin. com., 1957-64; chmn. women's sect. Douglas County Rep. Fin. Com., 1955, vice chmn. com., 1958-60; v.p. Omaha Woman's Rep. Club, 1957-58, pres., 1959-60; alt. del. Nat. Conv., 1956, 72, del., 1980, 84, 88; mem. Rep. Nat. Com. for Nebr., 1964-70; asst. chmn. Douglas County Rep. Ctrl. Com., 1971-74; 1st v.p. Nebr. Fedn. Rep. Women, 1971-72, pres., 1972-74; chmn. Nebr. Rep. Com., 1975-79; vice-chmn. Bldg. Fedn. Rep. Women, 1998—; mem. Nebr. State Bldg. Commn., 1979-83; Rep. candidate for lt. gov., 1974. Sr. v.p. Nebr. Founders Day, 1958; trustee Hastings Coll., 1977—; bd. dirs. YWCA, 1983-89, Omaha Libr. Found., 1991-2000, Libr. Found., 2000—; past trustee Brownell Hall, Vis. Nurse Assn.; past pres. Nebr. chpt. Freedoms Found. at Valley Forge; chmn. fin. George Bush for Pres., Nebr., 1987-88; apptd. Kennedy Ctr. Performing Arts, 1989, 94, Pres.' Adv. Com. on the Arts, 1990-92, Nat. Com. for the Performing Arts, 1992—; mem. Nebr. Rep. State Fin. Com., 1990, Nat. Fin. Com. Bush-Quayle, 1992; active Omaha Meth. Hosp. Found., Brownell-Talbot Sch. Found.; mem. Uta Halee Home for Girls, 1980—. Elected to Nebr. Rep. Hall of Fame, 1984; named Citizen of the Yr. Midlands Coun. Boy Scouts Am., 1997; recipient Silver Beaver, Boy Scouts Am., Spirit award Uta Halee Home for Girls, 1999. Mem. Mayflower Soc., Colonial Dames, P.E.O., Nat. League Pen Women Omaha Country, Omaha, Halee Spirit of Youth. Presbyterian. Home: 6875 State St Omaha NE 68152-1633

BATCHELOR, KAREN LEE, English language educator; b. Oregon City, Oreg., June 17, 1948; d. Jewel Elaine Durham; m. Luis Moncado, Mar. 17, 1978 (div. Aug. 1988); children: Virginia, Travis. BA in English, San Francisco State U., 1971, MA in English, 1980. Vol. U.S. Peace Corps, Andong, South Korea, 1972-74; tchr. English as second lang. City Coll. San Francisco, 1975—; tchr. trainer U. Calif., Berkeley, 1986—; acad. specialist USIA, 1991—; lectr. English Sonoma State U., 1999—. Speaker in field. Co-author: (textbooks) Discovering English, 1981, In Plain English, 1985, More Plain English, 1986, The Writing Challenge, 1990, The English Zone, Books 1-4, 1998; contbr. articles to profl. jorus. Mem. Tchrs. English to Speakers of Other Langs., Calif. Tchrs. English to Speakers of Other Langs. Office: City Coll San Francisco 50 Phelan Ave San Francisco CA 94112-1821

BATEMAN, ANDREA R. insurance agent; b. Park Ridge, Ill., Oct. 17, 1975; BS, Roosevelt U., 2000. Cert. Lic. Ins. Agent Ill. Ins. agent/owner Dave Rundblad, Inc./Allstate, Park Ridge, Ill., 1996—. Home: 545 N Rose Ave Park Ridge IL 60068 Office: Allstate Ins 1580 N Northwest hwy #15 Park Ridge IL 60068

BATEMAN, JEAN BUDINGTON, writer, poet, home furnishings consultant; b. Springfield, Mass., Oct. 24, 1923; d. Harold Fairchild and Josephine Elizabeth (Eckel) Budington; m. John Travis Lisenby Jr., Nov. 9, 1944 (div. Aug. 1961); children: Jo, John Travis III; m. E. Wallace Bateman, Mar. 11, 1967 (dec.). Student, Syracuse U., 1941-45. Supr., textile designer M. Lowenstein, N.Y.C., 1961-67; color coord. Celanese Corp., N.Y.C., 1967-68; outside saleswoman Jens Risom Design, N.Y.C., 1968-70, Jack Lenor Larsen, N.Y.C., 1970-78, Design Solution, Phoenix, 1985-89; sales rep. Judy Wilson & Assocs., Phoenix, 1989-91; owner, rep. Jean Bateman Assocs., Phoenix, 1991-94; home furnishings cons. Phoenix, 1994—. Pub. Mile High Poetry Society, Spectrum, Verses, Sheila.Na.Gig., Art.Rage.Us. Fellow Internat. Furnishings and Design Assn. (pres. Ariz. chpt. 1986-87, chmn. Nat. Ednl. Found. 1993) Avocations: swimming, travel, photography, reading, writing. Home and Office: 3046 N 32nd St Unit 320 Phoenix AZ 85018-6842

BATEMAN, JEANNINE ANN, county official; b. Hillsboro, Kans., July 6, 1945; d. Forrest Edward and Alvina (Bernhardt) Skibbe; m. Rufus J. Bateman, Apr. 25, 1965; 1 child, Kristine Kay. AS in Bus., Butler County Cmty. Coll., El Dorado, Kans., 1996; student, Baker U., Baldwin City, Kans., 1963-64, Wichita State U., 1997—. Bookkeeper Marion County Coop., Marion, Kans., summer 1963; abstract asst. Hannaford Title Co., Marion, 1964-74, 79-84; clk., dep. Marion County Treas. Office, Marion, 1984-94, treas., 1994—. Treas. Marion Warrior Boosters, 1993, 1st Dist. Rep. Women, Kans., 1997—; bd. dirs. Leadership Marion County, 1994-95, sec., treas., 1995-96, v.p., 1996-97. Mem. North Ctrl. Kans. County Treasurers (sec., treas. 1996-97, v.p. 1997-98, pres. 1998-99), Kans. County Treasurer's Assn. (sec. 1999, v.p. 2000, pres. 2001), Marion County Rep. Women, Marion County Rep. Party, Order of the Purple, Kiwanis Club Marion, Phi Theta Kappa, Phi Kappa Phi. N.Am. Baptist. Avocations: walking, hiking, reading, basketball, football. Office: Marion County Treas PO Box 257 Marion KS 66861-0257

BATEMAN, SHARON LOUISE, public relations executive; b. St. Louis, Oct. 18, 1949; d. Frank Hamilton and Charlotte Elizabeth (Hogan) Bateman. Student, Drury Coll., 1967-69; BJ, U. Mo., 1971. Asst. dir. pub. rels. Cardinal Glennon Hosp. Children, St. Louis, 1971-76; staff asst. pub. rels. Ozark Air Lines, St. Louis, 1976-80; mgr. corp. rels. Kellwood Co., St. Louis, 1980-83; mgr. corp. comm. May Dept. Stores Co., St. Louis, 1983-86, dir. corp. comm., 1986-94, v.p. corp. comms., 2000—; mgr. comm. Arthur Andersen, St. Louis, 1995-96; mgr. editl. and adminstrv. svcs. Falk Design Group, St. Louis, 1996—2000. Bd. dirs. St. Michael's Houses, 1996—97, Gateway Greening, 1999—2001. Recipient Best Regional Airline Employee Publ. award, Editor's Assn. Am. Transp. Assn., 1978. Mem.: Pub. Rels. Soc. Am. (sec.St. Louis chpt. 1983, bd. dirs. 1988—90, v.p. 1991), Internat. Assn. Bus. Comms. (pres. St. Louis chpt. 1977). Office: May Dept Stores Co 611 Olive St Saint Louis MO 63101-1721

BATES, BARBARA J. NEUNER, retired municipal official; b. Mt. Vernon, N.Y., Apr. 8, 1927; d. John Joseph William and Elsie May (Flint) Neuner; m. Herman Martin Bates, Jr., Mar. 25, 1950; children: Roberta Jean Bates Jamin, Herman Martin III, Jon Neuner. BA, Barnard Coll., 1947. Confidential clk. to supr. Town of Ossining, N.Y., 1960-63, receiver of taxes, 1971-90; ret.; pres. BNB Assocs., Briarcliff Manor, N.Y., 1963-83, Upper Nyack Realty Co., Inc., Briarcliff Manor, 1966-71. V.p. Ossining (N.Y.) Young Rep. Club, 1958; pres. Young Womens Rep. Club Westchester County (N.Y.), 1959-61; regional committeewoman N.Y. State Assn. Young Rep. Clubs, 1960-62; mem. Westchester County Rep. Com., 1963-95; mem. Ossining Women's Rep. Club, 1960-92, pres., 1984-85; mem. Westchester County Women's Rep. Club, 1957-92. Mem. DAR, Jr. League Westchester-on-Hudson, Receivers Taxes Assn. Westchester County (legis. liaison, v.p., pres. 1984-85), Hackley Sch. Mothers Assn. (pres. 1968), R.I. Hist. Soc., Ossining Hist. Soc., Westchester County Hist. Soc., Landmark Preservation Soc. of S.E., Ossining Woman's Club. Home: 23 Bloomer Rd Brewster NY 10509-1026 also: 663 Reynolds Rd Chepachet RI 02814-1629

BATES, BEVERLY JOYCE, retired educator and computer professional; b. San Francisco, Sept. 5, 1930; d. Ezra John Hughes and Lois Ruth (Barr) Bates; m. Truman Winfield Massee, Sept. 8, 1953 (div. Mar. 1978); m. Udo D. Ohrer, Dec. 19, 2003; children: Rebecca Lynn and Rachel Dorian (twins), Daniel L. BS in Home Econs., Oreg. State U., 1952; postgrad., Idaho State U., 1965-66; AA in Interior Design, Cañada Coll., 1982, computer cert., 1985. Tchr., substitute tchr. Sch. Dist. 411, Twin Falls, Idaho, 1965-70; rancher Jerome, Idaho, 1970-78; interior designer Menlo Park, Calif., 1978-83; bookkeeper Redwood City, Calif., 1980-85; computer specialist Stanford Linear Accelerator Ctr., Menlo Park, 1985-89; ret., 1989.

Designer, creator Tawanka Indian crafts. Vol. Eugene (Oreg.) Free Network, 1996. Mem. Oreg. Geneal. Soc. Avocations: biking, swimming.

BATES, CHERYL A, university educator; b. Oklahoma City, Okla., Nov. 20, 1959; d. Charles S and Marguerite H Miller; m. Don R Bates, Oct. 16, 1982; 1 child, Colin T. MusM, U. of Houston, Houston, TX, 1984—88; MusB, U. of Okla., Norman, OK, 1978—82. Texas Teacher Certification Tex. Edn. Agy., 1987. Music specialist Epps Island Elem., Houston, Tex., 1988—92; choir dir. Bammel Mid. Sch., Houston, 1992—98; adj. prof. Houston CC, Houston, Tex., 1991—92; tchg. fellow U. of Houston, Houston, Tex., 1986—87, 1998—2000; assoc. prof. Tomball Coll., Houston, Tex., 2000—. Bd. of directors The Regional Arts Coun., Tomball, Tex., 2000—02; clinician Tex. Music Educators Assn., San Antonio, 2001, San Antonio, 02. Dir.: (choral conducting) UIL Competitions (Four UIL Sweepstakes Awards for Outstanding Concert and Sightreading Performance, 97-8), American Classics Music Festivals (Two Outstanding Performance and Best in Class Awards, 97-8), Splashtown Choral Festivals (Two Best in Class Awards, 97-8); singer: (concert) Andre Bocelli in Concert at the Compaq Center, John Rutter conducts Brahm's German Requiem. V.p. North Houston Gamma Phi Beta Alumni, Houston, Tex., 1992—94. Fellow, U. of Houston Sch. of Music, 1986-87 and 1998-2000; grantee Innovative Project Grant, Tomball Coll., 2002; scholar Piano Scholarship, U. of Okla., 1978-1982. Mem.: Music Educators Nat. Conf., Am. Choral Directors Assn., Tex. Choral Directors Assn., Coll. Music Educators, Tex. Music Educators Assn., Mu Phi Epsilon, Gamma Phi Beta. Home: 11902 Quail Creek Houston TX 77070 Office: Tomball College 30555 Tomball Parkway Tomball TX 77375 E-mail: cheryl.a.bates@nhmccd.edu.

BATES, KATHY, actress; b. Memphis, June 28, 1948; d. Langdon Doyle and Bertye Kathleen (Talbot) Bates; m. Anthony Campisi, 1991 (div. 1997). BFA, So. Meth. U., 1969. Film appearances include Taking Off, 1971, Straight Time, Come Back to the Five and Dime, Jimmy Dean, Jimmy Dean, Summer Heat, Arthur 2: On the Rocks, Signs of Life, High Stakes, Men Don't Leave, Dick Tracy, White Palace, Misery, 1990 (Acad. award for Best Actress 1990, Golden Globe award), At Play in the Fields of the Lord, 1991, Fried Green Tomatoes, 1991 (Golden Globe nomination, BAFTA nomination), The Road to Mecca, 1992, Prelude to a Kiss, 1992, Used People, 1992, A Home of Our Own, 1993, North, 1994, Curse of the Starving Class, 1994, Dolores Claiborne, 1994, Angus, 1995, Diabolique, 1996, The War at Home, 1996, Primary Colors, 1998, Swept from the Sea, 1998, Titanic, 1998, The Waterboy, 1998, Baby Steps, 1999, Dash and Lilly, 1999, My Life as a Dog, 1999, Bruno, 2000, Rat Race, 2001, American Outlaws, 2001, About Schmidt, 2002, Love Liza, 2002; stage appearances include Vanities, 1976, Semmelweiss, Crimes of the Heart, The Art of Dining, Goodbye Fidel, 1980, Chocolate Cake and Final Placement, 1981, 5th of July, 'night, Mother, 1983 (Tony nomination, Outer Critics Circle award), Two Masters: The Rain of Terror, 1985, Curse of the Starving Class, Frankie and Johnny in the Clair de Lune (ODIE award 1988), The Road to Mecca; TV appearances include (series) The Late Shift (Golden Globe award, Am. Comedy award, SAG award), The Love Boat, St. Elsewhere, Cagney & Lacey, L.A. Law, China Beach, Homicide, N.Y.P.D. Blue, (pilot) Fargo, (miniseries) Murder Ordained, The Stand, 1994, (movies of the week) Johnny Bull, No Place Like Home, Roe vs. Wade, Hostages, The West Side Waltz, 1995, The Late Shift, 1996 (Golden Globe, 1997), Annie, 1999, My Sister's Keeper, 2002, Six Feet Under, 2003, Bridge of San Luis Rey, 2004, The Ingrate, 2004, dir. Talking With, [illegible] (NBC) Office: Susan Smith & Assocs 121 N San Vicente Blvd Beverly Hills CA 90211-2303*

BATES, LURA WHEELER, retired trade association executive; b. Inboden, Ark., Aug. 28, 1932; d. Carl Clifton and Hester Ray (Pace) Wheeler; m. Allen Carl Bates, Sept. 12, 1954; 1 child, Carla Allene. BSBA, U. Ark., 1954. Cert. constrn. assoc. Sec.-bookkeeper, then office mgr. Assoc. Gen. Contractors Miss., Inc., Jackson, 1958-77, dir. adminstrv. svcs., 1977-98, asst. exec. dir., 1980-98; owner Ditty Bay Supply Co., 1987-98; ret., 1998. Adminstr. Miss. Constrn. Found., 1977-98; sec. AIA-Assoc. Gen. Contractors Liaisonship Coms., 1977-98; sec. Carpenters Joint Apprenticeship Coms., Jackson and Vicksburg, 1977-98. Editor NAWIC Image, 1968-69, Procedures Manual, 1965-66, Public Relations Handbook, 1967-68, Profl. Edn. Guide, 1972-73, Guidelines & Procedures Handbook, 1987-88; author digests in field. Sec. Marshall Elem. Sch. PTA, Jackson, 1962-64, v.p., 1965; sec.-treas. Inter-Club Coun. Jackson, 1963-64; tchr. adult Sunday sch. dept. Hillcrest Bapt. Ch., JAckson, 1975-82; dir. Bapt. Women WMU, 1987—, sec., 1992—; tchr. adult Sunday sch. dept. 1st Bapt. Ch., Crystal Springs, Miss., 1989-98; mem. exec. com. Jackson Christian Bus. and Profl. Women's Coun., 1976-80, sec., 1978-79, pres., 1979-80. Named Outstanding Woman in Constrn. Miss., 1962-63, 74, 75, 85, 86, 95, 96 Fellow Internat. Platform Assn.; mem. AAUW, NAFE, Nat. Assn. Women in Constrn. (life, chpt. pres. 1963-64, 76-77, 92-93, 2003-04, nat. v.p. 1965-66, 77-78, nat. dir. Region 5 1967-68, nat. sec. 1970-71, 71-72, pres. 1980-81, coord. cert. constrn. assoc. program 1973-78, 83-84, guardian-contr. Edn. Found. 1981-82, chmn. nat. bylaws com.1974-75, 82-83, 85-86, 95-96, nat. parliamentarian 1983-92, Named Outstanding Mem., 1964, 74-84, 85-86, 95-96, Miss Hospitality 2002-03), Nat. Assn. Parliamentarians, U. Ark. Alumni Assn. (life, pres. ctrl. Miss. chpt. 1992-95), Delta Delta Delta (50 Yr. Golden Cir. 2002). Home: 1007 Lee Ave Crystal Springs MS 39059-2546

BATES, MARCIA JEANNE, information scientist educator; b. Terre Haute, Ind., July 30, 1942; d. Robert Joseph and Martha Jane B. BA, Pomona Coll., 1963; MLS, U. Calif., Berkeley, 1967; PhD, U. Calif., 1972. Peace corps vol., Saraburi, Thailand, 1963-64, Nongkhai, Thailand, 1964-65; jr. specialist Inst. Libr. Rsch., U. Calif., Berkeley, 1968; acting instr. U. Calif., Berkeley, 1969-70; asst. prof. U. Md., College Park, 1972-76, U. Wash., Seattle, 1976-80, assoc. prof., 1980-81, U. Calif., Los Angeles, 1981-91, prof., 1991—, prof. and dept. chmn. libr. and info. sci. Cons. U.S. Libr. Congress, Washington, 1986, 91, 2002-03, Getty Art Hist. Info. Program, Santa Monica, Calif., 1988-91, Info. Access Co., Foster City, Calif., 1992-95; mem. editl. bd. Jour. of Asis &T, 1989—, Libr. Quar., 1993-2001. Co-author: For Information Specialists, 1992; contbr. articles to profl. jours. Recipient Distinguished Lectureship award N.J. Am. Soc. for Info. Sci., New Brunswick, 1991. Fellow AAAS (sect. T electorate nominating com. 1980-84, chmn. 1983-84, sect. T com. mem.-at-large, 2001-04), mem. ALA (Frederick G. Kilgour award, 2001), Am. Soc. Info. Sci. and Tech. (bd. dirs. 1973-74, Best Jour. Article Yr. award, 1980, 99, Rsch. award 1998), Assn. Records Mgrs. Adminstrs., Calif. Libr. Assn. (mem. task force on future of Libr. profession, 1993-95), Phi Beta Kappa. Achievements include design of information systems and interfaces for search and subject access in information retrieval systems. Office: Grad Sch Edn & Info Studies UCLA 405 Hilgard Ave Los Angeles CA 90095-1520

BATES, MARGARET P. historian; BA, Barnard Coll.; MA, Wash. U., St. Louis. Dir. Coun. Basic Edn., Washington. Internat. bd. advisors Monterey Inst. Internat. Studies; bd. trustees York Sch., Carmel/Monterey, Calif.; pres. pres.'s coun. Calif. State U. Monterey Bay; former trustee Barnard Coll.; former mem. Calif. State Bd. Edn.

BATES, PATRICIA C. state official; m. John Bates; children: Jason, J'Amy. BA in Psychology, Occidental Coll.; postgrad., Calif. State U., Long Beach. Bus. owner, 1973—; councilwoman; social caseworker; mayor, 1989; state assembly mem. Dist. 73 Calif. State Assembly, 1998—. Mem. budget com.; mem. health com.; mem. judiciary com.; mem. transp. com.; vice-chair appropriations com.; mem. Orange County Charter Commn., 1995; chair Rep. Women's Caucus. Laguna Niguel Rep. Women Federated; mem. Orange County Mentoring Program Task Force, 1997, Gang Suppression Task Force; Jr. League Orange County; mem. Saddleback C.C. Found. Bd.; mem. South Coast Med. Ctr. Found., Taxpayers for Responsible Planning Adv. Bd. Mem.: Conservative Women's Leadership Assn., C. of C. (pres.), Laguna Niguel Rotary Club. Republican. Mailing: Rm 6031 PO Box 942849 Sacramento CA 94249 Office: Ste 120 30012 Ivy Glenn Dr Laguna Niguel CA 92677

BATES, SHIRLEY GRAVES, music educator; b. Lawrenceburg, Tenn., Sept. 8, 1945; d. Olnie Clyde and Charlotte (Smith) Graves; children: Charlotte Bates Lynn, Caroline Bates Scudder, Camille Bates Mickle. BA, Belmont U., Nashville, Tennessee, 1964—67; MA, Mid. Tenn. State U., Murfreesboro, Tennessee, 1999—2000; Plus 30, Cumberland U., Lebanon, TN, 2002—03. Orff Schulwerk Music Memphis State U., 1985, Master Tchr. State of Tenn., Dept. of Edn., 1992. Fifth grade tchr. Gleneyrie Sch., Shelbyville, Ky., 1967—68; music tchr. Lakeside Elem. Sch., Chattanooga, Crossroads Elem. Sch., Lebanon, Tenn., 1977—79, Ramona Elem. Sch., Jacksonville, Fla., 1981—82; Orff music specialist Buena Vista Mid. Sch., Nashville, 1983—90, Glendale Mid. Sch., Nashville, 1990—2002; adj. faculty Motlow State C.C., Nashville, 2001—01; Orff music specialist Stanford Montessori Elem. Sch., Nashville, 2002—. Advocate for at-risk children, organizer tutoring classes ho. devels.; coord. mission effort at-risk children Christ Ch. Recipient Tchr. of the Yr., Nashville Mid. Sch. Assn., 1991, Career Ladder Master Tchr. Level III, State of Tenn. Dept. of Edn., 1992 to Present, Brotherhood Sisterhood Award, Nat. Coun. of Christians And Jews, 1993-95, 1997, 2002, SE Regional choral competition, Prodn. Co. of Broadway-based Joseph and the Amazing Technicolor Dreamcoat, 1995, 1997, First Runner-up Tchr. of the Yr., Tenn. Performing Arts Coun., 1996, Tchr. of the yr./ Stanford Montessori, Metro Nashville Pub. Schools, 2003; grantee Tchr. Study grant, HCA Project Pencil, 1993, Grant to Study Evolution of Cajun Music, Frist Found., 1997, Study Sabbatical, Metro Nashville Dept. of Edn., 1999, Grant to study Gullah Culture in Ga. Sea Islands, Frist Found., 2003. Mem.: Music Educators Nat. Conf. (assoc.). Pentecostal. Avocation: seamstress/designer.

BATESON, MARY CATHERINE, anthropology educator emerita; b. N.Y.C., Dec. 8, 1939; d. Gregory and Margaret (Mead) B.; m. J. Barkev Kassarjian, June 4, 1960; 1 child, Sevanne Margaret. BA, Radcliffe Coll., 1960; PhD, Harvard U., 1963; DHL (hon.), Fordham U., 1994, U. Redlands, 1996, DePaul U., 1998, Marygrove Coll., 1999, Mills Coll., 2000. Instr. Arabic Harvard U., 1963-66; assoc. prof. anthropology Ateneo de Manila U., 1966-68; sr. rsch. fellow psychology and philosophy Brandeis U., 1968-69; assoc. prof. anthropology Northeastern U., Boston, 1969-71; rschr. U. Tehran, 1972-74; vis. prof. Northeastern U., 1974-75; prof. anthropology, dean grad. studies Damavand Coll., 1975-77; prof. anthropology, dean social sci. and humanities U. No. Iran, 1977-79; vis. scholar Harvard U., 1979-80; dean faculty, prof. anthropology Amherst Coll., 1980-87, Clarence J. Robinson prof. anthropology and English George Mason U., 1987—2002, prof. emerita, 2002—. Pres. Inst. Intercultural Studies, 1979—; vis. prof. Spelman Coll., 1996, Harvard Grad. Sch. Edn., 2001-2004; scholar in residence, Radcliffe Inst. of Advanced Studies, Harvard U., 2000-2001. Author: Arabic Language Handbook, 1967, 2d edit., 2003, Structural Continuity in Poetry: A Linguistic Study of Five Early Arabic Odes, 1970, Our Own Metaphor: A Personal Account of a Conference on Consciousness and Human Adaption, 1972, 2d edit., 1991, With a Daughter's Eye: A Memoir of Margaret Mead and Gregory Bateson, 1984, 2d edit., 1993, Composing a Life, 1989, Peripheral Visions: Learning Along the Way, 1994, Full Circles, Overlapping Lives: Culture and Generation in Transition, 2000, Willing to Learn: Passages of Personal Discovery, 2004; co-author: Angels Fear: Towards an Epistemology of the Sacred, 1987, Thinking AIDS, 1988; co-editor: Approaches to Semiotics: Anthropology, Education, Linquistics, Psychiatry and Psychology, 1964. Fellow Ford Found., 1961-63, NSF, 1968-69, Wenner-Gren Found., 1972, Bunting Inst., 1983-84, Guggenheim Found., 1987-88. Mem. Am. Anthrop. Assn., Lindisfarne Assn., Phi Beta Kappa.

BATES-ROMEO, DELORES ALVENIA, music educator, consultant; b. L.A., June 9, 1928; d. Albert and Athaliah Lydia (Crone) Bates; m. Nick Romeo, Dec. 4, 1986. BS, Emporia State U., 1956; cert., Empire Sch. Piano Tuning, 1960. Music tchr. Emporia (Kans.) Pub. Schs., 1950—55; music supr. Junction City (Kans.) Pub. Schs., 1955—59; music tchr., 4th grade tchr., organist Episcopal Ch., LaMesa, Calif., 1959—60; music dir., classroom tchr. Lakeside (Calif.) Pub. Schs., 1960—86; owner, tchr. Bates Music Studios, LaMesa, Spring Valley, El Cajon, San Diego, Calif., 1962—; music instr. U.S. Sch. Music, N.Y.C., 1963—; music dir., coord. pvt. schs. La Mesa, 1970—72. Organist, choir dir. various chs.; cons. elem. tchrs. Junction City Pub. Sch., 1955—59; counselor tchr., students and future tchrs. various pub. and pvt. schs. Mem.: NEA (life), Music Educators Nat. Conf. (life). Avocations: art, reading, herbs, exercise, cooking. Office: Bates-Romeo Music and Arts Ctr 3295-B Greyling Dr San Diego CA 92123

BATES STOKLOSA, EVELYNNE (EVE BATES STOKLOSA), educational consultant, educator; b. Camden, N.J., Mar. 13, 1946; d. Linwood T. and Eve Mary (Widzenas) Bates; m. Leslie E. Stoklosa, Apr. 15, 1968; children: Phillip J., Kristine L. BS in Home Econs. Edn., Buffalo State U. Coll., 1968, MS in Home Econs. Edn., 1971, Cert. Advanced Studies, 1994. Cert. sch. dist. adminstr. Tchr. Parkside Elem. Sch., Kenmore, N.Y., 1968-69, Kenmore West High Sch., 1968-71, 73-75, Kenmore Jr. High Sch., 1977-80, Ken-Ton Continuing Edn., Kenmore, 1980-87, Kenmore Mid. Sch., 1981—2001. Owner, pres. EBS Decors, Tonawanda, N.Y.; edn. cons. Villa Maria Coll., Buffalo, 1980-2000; adv. bd. interior design dept.; facilitator student of the month award program Kenmore Mid. Sch., 1982—, active mem. sch. planning team, 1984—, facilitator design team, 1990—; participant Buffalo Summits, 1994; ind. fashion cons. Editor parent informational pamphlet, 1992, faculty informational newsletter, 1992-94. Vol., Frankl Loyd Wright Found. of the Martin House Restoration Corp., 1999—; vol. various charitable functions and events in and around Buffalo; mem. Amateur Chamber Music Players, 2000—, Buffalo Philharmonic Orch. Women's Com. Found., 2000—. Erie County Nutrition Assn. grantee. Mem. AAUW (bd. dirs. 1992-94), ASCD, DAR (life), Family and Consumer Scientists Am. (life), Am. Vocat. Assn., Am. Fedn. Tchrs., N.Y. State Home Econs. Tchrs. Assn. (Tchr. of Yr. 1992-93, Most Outstanding Leadership and Creativity award 1987), N.Y. State Assn. Family and Consumer Sci. Educators (life), N.Y. State United Tchrs., Western N.Y. Women in Adminstrn., Kenmore Tchrs. Assn. (bldg. rep.), Amatuer Chamber Mus Soc., Chautaqua Lit. and Sci. Cir. (life), Phi Delta Kappa, Phi Upsilon Omicron. Avocations: travel, singing, swimming, golf, piano.

BATHAEE, SOUSSAN, engineering technician; b. Tehran, Iran, Jan. 23, 1953; arrived in U.S., 1983; d. Mohammad Bathaee and Farokhlagha Hassanpour. BSCE, Calif. State U., Fullerton, 2002. Overseas supr. Atomic Energy Orgn., Tehran, Iran, 1972—80; overseas drafts person London, 1980—83; drafts person Earl Walls Assocs., San Diego, 1984—85; job capt. Rsch. Facilities Design, San Diego, 1985—90; engrng. svc. technician County of San Bernardino, Calif., 1991—2002, ret., 2002; freelance engr. LDIC, San Jose, Calif., 2002—. Moslem. Home: 42045 Kaffirboom Ct Temecula CA 92591

BATORY, JOAN ANNE, solid waste and environmental administrator; b. Phila., Sept. 2, 1944; d. Joseph John and Beatrice Elizabeth Thomas Trybala; m. Joseph Patrick Batory, Dec. 26, 1967. BA, Immaculata Coll., 1966; MA, Rowan U., 1972. Cert. secondary tchr., Pa. Tchr. Camden (N.J.) Pub. Schs., 1966-71; pres. Natural Resource Studies, Inc., Cherry Hill, Pa., 1973-74, Environ. Analysis Inc., Pennsauken, N.J., 1974-75; dir. Camden County Environ. Agy., 1975-85; project mgr. U.S. Dept. Interior, Nat. Pk. Svc., Phila., 1985-88; solid waste coord. Chester County, West Chester, Pa., 1988-98; recycling coord. City of Phila., 1998-2000; environ. cons. Phila., 2000—. Commr. N.J. Pinelands Commn., Pemberton, 1979-85; bd. dirs. Pa. Resources Coun., pres., 1997-98; bd. dirs. Newtown Square; stakeholder adv. com. Commonwealth of Pa. Waste Mgmt., 1996-97; founder Camden County Eco-Ctr., Cherry Hill, 1972-73. Contbr. numerous waste mgmt. plans. Bd. dirs. Girl Scouts of Am., Camden County, 1973-74; officer Newton Creek Conservancy, Collingswood, N.J., 1976-84. Recipient St. Catherine's medal Kappa Gamma Pi, 1965, Pollution Prevention award U.S. EPA, 1991, Outstanding Mcpl. Recycling award Pa. Resources Coun., 1996. Mem. Nature Conservancy, Pinelands Preservation Alliance, Rotary (West Chester bd. dirs. 1989-93, Phila. bd. dirs. 2000-02, v.p. 2002-04, pres. 2004-). Avocations: hiking, birding, gardening. E-mail: jbatory@verizon.net.

BATT, ALYSE SCHWARTZ, technical officer; b. Bronx, NY, Aug. 8, 1960; d. Irwin Aaron and Beryl (Leff) Schwartz; m. David Charles Batt, Feb. 14, 1993; children: Shannon Paige, Megan Brooke. AAS in Data Processing, SUNY, Farmingdale, 1980; BBA in Bus. Computers, Hofstra U., 1987; MS in Mgmt. Engrng., L.I. U., 1995. Programmer trainee State Ins. Fund, N.Y.C., 1980; programmer analyst cons. Bradford Nat. Corp., N.Y.C., 1981-83; programmer E.F. Hutton, N.Y.C., 1983; programmer analyst Chase Manhattan Bank, N.Y.C., 1983-87; sr. systems analyst Met. Life Ins. Co., N.Y.C., 1987-89; sr. programmer analyst Orion Pictures Corp., N.Y.C., 1989-91, JPMorgan Chase, N.Y.C., 1991—. Mem.: Ladies Aux. Massapequa Fire Dept. (pres., v.p., treas.), Greater L.I. Road Runners Club, N.Y. Road Runners Club, Massapequa Road Runners Club, Commack Skating Club, Bayshore Skating Club. Republican. Jewish. Avocations: roller skating, running. Home: 153 Massachusetts Ave Massapequa NY 11758-4111

BATTAGLIA, LYNNE ANN, judge; b. Buffalo, 1946; BA Intl Relations, Amer. Univ., 1967, MA, 1968; JD, Univ. of Maryland, 1974. U.S. atty., Md., 1993-2001; chief of staff Office of U.S. Sen. Barbara A. Mikulski, 1991—93; judge Md. Ct. Appeals, 2001—. Office: Md Ct Appeals Robert C Murphy Bldg 361 Rowe Blvd Annapolis MD 21401*

BATTEE, SHARON TAYLOR, not-for-profit developer; b. Olean, N.Y., June 11, 1950; d. Glenn Merle Taylor and Beulah Ellen Moore-Taylor; m. Ralph L. Battee, Feb. 2, 1974; children: Michael, Brian, John. Student, Cecil C.C., North East, Md., 1971—72, Internat. Corr. Sch., 1998. Substitute tchr. Cecil County Bd. Edn., Elkton, Md., 1971—72, 1974, 1985—86; writer Meml. Poems Gee Funeral Home, Elkton, Md., 1996—; writer greeting cards, typist Cards with Love, Elkton, Md., 2000—; pres., dir., grant writer Angles of Love Ministries, Elkton, Md., 2000—. Author: It Is All Right to Cry, 2000, poems. Election judge Cecil County Election Bd., Elkton, 2000, 2002. Recipient Govs. award, State Md. Dept. Edn., 1998. Republican. Avocations: crafts, writing, reading. Home and Office: Angels of Love Ministries 119 Milestone Rd Elkton MD 21921

BATTEN, KIMBERLY JANE, Olympic athlete; b. McRae, Ga., Mar. 29, 1969; Grad., Fla. State U., 1991. Winner 2d place NCAA 400 meter hurdles, 1990, 3rd place 400 meter hurdles, 1991, 1st place 400 meter hurdles Mobil/USA Championships, 1991, 5th place World Championships, 1991, 4th place, 1992, Silver medal 400 meter hurdles Atlanta Olympics, 1996, World Bronze medalist, 1997, World Cup Bronze medalist, 1998, competed in Sydney Olympics, 2000, 6-time U.S. outdoor champion. Office: USA T&F Sanction Process 1 RCA Dome Ste 140 Indianapolis IN 46225-1023

BATTERSBY, KATHERINE SUE, elementary school educator; b. Middletown, N.Y., Nov. 17, 1960; d. George William and Joanne Marie (Endrich) Blaha; m. Jeffery Aaron Battersby, Sept. 10, [illegible]; children: Kristin Sierra, Joanna Reye, Colon Muir. BS cum laude, SUNY, Potsdam, 1983; MEd, SUNY, New Paltz, 1992. Coord. internat. sch., Spanish instr. Christian Min., Reynosa, Mexico, 1983—85; receptionist Chase NBW Bank, White Plains, N.Y., 1985-86; adminstr. NYNEX Bus. Ctr., White Plains, N.Y., 1986-87; admin. asst. Rsch. Inst. Am., N.Y., 1987-88; tchr. Haldane Elem. Sch., Cold Spring, N.Y., 1989—. Singer: Crane Chorus, 1978—82, Lake Placid Winter Olympics, 1980. Mem. Crane Chorus SUNY, Potsdam, 1978—82. Mem. PTA, Am. Fedn. Tchrs., N.Y. State United Tchrs., N.Y. State Tchrs. Retirement System, Kappa Delta Phi, Sigma Tau Delta. Avocations: reading, hiking, photography, travel, spanish. Office: Haldane Elem Sch Craigside Dr Cold Spring NY 10516

BATTIN, PATRICIA MEYER, librarian; b. Gettysburg, Pa., June 2, 1929; d. Emanuel Albert and Josephine (Lehman) Meyer; m. William Thomas Battin, June 16, 1951 (div. 1975); children: Laura, Joanna, Thomas BA, Swarthmore Coll., 1951; MS in LS, Syracuse U., 1967. Asst. libr. SUNY-Binghamton, 1967-69, asst. dir. for reader svcs., 1969-74; dir. libr. svcs. Columbia U., N.Y.C., 1974-78, v.p., univ. libr., 1978-87; interim pres. Research Libraries Group, Palo Alto, Calif., 1982, also dir., 1974-87; pres. Commn. on Preservation and Access, Washington, 1987-94. Trustee Coun. on Libr. Resources, Washington, 1984-94, EDUCOM, Princeton, N.J., 1982-88, Lehigh U., 1989-98, CAUSE, Boulder, Colo., 1993-96; mem. adv. com. on coun. on libr. and info. resources Frye Leadership Inst. Contbr. articles to profl. jours., Co-author: The Mirage of Continuity: Reconfiguring Academic Information Resources for the 21st Century, 1998. Recipient Nat. Medal for the Humanities, 1999. Mem. ALA, Assn. Rsch. Librs. (trustee 1982-85), Cosmos Club, Phi Beta Kappa, Beta Phi Mu.

BATTISTE, JANICE LOUISE, editor, writer; b. Schenectady, N.Y., Feb. 17, 1958; d. Sylvester Bernard Battiste and Elizabeth Theresa Swider. BA, SUNY, New Paltz, 1982, L'Universita di Urbino, Urbino, Italy, 1983; MA, Hunter Coll., 1993. Sales mgr. Abitalia USA Corp., N.Y.C., 1985—90, Stefano Ricci USA Corp., N.Y.C., 1990—94; editor N.Y. Living Mag., N.Y.C., 1997—. Adj. prof. English Yeshiva U. Stern Coll. for Women, N.Y.C., 1994—96, Coll. New Rochelle, N.Y.C., 2000. Author short stories; contbr. articles to profl. jours. Vol. Am. Italian Cancer Found., N.Y.C., 1994—. Democrat. Roman Catholic. Avocations: bicycling, cross country skiing, hiking, antique collecting, travel in Italy. Home: 34-56 30th St Astoria NY 11106 Office: NY Living Mag 3 E 48th St New York NY 10017-1027

BATTISTE, MICHELE C. poet, literature educator; b. Schenectady, N.Y., Nov. 26, 1971; d. Mark Battiste and Erika Battiste Bedor. BA, L.I. U., 1993; MA, SUNY, Albany, 1995; postgrad., Wichita State U., 2002—. Dir. comm. Wildwood Programs, Schenectady, 1996—2000; comm. specialist Liverpool (N.Y.) Ctrl. Sch. Dist., 2000—01; assoc. dir. devel., creative writing instr. Chinese Am. Internat. Sch., San Francisco, 2001—02; English instr. Wichita (Kans.) State U., 2002—. Author poetry. Pres. Hudson Valley Writers Guild, Albany, NY, 1999—2000; reading series co-creator Bodega Writers Collective, Syracuse, NY, 2000—01. Named Best Spoken Word Artist of the Yr., Metroland Mag., 1999; recipient The End of the World As We Know It award, The Vault, 2001; grantee, N.Y. State Senate Arts Coun., 2001; SOS grantee, N.Y. Found. for the Arts, 1998. Personal E-mail: mcbattiste@hotmail.com. E-mail: mcbattiste@hotmail.com.

BATTLE, PAT, reporter; married; 2 children. BA in Journalism, U. Md. Newspaper reporter Asbury Park (N.J.) Press; gen. assignment reporter, backup anchor New Jersey Network News, Trenton; gen. assignment reporter, host pub. affairs program WCAU-TV, Phila.; gen. assignment reporter WCBS-TV, N.Y.C., 1991—96; gen. assignment reporter, N.J. Bur. NewsChannel4 NBC, N.Y.C., 1996—. Mem.: Nat. Assn. Black Journalists. Office: NBC 30 Rockefeller Plz New York NY 10112

BATTLE, WILLA LEE GRANT, clergywoman, educational administrator; b. Webb, Miss., Sept. 30, 1924; d. James Carlton and Aslean (Young) Grant; m. Walter Leroy Battle, July 4, 1941. Diploma, Northwestern Coll., Mpls., 1956; B.A. cum laude, U. Minn., 1975, M.A., 1979; Ph.D. summa cum laude, Trinity Sem., 1982. Ordained to ministry, 1959. Founder, pastor

Grace Temple Del. Ctr., Mpls., 1958— ; founder, pres., Willa Grant Battle Ctr., Mpls., 1980— ; founder House of Refuge Mission, Haiti, W.I., 1957— ; adminstr., dir. Kiddie Haven Pre-Sch., Mpls., 1982— . Mem. Interdenominational Ministerial Alliance (sec. 1986—), Mpls. Ministerial Assn., AAUW, AAUP, U. Minn. Alumni Assn. (life), NAACP, Nat. Council Negro Women, Christian Educators, Nat. Assn. Female Execs. Home: 220 E 42nd St Minneapolis MN 55409-1634 Office: Willa Grant Battle Ctr 1816 4th Ave S Minneapolis MN 55404-1844

BATTLES, ROXY EDITH, novelist, consultant, educator; b. Spokane, Wash., Mar. 29, 1921; d. Rosco Jirah and Lucile Zilpha (Jacques) Baker; m. Willis Ralph Dawe Battles, May 2, 1941 (dec. 2000); children: Margaret Battles Holmes, Ralph, Lara. AA, Bakersfield (Calif.) Coll., 1940; BA, Calif. State U., Long Beach, 1959; MA, Pepperdine U., 1976. Cert. tchr. English, adult basic edn. and elem. edn., Calif. Free-lance writer 50 nat. and regional mags., 1940—; tchr. elem. Torrance (Calif.) Unified Schs., 1959-85; tchr. adult edn. Pepperdine U., Torrance, 1969-79, 88-89; free-lance children's author, 1966—; mystery novelist Pinnacle Publs., N.Y.C., 1980; with Tex. A&M U., 1988. Instr. Mary Mount Coll., Harbor Coll., 1995; author-in-residence Young Authors Festival, Am. Sch. Madrid, 1991; lectr. in field. Author: Over the Rickety Fence, 1967, The Terrible Trick or Treat, 1970, 501 Balloons Sail East, 1971, The Terrible Terrier, 1972, One to Teeter-Totter, 1973, 2d edit., 1975, Eddie Couldn't Find the Elephants, 1974, reprints, 1982, 84, 88, What Does the Rooster Say, Yoshio?, 1978, reprinted in Swedish, German, French, 1980, The Secret of Castle Drai, 1980, The Witch in Room 6, 1987, 3d edit., 1989 (nominee Garden State, Nene, and Hoosier awards), The Chemistry of Whispering Caves, 1988, rev. edit., 1997, Computer Encryptions in Whispering Caves, 1997; playwright: Roxy, 1995, The Lavender Castle, 1996, mus. version, 1997, Sacred Submarine, 2000, Embarking on Rebellion, 2001. Active So. Calif. Coun. on Lit. for Children and Young People, 1973-80, 87—. Recipient Commendation UN, 1979; Hoosier award nominee, 1990; Garden State award nominee, 1990, Nene award nominee, 1992, 93. Mem. S.W. Manuscripters (founder), Surfwriters. Home: 560 S Helberta Ave Redondo Beach CA 90277-4353 E-mail: groxy@aol.com.

BATTS, DEBORAH A. judge; b. Phila., Apr. 13, 1947; d. James A., Jr. and Ruth Violet (Silas) Batts; 2 children. BA, Radcliffe Coll., 1969; JD, Harvard U., 1972. Summer atty. Foley, Hoag & Eliot, Boston, Mass., 1970, Kaye, Scholer, Fierman, Hays & Handler, N.Y.C., 1971; law clerk to Hon. Lawrence W. Pierce U.S. Dist. Ct. (so. dist.) N.Y., N.Y.C., 1972-73; assoc. atty. Cravath, Swaine & Moore, N.Y.C., 1973-79; asst. U.S. atty. criminal divsn. U.S. Dist. Ct. (so. dist.) N.Y., N.Y.C., 1979-84; assoc. prof. law Fordham U., 1984-94, adj. prof. law, 1994—; spl. assoc. counsel dept. investigation N.Y.C., 1990-91; commr. law revision com. State of N.Y., 1990-94; judge U.S. Dist. Ct. (so. dist.) N.Y., N.Y.C., 1994—. Bd. trustees Cathedral Sch., N.Y.C., 1990-96; mem. faculty Corp. Counsel Trial Advocacy Program, 1988-94. Contbr. articles to legal jours. Trustee Spence Sch., 1987-95. Mem. Second Cir. Fed. Bar Coun., Assn. Bar. City N.Y., Lesbian and Gay Law Assn. Greater N.Y., Met. Black Bar Assn. Office: US Courthouse 500 Pearl St Rm 2510 New York NY 10007-1316

BAUER, BARBARA A. financial consultant; Student, Syracuse U., 1973-75, Wilma Boyd Airline Travel Sch., 1975. Script editor various networks, L.A., 1976-88; v.p. You, Inc., Palos Verdes Estates, Calif., 1980-83; cons. Pub. Broadcasting Systems, L.A., 1981-89; fin. cons., pres. Fin. Diversified Mgmt., Laguna Niguel, Calif., 1989—. Founder Bauer Living Fulfillment Found., 1992—. sr. health homecare and estate cons., 1993-; sr. health and rehab. cons. svs., 1994-; mem., adv. Commn. Human Rights, 2003-. Fashion model at charitable events; adv. for Human Rights Devel. & Protection, 2003. Mem. NAFE, Orange County Bus. Women, Entrepreneurs of Am., Delta Delta Delta. Office: Fin Diversified Mgmt 28241 Crown Valley Pkwy Suite F-600 Laguna Niguel CA 92677-4441

BAUER, BARBARA ANN, marketing consultant; b. Fairfield, Ohio, Dec. 4, 1944; d. Charles P. and Grace J. (Peteka) B.; m. Joseph J. Strojnowski. AA, So. Sem. Jr. Coll., Buena Vista, Va., 1964; BA, Am. U., 1966. Pub. relations, advt. specialist Sta. WOR-AM-FM-TV, N.Y.C., 1966-67; pub. relations mgr. Continental Corp., N.Y.C., 1967-68; dir. corp. communications Am. Internat. Group, N.Y.C., 1968-80; dir. mktg. mgmt. infos. CIGNA Corp., Phila., N.Y.C., 1980-83; asst. v.p. Citicorp Credit Services Inc., N.Y.C., 1983-87; v.p., dir. mktg. Skandia Am. Group, N.Y.C., 1987-88, v.p. corp. communications, 1988-89; pres. Bauer Mktg. and Communications, Goshen, N.Y., 1989—. Mem. Reinsurance Cons. Network. Lifetime mem. Girl Scouts U.S. Mem.: Ins. Media Assn. (adv. bd.), Assn. Profl. Ins. Women (chair pub. rels., advisor bd. dirs.), Pub. Rels. Soc. Am. (accredited, counselors' acad.). E-mail: barbarabauer@pioneeris.net.

BAUER, BETH E. advocate, consultant; b. Terre Haute, Ind., May 4, 1960; BSBA, St. Mary of the Woods Coll., 1982. Unit mgr. Reuben H. Donnelley Corp., Terre Haute, Ind., 1983-87, directory processing mgr., 1987-93, mgr. composition support, 1993-95; appeals mgr. AdminaStar Fed., Indpls., 1995-97; project mgr. Anthem, Inc., Indpls., 1997—2001; cons. PeopleSoft, Inc., Pleasanton, Calif., 2001—. Mem. Indpls. Zool. Soc., Alumnae Assn. of St. Mary of the Woods Coll. Office: PeopleSoft Inc Two Westbrook Corporate Ctr Westchester IL 60154-5725 Office Phone: 317-698-2648. E-mail: bauer.beth@sbcglobal.net.

BAUER, CHERYL KRISTINE, music educator; b. Manitowoc, Wis., Feb. 13, 1950; d. Lloyd and Jeanette Wernecke; m. Cheryl Kristine Bauer; children: Charles, Carla. B of Music Edn., Silver Lake Coll., 1972, MA in Edn., 1996. Cert. tchr. Wis. Music educator Plymouth (Wis.) Area Sch. Dist., 1972—73, Kiel (Wis.) Area Sch. Dist., 1973—. Elem. choir dir. Kiel Area Sch. Dist., 1994—. Author: poems. Recipient Disting. Svc. award, Kiel Area Sch. Dist., 2003, Wis. Sch. Musicians Choice award, 1997. Mem.: Wis. Coalition for Music, Music Educators Nat. Conf., Kappa Delta Pi (chpt. pres. 1996—97). Home: 9911 County Rd C Newton WI 53063 Office: Kiel Area Sch Dist 416 Paine St Kiel WI 53042

BAUER, EVE, research scientist; b. Monte Vista, Colo., May 23, 1955; d. Walter Howard Worker and Beth Carlson; m. Bradley F. Bauer, July 16, 1977 (div. Oct. 1998); children: Francis Clarence, David Bradley, Brett Caleb. BS, Fort Lewis Coll., 1998. Rsch. asst., rsch. chemistry tech Los Alamos Nat. Lab., N.Mex., 1998—2003, rsch. chemistry tech 07, 2003—. Contbr. articles to profl. jours. Mem.: Am. Chem. Soc. Avocations: gardening, stained glass. Home: 3000 Trinity #66 Los Alamos NM 87544 Office: Los Alamos Nat Lab Bikkin Rd MS J514 Los Alamos NM 87545*

BAUER, IRENE SUSAN, elementary school educator; b. Elyria, Ohio; m. Robert D. Bauer; 1 child, Jacquelyn I. BS in Edn., Ohio U., 1973. Tchr. OBerlin Pub. Schs., Ohio; owner Puti's, Amherst; tchr. Country Day Sch., Charles Town, W.Va., head. Office: The Country Day Sch Rt 51 W PO Box 659 Charles Town WV 25414 E-mail: headofschool@citynet.net.

BAUER, JEAN MARIE, accountant; b. Morristown, N.J., Sept. 10, 1958; d. Earl F. and Patricia A. (O'Brien) W.; m. Ronald F. Bauer, Sr. AA in Acctg., County Coll. of Morris, 1978; BSBA, Coll. of St. Elizabeth, Convent Station, N.J., 1986. Sec. to payroll supr. Monroe Calculator, Morris Plains, N.J., 1979-80; clk. typist Stewart Title, Morris Plains, 1980-81; with BASF Corp., Mount Olive, N.J., 1981—, credit rep. chems. div. Parsippany, N.J., 1986-88, property acct. III Mount Olive, N.J., 1988—. Co-leader folk group Sacred Heart Ch. of Dover, N.J., 1981, adult leader youth group, 1982, eucharistic minister, 1993—, vol. religious edn. chr. St. Jude Ch., Budd Lake, N.J., 1993; spl. dep. registrar boro Mountain Lakes, N.J., 1976. Named one of Outstanding Young Women in Am., U.S. Jaycees, 1985. Mem. Cath. Daughters Am. (treas. Dover chpt. 1987-89, regent 1989-91). Republican. Avocations: needlepoint, cooking, travel, gardening. Home: HC 1 Box 1896 Tafton PA 18464-9718 Office: BASF Corp Property Acctg 3000 Continental Dr N Budd Lake NJ 07828-1234

BAUER, JUDY MARIE, minister; b. South Bend, Ind., Aug. 24, 1947; d. Ernest Camiel and Marjorie Ann (Williams) Derho; m. Gary Dwane Bauer, Apr. 28, 1966; children: Christine Ann, Steven Dwane. Ordained to ministry Christian Ch., 1979. Sec. adminstrv. asst. Bethel Christian Ctr., Riverside, Calif., 1975-79; founder, pres. Kingdom Advancement Ministry, San Diego, 1979—; co-pastor Bethel Christian Ctr., Rancho Bernardo, Calif., 1991—; coll. funding advisor, 2002—03. Trainer, mgr., cons. Tex., Ariz., Calif., Oreg., Wash., Alaska, Okla., Idaho, Rep. South Africa, Guam, Egypt, The Philippines, Australia, Can., Mozambique, Malawi, Mex., Zimbabwe, Poland, Guatemala, Israel, Scotland, Ireland, Japan, Eng., others, 1979—; pres. Witty Outerwear Distbrs. Internat., Inc., 1993—96; mktg. exec. Melalueca, 1999—2002; founder, co-pastor Bernardo Christian Ctr., San Diego, 1981—91; adult tchr. Bethel Christian Ctr., 1973—81, undershepherd minister, 1975—79, evangelism dir., 1978—81; chaplain La Mesa Fed. Penitentiary, Tijuana, Mexico, 1998—2001; bd. dirs. Strong Tower Rehab. Ministry, San Diego; pres., founder Bethel Christian Ctr., Ranco Bernardo, Calif., 1991—; condr. leadership tng. clinics, internat. spkr., lectr. in field. Author syllabus, booklet, tng. material packets. Pres. Bernardo Christian Ctr., San Diego, 1981-91. Mem. Internat. Conv. Faith Ministries, Inc. (area bd. dirs. 1983-88). Address: PO Box 501711 San Diego CA 92150-1711 also: Kingdom Advancement Min PO Box 501711 San Diego CA 92150-1711 E-mail: jbauer2@ix.netcom.com.

BAUER, LOUISE MAY, minister, educator; d. Michael Bauer and Theresa Mueller. BA in Theology, St. Benedict's Coll., 1981; MA in Pastoral Studies, Cath. Theol. Union, 1998. Coord. religious edn. Urban India Apostulate, 1981—86, Our Lady of Lourdes, Little Falls, Minn., 1986—96; pastoral min. Cath. Area Parishes, Benson, Minn., 1998—. Mem. evangelization and catechesis com. Diocese of New Ulm, 1999—; mem. adv. bd. Benson ministerium Prairie 5 Food Shelf. Avocations: gardening, walking, cooking.

BAUER, MARIA CASANOVA, computer engineer; b. Cienfuegos, Las Villas, Cuba, Jan. 1, 1954; came to U.S., 1979; d. Manuel José and Loida Eugenia (Ojeda) Casanova; m. Lawrence D. Bauer, Feb. 14, 1997; 1 child, Ingrid. BSEE cum laude, U. Miami, 1985; MS, U. Cen. Fla., 2000. Software engr. Martin Marietta Corp., Orlando, Fla., 1986-89; computer engr., mgr. software acquisition, Tng. Sys. divsn. Naval Air Warfare Ctr., Orlando, 1989-97; project dir. U.S. Army Simulation, Tng. and Instrumentation Command, Orlando, 1000—. Software arch. U.S. Army Simulation, Tng. and Instrumentation Command, Orlando, 1997-2000. Mem. IEEE, Golden Key, Sigma Xi, Tau Beta Pi, Eta Kappa Nu, Phi Kappa Phi. Achievements include co-development of weapons system for Desert Storm. Home: 3212 Lake George Cove Dr Orlando FL 32812-6844 E-mail: maria_bauer@stricom.army.mil.

BAUER, MARION DANE, writer; b. Oglesby, Ill., Nov. 20, 1938; d. Chester and Elsie (Hempstead) Dane; m. Ronald C. Bauer, June 25, 1959 (div. Dec. 1988); children: Peter Dane, Elisabeth Alison. AA, LaSalle-Peru-Oglesby Jr. Coll., 1958; student, U. Mo., 1958—59; BA in Lang. Arts, U. Okla., 1961, postgrad., 1961—62. Author: Shelter from the Wind, 1976 (Notable Children's Book ALA, 1976), Foster Child (Golden Kite Honor Book award Soc. Children's Book Writers, 1977), Tangled Butterfly, 1980, Rain of Fire, 1983 (Tchrs.' Choices award Nat. Coun. Tchrs. of English, 1984, Revs. Choice award ALA Booklist, 1983, Children's Book award Jane Addams Peace Assn., 1984), Like Mother, Like Daughter, 1985, On My Honor, 1986 (Newbery Honor Book, 1987, Notable Children's Book ALA, 1986, Best Books of 1986 Sch. Libr. Jour., Editors' Choice Booklist, 1986, Pub.'s Weekly Choice the Yrs.'s Best Books, 1986, Flicker Tale Children's Book award, N.D., 1989, Golden Archer award, Wis., 1989, William Allen White Children's Book award, Kans., 1989, BBY, IRA selection for Janusc Korczak Lit. Competition Poland, 1990), Touch the Moon, 1987, A Dream of Queens and Castles, 1990, (drama) God's Tears: A Woman's Journey, Face to Face, 1991 (Children's Book of Distinction, Hungry Mind Rev., 1992), What's Your Story? A Young Person's Guide to Writing Fiction, 1992 (Notable Children's Book ALA, 1992), Ghost Eye, 1992, A Taste of Smoke, 1993, A Question of Trust, 1994; editor: Am I Blue? Coming Out from the Silence, 1994, When I Go Camping With Grandma, 1995, A Writer's Story, From Life to Fiction, 1995, Alison's Wings, 1996, Our Stories, A Fiction Workshop for Young Authors, 1996, Alison's Puppy, 1997, If You Were Born a Kitten, 1997, Turtle Dreams, 1997, Alison's Fierce and Ugly Halloween, 1997, Bear's Hiccups, 1998, Christmas in the Forest, 1998, An Early Winter, 1999, Sleep, Little One, Sleep, 1999, Jason's Bears, 2000, Grandmother's Song, 2000, My Mother is Mine, 2001, If You Had a Nose Like an Elephant's Trunk, 2001, Frog's Best Friend, 2002, Love Song for a Baby, 2003, Runt, 2002, Land of the Buffalo Bones, 2003, Toes, Ears and Nose, 2003, Why Do Kittens Purr, 2003, Wind, 2003, Snow, 2003, Rain, 2004, Clouds, 2004, The Double-Digit Club, 2004, The Very Best Daddy of All, 2004; contbr. short stories to mags. and books in field. Mem.: Soc. Children's Book Writers and Illustrators, Authors League Am., Authors Guild. Democrat. Home: 8861 Basswood Rd Eden Prairie MN 55344-7407 Office: Clarion 215 Park Ave S New York NY 10003-1603 Personal E-mail: mdanebauer@aol.com.

BAUER, TRICIA, publishing executive, writer; m. Bill Bozzone; 1 child, Lia. Mng. editor Joshua Morris Pub., Inc., Wilton, Conn., 1988—89; fiction reader Redbook Mag., N.Y.C., NY, 1990—94; asst. editor The Millbrook Press, Inc., Brookfield, Conn., 1992—94, dir. spl. sales, 1995—98; dir. spl. mkts. The Rosen Pub. Group, N.Y.C., NY, 1998—. Author: Working Women and Other Stories, 1995, Boondocking, 1997 (selected by Barnes & Noble's Discover Great New Writers Program, 1997), Hollywood & Hardwood, 1999, Shelterbelt, 2000; contbr. fiction & poetry to profl. jours., columns in newspapers. Fellow, Fundación Valparaiso, Spain, 1998. Office: 29 E 21st St New York NY 10010

BAUGH, LISA SAUNDERS (LISA SAUNDERS BOFFA), research chemist; b. Houston, Aug. 27, 1969; d. James Robert Saunders Jr. and Diane Hussey Young; m. Alexander Bowman Boffa, June 7, 1991 (div. Oct. 2000); m. Simon David Peter Baugh, Sept. 15, 2001. BS in Chemistry with high honors, U. Tex., 1991; PhD in Chemistry, U. Calif., Berkeley, 1996. Vis. scholar polymer sci. and engring. dept. U. Mass., Amherst, 1994-96; sr. rsch. chemist Air Products and Chems., Allentown, Pa., 1996-97; sr. chemist ExxonMobil Rsch. and Engring., Annandale, N.J., 1997—. Lectr. in field. Editor: Transition Metal Catalysis in Macromolecular Design, 2000, Late Transition Metal Polymerization Catalysis, 2003; contbr. articles to profl. jours. Violinist/violist Ctrl. Jersey Symphony Orch.; prin. violist Hunterdon (N.J.) Symphony. Nat. Merit scholar U. Tex., 1987-91; fellow NSF, 1991-94; named Dean's Honored Grad., 1991. Mem.: Am. Chem. Soc. (polymer sci. engring. divsn. mem.-at-large 2000—05, sec-gen./program chmn. catalysis and surface sci. secretariat 2001, assoc. women chemists com. 2002—03, editl. adv. bd. Chemistry mag. 2003—, chair 2004), Alpha Chi Sigma, Phi Beta Kappa. Achievements include patents in field. Office: ExxonMobil Rsch & Engring Route 22 East LC124 Annandale NJ 08801 Business E-Mail: Lisa.S.Baugh@ExxonMobil.com.

BAUGHMAN, LEONORA KNOBLOCK, lawyer; b. Bad Axe, Mich., Mar. 21, 1956; d. Lewie L. and Jannette A. (Krajenka) K.; m. Jene W. Baughman, Dec. 5, 1981; children: Wesley J. and Adrianne J. Student, Cen. Mich. U., 1973-75; AB, U. Mich., 1977; JD, U. Notre Dame, 1981. Bar: Mich. 1981, U.S. Dist. Ct. (ea. dist.) Mich. 1982. Assoc. Foster, Swift, Collins & Coey, P.C., Lansing, Mich., 1981-86; staff atty. Chrysler Fin. Corp., Troy, Mich., 1987-97; v.p. gen. mgr. sales and underwriting U.S. East Chyrsler Ins. Co., Southfield, Mich., 1997—. Mem. ABA, Mich. Bar Assn., Nat. Assn. Women Lawyers, Am. Bankruptcy Inst., State Bar Mich. (sec. bus. law sect., speaker 4th ann. comml. law seminar). Office: Chrysler Ins Corp 27777 Franklin Rd Southfield MI 48034-2337

BAUM, ELEANOR, electrical engineering educator, academic administrator; b. Poland, Feb. 10, 1940; came to U.S., 1942; d. Sol and Anna (Berkman) Kushel; m. Paul Martin Baum, Sept. 2, 1962; children: Elizabeth, Jennifer. BSE.E., CUNY, 1959; M.E.E., Poly Inst. N.Y., 1961, PhD, 1964; DS (hon.), Union Coll., 1993, Notre Dame, 1995. Engr. Sperry Gyrosoope Co., N.Y.C., 1960-61; instr. Poly. Inst. N.Y., N.Y.C., 1961-64; asst. prof. elec. engring. Pratt Inst., N.Y.C., 1964-67, assoc. prof., 1967-71, prof., chmn. dept. elec. engring., 1971-84, dean Sch. Engring., 1984-87; dean Sch. Engring., Cooper Union for Advancement Sci. and Art, N.Y.C., 1987—; exec. dir. Cooper Union Rsch. Found., N.Y.C., 1987—. Cons. engring. to various corps.; accreditation visitor Accreditation Bd. Engring. and Tech., 1983—, bd. dirs., fellow, 1994; organizer career confs. for careers in engring., careers for women, N.Y.C., 1970—; chair bd. examiners Grad. Record Exam., 1984-90; bd. dirs. Alleghany Powers Systems, U.S. Trust Co., Avnet, Inc.; commr. Engring. Workforce Commn., 1990—; mem. engring. adv. bd. NSF, 1989-94; mem. adv. bd. Duke U., Rice U., U.S. Mcht. Marine Acad., 1992—; mem. U.S./Japan Engring. Edn. Task Force, 1994—. Contbr. tech. articles and articles on engring. careers and edn. to profl. jours. Recipient Disting. Alumnus award Poly. Inst. N.Y., 1986, Alumni Achievement award CCNY, 1986, Emily Warren Roebling award Womens' Hall of Fame, 1988, Achievement award Mich. State U., 1992, Outstanding Woman Scientist award, 1992 Assn. Women Sci. Fellow IEEE (Steinmetz award 1990), Soc. Women Engrs. (Upward Mobility award 1990, Achievement award engrs. joint com. L.I. 1995); mem. Am. Soc. Engring. Edn. (bd. dirs. 1989—, v.p. 1992-93, pres. 1995—, various nat. task forces), Nat. Engring. Deans Coun. (bd. dirs. 1987—, chair 1990-93), N.Y. Met. Deans Assn. (chmn. 1985-90), N.Y. Acad. Scis. (bd. govs. 1994—), Order of Engr. (bd. govs. 1985-92, competitiveness policy coun. subcom. critical techs. 1992—, nat. rsch. coun. bd. engring. edn. 1991-95), Eta Kappa Nu, Tau Beta Pi (Achievement award Mich. Tech. U. 1995).

BAUM, M(ARY) CAROLYN, occupational therapist; b. Chgo., Mar. 26, 1943; d. Gibson Henry and Nelle (Curry) Manville; 1 child, Kirstin Carol. BS, U. Kans., 1966; MA, Webster Coll., 1979; PhD, Washington U., 1993. Occupl. therapist U. Kans. Med. Ctr., 1966-67; staff occupl. therapist Rsch. Med. Ctr., Kansas City, Mo., 1967, dir. occupl. therapy, 1967-73, dir. phys. medicine and rehab., 1973-76; dir. occupl. therapy, clin. svcs. Washington U. Sch. Medicine, St. Louis, 1976—88. Dir. program in occupl. therapy Rehab. Inst. St. Louis; prof. occupl. therapy and neurology, 1988—; prof., 2004—; vis. prof. NYU, U. Mo., 1985—87; mem. adv. com. Nat. Ctr. Med. Rehab. Rsch. NIH; allied health rep. AMA Health Policy Agenda for Am. People; mem. com. on assessing rehab. sci. and engring. Inst. Medicine; bd. dirs. Rehab. Inst. St. Louis; pres. Occupl. Therapy Certification Bd., 1986—93. Author: Understanding the Prospective Payment System: A Business Perspective, 1986, Occupational Therapy: Overcoming Human Performance Deficits, 1991, Occupational Therapy: Enabling Function and Well Being, 1997, Measuring Occupational Performance: Supporting Best Practice in Occupational Therapy, 2001, Occupation-Based Practice: Fostering Performance and Participation, 2001; contbg. author: Occupational Therapy, 1978, 83; editor Jour. OTJR; Occupation, Participation and Health; contbr. articles to profl. jours. Coord. St. Louis Ind. Living Coun., 1980-81; mem. nominating com. Greater Kansas City Health Sys. Agy.; vice-chmn. Village Ch. Accessibility Task Force, 1974-76; bd. dirs. Rehab. Inst. St. Louis. Named Employee of Yr., Rsch. Hosp., 1974, Kans. Occupl. Therapist of Yr., 1975, Outstanding Alumni Sch. Allied Health U. Kans., 1999. Fellow Am. Occupl. Therapy Assn. (chmn. stds. and ethics commn. 1973-77, nat. v.p. 1978-82, pres. 1982-83, pres. 2004-2007, Eleanor Clarke Slagel Lectureship award 1980, award of Merit 1984); mem. Mo. Occupl. Therapy Assn. (Occupl. Therapy Clinician of Yr. 1985), Mo. Assn. Rehab. Facilities (bd. dirs.), St. Louis Med. Rehab. Soc. (pres. 1987). Office: Program Occupl Therapy Wash U Sch Medicine 4444 Forest Park Ave Saint Louis MO 63108-2212 E-mail: baumc@msnotes.wustl.edu.

BAUM, SANDRA BEATTIE, executive secretary; b. Buffalo, Oct. 9, 1948; d. Edwin Eugene and Margaret Virginia (Kinkead) Beattie; m. William Paul Baum, Nov. 30, 1968; 1 child, Robert B. Student, Lake Sumter C.C. Office mgr. C.L. Ossman Design, Buffalo, 1980-85; contracts specialist M/A Com, Inc., Burlington, Mass., 1985-89; exec. sec. Lake County Coop. Ext. Svc., Taveres, Fla., 1989—. Bd. dirs., sec., vice chmn. Keep Lake County Beautiful, Eustis, Fla., 1994—; sec. Agrl. Adv. Com., Tavares, 1989—. Mem. NAFE, Nat. Assn. Exec. Secs. Republican. Roman Catholic. Avocations: knitting, sewing. Home: Apt 72 2715 River Plaza Dr Sacramento CA 95833-3708

BAUM, SELMA, customer relations consultant; b. Bklyn., Jan. 15, 1924; d. Samuel and Tillie (Bayer) Goldman; m. Milton W. Baum, Jan. 19, 1947; children: Victor C., Cynthia Baum-Baicker. Student, NYU New Sch. for Social Rsch. Communications mgr. Sobel & Goldman, Inc., N.Y.C., 1941-48; pub. rels. cons., 1948-65; comparison shopper Gimbels, Valley Stream, N.Y., 1965-67, mgr. comparison shopping office N.Y. div., N.Y.C., 1967-75, dir. consumer affairs East div., 1975-84; dir. corp. customer rels. Saks Fifth Ave., N.Y.C., 1984-89; cons. customer rels., Palm Beach, Fla., 1989—; lectr., writer in field. Arbitrator Met. N.Y. Better Bus. Bur. Mem. NAFE, Am. Mgmt. Assn. (industry panelist), N.Y. & N.J. Retail Mchts. Coun. (v.p.), Women in Communication (award N.Y. chpt. 1984), Nat. Retail Mchts. Assn. (consumer affairs com.), Fashion Group, Am. Coun. on Consumer Interests, Soc. Consumer Affairs Profls. in Bus. (chpt. pres. 1981-82, nat. dir. 1983-86, bd. dir. Found. 1985-89; nat. treas., fin. chmn., v.p. 1986-87, award N.Y. chpt. 1983), Greater N.Y. WINS (regional affairs com.), Direct Mktg. Assn. (customer rels. coun. 1987-88). Home and Office: 3460 S Ocean Blvd Apt 715 Palm Beach FL 33480-5969

BAUM, SUSAN JEAN, vocalist, voice educator; b. Miami, July 12, 1950; d. Frederick Gilbert and Irma Jean Baum. BA, U. Fla., Gainesville, 1972. Mem. staff Direct Theatre, N.Y.C., 1974-76, Children's Television Workshop, 1976-77, Time-Life Films, 1977-79, Brit. Broadcasting Corp., 1994-97; pvt. practice The Personal Trainer for the Voice, 1991—. Mgr. Actors Connection, N.Y.C., 1990—, Actors Information Project, N.Y.C., 1985-89; mem. adv. bd. Cinewomen NY, N.Y.C., 1995. Actress: various films, TV commercials and theatre, 1975—; prodr., solo performer Taking A Chance, 1997; exec. prodr. Am. Shakespeare Project; dir. Julius Caesar, 1995; co-writer: (with James Harter) Under the Stone, 1989, What Goes Around..., 1990, Buried Treasure, 1991, Heart of the Nation, 1992; bus. mgr. and prodn. office coord. The Middletown Film Project, 1979-82, Pumping Iron II: The Women, 1983-84, Eugene Smith: Through A Glass Darkly, 1989; asst. prodn. mgr.: 3-2-1- Contact Season II, 1984; rschr., editl. asst. Hometown, 1982, The Great Getty, 1985, Where is Nicaragua, 1987. Mem. SAG, AFTRA, Actor's Equity Assn., Am. Shakespeare Project, Manhattan Assn. of Cabarets and Clubs (bd. dirs. 1998-2000), N.Y. Sheet Music Soc. (bd.dirs. 2001-03).

BAUMAN, SUSAN, communications executive; BA, U. Mich. With J. Walter Thompson, Jack Tinker and Ptnrs., Telpac; founder, pres. Broadcast Traffic and Residuals, N.Y.C., 1973—. Recipient Women Mean Bus. award, Chase Bank. Office: Broadcast Traffic and Residuals Inc 333 Seventh Ave New York NY 10001

BAUMAN, SUSAN JOAN MAYER, mayor, lawyer; b. N.Y.C., Mar. 2, 1945; d. Curt H. J. and Carola (Rosenau) Mayer; m. Ellis A. Bauman, Dec. 29, 1968. BS, U. Wis., 1965, JD, 1981; MS, U. Chgo., 1966. Bar: Wis. 1981, U.S. Dist. Ct. (we. dist.) Wis. 1981, U.S. Ct. Appeals (7th cir.) 1983, U.S. Dist. Ct. (ea. dist.) Wis. 1985. Tchr. Madison (Wis.) Pub. Sch., 1970-78; research asst. U. Wis. Law Sch., Madison, 1981; ptnr. Thomas,

Parsons, Schaefer & Bauman, Madison, 1981-84; sole practice Madison, 1984-85; ptnr. Bauman & Massing, Madison, 1985-87; pvt. practice, Madison, 1987-97; mayor City of Madison, 1997—2003; mem. Wis. Employment Rels. Commn., 2003—. Alderman Madison Common Coun., 1985-97, coun. pres., 1989-90; commr. equal opportunities com. City of Madison, 1985-89; mem. Econ. Devel. Commn., 1986-87, chmn. human resources com., 1987-90, mem. affirmative action com., 1988-93; mem. Cmty. Action Commn., 1988-97, pres., 1991-96; mem. Pub. Health Commn., 1991-97, Monona Terr. Conv. and Cmty. Ctr. Bd., 1993-97; pres. South Madison Health and Family Ctr., Inc., 1993-97; bd. visitors U. Wis. Coll. Letters and Scis., Madison, 1997—2003; mem. exec. com. Wis. Alliance Cities, 1996—2003; mem. adv. bd. U.S. Conf. Mayors, 1999—2003. Mem. Wis. Bar Assn., Dane County Bar Assn., Wis. Indsl. Rels. Alumni Assn. (pres. 1985-86), Madison Civics Club. Democrat. Avocations: knitting, reading, backpacking, cross-country skiing. Home: 125 N Hamilton St # 407 Madison WI 53703 Office: Wis Employment Rels Commn 18 S Thornton Ave Madison WI 53709 E-mail: sjmbauman@aol.com.

BAUMAN-BORK, MARCEIL, health services administrator; b. Sidney, Nebr., Sept. 15, 1957; BA, Midland Luth. Coll., Fremont, NE, 1979; MD, U. Nebr. Med. Ctr., Omaha, 1983. Bd. cert. Am. Bd. Psychiatry & Neurology. Resident Menninger Sch. Psychiatry & Mental Health, Topeka; dir. gen. residency program Menninger Clinic, Topeka; co-founder, psychiatrist Heritage Mental Health Clinic, Topeka, 2003—. Presenter in field. Mem.: Am. Acad. Child and Adolescent Psychology, Kans. Med. Soc., Am. Psychoanalytic Assn., Am. Psychiatric Assn. Office: Heritage Mental Health Clinic 2921 SW Wanamaker Dr Topeka KS 66614

BAUMANN, CAROL EDLER, retired political science educator; b. Plymouth, Wis., Aug. 11, 1932; d. Clarence Henry and Beulah Hanetta (Weinhold) E.; m. Richard Joseph Baumann, Feb. 28, 1959; children: Dawn Carol, Wendy Katherine. BA in Internat. Rels., U. Wis., 1954; PhD in Internat. Rels., London Sch. Econs./Polit. Sci., 1957. Chmn. internat. rels. major U. Wis., Milw., 1962-79; dep. asst. sec. Bur. of Intelligence and Rsch./Dept. of State, Washington, 1979-81; prof. U. Wis., Milw., 1972-95, dir. internat. studies and programs, 1982-88, prof. emeritus, 1995—; dir. Inst. of World Affairs, Milw., 1964-97, dir. emeritus, 1997—. Internat. edn. adv. coun. U. Wis. Milw., 2000—. Author: Program Planning About World Affairs, 1991, The Diplomatic Kidnappings, 1973; editor: Europe in NATO: Deterrence, Defense, and Arms Control, 1987, Western Europe: What Path to Integration?, 1967. Mem. Gov.'s Commn. on the UN, 1964-79, 82-89; Dem. candidate 9th Congl. Dist., 1968; mem. World Affairs Coun. of Milw., 1964-75; bd. dirs. Wis. World Trade Ctr., 1987-2001, Wis. Dist. Export Coun., 1987-2003, Ea. Shores Libr. Sys., 1999—, Inst. World Affairs, U. Wis., Milw., 2000—. Recipient Pub. Svc. Achievement award Common Cause, Wis., 1991, World Citizen of Yr. award Internat. Inst. Wis, 2004; Marshall scholar, 1954-57. Mem. Coun. on Fgn. Rels., Fgn. Policy Assn. (bd. dirs. 1990—, editl. adv. com. 1977-79, 82-88), Nat. Coun. World Affairs Orgns. (pres. 1977-79, bd. dirs. 1992-96), UN Assn. of USA (bd. dirs. 1977-79, 82-89), Soc. for Citizen Edn. in world Affairs (pres. 1977-79), Phi Kappa Phi, Phi Beta Kappa. Democrat. Lutheran. Avocations: walking, swimming, reading, travel, writing fiction. Home: W6248 Lake Ellen Dr Cascade WI 53011-1322 E-mail: cbaumann@excel.net.

BAUMANN, PRISCILLA, medieval art history educator, researcher; b. Phila., Mar. 19, 1937; d. William Ambrose and Julia Frances (Morris) Fitz Gerald; m. Roger-Henri Baumann, Jan. 20, 1961; children: Robert C., Philippe G., Caroline. BA in French Lit., Manhattanville Coll., 1958; MA in French Lit., Middlebury Coll., 1959; MSLS, Peabody Libr. Sch., 1960; PhD in Medieval Studies, Boston U., 1992. Reference libr. N.Y. Pub. Libr., N.Y.C., 1960-61; vis. lectr. Tufts U., Medford, Mass., 1989-90; instr. medieval art history Radcliffe Seminars, Radcliffe Coll., Cambridge, Mass., 1990—2002. Docent, lectr. Fogg Art Mus., Harvard U., 1982—; lectr. in field. Contbr. articles to profl. jours. Fulbright scholar, Paris, 1958-59. Mem. Coll. Art Assn., Medieval Acad., Am. Soc. Ch. History, Soc. Medieval and Renaissance Philosophy, Internat. Ctr. Medieval Art. Home: 26 Everett Ave Winchester MA 01890-3524

BAUMANN, REBECCA ELLEN, minister; b. Lewiston, Maine, Dec. 12, 1950; d. George Alexander and Martha McShane Baumann; children: Timothy O'Brien, Devin McShane O'Brien. BS, Framingham State Coll., 1973; AS, Laboure Coll., 1987; MDiv, Boston U., 1998; postgrad., Andover Newton Theol. Sch., Newton Ctr., Mass. Ordained to ministry United Meth. Ch., 2000. Mem. faculty Laboure Coll., Boston, 1987—97, Aquinas Coll., Milton, Mass., 1990—97; transcription supr. Harvard Cmty. Health Plan, Boston, 1986—93; owner and operator transcription co., Quincy, Mass., 1993—98; pastor Hatherly United Meth., Rockland, Mass., 1997—2000, Christ United Meth., Groton, Conn., 2000—. Cons. health info. mgmt. Joslin Clinic, Boston, 1993—96; protestant chaplain Westborough State Hosp., Mass., 1997—2000; mem. adv. bd. Faith in Action Parish Nurse Network, New London, Conn., 2000—; sec. Shoreline Cluster Chs., Southeastern, Conn., 2000—; mem. Commn. on Status and Role of Women New Eng. Ann. Conf. United Meth. Ch., 2002—. Author: Medical Terminology for Medical Office Employees, 1993. Mem.-at-large Multi-Regional Area Commn., Uncasville, Conn., 2002—, Dept. Social Svcs., Uncasville, 2002—. Grantee, United Meth. Found., 2002. Democrat. Home: 62 Johl Dr Groton CT 06340 Office: Christ United Meth Ch 200 Hazelnut Hill Rd Groton CT 06340 E-mail: rebpastor@juno.com.

BAUMBACH, LISA LORRAINE, research scientist; b. Miami, May 22, 1958; d. Robert William and Elly (Hering) Decker; m. Robert Reardon. BA with honors, U. Fla., 1980, PhD in Biochemistry, 1986. Postdoctoral fellow Baylor Coll. Medicine, Houston, 1986-89; clin. fellow U. Colo. Sch. Medicine, Denver, 1989-90; asst. prof. U. Miami Sch. Medicine, 1991—. Mem. sci. bd. South Fla. Huntington's Disease Assn., Fla. NFS Assn., UM Brain Endowment Bank, South Fla. Muscular Dystrophy Assn. Contbr. articles to profl. jours. and contbr. book chpts. Vol. student health svc. U. Fla., Gainesville, 1976-86, Shand's Hosp., U. Fla., Gainesville, 1977-78, South Broward Community Hosp., Hollywood, Fla., ARC, Hollywood Meml. Hosp. Emergency Rm., 1975-76, Hosp. Aux. Svc., Hollywood Meml. Hosp., 1974-76, ACORN Rural Health Clinic, Gainesville, 1979-80. Paula Ellis scholarship U. Fla. Coll. Medicine, 1983. Mem. AAAS, Am. Soc. Human Genetics, Am. Acad. Neurology, Am. Cancer Soc., N.Y. Acad. Scis. Avocations: running, sailing, skiing, dance. Office: U Miami Sch Medicine 1601 NW 12th Room 6020 PO Box 16820 Miami FL 33101-6820

BAUMER, BEVERLY BELLE, journalist; b. Hays, Kans., Sept. 23, 1926; d. Charles Arthur and Mayme Mae (Lord) B.; BS, William Allen White Sch. Journalism, U. Kans., 1948. Summer intern reporter Hutchinson (Kans.) News, 1946-47; continuity writer, women's program dir. Sta. KWBW, Hutchinson, 1948-49; dist. editor Salina (Kans.) Jours., 1950-57; commd. writer State of Kans. Centennial Year, 1961; contbg. author: Ford Times, Kansas City Star, Wichita (Kans.) Eagle, Ojibway Publs., Billboard, Modern Jeweler, Floor Covering Weekly, other bus. mags., 1962-69; owner and mgr. apts., Hutchinson, 1970—; broadcaster Reading Radio Room, Sta. KHCC-FM, Hutchinson, 1982—, columnist The Hutchinson (Kans.) Record, 1983-86; info. officer, maj. Kans. Wing Hdqrs. CAP, 1969-72; participant People to People Citizen Ambassador program, People's Republic of China, summer 1988. Mem. Republican Presdl. Task Force. Recipient Human Interest Photo award Nat. Press Women, 1956, News Photo award AP, 1952. Mem. Fellows Menninger Found., Suffolk County Hist. Soc., Nat. Fedn. Press Women, Kans. Press Women (Comm. Contest award 1986), Am. Soc. Profl. and Exec. Women, Am. Film Inst., Nat. Soc. Magna Charta Dames, Nat. Soc. Daus. Founders and Patriots Am., Nat. Soc. Daus. Am. Colonists, Kans. Soc. Daus. Am. Colonists (organizing regent Dr. Thomas Lord chpt., state chmn. insignia com.), Nat. Soc. Sons and Daus. Pilgrims (elder Kans. br.), D.A.R., Ben Franklin Soc. (nat. adv. bd.), Daus. Colonial Wars, Order Descs. Colonial Physicians and Chirurgiens, Colonial Dames 17th Century (chaplain, charter mem. Henry Woodhouse chpt.), Plantagenet Soc., Internat. Platform Soc., U. Kans. Alumni Assn., Nat. Geneal. Soc. Author book of poems, 1941; editor: A Simple Bedside Book for People Who Are Kinda, Sorta Interested in Genealogy, 1983. Home and Office: 122 Downing Rd Hutchinson KS 67502-4453

BAUMGARDT, JUSTI MICHELLE, professional soccer player; b. Federal Way, Wash., July 22, 1975; m. Tote Yamada. Student in sociology, U. Portland. Former mem. US Women's Nat. Soccer Team; mem. Wash. Freedom Women's United Soccer Assn., 2001, mem. N.Y. Power, 2002—. Named Athlete of Yr., Seattle Times, 1993, Player of Yr., State of Wash., 2-time H.S. All-Am., Most Valuable Player, U. Portland, 1994, WCC Player of Yr., 1996. Achievements include playing in Nike Victory Tour, St. Charles, Ill., 1997; Nordic Cup, Denmark, 1993; Germany, 1994. Office: US Soccer Fedn 1801-1811 S Prairie Ave Chicago IL 60616

BAUMGARTNER, CINDY SUE, secondary school educator; d. Herb D. and Carolyn J. (Schwegler) Konigsmark; m. Larry S. Baumgartner, Aug. 9, 1975; children: Amy, Angie, Adam. BA summa cum laude, U. No. Iowa, 1976, MAE summa cum laude, 1997. Tchr. West Delaware Mid. Sch., Manchester, Iowa, 1976—82; advt. salesperson Welcome Wagon Inc., Memphis, 1982—87; area sales mgr. Worldbook Ency., Chgo., 1987—89; youth devel. specialist Extension Svc., Iowa State U., Ames, 1990—98; FCS tchr. West Delaware H.S., Manchester, 1998—. Author: (curriculum) Boomerang! Character Education Program, 1998 (J.C. Penney Golden Rule award, 1996). Grantee, W.K. Kellogg Found. Mem.: Iowa State Edn. Assn., NEA, Phi Upsilon Omicron, Kappa Delta Pi. Avocations: travel, music. Office: West Delawre HS 701 New St Manchester IA 52057-1415

BAUMGARTNER, MARY ANNE SGARLAT, academic administrator, entrepreneur; b. Boston, Apr. 5, 1958; d. Francis Abbott and Elizabeth Maria (Paragallo) Sgarlat; m. Michael von Arx Baumgartner, Nov. 18, 2000. Grad., Milton Acad.; student, Roedean Sch., Brighton, Eng.; BA, Bennington Coll., 1979. Adminstr. Harvard U., Cambridge, Mass., 1979-86; pub. rels. dir. Graham Gund Architects, Cambridge, 1986-89; mktg. and comms. mgr. Elkus/Manfredi Architects, Boston, 1989-90; comms. mgr. Turan Corp., Boston, 1990-92; mktg. dir. The Design Partnership of Cambridge, 1992-97; mng. dir. The Bounty Group, 1997—; mktg. mgr. Yolles Ptnrship. Ltd., 1998-99, Bishoff Solomon Comms., 1999-2000; adminstr. Kennedy Sch. Govt., Cambridge, 2000—. Mem.: LWV, Mus. Fine Arts, Harvard U. Art Museums, Focus Internat., Bennington Coll. Alumni Assn. (regional dir. 1993—97, exec. com. 1986—93). Avocations: politics, music, dance, antiques, sailing. Office: Kennedy Sch Govt 79 JFK St Cambridge MA 02138

BAUMOL, HILDA, management consultant; b. New Haven, Jan. 6, 1923; d. Aaron and Sophie (Horowitz) Missel; m. William J. Baumol, Dec. 27, 1941; children: Ellen, Daniel. BA, Hunter Coll., 1942. Exec. dir. Twentieth Century Fund Performing Arts Study, Princeton, N.J., 1960-64; cons. Mathematica, Princeton, N.J., 1965-72; pres. Consultants in Industry Econs., Princeton, N.J., 1972-90. Co-editor: Inflation and the Performing Arts, 1984; contbr. chpts. to books, articles to profl. jours. Avocations: music, cuisine.

BAUMRIND, DIANA, research psychologist; b. N.Y.C., Aug. 23, 1927; AB, Hunter Coll., 1948; MA, U. Calif., Berkeley, 1951, PhD, 1955. Cert. and lic. psychologist, Calif. Project dir. psychology dept. U. Calif., Berkeley, 1955-58; project dir. Inst. of Human Devel., 1960—, also rsch. psychologist and prin. investigator family socialization and devel. competence project. Lectr. and cons. in field; referee for rsch. proposals Grant Found., NIH, 1970—, NSF, 1970—. Contbr. numerous articles to profl. jours. and books; author 2 monographs; mem. editorial bd. Devel. Psychology, 1986-90, Parenting: Science and Practice, 2000—. Recipient Rsch. Scientist award, NIMH; grantee NIMH, 1955-58, 60-66, Nat. Inst. Child Health and Human Devel., 1967-74, MacArthur Found., Grant Found., 1967—. Fellow Am. Psychol. Assn., Am. Psychol. Soc. (G. Stanley Hall award 1988), Soc. Research in Child Devel. Office: U Calif Inst of Human Devel 1217 Tolman Hall Berkeley CA 94720-1691

BAUNER, RUTH ELIZABETH, library administrator, reference librarian; b. Quincy, Ill. d. John Carl and M. Irene (Nutt) B. BS in Edn., Western Ill. U., 1950; MS, U. Ill., 1956; postgrad., So. Ill. U., 1974, PhD, 1978. Asst. res. libr. Western Ill. U., Macomb, 1950; tchr., libr. Sandwich (Ill.) Twp. High Sch., 1950-54; circulation dept. asst. U. Ill. Libr., Urbana, 1955; asst. edn. libr. So. Ill. U., Carbondale, 1956-63, acting edn. libr., 1963-64, edn. and psychology libr., 1965-93, assoc. prof. curriculum and instrn. dept., 1971-93; coord. freshman yr. experience program, vis. assoc. prof. Coll. of Liberal Arts, Carbondale, 1994-96. Dir. Grad. Residence Ctr. Librs., So. Ill. U., 1973-79; subject matter expert Learning Resources Svc. Interactive Video, Carbondale, 1990-91, also scriptwriter; faculty emeritus So. Ill. U., 2004—. Co-author: The Teacher's Library, 1966; contbr. articles to profl. jours. Pres. alumni constituency bd. Coll. Edn., Carbondale, 1988—89, mem. Carbondale Bd. Ethics, 1989—2001; tchr. I Can Read Program, 2001—03; mem. Carbondale Citizens Adv. Commn., 1999—2001; bd. dirs. So. Ill. U. chpt. UN, 1985—86, 1994—97, So. Ill. Learning in Retirement, So. Ill. U. Emeritus Assn., Jackson County AARP, 1997—99, 2001—03, So. Ill. U. Emeritus Faculty Assn., 2004—. Recipient Luck Has Nothing To Do With It award Oryx Press, 1993. Mem.: AAUW (univ. rep. Carbondale br. 1988—89), ALA, Ill. Libr. Assn., Assn. Coll. and Rsch. Librs. (chmn. edn. and behavioral scis. sect. 1976—77, Most Active Mem. award 1968—93), AAUP (v.p. So. Ill. U. chpt. 1972—73), Delta Kappa Gamma (Inter-Varsity Christian Fellowship award for svc. 1956—2001), Phi Kappa Phi, Phi Delta Kappa (Women of Distinction award 1999). Office: 1206 W Freeman St Carbondale IL 62901-2351

BAUR, SUSAN W. psychologist, writer; b. N.Y.C., Jan. 22, 1980; d. John Ireland Howe Baur and Louise Wells Chase; children: Scottland Hubbard, Louisa Schlee. AB, Vassar U., 1961; ALM, Harvard U., 1987; PhD, Boston Coll., 1990. Reporter Binghamton (N.Y.) Sun-Bull., 1964—66, Palm Beach (Fla.) Post-Times, 1967—68; psychologist Thorne Clinic, Pocasset, Mass., 1989—. Author: The Edge of an Unfamiliar World: A History of Oceanography, 1973; On Almost Any Wind: The Saga of the Oceanographic Research, 1978; author: Hypochondria: Woeful Imagings, 1988, The Dinosaur Man and Other Tales From the Back Ward, 1991, Confiding: A Psychotherapist and Her Patients Search for Stories to Live By, 1994, The Intimate Hour: Love and Sex in Psychotherapy, 1997, The Love of Your Life: What We Learn in the Grip of Passion, 2002; contbr. articles to profl. jours. Recipient Pfizer award, Pfizer Chem. Co., 1974; Mark Ethridge fellow, Ford Found., 1968.

BAUTZ, JENNIFER JEAN, music educator; b. Fond du Lac, Wis., Nov. 10, 1975; BA, Univ. Wis., 1998; MFA, Univ. Wis., Milw., Wis., 2004. Music tchr. Nathan Hale HS, West Allis, Wis., 1998—; piano, vocal tchr. pvt. practice, West Allis, Wis., 1998—; a. Music dir. West Allis (Wis.) Players, 1999, Nathan Hale HS, 1998—. Vol. Democratic Party, Milw., 2002—. Recipient Ednl. Grant, Skylight Opera Co., 1999. Mem.: Wis. state Music Assn., Music Educators Assn., Am. Choral Dir. Assn. Democrat. Penecostal. Avocations: music, theater, literature. Home: 6715 W Grant St West Allis WI 53219 Office: Nathan Hale HS 11601 W Lincoln Ave West Allis WI 53227

BAWDEN, NINA (MARY BAWDEN), author; b. Eng., 1925; Author: Who Calls the Tune (in U.S. as Eyes of Green), 1953, The Odd Flamingo, 1954, Change Here for Babylon, 1955, The Solitary Child, 1956, Devil by the Sea, 1957, Just Like a Lady (in U.S. as Glass Slippers Always Pinch), 1960, In Honour Bound, 1961, Tortoise by Candlelight, 1963, The Secret Passage (in U.S. as The House of Secrets), 1963, On the Run (in U.S. as Three on the Run), 1964, Under the Skin, 1964, A Little Love, A Little Learning, 1966, The White Horse Gang, 1966, The Witch's Daughter, 1966, A Handful of Thieves, 1967, A Woman of My Age, 1967, The Grain of Truth, 1968, The Runaway Summer, 1969, The Birds on the Trees, 1970, Squib, 1971, Anna Apparent, 1972, Carrie's War, George Beneath a Paper Moon, 1974, The Peppermint Pig, 1975, Afternoon of a Good Woman, 1976, Rebel on a Rock, 1978, Familiar Passions, 1979, Walking Naked, 1981, Kept in the Dark, 1982, The Ice House, 1983, The Finding, 1985, Circles of Deceit, 1987, Keeping Henry, 1988, The Outside Child, 1989, Family Money, 1991, Humbug, 1992, The Real Plato Jones, 1993, In My Own Time, 1994, A Nice Change, 1997, Off the Road, 1998, Ruffian on the Stair, 2001. Address: care Curtis Brown Ltd 10 Astor Pl New York NY 10003-6935 also: 22 Noel Rd London NI 8HA England also: 19 Kapodistriou Nauplion 21100 Greece E-mail: ninakrak@talk21.com.

BAX, DEBRA, real estate agent; m. Greg Bax; 1 child, Jeremy Malensky. Lic. real estate broker Mo., 1982. CEO, broker Dutchman Realty, St. Charles, Mo., 1982—. Bar com. 11th Jud. Cir., St. Charles, 2002. Mem.: St. Charles County Bd. Realtors, St. Charles County C. of C. Office: Dutchman Realty Inc Saint Charles MO 63301 E-mail: deebax@dutchmanrealty.com.

BAXLEY, LUCY, lieutenant governor; m. Bill Baxley (div.); children: Becky Nichols, Louis; m. Jim Smith. Licensed realtor; Treas. State of Ala., 1994—2002, lt. gov., 2002—. Vice chair Aerospace States Assn. Women's Philanthropy Bd. Auburn U. Mem.: Nat. Assn. Lt. Govs., Ala. Fedn. of Dem. Women (chair adv. coun.), U. Ala. XXXI. Office: Ste 725 11 S Union St Montgomery AL 36130

BAXTER, BARBARA MORGAN, Internet service provider executive, educator; b. Cleve., Apr. 14, 1939; d. James Clifford and Mildred Elizabeth (Button) Baxter; m. David S. Unkefer, Dec. 28, 1956 (div.); children: Rachel, Clifford David, Elizabeth, Monica, Todd James. BSBA in MIS, Bowling Green State U., 1977, MBA, 1979, postgrad. in psychology, 1984, Wright State U., 1984-85. Clk. J.C. Baxter Co., Minerva, Ohio, 1962-66; v.p., co-founder Sherwood Plastics, Inc., Fostoria, Ohio, 1966-75, pres., CEO, 1975-89, Compututor Inc/Internet of Sandhills, Southern Pines, N.C. Mem. adj. faculty Tiffin (Ohio) U., 1984-90; MIS cons. to small bus., 1984-90; adj. continuing edn. faculty Sandhills C.C., Pinehurst, N.C., 1992-93; adj. faculty St. Andrews Coll., Lauringburg, N.C., 1993; CEO, co-founder CompuTutor, Inc., Southern Pines, N.C., 1994—, Internet of the Sandhills ISP, 1996—. V.p. Carroll County Young Reps., 1960-61; mem. Carroll County Rep. Cen. and Exec. Com., 1961-65, Wood County Rep. Com., 1967-70; troop leader, troop organizer, badge cons. Girl Scouts U.S., 1967-81; vestrywoman, sr. warden Trinity Episcopal Ch., Fostoria., 1972-75; therapist Community Hospice Care Seneca County, Tiffin, 1987-89, also Carroll, Wood, Fostoria Counties; del. U.S.-China Trade Talks People to People, Spokane, Wash., 1988; adv. bd. Tiffin U. Students in Free Enterprise, 1986-87; tchr. applied econs. Jr. Achievement, 1988-89. Mem. Ladies Oriental Shrine N.Am., DAR, Alpha Lambda Delta. Avocation: classical music.

BAXTER, BETTY CARPENTER, educational administrator; b. Sherman, Tex., Oct. 10, 1937; d. Granville e. and Elizabeth (Caston) Carpenter; m. Cash Baxter; children: Stephen Barrington, Catherine Elaine. AA in Music, Christian Coll., Columbia, Mo., 1957; MusB in Voice and Piano, So. Meth. U., Dallas, 1959; MA in Early Childhood Edn., Stephens Coll., Columbia, 1972, MEd, 1979, EdD, 1988. Tchr. Riverside Ch. Day Sch., N.Y.C., 1966-71; headmistress Episcopal Sch., N.Y.C., 1972-87, headmistress emeritus, 1987—. Founding head Presbyn. Sch., Houston, 1988-94; dir. Chadwick Village Sch., Palos Verdes Peninsula, Calif., 1995—; head of sch. St. Margaret's Episcopal Sch., Palm Desert, Calif., 2001-02. Author: The Relationship of Early Tested Intelligence on the WPPSI to Later Tested Aptitude on the SAT. Mem. ASCD, Nat. Assn. Episcopal Chs. (former gov. bd., editor Network publ.), Nat. Assn. Elem. Sch. Prins., Ind. Schs. Assn. Admissions Greater N.Y. (former exec. bd.), Nat. Assn. for Edn. of Young Children, L.A. Assn. Sch. Heads, Nat. Assn. Elem. Sch. Prins., Assn. Supervision and Curriculum Devel., Kappa Delta Pi, Delta Kappa Gamma. Republican. Presbyterian. Office: 72-828 Joshua Tree St Palm Desert CA 92260 E-mail: baxterbuty@jps.net.

BAXTER, BEVERLEY VELONS, economic association administrator, educator; b. Eugene, Oreg., July 5, 1943; d. J. Clifford Baxter and O. Veloris Crenshaw; m. Doyle R. Dobbins, July 7, 1962; children: Kendall Reé Baxter Dobbins, Kalen Baxter Dobbins, Konlee Baxter Dobbins. Certificate, Graduate Sch. Ecumenical Studies, Bossey, Switzerland, 1965, William Temple Coll., Rugby, Eng., 1965; BS, Phillips U., 1966, MEd, 1967; MA, U. Del., 1971, PhD, 1976. Tchg. asst. U. Del., Newark, 1971—76; asst. prof. dept. English Temple U., Phila., 1977—79; real estate investor Wilmington, Del., 1979—83; dir. edn. programs First Unitarian Ch., Wilmington, 1983; exec. asst. to county exec. New Castle County, Wilmington, 1983—84; v.p. Blue Ball Properties, Wilmington, 1985—93; exec. dir. The Com. of 100, Wilmington, 1993—. Dir. Wilmington Area Planning Coun. Wilmington Initiatives Steering Com., 1995—; mem. Gov.'s State Planning Citizens Adv. Coun., Del., 1995—, Del. State C. of C. Small Bus. Alliance Legis. Com., 1997—; dir. Del. Bus. Pub. Edn. Coun., Wilmington, 1998—; mem. working group De. Dept. Transportation; mem. Del. Dept. Natural Resources & Environ. Control Regulatory Adv. com.; bd. dirs., treas. Wiley Coll., Marshall, Tex. Author: Diaries and Journals of Americans Held Prisoner During the Revolutionary War, 1976; editor: For Your Info., 1995. Pres. bd. dir. Montessori Cmty. Sch., Wilmington, 1996—2000; bd. dir. Unitarian Universalist Svc. Com., Cambridge, Mass., 1985—91; pres. First Unitarian Ch., Wilmington, 1979—82, bd. dir., 1979—82, Friends of Rockwood Mus., Wilmington, 1986—88. Recipient Economic Turnaround Cert. of Appreciation, Wilmington 2000, 1982, Disting. Svc. award, Unitarian Universalist Svc. Com., 1991, Liveable Cmty. award, Wilmington Area Planning Coun., 1998. Mem.: The Associates, The Bus. Group, New Castle County C. of C. (state affairs coun., county govt. coun.). Unitarian Universalist. Avocations: music, reading, gardening, skiing. Office: The Committe of 100 824 Market St Ste 612 Wilmington DE 19801

BAXTER, KATHLEEN BYRNE, academic administrator; b. Rockville Center, Jan. 31, 1976; d. Anthony Campbell and Margaret Regan Baxter. BA in English, Villanova U., 1997; MA in Higher Edn. and Student Pers. Adminstrn., Teachers Coll., Columbia U., 2000. Asst. dir. event planning Teachers Coll., Columbia U., N.Y.C., 1998—2000; asst. dir. programs MIT, Cambridge, 2000—02; dir. leadership and first yr. programs Simmons Coll., Boston, 2002—03; assoc. dir. Ctr. for Career Edn., Columbia U., N.Y.C., 2003—. Mem. Franciscan Children's Hosp. Young Profl. Coun., Brighton, Mass., 2000—03. Mem.: Assn. Coll. Pers. Adminstrs., Nat. Assn. Pers. Adminstrs., Kappa Delta Pi, Delta Delta Delta. R-Liberal. Catholic. Avocations: travel, running, reading. Personal E-mail: kathleenbaxter7@hotmail.com.

BAXTER, MYRTLE MAE (BOBBI BAXTER), artist; b. Weableau, Mo., Nov. 10, 1928; d. Maxwell and Maude Bell Dorrel; m. Clarence Edgar Baxter, Dec. 31, 1945; children: Kenneth Wayne, Gary Dee, Joyce Evelyn. Profl. cert., Nevada (Mo.) Beauty Sch., 1970; degree in art, Am. Art Sch., 1987. Hair stylist Beauty Box, Butler, Nev., 1993-96; tchr. art to children Baxter Art Gallery, Butler, 1993-95. Exhibited in group shows Roscoe (Mo.) Mus. Soc., 1978-79 (1st place best of show award), Iola (Kans.) Guild, 1985-86, 1st award), Cottey Coll., Nevada, 1985-86, Royal Arts Coun., Versailles, Mo., 1985-86, (1st, 2d, 3d. awards, Best of Show), Table Rock (Mo.) Art Assn., 1996-97 (Best of Show award), Stover (Mo.) Art Assn., 1990-91, Warrensburg Coll. Art Gallery, 1995, Image Art Gallery,

Carthage, Mo., 1997, Lamar (Mo.) Art League, 1996-97 (1st, 2d and 3d awards), Royals Arts Coun. Art Show, 1997 (Best of Show award), Harrisonville, Mo. Best of Show Fine Arts award, 1997; contbr. poetry On the Wing of Poetry. Leader, v.p. Summit 4-H Club, Butler, 1975-80; pres. Ladies Aid Club, Butler, 1985-86, in charge festival Roscoe (Mo.) Art Festival, 1996-97. Mem. Butler Art Club (pres. 1973-74), Tri-County Art Assn. (v.p., show chmn. 1980-81, bd. dirs. 1980, sec. 1980-81), Bates County Art League (mem. 1980-81, 89, show chmn. 1978-79), Harrisonville Art Assn. (v.p. 1995-96, program organizer), Mo. Coun. Arts (program organizer 1995), Warrensburg Art Assn., Greater Kansas City Art Assn., Nat. Mus., Women in the Arts, Bates County Art League. Democrat. Methodist. Avocations: painting on location, hiking, bicycling, exercising, attending art meetings. Home: RR 5 Butler 52 E Box 65 Butler MO 64730-1852

BAXTER, NANCY, medical writer; b. Grand Rapids, Mich., Oct. 3, 1950; d. Robert Emerson and Mary (Knoblauch) B. BA in Journalism, Am. U., 1972. Asst. dir. publs. Am. Speech, Lang. & Hearing Assn., Washington, 1973-77; mng. editor Biomedia, Inc., Princeton, N.J., 1977-79, Continuing Profl. Edn. Ctr., Inc., Princeton, 1981-82; editor A.M. Best Co., Oldwick, N.J., 1979-81; med. writer, editor Biomed Info. Corp., N.Y.C., 1982-83; pres. Baxter Med. Comms. Co., Warren, N.J., 1983—. Mem. Am. Med. Writers Assn. Home and Office: 18 Stiles Rd Warren NJ 07059-5413 E-mail: baxmedcomm@aol.com.

BAXTER, SANDRA L, government agency administrator; BA in English, Howard U.; M in Education, Loyola Coll.; Doctorate in Admin., Harvard Grad. Sch. of Education, 1995. Sr. evaluator. U.S. General Accounting Office; interim exec. dir. Natl. Inst. for Literacy, 2001—. Office: Nat Inst for Literacy 1775 I Street NW Ste 730 Washington DC 20006*

BAY, JOANN REEDER, financial planner; b. Williamsport, Pa., Sept. 29, 1926; d. Rollin A. and Esther Ellen (Costello) Reeder; m. John William Bay, Sr., Aug. 22, 1948; children: John William Jr., Neil Andrew. BA in English & Psychology, Bucknell U., 1948. Cert.: Inst. Paralegal Tng., Phila. (paralegal) 1973; fin. planner Coll. Fin. Planning. Analyst HAY Assoc., Phila., 1973—75, fin. planning cons., 1975—77; prin., owner J.R. Bay Assoc., Drexel Hill, Pa., 1978—. Adv. com. Upper Darby (Pa.) Sch. Bd., 1970—72; exec. v.p. Mother's Group Upper Darby HS, 1970—71, pres. Parent's Group, 1971—72; pro bono work for financially needy women; chmn. investment com. Cmty. Y Ea. Delware County, Upper Darby, 1992—97, Cmty. Y Found., Upper Darby, 1995—97. Named one of 200 Best Fin. Adv. in U.S., Money Mag. Silver Anniversary Issue, 1987. Mem.: Fin. Planning Assn. (llic. practitioner), Delaware County Estate Planning Assn., Philadelphia County Estate Planning Assn., Delaware Valley chpt. IAFP, Women in Transition. Democrat. Presbyterian. Avocations: piano, reading, concerts, museums. Office: JR Bay Associates 5022 Sylvia Rd Drexel Hill PA 19026

BAY, LIBBY, college administrator, English language educator; b. N.Y.C., Dec. 22, 1932; d. Abraham and Faye (Orkofsky) Goldstein; m. Morris Bay, Nov. 24, 1965; children: Robin Bay Gilenson, Beth. BA, Hunter Coll., 1954; MA, U. Chgo., 1955; postgrad., NYU, 1955-57. Lectr. Bklyn. Coll., 1957-61, Hunter Coll., 1961-65; prof. SUNY/Rockland, Suffern, N.Y., 1965—, English chair, 1975-93, humanities divsn. chair, 1993—; liberal arts faculty Regents Coll., Albany, N.Y., 1985—, chmn. Divsn. Humanities, Social and Behavioral Scis., 2003—. Guest lectr. local librs., Rockland and Orange Counties, 1990—; grant dir. NEH, Washington, 1970-72, Am. Assn. C.C., Washington, 1991-93; lay mem. 9th Jud. Grievance Com., N.Y., 1985-93. Contbr. chpts. to books and articles to mags. and jours. Commn. mem. Women's Commn. Rockland County Legis., 1988—; exec. bd. dirs. Hunter Coll. Alumni, Rockland Coll., 1975—, newsletter editor, 1978-90. Named Outstanding Adminstr. in Higher Edn., Nat. C.C. Charter Assn., 1994; Mellon fellow CUNY Grad. Ctr., 1986; summer study grants NEH, 1992, Ams. Communities grant, 1995-96; (2) Mellon fellowships CUNY, fellowship East-West Inst. Hawaii, 1996. Mem. Nat. Two-Yr. Coll. Assn. (assoc. chair 1992—), Assn. Depts. of English (exec. bd. dirs. 1993—), N.E. Regional English Assn. (exec. bd. dirs. 1980—). Avocations: writing, theater, opera, concerts, travel. Home: 1 Danville Rd Spring Valley NY 10977-4515 Office: SUNY/Rockland 145 College Rd Suffern NY 10901-3611

BAYAR, JULIA BERYL, interior designer; b. Washington, June 12, 1949; BA, Vassar Coll., 1971; MS, Boston U., 1972. Press aide Dem. Nat. Com., Washington, 1972-73, U.S. Ho. Reps., Washington, 1973-76, U.S. Senate, Washington, 1976-77; speechwriter U.S. Dept. Justice, Washington, 1977-79; cons. Jules Kroll Assocs., N.Y.C., 1980-81; interior designer, owner Interiors by Julia Bayar, Scarsdale, N.Y., 1984—. Home: 47 Lynwood Rd Scarsdale NY 10583-2701

BAYARD, SUSAN SHAPIRO, adult education educator, small business owner; b. Boston, Dec. 26, 1942; d. Morris Arnold and Hester Muriel (Blatt) Shapiro; m. Edward Quint Bayard, Jan. 4, 1969; children: Jeffrey David, Lucy Quint. BA, Syracuse U., 1964; MA, U. Calif., Berkeley, 1966; cert. in advanced grad. study, Boston U., 1984. Rsch. chemist Harvard Med. Sch., Boston, 1966; asst. scientist Polaroid Corp., Cambridge, Mass., 1966-67; instr. Boston U., 1968-70, Wheelock Coll., Boston, 1978-81; chmn. sci. dept. Tower Sch., Marblehead, Mass., 1981-85; dir., owner Bayard Learning Ctr., Marblehead, 1985—94; vis. lectr. Salem (Mass.) State Coll., 1994—2000, coord. Instrnl. Design Lab., 1995—2000, coord. PALMS presvc. program, 1998—2000; dir. Ctr. Tchg., Learning and Assessment N. Shore CC, Danvers, Mass., 2003—. Ednl. cons., workshop facilitator Swampscott (Mass.) Pub. Schs., Lynn (Mass.) Pub. Schs., Marblehead, Mass., 1986—96; instr., cons. N.E. Consortium, North Andover, Mass., 1986—94. Mem. Curriculum Evaluation Com., Swampscott, 1978—80, Mass. Ednl. TV Program Selection Com., 1979—87, Supt. Screening Com., Swampscott, 1987, Town Meeting, Swampscott, 1988—, Sch. Improvement Coun., Swampscott, 1988—89. Named Outstanding Woman Grad. Student, Boston U. Women's Guild, 1977; grantee, NSF, Syracuse U., 1962, 1964. Mem.: Nat. Sci. Tchrs. Assn., Pi Lambda Theta. Jewish. Avocations: tennis, reading, computers, piano.

BAYES, GINNY, public relations and advertising executive; b. Denver, Apr. 7, 1960; d. Peter Oxley and Mary Virginia (Gray) B. BA, Met. State Coll., 1984; MFA, U. Colo. Asst. dir., systems analyst Met. State Coll., Denver, 1985-87; assoc./mktg. dir. Lowe Assocs. Inc., Denver, 1987-90; newspaper columnist The Denver Post, 1990-93, Denver's Rocky Mountain News, Denver, 1994—. Cons. Human Svcs., Bldg. Owners and Mgrs. Assn., Denver, 1991-92, Community Food Share, Boulder, 1991; speaker in field. Bd. dirs., treas. Ch. of Christ Scientist, Denver, 1977-84. Met. State Coll. scholar, 1984. Mem. Women in Real Estate. Avocations: fine art, painting, outdoor sports, writing. Office: Bayes and Assocs PO Box 61227 Denver CO 80206-8227 also: Harvest Moon Pub 385 S Franklin St Denver CO 80209-2608

BAYLES, JENNIFER LUCENE, museum program director, educator; b. Tokyo, May 26, 1953; d. Lewis Allen Bayles and Rosemary (Beuhler) Fraser; m. Robert Steinfeld, July 4, 1992; children: Noah Isaac Steinfeld, Ezra Milton Steinfeld. BA in Art History with honors, Ind. U., Bloomington, 1976; MA in Art History, U. Mich., 1984, cert. in mus. practice, 1984. Curatorial apprentice Indpls. Mus. Art, 1976; mus. apprentice Portland (Oreg.) Art Mus., 1976-78, asst. curator edn., 1978-81; asst. curator photographic collection dept. art history U. Mich., Ann Arbor, 1981-83, rsch. and editl. asst. Mus. Art, 1982-83; intern dept. mus. edn. Art Inst. Chgo., 1983-84; curator edn. Albright-Knox Art Gallery, Buffalo, 1984—2001, from asst. curator edn. adult programs to educator spl. projects, 2001—. Horace H. Rackman Grad. scholar, 1981—83, Acad. scholar, U. Mich., 1982. Mem.: Am. Assn. Mus. (regional rep. edn. com. 1979—81). Office: Albright-Knox Art Gallery 1285 Elmwood Ave Buffalo NY 14222-1096

BAYLESS, BETSEY, state official; b. Phoenix; BA in Latin Am. Studies and Spanish, U. Ariz., 1966; MPA, Ariz. State U., 1974; DHL (hon.), U. Ariz., 2001. V.p. pub. fin. Peacock, Hislop, Staley & Given, Inc., Phoenix; asst. dir. Ariz. Bd. Regents; acting dir. dept. revenue State of Ariz., dir. dept. adminstrn., sec. of state, 1997—2003; dir. Ariz. Dept. Adminstrn., 2003—. Bd. suprs. Maricopa County, 1989-97, chmn. bd., 1992, 94, vice chair, 1997; mem. Ariz. Bd. Investment, 2003—; bd. dirs. Child Help Ariz.; mem. Nat.bd. dirs. U. Ariz. Coll. of Bus. and Pub. Adminstrn.; adv. bd. Ariz. State U. West.. Bd. dirs. Xavier Coll. Preparatory Found., Ariz. Ctr. for the Book; commr. Gov.'s Commn. Violence Against Women; mem. Ariz. Town Hall, Charter 100, Valley Leadership Class VI, Ariz. Rep. Caucus, Ariz. Women's Forum. Named to Hall of Fame, Ariz. State U. Coll. Pub. Programs; recipient Disting. Citizen award U. Ariz. Alumni Assn., Woman of Yr. award Capitol chpt. Bus. and Profl. Women, Disting. Achievement award NEH Fellowship, Achievement award Nat. Assn. Counties, 1993, Citizen award Bur. Reclamation, 1993, Woman of Achievement award Xavier Coll. Preparatory, 1995. Mem. Phi Beta Kappa (Freeman medal 1966). Republican.

BAYLOR, AMY L. educational technology educator; b. Boston, Jan. 5, 1968; d. Gary K. and Mary Anne Bergholtz. BA in Philosophy, Stanford U.; PhD in Ednl. Psychology, U. S.C., 1997. Asst. prof. ednl. tech. San Diego State U., 1997—99; asst. prof. instrnl. sys. Fla. State U., Tallahassee, 1999—. Office: Fla State U 307 Stone Bldg Tallahassee FL 32306 Business E-Mail: baylor@coe.fsu.edu.

BAYM, NINA, English educator; b. Princeton, N.J., June 14, 1936; d. Leo and Frances (Levinson) Zippin; m. Gordon Baym, June 1, 1958; children—Nancy, Geoffrey; m. Jack Stillinger, May 21, 1971 BA, Cornell U., 1957; MA, Harvard U., 1958, PhD, 1963. Asst. U. Calif.-Berkeley, 1962-63; instr. U. Ill., Urbana, 1963-67, asst. prof. English, 1967-69, assoc. prof., 1969-72, prof., 1972—, Jubilee prof. liberal arts and scis., 1989—, dir. Sch. Humanities, 1976-87, sr. Univ. scholar, 1985, assoc. Ctr. Advanced Study, 1989-90, permanent prof. Ctr. Advanced Study, 1997—, Swanlund Endowed chair, 1997—. Author: The Shape of Hawthorne's Career, 1976, Woman's Fiction: A Guide to Novels By and About Women in America, 1978, 2d rev. edit., 1993, Novels, Readers and Reviewers: Responses to Fiction in Antebellum America, 1984, The Scarlet Letter: A Reading, 1986, Feminism and American Literary History, 1992, American Women Writers and the Work of History, 1790-1860, 1995, American Women of Letters and the 19th Century Sciences, 2002; gen. editor: Norton Anthology of American Literature; sr. editor Am. Nat. Biography; also author essays, edits., revs.; mem. editl. bd. Am. Quar., New Eng. Quar., Legacy, A Jour. of 19th Century Am. Women Writers, Jour. Aesthetic Edn. Am. Lit., Tulsa Studies in Women's Lit., Am. Studies, Studies Am. Fiction, Am. Periodicals, Hemingway Rev., Resources for Am. Lit. Study, Am. Lit. History, Cambridge U.P. Studies in Am. Lit. and Culture; mem. editl. adv. bd. PMLA. Guggenheim fellow, 1975-76, AAUW hon. fellow, 1975-76, NEH fellow, 1982-83; rec pient Arnold O. Beckman award U. Ill., 1992-93, Hubbell Lifetime Achievement medal, Am. Let. Sect., 2000. Mem. MLA (exec. com. 19th century Am. Lit. divsn., chmn. 1984, chmn. Am. Lit. sect. 1984, Hubbell Lifetime Achievement medal 2000), Am. Studies Assn. (exec. com. 1982-84, nominating com. 1991-93), Am. Lit. Assn., Am. Antiquarian Soc., Mass. Hist. Soc., Nathaniel Hawthorne Soc. (adv. bd.), Western Lit. Assn., Mortar Bd., Phi Kappa Phi, Phi Beta Kappa. Office: U Ill Dept English 608 S Wright St Urbana IL 61801-3630 E-mail: baymnina@uiuc.edu.

BAYMILLER, LYNDA DOERN, social worker; b. Milw., July 6, 1943; d. Ronald Oliver and Marian Elizabeth (Doern) B. Student, U. Hawaii, 1962, Mich. State U., 1965; BA, U. Wis., 1965, MSW, 1969. Vol. Peace Corps, Chile, 1965-67; social worker Luth. Social Svcs. of Wis. and Upper Mich., Milw., 1969-77, contract social worker, 1978-79; dist. supr. Childrens Svc. Soc. Wis., Kenosha, 1977-78; social work supr. Sauk County Dept. Human Svcs., Baraboo, Wis., 1979-90; sales and relief mgr.-trainee Wal-Mart, 1992-93, cashier, 1993—. Author: (with Clara Amelia Hess) Now-Won, A Collection of Feeling Poetry, 1973. Bd. dirs. Zoo Pride, Zool Soc. Milwaukee County, 1975-77, Sauk County Mental Health Assn., 1979-84; mem. Harmony chpt. Sweet Adelines, West Allis, Wis., 1970-75, pres. chpt., 1971; pres. bd. dirs. Growing Place Day Care Ctr., Kenosha, 1977-78; mem. Baraboo (Wis.) Centennial Com., 1982; pres. bd. dirs. Laubach Literacy Coun., Baraboo, 1986-88; mem. Sauk County Humane Soc., 1987—, sec., 1988-90. Mem. NASW, Acad. Cert. Social Workers, AAUW (br. sec. 1982-84), U. Wis. Alumni Assn. (life), Am. Legion Aux., DAR, Nat. Soc. Magna Carta Dames, Eddy Family Assn. (life), Nat. Soc. Ancient and Hon. Arty. Co. of Mass. (life), Wis. Soc. Daus. of 1812 (rec. sec. 1994-96), Sauk County Hist. Soc., Internat. Crane Found. (patron), Daus. Colonial Wars, Daus. Am. Colonists, Zool. Soc. Milwaukee County (life), Am. Bus. Women's Assn., Order Eastern Star (grad. rep. Miss. in Wis. 1988-90), Order White Shrine of Jerusalem, Ladies Aux. of Fraternal Order Eagles, Cameo Club, Queen of Sheba Order Eastern Star, Alpha Xi Delta. Home: 332 4th Ave Baraboo WI 53913-2029

BAYNE, KATHRYN ANN LOUISE, veterinarian; b. Santa Monica, Calif., Feb. 4, 1959; d. Richard Harry and Loretta Mary Bayne; m. Mark Cofer Haines, May 19, 1990. BS cum laude, Calif. State Poly. U., 1979; MS, Wash. State U., 1982, PhD, 1986, DVM, 1987. Vet. behaviorist NIH, Bethesda, Md., 1987-94; sr. dir. Assn. for the Assessment & Accreditation of Lab. Animal Care, Rockville, Md., 1994—. Diplomate Am. Coll. Lab. Animal Medicine, pres.-elect bd. dirs. Inventor in field; author publs. in field. Comdr. USPHS. Recipient Foster award, USPHS commendaton and achievement awards, Garvey award AALAS; named Alumnus of Yr. award Westlake Sch. Mem.: Scientists Ctr. for Animal Welfare (past v.p. bd. dirs.), DC Vet. Med. Assn. (past pres.), Assn. Primate Vets. (past pres.), Am. Soc. Lab. Animal Practitioners, Animal Behavior Soc., AVMA (chair animal welfare com.). Avocations: gardening, birdwatching. Office: AAALAC International 11300 Rockville Pike Ste 1211 Rockville MD 20852-3040

BAYS, KATHRYN MICHELLE, interior designer, educator; b. Tucson, Ariz., Dec. 2, 1963; d. Donald Ray Bays and Joan Damaris Riley. BS in Design, Ariz. State U., 1987. Interior designer Arch. Interiors, Phoenix, 1987—88, Goodmans, Las Vegas, 1988—89, BSHA, San Diego, 1989—91; prin., owner Bays Design Concepts, Solana Beach, Calif., 1991—. Prof. Mesa C.C., San Diego, Calif., 2000—02. Mem.: Calif. Cert. Interior Design Assn. (cert. 1995), Internat. Interior Design Assn., Am. Aerobics Fitness Assn. Avocations: golf, skiing, jogging, travel, study of cetaceans. Office: Bays Design Concepts 124 1/2 E Cliff St Ste C2 Solana Beach CA 92075

BAZELIDES, DIANE, public relations executive; BS in Bus. Edn., U. Nebr. With dept. internal audit Enron Corp., Houston, 1976-80, with dept. pub. rels., 1980-83, comm. adminstr. dept. pub. rels., 1983-86, mgr. media rels., 1986-88, dir. media rels. dept. pub. rels., 1988-91, gen. mgr. dept. pub. rels., 1991-92, v.p. dept. pub. rels., 1992—98; mng. dir. mktg. comms. and pub. rels. Azurix, Houston, 1998—. Bd. dirs. Alley Theater, Houston, Houston Ballet; mem. exec. com., pres. bd. dirs. Alzheimer's Assn., Houston. Mem. Pub. Rels. Soc. Am., Internat. Assn. Bus. Communicators. Office: Azurix 0333 Play St Houston TX 77002

BAZIK, EDNA FRANCES, mathematician, educator; b. Streator, Ill., Dec. 26, 1946; d. Andrew and Anna Frances (Vagasky) B.; BSEd, Ill. State U, 1969; postgrad. Hamilton Coll., summer 1971, Ill. State U., 1972, Augustana Coll., summer 1973; MEd, U. Ill., 1972; PhD, So. Ill. U., 1976, gen. adminstrv. cert., 1980. Tchr. math. Northlawn Jr. High Sch., Streator, 1969-74; instr. math. edn. So. Ill. U., 1974-76; asst. prof. math. Concordia U., 1976-78; asst. prof. math. Ill. State U., Normal, 1978-85; assoc. prof. math. Eastern Ill. U., 1985-88; math. specialist, coord. Oak Park (Ill.) Pub. Schs., 1988-89; math coord. Hinsdale Sch. Dist. 181, 1989—; coord. inservice presentations, workshops for tchrs.; cons. to sch. dists. NSF grantee, 1980—. Presdl. award NSF, 1990. Mem. AAUP, Ill. State Bd. Edn. (mem. assessment team math. 1998—), Assn. Tchr. Educators, Ill. Assn. Tchr. Educators, Nat. Coun. Tchrs. Math. (chair elections com. 1990-91, Ill. Coun. Tchrs. Math. (governing bd., dir. coll. and univ. level), Math. Assn. Am., Nat. Coun. Suprs. Math., NEA, Ill. Edn. Assn., Sch. Sci. and Math. Assn., U.S. Metric Assn., Am. Ednl. Rsch. Assn., Assn. Supervision and Curriculum Devel., Ill. Assn. Supervision and Curriculum Devel., Ill. Standards Achievement Test Math Validation Com., Ill. State Bd. Edn. Math. Assessment Com., Assn. Childhood Edn. Internat., Coun. Exceptional Children, Ill. Curriculum Coun., Rsch. Coun. Diagnostic and Prescriptive Math., Kappa Delta Pi, Phi Delta Kappa (pres. Ill. State U. chpt. 1982-83), Pi Mu Epsilon, Delta Kappa Gamma, Phi Kappa Phi. Republican. Lutheran. Co-author: Elementary Mathematical Methods, 1978, Mind Over Math, 1980, Teaching Mathematics to Children with Special Needs, 1983, Step-by-Step: Addition, 1984, Step-by-Step: Subtraction, 1984, Step-by-Step: Multiplication, 1984, Step-by-Step: Division, 1984, Problem-Solving Sourcebook, 1985, Step-by-Step: Fractions, 1987, Step-by-Step: Decimals, 1988. Home: 1501 Darien Lake Dr Darien IL 60561-5069 Office: Hinsdale Sch Dist 181 100 S Garfield Ave Hinsdale IL 60521-4252 E-mail: ebazik@d181.dupage.k12.il.us.

BAZILE, ANITA MICHELE, psychologist, educator; b. East Saint Louis, Ill., Aug. 22, 1971; d. Alfred Bazile, Sr. and Trenier Gloria Bazile. BA cum laude, So. Ill. U., Carbondale, Ill., 1993; MS with distinction, Saint Louis (Mo.) U., 1998; cert. in U. Tchg. Skills, St. Louis (Mo.) U., 1998; cert. in Child Abuse and Neglect, U. Okla., 2000; PhD, Saint Louis (Mo.) U., 2000. Lic. clin. psychologist Ill., 2001. Intern in psychology U. Okla. Health Scis. Ctr., Okla. City, Okla., 1999—2000; post-doctoral fellow Ctr. Trauma Recovery U. Mo., St. Louis, 2000—01; clin. psychologist Alton (Ill.) Mental Health Ctr., 2001—, Chester (Ill.) Mental Health Ctr., 2002—03. Cpl. Nat. Guard U.S. Army, 1989—96. Mem.: Okla. Psychol. Assn. (Rsch. award 1999), Am. Psychol. Assn., Delta Sigma Theta. Avocations: fishing, travel, time with family. Office: Alton Mental Health Ctr 4500 College Ave Alton IL 62002 Office Phone: 618-474-3800.

BAZIRJIAN, ROSANN V. dean, librarian; b. N.Y.C., Sept. 5, 1952; d. Dickran and Rose V. Bazirjian; m. Patrick T. Burger; 1 child, Terence Burger. BA, Lehman Coll., N.Y.C., 1973; MS, Columbia U., 1980; MSSC, Syracuse U., 1993. Acquisitions libr. Syracuse U., NY, 1980—84, head acquisitions dept., 1990—91, head bibliog. svcs., 1991—95; head acquisitions and collections devel. U. West Fla., Pensacola, 1985—90; asst. dir. tech. svcs. Fla. State U., Tallahassee, 1995—99; asst. dean tech. and access svcs. Pa. State U., University Park, 1999—. Contbr. articles to profl. publs., chapters to books. Mem.: ALA (Leadership in Acquisitions award 2002), Assn. Library Collections and Tech. Svcs., Assn. Coll. and Rsch. Libraries, Phi Beta Kappa. Office: Pa State Univ Librs 507 Paterno Library University Park PA 16802

BAZZONE, THERESA (TERRY) A. sales executive; Student, Bentley Coll. Sales mgr. Corp. Software, Inc., 1987—92; dir. software product mktg. div. Tech Data Corp., Clearwater, Fla., 1992—96, v.p., gen. mgr. strategic bus. dev. unit, 1996—2002, sr. v.p. US sales, 2002—. Office: Tech Data Corp 5350 Tech Data Rd Clearwater FL 33760-3122

BEA, BARBARA ANN, legal secretary; b. Richmond, Va., Nov. 26, 1957; d. Arthur and Edith (Thompson) B.; 1 child, Michael T. Sec. IEEE, Washington, 1981-83, Greenhoot, Inc., Washington, 1983-85; legal sec. Friedlander, Misler, Friedlander, Sloan & Herz, Washington, 1985-88, Arnold & Porter, Washington, 1988-97, Dickstein, Shapiro, Morin & Olshinsky, Washington, 1997-99, Hale and Dorr, Washington, 1999-00, Littler, Mendelson PC, 2000—01, KMZ Rosenman, 2001—. Democrat. Mem. Seventh-Day Adventist Ch.

BEACH, JEAN MRHA, food products executive; BA, Wellesley Coll.; MA in Fin. and Acctg., U. Chgo. Sr. v.p. commodity and trading risk mgmt. Tyson Foods, Inc., Springdale, Ark., 2002—. Office: Tyson Foods Inc 2210 W Oaklawn Dr Springdale AR 72762-6999*

BEACH, LISA (ELIZABETH) FORSTER, artist, educator; b. Ypsilanti, Mich., Feb. 3, 1937; d. Ralph Dale and Mildred E. (Drake) Bruce; m. Donald M. Forster, Apr. 19, 1962 (div. June 1988); children: Alan, Kenneth, Susan; m. David E. Beach, Feb. 14, 1989. BS in Art Edn., Edinboro U. of Pa., 1959; MFA, Rochester Inst. Tech., 1987. Art instr. Mercer (Pa.) Sch. Sys., 1959-60, Irondequoit (N.Y.) Pub. Schs., 1961-62; painting instr. Meml. Art Gallery of U. of Rochester, Rochester, N.Y., 1983-85; tchg. asst. Edgar Whitney Painting Tours, 1983-84; art instr., dir. Topnotch Resport and Spa, Stowe, Vt., 1989-95; painting instr. Stowe Hollow Studio, 1989—; drawing and painting instr. Vt. Inst. Life Long Learning Elder Hostel, Stowe, 1992—; painting instr. C.C. Vt., 1997—. Ski instr. Stowe Mt. Resort, 1990—; mem. visual arts com. Helen Day Art Ctr., Stowe, 1988—; membership campaign chmn. Meml. Art Gallery of U. of Rochester, Rochester, 1971; chmn. art divsn. PBS Channel 21 Auction, Rochester, 1972. Mem. Nat. Watercolor Soc. (signature mem.), No. Vt. Artists, Profl. Ski Instrs. Am. (cert. level II). Avocations: skiing, hiking, tennis, reading, windsurfing. Office: Stowe Hollow Studio 288 Upper Pinnacle Rd Stowe VT 05672-4529

BEACH, NANCY ANN HELEN, special education educator, educator; b. Kansas City, Kans., Nov. 10, 1944; d. Charles Andrew and Victoria Virginia (Handzel) Nugent; divorced; children: Cathe, Denise, Michelle. AA, East Los Angeles Coll., 1964; BS, Calif. State U., L.A., 1966; postgrad., UCLA, 1966-70. Cert. English teaching credential (life). Tchr. Calif. Pub. Schs., San Gabriel Valley, 1966-77; recreation therapist State of Calif., Pomona, 1966-67; recreation supr. City of Baldwin Park (Calif.), 1967-70; restaurant owner Baldwin Park, 1977; instr. English So. Bay Coll., Baldwin Park, 1984-89; instr. English and success skills Eldorado Coll., West Covina, Calif., 1989-90; tchr. blind and retarded spl. edn. Los Angeles County Schs., 1990—. Author: Reading Skills, 1971. Bd. dirs. pub. rels. com. CAP, El Monte, Calif., 1960-64. Democrat. Avocation: race car driving.

BEACH, REGINA LEE, librarian; b. Georgetown, Ohio, Dec. 22, 1963; d. H. LeRoy and R. Jean (Wardlow) B. BSBA, BA, Ohio No. U., 1987; MLS, Kent State U., 1990; MS in Bus. Adminstrn., Miss. State U., 1999. Serials cataloger, libr. U. Mich., Ann Arbor, 1990-92; libr. Allen Correctional Inst., Lima, Ohio, 1993-94; serials cataloger, libr. Miss. State U., Mississippi State, 1994-99; head info. tech., libr. U. Ark., Little Rock, 1999—2001; head tech. svcs. and systems Tex. A&M U., Kingsville, 2001—. Mem. ALA, ASIS, Southeastern Libr. Assn., Ark. Libr. Assn. Avocations: walking, running, swimming, aerobics, camping. Office: MSC 197 Jernigan Libr Tex A&M U Kingsville TX 78363

BEAGLES, DOROTHY BOETTICHER, office administrator, homeopathic consultant; b. Garfield, N.J., Feb. 15, 1937; d. Rudolph Paul and Dorothy (Zibulsky) Boetticher; m. J. Keith Beagles, Apr. 23, 1960; children: Bradley Keith, J. Kevin. BS, Brigham Young U., 1961; D of Homeopathic Medicine, Brit. Inst. Homeopathy, London, 1995. Bd. cert.

naturopathic doctor. Homeopathic cons. Dolosos, Las Vegas, 1986-91; office mgr. Tri-Chiropractic Kinesiology, Las Vegas, 1991—. Instr. Environ. Stress Mgmt. Fellow Brit. Inst. Homeopathy; mem. Internat. Coll. Applied Kinesiology, Am. Naturopathic Med. Assn. Office: Tri Chiropractic Kinesiology 3750 S Jones Blvd Las Vegas NV 89103-2259

BEAL, CAROL ANN, lawyer; b. N.Y.C., Aug. 8, 1962; d. Harry Steven and Margot Sanders; m. Kenneth I. Beal, Dc. 4, 1988; children: Zachary, Eric. BA in Psychology, SUNY, Binghamton, 1983; JD, St. John's U., 1986. Bar: N.Y. 1987, U.S. Dist. Ct. (ea. dist.) Conn. Sr. assoc. A.F. Pennisi, Forest Hills, N.Y., 1986-88, jr. ptnr., 1988-90; ptnr. C.A. Beal, Forest Hills, 1990-93, Beal & Beal, Jericho, N.Y., 1993—. Lectr. on landlord-tenant law, co-operatives and condominums, wills, trusts and estates, 1986—. Named Bus. Woman of Yr., N.Y. State Bus. Adv. Counsel, 2003. Mem. Queens Bar Assn., Landlord Tenant Assn., Nassau Bar Assn., Syosset Tennis Acad. Avocations: tennis, skiing. Office: Beal & Beal 34 Birchwood Park Cres Jericho NY 11753-2343 E-mail: carolabeal@aol.com.

BEALE, GEORGIA ROBISON, historian, educator; b. Chgo., Mar. 14, 1905; d. Henry Barton and Dora Belle (Sledd) Robison; m. Howard Kennedy Beale, Jan. 2, 1942; children: Howard Kennedy, Henry Barton Robison, Thomas Wight. AB, U. Chgo., 1926, AM, 1928; PhD, Columbia U., 1938; postgrad., Sorbonne and Coll. de France, 1930-34. Reader in history U. Chgo., 1927-29; lectr. Barnard Coll., 1937-38; instr. Bklyn. Coll., 1937-39; asst. prof. Hollins (Va.) Coll., 1939-41, Wellesley Coll., 1941-42, Castleton (Vt.) State Coll., 1968-70; vis. assoc. prof. U. Ky., Lexington, 1970-72; professorial lectr. George Washington U., 1983-84. Author: Révellère-lépeaux, Citizen Director, 1938, 72, Academies to Institut, 1973, Bosc and the Exequatur, 1978, The Botanophiles of Angers, 1996; contbg. author Historical Dictionary of the French Revolution, 1985; also articles. Mem. Madison (Wis.) Civic Music Assn. and Madison Symphony Orch. League, 1958—; hon. trustee Culver-Stockton Coll., 1974—. Univ. fellow Columbia U., 1929-30. Mem. AAUW (European fellow 1930-31), Am. Hist. Assn., So. Hist. Assn., Soc. French Hist. Studies, Western Soc. French History (hon. mem. exec. coun.), Am. Soc. 18th Century Studies, Brit. Soc. 18th Century Studies, Reid Hall Club (Paris), Brit. Univ. Women's Club (London), Phi Beta Kappa, Pi Lambda Theta, Phi Alpha Theta, Pi Kappa Delta.

BEALE, SUSAN M. electric power industry executive; Degree, Mich. State U.; law degree, U. Mich. Law Sch. Atty. Consumer Power and So. Calif. Edison; with Detroit Edison, 1982-95; v.p., corp. sec. DTE Energy, 1995—. Mem.: Am. Soc. Corp. Secs., Am. Corp. Counsel Assn. Office: Detroit Edison Co 2002 2nd Ave Detroit MI 48226

BEALL, CYNTHIA, anthropologist, educator; b. Urbana, Ill., Aug. 21, 1949; d. John Wood and J. Alene (Beachler) Beall. BA in Biology, U. Pa., 1970; MA in Anthropology, Pa. State U., 1972, PhD in Anthropology, 1976. Asst. prof. Case Western Res. U., Cleve., 1976—82, assoc. prof. of anthropology, 1982—87, prof. anthropology, 1987—. Co-editor: Jour. of Cross-Cultural Gerontology, 1986—95; contbr. articles to profl. jours. Active Internat. Rsch. Exch. Program, 1990, 1991. Fellow Nat. Program for Advanced Study and Rsch. in China, NAS, 1986—87, 1997; grantee rsch., NSF, 1981, 1983, 1986, 1987, 1993, 1994, 1995, 1997, 2000, 2002, Am. [illegible] 1990, 1986—87, 1993, 1995. Fellow [illegible] Anthropology and Gerontology, Soc. for Study Human Biology, Human Biology Coun. (exec. com. 1989—92, pres. 1992—94), Am. Assn. Phys. Antrhopology (exec. com. 1989—92), Am. Anthrop. Assn., Am. Philo. Soc. Achievements include research in in Peru, Bolivia, Nepal, Tibet, Mongolia and Ethiopia. Office: Case Western Res U Dept Anthropology 238 Mather Memorial Bldg Cleveland OH 44106-7125 E-mail: cmb2@po.cwru.edu.

BEALL, PAMELA HONN, psychologist, consultant; b. Mattoon, Ill., Mar. 24, 1955; d. Kenneth Franklin and Dorothy Marie (Linder) Honn; m. Thomas Allen Beall IV, June 23, 1985; children: Christopher Allen, Brittany Alane. BS in Psychology, Evangel Coll., Springfield, Mo., 1976; MS in Edn., Ea. Ill. U., Charleston, 1979. Nat. cert. counselor; lic. clin. profl. counselor. Community care coord. East Ctrl. Ill. Area Agy. on Aging, Bloomington, 1979-80; outpatient therapist Iroquois Mental Health Ctr., Watseka, Ill., 1981-86, 90-91, cons., part-time outpatient therapist, 1987-89, 91-93; program psychologist Paxaton (Ill.) Community Hosp., 1986-87; coord. good beginnings program Ctr. for Children's Svcs., Danville, Ill., 1987-88; psychol. cons., Milford, Ill., 1993—. Instr. psychology Kankakee (Ill.) C.C., 1981-84, 89, Danville Area C.C., 1983-86; cons. evaluator Dept. Rehab. Svcs., Danville, 1981-85; mem. exec. bd. Tgn. and Edn. Coordinating Com., Champaign, Ill., 1985-93. Vol. reading programs sch. sys. Milford; tchr. religion Milford Christian Ch., 1992—2002, vocal soloist music and drama ministry, 1992—2002. Mem. ACA, Ill. Assn. Mental Health Counselors, Evangel Coll. Alumni Assn. Avocations: hiking, playwriting, costume design, set construction, mentoring. Home: RR 3 Box 52D Milford IL 60953-9431

BEALS, NANCY FARWELL, former state legislator; b. El Paso, July 21, 1938; d. Fred Whitcomb and Katharine Doane (Pier) Farwell; m. Richard William Beals, June 30, 1962; children: Katharine, Robert, Susannah. BA in Polit. Sci., Bryn Mawr Coll., 1960; MA in Teaching, Harvard U., 1961. Group leader Exptl. Internat. Living, Putney, Vt.; jr. high sch. tchr. Winceshter (Mass.) Pub. Schs., 1961-62; high sch. tchr. Hamden (Conn.) Pub. Schs., 1962-64; state rep. Conn. Gen. Assembly, Hartford, 1993—2003. Mem. state adv. coun. on spl. edn., 2000-02. Mem. various local and regional offices PTA, Chgo. and Hamden, 1970-83; local pres., state bd. dirs. LWV, Conn., 1979-92; mem., sec., chmn. Hamden Bd. Edn., 1983-92. Recipient Citizenship award for Conn. Philip Morris Corp., 1992, Hamden Notable award Friends of Hamden Libr., 1986, Children's Hero award Children's Trust Fund, 1995, Disting. Legislator award Conn. Assn. Bds. of Edn., 1998, Master Builder award Habitat for Humanity of Greater New Haven, 2002; named Legislator of Yr. Conn. Libr. Assn., 1994, Caucus of Conn. Dems., 1997, Conn. Coalition on Aging, 2002; Flemming fellow Ctr. for Policy Alternatives, 1995. Democrat.

BEAM, GAIL C. state representative; PhD, U. N.Mex. State rep. dist. 18 State of N.Mex., Santa Fe, 1996—. Vice chair Consumer and Pub. Affairs com. N.Mex. State Legis., Santa Fe, mem. Edn. com. Home: 425 Aliso Dr NE Albuquerque NM 87108 Office: N Mex State Capitol Rm 314C Santa Fe NM 87503

BEAMAN, COLLEEN K. education educator, choreographer; b. Teaneck, N.J., June 18, 1952; d. Fredric Norbert and Dorothy (Greenawalt) Kelly; m. James Russell Beaman, July 31, 1976; children: Brian James, Michael Henry, Kimberly Diane, Patrick Kelly. BFA, U. Ariz., 1974, MEd, 1982, student, 1993—. Tchr. Pace U., N.Y.C., 1969—71; tchr. ESL Casa Grande Union H.S., Casa Grande, 1974—75; head theatre dept. Palo Verde Theatre Tucson Unified Sch. Dist., Tucson, 1975—78; prof. Ctrl. Ariz. Coll., Gila River Reservation, Ariz., 1975; prof. musical theater U. Ariz.; choreographer Tucson Ballet Co.; tchr. math. & sci. Tucson Unified Sch. Dist., 1997—; tchr. of tchrs. U. Ariz., Tucson, 2000—. 2nd v.p. Fred Kelly Dance Studio, Inc., Oradell, NJ, 1970—81; choreographer Miss Am. Pagent, Pima County, Ariz., 1978; co-dir./choreographer So. Ariz. Lighthouse Corp., Tucson, 1984; adj. prof. Pima C.C., Tucson, 1998—; entertainer Scott's Oquange Lake, NY, 1985. Master of ceremonies : Nat. Tap Dance Day awards show, 2000. Founder Fred Kelly Found., 2000—; mem. U. Ariz. Theatre Arts Bd., 1995—. Recipient Ariz. Career Educator award, Ariz. Edn. Assn., 1975, Nat. Best Prodn. award, Intenrat. Thespian Soc., 1977. Mem.: Am. Fedn. Garden Indian Ridge (treas. 1976—), Pima County Bar Aux. (treas. 1976—), Disabled Am. Vets. Aux. (life), Pima County Rep. Club. Republican. Roman Catholic. Home: 3540 N Camino de Vista Tucson AZ 85745-9798

BEAMAN, JOYCE PROCTOR, retired secondary and elementary school educator, writer; b. Wilson, N.C., Apr. 27, 1931; d. Jesse David and Martha Pauline (Owens) Proctor; m. Robert Hines Beaman; 1 child, Robert David. BS, East Carolina Coll., 1951, MA, 1952. English and French tchr. Stantonsburg (N.C.) H.S., 1952-53, Snow Hill (N.C.) H.S., 1953-60, Saratoga (N.C.) Ctrl., 1968-78, French tchr., libr., 1968-72, libr., 1972-78, Elm City (N.C.) Mid. Sch., 1978-82, Spaulding Elem. Sch., Spring Hope, N.C., 1987-92. Mem. Competency Test Commn. N.C., Raleigh, 1983-84. Author: Broken Acres, 1971, All for the Love of Cassie, 1973, Bloom Where You Are Planted, 1975, You Are Beautiful: You Really Are, 1981, Teaching: Pure and Simple, 1998. Recipient Terry Sanford Creativity and Innovation in Edn. state award, 1977. Mem. Kappa Delta Pi, Delta Kappa Gamma (state chmn. 1978-80). Home: 8427 Piney Grove Church Rd Walstonburg NC 27888-9626

BEAN, ROSIE M. volunteer; b. Homer, La., Oct. 31, 1925; d. John T. Bean and Bammer Nolen-Bean. Student, Herzel/Crane City Coll., Northwestern U., 1947—51. Clk. Montgomery Wards, Chgo., 1944—47, Fed. Govt., Chgo., 1947—49; typist Sigel, Chgo., 1950—51; sec. Fed. Govt., Chgo., 1952—57; group worker Chgo. Youth Ctr., 1957—63, Mercy Newberry Urban League, Chgo., 1963—76, Asian Pac., Chgo., 1976—99. Vol. Boy Scouts Am., Under Writers Consumer Bd., Sr. Citizens Coun. Recipient Silver Beaver award, Boy Scouts Am. Mem.: Nat. Coun. Negro Women (life). Democrat. Baptist. Avocations: cooking, reading, tennis. Home: 1343 N Cleveland #203 Chicago IL 60610*

BEAN, VIRGINIA ANN (GINNY BEAN), marketing executive; b. Grand Rapids, Mich., June 23, 1952; d. John Theunis and Muriel Naughton (Reeves) B.; m. Ronald Eugene Daley, Nov. 7, 1986; children: Jackson Phillip Wesley Daley, Bryan Augustin Daley, Geoffrey Eugene Daley. BA in Theater, Hiram Coll., 1974; MBA, NYU, 1987. Dir. fiscal ops. Cultural Coun. for Arts, N.Y.C., 1980-86; exec. dir. creative mktg. devel. Swiss Colony, Monroe, Wis., 1987—; pres. Ginny's, Monroe, 1995—; v.p. creative mktg. rsch. Swiss Colony, Wis. Creator: (catalog) Ginny's, 1992—. Bd. dirs. Rainbow Day Care, Monroe, 1989-92. Avocations: theater, sewing, parenting. Office: Ginny's 1112 7th Ave Monroe WI 53566-1364

BEANE, JUDITH MAE, psychologist; b. Durham, N.C., Mar. 28, 1944; d. Joseph William Sr. and Antoinette Gwathmey (Dew) B. BA, Campbell U., 1967; MRE, Golden Gate Bapt. Theol. Sem., Mill Valley, Calif., 1972; PhD, Profl. Sch. of Psychology, San Francisco, 1988. Lic. psychologist, Calif. Home missionary So. Bapt. Home Mission Bd., Atlanta, 1967-69; loan officer Coop Credit Union, Corte Madera, Calif., 1969-70; emergency svcs. specialist Community Action Marin, San Rafael, 1976-78; program coord. Marin Treatment Ctr., San Rafael, Calif., 1980-85; church sec. St. Paul's Episcopal Church, San Rafael, 1979-81; psychol. intern Raleigh Hills Hosp., Redwood City, Calif., 1984; psychol. asst. Lic. Psychologists, San Anselmo, Calif., 1985-92; bd. dirs. The Open Door Ministries, Inc., Sausalito, Calif., 1971—, psychologist Mill Valley, Calif., 1992-93; mng. dir. Ch. Resource Svcs. Inc., Lancaster, Va., 1997-2001; deacon Kilmarnock Bapt. Ch., Lancaster, Va., 1996—99. Cons. Ross (Calif.) Hosp., 1991; guest [illegible] 1991 [illegible] domestic violence project [illegible], 2001—02, outreach therapist Youth and Family Svcs., 2002, mental health therapist II, 2002—, No. Neck-Mid. Peninsula Cmty. Svcs. Bd., 1995—97. Recipient award Marin County People Speaking, 1985. Mem. APA (assoc.), Calif. State Psychol. Assn., Am. Counseling Assn., Am. Assn. Christian Counselors. Baptist. Avocations: handcrafts, reading. Home: PO Box 172 Lancaster VA 22503-0172

BEANE, MARJORIE NOTERMAN, academic administrator; b. Adams, Minn., Oct. 3, 1946; d. Matthias Hubert and Anna Helen (Boegeman) Noterman. BA, Marillac Coll., St. Louis, 1969; MEd, U. Ariz., 1979; PhD, Loyola U., Chgo., 1988. Tchr. St. Alphonsus Sch., Prospect Heights, Ill., 1969-73; tchr., asst. prin. St. Raphael Sch., Chgo., 1973-75; prin. St. Theresa Sch., Palatine, Ill., 1975-84; pres. Mallinckrodt Coll. of the North Shore, Wilmette, Ill., 1986-90; sr. v.p. for adminstn. Loyola U., Chgo., 1991—. Trustee Mallinckrodt Coll. of the North Shore, 1980-90; cons. Jospehinum High Sch., Chgo., 1976, St. Viator High Sch., Arlington Heights, Ill., 1986. Mem. History of Women Religious, Fedn. Ind. Ill. Colls. and Univs. (exec. com. 1989), Wilmette C. of C., Sisters of Christian Charity (councilor 1980-88). Rotary. Roman Catholic. Avocations: sewing, bicycling, swimming, travel. Office: Loyola U 820 N Michigan Ave Fl 1 Chicago IL 60611-2196

BEAR, MARCA MARIE, business educator, management consultant; b. S. Bend, Ind., Nov. 29, 1966; BSBA, Ohio State U., 1989, MA in Bus. Adminstrn., 1991, PhD in Bus. Adminstrn., 1992. Assoc. prof. internat. bus. Rochester (N.Y.) Inst. Tech., 1993-2000; assoc. prof. bus. and mgmt. U. Tampa, Fla., 2000—. Dir. Ctr. Internat. Bus. & Econ. Growth Rochester Inst. Tech., 1996—. Mem. editl. bd. Jour. Tchg. Internat. Bus., 1993—, Competitiveness Rev., 1994—, Ann. Edits. Dushkin/McGraw-Hill, 1996—; contbr. articles to profl. jours. Fellow U.S. Dept. Edn., 1991. Mem. Acad. Internat. Bus., Acad. Mgmt., Internat. Mgmt. Devel. Assn., Beta Gamma Sigma. Avocations: guitarist, lyricist, running, skiing. Home: 7209 Granby Dr Hudson OH 44236-1725 Office: U Tampa 401 W Kennedy Blvd Tampa FL 33606-1450

BEARCE, JEANA DALE, artist, educator; b. St. Louis; d. Clarence Russell and Maria Emily Dale; m. Lawrence F. Rakovan, June 7, 1969; children: Barbara Emily, Luke, Francesca. B.F.A., Washington U., St. Louis, 1951; MA, N.Mex. Highlands U., 1954. Vis. artist, various lectureships, India, Pakistan, 1961-62, 93; founder art dept. U. Maine, Portland, 1965, chmn. and dept. rep., 1965-70, asst. prof. art, 1967-70, assoc. prof., 1970-81, prof., 1982—. Reflections South India sabbatical, 1992-93. Exhibited one-woman shows, Portland Mus. Art, Maine, 1958, U. Maine, Orono, 1958, 65, 69, 77, 80, Madras Govt. Mus., India, 1962, Gallery 65, Paris, 1964, Bristol Mus. Art, R.I., 1965, Center Gallery, N.Y.C., 1974, Benbow Gallery, Newport, R.I., 1979, Ctr. for the Arts, Chocolate Ch., Bath, Maine, 1988, USM Gallery, 1991, Main Gallery U. So. Maine, 1991, others, group show, Boston Mus. Art, Library of Congress, Phila. Print Club, Springfield Mus., Mo., Birmingham Mus. Art, Ala., others; represented permanent collection, St. Louis Art Mus., U.S. Edn. Found. in India, New Delhi, U. Maine, Orono and Portland, Bklyn. Mus. Art, Cornell U. Mus. Art, Calif. Coll. Arts and Crafts, Sarasota Art Assn., Fla., Bowdoin Coll., Brunswick, Maine; executed murals, N.Mex. Highlands U., Bowdoin Longfellow-Hawthorn Library, Brunswick, sculpture reliefs, St. Bartholomew, Cape Elizabeth, Maine, St. Charles Ch. Brunswick; retrospective, Maine Ctr. for the Arts, 1988. Mem. artist's com. Maine Art Gallery, 1957-75, 80-87; mem. Maine com. Skowhegan Sch. Painting and Sculpture, 1972— . Recipient various awards; recipient Fannie Cook award People's Competition, 1958, 59; sabbaticals to India: Return to India-Creative Paintings and Printmaking, 1987, South India-Painting and Printmaking, 1993, The Maine to India Series USM Environ. Studies Ctr., 1996, Tibet The Maine Art Gallery, Wiscasset, 1999, Summer Invitational, Ctr. for Maine Contemporary Art, 2002, Maine Coast Artists, Rockport, 2002. Mem. Bowdoin Coll. Mus. Assocs. Home: 327 Maine St Brunswick ME 04011-3310 Office: U So Maine College Ave Gorham ME 04038-1004

BEARD, ANN SOUTHARD, diplomat, oil company executive; b. Denver, Jan. 13, 1948; d. William Harvey and Cora Alice Cornelia (Caldwell) Southard; m. Terrill Leon Beard, Dec. 20, 1970 (div. Oct. 1980); 1 son, Jeffery Leon; m. Rainer G. Froehlich, Feb. 12, 1988 (div. 1992). BA, Willamette U., 1970; postgrad., U. Calif., San Diego, 1981-82. Exec. asst. Kidder Peabody & Co., San Francisco, 1970-72; adminstrv. aide Arthur Anderson & Co., Portland, Oreg., 1972-73; owner, mgr. Beard's Frame Shoppes, Inc., Portland, 1973-80; dir. mktg. Multnomah County Fair, Portland, 1979; owner, CEO Ann Beard Spl. Events, San Diego, 1980-82; pres. Frame Affair, Inc., San Diego, 1982-86, Jack Oil Co., Inc., Greeley, 1982—; chancellor Consular Corps. Coll., Phila., 2002—. Co-owner, v.p. Froehlich Internat. Travel, La Jolla, Calif., 1987-92; chief of protocol Mayor Susan Golding's Office, City of San Diego, 1993-2001; pres., CEO, Diplomacy & Internat. Protocol, San Diego, 2001--; chmn. 1st Nat. Protocol Officers Assn. conf. U.S. Dept. State, Washington; chmn. 1st Internat. Protocol Conf., Ottawa, Can.; advisor to Govt. of China in Beijng for 2008 Summer Olympic Games; v.p. 146 Co., Inc., Greeley, pres. 1970-88; mem. San Diego Consular Corps; lectr. World Trade Ctr., Alaska, Consular Corps, Alaska, 2002; cons. SBA, San Diego, 1980-85; facilitator internat. seminars, workshops, and retreats; prof. internat. bus. diplomacy and protocol, San Diego State U., 2002-. Active Civic Light Opera, Old Globe Theatre; bd. dirs. San Diego Master Chorale, 1981-92; mem. state bd. Miss. Calif. Pageant/Miss. Am., 1982-87; citizens adv. bd. Drug Abuse Task Force/Crime Prevention Task Force, San Diego, 1983-87; campaign coord. Bill Mitchell for City Coun., 1985; candidate for Congress; staff aide to dep. mayor, 1987; mem. Lead San Diego Alumni, 1988, Scripps Hosp. Aux., 1992—, Internat. Visitors Coun., 1993—, San Diego County Commn. on the Status of Women, 1993-96; mem. Internat. Affairs Bd., San Diego, 1993—; chancellor, Consular Corps Coll., Phila., 2001—; founder, nat. chmn. Nat. Protocol Resource Bd., USA, 2002—, founder, internat. pres. Protocol and Diplomacy Internat., U.S., 2002—; bd. dirs. La Jolla Rep. Women Fedn., 1992—. Mem. Am. Mktg. Assn., World Affairs Coun., San Diego C. of C., Save Our Heritage Orgn., Charter 100 San Diego, San Diego 1988 Alumna Willamette U., 1909 Univ. Club (bd. dirs. 1992—, pres. 1996—), Univ. Club San Diego (mktg., devel. and social dir. 1987-88), Pres., Protocol and Diplomacy Internat. (founder), Delta Gamma. Home and Office: 597 So Sierra Ave #59 Solana Beach CA 92075-7621

BEARD, BERNICE TALBOTT, writer, publisher; b. New Windsor, Md., Sept. 1, 1927; d. Edwin Warfield and Henrietta Alice (Snader) Talbott; m. Paul William Beard, Oct. 9, 1948; 1 child, Jeffrey Paul. BA cum laude, Western Md. Coll., 1974; M of Liberal Arts, McDaniel Coll., 2002. Stenographer, sec. Balt. Gas. and Elec. Co., 1944-51; feature writer Carroll County Times, Westminster, Md., 1956-57; asst. dir. admissions, counselor Western Md. Coll., Westminster, 1963-72, exec. asst. to pres. and elected sec. bd. trustees, 1972-89; freelance writer Westminster, 1989—. Campus rep. Am. Coun. Edn. Advancement of Women in Higher Edn., Western Md. Coll., 1979-85, sec. coll. corp., 1985-89. Author: At Your Own Pace: Traveling Your Way in Your Motorhome, 1997, 2d edit., 2003, Alaska at Your Own Pace: Traveling by RV Caravan, 1998, Colorado at Your Own Pace: Travelling by Motorhome with Friends, 1999, 301 Ways to Make RV Travel Safer, Easier, and More Fun, 2001; contbr. articles to mags. and newspapers. Mem. AAUW, Nat. Mus. Women in Arts (charter mem.). Republican. Mem. Ch. of Brethren. Avocations: travel, photography. Fax: (410) 857 3835.

BEARD, DEBORAH FAYE, accounting and finance educator; b. Caruthersville, Mo., Mar. 20, 1951; d. Roy Howard Jones and Alice Jewel (Chism) Jones Brock; m. Daniel Howard Beard, May 24, 1975; children: Brian Daniel, Laura Elizabeth. BS in Sec. Edn., S.E. Mo. State, 1973, MA in Tulsa, 1971, PhD in Bus. Adminstrn., U. Ark., 1987. CMA, 1989. Instr. [illegible] 1973-76, grad. asst. U. Ark., Fayetteville, 1981-84; instr., asst. prof. S.E. Mo. State U., Cape Girardeau, 1976-91, assoc. prof., 1991—, chmn. dept., 1991—2002. Mem. Golf Adv. Bd., 1998. Contbr. articles to profl. jours. Recipient Faculty Mem. of Yr. award Acctg. and Fin. Club, 1994, Hometown Hero award, Hardees/KGMO, 1994. Mem. Midwest AAA (steering com. 2003—), Mo. Soc. CPA's, Mo. Assn. Acctg. Educators (sec.-treas. 1994-2003), Inst. Mgmt. Accts. (faculty adv. 1995-2002), Phi Delta Kappa (v.p. membership 1992-94, pres. 1994-95), Phi Kappa Phi (pres. 2002-03). Baptist. Avocations: golf, reading.

BEARD, ELIZABETH LETITIA, physiologist, educator; b. New Orleans, Apr. 2, 1932; d. Howard Horace and Irene (Handley) B. BA in Biology, Tex. Christian U., 1952, BS in Med. Tech., 1953, MS in Med. Tech., 1955; postgrad., Smith Coll., 1953-54, Vanderbilt U., 1954-55; PhD in Animal Physiology, Tulane U., 1961. Instr. dept. biol. scis. Loyola U., New Orleans, 1955-58, asst. prof., 1958-62, assoc. prof., 1962-68, prof., 1969—, chmn. premed. com., 1978—; rsch. assoc. dept. physiology Sch. Medicine Tulane U., New Orleans, 1960-63, prof. biology med. reinforcement and enrichment program, 1968-94. Vis. prof. dept. physiology and biophysics Med. Sch. Harvard U., 1983-84, dept. neuropharmacology Scripps Rsch. Inst.,, La Jolla, Calif., spring 2001; vis. scientist Am. Indian Rsch. Opportunities Programs at Mont. State U., 1994. Contbr. articles on rsch. in physiology to profl. pubs. Project rev. com. New Orleans Health Planning Coun., 1974-77, bd. dirs., 1975-78, soprano soloist Holy Name of Jesus Ch., 1978—, pres. sch. bd., 1976-79; grad. rsch. com. La. chpt. Am. Heart Assn., 1970-72, 81-83, undergrad. rsch. com., 1978-81, 89-93; active Met. Mus. Art, New Orleans Mus. Art; participant med. mission Christian Med. and Dental Soc., Tepic Navjarit, Mex., 1993, La Esperanza, Honduras, 1994-95; with Med. Ministry Internat., Muisine, Ecuador, 1996, Tena, Ecuador, 1997, Med. Ministry Internat., San Jose de Los Matas, Domincan Rep., 1998, Riobamba, Ecuador, 1999, Otovalo, Ecuador, 2000, Lima, Peru, 2002, Latacunga, Ecuador, 2003. NIH grantee, 1962-64, 67-69, La. Heart Assn. grantee, 1966-67, Edward Schleider Found. grantee, 1974-77, New Orleans Cancer Assn. grantee, 1962-63; Libby Rsch. fellow Sch. Medicine Tulane U., 1961. Mem. AAUP, AAAS, Am. Physiol. Soc., Soc. Exptl. Biology and Medicine, Sigma Xi. Office: 6363 St Charles Ave New Orleans LA 70118-6143 Home: # 22 6363 Saint Charles Ave New Orleans LA 70118-6143 Business E-Mail: Beard@Loyno.edu.

BEARD, LILLIAN B. MCLEAN, pediatrician, consultant; b. N.Y. d. Johnie Wilson and Woodie (Durden) McLean; m. Delawrence Beard. BS, Howard U., 1965, MD, 1970. MD, 1970. Pvt. practice pediat. Lillian M. Beard, Washington, 1973—; assoc. prof. pediat. George Washington U., 1983—; asst. prof. cmty. medicine Howard U., 1983—; contbg. editor Good Housekeeping Mag., N.Y.C., 1989-95; health adv. WUSA-TV, Washington, 1993-95; health and med. contbr. ABC-TV, Washington, 2000—04. Comm. cons. to industry including: Nestle Nutritional Products; mem. bd. dirs. Nat. Women's Econ. Alliance, 1993-2000, Children's Hosp., 1993-2002. Recipient Disting. Leadership award Nat. Assn. Equal Opportunity in Higher Edn., 1993, Disting. Svc. award Nat. Med. Assn., 1990, Hall of Fame in Medicine award, 1994, Healthy Babies Project "Making a Difference" award, 1995, Howard U. Alumni Achievement award, 1996. Fellow Am. Acad. Pediat.; mem. Nat. Med. Assn., Am. Acad. Pediat. (physician recognition awards 1993—). Home: 10517 Alloway Dr Potomac MD 20854-1662 Office: 10801 Lockwood Dr Ste 260 Silver Spring MD 20901

BEARD, PATRICIA CLAIRE, minister, apparel designer; b. CommercE, Tex., Jan. 27, 1944; d. Herbert Alton and Laura Helen Stanford; m. Wayne Forrest Beard, Jr., Sept. 14, 1963; 1 adopted child, Trina Lynn Anderson. Student, Bus. Computer Sys., 1968; A in Practical Theory, Christ for the Nations Inst., 1978. 25 mastered competition pieces level Nat. Piano Competition. Keypunch oper. and supr. various maj. oil and banking cos., Dallas and Houston, 1968—76; min. Full Gospel Chs. and Min. Internat., Dallas, 1978—; owner, designer Cana Creations Design Co., Lake Dallas, Tex., 1980—. Costumer, head costumer Scarborough Renaissance Faire, Waxahachie, Tex., 1995—2000; lifestyle and family counselor Cana Creations, Dallas and Lake Dallas, 1980—. Precinct del. Dallas County Dem. Conv., 1988; alternate state del. Dallas County Rep. State Conv., Dallas, 1988; entertainer, singer USO, Dallas, 1960—62. Scholar, East Tex. State

U., 1962—63. Republican. Avocations: needlecrafts, painting. Home: # 14 501 E Hundley Dr Lake Dallas TX 75065-2673 Office: Cana Creations Ste 14 501 E Hundley Dr Lake Dallas TX 75065 Business E-Mail: pcbeard@centurytel.com.

BEARE-ROGERS, JOYCE LOUISE, former research executive; b. Pickering, Ont., Can., Sept. 8, 1927; d. Frederick John and Sarah May (Michell) Beare; m. Charles Graham Rogers, Dec. 30, 1961; 1 child, Anne Catherine. BA, U. Toronto, Ont., 1951, MA, 1952; PhD, Carleton U., Ottawa, Ont., 1966; DSc (hon.), U. Man., Winnipeg, Can., 1985, U. Guelph, Ont., 1993. Rsch. assoc. U. Toronto, 1952-54; instr. Vassar Coll., Poughkeepsie, 1954-56; chemist Food, Drug Directorate, Ottawa, 1956-65; rsch. scientist Health Can., Ottawa, 1965-75; rsch. mgr. Bur. Nutritional Scis., Ottawa, 1975-91. Adj. prof. U. Ottawa, 1980-92; cons. Food and Agrl. Orgn. UN, 1992-94; Hilditch lectr. U.K., 1994; trustee Nat. Inst. Nutrition (Can.), 1997-99. Editor: Methods for Nutritional Assessment of Fats, 1985, Fat Requirements for Development and Health, 1988; contbr. articles on dietary fats to profl. jours. Decorated Order of Can.; recipient Queen's Jubilee medal Govt. of Can., 1977, Medaille Chevreul award Inst. Corps Gras, 1984, Crompton award McGill U., 1986, Normann medal German Assn. for Fat Rsch., 1987, Commemorative medal for 125th Anniversary of Fedn. of Can., 1992, Queen's Golden Jubilee medal 2002. Fellow: Am. Inst. Nutrition, Royal Soc. Can. (panelist on food biotechnology 2000—01, hon. treas. 2000—04); mem.: Can. Biochem. Soc., Can. Soc. for Nutrition Scis. (pres. 1984—85, Bordon award 1971, McHenry award 1993), Internat. Soc. Fat Rsch. (pres. 1991—92), Am. Oil Chemists Soc. (pres. 1985—86, Lifetime Achievement award Can. sect. 1995). Avocations: hiking, canoeing, cross-country skiing, reading. Home: 41 Okanagan Dr Ottawa ON Canada K2H 7E9 E-mail: jbrogers@sympatico.ca.

BEASLEY, BARBARA STARIN, sales executive, marketing professional; b. Nashville, Dec. 31, 1955; d. Donald Francis and Martha Murry (Bridges) S.; m. Johnny Mark Beasley, Oct. 22, 1983; children: John Thomas, Cara Nicole. BFA, So. Meth. U., 1976. Cert. strategic mktg. mgmt., Harvard Bus. Sch. Producer Bill Stokes Assn., Dallas, 1976-80; Mary Kay Cosmetics, Inc., Dallas, 1980-93; sr. v.p. mktg., 1987-89; exec. v.p. sales, 1990-93; sr. v.p. mktg. Nest Entertainment, Dallas, 1994-99, sr. v.p. sales and mktg., 1999-2000; freelance writer, 2000—. Mem. Leadership Tex., 1986. Avocation: birdwatching.

BEASLEY, MARY CATHERINE, home economics educator, administrator, researcher; b. Portersville, Ala., Nov. 29, 1922; d. Albert Otis and Beulah Green (Killian) Reed; m. Percy Wells Beasley, Dec. 15, 1956 (dec. Dec. 1958). BS in Home Econs., Bob Jones U., 1944; MS, Pa. State U., State College, 1954, EdD, 1968. Tchr. Geraldine and Collinsville (Ala.) High Sch., 1944-45; vocat. home econs. tchr. Glencoe (Ala.) High Sch., 1945-48, Washington County High Sch., Chatom, Ala., 1948-51; home econs. tchr. Homewood Jr. High Sch., Birmingham, Ala., 1958-60; asst. supr. and subject matter specialist Ala. Dept. Edn., Montgomery, 1951-57; asst. prof. Samford U., Birmingham, 1960-62; instr. U. Ala., Tuscaloosa, 1951, asst. prof. then assoc. prof., 1962-68, dir. continuing edn. in home econs., 1968-84, prof., 1984-88, prof. emeritus consumer sci. Coll. Human Environ. Sci., 1988—. Author: (with others) Human Ecological Studies, 1986. Pres. Joint Legis. Coun. of Ala., 1973-75; dir. On Your Own Program, 1970-80; v.p. bd. dirs. Collinsville Cemetery Assn., 2000-02, pres., 2002—. Recipient Creative Programming award Nat. U. Extension Assn., 1979, Women of Achievement award, 2000; named N.E. Ala Woman of Distinction, Girl Scouts North Ala., Inc., 2002. Mem. Am. Home Econs. Assn. (chmn. rehab. com. 1973, 75, leader 1986), Southeastern Coun. on Family Rels. (pres. 1982-84, Disting. Svc. award 1988), Ala. Home Econs. Assn. (pres. 1961-63, leader 1985), Ala. Coun. on Family Rels. (pres. 1981-83, Disting. Svc. award 1987), Altrusa Club of Tuscaloosa (pres. 1988-89, exec. bd. Ft. Payne/DeKalb 1989-93, corr. sec. 1995-96), Collinsville Study Club (v.p. 1992-94, pres. 1996-98, 2002--, reporter 1998-2000, parliamentarian 2000-2002), Ala. Federated Womens Clubs (dir. dist. II 1999-00), Alpha Delta Kappa (treas. Tuscaloosa chpt. 1973-75), Phi Upsilon Omicron, Kappa Omicron Nu. Republican. Baptist. Home: PO Box 680596 Fort Payne AL 35968-1606

BEASLEY, MAURINE HOFFMAN, journalism educator, historian; b. Jan. 28, 1936; d. Dimmitt Heard and Maurine (Hieronymus) Hoffman; m. William C. McLaughlin, May 20, 1966 (div. 1969); m. Henry R. Beasley, Dec. 24, 1970; 1 child, Susan Sook. BA in History, U. Mo., 1958; MS in Journalism, Columbia U., 1963; PhD in Am. Civilization, George Washington U., 1974. Edn. editor Kansas City (Mo.) Star, 1959—62; staff writer Washington Post, 1963—73; from asst. prof journalism to prof. U. Md., College Park, 1975—87, prof., 1987—, grad. dir. Coll. Journalism, 2000—02; sr. lectr. Fulbright Jinan U., Guangzhou, China, 2000. Author: Eleanor Roosevelt and the Media: A Public Quest for Self-Fulfillment, 1987; author: (with others) Women in Media, 1977, The New Majority, 1988, Taking Their Place! Documentary History of Women and Journalism, rev., 2002 (Outstanding Acad. Books Choice, 1994, award Text and Academic Authors Assn., 2004); editor: White House Press Conferences of Eleanor Roosevelt, 1983; co-editor: Voices of Change: Southern Pulitzer Winners, 1978, One Third of a Nation, 1981 (hon. mention Washington Monthly Book award, 1982), Eleanor Roosevelt Encyclopedia, 2000 (Editor's Choice award Booklist, 2001); mem. adv. bd. Am. Journalism, 1983—, Jour. Mass Media Ethics, —, Mass Com. Rev., —; corr. editor: Journalism History, 1995—; contbr. articles to profl. jours. Violinist Montgomery County Symphony Orch., 1975—, Washington Conservatory Orch., 2001—; pres. Little Falls Swimming Club, Inc. 1988-89; bd. dirs. Sino-Am. Ctr. for Media Tech. and Tng., 2000—. Gannett Tchg. Fellowships Program fellow, 1977, Pulitzer Travelling fellow Columbia U., 1963; Eleanor Roosevelt studies grantee Eleanor Roosevelt Inst., 1979-80, Arthur Schlesinger rsch. fellow and grantee Roosevelt Inst., 1998; named one of nation's outstanding tchrs. of writing and editing Modern Media Inst. (Poynter) and Am. Soc. Newspaper Editors, 1981, most outstanding woman U. Md. Coll. Park Pres. Commn. on Women's Affairs, 1993; recipient Haiman award Speech Comm. Assn., 1995, Founders Disting. Sr. Scholar award AAUW Ednl. Found., 1999, Columbia U. Sch. Journalism Alumni award, 2000, Smith-Cotton H.S. Hall Fame award, Sedalia, Mo., 2000, Alumni award U. Mo., 2004. Mem.: AAUW (v.p. Coll. Pk. br. 2002—04), Am. Journalism Historians Assn. (pres.-elect 1988—89, pres. 1989—90, Kobre award for lifetime achievement 1997, Rsch. Paper award named in her honor 1998), Internat. Assn. Mass. Comms. Rsch., Soc. Profl. Journalists (chair nat. hist. site com. 1986—87, bd. dirs. Washington chpt. 1988—90, pres. 1990—91, dir. region 2, nat. bd. dirs. 1991—92, Disting. Local Svc. award 1994, First Amendment award with others 1998), Assn. Edn. in Journalism and Mass Comms. (sec. history divsn. 1986—87, vice-head 1987—88, head history divsn. 1988—89, chair profl. freedom and responsibility 1990—91, exec. com. 1990—91, nat. pres. elect 1992, pres. 1993—94, leader People-to-People delegation to China and Hong Kong 1994, exec. com. 1994—95, Outstanding Contbn. to Journalism Edn. award 1994, Disting. Leadership award 2001), Nat. Press Club, Women in Comms., Am. News Women's Club (bd. govs. 2001—03), Orgn. Am. Historians, Am. Hist. Assn., Omicron Delta Kappa, Phi Beta Kappa. Democrat. Unitarian Universalist. Home: 4920 Flint Dr Bethesda MD 20816-1746 Office: U Md Coll Journalism College Park MD 20742-7111 Office Phone: 301-405-2413. Business E-Mail: mbeasley@jmail.umd.edu.

BEATON, MEREDITH, enterostomal therapy clinical nurse specialist; b. Danvers, Mass., Oct. 5, 1941; d. Allan Cameron and Arlene Margaret (Jerue) Beaton; m. William Paul Hollingsworth, Nov. 19, 1983 (div.); 1 stepchild, Brendon R. Diploma, R.I. Hosp. Sch. Nursing, Providence, 1968; BS in Nursing, U. Ariz., 1976; MS in Human Resource Mgmt., Golden Gate U., 1984; postgrad., U. Tex., 1988; EdD, U. N.Mex., 1995; MS in Nursing, U. Phoenix, 1998. Cert. enterostomal therapy nurse, health edn. specialist. Commd. ensign USN, 1968, advanced through grades to lt. comdr., 1979, charge nurse, 1968-88; command ostomy nurse, head ostomy clinic Naval Hosp. Portsmouth, Va., 1985-88; pres., CEO Enterostomal Therapy Nursing Edn. and Tng. Cons. (ETNetc), Rio Rancho, N.Mex., 1989-99; mgr. clin. svcs. western area Support Systems Internat., Inc., Charleston, S.C., 1990-92; pres., CEO, [illegible] Internat., Inc., Rio Rancho, N.Mex., 1992—2001; sr. cons. enterostomal therapy nursing, edn., & tng. cons.; dir./provost N.Mex. Sch. Enterostomal Nursing, Rio Rancho, 1996-2000; enterostomal therapy nurse, clin. nurse specialist, educator Presbyn. Health Care Svcs., Albuquerque, 1992-95; sr. cons. Enterostomal Therapy Nursing Edn. & Tng. Cons. A Divsn. of Paumer Assocs., Rio Rancho, N.Mex., 1995—2001. Dir./provost N.Mex. Sch. ET Nursing, Rio Rancho, 1995—2000; clin. svcs. mgr. Paper Pak Products Inc., 2000—02; sch. nurse Colinas del Norte Elem. Sch., Rio Rancho Pub. Schs. Sys., N.Mex., 2002—; lectr. in field. Reviewer: RN Mag. Mem. adminstrv. bd. Baylake United Meth. Ch., Virginia Beach, 1980-83; chmn. bd. deacons St. Paul's United Ch., Rio Rancho, moderator, 2001-02, also vice moderator; active Am. Cancer Soc.; mem. adv. bd. Keep Rio Rancho Beautiful, 1998-2003; bd. dirs. Assn. Advancement of Wound Care, 1998-2002. Mem. Wound, Ostomy and Continence Nurses Soc. (nat. govt. affairs com., govt. affairs com. Rocky Mountain region, newsletter editor, pub. rels. com., regional pres. 1989-93, nat. sec. 1994-95), United Ostomy Assn., World Coun. Enterostomal Therapists (mem. editl. bd. 2003-), N. Mex. Health Care Assn., N. Mex. Assn. for Home Care, N.Mex. Assn. Sch. Nurses, N. Mex. Assn. for Continuity of Care, Assn. Advanced Wound Care (bd. dirs.). Republican. Avocations: hot air ballooning, gourmet cooking, flower arranging, interior design. E-mail: meredith60@earthlink.net.

BEATON, REBECCA ANDREA, psychotherapist; b. West Covina, Calif., Dec. 3, 1964; d. Allen Ethan and Joan Delores (Graybill) Brogan; m. Robert Gifford Beaton II, Sept. 4, 1993. BA Human Philosophy & Cultural Geography, U. Calif., Santa Barbara, 1986; MS in Cmty. Counseling, Ga. State U., 1995, specialist in edn., 1996, PhD in Counseling Psychology, 2000. Health counselor Bragg Health Sci., Santa Barbara, Calif., 1986-87; counselor intern Anxiety Disorders Inst./Atlanta Ctr. for Eating Disorders, 1994-95; counselor intern employee assistance program Lockheed Aero. Sys. Co., Marietta, Ga., 1994-95; psychotherapist Anxiety Disorders Inst. Atlanta, 1995-98; pvt. practice Ctr. for Psychotherapy and Healing Arts, 1998-2000; psychology resident Counseling and Testing Ctr. U. Ga., 1999-2000; pvt. practice Atlanta, 2000—. Grad. rsch. asst. Ednl. Rsch. Bur., Ga. State U., Atlanta, 1993-94, dept. counseling and psychol. svcs., 1993-96; therapy group leader Trauma Abuse and Resource Program, Atlanta, 1995-98; psychotherapist Atlanta Ctr. for Eating Disorders, Altanta, 1995-98; growth group leader Ga. State U., Atlanta, 1995-98, adj. faculty counseling and psychol. svcs. dept. and Counseling Ctr., 2000--; trainer Wellness Inst., 1997-2000; process group leader for med. interns Ga. Bapt. Med. Ctr., 1998-99; presenter in field. Contbr. articles to profl. jours. Vol. counselor Ga. Mental Health Inst., Atlanta, 1991-93; vol. rape crisis ctr. counselor, legal liaison Grady Meml. Hosp., Atlanta, 1992-98. Mem.: ACA, APA (divsn. 17, divsn. 38, divsn. 30), Assn. for Transpersonal Psychology, Am. Ednl. Rsch. Assn., Lic. Profl. Counselors Assn. Ga. (licentiate; bd. dirs., ethics chair 2001—). Avocations: wildlife photography, hiking, gardening, mountain bike riding, bird watching. Office: Bdlg 7 Ste 200 1827 Powers Ferry Rd SE Atlanta GA 30339-5621

BEATTIE, ANN, writer; b. Washington, Sept. 8, 1947; d. James and Charlotte (Crosby) B.; m. Lincoln Perry. BA, Am. U., 1969; MA, U. Conn., 1970; L.H.D. (hon.), Am. U., 1983. Vis. asst. prof. U. Va., Charlottesville, 1976-77, vis. writer, 1980; Briggs Copeland lectr. English Harvard U., Cambridge, Mass., 1977. Author: Chilly Scenes of Winter, 1976, Distortions, 1976, Secrets and Surprises, 1979, Falling In Place, 1980, Jacklighting, 1981, The Burning House, 1982, Love Always, 1985, Where You'll Find Me, 1986, Alex Katz, 1987, Picturing Will, 1990, What Was Mine, 1991, My Life Starring Dara Falcon, 1997, Park City: New & Selected Stories, 1998, Perfect Recall, 2000, The Doctor's House, 2002. Recipient Disting. Alumnae award Am. U., 1980, award in lit. Am. Acad. and Inst. Arts and Letters, 1980, PEN/Malamud award for excellence in short fiction, 2000; Guggenheim fellow, 1977. Mem. Am. Acad. and Inst. of Arts and Letters (v.p. lit., 1989-99), PEN, Authors Guild. Office: care Janklow and Nesbit 445 Park Ave New York NY 10022-2606

BEATTIE, DIANA SCOTT, biochemistry educator; b. Cranston, R.I., Aug. 11, 1934; d. Kenneth Allen and Lillian Francis (Barton) Scott; m. Benjamin Howard Beattie, June 30, 1956 (div. 1975); children: Elizabeth, Sara, Rachel, Ruth; m. Robert Nathan Stuchell, Feb. 6, 1976 (div. 1991). BA, Swarthmore Coll., 1956; MS, U. Pitts., 1958, PhD, 1961. Research assoc. U. Pitts., 1961-67, VA Hosp., Pitts., 1967-68; faculty Mt. Sinai Sch. Medicine, N.Y.C., 1968-85, prof. biochemistry, 1976-85; prof., chmn. dept. biochemistry W.Va. U. Sch. Medicine, Morgantown, 1985-2001, chmn. dept. biochemistry and molecular pharmacology, 2001—. Mem. grad. faculty biomed. sci. CUNY, 1968-86, biochemistry, 1971-85, biology, 1974-85; mem. grad. faculty biochemistry W.Va. U. Sch. Medicine, Morgantown, 1985—; vis. prof. U. Louvain, Belgium, 1982, U. Nairobi, Kenya, 1993, Shandong U., China, 2000; mem. ad hoc biochemistry study sect. NIH, 1976-77, 79-81, mem. phys. biochemistry study sect., 1981-85, 1993-97; chmn. phys. biochemistry study sect., 1983-85, 1995-97; mem. metabolic biology panel NSF, 1986-89; mem. basic sci. merit rev. panel VA, 1989-92. Contbr. articles to profl. jours.; mem. editorial bd. Archives of Biochemistry and Biophysics, 1975-78, 85-2000, Jour. Bioenergetics, 1975—. Recipient award Met. N.Y. chpt. Assn. for Women in Sci., 1979; grantee NSF, 1970-92, 97—2001, NIH, 1966—; Fogarty internat. fellow, 1982, Fulbright fellow, 1993. Mem. Am. Soc. Biol. Chemists (membership com. 1987-89), Am. Soc. Cell Biology, Biophysics Soc., Assn. Med. Sch. Depts. Biochemistry (exec. com. 1989-92, pres.-elect 1995, pres. 1996), Am. Assn. Med. Schs. (coun. acad. socs. 1989-2001, adminstrv. bd. 1994-99, chair 1998), Nat. Bd. Med. Examiners (biochemistry test com. 1991-93, chair 1994-95, cell biology test com. 1998-2001, mem. adv. com. for med. sch. programs 2003—), Nat. Caucus Basic Biomed. Chairs (vice chair 1991—). Home: 324 Dream Catcher Cir Morgantown WV 26508-9473 Office: WVa U Sch Medicine Dept Biochemistry Morgantown WV 26506 E-mail: dbeattie@hsc.wvu.edu.

BEATTIE, STEPHANIE SHANNON, social worker; b. Greenville, S.C., Aug. 19, 1968; d. Jerry Nelson and Judith Farley Beattie. BS, Presbyn. Coll., Clinton, S.C., 1990; MA in Counseling, Webster U., 1997, MA in Human Resources and Devel., 2003. Residential counselor Luth. Family Svcs., Pelzer, SC, 1990—92; drug/alcohol counselor Methodone Clinic, Greenville, 1992—94; social worker Dept. Social Svcs., Greenville, 1994—. Mem. consumer adv. bd. Greenville Mental Health, 1999. Roman Catholic. Avocations: golf, snow skiing, landscaping. Office: Dept Social Svcs Ste C 100 Miracle Mile Dr Anderson SC 29621

BEATTS, ANNE PATRICIA, writer, producer; b. Buffalo, Feb. 25, 1947; d. Patrick Murray Threipland and Sheila Elizabeth Jean (Sherriff Scott) B. BA with honors, McGill U., Montreal, Que., Can., 1966. Contbg. editor National Lampoon mag., N.Y.C., 1970-74; writer Saturday Night Live NBC, N.Y.C., 1975-80; creator, prodr. Square Pegs CBS, Los Angeles, 1982-83; co-exec. prodr. A Different World NBC, Los Angeles, 1987-88; exec. prodr. The Stephanie Miller Show, 1994-95. Writer, creative cons. Saturday Night Live 25th Ann. Spl., 1999; exec. story cons. (WETV) Committed, 2000-01; head writer WGA Awards, 2004; adj. prof. writing divsn. Sch. Cinema-TV, U. So. Calif., 2003-05. Co-editor: (humorous books) Titters, 1976, Saturday Night, 1977; co-author: (humorous books) Titters 101, 1984, The Mom Book, 1986; author book for Broadway mus. Leader of the Pack, 1985; humor columnist L.A. Times, 1997-98. Mem. AFTRA, SAG, Writers Guild Am. (award 1976, 77, 2001), Dirs. Guild Am., Women in Film, Dramatists Guild, NATAS (2 Emmy awards, 6 Emmy award nominations 1975-80, 2000).

BEATTY, BETTY JOY, library educator; b. Columbus, Ohio, Mar. 25, 1926; d. Lee E. and Gladys (Heffner) Howard; m. James Auerhan Hecht, May 6, 1950 (dec. July 9, 1974); children: James Auerhan (dec.), Timothy Lee, David Arthur; m. Benjamin M. Beatty, Dec. 19, 1975 (dec. Oct. 1997). BFA, Ohio State U., Columbus, 1947, MA, 1948. Branch librarian Warder Public Library (now Clark County Library), Springfield, Ohio, 1957-59; librarian, teacher Shawnee H.S., Springfield, 1959-66; acquisition librarian Wittenberg U., Springfield, 1966-72, head, technical svcs., 1972-84, acting dir. univ. libraries, 1983-84, assoc. prof. emerita, 1992—. Mem. bd. dirs. Faculty Devel. Orgn., Springfield, 1975-78 pres. Wittenberg U. Fed. Credit Union, Springfield, 1979-81, sec. 1984-87; pres. AAUP, Springfield, 1980. Treas. Springfield Symphony Women's Assn., 1974-76; sec. bd. dirs. Touch of Love AIDS Support, Springfield, 1988-95. Mem. Alpha Chi Omega Sorority (pres. 1964-66, sec. 1985-87, 94-96). Democrat. Roman Catholic. Avocations: painting, reading. Home: 615 Piney Branch Dr Springfield OH 45503-2315

BEATTY, FRANCES, civic worker; b. Chgo., Apr. 17, 1940; d. Pasquale and Rose (Brunetti) Calomeni; m. Robert Alfred Beatty, Aug. 24, 1963; children: Bradford, Roxanna Beatty Goebel. BA, Northwestern U., 1961; MA, U. Chgo., 1967. Tchr. math. Proviso West High Sch., Hillside, Ill., 1961-66. Active Oak Brook Dist. 53 Sch. Bd., 1979-85; mem. women's bd. Field Mus. Natural History, Chgo., 1985—, mem. founders coun., 1988—, treas. women's bd., 1991-93; mem. governing bd. Chgo. Symphony, 1985-92; trustee Chgo. Symphony Orch., 1992—; mem. women's bd. Ravinia Festival, Highland Park, Ill., 1987—, Northwestern U., Evanston, Ill., sec. women's bd., 1999—, mem. libr. bd., 1990-95; mem. women's bd. U. Chgo.; mem. coun. Wellness House, Hinsdale, Ill., 1994; com. mem. Chgo. Humanities Festival, 1999—. Mem.: Merit Sch. Music, Alumnae of Northwestern U. (pres. 1996—98), The Antiquarian Soc. Art Inst. Chgo., John Evans Club, Woman's Athletic Club Chgo. (3d v.p. 1985—87, 1st v.p. 1992—94, pres. 1994—96).

BEATTY, JOYCE, state representative; b. Dayton, Ohio; married; 2 stepchildren. BA in Speech, Ctrl. State U.; MS in Counseling Psychology, Wright State U.; PhD, Pacific Western U. Mgmt. cons.; state rep. dist. 27 Ohio Ho. of Reps., Columbus, 1999—, mem. civil and comml. law, fin. and appropriations, health, and rules and reference coms., mem. agr. and devel. subcom., asst. minority leader. Named Linden Pride Grand Marshall, 2000. Mem.: NAACP, Am. Soc. Tng. and Devel., Columbus Urban League (chmn. bd. dirs.), Ohio Legis. Black Caucus, Dem. Women's Caucus, The Links, Inc. (nat. endowment chair), United Negro Coll. Fund, Delta Sigma Theta. Democrat. Office: 77 S High St 14th fl Columbus OH 43215-6111

BEATY, DEBORAH JOYCE, music educator; b. Erick, Okla., July 16, 1952; d. Freddie Milton Gage and Mary Lee Henry - Gage; m. Fields Tom Beaty, July 3, 1971; children: Amy Joy Beaty - DeLeon, Julie Lynne Beaty - Knutson. BME, S.W. Okla. State U., Weatherford, 1974, MME, 1987. K-8 vocal music tchr. Crawford (Okla.) Pub. Schs., 1980—82; k-4 vocal music tchr. Cheyenne (Okla.) Pub. Schs., 1982—85, k-12 vocal music tchr., 1986—90, Mangum (Okla.) Pub. Schs., 1992—94; 1-12 vocal music tchr. Merritt Pub. Schs., Elk City, Okla., 1994—. Mem. and accompanist Western Okla. Choral Dirs., 1974—2003. Mem. and accompanist Singing Churchwomen of Okla., 1990—2003, 1st Bapt. Ch., Las Vegas, Nev., Cheyenne, Prairie View, Okla., Elk City. Republican. Avocations: walking, motorcycling, travel, theater, piano. Home: 301 Lakeshore Dr Elk City OK 73644

BEATY-GUNTER, SHARON E. music teacher; b. Marietta, Ga., Aug. 3, 1953; d. James Webster and Reba Jo (Marshall) Earley; m. Marcus Eugene Gunter, May 28, 1993; 1 child by previous marriage, John Kevin Beaty. Degree in Vocal Performance, Ga. State U., Atlanta; PhD in Music Edn., U. Wexford. Sr. ct. clk. Fulton County, Atlanta, 1971-74; adminstrv. sec. Northside Hosp., Atlanta, 1975-77; auto analyst Cigna Ins., Atlanta, 1977-82; office trainer Travelers Ins., Atlanta, 1992-95; dir., owner Strings & Keys, Inc., Cumming, 1976—. Office mgr., pers. dir. Main Source Germany, Cumming, 1995-96; music dir. Bethelview Meth. Ch., Cumming, 1982; youth choir dir. North Lanier Bapt. Ch., Cumming, 1989-91. Author, creator vocal instrn. video Share the Song in Your Heart, 1997; composer sacred inspirational music. Entertainment assoc. March of Dimes, Cumming, 1999, Am. Cancer Soc., Cumming, 1997-99, City of Cumming Meml. Day Svcs., 1996-98, City of Cumming Vietnam Moving Wall, 1998. Recipient award Literary Competition, Ga. Bd. Edn., 1971, Outstanding Choral award City of Cumming, 1998. Mem. Nat. Assn. Music Makers, Nat. Piano Tchrs. Guild, Music Tchrs. Nat. Assn., Ga. Music Tchrs. Assn. Office: Gunter Music Studio Inc 2210 Goldmine Dr Cumming GA 30040-4322

BEAUBIEN, ANNE KATHLEEN, librarian; b. Detroit, Sept. 15, 1947; d. Richard Parker and Edith Mildred Beaubien; m. Philip Conway Berry, Feb. 7, 2004. Student, Western Mich. U., 1965-67; BA, Mich. State U., 1969; MLS, U. Mich., 1970. Reference libr., bibliographic instr. U. Mich. Libr., Ann Arbor, 1971-80, dir. MITS, 1980-85, head coop. access svc., 1985—. Author: Psychology Bibliography, 1980; co-author: Learning the Library, 1982; contbg. articles to profl. jour., editor, conf. proc., 1987. Mem. vestry St. Clare's Episcopal Ch., Ann Arbor, 1986—89, 2002—03; pres. Ann Arbor Ski Club, 1978—79. Recipient Woman of Yr. Award, Ann Arbor Bus. and Profl. Women's Club, 1982; Disting. Alumnus Award; Sch. Info. and Libr. Studies, U. Mich., 1987. Mem. ALA, Assn. Coll. and Rsch. Librs. (pres. 1991-92). Avocations: skiing, bicycling, ballroom dancing. Office: U Mich Libr 106 Hatcher Grad Libr Ann Arbor MI 48109

BEAUDET-FRANCÈS, PATRICIA SUZANNE, photography editor; b. Chgo., Aug. 6, 1951; d. André Marcel and Helen Gertrude (Joiner) B.; m. Gérard Jean-Pierre Frances, June 27, 1997. Sr. photography editor Playboy Enterprises Inc., Chgo., 1970—. Contbg. photographer Rolling Stone Illustrated History of Rock and Roll, 1992; rschr., photo editor Playboy (photographs pub. 50 yrs.): The Playboy Book: Forty Years, 1994, Playboy: 50 Years The Photographs Featured; prodr. CD Instrumental Journey, 2002. Democrat. Roman Catholic. Avocations: photography, traveling, cinema, workouts, reading. Home: PO Box 31351 Chicago IL 60631-0351 Office Phone: 312-373-2715. E-mail: pattyb@playboy.com.

BEAUDRY, DIANE FAY PUTA, medical quality management executive; b. Manitowoc, Wis., Mar. 6, 1947; d. Ruben William and Gertrude Katherine (Novak) Puta. BSN, Alverno Coll., 1971; MS in Ednl. Adminstrn., U. Wis., Milw., 1979, PhD in Urban Edn., 1991. Staff nurse St. Mary's Hosp., Milw., 1971-72, St. Anthony's Hosp., Milw., 1972-74; nurse coord. Pvt. Initiative in PSRO, Wis., 1974-75; insvc. instr. Deaconess Hosp., Milw., 1975-77, insvc. coord., 1977-81; dir. nursing staff devel./quality assurance Good Samaritan Med. Ctr., Milw., 1981-84, dir. quality assurance, 1984-85, dir. utilization mgmt., 1985-88; mgr. quality mgmt. Sinai Samaritan Med. Ctr., Milw., 1988-89, dir. med. staff svcs. and quality mgmt., 1989-97, dir. quality mgmt., 1997—2002, St. Luke's Med. Ctr., 1997—. Author: (with others) Interdisciplinary QA: Issues in Collaboration, 1991; author poem. Mem. Nat. Assn. for Healthcare Quality, Alverno Coll. Alumnae Assn., U. Wis. Alumni Assn., Delta Epsilon Sigma, Kappa Gamma Pi. Avocations: ballroom dancing, motorcycle riding. Home: 11047 N Riverland Ct # 36W Mequon WI 53092-4900 also: St Luke's Med Ctr PO Box 2901 Milwaukee WI 53201-2901 Office Phone: 414-649-7138. E-mail: diane.beaudry@aurora.org.

BEAUFORD, SANDRA, registered nurse, data processing executive; b. N.Y.C., Feb. 7, 1950; d. Ethel Beauford; children: Gary, Michael, David Sumerlin-Beauford. A.S, Manhattan C.C., 1974; BSN, Herbert H. Lehman Coll., 1976. CCRN, cert. parish nurse. Critical care mgr. Botsford Hosp., Farmingnton, Mich., 1990—92; asst. mgr. Henry Ford Hosp., Detroit, 1992—96; clin. mgr. Taylor Ambulance, Detroit, 1996—98; o.r. quality coord. Oakwood Hosp., Dearborn, Mich., 1999—; parish nurse Oakwood Hosp. Greater Grace Temple, Dearborn, Mich., 2000—01. Author: On The Road to Your New Beginning, 2000 (Bravo award, 2001, 2002). Facilitator customer svc. enhancement program Oakwood Hosp., 2002—. Lt. USAF, 1974—78, Mclaughin Air Force Base. Mem.: Am. Heart Assn. (logistic com.), American Coll. Cardiology, Soc. Thoracic Surgeons. Pentecostal. Avocations: basketball, photography, reading. Office: 18101 Oakwood Blvd Dearborn MI 48124-4089 Personal E-mail: beaufors@oakwood.org.

BEAUMONT, MARY, artist, art educator; b. Phila., Nov. 24, 1956; d. Frank B. Stepler, Jr. and Margaret Beaumont Lapp. Diploma, Pa. Acad. Fine Arts, 1984; student, Frudakis Acad., 1983—87. Art tchr. Phila. Sketch Club, 1986—89, Delaware County C.C. Cultural Programs, Media, Pa., 1987—91, Chester County Art Assn., West Chester, Pa., 1991—. Co-author: West Chester: The First 200 Years, 1999. Mus. guide Chester County Hist. Soc.; bd. mem. Manayunk Art Ctr., Phila., 1991. Mem.: The Plastic (Arts) Club, Fellowship Pa. Acad. (bd. mem. 1989—91, Purchase award 1987), Phila. Sketch Club (R. Tait McKenzie medal 1988). Democrat. Mem. Soc. Of Friends. Home: PO Box 257 West Chester PA 19381-0257

BEAUMONT, PAMELA JO, marketing professional; b. Valentine, Nebr., July 30, 1944; d. William Henry and Phyllis Faye (Zersen) (Mott) Bostrom; m. Fred H. Beaumont, Apr. 17, 1971 (div. May 1981). BS in Bus., U. Colo., 1966, MBA, 1968. Asst. product mgr. Ore-Ida Foods, Boise, Idaho, 1969-71, product mgr., 1971-73, sr. product mgr., 1973-75, gen. mgr. sales and mktg. services, 1975; v.p. consumer affairs Albertson's Inc., Boise, 1975-76, v.p. mktg., 1976-87; ptnr. Forrest/Beaumont & Andrus, Boise, 1987—; chair Garden City Urban Renewal Agy., 1995—. Home: 9304 N Pebble Falls Ln Boise ID 83714 Office: 4948 Kootenai St Ste 201 Boise ID 83705-2082 E-mail: pamb@spro.net.

BEAUMONTE, PHYLLIS ILENE, retired secondary school educator; b. Seattle, Dec. 15; d. Albert Hendrix and Bessie Dorothy (Duford) Ratcliff; m. Pierre Marshall Beaumonte, Mar. 12, 1962 (div. Aug. 1974). BA in Polit. Sci., U. Wash., 1973, BA in Editl. Journalism, 1973, MPA, 1975; postgrad., N.W. Theol. Union, Seattle, 1990-92; M in Pastoral Studies/Theology, Seattle U., 2001. Cert. tchr. K-12 Wash. Adminstrv. intern Office of the City Coun., Seattle, 1974; guest lectr. Pacific Luth. U., Tacoma, 1975; tchr. Hebrew Acad., Seattle, 1979; instr./tchr. Seattle Ctrl. C.C., 1988; tchr. Seattle Pub. Schs., 1980—2000; coord. hs Bus. Ptnrs. in Pub. Edn., Seattle, 1989-92; social studies chairperson Rainier Beach HS, Seattle, 1992—2000; ret., 2000. Cons. RA Beau Enterprises, Seattle, 1987—; participant Ctr. R&D in Law-Related Edn. Wake Forest U., Winston-Salem, NC, 1994; adv. com. Wash. State Commn. Student Learning, Social Studies Acad. Learning Requirements, 1994—; part-time faculty South C.C., Seattle, 1998—99. Author: (poetry) Satyagraha; author, editor: Roses and Thorns, 1994, writer, pub.: Parent Guardian Handbook: A Guide to Understanding Public Education and Standardized Testing, 2002. Mem. King County Women's Polit. Caucus, Seattle, 1993—; v.p. Ch. Women United, Wash. and Idaho, 1976—78, pres., 2002—, Seattle Ch. Women United, 2001 [illegible] 1972—74; Seattle edn. sch. rep. Seattle Tchrs. Union, 1983—85; alumni advisor Grad. Sch. Pub. Affairs U. Wash., 1994—; pres. Black Heritage Soc. Wash. Scholar Minority Journalism, U. Wash., 1972. Mem.: NAACP (mem. exec. bd., v.p. state conf. Wash., v.p. state conf. Oreg., v.p. state conf. Alaska, state chair edn., Daisy Bates Adv. award), Edn. Social and Pub. Svcs. Assn. (pres.), Nat. Coun. Social Studies, Nat. Coun. History Edn. (cert. of appreciation 1993), Internat. Soc. Poets (life Internat. Poet of Merit award 1993), Mus. History and Industry, Sigma Gamma Rho. Baptist. Avocations: singing, writing, reading, teaching. Home: 10012 61st Ave S Seattle WA 98178-2333

BEAUSOLEIL, DORIS MAE, federal agency housing specialist; b. Chelmsford, Mass., Jan. 9, 1932; d. Joseph Honorious and Beatrice Pearl (Smith) Beausoleil. Student, State Tchrs. Coll., Lowell, Mass., 1949-51; BA in Sociology and Psychology, Goddard Coll., Plainfield, Vt., 1954; MA in Human Rels., NYU, 1957; postgrad., CUNY, N.Y.C., 1988-97. With divsn. human rights State of N.Y., N.Y.C., 1960-69, housing dir., 1966-68; housing cons. Nat. Com. Against Discrimination Housing, N.Y.C., 1969—70, Edwin Gould Found., N.Y.C., 1970—71; human resources cons. interfaith housing strategy com., housing cons. Fedn. Prot. Welfare Agys., Inc., N.Y.C., 1971—72; housing cons., 1972—74; equal opportunity compliance specialist N.Y./N.J. HUD, N.Y.C., 1975—2000, fed. women's program coord., 1975—79, pub. trust specialist, 2000—. Br. chief Title VI Sect. 109 compliance divsn. fair housing and equal opportunity region II HUD, N.Y.C., 1979—84, coord. sect. III N.Y./N.J., 1998—. Mem. adv. panel Housing Mag., 1979. Founding mem. N.Y. State HUD Com.; cons., examiner N.Y. State Civil Svc. Commn., 1970—93. Mem.: Citizens Housing and Planning Coun., Nat. Assn. Human Rights Workers, Goddard Coll. Alumni Assn. (sec. 1988—90), Rep. Bus. Women's Club (pres. 1985—88, bd. dirs. 1989—91). Unitarian Universalist. Home: 392 Central Park W Apt 14N New York NY 10025-5868 Office: 26 Federal Plz Rm 3532 New York NY 10278-0004 E-mail: doris_m._beausoleil@hud.gov.

BEAVER, BONNIE VERYLE, veterinarian, educator; b. Mpls., Oct. 26, 1944; d. Crawford F. and Gladys I. Gustafson; m. Larry J. Beaver, Nov. 25, 1972 (dec. Nov. 1995). BS, U. Minn., 1966, DVM, 1968; MS, Tex. A&M U., 1972. Instr. vet. surgery and radiology U. Minn., 1968-69; instr. vet. anatomy Tex. A&M U., College Station, 1969-72, asst. prof., 1972-76, assoc. prof., 1976-82; prof. Tex A&M U., College Station, 1982-86, prof. vet. small animal medicine and surgery, 1986—, chief medicine, 1990-99. Mem. vet. medicine adv. com. HEW, 1972-74, nat. adv. food and drug com., HEW, 1975, com. on animal models and genetic stocks NAS, 1984-86, 87-89, panel on microlivestock NRC, 1986-87, task force on animal use study Inst. Lab. Animal Resources, 1986, adv. com. for Pew Nat. Vet. Edn. Program, Pew Charitable Trusts, 1987-92, 10th symposium on Vet. Med. Edn. Com., 1988-89; Frank K. Ramsey lects. Iowa State U., 2004. Mem. editl. bd. Applied Animal Ethology, 1981-82, 83-84, VM/SAC, 1982-85, Applied Animal Behavior Sci., 1982-84, 84-86, 86-88, 88-2000, Bull. on Vet. Clin. Ethology, 1994-1999, Jour. Am. Animal Hosp. Assn., 1995—; contbr. articles to profl. jours. V.p. Brazos Valley Regional Sci. and Engring. Fair, 1974[00bf] 83, dir., 1983-85; bd. dirs. Brazos Valley unit Am. Cancer Soc., 1976-83, v.p., 1976-83. Named Citizen of Week, The Press, 1981, Outstanding Woman Vet. of 1982, Disting. Practitioner, Nat. Acads. Practice; recipient Friskies PetCare award Am. Animal Hosp. Assn., 2001, Bustad Human-Animal Bond award, 2001, Elanco Disting. Lectr. award, 2002, Frank K. Ramsey Lectr. award, 2004. Mem.: AVMA (exec. bd. 1997—2003, chair exec. bd. 2001—02, pres. 2004—, Animal Welfare award 1996), AAAS, Am. Horse Coun., Am. Quarter Horse Assn., Tex. Palomino Exhibitors Assn., Palomino Horse Breeders Am. (v.p. 1983—88, treas. 1984—85, pres.-elect 1988—89, pres. 1989—90), Nat. Acad. Practice, Am. Coll. Vet. Behaviorists (chair organizing com. 1976—91, pres. 1991—96, charter diplomate 1993—, exec. dir. 1996—), Animal Behavior Soc., Am. Assn. Bovine Practitioners, Am. Assn. Equine Practitioners, Am. Assn. Vet. Clinicians, Am. Vet. Soc. Animal Behavior (pres. 1975—80), Am. Animal Hosp. Assn., Brazos Valley Vet. Med. Assn., Tex. Vet. Med. Assn. (3d v.p. 1990, 2d v.p. 1991, 1st v.p. 1992, pres.-elect 1993, pres. 1994), Phi Delta Gamma (pres. 1974—75), Phi Zeta (nat. pres. 1979—81), Sigma Epsilon Sigma, Phi Sigma, Delta Soc. Office: Tex A&M Univ Coll Vet Medicine Vet Small Animal Medicine & College Station TX 77843-4474

BEAVERS, KAREN MARJORIE, small business owner; b. Laurel, Md., Nov. 2, 1947; d. James Walter and Marjorie Lois (Fullerton) McQuaid; m. George Edward Kowalski, Aug. 30, 1969 (div.); children: Eddie, Charlie, Bill; m. Edward George Beavers Jr., Feb. 14, 1991; stepchild, Edward. Student, Art Instrn. Sch., 1970; BS in Behavioral Sci., U. Md., 1994; postgrad., Loyola Coll., 1995. Receptionist Capitol Software, Laurel, 1988-89; new accounts devel. staff Focus Telecom., Burtonsville, Md., 1989-90; CSR & tng. asst. Encore Mktg. Internat., Lanham, Md., 1990-91; office mgr. Computer Image Svc., Laurel, 1991-94; pres., owner Gifts & More, Laurel, 1994-95, Gifts & More, Inc., Laurel, 1993-2000. Author: Tippy and Freckles Great Adventures, 1996; The Development of Children's Behavior, several theories of parenting, author of poetry. Hot-line counselor Domestic Violence Ctr., Howard County, Md., 1993-94; vol. art tchr., playground and lunchroom staff St. Marys of the Mills, Laurel; team mother Prince George Gymnastics, Beltsville, Md.; actress Ann Martin's Drama Guild, Laurel. Mem. APA (grad. affiliate), AAUW, Internat. Soc. Poets, Psi Chi. Roman Catholic. Avocations: gardening, doll collecting, antique shopping.

BEBKO-JONES, LINDA, state legislator; Student, Erie Bus. Acad., 1964-65. Legal sec. Silin, Eckert & Burke, Erie, Pa., 1964-66; office mgr., legal sec. Atty. Joseph Knowacki, Erie, 1975-83; adminstrv. asst. Hon. A. Buzz Andrezeski Pa. Senate, Erie, 1984-89; dir. Women Against Sexual Harassment, Erie, 1989-92; caseworker Community House for Women, Erie, 1990-92; caseworker Hon. Harris Wofford U.S. Senate, Erie, 1991-92; mem. Pa. Ho. Reps., Harrisburg, 1993—, sec. mil. and vets. affairs, mem. health and welfare com., state govt. com., aging and youth com., task force on violence as health concern, mem. firefighters caucus, freshman nonpartisan caucus, Northwest caucus, substance abuse caucus, tax reform caucusm women's caucus. One on one reporter Presque Isle Mag., 1991-92; mem. adv. bd. Soldiers and Sailors Home; resident asst. Edmund Thomas Detention Hall; Erie County coord. Children's Lobby Kid Pix Program; apptd. to Pa. Commn. for Women; coord. Pa. Children's Legis. Conf./Coun. State Govts.; del. East Side Fedn. Mem. Dem. Exec. Com. Erie County, Dem. Women's Coun. Erie County; trainer in-svc. tng. program Mcpl. Police Officer's Edn. and Tng. Commn. Recipient Erie Woman of Yr. award, 1994. Mem. Am. Bus. Women's Assn., Slovsk Nat. Club (life). Home: 460 E 26th St Erie PA 16504-2802 Office: Pa Ho of Reps 112 South Office Bldg PO Box 202020 Harrisburg PA 17120-2020

BECERRA, ROSINA MADELINE, social welfare educator; b. San Diego, Mar. 6, 1939; d. Ray and Ruth (Albanez) B. BA, San Diego State U., 1961, MSW, 1971; PhD, Brandeis U., 1975; MBA, Pepperdine U., 1981. Mathematician United Tech. Corp., Sunnyvale, Calif., 1962-63; with Peace Corps, Washington, 1963-65; probation officer San Diego County Probation Office, 1965-69; research assoc. Brandeis U., Waltham, Mass., 1973-75; assoc. prof. UCLA, 1975-81, prof., 1981—, acting dean, 1989 90, assoc. dean, 1986-89, 92, dean, 1992—, assoc. vice chancellor faculty diversity, 2002—. Author: Defining Child Abuse, 1979, Hispanic Veterans Seek Health Care, 1982, The Hispanic Elderly, 1984 (Choice Mag. Book award 1986); editor: Hispanic Mental Health, 1981; contbr. articles to profl. jours. Ford Found. award, 1980.

BECERRA-FERNANDEZ, IRMA, electrical engineer, researcher, educator; b. Havana, Cuba, Mar. 28, 1960; came to U.S., 1960; d. Daniel Ivan Becerra and Irma Maria Peiteado; m. Vicente L. Fernandez, June 29, 1985; children: Anthony John, Nicole Marie. BSEE, U. Miami, Coral Gables, Fla., [illegible] tng., Fla., 1982. Engr., corp. instr. Fla. Power and Light, Miami, 1983-90; rsch. assoc. Fla. Internat. U., Miami, 1990—94, dir., vis. prof. Coll. Engring., 1994—98, asst. prof. Coll. Bus. Adminstrn., 1998—2003, assoc. prof., 2003—. Scholar Nat. Hispanic Scholarship Fund, Miami, 1982, Unico Nat. Soc., Miami, 1978; Women's History Month honoree Coalition Hispanic Am. Women, 1997. Mem. IEEE, Assn. Cuban Engrs. (v.p. 1994-96, pres. 1996, Student of Yr. 1993, faculty advisor), Soc. Women Engrs. (faculty advisor), Eta Kappa Nu (v.p. 1981-82, Most Valuable Mem. 1982), Tau Beta Pi, Phi Kappa Phi. Roman Catholic.

BECHLER, SUSAN KEIFER, music educator; b. Sept. 12, 1950; d. William L. and Rosalyn C. Keifer; m. Karl P. Bechler. MusB, Fredonia U., 1972. Cert. Music & Elem. Edn. Tchr. N.Y., 1972. Music tchr. Hendrick Hudson Ctrl. Sch., Montrose, NY, 1972—80; string tchr. Victor Ctrl. Sch., Victor, NY, 1980—. Mem.: Am. String Tchr. Assoc. (ASTA), Nat. Sch. Orch. Assoc.(NSOA), N.Y. State Sch. Music Assn., Suzuki Assn. Am. Avocations: gardening, reading, fiddling. Office: Victor Central School High St Victor NY 14564

BECHTEL, KATIE ELLEN, art educator, artist, writer; b. Indpls., Aug. 3, 1948; d. Robert Howard and Jacqueline LaRue Burford; m. Terrance Edward Bechtel, Apr. 10, 1971; children: Ashleigh Elizabeth, Graham Hudson, Molly Kathryn. BS in Art Edn., Ind. U., 1970. Cert. tchr. Ind., 1970, Colo., 1974, Ariz., 1993. Art specialist Ea. Hancock Sch. Corp., Wilkinson, Ind., 1970—72; ind. word processor Denver, 1973—78; word processor Streich Lang, PA, Phoenix, 1988—93; art tchr. Scottsdale (Ariz.) Unified Sch. Dist., 1993—94; mid. sch. art tchr. Paradise Valley Unified Sch. Dist., Phoenix, 1994—. Rsch. grant group mem. Ariz. State U., Tempe, 1999—; adv. bd. Paradise Valley Unified Sch. Dist., 1996—97. Painting, interior drawings for book, Access Your Brain's Joy Center; author: Expanding Horizons; editor (co-author): You Can Do It, The Next Step; author: Knot Just another Book; editor (co-author): Sounds of Clay. Chair Odyssey of the Mind, Phoenix, 1986—92; fundraiser Casa Shelter for Battered Women, Phoenix, 1999—2002, Cystic Fibrosis, Phoenix, 1993. Mem.: Ariz. Art Edn. Assn. (mid. sch. rep. 2000—03, workshop presenter 1995—, Mid. Sch. Art Educator of Yr. 2002), Nat. Art Edn. Assn. (workshop presenter 1996—, Pacific Region Med. Sch. Art Educator of Yr. 2002), Free Soul (sec. bd. 1998—2003). D-Liberal. Avocations: reading, knitting, swimming, travel, crocheting. Home: 5032 E Earll Dr Phoenix AZ 85018

BECHTEL, SHERRELL JEAN, psychotherapist; b. Birmingham, Ala., Sept. 23, 1961; d. Lewis Eugene and Sarah Rozelle (Sherrell) B. BS in Social Work, U. Ala., Birmingham, 1989; MSW, U. Ala., Tuscaloosa, 1990; DD, World Christianship Ministries, Fresno, Calif., 1997. Cert. addiction specialist; cert. group psychotherapist; lic. clin. social worker, Tenn., Ga.; ordained minister. Vol. counselor Planned Parenthood, Birmingham, 1986-88; intern Bradford Adult Chem. Dependency, Birmingham, 1989; rsch. staff asst. U. Ala., Tuscaloosa, 1989-90; intern counselor Bradford Adolescent Chem. Dependency, Birmingham, 1990; primary counselor The Crossroads, Chattanooga, 1990-92; owner S. J. Bechtel LCSW, CAS, Chattanooga, 1991—. Rschr. Ala. Commn. Youth, Montgomery, 1989-90; trainer Legal and Jud. Aspects Child Welfare, Decatur, Ala., 1989; presenter Ala. Victim Compensation, Mobile, 1990; speaker Limestone Correctional Facility, Huntsville, 1990; lectr. Grad. Sch. Social Wk., Tuscaloosa, 1990, U. Tenn., Chattanooga. Spkr. Victims of Crime and Leniency, Tuscaloosa, 1990; vol. ARC Disaster Mental Health/Direct Svcs.; broadcaster Power and Victory Ministry, 2000—; subcom. mem. Atty. Gen. Alliance Against Drug Abuse, Birmingham, 1989; mem. Tenn. Coun. on Children and Youth-Legis./Policy; planning com. Holistic Health Retreat, Birmingham, 1988. Mem. NASW (pres. student orgn. 1986-89), Tenn. Alcohol Drug Assn., Jewish Community Ctr., Phi Kappa Phi. Avocations: tennis, woodworking, softball, bowling, water sports. Office: 109A Jordan Dr Chattanooga TN 37421-6732 E-mail: sb4jc1@aol.com.

BECK, BARBARA NELL, elementary school educator; b. Corpus Christi, Tex., Oct. 25, 1940; d. Marshall Joseph and Madie Ann (Spence) Robertson; m. Joel J. Beck, June 23, 1973. BA, Baylor U., 1964. Tchr. Killeen (Tex.) Ind. Sch. Dist., 1964-2001. Sunday sch. tchr., 1967—, co-treas., 2000—, ch. clk. First Bapt. Ch. of Nolanville. Mem. NEA, Tex. State Tchrs. Assn. (life), Tex. Assn. for the Gifted and Talented, Killeen Edn. Assn. (treas., past pres., bd. dirs.), Clifton Park PTA (past treas.). E-mail: jbeck1@hot.rr.com.

BECK, CHRISTINE SAFFORD, photographer, publisher, volunteer; b. Phila., July 10, 1943; d. Elisha Jr. and Margaret (Tramdack) Safford; m. Leif Christian Beck, Nov. 21, 1964; children: C. Lars, Eric S., Anders. BA in German and French, Queens Coll., 1964; MA in German Lit., Bryn Mawr Coll., 1969; postgrad., N.Y. Inst. Photography. Co-founder, pres. Nat. Jr. Tennis League of Phila., 1969-79; pres., CEO Nat. Jr. Tennis League, N.Y.C., 1979-83; owner, photographer Christine S. Beck Photography, Villanova, Pa., 1990—; pub., owner Prism Light Press, Bryn Mawr, Pa., 1995—; stock photographer Garden Image Agy., Montreal, 1999—2002; v.p. Advisory Publs., 2001—03. Pres. Phila. Tennis Patrons Assn., 1985-95, mem. adv. bd., 1995—; pres. Arthur Ashe Youth Tennis Ctr., Phila., 1985-95; chair adv. coun. Esperanza Health Ctr., Phila., 1994-97. Photographer (books): Beyond Me. Voices of the Natural World, 1993, Spirit of Summit County, Colorado, 1996; producer Broadway Comes to Queens benefit concert, Charlotte, N.C., 1999. Bd. dirs. Habitat for Humanity, Phila., 1988-90; coord. vols. Jimmy Carter Workcamp, North Phila., 1988; chair stewardship campaign Bryn Mawr Presbyn. Ch., 1992; trustee Queens U. Charlotte, N.C., 1995—; trustee Gesu Sch., Phila., 1996—2003, chair devel., 2000-2003, pres., 2003—,; chair fundraising campaign Arthur Ashe Youth Tennis Ctr., 2000—; chair alumni phase fundraising campaign Queens U. Charlotte, N.C., 2000-02; trustee Penn Coun. for Relationships, 2000-02. Recipient Kennedy award Robert F. Kennedy Pro Celebrity Tennis Tournament, 1975, Jimmy Carter Hammer award Habitat for Humanity, 1988, Merit award for women Internat. Tennis Hall of Fame, 1988, Svc. Bowl, U.S. Tennis Assn., 1991, Take the Lead award Girl Scouts of Greater Phila., 1992, First Phila. Youth Tennis Jerome Laroque award, 1999. Mem. U.S. Tennis Assn. Middle States (treas. 1986-89, Mangan award 1990, Coren award 1973), N.Am. Nature Photographers Assn. (charter mem.), Nikon Profl. Svcs. Avocations: golf, tennis, hiking. Office: Prism Light Press 224 Broughton Ln Villanova PA 19085-1914 Home: 6 Deggs Cir Newtown Square PA 19073-1906

BECK, COLLEEN MARGUERITE, archaeologist; b. San Jose, Calif., Feb. 21, 1951; d. William Robert and Willa Rose (Moore) Beck; m. William Keith Kolb; children: William Logan Kolb, Alexa Rose Kolb. BA, U. Calif., Berkeley, 1973, MA, 1974, PhD, 1979. Dir. Agy. for Conservation Archaeology, Eastern N.Mex. U., Portales, 1980-83, asst. prof., 1983-84; rsch. assoc. Lowie Mus. Anthropology, Berkeley, 1985-89; asst. rsch. prof. Desert Rsch. Inst., Las Vegas, 1990-92, dep. dir. quaternary scis. ctr., 1992-98, assoc. rsch. prof., 1993-98, rsch. prof., exec. dir., 1999—. Postdoctoral fellow Carnegie Mus. Natural History, Pitts., 1979-80; mem. N.Mex. Hist. Preservatio Adv. Bd., Santa Fe, 1981-86; mem. San Joaquin County Historic Records Commn., Stockton, Calif., 1986-89. Author: Ancient Roads on the North Coast of Peru, 1979; editor: Views of the Jornada Mogollon, 1984; author articles. Mem. tech. adv. bd. Las Vegas Sch. Dist., 1994-96; mem. tech. adv. bd. Bur. Land Mgmt., 1995 , Las Vegas Historic Preservation Commn., 1996—. NSF fellow, 197-76; Tinker Found. grantee, 1974-77. Fellow Am. Anthropology Assn. (life); mem. Soc. for Am. Archaeology, Nev. Archaeology Assn. (bd. dirs. 1993—, pres. 1995—), Archaeo-Nev. Soc., Nat. Trust for Hist. Preservation, Inst. Andean Studies (life), Nev. State Mus. Hist. Soc. Avocation: piano playing. Office: Desert Rsch Inst 1055 E Tropicana Ave Ste 450 Las Vegas NV 89119-6644

BECK, DORIS OLSON, retired library media director; b. Kingsville, Tex., June 4, 1930; d. Thomas Leon and Estelle (Fosselman) Olson; m. John Roland Beck, Feb. 9, 1951; children: Elizabeth Joan, Thomas Roland, Patricia Lind, John William. BS in Chemistry, Tex. A & I Coll., 1949, BSChemE, 1950; MLS, Wayne State U., 1975. Cert. secondary educator with libr. endorsement, Ariz. Chemist Patterson's Lab., Harlingen, Tex., 1950-51; asst. libr. Tex. A & I Coll., Kingsville, Tex., 1951; chemist U.S. Geol. Svc., Stillwater, Okla., 1951-53; bookkeeper, nurse's aide McKenzie Co. Hosp., Watford City, N.D., 1953-54; math. tchr. Prescott Jr. High, Corpus Christi, Tex., 1954; chemist U.S. Geol. Svc., Columbus, Ohio, 1957-58; math. tchr. Christiansberg (Va.) High Sch., 1967-69; sci. tchr. East Jr. High Sch., Farmington, Mich., 1969-70; sci./math. tchr. Jane Addams Jr. High Sch., Royal Oak, Mich., 1970-78; math support Oakland Vocat. Sch., Royal Oak, 1978-79; head libr. S.W. Bapt. Coll., Pontiac, Mich., 1977-79; libr. media dir. Humboldt (Ariz.) Jr. High, 1979-87, Bradshaw Mt. Jr. High, Dewey, Ariz., 1987-95; ret., 1995. Site based com. Bradshaw Mt. Jr. High Sch., Dewey, Ariz., 1992-95. Vol. ch. libr., 1994-2002, Park View Middle Sch., Prescott Valley, Ariz., 1999—. Mem. Ariz. Libr. Assn., Alpha Delta Kappa. Republican. Baptist. Avocations: reading, needlework, travel. Home: PO Box 26566 3829 N Valorie Dr Prescott Valley AZ 86312

BECK, EMILIE PASCALE, actor, theater director, writer; b. Chgo., June 25, 1967; d. Bernard Beck and Alice Victoria Horevitz, Richard Paul Horevitz (Stepfather) and Sherry Beck(Stepmother); m. John Jacob Arky, Nov. 15, 1963. B in Speech, Northwestern U., 1989. Asst. to pres. production Paramount Studios, L.A., 2000—02; asst. to mng. dir. Center Theatre Group (Mark Taper Forum & Ahmanson Theatre), 2002—. Dir.: (plays) And Let the Skies Fall, 2003 (Critic's Pick, 2003); actor(writer): The Fantastic Lodge, 1991, Rats in the Coffeehouse, 1995, The Velveteen Rabbit, 1993, Chronicle of Piano Woman, 1991, Notebooks of Leonardo da Vinci, 1989, Processions, 1990, Mystery of the 4th Wall, 1989, Godiva, 1988, A Chorus Line, 1987, The Miss Firecracker Contest, 1992, The Merchant of Venice, 1996, Boom Chicago; dir.(writer): The Work of Talk.

BECK, EVA-CAROL, musician; b. San Antonio, Oct. 9, 1938; d. Carl Addison, Jr. and Seldon (Sandlin) B.; m. Jay Kenneth Friedman, 1962 (div. 1974); children: Erika Ann, David Jay. MusB magna cum laude, U. Houston, 1960; postgrad., Yale U., 1960-61; MusM, Ind. U., 1964. Prin. viola Fla. Symphony, Orlando, 1961; viola sect. Lyric Opera, Chgo., 1964-66, 71—, acting asst. viola, 1982; viola sect. Grant Park Symphony, Chgo., 1970—, acting asst. prin. viola, 1981; asst. prin. Symphony II, Chgo., 1989—. Del. Internat. Conf. Symphony Opera Musicians, 1984-97; mem. examining bd. Chgo. Fedn. Musicians, 1986-88; negotiator mems. com. Lyric Opera Orchestra, 1986-88, Grant Park Symphony, 1993. Mem. Mortarboard, Phi Kappa Phi. Democrat. Avocations: fitness, cooking. Home: 831 Hamlin St Evanston IL 60201-3205

BECK, IRENE CLARE, educational consultant, writer; b. N.Y.C., Dec. 18, 1944; d. James E. and Helen (Carroll) Clare; m. William J. Beck, Aug. 9, 1986; children: Daniel, James Chesire. BA, St. Mary's Coll., 1966; MA, Fairfield U., 1977; EdD, U. Rochester, 1982; Grad. Cert. Women's Studies, DePaul U., 1998. Cert. tchr., N.Y. Tchr. Elem. Sch., N.Y.C., 1966-68, Montessori Acad. N.Y., Bklyn., 1968-73; faculty Housatonic Community Coll., Bridgeport, Conn., 1975-77, Nazareth Coll., Rochester, N.Y., 1977-83; faculty dir. Sheppard Pratt Nat. Ctr. Human Devel., Balt., 1983-91; exec. dir. William & Irene Beck Found., 1987—. Cons. Headstart Programs, Rochester, 1980-83, Family Day Care Tng., Rochester, 1980-83; mem. women's studies faculty program DePaul U., 1999—; presenter workshops and seminars. Author: Expect Respect, Let Me Tell You (manuals), (No Hang Ups (telephone audiotape), 1987, In Tune With Teens (booklet), 1990; weekly news col. Parents and Teens, 1987-90; freelance writer, 1986—; contbr. articles to profl. jours.; sr. editor What's Working for Girls in Illinois, 1996-99. Mem. AAUW, Assn. Childhood Edn. Internat. Avocations: hiking, swimming, biking.

BECK, ISABEL HOLDERMAN, psychologist, consultant; b. Boise, Idaho, Mar. 17, 1916; d. Frank John Holderman and Beulah Beatrice Dennis; m. Lester Fred Beck, Dec. 22, 1956 (div. July 1969). AA in Journalism, L.A. Jr. Coll., 1939; BA in Psychology, Occidental Coll., 1941, MA in Psychology, 1949; PhD in Psychology, U. So. Calif., 1959. Cert.

psychologist, Calif.; lic. psychologist, Calif. Pers. technician Lockheed Aircraft, Burbank, Calif., 1943; psychologist L.A. City Schs., 1949-52; counselor, curriculum coord. L.A. Jr. Colls., 1953-66; sr. mem. profl. staff S.W. Regional Lab., Inglewood, Calif., 1966-68; pvt. cons. Inglewood, 1968-70; prof. psychology Santa Barbara (Calif.) City Coll., 1970-73; pvt. practice, 1973-94. Cons. Wexler Films, L.A., 1957-70, KCET-TV, L.A., 1967-69, Calif. State Colls. TV Project, Sonoma, 1974-75, L.A. C.C., 1969. Author: (monograph) Occupational Education: Foundation for a Master Plan, 1969; co-author: (jour.) Ednl. Tech. IX, 1969. Mem. grand jury Santa Barbara County, 1980-81, arts commn., 1985-91; mem. arts adv. com. Santa Barbara City, 1985-89, TV adv. com., 1983-85. Lt. USN, 1943-46. Named Arts Advocate of Yr., Santa Barbara Arts Coun., 1986. Avocation: volunteer work with arts organizations. Home: 2327 Edgewater Way Santa Barbara CA 93109-1922

BECK, LOIS GRANT, anthropologist, educator, author; b. Bogota, Colombia, Nov. 5, 1944; d. Martin Lawrence and Dorothy (Sweet) Grant; m. Henry Huang; 1 dau., Julia Huang. BA, Portland State U., 1967; MA, U. Chgo., 1969, PhD, 1977. Asst. prof. Amherst (Mass.) Coll., 1973-76, Univ. Utah, Salt Lake City, 1976-80; from asst. to assoc. prof. Washington U., St. Louis, 1980-92, prof., 1992—. Author: Qashqa'i of Iran, 1986, Nomad, 1991; co-editor Women in the Muslim World, 1978, Women in Iran from the Rise of Islam to 1800, 2003, Women in Iran from 1800 to the Islamic Republic, 2004. Grantee Social Scis. Rsch. Coun., 1990, NEH, 1990-92, 98, Am. Philos. Soc., 1998. Mem. Mid. East Studies Assn. (bd. dirs. 1981-84), Soc. Iranian Studies (exec. sec. 1979-82, edit. bd. 1982-91, coun. 1996-98). Office: Washington U Dept Anthropology 1 Brookings Dr Saint Louis MO 63130-4899 Office Phone: 314-935-5252.

BECK, MARILYN MOHR, columnist; b. Chgo, Ill, Dec. 17, 1928; d. Max and Rose (Lieberman) Mohr; m. Roger Beck, Jan. 8, 1949 (div. 1974); children: Mark Elliott, Andrea; m. Arthur Levine, Oct. 12, 1980. AA, U. So. Calif., 1950. Free-lance writer nat. mag. and newspapers, Hollywood, Calif., 1959-63; Hollywood columnist Valley Times and Citizen News, Hollywood, Calif., 1963-65; West Coast editor Sterling Mag., Hollywood, Calif., 1963-74; free-lance entertainment writer LA Times, Calif., 1965-67; Hollywood columnist Bell-McClure Syndicate, 1967-72; chief Bell-McClure Syndicate (West Coast bur.), 1967-72; Hollywood columnist NANA Syndicate, 1967-72; syndicated Hollywood columnist NY Times Spl. Features, 1972-78, NY Times Spl. Features (United Feature Syndicate), 1978-80, United Press abroad, 1978-80, Internat. Editors News and Features, Chgo. Tribune/NY Daily News Syndicate, 1980-97; Grapevine columnist TV Guide, 1989-92; creators syndicate, 1997—. Creator, host Marilyn Beck's Hollywood Outtakes spls. NBC, 1977, 78; host Marilyn Beck's Hollywood Hotline, Sta. KFI, LA, 1975-77; Hollywood reporter Eyewitness News, Sta. KABC-TV, LA, 1981, (TV program) PM Mag., 1983-88; on-air corr. E! TV, 1993-99, CompuServe Entertainment Authority, 1994-96, eDrive Internet Authority, 1996-97, e!online Internet Hollywood Authority, 1997—, Compuserve, 2000—, aeNTV.com, 2001-02; author: (non-fiction) Marilyn Beck's Hollywood, 1973, (novel) Only Make Believe, 1988; co-author: Unfinished Lives, What If...?, 1996. Recipient Citation of Merit LA City Coun., 1973, Press award Pub. Guild Am., 1974, Bronze Halo award So. Calif. Motion Picture Coun., 1982. Address: 4926 Delos way Oceanside CA 92056

BECK, RHONDA JOANN, paramedic, educator, writer; b. Hawkinsville, Ga., Apr. 20, 1965; d. Franklin Lamar and Ida (Scarborough) Woodard; m. Gary Wendell Bramlett, Apr. 9, 1983 (div. May 1995); 1 child, Gary Michael Bramlett; m. Kenneth Steve Beck, June 8, 1997. Gen. Banking Degree, Am. Inst. Banking. Cert. BTLS, CPR, PHTLS, ACLS, BLS instr. trainer, emergency med. technician-paramedic, instr. Collateral clk. Bank South, N.A., Perry, Ga., 1986-94; emergency med. technician Taylor Regional Hosp., Hawkinsville, 1993-94; paramedic Med. Ctr. Ctrl. Ga., Macon, 1994-99; emergency med. technician instr., paramedic instr. Ctrl. Ga. Tech. Coll., Macon, 1997—; paramedic Houston Med. Ctr., Warner Robins, Ga., 1997—. Instr. ACLS, Pediat. Life Support, PreHosp. Trauma Life Support, Basic Trauma Life Support, Am. Heart Assn.; reviewer Delmar Thomson, 1999—, Jones & Bartlett, 2000-, GEMS Faculty, 2003-present, Am. Geriatric Soc.; Brady, 2001—. Author: Emergency Care and Transportation of the Sick and Injured, student workbook, AAOS, 8th edit., 2001; pub. author, reviewer: Jones & Bartlett. Vol. firefighter Houston County Vol. Fire Dept., Hayneville, Ga., 1986-95. Recipient Heartsaver award Laerdal Med. Corp., 1994, Vol. Svc. award Am. Lung Assn. Ga., 1995. Democrat. Baptist. Avocations: reading, swimming, exercise, writing, coin collecting. Office: Houston County EMS Warner Robins GA 31093 E-mail: takai_sensei@yahoo.com.

BECK, RONNA LEE, judge; BA, U. Mich.; JD, Yale U., 1972. Law clk. to Judge Theodore R. Newman Jr., 1972-73; staff atty. Pub. Defender Svc., Washington, 1973-77; from assoc. to ptnr. Rogovin, Huge and Lenzner, Washington, 1977-85; pvt. practice Washington, 1985-95; assoc. judge Superior Ct., Dist. of Columbia, Washington, 1995—.

BECKER, BARBARA ANN STULAC (BOBBIE BECKER), small business owner; b. Chgo., Sept. 29, 1938; d. Josef Florian and Dagmar Adrienne Pakonen Stulac; m. Raymond August Becker (div. 1980); children: Raymond August, Jr., Renay Dagmar. AA, Florissant Valley (Mo.) C.C., 1980; BA, U. Mo., St. Louis, 1981. Pvt. instrumental music instr., St. Louis, 1977-80, Dallas, 1981-83, Columbia, Mo., 1984—, Boonville, Fayette, Mo., 1987—; owner Bobbie Becker Music, Franklin, Mo., 1992—, piano tuner, instrument repair profl., 1992—. Mem. Mid-Mo. Music Tchrs. Assn., Mo. State Old Time Fiddlers Assn., Mo. Folklore Soc. Avocations: painting, travel, violin, guitar, piano. Office: Bobbie Becker Music 3764 State Route J Franklin MO 65250-9592

BECKER, BARBARA LYNN, lawyer; b. Nov. 27, 1963; BA, Wesleyan U., 1985; JD, NYU, 1988. Bar: N.Y. 1989. Formerly ptnr. Chadbourne & Parke LLP; now ptnr. Gibson, Dunn & Crutcher LLP, N.Y.C. Mng. editor Rev. of Law and Social Change, 1984-85. Bd. dirs. Urban Pathways, N.Y.C. Mem. Phi Beta Kappa. Office: Gibson Dunn & Crutcher LLP 200 Park Ave New York NY 10166

BECKER, BRENDA L. federal agency administrator; Degree, Mich. State U.; MBA, Ctrl. Mich. U. Former v.p. congl. comm. Blue Cross Blue Shield Assoc.; asst. sec. legis. and intergovt. affairs U.S. Dept. of Commerce, Washington, 2001—. Office: US Dept of Commerce Legis and Intergovt Affairs 14th and Constitution Ave NW Washington DC 20230

BECKER, DOREEN DORIS, medical/surgical nurse; b. Elgin, N.D., May 22, 1944; d. Carl Ruff and Dorothy Buttmann; m. Glenn Alan Watson, Jan. 19, 2002; m. Roy Ernest Becker, June 5, 1964 (dec. Sept. 6, 1993); 1 child, Allen Roy. Degree in Nursing, U. Chgo., 1963. Nurse Columbia Hosp., Grand Forks, ND, 1976—77, surg. nurse, 1977—90; surg. nurse supr. Columbia HCA, Plano, Tex., 1990—92, med. records coder, 1993—2001, Baylor Hosp., Richardson, Tex., 2001—02, Med. City, Dallas, 2002—. Instr. HCA Med. Ctr., Plano, 1990—92. Instr. Red Cross, Braddock, ND, 1966. Recipient Medicorp award, Mott HS, 1962. Methodist. Avocations: marathon running, bicycling, fishing, fossils, rocks. Home: 616 Buffalo Bend Plano TX 75023

BECKER, DOROTHY LORETTA, education educator, librarian; b. Long Beach, Calif., May 27, 1933; d. Francis Ryan and Constance Marie Wolff; m. Paul Hermann Karl Heinz Peter Becker, Feb. 14, 1964 (div. Nov. 1971). BS, U. Calif., L.A., 1954; MLS, San Jose State U., 1981. Tchr. Monterey (Calif.) Peninsula Unified Sch. Dist., 1956—91, reading specialist, cons., 1966-78, sch. libr., 1978-81; supr. student tchrs. Chapman U., Monterey, 1991-99; reference libr. Monterey County Free Librs., Seaside, Calif., 1996—2003. Elder, Stephen min. First Presbyn. Ch., Monterey. Mem. Calif. Ret. Tchrs. Assn., Total Reading Assn. (cons. 1966—), Delta Kappa Gamma Soc. Internat. (Calif. corr. sec. 1993-95, Calif. state exec. sec. 1995-97, Chi state strategic plan ad hoc com. 1995-99, chmn. Chi state bylaws 1999—2001), Chi State Learning Is For Everyone Found. (pres. bd. dirs. 1999-2002, bd. dirs. 1999—). Democrat. Avocations: travel, reading, literacy advocate, flower arranging.

BECKER, GAIL ROSELYN, museum director; b. Long Branch, N.J., Oct. 22, 1942; d. Joseph and Adele (Michelsohn) B. BA, Vassar Coll., 1964. Exhibit project officer U.S. Info. Agy., Washington, 1967-87, chief devel. and prodn. exhibits, 1987-91; exec. dir. Louisville Sci. Ctr. (formerly Mus. History and Sci.), 1991—. Bd. dirs. Louisville Advanced Tech. Coun., 1993-2000, Louisville Com. Fgn. Rels., Main St. Assn., 1998—, Arts and Cultural Attractions Coun., 1999—; active Leadership Louisville. Recipient Presdl. Design awards Nat. Endowment for the Arts, Washington, 1984, 88, 92, Special Achievement award U.S. Info. Agy., Washington, 1988. Mem. Am. Assn. Mus. (bd. dirs. 1994-97), Assn. Sci.-Tech. Ctrs. (bd. dirs. 1992—2003, pres. 1999-2001), Vassar Coll. Alumnae Assn., Rotary. Office: Louisville Sci Ctr 727 W Main St Louisville KY 40202-2681

BECKER, GERALDINE ANN, psychology educator; b. Chgo., Oct. 14, 1945; d. Frank Joseph and Pauline Rose (Pichman) Fiefer; divorced; children: Rhonda Lynn, Patrick Richard. AA, Waubonsee C.C., 1987; BA, No. Ill. U., 1989, MA, 1992, PhD, 1995. Advanced teaching asst. No. Ill. U., DeKalb, 1992-94; asst. prof. Nat.-Louis U., Chgo., 1994—. Adj. faculty Waubonsee C.C., Sugar Grove, Ill., 1993-94; grad. coord. psychology program Nat.-Louis U., 1996—, social sci. rsch., 1992—, student advisor, 1994—; presenter in field. Cons. editor: Jour. Psychology, 1997—. Commr. Planning Commn., Aurora, Ill., 1983-94; bd. dirs. Unit Sch. Dist. #131, Aurora, 1981-85. Mem. Soc. Indsl./Organizational Psychologists, Phi Kappa Phi, Sigma Xi. Democrat. Avocations: reading, computers, friends. Office: Nat-Louis U 18 S Michigan Ave Chicago IL 60603-3200 Home: 2557 Pinehurst Dr Aurora IL 60506-6408

BECKER, GRACE CHUNG, lawyer; b. N.Y.C., Oct. 6, 1969; JD, Georgetown U., 1994; BA, U. Pa., 1991; BSE, U. Pa., Philadelphia, PA, 1991. Law clk. Judge Thomas Penfield Jackson, Washington, 1994—95; assoc. Williams & Connolly, Washington, 1995—96; law clk. Judge James L. Buckley, Washington, 1996—97; trial atty. Criminal Divsn. Dept. Justice, Washington, 1997—99; spl. asst. to Asst. Sec. of Army, U.S. Army, Alexandria, Va., 2000—01; asst. gen. counsel U.S. Sentencing Commn., Washington, 1999—2003; counsel to chmn. Orrin Hatch U.S. Senate Judiciary Com., 2003—. Bd. dirs., exec. v.p. Korean Am. Coalition, Washington, 2001—02. Office: US Sentencing Commn 1 Columbus Cir NE #2-500, South Lobby Washington DC Business E-Mail: gbecker@ussc.gov.

BECKER, HELANE RENÉE, securities analyst, financial executive; b. NYC, May 7, 1957; d. Arnold and Ella Florence (Feldman) Becker; m. George Paul Roukas, Sept. 6, 1980 (div.); children: Samuel Matthew Roukas, Hannah Beth Roukas. BA, Montclair State U., 1979; MBA in Fin., NYU, 1984. Options coord. Donaldson Lufkin & Jenrette, N.Y.C., 1979-81; mktg. coord. E.F. Hutton & Co., N.Y.C., 1981-82; securities analyst Prudential-Bache Securities, N.Y.C., 1982-86; v.p., analyst Drexel Burnham Lambert, N.Y.C., 1986-87; mng. dir., analyst Lehman Bros., N.Y.C., 1987-94, Smith Barney, N.Y.C., 1995-98; sr. v.p., prin. Buckingham Rsch. Group, N.Y.C., 1998—2003; prin., mng. dir. Benchmark Capital Advisors, N.Y.C., 2003—. Spkr. in field. Contbr. Corp. Travel Mag., 1990. Mem. Senate Commn. on Civil Tilt Rotor. Named to Investor All-Am. Rsch. Team, 1985-94, 5 Star Mine Analyst, Best Analyst, Wall St. Jour., 2000, 01. Mem. Soc. Airline Analysts (pres. 1996-98), Profl. Women in Bus., Wings Club, NYU Alumni Assn. NJ, Wyoming Club, Friends of Fencing (pres.). Avocations: skiing, tennis, swimming, golf. Office: Benchmark Advisors 750 Lexington Ave New York NY 10022

BECKER, JOANN ELIZABETH, insurance company executive; b. Chester, Pa., Oct. 29, 1948; d. James Thomas and Elizabeth Theresa (Barnett) Clark; m. David Norbert Becker, June 7, 1969. BA, Washington U., St. Louis, 1970, MA, 1971. CLU, ChFC, FLMI/M, CFA. Tchr. Kirkwood (Mo.) Sch. Dist., 1971-73; devel. and sr. devel. analyst Lincoln Nat. Life Ins. Co., Ft. Wayne, Ind., 1973-77, systems programming specialist, 1977-79, sr. project mgr., 1979-81, asst. v.p., 1981-85, 2d v.p., 1985-88, v.p., 1988-91; pres., CEO The Richard Leahy Corp., Ft. Wayne, 1991-93; pres. Lincoln Nat. Corp. Equity Sales Corp, Ft. Wayne, 1993-94; v.p. portfolio mgmt. group Lincoln Nat. Investment Mgmt. Co., Ft. Wayne, 1994-97; dir. investment mgmt. SVP, 1997—. Contbr. articles to profl. jours. Bd. dirs. Ind. Humanities Coun., Indpls., 1991-96, treas., mem. exec. com., 1994-95, mem. devel. com., 1995-96; bd. dirs. Auburn (Ind.) Cord Duesenberg Mus., 1995—, mem. devel. and exec. com., 1997—. Named Women of Achievement, YWCA, Ft. Wayne, 1986, Sagamore of Wabash, Gov. State of Ind., 1990. Fellow Life Mgmt. Inst. Soc. Ft. Wayne (pres. 1983-84, honors designation 1980); mem. Life Ins. Mktg. Rsch. Assn. (Leadership Inst. fellow, mem. exec. com. 1993-94, mem. fin. svcs. com. 1993-94), Am. Mgmt. Assn., Ft. Wayne C. of C. (mem., chmn. audit-fin. com. 1989—).

BECKER, KARLA LYNN, systems analyst; b. West Point, NY, Nov. 3, 1956; d. Fred D. and Margaret Erika (Buckmann) Spinks; m. Eric Louis Becker; children: Erika Margaret Augusta Ashmore, Eric Robert. BA, Ind. U.-Purdue U. at Indpls., 1982; MS, Ind. U., 1986. Cert. software quality engr. Mgr. Eastside Chiropractic Clinic, Indpls., 1978-80; English tutor univ. div. Ind. U.-Purdue U. at Indpls., 1980-82, composition instr. English dept., 1982-83, tech. writer computing services, 1983-84; tech. writer Ind. U. Adminstrv. Computing, 1984-87; mgmt. info. svcs. cons., writer, support adminstr. Simon Property Group, Indpls., 1987-97; sys. cons. KFORCE-.COM, Indpls., 1997-99; sr. sys. analyst Eli Lilly & Co., Indpls., 1999—. Author: Composing Technical Documents, 2000; contbr. articles, book revs., poems to various publs.; editor: Lit. Jour., Genesis, All-Am. Mag., Am. Collegiate Press Assn., 1983. Mem. Am. Soc. Quality, Soc. Tech. Communication (Cert. of Achievement 1985), Sigma Delta Chi, Pi Lambda Theta. Democrat. Roman Catholic. Avocations: singing, yoga. Office: Eli Lilly & Co Lilly Corp Ctr Drop Code 3118 Ctr Indianapolis IN 46285-0001 Personal E-mail: karla11@hotmail.com.

BECKER, KATHY GAIL, medical/surgical nurse; b. Lebanon, Mo., July 12, 1957; d. Cecil Julius and Mary Eveline (Walters) Newell; m. Randy Lee Waterman, Oct. 15, 1976 (div. 1991); 1 child, Brandon Lee Waterman; m. Michael Lee Becker, Mar. 6, 1992. Lic. LPN, Vo Tech. Sch., Waynesville, Mo., 1980; ADN, State Fair C.C., Sedalia, Mo., 1995. LPN charge nurse Lebanon Care Ctr., Lebanon, Mo., 1980-90; LPN staff nurse Cox Med. Ctr., Springfield, Mo., 1990-91, Citizens Meml., Bolivar, Mo., 1991-92, Lake Ozark Gen. Hosp., Osage Beach, Mo., 1992-96; RN supr. St. John's Breech Regional Med. Ctr., Lebanon, Mo., 1996—. Author (poems) The Day My Savior Died, 1989 (Golden Poet award 1989), Forgive Me, 1990, Yesterday, 1994 (Editor's Choice award 1994), A Tear Stained Face. Recipient Lake Ozark Gen. Hosp. scholar, 1994. Avocations: collecting cameos, writing poetry.

BECKER, MARY LOUISE, political scientist; b. St. Louis; d. W. R. and Evelyn (Thompson) Becker; divorced; children: James, John. BS, Washington U., St. Louis, 1949, MA, 1951; PhD, Radcliffe Coll., 1957; postgrad., U. Karachi, Pakistan, 1953-54. Intelligence rsch. analyst Dept. State, Washington, 1957—59; internat. rels. officer AID, Washington, 1959—64, cmty. rels. officer, 1964—66, sci. rsch. officer, 1966—71, UN rels. officer, 1971—91; pres. Internat. Devel. Enterprises, Washington, 1992—. Adviser U.S. dels. 19th, 21st, 23d, 24th, 26th, 28th, 30th, 32d, 34th Governing Coun. sessions UN Devel. Program; adv. U.S. del. 3d prep. com. meeting World Conf. UN Decade for Women; adviser U.S. dels. UNICEF exec. bd. sessions, 1987—91; mem. U.S. Com. for UN Fund for Women; lectr. internat. rels. civic orgn., student groups, 1954—. Author: Muhammad Iqbal, 1965; contbg. editor: Concise Ency. of Mid. East, 1973; contbr. articles to profl. jours. Mem. adv. bd. chmn. internat. student placement Washington Citizenship Seminar Nat. YMCA-YWCA, Washington, 1961—71. Named Blewett fellow, Washington U., 1951, Resident fellow, Radcliffe Coll., 1952—56, Fulbright scholar, U. Karachi, 1953—54. Mem.: AAUW, Nat. Press Club, Mo. Soc. Washington (sec. 1959—60), S. Asian Muslim Studies Assn. (v.p. 1992—), UN Assn. (bd. dirs. Nat. Capital area), Mid. East Inst., Asia Soc., Assn. Asian Studies, Soc. Internat. Devel., Am. Polit. Sci. Assn., Harvard Club (Washington), Chimes, Mortar Bd., Pi Sigma Alpha, Eta Mu Phi, Beta Gamma Sigma, Alpha Lambda Delta. Presbyterian. Home: 2301 E St NW Washington DC 20037-2829 Office: North Bldg Ste 700 601 Pennsylvania Ave NW Washington DC 20004-2601

BECKER, NANCY JANE, information science educator; b. Irvington, N.J., June 3, 1948; d. George Henry and Vida Jacqueline (Collins) B.; m. James Edward Weissinger, Sept. 4, 1971 (div. Aug. 1989); children: Jeffrey Michael, Erica Kathleen. BA, Seton Hall U., 1972; MLS with honors, Columbia U., 1992, EdD, 1999. Reference dept. intern Columbia U., N.Y.C., 1991-92, reference libr. Tchr. Coll., 1992-93, electronic info. resources libr., 1993-96; instr. info. sci. St. Johns U., Jamaica, N.Y., 1996-99, asst. prof., 1999—. Presenter in field. Contbr. articles to profl. jours. Mem. ALA, AAUP, Assn. Coll. and Rsch. Librs. (com. chair 1995-96, 98-99, sect. chair 1997-98), Am. Ednl. Rsch. Assn., Assn. Libr. and Info. Sci. Edn., Am. Soc. for Info. Sci. and Tech., (chair 2002-), Beta Phi Mu. Dem. Roman Cath. Avocations: hiking, reading. Office: St Johns Univ 8000 Utopia Pkwy Jamaica NY 11432-1343 E-mail: beckern@stjohns.edu.

BECKER, NANCY ANNE, state supreme court justice; b. Las Vegas, May 23, 1955; d. Arthur William and Margaret Mary (McLoughlin) Becker. BA, U.S. Internat. U., 1976; JD, George Washington U., 1979. Bar: Nev. 1979, D.C. 1980, Md. 1982, U.S. Dist. Ct. Nev. 1987, U.S. Ct. Appeals (9th cir.) 1987. Legis. cons. D.C. Office on Aging, Washington, 1979—83; assoc. Goldstein & Ahalt, College Park, Md., 1980—82; pvt. practice Washington, 1982—83; dep. city atty., prosecutor criminal div. City of Las Vegas, 1983; judge Las Vegas Mcpl. Ct., 1987—89, Clark County Dist. Ct., Las Vegas, 1989—99; now assoc. state supreme ct. justice Nev. Supreme Ct. Cons. MADD, Las Vegas, 1983—87. Contbr. articles to profl. jours. Pres. Clark County Pro Bono Project, Las Vegas, 1984—95. Mem.: NCCJ, Am. Businesswomen's Assn. (treas. Las Vegas chpt. 1985—86), Southern Nev. Assn. Women Attys. (past officer), Soroptimist Internat., Vietnam Vets. Am., Las Vegas and Latin C. of C. Office: Nevada Supreme Court Capital Complex 316 Bridger Ave Las Vegas NV 89101-5906

BECKER, NANCY MAY, nursing educator; b. Reading, Pa., July 28, 1949; d. Theodore R. and Minerva M. (Deiseroth) B. Diploma, Reading Hosp. Sch. Nursing, Pa., 1970; BS, Albright Coll., 1979; MS, U. Del., 1981. RN, Pa., Del. Nurse mgr. Cmty. Gen. Hosp., Reading, 1974-76; nurse educator Albright Coll., Reading, 1980-87; clin. nurse specialist Polyclinic Med. Ctr., Harrisburg, Pa., 1987-89; asst. prof. Lehigh Carbon C.C., Schnecksville, Pa., 1989-95, dir. nursing programs, 1995-97, dean allied health/dir. nursing, 1998—, dean profl. accreditation and curriculum, dir. nursing, 2001—, interim v.p. acad. affairs, 2001—02. Mem. ANA, Nat. League Nursing, Sigma Theta Tau.

BECKER, NANCY S. retired real estate broker, retired shop owner; b. Erie, Pa., June 14, 1928; d. Raymond Joseph and Anna Marie (Bechtold) Sanner; m. Eugene Thomas Becker, Nov. 1, 1947; children: Douglas, Kim, Jeffrey, Amy. Student, U. Maine, 1976—78. Lic. real estate salesperson and broker Fla. Owner Irish Import & Antique Shop, Bar Harbor, Maine, 1972—74, Irish Import Shop, Bar Harbor, Maine, 1972—74; asst. libr. St. Andrews, Canada, 1974—76; salesperson DeSantis Real Estate, Stuart, Fla., 1978—79; broker, owner Becker Real Estate, Stuart, 1980—84; proprietor Capt.'s House B & B, Thomaston, Maine, 1985—87; libr. Pittsfield, Maine, 1987—88, Holmes Beach, Fla., 1995—97. Active PTA, 1953—84; leader Girl & Boy Scouts, 1959—75; vol. ARC, 1955—72; asst. coach, supporter Little League, Pony League, 1955—65. Recipient Civic award, NATO, Izmir, Turkey, 1964, Papal Citation, Vatican City, 1964. Mem.: St. Petersburg (Fla.) Art Mus., Ringling Mus. of Art, Audubon Soc., Nat. Geog. Soc., Smithsonian Assocs., Art League (Bradenton, Fla.). Roman Catholic. Avocations: painting, gardening, sewing, fishing, cooking. Home: Bradenton, Fla. Died Feb. 28, 2001.

BECKER, PHYLLIS, systems analyst; b. Plainfield, N.J., Nov. 9, 1963; d. Stephen and Jean Mae Potasky; m. Andrew D. Becker, Feb. 14, 1993; 1 child, Samuel. BS in Computer Sci., Kean U., 1986; MS, Stevens Inst., 1998. Programmer ITT Def. Comms., Nutley, N.J.; sys. analyst AT&T, Somerset, N.J., CSC, Somerset. Republican. Jewish. Avocations: cat and dog care, sewing, needlework. Office: CSC 500 Atrium Dr Somerset NJ 08873 E-mail: pbecker@csc.com.

BECKER, SUSAN D. retired history educator; b. Cleve., Apr. 30, 1938; d. Kenneth George and Laura Jane (Biddlingmyer) Deubel; m. Edmund Heinz Becker, Dec. 1969 (div. Mar. 1972). AB, Ohio U., 1960; MA, John Carroll U., 1971; PhD, Case Western Res. U., 1975. Tchr. St. Joseph's Acad., Cleve., 1962-64, John Marshall High Sch., Cleve., 1964-69; from asst. to assoc. prof. history U. Tenn., Knoxville, 1974—99, prof. emerita, 1999—. Part time tchr. John Carroll U., Cleve., 1975—, Cleve. State U., 1975—. Author: The Origins of The Equal Rights Amendment, 1980, (with others) Decades of Discontent, 1983; co-author: (2 vols.) Discovering the American Past, 5th edit., 2002. Mem. Am. Hist. Assn., Am. Studies Assn., Orgn. Am. Historians, Coordinating Coun. Women in History, Phi Beta Kappa, Phi Alpha Theta.

BECKER, VANETA G. state representative; b. Alton, Ill., Oct. 7, 1949; m. Andrew C. Guarino. Attended, U. Evansville. Rep. dist. 75 State of Ind., 1981-91, rep. dist. 78, 1991—, ranking minority leader, 1991—; mem. pub. health & cities & towns coms.; mem. asst. minority caucus State of Ind.; realtor Don Cox & Assoc. Mem. bd. dirs. Albion Fellows Bacon Ctr., Patchwork Cent. Recipient Legis. Excellence award United Mine Workers, 1989; named Legislator of the Yr. Ind. Primary Health Care Assn., 1990. Mem. Nat. Assn. Realtors, Ind. Primary Health Care Assn., Evansville Zool. Soc., A Network of Evansville Women, Leadership Evansville, Crisis Prevention Nursery. Republican. Methodist. Home: 420 E Buena Vista Rd Evansville IN 47711-2720 Office: Ind Ho of Reps State Capitol Indianapolis IN 46204

BECKETT, VICTORIA LING, physician; m. Peter G.S. Beckett, 1954 (dec. 1974); 1 child, Paul T. (dec.); m. Joseph C. Sharp, 1996. BA, Mt. Holyoke Coll., 1945; MD, U. Mich., 1949; MA, St. Mary's U., 1995. Intern Mpls. Gen. Hosp., 1949-50; fellow Mayo Grad. Sch., 1951-55; clin. instr. Wayne State U. Sch. Medicine, Detroit, 1956-67; staff cons. internal medicine oncology svc. Henry Ford Hosp., Detroit, 1957-60; rsch. physician Darling Meml. Ctr., Detroit, 1965-69; rsch. assoc. rheumatology Trinity Coll. Dublin U., 1970-72, postgrad. tutor, 1972-73, dir., 1973-76; med. dir. Rochester (Minn.) Health Care Ctr., 1985—90; cons. physician in rheumatology Federated Dublin Vol. Hosps., 1973-76; staff cons. rheumatology Mayo Clinic, 1976-90, emeritus staff, 1990—; asst. prof. medicine Mayo Med. Sch., 1976-90. Fellow ACP; mem. Mayo Med. Alumni Assn., Am. Coll. Rheumatology (ret. mem.), Minn. State Med. Assn., Zumbro Valley Med. Soc., Phi Beta Kappa, Sigma Xi. Methodist. Avocations: teaching exercise class, creative writing.

BECK-HAFNER, JANENE M. assistant principal; b. Antigo, Wis., Nov. 23, 1968; d. Clement E. and Shirley M. Beck. MusB, U. Wis. Stevens Point, 1992, M in sci. edn., 1998; M in edn. leadership, Marian Coll., 2002. Music tchr. Birnamwood Elem., Wis., 1992—93; instrumental music tchr. Elcho (Wis.) Pub. Schs., 1993—2001; asst. prin. Antigo (Wis.) HS, 2001—. Office: Antigo HS 1900 10th Ave Antigo WI 54409

BECKINGHAM, KATHLEEN MARY, education educator, researcher; b. Sheffield, Yorkshire, Eng., May 8, 1946; came to U.S., 1976; d. Philip and Mary Ellen (Flint) B.; m. Alan Edward Smith, Oct. 7, 1967 (div. Oct. 1978); m. Robert Bruce Weisman, July 25, 1986; 1 child, Caroline Mary Weisman. BA, U. Cambridge, Eng., 1967, MA, 1968, PhD, 1972. Grad. student Strangeways Rsch. Lab., Cambridge, 1967-70; postdoctoral Inst. Molecular Biology, Aarhus, Denmark, 1970-72; rsch. assoc. Nat. Inst. Med. Rsch., London, 1972-76; rsch. assoc., instr. U. Mass. Med. Sch., Worcester, 1976-80; asst. prof. Rice U., Houston, 1980-85, assoc. prof. biochemistry, cell biology, molecular biology, 1985-92, prof., 1992—. Recipient award Camille and Henry Dreyfus Found., 1979. Office: Rice U Dept Biochemistry and Cell Biology PO Box 1892 Ms-140 Houston TX 77251-1892

BECKLAKE, MARGARET RIGSBY, epidemiologist, educator; b. London, May 27, 1922; d. James Thomas and Dorothy Mabel (Mills) B.; m. Maurice McGregor, Mar. 20, 1948; children: James, Margaret. MBBCh, U. Witwatersrand, 1944, MD, 1951, MD (hon.), 1974. Lectr. U. Witwatersrand, 1950-57; asst. prof. exptl. medicine McGill U., 1961-65, prof., 1967-96, prof. epidemiology and medicine, 1973-96, prof. emeritus, 1996—. Career investigator Med. Rsch. Coun. Can., 1968-93. Contbr. 160 articles to med. jours. Named hon. prof., U. Witwatersrand, 1984-85. Fellow Royal Coll. Physicians, Royal Soc. (Can.); mem. Am. Thoracic Soc. (Disting. Achievement award 1997, World Lung Health award 2001), Can. Thoracic Soc., Am. Physiol. Soc. Home: 532 Pine Ave W Montréal QC Canada H2W 1S6 Office: Montréal Chest Inst Respiratory Epidemiology Clin Rsch Unit 3650 St Urbain Office K1 33 H2X 2P4 Montréal Canada E-mail: margaret.becklake@mcgill.ca.

BECKLES, INGRID, mortgage banker; b. Washington, May 27, 1961; d. Frank Neville Beckles and Maria Beckles Jenkins; m. David Alan Fountain, July 3, 1981 (div. Jan. 1987); children: Kaiesha Nicole. BS, U. Md., 1988. Asst. br. mgr. Chevy Chase (Md.) Savs. Bank/B.F. Saul Mortgage Co., 1983-84, staff auditor, 1984-87, v.p., mgr. policies and procedures dept., 1989-91, v.p., mgr. ctrl. processing divsn., 1991, v.p. mgr., quality control dept., 1986-91; asst. v.p., regional ops. mgr. S.E. region PNC Mortgage Corp. Am., Vernon Hills, Ill., 1991-93, 2d v.p., underwriting mgr. Nat. Mortgage Ctr., 1993-96, mem. corp. fair lending initiatives staff, 1993—, v.p., chief underwriter, 1996-98, v.p., customer focused intiatives, 1998-99, v.p. credit policy and quality assurance, 1999—. Spkr. HUD and Joint Ctr. for Housing Studies, 1994, HUD Working Group for Underwriring and Bus. Practices, 1994—, Nat. Assn. Real Estate Brokers, 1995, Fannie Mae Nat. and Regional Risk Adv. Coun., 1995-96, VA Working Group on Underwriting and Bus. Practices, 1996—, Mortgage Bankers Assn., Nat. Underwriting Conf., 1997, Freddie Mac-Nat. Mgr.'s Meeting, 1998. Bd. dirs. Robert Taylor Boys and Girls Club, Chgo., 1998—. Mem. NAFE, Mortgage Bankers Assn. Am., Women in the Arts. Episcopalian. Avocations: horseback riding, piano, tennis, cycling. Office: PNC Mortgage Corp Am 75 N Fairway Dr Vernon Hills IL 60061-1846

BECKMAN, JUDITH KALB, financial counselor and planner, educator, writer; b. Bklyn., June 27, 1940; d. Harry and Frances (Cohen) Kalb; m. Richard Martin Beckman, Dec. 16, 1961; children: Barry Andrew, David Mark. BA, Hofstra U., 1962; MA, Adelphi U., 1973, cert., 1984. CFP; registered investment adviser, stockbroker. English tchr. Long Beach H.S., 1962-65; Promotion coordination pub. rels. Mandel Sch. for Med. Assts., Hempstead, N.Y., 1973-74; exec. dir. Nassau Easter Seals, Albertson, N.Y., 1974-76; dir. pub. info. Long Beach (N.Y.) Meml. Hosp., Long Beach, 1976-77; account rep. First Investors, Hicksville, N.Y., 1977-78; from sales asst. to acct. exec. Josephthal & Co. Inc., Great Neck, N.Y., 1978-81; v.p., fin. planner Arthur Gould Inc., Great Neck, N.Y., 1981-88; pres. Fin. Solutions (affiliated with Seco West Ltd., Goldner Siegfried Assocs. Inc.), Westbury, NY, 1988—2002; with Am. Portfolio Fin. Svcs., 2002—. Adj. instr. Adelphi U., Garden City N.Y., 1981-83, Molloy Coll., Rockville Ctr., N.Y., 1982-84; lectr. SUNY, Farmingdale, 1984-85; creater, presenter seminars, workshops on fin., investing, 1981—; adv. bd. L.I. Devel. Corp., 1993—; advisor investment clubs, 1996—. Fin. columnist The Women's Record, 1985-93; writer quar. newspaper The Reporter, 1987. Coord. meat boycott, L.I., 1973; mentor SUNY Old Westbury, 1989-93; co-founder, chair L.I. del. High Profile Men and Women, Colonie Hill, Hauppauque, N.Y., 1985; treas. L.I. Alzheimer's Found., 1989-93, trustee, 1993-95; apptd. to Nassau County Women's Adv. Coun. by County Exec., 1990; chief adv. coun. Ctr. for Family Resources, 1996-98; bd. dirs. L.I. Small Bus. Assistance Corp., (sec. 2003—), For Our Children (FOCUS), 20012— adviser to 4 investment clubs. Recipient citation for leadership Town of Hempstead, N.Y., 1986, 89, L.I. Press Club award, 1987, 92, Mentor award SBA, 1989, Fin. Svcs. award SBA, 1991, L.I. Assn. Fin. Svc. Advocate award, 1991, Woman of Distinction in Bus. award Women on the Job, 1989, Bus. Leadership citation Nassau County, N.Y., 1989, Supr. award Town of Hempstead, 1989, Pathfinder Bus. award, 1997, Bus. Adv. of Yr. N.Y. Dist. award U.S. SBA, 1998, Women's Bus. Advocate award, 1998, NAWBO LI Small Bus. Entrepreneur of the Yr. award, 1998; named one of 50 Leading Bus. Women, L.I. Bus. News, 2002, 2003, one of 90 Women in 90 Yrs. Making a Difference, Girls Scouts Nassau County, 2002. Mem. Nat. Assn. Women Bus. Owners L.I. (bd. dirs. 1987-89, membership chair 1996, v.p. membership 1996-98, v.p. edn. 1998-99, v.p. R&D 2002-03), Women's Econ. Developers of L.I. (bd. dirs. 1985-92), Internat. Assn. Fin. Planners, Inst. Cert. Fin. Planners, Fin. Planning Assn. L.I., L.I. Ctr. Bus. and Profl. Women (adv. coun. 1996-98, pres. 1984-86, Pres.' award 1992, Hall of Fame Achiever inductee 2001, steering com., co-founder L.I. Women's Agenda 1998, exec. v.p. Women's Agenda 1998-2000), Art League L.I. (bd. dirs. 2002—), Kiwanis (bd. dirs. 1994-97, chair fund raising 1994, chair cmty. svcs. 1995-97, v.p. membership 1996). Republican. Jewish. Avocations: theater, classical music, opera, reading. Home: 2084 Beverly Way Merrick NY 11566-5418 Office: Fin Solutions Fin Planning Office 2084 Beverly Way Merrick NY 11566-5418 also: 400 Post Ave Ste 200 Westbury NY 11590-2226 Office Phone: 516-333-1370. E-mail: jbeck0627@aol.com.

BECKMANN, KATHLEEN ANN, music educator; b. Binghamton, N.Y., Apr. 10, 1954; d. Eugene Stickle and Mary Catherine Baxter; m. Allan Graham, Jr. Beckmann, Aug. 16, 1975; children: Allan, Carolyn, Melinda. MusB, State U. Coll. Potsdam, N.Y., 1975; MusM, SUNY, Fredonia, 2003. Music tchr. Monticello (N.Y.) Ctrl. Sch., NY, 1975—78, Wappingers Ctrl. Sch., Wappingers Falls, NY, 1978—81, Hyde Park (N.Y.) Ctrl. Sch., NY, 1990—. Editor: Orchestrations, 1994—98. Recipient Crane Merit award, SUNY-Potsdam, 1975. Mem.: N.Y. State Sch. Music Assn. (string adjudicator), Nat. Sch. Orch. Assn. (exec. bd. 1994—98), Nat. Condrs. Guild, Am. String Tchrs. Assn., Music Educators Nat. Conf., Sigma Alpha Iota (parliamentarian). Avocations: tennis, travel, biking. Home: 3 Robin Ln Wappingers Falls NY 12590 Office: F D Roosevelt High Sch S Cross Rd Hyde Park NY 12538 Office Phone: 845-229-4020.

BECKMANN, NANCY BOURKE, retired elementary school educator; b. St. Louis, Aug. 30, 1940; d. Vernon Joseph and Janet Leahy Bourke; m. Vernal G. Beckmann, July 27, 1963; children: James Bourke, Janet C. Duckham. BS in English, St. Louis U., 1962; MA, Webster U., 1981. Elem. tchr. Ritenour Sch. Dist., Overland, Mo., 1962—64, Kirkwood (Mo.) Sch. Dist., 1964—67, Parkway Sch. Dist., Manchester, Mo., 1975—95; ret. Tchr. vol. English as a second lang. Rockwood Sch. Dist., Ballwin, Mo., 1995—97. Recipient English as Second Lang. Vol. Work award, Greater St. Louis Lit. Coun., 1997. Mem.: AAUW (v.p. membership 1998—2000, named gift honoree 2001). Roman Catholic. Avocations: swimming, book discussions, bridge, volunteer work. Home: 407 Sunnyslope Ballwin MO 63011

BECKWITH, BARBARA JEAN, journalist; b. Chgo., Dec. 11, 1948; d. Charles Barnes (dec.) and Elizabeth Ann (Nolan) Beckwith. BA in Journalism, Marquette U., 1970. News editor Lake Geneva (Wis.) Regional News, 1972-74; asst. editor St. Anthony Messenger, Cin., 1974-82, mng. editor, 1982—. Mem. Cath. Conf. Comm. Com., 1990—92. Mem.: Cath. Journalism Scholarship Fund (bd. dirs. 1993—, v.p. 1995—96, pres. 1996—99, 2001—), Nat. Cath. Assn. for Broadcasters and Communicators (bd. dirs. 1989—96, 1997—98), Fedn. Ch. Press Assns. of Internat. Cath. Union of the Press (3d v.p. 1989—92, pres. 1992—), Cath. Press Assn. (bd. dirs. 1986—96, v.p. 1988—90, pres. 1990—92, best interview 1982, best photo story 1985, St. Francis de Sales award for outstanding contbn. to Cath. journalism 1994, best poetry 1997). Office: St Anthony Messenger 28 W Liberty St Cincinnati OH 45202-6498

BECKWITH, MARY ANN, art educator; b. Phila., Pa., May 17, 1945; d. Raymond Leonard Liss, Leona Mary Liss; m. John Phillip Beckwith, Dec. 28, 1966; children: Susan Lynn Allen, Carl. BA, Marygrove Coll., 1967. With Mich. Bell Telephone, 1967—73; prof. art Mich. Tech U., Houghton, 1973—. Author: (bBook) Creative Water: A Step-by Step Guide and Showcase, 1997 (Signature Membership: National Watercolor Society, 2000). Mem.: Soc. Layeriest Multimedia, Midwest Watercolor Soc, (assoc.; pres. 1993—95). Office: 1400 Townsend Dr Houghton MI 49931-1200 Home Fax: 906-487-1841. Business E-Mail: mabeckwi@mtu.edu.

BECKWITH, SANDRA SHANK, judge; b. Norfolk, Va., Dec. 4, 1943; d. Charles Langdale and Loraine (Sterneberg) Shank; m. James Beckwith, Mar. 31, 1965 (div. June 1978); m. Thomas R. Ammann, Mar. 3, 1979. BA, U. Cin., 1965, JD, 1968. Bar: Ohio 1969, Ind. 1976, Fla. 1979, U.S. Dist. Ct. (so. dist.) Ohio 1971, U.S. Dist. Ct. Ind. 1976, U.S. Supreme Ct. 1977. Sole practice, Harrison, Ohio, 1969-77, 79-81; judge Hamilton County Mcpl. Ct., Cin., 1977-79, 81-86, commr., 1989-91; judge Ct. Common Pleas, Hamilton County Divsn. Domestic Rels., 1987-89; assoc. Graydon, Head and Ritchey, 1989-91; judge U.S. Dist. Ct. (so. dist.) Ohio, 1992—. Mem. Ohio Chief Justice's Code of Profl. Responsibility Commn., 1984, Ohio Gov.'s Com. on Prison Crowding, 1984-90, State Fed. Com. on Death Penalty Habeas Corpus, 1995—; pres. 6th Cir. Dist. Judges Assn., 1998-99; chair So. Dist. Ohio Automation Com., 1997—. Bd. dirs. Tender Mercies. Mem. Fed. Judges Assn., Am. Judges Assn., Am. Judicature Soc., Fed. Bar Assn. (exec. com.), Fed. Cir. Bar Assn. Office: Potter Stewart US Courthouse Ste 810 Cincinnati OH 45202

BECRAFT, CAROLYN HOWLAND, communications executive; b. San Antonio, Aug. 17, 1944; d. Donald Roe and Jeanne (Dady) Howland; m. Peter Michael Becraft, May 10, 1969; children: Peter Howland, Jeremy Cliffor. BS in Foods and Nutrition, U. N.D., 1966; MS in Adult Edn., U. So. Calif., 1978. Registered dietitian. Cons. dietitian Breckinridge Meml. Hosp., Harrisonburg, Ky., 1972-73; dir. Resource Ctr. U.S. Army, Bad Kreuznach, Germany, 1979-80; dir. mil. project Women's Equity Action League, Washington, 1982-87; rsch. assoc. Decision Resources Corp., Washington, 1987-89; ind. cons. Women's Rsch. and Ednl. Inst., Washington, 1990-91; dir. comms. Internat. Ctr. Rsch. on Women, Washington, 1991-92; sr. policy assoc. and cons. Women's Rsch. and Ednl. Inst., 1990, 1991, 1993; dep. asst. secy. personnel support, families and edn. Dept. of Defense, 1993-98; asst. secy for manpower and reserve affairs Dept. of the Navy, Washington, 1998—. Chair Army Family Action Com., Ft. Myer, Va., 1980-82. Contbr. chpt. to books, articles to mags. Pres. Burke (Va.) Sta. Swim Club, 1985-86; sec. Woodhirst Homeowners Assn., Burke, 1988-89. Capt. U.S. Army, 1966-71. Recipient Joyce Ott award Army Family Action Com., Alexandria, Va., 1982. Fellow Inter-Univ. Seminar on Armed Forces and Soc.; mem. Nat. Mil. Family Assn. (bd. dirs. 1983-86), Am. Soc. Assn. Execs., Am. Dietetic Assn., Women in Comms., Women in Def. (pres., treas. capital sect. 1989, 90, program chair nat. sect. 1988, 91). Episcopalian. Avocations: reading, skiing. Home: 8942 Kenilworth Dr Burke VA 22015-2175 Office: Dept of the Navy 100 Navy Pentagon Rm 4e7388 Washington DC 20350-0001

BEDELL, BARBARA LEE, journalist; b. Annapolis, Md., July 10, 1936; d. Royal Lee and Kathryn Rosalee (Alton) Sweeney; m. Raymond Lester Bedell, July 1, 1955 (div. 1979); children: Patricia Bedell Pulito, Barbara Ann Bedell Porrini, Raymond, Robert. DHL (hon.), Mt. St. Mary Coll., 2000. Dir. woman's programming, host daily talk show Sta. KLME, Laramie, Wyo., 1962-68, Sta. WKIP, Poughkeepsie, N.Y., 1968-70; asst. soc. editor, feature writer Poughkeepsie Jour., 1968-70; dir. comm. and publs. Spackenkill Sch. Dist., Poughkeepsie, 1970-73; columnist, reporter Times Herald-Record Newspaper, Middletown, N.Y., 1973—. Bd. dirs. Middletown Day Nursery, 1988 ; mem. steering com. Dr. Martin Luther King Jr. Cmty. Wide Celebration, 1992—; lectr. on various topics to civic, polit., religious, social orgns., 1961—. Mem. 75th Anniversary Com., Cheyenne, Wyo., 1965; mem. Rep. Precinct Com., 1961-68, Albany County Bd. Electors, 1966-68; mem. com. history and heritage collection Orange County C.C., Middletown, 1984; mem. 100th Anniversary Com., Middletown, 1983-88; bd. dirs. divsn. marshal 1988 Parade; apptd. del. Gov. Mario Cuomo's N.Y. State Conf. on Librs., 1981; campaign chair United Way, 1996; bd. dirs. Literacy Vols. of Am.; kettle chmn. Salvation Army, 1999. Recipient 1st in N.Y. feature writing award Am. Cancer Soc., 1973, Disting. Svc. award NAACP, 1980, 96, Hadassah Myrtle Wreath award, 1979, Cmty. Svc. award Boy Scouts Am., 1990, Humanitarian award Human Rights Commn., 1997, Orange County Agr. Soc. award, Svc. awards from numerous svc. clubs and lodges, chs., assns.; named Mrs. Wyo., Mrs. Am. Pageant, 1967, N.Y. State All-Am. Family, 1972, Lions Knight of the Blind award, 1999, Pinnacle award U.S. Harness Racing Hall of Fame, 2002, Masonic DeWitt Clinton award, 2002. Mem. Nat. Fedn. Press Women (8 awards for feature writing 1967-70, top Wyo. state award for radio script writing 1966), Elks (Mother of Yr. award 1989), SAR (Woman of Yr. award 1991), Kiwanis, Lions, Rotary. Home: PO Box 458 Walker Valley NY 12588-0458 Office: Times Herald-Record PO Box 2046 Middletown NY 10940-0558 E-mail: bbedell@th-record.com.

BEDELL, ELIZABETH SNYDER (BETTY BEDELL), editor-in-chief, marketing professional; b. Jacksonville, Fla., Mar. 26, 1940; d. Ralph Edward and Elizabeth Follin Snyder; m. David Thorpe Bedell, June 16, 1961 (div. Aug. 1974); children: Charles, Elizabeth Bedell Coyle, George. Student, Hollins U.; BA, U. North Fla. Founding editor Kalliope, A Jour. of Women's Lit. and Art, 1978—81; tchr. Stanton Coll. Prep., Venetia Elem., 1981—84; freelance writer, editor, 1984—93, 1997—; program developer St. Vincent's Found., Inc., 1993—98; editor Betty Snyder Bedell Editl. Svcs., Jacksonville, 1999—. Chmn. garden and grounds Ximenez-Fatio Mus. House, St. Augustine, Fla.; bd. dirs. Jr. League, Jacksonville. Mem.: Colonial Dames, Fla. Yacht Club Jacksonville. Home and Office: 4242 Ortega Blvd # 21 Jacksonville FL 32210 E-mail: ebedell@bellsouth.net.

BEDENBAUGH, ANGELA LEA OWEN, chemistry educator, researcher; b. Seguin, Tex., Oct. 6, 1939; d. Wintford Henry and Nelia Melanie (Fischer) Owen; m. John Holcombe Bedenbaugh, Dec. 27, 1961; 1 child, Melanie Celeste. BS cum laude, U. Tex., 1961; PhD in Organic Chemistry, U. S.C., 1967. Geol. mapping asst. Roland Blumberg Assocs., Seguin, summer 1958, 59; chemistry lab. instr. U. Tex., Austin, 1960-61; rsch. assoc. chemistry U. So. Miss., Hattiesburg, 1966-80, rsch. assoc. prof. chemistry, 1980—, bd. mem. women's studies program, 1996-97. Co-prin. investigator Bell South Found. grant, 1998; dir. website NASA grant, 1999-00. Author: Nomenplayture, 1998; co-author: (with John H. Bedenbaugh) Handbook for High School Chemistry Teachers, 1985, (with John H. Bedenbaugh) Teaching First Year Chemistry, 4th edit., 1993, (with John H. Bedenbaugh) Teaching Physical Science, Vols. 1 and 2; patentee in field. Adminstrv. bd. Parkway Heights United Meth. Ch., 1974-75, women's unit leader, 1973-75, women's unit treas., 1977, Wesleyan Svc. Guild v.p., 1970, Sunday Sch. tchr., 1973-74; bd. dirs. Forrest Stone Area Opportunity Inc., 1970-72, bd. dirs. exec. com., 1972, mem. com. to rewrite pers. policies and procedures, 1971, mem. Headstart monitoring com., 1971-72, mem. pers. screening com., 1971; mem. nat. Women's Polit. Caucus, 1976—; mem. Toastmasters Internat., 1986—, club. pres., 1993, area gov., 1994; adminstr., dir. Tchr. Mentoring Initiative through Bell South Found. Grant, 1998-2000; Miss. state coord. Bldg. a Presence for Sci. Recipient John and Angela Bedenbaugh award Coastal Miss. Assn. H.S. Chemistry Tchrs., 1996—; Rsch. grantee U.S. Dept. Energy, U. So. Miss., 1980, NSF, U. So. Miss., 1985, Adminstrv. Dir. Rsch. grant, 1988-91, 1993-96, 2001-04, NSF, 2000—, others. Mem. NSTA (nat. resource rev. panel for rev. of instrnl. materials), LWV, AAUW, Am. Chem. Soc. (chmn. 1984-85, program chmn. 1983-84, exec. bd. 1983—, Chemist of Yr. award 1991), Miss. Sci. Tchrs. Assn. (exec. bd. 1994—, pres.-elect 1998-2000, pres. 2000-02, state bldg. a presence for sci. coord. 2002—, Disting. Sci. Tchr. award 1994), Delta Kappa Gamma (pres. Miss. br. 1989-91, chmn. internat. rsch. com. 1980-82, chmn. internat. computer share fair at internat. conv. 1994, editor U.S. Forum Connection 2000-), Sigma Xi (charter, sec.-treas. 1967-69, treas. 1970, pres. 1973-74, program chmn. 1972-73). Democrat. Methodist. Home: 63 Suggs Rd Hattiesburg MS 39402-3639 Office: Univ So Miss PO Box 8466 Hattiesburg MS 39406-1000

BEDFORD, AMY ALDRICH, public relations executive; b. Pendleton, Oreg., July 13, 1912; d. Edwin Burton and Elsie (Conklin) Aldrich; m. J.M. Bedford (wid.); 1 child, Jacqueline Bedford Brown. BS, Oreg. State U., 1933. Mgr. comml. dept. East Oregonian, Pendleton, 1950-75, mgr. pub. rels., 1975—; corp. sec. East Oregonian Pub. Co., Pendleton, 1950-2000. Bd. dirs. Oreg. Status of Women Com., 1972-75, Oreg. Law Enforcement Commn., 1975-82; active Arts Coun. Pendleton. Recipient Pendleton First Citizen award C. of C., 1962, Gov.'s award for the Arts, 1988, Woman of Achievement award Oreg. Commn. for Women, 1998, Paul Harris award Rotary, 1993. Mem. Women in Communications, Oreg. Press Women, AAUW (pres. 1956-58, grantee 1965), LWV, Pendleton River Parkway Found., World Affairs Coun. Oreg., Altrusa. Avocations: reading, travel, music, theatre. Home: PO Box 1456 Pendleton OR 97801-0360 Office: East Oregonian Pub Co PO Box 1089 Pendleton OR 97801-1089 E-mail: jacbrown@eastoregonian.com.

BEDFORD, BARBARA J. Olympic athlete; b. Hanover, N.H., Nov. 9, 1972; Recipient Gold medal 4 x 100-meter medley (team) Sydney Olympics, 2000, 100-meter backstroke U.S. nats., Mpls., 1999; 3d pl. 100-meter backstroke Pan Pacific Championships, Gold medley relay, 1999, 7 time US Nat. Champion 5 100 backstroke, 1-200 backstroke, 1-50 free, Olympic Trials Champion, 2000, Pan Pacific Champion, 200-meters backstroke, 1993, Pan Am. Champion, 100-meter backstroke, 200-meter backstroke, 4X100 medley relay, 1995, World Championships 3d pl. 100-meter backstroke, 4th pl. 200-meter backstroke, 1994, Goodwill Games Champion 200-meter backstroke, 2nd pl. 100 backstroke, Gold winner on medley relay, 1994, World U. Games champion, 1st pl. 100-meter backstroke, 1st pl. 4X100 medley relay, 1991, 1st pl. 100-meter backstroke, 1st pl. 4X100 medley relay, 1993, World Championships Gold on free realy, Gold Preliminary Medley, 1998. Office: USA Swimming 1 Olympic Plz Colorado Springs CO 80909-5746

BEDFORD, FELICE L. psychologist, educator; b. Manhatten, N.Y., Dec. 9, 1960; d. Pauline (Allalouf) and Donald Bedford. BA, U. Pa., 1982, MA, 1983, PhD, 1988. Asst. prof. U. Ariz., Tucson, 1988—94; vis. scholar U. Calif., Berkeley, 1995—96, assoc. prof. Tucson, 1994—2002; rsch. fellow cognitive sci. program U. Ariz., Tucson, 2000—. Grant reviewer NSF, The Israel Sci. Found., and U.S. Air Force, 1990—; cons. USAF, 1993—95; chair undergrad. psychology curriculum U. Ariz., Tucson, 1997—; cons. Pub. Defender's Office and Dist. Attorney's Office, Tucson, 1997—; organizer cognitive sci. lectures series U. Ariz., Tucson, 1999—2000. Contbr. articles to profl. jours. Grantee, NSF, 1989—93, U. Ariz. Found., 2000—01, Social and Behavioral Sciences Rsch. Inst., 1994—95, 1998—99. Mem.: Rocky Mountain Psychol. Assn., Brain and Behavioral Sci., Am. Psychol. Soc., Sephardic Brotherhood Am., Phi Beta Kappa (life inducted 1982). Liberal. Avocations: dogs, genealogy, hiking, birdwatching. Office: Univ Ariz Dept Psychology Rm 312 Tucson AZ 85721 Office Fax: 520-621-9306. Business E-Mail: bedford@u.arizona.edu.

BEDICS, LYNN FAY, nurse; b. Scranton, Pa., May 13, 1947; d. Gerald Joseph and Esther Naomi (Sachse) O'Malley; m. Francis J. Bedics, Jr., Mar. 11, 1989. Grad., St. Luke's Hosp. Sch. Nursing, N.Y.C., 1968; BSN cum laude, Cedar Crest Coll., 1982. RN, Pa.; cert. comty. health nurse ANA Credentiality Ctr. Staff nurse emergency room Allentown Gen. Hosp., 1971; part-time charge nurse Phila. VA Hosp., 1971-72; critical care nurse St. John's Hosp., Tulsa, 1972-74; ICU nurse Allentown Osteo. Hosp., 1975-79, staff nurse VA Outpatient Clinic, Allentown, 1979-86; nurse mgr. Dept. Vets. Affairs, Outpatient Clinic, Allentown, 1986—. Instr.-trainer CPR, Am. Heart Assn., Allentown, 1980 89. Mem. coord. com. Combined Fed. Campaign, Lehigh Valley, Pa., 1984-86; bd. dirs. YWCA, Allentown, 1986-88, Korea-Vietnam Meml. Inc., Lehigh Valley, 1987—, sec., 1991-94, v.p. devel. 1997—; mem. Vietnam Vets. Health Initiative Commn., 1995-96. 1st lt. Nurse Corps, U.S. Army, 1967-70, Vietnam. Decorated Bronze Star medal; recipient excellence in Nursing award Dept. Vets. Affairs, 1989, VA Adminstr.'s Hands and Heart award Dept. Vets. Affairs Med. Ctr., Wilkes-Barre, Pa., 1989, Legion of Honor award Chapel of Four Chaplains, 1994, Lehigh County Disting. Svc. award. Mem. Assn. for Ambulatory Care Providers Ea. Pa. (v.p. 1987-89, pres. 1989-90, bd. dirs., chair edn. com. 1994-98), United Women Vets. Pa. VFW, Sigma Theta Tau, Beta Sigma Phi (internat. honr.). Republican. Avocations: ceramics, hiking, reading. Home: 1118 N 27th St Allentown PA 18104-2904 Office: 3110 Hamilton Blvd Allentown PA 18103-3630

BEDNAR, SUSAN GAIL, social worker, consultant; b. Chgo., Ill., May 28, 1949; d. Charles and Evelyn Bednar; m. Bruce Kevin Barnard, Nov. 15, 1988. BA in Sociology, U. Ill., 1973, MSW, 1996. LCSW Ill., cert. Domestic Violence Counselor III Nat. Assn. Forensic Counselors. Addictions therapist Prairie Ctr. Health Systems, Danville, Ill., 1997—98; clin. dir. DeWitt County Human Resource Ctr., Clinton, Ill., 1998—99; program coord. Shelby County Cmty. Svcs., Shelbyville, Ill.; clin. assoc. Dovetail Consulting, Crystal Lake, Ill., 2000—01; rsch. asst. Ind. U., Indpls., 2000—02; cons. Champaign, Ill., 2001—; clin. social worker in pvt. practice, 2003—. Dir. Mental Health Assn., Champaign, Ill., 1996—97. Contbr. Counseling Female Offenders and Victims, articles to profl. jours. Mem.: NASW, Am. Sociol. Assn., Assn. for Conflict Resolution, Nat. Assn. of Forensic Counselors. Avocation: horse owner. Office: Susan G Bednar LCSW 302 W Hill St Suite 103 Champaign IL 61820 Office Phone: 217-352-8502. Business E-Mail: sgbednar@advancenet.net.

BEDNARZ, NELL O'BRIANT, conservationist; b. Lubbock, Tx., Aug. 29, 1957; BS, Tex. Tech. U, 1980. Artist freelance, 1973—, writer, 1979—. Home: 23323 Millcross Ln Katy TX 77494 E-mail: mike_nell@ev1.net.

BEDNASH, GERALDINE POLLY, educational association administrator; b. San Antonio, May 6, 1943; d. David Anthony and Bernice (Brewer) Parrott; m. Thomas Francis Bednash, June 24, 1967; children: Thomas F. Jr., Joseph Andrew. B of Nursing, Tex. Women's U., 1965; M of Nursing, Cath. U. Am., 1977; PhD, U. Md., 1989. Cert. nurse practitioner. Nurse Binghamton (N.Y.) Gen. Hosp., 1967-69; instr. Broome County Community Coll., Binghamton, 1967-71; asst. prof. No. Va. Community Coll., Annandale, 1977-78, George Mason U., Fairfax, Va., 1978-86; dir. govt. rels. Am.

Assn. Coll. Nursing, Washington, 1986-89, exec. dir., 1989—. Co-chmn. Nat. Com. Nursing Implementation Project, Washington, 1990-91; cons. in field. Contbr. articles to profl. jours. Polit. action chmn. Va. Nurses Assn., 1979-83; nurse clinician So Others Might Eat, Washington, 1981-83. Capt. U.S. Army, 1963-67. Primary Care fellow Robert Wood Johnson Found., U. Md., 1981-82, Nat. Rsch. Svc. fellow, Washington, 1990-9[illegible] Acad. Nursing; mem. ANA, Sigma Theta Tau. Roman Catholic. Avocations: skiing, horticulture. Office: Am Assn Coll Nursing 1 Dupont Cir NW Ste 530 Washington DC 20036-1135

BEDRICK, BERNICE, retired science educator, consultant; b. Jersey City, Sept. 29, 1916; d. Abraham Lewis and Esther (Cowan) Grodjesk; m. Emanuel Arthur Bedrick, Dec. 25, 1938 (dec. 1967); children: Allen Paul, Jane Bedrick Abels; m. Samuel Milberger, Sept. 23, 1984 (dec. 1984); stepchildren: Susan Milberger Rafael, Stanford. BS, U. Md., 1938; MA, NYU, 1952. Cert. tchr., N.J. Tchr. Linden (N.J.) Pub. Sch. System, 1950-69, supr. sci. curriculum, 1969-79, sch. prin., 1979-87; ret., 1987. Co-author: A Universe to Explore, 1969; developer program of safety and survival N.J. Dept. Edn., 1975. Founder, mem., bd. dirs., v.p. edn. Temple Mekor Chayim, Linden; pres. bd. trustees Linden Pub. Libr., 1989-90, v.p., 1991; pres. Friends of Linden Libr., 1987-92, 95-97, coord. used books sales, 1990—, founder, 1987; bd. trustees Temple Beth-El Mekor Chayim, Cranford, N.J., 1999—, bd. edn., 1999—. Recipient Cmty. Vol. Svc. award B'Nai B'Rith, 1993, Outstanding Sr. Citizen of Yr., City of Linden, 1996; honored with Bernice Bedrick rm. at Sunnyside br. Linden Pub. Libr., 2001. Mem.: NEA (life), Nat. Sci. Tchrs. Assn., N.J. Sci. Tchrs. Assn., N.J. Prins. and Suprs. Assn., N.Y. Acad. Scis., Linden Edn. Found. (bd. dirs.), Am. Fedn. Sch. Adminstrs. (chpt. pres. 1984—86), Nat. Coun. Jewish Women (life), N.J. PTA (life), N.J. Edn. Assn. (life), Linden Ceramics Club (life; sec. 1991—92, 1995—99, pres. 2000—), Hadassah (life), Phi Kappa Phi, Alpha Lambda Delta, Alumni Assn. U. Md. (life). Home: 2016 Orchard Ter Linden NJ 07036-3719

BEDROSSIAN, URSULA KAY KENNEDY, editor; b. Austin, Tex., Dec. 8, 1948; d. Richard Arch and Ursula Marie (Jones) Kennedy; m. Carlos Wanes Bedrossian, Aug. 8, 1970; children: Vanessa, Richard, Robert. BS, Jacksonville U., 1972; MEd, Vanderbilt U., 1984; PhD, St. Louis U., 1991. Registered med. technologist and cytotechnologist Am. Soc. Clin. Pathologists. Med. technologist Del Oro Med. Lab., Houston, 1977-78; edn. coord., lab. supr. dept. family practice U. Tex. Med. Sch., Houston, 1978-81; rsch. asst. VA Med. Ctr., Nashville, 1981-84; clin. instr. dept. pathology St. Louis U., 1985-89; dir. edn. and quality I DMC Univ. Labs., Detroit, 1991-97. Mng. edtor Wiley-Liss, N.Y.C., 1989—. Mng. editor Diagnostic Cytopathology, 1984—; asst. editor The Prostate, 1992-95; contbr. articles to sci. jours. Dir. med. relief Armenian Gen. Benevolent Union, 1993-97. Recipient commendation U.S. Army 101st Workhorse Bn., Badhersfeld, Germany, 1985. Mem. Clin. Lab. Mgmt. Assn., Am. Soc. Cytotech. (liaison to Papunivolaou Soc. Cytopathology 1993—, scientist mem. Am. Soc. Cytopathology), Armenian Am. Bus. Coun., Brazilian Cultural Club. Avocations: geology, natural sciencies, travel, speaking spanish and portuguese. Office: Biomed Comm Oak Park IL 60302

BEE, ANNA COWDEN, dance educator; b. Feb. 17, 1922; d. Porter Guthrie and Marion Irene (McCurry) Cowden; m. Alon Wilton Bee, Oct. 21, 1942; children: Anna Margaret Bee Foote, Alon Wilton. AB, Samford U., 1944; student, Chalif Sch. Dance, N.Y.C., 1950-54. Mem. faculty Byram H.S., JAckson, 1945-52, Hinds Jr. Coll., Raymond, Miss., 1952—. Dir. Hi-Steppers, girls' precision dance group; chaperone Miss Mississippi to Miss Am. Pageant; condr. charm clinics for teenagers; judge beauty pageants. Prodr. half-time shows for Gator Bowl, 1958, 64, 81, Sugar Bowl, 1960, Hall of Fame Bowl, 1977-79, Mid-Am. Bowl, 1988, Sr. Bowl, 1988. Bd. dirs. Multiple Sclerosis Soc., Jackson, 1966-72; state chmn. Miss. Easter Seals Soc. campaign, 1966, 79; chmn. women's divsn. United Way, Jackson, 1973; commencement spkr. Hinds C.C., 1999. Recipient Hinds C.C. Svc. award, 1993, Miss Miss. Vol. of Yr. award, 1995, Miss Am. Vol. of Yr. award, 1995, Dance Tchrs. Unlimited Lifetime Achievement award, 1996, Dance Tchrs. United Achievement award in dance, 1996; named Woman of Achievement, Jackson Bus. and Profl. Women's Club, 1967-78, Outstanding Vol. Goodwill Industry Miss., 1997, Golden Isles Bowl Classic, 1997; Miss. Legislature commendation for contbn. to youth, 1981; Anna Cowden Bee Hall named in her honor Hinds C of C., bd. trustees, 1993; named Ageless Hero, Blue Cross/Blue Shield, 2001, Hometown Hero, WJTV, 2000; honored Legis., 2003. Mem. Nat. Faculty Dance Educators Am., Dance Masters Am., Miss. Edn. Assn., Miss. Assn. Health and Phys. Edn., Beta Sigma Omicron. Baptist. Home: 256 Azalea Ct Brandon MS 39047-7264 Office: Hinds Cmty Coll Box 10415 Raymond MS 39154

BEEBE, GAYLE L. music educator; b. Danville, Ill., Jan. 27, 1970; d. John A. McClatchey and Susan J. Daniels; m. Stephen M. Beebe, Mar. 30, 1996; children: Joel, Mitchell. Bachelor's Degree, Millikin U., 1992. Band dir. Marshall (Ill.) Schs., 1994—99; choir dir. Taylor Schs., Kokomo, Ind., 1999—. Musician: flute choir, 2002—03. Mem.: Music Educators Nat. Conf., Sigma Alpha Iota (Sword of Honor 1992, Ruby Sword of Honor 1992). Avocations: skydiving, swimming, flute. Office: Taylor Mid Sch 3794 E County Rd 3005 Kokomo IN 46902-9509

BEEBE, GRACE ANN, retired special education educator; b. Wyandotte, Mich., Feb. 16, 1945; d. Cecil Vern and Elizabeth Lucille (Tamblyn) B. BA, Ea. Mich. U., 1967; MEd, Wayne State U., 1970; postgrad., U. Mich., 1973-78; student, Meth. Theol. Sch., Ecumenical Theol. Sem. Cert. spl. edn. tchr., Mich. Tchr. POHI 1st grade Grand Rapids (Mich.) Pub. Schs., 1967-69; tchr. title VI Taylor (Mich.) Pub. Schs., 1970-73, tchr. Physically or Otherwise Health Impaired pre-kindergarten, 1973-79, tchr. POHI 1st-3rd grades, 1979-81, tchr. POHI pre-kindergarten, 1981-84, tchr., cons. POHI, 1984-2000; ret., 2000. Sem. student Ecumenical Theol. Sch., Detroit, 2000—01, Meth. Theol. Sch., Delaware, Ohio, 2001—. Area coord. Indian Trails Camp, Grand Rapids, 1979-97; Brownie troop leader Girl Scouts U.S., 1997-98. Recipient Recognition award 4-H Wayne County Handicapped Riding, 1986, Indian Trails Camp, 1990; Ronald McDonald Children's Charities grantee, 1990; State of Mich. Spl. Edn. scholar, 1966-67, Vocat. Rehab. scholar, 1969-70. Mem. SCADS (alt. rep.), N.Am. Riding for the Handicapped Assn., Mich. Fedn. Tchrs., Physically Impaired Assn. Mich., Taylor Fedn. Tchrs. (ancillary v.p. 1990-92), Taylor Handicapped Assn., Allen Park Assn. for Handicapped, Trenton Hist. Soc. (exec. bd. 1988-97), Coun. for Exceptional Children, Phi Delta Kappa, Alpha Delta Kappa. Democrat. United Methodist. Avocations: horseback riding, gardening, walking. Home: 2225 Emeline St Trenton MI 48183-3653 E-mail: Beebega@aol.com.

BEEBE, MARY LIVINGSTONE, curator; b. Portland, Oreg., Nov. 5, 1940; d. Robert and Alice Beebe. BA, Bryn Mawr Coll., 1962; postgrad., Sorbonne, U. Paris, 1962-63. Curatorial asst. Fogg Art Mus., Harvard U., Cambridge, Mass., 1966-68; apprentice Portland Art Mus., 1963-64, Boston Mus. Art, 1964-65; exec. dir. Portland Ctr. for Visual Arts, 1973-81; dir. Stuart Collection U. Calif., San Diego, 1981—. Cons. in field; mem. art steering com. Portland Devel. Commn., 1977-80; bd. dirs. Henry Gallery, U. Wash., Seattle, 1977-80; project cons. Nat. Rsch. Ctr. for Arts, N.Y.C., 1978-79; bd. dirs. Western Assn. Art Museums, Art Mus. Assn. San Francisco, 1978-84; bd. dirs., trustee Art Matters Inc., 1985—; trustee Russell Found., 1982-94; hon. mem. bd. dirs. Portland Ctr. for Visual Arts, 1984-91; mem. arts adv. bd. Centre City Devel. Corp., San Diego, 1982-94, art adv. bd. U. Calif. San Francisco Mission Bay, 1999—; panel mem., cons. Nat. Endowment Arts; juror numerous art exhbns. Nat. Endowment Arts fellow, 1979. Author: Landmarks: Sculpture Commissions for the Stuart Collection at the University of California, San Diego, 2001; contbr. articles to profl. jours. Recipient Allied Professions award AIA, 1992. Office: U Calif San Diego Stuart Collection 9500 Gilman Dr La Jolla CA 92093-0010 Office Phone: 858-534-2117.

BEEBE, SANDRA E. retired English language educator, artist, writer; b. March AFB, Calif., Nov. 10, 1934; d. Eugene H. and Margaret (Fox) B.; m. Donald C. Thompson. AB in English and Speech, UCLA, 1956; MA in Secondary Edn., Calif. State U., Long Beach, 1957. Tchr. English, Garden Grove (Calif.) High Sch., 1957-93, attendance supr., 1976-83, ret., 1993. Tchr. watercolor courses, Asilomar, Calif., 1997; jury chmn. N.W.S., 1997. Contbr. articles to English Jour., chpts. to books; watercolor artist; exhbns. include AWS, NWS, Okla. Watercolor Soc., Watercolor West, Midwest Watercolor Soc., Butler Inst. Am. Art, Youngstown, Ohio, Kings Art Ctr., Audubon Artists N.Y.; cover artist Exploring Painting, 1990, title page Understanding Watercolor, American Artist, 1991. Mem. faculty Asilomar, 1997; chmn. of jurors N.W.S. Open, 1997. Named one of the Top Ten Watercolorists The Artists Mag., 1994; recipient Best Watercolors award Rockport Press, 1995; chosen for Design Poster selection, 1995, 97. Mem. Am. Watercolor Soc. (dir. 1999—), Nat. Watercolor Soc., Midwest Watercolor Soc., Watercolor West, Allied Artists N.Y., Knickerbocker Artists N.Y., Audubon Artists N.Y., West Coast Watercolor Soc., Rocky Mountain Nat. Watermedia Honor Soc., Jr. League Long Beach, Kappa Kappa Gamma. Republican. Home: 239 Mira Mar Ave Long Beach CA 90803-3899 Address: 239 Mira Mar Ave Long Beach CA 90803-6153 E-mail: sebeebeaws@aol.com.

BEEDLE, DAWN DANENE, recruiting and training administrator; b. Mexico, Mo., July 16, 1968; d. Ronald Wayne and Delores Kay (Eastin) B. BA, William Woods Coll., 1990. Retail mgr. Kirlins Hallmark, Columbia, Mo., 1991-94, dist. mgr. Chgo./Milw., 1994, St. Louis, 1994-96, corp. tng. mgr. Quincy, Ill., 1996-2000; dir. recruiting and tng., 2000—. Pub. speaker, cons., Quincy, 1997—. Mem. NAFE. Republican. Presbyterian. Avocations: gardening, exercise, cooking, travel, family and friends. Home: 1307 Millbrook Ct Columbia MO 65203

BEEKS, CHERYL ELAINE, elementary school educator; b. Concord, NC, Aug. 28, 1946; d. Ray Edward and Maxine (Peterson) Barringer; m. Raymond Neil Beeks, July 12, 1971; 1 child, Alison Elaine Rios. B in Music Edn., So. Meth. U., Dallas, 1968. Tchr. Lamesa (Tex.) Ind. Sch. Dist., 1968—69, 1970—73, Loraine (Tex.) Ind. Sch. Dist., 1976—77, Highland Ind. Sch. Dist., Roscoe, Tex., 1980—. Coach 5th grade events Univ. Interscholastic League, Roscoe, 1980—, elem. poetry judge, 1995—. Pianist, organist Hermleigh (Tex.) United Meth. Ch., 1990—, treas., 1995—98; lay delegate United Meth. Northwest Conf., Lubbock, Tex., 1999—. Mem.: Tex. Assn. Cmty. Schs., Tex. Music Edn. Assn., Nat. Assn. Music Edn. Home: 206 Lowe Hermleigh TX 79526 Office: Highland Ind Sch Dist 6625 FM608 Roscoe TX 79545 Business E-Mail: cbeeks@highland.esc14.net.

BEELER, CHARLOTTE JEAN, oil and supply company executive, interior design business executive; b. Normal, Ill., Dec. 9, 1928; d. John William and Viola Maude (Walters) Geske: m. Charles Gilbert Beeler, Feb. 12, 1949; children: Judy Ann Kjellander, Mark Geske, David William. Student, Ill. Wesleyan U., 1946-48, Ill. State U., 1962, 75; degree in interior design, Ray Coll. of Design, Chgo., 1991. Gift buyer Dixie Truckers, McLean, Ill., 1967-78, gift buyer, mgr. Tuscola, Ill., 1978-80; adminstrv. mgr. travel stores Dixie Truckers Home, dba Shirley Oil and Supply Co., McLean and Tuscola, 1983-91; sec. bd. dirs. Dixie Truckers, McLean and Tuscola, 1985—. Owner, designer Creative Interiors, 1987—. Rep. precinct committeewoman, McLean, 1960-76; mem. bd. visitors Ill. Wesleyan U., 1980; trustee Wesley United Meth., Bloomington, 1986—, vice chmn., 1989; bd. dirs. YWCA, 1980-85, treas. bd. dirs., 1983-85; bd. dirs. Centrillio coun. Girl Scouts U.S.A., 1990-91, Route 66 Assn., 1994—, mem., 1990—; mem. McLean County Greenways Adv. Com., 1999. Mem.: Sigma Kappa, Ill. Wesleyan U. Alumni Assn. Avocations: reading, bridge, sculpture. also: Shirley Oil & Supply Co 401 E South St Mc Lean IL 61754-9701 Office: 2 Canterbury Ct Bloomington IL 61701-3401 Home: 124 Hawthorne Lake Rd Bloomington IL 61704-8530

BEEMAN, BARBARA, social work supervisor; b. Bayonne, N.J., Sept. 29, 1949; d. David and Jeanette (Agaman) B.; life companion Bill Bannon. BA, Jersey City State Coll., 1971. Lic. social worker, N.J. Reporter The Dispatch, Union City, N.J., 1971-73; social worker Hudson County Welfare, Jersey City, 1973-83, supr. social work, 1983—. Mem. steering com. Food and Shelter Coalition, Jersey City, 1990—. Singer, musician, bandleader: (with Barbara Beeman Band) Moving Day, 1986, So the Story goes, 1989, Spare Change, 2002; performer coffeehouses, bookstores. Performer Let's Celebrate "Race Against Hunger," Jersey City, 1985-93, Bayonne (N.J.) Hometown Fair, 1993, 94, 95, N.J. Seafood Festival, Belmar, N.J., 1991, 92, M.S. Race, Liberty Park, Jersey City, 1992-93, "Standdown" N.J. Homeless Vets. Conf., 1994. Democrat. Roman Catholic. Avocations: photography, writing. Home: 25 W 35th St Bayonne NJ 07002-3913 Office: Hudson Co Dept Social Svcs 100 Newkirk St Jersey City NJ 07306-3133 E-mail: bayonneb@aol.com.

BEER, CLARA LOUISE JOHNSON, retired electronics executive; b. Bisbee, Ariz., Jan. 14, 1918; d. Franklin Fayette and Marie (Sturm) Johnson; m. Philip James McElmurry, May 15, 1937 (div. July 1944); children— Leonard Franklin, Philip James Jr.; m. William Sigvard Beer, July 15, 1945 (dec. Aug. 1977); 1 son, Douglas Lee; m. Kenneth Christy Huntwork, May 1, 1982 (dec. Jan. 2003). Student, Merritt Bus. Sch., Oakland, Calif., 1935, Bus. Instrn. Sch., Palo Alto, Calif., 1955. Sec., artist M.R. Fisher Studios, Oakland, 1936-40; piano, organ instr. Anna May Studios, Palo Alto, 1948-50; pvt. piano, organ instr. Palo Alto, 1949-56; sec. Stanford Electronics Labs., Stanford U., 1955-58; corporate sec. and exec. sec. to chmn. bd. Watkins-Johnson Co., Palo Alto, 1958-88. Dir., sec. Watkins-Johnson Internat., 1968-88, Watkins-Johnson Ltd., 1971-88, Watkins-Johnson Assocs., 1977-88. Mem. Nat. Secs. Assn., Christian Bus. and Profl. Women's Coun. (sec. 1966-67, adviser 1968) Home: 24157 Hillview Rd Los Altos CA 94024-5222

BEERBOWER, CYNTHIA GIBSON, lawyer; b. Dayton, Ohio, June 25, 1949; d. Charles Augustus and Sarah (Rittenhouse) Gibson; m. John Edwin Beerbower, Aug. 28, 1971; children: John Eliot, Sarah Rittenhouse. BA, Mt. Holyoke Coll., 1971; JD, Boston U., 1974; LLB, Cambridge (Eng.) U., 1976. Bar: N.Y. 1975. Assoc. Cadwalader, Wickersham & Taft, N.Y.C., 1975-76, Simpson, Thacher & Bartlett, N.Y.C., 1977-81, ptnr., 1981-93; internat. tax counsel, dept. asst. sec. Dept. Treasury, Washington, 1993-96; chmn., CEO Reeve Ct. Ins. Ltd., 1997—2001; prin. The Quellos Group, N.Y.C., 2001—. Mem. ABA, Assn. Bar City N.Y., N.Y. State Bar Assn. (com. co-chmn. 1987-93). Presbyterian. Home: 720 Park Ave New York NY 10021-4954 Office: 667 Madison Ave New York NY 10021

BEERMAN, MIRIAM, artist, educator; b. Providence; d. William and Rose (Nochemsohn) B.; m. Julian F. Jaffe (dec. 1973); 1 child, William Jaffe. Student, Atelier 17, Paris, 1953; BFA, R.I. Sch. Design, 1945; postgrad., Art Students League, N.Y.C., 1945-46, New Sch. for Social Rsch., NYU. Prof. painting and drawing Queensborough C.C., CUNY, 1972—95; instr. Jersey City State Coll., 1973—75, Montclair (N.J.) Art Mus. Art Sch., 1974—90, Montclair State Coll., 1980—89. Artist-in-residence MacDowell Colony, 1959, Ossibaw Island, Ga., 1974, Camargo Found., Cassis, France, 1980—, Va. Ctr. for Creative Arts, Sweet Briar, 1983, 84, 86, 89, 90, 91, 92, 93, 94, 97, 98, 2000, 02, Leighton Artist's Colony, Banff Ctr., Alta., Can., 1986-87, Blue Mountain Ctr., N.Y., 1988, 93, 95, 97, Millay Colony for Arts, 1976, 91, Camargo Found., 1980, Mid-Atlantic Arts Found., 2000, Women's Studio Workshop, 2000. One-woman shows include Bklyn. Mus., 1971, Montclair Art Mus., 1974, 87-88, Graham Gallery, N.Y.C., 1972, 78, Mus. of St. John the Divine, N.Y.C., 1978, N.J. State Mus., Trenton, 1991, Klarfeld Perry Gallery, N.Y.C., 1993, Suffolk C.C., N.Y., 1993, Bergen Mus., Paramus, N.J., 1996, Jersey City Mus., 1997-00, [illegible] Wis., 2002, Chautauqua Ctr. Visual Arts, N.Y., 2004, also others; exhibited in group shows Inst. Contemporary Art, New Orleans, 1986, Newark Mus., 1985-86, Roanoke Mus. Fine Art, 1985, Bayly Mus., 1985, Corcoran Gallery of Art, Washington, 1994, Bergen Mus., Paramus, N.J., 1996, Montclair Mus., N.J., 1997, Ctr. for Book Arts, N.Y.C., 1996, 98, Women of the Book, 1997-2002, Bristol Meyers-Squibb Gallery, Lawrenceville, N.J., 2000, others; represented in permanent collections U. Del., Sterling Art Libr., Yale U., New Haven, Nat. Mus. Women in Arts, Washington, Israel Mus., Jerusalem, Israel, U. Oreg., Newark Mus., Whitney Mus., Am. Art, Bklyn. Mus., Montclair Art Mus., Arnot Art Mus., Morris Mus., Met. Mus. Art, N.Y., Mus. of Art, RISD, Providence, R.I., Queens Mus., N.Y., Jersey City Mus., Jewish Mus., N.Y.C., Women's Studio Workshop, Rosendale, N.Y., Allen Meml. Art Mus., Oberlin, Ohio, Skirball Mus., L.A., Spertus Mus., Chgo., Neuberger Mus., Purchase, N.Y., Bass Mus., Miami (Fla.) Beach, Kresge Mus., Lansing, Mich., Cocoran Mus., Wash., others. Recipient numerous awards including Childe Hassam Purchase award AAAL, 1977, prize 11th R.I. Arts Festival, 1969, Ives prize RISD, Disting. Artist award N.J. Coun. on Arts, 1987, Grand prize Am. Impressions Ben Shahn Galleries, Patterson U., 2003; grantee N.Y. State Coun. on Arts, 1971, N.J. Coun. on Arts, 1978, 83, 87, Womens Rsch. and Devel. Fund, CUNY, 1986, Rutgers Ctr. for Innovative Printmaking, 1987, 97, Joan Mitchell Found., 1994, Mid Atlantic NEA, 1996, Dodge Found. artist residency, 1998, 2000, 02, Pollock/Krasner Found., 2000, Midatlantic Arts Found., 2000, Womens Studio Workshop, Rosendale, N.Y., 2000, E.D. Found.; Fulbright fellow, Paris, 1953-55, Forest fellow Millay Colony, 1992, others.

BEERS, ANNE, protective services official; BA in Edn., Hamline U., 1975. Trooper trainee Minn. State Patrol, 1975-76, trooper East Metro dist. 2400, 1976-80, trooper 1, 1981-83, lt., 1984-88, capt., 1988-92, comdr. East Metro dist. 2400, 1993-95, maj., 1995-97, chief, 1997—. Named Woman of Yr. Women's Transp. Sem. of Minn., 1998. Mem. Minn. Chiefs of Police Assn., Internat. Assn. of Women Police, Internat. Assn. of Chiefs of Police, Law Enforcement Opportunities, Minn. Assn. of Women Police (Carolen Bailey Mentoring award 1992), Minn. Police and Peace Officers Assn. Office: Minn State Patrol 444 Cedar St Ste 130 Saint Paul MN 55101-2142

BEERY, BARBARA FAYE, secondary school educator; b. Flint, MI, Nov. 6, 1937; d. Ralph Lester and Anne Louise Rose; m. Carl Leonard Beery, Jan. 10, 1966 (dec. Sept. 1987); stepchildren: Julieanne, Elizabeth, Mary June, Deborah, John. BA in History, MA in Spl. Edn., Ariz. State U., 1971, DEd, 1992. Cert. paralegal Ariz., 1994. Tchr., coach Glendale (Ariz.) Union Sch. Dist., 1974—84, human resources adminstr., 1984—94. Adj. prof. No. Ariz. U., Flagstaff, Ottawa U., Phoenix. Home: PO Box 3548 Carefree AZ 85377-3548

BEETLE, KATE, designer, illustrator, calligrapher; b. East Orange, N.J., Mar. 6, 1951; d. Garrii LeClair and Lorraine Frances Ebert. BS in Geology, Richard Stockton Coll., Pomona, N.J., 1979. Exhibitions include Sunapee Crafts Fair, 1986—88, Sharon Arts Annual, 1989, 1994, League of N.H. Craftsmen Annual, 1993, Handed Down, Rivier Coll., 1994, ABC-The Letter Arts, 1996, WCA-NH Innaugural, 1996, juried exhibits, Sharon Arts Ann., 1989, 1994, League N.H. Craftsmen Ann., 1993, ABC-The Letter Arts, 1996, Handed Down, River Coll., 1994, WCA-N.H. Inaugural, 1996, Sunapee Crafts Fair, 1986—88. Vol. Manadnock Humane Soc. Recipient 2 Louie awards Internat. Greeting Card Assn., 1997. Mem. Granite Scribes (archivist), Sharon Arts Ctr., Nat. Mus. Women in the Arts. Democrat. Unitarian Universalist. Avocations: gardening, baking, piano, tatting. Office: 33 Longacre Ln Alstead NH 03602

BEGGS, ANNA TEA, special education educator; b. Miami, Fla., July 3, 1975; d. Rachelle and William Meissner; m. Timothy Philip Beggs, June 17, 2000. BS in spl. edn., Coll. of Charleston, 1993—97; MEd, Loyola Coll., 2000—03. Spl. Edn. Tchr. Md., 1997. Level v tchr. for students diagnosed emotionally disturbed Balt. County Pub. Schools, 1997—. Mem.: TABCO, NEA, Coun. for Exceptional Children.

BEGGS, PATRICIA KIRK, performing company executive; BA, Stephens Coll., 1970; MBA, U. Cin., 1984. Mktg. dir. Provident Bank, Cin.; with pub. rels. dept. Ctrl. Trust Co. (now PNC Bank), Cin.; dir. mktg. Cin. Opera, 1984-91, asst. mng. dir., 1991-97, mng. dir., 1997—. Office: Cin Opera Assn Music Hall 1241 Elm St Cincinnati OH 45210-2231

BEGLEY, CHARLENE, electronics executive; married; 3 children. BS in Bus. Adminstrn. magna cum laude, U. Vt., 1988. With transp. sys. GE, 1988—90, corp. audit staff, 1990—94, v.p. ops. capital mortgage svc., 1994—97, CFO transp., 1997, dir. fin. plastics, 1998—99, v.p. corp. audit staff, 1999—2001, pres., CEO transp. sys., 2001—. Office: GE Transp Sys 2901 E Lake Rd Erie PA 16531*

BEGLEY, JUNE ALICE, art educator; b. Chgo., June 25, 1946; d. Herbert Raymond and Edith Alice Nordby; m. Ronald Wayne Begley, Nov. 12, 1983; 1 child, Heather Ashlee. AA in Music, Citrus Jr. Coll., 1968; credential in bus. mgmt., U. Calif., Irvine, 1979; AA in Art, Victor Valey Coll., 1995; BA in Art, Calif. State U., San Bernardino, 1997. Cert. tchr. Bus. mgr. KMEX-TV, L.A., 1969—80, Pacific Video Post Prodns., L.A., 1980—82, KWIZ-AM/FM, Santa Ana, Calif., 1982—84, YID2-FM, Victorville, Calif., 1988—93; sec. Hesperia Unified Sch. Dist., Calif., 1993—98; tchr. art Rialto Unified Sch. Dist., Calif., 1998—. Mem.: AAUW (Scholarship award 1995), Nat. Art Educators Assn., Art Educators Network. Avocations: piano, cooking, gardening, watercolor.

BEGLEY, SHARON LYNN, journalist; b. Englewood, N.J., June 14, 1956; d. John Joseph and Shirley (Wintner) B.; m. Edward Groth III, July 24, 1983; children: Sarah, Daniel. BA, Yale U., 1977. Sci. editor Newsweek, N.Y.C., 1982—. Office: Newsweek 251 W 57th St New York NY 10019-1802

BEGUHN, SANDRA E. poet, writer; b. Kirksville, Mo., Nov. 3, 1942; d. Charles Elwin and Loeta Elaine (Payton) Funk; m. Lynn L. Beguhn, June 29, 1963; children: Kelly Lyn Beguhn Simpson, John Christopher. Student, MaryCrest Coll., Davenport, Iowa, 1962-63. Contbr. poetry to Capper's Weekly, Lyrical Iowa, Nat. Libr. of Poetry, Creative Arts and Enterprises. Mem.: Poetry Guild, Durango Colo. Poetry Gathering, Famous Poets Soc., Sparrowgrass Poetry Forum, Illiad Press, Mu Chi Sigma Soc. (pres.). Methodist. Avocations: travel, photography, writing. Home: 2115 W 34th St Davenport IA 52806-5301 E-mail: xalthim@mchsi.com.

BEHAR, JOY, television personality; b. Brooklyn, N.Y., Oct. 7, 1943; m. Joe Behar, 1965 (div. 1981); 1 child ; m. Steven Janowitz, 1982. BS in Sociology, Queens Coll.; MA in English, SUNY, Stony Brook. Teacher Lindenhurst H.S., Long Island, NY. Corrs. Comedy Cen.; host call-in radio show on WABC. Profl. actress: (tv series) Baby Boom, (tv pilot) The Rock, (guest appearances) Dr. Katze (CableACE award), (discussion panel) Politically Incorrect; (movies) Cookie, 1989, This is My Life, 1992, Manhattan Murder Mystery, 1993, Love Is All There Is, 1996, M Word, 1996; Broadway appearances include The Food Chain, The Vagina Monologues, Comedy Tonight; author Joy Shtick or What Is the Existential Vacuum and Does It Come with Attachments?, 1999; co-host The View, 1997-. Office: 320 W 66th St New York NY 10023-6304*

BEHLMAR, CINDY LEE, business manager, consultant, speaker; b. Smyrna, Tenn., July 4, 1959; d. James Wallace and Barbara Ann (Behlmar) Gribble. BBA, Coll. William and Mary, 1981; MBA, Old Dominion U., 1995. Cert. mgmt. acct.; cert. gen. mediator. Adminstrv. extern Hampton (Va.) Gen. Hosp., 1981-82; from mktg. rep. to supr. mktg. svcs. PruCare of Richmond, Va., 1983-85; exec. dir. PhysicianCare, Inc., Newport News, Va., 1986-89; provider rels. cons. Va. Health Network, Richmond, 1989-91; ind. cons. Tidewater Health Care, Virginia Beach, Va., 1991-92; COO Tidewater Phys. Therapy, Inc., Newport News, 1993-95; ind. cons. Yorktown, Va., 1996-97; contract mgr. Sentara Health Mgmt., Virginia Beach, 1998-99; state mgr. managed care Va. Oncology Assocs., 1999—. Sec., bd. dirs. Greater Peninsula Area Med.-Bus. Coalition, Newport News, 1987-89; symposium faculty mem. Am. Hosp. Assn., Orlando, Fla., 1987, Washington, 1988; profl. spkr. in field. Mem. ch. coun. St. Mark Luth. Ch., Yorktown, Va., 1988-91. Fin. Exec. Inst. scholar, 1993. Mem. Inst. Mgmt. Accts., Toastmasters Internat. (club pres. 1997-98, area gov. 1998-99, Club Toastmaster of Yr. 1997-98, Dist. Spirit Success award 1998, Dist. Area Gov. of Yr. 1998-99, Disting. Toastmaster 1999), Phi Kappa Phi, Beta Gamma Sigma. Avocations: reading, music theory and piano, art and fashion. Home: 922 Hanson Dr Newport News VA 23602-8910 Office: Va Oncology Assocs Bldg 200 895 Middle Ground Blvd Newport News VA 23606-4250 E-mail: CiLeBe@aol.com., cindy.behlmar@usoncology.com.

BEHNKE, DOLEEN, computer and environmental specialist, consultant; b. Alameda, Calif., Sept. 23, 1950; d. Charles Joseph Ziegler and Dola Faye (Cushing) Peterson; m. Glen A. Pellett, June 26, 1971 (div. 1986); children: Mark Dolan Pellett, Michael Jay Pellett; m. Danny L. Carr, Dec. 29, 1986 (div. 1996); m. Jon T. Behnke, June 28, 1996. BA, U. Wis., Madison, 1973. Notary pub. Mich. Budget analyst Ednl. Testing Svc., Princeton, N.J., 1979-80; tech. recruiter Uniforce Svcs., Inc., Rock Hill, S.C., 1983-84; mgr. tng. and documentation Electronic Data Systems Corp., Troy, Mich., 1985-87; tech. writer, trainer, analyst cons. CES, Inc., Troy, 1989-92; pres. D'Carr Co., Inc., Roseville, Mich., 1988-93; tech. writer, trainer, cons. Eaton Corp., Southfield, Mich., 1988-93; pres., CEO Carr-Ben Tech Ltd., Lake Orion, Mich., 1996—97, bd. dirs. Cons. Hazardous Materials Info. Exch., Washington, 1989—; installer, instr. Gt. Plains Acctg., Fargo, ND, 1990—; cons., tech. writer Saturn Corp., 1991—92, Blue Cross Blue Shield, Southfield, Mich., 1992—93, Southfield, 1995—96; tech. writer FANUC Robotics, N.A., Inc., Auburn Hills, Mich., 1993—95. Co-author: CIW-Weld Monitor, 1990, 1993. Mem.: NAFE, AAUP, Greater Trenton Musicians Union, Key Club (mktg. dist. chair 2002—03, dist. adminstr. 2003—), Oxford-Orion Kiwanis, Kiwanis Internat. (internat. com. K-Kids 2001—), Roseville Kiwanis (pres. 1995, lt. gov. elect 1996—97, lt. gov. 2001—02, cert. Kiwanis instr. 2002—), Am. Legion. Republican. Roman Catholic. Avocations: piano, swimming, computers, politics. E-mail: dfb876@charter.net.

BEHNKE, MARYLOU, pediatrician, educator; b. Orlando, Fla., Sept. 1, 1950; d. Ernest Edmund and Elizabeth (Kolb) Behnke. BS in Chemistry, U. Fla., 1972, MD, 1976. Diplomate Am. Bd. Pediatrics, Am. Bd. Neonatology-Perinatology. Intern dept. pediat. Coll. Medicine U. Fla., Gainesville, 1976-77, resident, 1977-79, chief resident, 1979-80, fellow in neonatology, 1981-83, asst. prof., 1979-81, 83-89, assoc. prof., 1989-99, prof., 1999, adj. asst. prof. Coll. Nursing, 1988-89, adj. assoc. prof., 1989-99, mem. senate-at-large, 1984-89, mem. grad. studies faculty, 1988-2000. Presenter nat. and internat. meetings, 1981—; med. dir. ICU Shands Hosp., Gainesville, 1983—89, [illegible] follow-up program, [illegible] ad hoc mem. spl. rev. com. human devel. rsch. NIH, 1991—96, chair, 1993, 94, mem. human devel. and aging-3 study sect., 1998—99; mem. BBBP-6 study sect., 1999—2002. Mem. editl. bd.: Death Studies, 1983—94; contbr. articles to profl. jours., chapters to books. Grantee, NIH, 1984—87, 1991—, Nat. Inst. Drug Abuse, 1991—, Ctr. Substance Abuse Treatment, 1993—95. Fellow: Am. Acad. Pediat. (sect. perinatal pediat. com. substance abuse); mem.: Am. Pediatric Soc., Fla. Soc. Neonatal Perinatologists, Fla. Interagency Coord. Coun. Infants and Toddlers, Soc. Pediatric Rsch., Nat. Perinatal Assn., Soc. Pediat. Rsch., Alachua County Med. Soc., Fla. Med. Assn. Republican. Mem. Ch. Of Christ. Avocation: reading. Home: 426 SW 40th St Gainesville FL 32607-2749 Office: J Hillis Miller Health Ctr Dept Pediatrics PO Box 100296 Gainesville FL 32610-0296 E-mail: behnkem@peds.ufl.edu.

BEHR, MARION RAY, artist, writer, business executive; b. Rochester, N.Y., Sept. 12, 1939; d. Justin Max and Sophie Gusta (Koffler) Rosenfeld. B.Art Edn., Syracuse U., 1961, M.F.A., 1962; m. Omri Marc Behr, June 24, 1962; children: Dawn Marcy Yael, Darrin Justin Mason, Dana Marisa Jana. Contbr. publs. for stories, crafts, mag. covers and toy designs to nat. mags. including McCall's, Good Housekeeping, Lady's Circle, 1962-77; one-woman shows include Douglas Coll., 1983, Pargot Gallery, 1989, Eldorado Gallery, 1992, Beamsderfer Gallery, 1992, Hunterdon Art Gallery, 1993; Hunterdon Mus. Art, 1998; Inst. Cultural Peruano Norteamericano, 1999, Johnson Gallery, 2002; exhibited in group shows at Contemporary Am. Artists, Scarsdale, N.Y., 1964, Douglass Coll., 1977, John Szoke Gallery, 1989, Kanagawa Prefectual Gallery, Yokohama, Japan, 1989, 80 Washington Sq. East Gallery, N.Y.C., 1990, Juniper Gallery, Napa, Calif., 1991, Eldorado Gallery, Colorado Springs, Colo., 1992, B. Beamsderfer Gallery, Highland Park, N.J., 1992, Artsquad Gallery, Easton, 1993, Lever House, 1995, Audubon Artists, 1995, 97, 99, Cork Gallery, 1996, Cheltenham Ctr. for Arts, 1996, Krasdale Gallery, 1998, Nat. Acad. Mus., 1998, Stark & Stark, 1998, Grounds for Sculpture, 2001, Zimmerli Art Mus., Rutgers U., New Brunswick; permanent print collection Smithsonian Instn. Nat. Mus. Art History, 1995, Jane Voorhees Zimmerli Art Mus., 1993, 96, 2002, Thai Royal Art Collection, Bangkok, 1995, Inst. Cultural Peruano Norteamericano, Peru, 1999; creator survey Women Working Home-the Invisible Workforce, 1978; pres. Women Working Home, Inc., Edison, N.J., 1980—; condr. workshops; author: (with others) Women Working Home: The Homebased Business Guide and Directory, 1981, 2nd edit., 1983; contbr. articles to popular mags., 1988-89, popular art jours., 1991-98, numerous articles to profl. jours.; illustrator Jewish Holiday Book, 1977; inventor (with Omri Behr) acid free, environmentally safe graphic etching process; installed Electrotech processor and taught first non toxic intaglio etching class at Stanford U., 1999; installed electroetch and established non-toxic etching in the Inuit Artists Holman Eskimo Co-op Art Center, Holman Island, NWT, Canada, 1999, U. Al Moutamid IBN Abbad, Asilah, Morocco, 2000, Howard U., Washington, Syracuse U., N.Y., 2001, U. Alaska, Juneau, U. Alaska, Fairbanks, 2001; extensive radio and TV appearances rep. Nat. Alliance Homebased Businesswomen. Mem. Kean for Gov. campaign, 1981; mem. White House Conf. on Free Enterprise Zones, 1982, Nat. Assn. of Women Artists, 1992, Soc. Am. Graphic Artists, So. Graphics Coun., 1992, Print Coun. N.J., 1993; trustee Women's Bus. Ownership Ednl. Conf., Inc., N.J., 1985; apptd. to N.J. Devel. Authority for Small, Minority and Women's Bus. Commn., 1986; Presdl. del. White House Conf. on Small Bus., 1986. Recipient N.J. Women in Bus. Advocate of the Yr. award SBA, 1984, Merit award Am. Artist Profl. League, Woman of Yr. in Bus. and Industry award, 1985, Audubon Artists Merit award, 1995; Syracuse U. alumni grantee, 1957; Arts and Humanities grantee Charles E. Lindbergh Fund, 1993-94. Mem. Nat. Alliance Homebased Businesswomen (pres. 1980-82, legis. chair 1982-85; originator, founder), Women's Caucus for Art, Audoban Artists. Jewish. E-mail: eee@electroetch.com., electroetch@prodigy.net.

BEHREND, BETTY ANN, municipal official; b. Canton, Mo., Feb. 26, 1948; d. James Marvin and Frieda Leora (Ludwig) DeWitt; m. Jerry Lee Behrend, Aug. 18, 1973; children: Jeffrey Lee, James Robert. BA in biology, Culver-Stockton Coll., 1970; MS in biology, U. N.Mex., 1972. Lab. technician Village of Los Lunas, N.Mex., 1983-88, wastewater supt., 1988-92, utilities dir., 1992—. Pres. N.Mex. Mcpl. Environ. Quality Assn., Santa Fe, 1997—; mem. Mid Rio Grande Tech. Adv. Com., Albuquerque, 1995—. Mem. Rio Grande Water Res. bd., vice-chmn. Water Providers Coun. Named Successful Woman of '90s Valencia News-Bulletin, 1993. Mem. N.Mex. Water/Wastewater Assn. (bd. dirs. 1984—, Outstanding Plant Ops. 1990, 91), Rocky Mountain Water Environment Fedn. (Analytical Merit award 1988), Solid Waste Assn. N.Am., Optimists (pres. Los Lunas club 1993). Republican. Methodist. Avocations: birdwatching and photography, gardening. Office: Village of Los Lunas 660 Main St NW PO Box 1209 Los Lunas NM 87031-1209 E-mail: behrendb@ciles-lunas.nm.us.

BEHRENS, BEREL LYN, physician, academic and healthcare administrator; b. New South Wales, Australia, 1940; MB, BS, Sydney (Australia) U., 1964. Diplomate Am. Bd. Pediatrics, Am. Bd. Allergy and Immunology. Intern Royal Prince Alfred Hosp., Australia, 1964; resident Loma Linda (Calif.) U. Med. Ctr., 1966-68; with Henrietta Egleston Hosp. for Children, Atlanta, 1968-69, T.C. Thompson Children's Hosp., Chattanooga, 1969-70; instr. pediatrics Loma Linda U., 1970-72, with dept. pediatrics, 1972—, dean Sch. Medicine, 1986-91, pres., 1990—, Loma Linda U. Med. Ctr., 1999—; pres., CEO Loma Linda U. Adventist Health Scis. Ctr., 1997—. Office: 11175 Campus St Loma Linda CA 92354 E-mail: myhanna@ahs.llumc.edu.

BEHRENS, ELLEN ELIZABETH COX, writer, counselor, educator; b. Fremont, Ohio, July 25, 1957; d. William Luther and Dorothy Cox. BA in English, Denison U., 1979; MFA in Creative Writing, Bowling Green State U., 1990. Writer in residence Ohio Arts Coun., 1991-94; ednl. devel. counselor Sch. Social Work Delphi Chassis Sys. facility U. Mich., Sandusky, Ohio and Flint, Mich., 1994-2000; mgr. instrnl. design and project mgr. Novations Learning Technologies, Lansing, Mich., 2000—. Adj. faculty Firelands Coll., Terra Tech. Coll., 1988-94; cons. Bowling Green State U., 1991-94. Author: None But the Dead and Dying, 1996; asst. editor: Mid-American Review, 1988-90, fiction editor, 1990-94, advisory editor, 1994—; contbr. short stories to anthologies, Wastelands Rev., Descant, Fiction, Echoes, Paragraph, other literary mags. Individual Artist fellow Ohio Arts Coun., 1992. Mem. Bowling Green State U. Creative Writing Alumni Assn. (bd. dirs. 1990—), Ohioana Lib. Assn. Office: Novations Learning Technologies MSU Rsch Park 3245 Technology Blvd Lansing MI 48910-8546 Office Phone: 517-336-8600 159. E-mail: ebehrens@novations.com.

BEHRENS, M. KATHLEEN, medical researcher; PhD in Microbiology, U. Calif., Davis. With Robertson Stephens Mgmt. Co., 1983—99, gen. ptnr., 1986-93; mng. dir. RS Investments, San Francisco, 1999—. Bd. dirs. Abgenix Inc., HealthTrio; mem. President's Coun. Advisors on Sci. and Tech. Mem. Nat. Venture Capital Assn. (pres. elect 1999—). Office: RS Investments 388 Market St San Francisco CA 94111 also: Abgenix Inc 7601 Dumbarton Cir Fremont CA 94555-3616

BEHRLL, CATHY G. special education educator; b. Peoria, Ill., July 25, 1951; d. James F. Lowery. BS in Edn., Bradley U., 1998; MS in Edn., Ill. State U., 2003. Cert. spl. edn. tchr. Ill., elem. edn. tchr. Ill. Tchr.'s asst. for spl. edn. of students with behavioral-emotional disabilities Peoria Pub. Schs., 1994—98, spl. edn. tchr. of students with behavioral-emotional disabilities, 1998—. Mem.: Coun. Exceptional Children (con.). Office: Peoria Public Schools Day Treatment 2900 W Heading Ave Peoria IL 61604

BEHRMANN, JOAN GAIL, newspaper editor; b. N.Y.C.; d. Jerome and Jeanette (Silberman) Metzner; m. Larry Jinks, Oct. 2, 1960 (div. 1970), children: Laura Jinks Kastigar, Daniel Carlton; m. Nicolas Lee Behrmann, Dec. 21, 1972. BA, Queens Coll., 1956; MS, Columbia U., 1958. Reporter Charlotte (N.C.) Observer, 1958-60, Miami (Fla.) Herald, 1960-64, Miami News, 1965-66; asst. prof. Miami Dade C.C., 1968-72; assoc. prof. Boston U., 1975-78; Sunday editor The Saratogian, Saratoga Springs, NY, 1979-80; editor Gannett Westchester, Westchester County, N.Y., 1981-83; page one editor, entertainment editor USA Today, Rosslyn, Va., 1983-87; exec. editor The Desert Sun, Palm Springs, Calif., 1987-95; arts editor The Detroit News, Detroit, 1996-2000; ret., 2000; freelance writer Trash or Treasure column, theater revs. Detroit News, Detroit, 2001—. Co-author: Questioning Media Ethics, 1978. Bd. dirs. Coll. of the Desert Found., Palm Desert, 1993-95, Jewish Family Svcs., Palm Springs, 1994-95, Palm Springs Opera Guild, 1989-91, Adult Well-Being Svcs., Detroit, Mich., 1997-2000, Mich. Opera Theatre, 2000—; founder Every Women's Coun., Glens Falls, N.Y., 1978-80. Recipient Athena award Palm Springs C. of C., 1991. Mem. Assn. Press Mng. Editors Orgn. (bd. dirs. 1991-96, com. chair 1996-97), Am. Soc. Newspaper Editors. Avocations: travel, reading. E-mail: jbehrmann@aol.com.

BEIDER, MARLYS ANNA, hotel executive, writer; b. Hannover, Germany, Feb. 7, 1945; d. Walter Schroeder and Elfriede (Ellen) Pallenberg-Schroeder; m. Harold Beider, Apr. 21, 1971 (dec.); children: Jacqueline Lee Shear, Kenneth Harry, Kelly Tema Rubin, Daniel Ayal. Bus., Buhmann Fachschule, 1960—63. V.p. Mid Am. Hotel Corp., Chgo., 1975—90, pres., 1990—. Author: (novels) Fateful Parallels, Continuum. Woman's bd. mem. North Shore Country Day Sch., Winnetka, Ill., 1981—91; adv. bd. The Theatre Sch. DePaul U., Chgo.; v.p. To Protect Our Heritage PAC, Chgo., 1985—90. Mem.: Royal Melbourne. Avocations: writing, opera, golf, hiking.

BEIDLEMAN, LINDA HAVIGHURST, biologist; b. Lakewood, Ohio, Apr. 23, 1948; d. John Graham and Mary Jane (Sagen) Havighurst; m. Jeffrey Stuart Price, Dec. 23, 1970 (div. Apr. 1983); adopted children: Joshua J., S. Benjamin; m. Richard Gooch Beidleman, June 3, 1991; stepchildren: Kirk, Janet B. Robson, Carol B. Tiemeyer. BA in Biology, Colo. Coll., 1970; MA in Biology, Rice U., 1975. Tchr. asst. Colo. Coll., Colorado Springs, 1969-70, instr., summer 1993; tchr. asst. No. Ariz. U., Flagstaff, 1970-71; self-employed prof. biologist El Cerrito, Calif., 1975—, Pacific Grove, Calif., 1991—. Instr. Rocky Mountain Nature Assn., Estes Park, Colo., summer 1995—, Aspen (Colo.) Ctr. for Environ. Studies, summer 1996—, Jepson Herbarium, Berkeley, Calif., 2000— Collaborator: (book) Marine Invertebrates of the Pacific Northwest, 1987; co-author: Plants of the San Francisco Bay Region, 1994, revised edit., 2003, Plants of Rocky Mountain National Park, 2000, The Annotated Bibliography of Colorado Vertebrate Zoology, 2000; contbr. articles to profl. jours. Soccer coach El Cerrito Soccer Club and H.S., 1977-88; soccer referee Alameda-Contra Costa (Calif.) Youth Soccer, 1978-95. Mem. Calif. Bot. Soc., Colo. Native Plant Soc. (v.p. plant sales 1985-92, mem.-at-large 1992-95), Calif. Native Plant Soc., Western Soc. Naturalists. Avocations: gardening, photography, hiking, reading. Home: 726 Richmond St El Cerrito CA 94530 Office: 766 Bayview Ave Pacific Grove CA 93950-2509

BEIDLER, MARSHA WOLF, lawyer; b. Bridgeton, N.J., Feb. 29, 1948; d. Benjamin and Esther (Lourie) Wolf; m. John Nathan Beidler, Aug. 18, 1974; children: Dora E., Evan A. BA, Dickinson Coll., Carlisle, Pa., 1969; JD, Rutgers U., Camden, N.J., 1972; LLM in Taxation, NYU, 1979. Bar: Pa. 1972, Fla. 1973, N.J. 1975; Fla. bar bd. cert. tax lawyer. Estate and gift tax atty. IRS, Phila., 1972-74, Trenton, N.J., 1974-76; atty. McCarthy & Hicks, Princeton, N.J., 1976-81; ptnr. Pinto & Beidler, Princeton, 1981-83; prin. Smith, Lambert, Hicks & Miller, Princeton, 1983-88; ptnr. Drinker, Biddle & Reath, Princeton, 1988—. Sec. Mercer County Estate Planning Council, 1977-86; prof. paralegal studies Rider Coll., Trenton, 1982; lectr. estate planning various corps. and univs. Bd. dirs. Birth Alternatives, Princeton, 1980; bd. dirs. Mercer Council on Alcoholism, Trenton, 1985-86. Fellow Am. Coll. Trusts and Estate Counsel; mem. ABA (taxation sect., real property, probate and trust sect.), Fla. Bar Assn., N.J. Bar Assn. (taxation sect.). Office: Drinker Biddle & Reath 105 College Rd E PO Box 627 Princeton NJ 08542-0627 E-mail: beidlemw@dbr.com.

BEIERSDORFER, ELIZABETH ANNE, music educator; d. Harold Dwayne and Miriam Jeanette Copp; m. Russell Alvin Beiersdorfer, Sept. 25, 1955; children: Corinne Nicole, Travis Michael, Adam Russell, Ethan Nathaniel. A in Applied Sci., Purdue U., West Lafayette, IN, 1977; B of Music Edn., No. Ky. U., Heighland Heights, 1993; MEd, Ind. Wesleyan U., Marion, 2003. Vet. technician Highland Heights Animal Hosp., Ky., 1978—84; music tchr. Oldenburg Acad., Ind., 1993—2002, fine arts dept. chair, 2002—. V.p. Harold Copp Farms, Inc., Columbia City, Ind., 2001—03. Mem.: Music Educators Nat. Conf., Sigma Alpha Iota (NKU Eta Psi chpt., charter pres. 1992—93, Sword of Honor 1993). Office: Oldenburg Acad 1 Twister Circle Box 200 Oldenburg IN 47036 E-mail: elizabeth_beiersdorfer@oa.batesville.k12.in.us.

BEILER, ANNE F. food company executive; m. Jonas Beiler; 2 children. Mgr. concession stand Md. Farmers Mkt., 1987; owner concession stand Farmers Mkt., Downingtown, Pa.; owner, chair, CEO Auntie Anne's, Gap, Pa., 1988—. Recipient Entrepreneur of Yr. award Inc. Mag., 1992, 94, Spirit of Achievement award Jr. Achievement Orgn. Ctrl. Pa., 1998; named one of 50 Pa.'s Best 50 Women in Bus., 1998. Office: Auntie Anne's Inc 160A Route 41 Gap PA 17527-9410

BEINECKE, CANDACE KRUGMAN, lawyer; b. Paterson, N.J., Nov. 26, 1946; d. Martin and Sylvia (Altshuler) Krugman; m. Frederick W. Beinecke II, Oct. 2, 1976; children: Jacob Sperry, Benjamin Barrett. BA, NYU, 1967; JD, Rutgers U., 1970. Bar: N.Y. 1971. Assoc., then ptnr. Hughes, Hubbard & Reed, N.Y.C., 1970—, chair, 1999—. Bd. dirs. First Eagle Funds, N.Y.C., 1996—, chair bd. dirs., 2004—; bd. dirs. ASTROM, 2001—. Bd. dirs. Merce Cunningham Found., N.Y.C., Jacob's Pillow Dance Festival, Lee, Mass., The N.Y.C. Partnership; mem. vis. com. Met. Mus. Art Watson Libr. Mem. ABA, Assn. Bar City of N.Y., River Club, Women's Forum. Office: Hughes Hubbard & Reed One Battery Park Plaza New York NY 10004-1466*

BEISCH, JUNE, freelance/self-employed writer, literature educator, poet; b. Ashland, Wis., Nov. 23, 1939; d. Theodore and Josephine Robertson; m. Charles Beisch, Sept. 5, 1964; children: Brooks, Leigh. BA, Harvard U., 1987, MA, 1991. Freelance writer, Boston, 1976—2001; journalist Boston Globe, 1976—90; interviewer Sta. WGBH, Boston, 1977—78; dir. Bus. Writing Program, Boston, 1984—87; instr. lit. Mass. Bay Coll., Wellesley, 1985—96, Emerson Coll., Boston, 1990—2000, Fisher Coll., Boston, 1992. Actress French Libr., 1992—97; poet-in-the-schs. Boston Schs., 1995—, Stonehan, Somerville. Author: (poetry book) Take Notes, 1990, Fatherless Woman, 2004; contbr. essays and fiction to mags. and jours. Recipient 1st pl. poetry, Middlesex CC, Boston, 1990; fellow, VA Ctr. for the Arts, 2002.

BEITZ, ALEXANDRA GRIGG, political activist; b. Cin., Oct. 15, 1960; d. Kenneth Andrew and Betty Ann (Carpenter) Grigg; m. Charles Arthur Beitz III, Oct. 17, 1987; 1 child, Madeleine Grigg Beitz. BA, Vassar Coll., 1982; MBA, Wake Forest U., 1985. Asst. buyer Bloomingdale's, N.Y.C., 1982-83, dept. mgr. Stamford, Conn., 1983; intern Ciba-Geigy Corp., Greensboro, N.C., 1984; retail sales promotion mgr. Hanes Hosiery, N.Y.C., 1985-86; market rep. May Co., N.Y.C., 1986-87; freelance polit. cons. Winston-Salem, N.C., 1990-98. Vol. Planned Parenthood, Winston-Salem, N.C., 1988-98, Southeastern Ctr. for Contemporary Art, Winston-Salem, 1992-98, exec. bd. dirs. Friends, 1983, v.p.-pres. elect, 1994, pres., 1995, exec. bd. dirs., 1995-98; vol. Am. Cancer Soc., Winston-Salem, 1992-94; bd. dirs. Planned Parenthood of the Triad, Winston-Salem, 1995-98. Avocations: photography, [illegible]

BEKAVAC, NANCY YAVOR, academic administrator, lawyer; b. Pitts., Aug. 28, 1947; d. Anthony Joseph and ELvira (Yavor) Bekavac. BA, Swarthmore Coll., 1969; JD, Yale U., 1973. Bar: Calif. 1974, U.S. Dist. Ct. (cen. dist.) Calif. 1974, U.S. Dist. Ct. (no. dist.) Calif. 1975, U.S. Ct. Appeals (9th cir.) 1975, U.S. Dist. Ct. (so. dist.) Calif. 1976, U.S. Surpeme Ct. 1979, U.S. Ct. Appeals (8th cir.) 1981. Law clk. at large U.S. Ct. Appeals (D.C. cir.), Washington, 1973-74; assoc. Munger, Tolles & Rickershauser, L.A., 1974-79, ptnr., 1980-85; exec. dir. Thomas J. Watson Found., Providence, 1985-87, cons., 1987-88; counselor to pres. Dartmouth Coll., Hanover, N.H., 1988-90; pres. Scripps Coll., Claremont, Calif., 1990—. Adj. prof. law UCLA Law Sch., 1982—83; mem. Calif. Higher Edn. Roundtable, 1996—; trustee Am. Coun. Edn., 1994—97. Bd. mgrs. Swathmore Coll., 1984—; trustee Wenner-Gren Found. Anthrop. Rsch., 1987—94; bd. trustees Am. Coun. Edn., 1994—97; chair Assn. Ind. Colls. and Univs., 1996—97. Recipient Human Rights award, L.A. County Commn. Civil Rights, 1984; fellow Woodrow Wilson fellow, Thomas J. Watson fellow, 1969. Mem.: Am. Assn. Ind. Calif. Colls. and Univs. (chair 1996), Sierra Club. Avocations: hiking, reading, travel. Office: Scripps Coll Office of Pres 1030 Columbia Ave Claremont CA 91711-3986*

BEKEY, SHIRLEY WHITE, psychotherapist; b. L.A. d. Lawrence Francis and Alice (King) White; m. George Albert Bekey, June 10, 1951; children: Ronald S., Michelle E. BA in Psychology, Occidental Coll., L.A., 1949; MSW in Psychiat. Social Work, UCLA, 1954; PhD in Edn. Psychology, U. So. Calif., 1980. Lic. clin. social worker, Calif.; cert. in pupil pers., parent-child edn. Caseworker outpatient svcs. Calif. State Dept. Mental Health, Montebello; caseworker Lowman Sch. for Handicapped, L.A. Unified Sch. Dist., North Hollywood, Calif., 1971-72; psychotherapist Hofmann Psychiat. Clinic, Glendale (Calif.) Adventist Hosp., 1973-75; pvt. practice Encino, Calif., 1980—2002; pvt. practice cons. Gifted and Talented, Relationship Counseling, Arroyo Grande, Calif., 2002—. Sprk. in field.; TV expert on children's emotional problems. 1st hosp. vol. candystriper in U.S., Hollywood Hosp, L.A., 1942; mem. World Affairs Coun., L.A., 1960—. Fellow Soc. for Clin. Social Work; mem. NASW, APA, Am. Ednl. Rsch. Assn., Nat. Assn. Gifted Children, Assn. Transpersonal Psychology, Inst. Noetic Sci., Assn. Ednl. Therapists, So. Calif. Soc. for Clin. Hypnosis, Analytical Psychology Club L.A., Nat. Assn. Poetry Therapy, Calif. Assn. for Gifted. Avocations: clinical hypnosis, gifted and talented, learning disabilities. Home and Office: 612 Via Belmonte Arroyo Grande CA 93420

BELAG, ANDREA SUSAN, artist; b. N.Y.C., Nov. 21, 1951; d. Julius Belag and Harriet (Goldberg) Belag-Lange; m. James Cole Bowness, Apr. 20, 1980 (div. Aug. 1989). Student, N.Y. Studio Sch., 1971-74. Lectr. visual arts program Princeton (N.J.) U., 1995; instr. Sch. Visual Arts, 1995—, SUNY., Purchase, 1992, Md. Inst. Coll. of Art, Baltimore, 1993; resident Bellagio Study Ctr. Curator Eight Painters, Jersey City Mus., 1980, 1981 Invitational, Selected Drawings, 1983, Ralph Hilton 1946-84, 1985, Mystery Show, 1985, The Mirror in Which Two Are Seen as One, 1989, Drawn Out, Kansas City (Mo.) Art Inst., 1987.; vis. artist N.Y. Studio Sch., 1983, Bard Coll., 1984, N.J. Coun. of Arts (fellowship juror), 1985, Kansas City Art Inst., 1987, N.Y. Feminist Art Inst., 1989, RISD, Providence, 1993, Hampshire Coll., 1999, Concordia U., Montreal, Que., Can., 1999. One-person shows include Jersey City Mus., 1979, N.J. State Mus., Trenton, 1984, John Davis Gallery, Akron, 1985, N.Y.C., 1987, 88, David Beitzel Gallery, N.Y.C., 1991, (monotypes), Richard Anderson Fine Arts, N.Y.C., 1992, 93, 94, Rutgers U., New Brunswick, N.J., 1995, Littlejohn Contemporary Art, N.Y.C., 1996, Bill Maynes Gallery, N.Y.C., 1998, 2000, 02, Galerie Heinz Holtmann, Cologne, Germany, 1998, 2000, 02, Bill Maynes Gallery, N.Y.C., N.Y., 2003; numerous group shows include Graham Modern, N.Y.C., 1991, Tibor de Nagy Gallery, N.Y.C., 1992, Galerie Bernhard Steinmetz, Bonn, Germany, 1992, 93, Newhouse Ctr. for Contemporary Art, Snug Harbor, N.Y., 1997, Michael Schneider Zeitgenossische Kunst, Bonn, 1997, 99, Rhona Hoffman Gallery, Chgo., 1997, Pratt Inst., Bklyn., U. Mich., Ann Arbor; represented in mus. collections including Newark Mus., N.J. State Mus., Moriss Mus. of Arts and Scis.; work represented in numerous publs. Fellow N.J. Coun. for Arts, 1984, Nat. Endowment for Arts, 1987, Mariposa Found. fellow Corp. of YADDO,

1994; grantee Blue Mountain Ctr., 1993; Guggenheim fellow, 1999, Bellagio Study Ctr. fellow Rockefeller Found., 2003. Studio: 137 W Broadway New York NY 10013

BELANGER, CHERRY CHURCHILL, elementary school educator; b. Berea, Ky., May 14, 1923; d. David Carroll and Anna El[illegible] ([illegible]) Churchill; m. Paul Adrien Belanger, Oct. 15, 1950 (dec. Feb. 1987); children: Peter Carroll, Karen Michelle Belanger-Magon. BA, Pomona Coll., Claremont, Calif., 1944; MA in Elem. Edn., Calif. State U., Northridge, 1983. Cert. tchr. early childhood edn. Actress Actor's Equity Assn., 1944-49; retail promotion asst. Bloomingdale's, N.Y.C., 1948-52; editor Living for Young Homemakers, N.Y.C., 1953-54, Bride-To-Be Mag., N.Y.C., 1955; off-camera editor NBC Home Show, N.Y.C., 1955-56; publicist home furnishing Alfred Auerbach, Bell & Stanton, N.Y.C., 1956-61; retail rep. Betsy Ross Martin Assocs., L.A., 1961-66; exec. sec. So. Calif. Assn. Bedding Mfrs., L.A., 1966-70; retail rep. Hercules Corp., L.A., 1971; tchr. early childhood edn. Carthay Nursery, Beverly Hills, Calif., 1971-78, L.A. Unified Sch. Dist., 1976-79, tchr. kindergarten and 1st grade, 1979-99. Den mother, treas., chmn., inst. rep. Boy Scouts Am., Beverly Hills, 1961-85; troop leader Brownies, Girl Scouts U.S., 1968-83. Recipient Silver Fawn award Boy Scouts Am., L.A., 1972, Elizabeth H. Brady Tchr. award So. Calif. Kindergarten Assn., 1997; honored Cherry Belanger Day in Beverly Hills, City Coun., 1976. Mem. DAR, AAUW, United Tchrs. of L.A. Avocations: drama, music, camping.

BELANGER, RANDI COLLEEN, special education educator; b. Penn Yan, N.Y., Dec. 27, 1962; d. William Wesley and Cheryl Ann Turner; m. Kenneth Donald Belanger, Sept. 4, 1988; children: Kendra Louise, Melissa Reed. B in Spl. Edn., Mansfield U., 1985. Cert. tchr. Ariz., 1986. Spl. edn. tchr. Steuben/Allegany BOCES, Bath, NY, 1985—86, LATCH Sch., Phoenix, 1986—87, Peoria (Ariz.) Unified Sch. Dist. #11, 1987—2002, Whitney Point HS, NY, 2002—. Nominee Disney Tchr. of the Yr., 2001. Mem.: Girl Scouts (assoc.; leader 2000—02, 15 yr. svc. pin 2002). Presbyterian. Office: Whitney Point High Sch 10 Kiebel Rd Whitney Point NY 13862

BELANGER, TRACI L. psychotherapist, writer; b. Whittier, Calif., Dec. 26, 1964; d. Ray Linn and Eleanor Lorraine (Guidas) Johns; m. Brian D. Belanger, Oct. 23, 1999. BA in Comm., Duquesne U., 1986; diploma of Social Svcs., Hesser Coll., 1993; MS in Counseling Psychology, Northeastern U., Boston, 1997. Lic. mental health clinician N.H., nat. cert. clinician. Asst. dir. continuing edn. Hesser Coll., Manchester, NH, 1990—95; house mgr. Moore Ctr. Svcs., Manchester, NH, 1995—97; emergency svcs. clinician Mental Health Ctr. Greater Manchester, 1997—. Mem. Cultural Diversity Task Force, Manchester, 2000—, Diversity Adv. Bd., Manchester, 2001—, N.H. State Diversity Task Force, 2001—; sec. Manchester Div. Task Force, 2002—. Mem.: N.H. Psychol. Assn. (bd. dirs. 1997—). Avocations: writing, reading, music. Home: 61 Theresa Ct Manchester NH 03103 Office: Mental Health Ctr Greater Manchester 401 Cypress St Manchester NH 03103

BELCHER, CAROLYN R. state representative; b. Lexington, Ky, Dec. 11, 1953; m. Danny Belcher. BS, Univ. of Ky, 1986. State Rep. House of Rep., Dist. 72, 1998—; Cert. Pub. Act. (CPA), 1991. Mem. State Gov., Econ. Devel. & Tourism; Vice chair Licensing & Oc.; mem. Sr., Mil. Affairs and Pub. Safety, Budget Rev. Subcommittee, Pub. Safety Subcommittee, Tobacco Task Force. Mem.: Chamber of Commerce (past pres.), DAV Aux., AICPA, KSCPA, KY Farm Bur., Christian Soc. Svc. Ctr. (past chair and current bd. mem.), Bath Co. Salvation Army (chair), Owingsville Woman's Club (past pres.), Kiwanis Club (pres. elect), Phi Kappa Phi Nat. Hon. Soc. Democrat. Christian. Office: Capitol Capitol Annex, Rm 351E Frankfort KY 40601 also: Dist PO Box 44 Preston KY 40366

BELCHER, DOROTHY S. state correctional department administrator; b. Macon, Ga., Sept. 3, 1954; d. Lawyer B. Stanley and Lena Mae Montgomery; divorced; children: Ayotunde Ronke Ware, Aziza Asha Belcher. BA, U. Wis., 1976. Cert. correctional probation officer, correctional officer inspector, Fla. Probation and parole officer I State of Fla. Dept. of Corrections, Miami, 1978-80, probation and parole officer II, 1980-83, pub. svc. officer, 1983-87, gold program coord., 1987-89, probation and parole supr., 1989-90, correctional probation sr. supr., 1990-91, correctional officer, sr. inspector, 1991-97, correctional probation sr. supr. Ft. Lauderdale, 1997-98, correctional probation dep. adminstr. Miami, 1998-99, correctional probation sr. cir. adminstr., 1999—. Fellow Eta Phi Beta; mem. 100 Black Women, Fla. Coun. on Crime and Delinquency, Criminal Justice Inst. (hon.). Democrat. Pentecostal. Avocations: reading, writing, singing, playing piano, gardening. Home: 17731 NW 32d Ave Opa Locka FL 33056 Office: State of Fla Dept Corrections Probation and Parole 3552 Okeechobee Rd Fort Pierce FL 34947-4597 Office Phone: 772-468-3933. E-mail: virtuousone1954@aol.com.

BELCHER, LA JEUNE, automotive executive; b. Chgo., Nov. 16, 1960; d. Lewis Albert and Dorthy (Brandon) B. BA, Northwestern U., 1982; postgrad., Am. Inst. of Banking, 1983-84; cert. paralegal, Roosevelt U., 1998. Notary pub.; securities lic.; ins. lic., Ill. Securities processor Am. Nat. Bank, Chgo., 1983, divisional asst., 1983-84; mgmt. trainee Toyota Motor Distbrs., Carol Stream, Ill., 1984-85, dist. parts mgr., 1985-90, sr. customer rels. adminstr., 1990-99; fin. rep. Waddell and Reed, 1992; from wholesale specialist, parts cons. to retail ops. cons. Toyota Motor Distbr., Aurora, Ill., 1998—2001, signature process mgr., 2002—. Rep. to Japan-U.S. Toyota Dealer Meeting, Tokyo, 1985; owner Crystal Clear Concepts. Author: (booklet) The Cutting Edge: 127 Tips to Improve Your Professional Image. Mem. alumni admissions coun. Northwestern U., Evanston, Ill.; bd. dirs. Boys and Girls Club; comty. docent Art Inst. Chgo. Mem. NAFE, NAACP, Northwestern Club Chgo., Toastmasters (edn. v.p. 1988, 94, 95, advt. v.p. 1989, pres. 1990-93), Delta Sigma Theta. Office: Toyota Motor Distbrs 2350 Sequoia Dr Aurora IL 60506-6211

BELCK, NANCY GARRISON, dean, educator; b. Montgomery, Ala., Aug. 1, 1943; d. Lester Moffett and Stella Mae (Whaley) Garrison; m. Jack Belck, May 27, 1976; 1 child, Scott Brian. BS, La. Tech. U., 1964; MS, U. Tenn., 1965; PhD, Mich. State U., 1972. Cert. tchr., La. State textile specialist coop. extension svc. U. Ga., Athens, 1965-67, chair, dir. Tucson, 1976-79; asst. prof./instr. Mich. State U., East Lansing, 1967-73; family econ. researcher USDA Agrl. Res. Svcs., Hyattsville, Md., 1973-75, nat. extension evaluation coord. Washington, 1978-79; dean, prof. Coll. Human Ecology U. Tenn., Knoxville, 1979-87; dean, prof. Coll. Edn. Cen. Mich. U., Mt. Pleasant, 1987—91, interim provost, v.p. acad. affairs, 1988-89; provost, vice chancellor academic affairs La. State U., 1991—93; chancellor So. Ill. U., Edwardsville, 1994—97, U. Neb., Omaha, 1997—. Author: Development of Egyptian Universities Linkages, 1985, Mid-Career Administrators, 1986, Textiles for Consumers, 1990. Mem. exec. com. Mich. Milescular Inst., Midland, strategic planning team Pub. Schs., Mt. Pleasant, 1989—; chair Women's Networking Group, Mt. Pleasant, 1990—. Mem. Am. Home Econs. Assn., Am. Assn. for Higher Edn., Am. Assn. for Colls. Tchr. Edn., Am. Home Econs. Assn., Rotary, Sigma Iota Epsilon, Omicron Nu, Phi Delta, Kappa, Omicron Delta Kappa, Phi Kappa Phi. Avocations: gardening, walking, internat. food tasting, traveling. Office: U of Nebraska at Omaha Office of the Chancellor Omaha NE 68182

BELDOCK, JOAN ELLEN, real estate broker; d. Paul Samuel and Blanche Coopersmith Fischbach; m. David N. Brahinsky, Nov. 25, 1984; children: Devra, Benard, John, Rachel. BS, degree in occupl. therapy, Tufts U., 1958. Occupl. therapist, N.Y., Mass., and Ill., 1958—72; real estate broker Beldock & Assocs., Metro Brokers, Denver, 1973—. Bd. dirs. Metro Brokers, Inc., Denver. Chairperson Park East Comty. Mental Health, Denver, 1985; sec. bd. Allied Jewish Apts., Denver, 2002; bd. dirs. Alzheimer's Assn., Denver, 1990. Democrat. Jewish. Avocations: golf, bowling, reading, swimming, painting. Home: 1561 S Krameria St Denver CO 80224 Office: Beldock & Assocs Metro Brokers # 300 1485 S Colorado Denver CO 80222 Office Phone: 303 753-1485. Personal E-mail: jeb1561@aol.com.

BELFER, NANCY B. design educator; b. Buffalo; d. Albert and Helen (S.) Barback; m. Bernard Belfer, Sept. 1, 1951; 1 child, Lauren Belfer Church. Diploma, Albright Art Sch., Buffalo, 1950; BS, SUNY, Buffalo, 1951; MFA, Buffalo State Coll., 1963. Prof. design SUNY, Buffalo, 1960—96. Author: Designing in Batik and Tie Dye, 1972, Designing in Stitching and Applique, 1972, Weaving: Design & Expression, 1974, Batik and Tie Dye Techniques, 1993; contbr articles to profl. jours.; solo exhbns. include Daemen Coll., Buffalo, 1994, Adams Art Gallery, Dunkirk, N.Y., 1995-96, Burchfield Penny Art Ctr., Buffalo, 2002, Arts in Embassies Program. Taipei, Taiwan, 2003; group shows include Am. Inst. NEA fellow, 1981; recipient numerous awards. Mem. Am. Craft Coun., Friends of Fiber Art Internat., Buffalo Soc. Artists. Avocation: photography. Office: SUNY Coll 1300 Elmwood Ave Buffalo NY 14222-1004

BELFORD, ROZ, real estate broker; b. Romania; came to U.S., 1950; d. Aaron and Marsha (Sax) Roth; m. Melvin Belford, Sept. 14, 1951 (dec. Nov. 1997); 1 child, Marsha. Baccalaureate, Heidelberg (Fed. Republic of Germany) U., 1949; student, Sorbonne U., Paris, 1949-50. Pvt. practice real estate and mortgage broker, Singer Island, Fla., 1984—. Mem. AAUW, Internat. Real Estate Inst., Am. Hotel and Motel Assn., Am. Technion Soc. (v.p. Palm Beach chpt.), Women's Am. ORT (v.p. chpt.). Jewish. Office: 2655 N Ocean Dr West Palm Beach FL 33404-4751 E-mail: rozbelford@attglobal.net.

BEL GEDDES, JOAN, writer; b. L.A. d. Norman and Helen (Sneider) Bel G.; m. Barry Ulanov, Dec. 16, 1939 (div. 1968); children: Anne, Nicholas, Katherine. BA, Barnard Coll. Columbia U., 1937. Researcher and theatrical asst. to Norman Bel Geddes, Inc., N.Y.C., 1937-41; publicity dir. Compton Advt., Inc., N.Y.C., 1942, new program mgr., 1943-47; pub. info. officer UNICEF, N.Y.C., 1970-76, chief editl. and publs. svcs., 1976-79, cons. devel. edn., promoter Universal Children's Day (over 100 countries), 1979-85, editor Almanac World's Children, 1985-90; editor Pate Inst. Bull., 1988-94. Tchr. drama Birch Wathen Sch., N.Y.C., 1950; mem. faculty Inst. Man and Sci., Rensellaerville, N.Y., 1969. Interviewer-hostess: weekly radio program Religion and the Arts, NBC, 1968; author: Small World: A History of Baby Care from the Stone Age to the Spock Age, 1964, How to Parent Alone: A Guide for Single Parents, 1974, To Barbara With Love--Prayers and Reflections by a Believer for a Skeptic (Catholic Press Assn. award 1974), Are You Listening, God?, 1994, Childhood and Children, a Compendium of Customs, Superstitions, Theories, Profiles, and Facts, 1998, Children Praying, Why and How to Pray with Your Children, 1999, (with others) Art, Obscenity and Your Children, 1969, American Catholics and Vietnam, 1970, The Future of the Family, 1971, Holiness and Mental Health, 1972, The Children's Rights Movement, 1977, And You, Who Do You Say I Am?, 1981; translator: (with Barry Ulanov) Last Essays of Georges Bernanos, 1955; editor: Magic Motorways (Norman B. Geddes), 1940, Earth: Our Crowded Spaceship (Isaac Asimov), 1974; editor in chief: My Baby mag, 1954-56, Congratulations mag, 1954-56. Rep. Balkan-Ji-Bar Internat. Orgn. for Child and Youth Welfare of the World, UN. Mem. Authors League Am., Assn. Former Internat. Civil Servants, The Coffee House, Teilard de Chardin Assn., Mcpl. Arts Soc. N.Y., Internat. Inst. Rural Reconstrn. (mem. internat. coun.), Thomas More Soc. (pres. 1966), Barnard Coll. Alumnae Assn. (class v.p. 1972-76, 92—, pres. 1976-82), N.Y. City Mission Soc., Guilford Friends of Music, Pate Inst. Human Survival (bd. dirs. 1989-95, editor bi-monthly bull. 1990-93), The Charles A. and Anne Morrow Lindbergh Fund, Citizens Against Govt. Waste. Roman Catholic. Home and Office: 60 E 8th St New York NY 10003-6514 Office: 60 E 8th St New York NY 10003-6514

BELICH, KAY S. music educator; d. Robert W. and Lorna O. Schoenfeld; m. Sam M. Belich, Aug. 16, 1975; children: Aaron F., Eva A. MusB, The U. of Wis., 1970—74; MusM, The Juilliard Sch., 1974—77. Lic. Teacher Dept. of Pub. Instrn., Wis., 1991. Singer NYC Opera Co., 1977—90; elem. sch. music tchr. Kenosha Unified Pub. Sch. Dist., Wis., 1991—96, West Allis/West Milw. Pub. Sch. Dist., 1996—; studio vocal and instrumental tchr. freelance, N.Y. and Milw., NY, 1968—, opera and concert singer N.Y. and Milw., 1972—; u. instr. Cardinal Stritch U., Milw., 1999—. Apprentice singer Ctrl. City Opera Co., Colo., 1975; union del. NYC Opera Touring Co., 1990; cooperating tchr. for student tchr. Carthage Coll., Kenosha, Wis., 1993—94; mentor West Allis/West Milw. Pub. Sch. Dist., 2001—02; cooperating tchr. for student tchr. Cardinal Stritch U., Milw., 2002—03. Singer performances include Cami Hall recital. Ch. coun. mem. Grace and St. Paul's Luth. Ch., NYC, 1980—81; various positions Mt. Hope Luth. Ch., West Allis, Wis., 1991—. Recipient Regional Finalist, Met. Opera, 1978, First Pl., Wis. Fedn. of Music Clubs, 1974; Full Tuition scholarship, The U. of Wis., 1970—74. Mem.: Am. Guild of Musical Artists, Take Off Pounds Sensibly (treas. 1998—). Lutheran. Achievements include Solo Debuts: with New York City Opera, 1982; with Music Under the Stars, 1991; with Skylight Opera Theatre, 1993; with Racine Symphony, 1996; with Waukesha Symphony, 1997. Avocation: organic gardening. Home: 2141 South 105 St West Allis WI 53227-1211 Office: Hoover School 12705 West Euclid Ave New Berlin WI 53151-4611 also: Cardinal Stritch Univ 6801 North Yates Rd Milwaukee WI 53217-3985

BELINSKY, ILENE BETH, lawyer; b. Boston, Jan. 30, 1956; d. Harry Lewis and Ann Natalie (Rubin) B. B.A., Simmons Coll., 1977; J.D. cum laude, New Eng. Sch. Law, Boston, 1980. Bar: Mass. 1980, U.S. Dist. Ct. Mass. 1981, U.S. Ct. Appeals (1st cir.) 1981, U.S. Supreme Ct. 1984. Reservitz, Steinberg & Belinsky P.C., Brockton, Mass., 1980-85; ptnr., 1985— ; bd. dirs. Southeastern Mass. Legal Assistance Corp., New Bedford, 1982-86. Bd. dirs. Brockton unit Am. Cancer Soc., 1983, 84. Mem. Mass. Bar Assn. (dir. young lawyers div. 1984-86), Mass. Women's Bar Assn., ABA, Plymouth County Bar Assn., Assn. Trial Lawyers Am., Mass. Acad. Trial Lawyers. Republican. Jewish. Office: 528 Pleasant St Brockton MA 02301-2515

BELK, JOAN PARDUE, English educator; b. Lancaster, SC, Oct. 4, 1933; d. William Hazel and Alfleda Steele Pardue; m. Joe Harvey Belk, Sr.; children: Joe Harvey Jr., Jennifer Elizabeth. Degree, Winthrop U., 1954; BA summa cum laude, U. Houston, 1957. Cert. tchr. Tex. Asst. to dir. librs. U. Houston, Houston, 1957—61; tchr. English Galena Park HS, Galena Park, Tex., 1961—62; tchr. English (advanced placement) Meml. HS, Houston, 1962—96; instr. English Houston C.C., Houston, 1996—2003. Musician, piano accompanist, piano tchr. Editor articles for profl. pubs. Mem. Chancel Choir, Royal Spring Civic Assn., Houston, 1989—, newsletter editor, 2002—; mem. Happy Hide-a-Way Civic Assn., Crosby, 1972—, Cancer Fighters Houston, Inc., 1998—, bd. dirs., 2003—; chmn. evaluations com. Expanding Your Horizons (conf. jr. HS girls), Houston, 1997—; accompanist children's choir, elder Spring Branch Presbyn. Ch., Houston. Recipient Friedheim Found. award, Winthrop U., 1954, Mrs. James P. Houstoun Found. award, U. Houston, 1957, Excellence in Tchg. award, So. Meth. U., 1992. Mem.: AAUW (com. chair 1997—), NEA, Spring Branch Ind. Sch. Dist. Minority Lit. Reading and Discussion Group (discussion leader 1990—96), U. Houston Reading and Discussion Group (sec. 1990—), Tex. Coun. Tchrs. English, Nat. Coun. Tchrs. English, Outstanding Lit. Book Club, Les Belles Lettres Club (pres. 1967—68), Shadow Oaks Garden Club (v.p. 1958—60, pres. 1960—61), En Amie Book Rev. Club, Phi Mu (award 1957), Kappa Delta Pi (award 1957), Phi Kappa Phi (treas. 1958—60, award 1957), Delta Kappa Gamma (rsch. com. chair 1998—2002). Presbyterian. Avocations: piano, bridge, travel, crocheting. Home: 2014 Southwick Dr Houston TX 77080 Office: Houston CC 1010 West Sam Houston Parkway North Houston TX 77043 Home Fax: 713-465-9535. Personal E-mail: joebelksr@aol.com.

BELKOV, MEREDITH ANN, landmark administrator; b. Chgo., Sept. 26, 1939; d. Louis and Sylvia (Charak) B. Student, U. Md. Recreation dir. Dept. Pks. and Recreation, Washington, 1960-69; outdoor recreation specialist Nat. Pk. Svc., Washington, 1971-73; chief disvn. recreation Golden Gate Nat. Recreation Area, San Francisco, 1973-75; chief interpretation and visitor svcs. Nat. Visitor Ctr., Washington, 1975-78, Dept. Interior Mgmt., Washington, 1978-79; supt. Chickamauga (Ga.) and Chattanooga (Tenn.) Nat. Mil. Park, 1979-87, Jean Lafitte Nat. Hist. Pk. and Preserve, New Orleans, 1987-90, Statue of Liberty, Ellis Island, N.Y.C., 1990—. Bd. dirs. N.Y. Conv. and Visitors Bur., Greater New Orleans Tourist and Conv. Commn., Inc., New Orleans Jazz and Heritage Found. V.p. Chattanooga Symphony and Opera, U. Tenn. Roundtable, Chattanooga Audubon Soc. Fellow NCCJ; recipient Freedom Found. award. Mem. Nat. Pk. and Recreation Assn., Hist. Soc., Mus. Coun. N.Y. Jewish.*

BELL, CAROLYN WILKERSON, English educator; b. El Paso, Tex., Nov. 16, 1943; d. Jack and Dorothy (Davenport) Wilkerson; m. Alexander Wayne Bell, June 11, 1966; 1 child, Stephen. AB, Randolph-Macon Woman's Coll., 1965; AM, U. Pa., 1966; PhD, U. Tex., 1972. Prof. English Randolph-Macon Woman's Coll., Lynchburg, Va., 1971—, Susan Duval Adams prof. English, 1992—. Usage panelist Am. Heritage Dictionary, 1987—; panelist NEH, 1980, 81; cons. Legacy Project, Inc., Lynchburg, 1995—. Author: Learning the Contradictions: A History of Randolph-Macon Woman's College 1950-93, 1998; contbr. articles to profl. jours. Precinct worker Dem. Party, Tex., Va., 1968—. Mem. Nat. Coun. Tchrs. English, Phi Beta Kappa, Omicron Delta Kappa. Democrat. Methodist. Avocation: gardening. Home: 42 N Princeton Cir Lynchburg VA 24503-1547 Office: Randolph Macon Woman's Coll 2500 Rivermont Ave Lynchburg VA 24503-1555

BELL, CHRISTINE MARIE, secondary educator; b. Bluefield, W.Va., Nov. 5, 1961; d. Robert Warren and Therese (Wolinski) Stroh; m. Harlin Lindel Bell, Aug. 3, 1991; children: Shelby Katherine. BA, Mary Washington Coll., Fredericksburg, Va., 1983; MEd, U. Va., 1986. Cert. history and social studies tchr., Va. Adminstrv. asst. U. Va. Hosp., Charlottesville, 1984-85; tchr., counselor Oakland (Va.) Residential Sch., 1986-87; tchr. social studies Hopewell (Va.) High Sch., 1987—, coord. computers for edn. program, 1991-93. (workshops) Va. Gov. Best Practice Ctr., 2001; (documentaries) Dept. of Edn. Hour, 2001. Advisor model exec. br. YMCA, Richmond, Va., 1991-92, advisor model gen. assembly, 1991—. Recipient YMCA service to youth award, YMCA, 1996, Resolution of Appreciation, Va. Dept. of Edn. Sch. Bd., 2001, Tchr. of the Yr., Hopewell City Sch., 2001. Mem. APA (affiliate), ASCD, Nat. Coun. for Social Studies, Va. Geog. Soc., New Va. Dept. of Edn. Database ofexemplary educators, Avocations: politics, reading, travel, swimming, jogging. Home: 96 Sand Hill Rd Williamsburg VA 23188-6600 Office: Lafayette High Sch Williamsburg VA 23188

BELL, CONSTANCE CONKLIN, child care association administrator; b. Columbus, Ohio, June 2, 1934; d. John Brevoort and Josephine (Suttles) Conklin; m. Robert Kilborne Hudnut, Sept. 12, 1957 (div. June 1975); children: Heidi A., Robert K. Jr., Heather E., Matthew C.; m. Gerald Duane Bell, June 25, 1977. BA, Ohio Wesleyan U., 1956; postgrad., Union Theol. Sem., 1956-57. Tchr. Cen. Presbyn. Ch. Nursery Sch., N.Y.C., 1956-59; ctr. coordinator Greater Mpls. Day Care Assn., 1973—, asst. dir., 1977, assoc. dir., 1982, exec. dir., 1991—95. Minn. Licensing Com., 1985—, Minn. Child Care LIcensing Com., 1986-87. Author: How to Start A Child Care Center, 1977, rev. edit., 1983, Sick Child Care, A Problem for Working Parents and Employers, 1983; (with others) Business and Childcare Handbook, 1981. Mem. social ministries com. Greater Mpls. Coun. of Chs., 1983-88, bd. dirs., 1988-92, strategic planning comm. 1993—, Mpls. Community Bus. Employment Alliance, 1984-85, Project Self-Sufficiency, Mpls., 1984—; mem. priorities com. United Way Mpls. Area, 1984-88, mem. mgmt. United Way Com. Success by Six, 1988—2002; elder St. Luke's Presbyn. Ch., 1978-81. Recipient special recognition award, City of Minn., 1995, Ruth Hathaway Jewson Disting. Service to families award, Coun. of family relations, 1995, Resolution of Commedation, Hennepin County commr., 1995. Mem. Minn. Assn. for Edn. of Young Children (area award 1987), Mn assn. for educ of young children (pres. 1990-93), Minn. Children's Lobby, Child Care Works Steering Com., Parents in the Workplace (co-dir. 1983—), Kappa Alpha Theta (pres. Delaware, Ohio chpt. 1955-56); bd. congregations concerned for children, 1990—. Democrat. Home: 4973 Devonshire Cir Excelsior MN 55331-9329 Office: Greater Mpls Day Care Assn 1628 Elliot Ave Minneapolis MN 55404-1620

BELL, DELORIS WILEY, physician; b. Solomon, Kans., Sept. 30, 1942; d. Harry A. and Mildren H. (Watt) Wiley; children: Leslie, John. BA, Kans. Wesleyan U., 1964; MD, U. Kans., 1968. Diplomate Am. Bd. Ophthalmology. Intern St. Luke's Hosp., Kansas City, Mo., 1968-69; resident U. Kans. Med. Ctr., Kansas City, 1969-72; practice medicine specializing in ophthalmology Overland Park, Kans., 1973—. Mem. AMA, Kans. Med. Soc. (pres. sect. ophthalmology 1985-86, spkr. house 1994-97), Am. Acad. Ophthalmology (councillor 1988-93, chmn. state govtl. affairs 1993-97, bd. trustees 2000-03), Kans. Soc. Ophthalmology (pres. 1985-86), Kansas City Soc. Ophthalmology and Otolaryngology (sec. 1984-86, pres.-elect 1988, pres. 1989). Avocations: photography, travel. Office: 7000 W 121st St Ste 100 Shawnee Mission KS 66209-2010 Office Phone: 913-498-2015. E-mail: cd2c@aol.com.

BELL, ELVA GLENN, retired secondary school educator, retired counseling administrator, interpreter; b. Phila., Sept. 3, 1922; d. Arthur Edward Glenn, Ruth Ann Marie Demby Glenn; m. Howard Wesley Bell, Sr.; children: Howard Bell, Jr., Linda Bell-Powell. BS in Edn., Cheyney State Coll., 1945; MS in Edn., Temple U., 1970. Case worker Dept. Pub. Assistance, Phila., 1945—51; tchr., guidance counselor Phila. Sch. Dist., 1956—71; guidance counselor Abington (Pa.) Sch. Dist., Pa., 1971—82; interpreter at Clivden - Hist. Mansion Nat. Trust Property, Germantown, Pa., 1987—. Sch./cmty. rep. human rels. adv. coun. Abington Sch. Dist., 1974—. Mem., chairperson ways and means com. United Neighbors, Willow Grove, 1975—; mem. Abington Coalition of Civics - Abington Township, 1996—; bd. mem., Unity Day chairperson, life mem. NAACP - Willow Grove, 1939—; Congl. sr. intern CLOSE-UP, Washington, 1997—. Recipient Cmty. Svc. and Leadership award, Citizens for Progress, 1976, Trailblazer award, Willow Grove NAACP, 1985, Cmty. Svc. and Leadership award, Optimist Club Lower Montgomery County, 1986, Ho. of Reps. citation, Pa., 1987, 1999, Martin Luther King award, Abington Twp., 1988, Svc. award, Willow Grove NAACP, 2001. Mem.: AAUW, Black Women's Ednl. Alliance (treas., fin. sec. 1980—86, newsletter editor, Svc. award 1986, Cmty. Svc. and Leadership award 1986), Zeta Phi Beta Sorority - Beta Delta Zeta Chpt. (vol.). Lutheran. Avocations: travel, church activities, community activist.

BELL, FRANCES LOUISE, medical technologist; b. Milton, Pa., Apr. 28, 1926; d. George Earl and Kathryn Robbins (Fairchild) Reichard; m. Edwin Lewis Bell II, Dec. 27, 1950; children: Ernest Michael, Stephen Thomas, Eric Leslie. BS in Biology cum laude, Bucknell U., 1948; MT, Geisinger Meml. Hosp., 1949. Registered med. technologist. Med. technologist Burlington County Hosp., Mt. Holly, N.J., 1949-50, Robert Packer Hosp., Sayre, Pa., 1950, Carle Hosp./Clinic, Urbana, Ill., 1951-52, St. Joseph Hosp., Reading, Pa., 1972-83. Vol. Crime Watch, City Hall, Reading, 1985-90, Am. Heart Assn., Reading, 1956-2000, March of Dimes, Reading, 1956-72, Am. Cancer Soc., Reading, 1956-71, Multiple Sclerosis, Reading,

1956-72, Reading Musical Found., 1985-90, Hist. Soc. Berks County; corr. sec. women's aux., 1986-90; fin. sec. aux. Albright Coll., 1988-95; hospitality co-chmn. women's com. Reading Symphony Orch., 1985-90, editor yearbook women's com., 1992-96; editor yearbook Reading Symphony Orch. League, 1996-2003; chmn. hospitality Reading-Berks Pub. Librs., 1988-91; mem. Friends Reading Mus., Berks County Conservancy. Mem. AAUW (assoc. editor bull. 1961-63, cultural interests rep. 1967-68), Woman's Club of Reading (treas. 1986-88, fin. sec. 1991—), United Meth. Women, World Affairs Coun. Berks County, Libr. Soc. Albright Coll., Phi Beta Kappa. Republican. Methodist. Avocations: music appreciation, photography, postcard art prints. Home: 1454 Oak Ln Reading PA 19604-1865

BELL, GLORIA JEAN, academic administrator, literature educator, dean; b. Greensboro, N.C., Oct. 10, 1939; d. John T. and Mary Ellen (Gray) Bell. BA, So. Wesleyan U., 1961; MA, U. N.C., 1963; PhD, U. Colo., 1982. English tchr. N.W. Guilford HS, Greensboro, 1962-63; tchr. Partlow State Sch., Tuscaloosa, Ala., 1963-64; English and reading tchr. Tuscaloosa HS, 1964-65; English instr. U. Ala., Birmingham, 1965-70; asst. prof. English Presbyn. Coll., Clinton, SC, 1974-77; faculty mem. So. Wesleyan U., Central, SC, 1977—, English prof., 1981—, chair divsn. humanities, 1981-93, acad. v.p., dean, 1993—. Mem. transfer adv. bd. Tri-County Coll., Pendleton, SC, 1993—98, chair, 1996—97. Contbr. articles to profl. jours. Ad hoc com. mem. Wesleyan Ch., 1997—; S.E. regional steering com. Conf. Christianity and Lit., 1985—88, 1994—96; mem. Clemson Area Leadership Program, 1995; judge Lt. Gov.'s Award for Composition, Pickens County, 1981. Recipient Govs. Disting. prof., Susan B. McWhorter Outstanding Woman Profl., 1998. Fellow: Coun. Christian Colls. & Univs. (exec. leadership inst.); mem. S.C. Women Higher Edn. (conf. steering com. 1983—84, 1996—97), Phi Delta Kappa. Avocations: travel, needlepoint, gardening, music. Office: Southern Wesleyan U PO Box 1020 907 Wesleyan Dr Central SC 29630-9748

BELL, JACQUELINE DELORES, management consultant; b. Cleveland, Ohio, Feb. 28, 1951; d. Gwendolyn Cherry Marks and William Glover; children: Corey, Shaun. AB, Atlanta Area Tech. Coll., 1970. Dir. bus. devel. Dreamsan, Inc., College Park, Ga., 2001—; mgr. customer svc. Denon Digital Industries, Madison, Ga., 1987—2001. Mem. Monticello City Coun., Monticello, Ga., 1992—2002; pres. 5th dist Ga. Mcpl. Assn., Atlanta, 2001—02; bd. dirs. Funderburg Park Commn., Monticello, Jasper County Family Connection, Monticello; mem. exec. bd. Ga. Assn. Black Elected Ofcls., Atlanta, 1998—2002; bd. dirs. Ga. Mcpl. Assn., Atlanta. Named One of 50 Most Influential Black Women in Ga., Ga. Informer News Publ., 2000-2001; recipient Racial Barrier Breaker - History Maker award, The James Wimberly Inst. Black Studies & History Inc., 2002. Mem.: Nat. League Cities (cmty. devel. policy com. 2002). Democrat. Avocation: travel. Home: 778 Funderburg Dr Monticello GA 31064 Office Phone: 404-559-9700.

BELL, JACQUELINE MICHELLE, marketing professional, public relations executive; b. Dallas, Oct. 3, 1961; d. Robert Moore Sr. and Rebecca Jane Bell; 1 child, Malcolm Bell-Yeldell. BFA, So. Meth. U., 1985; MS, Amber U., 1990. Min. of music Mt. Calvary Missionary Bapt. Ch., Dallas, 1980—; owner It Must Be Jamm!, Dallas, 1996—; grants writer Dallas Mus. Art, 1990-93; dir. devel., mktg. and edn. Jr. Black Acad. of Arts and Letters, Dallas 1993; coord. fed and found. rels. Paul Quinn Coll., Dallas, 1997-98; pub. info. mktg. Dallas Can Acad., 1991-93; ednl. devel. mktg. The Arts of African American Family Outreach So. Dallas, 2000—. Devel. chair The Women's Mus., Dallas, 2000—. Mem. Class of 2000, Leadership S.W., Dallas, 1999-00. Mem. Dallas-Ft. Worth Assn. Black Communicators, Internat. Assn. Bus. Communicators, Pub. Rels. Soc. Am., Delta Sigma Theta (Golden Life mem., chpt. pres., corr. sec., collegiate advisor, Outstanding Young Delta 1986, named one of Dallas Shakers and Movers, 2001, Amerigroup Healthy Heros award 2001). Democrat. Baptist. Avocations: reading, piano, gardening.

BELL, JEAN MARIE, music educator; b. Darby, Pa., May 3, 1964; d. Eugene Francis and Barbara Jean Fisher; m. Harold Stephen Bell, June 25, 1988; children: Jason Eugene, Benjamin Alexander. BS in Music Edn., West Chester U., 1987; postgrad., U. N.C., Pembroke, 2003—. Music tchr. K-6 Grafenwohr (Germany) Elem., 1990—91, Vilseck (Germany) Elem., 1990—91; music tchr. K-4 Ft. Bragg (N.C.) Schs., 1992—95; ch. pianist Arran Lake Bapt. Ch., Fayetteville, NC, 1992—; jr. high music tchr. Albritton Jr. H.S., Ft. Bragg, 1995—. Bd. dirs. Arran Lake Christian Acad., Fayetteville, Fayetteville State U. Edn. Recipient Mary E. Walker award, U.S. Mil., 1994, Crystal Apple award, Horace Mann Cos., 2002. Mem.: NEA, Fayetteville Edn. Assn., Music Educators N.C. Avocations: playing piano, volleyball, sailing, gardening, reading.

BELL, JOSEPHINE CRAWFORD, music educator; d. Willie Lee and Emma Mariner Crawford; m. James Robert Bell, Aug. 5, 1961; children: Bruce Irwin, Kimbra Aria, Kandice Allegra. BA, Talladega Coll., 1961; M in Music Edn., U. Ark., 1967; PhD, Kans. State U., 1976. Instr. Talladega (Ala.) County Schs., 1961—63, U. Ark., Pine Bluff, 1963—2002, chair dept. music, 1990—2003. Vocal soloist Sorority, Links, Inc. Mem.: Alpha Kappa Alpha (pres. 1990—92). Avocations: travel, interior decorating, singing. Home: 58 Westchester Ct White Hall AR 71602

BELL, KATHY DAWN, medical/surgical nurse; b. Camden, N.J., Apr. 15, 1967; d. Ernest and Carol (Henson) B. AS, Camden (N.J.) County Coll., 1993. LPN, N.J. Dietary aide Copper River Convalescent Home, Pennsauken, N.J., 1982-84; nurses aide Praza Med. Ctr., Camden, 1985-87; LPN Greenbriar Nursing Home, Woodbury, N.J., 1990-92, St. Mary's Cath. Home, Cherry Hill, N.J., 1992-94. Recipient George Miller award Preston Gunning, Camden, 1986. Mem. NAFE (adv. 1993—), Nat. League for Nursing (adv. 1990—). Baptist. Home: 1857 S 8th St Camden NJ 08104-3409

BELL, LEE PHILLIP, television personality, television producer; b. Chgo. d. James A. and Helen (Novak) P.; m. William Joseph Bell, Oct. 23, 1954; children: William J., Bradley, Lauralee. BS in Microbiology, Northwestern U., 1950. With CBS-TV, Chgo., 1952-86; pres. Bell-Phillip TV Prodns., 1985—. Bd. dirs William Wrigley, Jr. Co., Chgo. Bank Commerce, Phillips Flowers Inc. TV and radio shows include Lee Phillip Show, Chgo., from 1952, Lady and Tiger Show WBBM Radio, from 1962, WBBM TV from 1964; hostess Noon Break, numerous TV Spls. including Forgotten Children, The Rape of Paulette (nat. Emmy award, duPont Columbia award); Children and Divorce (Chgo. Emmmy award) co-creator: (with William Bell) The Young and the Restless CBS-TV daytime drama, 1973 (Emmy award); co-creator, exec. producer The Bold and the Beautiful, 1987—. Bd. dirs. United Cerebral Palsy, Chgo. Unlimited, Northwestern U. Hosp., Chgo. Heart Assn., Nat. Com. Prevention of Child Abuse, Mental Health Assn., Children's Home and Aid Soc., Salvation Army, Chgo., Family Focus; mem. Chgo. Maternity Ctr.; life mem. Northwestern U. Bd. Trustees. Recipient 16 Chgo. Emmys; Top Favorite Female award TV Guide mag., 1956, Outstanding Woman of Radio and TV award McCall's mag., 1957-58, 65, bd. govs. award Chgo. chpt. Nat. Acad. TV Arts and Scis., 1977, William Booth award for community svc. Salvation Army, 1990; named Person of Yr. Broadcast Advt. Club, Chgo., 1980. Mem. Am. Women Radio and TV (Golden Mike award 1968, Broadcaster of Yr. 1993), Acad. TV Arts and Scis. (bd. dirs.), Chgo. chpt. Acad. TV Arts and Scis., Women's Athletic Club of Chgo., Commercial Club, Delta Delta Delta. Home: 9955 Beverly Dr Beverly Hills CA 90210 Office: CBS c/o Bold and Beautiful 7800 Beverly Blvd Los Angeles CA 90036-2188 Office Phone: 323-575-4138. E-mail: dianemoss@boldandbeautiful.tv.

BELL, LINDA GREEN, psychology educator, therapist; b. Austin, Tex., July 12, 1944; d. Leslie Mason and Anna Violet Weber Green; m. David Chalres Bell, Dec. 27, 1965; children: Michael James, Eric Matthew, Claire Toshiko Ishikawa. BA, Oberlin (Ohio) Coll., 1967; MA, U. Tex., 1968; PhD, Duke U., 1973. Postdoctoral rsch. fellow U. Chgo., 1974-76; rsch. asst. Scientific Methods Inc., Austin, 1964-67; vis. rschr. Nat. Inst. of Mental Health, Ichikawa, Chiba, Japan, 1985-87; prof. psychology and family therapy U. Houston-Clear Lake, 1976—. Rchr. in field; presenter and workshops in family rsch. and family therapy. Contbr. articles to profl. publs. Vol. Peace Corps, Senegal, Liberia, 1968-70. Grantee, NIMH, 1976—77, 1977—83, Hogg Found. for Mental Health, 1978—82, Tex. Coord. Bd. for Higher Edn., 1998—2002. Fellow: APA, Nat. Coun. on Family Rels., Am. Family Therapy Acad., Am. Assn. for Marriage and Family Therapy. Democrat. Mem. Soc. Of Friends. Avocation: music.

BELL, M. JOY MILLER, financial planner, real estate broker; b. Enid, Okla., Dec. 29, 1934; d. H. Lee and M.E. Madge (Hatfield) Miller; m. Richard L.D. Berlemann, July 21, 1957 (div. Nov. 1974); children: Richard Louis, Randolph Lee; m. Donald R. Bell, Aug. 17, 1996; children: Jeri, Johnna, Nolan, Charles, Mary. BSBA, N.Mex. State U., 1956. CFP; grad. Realtors Inst.; fellow Life Underwriting Tng. Coun. Tchr. bus. and math. Alamogordo (N.Mex.), Las Cruces (N. Mex.) and Omaha Pub. Schs., 1956-63; tchr., dir. Evelyn Wood Reading Dynamics So. N.Mex. Inst., 1967-68; registered rep. Westamerica Fin. Corp., Denver, 1968-76; gen. agt. Security Benefit Life, Topeka, 1969—2001, Delta Life & Annuity, Topeka, 1969—; registered rep. AGF Sponsors, Inc., Denver, 1976—; pres., broker Fin. Design Corp. R.E. (name changed to Bell, Inc. 1997), Las Cruces, 1977—; with Allianz L.I. Co. N.Am., 2000—. Mrs. U.S. Savings Bonds ofcl. goodwill amb. U.S. Treasury, U.S. Savs. Bond Divsn., Washington, 1968-70. Contbr. articles to profl. jours. Vice pres. Dona Ana County Fedn. Rep. Women. Recipient Top Sales Person award Investment Trust and Assurance, 1976-77; named Outstanding Young Woman of N.Mex., 1970, Outstanding Young Women of Am., 1970. Mem. Nat. Assn. Realtors, Nat. Assn. Ins. and Fin. Advisors, Nat. Assn. Ret. Fed. Employees (v.p. programs local chpt.), Internat. Assn. Registered Fin. Planners, Fin. Planners Assn., S.W. N.Mex. Assn. of Ins. and Fin. Advisors (treas. 1990-91, pres.-elect 1991-92, pres. 1992-93), Las Cruces Assn. Realtors (bd. dirs.), Multiple Listing and Info., Inc. (pres.-elect), Las Cruces City Alumnae Panhellenic, Altrusa, Order Ea. Star, Delta Zeta. Presbyterian. Home: 4633 Lamar Rd Las Cruces NM 88005-3558 Office: Bell Inc PO Box 577 Las Cruces NM 88004-0577 E-mail: joybell@bellinc.com.

BELL, MAXINE TOOLSON, state legislator, librarian; b. Logan, Utah, Aug. 6, 1931; d. John Max and Norma (Watson) Toolson; m. H. Jack Bell, Oct. 26, 1949; children: Randy J. (dec.), Jeff M., Scott Alan (dec.). Assocs. in Libr. Sci., Coll. So. Idaho; CSI, Idaho State U., 1975. Librarian Sch. Dist. 261, Jerome, Idaho, 1975-88; mem. Idaho Ho. of Reps., 1988-. Bd. dirs. Idaho Farm Bur., 1976-77; rep. western states Am. Farm Bur. Women, 1990-93, vice chmn., 1993—; vice chmn. Am. Farm Bur., 1992—; mem. Jerome County Rep. Precinct Com., 1980-88. Home: 194 S 300 E Jerome ID 83338-6532

BELL, NANCY LEE HOYT, real estate investor, middle school educator, volunteer; b. L.A., Oct. 25, 1929; d. James and Mabel Ruth (Lockard) Hoyt; m. Ralph Rogers Bell, July 3, 1953; children: Linda Lee, John Curtis, James Hoyt, Nancy Lee. BA in History magna cum laude II, Mount St. Mary's Whittier Coll., 1940. Sun Jose State Coll. postgrad.; San Francisco State Coll., 1952, UCLA, 1953; MS in Edn., U. So. Calif., 1955. Tchr. John Adams Jr. H.S., Santa Monica, Calif., 1950-54, real estate investor. Pres. Santa Clarita Cmty. Concerts, Saugus, Calif., 1968-69; vol. worker USO, YWCA, 1944-45, Cancer Crusade, Calif. and Wash., 1960-90. Mem. AAUW (charter life; pres.), Big Bear Valley Hist. Soc. (life; sec.), DAR (charter life; treas.), Gen. Soc. Mayflower Descs. (life; bd. dirs.), Alpha Delta Pi. Republican. Methodist. Avocations: world travel, collecting antiques, genealogy researcher, music. Home: 615 Main St Apt B Edmonds WA 98020-3804

BELL, PATRICIA WRIGHT, music educator; b. Balt., Mar. 4, 1955; d. Henry Leroy and Mary Ann Wright; children: Mary Catherine, Joseph Christopher. Assocs. Degree, Anne Arundel C.C., Arnold, Md., 1977; BS in Music Edn., Towson State U., 1982; Master's Equivalency, Western Md. Coll., 1992. Advanced profl. cert. Anne Arundel County Pub. Schs. Music tchr. Old Mill Mid. Sch. South, Millersville, Md., 1984—94, Chesapeake Bay Mid. Sch., Pasadena, Md., 1994—. Chairperson Mid. Sch. All County Chorus for Anne Arundel County, 2000—03. Mem.: Music Educators Nat. Conf., Mid. Sch. Choral Dirs. Anne Arundel County (spokesperson 2000—03). Avocations: music, tennis, golf, boating, singing. Office: Chesapeake Bay Mid Sch 4804 Mountain Rd Pasadena MD 21122

BELL, REBECCA, psychotherapist, journalist; b. N.Y.C., Dec. 20, 1942; d. Hiram Charles Bluming and Mildred Ann Good; m. Martin Bell, Feb. 7, 1986 (div. Apr. 1993); children: Michael Sobel, Jessica Sobel. BA, UCLA, 1993, MSW, 1995. Lic. clin. social worker. Reporter Hollywood Citizens News, L.A., 1969-70; news writer Sta. KTLA-TV, L.A., 1970-71; assignment editor Sta. KHJ-TV, L.A., 1971-72; anchor, reporter Sta. WXYZ-TV, Detroit, 1972-76; reporter Sta. WCAU-TV, Phila., 1976-78; anchor Sta. WNET-TV, N.Y.C., 1978; corr. NBC, N.Y.C., 1978-86; corr. war coverage, White House reporter NBC Network, London, N.Y., Washington, 1978-86; pvt. practice as psychotherapist Beverly Hills, Calif., 1995—. Author: (book) The Strange Disappearance of Jimmy Hoffa, 1974. Recipient Emmy award Am. Fedn. Radio and TV Artists, 1983, Deadline award, 1978, Golden Mike award, 1974. Mem. NASW. Avocations: painting, horseback riding.

BELL, SANDRA KATHLEEN, special education educator; b. Miami, Fla., June 12, 1970; d. Bronwyn Janet and Albert Harry Bell. BS, Fla. Internat. U., 2001. Cert. tchr. Fla. Dept. of Edn., 2001. Varying exceptionalities tchr., grades 4-5 Miami-Dade County Pub. Schs., Miami, Fla., 2001—. Mem.: Phi Kappa Phi (hon.), Golden Key (life). Office: Miami-Dade County Pub Schs 1500 Biscayne Blvd Miami FL

BELL, SUSAN JANE, nurse; b. Columbus, Ohio, July 24, 1946; d. Donald Richard Bell and Martha Jane (McDowell) Nichols; m. Robert Earlin Ward, Oct. 24, 1964 (div. 1984); children: Duane Allen Ward, Melissa Jane Ward, Bryan Thomas Ward. Degree in nursing, Columbus Sch. Practical Nursing, 1986; ADRN, Columbus State C.C., 1989; student, Franklin U., 1993—. RN, Ohio; cert. CPR. Nurse's asst. Riverside Meth. Hosp., Columbus, 1970-80, Norworth Convalescent Ctr., Columbus, 1980-86; nurse, charge nurse Heartland Thurber Care Ctr., Columbus, 1986-89; staff nurse Am. Nursing Care, Columbus, 1989—; medicare home visitation, staffing and pvt. duty nurse Telemed, Columbus, 1989—; asst. head nurse Northland Terr., Columbus, 1989; supr. Elmington Manor, Columbus, 1989; staff nurse cardiac step down unit Grant Hosp., Columbus, 1989-92; nurse med. ICU, CCU and pediatric ICU, 1992-93; charge nurse critical-skilled unit Ford Cmty. Village Health Care Ctr., Columbus, 1992-95; supr., charge nurse St. Rita's Home. Pres. Bell Mktg. Distbrs., pvt. duty ALS ventilator patients Med. Pers. Poole. Sponsor Childreach mem. NAFE, ASPCA, World Wildlife Fund, Nature Conservancy, Ohio Hist. Found. (archives/libr. divsn.), Nat. Audubon Soc., Environ. Def. Fund, Nat. Wildlife Fedn., Humane Soc. U.S., Am. Assn. Individual Investors, Columbus Met. Mus. Art (supporting), Internat. Assn. Global Execs., Nat. Notary Assn., Nat. Mus. of Women in the Arts, Ohio Hist. Soc.-Archives Libr., Omtermat/ Exec. Guild, Rotary. Avocations: body building, power lifting, swimming, music, crocheting.

BELL, THERESA MARIE, music educator; b. Milw., Wis., Sept. 29, 1956; d. Henry Arthur and Mary Francis Welcer; m. Barry Stauffer Bell, May 1, 1982; 1 child, Gregory Stauffer. BMus in Vocal Performance, Fla. State U., Tallahassee, 1981. Cert. tchr. Ga., 2001. Soloist, choir mem. St. Paul's Episcopal Ch., Albany, Ga., 1986—; tchr., music and chorus Southside Mid. Sch., Albany, Ga., 1998—. Troop com. Boy Scout Troop 15, Albany, Ga., 1998—2003. Mem.: Ga. Music Educators Assn. (assoc.). Republican. Episcopal. Avocations: singing, white-water rafting, travel. Home: 826 W Third Ave Albany GA 31701 Office: Southside Middle Sch 1615 Newton Rd Albany GA 31701

BELLAMY, CAROL, international organization executive; b. Plainfield, NJ, 1942; BA with honors, Gettysburg Coll., 1963; JD, NYU, 1968. Asst. commr. Dept. Mental Health and Mental Health Retardation Svc., N.Y.C.; with Peace Corps., Guatemala, 1963—65; assoc. Cravath, Swaine & Moore, NYC, 1968—71; mem. NY State Senate, 1973—77; pres. NYC Coun., 1978—85; prin. Morgan Stanley & Co., NYC, 1986—90; mng. dir. Bear Stearns, NYC, 1990—93; dir. Peace Corps., Washington, 1993-95; exec. dir. UNICEF, 1995—. Fellow, Harvard U. Kennedy Sch. Govt. Mem.: Phi Alpha Alpha. Office: UNICEF Office of Exec Director 3 United Nations Plz New York NY 10017-4486*

BELLAMY, JENNIFER WIGGINS, artist; b. Clio, S.C., Aug. 9, 1944; d. Leland and Myrtle Lee (Wise) Wiggins; married; 1 child, Audrey Katherine Rollins. BA in Art & Performance magna cum laude, U. Tex., 1989, postgrad., 1992-93, 95-99. Cert. interior decorator 2002. Dist. sec. Corning Glass Works, Richardson, Tex., 1977-80; adminstrv. asst. The Chase Manhattan Bank, Dallas, 1981-85; owner The Bellamy Studio, Richardson, Tex., 1990—, Interiors by Jennifer Rachelle Wiggins, 2003—. Recipient tchg. assistantships U. Tex., Dallas, 1993. Mem. Phi Theta Kappa. Avocations: writing, gardening, cooking, walking. E-mail: jennw24121@cs.com.

BELLANTONI, MAUREEN BLANCHFIELD, manufacturing and retail executive; b. Warren, Pa., Mar. 18, 1949; d. John Joseph and Patricia Anne (Southard) Blanchfield; m. Michael Charles Bellantoni, Aug. 12, 1972; children: Mark Christopher, Melissa Catherine. BS in Fin., U. Bridgeport, 1976; MBA, U. Conn., Stamford, 1979. Fin. analyst Dictaphone Corp., Rye, N.Y., 1970-73, Gen. Telephone & Electronics, Stamford, 1973-74, Smith Kline Ultrasonic Products, now Branson, Danbury, Conn., 1974-77; fin. mgr. Gen. Foods, White Plains, N.Y., 1977-80; contr. Branson Ultrasonics Corp. div. Emerson Electric, Danbury, Conn., 1980-88, v.p. fin., 1988-90 v.p. fin., CFO Automatic Switch Co. divsn. Emerson Electric, Florham Park, NJ, 1990-93, PYA/Monarch, Inc. divsn. Sara Lee Corp., Greenville, SC, 1993-94; v.p. fin. CFO Meat Group Sara Lee Corp., Cordova, Tenn., 1994-97; pres., COO BilMar Foods divsn. Sara Lee Corp., 1997-98; exec. v.p., CFO Rohn Industries Inc., Peoria, Ill., 1999-2000; CFO divsn. Diageo Burger King Corp., Miami, Fla., 2000—01; sr. v.p. fin., 2001—02; sr. v.p., CFO CP Kelco, Chgo., 2003—. Vice chair Nat. Legacy Campaign Cancer Fund, Franciscan Sister of Poor Found. Mem. Fin. Execs., Inst., S.C.C. of C., Danbury C. of C. (leadership program 1989), Beta Gamma Sigma. Avocations: golf, tennis, racquetball. Office: 123 N Wacker Dr Chicago IL 60606 Office Phone: 312-554-7885. Business E-Mail: maureen.bellantoni@cpkelco.com.

BELL-BOWE, JACQUELINE, mental health nurse, consultant, nursing educator; b. Newark, Oct. 7, 1952; d. Fred and Claudia Bell; m. Franklin George Bowe, June 29, 1991; children: Jermaine Quenton Miller, Shaunagha Mia Bowe, Hakeemah Bowe, Hassanah Bowe-Pickney, Kigran Quincy Bowe. AS, U. Maryland, 1987; BS, U. Phoenix, 1999. RN psychiatic. clin. nurse specialist, ANCC, mental health screener, N.J., RN N.J., N.Y. Psychiat. clin. nurse specialist Essex Valley Health Care, East Orange, NJ, 1992—2002; advanced practice nurse pact tng. and tech. assistance Bridgeway Rehab. Svcs., Elizabeth, NJ, 2002—. Group facilitator EOF program Rutgers U., Newark, 1998; group facilitator SIDS Assn. NJ, Newark, 1998—99; cons. NJ Assn. Corrections, Trenton, 1997—; mentor Bd. Edn., East Orange, 1998—99. Grantee, Mental Svcs. Administrn., 1991—93. Mem.: Minority Nurse Leadership Inst., Chi Eta Phi. Batpist. Home: 1045 Kenyon Ave Plainfield NJ 07060 Office: Bridgeway Rehab Svcs 615 N Broad St Elizabeth NJ 07208 Office Phone: 908-352-0242.

BELLER, LUANNE EVELYN, accountant; b. Ft. Dodge, Iowa, Feb. 5, 1950; d. Gerald L. and Evelyn E. (Liston) Heyl; m. Stephen M. Beller, June 28, 1970; children: Clancy Dee, Corby Lu. BA, Oreg. State U., 1977, MBA, Rochester Inst. Tech., 1981. CPA, Ill. Plant acct. DuBois Plastic Products, Avon, N.Y., 1977-79; coll. acct. SUNY, Geneseo, 1979-81; gen. acctg. supr. M&M/Mars, Inc., Cleveland, Tenn., 1981-83, Hackettstown, N.J., 1983-84, sales rep. Jacksonville, Ill., 1984-86, terr. sales supr., 1986-88; gen. acctg. coord. Masterfoods USA (formerly Kal Kan Foods, Inc.), Columbus, Ohio, 1988-90, fin. info. coord., 1990-92, gen. acctg. supr., 1992-97, site svc. and fin. mgr., 1997—. Vol. Girl Scouts U.S.A., Jacksonville, 1985—88, Bexley, Ohio, 1988—; mem. sound control com. Bexley United Meth. Ch., 1989—2001, chair edn. com., 1998—2001, mem. edn. com., 1996—; LOGOS vol., 1996—2002, mem. diversity team, 2001—02; com. member. Meth. Theol. Sch. Ohio Partnership, 2001—02. Mem. Phi Kappa Phi, Beta Gamma Sigma, Beta Alpha Psi. Democrat. Avocations: children, pets, reading. E-mail: lbeller@columbus.rr.com.

BELLM, JOAN, civic worker; b. Alton, Ill., June 20, 1934; d. Harvey Jacob and Alma Lorene (Roberts) Goldsby; m. Earl David Bellm, Oct. 1, 1955; children: David, Lori, Michael. Bd. dirs. Drug Watch Internat., 1991-02, lifetime hon. dir., 1998—; exec. dir. Ctr. for Drug Info., 1998—; Editor Best of IDEA newsletter, 1991-96, Drug Watch World News, 1996-02; chmn. Drug Watch Internat. editnl. rev. com., 1996-02; columnist weekly newspaper, 1998—. Organist, dir. jr. choir St. Mary's Cath. Ch., 1958-78; mem. adv. bd. Carlinville (Ill.) Area Hosp., 1981-86; trustee Blackburn Coll., Carlinville, 1983-86; bd. dirs. Cath. Children's Home, Diocese of Springfield, Ill., 1986—; founder Drug Watch Internat., 1991, Internat. Drug Strategy Info., 1998—; founder Drug Watch Internat. Alliance, 1982-86, pres., 1987-89; bd. dirs., nat. networker Nat. Drug Edn. Alliance, 1982-86, pres., 1987-89; bd. dirs., nat. networker Nat. Fedn. Parents for Drug-Free Youth, Washington, 1984-86; mem. Ill. Gov.'s Adv. Coun. on Alcoholism and Substance Abuse, 1989-93; dir. Ctr. for Drug Info., 1998—; founder Drug Watch Internat., 1991, Internat. Drug Strategy Inst., 1993, invited participant Internat. Private Sector Conf. on Drugs, Seville, 1993, advisor U.N. Internat. Drug Ctrl. Program, 1994; numerous others. Recipient letter of endorsement Pres. of U.S., 1981, citation of recognition Ill. Dept., Am. Legion, 1981, Meritorious Svc. award, 1982, award Ill. Drug Edn. Alliance award, 1984, Southwestern Ill. Law Enforcement Commn., 1984, Carlinville Sch. Bd., 1985, Outstanding Svc. award Nat. Fedn. Parents, 1986, award Ill. Alcohol and Drug Dependence Assn., 1986, Optimist Internat., 1987, Ill. Drug Edn. Alliance, 1988, Outstanding Citizen award Blackburn U., 1989, Citizen of Yr. award, Carlinville, 1990; Leadership award Drug Watch Internat., 2001. Home: PO Box 227 Carlinville IL 62626-0227

BELLO, JUDITH HIPPLER, lawyer, trade association administrator; b. Alexandria, Va., May 31, 1949; BA in history summa cum laude, U. NC, 1971; JD, Yale Law Sch., 1975. Bar: D.C. 1975. Office legal adviser Dept. State, Washington, 1977-82; dep. to dep. asst. Sec. Commerce for Import Adminstrn., Washington, 1982-84 from dep. gen. counsel to gen. counsel, US trade rep. and chmn. Sect. 301 Com., 1985-89; ptnr. Sidley & Austin, Washington, 1989-96; joined Pharm. Rsch. and Mfrs. Am. (PhRMA), 1996—, exec. v.p. policy and strategic affairs, 1996—. Gen. counsel US Trade Rep.; mem. Pres. Commn. on Federal Ethics Law Reform; policy official and atty. Dept. Commerce and State; instr. Yale Law Sch., Woodrow Wilson Sch. Princeton U., Georgetown U. Law Ctr.; editnl. adv. bd. Am. Jour. Internat. Law, Georgetown Law and Policy in Internat. Bus., George Wash. Jour. Internat. Law and Econ.; adv. bd. and com. US Export-Import Bank,

Syracuse U. Maxwell Sch. Citizenship and Pub. Affairs, Atlantic Coun., Brookings Instn. Coun. on Pub. Policy Edn. Author: (with Alan F. Holmer) The Antidumping and Countervailing Duty Laws: Key Legal and Policy Issues, 1987, Guide to US-Can. Free-Trade Agreement, 1990; editor: North American Free Trade Agreement, 1994; contbr. numerous articles to profl. jours. Recipient Overall Excellence award DC Bar Com., 1985, Meritorious Pub. Svc. award USCG, 1978, named one of 100 Most Powerful Women in Wash., Washingtonian mag., 2001. Mem. ABA (internat. sect. co-chmn. trade com. 1986-90, couns. 1987-90), DC Bar (internat. sect., chmn. steering com. 1987-88; co-chmn. trade com. 1983-86), Am. Soc. Internat. Law (editl. adv. bd. 1982-89, coun. 1994-96, bd. dirs. 1995-2000), Coun. on Fgn. Rels., Phi Beta Kappa. Office: PhRMA 100 15th St NW Washington DC 20005 E-mail: jbello@phrma.org.*

BELLO, MARIA ELANA, actress; b. Norristown, Pa., Apr. 18, 1967; 1 child, Jackson Blue McDermott. BS in Polit. Sci., Villanova U. Actress: (off-Broadway plays) include The Killer Inside Me, Small Town Gals With Big Problems, Urban Planning; (films) Maintenance, 1992, Permanent Midnight, 1998, Payback, 1999, Coyote Ugly, 2000, Duets, 2000, Sam the Man, 2000, China: The Panda Adventure, 2001, Auto Focus, 2002, 100 Mile Rule, 2002, The Cooler, 2003, Nobody's Perfect, 2004, Secret Window, 2004; (TV films) The Commish: In the Shadow of the Gallows, 1995;(TV series) Mr. & Mrs. Smith, 1996, ER, 1997-98 (Screen Actors Guild award for outstanding performance by an ensemble in a drama series, 1997). Co-founder Dream Yard Drama Project for Kids, Harlem, N.Y.C. Office: Creative Artists Agy 9830 Wilshire Blvd Beverly Hills CA 90212

BELLOCK, PATRICIA RIGNEY, state legislator; b. Chgo., Oct. 14, 1946; d. John Dungan and Dorothy (Comiskey) Rigney; m. Charles Joseph Bellock, Nov. 8, 1969; children: Colleen, Dorothy. BA, St. Norbert Coll., 1968. With customer rels. 3M Corp., Chgo., 1968-69; tchr. jr. h.s. Milw. and Fairbanks, Alaska, 1970-72; v.p. sports corps. Dor-Mor-Pat Corp., River Forest, Ill., 1976-84; mem. DuPage County Bd. from Dist. 3, Wheaton, Ill., 1992-98, Ill. Ho. of Reps., Springfield, 1999—. Asst. treas. DuPage County Forest Preserve Dist. Mem. sch. bd. St. Isaac Jogues Sch., Hinsdale, Ill., 1989-91; bd. dirs. Hinsdale Cmty. House, 1987-89, U. Ill. Gerontology Rsch., 1988-91, Hinsdale Youth Ctr., 1987-90, DuPage County Bd. Health, Wheaton, 1990—, Care and Counseling Ctr., Downers Grove, 1977—, pres., 1986-89. Recipient award Ill. Health Dept., 1992, Woman of Yr. award Serenity House, Addison, Ill. Roman Catholic. Office: 6301 S Cass Ave Westmont IL 60559-3277 Home: 431 Canterbury Ct Hinsdale IL 60521-2825

BELLON, VENETIA ROCHELLE, financial consultant, educator; b. Beaufort West, Cape, South Africa, July 24, 1941; arrived in U.S., 1965; d. Michael and Roslyn (Sklaar) Bellon; m. Barry Fenroy Bass, Jan. 17, 1963 (div. Aug. 15, 1977); children: Tracey Bass Shilling-Hysjulien, Dayana Bass. Cert., U. Capetown, South Africa, 1960; BA in History, U. Tex., 1981, MA, LBJ, U. Tex., 1984. Tchr. Ellerton Jr. Sch., Capetown, 1961—63, Girls' HS, Pietermartizburg, South Africa, 1964; mktg. mgr. Austin Mag., 1978; officer corp. Bank Am., Va., 1987—91; mortgage cons. Penn Nat. Bancshares, McLean, Va., 1993—95, Access Nat. Mortgage, Reston, 1995—99, Countrywide Home Loans, Alexandria, Va., 2001—. Conf. coord. Third World Militarization, 1984; mem. Amnesty Internat.; mem. task force Gov. State of Tex., 1984. Mem.: AAUW, So. Poverty Law Ctr., Tex. Execs., Nat. Yiddish Book Ctr. Democrat. Jewish. Avocations: abstract expressionism, travel, crossword puzzles. Home: PO Box 1755 Alexandria VA 22313 Office: Countrywide Home Loans 5830 Kingstowne Ctr Alexandria VA 22315

BELLONI, ALESSANDRA, artistic director; b. Rome, July 24, 1954; came to U.S., 1971; d. Eugenio and Elvira (Rossetti) B. Student, Internat. Lyceum of Langs., Rome, NYU, Fiesole-Urbino, Italy. Artist in residence NYU, N.Y.C., 1981-91; artistic dir., co-founder I Giullari di Piazza, N.Y.C., 1982—; singer Carnegie Recital Hall, N.Y.C., 1985; dir., singer, actress Carnegie Hall, Pitts., 1986; dir., prodr. Walt Disney World, Orlando, Fla., 1985-86; dir., singer Lincoln Ctr.- Alice Tully, N.Y.C., 1985-88, 92-96; tchr., performer, dir. Caramoor Mus., Katonah, N.Y.; artist in residence Cathedral St. John the Divine, N.Y.C., 1993—. Tchr., spkr., lectr. N.Y. State Pub. Schs., N.Y.C., 1990—; performer adv. bd. Meditations on the Dark Mother, Santa Fe, 1993.dir. N.Y. State Dept. Cultural Affairs, 1985—, N.Y. State Coun. on the Arts, 1986—. Author, dir., singer (opera) 1492-1992: Earth, Sun and Moon, 1992, Stabat Mater: Donna de Paradiso, 1995-96, (concert) Dance of Ancient Spider, 1996; singer, percussionist (compact disk) Earth, Sun and Moon, 1995. Performing Arts grantee N.Y. State Coun. on the Arts, 1982—; recipient cert. appreciation Mayor of L.A., 1983; named Woman of Yr. Italian-Am. Women Orgn., 1996. Mem. Percussive Arts Soc. Roman Catholic. Avocations: horseback riding, swimming, mask making, research on folklore. Home: 500 W 111th St Apt 2G New York NY 10025-1972 Office: I Giullari Di Piazza c/o St John the Divine 1047 Amsterdam Ave New York NY 10025-1747

BELLOSPIRITO, ROBYN SUZANNE, artist, writer; b. Glen Cove, N.Y., Sept. 11, 1964; BA, L.I. U., 1986. Asst. Slide Libr. The Met. Mus. Art, N.Y.C., 1987-88, The Frick Art Reference Libr., N.Y.C., 1988-89; pub., editor The Exhibitioner Art Mag., Old Brookville, N.Y., 1993—, curator exhbns., 1994—. Exhbns. include Crystal Art Gallery, N.Y.C., 1988, Hutchins Gallery, Greenvale, N.Y., 1990, 91, Nassau County Mus. Art, Roslyn, N.Y., 1990, Sakura Gallery, Kennedy Airport, N.Y.C., 1992, PAAS Gallery, N.Y.C., 1992, Ward-Nasse Gallery, N.Y.C., 1992, 94, Outrlimits Art Gallery, Franklin Square, N.Y., 1993, Sea Cliff (N.Y.) Gallery, 1993, 94, Prince St. Gallery, N.Y.C., 1994, Foster Freeman Gallery, San Antonio, 1994, UN 4th Conf. on Women, Beijing, 1995, Tichenor Gallery/Harvard U., 1996, Fine Arts Mus. L.I., Hempstead, 1996, Islip (N.Y.) Art Mus., 1996, Galerie Observatoire 4, Montreal, 1996, Hillwood Art Mus., Brookville, N.Y., 1997, Fitton Ctr. for Creative Arts, Hamilton, ohio, 1997, Ghost Fleet Gallery, Nags Head, N.C., 1997, Watchung (N.J.) Arts Ctr., 1997, Barnes & Noble, N.Y.C., 1998, Soc. Illustrators, N.Y.C, 2001, IMAC, Huntington, NY, 2002, Oyster Bay Hist. Soc., N.Y., 2003-2004, others; permanent collections include Nat. Mus. Women in Arts, 1-800-Flowers, Inc., and pvt. homes. Grantee Puffin Found., 1997.

BELLOVARY, CATHY, aging services administrator, volunteer; b. Milw., Feb. 18, 1947; d. John Randolph and Florence Agnes Melster; m. Frank David Bellovary, Apr. 24, 1971; children: Anthony, Nicholas. BS, Purdue U., 1969; postgrad., Dominican Coll., U. Wis., Milw. Speech and lang. clinician Racine (Wis.) Unified Sch. Dist., 1969-74; dir. speech and lang. svcs. Racine Unified Schs., 1974-77; facilitator support groups Waukesha County Tech. Coll., Pewaukee, Wis., 1983-93, Family Svc. Waukesha, Wis., 1993-98; exec. dir. Waukesha County Food Pantry, Waukesha, 1990-97; dir. aging svcs. Waukesha County, 1997—. Mem. Women's Health Svcs., Waukesha, 1991—; exec. bd. mem. United Way-Waukesha County, 1996—; aging svcs. rep. Waukesha County Health Coun., Waukesha, 1997—; mem. sr. health ctr. adv. com. Waukesha Meml. Hosp.; chmn. Waukesha County Nutrition Coalition, Waukesha, 1998—; mem. County Execs. Cabinet, 1998—; spkr. in field. Contbr. articles to newsletters. Fundraiser, mem., com. chair Jr. League, Racine, Milw., 1973-83; past pres., v.p., sec., treas., com. chair Waukesha Svc. Club, 1981—; past pres., v.p. Friends of the Libr., Waukesha, 1989-96; past pres., v.p., sec., treas. Waukesha Tng. Ctr., 1991-98. Named Woman of Achievement, Altrusa Club, Waukesha County, 1991, Woman of Distinction, YWCA Waukesha County, 1993, Most Powerful Woman in Waukesha County, Waukesha Freeman, 1993. Mem. Wis. Aging Dirs., Waukesha County Mental Health Assn., Southeastern Wis. Area Agy. on Aging (Waukesha County dir.), Westwood Health Club, Antique Comb Collector's Club, Purdue Alumni Assn. Republican. Episcopalian. Avocations: volunteering, antique collecting, reading, traveling. Home: S28w29541 Pamela Cir Waukesha WI 53188-9519 Office: Waukesha County Dept Aging Svcs 1320 Pewaukee Rd Ste 130 Waukesha WI 53188-3878

BELLOW, ALEXANDRA, mathematician, educator; b. Bucharest, Romania, Aug. 30, 1935; d. Dumitru and Florica Bagdasar; m. Cassius Ionescu Tulcea, Apr. 1956 (div. 1969); m. Saul G. Bellow, Oct. 1974 (div. 1986); m. Alberto P. Calderon, Sept., 1989 (dec. 1998). MS in Math, U. Bucharest, 1957; PhD in Math., Yale U., 1959. Research assoc. Yale U., New Haven, Conn., 1959-61, U. Pa., Phila., 1961-62, asst. prof., 1962-64; assoc. prof. U. Ill., 1964-67; prof. Northwestern U., Evanston, Ill., 1967-96, prof. emeritus, 1996—. Emmy Noether lectr., 1991. Author: (with C. Ionescu Tulcea) Topics in the Theory of Lifting, 1969; assoc. editor: Annals of Probability, 1979-83, Advances in Math., 1979— . Recipient Sr. Disting. Scientist award Alexander von Humboldt Found., 1987; Fairchild Disting. scholar Calif. Inst. Tech., 1980; NSF grantee Mem. Sigma Xi. Office: Northwestern U Dept of Math 2033 Sheridan Rd Evanston IL 60208-2730 E-mail: a_bellow@math.northwestern.edu.

BELLVILLE, MARGARET (MAGGIE BELLVILLE), communications executive; B in Social Scis., SUNY, Binghamton; grad. advanced mgmt. program, Harvard U. With GTE Wireless/Contel Cellular, Inc., 1986—93; sr. v.p. Century Comm., L.A., 1993—95; from v.p. ops. to exec. v.p. ops. Cox Comm., Inc., 1995—2001; pres., CEO Incanta, Atlanta, 2001—02; exec. v.p. ops. Charter Comm., Inc., St. Louis, 2002—03, exec. v.p., COO, 2003—. Mem. exec. vom., bd. dirs. Calif. Cable TV Assn.; bd. dirs. Cable Positive, Women in Cable and Telecomm. Found.; advisor Nat. Cable and Telecomm. Assn. Task Force on Diversity. Named Woman of Yr., Women in Cable, Calif. chpt., Woman to Watch, Women in Cable, Atlanta chpt., Woman of Yr., Women in Cable nat.; named one of Top 10 Women in Bus. in Atlanta. Office: Charter Comm Inc 12405 Powerscourt Dr Saint Louis MO 63131

BELL WILSON, CARLOTTA A. state official, consultant; b. Detroit, Dec. 7, 1944; d. Albert Powell (dec.) and Elfrieda (Bertram) Bell; divorced; children: Lizette C. Wilson, SaMia M. Wilson, Shira M. Ingram. AA, Wayne County C.C., Detroit, 1975; BS, Wayne State U., 1979; MEd, Bowling Green State U., 1983. Dental asst. Fred Colvard, DDS, Detroit, 1968-73; edn. coord. Merrill Palmer Inst., Detroit, 1979-81; head start evaluator Cmty. Devel. Inst., Wayne County, 1981; grad. asst. Bowling Green (Ohio) State U., 1981-83; child care worker Meth. Children's Village, Detroit, 1984-85; tchr. New Calvary Head Start, Detroit, 1985; child welfare specialist Mich. Dept. Social Svcs., Detroit, 1985-93; resource program analyst teen parent program Family Independence Agy., Lansing, Mich., 1993—2002. Conf. presenter U. Mich., Ann Arbor, 1995, Mich. Assn. Cmty. and Adult Edn., Bellaire, 1995, Baker Coll., Flint, Mich., 1996. Mem. Mich. Profl. Soc. on Abuse of Children, Internat. Assoc. Infant Massage (cert. infant massage instr.). Roman Catholic. Avocations: gardening, pottery, cultural activities, travel. Home: 2110 Chene Detroit MI 48207

BELMONTEZ, DEBORAH LYNN GROVES, poet, editor; b. Newark, May 14, 1955; d. Howard and Edna (Loveday) Groves; m. Samuel Belmontez, Aug. 27, 1983; 1 adopted child, Maryann Rose. Grad., Heritage Bible Inst., 1982; leadership tng., WCTU, Evanston, Ill., 1982. English tchr. Heritage Acad., N.J., 1980-81; editor White Ribbon News, WCTU, N.J., 1980-82, 91—. Contbr. poems to a dozen poetry anthologies. Recipient WCTU Nat. Reading award, N.J., 1981, Writing Appreciation award, Am. Rescue Workers, 1982, Publisher's Choice award, Watermark Press, 1990. Mem. WCTU (editor White Ribbon News). Republican. Avocations: writing, traveling, collecting paintings and santini's statues. Mailing: 21 Almond Pass Dr Ocala FL 34472-8729

BELOFF, ZOE, filmmaker, educator, photographer; b. Edinburgh, Scotland; arrived in N.Y.C., 1980; Student, Edingburgh (Scotland) U.; MFA in Film, Columbia U., 1983. Tchr. digital media Pratt Inst.; adj. prof. City Coll. N.Y., 1989—, Coll. SI. Prodr.: (CD-ROM) include The Vanishing Machine of Miss Natalija A., Illusions, Where There There There Where, Beyond (First prize Apple QuickTime VR Competition, 1998); (film performances) include Claire and Don in Slumberland, A Mechanical Medium, Lost, Life Underwater; (films) include Echo, A Trip to the Land of Knowledge, Shadow land or light from the other side, Lost, Wonderland USA, Nightmare Angel. Work has been exhibited at MoMA, N.Y. Film Festival, Rotterdam Film Festival, Pacific Film Archives, Pompidou Ctr., others. Recipient Finishing Funds Award, Experimental TV Ctr., 1996, 2000, 2002, Found. Contemporary Performance Arts Fellowship, N.Y. Found. for the Arts, 1997; grantee, Art Matters Inc., 1986, 1989, 1997, The Jerome Foundations Inc., Apparatus Prodns., 1992, Nat. Endowment for the Arts, 1993, Individual Artist Grant, N.Y. State Coun. for the Arts, 1996, 2001, Guggenheim Found., 2003.

BELT, BETH MARIE, music educator; d. Ronald Leo Dippel and Laura Ann Stollard, John Patrick Stollard (Stepfather) and Debra Dippel(Stepmother); m. Brandon Dean Belt, June 1, 2002. MusB Edn., U. Ill., 1999. Cert. std. elem. tchg. grades K-9 State Ill. Tchr. Certification Bd., 1999, spl. K-12 tchg. cert. State Ill. Tchr. Certification Bd., 1999. Gen. music tchr. and band/choir dir. Shiloh (Ill.) Valley Sch., 1999—2000; choral dir. and asst. band dir. Mascoutah (Ill.) Unit Sch. Dist., 2000—01; orch. dir., asst. band and choir dir. O'Fallon (Ill.) Twp. H.S., 2001—. Dir. Smith Walbridge Drum Major Clinics, Charleston, Ill., 1994—; pres., choreographer Cutting Edge Show Choir U. Ill., Urbana, 1995—98, drum maj., flag corps, clarinet line Marching Illini, 1995—98; choral chairperson Music Edn. Day at the Capitol, Springfield, Ill., 1996—98; homecoming and panhellenic pride chairperson Chi Omega Frat. - Omicron Chpt., Champaign, Ill., 1996—99; undergraduate rep. U. Ill. Sch. Music Alumni Assn. Bd. Dirs., Urbana, 1997—98. Musician Belleville (Ill.) Am. Legion Band, 1993—95; boys' and girls' club vol. Don Moyer Boys and Girls Club, Champaign, 1995—98; vol. Read-A-Loud, Champaign, 1996—98; mem. promotion com. Greeks Advocating the Mature Mgmt. of Alcohol, Champaign, 1997—98; guest clinician Franklin and Eisenhower Schs., Champaign, 1996—98. Mem.: Am. Choral Dirs. Assn. (parliamentarian 1996—98), Ill. Music Educator's Assn., Music Educator's Nat. Conf., U. of Ill. Alumni Assn. (life), Phi Eta Sigma, Epsilon Delta, Kappa Delta Pi (hon.), Mu Phi Epsilon. Avocations: photography, hiking, travel, music, research. Home: 642 Rain Hollow Dr O Fallon IL 62269 Office: O'Fallon Township High School 600 S Smiley St O Fallon IL 62269 Office Phone: 618-632-3507. Personal E-mail: asuperangel@yahoo.com. E-mail: beltb@oths.k12.il.us.

BELT, JEAN RAINER, art gallery owner; b. Selma, Ala., Sept. 12, 1942; d. Sterling Price and Saidee (Crook) Rainer; m. Kemplin C. Belt, Aug. 31, 1963; children: Keven Curtis, Kelly B. Jones. BS in Math., U. Ala., 1964. Founder, ptnr. Corp. Art Source, Montgomery, Ala., 1983-92, owner, 1992—, CAS Gallery & Frames, Montgomery, Ala., 1994. Juror Jubilee Galleria Art Show, Montgomery, 1987, Riofest, Harlingen, Tex., 1989-90, BCA on My Own Time, Montgomery, 1990; guest lectr. Riofest, 1990; dir. Armory Gallery Arts Coun. Montgomery, 1989-91; advisor Montgomery Bus. Com. Arts, 1990-94, 97— (Bus. in Arts award 1989); curator Armory Gallery, Montgomery, 1989. Bd. dirs Arts Coun. Montgomery, 1980-94, 97—, pres., 1985-87, 92-93; mem. adv. bd. Montgomery Symphony Assn., 1993—; pres. Jr. League Montgomery, 1984, treas., 1981; Stephen min. 1st United Meth. Ch., Montgomery, 1992-94, mem. adminstv. bd., 2000—; bd. dirs. Vol. Info. Ctr., 1997—, mem. exec. bd., sec., 1998-2000, v.p. 2000-02, pres. bd. dirs., 2002—; bd. dirs. Arts Coun. of Montgomery. Named Vol. Action Ctr. Vol. of Yr., 1989; recipient Bus. in the Arts award Montgomery Bus. Com. for the Arts, 1989, Disting. Vol. in the Arts award Art Coun. Montgomery, 1996. Mem. Am. Soc. Appraisers (v.p. Ala. chpt. 2001—), Montgomery C. of C., U. Ala. Alumni Assn. Avocations: tennis, painting, gardening. Office: Corp Art Source 2960 Zelda Rd # F Montgomery AL 36106-2649

BELTZNER, GAIL ANN, music educator; b. Palmerton, Pa., July 20, 1950; d. Conon Nelson and Lorraine Ann (Carey) Beltzner. BS in Music Edn. summa cum laude, West Chester State U., 1972; postgrad., Kean State Coll., 1972, Temple U., 1972, Westminster Choir Coll., 1972, Lehigh U., 1972. Tchr. music Drexel Hill Jr. H.S., 1972-73; music specialist Allentown (Pa.) Sch. Dist., 1973—; tchr. Corps Sch. and Cmty. Devel. Lab., 1978-80, Corps Cmty. Resource Festival, 1979-81, Corps Cultural Fair, 1980, 81. Mem. bd. assocs. Lehigh Valley Hosp. and Health Network. Mem. Mus. Fine Arts, Boston, aux. Allentown Art Mus., aux. Allentown Hosp.; mem. woman's com. Allentown Symphony, The Lyric Soc. of the Allentown Orch.; mem. Allentown 2nd and 9th Civilian Police Acads.; bd. dirs. Allentown Area Ecumenical Food Bank, Allentown Arts Commn; mem. Growing with Sci. partnership—Air Products and Chems., Inc. and Allentown Sch. Dist., Good Shepherd Home Aux.; bd. assocs. Lehigh Valley Hosp. and Health Network. Decorated Dame Comdr., Ordre Souverain et Militaire de la Milice du St. Sepulcre; recipient Cert. of Appreciation, Lehigh Valley Sertoma Club; Excellence in the Classroom grantee Rider-Pool Found., 1988, 91-92. Mem. AAUW, NAFE, ASCD, Am. String Tchrs. Assn., Am. Viola Soc., Internat. Reading Assn., Internat. Platform Assn., Allentown Edn. Assn., Music Educators Nat. Conf., Pa. Music Educators Assn., Am. Orff-Schulwerk Assn., Orgn. Am. Kodaly Educators, Am. Recorder Soc., Phila. Area Orff-Schulwerk Assn., Soc. Gen. Music, Am. Assn. Music Therapy, Internat. Soc. Music Edn., Internat. Tech. Edn. Assn., Assn. for Tech. in Music Instrn., Civil War Roundtable Ea. Pa., Choristers Guild, Lenni Lenape Hist. Soc., Lehigh Valley Arts Coun., Allentown Symphony Assn., Midi Users Group, Pa.-Del. String Tchrs. Assn., Nat. Sch. Orch. Assn., Lehigh County Hist. Soc., Confedn. Chivalry (life mem. of merit, grand coun.), Maison Internat. des Intellectuels Akademie, Order White Cross Internat. (apptd. dist. comdr. for Pa./U.S.A. dist., nobless of humanity), Airedale Terrier Club of Greater Phila., Kappa Delta Pi, Phi Delta Kappa, Alpha Lambda. Republican. Lutheran. Home: PO Box 4427 Allentown PA 18105-4427

BELZER, ELLEN J. negotiations and communications trainer, consultant; b. Kansas City, Mo., May 22, 1951; d. Meyer Simmon and Fay (Weinstein) B. Student, U. Okla., 1969-70, U. Ibero-Americana, Mexico City, 1971; BA, Northwestern U., 1973; MPA, U. Mo., Kansas City, 1976. Rsch. asst. dept. polit. sci. Northwestern U., Evanston, Ill., 1970-73; adminstrv. asst. Ctrs. for Regional Progress Midwest Rsch. Inst., Kansas City, 1974; various positions to dir. socioecons. div. Am. Acad. Family Physicians, Kansas City, 1974-86; pres. Belzer Seminars and Cons., Kansas City, 1986—, Healthcare Collaborator, Inc., Kansas City, 2000—03. Instr. communication Avila Coll., Kansas City, 1987-92, dept. continuing edn. U. Kans., Lawrence, 1989-92; spkr. on negotiation strategies, conflict resolution techniques, communication skills, 1986—; mediator for hosps., physician groups, state health depts., cmty. health ctrs., others. Contbr. articles to profl. publs. and mags. including Working Women, Hospital Practice, and Family Practice Management, also monographs. Campaign vol. for local candidate, Kansas City, 1970, 82, 99. Democrat. Home and Office: 21 W Bannister Rd Kansas City MO 64114-4009

BEMIS, MARY FERGUSON, magazine editor; b. N.Y.C., Dec. 28, 1961; d. Edmund Augustus and Anne Adoian (Nalbandian) Bemis. BFA in Writing, Johnson State Coll., 1983. Co-editor, co-pub. Ave. Literary Rev. Ave. Publs. Inc., Burlington, Vt., 1983-85; editor Unique Hair and Beauty Mag., 1994; editor Lady's Circle Mag. Lopez Publs., N.Y.C., 1987-94, editor, 1989-94; freelance editor, writer Mus. Sci., Boston, 1991-93; freelance editor Woman's Day Spl. Interest Publs., 1996—98; sr. editor Am. Salon and Am. Spa Mags., 1988—; editor-in-chief Am. Spa Mag., 1998—; bd. dirs. Internat. Spa Assn., 2003. Co-editor: The Green Mountain Rev., 1982—83, Nature Through Her Eyes: Art and Literature by Women, 1994, Journey Into the Wilderness, 1994. Mem.: Am. Soc. of Mag. Editors. Democrat. Unitarian Universalist. Home and Office: 532 W 25th St #Fl2 New York NY 10001-5502 E-mail: MFBEMIS@aol.com.

BEMROSE, WENDY A. music educator; b. Salem, Oreg., Nov. 19, 1958; d. Kraig Arthur and Deanna S. Gately; m. Jeffrey J. Bemrose, July 14, 1984; children: Jordan, Nicholas. BS in Edn., Western Oreg. State Coll., 1983, MusM, 1993. Lic. adminstr. Oreg. Tchr. Oreg. Pub. Schs., Monmouth, 1984—. Dir. choirs United Meth. Ch., Salem, Oreg., 1985—97, Luth. Ch., Salem, Oreg., 1997—99; dir. Summer Music Camp for Children, Monmouth, Oreg., 1996—; coord. 21st Century Cmty. Learning Ctrs., Monmouth, 2001—, mem. adv. bd., 2001—. Ch. coun. mem. local Luth. ch., Dallas, Oreg., 2002—; local leader Stephen Ministries, Dallas, 2003. Recipient award for contbns. in the arts, Monmouth-Independence Cmty. Arts Assn., 1999. Mem.: NEA, Cmty. Arts Assn. (mem. scholarship com. 2001—), Oreg. Music Educators Assn. (chairwoman dist. IV 1986—90, 2000—), Music Educators Nat. Conf., Am. Choral Dirs. Assn., Kappa Delta Pi. Democrat. Avocations: travel, concerts, walking, singing.

BENAMOU, CATHERINE LAURE, filmmaker, educator; b. Paris, June 13, 1956; d. Jean Michel Benamou and Gerane (Siemering) Heinreich; m. Agustin Lao Montes, May 1, 1993 (div.); children: Aiyana Maya Lao, Emma Ursula Lao. Student, Reed Coll., 1974—75; BA, U. Wis., 1978; MA, NYU, 1982, MA, 1988, PhD, 1997. Asst. rsch. scientist N.Y. Rsch. Program in Inter-Am. Affairs NYU, 1984—86; adj. lectr. CUNY, S.I., 1992—96; vis. asst. prof. Duke U., Durham, NC, 1996—98; asst. prof. Film and Video Studies U. Mich., Ann Arbor, 1998—. Curator Latin Am. Film and Video, N.Y.C., 1983—92; adv. panelist Film and Media Grants N.Y. Coun. for Humanities, 1988; cons., rsch. coord. Film and Video Ctr. Nat. Mus. Am. Indian, N.Y.C., 1993—95. Co-prodr.: Latinos en Accion, 1990—92; contbr. articles to profl. jours. Bd. dirs. Alafia Arts Orgn.; co-founder Women Make Movies, Inc., N.Y.C., 1983—85. Recipient Recognition of Spl. Achievement, Smithsonian Instn., 1996; grantee, U. Mich., 2002. Mem.: Soc. Cinema and Media Studies (co-chair Latino Caucus 1999—2001), Latin Am. Studies Assn., Phi Beta Kappa. Avocations: photography, poetry, bicycling, piano, sailing. Office: Univ Mich Film and Video Studies 105 S State St #2512 Ann Arbor MI 48109

BEN-ARIEH, JOSEFA, language educator; arrived in U.S.A., 1990; d. Hoshe Kelner and Silvia Iosepovici; m. David H. Ben-Arieh, Sept. 25, 1973; children: Hila, Idan, Shanee. BA, Ben-Gurion U., 1978; MS in Edn., U. Kans., 1998, PhD, 2003. Tchr. English HS, Israel, 1976—82; tchr. Hebrew Torah Acad. Hebrew Sch., Columbus, Ohio, 1985—87; asst. to exec. Ben-Gurion U., Israel, 1987—90; tchr. Hebrew Manhattan (Kans.) Jewish Congregation, 1991—93; instr. Kans. State U., Manhattan, 1993—96; post doctorate Juniper Gardens Rsch. Inst., Kans. City, Kans., 2003—. Cons. spl. edn. U. Kans., 2000—03. Mem. Coun. Exceptional Children, 2000—03. Scholar, U. Kans., 2000—03, GRace M. Phinney scholarship, 2002. Mem.: Pi Lambda Theta.

BENARIO, JANICE MARTIN, retired classics educator; b. Feb. 19, 1923; m. Herbert W. Benario, Dec. 23, 1957; children: Frederick M., John H. AB in Latin, Goucher Coll., 1943; AM in Classical Lit., Johns Hopkin's U., 1949, PhD in Classical Lit., 1952. Teaching intern St. John's Coll., 1953-54; from instr. to assoc. prof. Sweet Briar Coll., 1954-60; asst. prof. classics Ga. State U., 1960—62, assoc. prof., 1962-84, assoc. prof. emerita fgn. langs., 1989; co-prof. in charge Intercollegiate Ctr. for Classical Studies, Rome, 1984-85; assoc. prof. Emory U., 1989-94, Agnes Scott Coll., 1997, ret., 1997. Editor: Vergilius, 1960-63, 73-79, mem. editorial bd., 1963-73; book rev. editor: Arch, 1964-69; editor: Ga. Classicist, 1981-83. Lt. (j.g.) USNR, 1943—46. Ford Found. grantee 1953-54,

Fulbright grantee, 1957. Mem. Classical Soc. of Am. Acad. in Rome (treas., v.p., pres. 1963-69), Classical and Modern Fgn. Lang. Assn. (pres. 1969-71), Atlanta Soc. Archaeol. Inst. Am. (pres. 1979-80), Ga. Classical Assn. (pres. 1985-87), Vergilian Soc. Am. (co-exec. sec. 1992-93).

BENATAR, PAT (PAT ANDRZEJEWSKI), rock singer; b. Bklyn., 1953; m. Neil Geraldo; 1 child, Haley. Albums include: In the Heat of the Night, 1979, Crimes of Passion, 1980, Precious Time, 1981, Get Nervous, 1982, Live From Earth, 1983, Tropico, 1984, Seven the Hard Way, 1985, Wide Awake in Dreamland, 1988, Best Shots, 1989, True Love, 1991, Gravity's Rainbow, 1993, All Fired Up: The Very Best of Pat Benatar, 1994, Heartbreaker: 16 Classic Performances, 1996, Innamorata, 1997, 8-15-80, 1998, Synchronistic Wanderings: Recorded Anthology 1979-99, 1999, Live at Electric Ladyland, 2002, Greatest Hits Live, 2003, Go, 2003; popular recs. include Treat Me Right, Hit Me With Your Best Shot, Love is a Battlefield, Hell is for Children. Recipient Grammy award for best female rock vocal performance, 1981, 82, 83, 84 Office: 584 N Larchmont Blvd Los Angeles CA 90004 also: Gold Mountain Mgmt care Danny Goldberg 2575 Cahuenga Blvd W # 470 Los Angeles CA 90068-2102*

BENAVIDES, DEBORAH ANN, academic advisor; d. Willie A. and Theresa L. Benavides. BA in Theatre, Incarnate Word Coll., 1983; MA in Edn., U. Tex., San Antonio, 2002. Bldg. supr. univ. ctr. ops. office U. Tex., San Antonio, 1988—96, internat. student program coord. office multicultural programs, 1996—99, academic advisor Coll. Liberal and Fine Arts, 1999—2002, academic advisor Sch. Arch., 2002—. Vol. Esperanza Peace and Justice Ctr., San Antonio, 1995—2001. Mem.: Tex. Academic Advisors Network. Avocations: music, reading, art, photography. Office: U Tex 501 W Durango Blvd San Antonio TX 78207 Office Phone: 210-458-3010. E-mail: dabenavides@utsa.edu.

BENAVIDES, GRETA LOUISE, elementary school educator, entrepreneur; b. Denver, July 28, 1956; d. Edwin M. and Mariam Jayne Randall; m. Francisco Vega Benavides, July 3, 1994; children: Robyn G. Fredericksen, Masi Brede Fredericksen. BA with hons., Fullerton U., 1996; MA in Edn., Biola U., 2000. Cert. tchr. Calif. 2d grade tchr. South Whittier (Calif.) Sch. Dist., 1997—; supr. Herbalife, L.A., 2003—. Supr. Home Sch., Buena Park, Calif., 1984—, young adult fine art instr. 1994—2003; tutor disabled students South Whittier Sch. Dist., 1999—2003. Exhibitions include Santa Ana Coll., 1984, Irvine Fine Arts Ctr. 1986; prodr.: (compact disc) Sing the Wondrous Story, 2003. Union rep. Calif. Tchrs. Assn., Whittier, 1997—2003; mem. chorus St. Linus Ch., 2000—03. Recipient Best in Show award, 1984; advanced classroom instrn. grantee, Whittier Credit Union, 2002. Democrat. Roman Catholic. Achievements include original research in the effects of reading comprehension on colored paper for persons with scotopic sensitivity. Avocations: painting, photography, promoting healthy nutrition, promoting public awareness of important political issues. Office: Los Altos Sch 12001 Bona Vista Ln Whittier CA 90605 Personal E-mail: teacher714@hotmail.com, gretafrancisco@adelphia.net.

BENBOW, CAMILLA PERSSON, psychology educator, researcher; b. Lund, Sweden, Dec. 3, 1956; came to U.S., 1965, naturalized, 1985; m. David Lubinski; children: Wystan R., Bronwen G., Trefor A., Evan M., Lovisa D., G. Byron, Lena C. BA in Psychology with honors, Johns Hopkins U., 1977, MA in Psychology, 1978, MS in Edn. of the Gifted, 1980. Dir. with distinction in Edn. of Gifted, 1981. Dir. Office of Precollegiate Programs for Talented & Gifted Iowa State U., 1977-80, assoc. prof. with distinction in Edn. of Gifted Johns Hopkins U., Balt., 1977-79, asst. dir. Study of Mathematically Precocious Youth, 1979-81, assoc. dir., 1981-85, co-dir., 1985-86, dir., 1986—, assoc. rsch. scientist dept. psychology, 1981-86, asst. prof. sociology, part-time, 1983-86; assoc. prof. psychology Iowa State U., Ames, 1985-90, prof. psychology, 1990-95, chair dept. psychology, 1992-98, disting. prof., 1995-98, interim dean coll. edn., 1996-98; dean Peabody Coll. of Edn. and Human Devel., Vanderbilt U., Nashville, 1998—. Sr. editor: Academic Precocity: Aspects of Its Development, 1983, Intellectual Talent: Psychometric and Social Issues, 1996; contbr. articles to profl. jours. Recipient John curtis gowan prize Nat. assn. Gifted children, 1980, 81; Rsch. award Am. Ednl. Rsch. Assn., 1982; Spencer fellow, alt., 1984, 85, 86, Rsch. paper award Mensa, 1985, 86, 89, 94, 95; Early Scholar award Nat. Assn. Gifted Children, 1985, Disting. Scholar award 1992, George A. Miller award, APA, 1999. Mem. Johns Hopkins Soc. Scholars, Phi Beta Kappa, Sigma Xi. Office: Vanderbilt Univ Peabody Coll Edn/Human Devel Deans Office Box 329 Peabody Sta Nashville TN 37203 E-mail: camilla.benbow@vanderbilt.edu.

BENCH, BARBARA ANNE, chemist; b. Trenton, N.J., Nov. 11, 1963; d. Steven and Joan Bench; m. Luis Moral-Noranjo, Aug. 19, 2003; 1 child, Isabel. BA, Rutgers U., 1985; PhD, Brown U., 2001. Cert. sci. tchr. grades K-12 N.J. Sci. tchr. Manalapan (N.J.) H.S., 1986—90; chemist Am. Cyanamid, Princeton, NJ, 1990—94; assoc. scientist Girindus Am. Inc., Cin., 2002—. GAANN fellow, U.S. Dept. Edn., 1994—95, 1998—2000. Mem.: Am. Chem. Soc. Achievements include patents for methods for safening herbicides in cereal crops using 5-Aryloxy-1,2- (disubstituted) benzene compounds. Avocation: quilting. Home: 1021 Timber Trail Cincinnati OH 45224 Office: Girindus Am Inc 8560 Reading Rd Cincinnati OH 45215

BENCINI, SARA HALTIWANGER, concert pianist; b. Winston Salem, N.C., Sept. 2, 1926; d. Robert Sydney and Janie Love (Couch) Haltiwanger; m. Robert Emery Bencini, June 26, 1954; children: Robert Emery, III, Constance Bencini Waller, John McGregor. Mus. B., Salem Coll., 1947; postgrad. grad. Juilliard Sch. Music, 1948-50; M.A., Smith Coll., 1951; D In Mus. Arts, U. N.C., Greensboro, 1989. Head piano dept. Mary Burnham Sch. for Girls, Northampton, Mass., 1949-51; pianist, composer dance and drama dept. Smith Coll., 1951-52; head music dept. Walnut Hill Sch. for Girls, Natick, Mass., 1952-54; pvt. piano tchr., High Point, N.C., 1954-66; concert pianist appearing in Am. and Europe, 1948—; duo-piano performances with PBS-TV, Columbia, S.C., 1967, Winston Salem Symphony, N.C., 1964-68, Ea. Mus. Festival, Greensboro, N.C., 1969. Democrat. Presbyterian.

BENCKENSTEIN, EUNICE R. foundation administrator; b. Thomas, Okla., June 6, 1908; d. Walter Sloan Robinson and Annie Florence Williams; BS in Indsl. Arts, Tex. Woman's U., 1929. Tchr. bus. Orange H.S., Orange, Tex., 1929—36; acct. Vinton Petroleum Co. of Tex., Orange, 1936—65; asst. Nelda C. Stark Offices, Orange, 1959—99; exec. dir. N.C. and H.J.L. Stark Found., Orange, Tex. Bd. dirs. Orange Savs. Bank, Orange. Methodist. Avocations: history, ornithology. Office: NC & HJL Stark Found PO Box 909 601 Green Ave Orange TX 77630

BENDER, BETTY BARBEE, food service professional; b. Lexington, Ky., Apr. 29, 1932; d. Richard Carroll and Sarah Elizabeth (Rodes) Barbee; m. David H. Bender, Dec. 14, 1957; children: Bruce, Carroll. BA in Home Econs., Mont. State U., 1954; MS in Food Service Mgmt., Miami U., Oxford, Ohio, 1980. Adminstrv. dietitan Mass. Gen. Hosp., Boston, 1955-56; asst. chief dietitan Meth. Hosp., Indpls., 1957-61; chief dietitan Community Hosp., Indpls., 1961-63; supervising dietitian Chgo. Area ARA, 1963-67; asst. food service supr. Dayton (Ohio) Bd. Edn., 1969, mgr. food service, 1969-92. Cons. Nat. Frozen Food Assn., Washington, 1983, Crescent Metal Products Co., Cleve., 1985; nat. food svc. mgr. Meat Inst., 1998-2003; clin. nutritioni Jessamine County Health Dept., 2003. Contbr. articles to profl. jours. Recipient 26th Ann. Foodsvc. Facilities Design award Instrs. Mag. for Commissary Design, 1972, Silver and Gold Plate awards Internat. Foodsvc. Mfrs. Assn., 1985, Pres.'s award Ohio Sch. Food Svc. Assn., 1987, FAME Golden Star award, 1992; recognized for outstanding contbns. to child nutrition program Ohio Ho. of Reps., 1972,

84. Mem. Am. Sch. Food Svc. Assn. (nat. pres. 1983, chmn. 1978-80, maj. city sect.), Ohio Sch. Food Svc. (pres. 1977), Dayton Sch. Adminstr. Assn., Dayton Sch. Mgmt. Assn. (pres. 1993-94), Am. Dietetic Assn. (cert., chair dietary practice group 1990-91, award for Excellence in Mgmt. Practice 1992, Food Svc. Dir. Yr. 1994), Ohio Dietetic Assn., Dayton Dietetic Assn., Soc. Nutrition Edn. (panel 1983). Democrat. Avocations: bridge, golf, swimming. Home: 1953 E Hickman Rd Nicholasville KY 40356-8838

BENDER, BETTY WION, librarian; b. Mt. Ayer, Iowa, Feb. 26, 1925; d. John F. and Sadie A. (Guess) Wion; m. Robert F. Bender, Aug. 24, 1946. BS, N.Tex. State U., Denton, 1946; MA, U. Denver, 1957. Asst. cataloger N. Tex. State U. Library, 1946-49; from cataloger to head acquisitions So. Meth. U., Dallas, 1949-56; reference asst. Ind. State Library, Indpls., 1951-52; librarian Ark. State Coll., 1958-59, Eastern Wash. Hist. Soc., Spokane, 1960-67; reference librarian, then head circulation dept. Spokane (Wash.) Public Library, 1968-73, library dir., 1973-88. Vis. instr. U. Denver, summers 1957-60, 63, fall 1959; instr. Whitworth Coll., Spokane, 1962-64; mem. Gov. Wash. Regional Conf. Libraries, 1968, Wash. Statewide Library Devel. Council, 1970-71 Bd. dirs. N.W. Regional Found., 1973-75, Inland Empire Goodwill Industries, 1975-77, Wash. State Library Commn., 1979-87, Future Spokane, 1983-88, vice chmn., 1986-87, pres., 1987-88. Recipient YWCA Outstanding Achievement award in Govt., 1985 Mem. ALA (mem. library adminstrn. and mgmt. assn. com. on orgn. 1982-83, chmn. nominating com. 1983-85, v.p./pres.-elect 1985-86, pres. 1986-87), Pacific N.W. Library Assn. (mem. circulation div. 1972-75, conv. chmn. 1977), Wash. Library Assn. (v.p./pres.-elect 1975-77, pres. 1977-78), AAUW (pres. Spokane br. 1969-71, rec. sec. Wash. br. 1971-73, fellowship named in honor 1972), Spokane and Inland Empire Librarians (dir. 1967-68), Am. Soc. Pub. Adminstrn. Clubs: Zonta (pres. Spokane chpt. 1976-77, dist. conf. treas. 1972). Republican. Lutheran. Home: 221 E Rockwood Blvd Apt 504 Spokane WA 99202-1274

BENDER, CAROL TILL (PINKY BENDER), minister; b. Charleston, S.C., Apr. 21, 1937; d. Wallace Conrad and Erna Louise (von Postel) T.; m. Michael Swift Bender; children: Louise, Katherine, David. BA in Journalism, Winthrop U., 1960; MDiv, Erskine Theol. Sem., 1984; DMin, Columbia Sem., 1993. Writer Presbyn. Ch. (USA), Louisville, 1983—; prof. Queens Coll., Charlotte, N.C., 1985-93; pastor McQuay Meml. Presbyn. Ch., Charlotte, 1986-97; parish assoc. Plz. Presbyn. Ch., Charlotte, 1998—2002. Chair ARC Blood Svcs., Charlotte, 1991-95, Clergy Assn. Bd., Charlotte, 1995-96. Author (curriculum) Bible Discovery, 1983-93; editor (study books) Presbyterian Women, 1990-92. Mem. bd. mgrs. Harris YMCA. Mem. AAUW (life, Ednl. Found. Program grantee 1983), Presbyn. Writers Guild. Home: 5001 Belford Ct Charlotte NC 28226-7801

BENDER, CAROLINE HELEN, senior technical trainer; b. Missoula, Mont., Nov. 6, 1974; d. Ronald James and Jeanne Matthews Bender. BA in Psychology, Women's Studies, U. Wis., 1997. Tech. edn. cons. U. Wis.-Do IT, Madison, 1997; sr. applications trainer New Horizons, San Diego, 1997—99; sr. tech. trainer Document Scis., Carlsbad, Calif., 1999—.

BENDER, JACQUELINE, music educator; b. Frankfurt, Ky., Mar. 15, 1954; d. William Lee and Adele Wylde Earls; m. Dennis R Bender, Sept. 4, 1952; children: Stephanie Denise Langdon, Samantha Leigh. MusB in Edn., U. of Cin., 1982, MusM in Flute Performance, 1987. Music tchr. Lawrenceburg (Ind.) Cmty. Schs., 1982—84, Wyo. (Ind.) City Sch., 1987—91; mem. Cin. Fairfield (Ohio) City Sch. district; prin. flute The Only White Oaks Opera Co., Middletown, Ohio, 1997 to present Springfield (Ohio) Symphony Orch., 1991—92; prin. flute The Hamilton-Fairfield Symphony Orch., 1990—. Mem.: Nat. Educators Assn., Ohio Music Educators Assn. Office: Fairfield High School 8800 Holden Blvd Fairfield OH 45014 E-mail: bender_j@fairfield-city.k12.oh.us.

BENDER, JUDITH, journalist, editor; d. Samuel and Edith Bender. BA, U. Mich., 1954; MS, Columbia U., 1964. Reporter Passaic Herald News, Clifton, NJ, 1964—66, Knickerbocker, Albany, NY, 1966—69; reporter, editor Newsday, Melville, NY, 1969—2000; freelance writer, 2000—03; consulting editor Columbia Journalism Rev., 2002—. Recipient award for Washington corr., Soc. for Profl. Journalists, 1982, Pub. Svc. award, N.Y. State Pubs. Assn., 1974. Mem.: Alumni Assn. Grad. Sch. Journalism Columbia U. (treas. 2002—). Office: Columbia Journalism Rev Grad Sch Journalism 2950 Broadway New York NY 10027

BENDER, VIRGINIA BEST, computer scientist, educator; b. Rockford, Ill., Feb. 10, 1945; d. Oscar Sheldon and Genevieve Best; m. Robert Keith Bender, July 19, 1969; children: Victoria Ruth, Christopher Keith. BS in Chemistry, Math., No. Ill. U., 1967; postgrad., U. Ill., 1967-69; MBA, Loyola U., Chgo., 1973. Cert. computer profl. Sr. sys. rep. Burroughs Corp., Chgo., 1969-73; sys. analyst Marshall Field & Co., Chgo., 1973-74; project leader Fed. Home Loan Bank, Chgo., 1974-76; sr. sys. analyst United Air Lines, Elk Grove Village, Ill., 1976-78; supr. Kemper Group, Long Grove, Ill., 1978-82; prof. computer info. sys., coord. computer info. sys. William Rainey Harper Coll., Palatine, Ill., 1982—2002, prof. emeritus, 2002—. Spkr. Midwest Computer Conf., DeKalb, Ill., 1988, moderator, 91; exch. prof. Maricopa CC, Mesa, Ariz., 1990, rsch. sabbatical, 93, 98; spkr. conf. info. tech. League for Innovation, Kansas City, Mo., 1995; steering com. Midwest Computer Conf., 1995—99; facilitator ToolBook User's Conf., Colorado Springs, Colo., 2000, presenter, Colo. Springs, 2001—03; adj. prof. SUNY, Valhalla, 2003—, SUNY/Westchester CC, Valhalla, 2003—. Nat. chief mother-dau. group Indian Maidens YMCA, Des Plaines, 1982—83; mem. Vols. Pks. Environ. Edn. Westchester County Dept. Pks., Recreation and Conservation, NY, 2002—; mem. choir Kingswood United Meth. Ch., Buffalo Grove, Ill., 1982—2002, asst. organist, 1982—89; mem. choir 1st Congl. Ch., Chappaqua, NY, 2002—, mem. bell choir, 2003—. Named Tchr. of the Month, Burroughs Corp., Chgo., 1972. Mem.: No. Ill. Computer Soc., Ill. Assn. Data Processing Instrs., Inst. Cert. Computer Profls. (life), No. Ill. Alumni Assn. (life), Mortar Bd., Sigma Zeta, Phi Theta Kappa. Avocations: swimming, sewing, needlecrafts, reading, playing piano. Office: William Rainey Harper Coll 1200 W Algonquin Rd Palatine IL 60067-7373 E-mail: vbender@hotmail.com.

BENDHEIM, LEONORE CAROLINE, psychotherapist; b. Amsterdam, The Netherlands, Oct. 26, 1921; came to U.S., 1943; d. Martin and Alice Sofia (Mayer) B. B. in Art Edn. and Art Therapy, Kans. U., 1970; B in Social Work, Washburn U., 1972; MS in Clin. Counseling/Art Therapy, Emporia State U., 1974; MS in Clin. Gerontology, Kans. State U., 1983. Interior designer Mehagians, Phoenix, 1950-59; pvt. practice interior design Phoenix, 1959-63; rsch. vol. Menninger Rsch., Topeka, 1963-66; art therapy vol. Topeka State Hosp., 1966; vol. vocat. rehab. Ctr. for the Blind, Topeka, 1967; psychiat. evaluation team mem. Kans. Psychiat. Diagnostic Ctr., Topeka, 1970-73; counseling in psychotherapy Colmery-O'Neil VA Med. Ctr., Topeka, 1973-83, Phoenix South Mental Health, 1987-89; pvt. practice psychotherapist Scottsdale, Ariz., 1989-93. Edn. coord. Ashram Assn., Topeka, 1970-73; pres. Unitarian-Universalist Fellowship, Topeka, 1973-75, program chmn., 1975-78, chmn. bd. dirs., 1978-80.

BENDIG, JUDITH JOAN, information systems specialist, computer company executive; b. Erie, PA, Oct. 28, 1955; d. Richard W. and Rhea Agnes (Hain) B. BS magna cum laude in music edn., Edinboro State Coll., 1977. Tech. cons. Inco, Inc., Washington, 1982; sr. systems analyst Deena Sci. Services, Inc., Arlington, 1982-85; dir. computer systems ADEENA Corp., Arlington, Va., 1985-86; prin. cons. Pricewaterhouse Coopers, Fairfax, Va., 1995—; prin. cons., integration mgr. WANG Labs., Inc., Bethesda, Md., 1986-95; v.p. F&B Computer Assocs., Bethesda, Md., 1986-95; prin. cons. Price Waterhouse Coopers, Fairfax, Va., 1995—. With USN, 1978-82, served to Capt., USNR, 1978—; mem. Arlington Commu-

nity Band, 1986—. Mem. NAFE Assn. Computing Machinery, IEEE (assoc.), Naval Res. Assn. Republican. Roman Catholic. Home: 7733 Vinewood Ct Gainesville VA 20155-2852

BENDIX, HELEN IRENE, lawyer; b. N.Y.C., July 24, 1952; d. Gerhard Max and Eva Gabriela (Sternberger) B.; m. John A. Kronstadt, Nov. 29, 1974; children: Jessica Claire Kronstadt, Erik Bendix Kronstadt, Nicola Eva Kronstadt. BA, Cornell U., 1973; JD, Yale U., 1976. Bar: Calif. 1976, D.C. 1978, U.S. Dist. Ct. D.C. 1980, U.S. Dist. Ct. (ctrl. dist.) Calif. 1986, U.S. Ct. Appeals (D.C. cir.) 1981, U.S. Ct. Appeals (9th cir.) 1987, U.S. Dist. Ct. (so. dist.) Calif. 1990. Law clk. to Hon. Shirley M. Hufstedler U.S. Ct. Appeals (9th cir.), L.A., 1976-77; assoc. Wilmer Cutler & Pickering, Washington, 1977-79; asst. prof. law UCLA, 1979-80; from assoc. to ptnr. Leva Hawes Symington Martin & Oppenheimer, Washington, 1980-85; of counsel Gibson Dunn & Crutcher, L.A., 1986-89; ptnr. Heller Ehrman White & McAuliffe, L.A., 1989-96; sr. v.p., gen. counsel KCET Cmty. TV of So. Calif., 1996—; judge Ct. L.A. Jud. Dist., 1997-2000, Superior Ct. L.A., 2000—. Vis. prof. law UCLA, 1985-86; chair ADR com. L.A. Superior Ct., 2004. Co-author: Moore's Federal Practice, Vols. X and XI, 1976, Vols. XII and XIII, 1979; contbr. articles to profl. jours. Violinist Palisades Symphony, Pacific Palisades, Calif., 1989—. Mem. European Union Ctr. of Calif. (mem. exec. adv. bd., 2003—), D.C. Bar Assn., Calif. State Bar Assn. (chairperson internat. law sect. 1990-91), Calif. Judges Assn., L.A. County Bar Assn. (past pres. dispute resolution svcs.), Jud. Coun. Calif. (mem. ad hoc com. on canon 6D 1998, working group on mediator ethics 2000, mem. access and fairness adv. com.), Nat. Charity League (past chmn. 12th grade class), Chancery Club, Phi Beta Kappa. Office: Dept 18 111 N Hill St Los Angeles CA 90012-3014 E-mail: hbendix@lasuperiorcourt.org.

BENDIX, JANE, artist, author, anthropological illustrator; b. Lansing, Mich., Oct. 20, 1920; d. Helmer and Violet Walstrum; m. Reinhard Bendix, July 5, 1940 (dec. Feb. 1991); children: Karen, Erik, John. BA, U. Chgo., 1941; postgrad., Art Inst. Chgo., 1941-43. Freelance artist, 1941—. Author: Mi'ca, 1987 (Kinderbuch prize 1987), Mi'ca, Buffalo Hunter, 1992, Türkishöhle, 1990, Chaco: The Anasazi Mystery, 1997, The Secret Map, 2000; exhbns. San Francisco, 1988, Oakland, Calif., 1979, Goldern, Switzerland, 1965, Oxford, Eng., 1966, Washington, 1975, Berlin, Germany, 1990. Mem. Calif. Watercolor Assn. Home: 3 Orchard Ln Berkeley CA 94704-1821

BENDO, AUDRÉE ARGIRO, anesthesiologist, educator; b. N.Y.C., Jan. 24, 1953; BS, Cornell U., 1974; MS, Columbia U., 1977; MD, U. Health Scis./Chgo. Med. Sch., 1981. Bd. cert. in anesthesiology. Rotating intern St. Lukes Hosp., N.Y.C., 1981-82; resident in anesthesiology SUNY Health Sci. Ctr., Bklyn., 1982-84, fellow in neurosurg. anesthesiology, 1984-85. Assoc. prof., vice chair edn. SUNY, Bklyn. Mem. Am. Soc. Anesthesiologists, Internat. Anesthesia Rsch. Soc., N.Y. Acad. Medicine, N.Y. State Soc. Anesthesiologists, Soc. Neurosurg. Anesthesia and Critical Care. Office: SUNY Dept Anesthesiology Box 6 450 Clarkson Ave Dept Brooklyn NY 11203-2056

BEN-DOR, GISSELLE, conductor, musician; b. Montevideo, Uruguay; came to U.S., 1982; m. Eli Ben-Dor; children: Roy, Gabriel. Student, Acad. of Music, Tel Aviv; artist diploma, Rubin Acad. Music, Tel Aviv; M, Yale Sch. of Music, 1982. Music dir. Annapolis Symphony, Md., Pro Arte Chamber Orch. of Boston; condr. Norwalk (Conn.) Youth Symphony; conducting fellow L.A. Philharm., 1986, Tanglewood Music Ctr., 1983; resident condr. Houston Symphony, 1988; music dir. Santa Barbara Symphony, Calif., 1994—. Resident condr. Houston Symphony; condr. variety conducting activities including prestigious summer festivals, competitions, 1983-87, Hungarian Nat. Symphony, Budapest Philharm., others; guest condr. orchs. in Uruguay, Ea. Europe, Israel and U.S. including Bavarian Radio Orch., Boston POPS, New World Symphony, Women's Philharm, San Francisco, Minn. Orch. in Summerfest Festival, 1986, N.Y. Philharm., 1993, 95, Orquestra del Teatro Nacional, Brazil, Ulster Orch., Israel Philharm., 1991, Carnegie Hall, 1997, others; past music dir. Houston Youth Symphony; past acting orch. dir. Shepherd Sch. Music Rice U.; music dir. Boston ProArte Chamber Orch., Annapolis Symphony. Condr. Israel Philharm. Orch. (play) The Rite of Spring; recs. with London Symphony, Israel Chamber Orch., (CD) London Symphony Orch., Sofia Soloists, Boston ProArte Chamber Orch.; numerous TV appearances. Am.-Israel Cultural Found. scholar, Frances Wickes scholar; Leonard Bernstein fellow; recipient Bartók prize Hungarian TV Internat. Condrs. Competition, 1986. Office: Santa Barbara Symphony Orch Arlington Theatre 1900 State St Ste G Santa Barbara CA 93101-8424 also: Del Rosenfield Assoc 714 Ladd Rd Bronx NY 10471-1204 E-mail: delrosdra@aol.com.

BENEDEK, MELINDA, television executive; BA, Oxford U., 1972; JD, Columbia U., 1977; French Law Degree, 1974. Owner High Wire Ltd., 1981—84; ptnr. Pollock, Bloom & Dekom; exec. v.p. Imagine Films; exec. v.p. bus. affairs Twentieth Century Fox, L.A.; exec. v.p. bus. affairs and prodn. Showtime Networks, L.A. Office: ShowtimeNetworks 1633 Broadway Fl 37 New York NY 10019-6708 also: Showtime Networks Inc Ste 1600 10880 Wilshire Blvd Los Angeles CA 90024-4116 Fax: 310-234-5397.

BENEDICT, CHEYANN, apparel designer; Student, Mesa Coll. Actress, photographer, N.Y.C.; store mgr. Calypso, L.A.; co-founder C&C California, 2003—. Address: c/o Lela Tillem #705 127 E 9th St Los Angeles CA 90015*

BENEDICT, Mrs. COLEMAN HAMILTON See WOLFE, ETHYLE

BENEDICT, ELISE, moving company executive; div.; 1 child, Steve; m. Marvin Howard; children: Kris, Kim Howard Parks. Grad. in journalism and mktg./acctg. Dispatcher, commn. saleswoman, claims mgr., sales mgr. Univ. Moving & Storage Co., Farmington Hills, Mich., gen. mgr., v.p., pres., CEO, 1986—; co-owner Univ. Bus. Interiors, 1996—. Office: Univ Moving & Storage Co 23305 Commerce Dr Farmington Hills MI 48335-2727 Fax: 810-615-4715.

BENEDICT, GAIL CLEVELAND, music educator; b. Rockville Ctr., N.Y., Dec. 15, 1942; d. Walter Charles and Louise Cleveland; m. Donald Alexander Davis, July 4, 1967 (div. Apr. 14, 1980); 1 child, Scott Paul Davis; m. Robert Lorin Benedict, July 6, 1983. BS in Music Edn., SUNY, Fredonia, 1964; MS in Adminstrn. and Supervision, Nova U., 1980; EdD, U. Sarasota, Fla., 1982. Cert. tchr. Fla. N.Y. Music tchr., dept. chair North Country Elem. Sch., Stony Brook, NY, 1964—66; vocal music tchr. Narimasu Elem. Sch., Tokyo, 1966—67; vocal music tchr. Mineral Wells (Tex.) H.S., 1967—68; music tchr., chorus dir. Park Ave. Elem. Sch., Amityville, NY, 1968—70; music tchr., resource tchr. Magruder Elem. Sch., Newport News, Va., 1970—72; music specialist Skyview Elem. Sch., Pinellas Park, Fla., 1979—; adj. instr. Nova Southea. U., Tampa, Fla., 1991—. Gen. mgr. V.I. Properties, St. Petersburg, Fla., 1989—. Author: (book) Cruzan Child, 2002. Grantee, Pinellas County Arts Coun., 2001. Mem.: Pinellas Co. Music Educators Assn. (vocal chair 1980—83), Fla. Elem. Music Educators Assn. (chair Dist. III 1979—84), Music Educators Nat. Conf. Avocations: travel, reading, history, writing. Home: 6712 Cardinal Dr S Saint Petersburg FL 33707 Office: Skyview Elem Sch 8601 60th St N Pinellas Park FL 33782 E-mail: drmommusic@aol.com.

BENEDICT, KENNETTE MARI, foundation executive, researcher; b. NYC, Jan. 19, 1948; d. Donald LaVerne Benedict and Ann Kennette Cnare; m. Jonathan David Casper, Aug. 2, 1980 (div. 2002); 1 child, Sarah Casper.

AB, Oberlin Coll., 1971; PhD, Stanford U., 1981. Rschr. Gov.'s Com. Law Enforcement/Adminstrn. Criminal Justice, Boston, 1971; asst. prof. Rutgers U., New Brunswick, N.J., 1980-81, U. Ill., Urbana-Champaign, 1981-85; dep. dir. peace and internat. cooperation MacArthur Found., Chgo., 1989-92, dir. internat. peace and security, 1992—, sr. advisor on philanthropy, 2002—. Cons. Compton Found., Menlo Park, 1998-2000, bd. dirs.; adv. [illegible] Iowa, 2001—, Ctr. for Effective Philanthropy, 2003—; advisor Rockefeller Bros. Fund, NYC, 1996-97, com. mem. Leonard Rieser Prize, Chgo., 2000— Contbr. articles to profl. jours. Bd. trustees mem. Oberlin Coll., 2004—; bd. dirs. Compton Found., 2003—. Lena Lake Forrest fellow Bus. and Profl. Women's Found., 1977-78. Mem. Coun. on Fgn. Rels., Internat. Inst. Strategic Studies, Chgo. Coun. on Fgn. Rels. Avocations: hiking, music. Office: MacArthur Found 140 S Dearborn St Chicago IL 60603

BENEDIS, SHEILA MEYER, sculptor; b. Norwich, Conn., June 5, 1936; d. Maurice William and Tessie Y. Meyer; m. Howard Benedis, Sept. 1969; 1 child, Greg. BA, Mt. Holyoke Coll., 1958; MS, Pace U., 1987. Judge Westchester County Womens Clubs, Pocantico, N.Y., 1996; lectr. in field; artist resident Va. Ctr. for Creative Arts, Sweet Briar, 1996, Valparaiso Found.,, Almeria, Spain, 1997. One-woman shows include Interchurch Ctr., N.Y.C., 1996, St. Peters Ch., Citicorp, N.Y.C., 1997, Sarah Lawrence Coll., Bronxville, N.Y., 1997, Chappaqua (N.Y.) Libr., 1998, Anthropomorphism: the Artist Book, Ceres Gallery, N.Y., 2002; exhibited in group shows at Castle Gallery, 1993, 95, Gallery of Hastings, N.Y., 1993, 95, 97, Corvallis (Oreg.) Ctr., 1994, Paramount Ctr., Peekskill, N.Y., 1994, 97, Arka Gallery, Vilnius, Lithuania, 1994, Interchurch Ctr., 1994, Neuberger Mus., Purchase, N.Y., 1994, 95, Pace U., Pleasantville, N.Y., 1995, Manhattanville Coll., Purchase, N.Y., 1997, Beyond Reading: Sculptural Book Arts, Ellipse Arts Ctr., Arlington, Va. 2003; represented in permanent collections at Neuberger Mus., 1995, Mus. Applied Arts, 1994 Recipient Internat. award Women in Design, 1983, Purchase award Channel 13 Art Auction, 1984; program on her work TCI Cable, 1996. Avocations: hiking, walking in woods. Home and Office: 22 Forest Ave Hastings Hdsn NY 10706-1204

BENEPE, VIRGINIA LYNN, medical/surgical nurse, oncological nurse, educator; b. Oak Park, Ill., Mar. 30, 1964; d. Irvin Guy and Marilyn Sherwood (Warner) Goodman; m. John Gregory Benepe, Aug. 30, 1986; children: David Irvin, John Wesley. BSN, Tex. Christian U., 1986. RN, Tex.; cert. chemotherapy therapist, nurse med.-surg. nursing, diabetes educator, gerontology nurse, pediatric nurse. Staff nurse Breckenridge Hosp., Austin, Tex., 1986-87; staff nurse, relief charge nurse Harris Hosp. Ft. Worth, 1987—97; staff nurse Cook Children's Hosp., Ft. Worth, 1997—. Bd. dirs. Greater Tarrant County chpt. Juvenile Diabetes Rsch. Found. Mem. Am. Diabetes Assn. (bd. dirs. Greater Tarrant County chpt.), Am. Assn. Diabetes Educators (cert.), Tex. Nurses Assn. Home: 7614 Dijon Lake Dr Corpus Christi TX 78413-5245

BENERIA, LOURDES, economist, educator; b. Boi, Lleida, Spain, Oct. 8, 1939; came to U.S., 1964; d. Agusti Beneria and Josepa Farre; children: Jordi, Marc. Licenciatura, U. Barcelona, Spain, 1961; MPhil, Columbia U., 1974, PhD in Econs., 1975. Coord. program on rural women ILO, Geneva, 1977-79; asst. prof. Rutgers U., New Brunswick, N.J., 1975-81, assoc. prof., 1981-86; prof. city and regional planning and women's studies Cornell U., Ithaca, NY, 1987—, dir. program on gender and global change, 1987—92, 2000—03, dir. Latin Am. studies program, 1993—97; pres. Internat. Assn. for Feminist Economy, 2003—. Recipient Narcis Monturiol award for rsch. in the social scis., Barcelona. Office: Cornell Univ CRP W Sibley Hall Ithaca NY 14853-2148

BENERITO, RUTH ROGAN (MRS. FRANK H. BENERITO), chemist; b. New Orleans, Jan. 12, 1916; d. John Edward and Bernadette (Elizardi) Rogan; m. Frank Henshaw Benerito, Aug. 22, 1950. BS, H. Sophie Newcomb Coll., 1935; postgrad., Bryn Mawr Coll., 1935-36; MS, Tulane U., 1938, DSc (hon.), 1981; PhD, U. Chgo., 1948. Instr. chemistry Randolph-Macon Woman's Coll., Lynchburg, Va., 1940-43, Newcomb Coll., New Orleans, 1943-47; asst. prof. chemistry Tulane U., New Orleans, 1947-53, mem. grad. faculty, 1945—86, adj. prof. dept. biochemistry Med. Sch., 1960-86, prof. emeritus, 1986; phys. chemist fat emulsion program So. Regional Lab., USDA, New Orleans, 1953-58, supervisory phys. chemist, head phys. chem. investigations natural polymers lab., 1958-86; cons. phys. chemistry of cellulose, adj. prof. chemistry U. New Orleans, 1986-96. Contbr. articles to profl. publs. Recipient Disting. Svc. USDA award, 1970, New Orleans Fed. Exec. Assn., 1967, Fed. Woman's award U.S. CSC, 1968; named one of 75 Most Important Women in U.S., Ladies Home Jour., 1971. Fellow Am. Inst. Chemists (Honor Scroll L.A. chpt. 1977); mem. AAAS, Am. Chem. Soc. (So. Chemist award 1968, Garvan medal 1970, S.W. Regional award 1972, Lemelson MIT Lifetime Achievement award 2002), Am. Oil Chem. Soc., Am. Assn. Textile Chemists and Colorists, Sci. Rsch. Soc. Am., Sigma Xi, Sigma Delta Epsilon, Delta Kappa Gamma (hon.), Iota Sigma Pi (hon.). Home: 4733 Marigny St New Orleans LA 70122-5020 Office: USDA PO Box 19687 New Orleans LA 70179-0687

BENFIELD, ANN KOLB, lawyer; b. Reading, Pa., May 1, 1946; d. Curtis Kepler and Stella (Kolb) B. BA, George Washington U., 1969, MA, 1974; JD, U. Ky., 1983. Ky. 1983, U.S. Ct. Appeals (6th cir.) 1985, U.S. Supreme Ct. 1987; cert. mental health consumer cons./educator; cert. trained mediator. Probation officer Superior Ct. of D.C., Washington, 1973-78; jud. law clk. to chief judge U.S. Dist. Ct. (we. dist.) Ky., Louisville, 1983-86, jud. atty. to fed. sr. judge, 1989-95; trial atty. Ogden, Welsh and Newell (formerly Ogden & Robertson), Louisville, 1986-89; pvt. practice Louisville, 1995—2001; ret., 2001. Adj. prof. U. Louisville Sch. Law, 1993. Mem. exec. com., bd. dirs. Ky. chpt. ACLU, 1988-89, 91—, nat. bd. dirs., 1992-94, sec., 1995-96, treas., 1996-98, mem. legal panel, 1988-2002; mem. Reproductive Freedom Adv. Com., 1994-2001; mem. steering com. Fellowship Reconciliation, Louisville, 1997-2002; mem. governing coun. U. Louisville Women's Ctr., 1998-2001; rape crisis advocate Ctr. for Women and Families, 1997—, domestic violence advocate, 1998-; bd. dirs., gen. counsel Depressed Self-Help Svcs., Inc., 1998-2000. Fellow: Ky. Bar Found. (bd. dirs. 1994—96, charter mem.); mem.: Louisville Women's Law Assn., Louisville Bar Assn., Ky. Bar Assn. (Donated Legal Svcs. Recognition award 2000, 2001, 2003), Ky. Paso Fino Horse Assn. (sec. 2000—01), Phi Beta Kappa, Order of Coif. Home and Office: 1113 Holly Springs Dr Louisville KY 40242-7762 E-mail: akbenfield@msn.com.

BENGALEE MILLER, AMATUL-MANNAN Q. KATHERINE, activist; b. Chgo., Apr. 21, 1937; d. Muti-Rahman Bengalee and Amatul-Rahim Attiyyah Amad Bengalee; m. Rashid Ahmad, Oct. 11, 1957 (div. Mar. 1968); children: Nadim L. Ahmad, Mueen A.J. Ahmad; m. Robert J. Miller, Mar. 13, 1971 (dec. Aug. 1988); children: Kent C.J. Miller, Amelia B. Miller. Student, Jamla Nasrat for Women, Punjab, India, 1954—56, Truman Coll., 1984—88. Dept. store clk. Md. and Va., 1963—71; candidate for Pres. of U.S., 1985—88. Recipient Hon. Mention for oil painting, 1985. Mem.: NAFE, NOW, World Affairs Coun., Am. Film Instn., Nat. Women Mus. Arts. Avocations: knitting, painting, writing, decorating, cooking. Home: 914 19th St S Arlington VA 22202

BENHAM, HELEN, music educator; b. N.Y.C., Dec. 4, 1941; d. Charles Mead and Dorothea Wheaton Benham; m. Samuel S. Kim, June 12, 1965; 1 child, Sonya Wheaton Kim Guardo. MusB, Oberlin Conservatory Music, 1962; BA, Oberlin Coll., 1963; MS, The Juilliard Sch., 1965; PhD, Rutgers U., 2001. Music faculty Diller-Quaile Sch. Music, N.Y.C., 1964-75, Mannes Coll. Music, N.Y.C., 1966-82, Monmouth Conservatory Music, Red Bank, N.J., 1967—; prof. music Brookdale C.C., Lincroft, N.J., 1973—. Concert artist, piano and harpsichord. Author: Piano for the Adult Beginner Books I and II, 1977. Trustee, sec. A. Louis Scarmolin Trust. Named Outstanding Young Women of Am., 1978. Mem. Music Tchrs. Nat. Assn., Nat. Guild Piano Tchrs., Am. Musicological Soc., Composers Guild N.J., Shore Music Educators Assn. Avocations: swimming, walking. Home: 960 Elberon Ave Long Branch NJ 07740-4709 Office: Brookdale CC Music Dept 765 Newman Springs Rd Lincroft NJ 07738-1597

BENING, ANNETTE, actress; b. Topeka, May 29, 1958; m. Steven White, 1984 (div. 1991); m. Warren Beatty, 1992; children: Kathlyn Bening Beatty, Benjamin Beatty, Isabel Ashley Ira Beatty, Ella Corinne Beatty. Student, Mesa Coll.; theatre degree, San Francisco State U.; studied at, Am. Conservatory Theatre. Films include The Great Outdoors, 1988, Valmont, 1989, The Grifters, 1990 (Acad. award nomination best supporting actress 1990), Postcards from the Edge, 1990, Guilty by Suspicion, 1991, Regarding Henry, 1991, Bugsy, 1991, Love Affair, 1994, Richard III, 1995, The American President, 1995, Mars Attacks!, 1996, The Siege, 1998, American Beauty, 1999 (Acad. award nom. best actress), In Dreams, 1999, What Planet Are You From, 2000, Open Range, 2003; stage appearances Coastal Disturbances, 1986, (Tony award nomination 1986, Clarence Derwin award 1987, Theatre World award 1987), Spoils of War, 1988, Hedda Gabler, 1999; TV movies: Manhunt for Claude Dallas, 1986, Hostage, 1988; TV series: Liberty's Kids (voice only); TV appearances: Sesame Street, 1969, Miami Vice, 1987, Wiseguy, 1987. Avocation: scuba diving. Office: Creative Artists Agy c/o Kevin Huvane 9830 Wilshire Blvd Beverly Hills CA 90212-1804

BENJAMIN, ADELAIDE WISDOM, community volunteer and activist, retired lawyer; b. New Orleans, Aug. 23, 1932; d. William Bell and Mary (Freeman) Wisdom; m. Edward Bernard Benjamin Jr., May 11, 1957; children: Edward Wisdom, Mary Dabney, Ann Leith, Stuart Minor. Student, Hollins Coll., 1950-52; BA in English, Newcomb Coll., 1954; JD, Tulane U., 1956; student, Loyola U., New Orleans, 1980-81; grad. extension program Sewanee Theol. Sch., U. South, 1982. Assoc. Wisdom, Stone, Pigman and Benjamin, New Orleans, 1956-58; tchr. ext. courses Sewanee Theol. Sem., 1984-88; ret. attorney; ret., 1959. Spkr., panelist on sch. issues various local and nat. groups. Mem. Tulane Law Rev., 1954-56; compiler, editor, pub. Trinity Ch. supplemental songbook, 1980. Trustee Mary Freeman Wisdom Charitable Found., sec., 1987—92, pres., 1990—94, treas., 1994—, pres., 2000—; sec. bd. dir. YWCA, New Orleans, 1967—68, 1st v.p., 1968—69; bd. dir. Kingsley House, New Orleans, 1971—77; trustee Metairie Pk. Country Day Sch., 1971—79, sec., 1976—79; mem. adv. bd. Tulane Summer Lyric Theatre, Tulane U., 1972—, pres. adv. bd., 1977—79; pres. PTA, 1975—76; bd. dir. Children's Hosp., New Orleans, 1976—79; mem. adv. bd. Pub. Radio Sta. WWNO, 1980—; bd. dir. Parenting Ctr., 1981—; pres. E&A Charitable Found., New Orleans, 1983—; pres. bd. New Orleans Symphony, 1984—89; mem. Loving Cup selection com. New Orleans Times Picayune, 1985; bd. dir. La. Mus. Found., New Orleans, 1989—, S.E. La. coun. Girl Scouts US, New Orleans, 1989—97, Loyola U., New Orleans, 1989—99, mem. exec. com., 1996—99, hon. bd. mem., 2003—; bd. dir. Louise S. McGehee Sch., New Orleans, 1990—97, v.p., 1991—97, hon. bd. dir., 1991; pres. New Orleans Mus. Art Fellows Forum, 1991—; mem. exec. com. La. Mus. Found., New Orleans, 1991—; bd. dir. Newcomb Children's Ctr., New Orleans, 1991—94; mem. adv. bd. dept. psychiatry La. State U. Med. Ctr., 1992—; mem. exec. bd. La. Philharm. Orch., 1992—; mem. Newcomb Dean's Coun., 1997—, pres., 2002—; bd. dir. Nat. D-Day Mus., New Orleans, 1998—2002; sec. parish coun. Trinity Episc. Ch., New Orleans, 1973—75, sec. vestry, 1975—79, active, leader Trinity Quartet, 1979—84. Recipient Weiss Brotherhood award Nat. Conf. Christians and Jews, 1986, Outstanding Philanthropist, Nat. Soc. Fundraising Exec., 1986, Volunteer Activist Award, St. Elizabeth Guild, 1986, Jr. League Sustainer award, 1987, Disting. Alumna award McGehee Sch., 1987, George Washington Honor Medal for Individual Achievement, Freedom Found. at Valley Forge, 1988, Living and Giving award Juvenile Diabetes Found. 1991, Outstanding Citizen New Orleans award La. Colonials, 1994, Jacques Yenni award Outstanding Cmty. Svc. Sch. Bus. Adminstrn. Loyola Univ., 1994, Integritas Vitae award for outstanding cmty. svc. Loyola U., 1994, Classical Arts Patron award Tribute to the Classical Arts, 1998; named Goodwill Ambassador for Louisiana Gov.'s Commn. Internat. Trade, Industry and Tourism, 1987, Sweet Art, Contemporary Arts Ctr., 1988, Significant Role Model, Young Leadership Coun., 1988, Woman of Distinction S.E. La. Girl Scout Coun., 1992. Mem. ABA, LWV, La. Bar Assn., New Orleans Bar Assn., Jr. League New Orleans (exec. com. 1971-72, bd. dir. 1967-72), Ind. Women's Orgn., Com. 21, Am. Symphony Orch. League, Quarante Club (2d v.p. 1978-79), Debutante Club, Le Debut des Jeunes Filles Club, New Orleans Town Gardners (pres. 1979-80), Thomas Wolfe Soc. (life mem.). Home: 1837 Palmer Ave New Orleans LA 70118-6215

BENJAMIN, ANN WOMER, former state legislator, lawyer; m. to David M. Benjamin; children: Katherine, Johanna. BA magna cum laude, Vandberbilt U., 1975; JD, Case Western Reserve U., 1978. Bar: Ohio. Counsel Arter & Hadden, Cleve., 1984—; mem. Ohio Ho. Reps., Columbus, 1995—2002; dir. Ohio Dept. Ins., Columbus, 2003—. Adj. prof. law Case Western Reserve U., Cleve. Producer: Aurora (Ohio) Cmty. Theatre; contbr. articles to Estate Planning. Trustee, advocate Broadway Sch. Music and Arts; former chmn. Aurora (Ohio) Civil Svc. Commn. Mem. Ohio Bar Assn., Cleve. Bar Assn., Portage County Bar Assn., Phi Beta Kappa. Office: Ohio Dept Ins 2100 Stella Ct Columbus OH 43215-1067

BENJAMIN, LORNA SMITH, psychologist; d. Lloyd Albert and Esther Smith; children: Laureen, Linda. AB, Oberlin Coll., 1955; PhD, U. Wis., 1960. NIMH fellow dept. psychiatry U. Wis., 1958-62, clin. psychology intern, 1960-64, asst. prof., 1966-71, assoc. prof., 1971-77, prof. psychiatry, 1977-88; prof. psychology U. Utah, 1988—. Adj. prof. psychiatry U. Utah, 1988-; rsch. assoc. Wis. Psychol. Inst., Madison, 1962-66. Contbr. articles to profl. jours. Mem.: APA, Soc. Psychotherapy Rsch., Phi Beta Kappa. Office: Univ Utah Dept Psychology 380 S 1530 E Salt Lake City UT 84112-8934 E-mail: lsb_3@msn.com.

BENJAMIN, REGINA MARCIA, physician, administrator; b. Mobile, Ala., 1956; B in chemistry, Xavier U., New Orleans, 1979; MD, U. Ala., Birmingham, 1984; MBA, Tulane U., 1991. Internship and residency Med. Ctr. of Ctrl. Ga., Macon; med. dir. nursing homes, 1990—95; founder, adminstr. Bayou La Batre (Ala.) Rural Health Clinic, Inc., 1990—; assoc. dean rural health U. South Ala. Coll. Medicine. Med. mission, Honduras, 1993. Recipient Nelson Mandela Award for Health and Human Rights, Kaiser Family Found., 1997, Nat. Caring Award, Caring Inst., 2000, President's Award, U. Ala. Birmingham, 2001. Fellow: Am. Acad. Family Physicians; mem.: Med. Assn. State of Ala. (pres. 2002—03), NAS, AMA (Women in Medicine Panel 1986—87, pres. Edn. and Rsch. Found. 1997—98). Achievements include First African Am. woman to become pres. of a state med. soc. in the US, 2002; featured in Nat. Libr. Medicine exhibit Changing the Face of Medicine honoring women physicians, 2003. Office: 318 Patrician Dr Spanish Fort AL 36527-9461

BENJAMIN, SUSAN SELTON, elementary school educator; b. N.Y.C., June 3, 1946; m. Robert F. Benjamin, Nov. 30, 1968; children: Joshua, Alana. BS, Cornell U., 1968; MEd, Tufts U., 1969. Tchr. Wakefield (Mass.) Schs., 1969-73, Los Alamos (N.Mex.) Schs., 1973—. Resource tchr. Montessori Sch. House, San Diego, 1986; tchr. U. N.Mex., Los Alamos, 1989, 90; cons. Activities Integrating Math. and Sci. (AIMS) Nat. Leadership, Fresno, Calif., 1992—. Chair leadership Hadassah, Los Alamos, 1991—. Named Outstanding Women of N.Mex., 1980, N.Mex. State Tchr. of Yr., 2002; recipient Presdl. award for excellence in math. tchg. N.Mex. State, 1990, 92, Leadership award Hadassah, 1996. Mem. Nat. Coun. Math. Tchrs. Avocations: hiking, travel, tennis, aerobics. Home: 315 Rover Blvd Los Alamos NM 87544-3559

BENKO, LINDSAY, Olympic athlete; b. Elkhart, Ind., Nov. 29, 1976; Degree in comms., U. So. Calif., 1999. Recipient Gold medal 4 x 200-meter freestyle (team) Sydney Olympics, 2000, Silver medal 4 x 200-meter relay (team) World Championships, 1998, 200-meter backstroke, 400-meter freestyle summer nats., 1999, Silver medal 200-meter and 400-meter freestyle Pan Pacific Championships, 1999, gold medal 200m free at Pan Pacific Championships, 2002; winner NCAA title in 500-meter freestyle and 200-meter backstroke, 1996, 97, 500-meter freestyle; broke world record in 400m freestyle for short course meters at the World Cup stop in Berlin, 2003, broke world record in 200m at Short course World Championships; also won gold 200m back and swam on 3 Am. record breaking relays; world record holder in 200m and 400m free; Kiputh award winner, Spring Nat., 2003; inducted into Ind. swimming Hall of Fame, 2003 Spring Nat. Avocations: surfing, basketball, volleyball, reading, skiing. Office: USA Swimming 1 Olympic Plz Colorado Springs CO 80909-5746

BENNER, MARY WRIGHT, event planner; b. Chgo., Aug. 4, 1956; d. Robert V.L. and Sara Helen (Beeler) W.; m. Thomas G. Benner, Aug. 8, 1987; children: Sara Eleanor, Robert Fox. BA, Conn. Coll., 1979; MBA, Columbia U., 1983. Rsch. assoc. Acad. for Contemporary Problems, Washington, 1979-81; rating specialist Standard & Poor's, N.Y.C., 1983-84; asst. adminstr. Twp. of Princeton, N.J., 1984-86; v.p. Fin. Guaranty Ins. Co., N.Y.C., 1986-99, mgr. dept. govt. affairs, 1997-99; cons., 1999—. Bd. dirs. Nat. Com. for Pub./Pvt. Partnerships, 1997-99; mem. sponsor adv. com. Women Exec. in State Gov., 1998-99; mem. steering com. Rebuild Am. Coalition, 1997-99; co-chair Uniting Citizens for Housing Affordability in Newton, 2000—; chair out reach commn. Eliot Ch. of Newton, 2001—. Mem. Pub. Works Forum (bd. dirs. 1986-88), Assn. for Govtl. Leasing and Fin. (bd. dirs. 1991-95, treas. 1994-95), Assn. Fin. Guaranty Insurers (chmn. com. govt. affairs 1997-99), Rebuild Am. Coalition (exec. bd. dirs. 1998-88), Cape Cod Chamber Mus. Festival, (v.p., bd. dirs. 2000-03), The Conf. Bd. (program dir. 2002—). Congregationalist. Avocation: cooking. Home and Office: 136 Washington St Newton MA 02458-2250

BENNERUP, BROOKE CLARA, poet, writer; b. New Haven, Conn., Jan. 25, 1977; d. Pierre Robert Bennerup and Susan J. Sawicki. BA in Cinema and TV Prodn., U. So. Calif., 1999. Asst. to prodr. Beacon Comm., L.A., 1997—98; asst. to mgr. product placement The Shooting Gallery, N.Y.C., 1998; asst. to poet/prof./writer Carol Muske-Dukes U. So. Calif., L.A., 1999—2000; asst. to dir. Propaganda Films, L.A., 2000; founder artists' and writers' cmty. The Dulcinea Corp., Barga, Italy, 2002—. Author: (book of poetry) Straw Beneath the Loom. Fundraiser Greenpeace, L.A., 2001—02; mid. sch. tutor Teamworks L.A., Watts, L.A., 1997—99; tutor, tchr. Joint Edn. Project, L.A., 1996—98. Grantee Summer Art Residency Program, Marie Walsh Sharpe Art Found., 1995; scholar, Cambridge U. Medieval Studies, 1995. Mem.: Phi Kappa Phi, Golden Key. Democrat. Avocations: organic gardening, art, travel, rowing, archaeology. Home: Barghigiani 1 55051 Barga Italy Office: The Dulcinea Corp 1829 Orchard Rd Berlin CT 06037 E-mail: bennerup@yahoo.com.

BENNETT, AMANDA, editor; Grad. cum laude, Harvard U., 1975. Reporter Wall St. Jour.; mng. editor projects The Oregonian, 1998—2001; editor, v.p. Lexington Herald-Leader, 2001—03; editor, exec. v.p. Phila. (Pa.) Inquirer, 2003—. Mem. Pulitzer Prize Bd., 2002—. Author: In Memoriam, 1998; co-author: (with Terence B. Foley) The Man Who Stayed Behind, (with Sidney Rittenberg) Death of the Organziation Man, 1991. Recipient Pulitzer prize, The Oregonian, 2001. Mem.: Pulitzer Prize Bd. Office: Philadelphia Inquirer PO Box 8263 400 N Broad St Philadelphia PA 19101

BENNETT, ANNE MARIE, nursing administrator; b. Savannah, Ga., July 29, 1968; d. Rex and Sherry Louise (Edenfield) Duggar; m. Joseph Cleveland Bennett, Jr., Dec. 18, 1992. BSc with honors, Armstrong Atlantic State U., 1992; MSc, U. Mobile, 1996. Cert. critical care nurse, registered nurse, Ga., Miss., La., Ala. Charge nurse Bulloch Meml. Hosp., Statesboro, Ga., 1992-94; critical care clinical specialist Springhill Meml. Hosp., Mobile, Ala., 1994-98; dir. critical care Thomas Hosp., Fairhope, Ala., 1998-99, dir., 1999—. Adj. faculty U. Mobile, Ala., 1995-96; cons. in field. Reviewer Jour. Nursing Staff Devel., 1998. Big Sister Big Brothers/Big Sisters, Savannah, 1989-91; medical missionary, Nicaragua, 1995; team captain Am. Cancer Soc., Mobile, 1997, Healthcare Olympics, Mobile, 1997; bd. dirs. Ala. Southern Cmty. Coll. Nursing Bd., Monroeville, 1996-97. Recipient Lamplighter award Ala. League for Nursing, Mobile, 1997, Nurse Educator of Yr. award Nurse's Soc., Mobile County, 1997. Mem. Am. Assn. Critical Care Nurses (sec. Mobile Bay Area chpt. 1993—, Circle of Excellence award 1997), Am. Nurses Assn., Emergency Nurses Assn., Mensa, Sigma Theta Tau (Virginia Henderson fellow 1997). Home: 139 Altama Connector Brunswick GA 31525-1881

BENNETT, BETTY T. English literature educator, university dean, writer; b. N.J. children: Peter, Matthew. BA, Bklyn. Coll., 1962; MA, NYU, 1963, PhD, 1970. Adj. asst. prof. dept. English and comparative lit. SUNY, Stony Brook, 1970-75, asst. chmn. comparative lit., 1971-72, asst. to dean Grad. Sch., 1970-79, adj. assoc. prof., 1975-79; assoc. prof. English and humanities Pratt Inst., Bklyn., 1979-81, prof., 1981-85, dean Sch. Liberal Arts and Scis., 1979-85; dean Coll. Arts and Scis. Am. U., Washington, 1985-97, disting. prof. lit., 1997—. Fellowship reader Danforth Found., 1978-79; edn. liaison officer N.Y. State, 1977-80; co-dir. NEH Inst., 1989-90. Author: British War Poetry in the Age of Romanticism: 1793-1815, 1976, The Letters of Mary Wollstonecraft Shelley, Vol. I, 1980, The Letters of Mary Wollstonecraft Shelley, Vol. II, 1983, The Letters of Mary Wollstonecraft Shelley, Vol. III, 1988, Mary Diana Dods: A Gentleman and a Scholar, 1991, Mary Diana Dods: A Gentleman and a Scholar, paperback edit., 1994, Mary Wollstonecraft Shelley: An Introduction, 1998; editor (with Donald H. Reiman and Michael Jaye): The Evidence of the Imagination, 1978; editor: (with Charles Robinson) The Mary Shelley Reader, 1990; editor: Proserpine and Midas and Relation of the Cenci, 1992, The Selected Letters of Mary Wollstonecraft Shelley, 1995, Lives of the Great Romantics III: Mary Shelley, 1999; editor: (with Stuart Curran) Mary Shelley in Her Times, 2000; cons. editor and author gen. intro.: The Novels and Selected Works of Mary Wollstonecraft Shelley, 1996, book rev. editor: Keats-Shelley Jour., 1976—94. Keats-Shelley Assn. Am. Disting. scholar, 1992; NEH fellow, 1974-75, Henry E. Huntington Libr. fellow, 1976, Am. Coun. Learned Socs. fellow, 1977-78; Am. Philos. Soc. grant, 1980-81, NEH grant, 1984-87. Mem. MLA, Byron Assn., Keats-Shelley Assn. Am. (bd. dirs.), Soc. for Textual Scholarship (exec. com. 1993—), NYU Alumni Assn., Phi Beta Kappa (founding pres. Zeta chpt. of D.C.). Office: Am U Dept Lit Coll Arts and Scis 4400 Massachusetts Ave NW Washington DC 20016-8001 E-mail: bbennet@american.edu.

BENNETT, BROOKE, Olympic athlete; b. Tampa, Fla., May 6, 1980; Grad., Durant HS, Plant City, Fla., 1998. Swimmer; winner gold and silver medals Pan-Am Games, 1995; winner gold medal Pan Pacific Games, 1995, 97; gold medalist 800m freestyle Olympic Summer Games, 1996; sponsor swim team Brower Aquatic Suns, Davie, Fla.; gold medalist 400m freestyle, Sydney, 2000, 800m freestyle, Sydney, 2000. Recipient Spring Nationals Kiphuth award, 1996, Spring Nationals Phillips Performance award, 1996, USOC Sports Woman of the Yr. for swimming, 1995. Avocation: horseback riding. Office: c/o USA Swimming 1 Olympic Plz Colorado Springs CO 80909-5746

BENNETT, C. LYNN, educational consultant; b. Morgantown, W.Va., May 21, 1947; d. Warren G. and Dortha M. Wiley; m. Ben P. Bennett, Nov. 30, 1981 (dec.). BA in Secondary Edn., Shepherd Coll., 1969. Cert. ednl. tech. leadership Salem Internat. U., 1998. Dir. program devel. North Ctrl. Regional Edn. Svc. Agy. (RESA VII), Clarksburg, W.Va., 1990—2003; ednl. cons. Bennett Ednl. Consulting, Bridgeport, W.Va., 2003—. Recipient

Profl. Courage award, W.Va. Edn. Assn., 1990; Regional Electronic Alternative Learning grantee, U.S. Dept. Commerce - TIIAP, 1996, Character Edn. grantee, W.Va. Dept. Edn., 2001—, NEH grantee, Tchg. Am. History grantee, U.S. Dept. Edn., 2003—. Mem.: ASCD, Nat. Assn. Regional Media Ctrs. (pres. 1997—98), Phi Delta Kappa. Methodist. Home: 18 Meadow Ln Bridgeport WV 26330 Office: Bennett Educational Consulting 18 Meadow Ln Bridgeport WV 26330 E-mail: lynnben@iolinc.net.

BENNETT, CAROL(INE) ELISE, retired reporter, actress; b. New Orleans, Dec. 27, 1938; d. Gerald Clifford Graham and Edna Doris (Toennies) Kerr; m. Ralph Decker Bennett, Jr., Feb. 27, 1966; children: Ralph Decker III, Katherine Elise. BA, U. B.C., Vancouver, Can., 1960; BLS, McGill U., Montreal, Que., Can., 1962. Libr. various locations, 1962-76; reporter TV/radio Washington-Ala. News Report, Washington, 1981-2001; ret., 2001. Actor: (plays) Girl in My Soup, 1978; (films) Prime Risk, 1984; host (TV series) Modern Maturity, 1986—88. Vol. reader Rec. for Blind, Washington, 1985—. Mem.: AAUW, AFTRA, SAG, Nat. Press Club, Soc. Profl. Journalists. Avocation: tennis. Home: 115 Southwood Ave Silver Spring MD 20901-1918

BENNETT, CATHERINE JUNE, information technology executive, educator, consultant; b. Augusta, Ga., June 19, 1950; d. Robert Stogner and Catherine Sue (Jordan) Robinson; m. Danny Marvin Bennett, Sept. 5, 1971; children: Timothy Jordan, Robert Daniel. BS in Stats., U. Ga., 1971, MA in Bus., 1973. Cert. project mgmt. profl. Project Mgmt. Inst., rational cert. cons., fellow Life Mgmt. Inst. Programmer William M. Shenkel & Assocs., Athens, Ga., 1971-73; sys. analyst U. Ga., Athens, 1973-76; product cons. ISA/SUNGUARD, Atlanta, 1976-78, mgr. product support, 1980-85, hotline mgr., sr. fin. specialist, 1986-88, mem. edn. staff Investment Client Support, 1988-90, mgr. investment reporting, 1991-93, mgr. devel., 1993-95; dir. Fin. Reporting Solutions, 1998-99; project mgr. CGI, Atlanta, 1999, dir. cons. svcs., 1999—2002, dir. outsourcing svcs., 2002—. Presenter in field. Den leader Cub Scouts, 1989-90, treas., 1990-95; head ofcl. Duluth Thunderbolts, 1994; mem. Gwinnett Swim League (sec. 1995-2003). Avocations: bridge, swimming, travel. Office: CGI 3740 Davinci Ct # 400 Norcross GA 30092-2670 E-mail: cathieben@worldnet.att.net., cathie.bennett@cgi.com.

BENNETT, CATHERINE MARGARET, music educator; b. Antwerp, Belgium, Jan. 23, 1970; d. George William and Betty Louisa Eberling; m. Chad Baylus Bennett, May 20, 2000; 1 child, Chase Baylus George. B, S.W. Tex. State U., 1993. Asst. band dir. Crowley (Tex.) H.S., 1993—94, Pflugerville H.S.; assoc. dir. bands James Bowie H.S., Austin, Tex., 1998—. Recipient Citation of Excellence, John Phillip Sousa Found., 2003. Mem.: World Assn. Symphonic Bands and Ensembles (assoc.), Nat. Assn. Music Edn. (assoc.), Tex. Music Educators Assn. (assoc.), Tau Beta Sigma (assoc.). Home: 9245 Vigen Cir Austin TX 78748 Office: James Bowie HS 4103 W Slaugher Ln Austin TX 78749 Personal E-mail: cb52000@flash.net. E-mail: ceberlin@austin.isd.tenet.edu.

BENNETT, COLLEEN T. music educator; d. Charles J. and Marygrace Z. Blair; m. David P. Bennett, 1986; children: Michael, Andrew. MusB, Marywood Coll. Founder and music dir. Colleen's Sch. Music, Hinckley, NY, 1986—2003; founder and dir. Colleen's Musical Nursery Sch., Hinckley, 1991—2003; founder, exec. dir., CEO KEYS Corp., Oneida, NY, 1991—. Early childhood music cons. Nat. Early Childhood Orgn., 1991—; music cons. for spl. needs orgns. Nat. Spl. Needs Orgns., 1997—; cons. arts coalition com. Ctrl. N.Y. Cmty. Arts Coun., Utica, 2002—. Musician: (children's concerts) Making Music with Mrs. G Clef (Outstanding Contbr. to Early Childhood Edn., 1997); author (music book) ; singer: (soloist for pro tour truck series) Nat. Anthem. Judge and steering com. sec. Oneida City Youth Ct., 1979—84. Recipient Cmty. Svc. award, Miss Nat. Teenager Scholarship Program, 1984. Mem.: N.Y. State Assn. for Edn. of Young Children, Family Child Care Assn., N.Y. State Sch. Music Assn., Music Educators Nat. Conf., Mid York Child Care Coord. Coun., Oriskany-Whitestown Rotary (exch. student counselor 2002—03), Sports Car Club Am., Zonta Club, St. Cecelia's Soc. (sec. 1985—86). Roman Catholic. Avocations: motorsports, song writing, travel. Home: PO Box 923 Oneida NY 13421 Office: KEYS Box 923 Kenwood Station Oneida NY 13421 E-mail: keysprogram@aol.com.

BENNETT, DEMARA B. psychologist; b. Gainsville, Fla., Dec. 9, 1967; d. Dana Collin and Betty Jo Barbour; m. Mathew Gerald Bennett, Feb. 14, 1996; children: Delaney Jo, Chase Riley. BS, Fla. Inst. of Tech., Melbourne, Fla., 1988, MS, 1993, Psy.D Psychology, 1994. Lic. psychologist Fla., 1996, Wis., 2000. Predoctoral psychology internship Counseling Ctr. for Human Devel., Univ. So. Fla., Tampa, Fla., 1993—94; external rotation Child Devel. Ctr., Univ. So. Fla., Tampa, Fla., 1994; therapist Womens Program, Charter Hosp. of Tampa Bay, Tampa, Fla., 1993—94, Codependency Group, Charter Hosp. of Tampa Bay, Tampa, Fla., 1993—94; neurobehavorial cons./postdoctoral residency Colo. Ctr. for Neurol. Rehab., Englewood, Colo., 1994—95; program supr./postdoctoral residency Mila Elem. Sch. Program, Melbourne, Fla., 1995—96; therapist Chlid/Adolescent Partial Hospitalization Program, Charter Behavioral Health Sys. of Tampa Bay, Tampa, Fla., 1996; dir./clin. psychologist Charter Brandon Counseling Ctr., Brandon, Fla., 1996—97; program dir. Sunshine Behavorial Health Svcs., Clearwater, Fla., 1997; pvt. practice clin. psychologist Clearwater, Fla., 1997—98; psychologist/EAP coord. Northside Mental Health Care, Tampa, Fla., 1998—2000; lic. psychologist Sacred Heart-St. Mary's Hosp., Psychol. Assoc., Rhinelander, Wis., 2000—. Contbr. scientific papers presented at many conf. Bd. dirs. Greener Pastures, Rhinelander, Wis., 2003. Mem.: APA. Avocations: horseback riding, bicycling, hiking, skiing, boating. Office: Psychol Assoc 203 Schiek Plaza PO Box 1146 Rhinelander WI 54501

BENNETT, GENEVIEVE, artist; b. Chgo., Feb. 11, 1927; d. Joseph and Mary Sieczka; m. William A. Bennett, Jan. 31, 1953; children: William George, J. Daniel, Gordon Dean. BA, Calif. State U., Fullerton, 1974; MA, Calif. State U., Long Beach, 1978. Artist, Anaheim, Calif. Tchr. art Ebell Club Anaheim, 1985-97, Whittier and Anaheim, Calif.; lectr. N.Am. temple mound builders. One-woman shows include Calif. Poly. U., Pomona, 1995, Orange County Fair, Calif., 1995, Anaheim Mus., 1997, exhibitions include Hotel-Restaurant La Musardiere, Giverny, France, 2002, Anaheim Arts Coun. Annual Souree, 2004 (Artist Honoree). Recipient Grumbacher Gold medal, 1999, Celebrating Remarkable Women Among Us award Orange County chpt. Nat. Assn. Women Bus. Owners, 1999, Cert. Spl. Congl. Recognition, Loretta Sanchez, 1999, Beyond the Call award Anaheim (Calif.) Arts Coun. and Arts in Pub. Places, 2002. Mem. Am. Internat. Culture and Art Assn., Nat. League Am. Pen Women (state v.p. 1997-98, Am. Internat. Culture and Art Assn., Orange County br. pres. 1997-98, recipient State Women of Achievement award, 1998), Calif. State U. Art Alliance, So. Calif. Women's Caucus for Art, Orange County Fine Arts, Phi Delta Gamma (Phi chpt.). Avocations: archaeology, piano, music, travel, art meetings. Home: 2026 W Judith Ln Anaheim CA 92804-6511

BENNETT, JEAN LOUISE MCPHERSON, physicist, research scientist; b. Kensington, Md., May 9, 1930; d. Archibald Turner and Margaret Fitch (Willcox) McPherson; m. Harold Earl Bennett, Aug. 17, 1952 (div. Nov. 1984). BA summa cum laude, Mt. Holyoke Coll., 1951, DSc (hon.), 1992; MS, Pa. State U., 1953, PhD in Physics, 1955. Physicist Wright Air Devel. Ctr., Dayton, Ohio, 1955-56, Naval Ordnance Test Sta. (now Naval Air Warfare Ctr. Weapons Div.), China Lake, Calif., 1956-85, sr. research scientist, 1987-93, 95; vis. prof. U. Ala., Huntsville, 1986-87, Mt. Holyoke Coll., South Hadley, Mass., 1994-95; ret., 1996—. Mem. NRC Evaluation Panel Nat. Bur. Stds., Ctr. for Radiation Rsch., 1979-85, Nat. Inst. Stds. and Tech. Mfg. Engring. Lab., 1988-94, U.S. Nat. Com. for Internat. Commn. for Optics, 1984-85, 88-95; vis. scientist Inst. Optical Rsch., Royal Inst. Tech., Stockholm, Mar.-Sept., 1988, 98, 99, 2000, 01. Author: (with Lars Mattsson) Introduction to Surface Roughness and Scattering, 1989, revised 1999; author: Surface Finish and Its Measurement, 1992; contbr. sci. articles to profl. jours.; patentee in field. Recipient Tech. Achievement award Soc. Photo-Optical Instrumentation Engrs., 1983, L.T.E. Thompson award Naval Weapons Ctr., 1988, Women in Sci. and Engring. Lifetime Achievement award, 1993, Outstanding Sci. Alumni award Pa. State U., 1999; named sr. fellow Naval Weapons Ctr., 1989, Disting. Fellow, 1994. Fellow Optical Soc. Am. (v.p. 1984, pres.-elect 1985, pres. 1986, past pres. 1987, chmn. book publ. com. 1991-94, David Richardson medal 1990); mem. Am. Inst. Physics (subcom. on books 1990-94), Phi Beta Kappa, Sigma Xi, Sigma Delta Epsilon, Iota Sigma Pi, Pi Mu Epsilon, Sigma Pi Sigma. Achievements include being the first woman to receive PhD in Physics at Pa. State U., 1955; first woman pres. Optical Soc. of Am. Home: 1275 Sage Ct Ridgecrest CA 93555-2622 Office: Code 4T41A0D Michelson Lab Naval Air Warfare Ctr Stop 6302 1900N Knox Rd China Lake CA 93555 E-mail: jbennett@ridgenet.net.

BENNETT, JOAN HIERHOLZER, artist; b. Grand Rapids, Mich. d. Frank R. and Bernice H. (Cooper) Hierholzer; m. John Pine Bennett (div.); children: David Pine, Charles Cooper. BFA, U. Tex., 1952; MFA, Rutgers U., 1969. Solo shows include Phoenix Gallery, N.Y.C., Rutgers Art Gallery, New Brunswick, N.J., Drew Chem. Corp., Boonton, N.J., Ednl. Testing Svc., Princeton, N.J., AT&T, Basking Ridge, N.J., Alba Vineyard Gallery, Finesville, N.J., Nat. Arts Club, N.Y.C.; group shows include Arc Gallery, Chgo., Montclair (N.J.) Art Mus., Mus. of S.W., Midland, Tex., N.J. State Mus., Trenton, Witte Mus., San Antonio, Dallas Mus. Fine Arts, Bodley Gallery, N.Y.C., Richmond (Ind.) Art Mus., Nat. Acad., N.Y.C., Kimball Art Ctr., Park City, Utah, Goddard Ctr. for Visual Arts, Ardmore, Okla., many others; permanent collections include Exxon, N.J., Schering-Plough, N.J., Deloitte, Haskin & Sells, N.J., NASA Gallery, Kennedy Space Ctr., Fla., Johnson & Johnson, N.J., Bristol-Meyers Squibb, N.J., many others. Trustee, mem. arts adv. coun. Hunterdon Art Ctr., 1980—. Fellow MacDowell Colony. Mem. Nat. Assn. Women Artists, Nat. Arts Club, Artists Equity, Hunterdon Art Ctr. Avocations: home designing, advertising. Home: 760 County Road 513 Pittstown NJ 08867-5164

BENNETT, JUDY A. music educator; b. Madison, S.D., Apr. 10, 1952; d. George Raymond and Berthein Cary Gannon; m. Jeffrey A. Bennett, June 15, 1974; children: Don Dean, Christopher Lee, Alexander Jeffrey. BS, Dakota State U., 1978. Vocal/gen. music tchr. Uinta County Sch. Dist. #1, Evanston, Wyo., 1978—92, Sch. Dist. La Crosse, Wis., 1992—96, Galena (Ill.) Pub. Schs., 1996—98, Albany (Wis.) Pub. Schs., 1998—2001; H.S. vocal music tchr. Sch. Dist. Monroe, Wis., 2001—. Composer songs. Dir. Cmty. Choir, Evanston, 1978—86, Hazel Green, Wis., 1998; bd. dirs. Monroe Theatre Guild, 2000. Mem.: NEA, Monroe Edn. Assn., Wyo. Edn. Assn., Music Educators Nat. Conf. Home: 1706 23rd Ave Monroe WI 53566 Office: Monroe High School 1600 26th St Monroe WI 53566 Personal E-mail: j_bennett@charter.net. E-mail: judy.bennctt@monroe.k12.wi.us.

BENNETT, KATHLEEN MAROURNEEN, elementary school educator; b. Harlingen, Tex., Jan. 26, 1943; d. Owen James Bennett and Betty Margaret Bell. BS, No. Mich. U., 1966. Cert. elem. edn. Mich. Tchr. Head Start, Iron Mountain, Mich., 1966, Iron Mountain Pub. Schs., 1966, Gladstone (Mich.) Area Schs., 1967. Chair Sch. Improvement Team, Gladstone, Mich., 1988—90; dir. musicals various elem. schs. Actor: Area Children's Theatre. Active Recreation Adv. Bd., Escanaba, Mich., 1980—82; dir. children's musicals; actor children's theater. Named Disting. Alumni, No. Mich. U., 1988. Mem.: AAUW (pres., Outstanding Educator Escanaba br. 1980), Mich. Edn. Assn. (sec. 1977—79, Outstanding Person in Edn. award 2003). Democrat. Episcopalian. Avocations: reading, walking, movies, interior decorating, travel. Home: 321 S 6th St Escanaba MI 49829

BENNETT, LENA M. special education educator; b. DeBerry, Tex., Dec. 20, 1951; d. Marvin T. and Ruby V. Bennett; 1 child, Martise V. Easter. AA, Texarcana (Tex.) C.C., 1973, Chaffey Coll., 1993; BA in Libr. Studies, Calif. State U., 1997; EdM, Calif. Polytech. Inst., 2001. Cert. tchr., spl. edn. Paraprofl. San Bernardino (Calif.) County Schs., 1998; tchr. spl. edn. Pomona (Calif.) Unified Sch. Dist., 1998—. Mem.: Autism Soc. Am. Democrat. Baptist. Avocations: dance, painting, drawing, sports.

BENNETT, LINDA LOU, school librarian, educator; b. Sidney, Ark., Nov. 17, 1941; d. Charles Orbra Richardson and Thelma Camilla Marchant Richardson; m. John Allan Bennett, Nov. 12, 1960; children: Dawn Denise McCoy, Tracy Lynne Royer. BS in Edn., S.E. Mo. State U., Cape Girardeau, 1968; MLS, U. Mo., 1995. Cert. tchng. Mo., 1968. Libr. staff Kent Libr. S.E. Mo. State U., Cape Girardeau, 1968—69; libr. Pattonville Sr. HS, Bridgeton, 1969—71; instr. Festus Pub. Sch. Dist., Mo., 1971—75; edn. rsch. and devel. project Ark. Dept. of Edn., Little Rock, 1989—91; libr. dir. U. Ark C.C., Batesville, 1991—. Author: Teamwork: The Name Of The Game In Recruitment; Retention: A Game Plan, 1991. Com. mem. Rep. Party, Batesville, 1986; chairperson The Ark. State Libr. Bd., Little Rock, 2002. Mem.: ALA (assoc.), Ark. Libr. Assn. (assoc.; com. mem.). Baptist. Avocations: reading, watercolor painting, travel, family activities. Home: 3120 Alice Dr Batesville AR 72501 Office: U of Ark Community Coll 2005 White Drive Batesville AR 72501

BENNETT, LISA, artist; b. Eng., Aug. 3, 1922; came to U.S., 1927; d. Reuben and Hannah Dora (Hacker) Bernstein. BA, Goddard Coll., MA, 1976. Instrl. coord. Walnut Creek (Calif.) Civic Arts, 1964-76; critic, art reviewer, essayist, reporter West Art, 1964-79, San Francisco Territorial News, 1962, 63; freelance writer Washington, 1980-81; adminstrn. coord. Gesell Inst., New Haven, 1982-84; owner, lectr. bur. Bennett Programs, San Francisco, 1985-86, freelance bus. writer, 1987-89; arts lectr. Oxford U., 1990-93; spl. editor Oxford U. Press, 1990-91; adj. lectr. Hunter Coll., N.Y.C., 1992. Freelance lectr. San Francisco State U., 1974-79, U. Calif., Dominican Coll., St. Mary's Coll., San Quentin Prison (Coll. of Marin), Hayward State Coll. One-woman shows include Lincoln Gallery, 1960, Firehouse Gallery, Cowell, Calif., 1966, Womens Resource Ctr., Sarasota, 1995, Sheraton Hotel, Boston, 1995, U.S. Garage, Sarasota, 1996, Am. Inst. Arch. Hdqs. Gallery, Washington, 1998, Barret Ho., Va. Found. Arch., Richmond, 1999, Flat Iron Gallery, Peekskill, N.Y., 2000, Temple Israel, Croton, N.Y., 2001; exhibited in group shows at Art Students League, 1955, Golden Gate Gallery, San Francisco, 1961, Civic Arts, Walnut Creek, 1966, St. Edwards Art Gallery, Oxford, 1991, U.S. Garage, Sarasota, 1993, Sarasota Visual Art Ctr., 1994, Sur-la-Mer Gallery, Sarasota, 1995, Francesca Armijo Presents Gallery, 1996, Fulton-Burt Gallery, Sarasota, 1997, Gallery-at-Crystal Bay, Peekskill, 1997, Bedford Gallery, Dean Lesher Regional Ctr. Arts, Walnut Creek, Calif., 1998, Paramount Ctr. Arts, Peekskill, 1999, Peekskill Art Supply Gallery, 1999, Westchester C.C., Valhalla, N.Y., 2000, Katonah Mus. Artists' Assn., North Westchester Ctr. Arts, Mt. Kisco, N.Y., 2000, Westchester Arts Coun., White Plains, N.Y., 2001, Smithtown Twp. Arts Coun., St. James, N.Y., 2002, Hendrick Hudson Free Libr., Montrose, N.Y., 2002, Ceres Gallery, N.Y.C., 2002, 2003, Chapel H ill Estates, Peekskill, 2002; pub. and pvt. collections include Bryn Mawr (Pa.) Coll. Study Collection, Am. Inst. Archs. Found., Metromedia Fiber Networks, White Plains, Ginsburg Devel. Arch., Hawthorne, NY. Recipient Spl. Opportunity stipend, State of N.Y., 1998, Artists' Showcase award, Manhattan Arts Internat., 1999, Internat. Grant award, Pollock-Krasner Found., N.Y., 2000. Mem. Nat. Mus. for Women in the Arts, Mus. Archives, Artists Equity. Address: 951 Main St Apt 2E Peekskill NY 10566-2932

BENNETT, LORRAINE MARTIN, editor; b. Portsmouth, Va., May 24, 1943; d. Albert Jewell Martin and Thelma Talaitha Elkins; m. Thomas Joel Bennett, Dec. 18, 1966. AA, Brevard (N.C.) Coll., 1963; BA in Journalism, U. N.C., 1965. Gen. assignment reporter Atlanta Jour., 1965—70; pub. rels. dir. Atlanta U., 1970—72; Orange County feature writer L.A. Times, 1974—80, Riverside-San Bernardino counties bur. chief, 1980—82; writer, copy editor, prodr. CNN, Atlanta, 1983—94, sr. editor, editl. mgr., 1995—99; dep. mng. editor Web MD, Atlanta, 1999—2002; news copy editor CNN Internat., Atlanta, 2002—. Bd. visitors U. N.C. Sch. Journalism, Chapel Hill, 1998—; co-pres. Fulton County Vol. Probation Officers, Atlanta, 1970. Recipient Ga. AP Pub. Svc. award, 1968, Quill award, Sigma Delta Chi, 1968, Ga. Sweepstakes award, Ga. Press Assn., 1968. Mem.: Soc. Profl. Journalists, Nat. Freedom of Info. Coalition, Atlanta Press Club. Democrat. Baptist. Avocations: music, photography. Office: CNN 1 CNN Ctr Atlanta GA 30348

BENNETT, MARGARET AIROLA, lawyer; b. San Francisco, Calif; AB cum laude, U. Calif., Berkeley, 1972; JD, U. San Francisco and Loyola U., 1976. Bar: Ill.1976, US Dist. Ct. (no. dist.) Ill. 1977, US Ct. Appeals (7th cir.) 1983. Intern Cook County State's Atty.'s Office, Chgo., 1975-76; assoc. Dunlap, Thompson & Boyd, Ltd., Libertyville, Ill., 1977-79; ptnr. Bennett & Bennett, Ltd., Oak Brook, Ill., 1980-96; pvt. practice The Law Offices of Margaret A. Bennett, Oak Brook, Ill., 1997. Atty. rep. McDonald's Corp., Oak Brook, 1982—, County of DuPage, Wheaton, Ill., 1990-95. Counsel fo DuPage Ill. Fair and Exposition Authority, County of DuPage, 1991-95, co-chmn. next generation com.; mem. devel. coun. Good Samaritan Hosp., 1988-92. Mem. DuPage County Bar Assn. (chmn. real estate law com. 1994-95, Cert. of Appreciation 1989, Bd. Dir. award 1998, chmn. profl. responsibility com. 1996-97, chmn. family law com. 1997-98), Ill. State Bar Assn. (assembly mem., 1996-2000, Cert. of Appreciation 1990, real estate sect. counsel 1996-2002, jud evaluation com. 1998—), Womens Bar Assn. DuPage County, Evang. Health Found. (bd. sponsors 1988-92). Republican. Episcopalian. Avocations: golf, reading, skiing, travel. Office: Ste 718 1200 Harger Rd Oak Brook IL 60523 1908

BENNETT, MARGARET ANN, cook; b. Grand Rapids, Mich., Nov. 19, 1933; d. John Phillip and Harriet Marie (DeKruyter) Kremer; m. Roscoe Dudley Bennett, Aug. 27, 1955; children: Paul Dudley, Martha Leigh Lanewala, Sarah Wyatt Gregory. AA, Grand Rapids Jr. Coll., 1954; BA, Newark State Coll., 1971. Cert. preschool teacher, N.J. Mgr. Animal Hosp., Grand Rapids, 1949-54; personal sec. Second Nat. Bank, New Haven, 1955-56; tchr. Happytime Sch., West Caldwell, N.J., 1964-67, adminstr., tchr., owner, 1967-95; baker McDonoughs Mkt., Beaver Island, Mich., 1996-97; prep cook Dalwhinnies, Beaver Island, 1997-98, Beaver Lodge, 1998—. Mem. Edn. Young Child (pres. Essex-Hudson), Assn. Edn. Young Child (sec. N.J.), bd. Beaver Island Preservation Assn., 1999—. Democrat. Episcopalian. Avocations: walking, gardening, singing, knitting, photography. Home: 30930 E Side Dr Beaver Island MI 49782-9748

BENNETT, OLGA SALOWICH, civic worker, graphic arts researcher, consultant; b. Detroit, June 30, 1925; d. Nicholas Stefanovich and Maria Elarionovna (Mikuliak) Salowich; m. Robert William Bennett, Dec. 20, 1947; 1 child, Susan Roberta. Student, U. Mich., 1943-45, Parsons Sch. Design, 1948, U. Md., Nagoya, Japan, 1959; BA, NYU, 1975. Graphic artist Silver & Co., N.Y.C., 1948-50; editor, pub. Bull., organizer radio series LWV, Pitts., 1950-55; instr. Nanzan U., Nagoya, 1959; aide, cons. to U.S. hon. consul, Safi, Casablanca, Morocco, 1962-65; chmn. internat. affairs LWV, Montclair, N.J., 1966-73; conf. coord. UN Assn., Madison, N.J., 1974; weekly broadcaster LWV, San Juan, P.R., 1976-81; lectr. color theory Cunard, Ltd., London, Miami, Fla., 1985-88. Bd. dirs., docent Ctr. Fine Arts, Miami, 1990-92; docent Bass Mus. Art, Miami Beach, Fla., 1990-92, Vizcaya Mus. Art, Miami, 1983—; cons. on corp. overseas placement. Author artist brochures, ednl. pamphlets; translator Russian-Am. Conf., Miami, 1990. Mem. panel theater award com. New Theater, Miami, 1991; mem. Nat. Mus. of Women in the Arts; bd. dirs. Kings Creek South Condominium Assn., 1996-99. Mem. AAUW, LWV, UN Assn., NYU Alumni Assn., New Sch. Alumni Assn., Fgn. Policy Assn., Great Decisions Program. Democrat. Russian Orthodox. Home: Kings Creek S Apt A1-402 7727 SW 86th St Miami FL 33143-7283

BENNETT, PATRICIA ANN, radio executive; 1 child, Jessica. BA in Communications, Sangamon State U., 1978, MA in Communications, 1981. Vol. coord. Sta. WSSR-FM, Springfield, Ill., 1977-79; sta. mgr. Stas. WRRS, KMUW, Wichita, Kans., 1979-85; gen. mgr. Sta. KGOU, Norman, Okla., 1985-87; mgr. sta. grant programs Corp. for Pub. Broadcasting, Washington, 1987-89; dir., gen. mgr. Sta. KWMU-FM, St. Louis, 1989—. Bd. dirs. NPR, 1992-94, 95-97; participant NPR Pub. Radio Conf., 1979-90, Pub. Broadcasting Svc. Conf., 1987-89, Corp. for Pub. Broadcasting Conf., 1977-80, Rocky Mountain Pub. Radio Meetings, 1987-89, SECA Meetings, 1987-89; bd. dirs. Pub. Radio in Mid-Am. Conf., 1986-88; mem. gerontology faculty Wichita State U., 1983-84; promotion and pub. svc. announcer Sta. KPTS-TV, Wichita, 1979 80; judge coord. Ohio State Awards, 1986-87. Mem. adv. com. for handicapped svcs. Wichita State U., 1980-82. Mem. Pub. Telecommunication Fin. Mgmt. Assn. (bd. dirs. 1990—), Alpha Epsilon Rho (pres. 1979-84, advisor 1990). Office: Sta KWMU-FM U Mo-St Louis 8001 Natural Bridge Rd Saint Louis MO 63121-4401

BENNETT, PEGGY ELIZABETH, librarian, library director, educator; b. Columbus, Ga., Aug. 22, 1935; d. William Osborne and Ola Lee (McMahan) B. BA in Chemistry, So. Coll., 1956; cert. med. technologist, Glendale Sch. Med. Tech., Glendale, 1957; MS in Libr. Sci., Fla. State U., 1971. Med. technologist Glendale (Calif.) Hosp., 1957-59, Columbus (Ga.) Med. Ctr., 1960-61; sec. Seventh-Day Adventists Ch. Orgns., various, 1961-67; med. technologists Warm Springs (Ga.) Found., 1967-69, Thrash Labs., Columbus, Ga., 1969-70; libr. So. Coll. Seventh-Day Adventist, Collegedale, Tenn., 1971—; dir. librs. So. Coll. of Seventh-Day Adventist, Collegedale, 1986—. Presenter in field, 1979-87; developer Processing Ctr. for Southeastern Adventist Sch. Librs., 1981; cons. Adventist Network of Gen. Ednl. Librs., Collegedale, 1981—, Girl's Preparatory Sch., Chattanooga, 1984-85; mem. Sirs Mandarain Adv. Bd. Author: Library Pathfinder for MIT, 1972; contbr. articles to profl. jours. Mem. ALA, Assn. of Seventh-Day Adventists Librs. (v.p. 1981-82, pres. 1982-83), Southeastern Libr. Assn., Chattanooga Area Libr. Assn., Solinet Lambda Users' Group (exec. com. 1984, steering com.), Beta Phi Mu. Seventh Day Adventist. Avocations: tennis, aerobic walking, crafts. Office: So Adventist U Industrial Dr Collegedale TN 37315

BENNETT, SUE ELLEN, director; b. La Vale, Md., Aug. 20, 1963; Assoc. Sci., Allegany Coll. Md., 2001. Customer svc. rep. AT&T, La Vale, Md., 1986—94; info. ctr. supr. Allegany Coll. Md., Cumberland, 1996—2001; coll. housing mgr. Willowbrook Woods, Allegany Coll., Cumberland, 2001—; asst. pastor God's Little Chapel, LaVale, 1982—. Recipient All Am. Scholar, U.S. Achievement Acad., 2001, All USA Acad. Team, 2001. Office: Willowbrook Woods 10300 Willow Woods Ct SE Cumberland MD 21502 Home: 89 LaVale Blvd LaVale MD 21502

BENNETT, TERESA ANN (TERRI), social worker, counselor; d. Duane Waldo and Frances Anne Cooley; m. Neal Thomas Bennett, Mar. 5, 1988; children: Michael Thomas, Ashley Anne. M in Social Work, U. Kans., 1995. LCSW. House parent Buchanan County Children's Home, St. Joseph, Mo., 1983—84; program supr. Minute Cir. Friendly House, Kansas City, Mo., 1984—85, childcare dir., 1985—86, dir. cmty./neighborhood, 1986—88; case mgr. City Union Mission, Kansas City, Mo., 1989—90, dir. counseling and edn., 1996—99, Christian counselor, 2001—. Chairperson Homeless Svcs. Coalition, Kansas City, Mo., 1995—97; bd. mem. Homeless Svcs. Coalition Adv. Bd., Kansas City, Mo., 1995—98. Mem.: Am. Assn. Christian Counselors, North Am. Assn. Christians in Social Work, Nat.

Assn. Social Workers. Avocations: gardening, cooking, camping, jail ministry, church activities. Office: City Union Mission 1310 Wabash Kansas City MO 64015 Home: 617 NW Cortland Dr Blue Springs MO 64015 E-mail: terri@comission.org.

BENNETT, VIRGINIA COOK, music educator, consultant; d. Leland LeRoy and Janet Roberts Cook; m. Edward James Bennett, Jan. 30, 1965; children: Susan Elizabeth, Edward James. MusB in Edn., Drake U., 1965, MusM. in Edn., 1978; PhD, U. Iowa, 1991. Instr. music and choirs Cedar Rapids (Iowa) Schs., 1965—66; instr. Newton (Iowa) Cmty. Schs., 1967—68, instr. elem. music, 1974—79; lectr. music edn. Drake U., Des Moines, 1979—80; chair music dept. and choir dir. Des Moines Area C.C., Ankeny, Iowa, 1984—97; assoc. prof. and chair, music edn. area Drake U., Des Moines, 1997—. Cons., curriculum and assessment various sch. dists., Iowa, 1998—; clinician Nebr. Music Educators State Conf., Lincoln, 2000, Ohio Music Educators State Conf., Cinn., 2000, Wis. Music Educators State Conf., Madison, 2001, N.D. Music Educators State Conf., Fargo, 2001, Minn. Music Educators State Conf., Mpls., 2001, Mich. Music Educators Ann. Conf., Ann Arbor, 2002, S.D. Music Educators Ann. Conf., Brookings, 2002, National Assn. For Music Edn. Nat. Conf., Nashville, 2002—, Mountain Lake (Va.) Symposiam on Tchg. Music Methods, Mountain Lake, Va., 2003. Contbr. articles to profl. jours. Mem. Governors Adv. Com. on Intergovernmental Affairs, Iowa, 1985—87; founding bd. mem. Newton Cmty. Edn. Found., Iowa, 1986—91; co-chair c.c. campaign United Way, Ankeny, Iowa, 1993—97; v.p. Newton Cmty. Schools Bd. Edn., Iowa, 1984, mem., 1984—91, pres., 1985—86. Mem.: Music Educators Nat. Conf., Iowa Alliance Arts Edn., Iowa Choral Dirs. Assn., Am. Choral Dirs. Assn., Iowa Music Educators Assn. (pres. 1996—98, Disting. Svc. Award 2001), Nat. Assn. Music Edn. (north ctrl. divsn. pres., nat. exec. bd. mem. 2000—02), Pi Kappa Lambda, Kappa Alpha Theta, Mu Phi Epsilon. Methodist. Avocations: reading, travel. Home: 203 Foster Dr Des Moines IA 50312 Office: Drake University 25th and University Des Moines IA 50311 Personal E-mail: vandjbenn@aol.com. E-mail: virginia.bennett@drake.edu.

BENNETT-HAMMERBERG, JANIE MARIE, small business owner, writer, consultant, administrative assistant; b. Chgo., Oct. 25, 1945; d. John Raymond Harvey and Violet Cleora (Yancey) Bennett-Harvey; m. Richard Arndt Hammerberg, May 9, 1964; children: Susan Jean, Richard John. Student, Joliet (Ill.) Jr. Coll., 1972-73, Lewis U. Sec. Valley View Sch. Dist., Romeoville, Ill., 1972—83; sec., adminstrv. asst. Babson Bros. Chem. Divsn., Romeoville, 1987-90; owner, operator real estate Hammer-Smith Mgmt., Romeoville, 1986—, St. Charles Pastoral Ctr., Romeoville, 1997—2001. Adminstrv. asst. Lewis U., 1995-; freelance cons. Contbg. author numerous poetry anthologies; freelance writer. Vol. numerous charitable founds., including AIDS Found., Chgo., 1983—, Muscular Dystrophy Assn., Chgo., 1983—, March of Dimes, Chgo., 1983—, Walk for Babies, Chgo., 1983—, Am. Cancer Soc., Chgo., 1983—, AHA Soc., Chgo., 1983—, Parkinson's Disease, Chgo., Avon Breast Cancer 60 Mile Walk, Chgo., 1983-, Officer friendly programs UIC, Chgo., Neighbor Newspaper Reporter, Plainfield, 2000-; hon. heart and sole vol. Muscular Sclerosis Found., Chgo., 1983-95; officer friendly programs U. Ill. Hosp., 1982-90; mem. bd. Homeowners Assn. Recipient several employee, Hon. Mention and Pres.'s awards, Editor's Choice awards Nat. Libr. of Poetry, Owings Mills, Md., Dickinson award The Amherst Soc., Balt., 1991, Golden Poet awards, Dickinson Recognition award, Best & Outstanding Poem awards, 1995, 96, 97, 98, Poet of yr., !SP, 2000-2002, Pres.'s award Lit. Excellence NAR, Illiad Press, 2002, Twentieth Century award Achievement, Life fellow award, 21st Century award Achievement, Noble prize United Cultural Conv.; named Outstanding Poets Best Poems of 90's Selected Works World's Best Poets, 1994-98, Intellectuals of the 20th Century, Leading Intellectuals of World, Internat. Women of the Millenium, Woman of the Yr., 2000, Internat. Amb.; honored laureate Verses Mag. Summer Prose, 1999, Wall of Tolerance Nat. Campaign Tolerance, 2001; named to Ill. and Nat. Poetry Soc., Internat. Poetry Hall of Fame, Am. Biog. Inst.'s Hall of Fame; nominated Outstanding People of the 20th Century, 2000, Outstanding Women of the 20th Century, 2000. Mem. Ill. State Poetry Soc., ABWA, Internat. Poetry Hall of Fame, Am. Poetry Soc., Internat. Soc. of Poets (charter, life), Nat. Authors Registry, Acad. Am. Poets, Nat. Multiple Sclerosis Soc., Fedn. State Poetry Soc., Am. Bus. Womens Assn., others. Avocations: walking, running, exercise, crafts, music. Home: 21307 Silktree Cir Plainfield IL 60544-9360

BENNETT MINNERLY, DENISE PATRICIA, artist, art educator; b. Cleve., Sept. 24, 1960; d. Gordon W. and Yvonne L. (Debegasa) Bennett; m. Barry H. Minnerly, May 9, 1987; children: Sarah Anne, Gillian Catherine. BS, BA cum laude, U. Vt., Burlington, 1984. Cert. tchr. K-12. Pub. rels. profl. Royal Copenhagen, N.Y., 1985-87; art tchr. Stamford (Conn.) Schs., 1987-88, After Sch. Art Program, Darien, Conn., 1988-92, Rowayton, Conn., 1988-95. Founder, dir. Rowayton Civic Assn., 1987-2003, Darien Arts Coun., 1988. Author, illustrator: (children's book) Color Tree, 1991; author: Molly Meets Mona & Friends, 1995. Vol. Women's Crisis Ctr., Norwalk, Conn., 1982—. Avocations: tennis, paddle, running, dance. Home: 183 Highland Ave Norwalk CT 06853-1109

BENNETT-WILKES, THERESA WILLIAMS, writer, educator; b. Yakima, Wash., Jan. 1, 1950; d. Everett Pendleton Williams Sr. and Blanche Madelyn Williams; m. Willie Lee Wilkes, Nov. 7; m. Frank L. Bennett, Sept. 24, 1977 (dec. Mar. 1978); 1 child, Kamilah M. Bennett. BA in Social Studies, Bennett Coll., 1972; M in Urban Planning, U. Wash., 1978. Planner San Bernardino County, San Bernardino, Calif., 1979—84; cmty. planner 63 CES, Norton AFB, Calif., 1986—88; sr. planning officer Ipswich (Eng.) Borough Coun., 1989—92; planner II zoning City of High Point, NC, 1996—97; exec. dir. Empowerment and Enterprise Devel. Corp. Bennett Coll., Greensboro, NC, 1998—99; instr., adj. prof. Guilford Tech. C.C., Jamestown, NC, 1998—. Cons. in field. Author: A Taste of Theresa..., 1999. Active Greensboro Housing Coalition, 1998—99, Martin Luther King Statue Com., San Bernardino, Calif., 1981, Co. Ctrl. Com., San Bernardino, Calif., 1983—84; hon. life mem. Md. Congress Parents and Tchrs., Inc., 1996—. Named Disting. Alumna, Nat. Assn. for Equal Opportunity in Higher Edn., 1984; named one of Outstanding Young Women of Am., 1979, 1982; recipient Martin Luther King Jr. award, 1968. Mem.: Royal Town Planning Inst. (chartered). Avocations: writing, reading, travel, cultural events, music. Office: Holly Tree Publ LLP PO Box 1113 High Point NC 27261

BENNING, MARY ETZOLD, interior designer; b. El Paso, Mar. 8, 1957; d. David Enberg and Mary (Francis) Etzold; m. George Henry Benning III, Nov. 2, 1985; children: Mary Francis, Lucy Alexander. AA, Stephens Coll., 1977, BFA, 1979. Lic. interior designer Tex. Designer Bus. Products & Svcs., Inc., El Paso, 1979-80; display designer Popular Dept. Store, El Paso, 1980-83; residential designer Reinharts Fine Furniture, El Paso, 1983-85; comml. designer FLooring Systems, Inc., El Paso, 1985-86, Charlotte's Comml. Interiors, El Paso, 1986-88; comml. interior designer N.Mex. State U., Las Cruces, 1988-94, Henry Benning Assocs., Inc., El Paso, 1994—. Cons. in field. Bd. dirs. Epilepsy El Paso, 1987-90. Mem.: AIA, Tex. Assn. Interior Designers, Am. Soc. Interior Designers, Pan Am. Soc. Am., El Paso Symphony Guild, Jr. League El Paso, Magna Carta Dames Am. (life), Colonial Dames Am. (life). Republican. Epsicopalian. Episcopalian. Avocations: reading, sewing, walking, gourmet cooking, travel. Office: 1205 Myrtle Ave El Paso TX 79901

BENNINGFIELD, CAROL ANN, lawyer; b. San Antonio, Dec. 8, 1952; d. Gordon Lane Benningfield and Ann Benningfield McCraw. BA in Polit. Sci., S.W. Tex. State U., 1975; JD, U. Tex., 1979. Bar: Tex. 1979, U.S. Dist. Ct. (so. dist.) Tex. 1995. Staff atty. Tex. Dept. Labor and Stds., Austin, 1979; staff counsel Tex. Chem. Coun., Austin, 1979-80; assoc. Wiley, Garwood, San Antonio, 1981-83; account exec. Dean-Witter Reynolds, San Antonio, 1983-89; pvt. practice, Rockport, Tex., 1990—. Gala com. San Antonio Stock Show and Rodeo, 1981-83; mem. Target 90 Goals for San Antonio, 1984-85; deacon First Presbyn. Ch., Rockport, 1992-95, choir, 1990 96; active Rockport Art Assn., 1990—; trustee Aransas County Ind. Sch. Dist., Rockport, 1993-96 [illegible] Tex. Bar Found. Tex., mem. San Antonio Young Lawyers (membership chmn. 1982), Rockport Fulton C. of C. (dir. 1992-94, awards com. chmn., v.p. 1993), Rotary. Mailing: PO Box 2389 Rockport TX 78381 E-mail: ladylawyer@sbcglobal.net.

BENOIT, MARILYN B. psychiatrist, medical association administrator; b. Trinidad & Tobago, 1943; MD, Georgetown U., 1973; cert. Specialist Health Svcs. Adminstrn., George Washington U., 1993. Diplomate Am. Bd. Psychiatry and Neurology with subspecialty in child and adolescent psychiatry. Resident in psychiatry Geworgetown U., Washington, 1973—75, resident in child psychiatry, fellow in child psychiatry, 1975—77, clin. assoc. prof. psychiatry; med. dir., exec. dir. Devereux Children's Ctr., 1993—98. Part-time pvt. practice psychiatry. Fellow: Am. Acad. Child and Adolescent Psychiatry (pres. 2001—03); mem.: AMA, Am. Psychiat. Assn. Home: 43 Prospect Bay Dr W Grasonville MD 21638 Office: 1015 33d St NW Washington DC 20007

BENOIT, NANCY LOUISE, former state legislator, secondary school educator; b. New Haven, Jan. 25, 1944; d. James Michael and Florence Louise (Bray) Wynne; m. Raymond George Benoit, Aug. 8, 1970; children: Michael, Patrick. BA, Albertus Magnus Coll., 1965; MEd, Wayne State U., 1969. Tchr. St. Vincent de Paul High Sch., Detroit, 1965-69; community organizer Social Progress Action Corp., Woonsocket, R.I., 1969-71; dir. Little Shavers Day Care Ctr., Woonsocket, 1971-73; edn. coordinator Northwest Head Start, North Providence, RI, 1978—84; mem. R.I. Ho. of Reps., 1985—2000, chair joint legis. commn. on child care, 1985—2000, mem. adult edn. commn., 1985-88, mem. health, edn. and welfare com., 1986-88, mem. fin. com., 1989-92, dep. majority whip, 1991-92; tchr. St. Raphael Acad., Pawtucket, RI, 1989—. Chair permanent legis. oversight commn. Dept. for Children, Youth and Families; chair House com. on Health, Edn. and Welfare, 1993—2000. Bd. dirs. Woonsocket Head Start and Day Care, R.I. affiliate Literacy Vols. of Am., 1985-88; mem. bd. mgrs. Woonsocket Family and Child Care Svcs., 1973-87, 2003—; bd. dirs. Health Svcs., Inc., Woonsocket, 1974—; founder Women for Women, 1983—90; vol. coord. Vols. in Action, Providence, 1984-86; grant coord. C.C. R.I., Lincoln, 1986-87. Named one of Outstanding Young Women in Am., Woonsocket and E.I. Jaycees, 1980, Legislator of Yr. United Way of Southeastern New England; recipient Francesco Cannistra Svc. award Health Svcs., Inc., 1986, Outstanding Svc. award R.I. Day Care Dirs. Assn., 1986. Mem. Common Cause, Sierra Club, Audubon Soc. Democrat. Roman Catholic. Avocations: travel, gardening. E-mail: NancyLBenoit@aol.com.

BENSHOOF, JANET LEE, lawyer, association executive; b. Detroit Lakes, Minn., May 10, 1947; m. Richard Klein; children: David, Eli. BA summa cum laude, U. Minn., 1969; JD, Harvard U., 1972. Dir. law reform South Bklyn. Legal Svcs., 1972-77; dir. reproductive freedom project ACLU, N.Y.C., 1977-92; founder, pres. Ctr. Reproductive Law & Policy, N.Y.C., 1992—. Guest lectr. Yale U., Columbia U., Rutgers U., Case Western Reserve U. Contbr. articles to profl. jours. Recipient Margaret Sanger award, 1986, Christopher Tietze Humanitarian award Nat. Abortion Fedn., 1988, Gloria Steinem award Ms. Found. Women, N.Y.C., 1989, 10 for 10 award Ctr. Population Optiums, 1990; named one of 100 Most Influential Lawyers in Am. Nat. Law Jour., 1991, 94; MacArthur Found. Fellowship grant, 1992—. Mem. ABA, Am. Pub. Health Assn., N.Y.C. Bar Assn. Office: Ctr Reproductive Law & Policy 120 Wall St New York NY 10005-3904

BENSMAN, HARRIET LANDSMAN, speech pathology/audiology services professional; b. Chelsea, Mass., June 17, 1942; d. Eli A. and Betty R. Landsman; m. Marvin Robert Bensman, Aug. 21, 1965; children: David Andrew, Lauren Joy Bensman Adkins. BS, Boston U., 1963; MS, U. Wis., Madison, 1965. Speech pathologist pvt. practice, Memphis, 1972—, St. Joseph Hosp., Memphis, 1985—95, U. Tenn., Memphis, 1990—95, St. Francis Hosp., Memphis, 2001—. Bd. dirs. Staff Bldrs., 1999. Bd. dirs. Playwright's Forum, Memphis, 2000—. Mem.: Am. Speech Lang.-Hearing Assn. (cert. clin. competence, med net 1999—). Avocations: theater, needlecrafts, cooking. Home: 8391 Westfair Cir N Germantown TN 38139 E-mail: mbensman@memphis.edu.

BENSON, A. LEGRACE GUPTON, humanities educator, researcher; b. Richmond, Va., Feb. 23, 1930; d. Herbert Lee and Frances Lillian W. (Covalt) Gupton; m. Thomas Fawcett Benson, Aug. 9, 1952 (dec. Feb. 1976); children: Thomas Lauck, Lawrence Thane, Theodore Lloyd. BA, Meredith Coll., 1951; MFA, U. Ga., 1956; PhD, Cornell U., 1974. Asst. prof. Cornell U., Ithaca, N.Y., 1968-72, Wells Coll., Aurora, N.Y., 1972-75, assoc. dean, 1975-77; assoc. dean Empire State Coll. SUNY, Albany, 1977-80, coord. arts, humanities, comms. Ctr. Distance Learning Saratoga Springs, N.Y., 1981-83, prof. Ctr. Distance Learning, 1985-93, prof. emerita Ctr. Distance Learning, 1993—. Ind. scholar Haitian studies, Ithaca, N.Y., 1994—; dir. Arts of Haiti Rsch. Project, Ithaca, 1996—; civic fellow Cornell U., 2003-. Author: (textbook) Understanding the Visible World, 1984; co-author: (textbook) Educational Planning: A Guide for Adult Distance Learners, 1985; mem. editl. bd. Prologue, Golden Hill literary mags., Jour. Caribbean Assn. Profls. and Scholars, 1981-93, Jour. Haitian Studies; contbr. articles to mags. Chair, vice chair so. tier regional plan City of Ithaca (N.Y.) Planning Bd., rep. ward IV Tompkins County Bd. Reps., N.Y., 1973-77; vol. tchr. Literary Vols. Am., Ithaca, N.Y., 1994—. Vis. scholar NEH Cornell U., 1985. Mem. Coll. Art Assn., African Studies Assn., Arts Coun. African Studies, Haitian Studies Assn., Can. Assn. for Latin Am. and Caribbean Studies, Latin Am. Studies Assn. Democrat. Roman Catholic. Home and Office: 314 E Buffalo St Ithaca NY 14850-4227

BENSON, BETTY JONES, retired school system administrator; b. Barrow County, Ga., Jan. 11, 1928; d. George C. and Bertha (Mobley) Jones; m. George T. Benson; children: George Steven, Elizabeth Gayle, James Claud, Robert Benjamin. BS in Edn., N. Ga. U., Dahlonega, 1958; MEd in Curriculum and Supervision, U. Ga., Athens, 1968, edn. specialist, 1970. Tchr. Forsyth County (Ga.) Bd. Edn., Cumming, 1956-66, curriculum dir., 1966—; asst. supt. for instrn. Forsyth County Schs., 1981—2003; ret., 2003. Mem. media com. Lanier Tech. Inst. Active Alpine Ctr. for Disturbed Children; chmn. Ga. Lake Lanier Island Authority; mem. North Ga. Coll. Edn. Adv. Com., Ga. Textbook Com.; adv. Boy Scouts; Sunday Sch. tchr. 1st Bapt. Ch. Cumming; active Forsyth County Substance Abuse Commn., Forsyth County Drug Task Force, Forsyth County Vision 20/20 Com., Forsyth County Drug Commn., Forsyth County Interagy. Coun. for Children and Youth, Forsyth County Health Dept. Bd., local coord. coun. Family and Children Svcs., Blue Ridge Cir. Ct.-Cherokee/Forsyth County Youth Shelter Com.; mem. literacy com. Forsyth County, Ptnrs. in Edn. program. Mem. NEA, ASCD, Am. Heart Assn., Ga. Assn. Educators (bd. dirs.), Ga. Assn. Supervision and Curriculum Devel. (pres.), Assn. Childhood Edn. Internat., Bus. and Profl. Women's Club, Internat. Platform Assn., Ga. Future Tchrs. Adv. Assn. (pres.), Profl. Assn. Ga. Educators, Ga. Assn. Ednl. Leaders (bd. dirs.), Headstart Dirs. Assn., Forsyth County Hist. Soc., Forsyth County Youth Shelter, Sawnee Mt. Cmty. Ctr. Assn., Ga. Cumming/Forsyth County C. of C. (edn. com.), Mt. Local Coord. Coun., Piedmont Learning Ctr. Coord. Coun. Home: 1235 Dahlonega Hwy Cumming GA 30040-4525 E-mail: bettybenson@adelph.net.

BENSON, ELIZABETH POLK, art specialist; b. Washington, May 13, 1924; d. Theodore Booton and Rebecca Dean (Albin) Benson. BA, Wellesley Coll., 1945; MA, Cath. U. Am., 1956. Mus. aide, curator Nat. Gallery of Art, Washington, 1946-60; curator Pre-Columbian Collection Dumbarton Oaks, Washington, 1962-79, dir. Ctr. for Pre-Columbian Studies, 1971-79; rsch. assoc. Inst. Andean Studies, Berkeley, Calif., 1980—. Lectr. Cath. U. Am., Washington, 1968—69; adj. prof. Columbia U., N.Y.C., 1973, sr. lectr. U. Tex., Austin, 1985; Andrew S. Keck disting. vis. prof. Am. U., Washington, 1987; cons. Montreal Mus. Fine Arts, 1990—91, 1990—92; mem. adv. bd. L.Am. Indian Lits. Jour., Pitts., 1989—; co-curator traveling exhbn. Birds and Beasts of Ancient L.Am., 1995—98. Author: The Maya World, 1967, 1972, 1977, The Mochica, 1972, Birds and Beasts of Ancient Latin America, 1997; co-editor: Olmec Art of Ancient Mexico, 1996, Ritual Sacrifice in Ancient Peru, 2001. Mem.: Coll. Art Assn., L.Am. Indian Lits. Assn. (v.p. 1989—), The Lit. Soc., Soc. Women Geographers (co-chair mus. com. 1994—). Home and Office: 8314 Old Seven Locks Rd Bethesda MD 20817-2005

BENSON, JEANNE P. music educator; b. Taylorville, Ill., July 21, 1948; d. George A. Pranske and Rosetta S. Strohl; m. Wayne A. Benson, Nov. 29, 1969; 1 child, Jennifer Leigh. BS Edn., Eastern Ill. U., 1970. Vocal dir. Cissna Park Sch., Ill., 1970—72; vocal/piano instr. Kankakee Sch. Dist., Ill., 1982—. Vocal dir. New Park Singers, Kankakee, 1988—; vocal dir., mgr. Kankakee Orch. Chorus, 1986—; vocal dir. Kankakee Vly. Theatre, 1978—. Mem.: Ill. Music Educators, Music Educators Nat. Conf.

BENSON, JOAN, musician, music educator; b. St. Paul; d. John Raymond and Frances (Ostergren) B. MusM, U. Ill., 1952; performer's cert., Ind. U., 1953; pvt. studies with Edwin Fischer, Switzerland, 1953-57; pvt. studies with Fritz Neumeyer, Fed. Republic Germany, 1958-59; pvt. studies with Santiago Kastner, Portugal, 1960. Concert musician, worldwide, 1962—; lectr. early keyboard Stanford U., Palo Alto, Calif., 1970-76; asst. prof. U. Oreg., Eugene, 1976-82. Mem. artist faculty Aston Magna Acad., Mass., 1980, 82; adj. prof. U. Oreg., 1982—; artistic advisor Boston Clavichord Soc., 1996—. Albums: Repertoire, 1962, Music of C. P. E. Bach for Piano and Clavichord, 1972, Pasquini and Haydn on Clavichords of the Boston Museum of Fine Arts, 1982, Kuhnau and C.P.E. Bach on Clavichord, 1988; contbr. music notes to Titanic and Focus record labels; contbr. articles to internat. profl. jours. Recipient Kate Nell Kinley award. Mem. Am. Musicol. Soc. Home: 2795 Central Blvd Eugene OR 97403-2528

BENSON, JOANNE C. state legislator; b. Roanoke, Va,, Mar. 11, 1941; BS, Bowie State Coll., 1961; MA, Cath. U. Am., 1972; postgrad., George Washington U. Del. Dist. 24 State of Md., Annapolis, 1991—; sch. prin. Mem. Const. and Adminstrv. Law Com., 1991-92, Environ. Matters Com., 1992-93, Commerce and Govt. Matters Com., 1994—, Md. Legis. Black Caucus. Recipient Outstanding Minority Leader award, Outstanding and Dedicated Svc. to Children, Outstanding Cmty. Svc. award Las Amigas, Inc.; named Citizen of Yr. Omega Psi Phi. Mem. NEA, Md. State Tchrs. Assn., Prince George's County Educators Assn. (Outstanding Educator award). Office: Md Ho of Reps 204 Lowe House Office Bldg 84 College Ave Annapolis MD 21401-1991

BENSON, JOANNE E. former lieutenant governor; b. Jan. 4, 1943; m. Robert Benson; 2 children. BS, St. Cloud State U. Mem. Minn. Senate, St. Paul, 1991-94; lt. gov. State of Minn., St. Paul, 1994-98.

BENSON, LUCY WILSON, political and diplomatic consultant; b. N.Y.C., Aug. 25, 1927; d. Willard Oliver and Helen (Peters) Wilson; m. Bruce Buzzell Benson, Mar. 30, 1950 (dec. Mar. 1990). BA, Smith Coll., 1949, MA, 1955; LHD (hon.), Wheaton Coll., Norton, Mass., 1965; LLD (hon.), U. Mass., 1969; LHD (hon.), Bucknell U., 1972; LLD (hon.), U. Md., 1972; LHD (hon.), Carleton Coll., 1973; LLD (hon.), Amherst Coll., 1974, Clark U., 1975; HHD, Springfield Coll., 1981; L.H.D. (hon.), Bates Coll., 1982; L.L.D. (hon.), Lafayette Coll., 1999. Mem. jr. exec. tng. program Bloomingdale's, N.Y.C., 1949-50; asst. dir. pub. rels. Smith Coll., 1950-53; rsch. asst. dept. Am. studies Amherst Coll., 1956-57; pres. Amherst LWV, Mass., 1957-61, pres. Mass., 1961-65, nat. pres., 1968-74; mem. Gov.'s cabinet and sec. human svcs. Commonwealth of Mass., 1975; mem. spl. commn. on adminstrv. rev. U.S. Ho. of Reps., Washington, 1976-77; under sec. State Security Assistance, Sci. and Tech. U.S. Dept. State, Washington, 1977-80; cons. U.S. Dept. State and SRI Internat., Washington, 1980-81; pres. Benson and Assocs., Amherst, 1981—. Vice-chair Citizen Network for Fgn. Affairs; bd. dirs. Dreyfus Fund and other Dreyfus mut. funds, Internat. Exec. Svc. Corps. Steering com. Urban Coalition, 1968, exec. com., 1970-75, 80-84, co-chair, 1973-75; mem. Gov. Mass. Spl. Com. Rev. Sunday Closing Laws, 1961; mem. spl. commn. Mass. Legislature to Study Budgetary Powers of Trustees U. Mass., 1961-62; mem. Gov. Mass. Com. Rev. Salaries State Employees, 1963, Mass. Adv. Bd. Higher Ednl. Policy, 1962-65, Mass. Bd. Edn. Adv. Com. Racial Imbalance and Edn., 1964-65, Mass. adv. com. U.S. Commn. Civil Rights, 1964-73; vice-chair Mass. Adv. Coun. Edn., 1965-68; mem. Mass. Com. Children and Youth Com. to Study Report by U.S. Children's Bur., Mass. Youth Svc. Div., 1967; mem. pub. adv. com. U.S. Trade Policy, 1968; vis. com. John F. Kennedy Sch. Govt.; mem. Trilateral Commn., Coun. Fgn. Rels.; mem. town meeting, Amherst, 1957-74, 2000, mem. fin. com., 1960-66; trustee Edn. Devel. Center, Newton, Mass., 1967-72, Nat. Urban League, 1974-77, Smith Coll., 1975-80, Brookings Instn., 1974-77, Alfred P. Sloan Found., 1975-77, 81-2000, Bur. Social Sci. Rsch., Inc., 1985-87; bd. dirs. Catalyst, 1972-90, Atlantic Coun. of U.S., 1988—, vice-chair, 1993-2000; former bd. govs. Am. Nat. Red Cross, Common Cause, Women's Action Alliance; bd. govs. Internat. Ctr. on Election Law and Adminstrn., 1985-87; trustee Lafayette Coll., 1985-2000, vice-chair, 1990-2000, trustee emeritus, 2000—. Recipient Achievement award Bur. Govt. Research, U. Mass., 1963; Distinguished Service award Boston Coll., 1965, Smith Coll. medal, 1969, Distinguished Civil Leadership award Tufts U., 1965, Distinguished Service award Northfield Mount Hermon Sch., 1976; Radcliffe fellow Radcliffe Inst., 1965-67. Mem. NAACP, ACLU, Nat. Acad. Pub. Adminstrn., UN Assn., Urban League, Assn. Am. Indian Affairs, East African Wildlife Soc., Jersey Wildlife Preservation Trust Channel Islands, Internat. Inst. Strategic Studies. Home and Office: 46 Sunset Ave Amherst MA 01002-2097

BENSON, MARIE CHAPMAN, insurance agent; b. Geneva, Ala., June 1, 1909; d. Charles Daniel and Lollie (Pilley) Chapman; m. Wilfred Tyner Benson, June 28, 1933 (wid. Mar. 1984); children: Laurie Lynn Benson Morris, Beverly Ree Benson, Joseph Daniel Benson; 1 foster child: Juan Manuel Hernandez. BS in Piano, Cert. in Pub. Sch. Music, Huntingdon Coll., 1930; postgrad., U. Va. Lic. ins. agt.; cert. music instr., Ala. Instr. of piano, Geneva, 1930-32; organizer/instr. music Geneva Elem. Sch., 1930-32; attendance officer Geneva County Schs., 1932-33; v.p. Benson Wholesale Co., Geneva, 1956-74, v.p. of leasing co., 1964-74; v.p., dir. Dixieland Foodstores, Geneva, 1956-74, Brundidge (Ala.) Mfg. Co., 1961; ins. agt. Security Ins., Geneva, 1963—. Pianist/organist Meth. Ch., Geneva, 1919-79; ptnr. C.D. Chapman Co., Geneva, 1930—. Vice-pres. PTA, Geneva, 1947-48, pres. Geneva Garden Club, 1954-56; bd. dirs. Geneva Recreation Ctr.; pres. United Meth. Women, Dothan (Ala.) Dist., 1956-60, organizer dist. prayer groups; sec. Christian Personhood/Ala.-W. Flor. Meth. Conf., Montgomery, 1962-64; mem. Rep. Presdl. Club, Washington; endowed chmn. Christian faith and philosophy Huntingdon Coll., Montgomery, 1991; elected del. to 4th Assembly, Dothan Dist. Soc. Christian Svc., Milw., 1960; others. Hon. Mother of Yr., Am. Mothers Com., State of Ala., Birmingham, 1971; Paul Harris fellow Geneva Rotary Club, 1979. Mem. Athenaeum Federated Club (pres. 1955-57, pres. 1968-70, Merit Mother award 1968), 6th Dist. Federated Club of ALA (treas.). Avocations: growing roses, gardening, reading, travel, writing. Address: PO Box 1382 Dothan AL 36302

BENSON, MELVOID J. state legislator; b. Jackson, Tenn., Feb. 13, 1930; Widow. BA, Lane Coll., 1951; student, Fisk U., 1954, R.I. Coll., 1963. Mem. R.I. Ho. of Reps.; educator North Kingstown; retired. Bd. dirs. Mktg.

St. Sch.; dep. majority leader R.I. Ho. of Reps., mem. labor com. and joint com. on vet. affairs; mem. North Kingstown Dem. Com. Mem. Kingstown Bus. and Profl. Women, Fleet Residence Ladies Aux., Alph Kappa Alpha, Delta Kappa Gamma. Address: 70 Shore Acres North Kingstown RI 02852-4526

BENSON, SALLY M. atmospheric scientist; BA in Geology, Barnard Coll., 1977; MS, PhD in materials sci. and mineral engring., U. Calif, Berkeley, 1988. With Lawrence Berkeley Nat. Lab., 1977—, dir. earth scis. divsn., 1993—97, assoc. lab. dir. for energy scis., 1997—2001, dep. dir. ops., 2001—. Office: Lawrence Berkeley Nat Lab 1 Cyclotron Rd Bldg 50E Berkeley CA 94720 E-mail: smbenson@lbl.gov.

BENSON, SARA ELIZABETH, real estate broker, real estate appraiser; b. Columbia, S.C., Nov. 29, 1960; d. Herbert Lankford Benson and Anna Marian (Stanley) Tucker; m. Donald Joseph DeBat, Aug. 20, 1994; children: D. Edward, Herbert L. Benson IV. Student, U. S.C., 1977, Am. Conservatory Music, Chgo., 1978-81. Lic. real estate broker, Ill., S.C.; designated cert. real estate brokerage mgr.; approved ind. fee appraiser; cert. real estate appraiser, Ill. Pres., owner Benson Stanley Realty, Chgo., 1990—; owner Sara Benson Cons., Inc., Chgo., 1992—. Fee appraiser FHA, HUD, Chgo., 1986—; speaker, author in field. Bd. dirs. Chgo. Child Care Soc. Mem. NAFE, Nat. Assn. Realtors, Assn. Fed. Appraisers, Real Estate Buyer's Agt. Coun., Ill. Assn. Realtors, Chgo. Assn. Realtors (chair profl. standards com.), North Shore Bd. Realtors, Real Estate Brokerage Mgrs. Coun., MLS No. Ill., Nat. Assn. Ind. Fee Appraisers, Bus. Execs. Assn. Chgo., Chgo. Child Care Soc. (bd. dirs. 1997—). Avocations: piano, literature, interior design. Office: Benson Stanley Realty 980 N Michigan Ave Ste 1400 Chicago IL 60611-7500 E-mail: sepbenson@aol.com.

BENSUR, BARBARA JEAN, art educator, researcher; b. Erie, Pa., Feb. 11, 1950; d. Jean Elizabeth and Durker William Braggins; children: Adele, Rebecca. BA, Mercyhurst Coll., 1972; MA, U. Md., 1992, PhD, 1995. Cert. art tchr. grades K-12, adminstrv. endorsement. Art tchr. St. Mary's County Pub. Schs., Leonardtown, Md., 1989—98; instr. Frostburg (Md.) State U., 1996—98; asst. prof. Millersville (Pa.) U., 1998—. Exhibitions include Delaware County C.C., 2001 (Purchase award, 2001), 30th Ann. Spring Arts Festival, 2001, Lancaster Open Award Exhibit, 2001, Millersville Faculty Art Show, 2001; contbr. articles to profl. jours. Cons. Demuth Found., Lancaster, 2000—01. Mem.: Am. Edn. Rsch. Assn., Pa. Art Edn. Assn., Nat. Art Edn. Assn. Roman Catholic. Avocation: jogging. Home: 743 Steeplechase Rd Landisville PA 17538 Office: Millersville Univ Art Dept PO Box 1002 Millersville PA 17551 Home Fax: (717) 871-2004; Office Fax: (717) 871-2004. Personal E-mail: barbara.bensur@millersville.edu. Business E-Mail: barbara.bensur@millersville.edu.

BENTAS, LILY HASEOTES, retail executive; Chmn, pres. Cumberland Farms, Canton, Mass., 1989—, pres., CEO, 1991—. Office: Cumberland Farms Inc 777 Dedham St Canton MA 02021 1484

BENTEL, CAROL RUSCHE, architect; m. Paul Bentel, 1987. BArch, Washington U., St. Louis, 1979; MArch (with hons.), NC State U., 1981. Registered Mass., NY. Asst. prof. architecture Ga. Inst. Tech., 1984—85; ptnr. Bentel & Bentel, Locust Valley, NY, 1987—. Tchg. asst. NC State U., 1980—81; vis. assoc. prof. NY Inst. Tech., 1999—; juror architecture Fulbright Found., 1996—98; vis. adj. prof. City Coll. NY, 1997; lectr. in field. Recipient First prize, Mcpl. Arts Soc., 1985, Disting. Alumni award, Washington U . St. Louis, 1999; fellow, Partitions, Inc., 1980, Samuel Kress Found., 1993—94, Am. Acad. Rome, 1993—94; grantee, Fulbright-Hays, 1985—86; scholar, Washington U., 1974—79, Fulbright scholar, U. Venice, 1985—86. Fellow: AIA (nat. com. design, chair Rome conf. 2001, scholar 1977—81); mem.: NY State Assn. Archs. Office: 22 Buckram Rd Locust Valley NY 11560 Office Phone: 516-676-2880. E-mail: crb@beltelandbentel.com.

BENTLEY, DIANNE H. GLOVER, minister, consultant; b. Bradford, Pa., Oct. 2, 1954; d. Harris William and Virginia Allen Edmonds Helenbrook; m. Christopher Bentley; 1 child, Cody Christopher ; children from previous marriage: Lucinda Marie Glover, Andrew Kirk Glover. BA, Drew U., 1976; MDiv, Drew Theol. Sch., 1997. LCSW HIV prevention counselor Pa. Dept. Health, 2003. Mgr. advt. The Rocket-Courier, Wyalusing, Pa., 1985—88; libr. Susquehanna County Libr., Montrose, 1989—91; editor The Villager, Moscow, 1991—93; pastor United Meth. Ch., Hollisterville-Sterling, 1994—97, First United Meth. Ch., Sayre, 1997—; edn. coord. HIV/Aids Support Network, Guthrie Health, 2002—. Dir. Ministry Resource Libr., Madison, NJ, 1994—97; pres. Bridge of Penn-York Valley Churches, Sayre, 1999—2002; chair Poverty Task Group, 2000—, Teen Pregnancy Prevention Task Force, 2002—; mem. Youth Activating Potential, 2003—. Author: (plays) Life In The Parsonage, short stories; actor: (plays) Anything Goes; composer: (songs) The Touch of God. Mentor Prudential Youth Leadership Inst., Wyo. Ann. Conf. United Meth. Ch., 1999; mem. com. Status and Role Women, Pa. Recipient Edwin A. Lewis Theology award, Drew Theol. Sch., 1997. Mem.: Binghamton Dist. Pastors' Assn. Methodist. Home: 77 Murray St Sayre PA 18840 Office: First United Meth Ch 200 W Lockhart St Sayre PA 18840

BENTLEY, EDITH LOUISE, secondary school educator; b. Eustis, Fla., Sept. 19, 1966; d. William Olin and Claudia Lucile Bradshaw; m. Christopher James Bentley. B Music Edn., Stetson U., 1988; MEd, U. Ctrl. Fla., 1991. Band dir. Trinity Christian Sch., Apopka, Fla., 1988—. Sponsor Trinity Christian Sch. Jr. Beta Club, Apopka, Fla., 1991—; mid. sch. lead tchr. Trinity Christian Sch., Apopka, Fla., 2002—. Mem.: Music Educators Nat. Conf., Fla. Bandmasters Assn., Kappa Delta Pi. Office: Trinity Christian Sch 1022 S Orange Blossom Trail Apopka FL 32703 Personal E-mail: EBentley00@aol.com.

BENTLEY, JOYCE ELAINE, customer service officer; b. Bartow, Fla., Dec. 25, 1955; d. Charlie and Nola Mae (Brown) Turner. BSBA, Fla. Meml. Coll., 1978; postgrad., Webster U., 1998—. Purchasing clk. Polk County Sheriff's Office, Bartow, 1978; acct. I Heartland Pvt. Industry Co., Bartow, 1978-80, internal auditor, 1980-83, sr. acct. exec. Lakeland, Fla., 1983-88, sr. auditor, 1988-89; mgr. Heartland Pvt. Industry Coun., 1989-91, dir. career specialist, 1991-94, human resource dir., 1994-96; customer svc. officer Polk County Work Force Devel. Bd., 1996—. Co-woenr, social affairs cons. JoyLynn's Memories, Bartow, 1986—. Chair Agy. Coun. for Emplyment and Tng., Lakeland, 1986-88, U.S. Census, Polk County, 1989—; bd. dirs. The Econ. Devel. Bd.; adv. bd. Women in the Workforce, 1992—; grad. leadership Bartow; mem. quality improvement coun. Floral Ave. Elem. Sch.; chair audit com., mem. budget com., mem. choir Burkett Chapel Primitive Bapt. Ch. Recipient Oustanding Citizen award of the Polk County Opportunity Coun., 1991, Angel awrd Early Childhood Resources, Extra Ordinary Cmty. Svc. award Polk County chpt. FAMU Alumni, 1998. Mem. NAACP (exec. bd. dirs., treas., Freedom Fund banquet chair), Bartow C. of C. (Can Do award), Am. Bus. Women's Assn., Internat. Assn. Pers. for Employment Security, Toastmasters, Fla. Meml. Alumni (treas. 1986-91, pres. 1991—), Order Eastern Star, Delta Sigma Theta (project chair 1988—). Democrat. Avocations: bike riding, horseback riding, cooking, shopping, traveling. Home: PO Box 923 Bartow FL 33831-0923

BENTLEY, KAREN GAIL, elementary school educator; b. Salina, Kans., Oct. 21, 1956; d. John Kennedy and Merle Lynn Blundon; m. Rodney Ray Bentley, Feb. 17, 1984 (dec. Sept. 1996). MusB cum laude, U. Mo., 1978; MusM, So. Ill. U., 1981. Grad. asst. So. Ill. U., Edwardsville, 1980—81; dir. music Ind. Congrl. Ch., St. Louis, 1978—81; tchr. elem. music Western Hghts. Schs., Oklahoma City, 1981—. Bd. dirs. Civic Music, 1985—, Orch. League, 1994—; bd. rep. PTA, 1992—; cantor Christ the King Cath. Ch., 1985—95. Republican. Episcopalian. Avocations: theater, raising Great Danes. Home: 11117 Quail Creek Rd Oklahoma City OK 73120 Office: John Glenn Elem Sch 6500 S Land Oklahoma City OK 73159

BENTLEY, LISA, publisher; married; 2 children. BA in English, U. Iowa. Acct. exec. Bozell; with SW Media Corp., Dallas, NY; sales exec. People and Life mag., L.A., NY; regional mgr. info. tech. Time mag., 1992—99; founding pub. Bus. 2.0 Mag. (formerly eCompany Now), 1999—. Office: One California St 29th Fl San Francisco CA 94111

BENTLEY, LISSA FRANCES, elementary school educator; b. N.Y.C., June 30, 1963; d. George Albert III and Nancy Ann (McNamara) B.; m. Matthew Levy, July 27, 2002. AB, Smith Coll., 1985; MA, Columbia U., 1988, MEd, 1997. Legal asst. Davis Polk & Wardwell, N.Y.C., 1985-87; presch. tchr. Episcopal Sch., N.Y.C., 1988-89; elem. tchr. Greenwich (Conn.) Pub. Schs., 1989—. Lector, eucharistic min. St. Mary Ch., Greenwich, 1991—. Mem. Greenwich Edn. Assn. (rep. profl. rights and responsibilities com. 1994-97), Greenwich-Stamford Smith Club (alumnae admissions coord. 1989-99), Kappa Delta Pi. Avocations: reading, biking, bird watching. Office: North Street Sch 381 North St Greenwich CT 06830-3999

BENTLEY, MARGARET ANN, librarian; b. Tawas City, Mich., June 13, 1956; d. Rupert A. and Joy A. (Bills) B. AB in English, Gordon Coll., 1978; MA in Libr. Sci., U. Mich., 1979. Cert. libr., Mich. Adult svcs. libr., asst. dir. Shiawassee Dist. Libr. (formerly Owosso Pub. Libr.), Owosso, Mich., 1979—. Mem.: AAUW (treas. 1984—2004), Mich. Libr. Assn., Phi Alpha Chi, Lambda Iota Tau, Beta Phi Mu. Avocations: reading, crafts, camping. Office: Shiawassee Dist Libr 502 W Main St Owosso MI 48867-2607

BENTLEY, MARJI, music educator; b. Louisville, Feb. 9, 1925; d. Frank Loyd and Sara Elizabeth (Hazlewood) Tullis; m. Richard Raymond Bentley, June 14, 1947; children: Richard R. Jr., Beth Ann, Martha Jane. B of Music Edn., Cornell Coll., 1946; MA, Tex. Woman's U., 1972. Supr. music Arlington Heights (Ill.) Pub. Schs., 1946-47; orch. dir. Redfield (S.D.) Pub. Schs., 1947-50; pvt. tchr. violin, viola Winfield, Kans., 1955-56, Napa, Calif., Denton, Tex., 1965—, Ardmore, Okla., 1973-88. Dir. children's and adult choirs, L.A., 1950-55; performed with U. So. Calif. Opera Orch., L.A., 1950-55, Southwestern Coll. Orch. and Faculty String Quartet, 1955-56, Napa Cmty. Symphony Orch. and Faculty String Quartet. Contbr. articles to profl. jours. Vol. Cross Timbers Coun., Girl Scouts Am. Mem. Music Educators Nat. Conf., Am. String Tchrs. Assn., Music Tchrs. Nat. Assn., Nat. Fedn. Music Clubs (founder Napa chpt.), Am. State Tchrs. Assn. (S.D. pres. 1948-49), Tex. Music Educators Assn., Tex. Music Educators Conf., Tex. Am. String Tchrs., Dallas Music Tchrs. Assn. Methodist. Avocations: reading, biking. Home: 2907 Foxcroft Cir Denton TX 76209 7809

BENTLEY, SARA, newspaper publishing executive; Pres. Gannett Northwest Newspaper Group, Salem, Oreg., 1988-95; pub. Statesman-Jour., Salem, 1988—. Office: Statesman-Jour Co Inc 280 Church St NE Salem OR 97301-3734

BENTLEY-MIXON, CHARMAINE CLARK, secondary school educator; b. Austin, Dec. 15, 1954; d. Harold Roy and Maria Rafaela Bentley; m. Charles Oliver Mixon, May 4, 1980; 1 child, Charlotte Farrar Mixon. BA in Anthropology, BS in Geological Sci., U. Tex., 1977; BS in Computer Sci., SW Okla. State U., 1984, MEd in Math., 1988. DATA engr. Dresser Industries, Magcobar DATA, Oklahoma City, 1972-82; tchr. Dallas Ind. Sch. Dist., 1988—, tchr., technologist F.D. Roosevelt H.S., 1992—2003, chmn. computer sci. curriculum com., 1997-98. Sec. F.D. Roosevelt H.S. Site Base Decision Making com., 1999—2001; mem. SBDM com., 1999—. Asst. troop leader Girl Scout U.S., Farmers Branch, Tex., 1992-95, Sunshine Literacy Project Coord., 1989-91; v.p. IB Parent Booster com. Clark H.S., Plano, Tex., 1995-96, sec., 1996-97; troop chmn. Boy Scout Am., Elk City, Okla., 1986-87; mem. F.D. Roosevelt H.S. Site Based Decision Com., 1998—, sec., 1998-2001. Recipient Award of Appreciation, City of Farmers Branch, 1990; F.D. Roosevelt HS local Tandy scholar, 1992, 94. Mem. Am. Assn. Petroleum Geologists, Nat. Coun. Tchrs. Math., Internat. Soc. Tech. Edn., Tex. Coun. Tchrs. Math., Tex. Computer Edn. Assn., Assn. Tex. Profl. Educators, Tex. Computer Edn. Assn. Computer Sci. Spl. Interest Group (area 5 rep. 2000-2002, sec./treas. 2002—), ISTE Computer Sci. Spl. Interest Group, TCEA Campus Technologist Spl. Interest Group, Assn. Computing Machinery. Episcopalian. Avocations: reading, woodwork, photography, gardening, pocket watches.

BENTON, KAY MYERS, sales executive; b. Balt. d. Brenton Ellsworth and Kevera (Hauf) Myers; m. Gregory W. Lewis, June 29, 1962 (div. Sept. 1986); children: Stacy Kay French, Gregory Lawrence; m. Robert David Benton, Nov. 19, 1988. BA, U. Md. Profl. model, Washington, 1971-76; sr. mgr. Unisys, McLean, Va., 1976-86; dir. bus. devel. Planning Rsch. Corp., McLean, 1986-87, Baxter Travenol, Reston, Va., 1987-88; real estate assoc. Prudential, Potomac, Md.; dir. bus. devel. ISN Corp., 1989-91, TRW, 1991-95; global strategic sales mgr. Sun Microsys., McLean, Va., 1995—. Cons. Andersen Cons., Washington, 1988-89. Contbr. articles to profl. publs. Mem. AIAA, Am. Assn. Airport Execs., Airports Cons. Coun., Air Traffic Control Assn., Industry Adv. Coun., Washington Transp. Seminar, Md. Realtors Assn., Montgomery County Bd. Realtors, Washington Club, The City Club, Army-Navy Country Club, Congl. Country Club, Kappa Delta. Republican. Methodist. Avocations: golf, tennis, travel. Home: 8031 Cobble Creek Cir Potomac MD 20854-2732

BENTON, MARJORIE CRAIG, federal agency administrator; m. Charles William Benton, three children. LHD, Nat. Coll. Edn., 1981, Lincoln Coll., 1982, Columbia Coll., 1983, Northwestern U., 1983; LLD (hon.), John Marshall Law Sch., 1984; D of Pub. Svc. (hon.), St. Xavier Coll., Chgo., 1987; PhD (hon.), Mundelein Coll., 1988. Pub. del. U.S. Mission to UN, 1977, del. spl. session on disarmament, 1978; mem. commn. UN Assn., 1978-79; spl. adv. UN Disarmament Commn., 1979; U.S. rep. UNICEF, 1980-83; mem. Commn. on White House Fellowships, Washington, 1993, chmn. bd. dirs., 1994—. Vice chair Pub. Media, Inc., Chgo.; bd. dirs. Royal Packaging Industries, Van Leer, The Netherlands; co-chair Am. for Strategic Arms Limitation Talks, 1977-79; U.S. Commr. Internat. Yr. of Child; mem. adv. com. Agy. Internat. Devel. Private Voluntary Orgns., 1981-82; co-chair Symphony for Survival, Chgo., 1982. Co-founder The Peace Mus., Chgo., Chgo. Found. for Women, Women's Issues Network, Chgo.; hon. chair Save the Children Fedn., N.Y.; pres. Chapin Hall Ctr. for Children U. Chgo.; chair bd. dirs. Coun. on Founds., Washington, 1994-96; mem. com. on univ. resources Harvard U., Cambridge, Mass., Internat. Humn Rights Law Inst. DePaul Coll. of Law, Chgo., Inst. Social & Econ. Policy in the Middle East, Harvard U., Middle East Policy Coun., Washington; mem. Bernard Van Leer Foundation, The Netherlands, The Van Leer Group Foundation, The Netherlands; trustee Benton Foundation, Washington, DC; del. Dem. Nat. Conv., 1972, 76, 82, 88, 92; commn. del. selection Dem. Nat. Com., 1973, 88; del. Dem. Mid-Term Conv., 1974, 78, 83; mem. procedures com. Dem. Nat. Conv., 1978; mem. Ill. Dem. Platform com., 1975; Ill. co-chair Inaugural Com., 1977; mem. rules com. Dem. Nat. Conv., 1980, 87; mem. affirmative action com. Ill. Dems., 1984; del.-at-large Dem. Nat. Conv., 1984. Recipient Oustanding Pub. Svc. award UNICEF, 1978, Alumni Svc. award Nat. Coll. Edn., 1979, Woman of Achievement award, Cleve. City Women's Club, 1980, Adlai Stevenson award, 1981, Outstanding Achievement in Cmty. Leadership award YMCA, 1982, Better Govt. Assn. award, 1983, Lincoln award Ill. Citizenx for Handgun Control, Louis Lerner Disting. Svc. award Ill. Pub. Action Coun., Leadership award Chgo. Chpt. Nat. Assn. Fundraising Execs., Woman of Achievement award, Girl Scouts of Am., Chgo., Jane Addams Internat. Women's Leadership award, 1991, Full Circle award, 1993; Co-recipient Disting. Grantmaker Award, Coun. on Founds., 2004; Midwest Women's Ctr. 10th Anniversary Honoree, 1986. Mem. Chgo. Pediat. Soc. (hon.), Am. Orthopsychiatric Assn., Arts Club Chgo., Econ. Club Chgo., River Club N.Y.

BENTON-BORGHI, BEATRICE HOPE, secondary school educator, consultant, writer, director; b. San Antonio; d. Donald Francis and Beatrice Hope Benton; m. Peter T. Borghi; children: Kathryn Benton Borghi, Sarah Benton Borghi. BA in Chemistry, North Adams State Coll. (now known as Mass. Coll. Liberal Arts); MEd, Boston U. Tchr. chemistry Cathedral H.S., Springfield, Mass.; tchr. chemistry and history Munich (W.Ger.) Am. H.S.; tchr. English Tokyo; tchr. chemistry and sci. Marlborough (Mass.) H.S.; project dir., adminstr. ESEA, Marlborough Pub. Schs.; CEO, pres., chmn. bd. dirs. Open Minds, Inc. Project dir., proposal writer Title III, Title IX, U.S. Dept. Edn.; evaluation teams New Engl. Assn. Schs. and Colls.; mem. regional dept. edn. com.; ednl. cons., lectr. Author: Project ABC (Access By Computer), Kathryn Borghi Digital Libr., Alternative Funding/Recycling Project, Down the Aisle, Best Friends, A Thousand Lights, Whoa, Nellie!, Best Friend Jour., Down the Aisle Jour., Whoa, Nellie! Jour., A Thousand Lights Jour., Best Friend: Teacher and Parent Guide, Whoa Nellie! Teacher and Parent Guide, Down the Aisle: Teacher and Parent Guide, Subtle Inclusion Through Literature, Kathryn Borghi Digital Library with Accessible Technology Center Model, 2001, others; contbr. articles to profl. jours. Energy conservation rep. Marlborough's Overall Econ. Devel. Com., 1976; mem. strategic planning com. Upper Arlington Sch., Ohio, 1994, 1999, tech., 1999; chmn. Marlborough's Energy Conservation Task Force, 1975; dir. Walk for Mankind, 1972; sec. Group Action for Marlborough Environment, 1975—76; pres. Sisters, Inc., dba Open Minds Inc.; with Project Digital Jones Mid. Sch., Upper Arlington, Ohio, 2001—03; bd. dirs. Girls Club, Marlborough, 1979. Mem. AAUW, Coun. for Exceptional Children, Nat. Women's Health Network. Home: 2449 Edington Rd Columbus OH 43221-3047 Office: Open Minds Inc PO Box 21325 Columbus OH 43221-0325

BENTON-HARDY, LISA RENEE, psychiatrist, educator; BA, Stanford U., 1988; MD, U. Calif., San Francisco, 1992. Diplomate Nat. Bd. Med. Examiners, Am. Bd. Psychaiat. and Neurology. Intern U. Calif. Davis-East Bay, Oakland, CA, 1992-93; adult psychiatry resident Stanford (Calif.) U. Med. Ctr., 1993-96, child and adolescent psychiatry fellow, 1995-97; staff psychiatrist Alliance for Cmty. Care, San Jose, Calif., 1994—. Calif. Wellness Found. Violence Prevention Initiative acad. scholar, Stanford U. Med. Ctr., 1995-97; presenter in field. Contbr. articles to profl. jours., chpt. to book. Laughlin fellow Am. Coll. Psychiatrists, 1997. Mem. AMA, Am. Psychiat. Assn. (Program for Minority Rsch. and Tng. in Psychiatry mini-fellowship award 1996), Am. Acad. Child and Adolescent Psychiatry (Presdl. Scholar award 1996, Charter fellow, leadership award 1994), No. Calif. Psychiat. Soc. Office: Childrens Hosp Oakland Dept Psychiatry 747 52nd St Oakland CA 94609-1809

BENYEI, CANDACE REED, psychotherapist; b. N.Y.C., Feb. 25, 1946; d. Harlow John and Jacqueline de la Valtaire (Smyth) Reed; m. Curt Christian Benyei, July 1, 1967; children: Tara Elaine, Christian Harlow. BA in Chemistry, Colo. Coll., 1967; MS in Sch. Psychology, So. Conn. State U., 1985; MS in Marriage and Family Therapy, U. Bridgeport, Conn., 1987; PhD in Clin. Psychology, Union Inst., Cin., 1988; MPS, N.Y. Theol. Sem., 1994. Lic. marriage and family therapist, Conn. Rsch. assoc. Cornell U., Ithaca, N.Y., 1967-68; rsch. asst. Yale-New Haven Hosp., 1968-70, Clairol Inc., Stamford, Conn., 1970-71; asst. chaplain So. Conn. State U., New Haven, 1984-85; adj. prof. U. Bridgeport, 1988-89; cons. family svcs. div. Danbury (Conn.) Superior Ct., 1990-91; mgr., pres. Whimsy Brook Farm, Ltd., Redding, Conn., 1972—; dir. Inst. for Human Resources, Redding, 1985—. Lectr. So. Conn. State U., 1990—97; adj. prof. Fairfield U., 1990—97; acting exec. dir. Burning Tree, Inc., 1998—; founder, tchg. elder Congregation of the Way, 2000—; adminstr. Schulhof Animal Hosp., 1999—. Author: Called to Be Lonely: A Company of Clowns, 1984, A Cape Cod Journal, 1985, Understanding Clergy Misconduct in Religious Systems: Scapegoating, Family Secrets and the Abuse of Power, 1998, How to Get There From Here: Creating God Among Us, 2002; contbr. poetry to jours. Pres. Fairfield Coop. Ext. Coun., 1975-78; mem. Redding Bd. Edn., 1978-86; lic. lay reader Episc. Diocese Coun., 1982-91, mem. diocesan com. on spiritual direction, 1985-87; assoc. Order of Holy Cross, 1986—; mem. adv. com. Ellis Clark Regional Agri-Sci. and Tech. Ctr. Mem.: Nat. Ctr. Homeopathy, Conn. Holistic Health Assn., Conn. Assn. Marriage and Family Therapists (clin mem., approved supr.), Am. Assn. Marriage and Family Therapists (approved supr.), Conn. Psychol. Assn., Conn. Farm Bur. (bd. dirs.), Am. Quarter Horse Assn. Democrat. Avocations: photography, gardening, writing poetry. Office: Inst Human Resources 29 Giles Hill Rd Redding CT 06896-2511 Office Phone: 203-938-9309.

BERANEK, KIM MARIE, music educator; b. Racine, Wisc., Mar. 13, 1962; d. Donald L. Frosland and Naomi B. Larrabee Frosland; m. David John Beranek, Dec. 20, 1985; children: Jonathan, Timothy, Samuel, Daniel. BA in Music Edn., Northwest Nazarene U., 1985; MA in Music Edn., U. Oreg., 1992. Lic. tchr. Oreg., Idaho. Music tchr. Medford (Oreg.) Sch. Dist., 1985—90, Eugene (Oreg.) Sch. Dist., 1990—91, Salem-Keizer Sch. Dist., Salem, Oreg., 1991—. Accompanist Rogue Valley Choral, 1985—90, S-KHONOR Choir, 1990—94; specialist Weather's Music Corp., Salem, 1994—; cons. Oregon Dept. Educators Music Educators, Salem, 1985—90; coord. North by Northeast Homeschoolers, Salem, 1996—. Mentor Music Specialists, Oreg., 1985—; cert. mem. Harmony Road and Music in Me, 1995—2004; choir dir. South Salem Nazarene Ch., Salem, 2002—03, mem. music com., 1991—. Mem.: Friends of Music, Oreg. Music Educators Assn., Northwest Nazarene U. Alumni Assn., Nazarene Mission Soc. Republican. Nazarene. Avocations: reading, travel, homeschooling, piano, teaching. Home: 842 Maine Ave NE Keizer OR 97303-4650

BERARD, MARIA DOLORES, clothing designer; b. Havana, Cuba, June 10, 1960; came to U.S., 1960; d. Pedro and Maria Luisa (Olagorta) Barquin; m. Roger Ernest Berard, Apr. 23, 1983; children: Jason Anthony, Roger August, Lucas Adrian, Sophia Anastasia. Student, U. Vt., 1979-83; BA in Psychology, Johnson State Coll. Designer, pres. Loli of Vt., Inc., St. Albans, 1987—97; tchr. City Elem., St. Albans, 1997—99, Bellows Free Acad. HS, St. Albans, 1999—2000; tutor Fairfield Ctr. Schs., 2000; substitute tchr. BFA HS, St. Albans, 2000—03, after sch. coord., 2000—04; tchr. Johnson State Coll., 2002—. Lifetime mem. PTA, City Elem., St. Albans, 1992—; religious educator St. Mary's Cath. Ch., St. Albans, 1993. Recipient award as Woman of Achievement, Bus. and Profl. Women Franklin County, 1994; Vt. Tchr. Diversity scholar 2003. Democrat. Roman Catholic. Avocations: dance, cooking, sewing.

BERCEAU, TERESE L. state representative; b. Green Bay, Wis., Aug. 23, 1950; m. Stuart Levitau. BS, U. Wis., 1978, postgrad. Mag. editor Wis. Counties Assn., 1981—83; career placement specialist U. Wis.-LaFollett Inst., 1983—88; state assembly mem. Wis. State Assembly, Madison, 1998—, mem. colls. and univs., family law, law revision, and urban and local affairs coms. Supr. Dane County Bd., Wis., 1992—2000; commr. Cmty. Devel. Authority, Wis., 1982—92; various task forces and city coms. Mem.: Nat. Women's Polit. Caucus, 1000 Friends of Wis., NOW. Democrat. Roman Catholic. Office: State Capitol Rm 208N PO Box 8952 Madison WI 53708-8952

BERCH, REBECCA WHITE, state supreme court justice, lawyer; b. Phoenix, June 29, 1955; d. Robert Eugene and Janet Kay (Zimmerman) White; m. Michael Allen Berch, Mar. 9, 1981; 1 child, Jessica. BS summa cum laude, Ariz. State U., 1976, JD, 1979, MA, 1990. Bar: Ariz. 1979, U.S. Dist. Ct. Ariz., U.S. Ct. Appeals (9th cir.), U.S. Supreme Ct. Assoc., ptnr.

McGroder, Tryon, Heller, Rayes & Berch, Phoenix, 1979-85; dir. legal rsch. and writing program Ariz. State U. Coll. Law, Tempe, 1986-91, 94-95; solicitor gen. State of Arizona, Phoenix, 1991-94, 1st asst. atty. gen., 1996—98; judge Ariz. Ct. Appeals, 1998—2002, Ariz. Supreme Ct., Phoenix, 2002—. Co-author: (Book) Introduction to Legal Method and Process, 1985, 2002, Teacher's Manual for Introduction to Legal Method and Process, 1992, 2002, Handling Complex Litigation, 1986; Bd. editors Jour. Legal Writing Inst., 1993—2002; contbr. articles to profl. jours. and newspapers. Bd. dirs. Tempe-Mesa chpt. ACLU, 1984—86, Homeless Legal Assistance Project, Phoenix, 1990—98. Mem. Ariz. Women Lawyer's Assn., Ariz. State Bar Assn. Republican. Methodist. Avocations: reading, travel. Office: Ariz Supreme Ct 1501 W Washington St Phoenix AZ 85009-3831

BERENATO, AGNUS MCGLADE, women's basketball coach; b. Dec. 9, 1956; m. Jack Berenato; children: Theresa Marie, Andrew, Joey, Clare, Christina. Student, U. N.C., 1976-77; BA in Sociology, Mt. St. Mary's Coll., Emmitsburg, Md., 1980, DHL (hon.), 1995. Profl. basketball player Entente Senonaise, Sens, France, 1975-76; head coach Rider Coll., 1981-85; asst. coach Ga. Tech U., 1986-88, head coach women's basketball, 1988—2003, U. Pitts., 2003—. Recipient Disting. Alumni award Mt. St. Mary's Coll., 1984; named Ga. Win Coll. Coach of Yr., 2000, Divsn. I Ga. Coach of Yr., 2002, Coach WBCA All Star Challenge, 2002; Sports Ethics fellow Inst. Internat. Sports, 1996; inducted into Rider Coll. Hall of Fame, 2002. Mem. Atlanta Tip-off Club (nat. adv. bd.), Atlanta Women's Network Inc., Women's Basketball Coaches Assn., Ga. Women's Intersport Network, Atlanta Women in Sports, Naismith Hall of Fame. Office: U Pitts PO Box 7436 Pittsburgh PA 15213 Business E-Mail: aberenato@athletics.pitt.edu.

BERENBAUM, MAY ROBERTA, entomology educator; b. Trenton, N.J., July 22, 1953; BS, Yale U., 1975; PhD, Cornell U., 1980. Asst. prof. entomology U. Ill., Urbana-Champaign, 1980-85, assoc. prof. entomology, 1985-90, prof. entomology, 1990-95, head dept., 1992—, Swanlund prof. entomology, 1996—. Assoc. editor Am. Midland Naturalist, 1982-85; mem. editl. bd. Jour. Chem. Ecology, Chemoecology, Proceedings of the Nat. Acad. Scis. USA. Recipient Presdl. Young Investigator award NSF, 1984, Founder's award Entomol. Soc. Am., 1994. Mem. AAAS, NAS, Am. Philos. Soc., Am. Assn. Arts and Scis., Entomol. Soc. Am. (fellow 2002), Ecol. Soc. Am., Phytochem Soc. Am., Internat. Soc. Chem. Ecology, Sigma Xi. Achievements include research in chemical aspects of insect-plant interaction, evolutionary ecology of insects, phototoxicity of plant products, host-plant resistance. Office: U Ill Dept Entomology 320 Morrill Hall 505 S Goodwin Ave Urbana IL 61801-3707

BERENS, BETTY KATHRYN MCADAM, community program administrator; b. Wheeling, W.Va., Dec. 17, 1927; d. Will and Elizabeth Margaret (Wickham) McAdam; m. Alan Robert Berens, June 18, 1949; children: Robert Seton, Kathryn Elizabeth. Student, Radcliffe Coll., 1945-47; BA cum laude, Case Western Res. U., 1949; postgrad., Kent State U., 1967. Vol., various cities, Ohio, 1963-88; founder Western Res. Human Svcs., Akron, Ohio, 1975-84; cons. Hudson (Ohio) Local Schs., Addison County, Vt., 1968-88, coord. cmty./sch. vol. program (VIP); pres. aux. bd. Porter Med. Ctr., Middlebury, Vt., 1990-92. Vol. Hawthornden State Hosp., Cleve., 1963-65; vol. probation officer Mcpl. Ct., Cuyahoga Falls, Ohio, 1973-74; comm. chmn. Elderly Svcs. Inc., Middlebury, 1990-95; cmty. sch. vol. cons. Ohio Dept. Edn., Columbus, 1984-88; bd. dirs. Addison County Home Health Care Agy., 1995-2001, Champlain Valley Agy. on Aging. Bd. dirs. Porter Med. Ctr., 1990-92; bd. dirs. Internat. Inst., Akron, 1983-88, pres., 1986-87; mem. Summit County Bd. Edn., Akron, 1977-88, pres., 1981, 86; chmn. Hudson Cares, 1974-76; comm. chmn. Addison County United Way. Recipient Cmty. Svc. award Hudson Jaycees, 1984, Commendation for Outstanding Svc. in Edn., Pres. Ronald Reagan, 1988. Mem. Phi Delta Kappa (Leader in Edn. 1977, 88). Avocations: volunteering, family, knitting, cross-country skiing, canoeing. Home: 10 S Gorham Ln Middlebury VT 05753

BERENSON, ABBEY BELINA, gynecologist, educator, researcher; b. Nashville, Aug. 19, 1958; d. Leon and Florence (Keiles) B.; m. Steven Mitchell Kornblau, Nov. 24, 1983; children: Ilyse Samantha, Jake Alexander. BA summa cum laude, U. Tex., 1980; MD, Baylor U., 1984. Lic. gynecologist, Tex. Resident in ob-gyn. Baylor Coll. Medicine, Houston, 1984-88; fellow in pediat. gynecology Queen Charlotte's and Chelsea Hosp., London, 1991; asst. prof. U. Tex. Med. Br., Galveston, 1989-93, assoc. prof., chief divsn. pediat. and adolescent gynecology, 1993-98, prof., chief divsn. pediat. and adolescent gynecology, 1998—. Reviewer: Jour. Adolescent Health, Pediats., Obstetrics and Gynecology, Archives of Pediats. and Adolescent Medicine, Jour. Reproductive Medicine; contbr. numerous articles to profl. publs. including Jour. Adolescent Health, Adolescent Pediat. Gynecology, Pediats., Am. Jour. Ob-Gyn. James and Minnie Edmonds scholar. Fellow ACOG (bd. cert.), Ctrl. Assn. Obstetricians and Gynecologists (pres. elect), Soc. Adolescent Medicine; mem. Internat. Fedn. Gynecologists Obstetricians (expert adv. panel 1997—), Soc. Gynecologic Investigation, N.Am. Soc. Pediat. and Adolescent Gynecology (abstract rev. com. 1992-93, com. position statements 1996). Achievements include research on appearance of external genitalia in prepubertal girls; physical abuse in pregnancy; contraceptive compliance in adolescents; drug abuse in pregnancy.

BERES, AMY LYN, director; b. Miami, Fla., June 15, 1974; d. Dennis Elijah and Ann Beres. B of Music Edn., Fla. State U, 1996. Dir. bands Mebane Mid. Sch., Alachua, Fla., 1996—2003; asst. dir. bands Santa Fe High Sch., 1997—2003. Mem.: Fla. Bandmasters Assn. (dist. chair 2001—03), Music Educators Nat. Conf. Avocations: cooking, baking, art, art, crafts, gardening.

BERES, MARY ELIZABETH, management educator, organizational consultant; b. Birmingham, Ala., Jan. 19, 1942; d. John Charles and Ethel (Belenyesi) Beres. BS, Siena Heights Coll., Adrian, Mich., 1969; PhD, Northwestern U., 1976. Joined Dominican Sisters, 1960. Tchr. St. Francis Xavier Sch., Medina, Ohio, 1962-64, St. Edward Sch., Medina, Ohio, 1964-67, Our Lady of Mt. Carmel Sch., Temperance, Mich., 1967-69, asst. prin., 1968-69; tchr. math. St. Ambrose H.S., Detroit, 1969-70; vis. instr. Cornell U., 1973-74; assoc. prof. orgn. behavior Temple U., Phila., 1974-84; assoc. prof. mgmt. Mercer U., Atlanta, 1984-91; founder, sr. assoc. Leadership Sys., Atlanta, 1988—. Mem. World Pilgrims, 2002—; bd. dirs. Aquinas Ctr. Theology, 2001—. Contbr. chpts. to books; organizer of symposia in areas of corp. leadership, orgn. change and cross-cultural comm. Bd. dir. Ctr. for Ethics and Social Policy, Phila., 1980—84, Assn. Global Bus., 1989—91; mem. program planning com. of interdepartmental group in bus. adminstrn. U. Ctr. in Ga., 1987—91, chair, 1988—90; trustee Adrian Dominican Ind. Sch. Sys., Adrian, Mich., 1971—79; pres. bd. dirs. New Ventures Network, 1998—2001; mem. Atlanta Clergy and Laity Concerned, 1986—95; econ. pastoral imlementation com. Archdiocese of Atlanta, 1988—89, Atlanta Archdiocesan Planning and Devel. Coun., 1991—93; episcopal moderator women Religious Archdiocese of Atlanta, 1993—97, Atlanta Conf. Sisters, 1984—, pres., 1993—97, 2001—; vicar Religious Archdiocese of Atlanta, 2001—, World Pilgrims of Atlanta, 2002—. Recipient Legion of Honor membership Chapel of the Four Chaplains, Phila., 1982, Disting. Tchg. award Lindback Found., 1982, Cert. for Humanity Mercer U, 1985. Mem. NAFE, Acad. of Mgmt., Dominican Sisters of Adrian, Mich. (strategic planning com. 2000-01). Democrat. Roman Catholic. Office: Leadership Sys PO Box 76475 Atlanta GA 30358-1475 E-mail: LeadSys@aol.com.

BERESFORD, ANNETTE DIANA, researcher; b. Bethesda, Md., Feb. 26, 1958; d. Spencer Moxon and Ann Lincoln Beresford; children: Conner Crossman, Mekha Schmidt. BS summa cum laude, U. So. Miss., 1991; M Pub. Policy and Adminstrn., Jackson State U., 1997; PhD in Pub. Adminstrn., Fla. Atlantic U., 2002. Analyst Hancock Bank, Gulfport, Miss., 1985-93; program mgr., planner Bd. Trustees of State Instns. of Higher Learning, Jackson, Miss., 1993—97; fin. specialist divsn. securities and investor protection Office of Contr., West Palm Beach, Fla., 1997—2002; vis. instr. Fla. Atlantic U., Jupiter, Fla., 2002—03; rsch. assoc. Nat. White Collar Crime Ctr., Morgantown, W.Va., 2003—. Bd. dirs. Mayan Towers, Palm Beach Shores. Contbr. articles to profl. jours. Named to Am. Acad. Disting. Students, Am. Ctr. for Grad. Edn., 1996-97; Breland scholar U. So. Miss., 1990-91; Newell doctoral fellow Fla. Atlantic U., 2000-2001. Mem. Am. Soc. for Pub. Adminstrn., Pub. Adminstrn. Theory Network, Phi Kappa Phi, Pi Alpha Alpha. Office: Nat White Collar Crime Ctr 12 Roush Dr Morgantown WV 26505

BERESFORD, MADELEINE ROSAMOND SYLVIA, theater director, puppeteer; b. N.Y.C., Jan. 28, 1959; d. John Spencer Beresford and Myriam Ruth (Cohn) Hartog; m. Jeffrey Allen Burger, May 1, 1994; children: Andre Beresford Burger, Myriam Arianna Burger. Mime student, Etienne Decroux, Paris, 1977; BA in Theater Arts, Oberlin Coll., 1981; apprentice, Salzburg Marionette Theater, Austria, 1980; student of Lee Tien-lu, Taipei, 1989. Sound technician Ridiculous Theatrical Co., N.Y.C., 1978; puppeteer, puppetmaker Ragabash Puppet Theater, N.Y.C., 1981-87; performer, workshop leader Shadowbox Theater, N.Y.C., 1985-92; puppetry tchr. Columbia Grammar Sch., N.Y.C., 1986-88; writer, dir., performer, puppetmaker Nassau County Puppetry Program, Mineola, N.Y., 1990-91; dir. Chinese Hand-Puppetry Project, N.Y.C., 1992; artistic dir., co-founder Galapagos Puppet Theater, Ridgewood, N.J., 1987—; artist in residence N.J. State Coun. on Arts, 2002—, 2003—. Actor Arts Horizens, 2002, tchr., 2002—. Prodr.: (film) Theater of the Palms: The World of Puppet Master Lee Tien-lu, 1989; performer, writer puppet shows, 1987—. Grantee Henson Found., 1991. Jewish. Avocations: travel, reading, swimming, sewing, cooking. Home and Office: 158 Hope St Ridgewood NJ 07450-4505

BERESFORD, MARY JO THERESA, theatre educator; b. Cin., July 13, 1949; d. William Dale and Coletta Josephine (Megrew) B. BA, Edgecliff Coll., 1971; MFA, U. Cinn. Conservatory of Music, 1977. Teaching asst. U. Cin., 1975-77; lectr. Edgecliff Coll., Cin., 1978-80; choreographer Xavier U. Singers, Cin., 1973-86; lectr. U. Cin., 1980-84, No. Ky. Univ., Highland Heights, Ky., 1982—. Chair Golden Galaxy Awards Speech/Drama Com., Cin., 1992—; regional chair drama Cinergy Overture Awards; critic Ohio Cmty. Theatre Assn., Cin., 1987—. Dir. plays Assassins, 1994, Biloxi Blues, 1994, Tintypes, 1992, The Pajama Game, 1996, Smoke on the Mountain, 1996, Ruthless, 1997. Poll worker Hamilton County Bd. Elections, Norwood, Ohio, 1990-93. Mem. AAUW, S.E. Theatre Conf., Ky. Theatre Assn. Democrat. Roman Catholic. Avocations: crossword puzzles, needlework, cooking. Home: 5413 Carthage Ave Norwood OH 45212-1023

BERETS, EILEEN TOLKOWSKY, artist; b. Antwerp, Belgium, July 15, 1930; arrived in U.S., 1940; d. Marcel and Marthe Germaine (Kleinberg) Tolkowsky; m. Donald J. Berets, June 24, 1956 (dec. Feb. 2002); children: James Carl, Susan Lee. BA in Economics, Wellesley Coll., 1952; student, Art Student's League, N.Y.C., 1953-56; studied with Ethel Todd George, Stamford, Conn., 1983, 84, studied with Diane Faxon, 1984-92; student, Silvermine Guild, 1984-87. Cons. Stone Studio, Stamford, Conn., Our World Gallery, 1991—. One-Woman and duo shows include U. Conn., Stamford, 1984, Stamford Art Assn. Landmark Tower, 1986, New Canaan (Conn.) Art Assn. Waveny Carriage Barn, 1988, Greenwich (Conn.) Art Soc. Marsh & McLennan, 1989, Conn. Commn. Arts Legis. Bldg., Hartford, 1990, Our World Gallery, Stamford, 1991, Darien (Conn.) Libr., 1992, Art in the Garden, 1995, Conn. Ballet Ctr., 1997-98; exhibited in group shows at Nat. Arts Club, N.Y.C., 1984, Stamford Art Assn., 1984-98 (2d prize 1991, 1st prize 1997), Art Soc. of Old Greenwich, 1984-93, Conn. Art Ann. Competition Stamford Mus., 1985, 88, 91, 97, Greenwich Art Soc., 1985-2003 (Best Watercolor award 1989, Allan Bernard award 1996), New Canaan Soc. Arts, 1992-2003 (2d pl. prize in watercolor 1998), (invitational) AAUW Salute to Conn. Artists, 1983-88, Stamford Cmty. Arts Coun. Eight Watercolorists, 1985, Conn. Pub. TV Preview Exhbn., Hartford, New Haven, Stamford, 1990-91, Hartford Architecture Conservancy, 1991, Wellesley Coll., 1992, 97, Stamford Art Assn. Lucas Industries, 1992-93, Arts in the Garden, 1995, Faber Birren Nat. Color Award show, 1996, Arthur Ross Gallery, 1996, Caron Gallery, Chester, Conn., 2001-03; represented in permanent collections Stamford Art in Pub. Places Program, 1990-95, Lending Art Collection Greenwich Pub. Libr., Pres.'s Office Turner Entertainment Co., L.A., Pres.'s Office Conservation Mgmt. Inc., Washington; commissions include Fellowship for Jewish Learning, Conservation Mgmt., Inc., Washington. Dir., v.p., pres. LWV, Stamford; sec., dir. Family and Children's Svcs.; Stamford rep. South Western Regional Planning Agy.; chair task force mass transp. Stamford Area Commerce and Industry Assn.; dir. Stamford Art Assn., 1994—, pres., 1999-2000. Mem.: Nat. League Am. Pen Women. Home: 47 E Ridge Rd Stamford CT 06903-4337

BEREZIN, EVELYN, management consultant; AB, postgrad., NYU; Doctorate (hon.), Adelphi U., Ea. Mich. U. Computer hardware designer, 1951—69; founder, pres. Redactron Corp., 1969—80; pres. Greenhouse Mgmt. Co., 1980—87; mgmt. cons., 1988—. Dir. Intelli-Check, Inc., Woodbury, NY; bd. dirs. Brookhaven Sci. Assocs., Stony Brook Found. SUNY, Brookhaven Nat. Labs., Boyce Thompson Inst. Fellow, Atomic Energy Commn. Achievements include patents in field. Office: Intellicheck Inc 246 Crosswarp Park West Woodbury NY 11797

BEREZIN, TANYA, acting coach, educator, actress; b. Phila., Mar. 25, 1941; d. Maurice and Bettye (Shifrin) Berezin; m. Robert Leeming Thirkield, June 29, 1969 (div. June 1977); children: Lila Joy, Jonathon Schuyler; m. Mark Beers Wilson, Oct. 18, 1987. Student, Boston U., 1959-63. Co-founder Circle Repertory Co., N.Y.C., 1969, artistic dir., 1986-94, pvt. coach, studio class, seminars, 1994—; resident acting coach All My Children, One Life to Live ABC, N.Y.C., 1994-99; resident acting coach Another World NBC, N.Y.C., 1997-98; resident acting coach As the World Turns CBS, N.Y.C., 1998-99. Actor: (TV shows) St. Elsewhere, 1984, Law and Order, 1992—94, 2000—02; (plays) Angels Fall, 1983, Moundbuilders, 1975 (Obie award), Sympathetic Magic, 1997; (films) Awakenings, 1993; prodr.: Prelude to a Kiss, Destiny of Me, Three Hotels, Baltimore Waltz. Avocation: gardening. E-mail: berezin@bellatlantic.net.

BERG, BARBARA KIRSNER, health education specialist; b. Cin., Dec. 6, 1954; d. Robert and Mildred Dorothy (Warshofsky) Kirsner; m. Howard Keith Berg, Apr. 8, 1984; children: Arielle, Allison, Stacy. BA, Brandeis U., 1976; MEd, U. Cin., 1977. Cert. health edn. specialist Nat. Commn. for Health Edn. Credentialing, Inc., Mass. Health educator S.W. Ohio Lung Assn., Cin., 1977-79; coord. adminstrv. edn. N.E. Regional Med. Edn. Ctr., Northport, N.Y., 1979-81; patient health edn. coord. VA Med. Ctr., Buffalo, 1981-87; clin. asst. prof. SUNY, Buffalo, 1982-87; dir. comty. health edn. N.W. Hosp. Ctr., Balt., 1987-89; coord. law and health care program U. Md. Sch. Law, Balt., 1989-90; med. mgmt. cons. Dr. Howard K. Berg, Owings Mills, Md., 1990—. Cons. health edn. Edward Bartlett, Assoc., Rockville, Md., 1987-88; mem. adult edn. com. Chizuk Amuno Congregation, Balt., 1993-99, mem. bd. dirs., 1996-98, chair cultural arts com., 1996-98. Bd. dirs., mem. Am. Lung Assn. Western N.Y., Buffalo, 1983-86, Pumpkin Theater, Balt., 1990-91; chair domestic concerns com. Balt. Jewish Coun., 1994-96, chair govt. rels. com., 1996-98, sec., bd. dirs., 1996-98, 2d v.p. 1998-2000; sec. women's dept. Associated Jewish Charities, Balt., 1994-97; mem. sch. bd. nominating conv. Baltimore County, 1995—; pres. Pikesville Mid. Sch. PTA, 1998-2001. Mem. APHA, Soc. for Pub. Health Edn., Am. Jewish Com., Balt. Brandeis Alumni Assn. (pres.), Phi Delta Kappa. Jewish. Avocations: reading, travel, advocacy. Home and Office: 12116 Heneson Garth Owings Mills MD 21117-1629

BERG, DARLA GAYE, service representative; b. Wenatchee, Wash., Oct. 17, 1952; d. Edward Jay and Elsie Louise (Jackson) JOnes; m. Mark Allen Keer, June 12, 1970 (div. May 1972); m. Thomas Wayne Berg, May 19, 1978; 1 child, Mackenzie Marie. Student, Regents Coll. Mail room, service rep., personnel Pacific N.W. Bell, Seattle, Wash., 1970-80; dir., creator Americorps, 1993-94; dir. after sch. program St. Barnabas Ch., Bainbridge Island, Wash., 1994-96; grant writer, 1993—. Promoter Parenting Classes, Bainbrige Island. Co-author: Architectural Doc. Production, 1991; editor: The Technical Advisor. Personnel com. St Barnabas Day Sch.,, 1996-97; bd. v.p. St. Barnabas After Sch. Program, 1993-97; instr. Episcopal Ch., 1993-97; staff mem. St. Barnabas Ch., asst. pastoral care, tchr., 1991-97. Recipient numerous grants. Epsicopalian. Avocation: writing for adolescents. Office: St Barnabas Epsicopal Ch PO Box 10207 Bainbridge Island WA 98110-0207

BERG, FRANCINE JUDITH, music educator; b. Syracuse, N.Y., Dec. 5, 1948; d. Ira and Lynn Mitchell; m. Norton Barry Berg, Apr. 7, 1979; children: Mark David, Jennifer Lynn. BS, Crane Sch. Music, SUNY, 1971; MusM in Edn., SUNY, 1977. Cantor Temple Soc. of Concord, Syracuse, 1980—; music tchr. Syracuse (N.Y.) City Sch. Sys., 1987—. Choral dir. The Rainbow Kids, Syracuse, 1990—. Bd. mem. Inter Religious Coun., 2000—02; bd. dirs. Syracuse (N.Y.) Jewish Family Svcs., 2002—03. Named Outstanding Music Educator, Syracuse (N.Y.) Symphony Musicians, 1995, Post-Standard Woman of Achievement, Post Std. Newspaper, 2000; recipient Hannah G. Soloman award, 1996, Peace Action award, City of N.Y., 2002. Mem.: Signature Music (bd. mem. & pres. 2001—), Syracuse Jewish Fedn. (bd. mem.), Nat. Coun. of Jewish Women (life Hannah G. Soloman award 1996). Democrat. Jewish. Avocations: tennis, wine tasting, travel, cooking. Home: 114 Haverhill Drive Dewitt NY 13214 Personal E-mail: songberg@hotmail.com.

BERG, G. VIVIAN, artist; b. Worcester, Mass., Feb. 28, 1932; d. Emil Mauritz Mattson and Gunhild Maria Israelson; m. Kenneth George Berg, May 10, 1957; children: Donna Maria, Leah Christine. Tng. cert., Ward Sch. Airline Tng., Worcester, 1951; diploma, Worcester Sch. Bus., 1951. Sec. Ea. Airlines, N.Y.C., 1951-52; legal sec. Office of Russell W. Anderson, Worcester, 1953-61; tchr. art Worcester, 1976-2000. One woman shows include Ogunquit (Maine) Art Ctr., Shore Road Gallery, Boston, Harrison Conf. Ctr., Marlboro, Mass; group shows include Cultural Assembly Portrait Show, UN Conf. Women in Nairobi, 1985; represented in permanent collecions including Milford (Mass.) Fed. Bank, Milford Savs. Bank, 1st Svc. Bank, Pepperell, Mass., Merrimac Valley Credit Union, North Andover, Mass., Spencer Savs. Bank, Medway (Mass.) Nat. Bank, Unibank for Savs., Hoosac Savs. Bank North Adams, Mass., Medway Co-Operative Bank, Methuen (Mass.) Co-Operative Bank, Am. Eagle Credit Union, Manchester, Conn., TruNorth Fin., North Adams, N.E. Cmty. Credit Union, Haverhill, Mass., Haverhill Co-Op Bank, New Eng. Design Assocs., Worcester, Oxford (Mass.) Free Pub. Libr. Mem. Am. Soc. Marine Artists, Am. Mensa Ltd., Nat. Mus. Women in the Arts. Episcopalian. Studio: 8 Inwood Rd Auburn MA 01501-1115

BERG, LILLIAN DOUGLAS, chemistry educator; b. Birmingham, Ala., July 9, 1925; d. Gilbert Franklin and Mary Rachel (Griffin) Douglas; m. Joseph Wilbur Berg, June 26, 1950; children: Anne Berg Jenkins, Joseph Wilbur III, Frederick Douglas. BS in Chemistry, Birmingham So. Coll., 1946; MS in Chemistry, Emory U., 1948. Instr. chemistry Armstrong Jr. Coll., Savannah, Ga., 1948-50; rsch. asst. chemistry Pa. State U., University Park, 1950-54; instr. chemistry U. Utah, Salt Lake City, 1955-56; prof. chemistry No. Va. C.C., Annandale, 1974-96, 98—, adj. prof., 1998—. Mem. Am. Chem. Soc., Am. Women in Sci., Am. Guild Organists, Mortar Bd. Soc., Iota Sigma Pi, Sigma Delta Epsilon, Phi Beta Kappa. Avocation: music. Home: 3319 Dauphine Dr Falls Church VA 22042-3724

BERG, LORINE MCCOMIS, retired guidance counselor; b. Ashland, Ky., Mar. 28, 1919; d. Oliver Botner and Emma Elizabeth (Eastham) McComis; m. Leslie Thomas Berg, Apr. 27, 1946; children: James Michael, Leslie Jane. BA in Edn., U. Ky., 1965; MA, Xavier U., 1969. Tchr. A.D. Owens Elem. Sch., Newport, Ky., 1963-64, 6th dist. Elementary Schs., Covington, Ky., 1965-69; guidance counselor Twenhofel Jr. H.S., Independence, Ky., 1969-78, Scott H.S., Taylor Mill, Ky., 1978-84. Bd. dirs. Mental Health Assn., Covington, Ky, 1970-76, v.p., 1973 (valuable svc. award 1973); mem. Lakeside Christian Ch., Ft. Mitchell, Ky. Named to Honorable Order of Ky. Colonels, Hon. Admissions Counselor U.S. Naval Acad.; cited by USN Recruiting Command for Valuable Assistance to USN, 1981. Mem. Am. Assn. of Univ. Women, Covington Art Club, Retired Tchrs. Assn., Kappa Delta Pi, Delta Kappa Gamma, Phi Delta Kappa. Democrat. Avocations: oil painting, dance, reading, arts and crafts. Home: 11 Idaho Ave Covington KY 41017-2925

BERG, MICHELE, health services administrator; Degree in psychology, U. Kans.; degree in edn., Washburn U; degree learning disabilities, degree in spl. edn., Kans. State U. Jack Aaron prof. Karl Menninger Sch. Psychiatry & Mental Health Scis., 1995; dir. Menninger Ctr. Learning Disabilities, Topeka. Mem. Nat. Assn. Learning Disabilities, Coun. Learning Disabilities, Internat. Dyslexia Assn. (v.p. Kans./Western Mo. br.). Address: Menningers PO Box 809045 Houston TX 77280

BERG, OLENA, investment company executive, former federal official; b. Dec. 31, 1949; d. Clarence Millard and Anna Elizabeth (Schlegel) Nave; 1 child. BA in English summa cum laude, Calif. State U., 1974; MBA, Harvard U., 1984. Budget and estimates analyst State of Calif. Depts. Fin. and Benefits Payments, 1975-77; asst. to sec. State of Calif. Bus. and Transp. Agy., 1977-78; chief dep. dir. State of Calif. Dept. Housing and Community Devel., 1978-82; project mgr. McNeil Consumer Products, 1983; pres., COO Gerson Bakar and Assocs., 1984-88; exec. v.p. Lowe Assocs., 1988-91; chief dep. state treas. State of Calif., 1991-93; asst. sec. pension and welfare benefits adminstrn. Dept. of Labor, Washington, 1993-98; sr. adv. Fin. Engines Inc., Palo Alto, Calif., 1998—. Baker scholar Harvard U. Mem. Century Club. Office: Fin Engines Inc 1804 Embarcadero Rd Palo Alto CA 94303-3341

BERG, PATRICIA ELENE, molecular biologist; b. Dubuque, Iowa, Sept. 17, 1943; d. Clifford Jay and Dorothy Ruth (McKibben) Emerson; 1 child, Bridget K. Mora; m. Robert S. Weiner. SB in Math., U. Chgo., 1965; PhD in Microbiology, Ill. Inst. Tech., 1973. Postdoctoral fellow U. Chgo., 1973-78; dir. genetic engring. Bethesda Rsch. Labs., Rockville, Md., 1978-80; expert NIH, Bethesda, 1980-82, sr. staff fellow, 1982-85, Nat. Inst. Digestive Diseases and Kidney, 1985-91; assoc. prof. divsn. of pediatric hematology/oncology Sch. Medicine U. Md., Balt., 1991-98; assoc. prof. dept. biochem. and molecular biology George Washington U. Med. Sch., Washington, 1999—. Contbr. articles to profl. jours. Scholar, U. Chgo., 1961—65. Mem. AAAS, Am. Soc. Microbiology, Am. Soc. Hematology, Am. Assn. Cancer Rsch., Sigma Xi. Democrat. Methodist. Achievements include discovery of BP1, new gene expressed in over 80 percent of breast cancer patients. Office: George Washington U Med Sch Dept Biochem/Molecular Biol 2300 Eye St NW Washington DC 20037-2336 Office Phone: 202-994-2810.

BERG, PATTY, state legislator; b. Eureka, Calif. 2 children. BA in Sociology and Social Welfare, UCLA, 1967. Social worker; mem., dist. 1 Calif. State Assembly, 2002—. Mem. Agriculture Com., Appropriations Com., Higher Edn. Com., Water, Parks, and Wildlife Com.; vice-chair Aging and Long-Term Care Com. Democrat. Mailing: PO Box 942849 Rm 2137 Sacramento CA 94249 Office: 235 4th St Ste C Eureka CA 95501

BERGÉ, CAROL, writer; b. N.Y.C., 1928; d. Albert and Molly Peppis; m. Jack Bergé, June 1955; 1 child, Peter. Asst. to pres. Pendray Public Relations, N.Y.C., 1955; disting. prof. lit. Thomas Jefferson Coll., Allendale, Mich., 1975-76; instr. adult degree program Goddard Coll., 1976; tchr. fiction and poetry U. Calif. Extension Program, Berkeley, 1976-77; assoc. prof. U. So. Miss., Hattiesburg, 1977-78; vis. prof. Honors Ctr. and English dept. U. N.Mex., 1978-79, 87; vis. lectr. Wright State U., 1979, SUNY, Albany, 1980-81; tchr. Poets and Writers, Poets in the Schs. (N.Y. State Council on Arts), 1970-72, Poets in the Schs. (Conn. Commn. Arts). Summer writing confs. Squaw Valley, Ind. U., U. Calif., Santa Cruz, 1975-1980; propr. Blue Gate Gallery of Art and Antiques, 1988-2003. Author: (fiction) The Unfolding, 1969, A Couple Called Moebius, 1972, Acts of Love: An American Novel, 1973 (N.Y. State Coun. on Arts CAPS award 1974), Timepieces, 1977, The Doppler Effect, 1979, Fierce Metronome, 1981, Secrets, Gossip & Slander, 1984, Zebras, or, Contour Lines, 1991; (poetry) The Vulnerable Island, 1964, Lumina, 1965, Poems Made of Skin, 1968, The Chambers, 1969, Circles, as in the Eye, 1969, An American Romance, 1969, From a Soft Angle: Poems About Women, 1972, The Unexpected, 1976, Rituals and Gargoyles, 1976, A Song, A Chant, 1978, Alba Genesis, 1979, Alba Nemesis, 1979, (reportage) The Vancouver Report, 1965; editor CENTER Mag., 1970-84, pub., 1991—; editor Miss. Rev., 1977-78, Subterraneans, 1975-76, Paper Branches, 1987, LIGHT YEARS: The N.Y.C. Coffeehouse Writers and Multimedia Artists of the 1960s, 2005; contbg. editor Woodstock Rev., 1977-81, Shearsman mag., 1980-82, S.W. Profile, 1981; editor, pub. CENTER Press, 1970-93; pub.: Medicine Journeys (Carl Ginsburg), Coastal Lives (Miriam Sagan), 1991; co-pub.: Zebras (Carol Bergé). Nat. Endowment Arts fellow, 1979-80 Mem. Authors' League, Poets and Writers, MacDowell Fellows Assn., Nat. Press Women Home: 2070 Calle Contento Santa Fe NM 87505-5406 E-mail: carolberge@earthlink.net.

BERGEN, CANDICE, actress, writer, photojournalist; b. Beverly Hills, Calif., May 9, 1946; d. Edgar and Frances (Westerman) B.; m. Louis Malle, Sept. 27, 1980 (dec. 1995); 1 dau., Chloe; m. Marshall Rose, 2000. Ed., U. Pa. Model during coll. Films include The Group, The Sand Pebbles, 1966, The Day the Fish Came Out, Live for Life, 1967, The Magus, 1968, Soldier Blue, The Executioner, The Adventurers, Getting Straight, 1970, The Hunting Party, Carnal Knowledge, T.R. Baskin, 1971, 11 Harrowhouse, 1974, Bite the Bullet, The Wind and the Lion, 1975, The Domino Principle, The End of the World in Our Usual Bed in a Night Full of Rain, Oliver's Story, 1978, Starting Over, 1979, Rich and Famous, 1981, Gandhi, 1982, Stick, 1985, Miss Congeniality, 2000, Sweet Home Alabama, 2002, View from the Top, 2003, The In-Laws, 2003; TV appearances include What's My Line, 1965, Coronet Blue, 1967, The Muppet Show, 1976, The Way They Were, 1981, 2010 (voice), 1984, Trying Times, 1987, Seinfeld, 1990, Images of Life: Photographs that have Changed the World, 1996, The Human Face (miniseries), 2001, Murphy Brown: TV Tales, 2002, Sex and the City, 2002, TV series: Murphy Brown, 1988-98 (Emmy award, Leading Actress in a Comedy Series, 1989, 90, 92, 94, 95); TV films Arthur the King, 1985, Murder by Reason of Insanity, 1985, Mayflower Madam, 1987, Shelley Duvall's Bedtime Stories, Vol. 7, 1993, Mary and Tim, 1996; TV miniseries Hollywood Wives, 1985, Trying Times, Moving Day; author Knockwood; photojournalist credits include articles for Life, Playboy; dramatist: (play) The Freezer (included in Best Short Plays of 1968).

BERGEN, JEANNINE EVELYN, psychologist; b. New Hyde Park, NY, July 13, 1970; d. Virginia Elise and Joseph Bergen; m. Jon James Cerabone, Aug. 12, 2000. MS, CAS, SUNY, 1996, PsyD, 1999. Lic. School Psychologist NY, 2000. Sch. psychologist Questar III, Rensselaer, NY, 1997, Brittonkill Sch. Dist., Troy, 1997—98, H. Frank Carey H.S., Franklin Sq., NY, 1999—. Sch. psychologist Rothman Therapeutic Services, Plainview, NY, 2002—. Grant, Sewanhaka Ctrl. H.S. Dist., 2002—03. Mem.: APA, NASP, NY Assn. of Sch. Psychologists. Avocations: music, travel, theater. Office: H Frank Carey H S 230 Poppy Ave Franklin Square NY 11010

BERGEN, POLLY, actress; b. Bluegrass, Tenn. d. William and Lucy (Lawhorn) Burgin; m. Freddie Fields, Feb. 13, 1956 (div. 1976); children: Kathy, Pamela, Peter. Pres. Polly Bergen Cosmetics, Polly Bergen Jewelry, Polly Bergen Shoes. Author: Fashion and Charm, 1960, Polly's Principles, 1974, I'd Love To, But What'll I Wear, 1977; author, producer for TV: Leave of Absence, 1994; Broadway plays include Champagne Complex, John Murray Andersons' Almanac, First Impression, Plaza Suite, Love Letters, Follies (Best Supporting Actress Tony and Drama Desk nominee), The Vagina Monologues, Cabaret; films include Cape Fear, Move Over Darling, Kisses for My President, At War with the Army, The Stooge, That's My Boy, The Caretakers, A Guide for the Married Man, Making Mr. Right, Cry-Baby, 1990, Dr. Jekyll and Ms. Hyde, When We Were Colored, 1994; performed in one woman shows in Las Vegas, Nev., and Reno; albums: Bergen Sings Morgan, The Party's Over, All Alone By the Telephone, Polly and Her Pop, The Four Seasons of Love, Annie Get Your Gun and Do Re Mi, My Heart Sings, Act One Sing Too; numerous TV appearances including star of The Polly Bergen Show, NBC-TV; other TV appearances include The Helen Morgan Story, 1957 (Emmy award as best actress), To Tell the Truth, The Lightning Field, The Surrogate, For Hope; miniseries include The Winds of War (Emmy nomination), 79 Park Ave, War and Remembrance, 1988 (Emmy nomination); writer, prodr. NBC movie Leave of Absence, 1994. Bd. dirs. Martha Graham Dance Ctr., The Singer Co., Soc. Singers, Calif. Abortion and Reproductive Rights Action League, Show Coalition; hon. canister campaign chairperson Cancer Care, Inc., Nat. Cancer Found.; founder Nat. Bus. Coun. for ERA; mem. Planned Parenthood Fedn., Am. Bd. Advs.; mem. nat. adv. com. NARAL, Hollywood Women's Polit. Com. Recipient Fame award Top Ten in TV, 1957-58, Troupers award Sterling Publs., 1957, Editors and Critics award Radio and TV Daily, 1958, Outstanding Working Woman award Downtown St. Louis, Inc., Golden Plate award Am. Acad. Achievement, 1969, Outstanding Mother's award Nat. Mothers' Day Com., 1984, Best Achievement in New Jewelry Design award, 1986, Cancer Care award, 1989, Woman of Achievement award LWV, 1990, Extraordinary Achievement award Nat. Women's Law Ctr., 1991, Freedom of Choice award Calif. Abortion and Reproductive Rights Action League, 1992; Polly Bergen Cardio-Pulmonary Rsch. Lab., Children's Rsch. Inst. and Hosp., Denver dedicated, 1970. Mem. AFTRA, AGVA, SAG, Actors Equity. Office: 1746 S Britain Rd Southbury CT 06488-3200

BERGER, BARBARA PAULL, social worker, marriage and family therapist; b. St. Louis, June 18, 1955; d. Ted and Florence Ann (Vines) Paull; m. Allan Berger, Dec. 27, 1980 (dec.); children: Melissa Dawn, Tammi Alyse, Jessica Lauren. BS, U. Tex., 1977; MSSW, U. Wis., 1978. Diplomate Am. Bd. Clin. Social Work; lic. social worker, Tex., Ky., Ind.; lic. marriage and family therapist. Clin. social worker Child and Family Svcs., Buffalo, 1980-81, United Cerebral Palsy Assn., St. Louis, 1982-83; clin. social worker/coord. Jewish Family Life Edn. Jewish Family Svc., Dallas, 1984-85, 88-90; instr. Miss. Delta C. C., Greenville, 1991; child and adolescent therapist United Behavioral Systems, Louisville, 1993-94; therapist Inpsych, Louisville, 1994-98, Beacon Behavioral Health Group, Louisville, 1998-2000, Louisville Behavioral Health Sys., 2000—. Mem. NASW, Acad. Cert. Social Workers, Am. Assn. Marriage and Family Therapy, Phi Kappa Phi, Pi Lambda Theta, Omicron Nu. Home: 2719 Avenue Of The Woods Louisville KY 40241-6281 E-mail: bepberger@hotmail.com.

BERGER, BONNIE G. sport psychologist, educator; b. Champaign, Ill., May 20, 1941; d. Bernard G. and Mildred W. Berger; 1 child, Stephen Casher. BS, Wittenberg U., 1962; MA, Columbia U., 1965, EdD, 1972. Tchr. George Rogers Clark Jr. H.S., Springfield, Ohio, 1962-64; supr. phys. edn. Agnes Russell Elem. Sch., N.Y.C., 1964-65; asst. prof. SUNY, Geneseo, 1965-66, Dalhousie U., Halifax, N.S., Can., 1969-71, Bklyn. Coll., 1971-77, assoc. prof., 1978-82, prof., 1982-93, dir. Sport Psychology Lab., dep. chair dept. phys. edn., 1989-93; prof., assoc. dean Sch. Phys. and Health Edn. U. Wyo., Laramie, 1993-96, prof., assoc. dean Coll. Health Scis., 1996-99; prof., dir. Sch. Human Movement, Sport and Leisure Studies, Bowling Green (Ohio) State U., 1999—. Cons. in field. Author: Free Weights for Women, 1984, Foundations of Exercise Psychology, 2002; contbr. chpts. to books, articles to profl. jours. Fellow Assn. for Advancement of Applied Sport Psychology (exec. bd.) Am. Acad. Kinesiology and Phys. Edn.; mem. APA, AAHPERD, Internat. Soc. Sports Psychology, N.Am. Soc. Psychology and Phy. Activity. Home: 640 Pine Valley Dr Bowling Green OH 43402

BERGER, CAROLYN, judge; BA, U. Rochester, 1969; MEd, Boston U., 1971, JD, 1976. Bar: Del. 1976, U.S. Dist. Ct. Del. 1976, U.S. Ct. Appeals (3d cir.) 1981, U.S. Supreme Ct. 1981. Dep. atty. gen. Del. Dept. Justice, Wilmington, 1976-79; assoc. Prickett, Ward, Burt & Sanders, Wilmington, 1979, Skadden, Arps, Slate, Meagher & Flom, Wilmington, 1979-84; vice-chancellor Ct. of Chancery, Wilmington, 1984-94; justice Del. Supreme Ct., 1994—. Mem. ABA, Del. Bar Assn. Office: Carvel State Office Bldg 820 N French St Fl 11 Wilmington DE 19801-3509*

BERGER, DIANNE GWYNNE, family life educator, consultant; b. N.Y.C., Mar. 10, 1950; d. Harold and Mary Bell (Mott) Gwynne; m. Robert Milton Berger, Aug. 25, 1974 (dec. 2001); children: Matthew Robert Gwynne, Daniel Alan Gwynne BS, Cornell U., 1971; MS, Drexel U., 1974; PhD, U. Pa., 1992. Cert. home econs. tchr., sexuality educator, family and consumer sci. educator and family life educator, Pa.; cert. supervision, curriculum and instrn. Tchr. family and consumer scis., sexuality edn. Wallingford-Swarthmore Sch. Dist., 1972—. Cons., Swarthmore, 1986—, Swarthmore Presbyn. Ch., 1995, Elwyn Insts., Media, Pa., 1989-91, Phila. Task Force on Sex Edn., 1991-93. Cons. Trinity Coop. Day Nursery, Swarthmore, 1980-93, Renaissance Edn. Assn., Valley Forge, Pa., 1987-94, A Better Chance, Inc., Swarthmore, 1990-91; mem. sci. bd. Adolescent Wellness and Reproductive Edn. Found. Grantee Impact, Inc., 1990. Mem. NEA, Am. Assn. Family and Consumer Scis. (presenter), Soc. for Sci. Study of Sex (sec. ea. region presenter), Nat. Coun. on Famly Rels., Am. Assn. Sex Educators, Counselors and Therapists (chmn. Delaware Valley sect. 1996-98). Home: 304 Dickinson Ave Swarthmore PA 19081-2001

BERGER, GISELA PORSCH, psychotherapist; b. Milw., Mar. 3, 1962; d. Kurt Wilhelm Bernhardt and Gudrun Margarete (Wolf) Berger; m. Phillip James Townsend, May 20, 1984 (div. June 1993); children: Patrick Bernhardt and Margarethe Josephine. BA, Purdue U., 1984; MEd, The Citadel, Charleston, S.C., 1992; postgrad., U. Md., 1996 . Lic. profl. counselor, S.C., 1996, Va., 2004, Master Addictions Counselor, 1996, Nat. Cert. Counselor, 1996. Clin. counselor Berkeley County Commn. Alcohol and Drug Abuse, Moncks Corner, S.C., 1993-94, Cmty. Control Ctr., Charleston, 1995-96; program dir. Voca Corp., Washington, 1997-98; grad. asst. U. Md., College Park, 1997—2000; clin. counselor No. Va. Family Svcs., Falls Church, 2001—03. Pres. Company Grade Officers' Coun., Charleston AFB, 1986-87; adj. faculty Marymount U., Arlington, Va., 1999—. Capt. USAF, 1984-90. Mem. ACA, Nat. Assn. Alcoholism and Drug Addiction, Mensa (program chair 1995-96), Alpha Tau Chi (pres. 1991-93). Presbyterian. Avocations: mystery novels, crossword puzzles, walking, dogs. Office: Marymount U 2807 N Glebe Rd Arlington VA 22207 Office Phone: 703-284-1620.

BERGER, JOYCE MURIEL, foundation executive, author, editor; b. N.Y.C., Oct. 20, 1924; d. Samuel and Daisy (Lichtenstein) Zeitlin; m. Arthur Seymour Berger, Feb. 11, 1946. BA magna cum laude, N.Y. U., 1944, MA, 1946. Editor Theta Psychical Rsch. Found., Durham, N.C., 1978-80; sec.-treas., libr. Survival Rsch. Found., administr Internat. Inst. for Study of Death, Miami, Fla., 1980—. Convener confs. Internat. Inst. Study of Death, Miami, 1985, 87, Survival Rsch. Found., Miami, 1986. Co-author: Reincarnation Fact or Fable, 1991, Encyclopedia of Parapsychology, 1991, Fear of the Unknown, 1995; co-editor: To Die or Not to Die, 1990, Perspectives on Death and Dying, 1989; lectr. and seminar coord. in field. Right to Die conf. grantee Fla. Endowment of the Humanities, Tampa, 1987. Mem. Am. Soc. for Psychical Rsch., Soc. for Psychical Rsch., The Book Group of South Fla., Phi Beta Kappa. Avocations: bridge, tennis, travel, recording for the blind.

BERGER, MIRIAM ROSKIN, creative arts therapy director, educator, therapist; b. N.Y.C., Dec. 9, 1934; d. Israel and Florence Roskin; m. Meir Berger, July 16, 1967; 1 child, Jonathan Israel. Student, Barnard Coll., 1952-53; BA, Bard Coll., 1956; postgrad., CCNY, 1956-58; Dr. Arts, NYU, 1998. Alumni dir. Bard Coll., Annandale-on-Hudson, N.Y., 1958-59; dance therapist Manhattan Psychiatric Ctr., N.Y.C., 1959-60; performer, educator Jean Erdman Theater of Dance, N.Y.C., 1959-62; dir. adult program Hebrew Arts Sch., N.Y.C., 1981; faculty Dance Notation Bur., N.Y.C., 1974-75, 77; asst. prof. dance therapy program NYU, 1975—, acting dir. dance therapy program, 1991, dir. dance edn. program, 1993—2002; dir. creative arts therapies Bronx Psychiatric Ctr., N.Y.C., 1970-90. Workshop leader in field; tchr., Republic of Korea, 1999—2003, Sweden, 1999—2003, Poland, 1999—2003, Czech Republic, 1999—2003, Greece, 1999—2003, Netherlands, 1999—2003; keynote spkr. Israel Dance Conf., 2004. Prodr. off-Broadway The Coach with the Six Insides, 1962-63; author, prodr. Non-Verbal Group Process, 1978; co-editor Am. Jour. Dance Therapy, 1991-94; led dance therapy session Senate hearing on Aging, 1992; contbr. articles to profl. jours.; editl. bd. Arts in Psychotherapy, Jour. Dance Edn. Chair Nat. Coalition of Creative Arts Therapies Assns., 2002—; bd. dirs. Theater Open Eye, 1978—82, v.p. bd. trustees, 1982—89, pres., 1989—94. Recipient NYU scholarship, 1981, Best Paper award Med Art World congress on Arts and Medicine, 1992. Mem.: Acad. Registered Dance Therapists, Am. Dance Therapy Assn. (founder, bd. dirs. 1967—76, v.p. 1974—76, 1992, credential com. 1976, 1982, keynote speaker at nat. conf. 1991, pres. 1994—98, Marian Chace award 2002), Dance Libr. Israel (v.p.). E-mail: miriam.berger@nyu.edu.

BERGER, MOLLY, historian, educator; b. Cleve., Aug. 24, 1948; d. Milton and Minnie Sevel Winger; m. Stanley M. Berger, July 27, 1969 (div. Dec. 2001); children: Martha Kay, Carrie Rae, Brian Lewis, Andrew Michael. BS Edn., Miami U., 1969; MA, John Carroll U., 1984; PhD, Case Western Res. U., 1997. Lectr. Weatherhead Sch. Mgmt., Cleve., 1999—2001; instr. dept. history Case Western Res. U., Cleve., 2001—, asst. dean Coll. Arts and Scis., 2001—. Vis. asst. prof. Case Western Res. U., Cleve., 1997—98, 1999—2000, Oberlin Coll., 1999; contractor, writer Nat. Park Svc., Boston, 1998—99. Recipient Robinson prize, Soc. for History Tech., 1992; fellow, Smithsonian Inst., Washington, 1993, Am. Antiquarian Soc., Worcester, Mass., 1994. Mem.: Ohio Acad. History, Soc. History of Tech., Am. Hist. Assn., Orgn. Am. Historians, Am. Studies Assn. Office: Case Western Res U Dept History Cleveland OH 44106

BERGER, PATRICIA WILSON, retired librarian; b. Washington, May 1, 1926; d. Thomas Decatur Wood and Nina Hughes; m. George Hamilton Combs Berger, May 20, 1970. BA, George Washington U., 1965; MSLS, Cath. U. Am., 1974. Asst. libr., ops. rsch. office Johns Hopkins U., Chevy Chase, Md., 1949-51, asst. ops. rsch. analyst, 1951-54; head libr. CEIR, Washington, 1954-55; chief, tech. info. and libr. svcs. Human Rels. Area Files Yale U., Washington, 1955-57; tech. info. officer, chief libr. Inst. for Def. Analyses, Washington, Arlington, Va., 1957-67; dir. tech. info. and security programs Lambda Corp., Arlington, 1967-71; chief libr. U.S. Commn. on Govt. Procurement, Washington, 1971-72; head gen. ref. br., later dep. chief libr. U.S. Patent and Trademark Office, Arlington, 1972-76; chief libr. divsn. U.S. Nat. Bur. Stds., Gaithersburg, Md., 1976-78; dir. info. resources and svcs. U.S. EPA, Washington, 1978-79; chief libr. and info. svcs. U.S. Nat. Bur. Stds., Washington, 1979-83, chief info. resources and svcs., 1983-91, dir. Office Info. Svcs., 1990-92; ret., 1992. Cons. libr., info. and security matters, 1965-95; del. 1st White House Conf. on Librs. and Info. Svc., 1979; bd. dirs. Universal Serial and Book Exch., 1983-84; chmn. Nat. Info. Std. Orgn., Am. Nat. Std. Inst., 1981-83, elected Nat. Info. Std. Orgn. fellow, 1989. Mem. editl. bd. Sci. and Tech. Librs., 1979-92; contbr. articles to profl. jours. Apptd. by Govs. of Va. to Libr. of Va. Bd., 1986-90, 90-95, vice chair, 1992-93, chair, 1993-94; bd. dirs. Va. Commn. for Reenactment of Battle First Bull Run, 1960-61; bd. dirs. Freedom to Read Found., 1988-90, 92-94; apptd. U.S. Postmaster Gen's. Commn. Lit., 1990-92. Recipient Internat. Women's Yr. award Dept. Commerce, 1976, Bronze medal, 1980, Silver medal, 1984, Outstanding Adminstrv. Mgr. award, 1985, H.W. Wilson Pub. Co. award, 1980, Disting. Svc. award U. Richmond Librs., 1989, Cert. of Recognition, Gov. State of Va., 1989, Resolution of Esteem, Va. State Libr. Bd., 1988, award Coun. Libr. and Media Technicians, 1989; named Outstanding Alumnus in Libr. and Info. Sci., Cath. U. Am., 1988, 20th Century Nat. Libr. Adv., Am. Libr. Assn./Am. Libr. Trustees Assn. Nat. Adv. Honor Roll, 2000; Cert. of appreciation Martin Luther King Jr. Fed. Holiday Commission, 1996. Mem AAAS (elected assn. fellow 1992), Spl. Librs. Assn. (exec. bd. Washington chpt. 1970-71, pres. Washington chpt. 1977, elected assn. fellow 1987), ALA (coun. 1984-88, exec. bd. 1986-90, v.p./pres.-elect 1988-89, pres. 1989-90, immediate past pres. 1990-91), D.C. Libr. Assn. (Ainsworth Rand Spofford Pres.'s award 2001), Fed. Librs. Roundtable (pres. 1982-83, Achievement award 1985), Cosmos Club, Chi Omega, Beta Phi Mu. Episcopalian. Home: 105 Queen St Alexandria VA 22314-2610 E-mail: pberger@his.com.

BERGER, PEARL, library director; b. N.Y.C., Nov. 30, 1943; d. Baruch Mayer and Tova (Brandwein) Rabinowitz; m. David Berger, June 14, 1965; children: Miriam Esther, Yitzhak, Gedalyah Aaron. B in Religious Edn., Yeshiva U.; BA, Bklyn. Coll., 1965; MLS, Columbia U., 1974. Diploma tchr. Hebrew. Tchr. Hebrew & Jewish studies Yeshiva of Crown Heights, Bklyn., 1963-65; asst. libr. YIVO Inst. Jewish Rsch., N.Y.C., 1976-80; head tech. svcs. Librs. Yeshiva U., N.Y.C., 1980-81, head libr. Pollack Libr., 1981-83, head libr. main ctr. librs., 1983-85, dean librs., 1985—. V.p. Coun. Archives and Rsch. Librs. in Jewish Studies, 1984-86, pres. 1986-89. Assoc. editor: Jour. Judaica Librarianship, 1983—; first v.p. Met. Reference and Rsch. Libr. Orgn., 1996-99; contbr. articles to profl. jours.; compiler catalog Guide to Yiddish Classics on Microfiche, 1980. Recipient Benjamin Gottesman Libr. Chair Yeshiva U. Mem. Am. Libr. Assn., Metro. Ref. Rsch. Libr. Agency (trustee 1991—, sec. 1993-99, 1st v.p. 1996-99), Assn. Jewish Librs. (rsch., spl. librs. divsn., v.p. 1982-84, pres. 1984-86, voting rep. Nat. Info. Stds. Orgn. 1995-2000, v.p., pres.-elect 2000-01, pres. 2002-04). Office: Yeshiva U Dean of Libraries 500 W 185th St New York NY 10033-3299

BERGER, ROSIE M. state representative; b. Monroe, Wis., Jan. 7, 1955; m. Bob Berger. Student, U. Wis., 1976, Sheridan Coll., 1994; BS, Regis U., 1996. Agt., owner Brittain World Travel, 1978—92; dist. mgr. Bus. Travel Svcs., 1992—95; bus. mgr. Four Winds Ministries, 1997—98; event coord. Polo Ranch Cutting Classic, 1999—2001; state rep. dist. 51 Wyo. State Legis., Cheyenne, 2003—. Location scout Wyo. Film Commn., 1986—2002; commr. Wyo. Parks and Cultural Resources Commn., 1995—2001; bd. dirs. Sheridan Conv. and Visitor Bur., 1993—96. Dir. Dog & Cat Shelter, Reaching Higher Sch. Bd.; pres. Wyo. Theatre, 1991—92. Mem.: Sheridan C. of C. (pres. 1986—87). Republican. Home: PO Box 275 Big Horn WY 82833 Office: Capitol Bldg Wyo State Legis Cheyenne WY 82002

BERGER, TINA, hotel executive; Student, N.Y.C. C.C. Restaurant and Hospitality Sch., Mich. State U., Oakland U., Rochester, Mich. Cert. hotel adminstr. Hotel ops. cons., Nashville; asst. exec. housekeeper, asst. reservations mgr., reservations mgr. Hyatt on Union Sq., San Francisco, 1978—83; with The Sanderling, Duck, NC, 1983—, dir. ops., 1983—93, gen. mgr., 1993—. Pres., founder Parents for Advancement of Gifted Edn., 1992—93. Mem.: Outer Banks Hotel Assn. (bd. dirs. 1994—), Dare County C. of C. (bd. dirs. 1994—98), NC Restaurant Assn., So. Innkeepers, Internat. Resort Mgrs. Assn. (bd. dirs., founding bd. 2001—), NC Hotel Motel Assn. (bd. dirs. 1993—, NC Gen. Mgr. of Yr. 1997). Office: 1461 Duck Rd Kitty Hawk NC 27949

BERGER, VICKI, state representative; BA, U. Wyo., 1974. Owner West Salem Lazerquick; project mgr. regional mfg. firm; mem. Oreg. Ho. of Reps., 2002—. Mem. sch. bd., Salem-Keizer, 1988—92. Republican. Office: 900 Court St North East H-488 Salem OR 97301

BERGER-GRANET, NANCY SUE, nursing researcher; b. N.Y.C., Apr. 22, 1957; d. Morris H. and Marilyn (Resnick) B.; 1 child. BSN, U. Colo., 1988. RN 1977. Staff nurse intensive care Hosp. U. Pa., Phila., 1981-84; clin. rsch. nurse U. Colo. Health Sci. Ctr., Denver, 1985-90, VA Med. Ctr., Denver, 1989-90; dir. clin. rsch. U. Colo. Health Sci. Ctr., 1990-94; clin. rsch. assoc. Bayer Corp., Berkeley, Calif., 1994-97; clin. rsch. mgr. Cygnus, Inc., Redwood City, Calif., 1997—98, Roche Palo Alto, Calif., 1998—. Contbr. articles to profl. jours. Mem. Am. Assn. Urological Assocs., Assocs. Clin. Pharm., Sigma Theta Tau. Democrat. Jewish. Avocations: hiking, reading, cooking. Office: Roche Palo Alto 3431 Hillview Ave Palo Alto CA 94063

BERGER-GREENSTEIN, JORI ANN, psychologist; b. Vincennes, Ind., Apr. 3, 1970; d. Diane Lynn and Michael Berger; m. David Mark Greenstein, Apr. 27, 2003. BS in psychology, Bradley U., 1988—92; MA in clin. psychology, PhD in clin. psychology, Bowling Green State U., 1993—99. Lic. Clinical Psychologist Mass., 2002. Psychologist Boston Med. Ctr./BUSM, 1999—. Vol. Behavioral and Social Sci. Vol. Program, Boston, 1997—; instr. Boston U. Sch. of Medicine, 2002—. Mem.: APA, Assn. for the Advancement of Behavior Therapy, Soc. for Behavioral Medicine. Jewish. Avocations: cooking, reading, travel. Office: Boston University Sch of Medicine One Boston Med Ctr PlDowling 7N Boston MA 02176 E-mail: jori.berger@bmc.org.

BERGER-KRAEMER, NANCY, speech and language pathologist, artist; b. N.Y.C., Aug. 15, 1941; d. George G. and Ruth (Kirsch) Berger; m. Aaron Kraemer, July 10, 1966; children: Lea, Steven. BA, Adelphi U., 1963; MS in Edn., Queens Coll., 1968; cert. clin. competency in speech pathology. Lic. and cert. speech and lang. pathologist, N.Y., N.J.; permanent cert. speech and hearing for handicapped, N.Y. Speech therapist Dist. # 24 Sch. Sys., Valley Stream, L.I., 1962-64; dir. speech and lang., hearing/speech pathologist Port Chester Sch. Dist., Rye, N.Y., 1965-66; speech and lang. pathologist Roselle Park (N.J.) Sch. Sys., 1966-67, Willis Sch. for Educationally Handicapped, Plainfield, N.J., 1967-68, St. Barnabas Med. Ctr., West Orange, N.J., 1971-97; pvt. practice Maplewood, N.J., 1968—, Andover Twp., 1998—. Lectr., spkr. in field; cons. in field. One-woman shows include Romano Gallery, Blairstown, N.J., 2001, exhibited in group shows at N.J. Ctr. Visual Arts, Summit, City Without Walls, Newark, Bergen Mus., Jersey City Mus., Trenton City Mus., N.J. State Mus., Montclair Art Mus., Noyes Mus., Phoenix Gallery, Veridian Gallery, Newark Mus., Pindar Gallery, Gallerie Ambiente, Germany, William Carlos Williams Ctr. Arts, N.J., San Diego Art Inst., Stedman Art Gallery, New Brunswick, N.J., Fordham U.-Lowenstein Libr., N.Y.C., Johnson & Johnson, N.J., Cali Assocs., Bellemead Devel. Corp., AT&T, Nabisco Brands, Beneficial Ins. Co., Prudential Ins. Co., Pleiades Gallery, N.Y.C., Art Ctr. No. N.J., Art Assn. Harrisburg, Pa., Stamford Art Assn., Conn., Princeton (N.J.) Art assn., Bucknell U. Ctr. Gallery, Art Alliance 13th Ann. N.J. Statewide Exhibit, Skylands Ann. Art Exhibit, Sussex Arts, Heritage Coun., Sparta, N.J., Ceres Gallery, N.Y.C., Romano Gallery, Blair Acad., Blairstown, N.J., Gaelen Gallery, Whippany, N.J., Sussex C.C., Newton, NJ, Faith Ringgold Salon Exhibit, Englewood, NJ, ACA Gallery, N.Y.C., Anyone Can Fly Found., Inc., Hoyt Inst. Fine Arts, New Castle, Pa., others.

Mem. Am. Speech Lang. Hearing Assn., Auditory Verbal Internat. (charter, lectr. 1975-2000), Alexander Graham Bell Assn., N.J. Speech and Hearing Assn., Sussex Co. Judicial Ctr., Newton, N.J.

BERGERON, EARLEEN FOURNET, actress, b. New Orleans, Aug. 7, 1938; d. Earl Joseph Fournet and Lucia (Cuccia) Walsworth; m. James Ronald Bergeron Jr., June 17, 1961; children: Blanche Theresa, Michele Yvette, James Ronald Jr. B in Social Sci. in Theatre and Speech, Loyola U., 1960. Actor: (plays) The Secret Affairs of Mildred Wilde, 1977, The Boyfriend, 1977, The Shadow Box, 1979, California Suite, 1980, Hay Fever, 1985, Brighton Beach, 1986, Beyond Therapy, 1987, Steel Magnolias, 1988, 1989, Nunsense, 1990, Broadway Bound, 1991, The Women, 1993, Nunsense II, 1995, Stomping Grounds, 1995, 1996, Angels in America, Part I: Millenium Approaches, Part II: Perestroika, 1997, Spareribs, 1998, Come Back Little Sheba, 1999, The Cripple of Inishmann, 2001, Ancestral Voices, 2002, Our Town, 2002, (comml.) Goodwill, 1988, Schumpert Medical Center, 1991, Cunningham and McDonald, Plastic Surgeons, 1991, JB Cable Ads, 1995, Pierre Bossier Mall, 1996; (films) Man in the Moon, 1990; (TV series) Rescue 911, 1991. Bd. dirs. Port Players, Shreveport, La.; assoc. mem. Co. Repertory Theatre, Inc., Project Shakespeare in Schs.; active Shreveport Med. Aux., 1968—97, mem. exec. bd., 1976—78; mem. Shreveport Opera Guild, 1972—97; area leader fund dr. Am. Cancer Soc., Shreveport, 1985—89. Named one of Outstanding Team Capts., United Way Fund, 1969. Mem.: Shreveport Little Theatre Guild (bd. dirs. 1985—86), Strand Theatre, Majorie Lyons Playhouse, Shreveport Little Theatre. Roman Catholic.

BERGERSON, NANCY DAHL, life and health underwriter, paralegal; b. Waco, Tex., Sept. 18, 1954; d. Howard Edward and Gladys Marie (Haynes) Dahl; children: Russell Edward Johnston, Dennis Aaron Johnston. Student, U. So. Maine, Portland; cert., Nat. Acad. Paralegal Studies, 1991. Exec. sec. to state court adminstr. State of Maine, Portland, Maine, 1993-95; risk mgmt. technician UNUM Corp., Portland, Maine, 1996-99; life and health ins. underwriter, 1999—. Vol. Maine Audubon Soc. Mem. Greenpeace. Avocations: camping, winter sports. Home and Office: 302 Plaza Dr Apt 5 Dover NH 03820-2446

BERGESON, TERESA, school system administrator; b. Mass. BA in English, Emmanuel Coll., Boston, 1964; M in Counseling and Guidance, Western Mich. U., 1969; PhD in Edn., U. Wash. Tchr., j.h. sch. guidance counselor, Mass., Alaska, Wash.; exec. dir. Ctrl. Kitsap Sch. Dist., 1989-92, Wash. State Commn. on Learning, 1993-95; state supt. pub. instrn. Olympia, Wash., 1997—. V.p. Wash. Edn. Assn., 1981, pres., 1985—89. Mem.: Wash. Edn. Assn. (v.p. 1981—85, pres. 1985—89). Office: PO Box 47200 Olympia WA 98504-7200 Fax: 360-753-6712.

BERGFORS, CONSTANCE MARIE, artist, educator; b. Quincy, Mass., Feb. 8, 1931; d. Fred Eric Bergfors and H. Margaret Sandberg; m. Andrew E. Rice, Dec. 2, 1972; children: Stefan Andrej, Brandt Eric. BA, Smith Coll., 1952; postgrad., Concoran Coll. Art, Washington, D.C., 1956, postgrad., 1957, postgrad., 1981, postgrad., 1982, Acad. di Belle Arte, Palermo, Naples, and Rome, Italy, 1957—60. Dir. Cabin John Visual Studies Workshop, Cabin John, Md., 1970—75; founding mem. Gallery 10, Washington, 1974—78; tchr. sculpture dept. Corcoran Sch. Art, Washington, 1991—95. Judge art scholarships for h.s. srs., 1981—2001. One-woman shows include Peabody, Rivlin, Gore, Caldouhos and Lambert Law Firm, Washington, 1970, Gallery Modern Art, Fredericksburg, Va., 1974, Gallery 10, Washington, 1974, 1976, U.S. Govt., 1978, Langley, Va., 1985, Galleria Editalia, Rome, 1980, Strathmore Hall Arts Ctr., Rockville, Md., 1984, Capital Ctr. Gallery, Landover, Md., 1984, Plum Gallery, Kensington, Md., 1986, 1988, 1991, Cmty. Gallery Lancaster, Pa., 1988, South Shore Art Ctr., Cohasset, Mass., 1988, Urban Inst., Washington, 1996, Workshop Gallery, Cabin John, Md., 1997, Temple Sinai Commn., Washington, 1998, Renwick Alliance visits the Workshop Gallery, 2000, Arts Coun. of Montgomery County, 2000, exhibited in group shows at 14 Sculptors Gallery, N.Y.C., 1977, Art Barn, Washington, 1983, Georgetown Ct. Artists' Space, 1984, Arlington Arts Ctr., Va., 1984, 1985, Three Rivers Arts Festival, Pitts., 1984, Sculpture 84 Washington Square, Washington, 1984, Washington Women's Art Ctr., 1985, Audubon Naturalist Soc. Sculpture Show, Washington, 1985, Brandeis Coll. Art Exhibit, Rockville, Md., 1986, D.C. Sculpture Now Show Summer Sch. Mus., Washington, 1989, Bldg. Mus., 1989—90, Montgomery County Art Exhibit, Rockville, Md., 1990, Internat. Sculpture 90 Montgomery Coll., 1990, Washington Sculpture Group Show Summer Sch., Washington, 1990, Mus. Nat. de Belas Artes, Rio de Janeiro, 1991—92, Oxon Hill Manor Found., Oxon Hill, Md., 1992, Fairfax County Coun. Arts Northern Va. C.C., Annandale, Va., 1992, Washington Sculptors Group Exhbn., Bethesda, Md., 1992, Fairfax County Coun. Arts Northern Va. C.C., 1993, The Cutting Edge: 20 Years at Gallery 10, Washington, 1994, Corcoran Sch. Art Washington Square, 1994, Washington Sculptors Group Show Washington Square, 1995, Arts 901, 1996, Bldg. Mus., 1999—2000, Represented in permanent collections. Recipient Mary Lay Thom award for Outstanding Achievement in Sculpture, Washington, 1983, Montgomery County Purchase prize, Exec. Office Bldg, Rockville, Md., 1987, 3rd prize, Montgomery County Art Exhibit, Strathmore Hall, Rockville, Md., 1990. Avocations: travel, architecture, archaeology. Home: 6517 80th St Cabin John MD 20818-1208

BERGGREN-MOILANEN, BONNIE LEE, education educator; b. L'Anse, Mich., June 2, 1940; d. Alvin Carl and Emma Leola (Wandell) Lydman; m. Grant Lorns Berggren, Jr., Aug. 22, 1959; children: Grant Victor Berggren, Rex Alvin Berggren, Konnie Kay Berggren; m. Glenn Moilanen, 2003. BA, U. Hawaii, 1961; MA, Ea. Mich. U., 1988; MA in Ednl. Adminstrn., No. Mich. U., 1991. Tchr. home econs. Baraga (Mich.) Twp. Schs., 1960-61, L'Anse Twp. Schs., 1963-65, Spencerport (N.Y.) Cen. Schs., 1979-84; presch. tchr. NCA Sch., Cmty. Action Agy., Hermansville, Mich., 1971-73; circulation supr. Spring Arbor (Mich.) Coll. Libr., 1985-87; adj. prof., supr. student tchrs. No. Mich. U., Marquette, 1989—96; co-owner, co-mgr. Menominee (Mich.) Floral, 1993-96; curriculum and tng. coord./spl. project coord. Campus Crusade for Christ, Children of The World Dept., San Clemente, Calif., 1997-2000; sr. staff Internat. Student Resources Campus Crusade for Christ, Madison, Wis., 2000—. Tchr. trainer Negaunee Pub. Schs., Negaunee, Mich., 1988—90; leader workshop Republic-Michigamme Schs., Republic, Mich., 1989—90; mem. evaluation team Marquette Pub. Schs., 1991; mem. tchr. edn. adv. coun. No. Mich. U., Marquette, 1991—96, mem. Hoppes award com., 1990—92, mem. pers. com., 1992. Libr. bd. Republic-Michigamme Schs., 1988—91; spkr. Christian Women's Club, 1989—90; bd. regents Liberty U., 1990—91; active Operation Carelift to Russia, 1997, Operation Sunrise to Africa, 2002. Fellow: Roberts Wesleyan Coll.; mem.: AAUW, DAV Aux. (life; Mich. historian 1975), AAUP, Concerned Women Am., U. Hawaii Alumni Assn., Ea. Mich U. Alumni Assn., Univ. Women No. Mich. U., Phi Delta Kappa, Phi Kappa Phi. Baptist. Avocations: reading, travel, writing, crafts. Home: HC 2 Box 772A Lanse MI 49946-9517 E-mail: bonnielb@chorus.net.

BERGLIN, LINDA, state legislator; b. Oakland, Calif., Oct. 19, 1944; d. Freeman and Norma (Lund) Waterman; m. Glenn Sampson; 1 child, Maria. BFA, Mpls. Coll. Art and Design. Mem. Minn. Ho. of Reps., St. Paul, 1972-80, Minn. Senate, St. Paul, 1980—. Chmn. Health and Human Svcs. Com.; mem. senate judiciary com., family svcs. com., tax and tax laws com., others; mem. various legis. commns. including Econ. Status of Women, Healthcare Oversight Commn.; U.S. rep. U.S.-Japan Legis. Exch. Program; seminar participant health care reform U.S.-Sweden, also Austria, 1981; studied health care reform Great Britain, 1992; rep. Nat. Coun. State Legislatures Women's Network Del., Korea, 1989. Bd. dirs. Freedom House, Better Jobs for Women, founding mem., Cornerhouse, Whittier Alliance, founding, St. Stephen's Guild Hall, Orgnl. Industrialization Ctrs., Children's Theater; mem. scattered site housing com. Powderhorn Cmty. Coun., Food and Land Resource Ctr., Joint Urban Mission Project, Phillips Neighborhood Improvement Assn., numerous others; trustee Inst. Arts. Recipient Pub. Citizen of Yr. award Nat. Assn. Social Workers, 1980, Nursing Home Residents Adv. Coun. award, 1983, NAACP Cert. Appreciation, 1984, Common Space Mutual Housing award, 1984, Award of Excellence Minn. Dept. Human Svcs., 1986, Leadership award Hmong Cult. Ctr. Greater Mpls. C. of C., 1986, Children's Champion award Children's Defense Fund, 1987, March of Dimes award, 1988, Child Health Care citation Am. Acad. Pediatrics and Children's Defense Fund, 1988, Health Span Coalition award, 1989, Outstanding Achievement award Med. Alley, 1989, Minn. Psychol. Assn. award, 1990, Disting. Svc. award Minn. Assn. Edn. Young Children, 1991, Cert. of Merit Minn. Women's Consortium, 1992, Minn. Assn. Cmty. Mental Health Programs, Inc., 1993, others; named Outstanding Woman of Yr. YWCA, 1980, Legislator of Yr. ARC, 1989, Pub. Official of Yr. Minn. Homes for the Aging, 1991, many other honors. Mem. Dem.-Farmer-Labor Party. Office: Minn Senate 309 State Capitol 75 Constitution Ave Saint Paul MN 55155-1606

BERGMAN, ANNE NEWBERRY, civic leader; b. Weatherford, Tex., Mar. 12, 1925; d. William Douglas and Mary (Hunter) Newberry; m. Robert David Bergman, Aug. 17, 1947; children: Elizabeth Anne Bozzell, John David, William Robert. BA, Trinity U., San Antonio, 1945; postgrad., UCLA, 1946-47. Councilperson City of Weatherford, 1986-91, mayor pro tem, 1990-91; pres. Weatherford Libr. Found., 1987-97, bd. dirs., 1987—. Mem. heritage gallery com. Weatherford Pub. Libr. (Mary Martin collection), 1993-98. Founder Hist. Home Tour, Weatherford, 1972; co-chair Spring Festival Bd., 1976, Weatherford Planning and Zoning Commn., 1980—85; fundraising chair Weatherford Libr. Found., 1985—86; chair Tex. State Rev. Com. Cmty. Devel. Block Grants, 1987—91; pres. Tex. Fedn. Rep. Women, 1975—77; del.. Nat. Rep. Conv., 1988; pres. Episcopal Churchwomen's Cabinet, Diocese of Ft. Worth, 1999—2001; del. Episcopal Ch. Women Triennial, Episcopal Ch. U.S.A., 1997, 2000. Named Outstanding Rep. Woman, Tex. Fedn. Rep. Women, 1981. Mem. Parker County Rep. Women, DAR (Weatherford chpt.), Weatherford C. of C. (Outstanding Citizen of the Yr. 1988), Friends of Weatherford Pub. Libr. (life, charter pres. 1959-61, pres. 1973-74). Avocations: sailing, bridge. Home: 609 W Josephine St Weatherford TX 76086-4055

BERGMAN, JANET EISENSTEIN, food industry executive; b. N.Y., Jan. 28, 1959; d. T. Donald and Ellen (Roob) Eisenstein; m. David J. Bergman, July 14, 1985; 1 child, Jennifer Sarah. BA, Yale U., New Haven, Conn., 1981; MBA, Harvard U., Boston, 1985. Analyst asst. v.p. Putman Mgmt. Co., Boston, 1985-88; corp. v.p. Sara Lee Corp., Chgo., 1989—93, exec. dir., 1988—89, v.p., investor relations and corp. affairs, 1993—2001, sr. v.p., investor relations and corp. affairs, 2001—. Mem. Charted Finl. Analyst., Econ. Club (Chgo.). Avocations: reading, cooking.

BERGMAN, MARILYN KEITH, lyricist, writer; b. Bklyn. d. Albert A. and Edith (Arkin) Katz; m. Alan Bergman, Feb. 9, 1958; 1 child, Julie Rachel. BA, NYU; MusD (hon.), Berklee Coll. Music, 1995, Trinity Coll., 1997. Lyricist, collaborator (with Alan Bergman) (numerous pop, theatrical and film score songs, TV themes) Bracken's World, 1969—70, The Sandy Duncan Show, 1972, Maude, 1972—78, Good Times, 1974—79, The Nancy Walker Show, 1976, The Dumplings, 1976, Alice, 1976—82, In the Heat of the Night, 1988—94, Brooklyn Bridge, 1991—93, The Powers That Be, 1993, TV film lyrics The Hands of Time (from Brian's Song), 1971, Queen of the Stardust Ballroom, 1975 (Emmy award for best dramatic underscore and best musical material, 1975, score only), Sybil, 1976 (Emmy award for best dramatic underscore 1976, 1976), Too Many Springs (from Hollow Image), 1979, theatrical scores Something More, 1964, Ballroom, 1978 (Grammy award nominee for best cast show album, 1979), The Lady and the Clarinet, 1980, feature film songs The Marriage Go-Round, from The Marriage Go-Round, 1960, Any Wednesday, from Any Wednesday, 1966, Make Me Rainbows, from Fitzwilly, 1967, (score) In the Heat of the Night, 1967, The Windmills of Your Mind, from the Thomas Crown Affair, 1968 (Acad. award for best song, 1968, Golden Globe award best original song, 1969), His Eyes, Her Eyes, from The Thomas Crown Affair, 1968, You Must Believe in Spring, from Young Girls of Rochefort, 1968, Maybe Tomorrow, from John and Mary, 1969, Tomorrow Is My Friend, from Gaily, Gaily, 1969, There's Enough to Go Around, 1969, A Smile, A Mem'ry and an Extra Shirt, from A Man Called Gannon, 1969, Sugar in the Rain, from Stiletto, 1969, What Are You Doing the Rest of You Life?, from The Happy Ending, 1969 (Acad. award nominee for best song, 1969), I Was Born in Love With You, from Wuthering Heights, 1970, Sweet Gingerbread Man, from The Magic Garden of Stanley Sweetheart, 1970, Nobody Knows, 1970, Move, from Move, 1970, Pieces of Dreams (Little Boy Lost), from Pieces of Dreams, 1970 (Academy award nominee for best song, 1970), The Costume Ball, from Doctors' Wives, 1971, All His Children, from Sometimes a Great Notion, 1971 (Acad. award nominee for best song, 1971), Rain Falls Anywhere It Wants To, from the African Elephant, 1971, The Summer Knows, from Summer of '42, 1971 (Grammy award nominee for song of the year 1972, 1972), A Face in the Crowd, from Le Mans, 1971, Marmalade, Molasses and Honey, from The Life and Times of Judge Roy Bean, 1972 (Acad. award nominee for best song, 1972), Love's the Only Game in Town, from Pete and Tillie, 1972, Molly and Lawless John, 1972, The Way We Were, from The Way We Were, 1973 (Grammy award for song of the year, 1973, Acad. award for best song, 1973, Golden Globe award for best original song, 1974, Grammy award for best original score, 1974), Breezy's Song, from Breezy, 1973, In Every Corner of the World, from Forty Carats, 1973, Summer Wishes, Winter Dreams, from Summer Wishes, Winter Dreams, 1973, Easy Baby, from 99 and 44/100%, 1974, There'll Be Time, from Ode to Billy Joe, 1975, Evening Sun, Morning Moon, from The Yakuza, 1975, I Believe in Love, from A Star is Born, 1976 (Grammy award nomination best original score, 1977), I'm Harry, I'm Walter, from Harry and Walter Go to New York, 1976, Hello and Goodbye, from Noon to Three, 1976, Bobby Deerfield, from Bobby Deerfield, 1977, The Last Time I Felt Like This, from Same Time Next Year, 1978 (Acad. award nominee for best song, 1978), The One and Only, from The One and Only, 1978, There's Something Funny Goin' On, from ...And Justice For All, 1979, I'll Never Say Goodbye, from The Promise, 1979 (Acad. award nominee for best song, 1979), Where Do You Catch the Bus for Tomorrow, from A Change of Seasons, 1980, Ask Me No Questions, from Back Roads, 1981, How Do You Keep the Music Playing?, from Best Friends, 1982 (Acad. award nominee for best song, 1982), Think About Love, 1982, Comin' Home to You, from Author! Author!, 1982, Tootsie, from Tootsie, 1982, It Might Be You, 1982 (Acad. award nominee for best song, 1982, Grammy award nominee for best original score, 1983), If We Were in Love, from Yes, Giorgio, 1982 (Acad. award nominee for best song, 1982), Never Say Never Again, from Never Say Never again, 1983, Papa, Can You Hear Me?, from Yentl, 1983 (Academy award nomination best song, 1983), The Way He Makes Me Feel, 1983 (Acad. award nominee for best song, 1983), Will Someone Ever Look at Me That Way?, 1983 (Acad. award best original score and Grammy award nomination for best original score, 1984, Acad. award nominee for best original song, 1983), Yentl, 1983 (Acad. award for best original score, 1983), Little Boys, from The Man Who Loved Women, 1983, Something New in My Life, from Mickey and Maude, 1984, The Music of Goodbye, from Out of Africa, 1985, I Know the Feeling, from The January Man, 1989, The Girl Who Used to Be Me, from Shirley Valentine, 1989 (Acad. award nominee for best song, 1989, Golden Globe nominee for best original song, 1990, Grammy award nominee, 1990), Welcome Home, from Welcome Home, 1989, Most of All You, from Major League, 1989, Dreamland, from For the Boys, 1991, Places That Belong to You, from The Prince of Tides, 1991, It's All There, from Switch, 1991, Moonlight, from Sabrina, 1995 (Acad. award nominee for best original song, 1996, Golden Globe nominee, Grammy nominee), The Best of Friends, from Bogus, 1996, Love is Where You Are, from At First Sight, pop songs You Don't Bring Me Flowers, 1978 (Grammy award nominee for song of the year, 1978), In the Heat of the Night, The Summer Knows, Nice 'N' Easy (Grammy award nominee for song of the year, 1960), Someone in the Dark, L.A. Is My Lady, After the Rain, I Was Born in Love With You, That Face, Look Around, I Love to Dance Like They Used to Dance, What Matters Most, One Day, A Child Is Born, Sleep Warm, Sentimental Baby, Live It Up, If I Close My Eyes, Yellow Bird, Like a Lover, Where Do You Start?, On My Way to You, Ordinary Miracles (Cable Ace award and Emmy award for best original song), A Ticket to Dream (Emmy Awd. for best song), albums Never Be Afraid for Bing Crosby, The Ballad of the Blues for Jo Stafford, 1999, Barbra Streisand: The Concert (Ace nominee for writing of a spl.). Named to songwriters hall of Fame, 1980; recipient singers salute to songwriter award, Clooney Found., 1986, Aggie award, Songwriter's Guild, 1987; grantee Am. Film Inst., 1976. Mem.: ASCAP (pres., chmn. bd. dirs. 1994—). Office: ASCAP 7920 Sunset Blvd Ste 300 Los Angeles CA 90046

BERGMAN, NANCY PALM, real estate investment company executive; b. McKeesport, Pa., Dec. 3, 1938; d. Walter Vaughn and Nellie (Sullivan) Leech; m. Donald Bergman; 1 child, Tiffany Palm Taylor. Student, Mt. San Antonio Coll., 1970, UCLA, 1989-93. Corporate sec. U.S. Filter Corp., Newport Beach, Calif., 1965—. Pres. Jaguar Research Corp., L.A. and Atlanta, 1971[00bf] ; owner Environ. Designs, L.A., 1976—; pres. Prosher Corp., L.A., 1978-83; now pres., dir. Futura Investments, L.A.; CEO Rescor, Inc. Author: Resident Managers Handbook. Home: 1255 Benedict Canyon Dr Beverly Hills CA 90210 also: 23540 Tapatia Rd Homeland CA 92548 Office: PO Box 15246 Beverly Hills CA 90209

BERGMANN, BARBARA ROSE, economics educator; b. N.Y.C., July 20, 1927; d. Martin and Nellie Berman; m. Fred H. Bergmann, July 16, 1965; children: Sarah Nellie, David Martin. BA, Cornell U., 1948; MA, Harvard U., 1955, PhD, 1959; PhD (hon.), De Montford U., 1996, Muhlenberg Coll., 2000. Economist U.S. Bur. Labor Stats., N.Y.C., 1949-53; sr. staff ecomomist, cons. Council Econ. Advisors, Washington, 1961-62; sr. staff Brookings Inst., Washington, 1963-65; sr. econ. advisor AID, Washington, 1966-67; assoc. prof. U. Md., College Park, 1965-71, prof. econs., 1971-88; disting. prof. econs. Am. U., Washington, 1988-97, prof. emeritus, 1997—. Author: (with Chinitz and Hoover) Projection of a Metropolis, 1961; (with George W. Wilson) Impact of Highway Investment on Development, 1966; (with David E. Kaun) Structural Unemployment in the U.S., 1967; (with Robert Bennett) A Microsimulated Transactions Model of the United States Economy, 1985, The Economic Emergence of Women, 1986, Saving Our Children from Poverty: What the United States Can Learn from France, 1996, In Defense of Affirmative Action, 1996, Is Social Security Broke? A Cartoon Guide to the Issues, 1999, (with Suzanne W. Helburn) America's Child Care Problem: The Way Out, 2002; mem. editl. bd. Am. Econ. Rev., 1970-73, Challenge, 1978—, Signs, 1978-85; columnist econ. affairs N.Y. Times, 1981-82. Mem. Economists for McGovern, 1977; mem. panel econ. advisors Congl. Budget Office, Washington, 1977-87; mem. price adv. com. U.S. council on Wage and Price Stability, 1979-80. Mem. AAUP (coun. 1980-83, pres. 1990-92), Am. Econ. Assn. (v.p. 1976, adv. com. to U.S. Census Bur. 1977-82), Ea. Econ. Assn. (pres. 1974), Internat. Assn. for Feminist Econs. (pres. 1999), Soc. for Advancement of Socio-Econs. (pres. 1995-96). Democrat. Home: 5430 41st Pl NW Washington DC 20015-2911 E-mail: bbergman@wam.umd.edu.

BERGNER, JANE COHEN, lawyer; b. Schenectady, N.Y., Apr. 6, 1943; d. Louis and Selma (Breslaw) Cohen; m. Alfred P. Bergner, May 30, 1968 (dec. Sept. 24, 2002); children: Lauren, Justin. AB, Vassar Coll., 1964; LLB, Columbia U., 1967. Bar: D.C. 1968, U.S. Dist. Ct. D.C. 1968, U.S. Ct. Appeals (D.C. cir.) 1968, U.S. Ct. Fed. Claims 1969, U.S. Ct. Appeals (fed. cir.) 1969, U.S. Tax Ct. 1979, U.S. Supreme Ct. 1992. Trial atty. tax divsn. U.S. Dept. Justice, Washington, 1967-74; assoc. Arnold & Porter, Washington, 1974-76, Rogovin, Huge & Lenzner, Washington, 1976-83; of counsel Arter & Hadden, 1983-86; ptnr. Spriggs & Hollingsworth, 1986-89, Feith & Zell, P.C., 1989-93; pvt. practice Washington, 1993—. Mem. jud. confs. U.S. Ct. Fed. Claims, U.S. Tax Ct. Author: Tax Court Practice and Court of Federal Claims Practice, West's Federal Forms, 2004; contbr. articles to profl. jours. Bd. dirs. Jewish Social Svc. Agy., Washington; former mem. cmty. adv. bd. Sta. WAMU-FM, Washington. Fellow Am. Coll. Tax Counsel; mem. ABA (sect. taxation, govt. rels. com., ct. procedure com., civil and criminal penalties com., chmn. subcom. important devels. 1991-93, chmn. regional liaison meetings com. 1993-95, sect. litigation); Vassar Coll. Class Alumnae (chair spl. gifts com. 25th reunion), D.C. Bar (chair taxation sect. 1985-90, chair tax audits and litigation com. 1990-93, Outstanding Sect. award 1986, Cmty. Outreach award 1993), Fed. Bar Assn., Women's Bar Assn. D.C., Washington D.C. Estate Planning Coun., Women's Tax Luncheon Group, Columbia U. Law Sch. Alumni Assn., Svc. Guild Washington, Vassar Club. Office: Ste 650 1615 L Street NW Washington DC 20036 Office Phone: 202-626-8215. E-mail: jbergnerlaw@abanet.org.

BERGSTEDT, SONJA K. elementary school educator; b. Richardson, ND, Jan. 19, 1955; d. Paul E. and Ruby N. Paulson; m. Dean H. Bergstedt, May 26, 1978; children: Dena, Ann. BS in Choral Music Edn., U. ND, 1976. Choral music dir. grades K-12 Wall (SD) Sch. Dist., 1976—77; elem. music dir. grades K-6 Kildeer (ND) Sch. Dist., 1977—89, 1994—, asst. coach drill team, 2001—. Ch. organist, choir accompanist, cmty. soloist, Kildeer. Mem.: ND Music Educators Assn., Nat. Music Educators Assn. (bd. dirs. 1980). Lutheran. Avocations: fishing, boating, reading. Home: 68 Lincoln St NE Killdeer ND 58640 Office: Kildeer Pub Sch 200 W High St Killdeer ND 58640

BERGSTROM, BETTY HOWARD, consulting executive, foundation administrator; b. Chgo., Mar. 15, 1931; d. Seward Haise and Agnes Eleanor (Uek) Guinter; m. Robert William Bergstrom, Apr. 21, 1979; children: Bryan Scott, Cheryl Lee, Jeffrey Alan, Mark Robert, Philip Alan. BS in Speech, Northwestern U., 1952, postgrad., 1983, U. Nev., Reno, 1974. Dir. sales promotion and pub. rels. WLS-AM, Chgo., 1952-56; account exec. E.H. Brown Advt. Agy., Chgo., 1956-59; v.p. Richard Crabb Assocs., Chgo., 1959-61; pres., owner Howard Assocs., Calif. and Chgo., 1961-76; v.p. Chgo. Hort. Soc., 1976-90; pres. Bergstrom Assoc., Chgo. and Carefree, Ariz., 1990—; exec. dir. Ariz. Found. for Women, 1996-98. Mem. editl. bd. Garden mag., 1977-84, Glenview Cmty. Ch., 1977-89, Fourth Presbyn. Ch., 1990—, trustee, 1994-97; editor Garden Talk, 1976-86; contbr. articles on fund devel., horticulture, edn. advt. and agr. to profl. jours.; editor Ill. AAUW Jour., 1966-67. Del. Ill. Constl. Conv., 1969-70, mem. com. legis. reform, 1973-74, cts. and justice com., 1971-74; apptd. mem. Ill. Hist. Libr. Bd., 1970, Ill. Bd. Edn., 1971-74. AAUW fellowship grant named in her honor; recipient Communicator of Yr. award Women in Comm., 1983; named Outstanding Fundraising Exec., 1997. Mem.: LWV (state v.p. Ariz. 1999), AAUW (Pres.'s award 1988), Assn. Fund Raising Profls. (bd. dirs. 1983—92, sec. 1986, v.p. 1990—92, nat. bd. dirs. 1990—92, bd. dirs. 1996—, pres.-elect 1997, nat. del. assembly 1997—99, pres. 1999, internat. bd. dirs. 2000—, vice chmn. 2002—03, cert. fund raising exec., Outstanding Fund Raising Exec.-Ariz. 1997), U. So. Calif. Alumni Assn., Am. Assn. Bot. Garden and Arboreta, Ariz. Women's Coun. (pres. 1999), Nat. Women's History Mus. (chmn. nat. bd. dirs. 2000—02, nat. adv. coun.), Charter 100, Am. Assn. Museums, Garden Writers Am., Northwestern U. Alumni, Fortnightly Club (bd. dirs. 1994—96). Office: 111 E Chestnut St Apt 49C Chicago IL 60611-6020 Office Phone: 312-280-1248. E-mail: bhbergstrom@sbcglobal.net.

BERGSTROM, ELAINE, novelist; b. Cleve., Dec. 13, 1946; d. Howard and Eleanor Schmieler; m. Carl J. Bergstrom, 1974 (div.); children: Lenore Marie, Kriista. BA, Marquette U., 1970. Novelist Red Bird Studios; writing coach. Author: Shattered Glass, 1989, Blood Alone, 1990, Blood Rites,

1991, Daughter of the Night, 1992, Tapestry of Dark Souls, 1993, Baroness of Blood, 1995, (using psuedomym Marie Kiraly) Mina, 1994, Leanna, 1996, Madeline, 1996; work represented in Women Who Walk Through Fire, Daughters of Darkness, 1993, Tales of Ravenloft, 1994, The Door Through Washington Square, 1998. Office: Donald Maas Lit Agy 157 W 57th St New York NY 10019-2210

BERIRO, DEBORAH RAQUEL, real estate broker, investor; b. Madrid, Apr. 24, 1972; d. Albert Abraham Beriro and Maria del Carmen Fernandez de Arenas Gomez Mena. BA, Am. U., 1990—94. Lic. Real Estate Broker Dept. of Bus. and Profl. Regulation Divsn. of Real Estate, 2001. Asst. to pres. of spl. client services Sotheby's, NYC, 1994—96; real estate assoc. Cmty. Real Estate, West Palm Beach, Fla., 1996—99; real estate investor Debico, West Palm Beach, Fla., 1997—; pres., broker Citi Properties, Inc., West Palm Beach, Fla., 2000—. Chair Aspira Palm Beach, West Palm Beach, 2002—03. Mem.: Realtor's Assn. (licentiate). Avocations: travel, tennis, foreign languages. Office: Citi Properties inc 319 Clematis St Ste 118 West Palm Beach FL 33401 E-mail: citiproperties@msn.com.

BERKA, MARIANNE GUTHRIE, health and physical education educator; b. Queens, N.Y., Dec. 25, 1944; d. Frank Joseph and Mary (DePaul) Guthrie; m. Jerry George Berka, June 1, 1968; children: Katie, Keri. BS, Ithaca Coll., 1966, MS, 1968; EdD, NYU, 1990. Tchr. Northport H.S., 1966—67; prof. Health, Phys. Edn. and Recreation Nassau C.C., Garden City, NY, 1968—. Adj. assoc. prof. Hofstra U., Hempstead, NY, 1998—. Mem.: AAHPER, AAHPERD, Am. Coll. Sports Medicine (cert. health/fitness instr.), Am. Assn. Sex Educators, Counselors and Therapists (cert. sex educator), N.Y. State Assn. Health, Phys. Edn., Recreation and Dance (J.B. Nash scholarship com. 1983—2000, Nassau Zone Disting. Svc. award 1988, Nassau Zone Higher Edn. Tchr. of Yr. 2003), Assn. Women Phys. Educators N.Y. State (chpt. chmn. 1973—74, chpt. treas. 1980—84). Roman Catholic. Home: 90 Bay Way Ave Brightwaters NY 11718-2012 Office: P226 HPER Nassau Community Coll Garden City NY 11530 Office Phone: 516-572-8147.

BERKELEY, BETTY LIFE, gerontology educator; b. St Louis, May 25, 1924; d. James Alfred and Anna Laura (Voltmer) Life; m. Marvin Harold Berkeley, Feb. 7, 1947; children: Kathryn Elizabeth, Barbara Ellen, Brian Harrison, Janet Lynn. AB, Harris Tchrs. Coll., 1947; MA in Edni. Adminstrn., Washington U., 1951; PhD, U. North Tex., 1980. Tchr. St. Louis Pub. Schs., 1946-48, Clayton Pub. Schs., Mo., 1948-49, Lamplighter Pvt. Sch., Dallas, 1964-67; program devel. specialist Richland Coll., Dallas, 1980-84, instr., 1981. Adj. prof. U. North Tex., Denton, 1981, cons. Sch. Cmty. Svcs. Ctr. for Studies on Aging, 1981; pres. Retirement Planning Svcs., Dallas, 1984. Contbr. articles to profl. jours. Mem. Dallas Commn. on Status of Women, 1975-79; bd. dirs. Dallas Mcpl. Libr., 1979-83, Sr. Citizen Greater Dallas, 1986-92, Coun. on Adult Ministry Lovers Lane United Meth. Ch., 1982, trustee, 1997, dir. found., 1997. mem. bldg. com., 1999; charter mem., bd. dirs., life. mem. Friends U. North Tex. Libr.; mem. Pres.'s Coun U. North Tex., mem. vol. mgmt. edn. task force, 1978-82. Named Outstanding Alumna Coll. Edn. U. North Tex., 1992. Mem. AAUW (pres. 1973-75, Outstanding Woman of Tex. 1981), Women's Coun. Dallas County (v.p. 1977-79). Avocations: travel, cooking, needlework. Home and Office: 13958 Hughes Ln Dallas TX 75240-3510

BERKERY, ROSEMARY T, lawyer, investment company executive; b. 1955. JJA, Coll., AB, St. vineum, N.Y. ...nym... 1977... estamenter, ... 1980. Sr. v.p., assoc. gen. counsel Merrill Lynch & Co., Inc., N.Y.C., 1995—97, co-dir. global securities rsch. and econs. group, 1997—2000, sr. v.p., head U.S. pvt. client group mktg. and investment, 2000—01, exec. v.p., gen. counsel, 2001—. Office: Merrill Lynch and Co Inc 4 World Financial Ctr 32d Fl New York NY 10080

BERKEY-ABBOTT, KRISTIN LEE, language educator; b. Nancy, France, July 14, 1965; d. Thomas Stanton and Ina Lee (Roof) Berkey; m. Carl Alan Abbott, Aug. 13, 1988. BA, Newberry Coll., 1987; MA, U. S.C., 1989, PhD, 1992. Prof. Trident Tech. Coll., Charleston, SC, 1992—98, Art Inst. Ft. Lauderdale, Fla., 2002—. Adj. prof. Breward C.C., Pembroke Pines, Fla., 1998—99, U. Miami, 2000—01. Contbr. articles to profl. jours. Organizer 52% Womens Polit. Group, Charleston, SC, 1994—98; cmty. outreach worker Whaley St. U. Meth. Ch., Columbia, 1988—94. Office: Art Inst Ft Lauderdale 1799 SE 17th St Fort Lauderdale FL 33316-3000 E-mail: kristenlba@aol.com.

BERKLEY, EMILY CAROLAN, lawyer; b. Richmond, Va., Mar. 2, 1950; d. Charles Garvice and Edna Gray (Berkley) Broom; m. Richard E. Bird, Sept. 6, 1969 (div. Mar. 1988); children: Jessica A. Bird, Martel J. Bird. Student, Coll. of William and Mary, 1968-70; BS in Psychology cum laude, Tufts U., 1972; JD magna cum laude, Temple U., 1977. Ptnr. Ballard Spahr Andrews & Ingersoll LLP, Phila., 1977—. Seminar panelist Pa. Bar Inst., 1992, 98-2003, Practicing Law Inst., 1993-2004; mem. U.S. Sec. of State's adv. com. on ext. internat. law. Long range planning com. Performing Arts for Tredyffrin-Easttown Sch. Dist., Berwyn, Pa., 1989, chair subcom. on creativity, futures com., 1990; active United Way, 1989-91; bd. dirs. Devon-Strafford Little League, 1992-95. Fellow: Am. Bar Found. (life); mem.: ABA (chair task force on exporation of Uniform Comml. Code 1995—97, vice chair internat. comml. law subcom. 1997—99, vice chair com. on legal opinions 2002—), bus. law sect. liaison U.S. Sec. of State's adv. com. on pvt. internat 1998—2001, mem. Uniform Comml. Code com.), N.Y. TriBar Opinion Com., Phila. Bar Assn., Pa. Bar Assn. (bus. law sect., chair legal opinion task force, chair article 9 task force, treas.), Am. Law Inst., Am. Coll. Comml. Fin. Lawyers (bd. regents 1993—2001, pres. 2000). Office: Ballard Spahr Andrews et al 1735 Market St Ste 5100 Philadelphia PA 19103-7599 Office Phone: 215-864-8611. E-mail: berkley@ballardspahr.com.

BERKLEY, GAIL WINNICK, psychotherapist; b. Detroit, Feb. 21; d. Lawrence C. Winnick and Helen M. Caner Leytus; m. Daniel Theodore Berkley, Jan. 22, 1966 (div. Feb. 1989). MA in Orgn. and Leadership, U. San Francisco; MS in Psychology, San Francisco State U.; PhD in Psychology, Kensington U. Lic. marriage, family, child therapist. With San Francisco Unified Sch. Dist., 1971-81, Belmont (Calif.) Hills Psychiat. Hosp., Cmty. Counseling Ctr. San Mateo County, East Palo Alto, Calif.; pvt. practice Berkley Therapy & Mediation Ctr., San Mateo, Calif., 1981—. ASID allied designer Berkley Goods, San Mateo and San Francisco, 1969—; design cons. interior residential/comml. properties designer. Author: (book) Financial Planner, 1988, (manual) How to Handle Probate, 1988; pub. quar. mag. People in Transition, 1989. Commr., chair San Mateo County Juvenile Justice and Delinquency Prevention, San Mateo; commr. San Mateo Maternal Child and Adolescent Bd., Mem. AAUW (bd. dirs., women comty. rels.), San Francisco Legal Aux. (bd. dirs., charity), San Francisco Peninsula Humane Soc. (chair fundraising, spl. events chair), San Francisco Zool. Soc. (guardian mem. fundraising). Avocations: animal rights, children, humanitarian rights advocate.

BERKLEY, SHELLEY, congresswoman; b. N.Y.C., Jan. 20, 1951; BA, U. Nev., 1972; JD, U. San Diego, 1976. Mem. U.S. Congress from 1st Nev. dist., 1999—; mem. transp. and infrastructure com., internat. affairs com., vet. affairs com. Democrat. Office: US Ho Reps 439 Cannon House Office Bldg Washington DC 20515-0001 also: 2340 Paseo Del Prado Ste D-106 Las Vegas NV 89102*

BERKMAN, CLAIRE FLEET, psychologist; b. New Orleans, Dec. 5, 1942; d. Joel and Margaret Grace (Fishler) Fleet; m. Arnold Stephen Berkman, Apr. 27, 1975; children: Janna Samantha, Micah Seth Siegel. BA, Boston U., 1964; EdM, Harvard U., 1966; EdD, Boston U., 1970. Asst.

prof. Counseling Ctr. Mich. State U., East Lansing, 1971-75, assoc. prof., 1975-78, assoc. prof. dept. psychiatry, 1975-82, clin. assoc. prof.; 1986-87; pvt. clin. practice, 1975—. Cons. Cath. Family Social Service, Lansing, 1979-83; mem. adv. bd. Cir. Ct. Family Counseling Program, 1982-88. V.p. Kehillat Israel Synagogue, 1975-76, pres., 1992-94; bd. dirs. Jewish Welfare Fedn., Lansing, 1974-75, 84-87; mem. children's task force State Bar Mich., 1993-95. NDEA fellow, 1968-70. Mem. APA, Mich. Psychol. Assn., Mich. Soc. Forensic Psychologists, Nat. Soc. Arts and Letters (pres. Mid-Mich. chpt. 2000-02). Office: 4084 Okemos Rd Okemos MI 48864-3258 Office Phone: 517-349-8388.

BERKMAN, LISA F. public health educator; PhD, U. Calif., Berkeley, 1977. Prof., chair dept. pub. policy Harvard U., Boston. Contbr. articles to profl. jours. Mem.: Inst. of Medicine of NAS. Achievements include research in on psychosocial influences on health outcomes. Office: Harvard Univ Kresge Bldg Rm T09 677 Huntington Ave Boston MA 02115

BERKOWITZ, BOBBIE, medical educator; BS in Nursing, M of Nursing, U. Wash.; PhD in Nursing Sci., Case W. Res. U. Chief nursing svcs. Seattle-King County Dept. Pub. Health, 1986—93; dep. sec. Wash. State Dept. Health, 1993—97; dir. Turning Point Nat. Program Office Robert Wood Johnson Found.; prof. and chair dept. psychosocial and cmty. health Sch. Nursing U. Wash., St. Louis, 1996—. Adj. prof. dept. health svcs. Sch. Pub. Health and Cmty. Medicine U. Wash., St. Louis; mem. Wash. State Bd. Health, 1988—93; apptd. by gov. Wash. Health Care Commn., 1990—92; bd. dirs. Hanford Environ. Health Found. Mem. editl. adv. bd.: jour. Pub. Health Nursing. Recipient Sch. Nursing Disting. Alumni award, U. Wash.; scholar, Ctrs. for Disease Control and Prevention's Pub. Health Leadership Inst., 1993—94. Fellow: Am. Acad. Nursing; mem.: NAS (co-chair Inst. Medicine com. on pub. health performance monitoring). Office: U Wash Psychosocial and Cmty Health Box 357263 Seattle WA 98195-7263

BERKOWITZ, SUSAN J. investment banking executive; MBA, Duke U. Various mktg. and sales positions Chase Manhattan Bank, N.Y.C., 1987-92, J. Walter Thompson, N.Y.C., 1992-94, Spin mag., N.Y.C., 1994-96; in charge mktg., advt. sales and bus. devel. theglobe.com., N.Y.C., 1996-98; sr. v.p. mktg. internet investment banking Wit Capital Group, Inc., N.Y.C., 1998—. Office: Wit Capital Corp PO Box 722 New York NY 10276-0722

BERKSON, SADIE, volunteer; b. Winnipeg, Man., Can., June 18, 1913; came to U.S., 1927; d. Samuel and Minnie (Liss) Finkelstein; m. Isadore J. Berkson, Feb. 3, 1940 (dec. Oct. 1982). Exec. sec. Convenant Club, Chgo., 1929-40. Supr. blood bank ARC, WWII and Six Days War, Israel; past mem. bd. dirs. Fedn. and Jewish United Fund; charter, life bd. dirs. Louis A. Weiss Meml. Hosp., Brandeis Hadassah, B'nai B'rith, Art Inst. Chgo.; co-chmn. 1st founder women's br. Brandeis divsn., Chgo.; co-chmn. 1st women's gift divsn. Jewish Combined Jewish Appeal, 1947; founder 1st spl. women's gift divsn. Crusade of Mercy, 1970; bd. oversers Ill. Inst. Tech.-Chgo. Kent Coll. Law, 1992—. chmn. Consular Ball, 1993, 94; chmn. Rita Hayworth Ball for Alzheimer's Assn., Chgo., 1987, also bd. dirs. and co-chmn. Chgo. support group, hon. emeritus bd. dirs., 1996—. Recipient award of merit ARC, Woman of Yr. award Crusade of Mercy, 1970, Cartier Disting. Humanitarian award Alzheimer's Assn., 1992, Archtl. award for I.J. Berkson Res. Reading Room, Ill. Inst. Tech.-Chgo. Kent Coll. Law, 1992, Disting. Svc. award Ill. Inst. Tech.-Chgo.-Kent Coll. Law, 1994, honoree Chgo. Rita Hayworth Ball for Alzheimer's rsch., 1985, endowed I.J. Berkson Res. Reading Room, 1985 seeded, established I.J. and Sadie Berkson Scholarship Fund, Chgo.-Kent Coll. Law, 1992. Mem. Soc. Wills and Endowment for Alzheimer's Assn. (founding). Avocations: painting, golf, tennis, world travel. Home: 200 E Delaware Pl Apt 34A Chicago IL 60611-7710

BERKUN, ROSE, anesthesiologist; arrived in U.S., 1980; d. Gregory and Raisa Shershnevsky; m. Robert Berkun, May 20, 1995; children: Ryan, Jason;; 1 child, Benjamin. BA, SUNY, 1987, MD, 1992. Diplomate Am. Bd. Anesthesiololgy, 1999, lic. N.Y., 1992. Intern Millard Filmore Hosp., Buffalo, 1992—93; resident in anesthesiology SUNY, Buffalo, 1993—96; anesthesiologist Maple-Gate Anesthesiology, Amherst-Buffalo, NY, 1996—97, St. Joseph Hosp., Buffalo, 1998—. Mem.: AMA, N.Y. State Soc. Anesthesiologists, Am. Soc. Anesthesiologists. Democrat. Jewish. Office: St Joseph Hospital 2625 Harlem Rd Cheektowaga NY 14225 Office Phone: 716-891-2300.

BERLAGE, GAI INGHAM, sociologist, educator; b. Washington, Feb. 9, 1943; d. Paul Bowen and Grace (Artz) Ingham; m. Jan Coxe Berlage, Aug. 7, 1965; children: Jan Ingham, Cari Coxe. BA, Smith Coll., 1965; MA, So. Meth. U., 1968; PhD, NYU, 1979. Tchr. math. Piner Jr. High Sch., Sherman, Tex., 1968-69; asst. prof. sociology Iona Coll., New Rochelle, N.Y., 1971-83, assoc. prof., 1983-88, chmn. dept., 1981—90, 1996—2003, prof., 1988—. Coord. urban studies program, 1984-90, gerontology program, 1984-90, NCAA faculty athletic rep., 1996—. Author: Experience with Sociology: Social Issues in American Society, 1983, Understanding Social Issues: Sociological Fact Finding, 1987, 2d edit., 1990, 3d edit., 1993, Women in Baseball: The Forgotten History, 1994, Understanding Social Issues: Critical Thinking and Analysis, 1996, 6th edit., 2003; mem. editl. bd. Jour. Sport and Social Issues, 1990-94; contbr. articles to profl. jours. Commr. Wilton Commn. on Aging and Social Svcs., 1980-88, chmn., 1982-88; co-chmn. Wilton Task Force on Youth Coun., 1988; chmn. Wilton Task Force Com. for Outreach Program, 1981-82, Wilton Task Force on Day Care, 1983-88; mem. Wilton Task Force for Pub. Health Nursing Assn., 1981-82, Wilton Sport Coun., 1985-88; bd. dirs. Wilton Meals on Wheels, 1983-88; fellow N.Am. Faculty Network of Northeastern Univs. Ctr. for Study of Sport in Soc. Recipient Best Profl. Paper award Third Annual Cooperstown Symposium on Baseball and the Am. Cultre; named to Iona Coll. Women of Achievement, 1993. Mem. Am. Sociol. Assn., N.Am. Soc. Sociology of Sport (treas. 1992-93), Wilton Assn. for Gifted Edn. (pres. 1980-81), N.Am. Soc. for Sports History, Soc. for Am. Baseball Rsch., Women's Sport Found. (resources coun.). Office: Iona Coll Dept Sociology New Rochelle NY 10801 Office Phone: 914-633-2594.

BERLIN, DORIS ADA, psychiatrist; b. Newark, May 23, 1919; d. Samuel and Fanny (Lippman) B.; m. Saul R. Kelson (div.); children: Joel, Tamar; m. Lewis H. Acker. BS in Pharmacy, Columbia U., 1940; MD, Med. Coll. Va., 1948; MPH in Community Mental Health, U. Mich., 1966. Cert. Am. Bd. Psychiatry and Neurology; lic. psychiatrist N.Y., Va., Ohio, Mich., Tex., Calif. Intern Beth Israel Hosp., N.Y.C., 1948-49; resident in psychiatry Bellevue Hosp., N.Y.C., 1949-52; pvt. practice N.Y.C., 1952-57, Toledo, 1957-66, Fishkill and Poughkeepsie, N.Y., 1984—. Clin. asst. in psychiatry NYU Coll. Medicine, 1952-57; asst. in psychiatry U. Hosp., N.Y., 1952-53; clin. asst. vis. neuropsychiatrist Bellevue Hosp., N.Y., 1954-57; lectr. mental health Sch. Pub. Health U. Mich., 1966-68; dir. profl. edn. Toledo State Hosp., 1969-70; clin. assoc. prof. N.Y. Sch. Psychiatry, 1970-81; dir. residency program Hudson River Psychiat. Ctr., Poughkeepsie, 1970-83, others. Mem. citizens adv. bd. Lucas County (Ohio) Welfare Dept., 1963-67, chair, 1965-66; bd. dirs. Jewish Family Svc., Toledo, 1969-70; mem. policy coun., rehab. com. Toledo Area Program on Drug Abuse, 1970; bd. dirs. Dutchess County Assn. for Sr. Citizens, 1993-96. Grantee NEH, 1979. Fellow Am. Psychiat. Assn. (chair editl. bd. Hosp. and Cmty. Psychiatric Jour., 1979-80, task force on cmty. mental health ctrs., 1983-88, com. on advertisers and exhibitors 1989-92, vice-chair lifers caucus 1990-91, chair lifers orgn. 1992), Am. Coll. Psychoanalysis (Laughlin fellowship com. 1976-79); mem. Am. Acad. Psychoanalysis (com. on psychoanalysis and cmty. mental health 1967-68), Dutchess County Med. Soc. (psychiatrists' rep. to coun. 1985-95, treas. 1987). Home and Office: 66 Mitchell Ave Poughkeepsie NY 12603-3423

BERLIN, MEREDITH RISE, editor; b. Bronxville, N.Y., Nov. 22, 1955; d. Marvin and Seena (Goldsmith) Brown; m. Jordan Stuart Berlin, Aug. 13, 1988; children: Gregory Samuel, Lauren Julia, Connor David. BS, Emerson Coll., 1976. With circulation-subscription World Bus. Weekly, N.Y.C., 1978-79; feature editor Soap Opera Digest, N.Y.C., 1979-82, editor-in-chief, 1982-91; editor-at-large, 1991-96, Soap Opera Digest, N.Y.C., 1999—; editor-in-chief Seventeen Mag., N.Y.C., 1997-99; dir. devel. Promedia Consumer Magazines, 1999—. Exec. producer Soap Opera Awards NBC-TV, L.A., 1988-91; commentator WCBS-TV Noon News, 1987-96; commentator NBC's House Party; producer, journalist Afternoon TV Show, 1982. Columnist N.Y. Post, 1994-96. Recipient 3 Emmy nominations, 1988, 89; named N.Y. Alumni of Yr. Emerson Coll. Mem. NOW, AFTRA, Am. Soc. Mag. Editors.

BERLINCOURT, MARJORIE ALKINS, government official, retired; b. Toronto, Ont., Can., June 2, 1928; came to U.S., 1950, naturalized, 1956; d. Herbert John and Ellen Florence (Barker) Alkins; m. Ted Gibbs Berlincourt, Feb. 28, 1953; 1 child, leslie Berlincourt Yale. BA, U. Toronto, 1950; MA, Yale U., 1951, PhD, 1954. Editl. dir. tech. publs. Rocketdyne, 1956-59; lectr. classics U. So. Calif., 1959-61; assoc. prof. classical history Calif. Luth. Coll., 1961-67, Calif. State U., Northridge, 1967-71; prof. Met. State Coll., Denver, 1971-72; program dir. div. fellowships for summer sems., fellowships NEH, Washington, 1972-78, dir. state programs, 1983—91, dir. divsn. fellowships, seminars, 1991-94; ret., 1995. Vis. lectr. Georgetown U., 1972. Author: De Surprise en Surprise, 1953, Entrez Petits Amis, 1954, Victory as a Coin Type, 1973; contbr. articles to profl. jours. Sterling fellow Yale U., 1950-53; recipient Calif. Faculty Rsch. award, 1970. Mem. Am. Assn. Ancient Historians. Episcopalian.

BERLINER, BARBARA, retired librarian, consultant; b. Bklyn., July 14, 1947; d. Robert and Mildred M. (Sklar) Morris; 1 child, Stefanie Lauren. BA in Anthropology, NYU, 1969; MLS, Columbia U., 1970. Libr. N.Y. Pub. Libr., N.Y.C., 1970-81, sr. libr., telephone reference, 1981-86, supervising libr., tele. reference, 1986-92, head libr., Mid-Manhattan sci. and bus., 1992-93; coord. NYPL Express, N.Y.C., 1993—2002. Cons. John Wright, N.Y.C., 1991; bibliographer Collier's Encyclopedia. Author: The Book of Answers, 1990. Mem. ALA, Planetary Soc. Avocations: sports, astronomy. Home: 64 Meadowview Ct Leonia NJ 07605-2044

BERLINER, DANA, lawyer; b. 1967; d. Michael and Judith Berliner. BA in Psychology, Yale U., 1987; JD, Yale Law Sch., 1991. Bar: Pa. 1993, D.C. 1999. Law clk. U.S. Circuit Ct. (5th cir.), Judge Jerry Smith, Houston, 1991—92; sr. atty. Inst. Justice, Washington, 1994—. Achievements include won case saving elderly widow's home from condemnation for Donald Trump's casino across the street; co-represented a Mississippi family whose home was being condemned for Nissan; state withdrew the condemnation; won suit declaring New Orleans' prohibition on street vending of books a free speech violation; Won Case Declaring That Would-Be Limousine Drivers Had Been Subjected To An Unconstitutional Application Process By State Agency. Office: Inst Justice 1717 Pennsylvania Ave NW Ste 200 Washington DC 20006 E-mail: dberliner@ij.org.

BERLINER, RUTH SHIRLEY, real estate company executive; b. N.Y.C., June 20, 1928; d. Irving William and Florence (Tomback) Blum; m. Arthur Ivan Berliner, Sept. 23, 1948; children: Daniel Scott, Michael Robert, Eric Lance. BA, Empire State Coll., Westbury, N.Y., 1974; diploma, Wilsey Sch. Interior Design, Hempstead, N.Y., 1975; MBA, Adelphi U., 1980. Lic. real estate broker, N.Y. Sec. to dir. librs NYU, N.Y.C., 1948-50; sec. Paragon Mtgl Investment Inc, N.Y.C., 1950-57, v.p. Paragon Mtgl Investment Inc, N.Y.C., 1972-78; pres. Ruth S. Berliner, Inc., N.Y.C., 1978—. Pres. Allied Corp., 1983—; cons. E. 59th St. Assocs., N.Y.C., 1962-70, Amrep Corp., N.Y.C., 1968-75, FKRA Assocs., N.Y.C., 1977-84; mem. stores com. Real Estate Bd. N.Y., 1984-96. V.p. NYU Dental Sch. Parents Assn., 1974-76, bd. dirs. Hadassah, Hewlett, N.Y., 1978-87; advisor Citizens for Charter Change, N.Y.C., 1987—. Mem. Nat. Assn. Realtors, Real Estate Bd. N.Y. (store com. 1984-98, econ. devel. com. 1994-99), Inwood Club, Nat. Realty Club, Williams Club, N.Y. Athletic Club. Avocations: tennis, swimming, dance, painting.

BERLOWITZ, LESLIE, cultural organization administrator; BA in English with honors, NYU, 165; MA in English, Columbia U., 1967. Mem. dept. English NYU, N.Y.C., 1967-96, asst. dean U. Coll. Arts and Scis., Washington Square Coll. Arts and Scis., 1969-73, dir. acad. program devel., 1973-81, asst. v.p. acad. affairs, 1981-84, assoc. v.p. acad. affairs, 1984-88, dep. v.p. acad. affairs, 1988-91, v.p. instnl. advancement, 1991-96; exec. officer Am. Acad. Arts and Scis., Cambridge, Mass., 1996—. Founder, dir. The Humanities Coun., 1977-96, Faculty Resource Network, 1985-96; nat. dir. AmeriCorps, Project SafetyNet, 1995-96. Editor: (with Denis Donoghue and Louis Menand) America in Theory, 1988, Greenwich Village: Culture and Counterculture, 1990. Bd. dirs. Mass. Inst. Psychoanalysis; panelist Boston Jewish Film Festival; exec. bd. Corp. Yaddo; active Fund for Artists' Colonies, Inc., Coun. Internat. Edn. Exch., Urban Rsch. Ctr., Am. Jewish Congress, Fedn. Jewish Philanthropies, Joseph S. Gruss Found.; panelist NEH. Recipient Pacesetter award Tougaloo Coll., 1993. Fellow N.Y. Inst. Humanities; mem. MIA, Century Assn. (N.Y.). Office: Am Acad Arts and Scis Norton's Woods 136 Irving St Cambridge MA 02138-1929 Fax: (617) 576-5055.

BERMAN, ARIANE R. artist; b. Danzig, Mar. 27, 1937; m. Mario La Rossa, 1965. B.F.A., Hunter Coll., N.Y.C., 1959; M.F.A., Yale, 1962; AAUW and Found. des Etats-Unis fellow, U. Paris, 1962-63. Juror nat. screening com. Fulbright grants, 1976-77, chmn. screening com., 1977-78. One man shows at Center Gallery, Conn., 1963, Harry Salpeter Gallery, N.Y.C., 1966, Brentano's Art Gallery, N.Y.C., 1973, Graphic Art Gallery, Tel Aviv, 1973, Galleria San Sebastianello, Rome, 1973, Eileen Kuhlik Gallery, N.Y.C., 1971, 73, Pub. Mus., Oshkosh, Wis., 1974, Wustum Mus. Fine Arts, Racine, Wis., 1974, Fontana Gallery, Pa., 1963, 71, 74, Galleria d'Arte Helioart, Rome, 1974, Munson Gallery, Conn., 1975, Ward-Nasse Gallery, N.Y.C., 1975, 77, 80, Phila. Art Alliance, 1980, Silvermine Guild Artists, Conn., 1976, Kornblee Gallery, N.Y.C., 1982, Babson Coll., Mass., 1983, Northwood Inst., Mich., 1983, Westenhook Gallery, Mass., 1984, Phoenix Gallery, N.Y.C., 1985, 87, Concordia Coll., Bronxville, N.Y., 1989, Gallery 84 Inc., N.Y.C., 1992, L'Artisanat, Mass., 1992, others; exhibited in group shows at Galerie Atrium Artis, Geneva, Switzerland, 1975, F 15 Gallery, Norway, 1974, Galeries Raymond Duncan, Paris, 1964, Asso. Am. Artists, N.Y.C., 1971, Circle Galleries Ltd., N.Y.C., 1974, Margo Feiden Galleries, N.Y.C., 1972, Gallery 500, Pa., 1973, Van Straaten Gallery, Chgo., 1974, Genesis Gallery, N.Y.C., 1978, Marymount Coll., N.Y.C., 1983, NYU, 1982, Fairleigh Dickenson U., 1982, Allentown Art Mus., Pa., 1982, numerous others; represented in permanent collections at Am. Petroleum Inst., Israel Ministry of Tourism, USIA, McGregor-Doniger, Inc., Shipley Sch., Bryn Mawr, Pa., Readers Digest, N.J. Bd. Edn., Athena Gallery, New Haven, Charles E. Ellis Coll., Newton Square, Pa., Hearst Corp., Met. Mus. Art, Phila. Mus. Art, Phila. Art Alliance, Ms. mag., Seventeen, Redbook, Feminist Press, Duke U., Newspaper Advt. Bur., Purdue U., Phila. Child Guidance Ctr., others. Recipient Yale Painting prize, 1960, Purchase award Purdue U., 1964, Stella Drabkin Meml. award, ACPS Purchase prize, 1973, Catherine Lorillard Wolfe Arts Club Gold medal, 1973, Hon. mention Hudson River Mus., 1974, Artists Equity award, 1985. Mem. Am. Color Print Soc., Nat. Assn. Women Artists, Yonkers Art Assn., Women's Caucus for Art, Met. Painters and Sculptors, Pen and Brush, League of Present Day Artists, Sheffield Art League, Silvermine Guild of Artists, Soc. Women Artists (past corr. sec.), Hunter Coll. Alumni Assn. (Hall of Fame 1974) Home: 161 W 54th St New York NY 10019-5322

BERMAN, BARBARA, educational consultant; b. N.Y.C., Oct. 15, 1938; d. Nathan and Regina (Pasternak) Kopp; children: Adrienne, David. BS,

Bklyn. Coll., 1959, MS, 1961; adminstrv./supervision cert., Coll. S.I., 1971; EdD, Rutgers U., 1981. Tchr. N.Y.C. Pub. Schs., 1959—70; project coord., dir. fed. projects Rutgers U., New Brunswick, NJ, 1976—80; math. cons. B&F Cons., S.I., NY, 1978—2003, BB Consulting, S.I., NY, 2003—; dir. fed. math. project Ednl. Support Systems, Inc., S.I., 1981-94; dir. Foresight Sch., S.I., 1985—, Great Beginnings Infant and Toddler Ctr., 1989—. Cons. to sch. dists. for restructuring/sch. reform and math. staff devel. Co-author of many books and articles on teaching mathematics for elem. and jr. h.s. tchrs. Mem. Nat. Coun. Tchrs. Math., Nat. Staff Devel. Coun., N.Y. Acad. Scis., Nat. Coun. Suprs. Math. Avocations: reading, travel, theatre. Office: BB Consulting 446 Travis Ave Staten Island NY 10314-6149 Office Phone: 718-698-3636. Personal E-mail: BarbBerman@aol.com.

BERMAN, CAROL, commissioner; b. Bklyn., Sept. 21, 1923; d. Hyman and Sarah (Levy) B.; m. Seymour Jerome Berman, May 19, 1944; children: Elizabeth, Charles. BA, U. Mich., 1943. Trustee Bd. Edn., Lawrence, N.Y., 1973-77; senator State of N.Y., Albany, 1978-84; spl. rep. State Divsn. for Housing, Hempstead, N.Y., 1985-86; commr. N.Y. State Commn. on Lobbying, Albany, 1988-92, N.Y. State Commn. of Elections, Albany, 1992—. N.Y. co-chair Nat. Jewish Dem. Coun., 1988—, Met. Airport Noise Mitigation Rev. Commn., 1992—; del. Dem. Nat. Conv., N.Y., 1992; vice-chair Nassau Dem. County Com., Mineola, N.Y., 1970-72. Mem. Phi Beta Kappa, Phi Kappa Phi. Jewish. Avocations: grandchildren, golf. Home: 42 Lord Ave Lawrence NY 11559-1324 Office: NY State Bd Elections 40 Steuben St Albany NY 12207

BERMAN, CAROL WENDY, psychiatrist; b. N.Y.C., Sept. 14, 1951; d. Irving and Dora (Adler) B.; m. Martin Farber, Feb. 5, 1994. BA, U. Calif., Berkeley, 1972; MD, NYU, 1981. Diplomate Am. Bd. Psychiatry and Neurology. Intern, resident in psychiatry St. Lukes-Roosevelt Hosp., N.Y.C., 1982-85; rsch. fellow in psychiatry NYU Med. Ctr., N.Y.C., 1986-87, mem. attending staff, 1987—; pvt. practice, N.Y.C., 1988—. Contbr. numerous articles to med. jours.; patentee device to prevent drunk driving. Active legal problems of mentally ill, Bar Assn. City N.Y., 1993—. Recipient writing prize Psychiat. Annals, 1987. Mem. Am. Psychiat. Assn. Office: 866 U N Plz Rm 473 New York NY 10017-1822

BERMAN, CHERYL R. advertising company executive; b. Chgo. BA in Journalism, U. Ill., Urbana. Copywriter, various positions Leo Burnett Co., Chgo., 1974-99, chief creative officer, chmn. U.S. bd. dirs., 1999—. Composer advt. music for McDonald's, Hallmark, Kraft, Walt Disney World, Chgo. Bulls; songwriter/composer Remember the Magic, Celebrate the Future Hand in Hand. Named Ad Woman of Yr. Women's Advt. Club Chgo., 1997. Office: Leo Burnett Co 35 W Wacker Dr Ste 3710 Chicago IL 60601-1648 E-mail: cheryl.berman@chi.leoburnett.com.*

BERMAN, ELEANOR, writer; b. Birmingham, Ala., May 7, 1934; d. Abraham and Bertha (Sirote) Greenwald; children: Thomas, Eric, Terry Ellen. BA, Smith Coll., 1955. Author: The Cooperating Family, 1977, Re-entering, 1980, The Palm-Aire Spa 7-Day Plan, 1987, Entertaining for Business, 1990, Grandparenting ABC's, 1999, Away for the Weekend travel guides, 1982—2003, Traveling Solo, 1997, 1999, 2001—03, Recommended Bed and Breakfast Inns: New England, 1998, 2000, 2002, New York Neighborhoods, 1999, 2001, 2004, New York Top 10, 2002; contbr. Eyewitness Guide to New York, 1994 (Thomas Cook award, best travel guide of yr), articles to publs. Mem.: N.Y. Travel Writers (pres. 1995—96), Soc. Am. Travel Writers.

BERMAN, ELEANORE, artist; b. N.Y.C., Sept. 2, 1928; d. Isidor and Elsie (Goldstein) Berman; children: Deborah Nicholas, Jan Nicholas, Anthony Nicholas, David Lazarof. BA, UCLA, 1950. One-woman shows include Kirk De Gooyer Gallery, L.A., 1982, Kouros Gallery, N.Y.C., 1982, L.A. City Hall, 1984, Stuhr (Nebr.) Mus., 1984, U. Wyo. Art Gallery, 1984, U. Minn., Duluth, 1984, Gallery X Brussels, 1985, New Eng. Ctr. for Contemporary Art, Mass., 1985, Mcpl. Gallery, Kampen, The Netherlands, 1986, Mcpl. Gallery, Amstelveen, The Netherlands, 1986, Lisa Kurts Gallery, Memphis, 1989, Boritzer/Gray Gallery, Santa Monica, Calif., 1991, L.A. Art Core, 1996, Cruz L.A., Venice, Calif., 2000, Don O'Melveny Gallery, L.A., 2003; exhibited in group shows: LAART, N.Y.C., 1986, U. Hawaii, Hilo, 1986, L.A. County Mus. Art, 1981, Boston Ctr. for the Arts, 1981, Wesleyan Coll., Conn., 1980, Newport (R.I.) Harbor Mus., 1977, Nat. Acad. Western Art Traveling Exhbn., 1988, L.A.-U.K. Print Connection, 1989, Bonnie Fridholm Gallery, Asheville, N.C., 1989, San Bernardino County Mus., Calif., 1994, Wichita Falls (Tex.) Mus., 1995, No. Calif. Arts Ann. INternat., 2000, 8th Ann. Gt. Plains Nat., Hays, Kans., 2001, Calif. Poly. Pomona, 2003; represented in permanent collections: L.a. County Mus. Art, Bklyn. Mus., Milw. Art Ctr., Grunwald Graphic Art Ctr., UCLA, others. Mem. Nat. Assn. of Women Artists, So. Calif. Women's Caucus for the Arts, L.A. Printmaking Assn., Nat. Watercolor Soc., Artists Equity Assn. E-mail: eberman718@earthlink.net.

BERMAN, ELLEN SUE, energy and telecommunications executive, theatre producer; Student, U. N.C., Greensboro, 1960-62, U. N.C., Chapel Hill, summer 1961, U. Calif., Berkeley, summer 1962; BA in Russian, Barnard Coll., 1964. Legis. asst. Senator Joseph Tydings, 1965-66; rsch. assoc. Washington Poverty Program United Planning Orgn., 1966-70; pres. Consumer Energy Coun. Am. Rsch. Found., Washington, 1973—. Mem. Office Tech. Assessment Residential Energy Conservation Adv. Com., 1976-77, Magnetic Fusion Adv. Com., 1986-87, Aspen Inst. Energy Policy Forum; mem. coun. for the Arts MIT, 1995—; mem. Com. on Energy and Econ. Devel. NAACP; mem. German Marshall Fund Adv. Com. on Energy Efficiency in Swedish Bldgs. Co-author: A Decade of Despair, A Compendium of Utility-Sponsored Appliance Rebate Programs, Transportation, Energy and Environment: Balancing Goals and Identifying Policies, 1995, Restructuring the Electric Utility Industry: A Consumer Perspective, 1998; author: Equity and Energy: Rising Energy Prices and the Living Standards of Lower Income Americans, 1983, Oil, Gas or ..? A Guide to Saving Heating Dollars, The Consumer and Energy Impacts of Oil Exports, Operating Costs of Refrigerators/Freezers and Room Air Conditioners, If You Want to Lower Your Heating Bill, It's Time to Raise the Roof, A Comparative Analysis of Utility and Non-Utility Based Energy Services Companies, A State by State Compendium of Energy Efficiency Programs Using Oil Overchange Funds; (reports) The Consumer and Energy Impacts of Oil Exports, 1984, A Comprehensive Analysis of a Crude Oil Import Fee: Dismantling a Trojan Horse, 1982, A Comparison of Crude Oil Decontrol and Natural Gas Deregulation: An Analysis of the Impract of Immediate Decontrol of Crude Oil and Related Products on End Use Consumers, Natural Gas Deregulation: A Case of Trickle Up Economics, 1982; pub. The Quad Report, 1993—. Bd. dirs. Barnard in Washington, 1994—; bd. trustees Wider Opportunities for Women; bd. mgrs. Adas Israel Congregation, 1996—; chmn. bldgs. and gounds com. Woodley Park Towers condominium. Named Woman of the Eighties, Ladies Home Jour., 1979; grantee German Marshall Fund. Mem. Barnard Coll. Washington Alumnae Assn. (bd. dirs.), Cosmos Club. Home: 2737 Devonshire Pl NW Washington DC 20008-3479 Office: Consumer Energy Coun Am Rsch Found 2000 L St NW Ste 802 Washington DC 20036-4913

BERMAN, GAIL, broadcast executive; m. Bill Masters, 1980; 2 children. B in Theater, U. Md., 1978. Former exec. prodr. Comedy Channel, HBO; from v.p. TV to pres. and CEO Sandollar Prodns., 1991—97, advisor, 1997—98; founding pres. Regency TV, 1998—2000; pres. entertainment Fox Broadcasting Co., 2000—. Named one of 100 Most Powerful Women in Hollywood, Hollywood Reporter, 2003, 50 Most Powerful Women in Am Bus., Fortune Mag., 2003. Office: Fox Broadcasting Co 10201 W Pico Blvd Bldg 100 Los Angeles CA 90035

BERMAN, GIZEL, sculptor; b. Sobrance, Slovakia, Aug. 26, 1919; came to U.S., 1946; d. Armin and Margit (Kaufman) Herskovits; m. Nicholas Berman, Dec. 23, 1941; 1 child, Margaret. Student, Uzhorod Bus. Coll., Czechoslovakia, 1935-37, Nagay Design Sch., Budapest, Hungary, 1938, Inst. Michot, Brussels, 1939. Lectr. in schs. and orgns. Survivors of the Holocaust, Seattle, 1980-90. Exhibited bronze sculptures at galleries in Seattle, Portland, Oreg. and Vancouver, B.C., Can., 1950—. Mem. Survivors of the Holocaust, Seattle, 1950—; with Herzl-Ner Tamid Conservative Congregation. Recipient Holocaust Meml. award Jewish Fedn. Greater Seattle, 1981; participant Album Internat., Geneva, 1979. Mem. Hadassah (life). Democrat. Avocations: horseback riding, skiing, tennis, hiking. Home: Ph 2 1200 University St Seattle WA 98101-4245

BERMAN, KAREN JUDITH, theater director, educator; b. Columbia, S.C., Dec. 31, 1952; d. Jerome David and Betty Green Berman; m. Paul Guy Accettura, May 25, 1980. BA, George Washington U., 1974; MFA, Cath. U. Am., 1993. Freelance theater dir. various univs. and theaters, 1974—. Dir. casting Sourcecast, Source Theatre, Washington, 1988—; artistic advisor, adminstrv. dir. theatre program Georgetown U., Washington, 1993—, adj. prof., 1995—, Am. U., Washington, 1997—. Dir.: Chicago, 1987 (Best Dir., Best Prodn.), Revenge of the Space Pandas, 1991 (Best Dir., Best Prodn.), Ah, Wilderness!, Glass Menagerie, Six Characters in Search of An Author, A Dybbuk, Cantorial, A Girl's Guide to Chaos. Mem.: Assn. Theatre in Higher Edn. (v.p. advocacy 2001—03, dir. advocacy watch 1998—2001). Office: Georgetown Univ Dept Art Music & Theatre Washington DC 20057

BERMAN, LISA, advertising executive; Media dir., sr. v.p. Hill, Holliday, Connors, Cosmopulos, Inc., Advertising, Boston, 1988—. Office: Hill Holliday Connors Cosmopulos Inc Advertising John Hancock Tower 200 Clarendon St Boston MA 02116-5021

BERMAN, LORI BETH, lawyer; b. N.Y.C., June 27, 1958; d. George Gilbert and Sara Ann (Abrams) B.; m. Jeffrey Ganeles, Nov. 26, 1983; children: Caryn Elissa, Steven Aaron. BA magna cum laude, Tufts U., 1980; JD, George Washington U., 1983; LLM, U. Miami, 2002. Assoc. Margolies, Edelstein & Scherlis, Phila., 1983-84, White and Williams, Phila., 1984-87, Brownstein Zeidman & Schomer, Washington, 1987-89; v.p. legal & compliance Pointe Savs. Bank, Boca Raton, Fla., 1990-95; dist. rep. Congressman Robert Wexler, Boca Raton, 1997-99; assoc. Belson & Lewis, Boca Raton, Fla., 2002—. Mem., Jour. Internat. Law and Econs. Mem. exec. coun. United Jewish Appeal Fedn., Washington, 1987-89, Boca Raton, 1990—, Leadership Boca, 1992. Mem. ABA, D.C. Bar Assn., Fla. Bar Assn., Boca Raton C. of C. Democrat. Jewish. Office Phone: 561-750-7600. E-mail: lbernlaw@aol.com.

BERMAN, PATRICIA KARATSIS, arts specialist; b. San Francisco, Oct. 2, 1953; d. George Emanuel and Hermoine Linda (Foster) Karatsis; m. William Issachar Berman, May 15, 1979; children: Ian, Melissa, Benjamin. BS, Duke U., 1975; MA, NYU, 1977. Dir. Vorpal Gallery, N.Y.C., 1976-83; visual arts coord. East End Arts Coun., Riverhead, N.Y., 1983-89, program dir., 1989-94, exec. dir., 1994-97; dir. mem. svcs. Alliance on N.Y. State Orgns., 1997—, assoc. dir., 1999—. Cons. N.Y. State Coun. on Arts, N.Y.C., 1985—, Suffolk Assn. Jewish Schs., Huntington, N.Y., 1985; adj. lectr. dept. anthropology Bklyn. Coll., 1976-77, Drew U., 1977; adj. tech. asst. dept. instrn. Suffolk County C.C., 1992-93; bd. dirs. Riverhead Bus. Improvement Dist., chair. Contbr. articles to East End Arts News; host cable arts show, 1986-87. Adminstr. L.I. Baroque Ensemble, 1996—; Trustee Commack (N.Y.) Jewish Ctr., 1984—86. Mem. Duke U. Alumni (AAAC chair Suffolk County 1998—). Home: 22 Daisy Ln Commack NY 11725-4106 Office: Alliance NY State Arts Org PO Box 96 Mattituck NY 11952-0096 E-mail: pkbarts@aol.com.

BERMAN, PHYLLIS OCEAN, adult education educator; b. Bklyn., Dec. 20, 1942; d. Charles Solomon and Beatrice Brown Berman; m. E. Fred Sher, July 31, 1966 (div. May 1985); children: Joshua Simon Sher, Morissa Nili Sher; m. Arthur Ocean Waskow, June 22, 1986. BA in English and Philosophy, U. Wis., 1964; MA in Lit. and Edn., CUNY, 1968; EdM in TESOL, Columbia U., 1978. Tchr. trainer Counseling Learning Insts., 1978—; founding dir. Riverside Lang. Program, N.Y.C., 1979—; dir. summer program Elat Chayyim Spiritual Retreat Ctr., Accord, NY, 1992—2003. Chair bd. Prai Or Religious Fellowship, Phila., 1985—93; sec. bd. ALEPH: Alliance for Jewish Renewal, Phila., 1993—2002. Co-author: Getting Into It, 1976, Tales of Tikkun, 1996, A Time for Every Purpose Under Heaven, 2002. Recipient Eyshet Hazon (Woman of Vision) award, ALEPH: Alliance for Jewish Renewal, 1987, Leaders of ABE, Literacy Assistance Ctr., 2001. Avocations: baking, meditation, walking. Home: 6711 Lincoln Dr Philadelphia PA 19119 Office: Riverside Lang Program Inc 490 Riverside Dr New York NY 10027

BERMAN, RACHEL, dancer; b. Berkeley, Calif., Nov. 14, 1963; d. Ronald Berman and Judith Ellen Harding; m. Eric Charles Benz, Nov. 20, 1988. BFA, SUNY, Purchase, 1985. Dancer Ballet Hispanico of N.Y., N.Y.C., 1985-87, Joyce Trisler Danscompany, N.Y.C., 1987-89, May O'Donnel Concert Dance Co., N.Y.C., 1988, Paul Taylor Dance Co., N.Y.C., 1989—. Dancer benefit for Paul Newman's Hole in Wall Gang Camp for Children, 1995, Paul Taylor: Speaking in Tongues, PBS Dance in Am. TV program, 1991, Paul Taylor: The Wrecker's Ball, PBS Dance in Am. TV program, 1996; profiled in Vanity Fair mag., 1993, cover story in Dance mag., 1997. Active Dancers Responding to AIDS. Avocations: scuba diving, travel, swimming, sewing. Office: Paul Taylor Dance Co 552 Broadway Fl 2D New York NY 10012-3947

BERMAN, SHARI SPRINGER, film director, scriptwriter; b. N.Y., July 1964; m. Robert Pulcini. BFA in Film, Columbia U., 1995. Author: (screenplays) Am. Splendor, 2003 (Grand Jury prize Sundance Film Festival, 2003, Critics award Cannes Film Festival, 2003, Open Palm award IFP, 2003, The New Dir.'s award Edinburgh (Scotland) Internat. Film Festival, 2003, named Best Film, Montreal's (Can.) Comedia Festival, 2003, The Critics award Deauville Film Festival, 2003); co-dir.: (films) Off The Menu: The Last Days of Chasen's, 1997 (named one of Ten Best Movies of 1998, USA Today and CNN, 1998, Best Documentary Grand Jury award Hamptons Internat. Film Festival, Spl. Jury award Locarno Internat. Film Festival, Spl. Jury award Newport Film Festival), The Young and the Dead, 2000, Hello, He Lied, 2002.*

BERMAN-HAMMER, SUSAN, public relations executive; b. Buffalo, Sept. 12, 1950; d. Leonard and Judith H. (Goldenberg) Berman; m. Tony Hammer, Aug. 17, 1975; 1 child, Erik Jason. BA, Northwestern U., 1972, MS, 1975. Pub. info. asst. Sta. WBBM-TV, Chgo., 1972; news asst. exec. trailer Dem. Nat. Conv. ABC-TV News, Miami, Fla., 1972; writer Chgo. Conv. and Visitors Bur., 1973-75; Washington corr. Sta. WYEN, Des Plaines, Ill., 1975; sr. v.p. Herbert H. Rozoff Assocs., Inc., Chgo., 1976-82; pres., owner Susan L. Berman Assocs., Inc., Highland Park, Ill., 1982—; v.p. corp. communications Sheldon Good & Co., Chgo., 1988-89; exec. v.p. client svcs. OnDeckExecs.com, Highland Park, Ill., 2003—. Chair Chgo. Comm./10, 1982-83; media rels. dir. Chris Cohen for Congress Campaign, 1999. Author: (book) Churches, Jail, and Gold Mines...Mega-Deals from a Real Estate Maverick, 2003. Asst. regional dir. Nat. Movement for Student Vote, Chgo., 1972; spokesperson North Shore Sch. Dist. 112 Edn. Found., Highland Pk., Ill., 1995—2001, chmn., 1999—2001; bd. advisor North Shore Sch. Dist. 112 Ednl. Found., Highland Pk., Ill., 2001—03, hon. trustee, 2004—; mem. North Shore Sch. Dist. 112 Caucus, 1995, Edgewood Mid. Sch. PTA, Highland Pk., 1995—97; also Dist. 112 crisis intervention team advisor, 1997—98; founder, chair, exec. com. Safe Home program North Shore Sch. Dists. 112 & 109, 1994—99; Sherwood Sch. PTO liaison to North Shore Sch. Dist. 112 & CIC Legls. Com., Highland Pk., Ill., 1994—95; young women's exec. bd., v.p. cmty. devel., co-chair Trendsetter luncheon, co-chair insights com., nominating com., Shalom Chgo. com, mem. campaign Jewish United Fund Chgo., 1991—96; bd. dirs. nat. women's com. North Shore chpt. Brandeis U., 1991—93; exec. bd., v.p. programming, reenrollment and membership, nominating com. Tamarisk chpt. ORT, Deerfield, Ill., 1990—95; spokesperson, co-leader Parents Against Proposed Annexation of Deerfield subdivsns. from North Shore Sch. Dist. 112 into Deerfield Sch. Dist. 109, 1993—94; chair comm. com. North Shore Congregation Israel, Glencoe, Ill., 1993—94; bd. dirs. Chgo. Women in Broadcasting, 1972—76, Younger Set Jewish Fedn., Dallas, 1985—87; exec. bd., chair Safe Home, liaison to North Shore Sch. Dist. 112, 1195—1996. Recipient Recognition award City Coun. of Highland Park, Ill. Avocations: aerobics, tennis. Office Phone: 847-681-9030. E-mail: sbhsba@aol.com.

BERMANN, SANDRA LEKAS, English language educator; b. Chgo., Mar. 30, 1947; d. Clarence and Theria Belle (Pollard) Lekas; m. George Alan Bermann, Dec. 28, 1969; children: Sloan Douglas, Suzanne Evelyne, Grant Alexander. AB, Smith Coll., 1969; MA, Columbia U., 1971, PhD, 1976. Asst. prof. Princeton (N.J.) U., 1976-83, assoc. prof., 1983-94, prof., 1994—, chmn. comparative lit. dept., 1998—. Dir. undergrad. studies dept. comparative literature Princeton U., 1978-82, 83-84, master of Stevenson Hall, 1984-92, dir. grad. studies dept. comparative literature, 1993-95; visitor Inst. for Advanced Study, Princeton, fall 2001; fellow Columbia U. Inst. for Scholars at Reidl Hall, Paris, 2002. Author: The Sonnet Over Time, 1988; translator, introducer: Manzoni's On the Historical Novel, 1984; contbr. articles to profl. jours. Fellow Fulbright Commn., Italy, 1969-70, Mrs. Giles Whiting Found., Columbia U. and Paris, 1974-75. Mem. MLA, Internat. Comparative Literature Assn., Am. Comparative Literature Assn. (chair undergrad. com. 1987-90, adv. bd. 1989-92, chair constitution 1991-93). Avocations: dance, music. Office: Princeton Univ Dept Comparative Literature 325 E Pyne Princeton NJ 08544-0001 E-mail: sandralb@princeton.edu.

BERMUDEZ, EUGENIA M. **See DIGNAC, GENY**

BERN, DORRIT J. apparel company executive; BSc in Bus., U. Wash. Mem. staff Sears, Roebuck & Co.; pres., CEO Charming Shoppes, Inc., Bensalem, Pa., 1995—, Chmn., 1997—. Bd. dirs. So. Co. Atlanta. Mem. Active Keeping Kids Warm, Bensalem, Pa. Mem.: Atlanta C. of C. (bd. dirs.). Office: Charming Shoppes Inc 450 Winks Ln Bensalem PA 19020-5993

BERNABO, LOIS, social worker, educator; b. Bolivar, Pa., May 7, 1935; d. Anthony Bernabo and Dorinda Audra Muir. BA, Bethany Coll., 1959; MSW, Adelphi U., 1963; DSW, Yeshiva U., 1979. Social worker Kings County Hosp., Bklyn., 1963—65, Bronx (N.Y.) Lebanon Hosp., 1965—67; social worker, dir. social work L.I. Jewish Hosp., Queens (N.Y.) Hosp. Affiliation, 1967—89; assoc. exec. dir. Queens Hosp. Ctr., 1989—97; ret. Lectr. Adelphi U. Sch. Social Work, Garden City, NY, 1970—72, Yeshiva U. Sch. Social Work, N.Y.C., 1984—85; mem. adv. bd. Queens Field Instrn. Ctr., 1970—90. Contbr. articles to profl. jours. Mem.: NASW (lic.). Avocation: researching and writing family history. Home: 210-10 50 Ave Oakland Gardens NY 11364

BERNAL, HARRIET JEAN DANIELS, real estate agent; b. Cin., Sept. 28, 1931; d. Ernest Richard and Amy Lillian (Jeffries) Daniels; m. Gil Bernal, July 9, 1950; children: Gil Jr., Lisa, Nicholas, Colette, Michelle. AA in Theatre Arts, Los Angeles City Coll., 1949-62; student, Kimballs Real Estate Sch., Burbank, Calif., 1974; AA in Humanities, Glendale Coll., 1982; BA in Polit. Sci. Pre-Law, Calif. State U., Los Angeles, 1987. Lic. real estate agt. Dancer, entertainer Greek Theatre, Los Angeles, 1949-50; travel, reservation agt. Iver's Dept. Store, Los Angeles, 1970-73, editor, dept. store news letters, 1972-73; sec. to area supt. and social chmn. Los Angeles Bd. Edn., 1973-74; exec. sec. CBS-TV City, Los Angeles, 1974; real estate salesperson, relocation mgr. Century 21 Realty, Los Angeles, Pasadena, Calif., San Marino, Calif., 1974-86; real estate salesperson Coldwell Banker Residential, Pasadena, Calif., 1986-89, Glendale, Calif., 1989-91, John Douglas Co., Pasadena, Calif., 1991-93; real estate sales, leasing agt., loan cons. Bill Davis & Assoc., South Pasadena, Calif., 1993—. Contbr. articles on sch. sci. ctrs., schs. in Russia, and schs. for the handicapped for local sch. paper, Ann. awards. Pres. San Pascual Elem. Sch. PTA, L.A., 1969-70, hon. life mem., 1970—; first soprano Consortium Angeli, 1991-92; fundraiser various groups to elect Mayor Tom Bradley, L.A.; wedding hostess Pasadena (Calif.) Ch. of Angels, 1980-88, also lic. lay minister. Mem. Pasadena Bd. Realtors (local govt. com., polit. affairs com.), Met. Player Guild. Democrat. Episcopalian. Avocations: acting, singing, writing, jewelry making, painting. Home: 1075 Rutland Ave Los Angeles CA 90042-1536 Office: Dilbeck Betters Home & Gardens Realtors 1499 Huntington Dr South Pasadena CA 91030-4552

BERNARD, APRIL, poet, literature educator; BA, Harvard U. Former sr. editor Premiere, GQ, Vanity Fair; instr. Amherst Coll., Yale U.; prof. lit., MFA core faculty Bennington (Vt.) Coll., 1998—. Author: (novels) Pirate Jenny, (poetry) Blackbird Bye Bye, Psalms: Poems, 1993, Swan Electric: Poems, 2002; contbr. poems, literary essays, and articles to various publs. Guggenheim fellow, 2003. Office: Bennington Coll One College Dr Bennington VT 05201

BERNARD, BETSY J. former telecommunications industry executive; b. May 1955; BS, St. Lawrence U.; MBA, Fairleigh Dickinson U.; MS, Stanford U. Various positions in sales, mktg., opers. AT&T; pres., CEO Pacific Telesis Group Pacific Bell Comms., 1995-97; CEO AVIRNEX Comms. Group, 1997-98; pres. U S West Long Distance U S West, Inc., 1998; exec. v.p. retail markets U.S. West, Inc., Denver, 1998—2000; exec. v.p., nat. mass markets Qwest Comm. Internat., 2000—01; pres., CEO AT&T Consumer unit, 2001—02; pres. AT&T Bus. unit, 2002—03, AT&T Corp., Bedminster, NJ, 2002—03. Bd. dirs. Prin. Fin. Group, Zantaz.com; spkr. in field Featured in Eleven Commandments of Wildly Successful Women. V.p. comms. Internat. Women's Forum; bd. dirs. Mile High United Way; active Denver Cmty. Recognized as Most Influential Bus. Woman, San Francisco, 1996. Mem. Wise Women's Coun.

BERNARD, CATHY S. management corporation executive; b. Bronx, N.Y., Nov. 13, 1949; d Burton and Norma (Ebb) B. BBA, George Washington U., 1971, M of Pub. Adminstrn., 1978; MA, U. Miami, 1972. Cert. property mgr. Staff asst. HEW, Washington, 1970-74; evaluation specialist OEO, Washington, 1974; tchr. St. Patrick's Acad., Washington, 1975; asst. prof. No. Va. C.C., Woodbridge, 1976-78; adj. prof. Prince George's CC, 2002; staff dir. Dem. Nat. Conv., N.Y.C., 1976; pres., chief exec. officer CSB Assocs. Mgmt. Corp., Riverdale, Md., 1977—. Mem. Housing Opportunities Commn., Kensington, Md., 1979-93, chmn., 1988, vice chair, 1980, 87, chair pro tem, 1986, chair housing honor roll, 1985-88, Moderate Priced Dwelling Unit Commn.; mem. exec. coun. Inst. Real Estate Mgmt., Washington, 1982-87, cert. property mgr.; adj. prof. bus. Prince Georges C.C., 2002. Adv. coun. Suburban Hosp., Bethesda, Md., 1984-89; bd. dirs. Ivymount Sch. for Handicapped, Potomac, Md., 1984—, chmn. bd. dirs., 2003, chair property com., chair bldg. expansion project, 1999-2002; treas. Jewish Coun. on Aging, 1988; bd. dirs., chair property com. Jewish Found. for Group Homes, Rockville, Md., 1989-91; bd. dirs. Roundhouse Theatre, Wheaton, Md., 1994—, treas., 1995—; bd. dirs. McLean Sch. Md., 2001, trustee 2001—04, vice chmn., sec., site com. chair, 2002; bd. dirs. Bethesda's Imagination State, 2003—; trustee Temple Emanuel, Kensington, Md., 1994-97; candidate Md. State Legislature, 1986; pres. Cmty. Housing Res. Bd., 1985. Recipient Hughes award for property mgmt., 1980, Jewish Coun. award, 1989. Mem. Montgomery County C. of C. (bd. dirs., v.p. housing com. 1981-82), Apt. and Office Bldg. Assn. (bd. dirs., chmn. affordable housing com. 1990-99). Office: CSB Assocs Mgmt Corp PO Box 647 Riverdale MD 20738-0647

BERNARD, MARCELLE THOMASINE, physician; b. N.Y.C., Aug. 11, 1920; d. Rene Jules and Antoinette (Byrnes) Bernard. AB Magna cum laude, Coll. of St. Elizabeth, 1941; MD, N.Y. Med. Coll., 1944. Diplomate Nat. Bd. Med. Examiners. Intern Flower and Fifth Ave. Hosps., 1944—45; gen. practice medicine N.Y.C., 1947—75; attending phys. St. Francis Hosp., Bronx, NY, 1950—57, Union Hosp., N.Y.C., 1957—75; attending staff Frances Schervier Home and Hosp., N.Y.C., 1952—75; pres. med. bd., 1959—60; sec., 1962; attending staff St. Patrick's Home, N.Y.C., 1954—75; pres. med. bd., 1962. Mem. exec. com. Bronx Tb and Health Assn., 1956—60; hon. surgeon Life Sav. Svc., N.Y.C., 1959—62; v.p. Bronxboro Commn. on Aging, 1961—62. Mem. Ladies of Charity. Lt. USMC, lt. Women's Res. USN, 1945—47. Fellow: Am. Geriatrics Soc., Am. Acad. Family Practice.

BERNARD, MARILYN THOMAS, director, vocalist; b. New Orleans, Mar. 20, 1946; d. Merrill Howard and Blanche Edwards Thomas; 1 child, Jennifer Elizabeth. BA, Newcomb Coll., 1968; MFA, Tulane U., 1970. Asst. prof. music Xavier U., New Orleans, 1970—76; tchr. Isidore Newman Sch., 1977—92; tchr. voice, choral dir. Albuquerque Acad., 1992—96, chair performing arts dept., 1996—. Adj. prof. voice Tulane U., 1976—77, So. U., 1976—77. Singer: (soloist and choralist) Santa Fe Desert Chorale, (soloist) N.Mex. Symphony Orch., New Orleans Symphony. Mem. Mayor's Arts Com., New Orleans; trustee N.Mex Symphony Orch., Albuquerque, 2000—02; pres. N.Mex Symphony Orch. Chorus, 2000—02; mem. edn. com. N.Mex Symphony Orch., Albuquerque, 2000—03. Named Outstanding Woman, State of La. Mem.: Music Educators Nat. Conf., Am. Choral Dirs. Assn. (pres. N.Mex. chpt. 2003—). Avocations: reading, travel, Scrabble. Home: 5222 Vicksburg Drive NW Albuquerque NM 87120 Office: Albuquerque Acad 6400 Wyoming Blvd NE Albuquerque NM 87109 Personal E-mail: bernard@aa.edu. E-mail: bernard@aa.edu.

BERNARD, RUTH FAYE, artist, educator; b. New Haven, Conn., May 5, 1951; d. Edward Robert and Naomi (Rudnick) Bernard; m. Peter Jermain Moore, Oct. 14, 1973 (div. 1980); m. Henry White Welch, Jr., July 24, 1991. Cert. in Fine Art, Sch. of Worcester Art Mus., Mass., 1973; BFA, Mass. Coll. of Art, 1987; MFA, Queens Coll., CCNY, 1989. Vis. instr. Queens Coll., CUNY, 1989—90; instr. painting Pa. Govs. Sch. of Excellence in Art, Erie, Pa., 1989—90; instr. Pa. Sch. of Art and Design, Lancaster, 1989—90, 1991—93, asst. prof., 1992—96, assoc. prof., 1996—. Artist: selected exhibitions include: (solo and two person) Syracuse Women's Ctr., 1982, Mass. Coll. of Art Exit Show, Boston, 1986, Queens Coll. Theatre, Flushing, N.Y., 1989, Ward Lawrence Gallery N.Y.C, 1989, Pa. Sch. of Art & Design, Lancaster, 1991, Cultural Coun. of Lancaster County, 1994, Here to Timbuktu, Lancaster, 1991, 95, Gettysburg (Pa.) Coll., 1995, Pa. State U., Harrisburg, 1995, 98, Blue Mountain Gallery, 1998, The Art Works at Doneckers, Lititz, Pa., 1999, Lancaster Gallery,2001, Lancaster Musuem of Art,2001, Millersville U.,2003, Md. Coll. Art and Design, 1999, Blue Mountain Gallery, N.Y., 2001, Lancaster (Pa.) Mus. Art, 2001, Washington Art Assn., Conn., 2001, Millersville (Pa.) U., 2003; group shows: Sch. of Worcester Art Mus., 1973, Copley Soc., Boston, 1981-85, Kingston Gallery, Boston, 1986, North Hall Gallery, Boston, 1985, 86, Pa. Govs. Sch. for Arts, [illegible] U., 1988, [illegible] Coll., Pa., 1990, [illegible] Gallery, N.Y., 1992, 93, Nittany Lion Competitive Show, Reading, Pa., others; author: John David Wissler and His Work, 2003; represented in pvt. and corp. collections. Dir., designer Art Enrichment Program for Children with Learning Disabilities, 1992, 93; judge local art shows: WITF Children's Art Contest, 1991, 92, 93, Mount Gretna Art and Craft Show, 1993, Art Assn. of Lancaster County, 1994, Lancaster Outdoor Show, 1995. Recipient Liquitex award for excellence, 1989; scholar Profl. and Bus. Women's Assn. Orange, Conn., 1982; fellow Vt. Studio Ctr., Johnson, 1991, 1999, fellowship, Pa. Coun. on the Arts, 2000, 2001, 2003. Mem. Coll. Art Assn., N.Y. Artist's Equity, Harrisburg (Pa.) Art Assn. Home: 2120 Marietta Ave Lancaster PA 17603-2208

BERNAY, BETTI, artist; d. David Michael and Anna Gaynia (Bernay) Woolin; children: Manette Deitsch, Karen Lynn. Grad. costume design, Pratt Inst.; student, Nat. Acad. Design, N.Y.C., Art Students League. Exhibited one man shows at Galerie Raymond Duncan, Paris, France, Salas Municipales, San Sebastian, Spain, Circulo de Bellas Artes, Madrid, Spain, Bacardi Gallery, Miami, Fla., Columbia (S.C.) Mus., Columbus (Ga.) Mus., Galerie Andre Weil, Paris, Galerie Hermitage, Monte Carlo, Monaco, Casino de San Remo, Italy, Galerie de Arte de la Caja de Ahorros de Ronda, Malaga, Spain, Centro Artistico, Granada, Spain, Circulo de la Amistad, Cordoba, Spain, Studio H Gallery, N.Y.C., Walter Wallace Gallery, Palm Beach, Fla., Mus. Bellas Artes, Malaga, Harbor House Gallery, Crystal House Gallery, Internat. Gallery, Jordan Marsh, Fontainebleau Gallery, Miami Beach, Carriage House Gallery, Galerie 99, Pageant Gallery, Miami Beach, Rosenbaum Galleries, Palm Beach; exhibited group shows at Painters and Sculptors Soc., Jersey City Mus., Salon de Invierno, Mus. Malaga, Salon des Beaux Arts, Cannes, France, Guggenheim Gallery, Nat. Acad. Gallery, Salmagundi Club, Lever House, Lord & Taylor Art Gallery, Nat. Arts Gallery, Knickerbocker Artists, N.Y.C., Salon des Artistes Independants, Salon des Artistes Francais, Salon Populiste, Paris, Salon de Otono, Nat. Assn. Painters and Sculptors Spain, Madrid, Phipps Gallery, Palm Beach, Artists Equity, Hollywood (Fla.) Mus., Gault Gallery Cheltenham, Phila., Springfield (Mass.) Mus., Met. Mus. and Art Center, Miami, Fla., Planet Ocean Mus., Charter Club, Trade Fair Ams.; represented in permanent collections including Jockey Club Art Gallery, Miami, Mus. Malaga, Circulo de la Amistad, I.O.S. Found., Geneva, Switzerland, others. Bd. dirs. Men's Opera Guild, Project Newborn Neonatal unit Jackson Meml. Hosp.; mem. adv. bd. Jackson Meml. Hosp. Project Newborn; mem. women's com. Bascom Palmer Eye Inst., mem. adv. coun.; mem. working com. Greater Miami Heart Assn., Am. Heart Assn., Am. Cancer Soc., Alzheimer Grand Notable, 2d Generation Miami Heart Inst., Sunrisers Mentally Retarded, Orchid Ball Com., Newborn Neonatal Intensive Care Unit, U. Miami, Jackson Meml. Hosp.; founder Mt. Sinai Hosp., Miami; benefactor Miami Heart Rsch. Inst.; grand benefactor Neonatal Project Newborn, Jackson Meml. Hosp., Miami Opera, Am. Cancer Soc., Am. Heart Assn., Alzheimers Notable Care Unit, Greater Miami Opera Guild, March of Dimes, CancerLink, Sylvester Cancer Unit; adv. coun. Bascom Palmer Eye Inst.; founder Mt. Sinai Hosp. Recipient medal City N.Y., medal Sch. Art Leagues, N.Y.C., Prix de Paris Raymond Duncan, others. Mem. Nat. Assn. Painters and Sculptors Spain, Nat. Assn. Women Artists, Société des Artistes Français, Société des Artistes Independants, Fedn. Francais des Sociétés d'Art Graphique et Plastique, Artists Equity, Am. Artists Profl. League, Am. Fedn. Art, Nat. Soc. Lit. and Arts, Met. Mus. and Arts Center Miami, Pres.'s Club U. Miami, Palm Bay Club, Jockey Club, Turnberry Club, Club of Clubs Internat. Address: 10155 Collins Ave Apt 1705 Bal Harbour FL 33154-1629

BERNDT, ELLEN GERMAN, company executive; b. N.Y.C., 1953; BS, Denison U., 1975; JD, Capital U., 1984. Bar: Ohio 1984. Legal asst. Borden Inc., Columbus, Ohio, 1978-84, corp. atty., 1984-90, asst. sec., corp. atty., 1990-96, corp. sec., asst. gen. counsel, 1996—. Mem. Am. Corp. Counsel Assn., Ctrl. Ohio Corp. Counsel Assn. (pres. 1997). Office: Borden Inc 180 E Broad St Columbus OH 43215-3799 E-mail: eberndt@bordencapital.com.

BERNER, JUDITH, mental health nurse; b. Tamaqua, Pa., June 19, 1938; d. Ralph Edgar and Ethel Mary (Williams) B. Diploma in nursing, Temple U. Hosp., 1959; AS, Coll. of Ganado, 1975, MS in Cmty. Health, D of Med. Adminstrn. (hon.), Coll. of Ganado; BA, Stephens Coll., 1977; MEd, U. Ariz., 1980; LD (hon.), U. Iceland. RN, Ariz., N.Mex., Pa. Nursing adminstr. Project HOPE Internat. Office & Hosp. Ship, Washington, 1970-72; assoc. adminstr. Navajo Nation Health Found., Ganado, Ariz., 1972-79; clin. instr. psychiat. nursing Mo. So. State Coll., Joplin, 1986; nurse/therapist Presbyn. Kaseman Hosp., Albuquerque, 1986-93; emergency svcs. clinician for mental health svcs. Presbyn. Healthcare Sys., 1994-95, Heights Psychiat. Hosp., 1994-95, Charter Heights Behavioral Health Sys., Albuquerque, 1995-2000; regional clin. coord. Mental Health Svcs., Inc., 1995-97; psychiat. cons.-liaison nurse U. N.Mex. Health Scis. Ctr., 1996—2003, Medication Monitoring, Pathways, Inc., 2000—. Mem. ANA (cert. in psychiat. and mental health nursing), AACD, Internat. Acad. Behavioral Medicine, Counseling and Psychotherapy, Inc.

BERNER, MARY, publisher; Publisher, v.p. Glamour Mag., to 1999; pres., CEO Fairchild Publs., N.Y.C., 1999—. Office: Conde Nast Fairchild Publs Seven W 34th St New York NY 10001-8191

BERNER HARRIS, CYNTHIA KAY, librarian; b. Concordia, Kans, Aug. 31, 1958; d. William Clifford and Donna Darlene (Brown) B.; m. Dwight Harris, May 1, 1999. AA, Cottey Coll., 1978; BA, U. Kans., 1980; MALS, U. Denver, 1981. System cons. Panhandle Libr. Network, Scottsbluff, Nebr., 1981-82; dir. Winfield (Kans.) Pub. Libr., 1982-84; from Westlink br. mgr. to coord. ext. svcs. Wichita (Kans.) Pub. Libr., 1984-95, coord. adminstrv. svcs., 1995—2000, dir. of librs., 2000—. Editor Propeller mag., 1995-96 (Jr. League Wichita); editor (newsletter) LWV, Wichita Met., 1993. Pres. PEO Sisterhood (chpt. IM), Wichita, 1989—90; active Jr. League Wichita; project chair STARBASE, 1997—98, dir. cmty. rels., 1998—99; trustee at large Bibliog. Ctr. for Rsch., 2001—, exec. com., 2002—; tech. adv. bd. City of Wichita, 2000—; banking chair Nat. Conf. for Cmty. and Justice Walk, 2003. Mem.: ALA, Kans. Libr. Assn. (chair pub. libr. sect. 1988—89, mem. legis. com. 1997—2001, nominating com. 1998—99, mem. legis. com. 2002—), Mountain Plains Libr. Assn. (chair profl. devel. grants com. 1983—84, 1986—87, chair pub. libr. sect. 1988—89, chair intellectual freedom com. 1988—90, sec. 1996—97, mem. nominating com. 1998—2000), Pub. Libr. Assn. (dir. pub. libr. sys. sect. 1995—98, dir. pub. libr. sys. com. 1998—2001). Methodist. Home: 6418 Oneil St Wichita KS 67212-6327 Office: Wichita Pub Libr 223 Main St Wichita KS 67202

BERNHAGEN, LILLIAN FLICKINGER, retired school health consultant; b. Cleve., Oct. 1, 1916; d. Norman Henry and Bertha May (Rogers) Flickinger; m. Ralph John Bernhagen, Sept. 2, 1940; children: Ralph, Janet Elizabeth Darling, Penelope Anne Braat. Student, Ohio Wesleyan U., 1934-37; BS, RN, Ohio State U., 1940, MA, 1958; postgrad., LaVerne Coll., 1972-73. Cert. health edn. specialist; cert. holistic coach Journeys of Wisdom Inst. Asst. dir. Kiwanis Health Camp for Underprivileged Children, Steubenville, Ohio, summer 1940; asst. dir. nurses Jefferson Davis Hosp., Houston, 1940-41; ARC instr. Ohio State U., 1943, 63, elem. edn. lectr., 1970; dir. health services Worthington (Ohio) City Schs., 1951-76; health edn. instr. Ohio State U., 1976-77; spl. cons. venereal disease and sex edn. Ohio Dept. Health, 1976-82; sch. health cons., 1976-98; vice chmn. medicine/edn. com. on sch. and coll. health AMA, 1976-78, chmn., 1978-80. Author: Sex Education: Understanding Growth and Social Development, 1968, What A Miracle You Are-Boys, 1968, 3d rev. edit., 1986, What A Miracle You Are-Girls, 1968, 3d rev. edit., 1986, Toward a Reverence for Life, 1971, Personality, Sexuality and Stereotyping, 1974, (with others) Growth Patterns and Sex Education: A Suggested Curriculum Guide K-12, 1967; contbr. articles to profl. jours., mags. Bd. dirs. Hearing and Speech Ctr. of Columbus and Franklin County, [illegible]; mem. nat. adv. com. Nat. Ctr. for Health Edn., 1978-82; sec.-tres. Ohio Wesleyan U. Class of 38, 1968-78, 83-88; bd. dirs. V.D. Hotline Columbus and Franklin County, 1974-87, bd. expansion chmn., 1978-85, pres., 1985-86; mem. profl. adv. com. Ptnrs. Home Health Inc., 1991-97; mem. Worthington Hist. Soc., Doll Docent, 1982—; mem King Ave. United Meth. Ch., 1938—, mem. marriage counseling com., 1997-98, mem. choir, 1950—, pres., 1961-63, pastor/parish rels. com., 1985-88, bd. trustees, 1989-92, adminstrv. coun., 1992-98, homosexual study com., 1998-99, edn. commn., 1982-85, nominations and pers., 1992-94; treas. Franklin County Women's Golf Tournament, 1992. Recipient Centennial award Ohio State U., 1970, Outstanding Alumna award Ohio State U. Sch. Nursing, 1964, Disting. Service award Mich. Sch. Nurses Assn., 1972, hon. mention La Sertoma Internat. Woman of Yr., 1972, Alumni award of hon. Ohio Wesleyan U., 1998. Fellow Am. Sch. Health Assn. (v.p. 1974, pres. 1976, governing coun. 1973-88, chmn. health guidance in sex edn. com. 1963-67, 71-77, chmn. sr. adv. coun. 1983-89, Disting. Svc. award 1969, Howe award 1979, cert. of merit, 1985, mem. awards com. 1986-89, mem. hist. com. 1989—, constn. and bylaws com. 1997-99), APHA (chmn. com. on urban health problems 1972); mem. NEA (life, ret.), Sex Edn. and Info. Coun. of U.S., Worthington Edn. Assn. (v.p. 1961-62, Tchr. of Year 1972-73), Ctrl. Ohio Tchrs. Assn. (chmn. sch. health svcs. sect. 1963), Ohio State U. Women's Golf Assn. (chmn. 1973, parliamentarian 1988—), Ohio Wesleyan U. Alumni Assn. (bd. dirs., chmn. alumni recognition com. 1994-95, chmn. bylaws revision com. 1991-96, mem. orgn. com. 1994-95), Columbus Women's Dist. Golf Assn. (treas. 1985, sec. 1987, v.p. 1989, pres. 1990, adv. bd. 1991-98, parliamentarian 1996-98), Chi Omega (pres. Columbus Alumnae chpt. 1947-49, fin. adv. Ohio Wesleyan U. 1964-76, Outstanding Alumna of Yr. State of Ohio 1986), Pi Lambda Theta (citation award 1971, mem. program com. 1986-89, chmn. by laws revision com. 1990-00, parliamentarian), Journeys of Wisdom, Monnett Club, Worthington Women's Club, Sigma Theta Tau, Phi Delta Kappa. Home and Office: 5916 Linworth Rd Worthington OH 43085-3357 E-mail: Lfbern@aol.com.

BERNHARD, SANDRA, actress, comedienne, singer; b. Flint, Mich., June 6, 1955; d. Jerome and Jeanette B., 1 child Stand-up comedienne nightclubs, Beverly Hills, Calif., 1974-78; films include Cheech and Chong's Nice Dreams, 1981, The King of Comedy, 1983 (Nat. Soc. Film Critics award), Sesame Street Presents: Follow That Bird, 1985, Track 29, 1988, Without You I'm Nothing, 1990, Hudson Hawk, 1991, Truth or Dare, 1991, Inside Monkey Zetterland, 1993, Dallas Doll, 1994, Unzipped, 1995, Catwalk, 1995, Plump Fiction, 1996, Somewhere in the City, 1997, Lover Girl, 1997, The Apocalypse, 1997, An Alan Smithee Film: Burn Hollywood Burn, 1997, I Woke Up Early the Day I Died, 1998, Exposé, 1998, Wrongfully Accused, 1998, Dinner Rush, 2000, Playing Mona Lisa, 2000, The Third Date, 2003; also appears in Heavy Petting, 1988, Perfect, 1985, The Whoopee Boys, 1986, Casual Sex?, 1988; stage appearances (solo) Without You I'm Nothing, 1988, Giving Till It Hurts, 1992, I'm Still Here...Damn It, 1998-99; TV appearances (host) Living in America, 1990; regular guest The Richard Pryor Show, Late Night with David Letterman; TV series Instant Comedy with the Groundlings, The Hitchhiker, The Full Wax, Tales from the Crypt, Roseanne, Space Ghost Coast to Coast, The Larry Sanders Show, Clueless, Chicago Hope, Highlander, Comedy Central's The A-List, 1992-1993, Superman (voice), Ally McBeal, Hercules (voice), 1999, The Sandra Bernhard Experience (host), 2001-2002; (TV movies) Freaky Friday, 1995, The Late Shift, 1996; albums (co-author 8 songs) I'm Your Woman, 1985, Without You I'm Nothing, 1988, Excuses for Bad Behavior, Part I, 1994; books include Confessions of a Pretty Lady, 1988, Love Love Love, 1993, May I Kiss You On The Lips, Miss Sandra?, 1998. Office: Noe-Man Mgmt Scott Noe 26500 Agoura Rd Ste 575 Calabasas CA 91302-1952 also: Joanne Schwartz Mgmt 330 W 56 St New York NY 10019

BERNHARDSON, IVY SCHUTZ, lawyer; b. Fargo, N.D., Aug. 22, 1951; d. James Newell and Phyllis Harriet (Iverson) Schutz; m. Mark Elvin Bernhardson, Sept. 1, 1973; children: Andrew Schutz, Jenna Clare. BA, Gustavus Adolphus Coll., 1973; JD, U. Minn., 1978. Bar: Minn. 1978, U.S. Dist. Ct. Minn. 1978. Staff atty. Gen. Mills, Inc., Mpls., 1978-83, asst. sec. to bd. dirs., 1982-96, assoc. counsel, 1983-85, sr. assoc. counsel, 1985-96, v.p., 1988-2000; assoc. gen. counsel, sec., 1996-2000; shareholder Leonard, Street and Deinard, 2000—. Trustee Gustavus Adolphus Coll., 1989-98, Fairview Southdale Hosp., 1993—, chair, 1999—; dir. Fairview Healthcare Svcs., 1996—, vice chair, 1999—; bd. dirs. The Bush Found., 1997—. Mem. ABA, Am. Soc. Corp. Secs., Minn. Bar Assn., Hennepin County Bar Assn. Lutheran. Office: Gen Mills Inc 1 General Mills Blvd Minneapolis MN 55426-1348

BERNHARDT, VICTORIA L. director, researcher; d. Richard L. and Marilyn M. Bernhardt; m. James E. Richmond, June 10, 1990. BS, Iowa State U., Ames, 1974, MS, 1977; PhD, U. Oreg., Eugene, 1981. Rsch./evaluation N.W. Regional Ednl. Lab., Portland, Oreg., 1976—79; rsch. cons. Calif. Dept. of Edn., Sacramento, 1980—81; evaluation cons. Calif. Commn. on Tchr. Credentialing, Sacramento, 1981—86; dir., inst. for advanced studies Calif. State U., Chico, 1986—91, exec. dir. Edn. for the Future, 1991—. Author: (book) Using Data to Improve Student Learning in Elementary Schools, The School Portfolio Toolkit: A Planning, Implementation, and Evaluation Guide for Continuous School Improvement, Designing and Using Databases for Sch. Improvement, The Sch. Portfolio: A Comprehensive Framework for Sch. Improvement, First and Second Edition, Data Analysis for Comprehensive Schoolwide Improvement, 1st and 2d edits., Using Data to Improve Student Learning in Middle Schools, Using Data to Improve Student Learning in High Schools, Using Data to Improve Student Learning in School Districts; co-author: The Example School Portfolio, A Companion to the School Portfolio: A Comprehensive Framework for School Improvement. Achievements include development of school portfolio for continuous school improvement; data analysis for school improvement. Office: Edn for the Future 400 W First St Chico CA 95929-0230

BERNIARD, SUSAN K. business writer/editor; b. Little Rock, Sept. 26, 1951; d. Herman Joseph and Patricia Anne Kresse; m. Charles William Berniard, Sept. 16, 1972; children: Sam, Lindsay. BA in Journalism, U. Houston, 1974. Pub. rels. writer-editor Raymond Internat., Houston, 1975-79; pub. affairs writer-editor Gulf Oil Corp., Houston, 1979-84; mktg. writer-editor Exxon Co. USA, Houston, 1984-95; pub. affairs writer-editor Exxon Chem., Houston, 1995—. Recipient Gold Excalibur award Pub. Rels. Soc. Am., 1999. Mem. Internat. Assn. Bus. Communicators (Gold Quill 1991, Silver Quill 1999, Bronze Quill 1994, 98, 99). Avocations: sporting events, reading, gardening. Office: Exxon Chem 13501 Katy Fwy Houston TX 77079-1306

BERNICK, CAROL LAVIN, corporate executive; m. Howard Bernick; three children. BA, Tulane U., 1974. Mem. mktg. staff Alberto-Culver Co., Melrose Park, Ill., 1974-79, dir. new products, 1979-81, dir. new bus. devel. group, 1981-84, v.p., 1984-88; co-dir., 1984; group v.p. Alberto-Culver Co., Melrose Park, Ill., 1988-90, exec. v.p. worldwide mktg., 1990-92, exec. v.p., 1992—94; pres. Alberto-Culver USA, Melrose Park, Ill., 1994—98, vice chmn., pres. N.Am. Alberto-Culver Co., Melrose Park, 1998—2002; pres. Alberto Culver Consumer Products Worldwide, Melrose Park, 2002—. Founder Friends of Prentice; mem. women's bd. Resurrection Home Health Svcs., Boys and Girls Clubs of Chgo.; regent Lincoln Acad. Ill.; mem. exec. com. of adv. bd. Kellogg Sch., Northwestern U.; bd. dirs. Northwestern Meml. Healthcare. Recipient Leadership in Bus. award YWCA Met. Chgo., 1992, award for philanthropy Harvard Club of Chgo. Mem. World Pres. Orgn., Econ. Club Chgo., Exec. Club Chgo., Com. 200 Chgo. Network. Office: Alberto-Culver Co 2525 Armitage Ave Melrose Park IL 60160-1163 Office Phone: 708-450-3000.

BERNIER, TINA, artist; b. N.Y.C., Dec. 9, 1949; d. Buddy and Jo Bernier; m. John Aikin Crawford; children: Jonah Bernier Crawford, Jacob Bernier Crawford, Kate Alexandra Crawford. MEd, Columbia U., 1980. Exhibitions include William Woods U., Fulton, Mo., 2000—01, Bushnell Promenade Gallery, Hartford, Conn. Mem.: Am. Artist Profl. League (assoc.), Catharine Lorillard Wolfe Art Club (assoc.), Allied Artists of Am. (assoc.), Salmagundi Club (assoc.), Pastel Soc. West Coast (assoc.), Conn. Pastel Soc. (assoc.), Pastel Soc. Am. (assoc.). Avocations: hiking, bicycling, travel. Office: Tina Bernier PO Box 1233 Redding CT 06875 Personal E-mail: tinabernierart@aol.com.

BERNING, LOUISE JUSTINE, bank executive; b. Scott City, Kans., Nov. 16, 1949; d. Paul William and Leona Mae (Macy) Numruch; m. Terrence A. Berning, June 21, 1969 (div. Oct. 1983); children: Christopher Justin, Jonathan Tate, Nicholas Brandon, Elizabeth Brooke. BS in Econs., Tex. Woman's U., 1971. Asst. cashier Security State Bank, Scott City, Kans., asst. v.p., 1985-89, v.p., 1989—, asst. trust officer, 1989—. Bd. dirs. United Sch. Dist. #466 Bd. Edn., Scott City, 1991-95, v.p., 1993-94, pres., 1994-95; treas. Scott County Hist. Soc., Scott County Health Care Found. Mem. AAUW, KANZA Soc. of High Plains Pub. Radio (chmn.). Home: 902 Crescent Ave Scott City KS 67871-1323 Office: Security State Bank PO Box 170 Scott City KS 67871-0170

BERNITZ, FRANCINE S. marketing professional; b. N.Y.C., Apr. 13, 1961; d. Irwin and Rita Rappaport; m. Steven B. Bernitz, Sept. 3, 1989; children: Nathaniel Byron, Sophia Ilana. B Engring. Sci., Johns Hopkins U., 1983; MS, Northeastern U., Boston, 1986; MBA, MIT, Cambridge, 1988. Materials engr. U.S. Army Materials Tech. Lab., Watertown, Mass., 1983—86; sr. bus. planner corp. devel. FMC Corp., Chgo., 1988—90, sales ops. mgr. chem. products group Downers Grove, Ill., 1990—92, product mgr. alkali chems. divsn. Phila., 1993—94, industry mgr. alkali chems. divsn., 1994—95, mktg. mgr. chem. products group, 1996—97, corp. mktg. dir., 1997—99; v.p. mktg. and corp. comms. Ionics, Inc., Watertown, Mass., 1999—2003. Bd. dirs. The Boston Cecilia, 2003—, Friends of Lexington Music, Arts and Drama Students, Mass., 2003—. Vice chair Today's Girls, Tomorrows Leaders, United Way of Mass. Bay, Boston, 2001—02; trustee Har Sinai, Trenton, NJ, 1996; chair donor dinner, holiday marketplace Temple Isaiah Sisterhood, Lexington, Mass., 1997, 2002. Recipient Beneficial Hodson Merit scholarship, Johns Hopkins U., 1979—83, awards, Am. Bus. Communicators, 1999—2000, Bus. Mktg. Assn., 2001—02, League Am. Comms. Profls., 2002—03. Mem.: Internat. Desalination Assn., Assn. Women in Comms., Suzuki Assn. of Americas, The Boston Club. Avocations: classical music, Ashtanga yoga, travel, horseback riding, gardening. Home: 357 N Emerson Rd Lexington MA 02420

BERNMÚDEZ, CARMEN, trust company executive; b. Costa Rica, 1944; m. Thomas J. Feeney, 1986. Attended, Colegio Superior de Señprotas, Santa Monica City Coll. Bull fighter, Costa Rica, Mex. City, 1962—67; various positions TWA, 1967—85; chmn., treas. Marathon Asset Mgmt. Co., 1985—94; founder, chmn., CEO Mission Mgmt. & Trust Co., 1994—. Apptd. hon. consul of Costa Rica to US by Pres. of Costa Rica. Worked with Central Am. Free Trade Agreement (CAFTA). Recipient Woman of Enterprise, Avon, 2001, Leading Woman Entrepreneur, STAR Group (sponsored by IBM and Chase Manhattan Banking), 2001. Mem.: US Hispanic C. of C., Nat. Minority Supplier Devel. Coun., Nat. Law Ctr. for InterAmerica Free Trade. Achievements include first woman to run a Fiduciary Trust co. in US. Office: La Paloma Corp Ctr 3567 E Sunrise Dr Ste 235 Tucson AZ 85718-3203 Office Phone: 520-557-5559.*

BERNSON, MARCELLA S. psychiatrist; b. N.Y.C., Aug. 24, 1952; d. Maxwell Isaac and Priscilla Edith (Zuckerman) Bernson; m. Robert A. Foster, Aug. 7, 2001. BA in Biology summa cum laude, Hofstra U., 1973; MD, Albert Einstein Coll. Medicine, 1976. Diplomate Am. Bd. Psychiatry and Neurology. Resident in psychiatry Bronx (N.Y.) Mcpl. Hosp. Ctr., 1976-79; assoc. dir. med. student edn. in psychiatry U. Medicine and Dentistry N.J.-N.J. Med. Sch., Newark, 1979-81; pvt. practice psychiatry Westfield, NJ, 1981-86; cons. psychiatrist Healthwise EAP, Elizabeth, NJ, 1985-86; staff psychiatrist Elizabeth Gen. Med. Ctr., 1985—88, 1992—95, med. chief adult ambulatory svcs. dept. psychiatry, 1986-87, asst. dir. dept. psychiatry, 1987-88; dir. tng. psychiat. svc. VA Med. Ctr., East Orange, NJ, 1988-89; med. dir. partial care Occupl. Ctr. Union County, Roselle, NJ, 1989-92; cons. psychiatrist Union County Ednl. Svcs. Commn., Westfield, 1992-95; med. dir. Richard Hall CMHC, Bridgewater, NJ, 1995—99, staff psychiatrist, 2003—; with devel. disabilities ctr. Morristown (N.J.) Meml. [illegible] instr. U. Medicine and Dentistry N.J.-N.J. Med. Sch., Newark, 1979—81, asst. prof. clin. psychiatry, 1988—89; mem. human rights com. Divsn. Devel. Disabilities, State of N.J. Mem.: N.J. Psychiat. Assn. (Union County rep. 1989—90, Morris County rep. 2000—02), Am. Psychiat. Assn. Avocation: short fiction. Office: Richard Hall CMHC 500 N Bridge St Bridgewater NJ 08807

BERNSTEIN, BONNIE, sportscaster; b. Howell, N.J., Aug. 16, 1970; BS in Broadcast Journalism, U. Md. Sports and news dir. Sta. WXJN Radio, Lewes, Del., 1992-93; weekend news anchor Sta. WMDT-TV, Salisbury, Md., 1993; weekday sports anchor Sta. KRNV-TV and Sta. KRNV Radio, Reno, Nev., 1993-95; Chgo.-based corr. SportsCenter ESPN, 1995-98; sportscaster CBS, 1998—. Acad. All-Am. gymnast U. Md. Office: CBS Sports 51 W 52nd St 25th Fl New York NY 10019 E-mail: Bbernstein@cbs.com.

BERNSTEIN, ELIZABETH ANN, retired executive secretary; b. London, Aug. 13, 1928; arrived in U.S., 1960; d. Eugene and Ethel (Housley) Horsfall-Ertz; m. Alvin Bernstein, Mar. 5, 1975. Sec. various firms, 1948—58, Icelandic Airlines, Reykjavik, Iceland, 1958—59; legal and med. sec. various firms, 1960—82, 1982—89; ret., 1989. Author (poetry): Tsunami, 1994, Pull of the Tides, 1998, Many Moons Rising, 2002, numerous poems. Mem.: Bay Area Poets Coalition, Calif. State Poetry Soc. (1st pl. poems 1999). Democrat. Avocations: reading, writing, music, gardening, travel. Mailing: PO Box 94 Paradise CA 95967-0094

BERNSTEIN, FLORENCE HENDERSON See HENDERSON, FLORENCE

BERNSTEIN, GERDA MEYER, artist; Student, Art Inst. Chgo., MFA, 1978. Founder Artists, Residents of Chgo., 1973. One woman shows include Angeleski Gallery, N.Y.C., 1960, Artists, Residents of Chgo. Gallery, 1974, 75, 78, Elmhurst (Ill.) Coll., 1979, Karl Ernst Osthaus Mus., Hagen, West Germany, 1982, A.I.R. Gallery, N.Y.C., 1985, 89, Neuer Berliner Kunstverein, 1987, Bochum (Germany) Mus., 1987, Badischer Kunstverein, Karlsruhe, Germany, 1987, Rockford (Ill.) Coll., 1991, Beacon St. Gallery, Chgo., 1993, Fassbender Gallery, Chgo., 1994, 97, Robert F. DeCaprio Art Gallery, Moraine Valley Coll., Palos Hills, Ill., 1994, Alt. Mus., N.Y.C., 1995, Alternative Mus., N.Y.C., 1995, Ellis Island Immigration Mus., N.Y.C., 1996, Fassbender Gallery, Chgo., 1997, 2000, Reicher Gallery, Lake Forest, 2001, Fassbender-Stevens Gallery, Chgo., 2003, Kuusthaus Potsdam, Germany, 2003; exhibited in group shows at Art Inst. Chgo., 1954, 55, 56, 77, 82, 89, 92, 94, Isaac Delgado Mus., New Orleans, 1954, San Francisco Mus. Art, 1955, U. Chgo., 1961, U. Wis., Madison, 1962, 93, Whitney Mus. Am. Art, N.Y.C., 1973, Carleton Coll., Northfield, Minn., 1974, Sangamon State U., Springfield, Ill., 1974, Ill. State Mus. Art, Springfield, 1976, A.I.R. Gallery, 1977, 84, 88, 1134 Gallery, Chgo., 1977, U. Mo., St. Louis, 1977, U. Ill., Urbana and Chgo., 1977, Cultural Ctr., Chgo., 1978, 81, 89, Rutgers U., New Brunswick, N.J., 1979, Columba Coll., Chgo., 1981, Print Club Phila., 1981, Midwest Mus. Am. Art, Elkhart, Ind., 1981, Purdue (Ind.) U., 1981, Mus. Contemporary Art, Chgo., 1984, No. Ill. U., DeKalb, 1984, 90, Neuer Berliner Kunstverein, 1984, Women's Interart Ctr., N.Y.C., 1985, U.N. Conf. Women, Nairobi, Kenya, 1985, Ministerio de Cultura, Madrid, 1986, Chgo. Office Fine Arts, 1989, Franklin Furnace Gallery, N.Y.C., 1991, Peace Mus., Chgo., 1993, Spertus Mus., Chgo., 1994, Minn. Mus. Am. Art, St. Paul, 1995, Southeastern Ctr. Contemporary Art, Winston-Salem, N.C., 1995-96, Ellis Island, N.Y., 1996. Active Feminist Majority, Planned Parenthood, So. Poverty Law Ctr., Amnesty Internat., Holocaust Mus. Mem. NOW. Democrat. Avocations: reading, walking, music. Home: 1728 N North Park Ave Chicago IL 60614-5710 Studio: 1060 W Adams Chicago IL 60607

BERNSTEIN, HENRIETTA RUTH, publishing executive, writer; b. L.A., Feb. 9, 1926; d. Abraham and Anna Rosen; m. Norman Robert Bernstein, June 15, 1947; children: Alan, Bruce, Anna. BA, U. So. Calif., 1948; postgrad., Santa Monica (Calif.) Coll., 1968—69. Propr. Ryder Art Gallery, L.A., 1958—63, Beverly Palms Hosp., L.A., 1963—68; dir. Light Am. Wisdom, L.A., 2001—. Founder, chair Elec. Magnetic Energy and Elec. Magnetic Medicine confs., L.A., 1985; dir. Cabalah Rsch. Found., Bosque Farms, N.Mex., 1989—. Author: Cabalah Primer, 1984, The Crone Oracles, 1994, Ark of the Covenant-Holy Grail, 1998. Dir., chair Veritat Found. (affiliated with philosopher Manly P. Hall), L.A., 1985—96. Avocations: philosophy, American history, electromagnetic medicine.

BERNSTEIN, JAN LENORE, lawyer; b. N.Y.C., Apr. 24, 1957; d. James Hanley and Joan Mathilda (Wertheimer) B. BA magna cum laude, U. Pa., 1979; JD, Rutgers U., 1982. Bar: N.J. 1982, Pa.1983, N.Y. 1990. Law clk. to hon. Herbert S. Glickman, Newark, 1982-83; ptnr. Riker, Danzig, Scherer, Hyland and Perretti LLP, Morristown, N.J., 1983—. Mem. jud. performance com., jud. and prosecutorial appts. commn., econ. consequences of dissolution com., dis. X fee arbitration com. N.J. Supreme Ct.; mem. exec. com. family law sect.; past mem. family practice com.; presenter in field. Mem. editl. bd. N.J. Lawyer mag.; bd. dirs. N.J. Lawyer newspaper; contbr. articles to profl. jours. Dem. committeeperson; assoc. trustee U. Pa., chair woemn's atheltic bd., mem. trustee coun. Penn Women, bd. of athletic advisors. Mem. N.J. Bar Assn. (past chair women's rights sect.), Morris County (N.J.) Bar Assn. (family law com.). Office: Riker Danzig Scherer Hyland & Perretti LLP Headquarters Plaza Speedwell Ave Morristown NJ 07962 also: 50 W State St Ste 1010 Trenton NJ 08608-1220 Fax: 973-538-1984. E-mail: jbernstein@riker.com.

BERNSTEIN, LESLIE, academic administrator, biostatistician; BA, U. Calif., 1965; MS, U. So. Calif., 1978, PhD, 1981. Rsch. assoc. dept. preventive medicine U. So. Calif., L.A., 1981-82, asst. prof. biostats./epidemiology, 1982-88, assoc. prof. biostats./epidemiology, 1988-91, prof. biostats./epidemiology, 1991—, sr. assoc. dean faculty affairs, 1996—2003, AFLAC Inc. chair in cancer rsch., 1997—, vice provost med. affairs, 2003—. Sci. dir. U. So. Calif. Cancer Surveillance program, 1988—; mem. bd. sci. counselors Nat. Cancer Inst., 2001—; mem. sci. adv. panel Calif. Gov., 1989-92; mem. sci. com. Internat. Soc. Study Esophageal Diseases, 1994—; chair adv. com. L.I. Breast Cancer Cancer Study, Columbia U., 1994-2000; chair external adv. com. Nurse's Health Study Harvard U., 1995—; sci. adv. com. Registry for Rsch. on Transplacental Carcinogenesis, U. Chgo., 1997—; external adv. com. No. Calif. Cancer Ctr., Hawaii Cancer Ctr., 1997—. Contbr. over 250 articles to profl. jours. Office: U So Calif/Norris Cancer Ctr 1441 Eastlake Ave # 4449 Los Angeles CA 90033-0804

BERNSTEIN, MAUREEN ANN, theater educator, director; b. Modesto, Calif., Aug. 24, 1953; d. Francis Paul and Ann Bernice Abell; m. Lawrence A. Bernstein, Nov. 17, 1983; 1 child, Frankie Jonathan. BA in Theatre, U. Nev., 1976, MEd in Curriculum and Instrn., 1998. Cert. tchr. Nev., 1994. Student tchr. Eldorado H.S., Las Vegas, 1994—94; theatre dir. Valley H.S., 1994—97; grad. asst., urban tchg. partnership & instr. with nat. youth sports program as part of master's thesis project U. Nev., 1997—98; theatre dir. chair dept. performing and visual arts Desert Pines H.S., 1999—. Mentor Student Theatrical Adjudicated Rev. Shows, Las Vegas, 2001—, bd. dirs.; mentor Student/Tchr. Mentorship Program, Desert Pines H.S., 2002—. Dir.: (plays, original theatrical production) Hip Hop Goes the Shakespeare (State Adjudicated Show: Nev. State Thespians, 2002); author: (plays) (original theatrical production) Hip Hop Goes the Shakespeare; dir.: (playwrighting program) Playwright's Connection, (play by Nicholas Mickleby) Les Miserables; (plays) Scapin, The Tempest, Stand and Deliver, The Hobbit, Special Delivery New on Broadway, The Grinch Who Stole Christmas, Scrooge, Pippin, Evita, Peter Pan, Babes in Arms, Story Theatre, Alice in Wonderland, Dreamgirls, [illegible] Thespian Troupe 0125, dir., coach students Nev. State Thespian Conf. Recipient Supporting Actress award, Am. Coll. Theatre Festival, 1974; Devos Talent scholar, U. Nev., Las Vegas Theatre Dept., 1972—76. Mem.: NEA, Clark Clounty Edn. Assn., Clark County Assn. Theatre Teachers (v.p. 2002). Liberal. Achievements include research in Role Play in the Classroom; development of Music Theatre within yearly theatre curriculum; Contributed to the development of high school drama review program for the Clark County School District; development of Seminar Based Learning Program for the High School Theatre Classroom; design of Playwright's Connection a writing program for the stage for grades 9-12. Avocations: music, antiques. Office: Desert Pines High School 3800 E Harris Ave Las Vegas NV 89110 Personal E-mail: bthespian@aol.com. E-mail: maureen_bernstein@interact.ccsd.net.

BERNSTEIN, NADIA J. lawyer; b. Salford, Lancashire, Eng., Feb. 26, 1945; came to U.S., 1948; d. David Colin and Rose (Bolton) Cohen; m. David J. Adler, Mar. 1977 (div. 1992); m. Robert Bernstein, May, 1997. BA, CCNY, 1966; JD, NYU, 1973. Bar: N.Y. 1974, U.S. Dist. Ct. (so. and ea. dists.) N.Y. 1974, U.S. Ct. Appeals (2d cir.) 1975, U.S. Supreme Ct. 1983. Assoc. Rosenman Colin Freund Lewis & Cohen and predecessor firms, NYC, 1973-82; ptnr. Rosenman & Colin, NYC, 1983-87; v.p., gen. counsel Montefiore Med. Ctr., NYC, 1987-89, sr. v.p., gen. counsel, 1989-98; v.p., gen. counsel, corp. sec. C.R. Bard, Inc., Murray Hill, NJ, 1999—. Mem. legal affairs com. Greater N.Y. Hosp. Assn., N.Y.C., 1987-99; mem. bioethics task force, subcoms. on patient decision making, reproductive techs. and physician-assisted suicide, commn. women's equality Am. Jewish Congress, N.Y.C., 1989—; mem. bd. ethics Village Briarcliff Manor, N.Y., 1997—; conf. bd. Coun. Chief Legal Officers, 1999—; mem. N.J. Gen. Counsel's Group, 1999—. Bd. dirs. Berkeley-in-Scarsdale (N.Y.) Assn., 1989-91. Mem.: ABA (forum on health care, bus. law com., law practice mgmt. com.), Am. Soc. Corp. Secs., Am. Corp. Coun. Assn. (law mgmt. com. 2000—), Advanced Med. Tech. Assn. (legal com. 2002—), Women Bus. Leaders U.S. Health Care Industry, Exec. Women of NJ, NY State Bar Assn. (exec. com. health law sect. 1996—99, co-chair in-house counsel com. health law sect.), Am. Health Lawyers Assn., Assn. Bar of City of NY. Democrat. Office: C R Bard Inc 730 Central Ave New Providence NJ 07974-1199

BERNSTEIN, PENNY L. biologist, educator; b. Newark, Mar. 30, 1947; d. Arthur and Grace E. Bernstein; m. Lowell Thomas Lambert; 1 child, Christopher Lambert. BA, U. Pa., 1969, PhD, 1978. NIMH postdoctoral fellow Inst. of Animal Behavior, Rutgers U., Newark, 1978—80; rsch. assoc. Rutgers U., New Brunswick, NJ, 1984—85, Wetlands Inst., Stone Harbor, NJ, 1983—84; asst. prof. Kent State U., Canton, Ohio, 1994—2000, assoc. prof., 2000—; vis. rschr. Smithsonian Inst., Washington, 1981. Editl. bd. Anthrozoos, London, 2000—. Mem. Supt.'s Adv. Com., Canal Fulton, 1989—. Recipient Distinguished Teaching Award, 2000; grantee, NSF, 1995—98, Am. Philos. Soc., 1979, Edn. Conf. Grant, Martha Holden Jennings Found., 1998. Mem.: Internat. Soc. Anthrozoology (asst. newsletter editor 1999—2001, sec. 2001—), Soc. for Integrative and Comparative Biology, Am. Ornithol. Union, AAAS, Animal Behavior Soc. (chair edn. com. 2000—). Office: Kent State U Stark 6000 Frank Ave Canton OH 44720 Office Phone: 330-499-9600.

BERNSTEIN, PHYLISS LOUISE, psychologist; b. Balt., Nov. 27, 1940; d. Samuel Wilfred and Helen Dorothy (Gerson) Wilke; m. Robert Bernstein, June 7, 1964; children: Steve, Susan, David. BA in Psychology summa cum laude, Avila Coll., 1980, MS in Psychology summa cum laude, 1981; PhD in Couseling Psychology with high honors, U. Mo., Kansas City, 1986. Lic. psychologist Mo. Psychotherapist Community Counseling Ctr., Kansas City, Mo., 1983-85; assoc. psychologist Counseling and Human Devel. Svcs., Kansas City, Mo., 1985-86; psychologist in pvt. practice Kansas City, Mo., 1996—. Staff privileges Bapt. Med. Ctr., Menorah Med. Ctr.; dir. Jewish Vocat. Svcs., Kansas City, 1988—91, U. Mo. Edn. Dept., Kansas City, Jewish Family and Children Svcs., Jewish Cmty. Found. Contbr. Life mem. Nat. Coun. Jewish Women, Kansas City; bd. dirs. Avila Coll.; adv. bd. mem. Friendship House, 2001—. Mem.: APA, Greater Kansas City Psychol. Assn., Psi Chi, Pi Lambda Theta, Phi Kappa Phi. Avocations: scuba diving, bungy jumping, skiing, horseback riding.

BERNSTEIN, PHYLLIS J. financial consultant; b. N.Y.C., Oct. 10, 1955; d. Stanley and Esther Bernstein; m. Robert Kuchner, Dec. 10, 1978. BBA, Hofstra U., 1977. CPA NY. Staff auditor promoted to sr. Pantasote, Greenwich, Conn., 1977—79; sr. promoted to mgr., corp. auditing RCA (now GE), N.Y.C., 1979—85; tech. mgr., personal fin. planning AICPA, N.Y.C., 1985—88, sr. tech. mgr., personal fin. planning, 1988—91, dir., personal fin. planning, 1991—2001; pres. Phyllis Bernstein Consulting, Inc, N.Y.C., 2001—. Editl. adv. bd. mem. Jour. of Accountancy, Jersey City, 2002—; editl. adv. bd. The Tax Advisor, Jersey City, 2002—; adv. bd. mem. Personal Fin. Planning Monthly, Denver, 2002—, Fee-only Client Newsletters, Jericho, NY, 1998—; founder AICPA Ctr. for Investment Adv. Services, 1998—2000; creator and dir. AICPA Personal Fin. Specialist Designation Program, New York, NY, 1985—2001, AICPA Personal Fin. Planning Membership Sect., New York, NY, 1985—2001. Author: (trade book) Financial Planning for CPAs, 2000, Investment Advisory Relationships: Managing Client Expectations in an Uncertain Market, 2002; contributor and editor: book Guide to Registering as an Investment Advisor, 1997; editor: (newsletter) The Planner, 1985—. Sec. and concours chair Jaguar Touring Club, Monclair, NJ, 1995—98; mem. Young Leadersip Cabinet United Jewish Appeal, N.Y.C., 1994—2000; bd. dirs. Jewish Fedn. of Ctrl. NJ Endowment Found., Scotch Plains, 1998—2002; chair investment com. Jewish Fedn. Ctrl. N.J., 2002. Named Top 100 Most Influential Persons in Acctg., Acctg. Today, 1997—2001, Top 10 Names to Know in PFP, 1999—2002, One of four movers, shakers and decision makers, Fin. Planning mag. Mem.: AICPA (legis. and regulation task force pers. fin. planning sect. 2001—02), NY State Soc. of CPAs (fin. planning com. 2002), Fin. Planning Orgn., All-Star Fin. Group (v.p. 2002), Jaguar Touring Club (sec. and concours chair 2000). Democrat. Avocations: skiing, travel, shopping, dining, restoring Jaguars, gardening. Office: Phyllis Bernstein Consulting Inc 7 Penn Plaza Ste 1600 New York NY 10001 Personal E-mail: phyllis@pbconsults.com. E-mail: phyllis@pbconsults.com.

BERON, GAIL LASKEY, real estate analyst, appraiser, consultant; b. Detroit, Nov. 13, 1943; d. Charles Jack Laskey and Florence B. (Rosenthal) Eisenberg; divorced; children: Monty Charles, Bryan David. Cert. real estate analyst, Mich. Chief/staff appraiser Ft. Wayne Mortgage Co., Birmingham, Mich., 1973-75; pvt. practice fee appraiser S.C., Iowa, Mich., 1976-80; pres. The Beron Co., Southfield, Mich., 1980—. Cons. ptnr. Real Estate Counseling Group Conn., Storrs, 1983—, Real Estate Counseling Group Am., prin., 1984—; lectr. real estate confs. Recipient M. William Donnally award Mortgage Bankers Assn. Am., 1975. Mem. Appraisal Inst. (nat. faculty 1991-97), Soc. Real Estate Appraisers (bd. dirs. Detroit chpt. 1980-82, nat. faculty 1983-91), Am. Inst. Real Estate Appraisers (bd. dirs. Detroit chpt. 1982-86, nat. faculty 1984-91), Nat. Assn. Realtors, Detroit Bd. Realtors, Southfield Bd. Realtors, Women Brokers Assn. (treas. Southfield chpt. 1981-83), Young Mortgage Bankers (bd. dirs. 1974-75). Avocations: art, music, piano, reading. Home: 7008 Bridge Way West Bloomfield MI 48322-3527 Office: Beron Co Ste 28 33000 Covington Club Dr Apt 28 Farmington Hills MI 48334-1649

BERRES, FRANCES BRANDES, clinical psychologist; b. Chgo. d. Max and Anna (Gould) Brandes; m. George Berres, July 6, 1941 (dec.); 1 dau., Barbara Lo Monaco BA, UCLA, 1937, MA, 1940, PhD, 1967. Head remedial instrn., tchr. English Huntington Beach (Calif.) High Sch., 1940-44; psychologist tchr. Fernald Sch., psychology dept. UCLA, [illegible] 52, assoc. dir., acad. adminstr., lectr. learning disabilities, dept. psychology, 1952-71; coordinator child-related programs info. project Neuropsychiat. Inst., 1971-73; pvt. practice clin. psychology Santa Monica, Calif., 1976—. Lectr. ann. series concerning child behavior problems. Contbr. chpts. to books and profl. jous.; author: Deep Sea Adventure Series, 1959, 62, 67, 71, 79; A Survey of Child Related Programs, 1975 Past bd. dirs. Los Angeles Philharm. Soc. Women's Com.; past pres., bd. dirs. Marina del Rey Symphony Soc.; sec. bd. dirs. Internat. Children's Sch. Grantee, State of Calif., Dept. Edn., Div. Compensatory Edn., 1966-69, Office Edn., HEW, 1966-70, NIMH, 1970-72, Office Vice Chancellor, UCLA, 1970 Mem. APA, Calif. Psychol. Assn. Office: 2122 Wilshire Blvd Santa Monica CA 90403-5704

BERRESFORD, SUSAN VAIL, philanthropic foundation executive; b. N.Y.C., Jan. 8, 1943; d. Richard Case and Katherine Vail (Marsters) Berresford Hurd; m. David F. Stein (div.); 1 son, Jeremy Vail Stein. Student, Vassar Coll., 1961-63; BA cum laude in Am. History, Radcliffe Coll., 1965. Vol. UN Vol. Services, N.Y.C., summer 1962; sec. to Theodore H. White, summer 1964; program officer Neighborhood Youth Corps, N.Y.C., 1965-67; program specialist Manpower Career Devel. Agy., N.Y.C., 1967, human resources adminstrn. specialist, 1968; free-lance cons., writer Europe and U.S., 1968-70; program officer nat. affairs div. Ford Found., N.Y.C., 1970-80, program officer in charge, 1980-81, v.p., 1981-95, exec. v.p., COO, 1995-96, pres., 1996—. Office: Ford Foundation 320 East 43rd St New York NY 10017*

BERRIDGE, MARY LLOYD, photographer; BA in Arts and Ideas-Lit. & Photography, U. Mich., 1986; MFA in Photography, Yale U., 1991. Adj. instr. Concordia Coll., Bronxville, NY, 1992, Fairleigh Dickinson U., Rutherford, NJ, 1992—94, Nassau C.C., Garden City, NY, 1994—96, Sch. Visual Arts, N.Y.C., 1997; artist-in-residence, adj. instr. Coll. New Rochelle, NY, 1993; lectr. Princeton (N.J.) U., 1998—99. Exhibitions include The Ctr. for Photography, Woodstock, N.Y., 1991, Mus. Modern Art, N.Y.C., 1991, Berkshire Mus., Pittsfield, Mass., 1992, OPSIS Found., N.Y.C., 1992, Coll. New Rochelle, 1993, Midtown Y Photography Gallery, N.Y.C., 1993, Ind. Arts Gallery, Jamaica, N.Y., 1994, U. Rochester, N.Y., 1995, Blue Sky Gallery, Portland, Oreg., 1996, San Marino Mus. Photography, 1997, Robert Mann Gallery, N.Y.C., 1997, Soc. for Contemporary Photography, Kansas City, 1997—98, Mus. Fine Arts, Houston, 1997, M.H. de Young Meml. Mus., San Francisco, 1997, Cathedral of St. John the Divine, N.Y.C., 1997, Portland (Maine) Mus. Art, 1998, San Francisco Camerawork, 1998, U. Mich., Ann Arbor, 1999, Ctr. for Documentary Studies, Duke U., Durham, N.C., 1999, Pleasures and Terrors of Domestic Comfort, 1991, The Human Condition/Photography, 1995, 1996, Double Take, 1996—97, A Positive Life: Portraits of Women Living with HIV, 1997. Recipient The Ernst Haas award, Maine Photographic Workshops, 1996, The Dorothea Lange-Paul Taylor prize, Ctr. for Documentary Studies, Duke U., 1996, The Romeo Martinez Internat. award, Ministry of Culture of the Republic of San Marino, 1997; fellow Fellowship award, Soc. for Contemporary Photography, Kansas City, Mo., 1997, Artist's fellow, N.Y. Found. for the Art, 1996; John Simon Guggenheim Meml. fellow, 1997. Home: 29 Linden Ln Princeton NJ 08540-3827 E-mail: berridge@princeton.edu.

BERRIGAN, HELEN GINGER, federal judge; b. New Rochelle, Apr. 15, 1948; m. Joseph E Berrigan Jr. BA, U. Wis., 1969; MA, Am. U., 1971; JD, La. State U., 1977. Staff rschr. Senator Harold E. Hughes, 1971-72; legis. aide Senator Joseph E. Biden, 1972-73; asst. to mayor City of Fayette, Miss., 1973-74; law clk. La. Dept. Corrections, 1975-77; staff atty. Gov. Pardon, Parole and Rehab. Commn., 1977-78; prin. Gravel Brady & Berrigan, New Orleans, 1978-94, Berrigan, Litchfield, Schonekas, Mann & Clement, New Orleans, 1984-94; judge U.S. Dist. Ct. (ea. dist.) La., New Orleans, 1994—. Active La. Sentencing Commn., 1987. Active Com. of 21, 1989, pres., 1990-92, ACLU of La., 1989-94, Forum for Equality, 1990-94, Amistad Rsch. Ctr. Tulane U., 1990-95. Mem. La. State Bar Assn. (mem. fed. 5th cir. 1986—), La. Assn. Criminal Def. Lawyers, New Orleans Assn. Women Attys. Office: US Dist Ct 500 Camp St C-556 New Orleans LA 70130-3313

BERRIOS, LILY DEL CARMEN, architect; b. San Juan, P.R., Aug. 29, 1958; d. Luis Oscar Berrios and Lily Esther Orlandi; m. Walter Edward Miller, May 12, 1984; children: Marie Louise Miller, Margaret Andrea Miller. BArch, Cornell U., 1981. Registered architect, AIA. Intern Jorge Del Rio Assoc., San Juan, PR, 1980; assoc. Cesar Pelli & Assocs., New Haven, 1981—87; ptnr. Berrios Miller Archs., Atlanta, 1987—88; prin. Sizemore Group, Atlanta, 1988—. Contbr. articles. Mem. Buckhead Bus. Leadership, Atlanta, 2001; chair coun. ministries St. Mark United Meth. Ch., Atlanta, 1988—91, chair bldgs./grounds, 1992—96, chair restoration, 1997—. Co-recipient Design award, Progressive Arch., 1987. Mem.: Soc. Coll. Univ. Planning, AIA. Methodist. Avocation: photography. Home: 681 Upton Rd NW Atlanta GA 30318 Office: Sizemore Group 1700 Commerce Dr NW Atlanta GA 30318 E-mail: lilyb@sizemoregroup.com.

BERRY, ALICE ALLEN, retired music educator; b. Bowling Green, Ky., June 23, 1946; d. Oscar Ainsworth and Dorothy (Maddox) Allen; m. Thomas Kay Berry, June 18, 1967; 1 child, Carl Thomas. B in Music Edn. cum laude, Murray State U., 1968. Cert. tchr. Ky., tchr., supr. spl. K-14 Ill. Choral music tchr. McCracken County Pub. Schs., Lone Oak, Ky., 1968—69, Cmty. Unit Sch. Dist. #186, Murphysboro, Ill., 1969—2002. Guest festival choral dir. Jefferson County Music Tchrs. Assn., Ina, Ill., 1993; guest dir. Murphysboro Voices United, 1993; adjudicator music contests Ill. Grade Sch. Music Assn., 1996—, Ill. HS Assn., 1980—; guest choral dir. So. Ill. Grade Sch. Vocal Music Festival, 1998, 2000, 02; guest festival choral dir. Miss. Valley Conf., Belleville, Ill., 2005; guest pianist Walnut St. Bapt. Ch., Carbondale, Ill., 2003. Performer (singer): (guest soloist) Quad State Festival Chorus, 1965, All State Chorus, 1964. Vol. Meals on Wheels, Jackson County Sr. Citizens, Murphysboro, 2002—, So. Ill. U. Choral Union, Carbondale, 2003—; vol. music dir. Cmty. Ecumenical Vacation Bible Sch., Lebanon, Ill., 2003—; choral dir. 1st Bapt. Ch., Murphysboro, 1974—78, 1981—2001; choir dir. United Meth. Ch., Murphysboro, 1969—70; guest choral dir. Cantata United Meth. Ch., Murphysboro, 2002. Named Unsung Hero, Sta. WSIL-TV, 1996, Class Act, 2002. Mem.: NEA (life), Jackson County retired Tchrs. Assn., Am. Choral Dirs. Assn., Ill. Music Edn. Assn. (adjudicator 1983, choral chmn. dist. 6 1988—, 25-Yr. Recognition award 1995), Music Educators Nat. Conf., Ill. Ret. Tchrs. Assn., Sigma Alpha Iota. Home: 2019 Commercial Ave Murphysboro IL 62966 Personal E-mail: atberry@midwest.net.

BERRY, CAROL ANN, insurance company executive; b. Walla Walla, Wash., Sept. 8, 1950; d. Alan R. and Elizabeth A. Berry; m. Mark Brooks. BA, Wash. State U. Cert. compliance profl. Asst. mgr. L.A. reg. claims CIGNA, Santa Monica, Calif., 1981-83; reg. adminstr. Equicor, Sherman Oaks, Calif., 1983-89; dir. sys. for managed care Blue Cross of Calif., Woodland Hills, Calif., 1989-90; dir. field account svcs. Managed Health Network, L.A., 1990-93; pres. VertiHealth Adminstrs., Chatsworth, Calif., 1993-2000; cons., expert witness, 2000—01; sr. v.p. Claim Recoveries Unlimited, 2001—04; sr. project mgr. All Health Logic, 2004—. Lectr. in field. Mem. Pres.'s Commn. Status of Women. Mem.: NAFE, Health Care Adminstrs. Assn. (past pres. bd. dirs.), Health Fin. Mgmt. Assn., Assn. Info. Mgrs. Healthcare Industry, Wash. State U. Alumni Assn. Home: 6155 Lockhurst Dr Woodland Hills CA 91367-1203 E-mail: cberry@hasc.org., cberry8@slocglobal.net.

BERRY, CHERIE KILLIAN, commissioner; b. Newton, N.C. d. Earl and Lena (Carrigan) Killian; m. Norman Berry, Jr.; 4 children. Former bus. owner LGM, Ltd.; state rep., 45th dist. N.C. Ho. of Reps., 1993—2000; apptd. labor commr. State of N.C., 2001. Past chair welfare reform com., co-chair commerce com., mem. pensions and retirement, campaign fin. and election laws and mental health coms. N.C. Ho. of Reps.; mem. N.C. Econ. Devel. bd.; chair State Welfare Reform Study Commn.; mem. Blue Ribbon Task Force on issue of potential impact of fed. block grant funding; mem. various other adv. coms. and study commns. Recipient Friend of Working People award, N.C. AFL-CIO, 1997. Office: 4 W Edenton St Raleigh NC 27601

BERRY, CLARE GEBERT, real estate broker; b. Carlisle, Pa., Oct. 4, 1955; d. George Robert and Helen (Davis) Gebert; m. James Isaac Vance Berry Jr., June 16, 1977; 1 child, James Isaac Vance Berry III. BA, Auburn U., 1977. Advt. assoc., circulation mgr. The News-Gazette, Lexington, Va., 1977-79; sales and editorial asst. Ponte Vedra Recorder Newspaper, Fla., 1979-81; co-founder, bus. mgr. The Sun-Times Newspaper, Jacksonville Beach, Fla., 1981-82; mgr. Arvida-Clearview Cable TV, Ponte Vedra Beach, 1982-85; broker, agt. Watson Realty Corp., Ponte Vedra Beach, Fla., 1985-90, Marsh Landing Realty, Ponte Vedra Beach, 1990-93; founder, broker, owner Berry & Co. Real Estate, Ponte Vedra Beach, 1993—. Com. chmn. The Players Championship, Ponte Vedra Beach, 1982—; dir. Marsh Landing Homeowners Assn. Bd., Ponte Vedra Beach, 1989-90; dir. Ponte Vedra Pub. Edn. Found., 1994—, N.E. Fla. Regional Planning Coun., 2000—. Recipient Realtor of Yr., Realtors' Assn., 1992, Residential Mem. of Yr., 1998. Mem. Fla. Assn. Realtors, Nat. Assn. Realtors, N.E. Fla. Builders Assn. Sales and Mktg. Coun., N.E. Fla. Assn. of Realtors (bd. dirs. 1998-00, chmn. edn. com. 2000), Ponte Vedra Rotary. Avocations: writing, promotions, aviation, music, tennis. Home: 113 Linkside Cir Ponte Vedra Beach FL 32082-2032 Office: Berry & Co Real Estate 330 Hwy A1A Ste 200 Ponte Vedra Beach FL 32082-1824 Office Phone: 904-273-4800.

BERRY, DEBORAH, state representative; b. Sept. 1958; Mem. Iowa Ho. Reps., DesMoines, 2003—, mem. various coms. including edn., human resources and judiciary. Waterloo City councilwoman. Mem.: Commn. on the Status of African Ams. Democrat. Office: State Capitol East 12th and Grand Des Moines IA 50319 Home: 241 Madison St Waterloo IA 50703

BERRY, ESTER LORÉE, vocational nurse; b. St. Joseph, La., Sept. 19, 1945; d. Sim and Ruby Jordan; (div.); children: Roderick Bryant, Pamela Elaine. Assoc. degree in nursing and art, Calif. State U., 1996. Lic. vocat. nurse. Ward clk. Santa Fe Hosp., Compton, Calif., 1969-72; supr. J.C. Penney's, Carson, Calif., 1973-80; asst. mgr. Std. Comm., Carson, 1981-84; lic. vocat. nurse, nurse King Drew Med., L.A., 1984-94, medicine nurse Martin Luther Jr. Hosp., 1996-99; poet Nobles Theatre of the Mind, Paris, London, N.Y.C., 2004 . Contbr. poetry to Internat. Libr. Poetry; author Am. Poet Soc. Named hon. mem. Vets. Am., 1999-2001, Best Poet of Yr.; recipient Editors Choice award, 1999, 2000, 2001, Silver Internat. Poet of Merit, Bronze Commemorative Medallion, Best Poet award, 2002-03, Internat. Libr. of Poetry, Bronze Leader award, Disabled Am. Vets. Commanders Club, 2002-03, Outstanding Intellecutal of 21st Century award, 2004, Best Poet award Internat. Libr. Poetry, 2004. Avocations: fishing, sewing, photography, crocheting, outdoor camping. Home: Apt P230 27-700 Landau B Cathedral City CA 92234

BERRY, GAIL W. psychiatrist, educator; b. Kalamazoo, Mich., Nov. 7, 1939; d. Milton and Rose N. Wruble. BA, Kalamazoo Coll., 1960; MD, NYU, 1964; cert. in psychoanalysis, N.Y. Med. Coll., 1976. Lic. Am. Bd. Psychiatry and Neurology. Clin. instr. psychiatry Mt. Sinai Sch. Medicine, N.Y.C., 1969—76, asst. clin. prof. psychiatry, 1976—; tng. and supervising psychoanalyst Psychoanalytic Inst. N.Y. Med. Coll., Valhalla, NY, 1980—; assoc. attending psychiatrist Mt. Sinai Hosp., N.Y.C., 1981—. Adj. prof. psychiatry N.Y. Med. Coll., Valhalla, 1984—. Fellow: Am. Psychiat. Assn. (life; disting.); mem.: Am. Acad. Psychoanalysis (asst. editor jour. 1984—2002), Am. Acad. Psychoanalysis and Dynamic Psychiatry (consulting editor jour. 2002—). Office: 11 S 1474 Third Ave New York NY 10028

BERRY, GAYLE, state representative; b. Aug. 9, 1954; A, Colorado State Coll. State rep. State of Colo., 1996—, mem. govt. affairs com., 1993—94, mem. appropriations com., mem. local govt. com., mem. transp. and energy com. Mem.: Am. Legis. Exchg. Coun., Grand Junction Area C. of C., Mesa State Coll. Alumni Assn., Phi Theta Kappa. Republican. Roman Catholic. Avocations: golf, sewing, cooking. Address: 1305 Wellington #102 Grand Junction CO 81501 Office: State Capitol 200 E Colfax Ave Denver CO 80203 E-mail: galye.berry.house@state.co.us.

BERRY, HALLE, actress; b. Cleve., Aug. 14, 1966; d. Jerome and Judith (Hawkins) B.; m. David Christopher Justice, Jan. 1, 1993 (div.); m. Eric Benet, Feb. 7, 2001. BA, Cuyahoga C.C., Cleveland, 1986. Appeared in films Jungle Fever, 1991, The Last Boy Scout, 1991, Strictly Business, 1991, Boomerang, 1992 (Image award nominee 1992), Father Hood, 1993, The Program, 1993, The Flintstones, 1994, Losing Isaiah, 1995, The Rich Man's Wife, 1996, Executive Decision, 1996, Race The Sun, 1996, Girl 6, 1996, B*A*P*S, 1997, Bulworth, 1998, Why Do Fools Fall in Love, 1998, Victims of Fashion, 1999, Ringside, 1999, X-Men, 2000, Swordfish, 2001, Monsters Ball, 2002 (Best Actress Acad. Award 2002), Die Another Day, 2002, X2: X-Men United, 2003, Gothika, 2003; TV mini-series Queen, 1992, Solomon & Sheba, 1995, The Wedding, 1998, Introducing Dorothy Dandridge, 1999 (Outstanding Lead Actress in Miniseries or Movie Emmy 2000, Best Performance by Actress in Miniseries or Motion Picture Made for TV Golden Globe 2000, Actor award, Spl. award, Image award, SAG award and three NAACP Image awards 2000); TV series include Living Dolls, 1989, Knots Landing, 1992; also appeared in episodes of Amen, A Different World, They Came From Outer Space, Frasier (voice). Named Miss Teen All-Am., 1985, Miss USA first-runner up, 1986, Miss U.S.A., 1987. Office: William Morris Agy c/o Bill Butler 151 El Camino Dr Beverly Hills CA 90212*

BERRY, JANIS MARIE, lawyer; b. Everett, Mass., Dec. 20, 1949; d. Joseph and Dorothy I. Sordillo; m. Richard G. Berry, Dec. 27, 1970; children: Alexis, Ashley, Lindsey. BA magna cum laude, Boston U., 1971, JD cum laude, 1974. Bar: Mass. 1974, U.S. Dist. Ct. Mass. 1975, U.S. Ct. Appeals (1st cir.), 1980, U.S. Supreme Ct. 1982. Law clk. Mass. Supreme Jud. Ct., Boston, 1974-75; assoc. Bingham, Dana & Gould, Boston, 1975-80; asst. U.S. atty. Boston, 1980-81; spl. atty. dept. justice N.E. Organized Crime Strike Force, Boston, 1981-84; chief atty. dept. justice N.E. Organized Crime Drug Task Force, Boston, 1984-86; ptnr. Ropes & Gray, Boston, 1986-94; pvt. practice, 1995; ptnr. Roche, Carens & DeGiacomo, 1996-97, Rubin & Rudman LLP, 1997-2001; justice Mass. Appeals Ct., 2001—. Instr. Harvard Law Sch., 1983-86, Inst. Trial Advocacy, Boston, 1984-87; lectr. Dept. Justice Advocacy Inst., 1986; mem. Mass. Bd. of Bar Overseers, 1989-93; bd. mem. Mass. Housing Fin. Agy., 1995-2001, Franciscan Children's Hosp.; chmn. merit selection panel U.S. Magistrate, 1989, Mass. Jud. Nominating Coun., 1991-92; trustee Social Law Libr., 1999-2001. Author: Defending Corporations Public Contracts Jour., (with others) Federal Criminal Practice, 1987. Candidate Mass. Atty. Gen., 1994; mem. Mass. Com. for Pub. Counsel Svcs., Boston, 1986-91; v.p. Boston Inn of Ct., 1990-91; trustee Atlanticare Hosp., 1990-94, 2001-; bd. dirs. Franciscan Children's Hosp. Spl. Commendation award Dept. of Justice, Washington, 1983. Mem. Mass. Bar Assn., Boston Bar Assn., Am. Law Inst., Phi Beta Kappa. Office: Mass Appeals Ct 1500 New Courthouse Boston MA 02108

BERRY, JONI INGRAM, hospice pharmacist, educator; b. Charlotte, N.C., June 6, 1953; d. James Clifford and Patricia Ann (Ebener) Ingram; div.; children: Erin Blair, Rachel Anne, James Rosser. BS in Pharmacy, U. N.C., 1976, MS in Pharmacy, 1979, postgrad., 1999. Lic. pharmacist, N.C. Resident in pharmacy Sch. Pharmacy, U. N.C., Chapel Hill, 1977-79, adj. asst. prof., 1985—; pharmacist Durham County Gen. Hosp., Durham, N.C., 1977-79; coord. clin. pharm. Wake Med. Ctr., Raleigh, N.C., 1979-80; co-dir. pharmacy edn. Wake Area Health Edn. Ctr., Raleigh, 1980-85; pharmacist cons. Hospice of Wake County, Raleigh, 1980—; co-owner Integrated Pharm. Care Systems, Inc., 1995—. Mem. editorial adv. bd. Hospice Jour., 1985-91, 94—, Jour. Pharm. Care in Pain and Symptom Mgmt., 1992—; reviewer Am. Jour. Hospice Care, 1996-98; editor pharmacy sect. notes NHO Coun. Hospice Profls.; contbr. articles to profl. jours. Troop leader Girl Scouts U.S.A., Raleigh, 1987—, trainer, 1989-91, mgr. svc. unit, 1990-94; Sunday sch. tchr. St. Phillips Luth. Ch., Raleigh, 1990-92, 94-95, asst. min., 1995—, choir mem. 1998-2000. Recipient Silver Pinecone award Girl Scouts U.S., 1991, Golden Rule award J.C. Penney Co., 1991. Mem.: Wake County Pharm. Assn. (sec. 1982—85), N.C. Hosp. Pharmacists (bd. dirs. 1984—86, program com. 1988—91), N.C. Pharm. Assn. (mem. continuing edn. com. 1986—87, chair com. 1981—84, Don Blanton award 1985), Am. Pain Soc., Nat. Hospice Orgn., Am. Soc. Hosp. Pharmacists, Acad. Pharmacy Practice and Mgmt. (mem.-at-large 1996, chair specialized sect. 1999—2002), Am. Pharm. Assn. (hospice pharmacist steering com. 1990—), Nat. Coun. Hospice Profls. (pharmacy sect. leader 1998—), Rho Chi. Democrat. Avocations: gardening, weight lifting, aerobics. Office: Hospice Wake County 1300 Saint Marys St Raleigh NC 27605-1276 E-mail: momsberry@aol.com.

BERRY, KATHRYN-GRACE, geriatrics nurse; b. Linden, Tex., Sept. 28, 1929; d. Wright Allen and Gladys Bowden; m. Wayman Byron Berry, Jan. 6, 1947; children: Ron, James Byron, Celia Elizabeth Froehlig. Diploma in nursing, Univ. Ala., 1969. Cert. nursing Ala. Nurse, Huntsville, 1970—80; charge nurse various nursing homes, Pulaski, Tenn., 1980—85, Ardmore, Ala., 1987—90; tchr. GED program Huntsville, 1990—97. Active Christians Helping Others, Ardmore, 1985—95; mem. Friends Ardmore Libr., 1990—95; pres. United Meth. Women, 1985. Avocations: oragami, reading, boating, fishing, crafts, oil painting. Home: 809 Stuart Ln Brentwood TN 37027-5824

BERRY, LORRAINE L. state senator; b. St. Thomas, V.I., Nov. 15, 1949; d. Joseph and Emelda Ledee; m. Richard Berry; children: Roxanne, Kurt. Mem. V.I. Legis., 1982—, pres., 1997-99. Mem. econ. devel., agr., consumer protection, health, govt. and operation coms.; chair fin. com. Office: Capitol Bldg PO Box 1690 Saint Thomas VI 00804-1690

BERRY, MARTHA KATHERYN, artist; b. Tulsa, June 10, 1948; d. Grady L. and Katheryn Crews York; m. David V. Berry, Dec. 21, 1972; children: Christina R., Karen Berry Higa. Student, U. Tulsa, 1971—72. Cherokee beadwork artist Berry Beadwork, Tyler, Tex., 1993—2003. Presenter in field. One-woman shows include Cherokee Heritage Ctr., 2000. Registered tribal citizen Cherokee Nation, Tahlequah, 1948—2003; del. Cherokee Nation Constn. Conv., Tahlequah, Okla., 1999—99. Recipient Eight-time award winner, Cherokee Heritage Ctr. Mus., Tahlequah, 2000—03, award, Five Civilized Tribes Mus., Muskogee, Okla., 2003; Native Am. Cmty. Scholars grantee, Smithsonian Instn., 2000. Mem.: Cherokee Cultural Soc. Houston, Cherokee Nat. Hist. Soc., Cherokee S.W. Twp. Achievements include self-taught traditional Cherokee beadwork artist and teacher, and creator of traditional Cherokee beadwork patterns

BERRY, MARY FRANCES, federal agency administrator, history and law educator; b. Nashville, Feb. 17, 1938; d. George Ford and Frances Southall (Wiggins) B. BA, Howard U., 1961, MA, 1962; PhD, U. Mich., 1966, JD, 1970; hon. degree, Cen. Mich. U., Howard U., U. Akron, 1977, Benedict Coll., U. Md., Grambling State U., 1979, Bethune-Cookman Coll., Clark Coll., Del. State Coll., 1980, Oberlin Coll., Langston U., 1983, Marian Coll., Haverfod Coll., 1984, Colby Coll., CUNY, 1986, DePaul U., 1987. Bar: D.C. 1972. Asst. prof. history Central Mich. U., Mt. Pleasant, 1966-68; asst. prof. Eastern Mich. U., Ypsilanti, 1968-69, assoc. prof., 1969-70, U. Md., College Park, 1969-76; acting dir. Afro-Am. studies, 1970-72, dir., 1972-74, acting chmn. div. behavioral and social scis., 1973-74, provost div. behavioral and social scis., 1973-76; prof. history, prof. law U Colo. at Boulder, 1976-80, chancellor, 1976-77; prof. history and law Howard U., Washington, 1980—; asst. sec. for edn. HEW, Washington, 1977-80; vice chair Civil Rights Commn., 1980—82; chmn U.S. Commn. on Civil Rights, 1993—. Adj. assoc. prof. U. Mich., 1970-71; mem. com. visitors U. Mich. Law Sch., 1976-80; mem. nat. adv. panel on minority concerns Coll. Bd., 1980-84; mem. adv. bd. Feminist Press, 1980— ; mem. research adv. com. Joint Ctr. for Polit. Studies, 1981— ; mem. editorial adv. com. Marcus Garvey Papers, 1981— ; mem. adv. bd. Inst. for Higher Edn. Law and Governance, U. Houston, 1983— ; Geraldine R. Segal prof. of Am. social thought U. Pa., 1987—. Author: Black Resistance/White Law, 1971, Military Necessity and Civil Rights Policy, 1977, Stability, Security and Continuity, Mr. Justice Burton and Decision-Making in the Supreme Court, 1945-58, 1978, (with John Blassingame) Long Memory: The Black Experience in America, 1982; Why ERA Failed, 1986; asso. editor Jour. Negro History, 1974-78; contbr. articles, revs. to profl. jours. Bd. dirs. ARC, Washington, 1980— ; trustee Tuskegee U., 1980— ; mem. adv. bd. Project '87, 1978— ; mem. council UN U., 1986— Recipient Athena (disting. alumni) award U. Mich., 1977, Roy Wilkins Civil Rights award NAACP, 1983, Image award, 1983, Allard Lowenstein award, 1984, President's award Congl. Black Caucus Found., 1985, Woman of Yr. award Nat. Capital Area YWCA, 1985, Hubert H. Humphrey Civil Rights award Leadership Conf. on Civil Rights, 1986, Rosa Parks award SCLC, Black Achievement award Ebony Mag., Woman of Yr. award Ms. Mag., 1986. Mem. ABA, Nat. Bar Assn., D.C. Bar Assn., Nat. Acad. Public Adminstrn., Orgn. Am. Historians (exec. bd. 1974-77), Assn. Study of Afro-Am. Life and History (exec. bd. 1973-76), Am. Hist. Assn. (v.p. for profession 1980-83), Am. Soc. Legal History, Coalition 100 Black Women (hon.), Delta Sigma Theta (hon.) Independent. Office: Commn on Civil Rights Office of Chmn 624 9th St NW Ste 553 Washington DC 20425-0002

BERRY, MARYANN PARADISO, minister; d. Joseph and Mary Mainolfi Paradiso; m. Wayne Robert Berry, Jan. 4, 1975; children: Maria, John. BS in Bus. Adminstrn. cum laude, Marist Coll., 1975; cert. of studies, Faith Fellowship World, Sayreville, N.J., 1985, Sch. Bibl. Studies, Poughkeepsie, N.Y., 1996. Ordained min. Christian Faith Ctr., Bloomfield, NJ, 1990, Covenant Ministries, Sayreville, 1992. Co-owner Mid-Hudson Alarm Co., Poughkeepsie, 1975—80; children's music dir., elder, tchr. Bible Coll. Faith Fellowship Ministries, Sayreville, 1982—88; min. Christian Faith Ctr., Bloomfield, NJ, 1988—91; pastor, dean Sch. Bibl. Studies John 3:16 Christian Ctr., Poughkeepsie, 1991—. Author: Answered Prayer, 1984. Vol. father's day parade Dutchess County Health Families, 2003. Mem.: Covenant Ministries Internat., Assn. Faith Chs. and Ministries. Avocations: reading, hiking, piano, guitar. Office: John 3:16 Christian Ctr 696 Dutchess Tpk Poughkeepsie NY 12603 Office Phone: 845-473-3114.

BERRY, NANCY, recording industry executive; With Virgin Records, 1979—, now vice chmn., Virgin Music Group Worldwide, L.A., N.Y.C. and London. Office: Virgin Records Am Inc 338 N Foothill Rd Beverly Hills CA 90210-3611

BERRY, PRISCILLA MARIE BURCH, ophthalmologist; b. Fairfield, Ill., Mar. 27, 1942; d. Miller and Opal Burch; m. William L. Berry, June 24, 1967; children: Scott, Heather. BS, So. Meth. U., 1963; MD, U. Tex., Dallas, 1967. Cert. Am. Bd. Ophthalmology. Intern Meth. Hosp., Dallas, 1967—68; pres-residency fellow ophthalmology dept. U. Tex. Southwestern Med. Sch., Dallas, 1968—69, ophthalmology resident, 1969—72; fellow in pediat. ophthalmology Children's Med. Ctr., Dallas, 1974—76; pvt. practice in ophthalmology Wichita Falls, Tex., 1972—74; pvt. practice in pediat. ophthalmology Dallas, 1976—. Active cons. Eye Clinic, Scottish Rite Hosp., 1976. Contbr. articles to med. jours. Pres. Jr. Charity League Dallas, 1991—92. Mem.: ACS, Dallas County Med. Soc., Tex. Ophthalmology Assn., Tex. Med. Assn., Am. Assn. for Pediat. Ophthalmology and Strabismus, Am. Acad. Ophthalmology. Avocations: walking, bell choir at church. Office: Pediat Ophthalmology and Ctr for Adult Strabismus # 140A 8201 Preston Dallas TX 75225

BERRY, SHARON ELAINE, interior designer; b. Kansas City, Mo., May 27, 1945; d. Ralph Epping Hohmann and Ruth Justine (Sturm) Hohmann Gibson; m. Max Allen Berry, Apr. 8, 1984. Grad. high sch., Kansas City; grad, Pierce Sch. Interior Design, 1972. Designer Danie Dunn Interiors, Kansas City, 1972-76, 80-83; co-owner, operator Clift-Willard Interiors, Leawood, Kans., 1976-80; head decorating dept. Carpets by Johnson and Johnson, Overland Park, Kans., 1983-84; owner, operator Nouveau Interiors, Shawnee Mission, Kans., 1984-92; coord. Met. Orgn. To Counter Sexual Assault, Kansas City, 1994-96, mem. adv. bd. adult survivor program, 1996—; pres. Recovery Records, 1996-98; dir. funding and devel. Cypress Recovery, Inc., Olathe, Kans., 1999-2000, bd. dirs., 1998; dir. fund devel. Rick's Place Found., 2000—01; owner Wild Berry Interior Design, 2002—. Vol. Design Excellence Awards Com., Kansas City, 1982-88; designer Designers Showhouse, Kansas City, Mo., 1975-90; participant Design '81 Congress, Helsinki, 1981, Gourmet March of Dimes, 1988, 90; writer City Limits, entertainment mag., Family News mag. Editor newsletter Survivors United Reading Empowerment (S.U.R.E.); contbr. to anthology The Bridge Is Out But I Can Fly; co-writer, co-prodr. CD Who Will Save the Children; editor, writer, newsletter Cypress Recovery. Vol. exec. dir. Recovery Is For Everyone Found., Olathe, 1996; vol. dir. pub. rels. Women's Resource Network, Shawnee Mission, 2000-02; v.p. internat. tng. in comm. JoCo Club. Recipient 2 Telly awards, gold award Houston Internat. Film Festival, 2d place Kans. Film Festival, cert. of merit Internat. Film and Video competition for video Who Will Save the Children, 1995. Avocations: writing, painting, sewing, gardening. E-mail: wildberry@prodigy.net.

BERRY, TERESA E.S. adult education educator; b. Milford, Del., Mar. 17, 1962; d. Alfred Harrison and Primrose Ella Sturgis; m. Ronald B. Berry, Jr., May 3, 1985; children: Ronald B. III, Alonna Danielle, Ryan Harrison. BA, Del. State Coll., 1984, MA, Del. State U., 2000. Tchr., Yigo, 1986—87; substitute tchr. Gila Bend, Ariz., 1987—89; test ranger, 1987—89; tchr. Smyrna (Del.) H.S., 1991—93, Cape Henlopen H.S., Lewes, Del., 1993—94, Calvary Christian Acad., Dover, Del., 1994—95, Dorchester Bd. Edn., Mace's Ln. M.S., Cambridge, Md., 1995—; adult educator Polytech H.S., 2001—. Asst. mgr. Chess King, Dover; libr. asst. Dover State U.; active Nat. Youth Sports Program, Dover. Md. Learning fellow, Md. State Edn. Dept., 1998—. Mem.: Delta Sigma Theta. Democrat. Avocations: music, reading. Home: 1000 Woodlytown Rd Magnolia DE 19962

BERRY BODOH, EMILY, dancer, choreographer, educator; b. Alma, Mich., Jan. 22, 1975; d. Ralph Max and Linda Marie Berry; m. Devon Michael Bodoh, Aug. 8, 1998. B in Dance Arts, B in Gen. Studies, U. Mich., 1998; MFA, George Mason U., 2003. Cert. movement analyst Laban/Bartenieff Inst. Movement Studies, N.Y., 2003. Guest lectr. Oakland U., Rochester, Mich., 1998—98; adj. dance faculty George Mason U., Fairfax, Va., 2001—. Choreographer (dance concert) From the Third Wave, Women & Religion, Women [illegible] for the Arts Grant, 1997). Apptd. mem. of com. Ann Arbor (Mich.) City Coun. Commn. on Increasing Saftey for Women, 1995—96. Mem.: Nat. Dance Edn. Orgn., Laban/Bartenieff Inst. Movement Studies. Avocations: travel, downhill snow skiing. Home: 1530 Key Blvd #722 Arlington VA 22209

BERRYMAN, DIANA (KAPNAS), radio personality; b. Gary, Ind., Oct. 10; m. Patrick Berryman; 1 stepchild, Shannon. Radio host, morning program announcer, ops. dir. Sta. WMBI, Chgo. Office: WMBI 820 N LaSalle Blvd Chicago IL 60610

BERRYMAN, MARY ANNE PIERCE, elementary school educator; b. Morrilton, Ark., June 4, 1937; d. Homer Rowland and Margaret (Oldham) Pierce; m. James Cleo Berryman, Aug. 5, 1961; children: James Andrew, Cathryn Anne. BA in Interior Design, U. Okla., 1959; MS in Religious Edn., Southwestern Seminary, Ft. Worth, 1961; tchr.'s cert., Ouachita Bapt. U., Aradelphia, Ark., 1970. Salesperson Ellison's Furnishings, Ft. Worth, 1961-62; interior designer J.C. Penny Co., Ft. Worth, 1962-63; tchr. Arkadelphia Pub. Schs., 1970—2003; ret., 2003. Chmn. Arkadelphia Drive for Arthritis Found., 1977. Named Tchr. Yr., Arkadelphia C. of C., 1984-85, State of Ark. Exemplary Tchr. of Econs., 1991-92. Mem. AAUW (local pres. 1976-77, chmn. ark. state edn. found. 1977-78, lt. gov. 1985-86, gov. Ozark Dist. 1998 99, named. Disting. Gov., 2000), S.W. Reading Coun (pres. 1978-79), Civitan (lt. gov. Ozark dist. 1989-90), Civitan (local v.p., sec., pres.), Delta Kappa Gamma, Kappa Kappa Iota (pres. 1986-88, 94-96, state bd. pos. 2), Civitan Club (local v.p., pres. 1988-89).

BERSCHEID, ELLEN S. psychology educator, writer, researcher; b. Colfax, Wis., Oct. 11, 1936; d. Sylvan L. and Alvilde (Running) Saumer; m. Dewey Mathias Berscheid, Nov. 21, 1959. BA, U. Nev., 1959, MA, 1960; PhD, U. Minn., 1965. Market rsch. analyst Pillsbury Co., Mpls., 1960-62; asst. prof. psychology and mktg. U. Minn., Mpls., 1965-66, asst. prof. psychology, 1967-68, assoc. prof., 1969-71, prof., 1971-88, Regents' prof. psychology, 1988—. Mem. NRC Assembly Behavioral and Social Scis., 1973-77. Co-author: Interpersonal Attraction, 1969, 78, Equity: Theory and Research, 1978, Close Relationships, 1983, Psychology of Interpersonal Relationships, 2004, also numerous articles; mem. numerous editorial bds., past editorships. Recipient Disting. Scientist award Soc. Exptl. Social Psychology, 1993. Fellow APA (Donald T. Campbell award 1984, editor Contemporary Psychology Jour. 1985-91, Disting. Sci. Contbn. award 1997, Presdl. Citation 2003), Soc. Personality and Social Psychology (pres. 1985), Soc. for Psychol. Study Social Issues, Am. Acad. Arts and Scis.; mem. Internat. Soc. for the Study Personal Relationships (pres. 1990-92), Soc. Exptl. Social Psychology (exec. bd. 1971-74, 77-80, 85-89, Disting. Scientist award 1993), Gown-in-Town Club. Lutheran. Avocation: interior design. Home: 506 Grand Hl Saint Paul MN 55102-2613 Office: U Minn Dept Psychology N309 Elliott Hall Minneapolis MN 55455

BERSI, ANN, lawyer; BA, MA, San Diego State U.; JD, Calif. Western Sch. of Law; PhD in Higher Edn. Adminstrn., U. Conn. Past mem. law firms Morris, Brignone & Pickering, Lionel, Sawyer & Collins, Las Vegas; dir. employee rels. State of Nev., 1981-83; exec. dir. State Bar Nev., 1983-89; dep. dist. atty. civil divsn. Clark County Dist. Atty.'s Office, Las Vegas. Past instr. pub. adminstrn. Pace U., N.Y.; legal counsel Clark County Sch. Dist. Bd. Trustees, Clark County Bd. Equalizaiton; mem. State Jud. Selection Commn., 2000—. Mem. State Bar Nev. (pres. bd. govs. 1999-2000). Office: District Attorneys Office PO Box 552215 Las Vegas NV 89155-2215

BERT, CLARA VIRGINIA, retired home economics educator, school system administrator; b. Quincy, Fla., Jan. 29, 1929; d. Harold C. and Ella J. (McDavid) B. BS, Fla. State U., 1950, MS, 1963, PhD, 1967. Cert. tchr., Fla.; cert. home economist; cert. pub. mgr. Tchr. Union County High Sch., Lake Butler, Fla., 1950-53, Havana High Sch., Fla., 1953-65; cons. rsch. and devel. Fla. Dept. Edn., Tallahassee, 1967-75, sect. dir. rsch. and devel., 1975-85, program dir. home econs. edn., 1985-92, program specialist resource devel., 1992-96, program specialist, spl. projects, 1996-99, program dir. grants mgmt., 1999-2000; ret., 2000. Cons. Nat. Ctr. Rsch. in Vocat. Edn., Ohio State U., 1978; field reader U.S. Dept. Edn., 1974-75.

Author, editor booklets. Mem. devel. bd., mem. adv. bd. Fla. State U. Coll. Human Scis. Family Inst., 1994—; mem. nat. com. for the capital campaign Fla. State U. Found., 2002—. U.S. Office Edn. grantee, 1976, 77, 78; recipient Dean's award Coll. Human Scis., Fla. State U., 1995; named Disting. Alumna Coll. Human Scis., Fla. State U., 1994. Mem. Am. Home Econs. Assn. (state treas. 1969-71), Am. Vocat. Assn., Fla. Vocat. Assn., Fla. Vocat. Home Econs. Assn., Am. Vocat. Edn. Rsch. Assn. (nat. treas. 1970-71), Nat. Coun. Family Rels., Am. Ednl. Rsch. Assn., Fla. State U. Alumni Assn. (bd. dirs. home econs. sect. 1976-81, pres.-elect 1978-79, 79-80), Havana Golf and Country Club, Fla. State U. Ctr. Club, Kappa Delta Pi, Kappa Omicron Nu (chpt. pres. 1965-66), Delta Kappa Gamma (pres. 1974-76), Sigma Kappa (pres. corp. bd. 1985-91), Phi Delta Kappa.

BERTAGNOLLI, LESLIE A. lawyer; b. Bloomington, Ill., Nov. 11, 1948; BA, Ill. State U., 1970, MA, 1971; PhD, U. Ill., 1975, JD, 1979. Bar: Ill. 1979. Ptnr. Baker & McKenzie, Chgo. Office: Baker & McKenzie 130 E Randolph Dr Ste 3700 Chicago IL 60601-6342

BERTELSEN, DELORA PEARL, human resources professional, mayor; b. Provo, Utah, Apr. 7, 1936; d. Lave and Nellie (Evans) B. BA, Brigham Young U., 1958, MPA, 1985. Tchr. Las Palmas Jr. High, North Sacramento, Calif., 1958-60; ch. rep. LDS Ch., Paris, France, 1960-62; dept. sec. polit. sci. Brigham Young U., Provo, 1963-66; sec., legis. aide Litton Industries, Washington, 1966-69; office mgr., rsch. asst. Inst. Pub. Adminstrn., Washington, 1969-72; exec. sec. Supreme Ct. U.S., Washington, 1972-76; asst. to dean Marriott Sch. Mgmt. Brigham Young U., Provo, 1976-95, equality opportunity mgr., 1995—. Founding bd. mem. Springville (Utah) World Folkfest, 1985-90; bd. mem. Ctrl. Utah Water Conservancy Dist., Orem, Utah, 1988-89, Springville (Utah) Mus. Art, 1990-97; mem. city coun. Springville City, 1980-87, mayor, 1990-97; chair So. County Mayors, 1995-96; mem. Coun. Govts., 1990-97; chair Springville Arts Commn., 1949—; mem. Utah County Arts Com., 1998—; historian Springville Playhouse Bd., 1998—, mem. adv. bd. Incredible Journey Arts Found., 1998—. Mem. Mountainland Assn. Govts. (chair steering com. 1995, chair regional planning 1996-97), Kiwanis Club (membership com. 1990—). Mem. Lds Ch. Avocations: biking, reading, arts.

BERTELSEN, KARYN, school system administrator, principal; b. Standardville, Utah, Nov. 20, 1944; d. John and Edith Piccioni; m. Bruce Bertelsen; children: Kristy Lee, Kelly Ann. AS, Coll. Eastern Utah Price, Utah, 1965; BS, Utah State Univ., Logan, Utah, 1967; MEd, Brigham Young Univ., Provo, Utah, 1983; EdD, Univ. Utah, Salt Lake City, 2002—. Family & consumer sci. tchr. Allessandro Jr. High, Moreno Valley, 1967—68; FACS/P.E. tchr. Helper Jr. High, Helper, Utah, 1969—83; adult roles Davis Sch. Dist., Farmington, Utah, 1983—88, nutrition coord., 1988—89, asst. prin., 1990—96, prin., 1994—. Accreditation team facilitator Ut. State office of Edn.; accreditation team Univ. Phoenix; team jr. high rep. Gov. Leavitt's H.S. Requirements. Founder Teen Help-Line, 1995; rep. Bountiful City Improvement Com., 2000—. Recipient Utah Mid. Sch. Prin. of the Yr., UASSP, 2001, Davis County's Women of the Yr., 2002, Utah Vocat. Tchr. of the Yr., 1990. Mem.: Davis C. of C., Nation Assn. of Sec. Prin., Utah Middle Sch. Assn., League of Women Voters, Phi Delta Kappa. Avocations: reading, helping others. Home: 1827 Maple Lane Bountiful UT 84010 Office Phone: 801-402-7100. E-mail: kbertselsen@dsdmail.net.

BERTINI, CATHERINE ANN, international organization official; b. Syracuse, N.Y., Mar. 30, 1950; d. Fulvio and Ann (Vino) B.; m. Thomas Haskell, 1988. BA, SUNY, 1971; DSc (hon.), McGill U., Montreal, Can., 1997; DHL (hon.), SUNY, Cortland, 1999; DSc, Pine Manor Coll., 2000; DHL (hon.), Am. U. Rome, 2001; D in Pub. Svc. (hon.), John Cabot U., Rome, 2001; PhD (hon.), Slovak Agrl. U., Nitra, Slovak Republic, 2001. Youth dir. N.Y. Rep. State Com., 1971-74; with Rep. Nat. Com., 1975-76; mgr. pub. policy Container Corp. Am., 1977-87; dir. Office Family Assistance, U.S. Dept. Health and Human Svcs., 1987-89; acting asst. sec. U.S. Dept. HHS., 1989; asst. sec. USDA, 1989-92; UN panel mem. sec. gen.'s High Level Personalities on African Devel., UN, 1992-95; exec. dir. UN World Food Programme, Rome, 1992—2002; personal humanitarian envoy UN Sec. Gen., 2002; policy maker in residence Gerald Ford Sch. Pub. Policy U. Mich., 2002; chmn. U.N. Sys. Standing Com. on Nutrition, 2002—; under-sec. gen. U.N., 2002—. Mem. Ill. State Scholarship Comm., 1979-84; mem. Ill. Human Rights Comm., 1985-87; spl. envoy of Sec. Gen. to the Horn of Africa, 2000. Recipient Leadership in Human Svcs. award Am. Pub. Welfare Assn., 1990, Pub. Svc. award Am. Acad. Pediatrics, 1991, Leadership award Nat. Assn. WIC Dirs., 1992, Quality of Life award Auburn U., 1994, Disting. Alumni award Nelson A. Rockefeller Coll. Pub. Affairs and Policy, 1997. Fellow Harvard U., 1986. Office: UN Plaza First Ave at 46th St New York NY 10017 Business E-Mail: bertini@un.org.

BERTOIA, RÉNATE, special education educator; b. Frankfurt, Germany, June 20, 1942; d. Erwin Karl and Ursula E.A. Borchardt; m. Edwin G. Johnson, Feb. 10, 1962 (div. Sept. 1986); children: Michal S., Douglas R.; m. Richard Michael Bertoia, Aug. 16, 1992; 1 child, Kevin Michael Bartoy. Secretarial degree, Clover Park Inst. Tech., 1970,, 1980, AS Yakima Valley Coll., 1978; BA in Elem. Edn. cum laude, St. Martin's Coll., 1996. Various office positions Puget Sound Nat. Bank, 1981—88; asst. to bookkeeper Sta. KBSG-FM, 1988—89; aide to student (one-on-one) Tacoma Pub. Sch. Dist., 1989—94, site coord., 1994—. Grantee in field. Mem.: Elks. Democrat. Lutheran. Avocations: gardening, music, poetry, reading. Home: 12116-414th St Ct E Eatonville WA 98328 Office: Tacoma Pub Schs PO Box 1357 Tacoma WA 98405

BERTOLOZZI, VICTORIA MARGARET, program analyst, community planning and development; b. Chgo., May 14, 1948; d. Charles Victor and Olga (Giachetti) Bertolozzi. AA, U. Md., 1975, BA in Bus. and Mgmt., 1977; MBA, Savannah State U., 1986; Certificate of Pub. Mgmt., U. Ga., 1995; DBA, Nova Southeastern U., 1997; student, Ga. Acad. Econ. Devel., 2001, student, 2003. Job developer New Visions for Newport County, Newport, R.I., 1978, adminstrv. asst. to dir., 1978-80, program dir., 1980-82; mktg. dir. Charter Broad Oaks Hosp., Savannah, Ga., 1982-86; mgmt. analyst City of Savannah, 1987-91, program analyst, 1991-93, sr. program analyst, 1994—, interim adminstr., Savannah Entrepreneurial Ctr., 2003. Founder, pres., CEO Global Bus. Growth and Design Corp., 2000—. Mem.: ASPA, Ga. Planning Assn., Acad. Internat. Bus. Home: 213 Executive Park Cir Savannah GA 31406-3355 Office: City of Savannah PO Box 1027 Savannah GA 31402-1027

BERTONIERE, NOELIE RITA, research chemist; b. New Orleans, Oct. 17, 1936; BS, St. Mary's Dominican Coll., 1959; PhD in Organic Chemistry, U. New Orleans, 1971. Rsch. chemist textiles & food USDA So. Regional Rsch. Ctr., New Orleans, 1960—. Mem. AAAS, Am. Chem. Soc., Am. Assn. Textile Chemists and Colorists, Fiber Soc., Sigma Xi. Achievements include research in cellulose chemistry, durable press cotton fabric, pore size distribution, supramolecular structure of cellulose, photochemistry of small ring heterocycles and carbenes. Office: USDA So Regional Rsch Ctr ARS PO Box 19687 1100 Robert E Lee Blvd New Orleans LA 70179

BERTOZZI, CAROLYN R. chemistry educator; b. Boston, 1966; AB in Chemistry summa cum laude, Harvard U.; PhD, U. Calif., Berkeley, 1993. Summer intern Bell Labs, 1987; postdoc. fellow U. Calif., San Francisco, prof. of Chemistry Berkeley, 1996—. Contbr. articles to profl. jours. including J. Org. Chem., Chem. and Biol., Biochem. MacArthur fellow 1999—. Mem. Am. Chem. Soc. (Arthur C. Cope Scholar Award, 1999). Office: U Calif Berkeley Chemistry Dept 813A Latimer Berkeley CA 94720-0001

BERTRAM, ANNE, playwright, application developer; d. Barbara and Lee Bertram; m. Martin Schub. BA, U. of Ill., 1982—85; MA, Northwestern U., 1989—94. Mng. dir. Theatre Unbound, Mpls., 1999—. Author: (plays) Liability (Tenn. Williams One-Act Prize, 2002), St. Luke's (Sigma Theta Tau Int'l Regional Media award, 2001), The Donner Gold (Playwrights' Ctr. Jones Commn., 2000), Sherry's Basement (O'Neill Playwrights Conf. (finalist), 2003). Recipient Residency, The Corp. of Yaddo, 2000. Mem.: The Playwrights' Ctr. (assoc.; bd. sec. 1997), Dramatists' Guild (assoc.).

BERTRAM, CHRISTINE G. artist, painter, graphics designer; b. New Bedford, Mass., Dec. 28, 1952; d. Samuel David Doran and Marjorie Ruth (Dore) B.; children: Christian Allan, Michael Doran. BFA in Painting, Swain Sch. Design, 1974; MFA, Bklyn. Coll., 1976; BFA in Design/Typography magna cum laude, U. Mass., Dartmouth, 1995. Freelance scrimshaw artist, Mattapoisett, Mass., 1980-87; graphic designer New Bedford Std. Times, 1997—2002. Designer visual prevention program State of Mass. Lead Paint Prevention Program, 1995; designer Beth Soll Dance Inc., Boston, 1994-95; project mgr., rschr. Office of Hist. Preservation, New Bedford, 1978-80. Author: Palmers Light House, 1978; co-author: History of North Bedford, 1979; designer numerous posters, books, invitations, pamphlets, logos; exhibited in various art exhbns., 1974—. Vol. Tchrs. Ctr. Sch., Mattapoisett, 1989—2001, Boy Scouts Am., Mattapoisett, 1986—; Sunday sch. tchr. Congl. Ch., Mattapoisett, 1984—2002. U.S. govt. grantee for rsch. involved in New Bedford becoming a Nat. Park. Avocations: antique restoration, braided and hooked rugs, sewing, painting, gardening. Home: 124 Acushnet Rd Mattapoisett MA 02739-1221 E-mail: christieb43@aol.com.

BERTRAM, JEAN DESALES, writer; b. Burlington, Iowa, Sept. 28; d. Val Randall and Ruth Cecilia Bertram; 1 child, Larkin Bertram-Cox Montgomery . BA, U. N.C., Greensboro, 1942; MA, U. Minn., 1951; PhD, Stanford U., 1963. Reporter Greensboro News Record, 1942-43; founder dept. pub. rels. Burlington Industries, Greensboro, 1943-49; asst. to dean edn. U. N.C., Greensboro, 1949-50; instr. U. Minn., Mpls., 1950-51; dir. radio performance Mpls. Vocat. High Sch., 1951-52; dir. Children's Theatre Touring Co., Jr. League Mpls., 1951-52; prof. theatre arts San Francisco State U., 1952-88. Cons. Wadsworth Pub. Co., Belmont, Calif., 1966; dir. Readers' Repertory, San Francisco State U., 1967-72; dir. Jean De Sales Bertram Players, San Francisco, 1971-74; founder, developer storytelling program San Francisco State U., 1971-88; cons. Scott-Foresman, Chgo., 1983; senator acad. senate San Francisco State U., 1983-84, dir. com. for lectures, arts and spl. programs, 1985-87; tax preparer, 1994. Author: (textbooks) The Oral Experience of Literature, 1967, The Actor Speaks, 4 edits., 1981-87, Tell Me a Story!, 5 edits., 1982-88; author, dir. Girl Scout Nat. Convention pageant Finding Your Own Adventure, 1955; prodr., dir., adapter, editor: (religious plays) A Symphonetic Easter Drama, 1954, The Awakening, 1954, The Vision of Isaiah, 1970, The Cherry Tree, 1971; author, dir.: (plays) American Cameos, 1976, Jeremiah The Prophet, 1999; author: (poem) Cosmorama, 1971; actress one-woman show numerous women from Shakespeare's plays, 1971-88; author: (short story) The Giraffe and the Canary, 1999; contbr. articles to profl. jours. Stanford-Wilson fellow Stanford U., 1962-63. Mem. Found. Bibl. Rsch., Acad. Am. Poets, Phi Beta Kappa (sec. Omicron of Calif. chpt. 1977-79, 83-88, pres. 1979-81, v.p. 1981-83, ofcl. del. Triennial coun. 1979, 82). Avocations: sculpturing in clay, poetry writing, photography.

BERTRAM, SUSAN, rehabilitation counselor; b. Darlington, S.C., July 7, 1945; d. Ernest and Leigh (Ogburn) Lowry; m. John David Bertram, Dec. 7, 1980. BFA, U. Ga., 1966; MS, Ga. State U., 1993. Cert. rehab. counselor, nat. cert. counselor, Ga.; lic. profl. counselor, Ga. Social work/counselor State of Ga., Atlanta, 1967—95, rehab. counselor, 1995—. Mem. ACA, Nat. Rehab. Counseling Assn., Ga. Rehab. Assn. Avocations: travel, reading, yoga.

BERZON, MARSHA S. federal judge; BA, Radcliffe Coll., 1966; JD, Boalt Hall Sch. Law, 1973. Bar: Calif. 1973, D.C. 1975. Clerk Judge James Browning, 9th Cir., 1973—74, Justice William Brennan, 1974—75; atty. Woll & Mayer, Washington, 1975—77, Altshuler, Berzon, Nussbaum, Berzon & Rubin, San Francisco, 1978—2000; judge U.S. Ct. Appeals 9th Cir., 2000—. Office: US Ct Appeals 9th Cir PO Box 193939 San Francisco CA 94119-3939

BESCH, LORRAINE W. special education educator; b. Orange, N.J., June 27, 1948; d. Robert Woodruff and Minnie (Wrightson) B.; m. William Lee Gibson, July 10, 1982. AA in Liberal Arts, Mt. Vernon Coll., 1968; BA in Sociology, U. Colo., 1970; MA in Spl. Edn., U. Denver, 1973. Cert. handicapped thcr., N.J. Elem. resource rm. tchr. Beeville (Tex.) Ind. Sch. Dist., 1973-75; trainable mentally retarded tchr. Kings County Supt. Schs., Hanford, Calif., 1975-78; h.s. resource rm. tchr. Summit (N.J.) Bd. Edn., 1980-81, Westfield (N.J.) Bd. Edn., 1981-99, head coach field hockey, 1981-83, mem. crisis mgmt. team, 1982-87, in class support tchr. English, 1993-99. Named to Women's Inner Circle Achievement, 1996; recipient Internat. Sash of Academia, ABI, 1997. Mem. AAUW, Smithsonian Nat. Mus. Am. Indian (charter), Sky Meadows Cir. Nat. Mus. Women in Arts, CEC (learning disabilities divsn.), Westfield Edn. Assn. (del. 1983-90, tech. com. 1993-94, conf. funds com. 1994-99), Hartford Family Found. (v.p., sec. 1991-97, trustee 1997—), Wrightson-Besch Found. (sec.-treas. 1994-99, pres. 1999—), Archaeology Conservancy (life), 1892 Founders Soc., Morristown Meml. Health Found., Col. Williamsburg Burgesses, Nat. Trust Historic Preservation, N.J. Hist. Society. Avocations: traveling, reading, gardening, cooking, tennis. Home: 8 Lone Oak Rd Basking Ridge NJ 07920-1613

BESCH, NANCY ADAMS, county official; b. Lancaster, Pa., Nov. 12, 1926; AB in Psychology, Wilson Coll., 1948, LHD, hon. doctor of humane letters, 1989. Commr., vice chair Cumberland County, 1992-95, commr., chair, 1995—. Bd. dirs., publ. info. tng. com. chair County Commrs.' Assn. of Pa.; Capital Region Chamber of Commerce "Envision" Task Force; v. chmn. So. Ctrl. Assembly for Effective Governance; Capital Region Econ. Devel. Corp. Bd. Coun. mem. Camp Hill Borough, 1984-91; bd. dirs. Camp Hill Sch., 1975-81; commr. liaison Cumberland County Libr. Sys. Bd.; mem. exec. bd. Cumberland-Perry Mental Health/Mental Retardation; comm. mem. cmty. adv. bd. Harrisburg Acad. 1998-2001; mem. Capital Region Funders Collaborative, Cmty. Connections, Keystone Area Coun. Boy Scouts (exec. com., mem. Bd. of NE Coun. Boy Scouts of Am.), Fund Devel. Com. Hemlock Girl Scout Coun., Inc. 1980-99, Cmty. Devel. Block Grant Adv. Com. of Pa. Dept. of Cmty. and Econ. Devel., Cumberland County Children and Youth Svcs. Adv. Com., DUI Task Force, Domestic Violence Svcs. Cumberland and Perry Counties; polity com. Presbytery of Carlisle; personnel sub-com. Synod of The Trinity Presbyn. Church, USA. Recipient Outstanding Publ. Ofcl. award, Pa. Assn. County Human Svcs., 1998, Pa.'s Mem. of Yr. award County Commr.'s Assn., 1997, Dist. Daughters of Pa. award, awarded by Govnr. Ridge, 1997, Catalyst award Capital Region Econ. Devel. Corp. for Leadership in Support of Devel. in Harrisburg Region, 1994, Elected Ofcls. award Pa. Libr. Assn., 1993, Trustee award Dist. Svc. Wilson Coll., 1988, Dist. Alum. award, Wilson Coll. 1989, Hemlock award for Svc. Hemlock Girl Scout Coun., Ketchum, Inc. award for Leadership in Am. Philanthropy, "Thanks" Badge Girl Scouts of Am., hon. membership prog. agy. Presbyn. Church U.S.A.; fellow Am. Assn. State Psychology Bds., 1991, Silver Beaver award Keystone Area Coun. Boy Scouts Am., 1999; named to "Movers and Shakers in Central Pa." List Ctrl. Pa. Bus. Jour., 1998. Mem. Susquehanna Alliance, West Shore Chamber of Commerce, Cumberland Cty. Hist. Soc., Cumberland Cty. Transp. Authority. Home: 209 Willow Ave Camp Hill PA 17011-3653

BESHAR, CHRISTINE, lawyer; b. Paetzig, Germany, Nov. 6, 1929; came to U.S., 1952, naturalized, 1957; d. Hans and Ruth (vonKleist-Retzow) von Wedemeyer; m. Robert P. Beshar, Dec. 20, 1953; children: Cornelia, Jacqueline, Frederica, Peter. Student, U. Hamburg, 1950-51, U. Tuebingen, 1951-52; BA, Smith Coll., 1953. Bar: N.Y. 1960, U.S. Supreme Ct. 1971. Assoc. Cravath, Swaine & Moore, N.Y.C., 1964-70, ptnr., 1971—. Bd. dirs. Catalyst for Women Inc., 1977-94; trustee Colgate U., 1978-84, Smith Coll., [illegible] Nature Conservancy, N.Y., 1995-96. Inst. Internat. Edn. fellow, 1952-53; recipient Disting. Alumnae medal Smith Coll., 1974. Fellow: Am. Coll. Probate Counsel; mem.: Fgn. Policy Assn. (bd. dirs. 1978—87), UN Assn. (bd. dirs. 1975—89), N.Y. Bar Found. (bd. dirs. 1977—2001), N.Y. State Bar Assn. (ho. of dels. 1971—80, v.p. 1979—80), Assn. Bar City N.Y. (exec. com. 1973—75, v.p. 1985—86), Am. Bar Found., Gipsy Trail Club, Cosmopolitan Club. Office: Cravath Swaine & Moore 825 8th Ave 43d Fl New York NY 10019-7475 also: Stone House Farm PO Box 533 Somers NY 10589-0533 E-mail: cbeshar@cravath.com.

BESHUR, JACQUELINE E. special education educator; b. Portland, Oreg., May 8, 1948; d. Charles Daniel and Mildred (Domreis) Beshears. BA, UCLA, 1970; MBA, Claremont Grad. Sch., 1980; postgrad., City U., Seattle, 1989-90. Dir. and founder L.A. Ctr. for Photog. Studies, 1972-76; precious gem distbr. Douglas Group Holdings, Australia, 1976-78; small bus. owner BeSure Cleaning, 1981-90; animal trainer, exotic livestock farmer, writer, 1990-2000; activities and disadvantaged children's tutor, 2000—. Author: Good Intentions Are Not Good Enough, 1992. Dir. County Citizens Against Incineration, 1987—, Ames Lake Protection Com., 1989—. Mem. Bridges for Peace, Nature Conservancy, Wash. Wilderness Coalition, Issaquah Alps Club. Republican. Office: BeSure Tng PO Box 225 Carnation WA 98014-0225

BESS, ANGELA PAIGE, music educator; b. Hickory, N.C., Apr. 27, 1978; d. Thomas Lee and Karen Wright Bess. MusB in Music Edn., East Carolina U., 2003. Band dir. Jacksonville (N.C.) Commons Middle Sch., 2000—02; asst. band dir. White Oak H.S., Jacksonville, 2002—03; band dir. Crest H.S., Shelby, NC, 2003—. Camp counselor Ea. Carolina U. Summer Band Camp, Greenville, NC, 2001—. Mem.: Ea. Dist. Band Assn., Music Educators Nat. Conf., Profl. Educators N.C. Office: Crest High Sch 800 Old Boiling Springs Rd Shelby NC 28152

BESSANT, CATHERINE POMBIER, bank executive, marketing professional; b. Jackson, Mich. m. John E. Clay; 2 children. BBA in Fin., Mktg. and Eng. Lit., U. Mich. Joined NationsBank, 1982; pres., cmty. devel. bank Bank Am. Corp. (formerly NationsBank), 1998—2000; pres., consumer real estate banking Bank Am. Corp., 1999—2000, pres., Fla. ops., 2000—01, chief mktg. exec., 2001—. Trustee Enterprise Found. Bd. dirs. Children's Theatre Charlotte, Blue Cross Blue Shield Fla., Inc. Named one of Most Powerful Women in Banking, US Banker Mag., 2003. Office: Bank Am Corp 100 N Tryon St Charlotte NC 28255

BESSETTE, DIANE J. homebuilding company executive; V.p., contr. Lennar Corp, Miami, 1995—. Office: Lennar Corp 700 NW 107th Ave Ste 400 Miami FL 33172-3154

BEST, AMY L. education educator; d. Gary and Natalie Best; m. J. Christopher McCauley, 1998; 1 child, Elizabeth. BA in Sociology, Ithaca (N.Y.) Coll., 1992; MA in Sociology, Syracuse (N.Y.) U., 1995, PhD in Sociology, 1998. Asst. prof. sociology Syracuse (N.Y.) U., 1998—99; asst. prof. San Jose (Calif.) State U., 1999—2004; assoc. prof. sociology and anthropology George Mason U., 2004—. Faculty mentor program San Jose State U., 1999—. Author: (book) Prom Night: Youth, Schools and Popular Culture, 2000 (Critics' Choice award, 2002); reviewer (jour.) Jour. of Gender and Society, 2002—03, Social Problems, 2002—03. Mem. compliance com. Ams. with Disabilities Act, San Jose, Calif., 2000—; action planning team mem. Nex Am. Cmty. Svc., San Jose, Calif., 2000—01. Recipient Critics' Choice award, Am. Ednl. Studies Assn., 2002; fellow, Calif. State U., 2003; grantee Rsch. grant, San Jose State U., 1999, 2001, 2002, 2003, Career Devel. grant, Jr. Faculty, 2001. Mem.: Am. Sociol. Assn. (coun. mem. children's sect. 2003—). Democrat. Avocations: reading, quilting. Office: San Jose State U Dept Sociology One Washington Sq San Jose CA 95192-0122

BEST, LAURA, special education educator; d. Donna Kelley and Robert Lettkeman; m. Richard Best, June 1, 1996. BS, Ala. A&M U., 2002. Paraprofessional in multiple disability classroom Riverton Elem. Sch., Huntsville, Ala., 2000—01; substitute tchr. Huntsville (Ala.) City Schs., 2002—03; tchr. for children with specific learning disabilities Whitesburg Elem. Sch., Huntsville, Ala., 2003—03; tchr. for children with autism Blossomwood Elem. Sch., Huntsville, Ala., 2003—03; tchr. for children with specific learning disabilities Hampton Cove Mid. Sch., Huntsville, Ala., 2003—. Tutor and mentor Huntsville City Schs., 2000; vol. Nat. Children's Advocacy Ctr., Huntsville, Ala., 1995—96, Spl. Olympics, Huntsville, Ala., 1994—96. Recipient President's Cup, twice, Ala. A&M U. Mem.: NEA, Ala. Edn. Assn., Coun. for Exceptional Children (pres. of student chpt. 2001—02), Alpha Kappa Mu Nat. Honor Soc., Kappa Delta Pi.

BEST, MARCIA A. graphics designer, artist; b. Toledo, Jan. 17, 1954; d. Best F. Robert. BFA, Siena Heights U., 1976. Verification completion in graphic design Albuquerque Tech. Vocat. Inst., 1999. Owner BestGraphics, Albuquerque, 1984—. Graphic technician Albuquerque TVI, 1984—. Exhibitions include N.Mex. Expo Fine Arts Exhibit, N.Mex. State Hispanic Art Exhibit, Siena Heights Invitational Exhibit, Canton Art Inst. Mem.: N.Mex Watercolor Soc. (assoc.; editor 2000—03). Liberal. Avocations: travel, photography, reading, music. Office: BestGraphics 308 Escena SE Albuquerque NM 87123 E-mail: bestgraphics@starband.net.

BEST, SUSAN MARIE, artist, educator; b. Peoria, Ill., July 4, 1949; d. Robert H. and Shirley (Critchlow) Coyle; m. David G. Best, Sept. 12, 1970 (div. May 1987); children: Timothy, Molly, Abby, George; m. Richard J. Gualandi, Dec. 20, 1996. BPhar, U. Ill., Chgo., 1972; MA in Fine Arts, Ill. State U., Normal, 1988, MFA, 1991. Grad. pharmacist S&C Drugs, Peoria, 1972, Indian Hosp., Pine Ridge, S.D., 1974-76; instr. art Ill. State U., Normal, 1988-91, Bradley U., Peoria, 1992-93, Ill. Ctrl. Coll., Peoria, 1991-93; artist, 1970—. Gallery artist Struve Gallery, Chgo., 1991-93; active Longue Vue Mus. Art Program. Exhbn. Contemporary Art Ctr., Oleczyn, Poland. Bd. dirs. St. Thomas Sch., Peoria, 1980-83, Amateur Mus. Club, Peoria, 1982-84; bd. dirs. Peoria Art Guild, 1994—. Recipient Percent for Art award City of New Orleans, 1997, also various awards for art including 2 grants from Ill. Arts Coun. Access Program, 1995; Ill. State U. fellow, 1988-91. Mem. AAUP, AAUW, NOW, Contemporary Arts Ctr. of New Orleans, New Orleans Mus. Art, Chgo. Artists Coalition, Lakeview Art Mus., Sun Found., Planned Parenthood Assn. Democrat. Avocations: skiing, jogging, piano. Studio: 811 1/2 Opelousas Ave New Orleans LA 70114-2429

BESTEHORN, UTE WILTRUD, retired librarian; b. Cologne, Germany, Nov. 6, 1930; came to U.S., 1930; d. Henry Hugo and Wiltrud Lucie (Vincentz) B. BA, U. Cin., 1954, BEd, 1955, MEd, 1958; MS in Library Sci., Western Res. U. (now Case-Western Res. U.), 1961. Tchr. Cutter Jr. High Sch., Cin., 1955-57; tchr., supr. libr. Felicity (Ohio) Franklin Sr. High Sch., 1959-60; with libr. sci. dept. Pub. Libr. Cin. and Hamilton County, 1961-78, with libr. info. desk, 1978-91; ret., 1991. Textbook selection com., Felicity-Franklin Sr. High Sch., 1959-60; supr. Health Alcove Sci. Dept. and annual health lectures, Cin. Pub. Library, 1972-77. Book reviewer Library Jour., 1972-77; author and inventor Rainbow 40 marble game, 1971, Condominium game, 1976; patentee indexed packaging and stacking device, 1973, mobile packaging and stacking device, 1974. Mem. Clifton

Town Meeting, 1988—; mem. Bookfest 90 com. Pub. Libr. Cin. and Hamilton County. Recipient Cert. of Merit and Appreciation Pub. Library of Cin., 1986. Mem. Cin. Chpt. Spl. Libraries Assn. (archivist 1963-64, 65-70, editor Queen City Gazette bull. 1964-69), Pub. Library Staff Assn. (exec. bd., activities com. 1965, welfare com. 1966, recipient Golden Book 25 yr. service pin, 1986), Friends of the Library, Greater Cin. Calligraphers Guild (reviewer New Letters pub. 1986-88), Delta Phi Alpha (nat. German hon. 1951). Republican. Mem. United Ch. of Christ. Avocations: calligraphy, painting and sketching, writing, photography, violin. Home: 3330 Morrison Ave Cincinnati OH 45220-1440

BEST-GORING, CYNTHIA LOVALE, elementary school principal; b. Washington, Aug. 24, 1950; d. Alexander Henry and Annie Belle (Spruill) Best; m. Anthony Trevor Goring, Apr. 27, 1975; children: Alexis, Trevor. BA in Elem. ELdn., Columbia Union Coll., 1972; MEd, U. Md., 1975, M.Reading, 1981. Cert. std. profl. cert., advanced profl. cert., Md. Tchr. Prince George's County Pub. Sch. Sys., 1972-82; reading specialist Bladensburg (Md.) Elem. Sch., 1983-88; vice prin. Beltsville (Md.) Acad. Ctr., 1988-89; tchr. specialist Area Asst. Supt.s Office, 1989-92; prin. Berkshire Elem. Sch., Forestville, Md., 1992-94, Adelphi ATLAS Communities Elem. Sch., Adelphi, Md., 1994—2000, East Silver Spring (Md.) ES, 2000—. Staff devel. cons. Prince George's County, Md., 1989—; spkr. in field. Pianist Pennsylvania Ave. SDA Ch., Capital Hts., Md., 1984-94, Sligo SDA Ch., Takoma Park, Md., 1994—; mem. Oxford Roundtable, 2003. Targeted Poverty grantee, 1994-95, Sch.-Wide Improvement grantee, 1995-96; nominee Wash. Post Leadership award, 2004. Mem. ASCD, New Am. schs. Devel. Corp. Democrat. Avocations: piano, reading, cooking, mentoring. Home: 7208 Wingate Dr Glenn Dale MD 20769 Office: East Silver-Spring ES 631 Silver Spring MD 20910 Office Phone: 301-650-6420.

BESTON, ROSE MARIE, retired academic administrator; b. South Portland, Maine, Sept. 27, 1937; d. George Louis and Edith Mae (Archibald) Beattie; m. John Bernard Beston, Feb. 1, 1970 BA, St. Joseph's Coll., 1961; MA, Boston Coll., 1963; PhD, U. Pitts., 1967; cert. of advanced study, Harvard U., 1978. Mem. faculty St. Joseph's Coll., Maine, 1967-68, SUNY, Oneonta, 1968-69, S.E. Mo. State Coll., 1969-70, U. Queensland and Western Australian Inst. Tech., 1970-76, U. Hawaii, Manoa, 1976-77; assoc. acad. dean Worcester State Coll., Mass., 1978-80; dean for acad. affairs Castleton State Coll., Vt., 1980-84; dean Nazareth Coll. Rochester, NY, 1984-98; ret., 1998. Former mem. Neylan Commn., Assn. Cath. Colls. and Univs., Pres. Network of Campus Compact. Contbr. articles to profl. jour. Mem. AAUW.

BETANCOURT, ANNIE, state legislator; b. Havana, Cuba, Mar. 3, 1947; arrived in Fla., 1960. AA in Psychology, Miami-Dade C.C., Fla., 1972; BA in Psychology, U. Miami, 1974. Mem. Fla. Ho. of Reps., Tallahassee, 1994—. Vice-chair juvenile justice com.; mem. colls. and univs. com., water and resource mgmt. com.; adminstr. Miami-Dade Coll.; bd. dirs. South Fla. Water Mgmt. Dist. Bd. dirs. Rep. Nat. Bank; past pres. League of Women Voters, 1989-91. Recipient Phoenix award AAUW, 1990; named Activist of Yr., Dade County Dem. Cmty., Woman of Yr., Coalition of Hispanic-Am. Women, 1994. Democrat. Roman Catholic. Avocations: swimming, sailing, tennis. Office: Capitol Bldg Ho Office Bldg 1401 The Capitol 402 S Monroe St Tallahassee FL 32399-6526

BETANZOS, AMALIA V. social services administrator; b. N.Y.C., July 12, 1930; d. Deverino Miguel and Margarita (Hassel) Carcasio; m. Odon Betanzos, Mar. 21, 1953; 1 child, Manuel. BA, NYU, 1950, postgrad. Administrv. coord. Summer in the City Program, N.Y.C., 1966-68; chief exec. officer, administr. P.R. Community Devel. Project, N.Y.C., 1968-70; spl. asst. to Mayor for housing, neighborhood affairs, social svcs. N.Y.C., 1970; deputy administr., commr. Housing & Devel. Adminstrn. of City of N.Y., 1970-72; exec. sec. to Mayor of N.Y.C., 1972; commr. youth svcs., exec. dir. youth bd. Human Resources Adminstrn.-Youth Svcs. Agency, N.Y.C., 1972-73; commr. N.Y.C. Housing Authority, 1973-78; pres., chief exec. officer Wildcat Svc. Corp., N.Y.C., 1978—. Lectr. Lehman Coll., Bronx, N.Y., 1960-70; mem.-at-large N.Y.C. Bd. Edn. Retirement Bd., 1988-90; mem. N.Y.C. Bd. Edn., 1987-90; bd. dirs. Nat. P.R. Coalition, Inc., Washington. Edit. adv. com. El Diario/La Prensa. Trustee Cath. Charities, N.Y.C., St. Barnabas Hosp., P.R. Community Found., Fund for the City of N.Y., Pub. Edn. Assn.; mem. N.Y.C. Outward Bound Ctr., Alcoholism Coun. Greater N.Y., The Children's Fund, Citizens Union of the City of N.Y., Women's Forum, Inc., Citizens Commn. on AIDS, Charter Revision Commn. '82-'83, '87-'89, N.Y.C. Private Industry Coun., Com. Integrity in Govt., N.Y.C. Loft Bd., numerous others; bd. dirs. Bklyn. Navy Yard, Community Service Soc., Correctional Soc. N.Y., N.Y. Urban League, Vera Inst. Justice, Drug Abuse Coun., P.R. Community Devel. Project, St. Lukes Hosp., Fortune Soc.; chairperson Nat. P.R. Coalition, Inc., Social Devel. Commn. Archdiocese of N.Y., N.Y.C. Rent Guidelines Bd.; pres. Manhattan Valley Spanish Civic Assn., Nat. Assn. P.R. Civil Rights, N.Y.S. Industries for Handicapped; ptnr. N.Y.C. Partnership; sec. bd. overseers Ctr. New Social Rsch.; steering com. Nat. Urban Coalition; mem. adv. bd. Cath. Interracial Coun. of N.Y., Inc., Bureau Community Edn., Consumer Protection N.Y. Bar Assn.; mem. Mayor's adv. com. Police Mgmt. & Personnel Policy; mem. many other adv. bds., coms., couns. Recipient Pub. Edn. award Pub. Edn. Assn., 1990, Golden Palm award INTAR, 1990, Las Casas award NE Pastora Coun., 1982; named Woman of the Yr. Nat. Coun. P.R. Women, 1993. Democrat. Roman Catholic. Avocations: painting, sculpture. Home: 125 Queen St Staten Island NY 10314-5350 Office: 17 Battery Pl New York NY 10004-1207

BETH, JOYCE ELIZABETH, elementary school educator; b. Two Rivers, Wis. d. Erhardt W. and Viola E. Meineke; m. James E. Beth, June 27, 1964; 1 child, Christine. BS, U. Wis., Osh Kosh, Wis., 1962. Tchr. 2d grade West Milw.-West Allis Sch. Dist., Milw., 1962—63; tchr. 1st grade Two Rivers J.F. Magee Sch. Dist., Wis., 1963—2003, reading program, 2003—. Chmn., sr. vol. coord., Arbor Day chmn. J.F. Magee Sch. Active Lester Libr. Bd., Two Rivers, 2001—; bd. dirs. Salvation Army, Two Rivers Ednl. Horizons Found. Mem.: AAUW (sec., fund raiser, edn. chair, named honoree 1999), Cool City Garden Club (pres. 1988—2000), Order of Ea. Star (sec.), Wis. Garden Club Fedn. (dist. dir. 1993—95, 1999—2001, 2003—, Sheboygan Dist. 110% award 1998), Delta Kappa Gamma (chmn. membership). Avocations: gardening, travel, cultural events. Office: J F Magee Sch 3502 Glenwood St Two Rivers WI

BETHEL, JOANN D. computer programmer, analyst; b. Ardmore, Okla., Nov. 20, 1956; d. Dorvin and Marian (McKinney) B. Student, U. Okla., 1998—; AS in Computer Sci., AS in Math., Oklahoma City C.C., 1999. Computer operator Security Nat. Bank and Trust, Norman, Okla., 1978-84, programmer, 1984-87, programmer analyst, 1987-90, tech. svc. officer, 1990-95; programmer analyst C-TEQ, Oklahoma City, 1995-2000, v.p., 2000-2001; programmer InterCept, Inc., Oklahoma City, 2001—. Okla. Coun. Tchrs. of Math. scholar, 1996. Mem.: Golden Key Honor Soc., Tau Beta Pi, Phi Theta Kappa. Home: 3915 Bellwood Dr Norman OK 73072-3622 E-mail: JDBethel@ix.netcom.com.

BETHEL, MARILYN JOYCE, librarian; b. Detroit, Jan. 14, 1935; d. Thomas Agmey and Mary Helen (Lisek) Hepfner; m. Herschel Earl Bethel, June 20, 1960 (div. Mar. 1969); 1 child, Mary Joyce. BA in Edn., Fla. Atlantic U., 1974; MLS, La. State U., 1975, MEd, 1976; postgrad., Fla. Atlantic U., 1977-78. Cert. reading specialist, Fla. Cons. Fla. Diagnostic and Learning Resources, Ft. Lauderdale, 1979-80; libr. Cocnut Creek (Fla.) Elem. Sch., 1980-82; cons. Fla. Coll. Bus., Pompano, 1982-84; libr. Broward County Libr., Hallandale, Fla., 1983, cataloger Ft. Lauderdale, 1983-90, br. head Deerfield, 1990-92, libr. Pompano, 1992-95, Ft. Lauderdale, 1995-2000, ret., 2000. Cons. Fla. Diagnostic and Learning Resources, 1979-80; mem. behavioral objectives writing team Broward County Spl.

Edn., 1981. Advisor to periodical Biography Today, 1992—; writer newsletter Exceptional Student, 1979-80. Vol. crisis counselor Sexual Assault Treatment Ctr., Broward County, Fla., 1977-78; lectr., instr. New Covenant Ch., Pompano, 1984-87. With USAF, 1954-55. Recipient Cert. of Appreciation, Bd. County Commrs., Ft. Lauderdale, 1978. Mem. ALA (com. for cataloging for children 1989-95, liaison Freedom to Read 1979-80), Fla. Libr. Assn., Broward County Libr. Assn., Nat. Alzheimers Assn. Republican. Presbyterian. Avocations: floral arranging, snorkeling, swimming, reading. Home: 272 NE 39th Ct Pompano Beach FL 33064-3545

BETHLEN, ILONA R. designer, educator; b. Budapest, Hungary, Apr. 10, 1921; came to U.S., 1952; d. Dezso and Vilma Gizella (Laszlo) Szentimrey; m. Francis R. Bethlen, Oct. 7, 1948; children: Anna Maria Bethlen LaFontaine, Mihaly Antal. MS, U. Econ. Sci., Budapest, Hungary, 1945; MA, Liszt Acad. Music, Budapest, Hungary, 1947; BA, SUNY, Plattsburgh, 1982. Tchg. asst. Econ. Faculty Jozsef Nador U., Budapest, Hungary, 1943-46; lady driver, trainer Hungarian Horse Racing Assn., Budapest, 1946-48; supplier, artist Gath & Chaves Dept. Stores, Buenos Aires, 1949-52; trainer of standardbreds A. Miller Stables, E. Aurora, N.Y., 1952-56; decorator, art adv. Am. Wallpaper Co., Buffalo, 1956-61; art instr. St. Mary Acad., Champlain, 1962-68; prof. art Coll. Cont. Edn. SUNY, Plattsburgh, 1970-81; gallery mgr. Four Winds Gallery, Burlington, Vt., 1970-77; artist, exhibitor Holt & Renfrew Co., Lupton DuVal Co., others, Toronto and Montreal, 1982—. Chairperson disasters ARC, N.Y., 1965-75; bd. dirs., chair edn. progress Joint Coun. Econ. Opportunities, Plattsburgh, N.Y., 1980-88. Named Outstanding Lady-Horse Trainer Buffalo Courier Express, 1952. Mem. AAUW, Rotary (mem. bd. world cmty. svcs. 1985-97, del. Rotary Internat. 91st annual conv. Buenos Aires, 2000). Avocations: travel, painting, small gardening.

BETTERIDGE, FRANCES CARPENTER, retired lawyer, mediator; b. Aug. 25, 1921; d. James Dunton and Emily (Atkinson) Carpenter; m. Albert Edwin Betteridge, Feb. 5, 1949 (div. 1975); children: Anne, Albert Edwin, James, Peter. AB, Mt. Holyoke Coll., 1942; JD, N.Y. Law Sch., 1978. Bar: Conn. 1979, Ariz. 1982. Technician in charge blood banks Roosevelt Hosp. and Mountainside Hosp., N.Y.C., Montclair, N.J., 1943-49; sub. tchr. Greenwich (Conn.) H.S., 1978-79; intern and asst. to labor contracts office Town of Greenwich, 1979-80; vol. referee Pima County Juvenile Ct., Tucson, 1981-85; sole practice immigration law Tucson 1982-87; judge Pro Tempore Pima County Justice Cts., 1988-91. Commr. Juvenile Ct., Pima County Superior Ct., Tucson, 1985-87; hearing officer Small Claims Ct., Pima County Justice Cts., Tucson, 1982; mediator Family Crisis Svc., Tucson, 1982-85. vol. referee Pima County Superior Ct., 1981-85; lectr. Tucson Mus. Art, 1994—. Pres. H.S. PTA, Greenwich, 1970, PTA Coun., 1971; mem. Greenwich Bd. Edn., 1971-76, sec. 1973-76; com. chmn. LWV Tucson, 1981, bd. dirs., 1984-85; bd. dirs., sec. Let The Sun Shine Inc., Tucson, 1981—; bd. dirs. Ariz. St. Ass'n Judges and Ariz. Ass'n 2003—. Mem. ABA, Conn. Bar Assn., Ariz. Bar Assn., Pima County Bar Assn., Tucson Sr. Acad., Point o'Woods Club. Republican. Avocations: imports folk art from oaxaca, mex. Home and Office: 7659 S Vivaldi Ct Tucson AZ 85747 E-mail: FMotz@aol.com.

BETTERMANN, HILDA, state legislator; b. Oct. 22, 1942; m. William; two children., U. Minn., St. Cloud U., Moorhead U., Hamline U. Rep. Dist. 10B Minn. State Ho. of Reps., 1991-98, asst. minority leader, 1993-98; instr. Alexandria Tech. Coll., 1982—. Mem. Commerce Com., Econ. Devel. Com., Labor Mgmt. Rels., Agrl. & Higher Edn. Fin. Divsn. Coms.; mem. Minn. Dflt. Lead. Inst., 1991—; mem. Alexandria County Bd., Dough Mgmt. NEA, Minn. Edn. Assn., Am. Vocat. Assn., Minn. Vocat. Assn., Minn. Sec. Assn., Nat. Sec. Assn. Office: 8435 Sara Rd NW Brandon MN 56315-8351

BETTISON, CYNTHIA ANN, museum director, archaeologist; b. St. Louis, Sept. 8, 1958; d. William Leslie and Barbara Ann (Yunker) B. BA in Anthropology and Biology, Pitzer Coll., 1980, MA in Anthropology, Eastern N.Mex. U., 1983; ABD in Anthropology, U. Calif., Santa Barbara, 1986, PhD in Anthropology, 1998. Registered profl. archaeologist. Asst. curator dept. anthropology U. Calif., Santa Barbara, 1988-89, curator dept. anthropology, 1990-91; dir. Western N.Mex. U. Mus., Silver City, 1991—. Co-dir. Western N.Mex. U. Archaeol. Field Sch., 1992, 94, 95; lectr. Western N.Mex. U., 1992, 93, adj. asst. prof. dept. social scis., 1994—; various archaeol. positions, 1981—. Contbr. articles to profl. jours. Recipient Conservation Assessment Program grant, 1994-95, NEH, 1994; Gila Nat. Forest grantee, 1992, 94, 95, Mimbres Region Art Coun. mini grantee, 1992, Silver City Lodgers Tax Bd. grantee, Andrew Isabell Meml. Fund grantee U. Calif., 1990, SIMSE grantee, 1994-95, 95-96. Mem. AAUW, Am. Assn. Mus., Am. Anthrop. Assn., Am. Soc. Conservation Archaeology, N.Mex. Mus. Assn., Soc. for Am. Archaeology, Archaeol. Soc. N.Mex., N.Mex. Archaeol. Coun. (sec. 1993-94), Coun. Mus. Anthropology (sec. 1992-94), Mountain Plains Mus. Assn., Univ. Women's Club, Univ. Club, Optimist Club (sec. Silver City chpt. 1992), Silver City Rotary Club (v.p. 1999-2000, pres. elect 2000-2001, pres. 2001-2002), Silver City Grant County C. of C., Chpt. AG PEO, Phi Kappa Phi. Office: Western NM Univ Mus 1000 W College Ave Silver City NM 88061-4158 E-mail: bettisonc@iron.wnmu.edu.

BETTS, BARBARA STOKE, artist, educator; b. Arlington, Mass., Apr. 19, 1924; d. Stuart and Barbara Lillian (Johnstone) Stoke; m. James William Betts, July 28, 1951; 1 child, Barbara Susan (dec.). BA, Mt. Holyoke Coll., 1946; MA, Columbia U. 1948. Cert. tchr., N.Y., Calif. Hawaii. Art tchr. Walton (N.Y.) Union Schs., 1947-48, Presidio Hill Sch., San Francisco, 1949-51; freelance artist San Francisco, 1951; art tchr. Honolulu Acad. Arts, summer 1952, 59, 63, 85, spring 61, 64; libr. aide art Inst. of Hawaii, Honolulu, 1959; art tchr. Hanahauoli Sch., Honolulu, 1961-62, Hawaii State Dept. Edn., Honolulu, 1958-59, 64-84; owner Ho'olaule'a Designs, Honolulu, 1973—; art editor Scrapbook Press, 2002—; Portfolio Cons. of Hawaii, 1990—. Staff artist The Acadian newsletter, 2000—; illustrator: Cathedral Cooks, 1964, In Due Season, 1986, From Nowhere To Somewhere On A Round Trip Ticket, 2003; exhibited in Hawaii Pavilion Expo '90, Osaka, Japan, State Found. Culture and Arts, group shows since 1964, one woman shows 1991, 96, 99; represented in Arts of Paradise Gallery, Waikiki, 1990-2001, Hale Ku'ai, a Hawaiian Coop., 1998-2001; traveling exhbns. include Pacific Prints, 1991, Printmaking East/West, 1993-95, Hawaii/Wis. Watercolor Show, 1993-94. Mem. Hawaii Watercolor Soc. (newsletter editor 1986-90), Nat. League Am. Pen Women (art chmn. 1990-92, sec. 1992-94, 2000-02, nat. miniature art shows 1991, 92, 93, 95), Honolulu Printmakers (dir. 1986, 87), Assn. Hawaii Artists, scholarship aid programs, Mount Holyoke Club, Mary Lyon Soc., Rutgers Univ., Col. Henry Rutgers Soc. Republican. Episcopalian. Avocations: art, travel, writing, photography. Home: 1434 Punahou St Apt 1028 Honolulu HI 96822-4740 Office Phone: 808-955-7817.

BETTS, CHRISTINA PINKSTON, education educator; d. H. E. Pinkston Sr. and M. C. Pinkston. BA, Ohio Wesleyan U., 1977—81; MA, Ohio State U., 1981—83; PhD, Trinity Theol. Sem., 1983—84. Lectr. of English Ohio State U., 1982—83; substitute tchr. Del. City and County Schools, Ohio, 1984; vis. asst. prof. of african-american history and lit. Ohio Wesleyan U., 1984; instr. of English Ohio State U. Upward Bound Program, 1985; dir. comm. lab. and writing skills ctr. Ctrl. State U., Wilberforce, Ohio, 1985—86, asst. prof. of English, 1985—90, dir., freshman English program, 1985—90, asst. dean of the coll. of arts and scis. candidate, 1989—90; lectr. of English Ohio State U. at Newark, 1997, 1999—2000; guest lectr. South-Western City Schools, Grove City, Ohio, 2001; asst. prof. of English Hampton U., Va., 2001—. Advisor, Sigma Tau Delta Internat. English Honor Soc. Hampton U. Va., 2003—; mem. nat. creative writing com. Coll. Lang. Assn., Washington, D.C., 2003—; session chair, 63rd ann. conv., 2003. Min. of music and dir. of choirs Good Shepherd Bapt. Ch., Columbus,

Ohio, 1993—2001. Recipient Stewardship Svc., Good Shepherd Bapt. Ch., 1997; grant, Va. Found. for the Humanities and Pub. Policy, 2002, US HUD and Historically Black Colleges and Universities Program, 2003—, Full Grad. Fellowship, Ohio State U., 1981—83. Mem.: Va. Assn. for Teachers of English (assoc.), Nat. Coun. of Teachers of English (assoc.), Coll. Lang. Assn. (assoc.), Sigma Tau Delta Internat. English Honor Soc. (life) Phi Sigma Iota Romance Lang. Honor Soc. (life). Avocations: music, travel, language arts, fine arts, cooking. Office: Hampton University Hampton VA 23668 E-mail: christina.pinkston-betts@hamptonu.edu.

BETTS, DIANNE CONNALLY, economist, educator; b. Tyler, Tex., Sept. 23, 1948; d. Martine (Underwood) Connally; m. Floyd Galloway Betts Jr., Feb. 14, 1973. BA in History, So. Meth. U., 1976, MA in History, 1980; MA in Econ., U. Chgo., 1986; PhD in Econ., U. Tex., 1991. Affiliated scholar Inst. for Rsch. on Women and Gender/Stanford U., 1993—; economist, tech. analyst, fin. cons. Smith Barney, Dallas, 1994—2000; economist, fin. cons. Morgan Keegan, Dallas, 2000—. Mem. women studies coun. So. Meth. U., 1993-94, Fulbright campus interviewing com., 1992—; vis. asst. prof. 1990-92; faculty mentor U. honors first year mentoring program, adj. asst. prof. dept. econ. and history, 1992—, vis. asst. prof. 1990-92; faculty, Oxford, summer 1991-93, adj. instr. dept. history 1989-90, adj. instr. dept. econ. 1985-89, tchg. asst. dept. history, spring 1980; lectr. dept. polit. economy U. Tex., Dallas, summer 1988. Author: Crisis on the Rio Grande: Poverty, Unemployment, and Economic Development on the Texas-Mexico Border, 1994, Historical Perspectives on the American Economy: Selected Reading, 1995; contbr. articles to profl. jours. Rsch. Planning grant NSF, 1992; recipient Margureta Deschner Teaching award, 1991; Humanities and Scis. Merit scholar, 1978. Mem. Am. Econ. Assn., Am. History Assn., Econ. History Assn., Cliometric Soc., Social Science History Assn., N.Am. Conf. on British Studies, Nat. Coun. for Rsch. on Women (affiliate), Omicron Delta Epsilon, Phi Alpha Theta. Home: 6267 Revere Pl Dallas TX 75214-3099 Office: Morgan Keegan 5956 Sherry Ln # 2002 Dallas TX 75225-6531 Office Phone: 972-738-5088. E-mail: dcbetts@airmail.net.

BETTS, DORIS JUNE WAUGH, writer, English language educator; b. Statesville, N.C., June 4, 1932; d. William Elmore and Mary Ellen (Freeze) Waugh; m. Lowry Matthews Betts, July 5, 1952; children: Doris LewEllyn, David Lowry, Erskine Moore II. Student, Woman's Coll., U. N.C., 1950-53, U. N.C., 1954; DLitt (hon.), Greensboro Coll., 1987; DLitt, U. N.C., Greensboro, 1990, Queens Coll., 1995; LHD, Erskine Coll., 1994, DHL, Pembroke U., 1995. Newspaperwoman Statesville Daily Record, 1950-51, Chapel Hill (N.C.) Weekly and News-Leader, 1953-54; editorial staff Sanford Daily Herald, 1956-57, N.C. Democrat, 1961-62; editor Sanford (N.C.) News Leader, 1962; lectr. creative writing English dept. U. N.C., Chapel Hill, 1966-74, dir. freshman-sophomore English, 1972-76, assoc. prof., 1974-78, dir. fellows program, 1975-76, prof., 1978—, asst. dean Honors program, 1979-81, chmn. faculty, 1982-85, Alumni Disting. prof., 1983-2001, chair faculty, 1980-83, prof. emerita, 2001—. Vis. lectr. creative writing Duke U., 1971, staff Ind. U. Summer Writers Conf., 1972, 73; mem. bd. Assoc. Writing Programs, lit. panel Nat. Endowment for Arts, 1979-81, chmn., 1981. Author: (story collections) The Gentle Insurrection, 1954 (G.P. Putnam-U. N.C. Fiction award 1954), The Astronomer and Other Stories, 1966, Beasts of the Southern Wild and Other Stories, 1973 (National Book award nomination 1974); (novels) Tall Houses in Winter, 1957 (Sir Walter Raleigh award 1957), The Scarlet Thread, 1964 (Sir Walter Raleigh award 1965), The River to Pickle Beach, 1972, Heading West, 1981, Souls Raised from the Dead, 1994 (Southern Book Critics award, Southeastern Libr. Assn. award), The Sharp Teeth of Love, 1997; editor: Young Writers at Chapel Hill, 1968; contbr.: Three by Three: Masterworks of the Southern Gothic, 1985, others; appeared in dramatized version of The Ugliest Pilgrim as Violet (Academy award Tex. Film Festival; bibliography in The Home Truths of Doris Betts, 1992. Mem. N.C. Tercentenary Commn., 1961-62, Sanford City Sch. Bd., 1965-71; lit. com. NEA, 1979-82, chair, 1982; mem. ctrl. com. Morehead Found., 1978-93, chair 1992-93; bd. trustees Nat. Humanities Ctr., 1993-96, Union Theol. Seminary, Richmond, Va., 1993-97. Recipient Short Story prize Mademoiselle mag., 1953, N.C. medal for lit., 1975, John Dos Passos award, 1983, medal of merit in short story divsn. Am. Acad. Arts and Letters, 1989, Parker award for lit. achievement, 1982-85, John Caldwell award for svc. to humanities, 1992; Guggenheim fellow, 1958-59, Doctor of Letters (hon.) from Greensboro Coll., Queens Coll., UNC-Pembroke, UNC-Greensboro, Erskine Coll., U. of the South, Carolinian Awd., 1998; Thomas Jefferson Awd., 1999, Judge P.E.N. Hemingway Awds., 1999, Lifetime Achievement award Christianity and Literature, MLA, 2000; Betts Professorship in Creative Writing created in her honor, U. N.C., Chapel Hill, 2001. Mem. N.C. Writers Assn. Address: Dept English 795-B NC #902 Pittsboro NC 27312

BETTS, DOROTHY ANNE, elementary school educator; b. Washington, Nov. 3, 1946; d. Thomas Joseph and Elizabeth Anne (McGee) Salb; m. Jerold LeRoy Betts, July 14, 1975; 1 child, Ellen Marie. BS in Elem. Edn., U. N.Mex., 1968, MA in Edn., 1976. Cert. tchr. N.Mex. Tchr. Newman (Calif.)-Gustine Dist., 1968—69, Albuquerque Pub. Schs., 1969—79, 1980—84, 1999—, ended assn., 1993—99; co-owner Stork News N.Mex. Zuni Elem. Sch. coord. Pennies for Patients Leukemia and Lymphoma Soc., Albuquerque, 2001. Mem.: Delta Kappa Gamma (1st v.p 1982—84, pres. 1984—86, 2d v.p 2000—02). Roman Catholic. Avocations: travel, family outings, crafts. Home: 10118 4th St NW Albuquerque NM 87114

BETTS, ELAINE WISWALL, retired headmistress; b. Albany, N.Y., Aug. 24, 1925; d. Frank Lawrence and Clara Elizabeth (Chapman) Wiswall; m. Darby Wood Betts, June 2, 1951; children: Victoria, Catherine, Darby Wood Jr. BA, Smith Coll., 1947; MA, Holy Names Coll., Oakland, Calif., 1975. Head upper sch. Anna Head Sch., Oakland, 1971-78, Head-Royce Sch., Oakland, 1978-80; headmistress Albany Acad. for Girls, 1980-84, Dana Hall Sch., Wellesley, Mass., 1984-95; ret., 1995. Mem. Nat. Assn. Prins. Schs. for Girls, Headmistresses of East.

BETTS, KATHERINE, editor-in-chief, publisher; married; 1 son. Grad., Princeton U. Various positions including Paris editor Metropolitan Home, Internat. Herald Tribune, others, 1986-88; former reporter to bur. chief Fairchild Pubs., Paris, 1988-91; former fashion news dir. Vogue Mag., 1991-99; editor-in-chief, pub. Harper's Bazaar, N.Y.C., 1999—

BETTS, REBECCA A. lawyer; b. Memphis, Nov. 25, 1951; BA, Dickinson Coll., 1972; JD, W.Va. U., 1976. Bar: W.Va., U.S. Dist. Ct. (so. dist.) W.Va. 1976, U.S. Ct. Appeals (4th cir.) 1978, U.S. Supreme Ct. 1984. Assoc. Spilman, Thomas, Battle & Klostermeyer, Charleston, W.Va., 1976—77; asst. U.S. atty. U.S. Atty.'s Office, 1977—81, chief civil divsn., 1979—81; founding ptnr. King, Betts & Allen, Charleston, W.Va.; U.S. atty. U.S. Dist. Ct. So. Dist., W.Va., 1994—2001; ptnr. Allen Guthrie McHugh & Thomas PLLC, 2002—. Adv. com. on rules & procedures 4th Cir., 1995—; com. for local rules and subcom. on criminal rules So. Dist. W.Va., 1992, civil justice reform act adv. com., 91. Mem. editl. bd.: W.Va. Law Rev. Mem.: The Legal Aid Soc. of Charleston (bd. dirs.), W.Va. State Bar (past mem. com. on legal ethics), Order of Coif. Office: Allen Guthrie McHugh & Thomas PO Box 3394 Charleston WV 25333

BETZER, SUSAN ELIZABETH BEERS, physician, geriatrician; b. Evanston, Ill., Aug. 24, 1943; d. Thomas Moulding and Mary Ella (Waidner) Beers; m. Peter Robin Betzer, June 18, 1965; children: Sarah Elizabeth, Katherine Hannah. AB in Biol. Scis. magna cum laude Mt. Holyoke Coll., 1965; PhD in Oceanography, U. R.I., 1972; MD, U. Miami, 1978. Diplomate Am. Bd. Family Practice, Am. Bd. Geriat. Rsch. assoc. dept. marine sci. U. South Fla., St. Petersburg, 1973-74, rsch. scholar, scientist, 1975-76; resident in family practice Bayfront Med. Ctr., St.

Petersburg, 1978-81; pvt. practice St. Petersburg, 1982—; clin. asst. prof. dept. family medicine U. South Fla., Tampa, 1982—. Cons. physician Fed. Employee Health Clinic, Honolulu, 1981-82. Contbr. articles to profl. jours. Adv. com. St. Petersburg H.S., 1996—; bd. dirs. Fla. Orch., Tampa, 1983-86, 88—, pres., 1985-86, mem. exec. com., 1988—, vice-chair bd. trustees 1996-2002, sec., 2002—, founder, chair audience devel. com., St. Petersburg, [illegible] Mental Health, St. Petersburg, 1992-93; trustee Bayfront Health Found., 1996—, chmn., 2001-03; trustee Bayfront Med. Ctr.; trustee Bayfront Health Svcs., 1992-96, vice-chair, 1993-96; vol. physician St. Petersburg Free Clinic, 1979—. Named Woman of Distinction, Suncoast coun. Girl Scouts U.S., 1994, Suncoast chpt. Vol. of Yr., Assn. Fundraising Profls., 2003; recipient Golden Baton award, St. Petersburg Fla. Orch. Guild, 1994, Chmns. award, Fla. Orch., 1997, Svc. award, Pinellas County Med. Soc., 1999, Philanthropy Vol. of Yr., Tampa Bay chpt. Assn. Fundraising Profls., 2003. Mem.: Fla. Acad. Family Physicians (Dr. of the Day, Fla. Legislature 1995, 1996), Am. Med. Women's Assn., Am. Acad. Family Physicians (Mead Johnson award 1980), Mount Holyoke Alumnae Assn. (alumnae honor rsch. com. 1988—91, alumnae devel. com. 1996—2003, pres. 2003—, Alumnae medal of honor 2000), Phi Beta Kappa. Avocations: symphony, birding, cooking, reading. Home: 1830 7th St N Saint Petersburg FL 33704-3322 Office: 461 7th Ave S Saint Petersburg FL 33701-4818

BEUGEN, JOAN BETH, communications company executive; b. Mar. 9, 1943; d. Leslie and Janet (Glick) Caplan; m. Sheldon Howard Beugen, July 16, 1967. BS in Speech, Northwestern U., 1965. Founder, prin., pres. The Creative Establishment, Inc., Chgo., N.Y.C., San Francisco and L.A., 1969—87; founder, pres. Cresta Comm. Inc., Chgo., 1988—. Spkr. on entrepreneurship for women. Contbr. articles to profl. jours. Trustee Mt. Sinai Hosp. Med. Ctr.; del. White House Conf. on Small Bus., 1979; bd. dirs. Chgo. Network, Chgoland Enterprise Ctr., Girl Scouts Chgo. Named Entrepreneur of Yr., Women in Bus.; recipient YWCA Leadership award, 1985. Mem.: Overseas Edn. Fund Women in Bus. Com., Nat. Women's Forum, Com. of 200, Women in Film, Chgo. Film Coun., Chgo. Audio-Visual Prodrs. Assn., Midwest Soc. Profl. Cons., Chgo. Assn. Commerce and Industry, Ill. Women's Agenda, Nat. Assn. Women Bus. Owners (pres. Chgo. bhpt. 1979), Econ. Club Chgo. Office: The Cresta Group 1050 N State St Chicago IL 60610-7829

BEUTLER, SUZANNE A. retired secondary school educator, artist; b. Cin., Oct. 23, 1930; d. Robert and Marguerite (Pierson) Armstrong; m. Frederick J. Beutler, Jan. 5, 1969; children: Richard and Mark Ireland. BA, U. Wis., 1954; MA, U. Mich., 1966, PhD, 1974, BFA, 2000. Cert. tchr. Middle sch. tchr. Ann Arbor (Mich.) Pub. Schs. Vis. lectr. U. Mich., Ann Arbor; adj. lectr. Eastern Mich. U., Ypsilanti. Author 3 manuals with Lang. Art Projects; contbr. articles to profl. jours.; developed writing program using personal classroom experiences. Recipient Tchr. Recognition award, 1986; grantee in field. Mem. Phi Delta Kappa (Svc. Key award 1992). Home: 1717 Shadford Rd Ann Arbor MI 48104-4543 Office Phone: 734-663-4870. E-mail: sbeutler@umich.edu.

BEVC, CAROL-LYNN ANNE, accountant; b. Jam, N.Y., Oct. 6, 1952; d. Joseph F. and Dorothea Mae (Kirshe) Bova; m. Frank P. Bevc, May 11, 1974; children: Christine, Elizabeth. BA, U. Pitts., 1974; student in Pub. Adminstrn., U. Ctrl. Fla., 2002—. CFO Wordwise, Inc., Winter Park, Fla., 1989-2000; acct. exec. Inner/g, Winter Park, 2000—01. Leader Citrus coun. Girl Scouts U.S.A., 1986-96. Mem. AAUW (pres. Seminole County br. 1985-87, 95-97, bd. dirs., dir. comm. Fla. state 1998-2002), DAR. Avocations: reading, writing, swimming, learning. Home: 1511 Black Bear Ct Winter Springs FL 32708-3860 E-mail: clbevc@bellsouth.net.

BEVERLEY, CORDIA LUVONNE, gastroenterologist; b. Jamaica, W.I., Oct. 19, 1950; d. Hurdley Aston and Joyce Ruby (Baker) B.; B.A., Hunter Coll., 1971; M.D., N.Y. U., 1975. Diplomate Am. Bd. Gastroenterology, Am. Bd. Internal Medicine. Intern, Columbia U., Harlem Hosp. Center, N.Y.C., 1975-76, resident in medicine, 1976-78; clin. fellow div. gastroenterology N.Y. Hosp./Cornell U. Med. Coll., N.Y.C., 1979-82; asst. physician Rockefeller U. Hosp., N.Y.C., 1978-81. Nat. Inst. Alcohol Abuse and Alcoholism postdoctoral fellow, 1980-82. Mem. Women's Med. Assn. N.Y.C. Office: 1085 Park Ave New York NY 10128-1168 Home: 1365 York Ave Apt 29E New York NY 10021-4044

BEVERS, THERESE BARTHOLOMEW, physician, medical educator; b. Amarillo, Tex., Apr. 5, 1960; d. James Oliver Bartholomew and Ruth Ann Berg. BS, Tex. Woman's U., 1981; MD, U. Tex. Health Scis. Ctr., San Antonio, 1987. Intern, then resident U. Tex. Health Sci. Ctr., San Antonio/Bexar County Hosp., 1987-90; physician pvt. practice, Wichita Falls, Tex., 1990-91, Dallas, 1991-94; chief med.dir. Medi Clinic, Houston, 1994-96; asst. prof. clin. cancer prevention, med. dir. cancer prevention ctr. U. Tex., M.D. Anderson Cancer Ctr., Houston, 1996—2003; assoc. prof. clin. cancer prevention U. Tex. M.D. Anderson Cancer Ctr., 2003—. Chmn. expert panel Nat. Comprehensive Cancer Network Breast Screening and Diagnosis Com., Nat. Comprehensive Cancer Network Breast Cancer Prevention Com. Mem. editl. bd. Oncolog, Breast Diseases: A Year Book Quarterly. Regent Tex. Woman's U., 2001—. Mem.: TMA (task force on prevention), Tex. Acad. Family Physicians (com. health care svcs. 1992—96, com. clin. preventive medicine 1996—98, commr. pub. health and clin. affairs 1998—), Am. Acad. Family Physicians, Am. Cancer Soc. Tex. (breast cancer detection com., colorectal cancer detection com., health sci. adv. bd., bd. dirs.). Avocations: skiing, hiking, antiques, decorating, reading. Office: U Tex M D Anderson Cancer Ctr 1515 Holcombe Blvd # 336 Houston TX 77030-4009

BEVINS, ANN BOLTON, retired journalist, retired historian; b. Ashland, Ky., July 11, 1936; d. Charles James and Frances Lyon Bolton; m. William Bernard Bevins, Apr. 19, 1956; children: William Bernard, James Bolton, Frances Anne Williams, Hiram Clinton, Robert Lesley. Student, Georgetown Coll., 1954—57. Reporter Ashland Daily Ind., Ky., 1954—54; corr. Lexington Herald-Leader, 1955—75; cons. archtl. historian pvt. practice, Georgetown, 1970—; instr. hist. preservation Georgetown Coll., 1987—88; columnist News-Graphic. Editor Ky. heritage Ky. Jr. Hist. Soc., Frankfort, 1963—73. Author: A History of Scott County As Told By Selected Buildings, That Troublesome Parish: St. Francis Church of White Sulphur, Kentucky, First Christian Church of Georgetown, Kentucky: The First Christian-Disciples Church; editor (author): Scott County, Kentucky: A History. Organizing pres. Georgetown & Scott County Mus., 1990—95; bd. chair Cane Ridge Preservation Project, Paris, 1996—2000. Recipient Citizen of Yr. award, Georgetown-Scott County C. of C., 1974, Georgetown Coll., 1984. Mem.: Nat. Trust Hist. Preservation, Blue Grass Trust Hist. Preservation (Clay Lancaster award for Heritage Edn. 2001), Ky. Hist. Soc. (bd. mem. 1967—69), Ky. Trust Hist. Preservation (bd. mem. 2000—03), Disciples Christ Hist. Soc. (life). Disciples Of Christ. Avocation: swimming. Home: 1175 Lexington Rd Georgetown KY 40324 Personal E-mail: a.b.bevins@worldnet.att.net.

BEXTERMILLER METZGER, THERESA MARIE, architect, computer engineer; b. St. Charles, Mo., Feb. 9, 1960; d. Charles Frederick and Loretta Joan (Unterreiner) Bextermiller; m. Paul James Metzger III, Nov. 29, 2000; stepchildren: Jennifer, Michael, Stephen, Andrew. BArch, Kans. State U., 1983; MFA in Computer Graphics and Interactive Media, Pratt Inst., 1990, Exptl. Computer Sci. and Engring. Degree, 1993. Registered architect, N.Y., 1989, Mo., 1990; cert. Nat. Coun. Archtl. Regis., 1996; real estate salesperson, Mo., 1995-98, broker, 2000—. Grad. arch. Mackey/Mitchell Assocs., St. Louis, 1983-84, Fleming Corp., St. Louis, 1984-85; project arch., prototype mgr. Casco Corp., St. Louis, 1985-87; grad. arch. HBE Corp., St. Louis, 1987-88; with telecomm. Western Union, 1992-93, Lucent Techs. (formerly AT&T Network Sys.), 1993—94; contract arch. Washington Group Internat., 1994-95, Fru-Con Engring. Inc. and other firms, various locations, 1995-98; prin. TMB Architecture/Computer Graphics, 1997—, Theresa Marie Bextermiller Metzger, RA, MFA, NCARB, Broker, 2000—, Le Pique and Orne Archs.-Inc., 1998—, Hellmuth, Obata & Kassabaum, Inc., St. Louis, 1998—; planner Infante Assocs., LLC, 1999—; cons. to various [illegible] tchr. St. Louis Pub. Schs., 2001—02; freelance architect. Mem.: AIA. Roman Catholic. Avocation: real estate. Home: 1120 Blendon Pl Saint Louis MO 63117-1911

BEYER, BARBARA LYNN, aviation consultant; b. Miami, Fla., Feb. 16, 1947; d. Morten Sternoff and Jane (Hartman) B. BA, George Washington U., 1978. Supr. printing office Saudi Arabian Airlines, 1966-67; ops. coord. Modern Air Transport, Miami, Fla., 1968-70, acct. Berlin, 1970-72; rep. Johnson Internat. Airlines, Washington, 1974-75; v.p., bd. dirs. Avmark, Inc., Washington, 1975—, pres., 1989—; chmn., bd. dirs. Avmark Internat., London, 1985—; mng. dir. Avmark Asia Ltd., Singapore, 1988-89, also bd. dirs., chmn. bd. dirs. Hong Kong, 1989—; pub. Avmark Aviation Economist, London, 1986—. Mem. adv. bd. aviation bus. dept. Embry-Riddle Aero. U. Mem. Aviation Space Writers (award 1978, internat. bd. dirs. 1986-88), Nat. Bus. Aircraft Assn., Am. C. of C., Fgn. Corr. Club, Aero Club, Internat. Aviation Club, Nat. Press Club. Avocations: reading, horseback riding, home improvement. Office: Avmark Inc 1925 N Lynn St Ste 403 Arlington VA 22209-1707 E-mail: bbeyer@avmarkinc.com.

BEYER, ELIZABETH TERRY, state representative; b. Springfield, Oreg. m. Lee Beyer; 3 children. Mem. Oreg. Ho. of Reps., 2002—. Coach AYSO Soccer; pack leader Cub Scouts; mem., pres. Page Elem. and Hamlin Middle Sch. PTA, 1978—94; liaison Springfield Bicycle Commn.; liason Springfield Arts Commn., Springfield Planning Commn.; city coun. Springfield, 1993—99; mem. budget com., 1993—2001; pres. bd. dirs. McKenzie River Presch. Coop., 1984—85; mem. adv. com. TransPlan, 1995—99; mem. bd. dirs. Conv. and Vis. Assn. Lane County, 1993—99, Springfield Libr., 1995—99, Springfield Edn. Foudn., 1997—2002. Democrat. Office: 900 Court St NE H-374 Salem OR 97301

BEYER, LA VONNE ANN, special education educator; b. Estherville, Iowa, Mar. 24, 1925; d. (George) Harold and Florence Catherine (Mulvey) Schafer; m. Gerald P. Beyer, June 7, 1943; children: Gregg Allan Beyer, Douglas Lee Beijer, Jodie Lu Beyer, Michael E. Beyer, Stefan A. Beyer. BA, Calif. State U., Northridge, 1959, MA, 1974; EdD, U. So. Calif., 1985. Cert. spl. edn. tchr., Calif. Tchr., regular and spl. edn. L.A. Unified Sch. Dist., 1959-88; cadre mem. Beginning Tchr. Assistance Program Calif. State U., Northridge, 1992—. Faculty U. So. Calif. reading clinic, 1974-75, Valley C.C., Burbank, 1974-75, L.A. C.C. (ESL), 1976-78. Contbr. articles to profl. jours. Literacy tutor Laubach Literacy Internat. (Van Nuys, Calif. chpt.), 1967—; mem. steering com. Roosevelt Commn., 1988. Recipient Mayor's Cert. of Appreciation, L.A., 1970, Dir. of Vols. in Agencies award, Van Nuys, 1989, Community award L.A. Times, 1990. Mem. DAR, Coun. for Exceptional Children,Laubach Literacy Internat., Pi Lambda Theta (v.p., pres. 1985-91), Phi Delta Kappa. Avocations: volunteering, gourmet cooking, travel, genealogy.

BEYER, LISA, journalist; b. Lafayette, La., 1961; BJ, U. Tex., 1983. Sr. correspondent Asiaweek, Singapore, 1984-88; staff writer, assoc. editor Time Mag., N.Y.C., 1988-91, Jerusalem bur. chief, 1991—. Office: Time Mag Time & Life Bldg Rockefeller Plz New York NY 10020-2002

BEYER, SUZANNE, advertising agency executive; b. N.Y.C. d. Harry and Jennie Hillman; m. Isadore Beyer; children: Pamela Claire, Hillary Jay. Grad., Conservatory of Mus. Art, N.Y.C., 1947; student, Nassau C. C., N.Y.C., 1963-65. Singer, tchr. piano, N.Y.C., 1947-66; asst. to v.p. media dir. Robert E. Wilson, Advt., N.Y.C., 1967-72; media planner, media buyer frank J. Corbett div. BBDO Internat., N.Y.C., 1972-77, Lavey/Wolff/Swift divsn. BBDO Advt., N.Y.C., 1977-80; sr. media planner Lavey/Wolff/Swift (divn. BBDO Advt.), N.Y.C., 1980-83, media supr., 1983-94, Lyons, Lavey, Nichel, Swift, N.Y.C., 1995-96; pharm. advt. med. media cons., 1996—. Soprano Opera Assn., Nassau, N.Y., 1976-99; soprano United Choral Soc., Woodmere, L.I., 1970-99, soprano Armand Sodero Chorale, Baldwin, Long Is., 1980-86, soprano Rockville Ctr. Choral Soc., 1986—. Mem. Pharm. Advt. Coun., L.I. Advt. Club, Healthcare Bus. Women's Assn. Home: 66 Fonda Rd Rockville Centre NY 11570-2751

BEYER-MEARS, ANNETTE, physiologist; b. Madison, Wis., May 26, 1941; d. Karl and Annette (Weiss) Beyer. BA, Vassar Coll., 1963; MS, Fairleigh Dickinson U., 1973; PhD, Coll. Medicine and Dentistry N.J., 1977. NIH fellow Cornell U. Med. Sch., 1963-65; instr. physiology Springside Sch., Phila., 1967-71; teaching asst. dept. physiology Coll. Medicine & Dentistry N.J., N.J. Med. Sch., 1974-77, NIH fellow dept. ophthalmology, 1978-80; asst. prof. dept. ophthalmology U. Medicine and Dentistry N.J., N.J. Med. Sch., Newark, 1979-85, asst. prof. dept. physiology, 1980-85, assoc. prof. dept. physiology, 1986—, assoc. prof. dept. ophthalmology, 1986—. Vis. assoc. prof. dept. ophthalmology and vision sci. U. Wis., Madison, 1995—; cons. Alcon Labs. Contbr. articles in field of diabetic lens and kidney therapy to profl. jours. Chmn. admissions No. N.J., Vassar Coll., 1974-79; mem. minister search com. St. Bartholomew Episcopal Ch., N.J., 1978, fund-raising chmn., 1978, 79; del. Episc. Diocesian Conv., 1977, 78; long range planning com. Christ Ch., Ridgewood, N.J., 1985-87, vestry, 1994-95. Recipient NIH Nat. Rsch. Svc. award, 1978-80, Found. CMDNJ Rsch. award, 1980; grantee Juvenile Diabetes Found., 1985-87, NIH, NEI grantee, 1980-95, Pfizer, Inc. grantee, 1985-89, 93—. Mem. Am. Physiol. Soc., N.Y. Acad. Scis., Soc. for Neurosci., Am. Soc. Pharmacology and Exptl. Therapeutics, Assn. for Rsch. Vision & Ophthalmology, Internat. Soc. for Eye Research, AAAS, The Royal Soc. Medicine, Internat. Diabetes Found., Am. Diabetes Assn., European Assn. Study of Diabetes, Aircraft Owners and Pilots Assn., Sigma Xi. Home: 120 Ely Pl Madison WI 53705-4015

BEYERSDORF, MARGUERITE MULLOY, retired secondary school educator; b. Terry, Mont., Apr. 20, 1922; d. John William and Laura Agnes (Mahar) Mulloy; m. Curtis Alexander Beyersdorf, 1946; 1 child, Mary Jo Wright. Kindergarten-Primary Cert., Coll. St. Catherine, St. Paul, 1942; PhB, Marquette U., 1945; postgrad., Gonzaga U., Spokane, Wash., 1957-62, Ea. Wash. State U., 1977-79. Tchr. grade 3 Sacred Heart Sch., Oelwein, Iowa, 1942-43; tchr. grades 1 and 2 Jr. Mil. Acad., Chgo., 1943-44; tchr. history, English Fairfield (Wash.) High Sch., 1945-46; substitute tchr. Riverside High Sch., 1957; tchr. Mead (Wash.) Sch. Dist., 1958-75; owner/mgr. First Ave. Parking Lot, Spokane, Wash., 1977—. Vol. Spokane N.W. Communities Found., 1982—; active United Way Spokane, 1950—95, ARC, Am. Cancer Soc., Multiple Sclerosis Soc., others; vol. coord. Dominican Outreach Found. to Domicile Single Parent Families; canteen vol. Spokane Blood Bank, 1981—; vol. Miryam's House of Transition, 1989—. Recipient Vol. of Yr. Golden Rule award J.C. Penney Co., 1993; grantee NSF, Whitworth Coll., 1967. Mem. NEA, APGA, AAUW (bd. dirs. Spokane br., chmn. scholarship com.), Wash. Edn. Assn.-Retired (del. rep. assembly, mem. comm. com 1993—, chmn. comm. commn. 1993—), Mead Edn. Assn. (sec., exec. bd., former bldg. rep., mem. curriculum com.). Avocations: golf, travel, reading, needlepoint, walking, bridge, crossword puzzles.

BEYONCÉ, (BEYONCÉ GISELLE KNOWLES), vocalist; b. Houston, Tex., Sept. 4, 1981; d. Matthew and Tina Knowles. Mem. group Destiny's Child, Houston, 1990—. Spokesperson L'Oreal. Singer: (albums) Destiny's Child, 1998, The Writing's on the Wall, 1999 (Platinum album 7 times, Grammy awards: Best R&B Song for "Say My Name", 2000, Best R&B Performance By A Duo Or Group With Vocal, 2000), Survivor, 2001 (debuted at #1 Billboard Album Chart, Platinum 3 times, Grammy award: Best R&B Performance By A Duo Or Group With Vocal, 2001), 8 Days of Christmas, 2001, (solo album) Dangerously in Love, 2003 (Grammy awards: Best Female R&B Vocal Performance, 2003, Best R&B Performance By A Duo Or Group With Vocals for song "The Closer I Get To [illegible] Song for "Crazy in Love", 2003, Best Contemporary R&B Album, 2003, Best Rap/Sung Collaboration for song "Crazy in Love", 2003); actor: (films) Austin Powers in Goldmember, 2002, I Know, 2003, The Fighting Temptations, 2003. Named Pop Songwriter of Yr., ASCAP, 2001; recipient 4 Billboard Music awards, 2000, 2 Billboard Music awards, 2001, Am. Music award, 2000, 2 Am. Music awards, 2001, MTV Music Video award, 2001, 4 World Music awards, 2001, Image award, NAACP, 2000, 2001, Sammy Davis, Jr. award, 2000, Soul Train award, 2000. Office: Columbia Records 550 Madison Ave New York NY 10022-3211*

BEZROD, NORMA R. artist; b. Phila., May 17, 1938; d. Samuel Bezrod and Bessie Roffman; m. Arthur J. Cooperman, Aug. 22, 1959 (div. Apr. 1977); 1 child, Seth Alan Cooperman; m. William D. P. Riley, July 1, 1983 (dec. Oct. 1998). BA, Queens Coll., 1960, MS, 1974; EdD, Columbia U., 1986. Lic. fine arts tchr., N.Y. Art tchr. N.Y.C. Pub. Schs., 1960-77; exec. dir. art Sr. Ctr., Human Resources Adminstrn., N.Y.C., 1977-78; instr. art edn. Queens (N.Y.) Coll., 1978-79; edn. evaluator, case mgr. N.Y.C. Bd. Edn., 1980-88. Cons. N.Y. State Coun. on the Arts, 1977-79. Author: Don't Be Afraid of the Dark, 1977, (series) Lion and Pretty Bird, 1983-85; art critic Good Times, L.I., N.Y., 1971-75; paintings in collections of St. John's Univ. Libr., Queen's Coll. Mus. Teaching fellow Queens Coll., 1978-79. Home: PO Box 660125 Flushing NY 11366-0125

BHANDARI, RAJIKA, psychologist; b. New Delhi, Sept. 10, 1970; came to U.S., 1992; d. Arvind Bhandari and Sudha Anand. BA in Psychology with honors, U. Delhi, New Delhi, 1991; MS in Psychology, N.C. State U., 1994, PhD in Psychology, 1998. Sr. social rep. Social Aid, New Delhi, 1989-90; rsch. asst. Nat. Ctr. for Human Settlements and Environment, Bhopal, India, 1990-92; tchg. asst. dept. psychology N.C. State U., Raleigh, 1993-95, rsch. asst. dept. psychology, 1995—; instr. IBM, Research Triangle Park, N.C., 1994, 95. Presenter, rschr. in field. Contbr. articles to profl. jours. Vol. Nat. Svc. Scheme, Indraprastha Coll., New Delhi, 1988-89, pres. Women's Devel. Ctr., 1990-91. Internat. Grad. fellow N.C. State U. Alumni Assn., 1994, Kenan fellow Kenan Inst. for Sci., Engring. and Tech., 1995; Human Resource Devel. Fund Rsch. grantee Coll. of Edn. and Psychology Found., 1993; Bhagwanti Kapoor Meml. scholar, 1990, Nat. Merit scholar U. Delhi, 1991. Mem. AAUW (internat. grad. fellow 1995), Soc. for Cmty. Action and Rsch. (student affiliate), Human Rights Com., UN Assn.-U.S.A., Sigma Iota Rho, Psi Chi. Avocations: painting, creative writing, travel, reading. Office: NC State U Dept Psychology Box 7801 Raleigh NC 27606

BIANCHI, CARISA, advertising company executive; Formerly with Benton & Bowles, L.A., Doyle Dane Bernbach; with Chiat/Day L.A., 1989-97; mng. dir., pres., CEO TBWA/Chiat/Day, San Francisco, 1998—2002, mng. ptnr. Playa del Rey, 2002, chief strategy officer L.A., 2002—. Office: TBWA/Chiat/Day 5353 Grosvenor Blvd Los Angeles CA 90066-6319

BIANCHI, MARIA, critical care specialist, adult and acute care nurse practitioner, nursing administrator; Grad., Catherine Laboure Sch. Nursing, 1979, Fitchburg (Mass.) State Coll., 1985; grad. clin. specialist in nursing adminstrn., Russell Sage Coll., Troy, N.Y. Cert. post-anesthesia care nurse; critical care clin. specialist. Recovery as mgmt. educator; mktg. and recruitment cons.; cons. in critical care nursing; adminstr. dept. spl. svcs., mgr. critical care Baystate Med. Ctr., Springfield, Mass., 1980-89; recruitment adminstrn. and sr. faculty St. Francis Med. Ctr. Sch. of Nursing, Hartford, Conn., 1989-92; grad. faculty U. Mass. Med. Ctr., Worcester, 1995-97; per diem nurse practitoner dept. surgery U. Mass. Sch. of Nursing, Worcester, 1995-97, 99—, faculty Amherst; clin. faculty Am. Internat. Coll., Springfield; asst. prof. Grad. Sch. U. Mass., Amherst, 1998-99. Rsch. in pain, burn trauma, stress reduction, holistic methods for high risk individuals in maximum security penitentiary and critical care patients; nat. cons. for critical care/post anesthesia issues, pres. TransInternat. Healthcare; nat. lectr. AHI, Balt.; expert witness, Mass. and Conn.; medicolegal cons.; laser med. provider; lectr. on critical care and post anesthesia issues, empowerment, acute pain, holistic techniques, medicological documentation, trauma. Invited ambassador del. People's for People's, Fed. Govt. Mem. AACN, Am. Soc. Post-Anesthesia Nursing (Boston chpt. editl. cons.), Soc. Critical Medicine, Mass. Gen. Hosp. Alumni Assn., Catherine Laboure Alumni Assn., Sigma Theta Tau. Office: PO Box 614 Suffield CT 06078-0614

BIAS, SHARON G. state commissioner; Commr. of banking State of W.Va., 1992—. Office: Banking Divsn 1900 Kanawha Blvd E Rm 3 Charleston WV 25305-0009

BIBBO, MARLUCE, physician, educator; b. Sao Paulo, Brazil, July 14, 1939; d. Domingos and Yolanda (Ranciaro) B. M.D, U. Sao Paulo, 1963, Sc.D., 1968. Intern Hosps. das Clinicas, U. Sao Paulo, 1963; resident in morphology, 1964-66; instr. dept. morphology and ob-gyn U. Sao Paulo, 1966-68, asst. prof., 1968-69; fellow in cytology U. Chgo., 1969-70, asst. prof. sect. cytology dept. ob-gyn, 1971-73, assoc. prof., 1973-77, assoc. prof. pathology, 1974-77, prof. ob-gyn and pathology, 1978-92; assoc. dir. Cytology Lab., Approved Sch. Cytotech and Cytocybernetics, AMA-Am. Soc. Clin. Pathologists, 1970-91; dir. Cytology Lab., Phila., 1992; prof. pathology and cell biology Thomas Jefferson U., Phila., 1992—, Warren R. Lane prof. pathology & cell biology, 1993—. Mem. rsch. com. Ill. divsn. Am. Cancer Soc., 1976-91. Contbr. numerous articles to profl. jours. Fellow Internat. Acad. Cytology (pres.-elect, v.p. 1987, pres. 1992, dep. editor Acta Cytologica, editor 1995), Am. Soc. Clin. Pathologists (coun. on cytopathology); mem. Am. Soc. Cytology (exec. com., pres. 1982-83), U.S. Acad. Pathology, Can. Acad. Pathology, Soc. Analytical Cytology, Coun. Cytopathology. Home: 250 S 9th St Philadelphia PA 19107-5734 Office: Cytology Lab Rm 260 Main Bldg 132 S 10th St Philadelphia PA 19107-5244 E-mail: marluce.bibbo@mail.tju.edu.

BIBBS, CHERYL SUSHEEL, education educator, researcher; d. Altheia W and Carl Allen Bibbs. MusB in opera, Boston U., 1964—68; MusM in voice, New Eng. Conservatory of Music, 1968—70; MPhil, Sandeepany Sadhanalaya, 1977—79; PhD in commn., Breyer State U., 1999—. Performer, Chautauqua presenter including Opera Co. of Boston, LA Mozart Orch., Va. City Opera Ho., Las Vegas Civic Symphony, TV and Radio, various cities in U.S. and Internat., 1984—; radio prodr., dir. WGBH-Radio, Boston, 1973—75; exec. prodr., zoom WGBH-TV, Boston, 1975—77, prodr. arts edn. program, 1979—80; dir. of adj. program devel. Sandeepany West Inst. of Vedantic Studies and E. Indian Culture, Piercy, Calif., 1980—82; comm. mgr. Frank B. Hall and Co., Inc, Walnut Creek, 1982—84; lectr., tech. comm. U. of Calif., Berkeley (Interdisciplinary Studies), 1984—; pres. Daya Kay Comm., San Francisco, 1984—. Cons., tech. comm. for computer industry Daya Kay Comm. and Publ. Arts Network, San Francisco, Oakland, Los Angeles, 1984—86; ind. tv-media prodr. Daya Kay Comm. & KTOP-TV, San Francisco-Oakland, 1990—91; touring concert artist-soprano various venues, such as Alice Tully Hall, Yachats Music Festival, Crocker Mus., Gardner Mus., LA Mozart Orch., San Francisco Chamber Orch., Robert Schuller's Hour of Power, 1984—99; musical and dramatic chautauquan (presenter of mary ellen pleasant, mother of civil rights in ca) The Calif. Coun. for the Humanities, The Nat. Chautauqua Tour, The Nat. Parks Svc., various-San Francisco et al, Calif., 1994—; ind. documentary prodr. M.E.P Productions, div. of Daya Kay Comm., San Francisco, 2000—. Prodr. and performer : (tv-performance (documentary) An Unsung Muse: Classical Song of Black Composers

(ACE award finalist, 1991); exec. prodr.: (TV series) ZOOM (Nat. Emmy for best series for children, 1977); prodr.(also dir.): (syndicated national radio storybook for npr) The Spider's Web (best program and most innovative program from corp. for pub. broadcasting; best series, action for children's TV, 1975); author: (touring exhibit on Mary Ellen Pleasant and booklet) Mother of Civil Rights and Legacies of Mary Ellen Pleasant (highest commendation, supervisors of city and county of San Francisco, 1999); actor(author, rsch., prodr.): (dramatic and musical chautauquas) Meet Mary Pleasant and O Freedom; author: (book) Heritage of Power (Marie LaVeau to Mary Pleasant) (Reader's Digest SP book awards-cert. of merit, 1999). Acting program chairperson San Francisco African Am. Hist. and Cultural Soc., 1995—96; program grantee-mem. Nat. Parks Svc. Network to Freedom Program, Western Region and Nat.; sponsoree for filmmaking Film Arts Found., San Francisco. Grantee, The Nat. Parks Svc., 2002—03, The Calif. Coun. for the Humanities, 2001—02, African Am. Mus. at Oakland, 2003. Mem.: African Am. Hist. and Cultural Assn. (bd. member-acting program chair 1995—96), Film Arts Found. (filmmaker and fiscal non-profit sponsoree 2001—03), Self Pub. Assoc. Network (SPAN). Democrat-Npl. African Methodist Episcopal And African Traditional. Achievements include research in uncovered lost memoirs, papers, and letters of Mary Ellen Pleasant, the 19th century abolitionist-entrepreneur called Mother of Civil Rights in CA. These enabled revision of her life history; uncovered lost interviews and material that shed light on the life and religion of New Orleans most famous Voodoo queen, Marie Laveau and proved for the first time that she met Mary Pleasant; discovery of a model that Marie Laveau used for social change in Antebellum New Orleans and that she passed it to Mary Pleasant who used it in California to effect social change. Avocations: travel, martial arts, watercolor painting, meditation, walking. Office: MEP Productions/Publications/DKC 477 Arlington St San Francisco CA 94131 E-mail: mepleasant@aol.com.

BIBLIOWICZ, JESSICA M. financial analyst; b. 1959; d. Sanford and Joan Weill; 2 children. Grad., Cornell U. Formerly with assesment mgmt. divsn. Shearson Lehman Bros.; dir. sales and mktg. Prudential Mutual Funds, 1992—94; exec. v.p., oversees mutual funds and insured investor group Smith Barney, N.Y.C., 1994—97; pres., COO John A. Levin & Co., 1997—99; pres., CEO Nat. Financial Partners, N.Y.C., 1999—. Dir. Eaton Vance Mutual Funds, Gov. Com. Scholastic Achievement, Securities Industry Assn.; mem., hedge funds adv. group, investment com. Cornell U. Gov. Boys & Girls Club of Am.; regional chair, N.E. Region. Office: NFP 787 7th Ave, 49th Fl New York NY 10019*

BICHLER, ELIZABETH ANNE, secondary school educator, musician; b. Pompton Plains, N.J., Oct. 9, 1962; d. Leopold and Lois Ann Bichler. MusB, Hope Coll., Holland, Mich., 1984; MEd, U. Cen. Fla., 2003. Cert. tchr. Fla. Freelance musician, Orlando, 1988—; tchr. St. James Cathedral Sch., Orlando, 1988—97, Orange County Pub. Schs., Orlando, Fla., 1997—. Mem.: Fla. Orch. Assn., Music Educators Nat. Conf., Delta Omicron (life). Avocation: dog training. Home: 620 S Oxalis Ave Orlando FL 32807 Personal E-mail: bethbic@att.net. E-mail: bichlee@ocps.net.

BICK, KATHERINE LIVINGSTONE, neurobiologist, international liaison, consultant; b. Charlottetown, Can., May 3, 1932; came to U.S., 1954, d. Spurgeon Arthur and Flora Hazel (Murray) Livingstone; m. James Harry Bick, Aug. 20, 1955 (div.); children: James A., Charles L. (dec.); m. Ernst Freese, 1988 (dec. 1990). BS with honors, Acadia U., Can., 1951, MS, 1952; PhD, Brown U., 1957; DSc (hon.), Acadia U., 1990. Rsch. pathologist UCLA Med. Sch., 1959-61; asst. prof. Calif. State U., Northridge, 1961-66; lab. instr. Georgetown U., Washington, 1970-72, asst. prof., 1972-76; dep. dir. neurol. disorder program Nat. Inst. Neurol. and Communicative Disorders and Stroke, NIH, Bethesda, Md., 1976-81, acting dep. dir., 1981-83, dep. dir., 1983-87; dep. dir. extramural rsch. Office of Dir. NIH, 1987-90; sci. liaison Centro Studio Multicentrico Internazionale Sulla Demenza, Washington, 1990-95. Cons. Nat. Rsch. Coun., Italy, 1991-97, The Charles A. Dana Found., N.Y.C., 1993-98, Edn. Commn. of the States, 1996-99. Editor: Alzheimer's Disease: Senile Dementia and Related Disorders, 1978, Neurosecretion and Brain Peptides, Implications for Brain Functions and Neurol. Disease, 1981, The Early Story of Alzheimer's Disease, 1987, Alzheimer Disease, 1994, 2d edit., 1999, Alzheimer Disease: The Changing View, 2000; contbr. articles to profl. jours. Pres. Woman's Club, McLean, Va., 1968-69; bd. dirs. Fairfax County (Va.) YWCA, 1969-70; pres. Avenel Homeowner's Assn., 1998; pres. Emerson Unitarian Ch., 1964-66; mem. Bethesda Pl. Cmty. Coun., 1992-95, pres., 1993-94; mem. Dana Alliance for Brain Initiatives, 1993—; bd. dirs. Wilmington N.C. Child Advocacy Commn., 1998-2002; mem. vol. guild St. John's Mus. Art, Wilmington; chair Vol. Guild Cameron Art Mus., Wilmington, 2002-2003, Cameron Art Mus. bd.,2003-. Recipient Can. NRC award Acadia U., 1951-52, NIH Dir.'s award, 1978, Spl. Achievement award NIH, 1981, 83, Superior Svc. award USPHS, 1986, Presdl. Rank award meritorious sr. exec., 1989; Universal Match Found. fellow Brown U., 1956-57, Fed. Exec. Inst. Leadership fellow, 1980. Fellow AAAS; mem. Am. Neurol. Assn., Am. Acad. Neurology, Assn. for Rsch. in Nervous and Mental Disease, Internat. Brain Rsch. Orgn., World Fedn. Neurology Rsch. Group on Dementias (exec. sec. Am. region 1984-86, chmn. 1986-93), Alzheimer's Disease Internat. (sci. and med. adv. bd.), Soc. for Neurosci., Acad. of Medicine Washington, Dana Alliance for Brain Initiatives.

BICKEL, MINNETTE DUFFY, artist; b. New Bern, N.C., June 24, 1921; d. Richard Nixon and Minnette (Chapman) Duffy; m. William Croft, Jan. 3, 1947; children: Minnette B. Boesel, Susan B. Scioli. One-woman shows include, N.C., statewide portrait exhbns., (two 1st place awards), regional juried shows, (winner three internat. awards); portraits include Gen. Claude Larkin, Tyrone Power, Thomas Graham, James Beckwith, Arthur Rolander, Frederick E. Fox, Senator Jesse Helms, Rachel Carson, R. Bud Dwyer, William Genge, Allison Williams, Dennis O'Connor, Frank Cahouet, Dr. Robert Edwards, Robert Wilburn, Henry L. Hillman. Mem. Am. Soc. Portrait Artists (affiliated), Stroke of Genius Gallery, Washington Soc. of Portrait Artists and Portrait Inst., Portrait Soc. Am. Republican. Home: 816 Saint James St Pittsburgh PA 15232-2113

BICKERSTAFF, MINA MARCH CLARK, university administrator; b. Crowley, Tex., Sept. 27, 1936; d. Winifred Perry and Clara Mae (Jarrett) Clark; m. Billy Frank Bickerstaff, June 12, 1954 (div. 1960); children: Billy Mark, Mina Gayle Bickerstaff Basaldu. AA, Tarrant County Jr. Coll., 1982; BBA, Dallas Bapt. U., 1991. Dir. pers. svcs. Southwestern Bapt. Theol. Sem., Ft. Worth, 1976—. Mem. Coll. and Univ. Pers. Assn., Seminary Woman's Club (past treas.), Alpha Chi. Baptist. Avocations: reading, music, genealogy. Office: Southwestern Bapt Theol Sem PO Box 22000 Fort Worth TX 76122-0001

BICKFORD, MELISSA A. internet administrator; b. Oakland, Calif., Oct. 22, 1964; d. Palmer Marquis and Joyce Lenore (Beeson) Oliver; m. Robert Lee Bickford, July 28, 1984 (div. July 1997). BA in Liberal Studies, Calif. State U., Hayward, 1998. CS svcs. mgr. Bay Alarm, Oakland, Calif., 1984-90, spl. project mgr. Walnut Creek, Calif., 1990-96, mgr. adanced tech., 1996-99; gen. mgr. InReach Internet, Stockton, Calif., 1999—. Cons. Integrated Telecomm Solutions, San Jose, Calif., 1999. Avocations: kayaking, camping, swimming, backpacking. Office: InReach Internet 4635 Georgetown Pl Stockton CA 95207-6203

BIDDLE, CATHARINA BAART, artist; b. The Netherlands; m. Livingston L. Biddle, 1973. MFA, George Washington U., Am. U., 1981. Art tchr. Am. Sch., Libya, 1964-66, Washington Pub. Sch. Sys., 1967-73; vol. NEA, 1973-81. Works in mus. and pvt. collections in New York and Wash. D.C. Home: 3050 P St NW Washington DC 20007-3052

BIDDLE, FLORA MILLER, writer; BA, Manhattanville Coll., 1978. Pres. Whitney Mus. Am. Art, N.Y.C., 1978-85, chmn., 1985—95, hon. trustee. Mem. N.Y.C. Art Commn., 1980-90. Author: The Whitney Women and the Museum They Made, 1999. Office: 88 Kielwasser Rd New Preston Marble Dale CT 06777 Home: 17 E 97th St New York NY 10029 E-mail: floramil@earthlink.net.

BIDLACK, JEAN MARIE, pharmacologist, educator, medical researcher; b. Rochester, N.Y., Dec. 4, 1953; d. William Henry and Mary Louise (Naughton) Bidlack; m. Carl T. Helmers, Jr., Nov. 1, 2003. BA in Biology and Chemistry, Skidmore Coll., 1975; PhD in Biophysics, U. Rochester, 1979. Postdoctoral fellow U. Rochester, 1979-80, sr. instr. Ctr. Brain Rsch., 1980-81, asst. prof. brain rsch., 1981-87, assoc. prof. pharmacology, 1987-97, prof. pharmacology and physiology, 1997—. Cons. NSF, Washington, 1983—89, VA, Washington, 1986—88, Nat. Inst. Drug Abuse, Rockville, Md., 1987—, AIDS Study Sect., 1996—2002; mem. secretariat Internat. Narcotics Rsch. Conf., 1999, treas.-elect, 2003—. Contbr. articles to profl. jours. Recipient Sr. Sci. award, KO5 NIH, 1998—; U. Rochester fellow, 1975—79. Mem.: Soc. NeuroImmune Pharmacology (pres.-elect 1999—), Soc. Neurosci., Am. Soc. Pharmacology and Exptl. Therapeutics, Coll. on Problems of Drug Dependence Inc. Achievements include patents for immunossay of free kappa light chains for the detection of multiple sclerosis. Office: U Rochester/Sch Med and Dentistry Dept Pharm and Physiology 601 Elmwood Ave Rochester NY 14642-8711

BIEBER-ROBERTS, PEGGY EILENE, communications educator, editor, journalist, researcher; b. Mobridge, S.D., Jan. 8, 1943; d. John J. and Lenora (Schlepp) Bieber; m. Phil Roberts. BS, No. State U., Aberdeen, S.D., 1966; MA, U. Wyo., 1984; PhD, U. Wash., 1990. Vol. Peace Corps, Turkey, 1966-68; tchr. secondary pub. schs., Idaho, 1968-69, Pine Ridge (S.D.) Reservation, 1969-71; co-founder Medicine Bow Post weekly newspaper, 1977; legis. reporter various weekly newspapers, Wyo., 1980-82; owner, pub. Capitol Times mag., Cheyenne, Wyo., 1982-84; pub. Skyline West Press, 1983—; lectr. pub. rels. and advt. U. Wash., Seattle, 1986-88; rsch. analyst Elway Rsch./Jay Rockey Co., Seattle, 1989-90; asst. prof. mass media U. Wyo., Laramie, 1990-96; journalism faculty comm. tech. Higher Colls. of Tech., Dubai, United Arab Emirates, 1996-98; polit. campaign mgr. Phil Roberts gubernatorial campaign, Wyo., 1998; prof. journalism and mass comms. Am. U. in Cairo, 1999—2003, assoc. prof., 2001—03, chair dept. journalism and mass comm., 2000—02. Indexer McGraw/Hill, Bedford Books, also others, 1988—94. Author, editor: hist. almanacs for various states, 1984—87; contbr. articles to profl. jours., chapters to books. Publicity chmn. Laramie County Dem. Com., Cheyenne, 1982; publicity chmn., precinct committeewoman Albany County Dems., 1999—2000. Named Stout fellow, U. Wash., 1990; recipient 1st Place award for feature writing, co-1st Place award for editorials, Wyo. Press Assn., 1982, Alumni Assn. Faculty Growth award, U. Wyo., 1994. Mem.: Internat. Assn. Media and Comm. Rsch., Assn. Ednl. Journalism and Mass Comm. Office Phone: 307-745-8205.

BIEDEL, ALEXIS, actress; b. Houston, Sept. 16, 1981; d. Martin and Nanette Biedel. Attended, Page Parkes Ctr. of Modeling and Acting, NYU, NYC, 1999. Actor: (films) Rushmore, 1998, Tuck Everlasting, 2002, DyεEnchanted, 2004; (TV series) Gilmore Girls, 2000—. Office: c/o Flutie Entertainment 270 Layfayette St Ste #1400 New York NY 10012*

BIEGEL, EILEEN MAE, retired hospital executive; b. Eau Claire, Wis., Nov. 13, 1937; d. Ewald Frederic and Emma Antonia (Conrad) Weggen; m. James O. Biegel, Oct. 6, 1956; children: Jeffrey Allan, John William. Student, Dist. One Tech. Inst., 1974; corr. student, U. Wis., Madison; grad. mgmt. seminars; student, Upper Iowa U., 1984—. Cert. profl. sec. Exec. sec. to pres. Broadcaster Svcs., Inc., Eau Claire, Wis., 1969-74; exec. sec. to exec. v.p. Am. Nat. Bank, Eau Claire, 1975-77; exec. asst. to pres. Luther Hosp., Eau Claire, 1977—2000, asst. corp. sec., 1984—2000, mem. exec. staff, 1985—2000; asst. corp. sec. Luther Health Care Corp., 1984—2000; ret., 2000; sec. Dist. Atty. Offfic, 2002—. Mem. secretarial adv. council Dist. One Tech. Sch. 1975—; corp. sec. Northwest Health Ventures, 1988-92, bd. dirs. State pres. Future Homemakers Am., 1955; mem. governance com. Wis. Hosp. Assn.; sec. bd. dirs. Chestnut Properties; sec. Christ Ch. Cathedral, Eau Claire, 2001, dist. atty., Eau Claire, 2002. Mem. Eau Claire Womens Network (founder, mem. steering com.), Profl. Secs. Internat. (chmn. goals and priorities com., pres. Eau Claire chpt. 1982-83), Wis. Hosp. Assn. (gov. com.). Home: 4707 Tower Dr Eau Claire WI 54703-8717 Personal E-mail: ebiegel23@aol.com.

BIEHLE, KAREN JEAN, pharmacist; b. Festus, Mo., July 18, 1959; d. Warren Day and Wilma Georgenia (Hedrick) Hargus; m. Scott Joseph Biehle, Aug. 22, 1981; children: Lauren Rachel, Heather Michelle. Student of pre-pharmacy, U. Mo., Columbia, Mo., 1977-79; BS in Pharmacy, U. Mo., Kans. City, Mo., 1982. Reg. Pharmicist. Pharmacy res. U. Iowa Hosp. & Clinics, Iowa City, Iowa, 1982-83; pharmacist Jewish Hosp. of St. Louis, St. Louis, 1983-86; pharmacy mgr. Foster Infusion Care, St. Louis, 1986-88; staff pharmacist Cardinal Glennon Children's Hosp., St. Louis, 1988-90, pres. Lauren's Specialty Foods, Inc., St. Louis, 1988-89; pharmacy mgr. Curaflex Health Svcs., St. Louis, 1989-91; asst. dir. Cobb Hosp. and Med. Ctr., Austell, Ga., 1991-94; asst. dir. pharmacy Publix Supermarkets, Marietta, Ga., 1994-96; pharmacist Scottish Rite Children's Med. Ctr., Marietta, Ga., 1996—. Preceptor St. Louis Coll. Pharmacy, 1984-91, U. Ga. Sch. Pharmacy, 1992. Vol. March of Dimes Walk-a-thon, 1985-90. Recipient Roche Pharmacy Communications Award, Roche Pharmaceuticals, Kans. City, 1982, I Dare You Award, 4-H Club, Nevada, Mo., 1976. Mem. Am. Soc. Hosp. Pharmacists, Kappa Epsilon, Alpha Delta Pi (St. Louis Alumnae pres. 1989-90). Republican. Baptist. Avocations: tennis, horseback riding, swimming, cooking, golf. Home: 3200 Wicks Creek Trl Marietta GA 30062-4867 Office Phone: 404-785-2059.

BIEL, JESSICA, actress, model; b. Ely, Minn., Mar. 3, 1982; d. John and Kim Biel. Attended, Tufts U., 2000. Spokesmodel L'Oreal. Actor: (plays) Annie, Beauty and the Beast, Anything Goes, The Sound of Music; (TV series) 7th Heaven, 1996; (films) Ulee's Gold, 1997, I'll Be Home for Christmas, 1998, Summer Catch, 2001, The Rules of Attraction, 2002, The Texas Chainsaw Massacre, 2003. Office: Innovative Artists 1999 Ave of the Stars Los Angeles CA 90067*

BIENIAS, JULIA LOUISE, medical researcher, statistician; b. Chgo. d. Ignatius M. and Harriet L. (Huddy) B. BA in Psychology and History, MA in Psychology, Washington U., St. Louis, 1986; postgrad., U. Ill., 1986-88; ScD in Biostats., Harvard U., 1993. Rsch. asst. in gerontology and psychology Washington U., 1986; math. statistician U.S. Bur. Labor Statistics, Washington, 1987-88, U.S. Bur. Census, Washington, 1989-97; asst. prof. lectr. George Washington U., Washington, 1995-96; adj. asst. prof. U. Md., 1997—2003; asst. prof., sr. statistician Rush Coll Medicine, Chgo., 1997—2003, assoc. prof., 2004—. Contbr. articles to profl. jours. Mem. Spl. Svc. Area Commn., City of Chgo., 2003—; bd. dirs. Park West Condo. Assn., 1999—, v.p., 1999—2001, pres., 2001—. NSF grad. fellow, 1987-92, Harvard tchg. fellow, 1992-93. Mem.: Caucus for Women in Stats. (rep.-at-large 1995—97, pres. 2004—), Internat. Biometric Soc. (regional adv. bd. 2000—02, various coms.), Am. Statis. Assn. (various coms.), Phi Alpha Theta, Psi Chi, Pi Mu Epsilon, Phi Beta Kappa. Unitarian Universalist. Avocations: piano, tennis, computer programming, jewelry design, interior decorating. Office: Rush Inst for Healthy Aging 1645 W Jackson Blvd Ste 675 Chicago IL 60612-3227 E-mail: jbienias@alum.wustl.edu.

BIENSTOCK, CAROL COOK, finance educator; b. Athens, Ga., Dec. 10, 1948; d. William Thomas and Olivia Spence Cook; m. Steven Allen Bienstock, Mar. 24, 1970; children: Kenneth Richard, Lauren Ashley Bienstock Cartwright. BS, Med. Coll. of Ga., Augusta, 1970; MBA, Miss. State U., Starkville, 1991; PhD, Va. Poly., Blacksburg, 1994. Instr. bus. stats. Miss. State U., Starksville, 1990—91; instr. mktg. Va. Poly., Blacksburg, 1991—95; asst. prof. mktg. Valdosta (Ga.) State U., 1995—98, U. Memphis, Tenn., 1998—2003, Radford (Va.) U., 2003—. Author: Sales Forecasting Mgmt., 1998; contbr. articles to profl. jours., scientific papers. Mem.: Am. Mktg. Assn., Coun. of Logistics Mgmt. (round table v.p.), Acad. of Mktg. Sci. Office: Radford U Dept of Mgmt and Mktg Radford VA 24142 E-mail: cbienstoc@radford.edu.

BIERBAUM, JANITH MARIE, artist; b. Evanston, Ill., Jan. 14, 1927; d. Gerald Percy and Lillian (Sullivan) Turnbull; m. J. Armin Bierbaum, Apr. 17, 1948; children: Steve, Todd, Chad, Peter, Mark. BA, Northwestern U., 1948; student, Mpls. Art Inst., 1964; postgrad., St. Paul Art Inst., 1969-70. Rsch. asst. AMA, Chgo., 1948-49; tchr. Chgo. high schs., 1949-51; freelance artist Larkspur, Colo., 1951—. Exhibited in group shows at Foot Hills Art Ctr., 1985, 86, 87, Palmer Lake (Colo.) Art Assn., 1986-87, 88-89, Gov.'s Mansion, Bismarck, N.D., 1960; oil painting appeared in 1989 Women in Art Nat. calendar pub. by AAUW. Recipient 1st Place Purchase award U. Minn., Mpls., 1966, Coors Classic award Coors Beer, Golden, Colo., 1987. Mem. Colo. Artist Assn. Republican. Avocations: cross-country skiing, swimming, hiking. Home and Office: 1609 Ridgecrest Dr Loveland CO 80537-9073

BIERDEMAN-FIKE, JANE ELIZABETH, social worker, educator; b. St. Louis, Nov. 7, 1922; d. Arthur Edward and Adele Evelyn Bierdeman; m. Don G. Fike, Aug. 5, 1978 (dec. Jan. 22, 1989). BA, Maryville Coll., St. Louis, 1944; MSW, St. Louis U., 1949; LHD (hon.), William Woods U., Fulton, Mo., 2001. LCSW Mo. Adminstrv. asst. Social Planning Coun., St. Louis, 1948—55; psychiat. social worker St. Louis State Hosp., 1955—58, supr. social work, 1958—62; dir. psychiat. social work Fulton (Mo.) State Hosp., 1962—2000, cons., 2000—. Asst. prof. social work U. Mo., Columbia, 1971—78. Mem. social work adv. bd. William Woods U., Fulton, 1989—; Elected mem. Mo. Employees Retirement Bd., Jefferson City, 1974—90; gov. appt. bd. mem. Mo. Employees Healthcare Bd., Jefferson City, 1993—2001. Recipient Profl. Achievement award, Maryville Coll., 1971, Alumni Merit award, St. Louis U., 1991, Hon. Alumni award, U. Mo., 1991, Hon. Instr. Emeritus, U. Mo. Sch. of Social Work, 2000. Mem.: Mo. Assn. Social Workers (pres. 1977—78), Nat. Assn. Social Workers (Named Pioneer 1997). Avocations: golf, painting, writing poetry. Home: 1318 Cedarwood Dr Fulton MO 65251-2275 Office: Fulton State Hosp 600 E Fifth St Fulton MO 65251

BIERMAN, JANE, wood products company executive; Pres., founder Lincoln Wood Products, Inc., 1947—. Office: 701 N State St Merrill WI 54452-1355

BIERMAN, SANDRA, artist; b. Bklyn., N.Y., 1938; d. John Charles Riesberg and Martha Lee Blair; m. Arthur Bierman, Oct. 1, 1983; children: Cheryl, Steven, James. Represented by Contemporary S.W. Gallery, Santa Fe, 1994—, David Haslam, Boulder, Colo., 1992—, Gallery East, Loveland, Colo., 1996— , Jack Meier Gallery, Houston, 1997—, Augustine Arts, Lake Tahoe, Nev., 1997—, Bakersfield (Calif.) Mus., 2001; instr. workshop Am. Acad. Women Artists, Wickenburg, Ariz., 1997, Oil Painting with Sandra Bierman, Kauai, Hawaii, 2000. One-person shows include Nat. Ctr. for Atmospheric Rsch., Boulder, 1992, David Haslam Gallery, 1993, 94, 95, Contemporary S.W. Galleries, 1996, Lincoln Ctr. for the Arts, Ft. Collins, Colo., 1998, Jack Meier Gallery, 1998, Bakersfield (Calif.) Mus. Art, 2001; group shows include C.S. Lewis Summer Inst. Show on Tour, 1994, Queens Coll. Art Gallery, Cambridge, Eng., 1994, 99th Nat. Exhbn. Nat. Arts Club, N.Y.C., 1995, 67th Grand Nat. Show, Salmagundi Club, N.Y.C., 1995, Artistes Americaines, Maison du Terroir, Genouilly, France, 1996, Colo. History Mus., 1996, Clymer Mus., Ellensburg, Wash., 1996, Desert Caballeros Mus., Wickenburg, Ariz., 1997, Colo. Gov.'s Invitational Show, Loveland (Colo.) Mus., 1997-2002, Art Expo, N.Y.C., 1998-99; works in permanent collections at City of Loveland, CSI Ltd., Cambridge, Eng., El Pomar Found., Colorado Springs, Colo., Gilford, Inc., N.Y.C., Herzog & Adams, N.Y.C., Harlow Club Hotel, Palm Springs, Calif., Loveland Mus., Telluride Gallery of Fine Art, Colo., Kaiser Permanente, Denver, Kohn Family Trust, Balt., Mfrs.-Hanover trust, N.Y.C., Mayo Women's Clinic, Scottsdale, Penrose Conf., Ctr., Colorado Springs, Philip Chamberlan Inc., Madison, Conn.; featured in Southwest Art Mag., Art Trends Mag., Mountain Living mag., Woman's Mag., Radiance mag., Sun Storm Fine Art Mag., US Art, Art World News, Art Bus. News, others. Recipient Colo. Gov.'s Purchase award, Loveland, 1988, Best of Show award Western Images, Boulder, 1993, medal of honor award Am. Artists Profl. League, N.Y.C., 1995. Mem. Am. Artists Profl. League, Nat. Mus. of Women in the Arts, Oil Painters Am., Am. Acad. Women Artists (nominating juror, exec. bd. dirs. 1997—).

BIERY, EVELYN HUDSON, lawyer; b. Lawton, Okla., Oct. 12, 1946; d. William Ray and Nellie Iris (Nunley) Hudson. BA in English and Latin summa cum laude, Abilene (Tex.) Christian U., 1968; JD, So. Meth. U., 1973. Bar: Tex. 1973, U.S. Dist. Ct. (we. dist.) Tex. 1975, U.S. Dist. Ct. (so. dist.) Tex. 1977, U.S. Dist. Ct. (no. dist.) Tex. 1979, U.S. Ct. Appeals (5th cir.) 1979, U.S. Ct. Appeals (11th cir.) 1981, U.S. Supreme Ct. 1981. Atty. Law Offices of Bruce Waitz, San Antonio, 1973-76; mem. LeLaurin & Adams, PC, San Antonio, 1976-81; ptnr. Fulbright & Jaworski, San Antonio, 1981—, head bankruptcy, reorganization and creditors' rights sect., 1990—. Policy com. Fulbright & Jaworski, San Antonio, 1996-98; spkr. on creditors' rights, bankruptcy and reorganization law; lectr. Southwestern Grad. Sch. Banking, Dallas, 1980, La. State U. Sch. Banking, 1994; presiding officer, U. Tex. Sch. of Law Bankruptcy Conf., 1976, 94, State Bar Tex. Creditors' Rights Inst., 1985, 88, State Bar Tex. Advanced Bus. Bankruptcy Law Inst., 1985, State Bar Tex. Inst. on Advising Officers, Dirs. and Ptnrs. in Troubled Bus., 1987; mem. bankruptcy adv. com. 5th cir. jud. coun., 1979-80; vice-chmn. bankruptcy com. Comml. Law League Am., 1981-83; mem. exec. bd. So. Meth. U. Sch. Law, 1983-91. Editor: Texas Collections Manual, 1978, Creditor's Rights in Texas, 2d edit., 1981; author: (with others) Collier Bankruptcy Practice Guide, 1993. Del. to U.S./Republic of China joint session on trade, investment and econ. law, Beijing, 1987; designated mem. Bankruptcy Judge Merit Screening Com. State of Tex. by Tex. State Bar Pres., 1979-82; patron McNay Mus., San Antonio; rsch. ptnr. Mind Sci. Found., San Antonio; diplomat World Affairs Coun., San Antonio. Fellow: Am. Coll. Bankruptcy Attys. (v.p.), Soc. Internat. Bus. Fellows (v.p.), Tex. Bar Found. (life), San Antonio Bar Found. (life); mem.: San Antonio Young Lawyers Assn. (pres. 1979—80, Outstanding Young Lawyer award 1979), Tex. Assn. Bank Counsel (bd. dirs. 1988—90, 2001—02), Tex. Bar Assn. (chair bankruptcy com. 1982—83, chair corp., banking and bus. law sect. 1989—90), Zonta (Chair Z club com. 1989—90), Plaza Club San Antonio (bd. dirs. 1982—), Order of Coif. Office: Fulbright & Jaworski LLP 300 Convent St Ste 2200 San Antonio TX 78205-3720 also: 1301 Mckinney St Ste 5100 Houston TX 77010-3031 Office Phone: 713-651-5544.

BIES, SUSAN SCHMIDT, federal agency administrator; b. Buffalo, May 5, 1947; d. Louis Howard and Gladys May (Metke) Schmidt; m. John David Bies, Aug. 29, 1970; children: John Matthew, Scott Louis. BS, State U. Coll.-Buffalo, 1967; MA, Northwestern U., 1968, PhD, 1972. Banking structure economist FRS, St. Louis, 1970-72; asst. prof. econs. Wayne State U., Detroit, 1972-77; assoc. prof. Rhodes Coll., Memphis, 1977-80; tactical planning mgr. First Tenn. Nat. Corp., Memphis, 1980-81, dir. corp. devel., 1982-83, treas., 1983-84, sr. v.p., CFO, 1984-85, exec. v.p., CFO, 1985—95, exec. v.p. for risk mgmt., auditor, 1995—2001; mem. bd. govs. Fed. Reserve Sys., Washington, 2001—. Mem. fin. adv. com. City of Germantown, Tenn., 1978—, also budget com.; mem. investment adv. com. Tenn. Consol. Retirement System, Nashville, 1981-86; instr. MidSouth Sch.

Banking, 1985-86; bd. dirs. Memphis Ptnrs. Pres., bd. dirs. North Germantown Homewoners Assn., 1978-83; treas. Germantown Area Soccer Assn., 1985-86; treas. Fury Soccer Club, 1988—; vice chmn. task force Com. on 21st Century, Rhodes Coll., Memphis, 1986-87; mem. exec. adv. bd. Sch. Accountancy Memphis State U.; bd. dirs. Memphis Youth Initiative, 1988; mem. BAI Acctg. and Fin. Commn., 1988—. Fellow Ctr. for Urban Affairs, 1968-69, Fed. Res. Bank Chgo., 1970. Mem. Am. Bankers Assn. (exec. com. 1986-88), Nat. Assn. Bus. Economists, Am. Econ. Assn., Planning Execs. Inst., Fin. Execs. Inst., (bd. dirs. Memphis chpt. 1988—), Planning Forum (Managerial Excellence award Memphis chpt. 1986), Memphis Area C. of C. (bd. dirs. 1988—, tax com. 1988—, chair 1989—), Econ. Club Memphis (bd. dirs. 1986—, vice chmn. 1987-88, chmn. 1988-89), Omicron Delta Epsilon, Lambda Alpha. Episcopalian. Avocations: gardening, golf, soccer. Office: Fed Reserve System Bd of Gov 20th St & Constitution Ave NW Washington DC 20551*

BIESEL, DIANE JANE, editor, publishing executive; b. N.Y.C., Feb. 15, 1934; d. Douglas and Runa (Patterson) Stevens; m. Donald W. de Cordova, June 24, 1956 (div. July 1971); m. David Barrie Biesel, Sept. 25, 1982. BS, Trenton State Coll., 1956; MLS, Rutgers U., 1969; MA in Edn., Seton Hall U., 1974, cert. in supervision, 1976. Tchr., libr. Arlington (Va.) Bd. Edn., 1956-58; media specialist elem. schs., librs. River Edge (N.J.) Bd. Edn., 1958-91; lectr., instr. children's lit. Alphonsus Coll., Woodcliff Lake, NJ, 1969-72; series editor Scarecrow Press, Lanham, Md., 1992—; v.p., CFO St. Johann Press, 1994—. Field svc. cons. N.J. Dept. Edn., 1969—71; cons. new books preview Baker and Taylor Co., 1972—76; mem. com. academically gifted River Edge Bd. Edn., 1977—83, mem. study skills com., mem. affirmative action com., 1988—90; adj. prof. Seton Hall U., 1978—79; mem. award com. Rutgers U. Grad. Sch. Libr. Svc., 1978—79; mem. River Dell Librs. Coop., 1988—91; cons. Pro Libra Assocs., 1992—. Editor: School Library Media Series, School Librarianship Series. Mem. Child Devel. Ctr. Bd., 1999—; mem. choir All Saints Ch., Bergenfield, 1971—, lay reader, 1973—, del. Diocesan Conv., 1978—, vestrywoman, 1980—83; mem. ecumenical commn. Diocese of Newark, 1992. Mem.: Divsn. Sch. Media Specialists (nat. nominating com. 1978—79, coun. 1978—79, evaluation com. 1979, steering com. 1979—80, co-chmn. liaison com. with Am. Assn. Sch. Librs. 1979—83, nat. nominating com. 1980—82, mem. awards com. 1981—89, program com. 1982—84, bd. dirs. region II 1983—84, pres. 1986, co-author: Information Power 1988, mem. task force on librs. and info. sci., White House, writing com.), River Edge Tchrs. Assn. (pres. 1964—66), Bergen County Sch. Librs. Assn. (pres. 1966—68), Edn. Media Assn. N.J. (state chmn. recruitment 1968—69, state chmn. hospitality 1972—73, state chmn. county liaison 1973—74, co-pres. 1977—78), Bergen Button Buffs (founding grandmother 1993), N.J. Button Soc. (v.p. 1999—2002), Nat. Button Soc. Home: 315 Schraalenburgh Rd Haworth NJ 07641-1200 E-mail: d.biesel@worldnet.att.net.

BIGBY, JUDYANN, medical educator; b. Jamaica, N.Y., 1951; children: Kenan, Naima. BA, Wellesley Coll., 1973; MD, Harvard U., 1978. Henry J. Kaiser fellow in gen. internal medicine Harvard Med. Sch. and Brigham and Women's Hosp., Boston; primary care internal medicine resident U. Wash. Affiliated Hosps., Seattle; assoc. prof. medicine Harvard Med. Sch., Boston, dir. Ctr. of Excellence in Women's Health, mem. faculty, 1983—; med. dir. Cmty. Health Programs Brigham and Women's Hosp., Boston, attending physician, 1983—. Mem. com. Assuring the Health of the Pub. in 21st Century, Inst. Medicine; mem. minority women's health panel of experts Office on Women's Health, Dept. HHS. Mem. bd. dirs. Boston Pub. Health Commn. Recipient Edna W. Smith Pioneer in Cmty. Health Care award, 2000. Office: Brigham and Womens Hosp Women Family and Cmty Programs 1620 Tremont St Boston MA 02120

BIGELOW, KATHRYN, film director; b. San Carlos, Calif., Nov. 27, 1951; Student, San Francisco Art Inst., Whitney Mus. Ind. Study Program, Columbi U. Sch. Film. Former Gap model. Director: (films) The Loveless, 1982, Near Dark, 1987, Blue Steel, 1990, Point Break, 1991, Strange Days, 1995, The Set Up, 1998, The Weight of Water, 2003, (TV series) Homicide Life on the Street, 1993, (TV miniseries) Wild Palms, 1993; dir., prodr., K-19: The Widowmaker, 2002; script supr. Union City, 1980; author: (screenplays) (with Monty Montgomery) The Loveless, (with Eric Red) Near Dark, actor: Born in Flames, 1983 Office: First Light care Working title Films 9333 Wilshire Blvd Beverly Hills CA 90210-5408

BIGELOW, MARGARET ELIZABETH BARR (M.E. BARR), mycology educator; b. Elkhorn, Man., Can., Apr. 16, 1923; d. David Hunter and Mary Irene (Parr) Barr; m. Howard Elson Bigelow, June 9, 1956 (dec.). BA with honors, U. B.C., Vancouver, Can., 1950, MA, 1952; PhD, U. Mich., 1956. Rsch. attaché U. Montreal, Que., Can., 1956-57; instr. U. Mass., Amherst, 1957-65, asst. prof., 1965-71, assoc. prof., 1971-76, prof., 1976-89, prof. emeritus, 1989—. Author: Diaporthales in N.A., 1978, Prodromus to Loculoascomycetes, 1987, Prodromus to Nonlichenized Members of Class Hymenoascomycetes, 1990; contbr. articles to profl. jours. With Can. Women's Army Corps, 1942-46. Mem. Mycol. Soc. Am. (v.p. to pres. 1980-82, editor 1975-80, Disting. Mycologist Award, 1993), Brit. Mycol. Soc., Am. Inst. Biol. Sci. (gen. chmn. ann. meeting 1986). Avocations: gardening, reading. Home and Office: 9475 Inverness Rd Sidney BC Canada V8L 5G8

BIGELOW, MARTHA MITCHELL, retired historian; b. Talladega Springs, Ala., Sept. 19, 1921; children: Martha Frances, Carolyn Letitia. BA, Montevallo U., 1943; MA, U. Chgo., 1944, PhD, 1946. Assoc. prof. history Miss. Coll., Clinton, 1946-48, Memphis State U., 1948-49; Assoc. prof. history U. Miss., 1949-50; assoc. curator manuscripts Mich. Hist. Collections, U. Mich., Ann Arbor, 1954-57; prof. history Miss. Coll., 1957-71, chmn. dept. history and polit. sci., 1964-71. Dir. Bur. of History, Mich. Dept. State, 1971-90; sec. Mich. Hist. Commn., Mich. Dept. State, state historic preservation officer, 1971-90; coord. for Mich., Nat. Hist. Publs. and Recs. Commn., 1974-90. Contbr. articles profl. publns. Fellow, Ency. Britannica, 1944—45; scholar Julius Rosenwald scholarship, 1943—44, Cleo Hearson scholarship, 1944. Mem. Am. Assn. State and Local History (v.p. 1979-80, pres. 1980-81, fellow summers 1958, 59), Orgn. Am. Historians, Nat. Assn. State Archives and Recs. Assn., So. Hist. Assn., Mich. Hist. Soc., Miss. Hist. Soc. Home: 201 Jefferson St Clinton MS 39056-4237

BIGGERS, CORNELIA ANDERSON, musician; b. Iowa City, Iowa, Mar. 15, 1935; d. William Arthur Anderson and Ann Maria Riddell; m. James Wesley Biggers, Jr., May 31, 1958. BA summa cum laude, U. Iowa, 1957. 3rd bassoon and contra- bassoon Tampa Philharm., Fla., 1963—68; 3rd bassoon and contra-bassoon Fla. Gulf Coast Symphony, 1968—82; 3rd bassoon and contra- bassoon Fla. Symphony, Orlando, 1967—82, The Fla. Orch., Tampa, 1982—85; prin. bassoon The Richey Cmty. Orch., Hudson, 1991—, Hernando Symphony Orch., Spring Hill, 1996—97, 2000—; 3rd bassoon and contra -bassoon Imperial Symphony Orch., Lakeland, 1998—. Solo bassoon The Masonic Band, St. Petersburg, Fla., 1995—; substitute organist various chs.; bassoonist, mgr. Profl. Woodwind Ensembles, Clearwater. Author: The Contra-Bassoon: A Guide to Performance, 1977. Mem., officer Ind. Order Foresters Bounty Br., Clearwater; bldg. capt. Woodland Villas Condominium, Clearwater. Mem.: Internat. Double Reed Soc., Am. Fedn. Musicians (life), Mensa, Order Ea. Star, Phi Beta Kappa. Republican. Avocations: recorder, literature, Star Trek, ornithology.

BIGGERT, JUDITH BORG, congresswoman, lawyer; b. Aug. 15, 1937; d. Alvin Andrew and Marjorie Virginia (Mailler) Borg; m. Rody Patterson Biggert, Sept. 21, 1963; children: Courtney Ray, Alison Mailler, Rody Patterson, Adrienne Taylor. BA, Stanford U., 1959; JD, Northwestern U., 1963. Bar: Ill. 1963. Law clk. to presiding justice US Ct. Appeals (7th cir.), Chgo., 1963-64; sole practice Hinsdale, Ill., 1964—99. Rep. Ill. Gen. Assembly, 1993-98, asst. Rep. leader, 1995-98; mem. US Congress from 13th Ill. dist., 1999—, mem. fin. svcs. com., edn. and workforce com. stds. ofcl. conduct, chmn. sci. com. subcom. on energy, mem. bipartisan working group on youth violence, speakers task force for drug free Am. Mem. bd. editors Law Rev., Northwestern U. Sch. Law, 1961-63. Pres. Hinsdale Twp. HS Dist. 86 Bd. Edn., 1983-85; pres. Jr. League Chgo., 1976-78, treas., bd. mgrs., 1966—; chmn. Hinsdale Antiques Show, 1980; pres. Oak Sch. PTA, Hinsdale, 1976-78; pres.-treas. Chgo. jr. bd. Travelers Aid Soc., 1965-70; Sunday sch. tchr. Grace Episcopal Ch., Hinsdale, 1978-80, 82-85; chair, treas., 2d v.p. bd. dirs. Vis. Nurses Assn. Chgo., 1978; bd. dirs. Salt Creek Ballet, 1990-98. Recipient Servian award Jr. aux. U. Chgo. Cancer Rsch. Foun., Woman Yr. in Govt., Politics, and Civic Affairs DuPage YWCA, 1995, Hero of the Taxpayer, Am. for Tax Reform. 2000, 02, award for pub. svc., Am. Chem. Soc., 2003, Excellence in Edn., Nat. Assn. Coll. Admission Counseling, 2002, Friend of Edn., Ill. & Nat. Edn. Assn., 2002, Outstanding Leadership to Homeless and Victims of Domestic Violence, Chgo., Pub. Sch., 2002, Disting. Achievement for Protecting and Expanding Opportunities for Children and Youth Who Are Homeless, Chgo. Coalition for the Homeless, 2002, Spirit of Enterprise award US C. of C.; named one of 100 Women Making a Difference; inductee to Hinsdale Ctrl. HS Hall Fame, 1997. Mem. ABA, Ill. Bar Assn., DuPage Bar Assn., Coalition Women Legislatures. Republican. Office: US Ho of Reps 1213 Longworth House Off Bl Washington DC 20515-1313 also: 13th Dist of Ill 115 W 55th St Ste 100 Clarendon Hills IL 60514-1593 Office Phone: 202-225-3515.*

BIGGINS, J. VERONICA, bank executive; m. Franklin Biggins; children: Dawn, Kenzie. B, Spelman Coll.; M, Ga. State U.; postgrad., U. Md. Asst. br. mgr. Citizens and So. Nat. Bank, Atllanta, affirmative action officer, compliance mgr., employee relations mgr., mgr. Atlanta personnel, exec. v.p., dir. human resources. Lectr. in field. Bd. dirs., co-chmn. freedom fund dinner NAACP; bd. dirs. Atlanta chpt. Urban League; chmn. personnel com., bd. dirs. United Way; bd. dirs., chmn. student affairs com., vice chmn. fundraising Spelman Coll.; mem. governing bd., vice chmn. Zoo Atlanta Capital Campaign; mem. exec. com. Leadership Atlanta, 1983; mem. bd. visitors Grady Hosp.; mem. bd. trustees YWCA, Exodus, Inroads, Inc.; chmn. nominating com. NW Girl Scout Council; mem. Atlanta women's fund adv. com. Recipient Outstanding Performance award Inroads, Atlanta, 1986, Urban Bankers, 1987, trail blazer award Nat. Assn. Negro Bus. and Profl. Women's Clubs, Inc. Mem. Am. Bankers Assn. (chmn. human resource div.), Dogwood City Links, Chautaugua Circle. Episcopalian. Office: Citizens and So Ga Corp PO Box 4899 Atlanta GA 30302-4899

BIGHAM, WANDA DURRETT, religious organization administrator; b. Barlow, Ky., June 19, 1935; d. Herbert Martin and Ada Florene (Baker) Durrett; m. William M. Bigham, Jr., June 7, 1958; children: William M. III, Janet Kaye, Julia Lynn. BME, Murray State U., 1956; MM, Morehead State U., 1971, MHE, 1973; EdD, U. Ky., 1978; cert., Inst. For Ednl. Mgmt. -Harvard U., 1982; LittD (hon.), Loras Coll., 1989. Dir. TRIO programs Morehead (Ky.) State U., 1972-85, assoc. dean acad. affairs, dir. instructional sys., 1982-85, acting dean grad. and spl. acad. programs, 1984-85; exec. asst. to pres. Emerson Coll., Boston, 1985, v.p. for devel., 1986; pres. Marycrest Coll., Davenport, Iowa, 1986-92, Huntingdon Coll., Montgomery, Ala., 1993—2003; asst. gen. sec. for schs., colls. and univs. The United Meth. Ch., Nashville, 2003—. Bd. dirs. NAICU, 2002-03; bd. dirs., pres. Asia-Pacific Fedn. Christian Schs.; bd. dirs. Internat. Assn. Meth.-Related Schs., Colls. and Univs., Montgomery Symphony Orch., 1993-2003, Ala. Shakespeare Festival, 1996-2003, NASCUMC, 1996-2003; exec. com., pres. Univ. Senate United Meth. Ch., Ctrl. Ala. chpt. ARC, Montgomery, 1995; mem. Leadership Ala., 1994—; co-chair Quad Cities Vision for the Future, Davenport, 1987-92. Recipient Pres.'s award Davenport C. of C., 1988, Women of Spirit and Note award Cmty. Com. of Davenport, 1991, Hope for Humanity award Jewish Fedn. of QC, Rock Island, Ill., 1993, Women's Acad. of Honor award Ala. Bus. and Profl. Women's Found., 2004; named to Alumni Hall of Fame, Morehead State U., 1988, Disting. Alumna, Murray State Coll., 1988, Woman of Distinction award Girl Scouts South Ctrl. Ala., 2001. Mem. Am. Coun. on Edn. (mem. coun. of fellows, bd. dirs. 1994-97, fellow in higher edn. adminstrn. 1983-84), Internat. Assn. Univ. Pres., Montgomery C. of C., Com. of 100, Sigma Alpha Iota (Sword of Honor 1956), Phi Kappa Phi, Kappa Delta Pi. Home: 1393 Woodley Rd Montgomery AL 36106-2435 Office: United Meth Ch Bd Higher Edn and Ministry 1001 19th Ave S PO Box 340007 Nashville TN 37203-0007 Office Phone: 615-340-7406. Business E-Mail: wbigham@gbhem.org.

BIHARY, JOYCE, federal judge; b. Detroit, Oct. 24, 1950; BA, Wellesley Coll., 1972; JD, U. Mich., 1975. Bar: Ga. 1975. Atty. Alston, Miller & Gaines, 1975-77, Rogers & Hardin, 1977-79, ptnr., 1979-87; bankruptcy judge U.S. Dist. Ct., Atlanta, 1987—. Mem. Ga. Assn. Women Lawyers, Atlanta Bar Assn., Southeastern Bankruptcy Law Inst. (adv.); fellow Am. Coll. Bankruptcy, Lawyers Found. Ga., Ga. Consortium Personal Fin. Literacy, Coalition Debtor Edn. Office: US Bankruptcy Ct US Courthouse 75 Spring St SW Atlanta GA 30303-3309

BILANIUK, LARISSA TETIANA, neuroradiologist, educator; b. Ukraine, July 15, 1941; arrived in U.S., 1951; d. Yaroslav and Myroslava Zubal; m. Oleksa-Myron Bilaniuk, Nov. 14, 1964; children: Larissa Indira, Laada Myroslava. BA, Wayne State U., 1961, MD, 1965. Diplomate Am. Bd. Radiology, Am. Bd. Neuroradiology. Resident in radiology Hosp. of U. Pa., Phila., 1966-70; fellow Fondation Ophtalmologique, Paris, 1972; assoc. in radiology U. Pa. Sch. Medicine, Phila., 1973-74, asst. prof., 1974-79, assoc. prof., 1979-82, prof., 1982—; with Children's Hosp. of Phila., 1992—. Reviewer grants rsch. NIH, Washington, 1983—86; St. Göran lectr. Karolinska Inst., Stockholm, 1984; vis. prof. Grosshadem Clinics, U. Munich, 1988, Inst. Med. Radiology, Kharkiv, Ukraine, 1996; invited lectr. USSR, 1976, 90, China, 79, France, 1980—82, France, 1989, France, 94, France, 96, Japan, 84, Japan, 90, Sweden, 84, Sweden, 92, England, 85, The Netherlands, 85, Italy, 1986—87, Italy, 1990, Italy, 92, Germany, 87, Germany, 95, Chile, 93, Australia, 95, Thailand, 95, Malaysia, 95, Israel, 97, Austria, 98, Ukraine, 96; invited lectr., Ukraine, 98, Ukraine, 2000, Ukraine, 02. Co-editor: 3 radiology books; contbr. articles to profl. jours., chapters to books. Fellow Rsch., Cancer Rsch. Ctr., Heidelberg, Fed. Republic Germany, 1967—68. Fellow: Am. Coll. Radiology; mem.: Acad. Med. Sci. Ukraine (elected), Ukranian Med. Assn. N.Am., Soc. Pediatric Radiology, European Soc. Neuroradiology, Am. Soc. Neuroradiology, Radiol. Soc. N.Am., Sigma Xi. Avocations: downhill skiing, alpine hiking, glider flying, photography. Office: Childrens Hosp of Phila 324 S 34th St Philadelphia PA 19104-4345 E-mail: bilaniuk@email.chop.edu.

BILL, SUSAN ALMA, violist; b. Portland, Maine, Oct. 15, 1954; d. Charles Rufus and Muriel Jean (Quinn) Brown; m. Robert George Bill, July 13, 1985; children: Samuel Charles, George Arthur, Timothy Winston. BS, U. Maine, 1976; MusM, Boston Conservatory, 1993. Violist Nat. Orchestral Assn., N.Y.C., 1985; prin. violist Cape Cod Symphony, Hyannis, Mass., 1986-93; violist numerous orchs., Mass., 1986-93; music tchr. Sacred Heart Sch., Quincy, Mass., 1990-93, 2000—. Music dir. St. Chrysostom's Ch., Quincy, 1992-97; min. of music Holy Nativity Episc. Ch., Weymouth, Mass., 1997—. Mem. Am. String Tchrs. Assn., Pi Beta Phi, Pi Kappa Lambda. Democrat. Episcopalian. Avocation: knitting.

BILLAU, ROBIN LOUISE, engineering and consulting executive; b. Denver, Sept. 19, 1951; d. Emerson Roy and Catherine Louise (Brewster) Billau; m. Edward E. Adams. BA, Western State Coll., 1973; MS, Colo. State U., 1977. Cert. indsl. hygienist. Life sci., indsl. hygienist Mont. Energy Devel. & Rsch. Inst., Butte, 1977-79; indsl. hygiene supr. Mountain States Energy, Butte, 1979-81; asst. prof. Mont. Coll. Mineral Sci. Tech., Butte, 1981-83; indsl. hygiene supr. EG & G Idaho, Idaho Falls, 1983-85, unit mgr., 1985-87, group mgr., 1987-88, sr. tech. adv., 1988-90; cons. environ. mgmt., indsl. hygiene RLB Cons., Inc., Houghton, Mich., 1990-92; mgr. Jason Assocs. Corp., Idaho Falls, Idaho, 1992-94, Lockheed Martin Environ. Systems, Pocatello, Idaho, 1994-95; cons. environ. health and safety Indoor Air Quality $ Occupational Health, Bozeman, Mont., 1996—; owner Indoor Air Quality and Occupational Health, Bozeman, Mont., 2001—. Owner Ranch Goddess Brand, Inc., 2001, Indoor Air Quality & Occupant Health, 2000. Mem. Am. Bd. Indsl. Hygiene, ASHRAE. Democrat. Avocations: skiing, gardening, raising worms and poultry, mountain biking, reading. Home and Office: 174 Quinn Creek Rd Bozeman MT 59715-9635 E-mail: rlbillau@imt.net.

BILLAUER, BARBARA PFEFFER, lawyer, educator; b. Aug. 9, 1951; d. Harry George and Evelyn (Newman) Pfeffer. BS with honors, Cornell U., 1972; JD, Hofstra U., 1975; MA, NYU, 1982; cert. in risk scis. and pub. policy, Johns Hopkins U., 1999. Bar: N.Y. 1976, Fed. Dist. Ct. N.Y. 1977, U.S. Ct. Appeals (2d cir.) 1978, U.S. Supreme Ct. 1984. Assoc. Bower & Gardner, N.Y.C., 1974-78; sr. trial atty. Joseph W. Conklin, N.Y.C., 1978-80; assoc. dept. head Curtis, Mallet-Prevost, Colt & Mosle, N.Y.C., 1980-82; ptnr. Anderson, Russell, Kill & Olick, N.Y.C., 1982-86, Stroock & Stroock & Lavan, N.Y.C., 1986-90; ptnr., chair environ. and toxic tort practice Keck, Mahin, Cate & Koether, 1990-93; prin. Barbara P. Billauer & Assocs., Lido Beach, N.Y., 1993—. Vis. scholar Johns Hopkins U. Sch. Pub. Health, 1998-99; faculty SUNY Stony Brook Med. Sch.; adj. assoc. prof. NYU Grad. Sch., 1982-88; lectr. Rutger's U. Med. Sch.; jud. screening com. Coordinated Bar Assn., 1983-86; mem. spl panel Citywide Ct. Adminstrn. 1982-85; bd. dirs. Weizmann Inst., Am. Com. Co-author: The Lender's Guide to Environmental Law: Risk and Liability, 1993. Fellow Am. Bar Found.; mem. ABA (indoor air polution 1990-93), Met. Womens Bar Assn. (v.p. 1981-83, pres. 1983-85, chmn. bd. 1985-87), Nat. Conf. Womens Bar Assn. (bd. dirs., v.p. 1989-95), Internat. Coun. Shopping Ctrs. (environ. com.), Brit. Occupl. Hygiene Soc., Environment Toxic Torts. Home: 2555 Pennsylvania Ave Nw Apt 518 Washington DC 20037-1614 E-mail: omniscience@starpower.net.

BILLIG, ETEL JEWEL, theater director, actor; b. N.Y.C., Dec. 16, 1932; d. Anthony and Martha Rebecca (Klebansky) Papa; m. Steven S. Billig, Dec. 23, 1956 (dec. Aug. 1996); children: Curt Adam, Jonathan Roark. BS, NYU, 1953, MA, 1955; student, Herbert Berghof Studio, N.Y.C., 1955-56. Cert. elem. and high sch. tchr. Actress Washington Square Players, N.Y.C., 1950-55, Dukes Oak Theatre, Cooperstown, N.Y., 1955, Triple Cities Playhouse, Binghampton, N.Y., 1956, Candlelight Dinner Playhouse, Summit, Ill., 1970, 73, 77, 79, 90; mng. dir. Theatre 31, Park Forest, Ill., 1971-73; asst. mgr. Westroads Dinner Theatre, Omaha, 1973-76; mng. dir., actress Forum Theatre, 1973, 94; mng. dir., actress, producing dir. Ill. Theatre Ctr., Park Forest, 1976—; mng. dir., actress Goodman Theatre, Chgo., 1987, 95, Ct. Theatre, 1990, Wisdom Bridge Theatre, 1991; dir. drama Rich Ctrl. H.S., Olympia Fields, Ill., 1978-86. Del. League of Chgo. Theatres Russian Exchange to Soviet Union, 1989; actress Drury Lane, Oak Brook, Ill., 1989; cons. and lectr. in field. Appeared in films including the Dollmaker, Running Scared, Straight Talk, Stolen Summer; (TV series) Hawaiian Heat, Missing Persons, Untouchables. V.p. Nat. Coun. Jewish Women, Park Forest, 1968-70; sec. Community Arts Coun., Park Forest, 1984-86; pres. Southland Regional Arts Coun., 1986-92. Recipient Risk Taking award NOW, 1982; grantee Nebr. Arts Coun., 1975, Ill. Arts Coun., 1995, 96, 2000, Athena award Matteson Area C. of C., 1997, Abby Found. award, 1997; named to Park Forest Hall of Fame, 2000. Mem. AFTRA, SAG, Actors' Equity Assn., League Chgo. Theatres, Ill. Arts Coun. Theatre Panel, Prodrs. Assn. Chgo. Area Theatre (sec. 1988-89), Bus. in the Arts Coun. of C. of C. (charter), Rotary (bd. dirs. Park Forest chpt. 1988-97, sec. 2000, hall of fame 2000). Avocations: travel, antiques. Office: Ill Theatre Ctr PO Box 397 Park Forest IL 60466-0397 E-mail: ilthctr@bigplanet.com.

BILLINGS, JUDITH A. state education official; Supt. public instrn. State of Washington, 1988-97. Chairwoman Gov.'s Adv. Coun. on HIV/AIDS, Washington, 1998—.

BILLINGS, KATHY, national monument administrator; Supt. USS Arizona Meml., Honolulu. Office: USS Arizona Meml 1 Arizona Memorial Rd Honolulu HI 96818-3145

BILLINGS, PATRICIA JEAN, inventor; b. Clinton, Mo., Feb. 15, 1926; d. Chester Irwin and Zoe Elizabeth (Strieby) Billings; m. William Marlman, June 21, 1949; 1 child, Melanie Ann Runge. Student, Amarillo Coll., 1955. Med. rschr. on Histoplasma capsulation and TB USPHS, 1946-48; rschr. Kansas City T.B. Sanitarium, 1951; med. technologist, 1960-67; tuberculosis rschr. Kansas City County Hosp., 1967-71; rschr. Craftcote, 1971-73; pres. Geobond, 1989—, Craftcote Internat., Inc. Spkr. Simmons Coll., Boston, Fire Materials Conv., Egypt, 1988; interviewed numerous TV shows including The Unbelievable, Gordon Elliott Show, CBS This Morning, Fox 41 News, Am. Chem. Soc., Pub. TV, Boston, Dateline, 1998; inventor Geoboval Construction Material, 6 patents, featured in articles: People Magazine, Wall St. Journ., Automated Builder-internet MIT network (inventor of week). 4 patents. Mem. adv. bd. Mus. History of Women, Washington. Named Inventor of Week, MIT. Achievements include research in 20 products for use in construction field. Home: 8120 Lee Blvd Shawnee Mission KS 66206-1219

BILLINGSLEY, FLORENCE ILONA, nurse, case manager; b. Detroit, Dec. 27, 1943; d. John and Doris Fannie (Creighton) B.; 1 child, Marc Todd. LPN, Detroit Practical Nursing Ctr., 1963; ADN, Highland Pk. Cmty. Coll., 1973; BSN, Wayne State U., 1983. RN, Mich.; diplomate Am. Bd. Quality Assurance and Utilization Rev. Physicians; cert. case mgr. Nurse preceptor, staff nurse, charge nurse Harper Hosp., Detroit, 1964-76; pub. health nurse Detroit Health Dept., 1976-86; discharge planning coord. Detroit Receiving Hosp., 1985-86; clin. svcs. mgr. Med. Ctr. Healthcare, Detroit, 1985-88; spl. instr. JTPA Sch. Practical Nursing, Detroit, 1988-89; case mgr. AIDS Consortium of S.E. Mich., Detroit, 1989-90; liaison nurse Renaissance Home Health Care, Oak Park, Mich., 1990-91; alternative health svcs. case mgr. United Am. Healthcare Corp., Detroit, 1991-95; disability mgr. Travelers Ins. Co., Warren, Mich., 1995-99; case mgmt. cons. New Detroit Nursing Ctr., 2000—. Ind. case mgmt. cons., 1990-2000. Vol. for breast and prostate screening programs Mich. Cancer Found., Detroit, 1992—; hospice vol. Hospice of Mich., Detroit, 1993—; precinct sr. chairperson, Detroit Election Commn., 2000—. Recipient Minority Nurse grant for Grad. Studies in Cmty. Health Nursing, State of Mich., 1989-90. Mem. Mich. Nurses Assn. (del. to conv. 1994-97), Citizens for Better Care, Acad. of Case Mgrs., Wayne State U. Alumni Assn., Chi Eta Phi Lambda Chi. Avocations: reading autobiographies, alternative health care, volunteer work.

BILLNITZER, BONNIE JEANNE, nurse, gerontologist; b. Mar. 7, 1935; d. George Gottfried and Sarah Edna Elizabeth (Park) Haffelder; m. Harold R. Billnitzer, Apr. 28, 1956; children: J. Stephen, David A., John Mark, Timothy P., Michael M. BA in Psychology, U. Mich., 1977; ADN, U. Toledo, Ohio, 1989; BSN, Med. Coll. Ohio, Ohio, 1992. RN, Ohio; cert. gerontol. nurse, cert. cardiovascular nurse. Adminstrv. mgr. Med. Coll. Ohio Ambulatory Care Ctr., Toledo, 1972-79; cardiovascular nurse St. Vincent Med. Ctr., Toledo, 1988-92; case mgr. The Vis. Nurse Svc., Toledo, 1992-97; pvt. practice RN case mgr. Perrysburg, Ohio. Mem. credentialing com. for RN St. Vincent Med. Ctr., Toledo, 1991-92. Recipient Logan award for Clin. and Theoretical Excellence in Nursing, U. Toledo, 1989. Mem. AAUW, ANA, Ohio Nurses Assn., Toledo Dist. Nurses Assn. (1st v.p. 1995-96), Am. Holistic Nurses Assn., Am. Assn. Critical Care Nurses, Internat. Order St. Luke the Physician. Lutheran. Avocations: music, reading, antiques, quilting. Home: 1084 Eastbrook Dr Perrysburg OH 43551-1646

BINDER, AMY FINN, public relations company executive; b. N.Y.C., June 13, 1955; d. David and Laura (Zeisler) Finn; children: Ethan Max, Adam Finn, Rebecca Eve. BA with honors, Brown U., 1977; MBA, Columbia U. Freelance photographer, N.Y.C., 1977-78; account exec. Newton & Nicolazza, Boston, 1978-79, Agnew, Carter, McCarthy, Boston, 1979-80; dir. pub. relations City of New Rochelle, N.Y., 1980-82; dir. urban communications Ruder-Finn, N.Y.C., 1982-85, v.p., 1985-86, exec. v.p., 1986-87; pres. Ruder-Finn America, N.Y.C., 1987; CEO, exec. mng. dir. RFBinder Partners, Inc. Ruder Finn Group, 2001—. Photographer: Museum without Walls, 1975, The Spirit of Man: Sculpture of Kaare Nygaard, 1975, Knife Life and Bronzes, 1977, St. Louis: Sculpture City, 1988, The Triumph of the American Spirit: Johnstown, Pennsylvania, 1989. Mem. Internat. Ctr. of Photography (mem. pres. coun.), Pres. Assn. of Am. Mgmt. Assn. Democrat. Jewish.

BINDER, ELAINE KOTELL, associations consultant; b. Boston, Oct. 12, 1938; d. Maxwell and Florence (Blumsack) Kotell; m. Richard A. Binder, Aug. 28, 1960; children: Mark Stephen, Jonathan Stuart. AB, Radcliffe Coll., 1960; MA, U. Md., 1975. Tchr. City of Medford, Mass., 1960-62; project dir. Wider Opportunities for Women, Washington, 1971-75, Women's Equity Action League Fund, Washington, 1976-78; mng. ptnr. Binder, Elster, Mendelson, Wheeler, Bethesda, Md., 1978-80; adminstrn. dir. AAUW, Washington, 1980-85; exec. dir. B'nai B'rith Women, Washington, 1985-94. Pres. Binder Assocs., Bethesda, 1994—; prin. ptnr. Tecker Consultants, Trenton, N.J., 1994—; cons. Bethesda, 1975-76. Co-author: Careers for Peers, 1973; contbr. articles to profl. jours. Trustee Temple Shalom, Silver Spring, Md., 1974-76; pres., v.p. Montgomery County Commn. for Women, Rockville, Md., 1978-80; commr. Anti-Defamation League, N.Y., 1985—; bd. dirs. Jewish Coun. for the Aging, 1996—. Fellow Am. Soc. Assn. Execs. (bd. dirs. 1990-93, vice chmn. 1994), Greater Washington Soc. Assn. Execs. (com. chair 1989—). Democrat. Jewish. Avocations: music, art, collecting native american art and artifacts, reading. Office: Tecker Consultants 427 River View Exec Park Trenton NJ 08611 also: Binder Assocs 6704 Bradley Blvd Bethesda MD 20817-3045

BINDER, MADELINE DOTTI, retail executive; b. Chgo., Oct. 7, 1942; d. Martin and Anne (Sweet) Binder; children: Mark Nathan, Marla Susan. BEd, Nat. Coll. Edn., 1964, MS, 1972, MS in Human Svcs-Counseling, 1993. Tchr. Rochester Schs. (Minn.), 1963-64, Orange County Schs., Orlando, Fla., 1967-68; reading cons. Palatine (Ill.) Schs., 1972-73; instr. Parent Effective Tng., Wilmette, Ill., 1974-76; tchr. Effectiveness Tng., 1974-76; pres. Profls. Diversified, Wilmette, 1976-89; remedial and enrichment reading tchr. Waukegan (Ill.) Pub. Schs., 1986; pres. Lifeline, 1989-90; mgmt. cons. World Wide Diamonds Assn., Schaumburg, Ill., 1979-89; Pearl direct distbr. Amway Corp., Ada, Mich., 1976-94; exec. distbr. NU Skin, 1992; distbr. Starlight Internat., 1994—. Psychotherapist, 1993-97. Author: Organic Gardening, 1975, The Go-Getters Planner, 1986, Singles Guide to Chicagoland, 1995, Divorce: You and Your Child, 2003. Leader, Camp Fire Girls, Evanston, Ill., 1963, 75. Ednl. scholar Nat. Coll. Edn., 1971. Mem. Phi Delta Kappa, Alpha Delta Omega.

BINDER, SUZANNE, federal agency administrator; BS, McGill U.; MD, Tufts U. Med. Sch. Bd. certified in Internal Medicine. Commd. officer U.S. Pub. Health Svc.; officer, Epidemic Intelligence Svc. CDC, chief Childhood Lead Poisoning Prevention branch, assoc. dir. med. sci., Divsn. Parasitic Disease, Nat. Ctr. Infectious Diseases, dir. Injury Ctr., 2000—. Contbr. articles to profl. jours. Recipient Arthur S. Fleming award for Excellence in Mgmt. Office: CDC Nat Ctr Injury Prevention and Control 4770 Buford Hwy NE K02 Atlanta GA 30340

BINGAMAN, ANNE K. lawyer; b. Jerome, Ariz., July 3, 1943; d. William Emil and Anne Ellen (Baker) Kovacovich; m. Jeff F. Bingaman, Sept. 14, 1968; 1 child, John. BA in History, Stanford U., 1965; gen. course cert. with honors, London Sch. of Econs., England, 1964-65; LLB, Stanford U., 1968. Bar: Calif. 1969, N.Mex. 1969, Ariz. 1969, U.S. Dist. Ct. D.C. 1983. Atty. Brown & Bain, Phoenix, 1968-69, N.Mex. Bur. Revenue, Santa Fe, 1969-70, Modrall, Sperling, Roehl, Harris & Sisk, Albuquerque, 1970, N.Mex. Atty. Gen's. Office, Santa Fe, 1970-72; from asst. prof. to assoc. prof. U. N.Mex. Sch. Law, Santa Fe, 1972-76; founding ptnr. Bingaman & Davenport, Santa Fe, 1977-82; ptnr. Brown, Bain & Bingaman, Santa Fe and Washington, 1982-84, Onek, Klein & Farr, Washington, 1984-85, Powell, Goldstein, Frazer & Murphy, Washington, 1985-93; asst. atty. gen. anti-trust divsn. U.S. Dept. Justice, Washington, D.C., 1993-96; sr. v.p. LCI Internat., McLean, Va., 1997-98; chmn. bd. Valor Telecom, Irving, Tex., 1999—. Contbr. articles to profl. jours. Exec. com. Stanford Law Sch. Bd. Visitors, 1978-80, 88-90; mem. for N.Mex. of 10th Cir. Jud. Nominating Panel, 1977-80. Ford Found. fellow 1975; recipient Nat. Vol. award Stanford Assocs., 1989. Fellow Am. Bar Found.; mem. ABA, N.Mex. Bar (founder, vice-chair antitrust sect. 1982-85, chair com. to rewrite comm. property & other state laws to conform to ERA), Am. Law Inst. Democrat. Episcopalian. Office: Valor Telecom 1200 19th St SW 5th Fl Washington DC 20036-

BINGHAM, JINSIE SCOTT, broadcast company executive; b. Greencastle, Ind., Dec. 28, 1935; d. Roscoe Gibson and Alpha Edith (Robinson) Scott; m. Frank William Wokoun, Jr. (dec.); children: Douglas Scott, Richard Frank; m. Richard Innes Bingham, June 24, 1964. Student, DePauw U., Greencastle, 1952-53, Northwestern U., 1953, Coe Coll., 1953-54. Exec. sec. Ind. Young Dems., 1958-60; receptionist Ind. Ho. of Reps., Indpls., 1959; saleslady Avon Products, Greencastle, 1961-64; sales mgr. Sta. WJNZ (formerly WXTA), Greencastle, 1969-77, owner, pres., gen. mgr., 1977-94; owner Radio Greencastle, 1977—. Owner, pres. GM of WJNZ, 1977-94; former ptnr. Sta. WVTL, Monticello, Ill., Sta. KBIB, Monette, Ark.; speaker DePauw U. Comm. Seminar, 1981-85; vis. lectr., 1986—. Co-author: Putnam County Indiana Land Patents, 2004; featured in Trainblazing Women of Ind., 1999—. Com. chair Legis. Awareness Seminar, 1978—86; co-chair Greencastle Gaelic Festival, 1983—84; charter mem. Greencastle 2001, 1985—, Greencastle Civic League, 1984—, Greencastle Merchant's Assn., 1983—97, Cmty. Resources Com., 1982—87; charter mem., corp. sec. Main St. Greencastle, 1983—87, v.p., 1987—88, pres., 1989—90, chmn., 1990—91; v.p. United Way, 1996—97, campaign chair, 1996—97, campaign advisor, 1998—99; announcer Putnam County Fair Parade, 1977—, hon. bd. dirs., 2002—; co-chmn. centennial com. Putnam County Courthouse, 2001—; v.p. Putnam County Mus., 2002, pres., 2003—04; tour guide Putnam County Conv. and Visitors Bur., 1998—; active Putnam County Coun. on Aging and Aged, 1999—; pres. Putnam County Hist. Soc., 1996—97, sec., 1998—; bd. dirs., v.p., sec., pres. Putnam County Found.; co-founder Greencastle H.S. Alumni Assn., 1995, founding chmn. scholarship fund, 1995—; active Govs. Commn. for a Drug Free Ind., 1991—; v.p. West Ctrl. Ind. Econ. Devel. Coun., 2003—; mem. Lilly Scholar Selection Com., 1998—; vice chmn. Putnam County Dem. Ctrl. Com., 2001—; bd. dirs. Putnam County Comprehensive Ctr., 1994—2000, Opportunity Housing, 1995—2002; charter mem., bd. dirs. Greencastle Devel. Ctr., 1988—89, Greencastle Cmty. Child Care Ctr., 1983—87; v.p. Greencastle Zoning Bd. Appeals, 1985—88, pres., 1988—; charter mem., bd. dirs. Greencastle Vol. Fire Dept., 1986. Sagamore of the Wabash, Ind. Gov. Evan Bayh, 1995; Limestone State Seal, 1996, Seal of City, Greencastle, 1996; named Hoosier Know It All Champion, Sta. WTTV, Indpls., 1998; inducted into Ind. Broadcasters Hall of Fame, 1999; named one of 53 Trailblazing Women of Ind., 1999, Outstanding Citizen Greencastle Jaycees, 1981; name to Putnam County Agr. Hall of Fame Putnam County Farm Bur., 2002. Mem. AARP (Capital City task force 2000), Nat. Soc. DAR (Centennial chmn. Washburn chpt. 2002, sec. 1994-2003, chaplain 1988-2004, chpt. regent 2003—), Broadcast Pioneers (life), Putnam County Bd. Realtors, Am. Women in Radio and TV (pres. Ind. chpt. 1979-82, Lifetime Achievement award 1996), Indpls. Network Women in Bus. (charter), Women in Comm., Inc. (bd. dirs. 1983-84, MATRIX co-chair 1984, Frances Wright award 1993), Am. Legion Aux., Nat. Assn. Broadcasters, Soc. Profl. Journalists, Ind. Broadcasters Assn. (v.p. FM 1982), Putnam County Extension Adv. Coun. (4H), Natural Resources Svc. Land Use Study Group, Greencastle Bus. and Profl. Women's Club (pres. 1975-76, 78-79, Woman of Yr. 1994), Indpls. Ad Club, Women's Press Club Ind., Indpls. Press Club, Nat. Fedn. Press Women, Ind. Dem. Editl. Assn. (sec. 1987, v.p. 1988, pres. 1990), Ind. C. of C., Greencastle C. of C. (bd. dirs. 1979-83, pres. 1982, amb. 2001—. Citizen of Yr. 1997), VFW (pres. ladies aux. 1966-68), Ind. Geneal. Soc., Milestone Care Soc., Packard Club Ind., Ind. Soc. Pioneers, Daus of 1812 (pres. Tippecanoe chpt. 1981, state v.p. 1982), Daus. of the Union, Internat. Order Job's Daus., Soc. Descendants of Valley Forge, Rotary (bd. dirs., pres. 1994-95, bull. editor 1995—, dist. conf. planner 1997, Paul Harris fellow 1998, del. world conf. 1998), Order Ea. Star, Women of Moose, Milestone Car Soc., Delta Theta Tau, Sigma Delta Chi. Mem. Christian Ch. (Disciples Of Christ).

BINGHAM, JUNE, writer, playwright; b. White Plains, N.Y., June 20, 1919; d. Max J.H. and Mabel (Limburg) Rossbach; m. Jonathan B. Bingham, Sept. 20, 1939 (dec. July 1986); children: Sherry B. Downes, Micki B. Esselstyn (dec. 1999), Timothy, Claudia B. Meyers; m. Robert B. Birge, Mar. 28, 1987; 1 stepchild, Robert R. Student, Vassar Coll., 1936-38; BA, Barnard Coll., 1940; LittD (hon.), Lehman Coll., 2002. Writer, editor U.S. Treasury, Washington, 1943-45; editorial asst. Washington Post, 1945-46; writer Tarrytown (N.Y.) Daily News, 1946. Author: Do Cows Have Neuroses?, Do Babies Have Worries?, Do Teenagers Have Wisdom?, Courage to Change: An Introduction to Life and Thought of Reinhold Niebuhr, 1961, Courage to Change: An Introduction to Life and Thought of Reinhold Niebuhr, paperback edit., 1992, U Thant: The Search for Peace, 1970, (plays) Triangles, 1986, Eleanor and Alice, 1996, You and the I.C.U., 1990; author: (with others) The Inside Story: Psychiatry and Everyday Life, 1953, The Pursuit of Health, 1985; author: (mus.) Squanto and Love, 1992, Young Roosevelts, 1993, The Other Lincoln, 1995, The Strange Case of Mary Lincoln, 2001; contbr. articles to nat. mags., newspapers and profl. jours. Bd. dirs. Riverdale Mental Health Assn., 1983—, Woodrow Wilson Found., Princeton, N.J., 1959-64, 83-89, Lehman Coll. Found., 1983-90, Ittleson Ctr. for Childhood Rsch., 1958-90, Franklin and Eleanor Roosevelt Inst., 1992-2002; founder T.L.C.; trained liaison comforter Vol. Program of Presbyn. Hosp., N.Y.C. Named Alumna of the Yr., Rosemary Hall, 1976. Mem. Authors Guild (nominating com. 1987-90), Dramatists Guild, PEN, Cosmopolitan Club. Democrat. Avocations: tennis, golf, theatre, movies, reading. Home: 5000 Independence Ave Bronx NY 10471-2804

BINGHAM, NANCY F. government agency administrator; BA in Bioengrng., U. Calif. San Diego, 1978, MS in Bioengrng./Fluid Mechanics, 1979; MS in Mgmt., Stanford U., 1997. With NASA, Moffett AFB, Calif., 1982—87, project mgr., 1987—93, assoc. dir. Sys. Mgmt. and Planning, 1993—. Design engr. for control sys. Numerical Aerodynamic Simulation Facility, Moffett AFB, Fluid Mechanics Lab., Moffett AFB, High Reynolds Number Channel II, Moffett AFB; design engr. for electronic, telemetry and computer sys. Life Scis. Flight Experiments Program for Space Shuttle, Moffett AFB; mem. Internat. Space Sta. Alpha Ind. Assessment Panel, Moffett AFB, 1994, Joint Industry/Govt. Cost Team, Moffett AFB, 1994, Space Sta. Redesign Team, Moffett AFB, 1993, Program/Project Mgmt. Summer Study Group, Moffett AFB, 1991; chairperson ARC Strategy and Tactics com., Moffett AFB, 1985. Recipient Group Achievement award, NASA, 1996, 1995, 1994, Exceptional Achievement medal, 1993, Group Achievement award, 1999, 1998, Ames Honor award, 1990. Office: NASA Ames Rsch Ctr MS 200-1B Moffett Field CA 94035

BINGHAM, OUITA HYAMS, librarian; b. Shreveport, La., June 30, 1952; d. John Skipwith Hyams and Myrtis Juanita Temple; m. William Benjamin Bingham III, Apr. 10, 1982; children: Sarah S., Alexander H., Emily E. BS in Psychology, La. State U., 1975; MLIS, U. Tex., Austin, 1987. Cert. tchr. Tex. Libr. Austin Pub. Libr., Legis. Ref. Libr., Austin, 1998—2002; sch. libr. S.W. Tex. U., 2003; libr. Hermelinda Rodriguez Elem. Sch., Austin, 2003—. Libr. Festival com., Austin, 1999; cons., youth story-times and puppet shows, Austin, 1990—; mem. adv. bd. Austing Pub. Libr., 1990. Prodr., designer (slide shows) Closer Look at Looking, 1977, prodr., designer (various puppet shows). Chair nursery com. Dripping Springs (Tex.) Meth. Ch., 1996—99; fundraising chair First United Meth. Ch. Presch., Austin, 1998—2001. Mem.: ALA, Nat. Assn. Young Children, Tex. Libr. Assn. Methodist. Avocations: writing children's books, travel, puppets. Home: 755 Green Oak Dr Dripping Springs TX 78620 Office: Hermelinda Rodriguez Elem Sch 4400 Franklin Pk Rd Austin TX 78744 E-mail: ouitabingham@msn.com.

BINGHAM-NEWMAN, ANN MARIE, marriage and family therapist, educator; b. Coronado, Calif., Feb. 14, 1943; d. Carl Robert and Janie Bell (Bingham) Newman; m. Arthur J. Gonchar, July 11, 1976; children: Becky, Andy, Jon. BS, U. Wis., 1965, MS, 1971, PhD, 1974; MA, Calif. Family Study Ctr., 1980. Lic. marriage and family counselor, Calif. Dir. Rhoades Terrace Sch., Dallas, 1969-71; coord. U. Wis., Early Childhood Study Ctr., Madison, 1971-74; chmn. child and family studies dept. Calif. State U., L.A., 1974—99; coord. urban learning major Charter Coll. Edn., 1999—2001. Co-author: Piagetian Perspective for Preschools, 1984; contbr. articles to profl. jours. Mem. Am. Assn. Marriage and Family Therapists, Nat. Coun. Family Rels. Resources for Infant Educators. Office: Calif State U Charter Coll Edn 5151 State University Dr Los Angeles CA 90032-4226

BINION, GAYLE, political science educator; b. N.Y.C., Sept. 20, 1946; d. Samuel and Ruth (Brovich) B. BA, CCNY, 1967; MA, UCLA, 1969, PhD, 1977. Prof. polit. sci. U. Calif., Santa Barbara, 1976—, dir. Washington Ctr., 1994-96. Exec. dir. ACLU of So. Calif., L.A., 1986-87; vis. asst. prof. San Diego State U., 1974-76; ethics hearing officer APA, Washignton, 1993—; USIA Internat. lectr., Bangladesh, Pakistan, Nepal, Sri Lanka, 1993; chmn. systemwide academic senate U. Calif., 2002-03. Contbr. chpt. to biog. dictionary, articles to profl. jours. Founding pres. Santa Barbara Women's Polit. Com., 1987-89. U. Calif. Humanities Faculty fellow, 1990, Interdisciplinary Humanities Ctr. grantee, 1991. Mem. Law and Society Assn. (trustee 1993-96), Am. Polit. Sci. Assn. (chair ethics com. 1989-92), Western Polit. Sci. Assn. (exec. com. 1981-83). Avocations: reading, travel, running. Office: U Calif Dept Polit Sci Santa Barbara CA 93106

BINION, LINDA DIANE, computer systems research specialist; b. Birmingham, Ala., Apr. 21, 1948; d. James Marvin and Sara Meredith (Moore) Binion; m. Norman Willard Holman, June 20, 1981 (div. 1983); m. Paul Anthony DeLorenzo, Aug. 16, 1986. Student, U. Ala.-Tuscaloosa, 1966-67, U. Ala.-Birmingham; BS in Computer Info. Mgmt., Southwest U., 1992, MS in Computer Sci., 1996. Data base adminstr. Carraway Methodist Med. Ctr., Birmingham, Ala., 1970-78; mgr. systems and program Brookwood Health Services Inc., Birmingham, 1979-80; sr. v.p. Innovative Systems Inc., Birmingham, 1980-83; pres. Amitec Inc., Birmingham, 1983-85; dir. research-info. systems technologies Ala. Metal Industries Corp., Birmingham, 1986; pres. AMICO Research Corp., 1986-90; mgr. IEF EBSCO Industries, 1990-95; dir. customer svc. Salcris Sys., Birmingham, 1995—; dir. ops. Reynolds and Renolds-Birmingham, 1996—; cons. in field. Designer: (software system) Innovative Healthcare Support System, 1980. Guest speaker U. Ala. Sch. Community Allied Health Services, 1986, numerous others. Mem. C. of C. (Birmingham), Mensa, Assn. Systems Mgmt. (past pres.), Internat. Platform Assn. Democrat. Am. Baptist. Home: 2900 Kirkcaldy Ln Birmingham AL 35242-4117 Office: Reynolds and Reynolds 42 Inverness Pkwy Birmingham AL 35242

BINKOWSKI, SYLVIA JULIA, water transportation executive, consultant; b. Dearborn, Mich. d. Steve S. and Cecelia Maria (Kwiatkowski) B. BS in Psychology and Comms., Ea. Mich. U., 1978. Sr. project coord. U.S. Treas. Dept., Detroit, 1979-83; sr. legis. asst. Congressman William D. Ford, Washington, 1983-91; head purchasing Decision Support Sys., McLean, Va., 1991-93; cons. The Eagle Cos., Annandale, Va., 1993-95; data analyst Louis Berger Internat. Inc., Washington, 1995—; mgr., data analyst GWU Nat. Ports & Waterways Inst., Rosslyn, Va., 1995—. Coord. U.S. Congress/German Bundestag Staff Exch. Program, 1989; cons. STC, London, 1992-93. Fund raiser Senatorial Campaign Com., 1984—, Congl. Campaign Com., 1984—; vol. Alexandria (Va.) Jaycees, 1988. Mem. House Legis. Asst. Assn. (founder, pres. emeritus, award 1989). Roman Catholic. Avocations: photography, oil painting, music, writing, fund raising for charities. Home: 6493 Frenchmens Dr Apt 202 Alexandria VA 22312-3608 Office: GWU Nat Ports & Waterways Inst 1300 17th St N Ste 310 Arlington VA 22209-3801 Fax: 703-276-7101.

BINKS, REBECCA ANNE, communications executive; b. Oak Park, Ill., July 23, 1955; d. Donald Melvin and Elizabeth June (Lobdell) B.; m. Cary Emmett Donham, June 22, 1980; 1 child, Samuel Joseph Donham. Student, Goodman Sch. Drama, Chgo., 1973-76; BA in Liberal Arts, Columbia Coll., Chgo., 1983; MS in Mktg. Comm., Roosevelt U., 1993; MEd in Reading, St. Xavier U., 2003. Freelance lighting designer, theater tech., Chgo., N.Y.C., 1975-80; retail mgr. Coffee and Tea Exch., Chgo., 1981-84; sales assoc. K&S Photographies, Chgo., 1984-87; supr. client services AGS&R Communications, Chgo., 1987-88; mgr. Meeting Express Systems, Chgo., 1988-90; pres. Binks & Assocs. Inc., Chgo., 1990-95; co-dir. Northside Parents Network, 1996-97; reading specialist Ridge Lawn Sch., Chicago Ridge, Ill. Mem. faculty mktg. comm. Columbia Coll., Chgo., 1992-97; mem. faculty English Chgo. State U., 1995-2001; tchr. travel photography, Chgo., 1987. Designer: (cookbook) Kitchen Angst, 1993; exhibited in group and one-woman shows. Mem. internal communications com. Girl Scouts, Chgo., 1989-91, founding parent Sect. bd. dirs., Ridge Acad., 2000-01. Mem. ASCD, Internat. Reading Assn., Chgo. Coun. on Fgn. Rels., Ancona Sch. Soc. (bd. dirs. 1997-99), Kappa Delta Pi.

BINNEY, JAN JARRELL, publishing executive; b. Frankfort, Ind., Aug. 16, 1941; d. Robert and Susie (Meek) Jarrell; m. Joseph M. Binney, June 23, 1962; 1 child, Robert J. BS, Purdue U., 1962; MA, Coll. N.J., 1972. Speech-lang. pathologist pub. schs., various locations, 1962-84; pvt. practice speech pathology East Brunswick, N.J., 1982-85; pres. The Speech Bin, Inc. Pub., Vero Beach, Fla., 1984—. Editor profl. publs. Deacon Presbyn. Ch., 1985-87, elder, 1987-90; bd. dirs., chpt. chmn. ARC, Indian River Country, Fla. Fellow Am. Speech, Lang. Hearing Assn. (legis. councilor 1981-89, bd. dirs. pub. info. exch. 1987-89, com. on equality 1988-90, bd. dirs. polit. action com.), N.J. Speech, Lang. Hearing Assn. (pres. 1981-82, hon. 1984), Exch. Club Indian River (sec. 1998-99, bd. dirs. 2001-2002), Exch. Club Indian River Found. (charter, sec. 2002—), Pi Beta Phi Alumnae Club (treas.). Office: The Speech Bin Inc 1965 25th Ave Vero Beach FL 32960-3000 E-mail: jan@speechbin.com

BINSFELD, CONNIE BERUBE, former state official; b. Munising, Mich., Apr. 18, 1924; d. Omer J. and Elsie (Constance) Berube; m. John E. Binsfeld, July 19, 1947; children: John T., Gregory, Susan, Paul, Michael. BS, Siena Heights Coll., 1945, DHL (hon.), 1977; LLD (hon.), No. Mich. U., 1998; DHL (hon.), Mich. State U., 1998, Thomas Cooley Sch. of Law, 1999; LLD (hon.), Saginaw Valley State U., 2000, Lake Superior State U., 2000; DHL (hon.), U. Notre Dame, 2000, Grand Valley State U., 2000, DHL (hon.). County commr. Leelanau County, Mich., 1970-74, mem. Mich. Ho. of Reps., 1974-82, asst. rep. leader, 1979-81; del. Nav. Conv., 1980, 88, 92; mem. Mich. Senate, 1982-90, asst. rep. leader, 1979, 81; lt. gov. State of Mich., 1990-98. Mem. adv. bd. Nat. Park Sys. Named Mich. Mother of Yr., Mich. Mothers Com., 1977; Northwestern Mich. Coll. fellow; named to Mich. Women's Hall of Fame, 1998. Mem. Nat. Coun. State Legislators, LWV, Siena Heights Coll. Alumnae Assn. Republican. Roman Catholic. E-mail: Connieltgov@mailstation.com.

BINTLIFF, BARBARA ANN, law educator, library director; b. Houston, Jan. 14, 1953; d. Donald Richard and Frances Arlene (Appling) Hay; m. Byron A. Boville, Aug. 20, 1977 (div. 1992); children: Bradley, Bruce. BA, Cen. Wash. U., 1975; JD, U. Wash., 1978, MLL, 1979. Bar: Wash. 1979, U.S. Dist. Ct. (ea. dist.) Wash. 1980, Colo. 1983, U.S. Dist. Ct. Colo. 1983. Libr. Gaddis and Fox, Seattle, 1978-79; reference libr. U. Denver Law Sch., 1979-84; assoc. libr., sr. instr. Sch. Law U. Colo., Boulder, 1984-88, assoc. prof., libr. dir., 1989—2001, prof., 2001—, Nicholas Rosenbaum prof. law, 2002—. Legal cons. Nat. Ctr. Atmospheric Rsch., Environ. and Societal Impacts Group, Boulder, 1980; vis. prof. U. Wash., Seattle, 1996, chair U. Colo. Boulder, Faculty Assembly, 2003—. Editor: A Representative Sample of Tenure Documents for Law Librarians, 1988, 2nd edit., 1994, Chapter Presidents' Handbook, 1989, Representatives Handbook, 1990; assoc. editor: Legal Reference Svcs. Quarterly, Perspectives: Teaching Legal Research and Writing; contbr. articles to profl. jours. Recipient Boulder Faculty Assembly Excellence Svc. award, 2001; named Disting. Alumnus, Ctrl. Wash. U., 2000. Mem. Am. Assn. Law Librs. (v.p./pres.-elect 2000-01, pres. 2001-02), Am. Law Inst. (elected), Colo. Bar Assn., Colo. Assn. Law Librs. (pres. 1982), Southwestern Assn. Law Librs. (pres. 1987-88, 91-92). Episcopalian. Office: U Colo Law Libr 2405 Kittredge Loop Dr Rm 190 Boulder CO 80309-0402

BIONDI, FLORENCE, freelance/self-employed artist; b. N.Y.C., Sept. 25, 1924; d. Angelo and Frances Curreri; m. Albert Anthony Biondi, Apr. 15, 1951; children: Joseph, Albert, Thomas, Robert. Student, Bklyn. Mus. Art Sch., 1967-75, Art Student's League, New City, N.Y., 1976-79. Pen and ink illustrator Simplicity Patterns, N.Y.C., 1943-45, Reader Mail Inc., N.Y.C., 1948-86; draftsman W.L. Maxson & Co., N.Y.C., 1945-48; freelance artist, 1986—. Mem. chorus Conservatory of Music. Recipient Pen and Brush Club award, 2001. Fellow: Am. Artists Profl. League (various awards 1980—82, 1988, 2000); mem.: Catherine Lorillard Wolfe Art Club (Portrait Pastel award 1983, 1996, 2001), Pastel Soc. Am. (Kalkow award 1983), Nat. Assn. Women Artists, Audubon Artists. Roman Catholic. Avocations: music, gardening, sewing, reading, choral music. Home: 426 Mcdonald Ave Brooklyn NY 11218-2212

BIRBRAGHER-ROZENCWAIG, FRANCINE, art historian, critic, editor; b. Chgo., Feb. 24, 1965; d. Leon and Celia (Sredni) Birbragher; m. Leslie Alan Rozencwaig, Apr. 11, 1992; children: Sharon Rozencwaig, Arielle Rozencwaig, Mark Rozencwaig. BA in Comms., Pontificia U. Javeriana, Bogotá, Colombia, 1987; MA in Art History, U. Miami, 1996, postgrad. Corr. Arte en Colombia/Art Nexus, 1990—, asst. dir., 1991-92; internat., editl. coord. Art Nexus, North Miami Beach, 1992—. Bd. trustees Mus. Contemporary Art, North Miami, Fla., 1994—, co-chair edn. com., 1997—; curator annual art exhibit Women's Internat. Zionist Orgn., Miami, 1991—, fundraising advisor, 1997. Contbr. articles to profl. jours. Bd. dirs. PTA Hillel Day Sch., North Miami, Fla., 1997—; mem. women's aux. Temple Menorah, Miami Beach, 1995—. Mem. Internat. Assn. Art Critics, Coll. Art Assn., Assn. Lat. Am. Art. Jewish. Office: Art Nexus 12955 Biscayne Blvd Ste 410 North Miami FL 33181

BIRCHARD, CATHERINE SUZANNE SIEH, artist; b. New Rochelle, NY, Jan. 20, 1964; d. Theodore and Eleanor Anne Becker Sieh; m. Richard Edward Birchard, Oct. 9, 1987; 1 child, Dylan. BA, Cornell U., Ithaca, N.Y., 1985. Painting, Munch (1938), 1997, exhibited in group shows at Westbeth Gallery, NYC, 1998, Gallery 402, 1998, Erector Sq. Gallery, New Haven, Conn., 1998, Silvermine Guild Galleries, New Canaan, Conn., 1998, The Macy Gallery, Valhalla, NY, 1999, The Art Club Gallery, NYC, 2000, NY Law Sch. Gallery, 2000, The Gallery on the Hudson, Irvington, NY, 2001, Pelham Arts Ctr. Gallery, Pelham, NY, 2002, Phoenix Gallery, NYC, 2002, The Arts Exch. Gallery, White Plains, NY, 2002—, 2003, The Macy Gallery, Valhalla, NY, 2003, Iona Coll. Arts Ctr., New Rochelle, NY, 2003. Recipient Juror's Selection Award, 1998, Cresson Pugh Award for

Most Innovative, 1997; named Inaugural Westchester Biennial Artist, Castle Gallery, 1998. Mem. Mamaroneck Artists' Guild (bd. dir. 1998—, newsletter editor 1998-99, dir. programs 1998-2001, dir. publicity 2001-, membership juror 2001-), Orgn. Ind. Artists, Ctr. for Book Arts. Avocations: music, book collecting.

BIRCHER, ANDREA URSULA, mental health services professional; b. Bern, Switzerland, Mar. 6, 1928; arrived in U.S., 1947; d. Franklin E. Bircher and Hedy E. Bircher-Rey. Diploma, Knapp Coll. Nursing, Santa Barbara, Calif., 1957; BS, U. Calif., San Francisco, 1961, MS, 1962; PhD, U. Calif., Berkeley, 1966. RN. Staff nurse, head nurse Cottage Hosp., Santa Barbara, 1957—58; psychiat. nurse, jr., sr. Langley-Porter Neuropsychiatric Inst., San Francisco, 1958—66; asst. prof. U. Ill. Coll. Nursing, Chgo., 1966-72; prof. U. Okla. Coll. Nursing, Oklahoma City, 1972-93, prof. emeritus, 1993—. Contbr. articles to profl. jours. Mem.: NAFE, ANA, AAUP, Calif. Assn. Psychiat. Nurses in Advanced Practice, N.Am. Nursing Diagnosis Assn., Internat. Soc. Psychiat.-Mental Health Nursing, Am. Psychotherapy Assn. (diplomate), ANA/Calif., Ventura County Writers Club, Phi Kappa Phi, Sigma Theta Tau. Republican. Avocations: indoor gardening, cooking, reading, yoga, writing. Home: 1161 Cypress Point Ln Apt 201 Ventura CA 93003-6074

BIRCHETT, COLLEEN LUCILLE, editor; b. Detroit, Dec. 30, 1944; d. Wilbur James and Esther Bernice (Moore) B. BS, Wayne State U., 1967; MA, U. Mich., 1975, PhD, 1986. Cert. secondary English tchr., Mich. Instrnl. designer Coalition for the Use of Learning Skills, Ann Arbor, Mich., 1978-80, Reading and Learning Skills Ctr., Ann Arbor, 1980-82; instrl. designer Bell & Howell, Chgo., 1983-85; development editor Urban Ministries, Chgo., 1986-98. Part-time faculty Chgo. State U., 1982-83, Loyola U., Chgo., 1982-86; curriculum writer United Ch. Press, Cleve., 1990; adj. faculty McCormick Theol. Sem., Chgo., 1996-98; vis. asst. prof. Chgo. State U., 1995-98. Writer, editor: (mags.) Inteen, 1986-96, Young Adult Today, 1990-96; editor: How to Help Hurting People, 1990, How I Got Over, 1994, Africans Who Shaped Our Faith, 1995, When Black Men Stand Up for God, 1996, Falling in Love with God, 1997, others. Pres. Newness of Life Ministry Trinity United Ch. of Christ, 1997—, asst. Sunday sch. supt., 1987-90; dir. Christian edn. 2d Bapt. Ch., 1984-87. Named Miss Cinderella Cinderella Club, 1965. Avocation: filmmaking. Home: 1414 E 59th St Chicago IL 60637-2916

BIRD, CAROLINE, author; b. N.Y.C., Apr. 15, 1915; d. Hobart Stanley and Ida (Brattrud) B.; m. Edward A. Menuez, June 8, 1934 (div. Dec. 1945); 1 dau., Carol (Mrs. John Paul Barach); m. John Thomas Mahoney, Jan. 5, 1957 (dec. 1981); 1 son, John Thomas. Student, Vassar Coll., 1931-34; BA, U. Toledo, 1938; MA, U. Wis., 1939; LHD (hon.), Keene State U., 1988. Desk editor N.Y. Jour. Commerce, 1943-44; editl. rschr. Newsweek mag., N.Y.C., 1942-43, Fortune mag., N.Y.C., 1944-46; with Dudley-Anderson-Yutzy, pub. relations, N.Y.C., 1947-68; Froman Disting. prof. Russell Sage Coll., 1972-73; Mather prof. Case Western Res. U., Cleve., 1977. Author: The Invisible Scar, 1966, Born Female, 1968, rev. edit., 1970, The Crowding Syndrome, 1972, Everything a Woman Needs to Know to Get Paid What She's Worth, 1973, rev., 1982, The Case Against College, 1975, Enterprising Women, 1976, What Women Want, 1979, The Two-Paycheck Marriage, 1979, The Good Years, 1983, Second Careers, 1992, Lives of Our Own, 1995; chief writer: The Spirit of Houston, 1978; also articles in nat. mags. Mem. review bd. Dept. State, 1974. Mem. Am. Soc. Journalists and Authors, Am. Sociol. Assn. Home: 8118 Sawyer Brown Rd #B113 Nashville TN 37221-1402

BIRD, LINDA C. psychotherapist, educator; d. Warren J. and Mary-Jane Conley; m. James J. Bird, Aug. 17, 1968; children: Brittany L., Meaghan N. Diploma in Nursing, MSOE, 1968; BA summa cum laude, Oakland U., 1989; MSW, U. Mich., 91. RN; LCSW. Head nurse Cleve. (Ohio) Clinic, 1972—74, Ohio State U. Hosp., Columbus, Ohio, 1974—76; childbirth educator ASPO, Lockport, NY, 1978—86, Pitts., 1978—86; psychotherapist Oakland Family Svcs., Pontiac, Mich., 1991—94, Eastwood Clinics, Royal Oak, Mich., 1994—, Heron Ridge Assocs., Bloomfield Hills, Mich., 1997—. Mem.: NASW. Avocations: quilting, gardening, reading, bicycling. Office: Heron Ridge Associates 7457 Franklin Rd Ste 303 Bloomfield Hills MI 48098

BIRD, MARY FRANCIS, secondary school educator; b. Mesilla, N.Mex., July 19, 1941; d. A.D. and Mary Theresa (Veitch) Alexander; m. Willis Monroe Bird Jr., May 3, 1962; children: William Michael, Keith Alexander, Steven Wayne. AA, N.Mex. State U., Farmington, 1977; BS, N.Mex. State U., Las Cruces, 1988. Med. transcriptionist Ctr. for Phys. Therapy and Sports Rehab., Las Cruces, 1988-92; family and consumer scis. tchr. Zia Middle Sch., Las Cruces, 1992—. Bd. sec. Farmington Amateur Baseball Congress, 1977-80; pres. Jr. Women's Club, Farmington, 1979-80; charter sec. Burley (Idaho) Amateur Baseball Assn., 1982-84; chairperson Monument for San Albino Ch., Mesilla, N.Mex., 1992. Recipient Outstanding Svc. award City Coun. and Mayor, Burley, Idaho, 1984; named N.Mex. Outstanding Young Home Economist, N.Mex. Home Econs. Assn., Las Cruces, 1987. Mem. AAUW, Am. Vocat. Assn., Family and Consumer Scis. (N.Mex. pres. 2002-03, N.Mex. counselor 2003—). Avocations: singing, theatre performances, volunteering. Office: Zia Middle Sch 1300 W University Las Cruces NM 88005

BIRD, MARY LYNNE MILLER, professional society administrator; b. Buffalo, Feb. 25, 1934; d. Joseph William and Mildred Dorothy (Wallette) Miller; m. Thomas Edward Bird, Aug. 23, 1958; children: Matthew David, Lisa Bronwen. AB magna cum laude, Syracuse U., 1956; postgrad., Columbia U., 1956-58. Mem. rsch. staff Ctr. for Rsch. in Personality, Harvard U., Cambridge, Mass., 1959-62, Ctr. Internat. Studies, Princeton (N.J.) U., 1962-66, Inst. Internat. Social Rsch., Princeton, 1965, Sch. Internat. Affairs, Columbia U., N.Y.C., 1966-67, Coun. Fgn. Rels., N.Y.C., 1967-69, Twentieth Century Fund, N.Y.C., 1969-72; asst. to pres. World Policy Inst., N.Y.C., 1972-74; dir. devel. Fund for Peace, N.Y.C., 1974-78; dir. fellows program Exec. Council Fgn. Diplomats, N.Y.C., 1978-79; dir. devel. Assn. Vol. Surgical Contraception, N.Y.C., 1979-83; exec. dir. Am. Geog. Soc., N.Y.C., 1983—. Cons. Fedn. Am. Scientists, Washington, 1974-75. Trustee Bel Canto Opera Co., N.Y.C., 1975-90; bd. dirs. Finding a Way Project. Maxwell Citizenship scholar Syracuse U., 1952-56. Fellow AAAS; mem. NAS (com. on geography, liaison mem. 1984-2000), Assn. Am. Geographers, Soc. Woman Geographers, Inst. for Current World Affairs (trustee), Nat. Coun. Geog. Edn., 100-Yr. Assn. N.Y., Conf. Latin Americanist Geographers, Planning Com. for Nat. Assessment on Ednl. Progress in Geography, St. David's Soc., Colonial Dames Am., Mid-Atlantic club N.Y.C. (bd. dirs.), Princeton Club, Am. Assn. of Assoc. Execs., Phi Beta Kappa, Phi Kappa Phi, Eta Pi Upsilon. Avocations: singing, sailing. Office: Am Geog Soc 121 Wall St Ste 100 New York NY 10005-3904 E-mail: MLBird@amergeog.org.

BIRD, PATRICIA COLEEN, business owner; b. Wolf Point, Mont., May 10, 1953; d. Harry Sidney and Pearl Rose (Firemoon) B. AA in Fine Arts, Haskell Indian JUCO, Lawrence, Kans., 1974; student, Kans. U., 1974-78; CDC Cert., Deaconess Hosp., Glasgow, Mont., 1990. Partnership bus. owner Blue Feather Indian Store, Wolf Point, Mont., 1980—2000. Indian arts steering com. mem. Mont. Arts Coun., Helena, 1991. Exhibitions include Beauty, Honor, and Tradition: The Legacy of Plains Indian Shirts Exhibit, George Gustav Heye Ctr., N.Y., 2001. First responder ambulance Trinity Hosp., Wolf Point, 1991-92; drug and alcohol facilitator Frazer (Mont.) Sch. Dist. 2-2B, 1990-91; acting sec. Frazer Community Coun., 1991-92; N.W. accrediting assn. mem. Poplar (Mont.) Sch., 1990-91; coord. "The Longest Walk", Davis, Calif., 1978, concert dir., 1978, Outstanding Young Women of Am., Ala, 1986, 87. Named Miss Nat. Congress of Am. Indians, 1975, The Modern Ms., 1975, Miss Haskell, 1974, Oil Discovery Celebration Pres., 1974, Oil Discovery Celebration Princess, 1973, 72, 71. Achievements include design of Smithsonian Inst., Nat. Museum of the Am. Indian, ribbon shirt made in 1981 was selected to become part of the Smithsonian's permanent plains Indian shirts collection from the 19th and 20th centuries. Avocations: indian art and crafts, sewing, reading, painting, drawing.

BIRD, SHARLENE, clinical psychologist; b. N.Y.C., Sept. 3, 1957; d. Rubin and Dina Bird. BA in Psychology & Hispanic Studies, Vassar Coll., 1979; MA in Applied Psychology, Adelphi U., 1986; MA in Human Resources Mgmt., New Sch. for Social Rsch., N.Y.C., 1987; PsyD in Clin. Psychology, Yeshiva U., 1992. Lic. psychologist, N.Y. Clin. extern St. Mary's Children and Family Svcs., Syosset, N.Y., 1980-81; behavior modifier Flower Hosp./Terence Cardinal Cooke, N.Y.C., 1981-82; clin. psychology extern Met. Ctr. for Mental Health, 1986-87; clin. psychology intern NYU Med. Ctr./Bellevue Hosp., N.Y.C., 1989-90; postdoctoral fellow in human sexuality N.Y. Hosp./Cornell Med. Ctr., 1990-92; family therapist Roberto Clemente Family Guidance Ctr., N.Y.C., 1991-93, 96-98; healthcare planning analyst Inst. for Family and Community Care, N.Y.C., 1993-96; pvt. practice N.Y.C., 1994—. Supr. NYU Med. Ctr./Bellevue Hosp., N.Y.C., 1992—; part-time clin. instr. dept. psychiatry NYU Med. Ctr., 1995—; tng. cons. Inst. for Family and Cmty. Care, N.Y.C., 1993; weekly permanent radio talk show co-host Siempre a Tu Lado, Sta. WADO 1280 AM, 1992—95. Chair bd. dirs. Mothers of Childrens with AIDS, N.Y.C., 1991-93. Mem.: APA, Assn. for Advancement of Behavior Therapy (chair pub. edn. and media dissemination com. 1996—99), Am. Group Psychotherapy Assn., Counselors and Therapists, Am. Assn. Sex Educators, Assn. Hispanic Mental Health Profls. (bd. dirs., mem.-at-large 1995—97, v.p. 1999—2001), Am. Orthopsychiat. Assn., N.Y. State Psychol. Assn., Sigma Delta Phi. Office: 112 W 56th St Rm C Ste 15 S New York NY 10019-3841

BIRD, SUE, professional basketball player; b. Oct. 16, 1980; d. Herschel and Nancy. Degree comm., U. Conn., 2002. Profl. basketball player Seattle Storm, 2002—. Named Two-time All.-Am., Best Female Coll. Athlete, Epsy Awards, 2002, Player of Yr., Associated Press and Naismith, 2002; named to First Team All-WNBA, 2002, 2003, WNBA Western Conf. All-Star Team, 2002, 2003; recipient Wade Trophy, 2002. Achievements include member NCAA Division 1 National Championship Team, U. Conn., 2000, 02. Office: Seattle Sonics and Storm 351 Elliott Ave W Ste 500 Seattle WA 98119 Business E-Mail: StormFans@sonics-storm.com.

BIRDSALL, NANCY, economist; b. Feb. 6, 1946; BA in Am. Studies, Newton Coll. of the Sacred Heart, 1967; MA in Internat. Rels., Johns Hopkins U., 1969; PhD in Econs., Yale U., 1979. Social sci. analyst Smithsonian Inst., 1972-76; economist, various policy and mgmt. positions World Bank, Washington, 1979-93; exec. v.p. Inter-Am. Devel. Bank, Washington, 1993-98; sr. assoc., dir. Econ. Reform Project Carnegie Endowment for Internat. Peace, 1998—. Sr. adviser Rockefeller Found., 1988-89; active numerous coms. Nat. Acad. of Scis.; chair bd. dirs. Internat. Ctr. for Rsch. on Women; bd. dirs. Bd. of Population Coun., numerous others. Author numerous publs. on econ. devel. issues. Office: care Carnegie Endowment for Internat Peace 1300 New York Ave NE Washington DC 20002-1621

BIRDSONG, CYNTHIA PRICE, artist, art educator; b. Charleston, W.Va., Feb. 12, 1954; d. Joe Wesley and Mildred Wilcher Price; m. John Michael Birdsong, Sept. 6, 1980; children: Michael Andrew, Joseph Edward. BS in Studio Art, Vanderbilt U., 1977; EdM in Gifted Edn., Belmont U., 2002. Art instr. Cheeckwood Art Camps, Nashville, 1994—2002; art instr. grades 4-12 Nashville Christian, 1996—98; art instr. St. Henry Sch., Nashville, 1998—2000; art specialist grades 10-12 Mid. Coll. H.S., Nashville, 2000—. Art tchr. Internat. Mission Bd., St. Lucia, West Indies, 2000; art cons. for Tenn. Crayol/Binney-Smith, Nashville, 2000—; adj. prof. Nashville C.C., 2002—; pvt. art instr., Nashville, 2003—; presenter in field. Mem. edn. curriculum bd. Cheekwood Bot. Gardens and Fine Arts Ctr., Nashville, 2000—; participating artist Kids On the Block, Nashville, 2000, 2003; participant Tenn. Arts Acad., Belmont U., 2003. Mem.: Tenn. Art Edn. Assn., Nat. Art Edn. Assn., Kappa Delta Pi (pres. 2001—03).

BIRDWELL, MICHELLE MARIE, music educator; b. Panama City, Fla., Nov. 22, 1974; d. Bennie Gene and Darlene Carroll Burdett; m. Jamie Birdwell, Apr. 5, 1997. MusB Edn., Troy State U., 1997, MS in Edn., 1998. Professional Teacher Certification State of Fla., 2001, State of Ala., 1998. Adminstrv. grad. asst. to dir. bands Troy (Ala.) State U. Sch. Music, 1997—98; elem. music tchr. Enterprise (Ala.) City Schs., 1999—2001; choir dir. Surfside Mid. Sch., Panama City Beach, Fla., 2001—02, dir. bands, 2002—. Musician: Southeast Alabama Community Band. Com. mem. quality stds.-baseddDesign SERVE R&D Project, Panama City, Fla., 2002—; host John Philip Sousa Nat. Jr. Honors Band. Chancellor's fellow, Troy State U., 1996—97. Mem.: Nat. Band Assn., So. Assn. Colls. and Schs. (mem. sch. leadership team surfside mid. sch.), NEA, Fla. Bandmasters Assn., Music Educators Nat. Conf., Women Band Dirs. Internat., Phi Kappa Phi. Avocations: performing, gardening, traveling, reading, walking. Office: Surfside Middle Sch Band 300 Nautilus St Panama City Beach FL 32413 E-mail: birdwmm@mail.bay.k12.fl.us.

BIRMINGHAM, PAT, pageant director; Founder, CEO, pres. Miss Tourism Internat. Beauty Pageant, Inc., Palm Beach, Fla. Office: Miss Tourism Internat Beauty Pageant Inc PO Box 2527 Palm Beach FL 33480

BIRNBAUM, S. ELIZABETH, lawyer; b. Ft. Belvoir, Va., Jan. 20, 1958; d. Myron Lionel and Emma Jane (Steiner) Birnbaum. AB, Brown U., 1979; JD, Harvard U., 1984. Bar: Colo. 1984, D.C. 1985, U.S. Dist. Ct. D.C. 1987, U.S. Ct. Appeals (D.C. cir.) 1988, U.S. Ct. Appeals (10th cir.) 1988, U.S. Ct. Appeals (4th cir.) 1990, U.S. Supreme Ct. 1990. Clk. to Justice Dubofsky Supreme Ct. Colo., Denver, 1984-85; assoc. Dickstein, Shapiro & Morin, Washington, 1985-87; counsel to water resources program Nat. Wildlife Fedn., Washington, 1987-91; counsel com. resources U.S. Ho. Reps., Washington, 1991-99; spl. asst. to solicitor U.S. Dept. of Interior, Washington, 1999-2000, assoc. solicitor for mineral resources, 2000-2001; dir. govt. affairs American Rivers, Washington, 2001—. Editor-in-chief Harvard Environ. Law Rev., 1984. Bd. trustees Amphibian Conservation Alliance, 1997-99; mem. Arlington Co. Environ. and Energy Conseration Commn., 2002—. Mem. Am. Water Resources Assn. (v.p. nat. capital sect. 1999-2000), D.C. Bar (steering com. 1994-97, sect. environment, energy and natural resource law). Office: 1025 Vermont Ave NW Ste 720 Washington DC 20005

BIRNBAUM, SHEILA L. lawyer, educator; b. 1940; BA, Hunter Coll., 1960, MA, 1962; LL.B., NYU, 1965. Bar: N.Y. 1965. Legal asst. Superior Ct., N.Y.C., 1965; assoc. Berman & Frost, N.Y.C., 1965-70, ptnr., 1970-72; prof. Fordham U., N.Y.C., 1972-78, NYU, N.Y.C., 1978-86, assoc. dean, 1982-84; ptnr. Skadden, Arps, Slate, Meagher & Flom, N.Y.C., 1984—. Adj. prof. law NYU Sch. Law, 1984—; exec. dir. Second Cir. Task Force for Racial, Ethnic and Gender Fairness, 1994—97; mem. jud. conf. adv. com. on rules and civil procedure U.S. Supreme Ct., 1997—; chair, Commn. Fiduciary Appointments N.Y. State Court System, 2000; lectr. in field. Author: (with Rheingold) Products Liability, Law, Practice Science, 1974; co-author: Practitioner's Guide to Litigating Insurance Coverage Actions; columnist N.Y. Law Jour., Nat. Law Jour.; contbr. articles to profl. jours. Named one of 50 Most Powerful Women in Am. Bus., Fortune Mag., 100 Most Outstanding Members of the Legal Profession, Nat. Law Jour., 75 Most Influential Women in Bus., Crain's N.Y. Bus.; named to, Hunter Coll. Hall of Fame; recipient John J. McCloy Meml. award, Fund for Modern Courts, 2003, Florence E. Allen award, NYU Sch. Law and N.Y. Women's Bar Assn., Louis D. Brandeis award, Am. Jewish Congress. Mem. N.Y.C. Bar Assn. (mem. exec. com. 1978—, jud. com. 1977), ABA (chmn. product gen. liability, consumer land coms.), Assn. of Bar of City of N.Y. (exec. com. 1978—, 2d century com. 1981-86), Phi Beta Kappa, Phi Alpha Theta, Alpha Chi Alpha. Office: Skadden Arps Slate Meagher & Flom 4 Times Sq Fl 24 New York NY 10036-6595 E-mail: sbirnbau@skadden.com.

BIRO, KATHY, advertising executive; BS in English Edn., NYU, 1973, MA in Ednl. Adminstrn., 1975; MBA in Mktg. and Fin., Columbia U., 1979. Product devel. mgr. Card Products Divsn. Citicorp, N.Y.C., 1979-81; v.p. Mktg. and Sales, Electronic Banking Chase Manhattan Bank1, N.Y.C., 1981-86; 1st v.p. Nat. Mktg.; dir. Credit Resources Shearson Lehman Hutton, N.Y.C., 1986-89; ptnr. Bank St. Consulting Group, N.Y.C., 1989-90; sr. v.p. Mktg. and Product Mgmt., Global Info. Bankers Trust, N.Y.C., 1990-91; sr. v.p. Mktg. Bronner Slosberg Humphrey, N.Y.C., 1991-99, also bd. dirs., 1991-99; founder, pres. and CEO Strategic Interactive Group, 1995-99; vice chmn., pres. Digitas, 1999—. Office: Digitas 800 Boylston St Prudential Tower Boston MA 02199

BIRON, CHRISTINE ANNE, medical science educator, researcher; b. Woonsocket, R.I., Aug. 8, 1951; d. R. Bernard and Theresa Priscilla (Sauvageau) B. BS, U. Mass., 1973; PhD, U. N.C., 1980. Rsch. technician U. Mass., Amherst, 1973-75; grad. researcher U. N.C., Chapel Hill, 1975-80; postdoctoral fellow Scripps Clinic and Rsch., La Jolla, Calif., 1980; fellow U. Mass. Med. Sch., Worcester, 1981-82, instr., 1983, asst. prof., 1984-87; vis. scientist Karolinska Inst., Stockholm, 1984; asst. prof. Sch. Medicine Brown U., Providence, 1988-90, assoc. prof., 1990-96, prof., 1996—, Esther Elizabeth Brintzenhoff prof., 1996—, chair Dept. Molecular Microbiology & Immunology, 1999—, dir. grad. program in pathobiology, 1995-99. Mem. AIDS and related rsch. study sect. 3 NIH, 1991-93; mem. exptl. immunology study sect. NIH, 1993-97, immunology working group sci. rev. Assoc. editor Jour. Immunology, 1990—94, 2000, bd. editors: Procs. of Soc. for Exptl. Biology and Medicine, 1993—99, sect. editor: Jour. Immunology, 1995—99; editor: Jour. Nat. Immunity, 1994—98, Jour. Leukocyte Biology, 1999—2000; mem. editl. bd.: Virology, 2001—03; contbr. articles, revs. to sci. jours.; mem. adv. bd. editors: Jour. Exptl. Medicine, 2002—. Leukemia Soc. Am. fellow, 1981, Spl. fellow, 1983, scholar, 1987; grantee NIH, 1985—; rsch. grantee MacArthur Found., 1991-96. Fellow AAAS (scholar 2002—); mem. Am. Assn. Immunologists (co-chmn. symposium 1990, 94, 95, 96, 98, 99), Am. Soc. Virology, Am. Assn. Immunology (block co-chair nat. meetings 1996-99, program com. 1998-2000), Soc. Natural Immunity (co-chair program for 2001 meeting), Sigma Xi. Office: Brown U PO Box G-B618 Providence RI 02912-0001

BIRSTEIN, ANN, writer, educator; b. N.Y.C., May 27, 1927; d. Bernard and Clara (Gordon) B.; m. Alfred Kazin, June 26, 1952 (div. 1982); 1 child, Cathrael. BA, Queens Coll., 1948. Lectr. The New Sch. Queens Coll., N.Y.C., 1953-54; writer-in-residence CCNY, 1960; lectr. The Writers Workshop, Iowa City, 1966, 72; lectr. Sch. Gen. Studies Columbia U., N.Y.C., 1985-87; dir., founder Writers on Writing Barnard Coll., N.Y.C., 1988—. Adj. prof. English Hofstra U., L.I., 1980, Barnard Coll., N.Y.C., 1981-93; film critic Vogue mag. Author: Star of Glass, 1950, The Troublemaker, 1955, The Sweet Birds of Gorham, 1966, Summer Situations, 1972, Dickie's List, 1973, American Children, 1980, The Rabbi on Forty-Seventh Street, 1982, The Last of the True Believers, 1988, What I Saw at the Fair, 2003; co-editor: The Works of Anne Frank; contbr. articles to numerous mags. Nat. Endowment of Arts grantee, 1983; Fulbright fellow, 1951-52. Mem. PEN (former mem. exec. bd., former chair admissions com.), Authors Guild (former mem. coun.), Phi Beta Kappa (hon.). Democrat. Jewish. Home: 1623 3rd Ave # 27jw New York NY 10128-3638 Office Phone: 212-289-0346. Personal E-mail: abirstein@aol.com.

BISBEE, JOYCE EVELYN, utility company manager, retired; b. Portage, Wis., May 15, 1941; d. Orris Dean and Helen Paulina (Golz) B. BS, U. Wis., Stout, 1963; MEd, U. N.C., 1971. Cert. family and consumer sci. Ext. home economist U. Wis., Racine, 1964-68; tchr., dept. chair Oshkosh (Wis.) Pub. Schs., 1963-64, 68-74; mgr. ednl. rels. J.C. Penney, N.Y.C., 1974-78; v.p. Creamer Dickson Basford, PR, N.Y.C., 1978-81; consumer affairs rep. Bklyn. Union, Bklyn., 1983-85, consumer advocate, 1986-92, mgr. consumer outreach and edn., 1992-98; dir. consumer comm. and advocacy KeySpan Corp., Bklyn., 1998—2003; ret., 2004. Mem. consumer affairs com. Bar Assn. City N.Y., 1993-98. Mem. adv. com. N.Y.C. 4-H Youth Program, 1985-96; active East 60s Neighborhood Assn., N.Y.C., 1993—. Recipient Alumni Disting. Svc. award U. Wis.-Stout, 1978. Lutheran. Avocations: craft shows, cultural performances, cats, travel. Home: 245 E 63rd St New York NY 10021-7456

BISCEVIC, NANCY LUNSFORD, photographer; b. Cin., Jan. 9, 1937; d. Carlton A. and Lucille P. Lunsford; m. Kamilo R. Biscevic, Aug. 3, 1963 (div. 1981); children: Carlton, Richard, John, Camilla. BAA, U. Cin., 1958. Illustrator GE Co., Cin., 1958-65; tech. illustrator ATE Assocs. Inc., Alameda, Calif., 1981-82, data dept. mgr., 1982-88; desktop publ. supr. Fed. Res. Bank of San Francisco, 1988-89, office adminstr., 1989-95; owner NancyB...Cards, Vacaville, Calif., 1995—. Organist, choir dir. St. Margaret Mary's Ch., Oakland, Calif., 1977-87. Recipient awards Alameda Photographic Soc., No. Calif. Camera Club Coun., Photographers Forum. Mem. Alameda Photographic Soc., Delta Delta Delta (pres. alumnae chpt. 1961-63). Avocations: photography, walking, piano, drawing. Office: PO Box 483 Vacaville CA 95696-0483 Home: 1300 Burton Dr Apt 130 Vacaville CA 95687-3529

BISCHEL, MARGARET DEMERITT, physician, managed care consultant; b. Moorhead, Minn., Nov. 8, 1933; d. Connie Magnus Nystrom and Harriett Grace (Petersen) Zorner; m. Raymon DeMeritt, 1953 (div. 1958); 1 child, Gregory Raymon; m. John Bischel, 1961 (div. 1964); m. Kenneth Dean Serkes, June 7, 1974. BS, U. Oreg., Eugene, 1962; MD, U. Oreg., Portland, 1965. Diplomate Am. Bd. Internal Medicine, Nat. Bd. Med. Examiners. Resident, straight med. intern Los Angeles County/U. So. Calif. Med. Ctr., 1965-68, NIH fellow nephrology, 1968-70, asst. prof. renal medicine, 1970-74; asst. prof., instr. medicine U. So. Calif., 1968-74; instr. nephrology East L.A. City Coll., 1971-74; dir. med. edn. Luth. Gen. Hosp., Park Ridge, Ill., 1974-78, dir. nephrology sect., 1977-80, pres. med. staff, 1974-88; founding mem., med. dir., dir. med. svcs. Luth. Health Plan, Park Ridge, 1983-87; clin. assoc. prof. medicine Abraham Lincoln Sch. Medicine U. Ill., 1975-80; sr. cons. Parkside Assocs., Inc., Park Ridge, 1986-88; pvt. practice Chgo., 1974-88; physician Buenaventura Med. Clinic, Ventura, Calif., 1989-94, med. dir., 1992-94; prin. Apollo Managed Care Cons., Santa Barbara, Calif., 1988—. Trustee Luth. Health Care System, Park Ridge, 1986-90, Unified Med. Group Assn., Seal Beach, Calif., 1993-94; hon. lifetime staff mem. Luth. Gen. Hosp., Park Ridge; mem. formulary com. HealthNet, 1992-94, med. adv. com. TakeCare, 1993-94, quality assurance com. PacifiCare, 1993-94; mem. doctor's adv. network AMA, 1994-96; JCAHO advisor for behavioral health care providers. Mem. editl. adv. bd. Capitation Mgmt. Report; author 35 texts including Medical Review Criteria Guidelines for Managed Care, 2d edit., 2002, Managing Behavioral Healthcare, 2001, The Credentialing and Privileges Manual, 2001; contbr. articles to profl. jours., chpts. to books; editor: Med. Mgmt. Manual, Managed Care Bull. Fellow: ACP (Calif. Gov.'s advisor 1993—95); mem.: Am. Coll. Physician Execs. Avocations: real estate, gardening. Office: Apollo Managed Care Cons 860 Ladera Ln Santa Barbara CA 93108-1626 Office Phone: 805-969-2606. E-mail: mbischel@cox.net.

BISCHOFF, SUSAN ANN, newspaper editor; b. Indpls, July 31, 1951; d. Thomas Anthony and Betty Jean (Coons) Bischoff; m. Jim B. Barlow, June 20, 1975; 1 child, Samantha Lynn Barlow Martinez. BA, Ind. U., 1973.

Rschr., reporter Congl. Quar., Washington, 1973-74; city desk reporter Houston Chronicle, 1974-75, bus. reporter, 1975-79, asst. bus. editor, 1979-84, bus. editor, 1984-86, asst. mng. editor, 1986-2000, dep. mng. editor, 2000—03, assoc. editor, 2003—. Houston corr. Kiplinger, Tex. Letter, Washington, 1980-85. Mem. class policy Leadership Houston, 1992—94; mem. exec. com. Gulf Coast affiliate United Way, 1994—2002; bd. dirs. Houston Chronicle Employees Fed. Credit Union, 1980—87, San Jacinto Coun. Girl Scouts US, 1997—2003, Child Adv., US Olympic Festival VII, Houston, 1985—86, Gulf Coast Mar. of Dimes Birth Defects Found., 1989—2001, YES Coll. Prep. Sch., 1999—2002, AIDS Found., Houston, 2002—; founding bd. dir. Greater Houston Women's Found.; mem. bd. visitors Anderson Cancer Ctr. U. Tex. Named Outstanding Woman in Houston Journalism, YWCA, 1989, Fabulous Femme, Greater Houston Women's Found., 1994, Woman of Distinction, Crohn's & Colitis Found., 1996; recipient Outstanding Vol. Achievement award, Gulf Coast United Way, 1995, Outstanding Media award, Nat. Soc. Fund Raising Execs., 1997, Nat. Thanks award, San Jacinto Girl Scouts, 2001, Mayborn award, Cmty. Leadership Tex. Daily Newspaper Assn., 2001, honoree, Jewish Cmty. Ctr. of Houston Children's Scholarship Ball, 2002, Strong, Smart and Bold award, Houston Girls, Inc., 2003, Pulitzer prizes in journalism. Mem.: Am. Assn. Sunday and Feature Editors (named to Features Hall of Fame 2003), Am. Soc. Newspaper Editors (dir., juror 2004), Press Club of Houston Ednl. Found. (founding bd. dir.). Home: 2929 Buffalo Speedway # 112 Houston TX 77098 Office: Houston Chronicle 801 Texas St Houston TX 77002-2996 Office Phone: 713-362-7375. E-mail: susan.bischoff@chron.com.

BISCHOFF, THERESA A. not-for-profit association administrator, former medical center executive; b. Rockville Center, N.Y., Nov. 6, 1953; d. Robert and Collette (Burke) Peters; m. Paul Bischoff, May 19, 1984; 1 child, Craig. BS in Acctg. cum laude, U. Conn., 1975; MBA, NYU, 1991. Auditor Arthur Andersen, Stamford, Conn., 1975-79; mgr. corp. acctg. Great No. Nekoosa, Stamford, Conn., 1979-81; mgr. external reporting Squibb Corp., Princeton, N.J., 1981-83, dir. acctg. practices, 1981-84; sr. dir. acctg. svcs. NYU Med. Ctr., 1984-87, v.p. finance, 1987-93; clin. prof. health care mgmt. NYU Sch. Medicine, 1993—; dep. provost, exec. v.p. NYU Med. Ctr., 1993—98, pres., 1998—2003; CEO ARC in Greater NY, NYC, 2004—. Bd. dirs. First Option Health Plan of N.Y., Combined Coord. Coun., 1984—, VHA-Metro N.Y., 1993—; mem. curriculum rev. com. Robert F. Wagner Grad. Sch. Pub. Svc., NYU, 1993-94; mem. beneficiary hosp. adv. com. United Hosp. Fund, 1994—; mem. adminstrv. bd. Coun. of Teaching Hosps., 1995—. Mem. AAMC (mem. group instnl. planning 1989-93, group on bus. affairs 1984-94, mem. project subcom. publishing: Space Planning and Mgmt. in Acad. Med. Ctrs. 1991, north-east regional sec.-treas. 1994), Greater N.Y. Hosp. Assn. (mem. bd. dirs. 1994—, mem. fiscal policy com. 1987-93, mem. health care exec. forum 1987—, sec. 1990-92), Hosp. Fin. Mgmt. Assn., Hosp. Assn. N.Y. State (trustee 1994). Office: ARC in Greater NY 150 Amsterdam Ave New York NY 10023*

BISCONTI, ANN STOUFFER, public opinion research company executive; b. Chgo., Nov. 22, 1940; d. Samuel Andrew Stouffer and Ruth Rachel McBurney; m. Raffaele Ludovico Bisconti (dec. Oct. 19, 1999); children: Alessandra Ilus Wilkes, Giulia Rachel; m. Charles William Dyke, Oct. 13, 2002. Student, Harvard U., 1958—60; BA with honors, McGill U., 1962; PhD, The Union Inst., Cin., 1978. Assoc. study dir. Nat. Commn. on Allied [illegible], Washington, 1977—79; dir. Washington office Higher Edn. Rsch. Inst., 1979—80; ptnr. Human Resources Policy Corp., Washington, 1980; dir. Nat. Ctr. for Allied Health Leadership, Washington, 1981—83; v.p. rsch. Nuc. Energy Inst., Washington, 1983—96; pres. Bisconti Rsch., Inc., Washington, 1996—. Mem. adv. com., risk comm. program EPA, Washington, 1988; advisor tech. cooperation program in Malaysia IAEA, Vienna, 1990; mem. adv. com., risk comm. Orgn. for Econ. Cooperation and Devel., Paris, 1991. Author: College and Other Stepping Stones, 1980; co-author: Higher Education and the Disadvantaged Student, 1972, The Power of Protest, 1975, College as a Training Ground for Jobs, 1977. Pres. Congl. Award Coun., 8th Congl. Dist., Md., 1990—93; advisor long-range planning com. Town of Somerset, Chevy Chase, Md., 2002; career advisor Harvard U., Cambridge, 1996; rsch. advisor NASA Alumni League, Washington, 1998. Recipient Disting. Svc. Award, Am. Soc. Allied Health Professions (now Assn. Schs. Allied Health Profls.), 1983. Mem.: World Assn. Pub. Opinion Rsch., Am. Nuc. Soc. (bd. dirs. 1993—96, Best Paper award 1989, Outstanding Session award 1990, 1992), Am. Assn. Pub. Opinion Rsch. Avocations: geography/travel, foreign languages, gardening.

BISH, DEBORAH F. music educator; b. Meriden, Conn., Oct. 5, 1971; d. Robert Joseph and Brenda Faye Bish. MusB in Clarinet Performance, Fla. State U., 1993; MusM in Clarinet Performance, Ariz. State U., 1998, DMA in Clarinet Performance, 2004. Instr. of clarinet Henderson State U., Arkadelphia, Ark., 1999—2001; asst. prof. of clarinet Fla. State U., Tallahassee, 2001—; 2d clarinet Tallahassee Symphony Orch., Tallahassee, 2001—. Mem.: Music Tchrs. Nat. Assn., Internat. Clarinet Assn., Pi Kappa Lambda, Phi Kappa Phi, Sigma Alpha Iota. Office: Fla State U School of Music Tallahassee FL 32306-1180 E-mail: dbish@mailer.fsu.edu.

BISH, MELODY ANN, public administration professional; b. Kittaning, Pa., Nov. 26, 1964; d. Robert E. and Shirley J. (Campbell) B. BA, U. Pitts., 1986, MA, 1993. Legal asst. Wilder & Mahood, P.C., Pitts., 1987-89; dir. applicant rels. U. Pitts., 1989-94; pub. rels. mgr. Ebony Bull Capital Corp., Pitts., 1994-96; office adminstr. Abes-Baumann, P.C., Pitts., 1996—. Vol. Clinton-Gore '92, Pitts., 1992. Mem. NAFE, Am. Mgmt. Assn., Pa. Assn. Notaries, Pitts. Legal Adminstrs. Assn., Assn. Legal Adminstrs., Phi Alpha Theta. Presbyterian. Avocations: reading, civil war history. Office: Abes-Baumann PC 810 Penn Ave Ste 5 Pittsburgh PA 15222-3614 Home: 3 Oak Hollow Ln Sicklerville NJ 08081-3908

BISHOP, C. DIANE, state agency administrator, educator; b. Elmhurst, Ill., Nov. 23, 1943; d. Louis William and Constance Oleta (Mears) B. BS in Maths., U. Ariz., 1965, MS in Maths., MEd in Secondary Edn., 1972. Lic. secondary educator. Tchr. math. Tucson Unified Sch. Dist., 1966-86, mem. curriculum council, 1985-86, mem. maths. curriculum task teams, 1983-86; state supt. of pub. instrn. State of Ariz., 1987-95, gov.'s policy advisor for edn., 1995-97, dir. gov.'s office workforce devel. policy, 1996-2000; asst. dep. dir. Ariz. Dept. Commerce, 1997-2000; exec. dir. Gov.'s Strategic Partnership for Econ. Devel., 1997—2002; pres. The Vandegrift Inst., 2000—; exec. dir. Maricopa Health Found., 2002—. Mem. assoc. faculty Pima C.C., Tucson, 1974-84; adj. lectr. U. Ariz., 1983, 85; mem. math. scis. edn. bd. NRC, 1987-90, mem. new standards project governing bd., 1991; dir. adv. bd. sci. and engring. ednl. panel, NSF; mem. adv. bd. for arts edn. Nat. Endowment for Arts. Active Ariz. State Bd. Edn., 1984-95, chmn. quality edn. commn., 1986-87, chmn. tchr. crt. subcom., 1984-95, mem. outcomes based edn. adv. com., 1986-87, liaison bd. dirs. essential skills subcom., 1985-87, gifted edn. com. liaison, 1985-87; mem. Ariz. State Bd. Regents, 1987-95, mem. com. on preparing for U. Ariz., 1983, mem. high sch. task force, 1984-85; mem. bd. Ariz. State Community Coll., 1987-95; mem. Ariz. Joint Legis. Com. on Revenues and Expenditures, 1989, Ariz. Joint Legis. Com. on Goals for Ednl. Excellence, 1987-89, Gov.'s Task Force on Ednl. Reform, 1991, Ariz. Bd. Regents Commn. on Higher Edn., 1992. Woodrow Wilson fellow Princeton U., summer 1984; recipient Presdl. Award for Excellence in Teaching of Maths., 1983, Ariz. Citation of Merit, 1984, Maths. Teaching award Nat. Sci. Research Soc., 1984, Distinction in Edn. award Flinn Found., 1986; named Maths. Tchr. of Yr. Ariz. Council of Engring. and Sci. Assns., 1984, named One of Top Ten Most Influential Persons in Ariz. in Field of Tech., 1998. Mem. AAUW, NEA, Nat. Coun. Tchrs. Math., Coun. Chief State Sch. Officers, Women Execs. in State Govt. (bd. dirs. 1993), Ariz. Assn. Tchrs. Math., Women Maths. Edn., Math. Assn. Am., Ednl. Commn. of the States (steering com.), Nat. Endowment Arts (adv. bd. for arts edn.), Nat. Forum Excellence Edn., Nat. Honors Workshop, Phi Delta Kappa. Republican.

BISHOP, CAROLE C. elementary education educator, family therapist; b. LA, Feb. 3, 1933; d. Beverley Marshall and Marjorie (Fitch) Caister; m. David Burleson Bishop, June 16, 1956; 1 chld, Dale Brian. BS, U. So. Calif., 1955; MS, Azusa Pacific Coll., 1973. Cert. marriage and family therapist. Tchr. 3d grade Covina Unified Sch. Dist., Calif., 1955-57; tchr. 4th grade La Can. Unified Sch. Dist., La Can.-Flintridge, Calif., 1957-58, substitute tchr., 1960-66, 2000, 01, tchr. 2d and 3d grades, 1966-67, tchr. 4th grade, 1967-71, tchr. 5th and 6th grades, 1971-79, tchr. 5th grade, 1979-2000. Author: Bishop Speller, 1971. Recipient Founders Day award La Canada-Flintridge PTA, 1973, 93; honored by placement of brick at the Medal of Honor Grove, Valley Forge by Freedoms Found. Mem. Nat. Sci. Tchr. Assn., La Canada Tchr. Assn. (sec., Tchr. of Yr. 1987), Am. Assn. Marriage and Family Therapists, Am. Assn. Physics Tchr., Delta Kappa Gamma (corr. sec.). Avocations: hiking, travel, reading, cooking. Home: South Pasadena CA

BISHOP, CAROLYN BENKERT, public relations counselor; b. Monroe, Wis., Aug. 28, 1939; d. Arthur C. and Delphine (Heston) Benkert; m. Lloyd F. Bishop, June 15, 1963. BS, U. Wis., 1961; grad., Tobe-Coburn Sch., N.Y.C., 1962. Merchandising editor Co-Ed Mag., N.Y.C., 1962-63; advt. copywriter Woodward & Lothrop, Washington, 1963-65; home furnishings editor Co-Ed Mag., N.Y.C., 1965-68; editor Budget Decorating Mag., N.Y.C., 1968-69; home furnishings editor Family Cir. Mag., N.Y.C., 1969-75; v.p., pub., editorial dir. Scholastic, Inc., N.Y.C., 1975-80; owner Mesa Store Home Furnishings Co., Aspen, Colo., 1980-83; dir. pub. rels. Snowmass Resort Assn., Snowmass Village, Colo., 1983-86; pres. Bishop & Bishop Mktg. Comm., Aspen, 1986-93, Monroe, 1993-99; acct. supr. Hiebing Group, 1999—. Mem. media rels. com. Colo. Tourism Bd., Denver, 1987-90. Author: 25 Decorating Ideas Under $100, 1969; editor: Family Circle Special Home Decorating Guide, 1973. Bd. dirs. Aspen Camp Sch. for the Deaf, 1987-90. Recipient Dallas Market Editorial award Dallas Market Ctr., 1973, Dorothy Dawe award Chgo. Furniture Market, 1973, Guardian of Freedom award, Anti-Defamation League Appeal, 1974. Mem. Rocky Mountain Pub. Rels. Group (chmn. 1991-93), Pub. Rels. Soc. Am. (accredited, small firms co-chair counselors acad. 1992-93), Aspen Writers' Found. (bd. dirs. 1991-93), Tobe-Coburn Alumni Assn., U. Wis. Alumni Assn. Democrat. Office: The Hiebing Group 315 Wisconsin Ave Madison WI 53703-4102

BISHOP, CLAIRE DEARMENT, small business owner, former librarian; b. Youngstown, Ohio, Oct. 12, 1937; d. Eugene Howard and Ruth (Bright) DeArment; m. Carl R. Meinstereifel, 1956 (div. 1964; children: Paul, Dawn; m. Olin Jerry Dewberry, Jr., 1974 (div. 1979); m. J. Bruce Bishop, May 6, 1992. BS, Clarion State U., 1967; MLS, Ga. State U., 1977. Cert. libr. media specialist, Ga. Libr. Henry County, Stockbridge, Ga., 1967-69; head libr. Russell H.S., East Point, Ga., 1969-84, engring. libr. Rockwell Internat., Duluth, Ga., 1984-88; rep. Govt. Industry Data Exch. Program, Corona, Calif., 1984-88; libr. Raytheon Co., 1990, Missile Sys. Divsn., Bristol, Tenn., 1988-90; owner, mgr. Claire's Collectibles, rubber stamp store, St. Augustine, Fla. Author newsletter Grin and Stamp It. Sec. San Marco Avenue Mchts. Assn. Mem. St. Augustine IBM Users Group (sec.), Six-Ninety-Six Investment Club (fin. officer), Mensa. Democrat. Avocations: computers, writing, information broker. Office: Claire's Collectibles 78 San Marco Ave Saint Augustine FL 32084-3250 Office Phone: 904-829-1122.

BISHOP, DELORES ANN, artist, educator; b. Balt., May 27, 1946; d. Edward James Boyle, Sr. and Norma Delores Boyle; m. John James Bishop, Jr.; children: Denise Anderson, Christine. Grad. h.s., Balt. Elite, one stroke cert. instr., cert. William Alexander instr., Jenkins, cert. instr. art. Fgn. lang. lab. asst. Baltimore County Md. Pub. Schs., Balt., 1964—71; asst. mgr. Ben Franklin Crafts, Cockeysville, Md., 1982—99; freelance decorative artist Balt., 1999—2001. Program mgr. Premises Providers, Inc (Arundel Mills Mall), Hanover, Md., 2000. Painted sculpture, The Shopper, 2000, Bushel of Crabs, 2000, Bass, 2000. Holiday vol. Cowenton Vol. Fire Dept. Sta. 200, Balt., 2000—01; Vol., asst. leader Girl Scouts Am., Balt., 1960—80. Mem.: Md. Art League, Inc., Balt. (Md.) Watercolor Soc., Decorative Painters Soc. Personal E-mail: dabishop@dabitup.com.

BISHOP, FAIRA LEE, library educator; b. Hinds County, Miss., Dec. 15, 1942; d. Ansel Bruce and Dora Alma (Langley) Lee; m. Billy M. Bishop, July 11, 1965. BA with distinction, Miss. Coll., 1964; MLS, U. Miss., 1972; PhD, U. So. Miss., 1989. Cert. tchr., sch., libr., sch. adminstr., Miss. Tchr. secondary English pub. schs., Greenville and Jackson, Miss., 1964-68; acad. libr. Miss. Delta C.C., Moorhead, 1969-71; tchr. Latin and English pub. sch., Oxford, Miss., 1971-73; libr. ssecondary and elem. schs., Clinton, Miss., 1977-94; instr. U. So. Miss. Sch. Libr. and Info. Sci., Hattiesburg, 1990—96, asst. prof., 1996—98. Trustee Clinton Libr., 1976. Mem. AAUW (treas. 1996-97), Miss. Libr. Assn. (ad hoc com. 1984-85), U. Miss. Med. Ctr. Women's Club (rec. sec. 1995-96), Friends Rowland Med. Libr., U. Miss. Alumni Assn., Maids and Matrons Club (v.p. 1996-98), Jackson Symphony League, Phi Kappa Phi, Beta Phi Mu, Phi Delta Kappa. Baptist. Avocations: reading, travel, volunteering. Home: 342 Woodlands Dr Brandon MS 39047-8187

BISHOP, JENNIFER ANN, photographer; b. Cleve., May 1, 1957; d. Warner Bader Bishop and Katharine Sue (White) McLennan; m. Daniel Mark Epstein, Dec. 20, 1994; 1 child, Theodore John Epstein and Nathaniel David Epstein. BA, Johns Hopkins U., 1979. Staff photographer The Balt. News Am., 1980-81; freelance photographer, 1981—. Contbg. photographer City Paper, Balt., 1977-94; mem. Actuality Picture Agy., N.Y.C., 1992—; workshop tchr. Internat. Ctr. for Photography, N.Y.C., 1993-95. Recipient 3 City Arts grants Balt. City Arts Coun., 1987, 89, 91, 2 Photography fellowship grants Md. State Arts Coun., 1989, 93, award of excellence Soc. Publ. Designers, 1990, 96, award of excellence Comm. Arts mag., 1991, Cert. of Excellence award 11th Annual Am. Photography Competition, 1995. Office: 843 W University Pkwy Baltimore MD 21210-2911

BISHOP, KATHRYN ELIZABETH, film company executive, writer; b. Seattle, July 7, 1945; d. Wesley Thomas Bishop and Muriel (Robert) Leisher; divorced; 1 child, Zachary. BA, Wartburg Coll., 1966. Voice over talent Chgo. Bd. Edn. Radio Network, 1960-62; prodn. asst. Sta. CBS-TV, WBBM-TV, Chgo., 1961-63; disk jockey, engr., writer Sta. KWAR-FM, Waverly, Iowa, 1964-65; assoc. producer Bing Crosby Prodns. Inc., Chgo., 1966-69; producer Sedelmaier Films, Chgo., 1969-73; v.p., head prodn. Wakeford/Orloff Inc., L.A., 1977-78; founder, owner Stiles-Bishop Prodns. Inc., L.A., 1974—; co-founder, exec. prodr. The Colman Group Inc., L.A., 1982-87; co-founder, co-owner Rapport Films, Inc., Hollywood, Calif., 1987-92; feature film prodr., 1992—. Co-author: (screenplay) Millionaire's Club; screenwriter: Cinnamon Bear. Mem. TV Acad. Arts and Scis., Dirs. Guild Am. Avocations: pottery, sailing, skiing. Office: Stiles-Bishop Prodns Inc 12652 Killion St Valley Village CA 91607-1535 E-mail: kbishop@simple.net.

BISHOP, LOUISE WILLIAMS, state legislator; b. Cairo, Ga., June 27, 1933; d. Elijah and Sarah (Hines) Williams; m. James Alburn Bishop (div.); children: Todd James, Tabb Jody, Tamika Joy, James Alburn Jr. B in Communications and Radio Broadcasting, Am. Found. Dramatic Arts. Ordained min. Baptist Evangelist Ch., 1978. With Sta. WHAT; program host Sta. WDAS; mem. Pa. Ho. of Reps., Harrisburg, 1988—. Recipient numerous awards including Richard Allen award African Meth. Episc.Ch., Community Svc. award Missionary Baptist Pastors Conf., Outstanding Citizen award Phila. Mayor's Coun. on Youth Opportunity. Mem. Pa. Legis. Black Caucus (sec.), NAACP, Nat. Assn. Women Legislators, Nat. Polit. Congress Black Women, Nat. Assn. Women's Clergy, Bapt. Min.'s Conf., Afro-Am. Hist. and Cultural Mus. Democrat. Home: 2460 N 59th St Philadelphia PA 19131-1208 Office: 100 South St Ofc Harrisburg PA 17101-1210

BISHOP, RUTH ANN, coloratura soprano, voice educator; b. Homewood, Ill., Feb. 21, 1942; d. George Bernard and Grace Mildred (Hoke) Riddle; m. John Allen Reinhardt, June 9, 1962 (div. 1975); children: Laura, Jonathon; m. Merrill Edward Bishop, Aug. 16, 1975; stepchildren: Mark, Lynn. BS in Music Edn., U. Ill., 1962; M of Music in Voice, Cath. U. Am., 1972; postgrad., U. Md., 1975. Music tchr. Prince Georges County (Md.) Schs., 1963-71, Yamaha Music Co., College Park, Md., 1971-73; voice tchr. Prince Georges Community Coll., Largo, Md., 1972-75, U. Md., College Park, 1975; profl. lectr. voice Chgo. Mus. Coll. Roosevelt U., 1977-82; tchr. voice McHenry County Coll., Crystal Lake, Ill., 1978-97; instr. voice Elgin (Ill.) C.C., 1981-97; pvt. voice tchr. Crystal Lake, 1975-97, Charlottesville, Va., 1997—; tchr. chorus, music and drama Burley Mid. Sch., Charlottesville, Va., 1997; asst. prof. music Piedmont Va. C.C., 1998—. Dir. music Epworth United Meth. Ch., Elgin, 1984-86, Cherub choir 1st Congl. Ch., Crystal Lake, 1986-88; mem. Camerata Singers, Lake Forest, 1988, Arts Chorale of Elgin Choral Union; performer, vocal dir. Woodstock (Ill.) Mus. Theatre Co., 1983-97; soprano soloist Internat. Band Festival, Besana Brianza, Italy, 1993; pvt. voice tchr., Charlottesville, Va., 1997—. Soprano soloist, Oratorio- The Psalms of David, 1986, opera, The Light of the Eye, 1985-86, Children's Day at the Opera, Washington, 1972, U.S. Navy Band, The White House, 1969; soloist with Crystal Lake Cmty. Choir and Band, 1987-97, 1st Congl. Ch., 1975-97, also others; performer Heritage Repertory Theatre, Charlottesville, Va., 1998, 99. Bd. mem. Opera Soc. Charlottesville, 1998-2000. Ill. State scholar, 1959. Mem. Nat. Assn. Tchrs. Singing (chpt. rec. sec. 1984-86, bd. mem. Chgo. chpt. 1995-97), Music Tchrs. Nat. Assn., Sigma Alpha Iota, Pi Kappa Lambda, Kappa Delta. Methodist. Avocations: travel, camping, hiking, bicycling, wildlife. Home: 1363 Wimbledon Way Charlottesville VA 22901-0635 E-mail: rambishop@aol.com.

BISHOP, RUTH FRANCES, microbiologist, research scientist, educator; b. Melbourne, Victoria, Australia, May 12, 1933; d. Percival Charles William and Una Frances Armitage (Wilson) Langford; m. Geoffrey James Bishop, Dec. 8, 1956; children: Thomas Geoffrey, Anne Frances, Michael William. BSc, U. Melbourne, 1954, MSc, 1958, PhD, 1961, DSc, 1978. Rsch. fellow U. Liverpool, Eng., 1962-65, Royal Children's Hosp. Rsch. Found., Melbourne, 1968-74, CEO, 1990-91; rsch. fellow Nat. Health and Med. Rsch. Coun., Australia, 1975-79, prin. rsch. fellow, 1980-91, sr. prin. rsch. fellow, 1992-98, Murdoch Childrens Rsch. Inst., Melbourne, 1999—; profl. assoc. U. Melbourne, 1990-94, prof., 1995—. Dir. Australian Med. Rsch. and Devel. Co., Melbourne, 1991-92; mem. regional grants interview com. Nat. Health and Med. Rsch. Coun., Australia, 1991—; cons. WHO, Geneva, 1983—. Editorial bd. Revs. Infectious Diseases, 1989-99; contbr. articles to profl. jours., chpts. to books. Chmn. assocs. spl. activities 8th Asian Conf. ObGyn, Melbourne, 1979-81. Decorated officer Order of Australia. Fellow Australian Soc. Microbiology; mem. Am. Soc. Microbiology, Am. Soc. Virology, Pediat. Rsch. Soc. Australia (pres. 1972), Australian Soc. Med. Rsch., Australian Soc. Infectious Diseases, Nat. Assn. Rsch. Fellows Nat. Health and Med. Rsch. Coun. (sec. 1991-93). Avocations: reading, opera, tennis, gardening. Office: Royal Childrens Hosp Flemington Rd Dept Gastroenterology Melbourne VIC 3052 Australia Business E-Mail: r.bishop@mcri.edu.au.

BISHOP, SUE MARQUIS (INA SUE MARQUIS BISHOP), dean, psychiatric and mental health nurse educator, researcher; b. Charleston, W.Va., Sept. 30, 1939; d. Harold Edwin and Ina Mabel (Walkup) Marquis; m. Randal Young Bishop, Feb. 27, 1960: children: Jon Marquis, Heather Suzanne. RN, Norton Infirmary Sch. Nursing, 1960; BSN, Murray State U., 1963; MSN, Ind. U., 1967, PhD, 1983. RN, Ky., Ind., Fla., N.C. Ind. staff nurse psychiatry Norton Infirmary, Louisville, 1960-61; head nurse obstetrics, nursing supr. Murray (Ky.) Gen. Hosp., 1961-62; primary care nurse, crisis counselor infirmary Murray State U., 1962-63; staff nurse, clin. instr. Madison (Ind.) State Hosp., 1963-65; instr. through assoc. prof. Ind. U. Sch. Nursing, Indpls., 1967-89, developer child/adolescent psychiat., mental health nursing program, 1982-83, chairperson grad. dept., 1983-89; prof., asst. dean Coll. of Nursing U. South Fla., Tampa, 1989-91; dean Coll. Nursing U. N.C., Charlotte, 1992-95; dean U. N.C. Coll. of Nursing and Health Professions, Charlotte, 1995—, U. N.C. Coll. Health & Human Services, Charlotte, 2002—. Pvt. practice marital and family therapy, 1975-89; cons. in field. Founding editor-in-chief Jour. of Child and Adolescent Psychiatric and Mental Health Nursing, 1987-91; contbr. articles to profl. jours. Bd. dirs. Carolinas blood svcs. region ARC, 1997-2002, chmn. bd. dirs., 2000—. NIHM trainee Ind. U., 1965-67, USPHS profl. nurse trainee Ind. U., 1977-78; recipient Youth Advocacy award Ind. Advs. for Child Psychiat. Nursing, 1987, Disting. Svc. award Ind. U. Sch. Nursing Alumni Assn., 1989, Nat. Youth Advocacy award Advs. for Child Psychiat. Nursing, 1990, Disting. Alumni award Ind. U. sch. Edn., 2000. Fellow Am. Acad. Nursing; mem. ANA, Psychiat. Mental Health Nursing Coun., Soc. for Edn. and Rsch. in Psychiat. Mental Health Nursing (pres. 1988-90), Am. Assn. Marital and Family Therapy, So. Nursing Rsch. Soc., So. Piedmont Alzheimer's Assn. (bd. dirs. 1999-2000), New South Hospice of Charlotte and Lincoln County (bd. dirs. 1995—2004, chair 2002-04), Sigma Theta Tau. E-mail: isbishop@email.uncc.edu.

BISHOP, SUSAN KATHARINE, executive search company executive; b. Palm Beach, Fla., Apr. 3, 1946; d. Warner Bader Bishop and Katharine Sue (White) McLennan; m. Robert Uchitel, Dec. 27, 1973 (div. 1979); 1 child, Rachel. BA, Briarcliff Coll., 1968; MBA, Fordham U., 1985. Actress, N.Y.C., 1968-72; producer, hostess Sta. KIMO-TV, Anchorage, 1972-74; dir. programming Visions Pay TV, 1974-79; recruiter Joe Sullivan & Assocs., N.Y.C., 1980-82; prin. Johnson, Smith & Knisely, 1982-88; ptnr. Schmitt Bishop Tolette, N.Y.C., 1989-91; pres. Bishop Ptnrs., Ltd., N.Y.C., 1991—. Mem. Cable TV Adminstrn. and Mktg. Soc., Women in Cable, Assn. Exec. Search Cons. (bd. dirs.). Office: Bishop Ptnrs 708 3rd Ave New York NY 10017-4201

BISHOP, VIRGINIA WAKEMAN, retired librarian and humanities educator, small business owner; b. Portland, Oreg., Dec. 28, 1927; d. Andrew Virgil and Letha Evangeline (Ward) Wakeman; m. Clarence Edmund Bishop, Aug. 23, 1953; children: Jean Marie Bishop Johnson, Marilyn Joyce. BA, Bapt. Missionary Tng. Sch., Chgo., 1949, Linfield Coll., McMinnville, Oreg., 1952, MEd, 1953; MA in Librarianship, U. Wash., 1968. Ch. worker Univ. Bapt. Ch., Seattle, 1954-56, 59-61, pre-sch. tchr. parent coop presch., 1965-66; libr. N.W. Coll., Kirkland, Wash., 1968-69; undergrad. libr. U. Wash., Seattle, 1970; libr., instr. Seattle Cen. Community Coll., 1970-91; co-owner small bus. Seaside, Oreg., 1972—. Leader Totem coun. Girl Scouts U.S., 1962-65; pres. Wedgwood Sch. PTA, Seattle, 1964-65; chair 46th Dist. Dem. Orgn., Seattle, 1972-73; precinct com. officer Dem. Party, 1968-88, 96-2000; candidate Wash. State Legislature, Seattle, 1974, 80; bd. dirs. Univ. Bapt. Children's Ctr., 1989-95, chair, 1990-95; vol. Ptnrs. in Pub. Edn., 1992-96. Recipient Golden Acorn award Wedgwood Elem. Sch., 1966. Mem. AAUW of Seaside, LWV of Seattle (2d v.p. 1994-96), U. Wash. Grad. Sch. Libr. and Info. Sci. Alumni Assn. (1st v.p. 1986-87, pres. 1987-88). Baptist. Avocations: swimming, walking, reading. Home: 3032 NE 87th St Seattle WA 98115-3529 Office: 300 5th Ave Seaside OR 97138

BISHOP-GRAHAM, BARBARA, secondary school educator, journalist; b. Angwin, Calif., Apr. 22, 1941; d. Will Francis and Esther Clara (Blissérd) Bishop; children: Gregory Mark, Steven Bishop. BA in Journalism, BA in English, BA in Art History, BFA in Painting and Drawing, U. Hawaii, 1975; nat. cert. in journalism, Kans. State U., 1994; MA in Tech. Curriculum & Instrn., Calif. State U., Sacramento, 1999. Cert. tchr., Hawaii. Photography [illegible] art tchr. Hawaii Sch. for Girls, Honolulu, 197[illegible]-76, substitute tchr. English State Dept. Edn., Oahu, 1977-78; English and grammar instr. Hawaii Sch. for Bus., Honolulu, 1979-80; media dir., exec. asst., historian Oriental Treasures and Points West, Honolulu, 1981-82; legal asst. Goodsill, Anderson, Quinn, Honolulu, 1983-84; lang. arts and photography tchr. Lodi (Calif.) H.S., 1984-88, writing and lang. arts tchr., 1988-93, creative writing tchr., 1989-99, journalism adviser, 1993-95, lang. arts tchr., 1993—, Brit. lit. tchr., 1995—2001, tchr. rhetoric and European lit., 2001—03. Mem. curriculum coun. Lodi Unified Sch. Dist., 1989-92, 97-2000; liaison to PTSA Lodi H.S., 1991-92, mentor tchr., 1991-94; student literary mag. advisor Lodi H.S., 1989—. Sportswriter Oakland Tribune, 1957-60, Author Three Poems, 1998; contbr. articles to profl. publs. Fundraiser chmn. Big Bros. of Am., San Francisco, 1967; media dir. Clements (Calif.) Cmty. Cares, 1985-89. Recipient Edn. Contbn. award Masons 1988-92, 20th Century Achievement award Am. Biographical Inst., 1999; grantee Nat. Endowment of Arts, rsch. Japanese Lit. 1989; social rschr. grantee Brazil, U. So. Calif. grantee, 1992; grantee S. Joaquin County Office Edn., 1996-97; champion Hawaii State barrel racing, 1980. Mem. NEA, Calif. Tchrs. Assn. (Calif. state tchrs. coun. rep. 1996-97), Lodi Edn. Assn. (conf. fund chair 1989-97). Republican. Seventh-Day Adventist. Avocations: writing, dressage riding, growing roses. Office: Lodi HS 3 S Pacific Ave Lodi CA 95242-3020

BISHOPRIC, SUSAN EHRLICH, public relations executive; b. NYC; AAS, Fashion Inst. Tech., 1965. Exec.-in-tng. Bloomingdales, Abraham & Strauss; merchandise coord. Seventeen mag.; publicity dir. Germaine Monteil Cosmetiques; account exec. Rowland Co., 1968-69, account supr., 1969-73, v.p., 1973-75, sr. v.p., creative dir., 1975-78, exec. v.p., 1979-81; pub. rels. dir. Susan Gilbert & Co., 1984-86; head pub. rels. divsn. Beber Silverstein & Ptnrs., 1986-89; founder, pres. Bishopric Agy., Coral Gables, Fla., 1989-99, NYC, 1999—. Office: The Bishopric Agy 185 E 85th St #9M New York NY 10028 E-mail: sbishopric@nyc.rr.com.

BITHONEY, CARMEN C. D'AMBORSIO, artistic director; b. Pelham Manor, N.Y., July 16, 1956; d. Anthony and Marian Christine D'Ambrosio; m. William G. Bithoney, Apr. 9, 1998. BA, Manhattanville Coll., 1978, MA, 1982. Exec. dir., founder First Expressions, A Nonprofit Gallery for the Arts, Inc., Boston, 1992-97; dir. Boston Film Bur. in Mayor's Office of Cultural Affairs, 1994-96; project dir. D'Ambrosio Ecclesiastical Art Studio, Onc., Mt. Kisco, N.Y., 1998—. Editor: Production Guide for Film & Video in the City of Boston, 1995. Office: DAmbrosio Ecclesiastical Art Studio Inc PO Box 656 Mount Kisco NY 10549-0656 Home: 727 N 26th St Philadelphia PA 19130-2403 E-mail: c.c.bithoney@juno.com.

BITNER, JERRI LYNNE, information technology professional, consultant; b. York, Pa., May 11, 1951; d. Ernest Maclellan and Gertrude Pauline (Beck) B. BS, Pa. State U., 1974. Procurement agt. Def. Indsl. Supply Ctr., Phila., 1975-77; contracts specialist Navy Ships Parts Control Ctr., Mechanicsburg, 1977-81; procurement analyst, then supr. Navy Fleet Material Support Office, Ctrl. Design Agy., 1981-87, dir. procurement systems div., 1987-94, dir. APADE/C2/Reengineering divsn., 1994-96, tandem rehost project mgr., 1996-98, dep. dir. tech. support dept., 1998-2001, dir. IT group e-bus. ops. office, 2001—03; dir. solution devel. dept. Navy Info. Sys. Support Activity, 2003—. Avocations: skiing, tennis, golf, camping, kayaking. Office: NAVSISA Mechanicsburg PA 17055 Personal E-mail: jerri.bitner@navy.mal.

BITTEL, LINDA LEE, art educator; b. Hays, Kans., Sept. 18, 1949; d. Beverly Charles and Vida Mae (Schraeder) Irvin; m. Ronald J. Urban, May 30, 1970 (div. Apr. 1980); children: Amy M. Urban, Ryan J. Urban; m. Gerald J. Bittel, July 14, 1990. BS, Kans. State U., 1971; MA, Fort Hays State U., 1980. Cert. tchg. Kans. Tchr. USD 395, La Crosse, Kans., 1972—81, USD 428, Great Bend, Kans., 1981—2003. Sch. bd. USD 395, La Crosse, Kans., 1990—95. Mem.: Hays Arts Coun., Barton County Arts Coun., Kans. Art Edn. Assn. (treas. 2000—03, Art Educator of Yr. 2002—03). Avocations: crafts, ceramics, sculpting, quilting.

BITTEL, MURIEL ALBERS, managing editor; b. N.Y.C., Mar. 22; d. Ernest Henry and Helen Minnie (Seibel) Albers; m. Robert Gifford Walcutt, June 15, 1946; children— Lynn Lowell Walcutt, Mark James Walcutt, Judith Anne Walcutt; m. Lester Robert Bittel, May 8, 1973. B.A., Douglass Coll. Feature writer Daily Home News, New Brunswick, N.J.; editor Fawcett Pubs., N.Y.C., 1940-46; pub. relations dir. Electrovox/Walco Inc., East Orange, N.J., 1946-62; mng. editor Acad. Hall Pubs., Bridgewater, Va., 1974— . Mng. editor: Ency. Profl. Mgmt., 1978; Handbook Profl. Mgrs., 1985, A Surprise in Every Corner, 1994, Island Adventures, 1995. Home: 106 Breezewood Ter Bridgewater VA 22812-1433

BITTERMAN, MARY GAYLE FOLEY, foundation executive; b. San Jose, Calif, May 29, 1944; d. John Dennis and Zoe (Hames) Foley; m. Morton Edward Bitterman, June 26, 1967; 1 child Sarah Fleming. BA, Santa Clara U., 1966; MA, Bryn Mawr Coll., 1969, PhD, 1971. Exec. dir. Hawaii Pub. Broadcasting, Honolulu, 1974-79; dir. Voice Am., Washington, 1980-81, Dept. Commerce, Honolulu, 1981-83, E.-W. Ctr. Inst. Culture, Comm., 1984-88; cons. pvt. practice, 1989-93; pres., CEO KQED, Inc., San Francisco, 1993—2002, The James Irvine Found., 2002—03; Dtr. Osher Lifelong Learning Inst., 2003. Bd. dir. Bank of Hawaii, Honolulu, Honolulu, 1984—; vice chmn. TIDE 2000, Tokyo, 1984—93; bd. dir. McKesson Corp., San Francisco, 1995—99; trustee Am.'s Pub. TV Stas., 1997—2002; bd. dir. Bernard Osher Found.; bd. dirs. Barclays Global Investors; bd. dir. PBS, vice chmn. Producer: (film) China Visit, 1978; contbr. numerous articles on internat. telecomms. to various pubs. Bd. dir. United Way, Honolulu, 1986—93; chmn. Kuakini Health System, 1991—94. Recipient Candle of Understanding award Bonneville (Utah) Internat. Corp., 1985; named hon. mem. Nat. Fedn. Press Women, 1986; Doctor of Humane Letters (honoris causa), Dominican Coll. of San Rafael, 1999; Doctor of Public Svc. (honoris causa), Santa Clara U., 2003. Mem.: Pacific Forum, CSIS (bd. gov.), Commonwealth Club Calif. (bd. dir.), Nat. Acad. Pub. Admin. (fellow). Office: One Ferry Bldg San Francisco CA 94111 Address: 229 Kaalawai Pl Honolulu HI 96816-4435

BITTINGER, CYNTHIA DOUGLAS, foundation executive; BA in Govt., Wheaton Coll., 1968; MA, Columbia U., 1970. Social studies tchr. Ridgewood (N.J.) High Sch., 1970-73; govtl. mgr. Mayor's N.Y.C. Office for Aging, 1974-76; owner, mgr. gift shop Princeton, N.J., 1978-87; exec. dir. Calvin Coolidge Meml. Found., Inc., Plymouth, Vt., 1990—. Instr. history C.C. of Vt., White River Junction, 1992-94. Writer Valley Bus. Jour., 1989. Address: Calvin Coolidge Mem Found Box 97 Plymouth VT 05056

BIXENSTINE, KIM FENTON, lawyer; b. Providence, Feb. 26, 1958; d. Barry Jay and Gail Louise (Traverse) Weinstein; m. Barton Aaron Bixenstine, June 25, 1983; children: Paul Jay, Nathan Alexis. BA, Middlebury Coll., 1979; JD, U. Chgo., 1982. Bar: Ohio 1982, U.S. Dist. Ct. (no. and so. dists.) Ohio 1983, U.S. Ct. Appeals (6th cir.) 1983. Law clk. to presiding judge U.S. Dist. Ct. (so. dist.) Ohio, Cin., 1982-83; assoc. Jones, Day, Reavis & Pogue, Cleve., 1983-90, ptnr., 1991-99; sr. counsel TRW Inc., Cleve., 1999—2001, v.p., chief litig. counsel, 2002—03; v.p., dep. gen. counsel Univ.. Hosp. Health Sys., Cleve., 2003—. Chair comml. adv. coun. N.E. Ohio chpt. Am. Arbitration Assn., 2002—03; mem. comml. adv. coun. NE Ohio Chpt. Am. Arbitration Assn., 2000—, chair, 2002—03. Bd. dirs. Planned Parenthood Greater Cleve., 1991—99, sec., 1992—93, v.p., 1994—96, pres., 1996—98; chair corp. giving subcom. Cleve. Bar Found. Campaign, 2001—02; bd. dirs. Boys and Girls Club Cleve., 2001—03, chair pub. rels. com., 2002—03. Mem.: Cleve. Bar Assn. (commn. women in the law 1988—2001, bd. dirs. 1993—96, minority outreach com. 1993—95, chair standing com. lawyer professionalism 1994—96, bd. liaison to jud. selection com. 1996, nominating com. 1997—99, chair nominating com. 1998—99, long range planning com. 2002—03), Ohio Women's Bar Assn. (chair legis. com. 1994—95, trustee 1995—97). Avocations: jogging, reading. Office: Univ Hosps Health Sys WO Walker Ctr 10524 Euclid Ave STe 1100 Cleveland OH 44106 E-mail: kim.bixenstine@uhhs.com.

BIZON, EMMA DJAFAR, management consultant; b. Atlanta, July 22, 1958; d. H. and Aminah Djafar; m. Lawrence Walter Bizon, May 24, 1994; 1 child, Rimagene. BSc in City & Regional Planning cum laude, Bandung Inst. Tech., Indonesia, 1985; MBA, Harvard U., 1994. Planner, Indonesia, 1983—86; asst. dir. Investment Bd., Indonesia; team leader Amre, Inc., Livonia, Mich., 1994—97; cons. to fast food restaurants Mich., 1997—98. Avocations: sports, music, cooking, writing. Home: 10909 Melbourne Ct Allen Park MI 48101

BIZUB, JOHANNA CATHERINE, law librarian; b. Denville, N.J., Apr. 13, 1957; d. Stephen Bernard and Elizabeth Mary (Grizzle) B.; m. Scott Jeffrey Smith, 1992. BS in Criminal Justice, U. Dayton, 1979; MLS, Rutgers U., 1984. Law libr. Morris County Law Libr., 1981-83, Clapp & Eisenberg, Newark, 1984-86; dir. libr. Sills Cummis, 1986-94; libr. dir. Montville (N.J.) Twp. Pub. Libr., N.J., 1994-97; libr. dir. law dept. Prudential Ins. Co. Am., Newark, 1997—. Mem. ALA, N.J. Law Librs. Assn. (treas. 1987-89, v.p./pres.-elect 1989-90, 99-2000, pres. 1990-91, 2000-01, past pres. 1991-92, 2001-02), Am. Assn. Law Librs. (pvt. law librs. SIS, vice chair 1992-93, chair 1993-94, past chair 1994-95), N.J. Libr. Assn., Assoc. Libr. of Morris County (v.p. 1995, pres. 1996, treas. 1997-01), Spl. Libr. Assn. N.J. (treas. 1990-92), Am. Legion Aux. (treas. Rockden unit 175 1983-93). Democrat. Roman Catholic. Home: 11 Elm St Rockaway NJ 07866-3108 Office: Prudential Ins Co Am 22 Plz 751 Broad St Newark NJ 07102-3714

BJORKLUND, NANCY MARGARETTE WATTS, music educator; b. Maryville, Tenn., Aug. 14, 1942; d. Charles Burdett and Alma Pauline (Calhoun) Watts; m. Ralph Edward Bjorklund, June 14, 1963; children: James Andrew, Deborah Elisabeth, John Carl. AA, Manatee C.C., Bradenton, Fla., 1962; BA, Stetson U., Deland, Fla., 1964; MusB, Stetson Univ., 1964. Founder, dir. music, pianist First Bapt. Ch., Freeport, Grand Bahama Is., 1964—70; dir. Cmty. Chorus Choir, Freeport, Grand Bahama Island, 1964—70. Recipient Crystal Heart award, Girl Scouts Am., 1995. Mem.: Fla. State Music Tchr. Assn. (exec. bd. 1993—95, 1993—, pres. dist. 7 2001—), Manatee County Music Tchr. Assn. (chmn. music spectacular 2004, exec. bd. 1978—, chmn. Pianorama 1980, exec. bd. 1983—, pres. 1993—95, chmn. music spectacular 2001), Nat. Assn. Music Clubs (chmn. Fedn. Festival Manatee County 1980—), Manatee County Assn. Retarded Citizens, Fla. State Assn. Retarded Citizens. Republican. So. Bapt. Avocations: reading, crewel, swimming, cooking. Office: 1912 48th St W Bradenton FL 34209

BJORNCRANTZ, LESLIE BENTON, librarian; b. Jersey City, Mar. 1, 1945; d. David and Jeanne (Proctor) Benton; m. Carl Eduard Bjorncrantz, Aug. 31, 1968; 1 child, William. BA, Wellesley Coll., 1967; MLS, Columbia U., 1968. Rsch. libr. Alderman Libr. U. Va., Charlottesville, 1968-70; reference libr. Northwestern U. Libr., Evanston, Ill., 1974-78, curriculum libr., 1970—, edn. bibliographer, 1974—, psychology bibliographer, 1989—, core libr., 1989-97, mgmt. bibliographer, 1997—. Coeditor: (book) Curriculum Material Center Collection Policy, 1984, Guide for the Development & Management of Test Collections, 1985. Bd. dirs. Internat. Visitors Ctr., Chgo., 1973-76; class rep., fund raiser class of 1967, Wellesley (Mass.) Coll., 1987-92. Scholar Wellesley Coll., 1967. Mem. ALA, Assn. Coll. & Rsch. Librs. (sec. 1977-79, 85-87, chair curriculum materials com. 1984-85), Am. Bus. Libr. Dirs. Avocations: reading, travel, food and wine. Home: 2146 Forestview Rd Evanston IL 60201-2057 Office: Northwestern U Libr 1970 Campus Dr Evanston IL 60208-0821 Office Phone: 847-491-7602. E-mail: l-bjorncrantz@northwestern.edu.

BJORNSON, EDITH CAMERON, foundation administrator, communications consultant; b. Orlando, Fla., Sept. 12, 1937; d. Hilliard Francis and Edith Muriel (McBride) Cameron; m. Carroll N. Bjornson, Jan. 11, 1963; children: Lisa Carol, Karl Cameron (dec.). BA, U. Fla., Gainesville, 1953, MA, 1956; profl. cert., Ecole de Cuisine LaVerenne, Paris, 1983. Copywriter Sta. WGGG, Gainesville, Fla., 1953-54; exec. asst. Actors' Studio, N.Y.C., 1956-58; prodn. asst. Omnibus, N.Y.C., 1958-59; assoc. prodr. Robert Saudek Assocs., N.Y.C., 1958-60, ABC News Adlai Stevenson Reports, N.Y.C., 1960; asst. gen. mgr. Sta. WNDT-TV, N.Y.C., 1960-63; co-prodr. The Open Mind, N.Y.C., 1963-69; dir. local programming Telepromter, Inc., N.Y.C., 1979-80; corporate v.p. programming Westinghouse Broadcasting and Cable, N.Y.C., 1980-83; cons. Sta. WNYC-TV, N.Y.C., 1984-86; v.p., sr. program officer The Markle Found., N.Y.C., 1986-98. Mem. working group Carter Commn. on Radio and TV, Atlanta, 1992—96; mem. strategic planning bd. Conn. Pub. TV; bd. dirs. N.Y. New Media Assn., N.Y.C., 1998—2002, chmn., 2002; bd. dirs. Conn. Pub. TV and Radio, 1999—, bd. advisors to Culture Connect, 2003—; cons. in new media profit and non-profit orgns.; exec. dir. Fulfilling the Promise project on digital comm. Century Found. and Carnegie Corp., 1999—2001; sr. advisor, Morningside Ventures Columbia U., 1999—2001; project dir., website designer Fulfilling the Promise The Century Found. Carnegie Corp., 1999—2001; website editor Digital Promise Project, 2002—03; project dir., website designer The Open Mind Digital Archive Project, Columbia Tchrs. Coll., 2002—; sr. advisor Fathom.com Columbia U., 1999—2001; sr. advisor video oral history project Healthcare Chaplaincy, 2002—; dir. oral history project The Healthcare Chaplaincy, 2003—; prin. Recorded Oral Histories, LLC. Project advisor: (computer software) Voyager Co., 1993, SimHealth, 1994, (Internet software, multi-player online games) ReInventing America, 1995, President '96; contbr. articles to profl. jours. Vice chmn. bd. dirs. HealthCare Chaplaincy, N.Y.C., 1989-96; bd. dirs. Pro-Natura USA, N.Y.C., 1995-99; life trustee Health Care Chaplaincy, N.Y.C., 1997. Recipient Emmy award Acad. TV. Arts and Scis., 1960. Mem. Internat. Assn. Culinary Profls., Night Kitchen (computer software developers bd. dirs. 1996-98), Ocean Reef Club, Mortar Board, Delta Gamma. Republican. Avocation: cooking. Home: 34 E Lyon Farm Dr Greenwich CT 06831-4349 Office Phone: 212-481-3949.

BJORNSRUD, MARLENE, professional athletics manager; Tennis coach Grand Canyon U., Phoenix, 1984, asst. athletic dir.; dir. of athletics Santa Clara U.; gen. mgr. San Jose Cyber Rays Women's United Soccer Assn., San Jose, Calif. Office: San Jose Cyber Rays 1991 Park Ave San Jose CA 95126

BLACK, BARBARA ANN, publisher; b. Eureka, Calif., Dec. 11, 1928; d. William Marion and Letitia (Brunia) Black; m. Vinson Brown, June 18, 1950 (dec Dec. 1991); children: Tamara Pinn, Roxana Hodges, Keven Brown. BA, Western State Coll., Gunnison, Colo., 1950. Cert. tchr., Colo. Editor/proofreader Naturegraph Pubs., Los Altos, Calif., 1950-53, co-owner, mgr. San Martin, Calif., 1953-60, Healdsburg, Calif., 1960-76, owner/mgr. Happy Camp, Calif., 1976—. Author: Barns of Yesteryear, 1993; co-author: Sierra Nevada Wildlife, 1996, The Californian Wildlife Region, 1999; pub. over 100 titles on wildlife and Native Ams. Mem. Am. Booksellers Assn. Baha'i Faith. Avocations: gardening, backpacking, animal training. Home: PO Box 1045 3633 Indian Creek Rd Happy Camp CA 96039-9706 Office: Naturegraph Publishers Inc 3543 Indian Creek Rd Happy Camp CA 96039-9706 Office Phone: 530-493-5353.

BLACK, BARBARA ARONSTEIN, legal history educator; b. Bklyn., May 6, 1933; d. Robert and Minnie (Polenberg) A.; m. Charles L. Black, Jr., Apr. 11, 1954; children: [illegible] BA, Bklyn. Coll., 1953; LLB, Columbia U., 1955; MPhil, Yale U., 1970, PhD, 1975; LLD (hon.), N.Y. Law Sch., 1986, Marymount Manhattan Coll., 1986, Vt. Law Sch., 1987, Coll. of New Rochelle, 1987, Smith Coll., 1988, Bklyn. Coll., 1988, York U., Toronto, Can., 1990, Georgetown U., 1991. Assoc. in law Columbia U. Law Sch., N.Y.C., 1955-56; lectr. history Yale U., New Haven, 1974-76, asst. prof. history, 1976-79, assoc. prof. law, 1979-84; George Welwood Murray prof. legal history Columbia U. Law Sch., N.Y.C., 1984—, dean faculty of law, 1986-91. Editor Columbia Law Rev., 1953-55. Active N.Y. State Ethics Commn., 1992-95. Recipient Fed. Bar Assn. prize Columbia Law Sch., 1955 Mem. Am. Soc. Legal History (pres. 1986-90), Am. Acad. Arts and Scis., Am. Philos. Soc., Mass. Hist. Soc., Supreme Ct. Hist. Soc., Selden Soc., Century Assn. Office: Columbia U Sch Law 435 W 116th St New York NY 10027-7201 Office Phone: 212-854-5735.

BLACK, CAROLE, broadcast executive; b. Cin. BA in English lit., Ohio State U. With Procter & Gamble, Cin.; account supr., sr. v.p., mgmt. rep. DDB Needham, Chgo., 1983—86; v.p. worldwide mktg. home video Walt Disney Co., 1986—88, sr. v.p. mktg., TV, 1988—94; pres., gen. mgr. NBC 4, L.A., 1994—99; pres., CEO Lifetime Entertainment Svcs., 1999—. Recipient CTAM Hall of Fame Award, 2000, Nat. Breast Cancer Coalition Leadership Award, 2000, Muse Award, NY Women in Film & Television, 2000, Impact Award, Nat. Hispanic Media Coalition, 2001, Women Who Change the World Award, NY Women in Communications, 2002, Matrix Award, 2002. Office: Lifetime Entertainment Svcs 309 W 49th St New York NY 10019-7404*

BLACK, CATHLEEN PRUNTY, publishing executive; b. Chgo., Apr. 26, 1944; d. James Hamilton and Margaret (Harrington) Black; m. Thomas E. Harvey; children: Alison, Duffy. BA, Trinity Coll., 1966. Advt. sales rep. Holiday mag., N.Y.C., 1966-69, Travel & Leisure mag., N.Y.C., 1969-70, New York mag., 1970-72; advt. dir. Ms. mag., 1972-75, assoc. pub., 1975-77, New York mag., 1977-79, pub., 1979-83; pres. USA Today, 1983, pub., 1984-91; exec. v.p. mktg. Gannett Co., Inc., 1985—91, also bd. dirs.; pres., CEO Newspaper Assn. Am., Reston, Va., 1992-95; pres. Hearst Mags., N.Y.C., NY, 1996—. Bd. dirs. iVillage, Coca-Cola Co., 1990—91, 1993—, IBM, 1995—. Trustee U. Notre Dame. Named Pub. Exec. of Yr., Advt. Age, 2000; named one of Most Powerful Women in Am. Bus., Fortune mag., 100 Most Influential Bus. Leaders, Crain's N.Y. Bus., 2002; recipient Muriel Fox Award for Comm. Leadership Toward a Just Soc., NOW, 2000, Stephen P. Duggan Award, Inst. Internat. Edn., 2002. Mem.: Coun. on Fgn. Rels., Advt. Coun. (bd. mem.). Office: Hearst Mags 959 8th Ave New York NY 10019-3795

BLACK, COBEY, journalist; b. Washington, June 15; d. Elwood Alexander and Margaret (Beall) Cobey; m. Edwin F. Black; children: Star, Christopher, Noel, Nicholas, Brian, Bruce. BA, Wellesley Coll., 1944; postgrad., U. Hawaii. Exec. sec. to Irene, designer Metro-Goldwyn-Mayer, 1944; actress Fed. Republic Germany, 1945-46; women's editor Washington Daily News, 1947-50; columnist Honolulu Star Bull., 1954-65, Honolulu Advertiser, 1969-85. Cons. HEW, Peace Corps; bd. dirs. Pacific and Asian Affairs Coun., Honolulu Com. on Fgn. Rels., Soc. Asian Art of Hawaii, Honolulu Media Coun.; pres. Black & Black, Inc. Author: Birth of A Princess, 1962, Iolani Luahine, 1986, Hawaii Scandal, 2002; travel editor Bangkok World, 1968-69; publicist CBS-TV series Hawaii Five-O, 1978. Mem. Hawaii State Commn. on Status of Women, 1978-86. Mem. Nat. Press Club, Nat. Soc. Colonial Dames, Lady of Dumbarton, Royal Bangkok Sports Club, Outrigger Canoe Club, Waialae Country Club, Garden Club of Honolulu. Democrat. Episcopalian. Office: Black & Black Inc 3081 La Pietra Cir Honolulu HI 96815-4736

BLACK, CORA JEAN, evangelist, wedding consultant; b. Mt. Pleasant, Pa., July 30, 1941; d. Alfred John and Ruby Isabel (Waugaman) B.; m. Arthur Byron Everett, Mar. 27, 1974. Student, Greensburg Bus. Coll., 1962, Moody Bible Inst., 1966; DD, Internat. Bible Inst., 1972; postgrad., Seton Hill Coll., 1986. Cert. bereavement facilitatior, Am. Acad. Bereavement, 1999; ordained evangelist; notary public. Advt. display silk-screen artist West Penn Power Co., Greensburg, Pa., 1962-63; missionary to W.I. Gospel Light Ministry, New Stanton, Pa., 1964; pers. dir., Pa. state chair Assn. Internat. Gospel Assemblies of DeSota, Mo., 1970-80; founder, pres. America for Christ Ministry, New Stanton, 1974—; owner, founder Sea-Jay's All Faith Wedding Chapel, New Stanton, 1979—; chaplain Westmoreland County Prison, 1999-2001. Coord. Holy Land Tours, 1971—83; owner Sea-Jay All Pet Hotel, New Stanton; ordained mem. Internat. Pentecostal Holiness Ch. Pa. Conf. Author Christian literature; composer: (published and recorded Gospel music including) Christ is Coming! Are You Ready?, America for Christ, and the Joy of Life; (weekly radio programs). Mem. disaster action ARC, 2002—, vol. DAT- mass care response family svc.; mem. Internat. Critical Incident Stress Found., Inc., 2002—; dip. Clin. Forensic Counseling, 2000—. Recipient award, Nat. Notary Assn., 2001. Mem.: DAR (regent chpt. Pa. 76 chpt. 2001—), Assn. Civil War Women (pres. tent 156 2002—03), Women in Christ, Internat. Gospel Assemblies (pub. rels. dir. U.S. and more than 50 countries, Pa.), God and Country Nat. Heritage Soc. (v.p. 2000—), Women's Relief Corp., Tri-State Gospel Music Assn. (treas. 1998—2000), Assn. Internat. Gospel Assemblies, Internat. Platform Assn., Pa. Assn. Notaries, Am. Assn. Christian Counselors (charter, counselor), Ctrl. Westmoreland C. of C., Am. Acad. Bereavement Assn. (cert. bereavement facilitator), Am. Psychotherapy Assn. (cert.), Assn. Internat. Gospel Assemblies (internat. pub. rels. dir.), Am. Acad. Cert. Forensic Counselors, BMI, New Stanton Hist. Soc. (sec.-treas. 1995—), Westmoreland Hist. Soc., Ladies Grand Army Rep. (nat. chaplain 2001—), Aux. Sons. Union Vets. Civil War, Daus. Union Vets. Civil War 1861-1865 (chaplain). Republican. Avocations: travel, photography, decorating and designing, painting, animals. Home: 440 N Center Ave PO Box 192 New Stanton PA 15672-0192 Office: Sea-Jays 440 N Center Ave New Stanton PA 15672-9416 E-mail: sea.jay@mymailstation.com.

BLACK, DEBORAH, information technology executive; BS in Computer Sci., MSE in Computer Engring., U. Mich. With Bell No. Rsch.; from program mgr. to corp. v.p. Microsoft, Redmond, Wash., 1992. Office: One Microsoft Way Redmond WA 98052-6399

BLACK, DONNA RUTH, lawyer; b. Yuma, Ariz., Sept. 13, 1947; d. Roy Welch and Rosalie Edith (Harrison) B.; children: Gavin Lewis, Trevor Elias. BA in History with honors, U. Ariz., 1969; JD, UCLA, 1975. Bar: Calif. 1975, D.C. 1979, U.S. Dist. Ct. (ctrl. dist.) Calif., 1975, U.S. Dist. Ct. (no. dist.) Calif. 1987, U.S. Dist. Ct. (ea. dist.) Calif. 1989, U.S. Ct. Appeals (8th cir.) 1978, U.S. Ct. Appeals (9th cir.) 1983, U.S. Supreme Ct. 1994. Equity ptnr. Baker & Hostetler, L.A., 1975-95; equity ptnr. Manatt, Phelps & Phillips, L.A., 1995—. Author/editor: California Environmental Law Handbook. Mem. ABA (chmn. sect. natural resources, energy and environ. law, mem. nominating com. ho. of dels., chmn. sect. officers' conf. adv. com.), State Bar Calif., Los Angeles County Bar Assn., UCLA Law Alumni Assn. (bd. dirs. 1996—, v.p. 1998—, pres. 1999). Avocations: music, art, travel, poetry, writing. Home: 1130 Tower Rd Beverly Hills CA 90210-2131 Office: Manatt Phelps & Phillips 11355 W Olympic Blvd Los Angeles CA 90064-1614

BLACK, EILEEN MARY, retired elementary school educator; b. Bklyn., Sept. 20, 1944; d. Marvin Mize and Anne Joan (Salvia) B. Student, Grossmont Coll., El Cajon, Calif., 1964; BA, San Diego State U., 1967; postgrad., U. Calif., San Diego, Syracuse U. Cert. tchr., Calif. Tchr. La Mesa (Calif.)-Spring Valley Sch. Dist., 1967-2001, ret., 2001. NDEA grant Syracuse U., 1968. Mem.: AARP, Calif. Ret. Tchrs. Assn., Wilderness Soc., Greenpeace, San Diego Zool. Soc., Sierra Club. Roman Catholic. Avocations: reading, baseball, walking. Home: 9320 Earl St Apt 15 La Mesa CA 91942-3846 E-mail: eblack44@aol.com.

BLACK, GENEVA ARLENE, social services agency administrator; b. Dazell, S.C., Apr. 30, 1932; d. Isaac and Carrie Lee (Hollimon) Sanders; children: Ronald D., Robert J., Clarissa D. Black Wells, Michael A., Steven G. Diploma Soc. Svc. Adminstrn., Temple U., 1970-73; Diploma Bus. Adminstrn., U. Detroit, 1981-82. Housing coord. Haddington Leadership Orgn., Phila., 1970-73, exec. dir., 1973; co-founder, exec. dir. Haddington Multi Svcs. for Older Adults, Inc., Phila., 1975—. Host monthly radio program Sr.'s Hour, Sta. WDAS, 1996—. Pres., block capt. 5500 Block Poplar St.; chmn. Emergency Fund Coalition; mem. human svc. com. Empowerment Zone West Phila.; 192d legis. dist. chmn. Com. on Aging, trustee, treas. inspiration choir Vine Meml. Bapt. Ch., co-chmn. ch. anniversary com., sec. Fed. Credit Union; sec. West Phila. Planning Com.; sec. bd. dirs. Spectrum Health Svcs.; bd. dirs., v.p. Housing Assn. Authority Delaware Valley; bd. dirs. Mayor's Commn. on Svcs. to Elderly, 1996—; coord. sr. programs. Recipient numerous awards, including Leon S. Rosenthal award for humanitarian and cmty. svc. West Phila. C. of C., 1983, citation for outstanding cmty. svc. Pa. Ho. of Reps., 1985, 87, 90, 95, Cmty. Svc. award Phila. chpt. Nat. Assn. Negro Bus. and Profl. Women's Club, 1989, citation for outstanding cmty. svcs. gov. State of Pa., 1990, Pa. Senate, 1990, Cmty. Svc. award Emergency Fund for Older Philadelphians, 1991, Phila. Bapt. Ch., 1993, Allan Yaffe svc. award Phila. Corp. for Aging, 1994, cert. of appreciation U. Pa., 1995; named to Afro-Am. Hall of Fame, Drexel U., 1996; named Top Ladies of Distinction, Inc. Phila. Chpt., 1998; recipient Trail Blazer award 2000 Black Women, 1998. Mem. AARP (1st sec. Overbrook chpt. 1993-96), Phila. Corp. Aging (cert. mental health, 1987). Office: Haddington Multi Svcs for Older Adults Inc 5502 Haverford Ave Philadelphia PA 19139-1431

BLACK, JACKIE JOHN, artist; d. Lloyd and Dorine Turnbow; children: Cody R. Simonsen, Derek C. Simonsen. Attended, U.Utah, Salt Lake City, 1969—72. Graphic artist, art dir. Corker Sullivan Advt. Agy., Spokane, Wash., 1978—82, Coons, Corker, Sullivan Advt. Agy., Spokane, Wash., 1982—83; graphic artist, sr. art dir. Clark White and Associates, Spokane, Wash., 1983—86; freelance graphic artist Jackie Black Art, Bellingham, Wash., 1986—92, fine artist / painter Mukilteo, Wash., 1992—. Art instr. Jackie Black Art, Mukilteo, Wash., 1986—. Graphic artist (graphic arts) Printed Materials and Letterhead (MAX Award Of Merit, 1983), fine artist / painter (fine arts exhibit) Artist Association for University Women, Snohomish Arts Council, Single Person Exhibit - Vinilla Beans Coffee Shop Mukilteo, Washington, Featured Artist - Powell Street Gallery San Francisco, California, Featured Artist at Gallery Carla - San Francisco, California, Featured Artist at Jezebel Gallery, Santa Fe, New Mexico, Art Exhibit / Thomas Moxley Gallery Santa Fe, New Mexico, graphic artist (graphic art) Anheuser-Busch Complete Campaign (MAX Award Of Excellence, 1983), (graphic arts) McClain Clothiers Sales Promotion and Package Design (MAX Award Of Excellence, 1983), IRLC / [illegible] Public Service - Single Entry Point (MAX Award Of Merit, 1984), Playfair Transit Exterior (MAX Award Of Excellence, 1984), Northtown Mall Back To School Sale insert (MAX Award Of Merit, 1986), Direct Mail Campaign South Hill Medical Center (MAX Award Of Excellence, 1986), Northtown Transit (MAX Award Of Merit, 1987), Patricks Package Design (MAX Award Of Excellence, 1987), Vanilla Beans Coffee Shop, 2001, Powell St. Gallery, 2001—03, Gallery Carla, 2003—, Jezebel Gallery, 2003—, Thomas Moxley, 2001—. Office: Jackie Black Art 11013 55th Ave W Mukilteo WA 98275 E-mail: jackieblackjohn@verizon.net.

BLACK, KRIS SUSAN LYNN, marketing company executive, speaker, author, poet; b. Ladysmith, Wis., Sept. 19, 1950; d. Bruce Roger and Christine Mae (Sweet) B. AA with honors, Bakersfield Coll.; student, Phoenix Coll. Asst. mgr. jewelry dept. K Mart, Rapid City, S.D., 1965-68; beauty titilist, actress, model, tchr. Patricia Stevens, Phoenix, 1968-72; Country Musics' 1st lady internat. promotional dir. for TV series Hee Haw (Buck Owens), Bakersfield, Calif., 1972-76; dir. K.B. Properties, Dallas, 1976-78; v.p. Wynn Investments, Dallas, 1978—; pres. Sunflower Mktg., Dallas, 1982—. Cons. CBI Labs., Aloe Labs. of Tex., 1979—, Richard Simmons, 1983, March of Dimes, 1976; dir. mktg. Colibri Skin Care Coming Home, healing retreat ctr.; internat. spkr. on mktg. and bus., relationships, mental health and illness, bi-polar rsch., healing from rape to internat. prosecution; Reiki master. Author: Ring of Dolphins, Mystic Carribean; featured in Acting Naturally (Eileen Sisk). Mem. DAR, M.K. Gandhi Inst. for Non-Violence. Avocations: horseback riding, water sports, singing, human and animal rights, environment protection.

BLACK, LISA HARTMAN, actress, singer; b. Houston, June 01; m. Clint Black, Oct. 20, 1991. Grad., High Sch. Performing Arts, Houston. TV series: Tabitha, 1977-78, High Performance, 1983, Knots Landing, 1982-86, 2000 Malibu Rd., 1993; TV Movies: Murder at the World Series, 1977, Where the Ladies go, 1980, Gridlock (also released as The Great American Traffic Jam), 1980, Beverly Hills Cowgirl Blues, 1985, Roses Are for the Rich, 1987, Full Exposure: The Sex Tapes Scandal, 1989, The Operation, 1990, The Take, USA, 1990, Fire! Trapped on the 37th Floor, 1991, Not of This World, 1991, Red Wind, 1991, The Return of Elliot Ness, 1991, Without a Kiss Goodbye, 1993, Search for Grace, 1994, Someone Else's Child, 1995, Have You Seen My Son?, 1996, Out of Nowhere, 1997, Still Holding On: The Legend of Cadillac Jack, 1998; TV mini-series: Jacqueline Susann's Valley of the Dolls, 1981, Judith Krantz's Dazzle, 1995; films: Deadly Blessing, 1981, Where the Boys Are, 1984, also recorded Hold On I'm Comin', 1979, Til My Heart Stops, 1988; prodr. Have You Seen My Son?, 1996; TV guest appearances include Police Woman, 1974, Vega$, 1978, On Stage America, 1984, The Hitchhiker, 1983, Matlock, 1986. Office: Hartman Black 8489 W 3rd St Los Angeles CA 90048-4124

BLACK, MARGARET LOUISE, accountant, educator; b. Houston, Apr. 28, 1954; d. Laurence N. and Wilma (Mowery) B. BBA magna cum laude, Sam Houston State U., 1974; MDiv, So. Meth. U., 1981; MBA, U. Houston, Clear Lake, Tex., 2003. CPA, Tex. Auditor State of Tex., 1975-78; bookkeeper Green, Gilmore, et al, Dallas, 1978-80; min. United Meth. Ch., Houston, 1980-87; employment interviewer Tex. Employment Commn., Houston, 1987-91; job placement coord. San Jacinto Coll., Houston, 1991—99; acctg. instr. San Jacinto (Tex.) Coll., 2000—. Squadron comdr. CAP, Liberty, Tex., 1986-89, Baytown, Tex., 1996—. Avocations: aviation, gardening. Home: 396 CR4284 Dayton TX 77535-8758 Office: San Jacinto Coll N 5800 Uvalde Rd Houston TX 77049-4513

BLACK, MARILYN HAMMER, non-profit organization executive; b. Sioux City, Iowa, Apr. 25, 1923; d. Franklin Wilfred and Ruth Marie (Gray) Hammer; m. Albert Scott Black; children: Barbara Black Miller, William Scott, Patricia Black Thompson. BA, U. Without Walls, 1975; MS, U. Houston-Clear Lake, 1980; PhD in Philosophy, Summit U., New Orleans, 1998. Dir. religious edn. St. Francis Episcopal Ch., Houston, 1968-72; program dir. NCCJ, Houston, 1972-80; exec. dir. Support Ctr. Houston, 1982-86; dir. C.G. Jung Edn. Ctr., Houston, 1987-91. Mem. mission coun. St. Francis Episcopal Ch., Houston, 1982. Mem. ASTD, Non-Profit Mgmt. Assn., Nat. Soc. Fund Raising Execs. (bd. dirs. 1982). Home: 2929 Post Oak Blvd Apt 602 Houston TX 77056-6117

BLACK, MARSHA C. environmental scientist; BS in Comprehensive Sci., Converse Coll.; PhD in Ecology, U. Tenn. Acad. & postdoctoral rsch. U. Joensuu, Finland; asst. prof. zoology Okla. State U., Stillwater, Okla.; assoc. prof. environ. health scis. Coll. Agrl. and Environ. Scis.. U. Ga., Athens, Ga. Mem. exec. com. UGA River Basin Sci. & Policy Ctr. Reviewer (for several environ. toxicology pub.); mem. editl. bd.: Environ. Toxicol. Chemistry, 2000—02. Mem.: Soc. Environ. Toxicology and Chemistry (bd. dirs.). Office: Univ Ga 148 Environ Health Bldg Athens GA 30602

BLACK, MARY LEE, writer, educator; b. Brookings, S.D., Dec. 2, 1935; d. Robert Emmet and Kathryn Bonesteel Coffey; children: Katherine, Theodore, Douglas, Thomas. Student(hon.), U. Heidelberg Dolmetcher Inst., Germany, 1964; BA, Mary Hardin-Baylor, 1976; MA, U. Tex., 1983. Tchr. Belton (Tex.) Ind. Sch. Dist., 1980—2000, Salado (Tex.) Ind. Sch. Dist., 1976—80; music tchr. Salado, 1972—76; organist 2d Armored Divsn., Ft. Hood, Tex., 1967—72; sec. Collins Radio, Seattle, 1959—60, USAF, 1958—59, Turner Constrn. Co., Chgo., 1957—58; adj. prof. ESL Ctrl. Tex. Coll., 2004. Stringer Belton Jour., 1973—76. Author, dir., prodr.: mus. play Jack in the Bean Stalk, 1983, Christmas in a Bus Station, 1985; prodr., dir. : (maj. prodns.) Many Moons, 1991; Ransom of Red Chief, 1992; Charlotte's Web, 1993; Aladdin, 1994; Once Upon a Clothesline, 1995; editor, prodr. (puppet plays), 1995; dir. : (plays) The Lesson, 1977; The Importance of Being Earnest, 1978; Mrs. McWilliams and the Lightening, 1979; Comedy of Errors, 1980; actor: Of Thee I Sing, 1988, Annie Get Your Gun, 1990. Leader 4H, Salado, 1972—76. Mem.: Daus. of the U.S. Army (pres. 1964—65), Soc. Children's Book Writers and Illustrators, Ft. Hood Officers' Wives Club (program chmn. 1970—71, reporter, editor newsletter 1970—71). Republican. Christian Scientist. Avocations: horseback riding, golf, reading, crossword puzzles. Home: 18800 Kuykendall Branch Rd Salado TX 76571-5143 E-mail: mlblacktx@earthlink.net.

BLACK, MELODEE, marketing professional; b. Aug. 22, 1969; d. Kenneth Lee and Mary Ruth Unger; m. Timothy Black, June 3, 1989. BA magna cum laude, Calif. State U. L.A., 2000. Cert. in Sales and Sales Mgmt. Calif. State U. Fullerton, 1998. Program / project analyst SCE, Rosemead, Calif., 1996—2002, market mgmt. and comm. program mgr., 2002—. Mem. Edison Spkrs. Bur., Rosemead, 2001—, Toastmasters, Rosemead, 1998. Author: (song) When I Think of Heaven, (play) He's Always There. Bd. mem. Belivers' Ministry Internat., Rialto, Calif., 2003; sec./treas. New Life Ctr., Downey, Calif., 1997—98; mem. SCE Employee Contbns. Com., Rosemead, 2002—03. Mem.: Am. Mktg. Assn., Phi Kappa Phi. Mem. Pentecostal Ch. Avocations: travel, gardening, reading, boating. Office: SCE 2244 Walnut Grove Rosemead CA 91770

BLACK, NATALIE A. lawyer; b. 1949; AB, Stanford U., 1972; JD, Marquette U., 1978. Bar: Wisc. Group pres., gen. coun. Kohler Co., Kohler, Wisc. Mem. ABA. Office: Kohler Co Legal Dept 444 Highland Dr Kohler WI 53044-1515 Fax: 920-459-1583.

BLACK, PAGE MORTON, civic worker; b. Chgo. d. Alexander and Rose Morton; m. William Black, Mar. 27, 1962. Student, Chgo. Mus. Coll. Singer, pianist Pierre Hotel, N.Y.C., Warwick Hotel, One Fifth Ave. Sherry Netherland Hotel; singer radio show and comml. Chock Full O'Nuts Corp.; rec. artist Atlantic Records, [illegible] Page and William Black Post-Grad. Sch. Medicine, Mt. Sinai Med. Sch., 1965—; chmn. mem. exec. bd. Parkinsons' Disease Found., Columbia U. Med. Ctr.; mem. nat. vis. coun. Columbia U. Health Scis. Faculties; hon. chmn. Chock Full O' Nuts Corp., 1983—90; active Columbia Presbyn. Health Scis. Adv. Coun.; founding mem. ASPCA; mem. neurosci. com. Neurol. Inst. of N.Y. at Columbia Presbyn. Med. Ctr. Mem. neuroscience com. Columbia Presbyn. Health Sci. Adv. Coun. Recipient Ann. award, Parkinsons' Disease Found., 1987, Police Athletic League, 1992, Manhattan Mag. award, 1992, Lifetime Achievement award, Parkinson's Disease Found., 1997, Dean's award for Disting. Svc., Columbia U. Coll. Physicians & Surgeons, 1998. Home: Premium Pt New Rochelle NY 10801

BLACK, PATRICIA JEAN, medical technologist; b. Milw., Oct. 22, 1954; d. Dale B. and Geraldine L. (Milligan) Heywood; m. Robert S. Black, Oct. 14, 1978. BS, Millikin U., 1978; degree in med. tech., St. Mary's Hosp., 1978. Med. technologist Mercy Hosp., Urbana, Ill., 1978-85; biol. lab. technician No. Regional Rsch. Ctr., USDA Agrl. Rsch. Svc., Peoria, Ill., 1985-88; lab. mgr. Chapman Cancer Ctr., Joplin, Mo., 1989-96, Freeman Cancer Ctr., Joplin, 1996—2001, Freeman Cancer Inst., Joplin, 2001—. Patentee in field. Mem. Am. Soc. Clin. Pathologists (cert., assoc.), Clin. Lab. Mgmt. Assn., Zeta Tau Alpha (scholar chmn. 1976, house mgr. 1977), Sigma Zeta. Avocations: fishing, arts and crafts. Office Phone: 417-347-4014.

BLACK, REBECCA LEREE, special education educator; b. Pasadena, Calif., Sept. 15, 1954; d. James and Mary Black; m. Mario Isabella, Aug. 10, 1996. BA, San Diego State U., 1977, MA, 1987. Multiple subject tchg. credential Calif., cert. specialist credential-learning handicapped Calif., resource specialist. Substitute tchr. San Diego Unified Dist., 1978—80, Poway (Calif.) Unified Sch. Dist., 1978—79; resource specialist Coronado (Calif.) H.S., 1980—. Support provider Beginning Tchr. Support Assessment, Coronado, 2000—02; focus group leader Coronado H.S. Accreditation Com., Coronado, 2001—02. Club advisor Coronado H.S. Friday Night Live Club, Coronado, 1991—2001, Girls' Svc. Club, Coronado, 1980—83, Youth to Youth, Coronado, 1986—89. Scholar Anita Snow Meml., San Diego South County Selpa and Bonita Optimist Found., 2001. Mem.: Calif. Assn. Resource Specialists and Spl. Edn. Tchrs. Avocations: martial arts, golf, softball.

BLACK, RECCA MARCELE, elementary school educator; b. Marion, Ind., Feb. 4, 1964; d. Charles Lee and Jerry Ann Barbour. BA in Elem. Edn., Marion Coll., 1987, MEd; postgrad., Ind. Wesleyan U. Tchr. Marion (Ind.) Community Schs.; food svc. worker Marion Coll. Baldwin Food Svc.; casual clerk, cashier, sec. U.S. Post Office; audio-visual asst. VA Med. Ctr. Reporter Marion Newspaper. Contbr. numerous articles to profl. jours. Bd. dirs. YWCA. Recipient Freshman scholar, Shugar scholar. Mem.: NEA, AAUW (bd. dirs.).

BLACK, RITA DUTTON, media specialist; b. Bklyn. d. Roger and Edith Dutton; m. David M. Black, Oct. 3, 1975; 1 child, Lindsay Edith Jean. BS in History & Social Sci., Longwood Coll., 1970; M of Libr. & Info. Sci., U. S.C., 1995. Cert. tchr. SC. Bd. Edn., 1995, registered Nat. Tchg. Coun. Scotland, 1975. Tchr. Portsmouth Pub. Schools, Va., 1972—75; pub. rels. officer Crawley Borough Coun., England, 1978—81; dep. clk. U.S. Dist. Ct., Columbia, SC, 1982—84; tchr. Dundee Schools, Scotland, 1975—77; info. tech. specialist Richland County Sch. Dist. One, Columbia, 1996—. Adept tchr. evaluator Richland County Sch. Dist. One, 2003—, mem. website rev. com., 2001—. Author (webmaster): (website) St. Andrews Mid. Sch. (Computer Visual Literacy Festival 1st Pl. award, 1999). Usher capt. Union United Meth. Ch., Irmo, SC, 1999—; coach SAMS Fellowship Christian Athletes, Columbia, 2002—. Wayne S. Yenawine scholar, U. S.C. Coll. of Libr. & Info. Sci. Alumni Assn., 1993. Mem.: Palmetto State Teachers Assn. (assoc.), S.C. Assn. Sch. Librarians (assoc.; regional network coord. 1998—99, mem. jr. book award com. 1997—2000), Pi Gamma Mu, Beta Phi Mu (treas. 1998—99). Conservative. Methodist. Avocations: travel, boating, reading, jazz, ballet. Office: St Andrews Mid Sch 1231 Bluefield Rd Columbia SC 29210 E-mail: rblack@richlandone.org.

BLACK, RUTH IDELLA, museum curator; b. Aug. 16, 1911; BA, Hastings Coll., 1933; MA, U. Nebr., 1952. Supt. of schs. Chester (Nebr.) Pub. Schs., 1948-54; head edn. dept. Fairbury (Nebr.) Jr. Coll., 1954-70; curator Fillmore County Hist. Soc. Mus., Fairmont, Nebr., 1987—, also bd. dirs. Mem. Ret. Tchr. Assn., Nebr. State Hist. Soc., Delta Kappa Gamma Rho (chpt. pres. 1965-67, state parlimentarian 1968), Pi Gamma Mu.

BLACK, SHARON SUE GIBBONS, veterinary pathologist, educator; b. Jackson, Miss., Aug. 8, 1959; d. Mack Graham and Carolyn Sue (Bland) Gibbons; m. John Gaston Black, May 25, 1985; 1 child, John Casey. BS, U. So. Miss., 1981; DVM, Miss. State U., 1985, PhD, 1994; postgrad., U. Ga., 1989-91. Diplomate Am. Coll. Vet. Pathologists. Small animal practitioner Animal Clinic Oxford, Miss., 1985-86; diagnostic lab. veterinarian U. Ga., Tifton, 1987-88, Athens, 1990-91; asst. prof. Coll. Vet. Medicine Miss. State U., 1994—99, assoc. prof., 1999—2002; pathologist ANTECH Diagnostics, Starkville, Miss., 2002—. Presenter in field. Mem. editl. bd. Vet. Pathology, 1991-2001; contbr. articles to profl. jours. Named Alumnus of Yr., Coll. Vet. Medicine, Miss. State U., 2001. Mem. Am. Vet. Med. Assn., Miss. Vet. Med. Assn., Assn. Vet. Lab. Diagnosticians, Phi Zeta.

BLACK, SHAWN MORGADO, dancer; b. Tuscaloosa, Ala., Sept. 29, 1964; d. Hank Scott Jr. and Olivia Jane (Matthews) B.; m. Jeffrey R. Bornemann, July 7, 1988. Grad., Ala. Sch. Fine Arts, 1982. Prin. dancer Alabama Ballet, Birmingham, 1981-83; dancer Atlanta Ballet, 1983-84; mem. corps de ballet Am. Ballet Theatre, N.Y.C., 1984-91, soloist, 1991—; dancer Twyla Tharpe Dance Co., N.Y.C., 1993—. Performances with ABT include La Bayadere, Bruch Violin Concerto No. 1, Fall River Legend, The Rite of Spring, Rodeo, The Sleeping Beauty, Swan Lake, Symphonic Variations. Democrat. Lutheran. Avocations: horseback riding, sailing, canoeing, camping. Office: Am Ballet Theatre 890 Broadway New York NY 10003-1211

BLACK, SHIRLEY TEMPLE (MRS. CHARLES A. BLACK), former ambassador, former actress; b. Santa Monica, Calif., Apr. 23, 1928; d. George Francis and Gertrude Temple; m. John Agar, Jr., Sept. 19, 1945 (div. 1949); 1 dau., Linda Susan; m. Charles A. Black, Dec. 16, 1950; children: Charles Alden, Lori Alden. Ed. under pvt. tutelage; grad., Westlake Sch. Girls, 1945. Rep. to 24th Gen. Assembly UN, N.Y.C., 1969-70; amb. to Ghana Accra, 1974-76; chief of protocol White House, Washington, 1976-77; amb. to Czechoslovakia Prague, 1989-92. Mem. U.S. Delegation on African Refugee Problems, Geneva, 1981; mem. public adv. com. UN Conf. on Law of the Sea; dep. chmn. U.S. del. UN Conf. on Human Environment, Stockholm, 1970-72; spl. asst. to chmn. Pres.'s Coun. on Environ. Quality, 1972-74; del. treaty on environment USSR-USA Joint Commn., Moscow, 1972; mem. U.S. Commn. for UNESCO, 1973—; hon. U.S. Fgn. Svc. officer. Began film career at age 3 1/2; first full-length film was Stand Up and Cheer; other films included Little Miss Marker, Baby Take a Bow, Bright Eyes, Our Little Girl, The Little Colonel, Curly Top, The Littlest Rebel, Captain January, Poor Little Rich Girl, Dimples, Stowaway, Wee Willie Winkie, Heidi, Rebecca of Sunnybrook Farm, Little Miss Broadway, Just Around the Corner, The Little Princess, Susannah of the Mounties, The Blue Bird, Kathleen, Miss Annie Rooney, Since You Went Away, Kiss and Tell, 1945, That Hagen Girl, War Party, The Bachelor and the Bobby-Soxer, Honeymoon, 1947; narrator, actress: TV series Shirley Temple Storybook, NBC, 1958, Shirley Temple Show, NBC, 1960; author: Child Star: An Autobiography, 1988. Dir. Bank of Calif.; dir. Fireman's Fund Ins. Co., BANCAL Tri-State Corp., Walt Disney, Del Monte Corp.; Mem. Calif. Adv. Hosp. Council, 1969, San Francisco Health Facilities Planning Assn., 1965-69; Republican candidate for U.S. Ho. of Reps. from Calif., 1967; bd. dirs. Nat. Wildlife Fedn., Nat. Multiple Sclerosis Soc., UN Assn. U.S.A.; bd. dirs. exec. com. Internat. Fedn. Multiple Sclerosis Socs. Appointed col. on staff of Gov. Ross of Idaho, 1935; commd. col. Hawaiian N.G.; hon. col. 108th Rgt. N.G. Ill.; dame Order Knights Malta, Paris, 1968; recipient Ceres medal FAO, Rome, 1975, numerous other state decorations. Mem. World Affairs Coun. No. Calif. (dir.), Coun. Fgn. Rels., Nat. Com. for U.S./China Rels. Clubs: Commonwealth of Calif.

BLACK, SUSAN HARRELL, judge; b. Valdosta, Ga., Oct. 20, 1943; d. William H. and Ruth Elizabeth (Phillips) Harrell; m. Louis Eckert Black, Dec. 28, 1966. BA, Fla. State U., 1965; JD, U. Fla., 1967; LLM, U. Va., 1984. Bar: Fla. 1967. Atty. U.S. Army Corps of Engrs., Jacksonville, Fla., 1968—69; asst. state atty. Gen. Counsel's Office, Jacksonville, 1969—72; judge County Ct. of Duval County, Fla., 1973—75; judge 4th Jud. Cir. Ct. of Fla., 1975—79; judge U.S. Dist. Ct. (mid. dist.) Fla., Jacksonville, 1979—90, chief judge, 1990—92; judge U.S. Ct. Appeals (11th cir.) Fla., Jacksonville, 1992—. Faculty Fed. Jud. Ctr.; mem. U.S. Jud. Conf. Com. on Jud. Improvements; trustee Am. Inns Ct. Found. Trustee emeritus Law Sch. U. Fla.; past pres. Chester Bedell Inn of Ct. Mem.: ABA, Jacksonville Bar Assn., Fla. Bar Assn. Episcopalian. Home: 4626 River Point Rd W Jacksonville FL 32207-1104*

BLACK, SYLVIA SLOAN, business educator; b. Phila., Pa., Oct. 24, 1946; d. Maceo A. and Charlotte Kennedy Sloan; m. Frederick Harold Black; children: Frederick Harold Black, Jr., Shana Sloan. BS, Howard U., Washington, 1968; MS, U. N.C., Chapel Hill, 1974; PhD, Columbia U., 1997; MBA, U. Kans., Lawrence, 1981. Instr. Fayetteville (N.C.) State U., 1973—74; opers. mgr. Pacific Trade Group, Waipahu, Hawaii, 1981—83; asst. mgr., fin. analyst Cadet Store, West Point, NY, 1984—93; asst. prof. U. N.C. Kenan-Flagler Bus. Sch., Chapel Hill, 1993—2001, N.C. A&T State U. Sch. Bus. and Econs., Greensboro, 2001—. Faculty advanced leadership program U.S. Postal Svc., Potomac, Md., 1999—. Chair bd. advisors U.S. Army War Coll., Carlisle, Pa., 1997—2002. Mem.: Strategic Mgmt. Soc., Acad. Internat. Bus., Acad. Mgmt., Nat. Black MBA Assn. (life), Phi Kappa Phi, Phi Beta Kappa, Beta Gamma Sigma, Delta Sigma Theta (life). Lutheran. Avocations: travel, reading. Office: NC A&T State U 1601 E Market St Greensboro NC 27411 Office Fax: 336-334-7093. Business E-mail: ssblack@ncat.edu.

BLACK, VICTORIA LYNN, writer, artist; b. Whittier, Calif., Nov. 23, 1943; d. Raymond Witty and Dorothy Ada (Burnett) Davenport; m. Bruce Robert Black, Aug. 30, 1997; m. Richard Dee Bandlow, Sept. 16, 1961 (dec. Dec. 2, 1972); children: Lisa Lynn Bandlow Dobbins, Lincoln Dee Bandlow. Student, Glendale Coll., 1986—2002. Model/actress Dale Garrick Agy., Beverly Hills, Calif., 1959—78, Bronson of Calif., L.A., 1968—79; prodn. asst./casting Pub. Svc. Co., Irvine, Calif., 1979—80; theatrical agt. William Carroll Agy., Burbank, Calif., 1980—83; office mgr. Greenline, L.A., 1984—86, Napier, L.A., 1986—88, Shah Safari, L.A., 1988—93; writer, artist L.A. Author poetry, short stories, articles; artist paintings and drawings, exhibited in group shows at Verdugo Hills Art Assn., Montrose, Calif., 1999—2003, Glendale (Calif.) Coll., 1998—2003, ERA Castle, La Canada, Calif., 2002, Pasadena (Calif.) Libr., 2002. Convalescent Hosp. L.A., 1997—99. Named Miss Palm Springs, 1960, Miss North Shore Beach, 1961, Miss Ma-Ha-Ya Lani, 1961, Miss Typical Teen, 1961. Mem.: Utah State Poetry Soc., W.Va. Poetry Soc., Poetry Soc. Okla., Mo. State Poetry Soc., Fla. State Poets Assn., Calif. State Poetry Soc., Ariz. State Poetry Soc., Verdugo Hills Art Assn., Alpha Gamma Sigma (life). Avocations: long walks, reading, collecting, gardening, museums and art shows. Home: PO Box 959 Sugarloaf CA 92386

BLACKBURN, DEBBIE, elementary school educator, state representative; b. Woodward, Okla., Jan. 12, 1951; d. Norman and Laura Stevens; m. Bob L. Blackburn; 1 child, Beau. BA, Southwestern Okla. State U., 1973; postgrad studies in history, Okla. State U. Rep. Ho. Reps., State of Okla., Okla. City, 1995—. Bd, dirs. Paseo Redevelopment Corp.; chair subcom on edn, to appropriations and budget com. Okla. Ho. Reps., Okla. City, 1995—, mem. banking and fin., common edn., govt. ops., agy. oversight and adminstrv rules, human svcs. coms., 1995—. Mem. Neighborhood Alliance Okla. City. Mem.: LWV, Okla. City Leadership Alumni Assn., Okla. Acad. for State Goals, Downtown Rotary Club. Democrat. Office: 2300 N Lincoln Blvd Rm 301-A Oklahoma City OK 73105 Home and Office: 126 NW 22d St Oklahoma City OK 73103 E-mail: blackburnde@lsb.state.ok.us

BLACKBURN, ELIZABETH HELEN, molecular biologist; b. Hobart, Australia, Nov. 26, 1948; 1 child. BS, U. Melbourne, Australia, 1970, MS, 1971; PhD in Molecular Biology, Cambridge (Eng.) U., 1975; DSc (hon.), Yale U., 1991. Fellow in biology Yale U., New Haven, 1975-77; fellow in biochemistry U. Calif., San Francisco, 1977-78, from asst. prof. to assoc. prof. molecular biology Berkeley, 1978-86; prof. molecular biology, 1986-90; prof. U. Calif., San Francisco, 1990—, chair dept. microbiology and immunology, 1993-99. Recipient Eli Lilly award in microbiology, 1988, NAS award in molecular biology, 1990. Mem.: NAS (fgn. assoc. 1993), AAAS, Royal Soc. London (G.M. Sloan prize 2001), Am. Soc. Cell Biology (pres. 1998, Australian prize 1998, Gairdner prize 1998, Passano award 1999, Rosensteil award 1999, Keio prize 1999). Office: U Calif Biochem and Biophys Box 2200 San Francisco CA 94143-2200 E-mail: telomer@itsa.ucsf.edu.

BLACKBURN, GRETA JEANETTE, writer; d. William Leroy and Sarah Jeannette (Turk) B.; m. Gary Wood, Sept. 17, 1983 (div. June 1993); m. James Allen Frost, June 1996. BS, Calif. Coast Univ., 1998, postgrad., 1998—. Editor-in-chief Natural Body and Fitness mag., L.A., 1985-90, Ms. Fitness mag., L.A., 1990—. Founder FITCAMP, Retreats for Women, Big Bear, Calif. and Malibu, Calif., 1994—. Co-author: (with Cory Everson) Life Balance, 1998. Mem. adv. bd. City of Hope Workout with the Stars against AIDS, 1987; founder Fitness Against Drugs, L.A., 1987; developed The Kick Butt Boxer's workout; produced, co-hosted Pro-Celebrity Sno Games, 1987, Pro-Celebrity Winter Games, 1988; prodr. Tennis Tournament of the Stars, 1987-88, benefits for charity. Recipient Outstanding Support to the Sport of Bodybuilding World Cup of Natural Bodybuilding, 1989. Mem. AAUW, The So. Touch Food Products Coun. Avocations: photography, travel, tennis, skiing, motorcycles. Office: Fitcamp 18653 Ventura Blvd Ste 16 Tarzana CA 91356-4103

BLACKBURN, JOY MARTIN, librarian; b. Marietta, Ohio, Oct. 28, 1925; d. Jonathan George and Helen Joy (Smith) Martin; m. Paul Edward Blackburn, Dec. 18, 1948 (dec. Dec. 1996); children: Paul Conrow, Amy Joy. BA, Ohio Wesleyan U., 1947; MA, U. Minn, 1948. Student counselor Ohio State U., Columbus, 1948—54; editor/libr. Jones & Laughlin Steel Co., Pitts., 1955—57; rsch. libr. Tech. Mktg. Assn., Concord, Mass., 1964—66; mgr. corp. libr. Washington Nat. Ins., Evanston, Ill., 1966—85; systems libr. Luth. Gen. Hosp., Park Ridge, Ill., 1986—88; info. specialist C. Berger & Co., Carol Stream, Ill., 1989—93; retired. Rsch./editor U. Pitts. Med. Sch., 1959. Author: J&L Rsch. Bull., 1955—57. Vol. Chgo. Bot. Garden Libr., Glencoe, Ill., 1997—99. Mem.: U. Va. Libr. Assocs. (bd. dirs. 2001—, 2004—), Cook County Hort. Soc. (hon.), Phi Beta Kappa. Avocations: history, photography, Arctic art, culture, travel.

BLACKBURN, MARSHA, congresswoman; b. Laurel, Miss., June 6, 1952; married; 2 children. BS, Miss. St. Univ., 1973. Retail mktg.; senator Tenn. State Senate, Nashville, 1998—2002; mem. U.S. Ho. of Reps. from 7th Tenn. dist., 2003—. Del. Am. Coun. Young Polit. Leaders, S.E. Asia, 1993; appointed by Gov. Don Sundquist exec. dir. Tenn. Film, Entertainment and Music Commn., 1995; chmn. Gov.'s Prayer Breakfast, 1996; bd. dirs. Benton Hall Sch., Nashville Symphony Guild, Arthritis Found., Nashville Zoo Friends; appointed Econ. Coun. on Women, 1999. Mem. Nat. Acad. Rec. Arts and Scis., Country Music Assn., Rotary, C. of C. Republican. Office: 509 Cannon Ho Office Bldg Washington DC 20515-4305 E-mail: sen.marsha.blackburn@legislature.state.tn.u.

BLACKBURN, SADIE GWIN ALLEN, business executive; b. San Angelo, Tex., Oct. 14, 1924; d. Harvey Hicks Allen and Helen (Harris) Weaver; m. Edward Albert Blackburn Jr., Feb. 25, 1946; children: Edward III, Catherine Ledyard, Robert Allen. BA, Rice U., 1945, MA, 1975. Bookkeeper, trust dept. State Nat. Bank, Houston; tchr. elem. sch. Galveston, Tex.; mng. ptnr. Storey Creek Partnership, Houston, 1969—; spl. projects dir. San Jacinto State Park, San Jacin; dir. master plan State Historial Park. Lectr. in landscape design history; spkr. in field. Co-author: Houston's Forgotten Heritage, 1822-1914, 1991; contbr. articles to gardening publs. Newsheet chmn. Jr. League, Galveston, 1950-53, art chmn., Houston Jr. League, 1957-58, chmn. garden/design com., 1991-93, mental health study com., 1959-61, 2d v.p., 1962-63, provisional chmn., 1962-63, interview chmn., 1963-64; adv. bd. Bayou Bend Gardens chmn. Mus. Fine Arts, 1973-74, Bayou Bend adv. com., 1987-89; v.p. Mental HEalth Assn., 1957-62; asst. treas. Child Guidance Assn., 1962-65; mem. Rice U. Hist. Commn., 1974-75; pres. River Oaks Garden Club, Houston, 1975-76; mem. adv. com. Bayou Bend Gardens, 1991—; active Buffalo Bayou Partnership, Houston Nature Conservancy, 1993, Friends of Herman Park, 1994, Meml. Park Adv., 1995, Scenic Houston Bd., 1999. Named Scenic Visionary, Scenic Houston, 2003; recipient Sweet Briar Disting. Alumna award, 1991, award, Friends of Herman Park, 2003. Mem. Garden Club Am. (zone chmn. 1977-79, founders fund vice chmn. 1979-80, dir. 1980-82, rec. sec. 1982-84, v.p. 1984-86, archive co-chmn. 1986-87, 1st v.p. 1987-89, pres. 1989-91, Achievement medal 2002), Nat. Wildflower Rsch. Ctr. (bd. dirs.), Nat. Parks and Conservation Assn. Bd. (v.p. 1995-97, sec. 1997-99), San Jacinto Mus. History (pres. bd. 1975-77, bd. dirs.), Pi Beta Phi (Carolyn Herman Lichtenberg Crest award for disting. alumnae achievement 1998). Republican. Episcopalian. Avocations: gardening, fishing, hunting, bridge, golf. Home: 1030 Potomac Houston TX 77057-1916

BLACKBURN, SHARON LOVELACE, federal judge; b. Pensacola, Fla., May 7, 1950; BA, U. Ala., 1973; JD, Samford U., 1977. Law clk. to Hon. Robert Varner U.S. Dist. Ct. Ala., 1977-78; staff atty. Birmingham Area Legal Svcs., 1979; asst. U.S. atty. U.S. Atty's. Office, 1979-91; judge U.S. Dist. Ct. (no. dist.) Ala., Birmingham, 1991—. Mem. Birmingham Bar Assn. Office: US Dist Ct 730 Hugo L Black US Cthouse 1729 5th Ave N Birmingham AL 35203-2000

BLACKER, HARRIET, public relations executive; b. N.Y.C., July 23, 1940; d. Louis and Rebecca (Siegel) B.; m. Roland Algrant, Aug. 6, 1970 (div. Jan. 1981); m. Matthew E. Harlib, Aug. 25, 1988 (dec. 1994). BA, U. Mich., 1962. Exec. dir. publicity Random House, N.Y.C., 1974-79; East Coast v.p. Pickwick Maslansky Koenigsberg, N.Y.C., 1980-81; v.p. pub. relations Putnam Pub. Group, N.Y.C, 1981-85; pres. Harriet Blacker, Inc., N.Y.C., 1986-90; ptnr. Blacker Hunter Pub. Rels. Inc., N.Y.C., 1990—96; pres. Blacker Communications, N.Y.C., 1993—. Mem. Publishers Publicity Assn. (sec. 1973-75, treas. 1982-83, pres. 1983-85), Women's Media Group

BLACKHAM, ANN ROSEMARY (MRS. J. W. BLACKHAM), realtor; b. N.Y.C., June 16, 1927; d. Frederick Alfred and Letitia L. (Stolfe) DeCain; m. James W. Blackham Jr., Aug. 18, 1951; children: Ann C., James W. III. AB, St. Mary of the Springs Coll. (now Ohio Dominican U.), 1949; postgrad., Ohio State U., 1950. Mgr. br. store Filene & Sons, Winchester, Mass., 1950—52; broker Porter Co. Real Estate, Winchester, 1961—66; sales mgr. James T. Trefrey, Inc., Winchester, 1966—68; pres., founder Ann Blackham & Co. Inc. Realtors, Winchester, 1968—2001; v.p. Coldwell Banker, Winchester, 2001—. Bd. econ. advisors to Gov., 1969-74; participant White House Conf. on Internat. Cooperation, 1965; mem. Presdl. Task Force on Women's Rights and Responsibilities, 1969; exec. coun. Mass. Civil Def., 1965-69; chmn. Gov.'s Commn. on Status of Women, 1971-75; regional dir. Interstate Assn. Commn. on Status of Women, 1971-74; mem. Gov. Task Force on Mass. Economy, 1972; mem. Gov.'s Jud. Selection Com., 1972, Mass. Emergency Fin. Bd., 1974-75; bd. registration Real Estate Brokers and Salesman Commonwealth of Mass., 1991—, chmn. 1994—. Bd. visitors Ohio Dominican U., 1995—, nat. fund raising chair, 1998-99; corporator, trustee Charlestown Savs. Bank, 1974-84; corporator Winchester Hosp., 1983—, chair fund raising emergency room; bd. dirs. Winchester Hosp. Found., [illegible] Winchester [illegible] Commn.; design rev. commn. Town of Winchester, 1981-2003; bd. dirs. Phoenix Found., 1980-90, Bay State Health Care, Mass. Taxpayers Found., Speech and Hearing Found., Baystate Health Mgmt., Realty Guild Inc., v.p. 1995-96, bd. dirs. 1996-99, pres. 1997-98; regional selection panel White House Fellows, 1973-74; com. on women in svc. U.S. Dept. Def., 1977-80; 2d v.p. Doric Dames, 1971-74, founding mem., 1969; dep. chmn. Mass. Rep. State Com., 1965-66; sec. Mass. Rep. State Conv., 1970, del., 1960, 62, 64, 66, 70, 72, 74, 78, 90, 98, 2002; state vice-chmn. Mass. Rep. Fin. Com., 1970; alt. del.-at-large Rep. Nat. Conv., 1968, 72, del., 1980, 84, 88, 92, 96; Rep. State Committeewoman, 1996—; pres. Mass. Fedn. Rep. Women, 1964-69; v.p. Nat. Fedn. Rep. Women, 1965-79; pres. Scholarship Found., 1976-78, Mass. Fedn. Women's Clubs; alumnae liaison The Beaumont Sch. for Girls; mem. Women for Romney, 2002; mem. Gov. Romney Inaugural Com. Recipient Pub. Svc. award Commonwealth of Mass., 1978, Merit award Rep. Party, 1969, Pub. Affairs award Mass. Fedn. Women's Clubs, 1975; named Civic Leader of Yr. Mass. Broadcasters, 1962, Banker and Tradesman Leader Making a Difference, 1999; recipient Bus. Owner of Yr. award New England Women Bus. Owners, 1995, Disting. Alumnae award Ohio Dominican Coll., 1999, Disting. Service Citation Town of Winchester, 2003. Mem. Greater Boston Real Estate Bd. (hon., bd. dirs.), Eastern Middlesex Bd. Realtors (life mem. multi-million dollar club), Mass. Assn. Realtors (bd. dirs.), Nat. Assn. Realtors (women's coun.), Brokers Inst. (cert.), Coun. Realtors (cert., pres. 1983-84), Winchester C. of C. (bd. dirs.), Greater Boston C. of C., Nat. Assn. Women Bus. Owners, ENKA Soc. (treas. 2001—), Rotary Internat., Tequesta Fla. Country Club, Capitol Hill Club, Ponte Vedra Club, Winchester Boat Club, Winchester Country Club, Wychmere Harbor Club, Womens City Club, Winton Club (sec., bd. dirs.), Hyannis Yacht Club. Home: 60 Swan Rd Winchester MA 01890-3747 Office: Coldwell Banker 3 Church St Winchester MA 01890-2903 E-mail: ann.blackham@nemoves.com.

BLACKMAN, BRENDA, newscaster; Anchor UPN 9 News at 10 O'Clock, Secaucus, N.J. Office: WWOR-TV/BHC Communications Inc 9 Broadcast Plz Secaucus NJ 07094-2913

BLACKMAN, CINDY, musician, composer; b. Yellow Springs, Ohio, Nov. 18, 1959; BA, U. Hartford; MA, Berklee Coll. Music. Represented by Highnote Records, Inc. (formerly Muse Records), 1987—. Performer jazz clubs, N.Y., 1982—. Contbr. recording to (album) Verses; performed and recorded albums with Jackie McLean, Lenny Dravitz, Jacky Terrasson, others; albums include Arcane, 1988, Code Red, 1992, Trio+ two, 1992, Telepathy, 1994, Works on Canvas, In the Now, Oracle. Office: Highnote Records Inc 106 W 71st St New York NY 10023-4060

BLACKMAN, DRUSILLA DENISE, dean; b. Madison, Wis., Aug. 26, 1954; d. Leonard and June (Jones) Blackman; m. Steven Baumholtz, June 28, 1987; children: Lukas Baumholtz, Adam Baumholtz. BS, Brown U., Providence; MBA, U. Pa., 1982. Dean grad. admissions and fin. aid Harvard U., Cambridge, Mass.; dean admissions and fin. aid Columbia U., N.Y.C.; dean of enrollment Culinary Inst. Am., Hyde Park, NY. Coll. cons. Vanguard Cons. Democrat. Avocations: reading, music, modern dance, cooking. Office: Culinary Inst 1946 Campus Dr Hyde Park NY 12538

BLACKMAN, GHITA WAUCHETA, natural energy consultant; b. Chgo., Feb. 19, 1932; d. William Harveston Joseph Harris and Zelda (Booth) Harris; m. David Edward Blackman, June 7, 1953 (div. Oct. 1976); children: Anasa, Anthony, Cynthia, Tracy. Student, NYU, 1949-50, U. Dayton, 1952-53. Various secretarial positions U.S. Air Force, Dayton, Ohio, Am. Humanist Assn., Yellow Springs, Ohio, 1950-64; sec. Antioch Coll., Yellow Springs, 1964-66, Fels Rsch. Inst., Yellow Springs, 1966-70; cons. direct sales Fashion Two Twenty, Dayton, 1966-72; mem. sales staff Prophet & Friends Inc., New Britain, Conn., 1972-76; customer rels. clk. Conn. Natural Gas Corp., Hartford, 1976-80, natural energy cons., 1980-98. Mem. Dayton Jr. Philharm. Orch., 1947-53, second violin Springfield Symphony, Ohio, 1956-64; v.p. Conn. Capitol Area chpt. Older Women's League, Hartford, 1985-87; sec. Spiritual Assembly of the Baha'is of West Hartford, Conn., 1977-78; corr. sec. Spiritual Assembly of the Baha'is of Hartford, 1982—. Independent. Mem. Baha'i Faith. Avocation: music. E-mail: ghitab@aol.com., ghitab@juno.com.

BLACKMAN, JEANNE A. community program manager; b. Decatur, Ill., Sept. 23, 1943; d. Robert Russell and Elizabeth Irene (DeWolfe) Shulke; m. Gary L. Blackman, Apr. 16, 1963 (div. Aug. 1983); children: Jeffrey Lynn, Stephanie Sue; m. Bill Weitekamp, Nov. 21, 1995. BS Elem. Edn., Ind. U., 1965; MS in Edn. Adminstrn., Eastern Ill. U., 1979. Cert. tchr. and administr.; lic. real estate salesperson. Elem. tchr. Taylorville (Ill.) Community Sch. Dist., 1965-86; real estate salesperson Craggs-Adams Realtors, Taylorville, 1985-87; adminstrv. asst. to chief of staff Ill. Dept. of Aging, Springfield, 1986-87, consumer adv., 1987-89; lobbyist Ill. Guardianship and Advocacy Commn., Springfield, 1989-95; policy advisor Office of the Atty. Gen., Springfield, Ill., 1995-99; mgr. vol. program Ill. Commn. on Volunteerism and Cmty. Svc., Springfield, 1999—. Pres. Taylorville Edn. Assn., 1983-85; mem. adv. coun. Gov.'s Rehab., Springfield, 1987—; chmn. Springfield Civil Svc. Commn., 1995—. Co-founder, treas. Ill. Vol. Optometry Svcs. to Humanity, Taylorville, 1976—; pres. Capitol City Rep. Women's Club, 1988—; pres. Women in Mgmt., 1989—, pres.-elect, 1990; fundraiser, chairperson Ill. Women's Polit. Caucus, Springfield, 1985—; pres. Am. Field Svc. Student Exch. Program, Taylorville, 1985-87; bd. dirs. LWV Springfield chpt., 1984—; pres. bd. dirs. Mental Health Ctrs. Ctrl. Ill., 1994—; trustee Lincolnland C.C., 1989, vice chair 1992-93, chmn. 93-94, 96-97, bd. dirs.; pres. Ill. C.C. Trustees Assn., 1992; mem. Mayor's Commn. Internat. Visitors; chmn. Springfield (Ill.) Civil Svc. Commn., 1995-97; alderman City of Springfield, 1997-99; pres. Springfiled Vol. Ctr., 2002--; bd. dirs. Lincolnland C.C. Found., 2001--; alumnae bd. Leadership Springfiled, 2001--. Mem. AAUW (edn. chairperson Taylorville chpt. 1985—), DAR, Sister Cities Assn. Springfield, Ill. Women in Govt. (bd. dirs. 1988—, v.p. 1990—), Women's Legis. Network, Ill. Fedn. Rep. Women (v.p., bd. dirs. 1988—, ways and means com. 1987—, world affairs coun. 1990—), Greater Springfield C. of C., Rotary, Delta Delta Delta (pres. 2001). Presbyterian. Avocations: volunteer work, travel, reading. Home: 19 Washington Pl Springfield IL 62702-4634 Office: 535 W Jefferso Springfield IL 62702-1614

BLACKMAN, LANI MODICA, copy editor; d. Salvatore Modica; m. Ronald Lewis Blackman, Sept. 17, 1969; 1 child, Lezlie Bianca Hepburn. Student, Ind. U., 1952—53; BS in Bus. Adminstrn., Bryant Coll., 1957; postgrad., SUNY, New Paltz, 1965—67; MFA in Theatre Arts, Brandeis U., 1972. Columnist Onterora Record, Woodstock, NY, 1962—64; dir. acting workshops Nashua (N.H.) and Manchester (N.H.) Inst. Arts and Scis., 1970—72; instr. acting and directing Berkshire C.C., Pittsfield, Mass., 1976—77; copy editor SUNY Press, Albany, NY, 1984—; editl. dir., copy editor, owner Renaissance Style, Ontario, NY, 1986—; editor Greenhaven Press, Mpls., 1986—87; copy editor Macmillan Pub., N.Y.C., 1988—91. Lectr. on Shakers Old Chatham (N.Y.) Mus., 1973—75; writer, editor Connections Episcopal Diocese Rochester, 1991—93; artist-in-residence Dorset (Vt.) Colony House, 2002. Author poetry, plays. Vestry mem. St. Luke's Episcopal, Catskill, NY, 1987, conv. del. Fairport, NY, 1989—91. Democrat. Avocations: English riding and jumping, reading, gardening. Office: Renaissance Style 641 Haley Rd Ontario NY 14519

BLACKMAN, SHARON FORBES, music educator; b. Velasco, Tex., Jan. 5, 1949; d. Edward King Forbes and Ivah Terry Forbes Powell; m. Franklin Vaden Blackman, Dec. 1, 1973; 1 child, Jeffrey Vaden. B in Music Edn., Fla. State Univ., Tallahassee, 1972. Music tchr. Spring Lake Elem., Ocoee, Fla., 1972—86; choral dir. Ocoee Mid. Sch., 1986—. Pianist McCormick Rd. Bapt. Ch., Apopka, Fla., 1984—. Mem.: NEA, Fla. Vocal Assn., Music Educators Nat. Conf., Order of Eastern Star. Baptist. Office: Ocoee Mid Sch 300 S Bluford Ave Ocoee FL 34761

BLACKMAN, SUE ANNE BATEY, economics researcher; b. Hamilton AFB, Calif., June 21, 1948; d. Wayman C. and Lela M. (Fasgold) Batey; m. Martin R. Blackman, Apr. 7, 1977; 1 child, Emily Batey Blackman. BA in Polit. Sci., U. Colo., 1970. Econs. rsch. aide dept. econs. Princeton (N.J.) U., 1972-79, econs. rsch. asst. dept. econs., 1979-86, sr. rsch. asst. dept. econs., 1987—. Author: (with W.J. Baumol and E.N. Wolff) Productivity and American Leadership: The Long View, 1989, (with Baumol) Perfect Markets and Easy Virtue, 1991; contbr. articles to profl. jours. Office: Princeton U Dept Econs 101 Fisher Hall Princeton NJ 08544-1021

BLACK MCCOY, DEBRA MARLENE, sales executive; b. Pitts., Nov. 6, 1953; d. Donald T. and Doris A. (Porter) B.; m. Edward B. McCoy, Aug. 8, 1998. BA, Ky. Wesleyan Coll., 1975; MA, Western Ky. U., 1983. Cert. elem. tchr., kindergarten endorsement, Ky. Tchr. kindergarten Owensboro (Ky.) Ind. Schs., 1975-79, Owensboro-Daviess County Child Care, 1987-88; elem. tchr. Ohio County Bd. Edn., Hartford, Ky., 1979-80; substitute tchr. Owensboro Ind. Schs., 1980-86; tchr. kindergarten Daviess County Bd. Edn., Owensboro, 1988-91; preschool tchr. Mary Mitchell Preschool, Owensboro, 1992—96; sales assoc. Bacons Dept. Stores, 1991—98; area sales mgr. Famous Barr divsn. May Co., Owensboro, Ky., 1998—. Mem. Beta Sigma Phi (chpt. pres. 1988-91, Woman of Yr. award 1990). Republican. Presbyterian. Avocations: reading, cross-stitch, sewing.

BLACKMON, BARBARA MARTIN, state legislator, lawyer; b. Jackson, Dec. 7, 1955; BS, Jackson State U.; MBA, U. of Ala.; JD, U. Miss.; LLM, NYU. State senator Miss. State Senate, Jackson, 1992—. Vice chmn. insurance, constitution; mem. judiciary, finance, highways and transportation, public health. Mem. Miss. Bar Assn., Miss. Trial Lawyers Assn., N.Y. Bar Assn. Baptist. Home: 907 W Peace St Canton MS 39046-4126 Office: State Capitol Bldg PO Box 1018 Jackson MS 39215-1018 E-mail: bblackmon@mail.senate.state.ms.us.

BLACKSTOCK, VIRGINIA LEE LOWMAN (MRS. LEROY BLACKSTOCK), civic worker; b. Bixby, Okla., July 2, 1917; d. Joseph Arthur and Winifred (Lundy) Lowman; m. Leroy Blackstock, Dec. 29, 1939; children: Vincent Craig, Priscilla Gay Kurz, Burch Lee, Lore Anne Mitchell; 1 child, Trena Jan. Student, Tulsa Coll. Bus., 1935-37. Legal sec. law firm, Tulsa, 1937-41. Chmn. program Internat. Students in Tulsa, 1955-65; mem. Tulsa Council Camp Fire Girls, 1963-66; mem. youth com. Tulsa Philharmonic Soc., 1969-70; now mem. women's assn.; pres. Eliot Elementary P.T.A., 1961-62, Edison High Sch. P.T.A., 1971-72; mem. Tulsa Opera Guild. Co-chmn. Democratic precinct No. 132, 1960-67. Mem. Tulsa County Bar Aux. (pres. 1954-55, sec. 1962-63, chaplain 1966-67). Clubs: Petroleum. Baptist. Home: 7213 S Atlanta St Tulsa OK 74136

BLACKWELL, DOROTHY PATTON, artist; b. Columbia, S.C., May 6, 1949; d. Charles Shannon and Dorothy Mitchell (Kelly) B. BA in Cultural Geography, Macalester Coll., St. Paul, 1974; Cert. Moyen, French Lang./Lit., Sorbonne, Paris, 1977; postgrad., Escola de Artes Visuais, Rio de Janeiro, 1984-86; M in Internat. Adminstrn., Sch. for Internat. Tng., 1997. Owner Blackwell Studios, Camden, S.C., 1993—, Rio de Janeiro, 1982—96. Dorland Mountain Arts Colony residency, Temecula, Calif., 1994; art columnist Rio Life, 1987-89. One woman shows include: Sao Jose dos Campos, Brazil, 1987, Sao Paulo, Brazil, 1987, N.Y.C., 1988, Museu de Arte Contemporaneo, Goiania, Goias, Brazil, 1993, Brasilia, Brazil, 1993, Recife, Pernambuco, Brazil, 1993, Louisville, 1995, Camden, 1996; group shows in cities including Rio de Janeiro, Brasilia, Sao Paulo, Asheville, N.C., Salvador, Bahia, Brazil, Cairo, Camden, Burlingame, Calif., Boca Raton, Fla., Greenville, S.C., Charleston, S.C., Tegricigulpa, Honduras, Guatamala, Dona, Qatar,and private and corp. collections in U.S., France, Brazil and Japan, Guatemala, Teguciqalpa, Honduras, Doha, Qatar. Mem. S.C. Arts Alliance, Camden Tree Found. Episcopalian. Avocations: golf, travel, visiting museums, nature. Office: Blackwell Studios PO Box 399 Camden SC 29020-0399

BLACKWELL, JEANNINE, foreign language educator; b. Tyron, N.C., July 26, 1949; d. Benjamin and Lois (Turner) B.; m. Michael Taylor Jones, Dec. 18, 1987; 1 child, Bettina. BA, Duke U., 1971, MA, 1975; PhD, Ind. U., 1982. Asst. prof. German Mich. State U., East Lansing, 1983-85, U. Ky., Lexington, 1985-89, assoc. prof. German, 1989—. Assoc. dean arts & scis. U. Ky., 1992-94, dean Grad. Sch., 2003. Assoc. editor Colloguia Germanica jour., 1994—; co-editor (spl. issue) Cultural Contentions in Early Modern Germany, 1996. Fulbright fellow, 1989-90. Mem. Modern Lang. Assn. (discipline exec. com. 1995—), Coalition Women in German (steerimg com. 1985-88, pres. 2002-04). Office: U Ky German Dept 1055 Patterson Tower Lexington KY 40506-0001

BLACKWELL, KAREN ELAINE, music educator; b. Sacramento, Apr. 25, 1954; d. Karl Lamar and Iris Elaine (McDaniel) Blackwell. BA in Music Edn., U. New Orleans, 1977, BA, 1978. Band dir. Jefferson Parish Schs., Gretna, Terrytown, Metairie, La., 1978—84, 1990—91, Higgins H.S., Marrero, La., 1984—90, Worley Jr. H.S., Westwego, La., 1991—. Honor band dir. Plaquemine Parish Schs., Belle Chasse, La., 2002, Jefferson Parish Schs., 2003; mem. New Orleans Concert Band, Jefferson Cmty. Band; sec. Summer Pops, 1978; hon. band clinician St. Charles Parish Pub. Schs., 2003. Church accompanist. Named Worley Tchr. of Yr. Mem.: La. Band Assn., Women's Band Dirs. Nat. Assn., Nat. Band Assn., Jefferson Parish Music Educators Orgn., Dist. VI Band Dirs. Assn., La. Music Educators Assn., Music Educators Nat. Conf. Baptist. Avocations: reading, music, cross stitch, sports. Home: 4920 Bright Dr New Orleans LA 70127

BLACKWELL, MICHELLE S. media company executive; b. San Diego, June 22, 1971; d. Lizabeth and James; m. Ptah S. Shabaf; 1 child, Allahna. Prodn. assoc. DreamWorks SKG, Burbank, Calif., 1993—94; pub. rels. asst. Fox Broadcasting Co., L.A., 1994—98; CEO BDP Entertainment, L.A., 1998—. Program dir. SportZphere.com, Beverly Hills, Calif., 1999—2000. Prodr., writer: Good Sportz, 2002; author: Nubians - Special Agents, 2002. Youth activist Young People Against Violence, Long Beach, Calif., 1992—. Jewish. Office: BDP Entertainment/RadioSTR 468 N Camden Dr Ste 200 Beverly Hills CA 90210 E-mail: bdpentertain@aol.com.

BLACKWELL, PATRICIA MASSEY, middle school educator; b. Toccoa, Ga., July 8, 1951; d. John William and Annie Lanier Massey; m. Randall Loyd Blackwell, June 12, 1982; 1 child, Rhett Loyd. B in Music Edn., Troy State U., 1972. Music tchr. Bay Elem. Sch., Panama City, Fla., 1972; choral dir. Whitesburg Middle Sch., Huntsville, Ala., 1972—. Mem.: Hunstville Choral Dirs. Assn. (sec., treas., pres. 1972—, pres.-elect 2003—04), Ala. Vocal Assn. (dist. chair 1993—98, state treas. 1998—), Am. Choral Dirs. Assn., Delta Kappa Gamma (music chair 1997—). Baptist. Avocations: cross stitch, reading, crafts. Home: 1703 Emily Cir Huntsville AL 35802 Office: Whitesburg Middle Sch 107 Sanders Rd Huntsville AL 35802

BLACKWOOD, LOIS ANNE, elementary school educator; b. Denver, Sept. 18, 1949; d. Randolph William and Eloise Anne (Green) Burchett; m. Clark Burnett Blackwood, June 26, 1971; children: Anna Colleen, Courtney Brooke. BA, Pacific U., 1971; MA, U. Colo., 1997. Tchr. Forest Grove

(Oreg.) Pub. Schs., 1971-72, Clarksville (Tenn.) Pub. Schs., 1972-73, Dept. of Defense Schs., Frankfurt, Germany, 1973-76, St. Vrain Valley Schs., Longmont, Colo., 1977—, presenter insvcs. and symposia, 1977-97, also tchr. of tchrs. Cons. Brush Pub. Schs., 1985; presenter U. No. Colo. Symposium, 1987, Greater San Diego Math. Conf., 1992-99, rural math. connections project U. Colo., 1992-94, So. sect. Calif. Coun. Math. Tchrs., 1992-98; cons. Brighton Pub. Schs., 2000-01. Recipient sustained superior svc. award U.S. Army, Frankfurt, 1975, outstanding performance award, 1976; Presdl. award for excellence in math. tchg. State of Colo., 1991, 94, Outstanding Elem. Math. Tchr. award Colo. Coun. Tchrs. Math., 1993; named Outstanding Tchr. of Yr., Longmont Area C. of C., 1992. Mem. NEA, Colo. Edn. Assn., St. Vrain Valley Tchrs. Assn., Phi Delta Kappa. Republican. Avocations: water and snow skiing, camping, tennis, family activities. Home: 1175 Winslow Cir Longmont CO 80501-5225 Office: Cen Elem Sch 1020 4th Ave Longmont CO 80501-5356 E-mail: clblackwood@hotmail.com.

BLADE, MELINDA KIM, archaeologist, educator, research scientist; b. Jan. 12, 1952; d. George A. and Arline A. M. (MacLeod) Blade. BA, U. San Diego, 1974, MA in Tchg., 1975, EdD, 1986. Cert. secondary tchr. Calif., CC instr. Calif., registered profl. historian Calif. Instr. Coronado Unified Sch. Dist., Calif., 1975-76; head coach women's basketball U. San Diego, 1976-78; instr. Acad. of Our Lady of Peace, San Diego, 1976—, chmn. social studies dept., 1983—, counselor, 1984-92, co-dir. student activities, 1984-87, coord. advanced placement program, 1986-95, dir. athletics, 1990. Mem. archeol. excavation team U. San Diego, 1975—, hist. rschr., 1975—; lectr., 1981—. Contbr. hist. reports and rsch. papers to profl. jours.; editor: U. San Diego publs. Vol. Am. Diabetes Assn., San Diego, 1975—; coord. McDonald's Diabetes Bike-a-Thon, San Diego, 1977—78; bd. dirs. U. San Diego Sch. Edn. Mem.: ASCD, San Diego Hist. Soc., Register Profl. Archaeologists, Am. Hist. Assn., Medieval Assn. Pacific, Medieval Acad. Am., Assn. Scientists and Scholars, Soc. Bibl. Archeology, Calif. Coun. Social Studies, Nat. Coun. Social Studies, Internat. Shroud of Turin, Phi Delta Kappa, Phi Alpha Theta (sec.-treas. 1975—77). Office: Acad Our Lady of Peace 4860 Oregon St San Diego CA 92116-1340

BLAIN, CHARLOTTE MARIE, internist, educator; b. Meadeville, Pa., July 18, 1941; d. Frank Andrew and Valerie Marie (Serafin) Blain; m. John G. Hamby, June 12, 1971 (dec. May 1976); 1 child, Charles J. Hamby. Student, Coll. of St. Francis, 1958-60, DePaul U., 1960-61; MD, U. Ill., Chgo., 1965. Diplomate Am. Bd. Family Practic, Am. Bd. Internal Medicine. Intern, resident U. Ill. Hosps., 1967-70; fellow in infectious diseases U. Ill., 1968-69; pvt. practice specializing in internal medicine and family practice Elmhurst, Ill., 1969—. Instr. U. Ill. Hosp., 1969—70; asst. prof. Loyola U., 1970—71; mem. staff Elmhurst Meml. Hosp., 1970—; clin. asst. prof. Chgo. Med. Sch., 1978—95, U. Ill. Med. Sch., 1995—, Rush Med. Coll., 1997—. Contbr. articles to profl. jours., chapters to books. Bd. dirs., v.p. Elmhurst Art Mus. Fellow: ACP, Am. Acad. Family Practice; mem.: AMA, DuPage Med. Soc., Am. Profl. Practice Assn., Am. Soc. Internal Medicine, Univ. Club (Chgo.). Roman Catholic. Avocations: Hapki Do (Black Belt), Tae-Kwan-Do (Black Belt), skiing. Home: 320 Cottage Hill Ave Elmhurst IL 60126-3302 Office: 135 Cottage Hill Ave Elmhurst IL 60126-3330 Office Phone: 630-832-6633.

BLAIR, ANN, historian; BA, Harvard U., 1984; MPhil, U. Cambridge, 1985; MA, Princeton U., 1987, PhD, 1990. [illegible] 1992—96; prof. history Harvard U., 1996—. Fellow Postdoc. fellow, NSF-NATO, 1990—91, NEH, 1996, MacArthur Found. fellow, 2002. Office: Harvard U Robinson 216 Cambridge MA 02138

BLAIR, BONNIE, former professional speedskater, former Olympic athlete; b. Cornwall, N.Y., Mar. 18, 1964; d. Charlie and Eleanor Blair; m. David Cruikshank; 1 child, Grant B. Cruikshank Student, Mont. Tech. Univ. Mem. U.S. Olympic Team, Sarajevo, Yugoslavia, 1984; Gold medalist, 500m Speedskating, Bronze medalist 1,000m Calgary Olympic Games, 1988; Gold medalist, 500m Speedskating Albertville Olympic Games, 1992, Gold medalist, 1000m Speedskating, 1992; Gold medalist, 500m Speedskating Lillehammer Olympic Games, 1994, Gold medalist, 1000m Speedskating, 1994; pro tour speedskater, 1994-95; ret. from competitive speedskating, 1995; motivational speaker, 1995—. ABC sports commentator; motivational spkr.; founder Bonnie Blair Charitable Fund; active fundraiser Am. Brain Tumor Assn. Author: Bonnie Blair: A Winning Edge. Recipient James E. Sullivan award for Outstanding U.S. amateur athlete, 1993, Sportwoman of the Year, Sports Illustrated, 1994. Achievements include 1st American woman in any sport to win gold medals in consecutive Winter Olympics; 1st American speedskater to win a gold medal in more than one Olympics. Most decorated female Olympian of all time -- five gold medals, six total. Office: Advantage Internat Mgmt Inc 1751 Pinnacle Dr Ste 1500 Mc Lean VA 22102-3833

BLAIR, CYNTHIA, meteorologist, oceanographer, researcher; b. Syracuse, N.Y., Nov. 20, 1965; d. Robert Harley and Judith Anne (Scanlon) Van Ostrand; m. Charles Roy Blair, Aug. 16, 1992; 1 child, Jesse Warren. AS in Travel/Tourism Mgmt., Johnson and Wales Coll., Providence, 1985. Asst. head cashier Winn Dixie, Largo, Fla., 1987-90; joined U.S. Navy, 1990, meteorol. observer NTMOD, 1990-94, oceanographic technician NEMOD Sigonella, Sicily, Italy, 1994-97, meteorology trainee NAVTECHTRAU Keesler AFB, Miss., 1997-98, meteorol. technician, rsch. asst. FNMOC Monterey, Calif., 1998—9. Command photographer FNMOC, USN, Monterey, 1998—; rsch. asst. Naval Rsch. Lab., Monterey, 1998—. Author poetry. Tutor, adult literacy program Monterey County Free Libr., 1998, reader, children's reading program, 1998-99. Office: Fleet Numerical Meteorology and Oceanography Ctr Stop 1 7 Grace Hopper Ave # 52 Monterey CA 93943-5598

BLAIR, HILARY, actor, performing company executive, educator; b. Newport, N.H., Apr. 4, 1963; d. William Colfax and Catherine MacDonald (Pomeroy) Blair. BA, Yale U., 1985; MFA, Nat. Theatre Conservatory, Denver, 1994. Freelance tchr. numerous schs., Denver, 1993—96; tchr. Graland Country Day Sch., Denver, 1996—98; actor/voice over I Hear Voice People, Denver, 1997—; curriculum coord., tchg. artist & workshop dir. Denver Ctr. for the Performing Arts, 1998—; asst. artistic dir. Island Theatre Workshop, Oak Bluffs, Mass., 1999—. Mem. adv. bd. Denver Acad. Youth, 2001—03; pvt. cons. for pub. speaking Denver Ctr. Acad., 2002—. Dir. author, playwright: over 100 plays. Workshop leader Rainbow Alley, Denver, 2001—03. Mem.: ASSITEJ, Theatre for Youth. Avocations: mountain biking, running, collecting childrens books, writing, hiking, Karate. Home: 4128 Batavia Pl Denver CO 80220 Office: Denver Ctr for the Performing Arts 1050 13th St Denver CO 80204

BLAIR, JENNIFER MARIE, music educator, consultant; b. Columbus, Ohio, Feb. 19, 1978; d. Millard Franklin and Georgann Blair. MusB, Ohio Wesleyan U., Del., Ohio, 1996—2000. Cert. Tchg. State of Ohio, 2000. Tchr. Children's World Learning Centers, Reynoldsburg, Ohio, 1997—98, Rainbow Sta. Daycare Inc., Pickerington, Ohio, 1999—99; sales assoc. Colonial Music, Westerville, Ohio, 2001—02; music educator Westerville (Ohio) Schools, 2000—; rsch. cons. Integrity Press, Westerville, Ohio, 2003—. Pvt. music instr. pvt., Reynoldsburg, Ohio, 1996—; asst. marching band dir. Westerville Combined Marching Bands, Westerville, Ohio, 2002—03; rsch. cons. Integrity Press, Westerville, Ohio, 2003—. Mem.: Internat. Clarinet Assn. (assoc.), Music Educators' Nat. Conf. (assoc.), Ohio Music Edn. Assn. (assoc.), Ohio Edn. Assn. (assoc.), Mu Phi Epsilon (life). Home: 73 Barry Rd SW Reynoldsburg OH 43068

BLAIR, KATHIE LYNN, social services worker; b. Oakland, Calif., Sept. 29, 1951; d. Robert Leon Webb and Patricia Jean (Taylor) Peterson; m. Terry Wayne Blair, Dec. 29, 1970 (div. 1972); 1 child, Anthony Blair. Eligibility worker Dept. Social Services, San Jose, Calif., 1974-76; adult and family svcs. worker State of Oreg., Portland, 1977-90. Guest speaker welfare advocacy groups, Portland, 1987. Translator: Diary of Fannie Burkhart, 1991; contbr. articles to profl. jours.; developer word game for children. Mem. ACLU, AARP, Nat. Geog. Soc., A Brotherhood Against Totalitarian Enactments, Oreg. State Pub. Interest Rsch. Group, Nat. Headache Found., Clan Chattan Assn., Portland Highland Games Assn., Nature Conservancy, Nat. Wildlife Fedn., Harley Owners Group, Ladies of Harley, Sierra Club, Wilderness Soc., Defenders of Wildlife. Democrat. Avocations: history, women's studies, writing, photography, motorcycles. E-mail: good_foottoo@yahoo.com.

BLAIR, LUDIE MAE RILEY, retired furniture company executive; b. Ashland, Ala., Feb. 7, 1918; d. David Love and Ludie Ann (Shores) Riley; m. George Elston Blair, July 21, 1943; children: George Stanley, Elder Thomas. BA, Jacksonville (Ala.) State U., 1937-40. Tchr. 4th grade New Site Sch., Alexander City, Ala., 1940-43; bookkeeper A.V. Riley's Furniture Co., Alexander City, Ala., 1944-45; co-owner AAA Furniture Co., Birmingham, Ala., 1947-90; ret. AAA Furniture Co. (presently Blair Furniture Inc.), Birmingham, Ala., 1990. Baptist. Avocation: creative modern art works. Home: PO Box 26703 Birmingham AL 35260-0703 Office: Blair Furniture Inc 2205 2nd Ave N # D Birmingham AL 35203-3805

BLAIR, MARGARET MENDENHALL, research economist, consultant, law educator; b. Bartlesville, Okla., Nov. 8, 1950; d. Harold Leroy and Mary Winifred (Simmons) Mendenhall; m. Forrest Randall Blair, May 29, 1971 (div. Sept. 1979); m. Roger Lisle Conner, June 22, 1991; 1 child, Elizabeth LeeAnn Conner. BA, U. Okla., 1973; postgrad., Harvard U., 1982-83; MA, MPhil, PhD, Yale U., 1989. Reporter Houston Chronicle, 1973-75; reporter, bur. mgr. Fairchild Publ., Houston, 1975-77; corr. Bus. Week, Houston, 1977-79, bur. chief, 1979-82; economist Fed. Res. Bank N.Y., NYC, 1985; rsch. asst. Yale U., New Haven, 1985-86, lectr., 1986-87; rsch. assoc. Brookings Instn., Washington, 1987-94, sr. fellow, 1995-99; dir. Brookings Project on Corps. and Human Capital, 1996-99; co-dir. Brookings Project on Intangible Sources of Value, 1998-2001; rsch. dir., vis. prof. Sloan-GULC project bus. inst. Georgetown U. Law Ctr., 2000—. Mem. adj. faculty U. Md. Coll. Bus. and Mgmt., 1993—94; vis. prof. Georgetown U. Law Ctr., 1996—; mem. steering com., rapporteur Woodstock Seminar Series on Bus. Ethics, Washington, 1989—90; mem. subcoun. on capital allocation Competitiveness Policy Coun., 1993—96; rapporteur Salzburg (Austria) Seminar on Internat. Fin. Markets, 1989; mem. steering com. time horizons project Coun. on Competitiveness, Washington, 1990; mem. Task Force on Restructuring America's Labor Market Instns., MIT/Sloan Sch. Mgmt., 1997—2001; non-resident sr. fellow Brookings Instn., 2000—; bd. advisors George Washington U. Sloan Program on Bus. and Soc., 1998—; mem. World Econ. Forum Corp. Performance Coun., 1999—; bd. dirs. Sonic Corp., 2001—; trustee Woodstock Theol. Ctr., 2001—; mem. steering com. project on corp. responsibility Am. Acad. Arts and Sci., 2002—. Author: The Deal Decade Handbook, 1993, Ownership and Control: Rethinking Corporate Governance for the Twenty-first Century, 1995; co-author: Unseen Wealth: Report of the Brookings Task Force on Intangibles, 2001; editor: The Deal Decade: What Takeovers and Leveraged Buyouts Mean for Corporate Governance, 1993, Wealth Creation and Wealth Sharing: A Colloquium on Corporate Governance and Investments in Human Capital, 1996, Employees and Corporate Governance, 1999, The New Relationship Human Capital in the American Corporation, 2000; contbr. numerous articles to profl. and acad. jours. Vol. Big Sisters Washington Met. Area, 1989-92; organizer neighborhood watch group, Washington, 1990; mem. bd. advisors Ctr. for Cmty. Interest, 1993-98; mem. bd. dir. Christ Edn. Rock Spring United Ch. Christ, 2000-03; mem. Arlington County Adv. Coun. Instrn. Univ. fellow Yale U., 1983-86, Leo Model fellow Brookings Instn., 1987-88; rsch. grantee Boston U. Mfrs. Roundtable, 1990, Columbia U. Instnl. Investor Project, 1994, Alfred P. Sloan Found., 1995, 96, 98, 99. Mem. AAAS (mem. steering com. corp. responsibility project 2002—), Am. Econ. Assn., Am. Law Econs. Assn. Avocations: ballet, religious studies, cooking. Office: Georgetown U Law Ctr 600 New Jersey Ave NW Washington DC 20001-2075

BLAIR, MAUDINE, psychotherapist, communications executive, management consultant; d. Eugene Goode and Della Wright Blair. MA, U. Ga., Athens, 1964; PhD, Fla. State U., Tallahassee, 1969. Diplomate Am. Psychotherapy Assn.; CGP Nat. registry of Group Psychotherapists, cert. transactional analyst, lic. psychotherapist Fla. Assoc. dir. of counseling and pers. svcs. Fla. State U., Tallahassee, 1964—67; dir. and founder Blair's Counseling Svc., Tallahassee, 1970—, Blair's Counseling Satellite Ctr., Tifton, Ga., 1971—92, Tenn. Comm. & Mgmt. Inst., Townsend, Tenn., 1980—89, Blair's Lodge, Townsend, Tenn., 1981—89, Fla. Comm. & Mgmt. Inst., Tallahassee, 1972—. Co-editor: Transactional Analysis Rsch. Index vol. I, 1976, Transactional Analysis Rsch. Index vol. II, 1979, contbr. articles to profl. jours. Fellow: Am. Orthopsychiatric Assn.; mem.: Fla. Assn. Marriage and Family Therapy, Internat. Transactional Analysis (clin. mem., diplomate), Am. Psychol. Assn. (life), Am. Assns. Marriage and Family Therapy (life; clin. mem.), Am. Psychotherapy Assn., Am. Group Psychotherapy Assn. (clin. mem.). Avocations: reading, traveling, writing. Office: Blair's Counseling Svc PO Box 12697 Tallahassee FL 32317 Office Phone: 850-297-2190. E-mail: BlairCare@att.net.

BLAIR, PHYLLIS E. artist; b. N.Y.C., Oct. 5, 1922; d. Franz Joseph and Marian Jane (Burke) Emmerich; m. Thomas Slingluff Blair, Sept., 17, 1946 (dec. May, 2003); children: Joan Dix, George Dike, Hadden Slingluff. Student, Skidmore Coll., 1940-42, Art Students League, 1945, Westminster Coll., 1970-72, Bennington Coll., 1989. Asst. art dept. Skidmore Coll., Saratoga Springs, N.Y., 1940-42; art illustrator & engring. draftsman GE, Schenectady, N.Y., 1942-44, Bell Labs., N.Y.C., 1944-46; elem tchr. Clinton, Tenn., 1946-47. One-woman shows include Hoyt Inst. Fine Arts, New Castle, Pa., 1971, 93, Butler Inst. Am. Art, Youngstown, Ohio, 1982, Westminster Coll., New Wilmington, Pa., 1983, Butler Inst. Am. Art, Salem, Ohio, 1994, Cornell Mus., Delray Beach, Fla., 2004-05. Art curator Human Svcs. Ctr., New Castle, 1968-89, Jameson Health Sys., 1978-99, Jameson Care Ctr., Jameson Retirement Pl., 1978-99, Jameson Rehab Ctr., 1978-99, Almira Home, New Castle, 1990-99, Lawrence County Children and Youth Svcs., 2000, The Soup Kitchen, Boynton Beach, Fla., 2000; founding mem. Nat. Mus. of Women in the Arts, Washington, D.C. Recipient Benjamin Rush award Pa. Med. Soc., 1991. Mem. Hoyt Inst. Fine Arts (chair art com. & permanent collection 1967-99, trustee, 1967-99, Blair Sculpture Walkway named in her honor 1996), Am. Heart Assn. (Disting. Svc. award Lawrence County chpt. 1978). Avocations: golf, painting, sculpting. Home: 1611 Cold Spring Rd Williamstown MA 01267-2771

BLAIR, REBECCA SUE, English educator; b. Terre Haute, Ind., Mar. 26, 1958; d. Albert Eldon and Genevieve Virginia (Smith) B.; m. Richard Volle Van Rheeden, May 27, 1989. BA in English magna cum laud, U. Indpls., 1980; MA in Medieval Lit. with honors, U. Ill., Springfield, 1982; MA, Ind. U., 1986, PhD, 1988. Grad. asst. U. Ill., Springfield, 1980—82; dir. English language tng. Ind. U., Bloomington, 1982-83, assoc. instr., 1982-88; assoc. prof., chmn. dept. English Westminster Coll., Fulton, Mo., 1989-99, dir. writing assessment, 1989-99; assoc. prof. U. Indpls., 1999—2003, Wartburg Coll., Waverly, Iowa, 2003—. Vis. prof. Webster U., St. Louis, Mo., 1988-89; writing assessment cons. Pepperdine U., Malibu, Calif., 1995, others; exec. com. of the faculty Westminster Coll.; mem. Assessment Com., College-Wide Budget Com., Profl. Stds. Com., Pers. Com., Dean's Cabinet Coun. of Chairs and Dirs., Edn. Task Force, Task Force to Reorganize the Acad. Area, Enrollment Svcs. Task Force; women's studies rep. Mid-Mo. Am. Coun. of Univs.; faculty sponsor Alpha Chi Scholastic Hon. Soc.; faculty organizer awareness of rape/domestic violence Take Back the Night Rally; presenter, spkr. in field. Author: The Other Woman: Women Authors and Cultural Stereotypes in American Literature, 1988; contbr. articles to profl. jours. Bd. dirs. Am. Cancer Soc., Callaway County, Mo., 1989-92; mem. pastor nominating com. First Presbyterian Ch., Fulton, Mo., 1990-91, elder, 1990—, session mem., elected mem., 1990-93, 97-2000, chmn. nominating com., 1993-94, chmn. music search com., 1994-95; pulpit supply Mo. Union Presbytery, 1995—, com. on ministry, 1997-2000, stated clk., 1997—; mem. Greater Mo. Focus on Leadership, 1992; vol. Habitat for Humanity, Fulton, 1993—; bd. dirs., founding mem. Coalition Against Rape and Domestic Violence, Fulton, 1995-97; bd. dirs. Friends of the Libr., Fulton, 1995-98, pres., 1997-98; sec. Fulton Art League, 1996—. Named Outstanding Faculty Mem., Westminster Coll., Fulton, 1991-92, Panhellenic Faculty Mem. of Year, Westminster Coll., 1996-97. Mem. Nat. Coun. for Rsch. on Women, Nat. Coun. Tchrs. of English, Am. Studies Assn., Midwest Modern Lang. Assn., Modern Lang. Assn., Writing Prog. Adminstrs., Coll. Composition and Comm., Fulton C. of C. (vol. 1992-96), Kiwanis (bd. dirs. 1990—, founder Circle K Club 1994, v.p. 1995-96, pres.-elect 1996-97, pres. 1997-98). Presbyterian. Avocations: gourmet cooking, reading, trains, writing. Home: 1916 Rainbow Dr Cedar Falls IA 50613 Office: Wartburg Coll 100 Wartburg Blvd Waverly IA 50677 Office Phone: 319-352-8447. Personal E-mail: mb326@yahoo.com. Business E-Mail: rebecca.blair@wartburg.edu.

BLAIR, SHERRY ANN, psychotherapist, educator; b. Belleville, N.J., Dec. 17, 1961; d. Edward Joseph Blair and Barbara Ann Ingham; 1 child, Michael Joseph. BA, Rutgers U., 1997; MSW, Columbia U., 2000; postgrad., North Ctrl. U., Prescott, Ariz., 2003—. LCSW NJ. Transitional housing & fin. coord. Manavi, Inc, Union, NJ, 1998—99; social worker, psychotherapist Women's Counseling & Psychol. Svcs., Verona, NJ, 2000—01; social worker, therapist Delta T-Group, Iselin, NJ, 2000—02; psychotherapist, social worker Assocs. in Counseling, Tng. & Psychol. Svcs., Clifton, NJ, 2000—; case mgr., family violence clinician Women Rising, Inc., Jersey City, 2001; dir., adminstr. Horizon Behavioral Health Care, Prospect Park, NJ, 2001—. Corp. cons., dir. Starbound, Inc., Lanoka Harbor, NJ, 2000—; bus. cons. Synergy Life Coaching & Psychotherapy Svcs., Montclair, NJ, 2000—; adj. prof. Women's Studies Program Rutgers U., Newark, 2000—; organizer confs., workshops in field. Crisis responder-World Trade Ctr. Crisis Care Network-Delta T Group, Iselin, 2001, field organizer NASW-PACE N.J. Chpt., Hamilton, 2002. Recipient Beth Niemi award for work for women's studies, Rutgers U. Women's Studies Program, 1997; grantee Office on Women's Health, HHS, 1997. Mem.: NASW (clin. social work supr.), EMDR Inst., Internat. Critical Incident Stress Found., Am. Acad. Experts in Traumatic Stress (bd. cert. expert, diplomate), So. Poverty Law Ctr., Columbia U. Sch. Social Work Alumni Assn., Amnesty Internat., Phi Beta Kappa, Psi Chi. Office: Horizon Behavioral Health Care 316 N 6th St Prospect Park NJ 07508 Office Phone: 973-746-0333. Personal E-mail: synergycoach@juno.com.

BLAIR, SYLVIA H. computer project engineer, small business owner; BS in Physics, Lamar U., 1976. Computer resources project engr. on F-16 and F-22 fighter aircraft Ft. Worth divsn. Gen. Dynamics, 1979—89. Session chmn., tutorials chmn. AIAA/IEEE Digital Avionic Systems Conf., 1983—86; conf. chmn., tech. program chmn. AIAA Aerospace Engring. Conf. and Show, L.A., 1983—85; chmn. AIAA Digital Avionic Tech. Com., 1987—89. Min. Higher Way Ministries, Grapevine, Tex., 1995. Recipient Navy Superior Pub. Svc. medal, U.S. Dept. of the Navy, 1990. Avocations: writing, reading, fishing, travel. Office: Ambassador Consulting PO Box 3338 Grapevine TX 76099 E-mail: shblair@earthlink.net.

BLAIR, VIRGINIA ANN, public relations executive; b. Kansas City, Mo., Dec. 20, 1925; d. Paul Lowe and Lou Etta (Cooley) Smith; m. James Leon Grant, Sept. 3, 1943 (dec. July 1944); m. Warden Tannahill Blair, Jr., Nov. 7, 1947 (dec. Apr. 2002); children: Janet, Warden Tannahill III. BS in Speech, Northwestern U., 1948. Free-lance writer, Chgo., 1959-69; writer, editor Smith, Bucklin & Assocs., Inc., Chgo., 1969-72, account mgr., 1972-79, account supr., 1979-80, dir. pub. rels., 1980-85; pres. GB Pub. Rels., Chgo., 1985—. Judge U.S. Indsl. Film Festival, 1974, 75; instr. Writer's Workshop, Evanston, Ill., 1978; dir. Northwestern U. Libr. Coun., 1978-91, dir. alumnae bd., 1986—, John Evans Club bd., 1990-98. Author dramas (produced on CBS): Jeanne D'Arc: The Trial, 1961, Cordon of Fear, 1961, Reflection, 1961, If I Should Die, 1963; 3-act children's play: Children of Courage, 1967. Emmy nominee Nat. Acad. TV Arts and Scis., 1963; recipient Svc. award Northwestern U., 1978, Creative Excellence award U.S. Indsl. Film Festival, 1976, Gold Leaf merit cert. Family Cir. mag. and Food Coun. Am., 1977, cert. Excellence superior achievement in media rels. N.Am. Precis Syndicate, 1997, Ginny award Cremation Assn. N.Am., 2002. Mem. Pub. Rels. Soc. Am. (counselors acad.), Am. Advt. Fedn. (lt. gov. Ill. 6th dist.), Women's Advt. Club Chgo. (pres.), Publicity Club Chgo., Nat. Acad. TV Arts and Scis., John Evans Club (bd. dirs.), Woman's Club Evanston (pres.), Zeta Phi Eta (Svc. award 1978, 93), Alpha Gamma Delta, Philanthropic and Ednl. Orgn. (Ill. chpt. pres. dist. pres.). Home and Office: 2601 Central St Unit 206 Evanston IL 60201-1395

BLAKE, ALLISON, social worker, educator; b. New York, NY, June 28, 1962; d. Vincent and Kathleen Blake. BSW, U. of Dayton, 1980—84; MSW, Rutgers U., 1985—89; PhD, Fordham U., 1997—2003. NASW Acad. of Cert. Social Workers, 1993, LCSW NJ. Bd. of Social Work Examiners, 1996. Social worker Montgomery County Children Services Bd., Dayton, Ohio, 1984—85; family svc. specialist NJ Divsn. of Youth & Family Services, Hackensack, 1985—86, investigator, instl. abuse investigation unit Paterson, NJ, 1986—91, asst. regional supr. of investigations, instl. abuse investigation unit, 1991—2000, cmty. edn. coord. Trenton, NJ, 2000, exec. asst., office of intergovernmental affairs, 2000—03, interim adminstr., office of intergovernmental affairs, 2003—. Adj. prof. Bloomfield Coll., NJ, 1996—98, Ramapo Coll., Mahwah, NJ, 1998; adj. prof., grad. sch. of social svc. Fordham U., New York, 1999—2001; chair, children's com. NASW - NJ. Chpt., Hamilton, NJ, 2002—, sec., 2002—; del. NASW, Washington, 2002. Recipient Nicholas J. Langenfeld award for Outstanding Dissertation, Fordham U., 2003. Office: NJ Division of Youth & Family Services 50 East State St Trenton NJ 08625

BLAKE, CATHERINE C. judge; b. Boston, July 27, 1950; d. John Ballard and Jean Place (Adams) B. BA magna cum laude, Radcliffe Coll., 1972; JD cum laude, Harvard Law Sch., 1975. Bar: Mass. 1975, Md. Ct. Appeals 1977, U.S. Ct. Appeals (4th cir.) 1977, U.S. Dist. Ct. Md. 1977, D.C. 1979. Assoc. Palmer & Dodge, Boston, 1975-77; asst. U.S. atty. Dist. of Md., Balt., 1977-83, first asst. U.S. atty., 1983-85, 86-87, U.S. atty. (court-appointed), 1985-86; U.S. magistrate judge U.S. Dist. Ct. Md., Balt., 1987-95, U.S. dist. ct. judge, 1995—. Mem.: FBA, Fed. Judges' Assn., Nat. Assn. of Women Judges, Md. Bar Assn., Bar Assn. Baltimore City. Office: US Courthouse 101 W Lombard St Ste 7310 Baltimore MD 21201-2639

BLAKE, DARCIE KAY, radio news director, anchor; b. Worland, Wyo., Aug. 29, 1958; d. Jerry Haley and Helen Ileen (Kerbel) Bloom; m. Paul Henry Reifschneider, Aug. 30, 1980; children: Sara Jayne, Mathew James. BS in Journalism, U. N.D., 1979. Anchor, reporter Sta. KFYR Radio, Bismarck, N.D., 1979, Sta. WHB Radio, Kansas City, Mo., 1980-82; news dir. Sta. KUDL Radio/Sta. WHB Radio, Kansas City, 1982—. Bd. dirs. Harvestors-Food Bank, Kansas City, 1990, Girl Scouts U.S., Kansas City, 1990; vol. Arthritis Assn (citation 1989), United Minority Media Assn. (citation 1989). Mem. Kansas City Press Club (bd. dirs. 1984-85), Radio/TV News Dirs., Kansas City Media Profls., Kans. Assn. Broadcasters, Soc. Profl. Journalists. Episcopalian. Avocations: golf, tennis. Office: Sta KUDL/WHB 3101 Broadway St Ste 460 Kansas City MO 64111-2478

BLAKE, GRACE, cultural organization administrator; Former pres., bd. dir. Apollo Theater Found. Inc., N.Y.C., N.Y. Women in Film and TV Orgn., advisor. Prodr.: (live performance) A Harlem Tribute to Lionel Haptom, A Memorial for Ron Brown, Amateur Night at the Apollo. Bd. dirs. Mayor's Adv. Office Film, Theater & Broadcasting, N.Y.C., Cinema Arts Ctr., Caribbean Am. Ctr. N.Y., 125th St. Bus. Improvement Dist. of Harlem. Recipient Leaders in Action award for Bus., New Women in Leadership Symposium, Honoree, N.Y. Women in Film & TV Music. Office: 253 W 125th St New York NY 10001

BLAKE, JANE SALLEY, publishing, public relations, and management consultant; b. Tallahassee, Fla., Sept. 3, 1937; d. George Lawrence Salley and Eleanor (King) Hookham; m. Arthur Copeland Blake Jr., Sept. 5, 1959 (div. 1991); children: A. Copeland III, Tarrant Salley. BA in Fine Arts, Fla. State U., 1958. Exec. sec. Hist. Homes Found., Louisville, 1975-76; chair Ky. Heritage Weekend U.S. Bicentennial Celebration, Louisville, 1976; founder, pres., chmn. Arts Forum, Inc., Louisville, 1978-84; pres. Blake Publs., Inc., Louisville, 1983-86; pres., prin. The Center mag., Inc., Louisville, 1986—, J.S. Blake Communications Group, Louisville, 1986—. Designer, writer: website. V.p. Art Ctr. Assn., Louisville, 1967-72; bd. dirs., publicity chair Children's Theatre, 1968; v.p., bd. dirs. Crusade vs. Crime, 1972-74; bd. dirs. Farmington Hist. Home, 1973-75, 77-80; founder, chmn. Potpourri of the Arts, 1979-83; mem. pub. rels. com. Jefferson County Police, 1987-88. Recipient Gov.'s Arts award for media excellence, 1989. Mem. Pub. Rels. Soc. Am. (Landmark of Excellence award 1988, 89), Advt. Club Louisville (13 Louie awards for publs. 1981-84), Entrepreneur Soc. (mem. exec. com., bd. dirs. 1989-91, Above and Beyong the Call of Duty award 1990), Women's Club Louisville. Democrat. Avocations: reading, playwriting, nutrition. Office: JS Blake Comm Group PO Box 22312 Louisville KY 40252-0312

BLAKE, LAURA, architect; b. Berkeley, Calif., Dec. 26, 1959; d. Igor Robert and Elizabeth (Denton) B. BA in Art History, Brown U., 1982; MArch, UCLA, 1985. Employee The Ratcliff Architects, Berkeley, 1986-90; architect IDG Architects, Oakland, Calif., 1990-92; assoc. ELS/Elbasani & Logan Architects, Berkeley, 1992-2000, Mark Cavagnero Assocs., San Francisco, 2000—. Organizer charity ball Spinsters San Francisco, 1988, sec., 1988-89, mem. adv. bd., 1989-92; mem. San Francisco Jr. League, 1991-2003. Recipient Alpha Rho Chi bronze medal, 1985. Mem. AIA, Soc. Calif. Pioneers. Republican. Episcopalian. Avocations: travel, photography, sport, the arts. Office: Mark Cavagnero Assocs 1045 Sansome St Ste 200 San Francisco CA 94111-1315

BLAKE, RENÉE, broadcast executive; b. Yonkers, N.Y. BA, Goddard Coll., 1973. Announcer, prodr. WCBQ-AM, Oxford, NC, 1974, WANV-AM, Waynesboro, Va., 1974; talk show host, anchor WEEZ-AM, Chester, PA, 1974-75; reporter, anchor WWDB-FM, Phila., 1975, WMMR-FM, Phila., 1975-78; programming special projects Drake Chenault Enterprises, L.A., 1978-79; copywriter S.M. Newmark & Assoc., L.A., 1980-81; reporter, public affairs dir. WHLY-FM, Orlando, FL, 1981-83; news dir. WJYO-FM, Orlando, FL, 1983-86; program dir. WKXL-AM/FM, Concord, NH, 1986-91, KXCI-FM, Tucson, 1991-93; programmer Jerrold Comm., Concord, NH, Tucson, AZ, 1990-94; reporter, anchor Metro Networks, Phoenix, 1995-97, news bureau chief Albuquerque, 1997—; owner, CEO Media IQ, Albuquerque, 1996—. Interviewer, spkr. in field. Co-editor: Westside Rapper, 1970; columnist: The Drummer, 1976-77, Steppin' Out Magazine, 1983-86; creator, prodr. Music Zone Snowbank, 1988-89 (Golden Mike Merit NH Assn. Broadcasters 1988), This Island Earth, 1990 (Best of the Best 1st Place Golden Mike NH Assn. Broadcasters 1990), NH Veterans' Memorial Wall and Scholarship Committee, 1988-90 (1st Place Golden Mike NH Assn. Broadcasters 1989), Send Our Support Day, 1990; affiliate prodr. Human Rights Now, 1989 (1st Place Golden Mike NH Assn. Broadcasters 1989); contbr. articles to profl. jours. Avocations: animal rights, alternative health care, writing, social justice, voiceovers. Office: Media IQ 174 Calle Loma Parda NW Albuquerque NM 87120-3477 E-mail: mediaiq@email.com.

BLAKELEY, LINDA, psychologist, speaker; b. Bklyn., July 26, 1941; d. Charles and Blanche (Josephson) Berkow; m. Dec. 17, 1961 (div. 1983); children: Stacey, Scott. BA, UCLA, 1964; MA, Calif. State U., Northridge, 1977; PhD, Calif. Grad. Inst., 1985. Founder, dir. Parents Sharing Custody, Beverly Hills, Calif., 1984—87; pvt. practice self esteem, eating disorders, leadership stress mgmt. Positive Self Images, Beverly Hills, 1984—95. Producer, host interview/talk show. Author: ABC's of Stress Management, 1989, Do It with Love-Positive Parenting After Divorce, 1988, (audio tape) Success Strategies, 1992; one-woman show The Magic Dress, 1998. Mem. adv. bd. Nat. Coun. Alcoholism and Drug Abuse, 1991-92. Mem.: Calif. Psychol. Assn. (state bd. dirs. media com. 1989—92, chair-elect media divsn.), Bulimia Assn. Disorders, Nat. Assn. Anorexia, Beverly Hills C. of C. (pres. women's network 1989—90, chmn. health care com. 1989). Avocations: writing, dance, acting. Office: 420 S Beverly Dr Ste 100 Beverly Hills CA 90212-4410 Fax: (310) 578-2434. Office Phone: 310-286-9171. E-mail: Drlindablakeley@aol.com.

BLAKEMORE, KARIN JANE, obstetrician, geneticist; b. Stockholm, Nov. 10, 1953; d. William S. and Elaine Claire (Hoover) B.; 1 child, Joseph William. BA, U. Pa., 1975; MD, Med. Coll. Toledo, 1978. Diplomate Am. Bd. Med. Genetics, Am. Bd. Ob-gyn. Resident in ob-gyn. NYU, N.Y.C., 1978-82; fellow in clin. genetics Yale U., New Haven, 1982-85; fellow in maternal-fetal medicine Washington U., St. Louis, 1985-87; asst. prof. ob-gyn. Johns Hopkins U., Balt., 1987-93, assoc. prof. ob-gyn., 1992—. Dir. Prenatal Genetics Johns Hopkins U., Balt., 1992—, dir. Maternal-Fetal Medicine, 1994—. Author chpts. to books; guest editor Obstetrics and Gynecology Clinics of N.Am., 1993. Fellow Am. Coll. Ob-gyn., Am. Coll. Med. Genetics; mem. AMA, Am. Inst. Ultrasound and Medicine, Am. Soc. Human Genetics, Internat. Soc. Ultrasound in Medicine, Soc. for Maternal-Fetal Medicine, Soc. for Gynecol. Investigation, Am. Gynecol. and Obstet. Soc. Office: Johns Hopkins Hosp Ob/Gyn Houck 228 600 N Wolfe St Baltimore MD 21287-0005

BLAKENEY, BARBARA A. public health service officer; BS, MS, U. Mass.; diploma, Worcester City Hosp. Sch. of Nursing. Primary care nurse practitioner Amherst Med. Assoc., Amherst, Mass., Boston City Hosp., Boston; prin. pub. health nurse for homeless svcs., addiction svcs. Dept. Health and Hosp., Divsn. Pub. Health, Boston; currently dir. health svcs. for homeless Boston Pub. Health Comm. Recipient Pearl McIver Pub. Health Nurse award, Am. Nurses Assn., Theta Alpha Cptr. Ann Kibirck Nursing Leadership award, Sigma Theta Tau. Mem.: Am. Nurses Assn. (pres. 2002—). Office: Boston Pub Health Commn 1010 Mass Ave Boston MA 02118 Address: 600 Md Ave SW Ste 100 W Washington DC 20024

BLAKENEY, KAREN ELIZABETH, social service and community health program executive, consultant; b. Evanston, Ill., June 27, 1953; d. Elwood Francis and Irene Loretta (Filloon) Garlick; life ptnr. Ydalia Granado; children: Jesse Alan, Aaron Paul. Cert. in Christian edn., Angeles Bible Coll., L.A., 1972; BA in Anthropology, Calif. State U., Long Beach, 1978; MS in Counseling Psychology, Mt. St. Mary's Coll., LA., 1992; cert. in non-profit mgmt., U. So. Calif., 1998. Commd. pastor Hosanna Ministries, 1994. Archaeologist VTM Corp., Vandenburg AFB, Calif., 1979-81; archaeologist, Arroyo Grande, Calif., 1981-82; acct. Airport Datsun/Volvo, Santa Maria, Calif., 1982-83; adminstrn. mgr. Concord Sys., Reseda, Calif., 1983-86; ins. broker Prudential Ins. Co., Torrance, Calif., 1986-87; mgr. legal compliance dept. G.J. Sullivan Cos., L.A., 1987-92; psychotherapy intern Hosanna Ministries, Santa Monica, Calif., 1990-95; children's social worker Dept. Children and Family Svcs., L.A., 1994-96; dir. social work Internat. Foster Family Agy., Carson, Calif., 1996-97; dir. youth svcs. L.A. Gay and Lesbian Ctr., Hollywood, Calif., 1997-99; dir. programs Chinatown Svc. Ctr., L.A., 1999—2002; exec. dir. Schutrum-Piteo Found., Burbank, Calif., 2002—03; CEO, pres. Blackwolf, LLC Consulting, 2001—; exec. dir. Grace Ctr., Pasadena, 2003—. Lectr. Calif. Poly. Inst. Archaeol. Field Sch., Mission San Antonio de Padua, 1978-81; co-founder, exec. dir. Inst. for trauma Intervention, L.A., 1993-96. Author: (poetry) Sacred Journey, 1995, Ydalia's Song, 1998. Bd. dirs. Art To Grow On, San Pedro, Calif., 1992-94, Desert Stream Ministries/AIDS Resource Ministry, L.A., 1985-91; mem. parent-tchr. adv. bd. Park Western Elem. Sch., San Pedro, 1993-94; dir. mem. Consortium for Homeless Youth Svcs., Hollywood, 1997-99; rep. L.A. County Svc. Planning Area Dist. 4 Coun., 1999-2002; mem. Asian-Pacific Islander police adv. com. L.A. Police Dept., 2000; mem. Nat. Network of Youth, 1997-2000; mem. Calif. Child, Youth and Family Coalition, 1998-2003; bd. dirs. Coalition Against Slave Trafficking, 1999-2002, Coalition for Cmty. Health, 2001-03, Schotrom-Pited Found., 2003-; mem. Dept. Pub. Social Svcs. long-term self sufficiency steering com. L.A. County, 2000-02, bd. dirs. Schutrum-Piteo Found., 2003-. Mem. NAFE, Calif. Assn. Marriage and Family Therapists, Calif. Assn. Against Domestic Violence, Calif. Stat U.-Long Beach Anthropology Alumni Assn. (alumni bd. 1984-85). Avocations: artist, writing. E-mail: kb0001@msn.com.

BLAKENEY, KECIA L. elementary school educator; b. Balt., Jan. 21, 1964; d. Bobby Lee and Saran (Grasty) B.; children: Michael A. Barnes Jr., Ian M., Keiren C., Myles G. BA, Sojourner-Douglas, 1986. Sr. staff tchr. Maarifa Children's Ctr., Balt.; tchrs. aide Feagin Day Care Ctr., Balt. Disability examiner Social Security Adminstrn., 1989—. Named to Nat. Honors Soc. Mem. Metro Edn. Coalition. Avocations: sewing, creating toys for children, reading.

BLAKENEY, MARGARET ELIZABETH FLEMING, counselor, educator; b. McComb, Miss., Jan. 23, 1961; d. Hiram Lee Fleming and Lucy Joe Ann Fleming Curran; m. Ray Edward Blakeney, May 26, 1984; children: Matthew, Lacey. MEd, Miss. Coll., 1985, ednl. specialist degree in counseling, 2002. Tchr. Crystal Springs (Miss.) Elem., 1983—2002; acad. educator, counselor Miss. Job Ctr., Crystal Springs, 2002—. Southern Baptist. Avocations: travel, ocean, mountains, painting, reading. Home: 3055 Millsaps Rd Crystal Springs MS 39059 Office: Copiah County Schs 254 Gallatin St Hazlehurst MS 39083 E-mail: magsb47@hotmail.com.

BLAKEY, MARION C. federal agency administrator; b. Gadsden, Ala., Mar. 26, 1948; B Internatl Studies, Mary Washington Coll., U. Va.; postgead., Johns Hopkins U. With Dept. Commerce, Dept. Dept. Edn., NEH, Dept. Transp.; prin. Blakey & Assocs., Washington, 1993—2001; adminstr. Dept. Transp.'s Nat. Hwy. Traffic Safety Adminstrn., 1992—93; chmn. Nat. Transp. Safety Bd., 2001—02; adminstr. FAA, 2002—. Office: FAA 800 Independence Ave SW Washington DC 20591-0004

BLAKLEY, EARNESTINE, elementary school educator; b. Steele, Mo., June 6, 1952; d. Thomas Bob and Mary Anna (Jones) R.; m. Charles Vernon Blakley, July 31, 1976; children: Charles Vernon Jr., Andrew Harvey. BS Elem. Edn., Lincoln U., 1974; writing diploma, Inst. Children's Lit., 1981; MS Elem. Teaching, Northwest Mo. State U., 1986. Tchr. 2d grade Humboldt Elem. Sch., St. Joseph, Mo., 1974-78; tchr. 5th grade Edison Elem. Sch., St. Joseph, Mo., 1984-85, tchr. 2d grade, 1985-89, tchr. 3d grade, 1989-90, Bessie Elem. Sch., St. Joseph, Mo., 1990-93. Team writer Environ. Protection, Washington, 1992; edn. panel Energizer Battery, Washington, 1992; com. mem. America 2000, Kansas City, 1991-93; spkr. Scholarship Banquet Alton, Ill., 1993; creator at-risk program Ptnrs. in Edn., 1989-90, Parent involvement Children & Parents, 1989-93. Supt. St. Francis Bapt. Temple, St. Joseph, Mo., 1987-92; bd. dirs. Girl Scout Coun., 1992-93, Family Guidance Ctr., 1980; founder, dir. HOPE Outreach Ministries. Recipient Excellence in Edn. award East Side Human Resource Ctr., 1990; Apple Seed Mini grantee project Aware, 1991; nomine Walt Disney Am. Tchr. awards, 1992; named Mo. State Tchr. of Yr., 1991-92, St. Joseph Tchr. of Yr., 1991-92. Mem. St. Joseph Community Tchrs. Assn. (sec. 1986-88), Mo. State Tchrs. Assn., Student Mo. State Tchrs. Assn. (pres. 1973-74), Delta Kappa Gamma, Phi Delta Kappa, Kappa Omicron Phi (v.p. 1973-74). Avocations: writing, reading, fishing, sewing, biking.

BLALOCK, ANN BONAR, evaluation researcher; b. Parkersburg, W.Va., Apr. 16, 1928; d. Harry and Fay (Conley) Bonar; m. Hubert Blalock, Jr., 1951 (dec. 1991); children: Susan Blalock Lyon, Kathleen Blalock McCarrell, James W.; m. Gerhard E. Lenski, 1996. AB, Oberlin Coll., 1950; MA, U. N.C., 1954; MSW, U. Wash., 1978. Pvt. cons. Admiralty Inlet Consulting, Hansville, Wash. Cons. OECD, Paris, 1990, European Commn., Brussels, 1995. Sr. author: Introduction to Social Research, 2d edit., 1982; editor, reviewer: Evaluation Forum, 1986-97, Evaluating Social Programs, 1990; co-editor: Methodology in Social Research, 1968; contbr. articles to profl. jours. Past pres. bd. dirs. Cmty. Mental Health Clin.; mem. Gov.'s Task Force on Accountability in Govt. Recipient Rsch. award Partnership for Employment and Tng. Careers. Mem. NASW (past pres. Wash. State chpt.), Am. Eval. Assn. (past com. chair). Home: PO Box 409 Hansville WA 98340-0409

BLALOCK, CAROL DOUGLASS, psychologist, educator; d. Allan Martin and Mary Louise Douglass; m. Harvey Anthony Blalock, Aug. 27, 1976; children: Jeanne, Patricia, Elizabeth. BEd, U. S.D., 1968; MEd in Edn., EdS in Counseling, U. Fla., 1976, PhD in Curriculum and Instrn., 1980; postgrad., U. Md., 1980—81. Nat. cert. sch. psychologist Fla., 1990, lic. sch. psychologist Fla., 1990. Tchr. Metcalf Elem., Gainesville, Fla., 1968, Gainesville (Fla.) H.S., 1969; coord. environ. edn. Sante Fe C.C., Gainesville, 1974—78, adj. faculty, 1974—78; grad. rsch. fellow U. Fla., rsch. assoc., 1979; chmn. sci. dept. Oak Hall Prep. Sch., Gainesville, Fla., 1981—84; guidance counselor Trenton (Fla.) HS, 1984—87; psychologist Marion County Schs., Ocala, Fla., 1987—; adj. faculty U. South Fla., Tampa, 1990. Author: (chpt.) A Futures Perspective on Instructional Design, 1980; co-author: (conf. summary) Computer Conf. on the Future, 1979, (chpt.) Learning Networks: The Next Step, 1981. Aux. officer Gainesville (Fla.) Police Dept., 1985—95; mem. Holy Faith Cath. Ch., Gainesville, Fla., 1976. Mem.: Fla. Assn. Sch. Psychologists, Nat. Assn. Sch. Psychologists, APA, Phi Delta Kappa. Republican. Roman Catholic. Avocations: grandchildren, travel, music, art. Office: Marion County Sch Bd Ste 5 1517 SE 30th Ave Ocala FL 34471

BLALOCK, CLARA DODD, artist; b. Atlanta, July 29, 1041; d. John Aiken and Louise Julian (Efird) Dodd; m. Thomas Louis Blalock, Jr., Sept. 12, 1964; 1 child, Sarah Clayton Blalock Foggin. Assoc., Stratford Coll., Danville, Va., 1961; BFA, Atlanta Coll. Art, 1964. Asst. dir. admissions Atlanta Coll. Art, 1964—67; mem. consultations task force Episcopal Diocese Atlanta, 1985—90, accredited lead cons., trainer, chmn. task force, mem. dept. congl. devel., mem. stewardship dept. Mentor for edn. Ministry Group Sch. Theology, U. of the South, Sewanee, Tenn., 2003. Exhibitions include galleries, Atlanta, Boston, Camden, S.C., Jacksonville, Vero Beach, Fla., Omaha, one-woman shows include. Vol. Lynwood Park Thrift Shop, Family Planning at Grady Meml. Hosp., Atlanta, Atlanta Speech Sch., High Mus. Art, St. Luke's Episcopal Soup Kitchen, All Saint's Ch. Night Shelter, Atlanta History Ctr.; jr. warden, sr. warden Vestry of Episcopal Ch. of the Atonement, Atlanta, chmn. search com. for rector, 1985, 2001; curator monthly art exhibit Ch. of the Atonement Gallery, 1990—. Recipient numerous awards for artwork. Mem.: Atlanta Artists Ctr. (pres., bd. chair). Republican. Episcopalian. Home: 5145 Timber Trail S NE Atlanta GA 30342 Studio: Tula Art Ctr 75 Bennett St Atlanta GA 30309

BLALOCK, MARY WRIGHT, counselor; b. N.C. AAS with honors, Ctrl. Carolina C.C., Sanford, N.C., 1992; BAS, Campbell U., Buies Creek, N.C., 1994; MA, Campbell U., 1999. Dep. clk. of ct. Adminstrv. Office of the Cts., Raleigh, N.C., 1978-83; computer lab. asst., news reporter Campbell U., 1992-94, asst. to curriculum materials coord., 1994-95; tutorial coord. Ctrl. Carolina C.C., 1995-96; data entry staff N.C. Dept. Environ. Health, Raleigh, 1997; counseling intern North Harnett Elem. Sch., Angier, N.C., 1997-98. Interviewer, counselor Employment Security Commn., 1998-2000; admissions counselor Campbell U., 2000—. Mem. Cape Fear Friends of the Fine Arts, Buies Creek, 1996—. Mem. Omicron Delta Kappa, Delta Kappa Pi. Democrat. Baptist. Avocations: reading, singing, horseback riding, photography, computers. Home: PO Box 234 Buies Creek NC 27506-0234

BLALOCK, SHERRILL, investment advisor; b. Newport News, Va., June 9, 1945; d. David Graham and Martha Lee (Bennett) B.; m. Jonathan L. Smith, Oct. 27, 1985; 1 child, Graham C.G. BA, Smith Coll., 1967. Chartered fin. analyst. Investment broker Legg Mason & Co., Washington, 1968-77, Blyth Eastman Dillon, Washington, 1977-80; portfolio mgr., mng. dir. Mitchell Hutchins, N.Y.C., 1980-88; gen. ptnr., portfolio mgr. Weiss Peck & Greer, N.Y.C., 1988-95; gen. ptnr. Delphi Asset Mgmt., N.Y.C., 1995-98; founder, mng. mem. Chesapeake Asset Mgmt., N.Y.C., 1998—. Chair investment com., trustee Diocese of NY of Episcopal Ch., 2001—; trustee, vice chmn. bd. trustees, chair investment com. Estate and Property of Diocese Conv. of N.Y., 1996—2002; trustee Cathedral of St. John the Divine, 1998—, chair investment com., 1999—. Mem. Washington Soc. Investment Analysts, Inst. Chartered Fin. Analysts. Office: Chesapeake Asset Mgmt 1 Rockefeller Plz Rm 1210 New York NY 10020-2002 Office Phone: 212-218-4040.

BLANC, CARYN, retail executive; Sr. v.p. distbr. and store adminstrn. Kohl's Corp., Menomonee Falls, Wis. Office: Kohl's Corp 1700 Ridgewood Drive Menomonee Falls WI 53051-7026

BLANC, MAUREEN, public relations executive; Ptnr. Blanc & Otus Pub. Rels., Inc., San Francisco. Office: Blanc & Otus Pub Rels Inc 4 Embarcadero Ctr Lbby 8 San Francisco CA 94111-4112

BLANCHARD, KAREN MARIE, development professional; b. Holyoke, Mass., Sept. 30, 1965; d. Ralph Joseph and Nancy Louise (Lecnar) B. AS in Bus. Adminstrn., Holyoke (Mass.) C.C., 1985; BS in Human Svcs., Springfield (Mass.) Coll., 1995, MA in Human Svcs. Adminstrn., 2001. Adminstrv. asst. United Way, Holyoke, 1987-89; bus. mgr. Providence Ministries, Holyoke, 1989—. Bd. dirs. Volleyball Hall of Fame, 1998. Mem. Women in Devel. of Western Mass. (treas. 1995-96). Roman Catholic. Avocation: softball. Office: Providence Ministries Box 6269 51 Hamilton St Holyoke MA 01040

BLANCHARD, KIMBERLY STAGGERS, lawyer, educator; b. Ann Arbor, Mich., May 17, 1954; d. Theodore R. and Bette Lee (Clark) Staggers; m. John Sears Blanchard, May 31, 1980; children: Charles Stuart, Virginia Greene. BA, Dartmouth Coll., 1976; MS, U. Wis., 1978; JD, NYU, 1981. Bar: N.Y. 1982. Assoc. Paul, Weiss, Rifkind, Wharton & Garrison, N.Y.C., 1981-83, Haythe & Curley, N.Y.C., 1983-89, ptnr., 1990—. Adj. prof. NYU Sch. Continuing Edn., 1982-88. Pres. Pelham Pub. Libr. Mem. ABA, N.Y. State Bar Assn. (exec. com. tax sect. 1996—). Clubs: Pelham Country (Pelham Manor, N.Y.). Democrat. Avocation: golf. Home: 657 Ely Ave Pelham NY 10803-2401 Office: Haythe & Curley 237 Park Ave New York NY 10017-3140

BLANCHARD, MARGARET MOORE, author, educator; b. Columbus, Ga., Dec. 29, 1938; d. Robert Moore and Ann (Keller) B. BA, Incarnate Word Coll., 1960; MA, St. Louis U., 1962; PhD, Union Inst., 1990. Instr. St. Louis U., 1960-62, Grailville C.C., Cin., 1962-64, LeMoyne Coll., Syracuse, N.Y, 1964-66, U. Wis., Madison, 1967-69; asst. prof. Morgan State U., Balt., 1969-71; adminstr. Women's Growth Ctr., Balt., 1972-74; asst. prof. Towson State U., Balt., 1975-90; assoc. prof. Vt. Coll., Montpelier, 1990—; dir. The Grad. Program, Montpelier, 1995—; prof. The Union Inst. and Univ., 2000—. Author: Ten Irish-American Women Poets, 1987, The Rest of the Deer, 1993, From the Listening Place, 1997, (novels) Hatching, 2001, Wandering Potatoes, 2002; co-author: Restoring the Orchard, 1994, Duet, 1995; author of poems; contbr. articles to profl. jours. Mem. MLA, Nat. Assn. Poetry Therapy, Nat. Women's Studies Assn. (cmty. coord. 1993), Nat. Coun. Tchrs. English, Internat. Women's Writers Guild. Avocations: photography, stained glass artisan, cross-country skiing. Office: The MA Program Vt Coll Montpelier VT 05602

BLANCHARD, MARYANN N. state legislator; b. N.J., Oct. 12, 1942; d. Joseph Charles and Mary (Longo) Navatta; m. Raymond P. Blanchard, 1967; children: Mary Beth, Catherine Anne, Daniel, Frances Elizabeth. BA, St. Joseph's Coll., 1966. Mem. Rockingham County Dist. 26 N.H. Ho. of Reps., Concord, 1982-90, mem. dist. 33, 1996-2000, ranking minority mem., mem. resources, recreation and devel. com., mem. fin. com. Trustee Strawberry Banke, 1993-96, Portsmouth Pub. Libr., 1981-83; commr. Portsmouth Police Commn., 1991-96; mem. adv. coun. Coop-Ext., Rockingham, 1992-93; mem. Portsmouth Hosp. Guild; leader Swiftwater coun. Girl Scouts USA, 1978-82; mem. Portsmouth PTA; mem. Atlantic States Marine Fisheries Commn., 2001—. Mem. LWV (past pres., bd. dirs. 1967-71), Soc. Protection N.H. Forests, Audubon Soc., Parents Music Club. Roman Catholic.

BLANCHARD, PAMELA SNYDER, special education educator; b. Winston-Salem, N.C., Feb. 5, 1951; d. Roger Alexander and Marie Gobble Snyder; m. George Winborne Blanchard, July 26, 1975; children: Andrew Micah, Justin Warren, Nathan Winborne. BA in Elem. Edn., St. Andrews Presbyn. Coll., 1973; Cert. in Spl. Edn., U. Tenn., 1990; MA in Ednl. Tech., Bible, Johnson Bible Coll., 2000. Cert. tchr. N.C., edn. and spl. edn., and Career Ladder I tchr. Tenn. Title I math. tchr. Durham (N.C.) City Schs., 1973—75; algebra tchr. Davidson County Schs., Welcome, NC, 1976; Chpt. I reading and math. tchr. Knoxville (Tenn.) City Schs., 1976—79, 1980—85; ednl. cons. Discovery Toys, Knoxville, 1989—90; spl. edn. extended resource tchr. Sevier County Schs., Sevierville, Tenn., 1990—91; spl. edn. resource specialist Knox County Schs., Strawberry Plains, Tenn., 1992—. Mem. leadership com., sch. improvement team, tech. com., webmistress Carter Elem. Sch., 1999—. Vol. counselor Sexual Assault Crisis Ctr., Knoxville, 1991—92; chairperson missions bd. Seymour (Tenn.) United Meth. Ch., 1988—90, chairperson assimilation com., 1990—92, sec. adminstrv. coun., 2000, 2001—02; missionary Charleston, SC, 2001—02, Damascus, Va., 2001—03; missionary to Zimbabwe, 2003. Grantee Multicultural Cooking Unit, Knoxville Jr. League, 1994, Accelerated Reader Books, East Tenn. Edn. Found., 1995. Mem.: ASCD, NEA, Internat. Reading Assn., Knox County Edn. Assn., Tenn. Edn. Assn., Children with Attention Deficit Disorder, Learning Disabilities Assn., Divsn. Learning Disabilities, Coun. for Exceptional Children, Nat. Honor Soc. Democrat. Methodist. Avocations: reading, hiking, computers, travel. Home: 705 Forest View Ct Seymour TN 37865 Office: Carter Elem Sch 9304 College Ln Strawberry Plains TN 37871

BLANCHARD, ROSEMARY ANN, university program administrator, consultant, educator; b. Hartford, Conn., Oct. 15, 1946; d. Bernard Richard and Ann Rosemary (Kelly) B.; m. James W. Zion, Dec. 26, 1967 (div. June 1983); 1 child, Jeannette Blanchard Zion; m. Dimitsri Mihalas, June 20, 1995. BA in History cum laude, Trinity Coll., Washington, 1967; MA in Sociology, Johns Hopkins U., 1972; JD cum laude, U. Conn., 1972; postgrad., U. Ill., 1996—. Bar: Conn. 1972, Mont. 1973, Navajo Nation 1983, N.Mex. 1985. Staff atty. Mont. Legislature, Helena, 1973-74; asst. prof. sociology Coll. of Great Falls, Mont., 1974-76; gen. counsel Mont. Human Rights Commn., Helena, 1976-78; atty.-advocate Devel. Disabilities Mont. Advocacy Program, Helena, 1978-79; atty. Zion, Reynolds &

Taylor, Helena, 1978-81; ednl. policy analyst divsn. edn. Navajo Nation, Window Rock, Ariz., 1982-88; assoc. prof. social scis. U. N.Mex., Gallup, 1988-95; spl. asst. for disability issues office of affirmative actio U. Ill., Champaign, 1996—. Cons. Tech. Rsch. Svcs., Gallup and Albuquerque, 1988—, Navajo Area Sch. Bd. Assn., Window Rock, 1989-97; chair Dept. Human Svcs., Sociology and Tribal Studies, U. N.Mex., Gallup, 1988-95; mem. adv. coun. U. Ill. Champaign-Urbana Divsn. Rehab. Edn. Svcs., 1996—. Author: Legal Status of Homemakers in Montana, 1975; contbr. articles to profl. jours. Exec. dir. ACLU of Mont., Great Falls, 1974-76; mem. Young Dems., Helena, 1977-80; clk. Helena Friends Meeting, 1977-80; convenor Gallup Friends Worship Group, 1983-90; mem. Fighting Back Core Com., Gallup, 1992-93, Gov.'s Com. on Concerns of the Handicapped, Santa Fe, 1994—; recording clk. Intermountain Yearly Meeting, Durango, Colo., 1994; clk. peace and svc. com. Urbana/Champaign Friends Meeting, Champaign, 1996-97. TIIAP grantee U.S. Dept. Commerce, 1994. Mem. Assn. on Higher Edn. and Disability, Nat. Indian Edn. Assn. (non-Indian assoc.), Western Social Sci. Assn., Navajo Bar Assn., N.Mex. Bar Assn. Mem. Soc. Of Friends. Avocations: hiking, swimming, theater, music, creative writing. Office: U Ill Office Affirmative Action 601 E John St Champaign IL 61820-5711

BLANCHARD, SHIRLEY LYNN, primary school educator, consultant; b. Medford, Oreg., Sept. 5, 1954; d. Richard L. Grigsby, Helen L. Grigsby; m. John T. Blanchard, Sept. 6, 1975; children: Andrew Blanchard children: Martin Blanchard, Richelle Blanchard. BA in Edn., So. Oreg. State Coll., 1975, BS, 1978; MA in Edn., So. Oreg. U., 1985. Nat. bd. cert. tchr. Nat. Bd. Profl. Tchg. Stds., 2000. Music tchr. Jackson County Sch. Dist. #6, Central Point, Oreg., 1975—81, kindergarten tchr. Eagle Point, Oreg., 1983—99; primary tchr. Jackson County Sch. Dist. #9, Eagle Point, Oreg., 1999—. Home schooling parent educator RIGGS Inst., So. Oreg., 1987—91, reading cons. for home schooling parents, 1987—91; continuing edn. presenter early childhood literacy So. Oreg. U./Medford Sch. Dist. 549C, Medford, 1995—96; site based mgmt. team chmn., mem. Glenn D. Hale Elem. Scho., Eagle Point, 1996—98; contract bargaining team mem. Eagle Point Edn. Assn., Eagle Point, 1997—98. Leader Wynema Girl Scout Counsel, Medford, 1972—75; 4H leader Oreg. State Ext. Svc., Central Point, Oreg., 1997—98. Recipient Slice of Life award, Williams Bread & McKenzie Farms Bakery and KOBI-TV, 2002. Fellow: Nat. Kindergarten Alliance Network; mem.: NEA, Internat. Soc. for Tech. in Edn., Oreg. Edn. Assn., Nat. Assn. Edn. Young Children. Avocations: internet mentoring, horses, technology, writing music, birds. Home: 1939 Dry Creek Rd Eagle Point OR 97524 Office: Jackson County Sch Dist #9 PO Box 197 215 E Main Eagle Point OR 97524 Home Fax: (541) 826-3221; Office Fax: (541) 826-3221. Business E-Mail: blanchards@eaglepnt.k12.or.us.

BLANCO, KATHLEEN BABINEAUX, governor; b. Dec. 15, 1942; m Raymond S. Blanco, Aug. 8, 1964; 6 children. BS, U. La.at Lafayette, 1964. With La. State Legis. Dist. 45, 1984-88, mem. house edn. com., mem. house transp., hwys., and pub. works com., Pub. Svc. Commn., La., 1988-94, chair, 1993-95; lt. gov. State of La., 1995—2003, gov., 2004—. Democrat. Office: Office of Gov PO Box 94004 Baton Rouge LA 70804-9004

BLAND, ANNIE RUTH (ANN BLAND), nursing educator; b. Bennett, N.C., Oct. 14, 1949; d. John Wesley and Mary Ida (Caviness) Brown; m. Chester Wayne Bland; 1 child, John Wayne; stepchildren: Jason Tyler, Adam Mathew. BSN, East Carolina U., Greenville, N.C., 1971; MSN, U. N.C., 1974; PhD in nursing, U. N.C., 2003; RN, N.C.; cert. clin. specialist in adult psychiat./mental health nursing. Staff nurse VA Med. Ctr., Durham, N.C., 1974-75, 77-80; psychiat. clin. instr. Duke U. Med. Ctr., Durham, 1980-82, asst. head nurse, 1982-90, staff nurse, 1993—99; psychiat. clin. nurse specialist John Umstead Hosp., Butner, N.C., 1990-93; psychiat. lead nursing instr. Alamance C.C., Graham, N.C., 1994-96; asst. prof. Sch. Nursing, U. N.C., Greensboro. Asst. Sunday sch. tchr. Mt. Hermon Bapt. Ch., Durham, 1994, 96, 99-2000. Capt. USNR, 1971-97, ret. 1997. Recipient award for nursing excellence Great 100 Orgn., Raleigh, N.C., 1991, Letter of Appreciation Am. Heart Assn., Chapel Hill, 1992. Mem. ANA, N.C. Nurses Assn. (sec. dist. 11, 1981), Assn. Mil Surgeons U.S., U. N.C. Chapel Hill Alumni Assn. and Sch. Nursing, East Carolina U. Alumni Assn. and Sch. Nursing, Res. Officers Assn. Baptist. Avocations: tennis, swimming, water skiing, snow skiing. Home: 2534 New Hope Church Rd Chapel Hill NC 27514-8218 Office: U NC Greensboro Sch Nursing CPG PO Box 26170 Greensboro NC 27402-6170

BLAND, DOROTHY ANN, construction executive, real estate agent; b. Black Township, Pa., Jan. 12, 1945; m. Jonathan Lee Sharp, Sept. 28, 1963 (dec. Dec. 31, 1979); children: Deborah, Todd, Wade; m. Brian C. Bland, Nov. 2, 1985; stepchildren: Paulette, Kelli. Lic. Real Estate Agent, Utah. Beauty coll. recruiter, sec. Continental Coll. of Beauty, Salt Lake City, 1968-72; exec. sec. Vaughn Hansen Assoc., Salt Lake City, 1973-82; v.p., co-owner Bland Bros., Inc., West Jordan, Utah, 1985—; co-owner Blands Sand & Gravel, Utah, 1990—. Real estate agent Preferred Properties, Salt Lake City, 1982-90, Mansell, Salt Lake City, 1990—. Avocations: golf, travel. Office: Bland Brothers Inc 8630 Redwood Rd West Jordan UT 84088-9226

BLAND, EVELINE MAE, real estate broker, musician, music instructor; b. Hughesville, Pa., Aug. 24, 1939; d. Burton Anthony and Mary Margaret (Mack) Morgan; m. Theodore D. Bland; 1 child, Susanna Elisabeth. BA, Mansfield (Pa.) U., 1961; Orff Schulwerk cert., Royal Conservatory, Toronto, Ont., Can., 1976; MBA, Century U., 1992. Tchr. Newburgh (N.Y.) Jr. High Sch., 1961-62, Cedar Grove (N.J.) Bd. Edn., 1962-66, West Caldwell (N.J.) Bd. Edn., 1973-76, Covenant Christian Sch., North Plainfield, N.J., 1976-77; salesperson Janett Realtors, Verona, N.J., 1977-79; sales mgr. Degnan Boyle Realtors, Caldwell, 1979-88, Schlott Realtors, Montclair, 1988-91; realtor Coldwell Banker, Sarasota, Fla., 1992; mortgage broker Sarasota, 1992—; tchr. Faith Christian Sch., Sarasota, 1992-95, Sarasota Music Ctr., 1993-98. Prin. Camp Shawnee, Waymart, Pa., 1961-71, Melody One Music Studios Club, 1993—, Music Studio, 1995-2003; instr. Sarasota Fine Arts Acad., 1992; music arranger Mouse Mountain Toy Co., 2002-2003. Music dir. Players, Sarasota Broadway Goes to Hollywood; prof. vocal soloist, N.J., Pa. Opera, Oratorios, Broadway-type shows, 1971-91; apprentice Paper Mill Playhouse, Millburn, N.J., 1962-66. Organist, choir dir. 1st Congl. Ch., Verona, 1978-87; organist Venice 1st Bapt. Ch., 1992-95; accompanist Sarasota Bapt. Ch., 1991; trustee Montclair Hist. Soc., 1970-87; bd. dirs. State Repertory Opera, Montclair Kiwanis, 1990-91; mem. Sarasota Opera Guild, 1992. Mem. Nat. Assn. Tchrs. Singing, Nat. Realtors Assn. (cert.), N.J. Assn. Realtors (profl. stds. and edn. coms. 1987), West Essex Bd. Realtors (v.p., sec. 1985-86, pres. 1987, career trainer 1987, Realtor of Yr. 1987), Sarasota Bd. Realtors, Fla. Assn. Realtors, Music Tchrs. Nat. Assn., Fla. State Music Tchrs. Assn. (chmn. state conf. 2000, treas. 1999), Sarasota Music Tchrs. Assn. (treas. 2002, 2003), Christian Profl. and Bus. Women (project advisor 1992), Am. Guild Organists, West Essex C. of C., Montclair C. of C., FIABCI-USA, Gideons Aux. (various offices 1982-87), Kiwanis, Lambda Mu. Republican. Baptist. Avocations: golfing, tennis, painting, reading, gardening.

BLAND, JANEESE MYRA, editor; b. Evanston, Ill., Feb. 20, 1960; d. James Milton and Jeanette Malisa (Bryant) B. BA, U. Ark., 1980. Cert. tchr., Ark., Ill. Tutor counselor U. Ark., Pine Bluff, 1979; tchr. Pine Bluff High Sch., 1980, Chgo. Bd. Edn., 1981-84; editor, author, columnist, creator Beautiful Images Hollywood (Calif.) Gazette Newspaper, 1985—. VIP organizer People's Choice Awards, Beverly Hills, 1984—; exec. prodr. stas. Chgo. Access Corp., Century Cable Comms., L.A., BH-TV, Beverly Hills; hostess The Janeese Bland Show. Proof editor: Nursing Rsch. Jour., 1989. Polit. vol. Rep. Party, Santa Monica, 1988—; vol. organizer Windfeather, Inc., Beverly Hills, 1983—, United Negro Coll. Fund, L.A., 1984—, Sickle Cell Disease Rsch. Found., L.A., 1985—; pres., founder June Maria Bland Scholarship Found. Recipient Image award Fred Hampton Scholarship Found., 1983, Wiley W. Manuel award State Bar Calif., Cert. Merit, Bet Tzedek Legal Svcs., Ill. Cmty. Leader of the Yr. award Nat. Coun. Negro Women and Quaker Oats, 1998. Mem. SBA (pres.). Republican. Baptist. Home and Office: 269 S Beverly Dr # 420 Beverly Hills CA 90212-3807 E-mail: landofbland@aol.com.

BLAND, MARY GROVES, state legislator; b. Kansas City, Mo., Jan. 24, 1936; Student, Ottawa U., Penn Valley Coll., Pioneer C.C., Weaver Sch. Real Estate. Mem. Mo. Ho. of Reps. from 43rd dist., Jefferson City, 1980-98; cmty. specialist Lan Clearance for Redevel., Kansas City, 1971-79; mem. Mo. Senate from 9th dist., Jefferson City, 1999—. Vice-chmn. human rights and resources com., chair labor and indsl. rels. com., mem. aging families and mental health com., civil and criminal jurisprudence com., elections, vet. affairs and corrections com., pub. health and welfare com., health rev. com., cert. of need program com., joint com. on wetlands; free-lance cmty. cons., 1979—; exec. bd. Freedom, Inc. Active Mayor's Neighborhood Coun. on Crime Prevention; mem. S.E. Neighborhood Coalition, U.S. Commn. on Civil Rights; active Niles Home for Children. Home: 1632 Bushman Dr Kansas City MO 64110-3512 Office: Mo State Senate Rm 334 State Capitol Building Jefferson City MO 65101

BLANDFORD, VIRGINIA ROSE, music educator; b. Whitesville, Ky., Nov. 17, 1947; d. William Lester and Mary Elizabeth (Shively) Coomes; m. Kenneth Michael Blandford; children: Terry, Ryan, Robert, Jason. MusB, Brescia Coll., 1969; MA in Edn., We. Ky. U., 1984, degree in Edn., 1993. Prin., owner Blandford's Piano Studio, Owensboro, 1969—; music tchr. St. Pius X Elem. Sch., Owensboro, Ky., 1969—74; gen. music instr. St. Angela Merici Sch., Owensboro, 1975—. Piano tchr. Brescia Coll., Owensboro, 1969—73; mem. ednl. adv. bd. Riverpark Center, Owensboro, 2000—. Talent show coord. Davis County (Ky.) Fair, 1985—89. Mem.: Ky. Fedn. Music Clubs, Nat. Fedn. Music Clubs (pres. Saturday musicale 1986—88), Nat. Assn. Pastoral Musicians (south ctrl. coord. music edn. divsn. 2000—, bd. dirs., named Outstanding Music Educator of Yr. 1996). Office: St Angela Merici School 525 E 23rd St Owensboro KY 42303

BLANEY, DOROTHY GULBENKIAN, academic administrator; BA in Comparative Lit. with high hons., Cornell U., 1962; Woodrow Wilson Fellow Comparative Lit., U. Calif., Berkeley, 1963; PhD in English, SUNY, Albany, 1971. Asst. prof. English SUNY, Albany, 1968-71; coord. N.Y. State Doctoral Rev. Program, Albany, 1971-73; asst. commr. higher edn. planning and policy analysis N.Y. State Edn. Dept., Albany, 1973-78, dep. commr. higher edn. and professions, 1978-81; cons. Internat. Labor Office, Internat. Mgmt. Inst., Geneva, N.Y.C., Switzerland, U.S., 1981-82; exec. v.p. Pace U., N.Y.C., 1982-88; pres. Cedar Crest Coll., Allentown, Pa., 1989—. Co-author (with Ernst R. May): (book) Careers for Humanists, 1981; columnist for Times Mirrors, Morning Call, and, occasionally, U.S.A. Today, Phila. Inquirer, Atlanta Constitution; contbr. articles to mags. and jours. Office: Cedar Crest Coll Office of the President 100 College Dr Allentown PA 18104-6132

BLANK, JOAN GILL, journalist, illustrator; b. Buffalo, Apr. 3, 1928; d. Ralph C. and Miriam A. Epstein; m. Harvey Blank, Sept. 14, 1975; children: Robin, Susan, Prudence. AB, Sarah Lawrence Coll., 1949. Editor, art dir. Investment Sales Monthly, Coral Gables, Fla., 1964-68, Fla. Commentary, Hollywood, 1973-75, Communique, Miami, Fla., 1974-75; editor, designer [illegible] 1960, [illegible] in field, 1963—; pres. Grapetree Prodns., Inc., 1981—. Author: Give Your Whole Self, 1981, Key Biscayne, A History of Miami's Tropical Island & The Cape Florida Lighthouse, 1996; author, illustrator: Laugh Lines, 1982; contbr. articles and photo features to mags. and newspapers. Mem. Nat. Press Club, Phi Theta Kappa, Chi Delta Phi. Democrat. Address: 600 Grapetree Dr Apt 10cn Key Biscayne FL 33149-2704

BLANK, MARION SUE, psychologist, educator; b. N.Y.C., Dec. 20, 1933; d. Morris David and Tillie Jean (Sherman) Hersch; m. Martin Blank, July 3, 1955; children: Donna, Jonathan, Ari. BA, CCNY, 1955, MS in Edn, 1956; PhD, Cambridge (Eng.) U., 1961. Asst. prof. Albert Einstein Coll. Medicine, 1965-70, asso. prof., 1970-73; prof. dept. psychiatry Rutgers Med. Sch., Piscataway, N.J., 1973-83; mem. adj. faculty dept. psychiatry Columbia Coll. Physicians and Surgeons, N.Y.C., 1980-83; pres. PHAT Phonics, 2001—. Dir. reading disabilities rsch. inst., pvt. practice, cons., 1983—; Nat. Tour lectr. Speech Pathology Assn. Australia, 1996. Author: Teaching Learning in the Preschool - A Dialogue Approach, Preschool Language Assessment Instrument, 1978, (with Rose and Berlin) The Language of Learning, 1978, (with Marquis and Klimovitch) Directing School Discourse, 1994, Directing Early Discourse, 1995, Sentence Master, 1990-96, (with Berlin) A Parent's Guide to Educational Software, 1991, (with Marquis and Klimovitch) Directing School Discourse, 1994, Directing Early Discourse with Marquis and Klimovitch, 1995, Your Cure for the Reading Crisis, 2004. Pinsent-Darwin fellow, 1960; recipient award of commendation N.J. Speech and Hearing Assn., 1979, Spl. Edn. award Software Pubs. Am., 1990, N.J., USPHS Career Devel. award, 1965-73; named N.J. nominee Kleffner Lifetime Svc. award Am. Speech Lang. Hearing Assn., 1994, 95. Fellow APA; mem. Assn. for Children with Learning Disabilities. Home: 157 Columbus Dr Tenafly NJ 07670-1635 Office Phone: 201-567-0790. E-mail: msb5@columbia.edu., msblank@optonline.net.

BLANK, REBECCA MARGARET, economist; b. Columbia, Mo., Sept. 19, 1955; d. Oscar Uel and Vernie (Backhaus) B.; m. Johannes Kuttner, 1994; 1 child, Emily. BS, U. Minn., 1976; PhD, MIT, 1983. Cons. Data Resources, Inc., Chgo., 1976-79; asst. prof. econs. Princeton U., 1983-89; assoc. prof. econs. Northwestern U., Chgo., 1989-94, prof. econs., 1994-99; sr. staff economist Coun. of Econ. Advisors, Washington, 1989-90, mem., 1998-99; dean, Henry Carter Adams prof. Gerald R. Ford Sch. Pub. Policy, U. Mich., Ann Arbor, 1999—; co-dir. Nat. Poverty Rsch. Ctr., U. Mich. Author: It Takes A Nation: A New Agenda for Fighting Poverty, 1997, other books; contbr. articles to profl. jours. Vis. Professorships for Women grantee, 1988-89; Sloan Found. fellow, 1982-83; recipient Jr. Faculty Teaching award Princeton U., 1985, David Kershaw award Assn. Pub. Policy Analysis and Mgmt., 1993, Richard Lester award for best book on labor econs., 1997. Mem. Nat. Bur. Econ. Rsch., Am. Econs. Assn., Assn. of Pub. Policy Analysis and Mgmt., Indsl. Rels. Rsch. Assn. United Ch. of Christ.

BLANKENBURG, JULIE J. librarian; b. Madison, Wis., Dec. 22, 1956; d. Henry A. and Marjorie L. Blankenburg; m. Wayne I. Zimmerman. BA in Theatre, U. Wis., 1979, MA in LS, 1980. Asst. libr. USDA Forest Products Lab. Libr., Madison, 1988-93, libr., 1994—. Mem. ALA, Spl. Librs. Assn., Wis. Libr. Assn., Theatre Libr. Assn. Office: USDA Forest Svc Forest Products Lab Libr One Gifford Pinchot Dr Madison WI 53726-2398

BLANKENSHIP, DAWN OLIVIA, pediatric nurse; b. Dover, Del., Aug. 16, 1962; d. Bobby Joe Jones and Margaret Carolyn Fritts; m. Charles E. Blankenship, Oct. 27, 1981; children: Jon, Rebekah. Assoc., U. Ky., 1990; BS in Nursing, Bellarmine U., 2002, postgrad. RN, cert. pediatric nurse. Nurse King's Daus. Med. Ctr., Ashland, Ky., 1990—; with neonatal unit Cabell Huntington Hosp., W.Va., 1993—2002; line instr. Arrow Internat., 2003—. Nurse, assessor Life Plans, 2000—; per diem clin. instr. Morehead State U., 2003—. Home: 1514 Napier St Flatwoods KY 41139 Personal E-mail: missqueenie@hotmail.com.

BLANKENSHIP, JENNY MARY, museum administrator; b. Mpls., Nov. 15, 1955; AA in bus., Weatherford Coll.; cert. paralegal, Southern Meth. U.; BBS in Mktg., BBA in Journalism, U. Tex.; PhD, So. Meth. U., 1998. Mktg. coord. Fingerhut Corp., Minnetonka, Minn.; pub. rels. coord. Family Svcs. Inc, Ft. Worth, Tex.; pres. Gloss Mgmt. Inc, Weatherford, Tex.; editor The Shorthorn, Arlington, Tex.; v.p., editor Randy Keck & Co., Boston; editor-in-chief Community Press, Hico, Tex.; dir. pub. affairs Hico Chiropractic; pub. Tex. Spotlight; promoter Dallas Cowboy Legends Event, 1997; mus. programs adminstr. Sci. Mus. Minn., 1999—. Dir. pub. rels. Hope Inc., Mineral Wells, Tex.; dir. Randy Keck & Co.; fundraising cons. WICI, Waco, Tex., instr. seminars Ctr. for Profl. & Exec. Devel. U. Tex; promoter Dallas Cowboy Legends, 1997. Author: Poetry of the Old Testament, 1987, The Business of Life, 1988, Do Over, 1994, The Brains, The Club and The Sneak, 1999, Shadows of Hate, 1999; pub. Tex. Spotlight. Vol. merit badge counselor, dist. officer, dist. tng. chair Boy Scouts Am. Recipient Best Layout, Column, Page award Columbia U., 1987, 90, Best Upstart Weekly in the State award Southwest Journalism Conf., 1994, Best Sports award South Tex. Press, 1995, Best Layout award South Tex. Press, 1995. Mem. Women In Communication, Inc. (Best Feature award, Best Advt. Campaign, 1991, Best Broadcast Feature award, 1990), MENSA, NAFE (com. mem), Soc. Profl. Journalists, United Meth. Women (pres.), Kiwanis. Methodist. Avocations: painting, singing, collecting headwear. Office: PO Box 96 Glen Rose TX 76043-0096

BLANTON, FAYE WESTER, legislative staff member; b. Tallahassee, Nov. 9, 1946; m. Edwin F. "Ed" Blanton; children: Wade, Doug, Laurel McDaniel. Staff asst. govtl. efficiency com. Fla. Senate, Tallahassee, asst. to dir. mgmt. staff, asst. sec., sec., 1996—. Advisor, counselor Girls State, Boys State, YMCA Youth Legislature, Silver-Haired Legislature; pres. PTO Leon County Sch. Dist., mem. adv. bd. Mem. Am. Soc. Legis. Clks. and Secs. (exec. com., past assoc. v.p., mem. exec. and nominating com., chair, vice-chair, mem. various coms.) Baptist. Avocations: gardening, walking, reading. Home: 610 Summerbrooke Dr Tallahassee FL 32312 Office: Fla Senate 404 S Monroe St Tallahassee FL 32399-1100 Fax: 850-487-5174.

BLANTON, PATRICIA LOUISE, periodontal surgeon; b. Clarksville, Tex., July 9, 1941; d. Ben E. and Mildred L. (Russell) B. MS, Baylor U., 1964, PhD, 1967, DDS, 1974, cert., 1975. Diplomate Am. Coll. Bd. Oral Medicine. Teaching asst. Baylor Coll. of Dentistry, Dallas, 1963-67, asst. prof., 1967-70, spl. instr., 1970-73, assoc. prof., 1974-76; resident periodontics VA Hosp., Dallas, 1975; prof. emeritus Baylor Coll. of Dentistry, Dallas, 1976-85; prof. Baylor U. Grad. Sch., Dallas, 1976—; prof., chmn. Baylor Coll. of Dentistry, Dallas, 1983-85; prof. emeritus. Cons. VA Hosp., Dallas, 1979-82; adj. prof. Baylor Coll. of Dentistry, Dallas, 1985—; cons. Commn. on Dental Accreditation and Coun. of Dental Edn., 1981—; v.p. State Anatomical Bd., Tex., 1983-85; mem. ADA-AADS Liaison Com., 1983—; chmn. Nat. Insts. Health, Oral Biology and Medicine Study Sect. II, 1985-86. Author: Periodontics for the G.P., 1977, Current Therapy in Dentistry, 1980, An Atlas of the Human Skull, 1980 (1st place honors 1981). Invited participant Am. Coun. on Edn., Austin, 1984; mem. liaison com. Dallas County Dental Soc.-Am. Cancer Soc., Dallas, 1976-78; bd. dirs. Dallas Dental Health Programs, 1992-93, S.W. Med. Found., 1992-93; bd. devel. Hardin-Simmons U., 1995—. Named one of Outstanding Young Women in Am., 1976. Fellow Am. Coll. Dentists, Internat. Coll. Dentists; mem. ADA (alt. del., pres. 2002-2003), Tex. Dental Assn. (bd. dirs. 1995-97, v.p., pres.-elect 2003, pres. 2003—), Am. Assn. Anatomists, Am. Acad. Periodontology, Am. Acad. Oral Medicine, Am. Acad. Osseointegration, Tex. Soc. Periodontists (pres. 1998-99), S.W. Soc. Periodontology (pres. 1998-99), Dallas County Dental Soc. (pres. 1992-93), Xi Psi Phi, Omicron Kappa Upsilon (pres. 1992-93). Avocations: reading, travelling. Office: 4514 Cole Ave Ste 902 Dallas TX 75205-4172

BLANTON, PRISCILLA WHITE, social sciences educator, psychologist, researcher; b. Little rock, Ark., Aug. 13, 1947; d. Douglas Malcolm and Nell Chandler White; m. Horace Dewey Blanton, Aug. 4, 1984; children: Benjamin Douglas, Janelle Ruth. BS, Carson-Newman Coll., 1969; MS, U. Tenn., 1970, EdD, 1972. Lic. psychologist Tenn. Asst. prof. dept. child and famiy studies U. Tenn., Knoxville, 1972—77, assoc. prof., 1977—82, prof., 1982—. Dept. head U. Tenn., 1980—83, mem. faculty adv. com. Black Studies Program, 1972—76, mem. faculty adv. com. Women's Studies Program, 1979—91; program developer and leader Southea. Newspaper Pub.'s Assn. conf., Knoxville, 1979. Contbr. articles to profl. jours., chapters to books. Bd. dirs. East Tenn. Planned Parenthood, Oak Ridge, 1988—90. Grantee, Consortium for Clergy Families, 1993. Mem.: Nat. Coun. on Family Rels. (state treas. 1988—94). Avocations: gardening, golf, skiing. Home: 7324 Cresthill Dr Knoxville TN 37919 Office: U Tenn Dept Child & Family Studies JHB 115 Knoxville TN 37996

BLANTON, VALLYE J. elementary school educator; b. Valdosta, Ga., Sept. 4, 1953; d. Louie Sloan and Tomie Jean (Roberts) B. BS in edn., U. Ga., 1975; MEd, Valdosta State Coll., 1977, cert., 1977-79. Tchr. Lowndes County Sch. System, Valdosta, Ga., 1975-89; assessment specialist Coastal Plains Regional Assessment Ctr., Valdosta, Ga., 1989-90, tchr. Lowndes County Sch. System, Lake Park, Ga., 1990—. Bd. dirs. Ga. Partnership for Excellence in Edn., Atlanta, 1994—; tchr. adv. com. Southeastern Regional Vision for Edn., Greensboro, N.C., 1994—; editorial bd. Tchr. Learning Resource Ctr., Dayton, Ohio, 1994—; scholarship selection com. U.S. Space & Rocket Ctr., Huntsville, Ala., 1994—. Bd. dirs. Valdosta Jr. Svc. League, 1985—, Valdosta State U. Alumni Bd., 1993—, U. Ga. Booster Club, 1982—. Named Ga. Tchr. of Yr. Ga. Dept. Edn., 1994; recipient Milken Nat. Educator award Milken Family Found., 1994. Mem. Ga Assn. Educators (profl. devel. chmn. 1975-94), Profl. Assn. Ga. Educators, Ga. Coun. Tchrs. Math., Nat. State Tchrs. of Yr. Orgn., Kappa Delta Pi, Phi Delta Kappa. Baptist. Avocations: reading, walking, volunteer work. Home: 2832 Fawnwood Cir Valdosta GA 31602-4105 Office: Lake Park Elem PO Box 869 Lake Park GA 31636-0869

BLASE, NANCY GROSS, librarian; b. New Rochelle, N.Y. d. Albert Philip and Elsie Wise (May) Gross; m. Barrie Wayne Blase, June 19, 1966 (div.); m. Charles M. Goldstein, July 25, 1999; 1 child, Eric Wayne. BA in Biology, Marietta (Ohio) Coll., 1964; MLS, U. Ill., 1965. Info. scientist brain info. svc. Biomed. Libr., UCLA, 1965-66; libr. Health Sci. Libr., U. Wash., Seattle, 1966-68, Medlars search analyst, 1970-72, coord. Medline, 1972-79, head Natural Scis. Libr., 1979—. Mem. libr. adv. com. Elizabeth C. Miller Libr., Ctr. for Urban Horticulture, Seattle, 1986-90. Contbr. articles to profl. jours. Mem. Bet Chaverim, Seattle, pres., 1998—2000. NSF fellow interdept. tng. program for sci. info. specialists U. Ill., 1964-65. Mem.: Internat. Tng. in Comm. (pres. Pacific N.W. region 1994—95), Am. Soc. Info. Sci. (pres. personal computer spl. interest group 1993—94, chair constn. and bylaws com. 1994—97, chair med. informatics spl. interest group 1998—99, rsch. grantee Pacific N.W. chpt. 1984—85), Phi Beta Kappa (pres. U. Wash. chpt. 1993—97, pres. Puget Sound Assn. 2001—03, mem. com. on chpts. 2002—). Avocations: walking, reading. Home: 10751 Durland Ave NE Seattle WA 98125-6945 Office: U Wash Natural Scis Libr Box 352900 Seattle WA 98195-2900 E-mail: nblase@u.washington.edu.

BLASING, MUTLU KONUK, English language educator; b. Istanbul, Turkey, June 27, 1944; came to U.S., 1963; d. Mustafa Celal Konuk and Muzeyyen (Uzun) Dursunoglu; m. Randolph Charles Blasing, Aug. 21, 1965; 1 child, John Konuk. Student, Carleton Coll., 1963-65; BA, Coll. William and Mary, 1969; PhD, Brown U., 1974. Lectr. English U. Mass., Mass., 1974-76; asst. prof. Pomona Coll., Claremont, Calif., 1977-79, Brown U., 1979-83, assoc. prof., 1983-88, prof., 1988—. Dir. Copper Beech Press, Providence. Author: The Art of Life, 1977, American Poetry: The Rhetoric of Its Forms, 1987, Politics and Form in Postmodern Poetry, 1995; translator: Human Landscapes (N. Hikmet), 1982, Epic of Sheik Bedreddin (N. Hikmet), 1975, Things I Didn't Know I Loved, (N. Hikmet), 1975, Rubaiyat (N.Hikmet), 1985, Selected Poetry (N. Hikmet), 1986,

Poems of Nazim Hikmet, 1994, Human Landscapes from my Country (N. Hikmet), 2002, Poems of Nazim Hikmet, 2002. Fellow U. Mass., 1974-76. Office: Brown U English Dept PO Box 1852 Providence RI 02912-1852

BLASSENGALE, MICHELLE YVETTE, music educator; b. Suffolk, Va., May 19, 1968; d. Earl Sanders Blassengale and [illegible] B in Music Edn., Winthrop U., 1990, M in Music Edn., 1992. Tchr. choir Ronald E. McNair Jr. High, Lake City, SC, 1992—93; tchr. music/choir Alice Dr. Elem., Sumter, SC, 1993—97, Bates Mid., Sumter, 1997—99, Chestnut Oaks Mid., Sumter, 1999—2001, Kinsbury Elem., Sumter, 2001—. Mem. Tchr. Adv. Com., Sumter, 2001—, Sch. Improvement Coun., Sumter, 2001—. Mem.: S.C. Music Educators Assn., Music Educators Nat. Conf., Woman's Afternoon Music Club (historian 2001—03). Baptist. Avocations: reading, piano. Home: 695 White Pine Way Sumter SC 29154 Office: Kinsbury Elem 825 Kingsbury Dr Sumter SC 29154

BLATE, ALISSA, advertising executive; m. Andrew Jessup; children: Noah, Emmery. BA in psychology, Ithaca Coll.; attended, NYU. Exec. v.p. MWW Group, 1997—; sr. v.p. Rowland Co., N.Y.C. Office: MWW Group 1 Meadowlands Plz 6th Fl East Rutherford NJ 07073-

BLATTNER, FLORENCE ANNE, retired music educator; b. Rockford, Ill., Nov. 27, 1935; d. Keith F. and Grace L. (Turney) Perkins; m. Lewis Olof Blattner, Mar. 28, 1959; children: Gloria Grace Blattner Mundt, Gayle Mary Blattner Ludwig. BA, Carroll Coll., 1958; studied with, Vladimir Levitski, 1984—95, Weekly and Arganbright, U. Ind, 1993, 98, 2000, Joanne Tierney, 1995—2002. Elem. and jr. high sch. libr. Racine (Wis.) Pub. Schs., 1958—60, elem. substitute tchr., 1961—62, elem. and jr. high tchr., 1962; pvt. practice piano instr. Indpls., 1970—78; data processor OMS Internat., Greenwood, Ind., 1978; pvt. practice piano and theory instr. Des Moines, 1980—83; piano and theory instr. Prelude Piano Studio, Apple Valley, Minn., 1983—2003; ret., 2003. Duettist concerts duet lit., Racine, Wis., 1996, 1999, Apple Valley, Minn., 1996, 1998—2002, White Bear Lake, 1996, Dodge City, Kans., 2001, Bloomington, Minn., 1996—97, 2001, Godfrey, Ill., 1998, 2000, Alton, Ill., 1998, 2000, solo perfomer, Hot Springs Village, Ark., 2003. Ch. pianist, accompianist, 1970—; vol. Rep. Party-Minn., Apple Valley, 1992, 94, 96, 98. Mem. Music Tchrs. Nat. Assn., Minn. Music Tchrs. (assoc. cert., state ensemble festival chair 1994-97, cert. com. 1997-2001), South Suburban Music Tchrs. Assn. (1st v.p. 1995-97, pres. 1998-2000, newsletter editor 1995-2001, yearbook editor 2001-2002), Nat. Guild Piano Tchrs., Am. Fedn. Music Clubs. Avocations: canoeing, hiking, traveling, reading, piano. E-mail: flblattner@usfamily.net.

BLATTNER, MEERA MCCUAIG, computer science educator; b. Chgo., Aug. 14, 1930; d. William D. McCuaig and Nina (Spertus) Klevs; m. Minao Kamegai, June 22, 1985; children: Douglas, Robert, William. BA, U. Chgo., 1952; MS, U. So. Calif., 1966; PhD, UCLA, 1973. Rsch. fellow in computer sci. Harvard U., 1973-74; asst. prof. Rice U., 1974-80; assoc. prof. applied sci. U. Calif.-Davis, Livermore, 1980-91, prof. applied sci., 1991-99, prof. emeritus, 2000—; pres. Color Wheel Creations, 2001—. Adj. prof. U. Tex., Houston, 1977—99; vis. prof. U. Paris, 1980; program dir. theoretical computer sci. NSF, Washington, 1979—80. Co-editor: (with R. Dannenberg) Multimedia Interface Design, 1992; contbr. articles to profl. jours. NSF grantee, 1977-81, 93-99. Mem. Assn. Computing Machinery, Computer Soc. of IEEE. Office: Color Wheel Creations 850 S Durango Rd Ste 107 Las Vegas NV 89145 E-mail: meera.blattner@cvi.net.

BLATZ, KATHLEEN ANNE, judge, state agency administrator, state legislator; BA summa cum laude, U. Notre Dame, 1976; MSW, U. Minn., 1978, JD cum laude, 1984. Psychiat. social worker, 1979—81; mem. Minn. Ho. of Reps., St. Paul, 1979—93, chmn. crime and family law, fin. instns. and ins. coms., 1985—86; judge Dist. Ct., Henne Pin County, 1993—96; justice Minn. Supreme Ct., 1996—98, chief justice, 1998—. Office: 305 Minn Judicial Ctr 25 Rev Martin Luther King Jr Blvd Saint Paul MN 55155

BLATZ, LINDA JEANNE, management professional; d. William Edmund and Jeanne Grace (Hyman) B. BS, U. Md., 1972. Mgr. sales Milliken & Co., N.Y.C., 1972-81; retail market mgr. Greenwood Mills Mktg. Co., N.Y.C., 1981-89; dist. mgr. Steelcase Inc., N.Y.C., 1989-94, tng. cons., 1994-95, tng. mgr., 1995-2000, tng. dir., 2000—03, sales tng. cons., 2003; regional sales mgr. Nat. Bus. Furniture, N.Y.C., 2003—. Contbr. articles to profl. jours. Mem. N.Y.C. Ballet Guild; corr. sec., pres. PEO; mem. jr. com. N.Y.C. Ballet; v.p. membership, bd. mgrs. exec. com. N.Y. Jr. League (Outstanding Vol. award 1991-92); nominating dir. Assn. Jr. Leagues Internat., 1997, centennial adv. bd., 1999—. Recipient Outstanding Vol. of the Yr. award N.Y. Jr. League, 1992. Mem.: ASTD, AAUW, Am. Woman's Econ. Devel. Corp., N.Y. Women's Agenda, U. Md. Alumni Assn., Women's City Club N.Y., East River Rowing Club, Alpha Gamma Delta. Congregationalist. Avocations: ballet, aerobic dancing, swimming, reading. E-mail: ljbeje@aol.com.

BLAU, ELIZABETH ANNE, restaurant executive; b. N.Y.C., Aug. 31, 1967; BS in Govt., Georgetown U., Washington; MS in Restaurant Mktg., Cornell U. Sch. Hotel Admin., Ithaca, N.Y. Dir. devel. Le Cirque, N.Y.C.; chief confectioner, sr. mgr. Hand-Crafted Hilliards Candies, West Hartford, Conn.; scholarship program developer James Beard Found., N.Y.C.; co-owner The Butler Did It Catering, Washington; asst. catering dir. Blantyte Hotel, Lenox, Mass.; v.p. of restaurant development Mirage Resorts, Inc., Las Vegas. Avocations: hiking, climbing, horseback riding, skiing. Office: Mirage Resorts Inc PO Box 7777 Las Vegas NV 89177-0777

BLAU, HELEN MARGARET, pharmacology educator; b. London, May 8, 1948; (parents Am. citizens); d. George E. and Gertrude Blau; m. David Spiegel, July 25, 1976; children: Daniel Spiegel, Julia Spiegel. BA in Biology, U. York (Eng.), 1969; MA in Biology, Harvard U., 1970, PhD in Biology, 1975; Doctorate (hon.), U. Nijmegen, Netherlands, 2003. Predoctoral fellow dept. biology Harvard U., Cambridge, Mass., 1969-75; post-doctoral fellow div. med. genetics, dept. biochemistry and biophysics U. Calif., San Francisco, 1975-78; asst. prof. dept. pharmacology Stanford (Calif.) U., 1978-86, assoc. prof. dept. pharmacology, 1986-91, prof. dept. molecular pharmacology, 1991—99, prof. dept. microbiology and immunology, 2002—, chair dept. molecular pharmacology, 1997—2001, dir. gene therapy tech., 1997—, Donald E. and Delia B. Baxter prof., 1999—, dir. Baxter Lab. in Genetic Pharmacology, 2002—. Rolf-Sammet-Fonds vis. prof., U. Frankfurt, 2003; co-chmn. various profl. meetings. Mem. editorial bd. 14 jours. including Jour. Cell Biology, Somatic Cell Molecular Genetics and Exptl. Cell Rsch., Molecular and Cellular Biology, Genes to Cells, Molecular Therapy; contbr. articles to profl. jours. Mem. ad hoc molecular cytology study sect. NIH, 1987-88; mem. five-yr. planning com genetics and teratology br. NICHHD/NIH, 1989. Recipient Rsch. Career Devel. award NIH, 1984-89, SmithKline & Beecham award, 1989-91, Women in Cell Biology Career Recognition award, 1992, Excellence in Sci. award FASEB, 1999, McKnight Endowment Fund for Neurosci. award, 2001; Mellon Found. faculty fellow, 1979-80, William H. Hume faculty scholar, 1981-84; grantee NIH, NSF, Ellison Med. Found., Muscular Dystrophy Assn., March of Dimes, 1978—; Yvette Mayent-Rothschild fellow for vis. profs. Inst. Curie, Paris, 1995. Fellow AAAS; mem. NAS (del. to China 1991), Internat. Soc. Differentiation (pres. 2002—), Am. Soc. for Cell Biology (nominating com. 1985-86, program com. 1990), Soc. for Devel. Biology (pres. 1994-95), Inst. Medicine Nat. Acad. Scis., Am. Soc. Gene Therapy (bd. dirs. 1999-2002). Avocations: skiing, swimming, hiking, music, theatre. Office: Stanford U Sch Medicine 269 Campus Dr CCSR 4215 Stanford CA 94305-5175 Fax: (650) 736-0080. E-mail: hblau@stanford.edu.*

BLAUVELT, BARBARA LOUISE, nutritionist; d. Starr Chester and Dorothy (Schofield) Blauvelt. PhD, U. Mass., 1969. Nutrition program supr. divsn. pub. health nutrition Va. Dept. Health, Roanoke, 1970-95. Pvt. cons., 2002—. Co-author: Kitchen Memories, 1998

BLAXALL, MARTHA OSSOFF, economist; b. Haverhill, Mass., Feb. 2, 1942; d. Michael M. and Eve Joan (Kladky) Ossoff; m. John Blaxall, May 15, 1970 (div. 1989); children: Jenifer, Johanna. BA, Wellesley Coll., 1963; PhD, Tufts U., 1971. Economist Abt Assocs. Inc., Cambridge, Mass., 1965-68; budget examiner Office Mgmt. and Budget, 1969-72; sr. profl. assoc. Inst. Medicine NAS, 1972-76; dir. rsch. Health Health Care Fin. Adminstrn., U.S. HHS, 1976-79; dir. Office Utilization and Devel., Nat. Marine Fisheries Svc., Dept. Commerce, 1979-82; assoc. prof. dept. cmty. and family medicine Georgeteown U. Med. Sch., 1982; pres. BBH Corp., 1982-87; prin. Chase, Brown & Blaxall, Inc., 1983-87; v.p. ICF Inc., Washington, 1987-89; economist Hill and Knowlton Econs. Group, Washington, 1990-91; dir. agribus. trade and investment group Devel. Alternatives Inc., Bethesda, Md., 1991-93, dir. mktg. devel. group, 1993-95, v.p., 1995—2001; dir. Ctrl. Asia and Caucasus Project Yale U. Ctr. Study Globalization, 2001—02; vis. scholar Nitze Sch. for Adv. Internat. Studies John Hopkins U., 2002—03; strategic devel. officer econs. studies Brookings Inst., 2004—. Treas. Fedn. Orgns. Profl. Women, 1974—76, 1983—84, exec. coun., 1982. Co-editor: Women in the Workplace: The Implications of Occupational Segregation, 1976. Trustee Sheridan Sch., Washington, 1978—86, Coun. for Excellence in Govt., 1991—; mem. Inst. Women's Policy Studies, 1993—2002, chair, 1998—2002; active Woolly Mammoth Theatre Co., 1997—, vice chair, 1999—; active Leadershp Forum Internat., 2002—; bd. dirs. Washington-Moscow Exch., 1990—93, Children's Health and Environ. Ctr. NDEA fellow, 1964—65. Mem.: Nat. Economists Club (v.p. 1990—91), Am. Econ. Assn. Home: 3960 Birdsville Rd Davidsonville MD 21035 Office Phone: 202-797-6306. E-mail: moblaxall@aol.com.

BLAYDES, SOPHIA BOYATZIES, English language educator; b. Rochester, N.Y., Oct. 16, 1933; d. James George and Helene (Bougdanos) Boyatzies; m. David Fairchild Blaydes, June 4, 1961; children: Stephanie Anne, Jeffrey Glenn. BA, U. Rochester, 1955; MA, Ind. U., 1958, PhD, 1962. Teaching asst. English Ind. U., 1955-62; instr. to asst. prof. Am. Thought and Lang. dept. Mich. State U., 1962-65; instr. to prof. English W.Va. U., Morgantown, 1966-99, chair faculty senate, 1990-91, coord. program for sr. and retired faculty, 1994—; pres. Carolinas Symposium for British Studies, 1990-91. Co-dir. Lit. Discussion Group for Sr. Citizens, 1978—; mem. faculty Elderhostel, 1985, 87, 88, 90, 94; mem. ctrl. exec. com. Folger Inst., 1992-99; chair faculty senate, bd. advisors W.Va. U., 1990-91, rep. to adv. coun. to bd. trustees, 1993-99; state del. to the 1995 White House Conf. on Aging; bd. trustees Univ. Sys., 1998-99. Author: Christopher Smart as a Poet of His Time: A Re-Appraisal, 1966, (with others) Sir William Davenant, 1981, Sir William Davenant: An Annotated Bibliography, 1986; editor: (with others) Selected Papers from the W.Va. Shakespeare and Renaissance Association, 1976, The Literary Discussion Group, 1982, 85; contbr. chpts. to books, articles to profl. jours., encys., dictionaries, bibliographies. Mem. cen. exec. com. Folger Inst., 1992-99. Recipient Disting. Manuscript award Mich. State U., 1965, Gerontology Ctr. award, 1983; named Disting. West Virginian, W.Va. Gov., 1995; grantee W.Va. Found., 1973, W.Va. Humanities, 1980; W.Va. U. Senate rsch. grantee, 1984, 89; Folger fellow, 1981, Folger grantee, 1988, 91; recipient Sigma Tau Delta Outstanding Tchg. award, 1996. Mem. Am. Soc. 18th Century Studies, MLA, W.Va. Assn. Coll. English Tchrs. (pres. 1977), Shakespeare and Renaissance Soc. W.Va. (chmn. 1978, 84), Carolinas Symposium on Brit. Studies (chair program 1989, pres. 1990, conf. chair 1993). Home: 652 Bellaire Dr Morgantown WV 26505-2421 Office: W Va U PO Box 6296 Morgantown WV 26506-6296

BLAZEJ, PENNY ANNETTE, clinical social worker, writer, artist; b. San Francisco, Sept. 2, 1954; d. Edmond Hugo and Betty Rae (Marvin-Mallory) Realini; m. Roger Noel Bybee, May 28, 1978 (div. June 1983); m. Anthony John Blazej, Oct. 12, 1985; 1 child, Kathryn Anne (dec. Feb. 1989). BS in Biol. Sci., U. Calif., Davis, 1976; MSSW, MPH in Mgmt. and Policy, Columbia U., 1996. Cert. clin. social worker, N.Y., Conn., Calif.; LCSW Am. Bd. Examiners; bd. cert. diplomat. Chemist Seroyal Brands, Concord, Calif., 1976-78; chemist, salesperson, mgmt. specialist Varian Assocs., Concord, Calif., 1978-80; dir. Smith Kline Beckman, Berkeley, Calif., 1980-82; mgmt. cons. IBM, 1982-92; bereavement counselor Hospice Care, Inc., Stamford, Conn., 1991-92; clin. social worker Cancer Care, Inc., 1993-95, Four Winds Hosp., Katonah, N.Y., 1995-96, Family and Children's Agy., Norwalk, Conn., 1997—99; sch. social worker Westchester Jewish Cmty. Svcs., White Plains, N.Y., 1996-97; med. social worker Hospice Care, Inc., Stamford, Conn., 1997-99; pvt. practice Valley Center, Calif., 2003—. Vol. Hospice, 1989—. Contbr. articles to profl. jours. Vol. Hospice Care, Inc., Stamford, 1989-92, Cancer Care, Inc., Norwalk, 1994-95; vol., CCT tchr. St. John's Ch., Darien, Conn., 1992-93, program dir. for Reach Out, 1989-92; vol., bereavement counselor St. Alouisa Ch., New Canaan, Conn., 1989-91. Recipient 1st prize photog., Silvermine Gallery Show, 1999. Mem. NASW, Exec. Nat. Pub. Health Orgn., Nat. Hospice Orgn., Nat. Orgn. Aging., Families of Spinal Muscular Atrophy (vol. 1989—). Roman Catholic. Avocations: painting, writing, cooking, gardening, photography. Office Phone: 760-685-3403.

BLAZEJOWSKI, CAROL A. professional sports team executive, retired professional basketball player; b. Elizabeth, NJ, Sept. 29, 1956; Grad., Montclair State Coll., 1978. Player Montclair State U., 1974—78, Allentown Crestettes, Pa., 1978—80, NJ Gems, 1980-81; dir. licensing NBA, 1990—95, dir. women's basketball programs, 1995—96; dir. basketball devel. WNBA, 1996—97; promotional rep. Adidas; v.p., gen. mgr. NY Liberty WNBA, 1997—2000, sr. v.p., gen. mgr., 2000—. Named Kodak All-Am., Montclair State Coll., 1976—78, Converse Women's Player Yr., 1977, Women's Basketball Player Yr., 1978; named to Naismith Basketball Hall Fame, 1994, NJ Sports Hall Fame, 1995; recipient Wade Trophy, 1978. Achievements include All-Am. selection, 1976, 77, 78; single season and career women's basketball scoring records, 1976; mem. World Univ. Gold Medal team, Mexico City, 1979; Pan Am. Silver medal team, 1979; leading scorer Women's Basketball League, 1980-81. Office: New York Liberty 2 Penn Plz New York NY 10121-0101 also: c/o Basketball Hall of Fame PO Box 179 Springfield MA 01101-0179*

BLAZEK-WHITE, DORIS, lawyer; b. Easton, Md., Nov. 17, 1943; d. George W. and Nola M. (Buterbaugh) Defibaugh; children: Christine T., Judson M.; m. Thacher W. White. BA, Goucher Coll., 1965; JD, Georgetown U., 1968. Bar: D.C. 1969, V.I. 1969, U.S. Ct. Appeals (3d cir. 1969), U.S. Ct. Appeals (D.C. cir. 1971), Md. 1979. Gen. practice with Judge Warren H. Young, V.I., 1968-70; assoc. Covington & Burling, Washington, 1970-76, ptnr., 1976—. Mem. Am. Coll. Trust and Estate Counsel. Office: Covington & Burling 1201 Pennsylvania Ave NW Washington DC 20004 E-mail: dblazek-white@cov.com.

BLAZINA, CAROLE MARIE, nun; b. Braddock, Pa., July 27, 1959; d. John Frank Blazina and Helen Ruyechan. BSN, BTh, Carlow Coll., Pitts., 1981; MSN, U. Pitts., 1994; MA in Pastoral Studies, Aquinas Inst. Theology, St. Louis, 2000. RN Pa., 1981, cert. CRNP, Pa., 1994, FNP. From staff nurse to head nurse Forbes Regional Hosp., Monroeville, Pa., 1983—94; FNP Ptnrs. in Health, Levelgreen, Pa., 1994—98, Fuge Family Practice, Wilkins Township, Pa., 2001—; mentor temp. professed Sisters of Charity Seton Hill, Greensburg, Pa., 1996—98, dir. novices, 1998—. Team mem. Pitts. Vols. Appalachian Health, 1992—96; bd. dirs. St. Paul's Manor PCH, Pitts., 1995—98; trustee Seton Hill U., Greensburg, 1994—. Mem.: ANA, Religious Formation Conf., Am. Acad. Nurse Practitioners, Sigma Theta Tau. Roman Catholic. Home: Marian Hall 451 Mount Thor Rd Greensburg PA 15601

BLAZINA, JANICE FAY, transfusion medicine physician; b. Youngstown, Ohio, Apr. 20, 1953; d. Joseph and Cordelia Evelyn (Mitchell) B. BS, Youngstown State U., 1975; MD, Ohio State U., 1978. Diplomate Am. Bd. Pathology. Resident in anat. and clin. pathology U. Ala. Med. Ctr., Birmingham, 1978-82; assoc. pathologist various [illegible] 1982-83, High Plains Bapt. Hosp., Amarillo, Tex., 1983-84; fellow in blood banking Baylor U. Med. Ctr., Dallas, 1984-85; asst. prof. dept. pathology Ohio State U., Columbus, 1985-93, asst. prof. Sch. Allied Med. Professions, 1987-93. Asst. dir. transfusion svc. Ohio State U. Hosp., 1985-89, assoc. dir., 1989-90, dir., 1990-93, med. dir. histocompatibility, paternity, apheresis and phlebotomy svcs., 1987-93, divsn. med. tech., 1987-93; asst. med. dir. Carter Blood Ctr., Ft. Worth, 1993-95, med. dir., 1995-96. Contbr. articles to profl. publs. Grantee: Bremer Found., 1987. Mem. AMA, Am. Soc. Apheresis, Am. Soc. Histocompatibility and Immunogenetics, Am. Assn. Blood Banks (insp. 1987—), Ohio Assn. Blood Banks (trustee 1990-93, sec. 1992-93), Assn. Women Sci. Cen. Ohio (v.p. 1989-90, pres. 1990-91), Nat. Alliance Mentally Ill Tarrant County (sec. 2003). Mem. Church of Christ. Avocations: gardening, cats, african violets.

BLECHA, DIANE LOUISE, business consultant; b. Olean, N.Y., Aug. 1, 1949; d. Thomas Frank and Norma Mae (Suppa) B.; m. Tim Timmermann, May 23, 1980. Assoc. in Edn., SUNY, Cobleskill, 1969; BA in Edn., Buffalo State, 1971; N.Y. state permanent teaching cert., U. Buffalo, 1976; MA in Edn., Counseling, St. Bonaventure, 1980. Elem. tchr. Pioneer Elem., Delevan, N.Y., 1971-73; flight attendant Eastern Airlines, Miami, Fla., 1973-74; elem. tchr. Pioneer Elem., Arcade, N.Y., 1974-75; mid. sch. tchr. Pioneer Mid. Sch., Yorkshire, N.Y., 1975-82; co-owner counseling ctr. East Aurora (N.Y.) Counseling Group, 1982-85; bus. cons. Ridge Assocs., Cazenovia, N.Y., 1982-85, co-dir. New Eng. region Brookfield, Conn., 1985-94; co-founder, exec. v.p. Lockwood Leadership Internat., Holden Beach, N.C., 1994—. Cons. dir. Fortune 500, 1985—, writer, designer tng. programs, 1985—conf. speaker, 1986—, internat. cons., 1984—; dir. sr. trainer group Ridge Assocs., Cazenovia, 1991—; co-designer Interaction Styles Profile, 1998. Co-author: Modern Stress: Needless Killer, 1982. Counseling Curriculum grantee N.Y. State. Mem. Phi Beta Kappa. Avocations: interior design, golf, running, reading, entertaining. Office: Lockwood Leadership Intl 183 Swordfish Dr Holden Beach NC 28462-1825

BLEDSOE, LAURITA, small business owner, publisher; b. Detroit, July 23, 1955; children: Miranda, Curtis, Kia. Assoc., Highland Park C.C., 1978. Clk. U.S. Postal Svc., Detroit, 1986—; owner Just For You Boutique, Detroit, 1995—; pres. Bledsoe Enterprises Inc., Detroit, 1998—. Author: Straight from the Heart, 2000; contbr. poems to anthologies (Merit award); author: Tomorrow Never Knows, 1995. Activist for juvenile causes, Detroit, 1998—; min. gospel Praise and Worship Leader. Inductee Black Inventors Mus., 2001, Detroit 300 Yr. Almanac, 2002, Charles H. Wright Mus. African Am. History, 2002. Mem. Internat. Soc. Poets, Detroit Writers Guild, Phi Theta Kappa. Achievements include invention of talking pottie training chair. Avocations: reading, art, design, liturgical dance. Office: 17660 W 12 Mile Rd Ste 5 Southfield MI 48076-1911

BLEDSOE, LINDA KAY, psychologist, researcher; b. Louisville, Ky. A in Computers, U. Louisville, 1979, BA in Russian, 1993, PhD in Psychology, 1998. Assoc. mem., grad. faculty U. of Ky., Lexington, Ky., 1993—95; from psychology instr. to faculty U. of Louisville, 1995—2002, mem. faculty Nat. Resource Ctr. Child Welfare Tng. and Evaluation, 2002—. Mem. Domestic Violence Prevention Coordinating Coun., Louisville, 2002—. Contbr. articles to profl. jours. Grantee, Office of Justice Programs, U. S. Dept. of Justice, 1999—2001, 2002—03, Metro United Way, 2001—02. Mem.: APA, Ky. Psychol. Assn., Am. Psychol. Soc. Office: Kent School of Social Work University of Louisville Louisville KY 40292 Office Phone: 502-852-0421.

BLEEKER, LAURIE, state legislator; b. Lincoln, Nebr., Nov. 30, 1952; m. Harry Bleeker; 2 children. BA, Bethel Coll. Homemaker, Great Bend, Kans.; mem. Kans. Senate, Topeka, 1996—, mem. edn. com., mem. pub. health and welfare com., mem. fed. and state affairs com., mem. arts and cultural resources com. Republican. Office: 300 SW 10th Ave Rm 460-e Topeka KS 66612-1504

BLEES, JOAN MARGARET, music educator; b. St. Paul, Apr. 12, 1948; d. James Spotts and Margaret Elizabeth (Laufenberg) Travis; m. James Edward Blees. BA, U. Minn., St. Paul, 1970; MPS, Loyola U., New Orleans, 1991. Nationally cert. tchr. music, kindermusik cert. Owner, instr. Blees Music Instrn., Anchorage, 1973—, Blees Kindermusik, Anchorage, 1994—; organist, choir dir. Cath. Ch., Anchorage, 1973—; liturgical music cons. Archdiocese of Anchorage, 1987-94; music tchr. Anchorage Montessori Sch., 1996—. Choir dir. Archdiocese of Anchorage; adjudicator Am. Keyboard Tchrs. Assn., Am. Music Tchrs. Assn., 1985—. Named master cantor Nat. Pastoral Musicians, 1987. Mem. Anchorage Keyboard Tchrs. Assn. (mem. bd., 1974-77, 80-83, 93-95.

BLEIER, CAROL STEIN, writer, researcher; b. N.Y., Jan. 31, 1942; d. Shelley and Ruth (Brown) Stein; m. Michael Bleier, Oct. 9, 1966; children: Thomas, Lisa, Mark. BA in English Lit., Syracuse U., 1963; MLS, U. Pitts, 1986. Pub. info. specialist IRS, Washington, 1964-68; columnist Springfield (Va.) Ind., 1977-78; mktg. cons. Greater Pitts. Mus. Coun., 1986-88; pub. rels. dir. Greater Pitts. Literacy Coun., 1988-89; writer, 1985—. Author: (corp. history book) To Good Health and Life: L'Chaim A History of Montefiore Hospital of Pittsburgh, 1898-1990, 1997; co-author: (corp. history book) The Ketchum Spirit: A History of Ketchum Communications Inc., 1992; contbg. author: Encyclopedia of Library History, 1994; contbr. articles to periodicals. Mem. ALA, Beta Phi Mu. Democrat. Jewish. Avocations: reading, travel. Home: 214 Lynn Haven Dr Pittsburgh PA 15228-1821

BLENDELL, ELIZABETH A. lawyer; BA, Mt. Holyoke Coll., 1972; JD, Boston Coll., 1980. Bar: Calif. 1980. With Latham & Watkins, L.A., 1980—, ptnr., 1988—. Mem. faculty Practising Law Inst., 1990—. Mem.: ABA, Calif. Bar Assn. Office: Latham and Watkins LLC 633 W Fifth St Ste 4000 Los Angeles CA 90071*

BLESCH, K(ATHY) SUZANN, small business owner; b. Evansville, Ind., Dec. 14, 1951; d. Robert Lee McBride and E. Jean (Oliver) Schumacher; m. Larry J. Blesch, Aug. 17, 1974; children: Nicholas R., Spencer A., Clayton W. Grad. Grad. Realtors Inst., Ind. U., 1979; cert. residential specialist, Nat. Assn. Realtors, 1980. Waitress, hostess Skyway & Pete's, Evansville, Ind., 1971-73; operator, asst. mgr. Stecklers T.A.S., Evansville, 1969-71; salesperson, broker Midwest Realty, Evansville, 1973-78; broker, owner Blesch Realty, Evansville, 1978-80; broker, salesperson Brand Realty, Evansville, 1980-83; owner, operator Nick Nackery Pl., Evansville, 1985—. Bd. dirs. Hope of Evansville, 1976-79. Mem. Nat. Costumers Assn., Am. Taekwondo Assn. (1st degree black belt). Avocations: family, reading. Home and Office: 201 E Virginia St Evansville IN 47711-5529 Office Phone: 812-423-6425.

BLESSEN, KAREN ALYCE, freelance/self-employed journalist, artist; b. Columbus, Nebr. BFA, U. Nebr., 1973. Freelance illustrator, 1973-86; designer Dallas Morning News, 1986-89, freelance illustrator, designer, 1989—; owner, illustrator Karen Blessen Illustration, Dallas, 1989—; artist Times Square Bus. Improvement Dist., N.Y.C., 1994—. Illustrator Be An Angel, 1994, contbr. (art and articles) Dallas Morning News; commd. by Absolute to represent Tex. in Absolute Statehood series. Recipient Pulizer Prize for explanatory journalism, 1989, awards, N.Y. Art Dirs. Club, Soc. Newspaper Design, Dallas Press Club. Home and Office: Karen Blessen Illustration 6327 Vickery Blvd Dallas TX 75214-3348 E-mail: kblessen@aol.com.*

BLESSING, CAROL ANN, literature educator; b. Glen Ridge, N.J., Nov. 3, 1957; d. Hugh C. and Mary M. Snodgrass; m. George T. Blessing, May 20, 1978; 1 child, Daniel Nam Moon. BA in English, Messiah Coll., 1979; MA in English, Calif. State U., LA, Calif., 1985; PhD in English, U. of Calif., Riverside, CA, 1991. Asst. prof. of english Biola U., La Mirada, Calif., 1991—93; prof. of lit. Point Loma Nazarene U., San Diego, 1993—. Co-author: Reader's Guide to Women's Studies; editor: (online publication) New Horizons: Resources for Nazarene Women Clergy; contbr. articles to profl. jours. and mags. Fellow, Wesleyan Ctr., Point Loma Nazarene U., 1996. Mem.: MLA, Soc. for the Study of Early Modern Women, Shakespeare Soc. of Am., Conf. on Christianity and Lit. Protestant. Avocations: travel, reading, writing, popular culture studies, music. Office: Point Loma Nazarene University 3900 Lomaland Drive San Diego CA 92106-5954

BLESSING, CAROLE ANNE, human resources manager; b. Phila., Nov. 27, 1945; d. Walter Francis and Margaret Jane (Hindman) Thompson; m. William Blessing, May 26, 1991. BA, Temple U., Phila., 1978; MA Univ. Pa., 1986. Cert. occupational health and safety, Temple U., Villanova U. Asst. safety supr. Phila. Coke Co. Inc., Phila., 1969-71, safety supr., 1971-73, dir. personnel and safety, 1973-78; div. mgr. safety and security Kelsey Hayes Co., Phila., 1978-86, mgr. human resource, Heintz Corp., 1986-91; mgr. human resources Jefferson Smurfit-CCA, Phila., 1991—; exec. v.p., dir. Powell Envirn., Inc., 1988-93; pres., chmn. Data Research, Inc., Phila., 1983-91; dir. Affiliated Med., Phila., 1983-90; lectr. Drexel U., 1983-84; cons in field Contbr. articles to profl. jours. Chmn. first aid and safety programs ARC, Phila., 1974-76. Recipient safety achievement awards Phila. Safety Council. Mem. AAUW, NAFE, Am. Soc. Safety Engrs. (treas. Phila. chpt. 1978-79, 80), Nat. Safety Mgmt. Soc., Soc. for Human Resource Mgmt., Am. Mgmt. Assn. Republican. Home: 1602 Northview Blvd Plymouth Meeting PA 19462-2651

BLESSING, MAXINE LINDSEY, secondary school educator; b. Skirum, Ala., Mar. 27, 1920; d. John Amos and Lizzy Maude (Croft) Lindsey; m. Alvin Reed Blessing, June 24, 1939; 1 child, Deanna Dawn Blessing Gilbert. BS in Secondary English Edn., Jacksonville (Ala.) U., 1956; postgrad., Auburn U., 1974-75. Tchr. DeKalb County (Ala.) Schs., 1943-97; ret., 1997. Beta Club sponsor Crossville (Ala.) H.S., 1960—, drama dir. jr. and sr. plays, 1960—, interim counselor. Sunday sch. tchr., pianist, organist Skirum Bapt. Ch., Crossville. Mem. AAUW, NEA, Nat. Coun. Tchrs. English, Ala. Coun. Tchrs. English, Ala. Edn. Assn., DeKalb County Edn. Assn. (mem. English textbook com. 1988-89), Ea. Star (worthy matron 1944-45), Skirum Cmty. Club (various coms.). Democrat. Baptist. Avocations: music, church and community activities, bridge, reading, attending plays. Home: 2314 County Road 46 Dawson AL 35963-3400 Office: Crossville HS PO Box 38 Crossville AL 35962-0038

BLESSING-MOORE, JOANN CATHERINE, allergist; b. Tacoma, Wash., Sept. 21, 1946; d. Harold R. and Mildred (Benson) Blessing; m. Robert Chester Moore; 1 child, Ahna. BA in Chemistry, Syracuse U., 1968; MD, SUNY, Syracuse, 1972. Diplomate Am. Bd. Pediatrics, Am. Bd. Allergy Immunology, Am. Bd. Pediatric Pulmonology. Pediatric intern, then resident Stanford U. Sch. Medicine, Palo Alto, Calif., 1972-75, allergy pulmonology fellow, 1975-77; co-dir. pediatric allergy pulmonology dept. Stanford U. Children's Hosp., Palo Alto, Calif., 1977-84; clin. asst. prof. dept. pediatrics Stanford U. Sch. Medicine, Palo Alto, Calif., 1977-84, co-dir. pediatric pulmonology lab., 1977-84; clin. asst. prof. dept. immunology Stanford U. Hosp., 1984—; allergist Palo Alto Med. Clinic, 1984-90; pvt. practice allergy immunology-pediatric pulmonary Palo Alto, Calif., 1990—. Dir. ednl. program for children with asthma Camp Wheeze, Palo Alto, 1975—; cons. FDA, 1992-97; cons. in field. Author handbooks, camp program manuals; co-editor jour. supplements; mem. edit. bd. Allergy jours.; contbr. articles to sci. publs. Fellow Am. Acad. Allery, Asthma, Immunology (various offices 1980—, task force parameters of care asthma and allergy 1989—, Outstanding fellow 1998, Women in Allergy award 2000), Am. Coll. Chest Physicians (com. mem. 1980—), Am. Coll. of Asthma, Allergy and Immunology (regent 1995-98); mem. Am. Thoracic Soc., Am. Lung Assn., No. Calif. Allergy Found. (bd. dirs., pres.), Peninsula Women's Assn., Santa Clara and San Mateo County Med. Soc. (bd. dirs. 1999—), Chi Omega. Republican. Presbyterian. Avocations: music, sailing, skiing, horseback riding, scuba diving. Office: 780 Welch Rd Ste 204 Palo Alto CA 94304-1518 also: 101 S San Mateo Dr Ste 310 San Mateo CA 94401-3844 also: Stanford Univ Hosp Dept Immunology Palo Alto CA 94304

BLETHEN, SANDRA LEE, pediatric endocrinologist; b. San Mateo, Calif., May 16, 1942; d. Howard Albion and Laura Katherine (Wolf) B.; m. Fred I. Chasalow, Nov. 26, 1966. BS in Biochemistry, U. Chgo., 1961; PhD in Biochemistry, U. Calif., Berkeley, 1965; MD, Yeshiva U., 1975. Diplomate Am. Bd. Pediat. Fellow biochemistry Brandeis U., Waltham, Mass., 1965-68; instr. biochemistry U. Calif., San Diego, 1968-69; asst. prof. San Francisco State U., 1969-71; resident in pediat. Columbia Presbyn. Med. Ctr., N.Y.C., 1975-77; fellow pediatric endocrinology U. N.C., Chapel Hill, 1977-79; asst. prof. pediatrics Washington U., St. Louis, 1979-84; assoc. prof. pediat. SUNY, Stony Brook, 1985-96; assoc. attending pediatrician L.I. Jewish Med. Ctr., New Hyde Park, NY, 1984-90; attending pediatrician Univ. Hosp., Stony Brook, 1991-96; cons. Genentech, Inc., South San Francisco, Calif., 1985-96, sr. endocrinologist, 1996—99, assoc. dir. product experience, 1997-2000, sr. clin. scientist, 1999—2002; v.p. med. affairs metabolic endocrinology Serono, Inc., Rockland, Md., 2002—. Cons. Diagnostic Systems Labs., Webster, Tex., 1989-96. Mem. editl. bd. Steroids, 1990—, Jour. of Endocrinology and Metabolism, 1995-98; contbr. more than 90 articles to profl. jours. Predoctoral fellow NSF, 1961-63, Postdoctoral fellow USPHS, 1965-67. Mem. Am. Pediatric Soc. (program com. 1994), Endocrine Soc., Lawson Wilkens Pediatric Endocrine Soc. (membership chair 1994-95), Soc. for Pediatric Rsch., Phi Beta Kappa, Alpha Omega Alpha. Avocation: sailing. Office: Serono Inc 1 Tech Pl Rockland MA 02370 Personal E-mail: sandra.blethen@serono.com.

BLEVINS, AMY L. financial advisor, investment advisor; b. Salem, N.J., Aug. 28, 1976; d. James E. Blevins, Linda M. Blevins; life ptnr. George F. Boulton, Jr.. BS in Bus. Adminstrn., Rowan U., 1999; student, Am. Coll., 2003—. Series 7 Licensed, Securities, lic. Series 66, Series 31, Futures and Commodities, ins. license Life and Health Authorities in New Jersey. Outreach coord. USDA Farm Svc. Agy., Vineland, NJ, 1998—99; fin. advisor, investment advisor Morgan Stanley, Vineland, 1999—. Mem. adv. coun. Rowan U. Sch. Bus.; pres. N.J. chpt. King Lion of Pitman, 2003—04; zone chairperson Lions Club, Dist. 16c, NJ. Mem.: Lions Club (mem. various coms. 2000—), Phi Theta Kappa (sec. 1996—97), Sigma Beta Delta. Office: Morgan Stanley 226 Landis Ave Vineland NJ 08360 Office Phone: 856-690-5056. Office Fax: 856-692-4445. Business E-Mail: amy.blevins@morganstanley.com.

BLEVINS, PATRICIA M. state legislator; BA, Temple U. Mem. Dist. 7 Del. Senate, Dover, 1990—. Office: 209 Linden Ave Elsmere Wilmington DE 19805-2515 also: Del State Senate Legislative Hall PO Box 1401 Dover DE 19903-1401

BLEY, CARLA BORG, composer; b. Oakland, Calif., May 11, 1938; d. Emil Carl and Arlene (Anderson) Borg; m. Paul Bley, Jan. 27, 1959 (div. Sept. 1967); m. Michael Mantler, Sept. 29, 1967 (div. 1992); 1 dau., Karen. Student public schs., Oakland. Mem. adv. bd. Jazz Composers Orch. Assn. Freelance jazz composer, 1956—, pianist, Jazz Composers Orch., N.Y.C., 1964—, European concert tours, Jazz Realities, 1965-66; founder, WATT, 1973—, toured Europe with Jack Bruce Band, 1975; leader, Carla Bley Band, touring, U.S. and Europe, 1977—; composed, recorded: A Genuine Tong Funeral, 1967, (with Charlie Haden) Liberation Music Orch., 1969; opera Escalator Over the Hill, 1970-71 (Oscar du Disque de Jazz 1973), Tropic Appetites, 1973; composed: chamber orch. 3/4, 1974-75; film score Mortelle Randonnée, 1983; recorded: Dinner Music, 1976, The Carla Bley Band: European Tour, 1977, Musique Macanique, 1979, (with Nick Mason) Fictitious Sports, 1980, Social Studies, 1980, Carla Bley Live!, 1981, Heavy Heart, 1984, I Hate to Sing, 1985, Night Glo, 1985, Sexted, 1987, Duets, 1988, Fleur Carnivor, 1989, The Very Big Carla Bley Band, 1991, Go Together, 1993, Big Band Theory, 1993, Songs with Legs, 1995, Goes to Church, 1996, Fancy Chamber Music, 1998, Are We There Yet?, 1999, 4x4, 2000, Looking for America, 2003, The Lost Chords, 2004. Named winner internat. jazz critics poll Down Beat mag., 1966, 71, 72, 78, 79, 80, 83, 84; Best Composer of Yr., Down Beat Readers' Poll, 1984, composer/arranger of yr., 1985-92; Guggenheim fellow, 1972; Cultural Coun. Found. grantee, 1971, 79; Nat. Endowment for the Arts grantee, 1973, Oscar du Disque de Jazz (for Escalator Over the Hill) 1973; named Best in Field Jazz Times critics poll, 1990, Best Arranger, Downbeat Critics Poll, 1993, 94, Best Arranger, Downbeat Readers' Poll, 1994; recipient Prix Jazz Moderne from Academie du Jazz for The very Big Carla Bley Band album, 1992. Office: Watt Works PO Box 67 Willow NY 12495-0067 E-mail: watt@ulster.net.

BLIGE, MARY JANE, recording artist; b. Yonkers, N.Y., Jan. 11, 1971; d. Cora Blige. Albums include: What's the 411?, 1992, (double platinum award), My Life, 1994 (debuted at top of Billboard's R&B album chart), Mary Jane, 1995, Share My World, 1997, Mary, 1999, The Tour, 1999, No More Drama, 2001, Dance For Me, 2002, Love & Life, 2003; recordings include I'll Do For You, 1991, (duet) Changes, One Night Stand, Whenever I Say Your Name (with Sting), 2003 (Grammy award for Best Pop Collaboration With Vocals 2003). Recipient Soul Train Music award, 1993, N.Y. Music award, NAACP Image award. Office: MCA Records 1755 Broadway Fl 8 New York NY 10019-3743*

BLISSITT, PATRICIA ANN, nurse; b. Knoxville, Tenn., Sept. 23, 1953; d. Dewitt Talmadge and Imogene (Bailey) B. BSN with high honors, U. Tenn., 1976, MSN, 1985; PhD in Nursing, U. Wash., 2002; postgrad., U. Pa., 2003—. RN; cert. in case mgmt., trauma nurse core course, ACLS. Staff nurse neurosci. unit City of Memphis Hosp., 1976-78, head nurse neurosci. unit, 1978-79; physician's asst. Dr. John D. Wilson, Columbus, Miss., 1979-81; staff nurse med.-surg.-trauma ICU U. Tenn. Meml. Hosp., Knoxville, 1982-83, staff nurse neurosci. ICU Bapt. Meml. Hosp., Memphis, 1985-86, clin. nurse specialist neurosci., 1986-94, trauma coord., 1991-93, neuro case mgr., 1993-94; staff nurse neurosurg. ICU Harborview Med. Ctr., Seattle, 1994—2000, 2001—02; NIH postdoctoral fellow neuro critical care U. Pa., Phila., 2003—; neurotrauma staff nurse surg. ICU Hosp. U. Pa., 2003—. Nurse cons. neurosci. VA Hosp., Memphis, 1986; adv. com. Tenn. Bd. Nursing Practice; mem. test devel. com. Am. Bd. Neurosci. Nursing, 1996-2001, trustee, 2000-03, treas., 2002-03, chair test devel. com., 2003—. Author: (with others) Critical Care Nursing in Clinics of North America, 1990, Jour. Neurosci. Nursing, 1986, 92, 96, 2001, 03, Guidelines for Critical Care Nursing, Care Management, 2001; abstractor: Nursing SCAN in Critical Care, 1995-99; contbr. articles to sci. jour., chpt. to book; mem. editl. cons. bd. Focus on Critical Care, 1990-92. Mem. rev. com. Neurosci. Nursing Found./AANN Scholarship com., 2001. Grantee biobehavioral nursing tng. grantee, NIH/NINR/U. Wash., 1999—2002; scholar scholarship, AANN Scholar Com., 2001, Wash. State Nurses Found., 1998, Am. Assn. Neurosci. Nurses, 1999. Mem.: ANA (mem. coun. med.-surg. nurses, cert. med.-surg. clin. nurse specialist), AACN (life; pres.-elect Greater Memphis area chpt. 1989—90, mem. CCRN exam devel. com. 1989—92, pres. 1990—91, editl. cons. bd. 1990—92, past pres., chair nat. critical care awareness week 1990—93, chpt. cons. Region II 1991—93, NTI spkr. 1992, chpt. of yr. com. chair 1992—94, NTI spkr. 1993, chair-elect Puget Sound chpt. program 1995—96, chair program com. 1996—97, editor elect newsletter Puget Sound chpt. 1997—98, mem. program com. 1997—2003, newsletter editor Puget Sound chpt. 1998—99, pres.-elect 1999—2001, pres. 2002—03, Southea. Pa. chpt. edn. com. 2003—, publs. chair, newsletter editor 2003—, cert.), Soc. of Critical Care Medicine, Neurocritical Care Soc. (charter), Tenn. Nursing Congress (pres. 1990—94), Western Inst. Nursing, Tenn. Nurses Assn. (mem. com. on practice 1992—93), Wash. Nurses Assn., Am. Assn. Spinal Cord Injury Nurses, Am. Assn. Neurosci. Nurses (chair test devel. com. 2003—, pres. local chpt. 1989—90, program/seminar chair local chpt. 1990—93, program/seminar chair mid-South chpt. 1990—93, chair nat. resource devel. com. 1992—94, pres. Memphis chpt. 1995—98, editor newsletter 1998—2000, chair role delineation study task force 2000—01, editor newsletter 2001—02, cert. neursci. nurse, nat. lectr., mem., chmn. resource devel. com., nurse practice com., mem. contg. edn./ann. sci. program com.), Am. Assn. Neurol. Surgeons (assoc.), Sigma Theta Tau. Methodist. Avocation: music. Home: 1 Franklin Town Blvd Apt 408 Philadelphia PA 19103 Office Phone: 215-415-4388. Personal E-mail: blissitp@uphs.upenn.edu. Business E-Mail: pbliss@u.washington.edu.

BLITCH, PEG, state legislator; Former mem. Ga. Ho. of Reps.; judge Clinch County Probate Ct., 1976-80; exec. Clinch County Nursing Home; owner Ford Dealership; mem. Ga. Senate, Atlanta, 1992—; chmn. reapportionment com.; sec. corrections, correctional instn. and property com.; mem. appropriations, natural resources, rules coms. Rep. fed. preemption and state-fed. affairs com. So. Legis. Conf.; mem. reapportionment task force Nat. Donv. State Legis.; Ga. vice chair Am. Legis. Exch. Coun. Past co-convener Ga. Network Elected Women Officials; bd. dirs., former chairperson Ga. Student Fin. Commn.; former chair Clinch County Libr. Bd. Democrat. Office: Rm 121 State Capitol Atlanta GA 30334

BLITZ, PEGGY SANDERFUR, corporate travel management company official; b. Pitts., Apr. 12, 1940; d. Charles I. and Rebecca Polk (McBride) Wallace; m. Clark L. Blitz, Aug. 25, 1962 (div. Apr. 1974); children: Danette L., Jonathan D. BS, Ball State U., 1962; postgrad., No. Ill. U., 1976-77. Cert. speech therapist, spl. edn. tchr. Tchr. mentally retarded Anderson (Ind.) Pub. Schs., 1962-64; speech therapist Elgin (Ill.) Pub. Schs., 1964-66; pvt. practice speech therapy Elgin, 1966-68; tchr. mentally retarded Easter Seal Rehab. Ctr., Elgin, 1968-77; account exec. Whitehall Hotel, Chgo., 1977-79; regional mgr. IVI Travel Inc., Milw., 1979-85, sr. v.p. Dallas, 1985-88; pres. Travelmasters, Inc., Chgo., 1988-91; staff devel. Kemper Securities, Inc., Chgo., 1991-92; pres. Travel Mgmt. Cons., St. John, V.I., 1991—; property mgr. Short-Term Vacation Rentals, 1992—; exec. asst. Caneel Bay Resort, St. John, V.I., 1999—. Presbyterian. Home and Office: PO Box 8333 Cruz Bay VI 00831-8333 Office Phone: 340-776-6111. E-mail: pblitz@rosewoodhotels.com.

BLIZNAKOV, MILKA TCHERNEVA, architect, educator; b. Varna, Bulgaria, Sept. 20, 1927; came to U.S., 1961, naturalized, 1966; d. Ivan Dimitrov and Maria Kesarova (Khorozova) Tchernev; m. Emile G. Bliznakov, Oct. 23, 1954 (div. Apr., 1974). Architect-engr. diploma, State Tech. U., Sofia, 1951; PhD, Engring.-Structural Inst., Sofia, 1959; PhD in Architecture, Columbia U., 1971. Sr. researcher Ministry Heavy Industry, Sofia, 1950-53; pvt. practice architecture Sofia, 1954-59; assoc. architect Noel Combrisson, Paris, 1959-61; designer Perkins & Will Partnership, White Plains, N.Y., 1963-67; project architect Lathrop Douglass, N.Y.C., 1967-71; assoc. prof. architecture and planning Sch. Architecture, U. Tex., Austin, 1972-74; prof. Coll. Architecture, Va. Poly. Inst. and State U., Blacksburg, 1974-98, prof. emerita, 1998—; prin. Blacksburg, 1975—. Bd. dirs. founder Internat. Archives Women in Architecture, Va. Poly. Inst. and State U., The Parthena award, 1994. Prin. works include Speedwell Ave. Urban Renewal, Morristown, N.J., 1967—69, Wilmington (Del.) Urban Renewal, 1968—70, Springfield (Ill.) Ctrl. Area Devel., 1969—71, Arlington County (Va.) Redevel., 1975—77; author (with others): Utopia e Modernità, 1989, Reshaping Russian Archtecture, 1990, Russian Housing in the Modern Age, 1993, Nietzsche and Soviet Culture, 1994, New Perspectives on Russian and Soviet Artistic Culture, 1994, The Eastern Dada Orbit: Russia, Georgia, Ukraine, Central Europe, 1996, Signs of Times, Culture and the Emblems of Apocalypse, 1998, Women Architects in Eastern Europe: The Contributions of the Bulgarians, 1997, International Archive of Women in Architecture, 1997, 1999, 2001, 2002, Encyclopedia of Eastern Europe, 2000, Centropa, 2001; author: (with others), 2003; author: (with others) Women Architects in Japan, 2002, Housing in Russia: 20th Century, 2002; author: (with others) Encyclopedia of Twentieth Century Architecture, 2003. William Kinne scholar, 1970, vis. scholar Inst. Advanced Russian Studies, The Wilson Ctr. of Smithsonian Instn., 1988; NEA grantee, 1973-74, Am. Beautiful Found. grantee, 1973, Internat. Rsch. and Exch. Bd. grantee, 1984-93; Fulbright Hays rsch. fellow, 1983-84, 91; recipient Parthena award, 1994. Mem. Internat. Archive Women in Architecture (founder, chair bd. dirs.), Am. Assn. Tchrs. Slavic and East European Langs., Soc. Archtl. Historians, Nat. Trust Hist. Preservation, Am. Assn. Advancement of Slavic Studies, Assn. Collegiate Schs. of Planning, Inst. Modern Russian Culture (chairperson architecture, co-founder, dir.), Bulgarian Studies Assn., Assn. Collegiate Schs. of Architecture. Home: 2813 Tall Oaks Dr Blacksburg VA 24060-8109 Office: Va Poly Inst and State U Coll Architecture Blacksburg VA 24061 Business E-Mail: mbliznak@vt.edu.

BLOCH, JULIA CHANG, adult education educator; b. Mar. 2, 1942; came to U.S., 1951, naturalized, 1962; d. Fu-yun and Eva (Yeh) Chang; m. Stuart Marshall Bloch, Dec. 21, 1968. BA, U. Calif., Berkley, 1964; MA, Harvard U., 1967, postgrad. in Mgmt., 1987; DHL (hon.), Northeastern U., Boston, 1986. Vol. Peace Corps, Sabah, Malaysia, 1964-66; tng. officer East Asia and Pacific region, Washington, 1967-68, evaluation officer, 1968-70; mem. minority staff U.S. Senate Select Com. on Nutrition and Human Needs, Washington, 1971-76, chief minority counsel, 1976-77; dep. dir. Office of African Affairs U.S. Internat. Comm. Agy., Washington, 1977-80; fellow Inst. Politics Harvard U., Cambridge, Mass., 1980; asst. adminstr. Bur. for Food For Peace and Voluntary Assistance AID, Washington, 1981-87; asst. administr. Bur. for Asia and Near East, 1987-88; assoc. U.S.-Japan Rels. Program, Ctr. for Internat. Affairs Harvard U., Cambridge, Mass., 1988-89; amb. Kingdom of Nepal, 1989-93; group exec., v.p. Bank Am., San Francisco, 1993-96; pres. The U.S.-Japan Found., 1996-98; dir. Am. West Airlines, 1994-98, Penn Mut. Life Ins., 1997; prof. Am. studies Beida Univ., Beijing; amb. in residence U. Md., 2000—. Pres. U.S.-China Ednl. Trust; trustee Eisenhower Exch. Fellowship, 1995-97, Nat. Com. U.S. China Rels., 1998—; U.S. Senate rep. World Conf. on Internat. Women's Yr., Mex., 1975; advisor U.S. Del. to Food and Agr. orgn. Conf., Rome, 1975; rep. Am. Coun. Young Polit. Leaders, Peoples Republic China, 1977; charter mem. Sr. Exec. Svc., 1979; head U.S. del. Biennial Session World Food Programme, Rome, 1981-86, Devel. Assistance Com. Meeting on Non-Govtl. Orgns., Paris, 1985, Intergovtl. Group on Indonesia, The Hague, Netherlands, 1987, World Bank Consultative Group Meeting, Paris, 1987, mem. exec. women in govt., 1988-93, mem. coun. fgn. rels., 1991—; vis. prof. internat. rels. Peking U., 1998—; Starr sr. fellow U.S. China Rels. Fudan U., Shanghai, adj. prof. Author: A U.S.-Japan Aid Alliance, 1991; co-author: Chinese Home Cooking, 1986. Exec. bd. mem. Internat. Ctr. for Rsch. on Women, 1974-81; mem. adv. bd. Women's Campaign Fund, 1976-78; mem. nat. adv. coun. Experiment in Internat. Living, 1981-83; mem. U.S. Nat. Com. for Pacific Econ. Cooperation, 1984—, Nat. Presdl. Debate Forum, 1987-92; bd. trustees Atlantic counsel, 2004-; mem. presdl. adv. couns. Peace Corps, 1988-89; mem. com. to visit art mus. Harvard U., 1989; founder Women Fgn. Policy Group; mem. Am. Refugee Com. Bd., 1993; mem. Am. Himalayna Found. Bd., 1994; commr. Asian Art Mus., San Francisco, 1994; trustee bus. leadership cir., 1994—; bd. trustees Coun. Am. Ambs., 2003-, chmn. bd. dirs. T.Y. Chang Found. Hon Fulbright fellow, 1996, Woodrow Wilson fellow, 2000-; recipient Hubert Humphrey award for internat. svc., 1979, Humanitarian Svc. award AID, 1987, Leader for Peace award Peace Corps, 1987, Asian Am. LEadership award, 1989, Brotherhood/Sisterhood award Nat. Conf. on Christians and Jews, 1996; named Outstanding Woman of Color, Nat. Inst. for Women of Color, 1982, Woman of Distinction, Nat. Conf. for Coll. Women Student Leaders and Women of Achievement, 1987, Disting. Pub. Svc. award Nat. Assn. Profl. Asian Pacific Am. Women, 1989; Ford Found. Study fellow for internat. devel. Harvard U., 1966, Paul Harris award Rotary, 1992, Award of Honor Narcotic Enforcement Assn., 1992. Mem. Orgn. Cinese Am. Women (founder, chair 1977—, bd. dirs., Woman of Yr. 1987), Asia Soc. (pres. coun. 1989, trustee, 1994), Am. Studies Ctr. (vice-chair), Prytannean Honor Soc., Coun. Fgn. Rels., Mortar Bd., Cosmos Club. Republican. Avocations: ceramics, gourmet cooking, collecting art. E-mail: jcbloch@aol.com.

BLOCH, SUSAN LOW, law educator; b. N.Y.C. d. Ernest and Ruth (Frankel) Low; m. Richard I. Bloch; children: Rebecca, Michael. BA in Math., Smith Coll., 1966; MA in Math., U. Mich., MA in Computer Sci., PhC, 1972, JD, 1975. Bar: D.C. 1975. Law clk. to chief judge U.S. Ct. Appeals, Washington, 1975-76; law clk. to assoc. justice Marshall U.S. Supreme Ct., Washington, 1976-77; assoc. Wilmer, Cutler & Pickering, Washington, 1978-82; prof. Georgetown U. Law Ctr., Washington, 1983—. Legal analyst for impeachment procs. CBS, 1998; impeachment expert U.S. Ho. of Reps. Jud. Com., 1998. Author: Supreme Court Politics: The Institution and Its Procedures, 1994; contbr. Constl. Commentary, Duke Law Jour., Mich. Law Rev., Wis. Law Rev., Law and Contemporary Problems, Georgetown Law Rev., St. Louis U. Law Jour., ABA Jour., Supreme Ct. Preview, Voice of Am., Supreme Ct. Hist. Soc. Yearbook, 1987, Supreme Ct. Hist. Soc. Yearbook, 1992, Oxford Companion to the Supreme Ct. of the United States, 1992, Biology, Culture and Law, 1993. Active Common Cause, Women's Legal Def. Fund. Mem. ABA, Am. Bar Found., Am. Law Inst., D.C. Bar (Bicentennial of Constn., mem. ethics com., jud. evaluation com.), D.C. Cir. Judicial Conf. (prog. chair 1993, 96), U. Mich. Com. Visitors, 1982—, Inst. Pub. Representation (bd. dirs.), Order of Coif, Phi Beta Kappa, Sigma Xi. Home: 4335 Cathedral Ave NW Washington DC 20016-3560 Office: Georgetown U Law Ctr 600 New Jersey Ave NW Washington DC 20001-2075 Office Phone: 202-662-9063.

BLOCHOWIAK, MARY ANN, cultural organization administrator, writer; b. Shawnee, Okla., Dec. 18, 1943; d. Casimir Joseph Blochowiak, Mary Roberta Blochowiak. BA in History, U. Ctrl. Okla., 1979, MA in History, 1984. RN. Staff nurse Mercy and Deaconess Hosps., Oklahoma City, 1964—90; asst. editor Okla. Hist. Soc., Oklahoma City, 1988—89, asoc. editor, 1990—99, pub. divsn. dir., 1993—, editor The Chronicles of Oklahoma, 2000—. Book awards judge Okla. Ctr. for the Book, Oklahoma City, 1998—. Contbr. articles to profl. jours. Mem.: Okla. Mus. Assn., Okla. Assn. Profl. Historians, Okla. Hist. Soc., Western History Assn. Avocations: history, reading, needlecrafts. Office: Okla Hist Soc 2100 N Lincoln Blvd Oklahoma City OK 73105-4997 Office Fax: 405-/521-2492. Business E-Mail: mablochowiak@ok-history.mus.ok.us.

BLOCK, AMANDA ROTH, artist; b. Louisville, Feb. 20, 1912; d. Albert Solomon and Helen (Bernheim) Roth; m. Gordon J. Wolfe, June 16, 1931 (div. 1947); 1 child, Joseph G. Wolf; m. Maurice Block, Jr., July 15, 1949. Student, Smith Coll., 1930-31, U. Cin., 1933, Art Acad. Cin., 1933-40; BFA, Ind. U.-Purdue U., Indpls., 1960. Instr. Herron Sch. Art, Ind. U. Purdue U., Indpls., 1969-73; instr. lithography Indpls. Art Ctr., 1974. Adv. bd. Indpls. Art League Found., 1979-81. One-woman shows, 1444 Gallery, Indpls., 1962, Sheldon Swope Art Gallery, Terre Haute, Ind., 1963, 73, Park Avenue Gallery, Indpls., 1964, Harriet Crane Gallery, Cin., 1965, Talbot Gallery, Indpls., 1967, Merida Gallery, Louisville, 1967, Herron Mus. Art, Indpls., 1969, Editions Ltd. Gallery, Indpls., 1972, 79, Franklin (Ind.) Coll., 1973, Tucson Mus. Sch., 1977, Indpls. Art League, 1992; two-woman shows, Jason Gallery, N.Y.C., 1964, Orange County Coll., Middletown, N.Y., 1964, Washington Gallery, Frankfort, Ind., 1975, Edits. Ltd. Gallery, Indpls., 1983; exhibited in group shows, Chgo. Art Inst., 1941, Butler Inst. Am. Art, Youngstown, Ohio, Burr Gallery, N.Y.C., Hanover Coll., Wabash, Ind., De Pauw U., Soc. Am. Graphic Artists AAA Gallery, Purdue U., Istan

Gallery, Tokyo, Phila. Print Club, Pa. Acad. Fine Arts, 1969, Imprint Gallery, San Francisco, 1972, Van Straaten Gallery, Chgo., 1973, McNay Inst., San Antonio, 1972, Pratt Graphics, N.Y.C., 1976, Ind. State Mus., 1976, Indpls. Mus. Art, 1977, Tucson Mus. Art, 1978, internat. traveling exhbn., Soc. Am. Graphic Artists, 1974-75, traveling exhbn., 1977, 78; represented in permanent collections, Continental Ill. Bank, Chgo., De Pauw U., Ind. State Coll., Terre Haute, Ind., Med. Soc., Indpls., Sheldon Swope Art Gallery, Stevens Coll., Boston Public Library, USIA, Lafayette (Ind.) Art Center, Lippman Assos., architects, Indpls., J.B. Speed Mus., Louisville, IBM Bldg., Indpls., Phila Mus. Art, Bklyn. Mus., Cin. Art Mus., N.Y. Public Library, Columbua U. Gallery, N.Y.C., Biodynamics Inc., Indpls., Fidelity Bank, Carmel, Ind., Tuscon Mus. Art, Indpsl. Mus. Art, Indianapolis Art Ctr. Retrospective Print and Drawing Exhib., 1992. Recipient award Ben and Beatrice Goldstein Found., N.Y.C., 1971. Mem. Soc. Am. Graphic Artists. Jewish. Home: Villa Valencia 24552 Paseo de Valencia A631 Laguna Hills CA 92653 E-mail: minblock@cs.com.

BLOCK, BARBARA ANN, biology educator; b. Springfield, Mass., Apr. 25, 1958; d. Merrill and Myra (Winograd) B. BA, U. Vt., 1980; PhD, Duke U., 1986. Postdoctoral fellow U. Pa., Phila., 1986-88; asst. prof. organismal biology U. Chgo., 1988-93; asst. prof. biol. sci. Stanford U., 1993-97, assoc. prof., 1997—. Contbr. articles to profl. jours. Recipient Presdl. Young Investigator award NSF, 1989; MacArthur fellow, 1996, Pew Conservation fellow, 1997. Mem. AAAS, Am. Soc. Zoologists, Biophys. Soc. Democrat.

BLOCK, FRANCESCA LIA, writer; b. Hollywood, Calif., Dec. 3, 1962; d. Irving Alexander and Gilda Rona (Klein) B.; m. Chris Schuette; children: Jasmine Angelina Schuette, Samuel Alexander Schuette. BA in English Lit., U. Calif., Berkeley, 1986. Author: Weetzie Bat, 1989 (ALA Best Book award, 1989), Witch Baby, 1991 (Sch. Libr. Jour. Best Book award), Cherokee Bat and the Goat Guys, 1992 (ALA Best Book award, N.Y. Times Book Rev. Notable Book), Ecstasia, 1993, Missing Angel Juan, 1993 (ALA Best Book award, 1993), Primavera, 1994, The Hanged Man, 1994, Baby Be Bop, 1995 (Pub.'s Weekly Best Book award, 1995, ALA Best Book award, 1995), Girl Goddess # 9, 1996, Dangerous Angels, 1998 (L.A. Times Rev. Best Seller), I Was a Teenage Fairy, 1998; author: (with Hillary Carlip) Zine Scene, 1998, Violet and Claire, 1999 (L.A. Times Rev. Best Seller), The Rose and the Beast, 2000 (L.A. Times Rev. Best Seller, Pub.'s Weekly Best Book award, 2000), Nymph, 2000, Echo, 2002; author: Guarding the Moon, 2003 (L.A. Times Rev. Best Seller, 2003), Wasteland, 2003, Goat Girls, 2004, Beautiful Boys, 2004, various translations into French, Italian, German, Japanese, Czech, Danish, Finnish and Norwegian. Mem. Phi Beta Kappa. Democrat. Jewish. Office: c/o Lydia Wills Writers and Artists Agy New York NY 10019-5206

BLOCK, RUTH, retired insurance company executive; b. N.Y.C., Nov. 7, 1930; d. Albert and Celia (Shapiro) Smolensky; m. Norman Block, April 5, 1952. BA, Adelphi U., 1952. With Equitable Life Assurance Soc. of U.S., 1952-87, v.p., planning officer, 1973-77; sr. v.p. in charge individual life ins. bus., 1977-80; exec. v.p. individual ins. bus.'s; group life and health chief ins. officer, 1980—87; chmn., CEO Equitable Variable Life Ins. Co., 1980-84. Bd. dirs. of 55 ACM Mut. Funds; trustee Life Underwriter Tng. Coun., 1983-85; vis. exec. Mobil Co. U. Iowa, 1978. Bd. dirs. Stamford (Conn.) YWCA, 1977-80, Donaldson, Lufkin & Jenrette, 1983-86, Avon Products, 1985-91, BP Amoco, 1985-2001, ECOLAB Inc., 1985-2001, St. Lukes Cmty. Svcs., 1991-94; nat. chmn. Equitable United Way, 1978. Recipient Disting. Alumni award Adelphi U. Sch. of Bus., 1979, Catalyst award 1983, WEAL award, 1983, N.Y.C. YMCA award. Mem. Nat. Assn. Securities Dealers (gov. at large 1982-84), Com. of 200, Womens Econ. Round Table, Rsch. Bd. (emeritus), Bus. Execs. for Nat. Security, Women's Forum N.Y. and Conn. Office: PO Box 4653 Stamford CT 06907-0653

BLOM, CAROL BARNES, music educator; b. Wilmington, Del., Jan. 9, 1944; d. Russell Bates and Elizabeth Raughley Barnes; m. Kenneth Gordon Blom, Apr. 19, 1969; children: Amy Virginia, Rebecca Carol (Blom) Carle. MusB, Muskingum Coll., 1965; MFA, Ohio U., 1968. Cert. tchr. N.Y. Dir. jr. H.S. band Catskill (N.Y.) Ctrl. Sch., 1965—71; dir. secondary strings South Glens Falls (N.Y.) Ctrl. Sch., 1989—2002. Cons. Nat. Edn. Svcs., Amherst, Mass., 2001—, Ednl. Testing Svcs., Princeton, NJ, 2001—. Mem.: Music Educator Nat. Conf., Am. Assn. String Tchrs., Sigma Alpha Iota (life). Home: 1072 N Creek Rd Porter Corners NY 12859

BLOMDAHL, SONJA, artist; b. Waltham, Mass., Sept. 8, 1952; BFA, Mass. Coll. Art, 1974; postgrad., Orrefors Glass Skolen, Sweden, 1976. Owner, operator glass blowing studio, Seattle, 1983—. Bd. adv. Pratt Fine Arts Ctr., Seattle, 1991—; instr. Pilchuck Sch., Stanwood, 1985, Appalachian Ctr., Smithville, Tenn., 1986, Haystack Mountain Sch., Deer Isle, Maine, 1988, 92, 98; workshop leader Urban Glass, Bklyn., 1993. One-person shows include William Traver Gallery, Seattle, 1981-99, Mus. N.W. Art, LaConner, Wash., 1999, Butters Gallery, Portland, Oreg., 1998, R. Duane Reed Gallery, St. Louis, 1998, Gump's, San Francisco, 1997, Whatcom Co. Mus, Bellingham, Wash., 1992-95; exhibited in group shows King County Arts Commn., Seattle, 1993, Boston Mus. Fine Arts, 1997, Venezia Aperto Vetro, Venice, Italy, 1998, Holter Mus., Helena, Mont., 1999, Renwick Gallery, Nat. Mus. Am. Art, Smithsonian, Washington, 1999-2000, Fresno (Calif.) Art Mus., 2000, Ky. Art and Craft Gallery, Louisville, 2000, Koganezaki Glass Mus., Shizuoka, Japan, 2000; represented in mus. collections Am. Craft Mus., N.Y.C., Corning (N.Y.) Mus. Glass, Mus. Decorative Art, Prague, Czech Republic, Mus. Fine Arts, Boston, Renwick Gallery, Nat. Mus. Am. Arts, Smithsonian Instn., Washington, White House Collection of Am. Craft, Washington. Visual Artists Fellow grantee Nat. Endowment Arts, 1986, Artist's Trust Fellow grantee, 1987. Office: c/o William Traver Gallery 110 Union St Seattle WA 98101-2099

BLOMGREN, JUDY A, music educator; d. Eldon David and Helen Naomi Blomgren. BST cum laude, Mankato State U., 1972—76; MAEd, St. Catherines Coll., 2003. Orch. tchr. Champlin Pk. H.S., Minn., 1992—; choir/orch. tchr. Northdale Jr. High, Coon Rapids, Minn., 1978—93. Recipient Teachers Outstanding Performance award, Anoka Hennepin Dist. 11, 2001. Mem.: Am. Guild Organists (assoc.), Music Educators Nat. Conf. (assoc.).

BLONDELL, DEBRA BROWN, chemist, researcher; b. Binghamton, NY, May 31, 1961; d. James Warren and Sandra Carol Brown; m. Christopher Daniel Blondell, Oct. 4, 1986; children: Emily Marie, Ryan Christopher. AA in applied sci., Alfred State Coll., 1981—83; BS in forensic chemistry, State U. Coll., Buffalo, N.Y., 1983—85. Med. lab technician CMX Laboratories, Rochester, NY, 1986—87, U. of Rochester, 1987; lab. technician Huntingdon Analytical Services, Middleport, NY, 1987—91; rsch. chemist Eastman Kodak Co., Rochester, NY, 1992—. Mem.: North Am. Thermal Analysis Soc. (assoc.), Am. Chem. Soc. (assoc.). Avocations: travel, photography, crafts, bowling. Office: Eastman Kodak Company 1669 Lake Ave Rochester NY 14652-0132 Business E-Mail: debra.blondell@kodak.com.

BLONDIN, JOAN, nephrologist educator; b. Beaumont, Tex., Nov. 28, 1936; d. Joseph Albert and Ona Mae (Williamson) B. BS, La. Tech U., 1959; MNS, Cornell U., 1961; MD, La. State U., 1969. Diplomate Am. Bd. Internal Medicine. Instr. U. Ala., Tuscaloosa, 1961-62; rsch. assoc. Cornell U., Ithaca, N.Y., 1962-63; asst. specialist La. State U., Baton Rouge, 1963-65; intern Barnes Hosp., St. Louis, 1969-70, resident, 1970-72; fellow Washington U., St. Louis, 1972-74, asst. prof., 1974-78; ptnr. Nephrology Cons., Monroe, La., 1978-2000. Assoc. prof. La. State U. Sch. Medicine, Shreveport, 1978-98; adj. prof. human ecology La. Tech. U., 1988; prof. medicine La. State U. Health Scis. Ctr., 2000—; active staff St. Francis Med. Ctr., 1978-2001, North Monroe Cmty. Hosp., 1984-2000; adj. prof. Coll. Pharmacy, Northeast La. U., 1996. Contbr. articles to profl. jours. Bd. dirs. Central Bank; mem. adv. bd. Bank One; bd. trustees Nat. Kidney Found. of La., 1988-97; mem. La. Bd. Regents, 1989-94, chmn., 1992; med. dir. North La. Dialysis Ctr., 1992-97, Ruston Kidney Ctr. Fellow La. Cancer Society, 1966, NIH, 1968; recipient Disting. Svc. award La. Dietetic Assn. 1996. Mem. AAAS, ACP, End Stage Renal Disease (chmn. quality consensus com. 1994-96), Internat. Soc. Nephrology, Am. Soc. Internal Medicine, Am. Soc. Nephrology (bd. adv. 2003—), Am. Soc. Tropical Medicine and Hygiene, Am. Soc. Parenteral and Enteral Nutrition, Am. Heart Assn. (coun. on hypertension), Renal Physicians Assn. (bd. dirs., fin. com. 1991-94, chmn. quality care com.), NY Acad. Scis., La. Med. Soc. (del. 1988-2001), Ouachita Med. Soc. (pres.-elect 1998-99, pres. 1999-2000, immediate past pres., exec. com. 2000), Sigma Xi, Alpha Omega Alpha, Phi Kappa Phi, Omicron Nu. Republican. Episcopalian. Avocations: music, needlepoint, reading. Home: 5516 Bent Tree Dr Shreveport LA 71115-9564 Office: LSU HSC Shreveport LA E-mail: jblond@lsuhsc.edu.

BLONDIN-ANDREW, ETHEL D. Canadian government official; b. Tulita, N.W.T., Can., Mar. 25, 1951; d. Cecilia Modeste, adopted d. Joseph and Marie Therese Blondin; children: Troy Zanl, Tanya, Timothy Townsend. BEd, U. Alta., 1974, LLD, 2001. Tchr. Tuktoyaktuk, Ft. Franklin, Ft. Providence, 1974-81; tchr. lang. spl. dept. edn. Yellowknife, 1981-84, asst. dep. min., culture & comm., 1986—88; tchr. U. Calgary & Arctic Coll., 1983; mgr., then acting dir. Pub. Svc. Commn., Canada, 1984-86; sec. state tng. and youth Can., 1993-97, sec. state children and youth, 1997—. Mem. bd. dirs. Arctic Inst. N.Am., Nat. Steering Ctr., Aboriginal Lang. Policy Dvel.; chair Indigenous Lang. Devel. Rev. Ctr. Recipient Culture and Heritage Preservation award MLA, 1987, Hilroy Scholar award R.C. Hill Char. Found., 1982. Liberal. Roman Catholic. Office: Human Resources Devel Canada Pl du Portage 2 Phase IV 140 Promenade du Portage12fl Hull QC Canada K1A 0J9 also: Ste # 102 51 02-50 Ave Yellowknife NT Canada X1A 3S8 also: House of Commons Ottawa K1A 0A6 Canada

BLOOD, ELIZABETH R. research scientist; Rsch. scientist Jones Ecol. Rsch. Ctr., Newton, Ga.; adj. grad. prof. Inst. Ecology UGA. Mem. Joint Comprehensive Water Plan Study Com.; mem. Ga. Drought Mgmt. Planning Com.; founding mem., co-chair S.W. Ga. Water Resources Task Force and S.W. Ga. Water Resource and Health Initiative. Author: books and articles on water-related topics. Named one of One Hundred Most Influential Person in Ga., Georgia Trend, 2000. Mem.: S.W. Ga. Agribus. Assn. Office: Jones Ecol Rsch Ctr Rt 2 Box 2324 Newton GA 31770

BLOODWORTH, GLADYS LEON, elementary school educator; b. Natchitoches, La., July 9, 1946; d. Rudolph and Mary (LeRoy) Leon; m. John Edward Bloodworth, Aug. 14, 1971; children: John, Jeremy. BA, Southern U., Baton Rouge, 1968; MA, Calif. State U., Dominguez Hills, 1989. Nat. bd. cert. tchr. mid. childhood generalist NBCT/MC, 2001. Lang. arts tchr. grades 6-10 Natchitoches Parish Schs.; categorical program adviser L.A. Unified Schs., mentor tchr., 1999—, coord. gifted coord., 1988. Named Outstanding Math Tchr., 1987-88. Mem. NEA, United Tchrs. L.A., Calif. Tchrs. Assn., Women in Ednl. Leadership, Kappa Kappa Iota. Methodist.

BLOOM, CLAIRE, actress; b. London, Feb. 15, 1931; d. Edward Max and Elizabeth (Grew) B.; m. Rod Steiger, Sept. 19, 1959 (div. Jan. 1969); 1 child, Anna Justine; m. Philip Roth, Apr. 29, 1990 (div. Mar. 1995). Student, Badminton Sch., Bristol, Eng., Fern Hill Manor, New Milton, Eng., Guildhall Sch. Music and Drama, London. Disting. vis. prof. Hunter Coll., N.Y.C., 1989-90. Appeared as Ophelia, Stratford-Upon-Avon, 1948; plays include Ring Around the Moon, London, 1949-51, Romeo and Juliet, also as Juliet in Old Vic tour of U.S.; film roles in Limelight, Richard III, 1956, Alexander the Great, 1956, The Brothers Karamazov, 1958, Look Back in Anger, 1958, The Brothers Grimm, 1962, The Chapman Report, 1962, The Haunting, 1963, 80,000 Suspects, 1963, Alta Infidelita, 1963, Il Maestro di Vigeevano, 1963, The Outrage, 1964, The Spy Who Came in from the Cold, 1965, The Illustrated Man, 1969, Three into Two Won't Go, 1969, A Severed Head, 1971, A Doll's House, 1973, Islands in the Stream, 1976, Clash of the Titans, 1981, Always, 1984, Sammy and Rosie, 1987, Crimes and Misdemeanors, 1989, Daylight, 1995, The Book Eve, 2002, Imagining Argentina, 2002; Broadway prodns. include Rashomon, 1959; other theatre appearances include Duel of Angels, London, 1958, Altona, Royal Court Theatre, London, 1960, Ivanov, London, 1964, A Doll's House, Hedda Gabler, 1971, Vivat! Vivat Regina!, 1972; N.Y. appearance The Innocents, 1976; London appearances A Doll's House, 1973, A Streetcar Named Desire, 1974, Rosmersholm, 1977, The Cherry Orchard, 1981, These are Women, 1982-83, When We Dead Awaken, 1990, Daughters, Wives and Mothers, 1991, Silenced Voices, 1992, Women in Love, 1993, The Cherry Orchard, 1994, Long Days Journey into Night, 1996, Electra, 1998, Conversations After a Burial, 2000, A Little Night Music, 2001, A Little Night Music NYCO, 2003; many roles Brit. and U.S. TV including In Praise of Love, 1975, A Legacy, 1975, Henry VIII, 1979, Hamlet, 1979, The Ghost Writer, 1983, Cymbeline, 1983, King John, 1983, Brideshead Revisited, 1981, Shadowlands, 1984, Time and the Conways, 1985, miniseries Queenie, 1987, Anastasia, 1987, Shadow in the Sun, 1988, The Camomile Lawn, 1991, The Mirror Crack'd, 1992, Remember, 1993, Village Affairs, 1994, Family Money, 1996, When the Dead Man Heard, 1997, The Lady in Question, 1999; author: Limelight and After, 1982, Leaving A Doll's House, 1996. Recipient Evening Standard award, London, 1974, Brit. Film and TV award, London, 1984; nominee Tony award, 1998, 99. Office: Marion Rosenberg Agy 1345 N Hayworth Ave Ste 104 Los Angeles CA 90046 Home: 622 3rd Ave FL 7 New York NY 10017-0723

BLOOM, ELAINE, state legislator; b. N.Y.C., Sept. 16, 1937; m. Philip Bloom. BA, Barnard Coll., Columbia U., 1957. Mem. Fla. Ho. of Reps., Tallahassee, 1974-78, 86—, dep. majority leader, 1986-88, speaker pro-tempore, 1992-94. Mem. transp. com., health and human svcs. appropriations, health care svcs.; v.p. South Fla. Broadcasting Co., 1981-86; cons. govt. rels., lectr., 1981-85; asst. dir. Women's Inst. Fla. Internat. U., 1973-74. Radio talk show host Sta. WKAT, 1979-81, v.p. pub. affairs, 1982-81. Fla. devel. dir. Bar-Ilan U., Israel, 1990—. Recipient Hannah G. Solomon award Nat. Coun. Jewish Women, 1975, Ben-Gurion award State of Israel, 1979, numerous others. Democrat. Jewish. Avocations: walking, dance, boating, music, travel. Office: Capitol Bldg 402 S Monroe St Rm 212 Tallahassee FL 32399-6526 Also: 300 71st St Ste 504 Miami Beach FL 33141-3087

BLOOM, JANE MAGINNIS, emergency physician; b. Ithaca, N.Y., June 22, 1924; d. Ernest Victor and Miriam Rebecca (Mansfield) M.; m. William Lee Bloom, Mar. 31, 1944; children: David Lee, Jan Christopher, Carolyn Wells, Eric Paul, Joseph William, Robert Carl, Mary Catherine, Thomas Mark, Patrick Martin (dec.), Arthur Emerson. BS, U. Mich., 1968, MD, 1974. Bd. cert. Am. Bd. Internal Medicine, Am. Bd. Emergency Medicine. Rotating intern Wayne County Gen. Hosp., Eloise, Mich., 1974-75; resident in internal medicine St. Mary's Hosp., Rochester, NY, 1975-77; emergency physician Emergency Physicians Med. Group, Ann Arbor, 1986—2003. Fellow Am. Coll. Emergency Physicians (life); mem. AMA, Mich. State Med. Soc., Am. Coll. Physicians, Am. Med. Womens Assn., Am. Assn. Women Emergency Physicians, Washtenaw County Med. Soc., Am. Coll. Emergency Physicians. Avocations: bird watching, planting trees, classical music, walking. Home and Office: 537 Elm St Ann Arbor MI 48104-2515

BLOOM, KATHRYN RUTH, public relations executive; d. Morris and Frances Sondra (Siegel) B. BA, Douglass Coll.; MA, U. Toronto, Can. Dir. spl. projects United Jewish Appeal, N.Y.C., 1973-78; mgr. pub. affairs Bristol-Myers-Squibb Co., N.Y.C., 1978-86; mgr. pub. rels. pharm. and nutritional Bristol-Myers Squibb Co., N.Y.C., 1986-90, dir. pharm. and rsch. comms., 1990-91; dir. comms. Biogen Idec, Inc., 1992—2001, sr. dir. pub. affairs, 2001—. Overseer Beth Israel Deaconess Med. Ctr., 2000—; v.p., bd. dirs. N.Am. Conf. on Ethiopian Jewry, N.Y.C., 1985-93; overseer Boston Lyric Opera, 1995-2000. Mem.: Am. Technion Soc. (N.E. region bd. dirs. 2000—), The Boston Club, Phi Beta Kappa. Office: Biogen Inc 14 Cambridge Ctr Cambridge MA 02142-1401

BLOOMFIELD, CLARA DERBER, oncologist, medical institute administrator; b. Flushing, L.I., N.Y., May 15, 1942; d. Milton and Zelda (Trenner) Derber; m. Victor A. Bloomfield, June 11, 1962 (div. 1983); m. Albert de la Chapelle, Jan. 1, 1984. Student, U. Wis., 1959-62; BA, San Diego State U., 1963; MD, U. Chgo., 1968. Diplomate Am. Bd. Internal Medicine, Nat. Bd. Med. Examiners. Intern in medicine U. Chgo. Hosps. and Clinics, 1968-69, resident internal medicine, 1969-70, U. Minn., Mpls., 1970-71, med. oncology fellow, 1971-73, chief resident in medicine, Jan.-June, 1972, instr., 1972-73, asst. prof. medicine, 1973-76, assoc. prof., 1976-80, prof. medicine div. oncology, 1980-89, dir. fellowship program med. concology, 1987—89, mem. univ. senate, 1986-89, mem. all univ. Commn. on Women, 1988-89; prof. medicine, chief div. oncology SUNY, Buffalo, 1989—97; head dept. medicine Roswell Pk. Cancer Inst., Buffalo, 1989—97; William G. Pace III prof. cancer research Ohio State U. Coll. Med. & Pub. Health, 1997—, dir., div. hematology & oncology, dept. Internal Medicine, 1997—. Mem. Kettering selection com. GM Cancer Rsch. Found., 1986-87; cons. Office Tech. Assessment, U.S. Congress, 1988; participant, chair various coms. Internat. Human Gene Mapping Workshops, Helsinki, Finland, 1985, France, 1987, Internat. Workshops Chromosomes in Leukemia, Lund, Sweden, 1980, Chgo., 1982, Tokyo, 1984, London, 1987, Buffalo, 1991; mem. nat. and sci. adv. bds. NIH, 1977—, mem. bd. sci. counselors divsn. cancer treatment, 1991—, organizer Internat. Hodgkins Disease Symposium, 1981; bd. dirs. cancer and leukemia group B, 1982—, mem. other coms., 1973— sponsored clin. trial groups, Nat. Cancer Inst., cons. S.W. oncology group; mem. nat. and sci. adv. bd. Don and Sybil Harrington Cancer Ctr., Amarillo, Tex., 1979—, Med. Coll. Pa., 1988—; bd. trustees Berlex Oncology Found., 1992—; vis. prof. dept. medicine W.Va. U., 1973, U. Ariz., Tucson, 1979, U. Fla., Gainesville, 1979, Emory U., Atlanta, 1980, U. Chgo., 1982, George Washington U., Washington, 1982, U. Tex., San Antonio, 1982, Brown U., Providence, 1982, Mayo Clinic, Rochester, Minn., 1982, U. Zurich, Switzerland, 1983, U. P.R., 1984, U. Witwatersand, S. Africa, 1984, Nihon U., Tokyo, 1984, Leukemia Soc. Mass., 1991; frequent invited speaker, guest lectr. symposia, workshops, continuing edn. courses, seminars, med. congresses, univs. in U.S., Europe, S. Am., Scandinavia, Eng., Japan, Republic of South Africa, New Zealand. Author: (with others) Recent Advances in Bone Marrow Transplantation, Vol. VII, 1983, New Prospectives in Human Lymphoma, 1984, Neoplastic Diseases of the Blood, 1985, Current Therapy in Hematology/Oncology 1984-85, 1985, Medical Genetics: Past, Present, Future, 1985, Directions in Oncology, Vol. 1, 1985, Medical Oncology, Basic Principles and Clinical Management of Cancer, 1985, Tumor Aneuploidy, 1985, Malignant Lymphomas and Hodgkins Disease: Experimental and Therapeutic Advances, 1985, Current Therapy in Internal Medicine, 1987, Genetic Maps, Vol. 4, 1987; contbr. over 250 articles, abstracts to profl. jours.; editor ann. Adult Leukemia series in Cancer Treatment and Rsch., 1979-85; cons. editor Leukemia and Lymphoma Yearbook of Cancer, 1980—; assoc. editor Cancer Rsch., 1981-88, editor, 91, Leukemia Rsch., 1984-87, Leukemia, 1987-89; mem. editorial bd. Jour. Clin. Oncology, 1983-88, Cancer Genetics and Cytogenetics, 1983-87, Directions in Oncology, 1984-86, Cancer Rsch. Bull., 1984-85, Med. and Pediatric Oncology, 1987—, Blood, 1988—, Annals of Medicine, 1989—, Seminars in Oncology, 1989—; editorial bd. Am. Jour. Hematology, 1985, assoc. editor, 1988—; reviewer 23 med. jours. Recipient Nat. Bd. award Med. Coll. Pa., 1981, Past State Pres.' Bus. and Profl. Women award U. Tex. System Cancer Ctr., M.D. Anderson Hosp. and Tumor Clinic, Houston, 1987; prin. or co-prin. investigator 8 grants, NIH, 1975—, also ACS, 1980-84, Minn. State Spl. Coleman Leukemia Rsch. Fund, 1981-89, Coleman Leukemia Rsch. Fund Endowment, 1981—, Baltzar W.A. von Platen Found., 1984-85, Genentech/Hoffman -LaRoche, 1988—. Mem. ACP, AAAS, Am. Assn. Cancer Rsch., Am. Soc. Hematology, Am. Soc. Clin. Oncology (bd. dirs. 1991—), Am. Fedn. Clin. Rsch., Cen. Soc. Clin. Rsch., N.Y. Acad. Scis., Inst. Medicine, Internat. Assn. Comparative Rsch. Leukemia and Related Diseases, Med. Soc. Finland (external mem.), Phi Beta Kappa, Alpha Omega Alpha, Sigma Delta Epsilon. Office: Comprehensive Cancer Ctr 320 W 10th Ave Columbus OH 43210*

BLOOMFIELD, SARA J. museum director; BA in English Lit., Northwestern Univ.; MA in Education. V.p. Cleveland Financial Group; dep. dir. for ops. U.S. Holocaust Meml. Coun., Washington, 1986—88, exec. dir., 1988—94; assoc. dir. for mus. programs U.S. Holocaust Memorial Museum, Washington, 1994—98, acting dir., 1998—99, dir., 1999—. Established the first Learning Disability Program for the Shaker Heights City School System. Recipient of the Young Leadership award from the American Jewish Com., 1986, Jan Karski award from the Anti-Defamation League, Washington Chap. Bd. mem, Women's Political Caucus, the Cleveland City Club and the American Jewish Com. Office: US Holocaust Meml Mus 100 Raoul Wallenberg Pl SW Washington DC 20024-2126*

BLOOMGARDEN, KATHY FINN, public relations executive; b. N.Y.C., June 9, 1949; d. David and Laura (Zeisler) Finn; m. Zachary Bloomgarden; children: Rachel, Keith, Matthew. BA, Brown U., 1970; MA, PhD, Columbia U.; cert., East Asian Inst. Pres. Rsch. & Forecasts, N.Y.C.; pres., dir. Ruder-Finn, Inc., N.Y.C., 1988—98, pres., 1998—, co-CEO, 2001—. Mem. comm. com. Brown U. Mem. comms. com. Brown U., Providence. Recipient PR Industry's All-Star award. Mem.: Women's Forum, Fgn. Policy Assn., Coun. Fgn. Rels., Am. Mgmt. Assn. (bd. dirs.), Pub. Rels. Soc. Am. Jewish. Office: Ruder Finn 301 E 57th St New York NY 10022-2900*

BLOOMSBURG, ANNE ELIZABETH, small business owner, writer; b. Lewiston, Idaho, June 24, 1969; d. Joseph Walter Bloomsburg and Beverly Ruth Kyburz; m. John-Pierre Rafael Picardat, Oct. 1, 1994. BA in English, George Mason U., 1993, MFA in Creative Writing, 1999. Editor Douglas Pubs., Inc., Richmond, Va., 2001—02; restaurateur Davis & Main, Richmond, 2002—. Author: Water Bugs, 1998, Woman-Stepping-Into-Fire, 1999, In Search of Kurt Loder, 1999 (nominated Pushcart prize); singer: (albums) By the Ounce, 1998, Some Swim, 2000, Clean, 2003; editor: So to Speak: a Feminist Jour. of Lang. & Art, 1998—99. Fellow, George Mason U., 1995—97. Mem.: Greater Richmond (Va.) C.of C. Democrat. Avocations: snowboarding, travel. Home: 1806 Grove Avenue Richmond VA 23220 Office: Davis & Main 2501 W Main St Richmond VA 23220

BLOOSTON, ROSELEE, cultural organization administrator, writer; b. Washington, Sept. 29, 1952; d. Arthur and Leone Isaacs Blooston; m. Jerry Michael Mosier, Sept. 9, 1983; 1 child, Oliver Blooston Mosier. BA in Drama, Vassar Coll., 1973; MFA in Theater, Trinity U., 1975. Drama instr. Smithsonian Instn., Washington, 1976; acting instr. U. Tex., Austin, 1976—79; faculty New Sch. for Social Rsch., N.Y.C., 1982—83; master tchr., dir. Paper Mill Playhouse, Millburn, NJ, 1991—96; dir., tchg. artist N.J. Performing Arts Ctr., Newark, 1997; adj. faculty Montclair (N.J.) State U., 1992—2000; founder, dir. Tunnel Vision Writers' Project, Inc., Montclair, 1998—. Cons. Job Performance Seminars, Bklyn., 1984—89; dir., playwriting coord. The Gathering/Whole Theater, Montclair, 1988—89; head speech dept. Action Theater Conservatory, Clifton, NJ, 1995—97. Author short stories; prodr.: 5 plays. Mem. edn. com. Montclair Editors and Writers, 2001—; mem. spoken arts com. Montclair Art Mus., 2001—. Recipient Greer Garson Theater Arts award, Dallas Theater Ctr., 1974. Mem.: Internat. Womens Writers Guild, Dramatists Guild, Actors Equity Assn., Phi Beta Kappa. Office: Tunnel Vision Writers' Project PO Box 43323 Montclair NJ 07043

BLOS, JOAN W. author, critic, lecturer; b. N.Y.C., Dec. 9, 1928; m. Peter Blos, Jr., 1953; 2 children, 1 deceased. BA, Vassar Coll., 1950; MA, CCNY, 1956; DHL (hon.), Bank St. Coll. Edn., 2001. Asso. publs. div., mem. tchr. edn. faculty Bank St. Coll. Edn., N.Y.C., 1958-70; lectr. Sch. Edn., U. Mich., Ann Arbor, 1972-80; U.S. editor Children's Literature in Education, 1976-81. Author: "It's Spring!" She Said, 1968, (with Betty Miles) Just Think!, 1971, A Gathering of Days: A New England Girl's Journal, 1830-32, 1979 (Newbery medal ALA, Am. Book award 1980, Best Book of Yr., Sch. Libr. Jour.), Martin's Hats, 1984, Brothers of the Heart: A Story of the Old Northwest, 1837-38, 1985, Old Henry, 1987 (Honor book Boston Globe Horn Book award 1991), Lottie's Circus, 1989, The Grandpa Days, 1989, One Very Best Valentine's Day, 1990, The Heroine of the Titanic, 1991, A Seed, A Flower, A Minute, An Hour, 1992, Brooklyn Doesn't Rhyme, 1994, The Days Before Now, 1994, Hungry Little Boy, 1995, Hello, Shoes (Best Book award Bank St. Coll. Edn. 1999). Office Phone: 212-473-5400.

BLOSSOM, BEVERLY, choreographer, dance educator; b. Chgo., Aug. 28, 1926; d. Theodore and Florence (Pfeiffer) Schmidt; m. Roberts Blossom, 1966 (div.); 1 child, Michael. BA, Roosevelt U., 1950; MA, Sarah Lawrence, 1953. Dancer Alwin Nikolais Co., N.Y.C., 1952-62; instr. Adelphi U., L.I., N.Y., 1964-66; prof. dance dept. U. Ill., Urbana, 1967-90. Choreographer Festival Theatre, Krannert Ctr., Urbana, Radio Show, 1985, Quick-Step, 1985, Heartbeat, 1985, Interlude from Veranda, 1985; choreographer: Rehearsal for a Class Act, 1983, You Are Still With Me, Fred, 1983, Dad's Ties, 1983, Ordinary Heartbreak, 1984, Egg, 1984, Weatherwatch, 1986, Potpourri, 1986, Eye of the Beholder, 1986, Russian Tea Room, 1986, Entitled, 1987, Grass Widow, 1987, Inch, 1987, Castles in Spain, 1988, Swansong, 1989, ...Exit, 1990, The Cloak, 1990, Onward, 1991, Shards, 1993, Dead Monkey, 1996, Cynicism, 1996, Cello Lessons, 2003, others. Choreography grantee Nat. Endowment for the Arts, 1986, 87, 88, 89, 90, 92, 93, 94, 95, Ill. Arts Coun. Choreography grantee, 1980, 81, 82; recipient Bessie award, 1993. Mem. Am. Guild of Musical Artists (cert.), Screen Actors Guild (cert.), Union of Profl. Employees (cert.). Office Phone: 847-573-8759.

BLOUNT, DELORES OVERMAN, publishing executive; b. Goldsboro, N.C., Dec. 1, 1948; d. Joseph Aaron and Beatrice (Basden) Overman; m. Girard Martin Blount, Jr., Mar. 23, 1974. BA, U. N.C., 1971. Account exec. Sta. WKZQ, Myrtle Beach, S.C., 1973-81, sales mgr., 1981-86; pub. Strand Media Group, Myrtle Beach, 1986—. Amb., Myrtle Beach Conv. Bur. Named Career Woman of Yr., Bus. and Profl. Women's Club, 1982. Mem. C. of C. (bd. dirs. 1983-86, 90-92, 98-2000), Coastal Ad. Fedn. (bd. dirs. 1983, sec. 1984, v.p. 1985).

BLOWE, ARNETHIA, religious studies educator; b. Sussex County, Va., Aug. 4, 1924; d. Reverend Willie Green and Mary Lue Blowe. BS, Va. State Coll., Ettrick, 1947. Asst. dir. Christian edn. Am. Bapt. Conv. USA, 1962; cert. home econs. tchr. Va. State Dept. of Edn., 1947, tchr. K-8 N.J. Dept. of Edn., 1962, Storyteller Maplewood Adult Sch., 1991. Storyteller N.J. Storyteller's Guild, Montclair, NJ, 1990—, Nat. Black Storytellers Assn., Baltimore, Md., 1992—. Elem. tchr. Newark Pub. Sch. Sys., 1968—91. Performer: (storytelling) Black History Presentations (Black History Cert. of Appreciation, Elizabeth Urban League, 2002). Pres. Congress of Christian Edn. New Hope Missionary Bapt. Assn. Inc, Newark, 2000—. Recipient Cert. of Appreciation, Middlesex Ctrl. Bapt. Assn. N.J., 1993, award, Nat. Coun. Negro Women, 2003. Mem.: NAACP (life; exec. bd. mem. 1998—2002). Home: 930 Flora St Elizabeth NJ 07201

BLOXOM, MARGUERITE DORIS, bibliographer; b. Denver, Sept. 24, 1932; d. Rex and Helen Marguerite (Deibler) B. BA, U. Colo., 1954; MA, Ohio State U., 1956, U. Md., 1963, PhD, 1970. Rsch. asst. Bell Telephone Labs., Murray Hill, N.J., 1956-57; advt. rechr. AT&T, N.Y.C., 1957-59; testing asst. USN Pers. Rsch. Field Activity, Washington, 1959; rsch. asst. HumRRo, Washington, 1960-64; instr. U. Md., College Park, 1964-70; bibliographer Libr. of Congress, Washington, 1971-91, sr. bibliographic specialist, 1992-95. Author: Pickaxe and Pencil: References for the Study of WPA. Bd. dirs. Chincoteague Island Libr. Mem. Cmty. Tennis Assn. Chincoteague Va. (sec. 1991-96).

BLOYD, RUTHANNE, gifted and talented mathematics educator; b. Houston, Sept. 22, 1952; d. Ted and C. Ruth (Carson) Bloyd. BA, Stephen F. Austin State U., 1974; MA in Math. Edn., U. Houston, Clear Lake, 1980; doctoral studies, U. North Tex., Denton, 1993-97. Cert. secondary edn. educator in English, math., sociology, Tex. Tchr. math. Friendswood (Tex.) Ind. Sch. Dist., 1977-78, Columbia-Brazoria Ind. Sch. Dist., West Columbia, Tex., 1978-84, Cypress Fairbanks Ind. Sch. Dist., Houston, 1984-85, Birdville Ind. Sch. Dist., N. Richland Hills, Tex., 1985-89, Jasper (Tex.) Ind. Sch. Dist., 1989-90; tchr. gifted and talented math. Grapevine (Tex.)-Colleyville Ind. Sch. Dist., 1990-96. Advisor Colleyville Mid. Sch. Nat. Jr. Honor Soc., Colleyville, Tex., 1991-96, coord. Acad. Pentathlon, 1992-96, coach CMS Math./Sci. Club, 1990-96, mentor tchr., 1991-96, tchr. Cross Timbers Mid. Sch. gifted/talented math, Math Sci. club advisor, Nat. Jr. Hon. Soc. advisor, coordinator mentor tchr. Les Dix. Colleyville mid. sch. liaison to Colleyville C. of C., 1994-96. Recipient Colleyville Mid. Sch. Tchr. of Yr. award, 1994, Grapevine-Colleyville Ind. Sch. Dist. Tchr. of Yr., Grapevine C. of C., 1994. Mem. ASCD, Nat. Coun. Tchrs. Math., Phi Delta Kappa, Delta Kappa Pi. Baptist. Avocations: painting, music, sports. Home: 98 Regents Park St Bedford TX 76022-6558 Office: Cross Timbers Mid Sch 2301 Pool Rd Grapevine TX 76051-4273

BLUE, CATHERINE ANNE, lawyer; b. Boston, Feb. 17, 1957; d. James Daniel and Angela Devina (Savini) Mahoney; m. Donald Sherwood Blue, 1980 (dec. 2001); children: Mairead Catherine, Edward Pierce. BA, Stonehill Coll., 1977; JD, Coll. William and Mary, 1980. Bar: Pa. 1980, N.Y. 1999; Mass. 2000. Atty. Aluminum Co. Am., Pitts., 1980-83, Pa. Dept. Revenue, Harrisburg, 1983-85, State Workmen's Ins. Fund, Pitts., 1985-87, Met. Pitts. Pub. Broadcasting (now QED Comm. Inc.), 1987-91, gen. counsel, 1991-95; regional gen. counsel ctrl. region AT&T Wireless Svcs., Paramus, N.J., 1995-97, dir. N.E. region, 1997-98, chief counsel land use, 1998-2000, v.p. land and comml. transactions, 2000—. Mem. Pa. Bar Assn., Mass. Bar Assn. Democrat. Home: 44 Holiday Ct River Vale NJ 07675 Office: AT&T Wireless 15 E Midland Ave Paramus NJ 07652-2926

BLUE, CHRISTINE RENEE WESTLAKE, music educator; b. Nuremburg, Germany, Jan. 31, 1972; d. Thomas H. and Lorna J. Westlake; m. Timothy James Blue, June 17, 2000. BS, Case We. Res. U., 1994, MA in Music Edn., 2003. Profl. Tchg. Cert. Ohio, 2002, Orff-Schulwerk Level I Cleve. State U., 2001, Orff-Schulwerk Level II Cleve. State U., 2002. Tchr. music East Cleveland City Schs., Ohio, 1994—96; band dir., tchr. music Buckeye Local Schs., Ashtabula, Ohio, 1996—2002; tchr. music Mentor Exempted Village Schs., Ohio, 2002—. Dir. marching band Case We. Res. U., Cleve., 1995—96. Recipient Phoenix Award, Heather Hill Hosp., 1997. Mem.: Ohio Music Educators Assn., Am. Orff-Schulwerk Assn., Music Educators Nat. Conf. Avocations: travel, reading, music, theater. E-mail: bluecr@mentorschools.org.

BLUE, ROSE, writer, educator; b. N.Y.C., 1931; d. Irving and Frieda (Rosenberg) Bluestone. BA, Bklyn. Coll., 1953; postgrad., Bank St. Coll. Edn., 1967. Tchr. N.Y.C. Pub. Schs., 1967—. Writing cons. Bklyn. Coll. Sch. Edn., 1981-83. Author: A Quiet Place, 1969, Black, Black Beautiful Black, 1969, How Many Blocks Is The World, 1970, Bed-Stuy Beat, 1970, I Am Here (Yo Estoy Aqui), 1971, A Month of Sundays, 1972, Grandma Didn't Wave Back, 1972 (teleplay 1983), Nikki 108, 1973, We are Chicano, 1973, The Preacher's Kid, 1975, Seven Years from Home, 1976, The Yo Yo Kid, 1976, The Thirteenth Year, 1977, Cold Rain on the Water, 1979, My Mother The Witch, 1981 (teleplay 1984), Everybody's Evy, 1985, Heart to Heart, 1986, Goodbye Forever Tree, 1987, The Secret Papers of Camp Get Around, 1988, Barbara Bush First Lady, 1990, Colin Powell Straight to the Top, 1991, Barbara Jordan-Politician, 1992, defending Our Country, 1993, Working Together Against Hate Groups, 1993, People of Peace, 1994, The White House Kids, 1995, whoopi Goldberg Entertainer, 1995, Bring Me A Memory, 1996, Good Yontif, 1997, Who's That In the White House?, 1998, Staying Out of Trouble in a Troubled Family, 1998, Madeline Albright U.S. Secretary of State, 1999, You're the Boss: Positive Attitude and Work Ethic, 1999, Who Lived In The House Divided, 2000, Chris Rock, 2001, Benjamin Banneker--Mathematician and Stargazer, 2001, Monica Seles, 2002; lyricist: Drama of Love, 1964, Let's Face It, 1961, Give Me a Break, 1962, My Heartstrings Keep Me Tied To You, 1963, Homecoming Party, 1966; contbg. editor: Tchr. mag., Day Care mag. Mem. PEN, Authors Guild Am., Authors League Am., Mensa, Profl. Womens Caucus, Broadcast Music, Inc. Home and Office: 1320 51st St Brooklyn NY 11219-3552

BLUFORD, MICHELLE A. music educator; b. Sioux City, Iowa, Mar. 24, 1966; d. Grady L. Bluford, Harriet L. Bluford. B in Music Edn., Morningside Coll., 1988; M in Music M in Music Ministry, D of Ethnic Studies, Covington Theol. Sem. Dir. bands Ponca Pub. Sch., Ponca, Nebr., 1988—94; dir. instrumental activities Benson H.S., Omaha, 1994—2000; dir. bands Elkhorn H.S., Elkhorn, Nebr., 2000—. Mem.: NEA, Nebr. Bandmasters Assn. (sec. 1988—2002, concert band festival chair 2003—), Nat. Music Educators Assn., Alpha Delta Pi (sec., v.p. 1986—88), Phi Beta Mu. Avocations: reading, movies, weight training. Office: Elkhorn HS 711 Veterans Dr Elkhorn NE 68022 Office Phone: 402-289-4239.

BLUHM, BARBARA JEAN, communications agency executive; b. Chgo., Mar. 5, 1925; d. Maurice L. and Clara (Miller) B. Student Coll. William and Mary, 1943-45; BS, U. Wis., 1947. Exec. tng. program Carson Pirie Scott & Co., Chgo., 1947-52; home economist Lever Bros. Co., Chgo., 1952-57; field rep. The Merchandising Group, Chgo., 1957-62, v.p. N.Y.C., 1962-82, pres., 1982-87, chmn., 1987-90. Publicity chmn. James Lenox House Assn., N.Y.C., 1980—90; vol. Venice Hosp., Venice Little Theatre; mem. Coll. Club of Venice, Venice Art League, Venice Symphony, Venice Opera Guild, Friends of the Venice Libr. Mem. Venice Yacht Club, Venice Hist. Preservation League. Republican. Presbyterian. Home: 1470 Colony Pl Venice FL 34292-1550 E-mail: bbluhm@iopener.net.

BLUING-OSBORNE, KAREN LOUISE, executive assistant; b. Nashville, Nov. 18, 1962; d. Leroy and Alexander Sr. and Fredda Louisa (Foster) Bluing. BS, Trevecca Nazarene Coll., Nashville, 1990; AS, Nashville State Tech. Inst., 1988. Cert. nurse's tech. aide; notary pub.-at-large. Reservationist Hospitality Internat., Nashville; bookeeper II to III Rogers Group, Inc., Nashville; office mgr. Williams & Dinkins Attys., Nashville; exec. asst. to Richard A. Lewis, 2002; bus. mgr. Richard Allen Lewis Sr., 2002—. Mem. NAFE. Home: 377 Cedarcliff Rd Antioch TN 37013-1374

BLUITT, KAREN, information technology executive; b. N.Y.C., Oct. 25, 1957; d. James Bertrand and Beatrice (Kaufman) B.; m. Kenneth Mark Curry, Nov. 24, 1979 (div. Dec. 1991). BS, Fordham U., 1979; MBA, Calif. State Poly. U., 1982; postgrad., George Mason U., 1994-98; PhD, Kennedy Western U., 2000. Software engr. Hughes Aircraft Co., Fullerton, Calif., 1979-81; microprocessor engr. Beckman Instruments Co., Fullerton, 1981-82, Singer Co., Glendale, Calif., 1982-83; sr. software engr. Sanders Assoc., Nashua, N.H., 1983-85; software project mgr. GTE Corp., Billerica, Mass., 1985-86; sr. software engr. Wang Labs., Lowell, Mass., 1986-87; project task leader Vanguard Rsch., Lexington, Mass., 1987-88; program mgr. Applied Rsch. & Engring., Bedford, Mass., 1989-91, Sparta, McLean, Va., 1992-93; prin. software engr. Sci. Applications Internat., Arlington, Va., 1993-94; tech. mgr. CACI, Arlington, 1994, Booz Allen & Hamilton, Vienna, Va., 1995, MRJ Tech. Solutions, Inc., Fairfax, Va., 1996-97, Softek Systems, Inc., Fairfax, 1998—2001; pres. QSCI, Ashburn, Va., 2001—. 1st lt. U.S. Army, 1979-88. Scholar Gov. N.Y. Scholarship Com., 1975-79, Beta Gamma Sigma, 1978—. Mem. IEEE, AAUW, Am. Women in Sci., Am. Brokers Network, Assn. Computing Machinery, Soc. Women Engrs., Wash. Soc. of Engrs.

BLUM, BARBARA DAVIS, investor; b. Hutchinson, Kans. d. Roy C. and Jo (McKinnon) Davis; children: Devin, Hunter, Ragan, Davis. BA, Fla. State U., 1960, MSW, 1961. Founder, ptnr. Mid-Suffolk Ctr. for Psychotherapy, Hauppage, L.I., N.Y., 1965-67; v.p. Restaurant Assocs. Ga., Inc., Atlanta, 1967-75; dep. adminstr. U.S. EPA, Washington, 1977-81; mem. Pres.'s Interagy. Coordinating Coun.; chair, pres., CEO Abigail Adams Nat. Bancorp and Adams Nat. Bank, Washington, 1983-98; CEO BDB Investment Partnership, 1998—; chair Main St. Bank, 2003—. Chair U.S./Japan Environ. Agreement, 1977—81; head 1st U.S. Environ. Del. to China, 1978; chmn. Environ. Policy Inst., 1981—84; sr. advisor UN Environ. Program, 1981—84; pres. UN Univ. Peace, 1986—89; chair emeritus Ctr. for Policy Alternatives; trustee Fed. City Coun., 1988—99; nat. adv. bd. U.S. SBA, 1993—2001; chmn. D.C. Econ. Devel. Fin. Corp., 1986—2002. Del. UN Mid Decade Conf. on Women, 1980; Presdl. appointee trustee and treas. Inst. for Am. Indian Art; founder, chmn. Leadership Washington, 1989; trustee, treas. Southeastern U.; trustee, chmn. investment com. D.C. Retirement Bd.; dep. dir. Carter-Mondale U.S. Presdl. campaign, 1976; dir. Carter-Mondale Transition Team, Washington, 1976—77; panelist Clinton-Gore Econ. Conf., Little Rock and Atlanta; bd. dirs., chmn. performance com. Kaiser Health Plan of Mid Atlantic, 1989—; bd. dirs., chair exec. com. Kaiser Health Plan, Inc., 2001—, Kaiser Found. Hosp., 2001—; bd. dirs. Stimpson Ctr. Decorated comdr.'s cross Order of Merit W. Ger.; recipient Disting. Svc. award Federally Employed Women, Spl. Conservation award Nat. Wildlife Fedn., Orgn. of Yr. award Ga. Wildlife Fedn., 1974, Disting. Svc. award Americans for Indian Opportunity; named Bus. Woman of Yr. Nat. Assn. Bus. Women, Leukemia Soc., Assn. Women Contractors. Mem. Washington Women's Forum, Internat. Women's Forum, Cosmos Club. Democrat.

BLUM, BARBARA B. foundation administrator; Pres. Found. Child Devel., N.Y.C., 1986—, Manpower Demonstration Rsch. Corp., 1982-86, Am. Pub. Welfare Assn., 1985-87; commr. N.Y. Dept. Social Svcs. Chair adv. coun. Nat. Ctr. Children in Poverty; former mem. Nat. Commn. Children. Office: Found Child Devel 345 E 46th St New York NY 10017-3004 Fax: 212-697-2258.

BLUM, BARBARA MEDDOCK, retired association executive; b. Oil City, Pa., Nov. 8, 1938; m. Stuart Hollander Blum, Sept. 21, 1963. BA in Psychology, Allegheny Coll., 1960. Psychometrist, researcher Hofstra U., Hempstead, N.Y., 1960-62; adminstrv. asst., editor The Asia Soc., N.Y.C., 1962-66, exec. asst., 1966-72, adminstrv. officer, 1972-85, dir. adminstrn., 1985-88, ret. 1988.

BLUM, BETTY ANN, footwear company executive; Student, Vanderbilt U. Various positions Zayre Dept. Store, Framingham, Mass., 1970-75; divsn. pres. Mootsie Tootsies, pres. Jones N.Y., exec. v.p. Maxwell Shoe Co., Hyde Park, Mass., 1976-88, exec. v.p., 1988—. Mem. bd. women's study group Brandeis U., 1998. Trustee Dana Farber Cancer Inst., 1998; dir. 210 Internat. Found., 1991.

BLUM, EVA TANSKY, lawyer; b. Pitts., July 29, 1949; d. Harry and Jeanette N. Tansky; 1 child. BA, U. Pitts., 1970, JD, 1973. Bar: Pa. 1973. Atty. U.S. Dept. Commerce, Washington, 1973-76, U.S. Air, Washington, 1976-77; sr. v.p., dir. corp. risk mgmt. and compliance PNC Fin. Group, Pitts., 1990—. Mem. com. Pitts. Health and Welfare Planning Assn., 1985-89; bd. dirs. Family Health Coun., Pitts., 1987-94, Forbes Health Found., 1992-96, WQED, Pitts., 1994—, U. Pitts. Alumni Assn., 1992-98, 2000—, The Ellis Sch., 1996—; bd. dirs., sec. ARC Western Pa. chpt., 1992-94; trustee Am. Jewish Com., Pitts., 1977—. Mem. ABA, Pa. Bar Assn., Allegheny County Bar Assn. Office: PNC Fin Svcs Group One PNC Plaza 249 5th Ave Pittsburgh PA 15222-2709 E-mail: eva.blum@pnc.com.

BLUM, JOAN KURLEY, fundraising executive; b. Palm Beach, Fla., July 27, 1926; d. Nenad Daniel and Eva (Milos) Kurley; m. Robert C. Blum, Apr. 15, 1967 (dec. Apr. 2001); children: Christopher Alexander, Martha Jane, Louisa Joan. BA, U. Wash., 1948. Cert. fund raising exec. U.S. dir. Inst. Mediterranean Studies, Berkeley, Calif., 1962-65; devel. officer U. Calif., Berkeley, 1965-67; pres. Blum Assocs., Fund-Raising Cons., San Anselmo, Calif., 1967-92; ptnr. Philmark Australia, 1980—2001; pres. The Blums of San Francisco, 1992-2001, ret., 2001. Mem. faculty U. Calif. Extension, Inst. Fund Raising, S.W. Inst. Fund-Raising U. Tex., U. San Francisco, U.K. Vol. Movement Group, London, Australasian Inst. Fund Raising. Contbr. numerous articles to profl. jours. Recipient Golden Addy award Am. Advt. Fedn., Silver Mailbox award Direct Mail Mktg. Assn., Best Ann. Giving Time-Life award, others; decorated commdr. Sovereign Order St. Stanislas. Mem. Nat. Soc. Fund-Raising Execs. (dir.), Nat. Assn. of Hosp. Devel., Women Emerging, Rotary (San Francisco), Fund Raising Inst. (Australia), Tahoe Yacht Club. Office: 202 Evergreen Dr Kentfield CA 94904-2708

BLUM, LISA CARRIE, social worker, researcher; b. N.Y., Nov. 11, 1961; BA magna cum laude, Douglass Coll., 1983; MSW, Rutgers U., 1985, PhD, 1996. LCSW Bd. of Social Work Examiners, N.J., 1994. Clin. program coord. Women Aware, Inc. Abused Women's Svcs., New Brunswick, NJ, 1986—94; planning rsch. cons. Atlanta (Ga.) Jewish Fedn., 1994—98; grants evaluator Friedman Supporting Found., Atlanta, 1996—98; coord. outpatient geriatric svcs. Jewish Family and Vocat. Svc., Edison, NJ, 2000—03; trainer Women Aware, Inc. Abused Women's Svcs, 2001—; sr. program coord. Highland Park Sr./Youth Ctr., NJ, 2004—. Adj. faculty Sch. Social Work Rutgers U., New Brunswick, 1985—91; cons. in field. Adv. bd. Project SPAN, Edison, 1989—; commr. Middlesex County Commn. on Missing and Exploited Children, New Brunswick, 1990—92; mem. Middlesex County Child/Adult Protection Coalition, New Brunswick, 1986—94. Grantee, Fahs-Beck Found., 1992; scholar, Rutgers U., 1986—89. Mem.: NASW, N.J. Coalition Battered Women, Nat. Coun. Family Rels., Phi Beta Kappa. Achievements include development of National Model for Domestic Violence Response Teams now mandated under New Jersey Law. Office: Highland Park Sr Youth Ctr 220 S Sixth Ave Highland Park NJ 08904

BLUM, SARAH LEAH, nurse psychotherapist; b. Atlantic City, N.J., Dec. 5, 1939; d. David and Diana (Fedner) B.; m. Joseph J. McGoran, Aug. 24, 1970 (div. 1986); children: Lorna Hope Marie, Sean-David Justin. BSN, Seattle U., 1971; M in Nursing, U. Wash., 1976. Cert. clin. specialist. Nurse Atlantic City Hosp., 1960-62, Kaiser Found. Hosp., L.A., 1963-66; instr. nursing North Idaho Coll., Coeur D'Alene, 1972-74; pvt. practice Federal Way, Wash., 1977-85, Auburn, Wash., 1985—. Nurse psychotherapist Christian Counselling Svc., Tacoma, 1977-83; founder The Found. for Planetary Healing; creator Drums, Dreams and Re-Membering; hands-on emergency healer, tchr. techniques to Reiki Masters, Japan, 2002; cons. in field; presenter workshops. Contbr. articles to profl. jours. Creator Healing Day, 1985. Capt. Nurse Corps, U.S. Army, 1966-71, Vietnam. Fellow Am. Orthopsychiatric Assn.; mem. ANA, Nat. Nursing Hon. Soc., Internat. Transactional Analysis Assn., Inst. Developmental Edn. and Psychotherapy (bd. dirs. 1989-93, chair profl. membership com. 1991-94), Vietnam Veterans of Am. (bd. dirs. 1983-85, 1st woman mem.). Avocations: music, cross country skiing, sailing, Djembe and Japanese Taiko drumming. Home and Office: 303 O St NE Auburn WA 98002-4645 E-mail: sarahbarnp@earthlink.net.

BLUM, SUSAN DEBRA, anthropologist, educator; b. Ann Arbor, Mich., Jan. 7, 1957; d. George Lewis and Joyce Zuieback Blum; m. Lionel Millard Jensen, June 5, 1988; children: Hannah Neora Blum Jensen, Elena Oriana Blum Jensen. AB in Human Lang., Stanford U., 1980; MA in Far Ea. Langs. and Lit., U. Mich., 1986, MA in Anthropology, 1988, PhD in Anthropology, 1994. Lectr. Chinese, Okla. State U., Stillwater, 1988—92; adj. instr. anthropology U. Colo., Denver, 1992—95, asst. prof. anthropology, 1996—2000; adj. instr. anthropology U. Denver, 1992—94, vis. asst. prof. anthropology, 1994—95; asst. prof. anthropology U. Pa., Phila., 1995—96; assoc. prof. anthropology U. Notre Dame, Ind., 2000—, dir. Ctr. for Asian Studies, 2003—. Reviewer Modern China, 1999, Jour. Asian Studies, 2001, NSF, 2001, 02. Author: Portraits of Primitives: Ordering Human Kinds in the Chinese Nation, 2001; co-editor: China Off Center: Mapping the Margins of the Middle Kingdom, 2002; contbr. articles to profl. jours. Rsch. grantee, Am. Philos. Soc., 1995, rsch. fellow, NEH, 2002—03. Mem.: Soc. for Linguistic Anthropology, Assn. for Asian Studies, Am. Anthropol. Assn. Avocations: gardening, piano. Office: Univ Notre Dame Dept Anthropology 614 Flanner Hall Notre Dame IN 46556

BLUMBERG, ADELE ROSENBERG, volunteer; b. Harrisburg, Pa., Jan. 19, 1916; d. Robert and Mary (Katzman) Rosenberg; m. Leonard Blumberg, June 16, 1940; children: Joyce Kozloff, Bruce, Allen. AB, Dickinson Coll., Carlisle, Pa., 1937; grad. cum laude, Froelich Sch. Music, Harrisburg, 1932. Tchr. piano, various cities, 1933-47; with Pa. Dept. Pub. Assistance, Harrisburg, 1937—40; assoc. pubr. Somerset Star, Somerville, NJ, 1951-55; sec. Raritan Valley Pub. Co., Manville, NJ, 1951—55. Pres. coun. Girl Scouts U.S., 1954—55, pres. Rolling Hill coun., 1966—72; pres., sec., bd. dirs. Bridgewater (N.J.) Local Assistance Bd., 1957—94; bd. dirs. Somerset County Jewish Family Svc., 1980—89, Inst. Arts and Humanities Edn., NJ, 1983—94, People Care Ctr., Finderne, NJ, 1985—91, Arts Found. N.J., New Brunswick, 1986—93, George St. Playhouse, 1997—2000, Bridgewater Com. Creative Arts, 1995—, Brook Art Ctr., 2001—, Somerset County Cmty. Concerts, Opera Theater N.J., Jewish Home for Aged, Somerset County, 1995—99; chmn. Printmakers Coun. N.J., 1975—79; pres. Somerset chpt. Hadassah, 1950—52, Jewish Fedn. Somerset County, 1974—76. Named Adele Blumberg Day in her honor, Mayor of Bridgewater, 1983; recipient Hannah G. Solomon award, Nat. Coun. Jewish Women, 1969, Cmty. Patriot, Bridgewater Edn. Assn., 1976, Tercentenary award, Bd. Freeholders and Cultural and Heritage Commn. Somerset County, 1988, Good Scout award, Boy Scouts Am., 1993, Raritan award, Leonard and Adele Blumberg Edn. Found. Bridgewater, 1995, Citizen of the Yr. award, Somerset C. of C., 1998, Hon. award, Dickinsooon Law Sch., 1998. Mem.: AAUW, Zonta (v.p. 1970—71). Democrat. Jewish. Avocations: music, piano, needlework, travel, photography. Address: 1820 Woodland Ter Bound Brook NJ 08805-1449

BLUMBERG, BARBARA SALMANSON (MRS. ARNOLD G. BLUMBERG), retired state housing official, housing consultant; b. Bklyn., Oct. 2, 1927; d. Sam and Mollie (Greenberg) Salmanson; m. Arnold G. Blumberg, June 19, 1949 (dec. June 1989); children: Florence Ellen Schwartz, Martin Jay, Emily Anne. BA, De Pauw U., 1948; postgrad., New Sch. for Social Rsch., N.Y.C. Mem. pub. rels. dept. Nate Fein & Co., N.Y.C., 1948-51; freelance pub. rels. cons., 1960—; councilwoman North Hempstead, N.Y., 1975-82; adviser to energy com. N.Y. State Assembly, N.Y.C., 1982-84; dir. spl. needs housing Divsn. Housing and Cmty. Renewal, State of N.Y., 1984-89, ret., 1989. Mem. bd. visitors Pilgrim State Hosp. Pres. UN Assn. Great Neck, N.Y., 1967-69, chmn. China Study Workshop, 1966-67; pres. Shalom chpt. Hadassah, 1955-57; exec. v.p. Lakeville PTA, Great Neck, 1963-65, Great Neck South Jr. H.S., 1965-66; co-chair UNICEF, Great Neck, 1968-70, spkrs. bur., 1971—; v.p. Herricks Cmty. Life Ctr., 1976-77, B'nai B'rith, Lake Success, N.Y.; coord. 6th Congl. Dist., N.Y. McGovern for Pres.; bd. dirs. New Dem. Coalition Nassau, Am. Jewish Congress, Day Care Coun. Nassau County, Citizens Sch. Com., Great Neck; active Reform Dem. Assn. Great Neck; platform com. Nassau Dem. Com.; del. Dem. Nat.

Conv., 1992; adv. com. to spkr. N.Y. State Assembly; resource coun., housing devel. com. Cmty. Advocates; chair North Hempstead Housing Authority; trustee L.I. Power Authority, 1994-96. Recipient award Anti-Defamation League, New Hyde Park, N.Y., 1975, Alumni award DePauw U., 1977, Hadassah New Life award, 1980, Women's Pole of Honor, North Hempstead, 1994. Mem. North Shore Archeol. Assn. (chmn. study group), [illegible] Internat. Platform Assn., L.I. Womens Network (co-convenor), Interfaith Nutrition Network (v.p.), Cmty. Advocates (bd. dirs.), Mental Health Assn. Nassau County (bd. dirs.), North Shore NAACP, N.Y. Alumni Club DePauw U. (trustee), Alpha Lambda Delta. Home: 12 Birch Hill Rd Great Neck NY 11020-1309 Office Phone: 516-627-6433.

BLUMBERG, BETTY LOU, education educator; b. New Haven, July 20, 1936; d. Adolph and Sylvia (Levine) Perlroth; m. Joseph Richard Blumberg, Dec. 20, 1956; children: Nancy Mae, Debra Lee. BA, Vassar Coll., 1957; MS, So. Conn. State Coll., 1967; CAS, Wesleyan U., 1981, M.Humanities, 1995. Tchr. English Hillhouse H.S., New Haven, 1957-59; lectr. English Albertus Magnus Coll., New Haven, 1965-71; tchr. English Hamden Hall County Day Sch., Hamden, Conn., 1971—, dept. chair English, coord. 7-12, 1982-92, J. Hamden Hall chair, 1985. Tchr. docent com. Yale U./Brit. Art Mus., 1992—; student tchr. supr. Albertus Magnus/Hamden Hall, Yale U./Hamden Hall, 1973, 86; book reviewer Hadassah, Tower One, B'nai Jacob Synagogue, Hamden Libr. Bd. dirs. Tower One, New Haven, Conn., 1986; mem. bd. edn. B'nai Jacob Synagogue, 1990-91; lead tchr. New Haven Holocaust Tchr. Group; bd. dirs. Tower-One-Tower East. Shakespeare Studies fellow Yale U., summer 1958; recipient citation Women in Leadership, YWCA, 1991, Disting. Tchr. commendation Hamden Hall, 1983. Mem. New Haven Vassar Club (bd. dirs., alumni rep. to coun. 1986—), Cum Laude Soc. Hamden Hall (sec. 1986—). Democrat. Jewish. Avocations: reading, art, tennis, grandchildren. Office: Quinnipiac Univ Dept of Edn Hamden CT 06517

BLUMBERG, NAOMI, symphony musician, educator; b. Chgo. married. Student, Northwestern U., Juilliard Sch. Music; B in Mus. Edn., Roosevelt U., Chgo.; studied with Karl Fruh, Dudley Powers, Bernard Greenhouse, Frank Miller, Claus Adam. Cellist Oregon Symphony, Portland, 1965—; prin. cellist West Coast Chamber Orchestra, 1980-90, North Coast Chamber Orchestra, 1972-77; cellist Portland Opera Orchestra, 1973-84, prin. cellist, 1979-80; private instr. Community Mus. Ctr., Portland, 1965—, dir., coach chamber mus. program, 1985—; founder and cellist Trio Encore, Portland, 1992—. Instr. U. Portland, Pacific U., Portland State U., George Fox College; adjudicator OMTA Syllabus, and others. Recipient Gruber award Chamber Mus. Am., 1992. Mem. MNTA, Am. String Tchrs. Assn., Oregon Cello Soc. (co-founder, pres. 1984-96), Bd. Mem. Friends of Chamber Music 1998—. Office: Community Music Ctr 3350 SE Francis St Portland OR 97202-3066

BLUMBERG, SHERRY HELENE, Jewish education educator; b. Mar. 7, 1947; BA in Drama Edn., U. Ariz., 1969; MA in Librarianship, San Jose State U., 1973; MA in Jewish Edn., Hebrew Union Coll., L.A., 1976, PhD in Jewish Edn., 1991. Cert. Reform Jewish educator. Sr. reference specialist Stanford (Calif.) U. Libr., 1969-73; dir. edn. B'nai Israel, Sacramento, 1976-79, Temple Israel, Long Beach, Calif., 1979-85; assoc. prof. Jewish edn. Hebrew Union Coll.-Jewish Inst. Religion, N.Y.C., 1985-99; vis. assoc. prof. Jewish edn. Gratz Coll., York, Pa., 1999; dir. edn. Congregation Shalom, Milw., 1999—; adj. prof. St. Francis Sem., Milw., 2002—, lectr., 2002—. Participant 1st internat. sem. on interreligious dialogue, Beijing, 1998. Author: God: The Eternal Challenge, 1980, A Teacher's Guide To Rooftop Secrets and Other Stories of Anti-semitism, 1987; co-author: Death, Burial and Mourning in the Jewish Tradition, 1978, Divorce in the Jewish Tradition, 1979, Teaching About God and Spirituality: A Resource for Jewish Settings, 2002. Mem. exec. bd. Coalition for Jewish Learning, Milw., 2001—; mem. editl. and adv. bd. for women's Torah commentary project Women of Reform Judaism. Mem. Internat. Seminar on Religion, Edn. and Values, Assn. Profs. and Rschrs. in Religious Edn. (mem. nat. bd. 1993-96), Religious Edn. Assn. (exec. bd. 1991—, acting pres. 1995-96, pres. 1999-2000), Union Am. Hebrew Congregations (exec. bd. com. Jewish edn. 1997-2000), ASCD, Nat. Assn. Temple Educators, Coalition on Alternatives in Jewish Edn. Office: Congregation Shalom 7630 N Santa Monica Blvd Milwaukee WI 53217-3299 E-mail: blumberg@teacher.com., sherry@cong-shalom.org.

BLUME, DEBORAH DAVENPORT, music educator; d. John Charles and Minnie Ruth Davenport; m. Butch Blume, Apr. 24, 1982; children: Katherine Elizabeth, Amy Elise. AFA, Anderson (S.C.) Coll., 1978; BA in Piano Performance, Newberry Coll., 1980. Cert. tchr. S.C. Dir. choral activities Palmetto HS, Williamston, SC, 1993—98; music tchr. Spearman Elem. Sch., Piedmont, SC, 1998—. Musical dir. Heritage Players, Williamston, 2001—03; bd. dirs. Williamston Heritage and Arts Coun., 2002—. Scholar, Anderson Coll., Newberry Coll., 1976—80. Mem.: S.C. Music Educators Assn. Southern Baptist. Avocations: piano, singing, cross stitch, reading. Office: Spearman Elem Sch 2001 Easley Hwy Piedmont SC 29673 Personal E-mail: blumed@anderson1.k12.sc.us.

BLUME, JUDY, author; b. Elizabeth, N.J., Feb. 12, 1938; d. Rudolph and Esther (Rosenfeld) Sussman; m. John M. Blume, Aug. 15, 1959 (div. Jan. 1975); children: Randy Lee, Lawrence Andrew; m. George Cooper, June 6, 1987; 1 stepchild, Amanda. BA in Edn., NYU, 1960; LHD (hon.), Kean Coll., 1987, Endicott Coll., 1995. Author: (fiction) including The One in the Middle is the Green Kangaroo, 1969, Iggie's House, 1970, Are You There God? It's Me, Margaret (selected as outstanding children's book 1970), Freckle Juice, 1971, Then Again, Maybe I Won't, 1971, It's Not the End of the World, 1972, Tales of a 4th Grade Nothing, 1972, Otherwise Known as Sheila the Great, 1972, Deenie, 1973, Blubber, 1974, Forever, 1975, Starring Sally J. Freedman as Herself, 1977, Superfudge, 1980, Tiger Eyes, 1981, The Pain and the Great One, 1984, Just As Long As We're Together, 1987, Fudge-A-Mania, 1990, Here's to You, Rachel Robinson, 1993, others; (adult novels) Wifey, 1977, Smart Women, 1984, Summer Sisters, 1998, Double Fudge, 2002; (other writings) Letters to Judy: What Kids Wish They Could Tell You, 1986; exec. producer (25 min. film) Otherwise Known As Sheila The Great, Barr Films, 1988. Founder, trustee The Kids Fund, 1981. Recipient Carl Sandburg Freedom to Read award Chgo. Pub. Libr., 1984, The Civil Liberties award ACLU, 1986, John Rock award Ctr. for Population Options, 1986, Margaret A. Edwards for lifetime achievement ALA, 1996, numerous Children's Choice award, U.S.A., Europe, Australia. Mem. Authors Guild (bd. dirs.), Nat. Coalition Against Censorship (adv. bd.), Soc. Children's Book Writers (bd. dirs.). Jewish. Office: c/o William Morris Agy 1325 Ave of Ams New York NY 10019*

BLUMENTHAL, KAREN, newspaper executive; Bus. editor Dallas Morning News, 1992-94; dep. bur. chief Dallas bur. The Wall St. Jour., 1994-96, bur. chief Dallas bur., 1996—. Office: The Wall St Jour 1201 Elm St Ste 5050 Dallas TX 75270-2141

BLUMENTHAL, RONNIE, lawyer; b. Passaic, N.J., Nov. 27, 1944; d. Paul and Marga (Stern) B. BA, George Washington U., 1966, JD, 1969. Bar: D.C. 1969. Gen. atty. EEOC, Washington, 1969-71, spl. asst. to commr., acting chmn., 1971-78, sr. atty., 1978-82, dir. spl. svcs. staff, 1982-85, dir. compliance programs, 1985-91, acting dir. Office of Communications-Legis. Affairs, 1991-92; spl. asst. U.S. atty. Dept. Justice, Washington, 1992, dir. Office Fed. Ops., 1992-99, mediator, 1999—. Legis. fellow U.S. Senate, 1982; chmn. Performance Review Bd., Exec. Resources Bd; lectr., cons. in field. Mem. ABA, D.C. Bar Assn., Fed. Bar Assn., Exec. Women in Govt., Womens Bar Assn., Soc. Profls. in Dispute Resolution. Home: 853 Vanderbilt Beach Rd # 327 Naples FL 34108-8746

BLUMENTHAL, SUSAN JANE, psychiatrist, educator, public health official; d. Stanley and Eloyse Blumenthal; m. Edward John Markey. BA, Reed Coll., 1971; MD, U. Tenn., 1976; MPA, Harvard U., 1982; PhD (hon.), Trinity Coll., 1996; DSc (hon.), Pine Manor Coll., 1998. Diplomate Am. Bd. Psychiatry and Neurology. Intern. Stanford U. Sch. Medicine, 1976-77, residency and fellowship, 1977-80, [illegible] 1980-81, assoc. dir. Psychiatry Tng. Rev., head suicide rsch. unit and coord. of project depression, 1982-85, chief behavioral medicine program, 1985-93, chief behavioral and basic prevention rsch. br., 1991-93; clin. asst. prof. Tufts Med. Ctr., 1981-82; clin. asst. prof. psychiatry George Washington Sch. Medicine, 1982-86; clin. assoc. prof. psychiatry Georgetown Sch. Medicine, 1986-91, clin. prof. psychiatry, 1991—; first dep. asst. sec. women's health HHS, Washington, 1993—97, asst. surgeon gen., 1998—, sr. med. and e-health advisor, 2002—, sr. sci. advisor, 2002—, sr. med. advisor Office of Global Health Affairs, 2003—; clin. prof. psychiatry Tufts Sch. Medicine, 1995—; assoc. v.p. for health affairs George Washington U. Med. Ctr., 1998. Vis. prof. ob-gyn. George Washington U. Med. Ctr., 1998-99; disting. vis. prof. women's studies Brandeis U., 1999—; vis. prof. Stanford U., 2004-; chair NIH Coord. Com. on Health and Behavior, 1991-94; co-chair NIH Reunion Task Force, 1992-94; chair fed. coord. com. breast cancer, fed. coord. com. women's health and the environ., co-chair nat. breast cancer action plan, coord. com. women's health issues and domestic violence, HHS, 1994-98; mem. Pres.'s Interagy. Coun. on Women; sr. advisor for pub. health White House Coun. on Youth Violence, 2000-02, sr. advisor on pub. health and sci. to the sec., USDA, 2000-02. Editor: Suicide Over the Life Cycle, 1989, Premenstrual Syndrome, 1985; mem. editl. bds.: Jour. Women's Health, Depression, health columnist : Elle Mag., Ladies Home Jour., U.S. News and World Report; contbr. articles to sci. jours. Mem. Nat. Commn. on Sleep Disorders Rsch., workgroup on mental health Pres. Task Force on Health Care Reform; U.S. rep. global commn. on Women's Health WHO. Capt. USPHS, 1992-94, rear adm., 1994—. Recipient Outstanding Svc. medal, 1989, Commendation medal, 1990, Meritorious Svc. medal, USPHS, 1992, Surgeon Gen.'s Exemplary Svc. medal, 1997, Spl. Assignment Svc. medal, 1998, 2002, Achievement medal, 2002, Sec.'s Honor award for Domestic Violence, 1996, Asst. Sec. for Health's award for Breast Cancer, 1996, Am. Med. Writers award, 1996, Gretchen Poston award, The Nat. Race for the Cure, 1996, Founder's award, 1996, Pub. Svc. award, Nat. Alliance for the Mentally Ill, 1996, Gracie award, Assn. Women Radio and TV Profls., 1997, Inspiration Leader award, Pa. Diabetes Assn., 1997, Women of Distinction award, Nat. Assn. Women in Higher Edn., 1998, Woman of Valor award, United Jewish Fedn., 1999, Mosaic award, Komen Found., 2000, Founder's award, 2000, Feminist First award for Health, Feminist Majority, 2000, Congl. award, 2001, Congl. citation, 2002, Women's Ctr. Leadership award, 2003. Mem. AMA, Am. Psychiat. Assn. (cons. Joint Coun. on Pub. Affairs, Francis Braceland award for pub. svc. 1998), Am. Coll. Psychiatrists, Am. Med. Women's Assn. (past chair com. on publicity and pub. rels., Pres.'s citation, 1996), Congl. Club, Nat. Assn. Bus. and Profl. Women (Magnificent Seven award 1996), Internat. Club, Internat. Women's Forum, Am. Suicide Found. (past bd. dirs. Washington divsn., pres.), Starlight Found. (past chmn. sci. adv. bd.). Office: HHS Rm 727H 200 Independence Ave SW Washington DC 20201

BLUMER, DEBORAH, state legislator; BA (magna cum laude), Framingham State Coll., 1974; MBA, Simmons Coll., 1980. State rep. Mass. House, 2001—. Chair fin. com. Framingham City Coun.; mem. Framingham Town Mtg., Framingham Sch. Capital Planning Com. Trustee, former chair Metrowest Cmty. Health Care Found.; former dir. Framingham League of Women Voters; mem. Framingham Civic League, Friends of Saxonville, Framingham Edn. Found.; former trustee Danforth Mus. Art. Democrat. Office: Rm 134 State House Boston MA 02133

BLUMKIN, LINDA RUTH, lawyer; b. Aug. 25, 1944; d. Louis and Edith (Fortus) Blumkin. AB cum laude, Barnard Coll., 1964; LLB cum laude, Harvard U., 1967, LLM, 1973. Bar: N.Y. 1968, U.S. Dist. Ct. (so. dist.) N.Y. 1969, U.S. Ct. Appeals (2nd cir.) 1969, U.S. Supreme Ct. 1982. Assoc. Fried, Frank, Harris, Shriver & Jacobson, N.Y.C., 1967—71, ptnr., 1979—. Lectr. Boston U., 1971, asst. prof. mgmt., 1972—73; assoc. Breed, Abbott & Morgan, N.Y.C., 1973—77; asst. dir. Bur. Competition, Fed. Trade Commn., 1977—79. Mem.: ABA, N.Y.C. Bar Assn. Office: Fried Frank Harris Shriver & Jacobson 1 New York Plz Fl 24 New York NY 10004-1901

BLUMSTEIN, RENEÉ J. educational research consultant, grant writer, program developer; b. Bklyn., Apr. 1, 1957; d. Robert and Rosalie (Burak) B.; m. Vic DiVenere, May 12, 1996; children: Robert Victor DiVenere, Joseph Dante DiVenere. BA, Queens Coll., N.Y., 1978; MA, Columbia U., 1980, MEd, 1982, MPhil, 1984, PhD, 1986. Rsch. psychologist CCNY, 1980-85; rsch. cons. AT&T, N.Y.C., 1986; rsch. analyst Citibank, N.Y.C., 1986-87, ednl. rsch. cons., 1987—, rsch. and statis. cons. L.I.; adj. prof. rsch. methods CUNY, 1990—. Scholar Columbia U., 1981. Mem. Am. Psychol. Assn., Nat. Assn. Women Bus. Owners, Am. Edn. Rsch. Assn. Avocations: travel, biking, swimming. Home and Office: 14 Ingold Dr Dix Hills NY 11746-7804 E-mail: rjb@researchforeducation.com.

BLUMSTEIN, SHEILA ELLEN, former academic administrator, linguistics educator; b. N.Y.C., Mar. 10, 1944; d. Edgar and Bernice Marjorie (Heineman) B. BA, U. Rochester, 1965; PhD, Harvard U., 1970. Asst. prof. linguistics Brown U., Providence, 1970—76, assoc. prof., 1976—81, prof., 1981—91, Albert D. Mead prof. cognitive and linguistic scis., 1991—, dean of coll., 1987—95, interim pres., 2000—01, interim provost, 1998; research assoc. Aphasia Research Ctr., VA Med. Ctr., Boston, 1970—. Vis. scientist MIT, Cambridge, 1974, 77-78; mem. study sect. NIH, 1976-80, exec. com. Com. on Hearing, Bioacoustics, Biomechanics, NRC, 1980-82, sci. program adv. com. Nat. Inst. Neurol. and Comm. Diseases and Strokes, 1982-84; Henry R. Luce vis. prof. Wellesley Coll., Mass., 1982-83; mem. adv. coun. Nat. Inst. Deafness and Other Comm. Disorders, 1989-93; mem. sci. adv. bd. McDonnell-Pew Program in Neuroscis., 1989-2000. Author: A Phonological Investigation of Aphasic Speech, 1973, (with P. Lieberman) Speech Physiology Acoustics and Speech Perception, 1987; editor: (with H. Goodglass) Psycholinguistics and Aphasia, 1973; mem. editorial bd. Brain and Lang., 1978-83, Cognition, 1982-90, Applied Psycholinguistics, 1984-89; adv. editor Contemporary Psychology, 1981-83; contbr. articles to profl. jours., chpts. to books Recipient Javits neurosci. investigator award, 1985-92; Guggenheim fellow, 1977-78, Radcliffe Inst. fellow, 1977-78 Fellow Acoustical Soc. Am., Am. Acad. Arts and Scis.; mem. Linguistics Soc. Am., Acad. Aphasia, Am. Philos. Soc., Phi Beta Kappa, Phi Sigma Iota. Jewish. Avocations: tennis, piano, music, gardening. Home: 14 Broadview Dr Barrington RI 02806-4012 Office: Brown Univ PO Box 1978 Providence RI 02912-1978

BLUNT, KATHRYN LONDON, screenwriter, author; b. Aug. 31, 1934; Student, Midwestern U., Tex. Author screenplays including The Eighth Day, 1999, The Golden Luster, 1999, Vigil of Venus, 1999, Mountains of the Moon, 1999. Mem. Nat. Resources Def. Coun., World Wildlife Fund, Nature Conservancy, Guissepe Armani Sculptors.

BLUNTZER, CHISPA HERNANDEZ, artist, educator; b. Caracas, Venezuela, Mar. 31, 1932; came to the U.S., 1948; d. Jose Benigno and Anita (Espinal) Hernández; m. Robert Dougherty Bluntzer, Aug. 23, 1952; children: Mary Ellen, Christopher, Dianna. AAS in Interior Design, Nat. Art Sch., 1952; BFA in Painting with highest honors, Tex. A&M U., 1991; postgrad., NYU, 1995. Watercolor instr. Art Ctr. Corpus Christi, 1989, Victoria (Tex.) Art Assn., 1991,. Smith Art Workshops, Caracas, 1993, Ateliers san Frontiers, Les Cerqueux s/Passavant, France, 1998; gallery lectr. Art Mus. South Tex., Corpus Christi, 1991; instr. children's summer art program Creative Art Ctr., Corpus Christi, 1992; adj. prof. art Tex. A&M U., Corpus Christi, 1992, 95; trustee Art Mus. South Tex., Corpus Christi, 1986—. One-woman shows Corpus Christi Mus., 1981, Josek's of Tex., Corpus Christi, 1981, Bay Front Plaza Arts and Sci. Ctr., Corpus Christi, 1985, Thomason Gallery, Ft. Worth, 1985, Corpus Christi Pub. Libr., 1987, Corpus Christi State U., 1991, Art Ctr. Corpus Christi, 1993; group exhbns. include Bonner/White Gallery, Corpus Christi, 198[illegible] Austin, 1986, Zanesville (Ohio) Art Ctr., 1987, Western Colo. Ctr. for the Arts, Grand Junction, 1988, S.W. Craft Ctr., San Antonio, 1988, Art Mus. South Tex., Corpus Christi, 1992, U. Tex. Health Sci. Ctr., San Antonio, 1992, Weil Gallery Tex. A&M U., Corpus Christi, 1995, Multicultural Ctr., Corpus Christi, 1996, 97, 98, Art Mus. South Tex., Corpus Christi, 1997, 99, Rockport (Tex.) Art Ctr., 1998, 99, Tex. Inst. for the Arts, Corpus Christi, 1998, Wilhelmi/Holland Gallery, Corpus Christi, 1998; juried exhbns. include Art Ctr. Corpus Christi, 1995, 97, Transco Towers Galleries, Houston, 1995, Art Mus. South Tex., 1998, Cain Meml. Gallery, Del Mar Coll., Corpus Christi, 1999, 99, others; represented in permanent collections Art Mus. South Tex., Corpus Christi Mus. Sci. and History, Commerce Bank, Corpus Christi Bank & Trust, Corpus Christi Cathedral, Nations Bank, Corpus Christi, Saumur Oil, Corpus Christi, Porter Oil, Corpus Christi, Landmark Condominiums, Corpus Christi. Pres. PTA S. Cyril and Methodius Sch., Corpus Christi, 1962-63; leader Girl Scouts Am., Corpus Christi, 1969-70. Mem. Nat. Watercolor Soc., Watercolor Soc. South Tex. (pres. 1978-79), Soc. Layerists in Multi Media, Western Fedn. Watercolor Socs. Roman Catholic. Avocations: gardening, reading, traveling. Home: 230 Circle Dr Corpus Christi TX 78411-1233

BLUTH, B. J. (ELIZABETH JEAN CATHERINE BLUTH), sociologist, aerospace technologist; b. Phila., Dec. 5, 1934; d. Robert Thomas and Catherine Cecelia (Boxman) Gowland; m. Thomas Del Bluth, Aug. 20, 1960 (dec. Aug. 6, 1980); children: Robert Thomas, Richard Del. BA in Sociology (Washington semster fellow), Bucknell U., 1953; MA, Fordham U., 1960; PhD, UCLA, 1970. Teaching fellow in methods of social research Fordham U., 1957-58; reading instr. St. Margaret's High Sch., Tappahannock, Va., 1958-59; instr. history, civics and English, Rosary High Sch., San Diego, 1959-60; successively instr., asst. prof. sociology Immaculate Heart Coll., Los Angeles, 1960-65; prof. sociology Calif. State U., Northridge, 1965-87; grantee NASA Ames Research Ctr., Moffett Field, Calif., 1982-83; grantee space sta. program NASA, Washington, 1983-87, aerospace technologist system engring. div. space sta. program office Reston, Va., 1987-90, spl. asst. to dep. program dir. space sta. freedom program and ops., 1990-94, spl. tech. asst. to dir. edn. divsn., mgr. edn. evaluation Washington, 1994—2003, program mgr. on-line edn. evaluation program, 1994—. Cons. Immaculate Heart Cmty., L.A., 1967-69; engring. rsch. NASA Space Sta. design Boeing Aerospace Co., 1982-83; mem. Presdl. Citizens Adv. com. on Space, Coun. Nat. Space Policy, Nat. Tech. Com. on Soc. & Tech., UN team on relevance of space activities to econ. and social devel.; professor emeritus Calif. State U., 1987—; computational scis. and informatics inst. dir.'s search com. George Mason U., 1992-93. Editor: (with others) Search for Identity Reader, vol. I and II, 1973, (with S.R. McNeal) Update on Space, vol. I, 1961, Parson's General Theory of Action, 1982, Space Station Habitability Report, 1983, Soviet Space Station Analog, 1983, Space Station Human Productivity Study NASA, 1986, Russian Mir Space Station Analog, 1993, Marching with Sharpe, 2001; contbr. articles to profl. jours. Recipient Alpha Omega faculty awards, 1966, 1974. Fellow Am. Astronautical Soc.; mem. AIAA (chpt. award for outstanding program 1980), Am. Sociol. Assn., L5 Soc., Brit. Interplanetary Soc., Inst. Social Sci. Study of Space (acad. adv. bd.), Space Studies Inst., Internat. Acad. Astronautics (com. on space econs. and benefits), Phi Beta Kappa. Republican. Office: NASA Code N Office of Edn 300 E St SW Washington DC 20546-0005

BLY, CAROL MCLEAN, writer, educator; b. Duluth, Minn., Apr. 16, 1930; d. Charles Russell and Mildred Barr (Washburn) McLean; divorced; children: Mary, Bridget, Noah, Micah. BA in English, Wellesley Coll., 1951; DHL, Northland Coll., 1985. Instr. writing U. Minn., Mpls., 1981—. Vis. disting. Benedict prof. Carleton Coll., U. Minn., 1990; co-founder Collaborative Tchrs. & Sch. Social Workers, St. Paul, 1993; Edelstein-Keller disting. author Carleton Coll., U. Minn., 1998—99; bd. dirs. The Loft, Mpls.; founder Bly & Loveland Press, Mpls., 2003. Author: (book) Letters from the Country, 1981, 1999, My Lord Bag of Rice, 2000, Beyond the Writers' Workshop, 2001, Three Readings for Republicans and Democrats, 2003, others. Bd. dirs. Episc. Cmty. Svcs., Mpls., 1980. Democrat. Avocation: tree planting. Home: 1668 Juno Ave Saint Paul MN 55116-1415 E-mail: carolbly@visi.com.

BLY-MONNEN, APRIL M. quality assurance professional; b. Akron, Ohio, Apr. 15, 1949; d. Chester Thomas Monnen and Rita M. Cassinelli; m. Charles A. Bly. BS in Edn., Miami U., 1970; PhD in Instrnl. Tech., U. Va., 1983. Cert. ISO internal quality auditor. Sr. instrnl. designer Applied Sci. Assocs., Butler, Pa., 1986-92; tech. info. mgr., quality assurance mgr. INOVA Corp., Charlottesville, Va., 1995—. Mem. ASTD, Am. Soc. for Quality chmn. sect. 1108 Blue Ridge 2002--), Acad. Am. Poets, N.Y. Acad. Sci. Avocations: handcrafts, amateur botany. Home: 777-D Mountainwood Rd Charlottesville VA 22903 Office: INOVA Corp 11 Avon St Charlottesville VA 22902

BLYTH, ANN MARIE, secondary school educator; b. Sharon, Pa., June 18, 1949; d. Chester Stanley and Mary Clara (Romian) Kacerski; m. Lynn Allan Blyth, June 26, 1976 (dec. June 1983); 1 stepchild, Breton Alan Blyth; 1 child, Amanda Lynn. BS in Edn., Kent (Ohio) State U., 1971; postgrad., Loyola U., New Orleans, 1973-74; MS in Teaching, John Carroll U., 1978. Cert. comprehensive sci., maths. and physics tchr., Ohio. Jr. high math. tchr. New Philadelphia (Ohio) Bd. of Edn., 1971-72; high sch. sci. and math. tchr. Hubbard (Ohio) Exempted Village Bd. of Edn., 1972-76, Painesville (Ohio) City Local Bd. Edn., 1976—; head dept. sci. Harvey H.S., 2001—. Instr. math. Morton Salt, Painesville, 1979-80; part-time faculty Lake Erie Coll., 1992. Mem. Adv. Bd. Western Res. br. Am. Lung Assn. of Ohio, Painesville, 1986-89, sec, 1988-89, Northeastern br., Youngstown, Ohio, 1989-99; judge state level Nat. Pre-teen and Pre-Teen Petite Pageants, 1990. Martha Holden Jennings Found. scholar, 1984-85; named Tchr. of the Yr., Harvey High Sch. Key Club, 1981-82. Mem. NEA, Ohio Edn. Assn., Northeastern Ohio Edn. Assn., Painesville City Tchrs. Assn., Am. Assn. Physics Tchrs. (Ohio sect.), Nat. Sci. Tchrs. Assn., Cleve. Regional Coun. of Sci. Tchrs. Democrat. Episcopalian. Avocations: travel, gourmet cooking, baking, gardening, music. Home: 7243 Scottsdale Cir Mentor OH 44060-6408 Office: Thomas W Harvey High Sch 167 W Washington St Painesville OH 44077-3328

BLYTH, MYRNA GREENSTEIN, publishing executive, editor, author; b. N.Y.C., Mar. 22, 1939; d. Benjamin and Betty (Austin) Greenstein; m. Jeffrey Blyth, Nov. 25, 1962; children: Jonathan, Graham. BA, Bennington (Vt.) Coll., 1960. Sr. editor Datebook mag., N.Y.C., 1960-62, Ingenue mag., N.Y.C., 1963-68; book editor Family Health mag., 1968-71; book and fiction editor, then assoc. editor Family Circle mag., N.Y.C., 1972-78, exec. editor, 1978-81; editor-in-chief Ladies' Home Jour., 1981—2002, pub. dir., sr. v.p., 1987—2002, editor-in-chief, pub. dir., More Mag., 1998—2002, v.p., editl. dir., 2002—03; with new product devel. Meredith Corp., 2002—03; freelance writer. Mem. Pres.'s Commn. on White House Fellows; mem. adv. com. for ORIWH, NIH. Author: (novels) Cousin Suzanne, 1975, For Better and For Worse, 1978, (nonfiction) Spin Sisters, 2004; contbr. articles to New Yorker mag., New York mag., Redbook mag., Cosmopolitan mag., Readers Digest. Mem. nat. adv. bd. Susan G. Komen Breast Cancer Found.; active The Communitarians; Nat. Commn. on Am. Jewish Women.; bd. dirs. Child Care Action Campaign, N.Y.C., 1989. Recipient Headliner award Women in Comms., Inc., 1992, Human Rels. award, Am. Jewish Com.'s Pub. Divsn., 1992, Henry Johnson Fisher award,

1999. Mem.: Women's Forum, Women's Media Group, N.Y. Women in Comm., Inc. (past pres., Amb. of Excellence, Matrix award 1988), Am. Soc. Mag. Editors, Overseas Press Club (bd. govs.), Authors League.

BLYTHE, CAROLITA ANTOINETTE, writer; b. Kingston, Jamaica, Dec. 25, 1968; arrived in U.S., 1974; d. Orville Fraser Blythe and Audrey Constance Miller-Edie. BS in TV, Radio, Film, Syracuse U., 1989. Freelance assoc. prodr., LA, 1999; freelance script supr., 2000—. Author: The Crickets' Serenade, 2003; co-author: The Caribbean Writer, 1997. Tchr. adult literacy LA (Calif.) Pub. Libr., 1999—2000; audio recording for blind LA, 1997—98. Roman Catholic. Avocations: travel, tennis.

BLYTHE, CHRISTINA JOSEPHINE, business analyst, consultant; b. Orange, N.J., Apr. 5, 1963; d. Winthrop Augustus and Ilse B. (Niessner) B. BS in Acctg., Seton Hall U., 1985. Staff acct. E. F. Hutton, Inc., N.Y.C., 1985-88; acctg. mgr. Outback Clothing, Berkeley, Calif., 1988-90, Crescent Jewelers, Oakland, Calif., 1990-91, asst. controller, 1991-93, fin. analyst, 1993-95; cons. Acctg. Solutions, San Francisco, 1995—96; bus. analyst, cons. N.Y.C., 1996—. Democrat. Avocations: skiing, piano, cooking, baking. Home: 415 E 80th St #2A New York NY 10021 E-mail: cjblythe@hotmail.com.

BOAL, CARMINE, state official; b. Mt. Pleasant, Iowa, Feb. 1956; d. Edward and Wilma Roth; m. Steve Boal; children: Rob, Beth, Mike. Assoc. in Exec. Secretarial/Legal, Am. Inst. Bus., 1976; postgrad., Drake U., 1978. State rep., Iowa, 1999—. Mem. adminstrn. and rules com.; vice chair edn. com.; mem. judiciary com.; mem. local govt. com.; mem. ways and means com.; precinct chair, cen. com. mem. Rep. Party; del. county, dist., and state convs. V.p. Ankeny Sch. Bd., 1996; parent vol. Ankeny Schs.; Sunday sch. tchr. Republican. Office: State Capitol E 12th and Grand Des Moines IA 50319

BOAL, MARCIA ANNE RILEY, clinical social worker, administrator; b. Carthage, Mo., Sept. 29, 1944; d. William Joseph and Thelma P. (Simpson) Riley; m. David W. Boal, Aug. 12, 1967; children: Adam J. W., Aaron D. Boal. BA, U. Kans., 1966, MSW, 1981. Lic. clin. social worker. Child therapist Gillis Home for Children, Kansas City, Mo., 1981; social worker Leavenworth (Kans.) County Spl. Edn. Cooperative, 1981-84; sch. social worker, dir. health and social svcs. Kans. State Sch. for the Blind, Kansas City, Kans., 1984—. Pvt. practice adoption counseling and workshops, 1981—; field instr. Sch. of Social Welfare, Kans. U., 1986—. Author: Surviving Kids, 1983, Teaching Social Skills to Blind and Visually Impaired Children, 1987. Nat. networking chmn. Jr. League Kansas City, 1977-81; bd. dirs. Wyandotte House Inc., 1973-81, Kans. Action For Children, Topeka, 1981, Gov.'s Commn. on Parent Edn., Topeka, 1984—, Lake of the Forest, 1994— (sec.). Named Kans. Sch. Social Worker of Yr., 1989. Mem. Council Exceptional Children, Nat. Assn. Social Workers, Kans. Assn. Sch. Social Workers, Am. Orthopsychiat. Assn., Kans. Conf. Social Welfare, R.P. Found., Phi Kappa Phi. Home: Lake Of The Forest Bonner Springs KS 66012 Office: Kans St Sch for Blind 1100 State Ave Kansas City KS 66102-4411 E-mail: mboal@kssb.net.

BOALER, JO, education educator; BSc in Psychology, U. Liverpool, Eng., 1985; MA in Math. Edn., London U., 1991, PhD in Math. Edn., 1996. Tchr. secondary sch. math., Camden, London, 1986—89; dep. dir. math. assessment project King's Coll., London U., 1989—93, lectr., rschr. on math. edn., 1993—98; assoc. prof. Stanford (Calif.) U., 2000—. Mem. Math. Edn. Study Panel; bd. dirs. Gender and Edn. jour. Mem.: Internat. Orgn. for Women in Math. Edn. Office: Stanford U Sch Edn 485 Lasuen Mall Stanford CA 94305-3096

BOAM, MARY L. special education educator; b. Chicago Heights, Ill., Dec. 22, 1951; d. Anthony H. and Enes C. Grazioni; m. Fred M. Boam, June 22, 1985; 1 child, April. BA, Lewis u., 1974; M, DePaul U., 1981. Tchr. Sch. Dist. 168, Sauk Village, Ill., 1975—. Diagnostician Sch. Dist. 168, 1981—2000, mem. adv. bd. and coms., 1975—. Mem. adv. com. State Corg. Scully, Park Forest, Ill., 2000. Mem.: NEA, CHADD, Coun. Exceptional Children, Ill. Reading Assn. Roman Catholic. Avocations: reading, cooking.

BOARDMAN, CONNIE, former mayor, biologist, educator; BS, MS, Calif. State U., Long Beach. Prof. biology Cerriots C.C., Norwalk. Mem. econ. devel. com. Huntington Beach (Calif.) City Coun., mem. intergovernmental com., mem. animal care svcs. com., mem. comm. com.; alt. mem. Orange County Sanitation Dist.; coun. liaison Allied Arts Bd., Environ. Bd., Mobile Home Adv. Bd., Oakview Task Force, Sister City Assn.; mem. city coun. City of Huntington Beach, 2000—, mayor, 2002—03. Office: City of Huntington Beach 2000 Main St Huntington Beach CA 92648

BOARDMAN, ELIZABETH DRAKE, naval reserve officer; b. Columbus, Ohio, Oct. 14, 1955; d. Jack Martin and Marilyn Hawk Boardman; children: Melissa Grimsley, Stephanie Grimsley. BS Bus. Adminstrn., Ohio State U., 1977; BS in Computer Sci. summa cum laude, We. Ill. U., 2003; MS in Info. Assurance Program, Iowa State U., 2003—. Officer (lt., unrestricted line) U.S. Navy, Various, 1977—85; sr. computer software analyst Analysis & Tech., North Stonington, Conn., 1985—88; database adminstr. We. Ill. U., Macomb, Ill., 2000—02; tchg. asst. computer sci. Iowa State U., Ames, 2003. Mem., bd. of dirs. Girl Scouts Shining Trail Coun., Burlington, Iowa, 1995—99; fin. com. Trinity United Meth. Ch., Keokuk, Iowa, 2000—02; blue & gold officer U.S. Naval Acad., Annapolis, Md., 1992—94; vol. Girl Scouts of Am., various, 1990—99; life mem. Girl Scouts. Lt. NAVY, 1977—85, various, CDR (Intelligence) USNR, 1985—. Named Iowa Cmty. Hero Olympic Torch Bearer, Iowa Com. for Olympic Torch Run, 1996. Mem.: AAUW, Western Ill. Alumni Assn., Mil. Officers Assn. Am., The Ohio State U. Alumni Assn., Naval Res. Assn., Phi Kappa Phi, Upsilon Pi Epsilon, Chi Omega. Protestant. Avocations: volunteer work, computers, travel.

BOARDMAN, EUNICE, retired music educator; b. Cordova, Ill., Jan. 27, 1926; d. George Hollister and Anna Bryson (Feaster) Boardman. B. Mus. Edn., Cornell Coll., 1947; M. Mus. Edn., Columbia U., 1951; Ed.D., U. Ill., 1963; DFA (hon.), Cornell Coll., 1995. Tchr. music pub. schs., Iowa, 1947-55; prof. music edn. Wichita State U., Kans., 1955-72; vis. prof. mus. edn. Normal State U., Ill., 1972-74, Roosevelt U., Chgo., 1974-75; prof. mus. edn. U. Wis., Madison, 1975-89, dir. Sch. Music, 1980-89; prof. music, dir. grad. program in music edn. U. Ill., Urbana, 1989-98; ret. Author: Musical Growth in Elementary School, 1963, 6th rev. edit., 1996, Exploring Music, 1966, 3d rev. edit., 1975, The Music Book, 1980, 2d rev. edit., 1984, Holt Music, 1987; editor: Dimensions of Musical Thinking, 1989, Dimensions of Musical Thinking: A Different Kind of Music, 2002, Up the Mississippi: A Journey of the Blues, 2002. Named to MENC Hall of Fame, 2004. Mem. Soc. Music Tchr. Edn. (chmn. 1984-86), Music Educators Nat. Conf. Avocations: reading, antiques. E-mail: eunieb@mchsi.com.

BOARDMAN, MAUREEN BELL, community health nurse, educator; b. Hartford, Conn., June 11, 1966; d. Jack Russell and Mary Elizabeth (Brumm) Bell; m. Byron Earl Boardman, June 4, 1988; 1 child, Meghan Elizabeth. BSN, U. Maine, Orono, 1988; MSN, U. Tenn., 1991. RN, Tenn.; ACLS; cert. family nurse practitioner. Charge nurse med.- surg. divsn. Scott County Hosp., Oneida, Tenn., 1988-89, employee health nurse, 1989-92; nurse team leader Oneida Home Health, 1989, Quality Home Health, Oneida, 1989-90; FNP, Straightfork Family Care Clinic, Pioneer, Tenn., 1992-96, Huntsville (Tenn.) Family Care Clinic, 1996-98, Oak Grove Primary Care Clin., 1998-2001, Cmty. Health Ctr., Hanover, NH, 2001—; instr. cmty. and family medicine Dartmouth Med. Sch., Hanover, 2001—. Mem. child abuse rev. team Dept. Human Svcs., Huntsville, Tenn., 1993-2001; adj. prof. Coll. Nursing U. Tenn., 1997-2001. Med. advisor, liaison Scott County (Tenn.) Sch. Systems Sci. Fair Com., 1992-2001; bd. dirs., editor newsletter Appalachian Arts Coun., Oneida, 1993-2001, v.p., 1996-98, del., 1997; com. on health policy TNA, 1998-2000. Mem. Sigma Theta Tau (sec. Gamma Chi chpt. 1996-2000). Roman Catholic. Avocations: reading, biking, swimming, dance. Home: 72 Anderson Hill Rd Enfield NH 03748-3152 Office: Cmty Health Ctr 1 Medical Center Dr Lebanon NH 03756 Personal E-mail: maureen.b.boardman@hitchcock.org. Business E-Mail: maureen.b.boardman@dartmouth.edu.

BOATWRIGHT, CHARLOTTE JEANNE, marketing professional, public relations executive; b. Chattanooga, Dec. 12, 1937; d. Clifton Jerry and Veltina Novella (Braden) Blevins; m. Robert W. Boatwright; children: Lynn Kay, Janis Ann, Karen Jean, Mary Ruth, Melody Susan, April Celeste. Diploma, Erlanger Sch. Nursing, Chattanooga, 1963; BS, U. Tenn., Chattanooga, 1976, MEd, 1981; PhD, Columbia Pacific U., San Rafael, Calif., 1987; student in Ministry, U. South Sewanee. Diplomate Nat. Assn. Forensic Counselors, Nat. Bd. Addiction Examiners; cert. domestic violence counselor Nat. Assn. Forensic Counselors; mediator Mediation Assn., Tenn. Supreme Ct. Surgeon's asst. William Robert Fowler, M.D., Chattanooga, 1963-64; instr. med.-surg. nursing Baroness Erlanger Hosp. Sch. Nursing, 1964-67, instr. fundamentals nursing, 1971-74, chmn. dept. mental health-psychiat. nursing, 1977-81; staff nurse Meml. Hosp., Chattanooga, 1967—68, nursing supr., 1968—70; dir. inservice edn. Hutcheson Med. Ctr., Ft. Oglethorpe, Ga., 1970-71; youth work cons. Sewanee Dist. Episcopal Chs., Chattanooga, 1975-76; dir. spl. projects N. Pk. Hosp., Chattanooga, 1984-87, dir. mktg. and pub. rels., 1987—. Pres. CBB Comm.; freelance writer; expert witness in field. Founder, pres. Domestic Violence Coalition Greater Chattanooga, 1994; bd. dirs. Family Violence Shelter Com., Sexual Abuse Resource Ctr., Child Abuse Prevention Coun.; mem. Cmty. Ptnrs. Neighborhood Change-Crime and Neighborhood Safety; crisis intervention homes prevention com. Partnership Families, Children and Adults, residential adv. com.; mem. fair housing roundtable Chatanooga, Tenn.; mem. endeavors re-entry roundtable; mem. coalition eliminate homelessness Faith Cmty. Svc. Network, Chatanooga; mem. dept. youth work Episcopal Diocese Tenn., 1975—77, mem. violence in soc. resource team, pres. diaconate formation com., 2002; mem. crisis response team Episc. Diocese, Tenn.; bd. dirs. Partnership Families, Children and Adults, Opportunity Home, Chattanooga; mem. oversight bd. Hamilton County Domestic Violence Task Force; vice chmn. Brynewood Park Cmty. Assn., 1985, 1986. Recipient Liberty Bell award, Chattanooga Bar Assn., 1997, Advocacy for Children award, S.E. Tenn. Coun. Children and Youth, 2000. Mem.: Chattanooga C. of C., Chattanooga Press Assn., Tenn. Soc. Hosp. Mktg. and Pub. Rels., Tenn. Hosp. Assn., Am. Coll. Healthcare Execs. (nominee), U. Tenn. Alumnae Assn. Republican. Avocations: music, reading, gardening, travel.

BOBB, CAROLYN RUTH, science writer; b. Flint, Mich., Jan. 9, 1955; d. Clarence Edward Bobb and Martha Elizabeth Maxwell; m. David A. Bazzett, June 25, 1977 (div. Feb. 1980); m. Theodore D. Spear. BS, Mich. State U., 1979; postgrad., U. Mich., Flint. Lab. med. technician Furda Biochem. Biopsy, Lansing, Mich., 1979; lab. technician Mich. Dept. Agr., East Lansing, 1979-81; forensic scientist Mich. State Police, East Lansing, 1981-89; writer Flint, 1991—. Forensic cons., Lansing, 1988-89. Mem. NAFE. Avocation: piano. Home: 939 Major St Flint MI 48507-2564

BOBEK, NICOLE, professional figure skater; b. Chgo., Aug. 23, 1977. Competitive history includes: mem. of 1st place team Hershey's Kisses Challenge, 1997, placed 13th in World Championships, 1997, 3rd in Nat. Sr., 1997, 2nd (team) U.S. Postal Svc. Challenge, 1996, 3rd (team) Hershey's Kisses Challenge, 1996, 10th place Centennial on Ice, 1996, 1st place Starlight Challenge, 1995, 3rd in World Championships, 1995, 1st in Nat. Sr., 1995, 2d place, World Pro Championship, 2000, 3d place, Canadian Open, 2001, numerous others. Champions on Ice Tour, 2000-. Avocations: dance, drawing, writing poetry, modeling, designing clothes. Office: USFSA 20 1st St Colorado Springs CO 80906-3624*

BOBEL, MARY, video development company financial executive; Various financial positions Advanced Micro Devices, 1981-90; v.p., corp. contr. Adobe Sys., 1990-94; v.p., CFO, Ednl. Pub. Corp., 1994-96; exec. v.p., CFO, Genus, Inc., semicondr. mfrs., 1997-98; CFO, Digital Origin Inc., developer digital video, Mountain View, Calif., 1999—. Office: Digital Origin Inc 290 Donald Lynch Blvd Marlborough MA 01752-4710

BOBER, JOANNE L. lawyer; b. NYC, Dec. 14, 1952; BA, Wash. U., 1974; JD, Georgetown U., 1980. Bar: Tex. 1980. Assoc. Moore & Peterson, 1980—82, Jones, Day, Reavis & Pogue, 1983—88, ptnr., 1989—96; sr. v.p., gen. counsel, sec. Gen. Signal Corp., 1997—98; v.p., gen. coun. Chubb Corp., Warren, NJ, 1999—. Mem.: ABA, Tex. Bar Assn., Phi Beta Kappa. Office: Chubb Corp PO Box 1615 15 Mountain View Rd Plainfield NJ 07061*

BOBRUFF, CAROLE MARKS, radio producer, radio personality; b. N.Y.C., Nov. 11, 1935; d. Morris Frank and Harriet (Lehman) Marks; m. Jerome Bobruff, June 20, 1954 (div. 1986). Student, Quinnipac Coll., 1954-55, U. N.C., 1955-56; AS, U. New Haven, 1981; BS in Human Services, N.H. Coll., 1982. Founder, dir. Tyndall Air Force Daycare Ctr., Panama City, Fla., 1957-60; med. asst. Digestive Disease Assocs., New London, Conn., 1974-82; program coord. Pre-Trial Release Program, Norwich, New London, Conn., 1982-84; case mgr., counselor residential criminal justice program Cochegan House, Montville, Conn., 1984-85; exec. dir. Ret. Sr. Vol. Program So. New London County, 1984-91; producer, host nat. radio program A Touch of Grey, Groton, Conn., 1990-97; prodr., host Senior Focus Talk Am. Radio Network, Groton, Conn., 1997—; CEO Focus Commn. Treas. Dir. Vols. in Agys., New London, 1986—, Conn. RSVP Dirs., 1987; bd. dirs. Cochegan House, Widowed Persons Service, Waterford, Conn. Editor: Senior Citizens Guide to Discounts and Services, 1988; editor, author: RSVP Newsletter, 1984—; columnist: The Day, 1987. Pres. women's aux. New London County Med. Assn., 1986-87; bd. dirs. League Women Voters, New London, HOSPICE, New London, Am. Cancer Soc. New London County. Recipient Proclamation Community award Town of Waterford, 1989, Community Service award The Connection, Inc., 1987. Mem. Women's Network New London County, Children and Family Services, Pub. Relations Network, Nat. Assn. Female Execs., Brandeis U. Jewish. Home: 3 Pondside Ct Mystic CT 06355-3124 Office: 3 Pondside Ct Mystic CT 06355 Fax: 860-572-8239. E-mail: carole@atouchofgrey.com.

BOCCHINO, FRANCES LUCIA, retired oil company official; b. Bronx, N.Y., July 5, 1944; d. Pasquale and Mary Ruth (Lacerenza) B. Grad. high sch., Bklyn., 1962. Various positions Texaco Inc., N.Y.C., 1965-86, sr. analyst exec. dept. Harrison, N.Y., 1987-90, transfer agt., 1990-95; comms., 1995—. Active Whitestone (N.Y.) Taxpayers Assn. Mem. Corp. Transfer Agts. Assn. Republican. Roman Catholic. Home: 15-15 150th St Whitestone NY 11357-2530

BOCCIA, JUDY ELAINE STACY, home health agency executive, consultant; b. San Diego, Aug. 29, 1955; d. Robert Garrett and Jerry Athalee (Carruth) Stacy; 1 child, Jennifer Lynn. BSN, Calif. State U., San Diego, 1978. RN, Calif.; lic. pub. health nurse, Calif. Staff nurse Univ. Hosp., U. Calif., San Diego, 1978-80, 81-82, Moffitt Hosp., San Francisco, 1980-81, Humana Huntington, Huntington Beach, Calif., 1982-84; intravenous and hospice vis. nurse Town & Country Nursing, Garden Grove, Calif., 1984-85; vis. nurse Vis. Nurse Assn., Orange, Calif., 1985-86; v.p. Doctors and Nurse Med. Mgmt., Newport Beach, Calif., 1986-89; dir. nursing HMSS, So. Calif., 1989-90; pres. Premier Care, Irvine, 1990-91, Homelife Nursing & Staffbuilders, Lake Forest, Calif., 1991—96. Cons., Calif., 1987—1996; pres., adminstr. Homelife Nursing-Staff Builders, O.C., 1991-97; AIDS educator; presenter in field; guest radio spkr. Parish nurse. Mem. Oncology Nursing Soc., Intravenous Nurse Soc., Calif. Nurses Assn. Avocations: singing, walking, gardening. Home and Office: 22712 Wood Lake Ln Lake Forest CA 92630

BOCCIGNONE, LISA MARIA, phlebotomist; b. Glendale, Calif., June 2, 1974; d. James Louis and Andrea Boccignone. AA, Orange Coast Coll., Costa Mesa, Calif., 2000; RN student, GWC, Hungtington Beach, Calif., 2003—. Lic. phlebotomist Calif., 1996, cert. B.A.T. Calif., 1996, CMA Calif., 2000. Phlebotomist Pacific Hosp., Huntington, Calif., 1996—97, Kasier, Anaheim, Calif., 1997—98, St. Jude Hosp., Fullerton, Calif., 1998—2001, Kasier, Anaheim, Calif., 2000—03. Democrat. Avocations: photography, fitness, tatooing, body piercing. Home: 6772 Rook Dr Huntington Beach CA 92647

BOCHERT, LINDA H. lawyer; b. East Orange, N.J., May 13, 1949; BA, U. Wis., 1971, MS, 1973, JD, 1974. Bar: Wis. 1974. Dir. environ. protection unit Wis. Atty. Gen. Office, 1978-80; exec. asst. to the secy. Wis. Dept. Natural Resources, 1980-91; ptnr. Michael, Best & Friedrich, Madison, Wis., 1991—. Mem. ABA, Wis. State Bar Assn. Office: Michael Best & Friedrich PO Box 1806 Firstar Plaza 1 S Pinckney St Madison WI 53701-1806 E-mail: lhbochert@mbf-law.com.

BOCK, CAROLYN A. writer, small business owner; b. Jan. 25, 1942; d. Wilfred Ignatius and Marcella Mary (Birkemeier) Gerschutz; m. Donald Charles Bock, Sept. 7, 1974 (dec. Nov. 1997); 1 child, Jonathon Edward. Student, Notre Dame Coll., 1960—62, John Carroll U., 1962—66. With sales and purchasing depts. Schaffer Diversified Corp. and other cos., Cleve., 1962-74; columnist, writer, 1979—; owner Dynamic Living Assocs., 1986—. Author: Authors, Artists and Auras, 1988, Gerschutz Family History, 1989. Co-founder, trustee Cmty. Action Team, Westlake, Ohio, 1980—85; trustee, co-founder Westlake Arts Coun., 1983—84, pres., 1984—85, Westlake PTA Coun., 1980—82, Parkside Jr. High PTA, Westlake, 1983—84; active Boy Scouts Am., Clague Playhouse, Westlake Hist. Soc., 1985—98; chmn. Morning Sem., Rocky River, Ohio, 1981—85. Named hon. life mem., Ohio PTA, 1982; recipient Outstanding Svc. award, Boy Scouts Am., 1980. Mem.: Soc. Profl. Journalists, Word Works, Westfield Ctr. Hist. Soc. Unitarian-Universalist. Avocations: travel, reading, history, gardening. Home: 9183 S Leroy Rd Westfield Center OH 44251 also: PO Box 240 Lodi OH 44254-0240

BOCK, JANINE SCHMELZER, elementary school educator; b. Nelsonville, Ohio, June 14, 1963; d. Maurice David Schmelzer and Jeanne Marie Flemming; m. James David Bock, Sept. 6, 1953; children: Christopher David McCabe, LeeAnn Marie McCabe. MusB Edn., Ohio State U., Columbus, Ohio, 1985. Cert. tchg. Ohio, 1985. Band dir. Franklin Local Sch. Dist., Duncan Falls, Ohio; dir. of bands Licking Valley Local Sch., Newark, Ohio, 1991—2001, music tchr., 2001—. Guest condr., clinician Zanesville Meml. Concert Band, Zanesville, Ohio, 2001—; tuba soloist Women in Music, Columbus, Ohio. Musician: (concerto soloist) Tubby in Tubby the Tuba. Pres. St. Benedict Cath. Sch. Home & Sch. Assn., Cambridge, Ohio; mem. Rep. club of Guernsey County, Cambridge, Ohio, 1997—2003; sec., mem. Zanesville Meml. Concert Band, Ohio, 1996—2003. Mem.: Licking Valley Edn. Assn., Ohio Music Edn. Assn., Ohio State U. Marching Band TBDBITL Alumni Club. R Conservative. Roman Cath. Achievements include i dotter-first female to dot the i in the Script Ohio Marching manuever in a single script in front of a home football crowd while a member of The Ohio State Univ Marching Band, Fall 1984. Avocations: travel, sewing. Personal E-mail: jbock@muskingum.edu.

BOCKENKAMP, KAREN ANN, bank administrator; b. St. Louis, Dec. 19, 1960; d. Joseph John and Constance M. (Bernabe) Clifford; divorced; children: Megan Elizabeth Clifford, Mallory Anne Clifford; m. William L. Bockenkamp, Nov. 8, 1996. BA in Polit. Sci., St. Louis U., 1983; MA in Legal Studies, MBA, Webster U., 1996; cert. in paralegal studies, Meramec C.C., St. Louis, 1984; cert. in bus. leadership, St. Louis U., 1997. Legal asst. Husch, Eppenberger, St. Louis, 1986-88, Nat. Bus. Owners, St. Louis, 1988-92, Deutsche Fin. Svcs., St. Louis, 1995-96; contract adminstr. Spectrum Healthcare Svcs., St. Louis, 1997, Nations Bank, 1997—. Mem., vol. St. Louis Zoo Friends, 1990—; mem. St. Louis Art Mus., 1994—, St. Louis Sci. Ctr., 1994—, YWCA of Met. St. Louis, 1994—, St. Louis Ambs., 1992—, St. Louis Women's Polit. Caucus, 1997—; mem., leader Girl Scouts USA, St. Louis, 1989—. Mem. AAUW (chmn. St. Louis chpt. 1997—), Bar Assn. St. Louis, Ga. Assn. Legal Assts. (cert.). Democrat. Roman Catholic. Avocation: volunteering. Office: NationsBank NA 910 N 11th St Saint Louis MO 63101-2914

BOCKWITZ, CYNTHIA LEE, psychologist, psychology and women's studies educator; b. Hallock, Minn., Apr. 11, 1954; d. Rodney Lee and Jeanette Yvonne (Vilen) B. AA in Arts and Scis., Richland Coll., 1983; BA in Devel. Psychology, U. Tex., Dallas, 1985; MA in Counseling Psychology, Tex. Woman's U., 1992. Lic. profl. counselor, Ga.; registered play therapist and supr. Pers. adminstr. Automatic Data Processing, Miami, Fla., 1974-77; office mgr. G.A. Dexter Co., Atlanta, 1977-79; regional human resources mgr. No. Telecom, Atlanta and Dallas, 1979-84; mental health asst. Timberlawn Psychiat. Hosp., Dallas, 1984-85; acct. NEC Am., Dallas, 1986-87; asst. program dir. Arbor Creek Hosp., Sherman, Tex., 1989; lic. profl. counselor Trinity Counseling Ctr., Carrollton, Tex., 1989-93; pvt. practice Atlanta, 1993—. Adj. instr. psychology Tex. Woman's U., Denton, 1988—92, Ga. Perimeter Coll., Atlanta, 1993—; adj. faculty Argosy U., Atlanta; cons. The Resource Ctr., Atlanta, 1993—94; clin. team leader Laurel Hts. Hosp., 1994—2000; mem. exec. com. Women Clinicians Network, Atlanta, 1994—95; psychiat. assessments Emory Pkwy. Med. Ctr., 2001. Mem.: Lic. Profl. Counselors Assn., Ga. Assn. for Play Therapy (bd. dirs. 2000—), Internat. Assn. for Play Therapy, Ga. Marriage and Family Therapy Assn. (legis. com. 1993—94, mem. metro Atlanta chpt. bd. officers 1999—2000), Am. Assn. for Marriage and Family Therapy (affiliate), Am. Psychotherapy Assn. (diplomate). Democrat. Avocations: wilderness camping, photography. Home: 711 Tuxworth Cir Decatur GA 30033-5620 E-mail: clbockwitz@aol.com.

BOCOBO-BALUNSAT, DALISAY, librarian, journalist; b. Metro Manila, Philippines, Jan. 22, 1926; d. Jorge Bocobo; m. Anthony Anton Balunsat. PhB, U. Philippines, 1950. Faculty mem. Adamson U., Manila, 1950—53; corr., columnist Philippine-Am. press, 1953—; ref. libr. San Francisco Pub. Libr., 1958—84. Founder, dir. Philippine-Am. Cultural Celebration, San Francisco, 1973—2003, Filipino Artists, Writers and Performers, 1973—. Recipient Woman Warrior award, Pacific Asian Am. Women, John Cotton Dana Nat. Libr. award, ALA, 1975, U.S. Bicentennial award, Filipino Arts Fiesta, 1976, Salutes to Asian-Am., mayor, bd. suprs. San Francisco and Calif. Legislatures, 2002. Mem.: Phillipine-Am. Press Correspondants, Filipino Artists, Writers, Performers, ALA (Dana Nat. Libr. award 1975). Avocation: reading, writing, travel, movies, TV. Office: Filipino Artists Writers and Performers 1437 19th Ave San Francisco CA 94122

BODE, BARBARA, Internet entrepreneur, foundation executive, freelance/self-employed writer; b. Evanston, Ill. d. Carl and Margaret Emilie (Lutze) B. BA magna cum laude, MA, U. Md.; scholar, Ludwig-Maximillians-Universitat, Munich; English Speaking Union scholar, U. London; Bundesrepublik scholar, Goethe Institut, Lubeck, W. Ger.; postgrad. NDEA fellow, UCLA. Woodrow Wilson teaching intern N.C. Central U., Durham; pres. Children's Found., Washington, 1970-86, Council on Founds., 1986-89; v.p. Coun. Better Bus. Bur., 1990-95; exec. dir. Coun.

Bettter Bus. Bur. Found., 1990-95; founder Campaigns Online, Washington, 1998-2000; bd. mem. Children's Found., Washington, 1986—; founder CashCares.com., 2000—03. Bd. dirs. Children's Found., Rainbow TV Works, Disability Rights, 1974-99, Edn. and Def. Fund Partnership, 1993-2001, Women's Campaign Fund, 1984-88; founding mem. Women of Washington, 1992—, Leadership Washington, class of 1994, 94—; trustee [illegible] Woodrow Wilson Nat. Found. fellow, 1963-64. Episcopalian. Office: BodeCorp 2400 Sixteenth St NW Ste 504 Washington DC 20009 Home: 725 15th St NW Ste 505 Washington DC 20005-2109 E-mail: bb@cashcares.com.

BODE, DENISE ANNE, petroleum association executive; b. Bartlesville, Okla., Apr. 7, 1954; d. Paul Harold and Virginia Louise (Williard) Durham; m. John William Bode, May 21, 1977; 1 child, Sean. BA in Polit. Sci., U. Okla., 1976; JD, George Mason U., 1982; ML in Taxation, Georgetown U., 1984. Adminstrn. asst., energy & nat. resources Gov. David Boren, Oklahoma City, Okla., 1976-78; lobbyist, tax counsel Sen. David L. Boren, Washington, 1978-84; founding ptnr., tax counsel Gold & Leibengood Inc., Washington, 1984-91; pres. Ind. Petroleum Assn. Am., Washington, 1991-97; corporation commr. OK, Okla. City, 1997—. Chmn. Tax Coalition, Washington, 1982—. Bd.dirs. Performing Arts Assn. Alexandria, Va., 1990-91. Mem. Okla. State Soc. (treas.), 116 Club, City Club. Democrat. Avocation: skiing. Office: Corporation Commn PO Box 52000-2000 Oklahoma City OK 73152-2000

BODEM, BEVERLY A. state legislator; b. Wis., Feb. 22, 1940; m. Dennis Bodem; 3 children. Student, U. Wis. State rep. Mich. Ho. Reps., Dist. 106, 1991-98; constituent svcs. dir. Sen. Mike Goschka. Mem. tourism and recreation com., co-chair econ. devel. com., conservation, environ. and great lakes com. and pub. health com., chair task force tourism, mem. task force sr. policy, Mich. Ho. Reps. Bd. dirs. Boys and Girls Club of Alpena. Mem. Club Alpena, Lions.

BODENSTEINER, LISA M. utilities executive, lawyer; BSBA and Acctg., U. Nev., 1985; JD, Santa Clara U., 1989. Assoc. Thelen, Reid & Priest, 1994—96; assoc. counsel Calpine Corp., 1996—99, v.p., gen. counsel, 1999—2001, sr. v.p., gen. counsel, 2001—02, asst. sec., exec. v.p., gen. counsel, 2002—. Office: Calpine 50 W San Fernando St 5th Fl San Jose CA 95113

BODI, SONIA ELLEN, library director, educator; b. Chgo., June 24, 1940; d. Franz Frithiof and Elsa (Noren) Bergquist; m. Peter Phillip Bodi, July 30, 1966; 1 child, Eric Christopher; stepchildren: Glenn Peter, John Jeffrey. Student, U. Edinburgh (Scotland), 1960-61; BA, Augustana Coll., Rock Island, Ill., 1962; MA Libr. Sci., Rosary Coll., 1977; MA, Northwestern U., 1986. Tchr. English and history Gemini Jr. H.S., Niles, Ill., 1962-64, Nagoya (Japan) Internat. Sch., 1964-65; tchr. English, Old Orchard Jr. H.S., Skokie, Ill., 1965-67; reference libr. Wilmette (Ill.) Pub. Libr., 1977-79, Kendall Coll., Evanston, Ill., 1979-81; head reference and instructional libr. North Park U., Chgo., 1981—, asst. prof. bibliography, 1985-87, assoc. prof., 1988-92, prof., 1992—, chmn. divsn. humanities, 1988-99, interim libr. dir., 1996-98, libr. dir., 1998—. Contbr. articles to profl. jours. Pres. PTA, Lincolnwood, Ill., 1977—79; mem. Bd. Edn., Lincolnwood, 1980—91, sec., 1981—84, pres., 1984—87, LIBRAS, 2001—02; chair Ill. Coop. Collection Mgmt. Program, 2002—03; elder First Presbyn. Ch. of Evanston, 1989—, Stephen ministry leader, 1992—98; bd. dirs. Chgo. Libr. Sys., 1999—, ILCSO, 2003—. Mem. Ill. Libr. Assn., ALA, Am. Assn. Coll. and Rsch. Librs., Beta Phi Mu. Democrat. Avocations: reading, bicycling, opera, music, piano. Home: 6710 N Trumbull Ave Lincolnwood IL 60712-3740 Office: North Park U 3225 W Foster Ave Chicago IL 60625-4895 Office Phone: 773-244-5587. Business E-Mail: sbodi@northpark.edu.

BODIE, PHYLLIS JEAN, art educator, watercolorist; b. Beatrice, Nebr., Apr. 11, 1950; d. Donald Charles and Harriet M. (Wilms) Cacek; divorced; children: Brook C., Aaron B., Paige M. BS cum laude, Peru State U., Nebr., 1971. Tchr. Antilles Consol. Schs., P.R., 1972-73, Fajardo (P.R.) Acad., 1973-74; prof. artist Miami, Fla., 1971—; tchr. Tropical Christian Sch., Miami, 1988—; owner art gallery Coconut Grove, Fla., 1995-96. Exhibited work in shows in Miami and Miami Beach. Recipient Outstanding Educator's award Kappa Delta Pi, 1969, awards for watercolors Old Island Days, Fla., 1993, 97. Mem. One Ear Soc., Nat. Mus. Women in the Arts. Christian.

BODKIN, RUBY PATE, corporate executive, real estate broker, educator; b. Frostproof, Fla., Mar. 11, 1926; d. James Henry and Lucy Beatrice (Latham) P.; m. Lawrence Edward Bodkin Sr., Jan. 15, 1949; children: Karen Bodkin Snead, Cinda, Lawrence Jr. BA, Fla. State U., 1948; MA, U. Fla., 1972. Lic. real estate broker Fla. Banker Barnett Bank, Avon Park, Fla., 1943-44, Lewis State Bank, Tallahassee, 1944-49; ins. underwriter Hunt Ins. Agy., Tallahassee, 1949-51; tchr. Duval County Sch. Bd., Jacksonville, Fla., 1952-77; pvt. practice realty Jacksonville, 1976—; tchr. Nassau County Sch. Bd., Jacksonville, 1978-83; sec., treas., v.p. Bodkin Corp., R&D/Inventions, Jacksonville, 1983—; assoc. Brooke Shields Innovative Designer Products, Inc., Kendall Park, NJ, 1988-92. Author: 100 Teacher Chosen Recipes, 1976, Bodkin Bridge Course for Beginners, 1996, Class Conscious, 1999, (autobiography) Grandma Bodkin, 2000, Essay on Death, 2003; author numerous poems. Mem. Jacksonville Symphony Guild, 1985—; mem. Southside Bapt. Ch. Recipient 25 Yr. Svc. award Duval County Sch. Bd., 1976, Tchr. of Yr. award Bryceville Sch., 1981. Mem. Am. Contract Bridge League, Nat. Realtors Assn., Southside Jr. Woman's Club, Garden Club Sweetbriar (bd. dirs.), Riverside Woman's Club Jacksonville (fin. dir. 1991-92, 3rd v.p. social dir. WCOJ, 1992-99), UDC (Martha Reid chpt. #19), Fla. Edn. Assn. (pers. problems com. 1958), Duval County Classrooms Tchrs. (v.p. membership 1957), Woman's Club Jacksonville Bridge Group, Fla. Ret. Tchrs. Assn., Fla. Realtors Assn., N.E. Fla. Realtors Assn., Jacksonville Geneal. Soc. (practicing genealogist, family historian 1986—), Friday Musicale of Jacksonville, San Jose Golf Country Club, Jacksonville Sch. Bridge. Baptist. Avocations: reading, writing, genealogy, photography, club bridge. Home: 1149 Molokai Rd Jacksonville FL 32216-3273 Office: Bodkin Jewelers & Appraisers PO Box 16482 Jacksonville FL 32245-6482

BODNER, SUSAN RACHEL, marketing and communications executive; b. N.Y.C., Apr. 20, 1949; d. Milton Meyer and Muriel Ruby (Walash) Swersky; m. Lawrence Bodner, Oct. 25, 1970 (div. June 1975); children: Jennifer Lynn Bodner, Jason Ross Bodner. BA in Edn., U. Md., 1970; BA in English, 1971; paralegal cert., Barry Coll., 1980; MBA, Ga. State U., 1980. Tchr. devel. curriculum Solomon Shecter Hillel Community Day Sch., North Miami Beach, Fla., 1974-77; English tchr. Hebrew Acad. Atlanta, 1977-78; life underwriter, estate planner Life Va. Ins., Atlanta, 1978-79; paralegal, probate and estate mgmt. Abrams, Anton Robbins, Resnick, Schneider & Mager, Hollywood, Fla., 1980-81; svc. cons. mktg. dept. Southern Bell, Ft. Lauderdale, Fla., 1981-83; dir. community rels. The Jewish Home, Atlanta, 1984-87; dir. mktg. and comm. svcs. The United Jewish Fedn. Metrowest, Whippany, N.J., 1988-95; exec. dir. mktg. and comm. Jewish Fedn. Greater Phila., 1995—; pub.'s rep. The Jewish Pub. Group-The Jewish Exponent, 1995—. Pubs. rep., adminstr. The Metrowest Jewish News, Whippany, 1988-95; cons. strategic mktg., comms. and pub. rels. for philanthropic orgn. and beneficiary agys., Whippany, 1988-95; pub. Metrosource, community resource book, 1990—, Inside Quar., lifestyle mag., 1994. Life mem. Nat. Coun. Jewish Women, Millburn-Shorthills, 1984—; mem. Nat. United Jewish Cmtys.; adv. bd. Nat. Direct Mktg. Ctr., Nat. Mktg. Planning Adv. Group. Mem. NAFE, N.J. Press Women (state and nat. comm. award 1990, 91, 92, 93, 94), N.J. Exec. Women, Pub. Rels. Soc. Am., Am. Mktg. Assn. Office: Jewish Fedn Greater Phila 2100 Arch St Philadelphia PA 19103-1300

BODURTHA, JOANNE NORMA, genetics educator; BA, Swarthmore Coll., 1974; MD, MPH, Yale U., 1979; cert. path. biochemistry, Nagasaki (Japan) U. Pediatric intern, resident Children's Hosp. Phila., 1979-82; med. officer, pediatrician Indian Health Svc. PHS Hosp., Belcourt, N.D., 1982-84, fellow dept. human genetics Va. Commonwealth U., Richmond, 1984-86, [illegible] pediats., and ob-gyn., 1987-93, assoc. prof., 1993—. Asst. clin. instr. U. Pa., 1982; asst. clin. prof. pediats. U. N.D., 1983-84. Contbr. articles to profl. jours. Named Woman of the Yr. Greater Richmond YWCA, 1997; Lucretia Mott fellow Swarthmore Coll.. 1974; Summer Student Rsch. fellow Nat. Found.-March Dimes, 1975; Luce scholar Nagasaki U., 1976-77. Mem. Alpha Omega Alpha. Office: Va Commonwealth U Sanger Hall PO Box 980033 Richmond VA 23298-0033 Fax: 804-828-3760. E-mail: jnbodurt@hsc.vcu.edu.

BODWELL, LORI, lawyer; b. Oct. 1966; AB, Bowdoin Coll., 1988; JD, Boston Coll., 1991. Bar: Alaska 1992, Maine 1993, Mass. 1992, Dist. of Alaska (US Dist. Ct.) 1994, 9th Air 1995. Mem.: Tananeu Valley Bar Assoc., Nat. Assoc. of Criminal Def. Lawyers, Alaska Bar Assn. (pres. 2002—03). Address: 712 8th Ave Fairbanks AK 99701

BOE, DONNA H. state representative; b. San Angelo, Tex., Aug. 7, 1934; m. Roger Boe; children: Carl, Karen. BA in Social Studies, U. N.Mex., 1957; attended, U. Wash., 1964; postgrad., Idaho State U., 1965—. Substitute tchr., 1959—64; tutor, ESL Idaho Stgate U., 1995—2002; state rep. dist. 30A Idaho Ho. of Reps., Boise, 1996—, mem. edn., environ. affairs, judiciary rules and adminstrn., and ways and means coms. Joint legis. oversight com., 2000—02; jud. elections task force, 2002; millennium fund (tobacco settlement) com., 1999—2002; substance abuse oversight com., 2000—02. Cmty. vol., 1996—2002; census supr., campaign mgr.; mem. Ft. Hall Replica Commn., 1980—88; city councilwoman Pocatello City Coun., 1975—85; mayor Pocatello, 1977; nat. bd. United Meth. Ch. Mem.: NAACP, LWV, Zonta Internat., Silver Sage Girl Scout Coun., Regional Substance Abuse Authority Region 6, Pocatello Zool. Soc. Democrat. Methodist. Office: State Capitol PO Box 83720 Boise ID 83720-0038

BOEHLKE, CHRISTINE, public relations executive; b. Dover, N.J., Dec. 29, 1946; BA in Creative Writing, U. Pa., 1968. Acct. supr. D.J. Edelman, 1978-79, group v.p., 1979-81; v.p. client svcs. mgr. Burson-Marsteller, Chgo., 1981-83, v.p., gen. mgr. San Francisco, 1983-85, v.p., mgr. northern calif., 1985-86, sr. v.p. western regional mgr., 1986-87; prin. Phase Two Strategies, San Francisco, 1987—. Mem. Pub. Rels. Soc. Am. (counselor's acad.), Commonwealth Club of Calif. Office: Phase Two Strategies # 8th-Fl 111 Pine St San Francisco CA 94111-5602

BOEHM, PEGGY, state agency administrator; BA, Mount Holyoke Coll. Dir. Ind. Budget Agy., Indpls., 1997—2000; exec. dir. White River State Pk., Indpls., 2000—. Office: White River State Pk 801 W Washington St Indianapolis IN 46204

BOEHM, TONI GEORGENE, seminary dean, nurse, minister; b. New Kensington, Pa., Dec. 28, 1946; d. Sylvio Chipoletti and Eula Gene (Smittle) Fox; m. Raymond Stawinski, Dec. 11, 1965 (div. Sept. 1978); 1 child, Michelle Stawinski Ivy; m. Jay Thomas Boehm, Apr. 28, 1983; children: Jonathon, Kimberly, Allison Cole, Amanda. Diploma, Allegheny Valley Sch. Nursing, Natrona Heights, Pa., 1967; family nurse practitioner cert., U. Kans., 1976; BA in Edn., Ottawa (Kans.) U., 1978; MSN, U. Mo., Kansas City, 1981; grad., Unity Sch. of Christianity, Unity Village, Mo., 1989; PhD in Religious Studies, Am. World U., 1997. Ordained to ministry Assn. of Unity Chs.; cert. occupl. health nurse. Nurse Allegheny Valley Hosp., Natrona Heights, 1967-74; head nurse, dir. nursing Truman Med. Ctr., Kansas City, Mo., 1974-78; mgr. med. Hallmark Card Inc., Kansas City, Mo., 1978-85; sr. staff specialist ANA, Kansas City, Mo., 1985-87; dean of adminstrn. Unity Sch. Christianity, 1987—2001, dir. strategic initiatives, 2001—02, dir. retreats and outreach and spl. events, 2003, interim dir. ministerial sch., 2003—, dir. retreats, 2004. Nat. spkr. and freelance writer for ministry and self-unfoldment. Author: The Spiritual Entrepreneur, 2003, One Day My Mouth Just Opened: Reverie, Reflections and Rapturous Musings on the Cycles of a Woman's Life, 2001, Embracing the Feminine Nature of the Divine, 2002. Mem. nat. steering com. for fundraising Unity Sch. of Christianity; mem. women's coun. U. Mo. Recipient scholarships. Mem.: NCCJ, ANA, Assn. Unity Chs. (urban curriculum com. 1987—2001, ministerial edn. com. 1987—2001, field licensing com. 1990—2001), Mo. Nurses Assn. (bd. dirs. 1975—85), U. Mo. Sch. Nursing Alumni Assn. Republican. Avocations: travel, reading, music, writing. Home: 430 N Winnebago Dr Greenwood MO 64034-9321 Office: Unity Sch Christianity Unity Village MO 64065-0001

BOEHMER, RAQUEL DAVENPORT, newsletter editor; b. Bklyn., Feb. 24, 1938; d. John Joralemon Davenport and Fanny (Barberis) Allison; m. Peter Joseph Boehmer; children: Kristian Ludwig, Louisa Boehmer Wickard, Timothy Joralemon. BA, Wells Coll., 1959. Radio producer Maine Pub. Broadcasting Network, Bangor, 1977—; developer, editor consumer newsletter Seafood Soundings, Monhegan, Maine, 1986-92; columnist, editor newsletter New Monhegan Press, Monhegan, Maine, 1989-96, chief editor, 1995—. Speaker Seafare, L.A., 1986; keynote speaker Beyond Wells Day, Wells Coll., Aurora, N.Y., 1988; pres. bd. dirs. Monhegan Artists' Residency Corp., 1995—. Writer, prodr. (radio commentary) Whole Foods for All People, 1977-91; prodr., host (TV cooking program) Different Kettle of Fish, 1984; prodr./host TV cooking program Great Tastes of Maine, Maine Pub. TV, 1996; author: A Foraging Vacation, 1982, Raquel's Maine Guide to New England Seafoods, 1988, Raquel's Maine Guide to Northeast Winter Vegetables, 1993. Writer legislation, Maine legis., 1985, 87, 91; treas. Monhegan Plantation, 1970-72, chair bicentennial com., 1976; chair Monhegan Sch. Bd., 1973-74; co-chair Monhegan Solid Waste Com., 1988-98; commr. Maine State Liquor and Lottery Commn., 1996—; mem. edn. task force Nat. Alcohol Beverage Control Assn., 1998—. Recipient Pub. Svc. award Maine Nutrition Coun., 1987, Alumnae award Wells Coll., 1992; named Gt. New Eng. Cook, Yankee mag., 1986. Mem. Women's Fisheries Network (bd. dirs. N.E. chpt. 1992-94, sec. to nat. bd. dirs. 1994-97, v.p. 1997-98, pres. nat. bd. dirs. 1998-2000), Colonial Dames Am., Women's Strike for Peace. Avocation: long distance walking. Home and Office: 10 Lobster Cove Rd Monhegan ME 04852 E-mail: raquel@monhegan.com.

BOEKHOUDT-CANNON, GLORIA LYDIA, business education educator; b. Portsmouth, Va., Jan. 18, 1939; d. William and Clara (Virgil) Boekhoudt; m. George Edward Cannon, Dec. 27, 1959. AB in Sociology/Psychology, Calif. State U., San Diego, 1977; MA in Spl. Edn./Learning Disabilities, Calif. State U., Sacramento, 1981; EdD in Orgn. and Leadership of Higher Edn. and Curriculum and Instrn., U. San Francisco, 1989. Instr. bus. edn. Midway Adult Sch. extension San Diego City Coll., San Diego, 1974-78, San Diego City Coll., 1974-78; prof. bus. edn. Sacramento City Coll., 1979—. Author: Fundamentals of Business English, 1986. Mem. Women in Community Colls., Phi Delta Kappa. Democrat. Jewish. Avocations: golf, needlepoint. Office: Sacramento City Coll Dept Bus 3835 Freeport Blvd Sacramento CA 95822-1318

BOER, LINDA KAREN, medical/surgical nurse; b. Lynwood, Calif., Sept. 12, 1952; d. Tom and Aldora (Eichert) Ponder; m. Richard Boer, Sept. 19, 1970; children: Andrea, Sonja, Jennifer, Linda Rae. LVN with honors, Chaffey Coll., 1983, AS, 1985; ASN, U. State N.Y., 1987; BS in Health Sci., Chapman U., 1999. RN, Calif.; cert. adv. med./surg. care nurse. Nurse med./surg. unit Kaiser Perm Hosp., Fontana, Calif., nurse urgent care/emergency rm. addition medicine dept. Mem. United Nursing Assn. Calif.

BÖER, SUSANNE ELLA, secondary school educator, translator; b. Osnabrück, Germany, July 30, 1957; arrived in U.S., 1984; d. Dieter Wolfgang Böer and Hannelore Rose; m. Mark Alan Nelson, 1984 (div. 1999); children: Anna, Nils. MEd, Carl-von-Ossietzky U., Germany, 1984. Lic. tchr. Va., 1999. Tchr. HS Divsn., Lower Saxony, Germany, 1982—84; night coord. We Care, Inc., Orlando, 1984—86; recreation dir. Va. Correctional Ctr. for Women, Goochland, Va., 1986—88; instr. The German Sch., Richmond, 1989—98, J. Seargeant Reynolds C. C., Richmond, 1989—99, Va. Commonwealth U., Richmond, 1990—99; tchr. Midlothian HS, Chesterfield, Va., 1998—. Translator German to English, Richmond, 1984—. Pres. bd. The Cir. Sch., Richmond, 1989—. Mem.: YMCA, Fgn. Lang. Assn. of Va., Am. Assn. for Tchrs. of German. Democrat. Unitarian Universalist. Avocations: folkdancing, making stained glass, reading, outdoors. Home: 3006 Kensington Ave Richmond VA 23221 Office: Midlothian HS 405 Charter Colony Pkwy Midlothian VA 23114 E-mail: Susanne_Boer@ccpsnet.net.

BOERSMA, P. DEE, marine biologist, educator; b. Mt. Pleasant, Mich., Nov. 1, 1946; d. Henry W. and Vivian (Anspach) B. BS, Ctrl. Mich. U., 1969; PhD, Ohio State U., 1974; DSc (hon.), Ctrl. Mich. U., 2003. Asst. prof. Inst. Environ. Studies U. Wash., Seattle, 1974-80, assoc. prof., 1980-88, prof. environ. studies, 1988-93, prof. zoology, 1988—, adj. prof. women's studies, 1993—2003, assoc. dir., 1987-93, acting dir., 1990-91, prof. biology, prof. womens studies, 2003—; mem. sci. adv. com. for outer continental shelf Environ. Studies Program, Dept. Interior, 1980-83; prin. investigator Magellanic Penguin Project Wildlife Cons. Soc., 1982—. Evans vis. fellow U. Otago, New Zealand, 1995, Pew fellow in marine conservation, 1997-2000. Assoc. editor Ecological Applications, 1998-2001; exec. editor Conservation in Practice, 2000—; contbr. articles to profl. jours. Mem. adv. U.S. del. to UN Status Women Commn., N.Y.C., 1973, UN World Status Women Commn., N.Y.C., 1973, UN World Population Conf., Romania, 1974; mem. Gov. Lowry's Task Force on Wildlife, 1993; sci. adv. EcoBios, 1985-95; bd. dirs. Zero Population Growth, 1975-82, Washington Nature Conservancy, 1995-98; adv. bd. Walt Disney World Animal Kingdom, 1993—, Island press, 1999—, Compass, 2000—, ; bd. dirs. Peregine Fund, 1995—, Bullitt Found., 1996-2000, Islandwood, 2001—; mem. scholar diplomatic program Dept. State, 1977. Recipient Outstanding Alumni award Ctrl. Mich. U., 1978, Matrix award Women in Comm., 1983; named to Kellogg Nat. Leadership Program, 1982-85; recipient Top 100 Outsiders of Yr. award Outside Mag., 1987, Outstanding Centennial Alumni award Ctrl. Mich. U., 1993; sci. fellow The Wildlife Conservation Soc., 1982—, Aldo Leopold Leadership fellow, 2000-01. Fellow AAAS, Am Ornithol. Union (regional rep. Pacific seabird group 1981-85); mem. AAAS, Ecol. Soc. Am., Wilson Ornithol. Soc., Cooper Ornithol. Soc., Soc. Am. Naturalists, Soc. for Conservation Biology (bd. govs. 1991-94, pres-elect 1995-97, pres. 1997-99, past pres. 1999-2001), Gopher Brokers Club (pres. Seattle chpt. 1982-83). Office: U Wash Dept Biology PO Box 351800 Seattle WA 98195-1800 E-mail: boersma@u.washington.edu.

BOESCH, DIANE HARRIET, retired elementary education educator; b. Erie, Pa., July 3, 1942; d. William Jacob and Dorothy Gertrude (Call) B. BS, Edinboro (Pa.) State U., 1964; MA, Kent (Ohio) State U., 1968; postgrad., So. Ill. U., Carbondale, 1969, CUNY, 1972, Norwalk State Tech. Coll., 1979, Northeastern U., Boston, 1982, Fla. State U., 1988. Tchr. math. Iroquois Area Sch. Dist., Erie, 1964-67; grad. asst. Kent State U., 1967-68; tchr., writer Comprehensive Sch. Math. Project, Carbondale, Ill., 1968-70; tchr. math. Weston (Conn.) Pub. Schs., 1970-2000, dept. chmn. math., 1989-2000; math edn. cons., 2000—. Dir. Weston Tchr. Ctr., 1983-84; condr. workshops on math. and writing, Conn., 1970—. Contbr. articles to profl. publs. Vol. nat. elections, Erie, 1960, West Haven, Conn., 1972. Recipient Celebration of Excellence award Conn. State Dept. Edn., 1988, Presdl. award NSF, 1990. Fellow Conn. Acad. for Edn. in Math. and Sci.; mem. NEA, Nat. Coun. Tchrs. Math., Conn. Educator Talent Pool, Conn. Edn. Assn., Weston Tchr. Assn., Coun. Presdl. Awardees in Math., Pi Mu Epsilon, Kappa Delta Pi. Republican. Lutheran. Avocations: genealogy, writing, music, reading, atlanta braves baseball. E-mail: dhb703@aol.com.

BOETTGER, NANCY J. state legislator; b. Chgo., May 1, 1943; m. H. David Boettger; 4 children. BS, Iowa State U., 1965; BA, Buena Vista Coll., 1982. Owner farm, 1965—; spl. edn. tchr., 1965-66; tchr. jr. H.S., 1982-86; dir. edn. Myrtie Meml. Hosp., 1986-99; mem. Iowa Senate from 41st dist., 1994—; asst. majority leader, 1996-2000. Mem. Midwest Legis. Coun., 1996-2000. Mem. First Bapt. Ch., People Who Care; former bd. dirs. Harlan Cmty. Libr.; former mem. dean's adv. bd. Iowa State U. Ext. Mem. PEO, Am. Legis. Exchange Coun., Midwest Coun. State Govts. (chair health and human svcs. 1997-99), Coun. State Govts. (mem. drug task force 1998), Iowa Coun. Internat. Understanding Bd., Shelby County Found. for Edn. (former exec. dir.), Farm Bur., Pork Prodrs. Republican. Home: 926 Ironwood Rd Harlan IA 51537-5308 Office: State Capitol Dist 41 3 9th And Grand Des Moines IA 50319-0001 E-mail: nancy_boettger@legis.state.ia.us.

BOETTICHER, HELENE, lawyer; b. Syracuse, N.Y., Mar. 26, 1920; d. Ford and Emily (Bennett) Zogg; m. William Donald Boetticher, Oct. 18, 1958 (dec. July 1990); children: John, Amy, Sally. BA, U. Wis., 1941, LLB, 1943. Bar: Wis., Ill. Atty. NLRB, Chgo., 1951—57, OSHA Rev., Washington, 1972—73, Dept. Labor, 1973—95, counsel for litigation, 1978—95. Contbr. articles to profl. jours. Democrat. Episcopalian. Avocation: travel. Home: 15204 Carrolton Rd Rockville MD 20853 E-mail: hzb3099@att.net.

BOFFA, LISA SAUNDERS See BAUGH, LISA

BOGACZYK, KATHRYN, conversion specialist, executive, consultant; b. Warsaw, N.Y., Aug. 29, 1963; d. Charles Frederick and Mary Jane (Garbo) B. BA/BS in History of Art Am. Civilization, U. Pa., 1985. With William M. Mercer, Phila., 1982-90, recordkeeper, 1988—90; gallery asst. Helen Drutt Gallery, Phila., 1986-87; conversion specialist Corestates Bank NA, Phila., 1991-95, Bisys, Ambler, Pa., 1995-96; cons. SunGard, Phila., 1996-97; mgr. daily recordkeeping CoreStates Bank, N.A., 1997—99; cons. SunGard OmniPlus, 1999—; owner RomeAbout.com. Tutor Ctr. for Literacy, Phila., 1990-95. Office: Centre Sq Philadelphia PA 19102

BOGAN, MARY FLAIR, stockbroker; b. Providence, July 9, 1948; d. Ralph A.L. and Mary (Dyer) B. BA, Vassar Coll., 1969. Actress Trinity Sq. Repertory Co., R.I., Gretna Playhouse, Pa., Skylight Comic Opera, Milw., Cin. Playhouse, Playmakers' Repertory, N.C.; mem. nat. co. No Sex, Please, We're Brit.; also TV commls., 1970-77; acct. exec. E.F. Hutton & Co., Inc., Providence, 1977-86; act. v.p. Paine Webber, 1986-97; v.p. investments Prudential Securities, Providence, 1997—2003, Wachovia Securities, 2003—; econ. reporter Sta. WPRI-TV, 1982-85, Sta. WJAR-TV, 1987—. Recipient Century Club award, 1980, 81, 82, 83, 85, Blue Chip Sales award, 1983, 85, Pacesetter Sales award, 1986-90; named Woman of Yr. Profl. Bus. and Rep. Women's Assn. Mem. Univ. Club, Brown Faculty. Home: 18 Cooke St Providence RI 02906-2023 Office: Wachovia Securities 900 Fleet Ctr 50 Kennedy Plz Providence RI 02903-2393

BOGARD, CAROLE CHRISTINE, lyric soprano; b. Cin. d. Harold and Helen Christina (Whittlesey) Geistweit; m. Charles Paine Fisher, Dec. 30, 1966; children: Christine, Pamela. Student, San Francisco State U. Debuts include: Despina in Cosi fan Tutte (Mozart), San Francisco, 1965, Poppea in Coronation of Poppea (Monteverdi), Netherlands Opera, 1971; other appearances include, Boston Opera, N.E.T., orchs. Boston, Madrid, Minn., Phila., Pitts., San Francisco, summer festivals, Mostly Mozart, N.Y., Tanglewood, Carmel, Aston Magna, Gt. Barrington, Mass., appeared in concerts throughout Europe and with Smithsonian Chamber Players, 1976-; recorded numerous albums including 1st rec. of songs of John Duke for his 80th birthday, 1979, recital of Groupe des Six; premiered songs of Dominic Argento in, Holland, 1978, songs of Richard Cumming (in collaboration with Donald Gramm); regular participant rec. and scholarly projects, Smithsonian Instn.; judge regional auditions, Boston; tchr., with emphasis on technique as taught in last Century; recs. have been re-issued on CDs during the 1990s including Baroque Cantatas and Arias, Mozart C minor Mass, Mozart Coronation Mass., 2 CD collection American Songs, 2000; female lead 3 CD Handel opera Tamerlano, 2002. Mem. Sigma Alpha Iota Home: 161 Belknap Rd Framingham MA 01701-3886

BOGARD, MARGARET JOAN, nurse; b. New Castle, Pa., Apr. 5, 1933; d. Frank James and Anna Dorothy (Gonda) Smilek; m. John H. Bogard, Sept. 4, 1954; children: Cheryl Ann, Brian, Kenneth. RN, Providence Hosp., Beaver Falls, Pa., 1954. Med.-surg. nurse Providence Hosp., 1954-56, delivery rm. nurse, 1956-57; RN in home care, 1967-85; nurse continued edn. Harmerville (Pa.) Rehab., 1985, rehab. nurse, asst. phys. therapist to home care patients, 1986-94; office coord. in home care Med. Ctr., Beaver, Pa., 1994—2000, INCARE Home Health Agy., North Myrtle Beach, SC, 2000—.

BOGART, WANDA LEE, interior designer; b. Ashville, N.C., Feb. 26, 1939; d. Bob West and Virginia Elizbeth (Worley) McLemore-Snyder; m. Sterling X. Bogart, Feb. 12, 1962; children: Kevin Sterling, Kathleen Elizabeth. BA, San Jose (Calif.) State U., 1961. Cert. interior designer. Tchr. Redondo Beach (Calif.) Sch. Dist., 1962-65; free-lance interior designer Ladera, Calif., 1970-75; designer MG Interior Design, Orange, Calif., 1975-80; prin., pres. Wanda Bogart Interior Design Inc., Orange, 1980—. Contbr. articles to profl. jours. Named one of Top 20 Interior Designers in So. Calif. Ranch and Coast Mag., 1987. Mem. Internat. Interior Design Assn. (profl. mem., cert.), Am. Soc. Interior Design (profl. mem., cert.), Orange C. of C. Office: Wanda Bogart Interior Design Inc 1440 E Chapman Ave Orange CA 92866-2279 Office Phone: 714-997-5991.

BOGDAN, CAROLYN LOUETTA, financial specialist; b. Wilkes-Barre, Pa., Apr. 15, 1941; d. Walter Cecil and Ethna Louetta (Kendig) Carpenter; m. James Thomas Bogdan, May 5, 1961; 1 child, Thomas James. Grad. high sch., Kingston, Pa. Head bookkeeper Forty Ft. (Pa.) State Bank, 1959-63, U.S. Nat. Bank, Long Beach, Calif., 1963-65; office mgr. United Parts Exch., Long Beach, 1976-81; contract adminstr. Johnson Controls, Inc., Rancho Dominguez, Calif., 1981-88, credit coord., 1989-98; co-owner, acct. Bogdan Elec. R & D, Lakewood, Calif., 1981—. Mem. Radio Amateur Civil Emergency Svc., L.A. County Sheriff Dept., 1974—, records keeper, 1988—93, radio comm. officer, 1994—2002. Mem. Tournament of Roses Radio Amateurs (pin chmn. 1975—), Calif. State Sheriffs Assn. (assoc.), Calif. State Office Emergency Svcs. Republican. Avocations: crochet, gardening, electronics, advanced amateur radio lic. (HAM). Home: 3713 Capetown St Lakewood CA 90712-1437

BOGDANOWICZ, LORETTA MAE, artist, educator; b. West Palm Beach, Fla., Aug. 11, 1940; d. James Paul and Bessie Margaret (Smith) Cone; m. Lawrence Robert Bogdanowicz, July 10, 19[illegible]; children: Laura June Ford, Michael David, Denise Ann Pharris. AA, Ocean County Coll., 1982; BFA, U. Ariz., 1996. Cert. art tchr., Ariz. Art instr. Ariz. Theatre Co., Tucson, 1997-98, Catalina Foothills Cmty. Sch., Tucson, 1997-98, Tucson Mus. Art Edn., 1997—; incorporator Floorcloths and More, Inc., 2001, art instr. Pima CC, Vail, Ariz., 2002—. Exhibited in group shows. Vis. artist Devon Gables Health Care Ctr., Tucson, 1997-2001; instr. neighborhood classes; artist in residence Acacia Elem. Sch., Vail. Recipient Liquitex Paint Exch. award, 1996. Mem.: Tucson/Pima Arts Coun., Western States Art Fedn., Contemporary Art Soc. Tucson, Tucson Mus. Art, Phi Kappa Phi. Avocations: hiking, photography, gardening, reading, travel.

BOGENSCHNEIDER, GAYLE MUELLER, small business owner, interior designer; b. Cape Girardeau, Mo., Sept. 24, 1949; d. Ruben Marvin and Norman Arlene Mueller; m. Duane R., July 5, 1969 (div. Aug. 16, 1994). RN N.C. Vol. nurse World Brotherhood Exch., Sklekleka, Ethiopia, 1971—73; dir. inservice edn. and surveillance Southampton Meml. Hosp., Franklin, Va., 1973—76; sales rep. Abbott Labs., Raleigh, NC, 1976—80, sales mgr. Boston, 1980—89, nat. acct. mgr. Chgo., 1989—92, mktg. mgr., 1992—94, managed care regional sales mgr., 1994—96, long term care nat. mgr., 1996—2000; owner, pres. Creative Environs., Inc., 2002—. Democrat. Lutheran. Avocations: gardening, reading, interior decorating, teaching, spiritual growth. Office: Creatie Environs Inc 716 Brittany Ln University City MO 63130

BOGER, GAIL LORRAINE ZIVNA, reading specialist; b. Portland, Oreg., Sept. 15, 1946; d. Stephen Edward and Harriet Lucille (Laws) Zivna; m. Dan Calvin Boger, June 23, 1973; children: Gretchen, Gregory. BS in Edn., Oreg. State U., 1968; MA in Edn., Stanford U., 1973; MA in Reading, U. LaVerne, 1982. Cert. reading and lang. arts specialist, Calif. Elem. tchr. Monterey (Calif.) Peninsula Unified Sch. Dist., 1968-72, 73-75, lang. arts tchr., 1979-81; elem. tchr. San Ramon (Calif.) Unified Sch. Dist., 1976-79; Miller-Unruh reading specialist Monterey (Calif.) Peninsula Unified Sch. Dist., 1983—. Mem.: Reading is Fundamental Program, Monterey County Reading Assn., Calif. Reading Assn., Internat. Reading Assn., Delta Kappa Gamma (rec. sec. 1992—94, 2002—). Avocations: ballet, music, piano, reading, golf. Home: 27 Cramden Dr Monterey CA 93940-4145 E-mail: dngboger@sbcglobal.net.

BOGGS, BETH CLEMENS, lawyer; b. Dubuque, Iowa, July 28, 1967; d. Theodore Alan and Mary Ann (Fleckenstein) Clemens; m. T. Darin Boggs, Mar. 9, 1991. BA, Govs. State U., 1987; JD, So. Ill. U., 1991. Bar: Ill. 1991, Mo. 1992, U.S. Dist. Ct. (so. dist.) Ill. 1991, U.S. Dist. Ct. (ea. dist.) Mo. 1992, U.S. Dist. Ct. (we. dist.) Mo. 2002, U.S. Dist. Ct. (cen. dist.) Ill. 1997. Clk. R. Courtney Hughes & Assocs., Carbondale, Ill., 1990-91; lawyer Sandberg Phoenix & von Gontard, St. Louis, 1991-93; assoc. LaTourette, Schlueter & Byrne, St. Louis, 1993-95; mng. ptnr. Landau, Omahana & Kopka, P.C., St. Louis, 1995-99; mng. and founding ptnr. Boggs, Backer & Bates, LLC, St. Louis, 1999—. Adj. faculty Webster U., 1995—. Editor student articles So. Ill. U. Law Jour., 1991; contbr. articles to profl. jours. Mem. Young Lawyers divsn. of ABA (vice chair corp. counsel com. 1991-92, editor Corp. Counsel Newsletter 1991-92), Bus. Women St. Louis, Women Lawyers Assn., Lawyers Assn. St. Louis, Def. Rsch. inst., Mo. Orgn. Def. Lawyers. Avocations: tennis, softball, golf. Office: BBB 7912 Bonhomme Ave Ste 400 Saint Louis MO 63105-3512 E-mail: bbblawyers@aol.com.

BOGGS, CATHERINE J. lawyer; b. Denver, 1954; BA, U. Denver, 1976; MS, Mich. State U., 1977; JD, U. Denver, 1981. Bar: Colo. 1982, Oreg. 1991, Calif. 1993. Atty. Sherman & Howard, 1982—90, Stoel Rives, 1991—93, Baker & McKenzie, Chgo., 1993—. Trustee Rocky Mountain Mineral Law Found., 2001—. Mem.: ABA, Soc. Mining, Metallurgy and Exploration, Soc. Mining, Oreg. State Bar Assn., Northwest Mining Assn., Colo. Bar Assn., Calif. State Bar Assn. Office: Baker & McKenzie One Prudential Plz 130 East Randolph Dr Chicago IL 60601*

BOGGS, CORINNE CLAIBORNE (LINDY BOGGS), retired congresswoman; b. Brunswick Plantation, La., Mar. 13, 1916; d. Roland Philomen and Martha Corinne (Morrison) Claiborne; m. Thomas Hale Boggs, Jan. 22, 1938 (dec.); children: Barbara Boggs Sigmund (dec.), Thomas Hale Jr., Corinne Boggs Roberts, William Robertson (dec.). BA, Sophie Newcomb Coll., Tulane U., 1935, LLD (hon.); LittD, U. St. Thomas; DPub Svc. (hon.), Trinity Coll., Washington, 1975; hon. degree, St. Mary of Woods; LLD, Loyola U., Notre Dame U., Wesleyan U., Cath. U. Law Sch., Xavier U., St. Mary's Coll., St. Thomas Aquinas Coll., Univ. New Orleans, Our Lady of Holy Cross Coll., Notre Dame Sem., Coll. of St. Elizabeth. Tchr. history and English, St. James Parish, La., 1936-37; elected to 93d Congress to fill vacancy caused by death of husband, 1973; re-elected to 94th-101st Congresses from 2d La. Dist., 1973-91; ret., 1991; Ambassador to Rome Tulane U., New Oleans. Mem. appropriations com. majority mem. from Ho. of Reps., Am. Revolution Bicentennial Adminstrn. Bd., chmn. Commn. Ho. of Reps. Bicentenary; mem. campaign com. Dem. Nat. Com., 1974; first chairwoman Dem. Nat. Conv., 1976; mem. Com. on Bicentennial of U.S. Constn. Pres., Dem. Congl. Wives Forum, 1954, Womans Nat. Democratic Club, 1958-59, Congl. Club, 1971-72; co-chmn. Inaugural Balls for Presidents John F. Kennedy, 1961, Lyndon Johnson, 1965; mem. Nat. Hist. Publs. and Records Com.; bd. dirs. La. Council for Music and Performing Arts; hon. bd. dirs. Met. New Orleans chpt. Nat. Found. March of Dimes; bd. advisers. CLOSE-UP and Presdl. Classroom; regent emeritus Smithsonian Instn.; mem. president's council Tulane U. Recipient Weiss Meml. award NCCJ, 1974; Nat. Oak award La. Assn. Ind. Colls. and Univs., Disting. Service medal Saint Mary's Dominican Coll., 1976, Humanitarian award AMVETS Nat. Aux., Torch of Liberty award B'nai B'rith, 1976, Gala IV award Birmingham So. U., 1976, Eleanor Roosevelt Humanitarian award, 1977, E. Roosevelt Centennial award, 1984, 1st woman recipient Disting. Alumna award Tulane U., 1986; 1st woman recipient VFW Congl. award, 1986; bldg., rm. in U.S. Capitol bldg., energy bldg. Tulane U., U.S. Vets. Hosp. Unit, New Orleans, Challenger Space Ctr. and Mission Control Ctr., Baton Rouge, and dam named in her honor. Mem. Nat. Soc. Colonial Dames, LWV, Internat. Fedn. Cath. Alumni, Internat. Women's Forum. Avocations: flower arranging, dance. Address: Office of the President Tulane Univ New Orleans LA 70118-5665

BOGGS, JESSICA LYNN, creative director, web designer; b. Warsaw, Ind., Dec. 18, 1976; d. Kevin Lee Boggs and Ellen Marie Dwyer. BFA in Visual Comm. Design, U. Dayton, Ohio, 1999. Web designer UDRI Web Devel. Ctr., Dayton, 1997—99, CC Comms., Charlotte, NC, 1999—2000; co-founder, ptnr. Soloist Graphics, Charlotte, NC, 2000—01; creative dir. Alpha Zeta, Inc., Chgo., 2001—. Mem.: Chgo. Software Assn., Chgo. Interactive Mktg. Assn. (mktg. comm. chair), Internet Execs. Club. Avocations: wheel throwing, painting, drawing, world events. Office: Alpha Zeta Inc 8 S Michigan 37th Flr Chicago IL 60603

BOGGS, PAULA ELAINE, lawyer; b. Washington, May 2, 1959; d. Nathaniel Boggs Jr. and Janice C. (Anderson) Barber. BA, Johns Hopkins U., 1981; JD, U. Calif., Berkeley, 1984. Bar: Pa. 1986, D.C. 1988, Wash. 1992, U.S. Dist. Ct. (we. dist.) Wash. 1988, U.S. Ct. appeals (9th cir.) 1990, U.S. Ct. Appeals (D.C. and fed. cirs.) 1995. Sr. law clk. Office of Army Gen. Counsel, Arlington, Va., 1984-85, spl. asst. Office of Dep. Under Sec. of the Army, Arlington, 1985-86, staff atty. White House Iran-Contra legal task force, Washington, 1987-88; asst. U.S. atty. we. dist. U.S. Atty.'s Office, Seattle, 1988-93; staff dir. adv. bd. investigative capability dept. def. Dept. Def., Arlington, 1994; ptnr. Preston Gates & Ellis, Seattle, 1995—97; v.p. legal Dell Computer Corp., 1997—2002; exec. v.p., gen. counsel, sec. Starbucks, Seattle, 2002—. Mem. faculty Nat. Inst. for Trial Advocacy, 1995; adj. prof. law U. Wash., Seattle, 1993. Vol. instr. presdl. classroom for young Ams. Washington, 1991; bd. dirs. ctrl. dist. YMCA, Seattle, 1991-93, Greater Seattle YMCA, 1995[illegible] Johns Hopkins U. Second Decade Soc., Balt., 1995-96. With U.S. Army, 1981-88. Recipient Sec. Def. award for Excellence William J. Perry, 1994; Presdl. svc. badge Pres. Ronald Reagan, 1988; Def. Meritorious Svc. award, 1987, Spl. Achievement award Dept. Justice, 1990, 91. Mem. ABA (ho. of dels., litigation sect. co-chair bus. torts com., bus. crimes com., criminal justice sect. white collar crimes com., standing com. on constn. and bylaws), Nat. Bar Assn., Wash. State Bar Assn. (corrections com.), King County Bar Assn., Fed. Bar Assn., Wash. Women Lawyers (bd. dirs. 1991-93), Loren Miller Bar Assn. Avocations: running, cycling, reading. Office: Starbucks 2401 Utah Ave S PO Box 34067 Seattle WA 98134*

BOGHOSIAN, PAULA DER, computer business consultant; b. Watervliet, N.Y., Nov. 19, 1933; d. Harry and Osgi (Piligian) der B. BS magna cum laude, Syracuse U., 1964, MS, 1967; postgrad., SUNY, Oswego, 1972, SUNY, Albany, 1974. Cert. profl. sec. Asst. prof. Cazenovia (N.Y.) Coll., 1964-73; instr. Bd. of Coop., Syracuse, N.Y., 1973-76, dir. bus. careers, 1976-92; cons. computer bus., prin. Syracuse, 1984—. Zonta scholar, 1964; Jessie Smith Noyes grantee Syracuse U., 1965. Mem. Assn. Info. Systems Profl. (com. chmn.), Bus. Tchrs. Assn. of N.Y. State, Adminstrv. Mgmt. Soc., Eastern Bus. Tchrs. Assn., Assn. for Supervision and Curriculum Devel., Assn. of Am. Jr. Colls., Assn. of Am. U. Profs., Nat. Assn. for Armenian Studies and Rsch. Harvard U., Internat. Tng. Communications (v.p. 1985-86), Delta Pi Epsilon, Beta Gamma Sigma, Phi Kappa Phi, Pi Lambda Theta, Sigma Lambda Delta. Republican. Mem. Armenian Apostolic. Avocations: music, golf, water colors, designer, travel. Home and Office: 3181 Bellevue Ave Apt B6 Syracuse NY 13219-3156 Office Phone: 315-468-0581.

BOGHOSSIAN, JOAN THOMPSON, artist; b. Newport, R.I., Mar. 6, 1932; d. Joseph and Hope (Bliss) Thompson; m. Paul O. Boghossian Jr., 1952 (dec. July 1995); children: Carol Boghossian Spencer, Paul O. III, David M., Nancy Boghossian Staples. BS, U. R.I., 1953. One person shows at Attleboro Mus., Newton Libr. Gallery, Charlestown Gallery; two-person shows at Providence Art Club (J. Banigan Sullivan prize 1984), Dodge House Gallery; group exhbn. at RI Watercolor Soc. (1st in watercolor 1988, 91, Block Artists Merchandise award 1989, Grumbacher Gold Medallion 1990, 93, 94, Dr. Edwin Dunlop award 1997), Mystic Art Assn. (1st in watercolor 1990, 92, 93, 95, Mystic Manor spl. award for aquatint 1992), Wickford Art Assn. (1st in watercolor 1986, 1st in all-media 1993, 2d in oil 1995), South County Art Assn. (award 1987, Florence B. Kane award 1989, Herbert Richard Cross award 1992, C. Gordon Harris award 1993, 1st prize award 1997), Peel Gallery-Danby, Vt., New Eng. South Shore Artists (Best in Show 1986), Cape Cod Art Assn. (1st in watercolor 1987, 90, 1st in graphics 1987, 2d in watercolor 1988, 92, Juror's award of merit 1994), Warwick Arts Found. (1st in watercolor 1985); RI Watercolor Soc. David Marsland Meml. Award, Providence Art Club, Wm. S. Brigham Award and Juror's Choice Award, Warwick Mus.Open, Am. Frame Award, 2002; others. Mem.: others, New Eng. Watercolor Soc. (James W. Duffy award 1998), South County Art Assn. (1st prize Open Annual South County award 1997, Kinney award Best Floral Painting 1996, C. Gordon Harris award 1993, Herbert Richard Cross award 1992, Best Marine Painting Loring award 1990, Florence B. Kane award 1989, Art Assn. award 1987), Wickford Art Assn. (1st pl. in show 1996, 2nd pl. in oil 1994, 1st pl. all-medal 1993), Mystic Art Assn. (1st pl. watercolor Annual Regional Exhbn. 1990, 1992, 1993, 1995, Mystic Manor Spl. award for Aquatint 1992), R.I. Watercolor Soc. (Dr. Edwin Dunlop Meml. award 1997, Grumbacher gold medallion 1990, 1993, 1994, 1st pl. Watercolor Soc. Open 1987, 1988, 1991), Providence Art Club (Frederick Sisson award 1988), Copley Soc. Boston, Catherine Lorillard Wolfe Art Club (Anna Hyatt Huntington medal 1996, Mary Hill Meml. award 1998). Home: 640 East Ave Pawtucket RI 02860-6158 Studio: 7 Thomas St Providence RI 02903-1314

BOGIE, LANA CECIL, librarian; d. Matt Cecil, Jr. and Ruth Cecil; m. Garnett Coleman Bogie, June 7, 1969; children: Jennifer LeAnn Newell, Emily Dawn, Amy DeAnn Rogers. BS in Music Edn., Trevecca Nazarene Coll., 1975, postgrad. cert. in English, 1985; MLIS, Trevecca Nazarene U., 2002. English and reading tchr. Maplewood H.S.-Metro Nashville Schs., Nashville, 1985—92; mid. sch. music tchr. Carter Lawrence Sch.-Metro Nashville Schs., Nashville, 1992—2000; elem. music tchr. J.E. Moss Elem. Sch.-Metro Nashville Schs., Nashville, 2000—03; elem. libr. info. specialist Granbery Elem. Sch.-Metro Nashville Schs., Nashville, 2003—. Asst. choir dir. Trevecca Cmty. Ch. of the Nazarene, Nashville, 1998—. Choir mem. Trevecca Cmty. Ch. of the Nazarene, Nashville, asst. choir dir., 1998—. Grantee, Met. Nashville Schs. Mem.: Nat. Educator's Assn., Metro Nashville Ednl. Assn., Music Educators Nat. Coun. Nazarene. Avocations: walking, reading.

BOGSTAHL, DEBORAH MARCELLE, market research consultant; b. Irvington, N.J., June 5, 1950; d. Marcel and Helena Christina (de Jaroszynsky) Bogstahl; children: Alexandra Boman, Michelle Boman. BA in English Edn., The Coll. of N.J., 1972. Cert. tchr., N.J. Project dir. U.S. Testing Co., Hoboken, N.J., 1973-75; project dir. J. Walter Thompson Co., N.Y.C., 1975-77; rsch. account exec. Dancer Fitzgerald Sample, N.Y.C., 1977-80; group rsch. mgr. Bristol-Myers Co., N.Y.C., 1980-87; dir. rsch. Med. Econs. Co., Inc., Oradell, N.J., 1987-90; mktg. rsch. mgr. The Mennen Co., 1991-92, Reckitt & Colman, Inc., Wayne, N.J., 2000, Kraft Foods, 2000-. Contbr. poetry to anthology. Mem. Am. Mktg. Assn., Product Devel. and Mgmt. Assn. Democrat. Roman Catholic. Avocations: sailing, reading, writing, music. Address: 33 Winding Way West Orange NJ 07052

BOHAN, GLORIA, travel retail executive; BA, LLD, Marymount Manhattan Coll. Pres. Omega World Travel, Fairfax, Va., 1972—. Bd. dirs. Am. Bus. Conf., Greater Washington Bd. Trade, Va. C. of C., Va. Coll. Fund., Va. Found. Ind. Colls.; mem. women's travel adv. coun. Inter-Continental and Crowne Plaza Hotels and Resorts. Lectr. Georgetown U. Sch. Bus., vol. YWCA, Womens Ctr., Suited for Change. Recipient Woman Yr., Network Entrepreneurial Women, 1990. Mem. Nat. Assn. Women Bus. Owners, Am. Soc. Travel Agts., Soc. Govt. Travel Profls. (pres. 1986-87). Office: Omega World Travel Inc 3102 Omega Office Park Fairfax VA 22031-2400 Fax: 703-350-8880.

BOHANNON, JANICE GAIL TREADWAY, art educator, artist; b. McKinney, Tex., Apr. 21, 1952; d. Glen Dale and Wanda Jean Treadway; m. Michael David Bohannon, Jan. 25, 1972; children: Christopher Bradley, Matthew Bryan. BS in Edn., Tex. A&M U., 1982. Tchrs. aide Melissa (Tex.) ISD, 1975—79; tchr. Princeton (Tex.) ISD, 1983—. Mem.: Assn. Tex. Profl. Educators. Democrat.

BOHANNON, SARAH VIRGINIA, personnel professional; b. Roanoke, Va., Mar. 1, 1947; AA in Bus. Adminstrn. Mgmt., Nat. Bus. Coll., 1983. Pers. appointment clk. IRS, Richmond, Va., 1983—84; pers. technician Commonwealth of Va., Richmond, Va., 1985—97, pers. asst., 1997—98, pers. technician, 1999—2000, pers. adminstrv. specialist dept. human resource mgmt., 2001—02. Mem. Am. Biog. Inst. (life, dep. gov. 1991, mem. women's inner circle of achievement 1991). Home: 2220 Clarke St Richmond VA 23228-6049

BOHANON, KATHLEEN SUE, neonatologist, educator; b. Mpls., 1951; BA summa cum laude, U. Minn., 1973, MD, 1977. Diplomate Am. Bd. Pediat., Am. Bd. Neonatal-Perinatal Medicine. Commd. 2d lt. USAF, 1973, advanced through grades to col., 1995; resident in pediats. Case Western Res. U., Cleve., 1977-80; gen. pediatrician USAF, 1980-85; fellow in neonatology Wilford Hall Med. Ctr., San Antonio, 1985-87; neonatologist, [illegible] USAF Med. Ctr., Wright Patterson AFB, Ohio, 1987-95, chmn. dept. pediat., 1995-98, chief med. staff, 1998-2000; ret., 2000; locum tenens neonatologist, 2001—03; staff neonatologist St. Mary's Hosp. and Med. Ctr., Grand Junction, Colo., 2004—. Asst. clin. prof. pediat. U. N.D. Sch. Medicine, Grand Forks, 1981-82; assoc. Wright State U. Sch. Medicine, Dayton, Ohio, 1987-2000, Uniformed Svc. U. Health Scis., Washington, 1988-2000; mem. com. Infant Bio-Ethics Com., Dayton, 1990-2000. Mem. Am. Acad. Pediat.

BOHEN, DOLORES BOYLSTON, retired school system administrator; b. N.Y.C., Nov. 2, 1929; d. Adrian F. Boylston and Louise Montanez; m. John McGee Bohen (dec. Apr. 1979); children: Christina, Pamela, Kerry, Sean, Michele, Patricia. BA in English, Adelphi U., 1951; MEd, Tulane U., 1968; PhD, George Mason U., 2000. Elem. tchr., Leavenworth, Kans., 1966-67; tchr. mid. sch. New Orleans, 1967-68; tchr., chmn. dept. English Fairfax (Va.) H.S., 1968-75, resource tchr., 1975-76; lang. arts specialist K-12 Fairfax County Pub. Schs., 1976-80, instrnl. coord., 1981-82, spl. asst. to dep. supt., 1982-84, asst. supt. comm., 1984-98. Author textbook series McDougal, Littell Spelling Grades 1-8, 1982, 85, 90, 94; contbr. articles to profl. jours. Bd. dirs. Arts Coun. of Fairfax County, Va. Mem. ASCD, Assn. Ednl. Pubs., Phi Delta Kappa, Kappa Delta Pi Home and Office: 4505 Tempest Pl Annandale VA 22003-3968

BOHI, LYNN, state legislator; b. Cleve., Feb. 20, 1947; m. Charles W. Bohi. BA, Olivet Coll., 1970; postgrad., Plymouth State U. State rep. Vt. Ho. of Reps., 1989—90, 1993—98, 2001—; chair local govt. com., 1997—98; vice chair local govt. com., 2003. Active Conn. River Joint Commn. Upper Valley River Subcom., Human Svcs. Coun., 1987-89, United Way Upper Valley, 1981-88, Hartford Recycles, Workforce Investment Bd., Adult Edn. Coun., 1997-2003, Cmty. Partnership of Orange and Windsor Counties; trustee EarthRight, 1991-94. Mem. No. Light Quilting Guild, Hartford Garden Friends. Address: 156 Manning Dr White River Junction VT 05001-8075 E-mail: lbohi@leg.state.vt.us.

BOHLE, SUE, public relations executive; b. Austin, Minn., June 23, 1943; d. Harold Raymond and Mary Theresa (Swanson) Hastings; m. John Bernard Bohle, June 22, 1974; children: Jason John, Christine K. BS in Journalism, Northwestern U., 1965, MS in Journalism, 1969. Tchr. pub. high schs, Englewood, Colo., 1965-68; account exec. Burson-Marsteller Pub. Relations, Los Angeles, 1969-73; v.p., mgr. pub. relations J. Walter Thompson Co., Los Angeles, 1973-79; founder, pres. The Bohle Company, L.A., 1979—; pres., CEO The Bohle Co., L.A.; former exec. v.p. Ketchum Pub. Rels., L.A. Free-lance writer, instr. communications Calif. State U. at Fullerton, 1972-73; instr. writing Los Angeles City Coll., 1975-76; lectr. U. So. Calif., 1979—. Contbr. articles to profl. jours. Dir. pub. rels. L.A. Jr. Ballet, 1971-72; pres. Panhellenic Advisers Coun., UCLA, 1972-73; mem. adv. bd. L.A. Valley Coll., 1974-75, Coll. Communications Pepperdine U., 1981-85, Sch. Journalism U. So. Calif., 1987-95, Calif. State U., Long Beach, 1988-93; bd. visitors Medill Sch. Journalism Northwestern U., 1984—. Recipient Alumni Svc. award Northwestern U., 1995; Univ. scholar, 1961-64, Panhellenic scholar, 1964-65; named to Hall of Achievement, Medill Sch. Journalism, 1997, charter mem. Hall of Fame; named to 50 Top Women in PR, PR Week, mag., 2001. Fellow Pub. Rels. Soc. Am. (bd. dirs. L.A. chpt. 1981-90, v.p. 1983, pres. 1989, del. nat. assembly 1980, 94, 95, 96, co-chmn. long-range strategic com. 1990, pres.'s adv. coun. 1991, exec. com. Counselors Acad. 1984-86, sec.-treas. 1990, chmn. 1992, sec. Coll. Fellows 1993, vice chair 1994, chmn. 1995, Silver Anvil award 1994); mem. Worldcom PR Network (bd. dirs. 2002—), World Com., Women in Comm., Shi-ai, Delta Zeta (editor The Lamp 1966-68, Woman of Yr. award 1993), Kappa Alpha Tau. Office: 1900 Avenue of the Stars # 200 Los Angeles CA 90067-4301

BOHLKE, ARDYCE, state legislator; b. Omaha, Nov. 2, 1943; m. Jan Bohlke, 1967; children: Jon Jr., Jason. BS, U. Nebr., 1965. Mem. from dist. 33 Nebr. State Senate, Lincoln, 1992—, mem. com. on coms., natural resources and rules coms., vice chair edn. com. Past pres. Hastings Bd. Edn., Hastings YWCA. Mem. LWV (past pres.), Bus. and Profl. Women, Rotary. Office: 7 Village Dr Hastings NE 68901-2436

BOHN, DONNA MAY, music educator; b. Kans. City, Mo., June 22, 1965; d. Martin Lewis and Barbara Lee Bohn. BS, U.of Ala., 1983—87; MusM, Wichita State U., 1987—89; Mus D, U. of Ala., 1991—94. Percussionist/timpanist freelance, Kans. City, Mo., 1989—91; grad. tchg. asst. U. of Ala., 1991—94; adj. percussion instr. U. of Montevallo, Ala., 1991—94; asst. prof. of music Quincy U., Quincy, Ill., 1994—2000; [illegible] faculty Interlochen Arts Camp, Interlochen, Mich., 1993—; assoc. prof. of music Quincy U., Ill., 2000—. Timpanist Muddy River Opera Co., Quincy, Ill., 1995—, Quincy Symphony Orch., Ill., 1994—; percussionist Interlochen Festival Orch., Interlochen, Mich., 1993—, Tuscaloosa Symphony Orch., Tuscaloosa, Ala., 1991—94, Ala. Symphony Orch., Birmingham, Ala., 1991—93, Am. Heartland Theatre, Kans. City, Mo., 1989—91. Musician: (solo percussion performance) Quincy U. Faculty Recitals. Newsletter and program editor Muddy River Opera Co., Quincy, Ill., 1995—2000; chair, artistic adv. com. Quincy Symphony Orch., Ill., 1996—97. Mem.: Nat. Assn. of Coll. Wind and Percussion Instructors, Music Educators Nat. Conf., Coll. Music Soc., Percussive Arts Soc. (Ill. chpt. pres. 1999—2001). Avocation: tennis. Office: Quincy University 1800 College Ave Quincy IL 62301

BOHN, DONNA SCHUHMANN, accountant; b. Louisville, Feb. 5, 1959; d. George Nicholas and Helen Rachel (Flood) Schuhmann; m. Bruce Allen Bohn, Oct. 8, 1983; 1 child, Geoffrey Allen. BS in Acctg., U. Ky., 1981; MBA, Bellarmine Coll., 1986. Acct. Brown & Williamson Tobacco Corp., Louisville, 1982-84, supr., 1984-91, analyst market rsch., 1991-94, sr. fin. analyst, 1994—. Bd. dirs., treas. B & W Fed. Credit Union, Louisville, 1993-95. Vol. Vols. Am., Louisville, 1992-94. Mem. Inst. Mgmt. Accts. (bd. dirs. 1994-95), Toastmasters Internat. (pres., v.p., sec./treas.). Democrat. Roman Catholic. Home: 8099 Regency Woods Way Louisville KY 40220-3810 Office: Brown & Williamson Tobacco Corp PO Box 35090 Louisville KY 40232-5090

BOHNENKAMPER, KATHERINE ELIZABETH, library science educator; b. Wichita, July 20, 1955; d. William Eugene and Emily Jane (Yount) Miller; m. David Allen Bohnenkamper, May 29, 1994; 1 child, Daniel William. BS in Edn., Emporia State U., 1977; MEd, Wichita State U., 1981; MA, Kans. State U., 1988; MLS, Emporia State U., 1990. Tchr. high sch. Brown County Pub. Schs., Horton, Kans., 1978-79; substitute tchr. Wichita Pub. Schs., 1979-81, 86-90, tchr. jr. high sch., 1981-86; libr. Kans State Hist. Soc., Topeka, 1990-91; asst. prof. libr. sci. Drury U., Springfield, Mo., 1991—. Instr. 1st aid & CPR ARC, Wichita and Springfield, 1976—. Recipient Arnie H. Richards Meml. scholar Sch. Libr. and Info. Mgmt. Emporia State U., 1990. Mem. Mo. Libr. Assn. (officer-reference coun. 1995-98), Springfield Area Libr. Assn. (v.p. 1995-97), DAR (chpt. historian 1982-84, 94-98), Order Eastern Star. Presbyterian. Avocations: church choir, travel, reading, photography. Home: 1022 E Greenwood St Springfield MO 65807-3713 Office: FW Olin Libr Drury U 900 N Benton Ave Springfield MO 65802-3712 Office Phone: 417-873-7485.

BOHNER, KATE, correspondent; BA, U. Pa.; grad. degree in journalism, Columbia U. Corr. CNN Fin. News, N.Y.C.; assoc. editor, contbr. Forbes Mag.; corr. CNBC, Ft. Lee, N.J. Co-author: (with Donald Trump) The Art of the Comeback, 1997. Fellow Reader's Digest Lit. Found. Office: CNBC 2200 Fletcher Ave Fort Lee NJ 07024-5005

BOHOSKEY, BERNICE FLEMING, actress, dancer, model; b. Seattle, Feb. 9, 1918; d. W. R. and Katherine E. (Emmeluth) Blair; stepdau. E. Charles Fleming; m. Woodward Bohoskey, Aug. 6, 1942 (dec. 1979); children: Charles W., Katherine A., Michael J., Constance E. Student, Mills Coll., Oakland, Calif., 1935-36, Cornish Sch. Arts, Seattle, 1936-38. Model various newspapers. mags., 1936-39; splty. dancer Earl Carroll's Vanities; actress various radio shows, stage plays and movies, Hollywood, Calif.; ptnr., land owner, mineral lease owner Yakima Sheep Co., Yakima Mineral Lease Co. Composer: (hymn) Blessed Trinity, 1948, (song) God's on His Throne, 1948, (song) Just Give Me the Merry-Go-Round, 1949; contbr. articles to profl. jours. Founder, pres. Young First Voters Groups, 1940; spkr., organizer, Yakima County, Wash.; v.p. Young Reps. Club, Wash., 1940. Mem. Jr. League (sustaining), Women's Aglow Internat. Ministries. Republican.

BOICE, MARTHA HIBBERT, writer, publisher; b. Toledo, Oct. 1, 1931; d. George Wilfrid and Gladys (Harbage) Hibbert; m. William V. Boice, Nov. 26, 1955; children: Ruth Celeste Boice Oake, Thomas Wilson, Judith Lynette. BA, Ohio Wesleyan U., 1953; MSW, U. Mich., 1955. Caseworker Travelers Aid, Toledo, 1955-57; pub. Knot Garden Press, Dayton, Ohio, 1986—. Author, compiler: Shaker Herbal Fare, 1985, The Wreath Maker, 1987, The Herbal Rosa, 1990, Maps of the Shaker West, 1997 (award of excellence Ohio Assn. Hist. Societies and Museums 1998); organizer, compiler: A Sense of Place, 1977. Pres. Nat. Assn. Monnett Clubs Ohio Wesleyan U., Delaware, Ohio, 1971-72; chmn. Washington Twp. Zoning Appeals Bd., 1980; trustee Ohio Preservation Alliance, Columbus, 1988-94; chair lit. com. Celebrate Dayton '96, 1995-96. Recipient Disting. Svc. award Nat. Assn. Ohio Wesleyan Monnett Clubs, Delaware, 1974, Centerville Mayor's award for cmty. svcs., 1988; named Vol. of the Yr., Dayton-Montgomery County Park Dist., 1985. Mem.: Herb Soc. Am. (libr. chmn. 1988—90, curator rosemary collection 1997—), Western Shaker Study Group (program chair 1988—91, 1999—2000, sec. 2001—02, program chair 2003—), Nat. Trust for Hist. Preservation, Friends of White Water Shaker Village, Inc. (trustee 2002—, sec. 2003—), Centerville-Washington Twp. Hist. Soc. (landmark chair 1974—78, 1980—94, 1997—99), Landmarks Found. (trustee, sec. 1996, chair 1997—2001), Flower and Herb Exch., Cox Arboretum (vol.), Phi Beta Kappa. Avocations: gardening, slide lectures on gardens and historic preservation topics. Home: 7712 Eagle Creek Dr Dayton OH 45459-3414

BOISE, AUDREY LORRAINE, retired special education educator; b. Hackensack, N.J., Feb. 12, 1933; d. Paul George and Lillian Rose (Goedecker) B. BA, Wellesley (Mass.) Coll., 1955; MA, Fairleigh Dickinson U., 1977. Cert. tchr. K-8, learning disabilities, supervision. Tchr. Township of Berkeley Heights, N.J., 1958-67; learning cons. Borough of New Providence, N.J., 1978-82, 86-00, ret., 2000; learning cons. Scotch Plains/Fanwood, N.J., 1984-86; instr. Fairleigh Dickinson U., Madison, N.J., 1975-78. Several other short-term tchg. positions; supr. student tchrs., 1968, 1975-78, 2000-02; lectr. on fgn. countries in areas of U.S.; part-time travel agt. Life mem Rep. Nat. Com. (Pres. Club 2003-04); mem. Nat. Rep. Senatorial Com., Washington, Rep. Presdl. Task Force, Washington, Rep. Congl. Com., Washington, N.J. State Rep. Com., Trenton, Nat. Fedn. Rep. Women, Washington. Recipient Rep. of Yr. Gold medal, Nat. Rep. Congress, 2002, 2003. Mem. NEA, AAUW, N.J. Assn. Learning Cons., Assn. for Children with Learning Disabilities, N.J. Edn. Assn., Internat. Platform Assn., Fortnightly Club, Hist. Soc. Summit, Canoe Brook Country Club Methodist. Avocations: travel, photography.

BOISEN, MARY, special education educator, department chairman; b. LeSueur, Minn., Jan. 27, 1964; d. Gary Donevan and Judith Ann Boisen. BS, St. Cloud (Minn.) State U., 1988. Tchr. phys. edn./health Cummings Mid. Sch., Brownsville, Tex., 1989-92, Villareal Elem. Sch., Los Fresnos, Tex., 1992-94; coach Los Fresnos H.S., 1992-94, tchr. spl. edn., 1994—. Chair dept. phys. edn./health Cummings Mid. Sch., 1989-91; chair dept. spl. edn. Los Fresnos H.S., 1997—, mem. campus adv. com., 1998—; mem. dist. spl. edn. steering com. Los Fresnos Ctrl. Ind. Sch. Dist., 1998—; mem. regional spl. edn. steering com. South Tex. region, 1999—. Bd. dirs., vol. coord. Habitat for Humanity, Brownsville, 1997-99. Mem. AAPEHRD, Coun. Exceptional Children, Assn. Tchrs. and Profl. Educators. Avocations: sports, outdoor activities, community services. Office: Los Fresnos H S PO Box 309 Los Fresnos TX 78566-0309 Home: 1369 Squaw Valley Dr Unit B Brownsville TX 78520-9793

BOJSZA, JOAN E. elementary school educator; b. Orange, N.J., Jan. 3, 1949; d. Stephen William and Josephine Rosemary (Sulpy) Horkay; m. Walter Joseph Bojsza, June 20, 1970; children: Elizabeth Joy, Katherine Anne. BS in Early Childhood Edn., U. Md., 1971. Cert. elem. edn. and nursery tchr. N.J. Preschool tchr. Woodyard Rd. Ctr., Clinton, Md., 1971—72, YWCA [illegible] West Orange, NJ, 1982—91, 2d grade tchr. St. Bernard Sch., Riverdale, Md., 1972—73; title I tchr. Rockaway (N.J.) Twp. Schs., 1973—74, 4th grade tchr., 1974—75; 1st grade tchr. St. Thomas More Sch., Fairfield, NJ, 1975—77; kindergarten tchr. Newton St. Sch., Newark, 1991—99, Quitman St. Sch., Newark, 1999—2002, pre-kindergarten tchr., 2002—. Project, new beginnings tchr. Summer Inst., Newark, 1998; presenter in field. Co-author: Putting the Children First. Mem. coun., PTA officer, pres. various, West Orange, 1986—99; PTA officer pres. West Orange HS, 1995—98; comitteewoman West Orange Dems., 1991—96. Recipient Outstanding Leaders award, Girl Scouts U.S., 1990. Mem.: Comer Whole Sch. Reform Model (chairperson mem. parent/staff com. 2000—01), Newark Early Childhood Educators Assn. (v.p. 1993—2001, sec., newsletter editor), Essex Hudson Assn. Edn. Young Children (corr. sec. 2001—, program com. 2003—), Kappa Delta Pi. Democrat. Roman Catholic. Avocations: gardening, singing, crafts. Home: 25 Harvard Ter West Orange NJ 07052

BOK, JOAN TOLAND, utility executive; b. Grand Rapids, Mich., Dec. 31, 1929; d. Don Prentiss Weaver and Mary Emily Toland; m. John Fairfield Bok, July 15, 1955; children: Alexander Toland, Geoffrey Robbins. AB, Radcliffe Coll., 1951; JD, Harvard U., 1955. Bar: Mass. 1955. Assoc. Ropes & Gray, Boston, 1955-61; pvt. practice Boston, 1961-68; atty. New England Electric Sys., Westborough, Mass., 1968-73, asst. to pres., 1973-77, v.p., sec., 1977-79, vice-chair, 1979-84, pres., CEO, 1988-89, chair, 1984-98, chair emeritus, 1998—. Bd. dirs. ALTIComm., Inc. Past pres. bd. overseers Harvard U.; bd. dirs. Boston Adult Literacy Fund, Nat. Osteoporosis Found., Vt. Hist. Soc., Woods Hole (Mass.) Oceanog. Inst. Fellow Am. Bar Found.; mem. Boston Bar Assn., Am. Acad. Arts and Scis., Phi Beta Kappa. Unitarian Universalist. Home: 53 Pinckney St Boston MA 02114-4801 Office: 25 Research Dr Westborough MA 01582-0001

BOK, SISSELA, philosopher, writer; b. Stockholm, Dec. 2, 1934; d. Gunnar and Alva (Reimer) Myrdal; m. Derek Bok, May 7, 1955; children—Hilary, Victoria, Tomas BA, George Washington U., 1957, MA, 1958, LHD (hon.), 1986; PhD, Harvard U., 1970; LLD (hon.), Mt. Holyoke Coll., 1985; LHD (hon.), Clark U., 1988, U. Mass., 1991, Georgetown U., 1992. Lectr. Simmons Coll., Boston, 1971-72; lectr. Harvard-MIT Div. Health Scis. and Tech., Cambridge, 1975-82, Harvard U., Cambridge, 1982-84; assoc. prof. philosophy Brandeis U., Waltham, Mass., 1985-89, prof. philosophy, 1989-92; fellow Ctr. for Advanced Study, Stanford, Calif., 1991-92; Disting. fellow Harvard Ctr. Population and Devel. Studies, Cambridge, Mass., 1993—. Mem. ethics adv. bd. HEW, 1977-80; bd. dirs. Population Coun., 1971-77; mem. Pulitzer Prize Bd., 1988-97, chmn., 1996-97. Author: Lying: Moral Choice in Public and Private Life, 1978 (Melcher award, George Orwell award), Secrets: On the Ethics of Concealment and Revelation, 1982, Alva: Ett kvinnoliv, 1987, A Strategy for Peace, 1989, Alva Myrdal: A Daughter's Memoir, 1991 (Melcher award), Common Values, 1996, Mayhem: Violence as Public Entertainment, 1998; mem. editl. bd. Ethics, 1980-85, Criminal Justice Ethics, 1980—, Contention, 1990-96, Common Knowledge, 1991—, (with others) Euthanasia and Physician-Assisted Suicide, 1998. Bd. dirs. Inst. for Philosophy and Religion, Boston U.; mem. Pulitzer Prize Bd., 1989-97. Recipient Abram L. Sachar Silver medallion Brandeis U., 1985, Radcliffe Coll. Grad. Soc. medal, 1993, Barnard Coll. medal of distinction, 1995, centennial medal Harvard Grad. Sch. Arts & Scis., 1998. Fellow Hastings Ctr. (dir. 1976-84, 94-97); mem. Am. Philos. Assn.

BOLAND, ELIZABETH, social services company financial executive; BBS, U. Notre Dame, 1981. From mem. audit staff to sr. audit mgr. Price Waterhouse LLP, Boston, 1981-90; v.p. fin. The Olsten Corp., home-health care-temporary staffing svcs., Boston; CFO, The Visionaries Inc., ind. TV prodn. co., Boston, 1994-97, Bright Horizons Family Solutions, Inc., Watertown, Mass., 1997—. Office: Bright Horizons Family Solutions 200 Talcott Ave Watertown MA 02472-5705

BOLANDRINA, GRETHEL RAMOS, nurse; b. Reina Mercedes, Isabela, Philippines, Dec. 11, 1966; arrived in U.S., 1989; d. Teodolo Collantes and Estrella Luyun Ramos; m. Joseph Maximino Bolandrina, Jan. 11, 1991; children: Jessica Dawn, Gino Ray, Lilly Amber, Max Joseph. BSN, U. Santo Tomas, Manila, Philippines, 1987; BS in Creative Journalism, Harvard U., 2001. RN; CRRN; lic. notary pub., Mass. Charge nurse Philippine Gen. Hosp., Manila, 1988-89, St. John of God Hosp., Brookline, Mass., 1989-91, nursing supr., 1991-94, Milford Meadows, Milford, Mass., 1994-95; dir. quality imp. SunRise for Milford, 1995-99, charge nurse, 1999-2000; nurse mgr. SunBridge for Milford, 2002—; asst. mgr. Motyka Art & Frame Gallery Inc., Central Falls, RI, 2000—02. Mem. QA/QI Network Group, Newton, Mass., 1995-99. Contbr. numerous articles to profl. jours. Active parent Iskwelahang Pilipino, Boston, 1997-99; press rels. Philippine Cmty. N.E. Area, 1997, Mrs. Philippine Centennial, Found., R.I., 1998, Nat. Fedn. Filipo Am. Assns., 1998; leader, asst. troop 290 Brownies, 1997-99. Recipient Excellence award 10 yrs Girl Scouts USA, Milford, 1997. Mem. Philippine Nurses Assn. New Eng. (editor newsletter 1997, rec. sec. 1994-96, corr. sec. 1996-98, v.p. 1998-2000, Mem. of Yr. 2001). Avocations: oil painting, gardening, writing, arts and crafts, embroidery. Home: 14 Smith Hill Way Douglas MA 01516 Office: 79 Chestnut St Central Falls RI 02863-2005

BOLANOS, MARIA CECILIA MARUQEZ, medical association administrator; b. Quezon City, Manila, Philippines, Oct. 24, 1977; d. Wilfredo D. and Imelda M. Bolanos. BSBA, St. Louis U., 1999. Data analyst/ advt. coord. Missionary Assn. Mary Immaculate, Belleville, Ill., 1999—2000; mktg. coord./referral developer St. Alexius Hosp., Tenet Healthcare Corp., St. Louis, 2000—. Cons. NCADA, St. Louis, 2000—01. Mem.: Am. Mktg. Assn., St. Louis U. Young Alumni Assn., Gamma Phi Beta (life). Office: St Alexius Hosp Tenet Healthcare 2639 Miami St Saint Louis MO 63118 E-mail: cecilia.bolanos@tenethealth.com.

BOLAR, AMY LEIGH, music educator; b. Maysville, Ky., Nov. 17, 1972; d. Kenneth Allen and Cheryl Ann (Bierley) Souder; m. Keith Alan Bolar, Oct. 7, 1995. BA, Transylvania U., 1995; MA, Morehead State U., 2000. Cert. Nat. Bd. of Profl. Tchg. Standards, 2003. Music tchr. Flemingsburg (Ky.) Elem., 1995—. Edn. coord. Am. Guild English Handbell Ringers, 1998; component mgr. Flemingsburg Elem. Revision Com., 2001—. Dir. Flemingsburg Bicentennial Band, 1999; article writer Flemingsburg Elem., 1999—2000; accompanist local churches, Flemingsburg, 1995—. Recipient Golden Apple Recipient, 1999. Mem.: Music Educators Nat. Conf., Ky. Choral Dirs. Assn., Ky. Music Educators Assn., Chi Omega. Avocations: cats, candlemaking, stamp collecting, music. Home: 149 Mt Gilead Rd Flemingsburg KY 41041 Office: Flemingsburg Elem 245 W Water St Flemingsburg KY 41041

BOLDEN, MARION A. school system administrator; b. Apr. 26, 1946; 2 children. BA in Math Edn., Montclair State U., 1968, MA in Tchg., 1982. Tchr. math. Barringer H.S., Newark, 1968—82; dir. Office of Math., Newark Schs., 1989—96, assoc. supt. tchg. and learning, interim supt. for high schs., 1996—99, supt., 1999—. Avocations: antiques, collecting black memorabilia. Office: Newark Pub Schs 2 Cedar St Newark NJ 07102*

BOLDING, KANDY DENESE MYNEAR, special education educator; b. Pampa, Tex., Oct. 31, 1960; d. Carl Andrew and Eva Nell Mynear; m. Timothy Stewart Bolding, June 14, 1980; 1 child, Brandon Traye. A in Edn., Western Tex. Coll., 2000; BA in Humanities, U. Tex., Odessa, 2000, Tchg. Cert., 2002. Youth dir. Southside Bapt. Ch., Perryton, Tex., 1989—91; tchg. asst. Perryton H.S., 1991—94, Snyder (Tex.) Jr. H.S., 1994—98, James Brooks Mid. Sch., Midland, Tex., 1998—2000; spl. edn. tchr. Greenwood H.S., Midland, Tex., 2000—. Mem campus ednl. improvement com. [illegible] Brooks Mid. Sch., 1999—2000; mem. dist. ednl. improvement com. Greenwood H.S., 2000—. Mem.: ATPE, Coun. for Exceptional Children. Republican. Baptist.

BOLDOVITCH, GERRI, art educator; d. Joseph and Esther Boldovitch. AA, Miami Dade C.C., 1971; BA, Fla. Atlantic U., 1971—73; MS, St. Thomas U., 1980. Cert. profl. educator in art edn. K-12, prof. educator in specific learning disabilities K-12, profl. educator in varying exceptional edn. K-12, endorsement ESOL, educator English to spkrs. of other langs. Art instr. grades 10-12 Miami Norland Sr. H.S., Dade County Pub. Schs., Miami, 1973—74; art instr. K-6 Oak Grove Elem., Miami, 1974—78, Bay Harbor Elem., 1977—84; art instr. K-5 Greynolds Park Elem., Miami, 1984—87, Ojus Elem., Miami, 1987—89, North Beach Elem., Miami, 1989—91, Highland Oaks Elem., North Miami, 1991—94, Madie Ives Elem., Miami, 1994—2000, Hibiscus Elem., Miami, 1977—. Mem. PTA, Dade County Pub. Schs., Miami, 1977—2000; participant South Fla. State Comty. Safe Sch. Summit, Ft. Lauderdale, Fla., 1998. Etchings exhibited in London, sculpture exhibited in Mexico City, crafts exhibited in Can. Mem. Friends of the Everglades, Miami, 2003; contbr. United Way, Miami, 1973—2002. Mem.: PTA, NEA, Nat. Art Edn. Assn., United Tchrs. of Dade County. Avocations: theater, music, reading, art-related activities.

BOLDUC, DIANE EILEEN MARY BUCHHOLZ, psychotherapist; b. Elizabeth, N.J., May 1, 1953; d. Howard Robert and Barbara Ann (Bowen) Buchholz; m. David Vianney Buchholz Bolduc, May 21, 1977; children: Elizabeth, Katharine. BA cum laude in Psychology, U. N.H., 1975, MEd Counseling, 1976. Lic. clin. mental health counselor. Counselor, asst. supr., social worker III Divsn. Children & Youth Svcs., Manchester/Salem, NH, 1978—88; supr. Child Health Svcs., Manchester, NH, 1987—88; program coord. N.H. Task Force on Child Abuse & Neglect, Concord, 1988—91; dir. youth & family svcs. Luth. Social Svcs. New England, Concord, NH, 1992—94; home/sch. coord. Raymond Schs., NH, 1994—96; counselor Pelham H.S., NH, 1996—. Mem.: ACA, Am. Mental Health Counselors Assn., N.H. Sch. Counselors Assn., N.H. Mental Health Counselors Assn. (treas. 2001—), Women*Spirit*Song. Home: 189 Ray St Manchester NH 03104

BOLENE, ROSALIE STEELE (MARGARET BOLENE), bacteriologist, volunteer; b. Kingfisher, Okla., July 11, 1923; d. Clarence R. and Harriet (White) Steele; m. Robert V. Bolene, Feb. 6, 1948; children: Judith Kay, John Eric, Sally Sue, Janice Lynn, Daniel William. BS, U. Okla., 1946. Technican bacteriology dept. Okla. Dept. Health, Oklahoma City, 1946-48; asst. bacteriologist Henry Ford Hosp., Detroit, 1948-49; bacteriol. cons., also asst. bus. mgr. Ponca Gynecology and Obstetrics, Inc., 1956-92, ret. Organizing dir. Bi-Racial Coun., 1963; lay adviser Home Nursing Svc., 1967-68; mem. exec. bd. PTA, 1956-71; active various cmty. drives; sponsor Am. Field Svc.; patron Ponca Playhouse; bloodmobile vol. ARC; vol. Helpline; Rep. precint organizer, 1960. Mem. AAUW (treas. 1964-66), DAR (life, sec.-treas. 1961-67, 1st vice regent 1972-73, chpt. treas. 1974-84, chpt. chaplain 1991-2000, state schs. chmn. 1990-94), Kay-Noble County Med. Aux. (treas. 1957-58, 66-67), Ponca City Art Assn., Pioneer Hist. Soc., Okla. Heritage Assn., Okla. Hist. Soc., Friends Cultural Ctr., Mus. Found., Inc. (publicity chmn. 2000), Friends Md. Mansion, Daus. Founders and Patriots (life, state pres. 1980-84, registrar 1993-2001), Nat. Huguenot Soc. (corr. sec.), Hereditary Order First Families Mass. Daus. Am. Colonists (chpt. regent 1982-84, state flag chmn. 1990-92), Magna Charta Dames (treas. Okla. chpt. 1984, life), Plantagenet Soc., Order Colonial Physicians and Chirurgiens (life), Ancient and Honorable Arty. Co. Women Descs. Okla. Ct. (life, treas. 1983-84, registrar 1986-2001), Dames of Ct. of Honor, Colonial Dames of 17th Century, Daus. of Colonial Wrs (registrar 1998—), Colonial Daus. 17th Century, U. Okla. Assn. (life), Ponca City Music Club, Red Rose Garden Club (pres. 1983-84, treas. 1993-95), Twentieth Century Club (rec. sec. 1992-94), Wall St. Ladies Investment Club, Lambda Tau, Phi Sigma, Alpha Lambda Delta. Presbyterian (elder 1983-86, trustee 1998-2001). Home: 8722 NW 49th Dr Coral Springs FL 33067-1841 E-mail: rsbolene@bellsouth.net.

BOLES, LENORE UTAL, nurse psychotherapist, educator; b. N.Y.C., July 3, 1929; d. Joseph Leo and Dorothy (Grosby) Utal; m. Morton Schloss, Dec. 17, 1955 (div. May 1961); 1 child, Howard Alan Schloss; m. Sam Boles, May 24, 1962; children: Anne Leslie, Laurence Utal; stepchildren: Harlan Arnold, Robert Gerald. Diploma in nursing, Beth Israel Hosp. Sch. Nursing, 1951; BSN, Columbia U., 1964; MSN, U. Conn., 1977. Bd. cert. clin. specialist in adult psychiatry/ mental health nursing, advanced practice registered nurse. Staff nurse Beth Israel Hosp., N.Y.C., 1951, Kingsbridge VA Hosp., Bronx, N.Y., 1951-55; night supr. Gracie Square Hosp., N.Y.C., 1959-60; head nurse Elmhurst City Hosp., Queens, N.Y., 1960-62; nursing instr. Norwalk (Conn.) Hosp., 1966-74; asst. prof. U. Bridgeport, Conn., 1976-78; nurse psychotherapist Nurse Counseling Group, Ltd., Norwalk, 1979—2003, Changing Perspectives, LLP, Westport, 2003; nursing faculty Western Conn. State U., Danbury, 1978-80. Adj. asst. prof. Sacred Heart U., Bridgeport, Conn., 1983-89; adj. faculty Western Conn. State U., Danbury, 1994, 96-2000; lectr. Yale U. Sch. Nursing, 2000-02; nurse cons. Bradley Meml. Hosp., Southington, Conn., 1982, Lea Manor Nursing Home, Norwalk, 1982, St. Vincent's Hosp., Bridgeport, 1982-92; staff devel. nurse Silver Hill Hosp., New Canaan, Conn., 1980-86, 94; cons. in field, 1980—. Author: (book chpt.) Nursing Diagnoses for Psychiatric Nursing Practice, 1994. V.p. Sisterhood Beth El, Norwalk, 1969-71; bd. dirs. religious sch. Congregation Beth El, Norwalk, 1971-75, 79-80, rec. sec. bd. trustees, 1975-77, v.p. congregation, 1977-80, bd. trustees, 1980-83. Named Speaker of Yr., So. Fairfield County chpt. Am. Cancer Soc., 1976. Mem. ANA, Northeastern Nursing Diagnosis Assn. (chair N.E. region conf. 1985, chair planning com. 1984-85, chair nominating com. 1989-91), N.Am. Nursing Diagnosis Assn., Coun. Psychiat./Mental Health Clin. Specialists, Conn. Nurses Assn. (Del. to convs. 1975-2000, legis. com. dist. 3 1984-86, nominating com. 1988-90, Florence Wald award 1984, Conn. Nursing Diagnosis Conf. Group 1980-87), Conn. Soc. Nurse Psychotherapists (founding mem.). Democrat. Jewish. Avocations: travel, reading, gardening, spending time with grandchildren. Home: 173 E Rocks Rd Norwalk CT 06851-1715 Office: Changing Perspectives LLP 468 Post Rd E Ste A Westport CT 06880

BOLEY, DONNA JEAN, state legislator; b. Bens Run, W.Va., Dec. 9, 1935; d. Glen A. and Grace (Jones) Northcraft; m. Jack Edward Boley, 1956; children: Kari Lynn, Brian Lee. Student, W.Va. U., Parkersburg. Chmn. Pleasant County Rep. Exec. Com., 1978—; mem. W.Va. Senate, 1985—. Chmn. Rep. Platform. Com., W.Va.; 1st woman minority leader State Senate, 1991, 92, 93, 94, 95, 96. Mem. Nat. Rep. Platform Com. from W.Va., Houston, 1992, San Diego, 1996, Phila., 2000; exec. com. W.Va. Rep. Com., 1978—, W.Va. nat. committeewoman, 1992-2002; alt. del. Rep. Nat. Conv., 1984, del., 1988, 92, 96, 2000. Mem. St. Marys Women's Club (pres. 1972-74, 80-81). Republican. Methodist. Office: Rm 229W State Capitol Complex Charleston WV 25305

BOLGER, DOREEN, museum director; BA, Bucknell U., 1971; MA, U. Del., 1973; PhD, CUNY, 1983. Mem. curatorial staff Am. Wing Met. Mus. Art, N.Y.C., 1976—88, curator Am. painting and sculpture, 1989; curator painting and sculpture Amon Ctr. Mus., Ft. Worth, 1989-94; dir. RISD Mus., Providence, 1994-98, Balt. Mus. Art, 1998—. Panelist NEA, NEH; field reviewer Inst. for Mus. and Libr. Svcs.; curator women artists exhbn. for Govt. House, Annapolis, Md.; Ailsa Mellon Bruce vis. sr. fellow Ctr. for

Advanced Study in the Visual Arts Nat. Gallery of Art; lectr. in field. Bd. dirs. several orgns. Chester Dale fellow Met. Mus. Art; grantee NEH, Met. Mus. Art Office: Balt Mus Art 10 Art Museum Dr Baltimore MD 21218-3898

BOLGER, DORITA YVONNE FERGUSON, librarian; b. Sharon, Pa., Apr. 18, 1951; d. Harold Edward Ferguson and Pauline May McQueen Ferguson; m. Terrence James Bolger, Sept. 24, 1977; children: Sarah Catherine Pauline, Matthew Terrence. BA, Pa. State U., 1973; MLS, Clarion U., 1978. English tchr. Greenville (Pa.) Area Schs., 1974—75; libr. asst. Pa. State U., Sharon, 1975—81; ref. libr. Westminster Coll., New Wilmington, Pa., 1981—. Mem. industry review bd. Sage Pubs., Inc., Thousand Oaks, Calif., 2001—; book rev. editor, contbr. Jour. Interlibr. Loan, Document Delivery & Info. Supply Haworth Press, Binghampton, NY, 1999—. Co-author: (novels) Church and Social Action, 1990. Founding mem., chair Mercer County (Pa.) Commn. for Women, 1989—93. Mem.: ALA. Office: Westminster Coll McGill Libr 319 S Market St New Wilmington PA 16172 Office Phone: 724-946-7330.

BOLGER, MARY PHYLLIS JUDGE, special education educator; b. Newark, Aug. 19, 1926; d. Michael Francis and Loretta Margaret (Reinhardt) Judge; m. William Patrick Bolger, Nov. 27, 1948 (dec. May 1973); children: Loretta, Francis, Christopher, Michael. BA, Montclair State U., 1946; MA, Reading Specialist, Seton Hall U., 1973. Cert. reading specialist, tchr. English, social studies, Spanish, and reading, learning disabilities tchr., cons. Tchr. English Bd. Edn., Irvington, NJ, 1946-49; tchr. West Side HS, Newark, 1963-69; reading specialist Roosevelt Jr. HS, West Orange, NJ, 1969-77; learning disability tchr., cons. West Orange HS and Hazel Ave., 1977-91. Tchr. ESL South Orange (N.J.) Maplewood Adult Schs., 1949—64; adj. prof. edn. Seton Hall U., South Orange, 1974—96; cons. dept. curriculum and spl. svcs. West Orange Bd. Edn., 1987—2002, cons., workshop presenter, 2000—01; mem. adv. bd. Prospect Ho., East Orange, NJ, 1994—97; cons. to therapeutic friendship groups for retarded adults, 1999—; cons., workshop presenter Lifelong Learning Inst., Caldwell (N.J.) Coll., 2000—01; freelance lectr., workshop presenter. Editor: (book) Beyond Common Sense: The Art of Intelligent Living, 1992, doctoral dissertations Seton Hall U., 1993—97. Eucharistic min. St. Barnabas Hosp., Livingston, NJ, 1991—2001, Ward Homestead, Maplewood, NJ, 1992—2000; coord. eucharistic ministry to the homebound Our Lady of Sorrows, South Orange, NJ, 1989—2000, Homebound Ministry, 1989—2002. Mem.: Seton-Essex Reading Coun. (pres., v.p.), N.J. Reading Assn. (co-chairperson Reading/Learning Disabilities com.), South Orange Sr. Circle (rec. sec. 2001—), Rosary Altar Soc. Roman Catholic. Avocations: writing, travel, reading, watercolors. Home and Office: 34 Mitchell Ave Roseland NJ 07068-1306 E-mail: ga-ga@prodigy.net.

BOLIN, MARY JANE, director; d. Howard Leonard and Mary Irene (Ruther) Bolin. BA in Piano, Clarke Coll., 1970; MA, Columbia U., 1973, EdM, 1974, EdD, 1977. Cert. sch. adminstr. N.Y. Music tchr. Iowa City Grade Sch., 1968—70; instr. Bklyn. Coll., CUNY, 1971—73, prof., 1973—77; adminstr. N.Y.C. Bd. Edn., 1977—79, N.J. State Edn. Dept., Trenton, 1979—82; dir. N.J. State Sch. of the Arts, Montclair, 1982—86; supr. arts in edn. Nassau County BOCES, Garden City, NY, 1986—. Mem. bd. advisors WNET/12 PBS, N.Y.C., 1995—. Contbr. articles to profl. jours. Dir. Russian Am. Cultural Exch., L.I., NY, 1993—; honoree Russian Mission to the UN, N.Y.C., 1994; bd. dirs. N.Y. State Alliance for Arts Edn., Albany, 1987—91, L.I. Arts Coun., Freeport, NY, 1994—98. Named Educator of Yr., L.I. Arts Coun., 1998; grantee, N.Y. State Coun. on the Arts, 1987—98, U.S. Info. Agy./U.S. State Dept., 1991—99. Avocations: Russian studies, travel, theater, needlecrafts, writing. Office: BOCES of Nassau County 71 Clinton Rd Sea Cliff NY 11579

BOLLEN, SHARON KESTERSON, artist, educator; b. Cin., Apr. 27, 1946; d. Marc J. and Regina (Mills) Kesterson; m. Jerry H. Bollen, June 22, 1968; children: Heather, Christopher. BA in Art, Coll. of Mt. St. Joseph, Cin., 1968; MA in Art Edn., U. Cin., 1970, EdD in Art Edn., 1980. Tchr. art Marian H.S., Cin., 1968-77; prof. art Coll. of Mount St. Joseph, Cin., 1977—. Fabric surface design art works in juried and invitational regional and nat. exhbns.; book reviewer Nat. Art Edn. Assn. Women's Caucus newsletter, 1985—. Recipient Alumni Appreciation award Coll. of Mount St. Joseph, 1993, Disting. Teaching award, 1981. Mem. Nat. Art Edn. Assn. (Student Chpt. Sponsor award 1994, Outstanding Ohio Art Educator of Yr. 1990, Western Region Higher Edn. Art Educator of Yr. 2001), Ohio Art Edn. Assn. (Outstanding Art Educator 1988, Higher Edn. Art Educator of Yr. 2000), Nat. Surface Design Assn., Am. Crafts Coun., Nat. Mus. for Women in the Arts (charter), Georgia O'Keeffe Mus. Roman Catholic. Home: 1138 Cryer Ave Cincinnati OH 45208-2803 Office: Coll of Mount St Joseph Art Dept 5701 Delhi Rd Cincinnati OH 45233-1670

BOLLES, SUSAN, production designer; b. Boston, May 25, 1960; d. Peter Piper and Jacqueline Maoria (Gilmore) B. BA in Theater, U. Mass., 1982; MFA, NYU, 1985; cert., L'Univ. Cath. L'ouest, Angiers, France, 1980. Vis. lectr. Tisch Sch. of Arts NYU, 1997. Prodn. designer (feature films) The Suburbans, Myth of Fingerprints, His & Hers, Illtown, Denise Calls Up, Me & the Mob, Wide Sargasso Sea (AD), (TV) The Kids' Choise Awards, House of Buggin', ESPN's 2 Minute Drill, The MTV Beach House, The Rolonda Show, Inside the Comedy Mind, Night After Night, Turn It Up!, The Ben Stiller Show, Remote Control, also numerous Tn spls. and pilots. Recipient Broadcast Designers' award, 1989, 90. Mem. United Scenic Artists local 829 (exam judge 1986—, exam. com. 1991—), Art Dirs. Guild (local 876, nominated for excellence in prodn. design). Democrat. Unitarian Universalist. Fax: 213- 629-4692.

BOLLEY, ANDREA, artist; d. Hildo and Laura Pia (Maurino) B. BFA, U. Windsor, 1975. Tchr. Activity Ctr. Art Gallery Ont., 1979, 80, Arts Sake, Toronto, 1982. One-woman shows include IDA Gallery York U., 1976, Art Gallery Brant, 1977, Pollock Gallery, Toronto, 1977, 78, 80, Agnes Etherington Art Ctr., Kingston, 1981, Gallery One, Toronto, 1984, 85, 86, Klonaridis Gallery, Toronto, 1989, 90, 91, Upper Can. Brewing Co., 1993, Studio Show, 1994, 95, 96, 97, 98, 99, 2000, 2002, Masterworks Found., Bermuda, 2003; group exhbns. include Grapestake Gallery, San Francisco, 1980, Alta. Coll. Art, Calgary, 1980, Art Gallery Ont., 1981, Art Gallery Hamilton, 1981, Gallery One, 1984, 85, 86, Triangle N.Y., 1985, 91, Klonaridis Gallery, 1988, John Schweitzer Gallery, Montreal, 1989, Mississauga Civic Ctr. Art Gallery, 1990, Magnum Books, Ottawa, 1991, Bennington Coll., Vt., 1991, Upper Can. Brewing Co., 1992, Robert Kidd Gallery, Birmingham, Mich., 1999, Group of Ten Corkin-Shopland, Toronto, Can., 2003, McGill U., Montreal, 2003others; represented in permanent collections Can. Coun. Art Bank, Art Gallery Windsor, Labatt's Can. Ltd., Citicorp Ltd., Can., Can. Imperial Bank Commerce, Max Factor Ltd., Chatelaine Mag., J.E. Seagram Ltd., McGill Club, Imperial Oil, Citibank Can., Toronto-Dominion Bank, Casey House, Am. Express, Guaranty Trust, Abitibi Paper, Triangle, Toronto Sund, Arthur Gelgoot and Assoc., Premiere Mag., Bells & Whistles, and various pvt. collections. Grantee Ont. Arts Coun., 1975, 76, 78, 79, 84, 85, Can. Coun., 1976, 80; recipient Ont. Soc. Artists Purchase award J.E. Seagram and Son Ltd., 1980. Office: 132 Jarvis St Toronto ON Canada M5B 2B5 E-mail: andreabolley@hotmail.com.

BOLLMAN, PEGGY, art educator; b. Frankfurt, Germany, May 27, 1957; d. Julius and Renate Klimach; m. Leonard Ray Bollman, July 10, 1976; children: Melanie Lynn, Michael Brian, Jennifer Ann. BA in Art Edn., Ark. Tech U., 1990, MSE in Gifted Talented Edn., 1994. Cert. tchr. Ark. State Dept Edn., 1991. Art tchr. Lamar (Ark.) HS, 1991—. Evangilism chmn. Grace Luth. Ch., Clarksville, Ark., 2002—. Mem.: Ark. Art Educators Assn. (dir. 2002—, named Secondary Art Tchr. of Yr. 2001), Nat. Art Educators Assn. Lutheran. Home: 2427 County Road 3470 Clarksville AR 72830 Office: Lamar School District 301 Elberta St Lamar AR 72846 Personal E-mail: lamar_art@yahoo.com. E-mail: pbollman@lamar.wsc.k12.ar.us.

BOLLS, IMOGENE LAMB, English language educator, poet; b. Manhattan, Kans., Sept. 25, 1938; d. Don Q. and Helen Letson (Keithley) Lamb; m. Nathan J. Bolls, Jr., Nov. 24, 1962; 1 child, Laurel Helen. BA, Kans. State U., 1960; MA, U. Utah, 1962. Instr. French Kans. State U., Manhattan, 1959-60; instr. English U. Utah, Salt Lake City, 1960-62; instr. to prof. Wittenberg U., Springfield, Ohio, 1963—. Poet-in-residence, dir. journalism program Wittenberg U.; tchg. poet Antioch Writers' Workshop Antioch Coll., summers, 1992—93; intensive seminar poet Antioch Writers' Workshop Antioch Coll., summer, 1994; poetry tchr. Ohio Poet-in-the-Schs. program, 1972—82; poetry instr. acad. camp; state and nat. poetry judge. Author: (poetry) Glass Walker, 1983, Earthbound, 1989, Advice for the Climb, 1999, works represented in anthologies; contbr. more than 600 poems to mags. Recipient Individual Artist award Ohio Arts Coun., 1982, 90, Poetry prize S.D. Rev., 1983, Poetry award Kans. Quarterly, 1985, Ohioana Poetry award Ohioana Libr. Assn., 1995; finalist Vassar Miller Prize in Poetry, 1994; grantee Ireland, 1986, France, 1990, Am. Southwest. Mem. Acad. Am. Poets (assoc.), Poetry Soc. Am., Women in Comm. Avocations: Native American cultures, hiking, photography, music, travel. Address: PO Box 2917 Taos NM 87571

BOLSTER, JACQUELINE NEBEN (MRS. JOHN A. BOLSTER), communications consultant; b. Woodhaven, N.Y. d. Ernest William Benedict and Emily Claire (Guck) Neben; m. John A. Bolster, May 8, 1954. Studied, Pratt Inst., Columbia U. Promotion mgr. Photoplay mag., 1949—53; merchandising mgr. McCall's, N.Y.C., 1953—64; dir. promotion and merchandising Harper's Bazaar, N.Y.C., 1964—71; dir. advt. and promotion Elizabeth Arden Salons, N.Y.C., 1971—76; dir. creative svcs. Elizabeth Arden, Inc., 1976—78; dir. comm. Elizabeth Arden Salons, 1978—87; comm. cons., 1987—. Recipient Art Dir.'s award, 1961, 1966. Mem.: Fashion Execs. Roundtable, Fashion Group, Advt. Women N.Y. (life), Women's Nat. Rep. Club (life). Episcopalian. Home and Office: 8531 88th St Woodhaven NY 11421-1308 also: Halsey Neck Ln Southampton NY 11968

BOLSTERLI, MARGARET JONES, English educator, farmer; b. Watson, Ark., May 10, 1931; d. Grover Clevel and Zena (Cason) Jones; m. Mark Bolsterli, Dec. 30, 1953 (div. Dec. 1964); children: Eric, David. BA with honors, U. Ark., 1952; MA, Washington U., St. Louis, 1953; PhD, U. Minn., 1967. Asst. prof. Augsburg Coll., Mpls., 1967-68; prof. English, U. Ark., Fayetteville, 1968-93, prof. emeritus, 1993—, dir. Ctr. for Ark. and Regional Studies, 1984-87. Fulbright lectr., Portugal, 1986; vis. rsch. fellow Yale U., 1997-98; bd. dirs. Ark. Humanities Coun., 1992-94. Author: The Early Community at Bedford Park, 1977, Vinegar Pie and Chicken Bread, 1982, Born in the Delta, 1991, A Remembrance of Eden, 1993; contbr. articles and stories to Jour. Modern Lit., So. Quar., others. NEH Younger Humanist grantee, 1970-71; Ark. Endowment for Humanities grantee, 1980, 81 Mem. MLA (pres. women's caucus), South Cen. MLA. Democrat. E-mail: mbolster@alltel.net.

BOLT, DAWN MARIA, financial coach, stock trader; b. Bklyn., June 12, 1949; d. Gulick Arthur B. and Georgette Helen (Werner) Bolt-Wiggs; widowed; children: Robert B. Williams, Wesley A. Williams. BA, Bklyn. Coll., 1971. Cert. fin. planner, chartered fin. analyst. Fin. analyst Blyth Eastman Dillon, N.Y.C., 1971-77; rating agy. analyst Fitch Investors Svc., N.Y.C., 1977-78; bank analyst Merrill Lynch, N.Y.C., 1978-80; fin. analyst Moodys Investors Svc., N.Y.C., 1980-86; real estate sales agt. J.R. Silvers Realty, N.Y.C., 1987-95, Coldwell Banker Hunt Kennedy, N.Y.C., 1995-98; pvt. practice fin. planning and coaching, 1998—. Avocations: bowling, tennis, skiing, reading, coaching. E-mail: jodiedawn49@hotmail.com.

BOLT, EUNICE MILDRED DEVRIES, artist; b. Clifton, N.J., Oct. 31, 1926; d. Lambert H. and Cora DeVries; m. Maurice L. Bolt (dec. Nov. 1989); children: Macyn Bolt, Tamsen Bolt, Valerie Bolt Wegner. Grad., Pratt Inst. Art & Design, Bklyn., 1949; BA, Calvin Coll., 1952; MA, Western Mich. U., 1973. Book illustrator Fideler Pubs., Grand Rapids, Mich., 1952-53, Zondervan Pub. Co., Grand Rapids, Mich., 1953-56; prof. Calvin Coll., Grand Rapids, Mich., 1962-67, Grand Rapids C.C., 1968-91. Internat. art study tours coord. and guide, 1978—; fine art exhbn. juror, 1987—; lectr. art history, 1991—, presenter watercolor workshops, 1991—; artist-in-residence, 1995—. Exhibited in group shows at Grand Rapids Art Mus., Kalamazoo Inst. Art, U. Mich. Schlusser Gallery, Pitts. Ctr. for the Arts, Westmoreland Mus. Art, Detroit Inst. Art. Home and Studio: 2481 Autumn Ash Dr Grand Rapids MI 49512 Studio: 110 Arango Ct Bluffton SC 29909-4580 E-mail: eunboltstudio@aol.com.

BOLT, LYNDA ELAINE, alcohol/drug abuse services professional; b. Beverly, Mass., Feb. 5, 1941; d. Emil Henry and Gladys Evelyn (Crane) Forss; m. William Coventry Henderson II, Jan. 12, 1980 (div. Aug. 1989); m. Chris Bolt, Feb. 14, 1992. BSc in Mgmt. Studies, U. Md.; MSc in Counseling & Human Devel., Troy State U. Lic. mental health counselor Fla., cert. addiction profl. Fla., cognitive-behavioral therapist Nat. Assn. Cognitive Behavioral Therapy, registered addiction specialist Fla., cert. alcohol drug counselor Internat. Cert. & Reciprocity Consortium. Social svc. asst. USN, Naples, Italy, 1987—88, facilitator, 1988—89; from addiction counselor to program dir. Twelve Oaks, Navarre, Fla., 1989—94, program dir., 1994—95; outpatient program dir. APOGEE, Ft. Walton Beach, Fla., 1995—97; substance abuse coord. ALTACARE, Ft. Walton Beach, 1998—99; pvt. practice Destin Counseling, Destin, Fla., 1997—2003, Elen P. Gajo M.D. & Assoc., Ft. Walton Beach, 1999—; outpatient program mgr. N.W. Fla. Counsel Alcohol and Drug Dependencies, Ft. Walton Beach, Fla., 2000—02; dir. Lifestyle Solutions and Counseling Ctr., Navarre, Fla., 2000—03. Presenter in field. Mem.: Nat. Assn. Cognitive Behavioral Therapy, Fla. Counseling Assn., Fla. Mental Health Counselors Assn., Fla. Alcohol and Drug Abuse Assn., Gulf Coast Mental Health Counselors Assn., Am. Counseling Assn., Am. Mental Health Counselors Assn. Avocations: tennis, swimming. Office: 348 Miracle stry Parkway Fort Walton Beach FL 32548

BOLTON, BETTY J. medical/surgical nurse, poet; b. Lusedale, Miss., Sept. 2, 1952; d. Saul Jones and Mary Hurley Fairley; m. Joe N. Bolton, July 28, 1968; children: Terry, Benilda, Timiki; 1 child, Joe Jones. AAS, Miss. Gulf Coast Jr. Coll., 1986; postgrad., Coastal Tng., Pascagoula, Miss., 1989. Libr. ref. aide Pascagoula Libr., Miss., 1986—89; program specialist I Salvation Army Domestic Violence Women, Pascagoula, Miss., 1986—90; owner B&J Vending, Moss Point, Miss., 1990—92; home health nurse Profl. Home Health, Biloxi, Miss., 1992—97; supr. South Miss. Regional Ctr., Long Beach, Miss., 1997—99; pvt. duty nurse Jackson County and South Miss., 2000—03. Author (poetry): Best Poems of 2002, 2002 (Editors Choice award, 2002), Across the Abyss, 2002 (Editors Choice award, 2002), Best Poems of 2003, 2003 (Editors Choice award, 2003). Recipient Pres. award, Iliad Press, 2003. Mem.: Ri Rsch., Acad. Am. Poets, Internat. Soc. Poets. Ch. Of Christ. Avocations: arts and crafts, sewing, walking, creative cooking, poetry. Home: 3809 Jeffery Dr Moss Point MS 39562

BOLTON, ELIZABETH (MARGARET BOLTON), artist, poet; b. Cranston, R.I., Sept. 7, 1919; d. James Ewart and Pamela (White) Hill; m. Archer Leroy Bolton Jr., Nov. 29, 1941; children: Wendy, Daria, Pamela, James. Student, Colby Sawyer Coll., 1936-39. Sec. Dr. Augustus Thorndike, Boston, 1939-41; sec. rehab. orgn. Mass. Gen. Hosp., Boston, 1950-51; sec. NAS, Washington, 1957-60, Mitre Corp. Electronics, Burlington, Mass., 1961-62; exec. sec. Manpower, Burlington, 1961-69; sec. RCA, Burlington, 1962-63; substitute tchr. art pub. HS, various cities, Mass., 1970-81. Exhibited in group shows (2d and 3d prize, 1978, 1st prize, 1979); poet pub. in New Voices, 1981, Golden Treasury of Great Poems, 1989, Vol. II, 1989, Summer Treasury of Poems of America, 1992, Fall Treasury of Poems of America, 1992, America at the Millennium: Best Poems and Poets of the 20th Century, 2000; author: Safe in the Arms of Jesus, 2000, (poetry) New Song, 2001. Mem. Friends of the Libr., 1986—, Exeter Area Art Assn. Recipient 1st prize, Merrimack Valley Art Assn., 1979, Nashua Art Assn., 1986, Rockport Bd. Trade Show, 2001, Haverhill Art Assn., 2001, 2d prize, Newburyport Art Assn., 1977, Award of Merit Certs. (2), World of Poetry, 1988, Golden Poet award, 1989, World of Poetry, 1992, Editor's Choice award, Internat. Libr. Poetry, 2001. Mem. Christian Ch. Avocations: music, singing, writing, photography, bicycling, bird watching. Home: 12 Glen Dr Hampstead NH 03841-2242

BOLTON, MARTHA O. writer; b. Searcy, Ark., Sept. 1, 1951; d. Lonnie Leon and Eunice Dolores Ferren; m. Russell Norman Bolton, Apr. 17, 1970; children: Russell Norman II, Matthew David, Anthony Shane. Grad. high sch., Reseda, Calif. Freelance writer for various comedians, 1975-86; newspaper columnist Simi Valley Enterprise, Simi, Calif., 1979-87; staff writer Bob Hope, 1986—, The Mark and Kathy Show, 1995-96. Author: A Funny Thing Happened to Me on My Way Through the Bible, 1985, A View from the Pew, 1986, What's Growing Under Your Bed?, 1986, Tangled in the Tinsel, 1987, So. How'd I Get To Be in Charge of the Program?, 1988, Humorous Monologues, 1989, Let My People Laugh, 1989, If Mr. Clean Calls Tell Him I'm Not In, 1989, Journey to the Center of the Stage, 1990, If You Can't Stand the Smoke, Get Out of My Kitchen, 1990, Home, Home on the Stage, 1991, TV Jokes and Riddles, 1991, These Truths Were Made for Walking, 1991, When the Meatloaf Explodes It's Done, 1993, Childhood Is a Stage, 1993, Honey, It's Time To Weed the Carpets Again, 1994, Walk A Mile in His Truths, 1994, The Cafeteria Lady on the Loose, 1994, On the Loose, 1994, If the Pasta Wiggles, Don't Eat It, 1995, Bethlehem's Big Night, 1995, Club Family, 1995, When the Going Gets Tough, The Tough Start Laughing, 1995, Who Put The Pizza in the VCR?, 1996, And Now a World from Our Maker, 1997, A Lamb's Tale, 1998, (lyrics) Mouth in Motion, Sermon on the Stage, 1998, Never Ask Delilah For A Trim, 1998, (with Mark Lowry) Piper's Night Before Christmas, (with Gene Perret) Talk About Hope, The Twelve Plays of Christmas, 1999, Don't Jump to Conclusions Without a Bungee Cord, 1999, I Love You...Still, 2000, Didn't My Skin Used to Fit, 2000, Piper Steals the Show, 2000, The "Official" Book series, 2002—, I Think Therefore I Have a Headache, 2003. Pres. Vista Elem. Sch. PTA, Simi, 1980-81. Recipient Emmy nomination for outstanding achievement in music and lyrics, 1988, Internat. Angel award, 1990, 91, 2001, 02, Amb. award Media Fellowship Internat., 1995. Mem. ASCAP, NATAS, Nat. League Am. Pen Women (pres. Simi Valley br. 1984-86, 96-98, Woman of Achievement award 1984, Pen Woman of Yr. award 1995, pres. 1996-98), Writers Guild Am. West, Soc. Children's Book Writers. Avocation: travel. Office: PO Box 3046 Brentwood TN 37024 E-mail: marthabolton@aol.com.

BOLTUCK, MARY A. retired psychologist, educator; b. Yellow Springs, Ohio, Nov. 2, 1924; d. Clyde Stewart and Sarah (Walker) Adams; m. Charles J. Boltuck, July 16, 1950; children: Richard Dale, Jane Ellen. BA, Miami U., Oxford, Ohio, 1946; MA, State U. Iowa, 1948. Clin. psychologist Wichita Guidance Ctr., 1948-50; psychologist/probation Monroe County, Bloomington, Ill., 1950-53; clin. psychologist Galesburg (Ill.) State Residential Hosp., 1953-55, Kent (Ohio) State U., 1957-64; from asst. prof. to assoc. prof. psychology St. Cloud (Minn.) State U., 1964-90. Tchr., workshop facilitator, spkr., 1990—. Mem.: APA, AAUW (life), Assn. Prevention Elder Abuse, Assn. Prevention of Child Abuse, Minn. Women Psychologists, Minn. Psycol. Assn., Midwest Psychol. Assn., Nat. Coun. on Aging, Ctrl. Minn. Psychol. Assn., Psi Chi (life; psychol. hon. advisor 1978—90). Avocations: travel, reading, knitting, walking, conservation. Home: 2830 Edward Dr Saint Cloud MN 56301-9104

BOLTZ, MARY ANN, aerospace materials company executive, travel agency executive; b. Far Rockaway, N.Y., Jan. 12, 1923; d. Thomas and Theresa (Domanico) Caparelli; m. William Emmett Boltz; children: Valerie Ann Boltz Austin, Beverly Theresa, Cynthia Marie Boltz O'Rourke. Grad. high sch., Lawrence, N.Y., 1941. Publicist CBS, N.Y.C., 1943-48; mgr. Coast-Line Internat. Distbrs. Ltd., Lindenhurst, N.Y., 1961-80, v.p., 1980-86, pres., 1987-90, CEO, 1990—; chief exec. officer Air Ship 'N Shore Travel, Woodmere, N.Y. and Marco Island, Fla., 1978—. Pres. Bangor Realty, 1975. Formerly radio and TV editor local publs., writer Gotham Guide mag. Sec. Inwood Civic & Businessmen's Assn., 1952-64, pres., 1964-66, chmn. bd., 1967-68; pres. Lawrence Pub. Schs. System PTA, 1956-58; pres., life mem. Cen. Coun. PTA, 1958-60; founder Inwood Civic Scholarship Fund, 1964; v.p. Econ. Opportunity Coun., Inwood; mem. fundraising bd. yearly ball St. Joachim Ch., Cedarhurst, N.Y.; gift chmn. L.I. Bd. Boys Town of Italy; bd. dirs. Marco Island Cancer Fund Dr.; dir., promoter Marco Island Philharmonic Symphony; dir. polit. campaign William Sieffert, Oceanside, N.Y.; chmn. 30 yr. reunion Class of 41, 1971, 50 yr. reunion, 1991, 55th yr. Lawrence H.S. reunion Class of 1938, 39, 40, 41, 42; asst. chmn. 50 yr. reunion Class of 42, 1991, Lawrence H.S. 55th Reunion Class of 1941, 1996; fundraiser Stecker and Horowitz Sch. Music Dinner Com., 1978, Am. Bus. Women's Assn., Long Island charter chptr., Rockville Centre, N.Y., 1990-92, United Fund, Red Feather Ball, 1992. Recipient award Nassau Herald Newspaper, Cedarhurst, Inwood Civic Assn., PTA Life Membership award, 25 Yr. Silver Medallion Boys Town of Italy, gold medal, 1995, Citizen of Yr. Bronze Plaque award Inwood Civic Assn., 1996; named Woman of the Year Boys Town of Italy, 1997. Mem. Am. Bus. Women's Assn. (L.I. charter chpt.), Nissoquogue Golf Club, Sun 'N Surf Beach Club, Island Country Club (Marco Island, Fla.), Desert Mountain Country Club. Republican. Roman Catholic. Home: 149 Hempstead Ave Rockville Centre NY 11570-2904 Office: Coast-Line Internat Distbrs 274 Bangor St Lindenhurst NY 11757-3633 Office Phone: 516-226-0500.

BOMAR, BUNNYE M. secondary school educator; b. Jasper, Fla., Sept. 2, 1941; d. James Alton and Louise Hutcherson McLauchlin; m. James Ludlow Bomar, July 11, 1964; children: James Ludlow, Timothy. BS, Fla. State U., 1963; MEd, Rollins Coll., Winter Park, Fla., 1981. Tchr. Orange County Sch. Bd., Orlando, Fla., 1963—64, Leon County Sch. Bd., Tallahassee, 1964—67; tchr. advanced placement English Seminole County Sch. Bd., Sanford, Fla., 1983—. Reader English advanced placement Coll. Bd., Princeton, NJ, 2001. Adv. bd. Seminole County Libr., Sanford, 1984—88. Named Tchr. of the Yr., Lake Mary H.S., 1987—88. Mem.: NEA, AAUW, Fla. Edn. Assn., Fla. Coun. Tchrs. English. Methodist. Avocations: reading, boating, travel, shopping. Home: 17 Cardinal Dr Longwood FL 32779

BOMAR, LAURA BETH, music educator; b. Atlanta, Ga., Feb. 24, 1965; d. Alvie Troy and Mary Elizabeth Elliott; m. Robert Linton Bomar, June 27, 1987; 1 child, Sarah Beth. AA, Brewton-Parker Coll., 1985; BA, Tift Coll., 1987; MusM, Ga. State U., 1993. Music tchr. Butts County Schools, Jackson, Ga., 1987—. Team leader North Mulberry Elem. Sch., Jackson, Ga., 1999—, sch. coun. mem., 2003—. Mem.: Music Educators Nat. Conf., PA of Ga. Educators (bldg. rep. 2001—03). Protestant. Avocations: hiking, camping, biking, reading. Office: North Mulberry Elem Sch 820 N Mulberry St Jackson GA 30233

BOMBARDIERI, MERLE ANN, psychotherapist; b. Atlanta, Mar. 16, 1949; d. Sol and Sadie (Drucker) Malkoff; m. Rocco Anthony Bombardieri, Jr., Aug. 22, 1971; children: Marcella, Vanessa. B.A. in Psychology, Mich. State U., 1971; M.S.W., San Diego State U., 1976. Cert. clin. social workers, Mass., clin. hypnosis Am. Soc. Clin. Hypnosis; Diplomate Nat. Assn. Social Workers, Am. Bd. Examiners in Clin. Social Work. Crisis intervention worker and trainer Listening Ear, East Lansing, Mich., 1969-71; tchr. English as 2d lang. Instituto Brasil Estados Unidos, Rio de Janeiro, 1971-73; supr. infant unit Married Student Day Care Ctr., Mich. State U., East Lansing, 1973-74; psychotherapist/family life educator Family Svc. Assocs., San Diego, 1975-77; psychotherapist Dade Wallace Mental Health Ctr., Nashville, 1977-78; psychotherapist/workshop leader Met. [illegible] Mental Health Ctr., Waltham, Mass., 1980-81; pvt. practice psychotherapy, Acton-Belmont, Mass., 1982—; clin. dir. Resolve, Inc., infertility orgn., Belmont, 1982-84; clin. cons., 1984—; cons. HealthData Internat., Westport, Conn., 1983—, Open Door Soc., Newton, Mass., 1983—, First Day Film Corp., 1985—, Mass. Dept. Social Svcs., 1987; sec. Boston Fertility Soc., 1995, others; psychology seminar leader; radio and TV appearances. Author: The Baby Decision, 1981, (cassettes) Your Mind's Own Medicine, 1998; founder, editor, pub. Wellspring newsletter; contbr. articles to profl. and med. jours. N.Y. State Regents scholar, 1967; NIMH trainee, 1970. Mem. Acad. Cert. Social Workers, Phi Beta Kappa, Phi Kappa Phi. Home: 4 Broadview Rd Acton MA 01720-4202 Office: 33 Bedford St Lexington MA 02420-4319

BOMCHILL, FERN CHERYL, lawyer; b. Chgo., Feb. 25, 1948; BA, U. Mich., 1969; JD, U. Chgo., 1972. Bar: Ill. 1972, U.S. Dist. Ct. (no. dist.) Ill. 1972, U.S. Ct. Appeals (7th cir.) 1986. Ptnr. Mayer, Brown & Platt, Chgo. Mem. ABA, Fed. Bar Assn. (bd. dirs. Chgo. chpt.), Chgo. Coun. Lawyers, Law Club Chgo., Legal Club Chgo., The Menomonee Club for Boys and Girls (bd. dirs., pres. 1993-94). Office: Mayer Brown & Platt 190 S La Salle St Ste 3100 Chicago IL 60603-3441

BOMHAN, RUTH WALKER, social studies educator; b. Wilmington, N.C, Dec. 17, 1955; d. Robert Henry and Edna (Barritt) Walker; m. Kenneth Earl Bomhan (div.); 1 child, Kenneth Earl Jr. BA, U. N.C., Wilmington, 1984. Cert. tchr. social studies. Tchr. New Hanover H.S., Wilmington, 1984-85, Hoggard Night Sch., Wilmington, 1985-88, Lakeside H.S., Wilmington, 1988-2000, Roland-Grise Mid. Sch., Wilmington, 2000—. Mem. Smithsonian Instn., Civil War Trust, Nat. Geog. Soc., Mus. of Confederacy, World War II Meml., N.C. Coun. Social Studies, Libr. Congress, Nat. Trust Historic Preservation, Friends of Nat. Park Gettysburg, N.C. Assn. Educators, Nat. Honor soc. Polit. Sci., Colonial Williamsburg Found. Avocations: bowling, lapidary, reading, travel, martial arts. Office: Roland-Grise Mid Sch 4412 Lake Ave Wilmington NC 28403

BOMHOF, ROBYN, artist, educator; b. Chgo., June 19, 1952; d. Emmett Earl and Ruth Carolyn Miller; m. James Alan Bomhof, Dec. 27, 1974; children: Russell, Allyson, Jessica. BFA with honors, Kendall Coll. Art and Design, Grand Rapids, Mich., 1997; MFA, Western Mich. U., 2001. Youth program dir. West YMCA, Grand Rapids, 1968-72; program dir. Vic Tanny, Inc., Detroit, 1974-76; creative dir., artist Genesis Advt., Grand Rapids, 1977-79; artist self employed, Grand Rapids, 1970—; tchr. Western Mich. U., Kalamazoo, 1998—2001, asst. dir. exhbns., 1999—2001. Mem. exec. bd. Westside Christian Sch., Grand Rapids, 1988-91; charter mem. Rivertown Artists Guild, Grand Rapids, 1990—; dir. word fellowship Sunshine Ministries, Grand Rapids, 1988-89. One-woman shows include Kendall Coll. Art and Design, 1997, Riley Galleries/Rapture, 1999, Western Mich. U., 2000, Newago Coun. for Arts 2002, exhibited in group shows at Fine Arts Gallery, 1998, Great Lakes Regional Competition, 1997, 1998, 1999, 2000, Lowell Coun. for the Arts Regional Show, 1997, Ferris State U., 1996, Muskegon Mus. Art, 1998 (Curator's award), Festival Regional, Grand Rapids, 1999, ARC Gallery, Chgo., 1999, Battle Creek Ctr. for the Arts, 1999, Carnegie Ctr. for Arts, 1999 (Best of Show), Kalamazoo Inst. of Art, 2000, works in various pub. and pvt. collections. Recipient awards for art and design; Vt. Studio Ctr. grantee, 1999; Western Mich. U. grantee, 1999; travel grantee Dietre Heineke. Mem. AAUW, Coll. Art Assn., Grand Rapids Kennel Club (bd. dirs. 1976-85), Friesian Horse Assn. N.Am., Am. Driving Soc., Carriage Assn. N.Am., Mich. Horse Drawn Vehicle Assn. Avocations: reading, dogs, cats, Friesian horses, driving. Home: Black Oak Farm 1701 14 Mile Rd Sparta MI 49345

BONACORSI, MARY CATHERINE, lawyer; b. Henderson, Ky., Apr. 24, 1949; d. Harry E. and Johanna M. (Kelly) Mack; m. Louis F. Bonacorsi, Apr. 23, 1971; children: Anna, Kathryn, Louis. BA in Math., Washington U., St. Louis, 1971; JD, Washington U., 1977. Bar: Mo. 1977, Ill. 1981, U.S. Dist. Ct. (ea. dist.) Mo., U.S. Dist. Ct. (so. dist.) Ill., U.S. Ct. Appeals (8th cir.), U.S. Supreme Ct. 1995. Ptnr. Thompson Coburn, St. Louis, 1977—. Chairperson fed. practice com. eastern dist., St. Louis, 1987—, eight cir. jud. conf. com., St. Louis, 1987—. Mem. ABA, Assn. Trial Lawyers of Am., Mo. Bar Assn., Met. St. Louis Bar Assn., Am. Bd. Trial Advocates (assoc.), Order of Coif. Office: Thompson Coburn Firstar Plz Ste 3100 Saint Louis MO 63101 E-mail: mbonacorsi@thompsoncoburn.com.

BONANNI, VICTORIA, writer; b. Jersey City, N.J., Dec. 13, 1952; d. Joseph Salvatore and Dolores DiMaria (Aidala) B. BA in English/Secondary Edn., SUNY, Stony Brook, 1974. Cert. ESL tutor, electronics technician. Sec., retail newsletter editor Zayre, Inc., Framingham, Mass., 1974; temporary sec., adminstrv. asst. Manpower, Inc., Salem, Mass., 1975; reporter/photographer The Beverly (Mass.) Times, 1976; mktg. comm. coord. United Shoe Machinery Corp., Middleton, Mass., 1977-79; adminstrv. writer HBH Co., Rosslyn, Va., 1979-80; technical writer Teradyne, Inc., Boston, 1981-89; sr. technical writer Panametrics, Inc., Waltham, Mass., 1989, EMC Corp., Hopkinton, Mass., 1991; owner, prin. writer VB Documentation Enterprises, Natick, Mass., 1991—; part-time customer svc. rep. May Dept. Stores Co. (Filene's), Natick, 1998—. Author, editor: A Blue Perfume, 1993; editor: Dolorata: Looking To The Future (Dolores Fiore), 1995, Burning Heads (Lawrence Carradini), 1996, A Bowl of Cherries: Just Spit The Pits (Mark Willman), 1996, I Wish That My Room Had a Floor Living With An Emotional Disorder (Rafael Woolf), 1996, A Pen Is Like A Piece (Gary Hicks), 1997, Hot Moon Night (Ann Murphy Fletcher), 1998, Of Rare Design (William J. Barnum), 1999; author: Ad Vivum, 2001. Direct mail fund raiser-coord. Kennedy Sr. Ctr., Natick, 1997. Recipient honorable mention "Writer's Digest", Cin., 1993, 2001, 80 Hrs. Cmty. Svc. award Natick Vis. Nurse Assn., 1996; recipient Cambridge Poetry Award, 2nd prise, Mass., 2001. Mem. NAFE, Soc. Am. Poets, Natick Ctr. Assocs. Roman Catholic. Avocations: original greeting cards, miniatures, historical perspectives, theology, songwriting.

BONANNO, THERESA M. nursing administrator; Exec. dir. Mass. Bd. of Registration Nursing, Boston. Office: Mass Bd Registration in Nursing 239 Causeway St Boston MA 02114-2130

BONASSI, JODI, artist, marketing consultant; b. LA, Aug. 22, 1953; d. Julian and Sara (DeNorber) Feldman; m. Raymond Gene Bonassi, June 7, 1986; 1 child, Spencer. Student, Otis Art Inst., L.A., 1972, Calif. State U., 1983-85, Calif. State U., Northridge, 1985-86. Participating artist Concern Found. and World Cup Soccer Gala Event for Cancer Rsch., Beverly Hills, Calif., 1994; lectr., guest spkr. L.A. Pub. Libr., Canoga Park, 1999, Pierce Coll., 2003; mem. adv. bd. Park LaBrea Art Coun.; guest spkr. Pierce Coll., 2003; art tchr. Learning Tree, Chatsworth, Calif., 2004. Artist, Creative With Words Publs., 1987, greeting cards, 1994—; one-woman shows include Pt. Adesa Gallery, Rancho Mirage, Calif., 1996, Orlando Gallery, 1999, Performing Arts Gallery, Calif. State U., Northridge, 2002; exhibited in group shows at Bowles-Sorokko Gallery, Beverly Hills, 1994, ChaCha-Cha, Encino, Calif., 1994—, Lyn/Bassett Gallery, L.A., 1994, Topanga (Calif.) Canyon Gallery, 1994, Hartog Fine Art Gallery, L.A., 1995, Charles Hecht Gallery, Tarzana, Calif., 1995, New Canyon Gallery, Topanga, 1995, Made With Kare, West Hills, Calif., 1995, Gail Michael Collection, Northridge, 1995, Mythos Gallery, Burbank, 1995-96, Nicole Brown Simpson Found., 1996, Orlando Gallery, Sherman Oaks, Calif., 1998, West Gallery, U. Calif., Fullerton, 1998, The Century Gallery at Mission Coll., 1998, Orlando Gallery, 1998-99, Christie's Beverly Hills Silent Auction, 1999, Palos Verdes Art Ctr. Gallery, 1999, White Meadows Gallery, 2000, St. Louis Artist Guild Gallery, 2000, Bank of Am., Laguna Beach, 2000, Almost Paradise Gallery, Laguna Beach, 2d City Gallery, Long Beach, 2002-03, Cambridge Nat. Prize Show, 2002-03, Beckstrand Gallery, Palos Verdes, 2003, Pierce Art Gallery, Woodland Hills, Calif., 2003, Lankershim Art Gallery, North Hollywood, Calif., 2003, [illegible] Art Gallery, West Hills, Calif., 2004, others; represented in pvt. collections; commd. works include Von's Corp., Alhambra Bus. Assn., North Hollywood Revitalization Program, MTA of N. Hollywood Fence Panel Project, 2003; illustrator All About Us, 1996; featured in books including Living Artists, 13th edit., 2003, New Art Internat., 4th edit., 2003, Community of Angels Book, 2001; featured in articles and art revs. including Pasadena Star News and Pasadena Weekly, The Chronicle Rev., LA Daily News, Harpers Mag., Boston Globe, 2003, also Showtime Cable-TV Film: Trust Me, 1997, Chandler Outdoor Gallery Documentary, 2002, others; featured artist in Living Artist, 2003. Art tchr. K-12 West Valley Christian Ch. Schs., 1997—. Recipient Best Banner 2d prize LA County Mus. Art, Park LaBrea Arts Couns. for PLB/LACMA Family Art Fund, 1997, World Peace Tour, 1997, Spl. Judges Art award Park LaBrea Art Coun., 1998, nat. prize Cambridge Art Assn., 2002, Outstanding Painting award Nat. Portrait Gallery, Washington, 2003, Smithsonian Nat. Portrait Gallery. Mem. Calif. Women Bus. Owners, L.A. Mcpl. Art Gallery Registry, So. Calif. Women's Caucus for Art, Soc. Children's Bookwriters and Illustrators. Avocations: hiking, reading, swimming. E-mail: jbonassi@aol.com.

BONAVENTURA, CELIA JEAN, biochemist, researcher; b. Silver City, N.Mex., June 19, 1941; d. Rolan James and Ruth (Hale) Taylor; m. Joseph Bonaventura, Aug. 20, 1960; children: Marina Celeste, Michelle Celia. BA, San Diego State U., 1964; PhD, U. Tex., 1968. Rsch. assoc. Duke U. Med. Ctr., Beaufort, N.C., 1972-75, asst. med. rsch. prof., 1975-84, assoc. prof., 1984-90, prof., 1990—; co-dir. Duke U. Marine Biomed. Ctr., Beaufort, 1978—. Mem. Gov.'s Task Force on Aquaculture, 1987-88. Mem. editorial bd. Hemoglobin, 1977-89; contbr. over 100 articles on structure, function and assembly of respiratory proteins to profl. jours. Mem. adv. bd. Vocat. Edn. Program, Carteret County, N.C., 1990—. Rsch. grantee NIH, NSF, Office of Naval Rsch., Nat. Oceanography and Atmospheric Adminstrn., others, 1972—. Mem. AAAS, Am. Chem. Soc., Biophys. Soc. (chmn. human rights com. 1990—). Achievements include development of new concepts in the allosteric control of respiratory proteins; establishment of Marine Biomedical Center to explore the relationships between the marine environment and the human species; research in protein engineering. Office: Duke U Marine Lab Pivers Island Beaufort NC 28516

BONAZZI, ELAINE CLAIRE, mezzo-soprano; b. Endicott, N.Y. d. John Dante and Zina (Rossi) B.; m. Jerome Ashe Carrington, Sept. 21, 1963; 1 child, Christopher. BM (George Eastman scholar), Eastman Sch. Music. Currently artist-in-residence SUNY, Stonybrook; pvt. voice studio N.Y.C. Past faculty Peabody Conservatory; vis. prof. Eastman Sch. Music, Rochester, N.Y., 1979; judge nat. and internat. competitions. Debuts, Santa Fe Opera, 1958, Opera Soc. Washington, 1960, N.Y.C. Opera, 1965, Opera Internacional, Mexico City, Mexico, 1966, Metropolitan Opera at the Forum, 1973, Europe, West Berlin Festival opera, 1961, Spoleto (Italy) Festival, 1974, Castel Franco Festival Venetian Music, Venice, Italy, 1975, Berlin Bach Festival, 1976, Pks. Radio TV Difusion, 1980—; Netherlands Opera, 1978, Minn. Opera, 1985, Artpark Festival, 1987, Opera Theater of St. Louis, 1988, New Orleans Opera, 1988, Paris, 1979, Spoleto-Charleston Festival, 1981, Edmonton Opera Can., 1990, New Orleans Opera, 1990, Winnipeg Opera, 1993, Edmonton Opera, 1992; frequent Libr. of Congress concerts; title role in Pique Dame, Washington Opera, 1989, in Vanessa, Opera Theatre of St. Louis, 1988, Carlson's Midnight Angel, Opera Theatre of St. Louis, 1993, Glimmerglass Opera La Calisto, 1995; lead N.Y.C. Opera; soloist N.Y. Philharmonic, Phila. Orch., Boston Symphony, Cleve. Orch., Canadian Broadcasting Corp., PBS NET Opera Theatre, NBC, ABC, CBS TV networks, recs. on, Candide, Columbia, Vanguard, CRI, Folkways, Vox, Grenadilla, Pro Arte and Nonesuch Records; over 40 world premiers of major works by leading composers with major orchs. and opera cos. Named 1 of 6 honored alumni 50th Anniversary Year, Eastman Sch. Music, 1971, Trustees Council U. Rochester, 1976, Recital in honor of 75th Anniversary of Eastman Sch. of Music, 1996; formerly William Matheus Sullivan grantee; recipient Concert Artists Guild award, 1960; more operatic premiers than any other living Am. singer. Mem. Mu Phi Epsilon. Achievements include being chosen by Stravinsky, Hindemith, Menotti, Chavez, Rorem, Thomson, Argento, Pasatieri, Diamond, Elliott Carter for premieres of their works, master classes Europe and U.S. Office: trawick Artists Inc P O Box 1378 Lynn Haven FL 32444-6178

BONCHER, MARY, talent agent; b. Green Bay, Wis. d. Anthony Peter and Bernice Mary (Lannoye) Williams; m. Joseph Phillip Boncher, Jan. 7, 1967; children: Yvette, Noelle. Diploma, Rosemary Bischoff Sch. Modeling, Milw., 1965. Dir. Mary Boncher Model Agy. & Sch. Ltd., Bloomington and St. Charles, Ill., 1970—76, Mary Boncher Model Agy. Ltd., St. Charles, 1976—84, Mary Boncher Model Mgmt. Ltd., Chgo., 1985-91; ptnr. ARIA Model & Talent Mgmt. LLC, Chgo., 1992—2001; sec., treas.; owner, mem., v.p., sec. ARIA Model & Talent Mgmt. LLC, Chgo., 2001—. Fashion reporter TV and radio Men's Fashion Assn., N.Y.C., 1975—80, Eleanor Lambert's Am. Designer, NY Fashion Press, N.Y.C., 1975—80; fashion corr. Green Bay Daily News, 1975—76. Lector Cath. mass, 1983-90, 92—; registered lobbyist, Ill.; mem. Rep. Nat. com., 1994-98. Mem. Am. Security Coun. (nat. adv. bd.), Ams. for Responsible TV and Radio, Ill. Creative Cmty. (pres. 1996-99), Washington Morgan Garage Condo Assn. (bd. dir. 2002—), Acorn Lofts Condo Assn. (bd. dir. 2002—). Republican. Roman Catholic. Office: ARIA Model & Talent Mgmt LLC 1017 W Washington St Ste 2C Chicago IL 60607-2119 Home: 3N874 John G Whittier Pl Saint Charles IL 60175

BOND, CHRISTINA M. magistrate, lawyer; b. Washington, Dec. 9, 1967; d. Eugene M. and Ann Marie (Berik) Bond. BA, Youngstown State U., 1989; JD, U. Akron, Ohio, 1989-92. Cert. to serve as co-counsel on death penalty cases. Clk. CIA, Langley, Va., 1990-91; rsch. asst. U. Akron, 1991-92; paralegal instr. Bus Sch., Ravenna, Ohio, 1993-95; hearing officer, trial and appellate Child Support Enforcement, Youngstown, Ohio, 1995-97; magistrate Mahoning County Ct. of Common Pleas, Youngstown, 1997—. Named to Outstanding Young Women of Am., 1997. Mem. ABA, Ohio Bar Assn. (bd. govs. Women in the Profession and Young Lawyers), Mahoning County Bar Assn. (newsletter editor 1995—), Ohio Assn. Magistrates, Youngstown Panhellenic Assn., Youngstown Women's Polit. Caucus, Cleve. Mus. Art, Butler Mus. Art, Friends of Nat. Zoo, Delta Zeta (newsletter editor). Office: Ste 200 1040 S Commons Pl Youngstown OH 44514-1959 Home: 1810 E Pinecrest Rd Spokane WA 99203-3938

BOND, FRANCES CURTIS, retired editor; b. Chgo., Feb. 9, 1909; d. Vine Harlan Sr. and Frances Lay (Watson) Curtis; m. Bradford Austin Bond, Mar. 8, 1940 (dec. Nov. 1991); 1 child, David Bradford (dec. Oct. 1997). B Journalism, U. Mo., 1932. Editor Nutrilite News Mytinger & Casselberry, Inc., Long Beach, Calif., 1948-58; dir. pub. info. and cmty. rels. Long Beach Commn. on Econ. Opportunities, 1967-77; cmty. editor Long Beach Rev. mag., 1978-90; ret., 1990. Bd. dirs., historian Ch. Women United, Long Beach, 1996; mission coord. United Meth. Women, Long Beach, 1996; mem. adminstrv. bd. Grace United Meth. Ch., Long Beach, 1996; former bd. dirs., exec. com. Pacific Coast Press Club; former adv. coun. com. on aging United Way; former mem. Calif. Atty. Gen.'s Adv. Com. on Consumer Info. and Crime Prevention for Sr. Citizens; former bd. dirs., sec. Calif. Dirs. Aging Programs; former mem. adv. bd. Sr. Opportunities and Svcs. Elderly Nutrition Program; former mem. adv. bd. Long Beach Children's Mus.; former bd. dirs. Internat. Cmty. Coun. of Calif. State U., Long Beach, Long Beach Ballet; former bd. dirs., exec. com. South Bay Indian Svcs., NAACP, Long Beach, Pacific Coast Press Club; docent, vol. Long Beach Aquarium of the Pacific, 1998—. Recipient 4 1st Pl. and 3 2d Pl. awards Internat. Indsl. Publs. Contest, 1951, Blue Pencil award for Outstanding Govt. Publs., Fed. Editors Assn., 1974, 75, 1st and 2d Pl. award Calif. Cmty. Action Exec. Dirs. Assn., 1976, Merit award Pacific Coast Press Club, 1988, Mission Recognition award United Meth. Ch., 1990, named Safe Driver of Yr. Long Beach, Nat. Safety Coun., 1963, Vol. of Mo., Long Beach Sr. Ctr., 1991, Lay Person of Yr., Grace United Meth. Ch., 1996. Mem. DAR (life, bd. dirs. Susan B. Anthony chpt. 1989-90), NAACP (life), Fulton County Ind. Hist. Soc. (life), Ind. Hist. Soc., Soroptimist Internat. (life, Soroptomist of Long Beach Hall of Fame 1997), Soc. Mayflower Descendants. Democrat. Avocations: photography, geneology, volunteering, writing. Home: 1625 E Appleton St Apt 3-J Long Beach CA 90802-4026

BOND, FRANCES TORINO, academic administrator, consultant; b. Balt., Jan. 8, 1939; d. Michael Torino and Josephine Baccacchione; widowed; children: William, Michael, Geoffrey, James. BS, Towson State U., 1955, MEd, 1963; PhD, U. Md., 1973. Faculty Towson (Md.) State U., 1962-74, chairperson early childhood, 1975-81, assoc. dean, 1982-94; assoc. dir. Fellows Program Peace Corps, Washington, 1994—99; spl. asst. to U.S. Sec. of Edn., 1999—2001; dir. profl. devel. PBS Ready to Learn, Alexandria, Va., 2001—. Creator, host, writer (video series) First Steps, 1987—; co-author (booklet) Reading to Your Child, 1985. Democrat. Roman Catholic. Home: 6901 Avondale Rd Baltimore MD 21212-1934 Office: PBS 1320 Braddock Pl Alexandria VA 22314

BOND, VICTORIA ELLEN, conductor, composer; b. L.A., May 6, 1945; d. Philip and Jane (Courtl) B.; m. Stephan Peskin, Jan. 27, 1974. B Mus. Arts, U. So. Calif., L.A., 1968; M Mus. Arts, Juilliard Sch. Music, 1975, D Mus. Arts, 1977; DFA (hon.), Washington and Lee U., 1992, Hollins Coll., 1995, Roanoke Coll., 1995. Condr., composer. Mem. N.Y. State Coun. Arts Music Panel, 1987-90; bd. dirs. N.Y. Women Composers. Guest condr. Cabrillo Music Festival, Calif., 1974, White Mountains Music Festival, N.H., 1975, Aspen (Colo.) Music Festival, 1976, Shenandoah Music Festival, W.Va., 1977, Colo. Philharm., 1978, Houston Symphony, 1979, 86, Buffalo Philharm., 1979, Pitts. Symphony, 1980, N.W. Chamber Orch., Seattle, 1980, Anchorage Symphony, 1980, 82, Ark. Symphony, 1981, Hudson Valley Philharm., N.Y., 1981, 98, Newton Symphony, Boston, 1982, Hartford Symphony, 1982, RTE Symphony, Dublin, Ireland, 1983, Albany Symphony Orch., 1984-85, Houston Symphony Orch., 1986, Richmond Symphony Orch., 1987, Williamsburg Symphony Orch., Greenville Symphony Orch., Des Moines Symphony Orch., Utah Symphony Orch., Cape Cod Symphony Orch., Tallahassee Symphony Orch., Va. Symphony Orch, 1988-90, Shanghai Symphony, 1993, 94, Erie (Pa.) Philharmonic, 1995, Amarillo (Tex.) Symphony, 1996, Opera Carolina, N.C., 1997, 99, Harrisburg (Pa.) Opera, 1997, 98, 99, 2000, 2001, 2002, Norwalk Symphony, 2002, Cutting Edge Concerts, 2002, Wuhan Symphony, China, 1997, 99, Hunan Symphony, Changsha, China, 1998, Honolulu Symphony, 1998, Louisville Symphony, 1998, Flagstaff Symphony, 1998, Greenville Symphony, 1998, 1998, Ray Charles 70th Birthday Concert, Warsaw (Poland) Symphony, York (Pa.) Symphony, Music from Penn's Woods (Pa.), 1999-2000, NY City Opera Showcasing Am. Composers, 2001, Norwalk Symphony, 2002, Da Corneto Opera Co., 2003, Dallas Symphony Ray Charles Concert, 2003; artistic dir. Cutting Edge Concerts, N.Y.C., 1999-, Hanisburg Opera, 1998-2003; music dir. New Amsterdam Symphony Orch., N.Y.C., 1978-80, Pitts. Youth Symphony Orch., 1978-80, Empire State Youth Orch., 1982-86, Southeastern Music Ctr., 1983-84, Bel Canto Opera, 1983-86, Roanoke (Va.) Symphony Orch., 1986-95; artistic dir. Bel Canto Opera Co., 1986-88, Harrisburg Opera, 1998-2003; artistic adv., Wuhan Symphony (China), 1997—, Opera Roanoke, 1989-95; Exxon/Arts Endowment condr., Pitts. Symphony, 1978-80, recs. include Twentieth Century Cello, Two American Contemporaries, The Frog Prince, An American Collage, Live from Shanghai, Victoria Bond: Compositions, The American Piano Concerto, Yes, 2003; commd. by Pa. Ballet, 1978, Jacob's Pillow Dance Festival, 1979, Am. Ballet Theater, 1981, Empire State Inst. Performing Arts, 1983, 84, Stage One, Louisville, 1986, Ga. State U., 1986, L'Ensemble, 1990, Renaissance City Winds, 1990, Audubon String Quartet, 1990, Women's Philharm., San Francisco, 1993, Va. Explore Park and The Shanghai Symphony, 1994, D Day Found., 1994, Linda Plaut, 1994, The Billings (Mont.) Symphony, The Elgin (Ill.) Symphony, The Elements String Quartet, The Indpls. Chamber Orch., The Composers' Conf., The Jade String Trio; others. Bd. dirs. Am. Music Ctr. Recipient Victor Herbert award 1977, Perry F. Kendig award, 1988, ASCAP Composition award 1973—; Nat. Inst. for Music Theater grantee in opera conducting N.Y.C. Opera, 1985, Martha Baird Rockefeller grantee, 1978-79, Meet-The-Composer grantee in Composition, 1973—; Juilliard scholar, 1972-77; Juilliard fellow, 1975-77, Aspen Music Festival fellow, 1973-76; named Exxon/Arts Endowment Conductor, 1978-80, Woman of Yr. in Va., 1990, 91; featured on NBC Today show, 1990, profiled in C.S. Monitor, 1987, Wall Street Jour., 1987, other mags. and shows. Mem. ASCAP (awards 1975—), Am. Symphony Orch. League, Am. Fedn. Musicians, Condrs. Guild (bd. dirs. 1994—98), Internat. Alliance Women in Music, N.Y. Women Composers, Mu Phi Epsilon. Avocations: horseback riding, sailing, hiking. E-mail: victoriabond@earthlink.net.

BONDAREFF, JOAN M. retired government official, lawyer; b. Utica, N.Y., Jan. 7, 1944; 1 child. Student, Cornell U., 1961-64; BA in Polit. Sci. cum laude, George Washington U., 1965; JD magna cum laude, Am. U., 1975. Bar: Md. 1975, D.C. 1978, U.S. Supreme Ct. 1979. Clk. Md. Ct. Spl. Appeals, 1975; atty. advisor for legis. and regulation Office Gen. Counsel, Dept. Commerce, Washington, 1975-76, atty. on detail to Dept. Justice, 1976-77; staff atty. NOAA, Washington, 1977-80, sr. counsel to nat. earth satellite svc., 1980-82, asst. gen. counsel for adminstrn., 1981-82, asst. gen. counsel for ocean svcs., 1982-87; sr. counsel Coast Guard and Mcht. Marine group U.S. Ho. of Reps. Mcht. Marine and Fisheries Com., Washington, 1987-94; chief counsel and acting dep. maritime adminstr. Maritime Adminstn., Dept. Transp., Washington, 1994—99; counsel maritime/marine dept. Dyer Ellis & Joseph, Washington, 2001—02; counsel maritime/marine transp. group Blame Rome LLP, Washington, 2003. Legal counsel Nat. Safe Boating Coun. Contbr. articles to law jours., including Territorial Sea Jour., Coastal Mgmt. Jour., Internat. Ship Registry Rev. Former chmn. Women's Aquatic Network. Mem. ABA (marine resources com. 1989—). Avocations: hiking, running, music, travel. Office: Blank Rome LLP 600 New Hampshire Ave NW Washington DC 20037*

BOND-BROWN, BARBARA ANN, musician, educator; b. Kansas City, Mo., July 1, 1955; d. John Bartley, Jr. and Tressie Laverne (Nichols) Bond; m. Lance Elliott Brown, Mar. 11, 1979. Student, Ctrl. Mo. State U., 1973-74, 75-77, U. Mo., 1974, William Jewell Coll., 1975; studies with Karen Halverhout, Prarie Village, Kans., 1995—. Dist. accompanist Kansas City Pub. Schs., 1979-82; ind. music tchr. Independence, Mo., 1982-84; ind. music tchr., accompanist San Francisco, 1984-92; ind. music tchr. Barbara Bond-Brown Music Studio, Lee's Summit, Mo., 1992—. Developer method for young music beginners; spkr. at workshops and confs.; active adjudicator for competitions and auditions. Mem.: Federated Music Tchrs., Las Vegas Music Tchrs. Assn., Nev. Music Tchrs. Assn., Music Tchrs. Nat. Assn., Mo. Music Tchrs. Assn. (chmn. honors auditions 1993—, officer 1995—), Kans. City Music Tchrs. Assn. (v.p. achievement auditions 1994—, v.p. fall festival 1994—, chmn. pre-coll. honors auditions 1995—). Avocations: reading, writing, cooking, traveling. Home: Ste 2-249 9811 W Charleston Blvd Las Vegas NV 89117 E-mail: fridaybrown@yahoo.com.

BONDINELL, STEPHANIE, counselor, academic administrator; b. Passaic, NJ, Nov. 22, 1948; d. Peter Jr. and Gloria Lucille (Burden) Honcharuk; m. Paul Swanstrom Bondinell, July 31, 1971; 1 child, Paul Emil. BA, William Paterson U., 1970; MEd, Stetson U., 1983. Cert. elem. educator Fla., guidance counselor grades K-12 Fla. Tchr. Bloomingdale (N.J.) Bd.

Edn., 1971-80; edn. dir. Fla. United Meth. Children's Home, Enterprise, 1982-89; guidance counselor Volusia County Sch. Bd., Deltona, Fla., 1988—. Coord. sch. improvement svcs., Deltona Lakes, 1996—98, Deltona Lakes, 2002—04, Deltona Lakes, 2002—04. Sec. adv. com. Deltona Jr. HS, 1996—98, sec. PTA, 1982; vice-chmn. adv. com. Deltona Mid. Sch., 1988, chmn., 1991—92, 1991—92; mem. adv. com. Deltona HS, 1995—96; secondary sch. task force Volusia County Sch. Bd., 1986—; team leader Volusia County Sch. Accreditation Quality assurance Team, 2003—04; mem. exec. com. Volusia County Sch. Reps.; mem. Rep. Presdl. Task Force; mem. state adv. bd. Fla. Future Educators Am., 1990—92, 2003—04. Named Deltona Lakes Tchr. of Yr., Volusia County Sch., 1991, 1996, Volusia County Schs. Dist. Sch. Accreditation Steering Com. Team Leaders, 2003—04; recipient Outstanding Ednl. Partnership award, S.W. Volusia C. of C., 1998, Sunshine State Medallion award, Fla. Pub. Rels. Assn., 1998, award, Volusia/Flagler Alcohol and Drug Abuse Prevention Coun., 1998—2004, Fla. Lottery Creative Tchg. award, 2002; Acad. scholar, Becton, Dickinson & Co., 1966, N.J. State scholar, 1966—70. Mem.: AAUW, ASCD, Internat. Platform Assn., Volusia Tchrs. Orgn., N.J. Edn. Assn., Fla. Assn. Counseling and Devel., Disvn. Learning Disabilities, Coun. Exceptional Children, Stetson U. Alumni Assn., Deltona Civic Assn., 4 Townes Federated Rep. Women's Club (sec., v.p.), Deltona Rep. Club (v.p. 1991—93). Avocations: painting, creative writing, dance. Home: 1810 W Cooper Dr Deltona FL 32725-3623 Office: Volusia County Sch Bd 2022 Adelia Blvd Deltona FL 32725-3976 E-mail: sbondine@mail.volusia.k12.fl.us.

BONDURANT, AMY LAURA, retired corporate financial executive; b. Union City, Tenn., Apr. 20, 1951; m. David E. Dunn III; 1 child. BA, U. of Ky., Lexington, 1974—78. Bar: D.C. 1978, Ky. 1978. Legislative aide Office of Senator Wendell Ford, Washington, 1975—78; sr. counsel Senate Com. on Commerce, Sci. & Transp., Washington, 1978—88; sr. shareholder (ptnr.) Verner, Liipfert, Bernhard, McPherson & Hand, Washington, 1987—97; amb. Orgn. for Econ. Cooperation and Devel., Paris, 1997—2001; mng. dir. Bozman Partners, Paris, France / Washington, DC, 2001—. Chmn., mem. comml. space transp. adv. com. Dept. Transp. Author: (article) Wired News, Director's Monthly, The Ambassador's Review. Mem., adv. bd. Forum 21 Conf. on Transatlantic Dialogue (yearly), Washington, D.C. & Paris, France (incl. Monaco), 2001—02; mem. of vestry Am. Cathedral of Paris, Paris, France (incl. Monaco), 2002—02; mem., bd. of governors Am. Hosp. of Paris, Paris, France (incl. Monaco), 2001—02. Mem.: Coun. of Am. Ambassadors, Coun. on Fgn. Rels., Cosmos Club. D-Conservative. Episcopalian/ Christian. Avocations: traveling, traveling, traveling, traveling, golfing. Home: 2 Avenue Bugeaud Paris 75116 France Office: Bozman Partners 2550 M Street NW Washington DC 20037 Home Fax. 01 45 00 19 56. Personal E-mail: albond@attglobal.net.

BONEMERY, ANNE M. language educator; b. Springfield, Mass., Nov. 1, 1950; d. Alley and Radie Bonemery. BA, Am. Internat. Coll., 1972, MAT, 1974; AS, Springfield Tech. C.C., 1993. Cert. tchr. in English and Bilingual English Mass., tchr. French and Bilingual French Mass., tchr. Spanish and Bilingual Spanish Mass. Tchr. Northampton Pub. Schs., Mass., 1972—85; prof. Springfield Tech. C.C., 1985—; acct., office mgr. Emery Devel., Ltd., Mass., 1985—. English lang. cons. Springfield Instn. Savings (now First Mass. Bank), 1996—97; treas. Emery Devel., Ltd., 1985—, bd. dirs. Vol. U.S. citizenship studies and English lang. studies Springfield Literacy Network, 1987—; bd. dirs. Am. Internat. Coll. Alumni Bd., Mass., 1997—2000, bd. dirs. Springfield chpt., 2000—. Recipient Nat. Inst. Staff and Orgnl. Devel. Excellence award, U. Tex. Austin, 1997, 2000, Ptnr. in Philanthropy award, We. Mass. chpt. Assn. Fundraising Profls., 2001. Mem.: TESOL, MLA, NEA, Springfield Tech. C.C. Profl. Assn. (bldg. rep.), We. Mass. Fgn. Lang. Assn., Mass. Fgn. Lang. Assn., Mass. Assn. TESOL, Mass. Tchrs. Assn., Am. Coun. Tchg. Fgn. Langs., Am. Assn. Tchrs. French, Springfield Libr. and Mus. Assn., Sigma Lambda Kappa (sec. 1985—2000). Avocations: travel, reading, photography, hiking. Office: Springfield Tech CC One Armory Sq Springfield MA 01105

BONFANTE, LARISSA, classics educator; b. Naples, Italy; arrived in U.S., 1939, naturalized, 1951; d. Giuliano and Vittoria (Dompé) B.; m. Peter B. Warren, Sept. 1950 (div. 1962); children: Sebastian Raditsa, Alexandra Bonfante-Warren; m. Leo Ferrero Raditsa, May 2, 1973 (dec. 2001). Student, Radcliffe Coll., 1950, U. Rome, 1951; BA, Barnard Coll., 1954; MA, U. Cin., 1957; PhD, Columbia U., 1966. Mem. faculty NYU, 1963—, prof., 1978—, chmn. dept. classics, 1978—84, 1987—90. Cons. in field; vis. mem. Inst. for Advanced Study, 1980. Author: Etruscan Dress, 1975, paperback, 2003, Out of Etruria, 1981, Reading the Past, Etruscan, 1990; author: (with Giuliano Bonfante) The Etruscan Language (transl. into Italian 1985, into Romanian 1995), 1983, 2d edit., 2002; author: Corpus Speculorum Etruscorum, N.Y. The Metropolitan Museum of Art, 1997; editor: Etruscan Life and Afterlife: Handbook of Etruscan Studies, 1986; translated to Romanian, 1996; editor (with Francesco Roncalli): Antichità dall'Umbria a New York, 1991; editor: (with Judith Sebesta) The World of Roman Dress, 1994; translator: Chronology of the Ancient World (E.J. Bickerman), 1967, The Plays of Hrotswitha of Gandersheim, 1979; editor (with Vassos Karageorghis): Italy and Cyprus in Antiquity: 1500-450 BC, 2000; contbr. articles to profl. jours. Mem. Archaeol. Inst. Am. (gov. bd. 1982-88), Istituto di Studi Etruschi (fgn.), German Archaeol. Inst. (corres. mem.). Home: 50 Morningside Dr New York NY 10025-1739 Office: NYU Classics Dept 25 Waverly Pl New York NY 10003-6701 E-mail: lb11@nyu.edu.

BONFILS, DARCY REYNE, television producer; b. Washington, Sept. 20, 1957; d. James Robert and Marjorie (Stemm) Bonfils. BA, Middlebury Coll., 1979; MA, U. Colo., 1983. Exec. asst. Internat. Student Movement of UN, Geneva, 1980; anchor, reporter KYCU-TV, Cheyenne, Wyo, 1984-86; asst. news dir. WUFT-TV, Gainesville, Fla., 1986-87; prodr. WPEC-TV, West Palm Beach, Fla., 1987-89, WFSB-TV, Hartford, Conn., 1989-91, WBBM-TV, Chgo., 1991-92, WCBS-TV, N.Y.C., 1992-95; sr. prodr. Court TV's: Inside Am.'s Cts., N.Y.C., 1995-97; prodr. WABC-TV, N.Y.C., 1997—. Co-author: The Elvis Presley Family and Friends Cookbook, 1999; prodr.: (documentaries) Elvis: Precious Memories, 2000, (news feature) Grounding of the Golden Venture, 1993 (Emmy nomination, 1993), (news spls.) Hurricane: Eyewitness to a Storm, 2000 (Writers Guild Am. award, 2001, Emmy nomination, 2001). Mem.: NATAS, Am. Women in Radio and TV, Writers Guild Am. E-mail: darcylbon@aol.com.

BONIFACHO, BRATSA, artist; b. Belgrade, Yugoslavia, 1937; arrived in Can., 1973, naturalized, 1976. Student, Sumatovachka Sch. Art, Belgrade, 1957-59, U. Belgrade, 1960-65, Acad. di Belle Arti, Italy, 1966-68, Atelier Kruger, West Germany, 1966-68. Tchr. painting and drawing Sch. Fine Arts, Belgrade, 1967-68; pvt. tutor, 1979-87. One-person shows Gallery Scollard, Toronto, 1978, Contemporary Art Gallery, Vancouver, 1979, Richmond (B.C.) Art Gallery, 1982, 93, 97, Heffel Gallery Ltd., Vancouver, 1988, 90, 91, Quan-Schieder Gallery, Toronto, 1989, 90, Fran Willis Art Gallery, Victoria, B.C., Can., 1992, 93, 94, 95, 2000, Patrick Doheny Fine Art Gallery, Vancouver, 1992, 93, 94, Artropolis, 1993, Seattle Art Fair, 1993, Threshold Gallery, Vancouver, 1993, Bau-Xi Art Gallery, Vancouver and Toronto, 1995, 96, 99, 2001, 02, 03, Kimzey Miller Gallery, Seattle, 1996, Mus. History and Art, Anchorage, 1997, Gallerijk Progres, Belgrade, 2000, Contemporary Art Gallery, Zrenjanin, Yugoslavia, 2001, Gallery of the Matica Srpsick, Novi Sad, Yugoslavia, 2002; juried group exhibits in B.C., 1974-93; represented in numerous pub. and pvt. collections. Grantee, B.C. Arts Coun., 1996, 1998, 2000; travel grantee, Can. Coun., 2000, 2001, 2002, B.C. travel grantee, 1999. Office: PO Box 549 Sta A Vancouver BC Canada V6C 2N3 E-mail: preview@portal.ca.

BONIN, SUZANNE JEAN, artist; b. Oakland, Calif., Nov. 12, 1955; d. Charles Freeman and Dorice Ruth (Brown) B.; m. Donald George Winchester, May 16, 1986 (div. Nov. 1990); m. Joseph Bogusis, Nov. 2, 1996. Grad. h.s., Alton, N.H. Owner, mgr. Bonin Gallery, Wolfeboro, NH, 1983-94, Bonin Studio, Wolfeboro, NH, 1994—. Spl. needs art instr. Kingswood Regional Sch. System, Wolfeboro, 1982. Designer logo Audubon Soc. of NH, 1982; exhbn. The Art Place, Wolfeboro; illustrator: The Best Plants for New Hampshire Gardens and Landscapes, 2003. Charter mem. Gov. Wentworth Arts Coun., Wolfeboro, 1980, vol., 1980—; donor N.H. Public TV, Durham, N.H.; initiator of art collection for silent auction Hospice, Wolfeboro, 1982—; donor Lakes Region Humane Soc., 1999—; mem. Cmty. Ch. of Alton, 1962—. Mem. League of NH Craftsmen, Washington Area Printmakers, No. NH Arts Alliance. Avocations: gardening, fishing, swimming, cross-country skiing, basketball. Studio: Bonin Studio 713 Beach Pond Rd Wolfeboro NH 03894-0801

BONINA, MARY, poet; b. Worcester, Mass., Nov. 2, 1950; d. Biagio John Bonina and Mary Cecilia Feeherry; m. Mark Joseph Pawlak, Aug. 21, 1982; 1 child, Gianni Bonina-Pawlak 1 stepchild, Andrai Pawlak Whitted. AB in English Lit., Anna Maria Coll., Paxton, Mass., 1972; MFA in Creative Writing, Warren Wilson Coll., 1985. Cert. tchr. Mass. Co-editor, writer The Little Apple (mag.), Worcester, 1975—82; tchr. English and social studies secondary schs., Worcester, 1978—81; instr. comm. skills Quinsigamond C.C., Worcester, 1981; statewide dir. Mass. Conservation Assistance Fund Office Cmtys. and Devel., Commonwealth of Mass., Boston, 1982—85; workplace instr. English Lang. Interchange, Inc., Concord, Mass., 1988—90; program developer, dir. Pub. Libr.: The Literacy Project, Cambridge, Mass., 1990—98; writer, 1999—. Poet in the Schs. resident Worcester County Poetry Assn., 1974—76; poet in residence Cambridge Pub. Libr./Schs./Mass. Bd. Libr. Commrs., Cambridge, 1988; cons. Oksner, Inc., N.Y.C., 1992. Author (poetry collections): Hanging Loose, 1991, Red Brick Review, 1992, City River of Voices, 1992. Founding com. mem. Abby's House (women and children's shelter), Worcester, 1975; selection and organizing coms. Oxfam, Am., Harvard U., 1988—89; rschr., writer, prodr. Mental Health Care for Women (radio documentary), 1977. With VISTA, 1972—74. Fellow Fiction Writing, Vt. Studio Ctr. Colony, Johnson, Vt., 1990. Fellow: Va. Ctr. Creative Arts; mem.: Nat. Writers Union (Boston local), PEN New Eng., Acad. Am. Poets. Avocations: photography, creative gourmet cuisine, hiking, canoeing. Home: 44 Thingvalla Ave Cambridge MA 02138

BONINO, FERNANDA, art dealer; b. Torino, Italy, Jan. 5, 1927; came to U.S., 1963; d. Francesco Pogliani and Marina Collino; m. Alfredo Bonino, July 29, 1925 (dec. Jan. 1981). M in Art, U. Italy, Torino, 1942. Dir. Galeria Bonino Ltd., N.Y.C., 1963-90, dir., pres., 1981—. Mem. Art Dealers Assn. Am. Office: Galeria Bonino Ltd 48 Great Jones St New York NY 10012-1133 Office Phone: 212-598-4262.

BONN, ETHEL MAY, psychiatrist, educator; b. Cin., Oct. 14, 1925; d. Stanley Ervin and Ethel May (Cliffe) B. BA, U. Cin., 1947; MD, U. Chgo., 1951. Asst. chief, then chief women's neuro-psychiat. services VA Hosp., Topeka, 1956-61, chief north service, 1961-62; assoc. dir. for clin. services Ft. Logan Mental Health Ctr., Denver, 1962-67, dir., 1967-76; clin. instr. psychiatry U. Colo. Sch. Medicine, 1963-76; field rep. Joint Commn. on Accreditation of Hosps., 1976-78, assoc. clin. prof. psychiatry UCLA Sch. Medicine, 1978-81; chief of quality assurance VA Med. Ctr.-Brentwood, L.A., 1978-81; chief psychiatry service VA Med. Ctr., Albuquerque, 1981-89, assoc. prof. psychiatry U. N.Mex. Sch. Medicine, 1981-89, prof. emeritus psychiatry sch. medicine U. N.Mex., 1989—. Cons. Fitzsimons Army Hosp., Denver, 1963-67, U. Calif. Dept Biobehavioral Scis., Los Angeles, 1978-81, VA Hosps., Ft. Lyon, Colo., Sheridan, Wyo., Tuscaloosa, Ala., 1963-67. Contbr. chpts. to books, articles to profl. jours. Recipient Dirs. commendation, VA, 1962, 81, 89, Psychiat. Adminstrs. award Am. Assn. Psychiat. Adminstrs., 1976. Fellow Am. Coll. Psychiatrists (emeritus), Am. Psychiat. Assn. (life; program com. insts. for hosp. and cmty. psychiatry 1977-81), Am. Coll. Mental Health Adminstrn. (founding), Am. Coll. Utilization Rev. Physicians; mem. AMA, Am. Hosp. Assn. (chmn. psychiat. sect. 1972-74). Avocations: travel, gardening, oil and watercolor painting, collecting rocks and minerals, photography.

BONNELL, GAYLA, art educator; b. Wilmington, Ohio, Aug. 14, 1943; d. Harry Herman and Mary Frances (Rosher) Rudy; m. William E. Bonnell, Mar. 21, 1964; children: Matthew T., Traci M. BS, Wilmington Coll., Ohio, 1971; M in Mgmt., U. Phoenix, 1986. Elem. art tchr. Berkely Co., Martinsburg, W.Va., 1964—68; jr. H.S. art tchr. Colrain Sch. Dist., Cin., 1971—72; art tchr. Turkey Foot Jr. H.S., Kenton County, Ky., 1972—75, Thomas Jefferson H.S., Louisville, 1975—79, Shadow Mountain H.S., Phoenix, 1980—2003. With Project Challenge, Phoenix, 2002—. Recipient Alumni citation for Edn., Wilmington Coll., 2002. Mem.: Ariz. Watercolor Assn., Ariz. Art Edn. Assn., Nat. Art Edn. Assn. Avocations: painting, printmaking, bookmaking. Home: 2360 E Cheryl Dr Phoenix AZ 85028

BONNELL, VICTORIA EILEEN, sociologist, educator; b. N.Y.C., June 15, 1942; d. Samuel S. and Frances (Nassau) B.; m. Gregory Freidin, May 4, 1971. BA, Brandeis U., 1964; MA, Harvard U., 1966, PhD, 1975. Lectr. politics U. Calif., Santa Cruz, 1972-73, 74-76, asst. prof. sociology Berkeley, 1976-82, assoc. prof., 1982-91, prof., 1991—. Chair Berkeley Ctr. for Slavic and East European Studies, U. Calif.-Berkeley, 1994-2000, dir. Inst. Slavic, East European, and Eurasian Studies, 2002-04. Author: Roots of Rebellion: Workers' Politics and Organizations in St. Petersburg and Moscow, 1900-1914, 1983; editor: The Russian Worker: Life and Labor Under the Tsarist Regime, 1983, (with Ann Cooper and Gregory Freidin) Russia at the Varricades: Eyewitness Accounts of the August 1991 Coup, 1994, Iconography of Power: Soviet Political Posters Under Lenin and Stalin, 1997, Identities in Transition: Eastern Europe and Russia After the Collapse of Communism, 1996, Beyond the Cultural Turn: New Directions in the Study of Society and Culture, 1999, (with George Breslauer) Russia in the New Century: Stability or Disorder, 2004; (with Thomas Gold) New Entrepreneurs of Europe and Asia: Russia, Eastern Europe and China, 2004; contbr. articles to profl. jours. Recipient Heldt prize in Slavic women's studies, 1991; AAUW fellow, 1979; Regents Faculty fellow, 1978, Fulbright Hays Faculty fellow, 1977, Internat. Rsch. and Exch. Bd. fellow, 1977, 88, Stanford U. Hoover Instn. nat. fellow, 1973-74, Guggenheim fellow, 1985, fellow Ctr. Advanced Study in Behavioral Scis., 1986-87, Pres.' Rsch. fellow in Humanities, 1991-92; grantee Am. Philos. Soc., 1979, Am. Coun. Learned Socs., 1976, 90-91. Mem. Am. Assn. Advancement Slavic Studies.

BONNELL-MIHALIS, PAMELA GAY, library director; b. Monterey, Calif., Feb. 2, 1948; d. Dewey L. and Marlyce I. (Hansen) Scoggins; m. Verneil S. Henerson, June 18, 1966 (div. 1971); 1 child, V. Samuel Henerson III; m. Chrisman E Bonnell, Mar. 2, 1974 (div. 1983); m. Hugh R. McElroy, Nov. 10, 1990 (div. 1996); m. Stephan S. Mihalis, Oct. 5, 2002. BA, Cameron U., Lawton, Okla., 1972; MLS, U. Okla., 1972-73; CPM, S.W. Tex. State U., 1998. Libr. Met. Libr. Sys., Oklahoma City, 1974-75, Office of City Mgr., Dallas, 1977-80; dir. audience devel. Dallas Symphony Orch., 1980-81; libr. Dallas Morning News, 1981-83; libr. mgr. Plano (Tex.) Pub. Libr. Sys., 1983-91; dir. libr. svcs. Waco-McLennan County Libr. System, Waco, Tex., 1992—2001; exec. dir. Elyria (Ohio) Pub. Libr., 2002—. Author: (book) Fund Raising for Small Libraries, 1983; contbr. chapters to books, articles to profl. jours. Gala chair Easter Seal Soc., Dallas, 1988; bd. dirs. Women's Shelter, Plano, 1991; exec. bd. Am. Heart Assn., 1997—99; chmn. Lorain County Librs. Coun., 2003—; trustee Dallas Symphony Orch., 1981, Freedom to Read Found., 1999—; pres. Townbluff Homeowners Assn., Plano, 1984—90, Hippodrome Theatre Guild, 1996; treas. YWCA, 1995—96. Recipient Telecom. Excellence award, Ctrl. Tex. Edn., 1997. Mem.: ALA (councilor-at-large 1990—99, pres. Intellectual Freedom Round Table 1993—94, constn. and bylaws chair 1994—97, Shirley Olofson Meml. award 1974, cert. of Spl. Thanks 1986, John Phillip Immroth award 1990), Ctrl. Tex. Women's Alliance (bd. dirs. 1992—96), Tex. Libr. Assn. (chmn. Adminstrs. Roundtable 1994—95, trustee Leroy C. Merritt Trust Fund 1997—2000, chair intellectual freedom com. 2000—02, SIRS Intellectual Freedom award 1990), Tex. Mcpl. Librs. Dirs. (pres. 1994—95), Jr. League, Leadership Waco Alumni Assn., Rotary. Avocations: reading, travel. Home: 164 Arrow Ct Elyria OH 44035 Office: Elyria Pub Libr 320 Washington Ave Elyria OH 44035 E-mail: pbonnell@elyria.lib.oh.us.

BONNER, BESTER DAVIS, school system administrator; b. Mobile, Ala., June 9, 1938; d. Samuel Matthew and Alma (Davis) Davis; m. Wardell Bonner, Nov. 28, 1964; children: Shawn Patrick, Matthew Wardell. BS, Ala. State Coll., 1959; MS in Library Sci., Syracuse U., 1966; PhD, U. Ala., 1982. Cert. tchr. Librarian Westside High Sch., Talladega, Ala., 1959-64; librarian, tchr. lit. Lane Elem. Sch., Birmingham, Ala., 1964-65; head librarian Jacksonville (Ala.) Elem. Lab. Sch., 1965-70; asst. prof. library media Ala. A&M U., Huntsville, 1970-74; adminstv. asst. to pres. Miles Coll., Birmingham, 1974-78, chmn. div. edn., 1978-85; specialist media Montgomery County Pub. Schs., Md., 1987-88; dir. libr. and media svcs. div. curriculum and ednl. tech. Dist. of Columbia Pub. Schs., 1988—. Forum leader Nat. Issues Forum, Domestic Policy Assn. U. Ala., Birmingham, 1983-84; mem. Libr. Svcs. Construction Act Adv. Com. Contbr. writer The Developing Black Family, 1975. Chmn. ethics commn. St. Ala., Montgomery 1977-81; radiothon sire coordinator United Negro Coll. Fund, Birmingham 1981. Mem. ALA, Ala. Instructional Media Assn. (pres. dist. II 1971-72), Assn. Women Deans and Adminstrs., Com. 100, D.C. Assn. Sch. Librs., D.C. Libr. Com., Am. Assn. Sch. Librs., Nat. Assn. State Ednl. Profls. Democrat. Methodist. Avocations: writing, speaking, consulting, piano. Home: 9601 Burgess Ln Silver Spring MD 20901-4701

BONNER, BRIGID ANN, marketing professional; b. Mpls., Apr. 27, 1960; d. John Patrick and R. Jeanne (Crahan) B. BS in Journalism and Indsl. Adminstrn., Iowa State U., Ames, 1982; MBA, Harvard U., 1988. Mktg. statistician Fingerhut, Minnetonka, Minn., 1982-83; mktg. rep. IBM Corp., Mpls., 1983-88, exec. cons., 1988-90, mktg. mgr., 1990-92, sector mgr., 1992—. Mem. com. United Way of Minn., Mpls., 1989—. Mem. Harvard Bus. Sch. Club Minn. (bd. dirs. Mpls. chpt. 1989, pres. 1992—, mgmt. assistance program cons. 1990—). Republican. Roman Catholic. Avocations: travel, running, tennis, bicycling. Home: 25 Willow Woods Dr Excelsior MN 55331-8426 Office: IBM Corp 650 3rd Ave S Ste 500 Minneapolis MN 55402-4300

BONNER, CATHY, foundation administrator; b. Dallas; Grad., U. Tex., Austin. Owner, op. Bonner Inc.; exec. dir. Tex. Dept. Commerce, 1991—94; pres. bd., founder Found. for Women's Resources, The Women's Mus.: An Inst. for the Future, Dallas, Leadership Tex., Dallas, Leadership Am. Bd. dirs. Lone Star Girl Scout Coun., Austin (Tex.) Area Rsch. Orgn. Recipient award, Women in Comm., Inc., Tex. Pub. Rels. Assn., Am. Coun. Econ. Devel. Office: 3800 Parry Ave Dallas TX 75226

BONNES, KAREN L. clinical social worker; b. Chgo., Feb. 1, 1962; d. Walter and Katherine (Ray) B. BMus, BA in Social Work, Ill. State U., 1985; MA in Social Work, U. Chgo., 1990. Lic. clin. social worker, Ill., Ind. Counselor Lighthouse Detoxification, Normal, Ill., 1984-86; case mgr. United Charities-Met. Family Svcs., Chgo., 1986-89, Oak Pk. (Ill.) Twp., 1989-90; med. social worker Hospice, Matteson, Ill., 1990-94; clin. social worker Bonnes and Vasquez PC, Blue Island, Ill., 1994—. Mem. NAFE, NASW. Democrat. Lutheran. Avocations: coin collecting, bowling. Office: Bonnes and Vasquez PC 13152 Cicero Ave Ste 260 Crestwood IL 60445-1470

BONNIN, JERI W. education educator; b. Bossier City, La., Nov. 15, 1956; d. Thomas Marshall and Nell Hurley Walker; m. Scott A. Bonnin; children: Elizabeth Anne, Daniel Scott, Katherine Suzanne. BME, La. State Univ., Baton Rouge, La., 1979; MME, Univ. La., Lafayette, La., 1983; PhD, Univ. Okla., Norman, Okla., 2003. Cert. Kodaly Concept of Music Edn. Univ. Okla., 1996. Tchr. music specialist 5-8 Acadia Parish Sch., Cameron, La., 1979—80, Meadowbrook Christian Sch., Ft. Worth, Tex., 1985—91, Ft. Worth Cath. Diocese, Tex., 1990—92; instr. music edn. Cameron Univ., Lawton, Okla., 1997—98; tchr.- music specialist K-12 Lawton Pub. Sch., Okla., 1992—97; asst. prof. Univ. Mont.-Western, Dillon, Mont., 2002—. Faculty sponsor Collegiate Music Edn. Nat. Conf., Dillon, Mont., 2002—; tchr. Rural Edn. Integrated Block, Dillon, Mont., 2002—; com. mem. Tchr. Edn. Program Interview Team, Dillon, Mont., 2002—. Bd. mem. SW Mt Arts Coun., Dillon, Mont., 2002—. Mem.: Mont. Gen Music Tchrs. Assn., Orgn. of Am. Kodály Educators, Mont. Music Educators, Music Educators Nat. Conf. Avocations: gardening, reading, fishing, hiking.

BONO, MARY WHITAKER, congresswoman; b. Cleve., Oct. 24, 1961; d. Clay and Karen Whitaker; children: Chesare Elan, Chianna Maria; m. Glenn Baxley, Nov. 2001. BFA in Art History, U. So. Calif., 1984. Cert. personal fitness instr. Mem. U.S. Congress from 44th Calif. dist., 1998—; mem. energy and commerce com. Bd. dirs. Palm Springs Internat. Film Festival. Active D.A.R.E. Program, Olive Crest Home Abused Children, Tiempos de Los Ninos. Named Woman of the Yr., San Gorgonio (Calif.) chpt. Girl Scouts U.S., 1993. Republican. Avocations: outdoor activities, computer technology. Office: US House of Reps 404 Cannon Ho Office Bldg Washington DC 20515-0545*

BONOMI, FERNE GATER, public relations executive; b. Council Bluffs, Iowa, July 27, 1923; d. Roy Winfield and Leona Hazel (Bays) Gater; m. Robert Foch Bonomi, Sept. 3, 1949 (div. 1974); children: Robert Duff, David Scott; m. Wayne P. Davis, Apr. 20, 1991. BA magna cum laude, U. Iowa, 1948. Editor Silver City (Iowa) Times, 1940-41; reporter, photographer, Sunday editor Cedar Rapids (Iowa) Gazette, 1943-47; dir. pub. info. Iowa Devel. Commn., Des Moines, 1950-51; pub. info. officer Gov. William S. Beardsley, Des Moines, 1951-53; v.p. Bonomi Assocs. Inc., Des Moines, 1954-72; adminstr. Mid-Iowa Drug Abuse Coun., Des Moines, 1972-74; cons. Plain Talk Pub. Co., Des Moines, 1974-75; communications dir. Iowa Assn. Sch. Bds., Des Moines, 1975-86; owner, operator Bonomi & Co., Des Moines, 1986—. Chmn. pubs. evaluation Am. C. of C. Execs., Washington, 1977-81; mem. Universal Accreditation Bd., 2003—; presenter in field. Author: Show Me A Man, 1969; editor Iowa Sch. Bd. Dialogue, 1975-86; assoc. editor Leader's Mag., 1964-72. Active Gov.'s Com. on Employment Handicapped, 1968—74; chmn. comms. Des Moines Area Religious Coun., 1980—82. Named Iowa Sch. Communicator of Yr., Iowa Sch. Pub. Rels. Assn., 1997. Fellow Pub. Rels. Soc. Am. (developer mentoring program 1994-97, chmn. 1995, pres. Iowa chpt. 1980-82, chmn. accreditation 1982-2001, writer nat. curriculum for accreditation 1998, rev. 2003, Outstanding Contbr. award 1983, commendation for meaningful rsch. Bronze Anvil competition 1997); mem. Nat. Sch. Pub. Rels. Assn. (cert., Gold medallion 1987), Phi Beta Kappa, Alpha Delta Pi (nat. editor 1959-62, Outstanding Alumna award 1977). Mem. United Ch. Christ. Avocations: canoeing, horseback riding, church choir, dance, theater. Office: Bonomi & Co 1003 Kennedy St Ames IA 50010-4247

BONOSARO, CAROL ALESSANDRA, professional association executive, former government official; b. New Brunswick, N.J., Feb. 16, 1940; d. Rudolph William and Elizabeth Ann (Betsko) B.; m. Donald D. Kummerfeld, Sept. 8, 1962 (div. Jan. 1970); m. Athanasios Chalkiopoulos, Nov. 21, 1976 (div. Dec. 1991); 1 child, Melissa. BA, Cornell U., 1961; postgrad., George Washington U., 1961-62. Analytical statistician Office Mgmt. and Budget, Exec. Office of Pres., Washington, 1961-66; asst. dir. fed. programs div. U.S. Commn. on Civil Rights, Washington, 1966-68, dir. Office Fed.

Programs, 1968-69, dir. tech. assistance div., 1969-71, spl. asst. to staff dir., 1972, dir. women's rights program, 1972-79, asst. staff dir. for program planning and evaluation, 1979-80, asst. staff dir. congressional and public affairs, 1980-86; pres. Sr. Execs. Assn., Washington, 1986—. Mem. adv. com. Asian Am. Govt. Execs. Network, 1996—, mem. Nat. Partnership Coun., 1997-2001. Vice chmn. Nat. Com. on Asian Wives of U.S. Servicemen, 1973-83; pres. Catholics for a Free Choice, 1980-83; chmn. bd. dirs. William Jump Found., 2003—. Mem. Exec. Women in Govt., Sr. Exec. Assn. (dir. 1981-86, chmn. bd. dirs. 1983-86) Democrat. Home: 5504 Jordan Rd Bethesda MD 20816-1366 Office: Sr Execs Assn PO Box 44808 Washington DC 20026-4808

BONSACK, ROSE MARY HATEM, state legislator, physician; b. Havre de Grace, Md., Oct. 24, 1933; d. Joseph Thomas and Nasma (Joseph) Hatem; m. James P. Bonsack, Aug. 24, 1957; children: Jeanette, Karen, Thomas, David, James J. BS in Chemistry cum laude, Washington Coll., 1955; MD, Med. Coll. Pa., 1960. Intern Easton (Pa.) Hosp., 1961; physician outpatient clinic Kirk Army Hosp., Aberdeen Proving Ground, Md., 1962-74, chief outpatient clinic, 1968-72, chief dept. hosp. clinics, 1972-74; contract physician Harford County Dept. Health, Md., 1975-78; utilization rev. officer Harford Meml. Hosp., Havre de Grace, 1981-82; pvt. practice Aberdeen, Md., 1981—; mem. Md. Gen. Assembly, 1991-99, chmn. house rules and exec. nominations com., 1991-94, mem. house ways and means com., 1995-99. Coord. clinics Hypertensive Coun. Md., 1977-81; reviewer quality assurance for nursing homes in Harford County, Md. Licensing Div., 1977-81; utilization rev. officer Harford Meml. Hosp., Havre de Grace, 1981-82; med. dir. Ashley Alcoholic Rehab., Havre de Grace, 1983-84; mem. Bd. Med. Examiners Md.; mem., exec. sec. Commn. on Med. Discipline, 1985-88. V.p. St. Joan of Arc Home-Sch. Assn., 1968, pres., 1969, mem., 1968-85; v.p. No. Md. Heart Assn., 1969, pres., 1970, bd. dirs., 1973; bd. dirs. Mann House, Bel Air, Md., 1973-82, Harford County Cancer Soc., 1973-86; mem. John Carroll Home-Sch. Assn., 1974—, 1st v.p., 1975, pres., 1975; bd. dirs. John Carroll H.S., 1975—, pres. bd. dirs., 1979-85; mem. Harford County Dem. Cen. Com., 1987-90; mem. chief exec.'s coun. Harford C.C., 1990; trustee Washington Coll., 1992-99, Harford C.C., 1999—. Recipient Outstanding Contbn. to Md. Traffic Safety citation State of Md., 1969, Cert. of Merit for svc. Md. Cancer Soc., 1977, Women Helping Women award Soroptomists Harford and Cecil Counties, 1983-84, V. McCrory award for significant contbn. to enhancement of eye care in Md., Md. Optometric Assn., 1995, Alumni Citation for outstanding achievement and svc. in field of pub. svc. Washington Coll., 2000; named one of Top 100 Women in Md., Daily Record, 1996. Mem. Am. Acad. Family Physicians (bd. dirs. 1997-99, alt. del. 1990-94, del. from Md. 1994-96, chmn. chpt. affairs com. 1992—, commn. on regulations 1993-96, found. bd. dirs. 1999—), Med. Chirurgical Fac. Md., Harford County Med. Soc. (sec. 1967, pres. 1968, v.p. 1978, Outstand Cmny. Svc. citation 1979), Md. Acad. Family Physicians (v.p. 1987, pres. 1988).

BONTEMPO, ELAINE, language educator; b. Lima, Peru, May 19, 1946; came to U.S., 1948; d. H. Ellis and Esther Plyler; m. Blaine Bontempo, Jun. 15, 1968; children: Brian, Kari. BA, Baldwin-Wallace Coll., 1968; MS in Edn., N. Ill. U., 1994. Coord. Spanish-English lang. prog. Metropolitan Life Ins. Co., N.Y.C., 1968-71; ESL tchr. Project Lift, Dallas, 1978-80, Literacy Vols. of Am., Norwalk, CT, 1984-86, Ctrl. Piedmont C.C., Charlotte, NC, 1989-90; non-native literacy tchr., workforce ESL tchr. William Rainey Harper Coll., Palatine, IL, 1991—. Presenter IL/TESOL Conv., Chgo, 1999, Adult Learning Resource Ctr./Adult Edn. Conf., Rosemont, Ill., 1999; missionary Vols. in Mission, various locations in S. Am., 1999. Mem. Hunter's Ridge Homeowners Assn., Ill., (treas. 1991-93, social chair 1997-99). Mem. New Oratorio Singers (bookkeeper 1990—), Elgin Choral Union, Four Seasons Garden Club (membership chair 1990—), Ill. TESOL. Christian. Office: William Rainey Harper Coll Workforce ESL 1200 W Algonquin Rd Palatine IL 60067-7373

BONVICINI, JOAN M. university women's basketball coach; b. Bridgeport, Conn., Oct. 10, 1953; Grad., So. Conn. State U., 1975. Coach Calif. State U., Long Beach, 1980-91; head coach U. Ariz., Tucson, 1992—. Spkr. basketball seminars and camps; mem. NCAA Rules com. Bd. dirs. Tucson Area Girl Scouts, Boys and Girls Club of Tucson. Named to Hall of Fame So. Conn. State U., 1989, Conn. Women's Basketball Hall of Fame, 1994, Hall of Fame Long Beach State U., 1996, Coach of Yr., NCAA, 1981, PAC-10, 1998. Mem. Women's Basketball Coaches Assn. (pres. 1988). Office: U Ariz 236 Mckale Ctr Tucson AZ 85721-0001

BONVILLIAN, PAULINE, artist; m. Lynn Bertaut. AA, Tulane U., 1991. One-man shows include Sioux Indian Mus. U.S. Dept. Interior, 1980, exhibitions include Ft. Walton Beach Art Mus. 15th Ann. Art Show (Fourth Pl. Merit award, 1996), Associated Women in the Arts 8th Juried Exhbn. (Grumbacher award, 1996), Fragments: An Invitational. Enrolled tribal mem. Oglala Sioux, Pine Ridge Reservation, Pine Ridge, SD. Home: 1005 Elmeer Ave Metairie LA 70005

BOO, KATHERINE, newswriter; AB (summa cum laude), Columbia U., 1988. Writer, editor Wash. City Paper, 1988—92, Wash. Monthly, 1988—92; staff writer Wash. Post, 1992—; writer New Yorker. Recipient Pulitzer prize, 2000; fellow MacArthur Found. fellow, 2002. Office: Washington Post 1150 15th St NW Washington DC 20071

BOOHER, ALICE ANN, lawyer; b. Indpls., Oct. 6, 1941; d. Norman Rogers and Olga (Bonke) B. BA in Polit. Sci., Butler U., 1963; LLB, Ind. U., 1966, JD, 1967. Bar: Ind. 1966, U.S. Dist. Ct. (so. dist.) Ind. 1966, U.S. Tax Ct. 1970, U.S. Ct. Customs and Patent Appeals 1969, U.S. Ct. Mil. Appeals 1969, U.S. Ct. Appeals (D.C. cir.) 1969, U.S. Supreme Ct. 1969; cert. tchr., Ind. Rsch. asst., law clk. Supreme and Appellate Cts. Ind., Indpls., 1966; legal intern, atty., staff legal advisor Dept. State, Washington, 1966-69; staff legal adviser Bd. Vets. Appeals, Washington, 1969-78, sr. atty., 1978—, counsel, 1991—. Former counselor D.C. Penal Facilities and Shelters. Author: The Nuclear Test Ban Treaty and the Third Party Non-Nuclear States, also children's books; contbr. articles to various publs., chpts. to Whiteman Digest of International Law; exhibited crafts, needlepoint in juried artisan fairs; originator U.S. postage stamps Women in Mil. Svc., 1980-97, POWs/MIAs, 1986-96. Bd. dirs. community groups including D.C. Women's Commn. for Crime Prevention, 1980-81, Friends of Nat. Vets Mus.; pres., legal adviser VA Employees Assn.; mem. sec.'s mus. task force Dept. VA. Recipient various awards; named Ky. Col., 1988. Mem. DAV (life), VFW Aux. (life), D.C. Sexual Assault Coalition (chmn. legal com.), Life Mem. Judge Advocates Assn., U.S. Supreme Ct. Hist. Soc., U.S. Naval Inst., Nat. Mus. Women in Arts, Kennedy Ctr. Stars, Sackler/Freer Galleries (patron), Women in Mil. Svcs. to Am. Found., Bus. and Profl. Women (pres. D.C. 1980-81, nat. UN fellow 1974, nat. bd. dirs. 1980-82, 87-94, Woman of Yr. award D.C. 1975, Marguerite Rawalt award D.C. 1986), USO, Navy League U.S.A. (life), Am. Legion Aux. (life), Women Officers Profl. Assns., Nat. Vets. Mus. Task Force, Nat. Task Force on Women of the Mil. and Women Mil. POWS (chair Esther Peterson Tribute 1995, panel, paper moderator conf. 1997, book reviewer, contbr. to Stars & Stripes, Ex POWs Bull., others), Assn. Former Intelligence Officers (assoc.), Army Women Officers Profl. Assn., Am. News Womens Club, Cons., Saigon Tourist, Inc., Alliance Nat. Def. (editor Advocate).

BOOKER, BETTY MAE, poet; b. Allentown, Pa., Nov. 26, 1948; d. Harold George and Bessie (Bealer-Miller) Bartholomew; m. Samuel Efford Booker III, June 27, 1970 (dec. May 1998); children: Liesel Tamarah, Dacey Justin, Jaeson Bartholomew. BA in English, Millersville (Pa.) State Coll., 1970. Contbr. poetry to jours. and lit. mags., including Plainsong, America, Christian Century, Poetry Now. Home: 27826 Island Dr Salisbury MD 21801-2350 E-mail: sebefford@aol.com.

BOOKER, NANA LAUREL, art gallery owner, honorary consul; b. Waco, Tex., Aug. 5, 1946; d. Karl and Helen Dorothy (Keene) B. BA, Baylor U., 1968; MA, U. Fla., 1970; MBA, Pepperdine U., 1980. Asst. prof. comm. U. New Orleans, 1970-74, 1977-78; pub. rels. cons. New Orleans, 1974-78; dir. pub. rels. Touro Infirmary, New Orleans, 1976-78; dir. comm. Lifemark Corp., Houston, 1978-81; pres. C[illegible], Houston, 1981-82, dir. internat. rels., comm. Mayor's Office, City of Houston, 1982-84; pres. Nana Booker & Assocs. (now Booker/Hancock & Assocs.), Houston, 1984—; owner Booker-Lowe Gallery of Australian Aboriginal Art, 2002—. Hon. consul of Australia, State Tex., 1999—. Co-author: Introduction to Theatrical Arts, 1972. Mem. South Tex. Dist. Export Coun., Houston, 1988-92; press aide campaign K. Whitmire for Mayor, Houston, 1982; mem. exec. adv. bd. coll. bus. adminstrn. U. Houston, 1990-95; bd. dirs. Escape Ctr., 1990-93, YWCA, Houston, 1991-92, Greater Houston Partnership, 2003—, Asia Soc. Tex., 1999—. Recipient Internat. Assn. Bus. Communicators awards, Women in Comms. awards, Crystal award Am. Mktg. Assn., Outstanding Pub. Rels. Practitioner award Tex. Pub. Rels. Assn., 1996, Vol. of the Yr. award Houston Area Women's Ctr., 1998. Mem. Pub. Rels. Soc. Am. (accredited, chairperson internat. sect. 1993-95, Excalibur award 1988, Cert. of Appreciation 1993, 94, 95; mem. U.S. coun. 1994-96), Internat. Pub. Rels. Assn., Houston World Trade Assn. (bd. dirs. 1986—), Houston-Shenzhen Sister City Assn. (bd. dirs. 1987-94), Swiss-Am. C. of C. (bd. dirs. 1987-90), River Oaks Breakfast Club (bd. dirs. 1997), The Asia Soc. of Tex. (bd. dirs. 1995—). Avocations: hot air ballooning, photography, design, collecting art. E-mail: bookerlowegallery@houston.rr.com.

BOOKMAN, ANN EDITH, director; b. N.Y.C., Apr. 28, 1948; d. John Jacob and Ruth Louise (Lowe) B.; m. Eric P. Buehrens, July 5, 1981; children: Nicholas, Emily. BA with honors, Barnard U., 1970; MA, Harvard U., 1973, PhD, 1977. Asst. dir. The Bunting Inst./Radcliffe Coll., Cambridge, Mass., 1983-89; rsch. assoc. in child and family policy Lesley Coll., Cambridge, 1990-92; dir. Ctr. for Interdisciplinary and Spl. Studies Coll. of the Holy Cross, Worcester, Mass., 1992-93, 96—; policy and rsch. dir. U.S. Dept. Labor-Women's Bur., Washington, 1993-96; exec. dir. Commn. on Family and Med. Leave, Washington, 1995-96. Editor: Women and the Politics of Empowerment, 1988. Gubernatorial appointee Commn. on TDI and Ins., Boston, 1988-89, Gov.'s Day Care Partnership Task Force, Boston, 1991-92; presdl. appointee U.S. Dept. Labor, Washington, 1993-96. Fellow Am. Anthropol. Assn. Democrat. Jewish. Avocation: gardening.

BOOKS, ROBERTA PAULA, real estate finance executive; b. Boston, Apr. 4, 1943; d. Leonard and Mary (Karsh) Books; m. Jay S. Negin, May 20, 1973; children: Martha Alice Books Negin, Samuel Benjamin Books Negin. AB in Math., Bryn Mawr Coll., 1964, AM in Physics, 1969; MBA, Harvard U., 1971; postgrad., NYU, 1966. Acct. mktg. rep. IBM, N.Y.C., 1966-69; v.p. Morgan Stanley, N.Y.C., 1971-81; spl. asst. to comptroller Office of the Comptroller of the Currency, Washington, 1977-79; mng. dir. Prudential Ins. Co. Am., Newark, 1982-86; v.p., co-head real estate capital markets Salomon Bros., N.Y.C., 1986-90; v.p. Citicorp Real Estate, N.Y.C., 1991-94; mng. dir. Chem. Bank, N.Y.C., 1994-96, Landauer Assoc., 1997—99; pres. Books Realty Capital, 1999—. Author pamphlet. Bookshop chair Bryn Mawr Club NY; mem. adv. bd. fin. and admissions coms. Green Meadow Waldorf Sch., Spring Valley, NY, 2001—. Mem.: Comml. Mortgage Securitization Assn., Fin. Women's Assn. N.Y. Office: Books Realty Capital 6 Demarest Ct Englewood Cliffs NJ 07632-1904

BOONE, CELIA TRIMBLE, lawyer; b. Clovis, N.Mex., Mar. 3, 1953; d. George Harold and Barbara Ruth (Foster) T.; m. Billy W. Boone, Apr. 21, 1990. BS, Ea. N.Mex. U., 1976, MA, 1977; JD, St. Mary's U., San Antonio, 1982. Bar: Tex. 1982, U.S. Ct. Appeals (5th cir.) 1985, U.S. Supreme Ct. 1986; cer. family law Tex. Bd. Legal Specialization, 1987, family law examination commn., 2002. Instr. English Ea. N.Mex. U., Portales, 1977-78; editor Curry County Times, Clovis, 1978-79; assoc. Schultz & Robertson, Abilene, Tex., 1982-85, Scarborough, Black, Tarpley & Scarborough, Abilene, Tex., 1985-87; ptnr. Scarborough, Black, Tarpley & Trimble, Abilene, Tex., 1988-90, Scarborough, Black, Tarpley & Boone, Abilene, Tex., 1990-94; of counsel Scarborough, Tarpley, Boone & Fouts, Abilene, Tex., 1994-96; prin. Law Office of Celia Trimble Boone, Abilene, Tex., 1996—. Instr. legal rsch. and writing St. Mary's Sch. Law, 1981-82; mem. family law exam. com. Tex. Bd. Legal Specialization, 2002--. Legal adv. bd. to bd. dirs. Abilene Kennel Club, 1983-85; landmarks commn. City of Abilene, 1989-90. Recipient Outstanding Young Lawyer of Abilene, 1988. Mem. ABA, State Bar Tex. (disciplinary rev. com. 1989-93), Am. Trial Lawyers Assn., Tex. Trial Lawyers Assn., Tex. Criminal Def. Lawyers Assn., Tex. Acad. Family Law Specialists, Abilene Bar Assn. (bd. dirs. 1985-88, sec.-treas. 1985-86), Abilene Young Lawyers Assn. (bd. dirs. 1985-89, treas. 1985-86, pres.-elect 1987-88, pres. 1988-89). Avocations: needlework, gardening. Office: 104 Pine St Ste 316 Abilene TX 79601-5930 Office Phone: 325-695-6800. E-mail: mail@celia.net.

BOONE, DEBORAH ANN (DEBBY BOONE), singer; b. Hackensack, N.J., Sept. 22, 1956; d. Charles (Pat) Eugene and Shirley (Foley) Boone; m. Gabriel Ferrer, 1979; children: Gabriella, Dustin Boone, Tessa Rose. Student Calif. schs. Singer: with father, Pat Boone, and family group, 1970—; profl. rec. artist, 1977—, numerous appearances (TV series) TV talk and variety programs, appeared (ABC-TV Movie of the Week TV films) Sins of the Past, 1984, star children's video Hug Along Songs; author: Debby Boone--So Far, 1988, (children's book) Bedtime Hugs for Little Ones, 1988; co-author: Tomorrow is a Brand New Day, 1989; starred in nat. tour (Broadway plays) Seven Brides for Seven Brothers, 1981—82, nat. tour Sound of Music, 1987—88. Named Singing Star of Yr. AGVA, 1978, Working Mother of Yr., 1982; recipient Am. Music award (Song of Year), 1977, Grammy award (Best New Artist), 1977, Grammy award for best inspirational performance, 1980, Grammy award for best Gospel performance for Keep the Flame Burning, 1984, Nat. Assn. Theatre Owners award (Best New Personality), 1980, Dove award, 1980, Dove award for album Surrender, 1984, Country Music award for Best New Country Artis, 1977. Mem.: Ch. on the Way. Address: 4334 Kester Ave Van Nuys CA 91403-4135

BOONE, DONNA CLAUSEN, physical therapist, biostatistician, researcher; b. Nebraska City, Nebr., Dec. 12, 1932; d. Otto Ralph and Hallie Rae Clausen; m. Robert William Boone, Apr. 3, 1965. BA in Zoology, U. Wyo., 1954; MS in Phys. Therapy, U. So. Calif., 1980, MS in Biometry, 1983. Lic. phys. therapist, Calif. Phys. therapist Ill. Hosp. Sch., Chgo., 1955-59, Calif. Hosp., L.A., 1959-63; hemophilia specialist in phys. therapy Orthopaedic Hosp., L.A., 1963-78, rschr., project dir. Hemophilia Ctr., 1967-78; rsch. methods instr. U. So. Calif., L.A., 1982-83, Calif. State U., Long Beach, 1982-83; biostatistician immunulogy U. So. Calif., L.A., 1983-87, coord., statistician Nat. Clin. Trial, The Silicone Study, 1987-93; phys. therapist Huntington Meml. Hosp., Pasadena, Calif., 1993-98; cons. Hemophilia, Continuous Quality Improvement, Lompoc, Calif., 1998—. Internat. lectr., cons. World Fedn. Hemophilia, Montreal, Can., 1970-78; cons. biostatis. dentistry and pharmacology U. So. Calif., L.A., 1982-83, cons. orthopaedics, U. Buffalo, 1982-83; continuous quality improvement coach Doheny Eye Inst., L.A., 1990-92, Huntington Meml. Hosp., Pasadena, Calif., 1993-97; cons. physical therapy working group Nat. Hemophilia Found., 2000—. Editor: Comprehensive Management of Hemophilia, 1976, (internat. newsletter) World Hemophilia AIDS Ctr., 1984-93; contbr. articles to profl. jours. including Phys. Therapy, Archives Phys. Medicine, Bone and Joint Surgery, Western Medicine, Pharmacology, Diagnostic Immunology, Ophthalmology, Archives of Ophthalmology, Controlled Clin. Trials; mem. editl. bd. Am. Phys. Therapy Assn., 1975-82. Co-chair United Way Campaign Orthopaedic Hosp., L.A., chair, 1975—75; mem. Lompoc Rep. Women, 1998—, legis. chair, 2000—; vol. Rep. Campaign for Ho. of Reps., Glendale, Calif., 1996; recording sec. Santa Barbara County Rep. Women, 2000—01; lay leader St. Mary's Episcopal Ch., 1998—; bd. dirs. World Hemophilia Alliance, sec., 1996—; mem. alumni com. U. Wyo., 1999—; mem. med. adv. bd. Hemophilia Found. So. Calif., L.A., 1974—78. Grantee Fed. Govt. Agys., 1967, 73; recipient Dr. Murray Thelin award Nat. Hemophilia Found., 1976, Disting. Alumna award U. Wyo., 1979, Achievement award Alpha Chi Omega, 1980, Spl. Achievement award for treatment advances 50th Anniversary of the Nat. Hemophilia Found., 1998, Donna Clausen Boone ann. award Nat. Hemophilia Found. to Phys. Therapist, 1999—. Mem. Village Country Club, Antique Automobile Club. Republican. Episcopalian. Avocations: gardening, antique autos, travel, reading, jazz music clubs. Office: Hemophilia Continuous Quality Improvement 266 Oakwood Cir Lompoc CA 93436-1300 E-mail: boone266@impulse.net.

BOONE, ROSEMARY, music educator; b. Greenwich, Conn., Feb. 26, 1969; d. Thomas F. and Catherine C. Boone. MusB, Westminster Choir Coll., 1992; MusM in Edn., U. of Hartford, 1999. Lic. tchr. Conn., 2003. Music tchr. New Haven (Conn.) Bd. of Edn., 1992—93, Westport (Conn.) Bd. of Edn., 1993—94; gen., vocal music tchr. Bridgeport (Conn.) Bd. of Edn., 1994—98; vocal music tchr. Milford (Conn.) Bd. of Edn., 1998—. Choir dir. Ch. of St. Mary, Norwalk, Conn., 1992—95; dir. choirs Huntington Congl. Ch., Shelton, Conn., 1995—96; dir. children's and youth music Norfield Congl. Ch., Weston, Conn., 2000—. Choir mem. Westminster Symphonic Choir, 1988—92, Westminster Singers (two nat. tours), 1990—92; dir. Milford (Conn.) Area Youth Choir, 2000—02; choir mem. Weston (Conn.) Summer Chorus, 2003; christian edn. com. mem. Norfield Congl. Ch., Weston, Conn., 2000—; class agt. Westminster Choir Coll., Princeton, NJ, 2002; vol. libr. Family History Ctr., Woodbridge, Conn., 2002—03. Grantee, Bridgeport (Conn.) Edn. Fund, 1996. Mem.: Am. Choral Dirs. Assn. Republican. Roman Catholic. Avocations: genealogy, travel, gardening.

BOONSHAFT, HOPE JUDITH, public affairs executive; b. Phila., May 3, 1949; d. Barry and Lorelei Gail (R ienzi) B. BA, Pa. State U., 1972; postgrad. Del. Law Sch, Kellogg Inst. Mgmt. Tng. Program writer Youth Edn., N.Y.C., 1972; legal aide to judge Phila., 1975; dir. spl. projects Guiffre Med. Ctr., Phila., 1975; senatorial campaign fin. dir. Arlen Specter, Phila., 1975; presdl. campaign fin. dir. Jimmy Carter, Atlanta, 1976; fin. dir. Dem. Nat. Com., 1977—79; dir. devel. World Jewish Congress, N.Y.C., 1978, Yeshiva U., L.A., 1979; dir. comm. Nat. Easter Seal Soc., Chgo., 1979-83; CEO Boonshaft-Lewis & Savitch Pub. Rels and Govt. Affairs, L.A., 1983-93; sr. v.p. Edelman Worldwide, 1993-95; exec. v.p. external affairs Sony Pictures Entertainement, L.A., 1995—. Spl. adv. cmty. rels. The White House, 1977-80; guest lectr. U. Ill., 1982, May Co.'s Calif. Women in Bus. Bd. dirs. L.A. Arts Coun., Los Angeles County Citizens for Economy and Efficiency in Govt. Commn., Calif. Film Commn., Spkrs. Commn. Calif. Initiative. Home: 1967 Mandeville Canyon Rd Los Angeles CA 90049-2235 Office: Sony Pictures Entertainment 10202 Washington Blvd Culver City CA 90232-3119

BOOTH, BARBARA RIBMAN, civic worker; b. N.Y.C., May 2, 1928; d. Benjamin C. and Ceclia (Lowe) Ribman; m. Mitchell B. Booth, July 13, 1952; 1 child, Brian S. AA, Centenary Jr. Coll., Hackettstown, N.Y., 1948; BA, Barnard Coll., 1950. Pres. women's alliance, chmn., Christmas fair 1st Congl. Ch. of City of N.Y., 1959-63; mem. vol. com. Sheltering Arms Children's Svc., N.Y.C.; vol., coord. high sch. visits, pres. aux. N.Y. Hosp., 1989-91, co-chmn., 1995—; trustee Florence K. Griswold Meml. Fund. Com., All Souls Unitarian Ch., N.Y.C., United Hosp. Funds Auxiliary for N.Y. Hosp., 1996; bd. dir. women's div. Jefferson Dem. Club. N.Y.C.; committeewoman N.Y. County Dem. Com.; bd. govs., v.p. N.Y. Fruit and Flower Mission, Inc.; del. city conv., chmn. East Manhattan br. LWV. Recipient Auxilian of N.Y. Hosp. award, 1996. Mem. City Gardens Club N.Y.C. (mem. grants com.). Home: 75 E End Ave New York NY 10028-7909

BOOTH, BETTY JEAN, retired daycare administrator, poet; b. St. Louis County, Mo., Dec. 27, 1944; d. Richard Augustus and Leoma Thelma (Atchison) Woods; m. Alfred Lee Pope Jr., Aug. 20, 1962 (div. Apr. 14, 1975); children: Wayman Maurice Woods-Pope, Aundrea Denise Woods-Pope, Juanita Rosetta Pope-Miller, Victoria Lynn Pope, Daniel Jerome Pope, Alfred Lee III Pope; m. Robert Lee Booth, Mar. 3, 1984; 1 stepchild, David Lee Griffin. Cert., United Bus. Coll., North St. Louis, Mo., 1987. Baby nurse, Ladue, Mo., 1984—89; home care worker and provider Clayton, Mo., 1989; adminstrv. asst. Grateful Home Homeless Shelter, Detroit, 1992; day care asst. Time for Happy Land Care, Detroit, 1999—. Contbr. poetry Internat. Poetry Hall of Fame Mus. Exhibit Nat. Libr. of Poetry, Phila., 1997—2001, poetry numerous anthologies, Poetry.com. Recipient numerous awards for poetry. Avocations: writing, gardening, taping, reading, creating. Home: 14503 Hazelridge St Detroit MI 48205-3619

BOOTH, DIRIE MURPHY DEE, music educator, musician; b. Altavista, Va., May 12, 1947; d. Prentis Allen and Margaret Delilah (Swain) Murphy; m. Raymond Addison Booth, Feb. 9, 1969; children: Sherry Lynn Booth Gray, Vickie Marie Booth Lagos, Kevin Addison. BS in Elem. Edn., Radford U., 1969; cert. of major in music, Randolph-Macon Women's Coll., 1995. Organist-music dir. Randolph Meml. Bapt. Ch., Madison Heights, Va., 1971-78, White's United Meth. Ch., Rustburg, Va., 1986-88; piano and organ tchr. Lynchburg, Va., 1986—; organist First Ch. Christ Scientist, Lynchburg, Va., 1988-89; music dir. Madison Heights Christian Ch., Lynchburg, Va., 1989-90; music edn. tchr. James River Day Sch., Lynchburg, Va., 1992-93; organist, pianist Keystone Bapt. Ch., Lynchburg, Va., 1992-94; organist Beulah Bapt. Ch., Lynchburg, Va., 1995—. Vol. musician Lynchburg Christian Women's Club, 1986—. Mem. Nat. Fedn. Music Clubs, Am. Guild Organists, Nat. Guild Piano Tchrs. (dist. ch. 1992-97, pres. 1998—), Music Tchrs. Nat. Assn., Ctrl. Va. Music Tchrs. Assn. (v.p. 1985—), Va. Music Tchrs. Assn. Avocations: aerobics, reading, cross-stitch. Home and Office: 206 Dean St Lynchburg VA 24502-2414

BOOTH, JANE SCHUELE, real estate company executive, real estate broker; b. Cleve. d. Norman Andrew and Frances Ruth (Hankey) Schuele; m. George Warren Booth, Dec. 6, 1968. AA, Stephens Coll., 1946; student, U. Mo., 1946-47. Lic. real estate broker, Fla. Assoc. J.M. Mathes Inc., N.Y.C., 1947-48; dept. supr. Lord and Taylor, Scarsdale, N.Y., 1948-50; art coord. J. Walter Thompson, Inc., N.Y.C., 1953-58; art buyer SSC&B Inc. Advt., N.Y.C., 1959-80; pres. Jane Schuele Booth Realty, Ocala, Fla., 1982—. Mem. Fla. Thoroughbred Fillies, Ocala, 1980—; charter mem., trustee Royal Dames for Cancer Rsch., Inc., Ocala, 1986—; treas. Ladies Aux. Fla. H.C.H. Inc., Ocala, 1986-90; bd. visitors Fla. Horsemen's Children's Home, Inc., 1983-90. Mem. Ocala/Marion County Assn. Realtors, Ocala/Marion County C. of C. (agribus./equine com.), Nat. Assn. Realtors, Fla. Assn. Realtors, Estates Club. Home: 1771 SW 55th Street Rd Ocala FL 34474-5933 Office: PO Box 5538 Ocala FL 34478-5538 E-mail: janeschuelebooth@aol.com.

BOOTH, MARGARET A(NN), communications company executive; b. N.Y.C., Dec. 25, 1946; d. Herbert and Alice (Traum) B.; m. Marvin E. Schechter, Jan. 22, 1984. BS, U. Wis., 1968. Editl. asst. Bantam Books, N.Y.C., 1968-70; publicity asst. Ruder & Finn Inc., N.Y.C., 1970-71, dir. radio and TV, 1971-76, v.p., 1974-76; pres. Pub. Interest Pub. Rels., N.Y.C., 1976—, M. Booth & Assocs., Inc., N.Y.C., 1983—. Author: Promoting Issues and Ideas, 1987; contbr. articles to profl. jours. Bd. govs. Eugene Lang Coll. New Sch. for Social Rsch.; bd. dirs. N.Y. Found. Recipient YWCA Salute to Women Achievers, City of N.Y., 1985. Mem. Pub. Rels. Soc. Am., Women in Comm. (Matrix award for Pub. Rels. 1987), Women Execs. in Pub. Rels. Office: M Booth & Assocs Inc 470 Park Ave S # 10N New York NY 10016-6819

BOOTH, PENELOPE PARTRIDGE, secondary school educator, writer, principal; b. Niskayuna, N.Y., Dec. 7, 1943; d. Leonard Charlton and Elizabeth Jane (Russ) Partridge; m. John Robert Booth, Sept. 10, 1966 (div. 1975); children: Elizabeth Ashley, Patricia Anne. BS in Math., Mary Washington Coll., 1965; EdM, Towson State U., 1981. Comml. supr. Chesapeake & Potomac Tel. Co., Washington, 1965-66, Richmond, Va., 1967-68; math. tchr. Havelock (N.C.) H.S., 1966-67, Jack Jouett Jr. H.S., Charlottesville, Va., 1968-70, Baltimore County Pub. Schs., Towson, Md., 1974-81, supr. math., 1987-93; prin. Catonsville (Md.) Mid. Sch., 1993-96; tchr. gifted and talented resource Office Of Math., Towson, 1981-84; chmn. math. dept. Hereford Mid. Sch., Monkton, Md., 1984-87; coord. office of math. Baltimore County Pub. Schs., Md., 1996—. Instr. Baltimore county Pub. Schs., 1976-88, Md. Acad. Scis., Balt., 1984-86, Inst. for the Gifted Talented, Towson, 1983-85; cons. Md. State Dept. Edn., Balt., 1981—, Sylvan Learning, 2002-; adj. prof. Johns Hopkins U., 1996—, Coll. Notre Dame Md., 1997—, Loyola Coll. Md., 2002-; co-owner Conversation Pieces, 1997—. Author: Essentials of Mathematics, 1988, Consumer Mathematics, 1988, Foundations of Algebra and Geometry, 1998, (booklet) First Book of Testing. Adult leader troop 336, Girl Scouts U.S.A., Towson, 1972-88; mem. Lutherville (Md.) Recreation Coun., 1979-89; cons. Md. Math. League, 1982-87; chmn., co-founder Christa McAuliffe Scholarship Found., 1986—; mem. alumni adv. coun. Towson State U.; mem. adv. bd. MAT Program Johns Hopkins U., 1992-2002. Recipient Presdl. award NSF, 1985, Disting. Alumni award Towson State U., 1989, Educator of Yr. award Md. Coun. Tchrs. of Math., 2002. Mem. ASCD, Nat. Coun. Suprs. Math. (sec.-treas. Md. coun. 2000—), Nat. Coun. Tchrs. Math., Coun. Presdl. Awardees (scholarship chmn.), Nat. Assn. Secondary Sch. Prins., Optimists, Phi Delta Kappa, Delta Kappa Gamma (v.p.). Republican. Presbyterian. Avocations: traveling, needlepoint. Home: 135 Greenridge Rd Lutherville Timonium MD 21093-6124 E-mail: pbooth@bcps.org.

BOOTH, RACHEL ZONELLE, nursing educator; b. Seneca, S.C., Feb. 10, 1936; m. Richard B. Booth, Feb. 13, 1957; 1 child, Kevin M. Student, Furman U., 1953-54; diploma in nursing, Greenville (S.C.) Gen. Hosp., 1956; student, U. Alaska, 1964-66; BS in Nursing, U. Md., Balt., 1968; MS in Nursing, U. Md., 1970, PhD in Adminstrn. Higher Edn., 1978; D of Nursing Sci. (hon.), Chiang Mai U., Thailand, 1999. RN. Staff nurse VA Hosp., Murfreesboro, Tenn., 1956-57, U. Colo. Med. Ctr., Denver, 1957-58; nurse psychiatry dept. Patton State Hosp., Calif., 1958-59; staff nurse USAF Dispensary, Iraklion, Greece, 1959-60; charge nurse psychiatry Santa Rose Med. Ctr., San Antonio, 1961; staff nurse Shannon S.W. Tex. Meml. Hosp., San Angelo, 1962; supervisory clin. nurse, head nurse U.S. Dept. Health, Edn., and Welfare/USPHS/Indian Health Service, Anchorage, 1962-66; staff nurse U.S. Dept. Health, Edn., and Welfare/USPHS, Balt., 1966, 68; assoc. dir. dept. nursing U. Md. Hosp., 1970-76, dir. primary care nursing svc., 1976-81; asst. prof. Sch. Nursing U. Md., 1972-76, asst. prof. Sch. Pharmacy, 1972-80, acting assoc. dean Sch. Nursing, 1979-81, assoc. prof. Sch. Nursing, 1979, assoc. prof. clin. pharmacy, 1980-83, assoc. dean for undergrad. studies Sch. Nursing, 1981-83, co-dir. nurse practitioner program Sch. Nursing, 1972-76, chairperson grad. program dept. primary care, 1974-79; dean, Sch. of Nursing and asst. v.p. for health affairs Duke U., Durham, N.C., 1984-87; dean Sch. Nursing U. Ala. at Birmingham, University Station, 1987—. Instr. Sch. Medicine U. Md., 1972-83, program dir. primary care nurse practitioner program continuing edn., 1976-82, project dir. Robert Wood Johnson Nurse Faculty Fellowship program, 1977-82; mem. joint practice com. Med. and Surg. Faculty Md., 1974-77, mem. tech. adv. com. for physician's assts. Bd. Med. Examiners Md., 1975-80; mem. adv. [illegible] Coll. Balt., 1976-79; mem. Joint Commn. on Accreditation of Hosps., pres. Md. Council Dirs. of Assoc. Degree, Diploma, and Baccalaureate Programs, 1982-83; mem. adv. bd. nursing Essex Community Coll., 1983; mem. peer rev. panel advanced nurse edn. nursing div. U.S. Dept. Health and Human Services, 1987—. Editor (with others) Hospital Pharmacy, 1971-72; asst. editor Jour. Profl. Nursing, 1984-87; contbr. articles on nursing to prof. jours. Bd. dirs. Health and Welfare Coun. Ctrl. Md., Inc., 1974-78, v.p., 1975-78; mem. health adv. com. to Pres. of Pakistan, 1981—. Recipient numerous grants for nursing adminstrn., 1972—. Mem. ANA (mem. nat. rev. com. 1975-78, v.p. 1977, chair 1978), Internat. Coun. Nurses (observer conf. 1981), Nat. Acad. Practice for Nursing (vice chairperson 1984-89), Nat. Orgn. for Nurse Execs., Nat. League for Nursing, Coun. Nat. Acad. Practice, Am. Assn. Colls. in Nursing (dean's summer seminar com. 1984-85, edn. and credentialing com. 1985-86, nominating com. 1986-87, bd. dirs. 1989-96, pres.-elect 1992-94, pres. 1994-96), N.C. Orgn. Nurse Execs. (bd. dirs. 1986-87), So. Coun. Collegiate Edn. for Nursing (exec. com. 1986-91, v.p., bd. dirs. 1991-94, pres. 1997-99), Sigma Theta Tau (chairperson nominating com. 1974, mem. 1975, rec. sec. 1980-83). Avocations: genealogy, travel, swimming. Office: U Ala at Birmingham 1530 3rd Ave S Birmingham AL 35294-0002

BOOTH, SUSAN, educational association administrator, product designer, marketing professional, researcher; d. Kyung Hi Yang and John Kent Booth; m. Martin Johnson, Jan. 4, 2002; 1 child, Makani Booth Johnson. BS, Lewis and Clark Coll., Portland, Oreg., 1984; MEd, Lesley Coll., Cambridge, Mass., 1988. Cert. elem. edn. Mass., 1988. Edn. and tech. devel. specialist Coun. for Advancement and Support of Edn., Washington, 1993—98; mgr., edn. tech. programs Nat. Sch. Bds. Assn., Alexandria, Va., 1998—2000; dir. of products and svcs. devel. Nat. Assn. of Ind. Schs., Washington, 2000—. Mem.: Am. Mktg. Assn., Greater Wash. Soc. of Assn. Exec., Am. Soc. of Assn. Exec.

BOOTH, SUSAN VIRGINIA, theater director; b. June 5, 1963; m. Max Leventhal. BA in Performance, Denison U., 1985; MA, Northwestern U., 1987. Dir. new play devel. Goodman Theatre, Chgo., 1993—2001; artistic dir. Alliance Theatre Co., Atlanta, 2001—. Co-artistic dir. Chgo. Summer Theatre; assoc. artistic dir. Northlight Theatre; tchr. Northwestern U., DePaul U., Art Inst. Chgo.; bd. dir. Regional Arts Alliance, Atlanta, Theatre Comms. Group; mem. Nat. Theatre Conf. Fellow, Nat. Critics Inst., 1990. Office: Alliance Theatre Co Woodruff Arts Ctr 1280 Peachtree St NE Atlanta GA 30309 E-mail: susan.booth@woodruffcenter.org.

BOOTH, TAMI, editor; Editor health and medicine category Little Brown, 1994—97; exec. editor health and lifestyle books IDG Books, N.Y.C. and Chgo., 1997—2000; dir. new title devel. Rodale, Inc., N.Y.C., 2000, exec. editor Women's Health Books, 2000—01, editor-in-chief Women's Health Books, 2001—. Office: Rodale Press 733 3d Ave New York NY 10017*

BOOTH, TERRI LYNNE, music educator; b. Jacksonville, Fla., Aug. 26, 1957; d. Fred Jay and Yvonne Mae-Lumpkin Morrow; m. Michael Stuart Booth, Apr. 28, 1978; children: Lea Michelle, Michael Travis. AA, Fla. Jr. Coll., Jacksonville, 1977; B in Music Edn., Jacksonville U., 1979. Cert. tchr. Fla. Band dir. Southside Jr. H.S., Jacksonville, 1980—84; tchr. music, phys. edn. St. Patrick's Cath. Sch., Jacksonville, 1990—96; band and choral dir. Bishop Kenny H.S., Jacksonville, 1996—. Softball rep. San Mateo Little League, Jacksonville, 1993—95. Mem.: Nat. Cath. Band Dirs. Assn., Fla. Vocal Assn., Fla. Bandmasters Assn., Fla. Music Educators Assn. (state Tri-M com.). Republican. Avocations: camping, canoeing, travel. Home: 13771 Grover Rd Jacksonville FL 32226 Office: Bishop Kenny HS 1055 Kingman Ave Jacksonville FL 32207 Personal E-mail: mstlbooth@aol.com.

BOOZ, GRETCHEN ARLENE, marketing executive; b. Boone, Iowa, Nov. 24, 1933; d. David Gerald and Katherine Bevridge (Hardie) Berg; m. Donald Rollett Booz, Sept. 3, 1960; children: Kendra Sue (dec.), Joseph David, Katherine Sue. AA, Graceland Coll., 1955. Med. asst. Robert A. Hayne M.D., Des Moines, 1955-61; mktg. dir. Herald Pub. House, Independence, Mo., 1975—. Author: (book) Kendra, 1979. Mem. Citizens Adv. Bd., Blue Springs, Mo., 1979-91, Independence Mayor's Christmas Concert Com., 1987-91; bd. dirs. Comprehensive Mental Health, 1981-83, Child Placement Svcs., Independence, 1987-94, Hope House, Inc., Independence, 1987-91, Ctr. for Profl. Devel. and Life-long Learning, Inc., 1995-96; trustee Graceland U., Lamoni, Iowa, 1984-96. Mem. Leadership Edn. Action Devel. (L.E.A.D.), Independence C. of C. (diplomat, Outstanding Mem. award 1981), Rotary. Republican. Mem. Community of Christ Ch. Avocation: writing and presenting monologues of women in history. Home: 1200 Crestview Dr Blue Springs MO 64014-2312 Office: Herald Pub House 1001 W Walnut PO Box 390 Independence MO 64051-0390 E-mail: gbooz@heraldhouse.org., gbooz3@comcast.net.

BOQUIST, DIANA D. mayor, real estate agent; b. Columbus, Ohio, Mar. 26, 1940; d. Cleo Lewis and Elizabeth Katherine (Fry) Dumaree; m. Edwin Russell Boquist, June 9, 1961; children: Kimberly, Kelly, Kerry. BSc in Edn., Ohio State U., 1961. 4th grade tchr. Long Beach (Calif.) Unified Sch. Dist., 1961-63; real estate sales staff Schlott & Coldwell Banker Realtors, Bernardsville, N.J., 1983-95; mgr. real estate office Coldwell Banker, Basking Ridge, N.J., 1995-98; asst. mgr. Weichert Realtors, Bernardsville, N.J., 1998—. Pres. Boeing Wives Club, Cape Canaveral, Fla., 1967, PTA, Greensburg, Pa., 1973, Welcome Wagon, Somerset Hills, 1978, Sch. Bd., Bernards Twp., 1986, 87; coun. woman Town Coun., Bernards Twp., 1992—, mayor, 1995, 99; elder Basking Ridge Presbyn. Ch., 1999—. Named Woman of Yr., Bus. and Profl. Women, Bernardsville, 1995, Basking Ridge, 1995. Mem. N.J. Assn. Realtors (Disting. Realtor award 1993). Republican. Avocations: bridge, travel, golf. Home: 39 Kensington Rd Basking Ridge NJ 07920-2505 Office: Weichert Realtors 62 Morristown Rd Bernardsville NJ 07924-2305 also: Collyer Ln Basking Ridge NJ 07920

BORAS, KIM, lawyer; BA, Rollins Coll., 1986; JD, Harvard U., 1989. Bar: Calif. 1989, Fla. 1990, N.Y. 2001. Jud. clk. to Hon. Peter T. Fay, Judge, U.S. Ct. Appeals (11th cir.), 1989—90; with Latham & Watkins, L.A., 1990—, ptnr., 2001—. Office: Latham and Watkins LLC 633 W Fifth St Ste 4000 Los Angeles CA 90071*

BORCHARDT, BETSY OLK, artist; b. Clintonville, Wis., June 5, 1953; d. James Howard and Bernice Durben (Olk); m. Andrew Peter Borchardt, Dec. 27, 1980. Student, Lawrence U., 1971; BA in Sociology, St. Norbert Coll., De Pere, Wis., 1980; postgrad., U. Tenn., 1981. Home health aide Upjohn, Oshkosh, Wis., 1989, Oshkosh, 90; pvt. practice, Omro, 1990—93; program aide United Cerebral Palsy, Oshkosh, 1996—97; participant electronic tranmission art Ariz. State U. project shown at UN 4th World Conf. on Women, Beijing, 1995; recruiting asst. U.S. Census Bur., Stevens Point, Wis., 2000; line therapist Autism and Behavioral Cons., Fond du Lac, Wis., 2002—03. Author: (poetry) A Personal Struggle, 1987; solo exhbn. U. Wis. Ctr., Marinette, Wisc., 2003;one woman show at U. Wis. Ctr.-Marinette, 2003; exhibited in groups shows at Kansas City Kans. Civic Ctr., Pub. Libr., The Country Club Plz., Kansas City, Mo., 1987-88, Neville Pub. Mus., Green Bay, Wis., 1990, The Art Barn Gallery, Green Lake, Wis., 1995, Wis. Ctr., Madison, 1996, Our Savior Luth. Ch., Oshkosh, Wis., 1998, Art for All, Menominee, Mich., 2002. Vol. Franklin Ctr. Coffee Shop, Kansas City, 1984; activity aide Omro Care Ctr., 1988—89; visual arts leader Winnebago County 4-H, Omro, 1991, 1992; vol. tutor Redgranite Elem. Sch., 1995—2000; mem. chorus, drama cast, handbell choir Maestro Prodns., Inc., Oshkosh, 1991—2000; scientist pen-pal Sci. By Mail Mus. Sci., Boston, 1996—2000; founding mem. Wildlife Land Trust Humane Soc. U.S., Wildlife Guardian for Defenders of Wildlife, 1999—; mem. and legis. activist Nat. Wildlife Fedn., 2000—; charter mem. Smithsonian Nat. Mus. of Am. Indian, 2000—. Mem. Nat. Mus. Women in Arts (charter), Philanthropy Soc., Wis. Regional Artists Assn. (Kenneth and Marie Kuemmerlein award 1992, Obermiller Edn. award, 1996), Wis. Regional Writers Assn., Lions (sec. 2001—). Avocations: reading, camping, fishing, bird watching. Home: 231 Wood St Redgranite WI 54970-9342 E-mail: betsyborchardt@hotmail.com.

BORCHERT, CATHERINE GLENNAN, minister; b. L.A., Dec. 6, 1936; d. Thomas Keith and Ruth Haslup Adams Glennan; m. Frank R. Borchert Jr., Sept. 12, 1959 (dec. Sept. 1997); children: Frank R. III, Anne Matthews, Thomas Adams. BS, Swarthmore Coll., 1958; MSLS, Western Res. U., 1959; MDiv, McCormick Theol. Sem., 1991; postgrad., Case Western Res. U. Ordained to ministry, Presbyn. Ch., 1991. Serial records libr. U. Chgo. Libr., 1959-61; ref. libr., head outreach Cleveland Heights (Ohio) Pub. Libr., 1979-86; stated clk. Presbytery of Western Res. U., Cleve., 1984-94; interim pastor Lyndhurst (Ohio) Cmty. Presbyn. Ch., 1993-94; coord. adv. com. social witness policy Gen. Assembly of Presbyn. Ch., Louisville, 1994-97; adj. faculty McCormick Theol. Sem., Chgo., 1987—, interim dean doctoral programs and continuing edn., 2000-01. Mem. exec. com. Permanent Judicial Commn. Contbr. articles to profl. jours. Bd. dirs. United Protestant Campus Min., Cleve., 1999—2002, History Assocs., Cleve., 1999—; mem. steering com. Woman 2000 Case Western Res. U., 1998—2000; alumni interviewer Swarthmore (Pa.) Coll., 1965—; mem. exec. com. Chs.' Ctr. for Theology and Pub. Policy, Washington. Mem.: Mortar Bd., Phi Alpha Theta, Beta Phi Mu. Democrat. Avocations: reading, birdwatching, choir, bike riding. Home: 13415 Shaker Blvd #9C2 Cleveland OH 44120

BORDA, DEBORAH, symphony orchestra executive; b. N.Y.C., July 15, 1949; d. William and Helene (Malloy) B. BA, Bennington Coll., 1971; postgrad., Royal Coll. Music, London, 1972-73. Program dir. Mass. Coun. Arts and Humanities, Boston, 1974-76; mgr. Boston Musica Viva, Boston, 1976-77; gen. mgr. Handel and Haydn Soc., Boston, 1977-79, San Francisco Symphony, 1979-86; pres. St. Paul Chamber Orch., 1986-88; exec. dir. Detroit Symphony Orch., 1988-90; pres. Minn. Orch., Mpls., 1990-91; exec. dir. N.Y. Philharm., N.Y.C., 1991-99; exec. v.p., mging dir. Los Angeles Philharmonic Assoc., 1999—. Office: Los Angeles Philharmonic Assn 135 N Grand Ave Los Angeles CA 90012

BORDALLO, MADELEINE MARY (MRS. RICARDO JEROME BORDALLO), congresswoman; b. Graceville, Minn., May 31, 1933; d. Christian Peter and Mary Evelyn (Roth) Zeien; m. Ricardo Jerome Bordallo, June 20, 1953; 1 daughter, Deborah Josephine. Student, St Mary's Coll., South Bend, Ind., 1952; AA, St. Katherines Coll., St. Paul, 1953; AA hon. degree for community service, U. Guam, 1968. Presented in voice recital Guam Acad. Music, Agana., 1951, 62; mem. Civic Opera Co., St. Paul, 1952-53; mem. staff KUAM Radio-TV sta., Agana, 1954-63; freelance writer local newspaper, fashion show commentator, coordinator, civic leader, 1963; nat. Dem. committeewoman for Guam, 1964—2003; 1st lady of Guam, 1974-78, 81-85; senator 16th Guam Legislature, 1981-82, 19th Guam Legislature, 1987-88, 20th Guam Legislature, 1989-90, 21st Guam Legislature, 1991-92, 22nd Guam Legislature, 1993-94; Dem. Party candidate for Gov. of Guam, 1990, lt. gov. of Guam, 1994; lt. gov. of Guam, 1994—2002; at-large repr. U.S. Ho. of Reps. from Guam, 2003—. Del. Nat. Dem. Conv., 1964, 68, 72, 76, 80, 84, 88-92, 96, pres. Women's Dem. Party Guam, 1967-69; rep. Presdl. Inauguration, Washington, 1965, 77, 85; del. Dem. Western States Conf., Reno, 1965, L.A., 1967, Phoenix, 1968, conf. sec., 1967-69; del. Dem. Women's Campaign Conf., Wash., 1965, Dem. Inauguration, 1992. Pres. Guam Women's Club, 1958-59; del Gen. Fedn. Women's Clubs Convs., Miami Beach, Fla., 1961, New Orleans, 1965, Boston, 1968; v.p. Fedn. Asian Women's Assn., 1964-67, pres., 1967-69, pres. 1996-98; pres. Guam Symphony Soc., 1967-73, del. convs., Manila, Philippines, 1959, Taipei, Formosa, 1960, Hong Kong, 1963, Guam, 1964, Japan, 1968, Taipei, 1973; chmn. Guam Christmas Seal Drive, 1961; bd. dirs. Guam chpt. ARC, 1963, sec., 1963-67, fund dr. chmn., 2000; pres. Marianas Assn. For Retarded Children, 1968-69, 73-74, 84—; bd. dirs. Guam Theatre Guild, Am. Cancer Soc.; mem. Guam Meml. Hosp. Vols. Assn., 1966—, v.p., 1966-67, pres., 1970-71; chmn. Hosp. Charity Ball, 1966; pres. Women for Service, 1974—, Beauty World Guam Ltd., 1981—, First Lady's Beautification Task Force of Guam, 1983-86; pres. Palace Restoration Assn., 1983—; nominee Dem. party for Gov. of Guam, 1990. Mem. Internat. Platform Assn., Guam Rehab. Assn. (assoc.), Guam Lytico and Bodig Assn. (pres. 1983-98), Spanish Club of Guam, Inetnon Famalaoan Club (pres. 1983-86), Guam Coun. of Women's Club (pres. 1993-95), Nat. Conf. Lt. Govs. (exec. com. 1998—). Democrat. Home: PO Box 1458 Hagatna GU 96932-1458 Office: 427 Cannon Ho Office Bldg Washington DC 20515-5301 Office Phone: 202-225-1188. E-mail: Madeleine.Bordallo@mail.house.gov.

BORDELON, CAROLYN THEW, elementary school educator; b. Shelby, Ohio, Dec. 28, 1942; d. Burton Carl and Opal Mae (Harris) VanAsdale; m. Clifford Charles Spohn, Aug. 28, 1965 (div. Feb. 1982); m. Al Ramon Bordelon, Oct. 26, 1985. BA in History and Polit. Sci., Otterbein Coll., 1966; MA in Edn., Bowling Green State U., 1972; postgrad., Ohio State U., 1986—. Cert. tchr. grades 1-8, Ohio. Elem. tchr. Allen East Schs., Harrod, Ohio, 1966-68, Marion (Ohio) City Schs., 1968-78, chpt. I reading tchr., 1978-86, reading recovery tchr., 1986-88, Dublin (Ohio) City Schs., 1988—. Adj. instr. reading dept.grad. studies Ashland (Ohio) U., 1996. Author: The Parent Workshop, 1992, Octopus Goes to School, 1995. Vol. Am. Heart Assn., Worthington, Ohio, 1991; mem. Rep. Nat. Com., Washington, 1994-95; mem. Royal Scots Highlanders, Mansfield, Ohio, 1976—. Recipient Excellence in Edn. award Dublin City C. of C., 1991-93, 96, 97; Dublin City Schs./Ohio Dept. Edn. Tchr. Award grantee, 1993; Martha Holden Jennings Found. scholar, 1978. Mem. Archaeol. Inst. Am., Ohio Edn. Assn., Reading Recovery Coun. N.Am., Opera/Columbus, Mus. of Art, Columbus, Phi Delta Kappa, Phi Alpha Theta. Presbyterian. Avocations: bagpiping and scottish activities, archaeology, interior design, harpsichord. Home: 3958 Fairlington Dr Columbus OH 43220-4531 Office: Griffith Thomas Elem Sch 4671 Tuttle Crossing Blvd Dublin OH 43017-3575 E-mail: cbordelonread@aol.com.

BORDELON, DENA COX YARBROUGH, retired special education educator, director; b. Gorman, Tex., June 20, 1933; d. William Thomas and Imogene (Dunlap) Cox; m. James Edgar Yarbrough, June 20, 1950 (dec.); m. Cecil J. Bordelon, Sept. 24, 1999. BA, Nicholls State U., 1964, MEd, 1971, postgrad., 1978. Supr. profl. pers., prin. schs., elem. tchr. Terrebonne Parish Sch. Bd., Houma, La., 1964-79, dir. spl. edn. svcs., 1980-91; ret., 1991. Mem. La. Ret. Tchrs. Assn. Democrat. Methodist. Avocations: reading, theatre. Home: 202 White St Houma LA 70364-2934 E-mail: cbordelon@sw.rr.com.

BORDEN, DIANE LYNN, communications educator; b. Chgo., Jan. 25, 1947; d. H. Frederick and Vera L. Borden; m. Robert Easley (div. 1970). BA, Colo. State U., 1972; MA, Stanford U., 1989; PhD, U. Wash., 1993. Mng. editor Bellingham (Wash.) Herald, 1977-80; dep. mng. editor Tribune, Oakland, Calif., 1981-85; pres. Santa Fe (N.Mex.) New Mexican, 1986-87; assoc. prof. Temple U., Phila., 1993-95; project dir. Am. Soc. Newspaper Editors, Reston, Va., 1995-96; asst. prof. George Mason U., Fairfax, Va., 1996-98; prof. San Diego State U., 1998—. Gannett profl. in residence U. Kans., Lawrence, 1985-86; cons. and expert witness in communication law and ethics. Co editor: The Electronic Grapevine, 1997; co-author: Creative Editing, 4th edit., 2003; contbr. articles to scholarly and profl. jours.; editor: (book) Women and Language, 1997-99. Active NOW, Habitat for Humanity, World Wildlife Fund, Washington. Profl. journalism fellow Stanford U., 1980-81, fellow in telecomm. policy Annenberg Washington Program, 1995; rsch. grantee Temple U., 1994, San Diego State U., 1999, 2000. Mem. Assn. for Edn. in Journalism and Mass Communication, AAUW, Am. Journalism Historians Assn. Avocations: hiking, golf, reading biographies of women. Office: San Diego State U School of Jour 5500 Campanile Dr San Diego CA 92182-8000

BORDEN, MICHELLE, health facility administrator; b. Bklyn., Jan. 16, 1959; d. Ronnie Estelle Leigh, children: Cortnea Michelle Bryant, Christian David. Grad. h.s., Bklyn. Allen School N.Y. Direct care counselor New Hope, Bklyn., 1981—87, Herbert G. Birch, Ridgewood Queen, NY, 1988—. Stock clk. Abraham & Strauss, Bklyn., 1978—81. Contbr. poetry to books. E-mail: bord41@yahoo.com.

BORDER, GLADYS LOUISE, piano educator; b. Cleve., Feb. 11, 1926; d. Frederick August and Edith Elliot (Spellman) Schnell; m. Tondra Harrison Border, Nov. 16, 1946; children: David, Thomas, Calvin. Diploma, Wilcox Coll. Commerce, Cleve., 1944; student, Baptist Bible Inst., Cleve., 1944-46. Sales clk. part time F.W. Woolworth Co., Cleveland Heights, Ohio, 1942-44; office sec. part time Wilcox Coll. Commerce, Cleve., 1944; sec. Standard Oil Co., Cleve., 1944-47; temporary office work Ballou Svcs., Cleve., 1954; piano tchr. pvt. practice, Cleve., 1955-59, Hollywood, Fla., 1959—; sec. indsl. and pub. rels. Food Fair Offices, Miami, 1961-62; piano tchr. pvt. practice, Hollywood, Fla., 1997—. Ch. pianist First Brethren Ch., Cleveland Heights, Ohio, 1941-46; regular pianist Phi Gamma Fishing Club, Cleve., 1944-46; asst. pianist Youth For Christ, Cleve., 1945; 2nd v.p., corr. sec., awards chmn. Broward County Music Tchrs., Ft. Lauderdale, Fla., 1970-90; pianist in churches Nazarene, Bapt. Hollywood Christian Sch., Cleve., 1947-58; accompanist for band solos McArthur H.S., Driftwood Jr. H.S., Hollywood, Fla., 1961-69; regular pianist 1st Bapt. Choir and Ch., W. Hollywood, Fla., 1971-89, part time 1993—. Author: (life story) On the Life of Gladys Louise (Schnell) Border. Den mother Boy Scouts Am. Cub Scouts, Cleve., 1958-59; Sunday sch. tchr. Ch. of Nazarene, Cleve., 1947-48, 57-58; treas. Band Parents Driftwood Jr. H.S., Hollywood, Fla., 1962, 63; recording sec. Women;s Soc. 1st Meth., Hollywood, Fla., 1962, 64; Sunday Sch. tchr. 1st Meth., Epworth Meth., Hollywood, Fla., 1960, 71. Recipient Electronic Metronome McArthur High Band Soloists, Hollywood, Fla., 1967, Bowling trophies Bapt. Fellowship League, Hollywood, Fla., 1973-86, music min. plaques (2) 1st Bapt. W. Hollywood, Fla., 1980, 89; named Fairest of the Island Mother's Banquet 1st Bapt. W. Hollywood, Fla., 1994. Mem. Nat. Guild of Piano Tchrs., Jolly Srs., Fla. Fedn. Music Clubs, Broward County Music Tchrs. Assn. Republican. Baptist. Avocations: piano playing, reading, sewing, bowling, writing letters. Home: 7091 Scott St Hollywood FL 33024-3849

BORDNER, PATRICIA ANNE, insurance agent, writer; b. Red Wing, Minn., Mar. 29, 1946; d. Harold Arthur and Cecilia Helen Rodman; m. Thomas Ottis Bordner, May 18, 1981. AA, U. Minn., 1966. Cert. commercial rater U.S. Fidelity and Guaranty Co. Tchr. St. Albert the Great Elem. Sch., Mpls., 1967—68; tchr. Epiphany Edn. Ctr., Coon Rapids, Minn., 1968—70; comml. rater and acctg. clk. U. S. Fidelity and Guaranty Co., Mpls., 1971—85; comml. ins. rater Independent, Coon Rapids, 1985—. Author: (songs) (Poetry Book) Hands of Time, 2000; contbr. poems to poetry contests and mags. Named to Internat. Poetry Hall of Fame, 1996; recipient Golden Poet award, 1990, 1991, 1992, Editor's Choice award, 1993—98. Roman Catholic. Home: 1010 94th Ave NW Coon Rapids MN 55433-5501

BORELLI, CYNTHIA ANN, vocal educator, chorus director; b. Reading, Pa., Jan. 6, 1969; d. Terry Lee and Mary Louise Beard; m. Giuseppe Domenico Borelli, July 14, 1990; children: Anthony, Nicholas. MusB, West Chester (Pa.) U., 1990, MusM, 1995. Elem. vocal and choral tchr. Wilson Sch. Dist., West Lawn, Pa., 1990—2003. Ch. choir mem. St. Ignatius Loyola Ch., West Lawn, Pa., 1998—2001. Recipient Theodore Presser scholar, West Chester U., 1990. Mem.: Pa. State Edn. Assn., Music Educators Nat. Conf., Am. Orff-Schulwerk Assoc. Home: 810 Broadcasting Rd Wyomissing PA 19610-1408 Office: Wilson Sch Dist 2601 Grandview Blvd West Lawn PA 19609

BOREN, LYNDA SUE, gifted education educator; b. Leesville, La., Apr. 1, 1941; d. Leonard and Doris (Ford) Schoenberger; m. James Lewis Boren, Sept. 1, 1961; 1 child, Lynda Carolyn. BA, U. New Orleans, 1971, MA,

1973; PhD, Tulane U., 1979. Prof. Northwestern State U., Natchitoches, La., 1987-89; propr. Colony Country House, New Llano, La., 1992-94; tchr. of gifted Leesville (La.) H.S., 1992—. Vis. prof. Newcomb Coll., Tulane U., New Orleans, 1979-83, U. Erlangen-Nuremburg, Germany, 1981-82, Middlebury (Vt.) Coll., 1983-84, Ga. Inst. Tech., Atlanta, 1985-87, Srinakharinwirot U., Bangkok, 1989-90; mem. planning com. 1st Kate Chopin Internat. Conf., Natchitoches, La., 1987-89; Fulbright lectr. USIA and Bd. Fgn. Scholars, 1981-82, 89-90. Author: Eurydice Reclaimed: Language, Gender and Voice in Henry James, 1989; co-editor, author: Kate Chopin Reconsidered, 1992; contbg. author: Encyclopedia of American Poetry, 1998; contbr. numerous articles to profl. jours. Founding mem. John F. Kennedy libr. Recipient awards for watercolors; Mellon fellow Tulane U., 1977-78; NEH seminar fellow Princeton U., 1986. Mem. MLA, AAUW, DAR, AFT, Fulbright Alumni Assn. Avocations: painting, video film documentaries, photography. Home: 1492 Fords Dairy Rd Newllano LA 71461-4530 Office Phone: 337-239-3464. E-mail: alborn@peoplepc.com.

BORETZ, NAOMI MESSINGER, artist, educator; b. Bklyn. BA, Bklyn. Coll.; MA in Fine Arts, CUNY; MA in Art History, Rutgers U.; postgrad., Art Students League N.Y. Exhibitions include Westminster Arts Coun. Arts Ctr., London, 1971, Hudson River Mus., N.Y., 1975, Katonah Gallery, 1976, Condeso-Lawler Gallery, N.Y.C., 1987, Carnegie-Mellon Art Gallery, Pitts., 1989, The Nelson Atkins Mus. of Art, St. Louis, 1994, Westbeth Gallery, N.Y., 1996, Mishkin Gallery, Baruch Coll., 1997, Rutgers (N.J.) U. Art Gallery, 1998, Hillwood Art Mus., N.Y., 2000, Muhlenburg Coll. Art Gallery, 2002, others, Represented in permanent collections Met. Mus. Art, N.Y.C., Solomon R. Guggenheim Mus., Whitney Mus. Am. Art, Mus. Modern Art, DeLand Art Mus., Fla., Brit. Mus., London, Nat. Mus. Am. Art, Washington, Yale U. Art Gallery, Joslyn Art Mus., Omaha, Walker Art Ctr., Mpls., Miami U. Art Mus., Oxford, Ohio, Fogg Art Mus. Harvard U., Cambridge, Mass., Glasgow (Scotland) Mus., San Jose (Calif.) Art Mus., Asheville (N.C.) Art Mus., Princeton U. Graphic Arts Collection, N.J., Mus. S.W., Midland, Tex., Swope Art Mus., Terre Haute, Ind., others; contbr. to arts publs. Artist-fellow Va. Ctr. Creative Arts, 1973, 86, Ossabaw Found., 1975, Tyrone Guthrie Arts Ctr., Ireland, 1987, Writers-Artists Guild Can., 1988; grantee N.J. State Coun. on Arts, 1985-86. Studio: Princeton NJ

BORG, RUTH I. home nursing care provider; d. Axel Gunner and Charlotte (Benston) B. Diploma, West Suburban Sch. Nursing, 1956; tchr.'s degree, Chgo. Conservatory, 1958; BSN, Alverno Coll., 1981. Staff nurse Boath Meml. Hosp., Chgo.; head nurse psychiatry, head nurse long-term medicine VA North Chgo. Med. Ctr.; staff nurse, night supr. intermediate care VA Clement Zabiocki Med. Ctr., Milw.; pool nurse, in-home nursing care provider Milw. County Mental Health Complex; home nurse care provider Dr. Ghonsham Sooknandan, Kenosha, Wis., 1994—99. In-home nursing care provider. Contbr. articles to profl. jours. Recipient Mary D. Bradford Disting. Alumni award, 1998. Avocation: teaching and performing music.

BORGEN, IRMA R. music educator; b. McPherson, Kans., Jan. 15, 1911; d. Nels J.W. Nelson and Ida Elizabeth Shallene; m. Clifford E. Borgen, July 6, 1942 (dec. Oct. 1967); children: David John, Elizabeth Marie. BA, Gustavus Adolphus Coll., St. Peter, Minn., 1932; postgrad., U. Colo., 1964—65. Tchr. Am. Sch. for Dependents, Essen, Germany, 1950—51; pvt. music tchr. Colorado Springs, Colo., 1969—. Mem.: Mil. Widows, Fountain Valley Sr. Orgn. Democrat. Lutheran. Avocations: music, fitness classes. Home: 114 Harvard St Colorado Springs CO 80911

BORGER, GLORIA, journalist, editor; Grad., Colgate U., 1974. Journalist Washington Star, 1975-78; chief congrl. corr. Newsweek, Washington, 1976-86; asst. mng. editor U.S. News and World Report, N.Y.C., 1986-98, contbg. mng. editor Washington, 1998—. Office: US News & World Report Ste 1 1050 Thomas Jefferson St NW Washington DC 20007-3837

BORGNINE, TOVA, cosmetics executive; m. Ernest Borgnine. Model, actress, N.Y.C.; owner, cosmetologist Tova's Touch, N.Y.C.; pres. chair The Tova Corp, Beverly Hills, Calif. Active World Econ. Forum, Susan G. Homan Br. Cancer Found.; bd. dirs. Jr. Achievement, Am. Scandinavian Found. Office: The Tova Corp 192 N Canon Dr Beverly Hills CA 90210-5304 E-mail: dave@beautybytova.com.

BORHI, CAROL, data processing executive, finance company executive; b. N.Y.C., Oct. 23, 1949; d. Carl and Elsie Elizabeth (Varady) Chaky; m. Nicholas Anthony Borhi, Sept. 23, 1972; children: Christy Nicole, Nicholas James. Assoc. in Applied Sci., Manhattan Community Coll., 1970; student, Hunter Coll., 1967-68, 70-71. Programmer asst. N.Y. Telephone, N.Y.C., 1970-73, programmer, 1974-76, programmer analyst, 1976-83; staff analyst Nynex Svc. Co., N.Y.C., 1984-87; systems analyst Nynex Corp., N.Y.C., 1987, assoc. dir., 1987-90, staff dir., 1991—97, Bell Atlantic, 1997—2000; sr. staff cons. Verizon, 2000—. Pres. Personal Touch Computing, N.Y.C., 1981-86. Mem. Telephone Pioneers Am. (charter), Creative Investors Am. Clubs: Sacred Heart. Republican. Roman Catholic. Avocations: real estate investing, coin collecting, dance, guitar, piano. Office: Verizon Comms 1095 Ave of the Americas New York NY 10036

BORIS, RUTHANNA, dancer, choreographer, dance therapist, educator; b. Bklyn., Mar. 17, 1918; d. Joseph Jay and Frances (Weiss) B.; m. Frank W. Hobi (dec.) Student, Profl. Children's Sch., N.Y.C. Dir. Boris-Hobi Concert Co., 1955-57. Prin. dancer Am. Ballet, N.Y.C., 1934, Ballet Caravan, N.Y.C., 1936; prima ballerina Met. Opera Co., N.Y.C., 1939-41, Ballet Russe de Monte Carlo, N.Y.C., 1942-49; prima ballerina, choreographer-in-residence Royal Winnipeg Ballet of Can., 1957-59, dir. 1957-58; choreographer Ballet Russe de Monte Carlo, 1947, N.Y.C. Ballet, 1951; prof. dance U. Wash., Seattle, 1965-83, prof. emeritus, 1983—; adj. prof. psychiatry U. Wash., 1982; pres. exec. dir. Ctr. for Dance Devel. & Research, Albany, Calif., 1986— ; choreographer: Cirque de Deux, 1947, Quelques Fleurs, 1948, Cakewalk, 1951, Kaleidoscope, 1951, Will O' The Wisp, 1951, Pasticcio, 1955, Wanderling, 1957, Ragtime, 1975, Tape Suite, 1976, Four All, 1980. Mem. adv. bd. Seattle Psychoanalytic Inst., 1975-82. Mem. Am. Guild Mus. Artists (award 1964, gov. 1942-64), Am. Dance Therapy Assn. (pres. Calif. chpt. 1986-88, mem. dance therapy credentials com. 1990-92). Office: Ctr Dance Devel & Rsch Apt 1334 555 Pierce St Albany CA 94706-1009

BORKO, HILDA, education educator; BA in Psychology, UCLA, 1971, MA in Philosophy of Edn., 1973, PhD in Ednl. Psychology, 1978. Elem. tchg. credential Calif., specialization in mental retardation U. So. Calif. Asst. and assoc. prof. Coll. Edn., Va. Poly. Inst. and State U., 1980—85; assoc. prof. Coll. Edn., U. Md., College Park, 1985—91, Sch. Edn., U. Colo., Boulder, 1991—94; prof. Sch. Edn. U. Colo., Boulder, 1994—. Co-author (with M. Eisenhart): (book) Designing Classroom Research: Themes, Issues, and Struggles, 1993 (Outstanding article award, 1992); contbr. articles to profl. jours. and chpts. to books. Recipient grants in field. Mem.: APA, Nat. Coun. for Tchrs. of Math., Invisible Coll. for Rsch. on Tchg., Am. Assn. Colls. of Tchr. Edn., Am. Ednl. Rsch. Assn. (pres. 2003—), Pi Gamma Mu, Phi Beta Kappa, Phi Delta Kappa. Office: U Colo Sch Edn CB249 Boulder CO 80309

BORKOVEC, VERA Z. Russian studies educator; b. Brno, Czechoslovakia, Aug. 13, 1926; came to U.S., 1952; d. Josef Zanda and Jarmila (Tuscher) Martinasek; m. Alexej B. Borkovec, Aug. 29, 1951. BA, Charles U., 1949; MA, Hollins Coll., 1961, The Am. U., 1966; PhD, Georgetown U., 1973. Secondary sch. tchr. English, French Montgomery County Pub. Schs., Md., 1961-64; from asst. prof. to assoc. prof. Russian studies The Am. Univ., Washington, 1966-91, prof. emerita. Recipient Artis Bohemiae Amicis medal, Czech Ministry of Culture, 2003. Mem. Czechoslovak Soc. of Arts and Scis. (v.p. 1994—). Avocations: theater, music, poetry. Home: 12013 Kemp Mill Rd Silver Spring MD 20902-1515

BORLAND, KATHRYN KILBY, author; b. Pullman, Mich., Aug. 14, 1916; d. Paul Melbourne and Vinnie (Bensinger) Kilby; m. James Barton Borland, May 16, 1942; children— James Barton, Susan Lee. BS in Journalism, Butler U., 1937. Editor North Side Topics, Indpls., 1938-42. Author: (all with Helen Ross Speicher) Southern Yankees, 1960, Allan Pinkerton, 1962, Miles and the Big Black Hat, 1963, Everybody Laughed, 1964, Eugene Field, 1964, Phillis Wheatley, 1968, Harry Houdini, 1969, Clocks from Shadow to Atom, 1969, Good-Bye to Stony Crick, 1975, The Third Tower, 1974, Stranger in the Mirror, 1974, Good-bye, Julie Scott, 1975, To Walk the Night, 1976, These Tigers' Hearts, 1978, Irena, 1979, Pseudonyms: Alice Abbott, Jane Land. Co-recipient award for most distinguished children's book pub. by Ind. author Ind. U., 1969 Mem. P.E.O., Theta Sigma Phi, Kappa Alpha Theta. Home: 1050 S Maish Rd Frankfort IN 46041-3213

BORN, BROOKSLEY ELIZABETH, lawyer; b. San Francisco, Aug. 27, 1940; d. Ronald Henry and Mary Ellen (Bortner) Born; m. Alexander Elliot Bennett, Oct. 9, 1982; children: Nicholas Jacob Landau, Ariel Elizabeth Landau, Andrew E. Bennett, Laura F. Bennett, Peter J. Bennett. AB, Stanford U., 1961, JD, 1964. Bar: DC 1966. Law clk. U.S. Ct. Appeals, Washington, 1964—65; legal rschr. Harvard Law Sch., 1967—68; assoc. Arnold and Porter, Washington, 1965—67, 1968—73, ptnr., 1974—96, 1999—2002; chair U.S. Commodity Futures Trading Commn., Washington, 1996—99. Lectr. law Columbus Sch. Law, Cath. U. Am., 1972—74; adj. prof. Georgetown U. Law Ctr., Washington, 1972—73. Pres.: Stanford Law Rev., 1963—64. Chair bd. visitors Stanford Law Sch., 1987; trustee Ctr. for Law and Social Policy, Washington, 1977—96, Women's Bar Found., 1981—86; bd. dirs. Nat. Legal Aid and Defenders Assn., 1972—79, Washington Legal Clinic for Homeless, 1993—96, Lawyers Com. for Civil Rights Under Law, 1993—96, Am. Bar Found., 1989—99, Washington Lawyers Com. for Civil Rights and Urban Affairs, 1992—96; chair bd. dirs. Nat. Women's Law Ctr., 1981—96, 2003—; bd. dirs., 1997—2002. Mem.: ABA (chair sect. ind. rights and responsibilities 1977—78, chair fed. judiciary com. 1980—83, chair consortium on legal svcs. and the pub. 1987—90, bd. govs. 1990—93, chair resource devel. coun. 1993—95, chair coun. Fund for Justice and Edn. 1995—96, state del. from DC 1994—), Southwestern Legal Found. (trustee 1993—96), Am. Law Inst., DC Bar (sec. 1975—76, mem. bd. govs. 1976—79), Order of Coif. Office: Arnold & Porter 555 12th St NW Washington DC 20004-1206 E-mail: brooksley_born@aporter.com.

BORN, ETHEL WOLFE, religious writer; b. Kasson, W.Va., Jan. 6, 1924; d. Otto Guy and Nancy Grace (Nestor) Wolfe; m. Harry Edward Born, Apr. 4, 1944 (dec. Aug. 1992); children: Rosemary Ellen (dec.), Barbara Anne Born Craig. Student, Ecumenical Inst., Geneva, 1983; BA, Mary Baldwin Coll., 1991. Author: A Tangled Web--A Search for Answers to the Question of Palestine, 1989, By My Spirit, Methodist Protestant Women in Mission, 1879-1939, 1990, From Memory to Hope, A Narrative History of the Areas of the World Federation of Methodist Women, 2000; contbr. articles to religious publs. Va. pres. United Meth. Women, 1972-76; bd. dirs. United Meth. Gen. Bd. Global Ministries, N.Y.C., 1976-84, v.p. women's divsn., 1980-84, v.p. com. on relief, 1980-84, Mid. East cons. women's divsn., 1984-88; chmn. N.Am. Coordinating Com. for Non-govtl. Orgns. UN Symposium, N.Y.C., 1986, 87; pres. N.Am. area, asst. world treas. World Fedn. Meth. Women, 1986-91, archivist, 1992-2001; mem. United Meth. Gen. Comm. Christian Unity and Inter-Religious Concerns, N.Y.C., 1988-96; mem. interfaith commn. Nat. Coun. Chs. of Christ, 1996-2000; mem. Pan-Meth. Commn. on Cooperation, 1996-2000. Recipient Stanley S. Kresge award, 1995. Mem. AAUW, Nat. League Am. Pen Women, Nat. Assn. Parliamentarians. Avocation: crafts.

BORNHOLDT, LAURA ANNA, university administrator; b. Peoria, Ill., Feb. 11, 1919; d. John and Barbara (Kohl) B. AB, Smith Coll., 1940, MA, 1942; PhD, Yale U., 1945. Asst. prof. history Smith Coll., Northampton, Mass., 1945-52; internat. relations asso. AAUW, Washington, 1952-57; dean Sarah Lawrence Coll., Bronxville, N.Y., 1957-59; dean women, adj. prof. history U. Pa., Phila., 1959-61; dean coll., prof. history Wellesley (Mass.) Coll., 1961-64; v.p. Danforth Found., St. Louis, 1964-73; sr. program officer Lilly Endowment Inc., Indpls., 1973-76, v.p. for edn., 1976-84; dir. office univ.-sch. rels. U. Chgo., 1984-94. Nat. adv. com. on black higher edn. and black colls. and univs. Dept. Edn., 1977-82; mem. Yale U. Council, 1977-82; emerita life trustee Coll. of Wooster, Ohio, 1967-77; trustee St. Louis U., 1971-75. Recipient Yale U. Wilbur Cross medal, 1976, Smith Coll. Alumnae medal, 1987. Mem. Am. Assn. Higher Edn., Phi Beta Kappa. Home: 925 Juniper Pl Bloomington IN 47408-1285

BORNINO-GLUSAC, ANNA MARIA, mathematics educator; b. Naples, Italy, Apr. 2, 1946; came to U.S., 1946; d. Bruno and Anna Maria (De Simone) B.; m. Howard Keith Wolff, July 29, 1966 (div. 1971); 1 child, Francesca Yvonne Wolff Hatzakis; m. Ronald G. Glusac, Sept. 4, 1993. BA in Chemistry, Calif. State U., Dominguez Hills, 1968, MA in Edn. Adminstrv. Svcs., 1986. Cert. standard secondary tchr., Calif., preliminary adminstrv., Calif., TFAS instr.; Calif. BCLAD credential. Tchr. math. L.A. Unified Sch. Dist., 1968—, dept. chair, 1982-84, 90-92, sch. improvement coord., 1998—2002; math. coach Dist. K., Wilmington, Calif., 2002—. Editor: Accreditation Report, 1983. Mem. United Tchrs. L.A., Nat. Coun. Tchrs. Math., Calif. Math. Coun. Democrat. Roman Catholic. Avocations: needlework, travel, reading, music. Office: 1527 Lakme Ave Wilmington CA 90744-1526

BORNSTEIN, RITA, academic administrator; b. N.Y.C., Jan. 2, 1936; d. Carl and Florence (Gates) Kropf; m. Harland G. Bloland; children from previous marriage: Rachel, Mark, Per. BA in English, Fla. Atlantic U., 1970, MA in English, 1971; PhD in Ednl. Leadership and Instrn., U. Miami, 1975. Tchr., adminstr. Dade County Pub. Schs., Fla., 1971-75; adminstr. dept. edn. U. Miami, Coral Gables, Fla., 1975-81, adminstr. divsn. devel., 1981-85, v.p., 1985-90; pres. Rollins Coll., Winter Park, Fla., 1990—. Bd. dirs. tupperware Corp. Author: (book) Freedom or Order: Must We Choose?, 1976, Title IX Compliance and Sex Equity: Definitions, Distinctions, Costs and Benefits, 1981; contbr. articles to profl. jours. Mem.: So. Univ. Conf. (exec. com. 1998—2003, pres. 2001—02), So. Assn. Colls. and Schs. (commn. colls. 1998—2000, exec. coun. 1999—2000, appeals com. 2002—), Ind. Colls. and Univs. of Fla. (coun. pres. 1990—, chair 1997—98), Fla. Coun. of 100, Assoc. Colls. of the South (bd. dirs. 1992—2001, treas. 1993—95, sec. 1995—97, vice chair 1997—99, chair 1999—2001), Nat. Assn. Ind. Colls. and Univs. (bd. dirs. 1992—95, chair govt. rels. com. 1994—95), Am. Coun. on Edn. (com. leadership devel. 1991—93, bd. dirs. 1995—98), Annapolis Group (exec. com. 1999—2001). Office: Rollins Coll Office of Pres 1000 Holt Ave # 2711 Winter Park FL 32789-4499

BOROCHOFF, IDA SLOAN, artist; b. July 29, 1922; d. Louis and Eva (Bistrick) Sloan; m. Charles Zachary Borochoff, Jan 11, 1942 (dec. July, 1990); children: Lynn Borochoff Gould, Jean Sue Borochoff Shapiro, Toby Ann Borochoff Bernstein, Lance Mark. Student, U. Ga., 1939-40, Ga. State U., 1940, Chgo. Sch. Interior Decorating, 1966, Allegro Sch. Ballet, Chgo., Atlanta Ballet, 1948-54, Emory U., 1971-72. Investor, owner real estate, 1941—; v.p. Designs Unltd., Inc., Atlanta, 1964—; pres. Sloan Borochoff Gallery, Atlanta, 1970—; art lectr. Met. Ednl. Svc.; art tchr. Ga. Inst. Tech., 1991. Prodr. live talk health show on cable TV, Atlanta, 1983-87. One woman shows include Lovett Sch., 1972, 75, Ga. Inst. Tech., 1972, 75, Atlanta Mdse. Mart, Saginaw Art Mus., 1998-99; group shows include Gwinnett Art Mus., Duluth, Ga., 1999, Ind. U., 1999, Purdue U., Indpls., 1999; art rev. columnist Northside Neighbor Newspapers; columnist Around Ga. with Ida. Bd. dirs. Atlanta Ballet, 1950-57; bd. dirs. Atlanta Music Club, co-editor newsletter; hostess Atlanta Arts Festival; capt. Heart Fund, 1968-76, area chmn. dr.; elected to bd. dirs. Am. Cancer Rsch. Ctr. Atlanta chpt.; active various multi-media groups; artistic dir. Atlanta Playhouse Theatre, chmn., trustee; artistic dir. Little Miss Ga. Pageant, Little Mr. Dogwood Festival Pageant; judge 17th Internat. Dogwood Festival Art Show, 1989; mem. U.S. cong. adv. bd. Am. Security Coun., 1983—; archivist nat. oral history nat. Coun. Jewish Women, 1990—; Ga. dir., chairperson Levi Hosp. Art Auction, Hot Springs, Ark., 1993-94; with Archives Exhibit Atlanta Jewish Fedn., 1994; donor Borochoff Libr. of A.A. Synagogue; com. mem., patron AJCC Book Festival, 1995-96. Recipient several art awards including Caber award, 1984; named hon. alumnus Atlanta Art Inst., 1968, One of Ten Leading Ladies of Atlanta, J.C. Singles, 19876, honored by Barbara Bush, White House, Washington, 1989, 90; City grantee, 1985. Mem. Atlanta Press Club, Atlanta Writers Club (membership com.), Atlanta Artists Club, Atlanta Women's C. of C. (chmn. fine arts 1977-78), LVW, High Mus. Art, Ga. Writers Assn., Arts High Mus. (patron), Corcoran Gallery (patron), Nat. Mus. Women in Arts (charter mem.), Internat. Platform Assn., B'nai B'rith Women (pres. chpt. 1975, mem. S.E. regional bd.), Ga. Hist. Soc., AAUW, Women in the Arts, Jockey Club, Progressive Club, Capitol Hill Club (Washington). Home: 3450 Old Plantation Rd NW Atlanta GA 30327-2426 Office: 733 Glendale Rd Scottdale GA 30079-1409

BORODKIN, ALICE, state representative; Past dir. comm. N.Y.C. Office Econ. Develop.; past dir. mktg. N.Y.C. Met. Transp. Authority; co-founder Women's Network; past pub., editor-in-chief Women's Bus. Chronicle; state rep. State of Colo., 2002—, mem. bus. affairs and labor, mem. transp. and energy com. Named Women Entrepreneur of Yr., Nat. Found. Woman Legislators and SBA Office Bus. Ownership, 2000, Woman Owned Bus. of Yr., Colo. Bus. and Profl. Women, 2000, Legislator of Yr., Colo. Assn. Homes and Svcs. for Aging, 2001, Adv. of Yr., Small Bus. Develop. Ctr., 2001, Freshman Legislator of Yr., Colo. Sr. Lobby, 2001, Colo. Bankers Assn., 2001, Indep. Bankers Assn., 2001; recipient Athena award for Leadership, Alliance of Profl. Women, 2001; Fleming fellow, Ctr. Policy Alternatives, 2002. Address: 8101 E Darmouth Ave #112 Denver CO 80231 Office: State Capitol 200 E Colfax Ave Denver CO 80203 E-mail: alice.borodkin.house@state.co.us.

BOROWSKI, JENNIFER LUCILE, corporate administrator; b. Jersey City, Oct. 23, 1934; d. Peter Anthony and Ludwika (Zapolska) B. BS, St. Peter's Coll., 1968; postgrad., Pace Coll., 1976-77. Mgr. benefits Amerada Petroleum Corp., N.Y.C., 1951-66, Mt. Sinai Hosp., N.Y.C., 1966-67; mgr. payroll and payroll taxes Haskins & Sells, N.Y.C., 1967-74, Cushman & Wakefield, Inc., N.Y.C., 1975-89. Mem. Am. Payroll Assn. (bd. dirs. 1979-81, cert.), Am. Mgmt. Assn., Am. Soc. Payroll Mgrs., Internat. Platform Assn. (hon.), Am. Soc. Profl. Exec. Women, NAFE. Avocations: golf, opera, boating. Home: 36 Front St North Arlington NJ 07031-5822

BORREE, YVONNE, dancer; Student, Sch. Am. Ballet, 1985. Apprentice N.Y.C. Ballet, 1987—88, mem. corps de ballet, 1988—93, soloist, 1993—97, prin., 1997—. Dancer with Mikhail Baryshnikov (ballets) Duo Concertant, 1992, Apollo, Coppelia, The Four Temperaments, The Nutcracker, Stravinsky Violin Concerto, Symphony in Three Movements, The Sleeping Beauty, Romeo and Juliet, Mercurial Manoeuvres, The Chairman Dances, Sinfonia, Sleeping Beauty, Slonimsky's Earbox, Danses de Cour, Correlazione, 1994. Office: NYC Ballet NY State Theatre 20 LIncoln Ctr Plz New York NY 10023-6913

BORROFF, MARIE, English language educator; b. N.Y.C., Sept. 10, 1923; d. Albert Ramon and Marie (Bergersen) B. Ph.B., U. Chgo., 1943, MA, 1946; PhD, Yale U., 1956. Teaching asst. U. Chgo., 1946-47; instr. dept. English Smith Coll., 1948-51, asst. prof., 1956-59, asso. prof., 1959; vis. asst. prof. English Yale U., 1957-58, vis. asso. prof., 1959-6O, asso. prof. English, 1960-65, prof., 1965-71, William Lampson prof., 1971-92, Sterling prof. English, 1992-94; Sterling prof. English emeritus, 1994—; Phi Beta Kappa vis. scholar, 1973-74. Fellow Ezra Stiles Coll., Yale. Author: Sir Gawain and the Green Knight: A Stylistic and Metrical Study, 1962, (with J. B. Bessinger, Jr.); recorded dialogues read in Middle English, 1965, Sir Gawain and the Green Knight: A New Verse Translation, 1967, Pearl: A New Verse Translation, 1977, Language and the Poet: Verbal Artistry in Frost, Stevens, and Moore, 1979, Sir Gawain and the Green Knight, Patience and Pearl: Verse Translations, 2000, Stars and Other Signs: Poems, 2002; essay collection: Traditions and Rewewals Chaucer, the Gawain-Poet, and Beyond, 2003; editor: Wallace Stevens, A Collection of Critical Essays, 1963; videotaped lectures: To Hear Their Voices, Chaucer, Shakespeare and Frost, Assn. of Yale Alumni Great Tchrs. Series, Chapter Headings: Remarks Made at the Annual Initiation Ceremonies of Phi Beta Kappa, Alpha Chapter of Connecticut, 1989-1994, 1996. Bd. Govs. Yale U. Press, 1988-98. Recipient James Billings Fiske poetry prize U. Chgo., 1943; Eunice Tietjens Meml. prize Poetry mag., 1945; Margaret Lee Wiley fellow AAUW, 1955-56; Guggenheim fellow, 1969-70 Fellow Am. Acad. Arts and Scis.; mem. MLA, Acad. Am. Poets, Medieval Acad. Am., Phi Beta Kappa. Home: 311 St Ronan St New Haven CT 06511-2328 E-mail: marie.borroff@yale.edu.

BORUCK, HOLLY, artist; b. Redwood City, Calif., Dec. 15, 1955; d. Holbrook Boruck and JoAnn Baldwin; m. Nicholas Simone (div. Dec. 1988); children: Zoltan Simone, Dante Simone; m. Mark Kirkland, July 17, 1994 (div. Mar. 1999). BFA, Calif. Coll. Arts and Crafts, 1991. Artist BRC Imagination Arts, Burbank, Calif., 1991—93, Sony, Klasky Csupo, Calif., 1995—2002, Warner Bros. TV Animation, Sherman Oaks, Calif., 1996—2002, Calif., 1991—. Exhibited in group shows at Art Pic, North Hollywood, Calif., 2000—, Elemental Arts Gallery, Los Gatos, Calif., 2001—02, Internat. Invitational Artshow, Jamsa, Finland, 2002, Small Works 2002, Louisville, 2002, Internat. Invitational Artshow, Barcelona, Spain, 2002, Warner Bros. Studio, 2003, Gallery 825, L.A., 2004, d'Antonio & Assocs., 1992—, Lisa Lodeski Fine Arts, Aliso Viejo, Calif., 2001—, Robin Ficara Fine Arts, Beverly Hills, Calif., 2001—, Represented in permanent collections Borgata Casino, Atlantic City, N.J., GAO, Washington, Rutgers U., ESPN Zone Restaurant, Denver, Pleasanton Hotel Suites, Harrah's Casino, Chgo., ESPN Zone Restaurant, Las Vegas, Anaheim, UPS Corp. Hdqrs. Mem.: Lawyers For Arts, Nat. Mus. Women in Arts, Am. for Arts. Avocations: violin, ballet. Home and Studio: 131 S Parish Pl Burbank CA 91506 Office Phone: 818-955-8974.*

BORUT, JOSEPHINE, retired insurance company executive; b. Bridgeport, Conn., Aug. 3, 1942; d. Frank and Catherine (Russo) Occhipinti; m. Arthur Lee Borut, Nov. 22, 1963; 1 child, Adam Seth. BS in Art, Hofstra U., 1964, MA in Humanities, 1971; cert. in mgmt., Adelphi U., 1984. Cert. art tchr., N.Y.; cert. mtgs. profl. Art tchr. Cen. Islip (N.Y.) Elem., 1964-65; coord. art dept. Mineola (N.Y.) Jr. High, 1965-70; art tchr., coord. Brandeis Sch., Lawrence, N.Y., 1979-81; mgr. community rels. Empire Blue Cross/Blue Shield, N.Y.C., 1984-85, mgr. conf. planning, 1985—2003. Freelance artist, East Meadow, 1978-79; lectr. meeting planning. Contbr. articles to profl. jours. Recipient hon. mention L.I. Art Tchrs. Assn. Art Show,1966, 3d pl. art show Hofstra U., 1966, 2d pl. East Meadow Pub. Libr. Juried Art Show, 1979; Inst. II scholar, 1991, Profl. Edn. Conf. scholar, 1990, 97. Mem. NAFE, NOW, Am. Soc. Assn. Execs., Meeting Planners Internat. Greater N.Y. (bd. dirs., com. chmn., pres. 1992-93, Meeting Planner of Yr. 1991), Am. Soc. Profl. and Exec. Women, Ins. Conf. Planners. Home: 1823 Kent St Westbury NY 11590-5305

BORYSENKO, JOAN, psychologist, biologist; b. Boston, Oct. 25, 1945; d. Edward and Lillian Zakon; children: Natalia, Justin, Andrei. BA in Biology, Bryn Mawr Coll., 1967; PhD, Harvard Med. Sch., 1972. Lic.

psychologist. Asst. prof. anatomy and cellular biology Tufts U., 1973-78; instr. in medicine Harvard Med. Sch., Boston, 1981-88; pres., founder Mind/Body Health Scis., Boulder, Colo., 1988—. Author: Minding the Body, Mending the Mind, 1987, Guilt is the Teacher, Love is the Lesson, 1990, Fire in the Soul, 1993, (with Miroslav Borysenko) The Power of the Mind to Heal, 1994, Pocketful of Miracles, 1995, A Woman's Book of Life, 1996, Seven Paths to God, 1997, A Woman's Journey to God, 1999, Inner Peace for Busy People, 2001; others; mem. adv. bd. several jours. and Web sites in field. Achievements include pioneering work in the study of psychoneuroimmunology. Office: Mind/Body Health Scis 393 Dixon Rd Boulder CO 80302-9769 E-mail: luziemas@aol.com.

BORYSEWICZ, MARY LOUISE, editor; b. Chgo. d. Thomas J. and Mabel E. (Zeien) O'Farrell m. Daniel S. Borysewicz, June 11, 1955; children: Mary Adele, Stephen Francis (dec. 1997), Paul Barnabas. BA, Mundelein Coll., 1970; postgrad. in English lit., U. Ill, 1970-71; grad. exec. program, U. Chgo., 1981-82. Editor sci. publs. AMA, Chgo., 1971-73; exec. mng. editor Am. Jour. Ophthalmology, Chgo., 1973-95; media cons. Fox-Wahls Design, Chgo., 1999—; editl. svc. cons. A.T. Kearney, Chgo., 2004—. Asst. sec., treas. Ophthalmic Pub. Co., 1985—95; guest lectr. U. Chgo. Med. Sch., 1979, Harvard U. Med. Sch., 1978, Northwestern U. Med. Sch., 1979, Am. Acad. Ophthalmology, 1976, 81, Northwestern U. Joseph Medill Sch. Journalism, 2002. Editor: Opthalmology Principles and Concepts, 7th edit., 1992, 8th edit., 1996, Documenta Ophthalmologica History Issue, 1997, 98, A.T. Kerney Inc. 2004—; contbg. writer Chicago Shops, 2002, 03, 04; contbr. articles to sci. publs. Mem. Coun. Biol. Editors (bd. dirs. 1988-91, mem. fin. com. 1985-88, mem. teller com. 1992-95). E-mail: mbory@aol.com.

BOSCHOK, JACKIE, labor union administrator; b. Kansas City, Mo., Apr. 24, 1952; d. John and Margaret Robey; m. Alex Boschok, July 30, 1983. Student, Culver Stockton Coll., 1970—71; BS, U. Mo., 1977. Materials facilitator Boeing Comml. Airplane Group, Seattle, 1980—2001; bus. rep. Aerospace Machinists Dist. 751, Seattle, 2001—. Chair labor and trades campaign cabinet Snohomish County United Way, Everett, Wash., 1994—97; mem. Snohomish County chpt. ARC, Everett, 2000—01. Recipient Spirit of Labor award, Snohomish County United Way, 1998; fellow, U. Mo. Columbia Sch. Agr., 1977. Mem.: Snohomish County Labor Coun. (trustee exec. bd. 2000—03), Wash. State Labor Coun. (mem. women's com. 1994—2003), Coalition Labor Union Women (nat. exec. bd. 1991—2003, rec. sec. Puget Sound chpt. 1993—2003). Office: Aerospace Machinists Dist 751 8729 Airport Rd Everett WA 98204 Personal E-mail: jackieboschok@hotmail.com.

BOSCOLA, LISA M. state legislator; b. Bethlehem, Pa., Apr. 6, 1962; d. Richard J. and Anna A. Stofko; m. Edward Boscola, 1987. BA, Villanova U., 1984, MA, 1985. Mem. Pa. Ho. of Reps., Harrisburg, 1995-98, Pa. Senate, Harrisburg, 1998—. Recipient Dorn Blaser award Pa. Fedn. Dem. Women. Mem. Pa. Assn. Ct. Mgmt. (chmn. pub. rels. com. 1991-93, editor newsletter 1992-93, regional bd. dirs. 1993), Bethlehem C. of C., Phi Kappa Phi, Pi Sigma Alpha. Office: PO Box 203018 Harrisburg PA 17120-3018

BOSDELL, MELONY, special education educator; b. Prosperity, S.C., Apr. 22, 1958; d. Jacob Frank and Janie Blondell Bickley; m. Francis Alvin Bosdell Jr., Oct. 17, 1981; children: Francis Alvin III, Martina Lee, Melony Danielle. BA in Edn. cum laude, Clemson U., 1979, M in Reading, 1981. Tchr. educable mentally retarded Palmetto Mid. Sch., Williamston, S.C., 1981-82; tchr. trainable mentally retarded, 5th grade Lexington (S.C.) Intermediate Sch., 1982-86; tchr. educable mentally retarded Johnsonville (S.C.) Elem. Sch., 1986; tchr. trainable mentally retarded Pee Dee Regional Ctr., Florence, S.C., 1987, New Kent (Va.) Primary Sch., 1989-92; tchr. elem. emotionally disturbed Va. Randolph Spl. Edn. Ctr., Glen Allen, Va., 1998—. Lutheran. Home: 9133 Epps Rd Mechanicsville VA 23111-6018 Office: Va Randolph Spl Edn Ctr 2206 Mountain Rd Glen Allen VA 23060-2232 E-mail: bosdell@juno.com.

BOSKEY, ADELE LUDIN, biochemistry educator, researcher; b. N.Y.C., Aug. 30, 1943; d. Benjamin and Anne (Monoson) Ludin; m. James Bernard Boskey, June 30, 1970 (dec. 1998); 1 child, Elizabeth Rona. BA, Barnard Coll., N.Y.C., 1964; PhD, Boston U., 1970. Editor Cambridge Data Base, England, 1969-70; rsch. fellow The Hosp. Spl. Surgery, N.Y.C., 1970-71, asst. scientist, 1971-75, assoc. scientist, 1975-79, sr. scientist, 1985, chief mineralized tissue rsch. sect., 1984—, dir. rsch., 1993—2002, Starr chair in mineralized tissue rsch.; asst. prof. biochemistry Cornell U. Med. Coll., N.Y.C., 1975-78, assoc. prof. Ithaca, NY, 1978-85, prof., 1986—. Mem editl. adv. bd. jour. Orthop Rsch., J. Bone and Min. Rsch., Calcif Tissue Internat., Bone and Min., J. Dental Rsch. contbr. articles to profl. jours. Recipient Disting. Rsch. award Kappa Delta, 1979, Career Devel. award NIH-Nat. Inst. Dental Rsch., 1975, NIH merit award Nat. Inst. Dental Research, 1987. Fellow Am. Inst. Chemists; mem. Am. Chem. Soc., Orthopaedic Rsch. Soc. (mem. at-large, newsletter editor 1989—, pres. 1997), Internat. Assn. Dental Rsch. (chair constrn. com., Biol. Basic Rsch. award 1994), Am. Crystallographic Assn., Am. Acad. Orthopaedic Surgeons, Am. Soc. Bone and Mineral Rsch., NIH (Nat. Adv. Coun. 1993— and numerous other coms.) Sigma Xi. Avocations: music, theatre. Office: The Hosp Spl Surgery 535 E 70th St New York NY 10021-4872 Business E-Mail: boskeya@hss.edu.

BOSLEY, KAREN LEE, English and journalism educator; b. Beech Grove, Ind., Sept. 23, 1942; d. Lowell Holmes and Kathryn Gertrude (Drake) Foley; m. Norman Keith Bosley, Dec. 21, 1964; children: Mark Harold, Rachael Kathryn, Keith Lowell, Sidney Clark. AB in Lang. Arts summa cum laude, U. Indpls., 1965; MA in English, Northwestern U., 1967; MA in Journalism, Ball State U., 1984; postgrad. (Newspaper Fund fellow), U. Mo., 1973; postgrad., Ohio U., 1977. Copy editor, reporter Indpls. News, 1963-65; English tchr., yearbook adviser Beech Grove (Ind.) Jr. H.S., 1965-66; English tchr. So. Regional H.S., Manahawkin, N.J., 1967-68; prof. humanities, journalism, and English Ocean County Coll., Toms River, N.J., 1971—, student newspaper adviser, 1971—, yearbook adviser, 1999—. Part-time reporter Daily Times-Observer, Toms River, 1972-77, part-time copy editor, 1993. Contbr. articles to publs. in field. Trustee Long Beach Island Hist. Assn., Friends of Island Libr., 1975-79; pres. Long Beach I PTA; chmn. Long Beach Twp. Dem. Mcpl. Com., 1971-78; Dem. committeeman Long Beach Twp. Dist. 2, 1971-78, 85—; mem. Long Beach Twp. Recreation Commn., 1972-75; bd. dirs. Ocean County Red Cross, 1972-78, Ocean County Family Planning, Inc., 1972-78, Student Press Law Ctr., 1987-2002, sec., 1998-2000, mem. adv. coun., 2002—; chmn. Cub Scout pack 32, Ocean County Coun. Boy Scouts Am.; founder, bd. dirs. Long Beach I Hist. Assn., Island Dems., Inc.; mem. adminstrv. bd. First United Meth. Ch. Beach Haven Terrace (N.J.); So. Regional H.S. Band Parent Orgn., 1995-96, pres., 1996-97, corr. sec; So. Regional Jazz Band Parents Assn., charter mem., 2001—. Mem. AAUW (pres., dir. Barnegat Light Area br.), NEA, N.J. Edn. Assn., Ocean County Edn. Assn., Faculty Assn. Ocean County Coll. (v.p. 1984-85), Coll. Media Advisers, Inc. (disting. newspaper adviser for U.S. 2-yr. colls. 1978, dir., sec.), Assn. Edn. in Journalism and Mass Comms., C.C. Journalism Assn. (dir., v.p.), Soc. Profl. Journalists, Internat. Platform Assn., Sigma Delta Chi. Home: 9 E Old Whaling Ln Long Beach Township NJ 08008-2930 Office: Ocean CC PO Box 2001 College Dr Toms River NJ 08754-2001 E-mail: kbosley@mac.com.

BOSNIAK, KANTA, artist; b. Phila., June 22, 1950; d. Richard Dengler and Dorothy Geraldine Stine; m. Murray Eli Bosniak; 1 child, Joshua Joseph. Grad. h.s., Phila.; student, U. Penn.; DD, hypnotherapy, Omega Coll., 2003. Ordained to ministry Sanctuary of the Beloved, 1990; cert. clinical hypnotherapist N.Eng. Inst. Hypnotherapy, 2002. Artist-in-residence Omega Inst. for Holistic Studies, Rhinebeck, NY, 1999, 2000. Founder, dir. Alpha Learning Found., Woodstock, NY, 2003. Contbg. artist Beautiful Necessity: The Art and Meaning of Women's Altars, 1999; exhibited in solo shows at Urban Artware, Winston-Salem, Omega Inst., Heritage Ctr., Virginia Beach, Assn. for Rsch. and Enlightenment, U. N.C., Wilmington, others; contbr. articles to Magical Blend Mag., Studies in Edn., Point of Light and Sagewoman Mag.; presenter workshops in churches, healing ctrs., alternative ednl. instns., pub. and pvt. ednl. schs. Avocations: film studies, screenwriting mystery and suspense books. Office: Alpha Learning Fdn 209 N Main St Ste C Blacksburg VA 24060

BOSS, AMELIA HELEN, law educator, lawyer; b. Balt., Apr. 3, 1949; d. Myron Theodore and Loretta (Oakjones) B.; m. Roger S. Clark, Mar. 3, 1979; children: Melissa, Seymour, Edward, Ashley. Student, Oxford (Eng.) U., 1968; BA in Sociology, Bryn Mawr, 1970; JD, Rutgers U., 1975. Bar: N.J, Pa., U.S. Dist. Ct. (ea. dist.) N.J., U.S. Dist. Ct. (ea. dist.) Pa., U.S. Supreme Ct., U.S. Ct. Appeals (3d cir.). Law clk. Hon. Milton B. Cranford N.J. Supreme Ct., 1975-76; assoc. Pepper, Hamilton & Scheetz, Phila., 1976-78; assoc. prof. law Rutgers U. Sch. Law, Camden, N.J., 1983-87, Temple U., Phila., 1989-91; prof. law Temple U. Sch. Law, Phila., 1991—, Charles Klein prof. law, 1999—. Vis. prof. law U. Miami Sch. Law, Coral Gables, Fla., 1985—86; Leo Goodwin disting. vis. prof. law Nova U., Sch. Law, 1998; mem. coms. Nat. Conf. Commrs. on Uniform State Laws; U.S. rep. to UN Commn. on Internat. Trade Law; dir. Inst. for Internat. Law and Pub. Policy, 2001—. Author: (books) Electronic Data Interchange Agreements: A Guide and Sourcebook, 1993, ABCs of the UCC: Article 2A, ABCs of the UCC: Article 5; editor-in-chief The Data Law Report, 1993-97, The Business Lawyer, 1998-99, ABCs of the UCC; mem. permanent editl. bd. Uniform Comml. Code; contbr. articles to profl. jours. Named among top 50 women lawyers in U.S. Nat. Law Jour., 1998. Fellow Am. Bar Found.; mem. ABA (chmn. bus. law sect. 2000-01, chmn. sect. officers conf. 2001—), Internat. Bar Assn., Am. Law Inst. (coun. 2000—), Am. Bankruptcy Inst., Am. Coll. Comml. Fin. Lawyers, Nat. Assn. Women Lawyers. Home: 309 Westmont Ave Haddonfield NJ 08033-1714 Office: Temple U Sch Law 1719 N Broad St Philadelphia PA 19122-6002

BOSSE, MARGARET FISHER ISHLER, education educator; b. Bellefonte, Pa., Oct. 19, 1934; d. Fred Raymond Fisher and Margaret (Hoffmeister) Fisher Hess; m. Richard Eves Ishler, Dec. 27, 1956 (div. June 1978); children: Frederick, Theodore; m. Richard C. Bosse, June 26, 1999. BA in English Edn., Pa. State U., 1956, MA in English, 1960; EdD, U. Toledo, 1972. English tchr. Bald Eagle (Pa.) H.S., 1956-57, Marion (N.Y.) Ctrl. Sch., 1957-59, York (Pa.) Suburban H.S., 1959-60; adj. instr. English Pa. State U., York, 1962-64; instr. York Coll., 1964-65; adj. inst. English U. Toledo, 1966-68, grad. asst., 1968-71; from asst. prof. to prof. Bowling Green (Ohio) State U., 1972-90, dir. field experiences and stds. compliance, 1985-90; head dept. curriculum and instrn., prof. U. No. Iowa, Cedar Falls, 1990-96, prof. curriculum and devel., 1997-2000, acting dir, teacher edn., 1998-99, prof. emeritus, 2000—. Mem. Nat. Coun. for Accreditation of Tchr. Edn. Bd. Examiners, 1998—. Co-author: Creating the Open Classroom, 1974, Teaching in a Competency-Based Program, 1977, Dynamics of Effective Teaching, 5th edit., 2003; contbr. articles to profl. jours. Bd. dirs. Wittenberg (Ohio) U., 1984-86, Luth. Student Chapel, Bowling Green, 1988-91, Ohio Luth. Campus Ministry, Columbus, 1986-87, Christian Cmty. Devel. Bd., Waterloo, Iowa, 1992-96. Recipient Christa McAuliff Showcase for Excellence award, 1990. Mem.: Iowa Assn. Tchr. Educators (pres. 1992—94), Ohio Assn. Tchr. Educators (exec. sec. 1980—87, pres. 1982, Disting. Educator 1982), Am. Assn. Colls. Tchr. Edn. (rep. 1985—, [illegible] 2000—), Assn. Tchr. Educators (nat. pres. 1996—97, named One of 70 Top Tchr. Educators 1990), Mortar Board, Phi Gamma Mu, Pi Lambda Theta, Phi Kappa Phi. Avocations: travel, golf, poetry. E-mail: mishlerbosse@msn.com.

BOSSMANN, LAURIE, controller, hardware company executive; m. Jeff Bossmann; two children. BS, No. Ill. U. CPA, Ill. With KPMG Peat Marwick; gen. acctg. mgr. Ace Hardware Corp., 1986-90, asst. contr., 1990-94, contr., 1994—, v.p., 1997—, v.p. mdse., 2000—. Mem. AICPA, Ill. CPA Soc. Office: 2200 Kensington Ct Oak Brook IL 60523-2103

BOSSUAT, JUDY WEIGERT, music educator; d. Edward Raymond and Edith Mabel Weigert; m. Christophe Raphael Louis Bossuat, Nov. 13, 1978 (div. June 27, 1994); 1 child, Joshua Edward Joseph. MusB magna cum laude, SUNY, Potsdam, 1975; Master in Suzuki Method Pedagogy, Talent Edn. Inst., Matsumoto, Japan, 1978, postgrad., 1982. Eminence tchg. credential Calif. Suzuki violin tchr. Potsdam Suzuki Talent Edn., 1973—77; dir., tchr., condr., tchr. trainer Ecole de Musique Suzuki de Lyon, Lyon, France, 1978—94; lectr. in music edn. U. of the Pacific, Stockton, Calif., 1994—; dir., tchr. Bossuat Music Sch., Stockton, 1994—; string tchr. Pacific Sch., Lincoln Unified Sch. Dist., Stockton, 1995—2000; lectr. music edn., dir. String Project Calif. State U., Sacramento, 2002—. Numerous short term tchr. tng. and workshop positions, 1978—; founding mem., bd. dirs. European Suzuki Assn., 1979—94, Fedn. Musical Suzuki de France, 1980—94; v.p. Assn. Ecoles Musique Rhone, Lyon, 1984—90; European violin-viola rep. Internat. Suzuki Assn., Dallas, 1992—93. Author: (music book) Exercises for Left Hand Devel. (violin), 2000, 2003, Learning to Read Music for the Violin, 1991, numerous orchestral compositions and arrangements; contbr. articles to profl. jours. Recipient medal of honor for exceptional contbn. to edn., Nat. Assembly France, 1983, medals of the city, Marseille, France, 1983, Lyon, France, 1986, Duluth, Minn., 1993, 1st prize, Regional Youth Orch. Competition, France, 1993, 2d prize, 1994. Mem.: European Suzuki Assn. (hon. life), Fedn. Musical Suzuki de France (hon. life), Suzuki Assn. No. Calif., Suzuki Assn. Ams. (Suzuki method tchr. trainer), Calif. Music Educators Assn. (orch. rep. Bay sect. 2001—02), Am. String Tchrs. Assn. (Calif. state pres. 2003—). Achievements include discovery of effect of eye dominance on playing stringed instruments. Office: Calif State Univ Sacramento Capistrano Hall 127 6000 J St Sacramento CA 95819-6015 E-mail: jwbossuki@onebox.com.

BOSTAIN, NANCY S. psychologist, educator; b. Cin., Feb. 5, 1959; d. Claude Warren and Marie Gertrude Bostain; m. David Eugene Wood, June 16, 1990; m. Frank Thomas Addrisi, Dec. 5, 1981 (div. June 1985). BA, U. Cin., 1981; MS, Highlands U., 1986; PhD, Walden U., 2000. Lic. profl. counselor Colo., 1989. Psychiatric social worker Wyo. State Hosp., Evanston, Wyo., 1981—83; dir. Colo. West Regional Mental Health Ctr., Glenwood, Colo., 1984—89; substance abuse coord. Centennial Mental Health Ctr., Ft. Morgan, Colo., 1989—90; dir. Lockeed Martin, Denver, 1990—2001; orgnl. psychologist Apex Solutions, Pine, Colo., 2001—. Trustee Labors Cmty. Agy., Denver, 1991—2000. Book photographer: Cowboy & Gunfighter Collectibles, 1989. Recipient Deitweiler award, Colo. Employee Assistance Profl. Assn., 2000. Mem.: APA, Soc. Indsl. Orgn. Psychologists. Avocations: hunting, photography, camping, ATV riding. E-mail: nbostain@earthlink.net.

BOSTED, DOROTHY STACK, public relations executive; b. Newark, Apr. 6, 1953; d. Richard Joseph and Dorothy Marie (Irvin) Stack; divorced, 2000; 1 child, Danielle Whitney. Student, Lyndon State Coll., 1971-73; BA, NYU, 1975. Reporter The Daily Advance, Succasunna, N.J., 1974-75; producer, tech. intern Manhattan Cable TV, N.Y.C., 1975; editorial asst. Calif. Sch. Employees Assn., San Jose, 1975-76; news dir., anchor UA-Columbia Cablevision, Oakland, N.J., 1977-79; dir. pub. relations Overlook Hosp., Summit, N.J., 1981-84; pres. Dorothy Bosted Pub. Relations, Harding Twp., N.J., 1984-86; dir. pub. relations, communications Middlesex County Coll., Edison, N.J., 1986-88; mgr. corp. communications Hoechst Celanese Corp., Bridgewater, N.J., 1988-89. Ptnr. Bosted-Burton Assocs., Plantation, Fla., 1986—; cons. Plantation, 1986—. Co-author: Writing with Impact, 1986; contbr. articles to N.Y. Times, various mags. Seminar leader Kinnelon (N.J.) Enrichment Program, 1978; trustee Middlesex County Coll. Found., Edison, N.J., 1986-88; bd. dirs. Middlesex County Coll. Alumni Assn., 1986-88. Recipient News Program ACE award Nat. Cable TV Assn., 1979, Spectrum of Talent merit award Internat. Assn. Bus. Communicators, 1982, Percy award N.J. Hosp. Mktg. and Pub. Relations Assn., 1982, 84, Tribute to Women and Industry award YWCA, Ridgewood, N.J., 1979; Mennen Co. scholar, 1971, Neighborhood House scholar, 1971, KP scholar, 1971. Mem. Tribute to Women and Industry Mgmt. Forum (v.p. pub. rels. Ridgewood chpt. 1986-87, bd. dirs. cen. N.J. chpt. 1989-91), Pub. Rels. Soc. Am. (editor N.J. chpt. newsletter 1987-89, bd. dirs. N.J. chpt. 1989-91). Home: 485 N Pine Island Rd #204A Plantation FL 33324-1378 E-mail: dbosted@aol.com.

BOSTIC, MARY JONES, librarian; b. Durham, N.C., June 20, 1939; d. Isaac William and Jennie Mae (Edwards) Jones; m. Charles Thomas Bostic Sr., Aug. 4, 1970; 1 child, Precious Jennifer. BA, N.C. Ctrl. U., 1964, MLS, 1969; MS, L.I. U., 1975, cert. advanced studies, 1980. Sec. Randolph County Home Econs. Agt., Asheboro, N.C., 1958-60; adminstrv. asst. chief libr. N.C. Ctrl. U., Durham, 1964-69; asst acquisitions libr. L.I. U., Bklyn., 1969-75, acquisitions libr., 1975—. Contbr. articles to profl. jours. Active Coun. Bd. #13, Queens, 1975—. Mem. Assn. Coll. and Rsch. Librs., N.Y. Tech. Svcs. Librs., N.C. Libr. Assn., N.C. Ctrl. U. Sch. Lib. Sci. Alumni Assn., Palmer Grad. Libr. Sch. Alumni Assn., L.I. U. Faculty Fedn., Beta Phi Mu (Beta Mu chpt.), United Block Assn., Dem. Club (Queens). Presbyterian. Avocations: reading, writing, theater, bowling, walking. Home: 10416 198th St Jamaica NY 11412-1216 Office: Long Island Univ 1 University Plz Brooklyn NY 11201-5372 E-mail: mbostic@liu.edu.

BOSTIC, POLLY THOMAS, music educator; b. Atlanta, Nov. 23, 1949; d. Frank Hopkins and Patricia Willmon Thomas; m. Ronald David Bostic, June 27, 1971; children: Christopher, Benjamin, Suzanne. MusB, Stetson U., 1971; postgrad., Golden Gate Bapt. Theol. Sem., 1977—78; MusM, Southwestern Bapt. Theol. Sem., 1979. Staff accompanist various Bapt. theol. seminaries, 1971—78; lectr. Wingate (N.C.) U., 1980—98, instr., univ. accompanist, 1998—. Organist Wingate Bapt. Ch., 1996—. Mem.: Music Educators Nat. Conf., Coll. Music Soc., N.C. Educators Nat. Conf. Baptist. Avocation: swimming. Home: 104 Douglas Cir Wingate NC 28174 Office: Wingate U PO Box 3057 Wingate NC 28174

BOSTON, BETTY LEE, investment company executive, financial consultant, financial planner; b. Agana, Guam, Dec. 21, 1935; d. Homer Laurence and Bessie Margarete (Leech) Litzenberg; m. Filibert Roth Boston, Aug. 12, 1956; children: William Litzenberg, Beth Boston Tedesco, Brent Litzenberg. BA, U. Mich., 1958. CFP®. Stockbroker I.M. Simon & Co., Murray, Ky., 1976—78, 1st of Mich. Corp., Murray, Ky., 1978—86; fin. cons. J.J.B. Hilliard, W.L. Lyons, Inc., Murray, Ky., 1986—; v.p. Hilliard Lyons Inc., Murray, Ky., 1998—. Instr. adult edn. investment classes Murray State U., 1977—2000; investment commentator Sta. WKMS, Murray, 1987—. Fin. columnist Murray Ledger and Times, 2000—. Chmn. Inter-Faith Coalition Congregations, Ann Arbor, 1971-73; pres. Need Line Ch. and Cmty. Ministry, Murray, 1981-83; mem. Murray regional bd. Ky. Coun. on Econ. Edn., 1987—. Recipient Woman of Yr. award Murray Bus. and Profl. Women, 1988. Mem. AAUW (treas. Murray br. 1982-87, pres. 1991-97), Rotary (sec. Murray club 1990-95, pres. 1998-99, Paul Harris fellow). United Methodist. Home: 917 N 16th St Murray KY 42071-1523 Office: JJB Hilliard WL Lyons Inc 414 Main St Murray KY 42071-2059

BOSTON, BILLIE, costume designer, costume history educator; b. Oklahoma City, Sept. 22, 1939; d. William Barron and Margaret Emeline (Townsend) Long; m. William Clayton Boston, Jr., Jan. 20, 1962; children: Kathryn Gray, William Clayton III. BFA, U. Okla., 1961, MFA, 1962. Asst. to designer Karinski of N.Y., N.Y.C., 1966-67; prof. costume history Oklahoma City U., 1987—. Rep. Arts Coun., Oklahoma City, 1987-90, Arts Festival, Oklahoma City, 1972-80; dir. ETC Theater, Oklahoma City SW Coll., 1979-83; actress Lyric Theatre, Oklahoma City, 1979-81; designer Casa Mahara Theatre, Ft. Worth, 1998. Exhibited in group shows at Taos, N.Mex., Santa Fe; represented in permanent collections in Dallas, Taos, Santa Fe, Tulsa, N.Y.C., La Jolla; costume designer Ballet Okla., Oklahoma City, 1979-84, Agnes DeMillie's Rodeo Ballet Okla., 1982, Royal Ballet Flanders, 1983, Pitts. Ballet, 1983, BBC's Childrens Prodn., 1984, 86, Lyric Theatre, Oklahoma City, 1987-95, Red Oak Music Theatre, Lakewood, N.J., 1988, Winter Olympics, 1988, Miss Am. Pageant, 1988, for JoAnne Worley in Hello Dolly, San Francisco Opera Circus, 1991, Jupiter (Fla.) Theatre, 1991-92, Mobile (Ala.) Light Opera, 1992, The Boy Friend, Temple U., Japan, 1995, The Sound of Music, Lyric Stage, Dallas, 1995, Annie Get Your Gun, Guys and Dolls with Vic Damone, 1995, Westbury Flash Valley Forge Music Fair, Oklahoma and Sound of Music, Casa Manana, Theatre, Ft. Worth, 1997, Singing in the Rain, Lone Star Theatre, Galveston, Tex., 1997, Most Happy Fellow, Lyric Stage Dallas, 1997, To Gillian on her 37th Birthday, Watertower Theatre, Dallas, 1998, Carousel, Annie Get Your Gun, Cinderella, Casa Manana, 1998; designer Titanic, Irving, Tex., 2003, Specture Bridegroom, Irving, 2003, Opal, Lyric Stage, Irving, 2003. Rep. Speakers Bur. Oklahoma City for Ballet, 1979-85; judge State Hist. Speech Tournament, Oklahoma City, 1985-87; chmn. State of Okla. Conf. on Tchr./Student Relationships, Oklahoma City, 1981. Recipient Gov.'s Achievement award, 1988, Lady in the News award, 1987; Excellence in Costume Design award Kennedy Ctr. Am. Coll. Theatre Festival XXXIV, 2001; nom. Outstanding Costume Designer Southwest, Dallas Theatre League, 2003. Mem. Alpha Chi Omega (house corp. bd. 1986-90). Methodist. Avocation: watercolorist. Home: 1701 Camden Way Oklahoma City OK 73116-5121

BOSTON, GRETHA, actress, vocalist; b. Crossett, AK; B of Music, N Tex. State U., Denton; vocal study with vocal tech. and coaches, John Wustman, Bill Riley. Carnegie Hall debut Mozart's Coronation Mass, 1991, concert performances Beethoven's Ninth Symphony (Carnegie Hall), Handel's Messiah (Madison, Wis. & Arlington, Tex.), roles (Operas) Carmen in Bizet's Carmen, The Mother in Menotti's The Consul, Ciesca in Puccini's Gianni Schicchi, Delilah in Saint-Saens's Samson et Delilah, Maddalena in Verdi's Rigoletto (N.Y. Grand Opera), Amneris in Verdi's Aida, Azucena in Verdi's Il Trovatore, Queenie in Kern & Hammerstein's Show Boat (Tony award Best Supporting Actress in a Musical, 1995), Maria & Strawberry Woman in Gershwin's Porgy and Bess, 1993, It Ain't Nothin' But The Blues, 1999 (Tony award), appeared (TV series) Law and Order, Rosie O'Donnel, David Letterman, PBS, Today Show. Recipient 3rd place D'Angelo Young Artist Internat. Competition, 1984. Address: 250 W 57th St Ste 2223 New York NY 10107-2210

BOSWELL, STEPHANIE, newscaster; married; 2 children. Grad. in Broadcast Jouralism, Tex. A&M. Reporter, Shreveport, La., KXAS-TV, Dallas, WDSU News Channel 6, New Orleans, 1996—. Office: WDSU News Channel 6 846 Howard Ave New Orleans LA 70113

BOSWELL, SUSAN G. lawyer; b. El Paso, Tex., June 26, 1945; BA, U. Ariz., 1972, JD, 1976. Bar: Ariz. 1977, Nev. 1992. Dir. Tuscon (Ariz.) office Quarles, Brady, Streich, Lang, PC (formerly known as Streich & Lang P.C.), Phoenix, 1987—. Instr., faculty mem. Nat. Inst. Trial Advocacy, 1991; bd. vis. U. Ariz. Coll. of Law. Fellow Am. Coll. Bankruptcy; mem. State Bar of Ariz. (peer review com., assistance com.), Ariz. Women Lawyers Assn, Phi Kappa Phi. Office: Quarles Brady Streich Lang PC 1 S Church Ave Ste 1700 Tucson AZ 85701-1630

BOSWELL, VIVIAN NICHOLSON, protective services official; b. Brewton, Ala., Mar. 27, 1950; d. Nathaniel Irving Nicholson, Ethel Mae Nicholson; m. Leonard Boswell, Jan. 30, 1981. BA in Sociology, Stillman Coll., 1972. Correctional officer D.C. Dept. Corrections, Washington, 1973—2000. Recipient award of excellence, 9-5 Working Women's Assn.,

1997, Lifetime Achievement award, 9 to 5 Working Women, 2002. Mem.: Mothers Against Drunk Driving, AARP, NAACP, Women's World Peace Family, Working Women's Assn., Am. Assn. Retired Persons, Harriet Tubman Assn., Diabetic Assn. Democrat. Baptist. Avocations: singing, art, mentoring, cooking, philantropic activities. Home: PO Box 75 Pine Level AL 36065-0075

BOSWORTH, KATE, actress; b. L.A., Jan. 2, 1983; Actor: (TV series) Young Americans, 2000; (films) The Horse Whisperer, 1998, Remember the Titans, 2000, The Newcomers, 2000, Blue Crush, 2002, The Rules of Attraction, 2002, Wonderland, 2003, Advantage Hart, 2003, Win a Date with Tad Hamilton, 2004. Office: United Talent Agy 5th Fl 9560 Wilshire Blvd Beverly Hills CA 90212*

BOTSFORD, MARY HENRICH, retired ophthalmologist; b. Buffalo, Aug. 22, 1915; d. John William and Margarethe Ingeborg (Kähler) Henrich; m. Daniel Ray Botsford, Feb. 11, 1943 (dec. Dec. 1970); children: Daniel Jr., Janet B. Thrush, William H., Thomas H. BA, Mount Holyoke Coll., 1937; MD, U. Buffalo, 1941. Diplomate Am. Bd. Ophthalmology. Assoc. Ivan J. Koenig M.D., Buffalo, 1943-46, 56-60; pvt. practice Buffalo, 1960-84; retired, 1984. Staff St. Francis Hosp., Buffalo, 1962-72, Vets. Hosp., Buffalo, 1962-72, Gowanda State Hosp., Helmuth, N.Y., 1962-80, Buffalo Children's Hosp., 1943-96, Buffalo Gen. Hosp., 1943-96. Founding bd. dirs., vol. Habitat for Humanity, Buffalo, 1985-96; vol. Meals on Wheels, Buffalo, 1985-96, Am. Cancer Soc., Buffalo, 1985-96. Recipient Outstanding Achievement in Medicine citation, SUNY, Buffalo, 1984. Mem. Am. Acad. Ophthalmology, Buffalo Ophthal. Club, N.Y. State Ophthal. Soc., Common Cause. Democrat. Lutheran. Avocations: bridge, classical music, travel, theater, reading.

BOTSIS, BETH ANN, director; b. Holland, Mich., May 4, 1958; d. Robert Constantine and Joan Dorian (Van Dyke) B. Student, Western Mich. U., 1976-77; MusB, Hope Coll., 1980; MusM, U. Md., 1985. Records mgr. Am. Mining Congress, Washington, 1983-88; asst. to dir. Interstate Mining Compact Commn., Herndon, Va., 1988—. Singer opera chorus The Washington Opera, 1984-88, The Wolf Trap Opera, Vienna, Va., 1985, 86; solo recitalist, actor Washington met. area and Holland, Mich., 1985—. Mem. Am. Guild Musical Artists (bd. govs. 1989-94), Nat. Assn. Tchrs. Singing, Am. Assn. Christian Counselors. Republican. Avocations: volunteer youth leader, acrylic painting, short-term mission work, lay counseling ministry. Office: Interstate Mining Compact Commn 445A Carlisle Dr Herndon VA 20170-4802

BOTT, BOBBIE LEE, real estate broker; b. Fontana, Calif., May 23, 1949; d. William Wallace and Lucille Hazel Weatherly; m. Carl Regan Bott (div.); children: Jeanette Brazeal, Jeanelle Shearer. Lic. real estate broker. Broker, assoc. Prudential Real Estate, Chino Valley, Ariz., 1996—2001; broker/owner All Pro Real Estate, Chino Valley, 2001—. Bd. dirs. Chino Valley Recreation Found., 1997—2000. Recipient Rising Star award, Prudential Cmty. Champions, 2000. Mem.: Prescott Area Assn. Realtors, China Valley C. of C. (pres-elect 2003). Avocations: kayaking, horseback riding. Office: All Pro Real Estate 1120 S Hwy 89 #B Chino Valley AZ 86323

BOTT-GRAHAM, MICHELLE LYNN, behavior therapist; b. Spokane, Wash., Nov. 17, 1967; d. James Joseph Bott and Ann Marie (Harrington) McDowell; m. Preston Scott Graham, May 28; children: Justin Riley, William James. BA in Psychology, U. Idaho, 1989; MA in Psychology, Claremont U., 1992. Therapist, billing coord. Claremont Ctr. for the Rsch. and Treatment of Austin, 1989-90; rsch. asst. Kaiser Permanente, Pasadena, Calif., 1989-92; tchr. Tobinworld, Glendale, Calif., 1991-92; program coord. Grand Teton Svc. Group, Idaho Falls, Idaho, 1992-93; program dir. TBA, Inc., Pocatello, Idaho, 1993-94; psychologist extender, therapist The Ctr. for Human Rels., Pocatello, 1993-97; owner, founder, dir., behavior therapist The Advocacy and Learning Assocs., Pocatello, 1997—. Claremont Grad. U. rsch. grantee, 1990-91; U. Idaho scholar, 1988-89. Mem. ACA, Assn. for Behavior Analysis, Assn. for the Advancement of Behavior Therapy, Idaho Psychol. Assn., Autism Soc. of Am. Democrat. Methodist. Avocations: reading, traveling, family. Office: Advocacy and Learning Assocs 850 E Lander St Pocatello ID 83201-5763

BOTTI VILLEGAS, MARIA MARTA, artist, art educator; b. Buenos Aires, Argentina, Feb. 2, 1956; d. Alfredo Antonio Botti and Noemi Maria Recoder; m. Jorge Villegas, Mar. 12, 1993; children: Celeste Paz Villegas, John Nahuel Villegas. BFA, Escuela Prilidiano Pueyrredon, 1974—78. Artist-in-education Ark. Arts Coun., Little Rock, Ark., 1994—; art educator South Ark. Arts Ctr., El Dorado, 1995—. Mural, Venice, light and color, In Celebration of The City Of Prescott, The Voice Of Time Is The Poem Of Earth, Sounds Of Winter, They Came With Hope, public work, mural, The Natural Cycle Of The Wood, exhibitions include Watching The Circumstances Go, Vibrations On Stage. Recipient Excellence award, painting, Masur Mus., Monroe, LA, 1995, Hon. Mention, Ark. Art Show, Henderson U., Arkadelphia, AR, 1992; Recipient of the Art Scholarship, Ark. Com. of The Nat. Mus. of Women in The Arts in Wash. DC, 2001. Mem.: Mus. of Natural Resources (assoc.), South Ark. Arts Ctr. (assoc.), Nat. Mus. of Women in The Arts (assoc.). Avocations: body movement and expression, nutrition- health, environment. Home: 1009 West 4th St El Dorado AR 71730-4302 Personal E-mail: marjo@arkansas.net.

BOTTOMLY, THERESE, editor; BS in Journalism, U. Oreg., 1983. With Oregonian, Portland, Oreg., 1983—, sr. editor news and planning, mng. editor news, 1998—. Office: Oregonian 1320 SW Broadway Portland OR 97201*

BOTTONE, JOANN, health services executive; b. Bklyn., June 20, 1943; d. Anthony and Claire (Bisesti) B.; m. William Recevuto, Feb. 12, 1989; children: Matthew, Sandra. RN, Kings County Hosp. Ctr., Bklyn., 1963; BS, St. Francis Coll., Bklyn., 1980; MPA, Russell Sage Coll., Albany, N.Y., 1986; PhD in Pub. Adminstrn. magna cum laude, Kensington U., 1995. Bd. cert. Health Care Mgmt. Am. Coll. Health Care Execs., 1997. From staff nurse, head nurse, quality assurance coord. Victory Meml. Hosp., Bklyn., 1961-81; instr. infection control Community Hosp. Bklyn., 1981-82; dir. quality assurance Profl. Stds. Rev. Orgn., Bklyn., 1982-85; devel. and coord. HIV post-test counseling program Greater N.Y. Blood Ctr., N.Y.C., 1985-88; dir. HIV/AIDS programs Health Sci. Ctr. SUNY, Bklyn., 1988—2000. Tchr. SUNY Coll. Health Related Professions; mem. working group to develop statewide policies and procedures for health care workers involved in potential HIV exposures N.Y. State Health Commr., 1990; mem. tech. adv. group to develop guidelines for OSHA's bloodborne pathogen standard Greater N.Y. Hosp. Assn., 1992, N.Y.C. Mayor's HIV and Human Svcs. planning coun., 1999; lectr. in field. Contbr. articles to profl. jours. Mem. Am. Coll. Health Care Execs. (diplomate), Greater N.Y. Hosp. Assn. (tech. adv. group). E-mail: dr.jbr@msn.com.

BOTWAY, JACLYN COOPER, antiques dealer, consultant; b. St. Louis, Sept. 14, 1935; d. Sterling Ellis and Thelma Adeline (Kinder) Cooper; m. Clifford Alan Botway, July 29, 1950; children: Cooper Alan, Jill Robyn-Sterling. BA, MA, U. Ga., 1947; MSW, N.Y. Sch. Social Work, 1950. Med. social worker Met. Hosp., N.Y.C., 1950-55; owner, mgr. Jaclyn J. Inc. (doing bus. as Rainbarrel), Salt Point, N.Y., 1980—. Pres., dir. Hist. Hudson Valley Antiquity, Clinton Corners, N.Y., 1980—; dir. Dutchess County Hist. Roads, Poughkeepsie, N.Y., 1985—. Author: Finding Art Treasures at Home, 1979, Auctions Mania, 1980, Money in the Attic, 1985, The Ancients Collectively, 1986. Mem. Clinton Hist. Road Commn.; founder Clinton Hist. Soc., 1989; v.p. New Rochelle (N.Y.) League for Svc., 1955-81; vol. Internat. Garden Club, Pelham, N.Y., 1955—; sec. Women's Manor Club, Pelham, 1955-57; v.p. Little Guild of St. Francis for Animals, Key West, Fla., 1982—; founder Art and Hist. Soc., Key West, 1982, Martello Mus., Key West, 1982, Tennessee Williams Arts Ctr. and Theatre, Key West, 1982—. Named Rep. Woman of Dutchess County, Nat. Rep. Com., 1963. Mem. Oldest House Mus., Mus. Modern Art, Mus. Natural History, Clinton Hist. Soc., Phi Beta Kappa. Avocations: pilot, [illegible] skiing, fox hunting, scuba diving, sea mobile racing. Home: 460 Beechmont Dr New Rochelle NY 10804-4613 Office: Rainbarrel No 2 Salt Pt Tpke Salt Point NY 12514

BOUCHARD, KIMBERLEY A. performing arts educator; b. Vt., Dec. 2, 1952; d. Bernard Roy and Bevalie Catherine (Bonardi) Bouchard; life ptnr. Edwin R. Clark; children: Francisco Corrigan Clark Bouchard, Carmelinda Patricia Clark Bouchard. BA with honors, U. Lancaster, Eng., 1974; MFA, U. Idaho, 1993. Plumber, gen. constrn. Oakland (Calif.) Better Housing, Inc., 1976—78; cabinet maker, carpenter Parker Constrn. Co., Lake City, Colo., 1978—79; co. mem., performer Estudio Busqueda de Pantomima Teatro, Guanajuato, Mexico, 1981—86; performing artist, tchr. Artistic Svcs., San Miguel de Allende, Mexico, 1986—89; instr./adj. prof. U. Idaho, Moscow, 1989—94, edn. dir. Women's Ctr., 1993—95; theatre dir. Pullman Summer Palace Theatre Wash. State U., 1993—95; asst. prof. SUNY, Potsdam, 1995—2001, dir. gen. edn., 1999—2001, assoc. prof., chair drama program, 2001—. Dir.: (theatre) Orgasmo Adulto Escapes From the Zoo (Franca Rame), Diary of Anne Frank, Anna Karenina (Helen Edmundson based on the novel by Leo Tolstoy), Twelfth Night (William Shakespeare), The Imaginary Invalid (Moliere), Birds (Aristophanes), American Radio Plays, Promenade (Maria Irene Fornes), Machinal (Sophie Treadwell), As You Like It (William Shakespeare), Hot l Baltimore (Lanford Wilson), The Odd Couple, Female Version (Neil Simon), (musical) Pump Boys and Dinettes, Little Shop of Horrors (Ashman and Mencken), (premiere) Margarita Came Back to Life (Leonor Azcarate) (cert. of merit/directing KC/ACTF, 1996), (original adaptation) Beggar's Opera (John Gay), (Spanish theater) El delantal blanco by Vodanovic; author (performer): (touring presentation) Idaho Women and the Land (Spkrs. award Idaho Humanities Coun., 1993); prodr.: (musical) Cabaret (Kander and Ebb), (theatre festival) One-Act Plays; choreographer and performer Mapping; actor: What I Did Last Summer (A.R. Gurney); co. mgr. (youth theatre) Circle in the Square. Bd. dirs. St. Lawrence County Arts Coun., Potsdam, 2003; co-chair Potsdam Music Friends, Potsdam Ctrl. Sch. Dist., 2001—02; Dem. conv. del. Lewiston, Idaho, 1992; religious educator Unitarian Universalist Assn., Moscow, 1989—95, Unitarian Universalist Ch. of Canton, NY, 1996—2003. Nominee Irene Ryan Scholarship, 1991; named Vol. of Yr.-Reading Svc., North Country Pub. Radio, Canton, 2003; recipient Outstanding Svc. award, Student Govt. Assn., U. of Idaho, 1992; grantee, Idaho Coun. Arts, 1994; Nuala McCann Drescher fellow, Joint Labor Mgmt. Com., SUNY, 1999, AIDS Prevention and Edn. grantee, HHS, Idaho, 1993—95. Mem.: Am. Soc. Theatre Rsch., Theatre Comm. Group, Am. Theatre in Higher Edn. Avocations: skiing, travel. Office: SUNY Potsdam 44 Pierrepont Ave Potsdam NY 13676

BOUCHARD, LYNNE KATHERINE, music educator; b. L.A., June 24, 1955; d. Thomas Joseph and Anne Katherine (Gurmatakis) Bouchard; m. Daniel Ernest Winans, Apr. 6, 1985 (div.); children: Collette Jeanine Winans Engle, Ashley Anne Winans; m. Timothy Ervin Junette, May 2, 1997 (div.). Lic. practical nurse, Ariz. We. Coll., 1981. LPN; lic. Kindermusik instr. LPN Dr. David Buster, Yuma, Ariz., Dr. Abraham Injean, Yuma, Yuma County Health Dept.; pvt. piano instr. Yuma, 1987—99; tchr. music Grace Brethren Christian Sch., Waldorf, Md., 1999—2001, tchr. drama, 2000—03. Pvt. piano instr., Waldorf, 1999—. Mem.: Md. State Music Tchrs. Assn., Bowie Cmty. Theatre, Thespian Soc., Port Tobacco Players, Nat. Guild Piano Tchrs. Avocations: acting, interior decorating, gardening, antiques. Home: 4575 Grouse Pl Waldorf MD 20603

BOUCHEY, HEATHER ANN, psychologist; b. Ogdensburg, N.Y., Nov. 6, 1970; d. Mahlon A. and Deborah A. Bouchey; m. Thomas V. Delaney, Oct. 6, 2001. BS, Cornell U., 1992; MS, Ill. State U., 1995; PhD, U. of Denver, 2000. Preschool tchr. Little Learners, Liverpool, NY, 1993; adj. prof. Met. State U., Denver, 1998—99, U. of Denver, Denver, 1999—2000; postdoctoral fellow U. of Mich., Ann Arbor, Mich., 2000—02; asst. prof. of psychology U. of Vt., Burlington, Vt., 2002—. Dir. Relationships and Achievement Ctr., Burlington, 2002—. Co-author (chpts.): Blackwell Handbook of Adolescence; contbr. articles to profl. jours. Fellow U. Denver, 1995—98, Instl. Nat. Rsch. Svc. fellowship, NIH, 2000—02, Individual Nat. Rsch. Svc. fellowship, 2002; scholar Ora Bretall scholarship, Ill. State U., 1994, U. Club scholarship, 1994. Mem.: APA (Dissertation Rsch. award 1999), Internat. Soc. for the Study of Behavioral Devel., Soc. for Rsch. on Adolescence, Soc. for Rsch. in Child Devel. (Travel award 1999), Psi Chi. Avocations: reading, knitting, hiking, swimming, pets. Home: 40 Village Green Burlington VT 05401 Office: University of Vermont Department of Psychology Burlington VT 05405 Office Phone: 802-656-0882. E-mail: heather.bouchey@uvm.edu.

BOUDREAU, LYNDA L. state legislator; m. Jim Boudreau; 3 children. Rep. Minn. Ho. of Reps., 1994—, speaker pro tempore. Mem., NRA, MN Outdoor Heritage Alliance. Office: 550 State Office Bldg 100 Rev Martin Luther Ling Jr Blvd Saint Paul MN 55155

BOUDREAU, MICHELLE E. principal, consultant; d. Wilfrid Odina and Eileen Boudreau; life ptnr. James Howell. B in Music, U. Hartford, 1983; MA in Music Therapy, NYU, 1990; postgrad. in MEd sch adminstrn., spl. edn., Goucher Coll.; postgrad. in Prin., Spl. Edn. Adminstr., Pupil Svcs. Dir. coursework, Bridgewater STate Coll., U. Mass. Bd. cert. music therapist Am. Music Therapy Assn., cert. spl. needs, preK-12 Mass., cert. adminstr. I and II Md., cert. spl. edn. K-8 Md., cert. music edn., K-12, advanced profl. Md., cert. prin. R.I., Mass., Md. Dir. Creative Arts in Action, 1990—; music tchr. Montgomery County (Md.) Pub. Schs., 1994—2000; gen. and spl. edn. music and chorus tchr.; dir. Southbridge Alt. Mid./H.S., Mass.; spl. edn. and grade 11 English tchr., case mgr. grades 9-12 ORR HS, Mattapoisett, Mass., 2001—02; head tchr., spl. educator East Alternative HS/Amherst-Pelham Regional HS, Amherst, Mass., 2002—. Mem., appointee Mental Health Adv. Com., Rockville, Md., 1998, Montgomery County Com. on Hate and Violence, Rockville, 1998—; appointee Leadership Arts Mentoring Project, Rockville. Mem.: ASCD, Nat. Coalition Edn. Activists, Nat. Assn. for Multicultural Edn., Nat. Music Therapy Assn. (bd. cert.). Democrat. Roman Catholic. Avocations: baking, poetry, cooking, creative writing, photography. Home: 38 Valley Rd Chatham MA 02633

BOUDREAUX, ANGELA LOIS, elementary school educator; b. New Orleans, July 13, 1957; d. Wilbert Boudreaux, Sr. and Ruth Elizabeth Boudreaux; 1 child, Najjah Djer. BS, S.W. Adventist U., 1981. Tchr. elem. sch. Berean S.D.A. Sch., Baton Rouge, 1981—82, Ellender Meml. Sch., Houma, La., 1984—85, Bethesda S.D.A. Sch., Amityville, NY, 1985—88, Dupont Pk. S.D.A. Sch., Washington, 1988—90, Columbia Pk. Elem. Sch., Landover, Md., 1990—91, Emery Elem. Sch., Washington, 1992—2000, John F. Cook Elem. Sch., Washington, 2000—. Presenter in field. Recipient Elem. Educator Excellence award, Scottish Rite Masons, Washington, D.C., 1996. Democrat. Seventh Day Adventist. Avocations: writing, poetry, crafts, travel, reading. Home: 9103 Stacey M Lane Clinton MD 20735 Office: Dist of Columbia Public School 825 North Capitol St NE Washington DC 20002

BOUFFORD, JO IVEY, health and human services administrator; b. Durham, N.C., July 2, 1945; BA in Psychology magna cum laude, Wellesley Coll., 1965; MD with distinction, U. Mich., 1971; DSc(hon.), SUNY, Bklyn., 1992. Diplomate Nat. Bd. Med. Examiners, Am. Bd. Pediats. Resident in social pediats. medicine Montefiore Hosp. and Med. Ctr., Bronx, N.Y., 1971-74, asst. attending physician, 1975-97, co-dir. Inst. for Health Team Devel., 1975-82, dir. residency program in social medicine, 1975-82; adminstrv. dir. Valentine Lane Family Practice, Yonkers, N.Y., 1975-82; v.p. med. ops. N.Y.C. Health and Hosps. Corp., 1982-83, v.p. med. and profl. affairs, 1983-85, exec. v.p., 1985, acting pres., 1985, pres., 1985-89; internat. fellow in comparative health sys. mgmt. King's Fund Coll., London, 1989-91, dir., 1991-93; prin. dep. asst. sec. for health Dept. Health and Human Svcs., Washington, 1993-97; dean Robert F. Wagner Grad. Sch. of Pub. Svc., New York Univ., 1997—; prof. pub. admin., clin. prof. peds. New York Univ., 1997—; asst. prof. dept. pediats. Albert Einstein Coll. of Medicine, Bronx, N.Y., 1976-87, clin. assoc. prof. dept. epidemiology and social medicine, 1982-94. Acting Asst. Sec. Health, Jan.-June 1997; adj. prof. Lehman Coll. Nursing, Bronx, 1974-80; mem. Nat. Adv. Coun. for Health Professions Edn. US-DHHS, 1976-80; mem. tech. panel on the ednl. environ. Grad. Med. Edn. Nat. Adv. Coun., 1979-80; cons. on manpower programs divsn. medicine bur. Health Professions Edn. HRSA-DHHS, 1980-88; mem. N.Y. State Coun. on Grad. med. Edn., 1987-89, N.Y. State Commn. on Grad. Med. Edn., 1985-86; mem. adv. bd. residency program in gen. preventive medicine and occupl. health Mt. Sinai coll. Medicine, 1986-89; mem. Nat. Vis. Coun. for the Health Scis. Faculty Columbia U., N.Y.C., 1988-90; mem. vis. faculty The New Sch. for Social Rsch., 1989; rep. of U.S. on exec. bd. WHO, 1994-97; mem. joint coordinating com. for Radiation Health Effects Rsch., 1994-97; U.S. staff dir. Gore-Chernomyrdin Commn. Health Com., 1994-97; various consulting positions. Mem. editl. bd. Jour. Med. Edn., 1980-86; mem. editl. adv. bd. The New Physician, 1979-89; contbr. articles to profl. jours.; presenter in field. Mem. Nat. Adv. Coun. of Agy. for Healthcare Quality and Rsch., 2000—; bd. dirs. United Hosp. Fund, 1999—; chair sub-bd. on health, Open Soc. Inst., 1998—; mem. N.Y. State Coun. on Grad. Med. Edn., 1987-89. Fellow Am. Acad. Pediats.; mem. APHA, NAS Inst. Medicine Coun. (Robert Wood Johnson health policy fellow 1979-80), Am. Med. Women's Assn., Ambulatory Pediats. Assn., Soc. for Health and Human Values, Soc. Med. Adminstrs., Med. Adminstrs. Conf. Office: NYU Robert F Wagner Grad Sch Pub Svc 4 Washington Sq N New York NY 10003-6671 E-mail: jo.bouffard@nyu.edu.

BOUGHAN, ZANETTA LOUISE, music educator; b. Grantham, Eng., Mar. 22, 1959; arrived in U.S., 1964; d. Peter Leonard and Alyda Venita Maria (Bellord) Snowden; m. Robert William Boughan, Nov. 3, 1995. AS, Cochise Coll., 2003—. Pvt. piano and violin instr., Sierra Vista, Ariz., 1988—. Concertmaster Cochise Coll. Orch., Sierra Vista, 1999—2001, Pima Coll. Orch., Tucson, 2001—02; first violinist Sierra Vista Sym. Orch., 2001—02. Vol. Sierra Vista Police Dept., 2002—; ct. apptd. spl. adv. vol. State Ariz., 2002—; vol. in Police Svc., 2002—; mem. Citizens Police Acad. Assocs., 2003—; vol. Cochise County Juvenile Ct., 2003—. With USN, 1979—84. Mem.: Ariz. Music Tchrs. Assn., Nat. Music Tchrs. Assn., Cochise Music Tchrs. Assn. (chmn. fundraising com. 1997—, sec. 1998—2000, treas. 2001—03, pres. 2003—, Profl. Develop. grant 2001), Phi Theta Kappa. Home: 4924 Marconi Dr Sierra Vista AZ 85635 E-mail: zboughan@earthlink.net.

BOUGHMAN, JOANN ASHLEY, dean; b. Kokomo, Ind., May 4, 1949; d. Robert George and Lydia Ann (Ashley) B. BS in Med. Tech., Ind. U., Indpls., 1972, PhD in Med. Genetics, 1978. Diplomate Am. Bd. Med. Genetics. Asst. prof. Med. Coll. Va., Richmond, 1979-82; assoc. prof. U. Md. Med. Sch., Balt., 1983-90, prof., 1990—; assoc. v.p. for rsch. U. Md. Balt. County, Balt., 1992-95; dean grad. sch. U. Md., Balt., 1992—, v.p. for acad. affairs, 1995—. Sec. Am. Bd. Med. Genetics, 1992-94, v.p., 1995-96; cons. NIH, Bethesda, Md., 1982—, Gallaudet U., Washington, 1977—. Contbr. articles to profl. jours., chpts. to 19 books; author ednl. materials. Bd. dirs., officer Har Sinai Congregation, Balt., 1987—; mem. exec. com. High Tech Coun., Balt., 1992—; com. chair Info. Tech. Bd., Balt., 1994—; mem. speaker bur. Jewish Family Svcs., Balt., 1987—. Grantee RP Genetics Registry Ctr., 1978-82, NIH, 1985-94, 90-94; Edwards fellow, 1976. Fellow Am. Coll. Med. Genetics; mem. Am. Soc. Human Genetics (cert., com. chair 1994), Am. Assn. Dental Rsch., Am. soc. Clin. Pathologists, Exec. Women's Network. Office: U Md Balt 515 W Lombard St Baltimore MD 21201-1602

BOUGHTON, LESLEY D. library director; b. New Haven, Conn., Jan. 21, 1945; d. Robert and Marjorie (Anderson) D.; m. Charles E. Boughton, Sept. 5, 1964 (dec. 1991); children: Michael, James, Gregg. AB, Conn. Coll., 1971; MLS, So. Conn. State U., 1978. Dir. Platte County Library, Wheatland, Wyo., 1980-88, Carbon County Library, Rawlins, Wyo., 1988-93, Natrona County Pub. Library, Casper, Wyo., 1993—99; state libr. Wyo. State Libr., Cheyenne, 1999—. Mem. Gov's. Telecommunications Coun., Wyo., 1994—. Mem. ALA (chpt. councilor 1988, 91), Wyo. Library Assn. (pres. 1985, Disting. Svc. award 1991). Office: Wyo State Library 2301 Capitol Ave Cheyenne WY 82002

BOUKUS, ELIZABETH, state legislator; b. New Britain, Conn. BS, Conn. State U.; MS, U. Hartford. Mem. Conn. Ho. of Reps. Mem. Plainville Town Coun., 1989—, vice chair, 1989, chair, 1993-94; mem. Plainville Inland Wetlands Com. Office: 43 Hollyberry Ln Plainville CT 06062-2604

BOULDEN, JUDITH ANN, judge; b. Salt Lake City, Dec. 28, 1948; d. Douglas Lester and Emma Ruth (Robertson) Boulden; m. Alan Walter Barnes, Nov. 7, 1982; 1 child, Dorian Lisa. BA, U. Utah, 1971, JD, 1974. Bar: Utah 1974, U.S. Dist. Ct. Utah 1974. Law clk. to A. Sherman Christianson U.S. Cts., Salt Lake City, 1974; assoc. Roe & Fowler, Salt Lake City, 1975-81, McKay Burton Thurman & Condie, Salt Lake City, 1982-83; trustee Chpt. 7, Salt Lake City, 1976-82, Standing Chpt. 12, Salt Lake City, 1987-88, Standing Chpt. 13, Salt Lake City, 1979-88; sr. ptnr. Boulden & Gillman, Salt Lake City, 1983-88; U.S. Bankruptcy judge U.S. Cts., Salt Lake City, 1988—. Mem. Utah Bar Assn. Avocations: gardening, golf.

BOULTER, ELIZABETH CATHERINE, music educator; b. Greenville, S.C., Oct. 7, 1968; d. Kearney Isaac and Catherine Oliver (Jenrette) Smith; m. Richard Ottmuller Boulter II, Aug. 11, 1990; children: Isaac, Rachel. B in Music Edn., U. N.C. Chapel Hill, 1990. Lic. tchr. Music K-12 N.C. Tchr. mid. sch. music Piedmont Mid. Sch., Union County, NC, 1990—93; tchr. elem. music Yancey County Sch., NC, 1993—. Avocations: reading, writing, hiking, singing, playing recorders. Home: 404 Mandavilla Dr Burnsville NC 28714 Office: Yancey County Schs 100 School Cir Burnsville NC 28714*

BOULTON, BONNIE SMITH, assistant principal, special education educator; b. Galliano, La., June 27, 1960; d. Kenneth Joseph and Geraldine Ledet Smith; m. Ross E. Boulton, May 11, 2001. BA, Nicholls State U., 1982, EdM, 1985; PhD, La. State U., 2003. Spl. edn. tchr. Lafourche Parish Schs., Thibodaux, La., 1982—87, Jefferson Parish Pub. Schs., Metairie, La., 1987—90, St. Charles Parish Schs., Destrehan, La., 1990—99; grad. asst. La. State U., Baton Rouge, 1999—2000; edn. program coord. La. Dept. Edn., Baton Rouge, 2000—01; asst. prin., spl. edn. campus supr. Eanes Ind. Sch. Dist., Austin, Tex., 2002—. Bd. dirs. La. Dyslexia Assn., 1994—98. Named to, Outstanding Young Women Am., 1985. Mem.: ASCD, Coun. for Exceptional Children. Avocations: reading, travel, gardening, cooking. Home: 11007 Major Oaks Dr Baton Rouge LA 70815-5449

BOUMA, LYN ANN NICHOLS, music educator; b. Lincoln, Nebr., Jan. 5, 1963; d. Raymond Joseph Nichols and Margaret Ann Nicholas; m. Stephen George Bouma, Jan. 25, 1964; 1 child, Claire. BMus, Nebr. Wesleyan U., Lincoln, 1985; MMus, U. Nebr., Lincoln, 1991. Choral dir. West Point (Nebr.) Pub. Schs., 1985—93, Omaha Ctrl. HS, 1993—. Mem. music ad hoc com. Nebr. Dept. Edn., Lincoln, 2000. Mem. Omaha Chamber Singers. Recipient Outstanding Tchr. award, Alice Buffett Found., 1999, Outstanding Music Alumni award, Nebr. Wesleyan U., 2002. Mem.: NEA,

Music Educators Nat. Conf., Am. Choral Dirs. Assn. (life; Nebr. sec. 1992—94, chair Nebr. women's chorus 2000—03, conducted featured choirs at numerous state and regional convs., Outstanding Young Choral Dir. 1989). Democrat. Congregational/Meth. Avocations: fitness, contract bridge. Home: 5123 Decatur Omaha NE 68104 Office: Omaha Ctrl HS 124 N 20th St Omaha NE 68102

BOUNDS, SARAH ETHELINE, historian; b. Nov. 5, 1942; d. Leo Deltis and Alice Etheline (Boone) Bounds. AB, Birmingham-So. Coll., 1963; EdS in History, U. Ala., 1971, PhD, 1977. Tchr. social studies Huntsville City Sch., 1963, 65-66, 1971-74; residence hall adv., dir. univ. housing U. Ala., Tuscaloosa, 1963-65, 68-71; instr. history N.E. State Jr. Coll., Rainsville, Ala., 1966-68, U. Ala., Huntsville, 1975, 78-80,85—. Dir. Weeden House Mus., 1981-83, com. mem., 1981-2000; asst. prof. edn., supr. student tchr. U. North Ala., Florence, 1978. Mem.: AAUW, NEA, Assn. Tchr. Educators, Huntsville Music Study Club, Historic Huntsville Found., Huntsville Hist. Soc., Aladdin Club (pres. 2004—), Huntsville Pilot Club (pres. 1990—91, club builder 1991—93, Ala. dist. lt. gov. 1995—96, Ala. dist gov. elect 1996—97, Ala. dist gov. 1997—98), Phi Alpha Theta, Kappa Delta Pi, Alpha Delta Kappa (state pres. Ala. 1990—92, regional sec. 1991—93, mem. internat. com. 1993—97, chmn. internat. com. 1995—97). Methodist. Home: 1100 Bob Wallace Ave SE Huntsville AL 35801-2807

BOUNDS-SEEMANS, PAMELLA J. artist; b. Milton, Del., Nov. 5, 1948; d. James Wilson Bounds and Marguerite Edna (Rickards) Bounds Carey; m. Jeffrey Wayne Seemans, Mar. 20, 1984; children: Misty Autumn, Sterling Hunter, Jordan Windsor. BA, N.Mex. Highlands U., 1971, MA, 1972. Tchr. elem. art Indian River Sch. Dist., Frankford, Del., 1973-79. Lectr. U. Md., 1981, U. Del., 1986, Del. Tech. and C.C., 1988, 75th Del. Women's Day Conf. at U. Del., U. Del. Coll. Arts and Mineralogy, 1999. Exhibited in group shows including Rehoboth (Del.) Art League, 1980, 89, 90, 92, 93, Tideline Gallery, Rehoboth Beach, Del., 1980—, Greenville, Del., 1993, Wicomico Art League, 1980, Del. Tech. and C.C., Georgetown, 1981, U. Md., 1981, Bluestreak Gallery, Wilmington, Del., 1989—, Blue Streak Art Gallery, Wilmington, 1993, Jamison Gallery, Santa Fe, 1993—, Del. Art Mus., 1996, Biennal 96 and 98 Del. Art Mus., U. Del., 1999, Am. Mus. Visionary Arts, Balt., 2000, numerous others; represented in permanent collections including Wilmington (Del.) Trust Co., Del. Nat. Bank, Sussex County Courthouse, Del. Parks and Recreation Bldg., Del. State Folklore Collection, also numerous pvt. collections; poster for mayor's office Clifford Brown Jazz Festival, Wilmington, 1998; mem. cmty. adv. editl. bd. News Jour., Gannett Papers, Wilmington, 1997-98; artist Dino Doys Rennaissance Corp. Donated art work to oncology ctr. Beebe Hosp. Found., 1995, Multiple Sclerosis Found. Del., Ronald McDonald House Del.; mem. cmty. adv. bd. News Jour. editl. Staff, 1997—. Recipient award for outstanding body of work Torpedo Factory, Alexandria, Va., 1982; fellow State of Del. Divsn. of the Arts, 1995. Mem. Nat. Mus. of Women in the Arts, Del. Art Mus., Tunnel 2d place award for most outstanding work in exhibit 1990, Popular Vote award 1980, 93, 94, 95, 96, 1st place award 1993, hon.), Del. Ctr. for Contemporary Arts, Del. Ctr. for Creative Arts, Newark Arts Alliance, Del. Nature Soc., Mothers Multiple Births (v.p. 1987), Wicomo Art League (hon. mention 1981), Univ. and Whist Club (Wilmington). Avocations: criminology, fashion, study of primitive art, psychology, gourmet cooking. Home: 1203 Greenbank Rd Wilmington DE 19808-5842

BOURDEAU, STEPHANIE, state representative; b. Burlington, Vt., Mar. 26, 1951; m. Andre P. Bourdeau. State rep. Vt. Ho. of Reps., 1996—. Mem. Lamoille County Planning Commn., 1992—; sec. Hyde Park Rep. Com. Roman Catholic. Office: 1 N Hyde Park Rd Hyde Park VT 05655-9558

BOURDON, CATHLEEN JANE, professional society administrator; b. Sparta, Wis., July 13, 1948; d. Cletus John and Josephine Marie (Bourdon) Scheurich; children: Jill Krzyminski, Jeff Krzyminski. BA in Polit. Sci., U. Wis., 1973, MLS, 1974. Tchr. Peace Corps, Arba Minch, Ethiopia, 1969-72; asst. prof., dir. Alverno Coll. Libr., Milw., 1974-83; dep. exec. dir. Assn. Coll. and Rsch. Librs., Chgo., 1983-93; exec. dir. Ref. and User Svcs. Assn. divsn. ALA Assn. Specialized and Coop. Libr. Agys., Chgo., 1993—. Mem. ALA (pres. Staff Assn. 1987-88). Avocations: reading mystery fiction, 1940s movies, building model doll house furniture. Office: Assn Specialized & Coop Libr Agys 50 E Huron St Chicago IL 60611-5295 E-mail: cbourdon@ala.org.

BOURG, MARIE HILDA, retired principal; b. Baton Rouge, La., May 26, 1937; d. Gabriel Levy and Corinne Marie Scioneaux; m. Jerry Henry Bourg; children: Denise, Kevin. BS, La. State U., 1959, MS, 1962; student, Lorenzo Walker Inst. Tech., Naples, Fla., 1998—99. Tchr. Isidore Newman Sch., New Orleans, 1959—60, E. Baton Rouge Sch., 1960—62; tchr., dept. chair U.S. Dept. Def., Bermuda, 1962—63; tchr. Montgomery County Sch. Dist., Rockville, Md., 1963—64, dept. chair., tchr., 1965—70; tchr., dir. drum and bugle corp Port Arthur (Tex.) Ind. Sch. Dist., 1964—65; tchr. Montgomery Coll., Silver Springs, Md., 1970—75; recreational dir. County Govt., Hancock County, Miss., 1988—93; organizer, head mistress Royal Palm Acad., Naples, 1998—99; dir Diamondhead Continuing edn., 2003. Author: This is Hancock County, 1984, 1978-88: A Ten-Year Study of Education in Hancock County, 1989. Pres., bd. dirs. United Way S. Miss., Hancock/Harrison/Pearl River Counties, 1980—98; sec., bd. dirs. Hancock County Pk. Commn., Hancock County, 1980—88; pres., sec., bd. dirs. Miss. Coast Crimestoppers, Inc., Hancock and Harrison Counties, 1984—2000; bd. dirs., mem. adv. com. Goodwill Industries of S. Miss., Gulfport, 1988; sec., bd. dirs. Hancock Med. Ctr. Found. Bd., Bay St. Louis, 1990—98. Mem.: Pearls' Red Hat Soc., Diamondhead Women's Club, Am. Legion Aux. Roman Catholic. Avocations: tennis, travel, bridge, bowling.

BOURGEOIS, LOUISE, sculptor; b. Paris, 1911; came to U.S., 1938, naturalized, 1953; Student, Sorbonne U., 1932-35; baccalaureate, Ecole des Beaux Arts, 1936-38; postgrad., Ecole du Louvre, 1936-37, Acad. Grande Chaumiere; D.F.A. (hon.), Yale U., 1977, Calif. Coll. Arts and Crafts, 1988, Moore Coll. Art, Mass. Coll. Art, 1983, Md. Art Inst., 1984, The New Sch., 1987. Instr. Md. Art Inst., Balt., 1984, New Sch. Social Rsch., N.Y.C., 1987. One-woman shows include Norlyst Gallery, 1947, Peridot Gallery, 1949, 50, 53, Allan Frumkin Gallery, Chgo., 1953, White Art Mus., Cornell U., Ithaca, N.Y., 1959, Stable Gallery, 1964, Rose Fried Gallery, 1963, 112 Greene St., N.Y.C., 1974, Xavier Fourcade Gallery, N.Y.C., 1978-80, Max Hutchinson Gallery, N.Y.C., 1980, Renaissance Soc., 1981, Mus. Modern Art, N.Y.C., 1982, retrospective Contemporary Art Mus., Houston, 1983, Daniel Weinberg Gallery, L.A., 1984, Robert Miller Gallery, 1982, 84, 87-89, 91, Serpentine Gallery, London, 1985, Maeght-Lelong, Zurich, 1985, Paris, 1985, Taft Mus., Cin., 1987-89 (travelled to The Art Mus. at Fla. Internat. U., Miami, Fla., Laguna Gloria Art Mus., Austin, Tex., Gallery of Art, Washington U., St. Louis, Henry Art Gallery, Seattle, Everson Mus. Art, Syracuse, N.Y.), Mus. Overholland, Amsterdam, The Netherlands, 1988, Dia Art Found., Bridgehampton, N.Y., retrospective Frankfurter Kunstverein, Frankfurt, Fed. Republic Germany, 1989 (travelled to Städtische Galerie im Lenbachhaus, Munich, 1990, Riverside Studios, London, 1990, Musée d'Art Contemporain, Lyon, 1990, Fondacion Tapies, Barcelona, Spain, Kunstmuseum, Berne, Switzerland, Kröller-Müller Mus., Otterlo, The Netherlands), Linda Cathcart Gallery, Santa Monica, Calif., 1990, Barbara Gross Gallerie, Munich, 1990, Karsten Schubert, London, 1990, Galerie Krinzinger, Vienna, 1990, Karsten Greve Gallery, Cologne, 1990, Ginny Williams Gallery, 1990, Monika Sprüthe Galerie, Cologne, 1990, Robert Miller Gallery 1986, 1987, 1988, 1989, 1991, Galerie Lelong, Zurich, 1991; solo exhbns. include Parrish Art Mus., Southampton, N.Y., 1991, Ydessa Hendeles Found., Toronto, 1991, 92, Milwaukee Art Mus., 1992, The Fabric Workshop, Phila., Galerie Karsten Greve, Paris, Linda Cathcart Gallery, Santa Monica, Calif., Second Floor, Reykjavik, Iceland; exhibited in numerous group shows, U.S., Europe including Sculpture Ctr., 1997, Jim Kempner Fine Art, 1997, Steinbaum Krauss Gallery, 1998, Mary Boone Gallery, 1998, Am. Craft Mus., 1998; represented in permanent collections Mus. Modern Art, N.Y.C., Whitney Mus., Met. Mus. Art, Hirshorn Mus., Musée Nat. D'Art Moderne, Paris, R.I. Sch. Design, NYU, Albright-KnAustralian Nat. Gallery, Canberra, Musée d'Art Moderne, Paris, Mus. Fine Arts, Houston, Guggenheim Mus., N.Y.C., Kunstmus. Bern, stmus. Lucerne, Albertina, Vienna, Mus. Modern Art, Vienna, Walker Art Ctr., Mpls., Storm King Art Ctr., Mountainville, N.Y., New Mus. Contemporary Art, N.Y.C., DC Moore Gallery, N.Y.C., Cheim & Read Gallery, N.Y.C.; appeared in Limited Edition Artists Books 1990—. Recipient Outstanding Achievement award Women's Caucus, 1980, Pres.'s Fellow award R.I. Sch. Design, 1984, Skowhegan medal sculpture Skowhegan (Maine) Sch. Painting, and Sculpture, Gold medal of honor Nat. Arts Club, 1987, Creative Arts Medal award Brandeis U., 1989, Grand Prix Nat. de Sculpture French Ministry of Culture, 1991, Nat. medal arts, 1999, Wolf prize, 2003; recipient Lifetime Achievement award Coll. Art Assn., 1989, Internat. Sculpture Ctr., 1991; named Officer of Arts and Letters French Ministry of Culture, 1984. Fellow Am. Acad. Arts and Scis.; mem. Am. Acad. and Inst. Arts and Letters, Sculptors Guild, Am. Abstract Artists, Coll. Art Assn. (Disting. Artist award for lifetime achievement 1989). Office: Robert Miller Gallery 524 W 26th St Ground Fl New York NY 10001-5541

BOURGEOIS, PATRICIA MCLIN, women's health and pediatrics nurse, educator; b. Hammond, La., Mar. 12, 1941; d. Lannie McLin and Mary (Lossett) Nicolay; m. Charles Bourgeois, June 10, 1962; children: Deborah, Cynthia, Terry Kay, Lori, Betsy. BSN, McNeese State U., 1962; MSN, Northwestern State U., Natchitoches, La., 1980. Cert. clin. nurse specialist, nursing child assessment, La. Office nurse pediatrics Green Clinic, Ruston, La., 1962-63; staff nurse ob-gyn. Lincoln Gen. Hosp., Ruston, 1963-64; staff nurse nursery St. Francis Cabrini Hosp., Alexandria, La., 1966-67; prof. maternal/child nursing La. Tech. U., Ruston, 1975—. Part-time office nurse Green Clinic, 1975-93; part-time resident nurse Methodist Children's Home, Ruston, 1990-97. Vice chairperson La. Coalition for Maternal/Infant Health, Baton Rouge, 1989-91; pres. Ruston Civic Guild, 1990. Mem. ANA (del. 1991-93), La. State Nurses Assn. (sec. 1991-93, pres. 1994-95), La. State Bd. of Nursing (apptd. mem.). Democrat. Roman Catholic. Office: La Tech Univ PO Box 352 Ruston LA 71272-3178

BOURGEOIS, PRISCILLA ELZEY, educational administrator; b. Natchez, Miss., Oct. 4, 1952; d. John Patrick and Patsy Ruth (Broussard) Elzey; 1 child, Stephanie Priscilla. BA, U. Southwestern La., 1974; MEd, U. New Orleans, 1979, postgrad., 1982. Cert. elem. tchr., mentally retarded, learning disabled, supr. student tchrs., socially maladjusted and emotionally disturbed edn., prin., parish or city sch. supr. instrn., reading specialist, spl. sch. prin., mild, moderate elem. and secondary edn., severe-profound parish or city sch. supr., La. Prin. John Martyn Sch., Jefferson Parish Sch. System, Metairie, La., ednl. strategist, former prin. Waggaman (La.) Sch.; prin. Kehoe-France Northshore, 1996—. Active community orgns. Recipient appreciation award Coun. for Exceptional Children, 1984, 89. Mem. NAESP, La. Assn. Sch. Execs., Phi Delta Kappa. Office: Kehoe-France Northshore 25 Patricia Dr Covington LA 70433-1116

BOURGEOIS, SHARON E. mechanical engineer; b. Beverly, Mass., June 11, 1955; d. Perry Bradford and Claire Arnold; m. Edwin H. Griffen, Apr. 12, 1977 (div.)l children: David, Michelle. BSME, U. New Orleans, 1981. Assoc. engr. La. Power & Light, New Orleans, 1981-84, engr., 1985-88, maintenance engr., 1988-90, Va. Power, Mineral, 1990-92, staff engr., 1992—. Served with U.S. Army, 1976-79. Mem. ASME (assoc.). Avocations: painting, home renovation, skiing. Home: 6909 W 34th St Little Rock AR 72204-4724

BOURGUIGNON, ERIKA EICHHORN, anthropologist, educator; b. Vienna, Feb. 18, 1924; d. Leopold H. and Charlotte (Rosenbaum) Eichhorn; m. Paul H. Bourguignon, Sept. 29, 1950. BA, Queens Coll., 1945; grad. study, U. Conn., 1945; PhD, Northwestern U., 1951; DHL, CUNY, 2000. Field work Chippewa Indians, Wis., summer 1946; field work Haiti; anthropologist Northwestern U., 1947-48; instr. Ohio State U., 1949-56, asst. prof., 1956-60, assoc. prof., 1960-66, prof., 1966-90, acting chmn. dept. anthropology, 1971-72, chmn. dept., 1972-76, prof. emeritus, 1990—; dir. Cross-Cultural Study of Dissociational States, 1963-68. Bd. dirs. Human Relations Area Files, Inc., 1976-79 Author: Possession, 1976, rev. edit., 1991, Psychological Anthropology, 1979, Italian transl., 1983; editor, co-author: Religion, Altered States of Consciousness and Social Change, 1973, A World of Women, 1980; co-author: Diversity and Homogeneity in World Societies, 1973; adv. editor: Behavior Sci. Rsch., 1976-79; assoc. editor Jour. Psychoanalytic Anthropology, 1977-87; mem. editl. bd. Ethos, 1979-89, 97—, Jour. Haitian Studies, 2000—, Anthropology of Consciousness, 2002—; editor: Margaret Mead: The Anthropologist in America—, Occasional Papers in Anthropology, No. 2, Ohio State U. Dept. Anthropology, 1986; (with Barbara Rigney) Exile: A Memoir of 1939 by Bronka Schneider, 1998; contbr. articles to profl. jours. Fellow Am. Anthrop. Assn.; mem. Ctrl. State Anthrop. Soc. (treas. 1953-56, exec. com. 1995-98), Ohio Acad Sci., World Psychiat. Assn. (transcultural psychiatry sect.), Am. Ethnol. Soc., Current Anthropology (assoc.), Soc. for Psychol. Anthropology (nominations com. 1981-82, bd. dirs. 1991-93, lifetime achievement award 1999), Soc. for the Anthropology of Religion, Phi Beta Kappa, Sigma Xi. E-mail: bourguignon.1@osu.edu.

BOURKE, DALE HANSON, publishing company owner; b. Harvey, Ill., Nov. 29, 1953; d. Allan Dale and Irene (Kornafel) Hanson; m. Thomas Krebs Bourke, May 27, 1977; children: Chase Hanson, Tyler Jackson. BA, Wheaton (Ill.) Coll., 1975; MBA, U. Md., 1979. Dir. pub. relations Christian Coll. Consortium, Washington, 1975-77; cons. Continental Mktg. Assn., Washington, 1977-79; v.p. Internat. Mktg. Group, McLean, Va., 1979-82; pres. Publishing Directions Inc., Washington, 1982—; pub. Religion News Svc., Washington. Author: You Can Make Your Dreams Come True, 1985, Everyday Miracles, 1989; editor Today's Christian Woman Mag., Washington, 1979—; pub. Possibilities Mag., Washington, 1983—. Bd. govs. Nat. Women's Econ. Alliance, 1985—. Named Young Woman of Promise Good Housekeeping Mag. Mem. Women's Econ. Alliance (bd. govs.) Evangelical Christian Pubs., Evangelical Press Assn. (treas. 1983-85), Direct Mktg. Assn. Presbyterian. Office: Religion News Svc 1101 Connecticut Ave NW Ste 350 Washington DC 20036-4378

BOURNE, CAROL ELIZABETH MULLIGAN, biology educator, phycologist; b. Rochester, N.Y., May 4, 1948; d. William Thomas and Ruth Townsend (Stevens) Mulligan; m. Godfrey Roderick Bourne, Dec. 21, 1968. BA in Botany/Bacteriology, Ohio Wesleyan U., 1970; MS in Botany, Miami U., Oxford, Ohio, 1978; PhD in Natural Resources, U. Mich., 1992. Lab. asst. Ohio Wesleyan U., Delaware, 1968-70; biol. lab. tech. USDA-Forest Svc., Delaware, 1970-73; grad. rsch. asst. botany dept. Miami U., Oxford, 1973-75; electron microscopist coll. medicine U. Cin., 1975-76; rsch. asst. sch. pub. health U. Mich., Ann Arbor, 1978-80, rsch. assoc. coll. medicine, 1981-83, grad. rsch. asst. sch. natural resources, 1983-86, grad. teaching asst. dept. biology, 1987; postdoctoral scientist U. Fla., Ft. Lauderdale, 1990-92; adj. instr. ecology Fla. Atlantic U. Coll. Liberal Arts, Davie, 1992-93. Adj. asst. prof. dept. biology U. Mo., St. Louis, 1994—, Washington U., St. Louis, 1994—2000, Pierre Laclede Honors Coll., U. Mo., St. Louis, 1997—; bd. dirs. CEIBA Biol. Ctr., Inc.; mem. Pierre Laclede Honors Coll. Governing Bd. Coun., 2004—. Contbr. articles to scholarly jours. Grantee NSF, 1987-89. Mem.: Pierre Laclede Honors Coll. Governing Bd. Coun., Soc. for Study of Evolution, Internat. Soc. for Diatom Rsch., Phycological Soc. Am., Am. Inst. Biolog. Scis. Office: U Mo at St Louis Dept Biology 8001 Natural Bridge Rd Saint Louis MO 63121-4499 E-mail: BourneC@msx.umsl.edu.

BOURQUE, SUSAN CAROLYN, political science educator; b. Detroit, Oct. 9, 1943; d. Joseph Edward and Helen Jeanette (Cooney) B. B.A., Cornell U., 1965, Ph.D., 1971. Asst., then assoc. prof. Smith Coll., Northampton, Mass., 1970-81, prof., 1981—94, dean academic devel., 1994-97, provost, dean academic faculty, 1997; cons. Pathfinder Fund, Boston, 1980-84, Harvard Inst. Internat. Devel., 1982; dir. Project Women and Social Change, 1978—94 . Author, editor: Women Living Change, 1985, Women on Power, 2001. Author: Women of the Andes, 1981 (Hamilton Prize 1979). Fulbright Hayes fellow, 1968; grantee Mellon Found., 1978-84. Mem. Am. Polit. Sci. Assn., New Eng. Council Latin Am. Studies, New Eng. Council Am. Studies (exec. council, v.p. 1981-82, pres. 1982-83).

BOUSKA LEE, CARLA ANN, nursing and health care educator; b. Ellsworth, Kans., Nov. 26, 1943; d. Frank J. and Christine Rose (Vopat) Bouska; m. Gordon Larry Lee, July 8, 1967. RN, Marymount Coll., Salina, Kans., 1964; BSN, U. Kans., 1967; MA, Wichita State U., 1972, EdS, 1975, M in Nursing, 1984; PhD, Kans. State U., 1988. RN, cert. family and adult nurse practitioner, health edn. specialist, advanced nurse adminstr. Staff, charge nurse Ellsworth (Kans.) County Vet. Meml. Hosp., 1964—65; critical, coronary, and surg. nurse Med. Ctr. U. Kans., Kansas City, 1966—67, Watkins Meml. Hosp. and Student Health Ctr., 1965—66; asst. dir., chief instr. Wesley Sch. Nursing, Wichita, Kans., 1967—74; asst prof., chair nurse clinician/practitioner dept. Wichita State U., 1974—84, asst. prof. grad. health adminstrn. program, 1984—92; assoc. prof., dir. nurse practitioner program Ft. Hays State U., Hays, Kans., 1992—95; assoc. prof., coord. postgrad. nursing studies Clark Coll., Omaha, 1995—, nursing health svcs. mgmt. and allied health, 1994—; cons., v.p. devel. GRCIs Industries, Inc., 1994—; coord. nurses continuing edn. Providers - Kans. Mo. Nurses Assn. EMT, physician asst. HCA; lectr. Wichita State U., 1972—74, mem. grad. faculty, 1993—95; cons. Hays Med. Ctr.-Family Healthcare Ctr., 1993—96, Baker U., Northeastern U., Boston; mem. adv. coun. Kans. Newman Coll.; mem. adv. bd. Kans. Originals, Kans. Dept. Econ. Devel. Project, Wilson; mem. grad. faculty U. Kans., 1993—95; rschr. in field; bd. advisors Who's Who in Am. Nursing; bd. rsch. advisors Internat. Biog. Ctr., Cambridge, England. Author (with Ig & Barrett): Fluids and Electrolytes: A Basic Approach, 1996; author: Delman's Fundamental and Advanced Nursing Skills, 2000, (poetry) Seasons: Marks of Life, 1991 (Golden Poet award, 1991); actor: (poetry) Winter Tree, 1995 (Internat. Poet of Merit award, 1995); author: (booklet) Czechoslovakian History, 1988 (honor room Czech Mus. and Opera House, Wilson); author: (and editor) History of Kansas Nursing, 1987; contbr. articles to profl. jours. Co-founder Kans. Nurses Found., pres., trustee, 1978—93; vol. ARC, 1967—92, bd. dirs., 1977—90; mem., rschr. Gov.'s Commn. Health Care, Topeka, 1990; vol., lectr. Am. Heart Assn., 1967—, Am. Cancer Soc., 1967—; chair Nat. Task Force on Core Competence of Nurse Practitioners, 1994—95; mem. State of Kans. health care agenda Kans. Pub. Health Assn., 1995; city coord. campaign Sec. State, 1986; election judge Sedgwick County, Kans., 1989—94. Named Outstanding Cmty. Leader, Jaycees, Alumnus of Yr., Kans. U., 1979, Marymount Coll., 1987, Poet of the Yr., 1995; recipient Tchr. award, Mortar Bd.; grantee Nurse Practitioner Tng. grantee, U.S. Health and Human Svcs., 1966—67. Fellow: Am. Acad. Nursing, Am. Acad. Nursing; mem.: Internat. Soc. Poets (disting.), Gt. Plains Nurse Practitioners Soc. (founder, pres. 1993—), Kans. Nurse Found. (pres., dir., dist. alt. rep. 1978), Kans. Alliance Advanced Nurse Practitioners (founder, pres. 1986—, pres., dir., dist. alt. rep. 1992), Kans. Nurses Assn. (bd. dirs., treas.), Nat. Commn. on Credentialing of Health Edn. Specialists, Am. Bus. and Profl. Women's Assn. (Hall of Fame 1999), Am. Acad. Nurse Practitioners, Nat. League Nursing, ANA (nat. and site visitor ANCC), Sigma Theta Tau (Internat. Woman of the Yr. 1998), Alpha Eta (pres. chpt.). Republican. Roman Catholic. Avocations: poetry, music, gardening, writing, sewing. Home: 1367 N Westlink Ave Wichita KS 67212-4238 Office: Holy Names College Dept Nursing 3500 Mountain Blvd Oakland CA 94619-1699 Fax: 510-436-1376. E-mail: lee@hnc.edu.

BOUSLOG, ROBBIN RAYE, performing arts educator, art educator; b. Fullerton, Calif., July 17, 1952; d. Roger Leslie and Wanda Lee (Culpepper) Acton; m. Richard Bouslog, Mar. 28, 1998; 1 stepchild, Summer Nicole ; m. Allan Lee Morrow, June 26, 1971 (div. Dec. 17, 1997); children: Samuel Eli Morrow, Israel Allan Morrow. AA, San Jacinto (Calif.) C.C., 1985; BA in Liberal Studies, Calif. State U., San Bernardino, Calif., 1987; MA in Edn., Claremont (Calif.) Grad. Sch., 1989. Cert. Collaborative Design Inst., 2003. Musician and choir dir. Canyon Lake (Calif.) Cmty. Ch., 1982—87; worship leader and musician Elsinore Valley Friends Ch., Lake Elsinore, Calif., 1987—97; elem. tchr. Lake Elsinore Unified Sch. Dist., 1987—96; adj. prof. Edn. dept. Hope Internat. U., Fullerton, 2001; mid. sch. tchr. Lake Elsinore Unified Sch. Dist., 1996—. Presenter visual and performing arts Lake Elsinore Unified Sch. Dist., 1987—; presenter Calif. League of Mid. Schs., San Francisco, 1996—, San Diego, 1996—. Author: (projects) Weaving in the Arts, 2000, LEUSD Visual and Performing Arts Stds., 2001. Com. mem. Tuscany Hills Homeowners Assn., Lake Elsinore, 2001; dir. Canyon Lake Choraleers, Canyon Lake, 1992. Nominee Bravo award, L.A. Music Ctr. Edn., 1994, 2002; scholar Tchrs. Honor Soc., San Jacinto C.C., 1985; Apple grant, Claremont Grad. Sch., 1987. Mem.: Calif. Music Edn. Assn., Calif. Tchrs. Assn., Calif. Art Project. Republican. Achievements include direction of nationally recognized mid. sch. choirs. Avocations: acting, music, hiking, travel, reading. Home: 30 Villa Valtelena Lake Elsinore CA 92532 Office: Lake Elsinore Unified Sch Dist 545 Chaney St Lake Elsinore CA 92530 E-mail: rickandrobbin@verizon.net.

BOUTELLE, ANN EDWARDS, poet, educator; b. Aberfeldy, Scotland, Oct. 8, 1943; arrived in U.S., 1965; d. Alexander Wishart and Jean Fulton Edwards; m. William E. Boutelle, June 17, 1967; children: Jonathan, Laura, Alexander. MA, Univ. St. Andrews, Scotland, 1965; PhD, NYU, 1972. Vis. assoc. prof. Mt. Holyoke Coll., South Hadley, Mass., 1980—84; sr. lectr. Smith Coll., Northampton, Mass., 1984—, founder, chair Poetry Ctr., 1997—. Author: (book) Thistle and Rose: A Study of Hugh MacDiarmid's Poetry, 1980; contbr. poems to profl. jours. Founder Poetry Ctr. Smith Coll., 1997; trustee First Congl. Ch., Chesterfield, Mass., 2001—. Finalist Walt Whitman award, Acad. Am. Poets, 1999, Kathryn A. Morton prize, Sarabande Books, 2001; recipient German medal, U. St. Andrews, 1964. Mem.: MLA. Avocation: painting. Office: Smith College Elm St Northampton MA 01063

BOUTELLE, JANE CRONIN, fitness consultant; b. Arlington, Mass., Nov. 3, 1926; d. William Francis and Sara (Gillis) Cronin; m. G. William Boutelle, 1953 (dec. 1973); children: Jeanne E., William R., James G. BS, Boston U., 1948; MA, Columbia U., 1953. Cert. tchr., Mass. Tchr. dance and health edn. Newton (Mass.) H.S., 1948-51, Scarsdale (N.Y.) H.S., 1951-55, Marymount Coll., Tarrytown, N.Y., 1955-58, Manhattanville Coll., Purchase, N.Y., 1958-59; pres., fitness cons. The Boutelle Method, Inc., Greenwich, Conn., 1973—. Author: Lifetime Fitness for Women, 1978; contbr. articles to mags. Mem. nat. alumni bd. Boston U., 1981—85, mn. 40th reunion; pres. Westchester Dance Coun., Westchester County, NY, 1956—57; mem. woman's com. Lighthouse, Westchester County, 1983. Recipient Bravo award Greenwich YWCA, 1978. Mem.: AAUW (chmn. edn. 1963—68), Greenwich Assn. Pub. Schs. (chmn. 1968—73), Assn. Women in Phys. Edn., Soroptimist Internat. (chmn. scholarship com.), Greenwich Woman's Club Gardeners (chmn. 1996—2000). Office: The Boutelle Method Inc 6 Huckleberry Ln Greenwich CT 06831-3341

BOUTIETTE, MARY ANTONIA, language educator; b. Mishawaka, Ind., May 16, 1943; d. Ralph and Antonetta Giannuzzi; m. Darwin Garth Boutiette, June 17, 1972; children: Damien, Andreaa. BA, We. Mich. U., 1965; MA, U. Notre Dame, 1968. Spanish tchr. John Adams H.S., South Bend, Ind., 1965—72, Bloomington (Minn.) H.S., 1988—89; Spanish instr. North Hennepin C.C., Brooklyn Park, Minn., 1989—. Sec. Faculty Assn.,

South Bend. Mem. campaign coms. DFL Party, Thief River Falls, Minn., 1970—80. Named one of Young Profl. Women of Yr., Mishawaka (Ind.) Bus. Women. Mem.: Delta Kappa Gamma (pres. 1981—84). Home: 17088 Saddlewood Trail Minnetonka MN 55345 Office: North Hennepin Cmty Coll 7411 85th Ave N Brooklyn Park MN 55445 E-mail: mary.boutiette@nhcc.mnscu.edu.

BOUTROS, LINDA NELENE WILEY, medical/surgical nurse; b. New Orleans, Aug. 31, 1951; d. Robert Vernon and Marye Dell (Adcock) Wiley; m. Eddy Boutros, Dec. 23, 1972; children: Scott, Mark, Natalie. BS in Nursing, U. S.W. La., 1973. Cert. health care risk mgr. RN, relief charge, charge nurse, med./surgical flr. Bap. Hosp., Beaumont, Tex., 1973—76; RN, coord./supr. of nursing Kelsey Seybold Clinic, Missouri City, Tex., 1982-86; RN, head nurse S.W. Pediatric Ctr., Sugarland, Tex., 1986-87; RN, nursing supr. Westshore Hosp., Tampa, Fla., 1988-89; med.-surg. nurse Centurion Hosp., Carrollwood and Tampa, 1989-90, asst. head nurse med., 1990-91, relief supr., 1991, dir. surg. nursing svcs., 1992-93; nurse mgr. surg. floor, relief house supr. Univ. Cmty. Hosp. Carrollwood, Tampa, Fla., 1993-99, RN adminstrv. supr., 1999—. Mem. ANA, Fla. Nurses Assn., Fla. Soc. Health Care Risk Mgrs. Office: Univ Cmty Hosp Carrollwood 7171 N Dale Mabry Hwy Tampa FL 33614-2670 E-mail: lwboutros@hotmail.com.

BOUTWELL, SHARON MARIE, school system administrator, educator; 2 children. BS in Secondary Edn., U. Tex., 1973; MEd in Curriculum and Instrn., U. Houston, 1981, EdD in Adminstrn. and Supervision, 1995. Cert. English, history, gifted and talented tchr., mid-mgmt., supt. Tex. Tchr. Spring Branch Ind. Sch. Dist., Houston, 1974—92, 1993—95, dir. tech., 1992—93, grad. sch. facilitator, rsch. and evaluation staff appraisal, staff devel., 1995—96, facilitator, staff and orgnl. devel., 1996—99, lead area instrnl. specialist Stratford Learning Cmty., 1999—2002, adminstr. strategic planning, 2002—. Cons. Ministry of Edn., Singapore, 1998; adj. prof. Houston Bapt. U., U. St. Thomas, Tex. A&M; pres. Region IV Tex. Coun. Women Sch. Execs., 2003—; presenter in field. Author, co-dir. (video) Learning Organization Initiative, 1996 (Matrix award, 1996). Chair h.s. drill team events, Houston, 2000—04; mem. ch. leadership Meml. Drive United Meth., Houston, 1997—2001. Mem.: Tex. Assn. Gifted and Talented, Tex. Assn. Sch. Adminstrs., Nat. Staff Devel. Coun., Phi Delta Kappa. Methodist. Avocations: gardening, decorating, antique collecting, reading. Office: 955 Campbell Rd Houston TX 77024 Office Phone: 713-464-1511.

BOVE, PATRICE MAGEE, elementary school educator; b. Fort Madison, Iowa, Apr. 29, 1946; d. Claude and Susie T. Magee; m. Roger E. Bove, Aug. 6, 1983; 1 child, Jonna. MusB, U. Iowa, 1968; M of Music Edn., Temple U., 1976. Tchr. elem. instrumental music Birmingham (Mich.) Sch. Dist., 1968-69; tchr. elem. music T-E Sch. Dist., Berwyn, Pa., 1969—. Co-author: Philadelphia Orchestra Student Concert Books, 1994—; contbr. MENC (Strategies for Teaching Elementary Music), 1996. Educator, writer edn. adv. com. Phila. Orch., 1994—; accompanist chorus, Wayne, Pa., 1995, Suzuki Concerts, Immaculata, Pa., 1994-97. Mem. AAUW, Nat. Assn. Music Therapy, Music Tchrs. Assn., Gordon Inst. Music Learning, Suzuki, Kodaly, Orff, Pa. Music Edn. Assn. (dist. 12 co-host elem. songfest 1995), Music Educators Nat. Conf. Avocations: reading, computers, cooking. Home: 325 Holly Rd West Chester PA 19380-4614

BOWDEN, SALLY ANN, choreographer, educator, dancer; b. Dallas, Feb. 27, 1943; d. Cloyd MacAnally and Sally Estelle. Student, Boston U., 1960-62. Mem. Paul Sanasardo Dance Co., N.Y.C., 1963-67; pvt. tchr., choreographer N.Y.C., 1968-70; faculty Merce Cunningham Dance Studio, N.Y.C., 1971-76; faculty, co-dir. Constrn. Co. Dance Studio, N.Y.C., 1972-77; choreographer Constrn. Co. Theater/Dance Assocs., N.Y.C., 1972—. Artist-in-residence U. Wis., Madison, fall, 1975, N.C. Sch. of Arts, winter, 1978, U. Minn., Duluth, 1979, 1981-82, Kenyon (Ohio) Coll., fall 1980 Choreographer: Three Dances, 1969, Sally Bowden Dances and Talks at the New School, 1972, The Ice Palace, 1973, White River Junction, 1975, The Wonderful World of Modern Dance or The Amazing Story of the Plie, (1976) Wheat, 1976-77, Kite, 1978, Voyages, 1978, Morningdance, 1979, Crescent, 1980, Diverted Suite, 1983, Baby Dance, 1984. Recipient Creative Artists Public Service award for choreography, 1976-77; Nat. Endowment for the Arts Choreography fellow, 1975 Office: Theater/Dance Assocs 41 E 1st St New York NY 10003-9307

BOWDEN, VIRGINIA MASSEY, librarian; b. Houston, Tex., July 22, 1939; d. Calvin Scott and Juanita Barlow Massey; m. Charles Lee Bowden, July 2, 1960; children: Sharon Scott Bowden Davis, Ellen Maureen. BA, U. Tex., 1960, PhD, 1994; MSLS, U. Ky., 1970. Programmer Texaco Inc., Houston, 1960-64; sr. programmer AMA, Chgo., 1964-65, C.E.I.R. Inc., N.Y.C., 1965-66, Bambergers, Newark, 1967-68; systems analyst, asst. to dir. U. Tex. Health Sci. Ctr., San Antonio, 1970-78, assoc. libr. dir., 1978-85, libr. dir., 1985—. Author: (with others) Handbook of Medical Library Practice, 1983; contbr. articles to profl. jours. Prse. Friends Pub. Libr., San Antonio, 1989-90. Recipient numerous grants Nat. Libr. Medicine, 1982-2000; fellow Coun. Libr. Resources, 1978-79. Fellow Med. Libr. Assn. (Louise Darling medal 1990); mem. ALA, LWV (bd. dirs. 1983-85), Acad. Health Info. Profls, Assn. Acad. Health Sci. Libr. Dirs. (bd. dirs. 1995-98), Nat. Network Librs. Medicine (bd. dirs. South Ctrl. region 1995-97), Amigos Bibliographic Coun. (trustee 1986-89), Nat. Libr. Medicine (cons. 1983-88), Tex. Libr. Assn., Coun. Rsch. and Acad. Librs. (pres. 1986-87), Tex. Coun. State Univ. Librs. (pres. 1996-98), Daus. Rep. Tex., South Ctrl. Acad. Med. Librs. (sec., 1996-98), Phi Beta Kappa (pres. 1979). Unitarian Universalist. Office: U Tex Health Sci Ctr 7703 Floyd Curl Dr San Antonio TX 78229 Home: PO Box 2968 Canyon Lake TX 78133-0016 E-mail: bowden@uthscsa.edu.

BOWEN, ALICE FRANCES, school system administrator; b. Worcester, Mass., Apr. 14, 1948; d. Vincent Francis and Alice Frances (Gray) B. BS in Edn., Worcester State Coll., 1971, MS in Math. Edn., 1973, MS in Computer Sci. Edn., 1985. Cert. prin., math. and social studies tchr., Mass. Tchr. math. Worcester Pub. Schs., 1971-83, tchr. computer sci., 1983-92, asst. prin., 1992—. Instr. SAT prep. Ctrl. New Eng. Coll., Worcester, 1980-85; mem. Greater Worcester Urban Math. Collaborative Alliance for Edn., 1992-95. Leader Montachusetts coun. Girl Scouts U.S.A., 1968-85. Recipient St. Anne award Montachusetts coun. Girl Scouts U.S.A., 1978. Mem. ASCD, AAUW (bd. dirs. Worcester br. 1972-75, 90-96, Eleanor Roosevelt tchr. fellow 1991, Turtle award Worcester br.), Alliance for Edn., Delta Kappa Gamma, Phi Delta Kappa (Adminstr. of Yr. 2002). Democrat. Roman Catholic. Avocations: travel, crafts, reading. Home: 43 Sheridan Dr Shrewsbury MA 01545-3865 Office: Burncoat Mid Sch 135 Burncoat St Worcester MA 01606-2405

BOWEN, CHIEH-CHEN, psychology educator, consultant; b. Peng-hu, Taiwan, June 24, 1963; d. Hui-gen Chang and Yu-ing Huang-Chang; m. William M. Bowen, Aug. 15, 1996; children: Ted, Tim, Kingsley. PhD, Pa. State U., 1993. Assoc. prof. of human resource mgmt. Nat. Sun Yat-Sen U., Kaohsiung, 1993—96; asst. prof. of psychology Cleve. State U., Cleve., 1997—. Cons. various pub. and pvt. sectors, Koahsiung, Taiwan, 1993—96. Mem.: Soc. of Indsl. and Orgnl. Psychology (corr.; membership rev. com. 2002—). Achievements include research in Faking in personality questionnaires for selection, and women's issues in the workplace. Office: Cleve State U 2121 Euclid Ave Cleveland OH 44115

BOWEN, CLOTILDE MARION DENT, retired career officer, psychiatrist; b. Chgo., Mar. 20, 1923; d. William Marion Dent and Clotilde (Tynes) D.; m. William N. Bowen, Dec. 29, 1945 (dec.). BA, Ohio State U., 1943, MD, 1947. Intern Harlem Hosp., N.Y.C., 1947-48; resident and fellow in pulmonary diseases Triboro Hosp., Jamaica, L.I., 1948-50; resident in psychiatry VA Hosp., Albany N.Y., 1959-62; asst. resident in psychiatry Albany Med. Ctr. Hosp., 1961-62; pvt. practice N.Y.C., 1950-55; chief pulmonary disease clinic, 1950-55; asst. chief pulmonary disease svc. Valley Forge Army Hosp., Pa., 1955—59; chief psychiatry VA Hosp., Roseburg, Oreg., 1962-66, acting chief of staff, 1964-66; asst. chief neurology and psychiatry Tripler Gen. Hosp., Hawaii, 1966-68; psychiatr. liaison and dir. Rev. D., Office Civil Health and Med. Program Uniform Svcs., 1968-70; commd. capt. U.S. Army, 1955, advanced through ranks to col., 1968, neuropsychiat. cons. USA Vietnam Medcom, 1970—71, chief dept. psychiatry Fitzsimons Army Med. Ctr., 1971-74, chief dept. psychiatry Tripler Army Med. Ctr., 1974-75; assoc. clin. prof. psychiatry U. Hawaii, 1974-75; comdr. Hawley Army Clin., post surgeon U.S. Army, Ft. Benjamin, Harrison, Ind., 1977-78, chief dept. primary care and cmty. medicine, 1978-83, chief psychiat. consultation svc. Fitzsimons Army Med. Ctr., 1983-85; chief psychiatry svc. med./regional office ctr. VA, Cheyenne, Wyo., 1987-90; staff psychiatrist Denver VA Satellite Clin., Colorado Springs, Colo., 1990-96; ret., 1996. Locum Tenens practice psychiatry, 1996—; surveyor Joint Commn. on Accreditation Healthcare Orgns., 1985-92; assoc. clin. prof. psychiatary U. Colo. Med. Ctr., Denver, 1971—; spkr. Vietnam Vets. Meml. Wall, 2001. Decorated Legion of Merit, others; recipient Colo. Disabled Am. Vets. award, 1994-95, Pres.'s 300 Commencement award Ohio State U., 1987, Profl. Achievement award Ohio State U. Alumni Assn., 1998, Cert. of Appreciation, VFW, 2000, Am. Assn. Emergency Psychiat. award, 2001. Fellow Am. Psychiat. Assn. (disting. life), Acad. Psychosomatic Med.; mem. AMA, Nat. Med. Assn., Menninger Found (charter), Ctrl. Neuropsychiat. Assn. (Peter Bassoe fellow). Home: 1020 Tari Dr Colorado Springs CO 80921-2257

BOWEN, DEBRA LYNN, lawyer, state legislator; b. Rockford, Ill., Oct. 27, 1955; d. Robert Calvin and Marcia Ann (Crittenden) Bowen. BA, Mich. State U., 1976; JD, U. Va., 1979. Bar: Ill. 1979, Calif. 1983. Assoc. Winston & Strawn, Chgo., 1979-82, Washington, 1985-86, Hughes Hubbard & Reed, Los Angeles, 1982-84; sole practice Los Angeles, 1984-93; mem. Calif. State Assembly, 1992—98, Calif. State Senate, 1998—. Gen. counsel, State Employee's Retirement System Ill., Springfield, 1980-82; adj. prof. Watterson Coll. Sch. Paralegal Studies, 1985. Exec. editor Va. Jour. Internat. Law, 1977-78; contbr. articles to profl. jours. Mem. mental health law com. Chgo. Council Lawyers, 1980-82. Rotary Internat. fellow Internat. Christian U., Tokyo, 1975; Wigmore scholar Northwestern U. Sch. Law, Chgo., 1976; recipient James Madison Freedom of Information award No. Calif. chpt. Soc. Profl. Journalists, 1995. Mem. Calif. Bar Assn. (exec. com. pub. law sect. 1990-94), Mortar Bd., Phi Kappa Phi. Office: Calif Senate State Capitol Sacramento CA 95814-4906 also: Dist Office 2512 Artesia Blvd Ste 200 Redondo Beach CA 90278-3210

BOWEN, FERN CHAMBERS, artist, educator; b. Orange Cove, Calif., May 3, 1917; d. Robert Malcolm Chambers and Mary Ether Montgomery; m. Howard Clee Willcox, Dec. 24, 1935 (div.); m. Walter Johnson Bowen, Feb. 19, 1946 (dec. Mar. 29, 1985); 1 child, Stephen Llane. Student, Soldini Sch. Art, Long Beach, Calif., 1957—67, Laguna Beach (Calif.) Sch. Art, 1968—80, Calif. State U., Chico, 1967—76, Calif. State U., San Diego, 1977, Inst. San Miguel de Allende, Mex., 1981; studied with Arnold Schiffrin, Italy, 1970—71. Artist, Bellflower, Calif., 1960—83; artist, lectr. for internat. travel L.A. County Mus. Art, 1972—81; dir. arts and crafts Cunard Princess Lines, NJ, 1984—85; art history lectr. local svc. clubs L.A., 1975—85. With prodn. illustration/engring. dept. U.S. Mil., Long Beach, Calif., 1942—43. One-woman shows include Long Beach Cmty. Playhouse Gallery, 1968, San Diego State U. Exhbn., Malcolm Love Libr., 1970, exhibitions include Pacific Asia Mus., 1974, Long Beach Mus., 1976, Downey Mus. Art, 1977—78 (1st Pl. award, 1977), Palm Springs Desert Mus. Art, 1984—85, Represented in permanent collections Long Beach Mus. Art. Mem. Civic Art Assn. Palm Springs Desert Mus., Nat. Trust for Hist. Preservation. Named Esteemed Artist, Westminster (Eng.) Gallery award, 2001; recipient Award of Excellence, Cerritos Coll., 1970, 1972, Best of Show award, Arteasel.com., Inc., 2001, 1st Pl. award, Nat. Acrylic Painters' Assn., 1998. Mem.: Nat. Mus. Women in Arts, L.A. Art Assn., Women Painters West. Home: Unit 109 1750 E Ocean Blvd Long Beach CA 90802

BOWEN, GINGER ANN, artist; b. Amarillo, Tex., Feb. 16, 1953; d. Emmitt Lewis and Rose Hales; m. James A. Bowen; 1 child, Christian. Grad. h.s., Amarillo. Dir. adminstrns. Warner Bros. Records, Nashville, 1980—84. Exhibited in group shows at Ctrl. South Art Exhibit, 1994 (Chromatic Photo-imaging Svc. award), Catherine Lorillard Wolfe Art Club, 1995, Am. Artist Profl. League, 1995 (award, 1995), 2000—01 (Honorable Mention, 1999, Frank C. Wright Meml. award, 2001), Art Maui, 1997—98 (Purchase Pledge award, 1997), San Bernadino County Mus., 1999 (Honorable Mention, 2001). Recipient First Pl. Profl., Scottsdale Artist Sch Best and Brightest Competition, 2003. Mem.: Nat. Mus. Women in Arts, Am. Artist Profl. League, Oil Painters Am. (assoc.), Calif. Art Club, Catherine Lorillard Wolfe Art Club. Avocations: travel, music. E-mail: gbowen7@cox.net.

BOWEN, JEAN, retired librarian, consultant; b. Albany, N.Y., Mar. 23, 1927; d. John W. and Grace Lester (Quier) B.; m. Henry F. Bloch, June 26, 1962; 1 child, Pamela A. Bloch. AB, Smith Coll., 1948, AM, 1956; MS, Columbia U., 1957. Curator Rodgers & Hammerstein Archives of Recorded Sound, N.Y.C., 1962-67; asst. chief music divsn. N.Y. Pub. Libr., N.Y.C., 1967-85, chief music divsn., 1986-96, dir. Humanities and Social Scis. Libr., 1996-2000. Cons. Rockefeller Bros. Found., N.Y.C., 1963, 67, N.Y. Philharm., N.Y.C., 1984, Schubert Archives, N.Y.C., 1982; mem. faculty Rare Book Sch. Columbia U., N.Y.C., 1984, 87, 91; bd. dirs. Amphion Found., N.Y.C. Contbr. articles to High Fidelity, Opera News, Am. Record Guide, Saturday Rev., MLA Notes, New Grove Dictionary of Am. Music. Mem.: Rare Book Sch. (mem. faculty, Columbia U., NYC 1984, 1987, 1991), Amphion Found. (NYC).

BOWEN, JEAN ANN, school system administrator; d. John W. and Helen T. Gerber; m. Gary K. Bowen, June 13, 1964; children: John Timothy, David Andrew. BA, Millikin U., 1964; MEd, U. Ill., 1968; EdD, Loyola U., Chgo., 2000. Tchr., Decatur, Ill., Champaign, Elgin; counselor Champaign, Elgin. Dir. pupil pers. svcs., Elgin; asst. prin., fine arts divsn. Larkin H.S., 1993—. Contbr. articles to profl. jours. Mem. Beautification Commn., Elgin. Named Outstanding Young Woman, Elgin Jr. Womens Club, 1975. Mem.: ASCD, Ill. Principals Assn. (bd. dirs. 1995), Phi Delta Kappa. Office: Larkin High Sch 1475 Larkin Ave Elgin IL 60123 E-mail: bowen_j/lhs@dns.u46.k12.il.us.

BOWEN, LINDA FLORENCE, pharmaceutical executive; b. Trenton, N.J., Apr. 21, 1960; d. Joseph John and Audrey (Würfel) Kish; m. Chris Bowen, Dec. 8, 1998. BA in English, Rutgers Coll., 1982; BS in Microbiology, Rutgers U., 1982; MS in Drug Regulatory Affairs, L.I. Univ., 1996. Cert. US Regulatory Affairs, 2001, EU Regulatory Affairs 2003. Microbiologist Kalipharma-Purepac Pharm., Elizabeth, N.J., 1983-85; quality assurance and regulatory affairs positions to assoc. dir. GlaxoSmithKline (formerly Block Drug Co.), Jersey City, 1985—2003. Adj. prof. grad. QA/RA program Temple U., 1998—; mem. bd. editors Fundamentals in Can. Regulatory Affairs, 2003—04; assoc. dir. regulatory affairs Bayer Healthcare, 2004—. Bd. dirs. Theatre Guild of Old Bridge, 1993—. Mem.: Drug Info. Assn., Regulatory Affairs Profl. Soc., Rho Chi. Avocations: community theater, traveling, deltiology, local history. E-mail: LKish@aol.com.

BOWEN, LINNELL R. director; b. Orlando, Fla., June 16, 1940; m. Paul Ivan, Jr. Bowen; children: Julia Anne, Paul Ivan III. Student, U. Md., 1962; fundraising and devel. mgmt. program, Goucher Coll., 1990; leadership tng. course, Nat. Trust for Hist. Preserve, 1991. Tchr. U.S. history Annapolis H.S., 1962—65; dir. devel./pub. rels., dir. edn., ednl. cons. Hist. Annapolis Found., 1976—94; adj. tchr. Colonial Md. Experience Anne Arundel C.C., 1989—91; adj. tchr. fundraising for hist. preservation Goucher Coll. Ctr. for Continuing Studies, 1993—95; exec. dir. Annapolis 300, A Capital Celebration, 1994—95, Md. Hall for Creative Arts, 1996—. Bd. pres. Cultural Arts Found. Anne Arundel County, 1995—96, Jr. League Annapolis Adv. Bd., [illegible]; county elec. appt. Scenic and Hist. Rds. Commn., 1986—96, pres. Scholarship for Scholars Inc., 1991—93; mem. steering com. Millennium Legacy Trail Art Competition, City of Annapolis Whitbread Race; mem. Cultural Heritage Alliance Com.; bd. dirs. Scholarship for Scholars Inc., 1991—93; bd. dirs. Annapolis and Anne Arundel County Conf. and Visitors Bur.; mem. adv. com. Mitchell Gallery at St. John's Coll., 1995—98. Named one of Md.'s Top 100 Women, 1998, 2001; recipient City of Annapolis award of commendation, Annapolis 300 Celebration, 1995, Cmty. award for Annapolis 300 Celebration, Hist. Annapolis Found., 1996, Leadership Anne Arundel Cmty. Trustee award, 1996, Lifetime Achievement award, Pub. Rels. Soc. Annapolis and Anne Arundel County, 1999; fellow Paul Harris fellow, Rotary Found., 1997. Mem.: Annapolis/Anne Arundel County (chpt. trustee), Pub. Rels. Soc. Am., Annapolis and Anne Arundel County C. of C., Anne Arundel Trade Coun., Annapolis and Anne Arundel County C. of C. Office: 801 Chase St Annapolis MD 21401

BOWEN, MARY LU, ecumenical administrator; b. Wheeling, W.Va., Feb. 14, 1930; d. Walter Philip and Helen Elizabeth (Luthy) Wagenheim; m. Robert Edward Bowen, June 13, 1953; children: Jeanne, Thomas, Robert, David. BS in Edn., Wittenberg U., 1952; MA in Social Scis., SUNY, Binghamton, 1989. Cert. tchr., Ohio, W.Va., Tex., N.Y. Various teaching positions, 1952-80; coord. ministry with the aging Coun. of Chs., Broome County, N.Y., 1979-82, adminstrv. asst., 1982-83, asst. dir., 1984-86; assoc. for ecumenical devel. N.Y. State Coun. of Chs., Albany, Syracuse, N.Y., 1990-94, regional dir. southern tier Albany, 1995-96; dir. of pub. policy N.Y. State Cmty. of Churches, 1997-98, exec. dir., 1998—. Sec. exec. cabinet N.Y. State Coun. Chs., Albany, Syracuse, 1986-91; synodical lay rep. Evang. Luth. Ch. in Am. Region VII Coun., Phila., 1987-91, churchwide leadership team Social Min. Project, Chgo., 1990-91, sec. constituting conv. Upstate N.Y. Synod, Syracuse, 1987. Author: Reclaiming Christianity's Feminist Heritage: Reflections on Patriarchal Teachings and Women's Problems, 1989, Handbook for Clergy on Child Abuse and Neglect, 1995. Active Broome County Coordinating Coun. Child Abuse and Neglect, 1986-88, 96-98, treas. 1997; mem. Luth. Statewide Advocacy Exec. Com., Albany, 1982-90, 2000—, chmn. exec. com., 1991-99; regional adv. bd. Citizen Action N.Y., Binghamton, 1994-98; co-chmn. Interreligious Health and Justice Coalition, N.Y. Ctrl. So. Tier Region, 1994-98; Evang. Luth. Ch. in Am. Coalition for Mission in Appalachia, 1996—, chair, 2000-2001. Recipient Citizen Action N.Y. Phoenix award, 1998, Upstate N.Y. Synod Lay Discipleship award, 1999; Sr. Congl. intern, 1997. Mem.: Nat. Assn. Ecumenical Staff. Democrat. Lutheran. Avocations: travel, reading. Home: 14 Overbrook Dr Apalachin NY 13732-4234 Office: NY State Cmty Chs 362 State St Albany NY 12210-1202 E-mail: marylubowen@aol.com., nyscoc@aol.com.

BOWEN, MELANIE, legislative staff administrator; m. Ronald S. Bowen; children: Elysa, Lindsey. BS in Polit. Sci. and History, Brigham Young U. Intern to Senator Orrin Hatch, Washington, 1977; dir. Ctrl. and Ea. Utah Office; dep. state dir., 1984; state dir.; dir. Office of Senator Hatch. Mem. U.S. Delegation Am. Swiss Leadership Conf., Geneva; co-chair State Rep. Platform com.; mem. State of Utah's Immunization Task Force, Utah Internat. Biomed. Conf. com., chair Utah Women's and Srs. Confs.; past pres. Salt Lake Coun. of Women. Office: Office of Senator Orrin Hatch 8402 Federal Bldg 123 S State St Salt Lake City UT 84138-1101

BOWENS, GLORIA FURR, educational administrator; b. Detroit, Apr. 15, 1927; d. Leon Lewis and Iva Rose (Talbot) Furr; B.S., Tufts Coll., 1947; Ed.M., State Coll. Boston, 1968; Ed.D., Harvard U., 1975; 1 dau., Stephanie T. Sci. tchr. Boston Pub. Schs., 1961-71, asst. to the dir. orientation for integration, 1971-73, acting dir. personnel mgmt., 1981-82, instr. med. tech., 1982— ; asst. supt. schs. Roosevelt (L.I., N.Y.) Sch. Dist., 1974-77; asst. dir. urban schs. collaborative Northeastern U., Boston, 1977-79, dist. IX coordinator curriculum and competency resources, 1979-81; ptnr. antique shop, Pickering Wharf, Salem, Mass., 1982—; pres. Horizons Extended Ednl. Consulting, 1992-98. Mem. Nat. Council Adminstrv. Women Edn. (exec. bd. 1970-73), Am. Assn. Sch. Adminstrs., North Shore Antiques Assn. (treas.), Phi Delta Kappa, Alpha Kappa Alpha.

BOWENS, THELLA, senior aviation director; b. Mount Enterprise, Tex. 2 children. BA, Barnard Coll, 1970; post grad., Texas Christian U. Budget adminstr. Dallas/Ft. Worth Internat. airport; dep. dir. of aviation Kansas City Internat. airport; sr. dir. of aviation San Diego Unified Port Dist., 1996—. Bd. dirs. george Washington Carver Neighborhood Ctr. and Day Care; mem. Lejardin Sr. Citizens Home; bd. dirs. San Diego United Way; mentor for Welfare to Work Program. Mem. Am. Assn. of Airport Execs., Econ. Steering Com. for Airports Coun. Internat. North Am., Natl. Forum for Black Pub. Adminstr. Avocations: tennis, reading hist. novels, enjoying arts and theatre productions. Office: San Diego Unified Port Dist San Diego Internat Airport PO Box 120488 San Diego CA 92112-0488

BOWEN-THOMPSON, FRANCES OCTAVIA, county official, nonprofit organization consultant; b. Jersey City, May 2, 1942; d. Roger and Marion Frances (Barbee) Howard; m. Walter Eugene Bowen (div. June 1975); 1 child, Glenn Scott Bowen ; m. Kenneth Edward Thompson, May 1, 1982. BA, Rutgers U., Newark, 1974, MPA, 1980; postgrad., Capella U., 1996. Exec. dir. House of Insight, Newark, 1980-83; placement dir. Fedn. of Handicapped, N.Y.C., 1983-85; mem. Jersey City Mcpl. Coun., Jersey City, 1985-89; propr. Klose to You Lingerie, Jersey City, 1987-89; employee assistance officer, benefits adminstr. Area Vocat. Sch., North Bergen, N.J., 1989-91; dir. minority and women bus. Hudson County Adminstrn. and Fin., Jersey City, 1993—. Cons. Howard, Bowen & Thompson Assocs., Jersey City, 1982—. ; c. Hudson County Dem. Com., Jersey City, 1989, vice chmn., 1994-95; std. bearer Frances O. Thompson Civic Assn., Jersey City, 1990, 97—; trustee Hudson County coun. Girl Scouts U.S.A., 1995; chmn. Bergen-Lafayette 4-H Club, 1994-96. Recipient cmty. svc. award Jersey City NAACP, 1985, Hoboken (N.J.) NAACP, 1987, Jersey City Martin Luther King Parade and Scholarship, 1995. Mem. Nat. Assn. Women Bus. Owners, Order Ea. Star. Baptist. Avocations: knitting, crocheting, sewing, painting t-shirts. Home: 27 Freedom Pl Jersey City NJ 07305-4101 Office: Hudson County Adminstrn and Fin 583 Newark Ave Jersey City NJ 07306-2301

BOWER, ANNE LIEBERMAN, English educator; b. N.Y.C., May 8, 1941; d. Frank J. Lieberman and Maxine (Scheuer) Donahue; m. Roger L. Bower, Dec. 1962 (div. Dec. 1987); children, Rachael, Aviva, Issac. BS in English, Columbia U., 1963; MA in English, W.Va. U., 1985, PhD in English, 1990. Exec. sec. Pitts. Psychoanalytic Inst., 1975-77; project mgr. Greene County Indsl. Devel., Waynesburg, Pa., 1977-79, Greene County Planning Ctr., Waynesburg, 1979-81; exec. dir. Wheeling (W.Va.) Creek Watershed Commn., Wheeling and Waynesburg, 1981-86; tchg. asst. English W.Va. U., Morgantown, 1983-85, 87-90; instr. in English Waynesburg Coll., 1985-87; assoc. prof. English Ohio State U., Marion, 1990—. Spkr. Ohio Humanities Coun., Columbus, 1994-96. Author: Epistolary Responses: The Letter in 20th Century American Fiction and Criticism, 1996; editor: Recipes for Reading: Community Cookbooks, Stories, Histories, 1997, The Historical Cookbook of the American Negro, repring, 2000; contbr. chpts. to books. Vol. Turning Point, Marion, 1994—, Pearl St. Sch., 2000—, Dollars and Sense Partnership, 2001—. Rsch. grantee Ohio State

U., 1991-92, Schlesinger Libr., Radcliffe Coll., 1992, Ohio State U., 1994, Ohio Humanities Coun., 1996. Mem. MLA, Midwest MLA, Nat. Coun. Tchrs. English. Office: Ohio State U - Marion 1465 Mount Vernon Ave Marion OH 43302-5628

BOWER, BARBARA JEAN, nurse, consultant; b. Akron, Ohio, Aug. 25, 1942; d. William Howard and Maxine (Goodykoontz) Sturm; m. Howard Bower, Aug. 25, 1961 (dec. 1989); children: Nancy, Janet. BA, Elmhurst Coll., 1974, postgrad., 1987—; diploma, Evang. Sch. Nursing, 1970; PhD, U. Chgo., 1993. RN. Critical care nurse, supr. nursing Loyola U. Med. Ctr.; critical care nurse Med. Staffing Services, Oak Park, Ill., 1978-84; pres. Heart Care Unltd., Oak Brook, Ill., 1982—. One of first ind. nurse contractors in Ill., Ind., Ariz. Creator ednl. programs for cardiac patients, families and staff, 1971—. Stephen min. Christ Ch. of Oak Brook, Ill.; Republican election judge, DuPage County. Mem. AAUW, ANA, Am. Assn. Critical Care Nurses, Am. Heart Assn., Elmhurst Coll. Alumni Assn., U. Chgo. Alumni Assn., Oak Brook Exec. Breakfast Club. Avocations: rose gardening, cooking, candymaking. Office: Heart Care Unltd PO Box 3275 Oak Brook IL 60522-3275 Office Phone: 630-920-1122. E-mail: bjb@hotmail.com.

BOWER, CATHERINE DOWNES, communications, management consultant; b. Balt., Dec. 29, 1947; m. Réjean Pierre Proulx, Apr. 28, 1990. BA, Kent State U., 1969. Editor East Ohio Gas Co., Cleve., 1971-74, Personnel Administrator mag., Berea, Ohio, 1974-79, dir. communications, 1979-84; v.p. communications, pub. Am. Soc. Pers. Adminstrn. (name Soc. Human Resource Mgmt.), Alexandria, 1984-86, v.p. communications and pub. relations, 1986-91; sr. ptnr. Tecker Cons., Trenton, N.J., 1991-96, prin. ptnr., 1996—; pres. Cate Bower Communications, Alexandria and West River, Md., 1991—. Project dir. Work in the 21st Century, 1984. Editor: Work Life Visions, 1987. Pres. Oak Cluster Community Council, Alexandria, 1985-89. Recipient Monument award Great Washington Soc. Assn. Execs., 1996. Fellow Am. Soc. Assn. Execs. (cert.; vice chmn. comms. sect. coun. 1986-87, chmn. 1987-88, planning com. 1989-91, bd. dirs. Found. 1989-93, chair rsch. com. 1995-96, chmn. strategic leadership forum 2003, Best Pub. Rels. Program award 1984); mem. Greater Washington Soc. Assn. Execs. (chmn. visibility task force 1994-95, Monument award 1996), West River Sailing Club. Avocations: sailing, gardening. Office: Cate Bower Comms 5109 Holly Dr West River MD 20778-9744 E-mail: cbower@tecker.com

BOWER, FAY LOUISE, academic administrator, nursing educator; b. San Francisco, Sept. 10, 1929; d. James Joseph and Emily Clare (Andrews) Saitta; children: R. David, Carol Bower Tomei, Dennis James, Thomas John. BS with honors, San Jose State Coll., 1965; MSN, U. Calif., 1966, DNSc, 1978. Cert. pub. health nurse, sch. nurse, Calif. Office nurse Dr. William Grannis, Palo Alto, Calif., 1950-53; staff nurse Stanford Hosp., 1964-72; asst. prof. San Jose (Calif.) State U., 1966-70, assoc. prof., 1970-74, prof., 1974-82, coord. grad. program in nursing, 1977-78, chairperson dept. nursing, 1978-82; dean U. San Francisco, 1982-89, v.p. acad. affairs, 1988-89, dir. univ. planning and instl. rsch., 1989-91; pres. Clarkson Coll., 1991-97; cons. in field, 1997—; chair dept. nursing Holy Names Coll., 2000—. Vis. prof. Harding Coll., 1977, U. Miss., 1976; lectr. U. Calif., San Francisco, 1975; nat. exec. adv. bd. Nurse Week, 1999—; spkr., cons. in field. Author: Approaches to Teaching Primary Care, 1981, The Newman Systems Model: Application to Nursing Education and Practice, 1982, Managing a Nursing Shortage: A Guide to Recruitment and Retention, 1989, Cracking the Wall: Women in Higher Education Administration, 1993, Nurses Taking the Lead..., 1999, Care and Management of Alzheimers, vols. 1-5, 2002, Developing and Managing a Career in Nursing, 2003; (with Em O. Bevis) Fundamentals of Nursing Practice: Concepts, Roles and Functions, 1978, (with Margaret Jacobson) Community Health Nursing, 1978, The Process of Planning Nursing Care, 3d edit., 1982, (with Mae Timmons) Medical Surgical Nursing, 1995, (with others) Concepts & Issues in Nursing, 3d edit., 1996, Creating Nursings' Futures: Issues, Opportunities & Challenges, 1999; contbr. articles to profl. jours. Fellow Am. Acad. Nursing; mem.APHA (Calif. chpt.), Nurses Assn., Western Gerontol. Assn., Jesuit Deans in Nursing (chair 1982-85), Rotary (Omaha), Sigma Theta Tau (internat.pres., 1993-95. Democrat. Roman Catholic. Home: 1457 Indianhead Cir Clayton CA 94517-1239 Office Phone: 510-436-1024. E-mail: fbower1@sbcglobal.net.

BOWER, JEAN RAMSAY, lawyer, writer; b. N.Y.C., Nov. 25, 1935; d. Claude Barnett and Myrtle Marie (Scott) Ramsay; m. Ward Swift Just, Jan. 31, 1957 (div. 1966); children: Jennifer Ramsay, Julia Barnett; m. Robert Turnbull Bower, June 12, 1971 (dec. June 1990). AB, Vassar Coll., 1957; JD, Georgetown U., 1970. Bar: D.C. 1970. Exec. dir. D.C. Dem. Ctrl. Com., Washington, 1969-71; pvt. practice Washington, 1971-78, 94—; dir. Counsel of Child Abuse and Neglect Office D.C. Superior Ct., 1978-94. Mem. Mayor's Com. on Child Abuse and Neglect, 1973-94, vice chmn., 1975-79; mem. Family Div. Rules Adv. Com., 1977-94; pres., bd. dirs. C.B. Ramsay Found., 1984—; cons. child welfare issues, writer. Contbr. poetry to In a Certain Place. Active D.C. Child Fatality Rev. Com., 1992-; bd. dirs. Friends D.C. Superior Ct., 1994—, pres. bd. dirs., 2002-, Family & Child Svcs., D.C., 1995-2003, bd. dirs., 2004-; Folger poetry bd. (chair 2002-), Folger Shakespeare Libr., 1998-. Named Washingtonian of the Yr. Washington Mag., 1978. Mem. Women's Bar Assn. (bd. dirs. 1993-96, found. 1986-91, Woman Lawyer of Yr. 1986), D.C. Bar Assn. (election bd. 1994-96, Beatrice Rosenberg award sect. com. 1994—), Women's Bar Assn. Found. (bd. dirs. 1986-91).

BOWERMAN, ANN LOUISE, writer, genealogist, educator; b. Branch County, Mich., June 4, 1933; d. George Allen and Mary (Thomas) Hubbard; m. Virgil Lee Bowerman, June 4, 1954 (div. 1977); children: William Lee, Sally Ann; m. Virgil Wayne Dunkel, Jr., May 23, 1987 (div. Dec. 1996). BA, Western Mich. U., 1966, MSLS, 1971, MA, 1976. Cert. tchr. K-8, Mich., libr. sci. Tchr. Bethel #6 Sch. Dist., Coldwater, Mich., 1953—55; tchr. kindergarten Union City (Mich.) Schs., 1963-64; children's libr. Sturgis (Mich.) Pub. Libr., 1971-72; libr./media specialist Coldwater H.S., 1972-91; field rep. U.S. Census Bur., 2000—02, 2003—; media specialist libr. Union City (Mich.) Schs., 2002—03; retired, 1991. Mem. programming com., mem. ann. scholarships telethon com., camera staff, video editor Cable TV Channel 31, Coldwater, 1983-90. Author: The Bater Book, 1987, A Bowerman Family History, 1998, Historic Howe, Indiana Walking Tour, 1998, The William (6) Bowerman Family of Conneaut Township, 1998; co-author: Recommendations for High School Media Centers in Michigan, 1980 (booklet); contbr. articles to profl. jours. Mem., chair governing bd. Woodlands Libr. Coop., Albion, Mich., 1973-74, 83-86; adv. coun. Calhoun and Branch Counties Regional Ednl. Media Ctr., Marshall, Mich., 1972-91; com. mem. So. Mich. Region of Coop., Albion, 1989-91; leader All Around 4-H Club, Union City, 1954-74; mem. Sullivan Lady's Aid Soc., Union City, 1955-74, Twin Lakes Cmty. Assn., 1997—; chair winter program com. Tibbits Arts Found., Coldwater, 1980-90; mem. Coldwater Hist. Preservation Assn., 1978-86; del. Mich. Rep. State Conv., Detroit, 1986; candidate for Branch County Commr., Coldwater, 1988; mem. Mich. Assn. for Computer Users in Learning, 1975-91; mem. cultural arts com., mem. walking tour com. Howe (Ind.) Cmty. Assn., 1996—, pres., 2003-2004. Recipient Cert. of Appreciation, Mich. Assn. for Media in Edn., 1980, 91, Golden Apple Retirement award Coldwater H.S., 1991. Mem. Soc. of Genealogists (London), New England Hist. Geneal. Soc., Descendants of Founders of Ancient Windsor, Ctrl. N.Y. Geneal. Soc., DAR (good citizen selection com., treas. Coldwater br. 1997-2002, registrar 2003-04), Mich. Assn. Ret. Sch. Pers., Schenectady County Hist. Soc., Old Brutus Hist. Soc., Union City Geneal. Soc., St. Joseph County Hist. Soc. (advisor to Land Office Mus. com. 1997—), Crawford County Geneal. Soc., Coldwater Edn. Assn. (sec. 1980-90), Howe Philomath Soc., Beta Phi Mu. Avocations: travel, coin collecting, tennis. Home: 1820 W 600 N Howe IN 46746-9406 E-mail: abowerma@ligtel.com.

BOWERS, BEGE K. English educator, academic administrator; b. Nashville, Tenn., Aug. 19, 1949; d. John and Yvonne Bowers. BA in English cum laude, Vanderbilt U., 1971; student, U. Mich., 1985; MACT, U. Tenn., 1973, PhD, 1984. Asst. loan officer Ctr. for Fin. Aid and Placement, Baylor U., Waco, Tex., 1975-76; editorial asst. Wassily Leontief, NYU, N.Y.C., 1976-78; instr. bus. English Florence-Darlington Tech. Coll., Florence, S.C., 1979-80; tchr. English and French St. John's High Sch., Darlington, S.C., 1980-82; teaching asst. dept English U. Tenn., Knoxville, 1982-84; asst. prof. English Youngstown (Ohio) State U., 1984-88, assoc. prof., 1988-92, prof., 1992—, composition coord. dept. English, 1985-94, acting chmn. dept., 1989, asst. to dean Coll. Arts and Scis., 1992-93, dir. profl. writing and editing, 1996-2000, assoc. to the dean Coll. Arts and Scis., 2001—02, asst. provost acad. programs and planning, 2002—. Part-time freelance editor MLA, N.Y.C., 1978-80; cons. Project Arete, Youngstown and Mahoning County Pub. Schs., 1984-87, Youngstown Pub. Schs., 1986, 87-88, 90-91, Macmillan Pub. Co., 1986, Trumbull (Ohio) County Schs., 1988, Akron Beacon Jour., 1994-95, Ohio Dept. Edn., 1998-2001, Ohio Bd. Regents, 2002—. Co-editor: CEA Critic, 1998-2002, CEA Forum 1988—, (with Barbara Brothers) Reading and Writing Women's Lives: A Study of the Novel of Manners, 1991, (with Chuck Nelson) Internships in Technical Communication, 1991, (with Mark Allen) Annotated Chaucer Bibliography 1986-1996, 2002; mem. editl. bd. South Atlantic Review, 1987-89; editor: of more than 40 pamphlets, 7 children's books, and 1 videoscript. Alumni Found. Rsch. fellow U. Tenn., 1978, dissertation fellow U. Tenn., 1983, Davis editl. fellow U. Tenn., 1984; Grad. Rsch. Coun. grantee Youngstown State U. Mem.: MLA, Gould Soc. (pres. faculty com. 1991—93), No. Ohio Soc. for Tech. Comm., Soc. for Tech. Comm. (Jay R. Gould award for excellence in tchg. tech. comm. 1999, Disting. Chpt. Svc. award 2001, Assoc. fellow award 2002), Assn. Tchrs. Tech. Writing, New Chaucer Soc. (asst. bibliographer 1986—), Coll. English Assn. Ohio, Coun. Editors of Learned Jours., Coll. English Assn. (exec. bd., Disting. Svc. award 1996), Phi Beta Kappa, Phi Kappa Phi (pres. 1991—92, sec. 1994—98, exec. bd. 1998—). Office: Youngstown State U Office of the Provost Youngstown OH 44555-0001 Office Phone: 330-941-1560. E-mail: bkbowers@ysu.edu.

BOWERS, GLORIA MILLS, secondary education art educator; b. Brookville, Pa., May 9, 1951; d. James Arthur and Geraldine Evelyn (Huffman) Mills; m. Ralph Gordon Bowers, July 2, 1977; 1 child, Amy Lynn. BS in Art Edn. with distinction, Pa. State U., 1973. Elem. art tchr. Jersey Shore (Pa.) Elem. Sch., 1973-76, secondary art tchr. Lock Haven (Pa.) H.S., 1982-95; secondary and elem. art tchr. Sugar Valley Elem. and H.S., Loganton, Pa., 1995-96; elem. art tchr. Woolrich (Pa.) Elem. Sch., 1995-96, Lamar Twp. Elem. Sch., Salona, Pa., 1995-96; secondary art tchr. Bald Eagle-Nittany H.S., Mill Hall, Pa., 1996—. Mem. AAUW, Pa. State U. Alumni Assn., Assn. Clinton County Educators, Pi Lambda Theta, Beta Sigma Phi (v.p. Jersey Shore chpt. 1982, pres. 1983, Woman of Yr. 1984, 85). Democrat. Avocations: antiques, drawing, reading, swimming, Pa. State U. football. Home: 402 W Water St Lock Haven PA 17745-1112

BOWERS, JANE MEREDITH, music educator; b. Mpls., Sept. 17, 1936; B in Music, Wellesley Coll., 1958; MA in Music History, U. Calif., Berkeley, 1962, PhD in Music History, 1971. Instr. U. N.C., Chapel Hill, 1968-72; asst. prof. dept. music history and musicology Eastman Sch. Music, Rochester, N.Y., 1972-73, 74-75; lectr., instr. women's studies, music and continuing edn. Portland (Oreg.) State U., 1976-80; instr. flute Reed Coll., Portland, 1979-81; from asst. prof. dept. music to prof. U. Wis., Milw., 1981—93, prof., 1993—2001, chmn. music history and lit. area, 1997—2001, mem. faculty senate, 1997—2000. Lectr. women's studies program Cornell U., Ithaca, N.Y., spring 1979; vis. asst. prof. dept. music Oreg. State U., 1980-81; lectr. in field, 1969—; flutist Am. Wind Symphony, summer 1958, Cabrillo Music Festival, 1963-64; asst. prin. flutist Oakland Symphony Orch., 1962-65; free-lance Baroque flutist, N.Y.C., 1975-77; numerous recitals and chamber music concerts on modern and Baroque flute, 1964-85. Editor: Michel de La Barre: Pieces pour la Flute Traversiere, 1978, Joseph Boden de Boismortier: Petites Sonates pour 2 Flutes Traversieres, 1993, (with Judith Tick) Women Making Music: The Western Art Tradition, 1150-1950, 1986, paperback edit., 1987 (Deems Taylor award ASCAP 1987, Pauline Alderman prize 1987), François Derenne's Nouvelle Méthode Théorique et Pratique pour la Flute, 1999; contbr. articles and revs. to profl. jours. and anthologies. Bd. dirs. Early Music Guild Oreg., 1981, Early Music Now, Milw., 1989-92. Alfred Hertz meml. travel scholar, 1965-66; postdoctoral fellow AAUW, 1973-74, 78-79, fellow Ctr. for 20th Century Studies, U. Wis.- Milw., 1982-83, Humanities Inst., 1988-89; grantee NEH, summers 1980, 84. Mem. Am. Mus. Instrument Soc. (rev. editor Jour. 1976-81, bd. govs. 1988-91), Am. Musicological Soc. (coun. 1982-84, chmn. performance com., 1998-2000, mem., chmn. Noah Greenberg award com. 1987-89), Coll. Music Soc. (sec. com. on status of women 1972-74, mem. com. 1992-96, tchr. Summer Inst. 1993), Soc. for Ethnomusicology (coun. 1995-98, chmn. constn. revision com. 1996-2000), Am. Women Composers (editl. bd. 1992-94), Internat. Assn. Women in Music (editl. bd. 1995-2002), Assn. Women in Edn. (vice chmn., chmn. U. Wis.-Milw. 1985-87). Home: 2516 E Stratford Ct Shorewood WI 53211-2634

BOWERS, LINDA, educational administrator; b. Lancaster, S.C., Aug. 11, 1950; d. Vernon Ray and Betty Elliott Bowers. BA in Elem. Edn., U. S.C., 1972, MA in Instnl. Design/Media, 1987. Cert. elem. tchr., S.C. Tchr. Orangeburg Sch. Dist., Springfield, S.C., 1972-73, Richland Sch. Dist., Columbia, S.C., 1973-86, elem. curriculum cons., 1986-97, dir. Richland Clicks!, 1998—. Adj. prof. U. Charleson, 1993, 94; cert. trainer Covey/Franklin; accelerated schs. project coach Stanford (Calif.) U., 1994; presenter in field. Author video script: Effective Teacher/Effective Teaching, 1996. Mem. Forest Hills Assn., 1987—; mem. testbook selection com. S.C. State Dept. Edn., Columbia, 1991; mem. violence prevention com. Columbia C. of C., 1989; mem. sch. improvement coun. A.C. Flora H.S., Columbia, 1994-96. Mem. S.C. ASCD, S.C. Coun. Tchrs. Math., S.C. Suprs. Math. (bd. dirs. 1994), Columbia Area Reading Coun. (bd. dirs. 1995-97), Delta Kappa Gamma, Phi Delta Kappa. Avocations: boating, photography, cooking, reading. Home: 225 Lake Vista Dr Chapin SC 29036-8471

BOWERS, MARTHA VASSAR, religious studies educator; b. Bowersville, Ga., June 27, 1930; d. John Richard and Clara Shiflet Vassar; m. Connie Mack Bowers, June 28, 1952; children: Richard, Holly B. Welborn, Julie B. Lassiter, Mack. AB, Ga. State Coll. for Women, 1951. Tchr. math. h.s., Elberton, Ga., 1951—52, Summerville, Ga., 1952—53; tchr. math. jr. h.s. Louisville, 1953—54; pianist Bardstown Bapt. Ch., Ky., 1954—56; min. music Mine City Bapt. Ch., Tenn., 1956—63; children's dir. Second Bapt. Ch., Chattanooga, 1963—67; missionary to Nigeria Bapt. Fgn. Mission Bd., 1966—87; ret. Min. of music, organist, pianist, tchr., writer, 1967—85; dir. TV and radio programs, Nigeria. Mem. Habitat for Humanity, 1995—; mem., dir. Hebron Baptist associational divsn. Ga. Bapt. Woman's Missionary Union, 1986—92, v.p., 1994—98; bd. dirs. Hebron Group Home for Children. Recipient Ethel Rae Mozo Stewart Comty. Svc. award, Ga. Coll. and State U., 2002, Inaugural Pres. award for svc. to Ga. Missionary Parents Fellowship, Bapt. Women's Missionary Union, 2003. Avocations: reading, gardening, time with grandchildren, writing family history. Home: 470 Air Line School Rd Bowersville GA 30516

BOWERS, PATRICIA ELEANOR FRITZ, economist; b. N.Y.C., Mar. 21, 1928; d. Eduard and Eleanor (Ring) Fritz. Student scholar, Goucher Coll., 1946-48; BA, Cornell U., 1950; MA, NYU, 1953, PhD, 1965. Statis. asst. Fed. Res. Bank N.Y., N.Y.C., 1950-53; lectr. Upsala Coll., East Orange, N.J., 1953-59; researcher Fortune mag., N.Y.C., 1959-60; teaching fellow NYU, N.Y.C., 1960-62, instr., 1962-64; mem. faculty Bklyn. Coll., CUNY, 1964-00, prof. econs., 1974-2000, chair dept. econs., 1996-99, prof. emerita, 2000—. Author: Private Choice and Public Welfare, 1974. Sec. Friends of the Johnson Mus., Cornell U., 1989-91. Mem. Am. Econ. Assn., Econometric Soc., Met. Econ. Assn. (sec. 1963-68, pres. 1974-75), Am. Statis. Assn. (univs. chmn. ann. forecasting confs. 1970-71, 71-72), Cornell Club N.Y., Kappa Alpha Theta. Home: 145 E 16th St Apt 11-L New York NY 10003-3405

BOWERS, PATRICIA NEWSOME, communications executive; b. Baton Rouge, June 21, 1944; d. Carl Allen and Sue Mayre (Powell) Newsome; m. Robert Lloyd Bowers Jr., Aug. 19, 1967 (div. Nov. 1979); children: Paige Ivy, Katherine Elizabeth. BJ, La. State U., 1967. Sr. writer, editor Litton Industries, Pascagoula, Miss., 1978-80; sr. presentations supr. Martin Marietta Aerospace, Orlando, Fla., 1980-81, mgr. presentations Balt., 1981-85, mgr. pub. rels., 1985-90; dir. pub. rels. and corp. comm. Contraves USA, Pitts., 1990-92; sr. mgr. sector comms. Harris Electronic sys. sector Harris Corp., Melbourne, Fla., 1992-95; dir. mktg. and pub. rels. Intracoastal Health Systems, Inc., West Palm Beach, Fla., 1995-99; dir. mktg. and comms. Northside Hosp., Atlanta, 1999-2000, The Bowers Group, Inc., 2000—01; chief comms. officer Atlanta Pub. Schs., 2001—. Coach Parkville Recreation Council, Balt., 1985-87; bd. dirs. Salvation Army, Human Resources Devel. Agy. Balt. County, Brevard Symphony Youth Orch.; adv. bd. Nat. Aquarium in Balt.; active Brevard Leadership; mem. corp. bd. Boys and Girls Club of Palm Beach County; mem. Osteoporosis Leadership Coun. Atlanta. Mem. Pub. Rels. Soc. Am. (bd. dirs. Chesapeake conf. 1987, Silver Anvil Judge, 1991, 92), Healthcare Forum for Strategic Planning and Mktg. Execs., Nat. Press Club, Navy League (bd. dirs. Balt. council 1986-87), Balt. County C. of C. (leadership program 1986-87), Pitts. Press Club, Forum Club of Palm Beach. Republican. Episcopalian. Avocations: golf, reading, photography.

BOWERS, ZELLA ZANE, real estate broker; b. May 24, 1929; Real estate broker Haley Realty Inc, Colorado Springs. Home: 128 W Rockrimmon Blvd Apt 104 Colorado Springs CO 80919-1876 Office: Haley Realty Inc 109 E Fontanero St Colorado Springs CO 80907-7494 E-mail: zane@zeebo.net.

BOWICK, SUSAN D. computer company executive; Bus. analyst Hewlett-Packard Co., Loveland, Colo., 1972-85, pers. mgr. Lake Stevens instrument divsn. Everett, Wash., 1985-89, group pers. mgr. computer sys. orgn., 1989-93, pers. mgr., 1993-95, pers. mgr. computer orgn., 1995-98, v.p. human resources. Office: Hewlett-Packard Co 3000 Hanover St Palo Alto CA 94304-1181 also: PO Box 10301 Palo Alto CA 94303-0890 Fax: 650-813-3003.

BOWIE, ANGIE, accounting company official; d. Anderson and Mary Alyce Baughman; m. David Bowie; children: Brooks, Courtney. BA in English lit., Talladega Coll., 1976; M Librarianship, Emory U., 1983; MBA, Case Western Res. U., 1993. On-line mtkg. specialist, N.Y.C.; rsch. asst. Fed. Res. Bank Atlanta; libr. asst.; tchr. jr. high Sch., dir. Cleve Rsch. Ctr., Cleve. Pub. Libr., 8 yrs.; established bus. and strategic analysis group Ernst & Young, Cleve., 1995, dir. Bus. and Strategic Analysis Ctr. for Bus. Knowledge, N.Y.C., 1995—. Mem. adv. bd. new publs. devel. Gale Rsch. Inc.; mem. networking forum steering com. Black Enterprise mag., Cleve.; mem. com. for recruitmand and retentionn of diverse workforce Ohio Librs. Coun.; mem. diversity initiative task force Greater Clevel. Roundtable. Trustee, elder Heights Presbyn. Ch.. Recipient Rosemarie Meschi award. Mem. Nat. Black MBA Assn. (adv. bd. Cleve. chpt.). Office: Ernst & Young LLP Bus-Strategic Analysis Ctr 787 7th Ave Fl 14 New York NY 10019-6085

BOWIE, JOANNE WALKER (JONI BOWIE), state legislator; b. Terre Haute, Ind., June 18, 1937; d. Philip and Iona Brown Walker; children: Michelle Elizabeth Bowie Gray, Amy Jo. BS, W.Va. U., 1960, MS, 1962. Former comm. specialist USDA; mem. N.C. Ho. of Reps., 1988—, vice-chmn pub. transp. and human resources coms., mem. various coms. Mem. Rail Passenger Svc. Task Force Com., 1991. Past mem. adminstrv. com. Nat. League Municipalities; city councilwoman Greens City Coun., 1977-88; pres. Guilford County Med. Aux., 1982; mem. State Bd. C.C., 1985; past mem. Guilford County Conv. and Visitors Bd.; active Mar. of Dimes, Symphony Guild, Greensboro Preservation Soc. Mem. Greensboro C. of C., Guilford County Rep. Womens Club, Rep. Women's Club. Roman Catholic. Home: 106 Nut Bush Rd E Greensboro NC 27410-5518 Office: NC State Senate 1206 Legislative Bldg 16 W Jones St Raleigh NC 27601-1096

BOWIE, PHYLLIS, secondary school educator; Tchr. secondary geography S.A.V.E. High Sch., Anchorage. Recipient Disting. Tchr. K-12 award Nat. Coun. for Geog. Edn., 1992. Office: SAVE HS 410 E 56th Ave Anchorage AK 99518-1244

BOWKER, LINDA BARBARA, lobbyist; b. Woodbury, N.J., July 31, 1948; d. Robert Keeley and Elizabeth Henrietta (Weatherby) B. BA in Polit. Sci., Drew U., 1971. Mgr. Nook of Knowledge Bookstore, Woodbury Heights, N.J., 1971-72; svc. rep. N.J. Bell Telephone, Woodbury, N.J., 1972-85; pres. NOW, Trenton, N.J., 1985-90; exec. dir. Shared Housing Resource Ctr., Phila., 1991; spl. projects organizer Feminist Majority, Haddonfield, N.J., 1992-93; campaign dir. Elect Women for a Change, Trenton, N.J., 1993; exec. dir. N.J. Divsn. on Women, Trenton, 1994. Vice-chmn. Camden County Commn. on Women, 1983-86. Candidate for Congress, N.J., 1990. Recipient award for Making a Difference for Women in Politics, Camden County Commn. Women, 1986, Woman of Achievement award Douglass Coll. of N.J. State Fed. Wo men's Clubs, 1995. Republican. Mem. Soc. Friends. Avocations: politics, computers, animals. Office: NJ Divsn on Women Box 801 101 S Broad St Trenton NJ 08608-2401

BOWKER, MARGARET SHEARD, artist; b. Dordrecht, South Africa, Oct. 31, 1938; BA, Tchr.'s U., Grahamstown, S. Africa, 1960. Tchr. Cape Edn. Dept., E. London, 1961—64, Natal Edn. Dept., Durban, 1965—97. Office: Margie Bowker Art 429 Monterey Rd Santa Maria CA 93055

BOWLER, MARIANNE BIANCA, federal judge; b. Boston, Feb. 15, 1947; d. Richard A. and Ann C. (Daly) B. BA, Regis Coll., 1967; JD cum laude, Suffolk U., 1976, LLD (hon.), 1994; LD (hon.), Regis Coll., 2003. Bar: Mass. 1978. Rsch. asst. Harvard Med. Sch., Boston, 1967-69; med. editor Mass. Dept. of Pub. Health, Boston, 1969-76; law clk. Mass. Superior Ct., Boston, 1976-77, dep. chief law clk., 1977-78; asst. dist. atty. Middlesex Dist. Atty.'s Office, Cambridge, Mass., 1978; asst. U.S. atty. U.S. Dept. of Justice, Boston, 1978-90, exec. asst. U.S. atty., 1988-89, sr. litigation counsel, 1989-90; magistrate judge U.S. Dist. Ct. Mass., Boston, 1990—2002, chief U.S. magistrate judge, 2002—. Chmn. bd. trustees New England Bapt. Hosp., Boston, 1990-95. Trustee Suffolk U., Boston, 1994—, Discovering Justice, 2003—; bd. dirs. The Boston Found., 1995—; dir. South Cove Nursing Facilities Found., Inc., 1995—; co-pres. Boston Coll. Inn of Ct., 1998—; bd. dirs. Discovering Justice, 2003-. Mem. Jr. League Boston, Suffolk Law Sch. Alumni Assn. (pres. 1979-80), Vincent Club, Isabel O'Neil Found., Save Venice. Democrat. Roman Catholic. Avocations: faux finishing, trompe l'oeil painting. Office: 1 Courthouse Way Ste 8420 Boston MA 02210-3010

BOWLER, SHIRLEY, state legislator; b. New Orleans, Oct. 2, 1949; d. Louis L. and Rose Clare (Mandina) Duvigneaud; m. Michael Joseph Bowler, June 11, 1971; children: Kathleen, Michael, Mary. BA, U. New Orleans, 1971. English tchr. Jefferson Parish Schs., Gretna, La., 1971-77; video producer D.H. Holmes Co., Ltd., New Orleans, 1980-87; alumnae coord. St. Mary's Dominican High, New Orleans, 1989-92; state legislator La. Dist. 78, Harahan, La., 1992—. Mem. textbook adoption and curriculum devel. coms. Jefferson Parish Schs. Dir. awards for (indsl. video) The

Sensormatic System, 1985; dir./writer (indsl. video) Benefits News, 1986; dir./writer-editor (indsl. video) Fashion Trends, 1986. Mem. Rep. Women's Club of Jefferson, 1991. Mem. Dominican High Alumnae Assn., Nat. Assn. Desktop Pubs., Harahan Rotary Club (bd. mem 1993). Republican. Roman Catholic. Avocations: tennis, reading. Office: Speakers' Office 1939 Hickory Ave Ste 203 Harahan LA 70123-2108 Address: 502 [illegible] River Ridge LA 70123-1401

BOWLES, BARBARA LANDERS, investment company executive; b. Nashville, Sept. 17, 1947; d. Corris Raemone Landers and Rebecca (Bonham) Jennings; m. Earl Stanley Bowles, Nov. 27, 1971; 1 son, Terrence Earl. BA, Fisk U., 1968; MBA, U. Chgo., 1971. Chartered fin. analyst. From bank official to v.p. First Nat. Bank of Chgo., 1968-81; asst. v.p. Beatrice Cos., Chgo., 1981-84; v.p. investor rels. Kraft Inc., Chgo., 1984—89; pres., founder The Kenwood Group Inc., Chgo., 1989—. Bd. dirs. Black & Decker Corp., Hyde Pk. Bank. Bd. dirs. Children's Meml. Hosp., Ga. Pacific Corp, Wis. Energy, and Dollar Gen. Corp. The Chgo. Urban League; mem. Grad. Sch. Bus. U. Chgo. Scholar United Negro College Fund, 1989. Mem. NAACP (life), Assn. Investment Mgmt. and Rsch., Chgo. Fisk trustee (1998-). Mem. United Ch. of Christ. Avocations: tennis, bridge. E-mail: kenwoodg@aol.com.

BOWLES, CRANDALL CLOSE, textiles executive; m. Erskine Bowles. B in Econ., Wellesley Coll.; MBA, Columbia U. Fin. analyst Springs Industries, Inc., 1973—78, exec. v.p. growth and devel., 1992, exec. v.p. textile prodn., 1993, pres. bath fashions group, 1995, pres., COO, 1997—98, CEO, chmn., 1998—; exec. v.p. Springs Co., 1978—82, pres., 1982; also bd. dirs. Bd. dirs. Deere & Co. Bd. trustees African Wildlife Found.; bd. dirs. Juvenile Diabetes Rsch. Found., Charlotte Inst. for Tech. Innovation. Mem.: Palmetto Bus. Forum, Bus. Roundtable, Bus. Coun., Am. Textile Mfrs. Inst., Excellence in Edn. Coun. Office: 205 N White St Fort Mill SC 29715-1654

BOWLES, EVELYN MARGARET, state legislator; b. Worden, Ill., Apr. 22, 1921; d. Ira Milton and Anna (Augustine) B. AA, Ill. State U., 1941; student, Greenville Coll., 1947, Southwest Photo Arts Inst., Dallas, 1945—46, Lewis & Clark C.C., 1984. Tchr. Livingston Elem. Sch., Edwardsville Elem. Sch., 1941—43, 1946—50; chief dep. County Clks. Office, Edwardsville, Ill., 1951-74; county clk. Madison County, Edwardsville, 1974—94; state senator Ill. Senate, Springfield, 1974—. Mem. Madison County Welfare Com., 1980—; meml. chmn. Cancer Soc., Edwardsville, Ill., 1980—; bd. dirs. Madison County Hospice, Granite City, sec., 1983-84; pres. adv. bd. Rape and Sexual Abuse Care Ctr., 1984-86; mem. voting systems som. Ill. Bd. Elections; pres. parish council St. Mary's Ch., mem. lector soc. Served with USMC, 1943-45, USCG. Recipient Alice Paul award Metro-East NOW, 1979. Mem. Ill. Assn. Clks., Recorders, Election Officials and Treas., Ill. Assn. County Officials, Ill. Fedn. Bus. and Profl. Women (Outstanding Working Women of Ill. 1986), Collinsville Bus. and Profl. Women (Boss of Yr. 1976), Edwardsville Bus. Profl. Women (pres. 1957-58, Woman of Achievement award 1978), Metro-East Women's Assn., Am. Legion. Avocations: reading, yard work, fishing. Address: M-103F Capitol Bldg Springfield IL 62706-0001 Also: 4 Club Centre Ct Edwardsville IL 62025-3518

BOWLES, LIZA K. construction executive; BA polit. sci., Mary Washington Coll.; M in urban affairs, Va. Tech. Pres. NAHB Rsch. Ctr., Upper Marlboro, Md., 1991—2002; gen. mgr. Newport Ptnrs., Davidsonville, Md., 2002—. Office: Newport Ptnrs LLC 3760 Tanglewood Lane Davidsonville MD 21035 E-mail: lbowles@nahbrc.org.

BOWMAN, BARBARA TAYLOR, early childhood educator; b. Chgo., Oct. 30, 1928; d. Robert Rochon and Dorothy Vaugn (Jennings) Taylor; m. James E. Bowman, June 17, 1950, 1 child, Valerie Bowman Jarrett. BA, Sarah Lawrence Coll., 1950; MA, U. Chgo., 1952; DHL (hon.), Bankstreet Coll., 1988, Roosevelt U., 1998, Dominican U., 2002, Gov.'s State U., 2002. Tchr. U. Chgo. Nursery Sch., 1950-52, Colo. Women's Coll. Nursery Sch., Denver, 1953-55; mem. sci. faculty Shiraz (Iran) U. Nemazee Sch. Nursing, 1955-61; spl. edn. tchr. Chgo. Child Care Soc., 1965—67; mem. faculty Erikson Inst., Chgo., 1967—, dir. grad. studies, 1978—94, pres., 1994—2002, prof. early edn., 2002. Mem. early childhood com. Nat. Bd. Profl. Tchg. Stds., 1992-2002; cons. early childhood edn., parent edn.; chair com. on early childhood pedagogy NRC, 1998-99. Contbr. articles to profl. jours. Bd. dirs. Ill. Health Edn. Com., 1969—71, Inst. Psychoanalysis, 1970—73, Ill. Adv. Coun. Dept. Children and Family Svcs., 1974—79, Child Devel. Assoc. Consortium, 1979—81, Chgo. Bd. Edn. Desegregation Commn., 1981—84, Bus. People in Pub. Inst., 1980—, High Scope Ednl. Rsch. Found., 1986—93, Gt. Books Found., 1988—, Cmty.-Corp. Sch., 1988—90; mem. Family Resource Coalition, 1992—96, mem. nat. bd. profl. tchr. stds., 1996—2002. Mem. Ill. Assn. Edn. Young Children, Nat. Assn. Edn. Young Children (pres. 1980-82), Chgo. Assns. Edn. Young Children (pres. 1973-77), Black Child Devel. Assn., Am. Ednl. Rsch. Assn. Achievements include research in early education teaching and school improvement. Office: Erikson Inst 420 N Wabash Ave Chicago IL 60611-3568

BOWMAN, DELORES, medical cost management administrator; b. Irmo, S.C., Aug. 7, 1948; d. Willie Bowman and Geneva Bowman-Nelson. AS, Allegheny C.C., 1970; BSN, NYU, 1975. RN; cert. risk mgr. Dir. HRA Medicaid/EPSDT Program/Medicaid HMO, 1978-80; project mgr., dir. Bradford Nat. Corp. McAuto Sys. Group, 1980-83; v.p. med. svcs. and programs NYLCARE Health Plan, 1983-98; cons. pres. Bowman Mgmt., 1998-99; v.p. PSI Medica, Elm Wood Park, N.J., 1999—. Home: 21-07 Greenwood Dr Fair Lawn NJ 07410-4537

BOWMAN, DOROTHY LOUISE, artist; b. Hollywood, Calif., Jan. 20, 1927; d. Bruce L. and Dorothy L. (Kalkman) B; m. Howard Hugh Bradford, Dec. 30, 1949 (div. 1965); children: Brock, Cyndra, Tal Scott, Heather, Delia, Callia. Student, Chouinard Art Inst., Calif., 1945-48, Jepson Art Inst., L.A., 1948-49; BA, Webster U., 1979. One-woman show Ventana Gallery, Big Sur, 1998; serigrapher, printmaker, painter: represented in permanent collections: Immaculate Heart Coll., L.A. County Mus., Bklyn. Mus., Long Beach Mus., Crocker Art Gallery, Mus. Modern Art, Phila., Mus. Fine Arts, San Jose State Coll., De Cordova and Danna Mus., Boston Pub. Libr., Boston Mus. Fine Arts, N.Y. Pub. Libr., Rochester Meml. Gallery, U. Wis., U. Hawaii, U. Ill., U. Kans., Santa Barbara Mus., Achenbach Found. Legion of Honor, Mus. Modern Art, Monterey, Calif., Libr. Congress, Calif. State Libr. Archives, Arquivos Historicos De Arte Contemporanea Museu De Arte Moderna, San Paulo, Brazil, Ch. of Latter Day Saints History Mus., Salt Lake City, 1987, Nat. Mus. of Women in the Arts, Washington, 2000—; twice juried internat. show 27 countries, 1987; creator animation films The Mobius World, 2000, Really O'Reiley, 2002, Never Seen Fox, 2003; Traveling show Smithsonian Inst., Nat. Collection of Fine Arts, 1952; movie prodr. hist. film, Big Sur, 2002. Address: Nat Mus of Women in the Arts Archives 1250 New York Ave NW Washington DC 20005-3970 Office Phone: 831-375-5170.

BOWMAN, HAZEL LOIS, retired English language educator; b. Plant City, Fla., Feb. 18, 1917; d. Joseph Monroe and Annie (Thoman) B. AB, Fla. State Coll. for Women, 1937; MA, U. Fla., 1948; postgrad., U. Md., 1961-65. Tchr. Lakeview H.S., Winter Garden, Fla., 1939-40, Eagle Lake Sch., Fla., 1940-41; welfare visitor Fla. Welfare Bd., 1941-42; specialist U.S. Army Signal Corps, Arlington Hall, Va., 1942-43; recreation work, asst. procurement officer ARC, CBI Theater, 1943-46; lab. technician Am. Cyanamid Corp., Brewster, Fla., 1946-47; instr., asst. prof. gen. extension divsn. U. Fla., Fla. State U., 1948-51; freelance writer, editor, indexer N.Y., Fla., 1951-55; staff writer Tampa (Fla.) Morning Tribune, 1956; staff writer, telegraph editor Winter Haven (Fla.) News-Chief, 1956-57; registrar, admissions officer U. Tampa, 1957-59; coll. counselor Atlantic States, 1959-60; registrar, freshman advisor Towson State Tchrs. Coll., Balt., 1960-62; dir. student pers., guidance, admissions Harford Jr. Coll., Bel Air, Md., 1962-64; instr., asst. prof. English, journalism York Coll., Pa., 1965-69; tchr. S.W. Jr. H.S., Lakeland, Fla., 1969-70; [illegible] Vanguard Sch., Lake Wales, Fla., 1970-82; libr. asst. Polk County Hist. and Geneal. Libr., Bartow, Fla., 1986-91. Editor, Tampa Altrusan, 1958-60, Polk County Hist. Calendar, 1986-90. Mem. Polk County Hist. Commn., 1992-99. Recipient Mayhall Music medal, 1933, Excellence in Cmty. Svc. award Nat. Soc. DAR, 1994, Outstanding Achievement award Fla. State Geneal. Soc., 2002. Mem. AAUW (hon. 50 yr. life), NOW, Nat. Geneal. Soc., Mortar Board, Imperial Polk Genealogical Soc., Alpha Chi Alpha, Chi Delta Phi. Home: 511 NE 9th Ave Mulberry FL 33860-2620

BOWMAN, KATHLEEN GILL, academic administrator; BS English & Spanish, U. of Minn., 1964, MA English Edn., 1967, PhD English Edn., 1977. Rsch. assoc. Legis. Adv. Coun. on the Econ. Status of Women, St. Paul, 1976-77; asst. dir. of grad. studies, asst prof. of edn. Reed Coll., Portland, OR, 1977-79, exec. asst. to the pres., dir. of spl. programs, 1979-82; assoc. dir., program officer Fred Meyer Charitable Trust, Portland, OR, 1982-84; assoc. v.p. for rsch. U. of Oreg., Eugene, OR, 1985-89, vice-provost for internat. affairs, 1989-94; pres. Randolph-Macon Woman's Coll., Lynchburg, VA, 1994—. Fullbright Sr. Scholar award, Japan & Korea, 1993. Office: Randolph-Macon Womans Coll Office of the Pres 2500 Rivermont Ave Lynchburg VA 24503-1555

BOWMAN, LAURA, artist; b. Oklahoma City, Jan. 4, 1967; d. Alfred and Loy Bowman; m. Matt McNeil, Jan. 22, 1970. AA, St. Gregory's U., Shawnee, Okla., 1987; BA, Coll. of New Rochelle, N.Y., 1991. One-woman shows include Modern Primitive Gallery, Station 29 Gallery, CAVU, exhibited in group shows at Melanee Cooper Gallery, Jules Pl., Modern Primitive Gallery, M.A. Doran Gallery, Art Miami, Studio E Gallery, Bennett St. Gallery. Mem. Save our Planet, Ocean Soc. Avocations: travel, cultural activities, reading. Personal E-mail: www.laurabowman.com.

BOWMAN, LEAH, fashion designer, consultant, photographer, educator; b. Chgo., Apr. 21, 1935; d. John George and Alexandra (Colovos) Murges; m. Veron George Broe, Aug. 31, 1954; 1 child, Michelle; m. John Ronald Bowman, Feb. 28, 1959 Diploma, Sch. of Art Inst., Chgo., 1962. Designer Korach Bros. Inc., Chgo., 1962-65; costume designer Hull House South Theatre, Chgo., 1966-67, Wellington Theatre, Chgo., 1966-67; from instr. to prof. emeritus Sch. of Art Inst., Chgo., 1967—2001, prof. emeritus, 2001—. Prodr. fashion performances and style exhbns.; vis. prof., cons. SNDT Women's U., Bombay, 1980, 85, 92, Ctrl. Acad. Arts and Design, Beijing, People's Republic of China, 1987; faculty sabbatical exhbn. Sch. of Art Inst., 1986, 93. Recipient Fulbright award Council for Internat. Exchange for Scholars, India, 1980, Pres. award Art Inst. Chgo., 1991, Honoror's award Sch. of Art Inst. Chgo., 1998. Office: Sch of Art Inst Chgo 37 S Wabash Ave Chicago IL 60603-3002

BOWMAN, MARGARET COON, retired public official, environmental educator; b. Rhinebeck, N.Y., Mar. 13, 1914; d. Ethan Allen and Alice Amelia (Traver) Coon; widowed. BA, Elmira Coll., 1936; cert., Clarke Sch. for Deaf, 1940. Tchr. Iowa Sch. for the Deaf, Council Bluffs, 1940-42, Alexander Graham Bell, Cleve., 1942-44; jr. exec. B. Altman & Co., N.Y.C., 1948-52; mgr. E. A. Coon & Co., Rhinebeck, N.Y., 1952-65; county commr. Indian River County, Vero Beach, Fla., 1982-92. Mem. Hutchinson Island Study Com., 1984-85, Treasure Coast Regional Planning Coun., Stuart, Fla., 1988-92, Ind. R. County Transp. Com., Vero Beach, 1986-92. Author: Where to Find Birds in Florida, 1977; contbr. articles to profl. jours. Mem. Jackson House Preservation; bd. dirs., editor Marine Resources Coun., 1990-96, sec., 1996-03; bd. dirs. LWV of Ind. River County, chmn. natural resources, 1992-02. Staff sgt. WAC U.S. Army, 1944-46; ETO. Mem. Fla. Audubon Soc. (bd. dirs., spl. commendation 1980, chpt. pres. of yr. award 1990), Pelican Island Audubon Soc. (charter mem., pres. emeritus, bd. dirs., sec. 1964-03), Friends of St. Sebastian River (bd. dirs., sec. 1992-03). Avocations: hiking, birding, writing, reading. Office: Pelican Island Audubon Soc Inc PO Box 1833 Vero Beach FL 32961-1833

BOWMAN, MARJORIE ANN, family practice physician, educator; b. Grove City, Pa., Aug. 18, 1953; d. Ross David and Freda Louise (Smith) Williamson; m. Robert Choplin; children: Bridget Williamson Foley, Skyler Weston Williamson Choplin. BS, Pa. State U., 1974; MD, Jefferson Med. Coll., 1976; MPA, U. So. Calif., L.A., 1983. Intern, then resident in family practice Duke U., Durham, N.C., 1976-79; med. officer USPHS, Hyattsville, Md., 1979-82; clin. instr. uniformed svcs. U. Health Scis., Bethesda, Md., 1980-83; dir. family practice residency, prof. Georgetown U. Sch. Medicine, Washington, 1983-86; chmn. dept. family practice, prof. Wake Forest U., Winston-Salem, N.C., 1986-96; chmn. dept. family practice U. Pa., Phila, 1996—. Author: (Book) Stress and Women Physicians, 1985, 1990, Women in Medicine: Life and Career, 2002; editor: Archives Family Medicine, 1992—2000, Jour. Women's Health, 2001—, Jour. Am. Bd. Family Practice, 2003—; contbr. articles to profl. jours. Fellow Am. Acad. Family Physicians; mem. AMA, Soc. Tchrs. Family Medicine (bd. dirs. 1984-88, bd. dirs. Found. 1984-99, v.p. 1988-91, pres. 1991-92), Am. Pub. Health Assn. Republican. Unitarian Universalist. Office: Univ Pa 2 Gates 3400 Spruce St Philadelphia PA 19104-4283 Office Phone: 215-662-3346. E-mail: bowmanm@uphs.upenn.edu.

BOWMAN-DALTON, BURDENE KATHRYN, education testing coordinator, computer consultant; b. Magnolia, Ohio, July 13, 1937; d. Ernest Mowles and Mary Kathryn (Long) Bowman; m. Louis W. Dalton, Mar. 13, 1979. BME, Capital U., 1959; MA in Edn., Akron U., 1967, postgrad., 1976-87. Profl. vocalist, various clubs in the East, 1959-60; music tchr. East Liverpool (Ohio) City Shcs., 1959-62, Revere Local Schs., Akron, Ohio, 1962-75, elem. tchr., 1975-80, elem. team leader/computer cons., 1979-85, tchr. middle sch. math., gifted-talented, computer literacy, 1981-92, dist. computer specialist, 1987-93, dist. statis. for standardize local testing, 1987-91, dist. tech. coord., 1993-98, ret., 1998. Local and regional dir. Olympics of Mind, also World Problem Captain for computer problem, 1984-86; cons., workshop presenter State of Ohio, 1987-91, dist. test. coord., 1991-98; coord. for Revere Schs., Ednl. Mgmt. Info. Sys., 1992-98; mem. Citizen Com., Akron, 1975-76; profl. rep. Bath Assn. to Help, 1978-80; mem. Revere Levy Com. 1986, Revere Bond Issue Com., 1991; audit com. BATH, 1977-79; vol. chmn. Antique Car Show, Akron, 1972-81; dist. advisor MidWest Talent Search, 1987-93; dist. statistician of standardized rech. test results. Martha Holden Jennings Found. grantee, 1977-78; Title IV ESEA grantee, 1977-81. Mem. Assn. for Devel. Computer-Based Instrnl. Sys. (dir. 1992-94), Ednl. Mgmt. Info. Sys. and Proficiency Test (coord. for Revere Schs. 1992-2003), Phi Beta. Home: 3347 Buckhaven Akron OH 44333

BOWNE, MARTHA HOKE, publishing consultant; b. Greeley, Colo., June 9, 1931; d. George Edwin and Krin (English) Hoke; children: Gretchen, William, Kay, Judith. BA, U. Mich., 1952; postgrad., Syracuse U., 1965. Tchr. Wayne (Mich.) Pub. Schs., 1953-54, East Syracuse and Minoa Cen. Schs., Minoa, N.Y., 1965-68; store mgr. Fabric Barn, Fayetteville, N.Y., 1969-77; store owner Fabric Fair, Oneida, N.Y., 1978-80; prodr., owner Quilting by the Sound, Port Townsend, Wash., 1987—2000, Quilting by the Lake, Cazenovia, NY, 1981—. Organizer symposium Am. Quilters Soc.; founder, pres. Quilter's Quest confs., 1994. Mem., pres. Minoa Library, 1960-75; mem. Onondaga County Library, Syracuse, 1968-71. Mem. Am. Quilters Soc. (editor Am. Quilter mag. 1985-95), North Idaho Quilters, New Eng. Quilt Mus. Avocations: reading, hiking, travel, bridge. Home: 478 Oden Bay Dr Sandpoint ID 83864-6499 E-mail: martyidaho@sandpoint.net.

BOWNE, SHIRLEE PEARSON, finance and housing consultant; b. High Shoals Twp., N.C., Mar. 11, 1936; d. Lloyd E. Pearson and Parnell (James) Garland; divorced; 1 child, Gregory Charles. Grad. h.s., Gaffney, S.C. Various secretarial positions, 1955-64; sales repr., pres. Real Estate Marketers, Inc., Tallahassee, 1964-80; chief exec. officer Shirlee [illegible] & Devel. Inc., Tallahassee, 1980-91; vice chmn. Nat. Credit Union Adminstrn., Washington, 1991-97. Cons. in field. Treas. Rep. Party Fla., 1988-91. Episcopalian. Avocation: bridge.

BOWSER, ANITA OLGA, state legislator, education educator; b. Canton, Ohio, Aug. 18, 1920; d. Nicholas B. Alby and Emile Stobbe. AB, Kent State U., 1945; LLB, William McKinley U., 1949; MS, Purdue U., 1967; MA, U. Notre Dame, 1972, PhD, 1976. Instr. Kent (Ohio) State U., 1945-46; prof. Purdue U. North Cen. Campus, Michigan City, Ind., 1950—; mem. Ind. Ho. Reps., 1980-92, Ind. Senate from 8th dist, 1992—. Mem. Delta Kappa Gamma. Office: Ind State Senate 200 W Washington St Indianapolis IN 46204-2728

BOWYER, JOAN ELIZABETH, medical technologist, realtor; b. Ellensburg, Wash., July 11, 1944; d. Chester Joseph and Rita Geneva (Newell) Howarth; 1 child, Suzanne Elise. BA, Ft. Wright Coll. Holy Names, 1966; grad., Real Estate Sch. Oreg., 1982. Lic. med. technologist. Med. technologist Lab. Clin. Medicine, Seattle, 1967-69, Sacred Heart Gen. Hosp., Eugene, Oreg., 1969-73, 74-76, McKenzie Willamette Hosp., Springfield, Oreg., 1976-77, Mid-Columbia Hosp., The Dalles, Oreg., 1977-82; realtor Red Carpet/Rick Hall Realty, Hillsboro, Oreg., 1982-85, Century 21 Columbia Realty, Portland, 1985-2001, John H. Scott Realty, 2001—; med. technologist ARC, Portland, 1982-89, Corning Nicholas Inst. formerly Physicians Med. Lab., 1989-95, East Moreland Hosp., 1985-2004. Co-editor: The Dalles Gen. Hosp. Newspaper, 1980-82. Pres. Wasco County Edn. Service Dist. Parents Group, The Dalles, 1978-82; founder, pres. Mid-Columbia Parents of Deaf, 1978-82; parental spokesperson Spl. Edn. Adv. Com., Salem, Oreg., 1980-82; activist parent for deaf/hearing impaired, 1977—. Mem. Med. Technologists Am. Soc. Pathologists, Nat. Assn. Realtors, Million Dollar Club. Democrat. Home: 704 SE 38th Ave Portland OR 97214-3206 Office: John H Scott Real Estate 2208 SE 182nd Ave Portland OR 97233-5608 E-mail: bowyerjoa@aol.com.

BOXER, BARBARA, senator; b. Bklyn., Nov. 11, 1940; d. Ira and Sophie (Silvershein) Levy; m. Stewart Boxer, 1962; children: Doug, Nicole. BA in Econ., Bklyn. Coll., 1962. Stockbroker, econ. rschr. N.Y. Securities Firm, N.Y.C., 1962-65; journalist, assoc. editor Pacific Sun, 1972-74; congl. aide to rep. 5th Congl. Dist. San Francisco, 1974-76; mem. Marin County Bd. Suprs., San Rafael, Calif., 1976-82, 98th-102d Congresses from 6th Calif. dist., mem. armed services com., select com. children, youth and families; majority whip at large; co-chair Mil. Reform Caucus; chair subcom. on govt. activities and transp. of house govt. ops. com., 1990-93; senator from Calif. U.S. Senate, 1993—, mem. banking, housing and urban affairs com., mem. budget com., mem. environ. and pub. works com. Pres. Marin County Bd. Suprs., 1980-81; mem. Bay Area Air Quality Mgmt. Bd., San Francisco, 1977-82, pres., 1979-81; bd. dirs. Golden Gate Bridge Hwy. and Transport Dist., San Francisco, 1978-82; founding mem. Marin Nat. Women's Polit. Caucus; pres. Dem. New Mems. Caucus, 1983. Recipient Open Govt. award Common Cause, 1980, Rep. of Yr. award Nat. Multiple Sclerosis Soc., 1990, Margaret Sanger award Planned Parenthood, 1990, Women of Achievement award Anti-defamation League, 1990. Democrat. Jewish. Office: US Senate 112 Hart Senate Office Bldg Washington DC 20510-0001*

BOXX, KAREN ELIZABETH, lawyer, educator; Of counsel Keller Rohrback LLP, Seattle; asst. prof. U. Wash., Seattle. Contbr. articles to profl. jours. Mem. adv. com. NCCUSL. Fellow: Am. Coll. Trust and Estate Counsel. Office: Keller Rohrback LLP 1201 3d Ave Ste 3200 Seattle WA 98101-3052 Business E-Mail: kboxx@kellerrohrback.com.

BOYCE, CAROLYN, political organization administrator; State chmn. Idaho Dem. Party, 2000—. Office: Idaho Democratic Party 988 Longmont Ave Ste 110 Boise ID 83706-3696

BOYCE, CORRIE MOSBY, music educator; b. Columbia, S.C., Apr. 7, 1953; d. Rufus Levi and Emma Jo Mosby; m. W. Ray Boyce, June 21, 1975; 1 child, Ray D'Mitry. BA, Columbia Coll., 1974; MEd, Cambridge Coll., 1995. Tchr. Richland Sch. Dist. 1, Columbia, 1974—; instr. Middle Sch. Sci. Enrichment Program, Benedict Coll., Columbia, 1996—. Cluster leader Keenan Cluster Sch.'s Music Program, Columbia, 1989—90; choral music curriculum com. Richland Sch. Dist. 1, Columbia, 1998; Curriculum Leadership in the Arts participant S.C. State Dept. Edn., Columbia, 2003. Rhomania co-chairperson Beta Epsilon Sigma chpt. Sigma Gamma Rho, 1991—2002. Named Outstanding Club Woman of Yr., S.C. Fedn. of Women and Youth Clubs, Inc., 1990, United Meth. Woman of Yr., I. DeQuincey Newman United Meth. Women, 1995, Living the Legacy honoree, Nat. Coun. Negro Women, Inc., 1998. Mem.: Music Educators Nat. Conf. and affiliates, NEA and affiliates (mem. S.C. del. assembly 1993—98). United Methodist. Home: 204 Torwood Dr Columbia SC 29203 Office: Richland County Sch Dist 1 1616 Richland St Columbia SC 29201 E-mail: corrie0407@aol.com.

BOYCE, DOREEN ELIZABETH, lecturer, civic development foundation executive; b. Antofagasta, Chile, Apr. 20, 1934; d. George Edgar and Elsie Winifred Vaughan; m. Alfred Warne Boyce, Aug. 11, 1956; children: Caroline Elizabeth, John Trevor Warne. BA with hons., Oxford (Eng.) U., 1956, MA with hons., 1960; PhD, U. Pitts., 1983; DHL (hon.), Westminister Coll., 1986, Washington and Jefferson Coll., 1993. Lectr. and tutor in econs. U. Witwatersrand, South Africa, 1960-62; provost and dean of faculty, Mary Helen Marks prof. econs. Chatham Coll., Pitts., 1963-79; prof. econs., chmn. dept. econs. and mgmt. Hood Coll., Frederick, Md., 1979-82; pres. Buhl Found., Pitts., 1982—. Dir. and vice chair DQE Duquesne Light Co., Dollar Bank, FSB, Orbeco Analytical Svcs. Inc., Coun. Ind. Colls.; co-founder, dir. Microbac Labs., Inc.; Pa. Gov.'s Sports and Exposition Facilities Task Force, 1995; del. White House Conf. on Small Bus., 1980; mem. Gov.'s Conf. Small Bus., 1979-82, chmn. bd. dirs. Trustee Franklin and Marshall Coll., 1982—, Frick Edn. Commn., 1980-94, Carnegie Sci. Ctr., 1982—; mem. Fed.Jud. Nominating Commn., 1977-79, Pa. Gov.'s Commn. on Financing of Higher Edn., 1983-85; bd. dirs. World Affairs Coun., 1984-96; mem. appeal com. Somerville Coll., Oxford, Eng., 1986—. Recipient Medallion of Distinction, U. Pitts., 1987; named Disting. Dau. Pa., 1996, Hon. Fellow Somerville Coll., U. Oxford, Women Who Make A Difference award, Internat. Women's Forum, 1998. Mem. Am. Econs. Assn., Am. Assn. Higher Edn., Grantmakers of Western Pa. (pres. 1984), Internat. Women's Forum, Assn. Governing Bds. Univ. and Coll. (coun. bd. chairs 2002—), Duquesne Club (bd. dirs. 2000—). Office: Centre City Tower 650 Smithfield St Ste 2300 Pittsburgh PA 15222-3912

BOYCE, EMILY STEWART, retired library and information science educator; b. Raleigh, N.C., Aug. 18, 1933; d. Harry and May (Fallon) B. BS, East Carolina U., 1955, MA, 1961; MS in Libr. Sci., U. N.C., 1968; postgrad., Cath. U. Am., 1977. Libr. Tileston Jr. H.S., Wilmington, NC, 1955-57; children's libr. Wilmington Pub. Libr., 1957-58; asst. libr. Joyner Libr. East Carolina U., Greenville, NC, 1959-61, libr. III, 1962-63; ednl. supr. II ednl. media divsn. N.C. State Dept. Pub. Instrn., Raleigh, 1961-62; assoc. prof. dept. libr. and info. scis. East Carolina U., 1964-76, prof., 1976-92, chmn. dept., 1982-89; retired, 1992. Cons. So. Assn. Colls. and Schs., Raleigh, 1975-92. Active Asheville YWCA, Mediation Ctr., Botanical Gardens, Literacy Coun. Buncombe County. Mem. ALA, AAUW, N.C. Libr. Assn., Assn. Libr. and Info. Sci. Educators, Spl. Librs. Assn. Democrat. Home: 30 Creekside Way Asheville NC 28804-1763 Personal E-mail: esboyce30@charter.net.

BOYD, ANN FISHER, office administrator; b. Corpus Christi, Oct. 2, 1933; d. King and Jewel (Tanner) Fisher; m. Waymon Lewis Boyd, July 8, 1956; children: Wayne Allen, Randy Lynn. Student, Durham Bus. coll., 1956. Operator Gen. Telephone Co., Port Lavaca, Tex., 1954-56; bookkeeper Champ Traylor Meml. Hosp., Port Lavaca, 1955-56; sec., payrol clk. King Fisher Marine Svc., Port Lavaca, 1956-58; sec., asst. sec., treas. King Fisher Marine Svc., Inc., Port Lavaca, 1961-64, asst. sec., treas., 1964—2001; ret. 2002. Home: PO Box 27 134 Harbor Dr W Port Lavaca TX 77979

BOYD, BARBARA, state legislator; m. Robert Boyd; 1 child, Janine. BS, St. Paul's Coll., 1965. Mem. Ohio Ho. of Reps., Columbus, 1992—. Named Officer of Yr. No. Ohio Police Benevolent Assn., 1989; recipient Black Women's History award, 1992. Mem. LWV, Delta Sigma Theta.

BOYD, BE (BELINDA) CAROLYN, theater educator; m. John Wayne Shafer. BS in Comm. and Theater, Austin Peay State U., 1982; MFA in Acting, U. Louisville, 1986. Voice/ acting instr. U. of Louisville, 1986—89; asst. prof. of theater U. of Vt., Burlington, Vt., 1989—91; assoc. prof. if theater U. N.C., Greensboro, 1991—98; assoc. prof. of theater Tex. Christian U., Ft. Worth, 1998—2002, U. of Ctrl. Fla., Orlando, 2002—. Dir., dir.: La Lorona; actor: (actor in fires in the mirror) Fires in the Mirror (Best Actress, 2000); author: (play) Dream Keeper, Mother Of Civil Rights, In Focus: A Recollection of Black Thought. Mem.: Ctrl. Fla. Performing Arts Alliance, Assn. for Theatre in Higher Edn., Voice and Speech Trainers Assn., Am. Coll. Theatre Festival, Actor's Equity Assn., Southeastern Theatre Conf. (culteral diversity com. 1998—2000), Dramatist's Guild (assoc.). Office: U Ctrl Fla PO Box 162372 Orlando FL 32816-2372

BOYD, BETTY, government official; b. Tulsa, Dec. 9, 1924; d. Theodore Wood and Victoria Marie (Fairchild) Carman; m. William Wray Boyd, Aug. 31, 1943; children: Beverlie J. Boyd Bryant, Barry Wray Boyd. Student, U. Tulsa, 1941-42, 45-46, Iowa State U., 1942-43. Broadcaster, pub. svc. dir. KOTV-Channel 6, Tulsa, 1955-65; broadcaster, pub. rels. dir. KTUL-TV-Channel 8, Tulsa, 1965-80; dir. pub. rels.-mktg. Tulsa County Area Vo-Tech. Dist., Tulsa, 1980-91; mem. Okla. Ho. of Reps., Dist. 23, Tulsa, 1991—. Author: Travelchatter: My Green Country, 1980, If I Could Sing I'd be Dangerous, 1983; contbr. articles to profl. jours. Bd. dirs. Tulsa Gridiron Trust, 1988—, Goodwill Ind. of Tulsa, 1985—, Osteopathic Found. of Tulsa Reg. Med. Ctr., 1989—; adv. bd. Okla. Alcohol & Drug Abuse Prevention and Life Skills Edn. Recipient Golden Mike for Pub. Svc., Am. Women in Radio & TV, 1970, Brotherhood award Nat. Conf. Christians & Jews, 1969. Mem. Am. Vocat. Assn. (Svc. award 1990), Nat. Coun. State Legislatures (edn. com.), So. Legis. Conf., Tulsa Coalition of Older People, Women in the Svcs. (def. adv. com.), Tulsa Press Club (bd. dirs. 1984—). Democrat. Baptist. Avocations: writing, travel, photography. Home: 11039 E 26th Pl Tulsa OK 74129-7519 Office: Okla House of Reps State Capital Oklahoma City OK 73105

BOYD, BETTY ANN, state representative; m. Douglas Boyd; children: James, Kirsten. BA in Sociology, Upsala Coll.; postgrad., Fairfield U. State rep., dist. 28 Colo. House Rep., Denver, 2002—. Mem. Judiciary Com., Health, Environment, Welfare and Instns. Com. Bd. dirs. Citizens for Lakewood's Future; mem. Colo. Social Legis. Com.; bd. dirs. Jeffco Action Ctr.; Lutheran Family Svcs. Colo. Mem.: AAUW, West Chamber Serving Jefferson County. Democrat. Lutheran. Avocations: singing, knitting, needlecrafts. Office: State Capitol 200 E Colfax Ave Denver CO 80203 Office Phone: 303-866-2923.

BOYD, CAROLYN PATRICIA, history educator; b. San Diego, June 1, 1944; d. Peter James and Patricia Mae (de Soucy) B.; m. Frank Dawson Bean, Jan. 4, 1975; children: Peter Justin Bean, Michael Franklin Bean. AB with great distinction and with honors in History, Stanford U., 1966; MA, U. Wash., 1969, PhD, 1974. Tchg. asst. dept. history U. Wash., 1970-71; from instr. to prof. dept. history U. Tex., Austin, 1973-95, prof., 1995-99, assoc. dean Office Grad. Studies, 1986-88, 90-92, chair dept. history, 1994-99; dir. univ. honors program, assoc. prof. dept. history U. Md., College Park, 1989-90; prof. dept. history U. Calif., Irvine, 1999—, chair dept. history, 2004—. Lectr. in field. Author: Praetorian Politics in Liberal Spain, 1979, La política pretoriana en el reinado de Alfonso XIII, 1990, Historia Patria: Politics, History and National Identity in Spain, 1875-1975, 1997, Spanish edit., 2000; mem. editl. bd. Essays, 1992-95; author chpts. to books; contbr. articles to profl. jours. Recipient Summer award U. Tex. Rsch. Inst., 1997; Woodrow Wilson hon. fellow, 1966, Fulbright-Hays fellow, 1966-67, NDEA Title IV fellow, 1968-72, AAUW fellow, 1972-73, ACLS fellow, 1985; ACLS Grant-in-Aid, 1977, Am. Philos. Soc. grant, 1978, URI Rsch. grant, 1985, New Del Amo Program grant, 2000-02; fellow Woodrow Wilson Internat. Ctr. for Scholars, 2002-03. Mem. Am. Hist. Assn. (James Harvey Robinson prize com. 1992-94, John Fagg prize com. 2001—03), Soc. Spanish and Portugese Hist. Studies (gen. sec. 2000—04, mem. exec. com. 1978-80, 83-85, 96-98, chair local arrangements, program chmn. conf. 1987), Coun. European Studies, Internat. Inst. in Spain. Office: U Calif Irvine Dept History Irvine CA 92697-0001 E-mail: cpboyd@uci.edu.

BOYD, DEBORAH ANN, pediatrician; b. Urbana, Ohio, Jan. 30, 1955; d. John A. Sr. and Juanita Jean (Routt) B. BA cum laude, Wittenberg U., 1977; MD, U. Cin., 1982. Diplomate Am. Bd. Pediatrics, Nat. Bd. Med. Examiners. Intern Children's Hosp. Med. Ctr., Cin., 1982-83, pediatric resident, 1982-85; pediatrician Nat. Health Svc. Corps, Springfield, Ohio, 1985-89; former pediatrician Community Hosp. Health Care Ctr., Springfield, 1989-97; staff pediat. primary care ctr., clin. faculty Children's Hosp. Med. Ctr., Cin., 1998—. Mem. Continuing med. edn. com. Mercy Med. Ctr., Springfield, 1989—, infection control com., 1987—. Adv. com. Miami Valley Child Devl. Ctr., Springfield, 1985—, New Parents as Tchrs., 1986—. Mem. Assn. of Clinicians for the Underserved, Am. Acad. Pediats., Ambulatory Pediat. Assn. Democratic. Avocations: bicycling, photography, basketball, music, church activities. Home: 12132 S Pine Dr Apt 240 Cincinnati OH 45241-1743 Office: Dept Gen Com Pediatrics Children's Hosp Med Ctr 3333 Burnet Ave Fl 4 Cincinnati OH 45229-3026

BOYD, HAZEL, minister; b. Huntingdon, Tenn., Sept. 09; d. Marion Homer Barnett and Lennie Victolia Hawkins; married; 6 children. Student in real estate, Columbus State Coll., Ohio. Ordained clergy Anderson Ind. Ch. of God, Ohio; cert. health aide Columbus State Coll., profl. activity dir. Cosmetologist, Columbus, Ohio; area commr. Columbus City Coun.; prison minister Columbus. Pres. PTA, 1960; judge Bd. Election; Sunday Sch. tchr., Bible tchr. Recipient various awards and citations, various orgns., including NAACP. Mem.: Greater SLAC, 50 Plus Club, Linden Kiwanis. Home: 1264 E 16th Ave Columbus OH 43211

BOYD, JANEGALE, state legislator; b. Reno, Nev., Nov. 30, 1952; m. Hines Boyd; children: Whit, Beth, Erin. ASN, Tallahassee (Fla.) C.C., 1975. Lic. ins. agt., life and health, Fla., Ga.; RN, Fla., Ga. Quality assurance coord., instr. critical care, head nurse Tallahassee Cmty. Hosp., 1979-85; adminstr. HMO Am., Inc., Tallahassee, 1986-87; exec. dir. Ga. Fla. Preferred, Inc. (Health Alliance of the South), Thomasville, Ga., 1987-92; dir. North Fla. ops. Family Health Plan of Fla., Inc., Tallahassee, 1992-93; area dir. Tallahassee market Humana/PCA Health Plans of Fla., 1993—; mem. Fla. Ho. of Reps., Tallahassee, 1996—. Vice chair water and resource mgmt. com.; mem. edn. com., utilities and comm. com., jt. legis. auditing com., fiscal responsibility coun., gen. appropriations com., procedural coun.; mem. Women's Caucus, Dem. Caucus, Blue Dawg Caucus; presenter in health care field. Chair United Way, Jefferson County; pres. Big Bend br. Am. Lung Assn., 1984-90; mem. exec. com. Monticello Opera House; mem. 1st United Meth. Ch., Monticello; grad. Leadership Tallahassee; mem. adv. bd. Tallahassee C.C. Sch. Nursing, 1988-92; instr., trainer BLS, Am. Heart Assn.; chmn. City of Monticello Planning Agy., 1989-96, Healthyways, Inc., 1989-96. Named 1 of Top 40 Legislators, Fla. C. of C., 1997, 98, 2000, Freshman Legislator of Yr., Fla. Sch. Bds. Assn., 1997, 98, Legislator of Yr., Fla. Assn. Dist. Sch. Supts., 1998; recipient Freshman Courage award Small Sch. Dist. Coun. Consortium, 1997, award Fla. Assn. HMO, 1997, 98, Legis. award Fla. Sheriffs Assn., 1997, Fla. Landscape Designers Assn., 1998, Regional I & II Correctional Officers, 1998, Small Sch. Dist. Coun. Consortium, 1998, Fla. Farm Bur., 1998, Quality Floridian award Fla. League of Cities, 1998, award Fla. Assn. Managed Care Orgns., Inc., 1999, cert. of appreciation Fla. Rural Health Assn., 1999, Outstanding Fla. Legislator award Fla. Nurses Assn., 1999, recognition for leadership and support Small County Coalition, 1999, Outstanding Leadership award Dept. Corrections, 1999, award Fla. Tchg. Profession-NEA Bd. Dirs., 1999, Friend of Edn. award, 1999, Spl. Recognition award Fla. Conf. Judges of Compensation Claims, 1999. Democrat. Avocations: swimming, reading, volunteer work. Office: House Office Bldg 402 S Monroe St Rm 212 Tallahassee FL 32399-6526

BOYD, LEONA POTTER, retired social worker; b. Creekside, Pa., Aug. 31, 1907; d. Joseph M. and Belle (McHenry) Johnston; m. Edgar D. Potter, July 16, 1932 (div.); m. Harold Lee Boyd, Oct. 1972. Grad., Indiana (Pa.) State Normal Sch, 1927; student, Las Vegas (N.Mex.) Normal U., 1933; student Sch. Social Work, Carnegie Inst. Tech., 1945, U. Pitts., 1956-57. Tchr. Creekside Pub. Schs., 1927-30, Papago Indian Reservation, Sells, Ariz., 1931-33; caseworker, supr. Indiana County (Pa.) Bd. Assistance, 1934-54, exec. dir., 1954-68, ret. Bd. dirs., hon. life mem. Indiana County Tourist Promotion; former bd. dirs. Indiana County United Fund, Salvation Army, Indiana County Guidance Ctr., Armstrong-Indiana Mental Health Bd.; cons. assoc. Cmty. Rsch. Assocs., Inc.; mem. Counseling Ctr. Aux., Lake Havasu City, Ariz., 1978-80; former mem. Western Welcome Club, Lake Havasu City, Sierra Vista Hosp. Aux., Truth or Consequences, N.M. Recipient Disting. Svc. award Indiana Jaycees, 1965, Bus. and Profl. Women's Club award, 1965. Mem. AARP, Daus. Am. Colonists. Lutheran. Home: 520 S Higley Rd Unit 126 Mesa AZ 85206-2274

BOYD, LISA BAKER, school media specialist; d. Charles and Ann Baker; m. Michael Richard Boyd, June 8, 1991. BS in Edn., Auburn U., 1981; MA in Edn., U. Ala., Birmingham, 1984. Cert. tchr. Ala., 1981, nat. bd. tchrs. 2003. Libr./media specialist Franklin Acad., Huffman, Ala., 1981—84, Pittman Mid. Sch., Hueytown, 1985—89; libr./media specialist and tech. coord. Bottenfield Mid. Sch., Adamsville, Ala., 1990—. Contbr. NECC Conf. Vol. Bruno's Meml. Classic, Birmingham, Ala., 1999—2004. Named Jefferson County Libr. Media Specialist of Yr., 1997, 2000, 2003; Promoting Reading in Daily Edn. grantee, Ala. Power Co., 1997, 2000. Mem.: Ala. Instrnl. Media Assn. (sec. 2003—, Carrie C. Robinson Award for Outstanding Sch. Libr./Media Program 1991). Office: Bottenfield Middle Sch 400 Hillcrest Rd Adamsville AL 35005 Personal E-mail: lboyd_bmc@yahoo.com.

BOYD, LYNNE KAPLAN, management consultant; b. Willimantic, Conn., June 17, 1951; d. Joseph and Rebecca Kaplan; m. William Randolph Boyd; 1 child, Joel. Student, U. Mich., 1970-71, BA with honors, [illegible] Coll., 1973; grad., Stanford U., 1999. Dist. mgr. Xerox Corp., Rosslyn, Va., 1973-85; dir. fed. sales Telic Corp., Rockville, Md., 1985-88; dir. sales Contel Fed. Sys., Fairfax, Va., 1988; sr. v.p. Uniplex Integration Sys., Inc., Dallas, 1988-93, pres., 1993-94; sr. v.p. Jetform Corp., Ottawa, Canada, 1994-99; v.p. worldwide sales Silanis Tech., Inc., Montreal, Canada, 1999—2002; prin. Mid-Atlantic Bus. Cons., 2002—. Mem.: NAFE, Assn. Info. and Image Mgmt., Buis. Forms Mgmt. Assn., Armed Forces Comms. and Elec. Assn. Avocations: youth soccer, gardening, sailing. Home and Office: 24 Yankee Point Dr Carmel CA 92923

BOYD, RHONDA CHERIE, psychologist, researcher; b. Phila., Apr. 20, 1970; d. Edward Ronald and Shirley (Channel) Boyd. BS, Brown U., 1992; MA, U. Iowa, 1995, PhD, 1998. Lic. psychologist Md., 1999, Pa, 2002. Instr. U. Pa, Sch. Medicine, Children's Hosp., Phila., 2001—. Mem. rsch., advocacy, & edn. com. Maternity Care Coalition, Phila., 2002—. Contbr. articles to profl. jours. Fellow, Johns Hopkins U., 1998—2000, AAAS, 2000—01, NIMH, Adminstrn. Children, Families & Youth, 2000—01, NIH, 2002; grantee, W.E.B. DuBois Collective Rsch. Inst. Mem.: APA, Soc. Prevention Rsch., Soc. Rsch. Child Devel., Soc. Rsch., Cmty., & Action (N.E. coord. 2002—), Delta Sigma Theta (pres. Iowa City-Cedar Rapids alumnae 1995—96, Jewel award 1996).

BOYDA, DEBORA, advertising executive; Sr. ptnr., acct. mgr. Tatham Euro RSCG, Chgo., mng. ptnr., 1997-99; v.p., acct. dir. Leo Burnett, Chgo., 1999-2000, sr. v.p., 2000—. Office: Leo Burnett 35 W Wacker Dr Ste 3710 Chicago IL 60601-1648

BOYDEN, JACLYNE WITTE, university vice dean; BA, Calif. State U., Hayward, 1970; MBA, Golden Gate U., 1982. Dept. mgr. dept. biochemistry and biophysics U. Calif., San Francisco, 1980-82, dept. mgr. dept. medicine, 1982-84, coord. adminstrv. policies Office of Pres., 1984-85, asst. dir. Cardiovasc. Rsch. Inst., 1985-88, vice dean for Adminstrn. and Fin. Sch. Medicine, 1992—; assoc. dean for Adminstrn. SUNY Sch. Medicine, Stony Brook, 1988-92. Mem. Med. Group Mgmt. Assn., AAMC Group on Instnl. Planning (steering com. 1991-93), AAMC Group Bus. Affairs (chmn. profl. devel. com. 1996, mem. steering com. 1997—, nat. sec. 1997, chairperson-elect 1998, chair 1999). Office: U Calif San Francisco Sch Medicine Office of Dean PO Box 410 San Francisco CA 94143-0001

BOYD-SCOTLAND, JOANN, college president; BA in Psychology and Music Edn., Tougaloo Coll.; MS in Edn./Guidance, Jackson State U.; PhD in Edn./Curriculum, Kans. State U. Exec. dir. S.C. Curriculum Congress; dean Sch. of Edn. Lander U., Greenwood, S.C., 1986-93; pres. Denmark (S.C.) Tech. Coll., 1993—. Benjamin E. Mays scholar Ind. U., 1986. Office: Denmark Tech Coll PO Box 327 Denmark SC 29042-0327

BOYEA, RUTHE W. retired educator; b. Waltham, Mass., Sept. 22, 1918; d. George Walter and Ethel Maude Wright; m. Douglas Paul Boyea, 1944; children: Ruthe Priscilla Boyea-Boiczyk, Douglas Paul. B Social Sci., Boston U., 1940; MEd, Ctrl. Conn. State U., 1960; cert. in polit. sci., Trinity Coll., 1970. Cert. elem. tchr., Conn. Dir. religious edn., Springfield, Mass., 1945; tchr. New Britain, Conn., 1945-51; prof. edn. Ctrl. Conn. State U., New Britain, 1951-65, dir., founder Women's Ctr., 1965-85, prof. emeritus, 1985, lectr. on women's issues. Adj. prof. Tunxis C.C., Mattatuck C.C., 1960-70. Commr. Human Rights and Opportunity, City of New Britain; vol., chair bd. dirs. ARC, New Britain; elected mem. Vets. Commn., City of New Britain, 1999. Lt. (j.g.) USN, 1942-45. Named Women's Educator of Yr., YWCA, 1975, Vol. of Yr. United Way, 1999; recipient Women Helping Women award Soroptimist Internat., 1982, Disting. Alumni award Boston U. Sch. Theology, 2002. Mem. AAUW (officer), LWV (bd. dirs.), Nat. Women's Mil. Meml. (founder), Nat. Women's Art Mus., Nat. Women's Hall of Fame. Mem. United Ch. of Christ. Office: Ctrl Conn State U Stanley St New Britain CT 06053 also: 126 New Britain Ave Apt Z2 Plainville CT 06062-2047

BOYER, ANNA MARIE, music educator; d. Joseph Elwood Boyer and Anna Marie Marnien. MusB, Chestnut Hill Coll., 1970; MMus in Edn., West Chester U., 1975. Cert. permanent cert. tchr. K-12 Pa. Music tchr. Fontbonne Acad., Phila., 1954—56; music tchr. 2d grade St. Patrick Elem. Sch., Kennett Square, Pa., 1956—60, Notre Dame Elem. Sch., Swarthmore, Pa., 1960—67; music tchr. West Cath. Girls H.S., Phila., 1967—70; music tchr., dept. head Cardinal Dougherty H.S., Phila., 1970—78; music tchr., head dept. St. Hubert HS, Phila., 1978—91; music tchr. St. Andrew Sch., Drexel Hill, Pa., 1991—. Cons. EQ project Coll. Bd., 1986—91; chairperson fine arts curriculum Archdiocese of Phila., 1981—88, chairperson Fine Arts Festival, 1984—88. Mem.: Music Educators Nat. Conf., Pa. Music Educators Assn., Nat. Pastoral Musicians, Sister of St. Joseph. Republican. Roman Catholic. Avocations: cooking, sewing, crossword puzzles. Home: 535 Mason Ave Drexel Hill PA 19026-2330 Office: St Andrew Sch 535 Mason Ave Drexel Hill PA 19026-2330

BOYER, HEIDI HILD, public policy consultant; b. Denver, Dec. 25, 1961; d. Leonard Gene and Marilyn Ann (Handrock) Hild; m. Samuel Ralph Boyer, Dec. 27, 1992; children: Elliott Gene Boyer, Ryan Stuart Boyer. BA, Colo. State U., 1985. Sr. ptnr. H. Earhart & Assocs., Denver, 1987-90; dir. comm. Colo. Assn. Commerce and Industry, Denver, 1990; dir. legis. affairs Rocky Mountain Farmers Union, Denver, 1990-93; pres. Colo. Capitol Preservation Fund, Denver, 1995-98; state fin. dir. Norton for Gov., Denver, 1997-98; sr. ptnr. Sq. Root Gardens, 2002—. Rsch. assoc. Gov.'s Unified Housing Task Force, Denver, 1987; cons. Planned Parenthood Rocky Mountains, 1988, Gov.'s Task Force on Homeless, 1989. Press sec. Sci. and Cultural Facilities Dist. Campaign, Denver, 1994; vol. Make-A-Wish Found., 1995-2000; mem. steering com. Colo. Open Lands, 1998—. Recipient Denver Post/Am. Newspaper Publs. Assn. Scholastic Journalist award, 1980. Mem. LWV, Inst. Internat. Edn., Colo. State U. Devel. Coun., Kappa Alpha Theta. Avocations: gardening, skiing, reading, traveling.

BOYER, KAYE KITTLE, association management executive; b. Peoria, Ill., July 5, 1942; d. Keith Howard and Evelyn Pearl (Benson) Kittle; m. Jon Frederick Boyer, Mar. 20, 1965; children: Tristan Boyer Binns, Kristine Monique Hitchens. Student, Merrill Palmer Inst., Detroit, 1964; BS in Home Econs., Pa. State U., University Park, 1964; MA in Sociology, Rutgers State U., New Brunswick, 1967. Cert. assn. exec.; cert. in family and consumer scis. Creative rschr. Nat. Inst. Drycleaning, Silver Spring, Md., 1963; extension home economist Md. Coop. Extension Svc., Westminster, 1964-65; coord. human resources N.J. Coop. Extension Svc., New Brunswick, 1966-67; instr. Douglass Coll., Rutgers U., New Brunswick, 1967-70; coord., instr. pilot project Urban Coalition of Met. Wilmington (Del.) Inc., 1972; asst. to chmn. 4-H Youth Devel. Dept., Cook Coll., 1973-74; feasibility study dir. Ocean County Coll., Toms River, N.J., 1975; exec. dir. N.J. Home Economics Assn., Manalapan, 1975-86; pres. Boyer Mgmt. Svcs., Manalapan, N.J. and Earleville, Md., 1984—, Earleville, Md., 1984—, Palm Coast, Fla., 1984—. Mgr. Costume Soc. Am., Palm Coast, Fla., 1984—; cons. Plumpton Pk. Zool. Gardens Rising Sun, 1988-89, bd. dirs., 1990-92; cons. N.J. White House Conf., Trenton, 1980, Baltimore County Med. Assn., 1995-96, Md. Acad. Family Physicians, 1994, 97, Textile Soc. Am., 1998—. Editor Exchs. Newsletter; resource dir., N.J. Programs and Svcs. Related to Adolescent Pregnancy. Mem. adv. com. dept. cmty. edn. Rutgers U., 1979-84; vol. Soroptomist Internat. of Elkton, Md., 1987-94; mem. Com. Libr. of Cecilton, pres., bd. dirs., 1986-92; player U.S. Pub. Links Amateur, 1986; trustee Cecil County Bd. Libr. Trustees, 1998-2002. Mem. AAUW (v.p. program devel. N.J. divsn. 1984-86), Am. Assn. Family and Consumer Scis. (cert., Ruth O'Brien project grantee), Am. Soc. Assn. Execs. (cert.), Fla. Soc. Assn. Execs., Profl. Conv. Mgmt. Assn. (edn. and profl. devel. com. 1996-2001, [illegible] working com., 2002), Internat. Assn. of Facilitators, Fla. Assn. Family and Consumer Scis., Profl. Conv. Mgmt. Assn. Edn. Found. (transition team product/svc., 2001, design task force 2000, learning ctr. task force 2000-2001, trustee 2000-2003), Penn State Alumni Assn.(chmn. strategic planning 2003—), Kappa Omicron Nu (v.p. fin. 1992-93, chair constn. and bylaws com. 1994-97). Democrat. Avocations: golf, sailing. Home and Office: 107 Front St Palm Coast FL 32137

BOYER, LILLIAN BUCKLEY, artist, educator; b. Paterson, N.J., Mar. 1, 1916; d. George and Adele (Roomy) Buckley; m. Floyd E. Boyer, Jr., Sept. 7, 1935; 1 child, Karen Boyer Lloyd. BA in Art Edn., U. Ky., 1975. Field interviewer Survey Rsch. Ctr., U. Mich., 1963-68; instr. art U. Ky., Lexington, 1976—2002. Ky. reporter for Sunshine Artists mag., 1976-85. Exhibited in group shows at Grand Theater, Frankfort, Ky., 1983, State Capitol, 1983, Lexington Art League, annually, —, Waller Gallery, Lexington, 1986, Headley-Whitney Mus., 1987—88, 1989, 1990, Gallery IO/IO, Knoxville, 1995, Living Arts and Sci. Ctr., Lexington, 1988, 1989, 1995, 1997, Artists Attic, 1989, Opera House Gallery, 1995, Owensboro Mus. Fine Arts, 2001, others. Crusade chmn. Am. Cancer Soc., Anaheim, Calif., 1958, Orange County, Calif., 1959; active, hon. life mem. PTA, 1950-62; mem. Lexington Arts and Cultural Coun., Ky. Citizens for the Arts, Friends of Ky. Ednl. TV, Headley Whitney Mus., Friends of Lexington Pub. Libr.; pres., life mem. Lexington Art League, 1976-80, 82-83, 84-86. Mem. U. Ky. Alumni Assn., Living Arts and Sci. Ctr., Friends of U.K. Art Mus., Nat. Mus. Women in Arts. Methodist. Address: 969 Holly Springs Dr Lexington KY 40504-3119 E-mail: labinart@aol.com.

BOYER, LISA, basketball coach;, Ithaca Coll., 1979. Asst. coach Davidson Coll., 1980-82, East Carolina, 1983-84, Miami of Ohio, 1984-95, Va. Tech., 1985-86; coach Bradley Univ., 1986-96, Phila. Rage. Named Gateway Conf. Coach of Yr., 1990. Office: 123 Chestnut St Fl 4 Philadelphia PA 19106-3051

BOYER, SISTER MARY VERONICA, nun, art educator; b. Phila., Dec. 5, 1938; d. Joseph Ellwood and Anna Marie (Marnien) Boyer. BA in Art Edn., Chestnut Hill Coll., 1972; MEd, Temple U., 1978. Joined Sisters of St. Joseph 1961. Tchr. music St. Matthew Sch., Conshohocken, Pa., 1963—65, Nativity of Our Lord Sch., Warminster, Pa., 1965—67, St. Mary, Star of the Sea Sch., Branchdale, Pa., 1967—72, St. Joseph the Carpenter Sch., Roselle, NJ, 1972—73; tchr. art, dept. chair Archbishop Ryan H.S., Phila., 1973—77; asst. prof. art Chestnut Hill Coll., Phila., 1978—81; tchr. art, dept. chair Mount St. Joseph Acad., Flourtown, Pa., 1981—91, Bishop McDevitt H.S., Wyncote, Pa., 1991—. Instr. Mayor's Commn. on Literacy, Phila., 1988; mem. Inter-Faith Choir for 9/11, 2002. Edn. for Justice-For Cath. Relief Svcs., 1981—83. Recipient Outstanding Educator award, Phila. Coll. Textiles and Scis., 1994, 1996, 1997. Mem.: Pa. Art Edn. Assn., Nat. Assn. Pastoral Musicians, Nat. Cath. Ednl. Assn., Nat Art Edn. Assn. Democrat. Home: 107 Old Soldiers Rd Cheltenham PA 19012 Office: Bishop McDevitt HS 125 Royal Ave Wyncote PA 19095 Office Phone: 215-887-5575.*

BOYER, PATRICIA ANN, social worker, educator; b. St. Paul, Feb. 13, 1934; d. Marvin Harold and Leslye Marilla (Smallidge) Adams; m. Edward Clair Boyer, May 25, 1968. BA, Mankato State Coll., 1958; MSW, U. Pitts., 1964. Lic. clin. social worker, marriage and family therapist, Wyo. Social worker Brown County Welfare Dept., New Ulm, Minn., 1958, Luth. Children's Friend Soc., Mpls., 1958-60, Armstrong County Children's Svc., Kittanning, Pa., 1960-62; psychotherapist Indiana (Pa.) County Guidance Ctr., 1964-65, Ctrl. Wyo. Counseling Ctr., Casper, 1965-70; program dir. Wyo. State Children's Home, Casper, 1975-76; assoc. prof. social work U. Wyo., Laramie, 1970-75, 76—. Marriage and family therapist Casper, 1976—; cons. Platte County Meml. Hosp., Wheatland, Wyo., 1996—, NMI Health Care, Casper, 1997—; instr. Cath. U. Washington, 1990-91, U. Denver, 1985—. Co-author: (with Jason Aronson) A Guide for the Family Therapist, 1984, 2d edit., 1994; contbr. numerous articles to profl. jours. Bd. dirs. Wyo. Med. Ctr., Casper, ethics forum, 1995—, cmty. ethics com., 1996—. Grantee LEAA, 1977-80. Mem. NASW (v.p., chmn. 1967, com. inquiry Wyo. divsn. 1996—, Wyo. Social Worker of Yr. 1987), Am. Family

Therapy Acad., Am. Assn. Marriage and Family Therapy (pres. Wyo. divsn. 1979-81, 90-92). Lutheran. Avocations: travel, swimming. Home: 1339 S Mitchell St Casper WY 82601-4436 Office: Univ Wyo Casper Coll Ctr 125 College Dr Casper WY 82601-4612

BOYETT, JOAN REYNOLDS, arts administrator; b. L.A., May 2, 1936; d. William Paris Reynolds and Jean Margaret (Howard) Hauck; m. Harry William Boyett, Oct. 5, 1956; children: Keven William, Suzanne Marie Boyett Liebherr. Student, Occidental Coll., 1954-55, Pasadena Playhouse, 1955-57. Mgr. youth activities L.A. Philharm. Orch., 1970-79; dir., founder edn. divsn. Performing Arts Ctr. L.A. County, 1979-2001, v.p. edn., 1988-2001. Mem. supt.'s task force on arts edn. Calif. State Dept. Edn., 1997; cons. NEA, Washington; chmn. arts edn. task force Calif. Arts Coun., Sacramento, 1993-95; arts edn. mem. Nat. Working Group, Washington, 1992-95; mem. U.S. Sec. of Edns. Com. on Am. Goes Back to Sch. Active various coms. and task forces, L.A., Sacramento. Named Woman of Yr. L.A. Times, 1976; recipient Labor's award of honor County Fedn. Labor, L.A., 1984, Susan B. Anthony award Bus. and Profl. Women, 1986, Gov.'s award Calif. Arts Coun. and Gov., 1989, R.O.S.E. Outstanding Svc. to Edn. award, U. So. Calif., 1999, Outstanding Arts Educator award Calif. Arts Coun., 2001, Music Ctr. Club 100 Spl. Tribute award, 2001, Women in Ednl. Leadership award, 2002, Ovation award for cmty. svc. Theatre League Alliance, 2002. Mem. Calif. Art Edn. Assn. (Behind the Scenes award 1985), Calif. Dance Educators Assn. (Svc. award 1985), Calif. Ednl. Theatre Assn. (Outstanding Contbn. award 1990, nominated for Nat. Medal Arts 1996, 97). Republican. Presbyterian. Avocations: reading, attending arts events, gardening, swimming. Home: PO Box 1805 Studio City CA 91614-0805 E-mail: jarboyett@earthlink.net.

BOYKIN, AMY WILLIAMS, librarian; b. Newport News, Va., Aug. 1, 1968; d. Edward Hamilton Williams, Lucy King Williams; m. Mark Julian Boykin. BA in English, Christopher Newport U., 1990; MS in Libr. Studies, U. N.C., Greensboro, 1993. Asst. reference libr. Christopher Newport U. Libr., Newport News, 1995—. Contbr. book Library Web, 1997, book Teaching Information Literacy Concepts, 2001, book Christopher Newpoa, 2003. Mem.: ALA, Ch. and Synagogue Libr. Assn., Mid-Atlantic Regional Archives Conf., Va. Libr. Assn., Beta Phi Mu. Baptist. Avocations: reading, cooking, crocheting. Office: Christopher Newport Univ Libr 1 University Pl Newport News VA 23606 Business E-Mail: awboykin@cnu.edu.

BOYKIN, ANNE J. dean; BSN, Alverno Coll., 1966; MSN, Emory U., 1972; PhD, Vanderbilt U., 1981. Asst. prof. Marquette U., Milw., 1973-74; assoc. prof., asst. dir. Valdosta (Ga.) State Coll., 1975-80; in-svc. educator Holy Cross Hosp., Ft. Lauderdale, Fla., 1980-81; assoc. prof. Fla. Atlantic U., Boca Raton, 1984—, dean Coll. Nursing, prof., 1996—. Dir. Christine E. Lynn Ctr. for Caring. Co-author: Nursing as Caring: a Model for Transforming Practice, 1993, 2d edit., 2001; editor: Living a Caring-Based Program, 1993, Power, Politics and Public Policy: A Matter of Caring, 1995; co-editor: Caring as Healing; Renewal through Hope, 1994; contbr. chpts. to books, articles to profl. jours. Mem. Internat. Assn. for Human Caring, Fla. Nurses Assn. (nursing educator award 1991), Sigma Theta Tau, Phi Kappa Phi. Office: Fla Atlantic U PO Box 3091 Boca Raton FL 33431-0991 Business E-Mail: boykina@fau.edu.

BOYKIN, GLADYS, retired religious organization administrator; b. N.Y.C., Dec. 10, 1929; d. Jacob Allen and Annie Mae (Alston) McClendon; m. Eugene S. Callender (div. 1963); 1 child, Renee Denise; m. John R. Strachan (dec. 1982); m. Elton Boykin, 1996. Student, NYU, 1947-49. Dep. asst. Presbyn. Ch. of East Africa, Nairobi, Kenya, 1964-67; assoc. for women's program Presbyn. Ch. of U.S., N.Y.C., 1970-83; exec. dir. United Presbyn. Women, N.Y.C., 1983-97; ret., 1997. Cons. Peace Corps, Nairobi, 1964-67, Operation Crossroads Africa, Nairobi, 1964-67, Afro-Am. Ednl. Inst., Teaneck, N.J., 1977-79, various women's orgns. in Asia, Australia, Europe, Africa. V.p. Addicts Rehab. Ctr. Bd., N.Y.C., 1957—; mem. N.Y. Coalition of 100 Black Women, N.Y.C., 1972—; v.p., bd. dirs. La. Internat. Cultural Ctr.; bd. dirs. aging resource ctr. Sister Cities of Louisville. Recipient Cert. of citation borough pres. N.Y.C., 1977, Harlem Peacemaking award Harlem Peacemaking Com., 1983, Vol. award Louisville Internat. Culture Ctr., 1996. Mem. La. C. of C., River City Assn. Bus. and Profl. Women. Avocations: music, reading, travel, needlepoint, theater. Home: 800 S 4th St Apt 2202 Louisville KY 40203-2132

BOYKIW, NORMA SEVERNE, retired nutritionist, educator; b. Coalmont, Ind., Feb. 3, 1918; d. Charles Edward Goble and Ressa Naomi Johnson; m. Russel Yaroslav Alexis Boykiw, 1948 (dec. Sept. 4, 1992); children: Russel Alexis II, Mark Emerson. BS, Ind. State U., 1941. Registered Med. Asst. 1950. Dietitian asst. Ind. State U., Terre Haute, Ind., 1939—40; tchr. home econ. Wawaka Sch. Sys., Wawaka, Ind., 1941—42; nutrition tchr. Crown Point Sch., Crown Point, Ind., 1942—43; mem. staff patient diabetic diets Wesley Meml. Hosp., Chgo.; writer of diet manuals Pa., 1945—48; office mgr. Russel Boykiw, MD, Clearfield, 1948—92, ret., 1992. Ombudsman Area Agy. on Aging, Clearfield, Pa., 1999—. Compilation author Genealogy for the Goble Family, 1976;, author diet manuals Hosps. Active cmty. devel. Pa. State U., Clearfield, Pa., 1959, 1966; den mother Presbyn. Ch., Clearfield, 1967. Named Woman of the Yr., Bus. and Profl. Women, 1974, Outstanding Citizen of the Yr., Clearfield Rotary Club, 1987; grantee, Ctrl. Pa. Dist. Libr. Bd., 1968—6879. Mem.: AAUW (Outstanding Woman award 1983), Nat. Soc. Daus. of Founders and Patriots of Am., Nat. Soc. DAR, Clearfield County Hist. Soc. (grant). Democrat. Avocation: yoga. Home: 364 Bailey Settlement Hwy Clearfield PA 16830-3505

BOYLAN, ELIZABETH SHIPPEE, academic administrator, biologist, educator; b. Shanghai, Nov. 29, 1946; d. Nathan M. and Elizabeth (Little) Shippee; m. Robert J. Boylan, Oct. 2, 1971; children: Elizabeth B., Emily A. AB, Wellesley Coll., 1968; PhD, Cornell U., 1972. Postdoctoral fellow U. Rochester (N.Y.) Sch. Medicine, 1972-73; asst. prof. Queens Coll. CUNY, Flushing, 1973-78, assoc. prof., 1978-82, prof. biology, 1983-95, acting asst. provost, 1988-89, asst. provost, 1989-90, assoc. provost, 1990-92; acting provost Queens Coll. CUNY, Flushing, 1992-93; assoc. provost acad. programs and planning Queens Coll., Flushing, 1994-95; provost and dean of faculty Barnard Coll., N.Y.C., 1995—, prof. biology, 1995—. Chmn. Queens Coll. Acad. Senate, 1985-88; mem. grad. faculty Grad. Ctr. CUNY, N.Y.C., 1977-95; vis. investigator Sloan-Kettering Inst. Cancer Rsch., N.Y.C., 1979-80; trustee N.Y. Met. Ref. and Rsch. Libr. Agy., Manhattan, 1989-97, chmn. fin. com. 1991-97; co-chmn. bd. trustees study com. on secondary edn. CUNY, 1987-88, co-chair vice chancellor's task force on sci., engring., tech. and math., 1988-89; panelist NSF grad. fellowship program, 1992-93; cons. to Nat. Cancer Inst., N.J. Commn. on Cancer Rsch., Endocrine Soc.; mem. breast cancer task force NCI, 1980-84; mem. adv. com. Am. Cancer Soc., 1981-85; Am. Coun. Edn. fellow Pace U., 1993-94; commr. Commn. on Higher Edn., Mid. States Assn. Colls. and Schs., 1999—. Contbr. and reviewer articles to profl. publs.; patentee in field. Grantee Nat. Cancer Inst., 1975-83, Am. Inst. Cancer Rsch., 1987-90, Am. Fedn. Aging Rsch., 1988-89. Mem. AAAS, AAHE, Soc. Devel. Biology, Am. Assn. Cancer Rsch., N.Y. Acad. Scis., Sigma Xi. Office: Barnard Coll Office of Provost 3009 Broadway New York NY 10027-6501

BOYLE, ANNE C. state commissioner; b. Omaha, Dec. 22, 1942; m. Mike Boyle; children: Maureen, Michael, James, Patrick, Margaret. Chmn., co-chmn. various polit. campaigns, Omaha, 1974-78; office coord. for U.S. Senator James Exon., 1979-81; corp. and polit. fundraiser, 1983-85, 88; campaign mgr. pub. rels. firm, Omaha, 1990-91; pres. Universal Rev. Svcs., Omaha, 1992—; mem. Nebr. Pub. Svc. Commn., Lincoln, 1996—. Active Clinton for Pres. Campaign, organizer fund raisers, host open house, Omaha, 1992; cons., lobbyist, 1994-95. Former nat. committeewoman Nebr. Young Dems.; chmn. Douglas County Dem. Ctrl. Com.; mem. jud. nominating com. for Douglas County Juvenile Ct.; chmn. inaugural ball invitation com. for gov. of Nebr., 1982; co-chmn. Midwestern Govs. Conf., 1984, Jefferson-Jackson Day Dinner, 1976, 82; del. Dem. Nat. Conv., 1988, 92, 96; mem. Nebr. Rev. com. for Fed. Appts. to U.S. Atty., U.S. Marshall and 8th Dist. Ct. Appeals Fed. Judgeship, 1993-95; mem. Nebr. Dem. Ctrl. Com., [illegible]. Coun. on Homeless, President's Adv. Com. on Arts, 1995; Nebr. authorized rep. '96 Clinton-Gore Campaign; Bd. dirs. Bemis Ctr. for Contemporary Arts, Omaha; chmn. Nebr. Dem. Party, 1999-2001. Mem. Nat. Assn. Regulatory Utility Commrs. and Mid-Am. Regulatory Commrs. Democrat. Office: PO Box 94927 Lincoln NE 68509-4927

BOYLE, ANTONIA BARNES, electronic learning consultant, writer; b. Detroit, May 21, 1939; d. James Merriam and Florence (Maiullo) B.; 1 child, Caitlin Merriam. BS in Speech, Northwestern U., 1962. Staff announcer WEFM-FM, Chgo., 1975-78; pres. Boyle Communications, Chgo., 1978-85; exec. producer Nightingale-Conant Corp., Chgo., 1985-90, Cassette Prodns. Unltd., Irwindale, Calif., 1990-92; pres. Antonia Boyle & Co., 1992—; v.p. content acquisition Youachieve.com, Inc., 1997—. Bd. dirs. WNUR-FM Alumni, Northwestern U., Evanston, Ill. Author: The Optimal You, 1990, Taping Yourself Seriously, 1991; co-author: (with Jay Gordon) Good Food Today, Great Kids Tomorrow, 1994 (with Scott McKain) Just Say Yes, 1994, (with William McCurry) Guerrilla Managing for the Imaging Industry, 1997. Chmn., bd. dirs. Horizons for the Blind, Chgo., 1984. Mem. Am. Fedn. Radio, TV Artists, Com.100 Northwestern U., NU Club, San Francisco Office: Youachieve dot com Inc 236 W Portal Ave San Francisco CA 94127-1423 Home: 3119A Lake Ave Wilmette IL 60091-1157 E-mail: aboyleco@earthlink.com., tboyle@youachieve.com.

BOYLE, BARBARA DORMAN, motion picture company executive; b. N.Y.C., Aug. 11, 1935; d. William and Edith (Kleiman) Dorman; m. Kevin Boyle, Nov. 26, 1960; children: David Eric, Paul Coleman. BA in English with honors, U. Calif., Berkeley, 1957; JD, UCLA, 1960. Bar: Calif. 1961, N.Y. 1964, U.S. Supreme Ct. 1964. Atty. bus. affairs dept, corp. asst. sec. Am. Internat. Pictures, L.A., 1960-65; ptnr. Cohen & Boyle, L.A., 1967-74; exec. v.p., gen. counsel, chief op. officer New World Pictures, L.A., 1974-82; sr. v.p. prodn. Orion Pictures Corp., L.A., 1982-85; exec. v.p. prodn. RKO Pictures, L.A., 1986-87; pres. Sovereign Pictures, Inc., L.A., 1988-92, Boyle and Taylor Prodns., 1993-99, Valhalla Motion Pictures, L.A., 2000—03; chair film, TV and digital media dept. UCLA, 2003—. Lectr. in field. Exec. prodr. (film) Eight Men Out, 1987, Bottle Rocket, 1995, Campus Man; prodr. (films) Mrs. Munck, 1995, Phenomenon, 1996, Instinct, 1999; exec. prodr. The Hi Line, 1998. Bd. dirs. UCLA Law Fund Com., L.A. Women's Campaign Fund; pres. Ind. Feature Project/West; founding mem. entertainment adv. coun. sch. law UCLA, co-chmn. 1979-80. Named UCLA Law Sch. Alumni of Yr, 1999, Women in Film Crystal award, 2000. Mem. Acad. Motion Picture Arts and Scis. (exec. com.), Acad. TV Arts and Scis. (exec. com.), Women in Film (pres. 1977-78), Hollywood Women's Polit. Com., Calif. Bar Assn., N.Y. State Bar Assn. Office: UCLA Sch of Theater Film & TV 203 E Melnitz Box 951622 Los Angeles CA 90095-1622 E-mail: boyle@tft.ucla.edu.

BOYLE, GERTRUDE, sportswear company executive; b. Augsberg, Germany, 1924; came to U.S., 1938; d. Paul and Marie Lanfrom; m. Neil Boyle, 1948; children: Tim, Kathy, Sally. BA in Sociology, Univ. Ariz., 1947. Pres., CEO Columbia Sportswear Co., Portland, Oreg., 1970-88, CEO, 1988-94, chmn. bd., 1994—. Named one of Best Mgrs. Bus. Week Mag., 1994, Am.'s Top 50 Women Bus. Owners Working Woman mag., Woman of Yr. Oreg. chpt. Women's Forum, 1987. Office: Columbia Sportswear Co 14375 NW Science Park Dr Portland OR 97229-5418

BOYLE, JANE J. lawyer; b. Sharon, Pa., Dec. 15, 1954; BS, U. of Tex., Austin, 1977; JD, So Meth. U., Dallas, 1981. Asst. dist. atty. Dist. Atty.'s Office, 1981-87; asst. U.S. atty. U.S. Dist. Ct. (no. dist.) Tex., 1987-90, magistrate judge U.S., 1990—2002, U.S. atty., 2003—. Office: 1100 Commerce St 3d Fl Dallas TX 75242-1027

BOYLE, KAMMER, estate planner, financial analyst; b. New Orleans, June 17, 1946; d. Benjamin Franklin and Ethel Clair (Kammer) B.; m. Edward Turner Barfield, July 23, 1966 (div. 1975); children: Darren Barfield, Meloe Barfield. BS in Mgmt. magna cum laude, U. West Fla., 1976; PhD in Indsl./Organizational Psychology, U. Tenn., 1982. Lic. psychologist, Ohio, Tenn.; reg. securities rep. InterSecurities, Inc., Nat Assn. Securities Dealers. Pvt. practice mgmt. psychology, Knoxville, 1978-81; tchg. and rsch. asst. U. Tenn., Knoxville, 1977-81; mgmt. trainer U.S. State Dept., Washington, 1978; cons. PRADCO, Cleve., 1982-83; pres., cons. Mgmt. and Assessment Svcs., Inc., Cleve., 1983-90; pres. Kammer Investment Co., Cleve., 1989-96; fin. advisor O'Donnell Securities Corp., Cleve., 1997-98. Registered securities prin., investment advisor rep. and retirement specialist Wealth Charter Group of InterSecurities, Inc., 1998-. Mem. editl. rev. bd. Jour. of Managerial Issues, 1987; author and presenter ann. Conf. APA, 1980, Southeastern Psychol. Conf., 1979, ann. Conf. Soc. Indsl./Orgnl. Psychologists, 1987, ann. conf. Am. Soc. Tng. and Devel., 1988. Mem. Jr. League Am., Pensacola, Fla., 1970-75; treas. Bar Aux., Pensacola, 1971. Recipient Capital Gifts Stipend U. Tenn., 1976-80; Walter Bonham fellow, 1980-81. Mem. APA, Cleve. Psychol. Assn., Orgn. Devel. Inst., Acad. of Mgmt., Soc. Advancement Mgmt. (pres. 1974-75), Am. Soc. Tng. and Devel. (chpt. rep. career devel. 1984-86), Cleve. Psychol. Assn. (bd. dirs. 1987-88), Real Estate Investor's Assn. (Cleve., trustee/sec. 1992-94), Mensa. Office: Wealth Charter Group Ste 200 6100 Oak Tree Blvd Independence OH 44131

BOYLE, LARA FLYNN, actress; b. Davenport, IA, Mar. 24, 1970; Actress: appeared in films made for TV and for movie house distbn.: Amerika, 1987, Poltergeist III, 1988, Terror on Highway 91, 1989, How I Got into College, 1989, The Preppie Murder, 1989, The Rookie, 1990, Mobsters, 1991, Wayne's World, 1992, Where the Day Takes You, 1992, The Temp., 1993, Three of Hearts, 1993, Red Rock West, 1993, Threesome, 1994, Baby's Day Out, 1994, The Road to Wellville, 1994, Three IFS and a Maybe, 1996, Dogwater, 1997, Twin Peaks, 1989, Dead Poets Society, 1989, Men in Black II, 2002; TV appearances include The Practice, 1997-; host Saturday Night Live, 2001. Office: Internat Creative Mgmt c/o Chris Andrews 8942 Wilshire Blvd Beverly Hills CA 90211-1934

BOYLE, PATRICIA JEAN, retired state supreme court justice; b. Detroit, Mar. 31, 1937; Student, U. Mich., 1955-57; BA, JD, Wayne State U., 1963. Bar: Mich. Practice law with Kenneth Davies, Detroit, 1963; law clk. to U.S. Dist. judge, 1963-64; asst. U.S. atty., Detroit, 1964-68; asst. pros. atty. Wayne County, dir. research, tng. and appeals, 1969-74; Recorders Ct. judge City of Detroit, 1976-78; U.S. dist. judge Eastern Dist. Mich., Detroit, 1978-83; assoc. justice Mich. Supreme Ct., Detroit, 1983-98, ret., 1999. Active Women's Rape Crisis Task Force, Vols. of Am. Named Feminist of Year Detroit chpt. NOW, 1978; recipient Outstanding Achievement award Pros. Attys. Assn. Mich., 1978, 98, Mich. Women's Hall of Fame award, 1986, Law Day award ABA, 1998, Champion of Justice award State Bar Mich., 1998. Mem. Women Lawyers Assn. Mich., Fed. Bar Assn., Mich. Bar Assn., Detroit Bar Assn., Wayne State U. Law Alumni Assn. (Disting. Alumni award 1979) Avocation: reading. Address: 10765 Oxbow Lake Shore Dr White Lake MI 48386

BOYLES, ELIZABETH KELLEY, psychologist, educator; b. Charlotte, N.C., Oct. 10, 1962; d. Jerry Thomas and Peggy Sue (Curd) Kelley. BA in Psychology with honors, U. N.C., Chapel Hill, 1984; MS in Sch. Psychology, Winthrop U., 1987, SSP in Sch. Psychology, 1988; PhD in Sch. Psychology, U. N.C., Chapel Hill, 1999. Nat. cert. sch. psychologist Nat. Assn. Sch. Psychologists, lic. sch. psychologist W.Va., N.C. Student svcs. specialist Charlotte-Mecklenburg Schs., Charlotte, NC, 1988—94; acad. cons., learning disabilities svcs. U. N.C., Chapel Hill, 1996—97, sch. psychology program mgr., 1997—98, vis. prof., 1999—2000; adj. faculty Alliance C.C., Graham, NC, 1995—2000; program dir., prof. sch. psychology Marshall U. Grad. Coll., South Charleston, W.Va., 2000—. Contbr. articles to profl. publs., chapters to books. Mem.: APA, W.Va. Sch. Psychologists Assn. (exec. bd. 2000—), Nat. Assn. Sch. Psychologists (program reviewer 2000—). Avocations: reading, quilting, gardening. Office: Marshall U Grad Coll 100 Angus E Peyton Dr South Charleston WV 25303-1600 E-mail: boyles@marshall.edu.

BOYSEN, MELICENT PEARL, finance company executive; b. Houston, Dec. 1, 1943; d. William Thomas and Mildred Pearl (Walker) Richardson; m. Stephen M. Boysen, Sept. 10, 1961 (dec. 1973); children: Marshella, Stephanie, Stephen. Student, Cen. Mo. State, 1973-75. Owner, pres. Boysen Enterprises, Kansas City, Mo., 1973-93; fin. cons., underwriter New Eng. Life Ins. Co., Kansas City, 1978-81; owner, pres. Boysen Agri-Svcs., Kansas City, 1984-94; pres. Boysen & Assocs., Inc., Kansas City, 1987—; stockholder, pres. Am. Crumb Rubber, Inc., Kansas City, 1996—; co-owner, v.p. Initiatives Worldwide, Inc., Kansas City, 2002—. Cons. San Luis Rey (Calif.) Tribal Water Authority, Wind River (Wyo.) Reservation, Cheyenne River (S.D.) Sioux, Iroquois Nations (N.Y.), 1983—; founding bd. dirs., pres. Am. Indian Youth Orgn., Visible Horizons, 1987—. Founding bd. dirs. Rose Brooks Ctr. Battered Women, Kansas City, 1979-87, treas., 1979-81; exec. dir. The Flame Spirit Run, 1992; citationist, 1993; mem. Pres.'s Vol. Action Awards Program; mem. Pres.'s Bus. Adv. Coun., 2001. Recipient Women of Conscience award Panel Am. Women of Greater Kansas City. Mem. DAR, Kans. C. of C. and Industry, Kansas City C. of C. Methodist. Avocations: stamp collecting, sports cars. Office: Boysen & Assocs 4112 Pennsylvania Ave Ste 202 Kansas City MO 64111-3057 E-mail: mboysen@boysencompanies.com.

BOZA, CLARA BRIZEIDA, marketing professional; b. Havana, Cuba, Apr. 18, 1952; came to U.S., 1957; d. Eduardo Otmaro and Hubedia Marta (Garcia) B. BA in English summa cum laude, Barry Coll., 1973, MA in Comm. Media, 1988. Program adminstr. Dade County Coun. Arts and Scis., Miami, Fla., 1980-82; dir. program devel. Nat. Found. for Advancement in Arts, Miami, 1982-85; exec. dir. Bus. Vols. for Arts/Miami, 1985-86; legal asst. supr. Steel Hector & Davis, Miami, 1978-80, dir. mktg., 1986-96; dir. practice devel. Arnold & Porter, Washington, 1996-98; chief mktg. officer Kirkpatrick & Lockhart, LLP, Washington, 1998—. S.E. regional cons. Arts and Bus. Coun., N.Y.C., 1986-88; panelist and spkr. various local, state and nat. orgns. and assns. Recipient ednl. scholarship Barry Coll., Miami, 1969-73, Fla. Bd. Regents, 1969-73. Mem. ABA (mem. commn. on advt. 1994-97), Legal Mktg. Assn. (bd. dirs. and officer 1993, 94, 96, bd. dirs. Mid-Atlantic chpt. 1997-99), Am. Mktg. Assn. (bd. dirs. Miami chpt. 1992-96), Fla. Bar (standing com. on advt. 1993-96). Office: Kirkpatrick & Lockhart 1800 Massachusetts Ave NW Washington DC 20036-1806

BRAASCH, BARBARA LYNN, banker, consultant; b. Santa Monica, Calif., Apr. 14, 1958; d. C. Duane and René Barbara (Siegel) B. Student, Golden Gate U., 1989-91. Cert. Compensation Professional, 1999. Ops. officer Bank of Am., Fresno, Calif., 1976-87; v.p., mgr. Wells Fargo Bank, San Fransisco, 1987-96; v.p., mgr. fin. MIS Bank of Am., San Fransisco, 1996-2000, catalyst bus. cons., owner, 2000—; mgr. investment sys.; mgr. devel. Wells Fargo Bank, 2000—. Mentor Jr. Achievement, L.A., 1980-83. 1st class scout Girl Scouts Am., 1976, leader, asst. leader, 1976-79, 84-87; vol. Open Hand, San Francisco, 1991-92, San Francisco AIDS Found., various women's groups, 1989—. Mem. Am. Compensation Assn., Bay Area Compensation Assn., Fin. Tech. Forum. Democrat. Jewish. Avocations: music, movies, theatre. Office: Wells Capital Mgmt 525 Market St 10 B Fl San Francisco CA 94105 E-mail: braascba@wellscap.com.

BRABEC, ROSEMARY JEAN, retail executive; b. St. Paul, Apr. 5, 1951; d. Peter Michael and Mary Jane (Nigro) Jacovitch; m. Loren W. Brabec, Sept. 16, 1972; children: Brenda Marie, Daniel Joseph. BS in Elem. Edn., St. Cloud State U., 1973. Tchr. Ind. Sch. Dist. 314, Braham, Minn., 1975-78; owner, mgr. Rosemary's Quilts and Baskets, Braham, 1988-97. Dir. Community Edn. Adv. Coun., Braham, 1978-95, chmn., 1992-95. Designer quilt block representing Minn. div. AAUW for display at Internat. Fedn. Univ. Women conv., Calif. Chmn. P.I.C.K. Immunization Clinic, Braham, 1978-85; vol. driver coord. Home Delivered Meals, Braham, 1984—; vol. coord. Com. to Build Robert Leathers Playground, Braham, 1985; mem. Braham City Park Bd., 2001—, chmn., 2002–. Mem. AAUW (sec.Cambridge Area Branch, 1985-87, 98-99, v.p. 1987-88, historian 1997-98, pres. 1999-2002), Minn. Quilters.

BRABENEC, STACEY MARIE, retail buyer; b. Detroit, Mich., Nov. 1, 1977; d. Frank Joseph and Kathy Ann Brabenec; m. Kevin Richard Etue, Aug. 0, 2003. BBA, Western Mich. U., 1995—99. Cert. Production and Inventory Management Am. Prodn. and Inventory Control Soc. (APICS), 2001. Buyer Tektronix, Inc., Portland, Oreg., 1999—2000; project mgr. Solectron Tech., Inc., Charlotte, NC, 2000—03; sr. buyer Ford Motor Co., Dearborn, Mich., 2003—. Vol. Am. Diabetes Assn., Kalamazoo, Mich., 1996. Recipient Disting. Leadership award, Western Mich. U., 1999; Academic scholarship, 1995. Mem.: Am. Prodn. and Inventory Control Soc., Alpha Gamma Delta Internat. Frat. (life; alumni club treas. 2001). Personal E-mail: sbrabene@ford.com. E-mail: sbrabene@ford.com.

BRACCO, LORRAINE, actress; b. Bklyn., Oct. 2, 1954; m. Harvey Keitel, 1982 (div. 1993); 1 child, Stella Keitel ; m. Edward James Olmos, Jan. 28, 1994 (div. 2002); 1 child, Margaux Guerard. Studied, Actors Studio; studied with Stella Adler, Ernie Martin, John Strasberg. Model in Europe. Films include The Pick-Up Artist, 1987, Someone to Watch Over Me, 1987, Sing, 1989, The Dream Team, 1989, Goodfellas, 1990 (Acad. award nominee for best supporting actress 1990, LA Film Critics Assoc. award for best sup. actress, 1990), Talent for the Game, 1991, Switch, 1991, Medicine Man, 1992, Radio Flyer, 1992, Traces of Red, 1992, (Showtime movie) Scam, 1993, Being Human, 1994, Even Cowgirls Get the Blues, 1994, The Basketball Diaries, 1995, Hackers, 1995, Les Menteurs, 1996, Ladies Room, 1999, Tangled, 2000, Your Aura is Throbbing, 2000, Riding in Cars With Boys, 2001, Tangled, 2001, Death of a Dynasty, 2003, Max and Grace, 2004; on TV in Getting Gotti, 1996, Lifeline, 1996, The Taking of Pelham One Two Three, 1998, Sex in our Century, 2001; (TV Series) The Sopranos, 1999- (SAG award for Outstanding Performance by an Ensemble in a Drama Series, 2000); off-Broadway play Goose and Tom-Tom; Broadway play The Graduate, 2002. Mem.: bd. of dir. Riverkeeper, NY Council for the Humanities. Office: Creative Artists Agy Inc 9830 Wilshire Blvd Beverly Hills CA 90212

BRACERAS, JENNIFER C. lawyer; BA Phi Beta Kappa, Magna Cum Laude, U. Mass., 1989; JD cum laude, Harvard Law Sch., 1994. Bar: Mass., Hispanic Nat. Atty. Ropes & Gray, Boston, 1996—2000; law clerk to the Hon. Ralph K. Winter, US Court of Appeals 2nd Circuit, 1995—96, to the Hon. William G. Young, US Dist Court, Dist Mass., 1994—95; staff asst. to Chief of Staff, VP Dan Quayle. Contbr. articles weekly column The Boston Globe, various profl. jours. Grantee Charles Hamilton Houston, Harvard Law Sch., 2000—01. Mem.: Nat. Adv. Bd of Indep. Women's Forum, Civil Rights Practice Group of Federalist Soc. Law & Pub. Policies Studies. Office: 624 9th St NW Washington DC 20425

BRACEY, COOKIE FRANCES LEE, minister; b. Phila., Mar. 14, 1945; d. John Daniels and Evelyn (Jarvis) Bracey. B in Social Work, Temple U., 1983; MDiv, Wesley Theol. Sem., 1990. Administrv. asst. United Meth. Ch., Phila., 1963—66, parish cmty. devel., 1984—86, local pastor Catonsville, Ellicott City, Md., 1986—90; chaplain Meth. Hosp., Phila., 1990—; pastor

St. Luke Snyder Ave United Meth. Ch., Phila., 1990—92, St. Matthews United Meth. Ch., Trevose, Pa., 1992—99; sr. pastor, dir. after sch. program Mt. Carmel United Meth. Ch., 1999—; chaplain Vet. Affairs Med. Ctr., Phila., 2003; vol. chaplain Battleship New Jersey, 2004, Am. Red Cross, 2004. Missionary, Brazil, 1988, Costa Rica, 1989, Dominican Republic, 1992, Zim Babwe, Africa, 1998, El Salvador, 1998; pastor St. Matthews United Meth. Ch., Trevose, Pa., 1992; Meth. mission tour, London, 1992, Israel, 1994; adj. faculty Ea. Bapt. Theol. Sem., Wynnewood, Pa., 1994—, Henry George Sch., Phila., 1996—; mem. faculty Phila. Sch. Devel. Mins., 1997, fac. mem. Sch. of Devel. Ministries, 1997; vol. reading specialist Howe Elem. Sch., Phila., Rowen Elem. Sch., Phila., 2001; supr. Pioneers Internat., Inc., Phila., 2001; chaplain VA Med. Ctr., Phila., 2003. Mem. Multi-Cultural Task Force, Phila. 1980, Victims and Crime Task Force, Phila. Ministers Law Enforcement Support Unit, Phila. Cmty. Assistance Network; del. World Meth. Conf., Rio Janero, Brazil, 1996; chaplain CAP Aux. USAF, 1996—, Phila. Prison Sys., 1996—; mem. Phila. Mayor's Commn. on Literacy, World Affairs Coun. of Phila., Spell Binders Storytellers; missionary Zimbabwe, Africa, 1998; faculty Phila. Sch. of Developing Ministries, 1997; bd. dirs. Archives and History United Meth. Ch., 1997; del. Clergywoman Convocation, Atlanta, 1997, San Diego, 2002; cert. mentor for supr. for ministry candidates; del. Billy Graham Conv., Amsterdam, 2000, World Meth. Conf., Brighton, Eng., 2001; bd. dirs. Youth Build Charter Sch. of Phila., 1999-; bd. mem. Youth Build, 2004, Met. Christian Coun. Phila., Experience Corps, 2004; participant Ministerial Exch. Program, 2004. Recipient Outstanding Clergywoman award Nat. Assn. Clergywomen, 1990, Peace & Justice award Ch. Women United, 1992, Ministry award Harry Hosier United Meth. Ch., 1992, Preacher of Yr. award, 1998. Mem. AAUW, Am. Assn. Christian Counselors, Temple Univ. Soc. Adminstrn. Alumni Assn., Asian Am. Youth Assn., Nat. Fellowship Local, Black United Meth. Preachers (v.p.), Black Clergy Phila. and Vicinity (corr. sec.), Phila. Police Clergy, Coalition Prison Evangelists, Good Shepherd Mediation Program, Chaplaincy Coalition of Greater Phila., Wesley Theol. Sem. Alumni Assn., Mil. Chaplains Assn. Democrat. Avocations: music, opera, historical researcher, board games, traveling. Home: 337 Christian St Apt 3 Philadelphia PA 19147-3219 Address: 5909 North Park Ave Philadelphia PA 19141

BRACKEN, PEG, writer; b. Filer, Idaho, Feb. 25, 1918; d. John Lewis and Ruth (McQuesten) B.; m. John Hamilton Ohman, June 15, 1991; 1 child from previous marriage, Johanna Bracken. AB, Antioch Coll., 1940. Author: The I Hate to Cook Book, 1960, The I Hate to Housekeep Book, 1962, I Try to Behave Myself, 1963, Peg Bracken's Appendix to The I Hate to Cook Book, 1966, I Didn't Come Here to Argue, 1969, But I Wouldn't Have Missed It for the World, 1973, The I Hate to Cook Almanack - A Book of Days, 1976, A Window Over the Sink, 1981, The Compleat I Hate to Cookbook, 1986, On Getting Old for the First Time, 1996.

BRACKENRIDGE, N. LYNN, not-for-profit developer; b. Youngstown, Ohio, Sept. 9, 1957; d. John Bruce Brackenridge and Mary Ann Rossi; m. Harry Lee Carrico, July 1, 1994. BA, Lawrence U., 1978; MS, Georgetown U., 1980. Tchg. asst. Georgetown U., Washington, 1979-81, admissions officer, 1984-85, editor, writer devel., 1985-87, asst. dir. devel., 1987-89; dir. devel. Cath. Charities U.S.A., Washington, 1989-91, Johns Hopkins U. Bologna (Italy) Ctr., 1991-92; dir. devel. and pub. rels. Nat. Ctr. for State Cts., Williamsburg, Va., 1993-97; v.p. for devel. Gateway Homes Greater Richmond (Va.), Inc., 1998-99, pres., 1999—. Vol. Richmond Ballet, 1990-96, Leukemia Soc. Am., Hampton Va. 1996—; bd. dirs. Nat. Alliance for Mentally Ill (Va. chap.), 2000-03, ChesterField Alternatives Inc., 2000—. Georgetown U. fellow, 1979-81; recipient diplome d'etudes Inst. d'Etudes Francaises de Touraine, 1976. Mem. Nat. Soc. Fund Raising Execs. (cert. fund raising exec., chmn. program com., pres. 1997). Democrat. Avocations: flying small aircraft, running, reading, films, languages. Home: 9303 Cragmont Dr Richmond VA 23229-7610 Office: Gateway Homes Greater Richmond Inc PO Box 11303 Richmond VA 23230-1303 E-mail: lbrackenridge@gatewayhomes.org.

BRADDOCK, NONNIE CLARKE, religious organization administrator; b. Rye, N.Y. d. Peter Benedict and Nora Bridget (Devins) Clarke; m. Eugene Stephen Braddock, Sept. 7, 1962; children: Stephen E., Brian B., Glenn C. Adminstr. Beaver Farm Retreat and Conf. Ctr., Yorktown Heights, N.Y.; deputy city clk. City of Rye, N.Y. Founder, pres. Celebrations; dir Security Enforcement Bur.; part-time therapist; with Marriage Encounter movement, co-founder, chmn. bd., team leader No. Westchester-Putnam (N.Y.) Interfaith Marriage Encounter, 1981-87. Vol. Boy Scouts Am., numerous polit. orgns. and cmty. groups, 1970—; chair Warmth for Christmas clothing drive, N.Y.C. shelters; facilitator mil. family support group; organizer food collections for needy, Heart to Heart, coord. Angel Fund; organizer, sponsor Weekly Cable TV program featuring peace, 1991; bd. dirs. Homeless Shelter; adv. com. Comty. Mem. Interfaith Clergy Coun. Rite Christian Initiation for Adults, Right to Life, North Am. Retreat Dirs. Assns., Pax Christi Metro, Westchester Assn. Vol. Adminstrs., Feminists for Life, Fedn. Christian Ministries, Internat. Platform Assn. Avocations: music, travel, reading. Office: Beaver Farm Retreat Ctr Underhill Ave Yorktown Heights NY 10598

BRADEN, BETTY JANE, legal association administrator; b. Sheboygan, Wis., Feb. 5, 1943; d. Otto Frank and Betty Donna (Beers) Huettner; children: Jennifer Tindall, Rebecca Leigh; m. Berwyn Bartow Braden, Nov. 5, 1983. BS, U. Wis., 1965. Cert. elem. tchr., Wis. Tchr. Madison (Wis.) Met. Sch. Dist., 1965-70, 71-72, sub. tchr., 1972-75; adminstrv. asst. ATS-CLE State Bar Wis., Madison, 1978, adminstrv. asst. Advanced Tng. Seminars-Continuing Legal Edn., 1979, coordinator, 1980, adminstr. coordinator, 1980-84, adminstrv. dir., 1984-87, dir. adminstrm., bar svcs., membership, 1987—; mem. rels. and pub. svcs. dir. Legal Edn., 1992—. Speaker Bar Leadership Inst. of ABA. Mem.: LWV, Nat. Assn. Bar Execs. (program chair 1995—96, sec. 1996—98, v.p. 1998—99, pres. elect 1999—2000, pres. 2000—01), Wis. Soc. of Assn. Execs., Am. Soc. of Assn. Execs., Am. Soc. for Personnel Adminstrn., Am. Mgmt. Assn., Adminstrv. Mgmt. Soc., Meeting Planners Internat. (sec. Wis. chpt. 1981—82, pres. 1982—83). Avocations: tennis, scuba diving, reading, skiing. Home: 41 Golf Pkwy Madison WI 53704-7003 Office: State Bar of Wis 5302 Eastpark Blvd Madison WI 53718-2101

BRADEN, MARTHA BROOKE, concert pianist, educator; b. Sturgis, Mich., July 19, 1936; d. Frederick Richard and Laura Clemens (Brooke) B.; m. Edmund Sanford Jones, Mar. 14, 1959 (div. Aug. 1983); children: Carrie Brooke, David Sanford, Christopher Braden, Charles Clemens, Mary Evelyn Reilley. Studied with Frances Oman Clark, Kalamazoo, 1942-60; student, Kalamazoo Coll., 1954-55; MusB, Westminster Choir Coll., Princeton, N.J., 1959 studied with Dr. Julius Hereford, N.Y.C., 1957-59; studied with, David Kraehenbuehl, Princeton, 1959-61, 84-97, Erno Balogh, Washington, 1976-79, Ross Lee Finney, N.Y.C., 1987-88, Madame Ming Tcherepin, 1979-91, Madeline Bruser, 1999-2000. Cert. directress Montessori primary edn. ages 2 1/2 to 6 Washington Montessori Inst.; cert. of attendance advanced course in Montessori edn. ages 6-12 State Ctr. for Montessori Studies, Bergamo, Italy. Piano tchr. Frances Clark Studios, Kalamazoo, 1951-54; piano faculty piano and prep. depts. Westminster Choir Coll., Princeton, 1956-60; founding faculty mem. New Sch. for Music Study, Princeton, 1960-61; co-founder, Montessori primary dir. Hope Montessori Sch., Annandale, Va., 1963-68; co-founder New City Montessori Sch., Washington, 1969-74; piano faculty New Sch. for Music Study, Princeton, 1978-80; piano tchr./coach Braden Piano Studio, Washington, 1975-78, N.Y.C., 1979—. Artistic dir. The David Kraehenbuehl Soc., 2001—. Featured artist Kalamazoo Symphony, South Bend (Ind.) Symphony, 1954; recitalist (with Doris Martin) Frances Clark Piano Workshops for Piano Tchrs., nationwide, summers 1948-58; N.Y. debut solo recital Carnegie Recital Hall, 1977, Lincoln Ctr. debut solo recital Alice Tully Hall,

1980; solo recitals include Carnegie Recital Hall, N.Y.C., 1979, Abraham Goodman House, N.Y.C., 1981, Merkin Concert Hall, N.Y.C., 1984, 85, NYU Maison Francaise, 1996; artist roster Circum-Arts Found., Inc., 1999—; (recs.) Ross Lee Finney, 1988, Alexander Tcherepin, 2002, David Kraehenbuehl, 2000, Pocketful of Music, 2003; author, pub.: (with Nancy M. Connors) David Kraehenbuehl, American Composer, 2000; editor, pub.: The Collected Works for Solo Piano by David Kraehenbuehl, 1999, Pocketful of Music, 2003; contbr. articles to Piano and Keyboard, Keyboard Companion. Performer benefit concerts UN Internat. Sch., N.Y. St. Luke's Sch., N.Y., 1999—, Kent Pl. Sch., N.J., 2002. Recipient 2d place award Bartok-Kabalevsky Internat. Piano Competition, Radford Coll., 1992; recipient Tcherepin award Ibla Internat. Piano Competition, Ragusa, Italy, 1993; grantee concert and tchg. tour of mainland China, Ministry of Culture and Conservatories of Music/The Tcherepnin Soc., 1982, Irving S. Gilmore Found., 1987, Warren Studios, 1998.. Mem.: MENC, Montessori Internat., Nat. Assn. for Music Edn., Music Tchrs. Nat. Assn. Avocations: family, friends, forests. Office: Martha Braden Studio 780 W End Ave Apt 7A New York NY 10025-5548 E-mail: martha@marthabraden.com.

BRADEN, SUSAN GERTRUDE, federal judge, lawyer, consultant; b. Youngstown, Ohio, Nov. 8, 1948; d. Orrin S. and Ernestine (Everett) B.; m. Thomas M. Susman, May 31, 1981; 1 child, Daily Lacey; stepchildren: Tara, Shana, Micah. BA, Case Western Res. U., 1970, JD, 1973. Bar: U.S. Supreme Ct. 1983, U.S. Dist. Ct. (no. dist) Ohio 1974, U.S. Dist. Ct. (ea. dist.) Mich. 1978, U.S. Supreme Ct. 1980, U.S. Dist. Ct. D.C. 1981, U.S. Dist. Ct. Md. 1985. Trial atty. antitrust div. Dept. of Justice, Cleve., 1973-78, sr. trial atty. Washington, 1978-80; sr. advisor FTC, Washington, 1980-83, spl. counsel, asst., 1983-85; former ptnr. Porter, Wright, Morris & Arthur, Washington; judge U.S. Ct. Fed. Claims, Washington, 2003—. Cons. Adminstrv. Conf. U.S., Washington, 1985—, spl. asst. atty. gen., State of Ala., 1990. Fed. Bar Assn. Disting. Service award, 1984. Mem. ABA, Fed. Bar Assn., D.C. Women's Bar Assn., Women in Govt. Relations., Case Western Res. Alumni Assn. (v.p. 1985-86). Republican. Methodist. Office: US Ct Fed Claims 717 Madison Pl NW Washington DC 20005

BRADFORD, ANNE HARDEN, director; b. Wilkinsburg, Pa., May 14, 1936; d. Boyd Harden and Ruth (Holmes); m. William Dalton Bradford, July 8, 1961; children: Scott Harden, Lisa Graham. AB, Randolph-Macon Woman's Coll., 1958. Rsch. asst. Lemuel Shattuck Hosp., Boston, 1958—65; reader, interviewer Office Undergrad. Admissions Duke U., Durham, NC, 1980—. Contbr. articles to profl. jours. Bd. trustees Providence Meml. Assn., Graham, NC, 1974—77, bd. chmn., 1975—76; pres. Hope Valley Garden Club, Durham, 1970—72, 1987—88, Durham-Orange County Med. Aux., 1978—79, Durham Coun. Garden Clubs, 1989—90; bd. dirs. Vol. Ctr. Greater Durham, 1987—94, pres., 1991—93; chmn. Debutante Ball Soc. Durham, 1995; bd. visitors Camp Sea Gull/Seafarer YMCA, Arapahoe, NC, 2001—; bd. govs. Elizabethan Gardens, Manteo, NC, 2002—. Named Vol. of Yr., Camp Sea Gull/Seafarer, 2002; recipient Dame, Hospitaller Order St. John of Jerusalem, 1997. Mem.: Durham Coun. Garden Clubs (life; pres. 1989—90). Avocations: tennis, painting, sewing, gardening, decorating. Home: 3724 Hope Valley Rd Durham NC 27707*

BRADFORD, BARBARA REED, lawyer; b. Cleve., June 13, 1948; d. William Cochran and Martha Lucile (Horn) B.; m. Warren Neil Davis, Oct. 9, 1976 (div. 1989); m. S. Jack Odell, Dec. 12, 1991. BA, Pitzer Coll., 1970; JD, Georgetown U., 1975, MBA, 1985. Bar: N.Y. 1976, D.C. 1976. Staff asst. Sen. Edward M. Kennedy, Washington, 1970-71; assoc. Breed, Abbott & Morgan, N.Y. 1975-76; atty. United Mine Workers Law Firm, Washington 1976-78; atty. AID, Washington, 1978-83; pres. Georgetown Export Trading, Inc., Washington, 1984-86; regional dir. U.S. Trade & Devel. Agy., Washington, 1986-2000, dep. dir., 2000—. Bd. dirs. Jr. League, Washington, 1977-78. Democrat. Avocations: art, golf, reading.

BRADFORD, BARBARA TAYLOR, writer, journalist; b. Leeds, Eng. came to U.S., 1964; d. Winston and Freda (Walker) Taylor; m. Robert Bradford, Dec. 24, 1963. Student pvt. schs., Eng.; D of Letters (hon.), Leeds (Eng.) U., 1990, U. Bradford, West Yorkshire, Eng., 1995; D of Humane Letters (hon.), Teikyo Post U., Waterbury, Conn., 1996. Women's editor Yorkshire (Eng.) Evening Post, 1951-53, reporter, 1949-51; editor Woman's Own, 1953-54; columnist London Evening News, 1955-57; exec. editor London Am., 1959-62; editor Nat. Design Center Mag., 1965-69; syndicated columnist Newsday Spls., L.I., 1968-70; nat. syndicated columnist Chgo. Tribune-N.Y. (News Syndicate), N.Y.C., 1970-75, Los Angeles Times Syndicate, 1975-81. Author: Complete Encyclopedia of Homemaking Ideas, 1968, A Garland of Children's Verse, 1968, How to Be the Perfect Wife, 1969, Easy Steps to Successful Decorating, 1971, Decorating Ideas for Casual Living, 1977, How to Solve Your Decorating Problems, 1976, Making Space Grow, 1979, Luxury Designs for Apartment Living, 1981, (novels) A Woman of Substance, 1979, Voice of the Heart, 1983, Hold the Dream, 1985, screen adaptation, 1986, Act of Will, 1986, To Be the Best, 1988, The Women in His Life, 1990, Remember, 1991, Angel, 1993, Everything to Gain, 1994, Dangerous to Know, 1995, Love in Another Town, 1995, Her Own Rules, 1996, A Secret Affair, 1996, Power of a Woman, 1997, A Sudden Change of Heart, 1999, Where You Belong, 2000, The Triumph of Katie Byrne, 2001, Three Weeks in Paris, 2001, Emma's Secret, 2003. Recipient Dorothy Dawe award Am. Furniture Mart, 1970, 71, Matrix award N.Y. Women in Comms., 1985, Spl. Jury prize for body of film Deauville Festival of Am.Film, 1994. Mem. Coun. Authors Guild, Nat. Soc. Interior Designers (Disting. Editl. award 1969, Nat. Press award 1971), Authors Guild Am. (mem. coun. 1989—), Am. Soc. Interior Designers. Office: Bradford Enterprises 450 Park Ave New York NY 10022-2605

BRADFORD, JUDITH LYNNELL, journalist, artist; b. Denver, Jan. 27, 1946; d. Robert Benjamin and Frances Mildred (Wolfe) B.; m. Gary Paul Zimmerman, Jul. 5, 1985; 1 child, Katherine. BA, East Carolina Univ. 1972. Columnist Keynoter, Fla., 1996—; freelance, 1988—; editor Fgn. Broadcast Info. Svc., 1994-95; weekly arts columnist Solares Hill Newspaper, Key West, 1988—96. Ptnr., sec. Guild Hall Gallery, 1987-98; adminstrv. asst., vol. coord. Durham Arts Coun., 1975-76; ind. tchr. painting at Images Art Camp, East Martello Mus., Key West, 1996-97; taught painting and drawing classes, 1991—; tchr. painting Audubon Ho. & Gardens, Key West, 2000—. Author: Lizard Licks: A Comic History of Key West, 2003; invented Lizard Licks, 1979, founder Key West Plein Air Painters, 2002; exhibits paintings at Pineapple Mus. Gallery, Key West, Audubon Ho. Mus. Gallery. Coord. Fantasy Fest Parade, 1995—, Chicken Fest Key West Parade, 2004; founded Pathfinders Bicycle Advocacy Group, 1992, Key West, coord. Street Arts Fair, Hemingway Days St Fair, 1994; bd. dirs. Waterfront Playhouse, Last Stand Environ. Group, Montessori Children's Sch., 1991-96. Named Mem. of Yr., Last Stand Environ. Group Key West Cultural Preservation Soc., 1995, Artist of Yr., 1985; recipient Non-Fiction award Am. PEN Women, 2002. Mem. Am. Mensa. Home and Office: PO Box 1844 Key West FL 33041-1844

BRADFORD, LOUISE MATHILDE, social services administrator; b. Alexandria, La., Aug. 3, 1925; d. Henry Aaron and Ruby (Pearson) B. BS, La. Poly. Inst., 1945; cert. in social work, La. State U., 1949; MS, Columbia U., 1953; postgrad., Tulane U., 1962, 64, La. State U., 1967; cert., U. Pa., 1966. Diplomate NASW, Am. Bd. Clin. Social Work; cert. social worker Acad. Cert. Social Workers. With La. Dept. Pub. Welfare, Alexandria, 1945-49, welfare caseworker, 1950-53, children's caseworker, 1957-59, child welfare cons., 1959-73, social svcs. cons., 1973-78, state cons. day care, 1963-66; dir. social svcs. St. Mary's Tng. Sch., Alexandria, 1978-2000; adoption splst. Vols. of Am., 2000—. Del. Nat. Day Care Conf., Washington, 1964; mem. early childhood edn. so. States Work Conf., Daytona Beach, Fla., 1968; mem. La. adv. com. 1970 White House Conf. on Children, also del.; mem. So. region planning com. Child Welfare League Am., 1970-73; mem. profl. adv. com. Cenla chpt. Parents Without Partners,

1970-95; adj. asst. prof. sociology La. Coll. Pineville, 1969-85; lectr. Kindergarten Workshop, 1970-72; mem. La. 4-C Steering Com.; social svcs. cons. La. Spl. Edn. Ctr., Alexandria, 1980-86; del. Internat. Conf. on Social Welfare, Nairobi, 1974, Jerusalem, 1978, Hong Kong, 1980, Brighton, 1982, Montreal, 1984. Bd. dirs. Cenla Cmty. Action Com., Alexandria, 1966-68; mem. kindergarten edn. Meth. Ch., 1967-87, ofcl. bd., 1974-75, 77-81, 83-85, 96-98, 2000-03. Recipient Social Worker of Yr. award, Alexandria br. NASW La. Conf. Social Welfare, 1974, Lifetime Achievement award, La. Chpt. Nat. Assn. of Social Workers, 2003. Mem.: DAR, NASW (Lifetime Achievement award, La. chpt. 2003), Ctrl. La. Pre-Sch. Assn. (dir. 1967—70), Am. Assn. on Mental Retardation (La. social work chair 1989—94, Meritorious Contbn. award 1999, La. chpt. Svc. award 2001, Region V Svc. award 2001), Internat. Coun. on Social Welfare, La. Conf. Social Welfare (George Freeman award 1987, Hilda C. Simon award 1987), So. La. Assn. Children Under Six, Acad. Cert. Social Workers, Alexandria Golf and Country Club, Lions. Home: 5807 Joyce St Alexandria LA 71302-2510

BRADFORD, MARIAH, elementary school educator, consultant; b. Bay Springs, Miss., Sept. 23, 1929; d. Glasco Hunter Bender and Georgianna Holloway; m. Demond Bradford, Sr., Apr. 15, 1960 (div. Sept. 1984); children: Anita, Demond Jr., Kelvin. BS in Home Econs., Jackson Coll., 1953; MS in Edn., Ind. U., 1973; LHD (hon.), Martin U., 1994. Cert. tchr. Miss., 1953, Ind., 1962, Ariz., 1997. Tchr. Scott County Pub. Schs., Forest, Miss., 1953—57, Meridian Mcpl. Separate Schs., Meridian, 1957, 1959—61; county ext. agent Coop. Ext. Dept., Kosciusko, 1958—59; tchr. Ind. Pub. Schs., Indianapolis, 1963—92; sub. tchr. Peoria and Dysart Unified Schs., Peoria and El Mirage, Ariz., 1997—. Sec., bd. dirs. Martin U., Indpls., 1989—94; mem. bd. dirs. Indpls. Edn. Assn., 1970—78; mem. desegregation task force Ind. State Tchrs. Assn., Indpls., 1975—80. Contbr. poems to literary pubs. and jours. (Editors' Choice award, 1996). Commr. Planning and Zoning, Surprise, Ariz., 1997—99; big sister Big Brothers/Big Sister, Indpls. and Phoenix, 1987—. Recipient Sagamore of the Wabash, State of Ind., Gov. Evan Bayh, 1994, Golden Apple award, Indpls. Power and Light Co. and Cmty. Leaders Allied for Superior Schs., 1992, Special Human Rights award, Indpls. Edn. Assn. Human Rights Com., 1963, Human Rights award, Indpls. Edn. Assn., 1983; grantee, Indpls. Pub. Schs. Found., 1986, DePauw U. and Dept. of Health Edn. and Welfare, 1977. Mem.: NAACP (life), Assn. Negro Bus. and Profl. Women's Clubs (founder, pres. Madame Walker chpt. 1979—89, Sojourner Truth award 1982), Ch. Nurses Auxiliary (first v.p., nat. missionary Bapt. Conv. Am., Svc. award 1998), Zion Rest Dist. Ch. Nurses Auxiliary (cons.), Household of Ruth (#6851, Grand United Order of Oddfellows). Democrat. Baptist. Avocations: writing, reading, traveling, sewing, volunteering. Home: 18019 N 145th Dr Surprise AZ 85374

BRADFORD, MARY ROSEN, lawyer; b. Chgo., Ill. d. Ralph John and Joan (McMahon) Rosen; m. William H. Bradford; children: Jennifer, Lillian. BA, U. Md.; MS in Mgmt., Stanford U., 1980; JD, Georgetown U., 1982; C. de S., U. Madrid. Bar: D.C. Pk. ranger Nat. Pk. Svc., various, Md.; atty. Washington; spl. asst. Dept. Interior, Washington; dep. regional dir. Nat. Pk. Svc., Santa Fe, assoc. dir., CFO Washington; prin. Cardinal Strategies, Washington. Adv. bd. Stanford U., Stanford, Calif.; dir. Ea. Nat., Pa., Global Govt. Strategies, DC. Co-founder Hands Across the Pks., Md.; co-chair Long Br. Revitalization Task Force, Silver Spring, Md.; bd. dir. Child Devel. Corp. Md.

BRADHAM, TAMALA SELKE, audiologist; b. South Bend, Ind., Oct. 5, 1969; d. David Allan and Janice Marie (Hayden) Selke; m. William Simons, Jr., May 14, 1994. BA in Math., Columbia Coll., 1992; M in Audiology, U. S.C., 1994, PhD, 1998. Cert. audiologist, S.C. Bd. Examiners; cert. clin. competence Am. Speech Hearing Assn. Grad. rsch. asst. U. S.C., Columbia, 1992-94, clin. fellow, audiologist, 1994-95, instr., 1997-98, asst. prof., 1998-2000; asst. prof., dir. Cochlear Implant Ctr. Med. U. S.C., Charleston, 2000—03; vice-chmn. First Sound, 2002—03; clin. rsch. asst. Vanderbilt U., 2004—; co-chair Nat. Steering Com. for Legis. & Policy, 2003—. Adv. bd. universal newborn hearing screening program S.C. State Interagy. Coord. Coun., Gov.'s Office, 2000—02. Treas. Nat. Student Speech, Lang., Hearing Assn., Columbia, 1993; pres. Palmetto Columbia chpt. Self Help Hard of Hearing (SHHH), 1995-96, librn., 1993-95; bd. dirs. S.C. chpt. A.G. Bell Assn. for the Deaf, 1996-98, pres., 2000-02; bd. dirs. S.C. Universal Newborn Hearing Screening Program, 1998-2003, vice chmn., 2002-03; bd. mem. State Interagy. Coordinating Coun., 1999-2002. Recipient Elizabeth Wade Meml. award for outstanding audiologist, S.C. Acad. Audiology, 2000, Focus on People award, Oticon, 2000; scholar Sertoma scholar, Carolina/West Region, 1993. Fellow Am. Acad. Audiology (Scholar award 1999); mem. Am. Speech, Lang., Hearing Assn. (spl. interest divsn. 9, 2000—, mem. legis. coun., Continuing Edn. award 1998, 2003), Am. Auditory Soc., Edul. Audiology Assn., Acad. Rehab. Audiology, Am Auditory Soc., S.C. Speech and Hearing Assn., S.C. Acad. of Audiology (pres. 1998). Roman Catholic. Avocations: backpacking, camping, canoeing. Office: MUSC Dept Otolaryngology 135 Rutledge Ave Rm 216 Charleston SC 29425 Home: 7208 S Colony Dr Nashville TN 37221-3931 Office: Vanderbilt Bill Wilkerson Ctr. 1114 19th Ave S Nashville TN 37221 E-mail: tamala.bradham@vanderbilt.edu.

BRADICK, ANGELLA VELVET, special education educator; b. Seattle, Sept. 5, 1945; d. George Andrew and Elizabeth Mary (Fath) B.; m. John Francis Raczkiewicz, June 28, 1986. BA, U. Pitts., 1968, MEd, 1969. Cert. tchr., Pa. Spl. edn. tchr. Allegheny Intermediate Unit, Pitts., 1969—. Mem. philosophy and goals self-study com. Brentwood H.S., 1997—, spl. edn. self-study com., 1997-98. Recipient Silver medal-Kata competition Traditional Karate Acad., 1997. Mem. NEA, Pa. State Edn. Assn., Allegheny Intermediate Edn. Assn., Allegheny Flute Assn., Tuesday Mus. Club, Nat. Mus. of Women in the Arts. Office: Brentwood High Sch 3601 Brownsville Rd Pittsburgh PA 15227-3196

BRADLEY, AMELIA JANE, lawyer; b. Columbia, S.C., Apr. 18, 1947; d. Hugh Wilson and Amelia Jane (Wylie) B.; m. Richard Bancroft Hovey, Apr. 1, 1977. BA, U. Va., 1968; MA, George Washington U., 1971. Bar: Va. 1976, D.C. 1985. Budget and mgmt. analyst NLRB, Washington, 1968-71, 72; clk. Cohen and Vitt, PC, Alexandria, Va., 1972-76; assoc. Cohen, Vitt & Annand, PC, Alexandria, 1976-80; White House fellow USDA, Washington, 1980-81, Office U.S. Trade Rep., Exec. Office of Pres., Washington, 1981, asst. gen. counsel, 1981-82, assoc. gen. counsel, 1982-84, legal advisor to U.S. GATT del. Geneva, 1984-87; prin. dep. gen. counsel Office U.S. Trade Rep., Exec Office of Pres., Washington, 1989-92; asst. U.S. trade rep. for dispute resolution Office U.S. Trade Rep., Exec. Office of Pres., Washington, 1994; assoc. dir. for global environment White House Office on Environ. Policy, Washington, 1994-95; assoc. dir. internat. trade and devel. Coun. on Environ. Quality, Washington, 1994—95; asst. U.S. trade rep. for monitoring, enforcement Exec. Office of Pres., Washington, 1996—2002; dep.dir. Inst. Internat. Econ. Law, Georgetown U. Law Ctr., Washington, 2004—. Chief negotiator U.S. GATT Uruguay Round Dispute Settlement Negotiating Group, 1986-87, 89-93; chmn. interagy. Sect. 301 Com., Washington, 1988-92; vis. rsch. assoc. Fletcher Sch. Law and Diplomacy, Tufts U., Medford, Mass., 1987-88; vis. rsch. Harvard U. Law Sch., Cambridge, Mass., 1988. Mem., chmn. Alexandria Human Rights Commn., 1975-80; pres., trustee Alexandria Law Libr., 1978-80; founding Lawyer Referral Svc., Alexandria, 1978. NEH fellow, 1978. Mem. ABA, Va. State Bar (mem., chmn. com. on legal edn. and admission to bar 1977-84), D.C. Bar (chmn. internat. trade com. 1989-90). Episcopalian.

BRADLEY, ANN WALSH, state supreme court justice; married; 4 children. BA, Webster Coll., 1972; JD, U. Wis., 1976. Tchr. HS; pvt. law practice; former judge Marathon County Circuit Ct., Wausau, Wis.; justice Wis. Supreme Ct., Madison, Wis., 1995—. Office: Wis Ct Sys PO Box 1688 Madison WI 53701-1688

BRADLEY, BARBRA BAILEY, musician, educator, accompanist; b. Windsor, Ont., Can., Dec. 27, 1944; d. Charles David Bailey and Mary Alice Calow; m. Joseph Patrick Bradley, Sept. 19, 1981. BA in Honours Music Edn., U. Western Ont., London, Can., 1967; A of Music in Piano, West. Ont. Conservatory Music, London, 1967; MM in Piano, Ind. U., 1969. Freelance performer, adjudicator, 1974-81; tchr. piano, performer Brigham Young U., Provo, Utah, 1973-74; accompanist concert tour Mu Phi Epsilon Found., various cities, 1974-76; tchr. piano, performer St. Clair divsn. Royal Hamilton Coll. Music, Windsor, Ont., 1975-79; tchr. piano, performer music dept. St. Clair Coll., Windsor, 1979-81; freelance performer piano and harp Washington, 1981—; tchr. piano, performer Leidzen Sch. Music, Fairfax, Va., 1987-88, Nat. Cathedral Sch., Washington, 1988—. Composer (music for children's theater): Cricket on the Hearth, 1989, Goldilocks and the Christmas Bears, 1991. Doctoral fellowship for grad. study Ind. U., Can. Coun., 1970. Mem.: Am. Fedn. Musicians, Fri. Morning Music Club (chamber music performer 1986—), Mu Phi Epsilon (pres. Washington alumni chpt. 1990—94, dist. dir. Atlantic-2 dist. 1994—96, internat. officer, alumni advisor 1996—2003, Sterling Staff Internat. Competition winner 1974). Mem. Lds Ch. Avocations: ballet, photography, walking, genealogy. Office: Nat Cathedral Sch Mount St Albans Washington DC 20016 E-mail: bradley@cathedral.org.

BRADLEY, CAROLYN ANN, social worker; b. Newark, N.J., Mar. 27, 1953; d. Joseph John and Dolores Caroline (Bersey) B.; m. Mickey Medlicott, Oct. 8, 1994. MSW, Fordham U., 1978. Lic. clin. social worker, N.J. Clinician St. Clares Cmty. Mental Health Ctr., Denville, N.J., 1974-79; med. social worker Jersey Shore Med. Ctr., Neptune, N.J., 1979-80, Jersey City Med. Ctr., 1980; pvt. practice Hazlet, N.J., 1980—. Student assistance counselor Middletown Twp. (N.J.) Bd. of Edn., 1980—; adj. instr. Monmouth U., West Long Branch, N.J., 1995-96, field instr., 1992—, Rutgers U. Grad. Sch. Social Work, New Brunswick, N.J., 1990—; presenter addiction tng. and gay and lesbian issues at profl. confs. Active Mcpl. Alliance, Middletown, 1990-96, choir Christ Ch., Middletown, 1994—. Grantee Withecombe Found., 1995-96. Mem. Assn. Student Assistance Profls. N.J. (pres. 1996-98, county chair 1994-96, corr. sec. 1992-94), Assn. for Marriage and Family Therapy, NASW, N.J. Edn. Assn., NEA. Democrat. Episcopalian. Avocations: reading, golf, tennis, travel. Office: 1 Bethany Rd Bldg 2 Ste 30A Hazlet NJ 07730-1659

BRADLEY, DEBORAH J. music educator; b. Frankfurt, Germany, Nov. 28, 1953; d. Chelse A. and Rose M. Bradley. B in Music Edn., Troy (Ala.) State U., 1975, MS in Edn., 1977, specialist degree in edn., 1999. Band dir. Clarke County H.S., Grove Hill, Ala., 1975—76; music sales rep. Art's Music Shop, Inc., Dothan, Ala., 1976—77; band dir. Calhoun County H.S., Edison, Ga., 1977—78, Valdosta (Ga.) Jr. H.S., 1978—88; asst. dir. Valdosta H.S. band, 1978—88; band dir., music dir. Patrick Henry State Jr. Coll., Monroeville, Ala., 1988—90; band dir. Clarke Ctrl. H.S., Athens, Ga., 1990—91, Max Bruner Jr. Mid. Sch., Ft. Walton Beach, Fla., 1991—92, Cook H.S., Adel, Ga., 1992—. Alumni pres. Sound of the South Alumni Band. Named to Sudler Order of Merit, John Philip Sousa Found., 1984. Mem.: Ga. Music Educators Assn. (dist. 8), Women Band Dirs. Internat. (indsl. chmn. 1975—2001, pres. elect 2004), Alumni Assn. South Ga. Troy State U. (pres. 1986—2001), Tau Beta Sigma (charter pres. Tau Beta Sigma chpt., Outstanding Svc. to Music award 2000). Avocations: travel, volleyball, tennis, bowling, golf. E-mail: booradlee@ureach.com.

BRADLEY, ELIZABETH CLAY, financial planner, educator; b. Dayton, Ky., Feb. 6, 1948; d. Glenn Washington and Margaret Elizabeth Clay; m. James D. McPhail, Aug. 16, 1970 (dec. Sept. 1990); m. Julian Bradley, May 4, 1996. BS in Home Econs., U. Ky., 1970; MS in Family Econs., Kans. State U., 1977. CFP. Tchr. Bourbon County Jr. H.S., Paris, Ky., 1970—71, Manhattan (Kans.) H.S., 1974—84; investment rep. Edward Jones, Cary, NC, 1984—2001; ret., 2001; cons. Wachovia Sec., Raleigh, NC, 2002—. Author: (workbook) Motivation Plus, 1982, The Good Life, 2001. Chair Expanding the Circle-Glenaire, Cary, 2001; trustee Glenaire Presbyn. Home, Cary, 2002; bd. dirs. Glenaire Found., Triangle Fin. Planning Assn., 2003—. Named Young Educator, Kans. Assn. Vocat. Home Econs. Tchrs., 1984, Small Businessperson of Yr., Cary C. of C., 1988. Mem.: Cary C. of C. (named Small Bus. Person of Yr. 1988). Presbyterian. Avocations: walking, writing, reading, quilting, designing clothes. Home: 1917 Olde Mill Forest Dr Raleigh NC 27606 Office Phone: 919-571-2830.

BRADLEY, JENNETTE, lieutenant governor; m. Michael C. Taylor. BA in Psychology, Wittenberg U. Lic. registered rep. Nat. Assn. Securities Dealers. Exec. dir. Columbus Met. Housing Authority; sr. v.p. pub. fin. banker Kemper Securities; sr. v.p., pub. funds mgr. Huntington Nat. Bank; councilwoman Columbus (Ohio) City Coun., 1991—2002, chair parks and recreation com., chair utilities and energy generation coms., chair safety com., mem. safety and judiciary com., mem. adminstrn. com., mem. recreation and parks com., mem. health, housing and human svcs. com., mem. zoning com.; lt. gov. State of Ohio, Columbus, 2003—. Dir. Ohio Dept. Commerce, 2003—; mem. fin., adminstrn. and intergovernmental rels. steering and policy coms. Nat. League Cities. Grad. Leadership Columbus; trustee Wittenberg U.; bd. mem., former chair Joint Columbus and Franklin County Housing Adv. Bd. Recipient Woman of Achievement award, YWCA. Republican. Office: 23rd Fl 77 High St Columbus OH 43215

BRADLEY, KIM ALEXANDRA, sales and marketing specialist; b. Glen Cove, N.Y., Aug. 27, 1955; d. Harold William and Helen Doris (Rosenthal) Shepard; m. Gary Morgan Bradley, Oct. 2, 1982; children: Hunter Morgan, Parker Davis, Preston Carter. BS, U. Ill., 1977. Media estimator Lee King & Ptnrs., Chgo., 1977-78; asst. buyer Grey North Advt., Chgo., 1978; broadcast negotiator J. Walter Thompson, Chgo., 1978-80; acct. exec. Katz Communications, Inc., Chgo., 1980-84, sales mgr., 1984-88, v.p. sales mgr., 1988-93; prin., pres. The Encore Group, Inc., Chgo., 1993; pres., owner Bradley Mktg. Group, Northbrook, Ill., 1993—2002; prin., owner Bradley and Thomas, Lake Forest, Ill., 2002—; exec. dir. sales tng. and devel. Tribune Broadcasting Co., Chgo., 2003—. Mem. mktg. com., bd. dirs. Child Abuse Prevention Svcs.; alliance mem. Art Inst. of Chgo.; vol. Infant Welfare Soc.; aux. bd. dirs. Juvenile Protection Assn. Mem.: Nat. Bur. Profl. Mgmt. Cons. (cert. profl. cons. to mgmtl.), Nat. Assn. Women Bus. Owners, Am. Mktg. Assn., Inst. Mgmt. Cons., Am. Mgmt. Assn., Rotary (pres.-elect Lake Forest/Lake Bluff chpts.), The Exec. Club, Broadcast Advt. Club (bd. dirs., v.p., exec. v.p., pres., chair for Child Abuse Prevention Svcs. charity com.). Home: 30 Barnswallow Ln Lake Forest IL 60045-2984 E-mail: kbradley@tribune.com.

BRADLEY, LEIGH A. government official, lawyer; b. Ft. Benjamin Harrison, Ind., Dec. 15, 1956; m. Douglas E. Wade, July 8, 1983; 1 child, Katie. BA in Polit. Sci. magna cum laude, U. Ala., 1978, JD, 1981. Prosecutor, def. counsel in spl. and gen. courtsmartial Air Force Judge Advocate Gen.'s Dept.; assoc. dep. gen. counsel Dept. of Def., 1987-93; spl. asst. U.S. atty. for mid. dist. Ala. Office of Sec. of Def., 1993-94; prin. dep. gen. counsel USN, 1994-98; gen. counsel Dept. VA, 1998—. Legal advisor Def. Adv. Com. on Women in the Svcs. Capt. USAF. Recipient Sec. of Def. medal for meritorious civilian svc., 1995, medal for disting. pub. svc., 1998. Mem. Phi Beta Kappa. Office: Dept VA 810 Vermont Ave NW Rm 1030 Washington DC 20420-0001

BRADLEY, LYNN HECHT, school librarian; b. Anderson, Ind. d. William Joseph and Pauline Roach Hecht; children: Carter, Will, Kate. AB, Coll. William amd Mary, 1970; MLn, Emory U., 1971; postgrad., Ga. State U., 1972—76. Children's libr. Atlanta Pub. Libr., 1970; lower/preschool libr. Lovett Sch., Atlanta, 1971—81; media specialist Douglas Co. Bd. Edn., Douglasville, Ga., 1988—93, Fulton County-Camp Creek Mid. Sch., Atlanta, 1993—. Salute to Schs. grantee, 3M Found., 2001. Mem.: ALA, Ga. Libr. Media Assn., Internat. Reading Assn. Presbyterian. Avocations: reading, walking. Office: Camp Creek Mid Sch 4335 Welcome All Rd College Park GA 30349

BRADLEY, MARILYNNE GAIL, advertising executive, advertising educator; b. Rockford, Ill., Apr. 12, 1938; d. Sherwin S. and Lillian (Leopold) Gersten; m. Charles S. Bradley, 1959 (div. Feb., 1994); children: Suzanne, Scott. BFA, Washington U., 1960; MAT, Webster U., St. Louis, 1975; MFA, Syracuse U., 1981; postgrad., St. Louis Tchrs. Acad., 1990. With Essayons Studio, St. Louis, 1968-69; tchr. Webster Groves (Mo.) H.S., 1970-98; instr. Webster Univ., Webster Groves, 1973-82, 97—, supr., 2002—; instr. U. Mo., 1980—, St. Louis U., 1978-99, Washington U., St. Louis, 1984-87. Sec. Mo. Art Edn., State of Mo., 1986-87; mem. Tchrs. Acad. 1990-92. Author, illustrator: Arpens and Acres, 1976, Packets on Parade, 1980, illustrator: St. Louis Silhouettes, 1977; editor: (videos) 12 Water Color Lessons, 1987, Techniques of American Watercolor, 1990, The Santa Fe Trail Series, 1993, Over Gauguin's Shoulder, 1994, Aboriginal Art Techniques, 1994, City of Century Homes, 1995, Australian Dreamings, 1996, Aboriginal Art - Past, Present and Future, 1996, Drawing and Painting Techniques, 1997, Line, Shape, Value, 1998, Molas, Snip and Sew: The Kuna Indians, Molas: Panamanian Traditions, 1999, The Katy Trail Series, 2000, Art Along the Katy Trail, 2000, Apre's Paris, 2001, Lewis and Clark Trail, 2001, It's Somewhere in St. Louis, 2002, St. Louis World's Fair, 2004. Bd. govs. Webster Groves Hist. Soc., 1965-72, 94—; mem. St. Louis Philharm. Soc., 1956-72; commr. City of Webster Groves, 1995—; co-chair Hist. Preservation Com., 2002, v.p., 2002—. Named Tchr. of Yr., 1987, Best of Show, Mo. Watercolor Soc., 2000. Mem.: Mo. Watercolor Soc. (bd. mem. 2001—), St. Louis Artist Guild (sec. 1985—86, pres. 1989—92, v.p. pres.'s coun. 1995—, Disting. Woman 1987), St. Louis Woman Artists, So. Watercolor Soc. (sec. 1978—80, v.p. 2002—, chair 26th ann. exhibit, Silver Brush award, Exceptional Salute to the Masters award), Monday Club (chmn. 1979—83). Avocations: music, art, travel. Home and Office: Bradley & Assocs 817 S Gore Ave Saint Louis MO 63119-4023 Personal E-mail: mgbrad@aol.com.

BRADLEY, PATRICIA ELLEN, professional golfer; b. Arlington, Mass., Mar. 24, 1951; d. Richard Joseph and Kathleen Maureen (O'Brien) B. Assoc. in Phys. Edn, Miami-Dade North Jr. Coll., 1971; BS, Fla. Internat. U., 1974. Mem. Sun-Star Japan-U.S. Team Matches, 1975-76, All-Am. Collegiate Team, 1971, U.S.A. Com., 1974, 76, Golf Mag.'s All Am. Team, 1976, 77-78, 79-81; qualified for Colgate Triple Crown Tournament, 1975, 76, 77, 78. Staff mem. Dunlop Golf Co.; under contract with Nabisco. Winner N.H. Womens Amateur Championship, 1967, 69, Fla. Collegiate Championship, 1970, Mass. Womens Amateur Championship, 1972, New Eng. Amateur Championship, 1972, 73, Colgate Far East Tournament, 1975, Girl Talk Classic Tournament, 1976, Bankers Trust Classic Tournament, 1977, Lady Keystone Open, Hoosier Classic, Rail Charity Classic, 1978, 91, J.C. Penny Classic, 1978, 89, Balt. Classic, Peter Jackson Classic, 1980, U.S. Womens Open, 1981, Du Maurier Classic, 1985, LPGA Pro-Am, 1985, Rochester Invitational, 1985, Turquoise Classic, 1990, Centel Classic, 1991, Safeco Classic, 1991, MBS Classic, 1991, HEALTHSOUTH Inaugural, 1995; recipient Most Improved Player award Golf Digest, 1976; named Player of Yr., 1986, Mazda Series, 1986, Vare Trophy, 1986; named to Ladies Profl. Golf Hall of Fame, 1991; mem. U.S. Solheim Cup Team, 1990, 92, 96, named capt., 2000; named one of the LPGA's top 50 players all-time, 2000. Mem. Ladies Profl. Golf Assn. Roman Catholic. Achievements include playing exhbn. golf match with Pres. Ford, Vail, Colo., 1976; first woman golfer to win all four USGA Womens Open, LPGA Championship, Du Maurier Classic and Nabisco/Dinah Shore Tournaments; leading money winner PGA, 1986, 91.*

BRADLEY, PAULA E. former state legislator; b. New Haven, Oct. 11, 1924; d. Richard Travis and Harriett (Bogenhagen) Elliott; m. William L. Bradley, 1947; children: James R. Choukas-Bradley, Dwight C., Paul W. BA, Hiram Coll., 1945; postgrad., Middlebury Coll., 1946, Hartford Seminary, 1963-64. Ret. rsch. assoc. univ. devel. Yale U.; mem. N.H. Ho. of Reps., 1992—98, 2000—02. Treas. Coos County Dem. Com., 1992—, Randolph Dem. Party, 1992—, Coos County Dem. Party, 1998—; chair bd. adjustment Town of Randolph, 2000—01, mem. planning bd., 2003; mem. Gorham (N.H.) Congregational Ch.; bd. dirs. Coos County Family Health Svcs., Berlin, NH, 1993—2001, Weeks Meml. Hosp., Lancaster, NH, 1993—95, No. Forest Heritage Park, Berlin, NH, 2001—, No. Country Coun., 2003—. Mem.: AAUW (Androscoggin br. 1990—), Randolph Mountain Club (bd. dirs. 1986—91, 1992—97, treas. 1989—91, pres. 1995—96). Democrat. Avocations: walking, gardening, choral singing. Office: 194 Randolph Hill Rd Randolph NH 03593 E-mail: wlb@ncia.net.

BRADLEY, VANESSA, music educator; d. James Allen and Olenia Smith; m. William Bradley, July 24, 2002; 1 child, William J. S. MusB, Howard U. Music-choral dir. Banneker H.S., Atlanta.

BRADLEY, VANESSA LYNN, management consultant; b. Saginaw, Mich., Apr. 8, 1967; BS in Indsl. Engring. magna cum laude, Northwestern U., 1989; MBA, U Pa., 1993. Project engr. Gen. Motors Corp., 1989—91; project cons. Ctr. for Applied Rsch., 1992—93; v.p. Bradley Automotive Group, Ann Arbor, Mich., 1996—98; prin. A.T. Kearney, Inc., Chgo., 1993—96, 1998—. Bd. trustees Sherwood Conservatory of Music, Chgo., Providence St. Mel Coll. Prep. Sch., Chgo. Mem.: NAFE, Northwestern Alumni Club of Chgo. Office: AT Kearney Inc 222 W Adams St Chicago IL 60606 Office Phone: 312-961-1219. E-mail: vanbrad67@aol.com.

BRADLEY, WANDA LOUISE, librarian; b. Havre de Grace, Md., June 6, 1953; d. William Smith and Josephine Viola (Miller) B. BA, U. Md., 1975; MSLS, Atlanta U., 1976; postgrad., Cath. U.; MPA (scholar), U. Balt., 1986. Libr. Harford County Pub. Libr., Bel Air, Md., 1976, Harford County Bd. Edn., Bel Air, Md., 1977-81, Nat. Grad. U., Arlington, Va., 1982, Md. State Dept. Edn., Balt., 1982-83, U.S. Dept. Labor, Washington, 1984, Balt. Gas and Electric Co., 1984-85, Morgan State U., Balt., 1985, Coppin State Coll., Balt., 1985-86, Montgomery County Pub. Sch. System, Rockville, Md., 1985-86, Community Coll., Balt., 1987-88; grant adminstr. Howard County Pub. Libr., 1988; libr., media specialist Balt. City Pub. Sch. System, 1992—. Acad. advisor George Mason U., Fairfax, Va., 1981-82. Dept. Edn. fellow, 1983-84; U. Balt. Merit scholar, 1984, Atlanta U. scholar, 1976, U. Md. scholar, 1971; Howard County Pub. Libr. grantee, 1988. Mem. ALA, ASIS, Md. Libr. Assn., Spl. Librs. Assn., Med. Libr. Assn. Methodist. Office: Dr Roland N Patterson Sr Acad Greenspring Ave Baltimore MD 21231

BRADSHAW, CLAUDETTE, Canadian government official; married; 2 children. Dir. girl's program Moncton's Boy's and Girl's Club, 1968-74; exec. dir. Moncton Headstart Early Family Intervention Ctr., 1974-97; mem. Ho. of Commons, Govt. of Can., 1997; parliamentary sec. to min. of internat. cooperation & min. responsible for the Francophonie Govt. of Can., Ottawa, 1997—98, min. of labour, 1998—, fed. coord. on homelessness, 1999—. Mem. parliament Moncton-Riverview-Dieppe, 1997-2000, re-elected, 2000—, Standing Com. of Fgn. Affairs and Internat. Trade, Standing Com. on Human Resources Develop. Recipient Muriel Fergusson award Greater Moncton C. of C, Ann Bell award N.B. Child Welfare Assn., Paul Harris award Moncton-West Riverview Rotary, Family Svc. Can.'s 1998 Leadership award. Office: Phase 2 11 Fl Place Portage 165 Hotel de Ville St Hull QC Canada K1A-OJ2

BRADSHAW, DOVE, artist; b. NYC, Sept. 24, 1949; d. David Nelson and Jean Katherine (Cormack) B. BFA, Boston Mus. Sch. Fine Arts, 1973. Co-artistic advisor The Merce Cunningham Dance Co., N.Y.C., 1984—. Artist in residence Pier Ctr., Orkney, Scotland, Sirius Art Ctr., Cork, Ireland, Statens Vaerksteder for Kunst, Copenhagen, 2000. One-man shows include Alan Stone Gallery, N.Y.C., 1979, S. Gering Gallery, N.Y., 1988-89, 91, 93, 95, 98, Graham Gallery, N.Y., 1979, Ericson Gallery, 1982, N.Y. Wave Hill, N.Y., 1983, PSI Mus., N.Y.C., 1991, Mattress Factory Mus., Pitts., 1990, 99, Pier Ctr., Orkney, Scotland, 1995, Stalke Gallery, Copenhagen, 1995, 96, 98-99, 2001, 2003, Barbara Krakow Gallery, 1997, Mus. Contemporary Art, L.A., 1998, Larry Becker Contemporary Art, Phila. 2000, Stark Gallery, N.Y., 2001, Baruch Coll., CUNY, N.Y., 2004, Volume Gallery, N.Y., Solway Jones Gallery, L.A., many others; group shows include Am. Ctr., Paris, Science Mus., Tokyo, 1982, Mus. Modern Art, N.Y.C., 1989, Carnegie Internat., Pitts., 1991, Met. Mus. N.Y., 1992, Art Inst. Chgo., 1992, 96, Aldrich Mus., Ridgefield, Conn., 1993, Phila. Mus., 1993, 98, 2000, Swiss Inst., N.Y.C., 1995, Baumgartner Gallery, Washington, 1998, Carnegie Mus. Art, 1997, Whitney Mus. Am. Art, N.Y., 1997, Millennium Film Theatre, 1998, Mus. Contemporary Art, L.A., 1998, U. Calif., San Diego, U. Mass. Amherst, 1999, UBU Gallery, N.Y.U., Baruch Coll., N.Y.C., Bayley Art Mus., U. Va., Charlottsville, 2000, Mus. Contemporary Art, Roskilde, Denmark, Rooseum Contemporary Art Ctr., Malmo, Sweden, Nikolaj Contemporary Art Ctr. Copenhagen, 2002, Baruch College,NY, Diferenca Gallery, Lisbon, Volckers and Friende Gallery, Berlin, Tanya Bonakdar, NY, 2003, others; represented in permanent collection at Met. Mus. Art, N.Y.C., Mus. Modern Art, N.Y.C., Bklyn. Mus. Art, Whitney Mus. Am. Art, Art Inst. Chgo., Phila. Mus. Art, Ark. Art Ctr., Little Rock, Fogg Art Mus., Cambridge, Mass., Harvard U., Getty Ctr., L.A., Mus. Contemporary Art, L.A., Nat. Gallery, Washington, Carnegie Mus Art, Pitts., Mattress Factory Mus., Pitts., Internat. Le Pompidou Ctr., Paris, Pier Ctr. Orkney, Scotland, Mus. Art, Bilboa, Spain, Kunst Mus., Dusseldorf, Germany, Moderna Mus., Stockholm, Oxygen, 2002, Self Interest, 1999; prodr., dir., artist: (film) Indeterminacy, 1995; prodr.: Metropolitan Mus. postcard, 1976-1992, Met. Mus. guerilla postcard, 1978; artist, prodr. handmade books, including Plain Air (installation with live birds 1969, 88, 91, documentation 1991), 1969-91; author: Indeterminacy, Contingency, Equivalents, Removal, Riverstone, 1991-99. Recipient Pollock-Krasner award, 1985; grantee Nat. Endowment Arts, 1975. Mem.: Volume Gallery, Larry Becker Contemporary Art Gallery (Phila.), Solway Jones Gallery, Les Yeux Monde. Avocations: meditation, yoga, running, reading. Home and Studio: 924 W End Ave New York NY 10025-3534 E-mail: dbradshaw1@nyc.rr.com.

BRADSHAW, MELISSA WAHLQUIST, art educator; b. Redlands, Calif., Aug. 2, 1970; d. Arvid Lee and Valerie Sue Wahlquist; m. Robert Keith Bradshaw, July 25, 1996. BFA, Va. Commonwealth U., 1988—93. Cert. tchr. SC. Visual arts instr. Ashley River Creative Arts Elem. Sch., Charleston, SC, 1994—2000; pres. and visual arts tchr. Wee Little Arts, LLC, Charleston, 2000—. Vol. Children's Mus. of the Lowcountry, Charleston, SC, 1998—. Mem.: Nat. Art Edn. Assn. Achievements include development of a three year visual arts curriculum for 3-5 year olds. Personal E-mail: weelittlearts@hotmail.com.

BRADSHAW, OTABEL, retired primary school educator; b. Magnolia, Ark., Oct. 27, 1922; d. Grover Cleveland and Mae (Staggs) Peterson; AA, Magnolia A&M Coll., 1950; BS in Edn., So. State Coll., 1953; MS in Edn., Henderson State U., 1975; postgrad. U. Ark.; PhD, Kensington U., 1983; m. Charles Howard Bradshaw, Aug. 14, 1948; children: Susan Charla, Michael Howard. Tchr., English and drama Walkers Creek Schs., Taylor Ark., 1945-46, primary grades Locust Bayou Schs., Camden, Ark., 1946-52, 2d grade Fairview Sch., Camden, 1962-73; tchr. 1st grade Harmony Grove Sch., Camden, 1973-83, coordinator Title IX, gifted children and handicapped; tchr. East Camden Accelerated Sch., 1983-96, ret., 1996; cons. econ. edn. workshop U. Ark., Fayetteville. Life mem., sec., historian chmn. bicentennial com. PTA; active vol. fund-raising drives Am. Cancer Soc., Birth Defects Soc.; leader Missionary Soc., Camden 1st United Methodist Ch.; mem. Camden and Ouachita County Library bd., 1974-77; active Boys Club Aux. Recipient Disting. Alumni Award So. Ark. U., 1981, Valley Forge Tchr. medal and George Washington Honor medal Freedom Found., 1973; Achievement citation Kazanian Found., 1969, citation for ednl. leadership Pres. of U.S., 1976, 77; profl. achievement citation Internat. Paper Co. Found., 1981. Mem. Assn. Supervision and Curriculum Devel. (speaker San Francisco conf.), NEA, Ark. Edn. Assn. (speaker 1969), Harmony Grove Edn. Assn. (pres. 1978-79), Nat. Council for Social Studies (mem. sexism com.), Am. Assn. Adminstrs., Alpha Delta Kappa (outstanding mem.). Club: Tate Park Garden (sec.). Home: 3188 Roseman Rd Camden AR 71701-5533

BRADSHAW, PHYLLIS BOWMAN, historian, historic site staff member; b. Cumberland, Ky., June 19, 1929; d. Lawrence David and Ann Rees Bowman; m. Glenn Lewis Bradshaw, June 30, 1949 (dec. Feb. 2000)); children: Charles Lewis, David Bowman. Student, Ctr. Coll., Danville, Ky., 1947-50, N.Y Sch. Speed Writing, 1967. Sec. to dir. and asst. dir. Shakertown, Pleasant Hill, Ky., 1967-68, asst. food dir., 1968-70, mus. dir. dept. interpretation, 1970-72; mus. hist. interpreter Old Fort Harrod State Pk., Harrodsburg, Ky., 1993-98. Rschr.: book Beyond Shenandoah, 2001. Mem. Harrodsburg Hist. Soc., Ky. Hist. Soc., Girl Scouts Am., Nat. Trust, Libr. Congress, Washington; tchr. Sunday sch. Harrodsburg Presbyn. Ch.; life mem. Women's Soc., Burgin Meth. Ch., bd. dirs., tchr./leader H.S. group; pres., sec. Burgin PTA; den mother cub scouts Boy Scouts Am.; life mem. Ky. PTA, Shakertown at Pleasant Hill; founding mem. Harlan (Ky.) Musettes; active Mercer County Blood Bank; assisted in creation of The Ky. Classic Sauces-Bluegrass Trade Assn. Mem. DAR (Jane McAfee chpt.), Lewis and Clark Assn., N.W. Territory Assn., Hite Family Assn., Ky. History Tchrs. Assn., Colonial Dames Ct. of Honor (Ky. chpt.), Ctr. Coll. Alumni Assn., Lions Club. mem. Va. Hist. Soc., 2002. Home: 876 Beaumont Ave Harrodsburg KY 40330

BRADY, ADELAIDE BURKS, public relations agency executive, giftware catalog executive; b. N.Y.C., June 27, 1926; d. Earl Victor and Audrey (Calvert) Burks; m. James Francis Brady, Jr., June 22, 1946 (div. 1953); 1 child, James Francis. BS, Boston U., 194. Exec. v.p. Media Enterprises, 1952—55; dir. group rels. Save the Children Fedn., N.Y.C., 1955-59; dir. pub. affairs divsn. Girl Scouts U.S.A., N.Y.C., 1959-69; pres. Comm. Internat., Inc., Washington, 1969-73, Burks Brady Comm., Washington, 1972—, Adelaide's Angel Shopper Catalog Inc., Wilton, Conn., 1976—. Exec. v.p. Arts in Parks Inc., Washington, 1971—. Past bd. dirs. Lenox Hill Hosp., N.Y.C., Achievement Rewards for Coll. Scientists Found.; pres. Animal Lovers Inc. Decorated comdr. Order of St. John of Jerusalem (Eng.); recipient Silver Reel award for film The Children of Now, Save the Children Fedn. Mem. NAFE, NEA, AAUW, Nat. Assn. Women Bus. Owners, Pub. Rels. Soc. Am., Am. Women in Radio and TV, Nat. Ednl. Broadcasters Assn., Am. Soc. Profl. and Exec. Women, Women Execs. in Pub. Rels., N.Y. Press Women, Nat. Fedn. Press Women (state pres.),Women's Econ. Roundtable, DAR, Capitol Hill Club (Washington), Yacht and Country Club (Fla.), MDW Officers Club (Washington). Republican. Episcopalian. Home: 312 Harvest Commons Westport CT 06880-3954 also: Yacht Country Club 3664 SE Fairway E Stuart FL 34997-6116 Office: 785 Park Ave New York NY 10021-3552

BRADY, DONNA ELIZABETH, performing arts company executive; b. Rockville Centre, N.J., Nov. 17, 1955; d. Frank A. and Dorothy Eleanor (Munden) B. BA, Knox Coll., 1976. Stage mgr., lighting designer Dance Edn. Svcs., Inc., Northport, NY, 1973-86; coord. Am. Dance Festival Tech.

Assistance Project, N.Y.C., 1981-85; exec. dir. Performing Arts Resources, Inc., N.Y.C., 1986—, also pres., bd. dirs. Project staff Tech. Assistance Group/TAG Found., Ltd., N.Y.C., 1980-81; treas. N.Y. Tech. Assistance Providers Network, 1995, 96, co-chair 1997; lighting designer, stage mgr. Solomons Co. Dance, 1978-81; asst. stage mgr. Pilobolus, 1978. Bd. dirs. Artists Cmty. Fed. Credit Union, 1992-2001, sec., 1993-2000; bd. dirs., treas. Acanthus Dance, 1997—. Mem. Am. Dance Guild (bd. dirs. 1980-87, treas. 1983-87).

BRADY, JEAN STEIN, retired librarian; b. Concord, Mass., Nov. 4, 1930; d. Walfred and Mary Selina (Jussila) Stein; m. Maurice Goodrich Klein, Feb. 22, 1957 (div. 1982); 1 child, Audrey Elaine; m. Lawrence Kevin Brady, Oct. 15, 1988. BS, Simmons Coll., 1952; cert. d'Etudes, U. Grenoble, France, 1954; MA, Northwestern U., 1957. Cert. pub. libr., N.Y. Sr. libr. N.Y. Pub. Libr., 1952-53, 57-60; cataloger Columbia U., N.Y.C., 1954-55; reference asst. Northwestern U., Evanston, Ill., 1955-57; cataloger U. W.Va., Morgantown, 1960-61; book reviewer ALA, Chgo., 1961-63; sr. cataloger Cleve. Pub. Libr., 1964-70; sr. catalog libr. Yale U. Libr., New Haven, Conn., 1970-92; cataloger Columbia U., N.Y.C., 1993-95; ret., 1995. Revision asst. Bibliographical Guide to Romance Langs. and Lits., 1956-57; reviewer: Booklist and Subscription Books Bulletin, 1961-63. Mem. Simmons Coll. Club of Cape Cod. Democrat. Episcopalian. Avocations: reading, travel, walking, swimming.

BRADY, KATHLEEN DEMING, psychologist, occupational therapist, educator; b. Enid, Okla., Jan. 8, 1920; d. Leon J. and Lola Faye (Hendryx) Deming; m. Roland Anderson (dec.); children: Virginia, Leon; m. Frederick S. Brady (dec. Jan. 1999); 1 child, Faye Lillian Burnaman. Student, William & Mary Coll., 1937-38, Arts Student League, NYC, 1938-39; BS cum laude, NYU, 1943; student, Pennsylvania U., 1945, Wayne State U., 1957-59; MA in Exceptional Edn., U. Fla., 1964, EdD in Psychology and Exceptional Edn., 1967. Registered Occupational Therapist, Phila., 1945; Cert. Sch. Psychologist, Occupational Therapist, Guidance. Art tchr., N.Y., Ohio and Mich.; occupational therapist U.S. Army Hosp., 1944-45; dir. occupational therapy Perry Point V.A. Hosp., 1946-55; coord. exceptional edn. program Brevard County, Fla., 1960-64; dir. guidance and counseling Satellite H.S., Brevard County, Fla., 1965-68; dir. guidence Brevard County, 1968-69; dir. guidance and counseling Orange County, 1969; psychologist Learning Disability Ctr. and Gateway Sch., 1970-72; dir. Pupil Personnel Services, High Point, N.C., 1972-73; psychologist Exceptional Edn. Program, Orlando, Fla., 1973-78; dir. Bureau Indian Affairs Special Edn. Program, Washington, 1978-80; psychologist Western Navajo Agency, Tuba City, Ariz., B.I.A. Eastern Navajo, 1983. Tchr. Brevard C.C. Fla., 1964-68, U. Fla. Gainesville, Fla., 1966-68, Fla. Ctrl. U. Orlando, 1969, U. So. Fla. Tampa, Fla., 1971-72, Rollins Coll. Orlando, 1976-77. Author: (booklet on VA tsch.) Occupational Therapy, 1950, Reflections Poems and Pictures, 2001, Renaissance Journey Poetry Book. Pres. Brevard County Coun. Exceptional Children, Brevard County Guidance Assn.; vol., greeter program James A. Haley VA Hosp. Scholar United Cerebral Palsy, U. Fla.; recipient Outstanding Achievement award Veterans Adminstrn. Mem. Nat. Assn. State Dirs. Special Edn. Home: 4000 E Fletcher Ave C-302 Tampa FL 33613-4890 E-mail: k63007@aol.com.

BRADY, KRISTYLYNNE, social worker, speech pathology/audiology services professional; b. Cocoa Beach, Fla., Oct. 20, 1965; d. Lon Garth and Mary Jo Brady. MSW, U. Utah, 1998, B.A. in Human Devel., 1996; BS in Psychology, Brigham Young U., 1991. LCSW Nat. Assn. of Social Workers Utah, 1998. Telecom. relay svcs. specialist Pub. Svc. Commn., Salt Lake City, 2002—; clin. dir. Counseling Ctr., Murray, Utah, 2001—; dir. crisis nursery Family Support Ctr., Salt Lake City, 2000—01, clin. dir., 1999—2000, therapist, 1997—2001; sign lang. interpreter Wasatch Front, Utah. Adv. bd. mem. Nat. Ctr. on Deafness Adv. Bd., Northridge, Calif., 2003—; adv. coun. mem. Utah Cmty. Ctr. for the Deaf and Hard of Hearing, Salt Lake City, 2003—; adv. bd. mem. We. Region Outreach Ctr. and Corsortia, Salt Lake City. Author of two chapters (book) The Deaf Way II Reader; actor: (theatrical performance in sign language) Woman at the Well; co-founder and performer (theatrical performance in sign language) Hands. Mem. State of Utah Strategic Mental Health Plan for Deaf and Hard of Hearing, Salt Lake City; cons. Utah State Bd. Mental Health Services for Deaf and Hard of Hearing, Salt Lake City, 2001—01; crisis response team co-leader for deaf cmty. tragedy Salt Lake Police Dept. and SWAT Team, Salt Lake City, 1999—99; stake primary pres. LDS Ch., Salt Lake City, 2000—03. Recipient Outstanding Young Alumni, Grad. Sch. of Social Work, 2001. Mem.: State of Utah Sch. Social Worker (assoc.; mem. 2001—03), Network on Juveniles Offending Sexually (assoc.; mem. 2001—03), Critical Incident Stress Mgmt. (assoc.; team mem. 2002—03). Mem. Lds. Achievements include invention of Innovative relaxation techniques with people who are deaf; research in Culturally Affirming Diagnosis with Individuals who are Deaf: It's All in the Axis III. Avocations: down hill skiing, volleyball, hiking, signing music, performing arts. E-mail: klbrady@utah.gov.

BRADY, M. JANE, state attorney general; b. Wilmington, Del., Jan. 11, 1951; m. Michael Neal. BA, U. Del., 1973; JD, Villanova U., 1976. Dep. atty. gen. Wilmington and Kent County, 1977—90; chief prosecutor Sussex County, 1987—90; solo law practice, 1990—94; atty. gen. State of Del., Wilmington, 1994—. Bd. dirs. Nat. Dist. Attys. Assn., Kent/Sussex Industries. Past chair Rep Attys. Gen. Assn.; bd. dirs. Nat. Org. Victim Assistance; founder KINfolk; bd. dirs. Del. Children's Trust Fund; advisory bd. Big Bros./Big Sisters Sussex County. Named Delaware's Top Fraud Fighter, AARP Delaware, 1998. Mem.: Nat. Assn. Attys. Gen. (exec. com.). Republican. Office: Office of Atty Gen Carvel State Office Bldg 820 N French St Wilmington DE 19801-3509 E-mail: jbrady@state.de.us.*

BRADY, MARY CLEMMER, medical association administrator, actress; b. Connellsville, Pa., Mar. 9, 1959; d. Norman Earl Clemmer and Mary Louise Fiesta; m. Timothy Scott Brady, Feb. 17, 1979 (div. Mar. 1983). Diploma, Connellsville Area HS, 1977. Asst. supr. State Nat. Bk., El Paso, Tex., 1978—80; admin. asst. U. Pitts., Dept. Surgery, Pitts., 1980—87; admin. supr. U. Pitts. Med. Ctr., 1987—. Choreographer Greensburg (Pa.) Ctrl. Catholic HS, 1987—92. Vol. Family House Shadyside, Pitts., 2001—. Avocations: movies, reading, puzzles, rowing. Home: 107 Pennwood Ave Pittsburgh PA 15218 Office: U Pitts Med Ctr 3811 O'Hara St Pittsburgh PA 15213 Office Phone: 412-246-6777.

BRADY, MARY ROLFES, music educator; b. St. Louis, Nov. 26, 1933; d. William Henry and Helen Dorothy (Slavick) Rolfes; m. Donald Sheridan Brady, Aug. 29, 1953; children: Joseph William, Mark David, Douglas Sheridan, John Rolfes, Todd Christopher. Student, Stanford U., 1951-54, UCLA, 1967, U. So. Calif., 1972-73; pvt. studies with, Roxanna Byers, Dorothy Desmond, and Rudolph Ganz. Pvt. piano tchr., L.A., 1955—; TV and radio performer. Pres. Jr. Philharmonic Com. L.A., 1975-76; legis. coord., bd. dirs. Philharmonic Affiliates, L.A., 1978-80. Life mem. Good Samaritan Hosp., St. Vincent Med. Ctr., L.A.; trustee St. Francis Med. Ctr., 1984-88; bd. dirs. Hollygrove-L.A. Orphans Home, Inc. Mem. Am. Coll. Musicians Club, Stanford Women's Club (past bd. dirs., pres. L.A. chpt. 1977—), The Muses, Springs Country Club.

BRADY, SISTER PATRICIA ANN, minister, director; d. John Anthony and Emily Jenny Brady. BA in English, Am. Lit., Poetry, Cath. U., 1965. Cert. Portugese Lang. Latin Am. Coll., Louvain, Belgium, 1991, Leadership Skills The Connolly Inst., 1991. Tchr. jr. h.s. Cath. Sch., Buffalo, 1962—63, 1965—68; h.s. prin., prof., missionary Schs. Various Countries, 1968—78; missionary, coll. and h.s. prof., religious educator Various Schools And Ch. Settings, Brazil, 1978—86; tchr. h.s., campus min. Mt. St. Mary Acad., Kenmore, NY, 1992—96; campus min. Canisius Coll., 1996—, dir. svc.-learning, 2003. Organizer young adult svc. Sisters of St. Mary, Mexico, 1990—2003; translator french, english Sisters St. Mary Namur, Belgium, 1989—2001, translator French, English, 1989—2001. Author: (poem) Cracked (First Pl. in the ann. Dr. Martin Luther King, Jr. Poetry contest at Canisius Coll., 2001). Mem. adv. bd. Friends Elderly, Youth Family Ctr., 1997—; religious vocation contact person Nat. Religious Vocation Conf., Buffalo, 2002—03. Recipient Dr. Martin Luther King, Jr. award, Canisius Coll., 2000. Mem.: Nat. Soc. for Experiential Edn., Regional Campus Mins. Assn. (bd. mem. 1999—), Assn. Jesuit Colls. U.S., DiGamma Honor Soc. (life). Roman Catholic. Avocations: reading, chess, egyptology, music. Home: 237 Lafayette Ave Buffalo NY 14213 Office: Canisius College 2001 Main St Buffalo NY 14208 Personal E-mail: bradyp@canisius.edu.

BRADY, TERRIE, political organization executive; Student, Polit. Leadership Tng. Sch., Washington, 1979, 85. Tchr., Jacksonville, Fla.; chair Fla. State Dem. Party, 1993—. Mem. Fla. State Dem. Platform Com., 1978, 80, 82, 89, 92; del. Nat. Dem. Conv., 1980, 84, 88, 92; mem. Dem. Nat. Com., 1989—; polit. dir., legis. liaison Duval Tchrs. United. Recipient Hubert H. Humphrey award for Fla.'s outstanding Dem., 1987, Golden Gavel award, 1989, 91, Frontier award Fla. Dem. Party, 1992, Mary Nolan award NOW, Jacksonville, 1996. Mem. Spina Bifida Assn., March of Dimes. Office: PO Box 1758 Tallahassee FL 32302-1758

BRADY-BORLAND, KAREN, retired reporter, columnist; b. Buffalo, Mar. 13, 1940; d. Charles A. and Mary Eileen (Larson) B.; m. Gregg Robinson Borland, Sept. 6, 1969 (div. July 1985); children: Caitlin Luise, Kristin Robinson, Leila Nell. BA in English, Daemen Coll., 1961; MS in Journalism, Columbia U., 1962. Summer reporter Buffalo News, 1961, reporter, 1965-68, columnist, 1968-81; editor Prentice-Hall, Inc., Englewood, N.J., 1962-65; press officer for Rep. Max McCarthy U.S. Ho. Reps., Washington, 1967; gen. assignment & features reporter Buffalo News, 1981—91, higher education reporter, 1991—2002; ret., 2002. Recipient numerous awards Buffalo Newspaper Guild, 1969-79, N.Y. State award for Major Dailies Mag. Writing AP, 1982, numerous community awards, Hilbert Coll. medal, 2002.

BRAGG, BEVERLY SMITH, volunteer; b. Montgomery, Ala., Apr. 3, 1932; d. Clarence Arnold and Dorothy Overton (Dabney) Smith; m. Wilbur Clark Bragg Jr., Nov. 12, 1954 (dec. Nov. 1997); children: Dabney Elizabeth, Martha Clarke, John Reneau. Student, Sweet Briar Coll, 1950—52; BA, U. Ala., 1952. Mem.: Music Study Club. Methodist. Avocations: writing, travel, reading. Mailing: PO Box 548 Fayette AL 35555

BRAGG, LYNN MUNROE, trade association administrator, former federal commissioner; b. Ft. Leonard Wood, Mo., June 15, 1954; d. Irving William and Elaine Frances (Heath) Munroe; m. Raymond Frank Bragg, Jr., Aug. 12, 1989; children: Hudson, Rachael, Braxton. BA in English, Mary Washington Coll., 1976; MS in Pub. Rels., Boston U., 1978. Speech and fin. writer Potomac Electric Power Co., Washington, 1978-80; legis. dir., legis. asst. Office of U.S. Senator Malcolm Wallop, Washington, 1981-91; dir. govtl. affairs Edison Electric Inst., Washington, 1991-94; commr. U.S. Internat. Trade Commn., Washington, 1994—2002, vice chmn., 1996-98, chmn., 1998-2000; pres. Chocolate Mfrs. Assn., McLean, Va., 2003—. Republican. Episcopalian. Avocation: golf. Office: Chocolate Mfrs Assn 7900 Westpark Dr Ste A-320 Mc Lean VA 22102*

BRAHAM, DELPHINE DORIS, accountant, government official; b. L'Anse, Mich., Mar. 16, 1946; d. Richard Andrew and Viola Mary Aho; m. John Emerson Braham, Sept. 23, 1967 (div. Aug. 1988); children: Tammy, Debra, John Jr. BS summa cum laude, Drury Coll., 1983; M in Mgmt., Webster U., St. Louis, 1986. Bookkeeper Cmty. Mental Health Ctr., Marquette, Mich., 1966-68; acctg. technician St. Joseph Hosp., Parkersburg, W.Va., 1972-74; material mgr. U.S. Army, Ft. Leonard Wood, Mo., 1982-86; acct., 1986-92; supervisory acct. Dept. Def., Indpls., 1992—. Instr., adj. faculty Columbia Coll., 1987-92, Park Coll., 1988-92. Leader Girl Scouts U.S., Williamstown, W.Va., 1972-74, Hanau, Germany, 1977-79. Mem. AAUW (treas. Waynesville br. 1986-90), Am. Soc. Mil. Comptrs., NAFE, Assn. Govt. Accts., Waynesville Bus. and Profl. Women's Orgn. Home: 2752 Pawnee Dr Indianapolis IN 46229-1418

BRAIL, KATRINA IRENE, epidemiologist; d. Robert Clinton and Debra Clinton Brail. Degree in Anthrop., U. Mo., 2000; MPH in Epidemiology, St. Louis (Mo.) U., 2002. Epidemiology specialist Mo. Dept. Health, St. Louis, 2000—02; epidemiologist St. Charles (Mo.) Dept. Health, 2002—. Avocations: running, pottery, travel, cooking, photography. Home: 440 Old Colony Rd Defiance MO 63341

BRAILEY, SUSAN LOUISE, quality analyst, educator; b. Omaha, Aug. 28, 1939; d. James Burt and Helen Frances B.; m. Hugh Pelham Whitt, Dec. 29, 1990. BS in Edn. with distinction, U. Nebr., Omaha, 1961; postgrad., U. Nebr., Lincoln, 1977-79; MA in Comm., U. Cin., 1970. Cert. quality analyst Quality Assurance Inst., Orlando, Fla. Instr., dir. debate Omaha Pub. Schs., 1965-67; tchr. Walnut Hills H.S., Cin., 1967-69, U. Cin., 1969-72, U. Nebr., Lincoln, 1978; dir. MIS Wayne (Nebr.) State Coll., 1979-80; sr. tech. writer, analyst 1st Data Resources, Omaha, 1981-82, supr. documentation, 1982-83, tng. specialist, 1983-85, sr. analyst quality assurance, 1988-92; tng. specialist Enron Corp., Omaha, 1985-86, sr. analyst quality assurance Houston, 1986-88. Mem. Dem. Nat. Com., 1995—, Dem. Congl. Campaign Com., 2000—. Mem. AAUW, Arthritis Found., Lupus Found, Pi Kappa Delta, Phi Delta Kappa, Phi Delta Gamma. Congregationalist. Avocations: reading, antiques, bridge, music, politics. Home: 9530 Davenport St Omaha NE 68114-3872

BRAINARD, CAROL LEE, realtor; b. Chgo., Dec. 13, 1933; d. Vernon Lee and Irene Jeanne (Glover) Kipp; m. John Howell Brainard, May 26, 1954; children: Laura Anne, Lynn Denise, James Howell. Attended, Conn. Coll. for Women, 1954; grad., Real Estate Inst., 1985. Cert. residential specialist Colo., 1985. Realtor RealTeam Realtors, Parker, Colo., 1976—. Avocations: tchg. music classes @ ch., 4-H horse program leader, skiing. Home: 8535 E Homestead Rd Parker CO 80138

BRAINARD, MELISSA, accountant; b. Buffalo, Jan. 11, 1969; d. Peter Anthony and Mary Agnes (Lazarus) Arena; m. Kevin Joseph Brainard, Sept. 25, 1993; children: Jacob Leon, Zachary Martin. BS, SUNY, Buffalo, 1991. CPA, N.Y., 1993. From staff mem. to mgr. KPMG, Buffalo, 1991-97; CFO Goodwill Industries Western N.Y., 1997-98; mgr. Deloitte & Touche, Buffalo, 1999—2002; cons. Albright-Knox Art Gallery, Buffalo, 2002—. Avocations: animals, family, collecting baskets. E-mail: mbrainard@albrightknox.org.

BRAINERD, MARY, small business owner; b. Denver, Apr. 25, 1963; d. John and Jane B. B in Music, U. Colo., 1985, M in M in Music, MBA, U. Colo., 1988. Freelance musician, Denver, 1975—; rsch. assoc. CSM, Golden, Colo., 1988-95; ind. prospect rschr. Colo. Pub. Radio, Children's Hosp., Mile High United Way, Denver, 1995-98; owner Golden Music Ctr., 1996—. Bd. dirs. Jefferson Symphony Orch., Golden, 1997-98. Office: Golden Music Ctr 2430 East St Golden CO 80401-2418 E-mail: goldenmusiccenter@home.com.

BRAININ, RISA, freelance/self-employed theater director; b. Chgo., July 3, 1960; d. Norman Herbert and Constance Spears Brainin; m. Michael Edward Klaers, Aug. 7, 1993. BFA, Carnegie-Mellon U., 1984. Dir. edn. SteppingStone Theatre Youth Devel., St. Paul, 1989—90; assoc. co. dir., resident dir., acting instr. Guthrie Theatre, Mpls., 1988—97; assoc. artistic dir. Ind. Repertory Theatre, Indpls., 1997—2000, Mo. Repertory Theatre, Kansas City; artistic dir. Shakespeare Santa Cruz, Calif., 2001—. Freelance dir., Minn., 1987—97; adj. instr. U. Minn., Mpls., 1992—96. Mem.: Theatre Comm. Group, Stage Soc. Dirs. and Choreographers. Personal E-mail: risab@ucsc.edu.

BRAISTED, MADELINE CHARLOTTE, artist, visual artist, retired financial planner, army officer; b. Jamaica, N.Y., Nov. 23, 1936; d. Melvin Vincent and Charlotte Marie (Klos) B. AAS, Nassau C.C., 1968; BA, Hofstra U., 1973, MA, 1975; grad., U.S. Command and Gen. Staff Coll., 1985. Cert. fin. planner, 1991. Reservations agt. Airline Industry, N.Y.C., 1957-64; reservations contr. Auto Lease Industry, N.Y.C., 1964-66; nuclear medicine technician Queens Gen. Hosp., Jamaica, N.Y., 1969-70; lab. mgr. CUNY, 1970-80; owner Energy Etcetera, Flushing, N.Y., 1979-85; active duty with U.S. Army Health Profl. Support Agy., Office of Surgeon Gen., Washington, 1980-92. Author, pub. Energy Etcetera catalog, 1981-85; artist On Shore painting (honorable mention 1974). Merit badge counselor Boy Scouts Am., Queens County, N.Y., 1980-83; active PTA, Jamaica, 1980-84. Served with USMC, 1954-57, from sgt. to maj. USAR, 1975-96. Decorated Legion of Merit, Army Commendation medal with one oak leaf, Army Achievement medal with one oak leaf cluster, expert field med. badge. Mem. NAFE, APHA, Am Acad. Med. Adminstrs., Fin. Planners Assn., Am. Assn. Individual Investors, Assn. Mil. Surgeons U.S., Res. Officers Assn., Ret. Officers Assn., Nat. Art League, Rockaway Artists Alliance, Queens Coun. Arts. Roman Catholic. Avocations: painting, sculpture.

BRAITERMAN, THEA GILDA, economics educator, state legislator, selectman; b. Balt., Sept. 11, 1927; d. Isaac E. and Clara (Fink) Bloom; m. Marvin Braiterman, Mar. 21, 1948; children: Kenneth, Marta, David. BS, Johns Hopkins U., 1949; MA, U. Md., 1966; PhD, Union Inst., 1977. Assoc. prof. econs. Balt. Coll. of Commerce, 1966-73; prof. econs. New England Coll., Henniker, N.H., 1973—; mem. N.H. Ho. of Reps., 1988-94. Cons. on retirement, 1988—; selectman Town of Henniker, 1997—. Author: Workbook on Economic Theory, 1966; contbr. articles to profl. jours. Sec., bd. govs. United Way of Merrimack County, Concord, N.H., 1984-90; v.p., bd. govs. Cmty. Svcs. Coun., Concord, 1980-84. Jane Addams Peace Assn. grantee, 1976-77; Gilmore grantee New Eng. Coll., 1988-90. Mem. Am. Econ. Assn., Ea. Econ. Assn. Home: PO Box 686 Henniker NH 03242-0686 Office: New England Coll Henniker NH 03242 E-mail: theabrait@conknet.com.

BRAITHWAITE, BARBARA J. secondary school educator; BA, Ctrl. Mich. U., 1959; MA, U. Mich., 1960. Geography tchr. grade 7 Pocono Mountain Sch. Dist., Swiftwater, Pa. Recipient 1st Place award Am. Express geography competition for tchrs., 1990, Outstanding Secondary Level Tchr. of the Year award Pa. Coun. Social Studies, 1992, Innovative Tchg. award State Farm Ins. Co., 1995. Mem. Pa. Geog. Alliance (steering com., tchr. cons.), Pocono Regional Geog. Alliance (co-founder, chairperson), Nat. Coun. Geog. Edn., Pa. Geog. Soc. (Tchr. Recognition award 1993, U.S., Russia, Ukraine Tchr. Excellence award 1997, Pa. Tchr. of Yr. 1999). Home: 65 Stones Throw East Stroudsburg PA 18301-9694 also: Pocono Mountain Sch Dist Swiftwater PA 18370-0200

BRAITHWAITE, MARGARET EVON, music educator; b. Savannah, Ga., Mar. 13, 1944; d. Collin and Lucille Peronica (McMoore) Tilson; m. Coleridge Alexander Braithwaite, June 10, 1978 (dec. May 27, 1995). Student, Savannah State U., Savannah, GA, 1961—63; BA, Armstrong Atlantic State U., 1988; MEd, Cambridge Coll., 1999, EdS, 2001. Cert. tchr. Ga. Tchr. Mercer Mid. Sch., Garden City, Ga., 1989—98; tchr. S.W. Mid. Sch. Savannah Chatham County Bd. of Edn., 1998—. Choir dir. Connors Temple Bapt. Ch., Savannah, 1981—84; min. of music/choir dir. Most Pure of Mary Cath. Ch., Savannah, 1984—90; min. of music Tilson's Temple, Savannah, 1992—. Bd. dirs. Savannah On Stage, 1999—2002; vocal music BRAVO, Savannah, 1997—2003, bd. dirs. music program, 1997—2003. Named Tchr. of Excellence, Savannah Morning News, 1998. Mem.: NEA, Music Educators Nat. Conf., A.E. Beach H.S. Nat. Alumni Assn. (life). Home: 106 Radick Dr Savannah GA 31406-3229 Office: Southwest Middle School 6030 Ogeechee Rd Savannag GA 31419 E-mail: mrgbrthwt@aol.com.

BRAITHWAITE, MARILYN JEAN, realtor; b. Winchester, Va., Jan. 24, 1948; d. Charles Wilson and Bette (Dickson) B. AS in English, Ferrum Coll., 1969; cert. in real estate, Merrill Lynch Inst., 1987; cert., Real Estate Sch. W.Va., 1992; grad. Realtor Inst., W.Va. U., 1995. Cert. residential specialist; accredited buyer rep. Acctg. officer Nat. Pub. Affairs Ctr. for TV, Washington, 1972-76; office mgr. Nat. Consumers Union, Washington, 1976-78; pers. dir. Urban Environment Conf., Washington, 1978-84; dir. of adminstrn. Human Rights Campaign Fund, Washington, 1984-87; realtor Barbara Held/City Sites, Washington, 1987-92, Long & Foster Real Estate, Martinsburg, W.Va., 1992-2000; with RE/MAX Enterprises, Hedgesville, W.Va., 2000—. Instr. real estate principles and law Shepherd Coll., Shepherdstown, W.Va., 1993-98; field trainer Long & Foster Real Estate, Martinsburg, W.Va., 1996-2000; chair Ea. Panhandle Bd. Profl. Standards Com., Martinsburg, 1999. Contbg. author: Patterns: An Anthology of Modern Poetry, 1970. Donation solicitor Shenandoah Women's Shelter, 1994—. Mem. Profl. Bus. Women's Assn. (founder), Ea. Panhandle Bd. of Realtors (pres. 2000), Nat. Assn. Realtors, W.Va. Assn. Realtors, Nat. Trust for Hist. Preservation. Democrat. Methodist. Avocations: reading, cooking, attending auctions, bird watching. Home: 765 Grade Rd Falling Waters WV 25419-4171

BRAKAS, NORA JACHYM, education educator; b. Schenectady, N.Y., Aug. 9, 1952; d. Thaddeus Michael and Theresa Mary (Patnode) J.; m. Jurgis Brakas, June 15, 1996. BS in Elem. Edn., Plattsburg State U. Coll., 1974; MS in Reading, SUNY, Albany, 1977, Cert. Advanced Study in Reading, 1986, PhD in Reading, 1990. Cert. elem. sch. tchr., reading tchr. Elem. sch. and reading tchr. Lee (Mass.) Ctrl. Sch., 1976-82; reading specialist Guilderland (N.Y.) Sch. Dist., 1988-89; rsch. asst., tchg. asst. SUNY, Albany, 1985-88, instr. reading dept., 1989-90; asst. prof. tchr. edn., reading specialist Southeastern La. U., Hammond, 1990-91, Marist Coll., Poughkeepsie, N.Y., 1991—. Presenter, spkr. in field. Contbr. articles to profl. jours. Student Literacy Corp. grantee U.S. Dept. Edn., 1991, IBM/Marist Joint Study Project grantee, 1992. Mem. Internat. Reading Assn., Soc. Children's Book Writers and Illustrators. Avocations: drawing, writing children's books, collecting antique children's books. Home: PO Box 176 Rhinecliff NY 12574-0176 Office: Marist Coll 388 F Dyson Poughkeepsie NY 12601 E-mail: Nora.Brakas@Marist.edu.

BRAKEBILL, ELIZABETH M. music educator; b. Camp Lejeune, NC, Feb. 14, 1965; d. Joseph J. and Martha Weaver Malloy; m. M. Merritt Brakebill, Aug. 25, 1984; children: Sara Blair(dec.), Jacob Wiley. MusB, Maryville Coll., Tenn., 1996. Music dir. Loudon H.S., Tenn., 1997—. Cheer coach Loundon H.S., Loudon, Tenn., 1997—2003. Named one of Outstanding Young Women of Am., 1992. Mem.: DAR, Music Educators Nat. Conf., East Tenn. Vocal Assn., Delta Omicron (pres. 1992). Avocations: reading, writing, hiking, skiing, swimming. Home: 135 Giffin Cir Loudon TN 37774 Office: Loudon H S 1039 Mulberry St Loudon TN 37774

BRAKEL, LISA ELAINE, multi-media specialist; b. Clinton, Ind., Jan. 16, 1959; d. Wayne Allen and Leona May Smith; m. Timothy Duane Brakel, July 2, 1988; children: Wayne Prentice, Brammer Christian. BS, Ind. State U., 1981, MEd, 1985; MLS, Ind. U., 1991. Gen. music tchr. Am. Sch. Kuwait, Kuwait, 1982—84; instrumental music tchr. E. Tipp Mid. Sch., Lafayette, Ind., 1985—97; pers. mgr. Bloomington (Ind.) Symphony Orch., 1997—98; music tchr. and libr. media specialist Christian Heritage Sch.,

Riverdale, Utah, 1998—2000; libr. media specialist Ctrl. Davis Jr. HS, Layton, Utah, 2000; instrumental music tchr. Bedford Pub. Schs., Temperance, Mich., 2000—01; libr. media specialist Monroe (Mich.) Mid. Sch., 2001—.

BRAME, MARILLYN A. hypnotherapist; b. Indpls., Sept. 17, 1928; d. [illegible] and Hilda (Kiley) Curtin; 1 child, Gary Mansour. Student, Meinzinger Art Sch., Detroit, 1946-47, U. N.Mex., 1963, Orlando (Fla.) Jr. Coll., 1964-65, El Camino Coll., Torrance, Calif., 1974-75; PhD in Hypnotherapy, Am. Inst. Hypnotherapy, 1989. Cert. and registered hypnotherapist. Color cons. Pitts. Plate Glass Co., Albuquerque, 1951-52; owner Signs by Marillyn, Albuquerque, 1952-53; design draftsman Sandia Corp., Albuquerque, 1953-56; designer The Martin Co., Orlando, 1957-65; pres. The Arts, Winter Park, Fla., 1964-66; supr. tech. publs. Gen. Instrument Corp., Hawthorne, Calif., 1967-76; pres. Camart Design, Westminster, Calif., 1977-86, Visual Arts, Lake Forest, Calif., 1978—; mgr. tech. publs. Archive Corp., Costa Mesa, Calif., 1986-90. Adj. instr. Orange Coast Coll., Costa Mesa, 1985-90; hypnotherapist, Mission Viejo, 1986—; bd. dirs. Orange County chpt. Am. Bd. Hypnotherapy. Author: Lemon and Lime Scented Herbs, 1994, (textbook) Folkdancing is for Everybody, 1974, Innovative Imagery, 1996, Changing Your Mood, 1997; inventor, designer dance notation sys. MS Method. Mem. bd. govs. Lake Forest II Showboaters Theatre Group, 1985-88; mem. City of Mission Viejo Cultural Arts Com., 1995—; bd. dirs. Orange County Fine Arts, v.p., pres., 2001. Mem. Soc. Tech. Communication (v.p. programs, 1987, newsletter editor 1986-87, newsletter prodn. editor 1985-86). Avocations: folkdancing, rock collecting, community theater, metaphysics. E-mail: visualarts@mindspring.com.

BRAMHALL, DEBRA A. information technology manager, consultant; d. Ronald C. Bramhall, Sr.; 1 child, Benjamin R. Solo. Assoc. Degree, Westmoreland County C.C., Youngwood, Pa.; Bachelor Degree, U. Phoenix, San Jose, Calif.; Masters Degree, Columbus U. Info. tech. sys. adminstr., contr. Syntrax, Provo, Utah, 1989—90; sys. mgr. Novell, San Jose, Calif., 1990—96; LAN mgr. Kaiser Permanente, Stockton, Calif., 1996—98; NSD mgr. Am. Century, Mountain View, Calif., 1998—2000; dir. Cyber Ctr. Qwest, Columbus, Ohio, 2000—02; ind. sr. cons. Columbus, 2002—. Mem.: NAFE, PTA. Avocations: volunteering, playing tenor saxophone.

BRAMLETT, SHIRLEY MARIE WILHELM, interior decorator, artist; b. Scottsboro, Ala., June 14, 1945; d. Robert David and Alta (Reeves) Wilhelm; m. Paul Kent Bramlett, June 5, 1966; children: Paul Kent II (dec.), Robert Preston. BS, David Lipscomb U., 1966; postgrad., U. Miss., 1966-68; pvt. study art, 1976—. Decorator The Anchorage House, Oxford, Miss., 1966-67, Interiors by Shirley, Tupelo, Miss., 1971-80; tchr. Oxford City Schs., 1967-69; decorator, buyer Donald Furniture, Tupelo, 1969-71; owner, importer Bramblewood Interiors & Antiques, Belden, Miss., 1976-80; owner, decorator, artist The Cottage on Caldwell, Inc., Nashville, 1980—. Sec.-treas. Kent Bramlett Found., Inc., 1992—. Represented in art galleries Hundred Oaks Castle, Winchester, Tenn., Lyzon Gallery, Nashville; introduced and presented painting House of Parliament, Luxembourg; commd. for watercolor print fortnightly Musicale of Miss., 1991-92; European representation by Internet Internat. Bd. dirs. Found. for Christian Edn., 1988—, Ea. European Missions, Vienna, Austria, 1986— (commd. for watercolor print used in internat. fundraising); del. Miss. Dem. caucus, 1970; fundraiser Agape Artist, 1991; sec., treas., bd. dirs. Kent Bramlett Found., Inc.; curator Hundred Oaks Castle, Winchester, Tenn. Named Woman of Decade, David Lipscomb Coll., 1986, one of Outstanding Young Women of Am., 1979; selected Centennial Artist, David Lipscomb U., Nashville, 1991, one of ten Master Tenn. Artists, Lyzon Gallery, Nashville, 1991. Mem. Nat. Mus. Women in Arts, Tenn. Watercolor Soc., Nat. Soc. Tole and Decorative Painters, Green Hills Garden Club (cover artist for nat. conv. garden clubs 1985), Assoc. Ladies Lipscomb (bd. dirs. 1991-92). Mem. Ch. of Christ. Avocation: restoring historic castle. Home: 930 Caldwell Ln Nashville TN 37204-4016

BRAMWELL, MARVEL LYNNETTE, mental health nurse, social worker; b. Durango, Colo., Aug. 13, 1947; d. Floyd Lewis and Virginia Jenny (Amyx) Bramwell. LPN, Durango Sch. Practical Nursing, 1968; ADN, Mt. Hood CC, 1972; BSN, BS in Gen. Studies cum laude, So. Oreg. State Coll., 1980; cert. in edn. grad. sch. social work, U. Utah, 1987, cert. in counselor alcohol, drug abuse, 1988, MSW, 1992. RN Utah, Oreg., Ind., Nev.; cert. social worker Utah, Ind., Nev., LCSW Nev., 2003. Staff nurse Monument Valley (Utah) Seventh Day Adventist Mission Hosp., 1973-74, La Plata Cmty. Hosp., 1974-75; health coord. Tri County Head Start Program, 1974-75; nurse therapist, team leader Portland Adventist Med. Ctr., 1975-78; staff nurse Indian Health Svc. Hosp., 1980-81; coord. village health svcs. North Slope Borough Health and Social Svc. Agy., Barrow, Alaska, 1981-83; nurse, supr. aides Bonneville Health Care Agy., 1984-85; staff nurse LDS Adolescent Psychiat. Unit, 1985-86; coord. adolescent nursing CPC Olympus View Hosp., 1986-87, 91; charge and staff nurse adult psychiatry U. Utah, 1987-88; nurse MSW Cmty. Nursing Svc., Salt Lake City, 1989-90, Willow Springs Ctr., Reno, 1996—2002; resident scvs. coord., dir. nursing Arden Ctrs., Reno, 1998-99—; med. social worker Meth. Home Health, Indpls., 1994-96; psychiat. nurse Willow Springs Ctr., 1996—2002; DON, resident svc. coord. Arden Ctrs., Reno, 1998-99; per diem nurse N. Nev. Med. Ctr., 2000—01; discharge planner Carson-Tahoe Hosp., 2003; lic. social worker, 2003—. Cons. design and constrn. 6 high tech. health clinics Alaska Arctic, 1982—83; per diem nurse Reno VA Med. Ctr., N. Nev. Med. Ctr., 1998—99; psychiat. nurse specialist Cmty. Nursing Svc. Contbr. articles to profl. jours. Active Mothers Against Drunk Driving Program U. Alaska Rural Edn., 1981—83. Recipient cert. appreciation, U.S. Census Bur., Colo., 1970, Barrow Lion's Club, 1983, others. Mem.: NASW, NOW, Assn. Women Sci. Avocations: watercolor painting, photography, hiking, horseback riding. Home: Apt 349 6200 Meadowood Mall Circle Reno NV 89502-6621 E-mail: anp3943@aol.com., marvel@bhr.reno.nv.us.

BRANAGAN, CAROLYN W. state representative; b. Windsor, Vt., June 5, 1954; m. Christopher Branagan; 3 children. BS, U. Vt., 1976, MEd, 1984. State rep. State of Vt., 2003—. Chair Ga. Sch. Bd.; mem. Ga. Town Moderator; treas. Ga. Bapt. Ch. Republican. Office: 1295 Ballard Rd Georgia VT 05478

BRANCH, BRENDA SUE, library director; b. Buffalo, Apr. 27, 1947; BS in Edn., SUNY, Cortland, 1969; MLS, postgrad., SUNY, Buffalo, 1972, S.W. Tex. State U., 1973-74, Stephen F. Austin State U., 1975-76; MPA, S.W. Tex. State U., 1985. Tchr. Kenmore Ind. Sch. Dist., 1969-70; asst. health scis. libr. SUNY, Buffalo, 1971-73; br. mgr. Austin Pub. Libr., 1973-75; acquisitions libr. Tex. Ea. U., 1975; humanities libr. Stephen F. Austin State U., 1975-76; dist. libr. coord. Longview Ind. Sch. Dist., 1976-77; program devel. coord. Austin Pub. Libr., 1977-80, supr. br. svcs., 1980-86, asst. dir. pub. svcs., 1986-91, dir., 1991—. Project mgr. reduction-in-force project City of Austin, 1988, co-chair customer svc. task force, coord. creativity program, 1990; mem. long range planning com. svcs. spl. populations Tex. State Libr., 1992. Mem. Austin Travis County Continuing Edn. Adv. Bd., Austin, 1981—, Tex. Mcpl. League, Mayor's Coalition Workplace Literacy, 1990, Literacy and Fundamental Edn. Speaker's Bur., 1991-93, Leadership Austin, 1991—, chair kids program, 1993; tutor, trainer Travis County Adult Literacy Coun., 1986-89; chair City of Austin Workplace Literacy Task Force, 1989—; mem. speaker's bur. United Way, 1990-92; mem. MPA adv. coun. S.W. Tex. State U., 1993; bd. dirs. Big Bros./Big Sisters, 1986-90, chair pub. rels. com., 1986-90, fundraiser, 1986-90, com. co-chair, 1986-90. Recipient Outstanding Achievement for Govt. Svc. award YWCA, 1991. Mem. ALA, Tex. Libr. Assn. (treas. dist. V 1976-77, mem. continuing edn. com. 1978-79, mem. membership com. 1986-89, mem. ann. conf. placement ctr. 1989, mem. literacy com. 1990, chair 1990-93, mem. resource sharing com. 1990—, mem. ad hoc property com. 1992, mem. minority recruitment com. 1992-93, co-chair legis. day 1992-93, chair-elect pub. libr. divsn. 1994-95, chair 1995-96), Austin Soc. Pub. Adminstrn. (chair membership com. 1984-89, newsletter editor 1984-89), Toastmasters (v.p., pres., newsletter editor). Office: Austin Public Library PO Box 2287 800 Guadalupe St Austin TX 78701-2314

BRANCH, DORI ALICE, music educator; b. Columbia, Md., Jan. 22, 1977; d. Carol Lynn Brain; m. William Ashley Branch, Dec. 28, 2001. MusB in Music Edn., East Carolina U., 1999. Coaching accreditation program level I. Music tchr. K-5 Howard County Pub. Schs., Columbia, 2000; piano/choral tchr. 6-8 Las Cruces (N.Mex.) Pub. Schs., 2000—; asst. coach women's varsity volleyball Mayfield H.S., Las Cruces, 2001—. Choreographer Las Cruces H.S., 2001—02; handbell dir. 1st Presbyn. Ch., Las Cruces, 2003—; youth coord. 9-11 meml. Mark Medoff (prodr. and author), Las Cruces, 2002. Mem.: Music Educators Nat. Conf., Am. Choral Dirs. Assn. Methodist. Avocations: volleyball, hiking. Home: 1630 Mountain View Ave Las Cruces NM 88001 E-mail: keplayer28@yahoo.com.

BRANCH, MICHELLE, musician; b. Flagstaff, Ariz., July 2, 1983; d. David and Peggy Branch. With Maverick Records, Beverly Hills, Calif., 2001—. Musician: (CD) Broken Bracelet, 2000, The Spirit Room, 2001, Breathe - The Remixes, 2002, Hotel Paper, 2003, (single) Everywhere, 2001, All You Wanted, 2001, Goodbye to You, 2003, Are You Happy Now, 2003, Breathe, 2003, (with Santana) The Game of Love, 2002 (Grammy award for Best Pop Collaboration with Vocals, 03). Recipient Grammy award for Best New Artist, 2003. Office: Maverick Recording 9348 Civic Center Dr Beverly Hills CA 90210*

BRANCIFORT, JANET MARIE, hospital administrator, respiratory therapist; b. New Britain, Conn., Dec. 3, 1956; d. Thomas Joseph and Ann Marie (Montanile) Thibodeau; 1 child, Jessica Marie Brancifort. AS in Respiratory Care, Manchester (Conn.) C.C., 1977; BS in Respiratory Care, Quinnipiac Coll., 1987; postgrad. in MPH program, U. Conn., 1991—. Cert. Nat. Bd. Respiratory Care, 1980, registerd, 1981, lic. respiratory care practitioner, Conn., 1995. Staff therapist New Britain Meml. Hosp., 1977-84, per diem respiratory therapist, 1981-84, asst. chief respiratory care, 1984-88; respiratory clin. specialist Hosp. for Spl. Care (formerly New Britain Meml. Hosp.), 1988-94, clin. outcomes mgr., 1994—. Chair-elect Conn. Pulmonary Care Respiratory Com., 1992, chair, 1993; presenter in field. Contbr. papers to profl. conf. procs. Asst. scout leader Conn. Yankee Girl Scouts Am., Berlin, 1992—. Recipient Conn. Yankee Girls Scout Leader award, 1993. Mem. Am. Assn. Respiratory Care (mem. ad hoc com. for pulmonary rehab. reimbursement, Dallas, 1993-94, mem. long term mech. ventilation task force 1993-95, clin. practice guidelines reviewer 1990-96), Nat. Bd. Respiratory Care, Conn. Thoracic Soc. (program com. 1994-95), Conn. Soc. Respiratory Care (legis. com. 1994-95), Conn. Pub. Health Assn., Alpha Sigma Lambda. Democrat. Roman Catholic. Avocations: reading, exercise, theater, basketball. Office: Hosp for Spl Care 2150 Corbin Ave New Britain CT 06053-2298

BRANCIFORTE, THERESA ALICE, retired business educator; b. Middletown, Conn., Sept. 11, 1930; d. Philip Orlacchio and Margaret Ilene Soule; m. John F. Branciforte, Apr. 23, 1955 (dec. Apr. 1985); children: Suzanne, John. BS, Tchrs. Coll. Conn., 1952; MA, Hofstra U., 1979. Tchr. Norwich (Conn.) Free Acad., 1952—54; instr. SUNY, Farmingdale, 1957—60, assoc. prof., 1977—93, ret., 1993. Contbr. articles (ref. book) Italian American of the 20th Century, 1999. Rec. sec., editor newsletter Sons of Italy in Am., Deltona, Fla., 1999—. Mem.: OSIA (Fla. chairperson Italian studies 1999—2001, editor newsletter The Floridian 2001—). Roman Catholic. Avocations: reading, travel, attending concerts and theater. Home: 784 Lake Como Dr Lake Mary FL 32746

BRAND, DONNA J. career consultant, mental health counselor; b. St. Louis; d. Richard Matthew and Esther (Shipley) Tully; m. Tom Krebs; children: Michelle, Todd, Kevin, Brian; m. Herb Brand, May 14, 1983. BA in Psychology, SUNY, Albany, 1987; MA in Counseling and Psychology Svcs., Marymount U., 1989. Cert. career counselor Nat. Bd. Cert. Counselors. Counselor Fairfax (Va.) County Pub. Schs., 1987-90, George Mason U., Fairfax, Va., 1990; career counselor Montgomery County Commn. for Women, Rockville, Md., 1990-95; owner consulting firm, career coach McLean, Va., 1995—. Cons., facilitator Women's Ctr. No. Va., Vienna, 1995—; guest commentator on career issues radio stas. WGAY-FM, WGTS-FM, WBIG-FM, Washington and met. area, 1990—. Bd. dirs. Pinecrest Cmty. Assn., Alexandria, Va., 1995—, Woodburn Mental Health Ctr., Fairfax, 1996, Vol. Emergency Families for Children, Fairfax, 1990-93. Recipient Women Making a Difference award Sta. WCOA-TV and Nat. Mus. Women in the Arts, 1995. Mem. Am. Counseling Assn. (cert.), Nat. Career Devel. Assn, Va. Counseling Assn., Psi Chi.

BRANDENBURG, LOIS SUE, special education educator; b. Bklyn., June 8, 1938; d. Bernard Robert and Audrey Esther (Cohen) Goldfinger; m. Harvey F. Brandenburg, Apr. 10, 1969; 1 child, Douglas Scott. EdB, U. Miami, 1960. Cert. handicapped tchr., N.J. Tchr. Dade County Elem. Sch., Miami, Fla., 1960-61, North. Merrick (N.Y.) Elem. Schs., 1961-71; substitute tchr. Uniondale (N.Y.) Schs., 1977-83, East Brunswick (N.J.) Schs., 1983-85, aide to retarded, 1985-88; tchr. Middlesex County Edn. Svcs. Com., Piscataway, N.J., 1988—. Tchr. parent effectiveness tng. YMCA, Freeport, N.Y., 1975-78. Com. woman Dem. ORgn., Forest Hills, N.Y., 1965-69; pres. N.F. of Ileitis & Colitis, Nassau County, N.Y., 1975-82; v.p. North Merrick Tchrs. Assn., 1969-71; treas. Middlesex County Edn. Svcs. Com. Assn., 1996—. Mem. NOW, NEA, N.J. Edn. Assn., B'Nai B'rith, Hadassah, City of Hope (life)., Am. Med. Ctr. (life). Avocations: travel, gourmet cooking, sports. Home: 10 Tall Oaks Dr East Brunswick NJ 08816-3402

BRANDES, DORIS, artist, art administrator, journalist; b. N.Y.C., Nov. 20, 1923; d. Robert Ralph Pratt and Grace Isabella Mott; m. Walter A. Spiro, July 24, 1948 (div. May 1971); children: Karen L., Pamela A. Gowers, Paul D., Amy E.; m. Gordon A. Brandes, June 13, 1971 (div. Aug. 1986); m. Tor Bjorn Polfelt, Sept. 11, 1993 (dec. Mar. 30, 2001). BFA, Pratt Inst., Bklyn., 1941; postgrad., Art Students League, 1942-43. Owner, ptnr. Witch Craft, N.Y.C., 1945-48; dir., tchr. Hidden House Creative Workshop, Jenkintown, Pa., 1964-69; printmaker, tchr. Abington Art Ctr., Jenkintown, 1971-79; dir. Cheltenham (Pa.) Art Ctr., 1979-81; founder, pub., editor Art Matters, Phila., 1981-93, dir. projects, 1981-93; founding bd. mem. Michener Art Mus., Doylestown, Pa., 1988—2004. Founding dir. Artsbridge, New Hope, Pa., Lambertville, N.J., 1993—; art columnist New Hope Gazette, 1994—, Lambertville Beacon, Hunterdon County, N.J., 1996-99; video script and prodn. Art of the River Towns, New Hope, 1996. Author: Artists of the River Towns, 2002; columnist: Artbuzz for Prime Time mag., feature writer: Bucks County Herald. Chairperson Alverthorpe Park Bd., Abington, 1964—65; founding mem. Ptnrs. in Progress, New Hope, 1996—98; adv. bd. Hepatitis B Found., Doylestown, Pa., 1994—99; advisor Artist in Residence, New Hope, 1998; bd. dirs. New Hope Hist. Soc. Recipient R. Tate McKenzie medal for svc. Phila. Sketch Club, 1985, Mayor's Citation City of Phila., 1986, 1st pl. for feature articles Pa. Press Assn., 1999, Cmty. Svc. award New Hope Pub. Libr., 1998. Democrat. Mem. Soc. Of Friends. Avocations: swimming, gourmet cooking, knitting, hiking, photography. Home and Office: 10 W Randolph St New Hope PA 18938-1326

BRANDES, JO ANNE, lawyer; BS, U. Wis., Eau Claire; JD, Willamette U. Assoc. Herz, Levin, Teper, Chernof & Sumner, SC, 1978—81; gen. counsel S.C. Johnson Comml. Markets, Sturtevant, Wis. Mem. bd. regents U. Wis., Wis., 1996—; mem. Gov.'s Commn. on Glass Ceiling; chmn. Wis. Child Care Coun.; past president Racine (Wis.) Area United Found. Office: SC Johnson Comml markets 8310 16th St PO Box 902 Sturtevant WI 53177-0902

BRANDLER, MARCIELLE Y. poet, educator; b. Riverside, Calif., June 27, 1950; d. Cecil U. and Luverne M. (Lieb) Parks. M of Profl. Writing, U. So. Calif. L.A., 1994; BA, U. Utah, 1981. Cert. lectr. L.A. C.C., 1988. Coll. educator Various colleges, Los Angeles, 1988—; dir. poetry workshop, mentor Performing Tree, Los Angeles, 2002—; vis. poet Calif. Poets in Schs., Los Angeles, 1988—2000. Author (singer, composer, producer): (cd poems with sound effects and voice) The Breathing House, poems published internationally; prodr.(featured singer/poet/emcee): (various benefit performances); author: (entertainment writer) Sierra Madre Vista & Creative Line Magazine, translator (poems transl. into Czech, French, Spanish, Arabic). Vol. Unitarian Universalist Ch., Pasadena, Calif., 1999—2003. Recipient First Pl. for poem, Eden, Mt. San Antonio Coll., 1997. Mem.: Am. Fedn. Tchrs. (assoc.), Alameda Writers Group (assoc.), Pasadena Opera Guild (assoc.; mem.). Unitarian Universalist. Achievements include Produced a film for American Film Institute; Produced a variety show for LA Coalition to End Hunger; Produced a benefit performance for the Literacy Campaign; Produced event to celebrate banned books. Avocation: poetry. E-mail: marcielle@dslextreme.com.

BRANDON, KATHLEEN ALMA, director; b. Cincinnati, Ohio, July 11, 1946; d. Arthur Hubert Brandon and Alma Martha Vorwerck; m. James Lee Frost, Apr. 15, 1987 (dec. June 13, 2000). BS, Ohio State U., 1969; MA, Calif. State U., Northridge, 1983, Calif. State U., L.A., 1997. Tchr., spl. edn. Franklin County Program for the Mentally Retarded, Columbus, Ohio, 1969—76, Atwater Ave. Sch., L.A., Calif., 1979—95, categorical program advisor, 1996—98; asst. prin. Los Angeles Unified Sch. Dist., L.A., Calif., 1998—99; coord. spl. edn., orthop. impaired L.A. Unified Sch. Dist., 1999—. Mem.: Computer Using Educators, Assn. Supervision and Curriculum Design, Coun. for Exceptional Children, Calif. Speech Lang. Hearing Assn., Am. Speech Lang. Hearing Assn. Avocations: reading, travel, decorating. Office: Los Angeles Unified Sch Dist 333 S Beaudry 17th Fl Los Angeles CA 90017 Personal E-mail: kate.brandon@lausd.net.

BRANDON, KATHRYN ELIZABETH BECK, pediatrician; b. Sept. 10, 1916; d. Clarence M. and Hazel A. (Cutler) Beck; children: John William, Kathleen Brandon McEnulty, Karen (dec.). MD, U. Chgo., 1941; BA, U. Utah, 1937; MPH, U. Calif., Berkeley, 1957. Diplomate Am. Bd. Pediats. Intern Grace Hosp., Detroit, 1941-42; resident Children's Hosp. Med. Ctr. No. Calif., Oakland, 1953-55, Children's Hosp., L.A., 1951-53; pvt. practice La Crescentia, Calif., 1946-51, Salt Lake City, 1960-65, 86—. Med. dir. Salt Lake City public schs., 1957-60; dir. Ogden City-Weber County (Utah) Health Dept., 1965-67; pediatrician Fitzsimmons Army Hosp., 1967-68; coll. health physician U. Colo., Boulder, 1968-71; student health physician U. Utah, Salt Lake City, 1971-81; occupational health physician Hill AFB, Utah, 1981-85; child health physician Salt Lake City-County Health Dept., 1971-82; cons. in field; clin. asst. U. Utah Coll. Medicine, Salt Lake City, 1958-64; clin. asst. pediatrics U. Colo. Coll. Medicine, Denver, 1958-72; active staff emeritus Primary Children's Hosp., LDS Hosp., and Cottonwood Hosp., 1960-67. Fellow APHA, Am. Pediat. Acad., Am. Sch. Health Assn.; mem. AMA, Utah Coll. Health Assn. (pres. 1978-80), Pacific Coast Coll. Health Assn., Utah Med. Assn., Salt Lake County Med. Soc., Utah Pub. Health Assn. (sec.-treas. 1960-66), Intermountain Pediat. Soc. Home and Office: PO Box 58482 Salt Lake City UT 84158-0482

BRANDON, LIANE, filmmaker, educator; Student, St. Lawrence U., U. Edinburgh, Scotland; exchange student, U. Moscow; AB, MEd, Boston U. Ski instr., Mt. Tremblant, Que., Can.; actress Children's Theatre, Cambridge, Mass.; film project dir. English dept. Quincy pub. schs., Mass.; prof. film-TV prodn. and media studies Sch. Edn. U. Mass., Amherst, 1973—; co-founder, mem. New Day Films, 1971—; co-dir. UMass Ednl. TV, U. Mass., Amherst, 1994—; dir. Sch. Edn. Ednl. Tech. Program, U. Mass., 1998—. Film cons. Mass. Gov.'s Commn. on Status of Women, 1974; cons. Mass. Artists Found., 1975, 82, WGBH-TV, 1992-97; judge Regional Student Acad. Awards, 1991, New Eng. Regional Emmy Awards,1992; trustee Theaterworks, 1981-83; bd. dirs. Boston Film-Video Found., 1983-87, ACLU of Mass., 1988-97; mem. adv. bd. Children's Media Found. Boston, 1993-97; guest lectr. various confs. on edn. and film to colls. and art schs. in U.S. Exhibited film, Mus. Modern Art, Whitney Mus. Am. Art, Chgo. Art Inst., Nat. Film Theatre, London, Internat. Womens Film Festival, Paris, Mus. Fine Arts, Boston, Libr. Congress, Washington, John F. Kennedy Ctr. Performing Arts, Washington; dir., prodr. (film) Anything You Want to Be, 1971 (Blue Ribbon Am. Film Festival award), Betty Tells Her Story, 1972, Once Upon a Choice, 1980 (Silver medal Houston Internat. Film Festival), How to Prevent a Nuclear War, 1987 (Blue Ribbon award Am. Film Festival 1988); prodr. (video) Goodnight Amherst, 1995, Fine Print, 1995, Try This At Home, 1998 (Judge's Choice award Hometown Video Festival 1999), Fresh Ink, 1998, Try This At Home: Nature Series, 2000 (award of Distinction, Communicator award); still photographer: Murder at Harvard, 2002, Act Your Age, 2002. Recipient Creative Artist award AAUW, 1975, Disting. Alumni award Boston U., 1985; Careth Found. grantee, 1988, Funding Exchange grantee, 1989, Mass. Found. for Humanities and Pub. Policy grantee, 1975, Film Fund grantee, 1985. Try this at Home: Nature Series (Award of Distinction, Communicator Awards), 2000 Mem. New Eng. Screen Edn. Assn. (v.p. 1972-83), Assn. Ind. Video and Filmmakers, Women in Film and Video New Eng. E-mail: brandon@educ.umass.edu.

BRANDT, DEBORAH, English educator; BA in English with highest distinction, Rutgers U., 1974; MA in English, Ind. U., 1981, PhD in English, 1983. Assoc. instr.dept. English Ind. U., 1979-81; asst. prof. dept. English U. Wis., Madison, 1983-90, assoc. prof. English, dir. intermediat composition dept. English, 1990—. Rep. Madison campus working group writing instrn. and assessment Alliance Undergrad. Edn., 1988-92; reviewer Harcourt Brace Jovanovich, So. Ill. U. Press, U. Wis. Press, U. Pitts. Press. Author: Literacy as Involvement: The Acts of Writers, Readers, and Texts, 1990, Literacy in American Lives, 2001; co-editor: Written Comm., 1993— (David H. Russell award Disting Rsch. Tchr. Eng. 1993); asst. editor: Coll. English, 1981-83; assoc. editor: First Labor, 1980; poetry editor: Indiana Writers, 1979; contbr. numerous chpts. to books, articles to profl. jours. Literacy vol. project Jamaa, Madison Urban League, Wis. Recipient Louisville Grawe Meyer award, 2003. Mem. Am. Fedn. Tchrs., Nat. Coun. Tchrs. English (exec. com. conf. on coll. composition and comm., Promising Researcher award 1984), Nat. Coun. Rsch. in English, Midwest Modern Lang. Assn. (Writing in Coll. sect. adv. com. 1986-89, sec., acting chair 1984-85). Office: U Wisconsin Dept English 6185 Helen C White Hall 600 N Park St Madison WI 53706

BRANDT, IRENE HILDEGARD, retired secondary school educator; b. Meriden, Conn., June 6, 1942; d. Walter M. and Hildegard E. Brandt. BS, Ctrl. Conn. State U., 1964, cert. 6th yr. degree, 1989, MS, 1969, postgrad., 1989. Cert. 7-12 math. tchr., K-12 adminstrn. and supervision, intermediate supervision, Conn. Tchr. math. Jefferson Jr. H.S., Meriden, 1964-67, Platt H.S., Meriden, 1967-99; ret., 1999. Substitute tchr. Platt H.S. Active Summit Club, Meriden, 1972-99. Yearbook dedicated to her Platt H.S., 1971, named Outstanding Tchr. by Srs., 1990, 91, 92, 96, 98, 99, 2000. Mem. ASCD, Nat. Coun. Tchrs. Math., New Eng. Math. Tchrs. Assn., Assn. Tchrs. Math. in Conn. (conv. presider 1990-98), Am. Fedn. Tchrs., Conn. Fedn. Tchrs., Meriden Fedn. Tchrs. (sec. 1982-90). Avocations: travel, reading, crossword puzzles, gardening. Home: 70 Genest St Meriden CT 06450-4538

BRANDT, KATHLEEN See WEIL-GARRIS BRANDT, KATHLEEN

BRANDT, LEOTA FAY, medical/surgical nurse; b. Hamburg, Iowa, June 22, 1940; d. Ralph Lester and Dorothy O. (Folkes) Melton; m. J. Merril Brandt, July 26, 1960; children: Forrest, Clifford, Merrilee, Stephen. ADN, Iowa Western Community Coll., 1985; student, Bethany Nazarene Coll., 1959, 86. RN, Iowa. Staff nurse Grape Community Hosp., Hamburg, Iowa, 1986-90, Glenwood (Iowa) State Hosp., 1987—.

BRANDT, NANCY G. education educator; b. Joliet, Ill., July 18, 1941; d. Robert Anthony Gordon and Alice Ryan; m. Charles C. Brandt, Oct. 23, 1965; children: Charles III, Elizabeth, Leslie. BS in Edn., St. Francis U., 1980; MS in Edn., Ind. U., Fort Wayne, 1984. Tchr., cons. Whitko Schs., Pierceton, Ind., 1981—. Lector Manchester (Ind.) Coll., 2001; chair NCA, 2001—03. Named Tchr. of Yr., LDIN, 1997. Mem.: Pi Lambda Theta (treas. 1998—2002). Roman Catholic. Avocations: gardening, reading, antiques. Home: 5334 Moonrock Ct Fort Wayne IN 46804

BRANDWEIN, RUTH ANN, social welfare educator, administrator, author; b. Bklyn., Apr. 24, 1940; d. Charles and Kate (Berkowitz) Solin; divorced; children: Lorena Lisa Epstein, Garth Whitman. BA magna cum laude, Bklyn. Coll., 1960; MSW, U. Wash., 1970; PhD, Brandeis U., 1978. Libr. trainee Bklyn. Pub. Libr., 1960-61; substitute tchr. N.Y.C. Bd. Edn., 1961-63; recreation dir. Seattle Park Dept., 1964-66; exec. dir. Cen. Seattle Commn. Coun., 1967-69; rsch. assoc. Harvard U./Lab. Comm. Psychiatry, Boston, 1971-72; asst. prof., chair, comm. org. Boston U. Sch. Social Work, 1973-78; dir., assoc. prof. U. Iowa Sch. Social Work, Iowa City, 1978-81; dean Sch. Social Welfare SUNY, Stony Brook, 1981-89, prof. Sch. Social Welfare, 1981—, dir. Social Justice Ctr., 2001—; commr. Suffolk County Dept. Social Svcs., Hauppauge, NY, 1989-93; holder Spafford Endowed chair U. Utah Sch. Social Work, 1994-96. Vis. prof. U. Wash. Sch. Social Work, 2000-01; co-founder Women's Rsch. Ctr. of Boston, 1971-78; co-dir. Women's Com. of 100, 1995—; cons. U.S. Senate Subcom. on Vets.' Affairs, 1971; guardian ad litem Family Ct., Middlesex County, Mass.; expert witness Grevatt vs. U. Minn., Duluth; vis. assoc. Inst. Policy Studies, 1986-87; lead reviewer Nat. Inst. Justice, 1997-98; spkr. nat. and internat. confs. Author: Battered Women, Children and Welfare Reform: The Ties That Bind, 1999; founding editor Affilia: Jour. of Women and Social Work; contbr. articles to profl. jours. and chpts. to books; mem. edtl. bds. Mem. Nat. Adv. Coun. Violence Against Women, 1997—2000; mem. steering com. L.I. Fund for Women and Girls, 1993—2000; mem. N.Y. Gov.'s Mental Health Coun., 1990—2002, chair, 1992—95, Suffolk County Exec. Task Force on Family Violence, 1988—94; bd. dirs., v.p. Kehillath Shalom Synagogue, Cold Spring Harbor, NY, 1987—90, bd. dirs., v.p., chair social action com., 2001—; bd. dirs. United Way of L.I., Melville, NY, 1982—88, mem. allocations com., 2002—; bd. dirs. Suffolk Cmty. Coun., Islandia, NY, 1981—97; bd. dirs., mem. exec. com. Am. Jewish Congress, L.I., 1989; bd. dirs. N.Y. Civil Liberties Union, 1994—98; adv. bd. L.I. Progressive Coalition, 1998—, bd. dirs. L.I. Cmty. Found., 1994—96, Hudson- Peconic Planned Parenthood, 1997—, Health and Welfare Coun. L.I., 1996—2001, Suffolk Coalition Against Domestic Violence, 2003—. Recipient Disting. Alumnus award U. Wash. Sch. Social Work, Seattle, 1989, Congrl. award Congressman Mrazek, Suffolk County, N.Y., Hon. Supporter award Women on the Job; Vol. Svc. award, Suffolk County Human Rights Commn., 2003. Mem.: NASW (bd. dirs. 1991—96, 2d v.p. 1994—96, pres.-elect NY state chpt. 1997—98, pres. 1998—2000, nat. com. on women's issues 2000—, Suffolk county nat. com. women's issues 2003, Suffolk County Social Worker of Yr. 1989, Lifetime Achievement award 2003), Huntington NY NOW (bd. dirs. 1982—91, chair 1988—91), Coun. Social Work Edn. (chair women's commn. 1980—83, bd. dirs. 1987—89, chair internat. commn. 1988—89), NY Pub. Welfare Assn. (bd. dirs. 1990—93), Phi Beta Kappa. Office: SUNY Stony Brook Sch Social Welfare Health Sci Ctr Level 2 Rm 093 Stony Brook NY 11794-0001

BRANESCU-HURT, ANA, music educator; b. Bucharest, Romania, Jan. 3, 1972; arrived in U.S., 1979; d. Paul Doru and Smaranda Ioana Branescu; m. William David Hurt, July 3, 1993; children: Maia Elizabeth Hurt, Elie Rose Hurt. BMus, Shenandoah U., 1998. Piano coach Brockwood Park Sch., Bramdean, England, 1988—90; music tchr. Concord Instn., Yellow-springs, W.Va., 1996—97; pvt. piano studio Winchester, Va., 1996—98; piano instr. Shenandoah Conservatory, Winchester, Va., 1998—; tchr. Winchester Acad., 2002—. Performer recitals Brockwood Park Sch., 1988—90, Shenandoah U., Winchester, Va., 1995, Shenandoah Arts Coun., Winchester, Va., 1996; bd. dirs., music tchr. Winchester Jr. Acad.; sec. bd. Windsor Jr. Acad. Counselor Cmty. Outreach. Grantee Marion Park Lewis Found., Shenandoah Arts Coun., 1992—96. Mem.: Music Tchrs. Nat. Assn., Nat. Fedn. Music Clubs (sr.; v.p.). Avocations: travel, hiking, working with orphans and the homeless. Home: 146 Margaret Ln Winchester VA 22603 Office: Shenandoah Conservatory Arts Acad 203 S Cameron St Winchester VA 22601

BRANHAM, LORRAINE E. literature educator, director; b. Phila., Dec. 7, 1952; d. Jesse T. Williams and Leona C. Green; m. Norris I. Branham, June 19, 1971 (div.); 1 child, Norris J. ; m. Melvin Williams, May 23, 1998. BA in Comm., Temple U., 1976; postgrad. Women in Mgmt. Program, U. Balt., 1982—83; John S. Knight fellow, Stanford U., 1985—86; postgrad., various Knight Ridder and API programs, and others. Reporter Phila. Tribune, Camden (N.J.) Courier-Post, Phila. Bull., Balt. Sun, 1977—83; night metro editor Balt. Sun; various editl. pos. to assoc. mng. editor for features Phila. Inquirer, 1987—96; sr. v.p., exec. editor Tallahassee Tem., 1996—99; asst. to pub. Pitts. Post Gazette, 2000—02; dir., G.B. Dealey Prof. Journalism U. Tex., Austin, 2002—. Tchr. news-writing and reporting Temple U., Phila., 1988—90; tchr. reporting and news-writing U. Calif., Berkeley, 1986; profl.-in-residence Poly-Tech, San Luis Obispo, Calif., 1991, U. Fla., 1993. Bd. dirs. Family Health Coun. We. Pa., 2002; exec. bd. United Way of the Big Bend, 1996—2000; bd. visitors Sch. Journalism, Fla. A&M U., 1996—98; bd. dirs. Tallahassee Police Athletic League, 1998—99. McCormick fellow, Northwestern U., 2001. Mem.: Nat. Assn. Minority Media Execs., AP Mng. Editors, Nat. Assn. Black Journalists, Am. Soc. Newspaper Editors, Assn. Educators in Journalism and Mass Communication. E-mail: lbranham@mail.utexas.edu.

BRANIGAN, HELEN MARIE, educational consultant, administrator; b. Albany, N.Y., Sept. 24, 1944; d. James J. and Helen (Weaver) B. BS in Bus. Edn., Coll. St. Rose, Albany, 1967, MA in English, 1972; postgrad., SUNY, Albany, 1973-81. Tchr., chair dept. bus. edn. S. Colonie Sch. Dist., Albany, 1968-81; assoc. Bur. Bus. Edn. N.Y. State Edn. Dept., Albany, 1981-87; assoc. Bur. Occupational Edn. Program Devel., Albany, 1987-91, Bur. Occupational Edn. Innovation and Quality, Albany, 1991-93, Cen./So. Regional Field Svcs., Albany, 1993-95, North Country/Regional Field Svcs., 1995-98, Regional Sch. Improvement Team, 1998—2003. Bd. trustees St. Catherine's Found., 1993-97; sr. cons. Internat. Ctr. for Leadership in Edn., Schenectady, N.Y., 1991—; facilitator Champlain Valley Ednl. Ctr., 2003-; cons. Inst. Learning Centered Edn., 2003-; bd. dirs. Adirondack Curriculum Project, 2003—. Editor: Glencoe Pub., 1986—; contbr. articles to profl. jours. Lay vol. Archdiocese of Anchorage, 1967-68; mem. N.Y. State Staff Devel. Coun. Mem. ASCD, Bus. Tchrs. Assn. N.Y. State, Delta Pi Epsilon. Roman Catholic. Avocations: skiing, mountaineering, golf, reading. Home: 540 New Scotland Ave Albany NY 12208-2318 E-mail: Hbranigan@aol.com.

BRANN, EVA TONI HELENE, archaeology educator; b. Berlin, Jan. 21, 1929; came to U.S., 1941; d. Edgar and Paula (Sklarz) B. BA, Bklyn. Coll., 1950; MA, Yale U., 1951, PhD, 1956; HHD (hon.), Whitman Coll., 1995, Middlebury Coll., 1999. Instr. archaeology Stanford (Calif.) U., 1956-57; tutor St. John's Coll., Annapolis, Md., 1957—, dean, 1990-97; mem. Inst. for Advanced Study, 1958. Mem. U.S Adv. Commn. for Internat. Edn., 1975-77; vis. prof. Whitman Coll., Walla Walla, Wash., 1978-79; honors prof. U. Del., Newark, 1984-86. Author: Protoattic Pottery from the Athenian Agora, 1962, Paradoxes of Education in a Republic, 1979, The World of the Imagination, 1991, What, Then, Is Time, 1999, The Ways of Naysaying, 2001, Homeric Moments, 2002, The Music of the Republic, 2004, Open Secrets, 2004; translator: Greek Mathematics and the Origin of Algebra, 1968; co-translator: Plato's Sophist, 1996, Plato's Phaedo, 1998. Mem. state adv. com. U.S. Commn. on Civil Rights, Md., 1988-96. Woodrow Wilson Ctr. fellow, 1976; NEH grantee, 1987. Mem. Phi Beta Kappa. Democrat. Jewish. Office: St John's Coll PO Box 2800 Annapolis MD 21404-2800 Office Phone: 410-268-0445.

BRANNAN, CLEO ESTELLA, retired elementary education educator; b. Turon, Kans., Feb. 22, 1924; d. Jesse Logan and Nancy Elma (Cox) Zink; m. Raymond Eugene Brannan, Aug. 4, 1946 (deceased); children: Raymond Eugene Jr., Nancy Estelle, Tricia Elaine. BS, Ft. Hays State U., 1964. Cert. elem. edn. educator, Kans. Elem. tchr. Pretty Prairie (Kans.) Schs., 1943-45, Meade (Kans.) Elem. Sch., 1945-48, 58-60, 61-87, substitute secondary sch. tchr., 1987; ret., 1987. Contbr. articles to Meadowlark mag. Trustee Meade Pub. Libr., 1961-65, 90-98, rustee, treas., 1990—; state bd. dirs. Friends of Kans. Librs., 1990-96; Silver Haired legislator, 1999—. Named Kans. State Libr. Friend of the Yr., 2002. Mem. AAUW (local pres. 1985-86), Kans. Ret. Tchr. Assn. (bd. dirs. 1991-99, state pres. 1996-97), Delta Kappa Gamma. Avocations: collecting china, traveling, reading, arranging flowers. Home: PO Box 13 Meade KS 67864-0013

BRANNICK, ELLEN MARIE, retired management consultant; b. Rochester, Minn., Aug. 10, 1934; d. Daniel Ryther and Grace Ellen (Mills) Markham; m. Thomas L. Brannick. BS in Health, Phys. Edn., MacMurray Coll., 1956, MS, 1959. Elem. phys. edn. Ritenour Consol. Sch. Dist., Overland, Mo., 1958-61; head tchr., summer dir. Civic League Day Nursery, Rochester, 1961-64; recreation therapist Rochester State Hosp., 1964-68; rehab. dir. Rochester State Hosp., 1968-70; rehab. therapist Napa State Hosp., Calif., 1971, indsl. therapy con., 1971-73, community liaison rep., 1973—2000; ret., 2001. Mem. Friends Napa County Libr., 1977. Mem.: Rogue Valley Geneal. Soc., Napa County Hist. Soc. Democrat. Avocations: antique post cards, stamp collecting/philately, bibliophily, military history, traveling. E-mail: ebrannick@medford.net.

BRANNON, PAT, poet; b. Morrilton, Ark., Nov. 6, 1953; d. Ben O. and Mary Ellen Baker; m. Howard Lynn Brannon, July 13, 1956; children: Jason Matthew, Shawn Christopher. Substitute sch. tchr. Amory Sch. Sys., Miss., 1988—99. Author: Walk Softly (You're Steppin' On My Heart), (poetry) Forgiven, 2001 (3rd Pl. Poetry Challenge winner Poetry of Today Pub., 2001), A Heart's Tug Away, 2001 (Adult World Reader's Choice award Poetic Lic. Mag., 2001), A Sacrificial Christmas, 2001 (Hon. Mention for Editor's Choice award Weems Concepts, 2001), Santa In His Place, 2001 (Hon. Mention for Editor's Choice award Weems Concepts, 2001) Vol. Stars Over Miss., Amory, 1994—2002; singer, musician, and revival choir mem. Beverly Health Care Nursing Home, Amory, 1986—2001; vol. Meals on Wheels, 1984—94; ch. clerical worker Food Pantry, Amory, 1996—98; vol. standardized testing Amory Sch. Sys.; band booster vol. & bus chaperone Amory H.S. Band; R.R. festival cmty.-wide ann. ch. svc. choir mem. City of Amory; pre-school dir. Meadowood Bapt. Ch., Amory, adult youth coun. rep., 1991—2001, mission action chairperson Women's Missionary Union, mem. adult choir, 1982, mission friends [illegible] youth Sunday sch. tchr. mem. adult fellowship com., 2001, publicity chairperson for Challenge to Build fin. bldg. campaign, publicity chairperson for the Faithful to the Future fin. bldg. campaign, dir. women on mission fundraising projects, numerous positions, 2001—02. Baptist. Avocations: reading, writing, music. Home: 212 Oakdale Dr Amory MS 38821 E-mail: wonderview@lycos.com.

BRANNON-PEPPAS, LISA, chemical engineer, researcher; b. Houston, Sept. 19, 1962; d. James Graham and Patricia Ann (Hightower) Brannon; m. Nicholas A. Peppas, Aug. 10, 1988. BS, Rice U., 1984; MS, Purdue U., 1986, PhD, 1988. Sr. formulations chemist Eli Lilly & Co., Indpls., 1988-91; pres., founder Biogel Tech., Indpls., 1991—2002; rsch. prof. dept. biomed. engring. U. Tex., Austin, 2002—, dir. Ctr. of Biol. and Med. Engring., 2003—. Author, editor: Absorbent Polymer Technology, 1990, mem. edtl. bd., Jour. Applied Polymer Sci., 1995—2001, Jour. Controlled Release, 1997—2001, Jour. Nanoparticle Rsch., 1998—, Biomaterials, 1999—, Drug Development and Industrial Pharmacy, 2003—. Vol. Indpls. Mus. Art, 1990—98, Humane Soc. Indpls., 1990—98, Indpls. Zoo, 1994—2000; trustee Chem. Engring. Found., 1999—2000. Recipient Harold B. Lamport award Biomed. Engring. Soc., 1989; named Outstanding Young Alumna, Kinkaid Sch., 1998-2000. Fellow Am. Inst. of Med. and Biol. Engring.; mem. AIChE (dir. 1998-2000, exec. bd. programming coun., dir. materials divsn., chmn. subcom. biomaterials divsn. 1990-93, dir.-at-large food, pharm. and bioengring. divsn. 1992-94, 2d vice chair materials divsn. 1994-95, 1st vice chmn. materials divsn. 1995-96, chmn. 1996-97, bd. dirs. 1998-2000), Am. Chem. Soc. (membership com. 1990—), Controlled Release Soc. (treas. 1995-98, internat. planning com. 1991, bd. govs. 1992-95), Jr. League Indpls. (bd. dirs. 1992-94). Avocations: fine art, dance, travel. Office: U Tex Austin CPE 3-168a Austin TX 78712 E-mail: peppas@mailutexas.edu.

BRANSCUM, CARLA JEANNE, special education educator; b. Sherman, Tex., Apr. 6, 1953; d. Carl Ellis and Bobbie Jeanne (Arnold) Little; m. Larry Marshall Branscum, July 19, 1975; children: Marshall Little, Larra Carljeanne. AA, Ea. Okla. State Jr. Coll., 1973; BS in Edn. in Spl. Edn., East Ctrl. State U., Ada, Okla., 1975, MEd in Learning Disabilities, 1977. Cert. tchr., Okla. Tchr. remedial reading Earlsboro (Okla.) Elem. Sch., 1975-77; tchr. spl. edn. Okemah (Okla.) Jr. H.S., 1977-79, Northwood Elem. Sch., Seminole, Okla., 1987-91; learning disabilities tchr. Bowlegs (Okla.) Elem. Sch., 1979-80; tchr. spl. edn. Bowlegs H.S., 1981-87; tchr. spl. edn., coach Odyssey of Mind, Seminole (Okla.) Mid. Sch., 1991-95; spl. edn. tchr. Butner Pub. Sch., 1996—. Bd. dirs. Seminole County Spl. Edn. Found., 1989-93. Mem. Seminole Arts Coun. Named Tchr. of Yr., Bowlegs Assn. Classroom Tchrs., 1985, Seminole County Tchr. of Yr., Seminole Edn. Assn., 1985, Butner Tchr. of Yr. Butner Edn. Assn., 2003; recipient Tchr. Today award The Masonic Fraternity Okla., 2003. Mem. NEA, AAUW (sec. 1990-92), Learning Disabilities Assn., Okla. Edn. Assn., Jasmine Moran Children's Mus., Beta Sigma Phi. Mem. Ch. of Christ. Avocations: special olympics, travel, reading, needlepoint. Home: 2804 Williams Blvd Seminole OK 74868-2429

BRANT, DORRIS ELLEN STAPLETON, bacteriologist, music educator; b. Southard, Mo., Jan. 21, 1933; d. John Ross Stapleton and Sylvia Cleo Boren; m. James Chesney Brant, Sept. 1, 1953; children: Solveig, Sonja Brant Betzen. BA, U. of Wichita, Wichita, KS, 1954, MS, 1956. Cert. tchr. Okla., 1966. Tchg. fellow Wichita U., Wichita, Kans., 1954—55; bacteriologist Hyde Pk. (Borden) Dairy, Wichita, Kans., 1955—56; asst. bacteriologist Wichita / Sedgwick Co. Dept. of Pub. Health, Wichita, Kans., 1956—59; educator Unified Sch. Dist. 382, Pratt, Kans., 1966—96; adj. prof. music St. Mary of Plains Coll., Dodge City, Kans., 1987—89. State bd. Kans. ORFF Assn., Kans., 1995—2000; exec. bd. Delta Kappa Gamma Soc. Internat., Kans., 1980—. Internat. chmn. of travel study com. Delta Kappa Gamma Soc., Kans., 1998—2000; nominating com. Delta Kappa Gamma Soc., Kans., 2002—; pres. Delta Kappa Gamma Soc., Kans., 1991—93; cmty. / foods leader Kans. Farm Bur. Youth Seminar, Manhattan, Kans., 1966—81; sr. counselor Pratt County 4-H Club, Pratt, Kans., 1960—90; pres. Pratt Regional Med. Ctr. Aux., Pratt, Kans., 2000—01; ctrl. com. mem. Rep. Party, Pratt, Kans., 1960—90, 1998—2002. Recipient Delta Epsilon (Hon. Sci.), Ft. Hays U., 1955, Phi State Achievement Award, Delta Kappa Gamma Soc. Internat., 2000, Golden Gift Leadership / Mgmt., Delta Kappa Gamma Soc. Internat., 1985. Mem.: Nat. Assn. of Parliamentarians, Pratt Music Club (pres. 1960—2002), AAUW (vice-president 1990—2002), AAUW (vice-president 1960—80), Phi Delta Kappa. R-Consevative. Methodist. Avocations: music, reading, geneology, ice skating (figure), cooking. Home: 70215 SE 100th Avenue Isabel KS 67065 Personal E-mail: jdbrant@havilandtelco.com.

BRANT, SANDRA J. magazine publisher; m. Peter M Brant. Pub., pres. Brant Publs., N.Y.C., 1985—. Publisher, Art in America, The Magazine Antiques, Interview. Office: Brant Publs 575 Broadway New York NY 10012-3230

BRANTLEY, WILLA JOHN, educational administrator; b. Carthage, Miss., Aug. 24, 1956; d. Rena John; m. Harlon Dwight Bell, May 15, 1974 (div. 1979); children: Chassidy Georgina, Gerrard Dwight; m. Nicky Paul Brantley, Jan. 5, 1985 (div. 1991). Student, East Cen. Jr. Coll., 1975, Wood Jr. Coll., 1975-76; BEd magna cum laude, Jackson State U., 1979; postgrad., Miss. State U., 1979-81, 83—. Cert. elem. tchr., Miss. Counselor Miss. Band Choctaw Indian, Philadelphia, Miss., 1979; elem. tchr. Standing Pine Sch., Walnut Grove, Miss., 1979-81, prin. Philadelphia, 1983-87; ednl. specialist Chocotaw Agy., Phila., 1981-83, 87—, acting agy. supr. for edn. Philadelphia, 1981-88, agt. supt. for edn. Phila., 1990—; tchr. evaluator Pa. Dept. Edn., Philadelphia, 1990—; dir. Choctaw Dept. Edn., Philadelphia, 1990—96; substitute tchr. Oxford Elem. Sch., Batesville Job Corp., Attalla County Sch. Dist., 1996—98; legis. analysis and rsch. asst. Office of Tribal Coun., 1998—2003, exec. adminstr., 2003—. Trainers of tng. Nat. Indian Sch. Bd., Philadelphia, 1987—; curriculum specialist Bur. Indian Affairs-Choctow, Philadelphia, 1987—, staff devel. coord., 1986—; chmn. bd. ESEA, 1991; bd. dirs. Southeastern Region Visions for Edn. Vol. program implementation Save the Children Fedn., Cherokee, N.C., 1981—; planning participant nat. issues forum Kettering Found., Dayton, Ohio, 1987; mem. task force com. Office of Indian Edn. Program, Washington, 1985. Recipient cert. of recognition Save the Children Fedn., 1986. Fellow Internat. Reading Assn., Miss. Staff Devel. Coun.; mem. ASCD, Minn. Edn. Computer Consortium, Choctaw Dept. Educators (bd. dirs.), Red Water Basketball Club, Red Water Community Devel. Club, Phi Theta Kappa. Democrat. Methodist.

BRANYAN, CHERYL MUNYER, museum administrator, consultant; b. Vincennes, Ind., Apr. 27, 1970; d. Edward A. and Janet E. Munyer; m. Richard R. Branyan, Oct. 4, 1997. BA, Ea. Ill. U., 1992, MA, 1993. Asst. curator Coles County Hist. Soc., Charleston, Ill., 1994-95; intern Nat. Pk. Svc., Natchez, Miss., 1995; asst. curator Manship Ho. Mus., Jackson, Miss., 1995-96, The Hermitage, Nashville, 1996-97; cons. Lower Lodge Conservation and Mus. Svcs., Natchez, 1997—; mus. adminstr. Rosalie Miss. State Soc. DAR, Natchez, 1999—; v.p. bd. dirs. Miss. Museums Assn., 2001—. Newsletter editor Historic House Museums Affinity Group, 2000—; bd. dirs. Natchez Hist. Soc., 2000—. Editor SERA News, 1998—, Hist. House Mus. Affinity Group, 2000—; copy editor, contbr. (newsletter) History at Eastern, 1995; co-founder, contbr. (jour.) Historia, 1992. Vol. Lincoln Meml. Gardens, Springfield, Ill., 1993, U. Fla., Gainesville, 1994, Miss. Arts Pavillion, Jackson, 1996; bd. dirs. Natchez Hist. Soc., 2001—. Mem. Am. Assn. Museums (Kay Paris Meml. award, registrar's com. 1997), Am. Assn. State and Local History (vol. Saratoga Springs, N.Y. 1995), Nat. Assn. Jr. Aux., Miss. Mus. Assn. (v.p. of bd. dirs. 2001—), Southeastern Registrars Assn. (comm. chair 1998—), Southeastern Museums Conf. (spkr.), Phi Alpha Theta, Sigma Tau Delta. Democrat. Lutheran. Avocation: visiting museums. Office: Rosalie House Mus MSDAR 100 Orleans St Natchez MS 39120-3452 E-mail: [illegible]

BRASEL, JO ANNE, pediatrician, educator; b. Salem, Ill., Feb. 15, 1934; d. Gerald Nolan and Ruby Rachel (Rich) B. BA, U. Colo., 1956, MD, 1959. Diplomate in pediatrics and pediatric endocrinology Am. Bd. Pediatrics. Pediatric intern, resident Cornell U. Med. Coll.-N.Y. Hosp., N.Y.C., 1959-62; fellow in pediatric endocrine Johns Hopkins U. Sch. Medicine, Balt., 1962-65, asst. prof. pediats., 1965-68; asst. prof., then assoc. prof. pediatrics Cornell U. Med. Coll., N.Y.C., 1969-72; assoc. prof., then prof. pediats. Columbia U. Phys. and Surg., N.Y.C., 1972-79; prof. pediats. Harbor-UCLA Med. Ctr./UCLA Sch. Medicine, 1979—, program dir. Gen. Clin. Rsch. Ctr., 1979-93, prof. medicine, 1980—; Joseph W. St. Geme, Jr. prof. pediats. UCLA Sch. Medicine, 1999—. Mem. adv. com. FDA, Rockville, Md., 1971-75; mem. nutrition study sect. NIH, Bethesda, Md., 1974-78; mem. select panel for promotion of child health HEW, Washington, 1979-80; mem. life scis. adv. screening com. Fulbright-Hays program, Washington, 1981-84; mem. digestive disease and nutrition grant rev. group NIADDK, 1985-89; mem. U.S. Govt. Task Force on Women, Minorities and the Handicapped in Sci. and Tech., 1987-89. Recipient Rsch. Career Devel. award NIH, 1973-77, Irma T. Hirschl Trust Career Sci. award, 1974-79, Sr. Fulbright Sabbatical Rsch. award, 1980. Mem. Soc. Pediatric Rsch. (sec.-treas. 1973-77, v.p. 1977-78, pres. 1978-79), Am. Fedn. Clin. Rsch., Endocrine Soc., Am. Soc. Clin. Nutrition, Am. Inst. Nutrition, Western Assn. Physicians, Lawson Wilkins Pediatric Endocrine Soc. (bd. dirs. 1972-74, v.p. 1991-92, pres. 1992-93), Western Soc. Pediatric Rsch., Phi Beta Kappa, Alpha Omega Alpha. Office: Harbor-UCLA Med Ctr Box 446 1000 W Carson St Torrance CA 90509-2910 E-mail: brasel@gcrc.rei.edu.

BRASH, SUSAN KAY, principal; b. Valparaiso, Ind., June 17, 1950; d. Loren Lewis and Naomi Louise (Mundy) Betz; m. Richard Allen Brash, July 8, 1970; children: Jennifer Lea, Julie Christine, Jill Reneé. BS, Ind. U., 1972, MS, 1976, Edn. Specialist, 1989. Cert. adminstrn. and supervision, elem. edn. grades K-8, reading grades K-12, gifted and talented grades K-12. Tchr. grade 1 Portage (Ind.) Twp. Schs., 1971-72; adult basic edn. El-Tip-Wa Vocat., Logansport, Ind., 1976-79; reading tchr. grades 6-8 Ea. Pulaski Schs., Winamac, Ind., 1979-80, reading tchr. grades 9-12, 1980-84, gifted/talented coord., 1984-87, elem. prin., 1987-89, Met. Sch. Dist. Lawrence Twp., Indpls., 1989—. Advisor St. Vincent's Stress Ctr., Indpls., 1993—; presenter and cons. in field. Named Adminstr. of Yr., Ind. Assn. Learning Disabilities, 1990; recipient City Coun./Mayor award, 1994. Mem. ASCD, Nat. Assn. Elem. Sch. Prins. (Nat. Disting. Prin. 1995), Ind. Assn. Sch. Prins. (Ind. Prin. of Yr. 1994), Phi Delta Kappa. Baptist. Office: Met Sch Dist Lawrence Twp 7601 E 56th St Indianapolis IN 46226-1310

BRASHER, TREASURE ANN KEES, physics educator; b. Maypearl, Tex., May 12, 1938; d. Leslie and Ora Odell (Segars) K.; m. Charles Albert Brasher, Sept. 5, 1959; 1 child, Cynthia Lynn Brasher Baker. BS, West Tex. State Coll., Canyon, 1960; MS, West Tex. State U., Canyon, 1967; postgrad., No. Ariz. U., Flagstaff, 1970, U. Houston, 1979, Tex. Tech. U., Lubbock, 1983. Cert. tchr. Tex. Instr. math. West Tex. State Coll., Canyon, 1961-62, tchg. asst. math., 1963-65, instr. physics, 1980—; physics/phys. sci. tchr. Canyon Ind. Sch. Dist., 1962-63, earth/life sci. tchr., 1965-66, physics/chemistry tchr., 1966-80. Dir. West Tex. A&M U. Regional Jets Contest, Canyon, 1983-99, dir. U. Interscholastic Sci. Contest Canyon, 1990—, coord. Pantex Dept. Energy, Canyon Sci. Bd., 1994—, dir. traveling chemistry show, Canyon, 1997-2000; dir. Panhandle JASON Project, 1998—; mem. Acad. Educator Devel. Tex. A&M U. Sys., 2000—. Author: Elementary Physics With Activities, 1995, Elementary Chemistry With Activities, 1995; contbg. editor: (with Gerald Skoog) Activities for Middle School Teachers, 1996. Sunday sch. tchr. First Bapt. Ch., Canyon, 1980—, mem. sanctuary choir, 1956—; mem. Panhandle chpt. Singing Women of Tex., 1992—. Named Eisenhower Tchr. Enhancement grantee, West Tex. State U., 1990—94, Eisenhower grantee, Tex. Edn. Agy., 1994—99, Sid Richardson Tchg. fellow, Tex. A&M U.Sys. and Tex. Edn. Agy., 1998—2000; recipient Outstanding Prof. award, Scribes/Mortar Bd., 1991—92, Outstanding Univ. Faculty award, Regl. Alliance Sci. Engring. Math., 2002; grantee, NSF, 1991—93, Amarillo Nat. Resource Ctr., 1996—98, ANRC, 1998—2000, New Century Energies, 2000—01, Xcel Energy Co., 2002—, W. Mem. NEA, Am. Assn. Physics Tchrs., Nat. Sci.

Tchrs. Assn., Tex. State Tchrs. Assn. (regional pres. 1978-80, state bd. dirs. 1983-87), Tex. Assn. Coll. Tchrs. (pres. 1986-88), Acad. for Educator Devel. Avocations: reading, needlecrafts, travel. Home: 83 Country Club Dr Canyon TX 79015-1821 Office: West Tex A&M U Dept Math Phys Scis & Engrin Canyon TX 79016-0001 E-mail: tbrasher@mail.wtamu.edu.

BRASSARD, VIRGINIA, elementary school educator; b. Clinton, Mass., Sept. 13, 1924; d. Patrick Francis and Anne Elizabeth (McIlveen) Hynes; m. Roland Ronald Brassard, Dec. 26, 1948; children: Anne Brassard Wharen (dec.), Patricia Brassard Small. BS, U. Mass., Boston, 1945; student, R.I. Coll., 1959, 61. Cert. tchr., Mass., R.I. Tchr. City of Boston, 1945-47; asst. to curator Mus. R.I. Sch. Design, Providence, 1947-49; tchr. City of Pawtucket, R.I., 1957-67; treas. Brassard & Co., Inc., 1972-85, ret.; internat. tchr. in San Salvador, Guatemala, Uruguay, Morocco Internat. Exec. Svcs. Corps, Stamford, Conn., 1985-96. Mem. Doric Dames State House, Boston, 1975-90. Mem. United Ostomy Assn. (treas. 1999—, membership chair 1999—), VFW Aux., KC Aux. (function chair 1999, KC aux. pres. 2000). Roman Catholic. Avocations: genealogy, world travel. Home: 3360 Sheffield Cir Sarasota FL 34239-6716 E-mail: VBrassard@aol.com.

BRASSEUR, IRMA FAYE, special education educator; b. Flint, Mich., Apr. 18, 1961; d. Ermen Massie and Gearldine Herbst; m. Curtis James Brasseur (div. Jan. 25, 1996); 1 child, Cali Jean. BS in Spl. Edn., Ctrl. Mich. U., Mt. Pleasant, 1984; MA in Spl. Edn., Eastern Mich. U., Ypsilanti, 1990; postgrad., U. Kans., 1998—. Cert. tchr. Mich. Tchr. Area Edn. Agy. #7, Waterloo, Iowa, 1984—86, Davison (Mich.) Cmty. Schs., 1986—98; project coord. U. Kans., Lawrence, 2000—. Student rep. Divsn. Learning Disabilities, 1999—2002, v.p., 2001—03, pres., 2003—04. Student Initiated grantee, Office Spl. Edn. Programs, 2001. Avocations: reading, bicycling, aerobics. Office: U Kans Ctr Rsch Learning 1122 W Campus Rd Lawrence KS 66045 Business E-Mail: ibrasser@ku.edu.

BRASSWEL, KERRY, tax accountant; d. J.D. Jr. and Kathryn Elizabeth (Rimmer) Braswell. Student, Occidental Coll., L.A., 1964-66. Cert. tax profl. Am. Inst. Tax Studies; qualified Ariz. and Calif. Superior Cts. and Fed. Ct. Bus. mgr. to entertainers Segal, Skaff and Co., L.A., 1968, Cary Harwin and Assocs., Beverly Hills, Calif., 1968-72, Bisgeier, Breslauer and Co., L.A., 1972-74, M. Klaiman Accountancy Corp., Beverly Hills, 1974-75, Michael L. Laney, CPA, Beverly Hills, 1975-77; pvt. practice Tucson, Ariz., 1977—. Owner Brasswel Arabians, L.A. 1966-76, Ka-BeAraby, Tucson, 1977—; appraiser St. Paul's Ins. Co., St. Paul, Minn.; equine, also accounting expert witness; lectr. herbal horse care. Author: Herbal Horse Handbook, 1989. Judge, leader 4-H Club, Tucson, 1981-84; travel del. Calif. Horsemens People to People Goodwill Tour, 1970. Mem. Nat. Soc. Tax Profls., Arabian Horse Registry Am., Internat. Arabian Horse Assn. (judge 1976-83), Am. Horse Show Assn. (judge 1976-83), Desert Show Horse Assn. (bd. dirs. 1980-83), So. Ariz. Arabian Horse Assn. (cert. appreciation 1978). Republican. Avocations: sidereal astrology, holistic herbalogy, organic gardening. Home and Office: 10151 W Picture Rocks Rd Tucson AZ 85743-9386 E-mail: kabearaby@surfree.com.

BRASWELL, JACKIE TERRY, medical, surgical nurse; b. Raleigh, N.C., Oct. 15, 1961; d. Charles Thurman and Laura (Russell) Terry; 1 child, Matthew Russell Braswell. BSN, U. N.C., 1983. Cert. BCLS, med. surgical nursing ANA. Staff nurse orthopedics/neurology unit Wake County Med. Ctr., Raleigh, staff nurse cardiac telemetry step-down unit; asst. head nurse orthopedics unit Raleigh Community Hosp., staff nurse telemetry unit; charge nurse vent unit IHS, Raleigh, 1993-95. Rschr. in field. Mem. ANA, NCNA. Home: PO Box 548 Knightdale NC 27545-0548

BRASWELL, JODY LYNN, gifted and talented educator; b. Cin., Aug. 30, 1955; d. Edward George and Willadene B. Kraemer; m. Jimmy Billings Braswell, Dec. 22, 1974; children: Cynthia, Gina. BS in Edn., West Tex. State U., 1985; MA in Edn., Sul Ross State U., 2000. Cert. elem. edn. grades 1-8, generic spl. edn. all levels, gifted/talented endorsement, reading specialist, master reading tchr. Tchr. spl. edn. Amarillo (Tex.) Ind. Sch. Dist., 1985—86; elem. tchr. Ector County Ind. Sch. Dist., Odessa, Tex., 1989—91, tchr. spl. edn., 1995—2000, curriculum specialist, 2000—01, gifted/talented program tchr., 2001—; elem. tchr. St. John's Episcopal Sch., Odessa, 1991—95. Lead mentor Ector County Ind. Sch. Dist., Odessa, 1998—, trainer, facilitator, 2000—. Vol. Home Hospice, Odessa, 1995—; pres. Permian Basin Reading Coun., Odessa, 2000—03; bd. mem. Read Odessa, 2003—. Recipient Lifetime Achievement award, PTA, Odessa, 2000. Mem.: Tex. Classroom Tchrs., Tex. Reading Assn., Internat. Reading Assn., Delta Kappa Gamma Iota (1st v.p. 2001—). Mem. Disciples Of Christ/Southern Baptist. Avocations: reading, music, needlecrafts, gardening. Home: 1514 E 10th Odessa TX 79761

BRASWELL, PAULA ANN, artist; b. Decatur, Ala., May 6, 1955; d. Andrew Leon and Dorothy Faye (Fretwell) B.; m. Roger Armand Robichaud, June 22, 1990. BA, Jacksonville State U., 1978; postgrad., New Orleans Acad. Fine Arts, 1987, U. New Orleans, 1987-88; MFA, Fla. State U., 1990. Instr. art Butler Sch., Marrero, La., 1984, Fla. Keys Coll., Tavernier, 1985; grad. instr. Fla. State U., Tallahassee, 1989-90; adj. prof. Calhoun Coll., Decatur, Ala., 1990, Chattanooga State Coll., 1991, Cleveland (Tenn.) State Coll., 1991; studio artist Knoxville, Tenn., 1991-96, Toronto, Ont., Can., 1996—. One-man shows include Contemporary Arts Ctr., New Orleans, 1992, ARC Gallery, 1997, Propeller Gallery, 2000, 2001, Loop Gallery, Toronto, 2002—03, Windsor (Ont.) Gallery Art, 2002, Kabat Wrobel Gallery, Toronto, 2003, WARC Gallery, Toronto, 2003, Kabuty Wrokel, Toronto, 2004, Loop Gallery, 2004, exhibited in group shows at Knoxville (Tenn.) Mus. Art, 1994—95, Combined Talents Fla. Nat., 1995, Transforming Tradition, 1996, New American Talent, 1996, Fla. State U., Mus. of the Arts., Washington, 1997, Mus. of the Ams., 1997, Mus. of Fine Arts, 1998, FSU Mus., 1998, Propeller Gallery, Toronto, 2000—02, WARC Gallery, 2000, 2003, Sculpture Soc. Can., 2000—01, Gallery 121, Toronto, 2000, Soul Ecology Exhibit, 2000, Propeller Ctr. for the Visual Arts, 2000—02, Sculpture Soc. Gallery, 2001, John B. Aird Gallery, 2001, John B. Aird Gallery 75th Anniversary juried exhibit, 2003. Grantee, Nat. Endowment Arts, 1991, Ont. Arts Coun., 1997, 2000, 2001—02, 2003, Can. Coun., 2002. Mem. AAUW, NOW, Women's Caucus for Arts (exhibitor), Knoxville Mus. Art (exhibitor), Knoxville Arts Coun. (exhibitor), Coll. Art Assn., Contemporary Arts Ctr. (exhibitor), People for Protection of Animals, Humane Soc. U.S. Democrat. Mem. Ch. of Christ. Avocations: gardening, environmental concerns, animal care, skiing, camping. Address: 221 Winona Dr Toronto ON Canada M6C 3S4 E-mail: paulabrasw@aol.com.

BRATCHER, JUANITA, journalist; b. Columbus, Ga. d. Benjamin Pickens and Tommie (English) Forte; m. Neal Archie Bratcher; children: Pamela, Angela, Sonya, Neal Jr. AA, Olive Harvey Coll.; BA in Journalism, Columbia Coll., 1976. News reporter South End Rev., Chgo., Roseland Rev., Chgo., Chgo. Defender; editor, publ. Southeast Alliance, Chgo., Copyline Mag., Chgo., 1990—. Bd. dirs. Provident Found.; host cable talk show One on One; host Internet talk show PCC Network. Author: Harold: The Making of a Big City Mayor, 1993, I Cry for a People: In Their Struggle for Justice, 1996, Crooked Curves: The Last of the Red Hot Mamas, 1999, A Celebration of Love, 2001, Love Me One More Time, 2001, The Best Poems and Poets of 2001, The Best Poems and Poets of 2002, The Best Poems and Poets of 2003, Sound of Poetry, 2003, Chasing the Good Times, 2003, Noble House: Theatre of the Mind, 2004, Noble House: Colours of the Heart, 2004; works appear in Nat. Libr. of Poetry Best Poems of 1997, A Celebration of Poets, 1998, The Best Poems and Poets of 2001, The Best Poems and Poets of 2003, Noble House Theatre of the Mind, 2004, Under a Quick Silver Moon, 2002, Great Poems of the Western World, 2004, recordings include Too Many Memories, 1996, Everything But Love, 1996, I'm Here for You, 1997, You've Been Gone Too Long, 1997, God Can Ease the Pain, 1999, Glorious Day in Heaven, 1999, America, The Land of Freedom, 1999, Freedom, Our Birthright, 1999, That Twinkle In Your Eyes, 2001, Overdose of Love, 2001, CD recordings include God Can Ease the Pain, 1999, A Glorious Day in Heaven, 1999, The Sound of Poetry, album recordings include America, The Land of Freedom, 1999, Freedom, Our Birthright, 1999, Everything But Love, 2001, That Twinkle in Your Eyes, 2001, An Overdose of Love, 2001, A Toast To Christmas, 2001, Can't Make It Without Him, 2001, CD recordings include The Sound of Poetry, 2002, mem. editl. com. One City, Chgo. Coun. Urban Affairs, The Sound of Poetry, 2004, guest panelist, guest host for numerous TV and radio programs. Mem. Regional Aux. Coun. Atlas Ctr.; press aide Cook County bd. campaign John S. Stroger; press aide Alderman Lorraine Dixon. Recipient certs. of merit Chgo. Pub. Schs., everyday hero award Ill. Sec. State George Ryan, 1993, Kizzy award The Kizzy Found., 1983, Probation Challenge Portraits of Achievers award, 1983, 87, Editor's Choice award (6) Nat. Libr. Poetry, svc. award Boy Scouts Am., U.S. Dept. Edn. Region V, Outstanding Support of Human Rights award Ill. Dept. Human Rights, 1985, Cmty. Svc. award Ada Park Adv. Coun., 1990, exemplary civic svc. award Dorcas Care Ctr., 1988, Excellence in Achievement award Zeta Phi Beta, Oustanding Svc. in Media and Telecomm. award Delta Sigma Theta, press award Chgo. and No. Dist. Assn. of Club Women, Inc., Par Excellence Journalism award Coalition for United Cmty. Action, 1987, Dedicated Svc. to Cmty. award Firefighters for Justice and Equality, 1987, The Good Spirit of Excellence award, 2000, From Whence We Came award, Allstate Ins., 2002.; named black bus. woman of yr. Parkway Cmty. House, Chgo., 1993; inductee Internat. Poetry Hall of Fame, Probation Challenge's Hall of Fame, 1991. Mem. Internat. Soc. Poets. Baptist. Home: 9026 S Cregier Ave Chicago IL 60617-3533 Fax: 773-375-7461. E-mail: JuanitaBratcher@yahoo.com., Copyfine.Magazine@oneononetelevision.com.

BRATER, ELIZABETH, state legislator; b. Boston, Apr. 12, 1951; BA, MA, U. Pa. City councilwoman City of Ann Arbor, 1988-91, mayor, 1991-93; state rep. Mich. Ho. Reps., Dist. 53, 1995—. Mem. conservations, environ. & great lakes, higher edn. & mental health coms., Mich. Ho. Reps. Office: 480 Roosevelt Bldg Lansing MI 48909

BRATHWAITE, HARRIET LOUISA, nursing educator, educator; b. Rye, N.Y., Aug. 28, 1931; d. James Pierce and Mattie (Collins) Bowling; m. Leroy L. Brathwaite, Feb. 18, 1950; 1 child, Helene Ann Brathwaite Ward. AAS in Nursing, CUNY, 1959; BSN, L.I. U., 1965; postgrad., Columbia U., 1965-68; MSN, Adelphia U., 1973. Staff nurse Kings County Hosp., Bklyn., 1959; head nurse City Hosp. at Elmhurst, Queens, N.Y., 1959-62; instr. Kings County Hosp. Sch. Nursing, 1963-65, Downstate Med. Ctr. Sch. Nursing, 1965-69; nurse community mental health South Beach Psychiat. Ctr., 1969-73; cons. psychiat. nursing service HEW and N.Y. State Health Dept., Albany, 1973-74; chief of service Creedmoor Psychiat. Ctr., Queens Village, N.Y., 1974-87; asst. prof. nursing L.I. U., 1987-92. Co-leader Allied Dems., Jamaica, N.Y., 1959-62; bd. dirs. South Queens Dems., Howard Beach, N.Y.; mem. adv. bd. Transitional Services, Queens, 1983-85; appointed Senatorial dist. coord. for U.S. Senator Charles Schumer, 1999; adv. bd. L.I. U. Sch. Nursing, Clara Barton Sch. Practical Nursing. Recipient Alumna of Yr. award Bkyn. Coll., 2000. Mem. AAUW, NAACP, Nat. Black Nurses Assn. (chmn. legis. com. Queens chpt. 1981—, Cert. of Appreciation 1989), N.Y. State Nurses Assn. (coun. on legislation 1990—, trustee Polit. Action Com. 1991—, 25 Yr. Membership award 1986, Legis. award 1988, Ruth W. Harper award for Disting. Svc. 1991, inducted into Leadership Inst. 1998, Maggie Jacobs award 1999), 100 Black Women of L.I., Bklyn. Coll. Alumni Assn. (bd. dirs. 1995), Knickerbocker Club (chmn. fin. and scholarship com.), Chi Eta Phi (Helen E. Miller award 1999), Kappa Eta, Sigma Theta Tau. Home: PO Box 1841 Cuffee Dr Sag Harbor NY 11963-3217

BRATRUD, LINDA KAY, secondary school educator; b. Salt Lake City, May 14, 1944; d. Milton Niels and Marian Lucy (Criswell) Peterson; m. Richard L. Settle, Sept. 10, 1965 (div. Sept. 1982); children: Courtney Settle Dodson, Dana R.; m. Jeffrey C. Bratrud, Aug. 27, 1990; children: Jennifer Bratrud Stauffacher, Jeff, John. 1st diploma, U. Grenoble, France, 1964; 2d diploma, U. Paris, 1965; BA, U. Wash., 1966; MBA, U. Puget Sound, 1987. Tchr. French, South H.S., Bakersfield, Calif., 1967-68, Peninsula H.S., Gig Harbor, Wash., 1984-93; instr. French, Tacoma C.C., 1970-71; owner bookstore Smith, Settle, Bingham & Wagner, Tacoma, 1980-82; client exec. asst. Frank Russell Co., Tacoma, 1981-84. Avocations: freelance writing, gardening, golf, tennis, cooking. Address: 353 Gran Via Palm Desert CA 92260-2169

BRATTEN, MILLIE MARTINI, editor-in-chief; m. John Bratten. With merchandising dept. Mademoiselle mag., 1975; assoc. editor Bride's mag. Conde Nast Pubs., N.Y.C., fashion coord. menswear Bride's mag., editor accessories, fashion and beauty assoc. Bride's mag., exec. editor Bride's mag., 1991—94, editor-in-chief Bride's mag., 1994—; editl. dir. Conde Nast Bridal Group, 2002—. TV appearances in Weekend Today, Good Morning Am., Good Day N.Y., Network News, Family Values, Weddings of a Lifetime; host Romance Classics A Day of Diana; interviewed in USA Today, N.Y. Times, Washington Post, Wall Street Journal, Boston Globe, Forbes, ABC Radio Network. Mem. Am. Soc. Mag. Editors and Fashion Group, Internat. Furniture and Design Assn. (bd. dirs.), Women in Comms., Inc. (program coun. N.Y., past bd. dirs., v.p. membership). Office: Conde Nast Pubs 4 Times Sq 6th Fl New York NY 10036

BRATTON, IDA FRANK, retired secondary school educator; b. Glasgow, Ky., Aug. 31, 1933; d. Edmund Bates and Robbie Davis (Hume) Button; m. Robert Franklin Bratton, June 20, 1954; 1 child, Timothy Andrew. BA, Western Ky. U., 1959, MA, 1962. Cert. secondary tchr., Ky. Tchr. math. and sci. Gottschalk Jr. H.S., Louisville, 1959-65; tchr. math. Iroquois H.S., Louisville, 1965-79; tchr. Waggener H.S., Louisville, 1979-2000, chair dept. math., 2000, ret., 2000. Mem. NEA, AAUW, Ky. Edn. Assn., Jefferson County Tchrs. Assn. Democrat. Methodist. Avocations: travel, needle crafts. Home: 304 Paddington Ct Louisville KY 40222-5541 Office: Waggener High Sch 330 S Hubbards Ln Louisville KY 40207-4099

BRATZLER, MARY KATHRYN, desktop publisher; b. Albuquerque, Sept. 16, 1960; d. William James and Nancy Jane (Hobbs) Colby; m. Zim Emig, May 30, 1987 (div. Nov. 1990); 1 child, Aeriel Kaylee Emig; m. Steven James Bratzler, Mar. 16, 1996, 1 child, Cody Benjamin. B of Univ. Studies, U. N.Mex., 1995. Comml. artist Modern Press, Albuquerque, 1978—80; asst. composition supr. Graphic Arts Pub., Albuquerque, 1980—84, composition supr., 1984—85, asst. plant mgr., 1985—86; typesetter Universal Printing and Graphics, Albuquerque, 1986—87, Bus. Graphics, Albuquerque, 1988—90; office asst. UNM Gen. Honors, Albuquerque, 1992—93; desktop pub., 1990—; computer specialist NEDA Bus. Cons., Inc., 1996—98; electronic prepress Acad. Printers, Albuquerque, 2002—03; pub. mgr. Albuquerque Acad., 2003—. Cons. Mary Kay Cosmetics, 1991—96. Participant N.Mex. Pub. Utilities Commn., Santa Fe, 1993; coord. clothing bank PTA, Zia Elem. Sch., 1995-96; parent rep. Unified Student Centered Classroom, 1996-98; gen. bd. mem. Albuquerque Acad. Parent Assn., 2000—. Mem. Golden Key, Phi Beta Kappa. Avocations: piano playing, bicycling, hiking, camping.

BRAUDY, SUSAN ORR, writer; b. Phila. d. Bernard and Blanche (Malin) Orr. BA cum laude, Bryn Mawr Coll.; postgrad., U. Pa., Yale U. Editor, writer The New Jour. Yale U., New Haven; assoc. editor Newsweek Mag., N.Y.C.; editor, writer Ms. Mag., N.Y.C.; freelance writer N.Y. Times, N.Y.C.; v.p. Warner Bros., N.Y.C., L.A., Michael Douglas Prodns., N.Y.C., L.A. Author: (novels) Between Marriage and Divorce, 1975, Who Killed Sal Mineo, 1984, What the Movis Made Me Do, 1984, This Crazy Thing Called Love, 1991, Family Circle: The Boudins and the Aristocracy of the Left, 2003; screenwriter : (films) Scorsese Co.; Am. Zeotrope; Ixtlan; Disney. Mem.: NOW, Writers Guild of Am., PEN Club Internat., Vet. Feminists Am., Nat. Bd. Rev., Bryn Mawr Alumni Club (class v.p.). Home: 910 Central Park S Apt 10D New York NY 10019-1413

BRAUER, CAMILLA THOMPSON (KIMMY THOMPSON BRAUER), civic leader; b. St. Louis, Apr. 8, 1946; m. Stephen F. Brauer; children: Blackford, Rebecca, Stephen Jr. Grad., Mary Inst., Bennett Coll., Millbrook, N.Y., 1966. Dir. St. Louis Arts & Edn. Coun., 1988—; dir., exec. com. Opera Theater of St. Louis, 1986—; dir. exec. com. Sheldon Arts Found., 1991—; trustee St. Louis Art Mus., 1989-94, chmn. bd. trustees, 1991-94, commr., 1996—; trustee Webster U., 1994—; exec. com., 1995—; chair Alexis de Tocqueville Soc., 1995, 96, 2001; v.p. exec. com. United Way of St. Louis, 1996—; bd. trustees St. Louis Symphony, 1994—, exec. com., 1995—. Recipient Internat. Barker award Variety Club, 2000; named St. Louis Post Dispatch Woman of Achievement, 1996. Mem. Naat. Soc. Fund Raising Execs. (Vol. of Yr. St. Louis 1994, Vol. of Yr. U.S. 1996), Variety Club (exec. bd. dirs. 1992—, Woman of Yr. 1992, Mo. Hist. Soc. (dir. 1991—, exec. com. 1991—). Home: 9630 Ladue Rd Saint Louis MO 63124-1311 Fax: (314) 994-1441. E-mail: camillabrauer@aol.com.

BRAULT, G. LORAIN, healthcare executive; b. Chgo., Jan. 3, 1944; d. Theodore Frank and Victoria Jean (Pribyl) Hahn; m. Donald R. Brault, Apr. 29, 1971; 1 child, Kevin David. AA, Long Beach City Coll., 1963; BS, Calif. State U.-Long Beach, 1973, MS, 1977. RN, Calif; cert. nurse practitioner. Dir. nursing Canyon Gen. Hosp., Anaheim, Calif., 1973-76; dir. faculty critical care masters degree program Calif. State U., Long Beach, 1976-79; regional dir.. nursing and support svcs. Western region Am. Med. Internat., Anaheim, Calif., 1979-83; v.p. Hosp. Home Care Corp. Am., Santa Ana, Calif., 1983-85; pres. Hosp. Home Health Care Agy. Calif., Torrance, 1986-92; v.p. Healthcare Assn. So. Calif., L.A., 1993—98; dir. student health svc. Fullerton Coll., 1999—. Invited lectr. China Nurses Assn., 1983; cons. AMI, Inc., Saudi Arabia, 1983; guest lectr. dept. pub. health UCLA, 1986—87; assoc. clin. prof. U. So. Calif., 1988—93; chair editl. adv. com. RN Times, Nurseweek, 1988—2000; advisor Nursing Inst., 1990—91; lectr. Calif. State U., L.A., 1996—99, Fullerton, Calif., 1999—2003; bd. dirs. Health and Human Svcs., Long Beach, Calif., 1997—, chmn., 2002—. Contbr. articles to profl. jours., chpts. to books. Commr. HHS, Washington, 1988. Grantee Health and Human Svcs. Advanced Nurse Tng. Mem. Women in Health Adminstrn. (sec. 1989, v.p. 1990), Nat. Assn. Home Care, Am. Orgn. Nursing Execs., Calif. Assn. Health Svcs. at Home (task force chmn. 1988, bd. dirs. 1988-93, chmn. bd. dirs. 1990-93), Calif. League Nursing (bd. sec. 1983, program chmn. 1981-82), Am. Coll. Health Care Execs., ASAE, Am. Orgn. Nurse Execs., HSACCC (sect. pres.2003-2004, state pres. 2004—), Phi Kappa Phi, Sigma Theta Tau, Soroptomist Internat. Republican. Methodist.

BRAUN, MARY LUCILE DEKLE (LUCY BRAUN), therapist, consultant, counselor, educator; b. Tampa, Fla. d. Guthrie "Gus" J. and Lucile (Culpepper) Dekle; children: John Ryan, Matthew Joseph, Jeffrey William, Douglas Edwin. AB, Brenau Coll.; MA, U. Cen. Fla.; EdD, U. Fla. Cert. disability mgmt. specialist, rehab. counselor, victim advocate; lic. mental health counselor; lic. marriage and family therapist; nationally cert. counselor. Coord. Orange County Child Abuse Prevention, Orlando, Fla., 1983-88; cons. Displaced Homemaker Program, Orlando, 1989-94, DCS, Oviedo, Fla., 1990-92. Adj. prof. U. Ctrl. Fla., Orlando, Troy State U.; clin. dir. Response Sexual Abuse Treatment Program, 1993—95; mem. adv. bd. Fla. Hosp. Women's Ctr., Orlando, 1989—; bd. dirs. Parent Resource Ctr., Orlando, Children With Attention Deficit Disorders, Orlando, 1989—91; cons. program devel. for children and adolescent treatment svcs., 1997—98; dir. clin. svcs. Rehab. and Indsl. Counseling, 1997—; cons., counselor contractor VA; counselor Share the Care Program. Author: Someone Heard, 1987, Humor Us Soup, 1989, Child Abuse and Neglect: Resource Guide for Orange County Schools, 1985, 2d edit., 1987; contbg. author: Death from Child Abuse, 1986, Personality Types of Abusive Parents, 1993, Why Children Fight, 1992. Sustaining mem. Jr. League of Greater Orlando. Program recipient Cmty. Svc. award Walt Disney World, 1987. Mem. ACA, Fla. Counseling Assn., Nat. Bd. Cert. Counselors, Phi Kappa Phi, Kappa Delta Pi, Chi Sigma Iota, Alpha Delta Pi. Avocations: scuba diving, sailing, puzzles.

BRAUN, SALLY A. elementary school educator, music educator; d. Verlin E. and Merry M. Braun; m. Terry L. Eklund, June 13, 1998 (div. June 13, 1999). AA in Audio Rec. Tech., Northest C.C., Norfolk, Nebr., 1990; MusB Edn., U. Nebr., 1998. Cert. tchr. Nebr. Optician Pearle Vision Ctr., Lincoln, Nebr., 1991—98; elem. music specialist Bellevue (Nebr.) Pub. Schs., 1990—99, beginning band instr., 1999—; mid. sch. band tchr. Plattsmouth (Nebr.) Pub. Schs., 1999. Webmaster Twin Ridge Elem. Sch., Bellevue, 2002—; north ctrl. assn. commn. on accreditation and sch. improvement steering com. mem. Twin Ridge Elem., Bellevue, 2003—; keyboard musician Plattsmouth Bapt. Ch., 2002—; pvt. music instr., Bellevue, 2003—. Transcriber (musical transcription) Concerto for Two Pianos, Winds and Percussion, compiler (instn. guide) How to use Overture Notation Software. Mem. Twin Ridge PTA, Bellevue, 1998—2003; praise and worship team mem. Plattsmouth Bapt. Ch., 2002—03, webmaster, 2003. Named Most Influential Tchr., Bellevue Optimist Club, 2003; recipient Hon. State Life award, Nebr. PTA, 2003. Mem.: Nebr. State Educators Assn., Nat. Music Educators Assn., Am. Orff-Schulwork Assn. Baptist. Avocations: quilting, crafts, bicycling, piano, computers. Office: Twin Ridge Elementary 1400 Sunbury Dr Bellevue NE 68005 Personal E-mail: claricat@hotmail.com. E-mail: claricat@hotmail.com.

BRAUN, SUSAN J. foundation administrator; married; 1 child, Alex. BA in English and Sociology with honors, George Mason U.; MA in Health Scis. with honors, U. Md.; postgrad. in Internat. Mktg., U. Muenster, Germany. Exec. Pracon Inc. and Ctr. Econ. Studies in Medicine; various positions, Oncology/Immunology Divsn. Bristol-Myers Squibb, Princeton, NJ; pres., CEO Susan G. Komen Breast Cancer Found., 1996—. Bd. mem., staff liaison Intercultural Cancer Coun. Mem. editl. bd.: Breast Jour., C.U.R.E. Mag. Active Americorps NCCC. Recipient Frances Williams Preston award for breast cancer awareness, Vanderbilt-Ingram Cancer Ctr., 2001. Mem.: Am. Soc. Clin. Oncology, World Soc. Breast Health, Am. Soc. for Breast Disease (chair pub. policy com.). Office: Susan G Komen Breast Cancer Found 5005 LBJ Freeway Ste 250 Dallas TX 75244*

BRAUNER, MARYGAIL K. engineer, systems analyst; BA in Math., U. Calif., L.A., 1969, MA in Math., 1970, PhD in Engring., 1986. Math. instr. Van Nuys Adult Sch., Van Nuys, Calif., 1972—75, Pierce Coll., 1975—81, Ventura Coll., Ventura, Calif., 1978—81; prof. mgmt. sci. Calif. State U., Northridge, Calif., 1981—84; ops. rsch. analyst RAND, Santa Monica, Calif., 1984—. Mem.: Inst. Ops. Rsch. & Mgmt. Sci. Office: RAND 1700 Main Street PO Box 2138 Santa Monica CA 90407-2138

BRAUNSTEIN, MARY, energy consulting company executive; AD in Elec. Engring., U. Cin., 1966. Project mgr. elec. & gas metering, customer billing; with Elec. distbn. & Engring.; mgr. info. tech. Cadence Networks, Cin. Trainer, mentor Rehab. Program Data Processing, U. Cin. Recipient J.H. Randolph award, 1993. Mem. Assns. Systems Mgmt. (past pres.). Office: Cadence Networks 105 E 4th St Ste 250 Cincinnati OH 45202-4006

BRAUTIGAN, JUNE MARIE, artist, poet; b. Syracuse, N.Y., Apr. 2, 1952; d. Ward Ernest Shaut and Frances Mary Craig; m. Thomas Francis Brautigan, Nov. 24, 1995; children: Timothy, Chad, Nathan, Crystal. Assoc. Degree, Corning C.C., Corning, N.Y., 1994. Author: (poetry) Goldenrod, 1993 (Winner in SCOP jour., 1993), Hometown, 1995, Perpetuate, 1997,

Seacast, 1997, Purgation, 1998, Reign, 1999, the coming of Age, 2000, Unify, 2001, I Can See Things I Cannot See, 2002, Weathering The Layoff, 2002, The Same Sameness, 2002, (short stories) A Room I Remember, 1992 (First place in Scop jour., 1992), Judgments, 2002, Red Light, Yellow Light, Green Light, 2003. Mem.: Internat. Poet Soc. Avocations: interior decorating, gardening. Home: 2850 Dunn's Mountain Rd Salisbury NC 28146 Office: 2850 Dunns Mountain Rd Salisbury NC 28146-8037 Personal E-mail: jmbrautigan@yahoo.com.

BRAVE, REBECCA S. LARSEN, curator; b. Albany, N.Y., Aug. 30, 1961; d. Oscar Wesley and Frances Burnett Larsen; m. Vincent P. Brave. BS in Anthropology, Bridgewater State Coll., 1985. Cert. archaeology and ethnology collections care and maintenance Nat. Pk. Svc., 1992. Curatorial asst. Peabody Essex Mus., Salem, Mass., 1989—91, project mgr., Native Am. Collection, 1991—94; registration technician Nat. Mus. Indians; Smithsonian Instn., N.Y.C., 1995—96; asst. curator Bklyn. Children's Mus., 1997—2000; curator/dir. George Peabody Ho. Mus., Peabody, Mass., 2000—. Mem.: New Eng. Mus. Assn., Am. Assn. State and Local Histories, Am. Assn. Museums, Crossroads Quilters (newsletter editor 2001—), Peabody Garden Club (exec. bd. 2000—, pres. 2002—), Garden Club Fedn. of Mass., Inc. (exec. bd., Wellesley Hills, Mass. 2001—02, chair historic preservation com. 2002—). Avocations: quilting, skiing. Home: 8a County Rd Essex MA 01929 Office: George Peabody House Mus 205 Washington St Peabody MA 01960 E-mail: drgnfly@mindspring.com.

BRAVO, DOMINIQUE, lawyer; b. 1962; BA, U. Calif.; JD, Northeastern U. Atty. Cohen, Weiss and Simon; nat. rep., staff counsel AFTRA, 1997—98, sr. nat. staff counsel, 1998—99, nat. dir. legal and legis. affairs, 2000—. Office: AFTRA Nat Office NY 260 Madison Ave New York NY 10016-2401*

BRAVO, ROSE MARIE, retail executive; b. N.Y.C., Jan. 13, 1951; d. Biagio and Anna (Bazzano) LaPila; m. William Selkirk Jackey, Oct. 9, 1983. BA in English, Fordham U., 1971. Exec. trainee, dept. mgr. A&S, Bklyn, 1971—74; assoc. buyer Macy's, N.Y.C., 1974—75, buyer, 1975—79, councilor, 1979—80, adminstr., 1980—84, group v.p., 1984—85, sr. v.p., 1985—88; chmn., CEO I. Magnin, San Francisco, 1988—92; pres. Saks Fifth Ave., Inc., N.Y.C., 1992—97; CEO Burberrys Ltd., London, 1997—. Bd. dirs. Tiffany & Co.

BRAWER, CATHERINE COLEMAN, foundation executive, curator; b. NYC, Feb. 19, 1943; d. Joseph A. and Beatrice R. Coleman; m. Robert A. Brawer, Sept. 7, 1962; children: Christopher Paul, Nicholas Andrew. BA, Sarah Lawrence Coll., 1964; MA in Art History, NYU, 1966. Publicity coord. Evehjem Mus. Art, Madison, Wis., 1970-75, curator Liebman Collection, 1974-75; mktg. mgr. Maidenform, Inc., NYC, 1975-78; ind. curator NYC, 1978; v.p. Ida and William Rosenthal Found., NYC, 1981-90, pres., 1990—; dir. pub. affairs Maidenform Inc., NYC, 1990-97, bd. dir., 1970-97. Curator Maidenform Mus., 1992-97; trustee Katonah (NY) Mus. Art, 1982-2000, Ind. Curators, Internat., NYC, 1989—, vice chmn., 1998—, Inst. Fine Arts, NYU, 1993—, Musica Viva, 1995-2002. Author: (catalogues) The Auspicious Dragon in Chinese Decorative Arts, 1978, Many Trails: Indians of the Lower Hudson Valley, 1983, Trade Winds: The Lure of the China Trade, 1985; (book) Making Their Mark: Women Artist Move into the Mainstream 1970-85, 1989, Chinese Export Porcelain from the Liebman Porcelain Collection, 1992. Trustee Plymouth (Mass.) Plantation, 2002—, Pk.-McCullough House, North Bennington, Vt., 2001—. Mem. NY Regional Assn. Grantmakers (mem. com. 1990-91), Art Table NY, Soc. Mayflower Descs. (sec. 2000--).

BRAXTON, TONI, popular musician; b. Severn, Md., Oct. 7, 1967; m. Keri Lewis; 1 child, Denim Lewis. Albums Toni Braxton, 1993, Heat, 2000, Snow Flakes, 2001, More Than a Woman, 2002, appeared in (films) Kingdom Come, 2000, contbr. Boomerang soundtrack, 1992, Secrets, 1997; actor: (Broadway musical) Aida, 2003. Recipient Grammy award Best Female R&B Vocal, 1994, 1995, 2001, Aretha Franklin Soul Train award, 2000, BET Black Oscar, 2000, 3 time Amer. Music award . Office: Arista Records care LaFace 6 W 57th St New York NY 10019-3999

BRAY, CAROLYN SCOTT, education educator; b. May 19, 1938; d. Alonzo Lee and Frankie Lucile (Wood) Scott; m. John Graham Bray Jr., Aug. 24, 1957 (div. May 1980); children: Caron Lynn, Kimberly Anne, David William. BS, Baylor U., 1960; MEd, Hardin-Simmons U., 1981; PhD, U. North Tex., 1985. Registered med. technologist. Dir. career placement Hardin-Simmons U., 1979-82, adj. prof. bus. comm., 1981-84, assoc. dean students, 1982-85; assoc. dir. career planning and placement U. North Tex., Denton, 1985-95, adj. prof. higher edn. adminstrn., mem. Mentor program, dir. Career Ctr., U. Tex. at Dallas, Richardson, 1995-2000, prof. edn., 2000—, tchr. devel. ctr. assessment officer, 2000—. Mem. Consortium State Orgn. Tex. Tchr. Edn., 1999—; mem. adv. bd. TxBESS, 2000—. Adult Bible study tchr, 1st Bapt. Ch., Richardson, Tex., 2000—. Mem.: North Ctrl. Tex. Assn. Sch. Pers. Adminstrs. and Univ. Placement Pers. (pres. 1987—88, sec. 1988—95), Nat. Assn. Colls. and Employers (co-chair nat. conf. planning com. 1996—98), Tex. Assn. for Employer Edn. and Staffing (v.p. 1986—87, pres. 1987—88), Am. Assn. for Employment in Edn. (bd. dirs. 1989—94, treas. 1994—95, nat. conf. com. 1999, conf. com. local arrangements 1999, Priscilla A. Scotlan award for disting. svc. 1999), S.W. Assn. Colls. and Employers (life; chair conf. registration 1991—92, vice chair ops. 1992—93, 4-yr. coll. dir. 1998—99, pres.-elect 1999—2000, co-chmn. tech. com.), Leadership Denton (co-dir. curriculum 1988—89, chair membership selection com., steering com. 1990, 1993—94), Denton C. of C. (pub. rels. com. 1988—95), Kappa Kappa Gamma (chpt. advisor, chair adv. bd. Zeta Sigma chpt. 1987—93). Republican. Avocations: skiing, tennis, golf, reading. Office: U Tex at Dallas PO Box 830688 GR22 Richardson TX 75083-0688 Office Phone: 972-883-2730. Business E-Mail: csbray@utdallas.edu.

BRAY, JOAN, state legislator; b. Lubbock, Tex., Sept. 16, 1945; m. Carl Hoagland; 2 children. BA, Southwestern U., 1967; MEd, U. Mass., 1971. Former tchr., journalist; former dist. dir. for Congresswoman Joan Kelly Horn; mem. dist. 84 Mo. Ho. of Reps., St. Louis, 1992—. Bd. dirs. Citizens for Modern Transit. Flemming fellow, 1995. Mem. PTO, Nat. Womens Polit. Caucus. Democrat. Home: 7120 Washington Ave Saint Louis MO 63130-4312 Office: Mo Ho of Reps Rm 412 State Capitol Building Jefferson City MO 65101-1556

BRAY, PATRICIA SHANNON, music educator, musician, small business owner; b. Elkton, Md., Sept. 4, 1953; d. Francis William Shannon and Mary Elizabeth Gardner; m. William Joseph Bray Jr., July 31, 1976; children: Mark William, Eric Joseph. BMEd magna cum laude, East Carolina U., 1975; MS summa cum laude, Med. Coll. Va., Va. Commonwealth U., 1995. Lic. tchr. Va. Tchr., dir. orch. Chesterfield County Pub. Schs., Chesterfield, Va., 1975—. Cellist Richmond Philharm. Orch., Va., 1975—82, Petersburg Symphony, Va., 1987—94, Lynchburg Symphony, Va., 1998—; chair dept. music Salem Ch. Mid. Sch., Richmond, 1998—; owner Talent Edn. Chesterfield, 2000—; adjucator Richard Bland Lions Club, Music Scholarship Competition, Chester, Va., 2000; adjucator Jr. Festival Va. Fedn. of Music Clubs, 2003; presenter in field, 00; co-presenter Suzuki Assn. of the Ams. Conf., 2002; presenter Chesterfield County Pub. Schs. Leadership Conf., 2002. Faculty sponsor Salem Music Boosters, Richmond, 1998—; sch. crisis team Chesterfield County Pub. Schs., 1995—, sch. improvement planning com., 2002—. Scholarship, Theodore Presser Publ. Co. Scholarship, 1973. Mem.: Va. Mid. Sch. Assn., NEA, Am. String Tchrs. Assn., Music Educators Nat. Conf., Suzuki Assn. Americas, Sigma Alpha Iota, Kappa Delta Pi, Phi Kappa Phi. Avocations: hiking, reading, gardening. Home: 918 Dawnwood Rd Midlothian VA 23114 Office: Salem Ch Mid Sch 9700 Salem Church Rd Richmond VA 23237 E-mail: intuitpsb@aol.com.

BRAZEAL, AURELIA ERSKINE, ambassador; b. Chgo., Nov. 24, 1943; BS, Spelman Coll., 1965; M of Internat. Affairs, Columbia U., 1967; postgrad., Harvard U., 1972. With Foreign Svc., 1968; consular and econ. officer U.S. Embassy, Buenos Aires, 1969-71; econ. reports officer Econ. Bureau U.S. State Dept., 1971-72, watch and line officer Office of Secretariat, 1973-74, desk officer Uraguay, Paraguay, 1974-77; review officer Office of Secretariat U.S. Dept. Treasury, 1977-79; econ. officer Tokyo, 1979-82; officer ECON Bur. U.S. Dept. State, 1982-84; dep. dir. Econ. Office Japan, 1984-86; mem. sr. seminar, 1986-87; min. counselor econ. affairs U.S. Embassy, Tokyo, 1987-90; U.S amb. to Micronesia, 1990-93; U.S. amb. to Kenya, 1993-96; deputy asst. sec. East Asian & Pacific Affairs, 1996-98; dean sr. seminar Fgn. Svc. Inst., Arlington, Va., 1998-99, dean leadership and mgmt. sch. and sr. seminar, 1999—2002; U.S. amb. to Ethiopia, 2002—. Office: Pub Affairs US Dept State 2201 C St NW Rm 2206 Washington DC 20520-2204

BRAZEAL, DONNA SMITH, psychologist; b. Greenville, S.C., Feb. 10, 1947; d. G.W. Hovey and Ollie Occena (Crane) Smith; m. Charles Lee Brazeal, June 27, 1970 (div. May 1980). BA, Clemson U., 1971, MEd, 1975; postgrad., Western Carolina U., 1974, Furman U., Greenville, 1977; PhD, Columbia Pacific U., 1994. Lic. sch. psychologist, S.C., N.C. Instr., head med. record dept. Greenville Tech. Coll., 1971-73; N.E. area chief psychologist Greenville County Schs., 1975-80; coord. psychol. svcs. Union County Schs., Monroe, N.C., 1980-97; ret., 1997; pvt. practice psychology, 1986-92. Mem. learning disabilities com. Greenville County Schs., 1978-79; co-founder, bd. dirs. Ctr. for Spiritual Awareness of N.C., Monroe, 1982—. Co-author, co-editor: School Psychologist, 1980. Child find program coord. Union County, 1980-85; mem. various coms. Assn. for Retarded Citizens, Monroe; mem. Union County Assn. for Retarded Citizens; mem. interagy. coun. Piedmont Mental Health, Monroe, 1983-97; mem. adult edn. com. River Hills Cmty. Ch., 1985-86. Catawba Bus. Women scholar, 1965; N.C. Dept. Pub. Instrn. Pre-Sch. Incentive grantee, 1984. Mem. Nat. Assn. Sch. Psychologists, N.C. Assn. Sch. Psychologist (mem. pub. relations com. 1984-85), Greenpeace, Humane Soc. U.S., Delta. Democrat. Interdenominational Christian. Home: PO Box 240173 Charlotte NC 28224-0173 E-mail: dsbrazeal@aol.com.

BRAZELL, KAREN WOODARD, Japanese literature educator; b. Buffalo, Apr. 25, 1938; d. Charles Cary and Josephine Mary (Bordonaro) Woodard; m. James Reid Brazell, Aug. 27, 1961 (div. 1978); children: Katherine Ann Brazell Rivera, Stephen Reid. Student, Coll. Wooster, 1956-58, Internat. Christian U., Tokyo, 1958-60; BA, U. Mich., 1961, MA, 1962; PhD, Columbia U., 1969; D Lit (hon.), Univ. Puget Sound, 1993. Asst. prof. Japanese lit. Princeton U., 1969-74; assoc. prof. Cornell U., Ithaca, N.Y., 1974-79, prof., 1979—, chmn. dept. Asian studies, 1977-82, dir. East Asia program, 1987-91. Vis. prof. U. Calif., Berkeley, 1984, Nat. Inst. Japanese Lit., Tokyo, 1988-89, vis. Shinchosha prof. Columbia U., 1996. Author: Confessions of Lady Nijo, 1973 (Nat. Book Award 1974), Noh as Performance, 1977, Dance in the Noh Theater, 1981; editor: 12 Plays of Noh and Kyogen Theaters, 1988; assoc. editor Jour. Japanese Studies, 1978—; contbr. articles and book revs. to profl. jours. Trustee Cornell U., 1979-83; bd. dirs. U.S.-Japan Soc. Ithaca, N.Y., Japan Soc. N.Y.C. Performing Arts Adv. Com., 1993—, Japan-U.S. Partnership for Performing Arts Inc., N.Y.C., 1994—. Fulbright-Hayes fellow, 1972-73, NEH fellow, summer 1974, Cornell U. Soc. Humanities fellow, 1976-77, Japan Found. fellow, 1978, 85, Nat. Inst. Japanese Lit. rsch. fellow, Tokyo, 1988-89. Mem. Assn. Asian Studies, Assn. Tchrs. of Japanese (exec. com. 1981-83, bd. dirs. 1989-92), Phi Beta Kappa (senator at large 1976-82, trustee found. 1977-82). Office: Cornell U Dept Asian Studies Ithaca NY 14853 Home: 376 Turkey Hill Rd Ithaca NY 14850-2943

BRAZIER, MARY MARGARET, psychology educator, researcher; b. New Orleans, Feb. 4, 1956; d. Robert Whiting and Margaret Long (Mc Waters) B. BA, Loyola U., New Orleans, 1977; MS, Tulane U., 1985, PhD, 1986. Assoc. prof. Loyola U., 1986—, chair dept. psychology, 1993—, acting assoc. dean Coll. Arts and Scis., 1997-98. Grantee, NSF, 1987, 1999. Mem.: APA, Southwestern Psychol. Assn. (coun. 1988—2000, pres. 2002—), So. Soc. Philosophy and Psychology (exec. coun. 1989—92), Southeastern Psychol. Assn., Am. Psychol. Soc. Roman Catholic. Avocations: gardening, sailing, new orleans cooking and culture, dance. Office: Loyola U Dept Psychology 6363 Saint Charles Ave Dept New Orleans LA 70118-6195 E-mail: brazier@loyno.edu.

BRAZIL, AINE M. engineering company executive; Student, Univ. Coll., Galway, Ireland; BS in Engring., U. Coll. Galway, Ireland, 1977; MS in Engring., Imperial Coll. Sci. and Tech., London, 1980. Structural engr. Thornton-Tomasetti Engrs., N.Y.C., 1982, sr. assoc., 1992—97, prin., 1997—. Adj. prof. dept. civil engring. and engring. materials Columbia U. Named one of Women of Achievement, Profl. Women in Constrn., 2001. Office: Thornton-Tomasetti 624 Commerce St Newark NJ 07102-4005

BRAZILE, DONNA, advocate; b. New Orleans; B, La. State U. Regional dir. Hands Across Am., 1985; nat. coord. housing Housing Now, 1989; founder, exec. dir. Nat. Polit. Congress Black Women; chief staff to Eleanor Holmes Norton, DC del. to US House Reps.; former host, prodr. A View From the Hill, Radio One News; campaign mgr. for Al Gore presdl. campaign, 2000. Adj. prof. Georgetown U.; sr. fellow James MacGregor Burns Acad. Leadership, U. Md.; at-large mem. Dem. Nat. Com. Nat. student coord. Martin Luther King, Jr. Holiday Com., 1981; nat. mobilization dir. 20th Anniversary Commemoration 1963 March on Wash., 1983; nat. chair Voting Rights Inst., 2003. Named one of Outstanding Young Achievers, Ebony mag., 100 Most Powerful Women in Wash., Washingtonian mag., 2001; recipient Congl. Black Caucus Youth award, Nat. Women's Student Leadership award. Office: Acad Leadership Univ Md College Park MD 20742-7715 Office Phone: 301-405-6100. Office Fax: 301-405-6402. Business E-Mail: dbrazile@academy.umd.edu.*

BRAZ-VALENTINE, CLAIRE, writer, playwright; b. San Francisco, July 22, 1939; d. George John Braz and Clara Roy; m. Richard Kier, Aug. 23, 1959 (div. 1972); children: Thomas Kier, Daniel Kier, Scott Kier; m. Jimmy Willins, 1973 (div. 1978). Grad., Immaculate Conception Acad., San Francisco, 1957. Asst. to chair U. Calif., Santa Cruz, 1979—93, writing instr., 1998. Guest lectr. Cabrillo Coll., Aptos, Calif., 1990—, Deanza Coll., Cupertino, Calif., 1997, Grand Valley State, Grand Rapids, Mich., 1997, Evergreen Coll., San Jose County, 2000; workshop tchr. William James Assn., Calif., 1990—2002; artist-in-sch. Cultural Coun., Santa Cruz County, Calif., 1990—99. Playwright: This One Thing I Do, 1989, Ashes, 2001. Vol. mother/infant program Calif. State Prison, Watsonville, 1997. Recipient Outstanding Woman in Santa Cruz award, Commn. for Status of Women, Santa Cruz, 1999. Mem.: NOW, Internat. League Women Playwrights, Writer's Union. Democrat. Avocations: writing, journalism, poetry.

BRDLIK, CAROLA EMILIE, retired accountant; b. Wuerzburg, Germany, Mar. 11, 1930; came to U.S., 1952; d. Ludwig Leonard and Hildegard Maria (Leipold) Baumeister; m. Joseph A. Brdlik; children: Margaret Louise, Charles Joseph. BA, Oberrealschule Bamberg, Fed. Republic Germany, 1948; MA, Bavarian Interpreter Coll., Fed. Republic Germany, 1949; Cert., Internat. Accts. Soc., Chgo., 1955. Interpreter, exec. sec. NCWC Amberg, Schweinfurt, Ludwigsburg and Munich, Fed. Republic Germany, 1949-52; exec. sec. Red Ball Van Lines, Jamaica, N.Y., 1952; interpreter Griffin Rutgers Inc., N.Y.C., 1952-53; office mgr., exec. sec. Rehab. Ctr. Summit Co., Inc., Akron, 1953-56; pvt. practice acctg. Cuyahoga Falls, Ohio, 1956-61, Uniontown, Ohio, 1961-81; sec., treas. Omaca, Inc., Uniontown and Deerfield Beach (Fla.), 1981-86, pres. Uniontown and Jupiter, 1986-2000, ret., 2000. Sec.-treas. Shipe Landscaping, Inc., Greensburg, Ohio, 1968-92, Sattler Machine Products, Copley, Ohio, 1981-88; asst. treas. Mar-Lynn Lake Park, Inc., Streetsboro, Ohio, 1969-97. Bd. dirs., trustee Czechoslovak Refugees, Cleve. and Cin., 1968. Mem.: Nat. Assn. Tax Profls., Nat. Soc. Accts. Roman Catholic. Avocations: sewing, swimming, travel. E-mail: ceb0311@bellsouth.net.

BREAKSTONE, KAY LOUISE, public relations executive; b. Allentown, Pa., Sept. 9, 1936; d. Morris H. and Mabel (Gruber) Senderowitz; m. Jules L. Breakstone, Dec. 3, 1960; children: Enid, Jessica. BS, N.Y.U., 1967. With N.Y. Conf. Bd., 1967-69, Bache, Halsey, Stuart, N.Y.C., 1969-70; securities analyst Dean Witter, N.Y.C., 1970-71; v.p. Burson Marsteller, Inc., N.Y.C., 1971-79, sr. v.p., 1981-87, exec. v.p., 1987-92; dir. investor rels. Kennecott Corp., Stamford, Conn., 1979-81; pres., CEO Ludgate Comm., N.Y.C., 1993—. Mem. Nat. Investor Rels. Inst. (pres. 1980-81). Office: Ludgate Comm 405 Lexington Ave New York NY 10174-0002

BREALL, SUSAN, judge; Chief criminal divsn. San Francisco Dist. Atty.'s Office, 1984—2001; judge Superior Ct. of Calif., County of San Francisco, San Francisco, 2001—. Mem. adv. bd. Nat. Network for Battered Immigrant Women. Office: Superior Ct of Calif Civic Ctr Courthouse 400 McAllister St San Francisco CA 94102-4519 Address: Volcano Press PO Box 270 Volcano CA 95689-0270

BREARLEY, CANDICE, fashion designer; b. Trenton, N.J., Jan. 2, 1944; d. Joseph William and Lillian (Mieler) Szalay; m. Purvis Brearley, Sept. 2, 1965. BFA, Mus. Sch., Phila., 1965, MFA, 1968; BFA, Parsons Sch. Design, 1975, New Sch. Social Rsch., 1975. Freelance portrait artist, Trenton, 1965-72; asst. designer Malcolm Starr, N.Y.C., 1974-75; designer Originala, N.Y.C., 1975-77, Vignette, N.Y.C., 1977-78; pres., designer Candice Brearley, Inc., Trenton, 1978—; pres. Wickford Corp. of N.J., Trenton, 1986—. Bd. dirs. Beta Con Corp., Lawrenceville, N.J. One-woman shows Nat. State Bank, N.J., 1971; exhibited in group show at N.J. State Mus., Trenton, 1970. Mem. devel. com. Restoration of "The Brearley House," Lawrenceville, N.J. Recipient award Lane Bryant Design Competition, 1974. Fellow Phila. Mus. Art, Met. Mus. Art, Princeton U. Mus., N.J. State Mus.; mem. Lawrence Hist. Soc. Roman Catholic. Avocations: collecting art, vintage cars, antique refinishing, opera, cooking. Office: Candice Brearley Inc 128 Buckingham Ave Trenton NJ 08618-3314

BREASURE, JOYCE M. counselor, educator; b. Milford, Del., May 4, 1951; d. John Ward and Effie Mae Breasure; BAAS, U. Del., Newark, 1973; M in Counseling, U. Del., Dover, 1977. Lic. profl. counselor mental health Del., 1995, cert. Nat. Cert. Counselor, Nat. Cert. Gerntol. Counselor Nat. Bd. Cert. Counselors, Nat. Cert. Clin. Mental Health Counselor Nat. Bd. Cert. Counselors. Pvt. practice counselor, Wyoming, Del., 1972—; educator Del. State U., Dover, 1974—2002, gerontol. counselor Genesis Health Care, Dover, 1990—; bd. dirs. Modern Maturity Ctr., Dover. Author: Nonverbal Communication Skills Handbook, 1982, (monograph) The Nuts and Bolts of Private Practice, 1997. Bd. dirs. Modern Maturity Ctr., Dover, Meals on Wheels, Del., 2002. Mem.: Nat. Bd. for Cert. Counselors (chair, mem. bd. 1985—91), Am. Mental Health Counselors Assn. (life; Counselor of Yr. 1983), ACA (life; Presdl. award 1996).

BREATHITT, LINDA K. federal commissioner; b. Hopkinsville, Ky. BA in Edn., U. Ky., 1975; cert. state-local govt. exec. mgmt. pro., Harvard U. Exec. dir. Washington Office, Commonwealth of Ky., 1980-92; commr. Ky. Pub. Svc. Commn., 1993-95, chmn., 1996-97; commr. FERC, 1997—. Bd. dirs. Martin Sch. Pub. Policy, U. Ky., Tata Energy Rsch. Inst. Regulatory Studies and Governance, New Delhi. Mem. Women Execs. in State Govt., U. Ky. Alumni Assn. Methodist. Avocations: photography, scuba diving, gardening. Office: Thelen Reid & Priest LLP 701 Pennsylvania Ave NW Ste 800 Washington DC 20004

BREBNER, KIMBERLY KAY, marketing professional; d. Rex and Patricia Lee Domaschofsky; married, Aug. 6, 1988; 1 child, Taryn Kay. BS in Mktg., Portland State U., 1987; MBA in Bus. and Mktg., U. Portland, 1997. Sales United Parcel Svc., 1987—92, mktg. mgr., 1993—97, mktg. mgr. segments, 1997—98, mktg. mgr. bus. planning Atlanta, 1988—99, air svcs., 1999—2000, e-commerce, 2001—03, dir. mktg., 2000—03. Mem.: Am. Mktg. Assn. Home: 1160 Beacon Hill Crossing Alpharetta GA 30005

BRECHT, SALLY ANN, quality assurance executive; b. Trenton, N.J., Aug. 5, 1951; d. Charles L. and Helen (Orfeo) B. BBA, Coll. William and Mary, 1973; MBA, Rider Coll., 1981. Cert. quality engr., software quality engr.; quality auditor, quality mgr., project mgr. Project Mgmt. Inst. Electronic data processing auditor McGraw Hill, Inc., Hightstown, N.J., 1976-79, State of N.J., Mercerville, 1979-80, NL Industries, Hightstown, 1980-84; systems tech. planning specialist Ednl. Testing Svc., Princeton, N.J., 1984-85, acting div. dir. application devel., 1985-87, mgr. computer standards and security, 1987-88, asst. dir. office corp. quality assurance, 1988-98; dir. software quality assurance Y2K Renovation, 1998—; portfolio project mgr. IT Project Mgmt. Office, 2000—02; project mgr. CMM Metrics Implementation, 2002—. Contbr. articles to popular publs. Mem. Am. Soc. for Quality Control (cert. quality engr., mgr., auditor and software quality engr.); pmi cert. project mgmt. profl. Avocation: dressage.

BRECHTEL, UNDA JURKA, library director; b. Riga, Latvia, Mar. 3, 1935; came to U.S., 1951; d. Aleksanders and Irene (Stesingers) Jurka; m. Philipp Jack Brechtel Jr., Sept. 3, 1960 (div. Aug. 1986); children: Philipp Jack III, Peter Kevin. BS in Psychology, St. Thomas Aquinas, 1981; MLS, L.I. U., 1982. Reference librarian Haverstraw (N.Y.) Pub. Libr., 1982-83; libr. dir. Sloatsburg (N.Y.) Pub. Libr., 1983-85, Wanaque (N.J.) Pub. Libr., 1985-88, Oakland (N.J.) Pub. Libr., 1988-2000; ret., 2000; libr. L.I. U., Sparkill, N.Y., 2000—. Mem. N.J. Libr. Assn., N.Y. Libr. Assn. Lutheran. Avocations: ballroom dancing, travel, gardening. Home: 1-16 Lawrence Pk Piermont NY 10968 E-mail: ubrechtel@yahoo.com.

BRECKEL, ALVINA HEFELI, librarian; b. Chgo., Dec. 6, 1948; d. William Christ and Liselotte (Herrmann) Hefeli; m. Theodore A. Breckel, Feb. 10, 1973. BFA cum laude, Bradley U., 1970; MALS, Rosary Coll. (now Dominican U.), 1973. Cert. art tchr., media libr., Ill. Tchr. art Chgo. Pub. Schs., 1971-84; libr. Oakton CC, Des Plaines, Ill., 1988—. Mem. North Shore Bd. of Gads Hill Ctr., corr. sec., 2000—; nat. seminar spkr. Early Am. Pattern Glass Soc., 1999; spkr. Mid-States conf. Early Am. Pattern Glass Soc., 2001; co-chmn. Winnetka Antiques Show, 1999, chmn., 2000, dealer chmn., 2000—; mem. Com. for Gallery 37 in the Schs., 2001—; mem. visual arts com. Chgo. Cmty. Trust Gallery, Northwestern U. Settlement Assn., 2001—. Author: Looking for Glass on the Internet, 1996; editor News & Notes, 1988-89. Rep. election judge New Trier Twp., Ill., 1988; com. mem. Villagers for a Safe Winnetka, 1989; mem. women's bd. Howard Area Cmty. Ctr., 1990-95; chmn. Fuller Lane Cir., Winnetka, 1991-92, 94-95; mem. Midwestern Antiques Club, 1993—; mem. women's bd. Winnetka Cmty. House, 1995—03, historian, 1997—2003, mem. steering com., 1999—. Mem. AAUW (bd. dirs. New Trier chpt. 1989-90), Sandwich (Mass.) Hist. Soc., Winnetka Hist. Soc., Art Inst. Chgo. (life), Nat. Greentown Glass Assn., Nat. Am. Glass Club (life, founding mem. James H. Rose chpt. sec. 1992-97), Greater Chgo. Glass Collectors Club (v.p. 1995-97, pres. 1998-2000, chmn. bylaws com. 2001, chmn. nominating com. 2002), Early Am. Pattern Glass Soc. (nominating com. 1998, spkr. Mid-States conf. 2001), Chgo. Area Shaker INterest Group, Pi Lambda Theta (life, art editor chpt. Notes 1977-84), Delta Zeta (v.p. Chgo.

North Shore chpt. 1987-90), Phi Delta Kappa. Avocation: collecting and researching early American decorative arts, especially glass. Home: 185 Fuller Ln Winnetka IL 60093-4212 Office: Oakton CC 7701 Lincoln Ave Skokie IL 60077-2800

BRECKENRIDGE, BETTY GAYLE, management development consultant; b. Austin, Tex., Dec. 8, 1945; BA, Baylor U., 1966; MA, So. Meth. U, 1984. Cons. Devel. Dimensions Internat., Pitts., 1984—, Bernard Haldane Assoc., Atlanta, 2003—, Children's Healthcare, Atlanta, 2003—. Office: 3447 N Druid Hills Rd Ste P Decatur GA 30033-3765 Office Phone: 404-321-1071. E-mail: mysteriouspa@mindspring.com.

BRECKENRIDGE, JOANNE, political organization administrator; Attended, Ctrl. Meth. Coll., Fla. U. Mem. Nat. Fedn. Rep. Women, 1975—, mem.-at-large, 1996-97, regent, 4th v.p., dir. region 6, 1988-99, 3d v.p. dir. region 3, 2000-01, regent, 1984-2002. Pres. Mo. Fedn. Rep. Women; club pres. St. Louis Rep. Women Com. Spkr. in field. Co-chair fundraisers for U.S. Congress, State Senate and House candidates; active Bush Campaign, 1996, Dole/Kemp Advance Team, 1996; alternate del. Rep. Nat. Conv., 1976, 84, 92; Mo. Rep. chmn. of youth for Reagan, 1980; pres. Mo. Fedn. Rep. Women, 1992-96, Rep. Women's Club South, 2000; mem. Rep. Com., Concord Twp., 2004—; active Kirkwood Bapt. Ch., mem. mission team to St. Lucia. Joanne Breckenridge Legis. Day scholarships named in her honor by Mo. Fedn. Rep. Women. Office: 5838 Five Oaks Pkwy Saint Louis MO 63128-1403 Fax: 314-416-1954.

BRECKENRIDGE, JUDITH WATTS, writer, educator; b. Knoxville, Tenn., Jan. 30, 1948; d. William Robert and Mary Kathryn (Ault) Watts; m. Rufus Gentry Breckenridge, June 26, 1977; children: Kathryn Suzanne, Mary Audra, Caroline Irene, Judith Gentry. BA in English, Carson-Newman Coll., 1970; MA in English, West Ga. Coll., 1972. Instr. Augusta (Ga.) Coll., Walter State C.C., Morristown, Tenn., 2002—; columnist Greeneville (Tenn.) Sun, 1993—; freelance writer. Author: Simple Physics Using Everyday Materials, 1993; author, creator (radio spots) Momtrax Minutes, 1999; author: (song) LA Cop: Cop of Lower Alabama, 1991. Mem.: First Families Tenn., Greeneville Arts Coun., Tuesday Morning Book Club. Baptist. Achievements include copyright Grammar Sticks; copyright Momtrax. Avocations: hiking, photography. Home: 506 Whisperwood Dr Greeneville TN 37743

BREECE, SHERRI LEE, education educator; b. Sacramento, Calif., Jan. 11, 1959; d. Sam Moss and Pamela Joyce Bell; m. Mark Alan Breece, Apr. 5, 2003; children: David, Jessica; life ptnr. Charles Keith Humble, Dec. 30, 1978 (div. May 1, 1995); children: Brian, Christy, Cassie. BE, Morehead St. Univ., Ky., 1981, MEd, 1990. Tchr. Magoffin County Bd. of Edn., Salyersville, Ky., 1984—2001, Russell Independ. Sch. Sys., Russell, Ky., 2001—. Mem. Coun. for Children with Behavior Disorders, 2001—03.

BREED, SARAH DUNFORD, elementary school educator, writer; b. Boston, Jan. 23, 1966; d. Putnam Pope Breed and Ramona Desmond; m. Augustine Musoke, Sept. 11, 1962; 1 child, Olivia Musoke. BA in Polit. Sci., Mt. Holyoke Coll., 1987; MA in Creative Writing, San Francisco State U., 1995. Editor Commerce Clearing House, San Rafael, Calif., 1988—91; educator, literacy specialist San Francisco Unified Sch. Dist., 1991—. Cons. Tchrs. Knowledge Project, Brattleboro, Vt., 2001—03; bd. dirs. Phoenix Rising Dance Club, San Francisco, 2000—. Author: Runaway Farm, 1995, Physical Landscape, 2002; editor: The Sage Intoning, 1992, Voices from Within, 1995. Black Dance scholar, Nat. Endowment Arts, 1991, Poetry grant, San Francisco Edn. Fund, 1992. Mem.: Mt. Holyoke Club. Avocations: dance, photography, travel. Office: Mystic Prodns PO Box 20272 Oakland CA 94607

BREEN, KATHERINE ANNE, speech and language pathologist; b. Chgo., Oct. 31, 1948; d. Robert Stephen and Gertrude Catherine (Bader) Breen. BS, Northwstern U., 1970; MA, U. Mo., Columbia, 1971. Cert. speech pathologist. Speech/lang. pathologist Fulton (Mo.) Pub. Schs., 1971-73; co-dir. Easter Seal Speech Clinic, Jefferson City, Mo., summer 1972, 73; speech/lang. pathologist Shawnee Mission (Kans.) Pub. Schs., 1973-96; staff St. Joseph's Hosp., Kansas City, Mo., 1978-81, Midwest Rehab. Ctr., Kansas City, 1985; pvt. practice speech therapy. Cons. East Ctrl. Mo. Mental Health Center; guest lectr. Fontbonne Coll., St. Louis. Vol., Mid Am. Rehab. Hosp. Mem. NEA, Am. Speech and Hearing Assn., Kans. Speech and Hearing Assn., Mo. State Tchrs. Assn., Kansas City Alumni Assn. of Northwestern U. (dir. alumni admissions coun., Outstanding Leadership award 1981, Svc. award 1991), Friends of Art Nelson/Atkins Art Gallery and Mus. (vol.), Nat. Trust Historic Preservation, Kansas City Hist. Found., Zeta Phi Eta. Methodist. Home: 8318 Mackey St Shawnee Mission KS 66212-2728

BREGOLI-RUSSO, MAUDA RITA, language educator, educator; b. Iesi-Ancona, Italy; came to U.S., 1965; d. Antonio Bregoli and Libe Maria Scipioni; m. Franco Gino Russo, June 27, 1964; 1 child, Antonella. Laurea, Bologna (Italy) U., 1963; PhD in Romance Langs., U. Chgo., 1978. Vis. asst. prof. Northwestern U., Chgo., 1981-83; asst. prof. U. Ill., Chgo., 1984-90, assoc. prof., 1990—. Author: Boiardo Lirico, 1979, Renaissance Italian Plays, 1984, Impresa Come Ritratto, 1990, Teatro D'Isabella D'Este, 1997. NEH grantee, 1981. Mem. MLA, Renaissance Soc. Am., Associazione Italiana per Gli Studi Di Lingua E Letteratura Italiana. Home: 100 E Walton St Apt 19de Chicago IL 60611-1448 Office: U Ill Chgo 601 S Morgan St Chicago IL 60607-7100 E-mail: mabrer@uic.edu.

BREHIO, RENEE MARIE, public relations executive, consultant; d. William and Marilyn Brehio. BA, Georgetown U., 1991, MA, 1992. Dir. pub. info. Am. Soc. Health-Sys. Pharmacists, Bethesda, Md., 1993—98; mgr. healthcare practice Burson-Marsteller, Washington, 1998—99; dir. comm. CFIDS Assn. Am., Charlotte, NC, 1999—2002; pub. rels. cons. Renee Brehio Healthcare Pub. Rels., Charlotte, 2002—. Contbr. articles to profl. jours. Therapy dog handler Therapy Dogs Internat., Charlotte. Tchg. fellow, Georgetown U., 1991—92. Mem.: Am. Med. Writers Assn., Pub. Rels. Soc. Am. Home: 3973 High Ridge Rd Charlotte NC 28270 Personal E-mail: reneebrehio@carolina.rr.com.

BREHM, SHARON STEPHENS, psychology educator, university administrator; b. Roanoke, Va., Apr. 18, 1945; d. John Wallis and Jane Chappel (Phenix) Stephens; m. Jack W. Brehm, Oct. 25, 1968 (div. Dec. 1979) BA, Duke U., 1967, PhD, 1973; MA, Harvard U., 1968. Clin. psychology intern U. Wash. Med. Ctr., Seattle, 1973-74; asst. prof. Va. Poly. Inst. and State U., Blacksburg, 1974-75, U. Kans., Lawrence, 1975-78, assoc. prof., 1978-83, prof. psychology, 1983-90, assoc. dean Coll. Liberal Arts and Scis., 1987-90; prof. psychology, dean Harpur Coll. of Arts and Scis. SUNY, Binghamton, 1990-96; prof. psychology and interpersonal comm., provost Ohio U., Athens, 1996—2001; chancellor Ind. U., Bloomington, 2001—, prof. dept. psychology, 2001—, adj. prof. sch. pub. and environ. affairs, 2001—. Vis. prof. U. Mannheim, 1978, Istituto di Psicologia, Rome, 1989; Fulbright sr. rsch. scholar Ecole des Hautes Etudes en Sciences Sociales, Paris, 1981-82; Soc. for Personality and Social Psychology rep. APA's Coun. of Reps., 1995-2000, finance com., 1999—; chair governing bd. Ohio Learning Network, 1998-99. Author: The Application of Social Psychology to Clinical Practice, 1976, (with others) Psychological Reactance: A Theory of Freedom and Control, 1981, Intimate Relationships, 1985, 2d edit., 1992, (with others) Social Psychology, 1990, 4th edit., 1999, also numerous articles, and chpts. Mem. APA (fin. com. 1999—). Office: Ind U 107 S Indiana Ave Bloomington IN 47405-7000*

BREHM-GRUBER, THERESE FRANCES, minister, consulting psychologist; b. Milw., July 6, 1932; d. Stanley Leo and Frances Hedwig (Kulasiewicz) Maternowski; m. James Monroe Brehm, Aug. 17, 1968 (dec. Feb. 1983); children: Frank X. Brehm, Gretchen Brehm Duran, Eric Brehm; m. Harold John Gruber, July 2, 1994. BS, Marquette U., 1961, MEd, 1963; D of Ministry, Grad. Theol. Found., 1993. Cert. state sch. psychologist, Wis.; ministerial cert. Fedn. Christian Mins. Counselor, sch. psychologist Germantown (Wis.) St. Sch. Dist., 1963-68; sch. psychologist Neenah (Wis.) St. Sch. Dist., 1968-91; lay min. Green Bay Diocese/Parish, Neenah, 1973—. Cons., Wis., 1990-94. Co-author: (with Irene Dill) The Sharing of Power in the Catholic Church, 1993. Vol. follow-up worker Best Friends, Neenah and Menasha, 1994-2000; dir. mem. bd. dir s. Big Bros./Big Sisters, screeners of vols., 1970-80. Named Dutch Uncle, Big Bros./Big Sisters, 1972, Vol. of Yr., 1975. Mem. Bd. Total Cath. Educators of Green Bay Diocese (bd. dirs., nominating com. 1993-99), Altrusa Club Neenah Menasha (pres. 1990-92). Democrat. Roman Catholic. Avocations: swimming, exercise programs, gardening, reading mystery books. Home: 711 Congress St Neenah WI 54956-3419

BREKKE, GAIL LOUISE, broadcasting administrator; b. Fargo, N.D., Dec. 9, 1949; d. Curtis Eugene Sr. and Geraldine Ann (Hughes) B. BS in Edn., U. N.D., 1971; AA in Retailing, Lucerne, Switzerland, 1972; MA, Webster Coll., 1981. News reporter WXIX-TV, Cin., 1973-74, KPLR-TV, St. Louis, 1974-75, in sales, 1975-77, sales mgr., 1977-80; gen. mgr. KRBK-TV, Sacramento, 1980-83, WNOL-TV, New Orleans, 1983-86, WGBO-TV, Chgo., 1986-87, KITN-TV, Mpls., 1987-93, WBNE, New Haven, 1996-99; dir. new sta. devel. LIN TV, 1997—99, dir. distbn. and spl. projects, 2003—; pres., gen. mgr. Sta. KXAN/KXAM/KNVA TV, Austin, Tex., 1999—2003. Owner, pres. Black Diamond Comm. Inc., 1994—. Mem. Nat. Alumni Leadership Coun., U. N.D., 1992—. Mem. Minn. Broadcasters Assn. (pres. 1991—), Women in Cable & Telecom. Midwest (bd. dirs. 1993-96). Avocations: sailing, aerobics.

BRELAND-NOBLE, ALFIEE MATIESE, psychologist, researcher; b. Annapolis, Md., Mar. 14, 1969; d. Allen Eugene and Mattie McLeod Breland; m. Richard Noble, III, Aug. 17, 2002. BA, Howard U., 1991; MA, NYU, 1993; PhD, U. of Wis., 1997; M of Health Scis., Duke U., 2003—. Counselor U. Settlement, N.Y.C., 1991—93, Young Adult Learning Acad., N.Y.C., 1992—93; cultural diversity specialist Madison Inner City Coun. on Substance Abuse, Inc., Madison, Wis., 1994—96; asst. prof. Mich. State U., East Lansing, 1997—2002; staff psychologist Meridian Profl. Psychol. Cons., East Lansing, 2000—02; nat. rsch. svc. award postdoctoral fellow Duke U. Med. Ctr., Durham, NC, 2002—03, Nat. Rsch. Svc. postdoctoral rsch. fellow dept. psychiatry, 2003—. Cons. Okemos (Mich.) Pub. Schs., 2001, Flint (Mich.) Pub. Schs., 2001, Iowa City (Iowa) Pub. Schs., 2001; editl. bd. mem. Jour. of Black Psychology, 2002—, Dimensions of Counseling: Rsch., Theory and Practice, Kalamazoo, 1998—2002, Jour. of Multicultural Counseling and Devel., 1998, assoc. editor, 1997—98. Co-author: (book chpt.) Elementary School Counseling in the New Millennium, Violence in American Schools: Practical Guidelines for Counselors; contbr. articles to profl. jours. Named one of Young Leaders Under 30, Ebony Mag., 1999; recipient Outstanding Undergraduate Student scholarship, Delta Sigma Theta, 1987, dissertation fellowship, U. of Wis., 1996; fellow R25 Mentoring and Edn. for Mental Health Svcs. Rsch., NIMH, Yale U. and UCLA, 2001—02, Leopold Scheep Found., 1993. Mem.: ACA (clin. rsch. network com. 2002—), APA, Soc. for Rsch. on Adolescence, Soc. for Rsch. on Child Devel., Kappa Delta Pi, Alpha Kappa Alpha (Kappa Psi Omega chpt. pres. 1993—94). Democrat. Roman Catholic. Achievements include Created model that addresses mental health disparities of African American adolescents with depressive disorders under-utilization of mental health services; research in color consciousness. Avocations: step aerobics, reading, weightlifting, travel. Office: Duke U Med Ctr Box 3516 Durham NC 27710 Personal E-mail: alfieeb@hotmail.com. E-mail: abreland@psych.mc.duke.edu.

BRELSFORD, MARY J. music educator; b. Osage, Iowa, Aug. 2, 1948; d. Robert Duane Mark and Marjorie June Saline; children: Jason E., Nathan E. MusB, Simpson Coll., 1970; MEd, Winona (Minn.) State U., 1998. Music tchr. Harmony (Minn.) Pub. Schs., 1975—76, Wabasha (Minn.)-Kellogg Pub. Schs., 1979—. Pvt. piano and voice tchr., 1966—; tchr. theatre and music (summers) Am. Sch., Leysin, Switzerland, 1980—84; music adjudicator Minn. State H.S. League, 1985—; music arranger, 1966—. Charter mem. River Junctions Arts Coun., Wabasha, 1980—; ch. organist St. Agnes Cath. Ch., Kellogg, Minn., 1st Bapt. Ch., Osage, Iowa, 1962—2000, United Meth. Ch., Kellogg, Minn., 1962—2000. Home: PO Box 103 Kellogg MN 55945 Office: Wabasha-Kellogg Pub Schs 2113 Hiawatha Dr E Wabasha MN 55981

BREMER, CELESTE F. judge; b. San Francisco, 1953; BA, St. Ambrose Coll., 1974; JD, Univ. of Iowa Coll. of Law, 1977; EdD, Drake U., 2002. Asst. county atty. Scott County, 1977-79; asst. atty. gen. Area Prosecutors Div., Iowa, 1979; with Carlin, Liebbe, Pitton & Bremer, 1979-81, Rabin, Liebbe, Shinkle & Bremer, 1981-82; with legal dept. Deere and Co., 1982-84; corp. counsel Economy Forms Corp., 1985-89; magistrate judge U.S. Dist. Ct. (Iowa so. dist.), 8th cir., Des Moines, 1984—; ed. D. Drake U. Sch. of Edn., 2002. Instr. Drake Univ. Coll. of Law, 1985-96. Mem. ABA, Fed. Magistrate Judge Assn., Nat. Assn. Women Judges, Am. Judicature Soc., Iowa State Bar Assn. (bd. govs., 1987-90), Iowa Judges Assn., Iowa Supreme Ct. Coun. on Jud. Selection (chmn. 1986-90), Iowa Orgn Women Attys., Polk County Bar Assn., Polk County Women Attys. Office: US Courthouse Ste 435 123 E Walnut St Des Moines IA 50309-2036

BREMER, NINA SHIPMAN, performing arts educator, actress; b. L.A., Aug. 15, 1938; d. Barry and Gwynne Shipman; m. Don Bremer, Dec. 24, 1975; children: Westerly Gardner, Lani Shipman. MusB, Cal State, Northridge, 1977; MA in Comm., Univ. La Verne, 1957; grad., Pasadena Playhouse, 1957. Contract actress 20th Century Fox, L.A., 1957—60; actress TV various, L.A., 1960—85; educator Univ. Hawaii, Hilo, Hawaii, 1988—2003. Bd. dir. Hilo (Hawaii) Cmty. Players, 1985—86; faculty adv. Comm. Club Univ. of Hawaii, Hilo, 1998—2003. Author: How To Become An Actor in TV, 1977; composer: (musical lyricist) Doraleen, 1980. Home: HC3 13006 Keaau HI 96749

BRENCHLEY, JEAN ELNORA, microbiologist, researcher, science administrator; b. Towanda, Pa., Mar. 6, 1944; d. John Edward and Elizabeth (Jefferson) B.; m. Bernard Asbell, July 21, 1990. BS, Mansfield U., 1965; MS, U. Calif., San Diego, 1967; PhD, U. Calif., Davis, 1970; hon. degree, Lycoming Coll., 1992. Rsch. assoc. biology dept. MIT, Cambridge, 1970-71; from asst. prof. to assoc. prof. microbiology Pa. State U., Univ. Pk., 1971-77, head. dept. molecular and cell biology, dir. Biotech. Inst. University Park, 1984-87, prof. microbiology, dir. Biotech. Inst., 1984-90, prof. microbiology and biotech., 1990—; assoc. prof., then prof. biology Purdue U., West Lafayette, Ind., 1977-81; research dir. Genex Corp., Gaithersburg, Md., 1981-84. Mem. Nat. Biotech. Policy Bd., 1990-93; trustee Biosis, 1983-88; vis. scholar NIH, 1991. Editor Applied and Environ. Microbiology, 1981-85; mem. editorial bd. Jour. Bacteriology, 1974-84, Butterworth Biotech. Series, 1988-92; editor Microbiol. Revs., 1992-97. Recipient Outstanding Alumni award Manfield U., 1983; Waksman award Theobald Smith Soc., 1985; named to Pa. Hall of Fame, 1988. Fellow AAAS (nominating com. 1990-92), Am. Acad. Microbiology; mem. NAS (bioprocess com.), Am. Soc. Microbiology (pres. 1986-87, ASM Found. lectr. 1975, Alice Evans award 1996), Assn. Women in Sci., Am. Soc. Biol. Chemists, Am. Chem. Soc., Found. for Microbiology (trustee 1988-95), Sigma Delta Epsilon (hon.).

BRENDAHL, MARCIA, artist, illustrator, designer; b. Battle Creek, Mich., Mar. 2, 1953; d. Ray LaVerne and Iris Donna (Hawkins-Eckhart) Leonard; m. Mark Eric Brendahl, Mar. 7, 1985; children: Mallorae E., Maureen E. AD in Liberal Arts, Lansing (Mich.) C.C., 1985. Ceramic tchr. Leonard's Ceramics, Lansing, 1972-83; fine artist Lansing, 1983—; art designer Lansing Sch. Dist./Kendon Elem. Sch., 1999 . Children's art tchr. Lansing Art Gallery, 1998-99, Lansing Parks and Recreation, 1999. Designer murals for stage performances, 1997—; fine art portraits of children and authors, 1989—. Vol. worker, artist Mich. Rep. Party, Lansing, 1999. Mem. Nat. Women of the Arts, Lansing Art Guild. Avocations: oil painting, writing short stories, photography. Home: 6888 Londal Cir Lansing MI 48911-7044

BRENKEN, HANNE MARIE, artist; b. Duisburg, Germany, July 6, 1923; arrived in U.S., 1977; d. Hermann and Luise (Werth) Tigler; m. Hans Brenken, Mar. 28, 1942 (div. 1985); children: Karin Brenken Schneider-Henn, Berndt; m. Ricardo Wiesenberg, May 20, 1986. Grad., Landschulheim, Holzminden, Germany, 1941; studied in pvt. art schs., Munich and Bonn, Germany. One-person shows include Contra Kreis Gallery, Bonn, Germany, 1958, Galerie Junge Kunst, Fulda, Germany, 1959, Universa-Galerie, Nurenberg, Germany, 1960, Galleria Monte Napoleone, Milan, 1961, Galerie Niedlich, Stuttgart, Germany, 1961, 63, Galerie am Jakobsbrunnen, Stuttgard, 1964, 67, Kunst und Kunstverein Mus. Pforzheim, Germany, 1969, Kunstverein Mus., Munich, 1972, Galerie Dorothea Leonhart, Munich, 1974, I.C.L. Gallery, East Hampton, N.Y., 1980, Anne Reid Gallery, Princeton, N.J., 1981, Adagio Gallery, Bridgehampton, N.Y., 1982, 84, Queens Mus., N.Y., 1983, Ericson Gallery, N.Y.C., 1984, 85, Benton Gallery, Southampton, N.Y., 1986, Vered Gallery, East Hampton, N.Y., 1988, Gallery Rodeo, Lake Arrowhead, Calif., Taos, N.Mex., Beverly Hills, Calif., 1990, Brian Logan Art Space, Washington, 1991, The Gallery, Leesburg, Va., 1992, Amerika Haus, Frankfurt, Germany, 1993, Ganser Haus Gallery, Wasserburg, Germany, 1993, Ann Norton Sculpture Gardens, West Palm Beach, Fla., 1994, Jean Chisholm Gallery, West Palm Beach, 1994, Okuda Internat. Gallery, Washington, 1995, Misia Broadhead Studio/Gallery, Middleburg, Va., 1996, Millennium Gallery, East Hampton, N.Y., 1997, Reynolds Gallery Westmont Coll., Santa Barbara, Calif., 1998, Svitozor Fine Arts, Santa Barbara, Calif., 2000, L.A. Artcore, Los Angeles, 2001; group shows include Duisburg (Germany) Mus., 1959, Baden-Baden Mus., Germany, 1961, 62, Haus der Kunst, Munich, 1963, 64, 69, 70, 71, 72, 73, Kunstgebäude, Stuttgart, 1963, 71, Acad. Fine Arts, Berlin, 1964, 73, Forum Stadtpark, Graz, Austria, 1965, Folkwang Mus., Essen, Germany, 1965, Munich City Mus., 1967, Karlsruhe (Germany) Kunstverein, 1967; permanent collections include Solomon R. Guggenheim Mus., New York, Queens Mus., Phoenix Art Mus., Guild Hall Mus, several mus. in Europe. Avocations: travel, visiting galleries and musuems, reading. Home: 184 Middle Rd Montecito CA 93108-2446

BRENNAN, CHRISTINE, journalist, columnist; b. Toledo; BA in journalism, Northwestern U., 1980, MA in journalism, 1981. Sports writer Miami Hearld, Washington Post. Appearences on ESPN, CNN, other network talk shows. Author: (book) Inside Edge, contbr. articles to profl. jours. Recipient Journalism award, Women's Sports Found., Woman of Achievement, Capital Press Women's, 1993; inductee Ohio Women Hall of Fame, 1998. Mem. Assn. Women Sports Media (pres. 1988). Office: USA Today 1000 Wilson Blvd Arlington VA 22229-0001

BRENNAN, DEBORAH ANN, artist; b. Dumas, Tex., Dec. 26, 1954; d. Ralph Elden and Mary Dell (Burros) Turner; m. Tracy Alan Brennan, Dec. 18, 1993 (div. Apr. 2002); 1 child, Shay Weston Turner. BS Interior Design, S.W. Mo. State U., 1977. Cert. draftsman Am. Design Drafting Assn., 1998, interior designer 1977. Adelstein dome, Addison Jewelry Store, 1981, stained glass, St. George & the Dragon, Van Buren, Mo., Breathe of the Spirit, Holy Trinity I & II, Father, Son & Holy Spirit, Piedmont, Mo., Mary & Child, Springfield, Grapes & Wheat, Mountain View, Mo., Yellow Ribbon window, Branson, Mo., Springfield-Cape Girardeau Diocese. Office: 1020 E Edgewood Springfield MO 65807

BRENNAN, DONNA LESLEY, public relations company executive; b. Washington, Mar. 13, 1945; d. Don Arthur and Louise (Tucker) B.; m. James L Bergey, Mar. 6, 1999. BA, Denison U., 1967. Tchr. Souderton Area H.S., Pa., 1967-69; mgr. media rels. Ins. Co. N.Am., Phila., 1969-72; dir. press rels. Colonial Penn Group, Phila., 1972-75, 1975-81, dir. comm., 1981-83; v.p. corp. comm. Norstar Bancorp, Albany, NY, 1983-85; v.p. comm. Meritor Fin. Group, Phila., 1986-87; prin. Donna Brennan Assocs., 1988—. Bd. dirs. W. Vincent Land Trust, Inc. Mem. Pub. Rels. Soc. Am. (pres. Phila. chpt. 1988), Phila. Women's Network (founder, bd. dirs.), Women's Assn. for Women's Alternatives (vice-chmn., bd. dirs.), Forum of Exec. Women (pres. 1992-93, bd. dirs. 1989-97). Office Phone: 610-469-8765. E-mail: brennanpr@comcast.net.

BRENNAN, FRANCES ANSTETT, artist; b. Wilkes-Barre, Pa., Aug. 29, 1907; d. Frank and Katherine (Schwalbach) Anstett; m. Thomas James Brennan, Dec. 15, 1937 (dec. 1953). RN, Mercy Hosp. Sch. Nursing, 1928; student, U. Pa., Coll. Misericordia. Dir. Georgetown Settlement House, Wilkes-Barre, Pa., ; art and craft instr. Wilkes U. One-woman shows Crespi Gallery, N.Y.C., Wilkes Coll., Wilkes-Barre; two-person shows Little Gallery-Wyoming Valley Art League, Wilkes-Barre; exhibited in group shows at Bergman's Dept. Store, Wilkes-Barre, 1952, Osterhout Libr., Wilkes-Barre, Misericordia Coll., Dallas, Pa., Everhart Mus., Scranton, Pa., Hazleton (Pa.) Art League, Pa. Dutch Festival, Kutztown, Franklin Marshall Coll., Reading, Pa., First Folklore Seminar, Bryden Wood, Woodmere Gallery, Phila., Great No. Hotel, N.Y.C., Plaza Galleries, N.Y.C., Grand Ctrl. Galleries, N.Y.C. (Grumbacher award of merit); retrospective exhibit at Hoyt Libr., Kingston, Pa. Vol. USO, Wilkes-Barre, 1940-45, ARC, 1940-45, War Bond Com., Wilkes-Barre, 1940-45. Recipient awards Dallas State Fair; Wilkes U. scholar. Mem. Internat. Soc. Poets, Nat. Mus. Women in the Arts (charter), Mus. Am. Indians Smithsonian Instn. (charter), Wyoming Valley Art League (charter), Libr. of Congress (charter).

BRENNAN, JOANN, photographer, educator; BFA in Photography, Mass. Coll. Art, 1986, MFA in Photography, 1988. Founder, instr. Progetto Perugia, Studio Arts in Perugia (Italy), 1987—99; photography gallery dir. U. R.I., Kingston, 1988—89, visual arts instr.; photography instr. Mass. Coll. Art, Boston, 1988, Worcester (Mass.) Art Mus., 1988—89; photography lectr. Princeton U., 1990—94, gallery curator program in women's study gallery, 1991—94; asst. prof. photography Coll. Ceramics SUNY, Alfred, 1994—98; asst. prof. photography U. Colo., Denver, 1998—. Photographer (one and two-person shows) Bausch and Lomb Gallery, Corp. Hqrs., Rochester, N.Y., 1998, So. Light Gallery, Amarillo (Tex.) Coll., 2001, Ironton Gallery and Studios, Denver, 2001, Knox Coll., Galesburg, Ill., 2002, 1708 Gallery, Richmond, Va., 2002, U. Arts, Phila., 2003, (group shows) Islep Mus. Art, Long Island, N.Y., 1996, Ball State U. Mus. Art, Muncie, Ind., 1997, Carol Keller Gallery, Denver, 1999, Vincent Price GAllery at E. L.A. Coll., 1999, Tex. Woman's U. Fine Art Gallery, Denton, Tex., 2001, Princeton Art Mus., 2002, Allegheny Coll., Pa., 2002, numerous others, (permanent collections) Danforth Art Mus., Princeton Art Mus., Paine Webber Collection, N.Y.C., N.Mex. State U., Las Cruces. Recipient Purchase award, Danforth Mus. Art, Framingham, Mass., 1992, Commn. award, Miller Performing arts Ctr., N.Y.S.C.C., Alfred, N.Y., 1997; fellow, John Simon Guggenheim Meml. Found., 2003. Mem.: Inst. Electronic Arts, Soc. Photographic Edn. (treas. N.E. region 1994—96, sec. N.E. region 1995—96, chair N.E. region 1996—98, chair S.W. region 2000—01, mem. portfolio rev. com. nat. conf. 2002, conf. com. nat. conf. 2002). Address: 6665 E Jamison Ave Englewood CO 80112

BRENNAN, LALLY, food service executive; Student, So. Meth. U. Operator Mr. B's, New Orleans, 1979—82; mng. ptnr. Commander's Palace, New Orleans, 1982—. Active Audubon Inst., New Orleans, Longue Vue House & Gardens, New Orleans, Herman Grima Found., New Orleans;

co-founder Les Dames des Escoffiers (New Orleans chpt.). Mem.: Women's Chefs and Restaurateurs, New Orleans Met. Conv. and Visitors Bur., La. Restaurant Assn., James Beard Found., Internat. Assn. Culinary Profls., New Orleans C. of C. Office: 1403 Washington Ave New Orleans LA 70130

BRENNAN, MARY M. state legislator; b. Valparaiso, Fla., May 17, 1954; d. Robert Vincent and Margaret Mary (Saville) B. Student, U. South Fla., 1973; BS, U. Fla., 1976; postgrad., U. South Fla., 1987. Journalist St. Petersburg (Fla.) Times, 1977-79; editor Pinellas Park (Fla.) Post, 1979-80; pub. Pinellas Park (Fla.) Press, 1980-82; legis. aide State Rep. Patricia Bailey, Pinellas Park, 1982-84; editor Pinellas Park (Fla.) News, 1984-86; pub. info. officer City of Pinellas Park, Fla., 1986-90; mem. Fla. Ho. of Reps., Pinellas Park, 1990-98. Bd. mem. Girls Inc. of Mid-Pinellas, Pinellas Park, 1979—; mem. pub. rels. Girls Club of Pinellas Park, Fla., 1982. Recipient Community Svc. to Children award Pinellas Emergency Mental Health Svc., 1992. Mem. Fla. Govt. Communicators, Pinellas Park Hist. Soc., Soroptimist Internat. Pinellas Park (Svc. award 1983, Women Helping Women award 1991), Greater Pinellas Park C. of C. (bd. mem. 1981-86, 90-92, Svc. award 1981, Outstanding Community Svc. award 1983). Democrat. Roman Catholic. Avocations: woodworking, sewing, photography, sailing, reading. Office: Fla House Reps 5827 77th Ave Pinellas Park FL 33781-3243

BRENNAN, MAUREEN, lawyer; b. Morristown, N.J., Aug. 7, 1949; BA magna cum laude, Bryn Mawr Coll., 1971; JD cum laude, Boston Coll., 1977. Bar: Pa. 1977, U.S. Dist. Ct. (ea. dist.) Pa. 1978, Ohio 1989. Atty. U.S. EPA, Washington, 1977-80; asst. dist. atty. Phila. Trial and Appellate Divs., 1980-84; in-house environ. counsel TRW, Inc., 1985-87; assoc. Baker & Hostetler, Cleve., 1987-91, ptnr., 1991—. Adj. prof. Case Western Res. U., Cleve., 1990-92, 2000-01. Active Cleve. Tree Commn., 1991-96, co-chair, 1993-95; trustee Clean-Land Ohio, 1990-2000; rep. Canal Heritage Corridor Com., 2000—; mem. Cuyahoga County Greenspace Working Group, 1999—; bd. dirs. Crown Point Ecology Ctr., 2001—. Recipient Bronze Medal for Achievement, U.S. EPA, 1980. Mem. ABA (natural resources and environ. sect., standing com. environ law 1996-98), Pa. Bar Assn. (environ. law com.), Ohio State Bar Assn. (environ. law com.), Cleve. Bar Assn. (environ. law sect., chair wetlands com. 1991-92, sect. chair 1996-97, mem. steering com. adv. OEPA on Brownfield regulations 1995-97). Office: Baker & Hostetler LLP 3200 Nat City Center 1900 E 9th St Ste 3200 Cleveland OH 44114-3475 E-mail: mbrennan@bakerlaw.com.

BRENNAN, NORMA JEAN, professional society publications director; b. Helena, Mont., Apr. 16, 1939; d. Harland Sanford Herrin and Elizabeth (Wardlaw) Brumfield; m. Anthony E. Brennan, Dec. 4, 1964 (div. Mar. 1986); children: Christopher E., Kimberly A. BA, U. Pacific, 1960. Editl. asst. Am. Rocket Soc., N.Y.C., 1961-62, asst. mng. editor, 1962-65; mng. editor AIAA, N.Y.C., 1978-80, publs. divsn. dir. N.Y.C., Washington, Reston, Va., 1980—. Mem. Young Republicans, Stockton, Calif., 1958-60; vol. Mt. Sinai Hosp., N.Y.C., 1962-64. Fellow: AIAA (Space Shuttle Flag award); mem.: Washington Women's Info. Network, N.Am. Serials Interest Group, Coun. Engring. and Sci. Soc. Execs., Assn. Am. Pubs., Coun. Sci. Editors, Soc. for Scholarly Pub. (bd. dirs.). Avocations: reading, travel, gardening. Home: 11551 Links Dr Reston VA 20190-4820 Office: AIAA 1801 Alexander Bell Dr Reston VA 20191-4344 E-mail: normab@aiaa.org.

BRENNAN, PATRICIA FLATLEY, nursing educator, systems engineer, educator; b. July 21, 1953; BSN, U. Del., 1975; MSN, U. Pa., 1979; MS in Indsl. Engring., U. Wis., 1984, PhD in Indsl. Engring., 1986. RN, Ohio. Staff nurse surg. ICU Lankenau Hosp., Phila., 1975-76; clin. nurse mgr./practitioner Friends Hosp., Phila., 1976-80; asst. prof. psychiat. nursing Marquette U., Milw., 1980-83; lectr. quantitative analysis U. Wis., Madison, 1984; asst. prof. nursing and systems engring. Frances Payne Bolton Sch. Nursing, Case Inst. Tech., Case Western Res. U., Cleve., 1986-89, assoc. prof., 1989-92; Lillian Moehlman-Bascom prof. nursing U. Wis., Madison, prof., indsl. engring. Mem. health care study sect. Nat. Ctr. Health Svcs. Rsch., 1989—; participant Coun. Nurse Researchers, 1981—, Nat. Conf. on Nursing Minimum Data Set, Milw., 1985, Nursing Use of Decision Support Workshop, Killarney, Ireland, 1988; guest lectr. Coll. Nursing, U. Wis., 1986, 89; mem. vis. faculty Campus for the Professions, U. Md., 1987, 89, 91, 92, U. Wis., 1989, U. Calgary, Alta., Can., 1989; presenter numerous profl. and ednl. orgns., 1981—. Mem. editorial bd. Computers in Nursing, 1988—; reviewer publs. Symposium on Computer Applications in Med. Care, 1982—, Rsch. in Nursing and Health, 1985—, Tech. MEDINFO86, 1985; contbr. articles to profl. publs. Mem. adv. bd. Sch. Nursing, U. Md., 1986—; active data consortium AIDS Commn. Cleve., 1989; vol. Am. Cancer Soc., 1983-86. Rsch. grantee Marquette U., 1981, Regner Fund, 1982, USPHS, 1982-86, Cleve. Found., 1987, NIH, 1987—, Mellon Found., 1987, Nat. Ctr. Nursing Rsch. 1988-91, Nat. Inst. on Aging, 1989—. Fellow Am. Acad. Nursing; mem. ANA, AACCN (mem. info. systems task force 1986-87), Ohio Nurses Assn. (mem. rsch. assembly, mem. GCNA), Am. Inst. Decision Scis. (mem. membership com., reviewer ann. meetings), Inst. Indsl. Engrs. (chpt. devel. chairperson 1987—), Inst. Medicine, The Mgmt. Sci. Inst.-Ops. Rsch. Soc. Am., Sigma Xi, Sigma Theta Tau. Office: U Wis-Madison Module K4 K6/340 Clin Sci Ctr 600 Highland Ave Madison WI 53792

BRENNAN, SUSAN MALLICK, utilities executive; BS, U.S. Air Force Acad., 1981; MBA, Nat. U., 1989. Fin. analyst and investor rels. analyst Nev. Power Co., Las Vegas, 1992—93, mgr. reogrn. project, 1993—94, mgr. performance mgmt. and analysis, 1993—95, dir. human resources, 1995—97, dir. industry restructuring and strategic planning, 1997—99; exec. dir. customer svc. and industry restructuring Sierra Pacific Resources, 1999—2001; v.p., chief info. officer Sierra Pacific Power and Nev. Power, 2001—. Active Leadership Las Vegas, 1998, Workforce 2010 Task Force; regional pres. Am. Diabetes Assn.; bd. mem. United Blood Svcs., Found. Bd. Opportunity Village. With USAF, 1981—88. Mem.: Las Vegas C. of C. Office: Sierra Pacific/Nev Power PO Box 10100 6100 Neil Rd Reno NV 89520

BRENNEMAN, AMY, actress; b. Conn., June 22, 1964; m. Brad Silberling; 1 child, Charlotte Tucker. BA, Harvard U., 1987. Mem. Cornerstone Theater Co. Appeared in films Bye, Bye Love, 1995, Heat, 1995, Casper, 1995, Fear, 1996, in TV programs Middle Ages, 1992, NYPD Blue, 1993-94 (Emmy award nomination for outstanding guest actress in a drama series 1994), Judging Amy, 1999, (TV film) Mary Cassatt: An American Impressionist, 1999, Things You Can Tell Just By Looking at Her, 2000, Off the Map, 2003; stage appearances Saint Joan of the Stockyards, 1992. Office: Creative Artists Agy 9830 Wilshire Blvd Beverly Hills CA 90212-1825 Address: Travel Entertainment 9171 Wilshire Blvd Ste 700 Beverly Hills CA 90211 also: PMK/HBH Pub Rels 8500 Wilshire Blvd Ste 700 Beverly Hills CA 90211*

BRENNER, ANNA (BONNIE) HURNYAK, music educator; b. Shenandoah, Pa., Aug. 20, 1948; d. Stephen C. and Anna Wargo Hurnyak; m. Peter R.K. Brenner, June 27, 1970; children: Erik Stephen, Timothy Peter. MusB in Edn., Wittenberg U., 1970; MusM, U. of Utah, 1988. Cert. tchr. Conn., 2002. Music specialist Bd. of Edn., Babylon, NY, 1971—72, Salt Lake City (Utah) Bd. of Edn., 1984—90, Holt (Mich.) Bd. of Edn., 1990—91, Grand Ledge (Mich.) Bd. of Edn., 1991—2001, Simsbury (Conn.) Bd. of Edn., 2001—. Chpt. pres. Mid-Mich. Orff Assn., Lansing, Mich., 1994—96; founding chpt. pres. Utah Orff Assn., Salt Lake City, 1989—90; adj. prof. U. Utah, Salt Lake City, 1986—88. Author: The Influence of Home Musical Environment and School Music Instruction on the Developmental Musical Aptitude of First Graders. Grantee, Michigan Assn. Inter Student Method awards, 1997. Mem.: Am. Orff Schulwerk Assn., Am. Kodaly Educators, Am. Guild of English Handbell Ringers (assoc.; festival coord. 1985—86, festival dir. 1982—83), Grand Ledge Cmty. Children's Choir (assoc.; co-founder and co-dir. 1998—2000), Sigma Alpha Iota (life). Congregational. Avocations: native american art, exercising, scrapbooks, organist, singing. Home: 40 Rainbow Trail Vernon CT 06066 Office: Central School 29 Massaco Simsbury CT 06067

BRENNER, BETH FUCHS, publishing executive; Grad., U. Vt., 1980. Sales promotion coordinator Chanel, Inc., 1980-83; promotion mgr. M mag., 1983-86; adv. sales rep. New York mag., 1986-91, adv. dir., 1991-93, SELF mag., 1993-94, pub., 1994-2001, v.p., pub., 2001—. Office: SELF Magazine 4 Times Sq New York NY 10036-6562*

BRENNER, ELIZABETH (BETSY BRENNER), publishing executive; b. Bellevue, Wash. m. Steven Ostrofsky. BJ, MBA, Northwestern U. City news reporter The Chgo. (Ill.) Tribune, 1977, bus. news reporter, columnist, 1978; with mktg. dept. The New York Times; with retail advt. and circulation posts Miami Herald, Rocky Mountain News, Denver, sr. v.p. sales and mktg., 1994—96; pub. Bremerton Sun, 1996—98, The News Tribune, Tacoma, 1998—. Bd. dirs. Econ. Devel. Bd, Tacoma, Mus. Glass, Greater Tacoma Cmty. Found., exec. coun.; mem. Tacoma adv. coun. U. Wash.; co-chmn. campaign Olympic Coll. Libr. Kitsap County. Office: The News Tribune 1950 S State St Tacoma WA 98405-2817 Mailing: PO Box 11000 Tacoma WA 98411 E-mail: betsy.brenner@mail.tribnet.com.

BRENNER, JANET MAYBIN WALKER, lawyer; b. Arkansas City, Kans. d. D. Arthur and Maybin (Gardner) Walker; children: Margaret Maybin Potthast, Theodore Kimball Jonas, Amanda Nash Freeman; m. Edgar H. Brenner, Aug. 4, 1979. AB, U. So. Calif.; JD, George Washington U., 1978. Bar: D.C. 1978, U.S. Dist. Ct. (D.C. cir.). Sponsor Brenner Women's Leadership com.; mem. women's com. Corcoran Gallery Art, Washington, 1969—, Pres.'s Cir., Planned Parenthood D.C., 1969—, Found. for Preservation of Hist. Georgetown. Mem. D.C. Bar Assn., Sulgrave Club (Washington). Home: 3325 R St NW Washington DC 20007-2310 also: Shadow Ridge Farm Washington VA 22747

BRENNER, MARCELLA SIEGEL, retired education educator; b. Balt., Dec. 5, 1912; d. Moses and Annie (Affachiner) Siegel; m. Morris Bernstein, July 1947 (dec. 1962); m. Abner Brenner, Oct. 1964. BS, Johns Hopkins U., 1934; MA, Am. U., 1949; EdD, George Washington U., 1962; DHL (hon.), Md. Inst. Coll. Art, 2001. Tchr. Balt. Pub. Schs., 1930-43; writer, editor USPHS, Washington, 1945-52; tchr. Lone Oak Elem. Sch., Md., 1952-54, prin., 1954-64; lectr. in edn. George Washington U., 1961, assoc. prof. Sch. Edn., 1965-83, assoc. dir. MA Tchg. Program, 1966-83, ret., 1983. Mem. staff Washington Sch. Psychiatry, 1962—; cons. U. Calif. Sch. Sys. of Washington, Tchr. Edn. and Profl. Standards Commn.; founder, dir. Mus. Edn. Program George Washington U., 1974-83; dir. Ctr. for Mus. Edn. George Washington U., 1976-79. Co-author: Interview Art and Skill, 1980, The Change Agent, 2000; contbr. articles to profl. jours. Bd. dirs. Boston Mus. Fine Arts, 1985—, Balt. Mus. Art, 1985—, B'nai Brith Klutznick Nat. Jewish Mus., 1985—, Project Interchange Dept. Am. Jewish Com., 1985—, George Washington U., 1985—; bd. Palestine Endorsement Fund, Israel Endowment Funds, Inc., 1985—. Brenner award established in her honor George Washington U., 1983; recipient Yakir Bezalel award Bezalel Acad. Arts and Design and Culture, 1988, award of appreciation State of Israel Min. Edn., 1991. Fellow Am. Orthopsychiatric Assn., Israel Mus. (hon.). [illegible] for U.S. citizenship reading for visually impaired. Home: 7204 Pomander Ln Chevy Chase MD 20815-3135

BRENT, ELIZABETH MARIA, education educator; b. Independence, Mo., May 12, 1954; d. Madora Belle and Charles Roland Kramer; m. Hal Chambers Brent, Feb. 14, 1999. BA, William Jewell Coll., 1973—76; MA, U. of Mo.-Kans. City, 1978, PhD, 1978—86; MPH, St. Louis U., 1994—96. Dean of students Rockhurst U., Kans. City, Mo., 1984—99, asst. dean of students, 1977—84, v.p. for student devel. and adminstrn., 1998—. Chmn., bd. of directors The Rehab. Inst., Kans. City, Mo., 2001—03. Avocations: travel, tennis, golf, swimming, bicycling. Office: Rockhurst University 1100 Rockhurst Rd Kansas City MO 64110

BRENT, HELEN TERESSA, school nurse; b. Grand Rapids, Mich., Oct. 4, 1946; d. William Henry and Anita Broyles Burress; m. Robert Lee Brent, June 10, 1967. AS, Grand Rapids C.C., 1966; diploma, Butterworth Hosp. Sch. Nursing, 1968; BSN summa cum laude, U. Mich., 1981; MPA, Western Mich. U., 1992. RN, Mich. Staff nurse Butterworth Hosp., Grand Rapids, Mich., 1968-69, head nurse psychiat. unit, 1969-72; DON Forest View Psychiat. Hosp., Grand Rapids, Mich., 1972-75; asst. DON, staff devel. coord. Kent Oaks Psychiat. Unit Kent Community Hosp., Grand Rapids, Mich., 1975-80; DON Kent Community Hosp. Complex, Grand Rapids, Mich., 1980-94; psychiat. nurse Pine Rest Christian Mental Health Svcs., Grand Rapids, 1994—; health planner Kent County Pub. Health Dept., Grand Rapids, 1996-97; sch. nurse Grand Rapids Pub. Schs., 1997—. Adj. faculty nursing divsn. Grand Rapids C.C., 1999—. Mem. adv. coun. Mich. Family Planning Mich. Dept. Cmty. Health, 1991-99, Family Outreach Ctr., Grand Rapids, 1980-95; mem. hospice care study panel United Way Kent County, 1984; vol. nursing health svcs. Kent County chpt. ARC, Grand Rapids, 1974—; vol. mediator West Mich. Dispute Resolution Ctr., 1995—. Recipient Outstanding Svc. award Family Outreach Ctr. Kent County Cmty. Mental Health, 1988, Helen Barnes award for outstanding vol. contbns. in nursing svcs. Kent County chpt. ARC, 1994, Eugene Browning Med. Svc. award Giants Orgn., Grand Rapids C.C., 1995. Mem. Vis. Nurses Assn. West Mich.(bd. dirs. 1991-2000), Nat. Black Nurses Assn. (local chpt. 1999—), Harambe Black Nurses Assn. Grand Rapids. Democrat. Avocations: travel, reading. Home: 3834 Old Elm Dr SE Kentwood MI 49512-9523 Office: Grand Rapids Pub Schs KEC Mayfield 225 Mayfield Ave NE Grand Rapids MI 49503-3768 E-mail: hbrent5558@webtv.net., BrentH@grps.k12.mi.us.

BRENTON, HATICE, painter, graphics designer; 1 child, Thomas. MFA, Goddard Coll., 2003. Fine artist, graphic designer Herbert F. Johnson Mus., Cornell U. Exhibitions include SUNY, Cortland, 1998, Tile-Tec Internat., 2000, Cornell U., 2001, exhibitions include Wessex-Bristol Gallery, 2003. Mem.: Nat. Mus. Women in the Arts, U.S. Holocaust Meml. Mus., Phi Kappa Phi. Green Party.

BRESCIA, ALICIA, science educator, vice principal; b. Reading, Pa., Jan. 19, 1947; d. Joseph John and Alice B. Heine; m. Frank J. Brescia, June 29, 1985. BA in Elem. Edn. and Biology, Coll. of St. Elizabeth, Convent Sta., NJ, 1969; MA in Sci. Edn., Columbia U., NYC, 1976. Profl. Diploma in Secondary Edn. Adminstrn. Fordham U., NYC, 1994. Tchr. Assumption Sch., Morristown, NJ, 1968—72, St. Teresa Sch., Summit, NJ, 1972—77; prin. St. Vincent Martyr Sch., Madison, NJ, 1977—81; tchr. biology and sci. Gov. Livingston HS, Berkeley Heights, NJ, 1982—85; faculty sci. in elem. edn. Coll. of St. Elizabeth, 1983—85; tchr. sci. and biology Somers (NY) HS, 1986—93; spl. GE tchr. program Ossining (NY) HS, 1993—94; vice prin. Port Chester (NY) HS, 1994—96, chair sci. dept., 1994—98; tchr. biology The Living Environment. HS mentor Anthony Foust and Great Potential mentoring program, Port Chester, 1994—; prin. summer sch. Port Chester HS, 1996—99, mem. scholarship com., 1994—, mem. sch. improvement com., 1999—, small learning cmtys. com., 2002—. Mem. vis. com. Mid. States Assn. Colls. and Schs., 1999; bd. dirs. Heritage Hills Condo 7, Somers, 1996—2002, pres. bd., 1991, sect. leaders chair, 1996—. Nominee Tchr. of Yr., Port Chester Tchrs. Assn., 2000; named an Outstanding Elem. Tchr. of Am., Outstanding Elem. Tchrs. Am., 1974; grantee studies in biology, chemistry and physics, CUNY, NSF, 1971, bereavement and grief related issues, Calvary Hosp., Bronx, NY, 2002. Fellow: Assn. Supervision and Curriculum Devel., Sci. Tchrs. of N.Y. State; mem.: N.J. Sci. Tchrs. Assn., Hastings Inst. of Ethics, United Fedn. Tchrs. Roman Catholic. Avocations: gardening, travel, cooking. Office: Port Chester High School 1 Tamarack Rd Port Chester NY 10573 Office Phone: 914-934-7952.

BRESLIN, EILEEN THERESA, women's health nurse; b. Palmerton, Pa., Oct. 14, 1954; d. Charles Bernard and Theresa Ann (Pollock) B. BSN, No. Ariz. U., 1977; MS, U. Ariz., 1983; PhD, U. Colo., 1992. RN, Ariz. Staff nurse Flagstaff (Ariz.) Med. Ctr., 1976-77; dir. client operation Planned Parenthood of Ctrl. No. Ariz., Phoenix, 1978-81; nurse practitioner ob-gyn. Planned Parenthood So. Ariz., Tucson, 1982-83; asst. prof. No. Ariz. U., Flagstaff, 1983-89, assoc. prof., 1989, chair, 1993-98; dean Sch. Nursing U. Mass., Amherst, 1998—. Pres. Ariz. Bd. Nursing, Phoenix, 1990-91, mem., 1986-91; mem. Ariz. Bd. Med. Examiners, Phoenix, 1981-90. Bd. dirs., pres. Ariz. Family Planning Coun., Phoenix, 1982-89, Hozhoni Found., Flagstaff, 1984-86, Flagstaff Women's Shelter, 1984-86. Recipient Outstanding Alumni award No. Ariz. U., 1989, Outstanding Tchr. award Associated Women's Students of No. Ariz. U., 1989, Outstanding Tchr. award Faculty Women's Assn., 1989. Mem. ANA, Ariz. Nurses Assn. (dist. pres. 1984-85), Nat. League for Nursing, Sigma Theta Tau. Roman Catholic. Avocations: reading, skiing, hiking, travel. Office: U Mass Amherst Sch Nursing PO Box 30420 Amherst MA 01003-0420

BRESLIN, EVALYNNE LOUISE WOOD-ROBERTSON, retired psychiatric nurse; b. Richmond, Ohio, July 7, 1931; d. Evan P. and Ada Augusta (Huscroft) Wood-Robertson; m. Donald Joseph Breslin, Jan. 30, 1954; children: Lisa Karen, Mark Nathaniel, Paul Andrew Scott. Diploma, Cleve. Met. Gen. Hosp., 1952; student, Case Western Res. U., 1953-55, Akron U.; HHD (hon.), London Inst. of Applied Rsch., 1973. Lic. RN, Ohio, Mass; RN, Ohio, Mass. Head nurse Cleve. Met. Gen. Hosp., 1952-55, Cleve. State Receiving Hosp., 1952-55; cons. mental illness and addictions Mass.; ret., 1986. Ret. bd. dirs. Triple Trouble; ret. vol. monitor state hosp. facilities Alliance for Mentally Ill; vol. nursing/psychiat. work wirh abandonded adolscents, 1968—2001; vol. tour guide Barefoot Beach Preserve, Inc.; tchr. ESL, 1999—.

BRESLIN, PEG M. judge; b. Ottawa, Ill., July 11, 1946; m. John X. Breslin, May 18, 1974. BA, Loyola U., Chgo., 1967, JD, 1970. Bar: Ill. 1971, U.S. Dist. Ct. (no. dist.) Ill. 1973. Mem. Chgo. Com. on Criminal Justice, 1970-71; atty. Allen and Narko, 1971-74, Ill. State Bd. Edn., 1974-76; mem. Ill. Ho. of Reps., 1976-90; pvt. practice, 1990-92; judge 3d Dist., Ill. Ct. Appeals, Ottawa, 1992—. Bd. dirs. Nat. Safe Workplace Inst. Recipient award Women's Bar of Ill., 1993; named Best Legis. 1990, Ill. Environ. Coun., Chgo. Tribune mag. Mem. Ill. State Bar Assn. (mem. coun. bench and bar sect. 1998), Ill. Cts. Commn. Roman Catholic. Avocations: art, gardening.

BRESLOW, ESTHER MAY GREENBERG, biochemistry educator, researcher; b. N.Y.C., Dec. 23, 1931; d. Harry Daniel and Lillian (Solomon) Greenberg; m. Ronald Charles David Breslow, Sept. 4, 1955; children: Stephanie Ruth, Karen Ann. BS with distinction, Cornell U., 1953; MS in Biochemistry, NYU, 1955, PhD in Biochemistry, 1959; postgrad., Radcliffe Coll., 1954-55. Postdoctoral fellow Cornell U. Med. Coll., N.Y.C., 1959-61, rsch. assoc., 1961-64, asst. prof., 1964-72, assoc. prof., 1972-78, prof. biochemistry, 1978—, acting chmn. dept. biochemistry, 1992-95. Mem. rev. panels NIH, Bethesda, Md., 1973—77, Bethesda, 1994—97, NSF, Bethesda, 1991—; mem. editorial bd. Jour. Biol. Chemistry, 1982-87, Internat. Jour. Peptide and Protein Rsch., 1981-97; contbr. articles to profl. jours. Mem. Englewood (N.J.) Bd. Health, 1986-94; mem. Dem. Mcpl. Com., Englewood, 1985-91. Eli Lilly fellow, 1954-55; USPHS fellow, 1959-61; NIH grantee, 1961—. Fellow AAAS; mem. Am. Soc. for Biochemistry and Molecular Biology, Am. Chem. Soc. (sec. div. biol. chemistry 1972-76), Harvey Soc., Sigma Xi. Home: 275 Broad Ave Englewood NJ 07631-4350 Office: Joan and Sanford I Weill Med Coll Cornell U 1300 York Ave New York NY 10021-4805 Business E-Mail: ebreslow@med.cornell.edu.

BRESLOW, MARILYN GANON, portfolio manager; b. Cleve., Apr. 23, 1944; d. Joseph M. and Edith (Rubin) Ganon; m. Jan L. Breslow, June 27, 1965; children: Noah J., Nicholas M. BA, Barnard Coll., 1965; MBA, Harvard U., 1970. Market rsch. analyst Polaroid Corp., Cambridge, Mass., 1965-68, project cons., 1973-78, bldg. W-4 mgr., 1978-80, dir. mktg. svcs., 1980-83; cons. Peat, Marwick, Mitchell & Co., Washington, 1970-71; assoc. ICF, Inc., Washington, 1971-73; cons. Brookline, Mass., 1983-84; v.p. Dillon, Read & Co., Inc., N.Y.C., 1984-90; gen. ptnr. Concord Ptnrs., 1984-90; portfolio mgr., analyst, pres. W.P. Stewart & Co., Inc., N.Y.C., 1990—; bd. dirs. W.P. Stewart & Co. Growth Fund, Inc., N.Y.C. Bd. dirs. Alteon, Inc., Ramsey, N.J. Mem. N.Y. Soc. Security Analysts, IEEE. Avocations: piano, skiing, gardening. Home: 10 Horseguard Ln Scarsdale NY 10583-2311

BRESSMAN, SUSAN BERLINER, health facility administrator; b. Bronx, N.Y., Jan. 29, 1951; d. Joseph and Dorothy Berliner. BA, Barnard Coll., 1973; MD, Columbia U., 1977. Cert. Am. Bd. Psychiatry and Neurology. Resident Columbia Presbyn. Med. Ctr., N.Y.C., 1978-81; prof. neurology Albert Einstein Coll. Medicine, N.Y.C.; chair Mirken dept. neurology Beth Israel Med. Ctr., N.Y.C. Movement Disorders fellow Neurol. Inst., Columbia Presbyn. Med. Ctr., 1981-83. Office: Beth Israel Med Ctr Phillips Ambulatory Care 10 Union Sq E Ste 2Q New York NY 10003

BRESTEL, MARY BETH, librarian; b. Cin., Feb. 5, 1952; d. John Wesley and Laura Alice (Knoop) Seay; m. Michael Charles Brestel, Aug. 3, 1974; 1 child, Rebecca Michelle. BS, U. Cin., 1974; MLS, U. Ky., 1984. Libr. asst. history and lit. dept. Pub. Libr. Cin. and Hamilton County, 1974-78, children's asst. Pleasant Ridge br., 1978-81, children's asst. Westwood br., 1981-84, reference libr. sci. and tech. dept., 1984-90, 1st asst. sci. and tech. dept., 1990-92, mgr. dept., 1992—. Mem. Ohio Libr. Coun., Columbus, 2001—03. Mem. United Methodist Ch. Office: Pub Libr Cin and Hamilton County Sci and Tech Dept 800 Vine St Cincinnati OH 45202-2071

BRETT, JAN CHURCHILL, illustrator, author; b. Hingham, Mass., Dec. 1, 1949; d. George and Jean (Baxter) Brett; m. Daniel Bowler, Feb. 27, 1970 (div. Jan. 1979); 1 child, Lia Bowler ; m. Joseph Hearne, Aug. 18, 1980. Student, Colby Jr. Coll., 1968-69, Boston Mus. Fine Arts Sch., 1970; DHL (hon.), Fitchburg State Coll., 1996. Mem. bd. overseers Boston Symphony Orch., 1991—99, trustee, 1999—, Thayer Acad., Braintree, Mass. Mem.: Nat. Soc. Colonial Dames Am., Chilton Club. Office: 132 Pleasant St Norwell MA 02061-2523 E-mail: janbrett@janbrett.com.

BRETT, NANCY HELÉNE, artist; BFA, Wayne State U., 1969; MFA, Cranbrook Acad. of Art, 1972. One-woman shows include Gallery Seven, Detroit, 1976, Ericson Gallery, N.Y.C., 1980, Harm Bouckaert Gallery, N.Y.C., 1982, Hillwood Art Mus., C.W.Post, Long Island U., N.Y., 1987, L'Ecole Gallery, N.Y.C., Victoria Munroe Gallery, N.Y.C., 1989, 91, 93, Victoria Munroe Fine Art, N.Y.C., 1993, Lake George Arts Project, N.Y., 1996, The Painting Ctr., N.Y.C., 1997, Cranbrook Art Mus., 1998, Hyde Collection Art Mus., Glen Falls, N.Y., 1999; group shows include Mich. Focus, Detroit Inst. of Art and Grand Rapids Mus. of Art (Catalog), 1974, Mus. of Modern Art, Touchstone Gallery, N.Y.C., 1979, Susan Caldwell, N.Y.C., 1979, Landscape Anthology, Grace Borgenicht Gallery, N.Y.C., 1988, Lines of Vision: Drawings by Contemporary Women, Blum Helman Warehouse and Hillwood Art Mus., Long Island U. Catalog, N.Y., 1989, Notions of Place: Paintings and Drawings, Victoria Munroe Gallery, N.Y.C., 1990, The Painters, 1991, Summer Salon, 1992, Celebrating Nature, Champion Internat. Corp. Collection Exhibit., Stamford, Conn., 1991,

Landscape Not Landscape, Gallery Camino Real, Boca Raton, Fla. Catalog, 1994, Bklyn. Mus. Art, Gasworks Gallery, London, Cornerstone Gallery, Manchester, U., Gallery Camino Real, Boca Raton, Fla., 1994, U. Art Mus., 1994, Gallery at Hastings-on-Hudson, Mcpl. Bldg., N.Y., 1995, West Eng., Bristol, 1996, Parsons Gallery, 1996, Bklyn. Mus. Art, 1997, Hyde [illegible], Exit Art/The first World, N.Y., 1999, Wendy Cooper Gallery, Madison, Wis., 2000, Williamsburg Art and Hist. Ctr., Bklyn., 2000, Akus Gallery, Ea. Conn. State U., Willimantic, Conn., 2000, Exit Art/The First World, N.Y.C., 2002, Sperone Westwater Gallery, N.Y.C., 2002, Courthouse Gallery, Lake George, N.Y., 2002, A.I.R., N.Y.C., 2002, numerous others; represented in pub. collections: J.P. Morgan, Morgan Guaranty Trust Co., N.Y., Champion Internat., Stamford, Conn., Amerada Hess Corp., GE, Manhattan Savings Bank, Milbank, Tweed, Hadley and McCloy, N.Y.C., Herbert F. Johnson Mus. of Art, Cornell U., Prudential Ins., Best Products, IBM, Morgan Stanley, N.Y.C., Cranbrook Acad of Art Mus., Kidder Peabody, Inc., Hosp. Corp. Am., Power Inst. of Fine Arts, Sydney, Australia, IBM, GE, Princess Cruise Lines, Marsh and McClennan Cos. Inc., Libr. of Congress, Washington. Studio: 457 Broome St New York NY 10013-2681

BRETZ, KELLY JEAN RYDEL, actuary, consultant; b. Wadena, Minn., Oct. 30, 1962; d. Edmund Leroy and Glenyce Clara (Andrie) B.; m. Daniel Mark Bretz Rydel; children: Michael Charles Bretz Rydel, Alexa James Bretz Rydel. BA in Math., Moorhead State U., 1984. CFA, Assn. for Investment Mgmt. and Rsch. Asst. actuary Northwestern Nat. Life Ins. Co. (now ING Reliastar), Mpls., 1984-92; assoc. actuary TMG Life Ins. Co. (now Sun Life), Fargo, ND, 1993-94, MSI Life Ins. Co., Arden Hills, Minn., 1994, MidAm. Mut. Life Ins. Co., Roseville, Minn., 1994-95; actuarial officer Fortis Fin. Group, Woodbury, Minn., 1996—2001; v.p. and sr. portfolio mgr. US Bank, Mpls., 2001—02; ind. cons. Minn., 2002—03; lead annuity pricing actuary Thrivent Financial for Lutherans, Mpls., 2003—. Grader Soc. Actuaries' Exam 220, 1992, 93. Contbr. articles to co. jours. Organizer blood drive Mpls. Blood Bank, 1992; meal deliverer Meals on Wheels, Fargo, 1993; meal server Sharing and Caring Hands, Mpls., 1992. Fellow Soc. Actuaries (mem. fin. and investment mgmt. practice edn. com. 1995-96); mem. Am. Acad. Actuaries, Twin Cities Actuarial Club, Life Ins. Mktg. and Rsch. Assn. (fin. mktg. and svcs. com. 1993). Avocations: scuba diving, outdoor and indoor physical activies. E-mail: kellybretz@aol.com.

BRETZFELDER, DEBORAH MAY, retired museum staff member; b. Hazelton, Pa., Sept. 21, 1932; d. Joseph and Rose (Smulyan) Hirsh; m. Robert Bretzfelder, Dec. 24, 1955; children: Karl, Marc. Student, Syracuse U., 1950-53. Textile colorist, designer Cohn-Hall-Marx, N.Y.C., 1954-55; fashion coordinator Hecht's Dept. Store, Washington, 1956; freelance artist Washington, 1956-58; exhibits technician Smithsonian Instn., Washington, 1958-59, supr. exhibits prodn., 1959-63, exhibits specialist Nat. Mus. Am. History, 1963-75, visual info. specialist, project mgmt. officer, 1975-83, acting chief design, 1983, chief design, 1983-87, assoc. asst. dir. exhibits and pub. spaces, 1987-88; ret., 1988. Cons. various firms., orgns., mus. personnel; instr. mus. programs; freelance photographer and exhibit designer; project dir. Contbr. works to various publs.; musician: violin sect. George Washington U. Orch., 2003, violin sect. Georgetown Symphony Orch., 2003—. Mem.: Nat. Mus. Women in Arts, Nat. Soc. Hist. Preservation, Am. Assn. Mus., Potomac Appalachian Trail Club, Tau Sigma Delta. Jewish. Home: 2748 Woodley Pl NW Washington DC 20008-1517

BREWER, AIDA M. treasurer; BS in bus., LeMoyne Coll., Syracuse. With Key Bank, 1976—83; investment officer, asst. investment officer Treasury Divsn., NY, 1983—2000; dep. treas. NY, 2000—; dep. commr., 2002—. Recipient First Woman Treas., N.Y., 2000. Mem.: Nat. Assn. State Treas., Assn. for Fin. Profls. Office: NY State Dept of Taxation and Fin Divsn Treasury PO Box 22119 Albany NY 12201-2119 E-mail: aida-brewer@tax.state.ny.us.*

BREWER, EDITH GAY, librarian, educator; b. Jacksonville, Tex., Aug. 14, 1944; d. Elige Ellis and Jimmie Lee (Durham) Alexander; m. Samuel David Brewer, May 23, 1964; children: Gayla Deeann, Michael David. AA, Tyler (Tex.) Jr. Coll., 1964; BA, Stephen F. Austin State U., 1966, MEd, 1970. Cert. libr., Tex. English tchr., speech tchr. Rusk (Tex.) H.S., 1966-71; English, math, journalism, speech tchr. Whitehouse (Tex.) H.S., 1973-75, libr., 1976—; dist. libr. coord. Whitehouse Ind. Sch. Dist., 1976—. Tech. bd. mem. Whitehouse Ind. Sch. Dist., 1994—; gifted and talented bd. mem. Region VII Edn. Svc. Ctr., Kilgore, Tex., 1996—. Contbr. articles to profl. jours. Bd. dirs. Whitehouse Cmty. Libr., 1985-87; Sunday sch. tchr. First Bapt. Ch., Whitehouse, 1984—, chmn. music com, 1994—, mem. sanctuary choir, 1984—, mem. handbell choir, 1995—; vol. Hospice, 1998—. Recipient Libr. Appreciation award Sunrise Rotary Club, 1994. Mem. Tex. Libr. Assn., Tex. Assn. of Libr. Adminstrs., Am. Libr. Assn. Baptist. Avocations: reading, music, gardening, interior decorating, church activities. Home: 12098 County Road 2175 Whitehouse TX 75791-5024 Office: Whitehouse Ind Sch Dist 108 Wildcat Dr Whitehouse TX 75791-3130

BREWER, JANICE KAY, state official, property and investment firm executive; b. Hollywood, Calif., Sept. 26, 1944; d. Perry Wilford and Edna Clarice (Bakken) Drinkwine; m. John Leon Brewer, Jan. 1, 1963; children: Ronald Richard, John Samuel, Michael Wilford. Med. asst. cert. Valley Coll., Burbank, Calif., 1963, practical radiol. technician cert., 1963; D in Humanities (hon.) L.A. Chiropractic Coll., 1970. Pres., Brewer Property & Investments, Glendale, Ariz., 1970—; mem. Ariz. Ho. of Reps., Phoenix, 1983-86, Ariz. Senate, 1987-96, majority whip, 1993-96; mem. Maricopa County Bd. Suprs., 1997-2002; sec. of state State of Ariz., Phoenix, 2003-. State committeeman, Rep. Party, Phoenix, 1970, 1983; legis. liaison Ponderosa Rep. Women, Phoenix, 1980; bd. dirs. Motion Picture & TV Commn. Active NOW. Recipient Freedom award Vets. of Ariz., 1994; named Woman of Yr., Chiropractic Assn. Ariz., 1983, Legislator of Yr., Behaviour Health Assn. Ariz., 1991, NRA, 1992. Mem. Nat. Fedn. Rep. Women, Am. Legis. Exch. Coun. Lutheran. Office: 7th Fl State Capitol 1700 W Washington Phoenix AZ 85007-2808

BREWER, JENNIFER A. respiratory care practioner; b. Hagerstown, Md., June 13, 1973; d. John Alan and Patricia Ann Brewer. BS in Respiratory Care, Shenandoah U. Cert. respiratory care practitioner Pa. State Bd. Medicine, Conn. Dept. Pub. Health, Va. Dept. Health Professions. Neonatal/pediatric respiratory care practitioner Thomas Jefferson U. Hosp., Phila.; respiratory care practitioner Jefferson Meml. Hosp., Ranson; neonatal/pediatric respiratory care practitioner Am. Mobile Healthcare, Cross Country Travelers Corp., 2003—. H. Kennedy Endowed Achievement scholar, H. Kennedy Estate, Acad. Achievement scholar, Shenandoah U. Mem.: Nat. Bd. for Respiratory Care.

BREWER, KAREN, librarian; b. Janesville, Wis., Apr. 29, 1943; d. Gordon A. and Charlotte (Warren) Schultz; m. Eugene N. Brewer, June 22, 1963. BA, U. Wis., 1965, MA, 1966; PhD, Case Western Res. U., 1983. Libr. Middleton Med. Libr. U. Wis., Madison, 1966-67; libr. Med. Libr. U. Tenn., Memphis, 1968-69; libr. Cleve. Health Sci. Libr. Case Western Res. U., Cleve., 1970-76; dir. libr. Coll. Medicine Northeastern Ohio U., Rootstown, 1976-88; dir. libr. Med. Ctr. NYU, 1988—. Mem. editorial bd. Ann. Stats. Acad. Health Sci. Libr., 1986-91. Fellow N.Y. Acad. Medicine; mem. Assn. Acad. Health Sci. Librs. (sec.-treas. 1986-89, pres. 1995), Med. Libr. Assn. (bd. dirs. 1991-94), Acad. Health Info. Profls. (disting. mem.), Am. Med. Informatics Assn. Office: NYU Med Ctr Libr 550 1st Ave New York NY 10016-6402

BREWER, NANCY ELLEN, communications executive, writer; d. William and Mary Brewer. BA in English, Miami U., 1996. Investor rels. mgr. LSI Industries Inc., Cin., 1978—91; project mgr., tech. writer The Sant Corp., Norwood, Ohio, 1996—98; dir. comm. Delta Zeta Sorority Nat. Hdqs., Oxford, Ohio, 1999—. Writer spl. projects Miami U., Oxford, Ohio, 1993—96, freelance writer, 1999—2002; editl. cons. and freelance writer Delta Sigma Pi Frat. Cul. Office, Oxford, 1999—2003. Author: A Century of Sisterhood: The Story of Delta Zeta Sorority [illegible] award/Pub. Rels. Soc. award of merit, 2003). Campaign cons. John Parks Candidate for Congress, Oxford, 2001—02. Recipient IABC Silver Quill award, Internat. Assn. Bus. Communicators, 1999, 2000, NIF award, No. Am. Interfraternity Found., 2001, Prism award, Pub. Relations Soc. Am., 2001. Mem.: Pub. Rels. Soc. Am., Coll. Frat. Editors Assn., Alpha Lambda Delta, Sigma Tau Delta, Phi Beta Kappa, Phi Eta Sigma (hon.), Delta Zeta Sorority. Avocations: creative writing, collecting hollywood memorabilia. Office: Delta Zeta Sorority National Headquarters 202 E Church St Oxford OH 45056 E-mail: neb@dzshq.com.

BREWER, NEVADA NANCY, elementary school educator; b. Balt., Jan. 21, 1949; d. Leo and Rebecca (Johnson) Brewer. BS, Coppin State Coll., 1973, MEd, 1974, MEd, 1981; postgrad., C.C. Balt., 1985. Cert. elem. tchr., spl. edn. tchr. Tchr. Balt. County Adult Edn., Towson, Md., 1973-88; coord. Just Say No to Drugs program Balt. City Sch. Sys., tchr., 2000—01, mgr. summer sch., 2000—02, acad. coach math. and sci., 2002—03, coord. math. elem. lab., 2003—04; lead tchr. adminstrv. team Dept. of Juvenile Svcs., 2004—. Coord. Heads Up Program, 1980, math-a-thon program St. Jude Rsch. Ctr., 1993—, 24 Challenge Math. Tournament, 1996—, elem. math. lab., 2003—, academic coach math. and sci. grades prek-5, 2002-03; supr. tchr. for student tchrs. Towson State U., Coll. Notre Dame, Coppin State Coll., 1989—; leadership tchr. STARS sci. program, 1995; participant in Project Future Search Phone-a-Thon to recruit minority students U. Md., College Park., Write to Learn Program, Balt. City Sch. Sys., 1990-91; acad. coach math and sci. grades Pre-K-5, 2002—. Coord. Echo Hill Outdoor Sch., 1988—, mem. adv. bd., 2003—. Recipient Freedom Found. award, 1974. Home: 1616 Wentworth Ave Baltimore MD 21234-6125 E-mail: nbrew@unlonnet.net.

BREWER, ROGENNA WYNNE, writer; b. Fon du Lac, Wis., Apr. 12, 1961; d. Roger Wayne Bean and Gloria Ann (Amend) Madien; m. Jeffrey Reagan Brewer, Jan. 22, 1986; children: Todd Eugene, Tyler Wayne, Troy Roger. Interior design diploma, Southern Coll., Orlando, Fla., 1984. Bookseller, reviewer, Colo., 1990—98; writer, 1998—. Author: (book) Midway Between You and Me, 2002, Sign, Seal, Deliver, 2001 (Romantic Times Top Pick, 2001), Seal It with a Kiss, 1999 (Romantic Times Top Pick, 1999, Romantic Times Reviewers Choice nominee, 2000, Booksellers Best nominee, 2000, 3d pl. Blue Boa, 2000), Aspen Gold, 2000 (1st pl. Long Contemporary, 2000), Heart of the Rockies (working title: Puss in Boots), 1997 (1st pl. Long Contemporary, 1997). With USN, 1980—85. Mem.: Colo. Romance Writers (pres. 1997), Heart of Denver Romance Writers (founding pres. 1998), Romance Writers of Am. Avocations: reading, gardening.

BREWINGTON, ELAINE SUE, social worker; b. Durango, Colo., June 26, 1950; d. Birl Joseph Brewington and Olive Prior King; m. Stephen Charles Love, Oct. 7, 2000. BSc, Colo. Coll., 1972; M in Social Work, Barry U., 1990. LCSW Colo. Rsch. asst., field supr. Behavioral Rsch. and Evaluation Corp., Boulder, Colo., 1973—79; mgr. fin., personnel Elan Vital, Miami, Fla., 1979—86; billing asst. Mershon, Sawyer, Johnston, Miami, 1989—90; site clinician Bertha Abess Children's Ctr., Miami, 1990—93; counselor youth group Health Crisis Network, Miami, 1991—94; therapist, asst. clinic dir. Children's Psychiat. Ctr., Miami, 1993—97; lead clinician Cigna Behavioral Health, Albuquerque, 1997—2000; employee assistance counselor, ind. contractor Grand Junction, Colo., 2001—. Mem.: NASW, LWV (1st v.p. 2002—, mem. bd. dirs., treas. 1985—87), Colo. Eating Disorder Coalition. Democrat. Avocations: gardening, yoga. Home: 1533-6 Crestview Way Grand Junction CO 81506

BREWSTER, ELIZABETH WINIFRED, English language educator, poet, novelist; b. Chipman, N.B., Can., Aug. 26, 1922; d. Frederick John and Ethel May (Day) Brewster BA, U. N.B., 1946; MA, Radcliffe U., 1947; BLS, U. Toronto, 1953; PhD, Ind. U., 1962; DLitt, U. N.B., 1982. Cataloger Carleton U., Ottawa, Ont., 1953-57; cataloger Ind. U. Library, Bloomington, 1957-58, N.B. Legis. Library, 1965-68, U. Alta. Library, Edmonton, Can., 1968-70; mem. English dept. Victoria U., B.C., 1960-61; reference libr. Mt. Allison U. Libr., Sackville, N.B., 1961-65; vis. asst. prof. English U. Alta., 1970-71; mem. faculty U. Sask., Saskatoon, Can., 1972—, asst. prof. English, 1972-75, assoc. prof., 1975-80, prof., 1980-90, prof. emeritus, 1990—. Author: East Coast, 1951, Lilloot, 1954, Roads, 1957, Passage of Summer, 1969, Sunrise North, 1972, In Search of Eros, 1974, Sometimes I Think of Moving, 1977, The Way Home, 1982, The Sisters, 1974, It's Easy to Fall on the Ice, 1977, Digging In, 1982, Junction, 1982, A House Full of Women, 1983, Selected Poems 1944-84, 2 vols., 1985, Visitations, 1987, Entertaining Angels, 1988, Spring Again, 1990, The Invention of Truth, 1991, Wheel of Change, 1993, Away from Home, 1995, Footnotes to the Book of Job, 1995, Garden of Sculpture, 1998, Burning Bush, 2000, Jacob's Dream, 2002. Recipient E.J. Pratt award for poetry U. Toronto, 1953, Pres. medal for poetry U. Western Ont., 1980, Lit. award Can. Broadcasting Corp., 1991, Lifetime award for excellence in the arts Sask. Arts Bd., 1995, Short List award Gov. Gen., 1996. Mem. League Can. Poets (life), Writers' Union Can., Assn. Can. Univ. Tchrs. English, Order of Can.

BREWSTER, LOUISE BOONE, artist, educator; b. Comanche County, Okla., July 5, 1925; d. Raymond Jennings and Annie Faye (Brazil) Wimple; m. Robert Lee Boone, July 8, 1969 (dec. Jan. 1982); m. Curtis Evan Brewster, July 19, 1992; children: James Dale Hall Jr., Margaret Elaine Heimlich, Lynda Louise Carnes. Student, Acad. Fine Arts, Vienna, 1982. Sales agt. Fidelity Life Ins., Irving, Tex., 1954-60; advt. mgr. Radio Sta. KVWC, Vernon, Tex., 1961-63; v.p. La Velle Labs., Oklahoma City, 1963-67; regional sales rep. Mr. Fine - Dallas, Sweet Adeline - Chgo., Midwest, 1967-70; art tchr. Rolla (Mo.) Sheltered Workshop, 1973-76; dir. Hobbit Hill Studio, Rolla, Mo., 1974—; actor Regional Opera Co., Newburg, Mo., 1989-92. Spkr. Rep. Women, Rolla, 1972-82. Mem. Philanthropic Ednl. Orgn., Order of Ea. Star (worthy matron 1973—). Baptist. Avocations: gardening, horsemanship. Home: HC 33 Box 101 Rolla MO 65401-9808

BREWSTER, MARGARET EMELIA, artist; b. Kaukauna, Wis., July 18, 1932; d. Eathen Edward and Emelia Josepha (Jennick) B. Attended, U. Wis., Fox Valley, 1951-53. Photographer, graphic artist Appleton Papers, Inc., Combined Locks, Wis., 1954-90. Exhbns. include Appleton Gallery Arts, 1965-94, Bank of Kaukauna, 1974-2003, Frances Hardy Gallery, Ephraim, Wis., 1984, 86, 93, 95, Neville Pub. Mus. Brown County, Green Bay, 1986-87, 90, 92-95, Minn. State Capital, St. Paul, 1987, Brown County Libr., Green Bay, 1988, Ctr. Visual Arts, Wausau, Wis., 1991, Milw. Art Mus., 1991-92, Outagamie County Hist. Mus., 1991-95, Bank One Lobby Gallery, Neenah, Wis., 1993-94, 96, Wis. Arts Bd. Gallery, 1994, U. Wis., Platteville, 1996, William F. Boniface Arts Ctr., Escanaba, Mich., 1996, Anderson Art Ctr., Kenosha, Wis., 1997, Atrium Gallery, Indpls., 1997, Mason St. Gallery, Green Bay, Wis., 1997-98, Colorado Springs Art Ctr., 1998, U. Wis., Marinette, 2000, Chgo. Windy City Artists, 2000, U. Wis., Oshkosh, 2001, White Bear Art Ctr., Minn., 2002, Portalwisconsin.org, 2002. Bd. dirs. Friends of the 1000 Islands Environ. Ctr., Kaukauna, 1986—, chair art fair, 1986-94, sec., 1988-93. Mem. Kaukauna Creative Artists Group (sec. 1991-2003, chair exhibit and publicity 1991—), Wis. Painters & Sculptors, Nat. Mus. Women in Arts, Bay Area Watercolor Guild. Avocations: photographer, needle arts, gardening, walking, nordic skiing. Studio: 400 W Division St Kaukauna WI 54130-1120

BREWSTER, OLIVE NESBITT, retired librarian; b. San Antonio, July 19, 1924; d. Charles Henry and Olive Agatha (Nesbitt) B. BA, Our Lady of Lake Coll., 1945, BS in LS, 1946. Asst. librarian aeromed. library U.S. Air Force Sch. Aviation Medicine, Randolph AFB, Tex., 1946-60; chief cataloger aeromed. library Sch. Aerospace Medicine, Brooks AFB, Tex., 1960-83, chief tech. processing, [illegible] Indexers, Mensa. Anglican. Home: 1906 Schley Ave San Antonio TX 78210-4332

BREWTON, MICHELE EILEEN, small business owner, consultant; b. Fresno, Calif., Feb. 16, 1973; d. Eduardo Salas and Victoria Marie Vizcarra. BA in Comms., U. So. Calif., 2000. Intern Buena Vista Pictures Distbn., Inc., Burbank, Calif., 1995; compliance mgr. Gemstar TV-Guide Internat., Inc., Hollywood, Calif., 1996—97; ops. mgr. Ctrl. Valley Tech. Ctr., Fresno, Calif., 1999—2000; project mgr. 30 Sixty Design, Inc., L.A., 2000—02; prin., owner Michele By Project, L.A., 2002—. Vol. PEW Hispanic Ctr., LA, 2003. Scholar, Mex. Alumni Assn., 1993—95, U. So. Calif., 1993—96. Mem.: Am. Inst. Graphic Arts, U. So. Calif. Alumni Assn., Mex.. Am. Alumni Assn., Latin Bus. Assn., Alpha Nu, Delta Gamma (pledge pres. 1992). Democrat. Avocations: tennis, skiing, vintage posters, interior decorating, environment. Home and Office: Michele By Project 429 S Sherbourne Dr 6 Los Angeles CA 90048 E-mail: michelebyproject@hotmail.com.

BRIAN, MARY H. librarian; b. Breckenridge, Tex., Dec. 17, 1929; d. Thomas Henry and M. Loyce Davis Hailey; m. Jack Brian, Dec. 26, 1953 (dec. Sept. 1983); children: Crystal Lee, Rosemary Hope, Tommy Wilson. BA, North Tex. State U., 1949; grad. in Libr. Sci., U. Tex., 1953. Tchr., libr. Dumas Jr. HS, Tex., 1949-94. Fin. chair Moore County Libr. Bd., Dumas, 1959-60, chair, 1960-62. Named among outstanding leaders in elem. & secondary edn., 1976; Defender of the constitution award. Mem. Tex. Ret. Tchr. Assn. (20th Century tchr. award 1997), Tex. Farm Bur.; Rep. Nat. Com., Eisenhower Commission, 2002, Nat. Rifle Assn., 2003. Republican. Baptist. Avocations: travel, opera, gardening, history. Home: 5278 Fm 722 Channing TX 79018-3312

BRICARD, YOLANDA BORRAS, music educator, music program administrator; b. Santo Domingo, Dominican Republic, Apr. 6, 1959; d. Alvaro Borrás and Ileana Viñas de Borrás; m. Philippe F. Bricard, Jan. 18, 1985; children: François, Henri. Bilingual secretarial studies, Louis Muñoz Rivera Coll., Santo Domingo, 1978; B in Music, Piano Performance, Peabody Conservatory Johns Hopkins U., Balt., 1985; MA in Ednl. Aminstrn., Columbia U., 1998. Head music tchr. Colegio Los Angelitos, Santo Domingo, 1980—81; elem. music tchr. Santo Domingo Conservatory, 1980; head music tchr. Atlanta Internat. Sch., 1985—87; head elem. music tchr. St. Ignatius Loyola, NY, 1988—89; part-time music tchr. Hong Kong Internat. Sch., 1992—93; vol. music tchr. Lycee Français Hong Kong, 1990—91; music tchr. Diller-Quayle Sch. Music, N.Y.C., 1997—99; program founder, adminstr. Mus. Kids, N.Y.C., 1999—. Vol. N.Y. Children's Concerts N.Y. Philharmonic, 1987—89. Mem.: Music Educators Nat. Conf., Orgn. Am. Kodaly Educators, Kappa Delta Pi. Roman Catholic. Avocations: reading, golf, skiing. Home: 1326 Madison Ave # 71 New York NY 10128

BRICCETTI, JOAN THERESE, theater manager, arts management consultant; b. Mt. Kisco, N.Y., Sept. 29, 1948; d. Thomas Bernard and Joan (Filardi) B. AB in Am. History, Bryn Mawr Coll., 1970. Adminstrv. asst., program guide editor Sta. WIAN-FM, Indpls., 1970-72; adminstrv. asst. T. Briccetti, condr., Indpls., 1970-72; dir. pub. rels. The Richmond (Va.) Symphony, 1972-73, mgr., 1973-80, St. Louis Symphony Orch., 1980-84, gen. mgr., 1984-86, chief oper. officer, 1986-92; ind. cons. for Arts & Edn., 1993—; mng. dir. Metro Theater Co., St. Louis, 1996—. Cons., panelist Arts Couns. Ohio, Va., Ky. Active orch. and planning sects., music programs Nat. Endowment fot the Arts, 1974-78, chmn. orch. panel, 1975-78, cons., evaluator, panelist, 1974—, mem. first challenge grant rev. panel, 1977, co-chmn. recording panel, 1983-84; mem. grant rev. panel Va. Commn. for the Arts, 1976-78; adv. bd. Eastern Music Festival, 1977-83, Richmond Friends Opera, 1979-80; adv. coun. Va. Alliance for Arts Edn., 1978, Federated Arts Coun. Richmond, 1979-80; steering com. BRAVO Arts, 1978-79 (gov.'s award); cons. Tenn. Arts Commn., 1979-80; bd. dirs. Theatre IV, Richmond, 1974-80, Am. Music Ctr, N.Y.C., 1980-84, St. Louis Forum, 1983—, New City Sch., St. Louis, 1987—, Metro Theatre Co., 1994—; mem. challenge grant evaluation panel Ky. Arts Commn., 1983; participant Leadership St. Louis, 1983-84, bd. dirs., 1987-89; commr. subdistrict Mo. History Mus., 1987—, sec., 1993; speaker, panelist, cons. numerous arts orgns. Mem. Am. Symphony Orch. League (chmn. orch. library info. svc. adv. com., recruiter, mem. final interview com., advisor mgmt. fellowship program), Regional Orch. Mgrs. Assn. (v.p. 1976, policy com. 1977-79), Women's Forum Mo. Office: Metro Theatre Co 8308 Olive Blvd Saint Louis MO 63132-2814

BRICKER, JOYCE LYNN, art educator; b. Chgo., Oct. 2, 1949; d. Andrew and Elizabeth Dobrick; m. Steven L. Bricker, Dec. 19, 1986. BS in Edn., Valparaiso U., 1971. Tchr. Sch. Dist. # 3, Park Forest, Ill., 1971—. Fellow: Nat. Art Edn. Assn., Ill. Art Edn. Assn. (Elem. Art Tchr. of the Yr. 2000). Lutheran. Avocations: drawing, painting, travel, gardening, art. Home: 212 N Locust St Frankfort IL 60423 Office: Park Forest Sch Dist # 163 Park Forest IL 60466

BRICKER, LISA G. marketing professional, not-for-profit fundraiser; b. Coldwater, Mich., Dec. 26, 1963; d. John Larry Bricker and Cona Rose Cameron. BA, Hillsdale (Mich.) Coll.; MA, Villanova (Pa.) U. Maj. gifts officer Hillsdale Coll., 1988—98; v.p. devel. Regent U., Va. Beach, Va., 1998—2000; v.p. cmty. rels. Clear Springs Land Co., Bartow, Fla., 2000—. Mem. bd. trustees Polk Mus. Art, Lakeland, Fla., 2001—. Vol. Am. Cancer Soc., Lakeland, Fla., 2002; campaign mgr. dist z Polk County Commn., Bartow, Fla., 2001. Republican. Methodist. Avocations: volleyball, golf, walking, bicycling. Home: 3125 New Jersey Rd Lakeland FL 33803 Mailing: 114 McDonald St Lakeland FL 33803-1179

BRICKER, VICTORIA REIFLER, anthropology educator; b. Hong Kong, June 15, 1940; came to U.S., 1947, naturalized, 1953; d. Erwin and Henrietta (Brown) Reifler; m. Harvey Miller Bricker, Dec. 27, 1964. AB, Stanford U., 1962; A.M., Harvard U., 1963, PhD, 1968. Vis. lectr. anthropology Tulane U., 1969-70, asst. prof., 1970-73, assoc. prof., 1973-78, prof., 1978—, chmn. dept. anthropology, 1988-91. Author: Ritual Humor in Highland Chiapas, 1973, The Indian Christ, The Indian King: The Historical Substrate of Maya Myth and Ritual, 1981 (Howard Francis Cline meml. prize Conf. Latin Am. History), A Grammar of Mayan Hieroglyphs, 1986, (with Gabrielle Vail) Papers on the Madrid Codex, 1997, (with Eleuterio Po'ot Yah and Ofelia Dzul de Po'ot) A Dictionary of the Maya Language as Spoken in Hocaba, Yucatan, 1998, (with Helga-Maria Miram) An Encounter of Two Worlds: The Book of Chilam Balam of Kaua, 2002; book rev. editor: Am. Anthropologist, 1971-73; editor: Am. Ethnologist, 1973-76; gen. editor: Supplement to Handbook of Middle American Indians, 1977—. Guggenheim fellow, 1982; Wenner-Gren Found. Anthropol. Rsch. grantee, 1971; Social Sci. Rsch. Coun. grantee, 1972; NEH grantee, 1990. Fellow Am. Anthrop. Assn. (exec. bd. 1980-83); mem. NAS, Am. Philos. Soc., Am. Soc. Ethnohistory (exec. bd. 1977-79), Linguistic Soc. Am., Seminario de Cultura Maya, Societe des Americanistes. Office: Tulane Univ Dept Anthropology New Orleans LA 70118

BRICKEY, KATHLEEN FITZGERALD, law educator; b. Austin, Tex., Sept. 16, 1944; d. Robert Bernard and Ina Marie (Daw) Fitzgerald; m. James Nelson Brickey, Aug. 22, 1969. BA, U. Ky., 1965, JD, 1968. Criminal law specialist/cons. Ky. Crime Commn., Frankfort, Cin., 1968-71; exec. dir. Ky. Judicial Conf. and Coun., Frankfort, 1971-72; adj. prof. law U. Ky., Lexington, 1972; asst. to assoc. prof. law U. Louisville, 1972-76;

assoc. prof. to prof. law Washington U., St. Louis, 1976-89, George Alexander Madill prof. law, 1989-93, James Carr prof. of criminal jurisprudence, 1993—, Israel Treiman faculty fellow, 2001—02. Cons. U.S. Sentencing Commn., 1988, 91; witness U.S. Senate Com. on Judiciary, Washington, 1986. Author: Kentucky Criminal Law, 1974, Corporate Criminal Liability, 1984, 2d edit., 1992-94, Corporate and White Collar Crime, 1990, 3d edit., 2002; contbr. articles to profl. jours. Mem. Am. Law Inst., Soc. for Reform of Criminal Law, Assn. Am. Law Schs. (sect. on criminal justice chair 1989, exec. com. 1985-91, 94-95). Office: PO Box 1120 Saint Louis MO 63188-1120 E-mail: brickey@wulaw.wustl.edu.

BRIDGE, BOBBE J. state supreme court justice; m. Jonathan J. Bridge; children: Rebecca, Don. BA magna cum laude, U. Wash; MA, PhD in Polit. Sci., U. Mich.; JD, U. Wash., 1976. Superior Ct. judge King County, Wash., 1990-1999; chief judge King County Juvenile Ct., Wash., 1994-97, asst. presiding judge, 1997-98, presiding judge, 1998-99; judge Wash. State Supreme Ct., 1999—; mem. faculty Wash. State Jud. Coll. Chmn. King County Criminal Justice Coun., King County Truancy Steerin Com., Juvenile Justice Operational Master Plan Oversight Com., Pub. Trust and Confidence Com. Bd. Jud. Adminstrn.; co-chmn. Unified Family Ct. Bench-Bar Task Force. Bd. dirs. YWCA, Seattle Children's Home, Families for Kids Permanency Oversight Com., Tech. Adv. Com. Female Juvenile Offenders, Adv. Com. Adolescent Life Skills Program, Street Youth Law Program, Northwest Mediation Svc., Woodland Pk. Zoological Soc., Wash. Coun. Crime and Delinquency, Women's Funding Alliance, Alki Found., Privacy Fund, Seattle Arts Commn., U. Wash. Arts and Sci. Devel., Greater Seattle C. of C., Metrocenter YMCA, Juvenile Ct. Conf. Com.; mem. King County Task Force on Children and Families, Wash. State's Dept. Social and Health Svcs. Children., Youth, Family Svcs. Adv. Com., Child Protection Roundtable, Govs. Juvenile Justice Adv. Com.; chmn. State Task Force on Juvenile Issues, Coun. Youth Crisis Work Group, Families-at-Risk sub-com., Bd. Dirs. Ctr. Career Alternatives, Candidate Evaluation Com. Seattle-King Mcpl. League, Law and justice Com. League Women Voters; co-chmn. Govs. Coun. on Families, Youth, and Justice; pres. Seattle Women's Commn., Seattle Chpt. Am. Jewish Com.,bd. dirs., asst. sec.-treas. Jewish Fedn. Greater Seattle, chmn., vice chmn. Cmty. Rels. Coun. Named Judge of Yr. Wash. Women Lawyers, 1996; recipient Hannah G. Solomon award Nat. Coun. Jewish Women, 1996, Cmty. Catalyst award Mother's Against Violence in Am., 1997, Women Making a Difference award Youthcare, 1998; honored "woman helping women" Soroptimist Internat. of Kent, 1999. Mem. Phi Beta Kappa. Office: Wash Supreme Ct PO Box 40929 Olympia WA 98504-0929

BRIDGES, BERYL CLARKE, marketing executive; b. NYC, Oct. 27, 1941; d. David and Edith (Foster) Clarke; m. R. Shaw Bridges, Sept. 2, 1962 (div. May 1985); children: Robert Shaw Jr., Margaret Clarke, John Morrison; m. Robert A. McMillan, July 25, 1992. BA in English, Philosophy, Wheaton Coll., 1963. Acct. exec. McMoran-Redington Pub. Rels., Greenwich, Conn., 1975-77; mgr. sales promotion Lindenmeyr Graphic Resource Ctr., Greenwich, 1977-79; corp. mgr. promotions Lindenmeyr Paper Corp., Greenwich, 1979-81; mgr. southeastern region Paper Sources Internat. subs. Lindenmeyr Paper Corp., 1981-83, v.p. mktg., 1983-84; pres. Zanders USA, Inc. (subs. Internat. Paper Co.), Wayne, N.J., 1984-95. Cons. and lectr. in field. V.p. Greenwich Hist. Soc., 1974-77; mem. Jr. League, Greenwich, 1971-78; founder Girls Inc. of No. N.J., 2002. Mem. AAUW. Democrat. Avocations: folk dancing, hiking, choral singing. Home: 18 Lake Dr Boonton NJ 07005-1047

BRIDGES, ELIZABETH ANN, project administrator; b. New Orleans, Sept. 13, 1950; d. Johnnie and Augustine Elmira (Calice) B.; 1 child, Elizabeth Alexis. BS, So. U., 1975, MS, 1977; MBA, Atlanta U., 1982; cert. of achievement, U. Oslo, 1983. Lic. broadcaster; cert. paralegal ABA. Resident dir. So. U., Baton Rouge, 1976-77, Spelman Coll., Atlanta, 1981-84; material analyst Xerox Corp., Webster, N.Y., 1977-80; edn. asst. Atlanta U., 1980-84; account exec. Inter-Urban Broadcasting, New Orleans, 1984-87; meml. counselor Stewart Enterprises, Metairie, La., 1987-89; mgr. pub. health City of New Orleans, 1989-92; dep. dir. Mayor's Office for Drug Affairs, New Orleans, 1992-94; dir. human resources, cons. Housing Authority New Orleans, 1994-95; mktg. cons. New Orleans, 1995—99; project dir. Edn. Talent Search, Dillard U., 1999—. Health educator chmn. Teen Screen Drug Awareness Summit, 1989; chmn. Inst. Pub. Leadership, 1990; mentor, career day spkr. Gregory Jr. H.S., 1992; adj. prof. U. Phoenix. Del. Dem. Nat. Conv., Atlanta, 1988; mem. Orleans Parish Exec. Com., New Orleans, 1991, La. Dem. Ctrl. Com., Baton Rouge, 1991; bd. dirs., com. chmn. YWCA, 1992-96; bd. dirs., vice chmn. New Orleans Job Corps, 1992-96; bd. dirs., past chmn. New Orleans Mental Health, 1993-95. Recipient award for outstanding profl. achievement New Orleans Health Dept., 1989; fellow Loyola U. Inst. Politics, New Orleans, 1989, Met. Area Com. Leadership Forum, 1989, Leadership La., 1990, Leadership Am., 1991, Vol. of Yr. award New Orleans Multicultural Network, 2001; named one of Outstanding Young Women of Am, Role Model, YWCA, 1998. Mem. Kappa Delta Epsilon. Avocations: travel, creative writing, public speaking, singing, community service. Home and Office: 2119 Sumpter St New Orleans LA 70122-3941

BRIDGES, JUDY CANTRELL, gifted and talented education educator; b. Dallas, Feb. 17, 1947; d. William and Jewel Alexandria (Autrey) C.; m. Gary L. Bridges, Aug. 17, 1969; children: John Drewry, Judith Alexandria. BA, Tex. Tech. U., 1969; gifted/talented endorsement, Sul Ross State U., Alpine, Tex., 1992, MEd, 1993; cert. in mid-mgmt., Sul Ross State U., 1994. Lic. secondary edn. math. and English. Tchr. New Deal (Tex.) Ind. Sch. Dist., 1969—70, Indpls. Pub. Schs., 1970, USDESEA, Zweibruecken, Germany, 1971—73, Lubbock (Tex.) Ind. Sch. Dist., 1973—76, Ector County Ind. Sch. Dist., Odessa, Tex., 1976-85, 87-90, tchr. gifted spl. edn., 1990—92, gifted/talented coord., 1992—97, dir. advanced acad. svcs., 1977—2001; ednl. cons., self employed Odessa, 2001—02; prin., dir. gifted programs Midland Ind. Sch. Dist., 2002—. Acct. Walter Smith CPA, Odessa, 1977—82; real estate appraiser Appraisal Assocs., Odessa, 1985—87; vis. lectr. Sul Ross State U., Odessa, 1994, Odessa, 1997—98, Odessa, 2001; mem. gifted/talented adv. com. Region 18 Edn. Svc. Ctr., Midland, Tex., 1993—2001. Author: (poem) Paradigm Shifts in the West Texas Sand, 1991. Advisor, officer Jr. League of Odessa, Inc., 1980—, treas./treas. elect, 1986—88; treas. Campaign to Elect County Judge, Odessa, 1991; mem. bd. Permian H.S. Football Booster Club, 1993; dir. region I Tex. Acad. Decathlon, 1999, 2000; bd. dirs. ECISD Edn. Found., 2002—; treas., asst. treas., bd. dirs. Odessa Symphony Guild, 1996—98, sec.-treas., 2002, bd. dirs., 1999—2000; dir. Tex. Assn. for the Gifted and Talented, 1999—2001; chairperson math. Gifted/Talented Performance Stds. Com. Tex., 2000; mem. State Bd. for Educator Cert. Math. Stds. Com., 2000; sec., treas. Tex. Assn. for the Gifted and Talented, 2002. Recipient Dept. of Def. Commendation, U.S. Dependent Edn. System, Zweibruecken, 1973, Cert. of Appreciation-Stop of Felony Odessa Police Dept., 1992. Mem. ASCD, NEA, Tex. State Tchrs. Assn. (treas. Ector County unit 1991-92), Tex. Assn. Gifted and Talented, Am. Creativity Assn., Nat. Coun. Tchrs. Math. Baptist. Avocations: snow skiing, flora design, reading, travel. Home: 4243 Lynbrook Ave Odessa TX 79762-7146 Office: 409 N Texas Ave Odessa TX 79761 E-mail: bridgesjc@hotmail.com.

BRIDGES, MARGARET ELIZABETH, physician; b. Brevard, N.C., Jan. 26, 1947; d. James Oliver B. and Mary Elizabeth Allison. BS, Coll. Charleston, 1969; MD, U. S.C., 1973. Intern Med. U. S.C., 1973-74, resident, 1974-76, fellow gastroenterology, 1977-79; physician Diagnostic Clin. Houston, 1979—; asst. clin. prof. Baylor Coll. Medicine, Houston, 1984—. Bd. trustees Diagnostic Hosp., Houston, 1994-97; vol. faculty Ben Taub Gen. Hosp., Houston, 1981—. Contbr. articles to profl. jours. Founder, advisor Lucky Livers Support Group, Houston, 1989—; bd. trustees Coll. Charleston (S.C.) Coll. Found., 1978-79. Fellow Am. Coll. Physicians; mem. Am. Assn. Study Liver Disease, Am. Coll. Gastroenterology, Am. Gastroen. Assn., Am. Soc. Gastroen. Endoscopy, Alpha Omega Alpha. Episcopalian. Avocations: scuba diving, bird watching, skiing. Home: 13114 Hermitage Ln Houston TX 77079-7201

BRIDGEWATER, DEE DEE, jazz singer, diplomat; b. Memphis, May 1927; Lead vocalist Thad Jones and Mel Lewis Orch., 1971-75; appeared in theatrical prodns. The Wiz (Tony award), Sophisticated Ladies, Lady Day (L. Oliver nomination), Carmen Jazz, others; albums include Afro Blue, 1974, Dee Dee Bridgewater, 1976, 1980, Just Family, 1977, Bad for Me, 1979, Live in Paris, 1986, In Montreux, 1990, Keeping Tradition, 1992, Love and Peace: A Tribute to Horace Silver, 1995 (Grammy award), Dear Ella, 1997 (Grammy awards), Victim of Love, 1998, Live at Yoshi's, 2000 (Grammy nomination), This is New, 2002. Amb. U.N. Food and Agr. Orgn., 2002—. Office: DDB Prodns 13428 Maxella Ave #554 Los Angeles CA 90292 Fax: 818-610-3952.*

BRIDGEWATER, PAMELA E. ambassador; b. Fredericksburg, Va., Apr. 1947; BA in Polit. Sci., Va. State U., 1968, LLD (hon.), 1997; MA in Polit. Sci., U. Cin., 1970; postgrad., Am. U., 1976. Tchr. Voorhees Coll., Denmark, SC, Bowie (Md.) State U., Morgan State U., Balt.; vice-consul Dept. of State, Brussels, labor attache/polit. officer Kingston, Jamaica, polit. officer Pretoria, South Africa, 1990—93, consul gen. Durban, South Africa, 1993—96, dep. chief of mission Nassau, 1996—99, mem., pres. 42nd Sr. Seminar, 1999—2000, U.S. amb. to Benin, 2000—. Office: DOS Amb 2120 Cotonou Pl Washington DC 20521

BRIER, BONNIE SUSAN, lawyer; b. Oct. 19, 1950; d. Jerome W. and Barbara (Srenco) B.; m. Bruce A. Rosenfield, Aug. 15, 1976; children: Rebecca, Elizabeth, Benjamin. AB in Econs. magna cum laude, Cornell U., 1972; JD, Stanford U., 1976. Bar: Pa. 1976, U.S. Dist. Ct. (ea. dist.) Pa., U.S. Tax Ct., U.S. Ct. Appeals (3d cir.), U.S. Supreme Ct. Law clk. to chief judge U.S. Dist. Ct. Pa. (ea. dist.), Phila., 1976-77, asst. U.S. atty. criminal prosecutor, 1977-79; from assoc. to ptnr. Ballard, Spahr, Andrews & Ingersoll, Phila., 1979-90; gen. counsel Children's Hosp. of Phila., Phila., 1990—. Legal counsel Womens Way, 1979—1999; lectr. U. Pa. Law Sch., 1988-95; lectr., speaker various orgns. and seminars. Editor Stanford Law Rev., 1974-76; contbr. articles to profl. jours. Bd. dirs. U.S. Com. for UNICEF, 1994—2000, vice chmn., 1998-2000. Fellow Am. Coll. Tax Counsel, Am. Law Inst.; mem. ABA (exempt orgn. com. on tax sect., chair 1991-93, mem. health law sect., bd. dirs. 1998-, chair 2003-), Pa. Bar Assn. (tax sect., health law sect., mem. com. charitable orgn., children's rights), Phila. Bar Assn. (tax sect., health law sect.), Am. Health Lawyers Assn. (bd. dirs. 1991-96). Home: 132 Fairview Rd Narberth PA 19072-1331 Office: Children's Hosp of Pa 34th St and Civic Ctr Blvd Philadelphia PA 19104

BRIERLEY, CORALE L. geological engineer; b. Mont. m. Jim Brierley. Student, Mont. State U.; BS in Biology, MS in Chemistry, N.Mex. Inst. Mining & Tech.; PhD in Environ. Scis., U. Tex., Dallas, 1981. With N.Mex. Bur. Mines; founder Advanced Mineral Techs., 1983 87; chief environ. process devel. Newmont Mining Co., 1989-91; founder, prin. Brierley Cons. LLC, Highlands Ranch, Colo., 1991—. Office: Brierley Consultancy LLC PO Box 260012 Highlands Ranch CO 80163-0012

BRIERRE, MICHELINE, artist; b. Jeremie, Haiti; d. Luc Brierre and Simone Lataillade; m. Charles Lopez (div.), children: Liza Lopez [illegible], Charles Lopez; m. Barry Kaplan. Studied with, Mr. Ramponeau, Haiti, 1951-53; student, Academie Nehemie Jean, Haiti, 1958-60, Miraflores Art Ctr., Peru. Author: I am Eve, 1980, Spanish translation, 1980; solo show Commonwheel, Manitou Springs, Colo., 1995; exhibited in group shows at Galerie Hotel Rancho, Haiti, 1961, Galerie Brochette, Haiti, 1962, Onze Femmes peintres, Haiti, 1963, Gallerie Brochette, Haiti, 1964, Brierre/Castera, Haiti, 1965, Musee d'Art, Haiti, 1980, Galeria 70, Bogota, Colombia, S. Am., 1980, Galeria San Diego, Colombia, 1980, Woman's Way, Miami, Fla., 1982, Un Regard Soleil, Port-au-Prince, Haiti, 1983, Reflection On The Past, Aureus, Miami, 1983, Un Mundo Para Compartir, Lima, Peru, 1983, Festival Arts Gallery, Port-au-Prince, 1984, An Evening With The Artists, Naples, Fla., 1986, 87, Art in Jewelry, Island House, Bayside, Fla., 1987, Mixed Media Studio Show, Miami, 1989, 91, Collective Show, Commonwheel, Manitou Spings, Colo., 1994, Douglas County Art Ctr., Roby Mills Gallery and Bus. of Art Ctr., 1995. Mem. Fine Arts Ctr. Colo. Springs, Bus. of Art Ctr., Commonwheel Co-op. Home: All Things Beautiful 8050 Woody Creek Dr Colorado Springs CO 80911-8332 E-mail: michelinbrierre@earthlink.net.

BRIERTON, CHERYL LYNN, lawyer; b. Hartford, Conn., Nov. 11, 1947; d. Charles Greenwood and Elizabeth (Grechko) Wootton; m. David Martin Black, Oct. 12, 1968 (div. 1978); m. John Thomas Brierton, Sept. 6, 1982 (div. 1988); 1 child, John Greenwood. BA, Wellesley Coll., 1969; JD, U. San Diego, 1982. Bar: Calif. 1983. Tchr., libr. Anglican High Sch., Grenada, West Indies, 1972-74; dep. dir. Transalpino Student Travel, Paris, 1975-76; asst. dir. adminstn. Project OZ, YMCA, San Diego, 1976-78; asst. coord. policy and advocacy Community Congress San Diego, 1978-81; field dir. Calif. Child, Youth and Family Coalition, San Diego, 1981-83; asst. exec. dir. Community Congress San Diego, 1984-85; exec. dir. Calif. Child, Youth and Family Coalition, Sacramento, 1985-86; gen. atty. Def. Logistics Agy., Def. Depot Tracy, Calif., 1986-88; atty.-advisor Dept. of the Navy, Mare Island Naval Shipyard, Vallejo, 1988-89; staff atty. San Diego Superior Ct., 1989—. Mem. faculty Nat. Juvenile Judges Conf. Dispositional Alternatives Serious Offenders, 1982, 6th and 7th Nat. Confs. Juvenile Justice, 1979-80; cons. San Diego Youth Involvement Project, 1983-84, San Diego Youth and Community Svcs., 1983-84, South Bay Community Svcs., Chula Vista, 1983. Mem. Juvenile Justice Commn., Golden Hill Neighborhood Justice Cen. Planning Bd.; mem. com. jud. process Regional Criminal Justice Planning Bd. Scholar U. San Diego 1979. Mem. MENSA. Avocations: yachting, travel. Home: 1329 Bancroft St San Diego CA 92102-2429

BRIGDEN, ANN SCHWARTZ, mediator, educator; b. East Aurora, N.Y., Oct. 15, 1932; d. John G. and Mildred (Glaser) Schwartz; m. John Kraig Brigden, June 17, 1953 (div. Nov. 1974); children: Nancy Brigden, Barbara Brigden Victor; m. Steve Nemeth, Dec. 31, 1983 (div. Nov. 1996); children: Kyra Nemeth Akins, Abel Nemeth. BS in Human Ecology, Cornell U., 1954; MA in Behavioral Scis., Calif. State U., Dominguez Hills, 1977, grad. cert. in negotiation/conflict res., 1991, MS in Marriage and Family Counseling, 1993. Cert. mediator, L.A. County. Dist. dir. Girl Scouts of Erie County, Buffalo, N.Y., 1954-55; recreation leader City of Phila., 1955-56; field dir. Angeles Girl Scout Coun., L.A., 1956-58, 69-79; dir. vols. Children's Home Soc. Calif., L.A., 1979-84, dir. Human Maturity Program, 1984-90; counselor-intern Dolores St. Sch., Carson, Calif., 1990-95; developer and dir. Conflict Resolution Programs Dolores and Catskill Schs., Carson, Calif., 1994—. Adv. bd. L.A. Unified Sch. Dist. Health Edn., 1985-87; chair Maternal, Child & Adolescent Health Coun. L.A. County West, L.A., 1988-93. Author (textbooks): Maturing as Humanly as Possible, 1986, Becoming a Teenager, 1988; co-author (jr. h.s. curriculum) Curriculum in Human Maturity, 1980, revised 1986, 94. Aux. mem. Children's Hosp. San Diego, 1962-68; Girl Scout leader, bd. mem. Girl Scout Coun. San Diego, 1964-68; com. chair Peninsula Action for Youth, Palos Verdes, Calif., 1971-76; vol. mediator L.A. County, 1992—; bd. dirs. Dispute Resolution Ctr. Calif. State U. Dominguez Hills/L.A. County, 1987—. Grantee Soc. Psychol. Study of Social Issues, 1994-96, L.A. County Dept. Edn., 1996—. Mem. So. Calif,. Mediation Assn., Calif. State U. Dominguez Hills Marriage, Family and Child Counseling Alumni Assn. Avocations: volunteering, piano, family, friends. Home: 3162 Crownview Dr Palos Verdes Estates CA 90275-6414

BRIGEOIS, EVELYNE BRIGITTE, artist, publisher; b. Troyes, Aube, France, Feb. 18, 1946; came to U.S., 1984. Student, B.E.P.C., Aix-en-Othe, France, 1961. Trilingual exec. sec., Eng., France, Germany, Spain, 1965-79; owner, mgr. Brigeois Pub., Vallejo, Calif., 1987—. Spkr. in field. One-woman shows include Lawrence Gallery, Portland, Oreg., 1984, Scott Gallery, Orinda, Calif., 1985, Leslie Levy Gallery, Scottsdale, Ariz., 1986, 89, Charleston Heights Art Ctr., Las Vegas, Nev., 1987, Horvath Gallery, Sacramento, 1993 ; exhibited in group shows at Transco Gallery, Houston, 1988; contbr. articles to profl. jours. Recipient numerous awards, including Robert Wiegand Meml. award La. Watercolor Soc., 1985, award Detroit Inst. Arts Drawing and Print Club, 1985, award of honor Birmingham Mus. Art, 1986, lst place award Assoc. Artists Southport, N.C., 1986. Mem. Nat. Watercolor Soc. (Helen Wurdeman award 1985), Ala. Watercolor Soc. E-mail: brigeoisfineart@fiberpipe.net., ebrigeois@fiberpipe.net.

BRIGGINS, VIKKI MARIE, medical/surgical nurse; b. Bronx, N.Y., Sept. 1, 1967; d. Lester L. and Lorraine M. Briggins. BSN, Bowie (Md.) State U., 2001. RN. Nurse VA Med. Ctr., Washington, 1994—. Mem.: Sigma Theta Tau (Extraordinary Nurse award Gamma Beta chpt. 2002), Chi Eta Phi (dean of pledgees Lambda Phi chpt. 2003—). Home: 14216 Hampshire Hall Ct Upper Marlboro MD 20772 Office: VA Med Ctr 50 Irving St NW Washington DC 20422 Office Phone: 202-745-8182.

BRIGGS, CYNTHIA ANNE, educational administrator, clinical psychologist; b. Berea, Ohio, Nov. 9, 1950; d. William Benajah and Lorraine (Hood) B.; m. Thomas Joseph O'Brien, Nov. 28, 1986; children: Julia Maureen, William Thomas. B Music Edn., U. Kans., 1973; MusM, U. Miami, 1976; D. Psychology, Hahnemann U., 1988. Lic. psychology, Mo.; bd. cert. music therapist. Music therapist Parsons (Kans.) State Hosp., 1973-74; grad. asst. U. Miami, Coral Gables, Fla., 1974-76; asst. prof., dir. Hahnemann U., Phila., 1976-85, asst. prof., 1985-91; psychology resident Assocs. in Psychol. and Human Resources, Phila., 1988-91; clin. dir. Child Ctr. of Our Lady, St. Louis, 1991—2004; faculty (full time) Maryville U., 2004—. Mem. editl. bd. Jour. Music Therapy, 1997-2001; adj. faculty LIndenwood U., 2000—; contbr. chpts. to books, articles to profl. jours. Mem. Am. Assn. Music Therapy (pres. 1987-89), Nat. Coalition Arts Therapies Assns. (chair 1991-93). Democrat. Avocations: cooking, piano, music, theatre. Office: Child Ctr of Our Lady 7900 Natural Bridge Rd Saint Louis MO 63121-4628

BRIGGS, DEBRA A. secondary school educator; d. George Robert Thompson and Dolores Carmella Cremeno-Thompson; m. Scott M. Briggs, Jan. 26, 1979; children: Beau Scott, Travis Owen, Lea Marie. AS, Seminole C.C., Sanford, Fla., 1997; BS in Edn., U. Ctrl. Fla., 1999; M in Varying Exceptionalities, Nova Southeastern U., 2002. Tchr. Winter Springs (Fla.) H.S. Recipient Literacy award, Sch. Adv. Coun., 2000, 2001, 2002, 2003. Mem.: NEA, Seminole Edn. Assn., Coun. for Exceptional Children. Home: 770 Glenwood Dr Lake Mary FL 32746 Office: Winter Springs HS 130 Tuskawilla Rd Winter Springs FL 32746

BRIGGS, ETHEL D. federal agency administrator; BA, N.C. Ctrl. U.; M in Counseling, U. N.C. Dir. adult svcs. Nat. Coun. on Disability, Washington, 1985—, dep. dir., acting exec. dir., exec. dir. Named One of Top 100 African-Am. Bus. and Profl. Women, Dollars and Sense Mag., 1989. Office: Nat Coun on Disability 1331 F St NW Ste 1050 Washington DC 20004-1138

BRIGGS, MARTHA WREN, publishing executive, writer; b. Princeton, N.J., May 30, 1933; d. Garland Baird Briggs and Mattie Williams. BA, Coll. William and Mary, 1955; MA, NYU, 1962. Art libr. C.W. Post Coll., L.I. U., Greenvale, NY, 1964—87; CEO, owner Dory Press, Sedley, Va., 1992—. Author: The Compass Windows of Blandford Church: A Tribute in Tiffany Glass, 1992, Circle and Square Tracts of the Nottoway Indians, 1995, The Little Ferry's Christmas, 1997, The Little Ferry Goes to the Paper Mill, 1998, The Little Ferry Meets the Colonial Ships, 1999, The Little Ferry, a Ham Sandwich and a Virginia Tradition, 1999, The Little Ferry and the Hiding Peanuts, 2000; contbr. articles to mags. and profl. jours. Mem. fund distbn. United Way Gtr. Williamsburg, Va., 2001—02. Mem.: United Daus. of Confederacy (Jefferson Davis medal 1994), DAR, Jamestown Soc., Omicron Delta Kappa (mem. Eta cir. 2001). Methodist. Avocations: birdwatching, gardening, trivia. Home and Office: Dory Press 13396 Wakefield Rd Sedley VA 23878

BRIGGS, SUSAN MILLER, surgeon; b. 1943; MD, Loyola U., 1974; MPH in Internat. Health, Harvard U., 1998. Assoc. dir. trauma svc. Matt. Gen. Hosp., attending gen. and vascular surgeon; asst. prof. surgery Harvard Med. Sch.; dir. Internat. Med. Surg. Response Team, Metro-Boston Disaster Med. Assistance Team; developer, dir. Harvard Med. Internat. Trauma and Disaster Inst., 2001—. Trauma cons. U.S. State Dept., Croatia and Bosnia, 1997. Co-editor: Advanced Disaster Medical Response: A Manual for Providers, 2003. Achievements include helping to direct on-the-scene trauma care at World Trade Ctr. disaster, Sept. 11, 2001; instrumental in relief efforts during 1999 earthquakes in Turkey. Office: Mass Gen Hosp 8 Hawthorne Pl Ste 114 Boston MA 02114*

BRIGHT, DEBORAH, artist, educator; b. Washington, Feb. 17, 1950; d. Albert Seymour and Lois Blanche (Jamison) B.; m. Hugh Reid Wilson, div. 1986. BA magna cum laude, Wheaton Coll., 1972; MFA, U. Chgo., 1975. Lectr. DePaul U., Chgo., 1979-86; asst. prof. U. Mass., Boston, 1986-88, RISD, Providence, 1989-93, assoc. prof., 1993—. Cons. NEA, 1992, 93. Exhibited in solo shows at SUNY Binghamton, 1988, Rutgers U., 1992, U. Calif., Irvine, 1992, Colgate U., 1995, Atlanta Coll. Art, 1997, Bernard Toale, Boston, 1998, 2002; exhibited in group shows at Nat. Mus. Am. Art, Washington, 1992, Museet for Fotokunst, Denmark, 1992, Victoria and Albert Mus., 1995, Art in Gen., N.Y., 1995, Jan Kesner Gallery, L.A., 1995, Can. Mus. Contemporary Photography, 1996, Inst. Contemporary Art, Boston, 1998, others; works in permanent collections at Whitney Mus., Victoria and Albert Mus., Nat. Mus. Am. Art, Mus. Art/R.I. Sch. Design, Calif. Mus. Photography, Ill. State Mus., Rose Art Mus., others; asst. editor The New Art Examiner, Chgo., 1985-86. Founding mem. Women's Cmty. Cancer Project, Cambridge, Mass., 1988; mem. Act-Up, Boston, 1989, Gay and Lesbian Caucus, CAA, N.Y.C., 1990—. Grantee New Eng. Found. for the Arts, 1992, Art Matters, Inc., 1994, Somerville Arts Coun., 1995 others; Mary Ingraham Bunting Inst. fellow, Cambridge, Mass., 1995—. Mem. Soc. Photographic Edn. (bd. mem. 1987-91), Coll. Art Assn. (program chmn. nat. conf. 1996). Democrat. Home: 1200 Washington St Apt 315 Boston MA 02118-2137 Office: RISD 2 College St Providence RI 02903-2784 E-mail: dbright@risd.edn.

BRIGHT, MARGARET, sociologist; b. Bentonville, Ark., Nov. 19, 1918; d. William Ray and Edna May (Woolwine) B.; m. Herman Binder, 1983. AB, U. Calif., Berkeley, 1941; MA, U. Mo., 1944; PhD, U. Wis., 1950. Lectr. rural sociology U. Mo., 1944-47; asst. project dir. U. P.R., 1950-51; acting assoc. prof. Cornell U., 1951-52; social affairs officer population br. UN, N.Y.C., 1952-54; research assoc. Bur. Applied Social Research Columbia U., N.Y.C., 1954-57; sociologist-demographer UN Tech. Assistance, Bombay, India, 1957-59; asst. prof. chronic diseases Johns Hopkins U., Balt., 1959-63, assoc. prof., 1963-68; dir. research Center for Urban Affairs, 1968-72, assoc. prof. behavioral scis., 1968-70, prof., 1970-83, prof. emerita, 1983—. Mem. U.S. Mission Coop. Health and Sanitation to, Brazil, 1960. Author: Cooperativas de Consumo de Puerto Rico: Análisis Socio-Económicó, 1957; co-author: Graduates of American Schools of Public Health, 1976; contbr. articles to profl. jours. Mem. Balt. Mayor's Task Force on Polit. Redistricting, 1971; mem. Rockefeller Commn. on Population and the Am. Future, 1970-72. Mem. Am. Pub. Health Assn. Democrat. Home: 3900 N Charles St Apt 1314 Baltimore MD 21218-1738 Office: 624 N Broadway Baltimore MD 21205-1900

BRIGHT, SHERYL ANN, special education educator; b. Hot Springs, Ark., Jan. 1, 1949; d. Alfred A. and Opal Owens; m. Darrell Lindrell Bright, Apr. 20, 1973; children: Victoria Ann, Elizabeth Angeline. BS in Phys. Edn., Henderson State Coll., 1969; MS in Spl. Edn., U. Ark., 1983. Cert. spl. edn. tchr., Ark., Ala. Placement specialists Dept. of Rehab., Industry and Bus., Little Rock, 1988-89; educator spl. edn. grades 1-5 Benton (Ark.) [illegible] counselor, adminstr. North Little Rock Alternative Sch., 1990-91; owner Bright Balloons and Baskets, North Little Rock, 1992-96; educator spl. edn. grades 10-12 Baldwin County Pub. Sch. Sys., Bay Minette, Ala., 1995-96; educator spl. edn. grades 10-12 mildly handicapped Mobile (Ala.) Pub. Sch. Sys., 1996—; educator elem. edn. grades 5-8 Atlantic Undersea Testing and Evaluation Ctr., Andros, Bahamas, 1998-99. Spl. edn. cons. Millcreek of Ark., Fordyce, 1988-89; chmn. unit family support group USAR, 1988-92; cons. to mgmt. team for choices program Southwestern Bell Telephone Co., Little Rock, 1988-89. Methodist. Avocations: snow skiing, scuba diving, decorating, designing, music. E-mail: sherylbright@hotmail.com.

BRIGHTMAN, SARAH, singer, actress; b. Berkhampstead, England, Aug. 14, 1960; d. Grenville and Paula (Hall) Brightman; m. Andrew Lloyd Webber (div. 1990). Student, Elmhurst Ballet Sch., Arts Edn. Sch., London. Stage appearances include (musicals) I and Albert, 1973, Cats (original cast), 1981, Nightingale, 1982, Song and Dance, 1984, Phantom of the Opera, 1986 (Drama Desk award), Aspects of Love, 1990, (requiem) Andrew Lloyd Webber's Requiem, 1985 (Grammy nomination), (operettas) Pirates of Penzance, 1983, Merry Widow, 1985; dancer, singer (dance group) Hot Gossip, 1978 (#1 record 1978); albums include: Dive, 1993, Timeless, 1997, Time To Say Goodbye, 1997, As I Came of Age, 1998, Fly, 1998, Surrender, 1998, Sings the Music of Andrew Lloyd Webber, 1998, Trees They Grow So High, 1998, Eden, 1998, La Luna, 2000, Harem, 2003. Avocations: singing, driving, swimming, writing. Office: A & M Records 825 8th Ave Fl 27 New York NY 10019-7416*

BRIGHTON, RUTH LOUISE, lay worker, educator; b. Harrisburg, Pa., Apr. 18, 1931; d. Paul Gerhard and Ruth Genevieve (Lee) Krentz; m. Carl T. Brighton, July 27, 1954; children: David, Susan, Andrew, Joel. BA, Valparaiso U., 1953; MS in Math., U. Wis., 1955. Cert. tchr. Tchr. Sunday sch., adult Bible class Christ Meml. Luth. Ch., Malvern, Penn., 1969—; coord. adult edn., Ea. dist. Luth. Ch.-Mo. Synod, Buffalo, 1986-89, bd. dirs., 1988-90. Bd. dirs. Concordia Pub. House, St. Louis, 1989—2001. Teaching fellow in math. U. Wis., 1953. Home: 14 Flintshire Rd Malvern PA 19355-1108

BRILL, MARILYN, community-based collaboration consultant; b. Inglewood, Calif., July 11, 1947; d. Glenn Edwin and Dorothea Maxine (Burling) Facka; m. David R. Brill, June 17, 1972. BA, Austin Coll., Sherman, Tex., 1969; MAT, Duke U., 1970; MA, Bloomsburg (Pa.) U., 1982. Pres. LWV of Pa., Harrisburg, 1987-91; bd. dirs. LWV of U.S., Washington, 1992-96, 1st v.p., 1996-98; ptnr., internat. observer 1996 Bosnia election Groupworks Cons., Lewisburg, Pa., 1998—. Sec., bd. dirs. Pa. Women's Campaign Fund, Harrisburg, 1991—. Deacon, Grove Presbyn. Ch., Danville, Pa., 1984—. Recipient Outstanding Woman award Columbia/Montour Counties Women's Conf., 1984. Mem. LWV of Danville Area (Anna E. Strawbridge honor 1991). Democrat. Avocations: running, tennis, swimming, biking. Office: 202 S 3rd St Lewisburg PA 17837-1912 Home: 570 Stein Ln Lewisburg PA 17837-8734 E-mail: MFBrillgroupworks@worldnet.att.net.

BRILL, YVONNE CLAEYS, engineer, consultant; b. St. Norbert, Manitoba, Canada, Dec. 30, 1924; d. August and Julienne (Carette) Claeys; m. William Franklin Brill, Dec. 15, 1951; children: Naomi, Matthew, Joseph. BS, U. Manitoba, Canada, 1945; MS, U. So. Calif., 1951. Mathematician Douglas Aircraft, Santa Monica, Calif., 1945-46; research analyst Rand Corp., Santa Monica, 1946-49; group leader Marquardt Corp., Van Nuys, Calif., 1949-52; staff engr. UTC Research, East Hartford, Conn., 1952-55; project engr. Wright Aeronautical, Wood Ridge, N.J., 1955-58; mgr. propulsion systems RCA AstroElectronics, Princeton, N.J., 1966-81, staff engr., 1983-86; mgr. solid rocket motor NASA Hdqrs., Washington, 1981-83; with space engring segment Internat. Maritime Satellite Orgn., London, 1986-91; cons. Brill Assocs., Skillman, N.J., 1991—. Mem. USAF Sci. Adv. Bd., Washington, 1982-83, Nat. Acad. Engring.; Com. on Internat. Orgns. and Programs, 1992-96; apptd. mem. aerospace safety adv. panel NASA, 1994-2001. Contbr. articles to sci. jours.; patentee in field. Recipient Engr. of Yr. award, Ctrl. Jersy Engring. Couns., 1979, Diamond Superwoman award, Harpers Bazaar/DeBeers Corp., 1980, Disting. Pub. Svc. medal, NASA, 2001, Judith A. Resnik award, IEEE, 2002. Fellow AIAA (Marvin C. Demlar award 1983, WYLD award in rocket propulsion 2002), Soc. Women Engrs. (dir. student affairs 1979-80, 83-84, treas. 1980-81, Engring. Achievement award 1986, Resnik Challenger medal 1993); mem. Nat. Acad. Engring., Internat. Astronautical Acad. (academician, edn. com. 1983-85), Sigma Xi, Tau Beta Pi. Home and Office: 914 Route 518 Skillman NJ 08558-2616

BRIMIJOIN, KAY ROTHGEB, education educator; b. Washington, June 13, 1945; d. Wade Lee and Marjorie Katherine (Miller) Rothgeb; m. Mark Pierce Brimijoin, June 23, 1967; children: William Armstrong II, Katharine Perry. BA, Conn. Coll., 1963-67; MEd, Lynchburg Coll., 1989; PhD, U. Va., 2002. Elem. tchr. Amherst Acad., Va., 1976-80, Amherst County Pub. Sch., 1982-88, coord. enrichment programs, 1988—2000. Adj. faculty U. Va., 1998—; mem. faculty Sweet Briar Coll., 2000—; mem. profl. devel. faculty ASCD. Contbr. articles to profl. jours. Grantee Va. Dept. Edn., 2000, 02, 03; Commn. Arts, 1994-96, U.S. Dept. Edn., 1989. Mem. ASCD, Assn. Tchr. Educators, Internat. Reading Assn., Am. Ednl. Rsch. Assn., Nat. Assn. Gifted Children (Nat. Curriculum award 1999, Doctoral Student Aaard 2002), Va. Assn. for Gifted (bd. dirs. 1989-98, sec. 1993-96, pres.-elect 1996-98, pres. 1998-99). Avocations: piano, cooking, hiking, reading, travel.

BRIMMERMAN, BARBARA JANE, language educator; b. Fremont, Nebr., Mar. 15, 1960; d. Lowell Oscar Nuetzmann and Wanda Ann Peery; m. Roger Dale Brimmerman, May 29, 1989; children: Alan James Callahan, Katie Lynn Callahan, Grant Davis. BA, Midland Luth. Coll., 1990; cert. in ESL, U. Nebr., 1996; EdM, Doane Coll., 1999. Secondary ESL tchr. trainer Omaha Pub. Sch., 1999—. Named Adm. in Gt. Navy, State of Nebr., 1999; recipient Key to the City of Omaha, Mayor Hal Daub, 1999. Mem.: Midland's Women, TESOL, Phi Delta Kappa. Lutheran. Avocations: gardening, interior decorating, travel. Home: 921 N Clarkson Fremont NE 68025 Office: Omaha Pub Sch 3215 Cuming St Omaha NE 68131

BRINDEL, JUNE RACHUY, writer; b. Little Rock, Iowa, June 5, 1919; d. Otto L. and Etta Mina (Balster) Rachuy; m. Bernard Brindel, Aug. 26, 1939; children: Sylvia Mina, Paul, Jill. BA, U. Chgo., 1945, MA, 1958. Prof. English Wright Coll., Chgo., 1958-81. Tchr. drama Nat. Music Camp, Interlochen, Mich., 1957—67. Author: Luap, 1971, Ariadne, 1980 (nominee Pulitzer prize), Phaedra, 1985, Nobody is Ever Missing, 1984; editor: Bernard Brindel, Who Wore at His Heart the Fire's Center, 1999; contbr. short stories to jours. Recipient C. S. Lewis prize, Ind. U., 1973, Lit. award, Ill. Arts Coun., Chgo., 1985; fellow, 1984, 1985. Mem.: The Writers, Soc. Midland Authors, Phi Beta Kappa. Home: 2740 Lincoln Ln Wilmette IL 60091-2234

BRINKEMA, LEONIE MILHOMME, federal judge; b. N.J., June 26, 1944; d. Alexander Juste and Modeste Leonie Milhomme; m. John Robert Brinkema, Dec. 22, 1966; children: Robert Aaron, Eugenie Alexandra. BA with honors, Douglass Coll., 1966; MLS, Rutgers U., 1970; JD with honors, Cornell U., 1976. Bar: D.C. 1976, Va. 1978. Trial atty. U.S. Dept. Justice, Washington, 1976-77, 1983-84; asst. U.S. atty. U.S. Atty's Office Ea. Va., Alexandria, 1977-83; prin. Leonie M. Brinkema Atty., Alexandria, 1984-85; U.S. magistrate judge U.S. Dist. Ct. (ea. dist.) Va., Alexandria, 1985-93, U.S. dist. judge, 1993—. Legal lectr. Va. State Bar Professionalism Faculty, 1990 92, No. Va. Criminal Justice Acad., 1984-85; guest lectr. Alexandria Bar Assn., Alexandria Women Attys. Assn., Va. Women Attys. Assn., U.S. Dept. Justice Advocacy Inst., Va. Law Found. Active Fairfax Choral Soc., Alban Chorale. Woodrow Wilson grad. fellow, 1966, Danforth Found. grad. fellow, 1966. Mem. ABA, Va. State Bar, D.C. Bar, Nat. Assn. Women Judges, Va. Women Attys. Assn., George Mason Inn of Ct. (master), Phi Beta Kappa. Avocation: singing. Office: US Dist Ct 401 Courthouse Sq Alexandria VA 22314-5704

BRINKER, NANCY GOODMAN, social service administrator; m. Norman Brinker; 1 child, Eric. Established Susan G. Komen Breast Cancer Found., 1982, Race for the Cure fitness/walk fundraising event, 1998—. Spkr. in field; advocate for women's health issues in Congress. Author: The Race is Run One Step at a Time; co-author: woman's Day's 1000 Questions About Women's Health. Bd. dirs. Physicians Reliance Network, Harvard Sch. Pub. Health, NYU Med. Sch. Found., Nat. Surg. Adjuvant Breast Project; mem. Nat. Cancer Adv. Bd.; bd. govs. Nat. Jewish Coalition. Recipient Jefferson award for Hero award Coping Mag., 1996, Pub. Svc. award Oncology Nursing Soc., 1996, Greatest Pub. Svc. by a Pvt. Citizen, Am. Inst. Pub. Svc., 1997, Lifetime Achievement award Nat. Breast Cancer Awareness Month, 1997, Albert Einstein's Sarnoff Vol. award, Humanitarian of Yr. award Mt. Sinai, James Ewing Layman's award Soc. Surg. Oncology, Humanitarian of Yr. award Rep. Women's Leadership Forum.

BRINKLEY, AMY WOODS, bank executive; b. Franklin, Va., Jan. 19, 1956; d. Samuel Baker and Iris (Lankford) Woods; m. Robert Gentry Brinkley, Jan. 2, 1988; 2 children. BA, U. NC, 1978. Credit analyst NCNB, Charlotte, NC, 1978-79, internat. banking officer, 1979-80, comml. banking officer Greensboro, NC, 1981-84, credit policy officer, 1985-87; sr. consumer credit policy exec. NationsBank (formerly NCNB), Greensboro, 1988—93; exec. v.p. NationsBank, 1990—99, mktg. group exec., 1993—99; pres. consumer prods. Bank Am. (formerly NationsBank), 1999—2001; chmn., risk policy Bank Am., 2001—02, deputy head, risk mgmt., 2001—02, chief risk officer, 2002—. Bd. dirs. Carolinas HealthCare Sys., Pvt. Export Funding Co. Bd. trustees Princeton Theol. Seminary; bd. advisors Partners in Out-of-Sch. Time, NC Dance Theatre, former chmn., bd. trustees; mem. U. NC bd. visitors. Mem. Women's Profl. Forum, Risk Mgmt. Roundtable, RMA Consumer Credit Execs., Phi Beta Kappa. Office: Bank Am 100 N Tryon St 18th Fl Charlotte NC 28255*

BRINKLEY, CHRISTIE, model, spokesperson, designer; b. L.A., Feb. 2, 1954; d. Don and Marge B.; m. Jean François Allaux, 1974 (div. 1981); m. Billy Joel, 1985 (div. 1994); 1 child, Alexa Ray; m. Ricky Taubman, 1995 (div. 1995); m. Peter Cook, 1996; children: Jack Paris, Sailor Lee. Attended, U. Calif., Northridge, La Grande Chaumiere. Model Elite Model Mgmt., Ford Models Inc., 1982—; co-owner Christie Brand Cosmetics, 1995—. Spokeswoman Nuskin Internat. Modeled for over 500 mag. covers incl. Sports Illustrated's annual swimsuit issue, 1979, 80, 81; product promotions incl. longest cosmetic contract with Cover Girl, Prell, Chanel No. 19 perfume; pub. Christie Brinkley's Outdoor Beauty and Fitness Book, 1983; appearance (film) National Lampoon's Vacation, 1983, Vegas Vacation, 1997, (video) Billy Joel's "Uptown Girl", River of Dreams, Keepin the Faith, Matter of Trust, (TV) Mad About You, 1994; designed album cover Billy Joel's "River of Dreams"; active infomercials Total Gym; past host Living in the 90's with Christie Brinkley CNN, others. Office: Ford Models Inc 142 Green St New York NY 10012 also: William Morris Agy 1325 Avenue Of The Americas New York NY 10019-6026

BRINKLEY, SUSAN, executive pastry chef; Student, Lynchburg Coll., 1985. Pantry position, Chapel Hill, N.C., 1985; pastry chef, 1989; exec. chef, 1990; asst. pastry chef Postrio, San Francisco, 1993, exec. pastry chef, 1998. Benefits participation in Meals on Wheels, Taste of Nations, Share Our strength, Project Open Hand. Mem. Womens Chefs and Restauranteurs, The Baker's Dozen. Office: Postrio 545 Post St San Francisco CA 94102-1228

BRINKMAN, PAULA H. music educator; b. Southampton, N.Y., June 17, 1949; d. Walter C. and Vivian Naimy Hackett; m. William J. Brinkman, Oct. 21, 1972; children: Michael C., Katherine L., Elissa J. BMusEd, SUNY, Fredonia, 1971. Choral dir. Niskayuna (N.Y.) HS, 1971—, Am. Music Abroad Red Tour, Haddonfield, NJ. Mem. Block Adv. Com., Niskayuna, NY, 2000—, Liaison Com., Niskayuna, NY, 2000—; prodr., music dir. Niskayuna HS musicals; guest condr. All-County Festivals, NY; mem. Saratoga-Potsdam Chorus, Saratoga Springs, NY, 1974—84; chairperson NYSSMA Choral Majors Festival, Niskayuna, NY, 2003—. Recipient S*t*a*r Award, GE, 1997. Mem.: Niskayuna Teachers Assn., NYSSMA, MENC. Home: 48 Pinewood Dr Scotia NY 12302 Office: Niskayuna High Sch 1626 Balltown Rd Niskayuna NY 12309 Personal E-mail: choir49@aol.com.

BRINSON, MONICA E. pharmaceutical sales representative; b. Hackensack, N.J., Feb. 19, 1971; d. Attichous and Gladys Brinson. BA, Rowan U., 1994. Lic. health and life ins. Acct. exec. Total Media, Hackensack, NJ, 1994—98; ins. sales rep. Aetna U.S. Health Care, Fairfield, NJ, 1998—99. Mem.: Women in Careers, Delta Zeta. Avocations: travel, golf, running. Home: Apt C 295 Essex St Hackensack NJ 07601 Office: Sanofi-Synthelabo Pharms 90 Park Ave New York NY 10016 Office Phone: 800-444-5052 3395. Personal E-mail: monbri201@aol.com.

BRISCAR-MARTEL, NANCY MARIE, agent, musician, educator; b. Cleve., Nov. 4, 1966; d. Richard Vincent and Rosanna Marie Briscar; m. Robert Michael Martel, Nov. 26, 1994. MusB, Baldwin Wallace Coll. Conservatory Music, 1990. Agt., mgr. Apollo String Quartet, Cleve., 1985—; pvt. instr. violin, viola and voice Cleve., 1986—; dir. Great No. Mall Christmas Choir, N. Olmsted, Ohio, 1988—91; pres., co-owner Tritone Prodns. Inc., Cleve., 1990—95; dir. music Rockport United Meth. Ch., Rocky River, Ohio, 1995—; adjudicator Omea Solo and Ensemble Competitions, Ohio, 1997—. Vocal soloist St. John's Cathedral, Cleve., 1987—89, Swing Time Big Band, Cleve., 1989—90; vocalist Cleve. Chamber Singers, 1996—97; violist in concert with Roberta Flack, Peabo Bryson, Jeffrey Osborne and Patty Austin, Cleve., 1992, in concert with Rosemary Clooney and Debby Boone, Erie, Pa., 1996, Apollo String Quartet, Cleve., 1985—2001, in concert with Roy Clark, Mansfield, Ohio, 1996, in concert with Yes, Richfield, 2001, in concert with Irish Tenors, Cleve., 2001; mem. symphony, Mansfield, Ohio, 1990—96, Wheeling, W.Va., 1990—96; violist in concert with Tony Bennett, 2002. Dir.: (theatrical production) Red, Hot and Cole, 1996, Anything Goes, 1997; author: numerous poems. Recipient Editor's Choice award, Nat. Libr. Poetry, 1999. Mem.: Nat. Assn. Music Educators, Ohio Music Educators Assn., Am. Fedn. Musicians, Nat. Assn. Women's Bus. Owners, Omicron Delta Kappa. Roman Catholic. Avocations: scrapbooks, rubber stamping, reading. Office: 3301 Wooster Rd Rocky River OH 44116-4181 Personal E-mail: nancy@apollostrings.com. Business E-Mail: RUMC44116@aol.com.

BRISCOE, ANNE M. retired scientist, educator; b. N.Y.C., Dec. 1, 1918; m. William A. Briscoe, Aug. 20, 1955 (dec. Dec. 1985); m. Theodore H. Heinly Sr., Jan. 21, 1989 (dec. Dec. 2002). MA, Vassar Coll., 1945; PhD, Yale U., 1949. From rsch. assoc. to asst. prof. Cornell U. Med. Coll., N.Y.C., 1950-56; faculty Columbia U. Coll. Physicians and Surgeons, N.Y.C., 1956—, prof. emeritus, 1987. Spl. lectr., 1987-89; lectr. Harlem Hosp. Center Sch. Nursing, 1968-77; adj. asst. prof. Hunter Coll., 1951-64, 73-75; mem. N.Y.C. Commn. on Status of Women, 1979-93, vice chair, 1982-93; non-govtl. orgn. del. to UN; adv. coun. Inst. Nuc. Power Ops., 1979-84. Contbr. articles to profl. jours. Sterling Jr. fellow, USPHS fellow, Yale U., 1949; recipient Yale medal, 1986, Susan B. Anthony award, 1989, Wilbur Cross medal Yale Grad. Sch. Sesquicentennial Convocation, 1997, Yale Fund Ch[illegible] 2000; Fellow [illegible] (mem. coun. 1982—85), chmn.'s award Yale Alumni Fund 2001), Assn. Women in Sci. (editor newsletter 1971—74, nat. pres. 1974—76), N.Y. Acad. Sci. (chair women in sci. com. 1978—92, bd. govs. 1981), Am. Inst. Chemists (sec. N.Y. chpt. 1981—83); mem.: ACS, Assn. Women in Sci. Ednl. Found. (pres. 1978—82), Fedn. Orgns. for Profl. Women (treas. 1978—80), Harvey Soc., Am. Fedn. Clin. Rsch., Am. Soc. Clin. Nutrition, Yale Grad. Sch. Alumni Assn. (pres. 1981—86), Assn. Yale Alumni (assembly rep. 1978—, bd. govs. 1982—85). Home: 2116 Sea Cres Ruskin FL 33570-6128 E-mail: drannieb@aol.com.

BRISCOE, MARY BECK, federal judge; b. Council Grove, Kans., Apr. 4, 1947; m. Charles Arthur Briscoe. BA, U. Kans., 1969, JD, 1973; LLM, U. Va., 1990. Rsch. asst. Harold L. Haun, Esq., 1973; atty.-examiner fin. divsn. ICC, 1973—74; asst. U.S. atty. for Wichita and Topeka, Kans. Dept. Justice, 1974—84; judge Kans. Ct. Appeals, 1984—95, chief judge, 1990—95; judge U.S. Ct. Appeals (10th cir.), Topeka, 1995—. Fellow: Kans. Bar Found., Am. Bar Found.; mem.: ABA, Women Attys. Assn. Topeka, Kans. Bar Assn. (Outstanding Svc. award 1992), Topeka Bar Assn., Nat. Assn. Women Judges, Am. Judicature Soc., U. Kans. Law Soc., Kans. Hist. Soc., Washburn Law Sch. Assn. (hon.). Office: US Ct Appeals 10th Cir 645 Massachusetts Ste 400 Lawrence KS 66044-2235 also: US Ct Appeals 10th Cir Byron White US Courthouse 1823 Stout St Denver CO 80257*

BRISKIN, MADELEINE, paleo-oceanographer, paleoclimatologist, micropaleontologist; b. Paris, Sept. 4, 1932; came to U.S., 1951, naturalized, 1956; d. Michel and Mina B. BS, CCNY, 1965; MS, U. Conn., 1967; PhD, Brown U., 1973. Prof. geology Geology-Physics Bldg., U. Cin., 1980—. Recipient award Rsch. Support, 1971-72, Support award NSF, 1978. Mem. AAAS, Am. Geophys. Union, Am. Quaternary Assn., Paleontologist Soc., Climap, Cin. Engrs. and Scientists Soc., Planetary Soc., Soc. Sci. Exploration, Woods Hole Oceanographic Instn., Lamont-Doherty Geol. Obs., N.Y. Acad. Scis., Sigma Xi. Achievements include discovery of 430,000 plus years astronomical cycle in deep-sea sediments; development of pulsating earth model. Office: U Cin Dept Geology Cincinnati OH 45221-0001 Home: 3346 Sherlock Ave Cincinnati OH 45220

BRISMAN, JENNIFER, event planning executive; BA in exercise and sport sci., George Wash. U. Event planner GANZI Prodns., Prodn. Group Internat., NYC; sr. conf. prodr. Internat. Comm. Mgmt., summit dir. fin., banking & ins. divsn.; founder, pres. jennifer brisman weddings newyork inc., NYC. Mem.: NY Women in Comm. Office: jennifer brisman weddings newyork inc 341 E 62nd St Penthouse on Six New York NY 10021*

BRISSETTE, MARTHA BLEVINS, lawyer; b. Salisbury, Md., Apr. 30, 1959; d. Reuben Wesley and Miriam Rebecca (Walters) Blevins; m. Henry Joseph Brissette III, May 24, 1980. BA, U. Richmond, 1981, JD, 1983. Bar: Va. 1983, U.S. Supreme Ct. 1987, Ill. 1997. Law clk. Supreme Ct. Va., Richmond, 1983-84; atty. Dept. Justice, Washington, 1984-88; staff atty. Office of the Exec. Sec., Supreme Ct. Va., Richmond, 1988; asst. atty. gen. Office of the Atty. Gen. of Va., Richmond, 1989-92; atty., v.p. counsel Lawyers Title Ins. Corp., Richmond, 1992-97; asst. counsel State Farm Ins. Cos., 1997-99; asst. atty. gen. Office of Atty. Gen. of Va., Richmond, 1999—. Mem. ABA, Phi Beta Kappa. Roman Catholic. Avocation: cake decorating. Home: 8307 Forge Rd Richmond VA 23228-3127 Office: 900 E Main St Richmond VA 23219-3513 E-mail: bmaahen@peoplecp.com.

BRISSON, HARRIET ELDREDGE, art educator; b. South Kingstown, R.I., Aug. 11, 1932; d. Lucus Gilbert and Harriet Hapgood (House) Eldredge; m. David Winslow Brisson, June 8, 1953 (dec. May 1982); 1 child, Erik. BFA, R.I. Sch. Design, 1953; MFA, Ohio U., 1955; MA in Teaching, R.I. Sch. Design, 1966. Instr. Auburn (Ala.) U., 1958-63, Providence Pub. Schs., 1966-69; from asst. prof. to prof. art R.I. Coll., Providence, 1969-98, Thorp prof. Faculty Arts and Scis. Thorp prof. artistic work R.I. Coll., 1986-87; pres. bd. trustees Studio Potter Orgn., Goffstown, N.H., 1990—. Contbr. articles to profl. jours. Recipient award R.I. Coll. Faculty of Arts and Scis. Mem. Nat. Coun. Edn. Ceramic Arts (dir.-at-large 1983-84), Internat. Sculpture Ctr. Home: 155 Green Hill Ave Wakefield RI 02879-6312 Office: RI Coll 600 Mount Pleasant Ave Providence RI 02908-1924

BRISTER, PAT, political party executive; m. Joe Brister; 5 children. Chmn. La. Rep. Party, 2000—. V.chmn. Tammany Parish Coun.; v.treas. La. State Museum bd., 1996-2000, chmn., bd. trustees Lasalle U., 1996-2002, chmn. La. Victory 2000; Nat. Committeewoman, La. Rep. Party, 1996-2000. Office: Republican Party of Louisiana 7916 Wrenwood Blvd, Suite E Baton Rouge LA 70809

BRISTO, MARCA, human services administrator; b. Albany, N.Y., June 23, 1953; d. Earl C. and Dorothy (Moore) B.; m. J. Robert Kettlewell, Oct. 15, 1988; children: Samuel Clayton Kettlewell, Madeline Elizabeth Kettlewell. BA in Sociology, Beloit Coll., 1974; BSN, Rush Coll. Nursing, Chgo., 1976. Cert. nursing. RN Rush Presbyn. St. Luke's Med. Ctr., Chgo., 1976-77, Northwestern Meml. Hosp., Chgo., 1977, family planning nurse specialist, 1978-79; exec. dir., co-founder Access Living Met. Chgo., 1979-84, pres., CEO, 1984—. Chair Nat. Coun. Disability, Washington, 1994-2002, Ill. Pub. Action Coun., 1989-94, U.S. delegate U.N. world summit on urban living and shelter, 1996, bd. dirs. Disability Funders Network, 2002-. Mem. Pres.'s Com. on Employment of People with Disabilities; mem. Pres.'s Task Force on Employment of Adults with Disabilities; bd. dirs. Rehab. Inst. Chgo.; mem. Leadership Greater Chgo.; mem. The Chgo. Network. Avocations: cooking, travel. Office: Access Living of Metropolitan Chicago 614 W Roosevelt Rd Chicago IL 61614

BRISTOR, KATHERINE M. lawyer; b. Hampton, Va., 1953; BA magna cum laude, Carleton Coll., 1975; JD, Columbia U., 1980. Bar: N.Y. 1981. Ptnr. Skadden, Arps, Slate, Meagher & Flom, N.Y.C. Harlan Fiske Stone scholar. Office: Skadden Arps Slate Meagher & Flom 4 Times Sq Fl 24 New York NY 10036-6595

BRISTOW, LOUISE ALICE, mental health nurse; b. N.Y.C., Mar. 9, 1943; d. Edward Frances and Elinore (Spuler) Leffert; m. Marshall Roger Bristow, May 31, 1970; 1 child, Christopher Darius. BS, Rutgers Coll. Nursing, 1966; MEd, Columbia U., N.Y.C., 1973. Nurse clinician Bellevue Hosp. Ctr., N.Y.C., 1967-69; cmty. mental health nurse South Beach Psychiat. Ctr., Bklyn., 1969-72; sr. psychiat. nurse NYU Med. Ctr., N.Y.C., 1974-79; clin. specialist Beth Israel Med. Ctr., N.Y.C., 1979-84; asst. prof. nursing Dalhousie U., Halifax, N.S., Can., 1973-74, CCNY, 1974-75; ind. med.-legal cons. N.Y.C., 1985-89; cons. ego devel. and child rearing, 1989—. Med.-legal cons. Commn. for Human Rights, N.Y.C., 1987-88. Active Dem. Nat. Com., N.Y.C., 1992—, LWV, N.Y.C., 1991—. NIMH scholar, Washington, 1965-72. Mem. ANA, N.Y. Nurses Assn. (mem. dist. 13 coms. 1990—). Roman Catholic. Avocations: orchid raising, painting, community activities. Home: 10 Waterside Plz New York NY 10010-2602

BRITT, MARGARET MARY, communications director; b. Rochester, NY, Jan. 26, 1962; d. James Gordon and Patricia Jean (Creedon) B. BS, Cornell U., 1983; MS in Environ. Studies, The Evergreen State Coll., 1990. Environ. scientist Monroe County Health Dept., Rochester, N.Y., 1984-87; environ. planner Wash. State Parks, Olympia, 1989-90, Wash. State Dept. Ecology, Olympia, 1990-93; asst. dir. Nat. Consortium for Environ. Edn.

and Tng., Ann Arbor, Mich., 1993-97, Mich. Sea Grant, Ann Arbor, 1997—. Adj. faculty U. Mich., 1995. Author: Evaluating Environmental Education Materials, 1994, Designing Community Education Programs, 1992. Coach, player, adv. Intramural Sports Summer League, Ann Arbor, 1993-95; capt., player Univ. Club Team, Olympia, 1987-92; organizer, co-capt. Rochester Womens Frisbee Team, 1986-87; vol. WEMU, Ann Arbor, 1995—; pres., bd. dirs., founding mem. Environ. Edn. Assn. Wash., 1989-93. Mem. N.Am. Assn. for Environ. Edn., So. Poverty Law Clinic, Three Cir. Ctr. for Environ. Edn. Avocations: cooking, hiking, reading, travel. Office: Michigan Sea Grant Coll Program 2200 Bonisteel Blvd Ann Arbor MI 48109-2099

BRITTAIN, NANCY HAMMOND, accountant; b. Athens, Pa., Oct. 29, 1954; d. Charles Avery Hammond and Leona May (Rolls) Mc Creary; m. Edward M. Brittain, Sept. 6, 1975. AS in Bus., Elmira Coll., 1989, BS in Acctg. summa cum laude, 1994. Legal sec. Friedlander, Friedlander, Reizes, Joch & Littman, P.C., Waverly, N.Y., 1973-84; bus. mgr., bd. dirs., pres. Foundry divsn. Ajax X-Ray, Inc., Sayre, Pa., 1984—; pres., bd. dirs. Ajax Leasing Corp. Mem. Athens Borough Zoning Bd., 1991-97. Mem. Inst. Mgmt. Accts., Alpha Sigma Lambda (mem. exec. com. Beta Tau chpt., various offices 1988-95). Republican. Methodist. Avocations: gardening, skiing. Home: PO Box 948 111 Vista Dr Sayre PA 18840-1107 Office: Ajax X-Ray Inc Foundry Divsn PO Box 98 Sayre PA 18840-0098

BRITTLE, LINDA VAUGHAN, reading and behavioral science educator; b. Suffolk, Va., Jan. 13, 1949; d. John Shelton Vaughan and Daphne (Williams) Dunn; m. M. Kenneth Brittle, Sr., July 24, 1971; children: Lorraine, Marshall. BS, Longwood Coll., 1971; MEd, U. Va., 1979; EdD, East Tenn. State U., 1994. 2d grade tchr. Spotsylvania County Pub. Schs., Fredericksburg, Va., 1971-74, 75-78; gifted instr. U. Va. Sch. for Gifted/Talented, Fredericksburg, Va., 1971-74, 75-78, 5th grade tchr. Henrico County Pub. Schs., Richmond, Va., 1979-80, 2d grade tchr., 1980-82; 1st grade tchr. St. Anne's Cath. Sch., Bristol, Va., 1983-90, 2d grade tchr., dir. enrichment, 1986-90; multi-age tchr. Bristol Va. City Schs., 1992-94, Chpt. I reading tchr., 1994-95, 1st grade tchr., 1995—; gifted tchr., 1996—99; asst. prin., gifted resource tchr., 1999—. Adj. asst. prof. dept. behavioral sci. King Coll., Bristol, 1996. With Bristol Hist. Bd. Dirs., 1998—, v.p., chmn. membership, 2001—02, pres., 2003—04. Recipient Doctoral fellowship East Tenn. State U., 1991, Tchr. of Yr. award Bristol Va./Tenn. Rotary, 1993, A. Margaret Boyd Internat., Delta Kappa Gamma, 1993. Mem. ASCD, Va. ASCD, Gifted Child Advocacy Assn., Va. Assn. for Edn. of Gifted (bd. dirs. 2001-), Assn. for Childhood Edn. Internat., Va. State Reading Assn., S.W. Reading Coun., Gifted Consortium (region VII 2002-, chmn. 2003), Phi Delta Kappa, Kappa Delta Pi, Gamma Beta Phi. Presbyterian. Avocations: music, art history. Home: 16 Long Crescent Dr Bristol VA 24201-3522 Office: Bristol Va City Sch 16 Long Crescent Dr Bristol VA 24201-3522

BRITTON, EMILY MADDOX, sales executive; b. Harris County, Ga., June 21, 1915; d. Charles Baker Maddox and Sara Brown Hudson; m. Joe Britton, June 25, 1935; children: Charles Wayne, Joe Maddox. Diploma, La Grange Bus. Coll., La Grange, Ga. Retail salesperson J.C. Penney, La Grange, Ga., Ala. Vol. with numerous church missions with United meth. Ch. Mem.: Paint Pushers Art Group, DAR, Anchorage Womans Club. Avocation: homemaker, family activities. Home: 1003 D St Anchorage AK 99501

BRITTON, MONICA ENA LOUISE, community health nurse, public health nurse; b. Manchester, Jamaica, July 30, 1933; came to U.S., 1967; d. Horatio Agustus and Advira (Campbell) Green; m. Frank Raphael Britton, Nov. 20, 1955. BSN, CUNY-Hunter Coll., 1977, MS in Cmty. Health Edn., 1982. RN, Fla., N.Y.; State Registered Nurse, State Cert. Midwife, Eng. Staff nurse, then sr. staff nurse N.Y.-Cornel Hosp., N.Y.C., 1967-71; staff nurse Vis. Nurse Svc., N.Y.C., 1971-72; pub. health nurse N.Y.C. Dept. Health, 1972-84, pub. health nurse supr., asst. clinics dir., 1984-92; pub. health nurse educator Renaissance Health Care, N.Y.C., 1992-95; regional nursing dir. Child Health Clinics, N.Y.C., 1995—. Mem. bd. occupational rev. N.Y.C. Dept. Health, 1984-88. Travel consult to Kenya, Ch. of God World Tour, Anderson, Ind., 1983, travel consult to Hong Kong, 1987; travel consult to Kenya and Uganda, Med. Missions Task Force, Anderson, 1993. Mem. Caring Ptnrs. Internat. (med. mission, Kenya 1997, 99). Democrat. Avocations: travel, reading, community activities, church activities, theatre. Home: 67 Park Ter E New York NY 10034-1445

BRITTON, RUTH ANN WRIGHT, elementary school educator; b. Ft. Smith, Ark., Apr. 4, 1943; d. Ralph M. and Margaret E. (Reising) Wright; m. Joseph D. Britton, Sept. 25, 1965; children: Beth, Meg, Jo. BA in Elem. Edn., Concordia Tchrs. Coll., River Forest, Ill., 1965; MS, Kans. State U., 1978. Cert. in reading K-12, elem. 1-6, developmental reading K-12, developmental edn. Tchr. 5th grade Pickens (S.C.) Sch. Dist., 1966-68; Tchr. grades 5 and 2 Manhattan (Kans.) City Schs., 1969, 77-78; Chpt. I reading tchr. Montgomery County Schs., Christianburg, Va., 1982-86; Dir. Jr. HS reading lab. Hillsborough County Schs., Tampa, Fla., 1986-92; Instr., dept. head Cochise Coll., Douglas, Ariz., 1993—. Co-author: Reading Handbook for Parents, Making Connections, a sociology and reading handbook. Recipient Helping Hands award for vol. svc. U.S. Army 7th Corps in Germany, 1980, Excellence in Edn. by Nat. Inst. for Staff and Organizational Development, 1997-98; named Outstanding Instr. Cochise Coll., 1999-2000, Tchr. of Yr. TCJS, 1989-90. Mem. Internat. Reading Assn., Literacy Vols., Coll. Reading and Learning Assn., Governor's Commn. for Svc. Learning and Volunteerism, 2002-. Office: Cochise Coll 4190 West Highway 80 Douglas AZ 85607

BRITZ LOTTI, DIANE EDWARD, investment company executive; b. York, Pa, June 15, 1952; d. Everett Frank and Billie Jacqueline (Sherrill) Britz; m. Marcello Lotti, Sept. 9, 1978 (dec. Apr. 1990); children: Ariane Elizabeth Lotti, Samantha Alexis Lotti. BA, Duke U., 1974; MBA, Columbia U., 1982. Asst. mgr. Columbia Artists, NYC, 1974-76; gen. mgr. Ea. Music Festival, Greensboro, NC, 1977-78; v.p. Britz Cobin, NYC, 1979-82; pres. Pan Oceanic Mgmt., Inc., NYC, 1983-90, Pan Oceanic Advisors, Ltd., NYC, 1988-94; chair Pan Oceanic Mgmt. Ltd., NYC, 1994-2001; mng. dir. Am. Capital Ptnr., Ltd., NYC, 1996—; chmn. Trinity Investors Fund Inc., NYC; mng. dir. ERAFO Ltd., NYC, 2000—; founding ptnr. Circle Fin. Group LLC, NYC, 2003—. Bd dirs Trinity Investors Fund Inc, Cir. Fin. LLC. Bd. advisors Turtle Bay Music Sch.; pres. Marcello Lotti Found.; trustee Lorne Weill Trust; mem. Nat. Com. Am. Fgn. Policy; bd. dirs. exec. com. Am. Acad. in Rome; chair Trinity bd. visitors Duke U. Mem.: Explorers Club (friend), Doubles Club, Columbia Bus Sch Club NY. Mem. Soc. Of Friends. Office: 45 Rockefeller Plz Ste 2077 New York NY 10111-0100

BRO, RUTH HILL, lawyer; b. Brookings, S.Dak., July 9, 1962; BA, Northwestern U., 1984; JD, U. Chgo., 1994. Atty. McBride Baker & Coles (now Holland & Knight), 1994—99, Baker & McKenzie, Chgo., 1999—2001, ptnr., 2001—. Editor: The E-Bus. Legal Arsenal: Practitioner Agreements and Checklists, 2004; co-author: Online Law, 1996, 6th edit., 2000; contbr. articles to profl. jours. Mem.: ABA (chmn. e-privacy law com., mem. coun., sci. and tech. law section, info. security com.), Ill. Bar Assn., Chgo. (Ill.) Bar Assn. (computer law com.). Office: Baker & McKenzie One Prudential Plz 130 East Randolph Dr Chicago IL 60601 Office Phone: 312-861-7985.

BROAD, BARBARA PRENTICE, retired real estate agent; b. Easton, Pa., Mar. 3, 1920; d. Donald Bishop and Mary Louise (Farnham) Prentice; m. Henry Sawyer Broad, Aug. 16, 1952 (dec. Mar. 1997); children: Louise Broad Lavine, Richard G., William G. BA, Wellesley Coll., 1941; postgrad., Northeastern U., 1951-52. Legal sec. Hutchins & Wheeler, Boston, 1946-48; sec. to Judge Charles Wyzanski U.S. Dist. Ct., Boston, 1948-52; real estate agt., 1975-2000; ret., 2000. Chmn. Princeton (N.J.) Nursery Sch.; pres. Wellesley Club Ctrl. N.J., Class of 1941 Wellesley; bd. dirs. Young Audiences N.J., 1978—93, pres., 1980—83. Lt. USNR, 1943—45. Democrat. Presbyterian. Avocations: singing in choir, tennis, bridge. Home: 33 Hedge Row Rd Princeton NJ 08540-5054

BROAD, CYNTHIA ANN MORGAN, special education educator, consultant; b. Toledo, Ohio, Apr. 19, 1947; d. James Glenn and Elaine Louise (Morris) Morgan; m. Alan Hugh Broad, Aug. 2, 1975; children: Travis Alan, Trevor Morgan. BS in Edn., Bowling Green State U., 1969, MEd, 1970, Accomplished Grad. (hon.), 1993. Cert. spl. edn. tchr., elem. tchr. Tchr. remedial reading ednl. therapy unit Toledo (Ohio) State Hosp., 1970; spl. edn. tchr. Green Elem. Sch. L'Anse Creuse (Mich.) pub. schs., 1970-81, spl. edn. tchr. Lobbestael Elem. Sch., 1982-95, spl. edn. cons., 1989-95, spl. edn. tchr. Higging Elem. Sch., 1995—. Contbr. articles to profl. jours.; developer talking animal idea telephone teachng tool, 1978. Fellow Masters Level Bowling Green State U., 1969-70; recipient Tchr. of Yr. State of Mich. Dept. Edn., 1989-90, Nat. Educator award Milken Family Found., 1990, Burger King Disting. Svc. to Edn. award, 1990. Mem. NEA, Mich. Edn. Assn., Mich. Reading Assn., Mich. Assn. Children with Learning Disabilities, Coun. Exceptional Children (Golden Nugget award 1989), Delta Kappa Gamma, Kappa Delta Pi. Avocations: technology, golf, biking, telecommunications, reading. Home: 71 S Deeplands Rd Grosse Pointe Shores MI 48236-2643 Office: L'Anse Creuse Higgins Elem Sch 29901 24 Mile Rd Chesterfield MI 48051-1760

BROAD, MARGARET CORBETT (MOLLY BROAD), academic administrator; b. Wilkes-Barre, Pa., Feb. 22, 1941; d. Stanley A. and Margaret (Kelly) Corbett; m. Robert William Broad, Aug. 25, 1962; children: Robert W. Jr., Matthew David. BA in Econs., Syracuse U., 1962, postgrad., 1971; MA in Econs., Ohio State U., 1965. Rsch. assoc. to comptr., v.p. finance Ohio State U., Columbus, 1963—65; budget and planning officer Syracuse U., NY, 1971—76; dep. dir. State Commn. Future of Postsecondary Edn. in N.Y., Albany, 1976—77; v.p. govt. and corp. rels. Syracuse U., 1977—85; exec. dir., chief exec. officer Ariz. Bd. Regents, Phoenix, 1985—92; sr. vice chancellor adminstrn. and fin. Calif. State U., 1992—93, exec. vice chancellor, COO, 1993—97; chair bd., CEO Calif. State U. Inst., 1994—97; pres. U. N.C., Chapel Hill, 1997—. Mem.: Beta Gamma Sigma, Phi Beta Kappa. Roman Catholic. Avocations: tennis, bicycling, gardening. Home: 400 E Franklin St Chapel Hill NC 27514-3707 Office: U NC Gen Adminstrn Bldg 910 Raleigh Rd Chapel Hill NC 27514-3916

BROADBENT, AMALIA SAYO CASTILLO, graphic arts designer; b. Manila, May 28, 1956; came to U.S., 1980, naturalized, 1985, d. Conrado Camilo and Eugenia de Guzman (Sayo) Castillo; m. Barrie Noel Broadbent, Mar. 14, 1981 (div. Apr. 1999); children: Charles Noel Castillo, Chandra Noel Castillo. BFA, U. Santo Tomas, 1978; postgrad., Acad. Art Coll., San Francisco, Alliance Francaise, Manila, Karilagan Finishing Sch., Manila Computer Ctr.; BA, Maryknoll Coll., 1972. Designer market rsch. Unicorp Export Inc., Makati, Manila, 1975-77; asst. advt. mgr. Dale Trading Corp., Makati, 1977-78; artist, designer, pub. rels. Resort Hotels Corp., Makati, 1978-81; prodn. artist CYB/Young & Rubicam, San Francisco, 1981-82; freelance art dir Ogilvy & Mather Direct, San Francisco, 1986; artist, designer, owner A.C. Broadbent Graphics, San Francisco, 1982—. Faculty graphic design and advt. depts. Acad. Art Coll., San Francisco. Works include: Daing na Isda, 1975, (Christmas coloring) Pepsi-Cola, 1964 (Distinctive Merit cert.), (children's books) UNESCO, 1973 (cert.). Pres. Pax Romana, Coll. of Architecture and Fine Arts, U. Santo Tomas, 1976-78, chmn. cultural sect., 1975; v.p. Atelier Cultural Soc., U. Santo Tomas, 1975-76; mem. Makati Dance Troupe, 1973-74; vol. spl. events San Francisco Mus. of Modern Art. Recipient Merit cert. Inst. Religion, 1977. Mem. Alliance Francaise de San Francisco. Roman Catholic. Office: 4380A Eagle Peak Rd Concord CA 94521-3427 E-mail: acbroad@aol.com.

BROADDUS, ANDREA LYNN, environmental policy advocate; b. Washington, D.C., Dec. 27, 1971; d. Ashton Gustave and Carolyn Edith (nee Viens) Broaddus. BS in Geology and Geophysics, U. N.C., 1996. Organizer trainee Green Corps, Madison, Wis., 1996—97; campaign coord. Wisconsin's Environ. Decade, Madison, 1997—98; state coord. New Transp. Alliance, Madison, 1997—99; Milw. mgr. Bicycle Fedn. Wis., Milw., 1999—2001; cons., Grassroots organizer Citizens for a better Environment, Milw., 1999—2000; self employed Environ. Law and Policy Ctr. of the Midwest, Chgo., 1999—2000. Bd. dirs. Am. Walks, Portland, Oreg., 2003—, Walk D.C., 2003—. Author: (report) Troubled Waters, 1997, The State of the Nation's Rail, 2004. Mem. Adv. Neighborhood Commn., 2002—; mem. steering com. Program Dane, Madison, 1996—97; bd. dirs. Pro-Rail, Madison, 1999—2000; pres. bd. dirs. Madison Hostel, 1999—2001. Sci. Opportunity Fellfellowo, U. N.C., 1995—96, Student Rsch. grantee, Am. Pub. Power Assn., Washington, 1995—96. Avocations: bicycling, running, swimming, yoga, chess. Office: Surface Transp Policy Project 1100 17th St NW 10th Fl Washington DC 20036

BROADRICK-ALLEN, SANDRA CAROL, retired city manager, consultant, civic worker; b. St. Louis, May 5, 1940; d. Charles Albert Jr. and Verna Catherine (Yount) Allen; m. King Woodard Broadrick, July 4, 1975. BS, Lindenwood Coll., 1962; MA, U. Denver, 1965; PhD, U. Ill., 1975. Cert. tchr. Ill., Mo. Tchr. home econs. Princeville (Ill.) H.S., 1962-65, guidance counselor, 1965-68; dean faculty, dean students Garland Jr. Coll., Boston, 1971—75, pres., 1975-76; adminstr. Office Arms Control, Disarmament and Internat. Security, Urbana, Ill., 1981-82; campaign mgr. for state rep. from 103d legis. dist. Ill. Ho. of Reps., 1982-84; city mgr. Village of Savoy, Ill., 1985-91; adminstrv.-exec. cons., Champaign, Ill., 1992—. Editor: County Banners of the Illinois Association for Home and Community Education, 2000; mem. editl. rev. bd. Nat. Assn. for Women Deans, Adminstrs. and Counselors Jour., 1972-74. Pres. Princeville High Sch. PTA, 1962—68; moderator Princeville Cmty. Coun., 1966—68; bd. dirs. U. YWCA, Champaign, 1983—89; mem. home econs. coun. Champaign County Coop. Ext. Svc., 1985—87, treas. unit coun., 1988—92; vice chmn., pres. Ext. Edn. Found., 1992—99, Ill. Assn. Home and Cmty. Edn., 1997—2000; mem. president's coun. U. Ill., 1998—, Busey Bank, 1998., 1998—; pres. Ill. Assn. Home and Cmty. Edn., 1997—2000; mem. precinct com. Champaign County Dem. Com, 1982—85; sr. high sch. youth fellowship advisor Princeville Presbyn. Ch., 1965—68. Recipient Leadership award Univ. YWCA, 1985, Outstanding Vol. award United Way Champaign County, 1986, cert. of recognition, Ill. Ho. of Reps., 1991; citizens lay advisor scholar Ritenour Sch. Dist., 1958-62, honors scholar Lindenwood Coll., 1958-62; grantee U.S. Office Edn., 1968-70. Mem. Assoc. Country Women of World (vice chmn. UN com. 1998-2001, chmn. 2001—, bd. dirs. 2001—), Scroll Soc., Rotary (charter pres. Savoy 1989-91, gov. dist. 6490 2001-02, coord. task force and adminstrv. coord. 2000-2001, dir. youth programs 2002-2003, chair R.I. Centennial Com. 2003—, Paul Harris fellow 1993, multiple Spirit of Paul Harris awards, others), Phi Delta Kappa, Kappa Omicron Phi. Avocations: international travel, archaeology of lost civilizations, earthwatch and global volunteer, gardening. E-mail: sandyba@net66.com.

BROADWATER, SHIRLEY MARIE, psychologist; b. Rosemont, W.Va., May 8, 1937; d. Robert Brooks and Erma Pearl (Wimer) Riffle; children: Cheryl Lynn Daugherty Johnson, Robert L. Daugherty Jr.; m. J. Rodney Broadwater, Aug. 28, 1982. Student, Indiana U. Pa., 1965, 66, U. Pitts., Johnstown, Pa., 1966-67, 68-69; AB in Secondary Edn. with highest honors, West Liberty State Coll., 1972; MS in Psychology, Shippensburg (Pa.) U., 1983. Cert. secondary tchr., Pa. Psychotherapist Contemporary Psychol. Svcs., Chambersburg, Pa., 1984-88; pvt. practice psychology Broadwater Psychol. Svcs., Chambersburg, 1988—. Psychologist to dep. coroner, Chambersburg, 1988-99. Vol. Piney Mountain Nursing Home, Fayetteville, Pa., 1981; telephone worker Contact Teleminsitry 24 Hour Hotline, Chambersburg, 1981-84, support worker, 1984-92; bd. dirs. Family Health Svcs., Chambersburg, 1984-89. Mem. APA (assoc.), Pa. Psychol. Assn. Republican. Methodist. Avocations: reading, racquetball, aerobic dancing, painting, piano, computer. Office: 394 Floral Ave Chambersburg PA 17201-3411

BROCK, ANGELA EULENE DOUGLASS, education educator; b. McMinnville, Tenn., Apr. 16, 1972; d. John Douglass, Shirley Eulene (McGee) Douglass; m. Tyson Lynn Brock, June 26, 1993; children: Allison Victoria, Jonathan Hunter. BS, Mid. Tenn. State U., 1993, MEd, 1995. Tchr. F.C. Boyd, Sr. Christian Sch., McMinnville, Tenn., 1994—99; adj. faculty Motlow State C.C., McMinnville, 2000—. Leader Girl Scouts U.S., 2002—; Bible tchr. Ctrl. Ch. of Christ, McMinnville, 1987—, event coord., 1998—. Mem.: DAR, AAUW. Avocations: camping, crafts, travel, sewing. Home: 1668 Fairview Rd Mc Minnville TN 37110

BROCK, DEE SALA, television executive, educator, writer, consultant; b. Covington, Okla., June 7, 1930; d. Lester Edward and Vera Mae (Bowers) Sala; m. Robert Wesley Brock, June 8, 1952 (div. 1979); children: Baron Sala, Bishop Chapman, Bevin Bowers. BA, U. North Tex., 1950, MA, 1956, PhD, 1985. Tchr. high sch. Dallas Ind. Sch. Dist., 1952-66; dir. Dallas Cowboy Cheerleaders, 1960-75; mem. faculty, adminstr. Dallas County Community Coll. Dist., 1966-74, telecourse writer, producer, adminstr., 1974-75, dir. mktg. info., 1975-80; dir., v.p. PBS, Washington, 1980-89, sr. v.p. edn. Alexandria, Va., 1989-90; pres. Dee Brock & Assocs., Plano, Tex., 1991-98; pub. FAQs Press, 1999—. Bd. dirs. Pub. Svc. Satellite Consortium, U.S. Basics; adv. bd. Learning Link, 1987-90, Telcon Industry, 1990-91; chair exec. coun. U. of the World, 1989-91; adv. coun. Triangle Coalition, 1989-91; spkr. in field. Author: Writing for a Reason: Study Guide, 1974; author: (with Jeriel Howard) Writing for a Reason, 1978; author: (with Laura Derr) The World of F. Scott Fitzgerald, 1980; author: (with Deborah Burkett and Carole Wilson) Troup Goes to War: World War II, A Collection of Memories, 1999; author: (with Linda Resnik) Food FAQs: Substitutions, Yields & Equivalents, 2000; author: (with JoAnna Lewis) 100 Great Fundraising Ideas Celebrating 100 Years of Texas Library, 2002; mem. editl. bd. : Am. Jour. Distance Edn., 1987—90; prodr.: (internat. teleconf.) Out of the Red, 1991; prodr., writer: TV series and workbook Communicating in English in the Healthcare Workplace, 1994; contbr. articles to profl. jours. Trustee Coun. for Adult and Experiential Learning, 1989—99; chair spl. task force Mcpl. Libr. Friends of Libr., 1996, pres., 1997—; lay rep. N.E. Tex. Libr. Sys., 1996—, chair planning to plan com., 1997—98, adv. coun., 1998—, vice chair, 1998—2000, chair, 2000—; chmn. Strategic Planning Com., 1999; fundraising co-chair Komen Tyler Race for the Cure, 1999; active PTA, Dallas; pres. Littera, 2002—, Friends of the Troup Libr., 1998—; chair Libr. Friends, Trustees and Advs., 2001—03; bd. dirs. Tyler Civic Theatre Ctr., Coalition for the Advancement of Citizenship, 1988—90. Reynolds Econ. fellow U. N.C., 1966; Literacy award N. Tex. Reading Coun., 1980, Nat. Person of Yr. award Nat. Coun. on Community and Continuing Edn., 1985, Award for Excellence in TV Programming NEA, 1986; recipient Outstanding Career Achievement award ITC Am. Assn. Community and Jr. Colls., 1990. Mem. NEH (nat. bd. cons. 1980-85), LWV (bd. dirs., v.p. cmty. rels. Tyler chpt. 2002-03, pres. 2003—), U.S. Distance Learning Assn. (bd. dirs. 1989-91, adv. bd. 1989), So. Assn. Colls. and Schs. (project 1990 task force 1984-86), Nat. Assn. Ednl. Broadcasters (steering com. 1979-81), Assn. Ednl. Comms. Tech., Nat. Coun. Tchrs. English (pres. S.W. regional coun. 1972-74), Tex. Libr. Assn. (legis. com. 1999—, chair roundtable 2001—). Multimedia achievements include being co-patentee video indexing system; design of and management of PBS Adult Learning Service and PBS Adult Learning Satellite Service. Home and Office: 3529 Woods Blvd Tyler TX 75707

BROCK, DOROTHY DIXON, psychologist, educator; b. St. Louis, Nov. 16, 1954; d. Arthur Roy and Dorothy Arnett Dixon. BS, Oral Roberts U., 1978; MEd, Ga. State U., 1980, PhD, 1991. Lic. psychologist Ga.; cert. tchr. Okla. Tchr. speech and English Clinton Jr. HS, Tulsa, Okla., 1978—79; co-founder Landmark Counseling Ctr., Norcross, Ga., 1981—83; contract therapist Rapha, Dunwoody, Ga., 1994—96; pvt. practice psychologist Norcross, Ga., 1995—97, 2001—; adj. instr. Toccoa Falls (Ga.) Coll., 1995—96, instr., 2001—02, asst. prof., 2002—, coll. counselor, 2003—; clin. coord. New Life Clinics, Smyrna, Ga., 1997—2000. Mem.: APA, Am. Assn. Christian Counselors. Office: Toccoa Falls Coll Toccoa Falls GA 30598

BROCK, KARENA DIANE, dancer, educator; b. L.A., Sept. 21, 1942; d. Orville DeLoss and Sallie Alice (Anderson) B.; m. Ted Kivitt, Apr. 16, 1965 (div. 1978); m. John Robert Carlyle, June 28, 1985; 1 child, Timothy John. Grad. H.S., Kansas City, Mo. Tchr. master classes Radford (Va.) Coll., U. Louisville, U. Tampa; staff tchr. Bklyn. Coll.; mem. faculty SUNY-Purchase; artistic dir., choreographer, tchr. and founder Hilton Head Dance Theater and Sch., Hilton Head Island, SC, 1985—. Guest tchr. S.C. Dance Inst., Columbia, 1993-94, Walnut Hill Sch., Boston, Savannah Ballet, Cleve. Ballet; tchr. master classes Florence, S.C., Columbia; guest choreographer Towson (Md.) U., 2000, Carolina Ballet Theatre, Greeville, S.C., 1998. Dancer, David Lichine Concert Group, L.A., 1960-61, Netherlands Nat. Ballet Co., Amsterdam, 1961-62, mem. corps, Am. Ballet Theatre, N.Y.C., 1963-68, soloist, 1968-73, prin. ballerina, 1973-79, artistic dir., prima ballerina, choreographer, Savannah (Ga.) Ballet Co., 1979-85; co-artistic dir. and choreographer Ballet South, Savannah, 1992-96; guest artist, Miami (Fla.) Civic Ballet, Macon (Ga.) Civic Ballet, Tampa (Fla.) Civic Ballet, U. Ill. Ballet Co., Champaign, San Jose (Calif.) Civic Ballet, Ballet de San Juan, P.R., Gala Ballet, Amarillo (Tex.) Civic Ballet, Maywood Ballet Co., Phila., U. Wis., Milw. Civic Ballet, Stars of Am. Ballet, various TV shows, White House, 1966, 69. Mem. adv. bd. S.C. Arts Commn., Columbia, 1988—; hon. mem. bd. dirs. Columbia City Ballet. Mem. AFTRA, AGVA, Am. Guild Mus. Artists. Office: Hilton Head Dance Theater and Sch 24 Palmetto Business Park Rd Hilton Head Island SC 29928-3234 Office Phone: 843-785-5477. Personal E-mail: timo7@hargray.com.

BROCK, KATHY, newscaster; married; 2 children. Degree in Journalism, Wash. State U. Anchor and reporter KWSU-TV, Pullman, Wash., KEPR-TV, Pasco, KCBI-YV, Boise, Idaho; weekend anchor and reporter KUTV-TV, Salt Lake City, 1984, anchor noon and 6pm news, 1985—90; co-anchor News This Morning and reporter WLS-TV, Chgo., 1990—93, co-anchor 6pm news, 1993—, co-anchor 10pm news, 2003—. TV Journalist (documentaries) Mali, West Africa, 1989 (Edward R. Murrow award, 1989, IRIS award, 1989). Office: WLS-TV 190 N State St Chicago IL 60601

BROCK, KATRINA RAE, music educator; b. Montgomery, Ala., Aug. 18, 1977; d. Kathreen Louis and Ray Von Straughn; m. Joey Thomas Brock. BA in Elem. Edn., BA in Early Childhood Edn., Huntingdon Coll., Montgomery, Ala., 2001. Cert. elem. tchr. Ala., 2001. Sales assoc. Big B/ Revco / CVS, Montgomery, Ala., 1995—98; work study Huntingdon Coll. Performing Arts Dept., Montgomery, Ala., 1995—98, Huntingdon Coll. Libr., Montgomery, Ala., 1997—98; camp counselor Strinfellows Camp - Huntingdon Coll. and Montgomery Symphony Orch., Montgomery, Ala., 1999—2000; choir singer St. John's Episcopal Ch., Montgomery, Ala., 1995—2001; libr. page Montgomery City/ County Libr., 1998—2000, libr. asst., 2001; music specialist at Brewbaker Primary Montgomery County Pub. Schs., Montgomery, Ala., 2001—. Tutoring Montgomery City County Pub. Libr., Montgomery, Ala., 2000—02; childress pastor's wife Bethel Assembly of God, 2002—, choir and praise team mem., 2001; camp counselor Assembly of God Camp, Springville, Ala., 2003; puppet team co-dir. Bethel Assembly of God, Wetumpka, Ala., 2002. Mem.: NEA, Montgomery County Edn. Assn., Ala. Edcation Assn., Music Educators Nat. Conf., Student Ala. Educators Assn., Collegate Music Educators Nat.

Conf. (treas. 1997—2000), Cir. K. Pentacostal. Avocations: singing, acting, puppetry, travel, teaching and tutoring. Home: 231 Landmark Dr Montgomery AL 36117 Office: Brewbaker Primary 4445 Brewbaker Dr Montgomery AL 36116 Personal E-mail: kat4cows@hotmail.com

BROCK, ROSLYN [illegible], association executive; BS magna cum laude, Va. Union U., 1987; M in Health Svcs. Adminstrn., George Washington U., 1989; MBA, Northwestern U., 1999. Dir. sys. fund devel. Sisters of Bon Secours Health Sys. Inc.; vice chair nat. bd. dirs. NAACP, Balt., 2001—. Vol. elem. sch. instr. Jr. Achievement; host local cable access program Cmty. Voices. Named a Future Leader, Ebony mag., 1989; named Outstanding Alumna, Va. Union U., hon. chairperson, Nat. Black Family Summit, Young Leaders fellow, Nat. Com. on U.S.-China Rels., 2003; named one of 100 Young Women of Promise, Good Housekeeping, 1987; recipient Martin Luther King, jr. medal for human rights, George Washington U. Mem.: APHA, Nat. Assn. Health Svc. Execs., The Links, Inc., Nat. Black MBA Assn., Alpha Kappa Alpha Sorority, INc. Office: NAACP 4805 Mt Hope Dr Baltimore MD 21215*

BROCKETT, FRANCESCA L. retail executive; BA, Harvard U., 1982; MBA, Stanford (Calif.) U., 1986. Cons. Booz-Allen and Hamilton, Atlanta, 1982—85, McKinsey and Co., Houston, 1986—92; with PepsiCo, New Eng., 1994—95, Irvine, Calif., 1995—97, Tricon Global Restaurants, Louisville, 1997—98; from sr. v.p. strategic planning and bus. devel. to exec. v.p. Toys "R" Us, Inc., Wayne, NJ, 1998—2000, exec. v.p. strategic planning and bus. devel., 2000—. Office: Toys R Us Inc 1 Geoffrey Way Wayne NJ 07470-2030 Business E-Mail: brocketf@toysrus.com.

BROCKHOFF, ELIZABETH KATHERINE, music educator; d. Bernard and Ruth Falksen; m. Merle Lee Brockhoff, Aug. 17, 1980; children: Carl Philip, Nyssa Elise. BA, Dana Coll., 1980; MusM, U. Nebr., 1998. Cert. tchr. Nebr. State Dept. Edn., N.Y. State Edn. Dept. K-12 vocal music tchr. Adams (Nebr.) Pub. Sch., 1986—91; 9-12 vocal music tchr. Pius X HS, Lincoln, Nebr., 1991—98, Lincoln HS, 1998—2001; elem. gen. music tchr. Chestnut Hill Elem., Liverpool, NY, 2001—02; vocal music tchr. Hannibal (N.Y.) Jr./Sr. HS, 2002—. Mem.: Oswego County Music Educators Assn. (treas. 2003—), VoiceCare Network, N.Y. State Sch. Music Assn., Am. Choral Dirs. Assn., Music Educators Nat. Conf.

BROCKIE, PAMELA, motion picture executive; BA, UCLA, 1972, JD, 1975. Mem. staff MCA; sr. v.p. bus. affairs ICM, Beverly Hills, Calif., 1984—. Mem. Next Generation Coun., Motion Picture and T.V. Fund Found. Mem. Women in Film (bd. dirs.). Office: ICM 8942 Wilshire Blvd Beverly Hills CA 90211-1934

BROCKWAY, LAURIE SUE, editor, journalist, author, minister; b. N.Y.C., Dec. 18, 1956; d. Lee L. and Shirley Ruth Brockway; 1 child, Alexander Kent Garrett. AA, Laguardia C.C., 1978; student in Arts, Hunter Coll. CUNY, 1978-81; MSC, The New Seminary, 1999. Features editor, crime reporter The Bklyn. Paper, 1978-81; editor-in-chief The Iniator, N.Y.C., 1982-83; pub., editor The Transformer, N.Y.C., 1983-84; co-prodr., writer The Brockway Good News Report, N.Y.C., 1984-85; N.Y. bur. chief Women's News, N.Y.C., 1983-85, Manhattan corr., 1985—2000, mng. editor, 1990; account supr. Brockway Assocs., Inc., N.Y.C., 1985-88. Tchr. women's sexuality, spirituality, 1990—; mem. faculty The Seminar Ctr., 1998—. Author: Network Your Way to Endless Romance, 1998, How to Seduce a Man and Keep Him Seduced, 1999, A Goddess Is a Girl's Best Friend, 2002. Recipient LaGuardia Meml. award, 1978, LaGuardia Student Coun. scholar, 1978, Expository Writing award, LaGuardia English Dept., 1978, Woman of Achievement award Women's News, 1997. Home and Office: 83-27 159th St Jamaica NY 11432

BRODA, C. DENISE, education educator; b. Wooster, Ohio, Apr. 15, 1960; d. Karen L. Warden Canankamp and David Canankamp(Stepfather); m. Martin P. Broda, Oct. 18, 1990; 1 child, Stefan Jeffery Bing. BA in Spanish, Coll. of Wooster, 1992—96; MA in Spanish summa cum laude, MA in edn., U. of Akron, 1996—98. Cert. Teaching K-12 Dept. of Edn., State of Ohio, 1998. Fitness instr. YMCA, Wooster, Ohio, 1986—96; payroll coord. Coll. of Wooster, 1989—92, rsch. asst. in anthropology, 1996—97, Spanish instr., 1997; tchr. Spanish Copley-Fairlawn Schools, Copley, Ohio, 1998—; adj. faculty U. of Akron, Ohio, 1998—2001; reader AP Spanish test Ednl. Testing Svc., Princeton, 2002—. Asst. speech and debate team coach Copley H.S., Ohio, 2000—, Spanish club adv.; tutor Coll. of Wooster, 1994—96. Contbr. articles (newspaper) The Daily Record. Vol. translator UN Guatemalan refugee camp, Quetzal-Edzna, Mexico, 1996; shelter vol. Every Woman's Ho., Wooster, Ohio, 1993—96; vol. big Big Bros. - Big Sisters, Wooster, Ohio, 1983—87; corp. challenge team capt. Coll. of Wooster, 1990; membership com. United Meth. Ch., Wooster, 1998—2001. Recipient Pablo Valencia prize Excellence in Spanish, 1996; Ohio Regents fellowship, Ohio Regents, 1996—98, Grad. fellowship, U. of Akron, 1996—98, Academic scholarship for grad. work, 1998, Leslie Gerding scholarship, Coll. of Wooster, 1995—96, Academic and Achievement award, 1992—96. Mem.: Am. Assn. of Teachers of Spanish and Portuguese, Ohio Fgn. Lang. Assn., Phi Beta Kappa. Avocations: travel, hiking, reading, writing. Home: 959 Marilyn Dr Wooster OH 44691 Office: Copley-Fairlawn Schools 3797 Ridgewood Rd Copley OH 44321 Personal E-mail: gringa@sssnet.com.

BRODBECK, MARY LOU, artist, furniture designer; b. Hastings, Mich., Nov. 25, 1958; d. Willard Nathan and Margaret Grace (Balduf) B.; m. John Joseph Schmitt, May 20, 1995; 1 stepchild, Jack. BFA, Mich. State U., 1982; MFA, Western Mich. U., 1999. Assoc. indsl. designer Haworth, Holland, Mich., 1985-90; freelance designer, Kalamazoo, 1990—. Cons. indsl. designer Steelcase, Inc., Grand Rapids, Mich., 1993-94 One-woman shows include Water Street Gallery, Saugatuck, Mich., 1992-93, UpJohn Corp., Kalamazoo, 1992, Deborah's Choice Gallery, Muskgeon, Mich., 1992, Kingscott Gallery, Kalamazoo, 1998, Carnegie Ctr. for the Arts, Three Rivers, Mich., 1998, Cmty. Arts Ctr., Hancock, Mich., 1999, New Moon Gallery, Benton Harbor, Mich., 2000, Oasis Gallery, Marquette, Mich., 2002, Lansing Art Gallery, 2003, Southwestern Mich. Coll., Dowagiac, 2003; patentee for furniture designs. Vol. leader Campfire Girls, Douglas, Mich., 1988-89; mem. Douglas (Mich.) Planning Commn., 1995-98. Recipient purchase award Holland Arts Coun., 1990, Krasl Art Ctr., St. Joseph, Mich., 1991, cash award Holland Friends of Art, 1990, cash award Artlink, Ft. Wayne, Ind., 2002, 3d Pl. Internat. Print Competition, Hollywood, Fla., 2002, Best Series award Peninsula Art Sch., Fish Creek, Wis., 2002; Bunka-Cho fellow Japanese Govt., 1998. Avocations: alto saxophone, swimming. Home: 471 W South St Apt 503 Kalamazoo MI 49007-4677 Office Phone: 269-344-6654.

BRODER, GAIL STEINMETZ, lawyer; b. Bklyn., Oct. 18, 1944; m. Samuel Broder, 1966. BA, CUNY, 1966; MA, U. Mich., 1971; JD with honors, George Washington U., 1979; MS in Clin. Counseling, Johns Hopkins U., 2002. Bar: Md., 1980. Pvt. practice, Rockville, Md., 1980-84; staff atty. Vet. Adminstrn., Washington, 1984-89; sr. atty. U.S. Dept. HHS, Washington, 1989-95; pres., founder, exec. dir. Cancer Survivorship Alliance of South Fla., Ft. Lauderdale, 1995—98. Office: 401 N Washington St Rockville MD 20850

BRODER, SHARI BRYANT, arbitrator, mediator; b. New Hyde Park, N.Y., June 10, 1955; d. Harold S. and Lorraine Natalie (Sidewitz) B.; m. Eric Joseph Bryant, Mar. 19, 1988; children: Andrea Rose Bryant, Eliza Anna Bryant. BA, U. Md., 1977; JD, U. Maine, 1986. Bar: Maine 1986. Legis. aide Rep. Olympia Snowe, Washington, 1979-83; law clk. Pierce, Atwood, Portland, Maine, 1985-86, Justice Sidney W. Wernick, Portland, Maine, 1986-87, Maine Superior Ct., Portland, Maine, 1986-87; assoc. lawyer Brann & Isaacson, Lewiston, Maine, 1987-91; arbitrator, mediator, hearing officer pvt. practice, Freeport, Maine, 1991—; hearing officer Maine Dept. Labor, Freeport, 1993—2002. Bd. dirs., pres. Maine Arts, Inc., Portland, 1991-96; clk., bd. dirs. The Children's Rainforest, Lewiston, 1988-2002. Recipient Disting. Graduate [illegible] U. Maine, 1986. Mem. Assn. for Conflict Resolution, Am. Arbitration Assn. (arbitrator), Maine State Bar Assn. (chair alternative dispute resolution sect. 1996-99), Maine Assn. Dispute Resolution Profls. (pres. 1997). Avocations: painting, ceramics, yoga, hiking, gourmet cooking. Office: PO Box 158 Freeport ME 04032-0158

BRODERSON, THELMA SYLVIA, marketing professional; b. St. Louis, Feb. 6, 1932; d. Harry and Lillian (Fishman) B. BA, U. Denver, 1953; postgrad., Washington U., St. Louis, 2001—. Marketer Marsh & McLennan, Inc., St. Louis, 1966-85; account exec. Daniel & Henry Co., St. Louis, 1985-87; marketer G. Steven DeMaster, Inc. at Crane Agy., St. Louis, 1987-99. Prodr. Harry Fender Program Sta. KMOX-CBS, St. Louis, 1968-74; columnist The Oil Can, 1972-75. Tchr. religious sch. United Hebrew Temple, St. Louis, 1956-63. Donor Harry Fender Memorabilia to St. Louis Pub. Libr. Media Archives and Rare Books Collection, 1997. Mem.: Phi Beta Kappa. Avocations: theater, arts.

BRODIE-BALDWIN, HELEN SYLVIA, retired college and human services administrator; d. Adolphus T. and Myrtilla Brodie; m. Wilmer Baldwin, Sept. 6, 1966; 1 child, Trevor Adolphus Avery Baldwin. BA, Hunter Coll., 1956; MA, Columbia U., 1963. Asst. prof. Queensborough C.C., Bayside, NY, 1965—82, dir. counseling-student pers.; asst. prof. CUNY, 1965—82; exec. dir. Minisink Town Ho. and Camp, N.Y.C., 1979—91; asst. to the pres. York Coll. CUNY, Jamaica, NY, 1993—94; exec. dir. The Harlem Cmty. Inc., N.Y.C., 1995—97; pres., ceo Catalyst Consulting Group Internat., N.Y.C., 1999—. Cons. Nat. Conf. of Black Mayors, Atlanta, 2001—; bd. dirs. Louis Aug. Jonas Found., Rhinebeck, NY; cons. Murphy Fine Arts Ctr. Morgan State U., Balt., 2002—; adv. coun. N.Y. Women's Found., N.Y.C., 1988—94. Prodr.: (films) Lucky Devil, 2002; author: Holly's Harlem, 2004; editor (founder): UPTOWN: The Voice of Ctrl. Harlem; prodr.: (plays) Show of Shows. Bd. dirs. Cmty. Bd. 10, N.Y.C., 1989—97; chmn. NYCMS Cadet Corps, Bronx, NY, 1970—79; com. chmn. N.Y.C. Mission Soc., The Cathedral Sch. of St. John the Divine, N.Y.C., YWCA-West Side, N.Y.C., 1970—74; nat. v.p. Am. Camping Assoc., 1988—90, 1992—99. Grantee, Hart Found., 1970, Am. Forum For African Studies, 1970; scholar, NYC Mission Soc., 1952—56. Mem.: Nat. Assn. Fgn. Student Advisors (com. chmn. 1970—77), Nat. Assn. Female Execs., Am. Women's Club, Delta Sigma Theta (life; v.p.rho chpt. 1954—56). Democrat. Avocations: writing, travel. Home and Office: Catalyst Consulting Group International POBox 250786 Columbia Univ Station New York NY 10025-1509 E-mail: hsbbest@msn.com.

BRODKIN, ADELE RUTH MEYER, psychologist; b. N.Y.C., July 8, 1934; d. Abraham J. and Helen (Honig) Meyer; m. Roger Harrison Brodkin, Jan. 26, 1957; children: Elizabeth Anne Brodkin Brauer, Edward Stuart. BA, Sarah Lawrence Coll., 1956; MA, Columbia U., 1959; PhD, Rutgers U., 1977. Lic. psychologist N.J. Sch. psychologist pub. schs., 1961—73; assoc. dir. Infant Child Devel. Ctr. St. Barnabas Med. Ctr., Livingston, N.J., 1977-79; clin. asst. prof. dept. psychiatry U. Medicine and Dentistry N.J., Newark, 1979-90, clin. assoc. prof., 1990-2001. Vis. scholar Hasting Ctr. for Life Scis., NY, 1979; sr. child devel. cons.; cons. Scholastic, Inc., 1988—. Author: Fresh Approaches to Working with Problematic Behavior, 2001, The Lonely Only Dog, 1998, Between Teacher and Parent, Supporting Young Children As They Grow, 1994; author: (with A.T. Jersild and E.A. Lazar) The Meaning of Psychotherapy in the Teacher's Life and Work, 1962; contbr. articles to profl. jours. Fellow, NIMH, 1962; Adelaide M. Ayer fellow, Columbia U., 1962—63, Louis Bevier fellow, Rutgers U., 1976—77. Fellow: Am. Orthopsychiat. Assn.; mem.: APA, Am. Sociol. Assn., N.J. Psychol. Assn. Home and Office: 2 Trevino Ct Florham Park NJ 07932-2724

BRODY, JACQUELINE, editor; b. Utica, N.Y., Jan. 23, 1932; d. Jack and Mary (Childress) Galloway; m. Eugene D. Brody, Apr. 5, 1959; children: Jessica, Leslie. AB, Vassar Coll., 1953; postgrad., London Sch. Econs., 1953-56. Assoc. editor Crowell Collier Macmillan, N.Y.C., 1963-67; writer Coun. Fgn. Rels., N.Y.C., 1968-69; mng. editor Print Collector's Newsletter, N.Y.C., 1971-72, editor, 1972-96, art writer, 1996—; dir., v.p. Picanet, Inc., N.Y.C., 1996—. Office: 2765 Deerfield Rd Sag Harbor NY 11963

BRODY, JANE ELLEN, journalist, researcher; b. Bklyn., May 19, 1941; d. Sidney and Lillian (Kellner) B.; m. Richard Engquist, Oct. 2, 1966; children: Lee Erik and Lorin Michael Engquist (twins). BS, N.Y. State Coll. Agr., Cornell U., 1962; MS in Journalism, U. Wis., 1963; HHD (hon.), Princeton U., 1987; LHD (hon.), Hamline U., 1993, SUNY Hlth. Sci. Ctr., 1999; LHD U. Minn. (hon.), 2000. Reporter Mpls. Tribune, 1963-65; sci. writer, personal health columnist N.Y. Times, N.Y.C., 1965—; mem. adv. council N.Y. State Coll. Agr., Cornell U., 1971-77. Author: (with Richard Engquist) Secrets of Good Health, 1970; (with Arthur Holleb) You Can Fight Cancer and Win, 1977, Jane Brody's Nutrition Book, 1981, Jane Brody's The New York Times Guide to Personal Health, 1982, Jane Brody's Good Food Book, 1985, Jane Brody's Good Food Gourmet, 1990; (with Richard Flaste) Jane Brody's Good Seafood Book, 1994, Jane Brody's Cold and Flu Fighter, 1995, Jane Brody's Allergy Fighter, 1997, The New York Times Book of Health, 1997, The New York Times Book of Women's Health, 2000, The New York Times Book of Alternative Health, 2001. Recipient numerous writing awards including Howard Blakeslee award Am. Heart Assn., 1971, Sci. Writers' award ADA, 1978, J.C. Penney-U. Mo. Journalism award, 1978, Lifeline award Am. Health Found., 1978 Jewish. Office: NY Times 229 W 43d St New York NY 10036-3913

BRODY-LEDERMAN, STEPHANIE, artist; b. N.Y.C. d. Maxwell and Ann (Rockett) Brody. Student, U. Mich.; BS in Design, Finch Coll., 1961; MA in Painting, L.I. U., 1975. One-person exhbns. Franklin Furnace, N.Y.C., 1979, Kathryn Markel Fine Arts, N.Y.C., 1979, 81, 83, Katzen/Brown Gallery, N.Y.C., 1988, 89, Real Artways, Hartford, Conn., 1984, Alfred U., 1990, Hal Katzen Gallery, N.Y.C., 1992, Hillwood Art Mus., Brookville, N.Y., 1992, Casements Mus., Ormond Beach, Fla., 1994, Broward Cmty. Coll., Ft. Lauderdale, Fla., 1994, Hebrew Home for the Aged, N.Y.C., 1994-95, Galerie Caroline Corre, Paris, 1995, La. State U., Shreveport, 1995, Marc Miller Gallery, East Hampton, N.Y., 1996, Pierogi 2000, Bklyn., 1996, Arlene Bujese Gallery, Easthampton, N.Y., 1997, 123 Watts Gallery, N.Y.C., 1998, Edison Coll., Ft. Myers, Fla., 2001, Arlene Bujese, E. Hampton, N.Y., 2001, Hudson Opera House, Hudson, N.Y., 2001, Arlene Bujese Gallery, East Hampton, N.Y., 2002, Cleary, Gottlieb, Steen & Hamilton Artists Program, N.Y.C., 2003; exhibited in numerous group shows including Newark Mus., 1983, Met. Mus. Art, N.Y.C., 1986, Queens Mus., 1989, Basel Art Fair, 1989, Caroline Corre, Paris, 1991, R.I. Mus. Art, 1991, Am. Acad. Arts & Letters, N.Y.C., 1992, Guild Hall Mus., East Hampton, N.Y., 1993, Ind. U, Terre Haute, 1993, Jewish Mus., N.Y.C., 1994, Nat. Mus. Women in Arts, Washington, 1994, Ronald Feldman Gallery, N.Y.C., 1995, Alternative Mus., N.Y.C., 1995, Eugenia Cucalon Gallery, N.Y.C., 1995, Rotunda Gallery, Bklyn., 1995, The Museums at Stony Brook, N.Y., 1996, Espace Eiffel-Branly, Paris, 1996, Fotouhi Cramer Gallery, N.Y.C., 1996, 123 Watts Gallery, N.Y.C., 1996, Mediatèque, Les Mureaux, France, 1996, San Francisco State U., 1997, Isis Conceptual Lab., West Branch, Iowa, 1997, Harper Collins Exhbn. Space, N.Y.C., 1997, Bklyn. Mus., 1997, Gasworks Gallery, London, 1997, Parrish Art Mus., Southampton, N.Y., 1998, Neuburger Mus., Purchase, N.Y., 1998, Librairie Nicaise, Paris, 1998, Connecticut Coll., New London, 1998, Montclair (N.J.) Art Mus., 1999, Kutztown State Coll., Kutztown, Pa., 1999, Mpls. Coll. Art, 1999, Musee Bourdelle, Paris, 1999—, U. of the Arts, Phila., 1999, Generous Miraeles Gallery, N.Y.C., 1999, Limn Gallery, San Francisco, Bklyn. Mus., N.Y.C., 2000, Eugenia Cucalon Gallery, N.Y.C., 2000, Arlene Bujese Gallery, East Hampton, 2000, N.Y. Sandusky Cultural Ctr., Sandusky, Ohio, 2000, Nassau Comty. Coll., Garden City, N.Y., 2000, Fla. Atlantic U., Boca Raton, Fla., 2000, [illegible], 2001, Hillwood Art Mus., LI, 2001, Hungarian Consulate, NYC, 2001, Coll. Art and Design, Bristol, Eng., 2001, Md. Art Place, Balt., 2002, Woodstock (NY) Guild, 2002, 450 Gallery, NYC, 2002, Metaphor Gallery, Bklyn., 2002, Topkapi Mus, Istanbul, 2002, Snug Harbor Culture Ct., Staten Island, N.Y., 2002, Gracie Mansions Booth, Javits Galleria, N.Y.C., 2003, Chelsea Art Mus., NY, 2003, Berliner Kunstproject, Berlin, 2003, OK Harris Gallery, N.Y.C., 2003, Nat. Mus. Woman in the Arts, Washington, 2003; represented in permanent collections Newark Mus., Mus. Modern Art, Prudential Ins., Bertelsmann Music Group, Guild Hall Mus., East Hampton, L.I., Chase Manhattan Bank, N.Y. Health and Hosp. Corp., Victoria & Albert Mus., London, Doubleday Books, Saks 5th Ave. Corp., Vero Beach Ctr. for the Arts, Vero Beach, Fla., Bklyn. Mus., Montclair Art Mus., N.J., Centre Du Livre D'Artiste, Verderonne, France, Hancock Info. Group, Orlando, Fla., 2002; commd. series of work on paper Cmty. Rsch. Initiative on AIDS, 1999; cover painting Paris Rev. Mag.; Cowparade pub. artwork, 2000; contbg. artist "Fresh" project, 2003; artist portfolio Gastronomica Mag., 2003. Recipient Hassam and Speicher purchase award Am. Acad. and Inst. Arts and Letters, 1988, purchase award Arts in Hosps., Richmond, Va., 1994; grantee Creative Artists Pub. Svc., 1977, Ariana Found. for Arts, 1985, Artists Space, 1987, E.D. Found., 1991, Lancaster Group., U.S. A. Comm. award, 1991, spl. opportunity stipend N.Y. State Coun. Arts, 1992, 94, Heuss House project Lower Manhattan Cultural Coun., 1992. Studio: 85 N 3rd St # 1D Brooklyn NY 11211-3944 Office Phone: 718-782-0310. E-mail: sbrodyl@aol.com.

BROE, CAROLYN WATERS, conductor, violist, music educator; b. Santa Monica, Calif., July 6, 1957; d. Warren Palmer and Lois Virginia Waters; m. Steve Broe, Apr. 26, 1980; children: JeanRené Waters Broe, Jasmine Elizabeth. MusB, Chapman Coll., 1979; MFA, Calif. State U., 1984; DMA, Ariz. State U., 2001. Co-prin. violist Mozart Camerata, Irvine, Calif., 1980-85; prin. violist Capistrano (Calif.) Valley Symphony, 1986-90; artistic dir. Capistrano Valley Chamber Players, Newport Beach, Calif., 1986-90; founder Orange County Four Seasons Orch., Newport Beach, 1990-93; condr., faculty violin Glendale (Ariz.) C.C., 1993—95; condr. Paradise Valley C.C., Phoenix, 1993—2003; condr., artistic dir. Four Seasons Orch., Scottsdale, Ariz., 1991—. Assoc. condr. master class Tanglewood (Mass.) Music Inst., 1995. Author: J.S. Bach's Treatment of the Viola, 1984; composer (chamber music score): Rebirth of the Goddess, 1992; prodr.(Four Seasons String Quartet): Wedding Album; dir., violist: ; author: The String Compositions of Louise Lincoln Kerr: Analysis and Edition of Five Solo Viola pieces; dir.: (Four Seasons Orch.), 2000 (nominated Grammy award, 2000); composer: (albums) Just Wishing On The Moon, 2000 (nominated Grammy award, 2000). Bd. dirs. Chapman Music Assn., Orange, Calif., 1985-86, Fiske Instrument Mus., Claremont, Calif., 1986-87, Capistrano Valley Symphony, 1987-88, Four Seasons Orch., Scottsdale, 1991—. Named Dream Catcher 1995, Indian Women in Progress, Phoenix, 1995; Cultural Arts grantee Scottsdale Cultural Arts Coun., 1995, 96, 2003. Mem. Am. String Tchr. Assn. Republican. Unitarian Universalist. Avocations: photography, roses, ancient history. Home and Office: Four Seasons Orch 4972 E Paradise Ln Scottsdale AZ 85254-9623

BROECKER, SHERRY, state legislator; b. Feb. 14, 1951; m. Jerry Broecker; 3 children. Student, U. Minn. Self-employed custom picture framer; rep. Dist. 53B Minn. Ho. of Reps., 1994—. Home: 1355 7th Ave SE Forest Lake MN 55025-2053

BROEDLING, LAURIE ADELE, human resources consultant, psychologist, educator; b. Plainfield, N.J., Aug. 1, 1945; d. Dana Adams and Olga (Goerke) Griffin; m. Timothy John Broedling, Sept. 9, 1967; children: Abigail, Emily. BA, Brown U., 1967; MA, George Washington U., 1969, PhD, 1973. Grad. teaching fellow George Washington U., Washington, 1967, prof., 1992—; social svc. worker Kern County Welfare Dept., Bakersfield, Calif., 1968-69; rsch. psychologist Naval Pers. R&D Lab., Washington, 1970-73, San Diego, 1973-74, supervisory pers. rsch. psychologist, 1975-84, head div., 1985-87, dir. dept., 1988-89; dep. undersec. def. Office Sec. Def., Washington, 1990-92; prof. San Diego State U., 1975-77; assoc. adminstr. for continual improvement Nat. Aeronautics and Space Adminstrn., Washington, 1992-95; sr. v.p. human resources and quality McDonnell Douglas Corp., 1995-97; v.p. people, sys. and employee involvement Boeing Co., 1997; pres.orgnl. cons. LB Orgnl. Consulting, 1998—. Editor: Perspective on Attitude Assessment, 1976, Military Productivity and Work Motivation, 1978; contbr. numerous articles to profl. jours. Recipient Rev. award Air U., 1977. Mem. Acad. Mgmt., Am. Soc. Quality, Deming Users Group San Diego (pres. 1985-86), Coun. for Excellence in Govt.

BROER, EILEEN DENNERY, management consultant; b. Phila., Sept. 7, 1946; d. Vincent Paul and Jane Dorothy (Knight) Dennery; m. Paul Alan Broer, Nov. 26, 1970 (div. 1980); m. Charles Kenneth ReCorr, Sept. 10, 1981 (div. 1991); 1 child, Matthew Vincent ReCorr; m. John Wayne Lipe, Dec. 2, 2001. BA, Coll. Mt. St. Vincent, 1969. Media dir. Merrill Anderson Adv. Co., N.Y.C., 1970-72; mgr. human resources McCall's Patterns and Publ., 1977-78; dir. human resources Notions Mktg., Inc., 1979-80; v.p. human resources Manhattan Life Ins. Co., N.Y.C., 1980-82, McM Corp., Raleigh, N.C., 1982-85; pres., org. devel. cons. Human Dimension, 1985—; sr. cons. PDS Consulting, Inc., Safety Harbor, Fla., 1990—; org. devel. cons., supr., exec. coach Lore Internat. Inst., Durango, Colo., 2002-; chair personnel com. Ctr. For Health Edn. Inc., Raleigh, 1990-92; adj. faculty NYU, 1975-78. Contbd. articles to profl. jourls. Recipient Leadership award, Assn. Psych. Type NC Chpt. (MBTI). Mem. Orgn. Devel. Network, Nat. Assn. Women Bus. Owners (pres. N.C. chpt. 1988-89). Mailing: 2275 Sandhurst Dr Castle Rock CO 80104-2397 Office Phone: 303-887-4891. Business E-Mail: ebroer@humandimension.org.

BROGAN, LISA S. lawyer; b. Chgo., Apr. 23, 1963; BA, Northwestern U., 1984, JD, 1987. Bar: Ill. 1987, U.S. Dist. Ct. (no. dist.) Ill. 1988, U.S. Ct. Appeals (fed. cir.) 1989, U.S. Ct. Appeals (7th cir.) 1994. Atty. Baker & McKenzie, Chgo., 1987—. Mem.: ABA, Ill. State Bar Assn., Chgo. (Ill.) Bar Assn. Office: Baker & McKenzie One Prudential Plz 130 East Randolph Dr Chicago IL 60601*

BROGAN-WERNTZ, BONNIE BAILEY, retired police officer, photographer; b. Pine Grove Mills, Pa., Mar. 28, 1941; d. Gilbert Chester and Rosalie Evelyn (Reed) Bailey; m. Donald M. Brogan, Aug. 12, 1960 (div. Oct. 1971); children: Donna Lynn Gregory, Rodney Marshall Brogan; m. Robert R. Werntz, Aug. 28, 1982 (dec. June 7, 1992). A in Criminal Justice, Ind. U., 1976, BS, 1981. Cert. instr. law enforcement tng., Ind. Stenographer South Bend (Ind.) Police Dept., 1970-73, police officer, 1973—, cpl. accident investigation, 1975-80, detective sgt., investigator sex crimes, 1980-85, lt., 1985-97, field tng. officer adminstr., shift comdr., 1985-88, dir. tng., 1988-92, investigative supr., 1992-96, juvenile supr. sex crimes, chld abuse supr., 1996-97; self-employed Golden Age Images Photography, South Bend, 1997—. Bd. dirs. Women's Com. on Sex Offenses, South Bend; vol., trainer rape crisis Sex Offense Svcs., South Bend, 1980-87; recorder, treas. Child Sexual Abuse Consortium, South Bend, 1982-85; mem. Giarretto Task Force/Family and Children Ctr., Mishawaka, Inc., 1985. Iniator ordinance St. Joseph County Funds for Examinations and Victims of Sex Crimes, 1983. Bd. dirs. Parents Anonymous, South Bend, 1982, Women's Shelter for Battered Women, South Bend, 1985, South Bend Credit Union Supervisory Commn., 1983; mem. Children and Adolescent Adv. Council, South Bend, 1984. Recipient Joseph J. Newman award Protective Bd./Council for Retarded St. Joseph County, 1982, Child Abuse Investigator award The Breakfast Exchange Club, 1982, award for

Exceptional Quality in Investigative Child Abuse/Neglect, Child Protective Services of St. Joseph County Dept. Pub. Welfare, 1983, Outstanding Service award Women's Com. on Sex Offenses, 1983, Outstanding Officer of Yr. award, St. Joseph County Council of Clubs, 1985, Police Officer of Yr. award, Ind. Council Fraternal Vets. and Social Scis., 1985, Outstanding Achievement award YWCA Tribute to Women, 1986. Mem. Internat. Assn. of Women Police (Hon. Mention Officer of Yr. 1985), Fraternal Order of Police. Democrat. Avocations: camping, photography. Home: 5776-51 Grape Rd #258 Mishawaka IN 46545 E-mail: bonwerntz@cs.com.

BROGDEN-STIRBL, SHONA MARIE, writer, researcher; b. Tuscaloosa, Ala., Sept. 3, 1948; d. Edward Henry Jr. and Esther Ruth (Coleman) Brogden; m. Robert Clark Stirbl, Mar. 30, 1990. BA, U. South Ala., Mobile, 1972; MA in English (Poetics), NYU, 1982. Adult protective social worker Mobile County Dept. Pensions and Security, 1972-74; child protection social worker Cumberland County Child Protective Svcs., Fayetteville, NC, 1975-76; cmty. placement specialist S.I. Devel. Ctr., 1976-78, Manhattan Borough Devel. Svc., NYC, 1978-80; adminstr. Coun. on Internat. Ednl. Exch., NYC, 1981, Office of Univ. Devel., Advt. and Pub. Affairs, NYU, NYC, 1982-85; dir. advt. Office of Advt. and Pub. Affairs, NYU, NYC, 1986; cons. Meml. Sloan-Kettering, NDRI, NYU, NYC, 1986-97. Patentee (photog. films with multiple ASA and associated camera). Voice recorder Book on Tape, Jewish Braille Inst., NYC, 1996; adminstrv. support Gay Men's Health Crisis, NYC, 1986; vol. Serendipity Sch. for Emotionally Disturbed Children, Sacramento, 1975, Strasberg Inst., 1977-1978; founding mem. Tell It Like It Was, 1999. Scholar NYU, 1978-82, U. So. Miss., 1966-68, Strasberg Theatre Inst., 1977-78. Christian. Avocations: poetry, art, acting, baroque violin, writing, options trading. Home and Office: 465 S Madison #109 Pasadena CA 91101 E-mail: s.brogden.1@alumni.nyu.edu.

BROGLE, JENNIFER LYNN, music educator, consultant; b. Lancaster, Ky., Sept. 16, 1965; d. Marion Leon Naylor and JoAnn Davis Amon; m. Thomas Dale Brogle, May 30, 1987; children: Katelyn, Seth, Hailey. AA in Sci., Somerset C.C., Ky., 1985; MusB Edn., Univ. Ky., Lexington, Ky., 1987, MusM Edn., 1989, rank I in Choral Music, 1996. Pvt. piano instr., Hustonville, Ky., 1985—2000; elem. music tchr. Danville City Sch., Ky., 1990—99; arts and humanities tchr. Boyle County Sch., Ky., 1999—2003. Youth music dir. Mt. Hebron Bapt. Ch., Bryantsville, Ky., 1990—2003; arts and humanities cons. Boyle County Sch., Danville, Ky., 2000—03. Contbr. articles to profl. jour., curriculm guide. Boyle County Com. United Way Campaign, Danville, Ky., 2000—02. Recipient Sallie Mae First Yr. Tchr., Danville City Sch., 1990; scholar McCracken Scholarship Music, Univ. Ky., 1986. Mem.: Ky. Music Educators Assn., Phi Kappa Lambda, Alpha Delta Kappa. Avocations: piano, sewing, reading. Home: 963 Jeffries Ln Hustonville KY 40437 Office: Boyle County H S 1637 Perryville Rd Danville KY 40422

BROGLIATTI, BARBARA SPENCER, television and motion picture executive; b. LA, Jan. 8, 1946; d. Robert and Lottie Spencer; m. Raymond Haley Brogliatti, Sept. 19, 1970. BA in Social Scis. and English, UCLA, 1968. Asst. press. info. dept. CBS TV, L.A., 1968-69, sr. publicist, 1969-74; dir. publicity Tandem Prodns. and T.A.T. Comm. (Embassy Comm.), L.A., 1974-77, corp. v.p., 1977-82; sr. v.p. worldwide publicity, promotion and advt. Embassy Comm., L.A., 1982-85; sr. v.p. worldwide corp. comm. Lorimar Telepictures Corp., Culver City, Calif., 1985-89; pres., chmn. Brogliatti Co., Burbank, Calif., 1989-90; sr. v.p. worldwide TV publicity, promotion and advt. Lorimar TV, 1991-92; sr. v.p. worldwide TV publicity, promotion and pub. rels. Warner Bros., Burbank, 1992-97; sr. v.p. corp. comm. Warner Bros., Inc., 1997-2000; sr. v.p., chief corp. comm. officer Warner Bros. Entertainment Inc., 2000—. Adv. com. acad. advancement program UCLA; bd. govs. UCLA Found., 2003—; Pub. Rels. in Entertainment vis. prof. U. So. Calif., 2004. Mem. bd. govs. TV Acad., L.A., 1984-86, UCLA Found., 2003—; bd. dirs. KIDSNET, Washington, 1987—, Nat. Acad. Cable Programming, 1992-94; mem. Hollywood Women's Polit. Com., 1992-93; mem. steering com. L.A. Free Clinic, 1997-98; mem. adv. bd. The Rape Found., 2004—. Recipient Gold medal Broadcast Promotion and Mktg. Execs., 1984. Mem. Am. Diabetes Assn. (bd. dirs. L.A. chpt. 1992-93), Am. Cinema Found. (bd. dirs. 1994-98), Dirs. Guild Am., Publicists Guild, Acad. TV Arts and Scis. (vice chmn. awards com.); adv. com. UCLA Acad. Advancement Prog. Office: Warner Bros Studios 4000 Warner Blvd Burbank CA 91522-0002 E-mail: barbara.brogliatti@warnerbros.com.

BROHAWN, VIRGINIA BRIDGEMAN, music educator; b. Lockport, NY, Feb. 8, 1943; d. Ross George Bridgeman and Helene Elizabeth Mac Donald; m. Philip Brohawn, Jr., June 13, 1964; children: Jennifer, Bridget. B in music edn., West Va. Wesleyan Coll., 1964. Cert. APC tchr. Md. Music tchr. Cambridge (Md.) HS, 1964—67; choir dir. St. Paul's United Meth., Cambridge, 1968—81; music specialist St. Claire Elem., Cambridge, 1970—72; music tchr. S. S. Peter and Paul Cath., Easton, Md., 1977—81; pvt. tchr. French horn Cambridge, 1980—87; dir. choral music Cambridge-South Dorchester HS, Cambridge, 1983—2004. Found., dir. Chorus of Dorchester, Cambridge, 1975—; adj. Md. All State MMEA, 1983—2004; music adv. coun. Chesapeake Coll., Wye Mills, Md., 1986 91. Recipient Md. State Eastern Region Choral award, Md. Music Educators Assn., 1997. Mem.: NEA, Md. State Tchrs. Assn., Ea. Shore Choral Dirs. Assn., Dorchester Educators, Dorchester Arts Ctr., Dorchester Garden Club, Cambridge Yacht Club, Alpha Xi Delta. Republican. Episcopal. Achievements include Govs. Salute To Excellence for the Md. You Are Beautiful Chorus Dir. 8 citations 1993-2001. Avocations: gardening, reading, cooking, genealogy. Home: 207 Oak St Cambridge MD 21613 Office: Cambridge-South Dorchester HS 2475 Cambridge Bypass Cambridge MD 21613 E-mail: brohawnv@dcpsmd.org.

BROKAW, MEREDITH A. women's health care company director; BA, English and Comm., U. S.D.; LLD (hon.), St. John's U. Founder Penny Whistle Toys, Inc., 1978-97; dir. Women First HealthCare, Inc., San Diego, 1998—. Dir. Gannett Co., Inc. Author 8 books on parenting and children's activities. Trustee Bank Street Coll. Edn., Ednl. Broadcasting Corp., Conservation Internat. Office: Women First HealthCare Inc 12220 El Camino Real Ste 400 San Diego CA 92130-2091 Fax: 619-509-1353.

BROKKE, CATHERINE JULIET, mission executive; b. Mpls., Dec. 25, 1926; d. Emil John and Alma (Brye) Eliason; m. Harold Joseph Brokke, Sept. 9, 1949; 1 child, Daniel. Diploma in nursing, Luth. Deaconess Hosp., Mpls., 1947; student, Concordia Coll., Moorhead, Minn., 1948-49, Bethany Coll. Missions, Mpls., 1949-51. RN, Minn. Sch. and occupational nurse Bethany Fellowship, Mpls., 1951-75; missions sec. Bethany Fellowship Missions, Mpls., 1963-86, dir., 1986-96; retired, 1996. Instr. Bethany Coll. Missions, 1950-88. Mng. editor Message of Cross, 1990-97; composer hymns. Organist Bethany Missionary Ch., Bloomington, Minn., 1956-89; trustee STEM Ministries, 1995-2000, bd. dirs. Mem. Evang. Fellowship of Mission Agys. (trustee 1987-93), Evang. Missions Info. Svc. (bd. dirs. 1994-96). Avocations: piano, organ. Office: Bethany Fellowship Missions 6820 Auto Club Rd Ste D Bloomington MN 55438-2849 E-mail: cathy.brokke@bethfel.org., cathybrokke@att.net.

BROMLEY, LYNN, state legislator; b. Burlington, Vt., Mar. 13, 1951; m. William Howard; 2 children. BA, Bridgewater State Coll., 1974; MSW, Boston Coll., 1991. Human resources mgr. Hannaford Bros. Co., 1978-84; sales rep. advt. Bride/Porter Comm., 1984-89; dir. support svcs. staff So. Maine Tech. Coll., 1991—; pvt. practice family therapy, 1995—; program dir., ednl. cons., 1995—; mem. Maine Senate from 30th Dist., Augusta, 2001—, mem. bus. and econ. devel., legal and vets. affairs com., 2001—, chair standing com. on engrossed bills, 2001—. Co-founder India St. Inst. for Solution Oriented Study; bd. dirs. Familyworks; co-chair Coalition for Women in Trade Tech.; bd. dirs. Jobs for Maine's Grads., 1999—; com. mem. TANF Adv. Bd., 1997—. Mem. NASW (Maine chpt. pres. 1993-95). Democrat. Congregationalist. Home: 102 Mitchell Rd South Portland ME 04106 Office: State House 3 State House Sta Augusta ME 04333 Office Fax: (207) 287-1585. E-mail: lynnbro@ibm.net.

BROMUND, ALICE A. retired elementary school educator; b. Mar. 24, 1943; d. Frank and Louise Vobora; m. Henry A. Cannon, Feb. 14, 1969 (div. July 1979); 1 child, Tracy Ann Young. BA in Humanities, Biola U., 1966. Primary grades tchr., Allendale, 1967—68; tchr. grades 1-2 San Ysidro Sch. Dist., Calif., 1968—70; tchr. sch. dist. grades 1-8 Gorman, Calif., 1970—76; tchr. grade 2 Alpharetta, Ga., 1976—77; kindergarten tchr. Menifee Sch. Dist., Sun City, Calif., 1980—96, 1997—2001; kindergarten tchr., bilingual resource tchr. North Sacramento Sch. Dist.; kindergarten tchr. San Bernardino (Calif.) Unified Sch. Dist., 2001—03; ret., 2003. Active mem. Arcade Ch., Sacramento. Nominee Walt Disney Tchr. Am., 1999. Mem.: NEA, Calif. Ret. Tchrs. Assn. Home: 2591 Millcreek Dr #79 Sacramento CA 95833

BRONDELLO, SANDY, professional basketball player; b. Australia, Aug. 20, 1968; B.Elem.Tchg., 1990. Guard Blazers, Australia, 1995-96, BTV Wuppertal, Germany, 1996-98, Detroit Shock, 1998-99, Miami Sol, 1999—. Mem. Australian Olympic team, 1988; participant World Championships, 1990, 94; guard Austrlian Nat. Team, Women's World Championship, Germany, 1998. Named Australian Intenrat. Basketball Player of the Yr., 1992, WNBL's Most Valuable Player, 1995; recipient European Cup Most Valuable Player, 1996. Office: Miami Sol Sun Trust Internat Ctr One SE 3rd Ave Ste 2300 Miami FL 33131

BRONKAR, EUNICE DUNALEE, artist, educator; b. New Lebanon, Ohio, Aug. 8, 1934; d. William Dunham and Helen Kate (Hypes) Connor; m. Charles William Bronkar, Jan. 26, 1957; 1 child, Ramona. BFA, Wright State U., 1971, M in Art Edn., 1983, postgrad. art studies, 1989, Dayton Art Inst., 1972. Cert. art tchr., Ohio. Part time tchr. Springfield (Ohio) Mus. of Art, 1967-77; adjunct instr. Clark State C.C., Springfield, 1974-84, lead tchr., 1984-94, adj. asst. prof., 1998-2000, asst. prof., 1989-94; ret., 1994; artist private practice, Urbana, Ohio, 1995—. Edn. chmn. Springfield Mus. Art, 1973-74; image banks participant, Ohio Arts Coun., Columbus, Visual Arts Network, Dayton, Ohio, 1994—; affiliated with The Art Ctr. of St. Augustine, Fla. Art Scene, Little Gallery, Springfield, Ohio, The Frame Haven Gallery and Frame Craft Gallery, Springfield, Ohio. One-woman shows include, Springfield, Ohio, Polo Club, Upper Valley Mall Cinema, Security Nat. Bank, Mr. C's Beauty Salon, Lakewood Beach, Springfield Mus. Art (awards, 1965, 1968, 2nd pastel, 1972, 1976, 1998, 1st drawing, 1976, 1986, 1990, 2000, 1992, Jurors award pastel, 1979, 3rd drawing, 1987, 2nd drawing, 1989, 2nd painting, 1991, 2003, 1st painting, 2002), Clark State C.C., Dayton, Ohio, Miami Valley Hosp., High St. Gallery, Stoeffer's Restaurant, Wegerzyn Garden Ctr., Meml. Hall, Wright State Univ., Urbana, Ohio, Champaign County Arts Coun., Urbana Cinema, South Charleston, Ohio, Cmty. Park Dedication, Phillip Caldwell spl. guest spkr., exhibited in group shows at Springfield Mus. Art, 1999, Zanesville Ohio Art Ctr., 2000, accepted in over 100 area, state, regional, and nat. juried exhibns. including Ohio Water Color Soc. Ann. Travelling shows, 1983—84, 1986—87, Wc. Ohio Watercolor Soc. (Hon. Mention, 1983, 2001, Chase Patterson award, 1985, Spl. Merit award, 1990, 1st, 1995, 2000, Merit award, 1997, 1998), Dayton Soc. Painters and Sculptors (Best of Show, 1974, 2001, 1st painting, 2nd painting, 3rd drawing, 1970, Hon. Mention, 1979, 3rd graphic, 1980, Best of Show drawing, 1981, 1st pastel, 1981, 1st drawing, 1991, 3rd painting, 1993, 2nd drawing, 1993, Spl. Merit award for balance, 2001, Merit award, 2001, 2003), Champaign County Fair (Best of Show drawing, 1968, 2003, 1st pastel, 1968, 1st painting, 2003), Wilson Gallery, Sidney, Ohio, Represented in permanent collections, drawings and paintings in Am. Artist Renown, 1981, Shades of Gray, 1983, 1984, 1986, 1987, 1990, 1991, 1993, 1994, 1997. Cleaned and restored art collections at Springfield Pub. Schs., Hist. Soc. in Springfield, Logan County Hist. Soc., Champaign County Hist. Soc., Warder Pub. Libr., Foos Manor Bed & Breakfast and the Masonic Temple, Penn House and Mus. of Art in Springfield, 1970-00, Calumet Antiques, Yellow Springs, Ohio, other groups and numerous pvt. collections, 1970—; mem. adv. com. comml. art, Clark County JVS Sch., Springfield, 1991-2003; judge more than 10 pub. h.s. art shows, 1970s-90s; judge Logan County (Ohio) Fair Fine Art Show profl. and amateur, 1998, Champaign County Fair Art Show, 2001. Recipient medal Bicentennial Com. and 4H Found. of Ohio, Springfield, 1976, Outstanding Tchr. award Clark State C.C., 1992, commd. to paint 2 past pres. Generals of the Natl. Soc. Daughters of the Amer. Revolution, which hangs in Continental Hall, Washington. Mem. Western Ohio Water Color Soc, Springfield (Ohio) Mus. of Art, Dayton Soc. Painters and Sculptors, Cin. Art Club, Ohio Water Color Soc., Nat. Mus. Women in Arts, Ohio Plein Air Painters, Audubon Artists Soc., Pastel Soc., St. Augustine (Fla.) Art Assn., Portrait Soc. Ames, others. Avocations: swimming, walking, sewing, flower arranging, travel to Europe, Caribbean, Russia, Israel and Ireland.

BRONKESH, ANNETTE CYLIA, public relations executive; b. Vineland, N.J., Dec. 18, 1956; d. Manasha and Miriam (Kutlan) B.; m. Steven Silver Schwartz, Aug. 18, 1985; children: Sarah, Emily, Julie. BA, NYU, 1979. Sr. editor Instnl. Investor, N.Y.C., 1979; chief editor McGraw-Hill, N.Y.C., 1980-85; dir. Am. Stock Exchange, N.Y.C., 1985-87; v.p. pub. rels. Nikko Securities, N.Y.C., 1987-90; pres. Bronkesh Assocs., Clifton, N.J., 1990—. Mem. 100 Women in Hedge Funds. Mem. Securities Industry Assn. (pub. rels. roundtable), Fin. Women's Assn. N.Y., Phi Beta Kappa. Avocation: playing piano. Office: Bronkesh Assocs 23 Virginia Ave Clifton NJ 07012-1222 also: 23 Virginia Ave Clifton NJ 07012-1222

BRONNER, KATHERINE ELIZABETH, high school counselor; b. Waverly, Iowa, Dec. 20, 1943; d. Wesley Neil and Mary Catherine (Berge) Bronner Hagerty. BS, Mankato (Minn.) State U., 1966, MS, 1971; postgrad., St. Thomas U., St. Paul, U. Minn., 1971—. Phys. edn. and health instr. Zumbrota (Minn.) H.S., 1966-67; phys. edn. instr. St. Paul Park (Minn.) Jr. High and Oltman Jr. High, 1967-70; resident advisor Gage Ctr. Mankato State U., 1970-71; counselor Rosemont (Minn.) H.S., 1971-76, Apple Valley (Minn.) H.S., 1976—2004. Counselor, instr. Women Sense of Identity program U. Minn., 1978-80. Contbr. to Teen Pregnance and Parenting Resource Handbook. Bd. dirs. Minn. Coalition of Orgns. for Sex Equality in Edn., St. Paul, 1980—; participant 2d Ann. Conf. for Drug Free Schs., Apple Valley, 1984; active Alanon, Mpls., 1980—. Mem. NEA, Minn. Edn. Assn. (bldg. rep.), Minn. Assn. Counseling and Devel. (govtl. chair), Minn. Sch. Counselor's Assn. (exec. bd. 1975-83, lt. chair 1975-80, govtl. rels. rep. 1975-80, treas. Dakota divsn. 1981-82, pres. 1982-83, facilities chair spring conf. 1992), Minn. Coalition of Sex Equality in Edn. (exec. bd. 1980-83, treas. 1982-83), Lake Area Counselors Assn. (facilities chair). Democrat. Methodist. Avocations: antique dealing, collecting antique marbles. Office: Apple Valley HS 14450 Hayes Rd Apple Valley MN 55124-6797

BRONNER, KATHLEEN M. not-for-profit fundraiser; b. Holyoke, Mass., July 13, 1956; d. Romeo Nelson and Kathleen (Mulvenna) Monat; m. Lenard M. Bronner, Sept. 8, 1979. BA, Mount Holyoke Coll., South Hadley, Mass., 1999. Asst. sec. of coll. Mount Holyoke Coll., South Hadley, 1993—96, sr. adminstrv. asst. to chief advancement officer, 1996—98, ann. and spl. gifts officer, 1998—2003, assoc. dir. ann. and spl. gifts, 2003—. Notary pub. State of Mass., 1995—; mem. Appeals Bd. for Town of Granby, Mass., 1995—. Mem.: Coun. for Advancement and Support of Edn. Democrat. Roman Catholic. Avocations: gardening, floral arrangement, swimming. Home: 46 Morgan St Granby MA 01033 Office: Mount Holyoke Coll 50 College St South Hadley MA 01075

BRONSON, CAROL E. health facility administrator; b. St. Louis, Sept. 11, 1944; d. Whitfield R. and Ruby E. (Graham) B.; m. Andre Pierre Duplessis, Sr. Nov. 16, 1980; children: Carl, Carol Lynne, Sterling, Andre, Jr., William, Andra, K'rin. BBA, Nat. U., San Diego, 1978; MA, U.S. Internat. U., San Diego, 1993; MA in Culture and Human Behavior, Calif. Sch. Profl. Psychology, San Diego, 2000; student, The Fielding Inst., Atlanta. Adminstrv. coord. Calif. Sch. Profl. Psychology, San Diego, 1989—2001; mgr., owner Any Necessary Typing Svc., San Diego, 1988-93; tchr. in bus. Calif. Comty. Colls.; tchr. San Diego City Schs., 2001. Instr. San Diego C.C., 1997, instr. 1979-2000; spkr. Cath. Diocese of San Diego, 1995, San Diego Black Nurses Assn., 1994. Author: (book) A History of Christ: The King Catholic Church 1932-95, 1996. Co-dir. nat. conf. comty. and justice, 1998-2001; probation asst. San Diego Dept. of Probation, 1994-95, tutor, 1987; children's advocate Voices for Children, San Diego, 1992-93; vol. coord. United Negro Coll. Fund, San Diego, 1985-95. Recipient 1st place runner-up award Writers Guild, San Diego, 1992. Mem. Nat. Assn. Multicultural Educators. Democrat. Roman Catholic. Avocations: reading, writing short stories.

BRONSTEIN, IRENA, science administrator, consultant; d. Jacob and Bella Bronstein; m. Eugene Albert Bonte, Dec. 17, 1972; 1 child, Benjamin Bronstein Bonte. AB, Bryn Mawr Coll., Penn., 1967; PhD, Johns Hopkins U., Balt., 1972. Scientist, tech. mgr., dir. Polaroid Corp., Cambridge, Mass., 1976—84; sr. staff scientist Allied Health & Sci. Products, Andover, 1984—86; founder, chmn. and chief sci. officer Tropix, Inc., Bedford, 1986—90, chmn. and CEO, 1990—96; v.p. and gen. mgr. Tropix, Inc., Divsn. of Applied Biosys., Bedford, Mass., 1996—2002. Cons. Applied Biosys., Newton, Mass., 2002—. Recipient Outstanding Woman of 1982, Am. Assn. for Women in Sci., 1982. Achievements include patents for chemistry and biotechnology. Home: 11 Ivanhoe Street Newton MA 02458-2715

BRONSTEIN, JAGODA EWA, pediatrician; b. Lublin, Poland, Sept. 26, 1962; came to the U.S., 1990; d. Zygmunt and Danuta (Celinska) O.; m. Glen Max Bronstein, Feb. 19, 1992; children: Lara Melanie, Sophie Milena. MD, Med. Acad., Lublin, Poland, 1990. Intern pediat. St. Vincent's Hosp. and Med. Ctr., N.Y.C., 1992-93; resident pediat. N.Y. Hosp.-Cornell Med. Ctr., N.Y.C., 1993-95; attending physician N.Y. Meth. Hosp., Bklyn., 1995-99, dir. primary care and gen. pediat., 1996-98; attending physician St. Joseph's Hosp. and Med. Ctr., Paterson, N.J., 1998—. Primary care faculty devel. fellow Mich. State U., East Lansing, 1992-98. Mem. AMA, Am. Acad. Pediat., Ambulatory Pediat. Assn. Office: St Joseph's at Willowbrook 57 Willowbrook Blvd Wayne NJ 07470-7045

BRONSTER, MARGERY S, state attorney general; b. N.Y., Dec. 12, 1957; married; 1 child. BA in Chinese Lang., Lit. and History, Brown U., 1979; JD, Columbia U., 1982. Assoc. Sherman & Sterling, NY, 1982—87; ptnr. Carlsmith, Ball, Wichman, Murray, Case & Ichiki, Honolulu, 1988—94; atty. gen. State of Hawaii, 1994—99; pvt. practice Honolulu, 1999—. Co-chair planning com. Citizens Conf. Jud. Selection, 1993. Mem.: Am. Judicature Soc. (bd. dirs., chair gov. com. on crime, VAWA planning com.). Office: Bronster Crabtree Hoshibata 23d Fl 1001 Biship St Pavahi Tower Honolulu HI 96813

BRONWELL, NANCY BROOKER, writer; b. Columbia, S.C., Oct. 11, 1921; d. Norton Wardlaw and Lucile Duty (Michaux) Brooker; m. Alvin Wayne Bronwell, June 21, 1943 (div. Mar. 1975); children: Betsy Randolph Bronwell Jones, Cynthia Alison (dec.). BS, Mary Washington Coll., 1942; postgrad., U. Ky., 1942-43, Tex. Tech. U., 1983, 87. Tchr. English, phys. edn. Louisville Pub. Schs., 1943-46; sec. edn. dept. Jos. S. Seagram & Sons Inc., Louisville, 1945-46; sec. to sales mgr. Marshall Field Corp., Chgo., 1946; sec. to dir. purchases Jos. E. Seagram & Sons., Inc., 1946-48; freelance writer Lubbock, Tex., 1978—. Author: Lubbock: A Pictorial History, 1980; contbr. articles to mags. Co-founder, bd. dirs. Young Women's Christian Assn., Lubbock, 1953; vol. Lubbock Jr. League, Lubbock Symphony Orch., Palsy Ctr., ARC, Tech. Mus., St. Paul's Ch. Mem. South Plains Writers Guild, Lubbock Heritage Assn. (Excellence award 1981), DAR, Huguenot Soc., Friends of Libr. (life). Republican. Episcopalian. Avocations: reading, word games. Home and Office: 4108 18th St # A Lubbock TX 79416-6009

BROOKER, LENA EPPS, human relations diversity management consultant; b. Lumberton, N.C., Oct. 13, 1941; d. Frank Howard and Grace Evelyn (Smith) Epps; m. James Dennis Brooker, July 30, 1966; children: Lora, Lindsey. AB, Meredith Coll., Raleigh, N.C., 1962. Cert. elem. sch. tchr., N.C. Elem. sch. tchr., Charlotte, Robeson County, N.C., Winchester, Va., Chevy Chase, Md., Raleigh, 1962-75; coord. human svcs. program N.C. Commn. Indian Affairs, Raleigh, 1975-78; planner, adminstr. human svcs. program N.C. Dept. Natural Resources and Community Devel., Raleigh, 1978-86; dir. diversity mgmt. The Women's Ctr., Raleigh, 1990-96; mgr. Diversity prog. First Citizens Bank, Raleigh, 1996-97; human rels. and diversity mgmt. cons., 1998-99. Developer model program U.S. Dept. Labor, Raleigh, 1976; presenter Pres.'s Commn. on Status of Women, Raleigh, 1979; facilitator Internat. Yr. of Woman, Winston-Salem, N.C., 1977; speaker on status of Am. Indians to univs., schs., chs. and orgns., 1975—. Contbg. writer The Carolina Call, The Carolinian. Chaplain, entertainment chmn. Dem. Women Wake County, Raleigh, 1989-91; mem. Task Force on Native Am. Ministry N.C. Conf. United Meth. Ch., chmn. ethnic minority local ch. concerns com., 1988-91, mem. bd. evangelism, 1986-91, audit com. coun. fin. and adminstrn., 1990-91, coun. ministries, 1992-94, mem. bishops task force on staff and structure, 1993-95; mem. Wake County Mammography Task Force, 1990-93; mem. cultural diversity com. Wake County Arts Coun., 1990; bd. dirs. Internat. Festival Raleigh, 1990-91, Triangle OIC, 1991-93, N.C. Civil Liberties Union, 1992-94, United Arts Coun. Wake County, 1996-97, sec. 1996; mem. steering com. for Yr. of native Am., N.C. Mus. Natural History, 1986; mem. city of Raleigh Human Resources and Human Rels. Commn., 1990-93; pres. bd. dirs. Women's Fund of N.C., 1993-97; bd. advisors Heritage Arts Found., 1993, N.Am. Health Edn. Fund, 1994-98, Women's Leadership Inst., Bennett Coll., 1995-96; mem. N.C. Coun. on Women, 1999—; bd. dirs. Carteret County Domestic Violence Program, 1999; mem. adminstrv. bd. Weaverville Univ. Med. Ctr.; lay spkr. Asheville dist. United Meth. Ch. Recipient Personal Advocacy for Women in N.C. Carpathian award N.C. Equity, 1993, Martin Luther King Jr. Light of Hope award Wake County Pub. Schs., 1998; grantee N.C. Arts Coun., Duke-Seminars Fine Arts Found., 1986. Mem. N.C. Natural Scis. Soc. (bd. dirs. 1987-90), Triangle Native Am. Soc. (past coord. spl. projects), Meredith Coll. Alumne Assn. (bd. dirs. 1994-95),The Women's Forum of N.C. Avocations: tennis, reading, writing, collecting american indian art and objects. Address: 120 Leisure Mountain Rd Asheville NC 28804-1117 E-mail: LBrooker00@cs.com.

BROOKER, SUSAN GAY, employment consulting firm executive; b. Washington, Sept. 4, 1949; d. Robert Morris and Mildred Ruby (Parler) B. BA, St. Mary's Coll., St. Mary's City, Md., 1971. News editor WPGC Radio, Lanham, Md., 1971; mgr. trainee Household Fin. Corp., Silver Spring, Md., 1972; career counselor Place-All, Bethesda, Md., 1972-73; exec. v.p. New Places, Inc./ Get-A-Job, Washington, 1973-89; employment cons., owner, pres. SGB Consultants, Reston, Va., 1989—. Mem. Emploibank, Washington, 1978-79; guest condr. LGCW 15th Aniv. Concert, 1999. Conservation chairperson Silver Spring Woman's Club, 1993—94; watch capt. Sawyer's Neighborhood, 1997—2001; crisis crew mem. Avon Breast Cancer, 2000; outreach vestry chair Grace Episcopal Ch., 1992—94. Recipient Cert. Appreciation U.S. Fish and Wildlife Assn., 1985, Cert. of Recognition Chaplaincy Assocs., Howard Gen. Hosp, Letter of Appreciation Pres. Bill Clinton, 1996. Mem. Pell-Capital Pers. Svc. Assn. (cert.), St. Mary's Coll. (Md.) Alumni Assn. (bd. dirs. 1987-91). Democrat. Avocations: swimming, travel, gardening, golf, snorkling. Home and Office: 2209 Coppersmith Sq Reston VA 20191-2305 Office Phone: 703-758-7111. Personal E-mail: suebrooker@aol.com.

BROOKES, RUTH HARDING, guidance counselor; b. prospect, ME, Mar. 14, 1915; d. Gerry Barker and Jennie Gertrude (Clifford) Harding; m. [illegible] Brookes, Dec. 27, 1938 (dec.); children: Gay, Gerry H., Kenneth C., Katherine H. BA with high distinction, U. Maine, 1935; MEd, Boston U., 1936. Cert. Guidance Counselor, Maine. Tchr. Bristol (Conn.) H.S., 1936-38; guidance counselor C Westboro (Mass.) H.S., 1955-60, Buker Jr. H.S., Augusta, Maine, 1961-64, Cony H.S., Augusta, 1965-75. Chmn. Direct Svc. to Patients, Damariscotta, Maine, 1976—; chmn. Adult Edn. Adv. Coun., U. Maine Sch. Union #74, 1980-98; vol. Miles Meml. Hosp., Damariscotta, Maine, 1976—; deacon Bristol (Maine) Congl. Ch., 1998—. Mem. Phi Beta Kappa, Phi Kappa Phi. Democratic. Avocations: traveling, swimming, reading, gardening, hiking. Home: 88 Seawood Park Rd New Harbor ME 04554-5003

BROOKNER, ANITA, writer, educator; d. Newson and Maude B. BA, King's Coll., 1946-49; Ed., U. London; PhD, Courtauld Inst., Paris, 1949-53. Vis. lectr. U. Reading, 1959-64; Slade prof. U. Cambridge, 1967-68; lectr. Courtauld Inst. of Art, 1964. Author: Watteau, 1968, The Genius of the Future, 1971, Greuze: The Rise and Fall of an Eighteenth Century Phenomenon, 1972, Jacques-Louis David, 1980, (novels) A Start in Life, 1981, Providence, 1982, Look At Me, 1983, Hotel du Lac, 1984 (Booker McConnell prize), Family and Friends, 1985, A Misalliance, 1986, A Friend From England, 1987, Latecomers, 1988, Lewis Percy, 1989, Brief Lives, 1991, Fraud, 1992, A Family Romance, 1993, A Private View, 1995, Altered States, 1996, Visitors, 1997, The Visitors, 1998, Soundings, 1998, Falling Slowly: A Novel, 1999, The Bay of Angels: A Novel, 2002; contbr. articles to mags.

BROOKS, ANGEL KIRSTIE, copy editor; b. Fitzgerald, Ga., Nov. 26, 1973; d. James Lee Brooks, Shirley Brooks. BS in Journalism, Fla. A&M U., 1996. Copy editor Phila. Inquirer, 1996—. Recipient Golden Eagle: Minority Journalism Scholarship award, Macon Telegraph & News, 1992. Mem.: Phila. Assn. Black Journalists, Am. Copy Editors Soc. Avocations: travel, reading, sports, music. Office: Phila Inquirer 400 North Broad St Philadelphia PA 19101 Business E-Mail: abrooks@phillynews.com.

BROOKS, ANITA HELEN, public relations executive; b. N.Y.C. d. Arthur and Bertha (Stewart) Sayle; m. Arnold Brooks, July 1, 1954 (div.). BA, Hunter Coll., 1950; MA, Columbia U., 1952, MLS, 1954. Tchr. Latin Hunter Coll. H.S., N.Y.C., 1955; publicity rep. WOR Radio, N.Y.C., 1955; writer King Features Syndicate, N.Y.C., 1955-59; pub. rels. exec. NBC-TV, N.Y.C., 1956; dir. pub. rels. N.Y. State Mental Health Fund Campaign, 1956, WMCA Radio, N.Y.C., 1957; account exec. various pub. rels. agys., N.Y.C., 1957-65; pres. Anita Helen Brooks Assocs., Pub. Rels., N.Y.C., 1965—. Lit. agt. Anita Brooks Lit. Agt., N.Y.C., 1956—. Writer radio-TV shows. Vice chmn. Sinatra for Meml. Sloan-Kettering Cancdr Hosp. Benefit; mem. patroness com. Harkness Ballet Found.; mem. benefit com. Mannes Coll. Music, N.Y.C.; mem. legis. adv. com. of Senator Roy M. Goodman, N.Y. State Senate. Decorated dame comdr. Knights of Malta; named hon. citizen Venezuela. Mem. Am. Women in Radio and TV, Pub. Rels. Soc. Am., Internat. Radio and TV Soc., Publs. Publicity Assn., Assn. Motion Picture Advertisers, Mystery Writers Am., Columbia U. Alumni Assn., Sisters in Crime Soc., Smithsonian Assocs., N.Y. Press Club, Eta Sigma Phi, Latin/Greek Honor Soc. Home and Office: 155 E 55th St New York NY 10022-4038

BROOKS, ARLENE SHEFFIELD, secondary school educator; b. High Point, N.C., Apr. 3, 1939; d. Sandy B. and Geneva M. (McCaskill) Sheffield; m. James Nash Brooks, July 18, 1964; children: James Timothy, Terry Sheffield. AB, Guilford Coll., 1961; MA, Longwood Coll., 1967. Tchr. social studies Bluestone Sr. High Sch., Skipwith, Va., 1961-64; tchr. Park View Sr. High Sch., South Hill, Va., 1964-67, 80—, Park View Jr. High Sch., South Hill, Va., 1976-80. Mem. Order Ea. Star, Delta Kappa Gamma (2d v.p. 1982-84, rec. sec. 1984-86, pres. 1992-94). Baptist. Avocations: reading, cross stitch, piano, travel. Office: Park View Sr High Sch 205 Park View Cir South Hill VA 23970-5031 Home: 3350 Trinity Church Rd South Hill VA 23970

BROOKS, CATHERINE COUCH, special education educator; b. Pensacola, Fla., June 20, 1964; d. John Alexander and Carolyn Barrett Couch; m. Lon Wayne Brooks, June 3, 1983; children: Natalie Marie, Carrie Susan. MEd in Interrelated Spl. Edn., State U. West Ga., 1998; BS in Biology, U. West Fla., 1986; AS, Pensacola Jr. Coll., 1984. Leadership Cert. Ga. Dept. of Edn., 2002, cert. Interrelated Spl. Edn. Ga. Dept. of Edn., 2000, Mental Retardation cert. Ga. Dept. of Edn., 2000. Tchr. spl. edn. Douglas County Sch. Sys., Douglasville, Ga., 1995—98, tchr., ednl. evaluator, 1998—. Sys. resource for specific learning disabilities Douglas County Sch. Sys., Douglasville, 2002—. Mem.: Profl. Assn. Ga. Educators, Coun. for Exceptional Children (v.p. - local level 2003).

BROOKS, DEBRA L. healthcare executive, neuromuscular therapist; b. Cedar Rapids, Iowa, Dec. 10, 1950; children: Brei, Benjamin, Bryan. BA, Coe Coll., 1973; MS, Clayton Coll., 1999, PhD, 2000. Cert. neuromuscular therapy Fla., natural therapeutics specialist N.Mex. Tchr. Cedar Rapids Cmty. Sch. Dist., 1973-92; COO NeuroMuscular Therapy Ctr., Walford, Iowa, 1994—. Educator Helping Hands Seminars, Cedar Rapids, 1992—2000, Debra Brooks' Seminars, Walford, 1993—; bus and educ consult Brooks Consults, Cedar Rapids, 1990—; mem Iowa Bd Examiners, 2001—03; chair adv. bd. ABLE, 2001—02; mem., chair Nat. Alliance State Bds., 2001—02; editl. bd. Momentum Media. Contbr. articles to profl jours and newsletters. Fundraiser, performer in musicals St Luke's Hosp, Cedar Rapids, 1978—91; fundraiser, performer in Follies Cedar Rapids Symphony, 1981—99; fundraiser, performer in telethons Variety Clubs Am, Cedar Rapids, 1989—91; mem Walford Community Develop, 1994—98; editl. bd. Tng. and Conditioning Mag. Named Outstanding Mentor of the Yr, YWCA, 2001; recipient First in Nation in Educ Award, State of Iowa, 1991, Tribute to Women of Achievement Award, YWCA, 2001. Mem.: Am. Coll. Healthcare Execs., Am. Massage Therapy Assn. (state v.p., edn. dir. 1992—94, nat. trustee Found. 1994—98, nat. bd. dirs. 1994—2002), Profl. Women's Network (chmn. 2002—03). Avocations: singing, painting, pianist, power walking, philosophy. Office: NeuroMuscular Therapy Ctr PO Box 8267 Cedar Rapids IA 52408-8267 E-mail: montanadebrabrooks@yahoo.com.

BROOKS, DIANE COX, music educator; b. Salisbury, NC, Sept. 26, 1951; d. Casey Edward and Francis Bradshaw Cox; m. Kenneth Eugene Brooks, Dec. 17, 1972; children: Michael Keith, David Eugene. BA in music edn., Gardner Webb U., 1971—73; AA in music edn., North Greenville Jr. Coll., 1969—71. Profl. Educator NC, 1973. Elem. music tchr. Cleve. County Schools, Shelby, NC, 1973—75, Rutherford County Schools, Spindale, NC, 1975—90; mid. sch. choral dir. Cleve. County Schools, Shelby, NC, 1990—. NC mid. sch. honor chorus coord. NC Music Educators Assn., Raleigh, NC, 1990—. Recipient NC Mid. Sch. Music Tchr. of the Yr., NC Music Educators Mid. Sch. Sect., 2000, Disting. Grad., Gardner Webb U., 2001. Mem.: Music Educators Nat. Conf., Am. Choral Directors Assn., NC Music Educators Assn. (mid. sch. honor chorus coord. 1990—2003). Bapt.

BROOKS, GLADYS SINCLAIR, retired public affairs consultant; b. Mpls., June 8, 1914; d. John Franklin and Gladys (Phillips) Sinclair; m. Wright W. Brooks, Apr. 17, 1941; children: Diane Brooks Montgomery, John, Pamela (Mrs. Jean Marc Perraud). Student, U. Geneva, Switzerland, 1935; BA, U. Minn., 1936; LLD, Hamline U., 1966. Dir. Farmer's and Mechanics Bank, 1973-82; pres. Brooks/Ridder & Assocs., 1983-94; ret. Lectr. world affairs, 1939—, lectr. on world tour as Am. specialist U.S. Dept., State, 1959-60; instr. continuing edn. for women U. Minn.; del. Rep. Nat. Conv., 1952; state chmn. Citizens for Eisenhower, 1956; founder, pres. Rep. Workshop. Mem. YWCA (pres. 1953-57, 62-65, mem. nat. bd., 1959-71, del. world mtg., Denmark), Mpls. Charter Commn., 1948-51, Mpls. City Coun., 1967-73, Coun. Ch. Women (pres. 1946-48), Nat. Coun. of Chs. (mem. gen. bd., v.p. 1961-69), Minn. Coun. of Chs. (1st woman pres. 1961-64, Christian service award 1967), Mpls. Coun. of Chs. (v.p. 1946-48), United Ch. Women (bd. mgrs.), Minn. UN Assn. (dir.), Nat. League Cities (human resources steering com. 1972-73, coun. fgn. rels.), U.S. Com. for UNICEF, 1959-68, Gov.'s Adv. Com. Children and Youth, 1953-58, Minn. Adv. Com. Employment and Security, 1948-50, Midwest adv. com. Inst. Internat. Edn., nat. com. White House Conf. Children and Youth, 1960, Midwest Selection Panel, White House Fellows, 1981; trustee United Theol. Sem., YWCA, Met. State U., Hamline U. Met. State U.; mem. pres.'s adv. coun. St. Catherine's Coll.; bd. dirs. Hamline U. Midwest China Ctr., Walker Health Services; chmn. Gov.'s Human Rights Commn., 1961-65, Minn. Women's Com. for Civil Rights, 1961-64, Mpls. Adv. Com. on Tourism, 1976-82, Ctr. Women in Govt., 1987-92, adv. com. Office World Trade, 1988-92; vice chmn. Nat. Community Partnerships Seminars, 1977-82; co-chmn. Mpls. Bicentennial Commn., 1974-76; dir. Citizens Com. Delinquency and Crime, 1969-93, Minn. Alumni Assn.; pres. Internat. Ctr. for Fgn. Students. Recipient Centennial Women of Minn. award Hamline U., 1954, Woman of Distinction award AAUW, Mpls., 1956, Outstanding Achievement award U. Minn., 1962, Woman of Yr. award YWCA, 1973, Brotherhood award NCCJ, 1975, State Bar award for community leadership, 1976, Service to Freedom award Minn. State Bar Assn., 1976, Community Leadership award YWCA, 1981, Svc. Beyond Self award Rotary, 1990. Mem. AAUW, World Affairs Coun. (pres. 1942-44), Minn. LWV (dir. 1940-45), Am. Acad. Polit. Sci., Minn. Women's Polit. Caucus, Minn. Women's Econ. Roundtable, Horizon 100, Women's Club, Delta Kappa Gamma (hon.). Home: 1023 Mount Curve Ave Minneapolis MN 55403-1126

BROOKS, HELENE MARGARET, editorial consultant; b. Jersey City, Apr. 1, 1942; d. Sinclair Duncan and Helen Margaret (McDermott) B.; m. Joseph F. Olivieri, Dec. 10, 1987 (dec. July 1991). BA, C.W. Post Coll., 1977; MBA, Dowling Coll., 1992; grad. cert. paralegal studies, Hofstra U., 1998. Asst. editor McCall's mag., N.Y.C., 1969-72, assoc. editor, 1972-75, editor features and travel, 1975-83; managing editor 50 Plus mag. Whitney Commn., N.Y.C., 1983; exec. editor 50 Plus mag. Whitney Comm., N.Y.C., 1983-87; editor in chief Network mag./Internat. Airlines Travel Agt. Network, N.Y.C., 1987-2000; dir. pub. affairs and prof. Coll. Aeronautics, LaGuardia Airport, Flushing, NY, 2000—. Editorial cons. Am. Hairdressing Industry, N.Y.C. 1983. Mem. Am. Soc. Mag. Editors, Delta Mu Delta, Phi Eta. Democrat. Presbyterian. Avocations: cooking, reading, piano, floral design. Home: 16 Vermont St Long Beach NY 11561-1410 Office: Coll Aeronautics LaGuardia Airport 86-01 23d Ave Flushing NY 11369 E-mail: hbrooks@aero.edu.

BROOKS, HILLARY AFTON, social worker; b. Radford, Va., June 10, 1947; d. Ray C. and C. Louise (Altic) Absher. BS, Madison Coll., 1970; MSW, Va. Commonwealth U., 1974. Lic. clin. social worker. Clin. social worker Cen. State Hosp., Petersburg, Va., 1970-76, So. Va. Mental Health Inst., Danville, 1976-77; social worker VA Med. Ctr., Salem, Va., 1977-80, Richmond, Va., 1980-86, Martinsburg, W.Va., 1988-98; coord. outpatient clinic St. John's Hosp., Richmond, 1987-88. Cons. Alcohol Safety Action Program, Richmond, 1981-82, appointed information security ofcr. for Martinsburg UAMC. Formed and organized Women's Spirituality Grp., 1992, initiated as priestess of Avalon of the Chalice Well in Glasdonbury, Eng., 1998. Mem. Nat. Assn. Social Workers, Acad. Cert. Social Workers. Avocations: music, reading, cross-stitch. Office: VA Med Ctr Martinsburg WV 25401

BROOKS, KATHLEEN, journalist; b. Atlanta, Jan. 25, 1957; d. William Chesley and Sara (Brooks) Howton. BA, Stephens Coll., Columbia, Mo., 1978. Mktg. asst. The Laitram Corp., New Orleans, 1978-79; reporter Daily Home, Talladega, Ala., 1979-80, copy editor, 1980-81; asst. wire editor, reporter Gastonia (N.C.) Gazette, 1981, wire editor, 1981-84; asst. wire editor Comml. Appeal, Memphis, 1984-88, Washington editor, 1988-91, nat. editor, 1991—. Methodist. Office: The Comml Appeal 495 Union Ave Memphis TN 38103-3221 E-mail: brooks@gomemphis.com.

BROOKS, LAURIE, playwright, educator; d. Dean Oliver Brooks and Marjorie Ianthe Gleason Brooks; children: Joanna McKenzie, Elizabeth Gollobin, Stephanie Gollobin. AA, Am. Acad. Dramatic Art, 1970; BA, Hofstra U., 1977; MA, NYU, 1991. Asst. prof. NYU Steinhardt Sch. Edn., 1997; playwright program in ednl. theatre NYU, 2001; lit. mgr. new plays for young audiences NYU Provincetown Playhouse, 2002. Panelist Nat. Endowment for the Arts, 2002; presenter in field. Author: (plays) Imaginary Friends, 1996 (John Gassner Meml. Playwriting award New Eng. Theatre Conf.), Selkie, 1996 (Disting. Play award Am. Alliance for Theatre and Edn., 1998), Deadly Weapons, 1998 (Charlotte Chorpenning cup Am. Alliance for Theatre and Edn., 2003), The Match Girl's Gift, 1998, Devon's Hurt, 1999 (Aurand Harris Meml. Playwriting award New Eng. Theatre Conf.), Franklin's Apprentice, 1999, The Wrestling Season, 2000 (Disting. Play award Am. Alliance for Theatre and Edn., 2000), The Tangled Web, 2000, Everyday Heroes, 2002, A Laura Ingalls Wilder Christmas, 2002, The 12:07, 2003. Aurand Harris grant, Children's Theatre Found. Am., 1999, FirstStage grant, AT&T and Theatre Comm. Group, 2001. Office: NYU Program in Ednl Theatre 82 Washington Sq E Rm 23 New York NY 10003

BROOKS, LILLIAN DRILLING ASHTON (LILLIAN HAZEL CHURCH), adult education educator; b. Grand Rapids, Mich., May 27, 1921; d. Walter Brian and Lillian Church; m. Frederick Morris Drilling, 1942 (div. Apr. 1972); children: Frederick Walter, Stephen Charles, Lawrence Alan, Lynn Anne; m. Richard Moreton Ashton, Aug. 25, 1973 (dec. 1990); m. Ralph J. Brooks, May 21, 1994. Student, Grand Rapids Jr. Coll., 1939-41, Wayne State U., 1941-42, Grand Rapids Art Inst., 1945-49, UCLA, 1964-69, Loyola Marymount Coll., Westchester, Calif., 1970-73; life tchg. credential, U. So. Calif., Long Beach, 1973. Life teaching credential, Calif. Decorator John Widdicomb Furniture Co., 1945-49; tchr. art Inglewood Sch. Dist., Calif., 1965-73; tchr. adult edn. art Downey Unified Sch. Dist., 1973-95; tchr. art Assn. Retarded Citizens and Mentally Disadvantaged Students Downey Cmty. Health Ctr., 2003—04. Art tchr. institutionalized adults ages 18 to 60, 2000-2004; lectr. Downey Art League, 1990-92, Whittier (Calif.) Art Assn., 1991, h.s. and mid. sch. lectr., 1994-95; judge Children's Art Exhibit, Downey, 1992; participant Getty Found., San Francisco, 1993, Getty Found., Cranbrook, 1994, Getty Conf. on Aesthetics, 1995, Cin. U., 1992, El Segundo, 1994; mem. state accreditation com. Inglewood and Downey United Sch. Dists., 1966-70, 75-80, 85—; owner A & B Furniture Svc. Ctr., 1995—. One-woman shows include El Segundo Mcpl. Libr., 1965, Pico Rivera Art Gallery, 1978, Downey Art Mus., 1999; exhibited in group shows at Fairlane Show, Dearborn, Mich., 1959, Jane Lessing Art Gallery, 1966, Westchester Mcpl. Libr., 1971, Inglewood City Hall, 1973, Aegina Sch., Greece, 1973, Downey Mus. Art, 1992, 99-2000; represented in permanent collection U. Mich., Calif. Senate Bldg. Pres. bd. dirs. Downey Art Mus., 1996-2002, dir. Mus., 1998, vol. dir., 1999, bd. dirs. 1998-2000; art commr. City of Dearborn, Mich., 1954-59; former pres. Dearborn Art Inst., Pacific Art Guild; pres. Downey Art League, 1991-94, v.p., 1999-2000; pres. Exhbn. Ch., 1995, v.p. 1996-98; vol. dir. Art Mus., 1998-99; lectr. on art as a career local Downey high and mid. schs.; juried children's art shows; vol. tchr. basic art; judge art shows. Recipient Certs. of Appreciation for contbn. of leadership Coord. Coun. Downey, Downey Governing Bd., Downey Bd. Edn., 1997, 2002, Cmty. Svc. award for Outstanding Svc. Downey Rotary, 1994, Cert. of Recognition Calif. State Assembly, 1999, Downey Coord. Coun., 1998-99, award 2002; named Tchr. of Yr., Masons, Downey, 1986; painting chosen to represent dist. in state capital, 1999-2001. Mem. Calif. Coun. on Art Edn. (parliamentarian Downey 1990-92, Calco Excellence in T[illegible] 1991) [illegible]). Avocations: reading, hiking, internat. travel, photography, painting. Home: 9318 Fostoria St Downey CA 90241-4020

BROOKS, LORRAINE ELIZABETH, retired music educator; b. Port Chester, N.Y., Mar. 10, 1936; d. William Henry Brooks and Marion Elizabeth Brooks. BS in Music Edn., SUNY, Potsdam, 1958; M of Performance, Manhattan Sch. Music, 1970; cert. in Religion EPS, Trinity Coll., 2001. Dir. Camp Spruce-Mountain Lakes, North Salem, N.Y., 1964-73; youth adviser St. Peter's Episcopal Ch., Port Chester, N.Y., 1964-65, St. Andrew's-St. Peter's Ch., Yonkers, N.Y., 1970-73; v.p. South Yonkers Youth Council, 1970-76; assoc. Sisters Charity of N.Y., Scarsdale, 1978—; eucharistic min., lector Our Lady of Victory Ch., Mt. Vernon, NY, 1981-93, 1981—93; asst. chaplain White Plains Hosp. Ctr., NY, 1981—2000; chaplain for renal patients St. Joseph's Med. Ctr., Yonkers, NY, 2000—. Cons. Quincy Tenants Assn., Mt. Vernon, 1986—; workshop presenter in kidney hemodialysis transplant; music educator cons., 2000—; chaplain for renal pts. St. Joseph Med. Ctr., Yonkers, NY, 2000—; choral dir. Elem. Middle Sch. Soloist Greenhaven Correctional Facility retreat, N.Y., 1994; recital St. Mary's Ch. Outreach Program, 1994. Vestrywoman St. Andrew's Episc. Ch., Yonkers, 1971-75; contralto soloist St. Peter's Episc. Ch., Port Chester, 1959-69, Cape Cod Roman Cath. Charismatic Conf., 1993; mem. Collegiate Chorale, N.Y.C., 1958-68; svc. team mem. Charismatic Cmty., Scarsdale, 1975-91; v.p. Willwood Tenant Assn., Mt. Vernon, 1981-82, pres., 1982-84; vol. speaker N.Y. Regional Transplant Program, 1992—; active Montefiore Med. Ctr. TRIO, 1991—, presenter kidney transplant program, 1995; active Teen/Twenty Encounter Christ, 1990-92; soloist concert Holy Spirit Episcopal Ch., Orleans, Mass.; facilitator Our Lady of the Cape, Brewster, Mass.; inspirational spkr. St. Joan of Arc, Orleans, Mass., 2002; lector, eucharistic min., workshop presenter, leader of prayer group, cons. St. Mary's Roman Cath. Ch., 1993—, facilitator RENEW program, 1994—, CORE team mem., 1996, coord. prayer group Day of Reflection, elected leader prayer group, 1998—, adviser young adults ministry, 1998-2002; asst. coord. RENEW, St. Mary's Ch., Mt. Vernon, N.Y., leader Charismatic Prayer Group, 1998-2000, cons. to Charismatic group, 2000—; coord. Life in the Spirit Program, 1997; trustee Edn. Parish Svc. Program, Trinity Coll., 2000; vol. chaplain for renal patients St. Joseph's M.C., Yonkers, N.Y., 2001—; team mem. Women's Cursillo-English, N.Y. Archdiocese; active Christopher Leadership course Gabriel Richard Inst., N.Y., 2000; vol. chaplain for renal patients St. Joseph's Med. Ctr., Yonkers, N.Y.; dir. EPS Local Task Force, 2003-. Mem. Westchester County Sch. Music Assn. (exec. bd.), Scarsdale Tchrs. Assn. (exec. bd.), Music Educators Nat. Conf., West Cmty. Sch. Music Assn (exec. bd. 1967-70). Democrat. Roman Catholic. Avocations: swimming, reading, walking, organic cooking, concerts. E-mail: Brookhem@aol.com.

BROOKS, MARION, newscaster; BA English, Spelman Coll. Weekend anchor Sta. WABG-TV, Greenville, Miss., anchor weekday 6 pm and 11 pm newscasts; gen. assignment reporter, morning anchor Sta. WJKS-TV, Jacksonville, Fla., 1991—93; gen. assignment reporter Sta. KTVI-TV, St. Louis, 1993—96, weekend anchor; anchor noon newscast, reporter 5 pm and 6 pm newscasts Sta. WSB-TV, Atlanta, 1996—98; co-anchor 5 pm and 10 pm weekend newscasts Sta. WMAQ-TV, Chgo., 1998—, co-anchor 4:30 pm and 5 pm weekday newscasts, healthwatch reporter. Mem.: Nat. Assn. Black Journalists. Office: NBC 454 N Columbus Dr Chicago IL 60611

BROOKS, Mrs. MEL See BANCROFT, ANNE

BROOKS, NORMA NEWTON, legal assistant; b. Granite, Okla., Oct. 30, 1936; d. Ralph David and Bessie M. (Elkins) Newton; m. Rex Dwain Brooks, May 16, 1964; children: Jonathan Douglas, Elizabeth Ann. Student, U. Okla., 1979, BS in Edn., 1970; MEd, Ctrl. State U., 1972. Cert. secondary sch. tchr., Okla. Legal asst. Rex D. Brooks Atty.-At-Law, Oklahoma City, 1974—. Mem. Am. Home Econs. Assn., Women in the Arts, Kappa Delta Pi. Baptist. Avocations: art, education. Home: 2323 N Indiana Ave Oklahoma City OK 73106-1632 Office: Rex D Brooks Atty-At-Law 1900 NW 23rd St Oklahoma City OK 73106-1202 Office Phone: 405-524-3525.

BROOKS, PATRICIA SCOTT, principal; b. St. Louis, July 19, 1949; d. John Edward and Doris Louise (Webb) Scott; m. John Robert Brooks, May 22, 1986; 1 child, Ollie. BS, W.Va. State Coll., 1971; MA, Marshall U., 1974; adminstrv. cert., Ind. U., 1990. Cert. tchr., Ind. Tchr. spl. edn. Huntington (W.Va.) State Hosp., 1971; tchr. elem. edn. Kanawha County Sch., Charleston, W.Va., 1971-78, Washington Twp., Indpls., 1979-82, tchr. mid. sch., 1982-90, adminstrv. intern, 1989-90, asst. coord., 1990, 92, asst. prin., 1990-93; prin. Pike Twp., Indpls., 1993-2000, New Pike Twp. Sch.-Snacks Crossing Elem., 2001. Participant Ind. U. Tchr. as a Decision Maker Program, Bloomington, 1989; mem. Human Rels. Com., Indpls., 1996; presenter U.S. Dept. Edn. Panelist State PTA Conv. Recipient Tchr. Spotlight award Topics Newspaper, 1983; named one of 100 Outstanding Black Women in State of Ind., Nat. Coun. Negro Women, 1990, Ctr. for Leadership Devel. award, 2002; Danforth fellow Ind. U., 1989. Mem. Ind. Assn. for Elem. and Mid. Sch. Prins., Phi Delta Kappa, Delta Sigma Theta. Methodist. Avocations: tennis, cooking, reading, dance. Home: 2432 Laurel Lake Blvd Carmel IN 46032-8902

BROOKS, PAULINE C. computer and networking services company executive; BA, George Washington U.; postgrad., Fitch Inst. Data Processing, London, Entrex Sch. Programming, Atlanta, USDA Grad. Sch., U. Md. Various positions to v.p. ops. Dynamic Data Processing, Inc., chief liaison with govt. contracting officer's tech. rep.; founder, pres., CEO, Mgmt. Tech., Inc., Clinton, Md., 1985—. Bd. dirs. Galloway Braintrust Group, Alexandria, Va. Mem. Commn. for Women Prince George's County, Md., Minority Bus. Enterprise Legal Def. and Edn. Fund, Inc. Named Greater Washington Entrepreneur of Yr. in wonan-owned bus. category, 1995; featured as one of top black women entrepreneurs Black Enterprise, 1996. Mem. NAFE, Entrepreneur of Yr. Inst., Am. Entrepreneurs for Econ. Growth, CEO's Club. Office: Mgmt Tech Inc 7700 Old Branch Ave Ste C200 Clinton MD 20735-1628

BROOKS, SHARON DIANE, lawyer; d. Bernard Edward and Alice Lillian Brooks. BA, U. Ill., 1984; MPH, Yale U., 1986; JD, Georgetown U., 2000. Bar: (Washington, D.C.) 2001, (Md.) 2000. Data base mgr./analyst Cardiac Arrhythmia Ctr., Wash. Hosp. Ctr., Washington, 1986—88; epidemiologist CSR, Inc., Washington, 1988—92; sr. data analyst U. Rsch. Corp., Bethesda, Md., 1992—94; policy analyst Project HOPE, Ctr. for Health Affairs, Bethesda, Md.; law clk. Am. Cancer Soc., Washington, 2000; atty. Olsson, Frank and Weeda, Washington, 2000—04, Paul, Hastings, Janofsky & Walker, Washington, 2004—. Contbr. reports to pub. health publs. Mem., instl. rev. bd. Project Hope, Ctr. for Health Affairs, Bethesda, Md., 1996—2003. Mem.: ABA, AAAS. Home: 329 1/2 Constitution Ave NE Washington DC 20002 Office: Paul Hastings Janofsky & Walker 1299 Pennsylvania Ave NW Washington DC 20004 Office Phone: 202-508-0457.

BROOKS, SUSAN W. prosecutor; Grad., Miami U.; JD, Ind. U. Ptnr. McClure, McClure & Kammen, 1985—88, Kammen & Brooks, 1989—97; dep. mayor Indpls., 1998—99; of counsel Ice Miller Law Firm, Indpls., 2000—01; U.S. atty. so. dist. Ind., 2001—. Office: 10 W Market St Ste 2100 Indianapolis IN 46204

BROOKS, SUZANNE RAYETTA, small business owner; b. Phila., Jan. 20, 1941; d. John Christian Lemon and Rayetta (Ortiga) Anderson. BA in English and Edn., La Salle U., 1975; MA in English and Creative Writing, Wash. State U., 1979; postgrad., Fielding Inst. Lic. pvt. investigator, Calif., tax preparer, Calif. Police woman juvenile aid divsn. Phila. Police Dept., 1965-72; dir. sci. supportive svcs. Wash. State U., Pullman, 1979-82; dir. affirmative action U. Nev., Reno, 1982-84, Pa. State U., University Park, 1984-89; dir. Multi-Cultural Ctr., Calif. State U., Sacramento, 1990-95; owner, cons. Creative Concepts/Systems, Sacramento, 1990—. Author: (poetry) Ins & Outs, 1983 (published in India), Ins&Outs, 2004, Escape Is Not an Option, 2004; jazz vocalist (2 CDs): Even Sad Memories are Sweet, 2004, Miles to Go Before I Sleep; contbr. short story to mag., poems, essays; hula dancer Hapa Haole Hula Dancers, Sacramento. Bd. dirs. Nat. Inst. Women of Color, Washington, 1981-92, Nev. Women's Fund, Reno, 1982-84, Washoe County Pers. Com., Reno, 1982-84, Bakari Homes for Boys, Sacramento, 1992—; assoc. Smithsonian Inst., Washington, 1985-89; mem. mayor's action network State Coll. Pa., 1986-89; mem. planning com. August Women's Peace Event, Sacramento, 1992. Recipient Racial Justice award YWCA, Sacramento, 1992; Danforth fellow, 1975, Andrew Kozak fellow Pa. State chpt. Phi Delta Kappa, 1987. Mem. AAUW, NAACP, NAFE, Internat. Assn. Women Color Day, Mensa. Democrat. Roman Catholic. Avocations: american sign language, spanish, international travel, civil rights. Office Phone: 916-483-9804. E-mail: creativesy@aol.com.

BROOKS, VELMA, entrepreneur, small business owner; Grad., Madam C.J. Walker Beauty Coll., Dallas, 1968; student, Bethune Cookeman Coll., Daytona Beach, Fla., Prairie View A&M U., Tex.; AA, El Centro C.C., Dallas, 1970; student, Internat. Aviation Travel Acad., Arlington, Tex., Loreal Sch. of Color, Paris, 1976. Cosmetology instr., ednl. dir. Madam C.J. Walker Beauty Coll., Dallas, 1974; salon owner, mgr. Velma B's Coiffures, Dallas; operator Neighborhood Beauty Salon, Dallas; tchr., technician Mme C.J. Walker Products Mfg. Co., Chgo.; artistic ednl. dir. Simpson's Labs., Houston; mktg. and sales dir. Diamite Direct Sales Corp., Santa Barbara, Calif.; outside sales rep. Mayo Travel Svcs., Dallas, Oak Cliff Travel Agy., Dallas. Named Legends in Bus., Ban of Am., 1997, Bus. Woman Against the Odds, Smithsonian Inst., Bus. Woman of the Yr., Theta Nu Sigma; recipient 1st place Rose D'or Championship, The Golden Rose Paris Festival, Vienna, Austria, 1974, Bus. Woman of the Yr., South Dallas Bus. and Profl. Women's Club, Pylon nat. Businessman's League, Psi Lambda, Trail Blazer award, Venture Advisors, Inc./Tex. State Assn. Beauty Culturist League, Outstanding Ednl. Contbn. award, Internat. Beauty Show Group/Advanstar Prodns., award for dedicated mentor and svc., Dallas Ind. Sch. Dist., 25 Yrs. Svc. in Indsl. Career Tech., Tex. Cosmetology Assn./Nat. Cosmetology Assn., Legacy award, Urban League Greater Dallas, 2004.

BROOKSHIER, ELAINE MARIE, counseling administrator, psychology examiner, social worker; d. William Junior and Elva Louise Sladek; m. Stephen Ray Brookshier, Oct. 21, 1988; children: Stephen William, Shane Leslie, Scott Alan, Sally Louise. BSc in History Edn., NE Mo. State U., 1975, MA in Guidance and Counseling, 1976; M in Social Work, U. Mo., 1994. LCSW Mo., 1993, cert. marriage and family therapist Am. Assn. Marriage and Family Therapists, 1994, lic. profl. counselor Mo., 1996; cert. secondary sch. tchg. Mo., 1975, sch. guidance counselor Mo., 1976, psychol. examiner Mo., 1996. Supr. crisis intervention programs Arthur Ctr., Mexico, Mo., 1991—96; jr. and sr. counselor, psychol. examiner Van-Far R-I Schs., Vandalia, Mo., 1996—; social worker Mo. Divsn. Family Svs., Montgomery City. Guidance counselor Lincoln County R-II Schs., Elsberry, Mo., 1976—79; h.s. counselor Bowling Green R-I, Mo., 1979—81; flood crisis counselor State Mo., Jefferson, 1993—94. Mem. Vandalia Area Optimist Club, 1997—99; mem. ann. conf. com. Mo. Assn. Social Welfare, Jefferson City, Mo., 1990—96. Recipient Mo. award foster parent recruitment video, Mo. State award, Mo. Flood Crisis Counseling; scholar Sch. Social Work, U. Mo.-Columbia Sch. Social Work, 1993. Mem.: Mo. Assn. Sch. Psychologists (licentiate), Mo. Assn. Coll. Admission Counselors (assoc.), Mo. Assn. Sch. Counselors (assoc.), Alethea Federated Mo. Club (assoc.; v.p. 1994), Unites Femme Club (assoc.; v.p. 2001—03), Alpha Phi Sigma (hon.), Phi Alpha Theta (hon. award 1974), Phi Delta Kappa (hon.; v.p. 1975—76), Delta Zeta (assoc.; rec. sec. 1973—74). Democrat-Npl. Baptist. Avocations: gardening, reading, sports. Office: Van-Far R-I HS 2200 West Hwy 54 Vandalia MO 63382 Personal E-mail: ebrookshier@vf.k12.mo.us.

BROOKS SHOEMAKER, VIRGINIA LEE, librarian; b. Oklahoma City, Sept. 16, 1944; d. Leo B. and Eloise Gilreath; m. Phil Ashley Brooks, Aug. 10, 1972 (dec. Oct. 1982); 1 child, Philip Brooks; m. Gene Darryl Shoemaker, Feb. 16, 1986; children: Rob, Julie, Donna, Gary. Student, Oklahoma City C.C., 1980; BS, U. Ctrl. Okla., 1988, M in Sch. Media, 1991, postgrad., 2000—. With Dept. Human Svcs., Oklahoma City, 1970-75, State Dept. Librs., Oklahoma City, 1980-87; substitute tchr. Oklahoma City Schs., 1989-91; vol. libr. Children's Libr., Children's Hosp., Oklahoma City, 1992—; libr. vol. Corpus Christi Sch. Libr., 1998—; vol. children's sect. First Bapt. Libr.; vol. Libr. for Blind. Sponsor World Vision, Seattle, 1994—; active cub scouts Boy Scouts Am.; active, life mem. Meth. Ch. of the Servant, women mission groups, Wesley Meth.; vol. Habitat for Humanity, Vista Care Hospice; vol. childrens sect. First Bapt. Libr.; reading sch. libr. tutor, First Bapt. Good Shepherd Children's Dental Clinic. project transformation, vista care volunteer. Recipient Adopt-a-Park awards, Oklahoma City Beautiful, Omniplex Sci. Mus., Oklahoma City, 1986-89. Mem.: Omniplex Sci. Mus. Zool. Soc. (Adpot-a-Park award 1986—89), Internat. Reading Assn. (reading tutor), Coun. Exceptional Children, Classen Alumni Assn., U. Ctrl. Okla. Alumni Assn. Baptist. Avocations: piano, reading, creative writing, dogs and cats, making greeting cards.

BROOKS-TURNER, MYRA, music educator; b. Knoxville, Tenn., Jan. 13, 1933; d. Paul David and Lilli Ray Brooks; m. Ronald J. Turner, June 11, 1960; children: Stacy Turner Steele, Cheryl Turner Walker, Teresa Turner Basler. Student of piano, voice and composition, Juilliard Sch. Music, 1945—51; BMus in Piano, So. Meth. U., 1955, MusM in Theory and Composition, 1956, postgrad. in Piano, 1957—58. Educator Dallas Indep. Schs., Tex., 1956—60; choral music specialist Knoxville City Schs., Tenn., 1960—65; composer-in-residence Birmingham Children's Theatre, Ala., 1965—68; music instr. Mercer U. Music Prep. Sch., Atlanta, 1975—77; instr. composition Maryville Coll. Pres. Sch. of the Arts, Tenn., 1978—80; music instr. U. Tenn., Knoxville, 1990—92; owner Myra Brooks Turner Studio of Music, Knoxville, Tenn., 1992—. Freelance writer, pub. MBT Productions, Knoxville, 1993—. Composer, producer : (musicals) Make Way for Love, 1955; Uh-Uh, 1956; Javaho Junction, 1958; composer, dir. The Green Dragon, 1965—68 (Seattle Nat. Playwriting First Place award); contbr. articles to profl. publs. and jours. Music worship leader Epis. Ch. of Ascension, Knoxville, Tenn., 1992—93. Recipient Cultural Arts award, Tenn. Arts Commn., 1982. Mem.: Tenn. Fed. Music Clubs (state jr. counselor 1978—88, officer, state bd. 1978—89, Ea. Tenn. divisional v.p. 2002—, officer, state bd. 2002—, East Tenn. divsn. jr. counselor 2002—, editor State Piano Competition Book 2003, 2004—06), Nat. Fed. Music Clubs (jr. festivals bulletin advisor 1982—90), Knoxville Music Tchrs. Assn. (sec., bd. mem. 2000—01, Composer of Yr. 1978, 2001), Tenn. Music Tchrs. Assn., Nat. Music Tchrs. Assn., Ossoli Circle, Knoxville Writer's Group, Tuesday Morning Musical Club (pres. 1990—91), U. Tenn. Faculty Women's Club, Pi Kappa Lambda Nat. Music Honorary, Mu Phi Epsilon Internat. Frat. (pres. 1973—74, pres. Atlanta Alumnae, Music Therapy award 1974), Alpha Delta Pi. Republican. Episcopalian. Achievements include published 350 original piano solos, duets, art songs and anthems from 1993 to 2003. Avocations: study of French, study of Italian, lessons in computer graphics and finale, interior decorating, photography.

BROOME, CLAIRE VERONICA, epidemiologist, researcher; b. Tunbridge Wells, Kent, England, Aug. 24, 1949; came to U.S., 1951; d. Kenneth R. and Heather C. (Platt) B.; m. John F. Head, Apr. 2, 1988; children: Gabriel K., Steven G. BA, Harvard U., 1970, MD, 1975. Diplomate Am. Bd. Internal Medicine. Dep. chief spl. pathogens br. Ctrs. for Disease Control, Atlanta, 1979-80, chief meningitis, spl. pathogens br., 1981-90, assoc. dir. sci., 1991-94, acting dir., nat. ctr. injury prevention and control, 1992-93, dep. dir., 1994-99, sr. advisor to dir. for health info. sys., 1999—. Cons. vaccine devel. AID, 1988—, WHO, NIH, various univs.; mem. steering com. on encapsulated bacterial vaccines, WHO, Geneva, 1989-91, chmn., 1992-96; mem. adv. com. on vaccines FDA, Washington, 1990-94; mem. sci. adv. group experts global program on vaccines and immunizations World Health Orgn., 1996—. Contbr. numerous articles to profl. jours. Recipient M. C. Rockefeller fellowship, 1970-71, Meritorious Svc. medal USPHS, 1986, Disting. Svc. medal USPHS, 1996, 2000, John Snow award Am. Pub. Health Assn., 2000; rsch. grants NIH, FDA, Dept. of State. Fellow Infectious Diseases Soc. Am. (Bristol-Myers Squibb award 1993); mem. ACP, Inst. of Medicine, Am. Epidemiologic Soc., Am. Soc. Microbiology, Common Cause, Phi Beta Kappa, Alpha Omega Alpha. Avocation: tennis. Office: Ctrs for Disease Control # D68 Atlanta GA 30333

BROOTEN, DOROTHY, nursing educator, former dean; b. Hazleton, Pa. married; two children. BSN, U. Pa., 1966, MSN, 1970, PhD in Ednl. Adminstrn., 1980. Assoc. prof. nursing Thomas Jefferson U., 1972-77; from asst. to assoc. prof. nursing U. Pa., 1977-88, prof. nursing, chair Health Care of Women & Childbearing, 1980-93, dir. Ctr. for Low Birthweight, Sch. Nursing, 1990-96, Overseers prof. perinatal nursing, 1990-96; dean, prof. Frances Payne Bolton Sch. Nursing Case Western Res. U., Cleve., 1998—2000; prof. Florida International Univ., 2001—. Cons. Sch. Medicine, U. Utrecht, The Netherlands, 1989, Ministry of Health, Malawi, Africa, 1991. Recipient Contbrn. to Nursing Sci. award ANA, 1988. Mem. Inst. Medicine-NAS, Am. Acad. Nursing (mem. gov. coun. 1988-91). Achievements include research on low birthweight prevention, postdischarge care of low birthweight infants, health care delivery. Office: Fl Internat U Rm ACII230 11200 SW 8th St Miami FL 33199

BROPHY, MARY O'REILLY, environmental scientist; b. N.Y.C., Aug. 3, 1948; d. Luke Edward and Regina (Mahoney) O'Reilly; children: Robert, Sara, Lena. Student, Fordham U., 1966-68; BS, U. Mich., 1970, MS, 1972, PhD, 1979. Rsch. asst. prof. Health Sci. Ctr., Syracuse, N.Y., 1979-84; environ. toxicologist Syracuse Rsch. Corp., 1984-86; pres. ARLS Cons., Inc., Syracuse, 1993—; sr. indsl. hygienist N.Y. State Dept. Labor, Syracuse, 1987-00; environ. specialist N.Y. State Dept. Transp., Binghamton, 2000—. Adj. asst. prof. SUNY Sch. Pub. Health, Albany, 1990—; adj. prof. chemistry LeMoyne Coll., 1998—; dir. Am. Bd. Indsl. Hygiene, Lansing, Mich., 1995—2001; mem. Z10 com. Am. Nat. Stds. Inst., 2001—; mem. adv. bd. N.Y. State Inst. for Health and the Environment, 2001—. Author: An Ergonomics Guide to VDTs, 1994, (with others) Occupational Ergonomics, 1996; contbr.: ILO's Encyclopedia of Occupational Health and Safety, 1998, Implications of Hormesis for Industrial Hygienists, 2003, Health Risk Assessment at Brownfield Redevelolpment Sites, 2003, 04, Ground Water Effects From Highway Tire Shred Projects, 2003, 04, others; contbr. articles to profl. jours. Mem. Am. Indsl. Hygiene Assn., Human Factors & Ergonomics Soc., N.Y. State Assn.Transp. Engrs. Avocations: Karate, fly-fishing, dance, folk harp. Home: 7705 Farley Ln Manlius NY 13104-9571 E-mail: mbrophy@dot.state.ny.us., Mary.Brophy@[illegible]

BROSELOW, LINDA LATT, medical office technician, aviculturist; b. Harrisburg, Pa., July 9, 1940; d. Herman and Ricci (Buch) Latt; m. Robert Joel Broselow, Nov. 26, 1966; children: Andrew M., Katherine, Jordan. BS, Pa. State U., 1962; MA, Columbia U., 1965. Vol. Peace Corps, Ankara, Turkey, 1962-64; office mgr. Robert J. Broselow, M.D., Lubbock, Tex., 1984-88, med. office technician, 1990-98. Vol. South Park Hosp., Lubbock, 1986-87, Ronald McDonald House, Lubbock, 1990-92. Mem. ASPCA, MADD, Am. Diabetes Assn., Am. Assn. Ret. Persons, Audubon Soc., Arkadashlar, Assn. of Univ. Women, League of Women Voters. Avocation: reading. Home: 4609 9th St Lubbock TX 79416-4710 Office: 4609 9th St Lubbock TX 79416 Fax: (806) 795-2005. E-mail: mamoollbb@sbcglobal.net.

BROSH, RITA, performing company executive; Trained with, Margaret Craske, Sallie Wilson, Ron Bostik, Patsy Swayze, Ron Sequoio, Robert Joffrey, Edith Stephen, Margo Marshall; student, Nat. Ballet Sch., Can. Asst. choreographer Beauty & the Beast Off Broadway, N.Y.C., 1976; artistic dir. S.W. Jazz Ballet Co., Houston, 1977—, choreographer, 1977—; artistic dir. Rita Brosh Sch. Dance, 1979—; dir. Am. in Concert Tours, 1980-92, Stars n Stripes, 1992-95. Performed in shows at Can. Nat. Exhbn., Edith Stephen Theatre Dance Co., Manhattan Festival Ballet Co., U.S. and Can. Nat. Tour, Balt. Ballet Co., Pocono's Equity Tour, San Antonio Festival Ballet, Ballet Western Reserve, U.S. Naval Acad., Miller Outdoor Theatre, numerous others. Office: SW Jazz Ballet Co PO Box 38233 720 1/2 Pinemont Dr Houston TX 77018-1518

BROSNAN, CAROL RAPHAEL SARAH, retired arts administrator, musician; b. Paterson, NJ, July 19, 1931; d. Basil Roger and Mary Ellen Carroll (McDonald) B. Piano student of, Iris Brussels, 1940-53; student, George Washington U., Washington, 1956-61, U. Va., 1975, U. Oxford (Eng.), 1975; BA in History, George Washington U., 1981, MA in History, 1987. Adminstrv. clk. Dept. of Army, Def., Pentagon, Office of asst. chief of staff intelligence, Washington, 1955-58; clk. fgn. sci. info. program NSF, Washington, 1958-60, adminstrv. clk., 1960-65, adminstrv. fellowship clk. grad. fellowship program, 1965-72; staff asst. to Jane Alexander, chmn. Nat. Endowment for the Arts, Washington, 1972-94; ret., 1994. Music tchr. piano, Paterson, 1945-53; piano recitalist U.S., Heidelberg, W. Ger. Served with WAC, 1953-55. Recipient Young People's Concerts award, 1945. Hon. fellow Harry S. Truman Libr. Inst. Nat. and Internat. Affairs, 1975. Mem. Am. Legion, Am. Hist. Assn., Nat. Assn. Uniformed Svcs., Acad. Polit. Sci. (contbg. 1978-81), Am. Classical League, Friends of Bodleian Libr. (Oxford U.), Luther Rice Soc. George Washington U. (life), Phi Alpha Theta. Home: 6030 Sunset Ridge Ct Centreville VA 20121-3051 Office: Nat Endowment for Arts 1100 Pennsylvania Ave NW Washington DC 20004-2501

BROSTOWSKI, GAYLE A. minister; b. Scranton, Pa., July 16, 1963; d. Joseph S. and Ruth L. Brostowski. BS in Bible, Valley Forge Christian Coll., 1985. Youth pastor Living Waters Assembly God, Greenfield, Mass., 1985—87, Spencerport (NY) Assembly God, 1987—88, First Assembly God, Tyrone, Pa., 1989—90, Cmty. Assembly God, Lowville, NY, 1990—91, Newburgh (NY) Assembly God, 1991—94; evangelist Gayle A. Brostowski Evangelistic Ministry, Taylor, Pa., 1994—. Avocations: Christian music, bicycling, walking.

BROTHERS, JOYCE DIANE, television personality, psychologist; b. N.Y.C. d. Morris K. and Estelle (Rapoport) Bauer; m. Milton Brothers, July 4, 1949; 1 child, Lisa Robin. BS, Cornell U., 1947; MA, Columbia U., 1950, PhD, 1953; LHD (hon.), Franklin Pierce Coll., Gettysburg Coll., Lehigh U., 1994, Mt. St. Mary Coll., 1998. Asst. in psychology Columbia U., N.Y.C., 1948-52; instr. psychology Hunter Coll., N.Y.C., 1948-52; ind. psychologist, writer, 1952—. Co-host: TV program Sports Showcase, 1956; appearances: TV program Dr. Joyce Brothers, 1958-63, Consult Dr. Brothers, 1960-66, Ask Dr. Brothers, 1965-75; hostess (TV syndication) Living Easy with Dr. Joyce Brothers, 1972-75; columnist TV syndication, N.Am. Newspaper Alliance, 1961-71, Bell-McClure Syndicate, 1963-71, King Features Syndicate, 1972—, Good Housekeeping mag., 1962— ; appearances Sta. WNBC, 1966-70; radio program Emphasis, 1966-75, Monitor, 1967-75, Sta. WMCA, 1970-73, ABC Reports, 1966-67, NBC Radio Network Newsline, 1975— ; news analyst radio program, Metro Media-TV, 1975-76, news corr., TVN, Inc., 1975-76, Sta. KABC-TV, 1977-82, Sta. WABC-TV, 1980-82,, 86-88, Sta. WLS-TV, 1980-82, NIWS Syndicated News Service, 1982-84, The Dr. Joyce Brothers Program, The Disney Channel, 1985, Sta. KCBS-TV News, 1987—; spl. feature writer Hearst papers, UPI; current affairs spl. corr. Fox TV Syndication, 1990-97; featured on A&E's Biography, 1999; author: Ten Days to a Successful Memory, 1959, Woman, 1961, The Brothers System for Liberated Love and Marriage, 1975, How to Get Whatever You Want Out of Life, 1978, What Every Woman Should Know About Men, 1982, What Every Woman Ought to Know About Love and Marriage, 1988, The Successful Woman, 1989, Widowed, 1990, Positive Plus: The Practical Plan to Liking Yourself Better, 1994. Co-chmn. sports com. Lighthouse for Blind; door-to-door chmn. Fedn. Jewish Philanthropies, N.Y.C.; mem. fund raising com. Olympic Fund; mem. People-to-People Program. Winner $64,000 Question TV Program, 1956, $64,000 Challenge, 1957; recipient Mennen Baby Found. award, 1959, Newhouse Newspaper award, 1959, Am. Acad. Achievement award, Am. Parkinson Disease Assn. award, 1971, Deadline award Sigma Delta Chi, 1971, Pres.'s Cabinet award U. Detroit, 1975, Woman of Achievement award Women's City Club Cleve., 1981, award Calif. Home Econs. Assn., 1981, award Distrubutive Edn. Clubs Am., 1981, Golden Gavel Excellence in Comm. award Toastmasters, 1982, Pub. Svc. award Ridgewood Women's Club, 1987, Women Who Make a Difference award Sen. Bill Bradley, 1990, Gt. Am. award Bards of Bohemia, 1993, Diamond award, 1994, George M. and Mary Jane Leader Healthcare Achievement award, 1995, Nat. Cmty. Svc. award McQuade Children Svcs., 1998. Mem. Sigma Xi. Office: NBC Westwood One Radio Network 1700 Broadway New York NY 10019-5905

BROTMAN, BARBARA LOUISE, columnist, writer; b. N.Y.C., Feb. 23, 1956; d. Oscar J. and Ruth (Branchor) Brotman; m. Chuck Berman, Aug. 28, 1983; children: Robin, Nina. BA, Queens Coll., 1978. Writer, columnist Chgo. Tribune, 1978—. Recipient Ill. Newspapers Column Writing award UPI, 1984, Peter Lisagor award Sigma Delta Chi, 1984. Avocation: broomball. Office: Chgo Tribune Co 435 N Michigan Ave Chicago IL 60611-4066

BROTMAN, PHYLLIS BLOCK, advertising and public relations executive; b. Balt., Mar. 23, 1934; d. Sol. George and Delma (Herman) Block; m. Don N. Brotman, Aug. 16, 1953; children: Solomon G., Barbara Brotman Kaylor. Student. Balt. Jr. Coll., U. Va., Mary Washington Coll. Assoc. Channel 13 TV, 1953-55; free-lance pub. rels., 1960-66; coord. pub. rels. Md. Coun. Ednl. TV, 1965-66; pres., CEO Image Dynamics, Inc., Balt., 1966—. Lectr., cons. Md. Gen. Assembly Legis. Info. Program, 1968-70; panelist TV and radio; bd. dirs., bd. trustees Notre Dame Coll., Md.; bd. visitors Elon Coll., N.C., Towson U., Md. Columnist Balt. Bus. Jour., 1965. State chair U.S. Olympics Com. Mid-Atlantic Region, 1989-92; chair, com. mem. Greater Balt. Com., 1985-87, econ. devel. coun., 1990-91; adv. bd. Nat. Aquarium Balt., 1988—; bd. dirs. Nat. Adv. Rev. Bd., 1988-89, Balt. Symphony Orch., 1989-2001, mktg. com. 75th ann. season, 1991; active Balt. Pub. Rels. Coun.; chair adv. bd. Children and Youth Trust Fund, 1989—; bd. dirs. Internat. Visitors Ctr., co-chair mktg. com., 1990—; founding mem. Chamber Symphony San Francisco, 1984, bd. dirs., 1984-91; pub. rels. com., pres. adv. coun. U. Md. Sys., 1988—; 20th ann. conf. com. Internat. Urban Fellows Program Johns Hopkins Inst. Policy Studies, 1989-90, cmty. resources bd. Jr. League Balt., 1982-87; bd. dirs. New Directions for Women, 1979, 87-90, Stella Maris Hospice Oper. Corp., 1985-87, Jewish Family and Childrens Soc., 1980-83, Nat. Coun. Jewish Women; mem. comm. United Way Ctrl. Md., 1981-83; mktg. and pub. rels. com. Balt. Mus. Art, 1982-84, hon. com. Joshua Johnson Coun. and Endowment Fund, 1988; active U. Md. Endowments Com., 1978-79; nat. commr. B'nai B'rith Youth Commn.; bd. electors Balt. Hebrew Congregation, pres. parents assn., religious sch. com., bd. congregation; past bd. dirs. Assoc. Placement and Guidance Bur., Levindale Home and Infirmary Ladies Aux., Sinai Hosp. Aux., Nat. Jewish Welfare Fund; chair Balt. County Econ. Devel. Commn., 1987-91; appointed commn., 1980; appointed Mayors Commn. Telecomm., 1987-90; appointed State of Md. Legis. Compensation Commn., 1979—, Mayor Balt. Bus. Delegation for Balt. Conv. Ctr., 1979; bd. trustees Loyola Coll. Balt., 1986-93, treas., 1981, 82-83; bd. adv. Towson State U., 1989—, bd. vis., mem. adv. coun. Sch. Bus. & Econs., 1983-85; Found. bd. dirs. Mary Washington Coll., 1985-87, 88-92, speaker jr. class ring ceremony, 1981; mem. exec. com. Inst. Politics and Govt. Coll. Continuing Edn. U. So. Calif.; commencement speaker U. Ky. Coll. Dentistry, 1982; chmn. panel State Dept. Edu., 2001-2002; mem. Bd. Edn. Visionary Panel, 2001—, chmn. support task force; bd. visitors Towson U.; chmn. Sch. Comms. Recipient Cert. Achievement, Young Womens Leadership Coun., Cert. Appreciation for svc. to Md. Gen. Assembly by Md. Senate, Cert. Achievement in profession Md. Ho. Dels., Legis. Info. Program Pub. Rels. Soc. Am. Md. Chpt., Cert. Appreciation pub. svc. Md. Area Residences Youth, Pub. Rels. award Great Chesapeake Balloon Race Pub. Rels. Soc. Am., Md. Chpt., Leadership award nat. svc. to profession Internat. Orgn. Women Execs., 1980, Dedicated Svc. award Jewish Family and Children, 1983, Pres. Citation pvt. sector initiatives, 1985, Guardian of Menorah Internat. award B'nai B'rith, 1986; named one of Balt. Most Powerful Women, Balt. Mag., Balt. Outstanding Women Mgts. WMAR-TV, U. Balt., 1983, Woman of Yr., Arlene Rosenbloom Wyman Guild-U. Md. Cancer Ctr., 1984, B'nai B'rith Internat., 1985, 94, Avon Products, Inc., 1990, Media Advocate of Yr. for Md. U.S. Small Bus. Adminstrn., 1985, Most Admired company Balt. Mag., 1987-89, Entrepreneur of Yr. Balt. County Econ. Devel., 1990, Save-A-Heart Humanitarian of Yr., 1991, Balt. County Woman of Yr., 2004. Mem. Am. Assn. Adv. Agencies (chair mid-Atlantic region 1981-82, gov. eastern region 1982-84, chair 1986-87, bd. dirs., gov. rels. com. 1982-87), Am. Assn. Polit. Cons. (pres. 1976-80, bd. dirs. 1974-76, 80—), Nat. Coun. Jewish Women (life, bd. dirs.), Pub. Rels. Soc. Am. (Md. chpt. nat. chair roundtable 1987-88, co-chair nat. conf. 1980, v.p. 1968, Silver Anvil award 1988, Lifetime Achievement award 1993), Am. Adv. Fedn. (co-chair pub. rels. com. 1986-88, nat. govt. rels. coun. 1982—, chair legis. com. 1981), Meeting Planners Internat. (co-chair pub. rels. 1978-80, task force election by-laws 1979), Adv. Assn. Balt. (bd. dirs. 1974-76), Md.-DC-Del. Press Assn. (co-chair assocs. sect. 1982-83), Am. Trauma Soc. (nat. bd. dirs. 1981-87, Md. bd. dirs. 1982-89), Balt. County C. of C. (co-chmn. pub. rels. 2003—, mem. legis. com., 2002—), Beta Gamma Sigma, Alpha Sigma Nu, Balt. Md. C. of C. (v.p. membership 1991—, v.p. leadership Md. bd. govs. 1992-93, v.p. ctrl. dist. 1985-91, legis. conf. chair 1990, exec. com. 1986—, bd. dirs. 1984—), Balt. County C. of C. (bd. dirs. 2004-, Woman of Yr. 2004), Ctr. Club Balt. (bd. dirs., comm. chair 1983—, pres. 2003—). Avocations: tennis, flying (cert. aviation solo flight single engine aircraft), wine tasting. Home: 8105 Mcdonogh Rd Baltimore MD 21208-1005 Office: Image Dynamics Inc 8105 Mcdonogh Rd Baltimore MD 21208-1005 Office Phone: 410-363-1565. E-mail: pbbrotman@comcast.net.

BROUGHTON, CAROLYN MILES, multimedia executive, public relations executive; b. Cambridge, Mass., Mar. 2, 1958; d. David Alan and Martha Jean (Butler) Miles; m. George C. Broughton, May 7, 1988; 1 child, Christiana Marie. AA, Am. Coll., Paris, 1979; BA in Radio and TV Communications, George Washington U., 1982; MA in Human Resources Devel., Webster U., 1996. TV reporter Sta. WHSV-TV3, Harrisonburg, Va., 1981-82, Sta. WJKS-TV17, Jacksonville, Fla., 1982-85, Sta. WJXT-TV4, Jacksonville, 1985-89; pub. rels. coord. City of Jacksonville, 1989—. Pres. Broughton & Assocs. Disabilities Cons., Jacksonville, Fla., 1994—. Vol. P.A.C.E. Ctr. for Girls, Jacksonville, 1989—, Gateway coun. Girl Scouts USA, 1999—. Recipient Cmty. Svc. Fla. Emmy award, 1987, Golden Palm award 1997 (2), 2000, Image award (3), 1998, Image Awds. (6), 1999, Silver Quill Awd., 1998, Image award (3), 2000, Mayor's award, 2001.

Mem. City County Communicators and Mktg., Fla. Govt. Communicators, Internat. TV and Video Assn., U.S. Fencing Assn. Avocations: internet, web content and design, photography, fencing, volunteerism. E-mail: brough@mediaone.net.

BROUGHTON, MARGARET MARTHA, psychiatric nurse practitioner; b. London, Ky., Feb. 1, 1926; d. Edward Broughton and Stella Alice Johnson; m. Louis Kurt Henkel, May 17, 1947 (div. Nov. 1957); children: Gretchen Maria Henkel Clark, Suzanne Henkel Guthrie, Elizabeth Henkel Stark, David Lawrence Henkel, John Arthur Henkel. RN, Christ Hosp. Sch. Nursing, Cin., 1947; BA in Religious Studies, U. Calif., Santa Barbara, 2003. Staff nurse, psychiatric nurse to asst. supt. psychiatric nurse and instr. Camarillo (Calif.) State Hosp., 1958—70; mental health nurse I and II, insvc. instr. Ventura County Mental Health, Calif., 1973—88; part-time spiritual group facilitator Hillmont Psychiatric Ctr., Ventura, Calif., 1995—. Democrat. Universalist Unitarian. Avocations: singing, reading, walking. Home: 980 Terracina Dr Santa Paula CA 93060 E-mail: phoenixrise@vcnet.com.

BROUN, ELIZABETH, art historian, museum administrator; b. Kansas City, Mo., Dec. 15, 1946; d. Augustine Hughes and Roberta Catherine (Hayden) Gibson. BA, U. Kans., 1968, PhD, 1976; cert. advanced study, U. Bordeaux, France, 1967. Curator prints and drawings Spencer Mus. Art, Lawrence, Kans., 1976-83; asst. prof. U. Kans., Lawrence, 1978-83; asst. dir. chief curator Nat. Mus. Am. Art, Washington, 1983-88, acting dir., 1988-89; dir. Smithsonian Am. Art Mus. (formerly Nat. Mus. Am. Art), Washington, 1989—. Author: exhbn. catalogues Prints of Zorn, 1979, Prints and Drawings of Pat Steir, 1983, Patrick Ireland; Drawings 1965-85, 1986, Albert Pinkham Ryder, 1989; co-author: Benton's Bentons, 1980, Engravings of Marcantonio Raimondi, 1981. Woodrow Wilson fellow, 1968-69; Ford. Found. fellow, 1970-72 Mem. Phi Beta Kappa Office: MRC 970 PO Box 37012 Washington DC 20013-7012

BROWAR, LISA MURIEL, librarian; b. N.Y.C., Jan. 22, 1951; d. Elliott Andrew and Shirley (Kahn) B. B in English Lit., Ind. U., 1973, MLS, 1977; M in English Lit., U. Kans., 1976; postgrad., Ind. U.-Purdue. U., Indpls., 2001—. Cert. in fund raising mgmt., 2001. Asst. curator Beinecke Libr. Yale U., New Haven, 1979-81, archivist Sterling Meml. Libr., 1981-82; curator spl. collections Vassar Coll. Libr., Poughkeepsie, N.Y., 1982-87; asst. dir. rare books and manuscripts N.Y. Pub. Libr., N.Y.C., 1987-96; dir. The Lilly Libr., Ind. U., Bloomington, 1996-2001; libr. for English and Am. lit., philosophy and film studies Main Libr., Ind. U., Bloomington, 2001—02; univ. libr. New Sch. U., N.Y.C., 2002—. Editor RBM: A Jour. of Rare Books, Manuscripts, and Cultural Heritage, 1999-2003. Mem. ALA, Assn. Coll. and Rsch. Librs. (sec. rare books and manuscripts sect. 1987-89, chair, 1994-95, editor 1999—), Soc. Am. Archivists, Bibliog. Soc. Am., Grolier Club. Democrat. Avocations: opera, theatre, photography. Office: Fogelman Libr 65 Fifth Ave New York NY 10011 Office Phone: 212-229-5304. E-mail: browarl@newschool.edu.

BROWN, ALICE ELSTE, artist; b. Balt., Nov. 5, 1922; d. Albert John and Anna Emily (Rosenbauer) Elste; m. Charles Hammond Brown, Nov. 30, 1946 (dec. Sept. 1994); children: Charles Hammond Jr., Barbara Brown Lander, Laurie Ellen. RN, U. Md., 1944; BS in Nursing Edn., Johns Hopkins U., 1949; BA in Art, Coll. Notre Dame, Balt., 1978; MA in Painting and Art Edn., Towson U., 1984. RN, Md. Nurse, head nurse U.S. Army Nurse Corps, U.S., Europe, 1944-46; pub. health nurse Balt. Health Dept., 1950-52; artist Balt., 1960—; artist-in-residence Pyramid-Atlantic Studios, Balt., 1987-92. Adj. instr. drawing and design Coll. Notre Dame, 1980. One-woman shows include Roland Park Libr., 1965, Greater Balt. Med. Ctr., 1964, exhibited in group shows at Md. Fedn. Art, 1970—79, Jewish Cmty. Ctr., 1970, Towson YMCA, 1960, Easton (Md.) Acad. Arts, 1977, Coll. of Notre Dame, 1980, Western Md. Coll., Westminster, 1990, Pyramid Atlantic, Washington, 1990, Rehoboth (Del.)Art League, 1996—. Home nursing tchr. ARC, Balt., 1950s; asst. leader, leader Girl Scouts Am., Balt., 1960s; vol. docent Balt. Mus. Art, 1970s. 1st lt., U.S. Army Nurse Corps, 1944-46. Recipient Pi Lambda Theta award Johns Hopkins U., 1949, Steinbugler award in art, Coll. Notre Dame, 1978. Mem. Nat. Mus. Women in the Arts (charter mem.), Md. Art Place, Rehoboth Art League (Thomas McFarland Skelly Meml. award 1998), Johns Hopkins U. Alumni Club. Democrat. Avocations: walking, biking, reading, archaeology, environmental concerns.

BROWN, ANGELA ROSE, social services speaker, educator; b. Alexandria, Va., Sept. 15, 1946; d. Andre John and Dorothy Loyola (Hinken) Polichnowski; m. Everett Delanel Brown Jr., Sept. 15, 1979 (dec. Feb. 15, 1992); m. David Eugene Warnick, June 12, 1993. AD in Abnormal Behavioral Problems, U. Paris, 1970. Spokesperson Women's Health, Bowie, Md., 1989—; facilitator Jacobs Inst. Women's Health, Washington, 1993—; ct. advocate for battered women Prince George's Mental Health, Bowie, 1994—; spkr., trainer, educator Awakening Women, Bowie, 1995—. Author: When All the Doors Close Look to the Windows, 1996; creator therapeutic dolls for abused children; creator healing cards. Mem. Montgomery County Cmty. Partnership, Rockville, Md., 1994—; presenter Prison program, 1996. Named Working Woman of 1998, WJLA TV7, 1998, Working Woman of 2002, Bus. and Profl. Women, 2002; recipient Vol. of Yr. award, Md. Juvenile Justice Authority, 1997, 1998, 1999, 2000, 2001. Mem. NOW (legal ct. watcher 1995-96), Nat. Polit. Caucus Black Women, Zonta Internat., Nat. Polit. Congress Black Women. Republican. Roman Catholic. Home: 15903 Pointer Ridge Dr Bowie MD 20716-1742

BROWN, ANGELIA, poet; b. Barnesville, Ga., Jan. 5, 1968; d. Charlie Fred and Elizabeth Brown; children: Demarius, Marcus, Jalessa Freeman, David Freeman. Poet: Nature, 1992, In Memory of Those We Love and Cherish, 1993, Love That Is Meant to Be, 1994, Love, 1997, Our Love, 1997, A Friendship, 1998 (Accomplishment of Merit award, 1998), Life, 1998 (Editors Choice award, 1998), All About Angelia and the Lord, 1998, Watch Them Dogs, 2003 (Editors Choice award, 2003). Mem.: Nat. Assn. Female Execs. Methodist. Avocations: gardening, art, baking, bookmaking. Home: 128 Roger Brown Dr Barnesville GA 30204

BROWN, ANN CATHERINE, investment company executive; b. St. Louis, Aug. 12, 1935; d. George Hay and Catherine Doratha (Smith) B. BA, Northwestern U., 1956; MBA, U. Mich., 1958. Copywriter Fred Gardner Advt. Co., N.Y.C., 1959-61, Batten, Barton, Durstine & Osborn, N.Y.C., 1961-63, Ogilvy & Mather Co., N.Y.C., 1963-64; copy group head Benton & Bowles Co., N.Y.C., 1964-66; pvt. investor, 1966-69; with Baker, Weeks & Co., Inc., N.Y.C., 1969-76, v.p., 1973-76; exec. v.p., dir. Melhado, Flynn & Assocs., Inc., N.Y.C., 1976-83; chmn., investment exec. A.C. Brown & Assocs. Inc., 1983—. Columnist Forbes mag., 1976-90. Home: 102 E Bay St Charleston SC 29401-2543

BROWN, ANN LENORA, community and business development professional; b. Austin, Tex., Aug. 29, 1955; d. William Alley and Ann Dyke (Shafer) B.; 1 child, Dancy Ann Lukeman. BArch, U. Tex., 1983. Main St. project dir. City of Brenham, Tex., 1983-86; owner, cons. TEXANA Cmty. Cons., La Grange, Tex., 1980—; dir. residential programs and arch. svcs. Galveston Hist. Found., 1988-91; urban planner City of Galveston, 1996; exec. dir. Colorado City Econ. Devel. Orgn., Inc., 1998-2000; bus. devel. and mktg. cons., La Grange, 2000—. Cmty. devel. cons. hist. neighborhoods and comml. dists., 1991-98; faculty mem. Coll. Arch., U. Houston hist. preservation program, 1991-93. Archtl. illustrator calendar U. Tex. Med. br., Galveston, 1991. Chair Broadway Redevel. Com., Galveston, 1990-93; founder, exec. dir. Galveston Cmty. Devel. Corp., 1991-96; bd. dirs., pres. Galveston Housing Fin. Corp., 1992-97; bd. dirs. Tex. Independence Settlement Heritage Tourism Trust, 2001—. Recipient Preservation award Tex. Hist. Commn., 1986. Mem. AIA (assoc., tri-chair urban design 1991, chair hist. resources 1990-93), Tex. Cmty. Devel. Assn. Tex. (steering com. Tex. Devel. Inst. 1991-92). Episcopalian. Avocations: antiques, needlework, photography. E-mail: texana@fais.net.

BROWN, ANN W. not-for-profit developer; m. Donald Brown, 1959; 2 children Student, Smith Coll., 1955-58; BA, George Washington U., 1959; LLD (hon.), Smith Coll., 2000. Past v.p. Consumer Fedn. Am.; chmn. bd. Pub. Voice, 1983-94; chmn. U.S. Consumer Product Safety Commn., 1994—2001, Safer Am. for Everyone, Palm Beach Gardens, Fla., 2001—. Nat. and local chmn. consumer affairs com. Ams. for Dem. Action; past chmn. adv. bd. Washington Consumer Protection Office. Named Washingtonian of Yr., Washingtonian Mag., 1989, Govt. Communicator of Yr., Nat. Assn. Govt. Communicators, 1995, Outstanding Alumna, George Washington U., 1996; recipient Champion of Safe Kids award, Nat. Safe Kids Campaign, 1994, Philip Hart Pub. Svc. award, Consumer Fedn. Am., 1999, Excellence in Pub. Svc. award, Am. Acad. Pediat., 2000, Nat. Working Parent award, Lokoff Found., 2000, Crystal Slipper award, 2002. Avocations: tennis, movies. Home and Office: SAFE Safer Am for Everyone 2734 Rhome Dr Palm Beach Gardens FL 33410 Office: SAFE Safer Am for Everyone 1776 I Street NW Ste 900 Washington DC 20006*

BROWN, ANNE SHERWIN, speech pathologist, educator; b. Denver, Oct. 15, 1952; d. John Frederick and Barbara Toft Sherwin; m. Max Dennis Brown, June 15, 1985; children: Jack Steven, Michael Patrick. BA, Adams State Coll., 1974, MA, 1975. Tchr. Aurora (Colo.) Pub. Schs., 1978—. Author: Adopt-A-Cop, 1994. Bd. mgrs. YMCA, Aurora, 1996-98. Pub. Svc. Co. grantee, Denver, 1996-97, 98-99; Excel Energy Found. grantee, 2002-03. Mem. ASCD, Aurora Edn. Assn., Internat. Reading Assn. Avocations: reading, dance, sewing, guitar, motorcycles. Home: 416 S Victor Way Aurora CO 80012-2447 Office: Aurora Pub Schs 395 S Troy St Aurora CO 80012-2472

BROWN, ARLENE PATRICIA THERESA See **BROWN, RENI**

BROWN, BARBARA SPROUL, retired librarian, consultant, writer; b. Salem, Mass., Jan. 12, 1934; d. Robert Hugh Sproul and Bernadette Elizabeth Marsolais; m. Bernard Peter Friesecke, Feb. 18, 1955 (div. Nov. 1975); children: Richardine, Rachel, Julie; m. Wallace Robert Brown, Jan. 16, 1988. AB magna cum laude, Boston U., 1967; MLS, Simmons Coll., 1971; cert. advanced grad. studies, Northeastern U., 1978. Cert. sch. libr. media specialist, instrnl. tech. specialist, Mass. Libr. Watertown (Mass.) Sch. Dept., 1969-97, profl. developer for faculty, 1990-96; instr. Watertown Adult Edn., 1983-87. Intern, cons. women's alcohol program CASPAR, Inc., Cambridge, Mass., 1977-79; cons. on database devel. Mindware Inc., Natick, Mass., 1982-83, Coleco Industries, Natick, 1983-84. Essay columnist Watertown Sun, 1990-02; author adult computer courses, 1983-96; contbr. short stories to lit. periodicals. Mem. Lexington (Mass.) Civil Rights Orgn., 1963-68; campaign worker Boston Dem. Com., 1985-93; bd. dirs. Coronado Unitarian Ch., 1999—. Mem. ACLU, Phi Beta Kappa, Beta Phi Mu. Democrat. Avocations: weight training, camping, motorcycling, competitive rifle shooting. Home: 1636 Donax Ave San Diego CA 92154-1003

BROWN, BARBARA HAYES, elementary school educator; b. Orlando, Aug. 9, 1954; d. James R. and Barbara J. Hayes; m. E.J. Brown, Aug. 17, 1979; children: Lori Presley, Matt. BS in Edn., Ga. So. U., 1977, MEd, 1979, EdS, 1982. Waitress, mgr. Vandy's BBQ, Statesboro, Ga., 1971—; tchr. Screven County Middle Sch., Sylvania, Ga., 1978—; rep. AVON, Statesboro, Ga., 1986—; instr. Ga. So. U., Statesboro, 1990—. Author: A Walk Through Time. Recipient Spl. Educator of Yr. award, GLRS, 1997. Mem.: Screven County Coun. Exceptional Children (treas.), Phi Delta Kappa (pres.), Pi Lambda Theta. Republican. Roman Catholic. Avocations: travel, reading, scrapbooks, cross stitch. Office: Screven County Middle Sch 126 Friendship Rd Sylvania GA 30467

BROWN, BARBARA JUNE, hospital and nursing administrator; b. Milw., Aug. 17, 1933; d. Carl W. and Nora Anne (Damrow) Rydberg; children: Deborah, Robert, Andrea, Michael, Steven, Jeffrey. BSN, Marquette U., Milw., 1955, MSN, 1960, EdD, 1970. RN, Wis.; cert. nurse adminstr. advanced. Adminstr. patient care Family Hosp., Milw., 1973-78; assoc. clin. prof. U. Wash., Seattle, 1980-87; assoc. adminstr. nursing Virginia Mason Hosp., Seattle, 1980-87; assoc. exec. dir. King Faisal Specialist Hosp., Riyadh, Saudi Arabia, 1987-91; adj. prof. Univ. Ariz., 2001—. Project dir. NIH, Sexual Assault Treatment Ctr., Milw., 1975-78; lectr., cons., 1974—. Founder, editor: Nursing Adminstrn. Quar., 1976—; editor-in-chief, regional v.p. Nurse Week, Mountain West, 2000—04. Vol. ski instr. for disabled, Winter Park, Colo. Fellow: Nat. Acad. Practice, Am. Acad. Nursing (governing coun.); mem.: ANA, Grand County Pub. Health and Emergency Svcs. (chmn. health adv. com. 1994—96), Nat. League Nursing (bd. dirs., bd. govs. 2002—), Am. Orgn. Nurse Execs., Sigma Theta Tau. Office Phone: 520-825-5629.

BROWN, BARBARA MAHONE, communications educator, poet, consultant; b. Chgo., Feb. 27, 1944; d. Loniel Atticus and Anne (Savage) Mahone. BA, Wash. State U., 1968; MBA, U. Chgo., 1975; PhD, Stanford U., 1988. Dir. corp. comm. NBC, N.Y.C., 1975-77; assoc. prof. dept. bus. adminstrn. and econs. Clark Coll., Atlanta, 1978-84; assoc. prof. depts. journalism and advt. U. Tex., Austin, 1988-91; assoc. prof. dept. mktg. San Jose (Calif.) State U., 1990—. Pres. Elbow Room Cons., 1994—; cons. The Fielding Inst., Santa Barbara, Calif., 1995—; evaluator Western Assn. Schs. and Colls., Oakland, Calif., 1993—; cons. KQED-TV (PBS), San Francisco, 1991; OBAC Poet, Orgn. Black Am. Culture, Chgo., 1970-75; mentor Ctr. for Devel. Women Entrepreneurs, 1995-97; founding faculty Fielding Inst. ODE Program, 1996. Author: (vol. poetry) Sugarfields, 1970; writer-rschr. pub. affairs documentary, WMAQ-TV (NBC Chgo.) 1973, WNET-TV (PBS N.Y.C.) 1971; contbr. articles to profl. acad. jours. Bd. dirs. Kids in Common, San Jose, 1997-98; trustee Hillbrook Sch., Los Gatos, Calif., 1995-98; vestry St. Edward's Episcopal Ch., San Jose, 1994-96; steering com. UN Mid-Decade of Women, Southeast Regional Conf., 1980. Regents fellow in comm., U. Tex. at Austin, 1989; tchr.-scholar San Jose State U., 1993. Mem. Delta Sigma Pi, Beta Gamma Sigma. Episcopalian. Avocations: art, literature, orchids, photography. Office: San Jose State U BT-750 One Washington Sq San Jose CA 95192-0069

BROWN, BERNICE LEONA BAYNES, foundation consultant, educator, consultant; b. Pitts., June 19, 1935; d. Howard Leon and Henrietta Lydia (Hodges) Baynes; m. James Brown, May 4, 1964; 1 child, Kiyeseni Anu. BFA, Carnegie Mellon U., 1957; MEd, U. Pitts., 1966. Tchr. Pitts. Pub. Schs., 1957-65; lectr. Carlow Coll., Pitts., 1964-67; edn. specialist Bay Area Urban League, San Francisco, 1967-68; asst. prof. San Francisco Coll. for Women, 1968-72; dean students Lone Mountain Coll., San Francisco, 1972-76; dir. San Francisco Pub. Schs. Commn., 1976; program exec. San Francisco Found., 1977-86; ednl. cons. San Francisco, 1987—; found. adminstr. Clorox Co. Found., 1989-91; dean of faculty and staff devel. City Coll. of San Francisco, 1991-98; dean Workforce Edn./Calworks Edn. and Tng., 1998—2002. Vis. scholar Stanford (Calif.) U., 1987-88. Mem. bd. govs. Calif. Cmty. Colls., 1975-81, Calif. Post Secondary Edn. Commn., Sacramento, 1978-80, State Supt's Adv. Com. on Black Am. Affairs, Calif., 1985—; chair Found. Cmty. Svc. Cable T.V., San Francisco, 1982-84; trustee Schs. of Sacred Heart, San Francisco, 1982-87; bd. dirs. Urban Econ. Devel. Corp., 1988-2000, High/Scope Ednl. Rsch. Found., 1990-98, Network for Elders, 1997—, Cmty. Bds., Inc., 2000—, Presidio World Coll., 2000—; trustee Howard Thurman Ednl. Trust, 1989-94, Uprising Cmty. Credit Union, San Francisco, 2001—. Recipient Milestone award Citizen's Scholarship Found. Am., 1995, Profl. Woman of Yr. award San Francisco Bus. and Profl. Women, Inc., History Makers award, 2002, Image award in Edn. Delta Sigma Theta, Inc., 2003. Mem. San Francisco LWV (bd. dirs. 2000-02), Women and Founds. Corp. Philanthropy (bd. dirs. 1985-87), Assn. Black Found. Execs. (bd. dirs. 1978-82), Commonwealth Club of Calif. (bd. govs. 1988-91). Home: 1271 23d Ave San Francisco CA [illegible] E-mail: bbrown@ccsf.edu.

BROWN, BETHANY JOY, advocate; b. Mineral Wells, Tex., Mar. 3, 1957; d. Richard Ewing Brown and Barbara Jean McCroskey; children: Caleb Joshua Ewing, Samuel Timothy Ewing, Joy Christine Ewing, Benjamin Paul Ewing, Grace Marie Ewing, Joel Peter Ewing. AA, Calif. State U., Fresno, 1978. Cert. therapeutic recreation Calif., 1978. Child support agt. adminstrv. law Dept. of Justice, Salem, Oreg., 1998—. Mem. diversity com. Dept. of Justice, Salem, 1997—2003. American Independent. Metaphysical. Avocations: paragliding, kayaking, public speaking, travel. Home: PO Box 688 Silverton OR 97381-0688 E-mail: bethany.brown@doj.state.or.us.

BROWN, BETSY ETHERIDGE, academic administrator; b. Statesville, N.C., Aug. 2, 1950; d. Guy Wetmore and Elizabeth (Hackney) Etheridge; m. Homer L. Brown, Aug. 13, 1972 (dec. Mar. 1987); 1 child, Elizabeth Leigh (dec. July 1992); m. Lawrence C. Timbs, Jr., July 30, 1995. BS in English, Appalachian State U., 1972; MA in English, Ohio State U., 1974, PhD in English, 1978. Cert. tchr., N.C. Asst. prof. English Pa. State U., University Park, 1978-85; asst. to v.p. Queens Coll., Charlotte, N.C., 1987-89, Winthrop U., Rock Hill, S.C., 1990-92, assoc. v.p., 1992-94, dean Coll. Arts and Scis., 1994—2001; assoc. v.p. acad. affairs U. N.C., Chapel Hill, 2001—. Bd. mem. Cmty. Bd. for Women's Svcs., Rock Hill, 1994—, WNSC Cmty. Adv. Bd., 1998—, Roanoke Island Commn., 2002—. Recipient Mgmt. Devel. Program award Harvard Grad. Sch. Edn., 1992, Forum award Am. Coun. on Edn.-Nat. Idenfification Program, 1995; Fulbright grantee, Bonn, Germany, 1994. Mem. AAUW, S.C. Women in Higher Edn. Adminstrn. (bd. sec. 1994—). Office: U NC Office of Pres PO Box 2688 Chapel Hill NC 27515-2688

BROWN, BETSY S. hotel executive; b. Raleigh, N.C. m. Reg Brown; children: Treg, Paige, Lance. Student, East Carolina U. Corp. sec. Hospitality Internat., Inc., Tucker, Ga., 1982—, treas., 1994—, pres., 1998—. Office: Hospitality Internat Inc 1726 Montreal Cir Tucker GA 30084-6809

BROWN, BETTY J. elementary school educator; b. Red Bluff, Calif., Apr. 19, 1934; d. Hugh Jerry and Lena Belle (Dobkins) Moran; m. Richard Owen Brown, Nov. 26, 1958; children: Karen, Gretchen, Heidi. BA in Edn., Calif. State U., Chico, 1956. Cert. tchr., Calif. Tchr. Gridley (Calif.) Elem. Dist., 1956-61; reading tchr. Richfield Elem. Dist., Corning, Calif., 1968, tchr., 1970—. Bd. dirs. Sch. Site Coun., Corning, 1990—; mem. County Lang. Arts Com., Red Bluff, 1987-99; mem., sec. Learning Coun., Red Bluff, 1995-99. Mem. Home Town Christmas, Corning, 1996-2000; vol. Shrine Hosp., Sacramento, 1998—; mem. adv. bd., mother adv. dep. Rainbow Girls, Corning, 1975-87. Recipient Nat. Educator award Milken Family Found., 1994, Literacy award Tehama County Reading Coun., 1995, 2001. Mem. AAUW, Tehama County Reading Coun. (pres. 1991-93), Corning C. of C., Order Eastern Star, Tehama County Shrine Club Wives (pres., treas.), Delta Kappa Gamma. Avocations: reading, biking, skiing, traveling. Home: 1406 Butte St Corning CA 96021-2408 E-mail: bjb@dm-tech.net.

BROWN, BETTY J. director; b. Lillington, N.C. d. Archie Leonard Johnson and Myrta Ruth Morgan; m. Robert Guy Brown, Sept. 5, 1952; children: Christopher Guy, Carolyn, Jennifer Ruth. BS in Philosophy and Psychology, Meredith Coll., 1949; MSW, U. N.C., 1956; MEd, U. Va., 1985. Tchr. child guidance clinic Duke U., Durham, NC, 1952—60; asst. head The Langley Sch., McLean, Va., 1963—79, headmistress, 1980—99; cons. in edn. Carney Sandae, Boston, 1999—2000; resource head The Words Acad., Bethesda, Md., 2000—. Area supr. Children's Friend & Svc., Providence, 1952—54; supr. children's svc. Durham County, Durham, 1954—56; dir. summer sch. The Langley Sch., 1963—79; spkr. in field. Named a bldg. in her honor, Langley Lower Sch., 1999. Episc. Avocations: reading, swimming, cooking, writing. Home: 1172 Foxhound Ct Mc Lean VA 22102

BROWN, BETTY MARIE, government agency administrator; b. Siler City, N.C., June 11, 1952; d. Ardentries and Emma (Peoples) Mason; m. Tommy E. Brown, Aug. 8, 1968 (dec.); 1 child, Christopher T.; m. Roger L. Cook, June 10, 1973 (dec. Feb. 1981); 1 child, Felicia M. AAS, Phila. Community Coll., 1981; BS, Drexel U., 1986. Cert. early childhood edn. tchr., elem. edn. tchr., Pa. Mgr. Mr. Gourmet Deli, Phila., 1977-80; pres. Parents, Friends and Vols. Community Svc. Orgn., Phila., 1983—; tchr. Phila. Sch. Dist., 1988-89; remittance perfection clk. IRS, Phila., 1990-92; account analyst IRS-Automated Collection Sys., Phila., 1992—; with Censur Bur./Dept. Commerce, 1980. Tchr. Mid City YWCA, Phila., 1983-88. Sec. support community outreach project Dept. Human Svcs., Phila., 1990-91. Recipient Community Svc. award Dept. Human Svc., 1988. Baptist. Avocations: reading, swimming, dance, flying, tennis. Home and Office: Parents of the 39th Dist PO Box 18707 1132 Easton Rd Apt B Philadelphia PA 19132 E-mail: BMBROWN52@go.com.

BROWN, BILLYE JEAN, retired nursing educator; b. Damascus, Ark., Oct. 29, 1925; d. William A. and Dora (Megee) B. BSNEd, U. Tex. Med. Br., Galveston, 1953; MSNEd, St. Louis U., 1958; EdD, Baylor U., 1975. Asst. prof. U. Tex. Med. Br. Sch. Nursing, 1958-60; assoc. prof. U. Tex. Nursing Sch., Austin, 1960-67, assoc. dean, prof., 1968-72, dean, prof., 1972-89; prof. emeritus Sch. Nursing U. Tex., 1989—; mem. Nat. Adv. Council Nurse Tng., 1982-87. Nat. League for Nursing fellow, 1957-58; recipient Alumni Merit award St. Louis U., 1981; Am. Acad. Nursing fellow, 1984. Mem. ANA, Am. Assn. Colls. Nursing (pres. 1982-84, Sister Bernadette Armiger award 1990), Tex. League Nursing, Tex. Nurses Assn. (Nurse of Yr. 1980), Sigma Theta Tau (pres. 1989-91, Internat. Mary T. Wright Founders award 1999), Phi Kappa Phi (life).

BROWN, BLANCHE Y. secondary education educator, genealogy researcher; b. Saint Mary's, W.Va., Feb. 2, 1918; d. Lewis Frederick and Edna Clara (Walker) Yost; m. Vincent Robert Brown, June 1, 1946; children: Susan Elizabeth, Roberta Ann Brown Pugh. BA, Marietta Coll., 1939; postgrad., Columbia U., 1946, 47. Cert. secondary tchr. in sci. and English. Pers. supr. Packard Electric divsn. Gen. Motors Corp., Warren, Ohio, 1940-44; tchr. bus. edn. New Matamoras (Ohio) H.S., 1945-49; fin. sec. St. Paul's United Meth. Ch., Houston, 1949-50; pers. dept. Olin Chem. Corp., Pasadena, Tex., 1951-53; tchr. biology Pasadena H.S., 1958-78. Co-editor: Grandview Township's First Trustees Journal--1803-1843, 1991; editor Matamoras Area Hist. Soc. Newsletter, 1987-99. Recipient First Families of Ohio award Ohio Geneal. Soc., 1989, Award of Achievement Ohio Hist. Soc. for Matamoras Area Hist. Soc. Newsletter, 1992. Mem. Tex. Ret. Tchrs. Assn. (life), Nat. Soc. DAR (Marietta, Ohio chpt. schs. chmn. 1988-94, corr. sec. 1995-99, nat. Photography award 1989), Matamoras Area Hist. Soc. (genealogy and local history coord. for Sesquicentennial Celebration 1846-1996, Bicentennial Celebration 1797-1997), VFW Aux. (life), AAUW. Republican. Methodist. Avocations: photography, artwork with shells, writing. Home: 733 Main St New Matamoras OH 45767-6013

BROWN, BOBBI, cosmetics executive; married; 3 children. Founder & CEO Bobbi Brown Cosmetics (div. Estee Lauder), 1992—. Beauty editor NBC's Today Show; frequent guest E! and Style channels; writer, nationally syndicated columns and advice features for Allure, Modern Bride, Working Mother, Prevention Mag. Author: Bobbi Brown Beauty, 1998, Bobbi Brown

Beauty Evolution: A Guide to a Lifetime of Beauty, 2002; co-author: Bobbi Brown Teenage Beauty, 2001. Office: Bobbi Brown Cosmetics, Inc 767 Fifth Ave New York NY 10153 Office Phone: 212-572-4200.*

BROWN, C. ALISON, counselor; d. William Thomas Wynn Jr. and Rose E. Wynn; m. Jim D. Brown, Nov. 22, 1986; children: Steven Brett Wallis, Aaron Thomas. BA in Psychology, U. Mo., St. Louis, MEd in Counseling, 1995. Lic. profl. counselor Mo., nat. cert. counselor. Domestic violence counselor Bridgeway Women's Ctr., St. Charles, Mo., 1995—2000; dir. Bridgeway Alternatives to Violence and Abuse Program, St. Charles, Mo., 2000—. Co-chairperson St. Charles County Family Violence Coun., 2001—; Mo. state bd. rep. Mo. Coalition Against Domestic Violence, St. Louis, 2003—. Mem.: Assn. for Batterer Intervention Providers (pres. 2002—). Office: Bridgeway Alternatives to Violence/Abuse Ste 102 3910 Old Hwy 94 S Saint Charles MO 63304 E-mail: avaprogram@sbcglobal.net.

BROWN, CAMPBELL, commentator; BA in Polit. Sci., Regis Coll. Polit. reporter KSNT-TV, Topeka, WWBT-TV, Richmond, Va., WBAL-TV, Balt., WRC-TV, Wash.; corr. NBC News, 1996—98, White Ho. corr., 1998—; co-anchor NBC Weekend Today, 2003—. Office: Weekend Today NBC News 30 Rockefeller Plz New York NY 10112

BROWN, CAROL, make-up artist; b. Stockholm, Nov. 26, 1949; d. Julius C. and Violet (Moten) B. Student, Mt. St. Mary's Coll., 1968-72, European Exch. Program, 1972-74, L.A. Valley Coll., 1974-76. Cert. make-up artistry tchr., Calif. Makeup-artist Spelling Entertainment, Paramount, Disney, NBC, others, L.A., 1977—; CEO Natural to Knockout.com., L.A., 1996—; founder, CEO Carol Brown Natural Empowerment Found., L.A., 2000—. Aesthetic cons. C.B. Enterprises, 1990—; instr. Fred Segal Beauty, 1990—; spkr. in field; mem. adv. bd. Denise Roberts Found.; mem. speakerservices.com. Author: Natural to Knockout Makeup Application Beauty Guide, 2001. Vol. L.A. Mission, 1989—, Jenesee Ctr., L.a., 1996—, Sickle Cell Disease Assn. Am., L.A., 1996—. Recipient Outstanding Tech. Achievement award L.A. Black Media Coalition, 1989. Mem.: NATAS (mem. Emmy awards com. 1985—90, mem. show com. 1985—90, mem. exec. peer group com. 1985—93, 3 Emmy awards, 7 Emmy award nominations), NAACP, Assn. Image Cons. Internat., Colour Soc. Australia, Internat. Alliance Stage and Theatrical Emmployees, Aesthetics Internat. Assn. Office: Carol Brown Natural Empowerment Found PO Box 79083 Los Angeles CA 90079

BROWN, CAROL ROSE, artist; BFA, Cornell U. Solo shows include The Witkin Gallery, N.Y.C., Charles Lucien Gallery, N.Y.C., Rettig Y Martinez, Santa Fe, The Little Gallery, Ithaca, N.Y., Korn Gallery, Drew U., Madison, N.J.; exhibited in group shows at Etherton-Stern Gallery, Tucson, Missoula (Mont.) Mus. Fine Arts, Parrish Mus., Southampton, N.Y., Provincetown (Mass.) Art Assn. and Mus., Whitney Mus. at Stamford (Conn.), The Torrey (Utah) Gallery; represented in collections U.S. Embassy, Athens, Greece, Rabat, Morrocco, Ashgabat, Turkmenistan. Individual fellow Nat. Endowment for the Arts, 1994. Office Phone: 505-474-8808. E-mail: carolrosebrown@aol.com.

BROWN, CAROLYN RICE, dancer, choreographer, writer, filmmaker; b. Fitchburg, Mass., Sept. 26, 1927; d. James Parker and Marion Burbank (Stevens) Rice; m. Earle Brown, June 18, 1950 (div.). BA cum laude, Wheaton Col., 1950; student, Marion Rice Studio of Dance, Fitchburg, Mass., 1931-46, Julliard, N.Y.C., 1952-53, Metropolitan Opera Ballet Sch., 1953-65, Merce Cunningham Studio, 1952-72; Doctor Fine Arts (honorary), Wheaton Col., 1974. Principal dancer Merce Cunningham Dance Co., N.Y.C., 1953-73; freelance choreographer and tchr. various cities and countries, 1973-90; self-employed filmmaker, 1975-78; choreographer Centre Choreographique, Anger, France, 1976; dean of dance Sch. of Arts, SUNY, Purchase, 1980-82; guest artist Die Palucca Schule, Dresden, East Germany, 1985, Bartholin Internat. Ballet, Copenhagen, Denmark, 1987; sr. fellow Dept. Theatre Arts U. Minn., Mpls., 1988-89, 90; regents lectr. Dept. Dramatic Art U. Calif., Berkeley; artistic dir. Cunningham Repertory Group, 2000—. Choreographer numerous works, 1967-90; contbr. articles to profl. jours.; dir., prodr. (film) Dune Dance, 1978. Recipient Dance Magazine award, 1969, 100th Anniversary Disting. Svc. award Wheaton Col., 1970, Choreography awards Nat. Endowment for the Arts, 1973, 75, 76, choreography fellowship John Simon Guggenheim Found., 1983. Mem. Merce Cunningham Dance Found., Phi Beta Kappa. Office: Cunningham Dance Found 463 West St New York NY 10014-2010

BROWN, CATHIE, city official; b. Seattle, Mar. 23, 1944; d. G. Warren and Dorothy (Patterson) Cryer; m. Tom Brown, July 1, 1967; children: Amy, James W. BA in Criminology, U. Calif., Berkeley, 1966; MPA, Calif. State U., Hayward, 1985. Juvenile probation officer Santa Clara (Calif.) County, 1967-72; founder, dir. Tri-Valley Haven for Women, Livermore, Calif., 1976-79; planning commr. City of Livermore, 1980-82, city coun. mem., 1982-89, mayor, 1989—; exec. dir. Alameda County Project Intercept, Hayward, 1986-92. Dir. Svcs. for Families of Inmates, Pleasanton, Calif., 1981-82; active County Justice System Adv. Group, Oakland, Calif., 1990—; co-founder Tri-Valley Community Fund, Pleasanton. Active Alameda County Mayors' Conf., 1989—; del. Assn. Bay Area Govts., 1982-89; founder Youth For Action, Livermore, 1984-86, Youth Task Force, Livermore, 1989-90. Named Woman of Yr. Calif. State Legislature, 1990. Mem. League Calif. Cities (pres. East Bay div. 1982-89), MPA Alumni Assn. (pres. Calif. State U. chpt. 1989—). Democrat. Avocations: music, racquetball, reading. Home: 1098 Angelica Way Livermore CA 94550-5701

BROWN, CLARE WINSLOW, accountant, writer; d. Colon Leroy and Phyllis Marie Winslow; m. Robert Malcolm Brown, Nov. 21, 1970; children: Bethany Rebekah Flanders, Penelope Marietta Greene, Meredith Jean, Lucas Tyler. BA, U. Maine, 1995. Sec./bookkeeper to supt. of schools Msad #7, North Haven (Island), Maine, 1985—89; computer telemarketer Taction, Waldoboro, Maine, 1991—97; bookkeeper Child Devel. Services, Rockland, Maine, 1992—93; acctg. mgr. MSAD #5 Sch. Dist., Rockland, Maine, 1988—99; exec. adminstrv. asst. MBNA Am., Belfast, Maine; bus. adminstr. Union 69 Sch., Hope, Maine, 2001—02. Chef Mr. and Mrs. Laurence M. Lombard, North Haven (summer home), Maine, 1967—89; acctg./computer cons. MSAD #8 Vinalhaven, Vinalhaven, Maine, 1998—99; peer tutor U. of Maine, Thomaston, Maine, 1989—96; guest poet Albany Poetry Workshop. Contbr. poetry to lit. jours. (Pres.'s award Iliad Press, 1998). Sec./treas. Fox Island Concerts, Inc., North Haven, Maine, 1985—87; treas. AFS North Haven Chpt., 1987—88. Mem.: ADS Computer User Group (sec./treas. 1986—90), Poetry Soc. Am., Maine Writers and Publishers Alliance, North Haven Grange (sec. 1980—85), Internat. Soc. of Poets, North Haven Alumni Assn. (sec./treas. 1975—82), Am. Legion Aux. # 33 (sec. 1981—82, pres. 1982—83). Republican. Home and Office: 9 Philbrick Ave Rockland ME 04841 Personal E-mail: clawryb@aol.com.

BROWN, COLLEEN, broadcast executive; BA bus admin and pol sci, U Dubuque, Iowa; MBA, U Colo. Gen. mgr. Sta. KPNX-TV, Phoenix, till 1998; v.p. broadcast Lee Enterprises, 1998-99, pres., 1999—2000; sr v.p. bus dev Belo Corp, Dallas, 2000—. Mem. March of Dimes. Mem. Young Press Assn. Office: AH Belo Corp 400 S Record St PO Box 655237 Dallas TX 75265-5237

BROWN, CORRINE, congresswoman; b. Jacksonville, Fla., Nov. 11, 1946; 1 child, Shantrel. BS, Fla. A&M U., 1969, MS, 1971; EdS, U. Fla., 1974. Prof. Fla. Community Coll., 1977—82, guidance counselor, 1982—92; mem. Fla. Ho. of Reps, 1982—92; del. Nat. Dem. Conv., 1988; mem. U.S. Congress from 3rd Fla. dist., 1993—; mem. transp. and infrastructure com., VA com. Mem. Sigma Gamma Rho. Democrat. Baptist. Home: 314 Palmetto St Jacksonville FL 32202-2619 Office: US Ho of Reps 2444 Rayburn Ho Office Bldg Washington DC 20515-0903*

BROWN, CRYSTAL JEANINE, writer; b. Bay Minette, Ala., Sept. 26, 1978; d. John M. Bolding and Kathy Lou Abbott; children: Megan Elizabeth, Ashland Victoria Bryan, Cassandra Jeanine Bryan. A in Social Sci., Faulkner State C.C., Bay Minette, 2000; student, Wash. State U., 2001—. Author: Embedded Dreams, 1997, A Prism of Thoughts; contbr. poetry to anthology. Vol. Deep South Coun. Girls Scouts of Am., Ala., 2001—02. Recipient Editors Choice award, Nat. Libr. Poetry, 1997. Avocations: poetry, genealogy, crafts, photography, sports. E-mail: tcbryan@earthlink.net.

BROWN, DALE PATRICK, retired advertising executive; b. Richmond, Va., Aug. 11, 1947; d. Thomas Windom and Helen (Curtis) Patrick. BA in Journalism, U. Richmond, 1968, MA in English, 1978. Reporter city news sect. Richmond Times-Dispatch, 1968-71; free-lance writer, 1971-73; v.p., supr. pub. rels. account The Martin Agy., Richmond, 1973-77, account supr. advt., v.p., 1977-79, v.p., supr. advt. account, then group v.p. and sr. v.p., 1983-89; mgr. communications svcs. Mobil Chem. Co., Richmond, 1979-81; mgr. communications Whittaker Gen. Med., Richmond, 1981-83; exec. v.p. The Stenrich Group, Richmond, 1989-90; pres., chief exec. officer Sive/Young & Rubicam, Cin., 1990-98. Trustee U. Richmond, 1992—, mem. exec. com., 1999-2001, vice chair acad. program com.; mem. devel. bd. Good Samaritan Hosp., 1992-95, Leadership Cin.; bd. dirs. Met. Growth Alliance, 1997-99, Downtown Cin. Inc., 1995-98, Midwest Strategic Trust, 1993-97, Ohio Nat. Life Ins. (exec. com.), bd. dirs. Frisch's Inc., 1998—, Mercantile Libr., 2000—, Cin. C. of C., 1995-98; chair Acad. Career Women of Achievement, 1996-2001; bd. govs. Cin. chpt. Am. Assn. Advt. Agys., 1990-98. Recipient 2 AAF Silver medals, 1988, 96, Richmond Advt. Person of Yr. award Advt. Club Richmond, 1988, Woman of Achievement award Cin. YWCA, 1993, Human Rels. award Am. Jewish Com., Cin. chpt., 1996, various others including Addy, Effie, Clio awards N.Y. Art Dirs. Club. Mem. Pub. Rels. Soc. Am., Advt. Club Cin., Queen City Club (bd. dirs.), Comml. Club of Cin. Avocations: reading, travel, arts. Home: 1231 Martin Dr Cincinnati OH 45202-1737

BROWN, DALE SUSAN, government administrator, educational program director, writer; b. NYC, May 27, 1954; d. Bertram S. and Beatrice Joy (Gilman) Brown. BA, Antioch Coll., 1976. Rsch. asst. Am. Occupational Therapy Assn., Rockville, Md., 1976-79; writer Pres.' Com. on Employment of People with Disabilities, Washington, 1979-82, program mgr. handicapped concerns com., 1982—85, program mgr. labor com., 1985, 96-98, program mgr. work environment and tech. com., 1988-94, program mgr. com. on libr. and info. svcs., 1984-86, youth devel com., 1986 88, new products devel. team, 1987-90, agy. rep., 1991-93, with interagy. tech. assistance coordinating team, 1992-94; program mgr. Job Accomodation Network, 1997-99; mgr. Nat. Conf. of Youth with Disabilities, 2000; policy advisor Office Disability Employment Policy Dept. Labor, 2001—, mem. youth team, 2002—. Cons. in field, gen. assembly speaker nat. conv. Gen. Fedn. Women's Clubs, 1981, mem. Rehab Svcs. Adminstrn. Task Force on Learning Disabilities, 1981-83. Author: Steps to Independence for People with Learning Disabilities, 1980, Pathways to Employment for People with Learning Disabilities, 1991, Working Effectively with People Who Have Learning Disabilities and Attention Deficit Hyperactivity Disorder, 1995, I Know I Can Climb the Mountain, 1996, Learning Disabilities and Employment, 1997, Learning A Living Guide to Planning Your Career and Finding A Job for People with Learning Disabilities, Attention Deficit Disorder and Dyslexia, 2000, Job-Hunting Tips for the So-Called Handicapped, 2001, (films) They Could Have Saved Their Homes, 1982; dir.: (videotape) Part of the Team People with Disabilities in the Workforce, 1990; co-editor: Learning Disabilities Quar. Americans with Disabilities Act and Learning Disabilities, 1992; mem. editl. bd. Perceptions, 1981—83, Learning Disabilities Focus, 1988—90, In the Mainstream, 1994—98; guest editor: Learning Disabilities Rsch. and Practice, 1990—96; guest editor Learning Disability and Career Development, 2002; guest editor: Career Planning and Adult Devel. Jour., 2002. Bd. dirs. Closer Look Nat. Info. Ctr., Washington, 1980—83; bd. dir. Am. Coalition for Citizens with Disabilities, 1985—86; congrl. task force Rights and Empowerment of Ams. with Disabilities, 1988—90; profl. adv. bd. Nat. Attention Deficit Disorder Assn., 1996—99; bd. dir. Coun. on Quality and Leadership, 2000—; adv. bd. Internat. Ctr. for Disability Resources on the Internet, 2003—; chair conf. on Info. Tech. for User With Disabilities, 1989; spl. asst. for people with disabilities Federally Employed Women, 1991—92; blue ribbon panel Nat. Telecomm. Access for People with Disabilities, 1989—94; pres. Assn. Learning Disabled Adults, Washington, 1979—80; del. Nat. Writer's Union, 1999; rep. com. on fed. govt. as model employer, com. on youth with disabilities Presdl. Task Force on Employment of Adults with Disabilities, 1999—2002; judge, Ten Outstanding Young Ams. U.S. Jr. C. of C. Jaycees, 2003. Named one of Ten Outstanding Young Ams., U.S. Jr. C. of C. Jaycees, 1994; recipient, Margaret Byrd Rawson award, 1989, Personal Achievement award Women's Program USDOL, 1989, Individual Achievement award, Nat. Coun. on Communication Disorders, 1991, Spl. Achievement award, Pres.'s Com. on Employment of People with Disabilities, 1991, Gold Screen award, Nat. Assn. Gov. Communicators, 1991, Arthur S. Fleming award, 1992; grantee, Found. for Children with Learning Disabilities, 1982. Mem.: Inter Agency. Com. on Handicapped Employees (rep. 1989—91), Learning Disabilities Assn. Am. (bd. dirs. 1986—91), Nat. Assn. Govt. Communicators (Blue Pencil award 1986), Nat. Network of Learning Disabled Adults (founder, pres. 1980—81, Rep. inter-agy. com. on comuter support handicapped employees 1998—99), ALA. Democrat. Office: Office Disability Employment Policy Dept Labor S1011 200 Constitution Ave NW Washington DC 20210

BROWN, DEAN NAOMI, state official, geologist; b. Fairbanks, Alaska, Mar. 9, 1944; d. James Heuston and Betty (Jefford) Alexander; m. Jim McCaslin Brown, Sept. 1, 1963 (div. 1987); children: Robin Wendy, Shelly Reneé. BS in Geology, U. Wis., 1967. Lectr. geology U. Ind., Kokomo, 1971-72; geologist, landman Amax Coal Co., Indpls., 1974; asst. and field constrn. engr. Trans-Alaska pipeline Fluor Alaska, Inc., 1975-76; environ. geologist Civil Engr./AK, Wasilla, 1977; various positions to acting dir. agr. Alaska Dept. Natural Resources, 1978-87; office mgr. Northwind Aviation, Anchorage, 1987-88; geologist Placer Dome U.S., Inc., Nome, Alaska, 1988; journeyman carpenter Ensearch Corp., Bradley Lake, Alaska, 1989; from no. regional mgr. div. land and water mgmt. to Dep. State Forester AK Dept. Natural Resources, Anchorage, 1990—2003, acting dir. agr., 2003—. Adj. prof. natural resource econs. Alaska Pacific U., 1991, 93; vice-chair Alaskan-Chinese Timber Commn., 1993, Gov.'s Mktg. Alaska Forest Products Coun.; del. Coun. Western State Foresters, 1994-95, Nat. Assn. State Foresters, 1994; co-chair Dept. Nat. Resources Computer Group, 1996—; des. Statewide Emergency Response Commission, 1997—; mem. AK Wildland Fire Coord. Group, 1996—2000, chair, 1999—, Gov.'s Transition Team-Valley, 2002. Vol. Iditarod Trail Com. Recipient cert. of appreciation City of Valdez, Alaska, 1976, Anchorage Sch. Dist., 1983, 4-H Leaders, Palmer, Alaska, 1987, cert. of achievement Susitna coun. Girl Scouts U.S.A., 1982, Outstanding Achievement award Alaska Dept. Natural Resources, 1986. Mem. Aircraft Owners and Pilots Assn., Alaska Airman's Assn., Pacific Rim Arabian Horse Assn. (charter mem. 1997—), Alaska Horse Breeders Assn. (bd. dirs. 1984-90), Ninety-Nines. Avocations: flying, horse breeding and showing, painting, photography, gold mining. Home: PO Box 870366 Wasilla AK 99687-0366 Office: Alaska Dept Natural Resources 550 W 7th, Ste 1450 Anchorage AK 99501-5925

BROWN, DEBORAH ELIZABETH, television producer, consultant; b. Aledo, Ill., Nov. 29, 1952; d. Kenneth M. and Mary Esther (Gilmore) B.; m. K. J. Lester, Nov. 28, 1975 (dec. Mar. 1982); children: Rebekah Jean, Aaron Mark, Jonathan Caleb. Student, Letourneau Coll., 1970; BA in Theater Arts, Sterling Coll., 1974; MA in Comm., Wheaton Coll., 1977. Producer, dir. Sta. WCFC-TV, Chgo., 1978-80; sales mgr. SNG Enterprises, St. Charles, Ill., 1980-82; pres., CEO Circle Family Video Stores, Niles, Mich., 1982-87; exec. producer Picture Radio Pictures, Naples, Italy, 1987-93, 98-2000; mgr. Computer Keyboard, Portland, Oreg., 1993-96, Michelle's Piano and Organ Co., Portland, 1996-98; exec. prodr. TV Napoli, Naples, 2000—02; exec. prodr., dir. Sabaoth Films, Milano, Italy, 2002—. Vis. prof. comm. Wheaton (Ill.) Coll., 1980; video cons. Spring Arbor Distbrs., Belleville, Mich., 1985, Gospel Films, Muskegan, Mich., 1985. Producer, dir., writer (TV program and book) Crafts With Emilie, 1979 (Spl. Emmy nomination); video contbg. editor Christian Booksellers Assn. jour., 1984-85; set decorator Cindy Williams Comedy Spl., 1993; prodr., dir. (Film) Sequestrato, 2003. Corp. sponsor Pregnancy Care Ctr., Niles, 1985-87; producer Four Flags Area Apple Festival, Niles, 1987. Mem. ISGI Internat. (dir. 1998—), Fellowship of Christians in Arts, Media and Entertainment, Christian Video Retailers Assn. (exec. dir. 1985-87). Evang. Home: via Chiesa Rossa 17 20143 Milano Italy Office: Sabaoth Films viale Liguria 5 20143 Milano Italy Fax: 503-408-1829.

BROWN, DEBORAH PARKE, art educator; d. Clinton Archebald and Rosemary Carolyn (Fisher) Parke; m. Douglas Mark Brown, Aug. 15, 1996. Diploma with honors, N. Ga. Tech./Vocat. Inst., Clarkeville, 1986; BFA, U. N.C., Charlotte, 2000. Cert. art edn. K-12. Tchr. art Cabarrus County Schs., NC, 2001—02, Cox Mill Elem. Sch., Concord, NC, 2002—. Mural, Jefferson Creekside, Charlotte, 1999, Jefferson at Carytowne, Cary, NC, 2000. Vol. cmty. beautification mural project, Charlotte, 1993. Mem.: NEA, Nat. Art Educator Assn., Profl. Educators N.C., Golden Key. Avocations: cooking, camping, art. Office: Cox Mill Elem Sch 1450 Cox Mill Rd Concord NC 28027

BROWN, DEBRA RAE, music educator; b. Joplin, Mo., July 22, 1955; d. Ramon R. and Lucinda L. Smith; m. Paul B. Brown, July 28, 1979; children: David R., Peter R., Benjamin J., Jacob M. BME, Baker U., Baldwin City, KS, 1973—77; MME, U. of Mo., Kans. City, Kansas City, Missouri, 1992—98. Cert. tchr. music Kans. State Bd. Edn., 1977. Educator music, secondary choral Osawatomie Unified Sch. Dist., Kans., 1977—79; educator music, elementary gen. music Big Rapids Sch. Dist., Mich., 1979—81; educator music, elem. gen. and choral music Olathe Unified Sch. Dist. #233, Kans., 1982—; educator music Johnson County C.C., Overland Park, 2000—. Singer: Kansas City Symphony Chorus; prodr.: (children's musicals). Dir. music First Christian Ch., Olathe, 1983—93; accompanist, music facilitator St. Joseph Cath. Ch., Shawnee, 1994—99; accompanist, choir dir. Holy Angels Cath. Ch., Basehor, 2000—03. Grantee, Olathe Sch. Dist., 1986, 1996; Glad Robinson Youse scholar, Baker U., 1975—77, Women's Coun. Rsch. grantee, U. Mo., Kans. City, 1998. Mem.: Nat. Educator's Assn. (assoc.), Music Educator's Nat. Conf. (assoc.), Phi Mu (assoc.; local v.p. 1975—76, Alumni Outstanding Sr. award 1977). R-Liberal. Roman Catholic. Avocations: collecting old recordings, sports, fitness activities, cooking, music. Home: 3414 N 154th Terr Ct Basehor KS 66007 Personal E-mail: debrown@jccc.net.

BROWN, DELORES RUSSELL, health management company official; b. Phila., Sept. 20, 1947; d. William and Jean (Nichols) Russell; children: Brendell F., William A. Jr. Student, Temple U., 1969-71; BA, Antioch U., Phila., 1988; MSW, U. Pa., 1991. Lic. real estate salesperson, Pa.; cert. residential appraiser, Pa. Real estate cons. Ball Real Estate, Inc., Phila., 1976-86; publ. word processor Magnavox (GAC), Wymoor, Pa., 1982-83; real estate closing clk. Merrill Lynch Relocation, Bala Cynwyd, Pa., 1983-84; med. and tech. sec. U. Pa., Phila., 1984-86, adminstrv. asst., 1986-89; social worker for aged Episcopal Community Svcs., Phila., 1989-90, dir. social svc., 1991-92; sr. svc. coord., rsch. interviewer Phila. Health Mgmt. Corp., 1992—, facilitator, 1992. Mem. Phila. Mayor's Adv. Bd. on Aging, 1987; tutor Phila. Mayor's Literacy Program, 1988; asst. dir. social svcs. Zion Cares Ministry, Phila., 1991—; mem. Zion Bapt. Outreach Ministry, 1985—; mem. family planning bd. Temple U., 1970-76. Recipient svc. award Temple U., 1988, Rosa Wessell Outstanding MSW award, U. Pa., 1991. Mem. Nat. Assn. Real Estate Brokers (2d v.p. women's coun. Washington 1991-92, Disting. Local Chpt. Presdl. award 1993), Phila. Women's Coun. of Assn. Real Estate Brokers (pres. 1991-93, Outstanding Presdl. award 1993), Alliance of Black Social Workers, Women of Color Coalition. Avocations: children and senior citizens rights, women's and community issues, bowling, christian education, fellowshipping. Home: 8101 Fayette St Philadelphia PA 19150-1214

BROWN, DENISE, poet; b. Chgo., Oct. 7, 1963; d. Earl L. and Dorothy Grier; married; 3 children. Author: (poetry) A Treasury of Great Poems, 1998, poems. Recipient Editor's Choice award, 1999, Cert. of Recognition, 2001, The Diamond Homer award, 1998.

BROWN, DENISE SCOTT, architect, urban planner; b. Nkana, Zambia, Oct. 3, 1931; arrived in U.S., 1958; d. Simon and Phyllis (Hepker) Lakofski; m. Robert Scott Brown, July 21, 1955 (dec. 1959); m. Robert Charles Venturi, July 23, 1967; 1 child, James C. Student, U. Witwatersrand, South Africa, 1948—51; diploma, Archtl. Assn., London, 1955; M of City Planning, U. Pa., 1960, MArch, 1965, DFA (hon.), 1994, Oberlin Coll., 1977, Phila. Coll. Art, 1985, Parsons Sch. Design, 1985; LHD (hon.), N.J. Inst. Tech., 1984, Phila. Coll. Textiles and Sci., 1992, Lehigh U., 2002; DEng (hon.), Tech. U. N.S., 1991; HHD (hon.), Pratt Inst., 1992; DFA (hon.), U. Pa., 1994; LittD (hon.), U. Nev., 1998; D. Arch. (hon.), U. Miami, 1997; DFA (hon.), Lehigh U., 2002. Registered architect, U.K. Asst. prof. U. Pa., Phila., 1960—65; assoc. prof., head urban design program UCLA, 1965—68; with Venturi, Rauch and Scott Brown, Phila., 1967—, ptnr., 1969—89; prin. Venturi, Scott Brown and Assocs. Inc., Phila., 1989—. Vis. prof. arch. U. Calif., Berkeley, 1965, Yale U., 1967—70; asst. prof. U. Pa., 1960—65, vis. prof. Sch. Fine Arts, 1982, 83; Eliot Noyes design critic in arch. Harvard U., Cambridge, Mass., 1989—90; mem. visitors com. MIT, 1973—83; mem. adv. com. dept. arch. Temple U., 1980—; cons. to dean search com. Sch. Arch. Washington U., St. Louis, 1992; mem. adv. bd. dept. arch. Carnegie Mellon U., 1992—96; mem. jury Prince of Wales Prize in Urban Design Grad. Sch. Design Harvard U., Cambridge, 1993; mem. bd. overseers U. Librs. U. Pa., 1995—. Author: Urban Concepts, 1990; co-author: Learning from Las Vegas, 1972, (rev. edit.), 1977, A View from the Campidoglio: Selected Essays, 1953-84, 1985, On Houses and Housing, 1992; contbr. numerous articles to profl. jours.; prin. works include campus plans U. Mich., Dartmouth Coll., prin. works include city plans Miami Beach, Memphis, plans for U. Pa. Perelman Quadrangle, Nat. Gallery, London, Hotel du Department de la Haute Garonne, Toulouse, France, Life Scis. Inst., U. Mich., exhibitions include retrospective on career and work at Phila. Mus. Art. Policy panelist design arts program NEA, 1981—83; mem. bd. adv. Architects, Designers and Planners for Social Responsibility, 1982—; mem. capitol preservation com. Commonwealth of Pa., Harrisburg, 1983—87; trustee Chestnut Hill Acad., Phila., 1985—89; mem. curriculum com. Phila. Jewish Children's Folkshul, 1980—86; bd. dirs. Ctrl. Phila. Devel. Corp., 1985—, Urban Affairs Partnership, Phila., 1987—91. Decorated chevalier de l'Ordre des Arts et des Lettres France, commendatore Order of Merit Italy; co-recipient The Phila. award, 1993; named to Germantown Hall of Fame, Germantown Hist. Soc., Pa., 2002; recipient Chgo. Architecture award, 1987, U.S. Presdl. award, Nat. Medal of Arts, 1992, Hall of Fame award, Interior Design mag., 1992, The Benjamin Franklin medal, Royal Soc. for Encouragement of Arts., Mfg. and Commerce, 1993, Topaz medal, Am. Coll. Schs. of Architecture/AIA, 1996, Giants of Design award, House Beautiful Mag., 2000, Joseph Pennell medal, Phila. Sketch Club, 2000, Vincent J. Scully Prize, Nat. Bldg. Mus., 2002, Edith Wharton Women of Achievement award for Urban Planning, 2002, Soc. for Environ. Graphic Design Fellow award, 2003, Visionary Woman award, Moore Coll. Art and Design, 2003, 2003. Mem.: Germantown Hist. Soc. of Phila. (Germantown Hall of Fame 2002, Soc. for Environ. Graphic Design Fellow award 2003), Royal Soc. Encouragement of Arts, Mfg. and Commerce, Soc. Archtl. Historians (bd. dirs. 1981—84), Soc. Coll. and Univ. Planning, Archtl. Assn. London, Am. Planning Assn., Archs. Designers and Planners for Social Responsibility, Am. Acad. Arts and Sculpt., Royal Inst. Brit. Archs., Athenaeum of Phila., Carpenters Co. of City and County of Phila., Internat. Women's Forum. Democrat. Jewish. Office: Venturi Scott Brown & Assocs Inc 4236 Main St Philadelphia PA 19127-1603

BROWN, DIANA L. elementary school educator; b. Bklyn., Oct. 9, 1946; d. Elva Jane Brown. AAS, N.Y.C. Community Coll., Bklyn.; BS, CCNY, 1980; postgrad., Nova U., Ft. Lauderdale, Fla. Cert. educator, Fla.; class cert. behavior analysis. Supr. outpatient clinics N.Y. Health and Hosps. Corp., N.Y.C.; asst. dir. Toddlers Country Club, Orlando, Fla.; tchr. Friends Sem., N.Y.C.; tchr. 3d grade Dover Shores Elem. Sch./Orange County Sch. Bd., Orlando, Fla.; 3d grade tchr. Shingle Creek Elem. Sch., 1993, 5th grade tchr., 1993-95, curriculum resource tchr., dean, 1995-97; alternative edn. tchr. Dover Shores Elem. Sch., 1997; 5th grade tchr. Tangelo Park Elem., 1997—2002; trainer for new tchrs., great beginnings induction Orange County Sch. Bd., 2001—; tch. applied behavior analysis Rock Lake Elem. Sch., 2002—, dean, 2002—. Sch.-based care team for students at risk; state sci. textbook adoption com., 1994-95; county sci. curriculum writing team, 1994-95.; trainer new tchrs. Great Beginnings Program, 2001—. Author: Afro-Amercan Artists: A Bio-Bibliographical Directory. Named Tchr. of Yr. Dover Shores, 1990-91; Coun. of Black Faculty and Staff scholar. Mem.: NEA, Nat. Sci. Tchrs. Assn. Office Phone: 407-245-1880 x2264.

BROWN, DONNA MARIE, educational consultant; d. Donald Frank and Shirley Roberta Corey; m. Nathan W. Brown Jr., Jan. 26, 1974 (div. Apr. 2002); children: Jason C., Dustin C., Sarah Jo. Family devel. credential, Cornell U., 2001. Cert. basic family literacy implementation. Family educator TST BOCES/Newfield Ctrl. Sch., Ithaca, NY, 1994—. Treas. Welcome Home Com., Ithaca, 1991; organizer Sarah Pines Free Food Pantry, 2002—03. Recipient Cert. of Appreciation, U.S. Army, 1991, Cmty. Action award, Tompkins Cmty. Action, 2002—03. Mem.: Nat. Assn. Edn. Young Children. Avocations: bowling, reading, volunteering, walking.

BROWN, DORIS JANE, medical technician; b. Mo., Dec. 6, 1934; d. Lowell Emmitt and Lottie Nancy (Downing) Heinrich; m. Thomas B. Brown, Aug. 12, 1958 (div. 1967); 1 child, Doris Ann. AA, Penn Valley Met. C.C., 1982. Accredited nurse aide, Mo. Clk. Western Auto, Kansas City, Mo., 1952-55; acctg. sec. Allied Signal, Kansas City, 1955-58; various positions K.C. Paper Box Co., Kansas City, 1958-61, Winn-Senter Constrn. Co., Kansas City, 1961-90, exec. sec., 1990-92; adminstrv. asst. Miller & Assocs., Lee's Summit, Mo., 1992-93; nurse aide Nat. Health Care, West Plains, Mo., 1994-2001, Beverly Health Care, West Plains, 2001, Beautiful Savior Home, Belton, Mo., 2001—, Jefferson Health Care, 2004, cert. medications technician. Contbr. articles. Vol. Vista, Kansas City, Mo., 1961. Mem. nat. health care coms. Avocations: volunteer facilitator project literacy, sports. Home: 725 NE Tudor Rd #3 Lees Summit MO 64086-5789 Office: Beautiful Savior Home Y Hwy and Cambridge Belton MO 64012 also: 615 SW Oldham Pkwy Lees Summit MO 64081

BROWN, DOROTHY M. academic administrator; Prof. history Georgetown U., Washington, 1966—98, interim provost, 1998—99, provost, 1999—. Former chair history dept. Georgetown U. Office: Georgetown U Office of the Provost Box 571014/ ICC 650 Washington DC 20057-1014

BROWN, EDNA, state representative; b. Toledo, Ohio, Apr. 7, 1940; widowed; 4 children. With CHP 1184, 1992, 2002; state rep. Ohio Ho. of Reps., Columbus, 1994—, minority leader, 1999—2001, ranking minority mem. human svcs. and aging com., mem. criminal justice, econ. devel. and tech., and ins. coms.; mayor Toledo, 2001. Councilwoman Toledo City Coun., 1994—. Mem.: AFSCME, NAACP, Dem. Women's Club. Democrat. Methodist. Office: 77 S High St 10th fl Columbus OH 43215-6111

BROWN, ELIZABETH A. librarian, multi-media specialist; b. Greensburg, Ind., Dec. 18, 1952; d. Robert Dale Brown and Rachel Hannah Taylor. BA, Purdue U., 1975, MS, 1982; MLS, Ind. U., 1985. Lic. sch. libr. scis. and audiovisual svcs. K-12 Ind. Tchr. Michigan City (Ind.) Area Schs., 1975-76; sch. libr. media specialist Valparaiso (Ind.) HS, 1976—. Coach speech and debate Valparaiso HS, 1989—96. Author: (book) Copyright and You, 1997. Advisor Model UN, 1990—96; mem. Friends of Ind. Dunes. Mem.: NEA, AAUW, ALA, Assn. Am. Sch. Librs., Assn. Ind. Media Educators, Friends of Ind. Dunes, Sierra Club, Alpha Delta Kappa. Avocations: hiking, travel, reading. Office: Valparaiso H S 2727 Campbell St Valparaiso IN 46385-2356 E-mail: brownliz@alumni.indiana.edu.

BROWN, ELIZABETH ANN, foreign service officer; b. Portland, Oreg., Aug. 15, 1918; d. Edwin Keith and Grace Viola (Foss) B. AB, Reed Coll., 1940; postgrad. (teaching fellow), Wash. State Coll., 1940-41; A.M., Columbia, 1943. Exec. asst. to chmn. 12th region WLB, Seattle, 1943-45; internat. affairs officer Dept. State, 1946-56; joined U.S. Fgn. Service, 1956; assigned Office UN Polit. Affairs, Dept. State, 1956-60; 1st sec. Am. embassy, Bonn, Germany, 1960-63; dep. dir. Office UN Polit. Affairs, 1963-65, dir., 1965-69; mem. State Dept. Sr. Seminar in Fgn. Policy, 1969-70; counselor for polit. affairs Am. embassy, Athens, Greece, 1970-75, dep. chief mission The Hague, Netherlands, 1975-78; sr. insp. Dept. State, 1978-79, cons., 1980—; ret., 1979. Adviser U.S. del. UN Gen. Assembly, 1946-50, 53, 55, 57-59, 64-65 Recipient 7th ann. Fed. Woman's award, 1967 Mem. Am. Fgn. Service Assn., Phi Beta Kappa. Home: 4848 Reservoir Rd NW Washington DC 20007-1561 Office: Dept State Washington DC 20007

BROWN, ELIZABETH SCHMECK, fashion historian; b. Ancon, Panama, Sept. 7, 1918; d. Henry Penuel and Pansy Blossom (Logan) Schmeck; m. Walter Daniel Brown, July 29, 1944; children: David Henry, Walter Daniel Jr., Edward Logan, Kenneth Maclin. Student, U. Tex., 1935—37; BS, Cornell U., 1940, MS, 1945; student, Art Students League N.Y. Cert. family and consumer scis. AAFCS. Instr. textiles and clothing, curator costume collection Coll. Home Econs. Cornell U., Ithaca, NY, 1941—45; assoc. home economist McCall Pattern Co., N.Y.C., 1963—65; assoc. Uno Pattern Co., N.J. and Pa., 1972—74; lectr. on hist. dress, 1972—; appraiser of hist. dress, 1978—. Contbr. articles to profl. publs.; curated exhbns., NJ Divsn. on Women, Trenton, Kemmerer Mus., Bethelehem, Pa., Antiques at the Armory, Phila., Rutgers Inst. for Rsch. on Women, New Brunswick, N.J., N.J. Hist. Commn. Mem. Montgomery Twp. Bd. Edn., Skillman, NJ, 1969—81, various offices, including pres., 1975—77; legis. chmn., pres. Somerset County Sch. Bds. Assn., Somerville, NJ, 1977—80; testified to State Legis. and Bd. Edn. for mandate of Family Life Edn.; active N.J. Network Family Life, 1983—2002; mem. adv. coun. Family, Career, and Cmty. Leadership Am., 2001—; bd. dirs. Costume and Textile Group N.J., 2001—; bd. dir. (former treas.) Wesley Found., 1984—, Princeton U.; mem. PTA, Pitts.; pres. Whittier Sch., Park Ridge, Ill.; founding com. River-Ridge Council, Broomall, Pa. Fellow: Costume Soc. Am. (treas. 1980—86, bd. dirs. several terms 1982—, Bd. of Dir., several terms 1982—2004, corr. sec. 1986—92, pres. region II 1993—97, v.p. internal rels. 1998—2003, parliamentarian, bd. dirs.); mem.: AAUW (pres. Princeton br. 1973—75), N.J. Assn. Family and Consumer Scis. (state pres.'s unit nom. com., divsn. chair, apparel and textiles, archives and history), Am. Assn. Family and Consumer Scis. (nat. leader 1992), Van Harlingen Hist. Soc. (former trustee), Hist. Soc. Princeton (collections com.), Internat. Textile and Apparel Assn., N.J. Assn. Mus., PTA Pitts. (various offices), Internat. Sewing Machine Collectors Soc., Am. Assn. State and Local History, Cornell Alumni Assn., Princeton YWCA (vol. Friday Club 1968—2000), Y Canoe Club, Cornell Woman's Club (Pitts.) (pres., chair sec. sch. com.), Friday (com. mem. 2000—), Cornell Woman's Club (Chgo.), Cornell Woman's Club (Phila.), Phi Kappa Phi, Kappa Omicron Nu, Alpha Lambda Delta. Achievements include testified to State legislature and Bd. of Edn. for mandate of Family Life Edn. in [illegible] 3-5 yrs. of giving my costume collection to the collection at the Coll. of Human Ecology there. Avocations: costume collection of over 2000 items, collecting antique paper patters, collecting antique sewing machines and other sewing items. Home and Office: 45 Whippoorwill Way Belle Mead NJ 08502 E-mail: ebrown@nerc.com.

BROWN, ELMIRA NEWSOM, retired elementary school educator; b. Proctor-Crittenden, Ark., May 31, 1907; d. Emanuel Newsom and Tennessee Johnson; m. James Jefferson Brown, Nov. 19, 1942. BS, U. Ark., Pine Bluff, 1950; MS, U. Ark., Fayetteville, 1954. Tchr. Wynoka (Ark.) Elem. Sch., 1930-34, Mildred Jackson Elem. Sch., Hughes, Ark., 1934-42; prin. McCrory (Ark.) Elem. Sch. (now Elmira N. Brown H.S.), 1943-50; tchr. Scipio A. Jones H.S., North Little Rock, Ark., 1950-53, Howard Elem. Sch., Ft. Smith, Ark., 1954-60, Goldstein Elem. Sch., Hot Springs, Ark., 1960-67, Langston H.S., Hot Springs, 1967-68; ret., 1968. Interim exec. dir. Coun. Econ. Opportunity, Hot Springs, 1968—. V.p. Woodland Shores Cmty. Action, Royal, Ark., 1983-92; mem. Dem. Nat. Com., Washington, 1992-97; chairperson task force Dem. Congl. Campaign Com., Royal, 1992-96; mem. women's missionary soc. African Meth. Episcopal Ch.; dir. connectional skill shops WMS, 1980. Mem. AAUW, LWV, Ch. Women United, U. Ark. Alumni Assn., Zeta Phi Beta. Mem. African Meth. Episcopalian Ch. Avocations: softball, basketball, fishing, boating, gardening.

BROWN, FAY, editor, writer; b. Patterson, La., Aug. 5, 1925; d. Alvan Paul Gautreau and Mari2 Stella Seghers; m. Hilton J. Brown, Aug. 12, 1950 (dec.); children: Patrick Ronald, Robert Allan(dec.). BA with highest distinction, U. Southwestern La., 1945. Editor weekly newspaper Franklin (La.) Banner Tribune, 1945-50; editor diocesan newsletter for older adults Diocese of La., Franklin, 1991—. Author: Franklin through the Years, 1972, St. Mary's Episcopal Church-Yesterday and Today. Past sec. St. Mary Landmarks; past chmn. St. Mary Coun. on Aging, Franklin, 1999—; mem. bd. St. Mary Literacy Coun., 1999—; mem. St. Mary Civil War Commn., 1999—. Recipient civic award Franklin Bus. and Profl. Women's Club, 1950. Republican. Episcopalian. Avocations: reading, music.

BROWN, FRANCES LOUISE (GRANDMA FRAN), artist, art gallery owner; b. Indpls., Oct. 19, 1925; d. Harley and Lenore (Spencer) Netherland; m. C.G. Clarkson, July 24, 1943 (div. Aug. 1967); children: James E. Clarkson, John B. Clarkson, Deborah L. Cromis. Thomas L. Currey, June 9, 1972 (dec. May 1978); m. George L. Brown, Jr., Mar. 3, 1982; 1 stepchild, Nancy Snow. BS in Edn., Miami U., 1968; MA in Edn., Ball State U., 1970. Elem. sch. tchr. Liberty (Ind.) Elem. Sch., 1968-71; tchr. Ball State U., Muncie, Ind., 1971-72; instr. Colby (Kans.) C.C., 1972-75; gallery owner, primitive artist Grandma Fran Art Gallery (formerly Currey Studio Gallery), Berryville, Ark., 1975—. Author: Now Hear This, 1974; works exhibited at Nat. Mus. Am. Art, Washington, Wichita (Kans.) Art Assn. Gallery, Ark. Coll., Batesville, South Ark. Art Ctr., El Dorado, Harding Coll., Searcy, Ark., U. Ark., Fayetteville, Eureka Springs (Ark.) Hist. Mus., Western State Coll. Colo., Gunnison, MacMurray Coll., Jacksonville, Ill., Colby (Kans.) Coll., Claremore (Okla.) Coll., Warren Hall Coutts, III, Meml. Art Gallery, Inc., El Dorado, Kans., Masur Mus. Art, Monroe, La., Nebr. State Hist. Soc. Mus., Lincoln, Ind. State Mus., Indpls., Ozark Folk Ctr., Mountain View, Ark., Ft. Smith (Ark.) Art Ctr., Ctr. for So. Folklore, Memphis, Rogers (Ark.) Hist. Mus., Albrecht Art Mus., St. Joseph, Mo., Shiloh Mus., Springdale, Ark., Internat. Ctr. Contemporary Art, Paris, John Judkyn Meml. Mus., Eng., Mykonos (Greece) Folklore Mus., Musees Royaux des Beaux-Arts de Belgique, Brussels, Setagaya Art Mus., Tokyo, Fukuoka (Japan) Art Mus.; represented in permanent collections Smithsonian Instn., Washington, Mus. Am. Folk Art, N.Y.C., Nebr. State Hist. Soc. Mus., Lincoln, Ind. State Mus., Indpls., Ozark Mountain Folk Ctr., Mountain View, Ctr. for So. Folklore, Memphis, Setagaya Art Mus., others; paintings recognized in various books, newspapers and articles. Avocations: pilot, sewing, reading, fishing, cooking. Home and Office: Grandma Fran Art Gallery 3331 Highway 62 W Berryville AR 72616-8948

BROWN, GERALDINE, nurse, freelance writer; b. Clemson, S.C. d. Isaac and Gladys (Patterson) B. AS in Nursing, U. D.C., Washington, 1973; real estate cert., Long and Foster Inst., College Park, Md., 1984; cert. in TV broadcasting, Columbia Sch., Bailey's Crossroads, Va., 1987; BSN, Bowie State U., 1989, MA in Comm., 1991, MSN, 1997; PhD, Howard U., 1994. RN, D.C., FCC Third Class License. Supr. staff nurse Walter Reed Hosp., Washington, 1970-76; supr. clin. nurse dept. Human Svcs., Washington, 1976-78, cmty. health nurse, 1978-84; nursing instr. Phillips Bus. Sch., Alexandria, Va., 1984-85; pvt. nurse Washington, 1973—; faculty Howard U. Coll. Nursing, 1994—. Dir. pub. affairs Bible Way Chs. Worldwide, Inc., Washington, 1978-91; soc. columnist As It Happens, Charlotte (N.C.) Post, 1964-66; soc. editor Washington Cafe Soc. mag, 1971; contbr. feature stories Capital Spotlight newspaper, 1978—; mem. faculty Coll. Nursing, Howard U., 1994—. Asst. organizer DC Mayor's United Nations Day, 1980; vol. Met. Boys and Girls Clubs, Washington, 1980—; vol. Nursing Instr., The Washington Saturday Coll., 1982-84; Co. ARC, 1973—, Big Sisters of the Washington Met. Area, 1988—. Recipient certs. of excellence Govt. of D.C., 1978-84; cert. of appreciation Mayor of D.C., 1980, Meritorious Pub. Svc. award, l980; svc. trophy Washington Saturday Coll., l984. Mem. ANA, NAACP, Nat. Coun. Negro Women, Smithsonian Inst. (assoc.), Nat. Black Nurses Assn., Washington Urban League, Chi Eta Phi, Sigma Theta Tau. Democrat. Avocations: stamp collecting, traveling, writing poetry. Office Phone: 202-244-0313. Business E-Mail: g.brown@enor10net.att.net.

BROWN, GERALDINE REED, lawyer, management consultant; b. L.A., Feb. 18, 1947; d. William Penn and Alberta Vernice (Coleman) Reed; m. Ronald Wellington Brown, Aug. 20, 1972; children: Kimberly Diana, Michael David. BA summa cum laude, Fisk U., 1968; JD, Harvard U., 1971, MBA, 1973. Bar: N.Y. 1974, U.S. Dist. Ct. (so. and ea. dists.) N.Y. 1974, U.S. Ct. Appeals (2d cir.) 1974, U.S. Supreme Ct. 1977, N.J. 1992, U.S. Dist. Ct. N.J. 1992, Pa. 1993. Assoc. White & Case, N.Y.C., 1973-78; atty. J.C. Penney Co., Inc., N.Y.C., 1978-88; pres. The Reed-Brown Cons. Group., Montclair, N.J., 1989—; counsel Spooner & Burnett, N.Y.C., 1993-98. Asst. prof. bus. law Montclair State Coll., 1990-92; adj. prof. bus. law Kean Coll. N.J., 1989-94; adj. prof. Law Sch. Seton Hall, 1995—; dir., sec., gen. counsel Renaissance Jr. Golf, Inc., Newark; instr. Hudson County C.C., Bergen C.C., Entrepreneurial Training Inst.; mem. com. on women and the cts. N.J. Supreme Ct. Bd. dirs. Coun. Concerned Black Execs., N.Y.C., 1977-88, Studio Mus. in Harlem, N.Y.C., 1980-81; mem. Montclair (N.J.) Devel. Bd., 1985-88, ad hoc com. on Montclair Econ. Devel. Corp., 1985-88; sec., bd. trustee Montclair YWCA, 1989-97, United Hosps. Med. Ctr., vice chmn., 1991-93, trustee, 1989-97, exec. com., chair bylaws com., chair strategic planning com., pers. com.; trustee, former sec. bd. trustees, chair human resources com. Ramapo Coll.; chair bylaws com., N.J. United Minority Bus. Brain Trust; trustee Essex County Ct. Apptd. Spl. Advocates, 1989-93, Jr. League of Montclair, Newark Mental Health Resources Ctr., Montclair, N.J., 1991-96; trustee, sec. Montclair Early Childhood Corp., 1997-98; trustee, sec. St. Marks United Meth. Ch., Pineridge Corp., United Meth. Homes. Mem. ABA (several coms. sect. corp., banking and bus. law, sect. internat. law and practice), N.J. Bar Assn. (mem. bus. orgns. com.), Essex County Bar Assn., N.Y. State Bar Assn. (continuing legal edn. com., legis. liason 1981-90, vice chmn. 1988-90, exec. com. of corp. counsel sect., chmn. com. on SEC, fin. corp. law and governance, chair com. atty. professionalism 1994-97, mem. task force on profession, com. rev. of cts. and professions), Assn. of Bar of City of N.Y. (corp. law com. 1978-81), N.Y. County Lawyers Assn. (corp. law com.), Exec. Women of N.J., Harvard Bus. Sch. Club, Harvard Law Sch. Assn. (trustee N.J. chpt.), Coalition 100 Black Women, Harvard Bus. Sch. Black Alumni Assn., Harvard Law Sch. Black Alumni Assn., Harvard Club (N.Y.C.), Phi Beta Kappa, Delta Sigma Theta (past chair social action com. Montclair alumnae [illegible] parliamentarian) Home and Office: The Reed-Brown Cons Group 180 Union St Montclair NJ 07042-2125 E-mail: rbcg1@aol.com.

BROWN, GERRI ANN, physical therapist; b. N.Y.C., May 1, 1948; d. S. Stanley and Corinne (Carlin) Schkurman; m. Michael Edward Brown, Oct. 2, 1971. BS in Phys. Therapy, Ithaca Coll., 1969. Registered phys. therapist, Colo., N.Y. Lectr. U. Colo. Med. Sch., Denver, 1970-81; dir. phys. therapy and team facilitator Wheatridge (Colo.) Regional Ctr., 1969-81; phys. therapist Ptnrs. Home Health Care, Lakewood, Colo., 1982-83, Mt. Evans Home Health Care, Evergreen, Colo., 1983-88, Western Home Health, Arvada, Colo., 1988-93, ICON Home Care, Lakewood, 1993-97, Vis. Nurse Assn., Denver, 1995—, 1995—. Lectr. U. Colo., Denver, 1970-81, U. No. Colo., Greeley, 1977-81; tchr., cons. ICON Home Care, Lakewood, 1993-97, Western Home Health Care, Arvada, 1988-93, Mt. Evans Health Care, 1983-88, Vis. Nurses Denver, 1996—; chairperson task force State of Colo., Denver, 1972-73. Mem. Citizens for Action, Idledale, Colo., 1975-76. Mem. Am. Phys. Therapy Assn. (sect. on geriatrics and home health care), Hiwan Golf Club. Avocations: golf, travel, music. Home: PO Box 88 Idledale CO 80453-0088 E-mail: bigboo49@aol.com.

BROWN, GLENDA ANN WALTERS, ballet director; b. Buna, Tex., July 22, 1937; d. Jesse Olaf and Kathryn Jeanette (Rogers) Walters; m. David Dann Brown, Dec. 13, 1958 (div. 1995); children: Kathryn, Jean, Vanessa Lea. Grad. h.s., Beaumont, Tex. Mem. Melody Maids, Beaumont, 1950-60; asst. tchr. Widman Sch., Beaumont, 1952-55; owner, tchr. Walters Sch. of Dance, Jasper, Tex., 1955-59; assoc. tchr. Emmamae Horn Sch., 1964-81, artistic dir., 1981—; assoc. dir. Allegro Ballet Houston, 1974-81, artistic dir., 1981—; owner, dir. Allegro Acad. Dance, Houston, 1981—. Dir. Regional Dance Am., Nat. Craft Choreography Conf., 1987—2001; mem. adv. bd. Dance Tchr. Mag., 1998—2003; founder, dir. Glenda Brown Choreography Project, 2002—. Dance panel Cultural Arts Coun., Houston, 1979, Tex. Commn. on the Arts, 1988-90; sec. Riedel Estates Civic Club, Houston, 1975-78; Rep. poll worker, Houston, 1970-81; bd. dirs. Austrian Alps Performing Arts Festival, 1996-98; coord. First Nat. Regional Dance Am. Festival, 1997, bd. dirs. Tanzsommer/Austria, 1998—. Mem. Dance Masters Am. (exam. chair chpt. 3 1980-86), Regional Dance Am. S.W. (exec. v.p. 1981-2001), Dance Am., Nat. Assn. Regional Ballet (bd. dirs. 1985-88), Regional Dance Am. (nat. bd. dirs., v.p. 1988-95, pres. 1995-2001). Methodist. Avocations: camping, singing, golf, travel. Office: Allegro Ballet and Dance Acad 1570 S Dairy Ashford St Ste 200 Houston TX 77077-3870 Office Phone: 281-496-4670. E-mail: glendabrown@allegroballet.com.

BROWN, GWENDOLYN (WILLIAMS), music educator; b. Danville, Ky., Aug. 3, 1945; d. Edward Pendleton Williams, Sr. and Mattie (Pride) Williams; m. Albert Sylvester Brown, Jr., Feb. 14, 1976; 1 child, Lydia Ruth ; m. John Davidson Reynolds, Aug. 4, 1964 (div. Aug. 1, 1968). BA, CSULA, Los Angeles, Calif., 1964—67, tchg. credential, 1994. Banker Wells Fargo Bank, Pasadena, Calif., 1968—75, Oakland, Calif., 1968—75, Berkeley, Calif., 1968—75; sales clk., music dept. Marshall Fields, Skokie, Ill., 1976—78; clerical substitute Arcadia Unified Sch. Dist., Arcadia, Calif., 1987—89; bible class, tchr. First A.M.E. Ch., Pasadena, Calif., 1989—92; substitute tchr. Pasadena Unified, Pasadena, Calif., 1989—93, Arcadia Unified, Arcadia, Calif., 1989—93; children's choir dir. First A.M.E. Ch., Pasadena, Calif., 1990—94; choral music tchr. Monsovia Unified Sch. Dist., Monsovia, Calif., 1993—. Soloist, opera workshop Merritt Coll., Oakland, Calif., 1971—75; western opera co. chorus San Francisco Opera, San Francisco, 1981; Phil Reeder Oakland Choraleers Oakland Choraleers, Oakland, Calif., 1986. Mem. First A.M.E. Ch., Pasadena, Calif., 1984—, First A.M.E. Heritage Com., Pasadena, Calif., 2000—. Recipient Outstanding Student Tchr., Calif. State Univ./Los Angeles, Calif., 1993—94, African Am. Artist award, First A.M.E. Ch., Pasadena Youth Usher Bd./ Calif., 2000. Mem.: Am. Choral Dir. Assn. (mem. 1994—), Music Educators Nat. Conf. (mem. 1994—), Kappa Delta Pi (mem. 1995—, v.p. 1996—98). Democrat. African Meth. Episc. Avocations: reading, photography, sewing, knitting, crocheting. Home: 44 W La Sierra Drive Arcadia CA 91007-4019 Office: 325 E Huntington Drive Monrovia CA 91016

BROWN, HELEN GURLEY, editor, writer; b. Green Forest, Ark., Feb. 18, 1922; d. Ira M. and Cleo (Sisco) Gurley; m. David Brown, Sept. 25, 1959. Student, Tex. State Coll. for Women, 1940—41, Woodbury Coll., 1942; LLD, Woodbury U., 1987; DLitt, L.I. U., 1993. Exec. sec. Music Corp. Am., 1942—45; exec. sec. William Morris Agy., 1945—47; copywriter Foote, Cone & Belding (advt. agy.), Los Angeles, 1948—58; advt. writer, account exec. Kenyon & Eckhardt (advt. agy.), Hollywood, Calif., 1958—62; editor-in-chief Cosmopolitan mag., 1965—97, Cosmopolitan Internat. Edits, 1997—. Named 1 of 25 most influential women in U.S., World Almanac, 1976—81; recipient Francis Holmes Achievement award for outstanding work in advt., 1956—59, Disting. Achievement award, U. So. Calif. Sch. Journalism, 1971, Spl. award for editl. leadership Am. Newspaper, Woman's Club, Washington, 1972, Disting. Achievement award in journalism, Stanford U., 1977, Matrix award in mag. category, N.Y. Women in Comm., 1985, Henry Johnson Fisher award, Mag. Pubs. of Am., 1995, Helen Gurley Brown Rshc. Professorship established name, Northwestern U. Medill Sch. Journalism, 1986, inducted into Pubs.' Hall of Fame, 1988. Mem.: AFTRA, Am. Soc. Mag. Editors (Hall of Fame award 1996), Authors League Am., Eta Upsilon Gamma. Office: Cosmopolitan The Hearst Corp 224 W 57th St New York NY 10019

BROWN, HELEN SAUER, fund raising executive; b. Findlay, Ohio, Feb. 7, 1923; d. Joseph Thomas and Mary Magdalene (Sweeney) Sauer; m. Thomas Francis Brown, June 10, 1944; children: Mary Helen Anne, Thomas F., Joachim J., Mary Christine, Mary Kathleen, Mary Elizabeth, Timothy J., Martin J., John Fitzgerald Kennedy. BA magna cum laude, Mundelein Coll. for Women, 1944, MA summa cum laude, 1970. V.p. T.F. Brown Co., Chgo., 1962-84; tchr. Nazareth Acad., La Grange Park, Ill., 1968-72; pastoral min. Ill., 1970—; dir. religious edn. Divine Savior Parish, Downers Grove, Ill., 1972-76; pres. Herself's Doings Ltd., La Grange, Ill., 1972—; retail store owner/mgr. Nettle Creek Shop, La Grange, 1976-85; dir. resource devel. Cmty. Family Svc. & Mental Health Assn., Lyons and Riverside Townships, Ill., 1986—. Cons., spkr. in field; pres. Religious Edn. Svcs., La Grange, 1972-86; adv. coun. U. Notre Dame Sch. of Theology, 1970-72. Author: Community and Social Justice, 1974. Trustee Mundelein Coll., Chgo., 1970-90; organizer ERA, Springfield, Ill., 1968—; peace activist, Washington, 1966—; commr. Lyons (Ill.) Mental Health Commn., 1978-80; commr. econ. devel. Village of La Grange, 1983-93; commr. program rev. Pvt. Industry Coun., Cook County, Ill., 1984-94; dir. Ill. Retirement Home Assn., Hinsdale, 1993—; chair Resident Coun., Bethlehem Woods. Named Woman of Century, West Suburban C. of C., 2002; recipient Welford award for disting. svc. to mental health, 1983; scholar Cardinal Meyer scholar, Archdiocese of Chgo., 1970. Mem. NAACP, AAUW, LWV, Nat. Soc. Fund Raising Execs. (cert. 1991), La Grange West Suburban C. of C. (chair pres.'s coun. 1985-96, pres. 1986-87, Woman of Yr. 1983), Women for Peace, Amnesty Internat., Bus. and Profl. Women/USA (Outstanding Working Woman Ill. chpt. 1993), Phoenix Soc., Women's Bd., Clergy and Laity Concerned for Justice and Peace, Gannon Ctr. Women and Leadership, Mundelein Coll. Alumnae, La Grange Cath. Women's Club, Kappa Gamma Pi. Democrat. Roman Catholic. Avocations: book reviewing, public opinion research, liturgical planning, philosophy, word puzzles. Home: 1571 W Ogden Ave Apt 2626 La Grange Park IL 60526-1769 E-mail: hsbtfb@msn.com.

BROWN, IFIGENIA THEODORE, lawyer; b. Syracuse, N.Y., Mar. 14, 1930; d. Gus and Christine Theodore; m. Paul Frederick Brown, Sept. 16, 1956; 1 child, Paul Darrow. BA, Syracuse U., 1951, LLB, JD, 1954. Bar: N.Y. 1956. Acting police justice Village of Ballston Spa, NY, 1960—62; sr. ptnr. Brown & Brown, Ballston Spa, 1958—95; ptnr. Brown Brown & Peterson Esqs, Ballston Spa, 1995—2000; of counsel Brown, Peterson and Craig, Ballston Spa, 2000—. Chmn. N.Y. State Bd. Real Property Svcs., Albany, 1996—. Mem. Charlton Sch. Bd., 1989-93, Ballston Spa Libr. Bd., 1991-94; founder, pres. Saratoga County Women's Rep. Club; vice-chmn. Saratoga County Rep. Com., 1958-72. Mem. N.Y. State Bar Assn., Saratoga County Bar Assn. (treas. 1983-84, pres. 1984-85), Zonta (pres. Saratoga County 1962, 90), Order Ea. Star. Republican. Greek Orthodox. Avocations: church choir, piano. Home: 42 Hyde Blvd Ballston Spa NY 12020-1608 Office: Brown Peterson and Craig One E High St Ballston Spa NY 12020

BROWN, J'AMY MARONEY, journalist, media relations consultant, investor; b. Oct. 30, 1945; d. Roland Francis and Jeanne (Wilbur) Maroney; m. James Raphael Brown, Jr., Nov. 5, 1967 (dec. July 1982); children: James Roland Francis, Jeanne Raphael. Student, U. So. Calif., 1963-67. Reporter L.A. Herald Examiner, 1966-67, Lewisville Leader, Dallas, 1980-81; editor First Person Mag., Dallas., 1981-82; journalism dir. Pacific Palisades Sch., L.A., 1983-84; freelance writer, media cons., 1984-88; media dir., chief media strategist Tellem Inc., 1990-92, comm. cons., issues mgr., 1992—. Press liaison U.S. papal visit, L.A., 1987; pres., CEO and owner PRformance Group Comm., 1995—; auction chmn. Assn. Pub. Broadcasting, Houston, 1974, 75; vice chmn. Dallas Arts Coun., 1976-80; vice chmn. Met. March of Dimes, Dallas, 1980-82; del. Dallas Coun. PTAs, 1976-80; bd. dirs., pres. continuing edn. adv. bd. Santa Barbara City Coll.; pres. bd. dirs. Montecito Assn., Women's Econ. Ventures, Santa Barbara Visual Arts Alliance; mem. core-coun. Santa Barbara Coun. on Self-Esteem; coord. specialist World Cup Soccer Organizing Com.; dir. J.M. Brown Charitable Found. Columnist: Santa Barbara News Press, 2004, Montecito Jour., 2004. Recipient UPI Editors award for investigative reporting, 1981. Mem. NAFE, Pub. Rels. Soc. Am. (accredited), Women Meeting Women, Women in Comm., Am. Bus. Women's Assn., Goleta Valley Art Assn., Santa Barbara C. of C. (media com.). Republican. Roman Catholic. Home: 1143 High Rd Santa Barbara CA 93108-2430

BROWN, JACQUELINE I. medical assistant; b. L.A., May 29, 1961; d. James I. and Carolyn Brown; m. Jonah I. Brown; 1 child, LaJuan D. Hines-Brown. Assoc. in Med. Asst., Cin. Met. Coll., 1987. Med. asst. Mt. Auburn Health Ctr., Cin., 1987—. Front desk clk. Anthony Munoz Pediats. Ctr., Cin., 1999—2003; clin. and med. records Mt. Auburn Health Ctr., Cin., 1987—. Avocations: Karate, team mom in sports. Home: 2321 Maplewood Ave Cincinnati OH 45219 Office: Mt Auburn Health Ctr 2415 Auburn Ave Cincinnati OH 45219 E-mail: jib52961@aol.com.

BROWN, JANE G. sports association executive; b. N.Y.C., Jan. 20, 1941; d. Samuel Hazard and Ruth (Reed) Gillespie; widowed; children: James, Serena; m. Ames Brown, July 14, 1978; 1 child, Ames. BA, Wellesley U., 1962. Exec. dir. Internat. Tennis Hall of Fame, Newport, R.I., 1981-85, pres., COO, 1991—; mng. dir. Women's Internat. Pro Tennis Coun., N.Y.C., 1986-91. Recipient David Gray award Women's Tennis Assn., 1991. Office: Internat Tennis Hall of Fame 194 Bellevue Ave Newport RI 02840-3515

BROWN, JANICE ROGERS, state supreme court justice; b. Laverne, AL, May 11, 1949; BA, Ca. St. U., Sacramento, 1974; JD, UCLA, 1977. Assoc. justice Calif. Supreme Ct., San Francisco, 1996—. Office: Calif Supreme Ct 350 Mcallister St Rm 1295 San Francisco CA 94102-4783

BROWN, JANIECE ALFREIDA, pilot; b. Ellensburg, Wash., May 23, 1956; d. Don Elmer and LaRhee Deloris (Montgomery) Lewis; m. David E. Brown, Oct. 10, 1993. AA, Big Bend C.C., Moses Lake, Wash., 1980-82; BS, Ctrl. Wash. U., 1982-84. Pilot AAR Western Skyways, Troutdale, Oreg., 1984-87; airline capt. N.P.A., Inc., Pasco, Wash., 1987-89; flight engr. airline pilot Alaska Airlines, Seattle, 1989—, 1st officer Boeing 727 and MD-80, capt. MD-80, 1996—; bus. mgr. David Brown & Assocs., 1994-99; airline capt. MD-80 Alaska Airlines, Seattle, 1996—. Owner, bus. mgr. Champagne Creek Cellars, Roseburg, Oreg., 2001—. Lobbyist Save Our Watershed, Roslyn, Wash., 1978-80; pres. Interlachen, Inc., A Homeowners Assn., 1998-2002. Recipient Scholastic award CleElum (Wash.) High Sch., 1974. Mem. Airline Pilot Assn., 1990- (mem. dangerous goods com., 1991-2002), Alpha Eta Rho (pres. Ctrl. Wash. U. chpt. 1983-84). Avocations: skiing, sewing, backpacking, contractor, remodeler of own home and rental. Home: 20912 NE Interlachen Ln Troutdale OR 97060-8731 Office: Alaska Airlines PO Box 61900 Seattle WA 98178

BROWN, JEAN WILLIAMS, state supreme court justice; b. Birmingham, Ala. m. E. Terry Brown; 2 children. Grad. with honors, Samford U., 1974; JD, U. Ala., 1977. Bar: Ala. 1977, U.S. Ct. Appeals (11th cir.), U.S. Supreme Ct. Law clerk Tucker, Gray & Thigpen; asst. atty. gen. criminal appeals divsn., chief extradition officer Ala. Atty. Gen.'s Office; judge Ala. Ct. Criminal Appeals, 1997-99; justice Supreme Ct. Ala., 1999—. Tchr. kindergarten Sunday sch. 1st Bapt. Ch. Mem. Montgomery Jr. League. Office: Ala Supreme Ct 300 Dexter Ave Montgomery AL 36104-3741

BROWN, JEANETTE GRASSELLI, retired university official; b. Cleve., Aug. 4, 1928; d. Nicholas W. and Veronica (Varga) Gecsy; m. Glenn R. Brown, Aug. 1, 1987. BS summa cum laude, Ohio U., 1950, DSc (hon.), 1978; MS, Western Res. U., 1958, DSc (hon.), 1995, Clarkson U., 1986; D Engring. (hon.), Mich. Tech. U., 1989; DSc (hon.), Wilson Coll., 1994, Notre Dame Coll., 1995, Kenyon Coll., 1995, Mt. Union Coll., 1996, Cleveland State U., 2000, Kent State U., 2000, Ursuline Coll., 2001; DSc, Youngstown State U., 2003, U. Pecs, Hungary, 2002. Project leader, assoc. Infrared Spectroscopist, Cleve., 1950-78; mgr. analytical sci. lab. Standard Oil (name changed to BP Am., Inc. 1985), Cleve., 1978-83, dir. technol. support dept., 1983-85, dir. corp. rsch. and analytical scis., 1985-88; disting. vis. prof., dir. rsch. enhancement Ohio U., Athens, 1989-95; ret., 1995. Bd. dirs. AGA Gas, Inc., USX Corp., McDonald Investments, BDM Internat., BF Goodrich Co., Nicolet Instrument Corp.; mem. bd. on chem. sci. and tech. NRC, 1986-91; chmn. U.S. Nat. Com. to Internat. Union of Pure and Applied Chemistry, 1992-94; mem. joint high level adv. panel U.S.-Japan Sci. and Tech., 1994-2001, Ohio Bd. Regents, 1995—, chmn., 2000-2002; vis. com. Nat. Inst. Stds. and Tech., 1988-91. Author, editor 8 books; editor: Vibrational Spectroscopy; contbr. numerous articles on molecular spectroscopy to profl. jours.; patentee naphthalene extraction process. Bd. dirs. N.E. Ohio Sci. and Engring. Fair, Cleve., Martha Holden Jennings Found., Cleve. Clinic Found., Sci. Svc. Inc.; chair bd. dirs. Cleve. Scholarship Programs, Inc., 1994-2000; trustee Holden Arboretum, Cleve., 1988—, Edison Biotech Ctr., Cleve., 1988-95, Cleve. Playhouse, 1990-96, Garden Ctr. Greater Cleve., 1990-93, Mus. Arts Assn., 1991—, Gt. Lakes Sci. Ctr., 1991—, Rainbow Babies and Children's Hosp., 1992-95, Nat. Inventors' Hall of Fame, 1993—, Ohio U., 1985-94, chmn. 1991-92; chair steering com. Mellen Ctr. Cleve. Clinic, 1996—; chair bd. dirs. ideastream, PBS, NPR. Recipient Disting. Svc. award Cleve. Tech. Soc. Coun., 1985; named Woman of Yr. YWCA, 1980; named to Ohio Women's Hall of Fame State of Ohio, 1989, Ohio Sci. & Tech. Hall of Fame, 1991, Humanitarian award Nat. Conf. Cmty. Justice, 2000, Medal of Honor, Ellis Island, 2002. Mem. Am. Chem. Soc. (chair analytical divsn. 1990-91, Garvan medal 1986, Analytical Chem. award 1993, Encouraging Women into Careers in Sci. award 1999), Soc. for Applied Spectroscopy (pres. 1970, Disting. Svc. award 1983), Coblentz Soc. (bd. govs. 1968-71, William Wright award 1980), Royal Soc. Chemistry (Theophilus Redwood lectr. 1994), Phi Beta Kappa, Iota Sigma Pi (pres. fluorine chpt. 1957-60, nat. hon. mem. 1987). Republican. Roman Catholic. Avocations: swimming, dance, music. Home: 150 Greentree Rd Chagrin Falls OH 44022-2424

BROWN, JEANETTE L. environmental protection administrator; BBA, Morgan State U., 1980; postgrad., Am. U., Washington. Intern Navy Regional Contracting Ctr., Washington, 1978; with Navy Automatic Data Processing Selection Office, Joint Cruise Missile Project/NAV AIR; dep. dir. Office of Small and Disadvantaged Bus. Utilization, EPA, Washington, dep. dir. Office of Acquisition Mgmt., dir. Office of Acquisition Mgmt.; dir. small and disadvantaged bus. EPA, Washington. Office: US EPA Small and Disadvantaged Bus 401 M St SW Washington DC 20460-0001 Fax: 202-401-1080.

BROWN, JESSICA BREE, secondary school educator, consultant; b. Indpls., Aug. 1, 1977; d. Barbara Jeanne Schoeppner and William Hicks; m. Joseph Brown, Mar. 1, 2003. BS in Psychology, U. South Fla., 1999; EdM, St. Leo U., 2003. Cert. profl. tchr. Fla. Dept. Edn., 2000. Educator Pasco County Schs., Land O' Lakes, Fla., 1999—, mainstream cons., 2002—. Dept. chairperson Exceptional Student Edn., Dade City, Fla., 2002—, Lang. Arts Dept., Dade City, Fla., 2003—; com. chairperson Mng. and Motivating Student Behavior, Dade City, Fla., 2002—. Mem.: Coun. Exceptional Children. Office: Pasco High Sch 36850 SR 52 Dade City FL 33525

BROWN, JO ETTA, elementary school educator, librarian; b. Akron, Iowa, Dec. 4, 1952; d. Ralph Marion and Edna Ophila (Lamoureux) Latham; m. Daryl Aaron Brown, Nov. 18, 1978; children: Ashlie Mae, Adam Edward BA in Edn., Wayne (Nebr.) State Coll., 1974; libr. and media endorsement, Kearney (Nebr.) State Coll., 1986; M in Edml. Adminstrn., U. Neb., 1998. Cert. tchr., Nebr. Elem. tchr. phys. edn. Brule (Nebr.) Pub. Sch., 1975—, libr. and media specialist, 1985—; asst. prin. Ogallala Elem. Schs. Mem. Community Improvement Assn., Brule, 1990—. Mem. NEA, AAHPER and Dance, Nebr. Assn. Health, Nebr. Assn. Elem. Sch. Principals, Neb. Assn. Sch. Adminstrs., Phys. Edn. and Dance, Nebr. Ednl. Media Assn., Villagers Club (pres. 1991-92). Democrat. Roman Catholic. Avocations: woodworking, reading, yard work, walking. Home: 1149 Rd West 50 Brule NE 69127-9756 Office: Ogallala Elem Sch 601 West B Ogallala NE 69153

BROWN, JOBETH GOODE, food products executive, lawyer; b. Oakdale, La., Sept. 15, 1950; d. Samuel C. Goode and Elizabeth E. (Twiner) Baker; m. H. William Brown, Aug. 4, 1973; 1 child, Kevin William. BA, Newcomb Coll. Tulane U., 1972; JD, Wash. U., 1979. Assoc. Coburn, Croft & Putzell, St. Louis, 1979-80; staff atty. Anheuser-Busch Cos. Inc., St. Louis, 1980-81, exec. asst. to v.p. sec., 1982-83, asst. sec., 1983-89, sec., v.p., 1989—. Trustee Anheuser-Busch Found., St. Louis, 1989—, St. Louis Sci. Ctr., Girls, Inc. of St. Louis; bd. dirs. Met. Assn. Philanthropy. Mem. ABA, Mo. Women's Forum, Mo. Bar Assn., Bar Assn. Met. St. Louis, Am. Soc. Corp. Secs. (pres. 1992), Algonquin Golf Club, Order of Coif. Republican. Presbyterian. Office: Anheuser-Busch Cos Inc 1 Busch Pl 202-6 Saint Louis MO 63118-1852

BROWN, JOY ALICE, social services administrator; b. Redmesa, Colo., Mar. 19, 1917; d. Ezra E. and Alice M. (Pinkerton) Walker; m. Clayton Henry Brown, Apr. 9, 1941; children: Kimleigh Clayton, Loraleigh Joy. BA, Highlands U., 1958; MA, U. No. Colo., 1967, EdD, 1970. Tchr. La Plata County, Colo., 1936-41, prin. Bayfield (Colo.) pub. schs., 1942-46; tchr. Aztec (N.Mex.) pub. schs., 1946-63; spl. edn. coordinator primary schs. Palmer, Alaska, 1963-67; lab. sch. supr. U. No. Colo., 1967-70; assoc. prof. edn. N.Mex. State U., 1970-75; dir. Open Door Center, Las Cruces, N.Mex., 1975—. Cons. Tex. Edn. Service Center, Roswell (N.Mex.) schs.; sec. Dona Ana Human Services Consortium, 1977. Contbr. articles on edn. to profl. jours. Recipient Community Service award Las Cruces Eastside Center, 1972; Outstanding Contribution award N.Mex. Council of Exceptional Children, 1977. Mem. NEA, Council for Exceptional Children, Nat. Assn. Retarded Citizens, Phi Delta Kappa. Home: 34081 Country Rd M Mancos CO 81328

BROWN, JOY WITHERS, music educator; b. Louisville, Ky., Jan. 29, 1955; d. Harold B. and Sarah B. Withers; m. Robert O. Brown Jr., Mar. 20, 1982; 1 child, Sarah Teresa. BA in Music & Christianity, Mercer U., 1976; M in Ch. Music, So. Bapt. Theol. Sem., 1980; postgrad., U. Louisville, 1981, Ga. State U., 1993; cert. in music, State U. W. Ga., 2000. Youth dir. YMCA, Waycross, Ga., 1976—77; music intern 2d Presbyn. Ch., Louisville, 1978—79; music therapist Children's Treatment Svcs., Louisville, 1979—81; program dir. YWCA Greater Atlanta, Riverdale, Ga., 1982—83; sr. caseworker Clayton County Dept. Family & Children's Svcs., Jonesboro, Ga., 1983—87; retirement counselor Tchrs. Retirement Sys. Ga., Atlanta, 1987—97; music tchr. Hickory Flat Elem. Sch., MCDonough, Ga., 1997—. Mem.: Ga. Music Educators Assn., Music Educators Nat. Conf. Baptist. Home: 107 Windsong Dr Stockbridge GA 30281-6423 Office: Hickory Flat Elem Sch 841 Brannan Rd Mcdonough GA 30253 Office Phone: 770-898-0107.

BROWN, JOYCE F. academic administrator; b. N.Y.C., July 7, 1946; d. Robert E. and Joyce Cappie Brown; m. H. Carl McCall, Aug. 13, 1983. BA, Marymount Coll., 1968; MA, NYU, 1971, PhD, 1980. Pres. Fashion Inst. Tech./SUNY, 1998—; univ. dean Ctrl. Office CUNY, 1983—87, vice chancellor, 1987—90, prof. clin. psychology, 1994—, acting pres. Baruch Coll., 1990; pres. Fashion Inst. Tech., 1998—. Dep. mayor pub. and cmty. affairs, N.Y.C., 1990. Dir. N.Y.C. Outward Bound Ctrl. Pk. Conservancy; trustee Marymount Coll.; dir. Boys Harbor Inc., 1987—. Office: Fashion Inst Tech Seventh Ave at 27 St New York NY 10001-5992

BROWN, JUDITH, academic administrator; BA, U. Calif., Berkeley, 1968, MA, 1971; PhD in History, Johns Hopkins U., 1977. Asst. prof. history U. Md., Balt. County, 1977—82, Stanford U., Palo Alto, Calif., 1982—92, prof., 1991—95; Allyn and Gladys Cline prof. history, dean Sch. Humanities Rice U., Houston, 1995—2001; v.p. acad. affairs, provost Wesleyan U., Middletown, Conn., 2001—. Author: In the Shadow of Florence: Provincial Society in Renaissance Pescia, 1982, Immodest Acts: The Life of a Lesbian Nun in Renaissance Italy, 1986. Office: Wesleyan U 3d Fl North Coll 237 High St Middletown CT 06459

BROWN, JUDITH OLANS, lawyer, educator; b. Boston, May 29, 1941; d. Sidney and Evelyn R. (Lefkovitz) Olans; m. James K. Brown, Oct. 5, 1969. AB magna cum laude with distinction, Mt. Holyoke Coll., 1962; LL.B. cum laude, Boston Coll., 1965. Bar: Mass. 1965. Law clk. Supreme Jud. Ct., 1965-66; assoc. Foley, Hoag and Eliot, Boston, 1966-69; chief counsel Mass. Dept. Community Affairs, Boston, 1969-70; atty. adv. Office of Regional Counsel, HUD, Boston, 1970, asst. regional counsel, 1971, assoc. regional counsel, 1971-72; instr. Boston U. Law Sch., 1971, Northeastern U. Sch. Law, Boston, 1972, assoc. prof., 1972-75, prof., 1975-98, prof. emerita, 1998—. Vis. prof. Law Sch., Boston Coll., 1992. Contbr. articles to legal jours.; article and book rev. editor: Boston Coll. Indsl. and Comml. Law Rev., 1964-65. Mem. steering com. Lawyers Com. for Civil Rights under Law (emeritus); trustee Kimball Union Acad.1993-2003. Loeb fellow, 1972-73 Mem.: Order of Coif, Phi Beta Kappa. Home: PO Box 82 Plainfield NH 03781-0082 E-mail: jbrown@fcgnetworks.net.

BROWN, JULIE M. state legislator; b. Worcester, Mass., Feb. 20, 1935; divorced; 4 children. Student, Worcester State Tchrs. Coll. Mem. N.H. Ho. of Reps., mem. children, youth and juvenile justice com. 1st woman chairperson Rochester (N.H.) Rep. City Com., 1974-76, vice chairwoman, 1976-78; ward 2 selectman Rochester, 1986-92; mem. Rochester Planning Bd., 1985-89; bd. dirs. Rochester Red Cross, 1985-90, Strafford County Cmty. Action Program, 1983-90, chmn. bd., 1991-98; crusade chair Am. Cancer Soc., 1976, bus. chair, 1977, profl. chair, 1978; dir 1st Ch. Congl. Youth Group, 1971-75. Recipient N.H. Voice for Children award, 1996. Avocations: reading, swimming. Home and Office: 414 Lilac City E Rochester NH 03867-4552

BROWN, JUNE DYSON, elementary education educator, administrator; b. Petersburg, Va., July 28, 1949; d. James Elmer Sr. and Clara (Foster) Dyson; m. Robert Wendell Brown, Apr. 10, 1971; children: Jason, Joshua, James-Robert. BA in English, Emory & Henry Coll., 1971; MEd in Early Childhood Edn., U. Ga, 1993; EdS, U. Ga, 1998. Cert. elem. tchr., Ga. Tchr. DeKalb County Schs., Decatur, Ga., 1971-72, 76-78, Newton County Schs., Covington, Ga., 1972-74, 80-84, 85-88, Henry County Schs., McDonough, Ga., 1984-85; tchr., grade mgr. Gwinnett County Schs., Berkeley Lake, Ga., 1988-90; tchr., learner support strategist Cobb County Schs., Marietta, Ga., 1990-96, asst. adminstr., 1996—2000; Prin. Lamar County Elem. Sch., 2000—; prof. Piedmont Coll., 2000—. Active North Ga. Conf. Min.'s Wives, Atlanta, 1990-93; pres. Atlanta/Marietta Min.'s Wives, 1991-93 Mem. ASCD, DAR, Internat. Reading Assn., Profl. Assn. Ga. Educators, Kappa Delta Pi, Phi Kappa Phi. Methodist. Avocations: sewing, reading, beachcombing. Home: 811 Avalon Rd Thomaston GA 30286-4011

BROWN, JUNE GIBBS, retired government official; b. Cleve., Oct. 5, 1933; d. Thomas D. and Lorna M. Gibbs; children: Ellen Rosenthal, Linda Windsor, Victor Janezic, Carol Janezic. BBA summa cum laude, Cleve. State U., 1971, MBA, 1972; postgrad., Cleve. Marshall Law Sch., 1973-74; JD, U. Denver, 1978; postgrad. Advanced Mgmt. Program, Harvard U., 1983. Cert. govt. fin. mgr., 1995; CPA, Ohio. Real estate broker, officer mgr. N.E. Realty, Cleve., 1963-68; staff acct. Frank T. Cicirelli, C.P.A., Cleve., 1970-71; asst. to comptr. S.M. Hexter Co., Cleve., 1971; grad. tchg. fellow Cleve. State U., 1971-72; dir. internal audit Navy Fin. Ctr., Cleve., 1972-75; dir. fin. sys. design Bur. of Land Mgmt., Denver, 1975-76; project mgr. Bur. of Reclamation, 1976-79; insp. gen. Dept. Interior, Washington, 1979-81, NASA, Washington, 1981-85; v.p. fin. and adminstrn. Sys. Devel. Corp., a Burroughs Co., 1985-86; assoc. adminstr. for mgmt. NASA, 1986-87; insp. gen. U.S. Dept. Def., Arlington, Va., 1987-90; dep. insp. gen. USN-CINCPACFLT, 1990; insp. gen. USN Pacific Fleet, Pearl Harbor, Hawaii, 1991-93, HHS, Washington, 1993-2001; inspector gen. HHS, SSA, Washington, 1995-96. Bd. dirs. Fed. Law Enforcement Tng. Ctr., 1984-85, Interagy. Auditor Tng. program Dept. Agr. Grad. Sch., 1983-85; chmn. interagy. com. on Info. Resource Mgmt., 1984-85; mem. bd. advisors Nat. Contract Mgmt. Assn., 1987-89, NIH Sci. Found., 2002—; mem. Pres.'s Coun. on Integrity and Efficiency, 1993-2001, vice chair, 1994-97, rep. Nat. Intergovtl. Audit Forum, 1994-98, (PCIE), 1998-2001, (HHS); mem. adv. coun. Govt. Auditing Stds., 1996-99; bd. dirs. Inspectors Gen. Auditor Tng. Inst.; mem. bd. advisors NSF, 2002—. Mem. bd. advisors Howard U. Sch. Bus., 1987-89, NSF, 2002—. Recipient award Am. Soc. Women Accts., 1969, 70, 71, Raulston award Cleve. State U., 1971, Pres.'s award Cleve. State U., 1971, Outstanding Achievement award U.S. Navy, 1973, Career Svc. award Chgo. region Fed. Exec. Bd., 1974, Outstanding Contbn. to Fin. Mgmt. award Denver region Fed. Exec. Bd., 1977, Donald L. Scantlebury award Joint Fin. Mgmt. Improvement Program, 1980, Outstanding Svc. award Nat. Assn. Minority CPA Firms, 1980, NASA Exceptional Svc. medal, 1985, Outstanding Achievement in Aerospace award, 1987, Woman of Yr. award, YWCA 1988, Bur. Land Mgmt., Dept. Interior, 1975, Disting. Pub. Svc. award Dept. Def., 1989, Meritorious Civilian Svc. award U.S. Navy, 1993, Nat. Capital Area chpt./Govt. Exec. Mag. award for leadership, 1994, George Washington U. Pi Alpha Alpha Pub. Svc. award, 1996; named Disting. Alumni Cleve. State U., 1990, named Outstanding Fellow of Coun. for Ethical Org. for Creating the Standards for Healthcare Compliance, 2001 Fellow Nat. Acad. Pub. Adminstrn. (standing panel exec. orgn. and mgmt., pub. svc. panel); mem. AICPAs, Assn. Govt. Accts. (nat. pres. 1985-86, nat. exec. com. 1977-87, vice chmn. nat. ethics com. 1978-80, 90, chmn. fin. mgmt. standards bd. 1981-82, service award 1973, 76, 93, outstanding achievement award 1979, Robert W. King Meml. award 1988, dir. Hawaii chpt. 1991-93, Nat. Pres.'s award 1999, Disting. Fed. Leadership award 1998), Hawaii Soc. CPAs (bd. dirs. 1991-93), Am. Accts. Assn., Nat. Contract Mgmt. Assn. (bd. advisors 1988-90), NASA Alumni Assn., Women in Aerospace, ASPA (at-large mem. nat. coun. 1994-98, Profl. Responsibility Exemplary Practice award 1990, pres.-nat. capital area chpt. 1989), Exec. Women in Govt., Beta Alpha Psi.

BROWN, KAREN, performing company executive; b. Augusta, Ga., 1955; Prin. ballerina Dance Theatre Harlem, N.Y.C., 1973—95; dir. edn. Atlanta Ballet Ctr. Dance Edn., 1995—97; founder, artistic dir. Karenina, 1997—2000; artistic dir. Oakland (Calif.) Ballet, 2000—. Cons. Internat. Assn. Blacks in Dance. Named Local Hero of Yr., KQED/Union Bank Calif., 2001; named one of Season's Top Performers, N.Y. Times, 1986, Ten Most Influential African Ams. in Bay Area, CityFlight Newsmagazine, 2001. Office: Oakland Ballet 130 Linden St Oakland CA 94607 Office Phone: 510-452-9288. E-mail: karen.brown@oaklandballet.org.

BROWN, KAREN KENNEDY, judge; b. Houston, May 23, 1947. BA, U. Pa., 1970; JD, U. Houston, 1973. Bar: Tex. 1974, U.S. Dist. Ct. (so. and we. dists.) Tex. 1975, U.S. Ct. Appeals (5th cir.) 1974, U.S. Ct. Appeals (11th cir.) 1981, U.S. Supreme Ct., 1980. Law clk. Judge John R. Brown, Houston, 1973-75, Judge Woodrow Seals, Houston, 1975-76, asst. fed. pub. defender So. Dist. Tex., Houston, 1976-82; pvt. practice, Houston, 1982-83; U.S. magistrate U.S. Cts. So. Dist. Tex., Houston, 1984-90; U.S. Bankruptcy Judge, 1990—. Mem. LWV. Episcopalian. Office: US District Court PO Box 61252 Rm 10501 515 Rusk Ave Houston TX 77208

BROWN, KAREN RIMA, orchestra manager, Spanish language educator; b. N.Y.C., Apr. 26, 1943; d. Alexander and Leona (Rosenfeld) Jaffe; m. Russell Vernon Brown, Aug. 13, 1966; children: Stephanie Leona and Gregory Russell. BA, Colby Coll., 1965; MA, U. Wis., 1966. Teaching asst. U. Wis., Madison, 1965-66, instr. Spanish Janesville, 1966-68, Baraboo, 1968-70, Eau Claire, 1970-71, Ohio U., Zanesville, 1978-98, assoc. prof., 1998—; mgr. Southeastern Ohio Symphony, New Concord, 1977-99. Lectr. Spanish Muskingum Coll., New Concord, 1984, 97-99; mem., music panelist Ohio Arts Coun., Columbus, 1979-83, 90-93; pres. S.E. Ohio Regional Arts Coun., Zanesville, 1978-80; mem. Univ. Internat. Coun. Ohio U., Athens, 2003-. Bd. dirs. Muskingum County Visitors and Conv. Bur., Zanesville, 1987-90, bd. sec., 1989-90; bd. dirs. Assn. of Two Toledos, 1984-87, Ohio Citizens Com. for Arts, Canton, 1979-84; mgr. emeritus Southestern Ohio Symphony Orch., 1999—. Mem. Am. Assn. Tchrs. Spanish and Portuguese, Ohio Valley Fgn. Lang. Alliance, Bus. and Profl. Women, Phi Beta Kappa, Phi Sigma Iota, Sigma Delta Pi (hon.). Democrat. Avocations: travel, consultant to arts organizations, mentor for gifted high school students. Office: Ohio Univ-Zanesville 1425 Newark Rd Zanesville OH 43701-2695

BROWN, KATE, state legislator; b. Torrejon de Ardoth, Spain, 1960; BA, U. Colo.; JD, Lewis and Clark Coll. Mem. Oreg. Ho. of Reps., 1991-96, Oreg. Senate, 1997—; atty. Democrat. Office: State Capitol Bldg 900 Court St NE S-323 Salem OR 97301-4075 E-mail: sen.katebrown@state.or.us.

BROWN, KATHLEEN, bank executive, lawyer; d. Edmund G. and Bernice Brown; m. George Rice (div. 1979); children: Hilary, Alexandra, Zebediah; m. Van Gordon Sauter, 1980; 2 stepsons. BA in History, Stanford U., 1969; JD, Fordham U. Sch. Law, 1985. Mem. L.A. Bd. Edn., 1975-80; with O'Melveny & Myers, N.Y.C., then L.A.; commr. L.A. Bd. Pub. Works, 1987-89; elected Treas. of Calif., 1990-94; exec. v.p. Bank of Am., L.A., 1994-99, pres. Pvt. Bank West, 1999—. Co-chmn. Capital Budget Commn., Washington, 1997—. Mem. Pacific Coun. on Internat. Policy, Stanford Inst. for Internat. Studies; dir. Children's Hosp. L.A., San Francisco Ballet. Democrat. Office: Bank of Am 555 S Flower St Fl 51 Los Angeles CA 90071-2300

BROWN, KATHRYN ANN, music educator; b. Tigerton, Wis., Feb. 3, 1972; d. Clarence Herbert and Janice Marie Natzke; m. Bryan Lee Brown; 1 child, Riley Michael. BA, U. Wis., Green Bay, 1995; M in Music Edn., U. Wis., 2001. Music educator intern Luxemburg-Casco (Wis.) Sch. Dist., 1995—96; music educator long term substitute W. DePere (Wis.) Sch. Dist., 1996; music educator, choral dir. Gillett (Wis.) Sch. Dist., 1996—; summer music camp instr. U. Wis., Green Bay, 1997—2002, summer music clinic instr., Madison, 1999. Dir.: Singing in Wisconsin, 2001; actor: Steel Magnolias, 1999, 1940s Radio Hour, 1999, Coping, 2000. Mem.: Wis. Choral Dirs. Assn. (summer music camp instr. 1996, membership chmn. 1999—2004), Wis. Music Educators Assn., Wis. Sch. Music Assn. (State Honor Treble Choir Sectional Coach 2000, 2001), Am. Choral Dirs. Assn., Main Str. Revue Cmty. Theater (bd. dirs. 2000—01). Avocations: scrapbooks, singing, choreography. Office: Gillett Secondary Sch 208 West Main St Gillett WI 54124 Office Fax: 920-855-6600. Business E-Mail: kbrown@gillett.k12.wi.us.

BROWN, KAY (MARY KATHRYN BROWN), retired state official, consultant; b. Ft. Worth, Dec. 19, 1950; d. H. C., Jr. and Dorothy Ruth (Ware) Brown; m. William P. Dougherty, Dec. 15, 1978 (div. 1984); m. Mark A. Foster, Aug. 24, 1991; 1 adopted child, Kathryn Yucui. BA, Baylor U., 1973. Reporter UPI, Atlanta, 1973-76; reporter, feature writer Anchorage Daily Times, 1976-77; reporter, co-owner Alaska Adv., Anchorage, 1977; aide, rschr. Alaska State Legislature, Juneau, 1979-80; dep. dir. divsn. of oil and gas (formerly divsn. minerals and energy mgmt.) Alaska Dept. Natural Resources, Anchorage, 1980-82, dir., 1982-86; elected Alaska Ho. of Reps., 1986-96; exec. dir. Alaska Conservation Alliance and Voters, 1997-2000; ret. Del. White Ho. Conf. Libr. and Info. Svcs., 1991. Co-author: (book) Geographic Information Systems: A Guide to the Technology, 1991; talk radio host, 1996—2000. E-mail: kaybrown@alaska.net.

BROWN, LANA WEISS, public relations executive; b. Kankakee, Ill., Jan. 11, 1948; d. Vern Aubert and Dorothy Violet (Breese) Weiss; m. James Michael Brown, Dec. 16, 1947; children: Heather, Justin, Blair. BFA in Drama, Ill. Wesleyan U., 1970; MEd, Northwestern U., 1985. Dir. pub. rels. educator Bradley Bourbonnais Dist. 307, Bradley, Ill., 1973—. Cons. and spkr. in field. Freelance writer Chgo. Tribune. Bd. dirs. YMCA, Kankakee, Ill., 1991-97, Jr. League, Kankakee, 1976-86, Kankakee Symphony Orch., 1984-95, Kankakee County Conv. & Visitor Bur.; founding bd. dirs. Exploration Sta. Children's Mus., Kankakee, 1990-94, Young Peoples Theatre, Kankakee, 1977-79; found. v.p. Tng. Ctr. Disabled, pastor parish dir. St. Mark Meth. Ch.; mem. Good Samaritan grant panel CBS. Office: Bradley Bourbonais Sch Dist 307 700 North St Bradley IL 60915

BROWN, LASHONDA DEJUAN, elementary school educator; b. Tuskegee, Ala., May 24, 1974; d. John Henry and Tujuana Denise Brown. MEd, Ala. A&M U., 1996; student, U. Ala., 2003—. Cert. tchr. Ala. State Bd. of Edn., 2001. Tchr. Huntsville (Ala.) City Schs., 1999—, tchr. social studies, 1999—. Freelance tutor. Fellow Nat. Alumni Assn. Grad. fellowship, U. of Ala., 2002. Mem.: NAACP (rep. 2003—), Ala. Edn. Assn. (rep. 1999—), Kappa Delta Pi (assoc.). Democrat. Baptist. Avocations: reading, research, cheerleading. Home: 3107 Adonna Drive Huntsville AL 35810 Personal E-mail: blashonda@aol.com.

BROWN, LENORE FRANCINE, music educator; b. Decatur, Ill., Dec. 15, 1956; d. Laurence Wiefel and Bernadine E. Hayes; m. Donald Eugene Brown, July 12, 1980; children: Daniel Thomas, David Eugene. AA, Richland C.C., 1977; MusB in Edn., Millikin U., 1980. Tchr. vocal, gen. music St. Thomas Sch., Decatur, Ill., 1981—89; nursery aide Macon Resources, 1989—94; tchr. vocal, gen. music Our Lady of Lourdes, 1996—. Choir dir. St. Thomas Apostle Ch., Decatur, 1986—. Singer Greater Decatur Chorale, 1994. Mem.: Zeta Tau Alpha, Sigma Alpha Iota. Roman Catholic. Avocations: singing, walking. Home: 1039 N Westlawn Decatur IL 62522 Office: Our Lady of Lourdes Sch 3950 Lourdes Dr Decatur IL 62526

BROWN, LILLIAN HILL, retired academic administrator; b. Newport News, Va., Nov. 24, 1932; d. Charlie Wyatt and Caroline Melinda (Rowlett) Hill; m. Louis Franklin Brown, June 30, 1956; children: Avery L., Colin H. BS, Va. State Univ., 1955; MS, U. Bridgeport, 1967, profl. 6th yr. degree, 1983; post grad., So. Conn. State Univ., 1985. Chmn. guidance and pers. svcs. Wilby H.S., Waterbury, Conn., team mem. student assistance team, coord. natural helpers program, proctor SAT coll. bds. prog. Mem. pres.'s adv. bd. Teikyo Post U.; admission advisor com. Naugatuck Valley Comty.-Tech. Coll.; adv. bd. to bd. govs. for higher edn. in Waterbury; adv. panel Racial Imbalance Regulations of Pub. Schs. in Conn.; regional adv. bd. dirs. Bank Boston. Bd. trustees St. Margaret's-McTernan Sch.; bd. dirs., chmn. nominating com. Waterbury Symphony Orch.; trustee, chair nominating com. The Antiquarian and Landmark Soc.; bd. dirs. Children's Comty. Sch.; chmn. bd. dirs. Waterbury chpt. ARC; bd. trustees, chmn. scholarship com. The Waterbury Found.; bd. mgrs., mem. The Waterbury Club; mem. devel. com. Waterbury Hosp. Health Network, Inc.-Waterbury Hosp.; mem. oral history project African Ams. in Waterbury; co-chair Leavenworth Soc./United Way; vestry bd., chalice bearer St. John's Episcopal Ch.; life mem. NAACP; mem. Waterbury chorale; co-founder In Search of Excellence A Scholarship Fund for African Am. Students; incorporator Child Guidance Clinic; co-chair United Way-Leavenworth Soc.; adv. regional bd. Bank Boston. Recipient Plaque for Outstanding Leadership in Cmty., Tribute to Conn. Women, Plaque for Outstanding Leadership in Cmty., Alpha Kappa Alpha, Achievement award Nat. Assn. Negro Bus. and Profl. Woman's Clubs, Inc., Cmty. Svc. award Waterbury Jaycees, 1991, St. John's Order of the Eagle, 1995, Humanitarian Svc. award Anderson's Boys Club, 1999, Cmty. Svc. Vol. of Yr. United Way CNV, 2001. Mem. NEA (life), Conn. Edn. Assn., Waterbury Tchr. Assn., Pupil Pers. and Guidance Assn., The Sch. Counselor (Conn. chpt.), Phi Delta Kappa (Plaque for Dedicated Svc. to U. of Conn. chpt. 1993), Delta Sigma Theta (charter mem. New Haven alumnae chpt., Waterbury alumnae chpt. v.p. 2001)., Waterbury Chorale (v.p.), The Links, Inc. (charter mem. Waterbury chpt.). Avocations: domestic and foreign travel, collecting lladro porcelain, chorale singing, collecting porcelain dolls of color. Home: 59 Timber Ln Waterbury CT 06705-3608

BROWN, LILLIE DELORIS, elementary school educator, adult education educator; b. Elizabeth, N.C., June 29, 1948; d. Miles and Lydia Pearl Brown; 1 child, Jadine Rashida Hampton. BS, Elizabeth City State U., 1970; MA, U. No. Colo., 1981. Tchr. Washington Arch, 1971—73, Fairfax (Va.) County Pub. Schs., 1973—2003, adult edn. adminstr., 1993—2003. V.p. Gum Springs HIst. Soc., Alexandria, Va., 1981—83. Mem.: AAUW, Delta Sigma Theta. Home: 3002 School St Alexandria VA 22303

BROWN, LILLIE HARRISON, music educator; b. Cin., July 7, 1937; d. James Albert and Lucille Elizabeth Harrison; m. Frederick Brown, Apr. 12, 1958 (dec. June 1996); children: Kevin Frederick(dec.), Gyll Renee Simpson, Carla Y. BS in Music Edn., U. Cin. Coll. Conservatory of Music, 1961. Music specialist Cin. Pub. Schs., 1961—91, 1999—2002; minister of music, ch. musician Bethel Bapt. Ch., Cin., 1956—. Nominating com. chmn. Coll. Conservatory Alumnae Bd., Cin., 1995—2001; music com. chmn. Hamilton County Ret. Tchrs., Cin., 1992—; mem. NAACP, 1994—. Mem.: Alpha Kappa Alpha (regional music chmn., dir., pres. 1972—76). Home: PO Box 12735 Cincinnati OH 45212-0735

BROWN, LILLIE MCFALL, elementary school principal; b. Feb. 29, 1932; d. Clayton and Septertee (Dewberry) McFall; m. Charles Brown, Oct. 4, 1958; 1 child, Eric McFall. BA in Home Econ., Sci., Langston Univ., 1956; MA in Spl. Edn., Chgo. Tchrs. Coll., 1964; MA in Adminstrn., Seattle Univ., 1976. Home econ. tchr. Altue (Okla.) Separate Pub. Schs., 1955-56, first grade tchr., 1956-57, fourth grade tchr., 1957-60; middle sch. tchr. Chgo. Pub. Sch.s, 1960-64; spl. edn. primary tchr. Seattle Pub. Schs., 1966-67, spl. edn. intermediate tchr., 1967-68, program coord., 1968-71, elem. asst. prin., 1971-76, elem. prin., 1976—. Mem. Project READ, Seattle, 1968; chairperson Eighteenth Coll. Fair, Seattle, 2001. Contbr. articles to profl. jours. Treas. African Am. Alliance, 1980—; historian Wash. Alliance Black Sch. Educators, 1991—; vol. Olympic Games, Seattle, 1990; participant First African-African Am. Summit, Ibidijan, Cote d'Ivoire, 1991-92; mem. rsch. bd. advisors Am. Biog. Inst., 1995—; chair 18th Coll. Fair, Seattle, 2001. Sears Found. grantee, 1967; recipient Disting. Alumni award Nat. Assn. for Equal Opportunity in Higher Edn., 1997. Mem. NAACP, Nat. Assn. Elem. Sch. Prins., Assn. Wash. Sch. Prins., Elem. Prins. Assn. Seattle Pub. Schs., Prins. Assn. Wash. State, Prin. Assn. Seattle Pub. Schs., Ednl. Leadership, Phi Delta Kappa, Kappa Delta Pi, Delta Sigma Theta. Democrat. Baptist. Avocations: swimming, dance, bicycling, travel, reading.

BROWN, LISA J. state legislator, educator; 1 child, Lucas. BA, U. Ill.; MA in Econs., PhD in Econs., U. Colo. Assoc. prof. econs. Eastern Wash. U., Cheney; mem. Wash. Senate, Dist. 3, Olympia, 1992—; chair energy, tech. and telecomms. com. Wash. Senate, Olympia, vice chair ways and means com., mem. edn. com. Recipient Woman of Distinction award Girls Scouts USA, Inland Empire Coun., Annual award for Saving Women's Lives Wash. State Pub. Health Assn., 1998, Achievement award Women's Club of Spokane, 1998, Child Care Champion award Child Care Workers Wash., 1998, Elected Ofcl. of Yr. Citizen's League of Greater Spokane, 1997, Random Acts Prevention award Greater Spokane Substance Abuse Coun.'s Prevention Ctr., 1997, Hunger Fighter award Anti-Hunger & Nutrition Coalition, 1997, Woman of Achievement Govt. award Spokane YWCA, 1997. Democrat. Avocations: reading, camping, bicycling. Office: 338 John Cherberg Bldg Olympia WA 98504-0001

BROWN, LOIS HEFFINGTON, health facility administrator; b. Little Rock, Mar. 28, 1940; d. Carl Otis and Opal (Shock) Heffington; M. Ivy Roy Brown, June 21, 1984; children: Carletta Jo Rice, Roby Lynn Rice, Pherby Allison Graham, Phelan Missy Graham. Student, Guilford Tech. Community Coll., Jamestown, N.C., 1974-75, 77, 80. Cert. hearing aid specialist. Sec. Berger Enterprises, West Memphis, Ark., 1962-65; office mgr. Beltone Hearing Aid Ctr., Greensboro, N.C., 1975-81; owner Hearing Care Ctr., Cullman, Ala., 1982-85, Miracle-Ear Ctr., Cullman, Decatur, Fultondale, Jasper and Birmingham, Ala., 1985-87; pres. L&I Corp., Cullman, Decatur, Fultondale, Jasper and Birmingham, 1987-90, L & I Corp. Miracle Ear Ctr., Cullman, Decatur, Jasper, Ala., 1991-93; owner Conway (Ark.) Hearing Aid Ctr., 1994—, Beltone Hearing Aid Ctr., Conway, 1995-96. Distbr. Showcase Distbg. Co., Conway, North Little Rock. Gov.-appointed Ala. Bd. Hearing, 1989-91. Mem. Nat. Hearing Aid Soc., Ark. Hearing Soc. (sec. 1996—), Ala. Hearing Aid Dealers Assn. (sec. 1984-86, 96-2002, v.p. 1986-88, bd. dirs. 1988-91), Ark. Hearing Aid Dealers Assn. (appt. by gov. to Ark. hearing aid bd. 2002—). Republican. Baptist. Avocations: music, swimming, gardening, tennis, golf. Home: 6 Ryan's Way Greenbrier AR 72058

BROWN, LORENE B(YRON), retired library educator, educational administrator; b. Plant City, Fla., Nov. 9, 1933; d. Benjamin and Sallie (Barton) Byron; m. Paul L. Brown, Aug. 1, 1974. BS, Fort Valley State Coll., 1955; MSL.S., Atlanta U., 1956; PhD, U. Wis., 1974. Cataloguer N.C. Central U., Durham, 1956-58, Gibbs Jr. Coll., St. Petersburg, Fla., 1958-60, Fort Valley State Coll., Ga., 1960-65, Norfolk State U., Va., 1965-70; assoc. prof., dean Atlanta U., 1970-89, prof., 1989—2003; dir. Info. Retrieval Workshops, Atlanta, 1976-78; evaluator Coop. Coll. Library Ctr., Atlanta, 1979-82; cons. United Bd. Coll. Devel., Atlanta, 1976-79. Mem. southeastern/Atlantic regional adv. coun. Nat. Network Librs. Medicine, 2001—03. Author: Subject Access for African American Material, 1995. Mem. Friends of Library, Atlanta, 1982. Recipient Rachel Schenk award Library Sch. U. Wis., Madison, 1971; So. Fellowship Found. fellow Atlanta, 1972-74 Mem. ALA, Am. Soc. for Info. Sci., Assn. Library and Info. Sci. Edn., Ga. Library Assn., Met Atlanta Library Assn., Beta Phi Mu. Democrat. Baptist. Home: 855 Flamingo Dr SW Atlanta GA 30311-2402

BROWN, LYN, newscaster; married; 2 children. With Sta. WSOC-Radio, Charlotte, NC, 1976—80; anchor, corr. Sta. WTNH-TV, New Haven, 1980—84, CNN, N.Y.C., 1984—88, CBS News, 1988—90; co-anchor Sta. WNYW-TV, N.Y.C., 1990—. Recipient Emmy, 1992. Office: WNYW 205 E 67th St New York NY 10021*

BROWN, LYNETTE RALYA, journalist, publicist; b. Beloit, Wis., Dec. 15, 1926; d. Lynn Louis and Ethel Clara (Meeker) Ralya; m. Donald Adair Brown, Jr., Dec. 20, 1947; children: Donald Adair III, Alison Laura, Julia Carol. BA in Journalism, Mich. State U., 1948; MA in Journalism, Michigan State U., 1985; MA in Mass Comm., Wayne State U., 1983. Actress, publicist Grand Traverse Playhouse, Traverse City, Mich., 1946 (summer), N.Y. Summer Playhouse, Mackinac Island, Mich., 1947 (summer); writer WILS Radio, Lansing, Mich., 1947-48; writer, performer WJBK Radio, TV, Detroit, 1948-49; editor Denby Ctr. News, Detroit, 1949-51; freelance writer Oakland County, Mich., 1952-78; editor Henry Ford Mus., Dearborn, Mich., 1979-81; writer, reporter Legal Advertiser Newspaper, Detroit, 1983-85; publicist Bloomfield (Mich.) and Birmingham (Mich.) Pub. Librs., 1986-89; freelance writer, publicist Lynette Brown Comm., Birmingham, Mich., 1989—. Columnist: (newspaper) At the Libraries, 1986-89; solo performer Elizabeth Cady Stanton, 1995—. Probation sponsor Dist. Ct. Mich., 1960-70; publicist Oakland County Vol. Bur., 1979-82; leader sr. high/jr. high youth group Drayton Ave. Presbyn. Ch., Oakland County, 1952-54, 62-66, Pine Hill Congl. Ch., Oakland County, 1968-71, Northbrook Presbyn. Ch., Oakland County, 1976-77; polit. campaign worker Rep. candidates and non-partisan jud. candidates, 1952—; Cub Scout leader Royal Oak Emerson Sch., Oakland County, 1961-64; Girl Scout troop leader Bloomfield Twp. Meadow Lake Sch., Oakland County, 1966-71; dir. Martha Griffiths Project, 1989-. Grantee N.Y. State's Thanks Be To Grandmother Winifred Found., 1996, Elizabeth Kummer Award AAUW Mich., 2002. Mem. AAUW (chair women's issues, pub. info. dir. 1995-2000, state projects dir. 2000—), Oakland County C. of C. (Athena award 1995), Mich. Women's Studies Assn. (bd. dirs. 1999—). Home and Office: 6120 Westmoor Rd Bloomfield Township MI 48301

BROWN, MABEL WELTON, lawyer; b. Geneseo, Ill., Dec. 7, 1916; d. Harry E. and Mabel (Welton) B. BA, Oberlin Coll., 1938; JD, U. Chgo., 1941. Bar: Ill. Ptnr. Brown and Brown, Geneseo, 1941-44; sole owner Brown & Brown, Geneseo, 1944-81; sr. ptnr. Brown and Ray, Geneseo, 1981—. Atty. Green River Spl. Drainage Dist., Henry and Bureau Counties, Ill.; chmn. Geneseo Planning Comm., 1961-68, bd. dirs. Geneseo Hist. Assn., 1987—. Mem. ABA, Ill. Bar Assn., Henry County Bar Assn. (pres. 1973-76). Republican. Methodist. Office: Brown and Ray 115 N State St Geneseo IL 61254-1345

BROWN, MARCIA JOAN, author, artist, photographer; b. Rochester, NY, July 13, 1918; d. Clarence Edward and Adelaide Elizabeth (Zimber) B. Student, Woodstock Sch. Painting, summers 1938, 39; student painting, New Sch. Social Research, Art Students League; BA, N.Y. State Coll. Tchrs., 1940; student Chinese calligraphy, painting, Zhejiang Acad. Fine Arts, Hangzhou, Peoples Republic China, 1985, 87; studied painting with Judson Smith, Stuart Davis, Yasuo Kuniyoshi, Julian Levi; LHD (hon.), SUNY, Albany, 1996. Tchr. English, dramatics Cornwall (N.Y.) High Sch., 1940-43; library asst. N.Y. Pub. Library, 1943-49; tchr. puppetry extramural dept. U. Coll. West Indies, Jamaica, B.W.I., 1953. Tchr. workshop on picture book U. Minn.-Split Rock Arts Program, Duluth, 1986, workshop on Chinese brush painting Oriental Brush Artists Guild, 1988; sponsor Chinese landscape painting workshops with Zhuo HeJun, 1988-89; sponsored workshops Chinese caligraphy with A. Wang Dong Ling, 1989-90, 92; invited speaker exhbn. illustrations, Japan, 1990, 94. Illustrator: The Trail of Courage (Virginia Watson), 1948, The Steadfast Tin Soldier (Hans Christian Andersen), 1953 (Caldecott Honor Book award), Anansi (Philip Sherlock), 1954, The Three Billy Goats Gruff (Asbjornsen and Moe), 1957, Peter Piper's Alphabet, 1959, The Wild Swans (Hans Christian Andersen), 1963, Giselle (Théophile Gautier), 1970, The Snow Queen (Hans Christian Andersen), 1972, Shadow (Blaise Cendrars), 1982 (Caldecott award 1983), How the Ostrich Got His Long Neck (Aardema, Mainichi Japan Picture Book award 1997, Translation Winner' prize Mainichi Newspapers and Sch. Libr. Assn. 1997), 1995, (with others) Sing a Song of Popcorn, 1988, Of Swans, Sugar Plums and Satin Slippers (Violette Verdy); author, illustrator: The Little Carousel, 1946, Stone Soup, 1947 (Caldecott Honor Book award), Henry Fisherman, 1949 (Caldecott Honor Book award), Dick Whittington and His Cat (retold), 1950 (Caldecott Honor Book award), Skipper John's Cook, 1951 (Caldecott Honor Book award), The Flying Carpet (retold), 1956, Felice, 1958, Tamarindo, 1960, Once a Mouse (retold), 1961 (Caldecott award), Backbone of the King, 1966, The Neighbors, 1967, The Bun (retold), 1972, All Butterflies, 1974 (Boston Globe Honor Book, Horn Book), The Blue Jackal (retold), 1977, Walk Through Your Eyes, 1979, (with photographs) Touch Will Tell, 1979; (with photographs) Listen to a Shape, 1979, Lotus Seeds; Children, Pictures and Books, 1985; (with others) From Sea to Shining Sea, 1993; translator, illustrator: Puss in Boots, 1952 (Caldecott Honor Book award), Cinderella (Charles Perrault), 1954 (Caldecott award 1955), How, Hippo!, 1969 (honor book Book World Spring Book Festival); author, photographer: film strip The Crystal Cavern, 1974; exhibited at Bklyn. Mus., Peridot Gallery, Hacker Gallery, Library Congress, Carnegie Inst., Phila. Print Club, Hammond Mus., North Salem, NY, 1988; one-woman show include: U. Albany, SUNY, 1997; represented in permanent collections Library of Congress, NY Pub. Library, Mazza Gallery Findlay (Ohio) Coll.; pvt. collections. Recipient Disting. Svc. to Children's Lit. award, U. So. Miss., 1972, Regina medal Cath. Libr. Assn., 1977, Disting. Alumnus medal SUNY, 1969, Laura Ingalls Wilder award, 1992; U.S. nominee Internat. Hans Andersen award illustration, 1966, 76; career rsch. material in spl. libr. collection, SUNY, Albany, de Grummond Collection, U. So. Miss., Hattiesburg, Kerlan Collection, U. Minn.; named Marcia Brown Rsch. Rm. in her honor SUNY, Albany, 2001. Fellow Internat. Inst. Arts and Letters (life); mem. Author's Guild, Print Coun. Am., Art Students League, Oriental Brush Artists Guild, Sumi-e Soc. Am, Am. Artists of Chinese Brush Painting.

BROWN, MARGARET DEBEERS, lawyer; b. Washington, Sept. 24, 1943; d. John Sterling and Marianna Hurd (Hill) deBeers; m. Timothy Nils, Aug. 28, 1965; children: Emeline Susan, Eric Franklin. BA magna cum laude, Radcliffe Coll., 1965; postgrad., Harvard U., 1965-67; JD, U. Calif., Berkeley, 1968. Bar: Calif. 1969, U.S. Ct. Appeals (9th cir.) 1971, U.S. Ct. Appeals (D.C. cir.) 1986, U.S. Ct. Appeals (2d cir.) 1987, U.S. Supreme Ct. 1972. Assoc. White, Hamilton, Wyche, Shell & Pollard, Petersburg, Va., 1968-70, Heller, Ehrman, White & McAuliffe, San Francisco, 1970-73; sole practice San Francisco, 1973-77, 98—; atty. Pacific Telephone (name changed to Pacific Bell), San Francisco, 1977-83, sr. atty., 1983-85; sr. counsel Pacific Telesis Group, 1985-98, ret. Elder, deacon, sec.-treas. of deacons Calvary Presbyn. Ch., San Francisco; bd. dirs. No. Calif. Presbyn. Homes and Svcs chmn. 2003-. Mem. Calif. State Bar (mem. com. bar examiners 1994-98, chair subcom. on petitions and litigation 1996-98), San Francisco Bar Assn. (chmn. corp. law dept. sect. 1993, judiciary com. 1993-96, nominating com. 1993), Harvard Club of San Francisco (v.p. schs. 1998—2003, bd. dirs.), Radcliffe Club of San Francisco (bd. dirs.), Phi Beta Kappa.

BROWN, MARGUERITE JOHNSON, music educator; b. El Paso, Tex., Mar. 31, 1940; d. Don Lee and Eloise (Watson) Johnson; m. R. Don Lumley, Dec. 1961 (div. July 1982); children: Jessica Lumley Rodela, Jeffrey Tate Lumley; m. Gilbert Bivins Brown, Oct. 27, 1989; 1 stepchild, Erich Michael. MusB in Piano Pedagogy with honors, U. Tex., 1962; M in Liberal Arts with honors, So. Meth. U., 1974. Tchr., group piano Dallas Ind. Sch. Dist., 1965-72; tchr. music theory Canal Zone Coll., Panama Canal Zone, 1977-79, musical theater accompanist, 1975-79; tchr. class piano Del Mar Coll., Corpus Christi, Tex., 1980-82; tchr., edn. dir. piano & keyboard Coast Music Co., Corpus Christi, Tex., 1982-87; tchr. class piano, theory Del Mar Coll., Corpus Christi, Tex., 1987-90, performance accompanist, 1993-94; owner, piano tchr. pvt. Studio 88, Corpus Christi, Tex., 1994—2001; resident music dir. Monastery St. Clare, Brenham, Tex., 2001—. Mem.: Nat. Guild Piano Tchrs. (adjudicator), Nat. Guild Piano Tchrs., Dallas Music Edn. Assn. (pres. piano divsn. 1969—71), Music Tchrs. Nat. Assn., Corpus Christi Music Tchrs. Assn. (pres. 1995—97), Nat. Fedn. Music Clubs. Office: Monastery Saint Clare 9288 Hwy 105 Brenham TX 77833-7269 Home: 9280 Highway 105 Brenham TX 77833-7269

BROWN, MARTA MACIAS, legislative staff member, executive assistant; b. San Bernardino, Calif., Nov. 29, 1944; m. George E. Brown Jr., Mar. 27, 1989. BA, Calif. State U., San Bernardino, 1970; postgrad., U. Calif., Riverside, 1971. Publ., editor El Chicano Cmty. Newspaper, San Bernardino, 1968-75; cmty. edn. specialist human resources agy. County of San Bernardino, 1972-73, dir. of info. and referral svcs., 1973-75; student affirmative action officer U. Calif., Riverside, 1975-80; exec. asst., dist. press sec. to Congressman George Brown, Calif., 1980-99; field rep. Senator Barbara Boxer, 1999—. Bd. dirs. Casa Ramona Inc., San Bernardino, Ramona Sr. Complex, San Bernardino; pres. George and Marta Brown Found. Mem. Senator Barbara Boxer's judicial appts. com., 1992-94; adv. bd., sponsor, Peacebuilders, 1994—; mem. Calif. Dem. Party Ctrl. Com., 1994-99, family preservation planning com. County of San Bernardino, 1995-99; adv. bd. Children's Spine Found. U. Calif. grad. fellow, 1970. Mem. LWV, Democratic Spouses, Kiwanis (bd. dirs. greater San Bernardino chpt. 1990—). Roman Catholic. Avocation: water gardens. Home: 873 Bernard Way San Bernardino CA 92404-2413 Office: Senator Barbara Boxer 201 N E St Ste 10 San Bernardino CA 92401-1517

BROWN, MARY ELLEN, former state legislator, accountant; b. Hartland, Maine, July 26, 1952; d. Justin O. and Ernestine (Garnett) Humphrey; m. Gary R. Brown, June 6, 1971; children: John A., Jessica I. AA, Franklin Pierce C.C., Concord, N.H., 1978. Pvt. practice Automated Bookkeeping Svcs., Pittsfield, N.H., 1976—. Author: Out of Season, Final Message, contbr. articles to newspapers, mags. State legislator, N.H., 1995-96; pres. Chichester (N.H.) PTO, 1979, Tax Payers Assn., 1996. Mem. Nat. Soc. Pub. Accts., N.H. Wildlife Fedn., Go N.H. (polit. group). Avocations: writing, fishing, gardening. Office: PO Box 216 Pittsfield NH 03263-0216

BROWN, MARY JANE, history educator; b. Columbus, Ohio, Mar. 25, 1939; d. Oreste and Clara (D'Andrea) Ricci; m. Michael W. Fallon, Aug. 5, 1961 (dec. Sept. 1971); children: Paul Matthew, Quinn Patrick, Kathleen Erin, Erin Suzanne; m. Donald L. Brown, Oct. 21, 1972; 1 child, Megan Elizabeth. BA summa cum laude, Otterbein Coll., Westerville, Ohio, 1987; MS, Ohio State U., 1989, PhD, 1998. Adj. faculty Otterbein Coll., 1992-96, Columbus State U., 1992—. Author: (book) Eradicating This Evil: Women in the American Anti-Lynching Movement, 1892-1940, 2000. Mem. adv. bd. United Healthcare, Columbus, 1993—. Mem. AAUW, Orgn. Am. Historians, Sybilla Soc. Avocations: gardening, water sports, skiing, reading, cooking.

BROWN, MARY ROSE, energy executive; B in Comm., S.W. Tex. State U. V.p. pub. rels. Atkins Agy., 1983—97, Valero Corp., San Antonio, 1997—, sr. v.p. corp. comm. Office: Valero Corp Hdqs One Valero Place San Antonio TX 78212-3186*

BROWN, MARY WILLOUGHBY, health facilities administrator; b. Louisville, July 7, 1950; d. Willoughby Randolph and Emma Madelein (Geissinger) B.; m. Richard Frederick Teichgraeber III, June 23, 1974; children: Rebecca Flynn, Erin Marie. Student, Smith Coll., 1968-70; BA, Williams Coll., 1972; MEd, Northeastern U., Boston, 1973; MBA, U. Pa., 1977. Mental health worker McLean Hosp., Belmont, Mass., 1973-74, asst. social worker, 1974-75; dir. adminstrv. services mental health ctr. Peninsula Hosp., Burlingame, Calif., 1977-79; resource adminstr. Ochsner Found. Hosp., New Orleans, 1979-81, adminstrv. assoc., 1981-83, asst. hosp. dir., 1983-86, assoc. hosp. dir., 1986-95, sr. v.p., hosp. COO, 1995—. Bd. dirs. Ochsner Home Health Services Inc., New Orleans. Bd. dirs. Hospice New Orleans, 1985-95, East Jefferson Cmty. Health Ctr. Mem. Am. Coll. Healthcare Execs. (regent at-large 1995—), New Health Care Mgrs. Assn. (bd. dirs. 1983-86), Women's Health Care Exec. Network (founding), Am. Hosp. Assn. (adv. panel clin. svcs. and tech. 1988—, faculty 1988—). Democrat. Episcopalian. Office: Ochsner Found Hosp 1516 Jefferson Hwy New Orleans LA 70121-2429

BROWN, MELISSA DAWN, band director, choreographer; b. Omaha, Nebr., Dec. 30, 1966; d. William Ray and Imogene Lorraine Cummins; m. Robert Scott Brown, July 16, 1994. BE Instrumental Music, NW Mo. State U., Maryville, MO, 1989; MusM Edn., SE Mo. State U., Cape Girardeau, MO, 1994. Dir. of bands Shennandoah H.S., Iowa, 1989—90, Smithville Pub. Sch., Mo., 1990—92; grad. asst., instrumental music SE Mo. State U., Cape Girardeau, Mo., 1992—94; dir. of bands Woodland R-4 Sch., Marble Hill, Mo., 1994—. Drill writer and coreographer various SE Mo. H.S., Mo., 1992—; instrumental music adjudicator Mo. State H.S. Activities Assn., Mo., 1994—; winter guard adjudicatior Mid-Continent Color Guard Assn., Mo., 2003—; summer music camp instr. NW Mo. State U., Maryville, Mo., 1999—. Mem.: Mo. Bandmasters Assn., Music Educators Nat. Confrence (dist. v.p. of jr. high bands 2000—02), PEO (treas. 2002—), Lions Internat. (v.p. 2003—, Lion of the Yr. 2002-2003), Kappa Delta Phi, Sigma Alpha Iota (life; treas. 1988—89). First Christian Disciples Of Christ. Avocations: reading, juggling, needlecrafts.

BROWN, MICHELLE ALISE, elementary school educator; b. Bronx, N.Y., June 17, 1966; d. Albert Charles Jr. and Sherry Ann (Arrington) B. BS, Cornell U., 1988; MA, Columbia U., 1991, EdM, 1993. Elem. tchr. N.Y.C. Bd. Edn., 1988-91; tchr. Teaneck Pub. Schs., NJ, 1991—99; adminstr. Englewood Bd. Edn., 1999—2002. Researcher in field. Mem. ASCD, Nat. Coun. Negro Women, Delta Sigma Theta.

BROWN, MYRA SUZANNE, university librarian; b. Gainesville, Fla., Jan. 6, 1949; d. Samuel Jackson and Myra Frances (Whiddon) B.; m. Roman Jonas Yoder, Jan. 5, 1973; m. Jeremy Gallaudet Hole, May 3, 1986. Student European divsn., U. Md., West Berlin, 1967-69; BA, U. South Fla., 1971; MSLS, Fla. State U., 1972; postgrad., U. Cin., 1974. Libr. asst. Strozier Libr., Fla. State U., Tallahassee, 1973, libr. serials dept., 1973, libr. sci. and tech. dept. Pub. Libr. of Cin. and Hamilton County, 1973-74; libr. assoc. II Coll. Design, Architecture and Art Libr. U. Cin., 1975-77; assoc. univ. libr. State U. Sys. of Fla. Extension Libr., St. Petersburg, Fla., 1979-81, Edn. Libr. U. Fla. Librs., Gainesville, 1982-84, head and edn. bibliographer, 1984-90; asst. dept. chair humanities and social scis. svcs. dept. Smathers Librs. U. Fla., Gainesville, 1990—92, head and edn. bibliographer Edn. Libr., 1992—2002, asst. edn. libr., 2002—, univ. libr., 2002—. Mem. reference liaisons discussion group Rsch. Librs. Group, Inc., 1990-92; reviewer Gale Rsch. Co., Inc., 1988—; participant rsch. panel Univ. Microfilms Internat., 1992; mem. nat. user group Libr. of Congress Cataloging Distbn. Svc., 1992-96; cons. Mus. Fine Arts Libr., St. Petersburg, Fla., 1981-82, Design, Architecture and Art Libr., U. Cin., 1975-77; participant focus group ISI, 1998, 99; participant rsch. panel, Libr. Supplies, 1999; cons. New Bus. Devel. Edn. titles Gale Rsch., 1998, 99. Contbr.: World Architecture Index: A Guide to Illustrations, 1991; contbr. chpts. to books, articles to profl. jours. Aux. mem., vol. Shands Hops. of U. Fla., Gainesville, 1993-96, nominating com., 1995-96, sustaining mem., 1997—; advocate for homeless; mem. outreach com. Holy Trinity Episcopal Ch.; advocate for animal rights; vol. Interfaith Hospitality Network, 2003-. Mem. ALA (chmn., planner, moderator preconf. and conf. program, mem. divsns. 2000—, reference svcs. in medium-sized rsch. librs. discussion group 1992—2001, presenter), Spl. Librs. Assn. (info. tech. divsn., 1979-93, edn. divsn. Fla. chpt. 1979—, discussion list mgr., developer 1994-2000, chair nominations com., 2004, presenter at ann. confs.), Am. Edn1. Rsch. Assn. (divsn. E counseling and human devel. 1989-90, 92—, divsn. K. tchr. edn. 1994—), Fla. Ednl. Rsch. Assn., U. Fla. Librs. Assn. (v.p. 1983-84), Phi Delta Kappa (historian 1993-94, NC & Fla. Chpt. & internat. orgn., 1985-), Editl. Bd. Edu. Libraries (reviewer, 1995-), George A. Smathers Libraries (sustained performance review for faculty, 2004), Univ. Fla. United Faculty Fla. (senator (UFF Senator), 2003-, FEH delegate, 2004, exec. bd.-sect., 2004). Democrat. Episcopalian. Avocations: animal welfare concerns, advocate for the homeless, artist, independent fashion consultant. Office: Smathers Librs of U Fla Edn Libr 1500 Norman Hall PO Box 117016 Gainesville FL 32611-7016 Office Phone: 352-392-0707.

BROWN, NANCY CHILDS, marriage and family therapist; b. Butler, Ga., Feb. 17, 1938; d. Preston Bussey and Essie Lou (Jones) Childs; m. Luther Edward Brown (dec. Oct. 6, 1988); children: Melanie B. Ketchum, Catherine B. Tucker, Anthony E. Brown. BA in English with honors, Mercer U., 1960, MS, 1998. Lic. assoc. marraige and family therapist. Stockbroker/sales asst. Evans & Co./Robinson-Humphrey Co., Augusta, Ga., 1961-64; real estate owner/mgr. Macon, Ga., 1975-98; exec. dir. Macon Arts Alliance, 1985-92; assoc. marriage and family therapist in pvt. practice, 1998—. Bd. leaders Atlanta Internat. Mus. Art and Design, 1994—; bd. dirs. Ga. Coun. for the Arts (gov. appointee), 1994-97. Treas. Hay House, 1995-96, adv. bd., 1996—; pres. Macon Heritage Found., 1979-80; mem. founding bd. City Club of Macon, 1989-91; v.p. legislation Assocs. to Ga., Soc. Ophthalmology, 1985; chmn. City of Macon Cmty. Devel. Inner City Adv. Com., 1979-82; bd. dirs. tourism devel. com. Macon Conv. and Visitors Bur., 1990-97; mem. MAPS (City of Macon) Policy Com. (mayoral appointee ward 3), 1994-99; former pres. Bibb County Med. Soc. Alliance; choir of Vineville United Meth. Ch., 1988—; bd. dirs. Macon Symphony Orch., 1998—. Recipient Macon Cultural award Macon Arts Alliance and City of Macon, 1992; named Woman of Achievement Career Women's Network, Macon, 1990; winner Algernon Sydney Sullivan award, 1960, Alumni Meritorious Svc. award Mercer U., 1977. Mem. Career Women's Network, City Club of Macon, Ga. Trust for Hist. Preservation, Am. Assn. for Marriage and Family Therapy, Phi Kappa Phi. Avocations: choral singing, golf, culinary arts, piano playing, travel. Home: 937 Walnut St Macon GA 31201-1918

BROWN, NANCY FIELD, editor; b. Troy, N.Y., Feb. 20, 1951; d. Robert Grant and Barbara Katherine (Field) B. BS in Journalism, Mich. State U., East Lansing, 1974. Asst. editor Mich. Am. Legion, Lansing, 1974-76, State Bar of Mich., Lansing, 1976-78, editor, 1976—, sr. dir. pubs., 1995-98, asst. exec. dir. publs., 1998—. Mem. Nat. Assn. Bar Execs. (cons. pubs. com. Chgo. chpt. 1989—), Mich. State U. Alumni Assn., Nat. Assn. Desktop Pubs., Am. Soc. Assn. Execs. Presbyterian. Avocations: reading, writing, photography, travel. Office: State Bar of Mich 306 Townsend St Lansing MI 48933-2012

BROWN, NANCY JANE, human resources specialist; b. Louisville, July 1, 1955; d. Charles Leonard and Melba Irene Brown. BA, Marshall U., 1977, MA, 1985, MS, 1988; postgrad., Va. Inst. Tech., 1998. Cert. nat. registered Safety Profls.; cert. tchr., W.Va., Ohio, first responder, Ohio. Human resources profl. Am. Elec. Power, Cheshire, Ohio, 1992-2000, safety and indsl. hygiene specialist, 1989-93, lab. tech., 1978-89; human resources and tng. specialist AKZO-Nobel Functional Chems. LLC, Gallipolis Ferry, W.Va., 2000—. Adj. prof. U. Rio Grande, Ohio, 1999—. EMT Pt. Pleasant Emergency Med. Svc., 1980-82; mem. adv. bd. U. Rio Grande, 1999-2000; pres. W.Va. chpt. Am. Soc. Safety Engrs., 1997-98; chair All-Ohio Safety Congress, Columbus, 1999-2001; hospitality com. Women's Internat. Network Utility Profls., Columbus, 1999-2001; mem. adv. bd. Gallipolis City Schs., 2001—. Named to Ohio Exemplary Women in Sci., 1985. Mem. DAR, ASSE, Am. Indsl. Hygiene Assn., Mid Ohio Valley Emergency Planning (pres. 1990), Soc. Human Resource Mgmt. Avocations: preventive medicine, nutrition, lapidary work, cultural activities, landscape gardening, dogs. Home: PO Box 939 Gallipolis OH 45631 Office: AKZO-Nobel Functional Chems LLC PO Box 1721 Gallipolis Ferry WV 25515-1721 E-mail: nancy.j.brown@akzo-nobel.com.

BROWN, OTHELIA VICTORIA, minister; b. Agricola, Va., Oct. 15, 1933; d. Henry Daniel and Mable Louise (Pryor) Robinson; m. Roscoe Brown (dec.); children: Sylvester, Roscoe, James, Wilhelmina, Charlotte. BA, Lake Cmty. Coll., Leesburg, Fla., 1985, Rollins Coll., Winter Pk., Fla; student, Va. Theol. Seminary and Coll.; grad., Internat. Seminary, 1992. Lic. 1991, ordained Gospel Ministry, 1992. Libr. N.Y. Libr., New Rochell, NY; sec. H.S., New Rochell; clk. Winter Pk. Tel. Co., NY, Sprint Tel. Co., Apopka, Fla.; pastor Mt. Zion Bapt. Ch., Leesburg, Fla.; assoc. min. Greater Mt. Carmel Bapt. Ch., Tangerine, Fla. Clergy Fla. So. Hosp., Orlando, Fla. Mem.: Order of the Eastern Star. Bapt. Achievements include organized youth ch. and was responsible for their training; invited to preach the Easter Sunrise Svc. April 19, 1992, for the Mt. Dora Ministrial Assn.

BROWN, PAM, state legislator; b. San Antonio, Tex., Sept. 12, 1952; m. F. Steve Brown; 1 child, Paul D. BA, U. Nebr., Lincoln. Mem. Nebr. Legislature from 6th dist., Lincoln, 1995—. Mem. Nebr. human genetics tech. commn. Bd. dirs. United Way of the Midlands, Westside Schs. Found. Office: State Capitol Rm 1012 Lincoln NE 68509

BROWN, PAMELA WEDD, artist; b. Cauderan, Gironde, France, Nov. 21, 1928; came to U.S., 1953; d. William Basil and Nora Marsh (van Nostrand) Wedd; m. Charles Freeman Brown, Nov. 29, 1952; children: Penelope Susan, Nicholas Wedd. Student, Ecole des Beaux Arts, Paris, 1947-48, Academie Julian, 1946-51. Free lance fashion illustrator, Paris, 1947-48; dir. arts and crafts YWCA, Toronto, Ont., Can., 1951; dir. Washington Womens Arts Ctr., 1987-88; dir., pres. Washington Printmakers Gallery, 1990-91; co-pres. Studio Gallery, 1992-94. Artist in residence The Art Barn, Washington, 1986. Designer book plate Nat. Mus. Women in Arts Libr., 1985; represented in permanent collections Libr. of Congress, NIH, Nat. Mus. Am. History, Nat. Mus. Women in Arts. Precinct capt. Bd. of Elections and Ethics, Washington, 1970-80. Recipient First prize drawing, Academie Julian, Paris, 1947, Purchase award, Jr. League, Newport News, Va., 1971. Mem. Studio Gallery D.C. (assoc.), Art League (Equal award 1980, 82, 85, 88, 2000, 02), Woman's Nat. Dem. Club. Avocations: music, tennis, sailing, dance. Home: 3500 Macomb St NW Washington DC 20016-3162

BROWN, PATRICIA A. customer service representative; b. Lynchburg, Va., Jan. 23, 1952; d. William Andrew Jr. and Josephine Jackson Paige; m. Arthur Landrum III, May 1, 1970 (div. Apr. 1977); 1 child, Michelle Evonne; m. Bobby G. Brown, Jr., Jan. 6, 1989; 1 child, Bobby Gordon III. A in Bus., Ctrl. Va. C.C., Lynchburg, 1979; cert. microcomputer applications, John Tyler C.C., Richmond, Va., 1994; B in Bus., Averette Coll., 1990. Operator AT&T, Richmond, 1976—. Job stewart Comm. Workers Am., Richmond, 1985—, social com. co-chair, 1995—; co-chair alliance AT&T, Richmond, 1986-97, chair Christmas children wish list, 1993. Active Chesterfield (Va.) Voters League, 1994; vol. Providence Elem., Richmond, 1995. Mem. Women With Vision (pres. 1997—). Democrat. Baptist. Avocations: travel, reading, volunteer work with children. Home: 1703 Winters Hill Cir Richmond VA 23236-2378

BROWN, PATRICIA DONNELLY, computer company executive; b. Plainfield, N.J., Sept. 6, 1954; d. Vincent Joseph and Rita Joan (Carroll) Donnelly; m. Douglas P. Brown, Oct. 17, 1986; children: Douglas, Christopher. BA in Liberal Arts, Rosemont Coll., 1978. Sales rep. Control Data Corp., Phila., 1978-81; dir. mktg. Columbia Software, Bryn Mawr, Pa., 1981-82; dir. tech. support Cullinet Software, Westwood, Mass., 1982-89; dir. engring. AT&T GIS/Teradata, San Diego, L.A., 1989-95; v.p. AT&T GIS, San Diego, 1995-96; v.p. strategic relationships HNC Software, San Diego, 1996-97, v.p. product mgmt. and software devel., 1998—2000; pres. Team Talent, 2001—. Vol. San Diego Urban League, 1994-95, Jackie Robinson YMCA, San Diego, 1994-95; exec. sponsor AT&T Alliance, 1994-96. Republican. Unitarian Universalist. Avocations: computers, skiing, hiking, reading.

BROWN, PATRICIA IRENE, retired law librarian, lawyer; b. Boston; d. Joseph Raymond and Harriet A. (Taylor) B. BA, Suffolk U., 1955, JD, 1965, MBA, 1970; MST, Gordon Conwell Theol. Sem., 1977. Bar: Mass. 1965. Libr. asst. Suffolk U., Boston, 1951-60, asst. libr., 1960-65, asst. law libr., 1965-85, assoc. law libr., 1985-92; ret.; human resources counselor Winthrop (Mass.) Sr. Ctr., 1993—. Author: A League of My Own: Memoir of a Pitcher for the All-American Girls Professional Baseball League, 2003. Dir. Referral/Resource Ctr., Union Congl. Ch., Winthrop, Mass.; vol. health benefits counselor Mass. Dept. Elder Affairs, 1994—. First Woman inducted into Nat. Baseball Hall of Fame, Cooperstown, N.Y., 1988, All- Am. Girls Profl. Baseball League, 1950-51. Mem. Assn. Am. Law Librs., Am. Congl. Assn. (bd. dirs. 1992—), Mass. Bar Assn. Avocations: television and movie history, walking, computers. Home: 1100 Governors Dr Apt 26 Winthrop MA 02152-3254

BROWN, PATRICIA MARY CLARE, health facility administrator; b. N.Y.C., Jan. 30, 1960; m. Joseph Paul Gill; stepchildren: Mallory R. Gill, Natalie R. Gill. BA, U. Richmond, 1982; JD, U. Balt., 1986. Asst. atty. gen. Office Atty. Gen., Dept. Health and Mental Hygiene, 1984—94; sr. counsel Johns Hopkins Health Sys., 1994—; acting pres. Johns Hopkins Health Care LLC, 2000, pres., 2000—, also bd. dirs. Sr. dir. managed care Johns Hopkins Medicine, 1997—2000; v.p. managed care Johns Hopkins Health Care LLC, 1997—2000; bd. dirs. Priority Ptnrs., Inc. Trustee Maryvale Prep. Sch., 1992—2000; bd. dirs. Glenwood Life Ctr., Inc., 1997—2000. Mem.: Am. Heart Assn. Md. Coun. (pub. policy and advocacy com. 1997—98), Md. State Bar Assn. (sec./treas. health care law sect. coun. 1993—94, vice chairperson health care law sect. coun. 1994—95, chairperson health care law sect. coun. 1995—96). Office: Johns Hopkins Healthcare LLC Adminstrn 204 600 N Wolfe St Baltimore MD 21287

BROWN, PATRICIA PEARL, principal, consultant; b. Wharton, Tex., Oct. 3, 1959; d. Kelly James and Lula Mae Long; m. Carlton Bennett Brown, Sept. 8, 1984; children: Xandrea Danielle, Zackery Bennett. BS, Tex. Womans U., 1981; EdM, U. Houston, 1990. Cert. elem. tchr. Tex., adminstrn. and supervision Tex. Pub. rels./advt. staff Dillards Dept. Store, Victoria, Tex., 1981—83; ops. mgr. Fair Stores, Beaumont, Tex., 1983—85; student advisor U. Houston, 1985—87; elem. sch. tchr. Houston Ind. Sch. Dist., 1987—89; elem. sch. tchr., adminstrv. Altef Ind. Sch. Dist., Houston, 1990—99; elem./middle sch. adminstr. Lamar Consol. Ind. Sch. Dist., Rosenberg, Tex., 2000—. Tchr./tng. cons., Missouri City, Tex., 1986—; mem. adv. bd. Youth Christian Bible Ch., Missouri City, 1998—2000. Sch. bd. pres. Christian Bible Acad., Houston, 1999—2003. Mem.: ASCD, Nat. Middle Sch. Assn., Tex. Middle Sch. Assn., Tex. Alliance Black Sch. Educators, Nat. Alliance Black Sch. Educators, Tex. Assn. Secondary Sch. Prins. Democrat. Baptist. Avocations: travel, reading.

BROWN, PAULA ANN, pre-school administrator; b. Hinton, Okla., July 19, 1962; d. Floyd H. and Cora Pauline Freeman; m. B. Roton (div. June 4, 2001); children: Michael Edward Roton, Daniel Keith Roton; m. Robert H. Brown, Sept. 27, 2002. BS, Okla. State U., 1985. Lead tchr. Head Start Action, Inc., Stillwater, Okla., 1985—88, area supr., 1988—91, disabilities mgr., 1991—98; disabilities/mental health mgr. Head Start United Cmty. Action Programs, Inc., Pawnee, Okla., 1998—. Chair SoonerStart Pers. Devel. Com., Okla., 1999—. Apptd. mem. Okla. Interagency Coordinating Coun., 1996—; pres. Okla. Family Resource Coalition, Oklahoma City, 2001—03; past pres., mem. Payne County Sheltered Workshop, Stillwater, 2001—02. Scholar, Okla. State U., 1980—81. Mem.: Coun. Earlychildhood Profl. Devel., Nat. Head Start Assn., Coun. Exceptional Children, Nat. Assn. Edn. Young Children (assoc.). Avocations: music, working out, reading. Home: 801 W Hartwood Stillwater OK 74075 Office: United Cmty Action Programs Inc 501 6th Pawnee OK 74058

BROWN, QUINCALEE, professional society administrator; b. Wichita, Kans., Nov. 9, 1939; d. Quincy Lee and Lorene (York) B.; m. James Parson Simsarian, June 24, 1978. BA, Wichita State U., 1961; MA, U. Pitts., 1963; PhD, U. Kans., 1975. Asst. prof. speech communications, dir. debate Wichita State U., 1963-69, Ottawa U., 1970-73; adminstrv. asst. Montgomery County (Md.) Commn. for Women, 1973-74, exec. dir., 1975-80; mgr. fed. women's program Govt. Printing Office, Washington, 1974-75; exec. dir. AAUW, Washington, 1980-85, Gen. Fedn. of Women's Clubs, 1986, Water Pollution Control Fedn. (name now Water Environment Fedn.), 1986—. Contbr. articles to profl. jours. Bd. dirs. Greater Washington Soc. Assn. Execs. Found., 1996-99, Am. Inst. for Pollution Prevention, 1996-97, Alexandria (Va.) Econ. Devel. Partnership, 1997-99. Recipient Contbn. to Pub. Svc. award Montgomery County Govt., 1975, Outstanding Contbn. to Sex Equity, 1979, Career Achievement award Profl. Fraternity Assn., 1981, Frances E. Willard award Alpha Phi Fraternity, 1994, ASAE Key award, 1995, Assn. Exec. of the Yr. award Assn. Trends, 1999. Fellow Am. Soc. Assn. Execs. (bd. dirs. 1985-88, vice chmn. 1990-91, chmn. elect 1991-92, chmn. 1992-93, cert. assn. exec.); mem. AAUW, Greater Washington Soc. Assn. Execs. (chmn. bd. dirs. leadership found. 1997-98), Speech Comms. Assn., Kappa Delta Epsilon (hon.), Zeta Phi Eta (Outstanding Svc. award 1975), Alpha Phi (Francis E. Willard award of achievement 1994). Office: WEF 601 Wythe St Alexandria VA 22314-1994

BROWN, RADIE LYNN, secondary school educator; b. Stuart, Fla., Nov. 14, 1962; d. Albert R. III and Martha Katherine (Brooks) Krueger; m. Richard G. Brown, Jan. 2000; 1 child, Travis. AB, Ga. Wesleyan Coll., 1984; postgrad., U. Ctrl. Fla. Tchr. English Brevard County Sch. System, Melbourne, Fla., 1984-86; bank officer, tng. dir. First Nat. Bank and Trust, Stuart, 1987-90; dir. Christian edn. 1st Presbyn. Ch., Stuart, 1990-91; prof. English, Indian River Community Coll., Ft. Pierce, Fla., 1990-91; employment comm. cons. Curtis and Assocs., Grand Island, Nebr., 1992-93; exec. dir. Community HelpCenter, Grand Island, 1993, Martin County Literacy Coun., Stuart, Fla., 1993-94; mgr. ednl. svcs. The Palm Beach Post subs. Cox Enterprises, Inc., West Palm Beach, Fla., 1994-95; with audiotext advt./programming dept. The Stuart (Fla.) News, 1995-96; lang. arts tchr. Southport Middle Sch., Port St. Lucie, Fla., 1996—2002; h.s. English tchr. Lincoln Park Acad., Ft. Pierce, Fla., 2002—. Republican. Episc. Avocations: gardening, golf, equestrian sports. Home: 3505 SW Buckskin Trl Okeechobee FL 34974 E-mail: writinggreyhounds@yahoo.com

BROWN, REBECCA, writer, educator; b. San Diego, Mar. 27, 1956; d. Vergil Neal Brown Jr. and Barbara Ann (Wildman) Brown; life ptnr. Christine Galloway. BA, George Washington U., 1978; MFA, U. Va., 1981. Tchr. Pacific Luth. U., Tacoma, 1997—98; writer-in-residence Hugo House, Seattle, 1997—99; tchr. MFA program Goddard Coll., Plainfield, Vt., 1999—. Author: (short stories) Annie Oakley's Girl, 1992, What Keeps Me Here, 1996, (fiction) The Dogs: A Modern Bestiary, 1998, (novels) The Gifts of the Body, 1994, The End of Youth, 2003, Excepts Froma Family Medical Dictionary, 2003. Recipient award, Boston Book Review, 1994, Pacific N.W. Booksellers, 1994, Wash. State Gov.'s Arts, 1995, Lambda Lit., 1995. Mem.: PEN West, Phi Beta Kappa. Democrat.

BROWN, RENEE, painter, art educator, minister; b. Buffalo, N.Y., Nov. 30, 1957; d. James Henry White and Edna Francis Corpening; m. Dwight Edward Brown, Dec. 21, 1985; children: Tiffany, Crystal. Student, State U. Coll. Buffalo Internat. Study Abroad Program, Siena, Italy, 1979; BFA in Painting, Rochester (N.Y.) Inst. Tech., 1982; MA, U. Buffalo, 1999. Cert. tchr. N.Y., 1988. Tchr. Buffalo (N.Y.) Bd. Edn., 1989—2000. Mem. Arts Commn., Buffalo, 1999—2003; art judge in field. Numerous art shows, 1999—. one-woman shows include The Olean (N.Y.) Pub. Libr. Gallery, 2003, The Dancer, Theodore Roosevelt Inaugural Nat. Historical Site, 1999, Joy Gallery, 1999. Founder Art Angels, Buffalo, 1986—; evangelist missionary New Mt. Ardrat Temple of Prayer, 1989—2003; co-founder Women's Ministry Temple of Prayer, Buffalo, 1985—, co-founder Youth and Family Outreach, 1985—. Recipient Urban League Artist award, 2003. Home: 315 Woodbridge Buffalo NY 14214 Office: New Mt Ararat Temple of Prayer 983 Jefferson Ave Buffalo NY 14204

BROWN, RENEE, sports association executive; b. Henderson, Nev. Grad., U. Nev., Las Vegas. Asst. coach women's basketball U. Kans., Stanford U., Calif., San Jose State U., Calif.; asst. coach USA Basketball Women's Nat. Team, Colorado Springs, Colo., 1995—96; dir. player pers. Women's Nat. Basketball Assn., N.Y.C., 1996—99, sr. dir. player pers., 1999—2000, v.p. player pers., 2000—. Office: Women's Nat Basketball Assn Olympic Tower 645 Fifth Ave New York NY 10022*

BROWN, RENI (ARLENE PATRICIA THERESA BROWN), artist; b. Jan. 3, 1953; d. William J. and Adelaide Elizabeth Brown. Student, Union Coll., 1971; BA Visual Comm., BA Occupl. Therapy, Kean Coll., 1980; student, Union Coll., $D71. Cert. personal trainer, health fitness instr. Am. Coll. Sports Medicine, water safety instr./swim instr., CPR, First Aid, workplace safety instr., Red Cross, yoga instr., yoga synthesis instr., yoga alliance registered. Owner, pres. Reni Co., Roselle Park, N.J., 1979—; profl. faux surface finishes artist residential and comml. Pvt. tchr. art, Glass and Mirror Abrasive Etching, comml. carved glass designs and creation, air brush artist designer, pinstripper metal and wood, crystal engraving and carving, Roselle Park, 1979—; owner Twinks Trademark and Associated Characters; performance nutrition specialist Internat. Sports Sci. Assn. Exhibited in The Children's Mus., Ind.; patentee in field. Recipient 3d Pl. award Custom Car and Van Show, Meadowlands, N.J., 1981, 2d Pl. award Custom Car and Van Show, Asbury Park, N.J., 1982. Mem. Graphic Artists Guild, Artists' Equity Assn., Summit Art Assn., Princeton Art Assn., Am. Women's Econ. Devel. Assn., Found. Christian Living, Positive Thinkers Club, N.J. Art Dirs. Club, Morris County C. of C., N.J. Jewelers Assn., Internat. Jet Sports Boating Assn. (standup womans' ski pts. champion 1996), Assn. Jensen Owners, Westfield Art Assn., Alumni Assn. Kean Coll. Address: 475 E Westfield Ave Roselle Park NJ 07204-2431 E-mail: R777eni@aol.com.

BROWN, RHONDA ROCHELLE, chemist, health facility administrator, lawyer; b. Shelbyville, Ky., July 13, 1956; d. Clifton Theophilus and Fannie Mae (Lawson) B. BA in Chemistry, U. Md., 1978; MA, Central Mich. U., 1983; JD, No. Va. Law Sch., 1992. Bar: Wash. 1998, D.C. 1994, U.S. Dist. Ct. D.C., U.S. Dist. Ct. Md. Analytical chemist Dept. Health and Mental Hygiene, Annapolis, Md., 1978-83, epidemiologist Balt., 1983-88; patent examiner U.S. Patent and Trademark Office, Xtal City, Va., 1989-90; freelance researcher New Carrollton, Md., 1990—; lawyer, pvt. practice Washington, 1998—. Mem. Am. Chem. Soc., Washington, 1978-82; mem., exec. bd. Nat. Lawyers Guild, Washington, 1987—; pres. Voucher Express, 1993—; mediator Superior Ct., Washington, 1993—; legal advt. mgr. Sentinel Newspaper. Subcommittee chmn. Anne Arundel County Task Force for Drug and Alcohol Abuse, 1979-80; pres., bd. mem. Md. Ornithological Soc., 1979-82; mem., exec. bd. Md. Condominium and Homeowners Assn., Rockville, Md., 1988-91. Named Outstanding Young

Women of Am., 1983. Mem. ABA, ATLA (family divsn. 1999—), Nat. Assn. Criminal Def. Lawyers, Superior Ct. Trial Lawyers Assn. (criminal and family divsn.), Nat. Intellectual Propery Law Assn., Anne Arundel County Tennis Assn., Sigma Iota Epsilon.

BROWN, RITA MAE, writer; b. Hanover, Pa., Nov. 28, 1944; d. Ralph and Julia Ellen B. AA, Broward Jr. Coll., 1965; BA, NYU, 1968; cinematography degree, Sch. Visual Arts, N.Y.C., 1968; PhD, Inst. Policy Studies, 1976; DLitt, Wilson Coll., 1992; LLD (hon.), William Woods U., Fulton, Mo., 2000; LLD (hon.), York (Pa.) Coll., 2003; LHD (hon.), Franklin Pierce Coll., 2002. Photo editor Sterling Pub., N.Y.C., 1969-70; lectr. Fed. City Coll., Washington, 1970-71; rsch. fellow Inst. Policy Studies, Washington, 1971-73; pres. Am. Artists Inc., Charlottesville, Va., 1980—. Vis. mem. faculty in feminist studies Goddard Coll., Plainfield, Vt., 1973—; mem. lit. panel NEA, 1978-81; Hemingway judge for 1st fiction PEN Internat., 1983; blue ribbon panelist Prime Time Emmy Awards, 1984, 86; tchr. Nebr. Summer Writers Conf., U. Nebr., Lincoln, 2003, 04. Author: (translator) Hrotsvitra: Six Medieval Plays, 1971, (novels) The Hand That Cradles the Rock, 1971, Songs to a Handsome Woman, 1973, In Her Day, 1976, Southern Discomfort, 1982, Sudden Death, 1983, High Hearts, 1986, Bingo, 1988, Venus Envy, 1993, Dolley, 1994, Paydirt, 1995, Riding Shotgun, 1996, Murder, She Meowed, 1996, Mrs. Murphy Mysteries, 2001, Outfoxed, 2000, Alma Mater, 2001, The Plain Brown Rapper, 1972, Rubyfruit Jungle, 1974, Six of One, 1977, Starting from Scratch, 1987, Wish You Were Here, 1989, Rest in Pieces, 1991, Murder at Monticello, 1993, Mrs. Murphy Series, annual novels, 2004, Loose Lips, 1998, Outfoxed, 2000, Hotspur, 2002, Full Cry, 2003; (poetry) The Poems of Rita Mae Brown, 1987; TV series include I Love Liberty, 1982, Long Hot Summer, 1985, My Two Loves, 1986, The Alice Marble Story, 1986, Southern Exposure, 1990, Cat on th Scent, 1999, Loose Lips, 1999, Outfoxed, 2000, Pawing Through The Past, 2000; TV films include The Firls of Summer, 1989, Selma, Lord, Selma, 1989, Passing Through, 1993, A Family Again, 1994, others; (cable TV) The Mists of Avalon, 1986, The Nat Turner Story-African American Anthology, 1993, The Wall, K-9, 1993; (films) Slumber Party Massacre, 1982, Sweet Surrender, 20th Century Fox, 1986, Table Dancing, 1987, Mary Pickford, 1998. Former exec. officer NOW; bd. dirs. Human Rights Campaign Fund, N.Y.C., 1986; co-founder Radical Lesbians; founder Redstockings Radical Feminist Group, Nat. Gay Task Force, Nat. Women's Polit. Caucus. Recipient Award for Best Variety Show on TV Writers Guild Am., 1982, Outstanding Alumni, Am. Assn. Cmty. Colls., 1999, Outstanding Alumna, Broward Cmty. Coll., 1999, Literary Lion award N.Y. Pub. Library, 1986, Emmy award nomination for The Long Hot Summer, ABC mini-series, 1985; Emmy nomination for best variety show I Love Liberty, 1982; named Charlottesville favorite author The Observer, 1990, Athlete of the Week, The Observer, 1990. Mem. PEN Internat., Oak Ridge Foxhunt Club (Master of Foxhounds). Office: care of The Wendy Weil Agy 232 Madison Ave Ste 1300 New York NY 10016-2901

BROWN, ROSELLEN, writer; b. 1939; BA, Barnard Coll., 1960; MA, Brandeis U., 1962. MS prof. in Am. and English lit. Tougaloo Coll., 1965—67; prof. creative writing Goddard Coll., Plainfield, Vt., 1976; vis. prof. creative writing Boston U., 1977—78; prof. creative writing U. Houston, 1982—85, 1989—96; prof. Grad. Creative Writing Program Sch. Art Inst. Chgo., 1997—. Author: The Autobiography of My Mother, 1976, Tender Mercies, 1978, Before And After, 1992, Civil Wars, 1994 (Janet Heidinger Kafka award for best novel), Half a Heart, 2000, short stories, poetry. Recipient award in Lit., Am. Acad. Arts and Letters; fellow, Radcliffe Inst., MacDowell Colony, Guggenheim Found., Ingram Merrill Found., Bunting Inst., Howard Found. Office: Sch Art Inst Chgo 4th Fl 37 S Wabash Chicago IL 60603-3103

BROWN, ROXANNE (JERENE ROXANNE BROWN), sales executive; b. L.A., July 5, 1947; d. John Phillip and Margaret Leona (Dalrymple) Ortiz; m. Terry Lee Wood, May 7, 1966 (div. Sept. 1969); 1 child, Tiffany Christine Wood Suraco; m. Christopher Corey Brown, July 17, 1984 (dec. Sept. 1984); children: Jason Michael and John Charles (twins); m. Richard L. Gibbs, Apr. 18, 1996 (dec. Feb. 2000). Student, Casper Coll., 1977. Info. operator Gen. Telephone, Baldwin Park, Calif., 1965-67, long distance operator Santa Maria, Calif., 1967-69; office mgr. Monroe Calculator, Las Vegas, Nev., 1972-74; mgr. Exch. Club, Salt Lake City, 1977-81, Pouches Inc., Salt Lake City, 1981-82; asst. producer KSTU TV 20, Salt Lake City, 1982-84; sec. ADVO - Sys., Inc., Orange, Calif., 1984-85, terr. sales rep., 1985-88, major account exec. Garden Grove, Calif., 1988-95; v.p. JRB & Assocs., Long Beach, Calif., 1995—. Cons. Rice - Urmana Advt., Huntington Beach, Calif., 1989-91. Bd. dirs. ACLU, Salt Lake City, 1977; precinct worker Voter Registrar, Huntington Beach, 1988, Long Beach, Calif., 1990; bd. dirs., sec. Alamitos Bay Beach Peninsula Preservation Group, 1996-98. Mem.: ACLU, SAG, Platform Speakers Assn., Alamitos Bay Garden Club (v.p., ways and means com. 1996—98). Avocations: sculpting, photography, sailing. Home: 77 Ximeno Ave Long Beach CA 90803-3056 E-mail: rocknsand@yahoo.com.

BROWN, RUTH ANN, pharmacist; b. Endicott, N.Y., Nov. 17, 1948; d. Herbert Matthew and Rose Marie (Murphy) B. BS in Pharmacy, Phila. Coll. Pharmacy & Sci., 1971; MBA in Health Adminstrn., Widener U., 1983. Lic. pharmacist, N.Y., Pa. Staff pharmacist Crozer Chester Med. Ctr., Chester, Pa., 1972-80, asst. dir. pharmacy, 1980-85, assoc. dir. pharmacy ops., 1985-91, acting dir., 1988-89; staff devel./QAI coord. pharmacy dept. Albert Einstein Med. Ctr., Phila., 1991-92; pharmacist, mgr. Willowcrest, Phila., 1992-97; pharmacy mgr. Taylor Hosp., Ridley Park, Pa., 1997—. Relief pharmacist Albert Einstein Med. Ctr., 1980-91; site coord. dept. ext. svcs. Phila. Coll. Pharmacy and Sci., 1988-90, continuing edn. adv. bd. 1988-90, clin. instr. pharmacy, 1982-91. Vol. LPGA Tournament to benefit Ronald McDonald Houses, 1987—. Mem. Am. Soc. Hosp. Pharmacists (ho. of dels. 1983, 9e-98), Pa. Soc. Hosp. Pharmacists (mem. Pa. pharmacy liaison group, mem. profl. affairs coun., mem. orgnl. affairs coun., mem. ctrl. office task force, mem. fin. com., chmn. policy rev. com. 1995-96, chmn. constn. and bylaws com. 1991-92, 95-96, DVSHP chpt. rep. to bd. dirs. 1990-92, presdl. officer 1992-95, other coms.), Ctr. for Proper Medication Use (chmn. bd. dirs. 1994—, chmn. subcom. on proper medication use in children 1995-96), Delaware Valley Soc. Hosp. Pharmacists (nominations com., mem. program com., sec. 1981-87, pres. 1988-89, chmn. bd. dirs. 1989-90, 96—, chpt. rep. to PSHP bd. dirs. 1990-92, Jonathan Roberts award 1991), Guild Phila. Hosp. Pharmacists, Delaware County Pharm. Assn., Alumni Assn. Phila. Coll. Pharmacy (various coms.), Am. Legion Aux., Ladies Ancient OrderHibernians, Lambda Kappa Sigma (grand v.p. for alumni 1986-88, grand pres. 1988-90). Roman Catholic. Office: Taylor Hosp Pharmacy Dept 175 E Chester Pike Ridley Park PA 19078-2284

BROWN, RUTH GEISLER, engineering supervisor; b. Beaver Falls, Pa., Mar. 17, 1924; d. Carl Charles and Emily (Pletz) Geisler; m. Stuart Fife Brown, Apr. 13, 1944. Student, Johns Hopkins U., 1960—70. Svc. rep. Bell. Tel. of Pa., Pitts., 1942—43; draftsman to group engr. Martin Marietta Co., Middle River, Md., 1944—49, 1950—63; design draftsman Bendix Radio, Balt., 1949—50; engring. staff assoc. missile programs and microelectronics Johns Hopkins U./Applied Physics Lab., Laurel, Md., 1963—75, sr. engring. staff, supr. hybrid ops., 1975—79, divsn. staff, 1979—81, electronic design supr., 1981—83, engring. design supr., 1983—90; ret., 1990. Mem.: NAFE, Internat. Electronic Packaging Soc., Internat. Soc. Hybrid Microelectronics. Republican. Home: 12628 W Parkwood Dr Sun City West AZ 85375-4626

BROWN, SANDRA, writer; Mgr. Merle Norman Cosmetics Studios, Tyler, Tex., 1971-73; weather reporter KLTV-TV, Tyler, 1972-75, WFAA-TV, Dallas, 1976-79; model Dallas Apparel Mart, 1976-87. Author: (romance novels) Breakfast in Bead, 1983, Heaven's Price, 1983, Relentless Desire, 1983, Tempest in Eden, 1983, Temptation's Kiss, 1983, Tomorrow's Promise, 1983, In a Class by Itself, 1984, Send No Flowers, 1984, Bittersweet Rain, 1984, Sunset Embrace, 1984, Words of Silk, 1984, Riley in the Morning, 1985, Thursday's Child, 1985, Another Dawn, 1985, 22 Indigo Place, 1986, The Rana Look, 1986, Demon Rumm, 1987, Fanta C, 1987, Sunny Chandler's Return, 1987, Adam's Fall, 1988, Hawk's O'Toole's Hostage, 1988, Slow Heat in Heaven, 1988, Tidings of Great Joy, 1988, Long Time Coming, 1989, Temperatures Rising, 1989, Best Kept Secrets, 1989, A Whole New Light, 1989, Another Dawn, 1991, Breath of Scandal, 1991, Mirror Image, 1991, French Silk, 1992, The Silken Web, 1992, Honor Bound, 1992, A Secret Splendor, 1992, Shadows of Yesterday (also published as Relentless Desire), 1992, Three Complete Novels, 1992, Charade, 1994, The Witness, 1995, "TEXAS!" series: Texas! Lucky, 1990, Texas! Sage, 1991, Texas! Chase, 1991, Texas! Trilogy, 1992, (as Laura Jordan) Hidden Fires, 1982, The Silken Web, 1982, (as Rachel Ryan) Love Beyond Reason, 1981, Love's Encore, 1981, Eloquent Silence, 1982, A Treasure Worth Seeking, 1982, Prime Time, 1983, (as Erin St. Claire) Not Even for Love, 1982, A Kiss Remembered, 1983, A Secret Splendor, 1983, Seduction By Design, 1983, Led Astray, 1985, A Sweet Anger, 1985, Tiger Prince, 1985, Above and Beyond, 1986, Honor Bound, 1986, The Devil's Own, 1987, Two Alone, 1987, Thrill of Victory, 1989, Exclusive, 1996, Fat Tuesday, 1997, Unspeakable, 1998, The Alibi, 1999, Stand Off, 2000, The Switch, 2000.

BROWN, SANDRA LEE, arts management consultant, watercolorist; b. Chgo., July 9, 1943; d. Arthur Willard and Erma Emily (Lange) Boettcher; m. Ronald Gregory Brown, June 21, 1983; 1 child, Jon Michael. BA in Art and Edn., N.E. Ill. U., 1966; postgrad., No. Ill. U. Cert. K-9 tchr., Ill. Travel agt. Weiss Travel Bur., Chgo., 1959-66; tchr. Chgo. Sch. Sys., 1966-68, Schaumburg (Ill.) Sch. Dist. 54, 1968-94, creator coord. peer mentoring program for 1st-yr. tchrs., 1992-96; cons. Yardstick Ednl. Svcs., Monroe, Wis., 1994—2003; exec. dir. Monroe Arts Ctr., 1996—2001, Monroe Area Coun. for the Arts, Madisonville, Tenn., 2002—03; arts mgmt. cons. Helping Hands, Non-Profit Consulting, Knoxville, Tenn., 2003—, Tenn. Arts Commn. Mem. adv. bd. Peer Coaching and Mentoring Network, Chgo. suburban region, 1992-94; peer cons. Schaumburg Sch. Dist. 54, 1988-94. Exhibited in group shows Court House Gallery, Woodstock, Ill., Millburn (Ill.) Gallery, Gallerie Stefanie, Chgo., Monroe Arts Ctr., 1997. Campaign chmn. for mayoral candidate, Grayslake, Ill., 1989; campaign chmn. for trustee Citizens for Responsible Govt., Grayslake, 1991. Mem. Lakes Region Watercolor Guild, Delta Kappa Gamma (chmn. women in arts Gamma chpt. Ill. 1992-94, Alpha Mu chpt. 1995-97), Cmty. Arts League (Athens, Tenn.). Avocations: gardening, musician for barn dances, pre-war Appalachian, blues and cajun music, research collecting 78 rpm records. Home and Office: Helping Hands Non-Profit Consulting PO Box 1456 Athens TN 37371

BROWN, SARA NORDHOLM, social work educator; b. Fergus Falls, Minn., Jan. 28, 1941; d. David E. and Sara Evelyn (Nelson) Nordholm; m. Dudley J. Brown, June 15, 1963; Sara (Brown) Dunlap, Kirsten Leona, Jesse Chanda. BA in Sociolgy, St. Olaf Coll., 1963; student, U. Beirut, Lebanon, 1962; MSW, Columbia U., 1965; PhD in Family Rels. and Child Devel., Okla. State U., 1982. Lic. social worker, Okla. Med. social worker St. Lukes Hosp., N.Y.C., 1965-66; instr. Mbereshi Secondary Sch., Zambia, 1970-73, U. Benghazi, Libya, 1974-77; tchg. assoc. Okla. State U., Stillwater, 1978-80, asst. prof., 1980-81; prof. Northeastern State U., Tahlequah, Okla., 1981—, chmn. dept., 1983-97. Adminstr. Child Welfare Tng. Grant, Tahequah, Okla., 1984-90, Child Abuse Prevention Rsch, Tahlequah, 1986-90; presenter, planner Cherokee Nation Women's Conf., Tahlequah, 1989. Contbr. articles to profl. jours. Founding mem. Child Abuse Prevention Task Force, Tahlequah, 1983; bd. dirs. Help-In-Crisis, Tahlequah, 1981-85, Habitat for Humanity, Tahlequah, 1990—, Tahlequah Food Pantry, 1998—; mediator Agr. Mediation, State of Okla., 1988—. Recipient Cert. Social Planning Aging Svc. Eastern Okla. Devel. Dist., Tahlequah, 1985, Appreciation award, Cherokee Nat. Employment & Tng., Tahlequah, Okla., 1986, Outstanding Alumni award, Okla. State U. Women's Coun., Stillwater, 1987; named Cherokee Nation Early Childhood Advocate of Yr., 1999; named to Muskogee (Okla.) Hall of Fame, 1984, NSU Faculty of the Yr. for Svc. Contbns., 1995. Mem.: NASW (v.p. 2001—, bd. dirs. Okla. chpt., Lifetime Achievement award 2000), AAUW (v.p. local br. 1988—89), Baccalaureate Social Work Program Dirs. Assn., Okla. Health and Welfare Assn. (bd. dirs. 1987—90), Okla. Lic. Social Workers, Coun. Social Work Edn., Columbia U. Sch. Social Work Alumni (bd. dirs.). Methodist. Office: Northeastern State U Dept Social Work Tahlequah OK 74464 also: PO Box 1412 Tahlequah OK 74465-1412 E-mail: browns@nsuok.edu.

BROWN, SHARI K. special education educator; b. Detroit Lakes, Minn., Nov. 5, 1973; d. Kermit and Marie Schultz; m. Christopher A. Brown, June 20, 1998. BA, Concordia Coll., 1996; postgrad., Moorhead State U., 1997. Lic. specific learning disabilities. Tchr. specific learning disabilities Moose Lake (Minn.) Cmty. Schs., 1997—98, Sebeka (Minn.) Pub. Schs., 1999—. Mem.: Edn. Minn.-Sebeka.

BROWN, SHARON WEBB, art educator; b. Whitesburg, Ky., Nov. 20, 1942; d. Chester and Doris Adams Webb; m. Bob Brown, May 19, 1973; children: Alyn, Ashley Susan. BA, Georgetown (Ky.) Coll., 1964. Art tchr. Jefferson County Schs., Louisville, 1964—72; art coord. Louisville City Schs., Louisville, 1972—73; tchr. fine arts, dept. chair Marshall County Schs., Benton, Ky., 1975—. Editor: Hallowed Hollows, 2001, Women in God's Word, 2001, God's Specialty, 2002; actor: (plays) Harvey, 2001, 2002, Do Not Go Gentle, 2002. Elder Presbyn. Ch., Calvert City, Ky. Mem.: Women in the Arts, Speed Mus. (bd. dirs. 1972—73), Commonwealth Yacht Club (rec. sec. 1993—2004). Republican. Avocations: travel, literature, painting. Home: POBox 641 Calvert City KY 42029 Office: Marshall County Schools 416 High School Road Benton KY 42025 Personal E-mail: sbrown@marshall.k12.ky.us.

BROWN, SHEBA ANN, elementary school educator; b. Miss., 1951; married; 1 child, Joshua. BS in Elem. Edn., U. So. Miss., 1973. Tchr. 4th grade Biloxi (Miss.) Pub. Schs., 1973-74; tchr. 3d grade Ferncrest Acad., New Orleans, 1974-75, Cifton Ganus Pvt. Sch., New Orleans, 1975-78; tchr. 4th grade Putnam County Schs., Palatka, Fla., 1986-87; tchr. multi-age primary class Biloxi Pub. Schs., 1987—. Condr. workshops; presenter in field. Recipient Beverly Briscoe award Biloxi Schs., 1990, Enhancement award City of Biloxi, 1995, Leo Seal Tchr. Recognition award, 1999; named Miss. Tchr. of Yr., 1995, Women at the Top Coast Mag., 1996. Mem. Internat. Reading Assn., Nat. Coun. Tchrs. English, Jeff Davis PTA (treas.), Delta Kappa Gamma. Home: 135 Travia Ave Biloxi MS 39531-5328

BROWN, SHERI LYNN, artist, poet, educator; b. Bluefield, W.Va., Nov. 22, 1968; d. James H. and Rosa B. Wilkes. BA in Comml. Art and Advt., Concord Coll., 1992. Owner T.J. Cool Advt., 1992—; writer Hill Top Records, Hollywood, Calif., 2001. Author numerous poems in anthologies. Mem. I Am His choir Scott St. Bapt. Ch., 1983—87. Mem.: Internat. Soc. Poets. Avocations: art, writing, trumpet, french horn, mellophone. Home: 120 Russell Terr Bluefield WV 24701-2932

BROWN, SHIRLEY ANN, speech-language pathologist; b. Bklyn., Oct. 9, 1935; d. Hyman and Lillian (Fuhrer) Rubak; m. Ronald Wallace Brown, Sept. 29, 1956; children: Abbie Howard, Daniel Mark. BA, Bklyn. Coll., 1956, MA, 1961. Lic. speech/lang. pathologist, N.Y., N.J. Speech pathologist Richmond County CP Treatment Ctr., S.I., N.Y., 1956-59, Coney Island Hosp., Bklyn., 1959-61, Mendham Boro Schs. and Chatham Twp. Schs., 1962-67; pvt. practice home care speech pathologist various hosps. and med. facilities, 1967-79; dir. speech pathology dept. Englewood (N.J.) Hosp., 1974-92; speech pathologist Holy Name Hosp., Teaneck, N.J., 1992-96, chief speech-lang. pathology dept., 1996-2000; speech pathologist Home Health Care Agys., Bergen County, 1992—. Clin. supr. comm. disorders grad. program Kean Coll., N.J., 1993—2000, Montclair State U., 1998—2000, project leader speech-lang. pathology Multiple Sclerosis Consortium website editl. bd., 1999—2001; website project dir. Consortium of Multiple Sclerosis Ctrs., 2001—. Editl. bd. Internat. Jour. Multiple Sclerosis Care, 1999—. Chair svc. and rehab. Am. Cancer Soc., Hackensack, N.J. Recipient Nat. Honor citation for Profl. Edn., Am. Cancer Soc., 1985, Crimson Sword award Am. Cancer Soc., 1989. Mem.: Nat. Multiple Sclerosis Soc. (Greater North Jersey chpt., clin. chpt. programs, adv. com. 1998—), N.J. Speech, Lang., Hearing Assn. (Disting. Svc. award), Am. Speech., Lang. Hearing Assn. (cert., congl. action com., state chair career info., Continuing Edn. award 1983—, Outstanding Clin. Achievement award 1985). Avocation: cooking. Home and Office: 6 Sisson Ter Tenafly NJ 07670-1810

BROWN, SHIRLEY JEAN, health care facility manager, nurse; b. Vallejo, Calif., Mar. 17, 1946; d. Celester Mackey and Lillie B. (Collins) Presley; m. Leo Brown, 1976; children: Vickie Hardin Williams, Altee Jr., Keith Hardin, La Tonya R. Brown. Diploma in nursing, Brackenridge Sch. Nursing, Austin, 1977; AA, Austin (Tex.) C.C., 1983; BA in Pub. Mgmt., Huston Tildtson Coll., 2000. RN Tex. ORT/RN Holy Cross Hosp., Austin, 1966-78; RN Austin Women's Clinic, 1978-80; dist. health svc. mgr. Health & Human Svcs. Dept., Austin, 1980—. Bd. mem. Child Inc. Health Care Adv. Bd. Co-chair Austin Interfaith, 1989—; mem. Nat. Forum Black Pub. Adminstrs. Recipient Boss III award of distinction Austin Met. Bus. Resource Ctr., 1990, Civic & Human Endeavors, 1994, Nurse of Yr. award Tex. Nurses Assn., 2001, Disting. Svc. award Mayor and City Councilmen, 2001. Mem. NAFE, Am. Coll. Health Care Execs., Brackenridge Hosp. Sch. Nursing Alumni Assn. Democrat. Baptist. Avocations: reading, walking, bowling. Home: 7207 Hartnell Dr Austin TX 78723-1518

BROWN, SHIRLEY MARGARET KERN (PEGGY BROWN), interior designer; b. Ellensburg, Wash., Mar. 30, 1948; d. Philip Brooke and Shirley (Dickson) Kern; m. Ellery Kliess Brown, Jr., Aug. 7, 1970; children; Heather Nicole Coco, Rebecca Cherise, Andrea Shirley Serene, Ellery Philip. BA in Interior Design, Wash. State U., 1973. Apprentice then interior designer L.S. Higgins & Assocs., Bellevue, Wash., 1969-72; interior designer ColorsPlus Interiors, Inc., Bellevue, Wash., 1972, Strawns Office Furniture & Interiors, Inc., Boise, 1973-75, Empire Furniture, Inc., Tulsa; owner Inside-Out Design Co., Ltd., Boise, 1973-82; interior designer Architekton, Inc., Tulsa, 1984-86, Johnson Brand Design Group, Inc., 1986-87, Ellery Brown & Assocs. Arch., 1987—, Seattle Design Ctr.-Visions & Studio Programs, Scottsdale, Ariz., 1998—, Mehagian's Fine Furniture, Scottsdale, Ariz., ASID Designers' Showhouse, 2000, Ladlows Fine Furniture, 2003—. Lectr. in field. Contbr. articles to profl. jours.; featured designer Ariz. Lifestyle mag., 2002. Pres. PTA, co-chair capital bond prin. sel. com., enrollment rev. com., 1989-95; bd. dirs. Paradise Valley Young Life; designer West Valley Child Crises Ctr., Inc.; contributing designer West Valley Child Crisis Ctr. Recipient Seattle Design Ctr. Marjorie Siegel award, 1997, Phoenix Home and Garden Mag. ASID Showhouse, 2000. Mem.: AAUW, Nat. Soc. Interior Designers, Am. Soc. Interior Designers (dir. chpt. 1976—77, presdl. citation Oreg. chpt. 1977, chmn. Boise subchpt. 1977—79, sec. 1980—81, chmn. Wash. chpt. step workshop chmn. 1993—97, NCIDQ chmn. 1993—97, Wash. state presdl. citation 1995, presdl. citation Oreg. chpt. 1995—96, Wash. state presdl. citation 1996, 1997, bd. dirs. North Ariz. chpt. 2003—, Showhouse Mehagian's Designer award Phoenix Home and Garden Mag. 2000, bd. dirs. Ariz. chpt. 2003—), Jr. League Phoenix, Wash. State U. Alumni Assn., Idaho Hist. Co., Jr. League Seattle, Zonta, Alpha Gamma Delta. Republican. Presbyterian. Office: Ladlows Fine Furniture 16000 N Scottsdale Rd Scottsdale AZ 85254 Office Phone: 480-315-8500. E-mail: az-browns@hotmail.com.

BROWN, SHIRLEY MARK, retired science administrator; b. Phila., Apr. 25, 1924; d. Paul and Bertha Evelyn (Zucker) Mark; m. Bernard Beau, Sept. 1, 1947; children: Eric Joel, Aimee Susan. BA, Temple U., Phila., 1945, MA, 1947. Rsch. chemist U. Mich., Ann Arbor, 1947-50; instr. Upsala Coll., East Orange, 1960-74; acad. planner Rutgers U., New Brunswick, N.J., 1974-80, assoc. dir. Waksman Inst., 1980-88; exec. dir. Rutgers Rsch. and Ednl. Found., New Brunswick, 1980-94; assoc. dir. Office of Corp. Liaison and Technol. Transfer Rutgers U., 1988-91, adminstr. corp. contracts, 1991-94. Ct. mediator Union County, 2003—04. Sec. Joint Civic Com. Westfield 1962-66, Com. for Human Rights Westfield 1967-70; publicity chairperson. PTA Westfield 1963-67; counselor State Health Ins. Program, Union County, 2000-04; vol. Zimmerli Art Mus., Rutgers U., 1994-2004, bd. dirs., 2003-04. Mem. LWV, Assn. Univ. Technol. Mgrs., Nat. Coun. Univ. Rsch. Adminstrs., Soc. Rsch. Adminstrs. Avocations: travel, theater, art history. Home: 146 Tudor Oval Westfield NJ 07090-2245 Personal E-mail: smb146@msn.com.

BROWN, TINA, journalist, television personality; b. Maidenhead, Eng., Nov. 21, 1953; d. George Hambley and Bettina Iris May (Kohr) Brown; m. Harold Evans, Aug. 20, 1981; children: George Frederick, Isabel Harriet. MA, Oxford U.; D (hon.), The London Inst., 2001. Columnist Punch Mag., London, 1978; editor in chief Tatler Mag., London, 1979—83, Vanity Fair Mag., N.Y.C., 1984—92; editor New Yorker mag., N.Y.C., 1992—98; chmn., editor-in-chief Talk Media, 1998—2002; weekly columnist The Wash. Post, 2003—, Salon.com, 2003—; host, Topic A with Tina Brown CNBC, 2003—. Author: (plays) Under the Bamboo Tree, 1973 (Sunday Times Drama award), Happy Yellow, 1977, (book) Loose Talk, 1979, Life As A Party, 1983. Named Most Promising Female Journalist, Young Journalist of Yr., 1978, Comdr. Brit. Empire, Her Royal Highness Queen Elizabeth, 2000; recipient Kathrine Pakenham prize, Sunday London Times, 1973, Mag. Editor of the Yr., Age Mag., 1988, USC Disting. Achievement in Journalism award, USC Journalism Alumni Assn., 1994. Office: Attn Betty Greif 447 E 57th St New York NY 10022*

BROWN, TOMMIE FLORENCE, social work educator; b. Rome, Ga., June 25, 1934; d. Phillip and Mary Louise (Murden) B. BA, Dillard U., 1957; MSW, Washington U., St. Louis, 1964; DSW, Columbia U., 1986. Social svc. supr. Tenn. Dept. Pub. Welfare, Chattanooga, 1964-67, dir. tng., 1967-71; asst. prof. sociology U. Tenn., Chattanooga, 1971-73, head social work dept., 1973-82, UC Found. assoc. prof. social work, 1982—; mem. Tenn. Ho. of Reps., Nashville, 1992—, mem. commerce, conservation and environ. coms., 1992-94, mem. edn. com., 1995—, sec. fin. ways and means com., 1995—. Named Nat. Social Worker of Yr., NASW, 1971. Democrat. Baptist. Home: PO Box 3258 Chattanooga TN 37404-0258 Office: Tenn Gen Assembly Legislative Plz Ste 36 Nashville TN 37243-0128

BROWN, TRISH EILEEN See VERNAZZA, TRISH

BROWN, TRISHA, dancer; b. Aberdeen, Wash., Nov. 25, 1936; BA in Dance, Mills Coll., Calif.; D (hon.), Mills Coll., 1997; PhD in Fine Arts (hon.), Oberlin Coll. Founder, artistic dir. Trisha Brown Dance Co., N.Y.C., 1970—; founding mem. Judson Dance Theater; choreographer Grand Union Improvisation Group, 1970-76. Lectr. Mills Coll., Calif., Reed Coll., Oreg., NYU, N.Y.C., Goucher Coll., Md., Carnegie Mellon U., Pa.; condr. workshops and seminars throughout world. Choreographer Untitled, 1961, Trillium, 1961, Lightfall, 1963, Untitled Duet, 1963, Part of a Tango, 1963, Target, 1964, Rulegame Five, 1964, Motor, 1965, Homemade, 1965, Inside, 1966, Skunk Cabbage, 1967, Saltgrass and Waders, 1967, Medicine Dance, 1967, Snapshots, 1968, Ballet, 1968, Falling Duet, 1968, Sky Map, 1969, Dance with Duck's Head, 1968, Yellow Belly, 1969, Leaning Duets, 1970, The Stream, 1970, Man Walking Down the Side of a Building, 1970, Accumulation 4 1/2, 1971, Walking on the Wall, 1971, Leaning Duets II,

1971, Falling Duet II, 1971, Rummage Sale and the Floor of the Forest, 1971, Planes, 1968, Roof Piece, 1971, Primary Accumulation, 1972, Accumulating Pieces, 1973, Group Accumulation, 1973, Roof and Fire Piece, 1973, Spanish Dance, 1973, Structured Pieces, 1973, Figure 8, 1974, Drift, 1974, Spiral, 1974, Pamplona Stones, 1974, Locus, 1975, Line Up, 1976, Water Motor and Splang, 1978, Glacial Decoy, 1979, Opal Loop, 1980, Son of Gone Fishin', 1981, Set and Reset, 1983 (N.Y. Dance and Performance award, 1984), Lateral Pass, 1985 (N.Y. Dance and Performance award, 1986), Carmen, 1986, Newark, 1987, Astral Convertible, 1989, For M.G.: The Movie, 1991, Astral Converted, 1991, Another Story as in Falling, 1993, If you couldn't see me, 1994, Foray Forêt, 1990, You Can See Us, 1995, M.O., 1995, Twelve Ton Rose, 1996; featured (TV series) M.O., Sta. WNET-TV, N.Y.C., Dance in America, Sta. WGBH-TV, Boston, Dancing on the Edge, Making Dances; exhibitions include Venice Biennale, Toulon Mus., exhibited in group shows at Musée de Marseille, Numerals: Math. Concepts in Contemporary Art, The Pluralist Decade, New Notes for New Dance, Art and Dance: Images From the Modern Dialogue. Mem. Nat. Coun. on Arts, 1994. Decorated chevalier Ordre des Arts et des Lettres; recipient Creative Arts award, Brandeis U., 1982, Dance Mag. award, 1987, Samuel H. Scripps Am. Dance Festival award, 1994, Prix de la Danse la Société des Auteurs et Compositeurs Dramatiques award, 1996, Nat. medal of Art, 2003; fellow, Guggenheim Found., 1975, 1984, NEA Creative Artists Svc. Program, 1977, 1981—84; grantee, NEA, N.Y. State Coun. on Arts; MacArthur fellow, 1991. Mem.: Am. Acad. Arts and Letters (Nat. medal of Art 2003). Office: Trisha Brown Co care Rebecca Davis 625 W 55th St New York NY 10019-3560

BROWN, TYESE ANDREA, music educator; d. Andrew Percy and Elois Smith Brown. B of Music Edn., Howard U., 1993; MA, NYU, 1999. Cert. tchr. music K-12. Telemarketer Americana Portraits, West Orange, NJ, 1992; substitute tchr. Orange Bd. Edn., Orange, NJ, 1994—95, South Orange and Maplewood (N.J.) Bd. Edn., 1994—95; music dir. Jersey Explorer Mus., East Orange, 1997—99; music tchr. K-4 Jersey City (N.J.) Bd. Edn., 1999—2000; music tchr. grades 3-5 Montclair (N.J.) Bd. Edn., 2000—02; music tchr. grades 7-8 North Plainfield (N.J.) Bd. Edn., 2002—; music tchr. grades K-7 Roselle (NJ) Bd. Edn., 2003—. Music competition judge NAACP ACT-SO Competitions, Charlotte, N.C. and Atlanta, Ga., 1996—98; soprano vocal judge Ctrl. Jersey Music Educators Assn. Jr. Competitions, 2002, NJ Music Educators Assn., 2002; music dir. Hillside's Traveling Troupe, Montclair, 2000—02. Composer: (songs) The Winds of Yesterday, 1984 (Instrns. Experience Exposures award, 1984), The Ancient Springs, 1985. Music dir. AmeriCorps, Jersey City, 1997—99. Named Gifted Musician of Essex County, Instrns. Experience Exposure, 1984; recipient Gifted Student scholarship, Geraldine R. Dodge Found., 1984, Musician of Yr. award, Newark Comty. Sch. Arts, 1982—88. Mem.: ASCAP (songwriter/pub. mem.), Music Educators Nat. Conf., NYU Alumni Assn., Howard U. Alumni Assn., Kappa Delta Pi, Pi Lambda Theta. Avocations: drawing, reading, composing music, swimming, bowling. Office: ASCAP 1 Penn Plz New York NY 10019 also: Roselle Bd Edn 710 Locust St Roselle NJ 07203

BROWN, VALERIE, writer; d. Vernon Thurman and Mildred Heaton Atkinson; m. Troy Brown, Oct. 5, 1996. BA, U. Tex., 1981; MA, S.W. Tex. U., 2002. Adminstr. Texlex, Inc., Austin, 1988—93; web coord. AMD, Austin, 1997—98, tech. analyst Sprint Paranet, Austin, Tex., 1998—2000 Author: Paralegal Guide to Intellectual Property, 1994, Legal Research Via the Internet, 2001. Habitat steward Nat. Wildlife Fedn. Mem.: Soc. Authors U.K., Authors Guild, Am. Acad. Poets. Avocations: gardening, calligraphy. Office: PO Box 1539 Kyle TX 78640 Office Phone: 512-791-1585.

BROWN, VALERIE ANNE, psychiatric social worker, educator; b. Elizabeth, N.J., Feb. 28, 1951; d. William John and Adelaide Elizabeth (Krasa) B. BA summa cum laude (fellow), C.W. Post Coll., 1972; MSW (Silberman scholar), Hunter Coll., 1975; PhD, Am. Internat. U., 1996. Diplomate Am. Bd. Examiners, Am. Bd. Clin. Social Work, Nat. Assn. Social Work; cert. addictions specialist; cert. master hypnotherapist; cert. psychophilogic integration therapist. Social work intern Greenwich House Counseling Ctr., N.Y.C., 1973-74, Metro Cons. Ctr., N.Y.C., 1974-75; sr. psychiat. social worker, co-adminstr. Essex County Guidance Ctr., East Orange, N.J., 1975-80; pvt. practice psychiat. social work, psychotherapy, 1979—. Sr. psychiat. social worker John E. Runnells Hosp., Berkeley Heights, N.J., 1980-86; dir. social work Northfield Manor, West Orange, N.J., 1987; clin. coord. Project Portals East Orange Gen. Hosp., 1987-88; asst. dir. ARS/Century House Riverview Med. Ctr., Red Bank, N.J., 1988-93; sr. clin. case mgmt. specialist Prudential Ins. Co., Woodbridge, N.J., 1993; clin. dir. Greenhouse-KMC, Lakewood, N.J., 1994-2000, Shoreline-KBH, Toms River, N.J., 1996-2000; tech. advisor Nat. Comm. Network, 1988—; mental health clinician III UMDNJ-UBHC, Edison, N.J., 2000—; instr. Brookdale Coll., 1991—; co-founder Women's Growth Ctr., Cedar Grove, N.J., 1979; counselor Passaic Drug Clinic, 1978-80; field instr. Fairleigh Dickinson U., Madison, N.J., 1981-86, Brookdale Coll., 1989-92; field supr. Union Coll., Cranford, N.J., 1986; instr. Sch. Social Work, NYU, N.Y.C., 1980-83, asst. prof., 1983-85; evaluator Intoxicated Driver Resource Ctr., Essex County, N.J., 1987-88. Alt. Monmouth County profl. adv. bd. Named Dist. Alumnae Mother Seton Regional H.S., Clark, N.J., 1997. Mem. NASW (Whittman Lifetime Achievement nominee 1997-98), Psi Chi, Pi Gamma Mu, Sigma Tau Delta. Avocations: reading, swimming, travel. Office: 20 Ellsworth Ct Red Bank NJ 07701-5403

BROWN, VIVIAN ANDERSON, retired government agency administrator; b. Manor, Tex., Aug. 27, 1920; d. Carl Robert Anderson and Edna Belle Elizabeth Johnson Anderson; m. Karl Patrick Brown, Aug. 29, 1970 (dec. July 1976); stepchildren: Patrick Thomas, Peggy Ann, David Brian. Student, U. Tex., 1938—39, Mayfair Taylor Secretarial Sch., 1940—42. Purchasing clk. USAF, Bergstrom AFB, Tex., 4357, contracting officer, 1957—73; ret., 1973. Contbr. articles to profl. pubs. (Outstanding award). Pres. women's orgn. Prince of Peace Luth. Ch., Austin, Tex. Recipient Vivian A. Brown Spl. Day honor, Mayor of Marshall, Tex., 1990, Gov. of Tex., 1990. Mem.: DAVA (state comdr. 1980—89), Nat. Assn. Ret. Fed. Employees (pres. 1979—81), Swedish Orgn. Carl-Widen Lodge (sec. 1998—2000). Democrat. Lutheran. Avocations: public speaking, reading, writing. Home: 7263 Creekside Dr Austin TX 78752

BROWN, WENDY ELAINE, communications consultant; b. Los Alamos, N.Mex., Apr. 28, 1956; d. Leon J. and Dorothy (Stern) B.; m. Richard Swanson; children: Tasmin Amanda Swanson, Nathaniel Richard Swanson. BA, Northwestern U., 1978. Software engr. Prime Computer Inc., Natick, Mass., 1978-80; systems programmer Dialcom, Silver Spring, Md., 1980-85; systems programmer, analyst APA, Falls Church, Va., 1985-86; mem. tech. staff Corp. for Open Systems, McLean, Va., 1986-89; cons. PSC Internat. Inc., McLean, Va., 1989-95, Digitalnet (formerly J.G. Van Dyke and Assocs.), Annapolis Junction, Md., 1995—. Author: OSI Dictionary of Acronyms, 1992. Democrat. Jewish. Avocations: sewing, electronic networking. Home: 9417 Russell Rd Silver Spring MD 20910-1445 Office: Digitalnet Ste 210 141 National Business Pkwy Annapolis Junction MD 20701-1003 E-mail: wendyb@starpower.net.

BROWN, WENDY WEINSTOCK, nephrologist, educator; b. N.Y.C., Dec. 9, 1944; d. Irving and Pearl (Levack) Weinstock; m. Barry David Brown, May 2, 1971 (div. Sept. 1995); children: Jennifer Faye, Joshua Reuben, Julie Aviva, Rachel Ann. BA, U. Mass., 1966; MD, Med. Coll. of Pa., 1970; MPH, St. Louis U., 1999. Diplomate Am. Bd. Internal Medicine. Intern U. Ill. Affiliated Hosps., Chgo., 1970-71; resident in internal medicine The Med. Coll. Wis. Affiliated Hosps., Milw., 1971-74; gen. practitioner Vogelweh (W. Germany) Health Clinics, 1975-76; fellow in nephrology Med. Coll. of Wis. Milw. County Med. Complex, Milw., 1976-78; staff physician St. Louis VA Med Ctr., 1978—2003, acting chief, hemodialysis sect., 1983-85, chief dialysis/renal sect., 1985-90, dir. clin. nephrology, 1990—2003; staff physician St. Louis U. Hosps., 1978—2003, St. Louis City Hosp., 1982-85, St Mary's Health Ctr., St. Louis, 1994—2003; chief of staff VA Tenn. Valley Healthcare Sys., Nashville, 2003—. Assoc. prof. internal medicine St. Louis U. Health Sci. Ctr., 1985—98, prof. internal medicine, 1998—2003; prof. medicine Meharry Med. Coll.. Vanderbilt Univ., 2003—. Reviewer Clin. Nephrology, Nephrology, Dialysis and Transplantation, Am. Jour. Nephrology, Am. Jour. Kidney Disease, Jour Am. Geriatric Soc., Jour. Am. Soc. Nephrology, Geriatric Nephrology and Urology, Kidney Internat.; med. editor NKF Family Focus; mem. editl. bd. Clin. Nephrology, Geriatric Nephrology, Internat. Urology and Nephrology, Advances in Renal Replacement Therapy; editor-in-chief: Advances in Chronic Kidney Disease, 2004-; contbr. articles to profl. jours. Mem. adv. coun. Mo. Kidney Program, 1985-91, chmn., 1988-89; numerous positions Nat. Kidney Found., 1984—, nat. chmn., 1995-97; bd. dirs. United Way, St. Louis, 1994-2003, Nat. Kidney Found. Ea. Mo. and Metro East, Inc., 1980-94; bd. dirs. Combined Health Appeal Greater St. Louis, Inc., 1988, pres., 1989-92; bd. dirs. Combined Health Appeal Am., 1991-98, sec., 1992-96, vice chmn., 1996-98. Named Casual Corner Career Woman of Yr., 1986, Combine Health Appeal of Am. Vol. of Yr., 1991, Olympic Torch Bearer, 1996, St. Louis Health Profl. of Yr., 1997; recipient Upjohn Achievement award, Med. Coll. Wis. Affiliated HOsps., 1972, Cert. of Leadership, St. Louis YWCA, 1989, Chmn.'s award, Nat. Kidney Found. of Ea. Mo. and Metro East, 1990, award of excellence, 2002, Chmn.'s award, Nat. Kidney Found., Washington, 1990, Martin Wagner award, Nat. Kidney Found., 1999, award of excellence, Nat. Kidney Found. Ea. Mo. and Metro East, 2002. Fellow ACP, AHA; mem. Am. Soc. Nephrology, Internat. Soc. Nephrology, Coun. on Kidney in Cardiovascular Disease, Am. Heart Assn., St. Louis Soc. Am. Med. Women's Assn., St. Louis Internists (v.p. 1983-84, pres. 1984-85), Women in Nephrology (pres. 2000-02), Internat. Soc. for Peritoneal Dialysis, Am. Geriatrics Soc., Soc. for Exec. Leadership in Acad. Medicine (bd. dirs., program chair 1999—), Alpha Omega Alpha. Office: VA Tenn Valley Healthcare Sys 1310 24th Ave S Nashville TN 37212-2637 Home: 1728 Glen Echo Rd Nashville TN 37215-2910 Office Phone: 615-327-5330. E-mail: wendy.brown@med.va.gov.

BROWN-DANIELS, PATRICIA, budget analyst, wedding consultant; b. Washington, June 25, 1953; d. Jesse and Katherine Austin; m. Joseph Lee Daniels, Aug. 25, 1990; children: Dionnah, James, Freddie. Assoc. in Bus. Adminstrn., Washington Saturday Coll., 1999; B in Ministry, Faith Christian U., Washington, 2002. Clk. typist IRS, Washington, 1972—75; procurement clk. U.S. GPO, Washington, 1975—78; acctg. technician Dept. of Navy - NSS, Washington, 1978—83, Dept. of Navy - BUMED, Washington, 1983—88; budget analyst Dept. of Navy - NNMC, Bethesda, Md., 1988—. Profl. wedding cons. Assn. Bridal Consultants, Stamford, Conn., 1999—; trustee, chair budget com. Mt. Rona Bapt. Ch., Washington, 1997—. Organizer Langdon / Woodridge Outreach Ministries, Washington, 2000—; founder Men 4 All Seasons Choir, Washington, 2002; debutante com. Shiloh Bapt. Ch., Washington, 1999—. Recipient Mary M. Bethune recognition Award, Nat. Coun. Negro Women, 1999-2001. Mem.: NAACP (sec. 1999—), Nat. Coun. Negro Women (membership chair 1999—), LJM Toastmasters Club (sec. 1997—, ATM-B 2000). Baptist. Avocations: mentor, tutor, model, choir member, children's advocate. Home: 2429 Hamlin Street NE Washington DC 20018 Personal E-mail: phdaniels0@aol.com

BROWNE, A. PAULINE, accountant, writer; b. Topeka, June 26, 1918; d. James Paul and Alice Bertha (Crabb) Sweeney; m. Raymond Smetzer, Jan. 4, 1948 (div. Jan. 1957); children: Jerry, Raymond, Jonathan, Patricia. BBA, U. Miami, 1975; JD, Atlanta Law Sch., 1980. Owner Smetzer Airport, Castalia, Ohio, 1948-58, Greenwood Inn, Castalia, Ohio, 1956-57; freelance legal sec., 1958-89. Owner Sweeney's Tax Svc., 1948—; legal word processor Steel Hector Davis, West Palm Beach, Fla., 1989-2003. Contbr. articles to profl. jours. Activist Fighting for Our Rights Under the Constitution, Alcoholics Anonymous. Mem. Women in Arts, U. Miami Alumni Assn. Avocations: golf, travel, whitewater rafting, hiking, scuba diving. Home: Apt D211 19417 Gulf Blvd Indian Shores FL 33785-2243

BROWNE, BONNIE ESTHER, minister; d. Howard Edward Browne and Mabel Leezer; 1 child, Deborah Dudley Zumberge. BS in nursing, U. of Cin., 1941—46; M in pub. adminstrn. health svcs., U. of Ariz., 1968—74. Registered Nurse, Ariz. and Ohio; Minister Living Bible Ctr., 1986, Interfaith Minister Emerson Theol. Inst., 2003. Counselor, children's clinic Arthritis Found., Tucson, 1973—74; hosp. co-founder and adminstr. American, Inc., Tucson, 1974—75; practitioner Religious Sci., Tucson, 1978—2003; ceo Sewage Treatment Rsch. & Devel., Tucson, 1979—81; facilitator/counselor Bonnie Browne Seminars, Tucson, 1983—2003; min. Celebration of Life Ctr., Tucson, 1988—2001; staff min. Cmty. Ch. of Positive Living, Tucson, 2001—; faculty and mentor Emerson Theol. Inst., Satellite Campus, Tucson, 2003—. Cons. - pain mgmt. U. Med. Ctr., Tucson, 1979—80; bd. mem. Governor's Adv. Bd. of So. Ariz. Mental Health Ctr., 1973—75; mem. of adv. com. to dir. Coll. of Nursing, U. of Ariz., 1967—68; chmn. Cmty. Coun. Health and Hosp. Planning Com., Tucson, 1961; fin. com. mem. Barry Goldwater Campaign, Tucson, 1964; vol. Am. Cancer Soc., Ariz. Heart Assn., Tucson Festival Soc., Women's Symphony Assn., Combined Hosp. Fund Dr., Kiwanis Women's Organizations, Asthmatic Found., Adv. Com. polit. candidates, Tucson, 1955—75; bd. mem. Ariz. Sch. of Acupuncture and Oriental Medicine, 2003—; sales dir. Mary Kay Cosmetics, Tucson, 1981—86. Del./officer LWV, Tucson, 1958—65; fundraising and candidates' vol. Rep. Party, Tucson, 1960—65. Recipient Outstanding Leadership award, Dale Carnegie, 1979. R-Liberal. Religious Science. Avocations: travel, reading, teaching, research.

BROWNE, DIANA GAYLE, artist, social worker; b. San Francisco, Aug. 31, 1924; d. Clarence Luther and Elsa Henrietta (Ericson) Sidelinger; m. Alfred B. Britton Jr., Sept. 2, 1942 (div. 1960); children: Alfred B. Britton III, Kathryn H. Lumbert, Patrick Luther Britton; m. James Stuart Browne M.D., May 19, 1963; children: Bruce Petter Browne, Julia Regina Browne. Student, Stanford U., 1947; BA with great distinction with honors, San Jose State U., 1949; MSW, U. Calif., 1958; BFA, San Francisco Art Inst., 1973. Lic. Clinical Social Worker, Calif. Clinical social worker Dept. Mental Health, Sacramento, 1958-59; clin. social worker U. Calif. Med. Ctr., San Francisco, 1960-61, Langley Porter Neuropsych. Inst., San Francisco, 1961-65, Napa State Hosp., 1980-85; postgrad. Inst. for Clin. Social Work, Berkeley, 1981-83; freelance artist Mill Valley, Calif., 1966-80, 1985—. Mem. Acci Gallery, Berkeley, 1977-91, Alliance Women Artists, 1988-89. Recipient Merit award Calif. State Fair Fine Arts Div., 1989, Marin Arts Guild, Larkspur, Calif., 1977-79, Art award Marin County Fair, 1977-78, 89-90. Mem. AAUW, DAR, Calif. Soc. Printmakers, Calif. Watercolor Assn. (signature mem., membership chmn. 1986-88, Merit award 1987), Marin Soc. Artists, Outdoor Art Club (Mill Valley), Alpha Chi Omega (pres. Santa Clara County alumnae 1949-51, Marin County alumnae 1966-68). Avocations: computer graphics, photography, geneology. E-mail: goldengate4@sbcglobal.net.

BROWNE, ELIZABETH PEDDLE, financial assistant; b. Bridgeport, Conn., Aug. 29, 1970; d. Joseph A. Jr. and Mary E. (Farrace) P.; m. Thomas F. Browne Jr., Dec. 1, 1996. AS summa cum laude, Sacred Heart U., 1990. Sec. Town of Fairfield (Conn.), 1987-88, exec. sec., 1988-93; adminstrv. asst. fin. City of Milford (Conn.), 1993—. Rec. sec. various bd. & commns., Fairfield, 1988—, rec. sec. Milford (Conn.) bd. fin., rec. sec. permanent sch. faculty bldg. com., 1997—. Vol. Fairfield Animal Control, 1991—; deputy dist. leader Rep. Town Com., Fairfield, 1995—; treas. Re-elect Dickman '96, Fairfield, 1996, 98; mem. Kennedy Ctr. Four Seasons Ball Com., 1997—; mem. RTC Adopt-A-Spot com. Mem. Gaelic-Am. Club, Delta Epsilon Sigma. Republican. Roman Catholic. Avocations: reading, walking, sports, local politics. Home: 200 Edgewood Rd Fairfield CT 06432-1716

BROWNE, JOY, psychologist, radio personality; b. New Orleans, Oct. 24, 1950; d. Nelson and Ruth (Strauss) B.; Carter Thweatt, June 9, 1966 (div. 1979); 1 child, Patience. BA, Rice U.; PhD, Northeastern U.; postgrad., Tufts U. Registered psychologist, Mass. With rsch./optics dept. Sperry Rand, Boston, 1966-68; engr. space program Itek, Boston, 1968-70; head social svcs. dept. Boston Redevel. Authority, 1970-71; staff psychologist South Shore Counselling Assocs., Boston, 1971-82; on-the-air psychologist Sta. WITS, Boston, 1978-82, Sta. KGO, San Francisco, 1982-84; host, news Sta. KCBS, San Francisco, 1984-85; on-air psychologist Sta. WABC, N.Y.C., 1985-87, ABC Talkradio, N.Y.C., 1987-92, WOR Radio Network, N.Y.C., 1992—, Sta. WABC-TV, 1995-97, Dr. Joy Browne Show, Syndicated Eyemark Entertainment, 1999—. On-air psychologist WCBS-TV Five O'Clock News, 1999; dir. Town of Hull Adolescent Outreach Program; cons. human sexuality PBS, 1994—. Author: The Used Car Game, 1971, The Research Experience, 1976, Nobody's Perfect, 1988, Why They Don't Call When They Say They Will and Other Mixed Signals, 1989, Dating for Dummies, 1998, 9 Fantasies That Will Ruin Your Life, 1998, It's a Jungle out There Jane! Understanding the Male Animal, 1999, Getting Unstuck: 8 Simple Steps To Solving Any Problem, 2002. Named One of 25 Outstanding Broadcasters USA Today, 1995-96, 100 Most Influential Talkers, Legend La., 1996, Best Female Talk Show Host, Nartash, 1996, 97, Female Talk Show Host of Yr., Vanity Fair Hall of Fame, 1996. Mem. APA (bd. dirs. 1994-97), Phi Kappa Phi (Communicator of Yr. award 1992). Office: c/o WOR Radio 1440 Broadway Fl 23 New York NY 10018-2390*

BROWNE, M. LYNNE, optician, artist; b. Houston, Sept. 15, 1958; d. Drew Arthur Browne and Marlena Kay Shofner. Student, Tex. Woman's U. Cert. dispensing optician. Optician Tex. State Optical, Lewisville, 1986-99; customer svc. Fed. Emergency Mgmt. Agy., Denton, Tex., 1999—. Freelance artist. Mem. Nat. Mus. Women in the Arts. Mem. NAFE. Avocations: reading, photography, flowers, animals. Office: Tex State Optical 1124 W Main St Lewisville TX 75067-3469

BROWNE, NICOLE N. elementary school educator; b. Bklyn., N.Y., July 11, 1972; life ptnr. Garrett Malcom Utley, Oct. 4, 2003. MEd, Hunter Coll., 1999. Elem. tchr. Bd. of Edn., Bklyn., 1997—. Mem.: Alpha Kappa Alpha. Democrat. Avocation: travel. Office: Pub Sch 114 Ryder Elem 1077 Remsen Ave Brooklyn NY 11236 Personal E-mail: nicolebrowne@earthlink.net.

BROWNE, RUTH, health science association administrator; Student, U. W. Indies; B, Princeton U.; MS in pub. health, MS in pub. policy, U. Mich.; PhD, Sch. Pub. Health, Harvard U., 2000. Asst. clinical prof. Coll. Health Related Professions, Dept. Preventive Medicine, SUNY Downstate Med. Ctr., exec. dir. Arthur Ashe Inst. Urban Health, 1993—. Investigator Nat. Cancer Inst.; cons. Internat. Program and Pub. Policy Funders Concerned About AIDS; rsch. cons. NY Task Force on Immigrant Health; mem. Nat. Coalition 100 Black Women/Cmty. Svcs. Fund, bd. dirs. Author: (papers included in) Task Force Report on Immigrant Health in NYC. Office: AAIUH 450 Clarkson Ave Box 1232 Brooklyn NY 11203-2098 Office Phone: 718-270-3101.*

BROWNELL, NORA MEAD, federal agency administrator; b. Erie, Pa., May 18, 1947; d. George J. and Mary E. (Burke) Mead; m. Frederic M. Brownell, Sept. 9, 1972 (div.); children: Samantha, Peter, Alexa. Student, Manhattanville Coll., 1965-66, U. Syracuse, N.Y., 1966-69. Auction dir. channel 12 Stas. WHYY, Phila., 1980-81; inaugural dir., campaign cons. Re-election Campaign for Gov. Thornburgh, Harrisburg, 1981-82; dep. exec. asst. Gov. Richard Thornburgh, Harrisburg, Pa., 1982-87; v.p. corp. community rels. Meridian Bancorp, Inc., Phila., 1987-92; sr. v.p. corp. affairs Meridian Bancorp, Inc., Corestates Bancorp., 1992-96; acting exec. dir. Regional Performing Arts Ctr. Inc., 1997; apptd. commissioner Pa. Pub. Utility Commission, 1997—2001; comnr. FERC, Washington, 2001—. Bd. dirs. NARUC, Times Pub. Co., Pa. Free Libr., Need Indeed, Please Touch Mus., Pa. Humanities Council, Susquehanna Art Mus., NRRI, Millennium Bank. Mem. Greater Phila. Cultural Alliance, Harmony House, Bus. Vols. for the Arts. Office: FERC 888 First St NE Washington DC 20426-4205

BROWNELL, PATRICIA JANE, social worker, educator; b. Platteville, Wis., July 14, 1943; d. Richard and Thelma (Rowe) B.; m. James Gale Collins, Mar. 5, 1996. BA, U. Wis., 1967; MSW, Fordham U., 1978, PhD, 1994. Cert. social worker, N.Y. Caseworker dept. social svcs. Human Resources Adminstrn., N.Y.C., 1967-73, project coord. office spl. housing svcs., 1973-77, project mgr. office adminstrv. svcs., 1977-78, grants mgr., rsch. asst., sr. planner policy/program devel., 1978-83, exec. asst. to exec. dep. and dep. commr. home care svcs., 1983-90, dir. spl. projects office exec. dep. commr. family support, 1990-94, dep. dir. non-residential svcs. domestic violence program, 1994, adv. to exec. dep. commr. family support adminstrn., 1995—; from instr. to adj. prof. Fordham U. Grad. Sch. Social Svc., N.Y.C., 1990-94, asst. prof., 1995—. Vis. prof. behavioral sci. dept. Police Acad./N.Y.C. Police Dept., 2001—; adv. bd. Mary's House, 2000—; sec. DW Fin. Mgmt. Agy., 1995-97; cons. N.Y.C. Dept. for the Aging, 1998—; rsch. assoc. Ctr. for Hispanic Mental Health Rsch., 2000—; ad hoc coord. Fordham-St. James Field Placement and Cmty. Practice Project, 2000—; steering com. Interdisciplinary Ctr. for Family and Child Advocacy, 1997—; dir. profl. devel. Interdisciplinary Tng. for Pub. Child Welfare Workers and Supr. to Improve Child Welfare Svcs., 1997-2000; liaison Influencing State Policy, 1997— Co-author: Work with Older People: Challenges and Opportunities, 1994, Helping Battered Women: New Perspectives and Remedies, 1996, Social Work in Juvenile and Criminal Justice Settings, 2d edit., 1997, Multicultural Perspectives in Working with Families, 1997; (with E.P. Congress and I. Abelman) Battered Women and their Families: Intervention and Treatment Strategies, 1998; (with J. Berman) To Grandmother's House We Go and Stay: Perspectives on Custodial Grandparents, 2000; (with M. Moch) Social Work in the Era of Devolution: Toward a Just Practice, 2001; mem. editl. bd. (newsletter) Victimization of the Elderly and Disabled: Preventing Abuse, Mistreatment and Neglect, 1997—; contbr. articles to profl. jours. Bd. dirs. Fund for the Advancement Social Svcs., 1998—; steering com. N.Y.C. Elder Abuse Coalition, 1995—. Faculty Rsch. grantee Fordham U., 1996-97, 99—, N.Y.C. Dept. for the Aging grant, 1999—; Ravazzin scholar Ravazzin Ctr. for Social Work Rsch. in Aging, 1998—; Rational Emotive Inst. fellow, 1995; recipient Linda Mills Meml. award N.Y. State Divsn. Parole, 1993, Faculty Merit award, 1996-2000. Mem. NASW (welfare reform task force N.Y. chpt. 1994—, nominating com., del. assembly 2000—), State Soc. on Aging N.Y. (nominating com. 1999—, exec. com., co-chair social policy com. 2001—) Avocations: reading, yoga, drawing. Office: Fordham U Grad Sch Social Svc 113 W 60th St New York NY 10023 E-mail: brownell@fordham.edu.

BROWNELL, SUSAN ELAINE, anthropologist, educator; b. Bethesda, Md., Oct. 8, 1960; d. Robert Burton Brownell and Claudia Strite. BA, U. Va., 1982; PhD, U. Calif., Santa Barbara, 1990. Vis. asst. prof. Middlebury Coll., Vt., 1990—91; lectr. U. Wash., Seattle, 1991—92, Yale U., New Haven, 1992—93, vis. assoc. prof., 2000; asst. prof. U. Mo., St. Louis, 1994—98, assoc. prof., 1998—, chair dept. anthropology, 2002—. Mem. rsch. coun. Internat. Olympic Com. Olympic Studies Ctr., Lausanne, Switzerland, 2000—. Author: Training the Body for China: Sports in the Moral Order of the People's Republic, 1995; co-editor: Chinese Femininities/Chinese Masculinities: A Reader, 2002.

BROWNER, CAROL M. former federal agency administrator; d. Michael Browner and Isabella Harty Hugues; m. Michael Podhorzer; 1 child, Zachary. Grad., U. Fla., 1977, JD, 1979. Gen. counsel govt. ops. com. Fla. Ho. of Reps., 1980; with Citizen Action, Washington; chief legis. aide environ. issues to Sen. Lawton Chiles, 1986—88; legis. dir. to Sen. Al Gore, Jr., 1988-91; sec. Dept. Environ. Regulation, Fla., 1991-93; administr. EPA, Washington, 1993—2001; principal The Albright Group L.L.C., 2001—. Mem. adv. coun. Harvard Med. Sch., Ctr. for Health and the Global Environment. Democrat. Office: The Albright Group 901 15th St NW Ste 1000 Washington DC 20005*

BROWNFIELD, SYBIL EDEN, trade association administrator, writer; b. Fontana, Calif., Jan. 2, 1966; d. John Petri Brownfield and Elise Charlotte Smiley; m. Richard Lawrence Edwards, Oct. 31, 1998; 1 child, Vivienne Eden. BA in creative writing, U. of Redlands (Calif.), 1989; MFA in English, U. Calif., Irvine, 1992. Notary pub. Calif. Adminstrv. asst. Swiss Life, Chgo., 1994; instr. Calif. CC and Calif. State U., 1995—2000; adminstrv. asst. global trade banking Union Bank of Calif., LA, 1998; exec. adminstrv. asst. to CFO Frederick's of Hollywood, 2000—02. Proofreader for pvt. investigator, Irvine, Calif., 1992, proofreader CINAHL, Glendale, Calif., 1998—99. Vol. Jobs for Youth of Chgo., 1994. Recipient 1st Pl., Acad. Am. Poets, Hon. Mention. Democrat. E-mail: redwards@usc.edu.

BROWN-GLOVER, PATRICIA, special education services professional; d. William Edward and Ruby Kenney Brown; m. E. L. Glover, Aug. 6, 1983; children: Brian B. Glover, Brennen B. Glover. BS, Old Dominion U., 1982; M in Spl. Edn., Va. Commonwealth U., 1990. Cert. spl. edn., adminstrn. and supervision Va. Dept. Edn., 2003. Tchr. King George (Va.) Pub. Schs., 1982—84, Richmond (Va.) Pub. Schs., 1984—89, transition planner, 1995—2001; tng. assoc. Va. Commonwealth U., Richmond, 1989—95; project coord. Coll. William and Mary, Williamsburg, Va., 2001—02; tchr./mentor Chesterfield (Va.) County Pub. Schs., 2002—04, mental disabilities liaison, 2004—; cons./owner Connection Plus Consulting, Richmond, 2002—. Contbr. chapters to books, articles to profl. jours. Amb.-vol. Leukemia and Lymphoma Soc. Va., Richmond, 2000; parent rep. sch. adv. com. Maggie L. Walker Governor's Sch., Richmond, 2002; mem. Parent Ednl. Advocacy Tng. Ctr., Springfield, Va., 2002. Mem.: NEA, Coun. Exceptional Children, Parent Tchr. Assn., Delta Sigma Theta. Home: 3200 Kenmore Rd Richmond VA 23225 Office: Instrn Divsn Ctr 2318 McRae Rd Richmond VA 23235 Office Fax: 804-560-9180. Personal E-mail: pbrownglover@cs.com. E-mail: pat_brownglover@ccpsnet.net.

BROWNING, CANDACE, corporate financial executive; B in History, Brandeis U., 1977; MBA in Mktg., Columbia U., 1979. Analyst airline industry; dep. dir. global rsch. product Pan-Europe MLEMEA Rsch. Mgmt., London, 2000—01; rsch. analyst Merrill Lynch and Co., N.Y.C., 1990, sr. v.p., head global securities rsch. and econs. group, 2003—, dir. equity rsch. for Ams. region, 2001—03. Mem.: Soc. Airline Analysts, Wings Club (bd. dirs.). Office: Merrill Lynch & Co Inc 4 World Financial Center New York NY 10080*

BROWNING, JANE LOUISE, social services administrator; b. Omaha, Dec. 7, 1947; d. Dale Paul and Esther Lucille (Quick) Schmidt; m. John William Browning III, July 29, 1978; children: John William IV, Paul Cornelius. Student, Northwestern U., 1966-68; BA in English Lit. cum laude, U. Tex., Dallas, 1978. Citizen advocacy coord. The Arc of Denver, 1972-74; pub. info. specialist The Arc of the U.S., Arlington, Tex., 1974-78; asst. dir. Ark. Endowment for Humanities, Little Rock, 1979-82, exec. dir., 1982-89; pres., CEO Word Work, Little Rock, 1989-90; dir. devel. The Arc of Md., Annapolis, 1991-95; exec. dir. Md. Coalition for Inclusive Edn., Balt., 1995-96; dir. divsn. membership & publs. NASW, Washington, 1997-98; exec. dir President's com. on mental retardation, Washington, 1999—2000; dep. dir. Nat. Assn. Women Judges, 2001; exec. dir. Learning Disabilities Assn., 2001—. Exec. com. Ark. Developmental Disabilities Coun., Little Rock, 1982-87; appointee, mem. Pres.'s Com. on Mental Retardation, Washington, 1994-2000; mem. nominating com. The Arc-U.S., The Arc-U.S. Congress States, 1997—. Co-author: (textbook) An Arkansas History for Young People, 1991, 3d edit., 2002. Mem. PEO, Am. Soc. Assn. Execs. Democrat. Episcopalian.

BROWNING, SINCLAIR, writer; b. Long Beach, Calif., Nov. 17, 1946; d. George William Sinclair, Rowena Mae Morse; m. William Docker Browning, Dec. 17, 1974; 1 child, Benjamin Sinclair stepchildren: Christopher, Logan, Courtenay; m. Allyn D. Bates, Sept. 2, 1966 (div. Aug. 1974). BA in Lit. and Creative Writing, U. Ariz., 1970. Judge Shamus Awards Pvt. Eye Writers, 2001; judge Edgar Awards Mystery Writers of Am., N.Y.C., 2002; judge best 1st novel St. Martin's Press, 2000; judge best novel Edgar, 2002, Shamus, 2002. Author: Enju, 1983, America's Best, 1995, The Last Song Dogs, 1999, The Sporting Club, 2000, Rode Hard, Put Away Dead, 2001, Crack Shot, 2002, Hot Biscuits, 2002, Tragedy Ann, 2003; co-author: Lyons on Horses, 1991, Hot and Sultry Night for Crime, 2003; editor: Feathers Brush My Heart, 2002. Nominee Ariz. Arts award, 2000. Mem.: Private Eye Writers of Am., Internat. Assn. of Crime Writers, Sisters in Crime, Mystery Writers of Am., Authors Guild. Avocations: horseback riding, reading. Mailing: PO Box 402 Sonoita AZ 85637

BROWNLEE, DELPHINE, actress, musician; b. Paris, July 19, 1930; d. John Donald and Carla (Oddone) B.; m. Dan Oluf Eriksen, Apr. 24,1954 (div. June 1958); 1 child, Lynn Michele; m. Theodore Robert Bashkow, Sept. 12, 1960. Grad., Neighborhood Playhouse, N.Y., 1949. Tchr. pvt. studio, 1977—; adj. prof. Montclair State U., 1981-84; faculty Conservatory Hackley Sch., 1985-90, Mt. Kisco Sch. Music. Several voice overs for TV and radio commercials, recitals at Carnegie Recital Hall, opera performances with Singers Theatre; original cast of Man of La Mancha, Fade-Out, Fade-In, Here's Love, Carnival, others. Mem. N.Y. Singing Tchrs. Assn., N.Y. State Music Tchrs. Assn., Nat. Coun. Jewish Women (past pres. No. Westchester sect. 1971-73), Actor's Equity Assn., Screen Actors Guild, Am. Federations TV and Radio Artists. Avocations: gardening, reading, birdwatching. Home: 92 Jay St Katonah NY 10536-3729

BROWNLEE, JUDITH MARILYN, priestess, psychotherapist, psychic; b. Beaumont, Tex., May 16, 1940; d. Alvin Maurice and Juanita M. (Whittington) B.; m. Theodore Blakey Peak, Apr. 12, 1974 (div. 1981); 1 child, Daniel David Brownlee Peak; m. Floyd S. Bond, Aug. 18, 1996. BA, Lamar U., Beaumont, Tex., 1962; postgrad., U. Denver, 1971; MA, Avalon Inst., Boulder, Colo., 1992; student, Our Lady Perpetual Responsibility, The Silent Cir., 1975-79. Wiccan priestess; cert. master tarot reader Am. Tarot Assn. Tchr. Deer Trail (Colo.) H.S., 1963-64, Lutcher Stark H.S., Orange, Tex., 1967-69; libr. technician Denver Pub. Libr., 1970-73; bus. exec. Weight Watchers Rocky Mtn., Denver, 1974; mail order divsn. mgr. Mile High Comics and Books, Denver, 1975-81; religious tchr. The Silent Cir., Denver, 1979-83; gov. employee Colo. Atty. Gen. Office, Denver, 1983-92; minister Fortress Temple, Denver, 1984-96; psychotherapist, 1992—; counselor Profl. Psychic Counselors Network, 1993-96, Morningstar Inc., 1997, Oracle Tree New Age Mall, 1997-2000, Astrological Health, 2001—03. Presenter, Am. Tarot Assn. Rocky Mountain Regional Conf., 1999; pub. spkr. Denver, 1988—, Spring Mysteries Festival, Seattle, 1988-92; workshop leader Spring Mysteries Festival, Seattle, 1988, 92, Dragonfest Pagan Festival, Denver, 1987-92; lectr. Isis Metaphys. Ctr., workshop leader, 1985—; lectr. Raven & Rose Bookstore, Ft. Collins Colo., 1992-93, Enchanted Chalice Bookstore, 1994-2000, Herbs & Arts Bookstore, 1996, Spirit Ways Bookstore, 1998; organizer Front Range Pagan Festival, 1985; guest spkr. Greeley (Colo.) Unitarian Fellowship, 1992, 1st Mennonite Ch., Denver, 2002; spkr. Rocky Mountain Fiction Writers Conv., 1993; creator, dir. Edn. for Pagan Youth com. Pagan Sch., 1990-94, 96-97; spkr. in field. Author: Pagan Parenting, 1987, The Wheel of the Year, 1988; contbr. articles to profl. jours.; participant Dedication to Faith, Images and Voices, 1999, Roundtable Discussions with Artist and Spiritual Leaders, 1999. Interviewee KOA Radio, 1984, 92, 95, 96, KNUS and KYBG, 1992, KUSA Channel 9, 1987, 90, Rocky Mountain News, Denver, 1992, Denver Post, 1996, 2000, 2001; cmty. prodr. Mile High Cablevision, 1987; tel. counselor Lifeline of Colo., Denver, 1988; field tng. supr. Iliff Sch. Theology, Denver, 1995-96; bd. dirs. Inst. for Interfaith [illegible] U. Denver, 1999-2003. Recipient Hart and Crescent Disting. Youth Svc. award Covenant of the Goddess, 1995. Mem. Colo. Assn. Psychotherapists, Assn. Past Life Rsch. and Therapy, Daus. of New Moon (founder, facilitator), Soc. for Creative Anachronism (Colo. founder, CEO 1970-73, treas. 1981-83), Denver Area Sci. Fiction Assn. (editor 1969-70, dir. 1974-75, conf. chmn. 1970-75), Denver Area Interfaith Clergy Conf., Covenant Unitarian Universalist Pagans. Avocations: reading, theatre, films, science fiction, internet. Office: PO Box 172271 Denver CO 80217-2271 E-mail: judith1152@aol.com.

BROWNLEE, KARIN S. state legislator; m. Doug Brownlee; 4 children. BS in Microbiology, Kans. State U. Co-owner Patrons Mortgage Co.; mem. Kans. Senate, Topeka, 1996—, mem. commerce com., mem. fin. instns. and ins. com., 1996—, mem. utilities com., mem. claims against the state com., mem. arts and cultural resources com. Mem. steering com. Leadership Olathe, 1994—; mem. QPA issues com. Olathe Sch. Dist., 1993; mem. adv. com. Mahaffie Farmsted; women's ministry leader Olathe Bible Ch.; del. Rep. Nat. Conv., 1996; vice chair Johnston Rep. Party, 1994-96; chair Olathe Rep. Party, 1992-94. Mem. Olathe Area C. of C. Republican. Office: 300 SW 10th Ave Rm 143-n Topeka KS 66612-1504

BROWNLEE, PAULA PIMLOTT, higher education consultant, former academic administrator; b. London, June 23, 1934; came to U.S., 1959; d. John Richard and Alice A. (Ajamian) Pimlott; m. Thomas H. Brownlee, Feb. 10, 1961; children: Kenneth Gainsford, Elizabeth Ann, Clare Louise. BA with honors, Somerville Coll., Oxford (Eng.) U., 1957, PhD in Organic Chemistry, 1959. Postdoctoral fellow U. Rochester, N.Y., 1959-61; rsch. chemist Am. Cyanamid Co., Stamford, Conn., 1961-62; lectr. U. Bridgeport, Conn., 1968-70; asst. prof., then assoc. prof. Rutgers U., N.J., 1970-76, assoc. dean, then acting dean Douglass Coll., 1972-76; dean faculty, prof. chemistry Union Coll., Schenectady, N.Y., 1976-81; pres., prof. chemistry Hollins U., Va., 1981-90; pres. Assn. Am. Colls. and Univs., Washington, 1990-98; prin. Pres.' Group, LLC, 1997—2003; founding prin. Nat. Acad. for Acad. Leadership. Bd. dirs. Acad. Search Consultation Svc. Author lab. manual; contbr. articles and chpts. to profl. publs. Sr. trustee U. Rochester; bd. dirs. Buena Vista U. Hon. fellow Somerville Coll., Oxford, Eng., 1996—. Mem. Am. Chem. Soc., Cosmos Club, Sigma Xi. Episcopalian.

BROWNMILLER, SUSAN, author, feminist activist; b. Bklyn., Feb. 15, 1935; Student, Cornell U., 1952-55. Asst. to mng. editor Coronet, N.Y., 1959-60; editor Albany Report, 1961-62; nat. affairs rschr. Newsweek, N.Y., 1963-64; staff writer Village Voice, N.Y., 1965; reporter NBC-TV, Phila., 1965; network newswriter ABC-TV, N.Y.C., 1966-68; free-lance journalist, 1968-70. Author: Shirley Chisholm, 1970, Against Our Will: Men, Women and Rape, 1975, Femininity, 1984, Waverly Place, 1989, Seeing Vietnam: Encounters of the Road and Heart, 1994, In Our Time: Memoir of a R2volution, 1999. Address: 61 Jane St New York NY 10014

BROWN-OLMSTEAD, AMANDA, public relations executive; b. Oct. 7, 1943; Founder ABOA (formerly a division of Shandwick PLC from 1998 to 1996), 1974; pres., CEO A Brown Olmstead Assocs., Atlanta. Mem. exec. com. Pub. Rels. Soc. Am. Counselors Acad.; mem. Pub. Rels. Soc. Am. Eligibility Bd., Atlanta Pub. Rels. Seminar Group. Bd. mem. Central Atlanta Progress, Councilors for The Carter Ctr., Atlanta Botanical Garden; mem. adv. bd. Sheperd Spinal Ctr., U. Miss. Bus. Sch.; mem. adv. guild Clark U.; mem. Emory Bd. Visitors, Georgia State Bus. Sch., Paralympics Congress Adv. Bd.; pres. Georgia chpt. Internat. Women's Forum; mem. Centennial Olympics Park Leadership Com. Named a Recognized Woman of Achievement, Internat. Women's Forum; named one of The Ten Outstanding Atlantans; named to Georgia Pub. Rels. Hall of Fame; recipient Gold Medal, N.Y. Film and TV Festival, Silver Anvil, Pub. Rels. Soc. Am.; fellow Pub. Rels. Soc. Am. Mem.: British Am. Bus. Group, Order of the Phoenix, Leadership Atlanta. Achievements include being featured in Mademoiselle magazine, Business Week, Savvy, Atlanta Weekly, Atlanta magazine, and Movers and Shakers in Georgia. Office: A Brown Olmstead Assocs 274 W Paces Ferry Rd NW Atlanta GA 30305-1167

BROWNSON, MARY LOUISE, counselor, educator, artist; b. Detroit, Dec. 8, 1927; d. Max Curt Poppe and Hilda Caroline Larson; m. Elwyn James Brownson, Dec. 30, 1950 (div. Sept. 1979); children: Elwyn James, Richard, Matthew, Mary. B of Design, U. Mich., Ann Arbor, 1950; MS, No. Mont. Coll., Havre, 1976. Cert. secondary sch. tchr. Mont., 1972. Instr. Wittenburg U., Springfield, Ohio, 1950—53, No. Mont. Coll., Havre, 1963—71; drug and alcohol counselor Alcohol Svcs. Ctr., Boise, Idaho, 1979—80; migrant career placement counselor Boise State U., Idaho, 1981—85; mgr. Ctr. Use, Boise Sr. Ctr., Idaho, 1985—88; employment counselor Fed. Cmty. Treatment Ctr., Boise, Idaho, 1988—90; mgr. activities Hillcrest Retirement Ctr., Boise, Idaho, 1990—94. Represented in permanent collections, Kent State U. Collection. Pres. PTA, Havre, Mont.; Dem. candidate for state legislature Havre, Mont. Mem.: AAUW (pres.), LWV (pres. 1999—2003). Democrat. Unitarian-Universalist. Avocations: gourmet cooking, swimming, reading, painting. Home: 3820 Sheringham Dr Boise ID 83704

BROWNSTEIN, BARBARA LAVIN, geneticist, educator, university official; b. Phila., Sept. 8, 1931; d. Edward A. and Rose (Silverstein) Lavin; m. Melvin Brownstein, June 1949 (div. 1955); children: Judith Brownstein Kaufmann, Dena. Asst. editor Biol. Abstracts, Phila., 1957-58; research fellow dept. microbial genetics Karolinska Inst., Stockholm, 1962-64; assoc. Wistar Inst., Phila., 1964-68; assoc. prof. molecular biology, dept. biology Temple U., Phila., 1968-74, prof., 1974-96, prof. emeritus, 1996—, chmn. dept., 1978-81, provost, 1983-90; sr. assoc. Ctr. Ednl. Rsch. U. Wash., Seattle, 1994—. Vis. scientist dept. tumor cell biology Imperial Cancer Rsch. Fund Labs., London, 1973-74; bd. dirs. Univ. City Sci. Ctr., Greater Phila. Econ. Devel. Coun., Forum Exec. Women; program officer NSF, 1992-93; sr. assoc. Inst. Ednl. Inquiry, Seattle, 1994—. Bd. dirs. Lopez Island Sch., 2001—. Recipient Liberal Arts Alumni award for excellence in teaching Temple U., 1980; recipient Outstanding Faculty Woman award Temple U., 1980 Fellow AAAS; mem. Am. Soc. Cell Biology, N.Y. Acad. Sci., Assn. Women in Sci., NSF (program officer 1992-93). Home: PO Box 835 Lopez Island WA 98261 Office: Inst Ednl Inquiry 124 E Edgar St Seattle WA 98102 E-mail: bbrownst@msn.com.

BROWN-WAITE, VIRGINIA (GINNY BROWN-WAITE), congresswoman; b. Albany, N.Y., Oct. 5, 1943; m. Harvey Waite; children: Jeannien Roxby Waite, Danene Mitchell, Sue Meaders, Lorie Sue. BS, SUNY, 1976; MS, Russell Sage Coll., 1984. Former commr. Hernando County; former legis. dir. N.Y. State Senate; mem. Fla. State Senate, 1992—2002, U.S. Ho. of Reps. from 5th Fla. dist., 2003—. Active W Hernando GOP, United Way; bd. dirs. Hernando County Spouse Abuse Ctr. Mem. Bus. and Profl. Women's Club, Suncoast MG Club. Roman Catholic.

BROWN-ZEKERI, LOLITA MOLANDA, elementary school educator; b. Stephens County, Mar. 15, 1963; d. James and Doris (Phillips) Brown; m. Austin Zekeri, Nov. 21, 1998; 1 child: Annabelle Lola. BS with honors, North Ga. Coll., 1985, MEd, 1989, EdS, 1994. Cert. tchr. Tchr., 2nd grade Jackson County Bd. Edn., Nicholson, Ga., 1985-87, chpt. 1 tchr., 1987—98, third grade tchr., 1998—. Chmn. grade level Jackson County Bd. Edn., 2002—03. Author: Exploring Blue Highways, 1995; co-author: Making Learning Funner, So People Want To Learn, A Longitudinal Study of Students' Perceptions About Schooling. Active Paradise AME Ch. trustee 1986-99, asst. Sun. Sch. sec. 1986-99, Sun. Sch. sec., 1999—, young adult choir mem. 1987-2001, Christian Edn. Youth Dept. 2d v.p. 1988—, Vacation Bible Sch. art coord. and tchr. 1986—. Mem. Ga. Edn. Assn., Assn. Childhood Edn. [illegible] Union Bd. (chmn. decorations/hospitality com. 1983-84, sec. 1984-85), Benton Parent/Tchr. Orgn.

BROYLES, BONITA EILEEN, nursing educator; b. Ross County, Ohio, Sept. 29, 1948; d. Arthur Runnels and Mary Elizabeth (Page) Brookie; m. Roger F. Broyles, Dec. 29, 1984; children: Michael Richard Brown, Jeffrey Allen Brown. BSN, Ohio State U., 1970; MA with honors, N.C. Cen. U., Durham, 1988; EdD summa cum laude, LaSalle U., 1996; PhD, St. Regis U., 2004. ADN instr., CPR instr. Piedmont C.C., Roxboro, N.C.; instr. nursing Watts Sch. Nursing, Durham; res. float staff nurse Durham County Gen. Hosp., Durham; dir. practical nursing edn., instr. Piedmont C.C., Roxboro, N.C.; maternity patient tchr. Mt. Carmel Med. Ctr., Columbus, Ohio. Second-level coord. assoc. degree nursing faculty Piedmont Community Coll., 1990—. Co-author: Test Manual for Bowden, Dickey, Greenberg Children and Their Families: The Continuum of Care, 1998; author: Clinical Companion for Ashwill and Droske Nursing of Children: Principles and Practice, 1997; author: (with Reiss and Evans) Pharmacological Aspects of Nursing Care, revised 6th edit., 2002; author: Dosage Calculation Practice for Nurses, 2003, Medical-Surgical Nursing Clinical Companion, 2004. Named ADN Educator of Yr. N.C. Assoc. Degree Nursing Coun., 1993; recipient nat. tchg. excellence award Nat. Inst. Staff Orgnl. Devel., U. Tex., Austin, 1998, Faculty Excellence award Piedmont Comty. Coll., 2001. Office: Piedmont CC Sch Nursing College St Roxboro NC 27573

BROYLES, CHRISTINE ANNE, art educator; d. H.C. and Dorothy E. Lippstreuer; m. Robert E. Broyles, Dec. 30, 1989. BFA, B in Art Edn., U. South Fla., 1981. Cert. tchr. Fla., Nat. Assn. Underwater Instrs. Intern Charlotte County Pub. Schs., Port Charlotte, Fla., 1981, sci. tchr. Lemon Bay H.S., 1981—83, art instr. grades 6-8 L. A. Ainger Mid. Sch. Rotonda West, Fla., 1984—; adult edn. tchr. (arts and GED) Charlotte County Adult and Cmty. Edn., Englewood, Fla., 1982—85; adult edn. tchr. (arts) Sarasota (Fla.) Vocat. and Tech. Sch., 1982—85, Venice (Fla.) Area Art League, 1982—86; freelancer, guest writer Suncoast Media Group, Venice, 1982—. Layout editor Charlotte County Lit. and Fine Arts Mag., Port Charlotte, 1999—2001; mem. supt.'s roundtable forum Charlotte County Pub. Schs., Port Charlotte, 1999—2001, secondary fine arts liason, 1998—, dept. head (elective subjects) L. A. Ainger Mid. Sch., Rotonda West, 2000—, EXCEL mentor tchr., Port Charlotte, 1999—, mem. code of student conduct com., 1999, mem. pupil progression plan com., 99, mem. student assistance team, 2000; trainer Beacon Learning Ctr., Panama City, Fla., 2001—; webmaster, co-creator, editor The Art Web; dir. instrnl. pers. Charlotte County Classified and Tchrs. Assn., Punta Gorda, 1995—96, v.p., 1996—98; mem. specification and validation com. Fla. Tchr. Certification Exam, 1984, 2004, tech. and lit. coun., 1999—; presenter in field. Author: (teacher resource book) Art Across the Curriculum. Named Educator of Yr., Sunshine Rotary of Englewood, 1998, Tchr. of Yr. (local), Wal-Mart, 1998, Sam's Club, 1998; recipient Best of Show award, Arts and Humanities Coun. Port Charlotte, 1999; grantee, Fla. Arts and Humanities Coun., 1996—98; scholar, Am. Legion Aux., 1975—80; arts program scholar, Fla. Ctr. for Tchrs., 2000. Mem.: Fla. Art Edn. Assn., Fla. League Tchrs., Nat. Art Edn. Assn. Avocations: scuba diving, travel, arts, antiquing. Office: L A Ainger Mid Sch 245 Cougar Way Rotonda West FL 33947

BROYLES, JUDITH ANN, accountant; b. Worcester, Mass., Aug. 21, 1947; d. Ernest Gunnar and Jane Kathryn Silverberg; m. William Eugene Broyles, May 25, 1966 (dec. May 1996); children: Ronald, Scott, Cynthia Wood, Kimberly. BBA, Kennesaw State U., 2000, MBA, 2003. Acct. Dixie Group Inc., Calhoun, Ga., 1999—2001; CEO Comp-U-Tax, Calhoun, 1970—2003, Comp-U-Rent, Calhoun, 2001—. Mem.: NAFE, Nat. Soc. Pub. Accts., Calhoun C. of C. Avocations: writing, gardening, art. Office: Comp-U-Rent 204 W Belmont Dr Calhoun GA 30701*

BROZOWSKI, LAURA ADRIENNE, mechanical engineer; b. Yokohama, Japan, May 12, 1960; arrived in U.S., 1961; d. John and Muriel Sydney (Jackson) Brozowski. BSME, U. Calif., 1982; MSME, Calif. State U., 1987; MBA, Pepperdine U., 1988. Registered profl. engr., Calif.; cert. profl. mgr. Inst. Cert. Profl. Mgrs. Engring. scientist Boeing Co., Canoga Park, Calif., 1982—. Author: in field. Recipient Space Achievement Mid Career award, Rotary Nat., Rotary Nat. award for Space Achievement, 2003, Stellar award, 2003. Fellow: Inst. Advancement Engring.; mem.: NSPE, ASME, Nat. Mgmt. Assn. Avocations: music, continuing education, dance.

BRUBACH, HOLLY BETH, writer; b. Pitts., Dec. 7, 1953; d. David J. and Dorothy Elizabeth (DeRusha) B. BA in English and History, Duke U., 1975. Freelance writer, 1975-78; staff writer Vogue mag., N.Y.C., 1978-82, contbg. editor, 1983-87; staff writer The Atlantic, Boston, 1982-87; fashion editor The New Yorker, N.Y.C., 1988—94, The New York Times Mag., N.Y.C., 1994—98; dir. sports clothing & home design Prada, N.Y.C., 1998—2001. Author: (with others) Choura: The Memoirs of Alexandra Danilova, 1986 (De La Torre Bueno award), Girlfriend: Men, Women and Drag, 1999, A Dedicated Follower of Fashion, 1999; scriptwriter Dance in America, 1980. Editorial adv. bd. Duke U. Alumni mag., 1986—. Recipient Nat. Mag. award Am. Soc. Mag. Editors, 1982. Mem. Dance Critics Assn., Writers Guild Am. Presbyterian.*

BRUBAKER, KAREN SUE, small business owner; b. Ashland, Ohio, Feb. 5, 1953; d. Robert Eugene and Dora Louise (Camp) B. BSBA, Ashland U., 1975; MBA, Bowling Green State U., 1976. Supr. tire ctr. ops. B.F. Goodrich Co., Akron, Ohio, 1976-77, supr. tire ctr. acctg., 1977-79, asst. product mgr. radial passenger tires, 1979-80, product mgr. broadline passenger tires, 1980-81, group product mgr. broadline passenger and light truck tires, 1981-83, mktg. mgr. T/A high tech radials, 1983-86; product mktg. mgr. B.F. Goodrich T/A radials The Uniroyal Goodrich Tire Co., Akron, Ohio, 1986-91; product mktg. mgr. Michelin performance tires Michelin Americas Small Tires, Akron, Ohio, 1991-95; ind. EcoQuest Internat. distbr. DBA Indoor Air Repair & Water, Fairlawn, Ohio, 1996—. Sect. chmn. indsl. divsn. United Way, Akron, 1983-86; mem. adv. coun. to trustees Coll. Bus. and Econs, Ashland U., 1990-92; vol. Hospice Vis. Nurses Svcs., 1995--; fund raiser Nat. Heart Assist and Transplant Fund/Judi Reali Transplant Fund, 1996. Recipient Alumni Disting. Service award Ashland Coll., 1986; Alpha Phi Clara Bradley Burdette scholar, 1975. Mem. Am. Mktg. Assn. (pres. Akron/Canton chpt. 1982-83, Highest Honors award 1983, nat. bd. dirs., v.p. bus. mktg. 1984-86, v.p. profl. chpts. 1987-89), Sales and Mktg. Execs. (v.p. membership, 1998-99), Akron Women's Network, Zonta Internat. (membership dir. 1987-94, 96—), Beta Gamma Sigma, Omicron Delta Epsilon. Home: 822 Village Pkwy Fairlawn OH 44333-3297 E-mail: airwaves@bigplanet.com.

BRUCE, BRENDA, pianist; b. Nov. 26, 1942; d. Leo Allen and Dorotha Mae (Russell) Bruce; m. Emmett W. Windham, Feb. 21, 1976 (div. Aug. 1988); m. Alvin Mark Fountain II, June, 2003. BMusic Edn., Ctrl. Meth. Coll., Fayette, Mo., 1964; MMus, New Eng. Conservatory, Boston, 1966; student piano master class, Claude Debussy Conservatory, St. Malo, France, 2000-01. Mem. faculty Dana Sch. Music, Wellesley, Mass., 1965-76, Campbell U., Buies Creek, N.C., 1977-79, Meredith Coll., Raleigh, N.C., 1979-90; pianist SAS Inst., Cary, NC, 1989—2001. Mem. adv. bd. Capitol Area Cmty. Chorus, Raleigh, 1999—; participant Master Class Pro Musica, St. Malo, France, 2000, 01. Performer, recitalist, 1964—, montage and piano, flute duo, 1992. Emerging Artists grantee City of Raleigh, 1992,

Emerging Artists grantee United Arts, 1995, State Arts Coun. grnatee, 1995—, regional artists grantee, 1999-2001, NCMTA grantee. Mem. Nat. Music Tchrs. Assn., Nat. Guild of Piano, Raleigh Piano Tchrs. Assn., Cary-Apex Piano Tchrs. Assn.; Pi Kappa Lampda. Methodist. Avocations: bicycling, travel, Polish dancing. Home: 101 Barbary Ct Cary NC 27511-5862 E-mail: brendabruce@mindspring.com.

BRUCE, MARY HANFORD, academic administrator, educator, writer; d. Francis Hamilton Baldy and Frances Lawson Waterfield; m. Guy Steven Bruce, Mar. 23, 1991; m. David Allan Terry, Oct. 7, 1962 (div. Jan. 8, 1980); children: David Hamilton Terry, John Hanford Terry. PhD, Ariz. State U., Tempe, 1986. Cert. tchr. Ariz., Tenn., Tex. Lectr. Memphis State U., 1968—69, Ariz. State U., Tempe, 1982—85; dir. reading program Monmouth Coll., Reading, England, 2001—04. Dir. Associated Programs of Midwest Program, Harare, Zimbabwe, 1995. Author: Holding to the Light, 1992, Dr. Sally's Voodoo Man, 2003, short stories, numerous poems. Grantee, Mellon Found. Global Ptnrs., Kenya, 2000, 2002, Mellon Found. Global Ptnrs., Tanzania, 2004—. Mem.: AAUP, Associated Writing Programs. Home: 511 E Boston Monmouth IL 61462 Office: Monmouth Coll 700 E Broadway Monmouth IL 61462 Office Phone: 309-457-2183.

BRUCH, CAROL SOPHIE, lawyer, educator; b. Rockford, Ill., June 11, 1941; d. Ernest and Margarete (Willstätter) B.; m. Jack E. Myers, 1960 (div. 1973); children: Margarete Louise Myers Feinstein, Kurt Randall Myers. AB, Shimer Coll., 1960; JD, U. Calif.-Berkeley, 1972; Dr. honoris causa, U. Basel, 2000. Bar: Calif. 1973, U.S. Supreme Ct. 1980. Law clk. to Justice William O. Douglas U.S. Supreme Ct., 1972-73; acting prof. law U. Calif., Davis, 1973—78, prof., 1978—2001, rsch. prof., prof. emeritus, 2001—, chair doctoral program in human devel., 1996—2001. Acad. vis. law dept. U. Munich, 1978-79, 92, U. Cologne, 1990, U. Cambridge, 1990, London Sch. Econs. and Polit. Sci., 1991, Kings Coll., London, 1991; vis. prof. U. Calif., Berkeley, 1983, Columbia U., 1986, U. Basel, 1994, vis. Fulbright prof. Hebrew U., Jerusalem, 1996-97; vis. fellow Fitzwilliam Coll., Cambridge, Eng., 1990, U. Calif. Humanities Rsch. Inst., Irvine, 1999, vis. scholar Inst. for Advanced Legal Studies (Univ. London), 1991; cons. to Ctr. for Family in Transition, 1981, Calif. Law Revision Commn., 1979-82, NOW Legal Def. and Edn. Fund, 1980-81; lectr., legis. drafting and testimony, 1976—; mem. U.S. del. 4th Inter-Am. Specialized Conf. on Pvt. Internat. Law, OAS, 1989. Contbr. articles to legal jours. Editor Calif. Law Rev., 1971; editorial Bd. Family Law Quar., 1980-87; Representing Children, 1995—, Am. Jour. of Comparative Law, 2001—; lectr. in field. Mem. adv. com. child support and child custody Calif. Commn. on Status of Women, 1981-83, child support adv. com. Calif. Jud. Coun., 1991-94, adv. com. on private internat. law U.S. Dept. State, 1989—, internat. child abduction steering com. Internat. Ctr. for Missing and Exploited Children (London), 1999—; host parent Am. Field Service, Davis, 1977-78. Max Rheinstein sr. rsch. fellow Alexander von Humboldt Found., Fed. Republic Germany, 1978-79, 92, Fulbright fellow, Western Europe, 1990, Fulbright Sr. Scholar, Israel, 1997, Disting. Pub. Svc. award U. Calif. Davis Acad. Senate, 1990. Mem. ABA, Calif. State Bar Assn., Am. Law Inst., Internat. Soc. Family Law (exec. coun. 1994-2000, 2002—), Order of Coif. Democrat. Jewish. Office: U Calif Sch Law 400 Mrak Hall Dr Davis CA 95616-5201

BRUCH, RUTH E. information technology executive; BA in fin., U. Iowa. [illegible] Davenport Bank and Trust Co., Iowa; with ctr. bus. innovation Ernst & Young; v.p. and dir. IT planning First Bank Sys. (now US Bank), St. Paul; v.p. and mng. dir. info. sys. Continental Bank (now Bank Am.), Chgo.; prin. JGA Consulting, Barrington, Ill., 1991—93; from dir. info. tech. strategic planning to v.p. and CIO Union Carbide Corp., Danbury, Conn., 1993—99; pres. and COO Zonetrader.com, Chgo., 1999—2000; v.p. and CIO Vistcon Corp., Dearborn, Mich., 2000—02; sr. v.p. and CIO Lucent Tech., Murray Hill, NJ, 2002—. Bd. dir. Mellon Fin. Corp., 2003—; tech. adv. bd. Blue Star Solutions. Home: Chgo. Office: Lucent Tech Inc 600 Mountain Ave Murray Hill NJ 07974*

BRUCKERHOFF, THERESA, business owner, educational researcher; b. Manchester, Vt., Apr. 9, 1961; d. Daniel Xavier Sr. and Alice Winifred Stannard; m. Charles E. Bruckerhoff, Dec. 21, 1986; children: Matthew Charles, Michael Charles. BS in Elem. Edn., Coll. St. Joseph, Rutland, Vt., 1983; MA in Curriculum and Instrn., Cleve. State U., 1991. Day care provider Sugar Maple Day Care, Rutland, 1979-83; classrm. tchr. Rutland Pub. Schs., 1983-85, Shaker Heights (Ohio) Pub. Schs., 1985-91; ops. mgr., asst. rschr. Curriculum Rsch. and Evaluation, Chaplin, Conn., 1995—. Chair SMSJ Sch. Family Assn., Willimantic, Conn., 1998—; pres. Storrs (Conn.) Cmty. Nursery Sch., 1994-95; treas. Beaver Pond Child Devel. Ctr., Chaplin, 1993-94. Office: Curriculum Rsch and Evaluation 237 Singleton Rd Chaplin CT 06235-2223

BRUCK LIEB PORT, LILLY, retired consumer advisor, broadcaster, columnist; b. Vienna, May 13, 1918; came to U.S., 1941, naturalized, 1944; d. Max and Sophie M. Hahn; m. Sandor Bruck, Mar. 7, 1943; 1 child, Sandra Lee (Mrs. John David Evans III); m. David L. Lieb, Dec. 7, 1985; m. Charles S. Port, Nov. 22, 1998. PhD in Econs., U. Vienna; postgrad., Sorbonne, Paris, Sch. of Econs., London, Sch. of Bus., Columbia U., 1941-42, Sch. of Social Work, NYU, 1964-66. Dir. consumer edn. Dept. Consumer Affairs, City of N.Y., 1969-78; project dir. Am. Coalition of Citizens with Disabilities, 1977-78; consumer advisor, broadcaster In Touch Networks, N.Y.C., 1978-90; consumer affairs commentator Nat. Pub. Radio, 1980-82; ret. Author: Access, The Guide to a Better Life for Disabled Americans, 1978; contbr. articles to disability and rehab. to books, ency. and mag. Presid. Scarsdale Hadassah, 1960-68. Chmn. Westchester county, Bonds for Israel, 1960-68; trustee Kol AMI-JCC, White Plains, N.Y.; assoc. Jewish Mus.; sponsor Lilly Bruck Lieb Creative Writing Program, Purchase Coll., SUNY; mem. pres.'s coun. White Plains (N.Y.) Hosp. Recipient Woman of Yr. award Anti Defamation League, 1972. Democrat. Home: 25 Murray Hill Rd Scarsdale NY 10583-2829 E-mail: lblone@aol.com.

BRUCKNER, MARTHA, academic administrator; Bachelor's degree, Master's degree, U. Nebr., Omaha; Doctorate, U. Nebr., Lincoln. Assoc. supt. for ednl. svcs. Millard (Nebr.) Pub. Schs.; tchr. h.s., asst. prin., prin. pub. schs.; assoc. prof., chairperson ednl. adminstrn. U. Nebr., Omaha. Contbr. articles to profl. jours. Recipient award, Nebr. Coun. Sch. Adminstrs., Nebr. Schoolmasters Orgn. Mem.: ASCD (pres.-elect 2003—, bd. dirs., budget liaison, organizer student chpt. U. Nebr., Omaha). Office: Don Stroh Adminstrn Ctr 5606 S 147th St Omaha NE 68137

BRUDNER, HELEN GROSS, social sciences educator; b. NYC; d. Nathan and Mae (Grichtman) Gross; m. Harvey Jerome Brudner, Dec. 18, 1963; children: Mae Ann, Terry Joseph, Jay Scott. BS, NYU, 1959, MA, 1960, PhD, 1973. Tchr. N.Y.C. Bd. Edn., 1959-60; instr. Pratt Inst., Bklyn., 1959-61; asst. prof. history N.Y. Inst. Tech., N.Y.C., 1961-63, dir. guidance, 1962-63; assoc. prof. Fairleigh Dickinson U., Rutherford, N.J., 1963-73, prof. history and polit. sci. Teaneck, N.J., 1974—, dir. Honors Coll. Rutherford, N.J., 1972-84, chmn. dept. social sci., 1980-88, pres. univ. senate, 1975-78, asst. provost, 1983—, dean, 1984, dir. grad. programs, assoc. dir. Sch. History, Polit. and Internat. Studies, 1995—, dir. lang. grad. studies, pres. acad. senate, 1996—; v.p. HJB Enterprises, Highland Park, N.J., 1970—. Vice chmn. bd. dirs. WLC Inc., Highland Park, 1990—; cons. auto ednl. systems, 1971—; participant bd. trustees F.D.U.; spkr. N.J. Com. for The Humanities. Contbr. articles to profl. jours. on constl. law, transfer of tech., futurism. Active women in politics project NSF, 1981; active consortium project women in Am. history NEH and Woodrow Wilson Found., 1980, Consortium on Global Interdependence, Princeton, 1984; bd. dirs. Options Spkrs. Bur., N.J. Credit Union League, N.J. Credit Union Shared Network, WLC Inc.; mem. Mcpl. Alliance Highland Park, Hist. Preservation Commn., Highland Park; chmn. bd. dirs. Fairleigh Dickinson U. Fed. Credit Union, 1987—; vice chmn. N.J. Adv. Com. on Women Vets., 1993—; design selection com. N.J. Korean Vets. Meml.; 2d v.p. bd. dirs. Casitas De Monte Corp., Calif. Recipient Woman of Yr. award Am. Businesswomen's Assn., 1980, Meritorious Svc. award N.J. Credit Union League, 1997, Cert. Spl. Congrl. Recognition, 2000. Mem. Am. Judicature Soc., Am. Hist. Soc., Acad. Polit. Sci., Phi Alpha Theta, Phi Sigma Alpha. Office: Fairleigh Dickinson U Sch History, Polit Internat Studies Teaneck NJ 07666

BRUENE, BARBARA JANE, artist, educator; b. Waterloo, Iowa, June 22, 1936; d. Hazen M. and Mary Lisle Fallgatter; m. Roger Julius Bruene, June 10, 1956; children: James, Bruce. BA, U. No. Iowa, 1958; MA, Iowa State U., 1978; MFA, Drake U., Des Moines, Iowa, 1986. Gallery dir. Coll. of Design Gallery, Iowa State U., Ames, 1988—98; faculty Dept. Art and Design, Iowa State U., Ames, 1975—98, assoc. prof. emerita, 1998—. One-woman shows include Calligraphic Paintings and Artist's Books, Ball State U., Muncie, Ind., 2000, exhibitions include Alpha Mark traveling exhbn., 1999—2001, Artist's Books, Corcoran Gallery of Art, Washington, 1999, numerous other group and solo exhbns. Avocations: reading, travel. Home: 2122 Greeley St Ames IA 50014

BRUESEWITZ-LOPINTO, GAIL C. marketing professional; b. N.Y.C., May 17, 1956; d. Arthur George and Blanche Juliana (Dobos) Bruesewitz; m. Joseph LoPinto, Sept. 1990; children: Frank Joseph, Joseph Arthur. BA in Eng. Lit., SUNY, Binghamton, 1978. Mem. promotion and artist devel. staff Columbia Records/CBS Records, Inc., N.Y.C., 1979-82, dir. nat. dance music mktg., 1982-89; nat. dir. Ear Candy Records, 1990-91; prodn. coord. AIG Risk Mgmt., Inc. divsn. Am. Internat. Group, Inc., N.Y.C., 1991-96, Swiss Reins. Am. Alternative Risk Transfer Div., N.Y.C., 1996-98; meeting and event specialist corp. comm. Swiss Re New Markets, N.Y.C., 1999-2000, Am. Home Assurance Co. AIG, 2004—. Rep. record divsn.Women's Orgn. coun. CBS, Inc., N.Y.C., 1980—82; mem. adv. bd. dance/music New Music Seminar, N.Y.C., 1989—; meeting and event planning cons., 2000—; co-chair catalog com. Grace Ch. Sch Scholarship Benefit Auction, 2002. Editor newsletter Brueser's Boogie Backpage, 1983-90. Bd. dirs. Mt. Tremper (N.Y.) Lutheran Camp and Retreat Ctr., 1976-78, Camp Wilbur Herrlich, Pawling, N.Y., 1990; active Big Sisters, Binghamton (N.Y.) Social Svcs. dept., 1975-78; asst. Sunday Sch. tchr. 1st Presbyn. Ch. Sag Harbor, N.Y., 2000—. Named N.Y. rep. for Mademoiselle mag., 1975. Democrat. Lutheran. Avocations: sailing, dance (jazz and ballet). Office Phone: 212-458-5815. E-mail: gail.lopinto@aig.com.

BRUETT, KAREN DIESL, sales and fundraising consultant; b. N.Y.C., May 15, 1945; d. Francis J. and Dorothy (Peterson) Diesl; m. William H. Bruett, Jr., Mar. 18, 1967; 1 child, Lindsey Diesl. BA in English, St. Lawrence U., 1966; MA, Hunter Coll., 1971. Tchr. English Freeport (N.Y.) pub. schs., 1966-70; exec. interviewer, researcher Louis Harris & Assocs., N.Y.C., 1970-72; dir. adult edn. West Side YMCA, 1972-76, mem. bd. mgrs., 1978-83; v.p. new bus. devel. Gaylord Adams & Assocs., Inc., N.Y.C., 1976-81; account exec. John Blair Mktg., N.Y.C., 1981-83, v.p. sales, 1983-84, sr. v.p., gen. sales mgr., 1984-86; ind. sales and fundraising cons. Bd. dirs. Resolution, Inc., S. Burlington, Vt., HMI, Inc., Norwood, Mass. Trustee St. Lawrence U., 1978—, vice chair trustees, 1995-2001, chair alumni fund, 1983-84, chair annual giving, 1984-88, chair planning com., 1987-88, chair presdl. search com., 1994-95, mem. exec. com., 1987—, chair devel. com., 1988-95, chair nominating com., 1999—, trustee Vt. Coun. on Arts, 1986-91, vice chair bd. trustees, chair devel. com., 1988-91; bd. advisors Somerset Hills Edn. Found., 1997—; del. Am.-Soviet Youth Forum, Baku, USSR, 1974. Mem. Internat. Women's Forum. Home and Office: 110 Mosle Rd Far Hills NJ 07931-2229

BRUGGE, JOAN S. medical educator; BA in Biology, Northwestern U.; PhD in Virology, Baylor U. Postdoctoral rschr. U. Colo. Med. Ctr.; mem. faculty SUNY, Stony Brook, 1979—88; prof. microbiology Sch. Medicine U. Pa., 1989—92; investigator Howard Hughes Med. Inst., 1989—92; sci. dir. ARIAD Pharm., Inc., Cambridge, Mass.; prof. dept. cell biology Med. Sch. Harvard U., Boston, 1997—. Mem.: NAS (mem. Inst. Medicine). Office: Dept Cell Biology Harvard Med Sch 240 Longwood Ave Boston MA 02115

BRUM, BRENDA, state legislator, librarian; b. Parkersburg, W.Va., Jan. 3, 1954; d. Carl Henry Ogilvie and Helen Mae (Camp) B. BS, W.Va. U., 1975, MA, 1978. Libr., tchr. English, Hamilton Jr. H.S., Parkersburg, 1976-85; libr. Parkersburg South H.S., 1985—; mem. W.Va. Ho. of Dels., 1991-92, 93-94. Bd. dirs. Wood County chpt. Am. Cancer Soc.; foster parent Try Again Homes; mem. adv. bd. Wood County Vocat. Nursing. Mem. LWV, Wood County Edn. Assn. (past treas., exec. com.). Democrat. Avocation: water and snow skiing. Home: 1717 20th St Parkersburg WV 26101-3509

BRUMELL, LISA MICHELLE, health facility administrator; b. Conway, S.C., May 8, 1973; d. James Allen and Patril Brumell. BS in Bus., U. S.C., 1995, MSW, 1998. LMSW; lic. real estate agent. Social worker IV S.C. Dept. Mental Health, Columbia, 1996—2000; clin. mgr. Companion Benefit Alternatives, Columbia, 2000—. Real estate agt. Hook & Assocs. Realty, Columbia, 2003—; notary pub., Columbia, 2000—. Recipient Cert. Appreciation, Phi Beta Lambda, 1996, Friendship Bapt. Ch., 1996. Avocations: tennis, racquetball, singing, reading, writing. Home: 14 Canterbury Ct Columbia SC 29210*

BRUMFIELD, DANA KRISTINE, music educator, medical transcriptionist; b. Jackson, Miss., Dec. 31, 1970; d. Barry Lynn and Linda Margaret (Melton) Lyall; m. Brian Keith Brumfield, May 27, 1995; children: Colby Kristine, Colin Keith, Ashton Margaret. B in Music Edn., Miss. Coll., 2000. Cert. music edn., vocal K-12 Miss. Med. transcriptionist MedScript, Clinton, Miss., 1994—; choral dir., gen. music tchr. Hillcrest Christian Sch., Jackson, Miss., 2002—. Presenter in field. Mem.: Miss. Music Educators Assn. (dist. VI chair-elect 2002—), Miss. Orff Assn. (v.p. 2002—), Music Educators Nat. Conf., Am. Choral Dirs. Assn., Am. Orff-Scheulwerk Assn. (Orff level I). Republican. Baptist. Avocations: swimming, reading, singing, travel. Office: Hillcrest Christian Sch 4060 S Siwell Rd Jackson MS 39212

BRUMIT, JO ANN, sheet metal manufacturing executive; 4 children. With KARLEE, 1982—, CEO & chmn. Recipient Entrepreneur of Yr. for Mfg. by INC. Mag., Ernst & Young, 1991, Amb. of Yr. Award, Hogan Ctr. for Performance Excellence, 1994, 1999, Dir. of Yr., Garland Chamber of Commerce, 1997, Athena Award, 2000, Malcolm Baldridge Nat. Quality Award, 2000. Mem.: Hogan Quality Roundtable, Garland Ind. Sch. Dist. (bus. sch. ptnr.), Richland Cmty. Coll. Middle Mgmt. Prog. (adv. bd. mem.), Baylor Healthcare System Found. (bd. dirs.), Sch. to Career Bd., Tex. Work (source bd. mem.), Tex. Quality Found. (adv. bd., Tex. Quality award 1999). Office: Karlee PO Box 461207 Garland TX 75046-1207

BRUMMEL, LISA, information technology executive; BA in Sociology, Yale U.; MBA, U. Calif., L.A. Sales mgmt. Prentice Hall Inc.; from mgr. to corp. v.p. home products divsn. Microsoft, Redmond, Wash., 1989, corp. v.p. home products divsn. Active Hopelink cmty.svc. programs; vol. U. Wash. Med. Ctr.; bd. dir. Wash. Acad. Performing Arts. Office: One Microsoft Way Redmond WA 98052-6399

BRUN, PAMELA ANN, special education educator; d. Ronald Peter and Patricia Mae Carzoli; m. Michael Eugene Brun, July 29, 1977; children: Michael, James, Angela. BA in Edn., St. Mary's Notre Dame, 1977; MA in Spl. Edn., U. Mo., Kansas City, 2003. Educator St. Ferdinands, St. Louis, 1977—78, Ctr. for New Ways, St. Louis, 1977—81, U. Sch. Nashville, 1981—86; spl. educator Infant Devel. Ctr., Shawnee, Kans., 1987—, Holy Spirit Cath. Sch., Overland Park, Kans., 1998—. Named Vol. of Yr., Johnson County Pks. and Recreation, 1999; named to Partnership for Children Honor Roll, Ewing Kaufman Found., 2000; recipient Richard Edmonds Exemplary Svc. award, 1996. Mem.: Nat. Cath. Tchrs. Assn., Coun. for Exceptional Children, Country Club Swim Assn. Kansas City (sec. 1996—98, pres. 1998—2000, Testimonial of Recognition 1996, 1999). Roman Catholic. Home: 9008 Wills St Overland Park KS 66210

BRUNE, EVA, fundraiser; b. Bklyn., Apr. 20, 1952; d. Paul Mass and Edythe Siegel; m. David H. Brune, Oct. 30, 1988; children: Jared Alexander, Isaac Nicolai. BFA, Calif. Coll. Arts and Crafts, Oakland, 1978. Visual arts dir. Sonoma (Calif.) County Arts Commn., 1980-82; assoc. dir. Visual Arts Ctr. of Alaska, Anchorage, 1982-83; program dir. Internat. Sculpture Ctr., Washington, 1983; dir. Pro Arts, Oakland, 1983-85; devel. dir. A Traveling Jewish Theater, San Francisco, 1985-88; mng. dir. INTAR Hispanic Arts. Ctr., N.Y.C., 1988-94; dir. ann. fund The Big Apple Circus, N.Y.C., 1994-96; exec. dir. CityKids Found., N.Y.C., 1996-98; nat. dir. instnl. advancement Young Audiences, Inc., N.Y.C., 1998-2001; dir. devel. Dance Theatre of Harlem, 2001—03; dep. dir. Eldridge St. Project, N.Y.C., 2003—. Instr. Calif. Coll. Arts and Crafts, Oakland, 1978-79. Past bd. dirs. Alliance Resident Theaters, N.Y.C., Citiarts, N.Y.C.; former panelist theater program Nat. Endowment for Arts, Washington, OPERA Am., Fla. State Coun. on Arts, Westchester County Coun. on Arts, N.Y.; panelist N.J. State Coun. on Arts. Recipient fellowships Nat. Endowment for the Arts, Washington, 1980, 82. Jewish. Avocations: piano, furniture building, writing. E-mail: evabrune@hotmail.com.

BRUNEAU, LISE, actor; b. Balt., May 19, 1966; d. George Irving Bruno, Jr. and Adele Ann (Molz) MacMillan. Degree in Drama, Royal Acad. Dramatic Arts, London, 1990. Cert. Brit. Bd. Fight Dirs. Lectr. Elder Hostels of Am., Ashland, Oreg., 1996; participant, poetry evenings Oreg. Shakespeare Festival, Ashland, Oreg., 1996; gala hostess Classical Action Against AIDS, San Francisco, 1995. Actor: (plays) Gertrude, in An Ideal Husband, Berkeley (Calif.) Repertory Theatre, 1995, Teacher, in School for Salomés, Chashama Theatre, N.Y.C., 2001, Rosalind, in As You Like It, Seattle Repertory Theatre, 2000, Sarah, in Patience, Wilmar Theatre, Phila., 2001, Ruth, in Blithe Spirit, Ctr. Stage, Balt., 2002, Hermione, in The Winter's Tale, Shakespeare Theatre, Washington, DC, 2003, Elizabeth I, in Mary Stuart, Ctr. Stage, Balt., 2003, Merteuil, in Les Liaisons Dangereuses, ACT, San Francisco, 2003. Recipient Outstanding Performance award, Dramalogue, 1994, Bay Area Theatre Critics Cir., 1994, 1997. Green Party. Home: 305 Ocean Ave # D1 Brooklyn NY 11225 Office: Actors Equity Assn 165 W 46th St New York NY 10036 E-mail: lise@lisebruneau.com.

BRUNELLO-MCCAY, ROSANNE, sales executive; b. Cleve., Aug. 26, 1960; d. Carl Carmello and Vivan Lucille (Caranna) B.; m. Walter B. McCay, Feb. 26, 1994; children: Angela Breanna, Mikala Bell. Student, U. Cin., 1978-81, Cleve. State U., 1981-82. Indsl. sales engr. Alta Machine Tool, Denver, 1982; mem. sales./purchases Ford Tool & Machine, Denver, 1982-84; sales/ptnr. Mountain Rep. Enterprises, Denver, 1984-86; pres., owner Mountain Rep. Ariz., Phoenix, 1986—; pres. Mountain Rep. Oreg., Portland, 1990—, Mountain Rep. Wash., 1991—, Mountain Rep. Calif., Sunnyvale, 1997—, San Clemente, 1998—, Port Clinton, Ohio, 1999—; we. regional sales mgr. Offshore Internat., Inc., Tucson, 2002—. Sec. Computer & Automated Systems Assoc., 1987, vice chmn., 1988, chmn., 1989. Active mem. Rep. Party, 1985—; mem. Phoenix Art Mus., Grand Canyon Minority Coun., 1994; vol. Make-A-Wish Found. fund raiser, 1995—. Named Mrs. Chandler Internat., Mrs. Ariz. Internat. [illegible], 1996, Mrs. East Valley U.S., 1997; finalist Mrs. Ariz. Internat., 1996, Ms. Ariz. 2000, Ms. U.S. Continental Pageant. Mem. NAFE, Soc. Mfg. Engrs. (pres. award 1988), Computer Automated Assn. (sec. 1987, vice chmn. 1988 chmn. 1989), Manufacturers and Agents Nat. Assn. (chair elect 2002), Nat. Hist. Soc., Italian Cultural Soc., Tempe C. of C., Vocat. Ednl. Club Am. (mem. exec. bd., pres. 1987—). Roman Catholic. Avocations: sports, aerobics, dance, skiing, golfing, tennis. Office: Mountain Rep Ariz 410 S Jay St Chandler AZ 85225-6253 E-mail: rosanne@mtnrep.com.

BRUNKE, DAWN BAUMANN, writer, editor; b. Madison, Wis., Nov. 6, 1959; d. Richard Joseph and Carol Edler Baumann; m. Bob Brunke, May 25, 1991; 1 child, Alyeska Isabela. BA, Lawrence U., 1977—81. Massage Therapist AMTA, Wash. D.C., 1985. Instr. Potomac Inst. of Myotherapy, Washington, 1986—88; massage therapist Gaithersburg, Md., 1986—88; editor Alaska Wellness Mag., Anchorage, 1995—; massage therapist Alaska Club, Wasilla, 2001—. Author: In God's Garden (Grand Prize; Anchorage Daily News/ U. of Alaska Creative Writing Contest, 1997), Before She Was the Queen of Syrup (Editors Choice, Anchorage Daily News/ U. of Alaska Creative Writing Contest, 1998), Animal Voices : Telepathic Communication in the Web of Life, 2002, Who Lives Here?, Awakening to Animal Voices: A Teen Guide to Telepathic Communication with All Life. Home: P O Box 877229 Wasilla AK 99687

BRUNNER, JANET LEE, physician assistant; b. Milw., Sept. 15, 1955; d. Donald Edward and Carol Louise (Radtke) B. BA in Biology, Luther Coll., 1977; MA in Edn., Ctrl. Mich. U., 1984; BS in Physician Assistance, U. Iowa, 1989. Cert. physician asst., Pa. Nat. Commn. on Certification of Physician Assts; registered med. technologist. Staff med. technologist St. Joseph's Hosp., Milw., 1977-79, 81-87, Hosp. Castañer (P.R.), 1979-81; physician asst. med. oncology Med. Coll. Wis., Milw., 1989-92, physician asst. bone marrow transplant, 1992-94, sr. coord. bone marrow transplant program, 1993-94; physician asst., sr. coord. bone marrow transplant program Thomas Jefferson U. Hosp., Phila., 1995—. Lab. cons. Am. Immediate Care, Chgo., 1984; guest lectr. Allentown Coll., Center Valley, Pa., 1996-99. Sec. bd. dirs. Wis. Interfaith Com. on Ctrl. Am., Milw., 1992-94; election observer U.S. Citizens Election Observer Mission, El Salvador, 1994; mem. coun. Prince of Peace Luth. Ch., 1997-99; mem. stds. com. The Nat. Marrow Donor Program, 2001—. Fellow Am. Acad. Physician Assts.; mem. Pa. Soc. Physician Assts. Avocations: aerobics, travel, bicycling. Home: 47 Lavister Dr Mount Laurel NJ 08054-2642 Office: Thomas Jefferson U Hosp 130 S 9th St Ste 400 Philadelphia PA 19107-5233 E-mail: j_brunner@lac.jci.tju.edu.

BRUNNER, LILLIAN SHOLTIS, nurse, writer; b. Freeland, Pa. d. Andrew J. and Anna (Tomasko) Sholtis; m. Mathias J. Brunner, Sept. 8, 1951; children: Janet Brunner Cramer, Carol Ann Brunner Burns, Douglas Mathias. RN, diploma, U. Pa., 1940, BS, 1945, LittD (hon.), 1985; MS in Nursing, Case-Western Res. U., 1947; ScD (hon.), Cedar Crest Coll., 1978. RN, Pa. Head nurse U. Pa. Hosp., Phila., 1940-42, operating room supr., 1942-44, head, fundamentals of nursing dept., 1944-46; asst. prof. surgical nursing Yale U. Sch. Nursing, New Haven, Conn., 1947-51; surgical supr. Yale-New Haven Hosp., 1947-51; Lillian Sholtis Brunner chair med.-surg. nursing U. Pa., 2001. Rsch. project dir. Sch. Nursing Bryn Mawr (Pa.) Hosp., 1973-77; co-founder History of Nursing Mus., Pa. Hosp., Phila., 1974; mem. bd. overseers Sch. Nursing U. Pa., 1982-88; bd. overseers emeritus, 1988—; chmn. nursing adv. Presbyn.-U. Pa. Med. Ctr., Phila., 1970-88, 90-93, trustee, 1976-88, 90-95, vice chmn. bd. trustees, 1985-88; mem. com. profl. advisory Vis. Nurse Assn., Lancaster, Pa., 1996-99; sec. Glen Coun., Willow Valley Manor North, 1997-2000. Author: Manual of Operating Room Technology, 1966, (with others) Lippincott Manual of Nursing Practice, 1974, 4th edit., 1986, Textbook of Medical and Surgical Nursing, 1964, 6th edit., 1988; editl. bd. Jour. Nursing and Health Care, Nursing 1978-1999, Nursing Photobook Series, 1978-90. Bd. dirs. Presbyn. Found. for Phila., 1995-99. Recipient Disting. Alumnus award Frances Payne Bolton Sch. Nursing, Case Western Res. U., 1980, Alumni award for merit Soc. Alumni Assns., U. Pa., and Am. Dream Achievement award Class of '45, U. Pa., 1995. Fellow: Am. Acad. Nursing (Living Legend award 2002); mem.: Nurses Alumni Assn. U. Pa. Hosp., Philanthropic Ednl. Orgn., Nat. League for Nursing (judge nat. writing contest 1982—84,

Disting. Svc. award 1979), ANA, Acad. U. Pa., Ben Franklin Soc., Internat. Old Lacers Soc., Nat. League Am. Pen Women (sec. Phila. chpt. 1972—76, nat. sec. 1984—86), Pi Lambda Theta, Pi Gamma Mu, Sigma Theta Tau. Home and Office: Apt J-411 645 Willow Valley Sq Lancaster PA 17602 4871 E-mail: LilalmaB@aol.com.

BRUNNER-MARTINEZ, KIRSTIN ELLEN, pediatrician, psychiatrist; b. Allentown, Pa., July 26, 1959; d. John Wilson and Ulla Brita (Arvide) Brunner; m. Fred F. Martinez. BS, Muhlenberg Coll., Allentown, Pa., 1981; DO, Phila. Coll. Osteo. Medicine, 1986. Diplomate Am. Bd. Pediatrics, Am. Bd. Psychiatry and Neurology in child and adolescent psychiatry and adult psychiatry. Resident U. Ky., 1992; dept. dir. Integra Health Family Devel. Ctr., Cedar Rapids, Iowa, 1993-98; with Hamot Inst. for Behavioral Health, Erie, Pa., 1998-2001; med. dir. Hamot Child and Adolescent Psychiat. Unit, Erie, 1999-2001, Sarah Reed Children's Ctr., Erie, 2001—. Fellow Am. Acad. Pediatrics; mem. AMA, Am. Acad. Child and Adolescent Psychiatry, Am. Psychiat. Assn. Avocations: cross country skiing, soccer (outdoor and indoor). Office: Sarah Reed Children's Ctr 1020 E 10th St Erie PA 16503

BRUNO, CAROL JEANETTE, library media specialist, gifted and talented education educator, innkeeper; b. Phila., Dec. 21, 1949; d. Everette Noble and Gertrude Mae (Weaver) Cliff; m. C. Gus Bruno, Aug. 28, 1971; children: Peter Everette, Jason Eugene. AA, Wesley Coll., 1969; BA, Davis & Elkins Coll., 1971; postgrad., St. Joseph's U., 1994—, Rowan U., 1997—. Elem. tchr. Ocean City (N.J.) Primary Schs., 1971-72; instr. Atlantic C.C., Mays Landing, 1979-80; reading tchr. Egg Harbor Twp. (N.J.) Schs., 1980-82; coord. gifted edn. Sea Isle City (N.J.) Pub. Schs., 1982—, adviser student yearbook, Nat. Jr. Honor Soc. Local pres., county pres., mem. state bd. dirs. N.J. PTA, Trenton, 1978-90; founder After-Sch. Care Program, Ocean City, 1984, Ocean City Safe Homes Project, 1984; den mother Boy Scouts Am., Ocean City, 1980-82; mem. Mayor's Task Force on Drug and Alcohol Abuse, Ocean City; pres., bd. dirs. Cape Ednl. Fund, Cape May County, N.J., 1980—. Named Role Model, Sun Newspaper, 1988, Cape May County Tchr. of Yr., 1993. Mem. ASCD, Sea Isle City Edn. Assn. (sec.). Avocations: reading, traveling, decorating bed and breakfast, cooking. Office: Sea Isle City Pub Sch 4501 Park Rd Sea Isle City NJ 08243-1896

BRUNO, CATHY EILEEN, management consultant, former state official, social sciences educator; b. Binghamton, N.Y. d. Martin Frank and Beverly Carolyn (Hamlin) Piza; m. Frank L. Delaney (div.); m. Paul R. Bruno, May 5, 1990. BA, SUNY, Binghamton; MSW, Syracuse U. Psychiat. social worker Broome Devel. Ctr., Binghamton, 1973-74, 76, congl. legis. aide, 1975; asst. dir. Bur. Program and Fiscal audits N.Y. State Office Mental Retardation and Devel. Disabilities, Albany, 1976-80; statewide coord. Intermediate Care Facilities for Developmentally Disabled, 1980; cert. coord. Western County Svc. Group, 1980-83, Upstate unit dir. Bur. Cert. Control, 1983-85; dir. ICF/DD Survey and Rev., 1985-89; area dir. Bur. Program Cert., 1989-95; dir. Bur. Transitional Svcs., 1995-97, mgmt. cons., 1997—. Adj. instr. SUNY Sch. Social Welfare, Albany, 1982-83; adj. faculty C.C. of Southern Nev., Las Vegas, 1998. Vol. U. Nev. Coop. Ext. Master Gardener program, 1997—; bd. dirs. Worldwide AIDS Movement, 2000—01. Mem. Am. Mgmt. Assn. Home and Office: 293 Canyon Spirit Dr Henderson NV 89012-3472

BRUNO, MIA NOELLE CLAUDIA, archaeological organization administrator; b. Erie, Pa., Dec. 23, 1970; d. Loretta Rose Nardo; m. John Joseph Bruno. BA in Bus. Mgmt., magna cum laude, Mercyhurst Coll., 2001, MS summa cum laude in Organizational Leadership, 2003. Office Coord. Mayor's Office, Erie, Pa., 1990—2001; office mgr. Mercyhurst Archaeol. Inst., Erie, 2001—. Mem.: Delta Mu Delta. Democrat. Lutheran. Avocations: travel, dance, theater, animals. Home: 210 Liberty St Erie PA 16507 Office: Mercyhurst Archaeol Institute 501 E 38th St Erie PA 16507 Personal E-mail: mbruno@ma.rr.com. Business E-Mail: mbruno@mercyhurst.edu.

BRUNS, CINDY MARIE, psychologist; b. Eugene, Oreg., Feb. 3, 1971; d. Robert O. Bruns and Judith Anne Hargreaves-Bruns. BS, U. of Oreg., 1994; MA, Calif. Sch. of Profl. Psychology, Alameda, 1997; PhD, Alliant Internat. Univ., San Francisco Bay, 2002. Lic. psychologist Tex. Dir. adult counseling svcs. Denton (Tex.) County Friends of the Family, 2000—03; staff psychologist Tex. Woman's U. Counseling Ctr., Dallas Ctr., 2003—. Contbr. articles to profl. jours. Recipient Dissertation Grant, Calif. Sch. of Profl. Psychology, 2000. Mem.: APA. Liberal. Episcopalian. Office: Tex Woman's Univ Counseling Ctr 1810 Inwood Rd Dallas TX 75235 E-mail: cbruns@mail.twu.edu.

BRUNS, PATRICIA ANN, art educator, consultant; b. Cinn., Jan. 26, 1951; d. Harry August and Anabel Louise Kase. B in Arts Edn., U. Ky., 1973; M in Arts Edn., Miami U., 1985. Cert. K-12 art edn. State of Ohio Dept. Edn., 1974. Art educator N.W. Local Sch. Dist., Cinn., 1974—. Owner Art Parts Framery & Gallery, Cinn., 1982—94; cons. Getty Ctr. for Arts in Edn., L.A., 1992—95, Smithsonian: Save our Sculpture, Washington, 1994, Contemporary Arts Ctr., Cinn., 1994—95, WCET Arts Connections, Cinn., 2000—; chair North Ctrl. Evaluation: Student Outcomes, Cinn., 1995. Contbr. articles to profl. jours. Mem. profl. develop. com. N.W. Local Sch. Dist., 2000—. Recipient Golden Apple Award, Ashland Oil Co., 1995; grantee, Greater Cin. Found., 1986. Mem.: N.W. Assn. Educators (pres. 1995—2003), Ohio Art Edn. Assn. (Art Educator of Yr. 1994), Nat. Art Edn. Assn., Ohio Edn. Assn. (life; congl. contact team mem. 2000—, regional coord. coun. 2001—03, del. 1983—), NEA (life; life del.). Home: 4540 Glenway Ave Cincinnati OH 45205 Office: Colerain High Sch 8801 Cheviot Rd Cincinnati OH 45251 Personal E-mail: pbruns@cinci.rr.com.

BRUNSWIG, JESSIE, executive assistant; b. Leone, Am. Samoa, Aug. 24, 1943; came to U.S., 1949; d. Harold Edwin Miller and Juliana (Toilolo) Copeland; m. William Lloyd Brunswig, July 17, 1989; children: Jennifer, Jeffrey, Eric, Kirk. Student, Washington State U., 1961, Lower Columbia Coll., 1964, Centralia Coll., 1988; diploma, Police Dept. Citizen's Acad., Centralia, 1996. Legal asst./paralegal Thurston County Prosecutor's Office, 1985-89; confidential sec. State Bd. of Health, 1989-91; adminstrv. asst. Wash. State Dept. Health, 1991-93; exec. asst. Wash. State Gov.'s Office, 1993-98. Staff Gov.'s Health Policy Group, 1993-98; spkr. Centralia Coll. Citizenship Class, 1997—; Mayor city of Centralia, Wash., 1997-99. Councilor Centralia City Coun., 1993-99; staff Gov.'s Task Force on Higher Edn., 1995-96, Exec.-Joint Legis. Task Force on Long Term Care, 1997-98; mem. Cascadia Mayor's Coun., 1998-99; pres. small cities adv. coun., 1997-99; bd. dirs. Lewis County Cmty. Network, 1995-96; com. Elect Gary Alexander Rep. 20th dist., 1995-97; mayor pro-tem Centralia City Coun., 1995-96; bd. dirs. Lewis County Econ. Devel. Coun., 1995-99; treas. Lewis County Children with Spl. Needs, 1997-99; Region VI adv. com. Wash. State Dept. Social and Health Svcs., 1997-98; chief police adv. panel, coun. liaison, 1995-97. Named Outstanding Young Woman in Am., 1973, Girl of Yr. Beta Sigma Phi Internat., 1978, Life Master Am. Contract Bridge League, 1976—, Wash. State Legal Sec. Yr. Wash. Assn. Legal Profls., 1990. Mem. Assn. Wash. Cities (nom. com. 1999), Nat. C. of C. (pres.'s adv. bd. 1997-99). Lutheran. Avocations: duplicate bridge, cooking, travel. Home: # 6 Liste Correos Colina Blanca El Zalate Playa 23451 Mexico

BRUSCINO, LEAH, state agency administrator; b. Laramie, Wyo. BS in Psychology, U. Wyo. Cert. bus. counselor. With Western Rsch. Inst., USDA Forest Svc., Wyo. Employee Fed. Credit Union, Lander Area C. of C., 1994, exec. dir., 1996; regional dir. N.W. region Wyo. Bus. Coun., Powell. Mem. Wyo. Econ. Devel. Assn. Office: Wyoming Business Council 143 S Bent Ste B Powell WY 82435

BRUSSEL, MARIKA H. writer, educator; b. N.Y.C., Aug. 18, 1968; d. Cabell Brussel and Tsurah August. MFA, Sarah Lawrence Coll., 1994. Adj. prof. Coll. of Santa Fe, 2000—, Inst. Am. Indian Arts, Santa Fe. Author: (novel excerpt) The Motion of Memory (S.W. Lit. Discovery prize, 2002, award Nat. League Am. Pen Women, 2003). Mem.: PEN [illegible]

BRUTON, REBECCA ANN, mayor, commissioner; b. Arkansas City, Kans., Dec. 12, 1949; d. Robert Thomas and Gloria JoAnn (Jackson) Bush; m. Ronald Dean Bruton, Sept. 23, 1973. BS, Southwestern Coll., Winfield, Kans., 1975; grad. Inst. Mcpl. Leadership, Wichita State U., 2001. Elem. tchr. USD #471, Dexter, Kans., 1977—88; owner, sec. Bruton's Towing and Salvage, Arkansas City, 1988—; mayor, city commr. City of Arkansas City, 1999—2003; founder A Piece of the Garden Ministries, 1989—. Bd. trustees S. Ctrl. Kans. Regional Med. Ctr., Arkansas City, 2000—03; bd. dirs. Strother Field Commn., Arkansas City, 2000—03. Preacher Medicalodge East, Arkansas City, 1992—2001. Named Vol. of Yr., Medicalodge East, 1999—2000. Mem.: Kans. Sunshine Coalition Open Govt. (charter mem.), Kans. Taxpayers Assn. Avocations: Bible study, reading. Office: Bruton's Towing and Salvage 1800 South Fourth Arkansas City KS 67005 E-mail: actycomm@ArkCity.org.

BRUTTOMESSO, KATHLEEN ANN, dean, nursing educator, researcher; b. Torrington, Conn., Apr. 28, 1935; d. Thomas F. and Margaret (Gleeson) McMahon; div.; children: Raymond I. Jr., Cheryl A., Robert I., Charles A., Douglas A. BS, St. Joseph Coll., West Hartford, Conn., 1956; MS, Boston Coll., 1959; DNSc, Boston U., 1987. RN, Conn., Mass., Ill., N.J. Staff nurse, head nurse, supr. Mass. Gen. Hosp., Boston, 1956-59; supr. Charlotte Hungerford Hosp., Torrington, 1963-64; instr. Seton Hall U., South Orange, N.J., 1975-77; assoc. prof. U. Conn., Storrs, 1977—, interim dean. Researcher in field. Contbr. articles to profl. jours. Boston U. scholar, 1980-81. Mem. ANA, Conn. Nurses Assn., Conn. Nurses Found. (charter mem.), Ea. Nursing Rsch. Soc., Sigma Theta Tau (Mu chpt. Gamma Nu chpt., charter mem.).

BRUVOLD, KATHLEEN PARKER, lawyer; BS in Math., U. Denver, 1965; MS in Math., Purdue U., 1967; JD, U. Cin., 1978. Bar: Ohio 1978, U.S. Dist. Ct. (so. dist.) Ohio 1978, U.S. Dist. Ct. (ea. dist.) Ky. 1979. Mathematician bur. rsch. and engring. U.S. Post Office, 1967; instr. math. Purdue U., West Lafayette, Ind., 1967-68, asst. to dir., tng. coord., programmer Administrv. Data Processing Ctr., 1968-71; instr. math. Ind. U., Kokomo, 1969-70; pvt. practice Cin., 1978-80; asst. dir. Legal Adv. Svcs. U. Cin., 1980-89, assoc. gen. counsel, 1989—2002; asst. atty. gen. State of Ohio, 1983—2002. Chair Ohio pub. records com. Inter-univ. Coun. Legal Advisors, 1980-84; presenter various confs. and symposiums. Active com. group svcs. allocation United Way and Community Chest; v.p. Clifton Recreation Ctr. Adv. Coun., 1983-84; vice chair Cin. Bilingual Acad. PTA, 1989-90. U. Denver scholar, Jewel Tea Co. scholar; Nat. Merit finalist. Mem. ABA, Nat. Assn. Coll. and Univ. Attys. (bd. dirs., co-chair taxation sect., com. ann. meeting arrangements, program com., publs. com., bd. ops. com., JCUL editl. bd. nominations com., honors and award com., intellectual property sect., com. continuing legal edn. 1992-2002), Cin. Bar Assn. (com. taxation, program chmn. 1985-86, sec. 1986-87, com. computer law). Home: 536 Evanswood Pl Cincinnati OH 45220-1527

BRUYN, KIMBERLY ANN, public relations executive, consultant; b. Grand Rapids, Mich., Jan. 25, 1955; BA in English, Calvin Coll., Grand Rapids, 1977; MS in Journalism, U. Kans., 1979. Advt. copywriter, acct. exec. Mendenhall, Jones & Leistra Advt., Grand Rapids, 1979-81; advt. copywriter Johnson & Dean Advt., Grand Rapids, 1981-82; pub. rels. analyst Amway Corp., Ada, Mich., 1982-84, sr. pub. rels. analyst, 1984-85, sr. pub. rels. specialist, 1986-87, pub. rels. supr., 1987-88, pub. rels. mgr., chief corp. spokesperson, 1988-93, sr. mgr. pub. rels., chief corp. spokesperson, 1993-98; v.p. comms. The Windquest Group, Grand Rapids, 1998-2000; exec. dir. Straightline Pub. Rels., 2000—01; sr. cons. The Grey Stone Group, Grand Rapids, Mich., 2001—. Mem. pub. rels. and mktg. com. Grand Rapids Symphony Orch., 1992; mem. planning com. Spl. Olympics Festival of Trees, Grand Rapids, 1990-92, Gerald R. Ford Presdl. Mus. 10th Anniversary Celebration, Grand Rapids, 1992; bd. dirs. Celebration on the Grand, 1989-96, co-chair, 1993, 94; co-chair pub. rels. Heart Ball, Am. Heart Assn., 1996-2001; chair pub. rels. Van Andel Arena Grand Opening, 1996, Presdl. Tribute to Gerald R. Ford, 1997. Mem. PRSA (Spectrum award 1990-98), Direct Selling Assn. (chair comm. com. 1997-98). Office: Greystone Group Inc 678 Front NW Ste 159 Grand Rapids MI 49504 E-mail: kimb@greystonegp.com.

BRUZEE, KRISTEN K. nursing administrator; b. Geneva, N.Y., Nov. 20, 1951; d. William LeRoy and Joan Louise (Conway) Bruzee. Diploma in Nursing, Willard State Hosp. Sch. Nursing, Willard, N.Y., 1972. RN N.Y., cert. psychiat. and mental health nurse. Staff nurse Willard State Hosp., 1972—73, head nurse, 1973—80; nurse adminstr. Willard Psychiat. Ctr., 1980—91, Elmira Psychiat. Ctr., NY, 1991—. Mem.: Chenung County Humane Soc., So. Tier Rose Soc., Syracuse Assn. of Psychiat. Nurses. Democrat. Avocations: watercolor artist, floral design, gardening, interior decorating. Home: 418 Euclid Ave Apt A Elmira NY 14905 Office: Elmira Psychiat Ctr 100 Washington St Elmira NY 14901

BRYAN, BARBARA DAY, retired librarian; b. Livermore Falls, Maine, May 20, 1927; d. Lorey Clifford and Olga Elvira (Bergquist) Day; m. Robert S. Bryan, June 24, 1950. BA in Psychology, U. Maine, 1948; MS in Library Sci., So. Conn. State U., 1964. Catalog dept. asst. Yale U. Library, New Haven, 1948-49; departmental library cataloger Harvard U., Cambridge, Mass., 1949-51; descriptive cataloger Yale U. Library, New Haven, 1951-52; cataloger Fairfield (Conn.) Pub. Library, 1952-54, reference librarian, 1954-57, asst. librarian, order librarian, 1957-65; asst. dir. libraries Fairfield U., 1965-74, university librarian, 1974-96, u. libr. emerita, 1996—. Mem. Conn. State Libr. Bd., Hartford, 1978—92, chair, 1987—92; bd. dirs. Bibliomation, Inc., Stratford, Conn., 1987—91. Pres. Friends Nyselius Libr., Fairfield U., 1998-2000, mem. exec. bd., 2001—; commr. Fairfield Hist. Dist. Commn., 2003—. Recipient Disting. Alumnus award So. Conn. State U. Sch. of Libr. Sci., 1979; named Conn. Libr. Assn. Libr. of Yr., 1988. Mem. ALA (life, Conn. chpt. councilor 1977-80), Assn. Coll. and Rsch. Librs. (constn. and by-laws com. 1986-90, mem. coll. libr. sect. stds. com. 1991-95), New Eng. Libr. Assn. (mem. com. 1981-85, coun. mem. 1975-77), Conn. Libr Assn., Fairfield Hist. Soc. (libr. vol.), Conn. Audubon Soc., Oak Lawn Cemetery Assn. (bd. dirs. 1994—), Assn. Conn. Libr. Bds. (bd. dirs., chair legis. com. 1996—), Inst. Ret. Profl. (adv. bd. 1998-2001), Fairfield U. Retirees Assn. (pres. 2003—), Phi Beta Kappa, Phi Kappa Phi. Democrat. Avocations: reading, walking. Home: 999 Merwins Ln Fairfield CT 06824-1919

BRYAN, KAREN SMITH, lawyer; BA in Psychology, Bryn Mawr Coll., 1972; MA, UCLA, 1973; JD, U. So. Calif., 1979. Bar: Calif. 1979. With Latham & Watkins, L.A., 1979—, ptnr., 1987—. Mem. planning com. U. So. Calif. Tax Inst. Mem.: ABA (corp. tax sect. and ind. income tax com.). Office: Latham & Watkins LLP 633 W Fifth St Ste 4000 Los Angeles CA 90071 Office Phone: 213-485-1234. E-mail: karen.bryan@lw.com.

BRYAN, MARY ANN, interior designer; b. Dallas, Nov. 16, 1929; d. William C. and Harriet E. (Carter) Green; m. Frank Wingfield Bryan, Aug. 31, 1957; children: Frank Wingfield, Elizabeth F. BS in Interior Design, U. Tex., 1950. Head of stock Foleys Dept. Store, Houston, 1952-53, asst. buyer, 1953-54, buyer, 1955-60; exec. tng. dir. Foleys Dept Store, Houston; owner, pres. The Bryan Design Assocs., Inc., Houston, 1961—2003. Mem. Tex. Bd. Archtl. Examiners, 1993—99. Mem. interior design adv. bd. Art Inst. of Houston, Houston C.C.; U.S. del. Friendship Among Women. Fellow Am. Soc. Interior Designers (nat. bd. dirs. 1984-86, 91-92; pres. Gulf Coast chpt. 1975), Chi Omega. Office: 5120 Woodway Dr Ste 8009 Houston TX 77056-1788 E-mail: maryannb@bryandesigns.com.

BRYAN, MARY JO W. realtor, artist, art educator; b. Dumas, Tex., Apr. 12, 1944; d. Edwin Franklin and Martha Lou (Workman) Williams; m. Gary W. Bryan, June 4, 1966; children: Mark William, Stacy Lynn. BS in Edn., Tex. Tech U., 1966; MEd in Guidance and Counseling, North Tex. U., 1969; MA in Art, West Tex. A&M U., 1994. Cert. tchr., all-level counselor, Tex. Tchr. Lubbock (Tex.) Ind. Sch. Dist., 1966, Irving (Tex.) Ind. Sch. Dist., 1966-68, Dallas Ind. Sch. Dist., 1968-69, counselor, 1969-71; bus. mgr. Gary W. Bryan, M.D., P.A., Amarillo, Tex., 1977—2002; artist Amarillo, 1994—; mgr. Prudential Ada Realtors, 2003—. Organizer Healthtreat, Med. Alliance, 1988; speakers chmn. Med. Alliance AIDS Program, 1992-96; mem. Leadership Amarillo, C. of C., 1989-90; Mem. Polk Street United Meth. Ch., class program com., 1988, 90, 93, 95, 96, chair Role and Status of Women feminist theology, 1995-2001; bd. friends Amarillo (Tex.) Pub. Libr., 1997-2003, v.p., 2001-02; bd. dir. Panhandle Art Ctr., 2003. Mem.: Amarillo Watercolor Assn. (pres. 2002—04), Lone Star Pastel Soc., Amarillo Fine Arts (chair Fall Art Show 2002), Potter-Randall County Med. Alliance (pres. 1988—89, sec.-treas. healthreat, Svc. award 1989), Tex. Med. Alliance (chair AIDS and sexually transmitted disease 1995—99), Am. Med. Alliance, Med. Mgrs. (v.p. 1989—90, Svc. award 1989).

BRYAN, SHARON ANN, lawyer; b. Kansas City, Mo., Dec. 18; d. George William and Dorothy Joan (Henn) Goll; children: Lisa Ann, Holly Renee. BJ, U. Mo., 1963; diploma, Stanford Radio and TV Inst., 1961; postgrad., NYU Sch. Arts and Sci., 1963-64; cert. personal fin. planning profl., UCLA, 1986; JD, U. So. Calif., 1989. Cert. specialist in family law. Proofreader, copy editor Cadwalader, Wickersham and Taft, N.Y.C., 1963-64; manuscript editor, writer nonsci. sects. N.Y. State Jour. Medicine, Med. Soc. State N.Y., N.Y.C., also mng. editor Staffoscope, 1965-66; manuscript editor Transactions, editor Perceiver Am. Acad. Ophthalmology and Otolaryngology, Rochester, Minn., 1969-72, hist. writer, 1972-82; atty. Burkley, Moore, Greenberg & Lyman, Torrance, Calif., 1989-91; with Christopher M. Moore & Assocs., 1991-99, Moore, Bryan & Schroff, 1999—. Writer publicity articles Ft. Lee (Va.) Cmty. Theatre; mediator Dept. 2 Superior Ct. of Calif., Ctrl. Dist. and Dept SWJ, S.W. Dist. Author: Pioneering Specialists: History of the American Academy of Ophthalmology and Otolaryngology, 1982. Vol. honor roll soc. Meml. Sloan-Kettering Cancer Ctr.; active N.Y. Hosp. Women's League, 1965-67; docent L.A. County Mus. Natural History, 1982-86; vol. Harriet Buhai Ctr., 1990-97; pres. Malaga Cove Homeowners Assn., 1999-2000. Mem.: NOW, ATLA, ABA, Assn. Cert. Family Law Specialists (bd. dirs. 2003—), South Bay Women Lawyers Assn. (rec. sec. 1994—95, pres. 1996—97), Los Angeles County Bar Assn. (exec. com. 1996—98, family law sect. exec. com. 2001—, del. to State Bar Calif.), Women's Lawyers Assn. L.A (bd. govs. 1991—97, chmn. family law sect. 1993—97), N.Y. Acad. Scis., Am. Med. Writers Assn. (editor conv. bull. 1966), Kappa Alpha Theta (chmn. membership com. N.Y. chpt. 1966), Kappa Tau Alpha. Home: 533 Via Del Monte Palos Verdes Estates CA 90274-1205 Office: 21515 Hawthorne Blvd Ste 490 Torrance CA 90503 E-mail: sharon@mbslawcorp.com.

BRYANT, ANNE LINCOLN, educational association executive; b. Jamaica Plain, Mass., Nov. 26, 1949; d. John Winslow and Anne (Phillips) B.; m. Peter Harned Ross, June 15, 1986; stepchildren: Charlotte Ross, George Ross. BA in English, Secondary Edn., Simmons Coll., 1971; EdD in Higher Edn., U. Mass., 1978. Intern U. Mass., Amherst, 1972; asst. to dean Springfield Tech. C.C., 1972-74; dir. Nat. Assn. Bank Women Ednl. Found., Chgo., 1974-86; v.p. P.M. Haeger, Chgo., 1978-86; exec. dir. AAUW, Washington, 1986-96, also exec. dir. Ednl. Found., Legal Advocacy Fund; exec. dir. Nat. Sch. Bds. Assn., Washington, 1996—. Contbr. articles to profl. jours. Mem. exec. com. Simmons Coll., Boston, 1971—; adv. commr. Edn. Commn. States, 1986—; mem. bd. govs. UNA of U.S.A., 1991—97, Ind. Sector, 1988-94, Hosp. Corp. Am., 1993-94. Recipient William H. Cosby Jr. award U. Mass., 1983; named Woman of Yr. for Edn., YWCA, 1976. Fellow Am. Soc. Assn. Execs. (bd. dirs. 1985-88, Key award 1992); mem. Am. Assn. for Higher Edn. (bd. dirs. 1980-87). Episcopalian. Avocations: tennis, skiing, reading, walking. Office: NSBA 1680 Duke St Alexandria VA 22314 E-mail: alb3@nsba.org.

BRYANT, BARBARA EVERITT, academic researcher, market research consultant, former federal agency administrator; b. Ann Arbor, Mich., Apr. 5, 1926; d. William Littell and Dorothy (Wallace) Everitt; m. John H. Bryant, Aug. 14, 1948; children: Linda Bryant Valentine, Randal E., Lois. AB, Cornell U., 1947; MA, Mich. State U., 1967, PhD, 1970; HonD, U. Ill., 1993. Editor art Chem. Engring. mag. McGraw-Hill Pub. Co., N.Y.C., 1947-48; editl. rsch. asst. U. Ill., Urbana, 1948-49, free-lance editor, writer, 1950-61; with continuing edn. adminstrn. dept. Oakland Univ., Rochester, Mich., 1961-66; grad. rsch. asst. Mich. State U., East Lansing, 1966-70; sr. analyst to v.p. Market Opinion Rsch., Detroit, 1970-77, sr. v.p., 1977-89; dir. Bur. of the Census, U.S. Dept. Commerce, 1989-93; rsch. scientist Sch. Bus. Adminstrn., U. Mich., 1993—. Author: High School Students Look at Their World, 1970, American Women Today & Tomorrow, 1977, Moving Power and Money: The Politics of Census Taking, 1995; contbr. articles to profl. jours. Mem. U.S. Census Adv. Com., Washington, 1980—86, Mich. Job Devel. Authority, Lansing, 1980—85; state editor LWV of Mich., 1959—61; bd. dirs. Roper Ctr. for Pub. Opinion Rsch., 1993—; mem. nat. adv. com. Inst. for Social Rsch., U. Mich., 1993—. Fellow: Am. Statis. Assn.; mem.: Am. Assn. Pub. Opinion Rsch., Am. Mktg. Assn. (pres. Detroit 1976—77, midwestern v.p. 1978—80, v.p. mktg. rsch. 1982—84, found. trustee 1993—2001), Rotary, Cosmos Club. Republican. Presbyterian. Avocation: swimming. Home: 1505 Sheridan Dr Ann Arbor MI 48104-4051 Office: U Mich Sch Bus Ann Arbor MI 48109-1234 E-mail: bryantb@umich.edu.

BRYANT, BERNICE R. speech pathology/audiology services professional; b. Honolulu, Aug. 7, 1959; d. Yvonne Adams; m. Kevin W. Bryant, June 15, 2002. BA, Lenoir Rhyne Coll., 1981; EdM, U. No. Fla., 1991. Tchr. Fla. Sch. Deaf & Blind, St. Augustine, Fla., 1981—88, speech-lang. pathologist, 1988—93, Ala. Sch. Deaf, Talladega, 1993—94, Levy county Sch Bd., Bronson, Fla., 1994—98, Pinellas County Sch. Bd., Clearwater, Fla., 1998—2001, pre-K tchr., 2001—03, speech-lang. pathologist, 2003—. Mem.: Am. Speech and Hearing Assn. Baptist. Avocations: crafts, sewing, counted cross stitch.

BRYANT, BERTHA ESTELLE, retired medical/surgical nurse; b. Va., Jan. 11, 1927; d. E.F. and Julia B. Diploma, Sibley Meml. Hosp., Washington, 1947; BS, Am. U., 1948; MA, Tchrs. Coll., Columbia U., 1962. Staff nurse, head nurse NIH, Bethesda, Md., 1954-59; asst. dir. nursing USPHS Alaska Native Hosp., Mt. Edgecumbe, 1959-61; instr. Sch. Nursing, U. Mich., 1962-64; chief div. clin. nursing Bur. Nursing, D.C. Dept. Public Health, Washington, 1964-65; commd. Nurse Corps, USPHS, 1965, nurse dir., capt., 1974—. Nurse cons., hosp. facilities services br., div. hosps. and med. facilities Bur. Health Services, HEW, Silver Spring; nurse cons., social analysis br., div. health services research and analysis Nat. Center Health Services Research, Health Resources Adminstrn., HEW, Rockville, Md.; nurse cons. div. extramural research Nat. Center Health Services Research, Office Asst. Sec. Health, HHS, Hyattsville, Md., 1977-81 Contbr. articles to profl. jours. Mem. AAUW, Assn. Mil. Surgeons U.S., Commd. Officers Assn. USPHS

BRYANT, BRENDA LOUISE, director, educator; b. Tacoma, Wash., Aug. 15, 1945; d. Charles Wilson Bryant and Vyra Alice Robinson. AB, Vassar Coll., 1967; MA, Cath. U., 1969; MPA, U. So. Calif., 1983, DPA, 1984. Dir. Andrews-Bryant, Inc., Washington, 1974—80; exec. v.p. Creative Assn. Internat., Inc., Washington, 1980—95; dir. Va. Women's Inst. Leadership

Mary Baldwin Coll., Staunton, Va., 1995—. Pres. Soc. Internat. Devel., Washington, 1991—93. Editor: The Leader, 1997—. Mem. leadership devel. com. Va. Bd. Edn., Richmond, Va., 2001—02. Mem.: Assn. Mil. Colls. and Schs. U.S. (pres. 2002—03). Avocation: physical fitness. Office: Mary Baldwin Coll 215 Market St Staunton VA 24401

BRYANT, DARYL LESLIE, painter, educator; b. L.A., Feb. 11, 1940; d. Colin Willis and Virginia Rouseau (Graves) Timmons; m. Dennis Rourke Murphy, 1960 (div. 1972); children: John Ashley, Sarah; m. Daniel Walster Bryant, 1985. Student, U. So. Calif., Acad. Arts, Florence, Italy; AA, Valley Coll., Van Nuys, Calif. Asst. designer Koret Calif., San Francisco, 1959-60; freelance artist Studiowork, Studio City, Calif.; art dir. Brentwood (Calif.) Publs., 1978-87; painter, graphic designer South Pasadena, Calif., 1987—; tchr. Creative Arts Group, Sierra Madre, Calif., 1996—. Works published in books and mags. Mem. Mid Valley Arts League (bd. dirs. 1993—), Nat. Watercolor Soc. (signature), Watercolor West (signature), Calif. Art Club (signature). Avocations: swimming, hiking, travel, journal keeping.

BRYANT, ESTHER, investment manager, retired correspondent; b. Chgo., Oct. 28, 1922; d. Joseph and Pauline (Smith) Gooder; m. Harold Bryant, Sept. 6, 1947; children: James, Janet. Typist, dictaphone operator Maremont Automotive, Chgo., 1942-44; salesperson Carson Pirie Scott & Co., 1945-47; coord. donations AMA, Chgo., 1979-81; corr. Rotary Internat., Evanston, Ill., 1982-88. Avocations: collecting antiques, rug hooking, singing. Home: 850 N Dewitt Pl Apt 8K Chicago IL 60611-7310

BRYANT, JANICE ANN, special education department administrator; b. Ada, OK, Mar. 11, 1955; d. Virgil and Corine Townsend; m. Larry Paul Bryant, Mar. 16, 1985; children: Samuel Paul, Mark Nathaniel. BS in Edn, E Ctrl Univ, Ada, OK, 1973—77, MEd, 1978—80. Cert. tchr. mental retardation OK, elem. edn. OK, 7th/8th gr. Social Studies OK, learning disabilities tchr. OK, reading specialist OK. Mem.: Oklahoma Dirs. Spl. Svcs. Baptist. Avocations: gardening, needlecrafts, cooking.

BRYANT, JOSEPHINE HARRIET, library executive; b. Oshawa, Ontario, Canada, Dec. 3, 1947; d. Donald Joseph and Margaret Mary (Quilty) B.; children: David Joseph, Michael Andrew. BA, U. Toronto, Ont., 1969, BLS, 1970, MLS, 1974; diploma in Pub. Adminstrn., U. Western Ont., London, 1988. Libr. Ont. Hydro, Toronto, 1970-74; libr. supr. Brampton Pub. Libr. and Art Gallery, Canada, 1974-77, br. head, 1977-79; regional dir. Fairview North York Pub. Libr., Canada, 1983-85, mgr. century libr., 1986, dep. dir., 1986-88, CEO, 1988-98; city libr. Toronto Pub. Libr., Canada, 1998—. Co-chair faculty info. sci. fundraising com., dean's adv. com. U. Toronto. Mem. ALA, Can. Libr. Assn., Ont. Libr. Assn., Inst. Pub. Adminstrn., Urban Libr. Coun., Bertelsmann Found., Can. Inst. for Hist. Micro-reprodns. Avocation: golf. Office: Toronto Pub Libr 789 Yonge St Toronto ON Canada M4W 2G8

BRYANT, KAREN WORSTELL, financial advisor, investment company executive; b. Cadillac, Mich., Sept. 7, 1942; d. Harley Orville and Rose Edith (Bell) Worstell; children: Lynda Jean Bashoor, Tracey Jo Taylor, Cynthia Jill Warren, Troy Thomas; m. Robert Melvin Bryant, Nov. 29, 1968. Student, Cen. Mich. U., 1963-67, Mich. State U., 1966, Johns Hopkins U., 1982-83, Loyola U., 1983. Sales rep. Xerox Corp., Southfield, Mich., 1972-74; [illegible] IBM World Trade Asia, The Policy Study Grp., Johnson & Johnson Internat., Tokyo, Japan, 1974-79; area sales mgr. Universal Plastics, McLean, Va., 1979-81; exec. product mgr. The Western Union Telegraph Co., Upper Saddle River, N.J., 1981-86; dir. mktg. and sales support The Nat. Guardian Corp., Greenwich, Conn., 1986-88; v.p., fin. cons. Salomon Smith Barney, Paramus, N.J., 1988-97; sr. v.p., fin. advisor Morgan Stanley, Pearl River, NY, 1997—. Guest lectr. for orgns.; guest on TV documentaries. Mem.: Nature Conservancy, Am. Lung Assn., World Wildlife Fedn., NY State Horse Coun. Avocations: horseback riding, power boating, decorating, horticulture. Home: Clermont on the Hudson One Main St 1301 Nyack NY 10960-3251 Office: Morgan Stanley Box 1726 One Blue Hill Plz 1st Fl Pearl River NY 10965-2535

BRYANT, MARIAN ALANNA, electric company consultant; b. Riverside, Calif., Apr. 5, 1955; d. Alan L. Bryant and Dorothea Sara Marie Ellington; children: Collin, Erin. BSBA, U. Ariz., 1983; MBA, U. Phoenix, 1990. Mgr. acctg. DM Fed. Credit Union, Tucson, Ariz., 1983-85; fin. analyst Carondelet Health Care, Tucson, 1985-93; fin. mgr. U. Med. Ctr., Tucson, 1993-97; internal bus. cons. Tucson Electric Power Co., 1997—. Bd. dirs. Tucson Urban League, 1997-99, Frontier Little League, Tucson, 1998-99; vol. mayoral campaign Bruce Wheeler, Tucson, 1995. Mem. Assn. of Internal Mgmt. Cons., Internal Mgmt. Accts. Avocations: hiking in mountains, weight lifting, racquetball, biking, swimming. Home: 6461 W Box Canyon Dr Tucson AZ 85745-9460 Office: Tucson Electric Power Co 220 W 6th St # Da314 Tucson AZ 85701-1093

BRYANT, RENEE TABOR, director, educator; d. Stephen C. Tabor and Gay Sallee Forsythe; m. Randy Bryant; 1 child, Sarah Elizabeth Clevenger. BS in Vocat. Edn., MS in Edn., U. Ky., 1993. Assoc. dean student affairs Hazard Cmty. and Tech. Coll., 2000—01; dir. retention svcs. Hazard C.C., 2001—. Bd. dirs. No Limits - MR/DD Svc. Provider, West Liberty, Ky., 1999—; charter mem. Leadership East Ky. Program, Hazard, 1999; co-sponsor student adv. coun. Hazard Tech. Coll., 1999—2001; mem. Ky. Appalachian Adv. Coun., Hazard, 2000—04; co-sponsor student amb. club Hazard C.C., 2001. Editor (author): (newsletter) Retention Review. Parent vol. Breathitt Youth Soccer League, Jackson, Ky., 1998, pub. rels. and interim sec., 2001, fundraising chair, 2003; vol. Repair Affair, Hazard, 1999; judge 4-H Talk Meet, Hazard, 2002, 2003; vol. Hampton United Meth. Ch., Jackson. Jane Venable Brown scholar, U. Ky., 1989. Mem.: Southeastern Counseling Assn., So. Poverty Law Ctr. - Nat. Campaign for Tolerance, Ky. Assn. Devel. Educators, Ky. Edn. Assn., Ky. Assn. Vocat. Edn. Spl. Needs Pers. (region 12 rep. 2003—), Ky. Paleontol. Soc., Hazard Lions Club, Phi Upsilon Omicron. Avocations: gardening, playing fiddle, travel. Office: Hazard Cmty & Tech Coll One Cmty Coll Dr Hazard KY 41701 E-mail: renee.bryant@kctcs.edu.

BRYANT, RHONA E. real estate company executive; d. Roosevelt William Bryant and Rhona M. Anthony-Bryant; m. Keith D. Howell, Jan. 23, 2004; 1 child, Rosetta Bryant Faulkner. Student in micro computer and bus. ops., Blake Bus. Sch., N.Y.C., 1990—91; grad., N.Y. State Constrn. Mgmt. Inst., 2003. Cert. real estate broker Realty Inst., 2000, loan officer NY State Cert. Tng. Ctr., 2001, real estate cons. Nat. Assn. Real Estate Cons., 2003. Lic. realtor/assoc. broker Century 21, Queens, NY, 1997—2002; chmn., CEO Lord & Bryant, Ltd., Queens, NY, 2002—. Exec. sec. Smith Barney Harris Upham & Co, Inc., N.Y.C., NY, 1991—93; adminstr. Pan Am. Caribbean Fin. Group, N.Y.C., NY, 1993—94; adminstrv. asst. Temp Positions, N.Y.C., NY, 1994—96; mktg. asst. S & S X-Ray Products, Bklyn., 1996—98. Mem. Cambria Heights (N.Y.) Civic Assn., 1997—99; supporter Realtors Polit. Action Com., N.Y.C., NY, 1999—2002; mem. Urban Bankers Coalition, N.Y.C., NY, 1995—96. Recipient Million Dollar Level, Century 21 Metro N.Y. / L.I. Brokers Coun., 2001. Mem.: Nat. Assn. Real Estate Cons. (consumer cert. real estate cons. 2003), Nat. Assn. Ind. Real Estate Brokers, L.I. Bd. of Realtors, Inc. (licentiate; realtor mem. 1997—2002), N.Y. State Assn. Realtors (licentiate), Christian Real Estate Network (assoc.; mem. 2002—04). Republican. Born Again Christian. Achievements include completion of Entrepreneurial Assistance Program/New York. Avocations: tennis, theater, volleyball, walking, mentoring. Office Phone: 800-320-0952.

BRYANT, RUTH ALYNE, banker; b. Memphis, Jan. 12, 1924; d. James Walter and Leola (Edgar) B. Student, Rhodes Coll. (formerly Southwestern Coll.), Memphis, 1941-43; LHD (hon.), U. Mo., St. Louis, 1990. Clk. Fed. Res. Bank of St. Louis (Memphis Br.), 1943-47, exec. sec., 1947-68, asst. cashier, 1968-69, asst. v.p., 1969-73, v.p., 1973-90. Trustee chancellor's coun. U. Mo., St. Louis, 1979—, chmn., 1985-88; pres. Premiere Performances, 1990-96, vice chmn., 1996-98, bd. dirs., 1998; mem. adv. bd. Salvation Army, St. Louis, 1983-91, DePaul Health Ctr., St. Louis, 1984-87; adv. coun. Hope Ctr., St. Louis, 1987, chmn., 1990-91; chmn. adv. coun. Riverway Sch., 1989-95; bd. dirs. Assocs. of St. Louis U. Librs., 1977—, pres., 1983-85; bd. dirs. The Vanderschmidt's Sch., 1980-86, Internat. Edn. Consortium, 1988-92; bd. dirs. St. Louis Merc. Libr., 1989—, sec., 1990-92, v.p., 1992-94, pres., 1994-2000; trustee Mo. Coun. on Econ. Edn., 1989-93; bd. dirs. Dance St. Louis, 1992—2003, v.p., 1993-94, English Lang. Sch., 1993-97; mem. devel. bd. U. Mo. Press, 2002—. Fellow: Winston Churchill Meml.; mem.: Bank Mktg. Assn. (dir. Mo.-Ill. chpt. 1976—79), English Speaking Union (bd. dirs. 1989—, 1989—, v.p. 1992—96, nat. bd. dirs. 1995—96, pres. 1997—, nat. bd. dirs. 1998—), Nat. Assn. Bank Women (editor Woman Banker 1959—62, v.p. so. region 1967—68, pres. 1970—71, trustee edn1. found. 1974—75), Mo. Bankers Assn. (mktg. and pub. rels. com. 1974—76), Am. Inst. Banking (nat. women's com. 1962—63, pres. Memphis chpt. 1968—69), Alliance Francaise of St. Louis (exec. v.p. 2001—03, pres. 2003—), Nat. Soc. Arts and Letters, Rhodes Coll. Internat. Alumni Assn. (exec. bd. 1999—2000), Univ. Club, St. Louis, The Venerable Order of St. John in Jerusalem (comdr.). Home: 625 S Skinker Blvd Apt 202 Saint Louis MO 63105-2301

BRYANT-WILBURN, ROSITA DOLORES, special education educator; b. Phila., , July 17; d. Roland and Lena Bryant; m. Ron Wilburn; children: Bryan D. Davis, Briana D. Wilburn. EdB, The Coll. of N.J., Trenton, 1979; MEd, Western Oreg. U., Fairbanks, 1999—99. Spl. edn. tchr. Burlington County Inst. of Tech., Medford, NJ, 1979—85, Willingboro Sch. Dist., NJ, 1986—88; resource tchr. Woodriver Elem. Sch., Fairbanks, Alaska, 1989—. Spl. edn. com. chair Fairbanks Edn. Assn., Fairbanks, Alaska, 2001—. Vol. Corinthian Bapt. Ch., Fairbanks, Alaska, 2003. Mem.: Alpha Delta Kappa (sgt. at arms 2002), Delta Kappa Gamma, Delta Sigma Theta. Christian. Avocations: travel, camping, sewing. Home: PO Box 82680 Fairbanks AK 99708 Personal E-mail: wilburn@ptialaska.net.

BRYFONSKI, DEDRIA ANNE, publishing company executive; b. Utica, N.Y., Aug. 21, 1947; d. Lewis Francis and Catherine Marie (Stevens) B.; m. Alexander Burgess Cruden, May 24, 1975 BA, Nazareth Coll., Rochester, N.Y., 1969; MA, Fordham U., 1970. Editorial asst. Dial Press, N.Y.C., 1970-71; editor Walker & Co., N.Y.C., 1971-73, Gale Research Co., Detroit, 1974-79, sr. editor, 1979, v.p., assoc. editorial dir., 1979-84, sr. v.p., editorial dir., 1984-86, exec. v.p., pub., 1986-94, pres., CEO, 1995-98; pres. Gale Pub. The Gale Group, Farmington Hills, Mich., 1999—. Author: The New England Beach Book, 1974; editor: Contemporary Literary Criticism, Vols. 7-14, 1977-80, Twentieth Century Literary Criticism, vols. 1-2, 1977-78, Contemporary Issues Criticism, vol. 1, 1982, Contemporary Authors Autobiography Series, vol. 1, 1984 Bd. dirs. Friends of Detroit Pub. Libr., 1980-89, pres., 1984-86; bd. dirs. Friends of Librs. U.S.A., 1995—. Mem. ALA, Assn. Am. Pubs. (chmn. libraries com. 1983-85, exec. council gen. pub. div. 1985-87, co-chmn. joint com. resources and tech. services div. 1983-85). Home: 546 Lincoln Rd Grosse Pointe MI 48230-1218 Office: The Gale Group 27500 Drake Rd Farmington Hills MI 48331-3535

BRYNER, F. JEANNE, medical/surgical nurse; b. Waynesburg, Pa., June 2, 1951; d. Willis B. Henderson and Wilma Ruth Stiles; m. David B. Bryner, Dec. 20, 1969; children: Gary Michael, Summar Leigh. BA, Kent State U., 1996. Bd. cert. emergency nurse, Emergency Nurses Assn., RN Ohio. Med-surg. nurse Forum Health, Trumbull Meml. Hosp., Warren, Ohio, 1979—80, pediats. nurse, 1980—81, ICU nurse, ER nurse, immediate care nurse, staff nurse, 2000—. Tchr. creative writing various locations, 1990. Author: (chapbook) Breathless, 1995, (book of poetry) Blind Horse, 1999, (book of short stories) Eclipse, 2003; contbr. poetry to anthologies. Tchr. creative writing cancer support group Beacon, Warren, 1999—2001; v.p. Friends of Libr., Newton Falls, Ohio, 1999—. Recipient Stan and Tom Wick Poetry scholarship, Wick Poetry Program, Kent State U., 1990, Younger Poets Seminar fellowship, Bucknell U., 1992, Individual Artist fellowship, Ohio Arts Coun., 1997, Outstanding Leadership for Nursing award, Forum Health, 1994, Resolution of Accomodation, Newton Falls Bd. Edn., 2000, Outstanding Comty. Svc. award, Newton Falls Libr. Bd., 1996. Mem.: Sigma Tau Delta, Sigma Theta Tau. Democrat. Avocations: quilting, bicycling, reading. Office: Forum Health Trumbull Meml Hosp Elm Rd Cortland OH 44410

BRYNILDSEN-SMITH, KRISTINE ANN, principal; b. Seattle, Feb. 24, 1950; d. Rudolph Wyman and Shirley Ann (Atkinson) Neuser; m. Richard Stephen Brynildsen, June 3, 1972 (div. 1980); 1 child, Erik Brynildsen; m. Albert Joseph Smith Jr., June 25, 1983; children: Gregory Smith, Margaret Smith. BA, U. Wash., 1972, MA, 1975; EdD, Seattle U., 1984. Cert. continuing adminstr./prin.; cert. continuing tchr. Tchr. Benson Hill Elem., Renton, Wash., 1972-81, Lake Ridge Elem., Renton, 1981-84, Hazen H.S., Renton, 1984-86; prin. St. Catherine Elem., Seattle, 1986-93, Holy Cross H.S. (now Archbishop Murphy H.S.), Everett, Wash., 1993—. Mem. assessment team Cath. Schs., Seattle, 1990-93; adj. prof. Pacific Luth. U., Tacoma, 1979-86; workshop designer, presenter Highline Sch. Dist., Burien, Wash., 1983; participant Cath. Prin.'s Acad., 1989; spkr. NEA Conf. on Human and Civil Rights, 1979. Conf. chair World Affairs Coun., Seattle, 1985; mem. adv. com. U. Wash. Coll. of Edn., Seattle, 1983-85; mem. human rels. commn. Wash. Edn. Assn., Federal Way, 1979-81; bd. dirs. Wash. Fedn. Ind. Schs., 1998--, bd. chair, 2000-01; sch. adminstr. profl. edn. adv. bd. Ctrl. Wash. U., 2001--; mem. exec. com. Nat. Cath. Edn. Assn. Dept. Secondary Schs., 2002--. Recipient 10 Yrs. Adminstrv. Svc. award Cath. Archdiocese of Seattle, 1996, Outstanding Svc. award Archdiocese of Seattle, 1987, Spl. Svc. Recognition award Wash. Edn. Assn., 1984. Mem. ASCD, Rotary, Phi Delta Kappa (charter mem.). Democrat. Roman Catholic. Avocations: reading, music, ballet, theater. Home: 2224 Broadway E Seattle WA 98102-4136 Office: 12911 39th Ave SE Everett WA 98208-6159

BRYSON, NANCY S. federal agency administrator; BA in History, Boston U.; JD, Georgetown U. Staff atty., asst. counsel for appellate litig. U.S. Dept. of Labor, Occupl. Safety and Health Divsn. Solicitor's Office, 1975—79; trial atty., asst. chief land and natural resources divsn. environ. def. sect. U.S. Dept. of Justice, 1979—84; ptnr. Crowell & Moring, Washington, 1998—2001; gen. counsel USDA, Washington, 2001—. Vol. mediator D.C. Bar. Office: USDA Gen Counsel 1400 Independence Ave SW Washington DC 20250

BUBB, KAREN DENISE, art association administrator, educator; b. Boise, Idaho, July 14, 1966; d. Ron Wilson Bubb and Marilyn Joyce (Sterns) Howard; m. Robert Henry Engbers, Aug. 1997. BFA, U. Oreg., 1990. Program mgr., preparator Exit Art/The First World, N.Y.C., 1990—94; program mgr., registrar Assn. Graphic Comms., N.Y.C., 1994—97; first night coord. Boise City Arts Commn., 1997—98, pub. arts mgr., 1998—. Cons. pub. art, Twin Falls, Moscow, McCall and Coeur d'Alene, Idaho, 1998—; presenter art and neighborhoods Seattle Arts Commn., 2000. Exhibitions include Boise State U., 1998, Esther Simplot Performing Arts Acad., Boise, 1999, J. Crist Gallery, 1999, Stewart Gallery, 2000, 2001, Boise Art Mus., 2001, Fulton St. Theater, Boise, 2001; contbr. articles to profl. publs. Guest lectr. Bishop Kelly H.S., Boise, 1997—; grant writer for individual women artists Boise, 1998—; mem. cmty. adv. bd. dept. art Boise State U., 1998—; mem. Boise 2000 Lasting Legacy Grant Com.; guest artist Work and Learn program, 2001—04. Recipient Most Creative Design award, Interior Design Assn., Boise, 2001, Accomplished Under 40 award, Idaho Bus. Rev., Boise, 2001. Avocations: painting, sculpting, reading, bicycling. Home: 2425 Ellis Ave Boise ID 83702 Office: Boise City Arts Commn PO Box 500 Boise ID 83701-0500 E-mail: kbubb@cityofboise.org.

BUC, NANCY LILLIAN, lawyer; b. Orange, N.J., July 27, 1944; d. George L. and Ethel Buc. AB, Brown U., 1965, LLD (hon.), 1994; LLB, U. Va., 1969. Bar: Va. 1969, N.Y. 1977, D.C. 1978. Atty. Fed. Trade Commn., Washington, 1969-72; assoc. Weil, Gotshal & Manges, N.Y., 1972-77, ptnr., 1977-78, Washington, 1978-80, 81-94, Buc & Beardsley, Washington, 1994—; chief counsel FDA, Rockville, Md., 1980-81. Mem. recombinant DNA adv. com. NIH, 1990-94; consensus panelist NIH Consensus Devel. Conf. on Effective Med. Treatment of Heroin Addiction, 1997; adj. prof. law Georgetown U. Law Ctr., 2000-2002. Mem. editl. bd. Food Drug and Cosmetic Law Jour., 1981-87, 94-97, Jour. of Products Liability, 1981-92, Health Span: The Jour. of Health, Bus. & Law, 1984-95. Mem. adv. com. on new devels. in biotech. 1986-89, mem. adv. com. on govt. policies and pharm. R & D, 1989-93, Office of Tech. Assessment, Washington, mem. com. to study drug abuse medications devel. and rsch., 1993-95; mem. com. on contraceptive R & D, Inst. Medicine, Washington, 1994-96; trustee Brown U., 1973-78, 1998—; fellow, 1980-92. Recipient Disting. Svc. award Fed. Trade Commn., Washington, 1972, Award of Merit FDA, Rockville, 1981, Sec.'s Spl. citation HHS, Washington, 1981, Ind. award Associated. Alumni of Brown U., 1991. Mem. ABA (mem. spl. com. to study FTC 1988-89), Com. of 200, Nat. Partnership for Women and Families (bd. dirs.). Office: Buc & Beardsley 919 18th St NW Ste 600 Washington DC 20006-5507 Office Phone: 202-736-3610. E-mail: nlb@bucbeardsley.com.

BUCCIARELLI, PATRICE DENICE, journalist; b. Chicago, Ill., July 24, 1953; d. Pasquale Antonio Raia and Yolanda Beatrice Verzani; m. Barry Ernesto Bucciarelli, Nov. 27, 2000. BA in Com., Rivier Coll., Nashua, NH, 1971—75. Exec. editor Leader Newspapers, Inc., Chicago, Ill., 1999—2001; v.p. Barraia Ltd. Pub., Monticello, Ky., 2001—. Writer Area Devel. mag., Westbury, NY, 2003—. Author: (poetry) Basic Italian. Recipient Best Lifestye Sect./Editl., Ill. Press Assn., 1998. R-Liberal. Roman Catholic. Achievements include design of Barraia Ltd. Greeting Arts. Avocations: archeology, music, game fishing, travel.

BUCCIERI, SHIRLEY H. lawyer; b. Terre Haute, Ind., Sept. 23, 1951; d. Mike and Dorothy Louise Hanna; m. Alexander C. Buccieri, Aug. 11, 1973; 1 child. BS in Maths., Purdue U., 1973; JD, U. Akron, 1982. Various positions GM Corp., Warren, Ohio, 1973-81, supt. indsl. engring., 1981-83; assoc. Gibson, Dunn & Crutcher, San Francisco, 1983-91, ptnr., 1991-95; sr. v.p., gen. counsel, sec. Transamerica Corp., San Francisco, 1995—. Mem. dean's adv. coun. Sch. Sci. Purdue U., 1999, West Lafayette, Ind., 1998—; mem. affil. leadership team Stanford U., Palo Alto, Calif., 1998—; old master Purdue U., 1999. Recipient Women in Leadership award San Francisco Bus. Times, 1997, 98, 99. Mem. Phi Beta Kappa. Roman Catholic. Office: Transamerica Corp 600 Montgomery St Ste 2300 San Francisco CA 94111-2770

BUCELLA, DONNA ANN, federal official; b. Bayside, N.Y., June 14, 1956; Student, St. John's U., 1974-76; BA in Sociology with distinction, U. Va., 1978; JD, U. Miami, 1983. Bar: Fla. 1984, U.S. Ct. Mil. Appeals 1985, Va. 1986. Paralegal Dickstein, Shapiro & Morin, Washington, 1978-80; criminal def. atty. U.S. Army Judge Advocacy Gen. Corps., Ft. Belvoir, Va., 1984-86, litigation atty. Washington, 1986-87; asst. U.S. Atty. So. Dist. Fla., 1987-93, dep. chief major crimes, 1992, dep. chief spl. investigations, 1992-93; dir. Office Legal Edn. Exec. Office U.S. Attys. U.S. Dept. Justice, Washington, 1993-94, prin. dep. dir., 1994-97, dir., 1997-99; interim U.S. Atty. Mid. Dist. Fla., 1994, U.S. Atty., 1999—. Lt. col. USAR Mem. ABA, Fla. Bar (mil. law com. 1985-87, 93), Phi Alpha Delta. Office: US Atty's Office 400 N Tampa St Ste 3200 Tampa FL 33602 4774

BUCEY, CONSTANCE VIRGINIA RUSSELL, retired elementary school educator, education educator; b. Miami, Aug. 22, 1936; d. Mose and Lillian (Jones) Russell; m. Henry Lee Bucey. BS Virginia State Coll., 1959, postgrad. U. Miami, 1961—63; postgrad. Fla. A&M U., Tallahassee, 1962—63; postgrad. UCLA, 1970; MA and Reading Specialist Credential, Pepperdine U., 1976. Tchr. J.R.E. Lee Elem. Sch., South Miami, Fla., 1959—67, Margaret Duff Elem. Sch., Rosemead, Calif., 1974—82, Hillcrest Elem. Sch., Monterey Park, Calif., 1982—95; ret., 1995; part-time prof. Calif. State U. Charter Sch. Edn., L.A., 1998—, univ. supr. in divsn. curriculum and instrn., 1998—. Bd. pres., v.p., dir. First Fin. Fed. Credit Union, 1973—82, dir., 1985—. Los Angeles Ct. juror docent. Recipient Vol. Achievement Filene award, 1997, awards for oil paintings, various exhbns. Mem.: AAUW, NEA, Nat. Assn. Credit Union Presidents, Ret. Tchrs. Calif., Garvery Sch. Tchrs., Calif. Tchrs. Assn., Reading Specialists of Calif., Women Aware, Southland Art Assn., Bus. and Profl. Womens Club, Am. Legion Aux., Alpha Kappa Alpha. Home: 871 Ashiya Rd Montebello CA 90640

BUCHANAN, EDNA, journalist; b. Paterson, N.J. Journalist Miami Beach (Fla.) Daily Sun, 1965-70; became journalist The Miami (Fla.) Herald, 1970. Author: Carr: Five Years of Rape and Murder, 1979, The Corpse Had a Familiar Face: Covering America's Hottest Beat, 1987, Nobody Lives Forever, 1990, Never Let Them See You Cry: More From Miami, America's Hottest Beat, 1992, Contents Under Pressure, 1992, Miami, It's Murder, 1994, Suitable for Framing, 1995, Act of Betrayal, 1996, Margin of Error, 1997, Pulse, 1998, Garden of Evil, 1999, You Only Die Twice, 2001; contbr. articles to popular mags. Recipient Green Eye Shade award Soc. Profl. Journalists, 1982, Pulitzer prize for gen. reporting, 1986. Mem. United Ch. of Christ. Office: care Don Congdon Assocs 156 5th Ave Ste 625 New York NY 10010-7002

BUCHANAN, GLORIA JEAN, sales executive; b. Bowling Green, Ky., Nov. 3, 1950; d. Albert M. and Lenora (Hayes)Paschal; m. Michael C. Moonan (div.); 1 child, Shelly; m. Andrew George. Mgr. Alexander Wallcovering, Falls Church, Va., 1976-81; decorator Duron Paints and Wallcovering, Beltsville, Md., 1982-84, sales rep., 1984-85, archtl. rep., 1985-86, dir., 1986-91; dir. archtl. sales dept. McCormick Paint Works Co., Rockville, Md., 1991-96; area sales mgr. PPG Industries Archtl. Finishes, Pitts., 1997—, sr. cons., 1999—. Bd. govs. Washington Bldg. Congress, 1994—. Mem. NAFE, Constrn. Specification Inst. (industry dir. 1993-94, membership chmn. 1993-94, v.p. 1995-97, pres. 1997-98, dir. region inst. 2000—, inst. dir. 2000), Interior Design Soc., Washington Sales and Mktg. Council. Republican. Episcopalian. Home: 5227 Blossom Hill Dr Haymarket VA 20169 Office: PPG Industries Inc 1 PPG Plaza Pittsburgh PA 15272-0001 E-mail: gbuchanan@ppg.com.

BUCHANAN, LOUISE, political organization worker, consultant; d. James Ellis and May (Hall) Buchanan. BA, Blue Mountain Coll., 1958; MA, Carver Sch. Missions and Social Work, 1960. Exec. dir. Bapt. Good Will Ctr., Charleston, SC, 1960—65; comty. organizer Inner City Meth. Coun., Louisville, 1965—66; neighborhood coord. Comty. Action Commn., Louisville, 1966—71; supr. comty. resources Ky. Dept. Child Welfare, Louisville and Frankfort, Ky., 1971—74; exec. asst. to Rep. Jack Kemp U.S. Ho. Reps., Washington, 1974—76, exec. asst. to Rep. Joe Early, 1976—93; cons. child advocacy Washington, 1993—; mem. adv. bd. Efforts from Ex-Convicts, Washington, 1978—96; exec. bd. pres. Life Pieces to Masterpieces, Washington, 1997—; mem. adv. bd. Congl. Chorus, Washington, 1989—. Organizer Capitol Hill Staffers for Hungry and Homeless, Washington, 1976—93; trainer benefit walks For Love of Children, Washington, 1988; active Arlingtonians for Better County, 1997; mem. Common Cause, 1989—; coord. Capitol Hill Women's Polit. Caucus,

Washington, 1976—83; mem., v.p. Park Spring Bd. Park Spring Condo Assn., 1999—. Recipient Keys to City of Worcester, Mass., Worcester City Coun., 1986, 1988, outstanding Svc. award, Efforts from Ex-Convicts, 1992, Leadership award, Life Pieces to Masterpieces, 2002. Democrat. Presbyterian. Avocations: music, writing, travel, tennis, being a loyal friend. Home: # 201 5075 7th Rd S Arlington VA 22204 Office: Consulting for Creative Change # 201 5075 7th Rd S Arlington VA 22204 Office Phone: 703-820-7293. Personal E-mail: lbuch44@msn.com.

BUCHANAN, MARGARET, publishing executive; Various mgmt. positions Rockford (Ill.) Register Star, Elmira (N.Y.) Star-Gazette; pub. Idaho Statesman, Boise, 1999—2003, Cin. Enquirer, 2003—. Office: Cin Enquirer 312 Elm St Cincinnati OH 45202

BUCHANAN, MARIAH SPANN, artist; b. Helena, Ark., Mar. 29, 1952; d. Levi and Rosie Bee Spann; m. Reuben William Buchanan, Dec. 30, 1984; children: David Allen, Johna Catrell, Reuben William Jr. BS in Edn., Ark. State U., Jonesboro, 1983; MFA, Ctrl. Mich. U., 2001. Glass engraver The Crystal Shop, Atlanta, 1984—86; sample maker J. Reynolds Designs, Atlanta, 1985—88; art tchr. Clayton County Bd. Edn., Jonesboro, Ga., 1992—. Artist Women's Caucus for Arts, Atlanta, 2000—, Nat. Art Assn., 1996—; pvt. art tchr., Clayton, Ga., 2002—. Childrens book, Bellfree's Leap to Better Grammer, 1996; illustrator: book My Life Story, 2000. Mentor Boys and Girls Club, Atlanta, 1997—2002; edn. specialist Clayton County Clean and Beautiful, 1998—. Named Artist of the Month, Clayton News Daily, 2002. Mem.: Clayton County Edn. Assn. (bd. mem., IPD chair 1992—, lobbyist 1998—). Home: 5981 Heatherwood Ln Riverdale GA 30296

BUCHANAN, MARY BETH, prosecutor; BA, U. Pa.; JD, U. Pittsburgh Sch. Law. Assoc. Strassburger, McKenne, Gutnick and Potter, Pittsburgh, 1987—88; asst. US Atty. Western Dist. of Pa., 1988—2001, US Atty., 2001—. Office: US Attorney 633 US Post Office & Courthouse Pittsburgh PA 15219

BUCHANAN, THERESA CARROLL, judge; b. Alexandria, Va., Aug. 27, 1957; BS, U. Va., 1979; JD, Coll. of William and Mary, 1982. Pvt. practice law, 1983-91; asst. U.S. atty. U.S. Dist. Ct. (ea. dist.) Va., Alexandria, 1991-96, magistrate judge, 1996—. Mem. Fed. Bar Assn., Va. State Bar Assn., Alexandria Bar Assn.

BUCHBINDER, BARBARA JOYCE, art and architectural historian; b. Bronx, N.Y., Dec. 23, 1944; d. Michael and Esther Buchbinder. BA cum laude, Vanderbilt U., 1965; PhD, Northwestern U., 1974. Teaching asst. Northwestern U., Evanston, Ill., 1967-68, lectr. Chgo., 1975; freelance researcher and writer Evanston, 1977—; editor GreenAssoc. Architects, Inc., Evanston, 1979-2000; cons. nomination forms Nat. Register of Historic Places, 1983—. Mem. architecture adv. com. Mus. Sci. and Industry, Chgo., 1980-86; trustee Evanston Hist. Soc., 1986-92, pres., 1988-90, trustee emeritus, 1999, mem. house walk com. 1981-83, 88-90, chmn., 1988-90, mem. restoration planning com., 1980-91, editor newsletter TimeLines, 1989-92; bd. dir. Heartland Alliance Women's Bd. Author: Lucy Fitch Perkins, 1984, Evanston: A Pictorial History, 1989; editor, compiler Evanstoniana, 1984; guest curator "Lucy Fitch Perkins" exhibit, 1983-84, "Photographs from Evanstoniana" exhibit, 1984-87; pub. photographer: Evanstoniana, 1984, Evanston: A Pictorial History, 1989, Victorian Details, 1990; history editor Chgo. Yacht Club Blinker, 1993-95; editor Cruising Sail Fleet, 1993-98, women's com., 1998-2000, race com., 1999-2000; contbr. articles to profl. jours. Founding mem. Preservation League Evanston, 1982; commr. Evanston Preservation Commn., 1981-89, chmn. preservations awards com., 1983-84, mem. evaln. com., 1978-92, chmn., 1985-89; mem. Citizen's Adv. Com. on Pub. Pl. Names, 1989-92; bd. dirs. Dewey Cmty. Conf., 1981-84, mem. exec. com., 1981-82, rec. sec., 1982-83. Univ. fellow Northwestern U., 1968-69, Dissertation Year fellow, 1969-70; Vanderbilt U. scholar, 1962-65. Mem. Victorian Soc. in Am. (bd. dirs. Chgo. chpt. 1978-81), Chgo. Architecture Found. Aux. Bd. (sec. 1990-91, exec. com. 1990-92, v.p. for cmty. affairs 1991-92), Archtl. Soc. Art Inst. Chgo., Soc. Archtl. Historians, Women's Archtl. League (v.p. 1980-82), Chgo. Maritime Soc., Nat. Trust for Hist. Preservation, Lake Forest Found. for Hist. Preservation, Tibetan Terrier Club Am. (Chgo. regional splty. chmn., 2001-02), Cliff Dwellers Club. Avocations: dogs, sailing, photography. Home and Office: 1026 Michigan Ave Evanston IL 60202-1436

BUCHER, MARY, school librarian; b. Olean, NY, June 16, 1952; d. Joseph Clinton and Myra Birdeen Bucher. BA in Polit. Sci., SUNY, Oswego, 1974; MLS, SUNY, Albany, 1976; MEd, St. Lawrence U., 1982. Records mgmt. specialist City of Oswego, NY, 1977—78; libr. SUNY Canton, NY, 1978—. Vis. libr. Bolton Inst. Higher Edn., England, 1987. Mem. St. Lawrence County Hist. Soc., Canton, Canton/Potsdam Hosp. Guild, Potsdam, NY. Recipient SUNY Chancellor's award for excellence in librarianship, SUNY, 1990. Mem.: AAUW (membership v.p. 2000—03), Soc. Am. Archivists, Assn. Coll. and Rsch. Librs., SUNY Librs. Assn., United U. Professions (chpt. sec. 1980, mem. N.Y. state/United U. Professions com. on tech. 1998—99, mem. N.Y. state/United U. Professions joint com. on health and safety 1999). Roman Catholic. Avocations: travel, photography, cooking. Office: SUNY Canton Cornell Dr Canton NY 13617

BUCHER, SUSAN A. elementary school educator, music educator; b. Ft. Morgan, Colo., Jan. 18, 1955; d. Elmer Wallace and Betty Mae Compton; m. Jon Arthur Bucher, May 30, 1993; children: Renee, Amy, Jon Aric, Julie, Desi, Tyler. B in Music Edn., Southwestern Coll., 1978; postgrad., Harding U., 1982. Activity dir. First United Meth. Ch., Searcy, Ark., 1980—81; music tchr. Searcy McRae Elem. Sch., 1982—. Pvt. piano tchr., Searcy, 1987—; music dir. Grace United Meth. Ch., Searcy, 1988—93; min. music First Presbyn. Ch., Searcy, 1993—98; music dir. St. Paul United Meth. Ch., Searcy, 1998—. Magic tchr. Fun, Unlimited-Harding U., Searcy, 1994—. Named Tchr. of the Yr., Optimist Club, 1996—97; recipient Searcy Tchr. of the Yr., VFW, 2001—02, Dist. Tchr. of the Yr., 2001—02, State Tchr. of the Yr., 2001—02. Mem.: MENC, Ark. Choral Dir. Assn., Brush VFW Aux., Internat. Brotherhood Magicians, Beethoven Club (mem. festival planning com. 1982—). Avocations: crafts, decorating, learning and playing different instruments. Home: 1718 Miranda Searcy AR 72143 Office: Searcy McRae Elem Sch 609 W McRae Searcy AR 72143

BUCHERT, STEPHANIE NICOLE, music educator; b. Seaford, Del., Sept. 2, 1976; d. John George and Connie Lee Chapis; m. Todd Michael Buchert; 1 child, Colby Skyler. student, BS in Music Edn., West Chester U., 1998. Cert. music tchr. Choir dir., asst. band dir. Cape Henlopen H.S., Lewes, Del., 1998—2002; choir dir., music tchr. Lewes Mid. Sch., 2002—03, Beacon Mid. Sch., 2003—. Mem. Delaware Jr. All State Chours Com., 2002—03. Mem.: Del. State Educators Assn., Del. Music Educators Assn. Avocations: singing, reading, drawing. Home: 18547 Whaleys Corner Road Georgetown DE 19947 Office: Beacon Mid Sch 19483 John J Williams Hwy Lewes DE 19958

BUCHHOLZ, DEBBY, lawyer; Bachelor's, U Calif San Diego; JD, Harvard Law Sch. Gen. counsel John F. Kennedy Ctr. Performing Arts, Washington; gen mgr La Jolla Playhouse, La Jolla, Calif., 2003—. Office: La Jolla Playhouse 2910 La Jolla Village Dr PO Box 12039 La Jolla CA 92039

BUCHIN, JACQUELINE CHASE, clinical psychologist; b. Providence, Nov. 27, 1935; d. Leslie Thurber and Mary Hillyer (Lyon) Chase; m. Stanley Ira Buchin, Sept. 14, 1957; children: Linda Chase Sullivan, David Lyon, Gordon Tomlinson. BA, Wellesley Coll., 1957; MEd in Counseling Psychology, Antioch U., 1979; PsyD, Mass. Sch. Profl. Psychology, Boston, 1990. Lic. clin. psychologist Mass. Dir., coord. emergency housing program Multi-Svc. Ctr., Newton, Mass., 1978-81; family therapy intern Newtom Guidance Clinic, 1981-82, Framingham (Mass.) Youth Guidance, 1982-84; psychology intern The Arbour Hosp., Boston, 1984-85, Solomon Carter Fuller Hosp., Boston, 1985-86, Behavior Assocs., Boston, 1986-90; staff psychologist Biobehavioral Treatment Ctr., Brookline, Mass., 1990—; fellow in clin. cognitive therapy program Mass. Gen. Hosp., Boston, 1993-95, clin. assoc., 1995—, rsch. clinician, 1995—. Clin. instr. Psychology Dept. Harvard Med. Sch., Boston, 1995—; faculty mem. Inst. Cognitive Therapy Mass. Gen. Hosp., Boston, 1996—99; founding mem. Acad. Cognitive Therapy, Boston, 2000. Pres. Wellesley Jr. Svc. League, 1972—73; mem., bd. dirs. Jr. League of Boston, 1975—77; bd. dirs. Wellesley Cmty. Chest and Coun., 1972—73, Wellesley Friendly Assoc., 1972—73, Family Counseling Region W, 1969; bd. dirs. Wellesley chpt. ARC; bd. dirs. Wellesley Cmty. Child Care, 1976, Human Rels. Svc.; trustee Mass. Sch. Profl. Psychology, chmn. human resources com., 1991—99. Mem.: APA, Mass. Psychol. Assn., Assn. for Advancement of Behavior Therapy. Episcopalian. Home: Union Wharf Boston MA 02109-1206 Office: Biobehavioral Treatment Ctr 1051 Beacon St Brookline MA 02446-3282

BUCHMANN, MOLLY O'BANION, choreographer, ballet educator; b. Baton Rouge, Nov. 22, 1949; d. James Dennis and Annie Laurie (Joffrion) O'Banion; m. Fred J. Buchmann, Aug. 23, 1969; children: F. Jason (dec.), Dennis Andrew. BS in Secondary Edn., La. State U., 1971, MS in Dance, 1973. Artistic dir. Baton Rouge Ballet Theatre, 1976—; choreographer Baton Rouge Little Theatre, 1983—; tchr. dance Baton Rouge Magnet H.S., 1979-85; owner, mgr. The Dancers' Workshop, Baton Rouge, 1973—; dir. dance Scotlandville Magnet H.S., 1986-98; dance dir., profl.-in-residence dept. theatre La. State U., Baton Rouge, 1999—. Vis. artist Arts and Humanities Council of Greater Baton Rouge, 1976; choreographer Aubin Lane Dinner Theatre, Baton Rouge, 1980-82; mem. cultural caucus steering com. La. State Div. of Arts, cons., 1986. Editor La. Dance News, 1976-77. Choreographer numerous ballets. State of La. Div. Arts Choreographic grant, 1982; Baton Rouge Alumni Fedn. scholar, 1967; recipient Mayor-Pres.'s award. Mem. Southwest Regional Ballet Assn. (bd. dirs., sec. 1984-88, parliamentarian 1993). Democrat. Roman Catholic. Avocations: performing, resting, reading. Office: Baton Rouge Ballet Theatre PO Box 82288 Baton Rouge LA 70884-2288 Office Phone: 225-578-4974.

BUCHSBAUM, JULIANNE, writer, educator; b. L.A., Jan. 6, 1970; d. Herbert Joseph and Linda Gail (Lampack) Buchsbaum. BA summa cum laude, Beloit Coll., 1993; MFA, U. Iowa, 1999; MLIS, U. Pitts., 2002. Copy editor J.D. Pub., Glendale, Wis., 1996—97; asst. poetry editor Iowa Rev., Iowa City, 1998—99; freelance tech. editor Iowa City, 2000—01; ref. libr. intern law libr. U. Pitts., 2002; libr. and tech. cons. Kenyon Coll., Gambier, Ohio, 2002—, tchr. creative writing, 2003—. Affiliated scholar dept. English Kenyon Coll., Gambier, 2002—. Author: Slowly, Slowly, Horses, 2001. Recipient Randall Jarrell Poetry prize, N.C. Writers Network, 1999; Writer's grantee, Vt. Studio Ctr., 1997, Paul Engle fellow, James Michener Found., 1999. Mem.: ALA, Assn. Coll. and Rsch. Libraries, Beta Phi Mu, Phi Beta Kappa. Office: Olin & Chalmers Library Kenyon Coll 103 College Dr Gambier OH 43022

BUCHSBAUM, KAREN FUSON, public relations executive, consultant; b. New Bern, N.C., Dec. 26, 1953; d. Robert Henderson and Amelia Carmen Fuson; m. Frederick Joel Buchsbaum, Nov. 23, 1979; 1 child, Ashley. BS in Comms., U. Tenn., Knoxville, 1975. Asst. dir., pub. info. dir. Greater Tampa (Fla.) Bicentennial Coun., 1975-76; dir. pub. rels. St. Francis Hosp., Miami Beach, Fla., 1977-79; dir. advt., comms. and pub. rels. Cedars Med. Ctr., Miami, Fla., 1979-84; prin., co-owner Comms. Strategies, Inc., Coral Gables, Fla., 1984—2002; comm. cons., 2002—. Bd. visitors U. Tenn. Coll. Comms., Knoxville, 1987—; mem. pub. rels. adv. coun. U. Miami, Coral Gables, 1997-2002. Advisor Crime Watch Am., 1994-95; pres. Epilepsy Found. South Fla., Miami, 2000-2002; pres. Carver Elem. Sch. PTA, Coral Gables, 1992-93; participant Leadership Miami, 1984; pub. rels. chair spl. events Gulliver Schs. Parents Assn., 2001-03; pub. rels. chair charity golf tournament Kidney Found. South Fla., 2002. Recipient award Nat. Health Info. Coun., 1999,2000, Pub. Rels. award, 1988-94, 98—, Fla. Hosp. Assn., 1978, 80, 81, 82, 83, 84, 86, 88, 89, 91, 92, 93, 96, 97, 98, 99, 2000, touchstone award Am. Soc. Hosp. Mktg. and Pub. Rels., 1986, Health and Medicine award for direct mktg. videos Telly Awards, 2000, Cardiovascular Comms. award Am. Heart Assn., 1998, 99, Health-care Mktg. Report awards 1988, 89, 90, 91, 92, 93, 94, 98, 99, 2000, 2001. Fellow Pub. Rels. Soc. Am. (accredited, chmn. Sunshine dist. 1989, pres. Miami chpt. 1983, MacEachern award 1986), South Fla. Hosp. Pub. Rels. and Mktg. Assn. (pres. 1979), Fla. Soc. for Healthcare Pub. Rels. and Mktg. (bd. dirs. 1979-84). Avocations: travel, reading, antiques, golf, dance. Home: 13627 Deering Bay Dr # 804 Coral Gables FL 33158

BUCHWALD, NAOMI REICE, judge; b. Kingston, N.Y., Feb. 14, 1944; BA cum laude, Brandeis U., 1965; LLB cum laude, Columbia U., 1968. Bar: N.Y. 1968, U.S. Ct. Appeals (2d cir.) 1969, U.S. Dist. Ct. (so. and ea. dists.) N.Y. 1970, U.S. Supreme Ct. 1978. Litigation assoc. Marshall, Bratter, Greene, Allison & Tucker, N.Y.C., 1968-73; asst. U.S. atty. So. Dist. N.Y., N.Y.C., 1973-80, dep. chief civil divsn., 1976-79, chief civil divsn., 1979-80; U.S. magistrate judge U.S. Dist. Ct. (so. dist.) N.Y., N.Y.C., 1980-99, chief magistrate judge, 1994-96, U.S. dist. judge, 1999—. Editor Columbia Jour. Law and Social Problems, 1967-68. Recipient spl. citation FDA Commrs., 1978, Robert B. Fiske Jr. Assn. William B. Tendy award, Outstanding Pub. Svc. award Seymour Assn., Columbia Law Sch. Class of 1968 Excellence in Pub. Svc. award, 1998. Mem. Fed. Bar Coun. (trustee 1976-82, 97-2000, v.p. 1982-84), N.Y. State Bar Assn., Assn. of the Bar of the City of N.Y. (trademarks and unfair competition com. 1988-89, mem. long range planning com. 1993-95, litigation com. 1994-96, ad hoc com. on jud. conduct 1996-99; prof., jud. ethics com. 2002-2004), Phi Beta Kappa, Omicron Delta Epsilon. Office: US Ct House Foley Square New York NY 10007-1316

BUCK, ANITA EMILY, newswriter; b. St. Paul, Aug. 25, 1925; d. Walter August and Hedwig (Hattie) Emily (Deppe) Albrecht; m. Eugene Caleb Buck, Jan. 16, 1954; children: Carol Marie Buck Cullen, Katherine Jean Buck Beal. BA, Hamline U., 1947. Sec., office mgr. Studebaker Corp., Mpls., 1947—49; asst. dir. Army Svc. Club, Seoul, 1949—50, dir. Camp Atterbury, Ind., 1951—52; dir. women's program Radio Sta. WAVN, Stillwater, Minn., 1952—57; editor family page Gazette, 1969—78, freelance columnist, 1978—88; columnist Courier News, 1988—. Bd. dirs. Carnegie Pub. Libr., Stillwater; pub. rels. Vets. Meml., 2002—; mem. adv. bldg. com. Carnegie Pub. Libr., 2002—. Author: Steamboats on the St. Croix, 1990, Jo Rollins & the Stillwater Art Colony, 1997, Behind Barbed Wire - POWS in Minn., 1998. Bd. dirs. Lakeview Hosp., Stillwater, 1987—94; chmn. Bi Centennial Celebration, 1996; bd. dirs. County Hist. Soc., 1977—97. Named Minnesotan of Yr., Minn. Territorial Pioneers, 2003. Mem.: Washington County Hist. Soc. (pres. 1979—81), Lakeview Hosp. Women's Aux. (pres. 1961—62). Avocations: painting, reading, hiking, writing. Home: 2511 Croixwood Blvd Stillwater MN 55082

BUCK, BERNESTINE BRADFORD, retired school counselor; b. Altheimer, Ark., July 25, 1924; d. Henry Walker and Dora Lois Bradford; BA, Stowe Tchrs. Coll., 1950; MEd, U. Mo., 1973; m. Joseph Wellington Buck, Oct. 1, 1950; children: Stanley W., Linda Carol, Debra Lois. Tchr. pub. schs., St. Louis, 1950-73, sch. counselor, 1973-87. Committeewoman, St. Louis 20th Ward, 1988-89; mem. U. Mo. scholarship com., 1974-84, Antioch Bapt. Ch. scholarship com., 1980-86, Coro Reinvest Program, 1988. Mem. Am., Mo. personnel and guidance assns., St. Louis Guidance Assn. (pres. 1979-80), Mo. Guidance Assn. (exec. council 1980-81, v.p. elem. sect.), Alpha Kappa Alpha. Baptist.

BUCK, JANE LOUISE, psychology educator; b. Reading, Pa., Mar. 10, 1933; d. C. Robert and Viola Louise (Berger) B.; m. Leo Laskaris, Oct. 7, 1954 (div. Aug. 1978); 1 child, Julie. BA, U. Del., 1953, MA, 1959, MEd, 1966, PhD, 1971. Instr. U. Del., Newark, 1964-66; rsch. assoc. Rsch. for Better Schs., Phila., 1967-68; asst. prof. Del. State U., Dover, 1969-73, assoc. prof., 1973-77, prof. psychology, 1977-98. Cons. in stats. E.I. duPont de Nemours, Wilmington, Del., 1983-93; vis. prof. Ctr. for Sci. and Culture, U. Del., 1986; bd. dirs. The Blvd. and Beyond, Wilmington. Author: Specifying the Risk, 1985; contbr. articles to profl. jours. Speaker, evaluator Del. Humanities Forum, 1980-88; pres. Del. Gerontol. Soc., Newark, 1987-88; mem. town coun. Chesapeake City, Md., 1998-2000; commr. parks and recreation, Chesapeake City, Md., 1998-99; bd. dirs. Friends of Cecil County Libr., 2000. Mem. AAAS (mem. sr. scientists and engrs.), AAUP (nat. coun. 1987-90, 93-99, pres. Del. State U. chpt. 1976-80, 95-98, chief negotiator 1982-98, mem. nat. com. on historically Black instns. and scholars of color 1988-91, 98-2000, interim sec. Del. Conf 1991-92, pres. Del. conf. 1993-2000, mem. nat. com. govt. rels. 1994-97, Sternberg award for collective bargaining 1994, nat. pres. 2000—), Am. Psychol. Soc., Coun. Tchrs. Undergrad. Psychology, Humanities and Tech. Assn., Am. Statis. Assn. (v.p. Del. chpt. 1999-2000), Danforth Assocs., Kappa Delta Pi, Psi Chi, Alpha Chi Omega. Avocations: classical music, reading, gardening, sewing, computer graphics. E-mail: buck@count.com.

BUCK, LINDA B. physician, medical educator; Assoc. prof. Med. Sch. Harvard U., Boston. Contbr. articles to profl. jours. Recipient Lewis S. Rosenstiel award for Disting. Work in Basic Med. Rsch., 1997. Office: Harvard Med Sch 25 Shattuck St Boston MA 02115-6027

BUCK, LINDA DEE, executive recruiting company executive; b. San Franciso, Nov. 8, 1946; d. Sol and Shirley D. (Setterberg) Press. Student, Coll. of San Mateo, Calif., 1969-70. Head hearing and appeals br. Dept. Navy Employee Rels. Svc., The Philippines, 1974-75; dir. human resources Homestead Savs. & Loan Assn., Burlingame, Calif., 1976-77; mgr. VIP Agy., Inc., Palo Alto, Calif., 1977-78; exec. v.p., dir. Sequent Pers. Svcs., Inc., Mountain View, Calif., 1978-83; founder, pres. Buck & Co., San Mateo, 1983-91. Publicity mgr. for No. Calif., Osteogenesis Imperfecta Found. Inc., 1970-72; cons. Am. Brittle Bone Soc., 1979-88; mem. Florence (Oreg.) Area Humane Soc., 1994—, Friends of Libr., Florence, 1994—; bd. dirs. Florence Festival Arts, 1995; bd. dirs., dir. women Rhododendron Scholarship Program, Florence, 1995. Jewish.

BUCK, SARAH BETH, educational association administrator, director; b. Thief River Falls, Minn., Mar. 16, 1948; d. Walter A. Ekeren and Lois M. (Schiager) Rand; m. Ray A. Boosinger, Sept. 20, 1969 (div. Nov. 1973); 1 child, David C. Boosinger; m. J. Ben Buck, June 7, 1975; stepchildren: Catherine, Kevin, Brian. BS in Indsl. Adminstrn., Iowa State U., 1981, MBA, 1995. Adminstrv. asst. Mary Greeley Med. Ctr., Ames, Iowa, 1972-80, dir. mktg. and info. svcs., 1980-87; instr. health care mktg. Iowa State U., 1987, mgr. Internat. Trade Svc., 1987-89; dir. devel./edn. and adminstrn. Iowa State U. Found., Ames, 1989-96, dir. $300 million campaign, 1995—2000, v.p., 2000—. Co-owner SafeGuard Films, Ames, 1983-91; spkr., guest lectr. U. No. Iowa, Cedar Falls, 1989, Iowa State U., 1989—; judge publ. competition Mo. Hosp. Assn., 1985. Mem. Golden Circle Internat. Visitors' Coalition, Des Moines, 1988-89, SAFE Coalition for Substance Free Cmty., Ames, 1995—; trustee Mary Greeley Med. Ctr., 1993—, chair bd. trustees 1998—; bd. dirs. Am. Heart Assn., Story County, 1985-87; v.p. St. Andrew's Luth. Ch., Ames, 1996, pres., 1997, treas., 1998. Mem. Coun. for Advancement and Support of Edn. (Regional Bronze award 1996, 99, Regional Gold award 1998, Nat. Seal of Excellence award 2000), Nat. Com. on Planned Giving, Am. Soc. Hosp. Mktg. and Pub. Rels. (cert., regional coun. coord. nat. publ. evaluation svc.), Nat. Assn. Hosp. Devel., Am. Hosp. Assn. (governance com., 2000-03, leadership devel. com., 2004—) Midwest Edn. Advancement Network, Iowa Soc. Hosp. Mktg. and Pub. Rels. (pres. various coms.), Mid-Iowa Planned Giving Coun., Ames C. of C. (various coms.), Iowa State U. Alumni Assn. (life, bd. dirs. 1993-94), Rotary Internat. Avocations: performing keyboard music, cooking, reading. Office: Iowa State U Found 2505 Elwood Dr Ames IA 50010

BUCKENMEYER, JANET, director, education educator, director; b. Toledo, Ohio, Nov. 2, 1962; d. William and Marjorie Staskiewicz; children: Laura, Michael. BS in Edn., Bowling Green State U., 1984; EdM, U. Toledo, 1998, PhD, 2001. Cert. elem. tchg. with endorsement in computer tech. Ohio, 2000, lic. tchg. K-12 spl. edn. Ohio, 2000. Grad. asst. to adj. prof. U. Toledo, 1997—2001; dir. master in edn. program Lourdes Coll., Sylvania, Ohio, 2001—. Grad. coun. mem. Lourdes Coll., Sylvania, Ohio, 2002—. N. Ctrl. assn. evaluation team mem. Sylvania Northview H.S., 2000—01; tech. planning com. mem. Monore (Mich.) Pub. Sch., 2001—02; sch. bd. mem. Sylvania Franciscan Acad., 2002—03. Mem.: Mich. Assn. Computer Users and Learning, Assn. Ednl. Comm. and Tech., Internat. Soc. Tech. in Edn., Pi Lambda Theta. Office: Lourdes Coll 6832 Convent Blvd Sylvania OH 43560 E-mail: jbuckenm@lourdes.edu.

BUCKINGHAM, BARBARA RAE, social studies educator; b. Union City, Ind., Jan. 27, 1932; d. Ray E. and Edith A. (Wagner) B. BA cum laude, Hanover Coll., 1954; MA, Ind. Univ., 1956. Tchr. City Sch. Dist., Marion, Ohio, 1956-64, social studies educator Rochester, NY, 1966—. Editor: Revonah, 1954; art work Aldelphean, 1959. Vol. Peace Corps, Ethiopia, 1964-66, Mary Cariola Children's Ctr., Christian Heritage Homes, Hope Hall, Congresswomen Louise Slaughter Campaign, 1996-97, 96-98; gov. bd. Rochester Returned Peace Corps Vols., 1968-76; election com. mem. Councilwoman Letvin, Gates, N.Y., 1980; steering com. Pub. Affairs Forum, Hanover, 1952, DAR. Mem. AAUW (pres. 1958-59), DAR, Nat. Peace Corps Assn., Friends of Ethiopia, Rochester Tchr. Assn., Pi Gamma Mu (Outstanding Grad. award 1954), Gamma Sigma Pi, Alpha Phi Gamma. Democrat. Presbyterian. Avocations: travel, art work. Home: 64 Lyellwood Pkwy Rochester NY 14606-4532

BUCKINGHAM, BETTY JO, library media consultant; b. Aug. 6, 1927; d. Irvin Amos and E(lsie) Dean (Webb) B. BA, Iowa State Tchrs. Coll., 1948; MS in Libr. Sci., U. Ill., Urbana, 1953; PhD, U. Minn., 1978. Tchr. English Earlham (Iowa) Cmty. Sch., 1948-50; tchr., libr. Harlan (Iowa) Cmty. Sch., 1950-54; libr. Ft. Madison (Iowa) Cmty. H.S., 1954-60, Kurtz Jr. H.S., Des Moines, 1960-64; cons. Iowa Dept. Edn., Des Moines, 1964—94. Lectr. U. Minn.-Mpls., 1970. Author, editor: Growth Notes for School Media Specialists, New Iowa Standards for Library Media Programs, 1989, Selection of Instructional Materials, A Model Policy and Rules, 1980, 1994; author: Weeding the Library Media Center Collections, 1984, Weeding the Library Media Center Collections, 1994, Planning the School Library Media Center Budget, 1984, Planning the School LIbrary Media Center Budget, 1994; editor: Iowa and some Iowans, 1995, Women at the Well, 1987, Plan for Progress in the Library Media Center, P-K12, 1991; joint compiler in field: ; contbr. articles to profl. jours.; author: History of Local Church, 1994, Church District, 2002, Lenten and Advent Dramas, 1996—. Mem. steering com. women's caucus Ch. of the Brethren, 1977-80, editor Cistern periodical, 1980-87, Femailings periodical, 1994-97, bd. dirs. No. Plains dist., 1984-91, 2002-, conf. moderator, 1990-91, conf. sec. 2002—. Mem. ALA, NEA, Am. Assn. Sch. Librs. (past sec., pres., councillor 1984-85), Iowa Ednl. Media Assn. (cons. 1973-83), Iowa Libr. Assn., Intellectual Freedom Found., Women's Fellowship Prairie City (past pres.), Beta Phi Mu, Kappa Delta Pi. Democrat. Avocations: reading, classical music, writing. Home: 10048 Highway F70 W Prairie City IA 50228-8471

BUCKINGHAM, DEIDRE LYN, writer, musician; b. Endicott, N.Y., Apr. 18, 1973; d. Richard Paul and Doris May (Mlynar) Moore; m. Jeff K. Buckingham, June 9, 1995. AA in Office Tech., Cedarville (Ohio) Coll., 1993, BA in Profl. Writing, 1995. Tech. writer Ont. Sys. Corp., Muncie, Ind., 1995-97. Author: Snapdragon's Dance, 2004. Caption editor Deaf Video Comm. Am., Lisle, Ill., 1997-99. Recipient Pres.'s award for lit. excellence Iliad Press, 1997, Editor's Choice award Internat. Libr. Poetry, 2003; Mari Heyduck scholar Women in Comm., 1994. Avocations: writing poetry and essays, recording original music.

BUCKINGHAM, LORIE, automotive executive; BA in Math. and Chemistry, SUNY, Potsdam. Dir. enterprise IT solutions Union Carbide Corp., Danbury, Conn., 1993—99; former chief info. officer Zonetrader.com, Chgo.; dir. global software solutions Visteon Corp., Dearborn, Mich., 2000—02, v.p., chief info. officer, 2002—. Office: Visteon Corp 1700 Rotunda Dr Dearborn MI 48120

BUCKINGHAM, VIRGINIA, editor; m. David Lowy; 1 child, Jack. B in Comms., Boston Coll., 1987. Dep. press sec., asst. press sec. to Gov. Weld and Lt. Gov.; press. sec. to Gov. Weld and Lt. Gov. Cellucci, 1994-95; campaign mgr. Gov. Weld's bid for U.S. Senate; chief of staff to Gov. Cellucci and Lt. Gov. Swift, 1997-2000; exec. dir., CEO Mass. Port Authority (Massport), East Boston, 2000—01; dep. editl. page editor Boston (Mass.) Herald, 2003—. Office: Boston Herald One Herald Square PO Box 2096 Boston MA 02106

BUCKLER, MARILYN LEBOW, school psychologist, educational consultant; b. N.Y.C., Mar. 18, 1933; d. Herman and Gertrude (Abolitz) Lebow; m. Sheldon A. Buckler, June 1, 1952 (div. 1978); children: Julie, Eve, Sarah Buckler Welcome. BS cum laude, NYU, 1954; MEd in Counseling, Northeastern U., 1970. Cert. ednl. psychologist, Mass.; sch. guidance counselor, Mass., sch. psychologist, Mass. Kindergarten tchr. Washington Pub. Schs., 1955-56, Stamford (Conn.) Pub. Schs., 1956-58; guidance counselor Framingham (Mass.) Pub. Schs., 1969-70; sch. psychologist, guidance counselor Carlisle (Mass.) Pub. Schs., 1970-95; parent program cons. Reach out to Schs. program Wellesley Coll.-Stone Ctr., 1993—. Tchr. parenting course Middlesex C.C., Bedford, Mass., 1990—, cons. LEAP program, 1992-93; workshop leader, creator parenting courses, various pvt. schs. and orgns., Mass., 1990—; spl. project cons., workshop specialist "Families First" Wheelock Coll., 1995—. Mem. ACA, Mass. Sch. Counselor Assn., Mass. Sch. Psychologists Assn., Pi Lambda Theta. Avocations: films, cooking, traveling, reading.

BUCKLES, JUDITH ANN, dental educator, program administrator; b. Francisville, Ind., Feb. 15, 1940; d. Lawrence Melvin and Mary Rosella Johnston; m. Edward Donald Buckles, Jan. 27, 1962; children: Dawn Marie, Erica Danielle, Erin Nichole. Cert. dental nurse, Elkhart (Ind.) U. Medicine and Dentistry, 1959; AAS, Purdue U., 1986, BS with honors, 1991. Cert. dental asst. Dental asst. Francis A Jones, DDS, Lafayette, Ind., 1959-69, Raymond Price, DDS, Lafayette, 1969-73; program supr., sr. instr. Ivy Tech. State Coll., Lafayette, 1973—. Religious instr. St. Ann Ch. and Shrine, Lafayette, 1980-95; asst. with fund raising St. Ann Rosary Soc., Lafayette, 1979—, St. Ann Social Club, Lafayette, 1994—, St. Ann Parish Coun., 2000-. Fellow Am. Dental Assts. Assn., Nat. Assn. Dental Assts., Ind. Dental Assocs. Assn., Lafayette Dental Assts. Assn., German-Am. Club, Phi Kappa Phi. Avocations: collecting antique depression glass ware, collecting cookbooks, collecting boyd bears and angels, collecting porcelain dolls, collecting german dishes. Office: Ivy Tech State Coll 3101 S Cressy Ln Lafayette IN 47905-6299

BUCKLEW, SUSAN CAWTHON, federal judge; b. Tampa, Fla., May 12, 1942; BA, Fla. State U., 1964; MA, U. So. Fla., 1968; JD, Stetson U., 1977; LLD (hon.), Stetson Coll. Law, 1994. Tchr. Plant H.S., 1964-65, 70-72, Seminole H.S., 1965-67, Chamberlain H.S., 1969; instr. Hillsborough C.C., 1974-75; corp. legal counsel Jim Walter Corp., 1978-82; county ct. judge Hillsborough County, 1982-86; circuit ct. judge 13th Jud. Circuit, 1986-93; judge U.S. Dist. Ct. (mid. dist.) Fla., 1993—. Mem. Gender Bias Study Commn., 1988-90, Fla. Bar Bench Bar Commn., 1990-92; bd. overseers Stetson Coll. Law, 1994—. Recipient award Disting Svc., Fla. Coun. Crime and Delinquincy, 1990, Disting. Alumnus award Stetson Lawyers Assn., 1994. Mem. ABA, Fla. Gar Assn., Fla. Assn. Women Lawyers, Hillsborough Assn. Women Lawyers (award Outstanding Pub. Svc. ADvancing Status Women 1991), Hillsborough County Bar Assn. (Robert W. Patton Outstanding Jursit award young lawyer's sect. 1990), Fla. State U. Alumni Assn., Am. Inns Ct. (LII, William Glenn Terrell chpt.), Athena Soc., Tampa Club, Delta Delta Delta Alumnae. Office: US Dist Ct 801 N Florida Ave Ste 109 Tampa FL 33602-3849

BUCKLEY, GRETA PAULA, auditor; b. Stanton, Calif., Sept. 8, 1963; d. Joseph Andrew Bertotti and Margarita Ann Marie (Lundgren) Helmut; 1 child, Gianna Marie Dossa; m. Steve Buckley, Nov. 7, 1998. BA, San Diego State U., 1991; Associate degree in Insurance, Insurance Inst. Am., 1997. Supr. Farmers Ins. Group, Carlsbad, Calif., 1991-96, auditor, 1996—. Mem. com. Children's Hosp. Safe Kids Coalition, San Diego, 1995—. Mem., tchr. Jr. Achievement, Carlsbad H.S., 1996—; mem. speakers bur. March of Dimes, San Diego, 1990—, mem. logistics com., 1995—; team leader Farmers Legis. Action Group, 1997; co-chmn. North County Walk Am., 1998. Mem. Inst. Internal Auditors, Western Ins. Inst. of Speakers. Avocations: camping, travel, biking, skiing, photography. Office: Farmers Ins Group 5815 El Camino Real Carlsbad CA 92008-8801

BUCKLEY, MAUREEN A. speech pathology/audiology services professional; b. Teaneck, N.J., Jan. 17, 1946; d. John and Grace Cahill; m. Joseph Buckley, Apr. 16, 1966; children: Kevin, Sean. AAS, Orange County C.C., Middletown, N.Y., 1976; BA, Dominican Coll., Blauvelt, N.Y., 1980; MS, William Paterson U., 1983. Cert. clin. competence in speech pathology. Presenter in field. Mem.: N.Y. State Hearing Lang. Assn., Am. Speech Hearing Assn. Avocations: tennis, boating, sewing, crafts. Home: 44 Deerpath Rd Tuxedo Park NY 10987 E-mail: joseph.l.buckley@verizon.net.

BUCKLEY, PRISCILLA LANGFORD, magazine editor; b. N.Y.C., Oct. 17, 1921; d. William Frank and Aloise (Steiner) B. BA, Smith Coll., 1943. Copy girl, sports writer UP, N.Y.C., 1944; radio rewrite staff mem. U.P., 1944-47, Paris corr., 1953—56; news editor Sta. WACA, Camden, S.C., 1947-48; reports officer CIA, Washington, 1951-53; with Nat. Rev. Mag., N.Y.C., 1956—, mng. editor, 1959-86, sr. editor, 1986-99. Mem. U.S. Adv. Commn. Pub. Diplomacy, 1984-91. Editor: The Joys of National Review, 1995; columnist One Woman's Voice Syndicate, 1976-80; author: String of Pearls, On the Newsbeat in New York and Paris, 2001. Mem. Sharon Country Club (Conn., sec. 1973-77, pres. 1978-80, 94-95). Home: Great Elm Sharon CT 06069 Office: Nat Review 215 Lexington Ave New York NY 10016-6023 E-mail: pbuckley@mohawk.net.

BUCKLEY, REBECCA HATCHER, allergist, immunologist, pediatrician, educator; b. Hamlet, N.C., Apr. 1, 1933; d. Martin Armstead and Nora (Langston) Hatcher; m. Charles Edward Buckley III, July 9, 1955; children: Charles Edward IV, Elizabeth Ann, Rebecca Kathryn, Sarah Margaret. BA, Duke U., 1954; MD, U. N.C., 1958. Intern Duke U. Med. Ctr., Durham, N.C., 1958-59, resident, 1959-61, pediat. allergist and immunologist, 1961—. Dir. Am. Bd. Allergy and Immunology, Phila., 1971-73, chair exam. com., 1971-73, co-chair bd. dirs., 1982-84; chair Diagnostic Lab. Immunology, 1984-88; mem. staff Duke U. Med. Ctr.; asst. prof. pediat. and immunology, 1968-72, assoc. prof. pediat., 1972-76, prof. pediat., 1976-79, assoc. prof. immunology, 1972-79, prof. immunology, 1979—, J. Buren Sidbury prof. pediat., 1979—. Contbr. articles to profl. jours. Fellow: AAAS (chair med. scis. sect. 2001—03); mem.: Nat. Acad. Sci., Inst. Medicine of NAS, Am. Pediatric Soc. (coun. mem. 1991—, pres. 1999—2000, chmn. immune deficiency found. med. adv. com. 2003—), Southeastern Allergy Assn. (pres. 1978—79), Am. Acad. Pediatrics (Bret Ratner award 1992), Soc. Pediatric Rsch., Am. Assn. Immunologists, Am. Acad. Allergy and Immunology (exec. com. 1975—82, pres. 1979—80, hon. fellow award 1999). Republican. Episcopalian. Home: 3621 Westover Rd Durham NC 27707-5032 Office: Duke U Med Ctr PO Box 2898 Durham NC 27710-2898 Office Phone: 919-684-2922. E-mail: BUCKL003@mc.duke.edu.

BUCKLEY, SUSAN, lawyer; b. Rockville Center, N.Y., Dec. 24, 1951; BA, Mt. Holyoke Coll., 1973; JD, Fordham U., 1977. Bar: N.Y. 1978, D.C. 1980. Ptnr. Cahill Gordon & Reindel LLP, N.Y.C., 1985—. Mem. ABA, N.Y. State Bar Assn. (com. on media law 1992-95), Bar Assn. N.Y.C. (com. comm. law 1986-89). Office: Cahill Gordon & Reindel 80 Pine St Fl 17 New York NY 10005-1790

BUCKLEY, VIRGINIA LAURA, editor; b. N.Y.C., May 11, 1929; d. Alfred and Josephine Marie (Manetti) Iacuzzi; m. David Patrick Buckley, July 30, 1960; children: Laura Joyce, Brian Thomas. BA, Wellesley Coll., 1950; MA, Columbia U., 1952. Tchr. English Bennett Coll., Millbrook, N.Y., 1954-56, Berkeley Inst., Bklyn., 1956-58; copy editor World Pub. Co., N.Y.C., 1959-69; children's book editor Thomas Y. Crowell, N.Y.C., 1971-80; editl. dir. Lodestar Books, N.Y.C., 1980-97; contbg. editor Clarion Books, N.Y.C., 1997—. Author: State Birds, 1986; contbr. articles to profl. jours. Mem. ALA Home: 33 Brook Ter Leonia NJ 07605-1504 Office: Clarion Books 215 Park Ave S New York NY 10003-1603 E-mail: vbuckley@worldnet.att.net.

BUCKLEY GREEN, DEBORAH FERN, nursing educator; d. James Sherman Buckley and Lily Mae Duffield; children: Daniel James Vail, Nathan James Vail. BC, RN, MS, U. Okla., Tulsa, 1996; postgrad. in PhD. program, Tex. Women's U., 1999—. Cert. med.-surg. nurse, ANCC, 1994. Staff nurse/instr. St. Johns Hosp., Springfield, Mo., 1986—95; course leader Rogers U., Claremore, Okla., 1995—98; instr. U. Okla., Lawton, 1998—99; clin. instr. U. Tex., Arlington, 1999—. Cons. nurse New Life Christian Sch., Tulsa, Okla., 1997—2002. Author (nurse educator): Drug Calculation/Orientation Booklet (Profl. Excellence in Nursing award, 1991). Bible studies tchr. United Pentecostal Ch., Euless, Tex., 2002. Mem.: ANA, Tex. Nurses Assn., Sigma Theta Tau (membership chair 2002—). Republican. United Pentecostal. Avocation: travel. Office: U Tex Arlington 411 Nedderman Dr Arlington TX 76019

BUCKLO, ELAINE EDWARDS, United States district court judge; b. Boston, Oct. 1, 1944; married. AB, St. Louis U., 1966; JD, Northwestern U., 1972. Bar: Calif. 1973, U.S. Dist. Ct. (no. dist.) Calif. 1973, Ill. 1974, U.S. Dist. ct. (no. dist.) Ill. 1974, U.S. Ct. Appeals (7th cir.) 1983. Law clk. U.S. Ct. Appeals (7th cir.), Chgo.; pvt. practice, 1973-85; U.S. magistrate judge U.S. Dist. Ct. (no. dist.) Ill., Chgo., 1985-94, judge, 1994—. Spkr. in field. Contbr. articles to profl. jours. Mem. jud. conf. com. on adminstrn. Magistrate Judge Sys., 1998—; mem. vis. com. No. Ill. U. Sch. Law, 1994—; mem. Northwestern U. Law Bd., 1996-99. Mem. ABA (standing com. law and literacy 1995-98), FBA (v.p. 1990-92, pres. Chgo. chpt. 1992-93), Women's Bar Assn. Ill. (bd. dirs. 1994-96), Chgo. Coun. Lawyers (pres. 1977-78). Office: US Dist Ct No Dist Everett McKinley Dirksen Bldg 219 S Dearborn St Ste 1988 Chicago IL 60604-1794

BUCKMAN, GAIL CHRISTINE, music educator; d. Charles Edward and Geraldine Clara (Herold) Buckman. BA, Notre Dame Coll., St. Louis, 1968; MusM in Edn., U. of Mo., Columbia, 1978. Cert. tchr. Mo. Classroom tchr. St. Martin of Tours Sch., Washington Park, Ill., 1968—70; music tchr. grades K-8 Our Lady of Sorrows Sch., St. Louis, 1970—77; vocal/instrumental music tchr. K-12 St. Paul Grade and H.S., Highland, Ill., 1977—78; vocal/instrumental music tchr. K-8 St. Peter/St. Cletus Sch., St. Charles, 1978—83; instrumental music tchr. 4-8 Consol. Schools Band, St. Charles, 1983—96, St. Gabriel the Archangel Sch., St. Louis, 1996—. Staff mem. Mo. Ambassadors of Music European Tour, St. Louis, Summer Music Camp at S.E. Mo. State U., Cape Girardeau, Mo.; asst. dir. St. Charles Mcpl. Band; dir. honor band DuBourg HS, St. Louis, 2001; coord. E. Desmond Lee Found. St. Gabriel Sch., St. Louis, 1999—; with Sch. Sisters of Notre Dame. Co-author: (music curriculum) Music Curriculum for the Archdiocese of St. Louis. Dir. holiday musical program Sch. Sisters of Notre Dame Resource Devel., St. Louis; bd. dirs. St. Charles Mcpl. Band Bd. Named Art Tchr. of the Yr., St. Louis Arts and Edn. Coun., 2003, Outstanding Music Educator, St. Louis Metro Dist. #8, 2002; recipient Merit Award, St. Louis Metro Dist., 1997. Mem.: Mo. Music Educators' Assn. (assoc.; dist. pres. 2000—02, treas. dist. 8 2002—03), Mo. Band Masters Assn. (assoc.), Music Educators' Nat. Conf. (assoc.), Nat. Cath. Band Assn. (assoc.), Nat. Cath. Educators' Assn. (assoc.), Phi Beta Mu (assoc.). Roman Catholic. Achievements include Established a consolidated band program between 4 schools and 3 parishes; Established the first Middle School Honor Band for the St. Louis Metro District of Missouri Music Educators. Avocations: travel, golf.

BUCKMAN, TRACEY ANN, political finance director; b. Berkeley, Calif., May 25, 1964; d. Charles Albert and Tracey (Tighe) B. BA, Vanderbilt U., 1986; student, Am. U., 1988. Adminstrv. asst. Majority Whip, U.S. Senate, Washington, 1987-89; cons. The Com. for a Dem. Consensus, Washington, 1989-90; fundraising asst. Cranston for Senate, Washington, 1989-90; fundraising cons. Women's Legal Def. Fund., Washington, 1990; dep. nat. fin. dir. Senator Daniel Akaka Campaign, Washington, 1990-91; dir. membership programs Dem. Senatorial Campaign Com., Washington, 1991-93; nat. fin. dir. Senator Richard Bryan Campaign, Washington, 1993-94; nat. dir. fin. Senator Max Baucus Campaign, Washington, 1994-97; nat. fin. dir. Dem. Senatorial Campaign Com., Washington, 1997-99, Senator Joseph Lieberman campaign, Washington, 1999—. Spl. events vol. D.C. Spl. Olympics, Washington, 1988-91; vol. park guide Smithsonian Nat. Zool. Park, Washignton, 1987-89; vol. Washington Humane Soc., 1995-98. Mem. NAFE, Nat. Dem. Club, Friends of the Nat. Zoo, Vanderbilt U. Washignton Alumni (bd. dirs. 1991-92). Avocations: tennis, skiing, bicycling, photography, softball, scuba diving.

BUCK-MOYER, SANDRA KAY, marriage and family therapist; b. Danville, Pa., Mar. 14, 1953; d. Franklin Adam and Martha (Bathurst) Moyer; m. David William Buck, Apr. 4, 1982; children: Lindsey, Paige. BS in English, Lock Haven U., 1975; MS in Edn. Exceptional Children, Pa. State U., 1976; Ma in Counseling, Calif. Poly U., 1985. Tchr. Santa Maria (Calif.) High Sch., 1976-85; tchr. St. Thomas (V.I.) Pub. Schs., 1982-83; counselor Calif. Poly U., San Luis Obispo, 1984-85; intern South County Mental Health Ctr., Arroyo Grande, Calif., 1985; counselor Paso Robles (Calif.) Schs., 1985—; therapist marriage & family pvt. practice, PAso Robles, 1993—. Part-time tchr. Calif. Poly U., 1989-91; therapist Family Svcs. Ctr., San Luis Obispo, 1993—; cons. in field. Bd. dirs. Big Bros. Program, Paso Robles, 1994; mem. Santa Margarita (Calif.) PTA, 1988—; vol. Atascadero (Calif.) Youth Soccer, 1987—. Pacific Gas & Elec. Mini grantee, 1990. Mem. NOW, NEA (local sec. 1980), Calif. Assn. Marriage & Family Therapists. Avocations: travel, bird raising, walking, reading. Home: 9547 Durango Rd Atascadero CA 93422-6128 Office: 801 NIblick Rd Paso Robles CA 93446 Office Phone: 805-237-3333 ext. 502. E-mail: sbuckmoyer@king.prps.k12.ca.us.

BUCKNER, GAIL, state legislator; m. Charles Buckner; children: Todd, Galyn, Lauren. AA in Edn., Clayton Jr. Coll.; postgrad., Ga. State U. Rep. Ga. House, Atlanta, 1991—. Bd. dirs. Reynolds Nature Preserve. Named Vol. of Yr. Clayton Clean and Beautiful. Mem. LWV, Ga. Congress Dem. Women, Mag. Assn. Ga., Coun. for Children, Hist. Jonesboro, Clayton County Grunaways Coun., Prevention PLUS, Elder Abuse Coun. Clayton County, Ga. PTA (hon. life). Home: 7324 Cardif Pl Jonesboro GA 30236-2543 Office: Legis Office Bldg Rm 601 Atlanta GA 30334 Fax: 404-657-7689.

BUCKNER, JENNIE, newspaper editor; b. Lexington, Ky. m. Steven Landers; 1 child Katie. BS in Journalism with honors, Ohio State Univ. Joined Detroit Free Press, 1969—78; features editor San Jose Mercury News, 1978—81, asst. mng. editor/features, 1981—82, asst. mng. editor/news, 1982—83, mng. editor/afternoon, 1983—89; v.p. news Knight-Ridder, Inc., 1989—93; v.p., editor The Charlotte (N.C.) Observer, 1993—. Bd. visitors Davidson Coll., 1994—. Mem. Am. Soc. Newspaper Editors (bd. dirs. 1998—). Office: The Charlotte Observer PO Box 30308 Charlotte NC 28230-0308 E-mail: jbuckner@charlotteobserver.com.

BUCKNER-DAVIS, ANNETT, professional volleyball player; b. Carson, Calif., Sept. 22, 1973; d. Cleveland Buckner; m. Byron Davis, 1996. Mem. Sydney Olympics Beach Volleyball Team, 2000. Named MVP and Offensive Player of the Yr., Bud Light Pro Beach Volleyball League, 1996, Rookie of Yr. and Sportsmanship awardee 1995; named to 1st Team NCAA All-American, 1993-94, others. Avocations: designing clothes, modeling. Office: USA Volleyball Bud Light Pro Volleyball 715 S Circle Dr Colorado Springs CO 80910-2368

BUCKNER-REITMAN, JOYCE, psychologist, educator; b. Benton, Ark., Sept. 25, 1937; d. Waymond Floyd Pannell and Willie Evelyn (Wright) Whitley; m. John W. Buckner, Aug. 29, 1958 (div. 1970); children: Cheryl, John, Chris; m. Sanford Reitman, Aug. 13, 1994. BA, Ouachita Bapt. Coll., 1959; MS in Edn., Henderson State U., 1964; PhD, North Tex. State U., 1970. Lic. psychologist, Tex., marriage and family therapist; cert. Nat. Registry Health Svc. Providers in Psychology; master trainer in imago relationship therapy. Assoc. prof. U. Tex., Arlington, 1970-80, chmn. dept. edn., 1976-78; pvt. practice psychology, Arlington, 1974—. Dir.(chief profl. officer): Southwest Inst. Relationship Devel.; author: (novels) Making Real Love Happen, The New Era of Intimacy; profl. speaker; appeared on internat. tv shows, including Oprah Winfrey Show. Mem. APA, Nat. Assn. for Imago Relationship Therapy (pres.), Nat. Speakers Assn., Am. Assn. Marital and Family Therapy. Avocations: dance, travel, art. Home: 2208 Farmer Rd Weatherford TX 76087-6964 E-mail: JoyBuckner@aol.com

BUCKSTEIN, CARYL SUE, writer; b. Denver, Aug. 10, 1954; d. Henry Martin and Hedvig (Neulander) B. BS in Journalism, U. Colo., 1976. Editor Rifle (Colo.) Telegram, 1976; corr. So. Colo. Pueblo (Colo.) Star-Jour. and Chieftain, 1977-84; corr. The Denver Post, 1985; staff editor Nat. Over-the-Counter Stock Jour., Denver, 1985-89; writer Rocky Mountain News, Denver, 1990-92, editor Urban Spectrum, Denver, 1993; contbg. writer Boulder (Colo.) County Bus. Report, 1992—. Bd. mem. Holiday Project, Denver, 1996; mem. exec. bd. Denver Newspaper Guild, 1998. Recipient 1st Place Gen. Assignment Bus. Articles, Colo. Press Women, Denver, 1985, 90, 91. Mem. Colo. Soc. Profl. Journalists (sec.-treas. 1988), Denver Newspaper Guild (bd. dirs. 1998). Avocations: inventing, writing. Home: 9995 E Harvard Ave Apt 0215 Denver CO 80231-3906 E-mail: dowrite@earthlink.net.

BUCKWALTER, KATHLEEN C. academic administrator, educator; BSN, U. Iowa; MA in Psychiatric/Mental Health Nursing, PhD in Nursing, U. Ill., Chgo. Assoc. dir. Gerontological Nursing Interventions Rsch. Ctr.; dir. Ctr. on Aging U. Iowa, Found. disting. Prof., assoc. provost health scis., 1997—. Contbr. over 200 articles to profl. jours., 75 chpts. to books; editor: Nursing Diagnosis and Intervention for the Elderly (Maas, M., Buckwalter, K.C., Hardy, M.A.), 1991, Geriatric Mental Health: Current and Future Challenges, 1992, others. Mem.: IOM. Office: U Iowa Coll Nursing 101 Nursing Bldg 234 CMAB Iowa City IA 52242

BUCOLO, GAIL ANN, biotechnologist; b. Port Chester, N.Y., July 27, 1954; d. Joseph Anthony and Jennie (Tomassetti) B. BS in French, Oneonta State Coll., 1976; MA in French, Middlebury Coll., 1977; postgrad., Columbia U., 1981-82; MS in Biotechnology, Manhattan Coll., 1995. Technician N.Y. Hosp., N.Y.C., 1983-86; rsch. technician NYU Hosp., N.Y.C., 1986; sr. rsch. technician Meml. Sloan Kettering, N.Y.C., 1986-88, Columbia U., N.Y.C., 1988-2001; tchr. Cathedral HS, N.Y.C., 2001—04. Corr. Scienceport, Rye, N.Y., 1994-96; adj. prof. Mercy Coll., Dobbs Ferry, N.Y., 1996—; summer rsch. intern Rockefeller U., 2003. Mem. AAAS, N.Y. Acad. Scis., Sigma Xi. Roman Catholic. Achievements include work on the factor VIII inhibitor and discovery that it inhibited reverse transcriptase of HIV; work on spinal cord injury and neuronal regeneration which was implemented at the Miami Project in Fla. Home: 3605 Kingsbridge Ave Apt 5L Bronx NY 10463 Office: 350 E 56th St New York NY 10022

BUCUVALAS, TINA, folklorist; b. Berwyn, Ill., Feb. 18, 1951; d. Theodore and Lorraine Bucuvalas; m. Charles A. Curran, May, 1987; children: Alexandra, Chloe. BA, U. Calif., Santa Cruz, 1973; MA, UCLA, 1976; PhD, Ind. Univ., 1986. Curator Hist. Mus. So. Fla., Miami, 1986-91; freelance folklorist Maine, Fla., Washington, 1991-95; folklorist Fla. Divsn. Hist. Resources, Tallahassee, 1996—. Bd. dirs. Cultural Resources Inc.; cons. Maine Indian Basketmakers, Portland Performing Arts. Author: Introduction to Arkansas Folklore: A Teacher-Student Guide, 1986, Native American Foodways and Recipes: Hopi, Navajo, Hualapai, Laguna, 1986. South Florida Folk Arts: A Teacher Guide, 1988, (with Peggy A. Bulgher and Stetson Kennedy) South Florida Folklife, 1994. Mem. Am. Folklore Soc., Fla. Folklore Soc. Office: Hist Resources Divsn 500 S Bronough St Tallahassee FL 32399-6504

BUDAK, MARY KAY, state legislator; b. Phila. m. Michael S. Budak, 1953; children: Kathy Budak Norred, Michael S. III, Patricia A. Budak Jones. Student, Temple U., 1950-51, Purdue U., 1968, 80. Owner, mgr. Budak Memls. Inc., 1960-81; sec. to campaign coord. Michigan City Mayor Campaign, Ind., 1966-79; mem. Ind. Ho. of Reps., 1980—, mem. various coms., ranking majority mem. judiciary com., former ranking Rep. mem. family and children com., asst. Rep. whip. Pres. Miss Ind. Scholar Pageant, 1970-74, former mem. exec. bd.; mem. exec. bd. Michiana Sheltered Workshop, 1981-86, Parents & Friends of Handicapped; asst. Rep. WAIP; bd. dirs. Stepping Stone for Spousal Abuse. Named Outstanding Woman in Politics, 1982, Outstanding Legislator, Fraternal Order Police and State Employees, 1983. Mem. LWV, LaPorte County Grange, LaPorte GOP Women's Club (v.p. 1979-81), Bus. & Profl. Women's Club, LaPorte Rep. Women's Club, LaPorte Homemakers Ext. Club, VFW Aux., Rotary. Roman Catholic. Home: 5144 N Pawnee Trl La Porte IN 46350-7565 Office: State House State Capital Indianapolis IN 46204

BUDD, BERNADETTE SMITH, lawyer, newspaper executive, public relations consultant; b. N.Y.C., Feb. 23, 1948; d. Stanley Allen and Toby (Percak) Smith; m. Thomas Witbeck Budd, July 4, 1988; children: Amanda Rose Kronin Castel, Karen Wendy Kronia Campisi, Paige Elizabeth Glickman, Kelly Lynn Budd Tinsley. BA in History and English, Bucknell U., 1964; MA in Liberal Studies, SUNY, Stony Brook, 1971; EdM, Columbia U., 1982; JD, Jacob D. Fuchsberg Law Ctr., 1998. Tchr. history N.Y., 1964-69; innovator pre-sch. programs, 1975-79; editor, pub. Cmty. Jour., Wading River, N.Y., 1978—, advt. mgr., 1978—; editor Shoreham-Wading River Newsletter, 1978-88; editor-in-chief Restatement Touro Law Ctr., 1997-98. Profl. breeder, shower A.K.C. golden retriever dogs; cons., workshop leader, 1979—; exec. dir. Suffolk County chpt. NYCLU, 1998-2000. Editor: C. of C. Directory, Shoreham, 1983, 84; contbr. articles N.Y. Times, Reader's Digest, Psychology Today Mag.om., 1979-82. Advisor Teen Recreation Adv. Com., Shoreham-Wading River, 1979-82; mem. Nuclear Emergency Evacuation Com., 1979-82; pres. PTA, Wading River,

1980-83; v.p. Spl. Edn. PTA, Wading River, 1979-80, Am. Civil Liberties Union Student Chpt. Touro Law Ctr.; active Com. Gifted and Talented Children, Wading River, 1979-80, Occupational Edn. Commn., 1979-80; mem. Suffolk County Human Rights Commn. Recipient Disting. Service award Am. Cancer Soc., 1982-83; award of merit N.Y. State Pub. Relations Assn., 1982-83; award of honor Nat. Sch. Pub. Relations Assn., 1981. Mem. Wading River C. of C. (bd. dirs. 1979-80), Suffolk County Bus. and Profl. Women's Assn., Women's Equal Rights Congress, East End Women's Network, N.Y.C. Press Assn., Rocky Point C. of C. (bd. dirs.), Soc. Profl. Journalists, L.I. Press Club, Sigma Delta Chi, Kappa Kappa Gamma. Roman Catholic. Home and Office: Cmty Jour PO Box 619 Wading River NY 11792-0619 E-mail: bernadettesbudd@aol.com.

BUDD, MARGARET JANE, retired physical therapist; b. Paterson, N.J., Nov. 28, 1931; d. Ralph Witbeck Budd and Marguerite Veronica Anderson. BA in Biology, Elmira Coll., 1953; cert. in phys. therapy, Columbia U., 1954; MEd, Seton Hall U., 1974. Registered phys. therapist N.J. Phys. therapist staff Mountainside Hosp., Montclair, NJ, 1954—63; chief phys. therapist Valley Hosp., Ridgewood, NJ, 1963—78, sr. staff phys. therapist, 1978—80; phys. therapist staff Hackensack (N.J.) Med. Ctr., supr. bedside care, 1985—95; ret. Mem.: AAUW, Am. Phys. Therapy Assn. Avocations: aerbocis, swimming, travel.

BUDDINGTON, OLIVE JOYCE, shop owner, retired education educator; b. Norwich, Conn., June 11, 1925; d. William and Viola Jane (Turnbull) B. BS, Ea. Conn. State U., 1947; MA, Columbia U., 1951. Cert. tchr. nursery-6th grade, Conn. Tchr. Bd. Edn., Greenwich, Conn., 1947-49, 51-84; tchr. Agnes Russell Ctr. Tchr.'s Coll. Columbia U., N.Y.C., 1949-51; owner, mgr. 1840 House-Antiques, Norwich, Conn., 1965—. Bd. dirs. TVCCA (pres.), Rose City Land Trust, Woman's City Club, Hist. Norwichtown Day, United Cmty. and Family Svcs., Inc.; bd. corporators Norwich Free Acad.; cons. part-time in early childhood edn.; pres. Thames River Family Program, Martin House Corp.; chmn. UCF Mktg. and Devel. Com., Tourism Com.; trustee Slater Museum. Photographer tourism and promotion, 1994. Chair Parking Commn. City Coun., Norwich, Conn., 1989-91, Tourism Commn., 1990—; chmn. environ. com., Norwich, 1989-91; vol. United Way, Am. Red Cross, Leukemia Soc., Am. Heart Assn., Am. Cancer Soc.; mem. Norwich Downtown Renewal Com., Norwich Slum and Blight Com., Norwich City Hall Renovations Com., UCF Health Svcs. Com., Rose Sr. Ctr. Bldg. Com. (chmn.), Dem. Town Com., Dept. Children and Families Regional Adv. Coun. Positive Youth Devel. Com., Sch. Breakfast Com., Sch. Readiness Com., Children's First Initiative, Norwich tourism Task Force; host (cable program) RSVP "WHY NOT READ??" Named Vol. of Yr., Citizen of Yr. Ea. Conn. C. of C., 1997; recipient Caroline Bidwell Award, Greenwich (Conn.) Assn. Pub. Schs., 1984, Svc. Above Help Norwich Rotary Club, 1995, Woman of Achievement award, Woman's Internat. Fed., 1997, Sam Walton Leadership award, 1998, Cmty. Svc. award, DAR, 1998, Successful Aging award, Conn. Cmty. Care, Inc., 2000, Pub. Svc. award, Conn. Sec. of State, 2002. Mem. Nat. Edn. Assn., Assn. Childhood Edn. Internat., Conn. Edn. Assn., Greenwich Edn. Assn., Kindergarten Assn. Conn., Kindergarten Assn. Fairfield County (pres., chmn. programs),Greenwich Hist. Soc., Norwich Tourism Task Force, Norwich Tourism Commn., Norwich Parking Commn. (chmn.), Norwich Commn. Sr. Affairs. Democrat. Avocations: reading, travel, knitting, photography, arts and crafts. Home and Office: 47 8th St Norwich CT 06360-3834

BUDDINGTON, PATRICIA ARRINGTON, engineer; b. Takoma Park, Md., Dec. 25, 1950; d. Warren and Elsie (Miller) B. BS, Northrop Inst. Tech., 1973; MS, Fla. Inst. Tech., 1986. With Air Force Systems Command, Edwards AFB, Calif., 1973-78; various positions Boeing Def. & Space Group, Huntsville, Ala., 1978-81, test engr. reaction control system inertial upper stage, 1981-86, lead engr. microgravity material processing facility, 1986-88, task leader advanced civil space systems, 1988-99; systems engr. ISS BRP Payload, 1999—. Mem. AIAA (assoc. fellow). Office: Boeing Spl Projects PO Box 240002 (JN-04) 499 Boeing Blvd SW Huntsville AL 35824-3001 E-mail: patricia.buddinton@hsv.boeing.com.

BUDIN, WENDY C. nursing educator, researcher; m. Arnold I. Budin, June 13, 1973; children: Barri, Sarah, Jill. BSN, Adelphi U., Garden City, NY, 1973; MSN, Seton Hall U., South Orange, NJ, 1986; PhD, NYU, N.Y.C., 1996. Cert. perinatal nurse, ANCC, 2002; Lamaze childbirth educator Lamaze Internat., 1998. Assoc. prof. nursing Seton Hall U. Coll. Nursing, South Orange, NJ, 1986—2002, program dir.-Lamaze childbirth educator program, 1994—, assoc. dean grad. nursing programs and rsch., 2002—; acad. dir. online MSN program SetonWorldWide-Seton Hall U., South Orange, NJ, 2001—. Co-chair nursing/ psychosocial adv. group N.J. State Commn. on Cancer Rsch., Trenton, 1994—; cons. rsch. in nursing Excelsior Coll., Albany, NY, 1996—; med. adv. bd. North Jersey Affiliate of Susan G. Komen Breast Cancer Found., Summit, NJ, 1999—; collateral reviewer Sigma Theta Tau Internat., Indpls., 2001—. Author (co-author with j. hott): (book) Notter's Essentials of Nursing Research (Brandon/Hill Selected List of Nursing Books for Rsch., 2000); author: (co-author with c. hoskins and j. haber) Breast Cancer: Journey to Recovery; editor (contributing editor): Journal of Perinatal Education; contbr. articles to profl. jours. Recipient Rudin Family Award for Doctoral Student Achievement, NYU, 1994, Arch award, NYU Sch. Edn., 1996, Sigma Theta Tau Internat. Regional Rsch. Dissertation Award, Sigma Theta Tau Internat., 1997, N.J. Gov.'s Nursing Merit Award for Nurse Rschr., N.J. Dept. of Health and Sr. Svcs., 1999; grantee Co-Investigator & Project Dir. Stress and Coping in Caregivers of AIDS Children, NIH - NINR, 1991, Am. Nurses Found., 1994, Co-Investigator and Nurse Interventionist for Breast Cancer: Edn., Counseling and Adjustment, AREA Grant - NINR, 1998, Fed. Nurse Traineeship, Divsn. of Nursing -Dept. of Health and Human Svcs., 2002-03; Doctoral scholarship, Sigma Theta Tau Internat., 1992, Erline P. McGriff Doctoral scholarship, NYU - Divsn. of Nursing, 1995, N.J. Breast Cancer Rsch. Vis. Scholar fellowship, N.J. Commn. on Cancer Rsch., 1996. Mem.: Oncology Nursing Soc., Assn. for Woman's Health, Obstet. & Neonatal Nursing-AWHONN, Ea. Nursing Rsch. Soc., Lamaze Internat. (certification coun.), Sigma Theta Tau (past president-gamma nu chpt.). Achievements include research in Adjustment to Breast Cancer. Office: Seton Hall Univ College of Nursing South Orange NJ 07079 E-mail: budinwen@shu.edu.

BUDNIAKIEWICZ, THERESE, writer; b. Mons, Belgium, Sept. 28, 1948; came to U.S., 1961; naturalized, 1967; d. Tadeusz Eugeniusz and Janina Antonina (Więckowska) B.; m. Bart S. Ng, July 6, 1972. BA in Math., U. Chgo., 1971; MA in Comparative Lit., U. Mich., 1972, PhD in Comparative Lit., 1986. Lectr. English, Ind. U.-Purdue U., Indpls., 1987-92. Author: Fundamentals of Story Logic, 1992; contbr. Ency. of Semiotics, 1998. Named Internat. Writer of the Yr., Internat. Biog. Ctr., Cambridge, Eng., 2003; recipient, 2004, 20th Century award. Mem. MLA, Semiotic Soc. Am., Can. Semiotic Assn., Internat. Assn. for Semiotics of Law, Internat. Assn. for Semiotic Studies. Avocation: publishing technologies. Home and Office: 5823 Dapple Trace Indianapolis IN 46228-1698 E-mail: tbudniakiewicz@math.iupui.edu.

BUDNY, LORRAINE, freelance writer, newspaper reporter; b. Chicopee, Mass., July 18, 1917; d. Marcel Girouard and Cecile Babineau; m. J. Travers Ward, Dec. 31, 1941 (div. June 1946); m. Bernard S. Budny, Aug. 15, 1947 (dec. Aug. 1981). Student, N.Y. Theater Sch. Dramatic Art, Traphagen Sch. Fashion Design, N.Y.C. Asst. designer to Bonnie Cashin Adler & Adler, N.Y.C.; publicist Claire McCardell, N.Y.C.; dir. fashion promotion Lord & Taylor, N.Y.C., 1945-47; fashion editor Harper's Bazaar, N.Y.C., 1947-48; fashion designer Lorraine Budny Inc., N.Y.C., 1948-55; publisher, editor, writer South Kent, Conn., 1987-97; columnist, freelance writer Housatonic Publs., New Milford, Conn., 1997—. Mem. adv. com. New Milford Bank and Trust. Roman Catholic. Avocations: art museums and galleries, reading, travel, travel writing, double crostic puzzles.

BUDOFF, PENNY WISE, retired physician, author, researcher; b. Albany, N.Y., July 7, 1939; d. Louis and Goldene Wise. BA, Syracuse U., 1959; MD, SUNY-Upstate Med. Sch., 1963. Intern St. Luke's Meml. Hosp., Utica, N.Y., 1963-64; practice medicine specializing in family practice, women's health, Woodbury, N.Y., 1964-85; clin. assoc. prof. family medicine SUNY, Stony Brook, 1980—97. Founder, dir. emeritus North Shore U. Hosp. Women's Healthcare (formerly Penny Wise Budoff, MD Women's Health Svcs.), 1985-97, Bethpage, N.Y., 1985, ground-breaking women's health care facility; attending dept. ob/gyn. North Shore U. Hosp., 1992-97; asst. prof. ob/gyn. Cornell U. Med. Coll., 1993-96, pres. Bonne Forme Vitamins and Skin Care, divsn. Vitamins for Women, Farmingdale, N.Y., 1983—; TV guest on women's medicine and health issues; mem. spl. menopause NIH, 1993; clin. rsch. on menstrual pain, premenstrual syndrome, menopause, breast cancer and osteoporosis. Author: No More Menstrual Cramps and Other Good News, 1980, No More Hot Flashes and Other Good News, 1983, No More Hot Flashes and Even More Good News, 1998, World Book Health and Medical Annual, 1994; med. reviewer Jour. JAMA; contbr. articles to profl. jours. Bd. dirs. Coalition Against Domestic Violence. Named Woman of Yr. C.W. Post Coll., 1981; recipient Nat. Consumers League award, 1983, Max Cheplove award Erie chpt. N.Y. State Acad. Family Physicians, 1983, Women of Distinction award Soroptomist Internat. of Nassau County, L.I., 1990, award for promoting better understanding of menopause N.Am. Menopause Soc., 1999; honoree Nassau County Coalition Against Domestic Violence, 1992. Fellow Nassau County Med. Soc., Am. Acad. Family Physicians (nat. com. on pub. rels.); mem. NOW (Equality award in Health 1988, Unsung Heroine award), Am. Med. Women's Assn. (co-chmn. nat. women's health com., liaison), Nassau Acad. Family Physicians (past pres.). E-mail: pennybudoff@bonneforme.com., pennybudoff@aol.com.

BUECHNER, MARGARET, composer, music educator; b. Hannover, Germany, May 27, 1922; came to U.S., 1951, U.S. citizenship, 1961; d. Wilhelm and Martha Voss; m. Werner Buechner, 1948 (dvi. 1972). MusM, U. Königsberg and U. Wuerzburg (Germany) and Conservatory, 1943; pvt. studies in composition and orch. with Otto Luening, Columbia U., 1954-55. Ind. composer, 1932—; choir dir., educator, 1946-87; founder, pres. Mich. Composers League, 1960-66. Host classical music ednl. radio programs, 1961-64; mem. Composers Conf., Bennington, Vt., 1954, 55. Composer, librettist numerous story ballets including The Key, Phantomgreen, The Legend of Alice, Mayerling, Elizabeth, The Erlking, stageless full-length Princess and the Pea Ballet, stageless Elf-King Ballet, stageless full-length Immensee ballet, stageless Adventures of Easter Bunny ballet; also various symphonies, tone poems, many chamber music works, concert performances; recs. with the Nürnberger Symphoniker (German Symphony Orch.), including Ballet Suite of Phantomgreen and the complete music of the evening-length ballet Elizabeth and the tone poem The Old Swedes Church, recorded with Royal Scottish Nat. Orch. Essay I and The Flight of the Am. Eagle, Symphonic Poem Erlkönig Symphonic Trilogy The Am. Civil War, Orchestral Choral Reminiscence The Liberty Bell, (ballet music of evening length) La Belle et la Bête (Beauty and the Beast) performances Grand Théatre de Bordeaux, France and in Genova, Italy; other recs. include Five Symphonic Classics, Symphonic Ballet Music, Sixteen Symphony Orch. Children's Recital Dances, The Key complete ballet music, Suites and others, also ednl. orchestral CD; many stage performances The Key, Phantomgreen; TV broadcasts The Key; collection of 71 recorded dramatic symphonic concert works on CDs. Avocation: gardening. Address: Mgmt Eldo Music Publisher Ste 104 4407 Gladding Ct Midland MI 48640-3383

BUEHLING, CYNTHIA GWYNNE, music educator; b. Paragould, Ark., July 12, 1952; d. Edward G. and Martel M. Ross; m. Henry F. Buehling; 1 child, Louis. BA, MA of Music Edn., Ark. State U., 1975. Cert. tchr. Ark. Music tchr. Blytheville Pub. Schs., 1975—78; asst. music libr. Interlochen (Mich.) Ctr. for the Arts, 1979—80; elem. music, h.s. choir tchr. St. Francis Cath. Sch., Traverse City, Mich., 1980—81; instr. music Northwestern Mich. Coll., Traverse City, Mich., 1982—86; elem. music tchr. Pulaski County Spl. Sch. Dist., Little Rock, 1986—87, Little Rock Sch. Dist., 1987—. Childrens choir dir. Pulaski Hts. United Meth. Ch., Little Rock, 1992—2000. Mem.: Classroom Tchrs. Assn. (sch. rep. 1990—91), Ark. Music Educator's Nat. Conf. (elem. rep. 1988—90), Music Educator's Nat. Conf., Tau Beta Sigma (life), Sigma Alpha Iota (life). Methodist. Avocations: reading, cross stitch, theater, concerts. Home: 19 Flourite Cove Little Rock AR 72212-2110 Office: Western Hills Elem 4901 Western Hills Ave Little Rock AR 72204 Personal E-mail: cbuehling@earthlink.net. E-mail: cynthia.buehling@lrsd.org.

BUELL, EVANGELINE CANONIZADO, consumer cooperative official; b. San Pedro, Calif., Aug. 28, 1932; d. Estanislao (C.) and Felicia (Stokes) Canonizado; m. Ralph D. Vilas, 1952 (dec.); m. Robert Alexander Elkins, July 1, 1961 (dec.); children: Nikki Vilas, Stacey Vilas, Danni Vilas Plump; m. William David Buell, Feb. 21, 1987. Student, San Jose State Coll., 1952—53; grad., U. San Francisco, 1978. With Consumers Coop. of Berkeley (Calif.) Inc., 1958—, edn. asst. for cmty. rels., 1964—73, supr. edn. dept., 1973—76, asst. to edn. dir., 1976—78, program coord. edn. dept, 1980—81, pers. tng. coord., 1981—92; ret. Events coord. Internat. House, U. Calif., Berkeley, 1984; also guitar tchr. Columnist Coop. News, 1964—; contbr. articles to profl. jours. and mags.; author, co-editor (anthology) Seven Card Stud with Seven Manangs Wild. Pres. Berkeley Cmty. Chorus and Orch.; co-chair Berkeley Art Commn., 1992—94; dir. various activities YMCA, YWCA, Oakland City Recreation Dept., Oakland, 1959—73; bd. dirs. Philippine Ethnic Arts and Cultural Exch.; mem. cmty. adv. com. Bonita House, Berkeley, 1974; mem. steering com. for cultural and ethnic affairs Guild of Oakland Mus., 1973—74; bd. dirs., v.p. Berkeley Art Ctr., pres., 1998. Recipient Honor award, U. Calif. Student Coop., 1965, Outstanding Staff award, U. Calif. Berkeley Chancellor, 1992, Nat. Philanthropy Disting. Vol. award, 1993, Outstanding Instrn. Program Support award, Cole Sch. Visual & Performing Arts, Outstanding Berkeley Woman award, Berkeley Commn. on the Status of Women, 1996, others. Mem.: Coop. Educators Network Calif., Filipino Am. Nat. Hist. Soc. (pres. East Bay chpt. 1996, Silver Arts & Music award 1994). Democrat. Unitarian Universalist. Home: 516 Santa Barbara Rd Berkeley CA 94707-1746 E-mail: vangiec@uclink.berkeley.edu.

BUEN, JAN YAGI, state legislator; b. Dec. 30, 1942; m. Rick Buen; children: Althea, Kristi, Michael. BS in Human Resources, U. Hawaii. Dir. spl. projects Maui Electric Co.; mem. Hawaii Senate, Dist. 4, Honolulu, 1998—; vice chair econ. devel. com., mem. ways and means com. Hawaiian Senate, Honolulu, mem. transp. and intergovtl. affairs com. Bd. dirs. March of Dimes, Maui United Way, campaign chair, 1997; co-founder, bd. dirs. Friends of Maui Meml. Med. Ctr.; mem. Maui Okinawa Kenjin Kai. Mem. U. Hawaii Alumni Assn. Democrat. Office: State Capitol 415 S Beretania St Honolulu HI 96813-2407

BUENAFLOR, JUDITH LURAY, secondary school educator; b. Phila., Mar. 11, 1949; d. James and Dorothy Tawney (Riley) Arnao; m. Michael Vincent Buenaflor, July 7, 1973 (dec. 1996); children: Amy, Katherine, Ryan. BA, Rosemont Coll., 1971; MA in English, Kutztown U., 1998. Tchr. Ctrl. Cath. High Sch., Allentown, Pa., 1991-97; adminstrv. asst. St. Thomas More Sch., Allentown, 1999-2000, principal, 2000—. Advisor Odyssey of the Mind, Allentown, 1989-91, Nat. Honor Soc., 1991-97; part-time prof. Allentown Coll.; Allentown Coll. MEd program, 1999. Author: (writing seminar) The Influential Writer, 1999. Mem. tower ball com. Sacred Heart Hosp., Allentown, Pa., 1987-89; pres. women's guild, St. Thomas More, Allentown, 1986; mem. bd. assocs. Sacred Heart Hosp. Mem. Nat. Assn. Tchrs. English, Women's Guild, Alpha Epsilon Lambda (hon.). Roman Catholic. Avocations: writing, historical fiction. Home: 1128 Valley View Dr Allentown PA 18103-6042 E-mail: JLBSTM@hotmail.com.

BUENDIA, IMELDA BERNARDO, health facility administrator, physician; b. Iloilo City, The Philippines, Nov. 12, 1944; d. Carlos P. and Coleta (De la Cruz) Bernardo; m. Arsenio G. Buendia, June 5, 1971; children: Mary Elaine, Joseph Carlo, Adrian Cesar. BS, U. The Philippines, 1964, MD, 1969. Diplomate Am. Bd. Family Practice. Resident in pediats. Philippine Gen. Hosp., Manila, 1969-71; resident in family practice St. Michael's Hosp., Milw., 1971-75; med. officer Talihina (Okla.) Hosp., 1975-78, Wewoka (Okla.) Indian Clinic, 1978-92, clin. dir., 1992-96; med. officer El Reno Indian Clinic, 1996—, clin. dir., 1997—. Active Phil-Am. Civic Orgn., Oklahoma City, 1978—. Recipient Dir. Excellence award USPHS, 1993. Fellow: Am. Acad. Family Physicians; mem.: Philippine Med. Assn. Okla. (treas. 1989, sec. 1990, 2000, pres.-elect 1994, pres. 1995). Home: 2105 Wyckham Pl Norman OK 73072-3042 Office: 1621A E Highway 66 El Reno OK 73036-5769

BUFFETT, SUSAN THOMPSON, investment company executive; m. Warren Buffett, Apr. 1952. Dir. Berkshire Hathaway, Omaha. Office: Berkshire Hathaway 1440 Kiewit Plz Omaha NE 68131

BUFFINGTON, ROSEMARY, secondary school educator; b. Springfield, Ill. d. Bernard Lawrence and Rita Margaret Layendecker; m. Rod Harris Buffington, July 16, 1983; children: Jeffrey, Tara, Jill. BS in Edn., Ill. State U., 1970. Tchr. Cmty. Unit Sch. Dist. # 16, New Berlin, Ill., 1970—. Adv. Students Against Destructive Decisions Cmty. Unit Sch. Dist. # 16, 1988, adv. Art Club, adv. Student Coun.; chmn. HS display Festival of Trees, Springfield, 1990—2000. Recipient Nat. Youth Art award, Craft and Watercolor Soc., 1980, Golden Apple award, WICS-TV, 1992; Fulbright grantee, 1979. Mem.: NEA, Ill. Art Edn. Assn. (membership pres. 1982—83), Ill. Edn. Assn., Nat. Art Edn. Assn., Delta Kappa Gamma (1st v.p., 2d v.p.). Roman Catholic. Avocations: photography, cooking, calligraphy, aquariums. Office: Cmty Unit Sch Dist # 16 300 Ellis St New Berlin IL 62670

BUFFLER, PATRICIA ANN, epidemiologist, educator, retired dean; b. Doylestown, Pa., Aug. 1, 1938; d. Edward M. and Evelyn G. (Axenroth) Happ; m. Richard T. Buffler, Jan. 20, 1962; children: Martyn R., Monique L. BSN, Cath. U. Am., 1960; MPH, U. Calif., Berkeley, 1965, PhD in Epidemiology, 1973. Prof. epidemiology sch. pub. health U. Tex. Health Sci. Ctr., Houston, 1979—91; prof. U. Calif., Berkeley, 1991—, dean sch. pub. health, 1991—98, dean emerita, 1998—. Mem. expert adv. panel on occupl. health WHO, 1985—; mem. environment, safety and health adv. com. U.S. DOE, 1992—95; mem. bd. on water sci. and tech. NRC, 1992—94; chair, bd. dirs. Mickey Leland Nat. Urban Air Toxics Rsch. Ctr., 1994—97, Societal Inst. of Math. Scis.; mem. Nat. Commn. on Superfund, Keystone Ctr., 1992—94; mem. adv. panel on mng. nuc. materials from warheads U.S. Congress Office Tech. Assessment, 1992—93; bd. sci. counselors Nat. Inst. for Occupl. Safety and Health, 1991—93; mem. sci. adv. bd. radiation adv. com. subcom. on cancer risks associated with electric and magnetic fields U.S. EPA, 1990—93, mem. sci. adv. bd., 1996—; mem. Nat. Adv. Coun. on Environ. Health Scis., 1995—98, NAS, Nat. Coun. Radiation Protection. Contbr. articles to profl. jours. Fellow: AAS, Inst. Medicine, Am. Coll. Epidemiology (pres.-elect 1990—91, pres. 1991—92); mem.: APHA (epidemiology sect. 1964—), Internat. Soc. for Environ. Epidemiology (pres.-elect 1989—91, pres. 1992—94), Soc. of Toxicology, Internat. Commn. on Occupl. Health, Internat. Soc. for Exposure Assessment (charter, bd. internat. councillors 1993—), Internat. Epidemiol. Assn., Soc. for Occupl. and Environ. Health, Am. Epidemiol. Soc., Soc. for Epidemiol. Rsch. (pres.-elect, pres., past pres. 1984—88), Collegium Ramazzini. Office: U Calif Sch Pub Health 714-F Univ Hall 140 Earl Warren Hl Berkeley CA 94720-0001

BUFORD, EVELYN CLAUDENE SHILLING, retired consumer products company executive; b. Ft. Worth, Sept. 21, 1940; d. Claude and Winnie Evelyn (Mote) Hodges; m. William J. Buford, Mar. 1982; children by previous marriage: Vincent Shilling, Kathryn Lynn Shilling LA Chapelle. Student, Hill Jr. Coll., 1975-76, Tarrant County (Tex.) Jr. Coll, 1992-93. With Imperial Printing Co., Inc., Ft. Worth, 1964-70, corp. sec., 1977-79, gen. sales mgr. coml. divsn., 1982—89; with Tarrant County Hosp. Dist., Ft. Worth, 1973-77, asst. to asst. adminstr., 1981-84; merch. asst. J.C. Penney Co., Hurst, Tex., 1989—96; ret., 1996. Mem. Exec. Women Internat. (life, dir., publs. chair, v.p. 1984, pres. 1985, chair adv. com. 1986-87, scholarship dir. 1988-93, corp. publ. com. 1988-89, dir. South ctrl. region 1993-94). Republican. Methodist. Home: 1025 Kenneth Ln Burleson TX 76028-2246

BUFORD-BAILEY, TONJA YEVETTE, Olympic athlete; b. Dayton, Ohio, Dec. 13, 1970; d. Georgianna Buford; m. Victor Bailey, Oct. 28, 1995. Grad., U. Ill., 1993. Mem. U.S. Olympic Team, Barcelona, 1992, Atlanta, 1996. Named winner 16 individual Big Ten Championships, U. Ill., winner 9 relay Big Ten Championships; recipient conf. title indoor awards for 55 and 200 dashes, 55 hurdles, conf. title outdoor awards for 100, 200, 400 and both hurdles, Bronze medal, Pan Am. Games, Havana, Cuba, 1991, Silver medal, Pam Am. Games, Argentina, 1995, Silver award, World Championships, Gothenburg, 1995, Bronze medal 400 meter hurdles, Olympic Games, Atlanta, 1996. Achievements include ranked 7th in world for 400 meter hurdles, 1992; ranked 5tj in the world 400 meter hurdles, 1993; ranked 2d in the world 400 meter hurdles, 1995; ranked 3d in the world 400 meter hurdles, 1996; ranked 6th in the world 400 meter hurdles, 1997. Office: USA Track and Field PO Box 120 Indianapolis IN 46206-0120

BUGBEE, JOAN BARTHELME, retired corporate communications executive; b. Galveston, Tex., Dec. 31, 1932; d. Donald and Helen (Bechtold) Barthelme; m. George A. Bugbee, Apr. 2, 1966; children: Richard, John. BA in Journalism, U. Colo., 1955. Pub. rels. rep. Philco Corp., Phila., 1957-60; account exec. Jacobs Keeper Newell Assoc., Houston, 1960-63; pub. rels. rep. Tex. Ea. Corp., Houston, 1963-66; assoc. editor Oil and Gas Digest Mag., Houston, 1978-79; mgr. corp. comms. Pennzoil Co., Houston, 1980-87, dir. corp. comms., 1987-90, v.p. corp. comm., 1990-96; ret., 1996; pub. rels. cons. Bd. dir., mem. bd. exec. com. Blue Ridge Pub. TV., mem. and publicity person, alternatives to War; book reviewer for The Roanoke Times. Mem. Radio Reading Svc., Sta. WVTF; publicity chmn. Roanoke chpt. Brady/Million Mom Mar. Recipient Outstanding Presentation award, Phila. chpt. Pub. Rels. Soc. Am., 1959. Mem.: Red Hat Soc., Phi Beta Kappa. Maronite Catholic.

BUGBEE-JACKSON, JOAN, sculptor, educator; b. Oakland, Calif, Dec. 17, 1941; d. Henry Greenwood and Jeanie Lawler (Abbot) B.; m. John Michael Jackson, June 21, 1973; 1 child, Brook Bond. BA in Art, U. Calif., San Jose, 1964, MA in Art and Ceramics, 1966; student, Nat. Acad. Sch. Fine Arts, N.Y.C., 1968-72. Instr. pottery Greenwich House Pottery, NYC, 1969-71, Craft Inst. Am., NYC, 1970-72, Cordova Ext. Ctr., U. AK, 1972-79, Prince William Sound Cmty. Coll., 1979—. Represented by B Street Artworks, Cordova. One-woman exhbn. in Maine, NYC, Alaska, Calif.; group exhbns. include Allied Artists Am., 1970-72, Nat. Acad. Design, 1971, 74, Nat. Sculpture Soc. Ann., 1971, 72, 73, Alaska Woman Art Show, 1987, 88, Cordova Visual Artists, 1991-96, Alaska Artists Guild Show, 1994, Am. Medallic Sculpture Nat. Travelling Exhbn., 1994-95, pres. Cordova Arts and Pageants Ltd., 1975-76; commns. include Merle K. Smith Commemorative plaque, 1973, Eyak Native Monument, 1978, Anchorage Pioneer's Home Ceramic Mural, 1979, Alaska Wildlife Series Bronze Medal, 1980, Armin F. Koernig Hatchery Plaque, 1985, Cordova Fishermen's Meml. Sculpture, 1985, Alaska's Five Gov., bronze relief, Anchorage, 1986, Reluctant Fishermen's Mermaid, bronze, 1987, Charles E. Bunnell, bronze portrait statue, Fairbanks, 1988, Alexander Baranof Monument, Sitka, Alaska, 1989, Wally Noerenberg Hatchery Plaque, Prince William Sound, Alaska, 1989, Russian-Alaskan Friendship Plaque (edit. of 4), Kayak Island, Cordova, Alaska and Vladivostok & Petropavlovsk-Kamchatskiy, Russia, 1991, Sophie-Last Among Eyak Native People, 1992, Alaska Airlines Medal Commn., 1993, Hosp. Aux. plaque, 1995, La Cirena, Mex., 1998, Alaska Vets. Monument lifesize bronze, Anchorage, 2001, Joe Redington, Sr. statue, Wasilla, 2003; J. Redington Sr., Father of the Iditarod, 2002, Alaska R.R.: Sheffield Plaque, 2002; also other portraits. Bd. dir. Alaska State Coun. Arts, 1991-95. Scholar, Nat. Acad. Sch. Fine Arts, 1969-72; recipient J.A. Suydam Bronze medal, 1969, Dr. Ralph Weiler prize, 1971, Helen Foster Barnet award, 1971, Daniel Chester French award, 1972, Frishmuth award, 1971, Allied Artists Am. award, 1972, C. Percival Dietsch prize, 1973, citation Alaska Legis., 1981, 82; named Alaskan Artist of Yr., 1991; Alaska Gov. Award, 2002. Fellow Nat. Sculpture Soc. Address: PO Box 374 Cordova AK 99574-0374

BUGGE, CAROLE ELIZABETH, writer, actress; d. Paul Rudolph Bowers and Margaret Katharine Simmons; m. Christopher Bugge, Aug. 27, 1978 (div. Oct. 1988). BA magna cum laude in Eng. and German, Duke U., 1976. Performer, writer Chgo. City Limits, N.Y.C., 1982—92; writing tchr. Gotham Writers Workshop, N.Y.C., 1992—2003. Author: (novels) The Star of India, 1998, Who Killed Blanche Dubois?, 1999, Who Killed Dorian Gray?, 2000, The Haunting of Torre Abbey, 2000, Who Killed Mona Lisa?, 2001, (short stories) Haunted America, 1991, Lovers and Other Monsters, 1992, More Masterpieces of Terror and the Unknown, 1993, Angels of Darkness, 1995, The Resurrected Holmes, 1996, Don't Open This Book!, 1997, The Confidential Casebook of Sherlock Holmes, 1997, Ultimate Halloween, 2001; playwright: Fool's Fair, 1990; actor: A Deconstructionists' Cinderella, 1990, Conversations in Hallways, 1991, The Tongue-Tied Tenor, 1994, Reflection of Evil, 1992, Counterpoint, 1996, House of the Seven Gables, 1996, Treason, 1997, Sherlock Homles, 2000. Vol. Head Start, Ohio, 1970; vol. reader Bookpals, N.Y.C., 2002. Recipient Citizenship award, DAR, 1972, Winner Eve of St. Agnes Poetry Competition, Negative Capability Mag., 1991, Winner Jean Paiva Meml. Fiction prize, Writer's Digest Competion-Essay Category, 1996, Writer's Digest Competion-Play Category, 1996, First prize, Maxim Mazumdar Playwriting Contest, 1996; grantee, N.Y. State Arts Coun., 1992, NEA, Lincoln Ctr. Reading, Poet's & Writers, 1993. Mem.: Actors Equity, SAG, Dramatists Guild. Avocations: horseback riding, bicycling, hiking, cooking, mushroom hunting. Home: 172 E 4th St New York NY 10009 Office: Gothic Prodns 172 E 4th St New York NY 10009 E-mail: CBugge@aol.com.

BUGGS, ELAINE S. financial analyst; b. Trenton, N.J., Aug. 18, 1954; d. Moses and Hattie (Mitchell) S.; m. Richmond Akumiah, Dec. 1982 (div. Aug. 27, 1987); m. James A. Buggs, Sr., Oct. 2, 1996; 1 child, James A., Jr. BS, Rochester Inst. Technol., 1976; MBA, Atlanta U., 1985. Mktg. rep. Mobil Oil Corp., 1976-77; mfg. analyst Reader's Digest, Pleasantville, N.Y., 1977-80; mgr. fin. instns. Am. Express, N.Y.C., 1980-83; sr. market analyst Ryder Systems Inc., Miami, 1985-86; dir. recruiting Atlanta U., 1986; cons. Consultants & Assocs., Washington, 1987-89; mgr. fin. analysis Blue Cross Blue Shield of Va., Roanoke, 1989-90; dir. group fin. reporting & analysis Blue Cross Blue Shield of Md., Owings Mills, 1990-93; sr. med. group analyst mid-Atlantic states region Kaiser Permanente, Rockville, Md., 1993-95; asst. mgr. Johns Hopkins U., Balt., 1995-98; mgr. bus. ops. Dingman Ctr. for Entrepreneurship, U. Md., College Park, 1998-2000; dir. fin. and adminstrn. Arts and Humanities Coll., U. Md., College Park, 2000—. Named IBM scholar, 1983. Mem. NAFE, Md. New Directions (bd. dirs. 1994-96), Internat. Soc. Strategic Planners, Nat. Assn. MBA Execs., Nat. Assn. of Black MBAs. Democrat. Methodist. Avocations: tennis, aerobics, antique hunting. Home: 8403 Gold Sunset Way Columbia MD 21045-7407 Office: Univ Md College Park Arts and Humanities Coll 1211B Art/Sociology Bldg College Park MD 20742 E-mail: eb148@wmail.umd.edu.

BUHAGIAR, MARION, editor, author; b. N.Y.C., Oct. 27, 1932; d. George and Mae (Pietrzak) B.; 1 child, Alexa Ragozin. BA cum laude, Hunter Coll., 1953; postgrad., Mt. Holyoke Coll., 1954. Economist U.S. Dept. Commerce, 1954-57; bus. reporter Time mag., 1957-59; assoc. editor Fortune mag., 1960-73, story devel. editor, 1970-73; text editor Time-Life Books, N.Y.C., 1973-76; v.p. Boardroom Inc., 1977-84; editor Boardroom Reports, 1977-84; exec. editor Bottom Line/Personal, 1980-84; pres. Expert Connections, N.Y.C., 1994—2002; editor Street Smart Investing, 1987-89; ret., 2003. Author: How to Build a College Fund for Your Child, 1989, Battle Plan for American Business, 1992, I-Power, 1992; editor: The Book of Secrets, 1989. Adv. bd. Scientists Inst. for Pub. Info., N.Y.C. E-mail: dorset2@aol.com.

BUHL, CYNTHIA MAUREEN, foreign policy educator and advocate; b. Los Angeles, Apr. 14, 1952; d. Albert Buhl and Dorothy Jane (Loth) Henry. BA, Lewis & Clark Coll., 1974. Dir. Resource and Counseling Ctr., Portland Youth Advs., Oreg., 1971-72; resource coordinator S.E. Youth Service Ctr., Portland Action Coms. Together, 1975-77; sec., asst. Human Rights Office Nat. Council Chs. Christ, N.Y.C., 1977-78; human rights coordinator Coalition for a New Fgn. and Mil. Policy, Washington, 1978-85; cons. Fgn. Policy Edn. Fund, Washington, 1986; nat. adv. bd. Caribbean Basin Info. Project, 1983-85; bd. dirs., legis. dir. Pax Am.'s/Priorities-PAC, 1986-90; legis. dir. Ctrl. Am. Working Group, 1990-93; dir. Indigenous Peoples Program, Bank Info. Ctr., 1994-96; legis. dir. U.S. Rep. James A. McGovern, 1997—. Author: Citizen's Guide to the Multilateral Development Banks and Indigenous Peoples: The World Bank, 1994, Spanish transl., 1995, Bahasa transl., 1996, Russian transl., 1996; co-editor: Central America 1985: Basic Information and Legislative History on U.S.-Central American Relations, 1985. Contbr. articles to various jours., mags. Co-chmn. Human Rights Working Group, Washington, 1978-81, chmn., 1982-85; chmn. Central Am. Lobby Group, 1983-85; mem. Commn. on U.S.-Central Am. Relations, 1983-85. Office Phone: 202-225-6101.

BUHLER, JILL LORIE, editor, writer; b. Seattle, Dec. 7, 1945; d. Oscar John and Marcella Jane (Hearing) Younce; 1 child, Lori Jill Moody; m. John Buhler, 1990; stepchildren: Christie Reynolds, Cathie Zatarian, Mike. AA in Gen. Edn., Am. River Coll., 1969; BA in Journalism with honors, Sacramento State U., 1973. Reporter Carmichael (Calif.) Courier, 1968-70; mng. editor Quarter Horse of the Pacific Coast, Sacramento, 1970-75, editor, 1975-84, Golden State Program Jour., 1978, Nat. Reined Cow Horse Assn. News, Sacramento, 1983-88, Pacific Coast Jour., Sacramento, 1984-88, Nat. Snaffle Bit Assn. News, Sacramento, 1988; pres., chief exec. officer Communications Plus, Port Townsend, Wash., 1988—; bd. sec. N.W. Maritime Ctr., 2001—, 2001—. Mag. cons., 1975—. Interviewer Pres. Ronald Regan, Washington, 1983; mng. editor Wash. Thoroughbred, 1989-90. Mem. 1st profl. communicators mission to USSR, 1988; bd. dirs. Carmichael Winding Way, Pasadena Homeowners Assn., 1985-87; mem. scholarship com. Thoroughbred Horse Racing's United Scholarship Trust; mem. governing bd. Wash. State Hosp. Assn., 1996-2000, mem. legis. policy com., 1999—, hosp. commr. Jefferson Gen. Hosp., 1995—, chair bd. dirs. 1997-2000, sec., 2004; mem. Jefferson County Bd. Health, 1997—, vice chmn., 1998, chmn. 2001; mem. Wash. State Health Care Leadership Com., 2003-. Recipient 1st pl. feature award, 1970, 1st pl. editorial award Jour. Assn. Jr. Colls., 1971, 1st pl. design award WCHB Yuba-Sutter Counties, Marysville, Calif., 1985, Photography awards, 1994, 95, 96. Mem. Am. River Jaycees (Speaking award 1982), Am. Horse Publs. (1st Pl. Editl. award 1983, 86), Port Townsend C. of C. (trustee, v.p. 1993, pres. 1994, officer 1996, 97, 98), Mensa (bd. dirs., asst. local sec., activities dir. 1987-88, membership chair 1988-90), Kiwanis Internat. (chair maj. emphasis program com., treas. 1992—), 5th Wheel Touring Soc. (v.p. 1970). Republican. Roman Catholic. Avocations: sailing, photography. Home: 440 Adelma Beach Rd Port Townsend WA 98368-9280 Personal E-mail: jillb@olypen.com.

BUHLER, LESLIE LYNN, museum director; BA in History and Art History with honors, Syracuse U., 1969; postgrad., New Sch. for Social Rsch., 1971, Am. U., 1980. Asst. for cmty. programs Met. Mus. Art, N.Y.C., 1970-72; program coord. resident assoc. program Smithsonian Instn., Washington, 1972-75; instl. devel. officer Nat. Archives and Records Svc., Washington, 1975-78; ind. cons., 1977—85; dir. devel., membership and mktg. Alban Inst., Inc., Bethesda, Md., 1985-88, dir. ops., 1988-89, exec. v.p., 1989-99, acting pres., 1994-95; exec. dir. Tudor Place Hist. House and Garden, Washington, 2000—. Grant reviewer Office of Mus. Programs, NEH, Washington, 1973-74. Bd. dirs. Mus. of City of Washington, 1980-84; vol. advisor Nat. Mus. for Bldg. Arts, Washington, 1977-79. Recipient cert. of appreciation Am. Revolution Bicentennial Adminstrn., 1976. Office: Tudor Place Found 1644 31st St NW Washington DC 20007

BUHR, FLORENCE D. county official; b. Strahan, Iowa, Apr. 7, 1933; d. Earnest G. and May (Brott) Wederquist; m. Glenn E. Buhr, 1955; children: Barbara, Lori Lynn, David. BA, U. No. Iowa, 1954. Precinct chair Polk County Dem. Ctrl. Com., Iowa, 1974-79; clerk, sec. Iowa Ho. Reps., 1974-79, 81-82; rep. dist. 85 State of Iowa, 1983-90, asst. majority leader Ho. Reps., 1985-90; state senator Iowa State Senate, 1991-95, asst. majority leader, 1992-95; Polk County supr. Des Moines, 1995—. Chairwoman Polk County Bd. Suprs., 1997. Democrat. Presbyterian. Home and Office: 4127 30th St Des Moines IA 50310-5946

BUHR-DUPREEZ, MARGARET ILSE, adult education educator; b. Kokstad, Natal, South Africa, Feb. 1, 1953; arrived in U.S., 1994; d. Wilhelm Heinrich Bernhard Buhr and Salomina Petronella Terblanche; children: Heinrich Christian, Frans Johan, Ilse. BA, U. Orange Free State, Bloemfontein, South Africa, 1974, EdB, 1975; MA, U. Pretoria, South Africa, 1994; PhD, Rand Afrikaans U., Johannesburg, South Africa, 2002. Tele interpreter Network Omni, Thousand Oaks, Calif., 1996—; instr. Golden State Coll., Oxnard, Calif., 1997—99; tchr. spl. edn. Adv. Schs., Camarillo, Calif., 1999—2001; instr. Simi Valley (Calif.) Adult Sch., 2001—, Conejo Valley Adult Sch., Thousand Oaks, 2002—. Bd. mem. First Luth. Sch., Camarillo, 2001—. Republican. Avocations: gardening, crafts, travel. Home: 1759 Marco Dr Camarillo CA 93010

BUI-BURTON, KIM LY, library director, poet; d. Duong An and Aurzella Boewe Bui; m. Steven Louis Silveria, Aug. 2, 1997; children: Katharine Burton, Robert Burton. BA in Lit. with honors, U. Calif., Santa Cruz, 1991; MLIS, San Jose State U., 1997. Reference /youth libr. Monterey County Free Librs., Seaside, Calif., 1995—96, br. mgr. Greenfield, Calif., 1996—97, supervising/mng. libr. Salinas, Calif., 1997—99; readers svcs. mgr. Monterey (Calif.) Pub. Libr., 1999—. Co-creator shelf to shore collaborative aquarium/pub. libr. access project Monterey Bay Aquarium and Monterey County Free Librs., Salinas, 1997—99; co-creator Guiding with Courage Multi-Media Writing Contest Monterey County Free Librs., Salinas, 1998—99; co-creator radio readers regional fm radio/webcast monthly book discussion program Monterey Pub. Libr. and Sta. KAZU-FM, Pacific Grove, Calif., 2000—02. Co-author: (anthologized poems) I am Becoming the Woman I've Wanted, 1994 (Nat. Book Award Before Columbus Found. Award recipient, 1995), Passionate Hearts: the Poetry of Sexual Love, 1996, Tilting the Continent: Southeast Asian American Poetry, 2000, The Body Eclectic: Poetry for Teens, 2002. Diversity trainer Nat. Coalition Bldg. Inst., Pacific Grove, 1993—2003; mem. awards selection com. Pacific Grove Arts Assn., 2001. Recipient Multi-Ethnic Recruitment award, Calif. State Libr., 1992, 1993; Edna Yelland Meml. scholar, Calif. Libr. Assn., 1992, 1993. Mem.: ALA (assoc.), Calif. Libr. Assn. (assoc.). Democrat. Avocations: gardening, reading. Office: Monterey Pub Libr 625 Pacific St Monterey CA 93940 E-mail: kimbb@sbcglobal.net.

BUILER, DOROTHY MARION, business owner; b. Athens, Wis., Apr. 20, 1925; d. Edwin Herman and Katherine Dorothy (Dick) Mueller; m. Donald J. Builer, May 24, 1947; 1 child, Thomas Edwin. Grad. h.s., Athens. Owner, ptnr. Builer's Sport Shop, Wausau, Wis., 1959—, Campers Haven, Heafford Junction, Wis., 1967—. Mem. Internat. Platform Assn., Bus. and Profl. Women Club (pres. Marathon county 1968-69, pres. Northwood dist. 1973-74), Wausau Womans Club (pres.-elect 1988-90, pres. 1990-91), Am. Legion Aux. (pres. local unit 1958-59, pres. 8th dist. 1963-64, chmn. State of Wis. aux. conv. 1964), Valley Garden Club, Wausau Wheelers Bike Club (organizer). Home: 3919 Pine Cone Ln Wausau WI 54403-2384

BUJOLD, LOIS MCMASTER, writer; b. Columbus, Ohio, Nov. 2, 1949; d. Robert Charles and Laura Elizabeth (Gerould) McMaster; m. John Fredric Bujold, Oct. 9, 1971 (div. Dec. 1992); children: Anne Elizabeth, Paul Andre. Author: (novels) Shards of Honor, 1986, The Warrior's Apprentice, 1986, Ethan of Athos, 1986, Falling Free, 1988 (Nebula award, 1989), Brothers in Arms, 1989, Borders of Infinity, 1989, The Vor Game, 1990 (Hugo award, 1991), Barrayar, 1991 (Hugo award, 1992, 1st place Locus poll, 1992), Mirror Dance, 1994 (Hugo & Locus awards, 1995), Cetaganda, 1996, Memory, 1996, Komarr, 1998 (Minn. book award, 1999), A Civil Campaign, 1999, The Curse of Chalion, 2001 (Mythopoeic award, 2002), Diplomatic Immunity, 2002, Paladin of Souls, 2003, (novellas) The Borders of Infinity, 1987, The Mountains of Mourning, 1989 (Nebula and Hugo awards, 1990), Labyrinth, 1989 (Best Novella/Novelette Analytical Lab., 1990), Weatherman, 1990 (Best Novella Analytical Lab., 1991); contbr. short stories to sci. fiction mags., articles to profl. jours. Mem.: Novelists, Inc., Sci. Fiction and Fantasy Writers Am. Office: Spectrum Literary Agency 320 Central Park W Ste 1D New York NY 10025-7659 E-mail: lois@dendarii.com.

BUKOWSKI, ELAINE LOUISE, physical therapist, educator; b. Phila., Feb. 18, 1949; d. Edward Eugene and Melanja Josephine (Przyborowski) B. BS in Phys. Therapy, St. Louis U., 1972; MS, U. Nebr., 1977. Lic. phys. therapist, N.J.; diplomate Am. Bd. Disabilities Analysts (sr. analyst, profl. adv. coun. 1995—). Clk. City of Phila., 1967; staff phys. therapist St. Louis Chronic Hosp., 1973, Cardinal Ritter Inst., St. Louis, 1973-74; dir. campus ministry musicals Creighton U., Omaha, 1974-75; tchg. asst. U. Nebr. Med. Ctr., Omaha, 1975-76; lectr. in anatomy U. Sci. and Tech., Kumasi, Ghana, 1977-78; chief phys. therapist Holy Family Hosp., Berekum, Ghana, 1978-79; coord. info. & guidance The Am. Cancer Soc., Phila., 1979-81; staff phys. therapist Holy Redeemer Vis. Nurse Assn., Phila., 1981-83, rehab. supr. Swainton, N.J., 1983-87; asst. prof. phys. therapy Richard Stockton Coll. N.J., Pomona, 1987-96, assoc. prof., 1996—2002, prof., 2003—. Bd. dirs. The Bridge, Phila., 1979-80; vacation relief phys. therapist, N.J., summer 1988—; mem. profl. adv. coun. Holy Redeemer VNA, Swainton, N.J., 1982-93, chmn., 1985-91, mem. pers. com., cons. hospice program, 1985-87, rehab. cons., 1987-88; legis. adv. coun. subcom. on edn. and health care Cape May & Cumberland Counties, 1988-90; utilization rev. cons. rehab. svcs., 1990; mem. fitness screening team N.J. State Legislature, 1990; mem. geriatric rehab. del. Citizen Amb. Program, China, 1992; middle states accreditation team evaluator, 1997-98. Co-author slide study program, (video) Going My Way? The Low Back Syndrome, 1976; author: Muscular Analysis of Everyday Activities, 2000. Vol. Am. Cancer Soc., Phila., 1979-82, Walk-a-Day-in-My Shoes prog. Girl Scouts Am., Cape May County, N.J., 1983-86; task force phys. therapy prog. Stockton State Coll., Pomona, N.J., 1985-88. U.S. Govt. trainee, 1971, 72; Physical Therapy Fund grantee, 1975, 76; recipient Vol. Achievement award Am. Cancer Soc., 1981. Mem. Am. Phys. Therapy Assn. (edn. sect., orthop. sect., vice chmn. so. dist. 1993-96, 99-2001, chmn. 1996-98, bd. dirs., ho. of dels. 1994-97, key contact voting dist. 2, mem. N.J. legis. network 1989-96, 1999-2002, mems. mentoring program 1998—, chair nominating com. 2002-04, key act voting dist., Phys. Therapy Club (sec. 1971-72), N.J. Phys. Therapy Assn. (rsch. com. 1995-97). Avocations: gardening, music, reading, poetry. Office: Richard Stockton Coll NJ Phys Therapy Program Jim Leeds Rd Pomona NJ 08240 Office Phone: 609-652-4416. Business E-Mail: elaine.bukowski@stockton.edu.

BUKTA, POLLY, state representative; b. Greenville, Pa., Apr. 3, 1937; m. Michael Bukta. BS, Mercyhurst Coll., 1962; postgrad., U. No. Iowa, 1967. Elem. tchr., Clinton, Iowa, 1967—2000; ret., 2000—; mem. Iowa Ho. Reps., DesMoines, 1997—, mem. various coms. adminstrn. and rules, edn., ethics and transp. Elected asst. minority leader, 2001—02, 2003—04. Former vice chair Clinton County Dems. Mem.: NEA, NACCP, AAUW, Clinton Area C. of C., Clinton Edn. Assn., Iowa State Tchrs. Assn., Clinton Womens Club, Delta Kappa Gamma. Democrat. Office: State Capitol East 12th and Grand Des Moines IA 50319 also: 604 S 32nd St Clinton IA 52732 Personal E-mail: pollyb03@msn.com.

BULGER, MARCIA S. physical education educator; d. Earl and D. Agnes Stearns; m. Charles Terry Bulger, Aug. 7, 1965 (dec. Sept. 21, 1999). BS, SUCC, 1965; MS, Syracuse U., 1993. Dir. HPEP, youth advisor YWCA, Cortland, 1965—72; exercise tchr. Trim n Tone, Cortland, 1972—73, YMCA, Cortland, 1973—75; local supr. H.A. Manning Co.-Vt., Cortland, NY and Wolsville, 1975—85; ednl. cons. City of Cortland Youth Bur., 1980—85; tchr. OCM Boces, Cortland, 1985—. V.p. Albcation team United Way Cortland Co., 1975—85; chair Consumer CoPlanel Cortland Co., 1976; mem. consumer com. N.Y. State Electric and Gas Co., Ctrl. Area, NY, 1977—85; mem. mental health subcom. Cortland Co. Legislature, 1988—2002; vice chair, co-chair Cmty. Svs. Bd., Cortland Co., 2003. Recipient Owl of Leaders, Girl Scouts Ctrl. N.Y., 1984, 1985, Thanks Badge, Girls Scouts Ctrl. N.Y., 1988. Mem.: AAUW (sec., pres., v.p. 1991—93, 1991—93), YWCA (life), Cortland Co. Burn Fund Inc. (treas. 1992—), City Cortland Fire Aux., Girl Scouts Am. (life; trainer 1995), Cortland Co. Fire Aux. (v.p.), Delta Kappa Gamma. Avocations: camping, swimming, crafts. Home: 8 Washington St Cortland NY 13045 Office: OCM Boces 1710 Rte 13 Cortland NY 13045

BULGER, PEGGY ANNE, cultural organization administrator; b. Albany, N.Y., Dec. 13, 1949; d. David J. and Hannah (Casey) B.; m. Douglas B. Leatherbury III, Apr. 21, 1979; children: (twins) Hannah Elizabeth and Meagan Chase. BA, SUNY, Albany, 1972; MA, Western Ky. U., 1975; PhD, U. Pa., 1992. Oral historian Bur. Cultural Affairs, Albany, 1975; rsch. and participants coord. Appalacian Mus., Berea, Ky., 1975-76; state folk arts coord. Fla. Dept. State, 1976-79; folklife programs adminstr. Bur. Fla. Folklife Programs, 1979-89; coord. Regional Folk Arts Program So. Arts Fedn., Atlanta, 1989-92, dir., 1992-99, Am. Folklife Ctr., Libr. Congress, Washington, 1999—. Chairperson Folk Arts Steering Com. Atlanta Com. Olympic Games Cultural Olympiad, 1992-96; cons. Marine Resources Coun. Fla., Nat. Folk Festival, Nat. Black Arts Festival; bd. dirs. Nat. Coun. Traditional Arts, 1992—. Editor: Musical Roots of the South, 1992; author: (with Tina Bucuvalas and Stetson Kennedy) South Florida Folklife, 1994; contbr. books The Steamboat Era in Florida, 1984, The Conservation of Culture: Folklorists and the Public Sector, 1988; guest editor: Southern Folklore, 1992; producer documentary videotapes and films for educl. TV, radio networks ans sound recordings, videotapes for PBS including Four Corners of Earth: Folklife of Seminole Women, 1984, Fishiing All My Days: Maritime Traditions of Florida's Shrimpers, 1985, Every Island Has Its Own Songs: The Tsinouris Family of Tarpon Springs, 1988, Music Mission and Rhythm Kings, 1993. Recipient Wayland D. Hand prize, 1991-92, Brit. Coun. fellow, Folklore Study Tour No. Ireland, 1992. Democrat. Episcopalian. Avocations: irish studies, guitar, running. Office: Am Folklife Ctr Libr of Congress 101 Independence Ave SE Washington DC 20540-0002

BULL, HELEN MAY, artist; b. Sweet Springs, Mo., Apr. 20, 1920; d. John Theodore Langewisch and Ethel Henrietta (Von Berkelo) Butemeyer; widowed; children: Jan Emerson Bull, Guy William Bull. BFA, Otis Art Inst., L.A., 1971; advanced certification Indsl. Rels., UCLA, 1983. Dir. Brazilian Primitive Painting Exhbn., L.A., 1972; pres. Bay West Assn. of Comty Assistance to Homeless Youngsters, L.A., 1973-74; artist, represented by Agora Art Gallery, N.Y.C. Panelist Inst. for Study of Women in Transition, 1976; nursing career devel. con., San. Antonio, Tex., 1978-80. Artist: Spl exhbn. of canvasses in Vista Rm., Faculty Ctr. UCLA, 1973, Art in Permanent Collections includes KTSC-TV, Pueblo, Colo, and framed mural of St. Luke, St. Luke's Luth. Ch., (Gold award 1993); one-person show Agora Gallery, 1999; exhibited group show at Agora Gallery, 1998. Recipient Cert. of merit, UCLA Juried Faculty Exhibit, 1960. Lutheran. Avocations: travel, hiking, coin collecting/numismatics. Office: Agora Art Gallery 560 Broadway New York NY 10012-3938

BULL, INEZ STEWART, special education, gifted music educator, coloratura soprano, pianist, editor, author, curator; b. Newark, Apr. 13, 1920; d. Johan Randulf and Aurora (Stewart) B. Diploma in piano, Juilliard, 1946; cert., Chautauqua Inst. Sch. Music, 1940-46; diploma, U. Oslo Grad. Sch., Norway, 1955; MusB, N.Y. Coll. Music, 1965; MA, NYU, 1972, EdD, 1979. Piano tchr. Juilliard Inst. Musical Art, NY, NY, 1942-43; chmn. music dept. Casement's Coll., Ormond Beach, Fla., 1949-50; dir. music Essex County Girls Vocat. & Tech. HS, Newark, 1953-57; dir. music, organist State of N.J. Institution for Retarded Girls North Jersey Tng. Sch., Totowa, NJ, 1953-68; spl. edn. gifted coord. Jefferson Magnet Sch. Pub. Sch. Sys., Union City, NJ, 1956-95; dir. Upper Montclair Music Sch., Montclair, NJ, 1945—, Ole Bull Music Sch., Potter County, Pa., 1952-68. Adjudicator Lycoming Coll., Williamsport, Pa., 1948—; conductor Whippany Symphony Orch., 1951-52; curator, builder Ole Bull Mus., Carter Camp, Pa., 1968—; dir. youth chorus Jefferson Sch., Union City, 1956-95; dir. Hudson County Elem. Choral Festival, 1971—; artist-in-residence, Union City; guest lectr. Columbia U., N.Y.C., Yale U. Grad. Sch. Music, Hartford, Conn., NYU, Lycoming Coll., Williamsport, Pa., Mansfield U., Pa., Princeton U., NJ, U. Scranton, Pa., Jersey City State Coll. Author: 27 books; editor: various newsletters and mag.; author: (song) Evening Prayer, 1934, I Will Bow and Be Humble, 1954, Voice of Am., 1952; recording artist Educo Records, soloist WFMB radio sta., Daytona Beach, Fla., 1949—50, NBC, Hartford, Conn., WNJR, Union, N.J., 1952—68, WNBT-ABC, Wellsboro, Pa., 1997—2003, Norsk Rikskringkasting, Oslo, Radio and TV Francaise, Paris, recitals, France, Norway, Eng., Switzerland, S. Am., US. Choir dir. First Congl. Ch., 1940-43, Holy Trinity Luth. Ch., Nutley Luth. Ch., 1953-55; organist, choir dir. North Jersey Tng. Sch. Chapel, 1952-68; founder, dir. Ole Bull Music Festival, 1952—; dep. gov. and mem. rsch. bd. advisors Am. Biog. Inst., Raleigh; US State Dept amb. of goodwill to Norway by order of Pres. Dwight D. Eisenhower, 1953, Norwegian Goodwill amb. to US by order of King Haakon VII, 1953. Recipient Freedom medal-Eisenhower medal, 1953, Sterling Silver plaque King Olav V of Norway, 1966, NJEA award, 1970, Performing Arts Prestige award in Edn., 1976, Olympic Gold medal Norwegian Govt., 1992, Silver medal of Honor, 1991, Gold medal of Honor, 1992, Pa. Senate Legis. citation, 1992, Outstanding Tchr. of the Handicapped in the U.S. Nat. Rsch. Coun., 1970, Woman of Distinction honorable mention award Girl Scout Coun. of Greater Essex County, 1996, Artisan award Oakeside Bloomfield Cultural Ctr., 1996, 50 Women You Should Know award Internat. YWCA, 1996, inducted into Millenium Hall of Fame, Am. Biog. Inst., 1998; named Am. Biog. Inst. World Laureate, 1999, St. Olav medal King Harald V (Norway), 1999, Outstanding Woman in Arts award World History Project/Twp. of Montclair, 2000, key to the City Renovo award, Pa., 2000, 2002, Am. Medal of Honor award Pres. of U.S., 2001, Nobel Peace prize, 2002, Congl. Medal of Merit, 2003, World Laureate Am. Biog. Inst., 1999, Congl. Medal of Excellence, Am. Biog. Inst., 2003; Fulbright scholar U. Oslo (Norway) Grad. Sch., 1955; film made in her honor A Child is Waiting, 1963. Mem. Ole Bull Hist. Soc. (pres. 1972—), Phi Delta Kappa (pres. 1984-86, newsletter editor 1984-92), Kappa Delta Pi (pres. 1984—, newsletter editor 1984—, counselor NYU Beta Pi chpt. 1996), Pen & Brush Club, Internat. Percy Grainger Soc. (v.p.), NYU Alumnae Club Inc. (bd. dirs., rec. sec., newsletter editor, 1979—). Republican. Avocations: concert pianist, soprano, writer. Home: 172 Watchung Ave Montclair NJ 07043-1737 Home (Summer): 79 S Cherry Springs Rd Galeton PA 16922 Office: Robert Waters Sch. 2800 Summit Ave Union City NJ 07087-2329

BULL, MARTHA, artist, educator; d. Charles and Phyllis Smead; m. James Bull, July 28, 1973; 1 child, Caitlin. EdB in Art Edn., No. Ill. U., Dekalb, 1975, MA in Studio Art Drawing, 1986, MFA in Studio Art Drawing, 1990. Exhibitions include Harper Coll. Art Show (Hon. Mention, 1987), Elgin CC Art Show (2nd Pl., 1988), Norris Cultural Vicinity Art Shows, Elgin Bubotto Salon, Campbell House Art Gallery, St. Charles Congl. Ch. Art Show, one-woman shows include McHenry County Coll. Grantee, Greater St. Charles Edn. Found., 2000, 2001. Mem.: St. Charles Edn. Assn. (assoc.), Ill. Art Edn. Assn. (assoc.), Nat. Art Edn. Assn. (assoc.). Office: Haines Mid Sch 305 S 9th St Saint Charles IL 60174

BULL, VIVIAN ANN, college president; b. Ironwood, Mich., Dec. 11, 1934; d. Edwin Russell and Lydia (West) Johnson; m. Robert J. Bull, Jan. 31, 1959; children: R. Camper, W. Carlson. BA, Albion (Mich.) Coll., 1956, DEcons (hon.), 1999; postgrad., London Sch. Econs., 1957; PhD, NYU, 1974; DHL (hon.), Drew U., 2003. Economist Nat. Bank Detroit, 1955-59; with Bell Telephone Labs., Murray Hill, N.J., 1960-62; dept. econs. Drew U., Madison, N.J., 1960-92, assoc. dean, 1978-86; pres. Linfield Coll., McMinnville, Oreg., 1992—. Bd. dirs. Chem. Bank N.J., Morristown; trustee Africa U., Zimbabwe; treas. Joint Expedition to Caesareu Maritima Archaeology, 1971—. Author: Economic Study The West Bank: Is It Viable?, 1975. Trustee, assoc. Am. Schs. Oriental Rsch., 1982-90; trustee Colonial Symphony Soc., 1984-92, The Albright Inst. of Archaeol. Record; commr. Downtown Devel. Commn., Madison, 1986-92; mem. Univ. Sen. United Meth. Ch., 1989-96, 2000-04, gen. bd. higher edn., 1988-92; mem. planning bd. Coll. Bus. Adminstrn., Africa U., Zimbabwe, 1990-91; exec. com. Nat. Assn. Commns. on Salaries, United Meth. Ch., 1986-92. Fulbright scholar, 1956, Paul Harris fellow Rotary Internat., 1988; named Disting. Alumna Albion Coll., 1979; recipient Salute to Policy Makers award Exec. Women in N.J., 1986, John Woolman Peacemaking award George Fox Coll., 1994, Equal Opportunity award Urban League of Portland, 1995. Mem. Nat. Assn. Bank Women, N.W. Assn. Colls. and Univs. (exec. com. 2000—), Phi Beta Kappa. Avocations: archaeology, traveling, music. Address: Linfield Coll Office of the Pres 900 S Baker St Mcminnville OR 97128-6808 Office Phone: 503-883-2234. Business E-Mail: bull@linfield.edu.

BULLARD, JUDITH EVE, psychologist, systems engineer; b. Oneonta, N.Y., Oct. 5, 1945; d. Kurt and Herta (Deutsch) Leeds; divorced; children: Nicholas A., Elizabeth A. BA in Polit. Sci., Spanish U., Oreg., 1966, MA in Psychology, 1973; MBA, George Washington U., 1994. Cert. Project Mgr. 1993, lic. realtor N.J. Supr. residential program Skipworth Juvenile Home, Eugene, Oreg., 1966-68; research asst. Oreg. Research Inst., Eugene, 1968-69, 83-85; supr. residential program Ky. Correctional Facility, Lexington, 1969-70; research asst. U. Oreg., Eugene, 1970-73; asst. dir. Regional Mental Health Clinic, Frankfort, Ind., 1974-76; dir. mental health Lane County Mental Health, Eugene, 1977-80; cons. Managerial Communications, Eugene, 1980-83; sys. engr. AT&T Bell Labs., Holmdel, N.J., 1985-91, mgr. strategic/tech. planning, 1992-95, mgr. reliability, customer satisfaction, process engring., 1996—; dir Lucent/Bus. Comm. Sys., 1998—2000; tech. mgr. Sys. Test Quality Configuration Processed, Alameda, Calif., 1999—2001; ret., 2001; cons., 2002. Mem. strategic task force Globa Bus. Comm. Sys., chairperson customer based panels edn. forum, 1991-95, mgr. forward looking work/tech. coord. tech. ptnr. program, 1994—, chairperson 2-day software symposium, tech. chmn. strategy conf., 1995, chmn. Breakthru Tech. project, 1996, software design project, 1999-2000, coord. planned and executed Rsch. Tech. Exch. Symposium, mem. leadership team Cultural Change project; exec. prodr. 13TV Broadcast Solutions, 1996, Art Tchr., St. Agnes, 2002- Prodr. (video) The World is Our Work Place, 1991. Bd. dirs. Asbury Park 10K, Jersey Shore 1/2 Marathon, 1985—, Women's Resource and Survival Ctr., Keyport, N.J., 1986—; chairperson Area Affirmative Action Com., 1990—; pres. Affirmative Action Diversity Coun.; active Alliance Neighborrs 9/11 Support Group, 2002—. Mem. Women's Profl. Network (trustee Holmdel br. 1987—), N.J. Bd. Realtors, Nat. Bd. Realtors, Nat. Art Collectors Assn., Partnership in Edn. & Bus., Corrections in Mental Health, Human Factors Soc. Avocations: running, biking, swimming, tennis, cooking.

BULLARD, LARCENIA J. state legislator; b. Allendale, S.C., July 21, 1947; m. Edward Bullard; children: Dwight M., Edwina Lynn, Vincent Brooker. BA, Antioch U., 1973; MA, Nova U., 1991. Former tchr., adminstr.; mem. Fla. Ho. of Reps., 1992—. Active South Dade Minority Cultural Arts Task Force, South Dade Alliance for Black Neighborhood Devel., Miami-Dade Criminal Justice Coun.; 1st v.p. Cmty. Concerts. Mem. NAACP, Nat. Coun. Negro Women, Dem. Power, Continental Soc., Inc., Greater South Dade-Miami C. of C., South Dade Civitan Club (bd. dirs. 1991-92), Delta Sigma Theta. Democrat. Baptist. Office: Fla House of Reps 407 House Office Bldg 10700 Caribbean Blvd Miami FL 33189-1232

BULLARD, MARCIA, publishing executive; b. Springfield, Ill., Aug. 28, 1952; d. Clark Wesley and Eileen (Kloppenburg) B. AA, Springfield (Ill.) Coll., 1972; BS, So. Ill. U., 1974; MBA, George Washington U. Reporter Democrat and Chronicle newspaper, Rochester, N.Y., 1974-79, mag. editor, 1979-82; dep. mng. editor Life sect. USA Today, Washington, 1982-85; mng. editor USA WEEKEND mag., Washington, 1985-89, editor, 1989—, pres., CEO, 1996. Tutor 2 schs. D.C., 1984-89, Literacy Vols., Washington, 1987. Mem. AP Mng. Editors, Newspaper Assn. Am., Am. Soc. Newspaper Editors. Office: USA WEEKEND 7950 Jones Branch Dr Mc Lean VA 22107*

BULLARD, MARY ELLEN, retired religious organization administrator; b. Elkin, N.C., Jan. 12, 1926; d. Roy Brannoch and Mattie Reid (Doughton) H.; m. John Carson Bullard Sr., Apr. 27, 1957; children: John Carson Jr., Roy Harrell. BS, U. N.C., Greensboro, 1947; postgrad., Union Theol. Sem., N.Y.C., 1956; MA, Troy State U., Montgomery, Ala., 1979. Dir. women's and girls' work Gilvin Roth YMCA, Elkin, 1947-49; dir. Christian edn. 1st United Meth. Ch., Salisbury, N.C., 1949-51, Charlotte, N.C., 1951-55; dir. youth ministry United Meth. Ch., Western N.C. Conf., 1956-57; dir. ednl. ministries, div. continuing edn. Huntingdon Coll., 1979-88; dir. U.S. office Bibl. Resources Study Ctr., Inc., Jerusalem, 1988-92. Bd. dirs. Ch. Women United Ala., 1970-71; del. World Meth. Coun., 13th World Meth. Conf., Dublin, 1976; mem. 15th World Meth. Conf., Nairobi, Kenya, 1986, 16th World Meth. Conf., Singapore, 1991, exec. com., 1991—, 17th World Meth. Conf., Rio de Janeiro, World Evangelism Inst., 1991—; del. Gen. Conf. United Meth. Ch., St. Louis, 1988, Louisville, 1992; del. Southeastern Jurisdictional Conf., United Meth. Ch., Lake Junaluska, N.C., 1988, 92, 96; mem. gen. coun. fin. and adminstrn. United Meth. Ch., 1992-2000. Bd. dirs. LWV, Montgomery, 1976-70, Am. Cancer Soc., Montgomery, 1975-81, Ala. Dept. Youth Svcs., Mt. Meigs Campus Chapel, 1984-86; mem. Montgomery Symphony League, 1984—; mem. adv. bd. Resurrection Cath. Mission, 1993—; mem. Nat. Vision 2000 Long-Range Dream Team, United Meth. Ch., 1995; del. Southeastern Jurisdictional Conf., The United Meth. Ch., 1988, 92, 96; bd. trustees Ala. West Fla. Con. The United Meth. Ch., 1995-96. Recipient award of recognition Bd. Edn. We. N.C. Conf. The United Methodist Ch., 1956, Christian Higher Edn., Ala.-West Fla. Conf. United Meth. Ch., 1975, Conf. Coun. on Ministries, Ala. West Fla. Conf., 1987, Candler Sch. of Theology, Emory U., 1990, Alice Lee award Ala. West Fla. Conf. United Meth. Ch., 1994. Mem. Christian Educators Fellowship, Kappa Delta Pi. Home: 3359 Warrenton Rd Montgomery AL 36111-1736

BULLARD, SARAH ELIZABETH, [illegible] Putnam, Conn., July 7, 1973; d. Edward Hill and Andrea Frances Bullard; m. Dennis Joseph Thibeault, Aug. 23, 2003. BA summa cum laude, U. Conn., 1995, MA, 1999, PhD, 2001. Psychology intern The Village for Families and Children, Hartford, Conn., 1999—2000; per diem clinician The Inst. of Living, Hartford, 2000—01; neurpsychology postdoctoral fellow Hartford Hosp./Inst. Living, 2001—03; clin. neuropsychologist Easter Seals Greater Hartford Rehab., Windsor, Conn., 2003—. Cons. China Yantai (China) Spl. Children's Ctr., 1999. Author: (children's book) Luigi the Llama: A Story for Children with Attachment Disorders, 2000, (neuropsychological test) The Biber Cognitive Estimation Test, 2003. Chairperson Chaplain Town Bd. Assessment Appeals, 1997—; alt. mem. Chaplin (Conn.) Town Conservation Commn., 2001—. Outstanding Woman scholar Coll. Liberal Arts and Scis., U. Conn., 1995. Mem.: APA, Internat. Neuropsychol. Soc., Nat. Acad. Neuropsychology, Phi Beta Kappa. Avocations: kayaking, travel, horseback riding, farming. Office: Easter Seals Greater Hartford Rehab Ctr 100 Deerfield Rd Windsor CT 06095 Office Phone: 860-714-9500.

BULLARD, SHARON WELCH, librarian; b. San Diego, Nov. 4, 1943; d. Dale L. and Myrtle (Sampson) Welch; m. Donald H. Bullard, Aug. 1, 1969. BS in Edn., U. Ctrl. Ark., 1965; MA, U. Denver, 1967. Tchr. libr. Humphrey pub. schs., Ark., 1965-66, libr., 1969-70; media splst. Adams County Sch. Dist. 12, Denver, 1967-69; catalog libr. Ark. State U., Jonesboro, 1970-75; head documents cataloging Wash. State U., Pullman, 1979-83; head serials cataloging Davidson Libr. U. Calif., Santa Barbara, 1984-88; head ACCESS svcs. Davidson Libr., 1988-98; head adminstrv. svcs., personnel U. N.C., Greensboro, 1998—. Cons. Ctr. Robotic Sys. Microelectronics Rsch. Libr., Santa Barbara, 1986, retrospective conversion project Calif. State Libr., 1987, ombudsman's office U. Calif., Santa Barbara, 1988; distributor Amway, 1985-91. Canvasser Citizens for Goleta Valley, 1985-86; adv. bd. Total Interlibr. Exch., 1994-96. Mem.: NAFE, ALA (chmn. heads circulation U. Calif. 1997—98, bldgs. for colls. and univs. com. 1998—2000, publs. com. 1998—2001, chair publs. com. 2000, program com. 2001—, bldg. cons. list com. 2002—, subcom. on advancement and promotion 1987—91, 1995—96, chmn. subcom. advancement and promotion 1996—97), Libr. Adminstrn. and Mgmt. Assn. (circulation/access svcs. com., equipment com. 1993—97), Assn. Col. and Rsch. Librs. (intern membership com. 1993—94, extended campus libr. sect. guidelines com. 1995—96), So. Calif. Tech. Processes Group (membership com. 1987), Libr. Assn. U. Calif. Santa Barbara, Calif. Libr. Assn. (tech. svcs. chpt. so. Calif. sect.), N.C. Libr. Assn. (planning commn. annual conf. 1998—99), Notis Users Circulation Interest Group (presenter meeting 1992, moderator meeting 1993—95, CIRC SIG steering com. 1993—97, chair elect 1994—95, chair 1995—96, program com. 1996—97), Pi Lambda Theta (sec. Santa Barbara chpt. 1990—91, hospitality com. 1991—92, exec. bd.). Avocations: walking, camping, white-water rafting, swimming. E-mail: sharon_bullard@uncg.edu., swbullard@aol.com.

BULLARO, GRACE RUSSO, literature, film and foreign language educator, speaker, book reviewer; b. Salerno, Italy, July 11, 1949; arrived in U.S., 1958; d. Salvatore and Carmela (Paciello) Russo; m. Frank John Bullaro, Sept. 19, 1971; children: Christian, Adrian Alexander. BA magna cum laude, CCNY, 1971; MA, SUNY, Stony Brook, 1989, PhD in Comparative Lit., 1993. Grad. tchg. asst. SUNY, Stony Brook, 1988-92; adj. asst. prof. SUNY-Nassau C.C., Garden City, N.Y., 1990—, CUNY-Lehman Coll., Bronx, N.Y., 1991-2000, adj. assoc. prof., 2000—02, asst. prof., 2002—; with Lincoln Ctr., N.Y.C., 1998; collaborative educator; asst. prof. CUNY-Lehman Coll., Bronx, 2002—. Mem. libr. com. CUNY, 1998, mem. acad. senate, 1997—; mem. faculty exec. com. Lehman Coll., Bronx, NY, 1999—, English dept. libr. acquisitions liaison, 2000—; mem. Tchr. of Yr. selection com.; mem. profl. adv. bd. Am. Biograph. Inst., 2002—; fgn. langs. acquisitions cons. Syosset (N.Y.) Pub. Libr., 2002—; book reviewer in field. Contbr. chpts. to books and articles to profl. jours. Acad. senate CUNY, Lehman Coll., 1997-99, 2001—, CUNY, 1998—, mem. Faculty Exec. Com., 1999—; liaison English Dept. Libr. Acquistions, 2000—; cons. Pub. Libr. Fgn. Lang. Acquisitions, Syosset, N.Y., 2002—; chair English Dept. Honors Com., 2004—; faculty advisor English Honors Program, 2004—. Recipient Chancellor and Pres.'s award for Excellence in Tchg., SUNY-Stony Brook, 1992, Adj. Tchr. of Yr. award, CUNY-Lehman Coll., 2001. Mem. MLA, PCA/ACA, NEMLA, Nat. Coun. Tchrs. English, Assn. Italian-Am. Educators, Inst. Français, Soc. Profs. Français, Phi Beta Kappa (sec. 2004—). Avocations: fitness trainer, tennis, travel, swimming, horseback riding. Office: CUNY Lehman Coll English Dept Bedford Park Blvd W Bronx NY 10468 Office Phone: 718-960-8362. Personal E-mail: gracerbullaro@msn.com.

BULLERDICK, KIM H. petroleum executive; b. 1953; BA, Wittenberg U.; JD, U. Va. Gen. coun. Giant Industries, Inc., Scottsdale, Ariz., v.p., sec., subs. officer. Office: Giant Industries Inc 23733 N Scottsdale Rd Scottsdale AZ 85255-3466

BULLETT, VICKY, professional basketball player; b. Oct. 4, 1967; Grad., U. Md., 1989. Forward-center, Italy, 1990—93, 1993—97, WNBA - Charlotte (N.C.) Sting, 1997—99, Washington Mystics, 1999—. Named to, Italian League All-Star Teams, 1992, 1995, 1996, 1997, Goodwill Games Team, 1989, World Championship Qualifying Team & USA Select Team, 1986, All-ACC Tournament Team, 1989, Kodak All-Am. Team, 1989; recipient U.S. Olympic gold medal, 1988, Bronze medal, 1992. Avocations: softball, tennis, tap dancing, keyboards, reading. Office: Washington Mystics MCI Ctr 601 F St NW Washington DC 20004-1605

BULLINGTON, GAYLE ROGERS, writer, researcher; b. Watsonville, Calif., May 17, 1923; d. Manley Duane and Gladyce Thelma (Horton) Rogers; m. Keith Charles Brown, Nov. 26, 1944 (div. Feb.4, 1963); children: Kendall Keith, Kevin Doran; m. Jack William Bullington, Dec. 23, 1978. BA, UCLA, 1949; postgrad. studies, Northridge U., 1962; MA, Calif. Luth. U., 1974. Cert. tchr., Calif. Tchr. Southgate (Calif.) Jr. H.S., 1947-48, Virgil Jr. H.S., L.A., 1948-50, North Hollywood (Calif.) H.S., 1950-52, Van Nuys (Calif.) H.S., 1953-54, Thousand Oaks (Calif.) H.S., 1963-79. Author: The Second Kiss, 1972, NAKOA's Woman, 1975—81, Gladyce With a C, 2000, Dark Corners, 2002, My Name Was Mary, 2003. Mem. ACLU, Pub. Citizen, Common Cause, Nation Assocs. Home: 23119 19th Ave NE Arlington WA 98223-7631 E-mail: gayle.rogers@verizon.net.

BULLIS, JO LOUISE, social services administrator, educator; d. Robert E. Bullis (dec.) and Mary M. Bullis Hoyt. BS in Phys. Therapy, U. N.D., 1976, JD, 1983. Bar: N.D. 1983, Mich. 1989. Program dir. Women's Resource Ctr., Traverse City, Mich., 1992—. Adj. instr. Northwestern Mich. Coll., Traverse City, 1995—; mem. Governor's Domestic Violence Law Implementation Task Force, Lansing, Mich., 1995—96, Best Practices for Law Enforcement Tng. - Violence Against Women Tng. Inst., Lansing, 1998—99, Mich. State Planning Body - Civil Legal Services for the Poor, Lansing, 2001—, Domestic Violence Trial Manual Com. - Pros. Attorney's Assn. of Mich., Lansing, 2002—03; mem. instrs. com. Mich. Law Enforcement Acad., Lansing, 1999—; peer reviewer Mich. Domestic Violence Prevention & Treatment Bd., Lansing, Mich., 2001—; mem. adv. group Safe Haven Supervised Visitation and Safe Exch. Nat. Demonstration Project, Traverse City, 2003—. Treas., chair fin. com. Addiction Treatment Services, Inc., Traverse City, Mich., 1998—. Named Woman of the Yr., Traverse City Zonta Club, 1997, Sarah Hardy Humanitarian of the Yr., Traverse City Human Rights Commn., 2000; recipient Domestic Violence Summit III Govs. award, Mich. Domestic Violence Prevention & Treatment Bd., 1997. Mem.: Women Lawyers Assn., Antrim-Grand Traverse-Leelanau Bar Assn., Order of the Coif, Phi Delta Phi (life Internat. Grad. of the Yr. 1983). Avocations: gardening, reading, travel, music. Office: Women's Resource Ctr Ste 2 720 S Elmwood Traverse City MI 49684 Personal E-mail: bullis@chartermi.net E-mail: [illegible]

BULLITT-JONAS, MARGARET MORLEY, priest, writer; b. Cambridge, Mass., Oct. 24, 1951; d. John Marshall Bullitt and Sarah (Cowles) Doering; m. Robert Alan Jonas, Oct. 25, 1986; 1 child, Samuel; 1 stepchild, Christy. BA, Stanford U., 1974; MA, Harvard U., 1977, PhD, 1984; postgrad., Shalem Inst., 1988; MDiv, Episcopal Divinity Sch., 1988. Tchg. fellow Harvard U., Cambridge, 1977-82; curate Christ Ch., Andover, Mass., 1988-91; assoc. priest Emmanuel Ch., Boston, 1991-92; priest assoc. Grace Ch., Newton, Mass., 1992-96; assoc. rector All Saints Parish, Brookline, Mass., 1996—. Lectr. pastoral theology Episc. Div. Sch., Cambridge, 1991-92, 94—; leader spiritual retreats and workshops in various dioceses, 1986—; chaplain Episcopal Ch. House Bishops, 1998-2000. Author: Holy Hunger, 1998, Christ's Passion, Our Passions, 2003; contbr. articles to profl. jours. including Anglican Theol. Review, Human Devel., also others. Active Commn. on Ministry, 1994-98, Examining Chaplain's Com., 1990-98; bd. dirs. MECA, 1992-96. Mem. Spiritual Dirs. Internat. (religious witness for the Earth), The Earth, Episcopal Peace Fellowship. Home: 105 Garfield St Watertown MA 02472-4914 Office: All Saints Parish 1773 Beacon St Brookline MA 02445

BULLOCK, ALICE GRESHAM, university dean; BA, Howard U., 1972, JD, 1975. Bar: Ga., D.C., U.S. Supreme Ct. Trial atty. Office of Chief Counsel IRS, 1975-79; prof.-in-residence Aetna Life and Casualty Co., summer 1981; of counsel Hart Carroll & Chavers, 1983-86; asst. prof. Howard U. Sch. Law, Washington, 1979-83, assoc. prof., 1983-87, prof., 1987—, assoc. dean Acad. Affairs, prof., 1988-92, acting dean, prof., 1990, interim dean, prof., 1996-97, dean, prof., 1997—. Bd. dirs. The Calvert Group; mem. profl. responsibility hearing com., 1995—; nat. dep. dir., 1992-94. Contbr. articles to profl. jours. Trustee The Levine Sch. Music. Fellow Am. Bar Found.; mem. ABA (com. on tchg. taxation 1992—), Coun. on Legal Edn. Opportunity (bd. dirs. 1994—), Soc. Am. Law Tchrs., Am. Law Inst., Nat. Bar Assn. Office: Howard U Sch Law 2900 Van Ness St NW Washington DC 20008-1100

BULLOCK, ANNA MAE See TURNER, TINA

BULLOCK, KAREN, social sciences educator; b. Warrenton, N.C., Sept. 9, 1965; d. James O. and Annie Mae Bullock; m. Joseph Walter Johnson, June 12, 1994; 1 child, Ramona Orlandra Bullock-Johnson. B Social work, N.C. State U., 1990; MS, Columbia U., 1992; PhD, Boston U., 1999. LCSW. Rsch. assoc. New Eng. Rsch. Inst., Watertown, Mass., 1993—99; asst. prof. Salem State Coll., 1994—99, U. N.C., Wilmington, 1999—2002, dir. undergrad. programs, 2001—02; asst. prof. U. Conn., 2002—. Diversity adv. coun. New England Rsch. Inst., 1994—99; mem. exec. bd. Amigos Internat., Wilmington, 1999—2002; chair diversity adv. coun. Carolinas Ctr. Hospice and End of Life Care, Cary, 2001—02. Youth activities coord. YMCA, Wilmington, 1999—2001. Recipient Disting. Vol., Brunswick County, 2001. Mem.: Boston U. Ctr. Minority Rsch., Gerontol. Soc. Am., Am. Pub. Health Assn. Avocations: travel, cross country running. Office: U of Conn 1798 Asylum Ave West Hartford CT 06117

BULLOCK, MARY BROWN, academic administrator; m. George Bullock; children: Ashley, Graham. BA, Agnes Scott Coll., Atlanta, 1966; MA in Chinese history, Stanford U., 1968, PhD in Chinese history, 1973. Profl. assoc. Com. on Scholarly Comm. with People's Republic of China, 1973—77; dir. Johns Hopkins U. Sch. Advanced Internat. Studies, Balt., 1977—88, lectr., 1988—95; dir. Asia program Woodrow Wilson Internat. Ctr. Scholars, Washington, 1988—95; pres. Agnes Scott Coll., Decatur, Ga., 1995—. Trustee China Med. Bd. of N.Y.; dir. Nat. Com. on U.S.-China Rels.; mem. adv. coun. on U.S.-China cooperation in sci., policy, rsch. and edn. NSF; chair Nat. Assn. of Ind. Coll. and U., 2002—; vice chair Women's Coll. Coalition; treas. Atlanta Regional Consortium Higher Edn. Bd. dir. Sun Trust Bank, Atlanta, Genuine Parts Co. Recipient Elizabeth Luce Moore Visionary Leadership award, Dist. Svc. award, NAS; fellow, Woodrow Wilson Internat. Ctr. Scholars, Rockefeller Conf. Ctr., Bellagio, Italy; grantee, Ford Found., Henry Luce Found., Rockefeller Found., NSF. Mem.: Coun. on Fgn. Rels., Carter Ctr. Bd. of Councilors, Decatur Found. Office: Agnes Scott Coll 141 E College Ave Decatur GA 30030*

BULLOCK, MOLLY, retired elementary school educator; d. Wiley and Annie M. Jordan; m. George Bullock; children: Myra A. Bauman, Dawn M. BS in Edn., No. Ariz. U., 1955, postgrad., 1958, LaVerne U., 1962, Claremont Grad. Sch., 1963, Calif. State U. L.A., 1966. Tchr. Bur. Indian Affairs, Kaibeto, Ariz., 1955-56, Crystal, N.Mex., 1956-59, Covina (Calif.) Valley Unified Sch. Dist., 1961-95, supervising master tchr. trainees LaVerne U. and Calif. State U. - L.A., 1961-71, mem. curriculum devel. adv. bd., 1977-79; ret., 1995. Cons. Bauman Curry Co., PR; mem. voting com. Excellence in Edn. awards Lawry's Foods; attendee reading conf. Claremont (Calif.) Grad. Sch. Author: (poems) A Tree (Golden Poet, 1991), What is Love (Golden medal of honor), The Change of Seasons (Dimond Homer trophy, 1999, Poet of the Yr. medallion). Vol. visitor area convalescent hosps.; mentor to former students. Mini grantee, Hughes/Rotary Club/Foothill Ind. Bank, 1986—90. Mem.: NAFE, Covina Unified Edn. Assn., Internat. Platform Assn., Internat. Soc. Poets (hon.). Avocations: poetry, collecting jewelry, dolls, paintings.

BULLOCK, SANDRA, actress; b. Washington, July 26, 1964; d. John and Helga B. Grad., Washington-Lee H.S., Arlington, Va., 1982. Appearances include (TV movies) Bionic Showdown: The Six-Million Dollar Man and the Bionic Woman, 1989, (TV series) Working Girl, 1990, (feature films) Fire on the Amazon, 1991, Love Potion #9, 1992, The Vanishing, 1993, Demolition Man, 1993, The Thing Called Love, 1993, Wrestling Ernest Hemingway, 1993, Speed, 1994 (Best Female Performance, Most Desirable Female MTV Movie awards), While You Were Sleeping, 1995 (Favorite Actress in a Motion Picture award People Choice Awards 1996), The Net, 1995, Two if by Sea, 1996, A Time to Kill, 1996, In Love and War, 1996, Practical Magic, 1998, Gun Shy, 1999, Forces of Nature, 1999, Exactly 3:30, 1999, 28 Days, 2000, Famous, 2000, Divine Secrets of the Ya-Ya Sisterhood, 2002; actor, prodr. Kate and Leopold, 1996, Murder By Numbers, 2002, Two Weeks Notice, 2002; actor, writer Making Sandwiches, 1996, Speed II, 1997; actor, exec. prodr. Hope Floats, 1998; voice Prince of Egypt, 1998. Recipient Best Actress MTV's Big Picture, 1994-95, Best Actress US Mag., 1995, Favorite Actress in a Comedy/Drama Theatrical and Favorite Actress-Comedy Video awards BlockBuster Entertainment Awards, 1996, Favorite Actress People's Choice award, 1997, 1999, ShoWest Female Star of the Year, 2001, Am. Comedy Award for Funniest Female Performer in a Motion Picture, 2001.

BULLY-CUMMINGS, ELLA M. protective services official; b. Japan; d. Daniel Lee Bully; m. William Cummings. BA with hons. in Pub. Adminstrn., Madonna State U., 1993; JD cum laude, Mich. State U., 1998. Bar: Mich. 1998. From police officer to chief police Detroit (Mich.) Police Dept., 1977—2003, chief police, 2003—; assoc. Miller, Canfield, Paddockand Stone, PLC, 1999—2000, Foley & Lardner, 2000—02. Mem.: Mich. Assn. Chiefs Police, Nat. Orgn. Black Law Enforcement Execs., Internat. Assn. Chiefs Police, Wolverine Bar Assn., Nat. Bar Assn. Office: Detroit Police Dept 1300 Beaubien Detroit MI 48226*

BUMA, JUDITH BERGESON, music educator; b. Worcester, Mass., Dec. 28, 1940; d. Harold Randolph Bergeson and Beatrice Mildred Larson-Bergeson; m. Frederick Sydney Buma, Jr., Feb. 3, 1968; children: Joanna

Ellen, Kristin Elizabeth. MusB, New England Conservatory Music, 1963; MMus, U. Mass, Lowell, 1993. Supr. music Sutton (Mass.)/Douglas Schs., 1964—70; tchr. Shrewsbury (Mass.) Schs., 1978—82, North Brookfield (Mass.) Schs., 1983—84, Sturbridge (Mass.) Schs., 1988—90, 1997—99; choral dir. Performing Arts Schs. Worcester, 1997—2001; fine arts dept. head, choral dir., internat. baccalaureate music educator Gateway H.S., Kissimee, Fla., 2001—. Composer: Mass of Celebration, 1999 (Mass. Composer of Yr., 1999). Mem.: Sigma Alpha Iota. Avocations: painting, sewing, writing. Home: 8751 Buena Pl # 12-301 Windermere FL 34786 Office: Gateway High Sch 93 Panther Paws Trail Kissimmee FL 34744

BUMANN, DANIELA, movement therapist, massage therapist; arrived in U.S., 1989; d. Alois Bumann and Emmely Affolter. Cert. movement therapist, Guggenbuel Inst., Switzerland, 1988. Holistic health practitioner Mannhart Wellness, Switzerland, 1982; adminstrv. sec. and adsst. Paribas Bank, Switzerland; occupl. therapist, movement Ballard Rehab., 1990; massage therapist Sirchbach, Spa Hotel and Casino, 1994; transformational coach, reikei master, owner Vibrant Living, Redlands, Calif., 1993—. Program dir., spkr., mentor For You Network; presenter in field. Avocations: swimming, reading, nature, animals, travel. Office: Vibrant Living PO Box 214 Redlands CA 92373 Office Phone: 909-235-8393. E-mail: daniela_freespirit@yahoo.com.

BUMANN, SHARON ANN, sculptor; b. Syracuse, N.Y., June 28, 1953; d. G. Bruce and Erma Jean (Gibbs) Stallknecht; m. George Charles BuMann, Aug. 26, 1972; children: George Bruce, Amy Beth. AAS in Graphic Arts with honors, Onondaga C.C., Syracuse, N.Y., 1975; BFA in Sculpture magna cum laude, Syracuse U., 1984; postgrad., U. Hartford, 1990, Lyme Acad., 2001. Owner, operator BuMann Sculpture Studio, Central Square, N.Y., 1977—. Adj. prof. Onondaga C.C.; lectr., juror and artist-in-residence, award winning sculptor; bronze conservator. Creator, bronze monuments, lifesize butter sculptures, exhibitions include butter sculptures N.Y. State Fair, 1996—2002, State Fair of Tex., 1997—2002, exhibitions include, 2004, exhibitions include butter sculptures Tulsa State Fair, 1998—2004, Erie County Fair, 1997—2001, Kans. State Fair, 2000—04; sculptor (monument restoration svc.) BuMann Scuplutre Studio, 2003—04. Bd. dirs., expansion chmn. Fort Brewerton (N.Y.) Hist. Expansion, 1997—. Mem. Nat. Sculpture Soc., Internat. Sculpture Ctr., Onondaga C.C. Alumni Assn. (pres., 1992-94). Avocations: equestrian activities, boating. Office: BuMann Sculpture Studio 90 Kellar Rd Central Square NY 13036-2122

BUMBRY, GRACE, soprano; b. St. Louis, Jan. 4, 1937; d. Benjamin and Melzia (Walker) B. Student, Boston U., 1954-55, Northwestern U., 1955-56, also fgn. countries, Music Acad. West, 1956-59; studied with, Lotte Lehmann, 1956-59; HHD (hon.), St. Louis U.; hon. doctorates in humanities, Rust Coll., Holly Spring, Miss., U. St. Louis, U. Mo.; MusD (hon.), Rockhurst Coll. Operatic debut, Paris Opera, 1960; debut Basel Opera, 1960, Bayreuth Festival, 1961, Vienna State Opera, 1963, Royal Opera House, Covent Garden, 1963, Salzburg Festival, 1964, Met. Opera, 1965, La Scala, 1964, Les Troyens, Paris, 1990, Turandot, Wembley Arena, 1991; has appeared all major opera houses worldwide, S.Am., Japan, U.S.; command performances The White House; recs. for Deutsche Grammophon, Angel, London and RCA. Recipient John Hay Whitney award, Richard Wagner medal, 1963, Grammy award, 1979, Royal Opera House medal, 1988, Puccini award, 1990, Commandeur de l'Ordre des Arts et Lettres, France, 1996. Mem. Zeta Phi Beta, Sigma Alpha Iota. Office: J F Mastroianni Assocs 161 W 61st St New York NY 10023-7400

BUMP, ELIZABETH BERTHA, music educator; d. Earl Harald and Lillian May Bump. BA in Music, Rivier Coll., Nashua, NH, 1978. Band dir., choir dir. Ascension Sch., Melbourne, Fla., 2002—03. Nominee Disney Tchr. of Yr., 2004. Mem.: Nat. Fedn. Music Clubs, Music Educators Nat. Conf., Nat. Cath. Edn. Assn.

BUMPAS, DIANE DEWARE, commissioner; Commr. Tex. Hist. Commn., Austin, 1999—. Mem. Dallas Cultural Affairs Commn.; sustainer, pres., mem. exec. com. Jr. League of Dallas; pres. Dallas Coun. on World Affairs.

BUNCH, CHARLOTTE, advocate; b. Ashe County, N.C., Oct. 13, 1944; d. Pardue and Marjorie Bunch. BA in History magna cum laude, Duke U., 1966; postgrad., Inst. Policy Studies, Washington, 1967-68. Founder Ctr. Women's Global Leadership Rutgers U., New Brunswick, NJ, 1989—, dir., disting. prof. women's and gender studies. Spkr. in field. Creator, editor: Quest: A Feminist Quar., 1974, 1980. Office: Ctr Womens Global Leadership Douglas Coll Rutgers U 160 Ryders Ln New Brunswick NJ 08901-8555 E-mail: cbunch@igc.org.

BUNDY-DESOTO, TERESA MARI, language educator, vocalist; d. Jose Jesus Avila-Carrillo and Maria del Pilar Lozano Avila; m. Glendon B. Bundy, Oct. 15, 1972 (div. May 20, 1987); children: Pete Hernandez Bundy, Angelita Dianne Bundy, Crystal Lorraine Bundy-Schwabenland, Ivan Glen Bundy; m. John B. Soto, Mar. 31, 1996. AA magna cum laude, Fresno City Coll., 1976; BA summa cum laude, Calif. State U., Fresno, 1978; Spanish and bilingual tchg. credential, 1979. Master tchr., trainer Proteus Adult Edn., Visalia, Calif., 1967—73; tchr. trainer Fresno City-County Manpower Commn., Calif., 1973—76; tchr. Spanish, mentor tchr. Ctrl. Unified Sch. Dist., Fresno, 1979—86; dept. chairperson Madera Unified Sch. Dist., Calif., 1986—89; tchr. Spanish, English Hoover HS/Fresno Unified Sch. Dist., 1989—. Rschr., trainer Office of Edn., Washington, 1968—74; adult edn. tchr. Chavez Adult Edn. Ctr.; alt. chief examiner ofcl. GED testing ctr. Gen. Ednl. Devel. Testing Svc., 1999—; spkr. in field. Singer: recorded 2 CDs and mus. videos under stage name Luz De Luna. Profl. radio announcer Spanish Radio Stas., Fresno, 1978—96; TV model Spanish TV Univision, Fresno, 1980; judge Miss Laverkin, Utah, 1982. Recipient Miss El Futuro C.U., 1967, 1972. Mem.: Am. Coun. on Edn., Calif. Tchr. Assn. Democrat. Mem. Lds Ch. Home: 1149 E San Bruno Ave Fresno CA 93710 Office Phone: 559-451-4000. E-mail: luzdeluna1@comcast.net.

BUNE, KAREN LOUISE, criminal justice official; b. Washington, Mar. 6, 1954; d. Harry and Eleanor Mary (White) B. BA in Am. Studies cum laude, Am. U., 1976, MS in Adminstrn. of Justice with distinction, 1978. Case mgr. Arlington (Va.) Alcohol Safety Action Program, 1979-94; victim specialist Office of Commonwealth's Atty., Arlington, Va., 1994—; cons. victim issues Dept. Justice/Office for Victims, 2001—. Case mgr. regional rep. of case mgmt. com. of Dirs. Assn. Commn. on Va. Alcohol Safety Action Program, Richmond, 1980-81, 84-85, 88-89, mem. subcom. studying treatment issues, 1988-94; chair career guidance subcom. alumni adv. com. Sch. Pub. Affairs Am. U., Washington, 1991-94; participant IACP Summit on Victims of Crime, 1999, nat. forum on terrorism, NCJA, 2002; adj. prof. George Mason U., Fairfax, Va., Marymount U., Arlington, Va. Recipient spl. achievement award Dept. Navy, 1973, merit award Arlington County, 1986, 97, Woman of the Yr. Am. Biog. Inst., 1990, Carl T. Earles meml. cmty. svc. award No. Va. Crime Prevention Assn., 1999, 2001, cert. of recognition for svc. to crime victims 3d Ann. Neighborhood Day, 1999, cert. of appreciation U.S. Dept. Justice, 2000; inducted into Hall of Fame for outstanding achievement in case mgmt. Mem.: AAUW (nat. and Arlington, Va. chpt.), APHA, NAFE, ASPA (pres. No. Va. chpt. 2003—), Internat. Assn. Forensic Mental Health Svcs., Am. Acad. Experts in Traumatic Stress, Assn. Traumatic Stress Specialists, Am. Sociol. Assn., Am. Pub. Human Svcs. Assn., Am. Profl. Soc. on Abuse of Children, Nat. Ctr. Women in Policing, Am. Probation and Parole Assn., Soc. for Study of Social Problems, Va. Assn. Female Execs., No. Va. Fraternal Order Police, No. Va. Crime Prevention Assn., Soc. Profl. Journalists, Va. Crime Prevention Assn., Internat. Narcotic Enforcement Officers Assn., Va. Sheriffs Inst., Am. Soc. Criminology, So. Criminal Justice Assn., Acad. Criminal Justice Scis., Am. Police Hall of Fame (cert. of appreciation 1985), Nat. Assn. Women Law Enforcement Execs., Nat. Ctr. Victims of Crime, Nat. Orgn. Victim Assistance, Nat. Criminal Justice Assn., Nat. Assn. Chiefs Police (award of merit 1986), Internat. Assn. Chiefs of Police (nat. adv. bd. on police-based victim response 2000—), Nat. Air Disaster Alliance Found., Washington Ind. Writers, World Affairs Coun., Am. U. Alumni Assn. (immediate past pres. sch. pub. affairs chpt. 1994—96), Nat. Press Club, Phi Delta Gamma (1st v.p. 1981—82), Phi Alpha Alpha, Phi Kappa Phi. Avocations: concerts, dance, travel, theatre, writing. Home: 926 16th St S Arlington VA 22202-2606

BUNGUM, CHERYL NANCY, music educator, director; b. Providence, May 9, 1963; d. Richard Leonard and Jean Wentworth Bratt; m. Brett Charles Bungum, Aug. 16, 1986; children: Samuel, Joshua. BA, Gustavus Adolphus Coll., St. Peter, Minn., 1981—85; EdM, St. Mary's U., Winona, Minn., 2000—02. Cert. tchg. K-12 Minn., 1985. Vocal music tchr. grades 5-12 Paynesville Area Schools, Paynesville, Minn., 1986—. Ch. choir dir. Paynesville Luth. Ch., Paynesville, Minn., 1994—; sect. leader Minn. All State Women's Choir, St. Peter, Minn., 2001. Author: (co-project planner for M) Fostering and Improving School Harmony, 2001—02. Planning com. mem. for new auditorium, Paynesville, Minn., 2000—01; dir. cmty. musical for Foodshelf, Paynesville, Minn., 1990—91. Recipient Tchr. of the Yr., Minn. Edn. Paynesville Area, 1996, Tchr. of Excellence, Minn. Edn., 1996. Mem.: Am. Choral Director's Assn., Music Educators Nat. Conf., Minn. Music Educators Assn. Lutheran. Achievements include 7th and 8th grade performing at Minn. Music Educators Assn. State Convention 1991. High sch. choir performing at Minn. Am. Choral Directors Assoc. State Convention 1991 and MMEA 1994. Avocations: singing, golf, reading, scrapbooks, camping. Home: 418 W Mill St Paynesville MN 56362 Office: Paynesville Area High Sch 795 Hwy 23 W Paynesville MN 56362 E-mail: cbungum@paynesville.k12.mn.us.

BUNKER, BERYL H. retired insurance company executive, volunteer; b. Chelsea, Mass., Aug. 18, 1919; d. Albert Crocker and Eva Agnes (Norris) Hardacker; m. John Wadsworth Bunker, Oct. 31, 1942. Student, Simmons Coll., 1936-38, Boston Coll. Law, 1948-49; grad., Bentley Sch. Acctg., Boston, 1958; BBA with highest honors, Northeastern U., 1962, MBA, 1967; D of Humane Svc. (hon.), Simmons Coll., 2001. CFA. Legal rsch. clerk Frank Shepard Co., N.Y.C., 1938-43; cost acct. Johns Manville Corp., Pittsburg, Calif., 1943-46; studio mgr. Wheelan Studios, Boston, 1946; clerical supr. Columbian Purchasing Group, Boston, 1946-48; office mgr. Wellesley (Mass.) Coll., 1948-51; statistician Eastman Kodak Co., Rochester, N.Y., 1951-53; investment officer John Hancock Mut. Life, Boston, 1953-74; sr. v.p. John Hancock Advisers, Boston, 1974-84. Nat. bd. dirs. YWCA of the U.S.A., 1988-94, hon. bd. dirs., 1998—, mem. World Svc. Coun., 1992 ; pres. bd. dirs. Boston YWCA, 1985-87, active 1977-96; chair bd. Vis. Nurses Assn. Cape Cod Found., South Dennis, Mass., 1995; bd. dirs. Old South Meeting House Mus., Boston, 1989-92; trustee Simmons Coll., 1994-2000, chair centennial com. 1999-2000, corporator, 2000—; mem. women's coun. Pine St. Inn, 1992—; bd. visitors Women's Edn. and Ind. Union, 2000—; adv. com. Boston Women's Fund, 2001—; mem. adv. com. On The Rise, 1997—; mem. Ct. for Women in Politics and Public Policy, Assocs. of the Boston Pub. Libr. Bd., The Coll. Club of Boston, 1998—, Cambridge YWCA, Neighborhood Assn. of the Back Bay; honoree Pine St. Inn Women's Coun., 2000. Recipient Philanthropy award Women in Devel., 1990, Disting. Alumni award Bentley Coll., 1994; named Woman of Achievement, Cambridge YWCA, 1991, Lifetime Service to Women award, On The Rise, 1998, Lifetime Achievement award, College Club, 1998, Outstanding Alumna Northeastern U., 2000. Mem. AARP, LWV, NOW, AAUW, Assn. Investment Mgmt. Rsch., Mass. Action for Women, Mass. Women Polit. Caucus, Boston Security Analysts Soc. (treas. 1973-76), Simmons Coll. Alumnae Assn. (pres. 1989-91, Alumnae Svc. award 1984, Planned Giving award 1993), Older Women's League, Harwich Hist. Soc., Project Vote Smart, Women's Edn1. and Indsl. Union, Friday Forum, Eire Soc., Wellesley Ctrs. for Women. Avocations: fundraising, theater, reading. Home: 790 Boylston St Apt 22F Boston MA 02199-7921 E-mail: berylb@mailstation.com.

BUNN, BARBARA JEAN, state legislator; m. William Bunn; 2 children. BS, Kans. State U. Mem. Ga. Ho. of Reps., 1992—; mem. def. and vet affairs com., indsl. rels. com., reapportionment com.; ret. educator. Republican. Presbyterian. Home: 2635 Stanton Rd SE Conyers GA 30094-2535 Office: Ga House of Reps 411 Legis Office Bldg Atlanta GA 30334

BUNT, KATHLEEN ANN, human resources specialist; b. Caldwell, Idaho, Aug. 12, 1965; d. Joseph Laverne and Judith Ann Bunt. BBA, Austin Peay State U., Clarksville, TN, 1988. Student asst. Austin Peay State U., Clarksville, Tenn., 1983-88; asst. mgr. Walgreens Co., Nashville, 1988-89; job specialist PENCIL Found., Nashville, 1989—. Author (program curriculum) Resume Writing, 1992. Advisor Jobs for Tenn. Grads. Tenn. Career Assn., Nashville, 1989—. Mem.: NAFE. Avocations: motor sports, com puters, music.

BUNTEN, BRENDA ARLENE, geriatrics nurse; b. Paris, Ill., May 7, 1947; d. Arthur Ray Sr. and Maxine L. (Bacon) B. A in Arts and Scis., Lakeland Coll., Mattoon, Ill., 1968; ADN, Kapiolani C.C., Honolulu, 1992. Charge nurse Meml. Med. Ctr., Springfield, Ill., 1968-76, Mattoon Health Care Ctr., 1977-79; agy. nurse Kahu Malama, Inc., Honolulu, 1983; charge nurse, staff devel. coord., infection control officer Hale Nani Health Ctr., Honolulu, 1979-93, also nursing staff scheduler, supr., 1979-93; unit mgr. Randal Mill Manor, Arlington, Tex., 1994—; supr. Heritage Oaks, Arlington, Tex., 1994—; dir. nursing Patriot Heights Health Care Ctr., 1998—; asst. dir. nursing Covenant Care Ctr., San Antonio, 1998—; staff nurse Warm Springs Rehab. Hosp., 1999—, Univ. Health Systems, San Antonio, 2002—. Fundraiser Challenger Run Hawaii, Honolulu, 1986—; co-owner, cons. retail sales Sunset Enterprises, Honolulu, 1982—. Named Am. Biog. Inst. Woman of the Year, 1997, dep. gov., 1997. Mem. USS Lancelot, Citizens Police Acad. Alumni Assn., Citizens Fire Acad. Alumni Assn. Avocations: marathon running, biking, baseball, football, circuit training. Home: PO Box 680743 San Antonio TX 78268-0743

BUNTING, ANNE EVELYN (EVE BUNTING), author; b. Maghera, Ireland, Dec. 19, 1928; came to U.S., 1958, naturalized, 1969; d. Sloan Edmund and Mary (Canning) Bolton; m. Edward Davison Bunting, Mar. 26, 1951; children— Christine Ann, Sloan Edward, Glenn Davison. Student, Meth. Coll., Belfast, Ireland, 1935-45, Queen's U., 1945-47. Lectr. UCLA, 1978-79, Chautauqua Writer's Conf.; bd. dirs. The Writer Mag., Soc. Book Writers and Illustrators. Author: over 100 children's books, including One More Flight, 1976 (Golden Kite award, Outstanding Sci. Book award), Ghost of Summer, 1977 (Jr. Lit. Guild selection), The Big Cheese, 1977, Winter's Coming, 1977, (with Glenn Bunting) Skateboards, How to Make Them, How to Ride Them, 1977, If I Asked You Would You Stay? (ALA best book award 1985), The Man Who Could Call Down Owls, 1985, Sixth Grade Sleepover, 1986, Ghost's Hour, Spook's Hour, 1987 (Booklist Best Book of Yr., Sch. Library Jour. best book award), The Wednesday Surprise, 1989 (ALA notable, Sch. Libr. Jour. best book award), Smoky Knight, 1990, The Wall, 1990, Someone is Hiding on Alcatraz Island, 1990, A Sudden Silence, 1990, (novel) The Two Giants, 1972. Recipient Edgar Allen Poe award, Mystery Writers of Am., Literacy award, PEN, Mark Twain award, State of Mo., Kerlan award, U. Minn., Regina medal, Cath. Libr. Am., Golden Kite award, Simon Weisenthal and Holocaust Mus. award, Commonwealth Club Calif. award, 25 state awards voted by children of each state. Mem. Author's Guild, Soc. Children's Book Writers (bd. dirs.), So. Calif. Council on Writing for Children and Young People. Democrat. Home: 1512 Rose Villa St Pasadena CA 91106-3525

BUNTING, CAROLYN ANNE, writer; b. Waltham, Mass., Sept. 17, 1949; d. Lawrence Earl and Josephine Ann (MacPherson) Rogers; m. Richard Dennis Bunting, Sept. 27, 1975; children: Dennis Richard, Christine Marie. Grad. high sch., Waltham, Mass. Author: (anthology books) Poem, 1986, 89, 90, 92, Poetic Song, 1989. Roman Catholic. Avocation: poetry. Home: 49 Nelson St # 3 Quincy MA 02169-4806

BUNZA, LINDA HATHAWAY, editor, writer, composer, institution director; b. Hartford, Conn., Feb. 23, 1946; d. Richard Collins and Alma C. Forest Hathaway, John Hennion Fisher and Eleanor Williston Chase; m. Geoffrey J. Bunza; children: Stephen, Matthew. BA, Bates Coll., 1968; MA, The Hartford Sem. Found., 1971; PhD, Syracuse U., 1974. Editl. asst. The Harvard Ednl. Rev., Cambridge, Mass., 1974—76; mng. editor The Andover Rev., Andover, Mass., 1976—79; dir. Columbia Rsch. Inst. Arts and Humanities, Portland, Oreg., 1998—2002. Editor Renaissance Mag., Hartford, 1963—64; editl. asst. Symposium Mag., Syracuse, NY, 1973—74; editor Soc. Arts, Religion, and Contemporary Culture, N.Y., NY, 1974—78; lectr. in field. Composer: (Classical Music Composition) There is Something Still Floating, 1999, Report From A Spiral, 1998, Snow Mountain, 2000, RiverMusic, 1995, Mythology of Clouds, 1993, Sphere, 1992, Cascadia, 1989, Widmanstatten Lines, 1987, View from a Mobius Strip, 1986, Sounds from the Olympic Peninsula, 1998, Electric Night, 1984, Odalisque, 1982, Awakening Night, 1981; editor: (Book) Adventures and Misadventures of Dr. Sonjee by Dr. Prasanna Pati, Snehalata Press, 2001, (Novel) Against Parched Winds by Kanta Luthra, (Book) Art of Literary Criticism, 2000; author: Theories of Modern Art-I, 1972, Theories of Modern Art-II, 1973, Theories of Modern Art-III, 1973; author: (catalog) Blue Note: The Art of Bruce Warner, 2000, Air, 2001, Where Art Reveals Itself in Symbols, Words are Hard to Find, 2001; mem. editl. bd. Anima Mag ., 1973—95. Bd. dirs. Fear No Music 20th Century Ensemble, 2000—02, Third Angle New Music Ensemble, Portland, 2000—03, Contemporary Art Coun., Portland Art Mus., 2001—03, Portland Baroque Orch., 2000—03; arts and culture com. City Club of Portland, 2000—03, arch. com., 1999—2002. Recipient Pres.'s award, Beaverton Arts Commn., 2000. Mem.: Portland Inst. Contemporary Art, European and Am. Art Coun., Portland Art Mus., Northwest Bookfest (program com.), Ancient Egypt Studies Assn., The Coll. Music Soc., Soc. Composers Internat., Friends William Stafford Assn. (life). Office: Columbia Rsch Inst Arts and Humanities PO Box 25316 Portland OR 97298 Personal E-mail: bunza@teleport.com. Business E-Mail: columbiaarts@aol.com.

BUONO, BARBARA, state legislator; b. July 28, 1953; JD, Rutgers Univ. Dem. Minority Parliamentarian assembly appropiatioans com., N.J., 1994—. Councilwoman Metuchen, 1993-94, police comm., 1993-94., co-chair McGreevey for Gov. Office: 1967 State Route 27 Ste 20 Edison NJ 08817-3262

BUPATHI, KAVITA K. pediatrician; b. Hyderabad, India, June 2, 1966; d. Venkateshwarlu and Saraswathi Pullakhandam; m. Kishor Bupathi, Aug. 15, 1992; children: Karthik, Sneha. MB, BChir, Gandhi Med. Coll., India, 1991. Diplomate Am. Bd. Pediat. Resident St. Marys Hosp., Waterbury, Conn., 1995—96, Jersey City Med. Ctr., 1996—98; pediatrician Jersey Pediat. Assocs., Woodbridge, NJ. Office: Jersey Pediat Assocs 900 Woodbridge Ctr Dr Woodbridge NJ 07095

BURATTI, BONNIE J. aerospace scientist; b. Bethlehem, Pa., Mar. 24, 1953; d. Ralph J. and Hildegard M. (Singles) B.; children: Nathan, Reuben, Aaron. MS, MIT, 1976, Cornell U., 1980, PhD, 1983. Summer intern Maria Mitchell Observatory, Nantucket, Mass., 1973; assoc. scientist Am. Sci. and Engring., Cambridge, Mass., 1974-76; rsch. asst. MIT, Cambridge, 1977-83; rsch. and teaching asst. Cornell U., Ithaca, N.Y., 1977-83; post-doctoral Jet Propulsion Lab. Calif. Inst. Tech., Pasadena, 1983-85, rsch. scientist Jet Propulsion Lab., 1985—. Cons. NASA, Washington, 1989—. Contbr. articles to profl. jours. Mem. MIT Ednl. Coun., Internat. Astro. Union, Am. Astro. Soc., Am. Women in Sci., Am. Geophys. Union. Office: Calif Inst Tech Jet Propulsion Lab 4800 Oak Grove Dr # 501 Pasadena CA 91109-8001

BURBANK, CLAUDIA, poet; b. New Haven, Conn., Feb. 24, 1954; d. Robinson Derry and Jeannette Bisson Burbank; m. Dennis Keith Hoover, Jan. 8, 1982. BA, Vassar Coll., 1975. Ops. mgr. Chem. Bank, N.Y.C., 1975—77; dist. mgr. AT&T, Bedminster, NJ, 1977—98; poet Bernardsville, NJ, 1999—. Contbr. poetry to lit. jours. Named Featured poet, Portland Rev. Web site, Featured Poet, Bellowing Ark; recipient Fellowship for Poetry, N.J. State Coun. on the Arts, 2003, Pushcart Prize nomination, Pushcart Press, 2004. Mem.: Poetry Soc. of Am., U.S. 1 Worksheets/Princeton Poets Coop., Poet's House. Avocations: opera, horticulture, cross-country skiing, foreign and silent film, local history. Home: 34 Prospect St Bernardsville NJ 07924-2520

BURBANK, JANE RICHARDSON, language educator; b. Hartford, Conn., June 11, 1946; d. John and Helen Lee (West) B.; m. Frederick Cooper, Sept. 3, 1985. BA, Reed Coll., 1967; MLS, Simmons Coll., 1969; MA, Harvard U., 1971, PhD, 1981. Asst. prof. Harvard U., Cambridge, Mass., 1981-85, U. Calif., Santa Barbara, 1985-86, assoc. prof., 1986-87, U. Mich., Ann Arbor, 1987-95, prof., 1995—2002, NYU, 2002—. Reviewer Kritika, 1983, Russian Rev., 1984, 98, Am. Hist. Rev., 1988, 91, 96, Jour. Modern History, 1989, 92, 94, Slavic Rev., 1990, Harvard Ukrainian Studies, 1991; presenter in field; dir. ctr. Russian E. European studies U. Mich., 1992-95, 98. Author: Intelligentsia and Revolution: Russian Views of Bolshevism, 1917-1922, 1986; editor: Perestroika and Soviet Culture, 1989, Imperial Russia, New Histories for the Empire, 1998; editor Kritika, 1978-80; mem. editl. bd. Ind.-Mich. Series in Russian and East European Studies, Kritika, 1990—; contbr. articles to profl. jours. Fulbright-Hayes Rsch. award, 1991, Krupp Found. fellow, Ctr. for European Studies, Harvard U., 1977-78, Whiting fellow, 1980-81, Am. Coun. Learned Socs. fellow, 1983-84, Hoover Inst. Postdoctoral fellow, 1990-91; grantee NEH, 1984, 97, Harvard U., 1982-84, Internat. Rsch. and Exchs. Bd., Acad. Exch. with the USSR, 1987-88, 91, U. Mich., 1990, 91, 93, 94, 97; fellow Ctr. for Advanced Study in the Behavioral Scis., 2002-03. Mem. Am. Hist. Assn., Am. Assn. for the Advancement of Slavic Studies, Social Sci. Rsch. Coun. (joint com. on Soviet studies 1988-93), Nat. Coun. for Eurasia and East European Rsch., Phi Beta Kappa. Office: NYU 53 Washington Sq South New York NY 10012 E-mail: jane.burbank@nyu.edu.

BURBANK, LYNDA A. painter; b. Burbank, Calif., Apr. 18, 1943; d. Norman Alfred and Glendora McComb Mactaggart. BA in Psychology, U. So. Calif. Prodn.designer (films) Born In East L.A., Quiet Cool, Sid And Nancy, The Wrestling Movie, Repo Man, The Slayer, Happy Birthday, Roadside Prophets, Highway To Hell, Body Rock, The Lady In Red, The Hitcher, Flicks, Losin' It, Walker, (TV Cable) True Tales, Love Kills, My Life As A Man, The Weathergirls, set decorator (TV series) Less Than Perfect, According To Jim, Geena Davis Show, Shasta Mcnasty, Mad About You, Ellen, John Ridley Pilot, Less Than Perfect Pilot, Bette Midler Pilot, Wish You Were Here Pilot, Over The Top Pilot, (TV films) The Taxman, Ride The Wind, When Love Kills, A Murderous Affair: The Carolyn Warmus Story, Running Mates, Alison Gertz Story, Keep The Change, Keeper Of The City, Call Me Anna (The Patty Duke Story), Rainbow Drive, Billy Crystal's Midnight Train To Moscow, A Summer To Remember, Doing time: Women In Prison. Home: 3205 Weldon Ave Los Angeles CA 90065

BURBIDGE, E. MARGARET, astronomer, educator; b. Davenport, Eng. d. Stanley John and Marjorie (Stott) Peachey; m. Geoffrey Burbidge, Apr. 2, 1948; 1 child, Sarah. BS, PhD, U. London; Sc.D. hon., Smith Coll., 1963, U. Sussex, 1970, U. Bristol, 1972, U. Leicester, 1972, City U., 1973, U.

Mich., 1978, U. Mass., 1978, Williams Coll., 1979, SUNY, Stony Brook, 1985, Rensselaer Poly. Inst., 1986, U. Notre Dame, 1986, U. Chgo., 1991. Mem. staff U. London Obs., 1948-51; rsch. fellow Yerkes Obs. U. Chgo., 1951-53, Shirley Farr fellow Yerkes obs., 1957-59, assoc. prof. Yerkes Obs., 1959-62; rsch. fellow Calif. Inst. Tech., Pasadena, 1955-57; mem. Enrico Fermi Inst. for Nuclear Studies, 1957-62; prof. astronomy dept. physics U. Calif. San Diego, 1964—90; [illegible] Castle), Hailsham, Eng., 1971-73; univ. prof. U. Calif., San Diego, 1984-91, prof. emeritus, 1991—, rsch. prof. dept. physics, 1990—. Lindsay Meml. lectr. Goddard Space Flight Ctr., NASA; Abby Rockefeller Mauze prof. MIT, 1968; David Elder lectr. U. Strathclyde, 1972; V. Gildersleeve lectr. Barnard Coll., 1974; Jansky lectr. Nat. Radio Astronomy Observatory, 1977; Brode lectr. Whitman Coll., 1986; Hitchcock lectr. U. Calif., Berkeley, 2001. Author (with G. Burbidge): Quasi-Stellar Objects, 1967; editor: Observatory mag., 1948—51; mem. editl. bd.: Astronomy and Astrophysics, 1969—85. Co-recipient Warner prize in Astronomy, 1959; recipient Bruce Gold medal, Astronomy Soc. Pacific, 1982, U.S. Nat. medal of Sci., 1984, Sesquicentennial medal, Mt. Holyoke Coll., 1987, Einstein medal, World Cultural Coun., 1988; fellow hon. fellow, Univ. Coll., London, Girton Coll., Lucy Cavendish Coll., Cambridge. Fellow: Royal Astron. Soc., Am. Acad. Arts and Scis., Nat. Acad. Scis. (chmn. sect.12 astronomy 1986), Royal Soc.; mem.: Internat. Astron. Union (pres. commn. 28 1970—73), Am. Astron. Soc. (v.p. 1972—74, pres. 1976—78, Henry Norris Russell lectr. 1984), Grad. Women Sci. (hon.). Office: U Calif-San Diego Ctr Astrophysics Space Scis Mail Code # 0424 La Jolla CA 92093 E-mail: mburbidge@ucsd.edu.

BURCH, CLAIRE RITA, writer; b. N.Y.C., Feb. 19, 1925; d. Albert I. and Dorothy (Denhoff) Cohen; m. Bradley A. Burch, Apr. 24, 1944 (dec. 1967); children: Laurie, Thomas (dec.), Emily, Elizabeth. BA, Washington Square Coll., N.Y.C., 1947. Editor, writer, N.Y.C., 1947-50; freelance writer, 1950-68; adj. prof. Union of Experimenting Colls., Antioch, N.Y., 1970-73; editor, freelance writer various nat. mags., N.Y.C., 1974-78; contbg. editor No. Calif. Psychiat. Network News, Berkeley, 1978-83; exec. dir. Art and Edn. Media Inc., Berkeley; pub. Regent Press, Oakland, Calif. Distbr. Facets Multimedia, Chgo., Tapeworm, Calif., Vast Vider, Astoria, N.Y.; conducted numerous workshops in field. Author: Stranger in the Family, 1972, You Be the Mother Follies, 1985, Goodbye My Coney Island Baby, 1988, Solid Gold Illusion, 1988, Shredded Millions, 1988, Homeless in the Nineties, 1990, Stranger on the Planet: The Small Book of Laurie, 1994; filmmaker (documentaries) James Baldwin: Patience and Shuffle the Cards, Entering Oakland (People's Choice award), Alfonia (People's Choice award), Thumbed a Ride to Heaven, Baby Don't Cry, Oracle Rising, People's Park Then and Now, Street Survivors, The Telegraph Ave., Street Calendar Live, Remembering the Summer of Love, Ghost of the S.F. Oracle Meets Tim Leary, How Timothy Leary Changed My Life; author (folk opera) Its' a Blues to Be Called Crazy When Crazy's All There Is; assoc. prodr. (film) Tim Leary's Dead, 1997. Recipient Carnegie award, 1981; grantee City of Berkeley, 1989-99, Calif. Arts Coun., 1991, 92, 93, Seva Found., 1996, San Francisco Found., 1999, Alameda Arts Coun., 1997, Puffin Found., 1999. Office: Art and Edn Media Inc 2747 Regent St Berkeley CA 94705-1212 Address: Regent press 60208 Adeline St Ste A Oakland CA 94608-1446 E-mail: info@claireburch.com.

BURCH, MARY SEELYE QUINN, law librarian, consultant; b. Worcester, Mass., Oct. 16, 1925; d. James Henry and Mary Seelye (O'Donnell) Quinn; m. Walter Douglas Burch, Aug. 18, 1972; children: Cathi, Andrew, David, John, Joan. BS, Suny, 1976; MLS, Pratt Inst., 1979. Law libr. N.Y. Supreme Ct., Troy, 1969-82; chief law libr. Office Ct. Adminstrn., Albany, N.Y., 1982-86; libr. N.Y. State Libr., 1986-89, ret., 1989; owner Mary S. Burch Law Libr. Svc., 1983—2003. Instr. legal rsch. SUNY, 1981; selected to meet with deans of law schs. in China for improvement of legal reference materials in China. Mem. N.Y. State Bar Assn. (lectr. 1980), Ulster County Bar Assn. (cons. 1980), Am. Assn. Law Librs., Assn. Law Librs. Upstate N.Y. (pres. 1971, v.p. 1981). Roman Catholic. Avocations: pilot, swimming, sewing. Home: 312 Diamond Rock Cir Troy NY 12182

BURCHAM, DARLENE, state agency administrator; 2 children. B in Psychology, Coll. William and Mary; M in Social Adminstrn., Va. Commonwealth U.; cert., Harvard U. Asst. county adminstr./acting county adminstr. James City County; dir. social svcs. City of Hampton, Va.; dir. human svcs. City of Norfolk, Va., 1987—89, asst. city mgr., 1989—2000, dep. city mgr., 1995—2000; city mgr. City of Roanoke, Va., 2000—. Pres. Va. Coun. on Social Welfare. Named Hampton Roads' Outstanding Profl. Women of Yr.; recipient Meritorious Svc. award, Va. Dept. Social Svcs., Woman of Distinction award, YWCA, Julian F. Hirst award for disting. svc., Hampton Roads chpt. ASPA. Office: City of Roanoke Rm 364 215 Church Ave Roanoke VA 24011

BURCHARD, RACHAEL C. literary critic, poet, playwright; b. Hendersonville, N.C., Aug. 27, 1921; d. Henry Homer and Olive (Gowan) Ballenger; m. Waldo W. Burchard, May 24, 1945 (dec. Dec. 1985); children: Gina Michel, Petrea Celeste, Margot Theresa, Stuart Gregory. BA, Linfield Coll., 1945; MA in English, No. Ill. U., 1966. Cert. secondary tchr., Calif. Tchr. English and history San Diego H.S./Jr. Coll., 1945-46; tchr. English and social studies Vallejo (Calif.) Jr. H.S., 1947-48; demonstration tchr. U. Calif., Berkeley, 1948; English tchr. El Cerrito (Calif.) H.S., 1948-50; tchr. English, drama Acalanes H.S., Lafayette, Calif., 1951-53; demonstration tchr. No. Ill. Univ., Dekalb, 1958-70, supr. instr., 1970-72; ednl. cons. Ill. Office of Edn., Dekalb, 1978-80. Adj. prof. Collin County C.C., Plano, Tex., 1989. Author: John Updike: Yea Sayings, 1971, Hallelujah Hopscotch, 1986, Green Figs and Tender Grapes, 1985, We the Real People I and II, 1991, 93, Troupers and Tramps, 1994; contbr. articles and poetry to numerous jours. Recipient Comm. Treasure award Portland Gen. Electric, Yamhill County, 1995; Oreg. Book awards finalist Literary Arts, Inc., Portland, 1994, Kay Snow awards finalist Willamette Writers, Portland, 1991, various poetry awards. Home: 1662 SW Bonnie Jean Pl Mcminnville OR 97128-5783

BURCHENAL, JOAN RILEY, science educator; b. N.Y.C., Dec. 11, 1925; d. Wells Littlefield and Bertha Barclay (Fahys) Riley; m. Joseph Holland Burchenal, Mar. 20, 1948; children: Elizabeth Payne Burchenal Paul (dec.), Joan Littlefield Burchenal Nycum, Barbara Fahys Burchenal Landers, Caleb Wells, David Holland, Joseph Emory Barclay; 1 stepchild, Mary Holland Burchenal Nottebohm. BA, Vassar Coll., 1946; MAT, Yale U., 1971; MA, Fairfield U., 1981. Sci. tchr. New Canaan (Conn.) Country Sch., 1968-69, Low Heywood Sch., Stamford, Conn., 1968-69, The Thomas Sch., Rowayton, Conn., 1972-73, Darien Bd. Edn., Conn., 1973-91, ret. Mem. panel on grants for tchrs. enhancement program NSF, 1987, 92; K-12 sci. curriculum com., 1994-2000. Hon. chmn. Darien Sci. Fair, 1986; mem. steering com. Holly Pond Saltmarsh Conservation Com., 1968—71; mem. acad. courses com. Darien Cmty. Assn., 1964—71, chmn., 1971; trustee Garrison Forest Sch., 1959—62; rep. Town Meeting Darien, 1993—2003, mem. edn. com., 1993—2003, chair edn. com., 1995—97, rules com., 2000—03; cmty. rep. K-12 Sci. Curriculum Com., 1994—2000; elder First Presbyn. Ch. of New Canaan, 1994—97, Stephen min., 1994—; bd. dir., chmn. standards com. A Better Chance, Darien, Conn., 1985—99; bd. dir. Darien Nature Ctr., 1975—91, Darien Audubon Soc., 1978—86, Darien LWV, 1951—62, Alumnae and Alumni Vassar Coll. Recipient Presdl. award for excellence in sci. teaching Nat. Sci. Tchrs. Assn., NSF, Washington, 1985. Mem. AAAS, N.Y. Acad. Sci., Assn. Presdl. Awardees in Sci. Teaching (nominating com. 1987-90), Cosmopolitan Club, Ausable Club, Phi Beta Kappa. Democrat. Presbyterian. Avocations: reading, travel, trekking, birding. Home: Kendal at Hanover #432 80 Lyme Rd Hanover NH 03755 E-mail: jhbjrb@aol.com.

BURCHETT, BRENDA JEAN HARNAGE, secondary school educator, writer; b. Orlando, Fla., Mar. 28, 1949; d. Lloyd A. and Mabel W. Harnage; m. E. Wayne Burchett, June 30, 1973 (dec. Jan. 17, 1993); children: Kara Renee(dec.), Rena Jayne(dec.). BA, Carson Newman Coll., 1971; MA, U. N.C., 1972; PhD, U. Md., 1985; student, U. Va., 1969—2003. Lic. tchr. Va. Grad. tchg. asst. U. N.C., 1971—72; admissions counselor Carson-Newman Coll., [illegible] Tenn., 1972—73; prof. No. Va. C.C., Annandale, Va., 1974—97, George Mason U., Fairfax, Va., 1995—97; tchr. First Acad., Leesburg, Fla., 1999—2000, Phillips, Annandale, Va., 2000—02, Osbourn HS, Manassas, Va., 2003, Manteo (N.C.) HS, 2003. Grad. tchg. asst. U. N.C., 1971—72, U. Md., 1979—80. Editor: Interpersonal Communication: A Reader, 1996, 1997. Named Outstanding Student in Speech, Carson-Newman Coll., 1971. Mem.: Met. Wash. Comm. Assn. (past pres.), Va. Speech Comm. Assn. (past pres.). Avocations: music, water sports, gardening. Home: 7625 Arlen Annandale VA 22003

BURDETT, BARBRA ELAINE, biology educator; b. Lincoln, Ill., Mar. 18, 1947; d. Robert Marlin and Klaaska Johanna Baker; m. Gary Albert Burdett, Sept. 27, 1968; children: Bryan Robert, Heather Lea, Amanda Rose. AA, Lincoln Coll., 1981; postgrad., Ill. State U. Edn. Core, 1982-83; BS, Millikin U., 1985; postgrad., Western U., 1994-95, U. Ill., Springfield, 1997, Quincy (Ill.) U., 1998. Cert. tchr., Ill. Tchr. advanced placement biology, botany and human physiology Brown County H.S., Mt. Sterling, Ill., 1985-95; tchr. zoology, botany, environmental sci. Pleasant Plains (Ill.) H.S., 1995-97; tchr. biology Quincy (Ill.) H.S., 1997-98; owner Wild Winds Pub. Co., 1999—. Dir. Drama Club, Brown County H.S., 1988-90, dir. sci. fairs; ednl. advisor Nat. Young Leaders Conf. Author: Misty White, 1991, Possums Sing, 1994; co-author: The Last Button on Gabe's Coat, 1999, Derthro—Meet Mrs. Claus, 1999. Sponsor Children, Inc., Richmond, Va., 1985—, Internat. Wildlife Coalition, North Falmouth, Mass., 1991—; commdr. club, silver leader., 1988—. Mem. ASCD, Nat. Assn. Biology Tchrs. (Biology Tchr. of Yr. in Ill. 1994), Ill. Sci. Tchrs. Assn., Phi Delta Kappa (newsletter editor 1990), Phi Theta Kappa. Episcopalian. Avocation: classical guitar.

BURDICK, GINNY, state legislator; b. Portland, Oreg., Dec. 3, 1947; BA, U. Puget Sound; M in Journalism, Oreg. U. Mem. Oreg. Legislature, Salem, 1996—. Democrat. Home: 4641 SW Dosch Rd Portland OR 97201-1244 Office: S-309 State Capitol Salem OR 97310-0001 E-mail: burdick.sen@state.or.us.

BURDICK, MARGARET SEALE (MARGE), interior designer; b. Ft. Worth, Tex., July 24, 1919; d. Walter Braton and Ivy (McCleskey) Seale; m. Donald K. Bennett (dec. May 1943); 1 child, Donald Jr.; m. William J. Walsh, Dec. 1, 1945 (div. June 1959); children: Susan S. Lynch, William J. Jr., Margaret J. Tannery; m. Lorence Connable Burdick, Oct. 21, 1961 (div. Aug. 1979); children: Michael, John, Timothy. Student, So. Meth. U., 1937-38. Interior redesigner Kalamazoo (Mich.) Country Club, 1948; interior desiger Child Guidance Ctr. Jr. League (formerly Service Club), Kalamazoo, 1956, designer nearly new shop, 1955; co-owner, interior designer Red Lion Inn, Vail, Colo., 1962-80; owner MSB Designs, 1980-2001; interior designer Outstanding Homes in Vail, 1981-99. Co-organizer 1st Sch. Bd. Vail, 1963; charter bd. dirs. Vail Inst Performing Arts, 1973-84; pres. Vail Inst., 1979-84, also hon. bd. dirs. 1984-87; mem. Art Selection Com. Vail, 1981-84; bd. dirs. Gerald R. Ford Commemorative Com., Vail, 1980-85; charter mem. bd. dirs. Bravo! Colo. Music Festival, Vail and Beaver Creek, 1987-95, adv. bd., 1995-2003; bd. dirs. Betty Ford Alpine Carden Found., 1986-97, nat. adv. bd., 1997-2001; bd. dirs. Vail Religious Found. Endowment Com., 1995-2003, Bravo! Music Festival Endowment Com., 1991-98, Ctr. for the Arts Com. (now Vilar Ctr.), Beaver Creek, Vail Valley Arts Coun., 1991—, pres., 1993-97. Honoree Bravo! Colo. Music Festival, 1997. Mem.: Racquet Club (charter), Homestead Ct. Club, Vail Athletic Club (charter). Republican. Episcopalian. Home and Office: PO Box 498 Edwards CO 81632-0498 E-mail: msb@vail.net.

BURFEIND, BETTY RUTH, science educator; b. Chgo., Feb. 10, 1947; d. William Frederick Burfeind and Ruth Pauline Amanda Batzer; m. Joseph Andres Ibanez, June 8, 1992. BS in Phys. Edn., Ea. Ill. U., 1969, MS in Phys. Edn., 1977; paralegal cert., Roosevelt U., 1982; type 75 adminstrv. cert., Govs. State U., 1994. Tchr. health and phys. edn. James Hart Jr. H.S., Homewood, Ill., 1969—80; tchr. sci. and phys. edn. Carl Sandburg H.S., Orland Park, Ill., 1980—83, Victor J. Andrew H.S., Tinley Park, Ill., 1983—. Coach swimming Victor J. Andrew H.S., Tinley Park, 1983—, coach water polo, 1998—; mem. governing bd,. Dist. 230 NEA, Orland Park, 1980—. Instr. ARC, Chgo., 1969—. Mem.: Nat. Sr. Games Assn., U.S. Water Polo Assn., Am. Swim Coaches Assn., Nat. Intercollegiate Swimming Coaches Assn. Lutheran. Avocations: softball, golf, bicycling, travel, writing. Home: 10601 Brookridge Dr Frankfort IL 60423 Office: Consol Sch Dist 230 15100 W 94th Ave Orland Park IL 60462 Office Phone: 708-342-5800.*

BURFORD, ANNE MCGILL, lawyer; b. Casper, Wyo., Apr. 21, 1942; d. Joseph John and Dorothy Jean (O'Grady) McGill; m. David Gorsuch, June 4, 1964 (div. 1982); children: Neil, Stephanie, J.J.; m. Robert Fitzpatrick Burford, Feb. 20, 1983 (dec. 1993). Student, Nat. U. Mex., 1955-56, 58, Regis Coll., Denver, 1959; BA, U. Colo., 1961, LLB, 1964. Bar: Colo. 1964, D.C. 1985. Asst. trust adminstr. 1st Nat. Bank of Denver, 1966-67; instr. Metro State Coll., 1966-67; asst. dist. atty. Jefferson County, 1968-71; dep. dist. atty. City and County of Denver, 1971—73; hearing officer Real Estate Commn., State Bds. Cosmetology, State Bd. Vet. Medicine, State Bd. Optemetric Examiners and Profl. Nursing, 1974-75; corp. counsel Mountain Bell Telephone Co., Denver, 1975-81; mem. Colo. Ho. of Reps., 1977-81, chmn. state affairs com., 1979-80, chmn. legal svcs. com., 1980; adminstr. EPA, Washington, 1981—83; lectr., author Washington, 1983—89; pvt. practice Denver, 1993—. Author: Are You Tough Enough, 1986. Del. Nat. Conf. State Legislators; mem. Nat. Conf. Commrs. on Uniform State Law, 1979, 80; presdl. del. to Kenya's Independence, 1983; loaned exec. mgmt. and efficiency task force Colo. Dept. Regulatory Agys., 1976; adminstr. EPA, Washington, 1981-83; former bd. dirs. YMCA. Fulbright scholar, Jaipur, India, 1964-65. Mem. Mortar Bd., Phi Alpha Delta, Delta Delta Delta. Republican. Roman Catholic. Home and Office: 3853 S Hudson St Denver CO 80237-1050

BURGE, CONSTANCE M. television producer; d. Phil. MFA in Playwriting, UCLA. Author: (TV series) Ally McBeal; prodr.: (TV series) Ally McBeal; author: (TV series) Boston Pub., Charmed; prodr.: (TV series) Charmed; author: (TV series) Ed; prodr.: (TV series) Savannah; author: The Power of Three: A Novelization, 1999, The Crimson Spell, 2000, Haunted By Desire, 2000, Kiss of Darkness: An Original Novel, 2000, Voodoo Moon, 2000, Whispers from the Past, 2000, Beware What You Wish, 2001, The Gypsy Enchantment, 2001, The Legacy of Merlin, 2001, Soul of the Bride, 2001, Charmed Again, 2002, Spirit of the Wolf, 2002.*

BURGESS, ANN DALTON, music educator; b. Ft. Payne, Ala., Mar. 18, 1955; d. James Simeon and Lillian Campbell Dalton; m. David Byron Burgess, Sept. 22, 1979; children: Laura JoAnn, Amanda Ruth. AS, N.E. Ala. State C.C., 1975; MusB in Edn. cum laude, Shorter Coll., 1997. Cert. level one Orff cert. Orff-Schulwerk Soc. Voice/piano tchr. Shorter Coll. Prep. Dept., Rome, Ga., 1999—2001; dir. children's choir 1st United Meth. Ch., Rome, 1998—2002; music specialist, tchr. McHenry Primary Sch., Rome, 1998—2002; choral dir. Armuchee (Ga.) Mid. Sch., 2002—03, Armuchee Mid. and H.S., 2003—. Music dir. Alton Holmn Heritage Arts Camp, Cave Spring, Ga., 2002, 03. Composer: (mus. vignette) Opera Girl, 2002. Recipient vocal competition winner, Am. Mothers, Inc., 2000, state winner women's classical divsn., Nat. Assn. Tchrs. of Singing, 1997. Mem.: Profl. Assn. Ga. Educators, Music Educators Nat. Conf., Am. Choral Dirs. Assn., Shorter Coll. Friends of Music, Met. Opera Guild, Rome Area Coun. for Arts, Mu Phi Epsilon, Pi Kappa Lambda. Democrat. Presbyterian. Avocation: musical theater. Home: 143 E Clinton Dr Rome GA 30165 Office: Armuchee Mid Sch 471 Floyd Springs Rd Armuchee GA 30105 Office Phone: 706-378-7924. E-mail: radburgess@comcast.net.

BURGESS, ANN WOLBERT, [illegible] prof. nursing U. Pa., Phila.; prof. of psychiat. and mental health nursing Boston Coll. Author: Advanced Practice Psychiatric Nursing, 1998, Psychiatric Nursing: Promoting Mental Health, 1997, Child Trauma I: Issues & Research, 1992, Community Mental Health: Target Populations, 1976, Rape: Victims of Crisis, 1974; co-editor: (with Robert K. Kessler and John E. Douglas) Sexual Homicide: Patterns and Movies, 1988, Rape and Sexual Assault II, 1985; co-author: (with Robert R. Hazelwood) Practical Aspects of Rape Investigation: A Multidisciplinary Approach, 3d edit., 1993, (with Robert Ann Prentsky) Forensic Management of Sexual Offenders, 2000, (with Robert R. Hazelwood and Park Elliott Dietz) Autoerotic Fatalities, 1983, (with Bruce A. Baldwin) Crisis Intervention Theory and Practice: A Clinical Handbook, 1981, (with Nicholas Groth and Suzanne M. Sgroi) Sexual Assault of Children and Adolescents, 1978. Mem.: Inst. Medicine, NAS. Office: Boston Coll Sch Nursing Cushing Hall 414 140 Commonwealth Ave Chestnut Hill MA 02467*

BURGESS, CAROL ANN, educational association administrator, literature educator; b. Detroit, Apr. 20, 1951; d. Charles Royal and Ann Timmons Burgess; m. Philip Mark Wonn, Dec. 27, 2000. B in english theater, Sarah lawrence Coll., 1972; M in english edn., Keene State Coll., 1983; EdD, U. Va., 2003. Cert. supr. admin. Va., admin. NY, Conn., supr. curriculum and instr. Team tchr. Bedford Mid. Sch., Westport, Conn., 1982—83; tchr. Weston (Conn.) HS, 1983—85, Daniel Morgan Mid. Sch., Winchester, Va., 1985—86, Clarke County HS, Berryville, Va., 1986—88; adj. faculty Shenandoah U., Winchester, 1990—92; tchr. John Handley HS, Winchester, 1988—97, lead tchr., 1997—98, asst. prin., 1998—2000; dir. curriculum Winchester (Va.) Pub. Schs., 2000—02; dir. of curriculum The Whitby Sch., Greenwich, Conn., 2002—. Bd. mem. Kids Voting, Winchester, 2000—02; dir. bd. mem. Very Spl. Arts, Winchester, 1995—98; mem., sec. Instr. Leaders, Reg. #4, Winchester, 2001—02. Contbr. articles various profl. jours. Vol. Red Cross, Winchester, 2000—02. Named Educator of Yr., Assn. Retarded Citizens, 1992; scholar George Bernard Shaw, NEH, 1988. Mem.: Assn. for Supr. and Curriculum Devel., Women Ednl. Leaders of Va., Phi Delta Kapp (pres. 2000—01, sec. 1989—92). Episcopal. Avocations: reading, old movies, golf, walking, theater. Home: 10 Three Season Ct Norwalk CT 06851 Office: Tuckahoe Free Sch Dist Sinawoy Blvd Eastchester NY

BURGESS, DEBORAH LEE, small business owner; b. South Bend, Ind., Dec. 15, 1949; d. Bruce Kent and Patricia Ann Burgess; m. Edilberto Marrero, May 14, 1968 (div. Oct. 1975); children: Micheal Marrero, Kimberly Marrero; m. David Shedd, June 26, 1978 (div.); children: Kristen Shedd, Amanda Shedd; m. Ed Northart, Oct. 16, 1992. BA, HI Loa Coll.; JD, Western State Coll. of Law. Cert. tax cons. 1992, real estate agent 2002. Examiner, tchr. IRS, L.A.; paralegal Harry Hicks JD, Newport Beach, Calif.; tax cons. Dynatax, Anaheim, Calif.; owner D&S Tax Svc., Sacramento. Organizer, canvasser Dem. Party, Sacramento, 1992—96; mem. El Dorado Grand Jury, Placerville, Calif., 1999—2000. Mem.: NOW, Amnesty Internat., Common Cause. Democrat. Office: D&S Tax 2267 Tulip Way Sacramento CA 95821 E-mail: dandstax@worldnet.att.net.

BURGESS, LYNNE A, lawyer; B, William Smith Coll.; JD, Fordham U. Asst. gen. counsel Am. Nat. Can Co.; of counsel Colier, Shannon, Rill & Scott, Washington, 1992—94; sr. v.p., gen. counsel Entex Info. Services, 1994—2000; gen. counsel and sec. governance com. Oliver, Wyman & Co. LLC, 2001—02; v.p., gen. counsel Asbury Automotive Group, 2002—. Office: ASbury Automotive Group 3 Landmark Square Stamford CT 06901

BURGESS, MARJORIE LAURA, retired protective services official; b. Whitakers, N.C., Nov. 24, 1928; d. Benjamin and Laura Lenora (Ford) Harrison; m. Bonus David Dixon, July 24, 1948 (div. Apr. 1970); children: David Kingsley (dec.), Terence David, Michael Jerome; m. William A. Burgess, June 6, 1970 (div. July 1976). AS in Correction Adminstrn., John Jay Coll. Criminal, Justice, N.Y.C., 1971; BA in Social Scis., John Jay Coll. Criminal Justice, N.Y.C., 1972, postgrad., 1973-75. Correction officer N.Y. State Dept. Correction, Bedford Hills, N.Y., 1959-67, correction sgt., 1967-73, correction lt., 1973-82, 86-90, capt., 1982-86; ret., 1990. Adv. coun. divsn. sr. svcs. Bergen County, 1997. Author: (poetry) Walking on the Road of Life, 1997, Life! It's More Than A Notion, libr. of congress Watermark press, 2000. Vol. intergenerational program Martin Luther King Srs. Ctr. Mem. AAUW, Am. Correctional Assn., Alumni Assn. John Jay Coll., The Smithsonian Assocs., Retired Pub. Employees Assn., AARP. Democrat. Baptist. Avocations: writing, singing, playing scrabble, reading.

BURGESS, MARY ALICE (MARY ALICE WICKIZER), publisher; b. San Bernardino, Calif., June 21, 1938; d. Russell Alger and Wilma Evelyn (Swisher) Wickizer; m. Michael Roy Burgess, Oct. 15, 1976; children from previous marriage: Richard Albert Rogers, Mary Louise Rogers Reynnells. AA, Valley Coll., San Bernardino, 1967; BA, Calif. State U., San Bernardino, 1975, postgrad., 1976-79, U. Calif., Riverside, 1976-79. Lic. real estate salesman, Calif.; real estate broker, Calif. Sec.-treas. Lynwyck Realty & Investment, San Bernardino, 1963-75; libr. asst. Calif. State U., San Bernardino, 1974-76, purchasing agt., 1976-81; co-pub. The Borgo Press, San Bernardino, 1975-99; owner MilleFleurs Info. Svcs., 2000—. Co-pub: (with Robert Reginald) Science Fiction and Fantasy Book Review, 1979-80; co-author (with M.R. Burgess) The Wickizer Annals: The Descendents of Conrad Wickizer of Luzerne County, Pennsylvania, 1983, (with Douglas Menville and Robert Reginald) Futurevisions: The New Golden Age of the Science Fiction Film, 1985, (with Jeffrey M. Elliot and Robert Reginald) The Arms Control, Disarmament and Military Science Dictionary, 1989, (with Michael Burgess) The House of the Burgesses, 2d edit., 1994; author: The Campbell Chronicles: A Genealogical History of the Descendants of Samuel Campbell of Chester County, Pennsylvania, 1989, (with Boden Clarke) The Work of Katherine Kurtz, 1992-93, (with Michael Burgess and Daryl F. Mallett) State and Province Vital Records Guide; editor: Cranberry Tea Room Cookbook, Still The Frame Holds, Defying the Holocaust, Risen from the Ashes: A Story of the Jewish Displaced Persons in the Aftermath of World War II, Being a Sequel to Survivors (Jacob Biber), 1989, Ray Bradbury: Dramatist (Ben P. Indick), 1989, Across the Wide Missouri: The Diary of a Journey from Virginia to Missouri in 1819 and Back Again in 1821, with a Description of the City of Cincinnati, (James Brown Campbell), Italian Theatre in San Francisco, Into the Flames: The Life Story of a Righteous Gentile, Jerzy Kosinski: The Literature of Violation, The Little Kitchen Cookbook, Victorian Criticism of American Writers, 1990, The Magic That Works: John W. Campbell and The American Response to Technology, 1993, Libido into Literature: The "Primĕra Época" of Benito Pérez Galdós, 1993, A Triumph of the Spirit: Stories of Holocaust Survivors, 1994, A Way Farer in a World in Upheaval, 1993, William Eastlake: High Desert Interlocutor, 1993, The Price of Paradise: The Magazine Career of F. Scott Fitgerald, 1993, The Little Kitchen Cookbook, rev. edit., 1994, An Irony of Fate: William March, 1994, Hard-Boiled Heretic: Ross Macdonald, 1994, We The People!, 1994, The Chinese Economy, 1995, Voices of the River Plate, 1995, Chaos Burning on My Brow, 1995; co-editor and pub. (with Robert Reginald) of all Borgo Press publs.; also reviewer, indexer, researcher and editor of scholarly manuscripts. Chmn. new citizens Rep. Women, San Bernardino, 1967; libr. San Bernardino Geneal. Soc., 1965-67; vol. Boy Scout Am., Girl Scouts U.S., Camp Fire Girls, 1960s. Recipient Real Estate Proficiency award Calif. Dept. Real Estate, San Bernardino, 1966. Mem. City of San Bernardino Hist. and Pioneer Soc., Calif. State U. Alumni Assn., Cecil County (Md.) Hist. Soc., Gallia County (Ohio) Hist. and Geneal. Soc., DAR (membership and geneal. records chmn. 1964-66, registrar and vice regent San Bernardino chpt. 1965-67). Avocations: genealogy, films, travel. Office: Mille-Fleurs PO Box 2845 Box 2845 San Bernardino CA 92406-2845

BURGESS, PAMELA SHAWNTA, music educator, director; b. Manning, S.C., Oct. 17, 1977; d. Ranie and Daisy Burgess. BS in Music Edn., S.C. State U., 1999. Band dir. Kingstree (S.C.) Jr. H.S., 2000—, athletic dir., 2002—. Mem.: Music Educators Nat. Conf., Kappa Delta Pi, Tau Beta Sigma (life; v.p. 1998—99, named Ms. Tau Beta Sigma 1998). Democrat. Baptist. Home: 525 Broomstraw Rd Laneq SC 29564 Office: Kingstree Junior High School 710 Third Ave Kingstree SC 29556 Personal E-mail: pamela.burgess@citadel.edu.

BURGESS, PAULA LASHENSKE, health facility administrator; b. Athol, Mass., Mar. 22, 1955; d. John Joseph and Lotta Catherine (Maroni) Lashenske; m. Jack Leland Burgess Jr., May 15, 1982; children: Jack Leland III, Brian Lane. AAS in Paralegal Studies, Durham (N.C.) Tech. C.C., 1988; Assoc. Risk Mgmt., Ins. Inst. Am., 1990; BSN, St. Anselm's Coll., 1977; MHA, Duke U., 1983. RN, N.C.; lic. real estate agt., N.C. Staff nurse Morton Plant Hosp., Clearwater, Fla., 1977-78, Duke U. Med. Ctr., Durham, 1978-86, risk mgr., 1984—; adminstrv. intern Durham County Gen. Hosp., 1982; dir. utilization rev. High Point (N.C.) Meml. Hosp., 1983-84. Co-author: Mapping Your Risk Management Course in Stand-Alone Hospitals, 1996; co-contbr.: Liability Issues in Perinatal Nursing, 1997; co-author newsletter N.C. Soc. for Healthcare, 1990. Mem. Durham County Rep. Women's Club, 1996—; vol. Duke Children's Classic, Durham; mem. N-Vestment Inc., Durham, 1996—. Mem. Am. Soc. Healthcare Risk Mgmt. (spl. projects com. 1994, nominating com. 1996, hist. com. 1998—), Risk and Ins. Mgmt. Soc. (Piedmont chpt. society dir. 1994-96, pres. 1990-91, Southeastern regional conf. com. 1990, 94, co-chair golf tournament 1992-93). Republican. Roman Catholic. Avocations: golf, tennis, basketball, investments, croquet. Home: 2013 Sprunt Ave Durham NC 27705-3251 Office: Duke U Med Ctr PO Box 3811 Durham NC 27702-3811

BURGESS, SANDRA JEAN, marketing consultant; b. Cleve., Sept. 26, 1953; d. Roy Thomas and Mary Lois (Ovardits) B. BA in Polit. Sci., Oakland U., 1975; MBA, Mich. State U., 1990. Project supr., publ. coord., asst. editor, writer William Beaumont Hosp., Royal Oak, Mich., 1977-86; editl. supr. St. Clair Health Corp., Detroit, 1986-88; owner Burgess Editl. Svcs., Troy, Mich., 1986—, Burgess Strategic Mktg. Svcs., Troy, 1996—. Bd. dirs. Mich. State U. Advanced Mgmt. Program Alumni Club, East Lansing, 1993-95, mktg. com. chair Boys and Girls Club Troy, 1992-93. Mem. Am. Advt. Fedn., Adcraft Club Detroit, Detroit Regional C. of C., Troy C. of C. (small bus. coun. mktg. com. 1995-96), Strategic Leadership Forum (v.p. pub. rels. Metro Detroit coun. 1997-99), The Strategy Forum (pres. 1999-2001), Internat. Acad. Comm. Arts and Scis. (faculty judges 1996—), Detroit Economic Club, Troy Democratic Club. Lutheran. Avocations: reading, golf, baseball, community service, photography.

BURGMAN, DIERDRE ANN, lawyer; b. Logansport, Ind., Mar. 25, 1948; d. Ferdinand William Jr. and Doreen Walsh Burgman. BA, Valparaiso U., 1970, JD, 1979; LLM, Yale U., 1985. Bar: Ind. 1979, U.S. Dist. Ct. (so. dist.) Ind. 1979, N.Y. 1982, U.S. Dist. Ct. (so. dist.) N.Y. 1982, U.S. Ct. Appeals (7th cir.) 1982, U.S. Ct. Appeals (D.C. and 2d cirs.) 1984, U.S. Supreme Ct. 1986, [illegible] to chief judge Ind. Ct. Appeals, Indpls., 1979-80; prof. law Valparaiso (Ind.) U., 1980-81; assoc. Dewey, Ballantine, Bushby, Palmer & Wood, N.Y.C., 1981-84, Cahill Gordon & Reindel, N.Y.C., 1985-92; v.p., gen. counsel N.Y. State Urban Devel. Corp., N.Y.C., 1992-95; dep. insp. gen. State N.Y., 1992-95; of counsel Vandenberg & Felieu, N.Y.C., 1995-99; cons. Salans, N.Y.C., 1999—2000, counsel, 2000—. Note editor Valparaiso U. law rev., 1978-79; contbr. articles to law jours. Mem. bd. visitors Valparaiso U. Sch. Law, 1986—95, chmn., 1989—92, mem. nat. coun., 2001—. Ind. Bar Found. scholar, 1978. Mem. ABA (trial evidence com. 1983-86, profl. liability com. 1986-89, ins. coverage litigation com. 1990-92), Assn. Bar City N.Y. (com. profl. responsibility 1988-91, com. profl. and jud. ethics 1991-95, mem. coun. jud. adminstrn. 1997-99), New York County Lawyers Assn. (com. Supreme Ct. 1987-94, chmn. 1990-93, bd. dirs. 1991-97, 2002-03, exec. com. bd. dirs. 1992-95, fin. and pers. com. 2003, mem. found., 2003-), N.Y. State Bar Assn. (mem. Ho. Dels. 1994-98, mem. com. on profl. stds. for atty. conduct 2002-). Home: 345 E 56th St Apt 5C New York NY 10022-3744

BURGOS, NORMA, former secretary of state; BA in Econs. with hons., U. P.R., 1978, MPA, 1982; postgrad., Ga. Inst. Tech.; D in Polit. Sci. (hon.), Caribbean U. Cert. housing mgr. Nat. Ctr. Housing Mgmt., profl. planner. With Govt. P.R., 1976; assoc. mem., chair, sec. of state P.R. Planning Bd., 1992. Pres., exec. dir. Old San Juan Devel. Corp., 1986-90; cons. dept. transp. pub. works, P.R.; spl. project Puerto Rico 2005, 1992; exec. dir. Gov.'s Coun. Econ. Productivity; bd. dirs. So. Growth Policy. Co-author: Transnationalization in the Decade of the 80's: An Opportunity to Export Knowledge, 1984, Public Administration in Puerto Rico and the New Century: The Experts' Opinion; contbr. articles to profl. jours. Recipient Eagle award Nat. Hispanic Heritage Leadership Conf.;named 1996 Disting. Citizen P.R., Pub. Servant of Yr., Encuantro Found. Office: State Dept Office of Gov PO Box 9023271 San Juan PR 00902-3271

BURGOS-SASSCER, RUTH, chancellor emeritus; b. N.Y.C., Sept. 5, 1931; m. Donald Sasscer, June 14, 1958; children: Timothy, James, Julie, David. BA, Maryville (Tenn.) Coll., 1953; MA, Columbia U., 1956; PhD, Fla. State U., 1987. Mem. faculty Inter-Am. U., P.R., 1968-71; dept. chair U. P.R., Aguadilla, 1972-76, dir. non-traditional programs Cen. Adminstrn. Regional Coll., 1976-81, dir., dean, chief exec. officer, 1981-85; v.p. faculty and instrn. Harry S. Truman Coll., Chgo., 1988-93; pres. San Antonio Coll., 1993-96; chancellor Houston C.C. Sys., 1996-2000; sr. fellow U. Houston Law Ctr. Inst. of Higher Edn Law and Goverance, 2001—. Bd. dirs. Nat. Hispanic Coun. C.C.s. Bd. dirs. Greater Houston Partnership, Houston Read Commn., City of Houston Ethics Com., Am. Assn. C.C., Internat. Consortium for Ednl. and Econ. Devel., Laredo Nat. Bank, Houston. Mem. Am. Assn. C.C., Internat. Consortium for Ednl. and Econ. Devel. Presbyterian. Home: 15115 Interlachen Dr Apt 403 Silver Spring MD 20908 E-mail: ruthburgossas@hotmail.com.

BURGOYNE, MOJIE ADLER, clinical social worker; b. Abilene, Tex., Apr. 26, 1942; d. Leonard A. and Mojie W. (Jennings) Adler; m. Wallace Carr Burgoyne, June 27, 1964 (div. Dec. 1974); children: Kristina, Pamela, Carr. BA, Tex. Woman's U., 1964; MSW, U. Houston, 1979. Lic. master social worker-advanced clin. practitioner, Tex.; diplomae Am. Bd. Cert. Managed Care Providers, Am. Bd. Examiners. in Clin. Social Work. Clin. social worker Post Oak Psychiatry & Assocs., Tomball, Tex., 1986-90, Raul R Gomez & Assocs., Tomball, 1990-91; owner, clin. social worker Affiliated Mental Health Svcs., Tomball, 1991—. Pres. Home Health Adv. Bd., Tomball, 1979-84. Contbg. author: Social Work Treatment with Abused and Neglected Children, 1985. Polit. activist Child Welfare Bd., Montgomery County, Tex., 1974-77. Named Woman of Yr., Montgomery County (Tex.) YWCA, 1981. Mem. NASW (diplomate in clin. social work). Avocations: reading, restoring an antique barn in farm country of south central texas. Office: Affiliated Mental Health Svcs Ste 2 701 W Main Tomball TX 77375-4451

BURGOYNE, SUZANNE, theater educator, writer; b. St. Joseph, Mich., Oct. 25, 1946; d. Leon Edward and Betty Louise Burgoyne. Cert., Belgian Nat. Theatre Inst. (L'INSAS), Brussels, 1969; BA, Mich. State U., 1968; MA, Ohio State U., 1970; PhD, U. Mich., 1975. Vis. asst. prof. theatre N.E. Mo. State U., Kirksville, 1973—74; head dept. dramatic art So. Sem. Jr. Coll., Buena Vista, Va., 1975—77; from asst. to assoc. prof. fine and performing arts Creighton U., Omaha, 1977—89; vis. prof. directing and dramaturgy L'INSAS, Brussels, 1986—87; assoc. prof. theatre U. Mo., Columbia, 1989—97, prof. theatre, 1997—. Dir.: (student-authored play) Survival Dance (show selected for performance at regional Kennedy Ctr. Am. Coll. Theatre Festival (KCACTF), 2003), (play) Oleanna (show selected for regional KCACTF-meritorious achievement award for directing (regional); Hon. Mention Award for Directing (Nat.), 1999), (and translator) La Vita Breve (by Paul Willems) (show selected for performance at regional KCACTF; Meritorious Achievement Award for Directing (regional), 1996); co-author: Teaching and Performing: Ideas for Energizing Your Classes, revised edit.; translator: (play) Paul Willems' The Drowned Land and La Vita Breve.; translator: (of 2 of 4 plays, vol. editor) Four Plays of Paul Willems: Dreams and Reflections; contbr. articles to profl. jours., chapters to books. Mem. INTERACT Teen-to-Teen Theatre, Columbia, Mo., 2001—03. Recipient Author of the Month awrd, Highlights for Children Mag., 1986; Kellogg Nat. fellow, W.K. Kellogg Found., 1981—84, Carnegie scholar, Carnegie Acad. for the Scholarship of Tchg. and Learning, 2000—01, Summer Rsch. fellow, U. Mo. Rsch. Coun., 1992, Summer salary and travel grantee, 1994, NEH Summer Seminar fellow, 1979, 1985. Mem.: Pedagogy and Theatre of the Oppressed, Kennedy Ctr. Am. Coll. Theatre Festival (regional playwriting awards chair 1978—80), Mid-America Theatre Conf. (v.p., pres. 1991—95), Assn. for Theatre in Higher Edn. (editor, theatre topics 1993—95, v.p. for profl. devel. 1999—2003, award as editor of Theatre Topics 1995, Outstanding Tchr. award 2003). Avocations: water aerobics, reading, gardening, swimming. Home: 103 Tracy Dr Columbia MO 65203 Office: Dept Theatre U Missouri 129 Fine Arts Columbia MO 65211 Personal E-mail: burgoynes@missouri.edu.

BURI, CAROLYN, management consultant; d. Melvin Cook and Irene Grace Orlandi; BS in Music Edn., Ohio State U., 1964; M in Consulting, Hubbard Coll. Adminstrn. Internat., 2000. Lic. master cons. World Inst. Scientology Enterprises. Tchr. music Ohio Schs., New Philadelphia, Ohio, 1964—69, Dept. of Def. Overseas Tchg. Sys., Clark Air Base, Philippines, 1969—72; mem. staff Scientology, Hollywood, Calif., 1972—96; exec. mgr. Manago Chiropractic Inc., Mission Viejo, Calif., 1997—98, Wiseman & Burke, Glendale, Calif., 1998—99; pvt. practice as cons. in pers. efficiency L.A., 1999—. Mem.: C. of C., World Inst. Scientology, Bus. Expansion Club (bd. dirs., Commendation award 2002). Avocations: hiking, swimming, movies, reading, writing poetry. Office: Mgmt Cons 10034 Samoa Ave Ste 5 Tujunga CA 91042 Office Phone: 818-353-1622. E-mail: managementconsultants@comcast.net.

BURINGRUD, LISA MARIE, music educator; b. Brawley, Calif., Jan. 16, 1961; d. Joseph Paul McKim and Mary Legakes-McKim; m. Joel Dean Buringrud, Nov. 30, 1991; children: Rebecca Danae, Deanna Marie. BA in Music with cert. in music therapy, Calif. State U., Long Beach, 1987; MusM in Instrumental Conducting, Calif. State U., Sacramento, 2001. Cert. profl. clear single No. 6 subject Calif., bd. cert. music therapy Calif. Bd. Music Therapy, tchg. credential in music Calif. Music therapist, band dir. L.A. GOAL, Santa Monica, Calif., 1986—90; music therapist Fairview Developmental Ctr., Costa Mesa, Calif., 1987—90, Stockton (Calif.) Developmental Ctr., 1990; music dir. Vanden H.S., Fairfield, Calif., 1993—99; band dir. Armijo H.S., Fairfield, 1999—2000; assoc. condr. wind studies dept. Calif. State U., Sacramento, 2000—01; instrumental music dir. Mendocino (Calif.) Unified Sch. Dist., 2001—03, band dir. Calaveras H.S., San Andreas, Calif., 2003—. Prin. flutist Solano Winds, Fairfield, 1995—2001; condr., artistic dir. North Coast Wind Symphony, Mendocino, 2002—03; assoc. condr. Opera Fresca, Mendocino, 2001—03; condr. children's concert series Symphony of the Redwoods, Mendocino, 2002—. Author: (book) American Women Composers of Band Music: A Biographical Dictionary and Catalogue of Works: An Addendum and Update, 2001. Music min. St. Marks Luth. Ch., Fairfield, 2000—01; bd. dirs. St. Marks Pre-Sch., Fairfield, 1999—2001. Recipient Cert. of Appreciation for Performance, Travis AFB, 1997. Mem.: Nat. Band Dirs. Assn., Calif. Music Educators Assn. (Hon. Recognition Band Concert/Clinic Pres. 2002), Calif. Band Dirs. Assn. (Hon. Recognition Band Concert/Clinic Pres. 1999, 2003), Women Band Dirs. Internat., Am. Sch. Band Dirs. Assn., Phi Kappa Lambda. Avocations: bicycling, jogging, reading, flute performance. Office: Calaveras H S PO Box 607 San Andreas CA 95249 Personal E-mail: jandlart@sbcglobal.net.

BURINI, SONIA MONTES DE OCA, apparel manufacturing and public relations executive; b. Havana, Cuba, Apr. 28, 1935; d. Francisco and Nilda (Diaz) Montes de Oca; m. Franco Burini, Apr. 5, 1959. Student, U. Havana, 1954-57, Georgetown U., 1958; BA in History cum laude, U. Miami, Coral Gables, Fla., 1971. Adminstr. Roma Fashions, Inc. D/B/A Franco B., Coral Gables, 1976-95; entrepreneur, pub. rels. exec., 1995—. Founder Nat. Parkinson Found., 1986—, v.p. Vizcayans Fund Raising Orgn., 1990—, chmn. fine arts events, 1993-95; co-chmn. 1st annual fund raising event Am. Cancer Soc. Winn-Dixie Hope Lodge Ctr.; mem. women with heart group Heart Assn. Greater Miami, Fla., 1981—; founder, bd. dirs. Cancer Link program U. Miami Comprehensive Cancer Ctr., 1987; chmn. spring fantasy luncheon Am. Cancer Soc., 1988; founding chmn. Rose Group, Am. Lung Assn., chmn. Rose Ball, 1989; amb. Mercy Hosp. Found., 1987-95; bd. dirs. Newborn program U. Miami, 1978, bd. dirs., 1982-87, amb. category years; vol. guide Viscaya Mus., Dade County, Fla., 1972-79, chmn. various coms., 1979—, found. bd. dirs., steering com., mem. com. of 100; bd. dir., Young Patroness of the Opera, 1979-87; grand patron Greater Miami Opera, 1986-95, bd. dirs., 1978—, chmn. opera gala, 1987, mem. opera guild, 1988; founding bd. mem. Ears Dears U. Miami, 1986—, chmn. 1990 gala; mem. Dade County Performing Art Ctr. Trust, 1993—; spl. chmn. fine arts events Vizcayans, 1993—; mem. sister cities com. Cities of Miami, Fla. and Nice, France, 1994—, Nat. Trust Hist. Preservation, 1997—. Named Oustanding Woman of Yr. Mayor of Dade County, 1986, Woman of Yr. Heart Assn. Greater Miami, 1986, named to Miss Charity Biscayne Bay Marriott Hotel and Marina, 1987, One of the Leading Ladies for the March of Dimes, 1998. Mem. Nat. Trust Historic Preservation, Ballet Soc. Miami (bd. dirs. 1979-80, named one of Miami's Oustanding Women 1986), Confrerie de la Chaine des Rotisseurs, NAFE, Nat. Found. Peace (bd. adv. 2001—), Opera Guild Fla. Grand Opera (bd. dirs. 2003—). Home: 5401 Collins Ave Apt 1016 Miami Beach FL 33140 Office: Roma Fashions Inc 3311 Ponce De Leon Blvd Coral Gables FL 33134-7210 also: Corregidor Aguirre 21 Las Palmas de Canaria Spain also: Burini Enterprises, Inc PO Box 347558 Coral Gables FL 33234-7374

BURKE, ANN THERESE, social worker, educator; b. Wilkes-Barre, Pa., Sept. 30, 1929; d. William Francis Burke and Anna Regina Forestal. BA in Sociology, Temple U., 1969; MSW, Rutgers U., 1972. LCSW. Mgr. art prodn. program The Grail, Cin., 1958—61, cmty. organizer, instr. Phila., 1962—70, program developer, adminstr. Cornwall-on-Hudson, NY, 1976—; cmty. organizer Lighthouse Settlement, Phila., 1972—76. Rschr. Grail-CETA Govt. Project, Cornwall-on-Hudson, 1977—78; mem. internat. presidency team Internat. Grail, Mulheim, Germany, 1980—88; social worker Cmty. Ctr. Newburgh (N.Y.) Ministry, 1989—94, bd. dirs., 1995—; rep. UN The Grail, N.Y.C., 1999—. Roman Catholic. Avocations: reading, gardening, cooking. Home: 90 Grand St Apt 8G Newburgh NY 12550 Office: The Grail PO Box 475 119 Duncan Ave Cornwall On Hudson NY 12520 Personal E-mail: atburke1@juno.com.

BURKE, BEVERLY J. lawyer, energy executive; BA, Brown U.; JD, George Washington U. Atty. D.C. Govt.; with Office Gen. Counsel Washington Gas & Light Co., 1992-96, dept. head, 1996-98, v.p., asst. gen. counsel, 1998—. Office: Washington Gas and Light Co 1100 H St NW Washington DC 20080-0002

BURKE, KAREN KEITH, county official; b. Picayune, Miss., July 15, 1966; d. Charles Herbert Keith and Janice (Carroll) Goss; m. Barry Gene Burke, Mar. 28, 1992. BFA in Graphic Design, Miss. U. for Women, 1988. Acct. exec., graphic designer Huff Advt.and Promotions, Meridian, Miss., 1988-94; pub. mgr., media liaison Cobb County Govt. Comm. Office, Marietta, Ga., 1994-2000; mktg. mgr. Homestead Village, Atlanta, 2000—. V.p. TipMasters, Meridian, 1990—94, Women in Comm., 1995—96, newsletter coord., 1995—96. Creative dir.: Cobb County Ann. Report, 1995. Active Seatbelt Safety Task Force, Marietta, 1996—; mentor Visions Youth Leadership, Meridian, 1993—94; mktg. com. United Way Cobb County, Marietta, 1996—2000; bd. dirs. Jr. Miss program, Meridian, 1989—94, Safe Path Child Advocacy Ctr., Marietta, 1996—2000. Named one of Outstanding Young Women of Am., 1991; recipient award of Excellence, Printing Industry Assn. of South, 1990, Merit award, Internat. Assn. Bus. Communicators, 1992, 1994, Silver Quill award, 1996, Golden Flame award, 1997, Silver Flame award, 1997. Mem.: Pub. Rels. Soc. Am. (pub. rels. com. Atlanta chpt.), Internat. Assn. Bus. Communicators, Women in Comms., Inc., Jaycees (bd. dirs. Greater Meridian chpt. 1989—94, bd. dirs. Miss. chpt. 1990—93). Republican. Presbyterian. Office: Homestead Village 2100 Riveredge Pkwy NW Fl 9 Atlanta GA 30328-4693

BURKE, KATHLEEN B. B. lawyer; b. Bklyn., Sept. 2, 1948; BA, St. John's U., 1969, JD, 1973. Bar: Ohio 1973. Ptnr. Jones, Day, Reavis & Pogue, Cleve. Chair Notre Dame Coll. of Ohio, 2002—. Pres. Cleve. Skating Club, 2000-2002. Named one of 29 Most Influential Women in Bus., Cleve. mag., 1997. Fellow Ohio State Bar Found. (pres. 2000); mem. Ohio State Bar Assn. (pres. 1993-94). Office: Jones Day Reavis & Pogue North Point 901 Lakeside Ave E Cleveland OH 44114-1190

BURKE, KATHLEEN J. foundation administrator; Exec. v.p., pers. rels. officer BankAmerica Corp., San Francisco, now vice chmn., pers. rel. officer; exec. dir. Stupski Family Found., Mill Valley, Calif., 2000—. Office: # 110 2 Belvedere Dr Mill Valley CA 94941-2418 E-mail: kathleen@stupski.com.

BURKE, KATHLEEN J. music director, writer; b. Detroit, Mich. d. Arthur Reginald and Lois Genevieve Brooks; married, Apr. 17, 1982; children: Sean Patrick, Conor Timothy. A in History, Butte Jr. Coll., Calif., 1975; BS in History, Calif. State U., Fullerton, 1977. Pub. rels. sports Burke Sports Mktg., Eugene, Oreg., 1977—79, Burke Comms., Irvine, Calif., 1983—90, pub. rels. gen. Mission Viejo, Calif., 1991—98, pub. rels. music, 1999—2002, Parodudes Inc., Pitts., 1999—2002, mgr. booking, 2001—02. Author, editor: PSA for Project Independence, 1988 (2d pl., Calif. Press Women, 1988). Vol. Rep. Party, Calif., 1991—92; vol. meals ministry S.V.C.C., Calif., 1991—2002, vol. christian missions, 2000—. Mem.: Recording Acad., Women in Comms., Nat. Mus. of Women in Arts, Nat. Assn. Rock Radio, Gospel Music Assn. Avocations: distance running, biking, hiking, triathlons. Office: Burke Comms 24161 Saiero Ln Mission Viejo CA 92691-4131 E-mail: music4filmbiz@cox.net.

BURKE, MARGARET ANN, computer and communications company specialist; b. N.Y.C., Feb. 25, 1961; d. David Joseph and Eileen Theresa (Falvey) B. BS in Computer Sci., St. John's U., Jamaica, N.Y., 1982; MBA, U. Md., 1994. Cert. data processor. Software specialist Bell Atlantic Corp., Washington, 1983—. Active Friends of Hillwood Mus., Washington. Mem. NAFE, Alliance Francaise, Nat. Fedn. Rep. Women, Am. Film Inst. Roman Catholic. Home: 6652 Hillandale Rd Unit A Bethesda MD 20815-6406 Office: Bell Atlantic 13100 Columbia Pike Silver Spring MD [illegible]

BURKE, MARIANNE KING, state agency administrator, financial executive, consultant; b. Douglasville, Ga., May 30, 1938; d. William Horace and Evora (Morris) King; divorced; 1 child, Kelly Page. Student, Ga. Inst. Tech., 1956-59, Anchorage C.C., 1964-66, Portland State U., 1968-69; BBA, U. Alaska, 1976. CPA, Alaska. Sr. audit mgr. Price Waterhouse, 1982-90; v.p. fin., asst. sec. NANA Regional Corp., Inc., Anchorage, 1990-95; v.p. fin. NANA Devel. Corp., Inc., Anchorage, 1990-95; sec.-treas. Vanguard Industries, J.V., Anchorage, 1990-95, Alaska United Drilling, Inc., Anchorage, 1990-95; treas. NANA/Marriott Joint Venture, Anchorage, 1990-95; v.p. fin. Arctic Utilities, Inc., Anchorage, 1990-95, Tour Arctic, Inc., Anchorage, 1990-95, Purcell Svcs., Ltd., Anchorage, 1990-95, Arctic Caribou Inn, Anchorage, 1990-95, NANA Oilfield Svcs., Inc., Anchorage, 1990-95, NANA Corp. Svcs., Inc., Anchorage, 1992-95; dir. divsn. ins. State of Alaska, 1995-99; pres. Marianne K. Burke Cons., 1999—. Cons. to Ins. Regulatory and Deve. Authority of India, 2002—; mem. State of Alaska Medicaid Rate Commn., 1985—88, State of Alaska Bd. Accountancy, 1984—87; cons. Bosnia and Herzegovina ins. sector Fin. Svcs. Vol. Corps, 2003; bd. dirs. Nat. Assn. Ins. Commrs. Edn. and Rsch. Found.; cons. internat. ins. domicile; chair Bd. Equalization Municipality of Anchorage, 2004—. Bd. dirs. Alaska Treatment Ctr., Anchorage, 1978, Alaska Hwy. Cruises; treas. Alaska Feminist Credit Union, Anchorage, 1979-80; mem. fund raising com. Anchorage Symphony, 1981. Mem. AICPA, Internat. Assn. Ins. Suprs. (funded mem.), Alaska Soc. CPAs, Govtl. Fin. Officers U.S. and Can., Fin. Execs. Inst. (bd. dirs.), Nat. Assn. Ins. Commrs. (bd. dirs.). Avocations: travel, reading. Home: 3818 Helvetia Dr Anchorage AK 99508-5016 Office Phone: 907-563-9790. Personal E-mail: mkburke@gci.net.

BURKE, MARJORIE TISDALE, retired special education educator; b. Chase City, Va., May 27, 1926; d. Henry and Sallie Keene; m. Willie Tisdale, 1948; children: Michael S., Carita F., Lydia R.; m. William C. Vaughn, 1966 (div. 1976); m. Faxie Burke, May 22, 1993. BS, Va. State Coll., 1956. Tchr. elem. edn. Newark (N.J.) Bd. Edn., 1951-53, tchr. spl. edn., 1954-64, Elizabeth (N.J.) Bd. Edn., 1964—92, Fauquier Bd. Edn., Warrenton, Va., 1992—; tutor, subs. tchr. Va.; ret., 1992. Cmty. parent advocate in spl. edn.; Mary Kay beauty cons., 1973—. Mem. Mt. Pleasant Bapt. Ch., Gainesville, Va., also choir mem., usher, sec., v.p. women's aux., pres. scholarship fund, asst. supt. Sunday sch., chairperson of greeters. Mem. AAUW, AARP, NAACP (chmn. edn. com. Prince William County 1994—), Nat. Coun. Negro Women (sr. caretaker), Garden Club Va., Nat. Congress Black Women, Inc. (Prince William chpt.), Housekeepers Club of Aldie (v.p.). Avocations: yoga, poetry, singing, volunteer work at hospital and church. Home: PO Box 3 Gainesville VA 20156-0003

BURKE, MICHELLE C. lawyer; b. Cleve., Oct. 2, 1952; d. Andrew L. and Catherine L. (Sedlak) Matlak; m. Michael E. Burke, Dec. 29, 1971. BA with honors, Lake Forest Coll., 1980; JD cum laude, Harvard, 1983. Bar: Ill., 1983; U.S. Dist. Ct. (no. dist.) Ill., 1984; U.S. Ct. Appeals (3rd. cir.), 1994. Assoc. Sidley & Austin, Chgo., 1983-86, McDermott, Will & Emery, Chgo., 1986-88, ptnr., 1989—. Mem. Phi Beta Kappa. Office: McDermott Will & Emery 227 W Monroe St Ste 3100 Chicago IL 60606-5096

BURKE, NANCY, psychologist, educator; b. Chgo., Feb. 13, 1957; d. Maurice Oscar and Elaine (Abelson) B. BA, Carleton Coll., 1979; MA, U. Chgo., 1984, PhD, 1990. Lic. clin. psychologist, Ill. Clin. psychologist in pvt. practice, Evanston, Ill., 1992; mem. med. staff Northwestern Meml. Hosp., Chgo., 1992; asst. prof. psychology Northwestern U. Sch. Medicine, Chgo., 1993—. Editor: Gender and Envy, 1998. Contbr. articles to profl. jours. Mem. APA, Chgo. Assn. for Psychoanalytic Psychology (coun. mem. 1994-96), MLA. Office: 222 E Erie St Ste 608 Chicago IL 60611

BURKE, SHEILA P. federal administrator; b. San Francisco, Jan. 10, 1951; d. George Abbott and Mary Joan (Winfield) B.; m. David Chew, Jan. 1983; children: Daniel, Kathleen, Sarah. BSN, U. San Francisco, 1973; MA in Pub. Adminstrn., Harvard U., 1982. Staff nurse Alta Bates Hosp., Berkeley, Calif., 1973-74; dir. student affairs Nat. Student Nurses Assn., NY, 1974-75, dir. program and field svcs., 1975-77; legis. asst. Senator Bob

Dole, 1977-78; profl. staff mem. Senate Com. Fin., U.S. Senate, 1979-82, dep. staff dir., 1982-85; dep. chief of staff Senate Majority Leader Bob Dole, U.S. Senate, 1985-86; chief of staff Senator Bob Dole, 1986-96; sec. U.S. Senate, Washington, 1995; undersec. Am. Mus. and nat. programs Smithsonian Instn., Washington, 2000—03, dep. sec., COO, 2004—. Adj. nursing faculty Georgetown U.; rsch. asst. J.F. Kennedy Sch. Govt. Harvard U. 1980-81, advisor to dean, 1996, exec. dean, lectr. pub. policy, 1996-2000, adj. lectr., 2000—. Republican. Address: 1323 Merrie Ridge Rd Mc Lean VA 22101-1826

BURKE, SUZANNE MAUREEN, art historian, dean; b. Commerce, Tex. d. John Emmett and Evelyn (Perkins) B. BA, Miss. U. for Women, 1977; MA, NYU, 1980, PhD, 1994; cert., Harvard Mgmt. Devel. Program, 1997. Cert. in mus. studies Met. Mus. Art and NYU, 1982. Ind. scholar, Rome, London, N.Y.C., 1983-92; from prof. to dean Savannah (Ga.) Coll. of Art and Design, 1992—98, dean academic initiatives, 1998—, founding dir., chief curator Newton Ctr. Brit.-Am. Studies, 2001—. Active confs. in field. Regional coord. Ga. Save Outdoor Sculpture, Savannah; adv. com. Nat. Trust Hist. Preservation Renaissance Soc. Am., Medieval Acad. Am., Internat. Ctr. Medieval Art. Fellow NEH, N.Y., 1978-81; Fulbright scholar Fulbright Commn., Rome, Florence, 1982-83. Mem. AAUW, Am. Assn. Mus., Coll. Art Assn., Phi Kappa Phi. Office: Kiah Hall PO Box 3146 Savannah GA 31402-3146

BURKE, TONI SCOTTO, primary school educator; b. Pensacola, Fla., May 18, 1954; d. Anthony Pasquel and Janet Alberta (Treadway-Stoddard) Scotto; m. John Michael Burke; children: Laurie, Patrick, Zachary. BS in Home Econs. Edn., Miss. U. for Women, 1975. Cert. tchr. with kindergarten endorsement Tex. Welfare worker Orleans Office of Family Svcs., New Orleans, 1976—77; adoption worker Orleans Regional Office, 1977—78; pre-sch. tchr., dir. My Tree House, Lindenhurst, Ill., 1983—88; teller 1st of Am. Bank, Libertyville, Ill., 1988—89; asst. tchr. Pope Elem., Arlington, Tex., 1995—96; kindergarten tchr. St. Maria Goretti Sch., Arlington, 1996—. Substitute tchr. E. Jefferson High Sch., New Orleans, 1975-76. Sec. Prince of Peace Parish Sch. Bd., Lake Villa, Ill., 1985-88; advisor Prince of Peace Youth Group, Lake Villa, 1980-88; adv. com. care and guidance children Lake County Area Vocat. Ctr., Coll. Lake County; sec. St. Joseph Parish Coun., 1990-91. Named Tchr. of Yr., Diocese of Ft. Worth, 1999—2000. Mem. Chgo. Assn. for the Edn. Young Children, Am. Assn. Univ. Women. Roman Catholic. Avocation: cake decorating. Home: 2903 Lucern Ct Arlington TX 76012 Office: St Maria Goretti Cath Sch 1200 S Davis Dr Arlington TX 76013 E-mail: toni_burke@hotmail.com.

BURKE, YVONNE WATSON BRATHWAITE (MRS. WILLIAM A. BURKE), lawyer; b. L.A., Oct. 5, 1932; d. James A. and Lola (Moore) Watson; m. William A. Burke, June 14, 1972; 1 child, Autumn Roxanne; 1 stepchild, Christine. AA, U. Calif., 1951; BA, UCLA, 1953; JD, U. So. Calif., 1956. Bar: Calif. 1956. Mem. Calif. Assembly, 1966-72, chmn. urban devel. and housing com., 1971, 72; mem. 93d-95th Congresses, 1973—79, House Appropriations Com.; chmn. Congl. Black Caucus, 1976; Los Angeles county supervisor 4th dist., ptnr. Jones, Day, Reavis & Pogue, L.A., 1979—80. Dep. corp. commr., hearing officer Police Commn., 1964-66; atty., staff McCone Commn. (investigation Watts riot), 1965; past chmn. L.A. Fed. Res. Bank; U.S. adv. bd. Nestle. Vice chmn. 1984 U.S. Olympics Organizing Com.; bd. dirs. or bd. advisers numerous orgns.; former regent U. Calif., Bd. Ednl. Testing Svc.; Amateur Athletic Found.; former bd. dirs. Ford Found., Brookings Inst.; mem. bd. supr's. 2d Dist., L.A. County Bd. of Supr's., 1992—, chair, 1993-94, 97-98, 2002-03; bd. govs. L.A. Met. Transp. Authority. Recipient Profl. Achievement award UCLA, 1974, 84; named one of 200 Future Leaders Time mag., 1974, Alumni of Yr., UCLA, 1996; recipient Achievement awards C.M.E. Chs.; numerous other awards, citations.; fellow Inst. Politics John F. Kennedy Sch. Govt. Harvard, 1971-72; Chubb fellow Yale, 1972 Office: 500 W Temple St Rm 866 Los Angeles CA 90012

BURKE-FANNING, MADELEINE, artist; b. New Orleans, Feb. 12, 1941; d. Henry Raymond Burke Sr. and Ella Mae Falgout-Burke; children: Denise Angele Duizend-Hargis, Michele Renee Duizend-Meyer, Jeanne Monet Duizend-Fillman; m. Joel Cornell Fanning, Mar. 28, 1981. Student, Pensacola (Fla.) Jr. Coll., 1988-96. Coord. New Orleans World Trade Ctr., Pensacola Cultural Ctr.; adj. prof. advanced watercolor Pensacola Jr. Coll.; tchr. nat. and internat. workshops; instr. advanced watercolor City of Pensacola, Vickrey Ctr., Fla. One-woman shows include Michele Dion Gallery, 1994, Soho Gallery, 1994, Wise Choice Gallery, 1996, The Wright Place, 1997, Awakenings, Gulf Breeze, Fla., 1997—98, The Shoppe Gallery, 1998, Pensacola Mus. Art, 1998—2003, Adams Street Gallery, 1998, Ducks Unltd., Pensacola, 1998, Right Angles Gallery, 1999, Kate Holmes-Branton Gallery, 1999—2002, The Art Market, Gulf Breeze, Fla., 2000, Art and Design Soc., Ft. Walton Beach, Fla., 2000, White Cloud Gallery and Gifts, Pensacola, 2000, Sam Houston Racetrack, Houston, 2001, Corner Copia, Orange Beach, Ala., 2000—03, N.W. Fla. Laser and Skincare Inst., Laurie Grizzard Gallery, 2001—, The MANE Event Expressions Gallery, Pensacola, 2001—, Laurie Grizzard Gallery, 2001—03, Kotlarz Gallery, Pensacola, 2002—, Stockamp Gallery, 2002—04, Woodcock Interiors and Gallery, Pensacola, 2003—, Roger Scott Tennis Ctr., 2003—04, exhibited in group shows at Pensacola Jr. Coll., 1988—96, Gnu Zoo, 1995—96, Eastern Shore Mus. Art, Fairhope, Ala., 1994—96, Pensacola Regional Airport, 1996, World Trade Ctr., 1996, Schmidt's Gallery, 1996, Pensacola Cultural Ctr., 1997, Adams Street Gallery, 1998, Artel Gallery, 1999—2003, Vickney Ctr., 1999—2003, Visual Art Ctr. of N.W. Fla., Panama City, 2001, The Avenue, St. Paul's Roman Cath. Ch., Pensacola, Fla., 2001—03, Woodcock Interior and Gallery, 2003, Eseambia County Equestrian Ctr., Pensacola, 2003—04; host (TV show) Art and Healing, 1997, (TV feature) Inside Scope, New Orleans, 1993, (TV show) Art Vision, 1994, Culture Center BLAB TV, 1996; host : (TV show) Everything Old is New Again, Pensacola Heritage Assn., 2002; TV appearance N.W. Fla. Arts Coun. Art Auction, Sanger Theatre, Pensacola, 2001; exhibitions include Sanger Theatre, 2003, Five Flags Stallion Assn. Horse Show, Pensacola, 2003, exhibited in group shows at Woodcock Gallery, 2003; contbr. articles Pensacola Opera League Publication. Art judge Just Say No Program, 1996—97, PTA Reflective Program, 1997—98; art chairwoman Pensacola chpt. Ducks Unltd., 1998; instr. Ctr. Ind. Living, Pensacola, 1998—2000, Vickery Ctr., Pensacola, 2000—03, Pensacola Jr. Coll., 2000—03. Recipient Rockport Pubs. award of distinction for inclusion in Best of Watercolor: Painting Texture, 1997, Collected Best of Watercolor, 2002. Mem.: Artel.Art with an Edge, Bay Cliff Watercolor Soc. (founder), Woodbine Figure Painters, Pensacola Mus. Art, N.W. Fla. Arts Coun., Tallahassee Watercolor Soc., La. Watercolor Soc., Fla. Watercolor Soc., Nat. Mus. Women in Arts, Am. Soc. Portrait Artists. Avocations: gardening, horseback riding, traveling, sailing, photography. Home: Palm Cottage Studio 4160 Rommitch Ln Pensacola FL 32504-4490 Office Phone: 850-434-3598.

BURKEMPER, SARAH B. state agency administrator; m. Ben Burkemper; 2 children. B Econs. and B Econs. and Bus. Adminstrn. Fin. cum laude, M Acctg., Truman State U., 1992; M Internat. Affairs, Washington U., St. Louis, 1997. CPA Mo. Pub. adminstr. Lincoln County, Mo., 1996—, also registered guardian. Active Trinity Luth. Ch.; bd. govs. Truman State U., 2001—. Office: 201 Main St Troy MO 63379

BURKEN, RUTH MARIE, utilities executive; b. Kenosha, Wis., Sept. 25, 1956; d. Richard Stanley and Anne Theresa (Steplyk) Wotjak; m. James H. Burken, Oct. 15, 1988. AAS, Gateway Tech. Inst., 1976; BA, U. Wis., Parkside, 1980; AAS, Coll. of DuPage, 1995. Transp. aide Kenosha Achievement Ctr., 1977; libr. clk. U. Wis.-Parkside, Kenosha, 1978-80, lifeguard, 1980; asst. mgr. K Mart Corp., Troy, Mich., 1980-88, regional office supr., 1988, internal auditor, 1989-92, sr. field auditor, 1992-98; gen. auditor Nicor Gas, Naperville, Ill., 1998-2000, billing splist., 2000—. Mem. Defenders of Wildlife, World Wildlife Fund. Mem.: NAFE, VFW, Am. Gas Assn., U. Wis.-Parkside Alumni Assn., Distributive Edn. Clubs Am. (parliamentarian 1976) Roman Catholic. Office: Nicor Gas 1844 W Ferry Rd Naperville IL 60563-9600 E-mail: rburken@nicor.com.

BURKE-SPENCE, BONNIE, psychologist, social worker, alcohol/drug abuse services professional; b. N.Y.C., Aug. 29, 1949; d. Jack Francis and Amy Lucia Spence; children: Kellie, Tammy, Cindy. MSW, M in Addiction Counseling, SUNY, Stonybrook; PhD, Adelphi U. Soup kitchen mgr. N.Y. Fedn., N.Y.C., social worker street outreach; news reporter This Week Newspaper, N.Y.C.; dental asst. for pvt. dentist N.Y.C.; office mgr. Health Force Home Care, N.Y.C.; with Winthrop Hosp. Nephrology S.W., N.Y.C.; pvt. practice psychotherapist Garden City, NY. Author poetry. Named 3 time Golden Poetry winner. Mem.: NASW. Roman Catholic. Home: 29 Tappanwood Dr Lattingtown NY 11560-1321

BURKET, DARLA EILEEN, music educator; b. Roaring Spring, Pa., June 3, 1947; d. Dean William and Erdene Ellmore Burket. BS in music edn., Geneva Coll., 1965—69; M in music edn., Ind. U. of Pa, 1970—74. Tchr. Cert. Pa. Dept. of Edn., 1972. Music tchr. and choral and band dir. Glendale Sch. Dist., Flinton, Pa., 1969—; girl scout camp dir. Girl Scouts of Am., Johnstown, Pa., 1984—87. Guest dir. for elem. song fest 1997and 2003 Pa. Music Educators Assn., Hamburg, Pa., 1996—. Young careerist Glendale Bus. and Profl. Women's Club, Coalport, Pa., 1973—90. Pa. Governor's Inst. for Arts, Pa, Dept. of Arts and the Humanities, 2002, Pa. Dept. of Arts and the Humanities, 2003. Mem.: Pa. Music Educators Assn. (leadership conf. participant 2001—02). R-Liberal. Lutheran. Avocations: swimming, painting, gardening, travel, sewing. Home: 402 Cherry St Roaring Spring PA 16673 Office: Glendale Sch Dist 1500 Beaver Valley Rd Flinton PA 16640 Personal E-mail: debsolo1@prodigy.net. E-mail: dburket@gsd1.org.

BURKEY, MARCIA B. engineering executive; Degree, Macalester Coll.; M, Columbia U. Various sr. fin. positions SBC Warburg (now UBS Warburg); various exec. fin. positions including regional mgr. Bechtel Enterprises Holdings Inc., San Francisco, 1996-2000, mng. dir., CFO, 2000—. Office: Bechtel Group PO Box 193965 San Francisco CA 94119

BURKHALTER, MYRA SHERAM, company official; b. Ringgold, Ga., Feb. 3, 1945; d. Benjamin Porter and Imogene (Bandy) Sheram; m. Alva Prentice Burkhalter, Dec. 19, 1965. BS, U. Ga., 1966; MEd, Auburn U., 1968; EdD, Fla. State U., 1981. Tchr. Barrow County Sch. Bd., Winder, Ga., 1965-66, Lee County Sch. Bd., Opelika, Ala., 1966-67, vocat. home econs. tchr., 1968-69; teaching asst. Auburn (Ala.) U., 1967-68; prof. interior design Ga. So. U., Statesboro, Ga., 1969-70; ednl. supr. State Fla. Dept. Edn., Tallahassee, 1971-77, chief cons. tchr. cert., 1977-81; adminstr. B.H. Margolis & Co., Houston, 1981-82; mktg. adminstr. petrolite Corp., St. Louis, 1984-89; adminstrv. mgr. Lifescapes, Inc., Atlanta, 1990-92; retired. Active Humane Soc., 1984—. Mem. U. Ga. Alumni Soc., Auburn U. Alumni Assn., Fla. State U. Alumni Soc., Phi Delta Kappa. Avocations: traveling, crafts. Home: 1300 Ten Mile Still Rd Bainbridge GA 39817

BURKHARDT, ANN, occupational therapist, clinical educator; b. Providence, Dec. 21, 1954; d. Kenneth Ralph and Betty Jane (Neale) B. BA in Psychobiology, Wheaton Coll., 1976; MA in Occupl. Therapy, NYU, 1979. Lic. occupl. therapist, N.Y., R.I., Mass. Staff therapist Charlton Meml. Hosp., Fall River, Mass., 1979; staff therapist, sr. therapist Columbia U.-Harlem Hosp., N.Y.C., 1979-84; staff therapist, burn specialist Cornell Med. Ctr.-N.Y. Hosp., N.Y.C., 1984-86; dir. occupl. therapy Greater Harlem Nursing Home, N.Y.C., 1986-87; chief occupl. therapist Meml. Sloan-Kettering Cancer Ctr., N.Y.C., 1987-92; asst. dir. occupl. therapy N.Y. Presbyn. Hosp.-Columbia Presbyn., N.Y.C., 1992-99, 1992—99, dir. occupl. therapy, 1999—; clin. instr. Columbia U., N.Y.C., 1993—, assoc. clin. instr., 1999—; pvt. practice N.Y.C., 1984—; clin. assoc. Mercy Coll., Dobbs Ferry, NY, 1998—. Del. Coll. of Occupl. Therapists, Edinburgh, Scotland, 1995, World Fedn. Occupl. Therapists, London, 1994, Montreal, Can., 1998, Stockholm, 2002; spkr. in field. Author: Occupational Therapy Intervention in Recreational Settings in Acute Care, 1993; co-editor, co-author: Stroke Rehabilitaton: A Function Based Approach, 1997; (pamphlet) Lymphedema: Self-Care and Treatment, 1992; co-author: A Therapists Guide to Oncology, 1996; contbr. articles to profl. jours., chpts. to books; columnist O.T. Week, The Sacred Fire Newsletter. Svc. award Touro Coll., N.Y., 1996. Fellow Am. Occupl. Therapy Assn. (cert., alt. rep. to rep. assembly 1992-94, polit. action com. 1994, dir., bd. dirs. 2002-, Recognition of Achievement award 1997, Svc. award 1997, 99, editor Quarterly adminstrn. and mgmt. spl. interest sect. 2001-2002); mem. Am. Occupl. Therapy Assn., N.Y. State Occupl. Therapy Assn. (alt. rep. 1992-94, pres.-elect. 1994-95, pres. 1995-99, Merit award 1990, Svc. award 1999, news editor 1999-), Metro N.Y. Dist. Occupl. Therapy Assn. (bd. dirs., sec. 1990-96, Abreu award 1998), Am. Congress Rehab. Medicine, N. Am. Soc. Lymphology, Internat. Soc. Lymphology, Am. Phys. Medicine, Am. Soc. Assn. Execs., Am. Med. Writers Assn., Am. Burn Assn., Congress of Rehab. Medicine. Avocations: kyacking, singing, theater going, traveling, writing. Home: 160 E 91st St Apt 4B New York NY 10128-2458 Office: Milstein Hosp Bldg 8 Garden North 407 177 Fort Washington Ave New York NY 10032-3713

BURKHARDT, DOLORES ANN, library consultant; b. July 28, 1932; d. Frederick Christian and Emily (Detels) Burkhardt. BA, U. Conn., 1955; MS, So. Conn. State Coll., 1960; postgrad., Cen. Wash. State Coll., 1962, Columbia, 1964—; 6th yr. diploma, U. Conn., 1972. Asst. librarian So. Conn. State Coll. Libr., summers 1960,62; sch. libr. tchr. Farmington High Sch., Unionville, Conn., 1955-65; libr. cons., media specialist East Farms Sch., Farmington, Conn., 1967-70; sch. libr. coord. K-12 Durham-Middlefield, Conn., 1970-72; media specialist Regional Dist. 10, Burlington-Harwinton, Conn., 1972-78, ednl. media cons., 1978—. Instr. Boston U. Media Inst.; spl. cons. Conn. Dept. Edn., 1965—. Mem.: NEA, AAUW (sec. 1956—58), New Eng. Sch. Devel. Coun., Am. Assn. Sch. Librarians, Conn. Sch. Libr. Assn. (2d v.p. 1965—, chmn. standards com. 1970—72, chmn. sch. libr. devel., chmn., instructional materials selection policy com. Region 10), New Eng. Sch. Libr. Assn. (pres. 1969—70), Conn. Edn. Assn., Phi Delta Kappa. Lutheran. Home and Office: 38 Center St Southington CT 06489-3105 E-mail: daburkhardt@msn.com.

BURKHARDT, MARY SUE D. secondary school educator; b. Frankfort, IN, Aug. 19, 1948; d. Marshall Clifton and Opal Marie Davis; m. Ronald John Burkhardt, June 13, 1970; children: John Thomas, Kristine Marie. BS, Purdue U., 1971, MS, 1974. Cert. Cert. family and consumer scis. Educator Twin Lakes H.S., Monticello, Ind., 1972—. Adj. faculty Ivy Tech State Coll., Lafayette and Logansport, Ind.; lectr. Purdue U., West Lafayette, Ind. Mem.: numerous profl. assns. Home: 1510 E 500 N West Lafayette IN 47906 Office: Twin Lakes High Sch 300 S Third St Monticello IN 47960

BURKHART, ELVIRA (JEAN), language educator, music educator; b. Knoxville, Tenn., Apr. 10, 1961; d. Dan Frances and Maureen Joan Sherrod; m. Jeffrey Alan Burkhart, June 26, 1982; children: Corey Alan, Wesley Adam. BS, U. Tenn., 1981, MA in Curriculum, 1992; Edn. Specialist in Supervision, Adminstrn. and Instrn., Lincoln Meml. U., 2000. English/vocal music tchr. Sevier County H.S., Sevierville, Tenn., 1984—85; travel and tourism prof. Draughon's Jr. Coll., Knoxville, Tenn., 1987—89; English/drama tchr. West H.S., Knoxville, Tenn., 1989—94; vocal/music tchr. Seymour H.S., Tenn., 1994—2003. Mem. leadership com. Cristin Sutphin Vocal-Music Scholarship, Tenn., 1999—; mem. leadership team Seymour H.S., Tenn., 2000—. Mem. Alzheimer's Assn. East Tenn., 1999—. Mem.: Music Educator Nat. Conf., East Tenn. Vocal Assn. (site choir person 2001—02). Avocations: gardening, mission work. Home: 354 Fallen Oak Cir Seymour TN 37865 Office: Seymour HS 732 Boyds Creek Hwy Seymour TN 37865

BURKHART, KATHERINE WEST, music educator, adult education educator; b. Roanoke, Va., Feb. 12, 1944; d. James Lemuel Wills and Kate Bradley West; m. Harold Eugene Burkhart, June 12, 1971; 1 child, Anna Katherine. BA in Music, Mary Baldwin Coll., 1966; MA in Humanities-Liberal Studies, Hollins U., 1976. Cert. basic literacy tchr. Literacy Vols. Am., ESL tchr. Literacy Vols. Am., collegiate tchr. Va. Freelance organist Va. Tech. Meml. Chapel, Blacksburg, 1964—2000, St. Luke's Anglican Ch., Rotorua, New Zealand, 1976—77; elem. sch. music tchr. Montgomery County Schs., Va., 1967—68, 1970—73; elem. music tchr. Virginia Beach (Va.) City Schs., 1968—69; ch. organist Blacksburg Presbyn. Ch., 1973—79, 1984—2000; pvt. piano tchr. Christiansburg/Blacksburg, 1973—84, 1990—; ESL program mgr. Literacy Vols. Am., Christiansburg, 1999—2000; ESL lead tchr. Rowe Furniture Co./Literacy Vols. Am., Elliston, Va., 2002—. Tutor, cons. Literacy Vols. Am., Christiansburg, 1999—. ESL cons., com. chair Task Force on Refugee Resettlement, Blacksburg, 1999. Mem.: Va. Music Tchrs. Assn. (Highlands chpt., pres. 1993—95), Nat. Guild Piano Tchrs., Am. Guild Organists (Highlands chpt., newsletter editor 1984—86, sub-dean 1992—93, Newsletter grant 1984). Presbyterian. Avocations: reading, foreign language films, travel, tutoring. Home: 1481 Mt Tabor Rd Blacksburg VA 24060 Office: Literacy Vols Am New River Valley 195 W Main St Christiansburg VA 24073 Office Phone: 540-951-0605.

BURKHART, SANDRA MARIE, art dealer; b. Cleve., Dec. 29, 1942; d. John Joseph Norris and Audrey Eleanor Kegg McGuire Marshall; m. Thomas Henry Burkhart, Oct. 29, 1960 (div. Sept. 26, 1979); children: Bryan, Brad, Lisa, Michelle. Student, Evergreen Valley Coll., San Jose, 1978-80, San Jose City Coll., 1978-80, West Valley Coll., Saratoga, Calif., 1978-79. Med. technician Eye Med. Clinic, San Jose, 1980-83; ind. corp. art salesperson San Jose, 1983-92; corp. sales dir. Phoenix Gallery, San Jose, 1986-88; v.p. mktg. Whittlers Mother, San Francisco, 1989-90; dir. Martin Lawrence Galleries, Santa Clara, Calif., 1990-97. Avocations: watercolors, crafts, tennis, skiing, horses. Home and Office: 1353 Greenwich Ct San Jose CA 95125-5964

BURKHOLDER, JOANN M. botany educator; BS in Zoology, Iowa State U., 1975; MS in Botany, U. R.I., 1981; PhD in Botany, Mich. State U., 1986. Asst. prof. dept. botany N.C. State U., Raleigh, 1986-91, assoc. prof. dept. botany, 1992—. Apptd. N.C. Marine Fisheries Commn., 1992—, Coastal Futures com., 1993-94; speaker Harvard, AAAS, Nat. Acad. Scis., NATO, Internat. Conf. on Modern and Fossil Dinoflagellates, others. Pew fellow in Conservation and Environment, 1997—; recipient Scientific Freedom and Responsibility award AAAS, 1998, Environ. Guardian award Charlotte Observer, 1996. Mem. Am. Soc. Limnology and Oceanography (chair sessions at annual meetings, bd. dirs. 1994-97), Internat. Soc. Study of Harmful Algae, Estuarine Rsch. Fedn., Phycological Soc. Am. (mem. editl. bd. 1995-97), Soc. Protozoologists, Sigma Xi. Achievements include research emphasizing in nutritional ecology of algae, hetortrophic dinoflagellates, and aquatic angiosperms, especially the effects of cultural eutorphication on both freshwater and estuarine/coastl blooms, and on seagrass disappearance; involved in discovery of a group of mixotrophic dinoflagellates resembling clay particles, which can dominate the plankton of turbid reservoirs, a severe inhibitory impact of water-column nitrite engrichment on Zostera marina, the dominant seagrass habitat species on the Atlantic Coast, a toxic dino-flagellate, Pfiesteri piscicida implicated as a major causative agent fo fish deeath and disease, with potential linkages to serious human health effects as well. Office: NC State U Dept Botany 4214 Gardner Hl Raleigh NC 27695-0001 Fax: (919) 515-3436. E-mail: burkholder@ncsu.edu.

BURKS, CHARLOTTE, state legislator; 3 children. Mem. Tenn. Senate, Nashville, 1999—. Democrat. Office: Tenn Senate 9 Legislative Plz Nashville TN 37243-0216

BURLESON, EMILY JANE, nursing administrator; b. Fayette, Ala., June 12, 1968; d. Paul Wilburn and Dianne Woods; children: Ashley, Alisyn. ADN, SUNY, 1995; BS in Mgmt. Human Resources, Faulkner U., 1999; postgrad., U. Phoenix, 2003. RN Ala., 1995. LPN scrub nurse Fayette (Ala.) Med. Ctr., 1993; clin. coord. and staff devel. coord. Fayette Med. Ctr. Home Care, 1994—2000. Mem.: ANA, Ala. Nurses Assn., Assn. Operating Room Nurses. Avocations: gardening, swimming, walking, water-skiing. Home: 149 2nd Ave SW Vernon AL 35592 Office: Lamar Healthcare Svcs Inc 49494 Hwy 17 South Sulligent AL 35586 Office Phone: 205-698-7111. Business E-Mail: emily@bamacomm.com.

BURLEY, BARBARA A. music educator; b. Ellsworth, Kans., Feb. 29, 1948; d. Victor and Elnora Ochs; m. John M. Burley, June 8, 1969; children: John C., Erin E. BS in Music Edn., U. Ill., Champaign, 1970, MS in Music Edn., 1975. Cert. level III ORFF U. Ill. Music specialist Windham Ex. Village Schs., Windham, Ohio, Champaign Pub. Schs., Cartwright Sch. Dist., Phoenix, Scottsdale Unified Sch. Dist., Madison Sch. Dist., Phoenix; with choral dept. Scottsdale Schs. Address: 10948 Scottsdale AZ 85259

BURMAN, DIANE BERGER, career management and organization development consultant; b. Pitts., Dec. 7, 1936; d. Morris Milton and Dorothy June (Barkin) Berger; m. Sheldon Oscar Burman, Dec. 15, 1926; children: Allison Beth, Jocelyn Holly, Harrison Emory Guy. BA, Vassar Coll., 1958; MA, Middlebury Coll., 1961. Tchr. of French Allderdice High Sch., Pitts., 1960-61, Mamaroneck (N.Y.) High Sch., 1961-64; personnel specialist G.D. Searle & Co., Skokie, Ill., 1972-77, orgn. devel. tng. cons., 1977-78; personnel and orgn. devel. cons. Abbott Labs., North Chgo., 1978-82; orgn. devel. cons., v.p., mgr. career devel. Harris Bank, Chgo., 1982-97; ind. mgmt. cons. in orgn. devel., career devel., 1997—; pres. Dee Burman & Assoc., Highland Park, Ill., 1997—, RetireRight Ctr., 2004—. Mem. edit. bd. Orgn. Devel. Jour., 1987. Bd. advisors Grad. Sch. Bus. No. Ill. U. Mem. ASTD (bd. dirs. Chgo. career devel. profl. practice area 1987—), Internat. Quality Leadership Inst. (sec., bd. dirs. 2000), Orgn. Devel. Network (founder, exec. dir. Chgo. chpt. 1986-89), Assn. Psychol. Type-Nat. Conf., Orgn. Devel. Inst. (adv. bd. 1987-91, chmn. nat. conf. 1990), Nat. Assn. Bank Women, Assn. Career Profls. Internat. (bd. dirs. Chgo. chpt. 1999-2001, co-chair pub. com. 1999), Am. Counseling Assn., Vassar Club (bd. dirs. 1975-80, 95—, chair career assistance com. 1997—, co-sec. 2000-2001, co-chmn. ann. scholarship benefit, 2002). Jewish. Avocations: biking, playing flute, traveling. Home and Office: 247 Prospect Ave Highland Park IL 60035-3357 E-mail: deeburman@aol.com.

BURMAN, SHEILA FLEXER ZOLA, special education educator; b. N.Y.C., May 1, 1935; d. Jack and Edna (Eagle) Flexer; m. Eugene Lee Zola, July 7, 1957 (div. Aug. 1973); children: Leslie Sheldon, Sharon Joanne; m. Milton Burman, Mar. 19, 1978 (dec. Apr. 1999). Student, Hunter Coll., 1952-55; BA in Edn., BS, UCLA, 1957, 85, spl. edn. cert. for learning handicapped, 1985; and severely handicapped; MS in Counseling, U. LaVerne, 1983; resource specialist cert., Calif. Luth. U., 1988. Cert. tchr., spl. edn. tchr., resource specialist, pupil pers. credential. Tchr. L.A. Unified Sch. Dist., 1957-62, tchr. 3rd grade gifted, 1977-81, spl. edn. tchr., 1981-88, mid. sch. resource tchr., 1987—89, elem. resource tchr., 1989—96, spl. edn. coord., 1997—2003. Cert. tchr., spl. edn. tchr., resource specialist, pupil pers. credential. Pres. L.A. chpt. Brandeis U. Nat. Women's Com., 2000-02, western region v.p. membership, 2000-04; buyer hardcover books Helping Hand Gift Shop, Cedar Sinai Hosp., 2003—; bd. dirs. U. Women, U. of Judaism. Grantee CTIP 1988, Computer 1989. Mem. Coun. for Exceptional

Children, Assn. Ednl. Therapists, United Tchrs. L.A., Calif. Tchrs. Assn., UCLA Alumni Assn., UCLA Grad. Sch. Edn. Alumni Assn., Hunter Coll. Alumni Assn., Pi Lambda Theta. Avocations: swimming, reading, needlepoint. Home: 15455 Hamner Dr Los Angeles CA 90077-1802

BURMASTER, ELIZABETH, school system administrator; b. Balt., July 26, 1954; m. John Burmaster; 3 children. B in Music Edn., U. Wis., 1976, M in Ednl. Adminstrn., 1984. Vocal music and creative dramatics dir. Longfellow Elem. and Sennett Middle Sch., Madison, Wis., 1976—78; choral and drama dir. East H.S., Madison, 1978—85; asst. prin. Marquette Middle Sch., Madison, 1985—88; fine arts coord. Madison Sch. Dist., 1988—90; prin. Hawthorne Elem., Madison, 1990—92, Madison West H.S., 1992—2001; state supt. pub. instrn. State of Wis., Madison, 2001—. Mem. Govs. Econ. Growth Coun., Coun. Chief State Sch. Officers, chair task force on early childhood learning, bd. dirs.; chair-elect Nat. Ctr. for Learning and Citizenship. Mem. bd. regents U. Wis.; mem. Edn. Commn. of the States, Wis. Tech. Coll. Sys. Bd., Ednl. Comms. Bd., Very Spl. Arts Wis., Gov.'s Work-Based Learning Bd.; bd. dirs. TEACH Wis. Mem.: Coun. of Chief State Sch. Officers, SAI-Music Assn., Tempo Internat., Assn. Wis. Sch. Adminstrs. Mailing: PO Box 7841 Madison WI 53707-7841*

BURNESS, MAUREEN O'LEARY, school system administrator, consultant; d. Robert and MaryKay O'Leary; m. Robert Canfield Burness, Dec. 21, 1969; children: Jessica O'Leary, Robert Todd O'Leary. BS, U. Calif., Davis, 1971; MS, Calif. State U., Sacramento, 1983. Cert. sch. counselor Calif., sch. psychologist Calif., ednl. adminstr. cert. Calif. Sch. psychologist/program specialist Winters (Calif.) Sch. Dist., 1983—89; dir. student svcs. Roseville (Calif.) City Sch. Dist., 1989—94; alternative edn. adminstr. Placer County Office of Edn., Auburn, Calif., 1994—96; asst. supt. Yolo County Spl. Edn. Local Plan Area, Woodland, Calif., 1996—2000, asst. supt. Placer Nevada Auburn, 2000—. Mem. faculty dept. edn. Calif. State U., Sacramento, 1995—2002; spl. edn. cons., Sacramento, 1997—. Contbr. articles to profl. jours. Named Spl. Edn. Adminstr. of the Yr., Calif. Coun. Exceptional Children. Mem.: Assn. Calif. Sch. Adminstrs. (chair spl. edn./pupil svcs. com. 1996—99, Spl. Edn. Adminstr. of the Yr. 1999), State Spl. Edn. Local Plan Area Adminstrs. (various offices 1998—2003). Avocations: travel, reading. Office: Placer Nevada SELPA 360 Nevada St Auburn CA 95603

BURNETT, BARBARA DIANE, social worker; b. Charleston, W.Va., Aug. 20, 1928; d. LeRoy Sparks and Hallie Catherine (Walker) Montague; m. Clyde Ray Burnett, Sept. 20, 1947 (div. Nov. 1972); children: Beverly O'Reilly, Pamela Van Scotter, Marcia Montague(dec.), Janet Summers, Craig. BS, U. Wis., 1949; MS, Pa. State U., 1963; MSW, Va. Commonwealth U., 1977. LCSW Fla. Spl. edn. tchr. Palm Beach County Sch. Bd., various locations, 1964-75, social worker Project Peace Elizabeth Falk Found., Boca Raton, Fla., 1977-78; social worker Cmty. Home Health, Boynton Beach, Fla., 1978-90, Hospice Care Broward Inc., Ft. Lauderdale, Fla., 1986-91; pvt. practice supr. MSW profls. Broward County, Fla., 1991—. Field instr. sch. social work Barry U., 1986—91, Fla. Internat. U., 1986—91, Fla. Atlantic U., 1986—91, Nova U., 1986—91. Active Dem. Party, Broward County, 1977—, crucible jr. hon., U. Wisc., 1948, mortar bd. sr. hon., 1949. Named Fla. Renal Social Worker of the Yr., Nat. Kidney Found., Tampa, 1998. Mem.: LWV, Common Cause, Nat. Kidney Found. (coun. nephrology social workers), Am. Assn. Kidney Patients (bd. mem.), Omicron Nu, Phi Lambda Theta. Democrat. Episcopalian. Avocations: reading, walking, swimming, attending grandchildrens special events traveling. Home: 104 SE 10th St Apt G101 Deerfield Beach FL 33441-5352 Office: Fresenius Med Care Plantation Artificial Kidney Ctr 849 Nob Hill Rd Plantation FL 33324

BURNETT, CAROL, actress, comedienne, singer; b. San Antonio, Apr. 26, 1933; d. Jody and Louise (Creighton) B.; m. Joseph Hamilton, 1963 (div.); children: Carrie Louise, Jody Ann, Erin Kate; m. Brian Miller, 2001. Student, UCLA, 1952-54. Introduced comedy song I Made a Fool of Myself Over John Foster Dulles, 1957; Broadway debut in Once Upon a Mattress, 1959; regular performer in Garry Moore TV show, 1959-62; appeared several CBS-TV spls., 1962-63; star Carol Burnett Show, CBS-TV, 1966-77, Carol & Co., 1990-91; appeared on Broadway, Once Upon a Mattress, 1960, Plaza Suite, 1970, I Do, I Do, (musical) 1973, Same Time Next Year, 1977, Moon Over Buffalo, 1995 (Tony nomination), co-wrote play (with Carrie Hamilton), Hollywood Arms, 2001; films include Who's Been Sleeping in My Bed, 1963, Pete 'n' Tillie, 1972, Front Page, 1974, A Wedding, 1977, Health, 1979, Four Seasons, 1981, Chu Chu and the Philly Flash, 1981, Annie, 1982, Noises Off, 1992, Moon Over Broadway, 1997, Get Bruce, 1999, The Trumpet of the Swan (voice), 2001; TV movies Friendly Fire, 1978, The Grass is Always Greener Over the Septic Tank, 1979, The Tenth Month, 1979, Life of the Party, 1982, Between Friends, 1983, Hostage, 1988, Men, Movies, and Carol, 1994, Seasons of the Heart, 1994, The Marriage Fool, 1998 (American Comedy award, 1998), Grace, 1998; club engagements, Harrah's Club, The Sands, Caesar's Palace, MGM Grand; TV specials Julie and Carol: Together Again, 1989, Happy Birthday Elizabeth: A Celebration of Life, 1997, Putting it Together, 2000, Carol Burnett: Show Stoppers, 2001; TV series Mad About You, 1996-1998; TV miniseries Fresno, 1986, A Century of Women, 1994; dir., writer The Universal Story, 1995, also prodr. Southern Star: Portrait of Atlanta, 1996; prodr. Fred Astaire: Puttin' On His Top Hat, 1980, Fred Astaire: Change Partners and Dance, 1980, Bacall on Bogart, 1988, Fred Astaire Songbook, 1991, Southern Star: A Portrait of Atlanta, 1996, others. Recipient outstanding comedienne award Am. Guild Variety Artists, 5 times; Emmy award for outstanding variety performance Acad. TV Arts and Scis., 5 times; Emmy award for best supporting actress in a comedy series for Mad About You, 1997; TV Guide award for outstanding female performer, 1961, 62, 63; Peabody award, 1963; Golden Globe award for outstanding comedienne of year Fgn. Press Assn., 8 times; Woman of Year award Acad. TV Arts and Scis.; 12 People's Choice awards ; 1st ann. Nat. TV Critics Circle award for outstanding performance, 1977; San Sebastian Film Festival award for best actress for A Wedding, 1978; 1st Ace award Best Actress Between Friends, 1983, Horatio Alger award Horatio Alger Assn. Disting. Ams., 1988; named One of 20 Most Admired Women Gallup Poll, 1977. Address: ICM 8942 Wilshire Blvd Fl 2 Beverly Hills CA 90211-1934*

BURNETT, DARLA MICHELE RUTHERFORD, psychologist, educator; b. Baton Rouge, Apr. 8, 1972; d. Michael Roy and Carolyn Elaine (Reeves) Rutherford; m. William Todd Burnett, Sept. 25, 1999. BS, La. State U., 1994; MA, U. So. Miss., 1996, PhD, 1999; MSCP, Calif. Sch. Profl. Psychology, 2002. Lic. clin. psychologist La. Psychologist I Jetson Correctional Ctr. for Youth, Baton Rouge, 1999—2000; psychologist IV forensic divsn. East La. Mental Health Sys., Jackson, 2000—; clin. psychologist Zachary (La.) Psychology Ctr., 2000—. Clin. asst. prof. Tulane U., New Orleans, 2003. Contbr. articles to profl. jours. Mem.: APA, La. Acad. Med. Psychologists (sec. 2002—), La. Psychol. Assn. (fed. advocacy coord. 2002—). Avocations: sports, cooking, travel, photography, reading. Home: 9966 W Summerfield Dr Denham Springs LA 70726 Office: ELMHS Forensic Divsn PO Box 498 Jackson LA 70748

BURNETT, ELIZABETH (BETSY BURNETT), counselor; b. Ohio; m. Gilbert C. Burnett, Jan. 2, 1973; children: Jeffrey, Stephanie. BS in Med. Tech. with honors, Rutgers U., 1976; MA in Counseling with honors, Denver Sem., 1992. Lic. prof. counselor, Colo.; nat. cert. counselor; master addictions counselor. Med. technologist various hosps., Denver and Plainfield, N.J., 1976-92; missions dir. Bear Creek Ch. and Family of Faith Ch., Denver, 1985-89; dir. Providence Counseling Ministry and Providence Homes, Denver, 1989-99; ind. counselor, psychology instr. C.C. Aurora, 1999—. Program cons. various urban counseling svcs. and rehabs., Denver, Colorado Springs, Mich., Calif., Australia, 1992—; urban ministry cons. Denver Sem., 1991-99; contract counselor So. Gables Ch., Littleton, Colo., 1992-96, presenter divorce recovery workshops, 1992-96; ministry ptnr. Mosaic Ch., 2002-2003; spkr. in field. Author: Handbook of Urban Christian Counseling, 1992. Children's dir. mothers of preschoolers, vacation Bible sch., and missions edn. program Bear Creek Ch., Denver, 1982-85; deaconess, lay leader So. Gables Ch., Littleton, 1992-96. Recipient med. tech. award Muhlenberg Hosp., 1976. Mem. Am. Assn. Christian Counselors, Am. Soc. Clin. Pathologists. Avocations: reading, needlework, painting, hiking. Office: 7475 W 5th Ave Lakewood CO 80226

BURNETT, IRIS JACOBSON, corporate communications specialist; b. Bklyn., Nov. 14, 1946; d. Milton and Rose (Dubroff) Groman; m. Allan Jacobson; 1 child, Seth Jacobson; m. David Burnett, Jan. 29, 1984; 1 child, Jordan Burnett. BS, Emerson Coll., 1968, MS in Commn. Theory, 1971. Instr. Boston U., 1971-73; dir. press and pub. rels. Dept. Parks and Recreation, Boston, 1975-77; dir. internat. visitors U.S. Dept. State, Washington, 1977-80; dir. security Dem. Nat. Conv., N.Y.C., 1980; sr. v.p. Arrive Unltd., Washington, 1980-84; pres. In Advance, Arlington, 1984-87; asst. prof. Am. U., Washington, 1987-90; pres. Sound Remarks, Arlington, 1990-92; exec. dir. Debates '92, Washington, 1992; chief staff USIA, Washington, 1993-96; sr. v.p. for corp. comm. USA Network, N.Y.C., 1997-99; prof. Am. U. Sch. Comm., 1999—. Co-founder, co-chair, pres. Count Mein for Women's Econ. Ind., 2002; pres. Kai Prodns. Author: Hart for Pres., 1984, Nat. Surrogate Schedule, 1984, Inauguration, Transition: Clinton Gore Campaign, 1992, (novels) Schlepper! A Mostly True Tale of Presidential Politics, 2004. Active McGovern presdl. campaign, Boston, 1972; mem. nat. staff Udall for Pres., Washington, 1974-76, Carter-Mondale '76, 1976-77; bd. dirs. Tap Am. Project, 1994—; official del. 4th World Conf. on Women; bd. gov.'s USO.; founder Broad Confidence in Chair Women; bd. dirs. Erase the Hate Found. Named Presdl. appt. to Bd. Govs. USO. Mem. Women's Fgn. Policy Group, Emily's List, Nat. Jewish Dem. Coalition.

BURNETT, JEAN BULLARD (MRS. JAMES R. BURNETT), biochemist; b. Flint, Mich., Feb. 19, 1924; d. Chester M. and Katheryn (Krasser) Bullard; B.S., Mich. State U., 1944, M.S., 1945, Ph.D. (Council fellow), 1952; m. James R. Burnett, June 8, 1947. Research assoc. dept. zoology Mich. State U., East Lansing, 1954-59, dept. biochemistry, 1959-61, acting dir. research biochem. genetics, dept. biochemistry, 1961-62, assoc. prof., asst. chmn. dept. biomechanics, 1973-82, prof. dept. anatomy, 1982-84, prof. dept. zoology, Coll. Natural Sci. and Coll. Osteo. Medicine, 1984— ; assoc. biochemist Mass. Gen. Hosp., Boston, 1964-73; prin. research assoc. dermatology Harvard, 1962-73, faculty medicine, 1964-73, also spl. lectr., cons., tutor Med. Sch.; vis. prof. dept. biology U. Ariz., 1979-80. USPHS, NIH grantee, 1965-68; Gen. Research Support grantee Mass. Gen. Hosp., 1968-72; Ford Found. travel grantee, 1973; Am. Cancer Soc. grantee, 1971-73; Internat. Pigment Cell Conf. travel grantee, 1980; recipient Med. Found. award, 1970. Mem. AAAS, Am. Chem. Soc., Am. Inst. Biol. Sci., Genetics Soc. Am., Soc. Investigative Dermatology, N.Y. Acad. Scis., Sigma Xi (Research award 1971), Pi Kappa Delta, Kappa Delta Pi, Pi Mu Epsilon, Sigma Delta Epsilon. Home: PO Box 805 Okemos MI 48805-0805 Office: Mich State Univ Dept Zoology Natural Sci Bldg East Lansing MI 48824

BURNETT, PATRICIA HILL, portrait artist, author, sculptor, lecturer; b. Bklyn. d. William Burr and Mimi (Uline) Hill; m. William Anding Lange, 1944 (div. 1947); 1 child, William Hill; m. Harry Albert Burnett III,, Oct. 9, 1948 (div. 1970); children: Harry Burnett III, Terrill Hill, Hillary Hill; m. Robert L. Siler, 1989. Student, U. Toledo, 1937-38, Goucher Coll., 1939-41, MA program Inst. D'Allende, Mex., 1967, Wayne State U., 1972; pvt. studies with, John Carroll, Detroit, 1941-44, Sarkis Sarkisian, 1956-60, Wallace Bassford, Provincetown, Mass., 1968-72, Walter Midener, Detroit, 1960-63. Actress Long Ranger and Green Hornet prgrams, Radio Blue Network, 1941-46; tchr. painting and sculpture U. Mich. Extension, Ann Arbor, 1965—. Lectr. N.Y. Speakers Bur., 1971—; propr. Burnett Studios, Detroit, 1962-88, mgr., 1962—; appt. to Mich. Quarter Commn. by gov. Engler, 2002. Numerous one-woman shows of paintings and sculptures include Scarab Club, Detroit, 1971, Midland (Mich.) Art Ctr., Wayne State U., Detroit, The Gallery, Ft. Lauderdale, Fla., Agra Gallery, Washington, Salon des Artes, Paris; numerous group shows include: Palazzo Pruili Gallery, Venice, 1971, Detroit Inst. of Arts, 1967, Butler Mus., Cleveland, 1972, Windsor (Ont., Can.) Art Ctr., 1973, Weisbaden (Germany) Gallery, 1976, Retrospective Show: Birmingham Bloomfield Art Assn., 1997; represented in permanent collections: Detroit Inst. Arts, Wayne State U., Wooster (Ohio) Coll., Ford Motor Co., Detroit, Bloomfield Art Assn., Bloomfield Hills, Mich., Henry Ford Hosp. Collection, Fed. Ct. Appeals in Washington, City-County Bldg., Detroit, Mich. State Capitol Bldg., Royal Acad. of Art, London, Moscow Mus., Moscow, Russia, Mich. State Capital, Lansing. Mich., Royal Palace of India, New Delhi, Palace of The Philippines, Manila, Mansion of Prime Minister, Greece; also pvt. collections: numerous portrait paintings including Indira Ghandi, Benson Ford, Joyce Carol Oates, Mrs. Edsel Ford, Betty Ford, Mayor Roman Gribbs, Princess Olga Mrivani, Lord John Mackintosh, Marlo Thomas, Viveca Lindfois, Betty Freidan, Gloria Steinem, Congresswoman Martha Griffiths, Margaret Papandreou, Valentina Tereshkova, Barbara Walters, Margaret Thatcher, Corazon Aquino, Violetta Chamarra, Jackie Joyner Kersee, Mayor Dennis Archer, Wayne U. pres. David Adamany, author Kate Millett, Michele Engler and triplets, Patricia Ireland, Rosa Parks, others; mem. editl. bd. Am. Portrait Soc.; author: True Colors: An Artist's Journey from Beauty Queen to Feminist. Chairwoman of Mich. Women's Commn., 1972—; pres. Detroit House of Correction Commn., 1975—; treas. Rep. Dist. 1 of Mich., 1973—; mem. Issues com., Rep. State Ctrl. Com., 1975-76; sec. Rep. State Ways and Means com., 1975—, Detroit Libr. Commn., 1980-85, Detroit Human Rights Comn., 1976-80, Detroit City Planning Commn., 1985-90; mem. Mich. State Adv. Coun. vocat. Edn.; mem. Mich. Arts in Edn. Coun., 1978—; mem. New Detroit Arts Com., 1979—; chmn. World Feminist Commn., 1974—; life mem. NAACP. Recipient Silver Salute award Mich. State U., 1976, Most Popular award San Diego Sculpture Show, 1971, First prize award Cape Cod Artists Show, 1968, State of Mich. award for creativity Gov. John Engler, 1999, Life Accomplishment award Mich. Women's Found., 2001; named Disting. Woman of Mich., Bus. and Profl. Women's Orgn., 1974, Disting. Woman Northwood Inst., 1977, Artist of Yr., Mich. Art Train, 1989, Disting. Woman award Mich. Bus. and Profl. Women Internat.; named to Ohio Hall of Fame, 1987, Mich. Women's Hall of Fame, 1988, one of Most Outstanding Women in Mich., Women in Advt., 1998, one of 10 People with Most Clout Outside of County, Detroit Free Press, 1998, one of 95 Most Powerful Women in Mich., Corp. Mag., 2002; elected to Internat. Hall of Fame, 2002. Mem. Mich. Women's Forum (founder 1989, bd. dirs. 1989-99), Internat. Women's Forum, bd. dirs. 1989-99), Detroit Inst. Arts (dir. membership com. 1958—), Nat. Assn. Commns. for Women (pres. 1976-78), Mich. Acad. of Arts, Detroit Soc. Women Painters and Sculptprs, Women in the Arts, Scrab Club (dir. 1962-63), Ibex Club (pres. 1951), NOW (nat. bd. 1971-75, del. UN conf. Mex., 1975, Feminist of Yr.), Coun. Leading portrait Painters (elect), Women's Econ. Club, N.Y. Portrait Club (nat. adv. bd. 1977—), French-Am. C.of C. (v.p.), Alpha Phi, Zonta, Detroit Econ. Club (bd. dirs.) Episcopalian. Home: 13 Oaks Ct Bloomfield Hills MI 48304-2120

BURNETT, SUSAN WALK, personnel service company owner; b. Galveston, Tex., Aug. 21, 1946; d. Joe Decker and Ruth Corinne (Lowe) Walk; m. Rusty Burnett, Dec. 27, 1973; stepchildren: Barbara, Sara. BA in Journalism, U. Ark., Fayetteville, 1968. Asst. pub. rels. mgr. Sta. KATV, Little Rock, 1968-69; speech writer Assoc. Milk Producers, Inc., Little Rock, 1969-70; mgr. Allied Personnel, Houston, 1970-74; owner, pres. Burnett Pers. Svcs., Houston, 1974—. Exec. bd. dirs. Arthritis Found.; bd. dirs. Goodwill, Better Bus. Bur. Recipient Appreciation awards Lyndon Johnson Space Ctr., NASA, 1983, State of Tex., 1984, Top Houston Woman Bus. Owner award Nat. Assn. Women Bus. Owners, 1996, Blue Chip award U.S. C. of C., Philanthrophy award Houston Bus. Jour.; named one of 10 Women on the Move in Houston, Houston Chronicle, 1996, Most Outstanding Woman in Bus. YWCA, 1997, Entrepreneur of Yr., Ernst & Young, 1998; named 2001 Woman Bus. Entrepreneur, Women's Bus. Enterprise Alliance; named to 2000 Women of Excellence, Women's Enterprise. Mem.: Am. Staffing Assn. (bd. dirs.), Houston Assn. Pers. Cons. (v.p. 1985, pres. 1986, Outstanding Contbn. to Placement Industry and Cmty. award 1995), Tex. Assn. Pers. Cons. (v.p. 1985), Nat. Assn. Pers. Cons., Chi Omega Alumnae. Avocations: reading, golf, travel. Office: Burnett Staffing Specialists Inc 9800 Richmond Ave Ste 800 Houston TX 77042-4548

BURNETTE, ADA M. PURYEAR, educational administrator; b. Darlington, S.C. d. Theodore and Floia (King) Peoples; m. Paul Lionel Puryear, March 27, 1954 (div. 1975); children: Paul Lionel, Jr., Paula Lynn. BA in Math., Talladega Coll., 1953; postgrad., Chgo. State U., 1954-56; MA in Reading, U. Chgo., 1958; PhD, Fla. State U., 1986; postgrad., Fla. A&M U., 1994. High sch. math tchr., Winston-Salem, N.C., 1953-54; elem. tchr. Chgo. Pub. Schs., 1954-58; reading clinician U. Chgo., 1958; dir. reading clinic, asst. prof. Norfolk State U., 1958-61, Tuskegee Inst., 1961-66; coord. freshman math., asst. prof. math. Fisk U., 1966-70; adminstr. early childhood basic skills and elem. edn. State of Fla. Dept. Edn., Tallahassee, 1973-88; assoc. prof., program dir., grad. studies dir. Bethune-Cookman Coll., Daytona Beach, Fla., 1988-90; dir., supt. Fla. A&M U. Devel. Rsch. Pub. Sch. Dist., Tallahassee, 1990-93; coord., prof., dept. chmn., dir. PhD program devel. Fla. A&M U., 1993-98, coord., prof., 1998—2003, prof., dir. Robert H. Anderson Ednl. Leadership Libr., 1998—2003, prof. emerita, 2003—, adj. prof., 2003—. Hostess radio talk show, 1977—79; sec.-treas. Afro-Am. Rsch. Assocs., 1968—74; tutor, diagnostician, lectr., cons., planner, 1958—; cons. Job Corps, N.C. Advancement Sch., pub. co.; lectr. univ. classes; trustee Fla. A&M U., 2003. Regular columnist profl. jours., 1974—; writer grants proposals; weekly columnist Capital Outlook, 1991-97; contbr. articles to profl. publs. Pres. PTA, 1975—76, v.p., 1983—84; edn. commentator Sta. WFSU, 1993—94; mem. NAACP, United Fund com., Leon County 4C Bd., Urban League; pres. Norfolk Women's Interracial Coun., 1960; del. state Dem. women's meeting, Fla., 1978, 1979; mem. Dem. Exec. Com. Leon County, 1981—88, 1991—93. Mem.: AAUW (pres. Tallahassee chpt. pres. 2004), Nat. Assn. African Am. Studies (coord. 1999—), Fla. Soc. Cert. Pub. Mgrs. (newsletter bd., pres. North Fla. chpt. 2004, pres. North Fla. chpt. 2004), Am. Assn. Sch. Adminstrs., Socs. Docta Inc. (sec. 1987—93), So. Assn. Colls. and Schs. (elem. and mid. sch. commn.), Assn. Childhood Edn. Internat., Leon Assn. Children Under Six (pres. 1977), So. Assn. Children Under Six, Fla. Assn. Children Under Six, Nat. Assn. Edn. Young Children, Nat. Assn. Elem. Sch. Prins., Internat. Reading Assn. (pres. Concerned Educators Black Students 1983—86, nat. early childhood com., nat. textbook com., libr./media com., nat. med. com., nat. awards com., nat. media com.), Fla. ASCD (regional dir. policy rev. jour. editl. bd. 1995—), Alliance of Black Sch. Educators, Assn. State Cons. on Early Childhood Edn., Fla. State Reading Assn., Fla. Coun. Elem. Edn., Fla. Assn. Suprs. and Adminstrs., The Holidays (nat. sec. fin. 1993—97, nat. v.p. 1997—2001, nat. pres. 2001—, pres., v.p.), Drifters (nat. membership chmn. 1977—79, Nat. Now Black Woman 1984, historian, reporter 1992—94, pres. 1994—99, cluster coord. 2000—), FAMU Ladies Art and Social Club (pres.), Alpha Kappa Alpha (treas., summer sch. dir., undergrad. adv., parliamentarian, sec.), Pi Lambda Theta, Phi Kappa Phi (pres. 1985—86, v.p. pub. rels. chair), Phi Delta Kappa. Presbyterian (deacon). Home: PO Box 38543 Tallahassee FL 32315-8543 Office: Fla A&M U Gore Edn Ctr C-204A Tallahassee FL 32307

BURNETTE, RUTH LEONA, retired finance company administrative assistant; b. Dayton, Ohio, Sept. 14, 1935; d. Charles J. and Velma Marie (Howard) Verness; m. William Robert Fuqua, Apr. 3, 1953 (div. Oct. 1955); children: Kathy J., Robert Michael; m. Richard Dale Burnette, Dec. 31, 1960 (dec.); children: Stephen Dale, David Wayne. Bookkeeper Commonwealth Loan Beneficial, Indpls., 1955—57, Seaboard Fin., Indpls., 1957—61; adminstrv. asst. Columbia Picture Distribution, Indpls., 1961—63, Assoc. Fin. Svc., 1963—99, mgr., 1973—96, ret., 1999. Mem.: Am. Bus. Women (pres., fund raiser, Woman of Yr. award 1988, 1995). Home: 69 N Tremont Ave Indianapolis IN 46222

BURNHAM, PATRICIA WHITE, consultant, advocate, writer, business executive; b. Omaha, July 30, 1933; d. William Max and Berniece Irene (Shockey) Orr; m. William L. White, June 18, 1955 (div. Nov. 1979); children: Lucinda, Christopher, Duncan; m. Robert A. Burnham, Feb. 23, 1980. BA in English, DePauw U., Greencastle, Ind., 1955; MA in English, Ill. State U., 1966, PhD in Adminstrn., 1977. Tchr. Morton Grove (Ill.) and Evansville (Ind.) pub. schs., 1955-60; instr. Ill. State U., Normal, 1963-71, dir. Nat. Student Exchange, 1971-74, acad. advisor and continuing edn. coord., 1974-76, asst. dean, 1976-79; assoc. dir. Ill. Bd. Higher Edn., Springfield, 1979-80; assoc. vice provost Ohio State U., Columbus, 1980-81; specialist bus. ins. Nationwide Ins. Co., Columbus, 1981-83; v.p. pvt. banking Chase Manhattan Bank, N.A., N.Y.C., 1983-88; pres. Transitions Group, Inc., East Burke, Vt., 1986—. Adj. prof. U. Vt., 1997—. Author: Life's Third Act, 1994; contbr. articles to publs. and seminars on successful aging, adult policies and programs. Pres. Cmty. Vt. Elders, 1994—99; mem. Vt. Health Resource Allocation Adv., 2004—; bd. dirs. Northeastern Vt. Hosp., St. Johnsbury, 1997—, bd. chair, 2000—04; bd. dirs. Vt. Cmty. Loan Fund, Vt. Assn. Non-Profit Orgns., 1998—2000, Dartmouth Hitchcock Alliance, 2004. Mem. Phi Beta Kappa, Phi Delta Kappa. Congregationalist. Avocations: hiking, literature, writing. Office: Transitions Assocs PO Box 43 Lower Waterford VT 05848 Home: 391 Copenhagen Road Waterford VT 05819 E-mail: pat.burnham@together.net.

BURNS, BARBARA, lawyer; b. Jersey City, May 12, 1951; d. Thomas Jr. and Regina (Trzanowska) Gangemi; m. Damon Williams, Jan. 4, 1977 (div. 1986); 1 child, Jacob Williams; m. Matthew Burns, Feb. 7, 1987; 1 child, Olivia Burns. BA, Newton Coll., 1973; JD cum laude, New Eng. Sch. Law, 1976. Bar: Mass. 1977, N.J., 1984, U.S. Dist. Ct. Mass. 1977, U.S. Dist. Ct. N.J. 1984, U.S. Supreme Ct. 1988. Corporate counsel Acton (Mass.) Corp., 1977-79; asst. gen. counsel Greater Media, Inc., East Brunswick, N.J., 1984-88, assoc. gen. counsel, 1988-93, v.p., gen. counsel, 1993-98, sr. v.p. law and adminstrn., 1999—. Mem. Am. Corporate Counsel Assn., Fed. Comm. Bar Assn., N.J. Bar Assn. Office: Greater Media Inc Two Kennedy Blvd East Brunswick NJ 08816

BURNS, BARBARA BELTON, investment company executive; b. Fredericktown, Mo., Dec. 10, 1944; d. Clyde Monroe and Mary Celestial (Anderson) Belton; m. Larry J. Bohannon; Mar. 27, 1963 (div.); 1 child, Timothy Joseph; m. Donald Edward Burns, Nov. 1, 1980; stepchildren: Brian Edward, David Keone (dec.). Student, Ohio State U., 1970-75. Dir. nat. sales Am. Way, Chgo., 1976-77; recruiter Bell & Howell Schs., Columbus, Ohio, 1978-80; pres., founder Bardon Investment Corp., Naples, Fla., 1980-90; founder Cambridge Mgmt. Co., Columbus, 1983-86; pres., CEO Charter's Total Wardrobe Care, Columbus, 1984-89; founder, exec. Phoenix Bus. Group, Inc., 1990—; founder, pres. Celestial Group Inc., Las Vegas, 1999—; pres., Bondtech Direct Nutraceuticals, 2002—. Treas. Vicace-Columbus Symphony, 1981—82; fundraiser Grant Hosp., Columbus, 1986; chmn. Impresarios/Opera Columbus, 1986—87; founding mem. Columbus Women's Bd., 1986—87; mem. devel. com. Babe Zaharias/Am. Cancer Soc.; auction chmn. Opera Ball-Opera/Columbus, 1989; tennis tournament chmn. NABOR Scholarship Fund, 1990—91; mem. Philharm. Chorale, Naples, Fla., 1992, First Presbyn. of Las Vegas Chancel Choir, 1998—; spokesman Diabetes Found. Collier County, Fla., 1992—, pres., 1994, Diabetes Found., 1994—; pres. CEO Bond Direct NutraCeuticals; elder Vanderbilt Presbyn. Ch., 1994. Named Entrepreneur of Yr. Arthur Young/Venture mag., 1988, Outstanding Vol. Opera Columbus, 1986, Vol. of Yr. Diabetes Found., 1994; recipient Design award Reynoldsburg C. of

C., 1988. Mem. Naples C. of C. (new bus. com. 1990—), Las Vegas C. of C. Republican. Avocations: tennis, boating, travel, music. Office Phone: 702-281-0780. Business E-Mail: info@essentialgroup.com.

BURNS, B(ILLYE) JANE, museum director; b. Yeager, Okla., Nov. 1, 1940; d. William O. and Berniece (Floyd) French; m. Richard D. Burns June 14, 1958 (div. 1990); children: Jennifer, Richard, Timothy, Daniel. AS, Okla. State U., 1960; BA in Bus., Goshen Coll., 1988. Treas. Woodlawn Nature Coun., Inc., Elkhart, Ind., 1975-82; cons. Am. art Midwest Mus. Am. Art, Elkhart, 1978-81, founding trustee, 1978—, dir., 1980—2003. Cons. Heritage Fine Arts, Elkhart; bd. dirs. Key Bank. Mem. Woodlaw Nature Coun., Inc., Elkhart, 4-Arts Club, Elkhart, Ind. Advs. for Art, Elkhart County Symphony; bd. dirs. No. Ind. Partnership Arts, 1997—, Elkhart Ctr., 1997—, Ind. U. Arts Found.; mem. Hoosier Millennium Com., 1999—. Mem. LWV (bd. dirs. 1985-2003, v.p. 1990-2003), Michiana Arts and Scis. Coun., Concert Club. Democrat. Methodist. Avocations: collecting art, antiques, skiing, curling, travel. Home: 2413 Greenleaf Blvd Elkhart IN 46514-4055 Office: MW Mus Am Art 429 S Main St Elkhart IN 46516-3210 E-mail: bjbfrench@aol.com.

BURNS, BRENDA, state senator; b. LaGrange, Ga., Nov. 22, 1950; 3 children. Mem. Ariz. Senate, Dist. 17, Phoenix, 1994—; pres. Ariz. Senate, 1996—2000. Nat. chair Am. Leg. Exch. Coun., 1999; exec. bd. Am. Legis. Exch. Coun. Republican. Office: State Capitol Legis Dist 17 1700 W Washington St Phoenix AZ 85007-2812

BURNS, CASSANDRA STROUD, prosecutor; b. Lynchburg, Va., May 22, 1960; d. James Wesley and Jeanette Lou (Garner) Stroud; m. Stephen Burns; children: Leila Jeanette, India Veronica. BA, U. Va., 1982; JD, N.C. Cen. U., 1985. Bar: Va. 1986, N.J. 1986, U.S. Dist. Ct. (ea. dist.) Va. 1987, U.S. Ct. Appeals (4th cir.) 1987, U.S. Bankruptcy Ct. (ea. dist.) Va. 1987; cert. in criminal law. Law clk. Office Atty. Gen. State of Va., Richmond, summer 1984; law intern Office Dist. Atty. State of N.C., Durham, 1985; staff atty. Tidewater Legal Aid Soc., Chesapeake, Va., 1987-89; asst. atty. Commonwealth of Va., Petersburg, 1989-90; assoc. atty. Bland and Stroud, Petersburg, 1990; asst. pub. defender City of Petersburg, 1990-91, Commonwealth's atty., 1991—. Founder BED Task Force on Babies Exposed to Drugs, 1991, Buddies of Petersburg Program, 1997—. Sec. Chesapeake Task Force Coun. on Youth Svcs., 1987-89; ch. directress and organist; mem. NAACP; chair Petersburg-Dinwiddie Cmty. Criminal Justice Bd. Mem. Va. Bar Assn. (mem. coun. 1993-99), Old Dominion Bar Assn., Va. Assn. Commonwealth Attys. (bd. dirs., mem. coun. 1993-2000), Legal Svcs. Corp. Va. (bd. dirs.), Nat. Bd. Trial Advocacy (cert.), Soutside Va. Legal Aid Soc. (bd. dirs.), Petersburg Bar Assn., Nat. Black Prosecutors Assn. (regional dir.), Petersburg Jaycees, Order Eastern Star, Peterburg C. of C., Kiwanis, Internat., Buddies Club, Phi Alpha Delta, Alpha Kappa Alpha. Democrat. Baptist. Avocations: piano, organ, volleyball, needlework, pets. Home: 326 N Park Dr Petersburg VA 23805-2442 Office: Commonwealth's Atty 150 N Sycamore St Petersburg VA 23803 E-mail: bossyda@aol.com.

BURNS, CORRINA JESSICA, marketing professional, public relations executive; b. Talpa, N.Mex., Aug. 1, 1977; d. Betheyla and Patrick Joseph Burns, Stephanie Burns (Stepmother). B in Bus. Adminstrn., U. N.Mex, 1999. Onsite meeting planner Deife Mktg. and Comm., Corrales, N.Mex., 1999—2000; pub. rels., mktg. mgr. Hyatt Regency Tamaya Resort and Spa, Santa Ana Pueblo, N.Mex., 2000—. Mem.: Am. Mktg. Assn. (v.p. pub. rels. 2002—), Pub. Rels. Soc. Am. (cumbre com. banquet chair 2002—03, Gold and Bronze awards for 2003 Cumbre awards 2003). Office: Hyatt Regency Tamaya Resort and Spa 1300 Tuyuna Trail Santa Ana Pueblo NM 87004 E-mail: cburns@tamaypo.hyatt.com.

BURNS, DIANN, newscaster; m. Marc Watts; 1 child. BA in Politics and Mass Comm., Cleve. State U., Ohio; MA, Columbia U. Grad. Sch. of Journalism, N.Y. Gen. assignment reporter Cleve. Plain Dealer; sports editor, photographer and reporter Cleve. Call and Post; field prodr. and reporter Ind. Network News of N.Y.; reporter to weekend anchor WLS-TV, Chgo., 1985—94, co-anchor 5pm and 10pm news, 1994—2003; co-anchor 5pm, 6pm and 10pm news WBBM-TV, Chgo., 2003—. Spokesperson Pediatric AIDS Chgo.; hon. co-chair Ricky Byrdsong Mem. Race Against Hate. Office: WBBM-TV 630 N McClurg Ct Chicago IL 60601

BURNS, DRUSILLA LORENE, microbiologist; b. Manhattan, Kans., Feb. 14, 1953; BS in Chemistry, Tulane U., 1975; PhD, U. Calif., Berkeley, 1980. Fellow lab cellular metabolism NIH, 1980-84; from sr. fellow to rsch. chemist FDA Ctr. for Biologics Evaluation and Rsch., Bethesda, 1984-94, chief lab. pertussis, 1994-99, chief lab. respiratory and spl. pathogens, 1999—. Ad hoc reviewer in field. Mem. editl. bd. Infection and Immunity, 1989-98, Jour. Biol. Chemistry, 1995-2000; editor Infection and Immunity, 1998—; contbr. articles to profl. jours. Recipient Am. Inst. Chemists award, 1975, FDA Commrs. Spl. Citation, 1989. Mem. AAAS, Am. Acad. Microbiology, Am. Soc. Microbiology (internat. activities com., pub. and sci. affairs bd. 1989-92, councilor divsn. B 1997-99), Phi Beta Kappa. Achievements include patents for process for isolation of the B oligomer of pertussis toxin, process for the purification of a 69,000 da outer membrane protein of Bordetella pertussis. Office: Ctr for Biologics Eval 8800 Rockville Pike Bldg 29 Bethesda MD 20892-0001 E-mail: burns@cber.fda.gov.

BURNS, ELIZABETH ANN, physician, educator; b. Detroit, Mich., Nov. 13, 1950; d. Vincent Paul Burns, Genevieve Elizabeth Burns; m. Roger Allen Zinser. BS magna cum laude, Marygrove Coll., 1972; MD, U. Mich., 1976; MA, U. Iowa, 1981. Diplomate Nat. Bd. Med. Examiners, Am. Bd. Family Practice. Robert Wood Johnson Found. faculty devel. fellow dept. family practice U. Iowa, Iowa City, 1979—81, asst. prof. family practice dept. family practice, 1981—86, assoc. prof. dept. family practice, 1986—92, assoc. dir. Family Practice Residency Program dept. family practice, 1985—89, program dir. Family Practice Residency Program dept. family practice, 1989—92; prof. dept. family medicine U. Ill., Chgo., 1992—2002, dept. head dept. family medicine, 1992—2000; prof. Sch. Medicine U. N.Dak., Grand Forks, ND, 2002—, chmn. Dept. Family Medicine, 2002—. Chair family practice dept. Mercy Hosp., Iowa City, 1989—90; bd. dirs. Assn. Family Practice Residency Dirs., Kansas City, 1990—91, Ill. Acad. Family Physicians, Lisle, 1995—99, Assn. Depts. Family Medicine, Kansas City, 1998—2000; presenter in field. Contbr. chapters to books, articles to profl. jours. Mem. adv. bd. Free Med. Clinic, Iowa City, 1986—92; U. Ill. Chgo. rep. Ill. State Senate/House Joint Task Force on Family Physician Shortages, Springfield, Ill., 1993—93; pub. health com. mem. Ill. State Med. Soc., Chgo., 1993—97; mem. health com. Oak Park (Ill.)/River Forest LWV, 2000; vol. staff physician Cmty. Health Clinic, Chgo.; bd. dirs., fundraising chair Domestic Violence Intervention Project, Iowa City, 1986—90; bd. mem. United Action for Youth, Iowa City, 1991—92. Recipient Listed in Top Doctors: Chgo. Metro Area, Castle Connelly, 2000, 2001; fellow Faculty Devel. Fellowship, Robert Wood Johnson Found. through the U. of Iowa, 1979-1981, Mar. of Dimes Fellowship for Intensive Course in Maternal Nutrtion, Mar. of Dimes at the U. of NC, 1985, Bishop/ACE, 2004—. Fellow: American Academy of Family Physicians; mem.: AMA, Am. Med. Womens Assn. (state dir. 1990—91), Physicians for Social Responsibility, Soc. Tchrs. Family Medicine (pres. 1999—2000), AOA. Office: DFM UNDSOM HS Box 9037 501 North Columbia Rd Grand Forks ND 58202-9037 Office Phone: 701-777-3255. Business E-Mail: eburns@medicine.nodak.edu.

BURNS, SISTER ELIZABETH MARY, hospital administrator; b. Estherville, Iowa, Mar. 3, 1927; d. Bernard Aloysius and Viola Caroline (Brennan) B. Diploma in Nursing, St. Joseph Mercy Sch. Nursing, Sioux City, Iowa, 1952; BS in Nursing Edn, Mercy Coll., Detroit, 1957; M.Sc. in Nursing, Wayne State U., 1958; Ed.D., Columbia U., 1969. Joined Sisters of Mercy, Roman Cath. Ch., 1946; nursing supr. Mercy Med. Center, Dubuque, Iowa, 1952-55; supr. orthopedics and urology St. Joseph Mercy Hosp., Sioux City, 1955-56; dir. Sch. Nursing, 1958-63; chmn. dept. nursing Mercy Coll. of Detroit, 1963-73; dir. health [illegible] Sisters of Mercy, Province of Detroit, 1973-77; pres., chief exec. officer Marian Health Center, Sioux City, 1977-87; sabbatical leave, 1988. Coord. life planning Sisters of Mercy, 1989-90, mem. province adminstrv. team, 1990-98; cons. Trinity Health, 2001—. Bd. dirs. Mercy Sch. Nursing of Detroit, 1968-77, Mercy H.S., Farmington Hills, Mich., 2000—; mem. exec. com. Greater Detroit Area Hosp. Coun., 1973-77; trustee St. Mary Coll., Omaha, 1981-82, Briar Cliff Coll., Sioux City, 1981-87, Battle Creek Health Sys., 2002—, Mercy Med. Ctr., Sioux City, Iowa, 2001—; chmn. Mercy Health Adv. Coun., 1978-80. Mem. Western Iowa League for Nursing (pres. 1960-62), Nat. League for Nursing, Sisters of Mercy Shared Svcs. Coordinating Com., Cath. Hosp. Assn. (trustee 1977-80), Sisters of Mercy Health Corp. (trustee 1988-90, governance coord. 1998-2001), Mercy Health Svcs. (chair bd. 1990-95, membership bd. 1995-98, historian 1998-2004). Address: 28554 Eleven Mile Farmington MI 48336-1507 E-mail: eburns@mercydetroit.org.

BURNS, ELIZABETH MURPHY, media executive; b. Superior, Wis., Dec. 4, 1945; d. Morgan and Elizabeth (Beck) Murphy; m. Richard Ramsey Burns, June 24, 1984. Student, U. Ariz., 1963-67. Promotion and programming sec. Sta. KGUN-TV, Tucson, 1967-68; programming and traffic sec. Sta. KFMB-TV, San Diego, 1968-69; owner, operator Sta. KKAR, Pomona, Calif., 1970-73; co-owner, pres. Evening Telegram Co. (parent co. Murphy Stas.); pres. Morgan Murphy Stas., Madison, Wis., 1976—. Bd. dirs. Nat. Guardian Life Ins. Co., Republic Bank, various media stas. and corps. Mem. Nat. Assn. Broadcasters, Wis. Broadcasters Assn., Madison Club, Nakoma Country Club, Northland Country Club (Duluth), Boulders Country Club (Carefree, Ariz.). Roman Catholic. Avocations: golf, travel. Home: 180 Paine Farm Rd Duluth MN 55804-2609 Office: Sta WISC-TV 7025 Raymond Rd Madison WI 53719-5053

BURNS, ELLEN BREE, federal judge; b. New Haven, Conn., Dec. 13, 1923; d. Vincent Thomas and Mildred Bridget (Bannon) Bree; m. Joseph Patrick Burns, Oct. 8, 1955 (dec.); children: Mary Ellen, Joseph Bree, Kevin James. BA, Albertus Magnus Coll., 1944, LLD (hon.), 1974; LLB, Yale U., 1947; LLD (hon.), U. New Haven, 1981, Sacred Heart U., 1986, Fairfield U., 1991. Bar: Conn. 1947. Dir. legis. legal svcs. State of Conn., 1949-73; judge Conn. Cir. Ct., 1973-74, Conn. Ct. of Common Pleas, 1974-76, Conn. Superior Ct., 1976-78, U.S. Dist. Ct. Conn., New Haven, 1978—, chief judge, 1988-92, sr. judge, 1992—. Trustee Fairfield U., 1978-85, Albertus Magnus Coll., 1985—. Recipient John Carroll of Carrollton award John Barry Council K.C., 1973, Judiciary award Conn. Trial Lawyers Assn., 1978, Cross Pro Ecclesia et Pontifice, 1981, Law Rev. award U. Conn. Law Rev., 1987, Judiciary award Conn. Bar Assn., 1987, Raymond E. Baldwin Pub. Svc. award Bridgeport Law Sch., 1992. Mem.: ABA, Conn. Bar Found., Conn. Bar Assn., New Haven County Bar Assn., Am. Bar Found. Roman Catholic. Office: US Dist Ct 141 Church St New Haven CT 06510-2030

BURNS, M. MICHELE, energy executive, former air transportation executive; B in bus. adminstrn. summa cum laude, M. Accountancy, U. Ga. Mgmt. Arthur Anderson, 1981-84, mgr., 1984-91, ptnr., 1991-99; v.p. corp. taxes, treas. Delta Airlines, 1999, sr. v.p. fin., treas., 2000, exec. v.p., CFO, 2000—04, Mirant Corp., Atlanta, 2004—. Mem. bd. dirs. Wal-Mart Stores Inc., Cisco Systems Inc., Ivan Allen Co., Atlanta Symphony Orch. Office: Mirant Corp 1155 Perimeter Ctr W Atlanta GA

BURNS, MARCELLINE, psychologist, researcher; BA in Psychology, San Diego State U., 1955; MA, Calif. State U., L.A., 1969; PhD, U. Calif., Irvine, 1972. Co-founder So. Calif. Rsch. Inst., L.A., 1973—. Cons., expert witness alcohol and drug effects on performance, FSTs, HGN, and drug recognition; lectr. in field. Contbr. articles to profl. jours. Recipient Public Svc. award U.S. Dept. Trans., 1993. Achievements include research on alcohol and drug effects, field sobriety tests and drug recognition. Office: So Calif Rsch Inst 11914 W Washington Blvd Los Angeles CA 90066-5816

BURNS, MARIAN LAW, human resources specialist; b. Pa., Jan. 10, 1954; d. Vincent Charles and Agatha M. Law; m. Lawrence Joseph Burns, Sept. 29, 1979; children: Peter Andrew, Rita Marie. Paralegal, legal sec. Tuso & Gruccio, Vineland, N.J., 1972-74; legal sec. Swartz, Campbell & Detweiler, Phila., 1974-80; adminstrv. mgr. Drinker Biddle & Reath (formerly Smith, Lambert, Hicks & Beidler, P.C.), Princeton, N.J., 1980-88; legal adminstr. Sherr, Joffe & Zuckerman, P.C., West Conshohocken, Pa., 1988-90, Groen, Laveson, Goldberg & Rubenstone, Bensalem, Pa., 1990—99; v.p. adminstrn. Brintnall & Nicolini, Inc., Phila., 1999—. Adj. prof. paralegal program Bucks County Cmty. Coll. Newtown, Pa. 1998—99, mem. paralegal studies adv. com., 1996-99. Mem.: Soc. Human Resources Mgmt. Office: Brintnall & Nicolini Inc 1880 JFK Blvd 16th Fl Philadelphia PA 19103 E-mail: marian.burns@brintnall.com.

BURNS, NOËLLE ANN, art educator; b. Elkhorn, Wis., Dec. 26, 1955; d. Robert F. and Christiane T. Marszalek; m. Edward William Burns, June 2, 1979; children: Amanda Louise, Cassandra Anne. BS, Carroll Coll., 1978; MS in Edn., U. Wis., Whitewater, 1993. Cert. tchr. K-12 Wis. Child care counselor II Wis. Sch. Deaf, Delavan, 1978—85, tchr. asst., 1985—90; tchr. Watertown (Wis.) Unified Sch. Dist., 1990—. Asst. troop leader Girls Scouts U.S., Lake Hills, Wis., 1989—; bd. dirs., CPA Jefferson Performing Arts Ctr., 2001—; tchr. St. Francis Xavier Ch., Lake Hills, 2000—. Recipient W. T. Graham award, W. T. Graham/Youth Art Month, 1997, 2003. Mem.: Watertown Arts Coun., Wis. Art Edn. Assn., Nat. Art Edn. Assn., Phi Kappa Phi. Republican. Roman Catholic. Avocations: travel, art, gardening, reading. Home: 219 Woodland Ct Lake Mills WI 53551 Office: Watertown Unified Sch Dist 111 Dodge St Watertown WI 53094 Personal E-mail: burns4@jefnet.com.

BURNS, PAT ACKERMAN GONIA, information systems specialist, software engineer; b. Birmingham, Ala., July 16, 1938; d. Richard Lee and Hattie Eugenia (Bragg) Ackerman; m. Robert Edward Gonia, June 4, 1957 (div. Jan. 1973); children: Deborah Hayes, Junita Grantham, Ronald Gonia; m. James Clayton Burns, June 23, 1984 (dec. Dec. 1989). BS in Math., U. Ala., 1970, postgrad., 1971-77. Cert. secondary tchr., Ala. Missionary United Meth. Bd. of Missions, Sumatra, Indonesia, 1961-64; homebound tchr. Huntsville (Ala.) City Schs., 1970-75; mem. tech. staff Gen. Rsch. Corp., Huntsville, 1975-79; rsch. scientist Nichols Rsch. Corp., Huntsville, 1979-84, mgr. personnel div., 1984-87, mgmt. info. systems dept. head, 1987-90, dir. info. systems div., 1990-95; program mgr. MIS and tech. MIS U.S. Army Space and Strategic Defense Systems, 1990-93; dir. info. sys. Trinity United Meth. Ch., Huntsville, 1996-98; exec. dir. Trinity Personal Growth Ctr., Huntsville, 1999-2000. Mem. adv. com. Drake Tech. Sch., Huntsville, 1988-94; program mgr. USASDC MIS//TMIS, 1990-94. Mem. PTA, Huntsville, 1994, Ch. Women United, Huntsville, Cmty. Chorus, Huntsville; bd. dirs. United Meth. Children's Home, Ala. and Fla., 2000—. Mem. IEEE, NAFE, Data Processing Mgmt. Assn., Assn. Pers. Adminstrs., Am. Computer Soc., Huntsville C. of C. (spkr. 1986-95). Democrat. Methodist. Avocations: travel, music, old movies. E-mail: burnspg@aol.com.

BURNS, REBECCA ANN, elementary school educator, librarian; b. Waynesboro, Pa., Dec. 28, 1946; d. John Albert and Betty Jane (Mason) Castelluccio; m. Terry Lee Burns, 1966; children: Todd Darin, Derick Jason. BS, Shippensburg U., 1968, postgrad., 1969, 70, 75, Pa. State U., 1973-74, 87, 89, U. Wyo., 1989. Cert. elem. tchr., libr. sci. tchr. Pa. Migrant educator Waynesboro (Pa.) Sch. Dist., 1971-72, elem. tchr., 1968-71, 74-79, Mifflin County Sch. Dist., Lewistown, Pa., 1972-74; test examiner Office Personnel Mgmt. U.S. Govt., State College, Pa., 1982-83; instr. Adult Basic Edn.- Gen. Edn. Devel. and Career Tng. Mifflin County Job Tng. Partnership Act, Lewistown, 1983-86; libr. State Correctional Inst.-Rockview, Bellefonte, Pa., 1983-85, Midd-West Sch. Dist., Middleburg, Pa., 1986-89; edn. adminstrn. assoc., pupil transp. specialist Pa. Dept. Edn., Harrisburg, 1989-90, edn. adminstrn. specialist, coord. non pub. sch. svcs., 1990-93, basic edn. assoc., youth edn. and employment coord., 1993-97, basic edn. assoc., work-based learning coord., 1997—2002; pvt. practice Harrisburg, 2002—. Lobbyist for stamp commemorating adult edn.; educator for women's rights devel. and implementation of regis. apprenticeships for youth in Pa. Mem.: AARP, Fedn. State Cultural and Ednl. Profl., Apprenticeship Assn., Pa. Fedn. Tchrs., Eastern Seaboard Apprenticeship Conf., Nat. Assn. State and Territorial Apprenticeship Dirs., Alliance Ret. Ams. (charter, charter Pa. chpt.), Aux. to Pa. Ret. State Police. Roman Catholic. Avocations: reading, collecting antique prints, travel. Home and Office: 4422 Saybrook Ln Harrisburg PA 17110-3477 E-mail: racb1228@aol.com.

BURNS, RED, academic administrator; 4 children. Joined, co-founder, interactive telecomms. program Tisch Sch. Arts NYU, 1979—, chair, interactive telecomms. program Tisch Sch. Arts, 1981—, Tokyo Broadcasting System Prof. Communications, 1997—. Bd. dirs. Media Lab Europe, The Visual Media Task Force, The Convergent Media Group; mem. adv. bd. The N.Y. Times Digital Company; juror On-Line Journalism Awards, Nat. Mag. Awards, Webby Awards; prin. investigator three on-going rsch. programs funded by Interval Rsch., Intel and Microsoft. Creator CD-ROM on chaos theory, Electronic Neighborhood. Bd. dirs. The Charles H. Revson Found.; ProBono.net; Ivrae Inst.; mentor The Ross Sch. Named one of 100 top leaders of N.Y.'s economy, Crain's N.Y., top 100 most influential women in bus., Top 25 Influential People on the Net, Newsweek's 50 for the Future, N.Y. Cyber Sixty, N.Y. Mag.; named to Silicon Alley's 100; recipient Matrix award, 1997, All-Star Educator award, Crain's, Award of Excellence in Sci. and Tech., Mayor of N.Y.C., Spl. Educator award, Art Dir. Club, Chrysler Design Award, 2002. Mem.: N.Y. New Media Assn. (founding mem.). Office: NYU Tisch Sch Arts 721 Broadway 4th Fl New York NY 10003-6807*

BURNS, ROBIN C(AROL), mathematics theoretician, accountant; b. L.A., Mar. 18, 1948; d. Kenneth and Jeanne C. (Murray) B.; m. Philip L. Benedict, Aug. 25, 1966 (dec 1968); m. Terrance R. Fuchek, Sept. 5, 1969 (div. 1988); children: Tracy, Bryan, Conni, Loren, Allan; m. William E. Pavone, July 6, 1991 (div. June 1993). Owner Math Pro Bus. Svcs., Tacoma, Wash., 1992—. Creator/producer pub. TV series: 9 Patch Palace, 1979-83, Robin's Nest, 1983-86; creator/owner WWW.MOMWIZ.COM; writer/producer songs: Cry on My Shoulder, Nothin' Average About Him, 1992-93; inventor in field; contbr. articles to profl. jours. Mem. Math. Assn. Am., Am. Assn. Profl. Bookkeepers, Alpha Sigma Lambda. Avocations: ethnic dance choreography, camping, songwriting, internet publishing. Home and Office: 2522 N Proctor St Tacoma WA 98406-5338

BURNS, ROSALIE ANNETTE, retired neurologist, educator; b. Phila., July 29, 1932; married. BA, Smith Coll., 1953; MD, Yale U., 1956. Intern in medicine Cornell Med. divsn. Bellevue Hosp., N.Y.C., 1956-57; resident in neurology Neurol. Inst. N.Y.-Columbia-Presbyn. Med. Ctr., 1957-60; asst. in neurology, fellow Nat. Cerebral Palsy Study, 1959-60; fellow in cerebral vascular disease NIH-dept. neurology Tufts U.-New Eng. Ctr. Hosp., Boston, 1960-61; asst. dir. 2d neurology divsn. Bellevue Hosp., N.Y.C., 1962-64; instr. neurology dept. medicine Cornell U. Sch. Medicine, 1962-64; asst. neurologist to outpatients N.Y. Hosp., N.Y.C., 1962-64; electroencephalographer The Inst. of Pa. Hosp., 1964-65; instr. in neurology Med. Coll. Pa., 1964-65, dir. neurology clinics, 1965-74, assoc. in neurology, 1965-66, head sect. neurology, dept. psychiatry and neurology, 1965-71, asst. prof. neurology, 1966-70, assoc. prof. neurology, 1970-74, acting chmn. dept. neurology, 1971-74, prof. neurology, 1974-95, chmn. dept. neurology, 1975-95; univ. prof., exec. dir. Ctr. for Clin. Neurosci. Med. Coll. Pa./Hahnemann Univ., 1995-98; clin. prof. neurology Thomas Jefferson U. Sch. Medicine, 1998—2000, hon. clin. prof. neurology, 2001—; ret., 2001. Program dir. NIH Devel. Grant Med. Coll. Pa., 1966-73; consulting physician in neurology Ea. Pa. Psychiat. Inst., 1965-76, Pathway Sch. for Learning Disorders, 1978-81, Phila. VA Med. Ctr., chief of neurology, 1975-77, attending physician in neurology, 1967-68; cons. staff Inglis House, 1967-93, Phila. Geriatric Ctr., 1985; half-time rsch. asst. neuropathology lab. Walter E. Fernald State Sch. Mental Retardation, Waverly, Mass., 1961-62; adj. attending neurologist dept. neurology Sloan-Kettering Cancer Ctr., 1986; presenter in field. Contbr. chpts. to books, articles to profl. jours. Nat. Found. fellow, 1955. Fellow Am. Acad. Neurology (edn. com. 1975-78, practice com. 1990-92, del. to Coun. of Acad. Socs. 1987-91, nominating com. 1993, 2d v.p. 1983-85, women's liaison officer 1991); mem. Am. Bd. Med. Specialties, Am. Bd. Psychiatry and Neurology (bd. dirs. 1993-2001, nominating com. 1993, rev. appeals com. 1992, credentials com. 1992, v.p. and chair neurol. coun. 2000 and many other coms.), Am. Neurol. Assn. (annals of neurology oversight com. 1993), v.p. & chair, 2000, Assn. Univ. Profs. Neurology (sec.-treas. 1983-88, pres.-elect 1988-90, pres. 1990-92), Phila. Neurol. Soc. (1st v.p. 1971, 2nd v.p. 1977, pres. 1979-80, chmn. nominating com. 1981, and other coms.), Smith Coll. Club Phila., Phi Beta Kappa, Sigma Xi, Alpha Omega Alpha (Delta chpt., chmn. membership com. 1980-81). E-mail: burnsr@comcast.net.

BURNS, SARAH CHLOE See GUNDERSON, SARAH

BURNS, SHIRLEY M. artist, educator; b. Kingsport, Tenn., Oct. 1, 1934; d. Kenneth MacDonald and Louise Gwendolyn (Cox) Cross; m. Richard Carroll Burns, Dec. 15, 1960; children: Jay Bradford, Kurt MacDonald. BS, East Tenn. State U., 1957, postgrad., 1957-86. Cert. tchr., Tenn., Va., Wash. Tchr. 3d grade Kempsville (Va.) Elem. Sch., 1955-56; tchr. art Princess Anne (Va.) H.S., 1957-58, Mt. Vernon Elem. Sch., Alexandria, Va., 1959-60, Harrisburg (Pa.) Jr. H.S., 1961; tchr. 6th grade art and social studies Silverdale (Wash.) Elem. Sch., 1967-70; tchr. art North Kitsap H.S., Poulsbo, Wash., 1978-84. Drawing instr. Harrisburg YMCA, 1961, pvt. lessons, Hawaii, 1964-65; docent Hall of Indians/Mus. Natural History, Smithsonian Instn., Washington, 1970-71; ptnr. The Art Cellar, Silverdale, 1971-75; instr. adult craft classes Olympic Coll., Bremerton, 1975-77; instr. pottery Bainbridge Island Park and Recreation Dist., 1984—2004, also adult sculpture classes, 1995—2004. Exhibited works in Bainbridge Arts and Crafts Gallery and Christmas Shows, 1991—, Studio Tour, Bainbridge Island, 1991-99, 2003, Bainbridge in Bloom, 1997-99; two-person show Collective Visions, 2001, 02; group show Collective Visions Gallery, Bremerton, Wash., 2001, Art Soup Gallery, Bainbridge Island, 2004; permanent disply of sculptural works at Seattle Aquarium, 1995—. Fundraiser, Friends of the Libr., Bremerton, Wash. Recipient awards for art. Mem. AAUW, PEO, Bainbridge Island Music and Arts, The Clay People, Bainbridge Arts and Crafts, Bainbridge Island Arts and Humanities, Seattle Art Mus. Methodist. Avocations: music appreciation, tennis, reading. Home: 8270 NE Meadowmeer Rd Bainbridge Island WA 98110-1241 E-mail: shrburns@aol.com.

BURNS, SUSAN RENEÉ, psychologist, educator; b. Topeka, July 11, 1975; d. Erwin Joseph and Linda Lou Ulses; m. Daniel Paul Burns, July 27, 1996; children: Isabella Reneé, Abigail Elaine, Noah Benjamin. BS in Psychology, Emporia State U., 1996, MS in Exptl. Psychology, 1998; PhD in Personality/Social Psychology, Kans. State U., 2002. Grad. tchg. asst. Emporia (Kans.) State U., 1996—98, Kans. State U., Manhattan, 1998—2001; asst. prof. Morningside Coll., Sioux City, Iowa, 2002—. Vis. prof. Washburn U., Topeka, 2001—02. Contbr. articles to profl. jours.

Mem.: APA, Soc. for Rsch. in Child Devel. Republican. Roman Catholic. Avocations: singing, flute, piano, guitar. Office: Morningside Coll 1501 Morningside Ave Sioux City IA 51106

BURNS, TONI ANTHONY, artist; b. L.A., Sept. 6, 1937; d. Earle Francis and LaVerne Myrtle (Holmberg) Anthony; m. George Orin Burns, May 14, 1965; children: Robert Anthony, James Randolph. BA in Fine Arts, Calif. State U., Long Beach, 1959, postgrad., 1960. Cert. secondary tchr., Calif. Interior decorator Ruth Connor Interiors, Downey, Calif., 1960-62; tech. illustrator N.Am. Rockwell Corp., Downey, 1962-64, McDonnell-Douglas Aircraft, Long Beach, Calif., 1964-65; graphic layout artist Beckman Instruments, Fullerton, Calif., 1968-70; owner, creator Original Art Rock Owls, San Juan Capistrano, Calif., 1970-78; custom jewelry designer Jewelry by Toni Burns, San Juan Capistrano, 1979-98; jewelry designer, ptnr. SuperNatural Art, San Juan Capistrano, 1999—; prin., owner Silver Dolls, San Juan Capistrano, 2003—. Wholesale exhibitor L.A. Gift Show, 1971-78, Beckman Handcrafts, L.A., 1982. Juried shows include Village West Gallery, Laguna Beach, Calif., summers 1971-75, Art-A-Fair Festival, Laguna Beach, 1984-86, Downey Art Mus., 1992, Fine Arts Pavillion, 1993. Recipient 1st pl. San Clemente Art Gallery, 1984, 99. Mem. Am. Craft Coun., Metal Arts Soc. So. Calif. Avocations: family genealogy, travel, photography. Office: SuperNatural Art 31412 Windsong Dr San Juan Capistrano CA 92675-2788 Office Phone: 949-388-4309. E-mail: info@supernaturalart.com.

BURNS, URSULA, printing company executive; BS, Polytech. Inst., 1980; MS in Mech. Engring., Columbia U., 1981. Joined Xerox, 1980, lead several bus. teams, 1992—2000, sr. v.p. corp. strategic svc., 2000—, pres. document sys. and solutions, 2001—. Bd. dirs. Hunt Corp., Banta Corp., U. Rochester Med. Sch. Mem.: Nat. Assn. Mfr. (bd. dirs.), Indsl. Mgmt. Coun. Rochester (bd. dirs.). Office: Xerox 800 Long Ridge Rd Stamford CT 06904*

BURNS, VIRGINIA, social worker; b. Boston, June 10, 1925; d. Thomas Patrick and Katherine Louise (Dempsey) Burns. AB in Sociology, Boston U., 1946, MSW, 1951; EDd honors, Wheelock Coll., 1994. Group work specialist Boston Children's Svc. Assn., 1951-58; group work cons. East London Family Svc. Units, 1958-59; assoc. exec. sec. group work coun. Welfare Fedn. Cleve., 1959-62; sr. staff mem. Office Juvenile Delinquency & Youth Devel. U.S. Dept. Health, Edn. and Welfare, Washington, 1962-67, asst. to asst. sec. cmty. svcs., 1967-69; sr. assoc. youth involvement study New Transcentury Found., Washington, 1969-70; assoc. prof., dir. social svc. project U. Chgo., Sch. Social Svc. Adminstrn., 1970-73; dir. cmty. svc., divsn. drug rehab. Dept. Mental Health, Boston, 1973-76; dir. cons. & edn. program Mass. Mental Health Ctr., Boston, 1976-82; lectr. mental health Harvard Med. Sch., Boston, 1978-82; dir. advocacy, Boston Children Svc. Assn. Mass. Soc. Prevention of Cruelty Children, Boston, 1983-94; instr. social welfare, coord. cmty. projects Smith Coll. Sch. Social Work, Northampton, Mass., 1994-99; instr. social welfare policy Salem (Mass.) State Coll. Sch. Social Work, 1993-99. Cons. in field. Contbr. articles to profl. jours., chpts. in books. Founding chair Children's Advocacy Network Mass., 1984—93, Latchkey Children's Coalition Mass., 1988—92, v.p. Mass. Human Svc. Coalition, 1984—99; legis. liaison Mass. Working Group on Women in Prison, 2000—; bd. dirs. Hispanic Office Planning and Evaluation, 1990—97, Here House, 1989—90, Parents Helping Parents, 2001—02, Inst. Health and Recovery, 2003—04; bd. advisors Aid to Incarcerated Mothers, 2002—04; active United Fair Economy, Boston, 1994—99, Tax Equity Alliance Mass., 1990—99; mem. adv. com. Wheelock Coll., 1999—. Named Alumna of Yr., Boston U. Sch. Social Work, 1968; scholar, Fulbright, 1958—58. Mem.: NASW (chair polit. action com. Mass. chpt. 1984—2001, award for greatest contbn. to social policy and change 1990, Lifetime Achievement award 2003—04), Boston U. Alumni Assn. (Disting.). Avocations: gardening, bicycling, cooking, flower arranging. Home: 41A Cushing St Cambridge MA 02138-4581 E-mail: Burns472@aol.com.

BURNSIDE, MARY BETH, biology educator, researcher; b. San Antonio, Apr. 23, 1943; d. Neil Delmont and Luella Nixon (Kenley) B. BA, U. Tex., 1965, MA, 1967, PhD in Zoology, 1968. Instr. med. sch. Harvard U., Boston, 1970-73; asst. prof. U. Pa., Phila., 1973-76, U. Calif., Berkeley, 1976-77, assoc. prof., 1977-82, prof., 1982—, dean biol. scis., 1984-90, chancellor prof., 1996-99, vice chancellor rsch., 2000—. Mem. nat. adv. eye coun. NIH, 1990-94; mem. sci. adv. bd. Lawrence Hall of Sci., Berkeley, 1983—, Whitney Labs., St. Augustine, Fla., 1993-97; mem. bd. sci. councillors Nat. Eye Inst., 1994—. Mem. editl. bd. Invest. Ophthalmol. Vis. Sci., 1992-94; contbr. numerous articles to profl. jours. Mem. sci. adv. bd. Mills Coll., Oakland, Calif., 1986-90; trustee Bermuda Biol. Sta., St. George's, 1978-83; dir. Miller Inst., Berkeley, Calif., 1995-98. Recipient Merit award NIH, 1989-99, Outstanding Alumna award U. Tex., 1999; rsch. grantee, NIH, 1972—, NSF. Fellow AAAS; mem. Am. Soc. Cell Biology (coun. 1980-84). Avocations: hiking, deserts, mountains, great danes. Office: U Calif MC # 3200 335 Life Scis Addn # 3200 Berkeley CA 94720-0001

BURR, MEGHAN LERA, researcher; b. Fort Scott, Kans., Dec. 10, 1962; d. James Leroy and Ramona Kathleen (Roberts) B. AA in Graphic Design, Rogers State Coll., Claremore, Okla., 1989; BS in Indsl. Tech., Northeastern State U., Tahlequah, Okla., 1991, MS in Indsl. Envrion. Mgmt., 1992; AA in Chemistry, Rogers State Coll., Claremore, Okla., 1994; student in Environ. Sci., Okla. State U., Stillwater, Okla., 1995—. Registered environ. profl., Nat. Registry of Environ. Profls. Grad. rsch. asst. Okla. State U., Stillwater, 1995—. Mem. lead steering com. Okla. Dept. Environ. Quality, Bartlesville, 1993-95. Mayoral appt. Select Oversight Com. on Lead and Cadnium, Bartlesville, Okla., 1992-95; head, chmn. Human Health Task Force, Bartlesville, Okla., 1993-95; mem., cons. Bartlesville (Okla.) Coalition, 1993-95. Mem. AAUW, Nat. Assn. Environ. Profls., Epsilon Pi Tau. Avocations: photography, quilting, shirt designing, reading, collecting. Office: Environmental Inst 201 Citd Stillwater OK 74078-0001 Home: Apt 101 248 N University Pl Stillwater OK 74075-3933

BURRELL, PAMELA, actress; b. Tacoma, Aug. 4, 1945; d. Donald A. and Mickey Rose (Curtiss) B.; m. Monty Silver, July 18, 1965 (div. 1978); children: Deirdre Paige, Emily Beth; m. Peter J. Gatto, Apr. 21, 1979. Studies with Sandy Miesner; student, San Francisco Ballet, N.Y.C. Ballet. Actress: (stage prodns.) Arms and the Man, 1967 (Theatre World award 1968), Where's Charley?, 1974, Berkeley Square, 1976, The Boss, 1976, Tatyana Repina, 1978, Biography, 1979, Strider, 1979, Sunday in the Park with George, 1985, also numerous regional stage appearances, 1967-86, (feature films) Da Duva, 1967, Popeye, 1980, (TV series) The Catlins, 1984-85, (TV episodes) Search for Tomorrow, Ryan's Hope, Spencer for Hire, 1986. Mem. Actors' Equity Assn., Screen Actors Guild, AFTRA. Office: Monty Silver Agy 200 W 57th St New York NY 10019-3211

BURRER, ARDATH ROSE, elementary school educator, music educator; b. Hettinger, N.D., Nov. 28, 1953; d. Fredrick Burrer and Flavia Virginia Akers. BS in Edn., Black Hills State Coll., 1981. Elem. classroom tchr. N.W. Sch. Dist., Lodgepole, SD, 1981—82, K-8 rural classroom tchr., 1996—98; substitute tchr. Hettinger Pub. Schs., 1992—95, 1998—2001; elem. music tchr. grades K-6 Hettinger Pub. Sch., SD, 2001—; substitute tchr. Bison (S.D.) Sch. Dist., 1992—95, 1998—2001, K-8 rural classroom tchr., 1995—96. Mem.: S.D. Edn. Assn. (local pres.), N.D. Edn. Assn., Music Educators Nat. Conf., Am. Choral Dirs. Assn. Republican. Evangelical Lutheran. Avocations: stamp collecting, sewing, needlecrafts, reading, cooking. Home: 12366 SD Hwy 75 Lodgepole SD 57640 Office: Hettinger Pub Schs Dist 13 Box 1188 209 8th St South Hettinger ND 58639

BURRI, BETTY JANE, research chemist; b. San Francisco, Jan. 23, 1955; d. Paul Gene and Carleen Georgette (Meyers) B.; m. Kurt Randall Annweiler, Dec. 1, 1984. BA, San Francisco State U., 1976; MS, Calif. State U., Long Beach, 1978; PhD, U. Calif. San Diego, La Jolla, 1982. Research asst. Scripps Clinic, La Jolla, 1982-83, research assoc., 1983-85; research chemist Western Human Nutrition Rsch. Ctr., USDA, San Francisco, 1985-99, Davis, Calif., 1999—; adj. prof. nutrition dept. U. Nev., 1993-98, U. Calif., 2000—; CRIS leader Davis, Calif., 2003—. Mem. steering com. Carotenoid Rsch. Interaction Group, 1994-97. Co-editor Carotenoid News, 1995-99; contbr. articles to profl. jours. Grantee NIH, 1982, 85, USDA, 1986, Spinal Cord Rsch. Found., 1998, Am. Chem. Soc., 1998-2002; affiliate fellow Am. Heart Assn., 1983, 84. Mem. Assn. Women in Sci. (founding dir. San Diego chpt.), N.Y. Acad. Sci., Carotenoid Rsch. Interaction Group, Internat. Carotenoid Soc. Office: Western Human Nutrition Rsch Ctr 229 Creuss Hall 1 Shields Ave Davis CA 95616 E-mail: bburri@whnrc.usda.gov.

BURRILL, KATHLEEN R. F. (KATHLEEN R. F. GRIFFIN-BURRILL), language educator; b. Canterbury, U.K., Mar. 8, 1924; d. William Henry and Ruby Amy (Webber) Griffin; children: Anne Ruth, Jane Ruth. AM, Columbia U., 1957, PhD, 1964; cert., Mid. East Inst., Columbia U, 1959. Officer of Brit. Coun., Ankara, Turkey, U.K., 1947-55; lectr. to prof. Middle East and Asian langs. and cultures Columbia U., N.Y.C., 1957-2000, prof. emerita, 2000—. Author: The Quatrains of Nesimi, Fourteenth-Century Turkic Hurufi Poet; co-editor Archivum Ottomanicum, 1984-95; contbr. articles to profl. jours. and encys. Recipient rsch. and travel award, Coun. Rsch. Humanities, 1966—67; fellow, Columbia U., 1957—59, Ford Found., 1959—60, Am. Rsch. Inst. in Turkey, summers, 1967, 1975. Fellow: Mid. East Studies Assn. (dir. 1974—76, founding fellow); mem.: Am. Assn. Tchrs. Turkic Langs. (pres. 1986—2002, hon. pres. 2003—), Mid. East Inst. (Washington), Brit. Soc. Mid. East Studies, Inst. Turkish Studies (governing bd. 1995—2001, founding assoc.), Turkish Studies Assn. (dir. 1974—76).

BURRIS, JANICE ELAINE, educational administrator; b. Omaha, July 3, 1964; d. Isreal and Pearlie Mae Beaugard; m. Lonnie Burris, June 29, 1991. BS, Creighton U., 1986, MS, 1999; MEd, Lesley Coll., Omaha, 1999. Cert. tchr., Nebr. Educator Omaha Pub. Schs., 1986-99, instructional facilitator, 1999-2000, counselor, 2000—. Mem. Met. Reading Coun. (rep.), Urban League, Alpha Kappa Alpha. Democrat. Home: 13020 Patrick Cir Omaha NE 68164-3938 E-mail: jebburris@aol.com.

BURRIS, LYNETTE SUE, music educator; b. Zanesville, Ohio, Feb. 8, 1961; d. Delbert Scott and Betty Laura Van Reeth; m. Jeffrey Dayel Burris, June 8, 1985; children: Elijah, Zane. MusB, Bowling Green State U., 1983; M in Tchg., Marygrove Coll., 2002. Cert. spl. K-12 music edn. Choral music tchr. Pleasant Local Schs., Marion, Ohio, 1986—2003. Martha Holden Jennings scholar. Mem.: Music Educators Assn. Home: 3580 Smeltzer Rd Marion OH 43302 Office: Pleasant Local Sch 1101 Ownes Rd W Marion OH 43302

BURRIS-SCHNUR, CATHERINE, minister, pastoral psychotherapist, medical/surgical nurse, nursing educator; b. Ft. Lee, Va., Nov. 22, 1961; d. Charlie Franklin and Geneva Mae (Melton) B. ADN, Eizabethtown C.C., 1981, BSN, U. Ky., 1984; postgrad., So. Bapt. Theol. Sem., Louisville, 1986—90; MDiv, Garrett Evang. Theol. Sem., Evanston, Ill., 1994, D of Ministry, Chgo. Theol. Sem., 2002. RN, Ill.; ordained to ministry Am. Bapt. Ch., 1997. Staff nurse Ctrl. Bapt. Hosp., Lexington, Ky.; rehab. specialist Intacorp, Louisville; nurse mgr. St. Anthony Med. Ctr., Louisville, nurse mgr., med.-surg. educator, continuing edn. adminstr., dir. ednl. svcs., 1986—91; clin. fellow pastoral psychotherapy tng. program Ctr. for Religion and Psychotherapy, Chgo., 1994—97; assoc. dir. admissions Garrett Evang. Theol. Sem., Evanston, 1995—97; pastoral psychotherapist, co-dir. edn. The Ctr. for Religion and Psychotherapy, Chgo., 1997—. Recipient various nursing scholarships; named to Outstanding Young Women of Am., 1991. Mem.: ANA, Mins.' Coun.

BURROW, NANCY KAY, special education educator; b. Toledo, Ohio, Oct. 25, 1953; d. Richard Allen and Norma Jean Rader; m. Paul Irving Burrow, Sept. 8, 1979; children: Rachel, Timothy. BS in Spl. Edn., St. Cloud (Minn.) State U., 1975. Tchr. Shelby-Tennant Schs., Shelby, Iowa, 1975—76, Oskaloosa (Iowa) Sr. H.S., 1976—, dept. head, special education, 1995—. Contbr. articles to profl. jours. Mem.: Delta Kappa Gamma (chpt. pres. 1998—2000). United Methodist. Avocations: music, needlework. Office: Oskaloosa Sr High Sch 1816 N 3d St Oskaloosa IA 52577-1898

BURROWS, BARBARA ANN, veterinarian; b. Columbia, S.C., Dec. 15, 1947; d. Robert Beck and Betty Elizabeth (Rabon) Burrows; m. Richard M. Duemmler, Aug. 31, 1968 (div. Aug. 1975); 1 child, Sandra Lynn. BA, Hartwick Coll., 1969; VMD, U. Pa., 1983. Bacteriologist Johnson & Johnson, North Brunswick, N.J., 1969-70; microbiologist Ciba-Geigy, Summit, N.J., 1973-79; veterinarian Amboy Ave Vet. Hosp., Metuchen, N.J., 1983-84, Black Horse Pike Animal Hosp., Turnersville, N.J., 1984-93, San Juan Animal Hosp., San Juan Capistrano, Calif., 1993-94; relief vet., 1994—. Mem. Am. Vet. Med. Assn., So. Calif. Vet. Med. Assn., Am. Assn. Feline Practitioners. Avocations: dance, racquetball, biking. Home: 25582 Breezewood St Dana Point CA 92629-2138

BURROWS, BERTHA JEAN, retired academic administrator; b. Brush, Colo., June 15, 1930; d. John and Marie Pabst; m. Leslie R. Burrows, Sept. 2, 1951; children: Paul Eric, Amy Susan, Julie Diane, David Arthur. BA in Bus., U. Colo., 1952. Sec. Dental Found. Colo., Denver, 1969—70, John Boswick, MD, Denver, 1970—72; adminstrv. cons. dept. contg. edn. U. Colo. Sch. Dentistry, Denver, 1975—76; asst. dir. vol. svcs. U. Colo. Health Sci. Ctr., 1977—80; sec. Denver Neurosurg. Assn., Denver, 1981—83, ret., 1983. Part-time bookkeeper Clark & Co., Denver, 1981—83; mem. various coms. U. Colo. Hosp., Denver, 1999—. Vol. U. Colo. Hosp., Denver, 1970—; treas., asst. mgr. U. Colo. Hosp. Gift Shop, 1997—, bd. mgrs., 1987—. Mem.: Colo. Assn. Healthcare Auxilians and Vols. (treas. 2000—01, chmn. gift shop 2002—03, pres.-elect 2003—04, pres. 2004—), U. Colo. Srs. Assn. (pres. 2002—). Home: 6911 E Iliff Place Denver CO 80224

BURROWS, ELIZABETH MACDONALD, religious organization executive, educator; b. Portland, Oreg., Jan. 30, 1930; d. Leland R. and Ruth M. (Frew) MacDonald. Certificate, Chinmaya Trust Sandeepany, Bombay; PhD (hon.), Internat. U. Philosophy and Sci., 1975; ThD, Christian Coll. Universal Peace, 1992. Ordained to ministry First Christian Ch., 1976. Mgr. credit Home Utilities, Seattle, 1958, Montgomery Ward, Crescent City, Calif., 1963; supr. Oreg. dist. tng. West Coast Tele., Beaverton, 1965; pres. Christ Ch. of Universal Peace, Seattle, 1971—, prof. religion, also bd. dirs.; pres. Archives Internat., Seattle, 1971—; v.p. James Tyler Kent Inst. Homeopathy, 1984-95; sec. Louis Braille Inst. for the Blind, 1995—. Author: Crystal Planet, 1979, Pathway of the Immortal, 1980, Odyssey of the Apocalypse, 1981, Harp of Destiny, 1984, Commentary for Gospel of Peace of Jesus Christ According to John, 1986, Seasons of the Soul, 1995, Voyagers of the Sand, 1996, The Song of God, 1998, Hold the Anchovies, 1996, Pilgrim of the Shadow, 1998, Maya Sangh and the Valley of the White Ones, 2001, The Secret Jesus Scroll, 2002, Poetry Chapbook, 2002, Visions, 2002, Maya Sangh and the Valley of the White One. Recipient Pres. award for literary excellence CADER, 1994, 95, 97, Diamond Homer award Famous Poets Soc., 1998, Pub.'s Choice award Poets of the New Era, 2002. Mem. Internat. Speakers Platform, Internat. New Thought Alliance, Cousteau Soc., Internat. Order of Chivalry, The Planetary Soc. Home: 10529 Ashworth Ave N Seattle WA 98133-8937 E-mail: Starbase2001@earthlink.net.

BURSLEY, KATHLEEN A. lawyer; b. Washington, Mar. 20, 1954; d. G.H. Patrick and Claire (Mulvany) B. BA, Pomona Coll., 1976; JD, Cornell U., 1979. Bar: N.Y. 1980, U.S. Dist. Ct. (ea. and so. dists.) N.Y. 1980, U.S. Ct. Appeals (5th and 11th cirs.) 1981, Fla. 1984, U.S. Dist. Ct. (mid. dist.) Fla. 1984, Tex. 1985, Mass. 1995. Assoc. Haight, Gardner, Poor & Havens, N.Y.C., 1979-81; counsel Harcourt Brace Jovanovich, Inc., N.Y.C. and Orlando, Fla., 1981-85, v.p. and counsel San Antonio and Orlando, 1985-92; assoc. gen. counsel pub. Harcourt Gen., Inc., Chestnut Hill, Mass., 1992—; gen. counsel Harcourt, Inc., Chestnut Hill, Mass., 1992—; v.p. Harcourt Gen., Inc., 1998—. Mem. Maritime Law Assn. (proctor). Address: 41 Dwight St # 3 Brookline MA 02446 E-mail: kbursley@harcourtgeneral.com.

BURSLEY-HAMILTON, SUSAN, secondary school educator; b. Redbank, N.J., May 6, 1955; d. Robert Kelly and Irene Magdolin (Connell) Bursley; m. Raymond Hamilton, June 20, 1981; 1 child, Robert. BA in Edn., No. Ariz. U., 1978, MA, 1988. Asst. prin. Kingman Jr. High Sch., Ariz. Order Eastern Star scholar. Mem. Am. Fedn. Tchrs.

BURSON, BETSY LEE, librarian; b. Olney, Tex., Dec. 16, 1942; d. James Hollis and Lora Elizabeth (Talbott) B.; m. Winston Rabb Henderson, June 26, 1976. BS in Edn., Kans. State Tchrs. Coll., 1964; MLS, Tex. Woman's U., 1967, PhD in Libr. Info. Studies, 1987. With Phoenix Pub. Libr., 1967-74; libr. dir. Glendale (Ariz.) Pub. Libr., 1974-75; project archivist Phoenix History Project, 1975-77; adj. faculty U. Ariz., Tucson, 1979, Tex. Woman's U., Denton, 1980; libr. cons. La. State Libr., Baton Rouge, 1982-85; libr. dir. El Paso (Tex.) Pub. Libr., 1987-90, Arlington (Tex.) Pub. Libr., 1990—. Named Librarian of the Yr. Tex. Library Assn., 1995. Office: Arlington Pub Libr 101 E Abram St Arlington TX 76010-1183

BURSTYN, ELLEN (EDNA RAE GILLOOLY), actress; b. Detroit, Dec. 7, 1932; m. Paul Roberts; m. Neil Burstyn; 1 child, Jefferson. LHD (hon.), Dowling Coll.; DFA (hon.), Sch. Visual Arts. Artistic dir. The Actor's Studio, N.Y.C., 1982-88. Actress: films include Gunfight in Black Horse Canyon, 1961, Alex in Wonderland, 1970, Tropic of Cancer, 1970, The Last Picture Shoe, 1971, The King of Marcin Gardens, 1972, The Exorcist, 1973, Harry and Tonto, 1974, Alice Dosen't Live Here Anymore, 1974, Same Time, Next Year, 1978, Resurrection, 1980, Silence of the North, 1981, In Our Hands, 1984, The Ambassador, 1984, Twice in a Lifetime, 1985, Hanna's War, 1988, Grand Isle, 1991, Dying Young, 1991, The Cemetery Club, 1993, The Color of Evening, 1994, Choosing One's Way: Resistance in Auschwitz/Birkenau (narrator, presenter), 1994, When a Man Loves a Woman, 1994, Roommates, 1995, The Baby-Sitters Club, 1995, How to Make an American Quilt, 1995, The Spitfire Grill, 1996, Deceiver, 1997, You Can Thank Me Later, 1998, Playing by Heart, 1998, Walking Across Egypt, 1999, Requiem for a Dream, 1999, The Yards, 1999, Divine Secrets of the Ya-Ya Sisterhood, 2002, numerous others; tv movies include: The People vs. Jean Harris, 1981, Acting: Lee Strasberg and the Actos Studio, 1981, Surviving, 1985, Into Thin Air, 1985, Something in Common, 1986, Act of Vengeance, 1986, The Ellen Burstyn Show, 1986, Hellow Actors Studio, 1987, Door America: Letters Home from Vietnam, 1987, Pack of Lies, 1987, When You Remember Me, 1990, Mrs. Lambers Remembers Love, 1991, Taking Back My Life: The Nacy Ziegenmeyer Story, 1992, Shattered Trust: The Shary Karney Story, 1993, Getting Out, 1994, Getting Gotti, 1994, Trick of the Eye, 1994, My Brother's Keeper, 1995, Follow the River, 1995, Timepiece, 1995, Our Son, The Matchmaker, 1996, Murder in the Mind, 1996, A Deadly Vision, 1997, Flash, 1998, The Patron Saint of Liars, 1998, (mini-series) A Will of Their Own, 1998, Night Ride Home, 1999; tv appearances include Cheyenne, 1955, Gunsmoke, 1955, Maverick, 1957, The Big Valley, 1965, The Time Tunnel, 1966, The Bold Ones: The Lawyers, 1969. Mem. individual artists grants and policy overview panels Nat. Endowment for the Arts, Theater Adv. Council City of New York. Mem. Actors Equity Assn. (pres. 1982-85) Office: Creative Artists Agy care Steve Tellez 9830 Wilshire Blvd Beverly Hills CA 90212-1804

BURT, GWEN BEHRENS, elementary school administrator; b. Clinton, Ind., Nov. 6, 1946; d. Henry Milum Allbright and Marjorie Evelyn (Muir) Wiot; m. Kurt Fredric Behrens, Mar. 28, 1970 (div. June 1984); m. Gary Orren Burt (dec. Sept. 1998), Sept. 5, 1996; 1 child, Amy Lynn. BS, Ind. State U., 1969, MS, 1974. Tchr. Center Grove Cmty. Schs., Greenwood, Ind., 1969-71; tchr. reading Vigo County Sch. Corp., Terre Haute, Ind., 1971-77; summer adminstr. Maercker Sch. Dist., Clarendon Hills, Ill., 1991-98, Title I dir., 1977-98; prin. Sauk Sch., Matteson (Ill.) Dist. 162, 1998—. Adj. lectr. Lewis U., Romeoville, Ill., 1996; presenter workshops and lectures, 1987—. Coord. single adult program, Grace United Meth. Ch., Naperville, Ill., 1992-95, coord. youth ministry program, 1985-87; vol. numerous charitable orgns. including Am. Cancer Soc., Am. Heart Assn., etc. Mem NEA (various offices Ill. and Ind. chpts.), AAUW, Internat. Reading Assn. (various offices Ill. and Ind. chpts.), Nat. Assn. Elem. Schs. Prins., AAUW, ASCD, Ill. Prins. Assn., Ill. Reading Coun., Ill. Women Adminstr., Ill. Title I coords., Adminstrs. and Reading Spl. Interest Coun., Delta Kappa Gamma. Republican. Avocations: power boating, golf, antiques, geneology, lighthouses. Home: 1245 Baythorne Dr Flossmoor IL 60422-1442 Office: Sauk Sch 4435 S Churchill Dr Richton Park IL 60471-1101 E-mail: gaboating1@cs.com., gburt@sd162.org.

BURTON, BARBARA, marketing executive; b. Plainfield, N.J., May 29, 1953; d. Frank James and Helen Sellmyer Wolf; m. Allen Craig Burton, June 21, 1986; children: Matthew James, Abigail Elizabeth. BA, Northwestern U., 1975; MLS, Rutgers U., 1977. Indexer N.Y. Times Info. Svc., Parsippany, N.Y., 1977-78, customer svc. rep., 1979-81, nat. tng. mgr., 1981-83; online mktg. coord. Dun & Bradstreet, Parsippany, 1983-84; account exec. Dow Jones & Co., Princeton, N.J., 1984-88, account devel. mgr., 1988-97, infopro alliance mgr., 1997—. Mem. Spl. Librs. Assn., Westfield Hist. Soc., Friends of Westfield Libr., Beta Phi Mu. Home: 620 Lenox Ave Westfield NJ 07090-2161

BURTON, BETTY JUNE, retired pastor; b. Muskegon, Mich., June 11, 1923; d. Bernard J. and Louise Ella (Weaver) Mulder; m. Harold Ver Berkmoes, June 4, 1943 (div. 1966); children: Suzanne, James, Michael, William, Judith, David (dec.); m. Eldon Franklin Burton, June 27, 1971 (dec. May 8, 2003). Student of music, psychology and religion, Hope Coll., 1941-45; student, Garrett Evang. Theol. Sem., 1984-85. Ordained to ministry United Meth. Ch., 1986. Librarian Vassar Hosp. Sch. Nursing, Poughkeepsie, N.Y., 1958-60, Hackley Pub. Library, Muskegon, 1960-64, Boyne City (Mich.) Pub. Library, 1972-74; reporter Ludington (Mich.) Daily News, 1975-81; caseworker Aid to Dependent Children Mich. Dept. Social Services, Hart, 1974-78; pastor various Meth. Chs., Norwood, Barnard and Charlevoix, Mich., 1981-83, Mears (Mich.) United Meth. Ch., 1985, 86; assoc. pastor United Meth. Centenary, Pentwater, Mich., 1986-90; pastor First Congl. Ch. of Central Lake, Mich., 1990-92, Thompsonville (Mich.) Congl. Church, 1982—83. Guest preacher, spkr. various chs. Sec. Pentwater Planning Commn., 1985; vol. chaplain Grand Tranverse Pavilions Nursing Home. Mem. NAFE, Internat. Platform Assn., Am. Platform Assn., Am. Assn. Christian Counselors, Nat. Christian Counselors Assn., Nat. Trust Hist. Preservation, Am. Mus. Natural History, Nat. Audubon Soc., Am. Acad. Ministry, Hist. Soc. Mich., Hist. Soc. U.S., Kappa Beta Phi (pres. 1943), Xi Gamma Beta (sec. 1970). Clubs: Women's of Pentwater (v.p. 1986—), Garden of Pentwater (pres. 1986—), Sierra. Republican. Avocations: writing, fishing, gardening, birding, travel. Home and Office: 3848 Silver Lake Rd Apt 108 Traverse City MI 49684-7005

BURTON, B.J. (BETTY JANE), playwright; b. Phila., Nov. 22, 1950; d. Robert Ellis and Barbara Elizabeth (Williams) Burton. BA in theatre, U. Mo., 1973; attended, Am. Conservatory Theatre, 1978; grad. in theatre, Villanova U., 1997; student MFA in creative writing, Rosemont Coll., 2003—. Playwright : Hunting Season, 1990; Buddy, 1992; Lunch on the [illegible], 1990; [illegible], 1998; [illegible], 1990; Green Benches, 2000; Marjorie and Helen, 2000; Room For Love, 2002. Grantee fellowship in playwriting, Pa. Coun. on the Arts, 1990, fellowship in scriptwriting, 2000; semi-finalist, Nicholl Fellowships in Screenwriting, 1998. Avocations: painting, photography. Office: PO Box 445 Wayne PA 19087 E-mail: bj_burton@hotmail.com.

BURTON, CHERYL, newscaster; b. Chgo. BS in Psychology and Biology, U. Ill., Champaign. Host Minority Bus. Report WGN-TV, Chgo., 1989; reporter WMBD-TV, Peoria, Ill., 1990; weekend anchor KWCH-TV, Wichita, Kans., 1990—92, host Viewpoint, 1990—92; weekend co-anchor and reporter WLS-TV, Chgo., 1992—2003, co-anchor and contbg. anchor 5 pm news, 2003—. Vol. Boys and Girls Club of Am., Rush-Presbyn./St. Luke's Fashion Show; motivational spkr. Chgo. Pub. Sch.; bd. mem. City Yr., Chgo. Recipient Kizzy Image and Achievement award, 1998, Phenomenal Woman award, Expo Today's Black Woman, 1997. Mem.: Nat. Assn. of Black Journalists, Chgo. Assn. of Black Journalists ((now named Russ Ewing award) 1996, 2003), Life with Lupus Guild, Delta Sigma Theta. Office: WLS-TV 190 N State St Chicago IL 60601

BURTON, KATHERINE GALE, music educator, recording industry executive, musician; d. James Richardson and Susie Smith; m. George Alfred Burton, Aug. 20, 1977 (div. Feb. 1997); children: George III, Desmond. BA, Temple U., 1997; MA, Arcadia U., 1998. Instrumental tchr. Phila. Sch. Dist., 1977—. CEO, pres. New Dawn Prodns., Phila., 1989—. Performer: CD recording I'll Fly Away, 1999. Mem.: Gospel Instrumental Music Assn., Gospel Music Workshop Am. (founder), Nat. Assn. for Music Edn., Am. String Tchr. Assn. Avocations: skating, reading. Home: PO Box 14149 Philadelphia PA 19138 Office: New Dawn Prodn PO Box 14149 Philadelphia PA 19138 Office Phone: 215-924-1336.

BURTON, LESLIE ANNE, psychologist; b. N.Y.C. BA, Queens Coll., 1977; MS, U. Chgo., 1983, PhD, 1985. Lic. psychologist, N.Y., Calif. Intern Columbia U. Coll. Physicians and Surgeons, N.Y.C., 1983-84; fellow in psychology Cornell U. Med. Coll., 1984-86; asst. prof. psychology in neurosci. Cornell U. Med. Coll./Burke Rehab. Hosp./N.Y. Hosp., White Plains, 1986-90; asst. prof. psychology Fordham U., Bronx, NY, 1994—, assoc. prof. psychology, 1999—. Adj. assoc. prof. psychology in neurosci. Cornell U. Coll. N.Y. Hosp., N.Y.C., 1995—. Contbr. articles to profl. jours. Mem. APA, Internat. Neuropsychol. Soc., Nat. Acad. Neuropsychology, Cognitive Neurosci. Soc., N.Y. Acad. Scis. Office: Fordham U Psychology Dept 441 E Fordham Rd Bronx NY 10458-9993

BURTON, R. JOHNNIE MEDINGER, state official, data processing executive, finance company executive; b. Birkadem, Algeria, Dec. 18, 1939; came to U.S., 1963; d. Georges Justin and Elise Rose (Pettinati) Medinger; m. Guy C. Burton Jr., Jan 21, 1966; children: Craig G., Valerie A. Licence-és-lettres, U. Sorbonne, 1962; MA, U. Wyo., 1974. Tchr. French Wantagh (N.Y.) Sch. Dist., 1963-65; lectr. Queens Coll., N.Y.C. U., 1965-66; tchr. Natrona County Sch. dist., Casper, Wyo., 1966-68; pres., CEO, Hotline Energy Reports, Casper, 1978-84; mem. Wyo. Ho. of Reps., Cheyenne, 1982-88; corp. v.p. Dwight's Energy Data, Dallas, 1984-89; dir. dept. revenue State of Wyo., 1995—2002; dir. Minerals Mgmt. Svc., Dept. of Interior, Washington, 2002—. Lectr. U. Ark., 1989-94. Mem. Natrona County Sch. Bd., Casper, 1976-82; adv. mem. Casper dist. Bur. Land Mgmt., 1986-88; bd. dirs. Wyo. Heritage Soc., 1986-88. Mem. Am. Assn. Tchrs. French, Société des Professeurs Francais en Amerique, Fgn. Relations Com. (Wyo. chpt.). Republican. Roman Catholic. Avocations: reading, needlepoint, folk arts and crafts. Business E-Mail: Johnnie.burton@mms.gov.

BURTON, SHEILA BELLE, music educator; b. Springfield, Ill., July 20, 1945; d. James Eugene Gurnsey, Hazel Belle Gurnsey; m. Charles Arlie Burton. B in Music Edn., Bradley U., 1968. Music instr. Chandlerville Unit Dist., Ill., 1968—70, Beardstown Unit Dist. #15, Ill., 1970—75; unit vocal and band instr. VIT, Table Grove, Ill., 1984—93; band instr. Schuyler Unit Dist. #1, Rushville, Ill., 1993—. Auxiliary/dance line dir. Schuyler Unit Dist. #1, Rushville, 1993—, girls golf coach, 1993—. Mem.: MENC - IMEA. Methodist. Avocations: golf, reading, gardening. Home: RR#2 Box 23 Rushville IL 62681 Office: Schuyler Dist #1 730 N Congress Rushville IL 62681 Office Fax: 217-322-2844. Personal E-mail: sburton@frontiernet.net. Business E-Mail: sburton@scud1.com.

BURTT, ANNE DAMPMAN, special education educator; b. Phila., Nov. 22, 1950; d. Elmer and Anne (Scott) Dampman; m. James Burtt, Aug. 5, 1972. BS in Edn. cum laude, Duquesne U., 1972; MEd, U. Pitts., 1976, Temple U., 1985. Cert. spl. edn., elem. tchr., reading specialist. Tchr. Pitts. Pub. Schs., 1972-77; tchr. Montgomery County (Pa.) Intermediate Unit, 1997—2000, Archdiocese of Phila. Schs., 2000—; archdiocese Phila. Schs., 2000—. Mem. PTO, 1972—, Chpt. Attention Deficit Disorders, 1989—, CHADD Bux-Mont. Divsn., Behavioral Disorders/Learning Disorders. Recipient Pius X award Archdiocese Phila., Most Successful Grad. 25th Yr. Reunion West Phila. Cath. Girls' H.S. Mem. Pa. State Edn. Assn., Coun. for Exceptional Children, Behavior Disorders and Learning Disabilities. Home: 131 Maple Ave Willow Grove PA 19090-2902

BURTT, LARICE ANNADEL ROSEMAN, artist; b. Phila., June 22, 1928; d. Milo A.J. Roseman and Anna Sterling; m. James C. Burtt, June 25, 1960; childen, James M., Kyleann S. BS in Biology, Bucknell U., 1950; MS in Nursing, Yale U., 1955; studied art with Dr. Selma Burke, studied with William A. Smith; cert., Katherine Gibbs Sec. Sch., 1951. Med. clinical instr. Jefferson Hosp., Phila., 1956-57; med. surgical instr. Rowan Meml. Hosp., Salisbury, N.C., 1958-59. Workshop leader Yale, New Haven Hosp. Pain Mgmt. Ctrs., New Haven, Ct., 1996, Attleboro Nursing Home, Langhorne, Pa., Chandler Hall, Newtown, Pa.; instr. Delaware Valley Schs., Pa., 1979—; profl. demonstrator in field, 1977—. Painter (three-dimensional stone painting), many locations, 1976-99; one person shows include Arnot Art Mus., Elmira, N.Y., 1987, Cannon Bldg., Washington, DC 1995, Yale Univ. Sch. Nursing, New Haven, Conn., 1996; exhibited in group shows at Immaculata Coll., Accent and Images Gallery, Lahaska, Pa., Designer Crafts on Main, Stroudsburg, Pa., 2000, Jane Anthony Gallery, Newtown, Pa., 2000, Abington (Pa.) Art Ctr., Louisa Melrose Gallery, Frenchtown, N.J., many area group exhbns., 1977—; represented in permanent collection Grand Canyon Nat. Pk. Mus. Mem. AAUW, Northhampton Hist. Soc., Middletown Grange, Bucks County Guild Craftsman (exhbn. at Franklin and Marshall Coll. 1979-96), James Michener Art Mus., Doylestown (Pa.), Artsbridge, Doylestown Art League, Pa. Guild. Avocations: tennis, piano, visual/performing arts, community affairs, service art shows. Home: 31 Beth Dr Richboro PA 18954-1901 E-mail: lariceburtt@aol.com.

BURZYNSKI, SUSAN MARIE, newspaper editor; b. Jackson, Mich., Jan. 1, 1953; d. Leon Walter and Claudia (Kulpinski) B.; m. James W. Bush, May 22, 1976 (div. 1989); children: Lisa M., Kevin J.; m. George K. Bullard, Jr., Mar. 21, 1992. AA, Jackson C.C., 1972; BA, Mich. State, 1974. Reporter Saratogian, Saratoga Springs, N.Y., 1974, Gongwer News Svc., Lansing, Mich., 1975, The State Jour., Lansing, 1975-79; Metro editor Port Huron (Mich.) Times Herald, 1979-82, mng. editor, 1982-86; asst. city editor Detroit News, 1986-87, Sunday news editor, 1987, news editor, 1988-91, asst. mng. editor/news, 1991-96, asst. mng. editor, recruiting and tng., 1996-98, asst. mng. editor, adminstr., 1998-2000, assoc. editor, 2000—. Roman Catholic. Avocations: swimming, skiing, tennis, biking. Office: Detroit News 615 W Lafayette Blvd Detroit MI 48226-3197

BUSARD, ROBERTA ANN, artist, educator; b. Muskegon, Mich., [illegible] 1952; d. Thomas Richard and Dolores Mae (Fisher) B.; m. William VonWemp Suchmann, Dec. 19, 1992; 1 child Katherine Susan Busard Suchmann. BFA, Mass. Coll. Art, 1977; attended, San Francisco Art Inst., 1970, 73, Art Inst. Boston, 1971, Silvermine Coll. Art, 1972; MFA, Wayne State U., 1998. Cert. art edn. K-12. Intern art tchr. Boston Pub. Schs., 1975, 77, The Internat. Sch. Genoa, Italy, 1976; art tchr., dir. The Kid's Art Studio, S. Burlington, Vt., 1990-91, The Women's Art Project, Ann Arbor, Mich., 1992-94; art tchr. Go Like The Wind Montesorri Sch., Ann Arbor, 1993-94. Guest lectr. u. Mich., Ann Arbor, 1992; mem., advisor, curator The Vt. Artist's Collective, Burlington, Vt., 1989-90; prof. artist in residence Ox-Bow Summer Sch., Art Inst. Chgo., 1995. Solo shows include Margolis Gallery, Vail, Colo., 1984, Hibberd-McGrath Galleries, Keystone, Colo., 1985, St. Mark's Gallery, N.Y.C., 1986, Lincoln Ctr., Ft. Collins, Colo., 1987, Reinike Gallery, New Orleans, 1988, Stowe (Vt.) Playhouse Gallery, 1988, Gallery One, Denver, 1988, Reinike Gallery, Atlanta, 1992, 95, Visual and Performing Arts Loft Gallery, Ann Arbor, Mich., 1995, Ford Amphitheater Gallery, U. Mich. Hosps., Ann Arbor, 1995, Chgo. Sch. Profl. Psychology, 1996; numerous group exhbns. include Woodstock (Vt.) Gallery, 1989, 90, Lone Pine Gallery, Newport Beach, Calif., 1989, 90, 91, Gallery One, Denver, 1989, 90, 91, Vt. Artists' Collective, Burlington, 1990, Burlington City Arts Coun., 1990, Reinike Gallery, Atlanta, 1990, 91, 92, 94, Art's Alive, Burlington, 1990, Impressions Gallery, Burlington, 1990, 91, 92, Stratton (Vt.) Arts Festival, 1991, U. Mich. Rackam Grad. Sch. Galleries, 1991, Art-Tech Gallery, Chgo., 1993, 94, Galleriea, Washtenaw Coun. for Arts, 1993, ARC Gallery, Chgo., 1994, Wells St. Art Festival, Chgo., 1994, Detroit Artists' Mkt., 1994, Chautauqua (N.Y.) Art Assn., 1994, Chgo.'s New EastSide Artworks, 1994, Anchorage Mus. History and Art, 1994-95, An Art Place Inc. Gallery, 1995, Art Inst. Boston, 1995, Elite Gallery and Russian-Am. Cultural Ctr., Moscow, 1995, Nat. Mus. of Women in the Arts, Washington, 1996, many others; permanent collections include Anchorage Mus. Art and History, Nat. Mus. Women in the Arts, Dieckmann & Assocs., Ltd., U.S. West Telecom. and many pvt. collections. Recipient Juror's Choice Mary Mellor Meml. Fund award for painting, mixed media and drawing San Francisco Women Artists Gallery, 1994, Juror's Choice award for painting Arts Alive, Burlington, 1990; Thomas C. Rumble Grad. fellow, 1996-97, 97-98. Mem. Nat. Women's Caucus for Art, Mich. Women's Caucus for Art (founder Mich. chpt. 1994, pres. 1994-95, co-pres. 1996—), Detroit Focus Gallery (exbhn. com. mem. 1994-95), Chgo. Artist's Coalition, Coll. Art Assn., Mich. Bus. and Profl. Assn., Nat. Mus. for Women in the Arts, Artists' choice Mus., Alumni Assn. of San Francisco Art Inst., Alumni Assn. of Art Inst. Boston, Alumni Assn. of Mass. Coll. Art. Avocation: snow skiing. Office: PO Box 130051 Ann Arbor MI 48113-0051

BUSBY, MARJEAN (MARJORIE JEAN BUSBY), retired journalist; b. Kansas City, Mo., Jan. 31, 1931; d. Vivian Eric and Stella Mae (Lindley) Phillips; m. Robert Jackson Busby, Apr. 11, 1969 (dec. Feb. 1989). B.J., U. Mo., 1952. With Kansas City Star Co. (Knight Ridder purchased 1997), 1952-2000, editor women's news, 1969-73, assoc. Sunday editor, People Sect. editor, 1973-77, fashion editor, 1978-81, feature and home writer, 1981-2000; ret., 2000. Mem. Fashion Group (1st recipient Kansas City appreciation award 1978), LSV, Mortar Board, Soc. Profl. Journalists, Friends of Art, Belle of Am. Royal Orgn., Kappa Alpha Theta (pres. Alpha Mu chpt. 1951-52) Presbyterian. Home: 9804 Mercier St Kansas City MO 64114-3860

BÜSCH, ANNEMARIE, retired mental health nurse; b. Ger. d. Jurgen Julius and Anna (Stark) B. RN, Anschar Sch. Nursing, Kiel, Fed. Republic Germany, 1954; student, Traverse City State Hosp., Mich., 1959, Wayne State U., 1962, Colby-Sawyer Coll., New London, N.H., 1981. Lic. nurse, N.H., Vt., Fed. Republic Germany. Asst. head nurse Univ. Eye Inst., Kiel, 1954-56; nurse aide, grad. nurse Ontario Hosp., London, Can.; staff nurse, charge nurse Grace Hosp., Receiving Hosp., Detroit, 1962-67; coll. health nurse Wayne St. U., Detroit, 1967-70; staff nurse Mary Hitchcock Meml. Hosp., Hanover, 1970-71, nurse mental health dept., 1978-82; charge nurse Dartmouth Coll. Health Svc., Hanover, N.H., 1971-77; staff nurse, charge nurse Hanover Health Terrace; staff nurse Temporary Nurses, Inc., Hanover, Vis. Nurse Alliance of Vt. and N.H., White River Junction, Vt.; ret., 1997. Camp nurse Nat. Music Camp InterLochen, Mich.

BUSCH, ANNIE, library director; b. Joplin, Mo., Jan. 6, 1947; d. George Lee and Margaret Eleanor (Williams) Chancellor; 1 child, William Andrew Keller. BA, Mo. U., 1969, MA, 1976. Br. mgr. St. Charles (Mo.) City Coun. Libr., 1977-84, Springfield/Greene County (Mo.) Libr., 1985-89, exec. dir., 1989—. Exec. bd. Mo. Libr. Network Corp., St. Louis, 1991-96. Adv. bd. Springfield Pub. Sch. Found., 1992—94, St. John's Health Sys., Boys and Girls Town, Good Cmty. Task Force, 1999—2002; pres. Ozarks Regional Info. On-Line Network, Springfield, 1993—98; active Gov.'s Commn. on Informational Tech., Cmty. Task Force, Springfield, 1993—98, Cmty. Partnership of the Ozarks, 1998; exec. bd. Mo. Rsch. and Edn. Network, pres., 1996—97; bd. dirs. Ozarks Pub. TV, 1994—2000, Every Kid Counts; task force Mo. Goals 2000, 1995, Mo. Census 2000 Complete Count Com., 1999—2000; coord. com. Springfield Vision 20/20; chair Sec. of State Adv. Coun., 2001—; adv. com. S.W. Mo. State U. Coll. Humanities and Pub. Affairs. Mem.: ALA, Springfield Rotary (pres. 1998—99), Springfield Area C. of C. (bd. dirs.), Pub. Libr. Assn., Mo. Libr. Assn. (exec. bd. 1990—94, pres. 1993—94), Forest Inst. Profl. Psychology (bd. dirs.). Office: Springfield-Greene Cty Libr PO Box 760 Springfield MO 65801-0760 Office Phone: 417-847-8120 ext 5. E-mail: annie@mail.sgcl.org.

BUSCH, BEVERLY GAIL, English language educator, literature educator, instructional resource center administrator; b. Boston, Oct. 27, 1948; d. Andrew Earl Thompson and Martha Bartlett; m. Peter Raymond Busch, Apr. 15, 1972; children: Cheyenne J., Carin S., Luke W. BA, U. Mass., 1970; MA, Middlebury Coll., 1978; MPhil, Drew U., 1981, PhD, 1986. Cert. English tchr. Mass., NJ. Adj. faculty mem. Coll. St. Elizabeth, Madison, N.J., 1981-83, Centenary Coll., Hackettstown, N.J., 1981-83; coord. ministries program Phillipsburg (N.J.) Alliance Ch., 1995-99; adj. prof. English Warren County Cmty. Coll., Washington, N.J., 1995-99; prof. English Somerset Christian Coll., Zarephath, NJ, 1999—, dir. Instructional Resource Ctr. Author poetry and inspirational articles; mem. editl. adv. bd.: Collegiate Press, 2002—. Mem. Greenwich Twp. Bd. Edn., Stewartsville, N.J., 1995-99; pres. Greenwich Twp. Parent Tchr. Orgn., 1989-92, Parents On Site, 1994-96. Mem.: MLA, NJ Coun. Tchrs. English, Nat. Coun. Tchrs. English, Drew U. Alumni Assn., Middlebury Coll. Alumni Assn., U. Mass. Alumni Assn. Republican. Avocations: walking, biking, crafts. Home: 113 Kennedy Mill Rd Stewartsville NJ 08886 Office Phone: 732-356-1595 126.

BUSCH, JOYCE IDA, small business owner; b. Madera, Calif., Jan. 24, 1934; d. Bruno Harry and Ella Fae (Absher) Toschi; m. Fred O. Busch, Dec. 14, 1956; children: Karen, Kathryn, Kurt. BA in Indsl. Arts & Interior Design, Calif. State U., Fresno, 1991. Cert. interior designer, Calif. Stewardess United Air Lines, San Francisco, 1955-57; prin. Art Coordinates, Fresno, 1982—, Busch Interior Design, Fresno, 1982—. Art cons. Fresno Community Hosp., 1981-83; docent Fresno Met. Mus., 1981-84. Treas. Valley Children's Hosp. Guidance Clinic, 1975-79, Lone Star PTA, 1965-84,; mem. Mothers Guild San Joaquin Mem. H.S., 1984-88. Mem. Am. Soc. Interior Designers. Clubs: Sunnyside Garden (pres. 1987-88). Republican. Roman Catholic. Avocations: gardening, art history. Office Phone: 559-447-1220.

BUSCH, SHARON LYNNE, elementary and secondary education educator; b. Beavercreek, Ohio, Nov. 16, 1952; d. James Earl and Lena Mae (Brown) B.; m. John Robert Busch, Oct. 8, 1977; 1 child, Brian Alexander. MusB, Miami U., Oxford, Ohio, 1976; postgrad., Wright State U., Fairborn, Ohio, 1991. [illegible] Studios, Fairfield, 1970-72, desk clk. YMCA, Fairfield, 1972-73; choir dir., accompanist Ch. of the Nazarene, Fairfield, 1972-74; tchr. music Albert Kirocofe Jr. High and Elem. Sch., Gratis, Ohio, 1976-77, Ankeney Jr. High Sch., Beavercreek, Ohio, 1977-98, Beavercreek High Sch., Beavercreek, 1978-98. Dir. Friends showchoir, Beavercreek, 1977-95, Guys and Dolls showchoir, Beavercreek, 1979—, dir. a capella choir and concert choir, 1977-98, dir. Nothing But Men group, 1997-98; dir. Beavercreek High. Sch. musicals, 1977-85; soloist Coventry Green Madrigal Group, Dayton, Ohio, 1982-85. Singer Dayton Philharm. Chorus, 1988—; chmn. North Cen. Vis. Team, Edgewood High Sch., Hamilton, 1989, Middletown High Sch., 1991, mem. North Cen. Vis. Team, Stebbins High Sch., Dayton, 1988. Named Outstanding Tchr. of Yr. Beavercreek Sch. Dist., 1991. Mem. Ohio Music Edn. Assn. (hon. choir dir. dist. 12), Am. Choral Dirs. Assn., Ohio Choral Dirs. Assn., Music Educators Nat. Conf., Ohio Music Educators Assn., U. Dayton Music Dept. (guest clinician, 1998). Republican. Avocations: composing music, swimming, bowling, singing. Home: 1363 Meadow Bridge Dr Beavercreek OH 45432-2602

BUSCHKOPF, DEBORA J. court reporter; b. Elkhorn, Wis., Aug. 24, 1956; d. Clyde D. and Irma G. (Ryder) Buschkopf. Adminstrv. secretarial diploma, Bryant & Stratton Bus. Coll., Milw., 1975; AA, Gateway Tech. Inst., Kenosha, Wis., 1982. Cert.: (profl. reporter) 1985, registered: 1991. Freelance ct. reporter, Atlantic City, 1987—95; ofcl. ct. reporter State of Nebr., Chadron, 1995—; dental asst., 2001. Recipient Queen for a Day award, Chadron Christian Women's Club, 2000. Mem.: International Order of Job's Daughters (Numerous in the organization 1972—76), Friends of Pets, Ivy Leaf Chapter #60, Order of the Eastern Star (Numerous in the organization 1996—), Business and Professional Women (2d v.p. 2001—02, 1st v.p. 2002—03). Methodist. Avocation: working with animals and local youth groups. Office: Dawes County Courthouse P O Box 630 Chadron NE 69337 Office Phone: 308-432-0112. Personal E-mail: dawescountycourtreporter@yahoo.com.

BUSCH-VISHNIAC, ILENE JOY, mechanical engineering educator, researcher; b. Phila., Jan. 28, 1955; d. Leonard and Ruth (Rudnick) Busch; m. Ethan Tecumseh Vishniac, June 13, 1976; children: Cady Anne, Miriam Rachel. BA in Math. magna cum laude, BS in Physics magna cum laude, U. Rochester, 1976; MSME, MIT, 1978, PhD in Mech. Engring., 1981. Mem. tech. staff acoustics rsch. dept. Bell Labs., 1980-82; asst. prof. mech. engring. U. Tex., Austin, 1982-86, assoc. prof., 1986-91, prof., assoc. chmn. mech. engring. for acad. affairs, 1991-95, Harry H. Power prof., 1994-98; dean Whiting Sch. of Engring. Johns Hopkins U., 1998—2003; prof., mech. engring. John Hopkins U., 2003—. Cons. AT&T Bell Labs., 1982-84, Nat. Inst. Justice, 1988, Body, Vickers, Daniels, 1989-93, to Tex. atty. gen., 1989-95; also others; mem. vis. com. dept. mech. engring. MIT, 1993-99; presdl. young investigator NSF, 1985; numerous presentations to profl. soc. mtgs., workships, confs.; numerous invited lectures; chmn. session on micro-automation, sensing and hardware issues Internat. Symposium on Robotics and Mfg., 1992, mem. mfg. program com., 1994; numerous others. Author: Electromechanical Sensors and Actuators, 1999; contbg. author: Handbook of Acoustics, 1992; contbr. numerous articles to sci. jours. Program mentor YWCA, 1989; speaker Tex. Energy Sci. Symposium for H.S.'s, 1989, Austin Sci. Acad., 1989, 90; speaker, session chmn. Expanding Your Horizons Workshop, 1991. Recipient Curtis McGraw rsch. award Am. Soc. for Engring. Edn., 1994, best paper award in mfg. Internat. Symposium on Robotics and Mfg., 1994; fellow Fannie and John Hertz Found., MIT, 1976-80, GM Found. Centennial tchg. fellow in mech. engring., 1985; grantee NSF, 1983—, Univ. Rsch. Inst., 1983-85, U. Tex. Bur. Engring. Rsch., 1983-85, Office Naval Rsch., 1985-87, Bosque Found., 1986-88, Semicondr. Rsch. Corp., 1987-90, GM, 1988-89, Tex. Instruments, 1989, Tex. Dept. Transp., 1994—; others. Fellow Acoustical Soc. Am. (v.p. 1997-98, tech. com. on engring. acoustics 1982—, tech. com. on noise 1982—, exec. com. 1988-91, com. on status of women in the Soc. 1992—, chmn. Austin chpt. 1986, nominating com. 1989, Lindsay award 1987); mem. ASME (micro-mech. sys. panel dynamic sys. and control div. 1992—, Outstanding Mech. Engring. Faculty Advisor award 1983), Inst. Noise Control Engring. (assoc.), Soc. Women Engrs. (Achievement award 1997), AAUW, Golden Key, Phi Beta Kappa. Achievements include patent on electret transducer with a selectively metallized backplate, with a variably charged electret foil, with a variable electret foil thickness, with a variable effective air gap, with a variable actual air gap; integrated capacitive microphone, electret transducer for blood pressure monitoring, six degree-of-freedom optical sensor. Office: John Hopkins U 223 Latrobe Hall 3400 N Charles St Baltimore MD 21218 E-mail: ilenebv@jhu.edu.

BUSER, CAROLYN ELIZABETH, correctional education administrator; b. St. Paul, June 14, 1946; d. Jerome Alfred and Ella Caroline (Anderson) B.; m. Richard John Ward, Sept. 17, 1977; children: John Jerome Buser Ward, Carl Alfred Buser Ward. BA in English, Carleton Coll., 1968; MS in Spl. Edn., U. Md., 1985, PhD in Ednl. Policy and Adminstrn., 1996. Correctional tchr. Md. Div. Correction, Hughesville, 1970-74, Balt., 1974-76; correctional edn. supr. Md. Dept. Edn. Md. Penitentiary, Balt., 1976-80, Md. Correctional Instn., Jessup, 1980-88; correctional edn. supr. Md. Dept. Edn., Md. correctional pre-release program Md. Correctional Instn. for Women, Jessup, 1988-94; field coord. correctional edn. Md. Dept. Edn., 1994-2001, dir. correctional edn., 2001—. Cons. Am. Correctional Assn., Laurel, Md., 1980; Md. state dir. Correctional Edn. Assn., Laurel, 1988-90; program supr. Prison Literacy, Nat. Inst. Corrections, Washington (designated exemplary program, 1986). Mem. editl. rev. bd. Jour. Correctional Edn., 2002—. Fellow Edn. Behaviorally Disordered Students, U. Md., 1985. Mem.: Md. State Use Indus. Coun., Md. Assn. Adult Cmty. and Continuing Edn., Correctional Edn. Assn. (sec. 1986, edit. bd. Jour. Correctional Edn. 2002—), Phi Kappa Phi. Office: Md State Dept Edn 200 W Baltimore St Ste 1 Baltimore MD 21201-2595 E-mail: cbuser@msde.state.md.us.

BUSER, ROSE M. elementary school educator; b. Port Washington, Wis., Oct. 2, 1948; d. Arthur Leo and Louise Angela Buser; children: Hajira, Rabiah, Joshua. BS in Edn., U. Wis., Whitewater, 1971, MS in Tchg., 1973; postgrad., Ohio State U., 1978—81. Lic. tchr. Dept. of Pub. Instrn., Wis., 1999. Tchr. Abbott Acad., Santo Domingo, Dominican Republic, 1972; instr. Briam Instituto de Idiomas, Madrid, 1973—74; Spanish tchr. Yellow Springs (Ohio) Schs., 1978—81; instr. U. Houston, 1981—82; immersion tchr. Milw. Pub. Schs., 1990—91; bilingual tchr. Christian Day Sch., San Juan, PR, 1991—92; ESL tchr. Oshkosh Area Sch. Dist., Oshkosh, Wis., 1995—. Coord., family cmty. ctr. Oshkosh Area Sch. Dist., 1999—; pub. spkr, Bhopal, India, 1983; bd. dirs. EvenStart Program, Oshkosh, Wis., 2002—, Lao Hmong Assn., Oshkosh, Wis., 2003—; diversity chairperson AAUW, Oshkosh, Wis., 2001—; at risk restructuring bd. Oshkosh Area Sch. Dist., 2003—; cooperating tchr. U. of Wis., Oshkosh, 2001—; vol. tchr. Newman Club, Chimayo, N.Mex., 1967—69, Orphanage La Esperanza, Mexico City, 1970; bilingual sec. Agencia Antillana, Santo Domingo, Dominican Republic, 1972. Recipient Tchr. of the Yr. award, Target Found., 1998; Healthy Nurturing grantee, Aurora Found., 2003, Assisting Endangered Langs. grantee, Alce Cozzi Found., 2003. Mem.: AAUW (diversity chair 2001—), Tchrs. of English to Speakers of Other Langs. (assoc.), Wis. Tchrs. of English to Speakers of Other Languages (assoc.), Wis. Edn. Assn. (assoc.), Delta Pi. Democrat. Roman Catholic. Office: Webster Stanley Elem Sch 745 Hazel St Oshkosh WI 54901 Office Phone: 920-424-0460. E-mail: busers@mac.com.

BUSEY, ROXANE C. lawyer; b. Chgo., June 15, 1949; BA cum laude, Miami U., 1970; MAT, Northwestern U., 1971, JD, 1975. Bar: Ill. 1975. Ptnr. Gardner, Carton & Douglas, Chgo. Mem. ABA (chmn. antitrust sect. 2001-2002, chair health com., antitrust sect. 1989-92, antitrust sect. coun. 1992-95, officer 1995-2003), Ill. State Bar Assn. (chair antitrust coun. 1984-85), Chgo. Bar Assn. (chair antitrust sect. 1990-91). Office: Gardner Carton & Douglas LLP 191 N Wacker Ste 3000 Chicago IL 60606 E-mail: rbusey@gcd.com.

BUSH, BARBARA PIERCE, former First Lady of the United States, volunteer; b. Rye, N.Y., June 8, 1925; d. Marvin and Pauline (Robinson) Pierce; m. George Herbert Walker Bush, Jan. 6, 1945; children: George Walker, Pauline Robin (dec.), John Ellis, Neil Mallon, Marvin Pierce, Dorothy Walker. Student, Smith Coll., 1943-44; hon. degrees, Stritch Coll., Milw., 1981, Mt. Vernon Coll., Washington, 1981, Hood Coll., Frederick, Md., 1983, Howard U., Washington, 1987, Judson Coll., Marion, Ala., 1988, Bennett Coll., Greensboro, N.C., 1989, Smith Coll., 1989, Morehouse Sch. Medicine, 1989. First Lady of the U.S., Washington, 1989—93; oper. & facilities div. Dept. Administration, Washington, 1992. Author: C. Fred Story, 1984, Millie's Book, 1990, Barbara Bush: A Memoir, 1994, Reflections: Life After the White House, 2003. Hon. chair adv. bd. Reading is Fundamental; hon. mem. Bus. Coun. for Effective Literacy; mem. adv. coun. Soc. of Meml. Sloan-Kettering Cancer Ctr.; hon. mem. bd. dirs. Children's Oncology Svcs. of Met. Washington, The Washington Home, The Kingsbury Ctr.; hon. chmn. nat. adv. coun. Literacy Vols. of Am., Nat. Sch. Vols. Program; sponsor Laubach Literacy Internat.; nat. hon. chmn. Leukemia Soc. of Am.; hon. mem. bd. trustees Morehouse Sch. of Medicine; hon. nat. chmn. Nat. Organ Donor Awareness Week, 1982-86; pres. Ladies of the Senate, 1981-88; mem. women's com. Smithsonian Assocs., Tex. Fedn. of Rep. Women, life mem.; hon. mem.; hon. chairperson for the Nat. Com. on Literacy and Edn. United Way, Barbara Bush Found. for Family Literacy, 1989-, Washington Parent Group Fund, Girls Clubs of Am., 10th anniversay Harvest Nat. Food Bank Network; hon. chmn. Nat. Com. for the Prevention of Child Abuse and Childhelp U.S.A.; hon. pres. Girl Scouts U.S; hon. chair Nat. Com. for Adoption; mem. bd. trustees Mayo Clinic Found.; hon. chair Read Am., Boarder Baby Project; mem. bd. visitors M. D. Anderson Cancer Ctr.; hon. chair Leukemia Soc. Am., Children's Literacy Initiative; hon. mem. Reading is Fundamental; ambassador at large Americares; honorary mem. Barbara Bush Found. for Family Literacy. Recipient Nat. Outstanding Mother of Yr. award, 1984, Woman of Yr. award USO, 1986, Disting. Leadership award United Negro Coll. Fund 1986, Disting. Am. Woman award Coll. Mt. St. Joseph, 1987, Free Spirit award Freedom Forum, 1995. Mem. Tex. Fedn. Rep. Women (life), Internat. II Club (Washington), Magic Circle Rep. Women's Club (Houston), YWCA. Episcopalian.*

BUSH, CHRISTINE GAY, dental hygienist; b. Toledo, Dec. 31, 1951; d. Jack G. and Virginia Aileen (Doyle) Tornga; m. John Howard Mosher, May 11, 1974 (div. July 1990); children: Heather Kristen, Andrew Jacob; m. Robert Milton Counts, July 5, 1991 (dec. Mar. 1993); m. Charles T. Bush II, June 16, 1998. BS in Dental Hygiene, U. Mich., 1974. Registered dental hygienist, Nat. Bd. Dental Examiners, Ind. State Bd. Dentistry, Fla. State Bd. Dentistry, Mich. State Bd. Dentistry. Asst. supr. dental hygiene Ind. U., South Bend, Ind., 1974-75; expanded functions hygienist South Bend Dental Ctr., 1975; periodontal hygienist Dr. John B. Lehman, South Bend, 1976-87 [illegible], Fla., 1980-81; Dr. Richard Altman, Orlando, Fla., 1984-85; dental hygienist Dr. H. Raymund Barcus, Winter Park, Fla., 1984—2000; periodontal hygienist Dr. Michael Abufaris, 2000—. Adj. instr. So. Coll., Orlando, 1984. Med./dental mission Wekiva Presbyn. Ch., Honduras, 1987, 89, Diocese of Orlando, Dominican Republic, 1994, 95, Fla. Hosp. Found., Jamaica, 1997; deacon Presbyn. Ch., 1992; mem. Festival of Orchs. League. Mem.: Greater Orlando Dental Hygiene Assn. (sec. 1986—87), Messiah Soc., Festival of Orchs. League, Shepherd's Hope, U. Mich. Club Orlando (treas. 1998—2001), Alpha Chi Omega (chpt. pres. 1995—97, Lyre editor 1997—98, 2000—01, pres. Gamma Upsilon Gamma chpt. 1998—99). Republican. Roman Catholic. Avocations: cross-stitch, playing piano, reading. Office: Dr Michael Abufaris Periodontics 201 N Lakemont Ave Ste 600 Winter Park FL 32792

BUSH, HOLLY NEWSOM, management consultant; BBA in Acctg., Tex. Christian U., 1984, MBA in Fin., 1990. CPA, Tex. Auditor Coopers & Lybrand, Ft. Worth, Tex., 1984-86; sr. auditor McCaslin Wright & Greenwood, Ft. Worth, 1986-88; sr. cons. Andersen Consulting, Dallas, 1990-93; prin. Booz Allen & Hamilton, Dallas, 1993—. Mem. AICPA, Tex. Soc. CPAs. Avocations: reading, biking, horseback riding, piano. Office: Booz Allen and Hamilton 1401 Bellefonte Ln Colleyville TX 76034 Fax: 214-712-6660.

BUSH, JILL A. medical educator; b. Point Pleasant, N.J., Sept. 29, 1971; d. John J. and Janet S. Bush; m. Luke C. Wallace, Aug. 9, 2003. BS, Rutgers U., 1993; MS, Pa. State U., 1995, PhD, 1999. Rsch. asst. Pa. State U., University Park, 1993—99; assoc. Baylor Coll. Medicine, Houston, 1999—2001; asst. prof. U. Houston, 2001—. Dir. Quality of Life & Fitness Testing Ctr., Houston, 2003—. Obesity & Phys. Activity grant, NIH, 2003—. Mem.: Am. Physiol. Soc., Nat. Strength & Conditioning Assn., Am. Coll. Sports Medicine, Am. Soc. Nutritional Sci. Avocations: exercise, reading, travel, singing, piano. Office: Univ Houston 3855 Holman St Rm 104 Houston TX 77204 E-mail: jbush@uh.edu.

BUSH, LAURA WELCH, First Lady of United States; b. Nov. 4, 1946; m. George Walker Bush, Nov. 5, 1977; children: Jenna, Barbara. BS in Edn., So. Meth. U., 1968; MLS, U. Tex., Austin, 1973. Tchr. Longfellow Elem. Sch., Dallas, 1968—69, John F. Kennedy Elem. Sch., Houston, 1969—72; libr. Houston Pub. Lib., 1973—74, Dawson Elem. Sch., Austin, 1974—77; First Lady State of Tex., 1995—2001; First Lady of the U.S., 2001—. Established Adopt-A-Caseworker programs, Tex., Rainbow Rooms, Tex.; launched National Book Festival, 2001. Republican. Address: The White House 1600 Pennsylvania Ave NW Washington DC 20500*

BUSH, LAUREN, model; b. 1984; d. Neil and Sharon. Student, Princeton U. Appeared in fashion mag. including Town and Country, Vogue; model Abercrombie & Fitch, Tommy Hilfiger clothing line, 2002—. Hon. spokesperson World Food Program, UN, 2004—. Office: Elite Modeling Agy 111 E 22nd St New York NY 10010*

BUSH, LINDA A. land use planner; b. Westfield, Mass., Dec. 4, 1951; d. Harold Arthur and Lucy (King) B. BS in Zoology, U. Mass., 1973; MS in Resource Mgmt., Antioch U., 1981. Planner Upper Valley-Lake Surapee Coun., Lebanon, N.H., 1980-81; local govt. advisor Tug Hill Commn., Watertown, N.Y., 1981-83; town planner Town of Wallingford, Conn., 1984—. Chmn. bd. YMCA, Wallingford, 1993-95; vice chmn. campaign United Way Meriden-Wallingford, 1995; treas. Habitat for Humanity of Wallingford, 1999—. Mem. Am. Inst. Cert. Planners. Office: Town of Wallingford 45 S Main St Wallingford CT 06492-4201

BUSH, LYNN JEANNE, judge; b. Dec. 30, 1948; BA, Antioch Coll., 1970; JD, Georgetown U., 1976. Assoc. Steptoe and Johnson, Washington, summer 1975; part-time law clk. Nat. Labor Rels. Bd., Washington, 1976; trial atty. comml. litigation br. Dept. of Justice, Washington, 1976-87; sr. trial atty. Naval Facilities Engring. Command, Dept. of Navy, Alexandria, Va., 1987-89, counsel engring. field activity, 1989-96; adminstr. judge Bd. of Contract Appeals HUD, Washington, 1996-98; judge U.S. Ct. Fed. Claims, Washington, 1998—. Mem. Nat. Bar Assn., Nat. Assn. Women Judges, Bd. of Contract Appeals Judges Assn., Bd. of Contract Appeals Bar Assn., Sr. Exec. Assn.

BUSH, ROBERTA B. psychotherapist, accountant; b. Watertown, NY, Dec. 23, 1937; d. Robert King and Barbara P. (Wiggins) Banks; m. Marvin D. Bush, Feb. 28, 1959 (div. 1977). BA, Glenville State Coll., 1977; MS, W.Va. U., Morgantown, 1985. Lic. profl. therapist W.Va. Acct. GE Plastics, Parkensburg, W.Va., 1959—77; lit. vol. Parkensburg, 1977—89; outpatient site head Abraxas, Parkensburg, 1989—95; psychotherapist Westbrook Health Svc., Parkensburg, 1996—97; ret., 1997. Pres., bd. dirs. Lit. Vol. Program of Wood City, Parkersburg. Mem.: Profl. Women's Assn. (pres., bd. dirs., Hall of Fame 1995). Episcoplian. Home: 111 Canterbury Dr Parkersburg WV 26104-8057

BUSH, SANDI TOKOA, elementary school educator; b. Albany, Ga., Aug. 1, 1953; d. Charlie and Beauty (Miller) Bush; 1 child, Allen. BS, Barry U., Miami, 1983; MS, Nova U., 1987; PhD, Union Inst., 2001, U. Cin., 2001. Cert. tchr. Fla. Counselor Health and Rehab. Svcs., Miami, Fla., 1979-86; tchr. Dade County Pub. Schs., Miami, 1986—. Tchr., tutor Ind. Children's Group, Miami, 1987—; co-chmn. Hall of Fame Dade County Sch. Bd., 1986—, world difference, 1987—. Author: (book) World of Poetry Anthology The Sun, 1991; co-author: Experiences with Discrimination: From Deep Within, 1998; contbr. articles to profl. jours. Mem.: Nova U. Assocs., Nova U. Alumni Assn. (mem. recruitment com. 1987—88, Recognition award 1988), Smithsonian Assocs. (Recognition award 1988), Am. Mus. Natural History (assoc.). Avocations: reading, classical music, walking, jogging, tennis.

BUSH, SHARON L, director; d. Clem and Dorothy L Adams; m. James M Bush, May 15, 1976. BS, U. of Houston Ctrl. Pk., 1980. Human resources adminstr. Pennzoil Co., Houston, 1972—89; ednl. outreach adminstr. Rice U., Houston, 1993—. Officer Tex. Assn. of Black Pers. In Higher Edn., Austin, Tex., 2003. Recipient Woman of the Yr., Holman St. Bapt. Ch., 1990. Mem.: Tex. Assn. of Black Pers. In HIgher Edn. (life; chair scholarship com. 2003). Office: Rice Univ 6100 Main St Houston TX 77005

BUSH, YVONNE, writer, counselor; b. Madelia, Minn., Jan. 29, 1935; d. Guy Pearl and Frances Louise (Traver) Burk; m. William Clarence Bush; children: Donald, Steven, Billie Jean Vogel, Thomas Bush Lovelace, Tami li Robbins, Christopher Clark. AA Edn., Yavapai Coll., 1985; BA, Prescott Coll., 1989, MA, 1999. Cert. EMT 1987, St. Joseph's Med. Center/Newborn,Child Normal Devel. 1983, Feeding and Swallowing Disorders of Infancy; Assessment and Mgmt. 1991, Fetal Alcohol Syndrome/Instructor 1993, Parenting the Teen Years 1987, Understanding Aids 1987, Failure to Thrive, Infant Mental Health 1988, Breast Cancer Self examination/Instructor 1983. Office mgr. Allen's New Way Retail Grocery Store, Prescott, Ariz., 1980—82; head cashier K Mart, Prescott, 1982—83; case mgr. Cath. Social Services of Yavapai, Prescott, Ariz., 1987—90, Ariz. Dept. of Econ. Security, Prescott, 1990—98. Trust com. The Acker Trust Bd., Prescott, 1983—85; organizer, co-leader Scholls Cmty. Orgn., Scholls, 1978—80; bd. dirs. Sierra Comm., Inc., Prescott; charter mem. Ariz. Pub. Svc. Project Voice, Phoenix; bd. dirs. Child Haven, Prescott Crisis Nursery; den mother Boy Scouts of Am., Rowland Heights, 1965—66; bd. dirs. Affordable Constrn., Inc. Prescott; leader women's ministries Alliance Bible Ch., Prescott, Ariz. Author: Bonding and Attachment, 2001, Beyond Tears, A Book To Encourage Women, 2002. Small claims hearing officer Prescott Justice Ct., 1998—2003. Mem.: Prescott Pub. Library/Friends of the Libr. Conservative.

BUSHEY, MARILYN, communications executive; Pres., CEO Power Performance and Comm., Inc., Dallas. Creator [illegible] Training Method. Recipient Internat. Silver Pyramid award, Promtional Products Assn. Mem.: Women's Bus. Coun. S.W. (mem. exec. bd.), Nat. Assn. Women Bus. Owners (pres. Dallas/Ft. Worth chpt. 2001—02). Office: Power Perf & Comm Inc Ste 936 1409 S Lamar Dallas TX 75215

BUSHKIN, KATHRYN A. foundation administrator; m. Arthur (Art) A. Bushkin. Grad. in speech and hearing therapy, Purdue U. Writer, researcher Kiplinger's Edn. Svc.; comm. dir., co-legis. dir. Senate office and Presdl. campaign Senator Gary Hart, 1976—84; dir. editl. adminstrn. newsroom mgmt., long-term strategy and online projects US News & World Report, 1985—96; sr. mng. dir. Hill and Knowlton, 1996—97; sr. v.p., chief comm. officer AOL, 1997—2001; sr. v.p. AOL Time Warner, 2001—03; pres. AOL Time Warner Found., 2001—03; exec. v.p., COO UN Found., 2003—. Former mem. bd. AOL Found. Co-founder (with husband) Stargazer Found., 1999—; bd. mem. Internat. Women's Media Found., Wolf Trap Nat. Park, Nat. Women's Law Ctr., Internat. Radio & TV Soc. Found., Share our Strength; bd. dirs. Internews. Named one of 100 Most Powerful Women in Wash., Washingtonian mag., 2001. Achievements include recognized as top comm. profl. in tech. industry and one of top women in comm./pub. rels., 1999. Office: UN Found 1225 Conn Ave NW 4th Fl Washington DC 20036 Office Phone: 202-887-9040. Office Fax: 202-887-9021.*

BUSHMILLER, ANN E. lawyer; BA cum laude, Bates Coll., 1979; JD, U. Chgo., 1982. Bar: D.C. 1982, U.S. Dist. Ct. D.C. 1983, U.S. Supreme Ct. 1989. Ptnr. Sidley & Austin, Washington. Mediator D.C. ct. sys., 10 yrs.; instr. Emory U. Law Sch. Trustee Bates Coll., Lewiston, Maine. Mem. Phi Beta Kappa. Office: Sidley & Austin 1722 E St NW Washington DC 20006 Fax: 202-736-8711. E-mail: Abushmil@sidley.com.

BUSHNELL, CANDANCE, columnist, writer; b. Conn., 1959; d. Calvin Camille Bushnell; m. Charles Askegard, July 4, 2002. Attended, Rice U. Writer Ladies' Home Journal, Good Housekeeping, Self, Mademoiselle, Cosmo Beauty and Fitness, Family Circle, GQ, Vogue; columnist New York Observer, 1994—98. Author: (novels) Sex and the City, 1996, (short stories) Four Blondes, 2000, (novels) Trading Up, 2003. Achievements include collection of columns for New York Observer, "Sex and the City", was made into HBO series of same name, 1998-2004. Office: c/o Atlantic Monthly Press 841 Broadway New York NY 10003*

BUSHNELL, PRUDENCE, diplomat, former management consultant, trainer; b. Washington, Nov. 26, 1946; d. Gerald Sherman and Bernice Edna (Duflo) B.; m. Richard Alan Buckley, Oct. 26, 1979. BA, U. Md., 1969; MS, Russell Sage Coll., 1980. Bi-lingual sec. Embassy of Morocco, Washington, 1969-70; chief sec. U. Md., College Park, 1970-72; tng. mgr. Legal Svcs. Tng. Program, Washington, 1972-76; dir. Cultural Learning Concepts, Dallas, 1976-81; mgr. adminstrv. ops. U.S. Consulate Bombay, U.S. Embassy, Dakar, 1982-86; dir. exec. devel. Fgn. Svc. Inst., Washington, 1986-89; dep. chief mission U.S. Embassy Dakar, Dept. State, Washington, 1989-92; dep. asst. sec. for African affairs Dept. State, Washington, 1993-96; U.S. amb. to Kenya Dept. of State, Nairobi, 1996-99, U.S. amb. to Guatemala, 1999—2002, dean Leadership and Mgmt. Sch., Fgn. Svc. Inst., 2002—. Avocations: gardening, walking, writing. Office: US Dept State 2201 C St NW Washington DC 20520*

BUSHONG, MARY FRANCES JULIA, music educator; b. Ridley Park, Pa., Apr. 23, 1963; d. Joseph Francis and Mary Catherine Bushong. MusB in Music Edn., Mansfield U., 1985; MA, Rowan U., 1997; ABD, Temple U., 1997. Choral dir. Richard M. Teitelman Sch., Cape May, NJ, 1986—87; elem. band dir. Wash. Twp. Sch. Dist., Sewell, NJ, 1987—; asst. marching band dir. Pitman (N.J.) H.S., 1990—96. Presenter in field. Mem.: Music Educators Nat. Conf., Pi Kappa Lambda, Sigma Alpha Iota (editor 2001). E-mail: mbushong@wtps.org.

BUSKA, SHEILA MARY, controller, writer, columnist; b. Brewer, Maine, May 9, 1941; d. George William Sanderlin and Margaret Owenita Harrah; m. Roland Michael Buska, Nov. 28, 1959; children: Bryan Michael, Craig William, Christine Mary, Paul Kevin. AA, U. San Diego, 1959; BS in Acct. magna cum laude with distinction, San Diego State U., 1984. Cert. mgmt. acct.; CPA, Calif. Sr. acct. Peak Health Plan, San Diego, 1984-86; legal entity acct. M/A-COM Govt. Sys., San Diego, 1986-87; sr. acct. Lois A. Brozey, CPA, San Diego, 1987-89; controller Soco-Lynch Corp. dba Crown Chem. Corp., Chula Vista, Calif., 1989-98; fin. mgr. Dermagraf & Joint Venture, 1998—99; controller Monarch Sch. Project, San Diego, 2003—. Author: (poem) Young America Sings, 1957, Sermons in Poetry, 1957, Time Out for Grown-Ups: 5 Minute Smile Breaks, 2003; contbr. columns to newspapers, 1997—, www.wordstoenjoy.com. Mem. Inst. Mgmt. Accts. (dir. membership acquisition 1995-96, treas. 1993-94, dir. corp. devel. 1992-93, dir. cert. mgmt. accts., 1989-90, v.p. membership and mktg. 1985-86, Most Valuable Mem. 1990-91), Hardhats Toastmasters (pres. 2000, v.p. pub. rels. editor Hardhats Herald 1998). Democrat. Roman Catholic. Avocations: travel, music, poetry, tennis, theater. Home: 509 Burgasia Path El Cajon CA 92019-2640 Office: Monarch School Project 808 W Cedar St San Diego CA 92101

BUSKIRK, PHYLLIS RICHARDSON, retired economist; b. Queens, N.Y., July 19, 1930; d. William Edward and Amy A. Richardson; m. Allen V. Buskirk, Sept. 13, 1950; children: Leslie, William, Carol (dec.), Janet. AB cum laude, William Smith Coll., 1951. Rsch. asst. W.E. Upjohn Inst. for Employment Rsch., Kalamazoo, 1970-75, rsch. assoc., 1976-83, sr. staff economist, 1983-87; co-editor Bus. Conditions in the Kalamazoo Area, Quar. Rev., 1979-84; asst. editor Bus. Outlook for West Mich., 1984-87; mem. civil svc. bd. City of Kalamazoo, 1977-91, chmn., 1981-91; trustee First Presbyn. Ch., Kalamazoo, 1984-87, chmn., 1985, 86, mgr. adminstrn. and fin., 1987-92, co-chair 150th ann., 1997-98, chair 150th ann., 1999-2000. Trustee Sr. Citizens Fund, Kalamazoo, 1984-88, exec. bd. 1986-88; bd. dirs. Heritage Cmty. Kalamazoo, 1988-2004, chair 1995-96, exec. com., 1997; Kalamazoo County Futures Coms., 1985-86, bd. dirs., 1987-89. Fellow Presbyn. Ch. Bus. Adminstrn. Assn.; mem. Nat. Assn. Ch. Bus. Adminstrn., P.E.O., Kalamazoo Network, YWCA; bd. dirs. Friends of Univ. Librs. Western Mich. U., 2000—. Mem.: Phi Beta Kappa. Home: 3324 Saint Antoine Ave Kalamazoo MI 49006-5522

BUSQUET, ANNE M. Internet company executive; BS in Hotel Adminstrn., Cornell U.; MBA, Columbia U. Mktg. mgr. Am. Express, 1978, sr. v.p., gen. mgr. Optima card divsn., 1988—92, sr. .vp., gen. mgr. mdse. svcs. bus., 1992—93, exec. v.p. consumer card group, 1993—95, pres. relationship svcs. divsn., 1995—2000, pres. interactive svcs. and new bus. divsn., 2000—01; pres. AMB Advisors, LLC; sr. advisor InterActiveCorp, 2003—04, CEO local svcs., 2004—. Office: InterActive Corp 152 West 57th St 42nd Fl New York NY 10019*

BUSS, JEANIE, professional sports team executive; d. Jerry Buss; m. Steve Timmons, Feb. 14, 1990 (div. 1993). Grad., U. So. Calif. Owner, gen. mgr. L.A. Strings, 1981—93; owner, pres. L.A. Blades, 1994—97; pres. Sports Forum Inc.; pres., dir. booking Great Western Forum, L.A., 1995—99; exec. v.p. bus. ops. L.A. Lakers, 1999—. Bd. dirs. L.A. Sports Coun., 1995—. Office: LA Lakers PO Box 10 3900 W Manchester Blvd Inglewood CA 90306*

BUSSABARGER, MARY LOUISE, mental health services professional; b. Chgo., Sept. 16, 1923; d. Joseph and Nellie Wheelen Sterling; m. Robert Franklin Bussabarger, May 11, 1946; children: Wendi Newell, David. BA, U. Mo., 1960, MA English Lit., 1963. Instr. English U. Mo., Columbia, 1960—2002; mental health commr. State of Mo., Jefferson City, 2001—. Instr. English as a fgn. lang. Indo-Am. Soc., Calcutta, India, 1961—62, 1968—69, tchr. Yoga, 1969—2002; [illegible] dir. Women's [illegible], 1974—77; regiohnal liaison officer Danforth Found., 1976—80. Commr. parks and recreation City of Columbia, 1975—77; mem. spkrs. bur. Internat. Women's Year, 1975—; mem. nat. steering com. Nat. Women's Polit. Caucus, 1974—75; pres. Columbia Women's Polit. Caucus, 1975—76; del. State Dem. Convs., 1968, 1972, alt., 1976; mem. state steering com. Mo. Women's Polit. Caucus, 1972—76. Mem.: AAUW, Modern Lang. Assn., Mo. State Tchrs. English, Delta Tau Kappa. Office: Dept Mental Health 1706 E Elm St PO Box 677 Jefferson City MO

BUSSERT, MEG, actress, educator; b. Chgo., Oct. 21, 1948; d. Martin Joseph Bussert and Rosemary Daly; m. Steve Newton Cochrane, Feb. 5, 1977 (div. 1986); 1 child, Rachel Kelly Cochrane ; m. Alexander Grasso, May 11, 1991 (div. 1999); 1 child, Nicholas Alexander Grasso. Student, U. Ill., 1966—70; BS, SUNY, Purchase, 1998; MA in Tchg., Manhattanville Coll., 1999. Mng. dir. theatre for YOung Audiences Westchester Broadway Theatre, 1996—97; tchr. English, drama Humanities H.S., NYC, 1999—2000; tchr. comm. arts Dobbs Ferry (NY) Middle Sch., 2000—01; dir. musical theatre Hoff-Barthleson, 2001; tchr. NYU, NYC, 2001—. Cons. in field; adj. instr. Manhattanville Coll., Am. Musical Dramatic Acad., NYC, 1988—91, NYU, NYC, 1992—2000, SUNY, Manhattan, 1998; guest lectr. Pace U., 1988. Actor: (plays) Applause, Lorelei, 1974, Irene, 1976—77, Something's Afoot, 1977, Gorey Stories, 1978, The Music Man, 1980 (Theatre World award, 1980), Brigadoon, 1980—81 (nominee Tony award, 1981), Camelot, 1981—82 (nominee Ace award, 1983), 1982—83, South Pacific, 1985, HMS Pinafore, 1987, Professionally Speaking, 1990, Damn Yankees, 1994—96, (TV appearance) The Today Show, 1980, Macy's Thanksgiving Day Parade, 1980, Jerry Lewis Muscular Dystrophy Telethon, 1985, Merv Griffin Show, 1985; (TV series) One Life to Live, 1990—96, All My Children, 1993, PBS Great Performances; (TV films) Camelot, 1983, Pete and Pete, 1995; performer: (albums) Irene, Phantom, Sousa for Orchestra, Songs of NY, Lost in Boston; dir.: (plays) Damn Yankees, 1997, Oklahoma!, 1998, Brigadoon, 1999, I Do, I Do, 1993, The Fabulous Fable Factory, 1997, Beauty and the Beast, 1997, Fiddler on the Roof, 1999. Performer Equity Fights AIDS, World Trade Ctr. Red Cross Benefit, 2001. Mem.: Ednl. Theatre Assn. Thespians, Internat. Music Theatre Training Symposium, Michael Chekhov Inst., NY Singing Tchrs. Assn., Am. Fedn. Radio TV Artists, Screen Actors Guild, Actors Equity Assn. Home: 7 Whitman St Hastings On Hudson NY 10706-1605 Office: NYU Dept Music 35 W 4th St New York NY 10012

BUSSINO, MELINDA HOLDEN, human services administrator; b. Boston, Apr. 20, 1946; d. Sharon Virtulan and Grace (Fitzgerald) Holden; m. Louis Logue Doyle, Feb. 14, 1974 (dec. Oct. 1980); children: Sarah, Joseph; m. Fred John Bussino, Sept. 22, 1998 (dec. Jan. 2000). BA in Psychology, U. N.H., 1968. Dir. outreach and tng. Stratford County Cmty. Action, Somersworth, N.H., 1968-73; trainer, cons. New Eng. Regional Commn., Boston, 1971-73; office mgr. Beacon Banjo Co., Westminster, Vt., 1980-88; asst. to pastor United Meth. Ch., Brattleboro, Vt., 1985-89; exec. dir. Brattleboro Area Drop In Ctr., 1989—; cons. Putney, Vt., 1994—. Chmn. Brattleboro Human Resource Coun., 1990—; bd. dirs., past pres. Vt. Affordable Housing Coalition, 1990—, Vt. Campaign to End Child Hunger, 1991-99; housing commr. Windham Regional Commn., Brattleboro, 1995—; organizer, bd. dirs. N.H. Low Income Advocacy Coun., 1972-73, Operation Low Income People, N.H., 1969-73; adv. coun., bd. dirs. Vt. Protection Advocacy, Montpelier, Vt., 1995-2001; vice chair Westminster (Vt.) Planning Commn., 2003—. Recipient Vt. Woman of Distinction award, 1996, Humanitarian award Brattleboro Pastoral Counseling Ctr., 2001. Democrat. Methodist. Avocations: gardening, cooking, grandchildren, skiing. Home: PO Box 387 Putney VT 05346-0387 Office: Brattleboro Area Drop In Ctr PO Box 175 Brattleboro VT 05302-0175 Office Phone: 802-852-4286 103. E-mail: badic@together.net.

BUSWELL, DEBRA SUE, small business owner, programmer, analyst; b. Salt Lake City, Apr. 8, 1957; d. John Edward Ross and Marilyn Sue (Patterson) Potter; m. Randy James Buswell, Aug. 17, 1985; 1 child, Trevor Ryan. BA, U. Colo., Denver, 1978. Programmer, analyst Trail Blazer Systems, Palo Alto, Calif., 1980-83; data processing mgr. Innovative Concepts, Inc., San Jose, Calif., 1983-86; owner Egret Software, Milpitas,

Calif., 1986—. Mem.: IEEE. Home and Office: 45701 Vineyard Ave Fremont CA 94539-4817 E-mail: dbuswell@ieee.org.

BUSWELL, JANE H. lay pastor; b. Penfield, N.Y., Aug. 27, 1922; d. Frank Siebert and Flora Euphemia (Waugh) Hermance; m. Robert Allen Buswell, Sept. 28, 1946; children: Don Robert, Sara Jane Fuller. AA, Ellen Cushing Jr. Coll. (formerly Bapbat Inst.). Lay pastor Tyson U.C.C. (formerly Tyson Congl.), Plymouth, Vt., 1947—2002; pastor Reading (Vt.) Christian Union Ch., 1971—72, Cavendish (Vt.) Baptist, 1979—80, Ludlow (Vt.) U.C.C., Weston (Vt.) U.C.C. Reporter Eagle Times, Ludlow, Vt. Justice of the Peace, Ludlow, Vt., 1967—2003; town auditor, 1967—82; leader Ninevah Brook 4H, Windsor, Vt., 1948—73; past mem. VFW Aux., Am. Legion Aux.; Sunday sch., Bible sch. Tyson Congl. Ch., 1947—98. Recipient Citizen of Yr., Ludlow Rotary Club, 1980. Mem.: VFW (hon.), Order Ea. Star (worthy matron, sec., chaplain, assoc. matron, 50 Yr. Pin 1999, 2 star points), Am. Legion (hon.). United Ch. Christ. Avocations: crocheting, youth groups, sewing, gardening. Home: 1552 Rt 100 N Ludlow VT 05149

BUTCHER, DEBORAH, public relations and communications consultant; b. Balt., Apr. 23, 1954; d. Robert Cleveland and Mildred Lois Butcher; m. Darwin Scott Bull, May 4, 1985; 1 child, Margeaux Gabrielle Bull. BS, Towson (Md.) U., 1988. Pub. rels. coord. Farm Credit Banks, Sparks, Md., 1981-83, pub. rels. mgr., 1983-85; v.p. Curry Comms. Group, Timonium, Md., 1985-89; account exec. Blue Cross/Blue Shield Md., Owings Mills, 1989-90, mgr. DARE Found., 1991; sr. coord. comms. Nat. Rural Electric Coop. Assn., Arlington, Va., 1992-96; owner, founder, pres. Deborah Butcher Pub. Rels./Bus. Comms., Hillsborough, N.J., 1997—. Vol., Somerset County Dem. Com., Somerville, N.J., 1999. Recipient award of merit Internat. Assn. Bus. Communicators, 1992, 93, 94, Cert. of Excellence, Am. Soc. Assn. Execs., 1993. Mem. Somerset County C. of C. (pub. rels. com. 1998-2000, legis. com. 1998-99). Avocations: gardening, golf. Office: Deborah Butcher Pub Rels/Comms 200 Hockenbury Rd Hillsborough NJ 08844

BUTCHER, DIANE, chaplain, bereavement facilitator; b. Passaic, N.J., Aug. 25, 1944; d. Richard William and Marion Rosalyn Butcher; m. William R. Schweitzer, Aug. 1975 (div. Oct. 1978); 1 child, Noreen Rozsa. BA, William Paterson Coll., Wayne, N.J., 1966, MA in Nat. History, 1972; postgrad., Montclair (N.J.) State U., 1975. Tchr. elem. edn. Bd. Edn., Kearny, N.J., 1966-68, Hasbrouck Heights, N.J., 1970-97; bereavement facilitator Four Seasons Hospice, Hendersonville, NC, 1997—, dir. Watchman program, 2001—. Mem. steering coun. Franciscan AIDS Hospitality House, Wallington, N.J., 1995-97. Named Vol. of Yr., Four Seasons Hospice, 1999. Mem. Assn. Profl. Chaplains, We. N.C. Aids Project, Asheville. Roman Catholic. Avocations: music, hiking, camping, pottery, watercolors. Home: 113 Rugby Dr Hendersonville NC 28791-9019

BUTCHER, DOROTHY, state representative; BSN, paralegal cert., U. So. Colo. State rep., dist. 46 Colo. House Rep., Denver, 2000—. Com. mem. Bus. Affairs and Labor, Info. and Tech. Democrat. Office: State Capitol 200 E Colfax Ave Denver CO 80203

BUTEL, JANET SUSAN, research scientist, virology educator; b. Overbrook, Kans., May 24, 1941; d. Floyd Charles and Berniece (Humbert) B.; m. David Yates Graham, Mar. 31, 1967; children: Susan Kathleen, David Peter. BS summa cum laude, Kans. State U., 1963; PhD with honors, Baylor U., 1966. Postdoctoral fellow Baylor Coll. Medicine, Houston, 1966-68; asst. prof. Houston, 1968-72; assoc. prof. Baylor U. Coll. Medicine, Houston, 1972-76, prof., 1976-95, head divsn. molecular virology, 1989-2000, disting. svc. prof., 1995—, Joseph L. Melnick prof. virology, 1986, chmn. dept. molecular virology and microbiology, 2000—. Mem. study sect. NIH, Bethesda, Md., 1980—84; mem. bd. sci. counselors Nat. Cancer Inst., Bethesda, 1980—84; mem. coun. Nat. Inst. Arthritis and Infectious Diseases, 1994—98; mem. external adv. coun. Am. Cancer Soc., 1998—2001. Contbg. editor: Lange Med. Microbiology, 1987—; contbr. sci. articles to profl. jours. Grad. fellow NSF, 1963-66; rsch. grantee NIH, 1973—. Mem. AAAS, Am. Assn. for Cancer Rsch., Am. Soc. for Cell Biology, Am. Soc. for Microbiology (div. chair 1990-91, group IV rep. 1993-95), Am. Soc. for Virology, Internat. Assn. Breast Cancer Rsch. (bd. govs. Lakewood, Colo. 1987-91), Sigma Xi. Office: Baylor Coll Medicine 1 Baylor Plz Houston TX 77030-3411

BUTENHOFF, SUSAN G. public relations executive; b. N.Y.C., Jan. 13, 1960; BA in Internat. Rels. with hons., Sussex U., Eng.; MPhil, Wolfson Coll., Cambridge U., Eng. Account exec. Ellen Farmer Prodns., 1984-85, Ketchum Pub. Rels., N.Y.C., 1988-90, v.p., account supr., 1990-91; prin., CEO Access Pub. Rels., San Francisco, 1991—, pres., CEO. Mem. Pub. Rels. Soc. Am. Office: Access Comm 101 Howard St Fl 2D San Francisco CA 94105-1629

BUTERA, ANN MICHELE, consulting company executive; b. Bayside, N.Y., Apr. 27, 1958; d. Gaetano Thomas and Josephine (Inserro) B. BA, L.I. U., 1979; MBA, Adelphi U., 1982. Dept. mgr. Abraham & Straus Stores, Huntington, N.Y., 1978-80; mgmt. cons. Chase Manhattan Bank N.A., Lake Success, N.Y., 1980-83, Nat. Bankcard Corp., Melville, N.Y., 1983-84; pres. Whole Person Project, Inc., Elmont, N.Y., 1984—. Bd. dirs. Nassau County coun. Girl Scouts U.S., 1985-95. Recipient Bus. Achievement award Women on the Job, 1990. Mem. NAFE, ASTD, Fin. Women Internat., L.I. Networking Entrepreneurs (pres. 1984-91), Inst. Internal Auditors, Assn. Govt. Auditors, L.I. Ctr. for Bus. and Profl. Women, World Futurists Soc. Republican. Roman Catholic. Avocations: tennis, dance, gardening. Home and Office: Whole Person Project Inc 82 Cerenzia Blvd Elmont NY 11003-3631 E-mail: annbutera@cs.com.

BUTHOD, MARY CLARE, school administrator; b. Tulsa, Aug. 20, 1945; d. Arthur Paul and Mary Rudelle (Dougherty) B. MA in Teaching, Tulsa U., 1969; M Christian Spirituality, Creighton U., 1981. Joined Order of St. Benedict. Asst. tchr. HeadStart, Tulsa, 1966; tchr. Madalene Parish Sch., Tulsa, 1968-69, Monte Cassino Pvt. Sch., Tulsa, 1969-79; prin. Monte Cassino Elem. Sch., Tulsa, 1979-86; dir. Monte Cassino Sch., Tulsa, 1986—. Mem. convent coun. Benedictine Sisters, Tulsa, 1975-88, dir. formation programs, 1983—; examiner Okla. Quality Found. Mem. State Congl. Ednl. Com., Tulsa, 1989-90; co-chair for edn. and human devel. Tulsa Coalition Against Illegal Use of Drugs, 1990-91; mem. adv. com. Okla. State Schs. Attuned, 2002—. Recognized for Excellence in Edn. U.S. Dept. Edn., 1993-94. Mem. Tulsa Reading Coun. (sec. 1975-77), Nat. Cath. Edn. Assn., Delta Kappa Gamma. Home: 2200 S Lewis Ave Tulsa OK 74114-3117 Office: Monte Cassino Sch 2206 S Lewis Ave Tulsa OK 74114-3109 Office Phone: 918-746-4112. E-mail: smc@montecassino.org.

BUTLER, BRETT, comedienne, actress; b. Montgomery, AL, 1958; d. Roland Decatur Anderson, Jr. and Carol; adoptive parent Bob Butler; m. Charles Wilson, 1978 (div. 1981); m. Ken Ziegler, 1987. Waitress, Houston, 1981-82; stand-up comedian, 1982—. Star, exec. prodr. TV series Grace Under Fire, 1993-98; appeared on TV in It's Just A Ride, 1994; in film Bruno, 1999; TV film It's Just a Ride, 1994. also: Martin Management 9229 W Sunset Blvd Ste 319 Los Angeles CA 90069-3403

BUTLER, CAROL GREEN, music educator; b. Alamosa, Colo., July 29, 1953; d. Joseph Franklin and Janie (Stowell) Green; m. Harold Lamont Butler; children: Amanda, Randy. BA in Music, William Jewell Coll., Liberty, Mo., 1975; MusM, Baylor U., 1977. Pvt. instr. piano Carol Butler Piano Studio, Nashville, 1977—2003; pvt. and class piano instr., choral union accompanist Free Will Bapt. Bible Coll., Nashville, 1993—2003. Piano accompanist for choirs and annual broadway dinner theater First Bapt. Ch., Nashville, 1988—2003. Piano arranger: published in collection of arrangements Come Celebrate! Contemporary Piano Arrangements for Worship, 2000. Mem.: Nat. Guild of Piano Tchrs., Nashville Area Guild of Piano Tchrs. (pres. 1993—94), Music Tchrs. Nat. Assn. (cert.), Tenn. Music Tchrs. Assn. (recording sec. 2001—03), Nashville Area Music Tchrs. Assn. (pres. 1997—99, Tchr. of Yr. 1997). Avocations: travel, videography. Home: 004 Darlington Pl Nashville TN 37211-5101

BUTLER, CAROL KING, advertising executive; b. Charlotte, N.C., May 29, 1952; d. Charles Snowden Watts and Marion (Thomas) King; m. James Rodney Butler, Aug. 12, 1972 (div. 1975). Student, U. N.C., Greensboro, 1970-72; BA in Theatre, U. N.C., Charlotte, 2000. Sales rep. Sta. WKIX, Raleigh, NC, 1978-82, N.C. Box Inc., Raleigh, 1982-84; radio sales account exec. Sta. WRAL-FM, Raleigh, 1984-88, team sales mgr., 1989; prin. Butler-Smith Assocs., Raleigh, 1988-89; ind. programming and video prodr. Raleigh, 1989-90; prin., freelance presentation/video script writer, 1991—. Sales mgr. BW Territory Lifetouch, 1996; creative cons. Creative Comms., 1997—98; writer, artist, digital photo-arts, companian photography, 2000; digital retoucher, playwright, 2003—; owner A Feral Cared Enterprise. Democrat. Mem. Unity Ch. Avocations: water-skiing, feral cat rescue, boating, photography, rollerblading. Home: 1948 Maryland Ave Charlotte NC 28209 E-mail: cbcats@comporium.net.

BUTLER, GLORIA SINGLETON, state legislator; children: Felicia, Leslie. AS in Bus. Adminstrn., Perimeter Coll. Fiscal acctg. asst. Health Scis. Ctr., Emory U., Atlanta; mem. Ga. State Senate, Atlanta, 1999—, sec. pub. safety com., mem. edn., retirement and transp. coms. Leg. asst. to U.S. Congresswoman Cynthia McKinney, Washington, 1992; mem. USIA Speaker program, South Africa, Zimbabwe, Swaziland, 1994; asst. to dir. AmeriCorps Team for Nat. Svc., 1996 Olympics and paralympics; dir. operation Big Vote, Coalition for Black Voter participation, 4th Congrl. Dist., DeKalb County, 1996; pub. rels. dir. Martin Luther King Jr. March com., 1997; mem. exec. staff, staff of intergovtl. rels. Office DeKalb County Sheriff. Mem. NOW, NAACP (exec. bd. DeKalb County chpt.), Nat. Coun. Negro Women, DeKalb Women's Polit. Caucus, Nat. Women's Polit. Caucus. Democrat. Office: Ste 420D State Capitol Atlanta GA 30334-9003

BUTLER, GRACE CAROLINE, medical researcher; b. Lima, Peru, Dec. 19, 1937;, (parents Am. citizens); d. Everett Lyle and Mary Isabella (Sloatman) Gage; m. William Langdon Butler, Dec. 28, 1961; children: Mary Dyer, William Langdon Jr. AA, Stephens Coll., 1957; BS in Nursing, Columbia U., 1960; postgrad., Union County Coll., 1984. Head nurse N.Y. State Psychiat. Inst., N.Y.C., 1960-61; clin. instr. Columbia U., N.Y.C., 1960-61; staff nurse, educator Vis. Nurse Service, Summit, N.J., 1962-63; health administr. Eagle Island Girl Scout Camp, Tupper Lake, N.Y., 1964; evening supr. Ashbrook Nursing Home, Scotch Plains, N.J., 1968-72; teaching asst. Scotch Plains-Fanwood (N.J.) Sch. System, 1975-78; staff nurse Westfield (N.J.) Med. Group, 1980-82, head nurse, 1982-83, supr., 1983-84; office administr. Harris S. Vernick, MD, PA, Westfield, 1984-86; corp. v.p., office adminstr., 1986-88, Assocs. in Medicine, Westfield, 1988-90; pvt. researcher, 1990—. Diabetes instr. Boehringer Mannenheim Diagnostics, 1994—, Eli Lilly and Co., Indpls., 1984—; microbiologist tester Med. Technol. Corp., Somerset, NJ, 1984—; computer advisor Cordis Corp., Miami, 1985—. Asst. leader Girl Scouts U.S., Fanwood, 1970—73; bd. dirs. PTA, Scotch Plains, Fanwood, 1973—79; religious instr. All Sts. Episcopal Ch., Scotch Plains, 1967—82, 1995—, mem. altar guild, 1994—, mem. vestry, 1999—, lay eucharistic min., 2001—. Mem.: Am. Soc. Notaries, League Ednl. Advancement RNs, Columbia U./Presbyn. Hosp. Sch. Nursing Alumni Assn. Republican. Episcopalian. Avocations: sewing, water sports, gardening, wood refinishing. Home: 125 Russell Rd Fanwood NJ 07023-1063

BUTLER, JANNETTE SUE, human resources professional; b. Eugene, Oreg., Mar. 15, 1960; d. Robert Eugene and Dorothy Marilyn (Irvin) Butler. BS in Hotel Adminstrn., U. Nev., Las Vegas, 1982. Cert. health promotion dir., sr. profl. in human resources. Pers. mgmt. trainee The Sheraton Corp., San Diego, 1982-83, dir. pers. Palm Coast, Fla., 1983-85, dir. human resources Dallas, 1985-89; corp. dir. human resources Hilton Reservations Worldwide, Carrollton, Tex., 1989-95; human resource cons. Symantec Corp., Eugene, Oreg., 1995-97; mgr. human resource Microsoft Corp., Redmond, Wash., 1997-99, sr. mgr. human resource, 1999—2000, group human resources mgr., 2000—01, human resource dir., 2001—. Mem., vol. Nat. Multiple Sclerosis Soc., Redmond Police Dept., 2001—; mem. steering com. Lane County Career Ctrs. Recipient Volunteerism award Lodging Industry Tng. Ctr., 1988. Mem. Soc. for Human Resource Mgmt., Northwest Human Resource Mgmt. Assn. (pres. elect 1997), Inst. for Internat. Human Resource Mgmt., Eugene C. of C. (edn. com.). Episcopalian. Avocations: boating, gardening, skiing. Office: Microsoft One Microsoft Way Redmond WA 98052

BUTLER, JESSIE D. community activist, retired educator and counselor; b. Conroe, Tex., Dec. 26, 1938; d. Floyd and Datchie (Walker) Davis; m. Franklin Delano Dismuke (div.); m. Lee Hayward Butler, Sr. (dec.). BA, Prairie View A&M U., 1962; MA, Atlanta U., 1969. Caseworker Crockett (Tex.) State Sch. for Girls, 1962-63; substitute tchr. Houston Ind. Sch. Dist., 1963-64; tchr. Sealy (Tex.) Ind. Sch. Dist., 1964-65; tchr., counselor Jasper County Pub. Schs., Monticello, Ga., 1965-67; guidance counselor Harrisburg (Pa.) Sch. Dist., 1968-97. Recipient cmty. svc. plaques; recipient Diamond Life award NAACP. Mem. NAACP (v.p. Pa. state 1991—, pres. Harrisburg 1991-96, Golden Heritage life mem.), NEA, NOW, ACLU, Am. Assn. Ret. Persons, So. Christian Leadership Conf., Am. Bus. Womens Assn. (v.p. 1999—), Prairie View A&M U. Alumni Assn. (life), Omnia Bona Inc. (co-founder, past pres. nat. sec.), Golden Heritage (life), Order Eastern Star, Phi Delta Kappa, Delta Sigma Theta (life). Democrat. Baptist. Avocations: travel, reading, volunteer work. Home: 3102 Schoolhouse Ln Harrisburg PA 17109-4628 E-mail: job798@aol.com.

BUTLER, KATHERINE E. lawyer; JD, Suffolk U.; LLM, Boston U.; BA, Smith Coll. With Digital Equipment Corp.; lead counsel GE Info. Svcs. Europe; sr. counsel GE Info. Svcs., Rockville, Md.; sr v.p., gen. counsel Software AG, Inc., Reston, Va., 1998—. Office: Software AG Inc 11190 Sunrise Valley Dr Reston VA 20191-5453

BUTLER, KATHLEEN MARIE, editor; d. Paul Evon and Jane Florence Butler. BS, U. Md., 1982; MS, U. New Haven, 2000; MA, So. Conn. State U., 2004. Cert. secondary English Conn. Sr. auditor br. and ops. divsn. Chase Manhattan Bank, N.A., N.Y.C., 1982—84; sr. auditor Nat. Bank Washington, 1984—85, corp. loan officer, 1985—88; analyst global credit tng. Chase Manhattan Bank, N.A., N.Y.C., 1988—89, assoc. Europe corp. fin. divsn. Paris, 1989, assoc. credit audit divsn. N.Y.C., 1989—91, assoc. multinational divsn., 1991—92, comml. loan mgr. St. Maarten, Netherlands Antilles, 1992—93, country mgr., 1993—97; mng. dir. K.I.S.S. Corp. Ltd., St. Maarten, 1997—99; spl. edn. intern Masuk H.S., Monroe, Conn., 1999—2000; student tchr. New Milford (Conn.) H.S., 2001; mng. editor Conn. Rev., New Haven, 2001—; instr. So. Conn. State U., New Haven, 2003—. Presenter in field. Author poetry. Recipient Eve Cummings Poetry prize 2nd pl., So. Conn. State U., 2002, Leslie Leeds Poetry prize; rsch. fellow, So. Conn. State U., 2001—02, rsch. grantee, 2002. Mem.: English Dept. Grad. Ensemble (pres. 2002—03, Outstanding Svc. award), Am. Mensa Soc.

BUTLER, KERRY, actress; Actor: (Broadway plays) Les Miserables, 1987—2003, Blood Brothers, 1993—95, Beauty and the Beast, 1994—95, Hairspray, 2002—03, Little Shop of Horrors, 2003— (nominated best actress Outer Critics Cir.), (regional stage shows) Prodigal, Le Passe Muraille, Bat Boy The Musical, The "I" Word, The Folsom Head, Bright Lights, Big City, State of Oklahoma. Office: Abrams Artists Agy 26th Fl 275 Seventh Ave New York NY 10001 Office Phone: 646-486-4600. Office Fax: 646-486-0100.*

BUTLER, MARGARET KAMPSCHAEFER, retired computer scientist; b. Evansville, Ind., Mar. 7, 1924; d. Otto Louis and Lou Etta (Rehsteiner) Kampschaefer; m. James W. Butler, Sept. 30, 1951; 1 child, Jay. AB, Ind. U., 1944; postgrad., U.S. Dept. Agr. Grad. Sch., 1945, U. Chgo., 1949, U. Minn., 1950. Statistician U.S. Bur. Labor Statistics, Washington, 1945-46, U.S. Air Forces in Europe, Erlangen and Wiesbaden, Germany, 1946-48, U.S. Bur. Labor Statistics, St. Paul, 1949-51; mathematician Argonne (Ill.) Nat. Lab. 1948-49, 51-80, sr. computer scientist 1980-92; dir. Argonne Code Ctr. and Nat. Energy Software Ctr. Dept. Energy Computer Program Exch., 1960-91; spl. term appointee Argonne Nat. Lab., 1993—. Cons. AMF Corp., 1956-57, OECD, 1964, Poole Bros., 1967. Author: Careers for Women in Nuclear Science and Technology, 1992; editor Computer Physics Communications, 1969-80; contbr. (chpt.) The Application of Digital Computers to Problems in Reactor Physics, 1968, Advances in Nuclear Sci. and Technology, 1976; contbr. articles to profl. pubis. Treas. Timberlake Civic Assn., 1958; rep. mem. nomination com. Hinsdale (Ill.) Caucus, 1961-62; coord. 6th dist. ERA, 1973-80; del. Rep. Nat. Conv., 1980; bd. mgr. DuPage dist. YWCA Met. Chgo., 1987-90; computer and info. sys. adv. bd. Coll. DuPage, 1987-95; industry adv. bd. computer sci. dept. Bradley U., 1988-91; vice chair Ill. Women's Polit. Caucus, 1987-90; chair voters svc. LWV, Burr-Ridge-Willowbrook, 1991-93; vol. Morton Arboretum, 1996—, Friends of Indian Prairie Pub. Libr., 2000-2002; mem. LaGrange Park Friends Librr., 2002—; bd. dir. Plymouth Place Resident's Coun., 2003—. Recipient cert. of leadership Met. YWCA, Chgo., 1985, Merit award Chgo. Assn. Technol. Socs., 1988; named to Fed. 100, 1991; named Outstanding Woman Leader of DuPage County Sci., Tech. and Health Care, 1992. Fellow Am. Nuclear Soc. (mem. publs. com. 1965-71, bd. dirs. 1976-79, exec. com. 1977-78, chmn. bylaws and rules com., 1979-82, profl. women in ANS com. 1991-93, reviewer for publs., spl. award math. and computer divsn. 1992); mem. Assn. Computing Machinery (exec. com., sec. Chgo. chpt. 1963-65, publs. com., nat. com. 1968, reviewer for publs.), Assn. Women in Sci. (pres. Chgo. area chpt. 1982, nat. exec. bd. 1985-87), Nat. Computer Conf. (chmn. Pioneer Day com. 1985, tech. program chmn. 1987). Independent. Home: 107 Brewster Lane La Grange Park IL 60526-6003

BUTLER, NANCY TAYLOR, gender equity specialist, program director; b. Newport, RI, Oct. 31, 1942; d. Robert Lee and Roberta Claire (Brown) Taylor; m. Edward M. Butler, Aug. 22, 1964; children: Jeffrey, Gregory, Katherine. AB, Cornell U., 1964. Asst. dir. Career Equity Assistance Ctr. for Tng. Coll. of N.J., 1990-98; owner Equity Resources, Tinton Falls, N.J., 1993—. Mem. N.J. Dept. Edn. Gender Equity Adv. Comm., 1995—, sec., 1996-2000, chair, 2000-03. Editor Equity Exch., 1991-2003. Monmouth County dist. ethics com. Supreme Ct. N.J., 1987-91; pres. Vol. Ctr. Monmouth County, Red Bank, 1985-89; mem. Cornell U. Coun., Ithaca, N.Y., 1987-91, 1994-2003, adminstrv. bd., 1996-2003, vice-chair, 2001-03; dir. Cornell Assn. Class Officers, 1991-97; chair Cornell Alumni Trustee Nominating Com., 1994. Recipient Woman of Achievement award Commn. on Status of Women, 1988, Women's History Tribute NOW-N.J., 1995, Woman Leader award N.J. Assn. Women Bus. Owners, 1996. Mem. AAUW (life; pres. N.J. chpt. 1988-90, Edn. Found. Named Gift 1982, 83, 84, 86, 87, 89, 91), Nat. Coalition for Sex Equity in Edn. Home: 20 Cedar Pl Tinton Falls NJ 07724-2807

BUTLER, OCTAVIA ESTELLE, free-lance writer; b. Pasadena, Calif., June 22, 1947; d. Laurice and Octavia Margaret (Guy) B. AA, Pasadena City Coll., 1968; student, Calif. State U., Los Angeles, 1969—. Free-lance writer, Los Angeles, 1975—. MacArthur fellow, 1995. Author: Patternmaster, 1976, Mind of My Mind, 1977, Survivor, 1978, Kindred, 1979, Wild Seed, 1980, Clay's Ark, 1984, Dawn, 1987, Adulthood Rites, 1988, Imago, 1989, Parable of the Sower, 1993, Bloodchild, 1995, Parable of the Talents, 1998; also sci. fiction short stories. Recipient fifth prize Writer's Digest Short Story Contest, 1967, Creative Arts Achievement award L.A. YWCA, 1980, Sci. Fiction (Hugo) Best Novelette award World Sci. Fiction Conf., 1985, Best Short Story award World Sci. Fiction Conv., 1984, Nebula Best Novelette award Sci. Fiction Writers Am., 1985, Locus Best Novelette award, 1985, Best Novelette award Sci. Fiction Chronicle Reader, 1985, Nebula award for Best Novel, Sci. Fiction and Fantasy Writers Am., 2000; fellow John D. and Catherine T. MacArthur Found., 1995. Mem. Sci. Fiction Writers Am., Nat. Writers Union. Address: PO Box 25400 Seattle WA 98165-2300

BUTLER, PATRICIA, protective services official; b. Salem, Mass., Aug. 13, 1958; d. Frank Arthur and Ruth Elizabeth (Bartlett) B. Paramedic degree, Davenport Coll., 1984, AA in Mgmt. of Emergency Med. Svcs., 1987; Mich. Law Enforcement Officers Tng. Coun. cert., Grand Valley State U., 1988; BA in MHR, Spring Arbor Coll., 1994. CEO Whispering Winds, Inc., L'Anse, Mich., 1985—; firefighter Grand Rapids (Mich.) Fire Dept., 1985; security, data entry clerk Lacks Industries, Grand Rapids, 1985-88; loss prevention officer Woodland Mall Security, Kentwood, Mich., 1988-89, Butterworth Hosp., Grand Rapids, 1989; police officer Lakeview Police Dept., 1989, Edmore (Mich.)-Home Mcpl. Police Dept., 1989-90, Coopersville (Mich.) Police Dept., 1989-90; chief police Lakeview Village Police Dept., 1990-94, State Police, 1994—. Mem. Mich. Paramedic, 1986-98. Mem. NAFE, Nat. Assn. Chiefs, Mich. Chief's Assn. (v.p. 1991-94), Internat. Assn. Women Police, Mich. Assn. Chief of Police, Women Police Mich. Avocation: freelance artist. Office: Mich State Police L'Anse Post 88 PO Box 100 Lanse MI 49946-0100

BUTLER, SUSAN BELINDA, environmental specialist; b. Mobile, Ala., Feb. 22, 1971; d. William Butler and Charlotte Virginia Tingle; m. William Daniel Kennedy, Feb. 29, 2000; children: Anna Corinne, Niamh Olivia. BS, Auburn U., 1992, MS, 1996. Rsch. staff Fla. Marine Rsch. Inst., St. Petersburg, 1996—97; biologist Crystal River Mariculture Ctr., 1997—2001; environ. specialist Progress Energy, St. Petersburg, 2001—. Guest spkr. in field. Mem.: Nat. Assn. Environ. Profls., Am. Fisheries Soc., Gamma Sigma Delta. Democrat. Roman Catholic. Avocations: swimming, running, aerobics. Office: Progress Energy PO Box 14042 BBIA Saint Petersburg FL 33733

BUTLER, TAMMY J. WILEY, medical, surgical, and pediatric nurse; b. Emporia, Va., Oct. 9, 1967; d. Danny Thomas and Joan (Evans) Wiley; m. Lawrence Graham Butler, July 20, 1991; children: Lawrencia Joan, Laren Talane, Leiara Lane. BSN, Med. Coll. Va., 1990; postgrad., Va. Commonwealth U., 1997-2001. RN Va., cert. ACLS, PALS, MSW. Charge nurse med./surg. and pediatrics Greensville Meml. Hosp., Emporia, 1990—, clin. coord., 1991—, quality assurance coord., 1993—. Baptist. Avocations: walking, reading, skating, outdoor summer games. Home: 736 Reedy Creek Rd Freeman VA 23856-2318 Office: Greensville Meml Hosp 214 Weaver Ave Emporia VA 23847-1224

BUTLER-HOPKINS, KATHLEEN MARGARET, musician, educator; d. Robert Ernest Butler and Kathleen Theresa Butler (Lawson); m. John Ray Hopkins, May 6, 1982; children: Christopher Sean Hopkins, Bryant Gregory Hopkins, Patrick Garrett Hopkins. Assoc. in Violin, Piano, Trinity Coll. of Music, London, 1969, Lic. in Violin, 1970, Fellow in Violin, 1971; student, Curtis Inst. of Music, Phila., 1971—72; MusB, The Juilliard Sch., N.Y.C., 1975, MusM, 1976; M of Mus. Arts, Yale U. Sch. of Music, New Haven, Conn., 1978, D of Mus. Arts, 1982. Asst. prof. of music U. Alaska, Fairbanks, 1979—83, assoc. prof. of music, 1983—90, prof. of music, 1990—. Concertmaster Arctic Chamber Orch., Fairbanks, Alaska, 1979—, Fairbanks Symphony Orch., Fairbanks, Alaska, 1980—; string coord. U.

Alaska Summer Fine Arts Camp, Fairbanks, 1982—2000; asst. concertmaster Boston Civic Symphony, 1988; chamber music coord. Fairbanks Suzuki Inst., Alaska, 1996—; jr. symposium coord. Fairbanks Symphony String Symposium, Alaska, 1996—; master tchr. Juneau Jazz and Classics, Alaska, 1999—. Guest soloist (arctic chamber orch. subscription series) Barber Violin Concerto, (fairbanks symphony subscription series) Solo Violin Recital, soloist with fairbanks youth orchestra (violin solo) Barber Violin Concerto, competitive selected presenter (nw division menc convention) Alaska Trio Recital, guest violin soloist (soloist with arctic chamber orchestra) Vivaldi The Seasons, guest soloist (arctic chamber orch. subscription series) Chamber Recital, Mozart Symphonie Concertante, guest artist Chamber Music Recital. Orch. rep. Fairbanks Symphony Assn., Alaska, 2000—. Recipient Fulbright scholarship, Fulbright-Hays, 1978-79, Disting. Svc. award, Usibelli Found., 2003; Summer Seminar fellow, Nat. Endowment for the Humanities, 1989. Mem.: Alaska String Tchrs. Assn. (sec./treas. 1979—83), Am. Fedn. of Musicians Local #248, Coll. Music Soc. (U. Alaska rep. 1979—2003), Music Educators Nat. Conf., Alaska Music Educators Assn. (Alaska String Tchr. of the Yr. 1999), Am. String Tchrs. Asssociation, Phi Kappa Phi. Home: 4978 Drake St Fairbanks AK 99709 Office: Dept of Music Univ Alaska Fairbanks AK 99775 E-mail: ffkmb@uaf.edu.

BUTLER YANK, LESLIE ANN, artist, writer, editor; b. Salem, Oreg., Nov. 19, 1945; d. Marlow Dole and Lala Ann (Erlandson) Butler; m. Howard Dennis Yank, July 4, 2001. Student, Lewis and Clark Coll., 1963-64; BS, U. Oreg., 1969; postgrad., Portland State U., 1972-73, Lewis and Clark Coll., 1991. Creative trainee Ketchum Advt., San Francisco, 1970-71; asst. advt. dir. Mktg. Systems, Inc., Portland, Oreg., 1971-74; prodn. mgr., art dir., copywriter Finzer-Smith, Portland, 1974-76; copywriter Gerber Advt., Portland, 1976-78; freelance copywriter Portland, 1983-84, 83-85; copywriter McCann-Erickson, Portland, 1980-81; copy chief Brookstone Co., Peterborough, N.H., 1981-83; creative dir. Whitman Advt., Portland, 1984-87; prin. L.A. Advt., 1987—; portrait artist. Bd. trustees Portland (Oreg.) Opera, 2001—03, Oreg. Human Soc., 2003—. Author: The Dream Road and Other Tales From Hidden Hills, 1997; arts and antiques editor Portland Living mag.; designer of fence featured in Better Homes & Gardens, 2000. Spokeswoman Nat. Alopecia Areata Found., San Rafeal, Calif.; Co-founder, v.p., newsletter editor Animal Rescue and Care Fund, 1972—81; mem. Friends of the Performing Arts Ctr., Portland Art Mus., Oreg. Humane Soc.; pres. OMSI; bd. dirs. Portland Opera Assn., 2001—. Recipient Internat. Film and TV Festival N.Y. Finalist award, 1985, 86, 87, 88, Internat. Radio Festival of N.Y. award, 1984, 85, 88, Hollywood Radio and TV Soc. Internat. Broadcasting award, 1981, TV Comml. Festival Silver Telly award, 1985, TV Comml. Festival Bronze Telly, 1986, AVC Silver Cindy, 1986, Los Angeles Advt. Women LULU, 1986, 87, 88, 89 Ad Week What's New Portfolio, 1986, N.W. Addy award Seattle Advt. Fedn., 1984, Best in the West award, 1985, Portland Advt. Fedn. Rosey Finalist award, 1986, Nat. winner Silver Microphone award, 1987, 88, 89. Mem. People for Ethical Treatment of Animals.

BUTO, KATHLEEN A. health products executive; BA, Rutgers U.; MPA, Harvard U. With Health Care Financing Adminstrn., 1982—2000; sr. health advisor Congl. Budget Office, 2000—02; v.p. for health policy, govt. affairs Johnson & Johnson, New Brunswick, NJ, 2002—. Office: Johnson & Johnson 1 Johnson & Johnson Plz New Brunswick NJ 08933

BUTT, ELIZABETH KATHRYN MOFFATT, journalist, photographer, newspaper editor; b. Harrisburg, Pa., Dec. 6, 1967; d. William Thomas and Kathryn Elizabeth (Gensler) M.; m. Jeffery S. Butt, June 6, 1998. BA in English Lit., U. Pitts., Johnstown, 1991; student in Nursing, Harrisburg (Pa.) C.C., 2003—. Reporter West Perry Sch. Dist., Elliottsburg, Pa., 1992; stringer Swank-Fowler Publs., Inc., Duncannon, Pa., 1991-92, staff and sports writer, photographer New Bloomfield, Pa., 1992—, assoc. editor Duncannon Record, 1994—. Reading tutor Perry County Literacy Coun., Newport, Pa., 1992-96, bd. dirs. 1993-95; mem. Laubach Literacy Action, 1993-96. Recipient 2d place award for writing, 1994, 95, 1st place for photograph, 1995. Mem. Women in Comm., Ea. U.S. Pipe Band Assn., Amateur Speedskating Union, Lions, Clan Moffatt Soc., Phi Theta Kappa. Republican. Lutheran. Avocations: playing highland bagpipes, short-track ice speedskating. Home: 512 Waverly Rd Harrisburg PA 17109-4033 Office: Duncannon Record 217 N High St # A Duncannon PA 17020-1319

BUTTE, AMY S. securities trader; BA in Polit. Sci. and Psychology, Yale U.; MBA, Harvard U. Various positions Andersen Consulting, Merrin Fin., Bridge Trading Co., Inc., Merrill Lynch; sr. mng. dir. Bear Stearns, 1999—2002; CFO, chief strategist fin. svcs. divsn. Credit Suisse First Boston, 2002—03; exec. v.p. N.Y. Stock Exch., N.Y.C., 2004, CFO, 2004—. Active N.Y. Women's Found.; mem. corp. adv. bd. N.Y.C. Ballet. Office: NY Stock Exch INc 11 Wall St New York NY 10005

BUTTERBRODT, PATRICIA ANN, music educator; b. Chattanooga, Tenn., July 12; d. Charles D. and Irene S. Groth; m. John F. Butterbrodt, Nov. 26, 1983; children: Patrick, Michael. MusB magna cum laue, Jacksonville (Fla.) U., 1981; MA in ednl. leadership, U. of North Fla., 2000. Cert. tchr. Fla. Dept. Edn., 2000. Elem. music tchr. Duval County Pub. Schs., Jacksonville, Fla., 1980—83, math tchr. HS, 1983—98, dist. music resource tchr., 1998—, acting supr. of music edn., 1998—. Ptnr. in edn. Kennedy Ctr. Duval County Schs. and U. of North Fla., Jacksonville, 2001—; bd. dir. Jacksonville (Fla.) Symphony Assn.; bd. dir., exec. bd. St. Johns River City Band, Jacksonville; mem. adminstrv. bd. Cathedral Arts Project, Jacksonville, 1999—2003. Choir mem. St. Johns Cathedral Choir, Jacksonville, 1990—2003. Scholar President's Academic scholarship, Luther Coll., 1977. Mem.: Fla. Music Educators Assn., Am. Soc. Choral Dirs. (Nat. Music Student award 1977), Fla. Music Supervisors Assn., Music Educators Nat. Conf. E-mail: butterbrop@educationcentral.org.

BUTTERFIELD, ANDREA CHRISTINE, elementary school educator, adult education educator, psychology educator; Student study abroad program, U. Md., Munich, Germany, 1973; BA in Childhood Edn., U. Fla., 1975; MEd in Reading, Beaver Coll., 1977; postgrad. reading supr. cert. program, Millersville U., 1985; DEd in Adult Edn., Pa. State U., 1995. Cert. supervisory I supr. reading, instrnl. II reading specialist-elem., Pa. Reading specialist Lauderdale Lakes Middle Sch., Fla., 1977-78; coord., oper. individual title I Roman Cath. H.S. for Boys Sch. Dist. of Phila., 1978-85; supr. of reading specialist interns and grad. instr., clin. practicum reading clinic Millersville U., Pa., 1985-86; reading specialist Ebenezer Elementary Sch. and Cedar Crest Middle Sch., Cornwall-Lebanon Sch. Dist., Lebanon, Pa., 1985—. Adj. instr. Camden County Coll., N.J., 1980; cons. to ednl. orgns., 1994—; part-time faculty ednl. psychology Pa. State U., Harrisburg, 1995—. Speaker in field. Planning commr., bd. officer Derry Township, Hershey, Pa., 1992—, design rev. bd. mem., 1994—. Mem. Am. Assn. Adult and Continuing Edn., Am. Planning Assn., Internat. Reading Assn., Pa. Assn. Adult Continuing Edn., Pa. Planning Assn., Keystone State Reading Assn., Phi Kappa Phi, Phi Kappa Delta. Home: 440 Leearden Rd Hershey PA 17033-2140

BUTTERFIELD, DEBORAH KAY, sculptor; b. San Diego, May 7, 1949; m. John Buck; 2 children. BA, U. Calif., Davis, 1971, MFA, 1973; DFA (hon.), Mont. State U., 1998, Rocky Mountain Coll., Billings, Mont., 1997. Asst. prof. sculpture U. Wis., Madison, 1975-76, Mont. State U., Bozeman, 1979-81, adj. prof., 1981-84. One-man shows include Lowe Mus. Art U. Miami, Coral Gables, Fla., 1992, San Diego Mus. Art, 1996, Yellowstone Art Mus., Billings, Mont., 2003-04, The Contemporary Mus. Art, Honolulu, 2004, Appleton Mus. Art, Ocala, Fla., 2004; exhibited in groups shows U. Mus. Berkeley, Calif., 1974, Whitney Mus. Am. Art, N.Y., 1979, Albright-Knox Gallery, Buffalo, 1979, Israel Mus., Jerusalem, 1980, Arco Ctr. Visual Art, 1981, Walker Art Ctr., Mpls., 1982, Dallas Mus. Fine Arts, 1982, Oakland, 1983, Chgo., 1985, Contemporary Art Ctr., Honolulu, 1986, Whitney Mus., 1988, Contemporary Art Mus., Honolulu, 1993, Seattle Mus. Art, 1994, The White House, Washington, Yale U., New Haven, 1997; represented in permanent collections Whitney Mus. Am. Art, N.Y., San Francisco Mus. Contemporary Art, Israel Mus., Jerusalem, Walker Art Ctr., Mpls., Met. Mus. Art, N.Y., Hirshhorn Mus., Washington, Seattle Art Mus., UCLA Sculpture Garden; commd. Copley Square, Boston, Portland (Oreg.) Airport, Denver Art Mus., Kansas City (Mo.) Zoo, White House, Washington, 2000, Monte Carlo, Monaco, 2000, Smithsonian Instn., Washington, San Francisco Internat. Airport. Nat. Endowment Arts grantee, 1977, 80, Guggenheim grantee, 1980; Commission Portland Internat. Airport.

BUTTERWORTH, RITAJEAN HARTUNG, broadcast executive; b. 1931; m. Fred R. Butterworth; 5 children. Bd. dirs. Corp. Pub. Broadcasting, Washington, 1992—. Chmn. bd. Corp. Pub. Broadcasting, 1995—96, vice chmn., 2001; treas., bd. dirs. Discovery Inst., 1990—2002. Mem. coun. Annenberg/CPB Project; active Children's Orthop. Hosp., Child Ryther Ctr., Seattle, 1989—91; mem. merit selection panel U.S. Dist. Ct. ea. dist., Wash.; Wash. state dir. Senator Slade Gorton, 1981—86, 1988—90; bd. trustees We. Wash. U., Bellingham, 1969—77, sec., vice chmn., chmn. bd.; mem. NPR Bd., 1977—85; sec., vice chmn.; mem. adv. bd. Sta. KUOW-FM, Seattle, 1985—88, KCTS, Seattle, 1989—. Recipient Lifetime Achievement Award, Corp Pub Broadcasting, 2003. Office: Corp Pub Broadcasting 401 9th St NW Washington DC 20004-2128

BUTTNER, JEAN BERNHARD, diversified financial services company executive; b. New Rochelle, N.Y., Nov. 3, 1934; d. Arnold and Janet (Kinghorn) Bernhard; m. Edgar Buttner, Sept. 13, 1958 (div.); children: Janet, Edgar Arnold, Marianne. BA, Vassar Coll., 1957; cert. bus. adminstrn., Harvard-Radcliffe program, 1958; Montessori diploma, Coll. Notre Dame, Belmont, Calif., 1967; D Bus. Adminstrn. (hon.), U. Bridgeport, 1994. Past v.p. Buttner Cos., Oakland, Calif.; pres. Value Line Inc. (subs. Arnold Bernhard & Co., Inc.), N.Y.C., 1985, chmn., pres., CEO, 1988—; chmn., CEO, pres. AB Properties, Inc., 1988—; chmn., pres. Compupower, 1988—, Value Line Securities, Inc., 1988—, Value Line Distbn. Ctr., Inc., 1994—, Value Line Pub., Inc., 1988—, Vanderbilt Advt., Inc., 1988—. Chmn., pres. Value Line Mut. Funds. Editor-in-chief Value Line Rsch. Ctr., The Value Line 600, The Value Line Investment Survey-Small and Mid-Cap Edition, The Value Line Mut. Fund Survey, The Value Line No-Load Fund Advisor, The Value Line Options Survey, The Value Line Convertibles Survey, The Value Line Spl. Situations Svc., Value Line Select, Value Line Investment Survey for Windows, Value Line Mut. Fund Survey for Windows, Value Line Daily Options, Convertibles Data File, DataFile and DataFile II, Estimates and Projections, Value Line on Microfiche. Past trustee Skidmore Coll.; past pres. Piedmont Sch. Bd.; past dir. Berkeley Montessori Sch.; mem. N.Y.C. Partnership, Com. of 200; past mem. adv. coun. Stanford Bus. Sch.; past mem. The Presdl. Roundtable, past vis. com. for bd. overseers Harvard Bus. Sch.; past bd. dirs. Harvard Bus. Sch. Club Greater N.Y.; past west coast admissions rep. Vassar Coll.; past trustee Radcliffe Coll., Harvard U., Williams Coll., Emma Willard Sch., Coll. Prep. Sch. Com. for Econ. Devel. Named one of N.Y.'s 75 Most Influential Women in Business, Crain's, 1996, One of N.Y.'s 100 Most Influential Women in Business, Crain's, 1999; recipient Alumni Achievement award, Harvard U. Grad. Sch. Bus. Adminstrn., 1995, Alumnae award Choate Rosemary Hall, Wallingford, Conn., 1995, Emma Lazarus award Associated Builders and Owners of N.Y., Inc., 1996; Life Achievement award Emma Willard Sch., 1998. Mem. Harvard Bus. Sch. Club Greater N.Y., Harvard Bus. Sch. Assn. (bd. dirs.). Republican. Congregationalist. Avocations: reading, swimming, biking, tennis, skiing. Office: Value Line Inc 220 E 42nd St Fl 6 New York NY 10017-5891 E-mail: jbb@valueline.com.

BUTTON, KATY, professional athletics manager; BS Sch. Fgn. Svc., Georgetown U. Policy advisor Hillary Rodman Clinton, 1994—2000; gen. mgr. Washington Freedom Women's United Soccer Assn., Washington, 2000—. Office: Washington Freedom 2400 E Capitol St SE Washington DC 20003-1749

BUTTON, RENA PRITSKER, public affairs executive; b. Providence, Feb. 15, 1925; d. Isadore and Esther (Kay) Pritsker; m. Daniel E. Button, Aug. 16, 1969; children by previous marriage: Joshua, Bruce, David Posner. Student, Pembroke Coll., 1942-45; BS, Simmons Coll., 1948; postgrad., Union U., 1968-69. Spl. asst. to U.S. Rep., 1967-69; spl. projects coord. United Jewish Appeal, 1971-74; exec. dir. Nat. Coun. Jewish Women, Inc., N.Y.C., 1974-76; pres. Button Assos., N.Y.C., 1976—; exec. v.p. Catalyst, N.Y.C., 1980-82; pres. Button & Button, Albany, N.Y., 1982—. Adv. coun. N.Y. State Senate Minority, 1980—; exec. dir. N.Y. State Coun. on Alcoholism and Other Drug Addictions, 1990-93; pres., founder Two Together, A Pilot Reading Program for Young People, 1997-2003. Co-producer, moderator: TV pub. affairs program Speak For Yourself, Albany, N.Y., 1963-66. Chair pub. affairs com. Marymount Manhattan Coll.; past bd. dirs. Albany YWCA, Albany Coun. Chs. Devel. Corp., World Affairs Coun., Planned Parenthood Assn. Albany; trustee Jerusalem Women's Seminar, Citizens for Family Planning, N.Y. Com. Integrated Housing, Hist. Albany Found. Ctr. for Counseling, Town of Bethlehem Pub. Libr., 1999; pres. Sr. Svc. Ctr. Albany Area, Two Together, 1997, bd. dirs. Com. Modern Cts.; exec. dir. N.Y. Head Injury Assn., 1993-96; candidate N.Y. State Assembly 102d Dist., 1996; trustee Albany Symphony Orch., 2002—. Mem. Siasconset Casino Club, Univ. Club. Clubs: Siasconset Casino (Siasconset, Mass.), Univ. (Albany). Home and Office: 16 Spruce Ct Delmar NY 12054-2614 E-mail: rbutton96@aol.com.

BUTTRAM, CHRISTINE RUTH, music educator; b. St. Louis, Mo., Oct. 12, 1973; d. Paul and Phyllis Huddleston; m. Virgil (Randy) Duran Buttram, Jr., Jan. 19, 2002. B in Music Edn., Kennesaw State U., 1997. Music tchr. Cobb County Pub. Schools, Marietta, Ga., 2001—03, Paulding County Pub. Schools, Dallas, Ga., 1998—2001; asst. choir master Rivercliff Luth. Ch., Atlanta, 1998—. Hope Scholarship, Ga. Lottery, 1994—97. Mem.: Music Educators Nat. Conf., Big Chicken Chorus Rooster Boosters (sec. 2003).

BUTTS, CAROL HENDERSON, human resources specialist, consultant; b. Anniston, Ala., Feb. 11, 1946; d. William Edward and Mary (Hill) Henderson; m. Robert Russell Butts, Feb. 12, 1976 (div. Mar. 1989); children: Jabe Bowden, Deborah Ann Miller. BA, Jacksonville State U., 1970. From pers. counselor to tng. dir. Norrell, Inc., Atlanta, 1971-77; creative dir. TV Tempo Stevens County, Toccoa, Ga., 1978-82; gen. mgr. Niermann Pers. Svcs., Atlanta, 1983-87; dir. tng. and continuing edn. KOT Pers., Atlanta, 1987-90; gen. mgr., v.p. med. divsn. Prestige Pers. Svcs., Norcross, Ga., 1990-94; dir. med. divsn. MedPro Pers., Atlanta, 1994-95; pres. MedStat, Inc., Alpharetta, Ga., 1995—. Pres. Habitat for Humanity, 1996—97. Recipient Editor's Choice award, Internat. Libr. Poetry, 2001—02, Poet of Merit award, 2002. Fellow: Nat. Assn. Pers. Cons., Am. Biog. Inst.; mem.: NOW, NAFE (pres. 1996—97), NAUW (pres. 1996—97), Ga. Assn. Pers. Cons. (chair, Disting. Cons. of Yr. 1978), Jacksonville State U. Alumni Assn. (Alumni fo the Yr. nominee 1997), Sigma Tau Alpha, Alpha Xi Delta. Avocations: reading, writing, poetry, fishing, water sports.

BUTTS, CHERIE LAVAUGHN, biomedical researcher; b. Baton Rouge, Feb. 13, 1971; d. Harry LeVaughn Butts and Linda Marie Sublet; m. Daniel Harris, Nov. 13, 1992 (div. Sept. 1999); 1 child: Daniel A. Harris. BA, Johns Hopkins U., 1992, MS, 1997; PhD, U. Tex., Houston. Rsch. asst. Johns Hopkins U., Balt., 1991-92, Morgan State U., Balt., 1995-96, U. Md., Balt., 1996-98; grad. rsch. asst. U. Tex. M.D. Anderson Cancer Ctr., Houston, 1998—. Trainee rep. M.D. Anderson Assocs., Houston, 1999—. Inventor Foster speculum, 1996; contbr. articles to profl. jours. Travel fellow 6th Biennial Symposium on Cancer, Minorities and the Underserved, Houston, 1998; fellow Am. Physiol. Soc., Nat. Inst. Diabetes and Digestive Disorders, Washington, 1998; Cancer Rsch. Tng. fellow Nat. Cancer Inst., Bethesda, Md., 1999. Mem. Am. Assn. for Cancer Rsch. (assoc.). Methodist. Avocation: biking. Home: 2121 Hepburn St Apt 806 Houston TX 77054-3220 Office: U Tex MD Anderson Cancer Ctr 1515 Holcombe Blvd # 67 Houston TX 77030-4009

BUTTS, MARY ELLEN F. secondary school educator; b. Hamilton Township, N.J., Apr. 17, 1955; d. Frederick John and Mary Rose Froehlich; m. Richard Lee Butts, Aug. 26, 1995; stepchildren: Nicolas Guy, Alice Marie. Student, Slippery Rock U., 1973—74; BS in Phys. Edn. with honors, U. Del., 1977; postgrad., U. Md., 1979—83, Hagerstown (Md.) C.C., 1990—96. Advanced profl. cert. Md. State Bd. Edn. Phys. edn. tchr. No. Middle Sch., Hagerstown, Md., 1977—, phys. edn. dept. coord., 1979—, unified and related arts team leader, 1986—, mem. sch. improvement team, 1986—. Dir. sch./cmty. recreation Washington County Pub. Schs., Hagerstown, 1978—81. Active membership drives YMCA, Hagerstown, 1978—84, mem. capital campaign drive, 1985; statistician Blue Ridge/Cascade Golf League, Fairfield, Pa., 1995—99, Mont Alto, Pa., 1995—99. Recipient award of excellence in edn., Hagerstown-Washington County C. of C., 1996, Unsung Heroes in Edn. award, Relia Star and No. Life, Hagerstown, 1999. Mem.: NEA, Washington County Tchrs. Assn., Md. State Tchrs. Assn. Democrat. Roman Catholic. Avocations: golf, walking, fishing, reading, tennis. Home: 14522 Water Company Rd Cascade MD 21719 Office: No Middle Sch 701 Northern Ave Hagerstown MD 21719

BUTZ, JANET AVERY, school system administrator; arrived in U.S., 1998; d. Ronald Alexander and Margaret Avery Currie; m. Craig Warner Butz, June 16, 1988; 1 child, Aanen. BA in Sociology, U. Sask., Saskatoon, Sask., Can., 1987, EdB, 1989; MA in Spl. Edn., CSUDH, Carson, Calif., 1992; adminstrv. credential, CSUDH, Carson, Calif.; EdD in Spl. Edn., U. Nev., Las Vegas, 1999. Professionally recognized spl. educator, sr. cert. grants specialist, cert. grant reviewer, bd. cert. behavior analyst. Spl. edn. tchr. L.A. Unified Sch. Dist., 1988—93, program specialist, 1993—96; spl. edn. tchr. Clark County Sch. Dist., Las Vegas, 1996—98, spl. edn. itinerant, 1998—2000, itinerant specialist, 2000—01; asst. prin. Odyssey Charter Sch., Las Vegas, 2001—03, dir. fed. programs, 2003—. Mem. charter schs. SFAC Nev. Dept. Edn., Reno, 2001—; pres. CARE LLC, Las Vegas, 2003—. Mem.: Nev. Assn. Sch. Adminstrs., Assn. Behavior Analysis, Coun. for Exceptional Children, Am. Ednl. Rsch. Assn. (assoc.). Avocations: travel, reading, sports. Home: 11001 Cliff Swallow Ave Las Vegas NV 89144 Office: Odyssey Charter Schs 6701 W Charleston Blvd Las Vegas NV 89146

BUVINGER, JAN, library director; b. Lampasas, Tex., Oct. 4, 1943; d. Orville Layne and Myriam (Hamer) Rogers; m. Robert C. Ward. BS, Coll. Charleston, S.C., 1965; MLS, Emory U., 1970. Childrens asst. libr. Charleston (S.C.) County Libr., 1970-71, reference libr., 1972-75, head reference dept., 1976-77, dep. dir., 1977-79, dir., 1979—. Mem. Am. Libr. Assn., S.C. Libr. Assn., S.E. Libr. Assn. Office: Charleston County Pub Libr 68 Calhoun St Charleston SC 29401-3508

BUXTON, GINA LEEANN, music educator; b. Wetumka, Okla., June 10, 1968; d. Jerry Lee Tynes and Glenda Sue Crews; m. Christopher David Buxton, June 12, 1999; 1 child, Sean Bailey. BS in Edn., S.W. Mo. State U., 1991; M in Music Edn., Northwestern U., 2001. Dir. bands Dixon (Mo.) H.S., 1991—92, Clearwater Schs., Piedmont, Mo., 1992—98, Fordland (Mo.) Schs., 1998—99, St. Vincent Schs., Perryville, Mo., 1999—2000; asst. dir. bands West Plains (Mo.) Sch., 2000—. Home: 720 Oakwood Dr Willow Springs MO 65793 Office: West Plains R-7 602 E Olden West Plains MO 65775

BUYANOVSKY, SOPHIA, linguist, educator; b. Moscow, Nov. 17, 1956; d. Michael and Lubor Yakobishvili; m. Lev Buyanovsky, Aug. 27, 1977; children: Michael, Paul, Daniel. BA, MA, Moscow State U. Tchr. of Russian S.I. Tech. H.S., N.Y.C., 1989—.

BUYSE, MARYLOU, pediatrician, geneticist, medical association administrator; b. N.Y.C., June 27, 1946; d. George J. and Barbara M. (Sauer) B.; m. Carl N. Edwards, Jan. 22, 1982. AB, Hunter Coll., 1966; MD, Med. Coll. Pa., 1970; MS in Med. Adminstrn., U. Wis., 1993. Diplomate Am. Bd. Med. Genetics. Intern U. Mich., 1970-71; resident in pediatrics L.A. County-U. So. Calif. Med. Ctr., 1971-73, fellow, 1973-75, Sch. Medicine Boston U., 1975-84; asst. prof. pediatrics U. So. Calif., 1973-75, Tufts U., 1976-84; coord. Myelodysplasia Clinic Tufts-New Eng. Med. Ctr., Boston, 1976-79; dir. Cystic Fibrosis Clinic, staff pediatrician Ctr. for Genetic Counseling and Birth Defects Evaluation, 1975-82; med. dir. Ctr. for Birth Defects Info. Service, 1978-82, dir. center, 1982-94; pres. Medx Ltd., 1985-94, Ctr. for Birth Defects Info. Scis., Inc., 1985-94; dir. clin. genetics Children's Hosp., Boston, 1985-86; mem. med. adv. bd. Mass. Cystic Fibrosis Found., 1977-79; med. dir. Ferald State Sch., 1988-94; assoc. med. dir. MassPRO, 1993-95; mem. Mass. Bd. Registration in Medicine, 1994-95; assoc. med. dir. Care Advantage Health Sys., Inc., med. dir., 1996-97, United Health Care of New England, 1997-98, consulting physician advisor, 1998-99, v.p. health affairs, 1999-2001; pres., CEO Mass. Assn. Health Plans, 2001—. Chair R.I. Folic Acid Coun., R.I. March of Dimes, 1999-2001; cons. in field. Assoc. editor Birth Defects Compendium, 2d edit., 1979; assoc. editor Syndrome Identification Jour., 1977-82, editor, 1982; editor Jour. Clin. Dysmortphology, 1982-86, Dysmorphology and Clinical Genetics, 1986-94; editor-in-chief Birth Defects Encyclopedia, 1990. Recipient Physicians Recognition award AMA, 1975, Alumni Achievement award Med. Coll. Pa., 1987; named to Alumni Hall of Fame, Hunter Coll., 1998. Fellow Am. Acad. Pediatrics, Mass. Med. Soc. (asst. sec.-treas. 1991-94, trustee 1991-2000, sec.-treas. 1994-96, v.p. 1996-97, pres.-elect 1997-98, pres. 1998-99); mem. Am. Med. Women's Assn. (pres. Mass. br. 39 1986-91), Am. Mgmt. Assn., Am. Soc. Human Genetics, AAAS, Am. Med. Writers Assn., Soc. Craniofacial Genetics (pres. 1986), Am. Coll. Physician Execs., Teratology Soc., Charles River Dist. Med. Soc. (pres. 1993-95), Alpha Omega Alpha. Office: Ctr Birth Defects Info Svcs Inc Dover Med Bldg Box 1776 Dover MA 02030

BUZALJKO, GRACE WILSON, retired editor; b. Cambridge, Mass., Nov. 4, 1922; d. Charles and Elizabeth (Douglas) Wilson; m. Ahmed Buzaljko, Mar. 9, 1963 (div. Mar. 1980). BA cum laude, St. Mary Coll., Leavenworth, Kans., 1944; postgrad., U. Pitts., 1945—46, New Sch. for Social Rsch., 1949—50. Promotions asst. Pitts. Press, 1945-48; manuscript editor John Wiley & Sons, N.Y.C., 1948-52, Harcourt Brace Jovanovich, N.Y.C., 1952-60, U. Calif. Press, Berkeley, 1960-67; adminstrv. editor Harcourt Brace Jovanovich, San Francisco, 1967-72; editor dept. anthropology U. Calif., Berkeley, 1973-88; ret., 1988. Editor: (books) Yurok Myths (A. L. Kroeber), 1976, Karok Myths (A. L. Kroeber and E. W. Gifford), 1980; contbr. articles to profl. jours. Co-clk. Berkeley Soc. of Friends Meeting, 1988—90. Mem.: AAUW (v.p., program chmn. Berkeley br. 1981—83, legis. chmn. 1988—94), Am. Anthrop. Assn., Miwok Archeol. Preserve of Marin. Avocations: gardening, walking. Home: 401 Santa Clara Ave Apt 219 Oakland CA 94610

BUZZELLI, CHARLOTTE GRACE, special education educator; b. Mar. 21, 1947; d. Edmund Albert and Sarah Agnes (Russo) Buzzelli. BS, U. Akron, 1969, MS in Edn., 1976. Tchr. St. Anthony Sch., Akron, 1969-76; program coord., tchr. Akron Montessori Sch. Continuing Edn. Program, Eastwood Ctr., Akron, 1976-77; dir. edn. Fallsview Psychiat. Hosp., Ohio Dept. Mental Health, Cuyahoga Falls, 1977-92, developer job tng. partnership grant program and spl. needs handicapped grant program, 1992-97; tng. coord. N.E. regional & program educator children svcs. Ohio Dept. Mental Health State Operated Svcs., 1992—97. Spl. edn. svcs. developer and educator cmty svcs. div. North Coast Behavioral Healthcare Sys., Ohio Dept. Mental Health, 1997-2002; tchr. adult basic lit. edn. program Akron City Sch. Dist., 1992—; developer Akron City Schs. Project Rise Homeless Youth Family Learning Literacy Program, 2001—; cons. in field; pioneered first spl. edn. program in Ohio for adult state psychiat. hosp.; developed 1st community-based adult basic edn. program in state instn. in Ohio; program cons. state operated svcs. State of Ohio; participant U. Hawaii Study Tours Rsch. Projects, Internat. Edn. and East Asia Pi Lambda Theta Orient Study Tour, Manoa campus, 1990, spl. edn. rsch. U. Akron, 1976. Developer literacy evaluation program Project Rise Homeless Youth, Akron, Ohio, 2000—; supr. Ctr. for Literacy, U. Akron Students Svs. Learners Program, Homeless Shelters Akron Pub. Schs. programs; supr. dept. ctr. lit. U. Akron; mem. gospel meets Symphony chorus Akron Symphony Orch. Gospel Choir, 1996—; mem. choir Diocese of Cleve., St. John's Cathedral, Mass of Jubilee Gospel Choir, 1998, 2000. Named Ohio Tchr. of Yr., 1979; recipient A Key award, U. Akron, Urban Light award for outstanding svc., 2001, Cmty. Svc. Achievement award, Italian Am. Soc., Cmty. Collaboration award, Summit County Housing Network, 2003, 2004. Mem. CEC (coun. pres.), ASCD, Assn. Children with Learning Disabilities, Internat. Reading Assn., U. Akron Alumni Assn., Univ. Club, Akron Women's City Club, Coll. Club of Akron, Pi Lambda Theta (pres.), Phi Delta Kappa, Delta Kappa Gamma, Gamma Beta (pres.), Kappa Kappa Iota. Avocations: pet therapy to children and adults with disabilities, reading, travel, writing, singing, creating community resources for spl. edn. students and mental health clients. Home: 662 Dayton St Akron OH 44310-2301 Office: Adult Basic Literacy Edn Profl Devel Acad 785 Carnegie Ave Akron OH 44314

BYAL, NANCY LOUISE, food editor; b. Plainfield, N.J., Mar. 12, 1944; d. Albert William and Anna Marie (Goering) Zeiner; m. Wayne Ole Byal, May 2, 1967; 1 child, Jason David. BS, Iowa State U., 1965. Cert. home economist; cert. culinary profl. Product counselor Gen. Mills, Inc., Mpls., 1965-67; assoc. food editor Better Homes & Gardens Books Meredith Corp., Des Moines, 1968-72, assoc. food editor Better Homes & Gardens, 1972-74, sr. food editor, 1974-83, sr. dept. head Food and Nutrition, 1983-86, exec. food editor Better Homes and Gardens, 1986—. Chair, com. mem. Iowa State U. Coll. Family and Consumer Scis. Adv. Com., Ames; chmn., exec. mem. Julia Child Cookbook Awards Com. Editor, author: Better Home and Gardens Fondue Cook Book, 1970, Better Home and Gardens Salad Book, 1969. Named Home Economist in Bus. of Yr., Iowa Home Economists in Bus., 1992. Mem. Internat. Assn. Culinary Profls., Am. Inst. Food and Wine (mem. tast and health com.), Am. Assn. Family and Consumer Scis., Luth. Women's Missionary League. Avocations: gardening, crafting, reading. Office: Meredith Corp 1716 Locust St Des Moines IA 50309-3023

BYARS, AMANDA, performing company executive, musician, educator; b. Spartanburg, S.C., Oct. 18, 1952; MusB, Converse Coll., 1974; MusM, So. Meth. U., 1977. Cert. tchr. piano. Piano tchr. Mountain View Coll., Dallas, 1975-80; asst. prof. So. Meth. U., Dallas, 1980-88; co-founder, dir. Dallas Music, 1988-92; ind. piano tchr. Dallas, 1992-98; dir. artist and educator rels. Steinway Hall, Dallas, 1998—. Piano adjudicator, 1985. Contbr. articles to profl. jours. Mem. Tex. Music Tchrs. Assn. (chmn. ind. music tchrs. 1997—), Dallas Music Tchrs. Assn. (pres. 1996-98, v.p. 1998—). Home: 10584 High Hollows Dr Apt 174 Dallas TX 75230-4714

BYARS, BETSY (CROMER), writer; b. Charlotte, Aug. 7, 1928; d. George Guy and Nan (Rugheimer) Cromer; m. Edward Ford Byars, June 24, 1950; children: Laurie, Betsy Ann, Nan, Guy. Author: Clementine, 1962, The Dancing Camel, 1965, Rama, the Gypsy Cat, 1966, The Groober, 1967, The Midnight Fox, 1968 (Am. Book of Yr. selection Child Study Assn. 1968, Lewis Carroll Shelf award 1970), Trouble River, 1969 (Am. Book of Yr. selection Child Study Assn. 1969), The Summer of the Swans, 1970 (Am. Book of Yr. selection Child Study Assn. 1970, John Newbery medal 1971), Go and Hush the Baby, 1971, The House of Wings, 1972 (Am. Book of Yr. selection Child Study Assn. 1972, Nat. Book award nomination 1973), The 18th Emergency, 1973 (Am. Book of Yr. selection Child Study Assn. 1973, New York Times Outstanding Book of Yr. 1973, Dorothy Canfield Fisher Meml. Book award Vt. Conress of Parents and Teachers 1975), The Winged Colt of Casa Mia, 1973 (Am. Book of Yr. selection Child Study Assn. 1973, New York Times Outstanding Book of Yr. 1973), After the Goat Man, 1974 (Am. Book of Yr. selection Child Study Assn. 1974), The Lace Snail, 1975 (Am. Book of Yr. selection Child Study Assn. 1975), The TV Kid, 1976 (Am. Book of Yr. selection Child Study Assn. 1976), The Pinballs, 1977 (Woodward Park School Annual Book award 1977, Child Study Children's Book award Child Study Children's Book Com. at Bank Street Coll. of Edn. 1977, Ga. Children's Book award 1979, Charlie May Simon Book award Ark. Elem. School Coun. 1980, Surrey School Book of Yr. award Surrey School Librs. of Surrey 1980, Mark Twain award Mo. Assn. of School Librs. 1980, William Allen White Children's Book award Emporia State Univ. 1980, Young Reader medal Calif. Reading Assn. 1980, Golden Archer award Dept. Libr. Sci. Univ. of Wis.-Oskosh 1982), The Cartoonist, 1978, Good-bye Chicken Little, 1979 (New York Times Outstanding Book of Yr. 1979), The Night Swimmers, 1980 (Am. Book of Yr. selection Child Study Assn. 1980, Best Book of Yr. School Libr. Jour. 1980, Am. Book award for Children's Fiction 1981), The Cybil War, 1981 (Tenn. Children's Choice Book award Tenn. Libr. Assn. 1983, Sequoyah Children's Book award 1984), The Animal, the Vegetable, and John D. Jones, 1982 (Parents' Choice award for Lit. Parents' Choice Found. 1982, Best Children's Book Sch. Libr. Jour. 1982, CRABbery award Oxon Hill Br. of Prince George's County Libr. 1983, Mark Twain award Mo. Assn. of School Librs. 1985), The Two-Thousand-Pound Goldfish, 1982 (New York Times Outstanding Book of Yr. 1982), The Glory Girl, 1983, The Computer Nut, 1984 (Charlie May Simon award 1987), Cracker Jackson, 1985 (S.C. Children's Book award 1988, Md. Children's Book award 1988), The Not-Just-Anbody Family, 1986, The Golly Sisters Go West, 1986, The Blossoms Meet the Vulture Lady, 1986, The Blossoms and the Green Phantom, 1987, A Blossom Promise, 1987, Beans on the Roof, 1988, The Burning Questions of Bingo Brown, 1988, Bingo Brown and the Language of Love, 1989, Hooray for the Golly Sisters, 1990, Bingo Brown, Gypsy Lover, 1990, Seven Treasure Hunts, 1991, Wanted...Mud Blossom, 1991, The Moon & I, 1992, Bingo Brown's Guide to Romance, 1992, McMummy, 1993, The Golly Sisters Ride Again, 1994, The Dark Stairs: A Herculeah Jones Mystery, 1994, Coast to Coast, 1994, My Brother, Ant., 1996, Tornado, 1996, Dead Letter: A Herculeah Jones Mystery, 1996; editor: Growing Up Stories, 1995, Death's Door, 1997, Ant plays Bear, 1997, Disappearing Acts, 1998. Recipient Regina medal Catholic Libr. Assn., 1987. Home: 401 Rudder Rdg Seneca SC 29678-2035

BYARS, LEISA, marketing professional, automotive executive; b. Warren, Ohio, 1967; m. Delfon McSpadden. BA in Econs. and Govt., Oberlin Coll.; MA in Pub. Policy, U. Mich.; MBA in Mktg. and Fin., U. Pa. From mem. staff to group mgr. Innovative Mktg. Solutions Group Ford Motor Co., Dearborn, Mich., 1995—2000, group mgr. Innovative Mktg. Solutions Group, 2000—. Recipient Outstanding Women in Mktg. and Comms. award, Ebony Mag., 2001. Office: Ford Motor Co 3900 Wyoming St Dearborn MI 48120

BYARS, MERLENE HUTTO, accountant, visual artist, writer; b. West Columbia, SC, Nov. 8, 1931; d. Gideon Thomas and Nettie (Fail) Hutto; m. Alvin Willard Byars, June 10, 1950 (dec.); children: Alvin Gregg, Robin Mark, Jay C., Blaine Derrick; m. Fred W. Klutzow, Dec. 10, 1999. Student, Palmer Coll., Midlands Tech., U. S.C., 1988—; diploma in Journalism, Internat. Corr. Sch., 1995, Longridge Writers Group, 1995. Acct. State of SC, 1964-93; ret., 1993; pres. Merlene Hutto Byars Enterprises, Cayce, 1993—. Designer Collegiate Licensing Co., US Trademark, 1989—; mem. Thinktank for Ret. Employees, U. SC Edn. Found., 1998-2003. Pub. Lintheads, 1986, Olympia-Pacific: The Way It was 1895-1970, 1981; Did Jesus Drive a Pickup Truck, 1993, Fate, Faith and Fortitude, 2003; The Plantation Era in South Carolina; pub., produr. (play) Lintheads and Hard Times, 1986; creator quilt which hung in SC State Capital for bicentennial celebration, 1988; designer Saxe Gotha Twp. Flag, 1993; author: The State of South Carolina Scrap Book, Orangeburg District, 1990, A Scrap Book of SC, Dutch Fork, Saxe Gotha, Lexington County, 1994, The Plantation Era of SC, 1996; exhibited art at Oxford (Eng.) U., 1997, Internat. Congress on Arts and Comm., 1997, Sonesta Hotel, New Orleans, 1998—; exhibited art and book From My Scrap Book of the State of SC; Xlibris publ. new book, 2003, Fate, Faith and Fortitude, Life of F.W. Klutzow, MD., Four Seasons, The Ritz, 1999—; exhibited genealogy and art work St. John's Coll., Cambridge U., 2001. Life mem. Women's Missionary Soc., United Luth. Ch., 1954—; mem. edn. found. U. SC, 1969-93; treas. Airport HS Booster Club, 1969-76; sec. Saxe Gotha Hist. Soc., Lexington County, 1994-96; mem. USC Edn. Found., Think-Tank for 2001 fundraising campaign/ret. faculty and staff, 1998-2001; rep. Cayce Hist. Com. at Am. Biographical Inst./Internat. Biographical Ctr. Congress, New Orleans, 1998. Recipient numerous awards for quilting SC State Fair, 1976—, Cert. for rose rsch. test panel Jackson and Perkins, 1982, Foremost Women in Comm. award, 1969-70, Cayce Amb. award, City of Cayce, 1994. Fellow Internat. Biog. Assn. (dep. dir. gen. 1999—), U. SC Caroliniana Soc., U. SC Thomas Cooper Libr. Soc.; mem. Cayce Mus. History (contbr. books, award for contribution 1987), SC State Mus., Town and Country Assn., Nat. Mus. Women in the Arts, Kiwanis Internat. Avocations: history, geneologist, reading, sewing, traveling. Home: PO Box 3387 West Columbia SC 29171-3387 E-mail: needle1@msn.com.

BYASSEE, MARGARET FOLEY, art educator, poet, vocalist; b. Newport, R.I., Jan. 17, 1922; d. Edward B. and May (Cruickshank) Foley; m. Ivan Byassee, Oct. 1, 1950 (dec.). Student, Wheaton Coll., 1947-49; BA, U. Tenn., Knoxville, 1952; MEd, U. Tenn., Chattanooga, 1984. Cert. tchr. Art tchr. Oak Ridge (Tenn.) City Sch. Sys., 1953-61, Chattanooga (Tenn.) City Sch. Sys., 1962-82, Sweetwater (Tenn.) City Schs., 1984-85, artist-in-residence. Author numerous poems; one-woman shows Gallery 210, Chattanooga, Ariel Galleries, N.Y., among others. Mem. Artist Guild, Newport, R.I., 1998-99, Newport Art Mus., 1998-99; pres. Chattanooga Civic Arts League, Authors and Artists, Chattanooga. Sgt. U.S. Army, 1943-46. Named to Internat. Soc. Poetry Hall of Fame, 1996; recipient Editor's Choice award Nat. Libr. Poetry, 1995, 96, 2000. Mem. Women in the Arts, Internat. Soc. Poetry, Assn. Visual Arts, Chattanooga Tenn. Authors and Artists. Avocations: tennis, golf, camping, soloist with island senior chorus, painting. Home: 2 Donna Dr Portsmouth RI 02871-1133 E-mail: MargarByas@aol.com.

BYEARS, LATASHA, professional basketball player; b. Aug. 12, 1973; Student, N.E. Okla. A&M Jr. Coll., 1992—94; grad., DePaul U., 1996. Basketball player Faenza, Italy, 1996—97, Beskijas, Turkey, 1996—97; basketball player Sacramento Monarchs Women's NBA, 1997—2000; basketball player LA Sparks WNBA, 2000—. Vol. Meals on Wheels. Office: Los Angeles Sparks Ste 100 2151 E Grand Ave El Segundo CA 90245

BYER, DIANA, performing arts company executive; b. Trenton, NJ, Aug. 31, 1946; d. Fred and Norma (Handis) B. Student, Juilliard Sch., 1964—66. Soloist Manhattan Festival Ballet, N.Y.C., 1972, Les Grands Ballet Canadiens, Montreal, Can., 1975; dir. Ballet Sch. of N.Y., N.Y.C., 1978—, N.Y. Theatre Ballet, 1978—. Dir., founder Project LIFT scholarship program for children living N.Y.C. homeless shelters, 1989—. Helen Weiselberg scholar Nat. Arts Club, 1988, 90, 93 Achievements include being subject of Lincoln Ctr. presentation Dreams on a Shoestring, 1992. Office: NY Theatre Ballet 30 E 31st St New York NY 10016-6825 E-mail: balletfore@aol.com.

BYERS, ELIZABETH, education educator; b. Cedar Rapids, Iowa, Mar. 22, 1964; d. Charles A. Byers and Mary Ann Hetherington-Byers. BA in Music, BA in English and Speech, Coe Coll., 1986; MA in Rhetorical Studies, U. Iowa, 1988, MA in English Edn., 2002. Tchg. asst. in pub. speaking U. Iowa, Iowa City, 1987—88, rsch. asst., 1987, tchg. asst. bus. and profl. speaking, 1987—88, art history teaching asst., 2000; English/speech instr. Kirkwood C.C., Iowa City, 1988—89; English and speech instr. Mt. Mercy Coll., Cedar Rapids, 1989—93; elem. edn. instr. Iowa Wesleyan Coll., Mt. Pleasant, 2001—. ESL tutor Kirkwood C.C., Iowa City, 1988—93, Mt. Mercy Coll., 1988—93; pub. speaking cons., Iowa City, 1988—93. Grad. student editor: Basil Blackwell Companion, 1989; editor: Communicating, 1992, author web page for postsecondary tchrs. Vol. Habitat for Humanity, Iowa City, 1999—2001, Cath. Worker House, Cedar Rapids, 1990—93. Mem.: DAR (Good Citizenship award 1982), Mu Phi Epsilon, Pi Lambda Theta (Teaching Excellence award 2001), Phi Beta Kappa. Home: PO Box 156 Morning Sun IA 52640-0156

BYERS, MARY MARGARET (PEG BYERS), systems educator; b. Munhall, Pa., May 20, 1953; d. Gerald J. B. and Florence B. (Luty) Byers-Steiner. BA, U. Pitts., 1982; MS, Nova U., 1993. Office conversion mgr. Franklin Interiors, Pitts., 1979-82; astrological cons. pvt. practice, Pitts., 1982-87; tng. cons. Elcomp Systems, Greentree, Pa., 1987-88; system sales Computer Renaissance, Pitts., 1988-89; instr. Duff's Bus. Inst., Pitts., 1989-91; bus. owner Byers Computer Svcs., Jeffersonboro, Pa., 1988-92; systems cons. pvt. practice, Jeffersonboro, Pa., 1993-96; systems coord. Mellon Bank, Pitts., 1996-97; dir. edn. Computer Learning Ctrs., Monroeville, Pa., 1997—. Mem. Hi-Tech. Coun., Pitts. Author: Introduction to Computers, 1994, PC Trouble Shooting, 1996; co-author: Into to Guidesign Using, 1996. Mem. NAFE, High Tech. Coun., Mensa. Avocations: reading, collecting music, astrology, metaphysics. Office: Computer Learning Ctrs Inc 777 Penn Center Blvd Fl 3D Pittsburgh PA 15235-5927

BYERS, NINA, physics educator; b. Los Angeles, Jan. 19, 1930; d. Irving M. and Eva (Gertzoff) B.; m. Arthur A. Milhaupt, Jr., Sept. 8, 1974 (dec.). BA in Physics with highest honors, U. Calif., Berkeley, 1950; MS in Physics, U. Chgo., 1953, PhD, 1956; MA, U. Oxford, Eng., 1967. Research fellow dept. math. physics U. Birmingham, Eng., 1956-58; research assoc., asst. prof. Inst. Theoretical Physics and dept. physics Stanford, 1958-61; asst. then assoc. prof. physics UCLA, 1961-67, prof. physics, 1967—. Mem. Sch. Math., Inst. Advanced Studies, Princeton, N.J., 1964-65; ofcl. fellow Somerville Coll., Oxford, 1967-68, Janet Watson vis. fellow, 1968-74; faculty lectr., mem. dept. theoretical physics Oxford U., 1967-74, sr. vis. scientist, 1973-74; official fellow and tutor in physics, Somerville Coll. John Simon Guggenheim Meml. fellow, 1964-65, Sci. Rsch. Coun. fellow Oxford U., 1978, 85. Fellow AAAS (mem-at-large physics sect., com. on freedom and responsibility 1983-86), Am. Phys. Soc. (councillor-at-large 1977-81, panel pub. affairs 1980-83, vice-chmn. forum on physics and soc. 1981-82, 2002--, chmn. 1982-83, vice-chmn. forum on history of physics 2002-03, chair-elect, 2003--); mem. Fedn. Am. Scientists (nat. coun. 1972-76, 78-80, exec. com. 1974-76, 78-80). Achievements include research in theory of particle physics and superconductivity; history of physics; contributions of 20th century women to physics. Office: U Calif Dept Physics Los Angeles CA 90095-0001

BYERS, TERESA ANN, music educator; b. Columbus, Ind., June 13, 1961; m. Brad William Byers, May 22, 1982; children: Hannah Rose, Adam William. MEd, Ind. State U., 1985. Elem. Adminstrn. and Supervision State of Ind., 2002. Tchr. Ctrl. Elem. Sch., Clinton, Ind., 1982—; tutor Student Acad. Svcs. Ctr. Ind. State U., Terre Haute, 1980—85. Co-dir. Parke County Relay for Life Am. Cancer Soc., Rockville, Ind., 2002—. Dir.(musician): (adult choir) Rockville Christian Ch. Treas. South Vermillion Edn. Assn., Clinton, 1985—87. Nominee Golden Apple Award, WTHI-TV, 1990. Mem.: NEA (assoc.), Music Educators Nat. Conf. (assoc.), Ind. State Tchrs. Assn. (assoc.), South Vermillion Edn. Assn. (assoc.), Ind. Music Tchrs. Assn. (assoc.; coord. of area 5 cir. the state with song event 2003—), Girl Scout Leader (assoc.; leader 1999—2003), Tri Kappa (assoc.). R-Consevative. Christian. Achievements include The Parke County Relay for Life was awarded a National Heart of Relay Award for the work done to honor cancer survivors. This award was presented in November of 2002. Avocations: reading, needlecrafts, crafts, antiques. Home: 6694 W Parkewood Rd Rosedale IN 47874 Office: South Vermillion Sch Corp 205 South 8th Street Clinton IN 47842 Personal E-mail: byersfamily1@aol.com. E-mail: tbyers@svcs.k12.in.us.

BYERS-PEVITTS, BEVERLEY, college administrator, educator; b. Ohio County, Ky., Aug. 15, 1939; d. Stanley Beveridge and Vera Elizabeth (Amos) Byers; m. Robert Richard Pevitts, June 12, 1966; 1 child, Robert Stanley. BA, Ky. Wesleyan Coll., 1961; MA, So. Ill. U., 1967, PhD, 1980. Dir. theatre and faculty Dept. English, Speech, Drama Young Harris (Ga.) Coll., 1966-69; dir. theatre and asst. prof. speech and theatre arts Western Carolina U., Cullowhee, N.C., 1969-71; coord. supplementary progr., asst. prof. Eng. and drama Pfeiffer Coll., Misenheimer, N.C., 1972-74; dir. and prof. speech and theatre Ky. Wesleyan U., Owensboro, 1974-86; chair theatre arts U. Nev., Las Vegas, 1986-89, prof. and dir. grad. studies in theatre arts, 1986-90; dean coll. of humanities and fine arts, prof. U. No. Iowa, Cedar Falls, 1990-95; v.p. acad. affairs Tex. Woman's U., Denton, 1995—2001; Pres., Park U., Parkville, Mo., 2001—. Lectr. in field; conductor workshops in field. Editor: Theatre Topics, 1990-93; contbr. articles to profl. jours.; author: (plays) Reflections in a Window, 1982, rev., 1983, Beauty and the Beast, 1982, Time and the Rock, 1981, Family Haven, 1979, Take Courage, Stand Beside Us, 1977, A Strange and Beautiful Light, 1976-77; co-author: Epilogue to Glory, 1966. Bd. dirs. Waterloo/Cedar Falls Symphony Orch., 1990-94, Iowa Citizens for the Arts, 1991-94; coord. spl. drama programs WeCan, Inc., Las Vegas, 1986; tchr. Elderhostel Program; program coord. NOW. NEH Seminar grantee U. Wis.-Milw., 1983, NYU, 1977; recipient Outstanding Alumni award Ky. Wesleyan Coll., 1983; named Disting. Woman Am. Theatre Assn., 1977; grantee Ford Found., Exxon Corp.; elected to Nat. Theatre Conf., 1992—. Mem. Assn. for Theatre in Higher Edn. (founding pres. 1986-87, bd. govs. 1986-89), Assn. for Communication Adminstrn. (exec. com. 1988-91), Univ. and Coll. Theatre Assn. of Am. Theatre Assn. (pres. 1985-86), League Profl. Theatre Women N.Y., Internat. Coun. of Fine Arts Deans, Coun. of Colls. of Arts and Scis., Order of Oak and Ivy, Alpha Psi Omega. Avocations: gourmet cooking, travel, collecting antiques. Office: Park University 8700 NW River Park Dr Kansas City MO 64152

BYERWALTER, MARIANN, academic administrator; BS, Stanford U., 1982; MBA, Harvard U., 1984. V.p. strategic planning & corp. devel. BankAmerica Corp.; v.p. BankAmerica Venture Cap. Corp.; CFO Eureka-Bank; ptnr., co-founder Am. First Fin. Corp.; CFO & v.p. bus. affairs Stanford U., Stanford, Calif., 1996—2000. Bd. dir. Schwab Funds, San Francisco, LookSmart, San Francisco, SRI Internat., Menlo Park, Calif., Stanford Hosp. & Clinics, Palo Alto, Redwood Trust & Am. First Co., Omaha; instr. Am. Bankers Assn. Calif. Banking Sch.; mem. Stanford Bd. Trustees, 1992—. Bd. dir. Lucile Salter Packard Children's Hosp. Stanford U., Palo Alto, Stanford Alumni Assn., Palo Alto, 1985—92. Recipient Fin. Woman of Yr. award, Fin. Women's Assn. San Francisco, 1998. Office: Stanford University mail code 2060 482 Galvez Mall Stanford CA 94305-2060

BYFORD, EMMA, rancher; b. Marlin, Tex., Jan. 30, 1918; d. Joseph and Emma (Conner) Watkins; m. Ray Homan Byford, Sept. 2, 1937 (dec. 1980). Stenographer, sec. Waco (Tex.)-McLennan County Health Unit, 1944-50; sec. to plant mgr. Owens-Illinois Glass Co., Waco, 1950-54; co-owner, office mgr. Byford Machine & Tool, Waco, 1956-76; owner Byford Ranch, Clifton, Tex., 1963—. Methodist. Home: 1108 Silver Creek Dr Desoto TX 75115-3726

BYMEL, SUZAN YVETTE, talent manager, film producer; b. Chgo. d. Howard Behr and Jacqueline Shirley (Richards) B. Student, U. Ill., Chgo. Exec. asst. Kenny Rogers Prodns., 1981; prodn. exec. Pinehurst Prodns., 1982; music mgmt. assoc. Frontline Mgmt., 1983; pres. Suzan Bymel & Assocs., 1985-94; oper. ptnr. Bymel/O'Neill Mgmt., 1995—, Meg Ryan Prodns. (a.k.a. Fandango Films), 1988-93, Bymel/O'Neill Mgmt., 1995-98; operating ptnr. Talent Entertainment Group, Beverly Hills, Calif., 1998—. Freelance screenwriter, actress. Mem. Hollywood Woman's Polit. Com., L.A. Office: Talent Entertainment 9111 Wilshire Blvd Beverly Hills CA 90210 Fax: 310-205-5385. E-mail: sbymel@mmbon.com.

BYNES, AMANDA, actress; b. Thousand Oaks, Calif., Apr. 3, 1986; d. Rick and Lynn Bynes. Actor: (films) Big Fat Liar, 2002, What a Girl Wants, 2003; (TV series) All That, 1996—2000 (nominee Cable Ace award, 1997), The Amanda Show, 1999—2002, (voice) Rugrats, 2002—04, What I Like About You, 2002—, (voice): (videos) Charlotte's Web 2: Wilbur's Great Adventure, 2003—; appeared as herself/guest panelist (TV series) Figure It Out, 1997—2000. Recipient Favorite TV Actress, Kid's Choice Awards, 2001, 2002, 2003, Favorite Movie Actress, 2003. Achievements include discovered at age 10 at a kid's comedy showcase at the Laugh Factory, LA and signed immediately by Nickelodeon for TV series All That. Office: Endeavor Talent Agy 9701 Wilshire Blvd 10th Fl Beverly Hills CA 90212*

BYNUM, GAYELA A. public affairs specialist; b. Sulphur, Okla., Oct. 28, 1945; d. Martin Cleveland and Birdie Burnett Sparks Word; m. Ronald Orr Bynum, June 6, 1965 (div. Apr. 1983); children: William Blaine, Bradley Word; m. Robert F. Hannon, Oct. 28, 1995. Student, U. Okla., 1963-66; BA, U. Ark., 1969; postgrad., George Washington U., 1991-93. Lic. real estate agt., legal asst. Supr. NAS, Jacksonville, Fla., 1972-79; mgmt. analyst Chief Naval Ops., Washington, 1979-85; pres. Gayela Bynum & Assocs., Washington, 1985-88, The Carpet Bagger, Ltd., Oklahoma City, 1997—; pub. affairs advisor HUD, Washington, 1988—2003. Treas. Globint, LLC, Carefree, Ariz., 199-2002, Globe Car, Ltd., Wilmington, Del., 1998-2002; exec. v.p. Sea Spur, Ltd., Wilmington, 1997—; internat. cons. Mideast Presdl. Candidate, Washington, 1988. Vice chmn. The Opera Camerata, Washington, 2001—02; fundraiser various polit. campaigns, 1985—88; mem. Congl. Steering Com., Washington, 1985—88; bd. govs. Summer Opera Theater, Washington, 2003—. Mem.: DAR, Nat. Press Club (mem. spkrs. com. 1996—2000, newsmakers com. 2001—02, bd. govs. 2002—). Avocations: running, sailing, aerobics, music, painting, crafts. Home and Office: 5902 Mount Eagle Dr Apt 408 Alexandria VA 22303-2516

BYNUM, MAGNOLIA VIRGINIA WRIGHT, retired secondary school educator; b. Waynesboro, Ga., Jan. 10, 1934; d. George and Edith Arilee (Williams) Wright; m. Marvin Bynum, Sept. 17, 1955 (dec. Oct. 1977). BS in Bus. Edn., N.C. A&T State U., Greensboro, N.C., 1956; postgrad., NYU, 1964—65; MS in Edn., CUNY, Bklyn., 1985, Adv. Cert. Guidance & Counseling, 1986. Engring. adminstr. Radio Receptor Co., Bklyn., 1957—59; data processing staff NYU, N.Y.C., 1959—64; tchr., dean, counselor Lincoln H.S., Jersey City, 1964—92; ret., 1992. Adj. prof. CUNY, Bklyn., 1986—90; asst. to Congressman Edolphus Towns, 10th Congl. Dist., Bklyn., 1982—90; counselor incentive program dept. human resources Bklyn. Coll., 1992—93; cons. Parent Advocacy, Medgars Evers Coll., Bklyn., 1984—85. Editor-in-chief (newsletter) Cornerstone Torch, 1993—97. Mem. Cmty. Coalition for Edn., Greensboro, NC, NAACP; spearheaded Hard of Hearing campaign, Bklyn.; women's day chairperson New Zion Missionary Bapt. Ch., Greensboro, NC; chairperson bd. dirs. Chama Child Devel., Bklyn., 1983—91, Cornerstone Day Care Ctr., Bklyn., 1991—97. Named to Faculty Achievement Hall of Fame, Lincoln H.S., 1981; recipient Outstanding Cmty. Svc. award, Bklyn. Coll. Grad. Students, 1984, citations, Congl. Record, 1990, 1997; scholar Myers Jacob Guidance & Counseling scholar, 1984. Mem.: Alpha Kappa Alpha, Phi Delta Kappa, Kappa Delta Pi. Baptist. Avocations: reading, travel, singing. Home: 563 Summerwalk Rd Greensboro NC 27455

BYRD, ALICIA D. minister, sociologist; d. William Lee and Myrtice Ernestine Byrd. BA, Wheaton Coll., Ill., 1975; MA, U. of Ill., Springfield, 1977; MDiv, Howard U., Washington, 1985; PhD, Am. U., Washington, 1988. Assoc. dean of students Gordon Coll., Wenham, Mass., 1977—79; sophomore counselor Boston U., 1979—82; assoc. dean of students Cath. U. of Am., Washington, 1982—85; dir. of theol. edn. Congress of Nat. Black Chs., Washington, 1987—97; vis. prof. Nazareth Coll., Rochester, NY, 1997—99; exec. dir. St. Stephens Econ. Devel. Corp, Elkridge, Md., 1998—; pastor St. Stephens AME Ch., Elkridge, 1988—; assoc. organizer Interfaith Action Communities, Seat Pleasant, Md., 2001—03; adj. prof. Wesley Sem., Washington, 2002—, Prince George's C.C., Landover, Md., 2003—. Cons. Coun. on Founds., Washington, 1987—95, Nat. Congress of Cmty. Econ. Devel., Washington, 1988—90, Lilly Endowment, Indpls., 1992—94, Ford Found., N.Y.C., 1995—97. Editor: (devotional bible) African American Devotional Bible, (book) Restoring Broken Places and Rebuilding Communities, Philanthropy and the Black Church. Chair St. Stephens Econ. Devel. Corp, Elkridge, Md., 1998—2003. Mem.: Alpha Kappa Alpha. Home: P O Box 8242 Elkridge MD 21075 Office: St Stephens AME Church 7741 Mayfield Ave Elkridge MD 21075 Personal E-mail: olivia_1953@yahoo.com. E-mail: olivia_1953@yahoo.com.

BYRD, CHRISTINE WATERMAN SWENT, lawyer; b. Oakland, Calif., Apr. 11, 1951; d. Langan Waterman and Eleanor (Herz) Swent; m. Gary Lee Byrd, June 20, 1981; children: Amy, George. BA, Stanford U., 1972; JD, U. Va., 1975. Bar: Calif. 1976, U.S. Dist. Ct. (ctrl., so. no., ea. dists.) Calif., U.S. Ct. Appeals (9th cir.). Law clk. to Hon. William P. Gray U.S. Dist. Ct., L.A., 1975-76; assoc. Jones, Day, Reavis & Pogue, L.A., 1976-82, ptnr., 1987-96; asst. U.S. atty. criminal divsn. U.S. Atty.'s Office, Ctrl. Dist. Calif., L.A., 1982-87; ptnr. Irell & Manella, L.A., 1996—. Mem. Calif. Law Revision Commn., 1992-97. Author: The Future of the U.S. Multinational Corporation, 1975; contbr. articles to profl. jours. Fellow: Am. Coll. Trial Lawyers, mem.: ADA (vice chmn. ADR Advocacy in Litig. 2003—), Assn. Bus. Trial Lawyers (bd. govs. 1996—99), 9th Jud. Cir. Hist. Soc. (bd. dirs. 1986—, pres. 1997—2002), Century City Bar Assn. (bd. govs. 2001—), Stanford Profl. Women L.A. County, Am. Arbitration Assn. (large and complex case panel 1992—, nat. energy panel 1998—, bd. dirs. 1999—), Women Lawyers Assn. L.A. County, L.A. County Bar Assn., Calif. State Bar (com. fed. cts. 1985—88), Stanford U. Alumni Assn. Republican. Office: Irell & Manella LLP 1800 Ave Of Stars Ste 900 Los Angeles CA 90067-4276 Business E-Mail: cbyrd@irell.com.

BYRD, ELLEN STOESSER, school nurse administrator; b. Dayton, Tex., Dec. 10, 1941; d. Edward Joseph and Nina Mae (Cannon) Stoesser; m. C. Robert Byrd, June 6, 1964; children: Byron, Preston, Aaron, Robyn. BSN, Baylor U., 1964. RN, Tex. Nurse Parkland Hosp., Dallas, 1964-65; nurse gyn. svcs. Baylor U. Med. Ctr., Dallas, 1965-66; charge nurse med./surg. Collin Meml. Hosp., McKinney, Tex., 1967-68; nurse newborn nursery St. Paul Hosp., Dallas, 1972; pvt. duty nurse Dist. 4 Tex. Nurse Assn., Dallas, 1976; sch. nurse Dallas Ind. Sch. Dist., 1989-90; home health nurse Rehab Home Care, DeSoto, Tex., 1994-98; dermatology nurse Dallas Bapt. U., 1999—2001, dir. health svcs., campus nurse, 2001—; sch. nurse Richardson (Tex.) Ind. Sch. Dist. Mem. adv. bd. Baylor U. Sch. Nursing, Dallas, 1994—, chmn. adv. bd. 1999—; advisor Baylor U. Woman's Coun., Dallas, 1995—, pres., 1994-95. Author: History of Dallas CPA Wives, 1983, Biography of Mae Stoesser, 1988, Byrd Family 25 Years, 1990. Program chmn. Freedom Found. Valley Forge, Dallas, 1986-89; centennial circle chmn. Dallas County Heritage Soc., Dallas; deacon Cliff Temple Bapt. Ch., 1988; v.p. DeSoto Svc. League, 1990; pres. Dallas CPAs Wives Club, 1984-85; mem. Richardson Jr. League. Recipient W.T. White Meritorious Svcs. award Baylor U. Alumni Assn., 1996. Mem. Richardson Jr. League, Presbyn. Presby Ptnrs. Repubican. Baptist. Avocations: european travel, grandchildren. Home: 304 Prince Albert Ct Richardson TX 75081-5059 Office: Dallas Bapt Univ 3000 Mountain Creek Pkwy Dallas TX 75211-9299 Fax: 972-234-8448.

BYRD, EMILY, newscaster; b. N.C. BS Meteorology, Carolina State U.; BFA, U. N.C. Meteorologist WXLV, Green, NC, 1996—97, NBC 17 - TV, Raleigh, NC, 1997—. Office: NBC 17 NBC 17 Studios 1205 1st St Raleigh NC 27609

BYRD, GWENDOLYN PAULINE, school system superintendent; b. Mobile, Ala., July 21, 1943; d. Marley and Frances (Ramsay) B. BS in History, Marillac Coll., St. Louis, 1966; MA in Sch. Adminstrn., DePaul U., 1975. Tchr. St. Matthias Sch., St. Louis, 1966-70; prin., tchr. Cathedral Elem. Sch., Natchez, Miss., 1970-74; prin. St. Francis De Sales Sch., Lake Zurich, Ill., 1974-77; curriculum coord. for sch. system Archdiocese of Mobile, 1977-83, sch. supt., 1983—. Chairperson Little Flower Liturgy Com., Mobile, 1980—; pvt. sch. rep. to adv. com. on tchr. edn. State of Ala., 1983—; adv. bd. Cath. Svc. Ctr., Mobile, 1989—; v.p. bd. dirs. Mobile Mental Health Assn., 1990—; bd. dirs. L'Arche Cmty., 1992—. Named Outstanding Career Woman, Gayfer's Career Club, 1985, Outstanding Supt., Ala. Assn. Learning Disabilities, 1988, Disting. Diocesan Leader Today's Cath. Tchr. Mag., 1992. Mem. Nat. Cath. Edn. Assn., Chief Adminstrs. Cath. Edn. (regional rep. and chair schs. adv. 1995), CACE (exec. com. 1996), Phi Delta Kappa. Office: Office Cath Schs PO Box 129 Mobile AL 36601-0129

BYRD, KATHRYN SUSAN, psychologist, educator; d. George Washington Byrd and Josie Beth Mayes. BA, Centenary Coll., Shreveport, La., 1974; MS, Northwestern State U., Natchitoches, La., 1977; PhD, U. Tex, Richardson, 1995. Coord. of academic advising, communication arts & tech. divsn. Eastfield Coll., Mesquite, Tex., 2001—, adj. faculty, 2001—. Acad. adv. Eastfield Coll., Mesquite, Tex., 1999—. Mem. of class of 2002, Eastfield Coll. rep. Leadership Garland, Mesquite, Tex., 2002. Mem.: APA, Bluebonnet Bebes Doll Collectors Club. Republican. Southern Baptist. Office: Eastfield College 3737 Motley Dr Mesquite TX 75150 E-mail: ksb4323@dcccd.edu.

BYRD, LISA MARIE, family nurse practitioner, lecturer; b. Jackson, MS, Sept. 1, 1964; d. Frank Ollie and Mary Sue Myers; m. Ricky D. Byrd, Nov. 1, 1960; children: Joshua, Sarah. A Nursing, Hinds C.C., Raymond, Miss., 1984; BN, Miss. Coll., Clinton, 1986; MN, Miss. U. for Women, Columbus, 1996. RN, CNOR, CFNP. Staff nurse, charge nurse-CCU U. Miss. Med. Ctr., Jackson, Miss., 1984—86; staff nurse, charge nurse-ICU St. Dominic Meml. Hosp., Jackson, Miss., 1986—90, staff nurse, charge nurse-surgery, 1990—94, nurse mgr. ambulatory surgery, 1994—96; nurse practitioner Miss. Family Drs., Bolton, Miss., 1996—2001; owner Bolton Family Clinic, Byrd Healthcare LLC., 2002—. Lectr. in field. Contbr. articles to profl. jours. Sunday sch. tchr. St. Francis of Assisi Catholic Ch., Madison, 1998—2001; ednl. chair Cmty. Orgn. Health Awareness, Jackson, 1997—2001; troop leader Girl Scouts of Am., Madison, 2001—02; tchr. Junior Achievement of Miss., Jackson, 1998—99. Recipient outstanding student in chemistry, Hinds Cmty. Coll., 2000. Mem.: Am. Geriatric Soc., Am. Coll. Nurse Practitioners, Miss. Nurses' Assn., Phi Kappa Phi Honor Soc., Sigma Theta Tau Internat. Nurses Honor Soc. Roman Catholic. Avocations: cooking, running, gardening. Home: 475 Cheyenne Ln Madison MS 39110 Office: Bolton Family CLinic 115 Madison Bolton MS 39041

BYRD, LORELEE, state treasurer; b. Bassett, Nebr., Apr. 14, 1956; m. Scott Byrd, 1976 (div.); children: Amy, Ryan. Auditor Mut. Protective Ins. and Mut. Ins.; aide to state and fed. lawmakers; unclaimed property admin., 1995; dep. state treas., 1995—2001; state treas., 2001—. Past mem. Rep. State Ctrl. Com., Douglas County Rep. Ctrl. Com.; past pres. Metro Right to Life; past mem. bd. dirs. Nebr. Right to Life; aide to Senator Sharon Beck Omaha; aide to Owen Elmer Indianola; aide to U.S. rep. Doug Bereuter. Office: PO Box 94788 Lincoln NE 68509-4788 E-mail: lbyrd@treasurer.org.*

BYRD, MARY JANE, education educator; b. Topeka, Apr. 21, 1946; d. Vernon Thomas and Mary Elizabeth (Caldwell) Wharton; m. Gerald David Byrd, June 24, 1965; children: Kari, Juli, Cori. BS, U. So. Ala., 1980, MBA, 1984; D of Bus. Adminstrn., Nova Southeastern U., 1991. Dental asst. Gerald E. Berger, DMD, Mobile, Ala., 1963-65; dental hygenist Robert P. Hall, DMD, Mobile, Ala., 1965-66; teller Am. Nat. Bank, Mobile, Ala., 1972-75; office mgr. Byrd Surveying, Inc., Mobile, Ala., 1975-80; div. acct. cafeteria Morrison, Inc., Mobile, Ala., 1980-82; mgmt. cons. pvt. practice Mobile, Ala., 1982-84; lectr. acctg. U. South Ala., Mobile, Ala., 1984; asst. prof. acctg. & mgmt. Univ. Mobile, Mobile, Ala., 1984-89; assoc. prof. acctg. and mgmt. Mobile Coll., 1989-95; prof. mgmt., 1995—. Reviewer Internat. Jour. Pub. Adminstrn., 1991—; dir. Nat. Assn. Accts., Mobile, 1986-89. Author: Supervisory Management Study Guide/Southwestern, 1993, 97, Small Business Management; An Entrepreneur's Guide to Success/Irwin, 1994, 4th edit. 2003, Human Resource Management, Dame, 1995; contbr. articles to profl. jours. Named Assoc. of the Month, Home Builders Assn., 1986, Charles S. Dismukes Outstanding Mem., Nat. Assn. Accts. Mem. AAUW, Acad. Mgmt., Am. Bus. Women Assn., Mortgage Lenders Assn., So. Acad. Mgmt. USASBE. Office: Univ Mobile PO Box 13220 Mobile AL 36663-0220 Office Phone: 251-442-2233. E-mail: janebyrd@free.umobile.edu.

BYRD, SWETTIE LEE, minister; b. Montgomery County, Ala., Mar. 22, 1939; d. N.D. and Lucille Effie (Gambles) Williams; m. Norman Byrd, Sept. 23, 1962; children: Norman David, Brenda Rachelle, Lionel Scott. Student, Youngstown State U., 1963-66. Cert. cmty. counselor. Sales clk. G.M. McKelvey Dept. Store, Youngstown, Ohio, 1957-66; choir dir., musician World Fellowship Ch., Youngstown, 1963-69, Oak Bapt. Ch., Youngstown, 1970-79; asst. pastor Good Shepherd Ministry, Youngstown, 1983-89, sr. pastor, 1989—. Sec., bd. overseers Greater Youngstown Coalition of Christians, 1995-2000; dir. Family Week, Concerned Christians for the Family, Youngstown, 1990—. Prodr. radio broadcast Joy of the Morning, 1993-96. Chairperson Ward 2, Am. Cancer Soc., Youngstown, 1980s. Recipient Barnabas award Women's Aglow, Youngstown, 1995, Rev. Swettie L. Byrd Day named in her honor City of Youngstown, 1994. Mem. Flame Fellowship Internat. (pres. 1983-88, chaplain Ohio chpt. 1989—), NAACP. Avocations: reading, writing, playing piano. Office: Good Shepherd Ministry 1902 Woodcrest Ave Youngstown OH 44505-3721

BYRD-BENNETT, BARBARA, school system administrator; m. Bruce Bennett, 1 child, Nailah Bennett. BA in English, L.I. U.; M in English Lit., NYU; MEd, Pace U.; Doctorate (hon.), John Carroll U., Notre Dame Coll. Elem. sch. tchr., Manhattan and Bronx, NY, 1965—75; adj. assoc. prof. Coll. of New Rochelle, 1975—91; spl. asst. to Manhattan Supt. for Curriculum, 1982—84; prin. PS 36, Manhattan, NY, 1984—92; adj. assoc. prof. CCNY, 1989—93; dep. exed. dir. for instrn. and profl. devel. N.Y.C. Schs., 1992—94; supt. Chancellor's Dist., N.Y.C. Sch. Sys., 1996—98; CEO Cleve. Mcpl. Sch. Dist., 1998—. Apptd. to edn. com. States Nat. Ctr. for Ednl. Accountability; apptd. to vis. com. Mandel Sch. Applied Scis. Recipient Cleve. Bus. Woman of Yr., 2001. Mem.: Urban Supts. Assn. Am. (v.p.), Internat. Women's Forum. Office: Cleve Mcpl Sch Dist 1380 E Sixth St Cleveland OH 44114*

BYRNE, ELEANOR, artist; b. Steubenville, Ohio, Jan. 16, 1921; d. Charles Bachelor and Bertha Droege McGowan; m. Horace Franklin Byrne, Nov. 4, 1948 (dec. Mar. 1999); children: Deborah, Charles, Malcolm. BA, U. S.C., 1977, MA, 1980, MFA, 1982. Grad. asst. dept. art U. S.C., Columbia, 1977—82; tchr. parent-child workshop Columbia Mus. Art, 1985—90. Exhibited in group shows at S.C. State Fair, 1980—99 (merit awards each yr.), nationally and internationally. Recipient Acad. Palm, French Legion of Honor, 1985. Episcopalian. Avocation: cooking. Home and Studio: 5A Exum Dr West Columbia SC 29169-7100

BYRNE, JUDY SUSANNE, writer, educator; b. Great Falls, Mont., Mar. 18, 1950; d. Patrick John and Lila Mae Byrne. Student, Coll. Litteraire U., Avignon, France, 1970; BA, Mont. State U., 1972, MEd, 1982. Mid. sch. tchr. Lewistown (Mont.) Sch. Dist. 1, 1972—97; substitute tchr. Fergus County Pub. Sch., Lewistown, 1997—; ret., 1997. Adj. instr. Coll. Gt. Falls, 1978—79, No. Mont. Coll., Havre, 1990—93, Carroll Coll., Helena, 2003, Mont. State U., 2001, mem. adv. coun., 1991—95, student tchr. supr., Billings, 2003; cons. in field; co-creator state stds. writing instrn. Mont. pub. schs. State Office Pub. Instrn., Helena, 1998; supr. student tchr. U. Mont., Missoula, 2002, Bozeman, 02. Contbr. articles to profl. jours., columns in newspapers; author: (newspaper column) A Class Act (Outstanding Media award, 1999); contbg. author (book) What America's Teachers Wish Parents Knew, 1993; editor: LEA Link Newsletter, 1985—95 (Outstanding Local Media award, 1992); dir., performer, co-author (plays) As the Whistle Blows, Lewistown, Mont., 1998; dir.: (plays) Centennial Story, 1999; actor: Annie, 2000, The Sound of Music, 2001; dir., actor (variety show) Luck o' the Irish, Lewistown, Mont., 1999, 2000; co-dir.: The Wizard of Oz, 2002. Student selection coord. Am. Field Svc., Lewistown, 1979—93; campaign chmn. Myers for Exec. Com. of the NEA, Great Falls, 1990—91; election judge Fergus County, Lewistown, 1997—2003. Grantee Title III Innovative Edn. Incentive grant, U.S. Dept. of Edn., 1976. Mem.: AARP, NEA (life), MEA-MFT, Mont. Theater Edn. Assn., Mont. Assn. Lang. Tchrs., Mont. Assn. Tchr. English Lang. Arts, Mont. State U. Alumni Assn. (life), Phi Delta Kappa, Delta Kappa Gamma. Avocations: skiing, golf, photography, reading, travel. Personal E-mail: judyb@lewistown.net.

BYRNE, LESLIE LARKIN, state legislator; b. Salt Lake City, Oct. 27, 1946; m. Larry Earl Byrne; children: Alexis S., Jason D. Student, U. Utah. Former del. 38th Dist. Fairfax County State of Va., 1986-92; mem. 103d Congress from 11th Va. dist., Washington, 1993-95; former pres. Quintech Assoc., Inc., 1985-92; dir. consumer affairs HHS, Washington, 1996-98; mem. Va. State Senate, 2000—. Mem. LWV. Home and Office: PO Box 2612 Falls Church VA 22042-0612

BYRNE, LORETTA DAUM, artist, writer; b. West Allis, Wis., July 28, 1932; d. Gerald Franklin and Esther Marie Daum; m. Eugene Thomas Daum, Feb. 19, 1955 (div. Apr. 1972); children: Laura Marie, Thomas Eugene, Maria Lynn, Michael Raymond; m. John William Byrne, Nov. 18, 1972; 5 stepchildren. Student, Layton Art Sch., 1950—53, various workshops, 1959—. Contbg. editor Decorating and Craft Ideas Mag., Ft. Worth, 1977—80, Crafts Mag., Jolier, Ill., 1978—90; contbg. editor, columnist Needlecraft for Today Mag., Ft. Worth, 1978—88; assoc. editor, contbg. editor Needle and Thread Mag., 1980—88; columnist Needlepeople News, Syosset, NY, 1980—83; contbg. editor Crafts 'n Things Mag., Park Ridge, Ill., 1988, Country Handcrafts Mag., Greendale, Wis., 1983—90; designer Walnut Hollow Farms, Dodgeville, 1985—87, Fibercraft Materials, Inc., Niles, Ill., 1988—95; owner Little Lotus Patterns, Ft. Worth, 1977—2002, Cambridge, Wis., 1977—2002; illustrator children's books, 2000—. Mem. Native Am. bd. Dallas Inter-Tribal Ctr., 1972—75, Ft. Worth Indian Ctr., 1976—79. Author: (designs and instructions) Pocket Pals, 1978, Anne Marie, 1983, Favorite Dolls, 1989; co-author: The Teddy Bear Book, 1985, Doll and Toy Collection, 1985, (short stories) Flowers Are Forever, 2000; numerous one-woman and group shows. Mem. bd. Glen Acres Home for Unwed Mothers, Dallas, 1960—64; active Inter-racial Adoptive Parents Group, Lake Bluff, Ill., 1966—68; mem. Socialworkers Bd. Inter-racialAdoption, Pitts., 1968—70; active Inter-racial Adoptive Parents Group, Denver, 1970—71, Friends Cambridge Libr., 1980—. Achievements include holder over 200 copyrights for articles and designs. Avocations: kayaking, camping, cooking, travel.

BYRNE, SUSAN M. investment company executive; Asst. treas. GAF Corp.; founder, chmn., CEO Westwood Mgmt. Group, Dallas, 1983—. Investment advisor, pres. The Gabelli Westwood Funds; bd. mem. U. Tex. Investment Mgmt. Co.; trustee City Dallas Employees Retirement Fund, Southwestern Med. Found.; chair investment com. First Presbyn. Ch. Dallas Found.; mem. Tex. Govs. Bus. Coun.; mem., former bd. mem. Com. of 200. Mem.: Dallas Soc. Securities Analysts, N.Y. Soc. Securities Analysts, Internat. Women's Forum (bd. mem. Dallas chpt.). Office: Westwood Holdings Group Inc Ste 1300 300 Crescent Ct Dallas TX 75201*

BYRNES, MAUREEN K. foundation administrator; Grad. magna cum laude, Le Moyne Coll.; MPA, U. N.C. Exec. dir. Nat. Comm. AIDS, 1989-91; dir. fed. rels. biomed. rsch. policy then v.p. Assn. Am. Univs., 1991-97; dir. health & human svcs. program Pew Charitable Trusts, Phila., 1997—. Office: Pew Charitable Trusts 2005 Market St Ste 1700 Philadelphia PA 19103-7017

BYRON, BEVERLY BUTCHER, retired congresswoman; b. Balt., July 27, 1932; d. Harry C. and Ruth Butcher; m. Goodloe E. Byron, 1952 (dec.); children: Goodloe E. Jr., Barton Kimball, Mary McComas; m. B. Kirk Walsh, 1986. Student, Hood Coll., 1962-64. Mem. 96th-102nd Congresses from 6th Md. dist., 1979-93; Presdl. appt. to base closing and realignment commn., 1993. Bd. dirs. McDonnell Douglas, Constellation Energy Group, Blue Cross/Blue Shield, UNC Corp., Farm and Mech. Nat. Bank, LMI, Def. Adv. Commn. on Women in the Mil.; exec. panel Chief of Naval Ops.; adv. bd. NASA, A.F. Meml. Found. State treas. Md. Young Dems., 1962, 65; bd. assocs. Hood Coll.; bd. visitors USAF Acad., 1980-87; trustee Mt. St. Mary's Coll.; bd. dirs. Frederick County chpt. ARC; sec. Frederick Heart Assn., 1974-79; mem. Frederick Phys. Fitness Commn.; chmn. Md. Phys. Fitness Commn., 1979-89; mem. Frederick County Landmarks Found.; bd. dirs. Am. Hiking Soc.; bd. dirs. Adventure Sports Inst., 1992—; bd. advisors Internat. Studies Frostburg State U., 1990—, Am. Volkssport Assn., 1991—; mem. bd. vis. U.S. Naval Acad., 1995—, chair, 1997-2002; chair TedCo. Recipient Pres.'s medal John Hopkins U. Democrat. Episcopalian. Home: 306 Grove Blvd Frederick MD 21701-4813

BYRON, E. LEE, real estate broker; b. Gt. Falls, Mont., Oct. 1, 1945; d. Chase and Mary Lee (Evans) Kimball; m. H. Thomas Byron Jr., May 18, 1966 (dec. 2000); children: H. Thomas Byron III, Chase K. (dec. June 2002), Lee-Hayes. AB, Smith Coll., 1967; MA, Monterey Inst. Fgn. Studies, 1971; Montessori cert., St. Nicholas. Ctr., London, 1971. Lic. real estate broker, Fla. Lectr. Monterey (Calif.) Inst. Fgn. Studies, 1971-72; founder, dir., owner Children's Sch. and Summer Dynamics, Auburn, Ala., 1975-79; instr. Child Study Ctr. Auburn U., 1973-79; hosp. dir. Fruitville Vet. Clinic, Sarasota, Fla., 1980-93, broker assoc. Michael Saunders & Co., Sarasota, 1993—. Founder, adv. bd. mem. Guaranty Bank, North Port, Fla., 1987-99; owner, ptnr. Lee Ventures Real Estate Partnership, Sarasota, 1984-99; presenter in field, organizer discussion panels. Co-author: Preschool Theme Lesson Plans, 1975. Bd. dirs. Jr. League, Sarasota, 1981-90; bd. dirs. Pine View Assn. PTA, 1981-90, chmn., 1984-85; bd. dirs. Teen Ct., Sarasota, 1990—, Fla. Sch. Bd. Assn., cert., 1993; bd. dirs. Taxpayers Assn. Sarasota County, 1995-99, pres., 1996-97; bd. dirs. Civic League Sarasota, 1995-2001, 2nd v.p., 1997-98, 1st v.p., 1998-99, pres., 1999-2000; chmn. Sarasota County Exceptional Student Edn. Sch. Adv. Bd., 1984-90; mem. Pine View Sch. Adv. Com., 1994-98, chmn., 1994-97; bd. dirs. Consortium for Children and Youth, Sarasota, 1986—, pres., 1993-97; vice chair Action Task Force Venice (Fla.) 20/20, 1995-97, Children and Youth Svcs. Adv. Com., 1993-2001, chair, 1996-98, vice chair, 1999-2000; bd. dirs. Sarasota County Human Svcs. Adv. Commn., 2002-; co-chmn. Pres.'s Spl. Com. Exceptional Edn. Fla. Sch. Bd. Assn., 1992-93; mem. Bishop's Com. Sexual Misconduct Cath. Diocese, Venice, 1994-95, Multi-Stakeholder's Group (Future Land Planning East Sarasota County), 1995-99; mem. adv. com. Fla. House Inst., 1998—; mem. Sarasota County Sch. Bd., 1990-94; bd. govs. Big Bros./Big Sisters of the Suncoast, 1998—, Fla. Women's Alliance, 1994-2000, Sarasota Women's Alliance, 2001—; eucharistic minister St. Patrick's Ch., 1995—. Recipient Sustainer of Yr. award Sarasota Jr. League, 1993, Cmty. Svc. award, 1995; Women of Power award Nat. Coun. Jewish Women, 1997; named one of 100 Vols. for 100th birthday, Internat. Assn. Jr. Leagues, 1996. Mem. Sarasota Assn. of Realtors (program com. 1995-99, govt. affairs com. 2001—), Nat. Assn. Realtors (Grad. Realtor Inst. 1996). Republican. Roman Catholic. Avocations: reading, swimming, skiing. Home: 653 Sinclair Dr Sarasota FL 34240-9367 Office: Michael Saunders & Co 5100 Ocean Blvd Sarasota FL 34242-1693 E-mail: lee@sarasota.com.

BYRUM, DIANNE, state legislator, small business owner; b. Mar. 18, 1954; d. Cecil Dershem and Mary D.; m. James E. Byrum; children: Barbara Anne, James Richard. AA, Lansing Cmty. Coll.; BS cum laude, Mich. State U. Rep. dist. 68 Mich. Ho. of Reps. from 68th dist., Lansing, 1991-94; mem. Mich. Senate from 25th dist., Lansing, 1995—; owner Blackhawk Hardware, Leslie, Mich., 1983—, Panther Hardware, Stockbridge, Mich., 1991—. Minority vice chair agr. and forestry, health policy and sr. citizens; mem. tech. and energy com., capitol com.; chair dem. caucus. Recipient Disting. Citizen award Ingham County Soil Conservation Dist., 1991, Disting. Alumnus award Lansing Cmty. Coll., 1993. Mem. Mich. Retail Hardware Assn., Lansing Regional C. of C., South Lansing Bus. Assn., South Lansing-Everett Kiwanis. Democrat. Office: Mich State Senate 125 W Allegan PO Box 30036 Lansing MI 48909-7536 E-mail: sendbyrum@senate.state.mi.us.

BYRUM, EDITH WARD, music educator; d. Cecil Thomas Ward, Sr. and Nora Lee (Rountree) Ward; m. James Lee Byrum, Jr., Dec. 18, 1960 (div. Sept. 1992); children: Steven Ward, Susan Yvonne. BS in Music Edn., Longwood Coll., 1960. Tchr. Deep Creek H.S., Chesapeake, Va., 1960—61, Rena B. Wright Elem., Chesapeake, Va., 1967—70, G.W. Carver Elem., Chesapeake, Va., 1970, Sparrow Rd. Elem., Chesapeake, Va., 1971—77; tchr. music G.A. Treakle Elem., Chesapeake, Va., 1977—86, Crestwood Elem., Chesapeake, Va., 1986—97, Deep Creek Elem., Chesapeake, Va., 1996—, Deep Creek Intermediate, Chesapeake, Va., 2001—03, Grassfield Elem., Chesapeake, Va., 2003—04. Pianist, organizer New Horizon Gospel Quartet, Chesapeake, 1993—97; Sunday sch. tchr. Deep Creek Bapt. Ch., Chesapeake, 1972—83, pianist, organist, 1975—98, fin. com., 1966—. Mem.: PTA (life). Avocations: cooking, gardening, travel. Home: 620 Brisa Ct Chesapeake VA 23322 Office: Deep Creek Elem 2809 Forehand Dr Chesapeake VA 23323 Office Phone: 757-558-5333.

BYSIEWICZ, SUSAN, secretary of state; b. New Haven, Conn. BA magna cum laude, Yale Coll., 1983; JD, Duke U., 1986. Corp. atty. White & Case, N.Y., 1986-88, Robinson & Cole, Hartford, Conn., 1988-92; with law dept. Aetna Life and Casualty, 1992-94; state rep. 100th dist. judiciary com. State of Conn., 1992-98, chair govt. adminstrn. and elections com., 1995-98, Sec. of State, 1998—. Author: Ella: A Biography of Governor Ella T. Grasso, 1984. Conn. Bar Assn., N.Y. Bar Assn. Democrat. Address: Rm 104 State Capitol Hartford CT 06106 E-mail: susan.bysiewicz@po.state.ct.us.*

CABALLERO, SHARON, academic administrator; m. Roger Caballero. BS Journalism/English, San Diego State U., 1968; MA Secondary Edn., U.S. Internat. U., 1976, EdD Ednl. Leadership, 1980. Dir. pub. rels. & mktg. Southwestern Cmty. Coll., Chula Vista, Calif., 1984—85; assoc. exec. dir. Calif. Assn. Cmty. Colls. (now Cmty. Coll. League Calif.), 1985—87; dean, commns. & fine arts Grossmont Coll., El Cajon, Calif., 1988—91; asst. supt. & v.p. acad. svcs. Rio Hondo Cmty. Coll. Dist., 1991—97; pres. San

Bernardino Valley Coll., 1997—2002, N.Mex. Highlands U., Las Vegas, N.Mex., 2002—. Mem. Arrowhead United Way, Bernardino Valley Coll. Found., Victor Valley Women's Club, KVCR-FM/TV Found.; San Bernardino C. of C.; chmn. journalism dept., instr. mass media, telecommunications coll. newspaper. Named Calif. Woman of Yr. 58th Dist., 1994 Mem.; Cailf. Cmty. Colls. Exec. Bd. (CEO mem. bd. 1995—), Mgmt. Devel. C——... f C.H. Wm.; Wl'li Pddiillmm. (llmll 190)—, Aiii. A&ii. Women in Cmty. & Junior Colls. (nat. v.p. for profl. devel 1987—89, nat. pres. 1989—91), Rotary. Office: NMex Highlands U 701 S Mt Vernon Ave San Bernardino CA 92410

CABANAS, ELIZABETH ANN, nutritionist, educator; b. Port Arthur, Tex., Oct. 27, 1948; d. William Rosser and Frances Merle (Block) Thornton. BS, U. Tex., 1971; MPH, U. Hawaii, 1973; Ph.D. Tex. Woman's U., 2001. Registered dietitian; cert. diabetes educator. Clin. nutritionist Family Planning Inst. Kapiolani Hosp., Honolulu, 1972-74; dietitian Kauikeolani Children's Hosp.-Pacific Inst. Rehab. Medicine, Honolulu, 1974-75; asst. food service administr. San Antonio Ind. Schs., 1975-89; coord. equipment and facilities Dallas Ind. Sch., 1990-91; nutritionist SureQuest Solutions in Software, Richardson, Tex., 1990-91; nutritionist div. endocrinology, metabolism and hypertension, clin. studies unit rsch. nutritionist, asst. prof. dept. health promotion & gerontology U. Tex. Med. Br., Galveston, 1991—2002. Lectr. nutrition U. Hawaii, Honolulu, 1974-75, St. Mary's U., San Antonio Coll., 1984-90; adj. faculty Tex. Woman's U., 1994; cons. nutritionist, 1980—; presenter in field. Contbr. papers to profl. jours. Vol. ARC, Brooke Army Med. Ctr., Saddle Light Ctr. for Therapeutic Riding, Habitat for Humanity. Recipient diabetes educator recognition Eli Lilly & Co., 1994. Mem. Am. Dietetic Assn., Am. Assn. Diabetes Educators (chair holistic care specialty practice group 1997-98), Assn. Sch. Bus. Ofcls. Internat., Nutrition and Food Svc. Mgmt. Com., Am. Diabetes Assn. (adv. com. U. Tex. Med. Br. children's diabetes mgmt. program 1993-98, mem. Galveston County diabetes support group 1991-99, Disting. Svc. award 1995, mem. Galveston County Outreach adv. com., UTMB rep. 1996-98), Coun. Nutritional Scis. and Metabolism (profl. sect., non-peer rev. com. 1993-94), Tex. Sch. Food Svc. Assn. (dist. bd. dirs. 1977-78), Tex. Nutrition Coun. (nominating com. 1996-97, 2d v.p. 1997-99, sports and cardiovasc. nutritionists practice group, Tex. gerontol. nutritionists practice group), Houston Area Dietetic Assn. (legis. network com. 1995-99), San Antonio Dietetic Assn., San Antonio Sch. Food Svc. Assn. (com. chmn. 1975-89), Tex. Assn. Sch. Bus. Ofcls., Tex. Restaurant Assn., San Antonio Area Food Svc. Administrs. Assn. (pres. 1989-90), Assn. Profls. in Positions of Leadership in Edn., Dallas Dietetic Assn. (cons. nutritionists practice group, chmn. 1990-91), Harris County Biofeedback Soc., San Antonio Mus. Assn., Randolph C. of C., Grand Opera House, Galveston (patron), Galveston Hist. Found., Phi Kappa Phi. Avocations: perpetuation of Hawaiian culture, nordic skiing, equestrian sports, art, dixieland jazz.

CABANISS, BARBARA LEE FERGUSON, counseling administrator; b. Houston, Miss., Apr. 14, 1946; d. James Walton and Ora Lee Ferguson; m. William M. Cabaniss, July 18, 1971; children: Melanie, Mark. BS, Delta State Coll., 1968; MEd, Augusta State U., 1999. Tchr. Fernwood Jr. High Sch., Biloxi, Miss., 1968—72, Oglethorpe County High Sch., Lexington, Ga., 1972—75, Oglethorpe County Elem. Sch., Lexington, 1986—91; recreation dir. Oglethorpe County, Crawford, Ga., 1995—97; counselor Oglethorpe County Elem. Sch., 1998—. Mem. Maxeys City Coun., Ga., 2001—; bd. dir. Oglethorpe County Libr., Lexington, Ga., 1996—. Recipient Vocational Achievement & Cmty. Svc. award, Oglethorpe County Rotary Club, 1998, Cmty. Svc. award, Concern Men of Oglethorpe County, 2000. Mem.; Profl. Assn. Ga. Educators, Ga. Sch. Counselors Assn., Am. Counseling Assn., Maxeys Women's Club. Avocations: photography, watching sports. Home: PO Box 710134 Maxeys GA 30671

CABANISS, CHARLOTTE JONES, library services director; b. Jefferson County, Ala., Apr. 13, 1951; d. Laurens Whipple Sr. and Sally Riddell Jones; m. Thomas Willard Cabaniss, Sept. 14, 1971 (div. Nov. 1998); children: Lauren Cabaniss Sellers, Amanda May, Willard Matthew. BA, Auburn U., 1973. English tchr. Rogers (Ark.) City Schs., 1984-92; libr. svcs. dir. Bay Minette (Ala.). Pub. Libr., 1994—. Dir. North Baldwin Cmty. Concerts, Inc., Bay Minette, 1995-98; mem. Baldwin County United, 1996—; chmn. bd. North Baldwin Literacy Coun., Bay Minette, 1995—; mem. adv. bd. Family Finders, 2000-02, Cath. Social Svcs., 2001; pres. bd. dirs. Jumbo Shrimp Theatre, 2002—; bd. dirs. Baldwin Co. United, 2003—, Ala. Ctr. for the Book, 2001—mem. steering com. Mobile/Baldwin United Envision, 2002—; founding mem. Fairhope Ctr. for the Writing Arts; mem. grant selection com. Ala. Arts and Humanities; founder Ala. Athenaeum Writers Series. Recipient Outstanding Svc. award Area Action Women's Group, 1998, Lynn Stuart Cmty. Svc. award, 2002; named among Women to Watch in South Ala., So. Cities mag., 2002. Mem. ALA, C. of C. (youth task force chair 1996-98, tourism com. chair, 1998), North Baldwin C. of C. (dir. 1996-99), Baldwin County Libr. Cooperative, Kappa Delta Pi, Phi Kappa Phi. Methodist. Avocations: reading, community volunteerism. Office: PO Box 249 Bay Minette AL 36507-0249

CABANISS, DALE, government agency administrator; BA, U. Georgia; JD, Columbus Sch. Law at Catholic U. Legislative asst. and dir. to Sen. Frank Murkowski; chief counsel Senate Govt. Affairs Subcommittee on Post Office and Civil Service; staff member Senate Appropriations Subcommittee; chmn. Federal Labor Relations Authority, 2001—. Office: FLRA 607 14th St NW Washington DC 20424*

CABAY, GINA GRACE ANGELA, lawyer; d. William Michael Bill and Martha Ellen Crum-Bill; m. Robert John Cabay, Aug. 8, 1993. AA, William Rainey Harper Coll., Palatine, IL, 1993; BA hons., Roosevelt U., Chgo., Ill., 1996; JD, Chgo.-Kent Coll. of Law - Ill. Inst. of Tech., Chgo., Ill., 2000. Bar: Ill. 2000, lic.: US Dist. Ct. for the No. Dist. of Ill. (Atty. and Counselor) 2000, bar: DC 2001. Legal analyst Markel Corp. - Shand Morahan & Co., Inc., Deerfield, Ill., 1999—2000, counsel, 2000—02, asst. gen. counsel, 2002—. Mem.: ABA, Ill. State Bar Assn. Office: Markel Corp - Shand Morahan & Co Inc 10 Pkwy N Deerfield IL 60015-2526 E-mail: gcabay@markelcorp.com

CABLE, SUSAN W. state legislator; m. Paul A. Cable; children: Mrs. Payton Cable Churchwell, Betsy. BA, Mercer U. Tchr. Bibb County (Ga.) Sch. Sys., Macon; mem. Ga. State Senate, Atlanta, 1998—, mem. agri. com., higher edn. com., ins. and labor com., spl. judiciary com. Mem. 1st Presbyn. Ch., Macon; past trustee Leadership Ga., Leadership Macon; mem. Macon 2000 Edn. Ptnrship, Ga. Pre-K Curriculum adv. com.; mem., pres. Bibb County Sch. Bd., 1988-96; founder United Parents for Excellence in Edn.; mem. Ga. Sch. Adv. panel, Ga. Sch. Improvement panel; mem. exec. com. Bibb County Reps. Mem. Ga. Bus. Forum. Republican. Office: State Capitol Legis Office Bldg 18 Capitol Sq SW Ste 304A Atlanta GA 30334-9003

CABOT, DIANA MARIE, marketing professional, travel and transportation executive; b. Phila., July 22, 1961; d. Walter Leon Cinkowski and Doris Irene Wojtkowiak. AS, Lab. Inst. Mdse., 1981; BS, Rowan U., 1983; postgrad., Purdue U., 1999. Asst. mgr. Jean Nicole, Cherry Hill, N.J., 1981-82; asst. buyer Hamrahn, Cresskill, N.J., 1984; fashion cons. Le Meilleur, Phila., 1984-86; reservation sales agt. Amtrak, Ft. Washington, Pa., 1986-87, sales cons., 1987-94, area sales mgr., 1994, mktg. mgr. Phila., 1994—. Mem. Evesham (N.J.) Twinning com., 1988; bd. dirs. Evesham Tri-Centennial com., 1988; mem. Greater Boston Conv. and Visitors Bur., Providence Conv. and Visitors Bur., N.Y. Conv. and Visitors Bur. Mem. NAFE, Am. Soc. Travel Agts., N.Y. Soc. Assn. Execs., Greater Washington Soc. Assn. Execs., Am. Bus. Assn., Am. Soc. Assn. Execs., Am. Travel

Mktg. Execs., Vt. C. of C., Evesham Hist. Soc., Evesham Twinning Soc. Avocations: antique collecting, skiing, biking. Home: 21 Creekwood Dr Bordentown NJ 08505-4802 Office: Amtrak 30th St Sta 5S Philadelphia PA 19104

CABRASER, ELIZABETH JOAN, lawyer; b. Oakland, Calif., June 22, 1952; AB, U. Calif., Berkeley, 1975; JD, U. Calif., 1978. Bar: Calif. 1978, U.S. Dist. Ct. (no., ea., cen. and so. dists.) Calif. 1979, U.S. Ct. Appeals (2d, 3rd, 5th, 6th, 9th, 10th, and 11th cirs.) 1979, U.S. Tax Ct. 1979, U.S. Dist. Ct. Hawaii 1986, U.S. Dist. Ct. Ariz. 1990, U.S. Supreme Ct. 1996. Ptnr. Lieff, Cabraser, Heimann & Bernstein LLP, San Francisco, 1978—. Contbr. articles to profl. jours. Named one of Top 50 Women Lawyers Nat. Law Jour., 1998, one of Top 100 U.S. Lawyers, 1997, 2000. Mem. ABA (tort and ins. practice sect., sect. litig. com. on class action and derivative skills, chair subcom. on mass torts), ATLA, Coun. Am. Law Inst., Calif. Constn. Rev. Commn., Nat. Ctr. for State Cts. (mass tort conf. planning com.), Women Trial Lawyer Caucus, Consumer Attys. Calif., Calif. Women Lawyers, Assn. Bus. Trial Lawyers, Nat. Assn. Securities and Comml. Attys., Bay Area Lawyers for Individual Freedom, Bar Assn. San Francisco (v.p. securities litig., bd. dirs.). Office: Lieff Cabraser Heimann & Bernstein LLP Embarcadero Ctr W 30th Fl 275 Battery St San Francisco CA 94111-3305 E-mail: ecabraser@lchb.com.

CACCAMISE, GENEVRA LOUISE BALL (MRS. ALFRED E. CACCAMISE), retired librarian; b. July 22, 1934; d. Herbert Oscar and Genevra (Green) Ball; m. Alfred E. Caccamise, July 7, 1974. BA, Stetson U., 1956; MLS, Syracuse U., 1967. Tchr. grammar sch., Sanford, Fla., 1956-57; tchr. elem. sch. Longwood, Fla., 1957-58; tchr., libr. Enterprise (Fla.) Sch., 1958-63; libr. media specialist Boston Ave. Sch., DeLand, Fla., 1963-83; head media specialist Blue Lake Sch., DeLand, 1983-87; ret., 1987. Author: Volusia County manual Instructing the Library Assistant, 1965, Echoes of Yesterday: A History of the DeLand Area Public Library, 1912-1995, 1995, A Quest for Beauty: A History of the Garden Club of DeLand, Florida, 1927-97, 1997, Index to Reflections: West Volusia County, 100 Years of Progress, 2002, (compilation) The Minutes and Memorials of the Old Settlers of DeLand, Fla., 1882-1916, 2003. Charter mem. West Volusia Meml. Hosp. Aux., DeLand, 1962-81; leader Girl Scouts U.S., 1955-56; area dir. Fla. Edn. Assn., Volusia County, 1963-65; bd. dirs. Alhambra Villas Home Owners Assn., 1972-75; trustee DeLand Pub. Libr., 1977-86, sec., 1978-80, v.p., 1980-82, pres., 1982-84; v.p. Friends of DeLand Pub. Libr., 1987-88, 98—, bd. dirs., 1987—, pres., 1989-90, 95-97, newsletter editor 1992-95, 99—; charter mem. Guild of the DeLand Mus. Art, 1988—, v.p., 1990, pres., 1991-92, co-rec. sec., 1997-98, mus. bd. dirs., 1991-95; co-orgn. chmn. Friends DeLand Mus. Art, 1993. Mem. AAUW (2d v.p. chpt. 1965-67, rec. sec. 1961-65, 78-80, pres. 1980-82, parliamentarian 1982-84), Assn. Childhood Edn. (1st v.p. 1965-66, corr. sec. 1963-65), DAR (chpt. registrar 1969-80, asst. chief page Continental Congress, Washington 1962-65), Fla. Libr. Assn., Bus. and Profl. Women's Club (corr. sec. DeLand 1968-71, 2d v.p. 1969-70), Stetson U. Alumni Assn. (class chmn. for ann. fund dr. 1968), Volusia County Assn. Media in Edn. (treas. 1977), Volusia County Ret. Educators Assn. (pres. Unit II 1988-90, scholarship chmn. 1992-95, corr. sec. 2003-), Soc. of Mayflower Descendants (lt. gov. Francis Cook Colony 1988-90), Pilgrim John Howland Soc., Colonial Dames XVII Century, Magna Carta Dames, Nat. Soc. New Eng. Women (v.p. Daytona Beach Colony 1990-91), Nat. League Am. Pen Women (corr. sec. 1996-98, 2000—, pres. 1998-2000), Hibiscus Garden Cir. (treas. 1988-89, v.p. 1990-93, 96-97, pres. 1997-99, treas. 2001-2003), Morning Glory Garden Cir., Nat. Soc. U.S. Daus. of 1812 (rec. sec. Peacock chpt. 1989-90), West Volusia Hist. Soc. (sec. 1996, libr. 1993—, v.p. 2000-02, pres. 2002-03, bd. dirs., Historian of Yr. 2003), Fla. Hist. Soc., DeLand Garden Club (corr. sec. 1993-95, editor newsletter 1993-95, v.p. 1997-99), Delta Kappa Gamma (pres. Beta Psi chpt. 1982-84). Address: PO Box 241 Deland FL 32721-0241

CACKENER, HELEN LEWIS, retired English educator, writer; b. Elmira, N.Y., July 4, 1926; d. Norman Pratt and Grace Genevieve (Oakes) Lewis; m. Daniel Glyndwr Lewis Jr., June 17, 1950 (div. Aug. 1959); children: Deborah Anne Poplasky, Elizabeth Laura Lewis-Michl, Margaret Grace Lewis-Price; m. Robert Millard Cackener, Apr. 17, 1960. BA in English Lit. magna cum laude, Oberlin Coll., 1948; MAT, Harvard U., 1950. Cert. secondary English tchr., N.Y. English tchr. Westbrook Coll., Portland, Maine, 1949-50, Schenectady (N.Y.) City Schs., 1950-51, 60, Hudson Falls (N.Y.) Sr. H.S., 1960-85. Contbr. articles to Glens Falls Today, Saratoga Style, and Schenectady Mag., 1985-88. Vol. PBS, Saratoga Performing Arts Ctr. John Hay fellow Ford Found., 1964. Mem. AAUW, P.E.O., Delta Kappa Gamma (Alpha Epsilon chpt., bd. mem. 1970-95, N.Y. state sec. 1983-87), Phi Beta Kappa. Republican. Presbyterian. Avocations: music, reading. Home: 49 Cedar Ct Queensbury NY 12804-8707

CADAMY, SHELLEY R. economic development professional; b. Oklahoma City, June 29, 1969; d. W. Jay Byram and Rita C. Cadamy. BA in Art History, U. Okla., 1992, M in Regional and City Planning, 1994. Rsch. asst. Okla. Dept. Commerce, Oklahoma City, 1994—96, bus. intelligence officer, 1996—99; dir. bus. devel. Edmond Econ. Devel. Authority, 1999—; coord. small bus. mgmt. Francis Tuttle Tech. Ctr., 2003—. Adj. prof. U. Ctrl. Oklahoma. Bd. dirs. Fine Arts Inst. Edmond. Mem.: Edmond Hist. Soc. (bd. dirs.). Office: 12777 N Rockwell Ave Oklahoma City OK 73142 E-mail: scadamy@francistuttle.com

CADDEN, JOAN, state legislator; b. Balt., Aug. 17, 1941; married; 4 children. Student, Marinello Sch. Cosmetology, 1967-69. Owner/operator cosmetology bus.; mem. Md. Ho. of Dels., Annapolis, 1991—, mem. constl. and adminstrv. law com., 1991-92, mem. appropriations com., 1992—, mem. spl. joint com. on pensions and legis. data sys. Mem. Stoney Creek, Roland Terrace and Lake Shore Dem. Club. Mem. LWV, Ploughmen & Fishermen. Home: Brooklyn Park 111 Cedar Hill Rd Baltimore MD 21225-3903 Office: Md Ho of Reps State Capitol Annapolis MD 21401

CADORA, KAREN MICHELE, application developer; b. Castle Air Force Base, Calif., May 15, 1970; d. Donald Frank and Mavis Lancene (Hart) C. BS, Cornell U., 1991; MS, Stanford U., 1993, MA, 1996, PhD, 1999. Software engr. Stanford (Calif.) U., 1997—. Instr. Stanford (Calif.) U., 1993—. Home: 4951 Noble Park Pl Boulder CO 80301-6313

CADWALLADER, GWEN NATALIE, elementary school educator, music educator; b. New Orleans, Feb. 18, 1962; d. Joseph Dale Cadwallader and Maria Natalie Lovoi. B in Music Edn., Southeastern La. U., 1984; MEd, Whitworth Coll., 1990. Cert. tchr. grades K-12 music, grades K-8 elem. edn. Wash., K-12 prin. Wash., kindermusik Kindermusik Internat., Orff, Kodaly. Elem. music specialist Ctrl. Valley Sch. Dist. #356, Spokane Valley, Wash., 1985—. Adj. faculty Whitworth Coll., Spokane, Wash., 1991—93; dir. Kindermusik with Gwen Cadwallader, Spokane, 1998—2002; presenter in field. Pres. Glenngill Ct. Homeowners Assn. Spokane Valley, 1999—. Mem.: NEA, Ctrl. Valley Edn. Assn., Wash. Edn. Assn., Wash. Assn. Sch. Prins., Wash. Music Educators Assn., Music Educators Nat. Conf., Kindermusik Educators Assn., N.W. Kodaly Educators, Orgn. Am. Kodaly Educators, Inland Empire Orff Chpt. (pres. 2001—03), Am. Off-Schulwerk Assn., Pi Lambda Theta, Delta Omicron (life). Republican. Avocations: music, swimming, reading, genealogy. Office: Progress Elem Sch 710 N Progress Rd Veradale WA 99037 Office Phone: 509-228-4500. Personal E-mail: gncad@icehouse.net.

CAFFEE, VIRGINIA MAUREEN, executive assistant; b. Kansas City, Mo., Feb. 25, 1948; d. Frederick Arthur Gladden and Ethel Elizabeth (Keithly) Courier; m. Marcus Pat Caffee, May 31, 1975; 1 child, Katheryn Elizabeth. Student, Ctrl. Mo. State U., 1966-73, Okla. State U., 1977-78;

BBA in Bus. Edn., Sam Houston State U., 1985. Cert. profl. sec., 1975. Land abstractor Johnson County Title Co., Warrensburg, Mo., 1967-68; dept. sec., bus. placement officer Ctrl. Mo. State U., Warrensburg, 1968-69; exec. sec. European Exchange System, Giessen, Germany, 1969-70; confidential sec. Consolidated Freightways, Kansas City, 1972-73; exec. sec. Rohmig Imment, II., un 1973-74; ser. admr. Tehniech Oil Co.Liel, Houston, 1979-84; exec. sec. St. Petersburg (Fla.) Hilton & Towers, 1989-90; adminstrv. mgr. Tampa Bay Engring., Clearwater, Fla., 1990-92; office mgr. WP trainer Marcus Caffee, Consulting, Largo, Fla., 1992-95; sr. adminstrv. asst. BMH Inc., Dallas, 1995-97; exec. sec. GTE Comms. Corp., Irving, Tex., 1997-2000, mem. Internet coun., 1999—2000; exec. asst. Verizon-ESG, 2000—02, human resources bus. ptnr., 2001—. Ad hoc instr. St. Petersburg (Fla.) Jr. Coll., 1993, Profl. Secs. Internat. chpt. liaison for CPS rev. course, 1993-94; presenter in field. Editor (performance programs) Suncoast Singers, 1991-94 (Cmty. Svc. award Arts Coun. Co-op 1993) Clearwater Cmty. Chorus, 1993-95, Ft. Worth Civic Chorus, Fall 1995, (newsletters) Clearwater Sparkler, 1992-93 (1st pl. award 1993), Fla. Divsn. The Secretariat, 1993-94; editor: Livin, Lovin, Laughin, 1995, Texana Newsletter, 1997-98; webmaster T-L Divsn., 1997—. Sec. Montgomery County Choral Soc., Conroe, Tex., 1986-88, publicity co-chmn., 1987-89; pres. Anona Meth. Ch. Choir, Largo, 1990-91; mem. adv. bd. Mountain View C.C., Dallas, 1999. Named Sec. of Yr. Profl. Secs. Internat. Inc. Clearwater chpt., 1994; recipient Mo. State Tchrs. scholarship Mo. Congress Parents and Tchrs., 1966. Mem. CPS Acad., Internat. Assn. Adminstrv. Profls. (chmn. secs. week, sec. Clearwater chpt. 1992-93, pres. 1994, chmn. seminar and v.p. Clearwater chpt. 1992-93, workshop spkr. Fla. divsn. 1993, program spkr. St. Petersburg chpt. 1993, alt. del. to internat. conv. 1993, 96, 98, del. to internat. conv. 1999, alt. del. to divsn. meeting 1993, 94, del. dist. conv. 1994, 98, Sec. of Yr. 1994-95, del. Fla. divsn. meeting 1995, program spkr. Trinity chpt. 1996, del. Tex.-La. meeting 1996, 97, 98, 99, divsn. treas. Tex.-La. divsn. 1996, v.p. 1997-98, pres.-elect 1998-99, pres. 1999-00, workshop spkr. internat. conv. Chgo. 2000), CPS Soc. Tex. (roster chmn. 1983-85); Soc. Human Resource Mgmt., Women's Assn. Verizon Employees. Republican. Methodist. Avocations: choral singing, sewing, movies, ensemble singing performances. Home: 218 Oakmont Dr Trophy Club TX 76262-5472 E-mail: gcaffee@mccinternet.com.

CAFFERTY, PASTORA SAN JUAN, public policy educator; b. Cienfuegos, Las Villas, Cuba, July 29, 1940; arrived in US, 1947; d. Jose Antonio and Hortensia (Horruitiner) San Juan; m. Michael Cafferty, Apr. 13, 1971 (dec. 1973); m. Henry P. Russe, Aug. 18, 1988 (dec. 1991). BA, St. Bernard Coll., 1967; MA, George Washington U., 1969, PhD, 1971; DHC, Columbia Coll., 1987. Instr. George Washington U., Washington, 1967-69; asst. to sec. U.S. Dept. Transp., Washington, 1969-70, U.S. HUD, Washington, 1970-71; asst. prof. U. Chgo., 1971-76, assoc. prof., 1976-83, prof., 1983—. Bd. dirs. Kimberly-Clark Corp., Dallas, Peoples' Energy Corp., Chgo., Waste Mgmt. Inc., Houston, Harris Fin. Corp., Chgo. Author: The Politics of Language: The Dilemma of Bilingual Education for Puerto Ricans, 1981, Backs Against The Wall, 1983, The Dilemma of American Immigration, 1983, Hispanics in the U.S.A., 1985, 2d edit., 1992, Hispanics: An Agenda for 21st Century, 1999, 2d edit., 2002. Bd. dirs. Lyric Opera Assn., Chgo., 1990—, South Univ. Med. Ctr., 1993— White House fellow U.S. Govt., 1969-70. Mem. Chgo. Yacht Club. Democrat. Roman Catholic. Office: U Chgo 969 E 60th St Chicago IL 60637-2677 Office Phone: 773-702-8959.

CAFFREY, MARGARET MARY, humanities educator, researcher; b. Wilkes-Barre, Pa., July 5, 1947; d. James Anthony and Louise Elizabeth (Keil) C. BA, Coll. Misericordia, 1969; MA, U. Tex., 1979, PhD, 1986. Lectr. U. Tex., Austin, 1986-87; instr. Austin C.C., 1988; asst. prof. Memphis State U., 1988-93; assoc. prof. U. Memphis, 1993—. Author: Ruth Benedict: Stranger in This Land, 1989 (Critics Choice award). Faculty Rsch. grantee U. Memphis, 1993; named Oustanding Young Rschr., Memphis State U. Coll. Arts & Scis., 1989-90. Mem. Orgn. Am. Historians & Affiliate Coord. Coun. for Women in History, Am. Studies Assn., So. Hist. Assn., Assn. Southern Womens Historians. Avocations: hiking, backpacking, canoeing, bird-watching. Office: U Memphis Dept History Memphis TN 38152-0001

CAFIERO, JENNIFER ANNETTE, academic administrator, educator; b. Bklyn., Jan. 8, 1975; d. Pasquale and Annette Rosemary Cafiero. Master's degree, Pace U., 2000. Cert. tchr. N.Y. Exec. asst. Pace U., N.Y.C., 1997—98, coord. of enrollment rsch., 1998—2000, dir. of enrollment planning and reporting, 2000—. Adj. prof. math Pace U., N.Y.C., 2002—. Mem.: Assn. for Instl. Rsch., Am. Motorcyclist Assn. Avocations: motorcycling, home improvement, travel, boating. Home and Office: Pace Univ 1 Pace Plz New York NY 10038 E-mail: jcafiero@pace.edu.

CAFRITZ, PEGGY COOPER, communications executive; b. Mobile, Ala., Apr. 7, 1947; d. Algernon Johnson and G. Catherine (Mouton) C.; married; 2 children. BA in Polit. Sci., George Washington U., 1968, JD, 1971. Bar: D.C. 1972. Founder Workshops for Careers in Arts, Washington, 1968; developer, chmn. bd. Duke Ellington Sch. Arts., Washington, 1968-84; dir. Arrowstreet, Architects and Planners Inc., Cambridge, Mass., 1972-74, Washington, 1972-74; spl. asst. to pres. Post-Newsweek Sta. Inc., Washington, 1974-77; programming exec., producer documentary films Sta. WTOP-TV, Washington, 1974-77. Cons. arts critic pub. TV show Around Town, 1986—. Cultural arts critic (PBS TV show) Around Town, 1986—. Mem. exec. com. D.C. Commn. Arts and Humanities, 1970-75, chmn., 1979-87, chmn. emeritus, 1987—; trustee Am. Film Inst., 1972-74, Pratt Inst., 1991; bd. govs. Corcoran Gallery Art, Washington, 1972-74; exec. dir. gt. issure program D.C. Bicentennial Commn. 1974; bd. dirs. Washington Performing Arts Soc., 1983—; Kennedy Ctr. Performing Arts, 1986—, Women's Project, 1987—, Nat. Guild Community Schs. of Arts, 1976-80, Pennsylvania Ave. Devel. Corp., Washington, 1979-87, Atlanta U., 1983-86, Washington, Am. Place Theater, N.Y.; co-chmn. Mayor's Blue Ribbon Task Force on Cultural and Econ. Devel., 1987-88; mem. exec. bd. Nat. Assembly State Arts Agys., 1979-86, planning com., 1986-87; mem. conv. staff Dem. Nat. Com., 1972, 76; mem. steering com. Carter-Mondale, Washington, 1976; mem. nat. panel Arts, Edn. and Ams., 1975-79; mem. internat. com. UNICEF, 1976-79; chair Smithsonian Cultural Edn. Com., 1989—; co-chair Smithsonian Cultural Equity Com., 1988—; mem. African-Am. Instnl. study adv. com. Smithsonian Instn., 1990— pres., D.C. St. Bd. of Education, 2001-. Fellow Woodrow Wilson Internat. Ctr. for Scholars, 1971; recipient John D. Rockefeller III award, 1972, George F. Peabody award U. Ga., 1976, Emmy award, 1977, 27th Ann. Broadcast Media award, 1977, Zeta Phi Beta award for outstanding contbn. in the arts, 1974, N.Y. Black Film Festival award, 1976, Women's Achievement award Pub. TV, 1984, Brava award for Outstanding Contbn. to Arts in Washington, 1988, Mayor's Art award for excellence in svc. to arts, 1991, 20th Malcolm X DayAnniversary award Arts Advocacy, 1991, Ann. Cultural Alliance award, 1992; named Washingtonian of Yr. Washingtonian mag., 1972, Woman of Yr. Mademoiselle mag., 1973, and numerous other awards. Mem. ABA, D.C. Bar Assn. Home and Office: 3030 Chain Bridge Rd NW Washington DC 20016-3410

CAGE, ALLIE M. communications executive; b. Memphis, Feb. 2, 1953; d. Ernest Hampton Sr. and Robie Lee (Bynum) Cage. BS, Cornell U., 1975; MBA, Tenn. State U., 1986. Pres., owner Profl. Svc., Inc., Memphis, 1981-83; dir. tutorial ctr. Tenn. State U., Nashville, 1984-85; rsch. assoc. Inst. African Affairs, Nashville, 1986-88; ptnr. Cage, Smith & Assocs., Nashville, 1988-91; mktg. dir. So. Colour, Inc., Brentwood, Tenn., 1994—; owner, pres. Cage Comm. Co., Madison, Tenn., 1988—. Bd. dirs. So. Colour, Inc. Author: (weekly publ.) Rap Sheet, 1983—86; co-author: (pub., cassette rec.) Arbitration, 1975; freelance reporter various newspapers, 1986—. Bd. dirs. Rainbow Coalition Davidson County, Tenn., 1984—, Nat. Coalition to Save Black Colls., Nashville, 1986—; pres. Lit. Soc., 1991—;

publicity coord., vol. coord. Unity Build Habitat for Humanity, project dir. Ecumenical Build 2002; publicity coord., vol. coord. Unity Build Bldg. Together for Christ, 1999—; min. in tng. St. Luke CME Ch., Nashville, min. Named to So. Women in Pub. Svc., Stennis Ctr. Pub. Svc. and Miss. U. for Women, 1992. Mem.: NAACP (life), Am. Mgmt. Assn., Nat. Hook-Up Black Women. Democrat. Avocations: travel, reading, tennis, volleyball, music. Office: 510 Heritage Dr Unit 25 Madison TN 37115-6001 E-mail: amcage@msn.com.

CAGLE, YVONNE DARLENE, astronaut; b. West Point, N.Y., Apr. 24, 1959; BA in Biochemistry, San Francisco State U., 1981; PhD in Medicine, U. Wash., 1985. Cert. ACLS instr.; flight surgeon. Intern Highland Gen. Hosp., Oakland, Calif., 1985; resident in family practice Ghent FP Ea. Va. Med. Sch., 1992; dep. project mgr. Kelsey-Seybold Clinics NASA-JSC Occupl. Health Clinic, 1994—96; tech. astronaut office ops. planning br. NASA Johnson Space Ctr., 1996—. Clin. asst. prof. U. Tex., Galveston; cons. in field. Active Boys and Girls Club Am.; vol. family practice clinical faculty U. Calif., Davis; active Third Bapt. Ch. With USAF. Named one of Outstanding Young Women of Am.; recipient Disting. Scientist award, Nat. Tech. Assn., Commendation award, Marin County Bd. Supr., Novato Sch. Bd. Mem.: Aerospace Med. Assn., Am. Acad. Family Physicians. Avocations: jigsaw puzzles, juggling, skating, hiking, music. Office: NASA Johnson Space Ctr Mailcode JA Houston TX 77058

CAHAN, CORA, not-for-profit developer; m. Bernard Gersten. Dancer; co-founder, exec. dir. The Feld Ballet, N.Y.C.; co-founder, v.p. Joyce Theater, N.Y.C., 1979—98; pres. The New 42nd St., Inc., N.Y.C., 1990—. Trustee emeritus Joyce Theatre. Recipient All-Star 2001 award, Crain's N.Y. Bus. mag., Ernie award, Dance/USA, 2002. Office: The New 42nd St Inc 330 W 42nd St 23rd Fl New York NY 10036*

CAHILL, ANNE PICKFORD, economist, demographer; b. Dayton, Ohio, Oct. 11, 1953; d. James H. and Margaret J. Pickford; m. Francis Patrick Cahill, Feb. 18, 1984; 1 child, Emily J. BS with honors in spl. edn., Va. Commonwealth U., 1975; MA in Econs., Va. Poly. Inst. and State U., 1983. Spl. edn. tchr. Nelson County Pub. Schs./Chelsea Sch., 1976-79; assoc. Robert R. Nathan Assocs., Washington, 1982-86; analyst Fairfax County Office of Rsch. and Stats., Fairfax, Va., 1986-88; br. chief Fairfax County Office of rsch. and Stats., Fairfax, Va., 1989-94; econ. and demographic rsch. supr. Fairfax County Office Mgmt. and Budget, 1994-99; demographic and econ. rsch. mgr. Fairfax County Dept. Sys. Mgmt. for Human Svcs., 1999—. Troop cookie sales coord. Girl Scouts U.S.A., Fairfax, 1996-97, 98-99, 99-00, troop svc. project coord., 1998-2000; mem. PTA, Fairfax, 1995—, sch. budget com., 1997-98, prin. selection com., 1999; bd. dirs., treas. Fairfax Plaza Civic Assn., 1983-85. Recipient Nat. Assn. Counties Achievement award, 1996, 2001, 2002. Mem. NAFE, Fairfax LWV (unit chair 86, budget chair 1995-96), Sierra Club (group chair, treas. 1987-90), Phi Kappa Phi. Avocations: reading, art. Home: 9353 Tartan View Dr Fairfax VA 22032-1207

CAHILL, CATHERINE M. orchestra executive; Gen. mgr. N.Y. Philharmonic, N.Y.C., 1994-98; exec. dir. Toronto Symphony, Can., 1998-99; exec. dir. cancer rsch. fund Damon Runyon-Walter Winchell Found., N.Y.C., 1999—. Office: Cancer Rsch Fund 675 3rd Ave Fl 25 New York NY 10017-5704

CAHILL, PATRICIA DEAL, radio station executive; b. St. Louis, Oct. 9, 1947, d. Richard Joseph and Dorothy (Deal) C.; m. children: Lindsay Cahill, Jessica Cahill Crump. BA, U. Kans., 1969, MA, 1971. Continuity dir. Sta. KANU-FM, Lawrence, Kans., 1970, audio reader dir., 1970-73; reporter Sta. KCUR-FM, Kansas City, Mo., 1973-75; news dir. Sta. KMUW-FM, Wichita, Kans., 1975, gen. mgr., 1976-87, Sta. KCUR-FM, Kansas City, 1987—. Asst. prof. communications studies U. Mo. Kansas City, 1987—; dir. Nat. Pub. Radio, 1982-88, exec. com., 1983-88, chair tech. and distbn., 1985-88. Chmn. Wichita Free U., 1979-81; v.p. Planned Parenthood Kans., 1986-87; bd. dirs. Kansas City Cultural Alliance. Recipient Matrix award Wichita chpt. Women in Commn., 1986, Alumni Honor citation U. Kans., 1993. Mem. Pub. Radio Mid. Am. (pres. 1979-80, 89-93), Radio Rsch. Consortium (bd. dirs. 1981—), Kans. Pub. Radio Assn. (bd. dirs. 1980-87). Office: Sta KCUR 4825 Troost Ave Ste 202 Kansas City MO 64110-2030

CAHILL, VERNA ELEANORE, writer; b. Nashua, N.H., Mar. 20, 1916; d. Edward Nazairre Dufault; m. Albert Pressey, Aug. 1936 (div. Oct. 1958); m. George Cahill (dec. Sept. 15, 1983). Student, Holy Cross Coll., 1973—79, U. N.H., 1958—60. Asst. editor Ins. mag., 1961—70. Editor: (poetry column) Sunday Union Leader; contbr. articles to numerous mags. and anthologies; author: But To The Hungray Soul Grant from Mass, 1985; host Edit, Talk Show, 1986. Mem.: Poetry Soc. N.H. (v.p., rec. sec., editor soc. publ., historian, bd. dirs., pres. 1964—). Avocations: interior decorating, landscaping, classical music.

CAHINHINAN, NELIA AGBADA, retired public health nurse, administrator; b. Laguna, Philippines, Sept. 20, 1939; d. Manuel Navarro and Milagros Agbay (Adea) Agbada; m. Rodolfo DeGuia Cahinhinan, Jan. 29, 1967; children: Rodney Paul, Roel James, Renee Ann, Nelie Rose. Diploma, U. Philippines, 1961; BSN, U. Guam, 1985. RN; cert. in nursing adminstrn. Pub. health nurse Dept. Health, Laguna, 1962-67, Dept. Pub. Health and Social Svc., Agana, Guam, 1967-73; pub. health nurse supr., home care Dept. PHSS, Mangilao, Guam, 1974-82; cmty. health nurse supr. Regional Pub. Health Ctr., Dept. PHSS, Tamuning, Guam, 1982-86; nursing and program supr. maternal child health Family Planning Program, Dept. PHSS, Mangilao, 1986-89; asst. nursing adminstr. Bur. Family Health and Nursing Svcs., Dept. PHSS, Mangilao, 1990-94. Mem. adv. coun. Coll. Nursing, U. Guam, Mangilao, 1994-95; mem. nursing asst. program adv. coun. Guam C.C., Mangilao, 1995-96; mem. profl. adv. bd. Clarke Home Nursing Svc., Tamuhning, 1995-97. Bd. dirs. Am. Cancer Soc., Agana, 1976—78; mem., sec., chair nursing and health svcs. com. ARC, 1980—83; mem. com. chair So. Tagalog Assn., 1980—2003. Recipient Centennial Leadership award Nat. League of Nursing, 1993, Outstanding Woman of Yr. award Govt. of Guam, 1996; named Guam Top Ten Suprs., Gov. of Guam, 1990. Mem.: Laguna Assn. Guam (pres. 2000—01, advisor 2002—04), Cath. Daus. of Ams. (treas. 1999—2001, 2004—), Guam Meml. Hosp. Vol. Assn. (com. chair 1998—2004, dir.-at-large 1999—2002), Guam Nurses Assn. (treas., dir. 1980, com. chair 1993—2003, pres. 1994—95, com. chair 2004, Svc. award 1983, Guam Nurse of Yr. 1985, Most Disting. Mem. award 1996), U. Philippines Alumni Assn. (pres. 1991—93, advisor 1994—2004, treas., dir., advisor 2004, Outstanding Svc. award 1993). Roman Catholic. Avocations: decorating, gardening, flower arrangement. Home: PO Box 11234 Tamuning GU 96931-1234

CAHN, RUTH PATRICIA, director, musician; b. McKeesport, Pa., Mar. 17, 1946; d. Thomas Allen and Vera Emilia (Schoeller) McLean; m. William L. Cahn, Sept. 9, 1968. BMus, Eastman Sch., 1968. Percussionist Rochester (N.Y.) Philharm., 1968—2000, devel. dir., 1993-94; tchr. Nazareth Coll., Rochester, 1972-76; instr. percussion Eastman Sch. of Music, Rochester, 1977—, dir. summer session, 2000—; artist in residence City Sch. Dist., Rochester, 1977—. Dir. music horizons Eastman Sch., Rochester, 1984-96. Bd. dirs. Operatheatre, Rochester, 1990-92, Rochester Philharm., 1988-92; pres. bd. dirs. Project UNIQUE, Rochester, 1995—. Grantee Arts for Greater Rochester, 1974. Mem. Percussive Arts Soc., Nat. Soc. of Fund Raising Execs., Mu Phi Epsilon (Musician of Yr. 1994). Avocation: study of world music. Office: Eastman Sch of Music 26 Gibbs St Rochester NY 14604-2599

CAI, MING ZHI, film producer; b. Changsha, China, Feb. 22, 1935; arrived in U.S., 1986; d. Xian Cai and Xian Jiao Du; m. Jing Yi Jin, Apr. 18, 1958; children: Ge Jin, Jun Jin. BS with hons. in Chemistry, Wu Han U., 1957. Rschr. Sch. Chemistry Ga. Inst. Tech., Atlanta, 1986—89; rschr. Dept. Chemistry U. Pitts., 1989—90, UCLA, 1991—93; freelance prodr. LA, 1994—. Prodr.: (video series for TV stas.) Local Conditions and Customs of America, 1998—; (films) The Stories of Chinese Americans, 2001—, Science and Education. Mem.: Sci. and Tech. Soc. China, Instrumental Measurement Soc. China, Chem. Soc. China, Nat. Mus. Women in Arts. Avocations: painting, photo design, travel, organic agriculture, volleyball.

CAIN, COLEEN W. writer, educator; b. Birmingham, Iowa, Sept. 2, 1916; d. Marida Irwin Cain and Effie Levina Walters; m. James Cazort McClurkin, Feb. 5, 1937 (dec. Jan. 1938); m. James Robert Cazort, Dec. 24, 1942 (div. Oct. 1970); 1 child, Sidney Cain ; m. Eugene Everett Bauer, Nov. 3, 1974 (div. Feb. 1984). BA in Journalism, U. Ark., 1938. Cert. real estate agt. Wash., 1946, Ark., 1948. Tech. writer Manpower, Inc., Huntsville, Ala., 1966—69; editor, arts reviews Huntsville Times, 1969—70; fgn. news corr. Beijing PRC Jour. Am., Bellevue, Wash., 1980—83; instr. Beijing Fgn. Langs. Inst., 1981—83; lectr. Continuing Edn. Bellevue & South Seattle C.C., 1983—88; pres., owner Cain-Lockhart Press, Issaquah, Wash., 1985; instr. Issaquah Cmty. Ctr., 1996, North Bellevue Cmty. Sr. Ctr., 1997—. Author: Beth Bauer's Enjoy China More, 1985, 1986, 115 Jet Stories for Your Briefcase, 2001, (novels) Wild Blue, 1st of WWII Series, 2002; : 2d edt., 2004, (novels) Glory After the War, 2004. Singer Seattle Symphony Chorale, New Orleans Opera Soc., Cascadian Chorale, Huntsville Cmty. Chorus; mem. 41st dist. Democrats, Bellevue, 1972; alt. del. King County Democrats, Seattle, 1992; election judge Westlake Precinct, Issaquah, 1991—98; mezzo soloist in choirs, chorales. Recipient cert. of excellence, City of Bellevue Parks and Cmty. Svcs. Dept., 2001. Mem.: Northwest Bookfest (author spkr. 2001), Seattle Free Lances (treas. 1997—98, advisor 2001), Pacific Northwest Writers Assn. (critique editor 1995—99, 3rd place nonfiction award 1976). Democrat. Presbyn. Avocation: music. Home: 19510 S E 51st St Issaquah WA 98027-9327

CAIN, KAREN MIRINDA, musician, educator; b. Anna, Ill., Feb. 25, 1944; d. James Paul and Margaret Camilla (Sinks) C. MusB, So. Ill. U., 1966, MusM in Voice and Choral Conducting, 1967; postgrad., Trinity Coll., Washington, 1985. Cert. music tchr., Md. Choral music tchr., Prince George's County, Md., 1969-71; music tchr. class piano Montgomery County, Md., 1972-89; music tchr., founder of studio Rockville, Md., 1972—; co-founder, dir., arranger, profl. madrigal ensemble The Renaissance Revelers, 1985—. Choral music dir. and soloist various chs. and synagogues, Rockville, Md., 1972-92; soprano soloist, sect. leader Grace Luth. Ch., Washington, 2000—; singer Paul Hill Chorale, Washington, 1982-90, mem. chorale staff, music theory instr., 1984-90; contbr. minstrel and history guilds, performer, mem., Md. Renaissance Festival, 1987—. Dir., editor: (CD) Renaissance Romance, 1994 (CD) Journey into Light, 2002; arranger choral works featured on Renaissance Romance, Journey Into Light; dir.: performances at The Lutheran Reformation Svc. held at The Washington Nat. Cathedral, 1995, The White House, Kennedy Ctr.; co-author (with John Sinks): Sinks: A Family History, 1980. Mem. AAUW, Md. Music Tchrs. Assn., Montgomery County Class Piano Tchrs. Assn., Mu Phi Epsilon. Home and Office: 862 College Pkwy # T-1 Rockville MD 20850-1558

CAIN, MADELINE ANN, mayor; b. Cleve., Nov. 21, 1949; d. Edward Vincent and Mary Rita (Quinn) C. BA, Ursuline Coll., 1973; MPA, Cleve. State U., 1985. Tchr. St. Augustine Acad., Lakewood, Ohio, 1973-75; clk. coun. legis. aide Lakewood City Coun., 1981-85; legis. liaison Cuyahoga County Bd. Commrs., Cleve., 1985-88; mem. Ohio Ho. of Reps., Columbus, 1989-95; mayor City of Lakewood, Lakewood, Ohio, 1995—. Mem. Cudell Neighborhood Improvement Corp., West Blvd. Neighborhood Assn.; trustee Malachi House. Mem. Lakewood Bus. and Profl. Women, Lakewood C. of C., City Club. Democrat. Roman Catholic. Office: Lakewood City Hall 12650 Detroit Ave Lakewood OH 44107-2891

CAIN, MARCENA JEAN BEESLEY, retail executive; b. Kingman, Kans., May 1, 1935; d. Albert Eugene and Stella Wanda (Ruthowski) Beesley; m. Kenneth B. Cain, Aug. 4, 1951 (dec. Aug. 2000); children: Kenneth Thomas, David Raymond. With AMVETS Thrift Stores, Washington, from 1971, asst. dir., 1971—87, exec. adminstr., from 1987; pres., asst. dir. AMVETS Value Village Thrift Stores, Balt. Ptnr. Bank St. Joint Venture Realty, Del-Mar Realty, Oakland Ctr. Partnership Ltd., 1987; pres. Familty Thrift Ctr., Inc.; v.p. 4 corps; chmn. bd. dirs. Alamo II Thrift Stores, 1993. DC area rep. PTA Valley Forge Mil. Acad. Named Woman of the Yr., Balt.'s Best BPW, 1981; recipient Disting. Citizen's citation, Howard Co., 1987, Gov.'s citation, State of Md., 1987, Dedicated Svc. award, Seat Pleasant, Md., 1987, Congl. cert. Merit, 1991, 1992, AMVETS Dept. Md. Freestate award, 1994, Silver Helmet Spl. award for cmty. svc., 2003, Nat. Amvet's Silver Helmet award. Mem.: DAV Aux. (past nat. historian), Affiliated Mchts. Assn. Balt. (past pres.), Govanstown Mchts. Assn. (rec. sec.), Highlandtown Mchts. Assn. (bd. dirs. 1980, pres. 1981, 1983—84, chmn. bd. dirs. 1982, 1984—85), Highlandtown Businessmen Assn., Bus. and Profl. Women's Club, Kiwanis. Republican. Christian Scientist. Died Aug. 17, 2000.

CAIN, SALLY H. federal agency administrator; m. David Cain. Edn. cons. NSF Tex. SSI Project; dir. edn. policy senate edn. com. Tex. State Senate; liaison for edn. cmty. to dept. U.S. Dept. Edn., sec.'s rep. region VI, 1993—. Office: 1999 Bryan St Ste 2700 Dallas TX 75201-6817

CAINE, VIRGINIA A. city health department administrator; BS, Gustavus Adolphus Coll., Minn., 1973; MD, N.Y. Upstate Med. Ctr., Syracuse. Resident U. Cin.; resident, infectious diseases U. Wash., Seattle; assoc. prof., medicine Ind. U. Sch. Medicine; dir. Marion Co. Health Dept., Indpls., 1993—. Mem., com. credentialing for pub. health workforce CDC, mem., bioterrorism and emergency preparedness com. Co-dir. Indpls. Campaign for Healthy Babies Initiative; bd. mem. Damien AIDS Ctr.; bd. mem., substance abuse Fairbanks Hosp.; bd. mem. Ind. AIDS Fund, Indpls. Alliance for Health Promotion, Ind. State Women's Health Com.; mem. Cmty. Drug Summit, Mayor's Commn. on Family Violence, City of Indpls. Mayor's Emergency Preparedness Task Force; mem. adv. bd. Women's Fund of Ctrl. Ind. Named one of Influential Women in Indpls., Indpls. Bus. Jour., The Ind. Lawyer; recipient Superstar award, Ind. AIDServe, 1998, Outstanding Svc. award, Indpls. Bus. Jour. Mem.: Ind. Pub. Health Assn., Nat. Med. Assn. (chair, infectious diseases, co-chair, AIDS sect., Internist of Yr. 1999), Nat. Assn. of County and City Health Officials, Am. Pub. Health Assn. (pres. 2004—, New Leadership award). Office: Marion Co Health Dept 3838 N Rural St Indianapolis IN 46205-2930

CAIRNS, ANNE MARIE, public relations executive; Pres. Cairns & Assocs., Inc., N.Y.C., 1982—. Office: Cairns & Assocs Inc 3 Park Ave 14th Fl New York NY 10016-5902

CAIRNS, SARA ALBERTSON, physical education educator; b. Bloomsburg, Pa., July 18, 1939; d. Robert Wilson and Sara (Porter) Albertson; m. Thomas Cairns, Apr. 13, 1968. BS in Edn., Pa. State U., 1961; MS in Edn., West Chester U., 1965. Cert. tchr., Pa., Del., prin., Del.; adaptive p.e. specialist. Phys. edn. tchr., coach Cen. Columbia County High Sch., Bloomsburg, Pa., 1961-64; phys. edn. tchr. Christina Sch. Dist., Newark, Del., 1964—, coord. adult edn., 1998—. Cons. U. Del., Newark, 1984—, coop. tchr., 1965—; area coord. New Castle (Del.) County Parks and Recreation, 1973—; presenter in field. Contbr. articles to profl. publs. Chair Leasure Elem. Sch. campaign United Fund, 1987-91. Recipient Outstanding Svc. award New CAstle County Parks and Recreation, 1985. Mem. NEA, AAUW, AAHPERD, Del. Assn. Health, Phys. Edn., Recreation and Dance (v.p. dance 1991-94, exec. bd.), Del. State Edn. Assn. Democrat. Presbyterian. Avocations: toy poodles, beach, walking. Home: 40 Vansant Rd Newark DE 19711-4839 Office: Leasure Elem Sch 1015 Church Rd Newark DE 19702-5102

CAKORA-NETZKY, LESLIE LYNN, photographer; b. Pekin, Ill., Aug. 24, 1960; d. Henry Joseph Cakora and Joy Christine Worman; m. Ric VanSickle, Oct. 19, 1991 (div. Feb. 1993); m. Barry Frank Netzky, Oct. 5, 1996; children: Mykah Skylar, Tasha Kayla. BS in Bus., We. Ill. U., 1982; postgrad., Columbia Coll., 1996—. Sales rep. assoc. Calvin Klein Activewear, Chgo., 1982—85; acct. coord. Prescriptives, 1985—87; freelance photo prop/set stylist & film stylist Chgo., 1997—98; freelance photographer, 1996—. Prop stylist Food Tales, 1989, Am. Girl Cookbooks and Craftsbooks, 1993; in solo and group exhbns. and permanent collecions. Mem.: Intiut Gallery, Mus. Contemporary Photography, Art Inst., Smart Mus., Photographic Soc., Mus. Contemporary Art, Women in Arts. Avocations: art, vintage costume jewelry. Home: 4118 Bordeaux Dr Northbrook IL 60062

CALABRESE, ROSALIE SUE, management consultant, writer; b. N.Y.C., Feb. 17, 1938; d. Julius and Florence (Tuck) Hochman; m. Anthony J. Calabrese, June 15, 1960 (div.); 1 child, Christopher. BA in Journalism, CCNY, 1959. Asst. news editor Electronic News, N.Y.C., 1960; asst. to publicist Abner Klipstein, N.Y.C., 1963; asst. to producer Leonard Field, N.Y.C., 1964; mgr. Am. Composers Alliance, N.Y.C., 1969-85, exec. dir., gen. mgr., 1985-94; dir. Rosalie Calabrese Mgmt., N.Y.C., 1983—. Music advisor Phyllis Rose Dance Co., N.Y.C., 1987—, also bd. dirs.; sec. bd. dirs. Am. Composers Orch., N.Y.C., 1987-93; pres., bd. dirs. 1st Ave. Ensemble, 1993—, Golden Fleece Ltd., 1994—; bd. dirs. Friends Am. Composers, treas., 1991-94; adv. bd. Downtown Music Prodns., 1991—, Joan Miller's Dance Players, N.Y.C., 1991-94, Copland House, 1996-97; mem. editl. adv. bd. New Music Connoisseur Mag., 2002-; mem. music com., Estate Project for Artists with AIDS, 2001-. Author, lyricist: (musicals) A Hell of An Angel, Simone, Not in Earnest, Murdering Macbeth, Pop Life, Does Anyone Here Speak Arabic?, Friends and Relations, Double-Play, C-R; assoc. prodr., treas. box office: (play) Courtyard, 1959, The Mime and Me; co-prodr.: various plays at White Lake (N.Y.) Playhouse, also packaged tours for Prodn. Assocs.; dir. The Bagel Baker's Daughter, 1999, night club acts for Florence Hayle; mem. editl. adv. bd. New Music Connoisseur Mag., 2002--; contbr. short stories and poetry to lit., nat. mags. and anthologies. Mem.: Poetry Soc. Am., Poets and Writers, Broadcast Music Inc., Dramatists Guild. Office: Rosalie Calabrese Mgmt PO Box 20580 New York NY 10025-1521

CALABRETTA, MARTI ANN, senator; b. Sandusky, Ohio, Dec. 14, 1940; d. Wilfred and Ida (Gerding) Beutler; m. Joseph Miller, Feb. 2, 1963 (div. Mar. 1976); m. Bennie G. Calabretta, Dec. 18, 1976; children: Joseph, Patrick, Rebecca, Debora, John, Ben, Lisa. Student, Case Western Res. U., 1961-63; BA, U. Utah, 1963, MSW, 1966; cert. mental health mgmt., U. Wash., 1981. Mental health specialist 4 Corners Mental Health Services, Moab, Utah, 1972-75, Idaho Mental Health Services, Coeur d'Alene, Idaho, 1975-81; sch. social worker Wallace (Idaho) Sch. Dist., 1981-85; state senator Boise, Idaho, 1984—. Pres. Valley Coordinating Corp., Kellogg, Idaho, 1982-86; mem. Pvt. Industry Council, Coeur d'Alene, 1984—, Idaho State Council on Developmental Disabilities, 1986—; vice chmn. Silver Valley Human Resources task force, Kellogg, 1982—. Mem. Idaho Edn. Assn. (del. 1983-84), Nat. Conf. State Legis. (health and welfare com.). Democrat. Episcopalian. Avocation: quilting. Home: Nuchols Gulch PO Box 784 Osburn ID 83849-0784

CALABRO, JOANNA JOAN SONDRA, artist; b. Waterbury, Conn., Dec. 2, 1938; d. Theodore Gruwien and Madeleine Elizabeth (Raynor) Reinhard; m. John Paul Calabro, Oct. 15, 1960; 1 child, Victor Theodore. Student, Paier Sch. Art, 1965-66, Mus. of Fine Arts Sch., 1976, Rice U., 1977; student of sculpture with, Bruno Lucchesi, Pietrasanta, Italy, 1982. Art instr. at gallery workshops, Houston, 1975-78; co-owner Archway Gallery, Houston, 1975-78, Fine Arts of Rockport, Mass., 1989—. One woman shows include Five Star Gallery, Houston, 1974-75, Roberts Gallery, Houston, 1977, Dayton (Ohio) Soc. of Painters, 1983, Wilmington (Ohio) Coll., 1983, Rockport Art Assn., 1989, 92; represented in permanent collections at Am. Embassy, Bratislava, Slovak Republic. Sculpture instr. for merit badge Sam Houston Area coun. Boy Scouts Am., Houston, 1978; juror for scholastic art shows, Tex., 1975, Ohio, 1982, numerous other art shows, Conn., Tex., Ohio, Mass., 1970—; mem. art coun. Bd. Selectmen, Rockport, 1994. Recipient numerous awards including 1st Place award Champions Art, 1974, Am. Pen & Brush Women, 1975, Conn. Classic Art, 1978, Martha Moore Meml. award, 1989, Richard Ricchia Meml. award, 1990, R.V. T. Steeves award, 1990, William N. Ryan award, 1991. Mem. Am. Artist Profl. League, Rockport Art Assn. (bd. dirs. 1992-93), Guild Boston Artists, The Copley Soc. of Boston, Am. Medallic Sculpture Assn., Federation Internat. de la Me'daille. Avocations: foreign travel, study of the arts. Studio: 32 Main St Rockport MA 01966-1532

CALABRO, SARA LOUISE, mental health therapist, consultant; b. Laredo, Tex., Sept. 11, 1966; d. Barry Alan and Patricia Louise (Hulse) Singleton; m. Gary Joseph Calabro, July 30, 1988 (div. June 1997); 1 child, Bethany Jordan. BA, U. Okla., 1988; MA, Nat. U., 1992. Lic. marital and family therapist, Tex., Okla.; master addictions counselor; cert. domestic violence counselor. Counselor Families First, Davis, Calif., 1990, Lighthouse Group Homes, Fairfield, Calif., 1990-91; marriage, family, child care counselor intern HIS Found., Vallejo, Calif., 1991-92, Vaca Valley CLC, Vacaville, Calif., 1994-95; clinician Peace River Ctr., Wauchula, Fla., 1995-96; case mgr. Tumbleweed Work Ctr., Altus, Okla., 1996-97; therapist Jackson COunty Meml Hosp. Counseling Ctr., Altus, 1997—. Cons. VVCLC Ch. Staff, Vacaville, 1994-95, Headstart, Wauchula, 1995-96; cons., case mgr. Tumbleweed Work Ctr., Altus, 1996-97; practitioner, cons. Jackson County Meml. Hosp., Altus, 1997—. Mem. Child Protection Team, Altus, 1997. Nat. U. scholar, 1990. Mem. Am. Assn. Marital and Family Therapy. Republican. Avocations: walking, shopping, reading, writing, playing piano. Office: 8104 Alderwood Dr Plano TX 75025-4030

CALAMAR, GLORIA, artist; b. N.Y.C., Sept. 7, 1921; d. Louis B. and Dina (Cotter) Calamar; m. R.L. Redgate, Aug. 22, 1950 (div. 1972); children: Chris James, Steven Clay, Michael Cotter. Cert., Otis Art Inst., L.A., 1943; student, Art Students League, N.Y.C., 1944-45; BA in Art History, State Univ. Coll. N.Y. at New Paltz, 1970. Instr. art history and painting Orange County (N.Y.) Community Coll., 1964-69; instr. art history Mt. St. Mary Coll., Newburgh, N.Y., 1968-69; instr. painting Santa Barbara City Coll., 1975-80. Judge Hallmark Art Contest, N.Y., 1968; lectr. Woodstock (N.Y.) Sch. Art, 1994; color slide lectr. throughout world. Artist in water color, oil, pen and ink, 1946—; one woman shows include Georgetown U., 1974, Portland (Oreg.) C.C., 1973, Willamette U., 1972, U. Oreg., 1971-72, U. Calif. at Berkeley, 1969, Santa Barbara (Calif.) Mus. Art, 1950, Musée d'Art Moderne de la Ville de Paris, 1967, Galèrie de la Madeleine, Brussels, Belgium, 1964, Landau Gallery, Beverly Hills, Calif., 1953, Parnassus Sq., Woodstock, N.Y., 1978, Ibiza, Balearic Islands, Spain, 1978, Santorini, Greece, 1980, Beaux Arts Ctr., Tunis, Tunisia, 1981, Alkamal Gallery, Jerusalem, Israel, 1981, Jaisalmer, India, 1984, Women's Cmty. Bldg., Santa Barbara, 1986, Jewish Cmty. Ctr., San Francisco, 1986; group shows include Delgado Mus., New Orleans, 1950, San Francisco Art Assn., 1953, L.A. County Mus. Art, 1954, Bertrand Russell Centenary Invitational, London, 1972-73, Woodstock Art Assn., 1978, Faulkner Gallery Santa Barbara, 1992, 93; curated Santa Barbara Visual Artists League Exhbn., 1993, 94; book, video Tar Pits Park Landmark Proposal, Portola Sycamore Tree Landmark Proposal, Carpinteria Airport Landmark

Proposal, Juarez-Hosmer Adobe Landmark Proposal, Leaping Greyhound Bridge Landmark Proposal, Los Clavelitos Landmark Proposal, Los Cruces Adobe Landmark Proposal, De la Cuesta Adobe Landmark Proposal; painted the facade of Wells Cathedral, 1999-00; producer video TV program; author: Traveling Artist, 1995; prodr. TV video series Traveling Artist; [illegible] prodn. (video) The Traveling Artist, 1996—. Curator Visual Artists League Exhbn., Santa Barbara, 1992, 93, 94, 95; mem. Santa Barbara County Hist. Landmark Adv. Commn. Nat. Endowment for Arts grantee, 1980-81; recipient Calif. Gov.'s Historic Preservation award Santa Barbara County Hist. Landmark Adv. Commn., 1999. Mem. Woodstock (N.Y.) Art Assn. (life), Alumni Assn. Otis Art Inst. (L.A.), Art Students League N.Y. (life), Santa Barbara Visual Artists League.

CALAME, KATHRYN LEE, microbiologist, educator; b. Leavenworth, Kans., Apr. 23, 1940; d. Jay O. and Marjorie B.; m. Byron Edward Calame, June 9, 1962; children: Christine Lee, Jonathan David. BS, U. Mo., 1962; MS, George Washington U., 1965, PhD, 1975. Asst. prof. biol. chemisty UCLA, 1980-85, assoc. prof., 1985-88, prof., 1988; prof. microbiology Coll. Physicians and Surgeons Columbia U., N.Y.C., 1988—. Mem. sci. rev. bd. Howard Hughes Med. Inst., 2002—. Exec. editor: Nucleic Acids Rsch., 1992-98; mem. bd. rev. editors: Sci. Mag., 1988-2000; assoc. editor Jour. Clin. Investigation; contbr. articles to profl. jours. Bd. trustees Leukemia Soc. Am., N.Y.C., 1992—, chair grant rev. com., 1992-96; bd. scientific counselors Nat. Inst. Child Health and Devel., 1999—. Recipient Stohlman award Leukemia Soc. Am., 1989, Faculty Alumni award U. Mo., Columbia, 1996; disting. lecture in basic sci., Columbia Physicians and Surgeons, 1998. Fellow: AAAS; mem.: Am. Acad. Arts & Sci., Am. Assn. Biochemistry and Molecular Biology (chair pub. com. 1992—93). Democrat. Avocations: cooking, gardening, reading, antiques. Office: Columbia U Dept Microbiology 701 W 168th St New York NY 10032-2704

CALDER, DIANE, artist, art educator, writer; d. William Macfarlane Calder and Elsie Barbara Koch; m. Alvin Christian Belsley, Sept. 21, 1957; children: Michael Scott Belsley, James Eric Belsley. BS in Edn., U. Ill., 1956; BA in Fine Arts, Calif. State U., Northridge, 1970, MA in Fine Arts, 1973; MFA in Art, Calif. Inst. Arts, 1989. Cert. tchr. grades K-12 Ill. Dir. arts and crafts George Williams Coll., Lake Geneva, Wis., 1965—72; instr. L.A. Pierce Coll., Winnetka, Calif., 1974—99; instr. internat. edn. program L.A. C.C., N.Y.C., 1975—93. Lectr. art Calif. State U., Northridge, 1986—99; writer, tour leader Kyoto Diary, L.A., 1994—2002, Kyoto and Tokyo, 1994—2002; writer, critic ArtScene, L.A., 1995—. Author: Mother Heard, 1975, Auntie Em, 1976; Exhibited in group shows at Eagle Rock Cultural Ctr., 1999, Contemporary Mus., Balt., 2000, P House Gallery, Tokyo, 2000, The Art Ctr., Art & Culture Found., Seoul, Republic Korea, 2001, Atelier Gym Gallery, Tokyo, 2001, ARC Gallery, Chgo., 2002, N.Y. Arts Gallery, 2003, others. Prodr. video on child care for pub. access TV The Woman's Bldg., L.A., 1987. Mem.: Internat. Assn. Art Critics (critic), Coll. Art Assn., Tree People. Unitarian. Avocation: gardening.

CALDERON, SILA M. governor; b. San Juan, Sept. 23, 1942; 3 children. B in polit. sci. with honors, Manhattanville Coll.; MPA, U. P.R. Worked for Sec. of Labor; spl. asst. econ. devel. and labor for Gov. Hernández Colón, 1974; chief of staff Gov. Hernández Colón, 1985, sec. interior, sec. state, 1988; mayor City of San Juan, 1996—2000; gov. PR, 2000—. Bd. dirs. Banco Popular P.R. Named Outstanding Woman of Yr., PR C. of C., 1975, 1985, 1987, Puerto Rican Products Assn., 1986, PR chpt. Am. Assn. Pub. Works, 1988. Mem.: Sister Isolina Ferré Found. Democrat. Office: Off de Gobierno Calle Fortaleza #52 PO Box 9020082 San Juan PR 00902-0082

CALDICOTT, HELEN, physician; b. Melbourne, Australia, Aug. 7, 1938; d. Philip and Mona (Coffey) Broinowski; m. William Caldicott; 3 children. MBBS, U. South Australia, 1962. Intern Royal Adelaide (Australia) Hosp., 1962-63; fellow in nutrition Children's Hosp. Med. Ctr., Boston, 1967-68; researcher Adelaide Children's Hosp., 1973-75; mem. faculty Harvard Med. Sch., 1975-80; pres. Physicians for Social Responsibility, 1978-83. Author: Nuclear Madness: What You Can Do!, 1979, Missile Envy: The Arms Race and Nuclear War, 1984. Fellow Royal Australian Coll. Physicians; mem. Women's Action for Nuclear Disarmament (founder).

CALDWELL, ANN WICKINS, academic administrator; b. Rochester, N.Y., Dec. 3, 1943; d. Ralph Everett and Constance Ann (McCoy) Wickins; m. Herbert Cline Caldwell, Sept. 17, 1966; children: Constance Haley Blacklow, Robert James. BA in English Lit., U. Mich., 1965. Reporter Democrat & Chronicle, Rochester, 1961-64; asst. to dean Harvard Grad. Sch. of Edn., Cambridge, Mass., 1965-70, editor alumni quarterly, 1968-71; freelance editor, writer Harvard U. and Radcliffe, Cambridge, 1971-73; assoc. sec. Phillips Acad., Andover, Mass., 1973—80; v.p. for planning and resources Wheaton Coll., Norton, Mass., 1980-90; assoc. dir. Mus. Fine Arts, Boston, 1990-91; v.p. for devel. Brown U., Providence, 1991-97; pres. MGH Inst. Health Professions, Boston, 1997—. Chair bicentennial com. Newburyport, Mass., 1974—76; citizens adv. com. Pub. Sch., Newburyport, 1979—80; bd. dirs. Am. Laryngological Voice Rsch. & Edn. Found.; trustee Women's Edn. and Indsl. Union, Boston, 1988—91, John Hope Settlement Ho., Providence, 1997—. Mem.: Women in Devel. Boston (founder, pres. 1984—86), Coun. for Advancement and Support of Edn. (trustee, sec. dist. 1 1985—87, trustee, sec. nat. 1987—89), Boston Club, Chilton Club, Phi Delta Kappa. Avocations: sailing, skiing, travel, reading. Office: Charlestown Navy Yard 36 First Ave Boston MA 02129-4724 E-mail: acaldwell@mghihp.edu.

CALDWELL, COURTNEY LYNN, lawyer, real estate consultant; b. Washington, D.C., Mar. 5, 1948; d. Joseph Morton and Moselle (Smith) Caldwell. Attended, Duke Univ., 1966-68, U. Calif., Berkeley, 1967, 1968-69; BA, U. Calif., Santa Barbara, 1970, MA, 1975; JD (hon.), George Washington Univ., 1982. Bar: D.C., 1984; Wash., 1986; Calif., 1989. Jud. clk. U.S. Ct. Appeals for 9th Cir., Seattle, 1982-83; assoc. Arnold and Porter, Washington, 1983-85, Perkins Coie, Seattle, 1985-88; dir. western ops. Edn. Real Estate Svc., Inc., Irvine, Calif., 1988-91, sr. v.p., 1991-98; ind. cons., Orange County, Calif., 1998—. Bd. dir. Univ. Town Ctr. Assn., 1994; bd. dir. Habitat for Humanity, Orange County, 1993-94, chair legal com., 1994. Named Nat. Law Ctr. Law Rev. scholar, 1981-82. Mem. Calif. Bar Assn. Avocation: fgn. languages. Home and Office: 140 Cabrillo St 15 Costa Mesa CA 92627 Personal E-mail: clcaldwell@earthlink.net.

CALDWELL, GAIL, book critic; b. Amarillo, Tex., Jan. 20, 1951; d. Bill M. and Ruby C. BA, U. Tex., 1978, MA in Am. Studies, 1980. Instr. U. Tex., Austin, to 1981; staff writer, critic Boston Globe, 1985—, book editor, 1992—95. Judge Radcliffe Bunting Fiction Fellowship; nominator Irish-Times/Aer Lingus Internat. Fiction Prize; mem. Pulitzer jury fiction, 1991 (chmn. of jury 1995 & 1997). Recipient Pulitzer Prize for criticism, 2001. Mem. PEN New Eng. (bd. dirs.), Nat. Book Critics Circle. Office: The Boston Globe PO Box 2378 135 Morrissey Blvd Boston MA 02125-3338*

CALDWELL, JUDY CAROL, advertising executive, public relations executive, consultant, writer, designer; b. Nashville, Dec. 28, 1946; d. Thomas and Sarah Elizabeth Carter; 1 child, Jessica. BS, Wayne State U., 1969. Tchr. Bailey Mid. Sch., West Haven, Conn., 1969-72; editorial asst. Vanderbilt U., Nashville, 1973-74; editor, graphics designer, field researcher Urban Observatory of Met. Nashville, 1974-77; account exec. Holden and Co., Nashville, 1977-79; bus. tchr. Federated States of Micronesia, 1979-80; dir. advt. Am. Assn. for State and Local History, Nashville, 1980-81; dir. prodn. Mktg. Communications Co., Nashville, 1981-83; ptnr. Victory Images of Tenn., Inc., Nashville, 1990-92; sr. tech. advisor UN, 2002; owner, pres., writer, designer Ridge Hill Corp., Nashville, 1983—. E-mail: ridgehillcorp@comcast.net.

CALDWELL, MARY ELLEN, English language educator; b. El Paso, Ark., Aug. 6, 1908; d. Clay and Mabel Grace (Coe) Fulks; m. Robert Atchison Caldwell, Feb. 22, 1936; 1 child, Elizabeth. PhB, U. Chgo., 1931, MA, 1933. Instr. English U. Ark., Fayetteville, 1940-42, U. Toledo, 1946-48; from instr. to asst. prof. to [illegible] Grand Forks, 1952-79, assoc. prof. emeritus, 1979—, prof. ext. divsn., 1979-2000. Author: North Dakota Division of the American Association of University Women, 1930-63, A History, 1964; co-author: The North Dakota Division of the American Association of University Women, 1964-84, 2d vol., 1984; contbr. revs. and articles to scholarly jours. Sec. citizen's com. Grand Forks Symphony Assn., 1960-66. Mem. AAUW (life, N.D. state pres. 1968-70), P.E.O., MLA (life), Soc. for Study of Midwestern Lit. (bibliography staff 1973-2002, MidAm. award for disting. contbns. to study of midwstern lit. 2000), Linguistic Cir. of Man. and N.D. (pres. 1981), Melville Soc. Democrat. Episcopalian. Home: 514 Oxford St Grand Forks ND 58203-2847

CALDWELL, NANCI, software company executive; b. Brockville, Can., Mar. 26, 1958; BA in Psychology, Queen's U.; diploma in Exec. Mktg. Mgmt. Program, U. We. Ont. With Xerox Corp.; from mem. staff to v.p. mktg. Hewlett Packard Co., 1982—2001, v.p. mktg. HP Svcs., 2001; sr. v.p, chief mktg. officer PeopleSoft Inc., Pleasonton, Calif., 2001—02, exec. v.p., 2002—, chief mktg. officer, 2002—. Office: PeopleSoft Inc 4460 Hacienda Dr Pleasanton CA 94588

CALDWELL, NAOMI RACHEL, library and information scientist, educator; b. Providence, Mar. 31, 1958; d. Atwood Alexander II and Juanita (Johnson) Caldwell; 1 child, William Earl Wood. BS, Clarion State Coll., 1980; MSLS, Clarion U. Pa., 1982; postgrad., Tex. A&M U., 1986-87, Providence Coll., 1990-92; PhD in Libr. and Info. Studies, U. Pitts., 2002. Cert. tchg. libr.; cert. libr. media specialist. Asst. dir., adult svcs. libr. Oil City (Pa.) Pub. Libr., 1984-85; microtext reference libr. Sterling C. Evans Libr., Tex. A&M U., College Station, 1985-87; libr. media specialist Nathan Bishop Mid. Sch., Providence, 1987-92; libr. sci. doctoral fellow dept. libr. sci. Sch. Libr. and Info. Sci. U. Pitts., 1992-94; sch. library media specialist Feinstein H.S. for Pub. Svc., Providence, 1994-99; asst. prof. U. R.I. Grad. Sch. Libr. Info. Studies, 2002—. Mem. discovery award com. U.S. Bd. on Books for Young People, 1994; mem. com. R.I. Children's Book Award, 1990—92, R.I. Read-Aloud, 1990—92; participant Native Am. and Alaskan Native Pre-Conf. to White House Conf. on Librs. and Info. Scis., Washington, 1991, George Washington U. Nat. Indian Policy Ctr. Forum on Native Am. Librs. and Info. Svcs., Washington, 1991; participant, del., spkr. Internat. Indigenous Librs. Forum, Auckland, New Zealand, 1999, Santa Fe, 2003; hon. del. White House Conf. on Libr. and Info. Svcs., Washington, 1991; bd. dirs. Ocean State Freenet; mem. exec. bd. R.I. Ednl. Media Assn., 1996—97; cons. Am. Coll. Testing, 1995—; mem. exec. bd. Native Am. child literacy program If I Can Read, I Can Do Anything, 2001—; mem. Coalition Libr. Advocates, 2002—; presenter in field; del., spkr. Internat. Indigenous Libr. Forum, Santa Fe, 2003. Mem. editl. adv. bd., reviewer : Multicultural Rev., 1991—; mem. adv. bd. Native Ams. Info. Dir., 1992, OYATE, 1992—, Gale Ency. Multicultural Am., Native N.Am. Ref. Libr.; mem. exec. bd.: OYATE, 2001—; reviewer Clarion Books, Greenwood Press, Random House, Harcourt Brace Trade Divsn., Browndeer Press, Oryx Press; contbr. articles to profl. jours. Mem. State of R.I. Libr. Bd., 1996-97, Spl. Presdl. Adv. Com. on Libr. of Congress, 1996-97; mem. nominating com. R.I. chpt. Girl Scouts of Am., 1998-99; enrolled mem. Ramapough Lenape Tribe. Mem.: ALA (councilor-at-large 1992—96, chmn. com. on status of women in librarianship 1995—97, nominating com. 1996—97, legis. assembly 1996—98, councilor-at-large 1996—2000, assembly on planning and budget 1998—99, presdl. task force spectrum program, com. on coms. 1999—2000, spectrum jury com. 2001—02, com. on diversity 2001—03, pres.'s adv.com. 2003—), R.I. Coalition of Libr. Advs. (sec. 2003), Native Am. N.E. Librs., Worcraft Cir. Native Writers and Storytellers, Windwalker Coalition, Libr. Adminstrn. Mgmt. Assn., Spl. Librs. Assn., Am. Assn. Sch. Librs., Am. Indian Libr. Assn. (new mems. round table publicity com. 1986, new mems. round table minority recruitment com. 1986—88, OLOS libr. svcs. for Am. Indian people subcom. 1986—88, ALCTS micropub. com. 1988—90, OLOS libr. svcs. for Am. Indian people subcom. 1990—91, pres. 1990—94, mem. coun. com. on minority concerns 1991—92, chmn. 1992—94, sec. 1994—96, mem. coun. com. on minority concerns 1994—96, book award task force 2002—03). Home: 475 Sowams Rd Barrington RI 02806-2745 Office: U RI Grad Sch Libr and Info Studies 11 Rodman Hall Kingston RI 02881 E-mail: inpeacencw@aol.com.

CALDWELL, SARAH, opera producer, conductor, stage director and administrator; b. Maryville, Mo., Mar. 6, 1924; Student, U. Ark., Hendrix Coll., New Eng. Conservatory, Berkshire Music Ctr., Tanglewood, Mass.; MusD (hon.), Harvard U., Simmons Coll., Bates Coll., Bowdoin Coll. Mem. faculty Berkshire Music Ctr.; dir. Boston U. Opera Workshop, 1953-57; created dept. music theater Boston U.; founded Boston Opera Group (later became Opera Co. of Boston), 1957, served as artistic dir. and condr., 1968—91; disting. prof. dept. music U. Ark., Fayetteville, 1999—. Asst. to Boris Goldovsky in direction of New Eng. Opera Co.; operatic directorial debut with Rake's Progress, Opera Workshop, 1953; operatic debut as condr. with Opera Group of Boston, 1957, Carnegie Hall debut with Am. Symphony Orch., 1974; condr. and/or dir. maj. opera cos. in U.S., including N.Y. Met. Opera, Dallas Civic Opera, Houston Grand Opera, N.Y.C. Opera; condr. with maj. orchs. including: Indpls. Symphony, Milw. Symphony, Am. Symphony, N.Y. Philharmonic; condr. at Ravinia Festival, 1976. Recipient Rogers and Hammerstein award. Achievements include 1st woman to appear as conductor with the Met. Opera, N.Y.C., 1976. Office: Univ Ark MB 201 Dept Music Fayetteville AR 72701 Address: 134 Pownal Road Freeport ME 04032

CALDWELL, SHIRLEY W. commissioner; b. Blairstown, Mo., June 23, 1935; BS, U. Mo. Owner, mgr. Lynch Line bookstore, 1990—; commr. Tex. State Hist. Commn., Austin, 1995—. Co-author: For 500 Years: The Shackelford County Courthouse. Chmn. Shackelford County Hist. Commn., 1972—79, Dallas County Hist. Commn., 1983—87. Mem.: Tex. State Hist. Assn. (pres.), Albany C. of C. (bd. dirs., Cornerstone award), Mortar Bd., Delta Delta Delta. Office: PO Box 12276 Austin TX 78711-2276

CALDWELL, TRACY ELLEN, surface chemist, researcher; b. Arcadia, Calif., Aug. 14, 1969; d. James and Mary Ellen C. BS, Calif. State U., Fullerton, 1993; PhD, U. Calif., Davis, 1997. Journeyman electrician J.C. Electric Co., Cherry Valley, Calif., 1987-92; environ. lab. asst. Rsch. and Instrml. Safety Office Calif. State U., Fullerton, 1990-93, rsch. asst. chemistry, 1991-93; tchg. asst. chemistry U. Calif., Davis, 1993-94, rsch. asst. chemistry, 1994-96, rsch. asst. physics, 1996-97, Camille and Henry Dreyfus postdoctoral fellow Irvine, 1997—; astronaut, 1998—. Contbr. articles to profl. jours. including Polyhedron, Jour. Am. Chem. Soc., Surface Sci., and Jour. Phys. Chemistry. Recipient NASA Superior Accomplishment Award, 2000, NASA Performance Award, 2001, 2003. Mem. Am. Chem. Soc., Am. Vacuum Soc. (Nellie Yeoh Whelton award 1996, Grad. Rsch. award 1996), Sigma Xi. Presbyterian. Achievements include mem. Russian Crusader Team, Office ISS Operations Branch, 1999; Crew Support Astronaut, 5th ISS Expedition crew, 2000. Office: NASA Johnson Space Ctr Astronaut Office Houston TX 77058*

CALDWELL, ZOE, actress, film director; b. Hawthorn, Victoria, Australia, Sept. 14, 1933; m. Robert Whitehead, 1968; 2 sons: Sam, Charlie. Attended, Meth. Ladies Coll., Melbourne, Australia. Dorothy F. Schmidt Vis. Eminent Scholar in Theatre, Fla. Atlantic U., 1989-93. Theater debut as mem. of Union Theatre Repertory Co., Melbourne, 1953; other appearances in The Madwoman of Chaillot, Goodman Theatre, Chgo., 1964, The Way of the World, The Caucasian Chalk Circle, Mpls., Slapstick Tragedy, N.Y.C., 1966 (Best Supporting Actress Tony award 1966), Antony and Cleopatra, Richard III, The Merry Wives of Windsor, Stratford, Ont., Can., Shakespeare Festival, 1967, The Prime of Miss Jean Brodie, 1967 (Best [illegible] Tony award 1968), Colette, N.Y.C., 1970, A Bequest to the Nation, London, 1970, The Creation of the World and Other Business, N.Y.C., 1972, Love and Master Will, Washington, 1973, The Dance of Death, N.Y.C., 1974, Long Day's Journey Into Night, N.Y.C., Washington, 1976, Medea, N.Y.C., 1982 (Best Actress Tony award), Lillian, 1986, Come A-Waltzing With Me, A Perfect Ganesh, 1993, Master Class, 1995 (Best Actress Tony award 1996); dir. (plays): An Almost Perfect Person, N.Y.C., 1977, Richard II, Stratford, Ont., 1979, These Men, off-Broadway, 1980, The Taming of the Shrew, Hamlet, Am. Shakespeare Theatre, 1985, Vita and Virginia, N.Y.C., 1995. Decorated Order Brit. Empire; recipient Theatre World award, 1966, John Gielgud award Shakespeare Guild/Folger Shakespeare Libr., 1998, Linda Wilson Lifetime Achievement award for Excellence in the Theatre U. Fla., 1998, Bernard B. Jacobs Excellence in the Theatre award/U.J.A. Fedn. N.Y., 1999, medal of distinction Barnard Coll., 1999. Address: Whitehead Stevens 1501 BroadwaySte 1614 New York NY 10036

CALDWELL-ANDREWS, ALISON AMELIA, psychologist, researcher; b. Provo, Utah, June 23, 1968; d. Nicholas Wayne Andrews and Anita Susanne Call; m. Ronald James Caldwell, June 19, 1999; children: Talia Nicole, Malachi Joshua; m. Charles Allen Kreutzkamp, June 25, 1988 (div. Jan. 31, 1994); 1 child, Charles Brandon. BS, Brigham Young U., 1990; MS, U. Ky., 1998, PhD, 2000. Lic. clin. psychologist Conn., 2002. Post doctoral fellow Sch. Medicine Yale U., New Haven, 2000—01, program mgr. rsch. Sch. Medicine, 2001—02, assoc. rsch. scientist Sch. Medicine, 2002—, program mgr. Yale Preoperative Anxiety Rsch. Group, 2002—. Contbr. articles to profl. jours. Avocations: music composing, writing, cooking, motherhood. Office: Yale University School Medicine TMP3 333 Cedar Street New Haven CT 06520

CALDWELL-SMITH, GAETANA LEE, writer; d. Ennis Combs Caldwell and Maria Esperanza Ilya-Salituri Sanchez Hill; children: Roark Smith, Terrence Smith, Douglas Smith. BA cum laude, San Francisco State U., 1994. Comml. ins. underwriter Fireman's Fund Ins. Co., San Francisco, 1978—84; account rep. Marsh & McLennan Ins. Co., San Francisco, 1984—97; theatre writer Socialist Action Newspaper, San Francisco, 1998—2002. Author: (solo performance plays) The Cynthia Trilogy: Part I, The Sign, 1996 (1st prize Dominican Players, San Rafael, Calif., 1998); actor: (solo perfornace) The Cynthia Trilogy: Part I, The Sign, 1996 (2nd prize Dominican Players, San Rafael, Calif., 1998). Mem.: Wild Plum (writer 2001—02), San Francisco Bay Area Theatre Critics Cir. (theatre writer 2001—02). Avocations: swimming, bicycling, hiking.

CALEGARI, MARIA, ballerina; b. N.Y.C., Mar. 30, 1957; d. Richard A. and Marion (Gentile) C. Student, DuPons Dance Studio, Queens, 1960-66, Ballet Acad., 1966-71, Sch. Am. Ballet, 1971-74. Mem. corps de ballet N.Y.C. Ballet, 1974-81, soloist, 1981-83, prin., 1983-94; guest artist Richmond Ballet, 1996—; artistic dir. dance Conn. Conservatory of the Performing Arts, New Milford, 2002—; artistic dir. The Maria Calegari Schl of Ballet, New Milford, Conn., 2003—. Artist-in-residence Richmond Ballet, Richmond Ctr. for Dance, State Ballet of Va., 1997—98, Conn. Cons. of Performing Arts, New Milford, 1999—. Dancer in N.Y.C. Ballet's Balanchine Celebration, 1993, Celebrating Balanchine, Kennedy Ctr., 1995. Repétiteur George Balanchine Trust. Recipient Alumni award Profl. Children's Sch., 1986. Address: 404 Richardsville Rd Carmel NY 10512-3771 E-mail: mcale50064@aol.com.

CALFEE, LAURA PICKETT, university administrator, photographer; b. Liberty, Tex., Oct. 30, 1952; d. Benjamin Ellis and Florence Ellen (Watson) Pickett; m. Gary Wayne Calfee, Dec. 21, 1981. BJ, U. Tex., 1979. Com. clk. Tex. Ho. of Reps., Austin, 1973-77; asst. to dir. Legis. Divsn. Ho. of Reps., Austin, 1977-83; com. coord. Tex. Ho. of Reps., Austin, 1983-87; spl. asst. for govtl. rels. Univ. Houston Sys., Austin, 1987-92, asst. vice chancellor, 1992—. Exec. prodr. Capitol Report, Sta. KUHT-TV, Houston, 1989—; moderator 1993. Co-author: (dance/theater) Chicken Tawk, performed at DIA Ctr. for Arts, N.Y.C., 1991; photographer: Gary's Best (hon. mention Best of Photography ann. 1992, Maria's Geese (hon. mention Best of Photography ann. 1994); permanent collections include Harry Ransom Humanities Rsch. Ctr. Photography Collection/U. Tex. at Austin, Tex. Midcontinent Oil and Gas Corp., Mus. Fine Art, Houston, Tex., Simon Gorsky Mus., Longview Mus. Art. Bd. dirs. Ctr. for Women and Their Work. Grantee: Tex. Hist. Commn., 1992-93; recipient Hon. Mention award Phoenix Gallery Ann. Juried Competition, 1994, State of the Art Nat. Juried Competition, 1994, State of the Art Nat. Juried Competition, Ithaca, N.Y., 1995, Grand award Govtl. Rels. Program, Coun. for Advancement and Support of Edn., Region IV, 1995, Santa Fe Workshops Project Competition, 1st pl./2d pl. Viewpoint 96 Bosque County Conservatory of Fine Art Competition, 1996, Best of Show award Gov.'s Exhbn., 1996. Mem. Tex. Fine Arts Assn., Tex. Photog. Soc. (bd. dirs.), Laguna Gloria Art Mus. Avocations: reading, gardening, golf, travel. Home: 19001 Fm 1826 Driftwood TX 78619-4201 Office: U Houston System 1005 Congress Ave Ste 820 Austin TX 78701-2487

CALHOUN, NANCY, state legislator; b. Suffern, N.Y., July 10, 1944; d. Andrew Felix and Paula Mathilda (Kusmitsch) Coleman; children: Richard, Kathy Calhoun Wells, Glenn. Student, Empire State Coll., 1981-84. Tax collector Washingtonville (N.Y.) Sch. Dist., 1976-84; adminstrv. aide Office of the Assessor, Town of Blooming Grove, 1978-81; mem. Council, Town of Blooming Grove, 1982-85, supr., 1986-90; assemblywoman N.Y. State Assembly, Albany, 1991—. State committeewoman N.Y. State Rep. Com., 1985-91. Named Citizen of Yr., Monell Engine Co., 1988. Office: 2011 D St Bldg 740 New Windsor NY 12553-8475

CALHOUN, RAMONA, human services administrator, academic administrator, consultant; b. Akron, Ohio, Sept. 2, 1950; d. Howell and Rebecca (Hammonds) C.; m. William J. Webb, Sept. 1969 (div. 1973); 1 child, Forrest J. Webb. BS, U. Akron, 1980; MS, SUNY, Oswego, 1988; PhD, Walden U., 2001. Sales corr./sec. Monsanto Co., Akron, Ohio, 1973-77; student instr./career guide U. Akron; instr. SUNY Delhi Coll., Delhi, 1980-82; Dept. chair-bus. SUNY Morrisville Edn. Opportunity Ctr., Syracuse, 1983-88; dir. program opns., Job Tng. Partnership Agy. City of Syracuse, 1988—91; dir., student svcs, grants Ivy Tech State Coll., 1991—95; acad. dir. Ctr. Ohio Tech Coll. Artist charcoal sketch Portrait in Bronze (Best of Show, 1990); writer-poet Rain Dance, 1979; contbr. poetry to African Am. Jour. Bd. dirs. YWCA of Syracuse and Onandaga, 1990-92, City/County Youth Bd., 1989-91; com. mem. N.Y. State Task Force on the Older Worker, Albany, 1990-91, N.Y. State Task Force for Career Pathways for Youth. Recipient Leadership award, SUNY Oswego, 1988. Mem. N.Y. Assn. Tng. and Employment Profls., Partnership for Employment and Tng. Avocations: reading, writing (short stories, poetry, novels), painting.

CALINESCU, ADRIANA GABRIELA, museum curator, art historian; b. Bucharest, Romania, Dec. 30, 1941; came to U.S., 1973; d. Nicolae and Tamara Gane; m. Matei Alexe Calinescu, Apr. 29, 1963; children: Irena, Matthew. BA, Cen. Lycée, Bucharest, 1959; MA in English, U. Bucharest, 1964; MLS, Ind. U., 1976, MA in Art History, 1983. Asst. prof. Inst. Theater and Cinema, Bucharest, 1967-73; rsch. assoc. Ind. U. Art Mus., Bloomington, 1979-83, Thomas T. Solley curator ancient art, assoc. scholar, 1992—. Vis. assoc. mem. Am. Sch. Classical Studies, Athens, Greece, 1984. Author: The Art of Ancient Jewelry, 1994; author, co-editor: Ancient Art from the V. G. Simkhovitch Collection, 1988; editor: Ancient Jewelry and Archaeology,

1996. NEA fellow, 1984; grantee Salzburg Seminar, 1970, NEA, 1987, 93, Kress Found., 1991, Internat. Rsch. and Exchanges Bd., 1991. Mem. Am. Inst. Archaeology, Classical Art Soc., Beta Phi Mu. Office: Ind U Art Mus E 7th St Bloomington IN 47405

CALISHER, HORTENSE (MRS. CURTIS HARNACK), writer; b. N.Y.C., Dec. 20, 1911; d. Joseph Henry and Hedvig (Lichtstern) C.; m. Curtis Harnack, Mar. 23, 1959; children by previous marriage: Bennet Hughes, Peter Heffelfinger. AB, Barnard Coll., 1932; LittD (hon.), Skidmore Coll., 1980, Grinnell Coll., 1986; LittD, Adelphi U., 1988. Adj. prof. English Barnard Coll., N.Y.C., 1956-57. Vis. lectr. State U. Iowa, 1957, 59-60, Stanford U., 1958, Sarah Lawrence Coll., Bronxville, N.Y., 1962, 67; adj. prof. Columbia U., N.Y.C., 1968-70, CCNY, 1969; vis. prof. lit. SUNY, Purchase, 1971-72, Brandeis U., 1963-64, U. Pa., 1965; Regent's prof. U. Calif., 1976; vis. prof. Bennington Coll., 1978, Washington U., St. Louis, 1979, Brown U., spring 1986; lectr., Fed. Republic of Germany, Yugoslavia, Rumania, Hungary, 1978; guest lectr. U.S./China Arts Exch., Republic of China, 1986. Author: (novels) False Entry, 1961, Textures of Life, 1962, The New Yorkers, 1969, Journal from Ellipsia, 1965, Queenie, 1971, Standard Dreaming, 1972, Eagle Eye, 1973, On Keeping Women, 1977, Mysteries of Motion, 1984, The Bobby-Soxer, 1986 (Kafka prize U. Rochester 1987), Age, 1987, (under pseudonym Jack Fenno) The Small Bang, 1992, In the Palace of the Movie-King, 1994, In the Slammer with Carol Smith, 1997; (novellas) The Railway Police, 1966, The Last Trolley Ride, 1966; short stories include In The Absence of Angels, 1951, Tale for the Mirror, 1962, Extreme Magic, 1963, Collected Stories, 1975, Saratoga Hot, 1985; autobiography: Herself, 1972; memoir: Kissing Cousins, 1988; contbr. short stories, articles, revs. to Am. Scholar, N.Y. Times, Harpers, Yale Rev., New Criterion, others. Guggenheim fellow, 1952, 55; Dept. of State Am. Specialists's grantee to S.E. Asia, 1958; recipient Acad. of Arts and Letters award, 1967, Nat. Council Arts award, 1967, Lifetime Achievement award Nat. Endowment for the Arts, 1989. Mem. Am. Acad. Arts and Letters (pres. 1987-90), PEN (pres. 1986-87). Office: 365 5th Ave #5406 New York NY 10016-4309*

CALKINS, SUSAN W. state supreme court justice; Grad., U. Colo.; JD, U. Maine. Staff atty., exec. dir. Pine Tree Legal Assistance; judge Maine Dist. Ct., 1980-90, chief judge, 1990—94; judge Maine Superior Ct., 1995—98; justice Maine Supreme Jud. Ct., 1998—. Office: Maine Judicial Center 65 Stone St Augusta ME 04330

CALKINS, SUSANNAH EBY, retired economist; b. Bucyrus, Ohio, Jan. 16, 1924; d. Samuel L. and Mae (McClure) Eby; m. G. Nathan Calkins, Nov. 19, 1949 (dec.); children: Helen E. (dec.), Margaret S. Van Auken, Sarah A. (dec.), Abigail Calkins Aguirre. AB, Goucher Coll., 1945; MS in Econs. (Univ. scholar 1946-47), U. Wis., 1947. Fiscal analyst U.S. Bur. Budget, 1945-50; economist U.S. Council Econ. Advisors, 1950-51, U.S. Office Price Stabilization, 1951-53, U.S. Bur. Budget, 1953-55; cons. U.S. Adv. Commn. on Intergovtl. Rels., Washington, 1972-73, 74-75, cons. on counter-cyclical aid programs, 1977-78, sr. analyst, 1979-87, exec. asst. to dir., 1987-89. Cons. revenue sharing Brookings Instn., Washington, 1973-74. Author: (with R. Nathan and A. Manvel) Monitoring Revenue Sharing, 1975. Sponsor S.S. Goucher Victory, Balt., 1945; bd. dirs. Bread for the City, 1994-2002. Mem. Am. Econs. Assn., George Towne Club (Washington), Phi Beta Kappa. Presbyterian. Home: 6504 Dearborn Dr Falls Church VA 22044-1115

CALL, DENISE HODGINS, curator, artist, freelance/self-employed writer; b. Philadelphia, Pa., Oct. 27, 1942; d. James Francis Hodgins and Catherine C. Whitney-Lear; m. Stephen M. Call, Jan. 22, 1994; m. Edward J. Gilhooly, July 16, 1966 (div.); children: Caitlyn Gilhooly Parker, Mairin Gilhooly Kuligowski, Edward J. Gilhooly, III, Bevin J. Gilhooly. BA in English with honors, Cabrini Coll., 1960—64; Grad. studies, University of Pa., 1964—66. Assoc. curator NJ. Ctr. for Visual Arts, Summit, NJ, 2000—; artist and freelance writer DHC Enterprises, Morristown, NJ, 1998—; jet fuel sales Exxon Co. Internat., Florham Park, NJ, 1988—87; v.p. of mktg. BA Internat., Morristown, NJ, 1984—86; tchr. of english Marylawn of the Oranges, South Orange, NJ, 1978—80; reader svc. editor Chilton Co./Food Engrng., Philadelphia, Pa., 1960—66. Dir. Artemis Group, Morristown, NJ, 1990—98. Mem.: Somerset Art Assn. Avocations: cross country skiing, hiking. Home: 20 Raven Dr Morristown NJ 07960 Office: New Jersey Center for Visual Arts 68 Elm St Summit NJ 07901 Personal E-mail: dhcall@aol.com.

CALLAGHAN, GEORGANN MARY, lawyer; b. Bklyn., June 25, 1944; d. George Louis and Jean (Russo) Carpenito; m. Matthew John Callaghan, June 7, 1969; children: Matthew, Michael, Christian. BS in Hist. Studies, SUNY Empire State Coll., 1994; JD, Pace U., 1999. Bar: Conn. 1999, N.Y. 2000, D.C. 2000. Adminstr. Wood & Scher, Scarsdale, 1986—99, atty., 1999—2001; assoc. Colucci & Umans, 2001—. Exec. com. Boy Scouts Am. Mem. ABA, N.Y. State Bar Assn., Westchester County Bar Assn., Conn. Bar Assn., D.C. Bar Assn., Westchester Women's Bar Assn., Scarsdale Town and Village Club. Home: 49 Carman Rd Scarsdale NY 10583-6328 Office: Colucci & Umans 670 White Plains Rd Scarsdale NY 10583

CALLAHAN, CHRISTINE H. state legislator; b. N.Y.C., Oct. 19, 1944; divorced; children: Mary, James. AA, Centenary Coll., 1964; BS, U. R.I., 1989. Mem. R.I. Ho. of Reps., Providence, 1986—, mem. fin. com., joint com. on small bus. Acct. R.I. Philharmonic Orch. Home: 5 Cedar St Middletown RI 02842-5305 Office: RI House of Reps State House Rm 106 Providence RI 02903

CALLAHAN, CONSUELO MARIA, federal judge; b. Palo Alto, Calif., June 9, 1950; married; 2 children. BA, Leland Stanford Jr. Univ., 1968—72; JD, McGeorge Sch. of Law, Univ. of the Pacific, 1972—75; grad LLM, Univ. of Va. Sch. of Law, 2002—. Bar: Calif. 1975. Dep. city atty. City of Stockton, Stockton, Calif., 1975—76; dep. dist. atty. Dist. Atty. Office, San Joaquin County, Calif., 1976—82, sup. dist. atty., 1982—86; ct. comm. Mcpl. Ct. of Stockton, Stockton, Calif., 1986—92; judge San Joaquin County Superior Ct., San Joaquin, Calif., 1992—96; Assoc. judge Ct. of Appeal, State of Calif., Calif., 1996—2003; judge, U.S. Court of Appeals (9th. cir.), 2003—. Recipient Award for Criminal Justice Programs, Gov., Susan B. Anthony Award for Women of Achievement, Stockton Peacemaker of the Yr., 1997, Mexican-Am. Hall of Fame, San Joaquin County, 1999. Office: US Ct Appeals 95 Seventh St San Francisco CA 94103

CALLAHAN, DEBRA JEAN, professional society administrator; b. Burbank, Calif., June 4, 1958; d. Robert Bascom and Betty Jean Callahan; m. Kenneth A. Cook. Student, Calif. State Poly. U., San Luis Obispo, 1976-79; BA magna cum laude, U. Calif., Santa Barbara, 1981. Legal asst. Loo, Merideth & McMillan, L.A., 1982-83; field staff Mondale for Pres., Washington, 1984; dep. state campaign mgr. Mondale-Ferraro Com., Kansas City, Mo., 1984; regional polit. dir. League of Conservation Voters, Portsmouth, N.H., 1985-86; dep. campaign mgr. Kent Conrad for U.S. Senate, Bismarck, N.D., 1986; exec. asst. to Senator Kent Conrad, Washington, 1986-87; dep. nat. polit. dir. Gore for Pres., Washington, 1987-88; exec. dir. Ams. for the Environment, Washington, 1988-90; campaign mgr. Re-election Rep. Howard Wolpe (D-Md.), 1990; policy cons. Nat. Toxics Campaign, 1991—; program dir. W. Alton Jones Found., 1992-95; exec. dir. Brainerd Found., Seattle, 1995-96; pres. League of Conservation Voters, Washington, 1996—. Polit. cons. League of Conservation Voters, 1988. Field dir. Hands Across Am., St. Louis, 1986; bd. dirs. World Resources Inst., 1998—, Earth Day Network, 1999-2003. U. Calif. Dept. Environ. Studies scholar, Santa Barbara, 1981, Alumni award, 1998. Avocations: travel, reading, scuba diving, cycling, music. Office: League of Conservation Voters 1920 L St NW Ste 800 Washington DC 20036-5045

CALLAHAN, JEAN M. personnel administrator; d. John Martin Hildebrandt and Catherine Mary Dore; m. Gerald Francis Callahan, July 11, 1969; 1 child, Christopher. BS, CUNY, 1967, MEd, 1969; MA in Labor Studies, SUNY, 1981; MS in Spl. Edn., Adelphi U., N.Y., 1983; diploma in adminstrn., Long Island U. CW Post, N.Y., 1989. Cert. home and careers, elem. edn. and spl. edn. N.Y. Tchr. home and careers various schs., Long Island, NY, 1971—83; consumer tchr. Ea. Suffolk Bd. Cooperative Svcs. Edn., Long Island, NY, 1985; spl. edn. tchr. Miller (N.Y.) Pl. Union Free Sch. Dist., 1985—96, adminstr. pupil personnel adminstr., 1994—. Chairperson spl. edn. Miller (N.Y.) Pl. Union Free Sch. Dist., 1994—96; ednl. cons. ACCES Partnerships, Long Island, NY, 1993—96, N.Y. Dirs. Com., 2001—. Mem.: Coun. Exceptional Children, Coun. Adminstrs. Spl. Edn. (Long Island Chpt.) (treas. 2000—). Avocations: fitness, swimming, reading. Office: Miller Pl Union Free Sch Dist 275 Rte 25A Miller Place NY 11764 E-mail: jcallaha@millerplace.k12.ny.us.

CALLAHAN, JENNIFER, state legislator, education educator; BA, BS, Boston U.; MS, U. Mass.; EdD, U. Mass. State rep. Mass. House, 2003—. Bd. dirs. Blackstone Valley C. of C.; mem. Blackstone Valley Vocational Regional Sch. Dist. Edn. Found., Ctrl. Mass. Labor Coun.; founding dir. Hunger Relief Program. Mem.: Mass Nurses Assn., Am. Bus. Womens Assn. (former v.p.). Democrat. Office: Rm 437 Mass House Boston MA 02133

CALLAHAN, PATRICIA R. bank executive; BSME, MIT; M of Mgmt. and Fin. Various mgmt. positions Crocker Nat. Bank, 1977—84, sr. v.p., mgr. corp. svcs., 1984—93; dir. human resources Wells Fargo & Co., 1993—97, exec. v.p. wholesale banking, 1997—98, exec. v.p., 1998, exec. v.p., dir. human resources, 1998—. Office: Wells Fargo & Co 420 Montgomery St San Francisco CA 94163

CALLAHAN, SUSAN JANE WHITNEY, accountant; b. Salt Lake City, Dec. 2, 1950; d. Nathaniel R. Jr. and Mary Jeanette (Schroeder) Whitney. BS in Acctg. and Bus. Adminstrn., Black Hills State U., Spearfish, S.D., 1973. Agt. IRS, Rapid City, S.D., 1979—. Pres., bd. dirs. Black Hills Chamber Music Soc., Rapid City, 1992—; active First Presbyn. Ch. Rapid City. Named Civil Servant of Yr., Fed. Exec. Bd. Minn., 1999. Mem. AAUW. Avocations: music, snow skiing. Home: 4925 Raven Cir Rapid City SD 57702-9018

CALLAN, JOSI IRENE, museum director; b. Yorkshire, Eng., Jan. 30, 1946; came to U.S., 1953; d. Roger Bradshaw and Irene (Newbury) Winstanley; children: James, Heather, Brett Jack; m. Patrick Marc Callan, June 26, 1984. BA in Art History summa cum laude, Calif. State U., Domingues Hills, 1978, MA in Behavioral Scis., 1981. Dir. community rels./alumni affairs Calif. State U., Dominguez Hills, adminstrv. fellow office chancellor Long Beach, assoc. dir. univ. svcs. office chancellor, 1979-85; dir. capital campaign, assoc. dir. devel. Sta. KVIE-TV, Sacramento, 1985-86; dir. project devel. Pacific Mountain Network, Denver, 1986-87; dir. mktg. and devel. Denver Symphony Orch., 1988-89; assoc. dir. San Jose (Calif.) Mus. Art, 1989-91, dir., 1991-99, Mus. of Glass, Tacoma, Wash., 1999—. Asst. prof. sch. social and behavioral scis. Calif. State U., Dominguez Hills, 1981—, mem. adv. com. Issues Facing Mus. in 1990s JKF U., 1990-91. Mem. com. arts policy Santa Clara Arts Coun., 1990-92; chair San Jose Arts Roundtable, 1992-93; active ArtTable, 1992—, Community Leadership San Jose, 1992-93, Am. Leadership Forum, 1994, bd. dirs., 2000—; mem. adv. bd. Bay Area Rsch. Project, 1992—; mem. Calif. Arts Coun., Visual Arts Panel, 1993-95, Santa Clara Arts Coun. Visual Arts Panel, 1993; bd. dirs. YWCA, 1993—. Recipient Leadership award Knight Found., 1995; Women of Vision honoree Career Action Ctr., 1998; fellow Calif. State U., 1982-83. Mem. AAUW, Am. Assn. Mus., Nat. Soc. Fund Raising Execs. (bd. dirs. 1991), Colo. Assn. Fund Raisers, Art Mus. Devel. Assn., Assn. Art Mus. Dirs., We. Mus. Assn., Calif. State U. Alumni Coun. (pres. 1981-83), Rotary Internat. Office: Museum of Glass 1801 E Dock St Tacoma WA 98402-3217

CALLANDER, KAY EILEEN PAISLEY, business owner, retired education educator, writer; b. Coshocton, Ohio, Oct. 15, 1938; d. Dalton Olas and Dorothy Pauline (Davis) Paisley; m. Don Larry Callander, Nov. 18, 1977. BSE, Muskingum Coll., 1960; MA in Speech Edn., Ohio State U., 1964, postgrad., 1964-84. Cert. elem., gifted, drama, theater tchr., Ohio. Tchr. Columbus (Ohio) Pub. Schs., 1960-70, 80-88, drama specialist, 1970-80, classroom, gifted/talented tchr., 1986-90, ret., 1990; sole prop. The Ali Group, Kay Kards, 1992—. Coord. Artists-in-the Schs., 1977-88; ednl. cons. Innovation Alliance Youth Adv. Coun., 1992—; cons., presenter in field, Producer-dir., Shady Lane Music Festival, 1980-88; dir. tchr. (nat. distbr. video) The Trial of Gold E. Locks, 1983-84; rep., media pub. relations liason Sch. News., 1983-88; author, creator Trivia Game About Black Americans; presenter for workshop by Human Svc. Group and Creative Edn. Coop., Columbus, Ohio, 1989. Benefactor, Columbus Jazz Arts Group; v.p., bd. dirs. Neoteric Dance and Theater Co., Columbus, 1985-87; tchr., participant Future Stars sculpture exhibit, Ft. Hayes Ctr., Columbus Pub. Schs., 1988; tchr. advisor Columbus Coun. PTAs, 1983-86, co-chmn. reflections com., 1984-87; mem. Columbus Mus. Art, Citizens for Humane Action, Inc.; upt.'s adv. coun. Columbus Pub. Schs., 1967-68; presenter Young Author Seminar, Ohio Dept. Edn., 1988, Illustrating Methods for Young Authors' Books, 1986-87; cons. and workshop leader seminar/workshop Tchg. About the Constitution in Elem. Schs., Franklin County Ednl. Coun., 1988; sponsor Minority Youth Recognition Awards, 1994. Named Educator of Yr., Shady Lane PTA, 1982, Columbus Coun. PTAs, 1989, winner Colour Columbus Landscape Design Competition, 1990; Sch. Excellence grantee Columbus Pub. Schs.; Commendation Columbus Bd. Edn. and Ohio Ho. of Reps. for Child Assault Prevention project, 1986-87; first place winner statewide photo contest Ohio Vet. Assn., 1991; recipient Muskingum Coll. Alumni Disting. Svc. award, 1995. Mem. ASCD, AAUW, Assn. for Childhood Edn. Internat., Ohio Coun. for Social Studies, Franklin County Ret. Tchrs. Assn., Nat. Mus. Women in the Arts, Ohio State U. Alumni Assn., U.S. Army Officers Club, Navy League, Liturgical Art Guild Ohio, Columbus Jazz Arts Group, Columbus Mus. Art, Nat. Coun. for Social Studies, Columbus Art League, Columbus Maennerchor (Damen sect.). Republican. Avocations: painting, photography, swimming, golfing, playing piano and organ. Home: 9131 Indian Mound Rd Pickerington OH 43147 Personal E-mail: pais16091@aol.com.

CALLARD, CAROLE CRAWFORD, librarian, educator; b. Charleston, W.Va., Aug. 8, 1941; d. William O. and Helen (Shay) Crawford; children: Susan Lynne, Annie Laurie. BA in Am. History, U. Charleston, 1963; MLS, U. Pitts., 1966; MA in Social Founds., Ea. Mich. U., 1978; grad., Nat. Inst. for Geneal. Rsch., 1997. Tchr. Blessed Sacrament Sch., South Charleston, W.Va., 1962-64; grad. trainee W.Va. Libr. Commn., Charleston, 1964-65; reference libr. Tompkins County Pub. Libr., Ithaca, N.Y., 1966-69; head libr. U.S. Embassy, Addis Ababa, Ethiopia, 1969-70; head govt. documents Haile Sellassie U., Addis Ababa, 1970-71; br. libr. Ann Arbor (Mich.) Pub. Libr., 1973-83; documents libr. U. Mich., Ann Arbor, 1983-84; pub. svcs. supr. Libr. of Mich., Lansing, 1984-95; depository libr. inspector Govt. Printing Office, 1995-96; libr. Allen Co. Pub. Libr., Ft. Wayne, Ind., 1996-97; specialist Libr. of Mich., Lansing, 1997—; instr. Nat. Inst. for Geneal. Rsch., 1999. Chair around the world, around the campus U. Mich. Faculty Women's Club, Ann Arbor, 1974-76; tchr. genealogy Holt Pub. Schs., Okemos Pub. Schs., 1990-92, Lansing Cmty. Schs., 2000, Washtenaw C.C., 1992-94; judge Mich. history Day, 1991, 93, 94; genealogy chair Abrams Found., 1997—; adj. prof. libr. info. sci. Wayne State U., Mich., 2003-. Author: Index to 150th Anniversary Issue Ithaca Jour., 1967, Guide to Local History, Sources in the Huron Valley, 1980; editor: Sourcebook of Michigan, 1986, Michigan Cemetery Atlas, 1991, Michigan 1870 Census Index, 1991-95, Michigan Cemetery Sourcebook, 1994, Government Documents for Genealogists Historians and Archivists, 1998; column editor Mich. History Mag. and Chronicle; contbr. articles to profl. jours. Membership chair LWV, Ann Arbor; v.p. Geneal. Soc. Washtenaw County, Mich., 1993, pres., 1993-94; v.p. Palatines to Am., 1987-90, Washtenaw Libr. Club, 1982-83; pres. Libr. Staff Assn., Lansing, 1985-86; pres. Govt. Documents Roundtable of Mich., pres., 1992-93; pres. Mich. Data Base Users Group, 1992-93; chmn. book sale Friends of Ann Arbor Pub. Libr. Recipient Notable Document award Govt. Documents Roundtable of Mich., 1991, Paul Thurston Documents award Govt. Documents Roundtable of Mich., 1993, Cert. of Merit Assn. State and Local History, 1995, Mich. Geneal. Coun., Libr. of Mich. Found. and Abrams Found. award, 1996, P. William Filby award for genealogy librarianship, 2003; grantee U. Pitts., 1966, prof. staff grantee Ann Arbor Pub. Schs., 1980, edn. found. grantee Mich. Libr. Assn., 1982. Mem. ALA (Godort state and local documents com., mem. genealogy com. 2000—, instr. genealogy pre-conf. 2001, 02, mem. local history com. 2002-, chmn. genealogy pre-conf. 2003—), AAUW (corr. sec., historian 1973-74, 82-83), DAR (corr. sec. Lansing chpt., 2002-03, libr., 2004—, Sarah Angell Caswell chpt. chair, registrar CAR Seimes Microfilm), Children of Am. Revolution, Internat. Soc. Brit. Genealogy (trustee 1994-96), Mich. Libr. Assn. (chmn. govt. documents sect. 1982-84, leadership acad. 1991-93), Spl. Librs. Assn., D.C. Libr. Assn., Va. Libr. Assn., Fedn. Genealogy Socs. (del., corr. sec. 1986-87, v.p. regional affairs 1989-92), Nat. Genealogy Soc. (instr. devel. com. 1988-90, chmn. instns. com. 1992—, archives and libr. com. 1993-94, P. William Filby award 2003), Mich. Geneal. Coun. (ofcl. good will ambassador 1995-), Mid-Mich. Genealogy Soc. (pres. 2003—, v.p. 2002-03, pres. 2003—), Beta Phi Mu. Avocations: storytelling, reading, travel, genealogy. E-mail: ccallard@michigan.gov.

CALLAWAY, JULIENNE MORRISS, financial consultant; b. N.Y.C., May 31, 1965; d. John Michael and Judy (Mauser) Morriss; m. John Patrick Callaway, Nov. 4, 1995; children: James Michael, Emeline Hanna, Madeleine Judy. BA, Georgetown U., 1987; MBA, Columbia U., 1993. Cert. CFA. Paralegal Davis Polk & Wardwell, N.Y.C., 1987—90; assoc. Taylor Rafferty Assoc., N.Y.C., 1990—91, Brown Bros. Harriman & Co., N.Y.C., 1993—94; equity rsch. Morgan Stanley & Co., Inc., N.Y.C., 1994—96; risk mgr. G.E. Capital Corp., Stamford, Conn., 1996—99; ret., 1999. Mem.: Georgetown U. Alumni Assn. (comm. chmn. 1997).

CALLAWAY, KAREN A(LICE), journalist; b. Daytona Beach, Fla., Sept. 5, 1946; d. Robert Clayton III and Alice Johnston (Webb) Callaway. BS in Journalism, Northwestern U., 1968. Copy editor Detroit Free Press, 1968-69; asst. woman's editor, features copy editor, news copy editor, asst. makeup editor Chgo. Am. and Chgo. Today, 1969-74; asst. makeup editor Chgo. Tribune, 1974-76, asst. news editor, 1976-81, assoc. news editor spl. sect., 1981-2000, assoc. news editor vertical publs., 1993-2000, asst. news editor spl. sect., 2000—. Adviser Jr. Achievement Tribune sponsored co., Chgo., 1976—77; editor Infant Mortality sect., 1989; vis. prof. student chpt. Soc. Profl. Journalists, Northwestern U., 1989. Chmn. Class of 1968 20th reunion Northwestern U., Evanston, Ill., 1989, seminar day com., 1989—90, chmn., 1991; alumni bd. Medill Sch. Journalism, Evanston, Ill., 1991—99, Northwestern U. Settlement Assn., Chgo. Mem.: Soc. Profl. Journalists, Chgo. Headline Club, Kappa Delta. Methodist. Avocations: swimming, cooking, travel. Office: Chicago Tribune 435 N Michigan Ave Ste 500 Chicago IL 60611-4041 Office Phone: 312-222-3515.

CALLAWAY, LINDA MARIE, special education educator; b. Upland, Calif., June 21, 1940; d. Elwyn T. and Fladger Idell (Flake) Bice; m. David Barry Callaway, May, 1957 (div. sept. 1962); children: Tess Callaway Tyler, Darren Francis. B in English, Calif. State U., Fullerton, 1975; MEd Adminstrn., Calif. State U., L.A., 1991. Cert. tchr. L.A. County Office Edn., 1984—88; resource specialist spl. edn. Pomona (Calif.) Unified Sch. Dist., 1990—. Presenter U. St. Petersburg, Russia, 2002. Mem. Soc. Of Friends. Avocations: traveling, jewelry making. Home: 2225 Brescia Ave Claremont CA 91711-1807 Office: Pomona HS Pomona Unified Sch Dist 475 Bangor St Pomona CA 91767-2449

CALLEN, PAULETTE MARIE, writer, advocate; b. Webster, S.D., July 24, 1947; d. Kenneth Lee and Marlys Louise (Magnus) Callen; m. Reeves John Cary, July 25, 1971 (div. 1977). BA in English, Concordia Coll., 1969. Coord. legis. affairs ASPCA, N.Y.C., 1995—97. Author: Charity, 1997; actor: numerous summer stock and off-off Broadway plays, (touring prodn.) Blithe Spirit; contbr. poems, stories and essays to pubs. Vol. staffer Pet Owners With AIDS Resource Svcs., N.Y.C., 1991—93. Recipient 1st place fiction award, Negative Capability Press, U. Ala., 1993.

CALLENDER, NORMA ANNE, psychology educator, counselor; b. Huntsville, Tex., May 10, 1933; d. C.W. Carswell and Nell Ruth (Collard) Hughes Bost; m. B.G. Callender, 1951 (div. 1964); remarried 1967 (div. 1973); children: Teresa Elizabeth, Leslie Gemey, Shannah Hughes, Kelly Mari; m. E Purfurst, June 1965 (div. Aug. 1965). BS, U. Houston, 1969; MA, U. Houston at Clear Lake, 1977; postgrad., U. Houston, 1970, Tex. So. U., 1971, Lamar U., 1972-73, U. Houston-Clear Lake, 1979, 87, 89-93, St. Thomas U., 1985, 86, Aerospace Inst., NASA, Johnson Space Ctr., 1986, U. Houston-Clear Lake, summer 98, San Jacinto Coll., 1988—99, postgrad., 1994, postgrad., 2001—03. Cert. profl. reading specialist, Tex.; lic. profl. counselor. Tchr. Houston Ind. Schs., 1969-70; co-counselor, instr. Ellington AFB, Houston, 1971; tchr. Clear Creek Schs., League City, Tex., 1970-86; owner, dir. Bay Area Tutoring and Reading Clinic, Clear Lake City, Tex., 1970—, Bay Area Tng. Assocs., 1982-98, Bay Area Family Counseling, 1995—; cons., LPC intern Guidance Ctr. Pasadena (Tex.) Ind. Sch. Dist., 1993-95. Part-time instr. San Jacinto Coll., Pasadena, 1980-81, 91-93; univ. adj. U. Houston, Clear Lake, 1986-91; founder, editor BATA Books Pub., 1997—; cons. in field. Contbr. poetry to profl. jours. State advisor U.S. Congl. Adv. Bd., 1985-87; vol., bd. dirs. Family Outreach Ctr., 1989-92; vol. Bay Area Coun. on Drugs and Alcohol, Nassau Bay, Tex., 1993-94; bd. dirs. Ballet San Jacinto, 1985-87; adv. bd. Cmty. Ednl. TV, 1990-92. Recipient Franklin award U. Houston, 1965-67; Delta Kappa Gamma/Beta Omicron scholar, 1967-68, PTA scholar, 1973, Berwin scholar, 1976, Mary Gibbs Jones scholar, 1976-77, Found. Econ. Edn. scholar, 1976, Insts. Achievement Human Potential scholar, Phila., 1987. Mem.: ACA, Internat. Reading Assn., Clear Creek Educators Assn. (past, honorarium 1976, 1977, 1985), Leadership Clear Lake Alumni Assn. (charter, program and projects com. mem. 1986—87, edn. com. 1985), U. Houston Alumni Assn. (life), Phi Theta Kappa, Phi Delta Kappa, Kappa Delta Pi, Psi Chi (life), Phi Kappa Phi (life). Mem. Life Tabernacle Ch. Office: 1234 Bay Area Blvd Ste R Houston TX 77058-2538

CALLINAN, PATRICIA ANN, legal secretary; b. Harrisburg, Pa., Dec. 29, 1943; d. Albert Frances and Gilda Mary (Cifani) Pugliese; 1 child, Tricia Ann Corder. Comml. diploma, Bishop McDevitt, 1961. Chief enforcement sec. Commonwealth of Pa., Harrisburg, 1961-66; supt. sec. Cape May (N.J.) County Vocat. Tech. Ctr., 1966-67; asst. br. mgr. Continental Title Ins., Wildwood, N.J., 1967-91; legal sec. Corino & Dwyer, Esqs., Wildwood, 1991—. Past. pres., treas. Cape May County Legal Sec., 1968-70, St. Ann's PTA, Wildwood, 1980-84; past pres. Wildwood Cath. Parent Guild, 1986-88; bd. sec. Wildwood Crest Tourism Commn., 1990-93. Mem. Cape May County Women's Rep. Club; apptd. commr. Cape May County Mcpl. Utilities Authority, 1999; sunshine chmn. Cape May County Rep. Orgn. Named Legal Sec. of Yr., Cape May County Legal Sec., 1970, 73. Mem. Victoria Village Homeowners (sec. 1994-96), Lower Township Rep. Club, Lower Township Rep. Orgn. (committeewoman 1994-96, 96—, mem. exec. com. rec. sec. 1994—), Cape May County Legal Secs. Assn.

Roman Catholic. Avocations: walking, dance, reading, plays. Home: 36 Canterbury Way Cape May NJ 08204-4268 Office: Corino & Dwyer Esqs 9700 Pacific Ave Wildwood NJ 08260-3334

CALLISON, JOJEAN FAYE, educational association administrator; b. Sioux Falls, South Dakota, U.S.A., Aug. 13, 1931; d. Adair Frazier and Sylvia Faye (Hansen) Callison; m. Thomas Joseph Chap; children: Peter Callison Chap, Eric Thomas Chap. BA., Augustana Coll., Sioux Falls, 1973; M. Ed., U. of Sioux Falls, Sioux Falls, 1993; Ed. D., U. SD., Vermillion, 2002. Tchr., Lockport, Ill., 1973—74, Stevens Point, Wis., 1974—78, Milford, 1979—80, Spencer, 1980—81, Ruthven, 1983—90, Sioux Falls, SD, 1990—2000; admin., 2000—. Office: Axtell Park Middle School 201 N West Ave Sioux Falls SD 57104

CALMENSON, STEPHANIE LYN, writer; d. Kermit and Edith Calmenson; m. Mark J. Goldman, June 13, 1998. BA, Bklyn. Coll., 1973; MA, NYU, 1976. Editor children's books Double Day & Co., N.Y.C., 1977—80; editl. dir. Parents Mag. Read-Aloud, N.Y.C., 1980—84; writer children's books Parents Mag. Book Club, N.Y.C., 1984—. Author, editor: Never Take a Pig to Lunch and Other Funny Poems about Animals, 1982; author: My Book of the Seasons, 1982, One Little Monkey, 1982, Barney's Sand Castle, 1983, Bambi and the Butterfly, 1983, The Three Bears, 1983, That's Not Fair!, 1983, The Kindergarten Book, 1983, Where Will the Animals Stay?, 1983, The Birthday Hat: A Grandma Potamus Story, 1983, Where is Grandma Potamus?, 1983, The Afternoon Book, 1984, Ten Furry Monsters, 1984, All Aboard the Goodnight Train, 1984, Waggleby of Fraggle Rock, 1985, Ten Items of Less, 1985, Rainy Day Walk, 1985, The Toy Book, 1986, What Babies Do, 1986, The Shaggy Bunny, the Shaddy Little Monster, the Little Chick, 1986, The Sesame Street ABC Book, 1986, The Sesame Street Book of First Times, 1986, Little Duck's Moving Day, 1986, Fido, 1987, Tiger's Bedtime, 1987, The Bambi Book, 1987, The Giggle Book, 1987, Where's Rufus?, 1987, One Red Shoe (The Other One's Blue!), 1987, Spaghetti Manners, 1987, The Busy Garage, Who Said Moo?, A Visit to the Firehouse, 1987, The Children's Aesop: Selected Fables, 1988, Little Duck and the New Baby, 1988, Ho! Ho! Ho! Christmas Jokes and Riddles, 1988, No Stage Fright for Me!, 1988, The Little Witch Sisters, 1989, What Am I? Very First Riddles, 1989, The Principal's New Clothes, 1989, Wanted: Warm, Furry Friend, 1990, Magellan's Hats, 1991, Hopscotch, the Tiny Bunny, 1991, Dinner at the Panda Palace, 1991, Come to My Party, 1991, Babies, 1992, Roller Skates!, 1992, It Begins with an A, 1993, The Little Witch Sisters, 1993, Race to Danger, 1993, Kinderkittens: Show-and-Tell, 1994, Marigold and Grandma on the Town, 1994, Rosie: A Visiting Dog's Story, 1994, Hotter Than a Hot Dog!, 1994, New, 1994, Kinderkittens: Who Took the Cookie from the Cookie Jar?, 1995, Engine, Engine, Number Nine, 1996, Who Am I?, 1996, My Dog's the Best, 1997, First Steps, 1998, Shaggy, Waggy Dogs (and Others), 1998, The Teeny, Tiny Teacher, 1998, The Frog Principal, 2001, Good for You!: Toddler Rhymes for Toddler Times, 2001, Perfect Puppy, 2001, Welcome Baby!: Baby Rhymes for Baby Times, 2002, (adaptation) Walt Disney Presents the Little Mermaid, 1991; author: (with others) All About Me: Featuring Jim Henson's Sesame Street Muppets, 1989; author: (with J. Cole) Safe from the Start: Your Child's Safety from Birth to Age Five, 1989, Crazy Eights and Other Card Games, 1994, The Gator Girls, 1995, Bug in a Rug: Reading Fun for Just-Beginners, 1996, Rockin' Reptiles, 1997, The Rain or Shine Activity Book: Fun Things to Make and Do, 1997, Get Well, Gators!, 1998; compiler with Joanna Cole: The Laugh Book: A New Treasury of Humor for Children, 1986; author (with J. Cole): Gator Halloween, 1999; author: (with J. Cole and M. Street) Marbles: 101 Ways to Play, 1998, Fun on the Run: Travel Games and Songs, 1999; compiler with Joanna Cole: The Read-Aloud Treasury for Young Children, 1987, compiler with J. Cole: Ready, Set, Read! The Beginning Reader's Treasury, 1990, Miss Mary Mack and Other Children's Street Rhymes, 1990, The Scary Book, 1991, compiler with Cole: The Eentsy, Weentsy Spider: Fingerplays and Action Rhymes, 1991, Pat-a-Cake and Other Play Rhymes, 1992, Pin the Tail on the Donkey and Other Party Games, 1993, Six Sick Sheep: 101 Tongue Twisters, 1993, Why Did the Chicken Cross the Road? And Other Riddles, Old and New, 1994; compiler with Cole A Pocketful of Laughs: Stories, Poems, Jokes & Riddles, 1995; compiler with Cole: Ready, Set, Read--and Laugh! A Funny Treasury for Beginning Readers, 1995, Yours Till Banana Splits: 201 Autograph Rhymes, 1995, Give a Dog a Bone: Stories, Poems, Jokes, and Riddles about Dogs, 1996. Mem.: SCBWI, PEN, Nat. Arts Club, Authors Guild.

CALO, TINA CAROL, school counselor; b. Cleve., June 3, 1939; d. Vincent J. Calo and Marie A. (Caruso) Feudo. BSEd, Ohio U., 1961, MEd, 1969; postgrad., Calif. State U., Sacramento, 1979-80. Cert. tchr., counselor, spl. edn. tchr. Tchr. Maple Hts. (Ohio) Schs., 1961-67; counselor Dept. Def. Schs., Okinawa, Japan, 1967-70, Berlin, 1970-71, Washington Schs., 1971-72, Dept. Def. Schs., Hahn AB, Germany, 1972-79, Rhein Main AB, Germany, 1980-95; sch. counselor Myrtle Beach (S.C.) AFB, 1991-92. Mem. NEA, ACA (mem. European br., sec., bd. dirs.), Am. Sch. Counselors Assn., Fed. Edn. Assn., Sons of Italy. Avocation: travel. Home: PO Box 15871 Surfside Beach SC 29587-5871

CALOOY, SONYA RENEE, advertising executive, consultant; b. Verdun, France, Feb. 6, 1961; naturalized U.S. citizen, 1961; d. Rudy A. and Frances (Rosales) C. BFA in Advt. Design with honors, North Tex. State U., 1983. TV studio mgr. Tex. Dept. of Mental Health/Mental Retardation, Denton, Tex., 1983-85; prodn. coord. Kim Dawson Agy., Dallas, 1983-91; art dir., owner Image by Design Group, Dallas, 1986-89; sr. art dir. The Promotion Network, Dallas, 1989-90; art dir., prin., founder, owner Calooy & Co., Dallas, 1990—; creative dir., prin., founder The Lucky Seven Project, Dallas, 1997-99; pres., CEO Creative Showcase, Inc., Dallas, 1998—; founder, pres. WebMacster.com, 1999—. Creative svcs. cons. Pepsico Creative Pool, Plano, Tex., 1995-98; vis. scholar, adj. faculty internet pub. and e-commerce techs. program El Centro C.C., Dallas, 2000—. Choral musician The Women's Chorus of Dallas, 1991-2001; mem. Dallas/Ft. Worth Minority Bus. Devel. Coun. Mem. North Tex. Women's Bus. Coun., Greater Dallas C. of C., Gamma Beta Phi. Democrat. Avocations: comedian, jazz musician, fine artist.

CALTAGIRONE, NORMA TOMASELLO, psychologist, educator; b. Tampa, Fla., May 27, 1948; d. Fred and Angelina (Langiotti) Tomasello; m. Sam Caltagirone, June 26, 1970 (div. Aug. 1985); children: Carla, Ciara. BA, U. South Fla., 1970; MEd, N.C. State U., 1977; postgrad., Person-Centered Expressive Arts Therapy Inst., Santa Rosa, Calif., 1991. Acad. advisor, editl. asst. U. N.C., Chapel Hill, 1970—76; counselor St. Petersburg Jr. Coll., Clearwater, Fla., 1978—81; counselor Career Planning and Placement U. Tampa, Fla., 1979—83; student activities specialist St. Petersburg Jr. Coll., Clearwater, 1984—86; counselor Hillsborough C.C., Tampa, 1987—91, prof. psychology, 1991—. Author (poetry): Galeria. V.p., bd. dirs. Stageworks Theater Co., Tampa; vol. Tampa Bay Performing Arts Ctr., 1988—. Recipient Fulbright-Hays Scholarship abroad (Brazil), 2002. Mem.: Assn. Humanistic Psychology, Fla. Assn. C.C. (judge, editor), Pan Am. Univ. Women (chaplain 1992—). Avocations: travel, acting, writing. Office: Hillsborough CC Ybor Campus 2112 15th St Tampa FL 33675*

CALTON, SANDRA JEANE, accountant; b. Portales, N.Mex., Feb. 3, 1945; d. Lloyd Paul and Nana Mae (Parris) Grant; m. Gary Jim Calton, Nov. 26, 1964; children: Deborah, April, Craig. BS, Ea. N.Mex. U., 1967, U. Md., 1984. CPA, Md. Comptr. Purification Engring. Inc., Columbia, Md., 1981-85, IBF Biotechnics Inc., Savage, Md., 1987-88; pres. Srchem, Inc., Elkridge, Md., 1988—; acct. Calton Rsch. Assocs., Elkridge, 1974—; v.p. Calwood Chem. Industries, Inc., Elkridge, 1991—, AuRx, Inc., Balt., 1996—, Calwood Nutritionals, Inc., Elkridge, 1999—; pres. Odorpro, Inc., Elkridge, 1999—. Treas. Howard Coun. Extension Homemakers Coun., Ellicott City, Md., 1984. Mem. AICPA, Nat. Soc. Tax Profls., Md. Assn. CPAs. Home: 5331 Landing Rd Elkridge MD 21075-5717

CALVANO, LINDA SUE LEY, insurance company administrator; b. [illegible], Ind., Nov. 27, 1949; d. Jiles Rex and Naomi Katherine (Van Horn) Riggs; m. Thomas Alan Ley Calvano, Feb. 28, 1987. BS in Edn. with distinction, Ind. U.-Purdue U., 1971, MS in Edn. with highest distinction, 1975. Cert. paralegal; lic. life, accident, health, property and casualty ins. agt., Ind.; cert. total quality mgmt.; project mgmt. profl. designation. Elem. tchr. Indpls. Pub. Schs., 1972-74, Center Grove Community Schs., Greenwood, Ind., 1974-81; dir. adminstrn. Brougher Agy., Inc., Greenwood, 1981-84; mgr. claims/customer svc. The Associated Group, Inc., Indpls., 1984-89; v.p. team ops. Key Benefit Adminstrs., Inc., Indpls., 1989-92; regional mgr. ops. & rev. projects Anthem Blue Cross Blue Shield, Indpls., 1992-97, quality assurance dir., 1997—. Mem. cotillion com. Humane Soc. Indpls., 1991; vol. Riley Run for Children, Indpls., 1985-92. Recipient Good Girl Citizenship award Women's Aux. of Am. Legion, 1968. Mem. Am. Mgmt. Assn., Nat. Assn. Life Underwriters, Nat. Assn. Health Underwriters, Inst. Internal Auditors, Indpls. Paralegal Assn., Project Mgmt. Inst., Toastmasters Internat. Republican. Episcopalian. Home: 6358 Bluff Acres Dr Greenwood IN 46143-9037 Office: Anthem Blue Cross Blue Shield 220 Virginia Ave Indianapolis IN 46204 Office Phone: 317-287-8160.

CALVERT, JEANNE ANNE, historian, educator; b. Paulding, Ohio, Dec. 30, 1943; d. Homer F. and Helen Grace Bennett; m. William L. Calvert, June 4, 1966; children: Jed, Jared, Jeven. BA, Ohio No. U., Ada, 1966; MS, Emporia State U., Kans., 1969. Prof. Luth. Coll., Ft. Wayne, Ind., 1993—98, U. St. Francis, Ft. Wayne, Ind., 1998—. Author: Oakwood: Past and Present, 1994, A Paulding Journal, 2002, Ancestors and Descendents of G.A. and Ida Bennett, 2003. Pres. Oakwood Libr. Assn., Ohio, 1999—2001; chair Oakwood Alumni, Ohio, 1998—2003. Mem.: DAR (pres. 1996—2001). United Methodist.

CALVERT, LOIS PRINCE, health facility administrator, geriatrics nurse; b. Lawrenceburg, Tenn., June 27, 1948; d. Virgil Miller and Beulah Mae (Fox) Prince; m. Albert Sidney Johnson, Sept. 26, 1970 (div. 1985); children: Kelly Nicole Johnson, Kristopher Scott Johnson; m. Malon Sherman Calvert, Oct. 19, 1990. Student, Bapt. Hosp. Sch. Nursing, 1966-67, Belmont Coll., 1966-67; ADN cum laude, Columbia State C.C., 1970; cert. in nursing home adminstrn., George Washington U., 1985. RN Ala., Tenn. Psychiat. nurse, staff RN Bapt. Meml. Hosp., Memphis, 1970-71; staff RN, psychiat. staff nurse VA Hosp., Memphis, 1971-73; DON svc. Lawrenceburg (Tenn.) Health Care Ctr., 1975-80, nursing home adminstr., 1980-85; case mgr., aide supr., staff RN Lawrenceburg Home Health Agy., 1985-86; staff RN, case mgr. home health patients, coord. home health Mid-South Home Health Agy., Florence, Ala., 1986-87; DON svcs. Lawrenceburg Manor, Inc., 1987-96, adminstr., 1996-98; gero-psychiatric nurse Lifesprings Unit, Hillside, Pulaski, Tenn., 1998-2000; nurse mgr. gero-psych lifespring unit Hillside Hosp., Pulaski, Tenn., 2000—. Paramed. examiner ASB-Meditest, Nashville, 1989—; mem. NCLEX panel, item reviewer LPN State Bds., 1993. Sustaining membership chmn. Lawrence County coun. Girls Scouts U.S., 1977—78; vol., bd. dirs. Lawrence County chpt. ARC, 1995, disaster health chmn.; mem. Lawrence County Health Coun., 1998—; pianist, dir. youth choir E. Edn. Meth. Ch., 1985—94; mem. choir Mt. Moriah Cumberland Presbyn. Ch.; v.p., founding mem. NG Family Support Group 1/115 FA Bn., 1996—97, publicity chmn., 1998. With Tenn. NG, 1997—98. Recipient Molly Pitcher award, NG Arty. Assn., 1998. Fellow: Am. Coll. Health Care Adminstrs. (profl. cert.); mem.: Nat. Assn. Dirs. Nursings Adminstrs. (founding mem. Tenn. chpt., corr. sec. 1995), Tenn. Employee Rels. Com., Beta Sigma Phi (Girl of the Yr. 1973, 1976). Avocations: piano, painting, cross stitch, basket weaving. Home: 800 Old Agnew Rd Pulaski TN 38478 Office: Hillside Hosp Lifesprings Geropsych Unit 1265 W College St Pulaski TN 38478-3640

CALVI, MARY, reporter; m. Michael J. Spano; 2 children. BJ magna cum laude, Syracuse U. Anchor Sta. WRKL-AM-FM; reporter TCI News, News 12 L.I., USA Networks; anchor Sta. WCBS-TV, N.Y.C., 1991—2002, exec. prodr., 1995, asst. news dir., 1999—. Office: CBS 524 W 57th St New York NY 10019

CALVIN, CAROLINA, apparel executive, designer; U.S. creative dir. Levi's Levi Strauss & Co., San Francisco, 2001—. Office: Levi Strauss & Co 1155 Battery St San Francisco CA 94111*

CALVIN, DOROTHY VER STRATE, computer company executive; b. Dec. 22, 1929; d. Herman and Christina (Plakmyer) Ver Strate; m. Allen D. Calvin, Oct. 5, 1953; children: Jamie, Kris, Bufo, Scott. BS magna cum laude, Mich. State U., 1951; MA, U. San Francisco, 1988, EdD, 1991. Mgr. data processing Behavioral Rsch. Labs., Menlo Park, Calif., 1972-75; dir. Mgmt. Info. Sys. Inst. for Profl. Devel., San Jose, Calif., 1975-76; sys. analyst, programmer Pacific Bell Info. Sys., San Francisco, Calif., 1976-81, staff mgr., 1981-84; mgr. applications devel. Data Architects Inc., San Francisco, Calif., 1984-86; pres. Ver Strate Press, San Francisco, Calif., 1986—. Instr., Downtown C.C., San Francisco, 1980-84, Cañada C.C., 1986-92, Skyline Coll., 1988-92, City Coll. of San Francisco, 1992—; mem. computer curriculum adv. coun. San Francisco City Coll., 1982-84. V.p. LWV, Roanoke, Va., 1956-58. Pres. Bulliss Purissima Parents Group, Los Altos, Calif., 1962-64; bd. dirs. Vols. for Israel, 1986-87. Mem. IEEE Computer Soc., Assn. Sys. Mgmt., Assn. Women in Computing, Phi Delta Kappa. Democrat. Avocations: computing, gardening, jogging, reading. Office: Ver Strate Press 1645 15th Ave San Francisco CA 94122-3523 E-mail: dcalvin2@aol.com.

CALVIN, JAMIE DUIF, interactive designer; b. Lansing, Mich., July 28, 1954; d. Allen David and Dorothy Viola Calvin; m. Craig Aaron Tovey, Mar. 23, 1980 (div. Oct. 1994); children: Kendl, David, Leo. BBA in Computer Info. Sys., Ga. State U., 1990. Pres. Strategy, Inc., Atlanta, 1982-94; sr. designer Jade River Designs, Atlanta, 1994-98; sr. tech. cons. interactive media IBM, Atlanta, 1998-99; v.p. global retail practice Scient, San Francisco, 1999—. Author: 6 Myths of Web Marketing, 1996, Marketing Manager's Plain English Guide to the Internet, 1998; columnist Chess Life Mag., 1996-97. Mem. ACM, Assn. Internet Profls., HTML Writers Guild (governing bd. 1998), U.S. Chess Fedn. (publs. com. 1996-97, Top 50 U.S. Women Chessplayers). Avocation: chess. Home: 454 Las Gallinas PMB 335 San Rafael CA 94903 Office: Scient One Market Spear Tower 36th Fl Ste 3646 San Francisco CA 94105- E-mail: dcalvin@scient.com.

CALVO, RHONDA LYNNE, special education educator; b. Upland, Calif., Jan. 31, 1960; d. Ronald Thurl and Marilyn Brown Smith; m. Chuck M. Calvo, May 30, 1981; children: C.J., Christian. BA in Social Sci., Azusa Pacific U., 1982; degree, Prescott Coll., 1994. Lic. tchr. Ariz., 1994, Nev., 1998. Spl. edn. tchr. Lake Havasu Unifed Sch. Dist., Lake Havasu City, Ariz., 1994—98, Clark County Sch. Dist., Boulder City, Nev., 1998—99, spl. edn. tchr. facilitator, 1999—. Adv. Nat. Jr. Honor Soc., Garrett, Miss., 1999—2002; mem. various com. Boulder City H.S., 2000—. Recipient Caring Enough to Make a Difference award, STOP DUI, 2002; grantee Least Restrictive Environ. grant, Clark County Sch. Dist., 2001—02. Republican. Avocations: boating, swimming, water sports. Office: Boulder City High School 1101 Fifth St Boulder City NV 89005

CAMAC, MARGARET VICTORIA, construction company executive; b. Wellington, New Zealand, Mar. 26, 1946; came to U.S., 1981; d. Paul and Cavel (Durnett) Leonard; m. Barry John Camac, June 1, 1968; children: Bianca, Karla, Paula, Victoria. BA, U. Manitoba, Winnipeg, Manitoba, Can., 1977; MEd, U. Manitoba, Winnipeg, Can., 1978. Tchr., New Zealand, 1966-69, 1969-76; vol. set up parent programs for handicapped children various bus., Rio Grande Valley, Tex., 1981-86; v.p. Wellington Constrn. [illegible], 1991-92; pres. Hadley J Design, 1992-2000; v.p. Concrete Pumping Co., 1998-2000. Child advocate. Vol. Ga. Coun. Child Abuse, Atlanta, 1990-91; developmental disabilities com. Atlanta Jewish Cmty. Ctr., 1998-2000. Mem. Jr. League Atlanta (named one of Twelve Outstanding Vols. in Atlanta, 1990-91, mem. fidelity trust 1991). Avocations: classical piano, flower judging and design, sewing, weaving, hiking. Home: 335 Mount Paran Rd NW Atlanta GA 30327-4605

CAMARA, MADELINE MARIA, humanities educator; b. Havana, Cuba, Aug. 26, 1957; arrived in U.S., 1992; d. Raimundo Cámara and Neida Betancourt; m. Ralph Hansen, Aug. 2, 1983 (div. Sept. 7, 1988); 1 child, Lena Hansen ; m. Bovalem Bouchama, June 9, 1999. BA, Universidad de La Habana, Cuba, 1982; MA, Colegio de México, 1992; PhD, SUNY, Stony Brook, 1996. Editor El Caimán Barbudo, Habana, 1984—86; vis. prof. Universidad de La Habana, 1984—89; editor Editl. Letras Cubana, La Habana, 1984—89; vis. instr. U. Ctrl. Fla., Orlando, 1996—97; asst. prof. San Diego State U., 1996—2002; assoc. prof. U. S. Fla., Tampa, 2002—. Bd. dirs. Inst. Cuban Studies, Miami, Fla. Reviewer: jour. Cuban Studies Jour., 1999—, columnist: newspaper El Nuevo Herald, 1996—; author: (book) Vocación de Casandra, 2001—; editor: Cuentos Cubanos Contemporaneos, 1998—, Cuba, The Elusive Nation, 2000—, La Letra Rebelde, 2002, La Memoria heelizada. Panel presenter CuBanas, Miami, 1998; spkr. Cuban Com. for Democracy, N.Y.C., 1994. Mem.: Fulbright Assn., S. Ea. Coun. on Latin Am. Studies, Assn. Letras Femeninas. Roman Catholic. Avocations: cats, movies, travel. Home: 12111 Wildbrood Dr Riverview FL 33569 Office: U S Fla East Fowler Ave 4202 Tampa FL 33620

CAMARDESE, AMY HOFFMAN, education educator; b. Massillon, Ohio, Sept. 5, 1950; d. Paul Wilbur and Anne Kelly Hoffman; m. Zachary Camardese, Dec. 22, 1973; children: Christina, Margaret, Stephanie. BS in Edn., Ohio U., 1972; MS in Edn., U. Pitts., 1975; PhD, Kent State U., 2002. Tchr. Keystone Oaks Sch., Pitts., 1972—75; tchr. spl. edn. Liberty Schs., Youngstown, Ohio, 1985—99; asst. prof. Geneva Coll., Beaver Falls, Pa., 1999—2001, Westminster Coll., New Wilmington, Pa., 2001—. Grant reviewer FIPSE, Washington, 2003; text reviewer Houghton-Mifflin Pub., 2003. Bd. dirs. Children's Internat. Summer Villages, 1994, Relay for Life, Am. Cancer Soc. Recipient Martin Luther King award, East Ohio Edison, 1995; Jennings scholar, Liberty Schs., 1995. Mem.: Coun. Exceptional Children, Delta Kappa Gamma, Phi Delta Kappa (sec. 2003). Methodist. Avocations: reading, walking, running. Home: 12 Redfern Dr Youngstown OH 44505

CAMBIO, BAMBILYN BREECE, state legislator; b. Johnston, R.I., Dec. 14, 1956; m. James V. Cambio. Cert. Am. Inst. Paralegal Studies. Mem. R.I. Ho. of Reps., Providence, mem. HEW com., joint com. on environ. and energy, vice chmn. ho. edn. welfare com. Commr. Exec. Dept. on Deaf and Hard of Hearing; sec. State Govt. Intern Commn.; freelance paralegal, title examiner. Chair North Providence Citizen's Environ. Com.; mem. North Providence Preservation Com., North Providence Women's Dem. Caucus, North Providence Dem. Town Com. Mem. Am. Polit. Item Collectors, R.I. Caucus Women Legislators, Nat. Order Women Legislators. Office: RI Ho of Reps State Capitol Providence RI 02903

CAMER, MARY MARTHA, retired secretary; b. McAdoo, Pa., Oct. 30, 1932; d. John Fiolich and Elizabeth (Chomo) Sussick; m. Kenneth Camer, Feb. 10, 1952; children: Kenneth, Curtis, Marybeth. AA in Bus. Mgmt., Bucks County Community Coll., 1982. Sch. sec. Neshaminy Sch. Dist., Langhorne, Pa., 1959-61; NCR bookkeeper Gen. Doors Corp., Bristol, Pa., 1962-65; jr. acct., NCR bookkeeper Lower Bucks Hosp., Bristol, Pa., 1965-68; office mgr., bookkeeper Archdiocese of Phila., Blessed J. Neumann Nursing Home, 1968-78; payroll coord. Warner Lambert Co. Alphamedics Divsn., Levittown, Pa., 1979-81, human resouces pers. coord., 1978-86; sec. Rohm and Haas, DVI, Bristol, 1988-95. Election judge Middletown, Pa., 2001. Recipient Outstanding Adult award Pa. Assn. for Adult Continuing Edn., 1991. Democrat. Roman Catholic. Home: 94 Queen Lily Rd Levittown PA 19057-1914

CAMERON, DONNA, artist, art educator; b. Mishawaka, Ind., Apr. 7, 1951; d. Donald Peter Benjamin Cameron and Carmela Barbara Milo; m. Phillip Emil Sloan, Jan. 12, 1975; 1 child, Andrew Cameron Sloan. BA in Fmil, Paingint and Drawing, RISD, 1974; BA in Film, Sch. of Art Inst. of Chgo., 1980; postgrad., Atelier Herbo, Paris, 1982—84. Fla. Keys corr. Miami (Fla.) Herald Newspaper, 1976—78; film artist Mus. Modern Art, N.Y.C., 1992—; sr. editor Manhattan Arts Internat. Mag., N.Y.C., 1995—. Adj. asst. prof. Tisch Sch. of Arts, N.Y.C., NY, 1994—. Author: more than 80 short films and videos; Fedn. Modern Sculptors and Painters, N.Y.C. Bd. dirs. NY Film and Video Coun., N.Y.C., 1998—; consw. mem. Univ. Coun. Arts Educators, N.Y.C., 1998—. Fellow, Art Students League NY, N.Y.C., 1984—86, Jerome Found., St. Paul, 1989, 1993, MacDowell Colony, Peterborough, NH, 1998, Macdowell Colony, Peterborough, NH, 1999, 2000, Rockefeller fellowship, 2004. Achievements include patents for cinematic paper emulsion. Avocations: gardening, bicycling, hiking, animal rights advocacy. E-mail: papercam@aol.com.

CAMERON, ELEANOR CRANSTON FOWLE, writer; b. Palo Alto, Calif., Nov. 22, 1909; d. William McGregor and Carol Edith (Dixon) Cranston; m. John Miller Fowle, June 19, 1929 (dec. Apr. 1983); children: Michael, Linda Fowle Burke; m. Donald Churchill Cameron, Aug. 25, 1984 (dec. Nov. 1996). Student, Stanford U., 1928-31. Author: Cranston, The Senator from California, 1980. Chmn. Dem. State Women, Calif., 1966-80; officer Dem. State Ctrl. Com., 1966-80; pres. Foothill-De Anza C.C. Found., 1980-90, bd. dirs., 1996-98; bd. dirs. Stanford U. Founding Grant Soc., 1980—; trustee Hidden Villa, Los Altos Hills, Calif., 1996—. Congregationalist. Avocations: travel, politics, community activist. Home: 501 Portola Rd Apt 8131 Portola Valley CA 94028-7604

CAMERON, HEATHER ANNE, publishing executive; b. Montreal, Quebec, Can., Mar. 12, 1951; came to U.S., 1981; d. Douglas George and Jeanne Sutherland (Thompson) C.; m. Ward Eric Shaw, Dec. 20, 1980; 1 child, Geoffrey Cameron. BA, Queen's U., Kingston, Ont., Can., 1973; MLS, McGill U., Montreal, 1977. Head reference and bibliography sect. Nat. Libr. Can., Ottawa, 1977-80; head editl. dept. Librs. Unltd., Inc., Denver, 1981-86; v.p. acquisitions and editl. devel. ABC-CLIO, Inc., Santa Barbara, Calif., 1986-92, pres., pub. Santa Barbara, Denver and Eng., 1992-97; v.p., gen. mgr. Westgroup, San Francisco, 1997—. Bd. dirs. Friends of Librs. U.S.A., v.p., 1996, pres., 1997—. Mem. ALA (com. chair 1993—), Friends of Librs., USA (dir. 1994—, pres. 1997-2000), Amnesty Internat., Phi Beta Mu. Office: West Group 50 California St Fl 19 San Francisco CA 94111-4624 E-mail: heather.cameron@thomson.com.

CAMERON, JOYCE, human factors and ergonomics specialist, music educator; b. Oakland, Calif., June 1, 1941; d. Dudley Alfred and Virginia Laing Cameron. BA, Pomona Coll., 1963; MusM, Ind. U., 1965; D of Musical Arts, U. Oreg., 1985; MA, U.Dayton, 1997. Tchr., 1979—94; intern Idaho Nat. Engring. Lab., Idaho Falls, 1994, Lexis-Nexis, Miamisburg, Ohio, 1994—95; human factors analyst HSIAC, Wright Patterson AFB, 1995—98; cons., sr. cons., assoc. Booz Allen Hamilton, Wright Patterson AFB, 1998—. Assoc. editor Keyboard Companion, L.A., 1990—2000. Mem.: Music Tchrs. Nat. Assn., Human Factors Ergonomics Soc. (local sec. 2000—01, nat. program chair 2000—02, chair test and evaluation tech. group 2002—), Pi Kappa Lambda, Phi Beta Kappa. Achievements include development of survey to assess worker body part discomfort. Office: Booz Allen Hamilton 1900 Founders Dr Ste 300 Dayton OH 45420 Office Phone: 937-781-2444. Business E-Mail: cameron_joyce@bah.com.

CAMERON, JUDITH LYNNE, secondary education educator, hypnotherapist; b. Oakland, Calif., Apr. 29, 1945; d. Alfred Joseph and June Estelle (Faul) Moe; m. Richard Irwin Cameron, Dec. 17, 1967; 1 child, Kevin Dale. AA in Psychol., Sacramento City Coll., 1965; BA in Psychol., German, Calif. State U., 1967; MA in Reading Specialization, San Francisco State U., 1972; postgrad., Chapman Coll.; PhD, Am. Inst. Hypnotherapy, 1987. Cert. tchr., Calif. Tchr. St. Vincent's Cath. Sch., San Jose, Calif., 1969-70, Fremont (Calif.) Elem. Sch., 1970-72, LeRoy Boys Home, LaVerne, Calif., 1972-73, Grace Miller Elem. Sch., LaVerne, Calif., 1973-80, resource specialist, 1980-84; owner, mgr. Pioneer Take-out Franchises, Alhambra and San Gabriel, Calif., 1979-85; resource specialist, dept. chmn. Bonita H.S., LaVerne, Calif., 1984; mentor tchr. in space sci. Bonita Unified Sch. Dist., 1988-99, rep. LVTV; owner, therapist So. Calif. Clin. Hypnotherapy, Claremont, Calif., 1988—. Bd. dirs., recommending tchr., asst. dir. Project Turnabout, Claremont, Calif.; Teacher-in-Space cons. Bonita Unified Sch. Dist., LaVerne, 1987-99; advisor Peer Counseling Program, Bonita High Sch., 1987—; advisor Air Explorers/Edwards Test Pilot Sch., LaVerne, 1987—; mem. Civil Air Patrol, Squadron 68, Aerospace Office, 1988-92; selected amb. U.S. Space Acad.-U.S. Space Camp Acad., Huntsville, Ala., 1990; named to national (now internat.) teaching faculty challenger Ctr. for Space Edn., Alexandria, Va., 1990; regional coord. East San Gabiel Valley Future Scientists and Engrs. of Am.; amb. to U.S. Space Camp, 1990; mem. adj. faculty challenger learning ctr. Calif. State U., Dominguez Hills, 1994, state sch. accreditation team, 2000, 2003, negotiating team, 1998-2003; rep. ceremony to honor astronauts Apollo 11, White House, 1994; exec. bd. Bonita Unfied tchrs. assoc., 1995— (negotiating team, 1998—); flight dir. mission control, Challenger learning ctr., Long Beach, Ca., 2002—. Vol. advisor Children's Home Soc., Santa Ana, 1980-81; dist. rep. LVTV Channel 29, 1991; regional coord. East San Gabriel Valley chpt. Future Scientists and Engrs. of Am., 1992; mem. internat. invesigation Commn. UFOs, 1991; field mem. Ctr. for Search for Extraterrestrial Intelligence, 1996; tchr., leader Ctr. for the Study Extraterrestrial Intelligence, 1997—. Recipient Tchr. of Yr., Bonita H.S., 1989, continuing svc. award, 1992; named Toyolaa Tchr. of Yr., 1994. Mem. NEA, AAUW, Internat. Investigations Com. on UFOs, Coun. Exceptional Children, Am. Psychol. Assn., Calif. Assn. Resource Specialists, Calif. Elem. Edn. Assn., Calif. Tchrs. Assn., Calif. Assn. Marriage and Family Therapists, Planetary Soc., Mutual UFO Network, Com. Sci. Investigation L5 Soc., Challenger Ctr. Space Edn., Calif. Challenger Ctr. Crew for Space Edn., Orange County Astronomers, Chinese Shar-Pei Am., Concord Club, Rare Breed Dog Club (L.A.), gardening club of Am., ctr. for the extraterrestrial intelligence, diplomat, 1997. Republican. Avocations: skiing, banjo, guitar, flying, astrophotography. Home: 3257 La Travesia Dr Fullerton CA 92835-1455 Office: Bonita High Sch 115 W Allen Ave San Dimas CA 91773-1437 Office Phone: 714-992-0360.

CAMERON, KAY, conductor, music director, arranger; b. Robbins, N.C.; d. Joe and Gladys (Hussey) C. MusB, U. N.C., 1972, MusM, 1973. Music dir. Kennedy Ctr. For the Performing Arts, Washington, 1994—; condr. Words and Music, Musicals in Concert; music supr. Sondheim Celebration. Tchr. Richmond Pub. Schs., Va., 1973-77; music dir., condr. broadway and nat. tours, N.Y., 1978-1996; arranger, orchestrator musicals and TV, 1979-1990, vis. lectr. U. N.C., Wilmington, 1997-98; condr. concert featuring Cy Coleman, Kennedy Ctr. Opera House Orch. Music dir., condr. State Fair, The Will Rogers Follies, Phantom, The King and I, On The 20th Century, Sugar Babies, Showboat, The Sound of Music, Salute To The Broadway Composer, The Sound Of Rodgers And Hammerstein, New Moon, La Cage Aux Folles (opera) Amelia Goes To The Ball, Candide, Die Fledermaus, Hansel and Gretel, The Medium, Madama Butterfly, The Telephone, others; arranger, orchestrator Show Boat on PBS, United Nations 40th Anniversary, Herman & Soundheim Together, (compositions) A Christmas Carol, Heroes, others. Mem. Am. Fedn. Musicians. Home: 121 Loder Ave Wilmington NC 28409 E-mail: kcameron@kennedy-center.org.

CAMERON, LUCILLE WILSON, retired dean; b. Nashua, N.H., Dec. 21, 1932; d. Hugh Alexander and Louise Perham (Baldwin) C.; m. James Robert Doris, Aug. 19, 1976; children: Glenn A. Browning, Gail W. Browning, Valerie B. Cruickshank. BA, U. R.I., 1964, MLS, 1972. Social case worker R.I. Dept. Pub. Assistance, Providence, 1964-70; asst. circulation libr. U. R.I. Libr., Kingston, 1970-72, reserve libr., 1972-73, reference/bibliographer, 1973-88, head reference unit, 1983-86, chair pub. svcs., 1988-89, interim dean, 1989-90, dean, 1990—, dean emerita. Bd. trustees North Scituate (R.I.) Pub. Libr., 1995, pres., 1996. Co-author: Labor and Industrial Relations Journals and Serials, 1989; contbr. articles to profl. jours. Bd. trustees North Scituate (R.I.) Pub. Libr., 1995—, pres., 1996—. Recipient Computerized Intergrated Libr. System award Champlin Founds., Providence, 1989, 90, 91, Coll. Tech. Libr. Program award U.S. Dept. Edn., Washington, 1990, Disting. Alumna award Grad. Sch. Libr. and Info. Studies, U. R.I., Kingston, 1991. Mem. ALA, Assn. Coll. and Rsch. Librs., Consortium R.I. Acad. and Rsch. Librs., Higher Edn. Libr. Info. Network (chair), Univ. Press New England (gov.), North Scituate (R.I.) Pub. Libr. Assn. (bd. trustees 1995—, pres. 1996—), Alpha Kappa Delta.

CAMERON, RITA GIOVANNETTI, writer, publisher; b. Washington; d. Joseph Angelo and Adeline Katherine (Fochett) C. BS with honors, U. Md., 1957; MEd, Am. U., Washington, 1962; DEd, Nova U., 1978. Tchr. D.C. pub. schs., Washington, 1959-64; prin. Prince George's County (Md.) Pub. Schs., 1964-73, 76-84; supr. instrn. K-12 Prince George's County pub. schs., 1973-76; free-lance writer ednl. materials Media, Materials Inc., Balt., 1965-75, Learning Well, Balt., 1995, World Class Learning Materials, Inc., Balt., 2000—; free-lance writer travel articles AAA, Washington, 1978-83; owner, pub. Sch. House Global Enterprises, Fort Washington, Md., 1980—. Presenter, cons. to sch. systems and ednl. orgns., 1985—. Author: Let's Learn About Maryland and Prince George's County, 1970, Let's Learn About Maryland, 1972, 95, Super Sub! Or How to Substitute Teach in Elementary School, 1974, AAA Travel articles and Traffic Safety Teacher Guide Grades 4-6, 1982, 83; author, pub.: The Master Teacher's Plan and Record Book, 1985, The School House Encyclopedia of Educational Programs and Activities, 1991; author, publisher and nat. marketer of 88 social studies and sci. ednl. materials for students grades 4-10; developer/owner School House Global Enterprises Pub. Co. Food preparer So Others Might Eat, Washington, 1985—, food preparer for Missions of Charity Home for AIDS Victims, Washington, 1992—, sponsor Christian Found. for Children and Aging, 1998—. Recipient Outstanding Citizenship award DAR, 1954, Nat. Tchr. award Expedition Nat. Tchr. Awards Program, 1960-61, Outstanding Tchr. Sci. award D.C. Coun. Engring. and Archtl. Soc. and Washington Acad. Scis., 1964, Outstanding Educator of Yr. award Prince George's County Bd. Edn., 1982-83, Am. Hist. award DAR, 1987, Outstanding Contbn. to Bicentennial Leadership Project award Couns. for Advancement of Citizenship, 1989. Mem. U. Md. Alumni Assn., Am. U. Alumni Assn., Nova U. Alumni Assn., Phi Kappa Phi. Roman Catholic. Avocations: art, music, theater, antiques, travel. Office: Sch House Global Enterprises PO Box 441028 Fort Washington MD 20749-1028 Office Fax: 301-292-9744. Business E-Mail: dawn@schoolhouseglobalenterprises.com.

CAMERON, SUSAN KAY, government and public relations executive; b. Carroll, Iowa, Mar. 15, 1960; d. Charles William and Lois JoAnn (Reser) Hutchins; m. Michael J. Cameron, Aug. 12, 1989; 1 child, Sarah Jo. BA, Buena Vista U., 1982. Mgr. news and edtl. svcs. Drake U., Des Moines, 1984-85; asst. dir. pub. rels. Buena Vista U., Storm Lake, 1982-84, dir. pub. rels., 1985-96; pres. Charles W. Hutchins & Assocs., 1997—. Chmn. com. career advancement for minorities and women Mid-Am. dist. Coun. Advancement and Support Edn., 1989, presenter leadership conf., sec., 90, student scholarship chairperson, 92, chairperson conf. program track, 1992—93, conf. program chairperson, 1994—95; participant Nat. CASE Commn. Philanthropy, 1995—97. Recipient Young Alumnus award, Buena Vista U., 1995. Mem.: Iowa Women in Pub. Policy (bd. dirs. 2001—), Storm Lake C. of C. (bd. dirs. 1992, amb. 1990—96, Profl. Leadership award 1993). Roman Catholic. Avocations: writing poetry, reading, golf.

CAMMACK, ANN, librarian, secondary school educator; b. Akron, Ohio, Sept. 24, 1947; d. Matthew John and Anna (Maxim) Klinovsky; m. Robert Floyd Cammack, Sept. 27, 1969; children: Lisa Ann, Holly Ann, Noël Ann, Monica Ann. BA, Youngstown State U., 1969; MLS, Tex. Woman's U., 1995, PhD, 2001. Cert. tchr. secondary sch. Ohio, elem. and secondary sch., Tex. English tchr. Struthers (Ohio) City Schs., 1969-83; asst. cataloger Amon Carter Mus., Ft. Worth, 1997, 2000—01. Life mem. Tex. Parent Tchrs. Assn., historian Arlington, 1991-92. Doctoral fellow Tex. Woman's U., 1996. Mem. AAUW, ALA, Ladies Aux. VFW, Tex. Libr. Assn., Youngstown State U. Alumni Assn., Beta Phi Mu. Avocation: golf.

CAMMARATA, JOAN FRANCES, Spanish language and literature educator; b. Bklyn., Dec. 22, 1950; d. John and Angelina Mary (Guarnera) Cammarata; m. Richard Montemarano, Aug. 9, 1975. BA summa cum laude, Fordham U., 1972; MA, Columbia U., 1974, MPhil, 1977, PhD, 1982. Preceptor Columbia Coll., NYC, 1974-82; adj. instr. Fordham U., NYC, 1980-81; adj. asst. prof. Iona Coll., New Rochelle, NY, 1982-84; asst. prof. Manhattan Coll., Riverdale, NY, 1982-90, assoc. prof., 1990-96, prof., 1996—. Author: Mythological Themes in the Works of Garcilaso de la Vega, 1983; editor: Women in the Discourse of Early Modern Spain, 2003; mem. editl. bd. Modern Lang. Studies; editl. reviewer D.C. Heath; contbr. articles and revs. to profl. jours. Fellow arts and sci. Columbia U., 1972-75; grantee Manhattan Coll., 1985, 91, NEH, 1987, 88, Spain's Min Edn. Culture, 1997—; Rsch. Fellowship grantee NYU Faculty Seminars, 1992, 94; named univ. assoc. Faculty Resources Network Program NYU, 1985—; Andrew Mellon Found. vis. scholar, 1990; scholar-in-residence NYU, 1991-92, 97-98. Mem.: MLA (mem. del. assembly), N.Y. State Assn. Fgn. Lang. Tchrs., Am. Assn. Tchrs. Spanish and Portugese, Assn. Internat. de Hispanistas, Renaissance Soc. Am., Inst. Internat. de Lit. Iberoamericana, South Atlantic, South Ctrl. and Midwest MLA, N.E. MLA (rsch. fellow 1991, v.p. 1997—98, pres. 1998—), Am. Coun. Tchg. of Fgn. Langs, Cervantes Soc. Am., Hispanic Inst. Roman Catholic. Avocations: piano, gardening, writing, needlework. Office: Manhattan Coll Bronx NY 10471

CAMMERMEYER, MARGARETHE, retired medical/surgical nurse; b. Oslo, Mar. 24, 1942; arrived in U.S., 1951; d. Jan and Margrethe (Grimsgaard) Cammermeyer; m. Harvey H. Hawken, Aug. 1965 (div. 1980); children: Matthew Hawken, David Hawken, Andrew Hawken, Thomas Hawken; life ptnr. Diane Divelbess. BS, U. Md., 1963; MA, U. Wash., 1976, PhD, 1991. RN Wash. Staff nurse VA Hosp., Seattle, 1970-73, clin. nurse specialist in neurology, epilepsy, 1976-81; clin. nurse specialist in neuro-oncology VA Med. Ctr., San Francisco, 1981-86, clin. nurse specialist in neuroscis., nurse rschr. Tacoma, 1986-96; ret., 1996. Asst. chief nurse, supr. Army Res. Hosp., Oakland, Calif., 1985—88; adv. bd. Sourcemenber's Legal Def. Network. Co-author: Neurological Assessment for Nursing Practice, 1984 (named Book of Yr. ANA), Serving in Silence, 1994; co-editor, contbg. author: Core Curriculum for Neuroscience Nursing, 1990, 1993; contbr. articles to profl. jours.; host radio-Internet talk show, 1999—2001. Hon. bd. Ctr. Study of Sexual Minorities in Mil. Svc. Mem.'s Legal Def. Network. Capt. to col. USAR, 1972—88, col. Wash. N.G. U.S. Army, 1988—97, capt. U.S. Army, 1961—68. Decorated Bronze Star; named Woman of the Yr., Woman's Army Corps Vets. Assn., 1984, Nurse of the Yr., VA, 1985; recipient Presdl. cert. for Outstanding Cmty. Achievement Vietnam Era Vets., 1979, Woman of Power award, NOW, 1993, 1998, Human Rights award, ANA, 1994, Disting. Alumna award, U. Wash. Nursing Assn., 1995. Mem.: Am. Vets. for Equal Rights. Home and Office: 4632 S Tompkins Rd Langley WA 98260-9695 Office Phone: 360-221-5882. Business E-Mail: grethe@cammermeyer.com.

CAMP, ALETHEA TAYLOR, executive and organizational design consultant; b. Wingo, Ky., Nov. 12, 1938; d. Wayne Thomas and Ethel Virginia (Austin) Taylor; children: Donna Paul, Sean Richard. BA, Murray State U., 1961; MA, So. Ill. U., 1975. Tchr. McLean and Hopkins (Ky.) County Schs., 1961-64; instr. homebound Harrisburg (Ill.) Community Sch. Dist., 1971-73; counselor evaluation Coleman Rehab. Ctr., Shawneetown, Ill., 1974-75; counselor corrections and parole Dept. Corrections, State Ill., Springfield, 1975-77, supr. casework, 1977, supr. parole, 1977-80, asst. warden programs Hillsboro, 1980-84, warden, 1984-91; correctional program specialist Nat. Inst. Corrections, Washington, 1991-95; exec. and orgnl. cons. Camp-Blair Consulting, Inc., 1995—2002, CAUCAsoft, Inc., 2003—. Mem.: NAFE, Assn. Women Execs. in Corrections (exec. dir. 1998—2001), Am. Correctional Assn. Avocations: gardening, sailing, traveling, extensive walking. E-mail: ataylorcamp@compuserve.com.

CAMP, CARMEN SUE, special education educator; b. Kilgore, Tex., Sept. 11, 1937; d. G.U. and Anna Bell (Graham) Yoachum; m. Frank Wesley Camp, Sept. 30, 1955; children: Frank Guy, Gay. BS, U. Houston, 1970; MEd, Tex. Tech. U., 1977. Cert. tchr., spl. edn. tchr., Tex. Tchr. spl. edn. Spring Branch Ind. Sch. Dist., Houston, 1971-72, Brownfield (Tex.) Ind. Sch. Dist., 1972—; tchr. adult edn. Region 17 Svc. Ctr., 1993—. Fundraiser for state and local Dem. politicians; mem. Dem. Nat. Coun. Mem. DAR, Tex. Assn. for Lit. and Adult Edn., Coun. for Exceptional Children, Parent-Tchrs. Orgn. (life), So. Poverty Law Ctr., Tex. Tech Ex-Students Assn., Phi Delta Kappa, Delta Kappa Gamma. Episcopalian. Home: PO Box 279 Kilgore TX 75663-0273

CAMP, DELPHA JEANNE, counselor; b. Yakima, Wash., Apr. 20, 1937; d. George Emerson and Emilie Loraine (Rivard) Stevens; m. George Ernest Mills, Aug. 13, 1960 (dec. 1975); children: Adriene Phillips, Stacey Harcus, Ryan, Tiffany; m. James Clell Camp, June 24, 1978; children: Catherine Thompson (dec.), Wayne (dec.), Darla Coolman, John, Janna Barnes. BEd, Gonzaga Univ., 1959; MS, Univ. Oreg., 1977. Lic. profl. counselor; cert. in death, dying and bereavement. Tchr. Riverside Sch. Dist., Milan, Wash., 1959-61, Cheney (Wash.) Sch. Dist., 1968-70; asst. prof. Univ. Oreg., Eugene, 1979-92; pvt. practice Eugene, 1992—. Mem. faculty Marylhurst (Oreg.) U., 1992—2002. Mem. Assn. for Death Edn. and Counseling (bd. dirs. 1990-93, co-chair conf. 1994, 2002, 1st v.p. 1998-99, pres. 1999-00, Svc. award 1990), Am. Mental Health Counselors Assn., Oreg. Mental Health Counselors Assn. Avocations: reading, classical music. Home: 440 E 39th Ave Eugene OR 97405-4722 Office: 317 W Broadway Ste 217 Eugene OR 97401-2890 E-mail: deljcamp@aol.com.

CAMP, HAZEL LEE BURT, artist; b. Gainesville, Ga., Nov. 28, 1922; d. William Ernest and Annie Mae (Ramsey) Burt; m. William Oliver Camp, Jan. 24, 1942; children: William Oliver, David Byron. Student, Md. Inst. Art, 1957-58, 62-63. Exhibitions include Susquehanna U. Lore A. Degenstein Gallery, Pa., 1994, Nat. League of Am. Pen Women Cork Gallery, Lincoln Ctr., N.Y.C., 1994, Suffolk Art League, 1994, 1996—2001, Town Hall Gallery, Epe, The Netherlands, 1999, Piedmont Art Assn, Martinsville, Va., 2000, one-woman shows include Ga. Mus. Art, Rockville Art Mus., Coll. Notre Dame (Balt.), U. Md., Balt. Vertical Gallery, Cleveland Meml. Gallery (Balt.), Unicorn Gallery, 1982, Hampton Ctr. for Arts and Humanities (Va.), 1985, Bendann Art Gallery, Balt., 1980, Cultural Art Ctr. On the Hill Gallery, Yorktown, Va., 1995, Cultural Art Ctr. on the Hill Gallery, Yorktown, Va., 2000—03, others; juried shows include Peale Mus., Balt., Muscarelle Mus. of Art Coll. of William and Mary, Williamsburg, Va., 1998—99, Wilmington (Del.) Fine Arts Ctr., Smithsonian Inst., City Hall Gallery, Balt., 1982, Balt. Watercolor Soc., 1983, 1994—95, Arts Club, Washington, 1987—96, Strathmore Hall Arts Ctr., Md., 1997—2004, Fells Point Gallery, Balt., 2000, 2002, Hampton Bay Days Raddison Hotel Gallery, 1988, Twentieth Century Gallery, Williamsburg, Va., 1989—2003, D'Art Ctr., Norfolk, Va., 1989, Virginia Beach Ctr. for Arts, 1990, Verona, 1991, William King Regional Arts Ctr ., Abingdon, Va., 1992, 2002, Lore A. Degenstein Gallery, Pa. Watercolor Soc., 1994, Longwood Ctr. Visual Arts, Farmville, Va., 1995, Fine Arts Ctr., Lynchburg, Va., 1996, Va. Watercolor Soc., Martinsville, Va., 2000, Yorktown Cultural Arts Ctr., 1991—2004, Furman U., 1992, Goucher Coll., Towson Md., Hermitage Found. Mus., Norfolk, 1994, 1998, 2000, Francis Land House Tidewater Artists Assn., Va. Beach, 1994, Salmagundi Club, N.Y.C., 1995, The Nat. League of Am. Pen Women; Miniature Art Soc. Fla., 1999, 2001—02, St. Petersburg Mus. Fine Arts, 2000, Dunedin Fine Arts Ctr., 2002, Gulf Coast Mus. Art, Fla., 2003, exhibitions include Seaside Art Gallery, Nags Head, NC, 2001—03, Miniature Painters, Sculptors and Gravers Soc. Washington, 1987—2003 (hon. mention, 1991). Recipient 3d prize Nat. Biennial Exhibit, Tulsa, 1966, 1st prize Md. chpt. Artists' Equity, 1967, St. Mary's County Art Assn., 1964, 67, 1st prize still life Cape May, N.J., 1969, Catonsville (Md.) C.C., 1969, Nat. League Am. Pen Women Exhibit at St. John's Coll., 1969, Best in Show York (Pa.) Art Assn. Gallery, 1972, 2nd award Md. Inst. Alumni Founding Chpt., Balt., 1976, Best in Show Three Arts Club, Balt., 1978, hon. mention Rehoboth Art League, Del., 1983, 93, Adelia E. Chiswell 2nd award, 1996, purchase award Old Point Nat. Bank, Hampton, Va., 1985, merit award Hampton (Va.) City Hall, 1986, Juror's Choice award Twentieth Century Gallery, Williamsburg, Va., 1987, first prize 1999; Award of Excellence Md. State Biennial Eliminations of Nat. League Am. Pen Women at Essex C.C., 1989, Montgomery Coll., Rockville, Md., 1987, hon. mention Nat. Miniature Show, Jackson, Tenn., 1991, Suffolk Art League, 1992, award Eagleton's Inc., 1996, 1st prize Virginia Heritage Exhibit, Yorktown Arts Found., 1998, hon. mention award Tidewater Art Assn., Norfolk, 1999, The Willows award Suffolk Art League Juried Exhibit, 1999. Mem. Nat. League Am. Pen Women (pres. Carroll branch 1968-70, editor The Quill 1975-76, Carroll br. 1982-83, rec. sec. nat. exec. bd. 1979-80, nat. nominating com. 1982, Md. art chmn. 1982, illustrator Nat. Roster 1990 and The Pen Woman mag. 1995), Rehoboth Art League (Adelia E. Chiswell 2d award 1996), Del. Hampton Arts League, Va. Watercolor Soc. (signature artist mem.), Balt. Watercolor Soc. (signature artist life mem., hon. mention 1982, sec. 1978-80), Peninsula Fine Arts Ctr., 20th Century Gallery (Williamsburg), This Century Gallery, Yorktown Cultural Arts Ctr., Tidewater Art Assn., Miniature Painters, Sculptors and Gravers Soc. of Washington, Hampton (Va.) Arts League, Miniature Art Soc. Fla., Pa. Watercolor Soc. Methodist. Home: 2 Bayberry Dr Newport News VA 23601-1006

CAMP, KIMBERLY N. museum administrator, artist; b. Camden, N.J., Sept. 11, 1956; d. Hubert E. and Marie (Dimery) C.; m. Seydou Coulibaly, Apr. 1997 (div.). BA, U. Pitts., 1978; MS, Drexel U., 1986. Dir. artistic design project City Camden, 1984-86; program dir. Pa. Coun. on Arts, Harrisburg, 1986-89; dir. exptl. gallery Smithsonian Instn., Washington, 1989-94; pres. Mus. African Am. History, Detroit, 1994-98; exec. dir., CEO Barnes Found., Merion, Pa., 1998—. Evaluator Am. Assn. Mus., Washington, 1994—; panel chair Nat. Endowment for Arts, Washington, 1991-92, vice chair, bd. dirs. Assn. Am. Cultures, Washington, 1987-89. One-woman shows include Clifton Art Ctr., N.J., Glouchester County Coll., Deptford Township, N.J., Passaic Count C.C., Paterson, N.J., Diggs Gallery, Winston-Salem, N.C., Galerie Francois, Washington, Banneker Douglass Mus., Annapolis, Md., 3d Bienniel Nat. Black Arts Festival, Atlanta, Manchester Craftsmen's Guilde, Pitts., Caribbean Cultural Ctr., N.Y.C., Jr. Black Acad. Arts and Letters, Dallas, Walt Whitman Ctr. Arts and Humanities, Camden, Longwood Gardens, Kennett Square, Pa., Art Mus. Western Va., Raonoke, Harrison Mus. African Am. Culture, Roanoke, 1994; represented in permanent collections J.B Speed Art Mus., Manchester Craftsmen's Guild, Reader's Digest, Camden Hist. Soc.; mng. editor Nat. Conf. Artists Phila. Chpt. newsletter, 1980-84. Bd. dirs. Bus. Vols. for Arts, 1994-97. Recipient Nat. Svc. award Nat. Conf. Artists, 1984, Arts Achievement award City of Camden, 1984, Cmty. Svc. award Assn/ Negro Bus. and Profl. Women, 1985, Builders of Cmty. award Camden County Cultural and Heritage Commn., 1986, Purchase award J.B. Speed Art Mus., 1988, Spirit of Detroit award Detroit City Coun., 1994; Arts Internat. grantee Ctr. Internat. Exch. Scholars, 1994, Roger L. Stevens Nat. Arts award Carnegie Mellon U. H. John Heinz Sch. Mgmt., 1999; fellow Kellogg Nat. Leadership Program, 1994-97. Mem. Assn. Am. Cultures (bd. dirs. 1989—), Am. Assn. Museums (bd. dirs. 1995-97), Links, Inc., N.J. Coun. on Arts. Office: The Barnes Found 300 N Latch's Ln Merion Station PA 19066-1729

CAMP, SHIRLEY A. nursing consultant, lawyer; b. Winnipeg, Man., Can., Oct. 24, 1955; m. Daniel Lloyd Camp, Aug. 1, 1976. BSN, Calif. State U., Long Beach, 1982; JD, Western State U., 1985. House supr. Kaiser Permanente, Anaheim, Calif., 1981-90; clin. coord., nurse exec. Smyrna (Ga.) Hosp., 1991-93; RN, cons. Loube Cons., Norcross, Ga., 1993-95; lawyer, exec. dir. State of Ga. Bd. Nursing, Office of Sec. of State, Atlanta, 1995—. Mem. Nat. Coun. State Bds. Nursing. Mem. Ga. Nurses Assn. Office: State Ga Bd Nursing 237 Coliseum Dr Macon GA 31217

CAMPAGNOLO, ANN-CASEY, retail executive; b. Newport, R.I., July 17, 1972; d. Eugene Louis and Kathleen Ellen (Laughlin) C. BS in Agr. and Resource Econs., U. Md., 1995. Asst. buyer petites Bloomingdale's, N.Y.C., 1995-96; asst. buyer Salon Z Saks Fifth Ave., N.Y.C., 1996-97, assoc. buyer sportswear, 1997-98, store planner casual, 1998-99, corp. planner ready-to-wear divsn., 1999-2001, dir. corp. merchandise planning, 2001—02, sr. dir. planning and allocation mens and cosmetics, 2002—03, sr. dir. planning and allocation designer, childrens and home, 2003—. Bd. dirs., treas. Saks Fifth Ave. Employee Fed. Credit Union, 2002—. Mem. Jr. League N.Y. Mem.: Order of Omega (Outstanding Chpt. Pres. award 1994), Gamma Phi Beta (Province collegiate dir. 1996—2001, sec. alumnae N.Y.C. chpt. 1995—96, pres. Beta Beta chpt. 1993—94). Republican. Roman Catholic. Avocations: cooking, reading, traveling. Office: Saks Fifth Ave 12 E 49th St 9th Fl New York NY 10017-1088

CAMPAS, ANNA PENELOPE, civil engineer, architect; b. Balt., Nov. 21, 1949; d. William and Katy (Hondros) Campas; children: Thomas William, Scott Stratton. BArch, Rensselaer Polytech. Inst., 1972; BSCE, Union Coll., 1977. Registered profl. engr., architect, N.Y.; accredited profl. leadership in energy and environ. design profl. Staff architect-engr. GE Co., Schenectady, N.Y., 1972-73; architectural designer Fay Evans, P.C., Troy, N.Y., 1974-75, Golub Corp., Schenectady, 1975-77, Einhorn, Yaffee, Prescott, P.C., Albany, N.Y., 1979-80; jr. engr. N.Y. State Office Gen. Svc., Design and Constrn. Group, Albany, 1980-82, asst. bldg. structural engr., 1982-87, sr. bldg. structural engr., 1987—, mem. green bldg. working group for NY State exec. order 111, team leader design & constrn. green bldg. coun. Bd. dirs. Montessori Sch. of Albany, 1990-92. Vol. Susan G. Komen Breast Cancer Race for the Cure. Mem. Bethlehem Music Assn. (membership chmn., treas., co-pres.). Home: 41 Darroch Rd Delmar NY 12054-3916 Office Phone: 518-473-8769. E-mail: penrose@nycap.rr.com.

CAMPASINO, ELLEN MARIE, elementary school educator; b. Titusville, Pa., Aug. 30, 1950; d. Frank and Helen (Lowicki) Campasino. BS in Elem. and Early Childhood Edn., Edinboro U., 1972, cert. in elem. and early childhood edn., 1978. 1st grade tchr. St. Titus Sch., Titusville, 1975-76, 4th grade tchr., 1976-77, 3rd grade tchr., 1977—. Coaching tchr. St. Titus Tchr. Induction Program, Titusville, 1989—90, asst. to prin., 1993—, 2003—04; mentor tchr., 2000—01. Mem. ministry tng. program Diocese of Erie; min. hospitality St. Walburga Parish, Roman Cath. Ch., Titusville. Recipient Svc. award, Diocese of Erie, 1988, 1990, 1996, 25 Yrs. of Svc. award, 2000—01. Avocations: reading, doll collecting, embroidery. Office: St Titus Sch 528 W Main St Titusville PA 16354-1598

CAMPBELL, ANDREA S. writer; b. Lakewood, Ohio, Jan. 3, 1949; AAS in Criminal Justice, Garland County C.C., Hot Springs, Ark., 1997. Diplomate Am. Coll. Forensic Examiners. Forensic sci. artist, 1999—; author, 1989—. Forensic artist Ark. State Crime Lab. Author: (book) Legal Ease: A Guide to Criminal Law, Evidence and Procedure, 2002, Making Crime Pay: A Writer's Guide to Criminal Law, Evidence, and Procedure, 2002, Perfect Party Games, 2001, Rights of the Accused, 2000; contbg. editor: The Simian Newsletter, First Draft Newsletter. Fellow: Am. Coll. Forensic Examiners; mem.: Sisters in Crime, Internat. Assn. for Identification (Ark. bd. dirs.), Mystery Writers of Am., Am. Soc. Journalists and Authors. Office Phone: 501-922-0050.

CAMPBELL, ANITA JOYCE, computer company executive; b. Jefferson City, Mo., Sept. 24, 1953; d. George Rigsby and Betty Jean (Heade) Sanders; m. Michael Joseph Campbell (div. 1986); children: Kim Erik Seaver, Daniel Joseph Campbell. AAS in Computer Sci., Lincoln U., Mo., 1985; BA in Psychology, Maryville U., 1998; MBA in Global Tech. Mgmt., 2004. Student lab. mgr. Lincoln U., 1985; integrated systems analyst Xerox Corp., St. Louis, 1988-89, ins. industry project mgr., western region ops. mgmt. staff, 1990-91, advanced product specialist, western regions ops. mgmt., 1991, advanced solutions tech. mgr., western region ops. mgmt., 1992-93, tech. market project mgr., rsch. & engring, integrated systems orgn., 1993-94, tech. mktg. mgr. integrated solutions, systems sales and support, 1994-95; tech. con., integrated document solutions Integrated Document Solutions, 1995-96; project mgr. state and local govt. Xerox Profl. Document Svcs., Bridgeton, Mo., 1996-97; project mgr. govt. practice Xerox Profl. Svcs., 1997-99, opportunity mgr. cons. and sys. integration, 1999—; program mgr. GraphicArts Solutions Xerox Document Svcs.; program mgr. graphic arts solutions Document Solutions Group; prin. document solutions practice Xerox Connect, St. Louis, 2000-01, solutions architect, 2001; IT rschr. Wyeth BioPharma, Berkeley, Mo., 2001—03; bus. analyst KV Pharms., 2003—. Co-developer Delta Plan, 1988. Office staff campaign mgr. for Carter-Mondale Reelection Com., Washington, 1989-90; waterfront dir. Spl. Olympics, Lake of the Ozarks, Mo., 1987; bd. dirs. ARC, Jefferson City, 1986. Avocations: reading, swimming. Home: 912 Leawood Dr Saint Louis MO 63126-1114 Office: KV Pharm 2503 S Handley Rd Saint Louis MO 63144

CAMPBELL, ANN MARIE, artist; b. Burbank, Calif., June 14, 1956; d. Stephen and Ann Marie (Luis) C.; children: Richard Arthur, Robert Campbell, Victoria Ann. BA in Painting, Sculpture, Graphic Arts, UCLA, 1980. Spkr. Mural Art Seminar, ASID Student Career Forum, 1995. Artist: (murals) The Pickle Barrel, 1992, Old World Sky with Angels, 1996, Cottage Garden, 1995, Two Street Window, 1996, Heather's Jazz Band, 1996, California Groaning Board, 1997, History of Virgin Records, 1997, Christ Crucufied, 2000, numerous others throughout U.S. and Can., San Francisco, N.Y., L.A., Las Vegas, Orlando, Fla., Dallas, Phoenix, New Orleans, Denver, Chgo., Columbus, Ohio, Miami, Fla., and Vancouver, B.C., Can., St. Anthony Ch., El Segundo, Calif. Mem. Nat. Soc. Mural Painters, Am. Soc. Portrait Artists, Alpha Lambda Delta. Roman Catholic. Office: PO Box 581 Folsom CA 95763-0581 E-mail: AmcArtist@aol.com.

CAMPBELL, BRENDA DIANNE, protective services official; b. Oklahoma City, Sept. 4, 1956; d. Jerry Glenn and Janice Gail Hall, Ronald Ross Stevenson; m. Joe Allen Lindsey, Aug. 30, 2003; children: Stephanne Suzanne Howery, Desiree' Nicole Lindsey, Donyae' Michelle Lindsey, Myles Gregory Lindsey. A of Police Sci., Okla. State U., 1997. Insp. Okla. City Police Dept., 1980—. Recipient Police Officer Yr., Kiwanis Club, 1990. Independent. Methodist. Office: Oklahoma City Police Dept 701 Colcord Dr Oklahoma City OK 73102 Personal E-mail: ladyheat@cox.net.

CAMPBELL, CLAIRE PATRICIA, nurse practitioner, educator; b. Jan. 10, 1933; d. Hugh Paul Campbell and Clara Louise Campbell. Student, So. Meth. U., 1956-57; BS in Nursing, U. Tex. Sch. Nursing, Galveston, 1959, Family Nurse Pracitioner, 1979, cert., 1984, 89, 99; MS in Nursing, Tex. Woman's U. Sch. Nursing, 1971. Staff nurse Parkland Meml. Hosp., Dallas County Hosp Dist., 1955-70; head nurse gen. surgery, chest surgery, neurosurgery orthopedics and internal medicine, until 1970; instr. nursing Tex. Woman's U. Sch. Nursing, Dallas, 1971-72; rschr. nursing diagnosis Dallas, 1972-77; FNP Otis Engring. Health Svc., Dallas, 1979-86; nurse pracitioner pain mgmt. program Dallas Rehab. Inst., 1986-95, HealthSouth SubAcute Unit, Dallas, 1995-97, HeathSouth Med. Ctr.-Rehab., Dallas, 1997—. Adj. asst. prof. U. Tex. Sch. Nursing, Arlington, 1976-98; cons. nursing diagnosis. Author: Nursing Diagnosis and Intervention in Nursing Practice, 1st edit., 1978, 2d edit., 1984. Mem.: ANA, Tex. Nurses Assn. Roman Catholic.

CAMPBELL, CYNTHIA, retail executive; From regional v.p. Bus. Svcs. Group Southeast Region to exec. v.p. Delivery Sales N.Am. Office Depot, Inc., Delray Beach, Fla., 1995—2003, exec. v.p. Delivery Sales N.Am., 2003—; v.p., gen. mgr. Info. Svcs. GTE Corp., 1976—95. Office: Office Depot Inc 2200 Old Germantown Rd Delray Beach FL 33445

CAMPBELL, DEBRA LYNN, marketing and new venture consultant; b. Phoenix, Apr. 8, 1954; d. Joseph David and Elaine Lucinda (Krueger) C.; m. J. Frederick Stillman III, Oct. 26, 1985; 1 child, J. Frederick Stillman IV. BS, U. Ariz., 1975; MBA, Harvard U., 1980. Brand mgr. Procter & Gamble Co., Cin., 1975-78; project mgr. Dunham & Marcus, N.Y.C., 1980-81; v.p. Cox, Lloyd Assocs., N.Y.C., 1981-83; cons. Am. Cons. Corp., N.Y.C., 1983-85, dir., 1985-87, dir., CFO, 1987-88, pres., COO, 1988-90; pres. DCA, 1990—2002; COO Hudson River Group, Valhalla, NY, 2002—. Pres. 173-175 Tenants' Corp.; Treas. Cathedral Guild St. John the Divine Ch. Recipient Reggie award Promotion Mktg. Assn. Am. (Reggie award 1986, 87, 90). Mem.: Nat. Sculpture Soc. (treas.). Avocations: travel, collecting American Indian art, golf, tennis. Office: Hudson River Group 465 Columbus Ave Valhalla NY 10595-1336

CAMPBELL, DOROTHY MAY, management consultant; d. George S. May. V.p. George S. May Intl Co Del, Park Ridge, Ill., 1962—; also bd. dirs. Office: George S May Intl Co Del 303 S Northwest Hwy Park Ridge IL 60068-4232

CAMPBELL, EILEEN M. oil industry executive; married; 2 children. Bachelor's, U. Md. Lobbyist Gov. NJ; with Nat. Assn. Mfrs.; lobbyist United Gas Pipe Line Co.; mgr. govt. affairs Marathon Oil Corp., Houston, 1991—98, v.p. human resources, 2000—; dir. state govt. affairs USX, 1998—2000. Office: Marathon Oil Corp Corp Hdqrs 5555 San Felipe Rd Houston TX 77056-2723*

CAMPBELL, ELIZABETH ROSE, astrologer, writer, videographer; b. Rocky Mount, N.C., Mar. 7, 1952; d. Walker Aylett Jr. and Sarah West (Davis) C. BA in Journalism, BA in Studio Art, U. N.C., 1975. Asst. editor The Sun: A Mag. of Ideas, Chapel Hill, N.C., 1977-82; dir. mktg., seminar prodr. Omega Inst. for Holistic Studies, Rhinebeck, N.Y., 1982-84; founder, counselor Wild Rose Cons., Carrboro, N.C., 1984—. Contbr. (anthology) The Best of the Sun, Vol. I, 1985, Vol. II, 1986, Dreams are Wiser than Men, 1988, Jo's Girls, 1997; videographer Pulses (winner PBS competition 1996); author: Intuitive Astrology-Follow Your Best Instincts to Become Who You Always Intended To Be, 2003. Fellow Edna St. Vincent Millay Colony, 1986, Cummington Cmty. of Arts, 1988, Va. Ctr. for Creative Arts, 1996, 97, Ragdale Found., 1998. Home: PO Box 449 Rhinebeck NY 12572-0449

CAMPBELL, ELSIE MAE, mathematician, educator; b. Grand Haven, Mich., Mar. 3, 1947; d. Harold Walter Oscar and Marjorie Leona (Reichelt) Gustafson; m. Edgar James Campbell, Nov. 23, 1974; children: James Harold, Victoria Mae. BA, Grand Valley State U., Allendale, Mich., 1968; MA, Western Mich. U., Kalamazoo, 1970, Specialist in Arts, 1971. Math. tchr. Spring Lake H.S., Mich., 1972—73; engr. GTE-Mich., Muskegon, Mich., 1973—74; traffic engr. GTE-S.W., San Angelo, Tex., 1974—76; math tchr. Wall Ind. Sch. Dist., Wall, Tex., 1990—97; math instr. Howard Coll., San Angelo, Tex., 1997—99; math tchr. Angelo State U., San Angelo, Tex., 1999—2003, profl. specialist, 2003—. Contbr. articles to profl. jours. Pres. Barrow Mus., Eola, Tex., 1998—2000, vice-president, 1997—98, mem., 1996. Mem.: Assn. of Tex. Profl. Educators, Tex. Acad. of Sci., Math. Assn. of Am. Lutheran. Avocations: billiards, sewing, hunting. Home: 19260 Fm 381 Paint Rock TX 76866 Office: Angelo State University 2601 W Avenue N San Angelo TX 76909 Personal E-mail: jvic@wcc.net. E-mail: elsie.campbell@angelo.edu.

CAMPBELL, HEATHER SUE, credit manager, religious studies educator; b. Santa Monica, Calif., Sept. 2, 1954; d. George and Leona Hoppen; m. John Rankin Campbell; 1 child, Meghan. Assoc. in Arts, SUNY, New Paltz, 1974; BA in Liberal Studies, Calif. State U., 1977; M in Sci. Edn., Nat. U., 1981. Bookeeper Law Offices of Eric Schnurmacher, Oakland, Calif., 1990; office mgr./bookkeeper Avalanche Snowboards, Benicia, Calif., 1990—92; office mgr. Cygnet Techs., Berkeley, Calif., 1992; office mgr., billing supr. Spinal Care Ctr., Benicia, Calif., 1992—94; collections specialist Pubs. Group West, Emeryville, Calif., 1994—97; dir. tng. and gen. adminstrn. RYNO Consulting, Inc., Benicia, Calif., 1997—99; credit mgr. Pubs. Group West, Berkeley, Calif., 1999—2001; Sunday School Teacher Congregation B'nai Israel, Vallejo, CA, 1999—2000. City clerk candidate City Coun., Benicia, 1992; pres. Congregation B'nai Israel, Vallejo, 1995—98, v.p., 1993—95; co-founder Benicia-Solano Jewish Women's Network, Benicia, 1989—2001; mem. com. Cultural Diversity Fair Com., Benicia, 1999. Recipient Tony Ubalde's People award, Tony Ubalde of Vallejo Times-Herald, 1997. Mem.: AAUW, Hadassah, Nat. Coun. Jewish Women (life; chmn. 1986—88). Democrat. Jewish. Avocations: cooking, reading, camping, hiking, travel. Personal E-mail: HeatherCam@aol.com.

CAMPBELL, HEIDI DENICE, communications educator; d. Thomas David and Stacy L Blossom; m. Chace D Campbell, July 29, 1995. BS, Bob Jones U., Greenville SC, 1994, MA in Broadcast Comm., 2001. Broadcast Certificate Assn. of Youth Devel./ Dominican Republic, 1990. Announcer WBJU, Greenville, SC, 1991—94; prodr. Audio Services, Greenville, SC, 1993—95; copywriter WSCQ-FM, Columbia, SC, 1995—96; prodr. of bill benton talk show WSCQ, Columbia, SC, 1995—96; program dir. Bible Broadcasting Network, Charlotte, NC, 1996—99; broadcast instr. Bob Jones U., Greenville, SC, 1999—, chmn. of dept. of radio & tv broadcasting, 2003—. Cons. Broadcast Organizations, Greenville, SC, Radio Light Ho., Antigua and Barbuda, Designs for Living Ministries, Danville, Pa., Spoken Word of God Ministries, Boca Raton, Fla., Convertidos a Cristo, Santo Domingo, Dominican Republic. Prodr.: (radio program) Today's Christian Teen; author: (seminar) Adventures in Announcing, (training program) Radio and the Internet; dir.(producer): (radio program) Club de Ninos; prodr.: Culto Dominical, Desde Mi Hogar al Suyo; dir.(producer): (seasonal radio program) Noticias de la Hora, (radio program) Historias de Grandes Himnos; author (producer): (seasonal radio program) Navidad Alrededor del Mundo, Christmas Around the World, The Candy Cane. Vol. coord. Rep. Party, Greenville, SC, 2002—02; dir. Cmty. Bible Church-First Impressions Ministry Team, Easley, SC, 2001. Recipient Best Talk Show of Columbia, The State, 1996. Mem.: Assn. for Edn. in Journalism and Mass Communication (assoc.), SC. Broadcast Assn. (assoc.), Nat. Religious Broadcasters (assoc.), Broadcast Edn. Assn. (assoc.). R-Consevative. Achievements include research in Radio and the Internet-The merging of the minds; Training the new generation of radio announcers. Avocations: reading, radio production, traveling, international communications. Office: Dept Radio & TV Broadcasting 1700 Wade Hampton Blvd Greenville SC 29614

CAMPBELL, JACQUELYN C. community health nurse; b. Camden, N.J., Aug. 2, 1946; d. Joseph and Dorothy (Cutler) Bowman; 1 child, Christina, Bradley. BSN, Duke U., 1968; MSN, Wright State U., 1980; PhD in Nursing, U. Rochester, 1986. RN, Mich. Instr. Sinclair Community Coll., Dayton, Ohio, 1976-79, Wayne State U. Coll. Nursing, Detroit, 1980-82, mem. faculty, 1984—, assoc. prof., 1988—; teaching asst. U. Rochester (N.Y.) Sch. Nursing, 1982-84; Anna D. Wolf Endowed Prof., Sch. Nursing Johns Hopkins U., associate dean for the Ph.D. program and res., Sch. Nursing. Bd. dirs. Family Violence Prevention Fund, House of Ruth; mem. violence rev. panel NIMH, Washington, 199—. Co-author: Nursing Care of Victims of Family Violence, 1984 (AJN Book of Yr.); author: To Have & To Fit, Cultural Perspectives on Wife Beating, 2d edit., 1999, Assessing Dangerousness: Violence by Sexual Offenders, Batterers and Child Abusers, 1994, Ending Domestic Violence: Changing Public Perceptions/Halting the Epidemic, 1997, Empowering Survivors of Abuse: Health Care for Battered Women and their Children, 1998, Family Violence and Nursing Practice, 2003, Nursing Care Survivors of Family Violence 2d edit., 1993; mem. editorial bd. to sci. jours.; contbr. articles to profl. jours. V.p., bd. dirs. Women's Justice Ctr., Ann Arbor, Mich., 1987—; pres. Coun. on the Status of Women, Detroit, 1988-92; support group facilitator My Sister's Place, Detroit, 1989-92; mem. adv. bd. Wayne County Adv. Bd. Interpersonal Violence, Detroit, 1991-92, adv. panel Robert Wood Johnson Found., Princeton, N.J., 1990-92; prin. investigator NIH, NCNR, 1990—; mem. Dept. Defense Task Force on Domestic Violence. Recipient First ward NIH, 1987-92; W.K. Kellogg Found., 1990-93. Mem. ANA (chair task force on violence 1991-92), APHA, Am. acad. Nursing, a.A.N. award 1988), Inst. Medicine, Midwest Nursing Rsch. Soc. (Helen Werley new investigator 1992), Nursing Rsch. Consortium on Violence and Abuse, Nursing Network on Violence Against Women. Democrat. Avocation: tennis. Office: Johns Hopkins Univ Sch Nursing 525 N Wolfe St Baltimore MD 21205-2110*

CAMPBELL, JANE LOUISE, mayor; b. May 19, 1953; d. Paul and Joan (Brown) C.; m. Hunter Morrison, Dec. 8, 1984; children: Jessica Elizabeth, Catherine Joanna. BA in History, U. Mich., 1974; MS in Urban Studies, Cleve. State U., 1980. Mem. State of Ohio Ho. of Reps. 11th dist., Columbus, 1984—92, majority whip, 1992—2000; mayor City of Cleve., 2001—. Apptd. mem. Nat. Com. on Welfare Reform; mem. Cuyahoga County Plan Commn., Fin. and Appropriations Com., Ways and Means Com., Aging and Housing Com.; active Nat. Coun. State Legislators, vice-chair Human Svcs. Com., Children, Families and Youth Com., past pres. Women's Network, mem. Federal Budget and Taxation Com.; chair Abused, Neglected Children Oversight Com.; vice-chair Select Com. on Child Abuse and Juvenile Justice, 1989; mem. gov. task force on Adolescent Sexuality and Pregnanacy, 1986, com. to Study Ohio's Sch. Found. Program Distribution of State Funds to Sch. Dists., 1991; exec. dir. Friends of Shaker Square, 1982-84; nat. field dir. ERAmerica, 1979-82; founding dir. Womenspace, 1975-79. Elder Heights Christian Ch. Recipient Legislative Leadership award Ohio Psychological Assn., 1986, Legislative award Ohio Hunger Task Force, 1987, Recognition award Ohio Primary Care Assn., 1987, Dean's Disting. Alumni award Cleve. State Univ., 1987, Hall of Fame award Nat. Senior Citizens, 1988, State Public Official of the Year award Ohio Chpt. Nat. Assn. of Social Workers, 1988, Found. award Ohio Chpt. ACLU, 1988, Legislative award Ohio Assn. of Counseling and Devel., 1989, Ohio Assn. of County Bds. of Mental Retardation/Developmental Disabilities award, 1989, Cancer Fighter award Ireland Cancer Ctr., 1990, Legislative award Ohio Human Svcs. Dirs. Assn., 1990, Hosephine Irwin award Womenspace, 1991, Spcl. Recognition award Providence House, 1991, Citizen award Ohio Assn. for the Edn. of Young Children, 1991, Legislator of the Year award Greater Cleve. Nurses Assn., 1991, Legilsative award Nat. Assn. of Sch. Psychologists, 1992, Outstanding Svc. award Public Children's Svcs. Assn., 1992., numerous others. Democrat. Office: Cleveland City Hall 601 Lakeside Ave Rm 202 Cleveland OH 44114

CAMPBELL, JANE TURNER, retired realtor, retired secondary school educator, retired adult education educator; b. Macon, Mo., July 8, 1931; d. Thomas Freeman and Rena Ellen (Vandiver) Turner; m. Duard Ray McDonald, Aug. 25, 1952 (div. 1955); m. Ian MacCallum Campbell, Mar. 28, 1958; children: Colin Turner, Clay Ian. BS in Edn., U. Mo., 1953; postgrad., San Diego State Coll., 1955-57, UCLA, 1958. Cert. secondary sch. tchr. Calif., Ill., N.J., lic. real estate salesperson, broker N.J., Pa., Mo. Tchr. Hallsville (Mo.) HS, 1953-54; co-owner McDonalds' Clothiers, Wewoka, Okla., 1954-55; tchr., class advisor Imperial (Calif.) HS, 1955-58, Temple City (Calif.) HS, 1958-59; prof. Coll. San Mateo, Calif., 1965-70, McHenry County Coll., Crystal Lake, Ill., 1972-76, Waubonsee Coll., Aurora, Ill., 1976-79; tchr., adminstr. Purnell Sch., Pottersville, NJ, 1980-86; realtor Sig Kuhne Realtors, Milford, NJ, 1986-89, Burgdorff Realtors, Inc., Pittstown, NJ, 1989-94, ret., 1994. Co-founder Audio, Verbal and Tutorial Ctr. McHenry County Coll., Crystal Lake, 1975—77. Author: Shorthand I, Shorthand II, Shorthand III, Office Procedures I, Bookkeeping I, Bookkeeping II, Bookkeeping III, Medical Secretary, Legal Secretary, Office Procedures II, Business Materials, Business Law, Office Machines I, Office Machines II. Chair Holland Twp. (N.J.) Hist. Preservation Commn., 1989—95; chairperson Delaware Valley Autumn Antique Show, Milford, 1988—93; chair Christmas Project, Hunterdon County, NJ, 1988—. Mem.: N.J. Assn. Realtors, Hunterdon County Bd. Realtors (Cmty. Svc. award 1988), Golden Talents (pres., v.p., trustee 1988—91), Holland Twp. Women's Club (chairperson Clarence Carter Night 1988), Pi Beta Phi (province pres.). Republican. Episcopalian. Avocations: swimming, boating, antiques. Fax: 435-946-3508.

CAMPBELL, JENNIFER BRADLEY, company official, social worker; b. Plattsburg, N.Y., Oct. 26, 1953; d. Monroe Marshall and Mary Evelyn (Hutchinson) Kissane; children: Jason Marshall Bradley, Jeffrey Scott. AA in Liberal Arts, Bay Path Jr. Coll., Longmeadow, Mass., 1973; BS in Edn., Norwich U., 1975. Dep. sheriff Lamoille Sheriff's Dept., Hyde Park, Vt., 1981-84; adminstrv. asst., coord. vol. svc., dir. fin. aid Johnson (Vt.) State Coll., assoc. dir. Upward Bound, case mgr. Reach Up, 1984-97; exec. asst. Ilco Tube Bending Inc., Rancho Dominguez, Calif., 1997—. Mem. adv. bd. Vol. Svc. Learning Project, Johnson, 1988-91, LINK Family Svcs., Morrisville, Vt., 1996; vol. Spl. Olympics. Republican. Avocations: crafts, writing, sailing. Home: 900 W 14th St Apt 5 San Pedro CA 90731-3938 Office: ILCO Industries 1308 W Mahalo Pl Rancho Dominguez CA 90220-5418

CAMPBELL, JILL FROST, university official; b. Buffalo, July 29, 1948; d. Jack and Elaine Mary (Hamilton) Frost; m. Gregory H. Campbell, May 31, 1969; children: Geoffrey, Kimberly, Kristina. BS, SUNY, Brockport, 1970, MSED, 1981; PhD, U. Buffalo, 1997. From acct. clk. bursar's office to asst. v.p. SUNY, Brockport, 1974—2003, asst. v.p. student affairs, 2003—. Chmn. web redesign com. SUNY, Brockport; mem. enrollment ops. group SUNY, Brockport, 1997-99, mem. metroctr. com. for student svcs., 1997-98, chair campus com. on profls.' roles and rewards, 1997-98, campus jud. officer, 1997-99, mem. coll. rev. panel, 1995—, coll. com. profl. evaluation, 1995—, strategic planning com., 1995-97, mem. retention com., 1998—, mem. presdl. scholars com., 1998-99, mem. strategic planning implementation com. on retention, 1999-2000, mem. strategic planning implementation com. on systemic change, 1999-2000, mem. alumni follow-up survey adv. com., 1999-2000, coord. alumni placement survey, 2000-, mem. transfer articulation group, 1999—, mem. acad. advisement task force, 2000-01, mem. enrollment mgmt. divsn. budget rev. com., 2000, chmn. alumni survey consulting group, 2000-02, mem. coll. tech. coun., 2003-. Mem. exec. com. Nativity Home Sch. Assn., Nativity Blessed Virgin Sch., Brockport, 1985-87, mem. sch. pub. rels. and mktg. com., 1985-88, mem. ch. festival com., 2001—; mem. Friends of Brockport Athletics, 1985-2000; coach Brockport Youth Summer Soccer, 1988-91; host family Assn. for Teen-Age Diplomats, 1995-96; mem. com. Chancellor's Award for Excellence in Profl. Svc., Brockport, 1989-90; liaison Brockport Child Care Ctr., 1995-96. Grantee United Univ. Professions, 1985, 90, 93, 94, 2000, 01. Mem. NAFE, Nat. Assn. Instl. Rsch. (mem. exec. com., co-originator and discussion leader books and current issues 1985-87, co-author profl. file, presenter papers, presenter panels 1979-87), SUNY Assn. Instl. Rsch. and Planning Officers (mem. exec. com., presenter papers, presenter panels 1984-87), North East Assn. Instl. Rsch. (mem. exec. com., sec. 1985-87, presenter papers, presenter panels 1978-87), Nat. Coun. Univ. Rsch. Adminstrs., Internat. Conf. for Women in Higher Edn. (presenter 1992), SUNY Brockport Alumni Assn., Brockport Profl. Women's Group, Rsch. Found. Cen. Office (users group 1987-90, sponsored program comm. com. 1990-97, 4-yr. rsch. coun. 1988-93, vice chmn. 1991, chmn. 1992, univ. colls. rsch. coun. 1993-97), N.Y. State Transfer Articulation Assn. (presenter 1998, 2003, mem. conf. com. 2001-03, nominations com., 2001-02, registration 2001-03), N.Y. State/United Univ. Professions (Excellence award 1990, 2003). Home: 5129 Redman Rd Brockport NY 14420-9601 Office: SUNY Brockport Seymour 224 350 New Campus Dr Brockport NY 14420

CAMPBELL, JOAN BROWN, religious organization executive; BA, MA, U. Mich.; DDiv (hon.), Bethany Coll., Coe Coll., Lynchburg Coll., Doane Coll. Ordained, Christian Ch., also Am. Bapt. Churches (USA). Assoc. exec. dir. Communited United Headstart, 1967-69; exec. sec. Welfare Action Coalition, Cleve., 1969-71; exec. dir. Coun. for Action in Pub. Edn., Ohio, 1971-73; program developer Roman Cath. Diocese, N.Y.C., Cleve., 1973; assoc. exec. dir. Greater Cleve. Interch. Coun., 1973-79; asst. gen. sec. Commn. Regional and Local Ecumenism, Nat. Coun. Chs., 1979-85; exec. dir. U.S. office World Coun. Chs., 1985-91; gen. sec. Nat. Coun. Chs. Christ in U.S.A., N.Y.C., from 1991; dir. dept. religion Chatuauqua Instn. Founder, 1st pres. WomenSpace, Cleve. Women's Ctr., 1974-76; v.p. Cleve. Urban League, 1975-79; pres. Nat. Assn. Ecumenical Staff, 1976-78; mem. steering com. U.S. Ch. Leaders, 1989—; bd. dirs. Ind. Sector, 1993—, Union Theol. Sem., 1993—; mem. adv. com. Pew Global Stewardchip Initiative, 1993—; trustee Nat. Religious Partnership for Environment, 1993—. Named to Women of Achievement, YWCA, Leadership Cleve., Martin Luther King Jr. Bd. Preachers, Sponsors and Collegium of Scholars, Morehouse Coll. Mem. NAACP (life, bd. dirs.), Coun. on Christian Unity, Christian Ch. (Disciples of Christ) (life), Mortar Bd., Phi Beta Kappa. Address: Chautauqua Institution Director Dept of Religion PO Box 28 Chautauqua NY 14722-0028

CAMPBELL, JOAN VIRGINIA LOWEKE, secondary school educator, language educator; b. Detroit, Nov. 8, 1942; d. George Paul and Lolamae (Weians) L.; m. James Bachelder Campbell, July 26, 1975; 1 child, James Bachelder Loweke. BA in German, French, Hope Coll., 1965; student, U. Cologne (Germany), 1964, U. Salzburg (Austria), 1968, U. Stuttgart (Germany), 1970-71, Sampere Inst., Madrid, 1982, Millersville (Pa.) State U., 1983, 84, 90, Va. Poly. Inst. and State U., 1976-77, 80-84, U. Va., 1996-97, 98-99. Cert. secondary tchr., Mich., Kans., Va. Tchr. French and German I, II Grand Haven (Mich.) Jr. H.S., 1965-69; asst. instr. elementary and intermediate German U. Kans., Lawrence, 1969-70, 71-72; tchr. German I, II Ctrl. Jr. H.S., Lawrence, Kans., 1972-74; tchr. French I, II, sr. English Oskaloosa (Kans.) H.S., 1974-75; tchr. German I-IV Highland Park H.S., Topeka, 1975-76; tchr. French I-V, Spanish I and II Blacksburg (Va.) H.S., 1977—. Tchr. French, Spanish YMCS, YMCA evening courses, Blacksburg, Va., 1976-80; mem. audio visual com. Montgomery County Fgn. Lang. Collaborative Group, Blacksburg, 1984-87; chaperone Am. Inst. Fgn. Study, Germany, France, Spain, 1968-82, area adminstr. summer and winter programs abroad, We. Mich., 1968-69; chaperone Ednl. Adventures,

Quebec City, Montreal, 1984, 90-91, 93-94, 98, Montgomery County Schs.; presenter in field. Author: The Gothic Cathedral, 1995. Mem. Internat. Host Family Orgn. Va. Poly. Inst. and State U., Blacksburg, 1977— Fulbright exch. fellow U. Kans., 1970-71, Fulbright fellow Goethe Insts., 1976, Rockefeller fellow Rockefeller Assn. and Nat. Endowment Humanities, 1986, NDEA fellow, 1966; recognized as Va. Gov.'s Sch. Outstanding Educator, 1990. Mem. Am. Assn. Tchrs. French (state and region IV U.S. Recognition effort, dedication and high scores on nat. French exams, 1988, 96, 97, founder La Soc. Hon. de Français for Outstanding Students in French Blacksburg chpt. 1977, state com., dist. adminstr. Le Grand Concours-Nat. French Exams 1980—), Am. Assn. Tchrs. Spanish and Portuguese, Am. Assn. Tchrs. German (life, Va. exec. com. sec. 1977-83, co-chmn. nat. German exams Va. chpt. 1984-87, state nominating com. 1984-87, chmn. 1984-85, life), Nat. Assn. Edn. (Blacksburg H.S. rep. 1980-82), Va. Assn. Edn., Montgomery County Assn. Edn., Assn. Supervision and Curriculum Devel., Fgn. Lang. Assn. Va. (life). Republican. Presbyterian. Avocations: flower gardening, hiking, mountain climbing, violin, art history. Home: 3003 Mclean Ct Blacksburg VA 24060-8110 Office: Blacksburg HS 520 Patrick Henry Dr Blacksburg VA 24060-3106 E-mail: jayhawk@vt.edu.

CAMPBELL, JOSEPHINE ANNE CONRAD, news service executive; b. Evansville, Ind., Jan. 31, 1927; d. Owen McIntyre and Josephine Anne (Greene) C.; m. Donald Herman Campbell, Mar. 15, 1946 (dec. Mar. 3, 1988); children: Kathleen Mary, Carolyn Margret, Deborah Jean. Cub reporter Daytona Beach (Fla.) News-Jour., 1944-45; copy boy Washington Post, 1945-46; copy editor World Report Mag., Washington, 1946-47; mem. pub. rels. staff AMVETS, Washington, 1952-53; pub. rels. person Govt. Pakistan, Washington, 1953-55; Washington and UN corr. Daily NAWA-I-WAQT, Lahore, Pakistan, 1955-56; writer, editor USIA, 1956-86; founder, CEO Ecotopics Internat. News Svc., Ocean City, Md., 1986-98, Willits, Calif., 1998—. Columnist Prince George's Jour., 1994-2000. Chair White House/Justice Dept. Task Force on Sex Discrimination USIA Press Svc.; active Gov.'s Task Force to Examine State Pension Investment in South Africa, 1987; v.p. Am. Fedn. Govt. Employees, AFL-CIO, Local #1812, 1969—78, del. nat. conv., 1974—76; del. founding conf. Coalition Labor Union Women, 1974; exec. com. Prince George's County NCCJ, 1980—84; rep. Ocean City State Coastal and Watershed Resources adv. Com., 1991—98; steering com., commr. Worcester County Commn. for Women, 1995—98; active Friends of Ocean City Libr., 1988—, Friends of Willits Libr., 1999—; citizen's adv. bd. Willits News, 1999—2000, op-ed writer, 1999—. Jefferson fellow, George Washington U., 1980—81. Mem. NAACP (3d v.p. Worcester County 1992-98; Sonoma County, Calif. br. 1999—), ACLU (Prince George County exec. bd. 1975-81, chair, 85-88, Mendocino County exec. bd. 2003—), Nat. Writers Union Local 3, Nat. Press Club, Dog Writers Assn. Am., Women's Inst. Freedom of Press, Conservation Voters, Worldwatch, Nat. Resources Def. Coun., Mendocino County Nat. Women's Polit. Caucus, Women's Club Ocean City (2d v.p. 1996), Marine's Meml. Club. Democrat. Roman Catholic. Avocations: photography, poetry writing, political activism. Fax: 707-456-0713. Office Phone: 707-456-0841.

CAMPBELL, JUDITH E. retired insurance company executive; BA, Chestnut Hill Coll., 1969. With Chem. Bank, N.Y., sr. v.p. consumer sales and svc. delivery, head ops. and adminstrn. consumer banking, sr. v.p., 1991—97; with Consumer Banking, 1992—97; sr. v.p., chief info. officer, bd. dirs. N.Y. Life Ins. Co., N.Y.C., 1997—. Bd. trustees Drew U. Office: NY Life Ins Co 51 Madison Ave New York NY 10010-1603*

CAMPBELL, KARLYN KOHRS, speech and communication educator; b. Blomkest, Minn., Apr. 16, 1937; d. Meinhard and Dorothy (Siegers) Kohrs; m. Paul Newell Campbell, Sept. 16, 1967 (dec. Mar. 1999). BA, Macalester Coll., 1958; MA, U. Minn., 1959, PhD, 1968. Asst. prof. SUNY, Brockport, 1959-63; with The Brit. Coll., Palermo, Italy, 1964; asst. prof. Calif. State U., L.A., 1966-71; assoc. prof. SUNY, Binghamton, 1971-72, CUNY, 1973-74; prof. comms. studies U. Kans., Lawrence, 1974-86, dir. women's studies, 1983-86; prof. comms. studies U. Minn., Mpls., 1986—, dept. chair, 1993-96, 99—. Inaugural Gladys Borchers lectr. U. Wis., Madison, 1974. Author: Critiques of Contemporary Rhetoric, 1972, rev. edit., 1997, Form and Genre, 1978, The Rhetorical Act, 1982, rev. edits. 1996, 2002, The Interplay of Influence, 1983, rev. edits., 1987, 92, 96, 2000, Man Cannot Speak for Her, 2 Vols., 1989, Deeds Done in Words, 1990, Women Public Speakers in the United States, 1800-1925: A Bio-Critical Sourcebook, 1993, Women Public Speakers in the United States, 1925—: A Bio-Critical Sourcebook, 1994; editor Quar. Jour. Speech, 2001--; co-editor: Guilford Revisioning Rhetoric series, 1995-2000; mem. editl. bd. Comm. Monographs, 1977-80, Quar. Jour. Speech, 1981-86, 92-94, editor, 2001—, Critical Studies in Mass Commn., 1993-99, Rhetoric and Pub. Affairs, 1997-2000, Philosophy and Rhetoric, 1988-93; contbr. articles to profl. jours. Recipient Woolbert Rsch. award, 1987, Winans-Wichelns Book award, 1990, Ehninger Rsch. award, 1991; Tozer scholar Macalester Coll., 1958, Tozer fellow, 1959; fellow Shorenstein Barone Ctr., JFK Sch. of Govt., Harvard, 1992; Disting. Woman scholar U. Minn., 2002. Mem. Nat. Comm. Assn. (disting. scholar award 1992, Francine Merritt award for significant contbns. to the lives of women in comm. 1996 Women's Caucus), Ctrl. States Speech Comm. Assn., Rhetoric Soc. Am., Phi Beta Kappa, Pi Phi Epsilon. Office: U Minn Dept Comm Studies 225 Ford Hall 224 Church SE Minneapolis MN 55455 E-mail: campb003@umn.edu.

CAMPBELL, KATHERINE MARIE LANGREHR, elementary and secondary education educator; b. N.Y.C., Dec. 4, 1947; d. Anton A. and Katherine (Batky) Langrehr; m. Frederick Augustus Campbell, Nov. 4, 1967; children: Julie Ann, Alicyn Katherine. BA in History, U. Bridgeport, 1970; MS in Lang. Arts Edn., Ctrl. Conn. State U., 1992. Tchr. grades 3 and 5 Holy Rosary Parochial Sch., Bridgeport, Conn., 1968-71; outreach worker Migratory Children's Program Vernon (Conn.) Bd. Edn., 1980-81; sales rep. Procter & Gamble, Wilton, Conn., 1982-86; reading/math tutor Bennet Jr. H.S., Manchester, Conn., 1986-87; tchr. lang. arts Elisabeth M. Bennet Mid. Sch., Manchester, Conn., 1987-96, dept. head lang. arts, 1994-96; tchr. grade 5 Verplanck Elem. Sch., Manchester, 1996—. Mem. content validation com. Nat. Bd. Profl. Teaching Stds., 1996; presenter in field. Mem. Gifted & Talented Bd. Vernon Bd. Edn., 1992-93; dir. Planning Bd. Emergency Shelter, Vernon, 1984-85; scout leader Girl Scouts Am., Vernon, 1979-80; treas., bd. dirs. PTO Vernon Elem. Sch., 1976-80. Recipient Celebration of Excellence award State of Conn., 1992; Conn. Writing Project fellow, 1989; nominee Heroes in Edn. award Readers Digest, 1999, Am. Tchrs. award Disney, 2001. Mem.: Internat. Reading Assn. Office: Verplanck Elem Sch 126 Olcott St Manchester CT 06040-2632

CAMPBELL, LEANNE HAYS, pastor; b. Providence, Rhode Island, May 7, 1949; d. Leopold Mozart Hays and Florence Robinson Peck; m. Robert Bruce Campbell, Aug. 5, 1978 (div. Nov. 1994); children: Jennifer Elizabeth, Joel Michael. Attended, Barrington Coll., R.I., 1967—69; BA in Christian edn., Scarritt Coll. for Christian Workers, Nashville, Tenn., 1975; MDiv, St Paul's Sch. of Theology, Kans. City, Mo., 1984. Pastor Sugar Creek United Meth. Ch., Sugar Creek, Mo., 1983—84, Oakley United Meth. Ch., Kans. City, Mo., 1984—85, Chillicothe Cir., Chillicothe, Mo., 1988—99; supply pastor Garrattsville United Meth. Ch., Garrattsville, NY, 1990—92; dir. of daycare and asst. pastor Cmty. United Meth. Ch., Holiday, Fla., 1993—97; pastor Tioga Ctr. and Smithboro United Meth. Ch., Tioga Ctr., NY, Plymouth and Larksville United Meth. Ch., Plymouth, Pa., 2002—. Mem. Plymouth Ministerial Assn., Plymouth, Pa., 2002—. Recipient The George Akers Award, United Meth Ch. Bb. of Ordained Ministry, 2001. Methodist. Achievements include being a creative and caring single parent. Avocations: singing, writing, horseback riding. Home: 240 W Main St Plymouth PA 18651 Office: First United Meth Ch 240 W Main St Plymouth PA 18651-2919 E-mail: revlhc@yahoo.com.

CAMPBELL, M. EDITH, writer, public relations consultant; b. Flint, Mich. d. Robert James and Lily (Bell) Brownlee. Grad. H.S., Flint. Advt. specialist Buick Motor Divsn. GM, Flint, 1957-87; exec. dir. Whaley Hist. Hous, Flint, 1995; free-lance writer Flint Jour., 1988-98; pub. rels. coord. Genesee County Humane Soc., 1990-97; pub. rels. dir. All Tech Engring., 1990-97. Owner Pub. Rels. Specialties, Flint, 1990-97; publicity/devel. cons., grant writer Christ Episcopal Lit. Ctr. Author: 50 Years of Industrial Businesswomen, 1984. Pres. bd. dirs. Vol. Action Ctr., Flint, 1984; Big Sister, Big Bros./Sisters, Flint; mental health group leader Recovery, Inc., Flint, 1968-73; para-profl. Flint Regional Emergency Svc. Crisis Ctr., 1972-77; pres. Indsl. Bus. Women, Flint, 1976-77; bd. mem. Genesee County Humane Soc., Flint, 1983-87, Whaley Childrens Ctr., Flint, 1992-95; paraprofl. Cmty. Mental Health Crisis Ctr.; ambulance attendant Mt. Morris Twp. Police; asst. chaplain McLaren Gen. Hosp. Recipient Liberty Bell award Genesee County Bar Assn., Flint, 1981, Woman of Achievement award YWCA, Flint, 1987, VIP award Pub. Rels. Assn., Heart of Gold award Vol. Action Ctr., Key to City, Outstanding Women Who Work award Greater Downtown Flint, Citizenship award VFW; named Big Sister of Yr., Big Bros./Sisters, Flint, 1986, Vol. of Yr., United Way, Flint, 1988. Mem. Pub. Rels. Assn. (pres. 1984-94), Nat. Assn. Women Bus. Owners (pub. rels. dir. Flint chpt. 1997, mem. steering com.), Flint Area Advt. Fedn., Sales and Mktg. Execs., GM Retirees, Flint Area C. of C., Flint Area Convention and Visitors Bur. Avocations: modeling, singing, rehabilitating dogs, teaching grooming-handicapped women. Home: 2551 Paducah St Flint MI 48504-7728

CAMPBELL, MARIA BOUCHELLE, lawyer, consultant; b. Mullins, S.C., Jan. 23, 1944; d. Colin Reid and Margaret Minor (Perry) C. Student, Agnes Scott Coll., 1961-63; AB, U. Ga., 1965, JD, 1967. Bar: Ga. 1967, Fla. 1968, Ala. 1969. Pvt. practice law, Birmingham, Ala., 1968-94; law clk. U.S. Cir. Ct. Appeals, Miami, Fla., 1967-68; assoc. Cabaniss, Johnston and Gardner, 1968-73; sec., counsel Ala. Bancorp., Birmingham, 1973-79; sr. v.p., sec., gen. counsel AmSouth Bancorp., 1979-84, exec. v.p., gen. counsel, 1984-94, AmSouth Bank, 1984-94; exec. asst. to rector Parish of Trinity Ch., N.Y.C., 1994-99; lawyer, mediator Sirote & Permutt, 1999-2001; cabinet ofcl., supt. of banks State of Ala., Montgomery, 2001—03; chmn. fin. svcs. SC& B Strategic Solutions, Montgomery, 2003—; of counsel Steiner Crum & Byars, Montgomery, 2003—. Bd. trustees Ptnrship for Women's Health Columbia U., 1996-2000; bd. dirs. Leake and Watts Childrens Svcs., Inc., 1997-99; lectr. continuing legal edn. programs, cons. to charitable orgns. Exec. editor Ga. Law Rev, 1966-67. Bd. dirs. St. Anne's Home, Birmingham, 1969-74, chancellor, 1969-74; bd. dirs. Children's Aid Soc., Birmingham, 1970-94, 1st v.p., 1988-90, pres., 1990-92; trustee Canterbury Cathedral Trust in Am., 1992—, Discovery 2000 Children's Mus., 1991-94, Soc. for Propagation of Christian Knowledge, 1991-93; bd. dirs. NCCJ, 1985-94, 99-2002, state chair, 1990-93; bd. dirs. Positive Maturity, 1976-78, Mental Health Assn., 1978-81, YWCA, 1979-80, Op. New Birmingham, 1985-87, pers. com., 1987-90, v.p., 1990-94; bd. dirs. Soc. for the Fine Arts U. Ala., 1986-89, Baptist Hospital Found. of Birmingham Inc., 1994-95, Alliance for Downtown N.Y., 1995-99, chair affordable housing initiative region 2020, 2000-01, Habitat for Humanity of Birmingham, 2000-02; commr. Housing Authority, Birmingham Dist., 1980-85, Birmingham Partnership, 1985-86, Leadership Birmingham, 1986—, program com., 1989-90, co-chair program com., 1990-91, mem.'s coun., 1999-2002; mem. pres. adv. coun. Birmingham So. Coll, 1988 92, chair bd. overseers Masters Program, 1990-94; mem. pres.'s cabinet U. Ala., 1990-95; trustee Ala. Diocese Episcopal Ch., 1971-72, 74-75, mem. canonical revision com., 1973-75, 89-91, liturg. commn., 1976-78, treas., chmn. dept. fin., 1979-83, 2000-03; mem. coun., 1983-87, chancellor, 1987-91, cons. on stewardship edn., 1981-94, dep. to gen. conv., 1985, 88, 91; mem. Standing Commn. on Constn. and Canons, 1988-94, mem. investment com., 2000—, vice chmn., 2003—; vestryman St. Luke's Episcopal Ch., 1991-94; bd. advisors So. region of Am. Soc. Corp. Secs., pres., 1992-94; cmty. advisor Jr. League Birmingham, 1992-93; mem. adv. bd. Cahaba River Soc., 1991-94; trustee St. Andrew's Sewanee Sch., 1998—; commr. Ala. Securities Commn., 2001-03; bd. dirs. Ala. Agrl. Commn., 2001-03; bd. dirs. Ala. Housing Fin. Authority, 2001-03; bd. regents Univ. of the South, 2002—; bd. dirs. Housing Enterprise Ctrl. Ala., 2003—, Fin. Investors of South, 2003—04. Named One of Top 10 Women in Birmingham, 1989, One of Top 5 Women in Bus., 1993. Mem. ABA, State Bar Ga., Fla. Bar, Ala. Bar Assn., Birmingham Bar Assn., Am. Corp. Counsel Assn. (bd. dirs. Ala. 1984-89), Assn. Bank Holding Cos. (chmn. lawyers com. 1986-87), Greater Birmingham C. of C. (bd. dirs. 1988-94, exec. com. 1992-94, vice chmn., gen. counsel 1993-94), Kiwanis, The Church Club N.Y., Order of St. John of Jerusalem, Summit Club. Office: PO Box 668 Montgomery AL 36101 E-mail: mcampbell@scbstrategic.com.

CAMPBELL, MARTA SMITH, librarian; b. Buffalo, June 25, 1941; d. Frank Lawrence Jr. and Alice (Bement) Smith; m. Harry William Campbell Jr., 1964 (div. 1981); children: Marta Christine, Jennifer Leigh. BA in English Lit., Bucknell U., Lewisburg, Pa., 1963; MLS, So. Conn. State U., New Haven, 1983. Libr. and head of collection mgmt. Westport (Conn.) Pub. Libr., 1983—. Democrat. Congregational. Home: 10 Bauer Pl Westport CT 06880 Office: Westport Pub Libr Westport CT 06880

CAMPBELL, MARTHA MADISON, educational administrator; b. Glen Ridge, N.J., May 9, 1941; d. Kenneth and Margaret Bruce (Macon) C.; m. Morton Park Iler, May 30, 1964 (div. July 1988); children: Douglas Gordon, Janet Madison, Bruce Campbell; m. David Malcolm Potts, March 25, 1995. BS, Wellesley Coll., 1963; MA, U. Colo., 1989, PhD, 1994. Statis. analyst A.C. Nielsen Co., N.Y.C., 1963; founder, dir. Population Speakout, Denver, 1988-93; mktg. cons. Specialized Comm., Denver, 1989-93; sr. program officer population David and Lucile Packard Found., Los Altos, Calif., 1994-99; lectr., co-dir. Ctr. Entrepreneurship Internat. Health & Devel., Sch. Pub. Health U. Calif., Berkeley, 2000—. Vis. scholar U. Calif. Berkeley, 1994; cons. Planned Parent Fedn. Am., 1990-91. Contbr. articles to profl. jours. Pres., founder Venture Strategies Health and Devel. Avocations: music, reading, hiking. Office: U Calif Sch Public Health 310 Warren Hall Berkeley CA 94720-7360

CAMPBELL, MARY KATHRYN, chemistry educator; b. Phila., Jan. 20, 1939; d. Henry Charles and Mary Kathryn (Horan) C. AB in Chemistry, Rosemont Coll., 1960; PhD, Ind. U., 1965. Instr. Johns Hopkins U., 1965-68; asst. prof. chemistry Mt. Holyoke Coll., South Hadley, Mass., 1968-74, assoc. prof., 1974-81, prof., 1981—; vis. scholar U. Paris VII, 1974-75; vis. prof. U. Ariz., 1981-82, 88-89. Mem. panel on grad. fellowships NSF, 1979-81 Author: Biochemistry, 1991, 4th edit., 2002; co-author: Understand! Biochemistry, 1999; contbr. articles to profl. jours. Fellow Woodrow Wilson Found., 1960, NSF, 1960-64, NIH, 1964-65; grantee in field Mem. Am. Chem. Soc., AAAS, AAUP, Sigma Xi Office: Mt Holyoke Coll 50 Coll St Dept Chemistry South Hadley MA 01075

CAMPBELL, MARY SCHMIDT, dean; b. Phila., Pennsylvania, Oct. 21, 1947; d. Harvey Nathaniel and Elaine Juanita (Harris) S.; m. George Campbell, Jr., Aug. 24, 1968; children: Garikai, Sekou, Britt Jackson. BA in Eng. Lit., Swarthmore Coll., 1969; MA in Art Hist., Syracuse U., 1973, PhD Humanities, 1982; ArtsD (hon.), Pace U., 1991; DFA (hon.), CCNY, 1992; PhD (hon), Colgate U., 1994; PhD (hon.), Coll. of New Rochelle, 2001. Art editor Syracuse New Times, NY, 1973—77; guest curator, curator Everson mus., Syracuse, 1974—76; exec. dir. Studio Mus. in Harlem, N.Y.C., 1977—87; commr. cultural affairs City of N.Y., 1987—91; dean Tisch Sch. Arts, NYU, N.Y.C., 1991—. Bd. mgrs. Swarthmore (Pa.) Coll., 1987-99; mem. fine arts vis. com. bd. overseers, Harvard Coll., Harvard U., Cambridge, Mass., 1991-95; mem. Tony nominating com., 1996-98, 2000-2002. Co-author: Harlem Renaissance: Art of Black America, 1987, Memory & Metaphor, 1991; prodr. (film) Sembene: A Biography, 1994. Mem. N.Y.C. Mayor's Adv. Commn. on Culture, 1991-94; co-chmn. subcom. on culture Dem. Nat. Conf., N.Y.C., 1992; bd. dirs. N.Y. Shakespeare Festival, 1993—, Harlem Sch. Arts, 1997-2001; bd. trustees Am. Acad. in Rome, 1999—, Bklyn. Mus. Art, 1999-2002, mem. bd. trustees, United Nations Internat. Sch., 2001-. Recipient George Arents award Syracuse U., 1993, Project of Yr. award N.Y. Coun. on Humanities; Tisch Sch. fellow Am. Acad. Arts & Scis. Democrat. Baptist. Avocations: jogging, writing. Office: NYU Tisch Sch of the Arts 721 Broadway 12th Flr New York NY 10003-6862*

CAMPBELL, MILDRED CORUM, business owner, nurse; b. Warfield, Va., Feb. 24, 1934; d. Oliver Lee and Hazel King (Young) Corum; m. Hugh Stuart Campbell, Dec. 2, 1972. BSN, U. Va., 1956; operating rm. mgr. cert., U.S. Army Med. Svcs. Sch., San Antonio, 1967; gen. mgr. cert., Cedars of Lebanon Med. Ctr., L.A., 1968. Head nurse plastic surgery U. Va. Med. Ctr., Charlottesville, 1956-58, head nurse cardio-surg., 1958-61; staff nurs operating rm. NIH Heart Inst., Bethesda, Md., 1961-62; supr. operating and recovery rms. Med. Univ. of S.C., Charleston, 1962-64; head nurse cardio operating rms. Meth. Hosp., Tex. Med. Ctr., Houston, 1964-67; supr. operating and recovery rms. Cedars of Lebanon Med. Ctr., L.A., 1967-68; product-nurse cons. Ethicon, Inc., Somerville, N.J., 1968-69; nurse cons. Johnson & Johnson, New Brunswick, N.J., 1969-70; gen. mgr. Ariz. Heart Inst., Phoenix, 1970-72; owner, pres., bd. dirs. Highland Packaging Labs., Inc., Somerville, 1983—2002; ret., 2002. Mem., moderator Nat. Assn. Operating Rm. Nurses, Denver, 1963-76; pres. Aux. Orgn., Muhlenberg Hosp., Plainfield, N.J., 1979-80; chmn. Assn. for Retarded Citizens Fund Raising Ball, Somerset County, N.J., 1982. Mem. Inst. Packaging Profls. Home: 29 Lambert Dr Princeton NJ 08540-2304 E-mail: hs.cam@verizon.net.

CAMPBELL, NAOMI, model; b. London; d. Valerie Campbell. With Elite Model Mgmt., N.Y., 1987-93, Elite Premier, London, Ford Models, Inc., Paris, 1991—, N.Y., 1993—, Women Model Mgmt., N.Y.C. Appearances include (T.V. series) The Fresh Prince of Bel Air, The Cosby Show, (videos) George Michael's Freedom, Michael Jackson's In the Closet, (book) Madonna's Sex, 1992, (films) Ready to Wear, 1994, Miami Rhapsody, 1995, Unzipped, 1995, To Wong Foo, Thanks for Everything, Julie Newmar, 1995, Catwalk, 1995, Girl 6, 1996, Invasion of Privacy, 1996, An Alan Smithee Film: Burn Hollywood Burn, 1997, Beautopia, 1998, Trippin, 1999, Prisoner of Love, 1999, Destinazione Verna, 2000, (TV film) Naomi Conquers Africa, 1998; author: Swan, 1994; album: Love and Tears, 1994. Achievements include first black model to appear on the cover of French Vogue. Office: Women Model Agy 2nd Fl 107 Greene St Fl 2 New York NY 10012-3803

CAMPBELL, NAUSHA COURY, speech pathology/audiology services professional, educator; d. William and Mary Magdalene Coury; m. Ronald Gene Campbell, Aug. 26, 1965; 1 child, Zachary G. BA, Marshall U., 1968, MA, 1971. Lic. speech pathologist W.Va. Tchr. Louisville (Ky.) Bd. Edn., 1969—75; speech lang. pathologist Cabell County Bd. Edn., Huntington, 1972—, Ironton (Ohio) Health Dept., 1975—84, Wayne County Bd. Edn., 1983—85, Geiger Easter Seals, Ashland, 1984, Wayne County (W.Va.) County Health Dept., 1985. Instr. Huntington Jr. Coll., 1980—, Marshall U., 1993—. Mem.: W.Va. Speech Hearing Lang. Assn., Am. Speech Hearing Assn. (cert.), Women's Club Huntington (dept. chair, Rookie of Yr. 1977). Avocations: crewel, ballroom dancing. Home: 778 Eastwood Dr Huntington WV 25705 Office: Cabell County Bd Edn 29th St 3rd Ave Huntington WV 25702

CAMPBELL, NELL, mayor; b. Walnut, Miss. d. Newton Alcy and Lula Elizabeth (Luker) Vinson; m. Robert Fred Campbell, May 24, 1946 (widowed, Oct. 3, 1976); children: Elizabeth Ann, Robert Fred Jr., Rose Marie. Student, Jackson State, 1978. Cert. flower arranging. Machine operator Corinth Mfg. Co., Miss., 1944-46, Adamsville Mfg., Tenn., 1953-64, Kimberly Clark Inc., Memphis, 1945-46; supr. H.I.S. Coro., Saltillo, Tenn., 1964-89; florist Enville, Tenn., 1989—; mayor Town of Enville, 1994—. City bd. mem. Town of Enville; bd. mem. C. of C. Ruritan Club. Democrat. Baptist. Avocations: quilting, sewing, gardening, traveling, reading, crafts. Home: 6805 Main St Enville TN 38332-5205

CAMPBELL, NEVE, actress; b. Guelph, Ont., Can., Oct. 3, 1973; m. Jeffrey Colt, Apr. 1995 (div. 1997). Student, Nat. Ballet Sch. Can. Actress (films) Scream, 1996 (Saturn award for Best Actress, MTV Movie award nomination, MTV Movie award for Best Female Performance), The Craft, 1996, Scream 2, 1997 (Blockbuster Entertainment award for Favorite Actress-Horror, MTV Movie award for Best Female Performance), 54, 1998, Wild Things, 1998, Three to Tango, 1999, Scream 3, 2000, Drowning Mona, 2000, Hairshirt, 2001, Investigating Sex, 2001, Lost Junction, 2003, Blind Horizon, 2004; writer, actor (films): the Company, 2003. Named one of 50 Most Beautiful People, People mag., 1998. Office: Creative Artists Agy 9830 Wilshire Blvd Beverly Hills CA 90212-1825

CAMPBELL, PATRICIA LINDSEY, mechanical engineer, lawyer; b. Little Rock, Oct. 16, 1952; d. Harvey Clay and Willie C. Pinkston; m. Dennis K. Campbell, July 3, 1971 (div. Oct. 1981); children: Casondra, Jeffrey; m. George O. Newsome, Mar. 14, 1991. AS in Engring., U. Ark., Little Rock, 1979; BS in Mech. Engring., Memphis State U., 1983; MS in Engring., U. Ark., 1989; JD, George Washington U., 1996. Registered profl. engr., Ark. Mech. engr. Entergy Ops./Ark. Power & Light, Russellville, Ark., 1983—91, U.S. Nuc. Regulatory Commn., Washington, 1991—97; assoc. Winston & Strawn, Washington, 1997; tech. asst. Entergy Operations, Inc., St. Francisville, La., 1997—2000; atty. Winston & Strawn, Washington, 2000—. Leader Girl Scouts, Russellville, Ark., 1990. Scholar Inst. Nuclear Power Ops., Atlanta, 1982-83. Mem.: Women's Coun. on Energy and Environ., Women in Nuc., D.C. Bar Assn., Md. Bar Assn., Am. Nuc. Soc., Tau Beta Pi. Methodist. Avocations: biking, rafting, roller-blading, running, crafts. Home: 442 Chauncey Ct Alexandria VA 22314-5764 Office: Winston & Strawn 1400 L St NW Washington DC 20005

CAMPBELL, RUTH ANN, retired budget analyst; b. La Plata, Md., Aug. 25, 1948; d. Lawrence Gilbert Pilkerton and Eleanor Garretter (Swann) Pilkerton-Grimm; m. Joseph Harvey Campbell, May 22, 1970 (dec. Oct. 1989); children: Joseph Lawrence, Timothy Craig. Clk.-stenographer Gen. Svcs. Adminstrn., Washington, 1966-68, sec., stenographer, 1968-70, program asst., 1970-71, adminstrv. asst. Mpls., 1971-72, Washington, 1974-75, program analyst, 1975-78, corr. specialist, 1978-79, program analyst, 1979, budget analyst, 1979—2004; ret., 2004. Sec. Fed. Women's Program/Gen. Svcs. Adminstrn., Washington, 1981—82, PTA, Waldorf, Md., 1981—83; treas. Cub Scout pack Boy Scouts Am., La Plata, Md., 1982—87, Athletic Boosters Club, 1993—94; sec. Warrior Stadium Steering Com.; team capt. Thursday Nite Mixed Bowling League, 1976—; mem. vestry Christ Ch., Wayside, 1990—94, 2000—, treas. Woman's Guild, 1990—. Mem. Am. Assn. Budget and Program Analysis. Episcopalian. Avocations: bowling, camping, horseshoes, travel, reading. Home: 7305 Saint Marys Ave La Plata MD 20646-3968 Office: Gen Svcs Adminstrn Bldg 4 Rm 1105 Washington DC 20406-0001 E-mail: no1nanie082548@cs.com.

CAMPBELL, SALLY JO, music educator, primary school educator; b. Longmont, Colo., Nov. 16, 1952; d. Vernette Russell and Goldamay Anderson; m. William Clair Campbell, July 2, 1983; children: Kenyon Charles, Kathleen Claire. B in Music Edn., U. No. Colo., 1975; MusM, Manhattan Sch. Music, 1978. Owner, prodr. Wayside Inn Dinner Theatre, Berthoud, Colo., 1983—93; pvt. voice tchr. Longmont, 1984—; voice tchr. U. No. Colo., Greeley; music tchr. grades K-3 St. Johns Cath. Ch., Longmont, 1994—95; chef Jesters Dinner Theatre, Longmont, 1999—2003; presch. music tchr. Gunbarrel Presch., Boulder, Colo.,

2002—; office asst. Divsn. 12 APA, Niwot, 2003—. Choir dir. 4-6 grades First Luth. Ch., Longmont, 1996—2003. Named Miss. Colo., 1972. Home: 7477 N 107th St Longmont CO 80504

CAMPBELL, SELAURA JOY, lawyer; b. Oklahoma City, Mar. 25, 1944; d. John Moore III and Clyde (Hallum) [illegible]; AA, Stephens Coll., [illegible]; BA, U. Okla., 1965; MEd, Chapel Hill U., 1974; JD, N.C. Cen. U., 1978; postgrad. atty. mediation courses, South Tex. Sch. of Law, Houston, 1991, Atty. Mediators Inst./Dallas, Dallas, 1992. Bar: Ariz 1983; lic. real estate broker, N.C.; cert. tchr. N.C. With flight svc. dept. Pan Am. World Airways, N.Y.C., 1966-91; lawyer Am. Women's Legal Clinic, Phoenix, 1987. Charter mem. Sony Corp. Indsl. Mgmt. Seminar, 1981; guest del. Rep. Nat. Conv., Houston, 1992; judge all-law sch. mediation competition for Tex., South Tex. Sch. Law, Houston, 1994. Mem. N.C. Cen. U. Law Rev., 1977-78. People-to-People del. People's Republic of China, 1987; guest del. Rep. Nat. Conv., Houston, 1992. Mem. Ariz. Bar Assn., Humane Soc. U.S., Nat. Wildlife Fedn., People for the Ethical Treatment of Animals, Amnesty Internat., Phi Alpha Delta. Republican. Episcopalian. Avocations: climbed Mt. Kilimanjaro, 1983, also Machu Pichu, Peru, Mt Kenya, Africa, horseback riding, photography. Home: 206 Taft Ave Cleveland TX 77327-4539

CAMPBELL, SUZANE EVA, computer graphics designer, freelance/self-employed interior designer; b. Greensboro, NC; d. Jack (John) Wilson and Eva Couch (Lou) Campbell. BA graphic design, Appalachian State Univ., Boone, NC, 1991. Cert. vol. Hospice/NC, 2002. Designer and computer artist Kester & Assoc., Charlotte, NC, 1990—95; art dir., computer artist Arts Engraving Co., Charlotte, NC, 1995—2003; computer artist Alcoa, So. Graphic Systems, Charlotte, NC, 2003—. Graphic designer freelance, Charlotte, NC, 1991—; cons., flexographic/printing fields, curriculum creation Ctrl. Piedmont Cmty. Coll., Charlotte, NC, 2001. Youth leader Forest Hill Ch., Charlotte, NC, 2000—03. Mem.: CSCA (mem. 2000—02), Supper Club. Christian. Avocations: decorative furniture painting, design, faux finishing, church activities, music, camping, yard scapes. Home: 2232 Lanier Avenue Charlotte NC 28205 Office: Southern Graphic Systems 9201A Forsyth Park Dr Charlotte NC 28273

CAMPBELL, TENA, judge; b. Twin Falls, Idaho, Dec. 11, 1944; BA, U. Idaho, 1967; MA in French Lit. with honors, Ariz. State U., 1970, JD, 1977. Bar: Utah 1977, U.S. Dist. Ct. Utah 1977, U.S. Ct. Appeals (10th cir.) 1982. Tchr. French Twin Falls (Idaho) Sch. Dist., 1967-69, Tempe (Ariz.) H.S., Phoenix Jr. Coll., 1972-73; assoc. atty. Johnson Durham and Moxley, Salt Lake City, 1977-79, Fabian and Clendenin, Salt Lake City, 1979-81; dep. county atty. Salt Lake County, Salt Lake City, 1981; asst. U.S. atty. criminal divsn. Office of U.S. Atty. Dist. Utah, 1981-95; judge U.S. Dist. Ct. Utah, 1995—. Mem. Utah Bar Assn., Ft. Douglas HIdden Valley Country Club. Office: US Dist Ct Utah Rm 235 US Ct House 350 S Main St Salt Lake City UT 84101-2106

CAMPBELL, VIRGINIA HOPPER, piano concert artist, composer, educator; b. Oklahoma City, Okla., June 3, 1930; d. James Robert and Emily (Hess) Hopper; m. Rev. Walter Erlin Campbell, Jr., June 3, 1950; children: Walter Erlin III, James Andrew, Mary Catherine, Anne Charlotte, Patricia. B Music in Piano Performance cum laude, Oklahoma City U., 1985, M Music, 1988; studied in Europe, with Jörg Demus. Adj. prof. Okla. City U., tchr. of piano to 30 students, 1945—; tchr. St. Luke's Meth. Sch. Cont. Edn.; empresaria, founder, pres. Piano Artist Series, Oklahoma City, 1984—. Performances and concerts in Austria, Germany, Mex., U.S., including Vienna, Salzburg, 1990—; primary ch. organist Episcopal Chs. in Okla. and Tex., 1978—; also performed at Hilton Hotel, Oklahoma City Golf and Country Club, Peroleum Club, Waterford Hotel; concerts in Oklahoma City, Norman, Edmond, Ponca City, Duncan, Durant and Guthrie, Okla.; pianist on CDs and cassettes including Virginia Live, 1993, Just Gershwin, 1998. Mem. Okla. Music Tchrs. Assn., Nat. Music Tchrs. Assn., Ladies Music Club (pres. composers divsn. 1990-99, program chair music appreciation 19977-99), Sigma Alpha Iota, Pi Kappa Lambda. Home: 1815 W Wilshire Blvd Oklahoma City OK 73116-4115

CAMPBELL, ZENITA A. D. environmental engineer, educator, safety engineer; b. Minot, N.D., Oct. 17, 1961; d. Ida Mae and Clayton Campbell; 1 child, James Dorris. AS in Fire Safety Engring. Tech., Ea. Ky. U., Richmond, 1997, BS in Occupl. Safety Engring., 1999, MS Loss Prevention and Safety, 2000. Cert. fire and explosive investigator 1998, fire and explosive instr. 1998. Maintenance planning tech. Kuparuk Maintenance Planning, Alaska, 1986—91; engr. Kuparuk Facility Engring., Anchorage, 1991—94; sr. safety specialist L-3 Commns., Lexington, Ky., 2000—. Adj. prof. Coll. Fire and Safety, Ea. Ky. U., Richmond, 1995—; supt. cert. Six Sigma Blackbelt Expert, Lexington, 2000—. Mem.: Nat. Assn. Fire Investigation, Nat. Safety Mgmt. Soc., Am. Soc. Safety Engrs. (student pres. 1998—99), Ky. Safety and Health Network, Inc. (labor cabinet, Robert V. Moyer award 1999), Alpha Phi Sigma. Home: 192 Plum Street Stanton KY 40380 Office: L-3 Communications 5749 Briar Hill Rd Lexington KY 40516 Personal E-mail: zenita.campbell@yahoo.com. Business E-Mail: Zenita.Campbell@SOFSA.mil.

CAMPION, JANE, director, screenwriter; b. Wellington, New Zealand; d. Richard and Edith Campion. BA in Anthropology, Victoria U., Wellington, 1975; Diploma of Fine Arts, Chelsea Sch. Arts, London, 1979; degree, Sydney Coll. Arts, 1979; Diploma in Direction, Australian Film and T.V. Sch., Sydney, 1984; DLitt (hon.), Victoria U., 1999. Adj. prof. Sydney Coll. Arts, 2000. Dir., screenwriter Peel: An Exercise in Discipline, 1982 (also editor, Palme d'Or short film category Cannes Internat. Film Festival 1986, Diploma of Merit Melbourne Film Festival, 1983, finalist Greater Union awards, Australian Film Inst. awards 1983-84), A Girl's Own Story, 1983 (with Gerard Lee, Rouben Mamoulian award 1984, Best overall short film Sydney Film Festival 1984, Unique Artist Merit Melbourne Film Festival 1984, Best Direction, Best Screenplay, Best Cinematography Australian Film Inst. 1984, First Prize Cinestud Amsterdam Film Festival, 1985, Best Film Cinestud 1985, First Prize Festival and Press prize), writer/dir. Mishaps of Seduction and Conquest, 1984-85, Passionless Moments (also prodr., dir., writer, with Gerard Lee and dir. photography, Unique Artist Merit Melbourne Film Festival 1984, Best Exptl. Film Australian Film Inst. 1984, Most Popular Short Film Sydney Film Festival 1985), screened at Cannes Un Certain Regard, 1986, After Hours, 1984 (XL Elders award Best Short Fiction, Best Short Fiction Melbourne Internat. Film Festival 1985), Dancing Daze (TV series), 1985, (TV movie) Two Friends, 1986 (Golden Plaque TV category Chgo. Internat. Film Festival 1987, Best Dir., Best Telemovie, Best Screenplay Australian Film Inst. awards 1987, screened at Cannes in Un Certain Regard, 1986, Edinburgh Film Festival, Sydney and Melbourne Film Festival, 1986), Sweetie, co-writer, dir. 1988, (Georges Sadoul prize Best Fgn. Film, Best Dir., Best Actress, Best Film Australian Critics awards 1990, New Generation award L.A. Film Critics, 1990, Best Fgn. Film Spirit of Independence awards 1990), An Angel at my Table, 1990 (Byron Kennedy award Australian Cinema 1990, Spl. Jury prize, Elvira Notari award Best Woman Dir., Agia Scuola Italian Min. Culture, Best Film Si presci award Panel Internat. Critics, Best Film O.C.I.C. award Christian journalists, Best Film for Young Audiences Cinema e Ragazzi Italian film critics prize, Critics award Toronto Film Festival, Most popular film in the Forum, Otto Debelius prize Berlin Film Festival, Best Fgn. Film, Spirit of Independence Awards, Venice Film Festival, World Premiere, 1990); writer, dir. The Piano, 1993 (Palme d'Or Cannes Internat. Film Festival 1993, Academy Award Best Original Screenplay 1994, Best Picture, Best Dir., Best Cinematography nominations, Acad. Awards, Australian Film Inst. awards, Australia Film Critics, Southeastern Film Critics Assn., others, Best Fgn. Film Chgo. Film Critics, Caesar awards (2000 WIN award, Wimfemme Film Festival Women's Image Network); composer: Feel the Cold, 1983, (play) The Portrait of A Lady, 1996, Holy Smoke, 1998-99 (Best Film Francesco Pasinetti award, pres. Internat. jury Mostra Internat. Art Cinematogrophy Festival Venice Film Festival, 1997, Nat. Union Film Journalists, nominated Best Costume Acad. awards 1997, nominated Best Supporting Actress Acad. awards 1997; dir. In the Cut, 2002-03. Office: HLA Mgmt Pty Ltd 87 Pitt St Redfern NSW 2016 Australia also: PO Box 1530 Strawberry Hills NSW 2012 Australia

CAMPOS, CHRISTINA RIVAS, finance officer, restaurant owner; b. Albuquerque, Nov. 1, 1964; d. Luz Ofelia (Gabaldon) Tuma; m. Jose A. Campos II, June 1, 1985; children: Analisa, Andrea, Jose III. BA in Latin Am. Studies, U. N.Mex., 1995. Owner Joseph's Restaurant, Santa Rosa, N.Mex., 1985—; chief fin. officer Guadalupe Health Svc., Santa Rosa, 1993-96. Cmty. health liaison Guadalupe County, Santa Rosa, 1993-94; mem. geog. access task force State of N.Mex., 1993-94. Mem. Presdl. Rural Health Care Panel, Bernalillo, N.Mex., 1993; bd. trustees U. N.Mex. Hosp., 1999—. Mem. Rotary Internat. (sec. 1993—), Santa Rosa C. of C. Democrat. Roman Catholic. Avocations: reading, gardening, golf, aerobics. Office: Joseph's Restaurant 865 Will Rogers Dr Santa Rosa NM 88435-2634 E-mail: josephs@etsc.net.

CAMPOS-PONS, MARIA MAGDALENA, artist; b. Matanzas, Cuba, 1959; Student, Nat. Sch. Art, Havana, Cuba, 1980, Higher Inst. Art, 1985, Mass. Coll. Art, 1988. Prof. aesthetic and painting Higher Inst. Art, Havana, Cuba, 1986-89; asst. curator The Space Gallery, 1992. Co-coord. aesthetic and fine art seminar Revolution and Culture Mag., Cuba, 1989—90; vis. prof. RISD, 1994, Mass. Coll. Art, Boston, 1995, Boston, 96, Sch. Mus. Fine Arts, Boston, 1997; juror numerous competitions; curatorial project Articule Gallery, Montreal, 1991, Inst. Contemporary Art, Boston, 1992. One-woman shows include Gallery L, Havana, 1985, Kennedy Bldg. Gallery Mass. Coll. Art, Boston, 1988, CAstle of Royal Force, Havana, 1989, Embassy Cultural House, London, Ont., 1990, Banff Ctr. Arts, Can., 1990, SOHO 20 Gallery, N.Y.C., 1991, Gallery Burning, Montreal, Can., 1991, Burnaby Art Gallery, B.C., Can., 1991, Gallery La Ctrl./Powerhouse, Montreal, 1992, Akin Gallery, Boston, 1993, Latin Am. Gallery, N.Y.C., 1993, Gallery North Miami Dade C.C., 1994, Bunting Inst. Radcliffe Coll., Mass., 1994, Martha Schneider Gallery, Chgo., 1996, The Caribbean Cultural Ctr., N.Y.C., 1997, The Photographers Gallery, Saskatoon, Can., 1997, U. Antioquia and Centro Colombo Am., Colombia, 1997, Ambrosino Gallery, Coral Gables, Fla., 1997, Martha Schneider Gallery, Chgo., 1997, Mario Diacono Gallery, Boston, 1997, Hallwalls, Buffalo, 1998, Mus. Modern Art, N.Y.C., 1998, exhibited in group shows at Ctr. Fine Arts, Miami, 1996, DNA allery, Provincetown, Mass., 1996, Craiger/Dane Gallery, Boston, 1997, Addison Gallery Am. Art Philips Acad., Andover, Mass., 1997, Smithsonian, Washington, 1997, 1998, Nat. Gallery Can., Ottawa, 1998, numerous others, Represented in permanent collections; performer: The Seven Powers Come by the Sea, 1992, La Voz del Silencio/The Voice of Silence, 1993, Letter to my Mother, 1994, 1995, 1996, others; reviewer in field, contbr. carticles to profl. jours. Office: care Schneider Gallery 230 W Superior St Chicago IL 60610-3595

CAMPOVERDE, REBECCA O. federal agency administrator; b. Ecuador;, naturalized, U.S. married; 1 child. Grad., Northwestern U. Reporter, Tex.; with Dallas Ind. Sch. Dist.; legis. asst. to Rep. Steve Bartlett Washington; chief of staff to two successive dep. secs. U.S. Dept. Edn., dep. chief of staff to sec. Lamar Alexander; dir. comm. U.S. Ho. of Reps., dep. staff dir. com. on edn. and the workforce; asst. sec. legis. and congl. affairs Dept. Edn., Washington, 2001—. Cons. trade matters; mem. Bush-Cheney transition team U.S. Dept. Edn. Office: Dept Edn Legislation and Congl Affairs 400 Maryland Ave SW Washington DC 20202-3100

CAMRON, ROXANNE, retired magazine editor, consultant; b. Los Angeles; d. Irving John and Roslyn (Weinberger) Spiro; m. Robert Camron; children: Ashley Jennifer, Erin Jessica. BA in Journalism, U. So. Calif. West Coast fashion and beauty editor, Teen mag., Los Angeles, 1969-70, sr. editor, 1972-75, editor, 1976-99, cons., 1999—; pub. relations rep. Max Factor Co., 1970; asst. to creative dir. Polly Bergen Co., 1970-71; ret., 1999. Lectr. teen groups; freelance writer. Active Homeowners Assn. Mem. Am. Soc. Exec. Women. Office: Teen Mag 6420 Wilshire Blvd Los Angeles CA 90048-5502

CANADY, ALEXA IRENE, pediatric neurosurgeon; b. Lansing, Mich., Nov. 7, 1950; d. Clinton Jr. and Hortense (Golden) C.; m. George Davis, June 18, 1988. BS, U. Mich., 1971, MD cum laude, 1975; DHL (hon.), Marygrove Coll., 1994, U. Detroit, 1997; DSc (hon.), Ctrl. Mich. U., 1999, U. So. Conn., 1999. Diplomate Am. Bd. Neurol. Surgery. Intern in surgery Yale U., New Haven, 1975-76; resident in neurosurgery U. Minn., Mpls., 1976-81; fellow in pediatric neurosurgery Children's Hosp. Pa., Phila., 1981-82; instr. neurosurgery U. Pa., Phila., 1981-82; staff neurosurgeon, instr. neurosurgery Henry Ford Hosp., Detroit, 1982-83; asst. dir. neurosurgery Children's Hosp. Mich., Detroit, 1986-87, chief of neurosurgery, 1987-97; assoc. prof. neurosurgery Wayne State U., Detroit, 1988-91, vice chmn. neurosurgery, 1991—2001; prof. neurosurgery, 1997—2001. Clin. instr. neurosurgery Wayne State U. Sch. Medicine, 1985, mem. internal rev. com. dept. anatomy, 1988, chmn. search com. dept. neurosurgery, 1989, internal rev. com. dept. neurology, 1991-92, 125th anniversary celebration com., 1992, internal rev. com. dept. pediat., 1993, chmn. search com. dept. ophthalmology, 1992-93, internal rev. com. dept. neurosurgery, 1994; chmn. neurobil. devices panel, FDA; vis. prof. Med. Coll. S.C., 1990; cons. neurol. devices panel Med. Devices Adv. Com., FDA, 1994; mem. surg. com. Children's Hosp. Mich., chmn. operating room subcom. surg. com., intensive care unit com., med. record com., med. exec. com.; mem. med. staff Children's Hosp. Mich., William Beaumont Hosp, Royal Oak and Troy, Mich., Harper-Grace Hosps., Detroit, Hutzel Hosp., Detroit, Sinai Hosp., Detroit, Huron Valley Hosp., Milford, Mich., Crittenton Hosp., Rochester Hills, Mich., St. John Hosp. and Med. Ctr., Detroit; presenter various profl confs. in U.S. and internat. Contbr. chpts. to books. Mem. Mich. Head Injury Alliance, Mich. Myelodysplasia Assn.; bd. dirs. Inst. Am. Bus., 1986-88. Recipient Citation Women's Med. Assn., 1975, Candace award Nat. Coalition 100 Black Women, N.Y., 1986, Golden Heritage award, 1989, Leonard F. Sain Esteemed Alumni award U. Mich., 1990, Disting. Alumni award Everett H.S., Pres.'s award Am. Med. Women's Assn., 1993, Variety Heart award for Med., Sci. and Tech. Variety Club, 1994, Shining Star award Colgate-Palmolive Co./Starlight Found., 1994, Golden Apple award Roeper Sch., 1995, Athena award Alumni Assn. U. Mich., 1995; named Outstanding Young Woman in Am., 1977, Top 100 Bus. & Profl. Women of Am., 1985, Woman of Yr. Detroit Club Nat. Assn. Negro Bus. & Profl. Women's Club, Inc., 1986; named to Mich. Woman's Hall of Fame, 1989; grantee Am. Cancer Soc., 1979, Minn. Med. Found., 1979, Am. Cancer Soc., 1981-82, Widman Found. Early Intervention Treatment and Follow-Up of Infants with Post-hemorrhagic Hydrocephalus, 1984-85, Neuropsychol. Recovery and Family Adaptation to CHI Children's Hosp. Mich., 1987-88, Hydrocephalus Induced Endocrinopathies: Morphologic Correlates Children's Hosp. Mich., 1989, 91. Mem. AMA, ACS, Am. Assn. Neurol. Surgeons, Congress Neurol. Surgeons, Am. Soc. Pediatric Neurosurgery, Nat. Med. Assn. Detroit Med. Soc., Mich. Assn. Neurol. Surgeons (sec. 1992-93, v.p. 1994-95, pres. 1995-96), Transplantation Soc. Mich. (adv. bd. 1993-94), Mich. State Med. Soc. (child abuse and neglect divsn. 1986), Southeastern Mich. Surg. Soc. (sec. 1986-87), Soc. Crit. Care Medicine, Wayne County Med. Soc. (ethics com., pub. affairs com., law com.), U. Mich. Med. Ctr. Alumni Soc., Delta Sigma Theta. Office: 6064 Forest Green Rd Pensacola FL 32505 E-mail: alexacanady@aol.com.

CANAHUATI, JUDY, lactation consultant; b. Phila., July 17, 1941; d. Max and Besse S. (Creshkoff) Weiner; m. Pedro Felipe Canahuati, Sept. 6, 1969 (dec. June 2001); children: Emilia, Pedro Cesar. BA, U. Pa., 1963; MPhil in Anthropology, Columbia U., 1974. Cert. Internat. bd. cert. lactation cons. Cmty. organizer Planned Parenthood, N.Y.C., 1966-67; instr. U. Nacional Honduras, San Pedro Sula, 1970-72; import-export mgr. Contessa Indsl., San Pedro Sula, Honduras, 1978-82; tech. adv. USAID, Tegucigalpa, 1982-85, Mgmt. Scis. for Health, Boston, 1986-88; bd. dirs. La Leche League Internat., Schaumburg, Ill., 1980, project dir., 1989-91; cmty. adv. Wellstart Internat., Washington, 1991-96; sr. nutrition advisor CARE USA, Atlanta, 2001—03; fellow internat. develop. John Hopkins in US Agy, 2004—. Cons. Centro de Apoyo a la Lactancia Materna, San Salvador, 1981-83, Ednl. Devel. Ctr., Boston, 1985, UNICEF, N.Y.C., Tegucigalpa, 1989, China, 1997; researcher Inst. Reproductive Health Georgetown U., Washington, 1990-92; cons. Wellstart Internat., Washington, 1996, World Relief, Tegucigalpa, Honduras, 1994, Catholic Relief Svcs., San Salvador, El Salvador, 1996, Project Hope, Managua, Nicaragna, 1996, CARE, Honduras, 1997, Acad. Ednl. Devel., 1997, others; dir. project to improve basic edn. World Bank, Honduras, 1998; supt. Escuela Internacional Sampedrana, Honduras, 1999-2001, CARE USA, 2001-03. Co-author: Community-based Breastfeeding Support: A Planning Manual, 1996; contbr. articles to profl. jours.; co-prodr.: (video) Investing in the Future: Women, Work, and Breastfeeding, 1995. Bd. dirs. Escuela Internacional Sampedrana, San Pedro Sula, Honduras, 1980-85, spt., 1999; bd. dirs. Soc. Pro-Musica, San Pedro Sula, 1975-76. Fellow Nat. Inst. Mental Health, 1968-69. Mem. Internat. Lactation Cons. Assn., Consumer's Edn. and Protective Assn., La Leche League Internat., World Alliance for Breastfeeding Action, Phi Beta Kappa. Avocations: reading, writing, cooking. Home: 13702 Modrad Way # 23 Silver Spring MD 20904 E-mail: jwc@theansible.net.

CANARY, LEURA, prosecutor; Grad., Huntington Coll.; JD, U. Ala. Asst. Atty. Gen. Ala. Atty. Gen. Office, 1981—90; trial atty. Dept. of Justice Civil Dist., Ala., 1990—94; asst. U.S. Atty. Middle Dist., Ala., 1994—2001, U.S. Atty., 2001—. Office: US Atty'sOffice One Ct Sq Ste 201 Montgomery AL 36104

CANARY, NANCY HALLIDAY, lawyer; b. Cleve., Apr. 21, 1941; d. Robert Fraser and Nanna (Hall) Halliday; m. Sumner Canary, Dec. 1975 (dec. Jan. 1979). BA, Case Western Res. U., 1963; JD, Cleve. State U., 1968. Bar: Ohio 1968, Fla. 1972, U.S. Dist. Ct. (no. dist.) Ohio 1975, U.S. Supreme Ct. 1974, U.S. Dist. Ct. (so. dist.) Fla. 1994. Law clk. to presiding judge Ohio Ct. Appeals, Cleve., 1968—69; ptnr. McDonald, Hopkins & Hardy, Cleve., 1969—83, Thompson, Hine, LLP, Cleve., 1984—2002. Trustee Beck Ctr. for Cultural Arts, Lakewood, Ohio, 1980—90, Ohio Motorists Assn., 1989—95, Ohio Chamber Orch.; trustee, mem. devel. adv. com. Fairview Gen. Hosp., Cleve., 1980—96; chairperson Sumner Canary Lectureship com. Case Western Res. U. Law Sch.; sec. bd. govs. Churchill Ctr., Washington, 2000—02; bd. dirs. Comerica Bank & Trust Co., F.S.B., 1993—2000. Mem. Ohio State Bar Assn., Cleve. Bar Assn., Palm Beach County Bar Assn., Estate Planning Coun. Cleve., Estate Planning Coun. Palm Beach County, Gulf Stream (Fla.) Golf Club, Westwood Country Club (Cleve.). Republican. Avocations: music, horseback riding, collecting Churchill books. Home: Unit 1806 12500 Edgewater Dr Cleveland OH 44107-1677 also: 200 N Ocean Blvd Delray Beach FL 33483-7126 Office: 125 Worth Ave # 117 Palm Beach FL 33480 Office Phone: 561-833-5900.

CANAVAN, CHRISTINE ESTELLE, state legislator; b. Dorchester, Mass., Jan. 25, 1950; m. Paul Canavan; 2 children. Grad., Massasoit C.C., 1983; BS summa cum laude, U. Mass., 1988. RN. Mem. Mass. Ho. of Reps., Boston, 1993—, vice chair joint healthcare, mem. steering policy and scheduling com., mem. spl. legis. com. on foster care. Mem. Brockton (Mass.) Sch. Com., 1990-94, vice chmn., 1992-2000. Mem. South Shore Nurses Assn., Polish White Eagles. Democrat. Roman Catholic. Home: 29 Mystic St Brockton MA 02302-2825 Office: Mass Ho of Reps Mass State House Rm 34 Boston MA 02133

CANCIO, MARGARITA R. infectious disease physician; b. Pinar del Rio, Cuba, Sept. 29, 1959; d. Jose and Maria Cabrera; m. Derry H. Cancio, June 6, 1982. BS magna cum laude, U. South Fla., 1979; MD. Am. Bd. Internal Medicine, Infectious and Tropical Medicine. Clin. assoc. prof. dept. internal medicine USF Coll. Medicine, 2001—; chief of staff dept. internal medicine Tampa Gen. Hosp.; epidemiologist Town & Country Meml., Vencor, Tampa and Saint Petersburg. Served numerous med. staff coms. at area hosps.; lectr. in field. Founder, med. dir. Internat. Traveelr's Clinic, Infectious Disease Assocs. Tampa Bay, Kidcare; mem. comty. Hillsborough County AIDS Coordination Coun., Suncoast AIDS Network Fla., Shadow program coll. medicine students, USF and USF-HRS AIDS Patient Care Clinic. Named physician of Yr. Tampa Bay Latin Am. Med. Soc., 1997, Hispanic Woman of Yr., 1998. Fellow ACP; mem. AMA, Hillsborough County Med. Assn., Infectious Disease Soc. Am. (pres. 1989—), Soc. Hosp. Epidemiology, Am. Soc. Microbiology, Fla. Infectious Disease Soc., Fla. Health Sci. Bd. (trustee), USF (trustee), Alpha Omega Alpha. Office: Infectious Disease Assoc 4 Columbia Dr # 820 Tampa FL 33606 Fax: (813) 254-6414. Office Phone: 813-251-8444. Business E-Mail: cfalcon@travelerclinic.com.

CANDARAS, GALE D. state legislator, lawyer; BS magna cum laude, Fairleigh Dickinson U.; JD. Mem. Mass. Ho. of Reps., Boston, 1997—, mem. govt. regulations com., mem. jud. com. Mem. planning bd. Town of Wilbraham, 1987-88, mem. fin. com., 1988-90, selectman, 1990-97. Mem. N.Y. Bar Assn., N.J. Bar Assn., Conn. Bar Assn., Mass. Bar Assn., Mass. Juvenile Bar Assn., Wilbraham Women's Club. Democrat. Office: Mass State Legis Rm 138 State House Boston MA 02133

CANDELARIA, ANGIE MARY, special education educator; b. Durango, Colo., July 13, 1939; d. Angelo and Lucia (Mattevi) Dallabetta; m. David Candelaria, Sept 24, 1958 (div. Mar. 1964); children: David D., Craig D.; m. Richard James McMullen, July 3, 1982 (dec. Mar. 1999). BA, Ft. Lewis Coll., Durango, 1965; postgrad., U. North Colo., 1997-99. Cert. tchr. spl. edn., Colo. Tchr. Sch. Dist. R25, Loveland, Colo., 1967-68; tchr. spl. edn. Sch. Dist. 9R, Durango, 1968-98, mem. profl. devel. com., 1990-97; ret., 1998. Ind. rschr. Josten Integrated Computer Edn. Co. Colo. Dept. Edn. spl. edn. grantee, 1966, cross-cultural inst. grantee, 1972-74, Sch. Dist. 9R grantee, 1992. Mem. ASCD, NEA, Colo. Edn. Assn., Durango Edn. Assn., Internat. Reading Assn., VFW Aux. (life), Am. Legion Aux., Elks, Colombo Lodge. Republican. Roman Catholic. Avocations: computers, travel, reading, animals. Home: 16B 1741 Tustin Ave Apt 16B Costa Mesa CA 92627-3294 also: PO Box 472 Durango CO 81302-0472

CANDIDO, VIOLA JEANE HEIMBERGER, writer; b. New Philadelphia, Ohio, Jan. 13, 1947; d. Walter and Clara Heimberger; m. Richard F. Candido, June 22, 1974; children: Anne Marie Candido Westbrook, Robert V. BA, U. Dayton, 1969, MA, 1972. Creative adminstr. E. F. MacDonald Incentive, Dayton, Ohio, 1969—70; bank mktg. mgr. 1st Nat. Bank, Dayton, 1972—74; freelance writer Columbus, Ohio, 1974—90; writer Columbus Dispatch/Dublin Villager, Columbus, 1993—95; novelist, Civil War historian Windstorm Creative Pubs., Pt. Orchard, Wash., 1995—. Author: (novels) Redemption of Corporal Nolan Giles, 1995, Shepherd's Song, 2001, (children's book) Levi, the Smartest Boy in the World, 1999, (PBS documentary) Call to Care; contbr. articles, stories, columns to mags. and jours. Mem. Ohio Hist. Soc., Columbus, 1998—, 1st Ladies Mus., Canton, Ohio, 1998—; religious edn. adminstr., tchr. St. Peter's Cath. Ch., Columbus, 1980—94. Named one of nat. winners, Ashland Chem. Bicentennial Essay Contest on Econs.; named to Top 100 Nat. Honorees, Writer's Digest, 1981. Avocations: piano, guitar, reenacting, quilting, needlecrafts.

CANDLAND, CATHERINE C. human resources executive; Founder, CEO Advantage Human Resourcing, Stamford, Conn., 1983—. Mem. Nat. Ethics Com., Nat. Assn. Temporary and Staffing Svcs.; bd. dirs. SACIA, Norwalk Cmty. Tech. Coll., Coun. Econ. Competitiveness and Tech.

Recipient Hot Young Entrepreneurs award, Fortune Mag., 1994, 40 under 40 list, Entrepreneurs Mag., Entrepreneur Yr. So. New England, Entrepreneur Mag., 1993, Top Woman Bus. Owners in Metro. D.C., Working Woman Mag., 1998, Saleswoman Advocate and Leader Yr. award, Nat. Assn. Profl. Saleswomen, 1993. Office: Advantage Human Res 1055 Washington Blvd Stamford CT 06901-2216 E-mail: advantage@advstaff.com.

CANDLIN, FRANCES ANN, psychotherapist, social worker, educator; b. Phila., July 18, 1945; d. Francis Townley and Wilma (David) C. BA magna cum laude, Loretto Heights Coll., Denver, 1967; MSW with honors, St. Louis U., 1971. Diplomate Am. Bd. Clin. Social Work; cert. social worker; lic. clin. social worker, Colo. Recreational therapist trainee Jewish Hosp., St. Louis, 1970-71; social worker trainee Jefferson Barracks VA Hosp., St. Louis, 1970-71; social worker Adams County Juvenile Probation, Brighton, Colo., 1972-74, Boulder (Colo.) County Social Svcs., 1974-75; sch. social worker Adams County Sch. Dist. #50, Westminster, Colo., 1975-80; workshop presenter Human Enrichment Cons., Denver, 1980-90; pvt. practice Denver, 1980—; dir. Madison St. Counseling Ctr., Denver, 1991-97; founder, dir. Women's Mysteries Tour Co., 1993, Enneagram Ctr. of Colo., 1997—. Cons. Mountain Plains Regional Ctr., Denver, 1981-85, Dept. Edn., Topeka, 1981-87, Dept. Spl. Edn., Nebr., Colo., Mo., N.Mex., Utah, 1982-86. Bd. dirs. Denver Sch. for Gifted, 1982-86, Weaver Found., 1985-86, St. Mary's Acad., Englewood, Colo., 1985-88. Recipient stipend NIMH, 1969, VA Social Work Trainee, 1970. Mem. NASW, NOW, Acad. Cert. Social Workers, Internat. Enneagram Assn., Assn. Transpersonal Psychology, Colo. Assn. Clin. Social Workers, Vajra Soc. (bd. dirs. 1990—). Avocations: world travel, women's issues, spiritual devel. Office: Enneagram Ctr Colo PO Box 933 Glenwood Springs CO 81602

CANDREIA, PEGGY JO, financial analyst; b. Pawhuska, Okla., Aug. 23, 1944; d. Joseph Leonard and Wilma Jane (Brook) C. Student, U. Ozarks, 1965. Supr. credit and collections Credit Bur. Bartlesville, Okla., 1965-69; credit rep. Shell Oil Co., Tulsa, Okla., 1969-88; owner, mgr. Gorgeous Car Care, Tulsa, 1988-90; date coord. H.A. Chapman Children's Ctr., Tulsa, 1990—; fin. analyst H.A. Chapman Inst., Children's Med. Ctr., Tulsa, 1990—, fin. coord. Children's Med. Network Telethon, 1994—2002; data coord. Hillcrest Healthcare Sys., Tulsa, 2002—03; asst. acctg. mgr. Preferred Pediat. Home Health Care, Tulsa, 2003—. Founder local chpt. Parents and Friends of Lesbians and Gays, Tulsa, 1988-90; v.p. Tulsa Oklahomans for Human Rights, 1988-89; bd. dirs. Follies Rev., Tulsa, 1993-97, Broken Arrow Cmty. Playhouse, 1998-99; mem. steering com., sec., treas., Names Project, Tulsa, 1990—, co-chmn. ctrl. region logistics, Washington, 1996. Recipient Honor of Ky. Col. Republican. Roman Catholic. Avocations: designing homes, travel, skiing, fundraising, drawing. Home: 1525 N College Ave Tulsa OK 74110-2719

CANDRIS, LAURA A. lawyer; b. Frankfort, Ky., Apr. 5, 1955; d. Charles M. and Dorothy (King) Sutton; m. Aris S. Candris, Dec. 22, 1974. AB with distinction in polit. sci., Transylvania Coll., 1975; postgrad., U. Pitts., 1975-77, U. Fla., 1977-78; JD, U. Pitts., 1978. Bar: Fla. 1978, U.S. Dist. Ct. (mid. dist.) Fla. 1978, U.S. Ct. Appeals (4th cir.) 1980, Pa. 1981, U.S. Dist. Ct. (we. dist.) Pa. 1982, U.S. Ct. Appeals (3d cir.) 1983. Assoc. Coffman, Coleman, Andrews & Grogan, Jacksonville, Fla., 1978-80, Manion, Alder & Cohen, Pitts., 1981-85, Eckert, Seamans, Cherin & Mellott, Pitts., 1985-86, ptnr., 1987-96, vice chmn. labor and employment law dept, mem. practice mgmt. com., mem. strategic planning com.; ptnr. Meyer Unkovic & Scott, LLP, Pitts., 1996—, chair labor, employment law and employee benefits sect., mem. litigation and transactions depts. Contbr. over 30 articles to profl. jours. including Compensation and Benefits Rev., Forum Reporter, Employment Law Inst. manuals, Ref. Manual for the 34th Ann. Mid-West Labor Law Conf. Dynamic Bus. Mem. O'Hara Twp. Coun., 1986—90, O'Hara Twp. Planning Commn., 1990; bd. dirs. Tri-State Employers Assn., 1991—93, Parent and Child Guidance Ctr., 1991—2001, v.p., 1998—99, mem. exec. com., 1998—2001, pres., 1999—2000, sec., 2000—01; treas., mem. exec. com. SMC Bus. Couns., 1993—94, bd. dirs., 1993—96, Big Bros. & Big Sisters Greater Pitts., 1998—, v.p. planning, 2001—02, mem. exec. com., 2001—, v.p. adminstrn., 2003—; bd. dirs. The Whale's Tale, 2000—01; bd. dirs., mem. exec. com. The FamilyLinks, 2000—01. Nat. Merit Found. scholar 1972-75; named Ky. Col., 1974. Mem.: ABA (EEO com. labor sect., labor and employment law com. litigation sect.), Pitts. Human Resources Assn., Allegheny County Bar Assn. (coun. on professionalism 1990—2000, employment and fed. cts. sect., mem. coun. 2003—, women in the law div., hqrs. com. and pers. subcom.), Pa. Bar Assn. (employment sect.), Fla. Bar Assn. Republican. Avocations: skiing, traveling, bicycling, reading. Office: Meyer Unkovic & Scott LLP 1300 Oliver Bldg Pittsburgh PA 15222 Office Phone: 412-456-2891. E-mail: lac@muslaw.com.

CAÑEDO, MARION, school system administrator; b. Marion, Man., Can. m. Angel Canedo; children: Eric Vosburgh, Dana Vosburgh. BE, Geneseo State Coll.; M, Cert. Advanced Studies in Curriculum and Supervision, Buffalo State Coll. Tchr. Buffalo Pub. Schs., 1968, prin., dir. early childhood ctrs. and acads., dir. reading, asst. supt. stds. and tchg. effectiveness, assoc. supt. curriculum, 1999—2000, interim supt., 2000—. Founder Invention Conv.; lectr. in critical and creative thinking, Egypt, 2000. Author: Inventive Thinking Curriculum Guide. Named N.Y. State Tchr. of Yr., 1979; named to We. N.Y. Women's Hall of Fame, 2001; recipient Nat. Excellence Edn. award, 1994, NCCJ Brotherhood/Sisterhood award in edn., 2002. Office: Buffalo Pub Schs 713 City Hall Buffalo NY 14202

CANFIELD, CINDY SUE, art educator; b. Farmington, Mo., June 22, 1960; d. Lee Roy and Dale Collins; m. John M. Canfield II, Aug. 2, 1987; children: Clara Seleena, Johnell Mckinlee, Macarthur. B in Art Edn., Coll. Ozarks, 1983; post grad., Drury, 1984; post grad, U. Va., 1992. Cert. tchg. Mo. Weaver Coll. Ozarks, Point Lookout, 1978—83; tchr H.S. art Steelville Pub. Schs., 1983—85, Miller Pub. Schs., 1985—86, Strafford Pub. Schs., 1986—92; educator elem. art Hollister Pub. Schs., Mo., 1992—. Arts basic program site coord. Hollister Pub. Schs., Taney County, 1992—, dir. cmty. art events, Hollister, 1992—, new sch. com. bond organizer, 1994—95; dir. pub. rels. Sch. Bond Issue, 1994—. Author: Southwest Arts Reference Directory, 1991, K-12 Sequential Art Curriculum Guide, 1991. Recipient Nat. Tchr. Inst. Excellence award, Robert Rauschenberg, 1994, Arts Alliance grant, Getty Found., 1992—94, Conservation award, Soil Water Co., 2001. Mem.: PTA, S.W Dist. Art Tchrs. Assn., Nat. Art Educator's Assn. Democrat. Baptist. Avocations: reading, writing, painting, sculpting, swimming. Home: 295 Quincy Rd Kirbyville MO 65679 Office: Hollister Pub Schs 1798 State Hwy Hollister MO 65672

CANFIELD, CONSTANCE DALE, retired accountant, retired medical/surgical nurse, retired military officer; b. Fairmont, W.Va., May 2, 1940; d. Robert Alman and Dorothy Jane (Motter) C. Flight nurse diploma, Sch. Aerospace Med., 1967; BS in Acctg., Rollins Coll., 1979; student, Stetson U., 1975-76, Fla. Inst. Tech., 1976-77; grad., Army Comd. Gen. Staff Coll., Ft. Levenworth Kans., 1991. RN Fla.; registered Nurse Fla. Prin. C. D. Canfield, Acct., Melbourne, Fla., 1979-90; acct. C.D. Canfield, Acct., Melbourne, Fla., 1991—2002; ret., 2002. Gov.'s appointee Women in Mil. for Am. Meml. Found., Washington, 1991; gov.'s escort Fla. Freedom Festival, Inc., Tallahassee, 1991; state coord. VietNam Women's Meml. Project, Inc., Washington, 1986—; adminstrv. bd. United Meth. Ch., Melbourne, 1987—; musician Melbourne Mcpl. Band, 1980-90, Space Coast Philharmonic Orch., 1986-87; vol. Habitat for Humanity. With USAF, 1963—70, with U.S. Army, 1970—75, lt. col. U.S. Army, 1989—2000. Decorated Air Force Commendation medal, Army Commendation medal, Fla. Meritorious Svc. medal. Mem. AACN, Nat. Soc. Tax Profls., Nat. Soc. Pub. Accts., Fla. Assn. Ind. Accts. (sec. space coast chpt. 1992-93), Internat. Biog. Assn. (life), VFW (life), Vietnam Vets. Am. (life), Vietnam Vets. of Brevard, Inc. (life), N.G. Officers Assn., Fla. Hist. Soc., U.S. C. of C., Internat. Lions Club (pres. local club). Republican. Avocations: fishing, camping, music, boating, jet skiing.

CANFIELD, JUDY S. psychologist; b. NYC, May 15, 1947; d. Arthur and Ada (Werner) Ohlbaum; m. John T. Canfield (div.); children: Oran David, Kyle Danya. BA, Grinnell Coll., 1963; MA, New Sch. Social Rsch., 1967; PhD, U.S. Internat. U., 1970. Psychologist Mendocino State Hosp., Talmage, Calif., 1968-69, Douglas Coll., New Westminster, BC, Can., 1971-72, Family & Childrens Clinic, Burnaby, BC, Can., 1971-72; psychologist, trainer, cons. VA Hosp., Northampton, Mass., 1972-75; dir. New England Ctr., Amherst, Mass., 1972-76; dir., psychologist Gateways, Lansdale, Pa., 1977-78; asst. prof., psychologist Hahnemann Med. Ctr., Phila., 1978-84; pres., dir. Inst. Holistic Health, Phila., 1978-85; psychologist, cons. Berkeley, Calif., 1986—. Mem. task force, tng. com. Berkeley Dispute Resolution Svc., 1986-89; mem. measure H com. Berkeley United Sch. Dist., 1987-88. Mem. APA, Nat. Register Health Svc. Providers in Psychology, Nat. Assn. Advancement Gestalt Therapy (steering com. 1990), Calif. Psychol. Assn., Alameda County Psychol. Assn. (info.-referral svc. 1989—), Assn. Humanistic Psychology. Avocations: piano, horseback riding, ice skating. Office: 2031 Delaware St Berkeley CA 94709-2121

CANFIELD, STELLA STOJANKA, artist, art gallery owner, educator; b. Varna, Bulgaria, Jan. 17, 1950; emigrated to W. Germany, 1980, came to U.S., 1985; d. Stamat and Pepa-Despenna (Blisnacova) Bogdanov; m. Peter Petrov, Feb. 28, 1971 (div. Mar. 1988); children: Nicoletta, Peter; m. Michael Canfield, Mar. 27, 1988; adopted children: Jennifer, Paul. M, U. Phys. Edn. and Sports, Sofia, 1973. Lic. sport phys. therapy, Bulgaria. Phys. edn. and sports pedagogue H.S., Tolbuhin, Bulgaria, 1974-75, Med. U., Sofia, Bulgaria, 1975-76, middle and H.S., Sofia, 1976-80; owner Stella restaurant, Dusseldorf, Germany, 1982-83; with Oberheid Ceramic Studio, Dusseldorf, 1983-85; retail sales rep. The Ltd., Walnut Creek, Calif., 1989-90; savs. rep. Calif. Savs. & Loans, Montclair, 1990-92; owner Stella Art Gallery, 1998—. Owner Stella gallery. Bd. dirs. Coupeville (Wash.) Arts Ctr., Coupeville, 1995-2001; found. Stellar Arts Found., 2000. Recipient 3 awards Tulip Festival, La Conner, Wash., 1994, 2 awards, 1995, 96, 2 awards, 1997, 1 award, 1998, 1st place mixed media, 1999. Mem. N.W. Watercolor Soc., AWS Assn. Avocations: languages, reading, travel, sports, rowing (Bulgaria Nat. Champion 1968-71). Home: PO Box 1676 5 NW 8th St Coupeville WA 98239

CANHAM, PRUELLA CROMARTIE NIVER, retired educator; b. Statesboro, Ga., Dec. 4, 1924; d. Esten Graham and Mary Lee (Jones) Cromartie; m. Robert E. Niver June 4, 1946 (div. 1965) m. David L. Canham July 26, 1985; 1 child, Peddy Niver Hayhurst Moran. BS in Bus. and Music, Ga. So. U., 1944; postgrad., various univs. tchr. voice, piano, chorus and bus. career maths. North Ft. Myers H.S., Fla.; former sec. Statesboro Air Base, Ga., Warner Robbins Air Base, Macon, Ga.; former tchr. Westside Sch., Bulloch County, Ga., Southside Sch., Opelika, Ala. Mem. Singers Club of L.I.; guest spkr., panelist various cultural orgns. in Fla. and so. states; soloist various chs. and schs.; music cons. local theater groups; mem. Fla. State Secondary Music Instructional Materials Coun. Nominee Gannett Found. Heart of Gold Humanatarian award, 1981; named Vocal Solo. Lit. Music Specialist State of Florida, Lee County Florida Tchr. of the Year, 1987, nominee Nat. Tchr. Hall of Fame, 1998; recipient Nat. Libr. Poet's Editor's Choice award, 1994; cert. Appreciation Nat. Park Trust, 1995, Lee County Sch. Dist. Fla., 1991, numerous awards in 2002, including: ABI Hall of Fame, Poet of Year, Internat. Poet Merit and Honored Mem., Living Legions, Worlds Lifetime Achievement award, Companion of Honor, Internat. Peace Prize, Am. Medal of Honor; Nobel Prize for Oustanding Achievement and Contbr. to Humanity, 2002; recipient Congl. Medal of Excellence, 2004. Mem. AAAS, Am. Ch. Dirs. Assn., Fla. Music Educator Assns., Music Educator's Nat. Conf., Lee County Alliance of the Arts (charter), Fla. Vocal Assn. (past coord., state bd.), Nat. Assn. of Tchrs. of Singing in Am. and Cand., So. Fla. Symphony and Chorus Assn., Am. Guild of Organists, Fla. League of the Arts (past pres. and bd. dirs., hon. life, 1998—), Lee County Retired Tchrs. Assn., Fla. Vocal Assn., Am. Choral Assn., Internat. Soc. Poets (disting. mem. 1994, merit award, 1995), Profl. Women's Adv. Bd., others. Home: 1271 Burtwood Dr Fort Myers FL 33901-8711

CANJA, ESTHER, foundation administrator; V.p. Am. Assn. Retired People, Washington, 1996-98, pres.-elect, 1998—; exec. dir. Area Agencies of Aging Assn. Mich. Bd. mem. Mich. State Health Coord. Coun., Fla. State Long-term Care Ombudsman Coun., Area Agency Aging, S. Ctrl. Fla.; founding mem. Quality Care Advocates, Inc. Office: Am Assn Retired People 601 E St NW Washington DC 20049-0001

CANN, SHARON LEE, retired health science librarian; b. Ft. Riley, Kans., Aug. 14, 1935; d. Roman S. and Cora Elon (George) Foote; m. Donald Clair Cann, May 16, 1964. Student, Sophia U., Tokyo, 1955-57; BA, Calif. State U., Sacramento, 1959; MSLS, Atlanta U., 1977; EdD, U. Ga., 1995. Cert. health scis. libr. Recreation worker ARC, Korea, Morocco, France, 1960-64; shelflister Libr. Congress, Washington, 1967-69; tchr. Lang Ctr., Taipei, Taiwan, 1971-73; libr. tech. asst. Emory U., Atlanta, 1974-76; health sci. libr. Northside Hosp., Atlanta, 1977-85, libr. cons., 1985-86; libr. area health edn. ctr., learning resource ctr. Morehouse Sch. Medicine, 1985-86; edn. libr. Ga. State U., 1986-93; dir. libr. svcs. Ga. Bapt. Coll. Nursing, 1993-99, ret., 1999. Author: Life in a Fishbowl: A Call To serve, 2003; editor Update, publ. Ga. Health Scis. Libr. Assn., 1981; contbr. articles to publs. Chmn. Calif. Christian Youth in Govt. Seminar, 1958. Named Alumni Top Twenty Calif. State U., Sacramento, 1959. Mem. ALA, Med. Libr. Assn. (hon. life; bookkeeper So. chpt. 1996-98, credentialing com. 1996-2000, nursing and allied health sect. continuing edn. chair 1998-2000), Spl. Libr. Assn. (dir. South Atlantic chpt. 1985-87), Ga. Libr. Assn. (spl. libr. divsn. chmn. 1983-85), Ga. Health Scis. Libr. Assn. (hon. life, chmn. 1981-82), Atlanta Health Sci. Libr. (chmn. 1979, 95), Am. Numis. Assn., ARC Overseas Assn., Audubon Soc., Women in Mil. Svc. for Am., Suncity Hilton Head Computer Club (v.p. 2003). Home: 69 Plymouth Ln Bluffton SC 29909-5062 E-mail: sharoncann@aol.com.

CANNELL, CYNDY MICHELLE, elementary school principal; b. Salt Lake City, Utah, July 27, 1948; d. Nick M. and Eugenie E. (Pfanmuller) Fasselin; m. Peter Anthony Cannell, Oct. 13, 1973; children: Peter John, David. BA, U. Utah, 1970, MA, 1973. Cert. adminstr., supr. severly handicapped, spl. edn., emotionally handicapped, gifted and talented. Tchr. Hab Ctr., 1973-74, Hill View Elem Sch., 1974-78; coord. spl. needs. Granite Sch. Dist., Salt Lake City, 1978-79, tchr. leader youth in custody, 1979-80, coord. spl. edn., 1980-84; asst. prin. Western Hills Elem. Sch., Salt Lake City, 1984-85; prin. Webster Elem. Sch., Salt Lake City, 1985-90, Plymouth Elem. Sch., Salt Lake City, 1990-95, Twin Peaks Elem. Sch., Salt Lake City, 1995—2000; field asst. Utah State Office Edn., 2000—01; coord. spl. edn. unit Cottonwood Heights Elem., 2002. Mem. state strategic planning com. for edn., 1990-91, elem. prin. adv. com., 1990-96, spl. edn. strategic planning com., 1990-91, exec. class size steering com., 1990, ptnrs. in edn. com., 1985—, sch. lunch com., 1989-91, emer. preparedness com., 1989-90; mem. Women's State Legis. Coun., Utah, 1991-92; co-coord. Corp. Games, 1988—. Contbr. articles to profl. mags. Prin. rep. to state PTA Community Involvement Commn., 1989-90, Oquirrh South PTA Coun., 1989; mem. Utah Youth Village Scholarship Com., 1996—. Named Outstanding Educator of Yr. Nat. PTA Phoebe Apperson Hearst, 1990, Outstanding Adminstr. Utah Congress of Parents and Tchrs., 1989-90, Region V PTA, 1988-90. Mem. Granite Assn. Elem. Sch. Prins. (sec. 1998—, Innovator of Yr. 1997-98), Granite Assn. Sch. Adminstrs. (sec., treas. 1990-91) Utah Assn. Sch. Adminstrs., Nat Assn. Elem. Adminstrs., Granite Assn. Sch. Adminstrs. Avocations: skiing, reading, tennis, golf, travel. Home: 10331 S 2375 E Sandy UT 84092-4422 Office: Cottonwood Heights Elem 2415 E Bengal Blvd Salt Lake City UT 84121

CANNISTRACI, DIANE FRANCES, sales account executive; b. Bronx, N.Y., Jan. 9, 1950; d. John and Dorothy (Romano) C. Student, Orlando (Fla.) Jr. Coll., 1968-70, Teiko Post Coll., 1991-92. Ea. regional sales mgr. Kierulff Airline/Internation Supply, 1979-86; western regional sales mgr. C & K Unimax, Wallingford, Conn., 1989-90; sales and mktg. rep. U.S. C. of C., 1990-91; store mgr. Petite Sophisticate, Manchester, Conn., 1991-92; internat. and airline mktg. Richey Cypress Electronics, Wallingford, 1992-96; sales account exec. Midway Indsl. Electronics, Plainview, NY, 1996—2000; Rep. coord. New Suffolk County Bd. Election, 2000—. Committeewoman Rep. Party, Huntington, N.Y.; fund raiser Am. Heart Assn., Rocky Hill, Conn., Am. Diabetes Assn., Rocky Hill; vol. Hartford (Conn.) Hist. Soc., With USNG, 1981-86. Recipient All Around Womanhood award PTA, Huntington Station, N.Y., 1968. Mem. Air Carrier Purchasing. Republican. Roman Catholic. Home: 345 Depot Rd Huntingtn Station NY 11746-3339

CANNISTRARO, CAROLYN MARIE, financial recruiter; b. Yonkers, N.Y., July 24, 1972; d. Philip Attilio and Diane Rose (Spinelli) C. BA in Psychology, Boston Coll., 1995. Fin. recruiter Robert Half Internat., White Plains, N.Y., 1996—; exec. recruiter Lindsey and Co., Inc., Darien, Conn., 1998—. Mgr. Millennium divsn. Millennium Staffing Accts. on Call; mktg. dir. human resources discipline, mktg. dir. fin. and acctg. divsn. Romac Internat.; self-expression coach Landmark Edn., N.Y. Classically trained opera singer. Mem. NAFE, Am. Soc. Women Accts. (mem. chair 1997-98, dir. membership, pub. rels. chair 1998—, High Profile Women of Month 1998), Women in Sales, Fairfield County Bus. Women's Network, Soc. for Human Resource Mgmt. Republican. Roman Catholic. Avocations: opera, racing cars.

CANNIZZARO, LINDA ANN, geneticist, researcher; b. S.I., N.Y., Aug. 4, 1953; BS, St. Peter's Coll., 1975; MS, Fordham U., 1977, PhD, 1981. Postdoctoral fellow Dartmouth U. Med. Sch., Hanover, N.H., 1981-83; fellow in human genetics Children's Hosp. Phila., 1983-84; co-dir. cytogenetics Milton S. Hershey (Pa.) Med. Ctr., 1984-86; dir. gene mapping S.W. Biomed. Rsch. Inst., Scottsdale, Ariz., 1986-89; asst. prof. Fels Inst. Temple U. Med. Sch., Phila., 1989-91; asst. prof. Jefferson Cancer Inst., Phila., 1991-93; assoc. prof. Albert Einstein Coll. Medicine, Bronx, NY, 1993—2001; dir. cancer and molecular cytogenetics Albert Einstein Coll. Medicine and Montefiore Hosp., Bronx, N.Y., 1993—; prof. pathology Albert Einstein Coll. Medicine, 2001—. Editor-in-chief Cytogenetics Cell Genetics, 1995—; contbr. articles to profl. jours. Grantee Am. Cancer Soc., 1989-90, 94-97; Kriser awardee in Lung Cancer Rsch., 1999-2001. Mem. AAAS, AAUW, Am. Soc. Human Genetics. Avocations: oil painting, hiking, reading, writing. Office: Albert Einstein Coll Med and Montefiore MC/Pathology 111 E 210th St Bronx NY 10467-2401 E-mail: cannizza@earthlink.net.

CANNON, ALICE GRACE, counselor; b. Greenville, N.C., Nov. 3, 1949; d. Carl William Hannah and Lula Estelle Briley; children: Mary Alice Cannon Blankenship, Laren Jay. PhD, DD, Progressive Universal Life Ch., 2000. Commd. 2d lt. USAF, 1973, advanced through ranks to staff sgt., 1980, ret., 1993; clk. U.S. Postal Svc., Norfolk, Va., 1994—97, ret.; min. Progressive Universal Life Ch., Sacramento, 2000—, counseling practitioner, 2001—; min., 2000; counselor practitioner, 2001. Staff sgt. USAF 1983 Greneda Invasion, staff sgt. USAF, 1991—92, Desert Storm. Mem. AARP, Air Force Meml. Assn., Disabled Vets. Assn. Avocations: Black Belt in Tae Kwon Do, reading, museums, travel, music. Home: 2618 Summitt Ridge Loop Morrisville NC 27560-6974 E-mail: snowy777@msn.com.

CANNON, CAROL ANN, painter; b. White Plains, N.Y., Aug. 19, 1954; d. Fillmore W. Cannon and Lily Jean Hansen; m. Mostafa A. Mostafa, Feb. 16, 1984 (div. May 8, 1989). BFA in Illustration, Sch. Visual Arts, N.Y.C., 1980; BFA in Creative Arts Therapy, New Sch. U., N.Y.C., 1999. Ordained Interfaith Min. 1996. Pub. rels., restorer Club Am. Collectors, N.Y.C., 1985—90; owner Cannon Enterprises, Astoria, NY, 1990—2003; mgr. Troubetzkoy Paintings, N.Y.C., 1990—98; tchr. Hut Humble, Flushing, NY, 1998—2001; bldg. restorer The Frick Collection, 2003—. Min. Becoming Celebration, Astoria, 1998—. Mem.: Holographic Re-Patterning Assn., Assn. Comprehensive Energy Psychology, Urantia Assn. Greater N.Y. (pres. 1999—2003). Avocations: travel, photography, meditation, yoga, chi gong. Home: 32-45 37th St Astoria NY 11103

CANNON, CHRISTINE ANNE, veterinarian; b. Chgo., Nov. 13, 1952; d. Joseph Phillip and Mildred Eileen (Toll) C.; divorced. BS in Animal Sci., Purdue U., 1974; BS in Vet. Medicine, U. Ill., 1975, DVM, 1977. Vet. Bellemore Animal Hosp., Granite City, Ill., 1977-79, Humane Soc. of Mo., St. Louis, 1979-81, Wheaton Way Vet. Hosp., Bremerton, Wash., 1981-82, Rose Hill Animal and Bird Hosp., Kirkland, Wash., 1982-83; relief vet. Wash., 1983-87; vet., owner Bird and Exotic Pet Care Clinic, Lynnwood, Wash., 1987-92; vet. owner A Pet Care Clinic, Mountlake Terrace, Wash., 1992—. Lectr. Pet Industry Joint Adv. Coun., 1996 . Asst. editor Avian Emergency Care A Manual for Emergency Clinics, 1990. Group leader Canine Coll., Kirkland, 1986-87; mentor Project Discovery, Edmonds, Wash., 1989, 95-96; leader Explorer scout troop Boy Scouts Am., St. Louis, 1981; chair King County Animal Control Citizens Adv. Com., 1991-97; bus. cons. Jr. Achievement, 1994-95, 95-96. Mem. AVMA, Assn. Avian Veterinarians (pub. rels. com. 1989-95, chmn. client edn. com. 1995-96), Wash. State Vet. Med. Assn. (editors and pub. com. newsletter), Seattle-King County Vet. Med. Assn. (rep. South Snohomish chpt. 1990—, chmn. ethics com. 1991-94, pres. 1995-97), Finch Lovers Puget Sound (co-founder, sec.-treas. 1987-91), Aviculturai Soc. Puget Sound, N.W. Exotic Bird Soc., Pacific N.W. Herpetological Soc., Rotary (charter Mountlake Terrace, sgt.-at-arms 1994-96, cmty. svc. dir. 1997-2000, Lake Forest Pk. chpt. 2000—, sgt.-at-arms, 2003—), Assn. N.W. Avian Vet. (co-founder 1989—, pres. 1994-96). Avocations: reading, camping, aquarium keeping, gardening, dog training. Office: A Pet Care Clinic 23502 56th Ave W Mountlake Terrace WA 98043-5204

CANNON, FAYE E. bank executive; b. Frederick, Md., 1949; m. Robert P. Cannon; 1 child, Jennifer Serenyi. BA, Shepherd Coll., 1971; postgrad., Frostburg State U. V.p. mktg. and bus. devel. F&M Nat. Bank, 1974—85; v.p. mktg. Hagerstown Trust Co., 1985—88; sr. ops. officer and v.p. First Bank Frederick, 1988—90; exev. v.p. retail banking F&M Bancorp., 1990—93, pres., CEO, 1993—. Bd. dirs. F&M Bancorp/F&M Nat Bank, Home Fed. Savs. Bank; vice-chair bd. trustees Hood Coll., 1996—97. Bd. mem. Christmas in April, Frederick County, 1994—96, The Jefferson Sch., Sheppard Pratt, 1996—97; chair pvt. industry coun. PIC-Frederick County, 1996—97; chair cmty. edn. coun. Frederick C.C., 1997—99. Named to Phenomenal Women Panel, Arthur Anderson; recipient Character Counts Support award, Frederick County YMCA, 1997, Youth Devel. award, F&M Bank Big Bros. and Big Sisters, 2000. Mem.: Md. Banking Assn. (chair Md. Banking Sch. 1997), Bank Mktg. Assn. (pres. 1997), Am. Bankers Assn. (chair govt. rels. coun. 1999—2000). Office: F&M Bancorp & Farmers and Mechanics Nat Bank 110 Thomas Johnson Dr Frederick MD 21702

CANNON, FRANK See MAYHAR, ARDATH FRANCES

CANNON, GRACE BERT, retired immunologist; b. Chambersburg, Pa., Jan. 29, 1937; d. Charles Wesley and Gladys (Raff) Bert; m. W. Dilworth Cannon, June 3, 1961 (div. 1972); children: Michael Quayle Cannon, Susan Radcliffe Cannon Antolin, Peter Bert Cannon. AB, Goucher Coll., 1958; PhD, Washington U., St. Louis, 1962. Fellow Columbia U., N.Y.C.,

1962-64, Columbia U. Coll. Physicians and Surgeons, N.Y.C., 1964-65; staff fellow NIH Nat. Cancer Inst., Bethesda, Md., 1966-67; cell biologist Litton Bionetics, Inc., Kensington, Md., 1972-80, head immunology sect., 1980-85; dir. sci. ImmuQuest Labs., Inc., Rockville, Md., 1985-88; pres. Biomedical Analytics, Inc., Rockville, Md., 1988-2001; mgr. ATLIS Fed. Svcs., Inc., Rockville, Md., 1991-95, dir. Silver Spring, Md., 1995-97; sr. [illegible] Bethesda, Md., 1998—2000. Mem. contract rev. coms. Nat. Cancer Inst., 1983-87. Contbr. articles to profl. jours. Mem. Pub. Svc. Health Club, Bethesda, Md., 1984—, sec., 1990-2000. Grantee USPHS, 1959-65, NSF, 1959. Mem. AAAS, Am. Assn. for Cancer Rsch., N.Y. Acad. Sci., Sigma Xi. Home and Office: 2708 Oak Rd # 36 Walnut Creek CA 94597

CANNON, KATHLEEN, lawyer, educator; b. Monterey, Calif., Nov. 11, 1951; d. Jack Dempsey and Virginia Ann Cannon; m. Richard Eiden, May 26, 1979; children: Joncannon, Katrina. BS, Mich. State U., 1973; JD, Southwestern Law Sch., L.A., 1977. Bar: Calif. 1977. Paralegal VISTA/Peace Corps, Pacoima, Calif., 1973-74; prosecutor L.A. City Atty.'s Office, 1977-78; lawyer Los Angeles County Pub. Defender's Office, L.A., 1978-89, San Diego County Pub. Defender's Office, San Diego, 1989—. Instr. Nat. Inst. Trial Advocacy, 1992—; prof. Calif. Western Sch. Law, San Diego, 1993—, U. San Diego, 1995; spkr. Continuing Edn. Bar, San Diego, 1995-97. Bd. dirs., treas. North County Forum, Vista, Calif., 1997—. Mem. Calif. Pub. Defenders Assn. (bd. dirs. 1999—, spkr.). Avocations: hiking, travel. Office: San Diego County Pub Defender's Office 400 S Melrose Dr Ste 200 Vista CA 92083-6632

CANNON, LILLIAN, retired editor; b. Jacksonville, Fla., Dec. 21, 1926; d. James Lawrence Irvin and Esther Boone; m. Bernard O. Johann, Aug. 21, 1947 (div. 1973); children: Karen, Susan, Glenn(dec.), Jeanne; m. John G. Cannon, Dec. 27, 1984. AA, Stephens Coll., 1946; BA in English, Jacksonville U., 1960. Social worker, Jacksonville, Fla., 1972—74; editor agy. newsletter Jacksonville Dept. Cmty. Devel., Jacksonville, 1974—76, supr. writing staff, 1974—96; ret., 1996—. Contbr. articles to Fla. Living; pub.: books for children, novel, short stories. Pres. Learn to Read, Inc., Fine Arts Forum, Leadership Jacksonville. Mem.: Nat. League Am. Penwomen, St. John's Book Club (pres.). Episcopalian. Avocations: gardening, travel. Home: 11339 Honeytree Ln N Jacksonville FL 32225

CANNON, NANCY GLADSTEIN, insurance agent; b. San Francisco; d. Richard and Caroline Gladstein; m. Robert L. Cannon; 1 child, Richard Michael. BA, San Francisco State U.; JD, U. West Los Angeles, 1980. Agt. State Farm Ins. Co., Pacific Palisades, Calif., 1984-99, Thousand Oaks, Calif., 1999—. Mem. bd. govs. Pacific Palisades Civic League, 1987—91, Cmty. Coun., 1988—89; bd. dirs. YMCA, Pacific Palisades, 1989—93. Mem.: Westlake-Thousand Oaks C. of C. Republican. Avocations: sailing, paddle tennis. Home: PO Box 1228 Agoura Hills CA 91376-1228

CANNON, PATRICIA ALTHEN, librarian, writer; b. Granite City, Ill., Feb. 26, 1947; d. Eugene and Miriam (Knowles) Althen; m. Marvin E. Watson Jr., June 26, 1967 (div. 1975); m. Thomas Milton Cannon Jr., Dec. 24, 1982. BS in Psychology, West Tex. State U., 1976, MA in Jr. Coll. Teaching, 1978; MLS, Tex. Woman's U., 1982, PhD in Library Sci., 1988. Area office mgr. SSS, Dallas Naval Air Sta., Tex., 1979-84; vocat. evaluation program dir. Goodwill Rehab. Ctr., Amarillo, Tex., 1979-80; researcher pers. dept. City of Ft. Worth, 1981; br. reference librarian Amarillo Pub. Library, 1981-82, br. dir., 1983-85; asst. librarian office products div. Xerox Info. Svcs., Dallas, 1982; grad. teaching asst. Sch. Library and Info. Studies, Tex. Woman's U., Denton, 1985-87; asst. prof. dept. library and info. studies Northern Ill. U., DeKalb, 1987—94; freelance writer.

CANO, LEAH MARIE, music educator, writer, musician; b. Glendale, Calif., Oct. 8, 1951; d. Oscar José and Conception (Ponce) Cano; m. José Rosales, Feb. 2, 1974 (div. July 15, 1986); 1 child, Gabriel Joseph Rosales. AA, Saddlebk Jr. Coll., Mission Viego, Calif., 1972; BA in Spanish, U. Calif., Irvine, 1989, Tchg. Credential, 1991; MEd, U. Calif., Santa Cruz, 1994. Tchr. Soquel Unified Sch. Dist., Santa Cruz, Calif., 1995—. Avocations: writing, guitar, piano, violin.

CANO, MARTA MENDENDEZ, securities company executive, financial consultant; b. Havana, Cuba, July 29, 1941; came to U.S., 1961; d. Jose F. and Maria C. (Llanio) Menendez; m. Peter J. Cano, Nov. 30, 1960 (div. Jan. 1982); children: Marta, Eileen, Marianne, Peter, Andres. BA in English cum laude, U. Havana, 1961; MEd, U. P.R., 1970. Lic. securities profl., mgmt., life and health ins., notary pub. Dir. ESOL program Colegio Rosa-Bel, Bayamon, P.R., 1966-75; v.p. import/export Distribuidora Delmar, Inc., Bayamon, 1975-79; advanced sales specialist Sun Life of Can., Morristown, N.J., 1980-87; sr. fin. cons. Smith Barney, West Palm Beach, Fla., 1987-94; v.p. investments Prudential Securities, Inc., North Palm Beach, Fla., 1995-97, Brinker Capital Securities, Inc., Coral Gables, Fla., 1997—. Speaker in field. Founder Hispanic Coalition, Palm Beach County; nominated bd. dirs. Pal, Beach County, 1994; participant Directions 94, 1994; bd. commrs. Palm Beach County Health Care Spl. Taxing Dist., 1993—, Housing Authorities, City of West Palm Beach, 1994—; bd. dirs. Citizens Adv. for Health and Human Svcs., Palm Beach County, 1993—, Palm Beach County Budget Task Force, 1991—; mem. St. Ignatius Cathedral Parish coun., 1989-91; mem. Healthy Start Coalition, 1991—, others. Mem. Internat. Businessmean's Assn. (v.p. 1989-93), Internat. Assn. Fin. Planners. Roman Catholic. Avocations: walking, reading, theater, charity. Fax: 561-691-9718. E-mail: martamcano@msn.com.

CANONIZADO, GLORIA M. choreographer, educator; b. San Antonio, Mar. 23, 1940; d. Noberto Pobre and Primitiva Pablo (Madarang) Canonizado; m. Jose Honrado Villanueva, June 6, 1965 (annulled 1968); 1 child, Mary Josephine Villanueva Frijas. BS in Elem. Edn., Philippine Normal U., Manila, 1961; BS in Phys. Edn., Nat. Coll. Phys. Edn., Manila, 1962; MA in Edn., East Carolina U., Greenville, N.C., 1976. Cert. tchr. Tchr. phys. edn. Assumption Convent, Manila, 1961-71; tchr. Palma Elem. Sch., Manila, 1961-63; thcr. phys. edn. Quezon City H.S., Manila, 1963-66, U. of the East, Manila, 1966-69; tchr. Terrell County Schs., Columbia, N.C., 1972-75; instr. U. N.C., Pembroke, 1976-81, Southeastern C.C., Whiteville, N.C., 1985-87; tchr. Pub. Schs. of Robeson County, Pembroke, 1981-86, Yonkers (N.Y.) City Schs., 1987-89, Inst. Human Dynamics, Bronx, N.Y., 1987-89, Pub. Schs. of Robeson County, Maxton, N.C., 1989—. In-charge nurse aide Allen County Health Ctr., Ft. Wayne, Ind., 1971-72; aerobic instr. Lumberton Recreation Ctr., 1976-85, ballroom dance instr., 1976-85; dir., choreographer, aerobic instr. Maharlika Dance Troupe, 1977—. Mem. Human Rels. Commn., Lumberton, 1994-97; amb. of goodwill Baranggay Folk Dance Troupe, Manila, 1958-71; active Girl Scouts, 1961-72, Eagle Scouts, 1961-63; religious instr. St. Francis de Sales Cath. Ch., 1992—; com. chair Entertainment Internat. Festival, Fayetteville, N.C., 1996—. Recipient various awards, including Coach of the Yr., Carolina Conf. UNCP, 1978, Cert. of Appreciation, Ft. Bragg, Fayetteville, N.C., 2002, 25th Yr. Svc. award Maharlika Dance Troupe, 2003. Mem. Fgn. Lang. Assn. N.C., Philippine-Am. Club of Fayetteville, N.C. (life, Outstanding Svc. and Leadership award 2001). Democrat. Roman Catholic. Avocations: reading, travel to historical and exotic places, dance, swimming, visiting museums. Home: 517 E 14th St Lumberton NC 28358-4706 Office: Pub Schs Robeson County PO Box 2909 Lumberton NC 28359-2909 E-mail: gcanonizado@aol.com.

CANTOR, LINDA C. retired history educator; b. N.Y.C., Nov. 25, 1947; d. Henry and Sylvia (Pepper) C. BA in History, Bklyn. Coll., 1968; MA in History, U. Ill., Urbana, 1969; MLS, Queens Coll., 1973. Tchr. history Sarah J. Hale H.S., Bklyn., 1969—99, ret., 1999; staff developer N.Y.C. (N.Y.) Bd. Edn., 1999—2002. Program chair S.J. Hale H.S., Bklyn., 1976—. Editor: (newsletter) LINEAGE (Jewish Genealogy Soc. L.I.), 1995-99. Mem. Jewish Genealogy Soc. L.I. (bd. dirs. 1988-90, sec. 1990-91, pres. 1992-94, past pres. 1995), Jewish Genealogy Soc. N.Y. (mem. exec. coun., 1999 2001, sec. 2001-), Assn. Jewish Genealogical Socs. (dir. 1995-97). Avocation: genealogy. Home: 205 W End Ave Apt 6L New York NY 10023-4818

CANTOR, NANCY, academic administrator; b. NYC; m. Steven Brechin; children: Maddy, Archie. AB, Sarah Lawrence Coll., 1974; PhD in Psychology, Stanford U., 1978. Faculty, chair dept. psychology Princeton (NJ) U., 1991—96; dean Horace H. Rackham Sch. Grad. Studies, vice provost for acad. affairs U. Mich., Ann Arbor, 1996—97, provost, exec. v.p. acad. affairs, 1997—2001; chancellor U. Ill.-Urbana-Champaign, 2001—. Mem. adv. bd. NSF; mem. com. on nat. needs in biomed. and behavioral sci. rsch. NRC, mem. com. on women in sci. and engring. Co-author (or co-editor): 3 books; contbr. 50 articles to profl. jours., chpts. to books. Recipient Woman of Achievement award, Anti Defamation League. Fellow: Soc. for Personality and Social Psychology, APA (Disting. Sci. award for early career contbn. in psychology), Am. Psychol. Soc.; mem.: Am. Assn. for Higher Edn. (vice chair bd. dirs.), Am. Acad. Arts and Sci., Inst. of Medicine of NAS. Office: Univ Ill-Urbana-Champaign 320 Swanlund Adminstrn Bldg 601 E John St Champaign IL 61820

CANTOR, PAMELA CORLISS, psychologist; b. N.Y.C., Apr. 23, 1944; d. Alfred Joseph and Eleanor (Weschler) C.; m. Howard Feldman, Sept. 11, 1969; children: Lauren Jaye, Jeffrey Lee. BS cum laude, Syracuse U., 1965; MA, Columbia U., 1967, PhD, 1972; postgrad., Johns Hopkins U., 1969-70, Harvard U., Boston, 1973-74. Assoc. prof. psycholoyg Boston U., 1970-80; instr. Radcliffe Inst., Harvard U., 1977-78; pvt. practice clin. psychology, South Natick, Mass., 1980—. Mem. faculty Med. Sch., Harvard U.; lectr. in field, also TV and radio appearances Author: Understanding a Child's World—Readings in Infancy through Adolescence, 1977; cons. editor Suicide and Life-Threatening Behavior; columnist For Parents Only; contbr. articles to profl. jours., chpts. to hanbooks. Mem. statewide adv. bd. Mass. Gov.'s Office for Children, 1980—; mem. adv. bd. Samaritans of Boston; pres. Nat. Com. Youth Suicide Prevention; mem. Presdl. Task Force on Youth Suicide, HHS. Mem. APA, Am. Assn. Suicidology (pres. 1985-86, bd. dirs.), Am. Orthopsychiat. Assn., Mass. Psychol. Assn. Home: 6 Phillips Pond South Natick MA 01760

CANTRELL, ANDREA E. library administrator; b. Springfield, Mo., Jan. 1, 1948; d. A.J. Cantrell and Wilma (Snowden) Cave; m. Stephen J. Chism, 1989; m. Robert L. Clark; m. James D. Hawkins; BA, Am. U., 1970; MLS, U. Md., College Park, 1971. Young adult svcs. libr. Thomas Jefferson Regional Libr., Jefferson City, Mo., 1971-72; reference libr. Springfield-Greene County Libr. (Mo.), 1972-74; coord. Libr. resources Mo. State Libr., Jefferson City, 1974-78; chief cons. svc. Wash. State Library, Olympia, 1978-79; dir. Joplin Pub. Libr. (Mo.), 1979-81; dir. libr. resources div. Okla. Hist. Soc., Oklahoma City, 1981-85; spl. collections libr. U. Ark., Fayetteville, 1985—. Author: Manuscript Resources for Women's Studies, 1989; contbr. articles to profl. jours. Mem. ALA (chmn. staff devel. com. 1977-78; genealogy com. 1983-85), Ark. Libr. Assn. (chmn. Coll. and Univ. div. 1986-87), Assn. Specialized and Coop. Libr. Agys. (chmn. 1978-79), Ark. & Mo. Libr. Assns. (mem. various coms.), Zeta Tau Alpha. Office: U Ark Librs Spl Collections Dept Fayetteville AR 72701 Office Phone: 479-575-5577.

CANTRELL, CAROL HOWE, municipal administrator; b. Martins Ferry, Feb. 10, 1947; d. Ferd A. and Geraldine (Hayne) Howe; m. William O. Cantrell, Dec. 29, 1968 (div. Oct. 1997); children: David, Paul, Emily. BS in Acctg. magna cum laude, U. Rio Grande, Ohio, 1982. Formerly cost analyst Holzer Med. Ctr.; formerly tax adminstr. Rio Grande, Ohio; adminstr. mcpl. income tax and ins. Village of Middleport, Ohio, 1988—. Vol. in orgns. that support children and teenagers; mem. First united Presbyn. Ch., Gallipolis. Mem. Greater Ohio Assn. Tax Adminstrs. Presbyterian. Home: 662 4th Ave Gallipolis OH 45631-1231 Office: Tax Dept 237 Race St Middleport OH 45760-1054

CANTRELL, CAROL WHITAKER, educational administrator; b. Cin., July 25, 1951; d. James Ross and Edna M. Whitaker; m. David F. Justus, Jan. 23, 1970 (div. May 1981); 1 child, Holly; m. Pierce E. Cantrell Jr., May 24, 1986; 1 child, Janette. BS, postgrad., West Tex. A&M U., 1973, Tex. A&M U., 1974, 88. Dir. adminstrn. and budgets Tex. Engr. Experiment Sta., College Station, 1984-87, asst. agt. dir., 1987-97, assoc. agy. dir., 1997—; asst. vice chancellor Tex. A&M U. Sys., College Station, 1987—. Regents life fellow Tex. A&M U. System, 1998—; grantee USIA, 1998. Mem. Soc. Rsch. Adminstrs., Nat. Coun. Univ. Bus. Officers, Tex. Assn. Sr. State U. Bus. Officers, Exec. Women in Govt., Nat. Coun. Univ. Rsch. Adminstrs., Mu Phi Epsilon. Avocations: music, piano. Office: Tex A&M U Sys Engr Experiment Station Werc Sta Rm 301 College Station TX 77843-0001 E-mail: c-cantrell@tamu.edu.

CANTRELL, GEORGIA ANN, realtor; b. Hall, Ky., May 26, 1950; d. Melvin Johnson and Liza Ann (Collins) Johnson; children: David Cantrell, Jr., Mary Elizabeth Cantrell Riley. Grad. h.s., Fedcreek, Ky. Cert. realtor Ky. Owner Cantrell Supply, Winchester, Ky., 1979—2000; realtor Coldwell Banker Mc Mahan, Winchester, Ky., 1995—. Recipient Leadership award, Winchester-Clark Co. C. of C., 1996. Mem.: Boonesboro Lions Club, Million Dollar Club (life). Baptist. Avocations: travel, reading, walking. Home: 330 Runnymeade Dr Winchester KY 40391 Office: Coldwell Banker Mc Mahan 920 Bypass Rd Winchester KY 40391 Personal E-mail: gcantrell@coldwellbanker.com .

CANTRELL, LANA, actress, lawyer, singer; b. Sydney, Australia, Aug. 7, 1943; d. Hubert Clarence and Dorothy Jean (Thistlethwaite) C. JD, Fordham Law Sch., 1993. Bar: N.Y. 1994. Former of counsel Ballon Stoll Bader & Adler, N.Y.C.; assoc. Sendroff & Assocs. PC, N.Y.C., 1996—. Singer supper clubs, TV programs, Australia, 1958-62; U.S. debut: TV show The Tonight Show, NBC, 1962; rec. artist RCA and Polydor Records, 1967— (Grammy award as Most Promising New Female Artist, Nat. Assn. Rec. Arts and Scis. 1967); recs. include Lana!, Act III, And Then There Was Lana, The Now of Then! Pres. Thrush, Inc.; U.S. rep. Internat. Song Festival, Poland, 1966, UN Internat. Women's Year Concert, Paris, France, 1975. Decorated Order of Australia, 2003; recipient 1st prize Internat. Song Festival Poland, 1966; 1st Internat. Woman of Yr. award Feminist Party, 1973 Office: 300 E 71st St New York NY 10021-5234

CANTRELL, SHARRON CAULK, principal; b. Columbia, Tenn., Oct. 2, 1947; d. Tom English and Beulah (Goodin) Caulk; m. William Terry Cantrell, Mar. 18, 1989; 1 child, Jordan; children from previous marriage: Christopher, George English, Steffenee Copley. BA, George Peabody Coll. Tchrs., 1970; MS, Vanderbilt U., 1980; EdS, Mid. Tenn. State U., 1986. Tchr. Ft. Campbell Jr. High Sch., Columbia, Tenn., 1970-71, Whitthorne Jr. High Sch., Columbia, Tenn., 1977-86, Spring Hill (Tenn.) High Sch., 1966—. Mem. NEA, AAUW (pres. Tenn. divsn. 1983-85), Maury County Edn. Assn. (pres. 1983-84), Tenn. Edn. Assn., Assn. Preservation Tenn. Antiquities, Maury Alliance, Friends of Children's Hosp., Rotary (bd. dirs.), Phi Delta Kappa. Mem. Ch. of Christ. Home: 5299 Main St Spring Hill TN 37174-2495 Office: Spring Hill High Sch 1 Raider Ln Columbia TN 38401-7346

CANTU, DELIA, training services executive; b. Anthony, N.Mex., Jan. 13, 1949; d. Jose Perea and Eusebia (Ostos) Montes; m. Theodore Oscar Almaguer, Jan. 4, 1969 (div. Apr. 1974); m. Robert V. Cantu, June 23, 1979; 1 child, Fernando. BA, N.Mex. State U., 1971, MA, 1973. Counselor coord. N.Mex. State U., Las Cruces, 1973-74, asst. dir., 1974-77, dir., 1977-79; mem. faculty U. Santa Clara, Ft. Knox, Ky., 1979; bus. owner Cantu Photography & Camera, Radvliff, Ky., 1979-88; fin. adminstr. Vogue Coll., Las Cruces, 1988-89; border ops. tng. coord. Johnson & Johnson Med., Inc., Juarez, Mex., 1989-93; regional staff svcs. officer Tex. Dept. Health, El [illegible] coord. Eureka, El Paso, 1996—2001; mem. faculty U. Phoenix, Santa Teresa, N.Mex., 1995-99, faculty curriculum coord., 1997—. Co-author: Counseling the Mexican American Student, 1972. Mem. workforce adv. bd. El. Paso C.C.; bd. dirs. Ysleta Learning Ctr., El Paso; mem. faculty adv. bd. U. Phoenix; chair El Paso Mfrs. Tng. Consortium, 2001; mem. Adult Bilingual Curriculum Inst, 2001. Mem. ASTD. Home: RR 1 Box 364 La Mesa NM 88044-9767 Office: Valeo Motors and Actvators 1335 Bermudez Ave La Mesa NM 88044

CANTÚ, NORMA V. law educator, former federal official; b. Brownsville, Tex., Nov. 2, 1954; BS summa cum laude, Pan Am. U., 1973; JD, Harvard U., 1977. Bar: Tex. 1978, U.S. Dist. Ct. (so. dist.) Tex. 1979, U.S. Dist. Ct. (we. dist.) Tex. 1981, U.S. Ct. Appeals (5th and 11th cirs.) 1982, Calif. 1985, U.S. Ct. Appeals (10th cir.) 1986, U.S. Dist. Ct. (no. dist.) Tex. 1992. Tchr. English, Brownsville, 1974, San Antonio, 1979; intern Office of Atty. Gen. Tex., 1977-78; atty. Mex. Am. Legal Def. and Ednl. Fund, 1979—93, regional counsel, 1985-93; asst. sec. for civil rights Office for Civil Rights U.S. Dept. of Edn., Washington, 1993—2001; prof. law and edn. U. Tex., Austin, Tex., 2001—. U.S. rep. OAS Commn. on Children, 1999—2001. Officer Avance Parent Child Tng. Program, 1990; bd. dirs. Hispanic Health Policy Devel. Program, 1992, MALDEF, 2001—02, Mex. Am. Leadership Coun., 2002—, Leadership San Antonio, 1992—. Named to San Antonio Women Hall of Fame, Women in Sports Edn. Hall of Fame. Office: U Tex at Austin Sch Law Townes Hall Rm 3118M 727 E Dean Keeton St Austin TX 78705 Home: 140 Twinleaf Ln San Antonio TX 78213

CANTWELL, MARIA E. senator; b. Oct. 13, 1958; d. Rose and Paul Cantwell. BA Public Policy, Miami U. of Ohio. State repr. Dist. 44, Wash., 1987—92; mem. 103rd Congress from 1st Wash. dist., Washington, 1993—2000; owner pub. rels. firm.; U.S. senator from Wash., 2001—. Democrat. Office: 717 Hart Senate Bldg Washington DC 20510*

CANULLA, THERESA, microbiologist; b. Fall River, Mass., Jan. 13, 1962; d. Raymond Joseph and Emily Morrow; m. Marcus Francis Canulla, July 24, 1987; children: Megan Elizabeth, Laura Emily. BSc, Salve Regina Coll., 1984. Mem.: N.E. Assn. Clin. Microbiology and Infectious Disease. Republican. Roman Cath. Avocations: gardening, reading, youth ministry.

CAPELL, CYDNEY LYNN, editor; b. Jacksonville, Fla., Dec. 20, 1956; d. Ernest Clary and Alice Rae (McGinnis) C.; m. Garrick Philip Martin, July 16, 1983 (div. Jan. 1988). BA, Furman U., 1977. Mktg. rep. E.C. Capell & Assocs., Greenville, S.C., 1977-80; sales rep. Prentice-Hall Publs., Cin., 1980-81; sales, mktg. rep. Benjamin/Cummings, Houston, 1981-83; sales rep. McGraw-Hill Book Co., Houston, 1983-85, engring. editor N.Y.C., 1985-87; acctg. and infosys. editor Bus. Pubs., Inc., Plano, Tex., 1988-89; sr. editor Gorsuch Scarisbrick Pubs., Scottsdale, Ariz., 1989-90; editor-in-chief rsch. dept. Rauscher, Pierce, Refsnes Stock Brokers, 1990-94; editor-in-chief, dir. mktg. Marshall & Swift, L.A., 1994-98; sr. mng. editor Pearson Custom Pub., Tulsa, 2000—. Editor Talon mag., 1972; news editor Paladin newspaper, 1977. Named Rookie of Yr. McGraw-Hill Book Co., 1985. Mem. NOW, NAFE, Women in Pub., Women in Comm., Mensa. Republican. Avocations: tennis, ballet.

CAPELLE, ELAINE M. financial planner; b. Green Bay, Wis., June 29, 1941; d. Stanley E. and Lena J. (DeValk) Van De Hey; m. Ralph Unsin, Sept. 3, 1958 (div. Sept. 1960); m. John J. Capelle, July 28, 1962; children: Debra Ann, Laura Marie. William Arthur. Student, U. Wis., Green Bay, 1999—. A/p specialist Shopko Gen., Green Bay, Wis., 1964-74; fin. specialist U. Wis., Green Bay, 1974-99; bookkeeper Comml. Laundry Sales, 2002—. Bd. dirs. United Way, Green Bay, 1990-94; chair NWPC, Northeastern Wis., 1994-96; income tax asst. UWGB- Acctg., 1990—; family fin. counselor Brown County Extension, Green Bay, 1989-90. Mem. Nat. Fedn. Bus. & Profl. Women, Wis. Fedn. Bus. & Profl. Women (past state pres.), Green Bay-De Pere Bus. & Profl. Women (past local pres. and rec. sec.), AAUW, NWPC. Democrat. Roman Catholic. Avocations: reading, knitting. Home: 2032 Deckner Ave Green Bay WI 54302-3532 E-mail: emcapella@greenbaynet.com.

CAPELLE-FRANK, JACQUELINE AIMEE, writer; b. Fond du Lac, Wis., Dec. 23, 1935; d. Ira Richard and Aimee Cecilia (Dignin) Capelle; divorced; children: P. Malachi, Tamara, Daria Frank-Weber. AA, Edison C.C., Naples, Fla., 1986; cert., U. Cambridge, Eng., 1991, U. Oxford, 1992, Paris Am. Acad., 1992; BA, Fla. Internat. U., 1994. Part-time instr. Internat. Coll., 1999. Author: (children's book) What's a Library, 1974, (anthologies) Poetic Voices of America, 1996, 97. Mem. adv. bd. Greater Naples Leadership, Inc., 1999—. Mem. AAUW, Nat. Mus. Women, Collier County Hist. Soc. (bd. dirs. 1994—, pres. 1997-2001), Nat. Trust for Hist. Preservation, Mus. Trustee Assn., Cooperstown Art Assn. Republican. Presbyterian. Avocations: reading, travel, country walks, gardening, swimming. Home: 143 4th Ave N Naples FL 34102-8421

CAPELLO, LINDA, artist; b. Bklyn., July 12, 1949; m. John Capello; 1 child, Joanna. AAS, Fashion Inst. Tech., N.Y.C., 1968. Art tchr. figure drawing; art tchr. Guild Hall's Young At Art Program; art tutor Empire State Coll.; art tchr., dept. head Bialik Sch., Bklyn., 1985-87; illustrator for children's newspaper The Waldo Tribune; artist Karl Mann studios, 1978-80; freelance fashion illustrator. Exhibited in group shows at ann. Guild Hall shows, East Hampton, ann. Goat Alley Gallery 725 shows, Sag Harbor, ann. Southampton Artists group shows, Adelphia U. Gallery, L.I., 1973, Belanthi Gallery, Bklyn., 1979-81, BACA Small Works show, Bklyn., 1986, AFA at Lever House, N.Y.C., 1989, Mark Humphries Gallery, Southampton, 1993, Goodman Deisgn Gallery, Southampton, 1993, Clayton-Libratore Gallery, Bridgehampton, N.Y., 1993, 51st Ann. Audubon Exhibit, N.Y.C., 1993, Ashwagh Hall, East Hampton, 1994, Catherine Lorillard Wolf Art Club ann. show, N.Y.C., 1994, Am. Pen Women show, Farmingville, N.Y., 1995, Sundance Gallery, Bridgehampton, 1995, EEAC Juried Show, Riverhead, N.Y., 1995, Jennifer Garrigues, Palm Beach, Fla., 2000, Hampton Rd. Gallery, Southampton, N.Y., 2003; oil paintings, drawings in pvt. collections; murals on pub. and pvt. walls. Mem. Southampton Artists, Artists Alliance East Hampton.

CAPERS, CYNTHIA FLYNN, dean, nursing educator; Diploma, Freedman's Hosp., Washington, 1965; BSN, U. Md., 1968; MSN, U. Pa., 1981, PhD in Culture and Nursing, 1986. Assoc. prof., course coord. Thomas Jefferson U., Phila., 1989-93; dir. undergrad. programs, assoc. prof. LaSalle U. Sch. Nursing, Phila., 1993-96, interim dean, assoc. prof., 1996-97; dean, prof. U. Akron Coll. of Nursing, 1997—. M. Elizabeth Carnegie vis. prof. in nursing rsch. Howard U., 1998; recipient Outstanding Achievement, Leadership and Svc. Med. Soc. of Ea. Pa., 1997, Disting. Nurse award Pa. Nurses Assn., 1995, Nurse Excellence award Pa. Nurses Assn., 1991; named Woman of Yr. YWCA of Germantown, 1992. Contbr. articles to profl. jours. Bd. trustees Am. Heart Assn., 1998-2000, Coming Together Project, Akron, 1998—, The Akron Cmty. Found., 1999—, Summa Health Sys. Hosp. Bd., 2000—; adv. bd. LaSalle U. Neighborhood Nursing Ctr., 1997-98, Coll. of Health, Edn., and Human Resources U. Scranton, 1992-96, Govs. Sch. of Health Care Professions in Pa., 1990-97; vice chmn. Pa. State Bd. of Nursing, 1991, chmn., 1992, 93; bd. mgrs. The Phila. Found., 1993-97. Office: U Akron Coll Nursing Mary E Gladwin Hl Akron OH 44325-0001 Fax: 330-972-5737.

CAPETILLO, CHARLENE VERNELLE, music educator, special education educator; b. Streator, Ill., Sept. 18, 1944; d. Miles Bryan and Lillian Mae Baker; m. Benjamin Capetillo, July 20, 1963; children: Christiana, Matthew Bryan, Susannah Carlina. Photography cert., Woodland Hills Occupl. Ctr., 1979; student, Pierce Coll., 1985, student, 1987. Sales staff Avon, Pasadena, Calif., 1963—78; pvt. seamstress Calabasas, Calif., 1963—; piano and voice tchr. pvt. and pub. schs., Conejo and L.A., 1978—; singer L.A. Opera, Opera Pacific, 1985—95, L.A. Camerata Orch., 1985—; owner, pres. Hollywood Angels Childrens' Photography, L.A., 1994—; spl. edn. tchr. L.A. Unified Sch. Dist., 1999—; dir. sales Neo-Life Diamite Health Products, 1985—. Actor: (poems and essays); performer: Carnegie Hall, 1999, 2001, 2003, (soloist) China Tour, 2003. Vol. performer various retirement homes, L.A., 1992—; soloist numerous chs., L.A.; choir mem. Grace Cmty. Ch., Sun Valley, Calif., 1994—96. Mem.: Phi Beta, Pi Alpha Theta. Achievements include 4th great grandaughter of Daniel Boone. Avocations: traveling, hiking, quilting, art. Home: 6519 W 87th Pl Westchester CA 90045

CAPITO, SHELLEY MOORE, congresswoman; b. Glen Dale, WV, Nov. 26, 1953; m. Charles L. Capito, Jr.; children: Charles, Moore, Shelley. BS in zoology, Duke U., 1975; MEd, U. Va., 1976. Career counselor West Va. State Coll.; dir. Ednl. Info. Ctr. West Va. Bd. Regents; mem. West Va. House of Delegates, 30th dist., 1996—2000, U.S. Ho. of Reps. from 2nd WV dist., 2001—; minority chair health and human resources committee; mem. judiciary committee., banking commitee, insurance committee. Mem. 107th Congress House Banking and Fin. Svcs. com., House Transportation and Infrastructure com., House Small Bus. com. Mem. YWCA (past pres.), Cmty. coun., Kanawha Valley, West Va. Interagency Coun. Early Intervention. Republican. Mem. First Presbyn. Ch. Office: 1431 Longworth House Office bldg Washington DC 20515-4802*

CAPLAN, ELINOR, former Canadian government official; b. Toronto, Ont., Can., May 20, 1944; m. Wilf Caplan; children: David, Mark, Zane, Meredith. Pres. Elinor Caplan and Assocs., 1973-78; alderman Ward 13 City of North York, 1978-85; mem. Ont. Legislature, 1985-97, chief opposition whip; minister Ministry of Health, Toronto, 1987-90; critic for health and women's issues; mem. Ho. of Commons Dist. Thornhill, Ont., 1997—; Min. of Citizenship and Immigration Canada, 1999—2002; Min. of National Revenue, 2002—03. Chmn. Mgmt. Bd. of Cabinet, chmn. of cabinet Peterson Govt.; minister Govt. Svcs., mem. Standing Com. on Health, Standing Com. on Pub. Accounts Past chmn. North York Coun. Com., Human Resources Adv. Coun., Rapid Transit Subcom.; past mem. North York Bd. of Health; past vice chmn. North York Interagy. Coun. Mem. North York Bus. Assn. (founder, past chmn. devel. and econ. growth com.). Office: House of Commons 658 Confederation Bldg Ottawa ON Canada K1A OA6

CAPLAN, JESSICA MARIE, small business owner, artist; b. Cleve., Aug. 11, 1969; d. Harry Walter Caplan and Susan Elaine Klein. BFA, Carnegie Mellon U., 1991. Asst. mgr. Crystal Dragon Gallery, Madrid, N.Mex., 1992—94; owner, dir. Humana Gallery, Madrid, 1994—96; owner, tchr. Sun Studios, Santa Fe, 1996—97; owner, pres. Jezebel, Inc., Santa Fe, 1997—. Spkr. Arts Coun. U. Pa., 1990. Inventor glass slumping process. Office: Jezebel Gallery 236 Delgado St Santa Fe NM 87501

CAPLAN, PAULA JOAN, actress, playwright; b. Springfield, Mo., July 7 1947; d. Jerome Arnold and Theda Ann (Karchmer) C.; children: Jeremy Benjamin, Emily Julia. AB in English cum laude, Harvard U., 1969; MA in Psychology, Duke U., 1971, PhD in Psychology, 1973. Clin. psychology intern John Umstead Hosp., Butner, N.C., 1972-73, N.C. Meml. Hosp., Chapel Hill, 1972-73; fellow neuropsychology divsn. Rsch. Inst. Hosp. for Sick Children, Toronto, Ont., Can., 1974-76; psychologist Toronto Family Ct. Clinic Clarke Inst. Psychiatry, Can., 1977-80; asst. prof. dept. applied psychology Ont. Inst. for Studies in Edn., 1980-81; prin. investigator Toronto Multi-Agy. Child Abuse Rsch. Project, 1979-84; asst. prof. psychiatry U. Toronto, 1979-95; assoc. dir. Ontario Inst. for Studies in Edn.'s Ctr. for Women's Studies in Edn., 1984-85; head Ctr. for Women's Studies in Edn. Ont. Inst. for Studies in Edn., 1985-87, assoc. prof. applied psychology, 1982-87, full prof. dept. applied psychology, 1987-95; vis. scholar Brown U. Pembroke Ctr., Providence, 1993—94, 1996—2000, adj. prof., 2001—03. Spkr., lectr. in field; appeared on TV and radio programs. Actor: (theatre) Native Tongues, Last Exit Before Toll, Arizona Anniversaries, You Have To Serve Somebody, Allelujah Yodelayheehoo, Gold, Hound of Baskervilles, Getting Out, Six Char. Srch. of Author, Showcase, Waiting for Odysseus, Under Milkwood, The Bad Seed, She Stoops To Conquer, Machinal, The Sins of Sor Juana; Author: The Myth of Women's Masochism, 1985, 93, German edit., 1986, Swedish edit., 1987, Between Women: Lowering the Barriers, 1981, Don't Blame Mother: Mending the Mother-Daughter Relationship, 1989, 90, Brazilian edit., 1990, German edit., 1990, Dutch edit., 1991, Lifting a Ton of Feathers: A Woman's Guide to Surviving in the Academic World, 1993, You're Smarter than They Make You Feel: How the Experts Intimidate Us and What We Can Do About It, 1994, German edit., 1995, They Say You're Crazy: How the World's Most Powerful Psychiatrists Decide Who's Normal, 1995, (with Jeremy B. Caplan) Thinking Critically About Research on Sex and Gender, 1994, (with Marcel Kinsbourne) Children's Learning and Attention Problems, 1979, Spanish edit., 1984; (plays) Call Me Crazy (2d place Arlene & William Lewis Nat. Contest 1997), Tikkun Olam; mem. editl. bd. Can. Jour. Cmty. Mental Health, 1990-93, Women and Therapy, 1992-95, Feminism and Psychology, 1993-95; editor Resources for Feminist Rsch., 1982-86, adv. bd. mem. 1986-87; reviewer of grant proposals Hosp. for Sick Children Found., Social Scis. and Humanities Rsch. Coun. Can.; contbr. articles to profl. jours. and chpts. to books. Mem. Brown U. Parents Coun., 1992-94. Recipient fellowship Nat. Inst. Mental Health, 1969-71, fellowship Nat. Inst. Child Devel., 1971-73. Fellow APA (Eminent Woman Psychologist 1996), Am. Orthopsychiat. Assn. (fellow program com. mem., reviewer conv. 1983-84, program com. mem., reviewer Women's Inst. 1984-85), Can. Psychol. Assn. (newsletter editor interest group on women and psychology 1979-80, inst. organizer sect. on women and psychology 1980-81, coord.-elect sect. on women and psychology 1981-82, mem. com. on status women 1982-84, coord. sect. on women and psychology 1982-83, past coord. sect. on women and psychology 1983-84, com. on nominations 1990-91); mem. Harvard-Radcliffe Club Toronto (schs. com. 1981-82).

CAPLOE, ROBERTA, magazine editor; b. Framingham, Mass., Mar. 24, 1962; d. Robert Coleman and Jeanne Adele (Goldburg) Caploe. BA, Barnard Coll., 1984. Sr. prodr. Phone Programs Inc., N.Y.C., 1985—88; exec. editor Soap Opera Digest Presents, N.Y.C., 1988—89; West Coast editor Soap Opera Digest, L.A., 1989—95; exec. editor Seventeen mag., N.Y.C., 1997—2000; editor-in-chief Youth Entertainment Group, Primedia, 2000—03; exec. editor Ladies Home Jour., N.Y.C., 2003—. Co-author (with Jamie Caploe): Melrose Confidential. Assoc. mem. Acad. TV Arts and Scis. Avocation: tennis. Office: Ladies Home Jour 20th Fl 125 Park Ave New York NY 10017

CAPODILUPO, JEANNE HATTON, public relations executive; b. McRae, Ga., May 3, 1940; d. Lewis Irby and Essee Elizabeth (Parker) Hatton; m. Raphael S. Capodilupo, Jan. 21, 1967. Grad., Dale Carnegie Inst., 1976. Sec. A.R. Clark Acct., Fernandina Beach, Fla., 1958-59; receptionist, girl Friday Sta. WNDT-TV, N.Y.C., 1960-62, Coy Hunt and Co., N.Y.C., 1962-69; clk. Woodlawn Cemetery, Bronx, N.Y., 1969-71, historian, cmty. affairs coord., 1971-84, editor newsletter, 1979—, asst. to pres., 1984-99, dir. pub. rels., 1984; grad. asst. Dale Carnegie Inst., 1977-78. Rschr. Woodlawn Cemetery's Hall of Fame; contbr. articles to Collier Encyclopedia, 1985; contbr. articles to profl. jours. Chmn. ann. Adm. Farragut Honor Ceremony, Bronx, 1976—; founder, chmn. Toys for Needy Children, 1983-97; bd. dirs. Bronx Mus. Arts, v.p., 1983-84; pres. Bronx Coun. Arts, 1987-90, Network Orgn. Bronx Women, 1997-98; adv. bd. Salvation Army, 1985, Bronx Arts Ensemble, 1985; bd. mgrs. Bronx YMCA, 1985, vice-chmn., 1989—; bd. dirs. Bronx Urban League, 1985, Bronx Coun. on Arts, 1985, pres. 1987-90; active Bronx Landmarks Task Force, 1994—. Recipient award citation VFW, 1976, Voice of Democracy Program judge's citation, 1980, Disting. Community Svc. award N.Y.C. Council, Il Leone di Sanmarco award Italian Heritage & Culture Com. Bronx, 1989, Lifetime Achievement Humanitarian award Bronx Coun. on Arts, 1999-2000; named Woman of Yr., YMCA, Bronx, 1986, Network Orgn. Bronx Women, 1986, Jeanne and Ray Capodilupo named as Mr. & Mrs. Bronx 1989-90 proclaimed by Borough Pres., named Pioneer of the Bronx, 1992, Citizen of Yr. Bronx Club, 1995; recipient cert. appreciation Dale Carnegie Inst., 1977, Outstanding Citizenship award Bronx N.E. Kiwanis Club, 1981, Service to Youth award YMCA of Bronx, 1983; recipient proclamation City Council of N.Y., Italian Heritage and Culture Com. of the Bronx, 1989; Outstanding Cemeterian award Am. Cemetery Assn., 1987-88; Citation of Merit Bronx Borough Pres.'s Office, 1988; Spl. Hons. for Outstanding Vol. Work Ladies Aux. Our Lady of Mercy Med. Ctr.; named Hon. Grand Marshall Bronx Columbus Day Parade, 1987-89, Bronx Meml. Day Parade, 1989; apptd. to commn. celebrating 350 yrs. of the Bronx by Borough Pres., recipient Pioneer award for Women's History Month for Outstanding Humanitarian Svcs., 1991, Lifetime Achievement award Bronx YMCA, 1999-2000, Role Model award Columbus Alliance, 2000; Jeanne Hatton Capodilupo Day proclaimed by Bronx Borough Presdl. Proclamation, 1999. Mem. Bronx County Hist. Soc., Network Orgn. Bronx Women (pres. 1997-99), Women in Communication, Bronx C. of C. (sec. 1988), YMCA (life mem.), N.Y. Press Club, Italian Big Sisters Club, Women's City Club, Order Eastern Star. Methodist. Office: Woodlawn Cemetery Webster Ave at 233 St Bronx NY 10470-0075 E-mail: smilerjean@aol.com.

CAPOGNA-MORAS, BARBARA JEAN, secondary school educator; b. Schenedctady, NY, Dec. 29, 1955; d. Victor and Gloria Jean Capogna; m. M. Shane Moras (div. Nov. 1998). B of Music Edn., SUNY, Potsdam, 1977; M of Music Edn., La. State U., 1985. Cert. tchr. Ga. Tchr. North Adams (Mass.) Mid. Sch., 1977—81, Lake Placid (N.Y.) H.S., 1981—84; grad. asst. La. State U., Baton Rouge, 1984—85; tchr. Fulton County Schs., Atlanta, 1985—88, 2000—, Cleveland (Tenn.) Mid. Sch., 1988—89, Destrehan (La.) H.S., 1995—2000. Music dir. Rivertown Rep. Theatre, Kenner, 1994—98; accompanist Jefferson Children's Choir, Metairie, La., 1993—95; performer various theatrical prodns., New Orleans, 1992—2000. Vol. Roswell (Ga.) Cultural Arts, 2003. Mem.: Music Educators Nat. Conf., Am. Choral Dirs. Assn., Internat. Assn. Jazz Educators. Republican. Roman Catholic. Avocations: musical theater, reading, fitness, dogs, drama. Home: 3217 Walton Way Roswell GA 30076 Office: Northview HS 10625 Parsons Rd Duluth GA 30097 E-mail: moras@fulton.k12.ga.us.

CAPONE, MARYANN, financial planner; b. Bklyn., July 25, 1952; d. Pasquale and Dorothy (Rizzo) Capone; m. Donald Walter Huebner, June 7, 1975; 1 child, Melissa Lauren. BA, Queens (N.Y.) Coll., 1974; MBA, St. John's U., Queens, 1980. Cert. financial planner, enrolled agent for the IRS 2001. Asst. to head rsch. F. Eberstadt, N.Y.C., 1975-78; asst. v.p. Merrill Lynch, N.Y.C., 1978-81; v.p. Integrated Resources, N.Y.C., 1981-84, Mid-Island Equities, Wesbury, N.Y., 1984-85, Am. Savs. Bank, N.Y.C., 1985-86, 1st v.p. Greater N.Y. Savs. Bank, N.Y.C., 1986-97; prin. MCH Fin Planning, Massapequa, N.Y., 1997—; enrolled agt. IRS Adj. prof. acctg. Molloy Coll., Rockville Centre, 2003. Instr. religious edn. St. James Roman Cath. Ch., Seaford, N.Y., 1988—, mem. adv. bd. religious edn., 1996—; mem. adv. bd. Women in Mgmt., C.W. Post U., Brookville, N.Y., 1995. Roman Catholic. Home and Office: MCH Fin Planning & Tax Svc 433 N Atlanta Ave North Massapequa NY 11758 E-mail: mcapone7@optonline.net.

CAPOTORTO, ROSETTE, small business owner, printing company executive, writer; d. Philip Vito Capotorto and Mary Cuffari-Capotorto; 1 child, Sophia. BA summa cum laude, Hunter Coll., 1986. Co-owner Full House Printing, Hoboken, NJ, 1988—. Tchr./cons. Hoboken (N.J.) Charter Sch., 1998—2003; cons. Bklyn. (N.Y.) Children's Mus., 1998—2001. Contbr. ; co-author: Are Italians White: How Race is Made in America, 2003, Italian American Writers on New Jersey, 2003. Mem. Future Forum Program, Englewood, NJ, 1999. Recipient A. Ginsberg Poetry award, Paterson Lit. Rev., 2000; fellow, Edward F. Albee Found., 1988, 1994. Mem.: Italian Am. Writers Assn., Malia Collective Italian Am. Women, Phi Beta Kappa. Avocations: photography, painting, travel. Home: 228 Jefferson St Hoboken NJ 07030 Office: 303 First St Hoboken NJ 07030

CAPPARELL, LORRAINE SUSAN, artist, sculptor, painter; b. Rochester, N.Y., July 26, 1947; d. Edmond Seth and Ruth Myrtle (Goettel) Spencer; m. James Capparell, Aug. 23, 1969 (div. 1995); m. Lars Speyer, July 26, 1997. BS, Cornell U., 1969. Exec. trainee McCurdy's, Rochester, 1969-70; prodn. artist Coakley-Heagerty, San Jose, Calif., 1971-73; freelance graphic designer Palo Alto, Calif., 1974—; photographer, 1978—; sculptor, painter, 1980—. Artist, creator Hands, 1982, The Three Ages of Women, 1986, Five Women: Tree of Life, 1994, Erato, 1995, Observer, 1996, Yin and Yang, 1997, Abhaya, 2001, Mahapajapati, 2002. Bd. dirs. Cult. Odyssey San Francisco, 1985—, Women's Caucus for the Arts, Palo Alto, 1986—. Mem. Kappa Kappa Gamma. Buddhist. Avocations: meditation, travel, writing, cooking, tai chi. Home: 698 Kendall Ave Palo Alto CA 94306-2723

CAPPEL, CONSTANCE, educational consultant, writer; b. Dayton, Ohio, June 22, 1936; d. Adam Denison and Mary Louise (Henry) C.; m. R.A. Montgomery Jr., June 16, 1962 (div. Apr. 1980); children: Raymond A. Montgomery III, Anson Cappel Montgomery. BA, Sarah Lawrence Coll., 1959; MA, Columbia U., N.Y.C., 1961; PhD, Union Inst. & Univ., Cin., 1991. Editor Newsweek, N.Y.C., 1961-63, Vogue, N.Y.C., 1964-66; grad. prof. Goddard Coll., Plainfield, Vt., 1975-79; founder, chief exec. officer, pub. Vt. Crossroad Press, Waitsfield, 1972-82; comml. realtor Investmark, Dayton, 1983—85; prin., founder, CEO Cappel Cons., San Francisco, 1986-94; bus. advisor U.S. Peace Corps, Lodz, Poland, 1994-96; mgr. Price Waterhouse Nieruchomości, Warsaw, 1996-97; dir. devel. Conflict Resolution Catalysts, Montpelier, Vt., 1997; tchr. trainer U.S. Peace Corps., Kazakhstan, 1998; pres. Newport (N.H.) Earth Inst., 1999; faculty Norman Rockwell Mus., 2000—02. Author: Hemingway in Michigan, 1966 (paperback 1977, 99), Vermont School Bus Ride, 1977, Utopian Colleges, 1999, Sweetgrass and Smoke, 2002, A Stairwell in Lodz, 2004, A union of Voices: Accounts of the Union Institute and University, 2004. Founder Women's Rights Project/ACLU, Vt., 1973-74; mem. grad. alumni/ae bd. The Union Inst. & Univ., 1992-94, 99—, sec., 1993; v.p. bd. Chief Andrew Blackbird Mus., 2003—, bd. dirs. 2002—, Harbor Springs Hist. Soc., 2002—, trustee, 2002—. McDowell Colony fellow, Peterborough, N.H., 1972, 74. Fellow: New England Antiquities Rsch. Assn.; mem.: Petoskey Audabon Soc., Archaeol. Conservancy, Audubon Soc., Mich. Hemingway Soc., Ernest Hemingway Soc., Great Lakes Lighthouse Keepers Assn., PEN Am. Ctr. Democrat. Episcopalian. Office: 524 Pine St Harbor Springs MI 49740

CAPPEL, LINDA GREENWOOD, education educator; b. Mt. Airy, N.C., Feb. 18, 1947; d. Howard Franklin and MaryLee (Tilley) Greenwood; m. Robert Francis Cappel, Jr., Mar. 17, 1973; 1 child, Stacy Leeann. ABT, High Point U., N.C., 1969; MEd, U. N.C., Greensboro, 1978. Tchr. Winston Salem/Forsyth pub. schs., 1969—. Prof. Wake Forest U., Winston-Salem, 1976—77; instr. Forsyth Tech. Coll., Winston-Salem, 1992—2000; adj. prof. High Point U., NC, 2001—; mem. Disting. Tchrs. Forum, Raleigh, 2001—03; gifted adv. com. Winston-Salem/Forsyth Schs., 1999—, mem. equity com., 1995—97. Fellow, R.J. Reynolds Nabisco fellow, 1988—90. Mem.: N.C. Assn. Educators (Terry Sanford Award for Creative Tchg. 1997), Zeta Tau Alpha (dist. pres. 1985—93, Cert. of Merit 1978, Honor Ring 1990), Delta Kappa Gamma. Home: 1026 Branchwood Dr Kernersville NC 27284

CAPPELLO, EVE, speaker, trainer, author; b. Sydney, Australia; d. Nem and Ethel Shapira; children: Frances Soskins, Alan Kazdin. BA, Calif. State U., Dominguez Hills, 1974; MA, Pacific Western U., 1977, PhD, 1978. Singer, pianist, L.A., 1956—76; profl. devel. and mgmt. staff tng. Calif. Inst. Tech., 1977—; instr. Calif. State U., St. Mary's Coll., U. So. Calif., Loyola Marymount U.; founder, pres. A-C-T Internat.; founder WIN Internat. Invited speaker World Congress Behavior Therapy, Israel, Melbourne U., Australia; newspaper columnist, 1976—. Author: Let's Get Growing, 1979, The Professional Touch, 1988, 3d edit., 2000, Dr Eve's Garden, 1984, Act, Don't React, 4th edit. 2000, The Game of the Name, 1985, The Perfectionist Syndrome, 1990, Why Aren't More Women Running the Show?, 1994, Great Sex After 50, 2d edit., More Great Sex After 50, 2003; contbr. articles to profl. jours. Named to Bus. and Profl. Women Internat. Hall of Fame, 1994. Mem. Internat. Platform Assn. (bd. dirs., affirmative action com., bd. govs.), Toastmasters, DTM (area gov.), Alpha Gamma. Office Phone: 626-432-1981. E-mail: dreve@earthlink.net.

CAPPETTA, PAMELA GUYLER, counselor; b. Huntington, Pa., May 16, 1949; d. Thomas Winslow and Lois Olene (Lukens) G.; m. Christopher John Boll, Aug. 16, 1969 (div. Aug. 1985); 1 child, Kirstin Boll Kochanek; m. Robert Christopher Cappetta, May 4, 1991. BS, Shippensburg U., 1971; MEd, Coll. William & Mary, 1980, EdD, 1990. Lic. profl. counselor, Va.; lic. marriage and family therapist, Va. Social worker York-Poquoson Social Svcs., Grafton, Va., 1981-84; coord. PACES family counseling ctr. Coll. William & Mary, Williamsburg, Va., 1984-87; family therapist TMJ rsch. ctr. Med. Coll. Va., Sch. Dentistry, 1984-88; clin. assoc., counselor Family Living Inst., Williamsburg, Va., 1985-88; clin. asst. prof. Med. Coll. Va., Sch. Dentistry, Richmond, Va., 1990-94; med. family therapist Norge Family Practice, Williamsburg, 1992-94; co-owner, counselor Family Living Inst., 1988-94; allied health prof. Williamsburg Place, 1993—; counselor pvt. practice, Williamsburg, 1995—. Dir. coord. Transitions, Williamsburg, 1992-94; holotropic breathwork practitioner, Williamsburg, 1996—; faculty Asheville (N.C.) Body-Mind Clinic, 1999—. Contbr. articles to profl. jours. Vol. Va. Breast Cancer Found., Williamsburg, 1995—; bd. dirs. Va. Cancer Pain Initiative, Richmond, 1996. Mem. ACA, Am. Acad. Pain Mgmt., Nat. Bd. of Cert. Counselors, Va. Counseling Assn., Assn. Transpersonal Psychology, Assn. for Holotropic Breathwork Internat. (cert.), Acad. for Eating Disorders, EMDR Internat. Assn. Democrat. Avocations: travel, reading, walking dogs. Office: 161-B John Jefferson Rd Williamsburg VA 23185-5640 Office Phone: 757-253-5708. E-mail: drpamm@mindspring.com.

CAPPIELLO, ANGELA, meeting and marketing manager; b. New Hyde Park, N.Y., July 6, 1954; d. Augustine and Angela (Tamburello) C. Cert. meeting and conv. mgmt., NYU, 1988, cert. assn. mgmt., cert. food and beverage mgmt., NYU, 1989, cert. travel mgmt., 1990, cert. hotel and motel mgmt., 1991, cert. in fin. controls, 1992, cert. mgmt. practices, 1998. Cert. meeting profl., assn. exec. Mgr. meetings and convs. N.Y. Libr. Assn., N.Y.C., 1987-89; conf. coord. ASCE, N.Y.C., 1989; mgr. meetings and confs. Coun. Cons. Orgns., N.Y.C., 1990-91; asst. to pres. Goodstein Devel. Corp., N.Y.C., 1991-93; asst. meetings mgr. Nat. Episcopal Ch., N.Y.C., 1993-96, dir. grants program, 1996-99; mgr. meetings SCT Comm./Cliggott Pub., N.Y.C., 1999—. Mem. Meeting Profls. Internat. (bd. dirs. N.Y. chpt. 1991-93). Home: 36 New Hyde Park Rd New Hyde Park NY 11040-4935 Office: Cliggott Pub 330 Boston Post Rd Darien CT 06820 E-mail: apcmeetings@worldnet.att.net.

CAPPIELLO, MIMI, elementary school educator; b. Atella, Potenza, Italy, Feb. 3, 1952; d. Giovanni Turro and Rosa Maria Palese; m. Gerard Cappiello; children: Jessica, Vera, Andrew John. Degree in bus. mgmt., Eckerd Coll., St. Petersburg, Fla., 2000. Cert. grade sch. tchr. Tchr. Scoula Elem. Statale, Atella, Italy, 1972—74; bus. mgr. All-lfemcare Ob-Gyn Ctr., Clearwater, Fla., 1983—96; sch tchr. Elem. Sch., 1992—. Mem.: Holy Sepulchre (Lady Commander 1992—2002). Roman Catholic. Avocations: gardening, painting, gourmet cooking, archaeology. Home: 1965 Lynnwood Ct Dunedin FL 34698 Personal E-mail: Anjeve @aol.com.

CAPPS, LOIS RAGNHILD GRIMSRUD, congresswoman, former school nurse; b. Ladysmith, Wis., Jan. 10, 1938; d. Jurgen Milton and Solveig Magdalene (Gullixson) Grimsrud; m. Walter Holden Capps, Aug. 21, 1960 (dec.); children: Lisa Margaret, Todd Holden, Laura Karolina. BSN with honors, Pacific Luth. U., 1959; MA in Religion, Yale U., 1964; MA in Edn., U. Calif., Santa Barbara, 1990. RN, Calif.; cert. sch. nurse, Calif.; jr. coll. instr., Calif. Asst. instr. Emanuel Hosp. Sch. Nursing, Portland, Oreg., 1959-60; surgery flr. nurse Yale/New Haven Hosp., 1960-62, head nurse, out patient, 1962-63; staff nurse Vis. Nurse Assn., Hamden, Ct., 1963-64; sch. nurse Santa Barbara (Calif.) Sch. Dists., 1968-70, 77-98; dir. teenage pregnancy and parenting project Santa Barbara, 1985-86; mem. U.S. Congress from 23rd Calif. dist., Washington, 1998—. Mem. commerce com., former mem. sci. com., internat. rels. com; mem U.S. Congress, campaign finance reform task force, budget task force, Calif. ISTEA task force, congrl. caucus women's issues, congrl. task force tobacco and health, diabetes caucus, congrl. caucus on the arts, House com. on the budget; instr. Santa Barbara City Coll., 1990—. Bd. dirs. Am. Heart Assn., Santa Barbara, 1989—, The Adoption Ctr., Santa Barbara, 1986-90, Family Svc. Agy., Santa Barbara, 1994—, Stop AIDS Now, Santa Barbara, 1994—, Santa Barbara Women's Polit. Com., 1991—; instr. CPR, first aid, ARC, Santa Barbara, 1985—; bd. dirs. Pacific Luth. Theol. Sem. Democrat. Lutheran. Office: US House of Reps 1707 Longworth Ho Office Bldg Washington DC 20515-0001 Home: 1216 State Street Suite 403 Santa Barbara CA 93101 Fax: 202-225-5632. E-mail: lois.capps@mail.house.gov.*

CAPRIATI, JENNIFER MARIA, professional tennis player; b. N.Y.C., Mar. 29, 1976; d. Stefano and Denise (Deamicis) Capriati. Profl. tennis player, 1990—. Mem. U.S. Wightman Cup Team, 1989, U.S. Fed Cup Team, 1990—91, 1996, 2000. Winner: (jr. singles) French Open, 1989, U.S. Open, 1989, (jr. doubles, with McGrath) Italian Open, 1989, Wimbledon, 1989, (doubles, with M. Seles) Italian Open, 1991, Grand Slams, Roland Garros, 2001, Australian Open, 2001, 02; winner 13 Career Singles Titles and 1 Career Doubles Title, WTA Tour; recipient Gold medal 1992 Olympics, Espy award as Comback Athlete of Yr., 2002; named Comback Player of Yr., WTA, 1996, Female Athlete of Yr., AP, 2001, Singles Champion of Yr., Internat. Tennis Fedn., 2001, Sportswoman of the Year by US Olympic Comm., 2001. Avocations: dance, swimming, reading, music, golf. Office: Internat Mgmt Group care Barbara Perry 22 E 71st St New York NY 10021-4975 Address: Ste 1500 One Progress Plaza Saint Petersburg FL 33701

CAPRONI, VALERIE E. government agency administrator; BA in Psychology magna cum laude, Tulane U., New Orleans, 1976; JD cum laude, U. Ga., 1979. Clk. Hon. Phyllis Kravitch, U.S. Ct. Appeals, 11th cir., 1979—80; assoc. litigation dept. Cravath, Swaine & Moore, N.Y.C., 1980—85; asst. U.S. atty. Criminal divsn. U.S. Atty.'s Office, Ea. Dist. N.Y., 1985—89; gen. counsel N.Y. State Urban Devel. Corp., 1989—92; chief of spl. prosecutions, chief organized crime and racketeering sect. U.S. Atty.'s Office, 1992—94, chief criminal divsn., 1994—98; regional dir. Pacific Regional office SEC, L.A. and San Francisco, 1998—2001; counsel Simpson Thacher & Bartlett, N.Y.C., 2001—03; gen. counsel Office of Gen. Counsel, FBI, Washington, 2003—. Office: FBI J Edgar Hoover Bldg 935 Pennsylvania Ave NW Washington DC 20535-0001*

CAPSHAW, KATE (KATHY SUE NAIL), actress; b. Ft. Worth, Nov. 3, 1953; m. John Capshaw (div.); 1 child: Jessica; m. Steven Spielberg, Oct. 12, 1991; children: Theo, Sasha, Sawyer, Mikaela, Destry. Student, U. Mo. Actress: (feature films) A Little Sex, 1982, Indiana Jones and the Temple of Doom, 1984, Best Defense, 1984, Dreamscape, 1984, Windy City, 1984, Power 1986 Spacecamp 1986, 'Til Death Do Us Part 1982, Black Rain, 1989, Love at Large, 1990, My Heroes Have Always Been Cowboys, 1991, Love Affair, 1994, Just Cause, 1995, How to Make an American Quilt, 1995, Duke of Groove, 1995, The Locusts, 1997, Life During Wartime, 1997, No Dogs Allowed, 1996; (TV series) The Edge of Night, Black Tie Affair, 1993, (TV movies) Missing Children: A Mother's Story, 1982, The Quick and the Dead, 1987, Her Secret Life, 1987, Internal Affairs, 1988, Next Door, 1994, Due East, 2002; (TV miniseries) A Girl Thing, 2001; actress, prodr.: The Love Letter, 1999. Mem. Screen Actors Guild, AFTRA. Office: Creative Artists Agy care Kevin Huvane 9830 Wilshire Blvd Beverly Hills CA 90212-1804*

CAPUCILLI, TERESE, performing company executive; b. Syracuse, N.Y. d. Dan and Theresa Capucilli; m. Bill Randolph. BFA in Dance, SUNY, 1978. From dancer to co-artistic dir. Martha Graham Ctr. Contemporary Dance, N.Y.C., 1978, co-artistic dir. Co-assoc. dir. Martha Graham Dance Co., N.Y.C.; assoc. founder Buglisis/Foreman Dance; tchr. Purchase Coll., The Julliard Sch. Office: Martha Graham Center Contemporary Dance 344 East 59th St New York NY 10022*

CAPUTO, ANNE SPENCER, knowledge and learning programs director; b. Eugene, Oreg., Jan. 14, 1947; d. Richard J. and Adelaide Bernice (Marsh) Spencer; m. Richard Philip Caputo, July 15, 1977 (dec. Sept. 1997); 1 child: Christopher Spencer Caputo. BA in History, Lewis and Clark Coll., Portland, Oreg., 1969; MA, U. Oreg., 1971; MALS, San Jose State U., 1976. Librarian San Jose State U., Calif., 1972-76; online instr. DIALOG Info. Svcs., Palo Alto, Calif., 1976-77, chief info. scientist Washington, 1977-85, mgr. classroom instrn. program, 1986-89, dir. acad. programs, 1990-96; sr. dir. prod. Knight-Ridder Info., Arlington, Va., 1996-97; sr. dir. acad. and profl. market devel. The Dialog Corp., Arlington, 1998; dir. info. pro and acad. programs Dow Jones Interactive Pub., Washington, 1998—. Asst. prof. info. sci. Cath. U. Am., Washington, 1978—2000; online cons. Nat. Com. Library-Info. Sci., Washington, 1980—82; adj. prof. U. Md. Coll. Info. Studies, 2000—. Author: Brief Guide to DIALOG Searching, 1979; contbr. articles to profl. jours. Named Info. Sci. Tchr. of Yr. Catholic U. Am., 1983. Mem.: ALA, Am. Assn. Sch. Librarians, D.C. Library Assn., Am. Soc. for Info. Sci. (officer, chair Potomac Valley chpt. 1985—86), Spl. Libraries Assn. (pres.-elect 2001). Episcopalian. Avocation: photographing architectural details on national trust buildings. Home: 4113 Orleans Pl Alexandria VA 22304-1618 Office: Factiva 1400 L St NW Ste 460 Washington DC 20005-3509 E-mail: anne.caputo@factiva.com.

CAPUTO, CARRIE DAWN, music educator, musician; b. Byron Lynn and Linda Harder; m. Andrew Vincent Caputo, Aug. 20, 1994 (div. Oct. 26, 2001); 1 child, Leah May. BA, N.E. Mo. State U., Kirksville, 1995; MA in Edn., Truman State U. Kirksville, 1996. Cert. tchg. Mo., 1991. Music tchr. Mary Immaculate Cath. Sch., Kirksville, Mo., 1993—95, Wilton Sch. Dist., Iowa, 1995—98; music dir. Shelby County C-1 Schools, Shelbyville, Mo., 1998—. Trumpeter Bethel (Mo.) German Band, Mo., 1998—; ch. choir mem. Shelbyville Christian Ch., 1998—, ch. organist, 1999—; contl. music coord. Tri-Rivers Conf., Shelbyville, 2003—. Mem.: Cmty. Tchrs. Assn. (assoc.), Music Educators Nat. Conf. (assoc.), Alpha Phi Sigma (assoc.), Sigma Alpha Iota (life).

CAPUTO, KATHRYN MARY, paralegal; b. Bklyn., June 29, 1948; d. Fortunato and Agnes (Iovino) Villacci; m. Joseph John Caputo, Apr. 4, 1976. AS in Bus. Adminstrn., Nassau C.C., Garden City, N.Y., 1989. Legal asst. Jacob Jacobson, Oceanside, N.Y., 1973-77; legal asst., office mgr. Joseph Kaldor, P.C., Franklin Square, N.Y., 1978-82, William H. George, Valley Stream, N.Y., 1983-89; exec. legal asst., office adminstr. Katz & Bernstein, Westbury, N.Y., 1990-93; sr. paralegal and office adminstr. Blaustein & Weinick, Garden City, N.Y., 1993—. Instr. adult continuing edn. legal sec. procedures Lawrence (N.Y.) H.S., 1992—. Spl. events coord. Bklyn.-Queens Marriage Encounter, 1981, 82, 83, 85, 86; mem. Lynbrook Civic Assn., St. Raymond's R.C. Ch. Pastoral Coun., 1999-2002, sec. 2000-02, Renew 2000, mem. rev. bd.; mem. St. Vincent DePaul Soc., sec., 2001—. Mem. L.I. Paralegal Assn. Avocations: traveling, reading, theatre, gardening. Office: Blaustein & Weinick 1205 Franklin Ave Garden City NY 11530-1629 E-mail: kacapbwparalgl@hotmail.com

CAPUTO, LISA M. finance company executive; b. Wilkes-Barre, Pa. d. A. Richard and Rosemary (Shea) C. BA in French and Polit. Sci. magna cum laude, Brown U., 1986; MS in Journalism with highest honors, Northwestern U., 1987. Press sec., fed. grants coord. U.S. Rep. Bob Traxler, Washington, 1987-89; press sec. nat. issues Dukakis-Bentsen Campaign, Boston, 1988; press sec. U.S. Senator Tim Wirth, Washington, 1989-92; dir. vice presdl. media ops. Dem. Nat. Conv., N.Y.C., 1992; press sec. to Hillary Rodham Clinton Clinton-Gore Campaign and Presdl. Transition, Little Rock, 1992; dep. asst. to Pres., press sec. to First Lady The White House, Washington, 1993-96; v.p. corporate comm. CBS, 1996—98; v.p., global comm. and synergy Disney Pub. Worldwide, 1998—99; pres., CEO, Women and Co. Citigroup Inc., 2000—, mng. dir., bus. ops. and planning, global consumer div., 2003—. Contbg. editor George Mag., 1997—2000; co-host, Crossfire CNN; co-host, Equal Time CNBC, MSNBC; mem. Coun. Foreign Relations, Fin. Women's Assn. Office: Citigroup Inc 399 Park Ave New York NY 10043*

CARACCIOLO, SANDRA NICOL, voice educator; b. Marysville, Ohio, Mar. 18, 1960; m. Stephen Jonathan Nicol; children: Matthew, Stephanie. Assoc. in Bus., Franklin U., 1980; MusB, Capital U., 1984. Tchr. choral Hamilton Mid. Sch., Columbus, Ohio, 1984—2002. Singer, vol. musicals and weddings. Recipient Columbus Symphony Music Educator award Secondary Edn., 2003. Mem.: NEA, Ohio Edn. Assn., Ohio Music Edn. Assn., Music Educators Nat. Conf. Lutheran. Avocations: baking, cross stitch, sewing, reading. Home: 5588 Reebok Dr Hilliard OH 43026 Office: Hamilton Mid Sch 775 Rathmell Rd Columbus OH 43207

CARAMELLI, IRAINA R. artist, educator; b. Bronx, N.Y., June 5, 1948; d. Raymond and Divina Acevedo; m. James V. Caramelli, Jr., June 16, 1973; children: Heather, Iraina Rose. Student, NYU, 1965—66, Pratt Inst., Bklyn., 1966—67; cert. in Graphic Design, Parson's Sch. Design, N.Y.C., 1969. Pvt. instr., painting and drawing, Pocono Lake, Pa.; represented Morgan Gallery of Fine Arts, Pocono Lake, Pa. Condr. cultural arts program Arrowhead Lakes Cmty., 1994—96; instr. adult painting/drawing classes Alliance of Queens Artists, 1984—90, program adminstr., 1986—90, exhbn. and workshop coord. libr. shows, 1986—90, coordr. and condr. children's workshops, 1983—90, lectr. 1981—90; mem. various jury coms., curator various exhbns.; asst. art dir. Norcross Cards, 1966—67; graphic designer/asst. to art dir. Dana Perfumes, 1968—74. One-woman shows include Mellon Bank, Stroudsburg, 1995, Tannersville, 1997, Pocono Cancer Ctr., 1997, Bar Assn., Stroudsburg, 1999, Morgan Gallery, Blakeslee, Pa., 1999, Clymer Libr., Pocono Pines, Pa., 2002, exhibited in group shows at Pen & Brush Open Media Shows, Pen & Brush Mem. Mixed Media Shows, Pen & Brush Mem. Oil Shows, MCAC Mem. Shows, Pocono Manor invitational, 1994, Pen & Brush Invitational, 1997—98, juried shows, Fed. Plz., N.Y.C., 1987, Tweed Gallery, City Hall, 1988, Fed.Hall, 1997. Represented in permanent collections Unitarian Universalist Fellowship, Huntington, N.Y., numerous other private collections. Recipient numerous art awards, including Alexander award, Met. Mus. Art, 1966, Margaret Sussman Meml. award, 1997. Mem.: Alliance of Queens Artists, Monroe County Arts Coun., Pen & Brush, Inc. (N.Y.C.). Democrat. Roman Catholic. Studio: HC 88 Box 566 Pocono Lake PA 18347

CARANGELO, LORI, writer, social activist, not-for-profit executive; b. New Haven, Apr. 3, 1945; 1 son. Student, Santa Barbara City Coll., Coll. of the Desert. Adminstrv. asst. Pvt. Industry Coun., Santa Barbara, Calif.; founder, pres. Americans for Open Records (AmFOR), Palm Desert, Calif., 1989. Author: The Ultimate Search Book 1997, 5th Ed. 2000, Missing Children: Billion Dollar Babies in America's Foster Care, Adoption and Prison Systems, 2002, Italian Restaurant Cookbook, 2001, Italian Tonight!, 2003; contbr. articles to profl. publs. Data reporting source Rights of the Child project UN, Hague Intercountry Adoption/Abduction Treaty Confs.; leader internat. adoption open records and anti-adoption movements. Mem. Lit. Guild of Palm Springs, Open Records Movement. Office: AmFOR PO Box 401 Palm Desert CA 92261-0401 E-mail: accesspress@yahoo.com.

CARBONELL, JOSEFINA, federal agency administrator; b. Cuba; 1 child, Alfredo. Student, Fla. Internat. U. With Little Havana Activities and Nutrition Ctrs., Dade County, Fla., 1972—, pres., CEO; asst. sec. for adminstrn. on aging Dept. HHS, Washington, 2001—. Recipient Citizen of Yr. award, Miami, 1992, Charles Whited Spirit of Excellence award, Miami Herald, 1993, Cmty. Svc. award, Nat. Alliance for Hispanic Health, 1995, Monsignor Bryan Walsh Outstanding Human Svc. award, United Way, 1997, Commrs. Team award, Social Security Adminstrn., 1997, Claude Pepper Cmty. Svc. award, 2001; fellow in health mgmt., John F. Kennedy Sch. Govt., Harvard U. Office: Dept HHS Adminstrn on Aging 330 Independence Ave SW Washington DC 20201

CARBOY, BEVERLY J. humanities educator; b. Pompton Plains, N.J., Aug. 7, 1943; d. James Francis and Glenna M. (Cullen) C. BA, William Paterson Coll., Wayne, N.J., 1965; MA, Seton Hall U., South Orange, N.J., 1969, William Paterson Coll., 1977. Cert. tchr. grades 7-12, N.J. Tchr. English Morris Hills H.S., Rockaway, NJ, 1965—98, adv. lit. mag., 1968-84. Adv. Helping Hands, 1985-90. Recipient Geraldine R. Dodge grantee Dodge Found., 1986. Mem. NEA, NJEA, Morris Hills Edn. Assn., Morris County Edn. Assn. (rep.) Avocations: reading, needlework, boating, traveling. Office: Morris Hills HS 520 W Main St Rockaway NJ 07866-3729

CARD, DEBORAH FRANCES, orchestra administrator; b. Pottstown, Pa., Sept. 30, 1956; d. Marshall Anthony and Winifred (Hitz) R. BA, Stanford U., 1978; MBA, U. So. Calif., 1985. Orch. mgr. L.A. Philharm., 1978-86; exec. dir. L.A. Chamber Orch., 1986-92, Seattle Symphony, 1992—. Bd. dirs. AIDS project L.A., 1985-92; active Jr. League L.A. 1982-92. Mem. Am. Symphony Orch. League, Assn. Calif. Symphony Orchs. (pres. 1988-91), Assn. N.W. Symphony Orchs. (bd. dirs. 1993—), Chamber Music Soc. L.A. (bd. dirs. 1987-92), Ojai Festival (pres.'s coun.). Democrat. Episcopalian. Avocations: skiing, tennis, gardening, reading. Office: Seattle Symphony Ctr House PO Box 21906 Seattle WA 98111-3906

CARDENAS, DIANA DELIA, physician, educator; b. San Antonio, Tex., Apr. 10, 1947; d. Ralph Roman and Rosa (Garza) C.; m. Thomas McKenzie Hooton, Aug. 20, 1971; children: Angela, Jessica. BA with highest honors, U. Tex., 1969; MD, U. Tex., Dallas, 1973; MS, U. Wash., 1976, MHA, 2001. Diplomate Nat. Bd. Med. Examiners, Am. Bd. Phys. Medicine & Rehab., Am. Bd. Electrodiagnostic Medicine. Asst. prof. dept. rehab. medicine Emory U., Atlanta, 1976-81; instr. dept. rehab. medicine U. Wash., Seattle, 1981-82, asst. prof. dept. rehab. medicine, 1982-86, assoc. prof. dept. rehab. medicine, 1986-92, prof. rehab. medicine, 1992—. Med. dir. rehab. medicine clinic U. Wash. Med. Ctr., Seattle, 1982—99; project dir. N.W. Regional Spinal Cord Injury Sys., Seattle, 1990—; mem. Accreditation Coun. for Grad. Med. Edn. Residency Rev. Com., 1995—96; chief of svc. rehab medicine U. Wash. Med. Ctr., 2002—. Editor: Rehabilitation & The Chronic Renal Disease Patient, 1985, Maximizing Rehabilitation in Chronic Renal Disease, 1989; acad. editor Archives of Phys. Medicine and Rehab., 1997-99; contbr. articles to profl. jours. Co-chairperson Lakeside Sch. Auction Student Vols., Seattle, 1991; bd. dirs. CONSEJO Counseling & Referral Svc. Mem.: Inst. of Medicine Nat. Acad. Sci. (com. on assessing rehab. sci. and engring 1996—97, com. on injury prevention and control 1997—99), Nat. Inst. Child Health and Human Devel. (rsch. subcom. 1996—99), Am. Assn. Electrodiagnostic Medicine, Am. Congress of Rehab. Medicine (chairperson rehab. practice com. 1981—83, bd. govs. 2003—, Ann. Essay Contest winner 1976), Am. Acad. Phys. Medicine and Rehab. (chairperson rsch. adv. and advocacy com. 1997—99), Am. Spinal Injury Assn. (chairperson rsch. com. 1990—94, bd. dirs. 1994—2000, co-chair internat. rels. com. 1995—98, chair internat. rels. com. 1999—2002, chair mktg. com. 2000—03), Assn. Acad. Physiatrists (chair awards com. 1993—99). Avocations: art collecting, sewing, painting. Office: Univ Wash Dept Rehab Med Box 356490 1959 NE Pacific St Seattle WA 98195-0001

CARDINALI, NOREEN SADLER, state agency administrator; b. Bklyn., May 7, 1955; d. John William and Mary Agnes (Henry) Sadler; m. Louis Joseph Cardinali, July 30, 1983 (div. Jan. 1998). BA, Fordham U., 1977. Mgr. Employer Trip Reduction program N.J. Dept. Transp., Trenton, 1994-97, chief mobility measures sect., 1997—. Mem. Assn. Commuter Transp. (v.p. 1984-85). Roman Catholic. Avocations: gardening, collecting antiques. Home: 28 Windingbrook Rd Bordentown NJ 08505-3150 Office: NJ Dept Transp PO Box 600 1035 Parkway Ave Trenton NJ 08625

CARDONE, BONNIE JEAN, freelance photojournalist; b. Chgo., Feb. 21, 1942; d. Frederick Paul and Beverly Jean Rittschof; m. David Frederick Cardone, June 9, 1963 (div. 1978); children: Pamela Susan, Michael David. BA, Mich. State U., 1963. Editorial asst. Mich. State Dental Assn. Jour., Lansing, 1963-64; asst. editor Nursing Home Administr. mag., Chgo., 1964-65, Skin Diver Mag., L.A., 1976-77, sr. editor, 1977-81, photographer, 1981—, exec. editor, 1981-97, editor, 1997-99; mystery novelist, 1999—. Author: Fireside Diver, 1993; co-author: Shipwrecks of Southern California, 1989. Named Woman Diver of Yr. Women's Scuba Assn., 1999; recipient Calif. Scuba Svc. award St. Brendan Group, 1999; named to Women Diver's Hall of Fame, 2000, Women's Scuba Assn. Mem. Calif. Wreck Divers Club (Wreck Divers Hall of Fame, 2003), Hist. Diving Soc. (bd. dirs. 1997-2001). E-mail: bjcardone@hotmail.com.

CARDUCCI, JUDITH WEEKS BARKER, artist, former social worker; b. Norwood, Mass., Feb. 25, 1935; d. Harold O. and Catherine E. (Stone) Barker; m. Dewey J. Carducci, June 22, 1961; 1 child, David E.B. BA, U. Maine, 1956; MS, Columbia U., 1958. Coor. psychiatry and social work programs Cleve. VA Med. Ctr., Brecksville, Ohio, 1964-94; now artist, 1994—. Instr. art workshops, Cuyahoga Valley Art Ctr., Cuyahoga Falls, Ohio. Mag., Am. Artists Mag., 1997, 2001, Artist's Mag., 1998, 2000, book, The Best of Portrait Painting, 1998, Internat. Artist, 1999, 2000, Pastel Artist Internat., 1999, 2001, mag., 2003, Pastel Jour., 1999, mag., 2003, book, Beautiful Things, 2000, Paint! Figure & Portrait, 2000, juried art shows include, State Tchrs. Retirement Sys., 1997, 1998 (Purchase award, 1997), Pastel Soc. Am., Nat. Arts Club, Am. Artists Profl. League, Salmagundi Club, Hilton Head Art League, Grand Exhbn., Akron, Portrait Soc. Am., Reston, Va., Degas Pastel Soc., New Orleans, Pastel Soc. of the West Coast, Calif., Butler Inst. Am. Art, Youngstown, Ohio, KLH Fine Art Competition, Bennington (Vt.) Ctr. Fine Art, Cahoon Mus. Am. Art, Mass., Lexington (Ky.) Art League (Best of Show), Cin. Art Club, one-woman shows include Gallery 732, Akron Women's City Club, 1997, Hudson (Ohio) Galleries, 1997, Akron Jewish Cmty. Ctr., 1997, Moos Gallery, Western Res. Acad., Ohio, exhibited in group shows at Churski Gallery, Bath, Ohio, 1996, 1997, 1998, 1999, 2000, 2001, 2002, Veerhoff Gallery, Georgetown, Va., exhibitions include Butler Inst. Am. Art, Youngstown, Ohio, Spaces Gallery, Cleve., Summit Art Space, Akron, Ohio, Represented in permanent collections Ohio Edn. Assn., State Tchrs. Retirement Sys., Rep. Sav. Bank, Hudson Libr. and Hist. Soc., Cuyahoga Valley Youth Ballet, Hudson C. of C., City of Hudson, Case-Barlow Hist. Farm, Cleve.

State U., Hosp. for Spl. Surgery., N.Y.C., U. Maine Mus. Art; author: (book) How Did You Paint That--100 Ways to Paint People, 2004 (Internat. Artist award), Artists of Distinction, 2004 (Internat. Graphics award). Recipient Best of Show nat. pastel competition award LaBond Gallanian Best of Oil Portrait Soc. Am. Internat. Competition, 1999, Lexington Art League Nat. Show. Mem.: Hudson Soc. Artists (pres. 1996—97), Am. Artists Profl. League, Portrait Soc. Am. (charter), Akron Soc. Artists (Best of Show award), Degas Pastel Soc. (award of Excellence 1998, Patrons Purchase award 2001, Pastel-Rowney award 2001, Merit award 2002), Pastel Soc. Am. (award of Merit 2003, Art Times award, David B. Korostoff Purchase award), Cin. Art Club (Internat. Artist award), Salmagundi Club, Phi Kappa Phi, Phi Beta Kappa. Home: 197 Sunset Dr Hudson OH 44236-3347 E-mail: djcarducci@aol.com.

CARDWELL, NANCY LEE, editor, writer; b. Norfolk, Va., Apr. 2, 1947; d. Joseph Thomas Cardwell and Martha (Bailey) Underwood BA in Econs., Duke U., 1969; MS in Journalism, Columbia U., 1971. Copy editor Wall Street Jour., N.Y.C., 1971-73, reporter, 1973-76, editor fgn. dept. and Washington bur., 1977-80, night news editor, 1981-83, nat. news editor, 1983-87, asst. mng. editor, 1987-89; sr. editor Bus. Week mag., N.Y.C., 1989-91; editor Habitat World, Habitat for Humanity Internat., Americus, Ga., 1991-94; freelance editor/writer, 1994—. Episcopalian.

CARDWELL, NINA FERN, special education educator; b. Queens, Aug. 25, 1960; d. Lazarus and Elizabeth Ann Cardwell. BA, Bennett Coll., 1982. Tchr. Durham County, Durham, NC, Conway (SC) Horry County Sch. Sys., Poughkeepsie City Sch. Dist., NY, Cumberland County, Fayeville, NC. Mem.: ASCD, PTA, NEA, Delta Sigma Theta (sec. 1990). Home: 980 S Hardin Southern Pines NC 28387

CARDWELL, SANDRA GAYLE BAVIDO, university admissions professional; b. Vinita, Okla., July 14, 1943; d. Amos Calvin Wilkins and Gretta Odell (Pool) Wilkins Kudlemyer; m. Phillip Patrick Bavido, Nov. 26, 1964 (div. Dec. 1973); 1 child, Phillip Patrick Bavido Jr.; m. Max Loyd Cardwell, Jan. 18, 1979 (div. Apr. 1992). AA, Tulsa Jr. Coll., 1973; BS cum laude, U. Tulsa, 1975. Sec. with various cos., 1966-69; sec. U.S. Dept. Fgn. Langs., West Point, NY, 1969-70; dep. ct. clk. civil divsn. Tulsa County Dist. Ct., 1975-76, dep. ct. clk. U.S. Passport Office, 1976-77; broker-assoc. Gordona Duca, Inc., Realtors, Tulsa, 1977-91; mem. admissions staff St. Francis Hosp., Tulsa, 1997—2000; univ. admissions profl. Oral Roberts U., Tulsa. Mem. Polit. Action Com., Tulsa, 1980—; vol. children's rights and child abuse legis. and statutes.; bd. of trustees Asbury United Meth. Ch., 2003—. Mem. AAUW, Tulsa Met. Bd. Realtors, Okla. Bd. Realtors, Tulsa Christian Women's Club (contact advisor 1988-89), Stonecroft Ministries (life publs. 1987-88), United Meth. Women (bd. dirs. 1986-87), Phi Theta Kappa (pres.), Pi Sigma Alpha (treas. 1974). Republican. Methodist. Avocations: piano, boating, gardening, reading, walking. Home: 3908 S St Louis Tulsa OK 74105-3317 Office: Oral Roberts U 7777 S Lewis Ave Tulsa OK 74171

CAREY, CATHERINE ANITA, artist, art educator; b. Washington, Sept. 27, 1960; d. Charles William Carey and Geraldine Elizabeth Sheil; m. Brian Elliot Sinofsky. Student, Corcoran Sch. Art, 1976—78; BFA, Va. Commonwealth U., 1982. Fine art painter, Escondido, 1982—; graphic artist Circuit City Stores, Inc., Richmond, Va., 1985—87, Circuit City stores, Inc., Walnut, Calif., 1987—89; art dir. W. Coast Cmty. Newspapers, Encinitas, Calif., 1989—91; freelance art dir. Elements Graphic Design, Escondido, 1991—; tchr. Art Methods and Materials Show, Pasadena, Calif., 1998—; workshop leader Golden Door, Escondido, 2001—; tchr., owner The Glass House Art Studio, Escondido, 2001—. Workshop leader Daler-Rowney Art Mfr., 1998—; workshop demonstration artist Savoir Faire, San Diego, 2000—. Exhibitions include Paintings from Giverny France, La Jolla, Calif., 2000, Paintings by Cathy Carey, Escondido, Calif., 2001, Impressions of Mission Trails, San Diego, 2002, Color Harmony and Contrast, Escondido, Calif., 2003, one-woman shows include Expressive Colors, Escondido Artists Gallery, 2003; author: The Philosophy of Color, 2003. Organizer art shows for children, Encinitas, 1990—91, San Diego, 1999—2000, 2000—01. Recipient Blue Ribbon, San Dieguito Art Club, 1990, Honorable Mention, San Diego Watercolor Soc., 2000, Escondido Art Assn., 2001. Master: Scripps Ranch Art Club (pres. 2000—01, founder 2000). Avocations: hiking, photography, swing dancing, gardening, cooking. Office: Glass House Studio 2048 Ridgecrest Pl Escondido CA 92029 E-mail: element@abac.com.

CAREY, ELLEN, artist; b. N.Y.C., June 18, 1952; BFA, Kansas City Art Inst., 1976; MFA, SUNY, Buffalo, 1978. Assoc. prof. of photography Hartford Art School, U. of Hartford, Hartford, CT. One woman shows include Concord Gallery, N.Y.C., 1985, Zone, Springfield, Mass., 1986, Real Art Ways, Hartford, Conn., 1986, Art City, N.Y.C., 1986, Simon Cerigo, N.Y.C., 1987, Internat. Ctr. of Photography, N.Y., 1987, John Good Gallery, N.Y.C., 1989, Schnider-Bluhm-Loeb Gallery, Chgo., 1990, Nat. Acad. of Scis., Washington, 1992, Jayne H. Baum Gallery, N.Y.C., 1992, 94, Gallery 954, Chgo., 1994, Nina Freudenheim Gallery, Buffalo, N.Y., 1995, Mus. Contemporary Photography, Chgo. 2002; exhibited in numerous group shows including Dayton (Ohio) Art Inst., 1993, The Dallas Mus. of Natural History, 1993, Rochester Mus. of Sci. Ctr., Rochester, 1993, L.A. Mus. of Natural History, Charles and Emma Frye Art Mus., Omniplex Sci. Ctr., Seattle, 1993, Fernback Mus. of Natural History, Atlanta, 1993, Calif. Acad. of Scis., 1993, Cleve. Mus. of Natural History, 1993, Tatischeff Gallery, N.Y.C., 1993, Mus. of Modern Art, 1994, U. N.C., Greensboro, 1993-94, Herter Gallery, U. Mass., Amherst, Mass., 1993-94, Palazoo de Exhbns., Rome, 1993-94, Art Inst. of Chgo., 1994, Caldwell (N.J.) Coll., Artspace, New Haven, Conn., 1994, Akron Art Mus., 1994, Ansel Adams Ctr. for Photography, San Francisco, 1994, Park Avenue Atrium, N.Y.C., 1994, Charter Oak Cultural Ctr., Hartford, 1995, Kingsborough Cmty. Coll. Art Gallery, Bklyn., 1995; represented in permanent collections Albright-Knox Art Gallery, Art Inst. of Chgo., Bell Atlantic, Bklyn. Mus. of Art, Chase Manhattan Bank, Coca Cola Corp., First Bank of Mpls., Fogg Mus., Harvard U., Internat. Ctr. of Photography, Mus. of Fine Arts, many others; contbr. articles to profl. jours. Office: Hartford Art School U of Hartford 200 Bloomfield Ave Hartford CT 06117-1545 Home: 155 Kenyon St Hartford CT 06105

CAREY, ERNESTINE GILBRETH (MRS. CHARLES E. CAREY), writer, lecturer; b. N.Y.C., Apr. 5, 1908; d. Frank Bunker and Lillian (Moller) Gilbreth; m. Charles Everett Carey, Sept. 13, 1930; children: Lillian Carey Barley, Charles Everett. BA, Smith Coll., 1929. Buyer R. H. Macy & Co., N.Y.C., 1930-44, James McCreery, N.Y.C., 1947-49. Carey writer and lectr. Book reviewer, 1949—, syndicated newspaper articles, 1951, (with Lillian Moller Gilbreth) (McElligott medallion Assn. Marquette U. Women 1966)￼; author: Jumping Jupiter, 1952, Rings Around Us, 1956, Giddy Moment, 1958, Off and Away, 1998, Blubby, 1999, (with Frank B. Gilbreth, Jr.) Cheaper by the Dozen, 1948 (Prix Scarron French Internat. Humor award 1951, more than 53 translations), Belles on Their Toes, 1950; contbg. author: Smith Voices—Selected Works by Smith College Women, 1990, 99; lifetime papers represented in collections at Smith Coll.; also mag. articles and book revs. Bd. dirs. Right to Read, Inc., 1968—, co-chmn., 1967; lay adv. com. Manhasset (N.Y.) Bd. Edns.; trustee Manhasset Pub. Libr., 1953-59, v.p., 1956-59; trustee Smith Coll., 1967-72; active in care-preservation and current student use of Frank B. and Lillian M. Gilbreth lifetime papers at Purdue U., Smith Coll. and internationally. Montgomery award Friends of Phoenix Pub. Libr., 1981; honored guest Ariz. Lib. Friends, 1994; recipient Internat. Mgmt. award: the Gilbreth Medal, Soc. for Advancement of Mgmt., 1996. Mem. Authors Guild Am.

(life mem., mem. guild council 1955-60), PEN, North Shore Club, Smith Coll. Club (asst. chmn. scholarship com. L.I. chpt. 1950-59), Smith Coll. Club (vice chmn. scholarship com. Phoenix chpt.). Home: 703 W Herbert Ave # 115 Reedley CA 93654-3946

CAREY, ERRON J. merchant banker, state representative; b. Brattleboro, Vt., Sept. 30, 1946; m. Gilbert Carey; 2 children. Banker; rep. Vt. State Ho. Reps., 2001—. Chmn. Chester Town Sch. Dirs., Chester Trustees Pub. Funds; justice of the peace; bd. dirs. The Rockingham Area Cmty. Land Trust, Chester-Andover Family Ctr. Republican. Home: 145 River Street Chester VT 05143

CAREY, JOANNA, financial consultant, writer; d. Daniel Bernard and Gail Marie Carey; m. Steven C. Kluth. AA, W. Shore CC, Scottville, Mich., 1993; BBA, Grand Valley State U., 1995. Mktg. & pub. info. coord. W. Mich. Mental Health, Ludington, 1996—98; fin. advisor Paine Webber, Grand Rapids, Mich., 1998—99; writer, motivational spkr., owner, founder Carey'D Away Enterprises, LLC., Wyoming, Mich., 1999—; relationship banker Bank One, Grand Rapids, 2003—. Mem. mktg. com. Women's Resource Ctr., Grand Rapids, 1999—. Author: (book) Rat Race Relaxer: Your Potential & The Maze of Life; prodr., show host (TV series) The Rat Race Relaxer Show. Mem.: Small Pubs. Assn. N.Am., Am. Mktg. Assn. (GVSU Student Mem. of The Yr. 1995), Sons of Italy Am. (state trustee 2002—03). Office: Carey'D Away Enterprises LLC 2455 Woodlake Rd SW Ste 4 Wyoming MI 49509 Personal E-mail: j.carey@att.net.

CAREY, KATHRYN ANN, foundation administrator, editor, consultant; b. LA, Oct. 18, 1949; d. Frank Randall and Evelyn Mae (Walmsley) Carey; m. Richard Kenneth Sundt, Dec. 28, 1980. BA in Am. Studies with honors, Calif. State U., L.A., 1971; postgrad., Georgetown U., Boston Coll. Cert. comml. pilot instrument rated, advanced cert. corp. cmty. rels. Tutor Calif. Dept. Vocat. Rehab., L.A., 1970; tchg. asst. U. So. Calif., L.A., 1974-75, UCLA, 1974-75; claims adjuster Auto Club So. Calif., San Gabriel, 1971-73; corp. pub. rels. cons. Carnation Co., L.A., 1973-78; cons., adminstr. Carnation Cmty. Svc. Award Program, 1973-78; pub. rels. cons. Vivitar Corp., 1978; sr. advt. asst. Am. Honda Motor Co., Torrance, Calif., 1978-84; exec. dir. Am. Honda Found., 1984—, Honda Philanthropy, Office of the Ams., 1996—. Adminstr. Honda Involvement Program; mgr. Honda Dealer Advt. Assns., 1978—84; cons. in field. Asst. editor: Friskies Rsch. Digest, 1973—78; editor: Vivitar Voice, 1978, Honda Views, 1978—84, Found. Focus, 1984—, Instrument Pilots' Survival Manual (Rod Machado), 1991; contbg. editor: Newsbriefs and Momentum, 1978—. Recipient Silver award, Wilmer Shields Rich award, Coun. Founds. Excellence in Comm., 1995, 2003, Gold award, 1997, 2001, award of Excellence, Soc. Tech. Comm., 1995, Merit award, 1996, 1997, 1999, 2001, Apex award, Excellence in Comm., 1997—2001, 2003; scholar, Calif. Life Scholarship Found., 1967. Mem.: Affinity Group on Japanese Philanthropy (pres.), Coun. on Founds., So. Calif. Assn. Philanthropy, Pub. Rels. Soc. Am., Advt. Club L.A., Calif. Advs. Nursing Home Reform (officer, sec./treas., treas. bd. dirs. 1997—), Elsa Wild Animal Appeal, Humane Soc. U.S., Am. Humane Assn., Ocicats Internat., Greenpeace, L.A. Soc. Prevention of Cruelty to Animals, Aircraft Owners and Pilots Assn., Am. Quarter Horse Assn., Ninety-Nines. Office: Am Honda Found 1919 Torrance Blvd Torrance CA 90501-2722 Office Phone: 310-781-4090. E-mail: kathryn_carey@ahm.honda.com.

CAREY, LOIS J. psychotherapist; b. Pitts., Aug. 7, 1927; d. Robert Gray Doeblin and Thelma (Pettit) Harris; m. David Carey, June 22, 1947; children: David, Norman, Arlene Keiser. BS, Columbia U., 1973, MS, 1974. Diplomate Am. Bd. Examiners, Am. Bd. Clin. Social Work. Pvt. practice, specializing in sand play therapy, Upper Grandview, N.Y., 1980—; dir. Ctr. for Sandplay Studies, East Coast Sandplay Assn. Workshop leader in U.S., Can., South Africa, Greece, Holland, Ireland; adj. prof. play therapy Hofstra Univ., 2003—. Author: Sandplay Therapy with Children and Families, 1999; co-editor: School-Based Play Therapy, Family Play Therapy; contbr. articles to profl. jours. Recipient Lifetime Achievement award N.Y. Assn. Marriage and Family Therapy, 1999. Mem. NASW, Am. Assn. Marriage and Family Therapy (past pres. West/Mid-Hudson), Assn. for Play Therapy (pres. N.Y. br.). Avocations: clay, writing. Home: 254 S Boulevard Nyack NY 10960-4125 E-mail: ljcarey@spyral.net.

CAREY, MARGOT BECKMANN, fundraiser; b. Cin., Feb. 22, 1960; d. Emil Hans and Beatrice Christina (Sciarra) Beckmann; m. David Mitchell Carey, Nov. 28, 1981 (dec. Oct. 2001); children: Cayelan, Spencer. BS, Skidmore Coll., 1983; postgrad., Ctr. on Philanthropy, Indpls. Program and devel. dir. Bethesda Episcopal Ch., Saratoga Springs, N.Y., 1989—. Trustee Bethesda Vestry, Saratoga Springs, Home of the Good Shepherd, Saratoga Springs; mem. Flower and Fruit Mission, Saratoga Springs, 1987, Caroline St. Home Sch. Assn., Saratoga Springs, 1995, Bethesda Altar Guild, Saratoga Springs, 1985; den mother cub scouts Boy Scouts Am., Caroline St. Sch., 1998-99; mem. Skidmore Coll., Saratoga Springs, 1986-99. Mem. Assn. Fundraising Prodls., Women in Devel. in the N.E. N.Y. Republican. Episcopalian. Avocations: tennis, aerobic exercise, swimming, sailing, reading. Office: Bethesda Episcopal Ch 41 Washington St Saratoga Springs NY 12866-4116

CAREY, SARAH COLLINS, lawyer; b. N.Y.C., Aug. 12, 1938; d. Jerome Joseph and Susan (Atlee) Collins; m. James J. Carey, Aug. 28, 1962 (div. 1977); 1 child, Sasha ; m. John D. Reilly, Jan. 27, 1979; children: Sarah Reilly, Katherine Reilly. BA, Radcliffe Coll., 1960; LLB, Georgetown U., 1965. Bar: D.C. 1966, U.S. Supreme Ct. 1977. Soviet specialist USIA/U.S. Dept. State, 1961-65; assoc. Arnold & Porter, Washington, 1965-68; asst. dir. Lawyers Com. for Civil Rights, Washington, 1968-73; ptnr. Heron, Burchette, Ruckert & Rothwell/predecessor firms, Washington, 1973-90; chair CIS Practice Steptoe and Johnson, Washington, 1990-99; chair CIS Practice, sr. ptnr. internat. Squire, Sanders & Dempsey, Washington, 1999—. Cons. Ford Found., 1975—83; bd. dirs. Yukos Oil Co., 2001—. Chair bd. dirs. Eurasia Found., 1994—; bd. dirs. Russia-Am. Enterprise Fund, 1993—95, Def. Enterprise Fund, 1994—2001, Georgetown U. Sch. Law Inst. Pub. Representation, 1971—85, Am. Arbitration Assn., 1975—82, Women's Fgn. Policy Group. Mem.: Atlantic Coun., Coun. Fgn. Rels. Democrat. Office: 1201 Pennsylvania Ave NW Washington DC 20004-2401 Office Phone: 202-626-6605. E-mail: scarey@ssd.com.

CAREY, SHIRLEY ANNE, nursing consultant; b. Syracuse, N.Y., Sept. 27, 1939; d. John Crotty and Eva Mae (Pratt) Walsh; m. John Paul Carey, July 23, 1966; children: Jason Leo, Jonathan Paul, Jennifer Anne. BSN, Nazareth Coll., 1961. RN Calif. Charge nurse surg. svcs. L.A. County Hosp., 1962-64; instr. nursing L.A. County-U. So. Calif. Med. Ctr. Sch. Nursing, 1964-70; rschr., developer nursing edn. films Concept Media, Irvine, Calif., 1971—2003, prodn. and sales coord., 1999—; cmty. health educator Huntington Beach Hosp. and Med. Ctr., Calif., 1983—; nursing cons., health educator, writer Huntington Beach, 1988—; dir. staff devel. Columbia Huntington Beach, 1995-99, Columbia San Clemente Hosp. and Med. Ctr., San Clemente, Calif., 1995-99. Bd. trustees Huntington Beach City Sch. Dist., 1990—2004, clk., 1993, 97, 2001, pres., 1993, 98, 2002, 03. Author (ednl. video): Impaired Mobility, 1993, Basic Patient Care, 1994, Infection Control, 1995, Elder Issues: Nutrition, Falls and Abuse, 2002; prodn. coord. : (films) Human Development: Conception to Neonate, 1992; Human Development: First 21/2 Years, 1992; coord. The Vulnerable Child, 2000; Birth to 2 1/2, 2001; Young Children With Developmental Challenges (Autism, ADHD), 2001; Nutrition in Young Child, 2002; Nutrition in Infant, 2002; coord.: films Infection in Elderly, 2003; coord. (films) Diabetes, 2004. Mem., past officer Orange County Adoptive Parents, Calif., 1975—80; active Girl Scouts Am., Costa Mesa, Calif., 1984—98, PTA, Huntington Beach, 1976—; bd. dirs. West Orange County Consortium Spl. Edn., Huntington Beach, 1991—92, clk., 1992; active Huntington Coalition Against Substance Abuse, 1999—2000, Orange County Com. on Sch. Dist. Orgn., 1994—, v.p., 1997, pres., 1998—; pres., bd. dirs. Harry W. Montague Basketball Meml. Scholarship Com., Huntington Beach, 1989—; sec., bd. dirs. Huntington Beach Sister City Assn., 1993—95; commr. Huntington Beach Cmty. Svcs. Commn., 1994—2000, v.p., 1996—97; active Huntington Beach Children's Needs Task Force, 1995—, chair, 2000—02; active Huntington Beach Collaboration, 1997—2001; exec. bd. dirs. Huntington Beach PRIDE/DARE Found., 1995—, v.p., 1998, 2002, chair, 2000—01; founder, coord. Substance Abuse and Violence Edn. Task Force, 2001—03. Recipient Hon. Svc. award PTA, 1989, 2d Pl. award Am. Jour. Nursing Film Festival, 1994, 96, Gold Svc. award Orange Svc. Ctr. Coun., 1994, 24th Ann. Telly award finalist Elder Abuse, 2003; named Finalist AMA Internat. Film Festival, 1996. Mem.: AAUW (exec. bd. dirs. Huntington Beach chpt. 1996—2001, co-pres. 1997—98, Calif. pub. policy com. 1998—2000, honoree Huntington Beach br. 1998), Calif. Sch. Bd. Assn. (legis. network 1990—, del. assembly 1993—, nomination com. 1999), Nat. Sch. Bd. Assn. (fed. rels. network 1993—97), Orange County Sch. Bds. Assn. (v.p. 2001, pres. 2002), AHA (bd. dirs. Huntington Valley divsn. 1996—98). Avocations: travel, music, working with children and teenagers. Home and Office: 21142 Brookhurst St Huntington Beach CA 92646-7407

CAREY, SUSAN M. psychologist; b. Chgo., Sept. 29, 1942; d. Malcolm Hall MacLeod and Elizabeth Frances Bailey; m. James Patrick Carey, Aug. 21, 1965 (div. May 1976); children: Kevin, Tim, Brian, Colleen. AB in English, French Edn., Marquette U., 1964; MS in Ednl. Psychology and Counseling, U. Wis., 1967; MA in Theology, MA in Clin. Psychology, Fuller Seminary, 1991, PhD in Clin. Psychology, 1999. Registered counselor, Wash. Tchr. 3d grade Milw. Schs., 1964-66; Montessori remedial Mary Linsmeier, Inc., Milw., 1967-71; tchr. presch. and Montesorri Kinderkamp, Mansfield, Ohio, 1971-72; rschr. Mansfield Schs., 1973; tchr. presch. and Montesorri Country Village Day Sch., Mercer Island, Wash., 1974-76; substitute, asst. gymnastics coach Mercer Island Schs., 1976-80; assessment specialist ESD 123, Wallawalla, Wash., 1980-81; tchr. French, English, and typing Lake Washington Jr. H.S., Kirkland, Wash., 1981-82; tchr. bus. edn. Quinault (Wash.) H.S., 1982; tchr. French and English Dallas Schs., 1982-83; sch. psychologist Peninsula Schs., Gig Harbor, Wash., 1983-85, Bremerton, Wash., 1985-86, Seattle Schs., 1986; pvt. practice psychology Seattle, 1997—. Author: (game) Hamunculus; author rsch. papers. Singer Folk Choir, Mercer Island, 1982-99; founding mem., bd. dirs. You Theater, Mercer Island, 1989; Eucharistic min. St. Monica's Ch., Mercer Island, 1982-88. Mem. APA, Nat. Assn. Sch. Psychologists, Wash. Assn. Sch. Psychologists (ethics com., writer ethics manual 1985-86), Wash. Edn. Assn. (Seattle Edn. Assn., Christian Assn. Psychol. Svcs., Coun. Exceptional Children. Avocations: dance, drama, skiing, tennis, writing. Home: 2500 81st Ave SE Apt 101 Mercer Island WA 98040-2244 E-mail: SMC7388@aol.com.

CAREY-SHULER, BARBARA, county commissioner; BA in Speech, Fla. A&M U., 1961; M in Comms. and Speech, Ohio State U., 1962; M in Guidance, U. Miami, 1969; EdD, U. Fla., 1978. Exec. dir. office of multicultural programs Dade County Pub. Schs., 1990-92, asst. supt., 1992-96; county commr. dist. 3 Miami Dade County, Fla., 1979—, chair. Office: 111 NW 1st St Miami FL 33128-1902

CARIDEO, MARGUERITE, painter; b. Mount Vernon, NY, May 27, 1954; d. Thomas Carideo and Mary De Orio. Studied painting and stained glass, Westchester Art Workshop, White Plains, N.Y.; studied Eastern Painting, with various prominent Chinese brush masters. Owner Studio 527 Artworks, Pawling, NY, 1999—. Tchr. oriental painting for beginners Croton/Cortlandt Ctr. for Arts, Cortlandt Manor, NY; co-founder Boone Dog Artists Group, Brewster, NY, 1999. One-woman shows include galleries in, NY, Conn., exhibitions include various shows, Cirque d'art, Bedford Hills, N.Y., 2004, Represented in permanent collections; featured artist Flatiron Gallery, Peekskill, NY. Recipient awards (8) for painting, various juried art shows, 1990—2001. Mem.: Oriental Brush Artists Guild (bd. dir.). Personal E-mail: mcarideo@earthlink.net.

CARIELLI, CAROL LEGGIO, guidance counselor; b. Bklyn., Oct. 27, 1956; m. Dominick Carielli, July 17, 1988. BA, Bklyn. Coll., 1977, MS, 1980, Long Island U., 1983; PhD, Fordham U., 1997. Cert. in sch. psychology, N.Y., supervision and adminstrn., N.Y. Tchr. comm. arts Bishop Ford Ctrl. Cath. High Sch., Bklyn., 1979-83, guidance counselor, 1984—. Adj. asst. prof. Kingsborough Cmty. Coll./CUNY, Bklyn. Teach grantee Prins. Cath. High Sch./Diocese of Bklyn. Mem. Cath. Secondary Sch. Counselors N.Y.C. (Svc. award, past pres. 1990-92, editor newsletter). Avocations: writing, photography, tennis, golf, furniture restoration. Office: Bishop Ford Ctrl Cath High Sch 500 19th St Brooklyn NY 11215-6204

CARINO, AURORA LAO, psychiatrist, hospital administrator; b. Angeles, Philippines, Jan. 11, 1940; came to U.S., 1967; d. Pedro Samson and Hilaria Sanchez (Paras) Lao; m. Rosalito Aldecoa Carino, Dec. 2, 1967; children: Robert, Edwin, Antoinette. AA, U. of the East, Manila, 1961; degree in Medicine, U. of the East, Quezon City, Philippines, 1966. Lic. psychiatrist N.Y., Va., Conn., Fla.; cert. Am. Bd. Psychiatry and Neurology. Resident in pediat. U. of the East-R.M. Meml. Hosp., Quezon City, 1966-67; rotating intern Stamford (Conn.) Hosp., 1967-68; resident in psychiatry Norwich (Conn.) Hosp., 1968-71, staff psychiatrist, 1971-75; staff psychiatrist, unit chief, acting clin. dir. Harlem Valley Psychiat. Ctr., Wingdale, NY, 1975-80; svc. chief Fla. State Hosp., Chattahoochee, 1982-83; unit chief Hudson River Psychiat. Ctr., Poughkeepsie, NY, 1983-89, dep. med. dir., acting clin. dir., 1989-90, asst. to clin. dir., 1990-93, dep. med. dir.-admissions, 1993-97. Cons. Dept. Mental Hygiene, Dutchess County, Poughkeepsie, 1976—. Mem. Am. Psychiat. Assn. Republican. Roman Catholic. Avocations: gardening, country music, recording/listening to spiritual enhancement. Home: 10 Millbank Rd Poughkeepsie NY 12603-5112

CARINO, LINDA SUSAN, business consultant; b. San Diego, Nov. 4, 1954; d. DeVona (Clarke) Dungan. Student, San Diego Mesa Coll., 1972-74, 89-90. With Calif. Can. Bank, San Diego, 1974-77, from ops. supr. to ops. mgr., 1977-82; asst. v.p. ops. mgr. First Comml. Bank (formerly Calif. Can. Bank), 1982-84; v.p. data processing mgr. First Nat. Bank, 1984-91; v.p. conversion adminstr. Item Processing Ctr. Svc. Corp., Denver, 1991-92; mgr. computer ops. FIserv, Inc., Van Nuys, Calif., 1992-93; v.p., data processing mgr. So. Calif. Bank, La Mirada, 1993-94, v.p. tech. support mgr., 1994-96; cons. First Nat. Bank of Ctrl. Calif., Salinas, 1996-97; project mgr. EDS Corp., Burbank, 1997-98, customer group mgr. Charlotte, NC, 1998-99, bus. svcs. rep., 1999-2000, project mgr., 2000—02; installation project mgr. Jack Henry & Assocs., Inc., Charlotte, 2003—. Democrat. Avocations: swimming, bicycling, camping, knitting, sewing. Home: PO Box 481084 Charlotte NC 28269 E-mail: lcarino@jackhenry.com.

CARISTO-VERRILL, JANET ROSE, international management consultant; b. Quincy, Mass., Jan. 30, 1945; d. John J. and Adelaide Caristo; m. Richard M. Verrill, Mar. 31, 1984 (dec. Feb. 1995). BS, Boston U., 1968; diploma in social anthropology, Lady Margaret Hall, Oxford, Eng., 1974; M in Internat. Mgmt., Am. Grad. Sch. Internat. Mgmt., 1982. Social studies tchr. Boston, Pembroke & Cohasset Schs., Mass., 1969-81; summer planner, reunions MIT Alumni Office, Cambridge, 1973-76; pres. Macro Projects Internat., Wayland, Mass., 1984—. Advisor Govt. Can., 1985, Nepal, 1986, Nizhny Novgorod, 1994, Algeria, 1994, Bosnia, 1996, 97, Ctr. for Religious Dialogue, Sarajevo, 1999-2001, Montenegro, 2000, Kosovo, 2002, Habitat for Humanity, Belfast Unltd., 1994-96; guest spkr. energy conf. Govt. Turkey, Ankara, 1997; NGO del. UN Sci. & Tech. Commn., N.Y.C., 1993; dir. ctr. macro projects & diplomacy, Roger Williams U., RI, 2003-. Author: Civilian Military Cons. Corps, 1992,96; contbr. Macro Problems and World Projects, 1998. Filmmaker, vol Mother Theresa's Hosps., Calcutta, India, 1980; vol. U.S. Peace Corps., Nigeria, 1964—66, U.S./China People's Friendship, Cambridge, 1982—83; treas. Internat. Sunsat Energy Coun., 1986—; adv. com. MIT Dewey Libr., Cambridge, 1993—2000; mem. dispute resolution forum Harvard Law Sch., 2000—; guest White House Conf. Trade & Devel. No. Ireland, 1995; participant Friends Raoul Wallenberg Conf., Stockholm, 1997. Mem.: World Boston, English Spkg. Union, World Citizens Orgn. (dir. 2000—), Macro Engring. (pres. Boston chpt. 1985—), Internat. Assn. Macro-Engring. Soc.s (dir. 1996—2002), Brookline Bird Club, Oxford & Cambridge Club New Eng., United Oxford & Cambridge U. Club (London). Roman Catholic. Avocations: poetry, birdwatching, gardener, music, art and literature. Office: Macro Projects Internat Inc 174 Pelham Island Rd Wayland MA 01778-2513 E-mail: passingpeace@comcast.net.

CARIUS, CHRISTINA MARIE, music educator, horse trainer; d. William Carl and Diane Marie Carius. BA in Music Edn., Augustana Coll., 2002. Vet. asst. Oakwood Vet. Sci., Colona, Ill., 1997—2000; wrangler Lake Mancos Ranch, Colo., 2000; vocal instr. Augustana Coll., Rock Island, Ill., 1999—2002; equestrian trainer Swanson Appaloosas, Ohio, Ill., 2001—; tchr. gen. music and choir dir. La Moille Cmty. Sch. Dist., Ill., 2002—. Mem. exec. talent show com. La Moille Town Bd., 2003. Mem.: Ill. Music Educators Assn., Music Educators Nat. Conf., Fedn. Tchrs. Democrat. Roman Catholic. Avocations: horseback riding, singing, archery, gardening, travel. Home: Green River Rd PO Box 171 Ohio IL 61349 Office: La Moille Cmty Sch Dist # 303 PO Box 470 La Moille IL 61330

CARL, JANET A. writing instructor, consultant; b. Omaha, Feb. 24, 1948; d. Chauncey Howard and Marynelle Holmes Carl; m. Gregory R. Johnson, Nov. 20, 1952; children: William Theodore Carl Johnson, Nicholas John Carl Johnson. BA, U. Iowa, 1970, MA, 1973. Dean of students Hood Coll., Frederick, Md., 1973—76; assoc. dean of students Grinnell (Iowa) Coll., 1977—80; Iowa state rep. Iowa Gen. Assembly, Des Moines, 1981—86; dir. ct.-apptd. spl. adv. program Supreme Ct. State of Iowa, Des Moines, 1986—87; resource devel. dir. Mid-Iowa Comty. Action, Marshalltown, Iowa, 1987—2000; instr. writing lab. Grinnell Coll., 2000—. Office: Grinnell Coll Grinnell IA 50112

CARL, SUSAN MARIE, photographer, photojournalist; b. Ft. Hancock, N.J., Oct. 2, 1966; d. William Paul and Dolores Ruth Carl. BA, Coll. William and Mary, Williamsburg, VA, 1994; MA, U. Ga., Athens, 1997. Photojournalist U.S. Navy, Norfolk, Va., 1984—92; photojournalist U.S. Naval Reserves, Washington, 1992—2001; asst. archeologist U. Ga., Carthage, Tunisia, 1992—97; undergrad. asst. Coll. William and Mary, Williamsburg, 1992—94; grad. asst. U. Ga., Athens, 1995—97; photographer European Stars and Stripes, Darmstadt, DC, Germany, 1996—96, Action Press, Sarajevo, Bosnia-Herzegovina, 1997—98; programme mgr. Ind. Bur. for Humanitarian Issues, Islamabad, Pakistan, 1998; photo editor The European & Pacific Stars and Stripes, Washington D.C., DC, 1999—2001; vol. U.S. Peace Corps Island Hospice, Harare, Zimbabwe, 2001; graphics designer Ft. Wainwright Morale, Welfare and Recreation, Fairbanks, Alaska, 2002—. Consulting Photographer Internat. Com. Red Cross, Sarajevo, 1998—98. Petty Officer 1st Class U.S. Navy, 1984—92, Norfolk, VA. Named Military Photographer of Yr., U.S. Military and Nat. Press Photographers Assn., 1996. Avocation: travel. Personal E-mail: SCARL49932@hotmail.com.

CARLEN, SISTER CLAUDIA, librarian, consultant; b. Detroit, July 24, 1906; d. Albert B. and Theresa Mary (Ternes) C. AB in Library Sci., U. Mich., 1928, MA in Library Sci., 1938; LHD (hon.), Marygrove Coll., 1981, Loyola U., Chgo., 1983, Sacred Heart Major Sem., 1989; LittD (hon.), Cath. U. of Am., 1983. Asst. libr. St. Mary Acad., Monroe, Mich., 1928-29, Marygrove Coll., Detroit, 1929-44, libr., 1944—68; on leave as index editor New Cath. Ency., 1963—67, Cath. Theol. Ency., 1968—70; libr. grad. div. Casa Santa Maria, N.Am. Coll., Rome, 1971—72; libr. St. John's Provincial Sem., Plymouth, Mich., 1972-80, libr. emeritus, 1980-82, scholar-in-residence, 1982-85, archivist, 1985-88; rschr. Bentley Hist. Libr., U. Mich., Ann Arbor, 1989-97. Supr. orgn. and servicing Community Ctr. Libraries staffed by vols.; bd. dirs. Corpus Instrumentorum, Inc., v.p., 1969-70; mem. instructional materials com. Mich. Curriculum Study; cons. McGraw Hill Ency. World Biography, 1968-72, World Book Ency., 1969-70; mem. working group on uniform headings for liturgical works Internat. Fedn. of Libr. Assns., 1972-75. Author: Guide to Encyclicals of the Roman Pontiffs, 1939, Guide to the Documents of Pius XII, 1951, Dictionary of Papal Pronouncements, 1958; editor: Papal Encyclicals, 1740-1981, 1981, Papal Pronouncements, 1991; editor: column At Your Service, Cath. Library World, 1950-52; Reference Book Rev. Sect., 1952-64, 66-72; Books for the Home column; monthly news release, Nat. Cath. Rural Life Conf., 1952-61; mem. adv. bd.: The Pope Speaks (quarterly periodical), 1953-88; contbr.: Catholic Bookman's Guide, 1961, Dictionary Western Chs, 1969, Ency. Dictionary of Religion, 1979, Translatio Studii Festschrift, 1973, Intellectual Life on the Michigan Frontier, 1985; contbr.: Vatican Archives: An Inventory and Guide, 1997. Trustee Marygrove Coll., Detroit, 1976-79, vice chmn. bd., 1977-79. Recipient Disting. Alumna award U. Mich. Sch. Libr. Sci., 1974, Domitilla award Marygrove Coll., 1991, Gabriel Richard award Mich. Cath. Libr. Assn., 1998. Mem. ALA (coun. 1958-61, 68-71), Cath. Libr. Assn. (chmn. com. membership 1946-49, chmn. Mich. unit 1952-54, chmn. coll. and univ. sect. 1954-56, chmn. publs. com. 1961-62, pres. 1965-67, Jerome award 1993), Mich. Libr. Assn. (chmn. coll. sect. 1956-57, chmn. recruiting com. 1959-60), Accademia Olubriense (Pietrabissara, Italy, charter), Am. Friends of Vatican Libr. (co-founder, v.p.), Phi Beta Kappa, Phi Kappa Phi, Beta Phi Mu. Home: 610 W Elm Ave #D208 Monroe MI 48162

CARLILE, JANET LOUISE, artist, educator; b. Denver, Apr. 26, 1942; d. Jessie Crawford and Alice Essie (Locker) Carlile. BFA, Cooper Union, 1966; MFA, Pratt Inst., 1971. Prof. Bklyn. Coll., CUNY, 1971—; prin., owner Red Mountain Gallery, Ouray, Colo., 2001—. Founder Incline Village (Nev.) Fine Arts Ctr., 1966—68; instr. Sch. Visual Arts, N.Y.C., 1968—70, Printmaking Workshop, N.Y.C., 1971, Scarsdale (N.Y.) Studio Workshop, 1971—73, SUNY-Stony Brook, L.I., 1976, Bard Winter Coll., Rhinebeck, NY, 1980; head printmaking, asst. dir. Bklyn. Mus. Art Sch., 1971—77; dir. Bklyn. Coll. Press, 1977—; cons. Woodstock (N.Y.) Sch. Art, 1980—84; judge Alpine Artists Show, Ouray, Colo., 1989; judge Landscape Painting Show Woodstock Art Assn., 1995; dir. Red Mountain Gallery, Ouray, Colo. One-woman shows include Blue Mountain Gallery, N.Y.C., 1980, Stetson U., Deland, Fla., 1995, Fairleigh Dickinson Coll., Teaneck, N.J., 1995, exhibited in group shows at Associated Am. Artists Gallery, N.Y., 1971—81, Bklyn. Mus., 1976, Ulster County Artists Show, N.Y. State Coun. Show, 1984, Alpine Artists Show Ouray County, 1987, IRT Bklyn. Mus. Sta. Sec. San Juan Vista Landowners Assn., Ridgway, Colo., 1980—86. Recipient Hirshorn Purchase prize, Soc. Am. Graphic Artists, 1969, Best of Show award, Alpine Artists Show Ouray County, 1987, Creative Incentive award, Rsch. Found., CUNY, 1992, 1996—, Pollack/Krasner Found. award, 2002—03; fellow, Pratt Inst., Bklyn., 1971; grantee NEA workshop, Colo. Coun. Arts; scholar full scholarship, Cooper Union, N.Y.C., 1962—66. Mem.: Ouray County Arts Assn. (pres. 1991—93). Avocation: Avocations: hiking, backpacking, skiing, yoga, rock climbing. Home: PO Box 1004 Ouray CO 81427-1004 Office: Brooklyn Coll Art Dept Bedford at Ave H Brooklyn NY 11210

CARLIN, BETTY, education educator; b. N.Y.C. d. Samuel and Rose Sara (Bernstein) Grossberg; m. Arthur S. Carlin, July 18, 1953 (dec.); children: Lisa Anne Skinner, James Howard. BA, UCLA, 1952; MA, U. Calif., Berkeley, 1955. Educator L.A. Sch. Dist., 1952-55; owner Carlin's Shoes, L.A., 1952-68; educator Berkeley (Calif.) Sch. Dist., 1957-58; master tchr. spl. programs Calif. State Coll., Hayward, 1967-84; educator U. Calif.,

Berkeley, 1984-86; tchr. demonstrator C.V.U. Sch. Dist.; student tchr. supr. Calif. State U., Hayward. Co-owner Art-Car Corp., 1978-88. Creator ednl. videos for children Study in Characteristics of an Effective and Loving Mother, Children's Play as Related to Intelligence, An Eclectic Approach to Teaching Reading. Mem. Nat. Tchrs. Assn., Calif. Tchrs. Assn., Commonwealth Club, San Francisco Opera Guild. Avocations: swimming, opera, theater, gardening, vocal study.

CARLIN, SYDNEY, state representative; b. Wichita, Kans., Nov. 20, 1944; m. John Carlin; 4 children. BS in Social Sci. City commr. City of Manhattan, Kans., 1993—96, mayor, 1996—97; state rep. Dist. 66, Kans., 2003—. Democrat. Roman Catholic. Office: 272-W State Capitol 300 SW 10th Ave Topeka KS 66612

CARLISLE, LILIAN MATAROSE BAKER (MRS. E. GRAFTON CARLISLE JR.), writer, lecturer; b. Meridian, Miss., Jan. 1, 1912; d. Joseph and Lilian (Flournoy) Baker; m. E. Grafton Carlisle, Jr., Jan. 9, 1933; children: Diana, Penelope. Student, Dickinson Coll., 1929-30, Pierce Coll. Bus. Adminstrn., 1930-31; BA, U. Vt., 1981, MA, 1986. Adminstrv. sec. RAF Ferry Command, Montreal, Can., 1942; exec. staff. mem. in charge collections, research Shelburne (Vt.) Mus., 1951-61; exec. sec. Burlington Area Community Health Study, 1963, coord., 1964; asst. coord. Vt. Mental Retardation Planning Project, 1965; project dir. 4-county Champlain Valley Medicare Alert, 1966; dir. publ. rels. Champlain Valley Agrl. Fair, 1968-77; lectr. U. Vt. Elder Hostel program, 1976-77. Mem. faculty Vacation Coll., 1980-83. Co-author: The Story of the Shelburne Museum, 1955, Profile of the Community, 1964, Environmental and Personal Health of the Community, 1964, Vermont Clock and Watchmakers, Silversmiths and Jewelers, 1970; also numerous catalogs on collections at Shelburne Mus.; editl. cons. Burlington Social Survey, 1967; editor: Historic Guide to Burlington Neighborhoods, 1991, vol. II, 1997, vol. III, 2003; contbr. articles to profl. jours. Pres., Burlington Comty. Coun. for Social Welfare, 1959-61, 1971-73; chmn. bd. Champlain Sr. Citizens, 1977-79, justice of peace, 1979-81; pres. Chittenden County Extension Adv. Com., 1977-78; chmn. publs. com. Vt. Bicentennial Commn., 1974-77; mem. Vt. Ho. of Reps., 1968-70. Recipient Community Coun. Disting. Citizen award, 1978, cert. of award for Excellence in Cmty. Svc. DAR, 1996. Mem. Vt. (trustee, chmn. mus. com. 1967), N.Y. (faculty seminar) Chittenden (pres. 1969-72, editor Heritage Series of 10 books about Chittenden County towns 1972-76) hist. socs., Vt. Old Cemetary Assn., Vt. Folklore So., League Vt. Writers (dir. 1962, v.p., pres. 1967-69), Am. Pen Women (pres. Green Mountain br. 1980-82), Order Women Legislators (pres. Vt. br. 1972-74), Meml. Soc. Vt. (pres. 1989-94), Zonta Club (pres. 1964-65), Chi Omega, Conglist. Home: 117 Lakeview Ter Burlington VT 05401-2901

CARLISLE-FRANK, PAMELA L. writer, researcher, consultant, management consultant; d. James E. and Barbara Carlisle; m. Joshua M. Frank, Mar. 13, 1988. BA with honors, U. Chgo., 1985, MA, 1986; PhD, U. Calif., Irvine, 1991. Rschr. The Hardiness Inst., Chgo., 1983-86, U. Chgo., 1983-86, U. Calif., Irvine, 1987-91, Eastern N.Mex. U., Portales, 1991-92; rsch. cons. Rsch. Inst. on Addictions, Buffalo, 1992; co-founder, pres. Found. Interdisciplinary Rsch./Edn. Promoting Animal Welfare, (FIRE-PAW), 1992—; self employed rsch. cons. San Francisco, NY, 1992—98; prof. Ea. N.Mex. U. Cons. Crisis Ctr., Clovis, N.Mex., 1991-92, Mental Health Resources, Clovis, 1992-93; adj. instr. Coll. San Mateo, Calif., 1997-98, Russell Sage Coll., Troy, N.Y., 1999; prof. Green Mountain Environ. Coll., 2000-01. Co-author: Addictive Behaviors in Women, 1994; contbr. articles to newspapers, mags., profl. jours. Vol. Homeless Teens, San Francisco, 1995—98. Regents fellow, 1998; U. Calif. Irvine rsch. fellow, 1990. Mem.: APA, Soc. for Study of Social Problems, Psychologists for Ethical Treatment of Animals, Am. Sociol. Assn. (sect. animals and soc.). Avocations: writing novels, hiking, painting. E-mail: firepaw@earthlink.net.

CARLOZZI, CATHERINE L. corporate communications consultant, writer; b. Berea, Ohio, July 25, 1953; d. Charles Henry and Carol Louise (Jones) Bader; m. Nicholas Carlozzi, Jan. 4, 1975. BA in English summa cum laude, Denison U., 1975; MA in English with distinction, U. Wis., 1976. Tchg. asst. U. Wis., Madison, 1976-77; editor Visual Edn. Cons., Madison, 1977-78; copywriter advt. Walnut Equipment Leasing, Ardmore, Pa., 1978-79; assoc. nat. dir. publs. Laventhol & Horwath, Phila., 1979-84; sr. assoc., mgr. spl. projects, v.p. Brown Boxenbaum, N.Y.C., 1984-91; prin. Carlozzi Comm. Cons., Cedar Grove, N.J., 1991—. Trustee Montclair, N.J. Art Mus., 1993—. Recipient Dir.'s award Montclair Art Mus., 1994. Mem. N.Y. Women in Comm. (Liz Hoover award 1999), N.Y. Women's Agenda, Phi Beta Kappa. Avocation: sailing. Home and Office: 334 Crestmont Rd Cedar Grove NJ 07009-1908

CARLSEN, JANET HAWS, retired insurance company executive; b. Bellingham, Wash., June 16, 1927; d. Lyle F. and Mary Elizabeth (Preble) Haws; m. Kenneth M. Carlsen, July 26, 1952; children: Stephanie L. Chambers, Scott Lyle, Sean Preble, Stacy K., Spencer J. Cert., Armstrong Bus. Sch., 1945; student, Golden Gate Coll., 1945-46. Office mgr. Cornwall Warehouse Co., Salt Lake City, 1950-55, Hansen's Ins., Newman, Calif., 1969-77; owner Carlsen Ins., Gustine, Calif., 1978-97, retired, 1997. Mem. city coun. City of Newman, 1980-82, mayor, 1982-94; bd. dirs. ARC, Stanislaus, Calif., 1982-83, Tosca, 1993-98; bd. dirs. Stanislaus County Area Agy. on Aging, 1995-2000, chairperson, 1996-99; bd. dirs. Calif. state com. TACC Commn. on Aging, 1996-98; grand marshal Newman Fall Festival, 1989; v.p. ctrl. divsn. League of Calif. Cities, 1989-90, pres. 1990, 91; bd. dirs. Sr. Opportunity Svc. Ctr., 1993-96, 97-98, Sr. Opportunity Svc. Program of Stanislaus County, 1995-96; chairperson Ctrl. Valley Opportunity Ctr., 1996-98; mem. Stanislaus County Vision Com., 1997-99; bd. dirs. Gt. Valley Ctr., 1997-99. Named Soroptimist Woman of Achievement, 1987, Soroptimist Woman of Distinction, 1988, Outstanding Woman, Stanislaus County Commn. for Women, 1989, Newman Rotary Club Citizen of Yr., 1993-94, Woman of Yr. Calif. State Assembly Dist. 26, 1994, Ambassador, City of Newman, 1997—, John T. Silver award Newman C. of C., 2000; recipient plaque Ctrl. Valley Opportunity Ctr., 2001. Mem. Booster Club (Newman) Soroptimist Club, Newman Women's Club, Newman Garden Club. Mem. Lds Ch. Home: 1215 Amy Dr Newman CA 95360-1003

CARLSEN, MARY BAIRD, clinical psychologist; b. Salt Lake City, Utah, Aug. 31, 1928; d. Jesse Hays and Susannah Amanda (Bragstad) Baird; m. James C. Carlsen, May 1, 1949; children: Philip, Douglas, Susan, Kristine. Student, St. Olaf Coll., 1946-47; BA, Whitworth Coll., 1950; MA, U. Conn., 1967; PhD, U. Wash., 1973. Profl. organist, piano tchr., Wash., Oreg., Ill., Conn., 1949-68; staff counselor Presbyn. Counseling Svc., Seattle, 1976-79; pvt. practice clin. psychologist, marriage therapist, cognitive, devel. psychology, career devel. Seattle, 1978-95; cons. creative aging Walla Walla, 1996—. Chmn. sr. adult adv. coun. Seattle Parks Dept., 1975-76; adv. bd. Northwest Ctr. for Creative Aging, 1995-98; mem. steering com. Quest Learning Inst., Walla Walla, Wash., 1997-2001, mem. faculty, 1997—; mem. nat. adv. bd. Ctr. for Creative Retirement, Asheville, N.C., 1998-2001. Author: Meaning-Making: Therapeutic Processes in Adult Development, 1988, Creative Aging: A Meaning-Making Perspective, 1991, 2d edit., 1996, Transformational Meaning-Making and the Practices of Career Counseling, 1991; contbr. chpts. to books and articles to profl. jours. Grantee PEO Rsch., 1972, U. Wash. Women's Guidance Ctr., 1972. Mem. APA, Am. Soc. Aging, Nat. Coun. on Aging.

CARLSON, ALISA M. secondary school educator; b. Michigan City, Ind., Feb. 21, 1975; d. Donald and Candice Hunt; m. Rodney L Carlson, May 22, 1999. BS, Purdue U., Westville, Ind., 1999. Med. ins. adjuster Med. Group, Michigan City, 1993—2000; tchr. Michigan City Area Schs., 2000—. Pvt. tutor, LaPorte, Ind., 2000—; interior decorator. Worship leader Countryside Christian Ch., Michigan City, 1997—2003. Recipient Pres.'s Award for Academic Excellence, Purdue U., 2000; grantee Dean's grantee, 1999—2000. R-Consevative. Avocations: decorating, walking my dog, bicycling, softball.

CARLSON, CYNTHIA JOANNE, artist, educator; b. Chgo. d. Ivan Morris and Ruth (Holmes) Carlson. BFA, Sch. Art Inst., Chgo., 1965; MFA, Pratt Inst., Bklyn., 1967. Instr. Phila. Coll. Art., 1967-72, U. Colo., Boulder, 1972-73; asst. prof. painting Phila. Coll. Art., 1973; assoc. prof. Phila Coll. Art., 1979-82; prof. Phila. Coll. Art., 1982-87, Queens Coll., CUNY, 1987—. One-woman shows include Allen Meml. Art Mus., Oberlin, Ohio, 1980, Milw. Art Mus., 1982, Pam Adler Gallery, N.Y.C., 1983, Albright-Knox Art Gallery, Buffalo, 1985, Queens Mus., Flushing, N.Y., 1990, Charles More Gallery, Phila., 1990—96, AIR Gallery, N.Y.C., 1992, Neuberger Mus., Purchase, N.Y., 1999, exhibited in group shows at Contemporary Art Ctr., Cin., 1980, Whitney Mus. Art, N.Y.C., 1980, Hayden Art Gallery, MIT, Cambridge, 1981, Jacksonville (Fla.) Art Mus., 1982, Represented in permanent collections Guggenheim Mus., N.Y.C., Bklyn. Mus. Art, Phila. Mus. Art, Richmond (Va.) Mus. Fine Arts, Denver Art Mus., Allen Meml. Art Mus., commn., L.A. Metro Rail Sys., 1992—93, Criminal Justice Ctr., Phila., Dept. Arts and Culture, 1995. Grantee, NEA, 1975, 1978, 1981, 1987, Creative Artists Pub. Svc., 1978. Home: 139 W 19th St New York NY 10011-4105 Office: CUNY Queens Coll Art Dept Klapper # 172 Flushing NY 11367-0904 Office Phone: 718-997-4800.

CARLSON, DALE BICK, writer; b. N.Y.C., May 24, 1935; d. Edgar M. and Estelle (Cohen) Bick; children: Daniel, Hannah. BA, Wellesley Coll., 1957. Lic. wildlife rehabilitator. Founder, pres. Bick Pub. House, 1993—. Founder, pres. Bick Pub. House, 1993—. Author children's books, adult books, Perkins the Brain, 1964, The House of Perkins, 1965, Miss Maloo, 1966, The Brainstormers, 1966, Dracula, 1967, Frankenstein, 1968, Counting Is Easy, 1969, Your Country, 1969, Arithmetic 1, 2, 3, 1969, The Electronic Teabowl, 1969, Warlord of the Genji, 1970, The Beggar King of China, 1971, The Mountain of Truth, 1972 (Spring Festival Honor book, named Am. Libr. Assn. Notable Book), Good Morning Danny, 1972, Hannah, 1972, The Human Apes, 1973 (named Am. Libr. Assn. Notable Book), Girls Are Equal Too, 1973; : 2d edit., 2000 (named Am. Library Assn. Notable Book), Baby Needs Shoes, 1974, Triple Boy, 1976, Where's Your Head?, 1971, The Plant People, 1977, The Wild Heart, 1977, The Shinning Pool, 1979, Lovingsex for Both Sexes, 1979, Boys Have Feelings Too, 1980, Call Me Amanda, 1981, Manners That Matter, 1982, The Frog People, 1982, Charlie the Hero, 1983—85, The Jenny Dean Science Fiction Mysteries, The Mystery of the Shining Children, The Mystery of the Hidden Trap, The Secret of the Third Eye, The James Budd Mysteries, The Mystery of Galaxy Games, The Mystery of Operation Brain, 1985, Miss Mary's Husbands, 1988, Basic Manuals in Wildlife Rehabilitation, 6 vols., 1993—94, Basic Manuals for Friends of the Disabled Series, 1995—96, Living With Disabilities, 1997, Wildlife Care for Birds and Mammals, 1997, Stop the Pain: Mediations for Teenagers, 1998 (N.Y. Pub. Libr. Best Books, 2000), Confessions of a Brain-Impaired Writer: A Memoir, 1998; Stop the Pain: Adult Meditations, 2000; editor: What Are You Doing With Your Life, 2001, In and Out of Your Mind: Teen Science, Human Bites, 2002, Who Said What? Philosophy Quotes for Teens, 2003, The Teen Brain Book, 2004. Mem. Authors League Am., Authors Guild. Address: 307 Neck Rd Madison CT 06443-2755 Office: Agent Hagenbach-Bender 20 Gutenbergstrasse Bern Switzerland Business E-Mail: bickpubhse@aol.com.

CARLSON, DESIREE ANICE, pathologist; b. Clinton, Iowa, June 10, 1950; d. Donald Richard and Bernice Elfriede (Jacobs) C. MD, Duke U., 1975. Diplomate in anat. and clin. pathology, blood banking and cytopathology Am. Bd. Pathology. Resident in pathology U. Wash., Seattle, 1975-76, N.E. Deaconess Hosp., Boston, 1976-77, Peter Bent Brigham Hosp., Boston, 1977-79; pathologist W. Roxbury VA Med. Ctr., Boston, 1979-82; med. dir. blood bank Univ. Hosp., Boston, 1982-90; assoc. chief pathology N.E. Meml. Hosp., Stoneham, Mass., 1990-93; chief pathology Brockton (Mass.) Hosp., 1993—, sec., treas. med. staff, 2001—02, v.p. med. staff, 2003—04. Asst. prof. pathology Boston U. Sch. Med., 1983—; cons. pathology Brigham and Women's Hosp., Boston, 1984-95; mem. adv. bd. ARC, Dedham, 1982-96. Contbr. chapters to books, articles to profl. jours. Recipient Outstanding Contbd. Article award Med. Lab. Observer, 1988. Mem. Coll. Am. Pathologists (N.E. regional commr. 1991—), Am. Med. Women's Assn., Am. Assn. Blood Banks, Mass. Med. Soc. (coms.), Mass. Pathology Soc., N.E. Pathology Soc. (sec. 1996-98, treas. 1998-2000, pres.-elect 2000-01, pres. 2001-02, joint sponsored activities coord. 2002-04). Republican. Presbyterian. Avocations: aerobic exercise, bicycling, hiking. Office: Brockton Hosp 680 Centre St Brockton MA 02302-3395 Office Phone: 508-941-7414. E-mail: dcarlson@brocktonhospital.org.

CARLSON, ELIZABETH BORDEN, historian, educator; b. Fall River, Mass., Oct. 5, 1937; d. Richard and Elizabeth McGinley Borden; m. William C. Badger, Sept. 14, 1957 (div. July 1974); children: Christopher C. Badger, Lisa A. Badger; m. Robert F. Carlson, May 5, 1985. Student, Radcliffe Coll., Cambridge, Mass., 1955—57; BA cum laude, Harvard U., 1975; MA with honors, U. Calif., Santa Barbara, 1983, PhD with honors, 1988. Assoc. and contbg. editor The Carlisle Gazette, Mass., 1975—80; head pub. relations Gregory Fossella Assocs., Boston, 1978—80; tchr. Westmont Coll., Santa Barbara, Calif., 1986—90; pres. The Ednl. Design Found., Norwich, Vt., 1991—. Contbr. over 100 articles to profl. jours. Mem. Master Planning Com., Carlisle, Mass., 1974—78; Carlisle rep. Master Planning Com. of Greater Boston, 1978—80; bd. dirs. The Fenn Sch., Concord, Mass., 1969—73; pres. PTA, Carlisle, 1967—69. Mem.: Soc. of Archtl. Historians. Avocations: reading, birdwatching, tennis, swimming, skiing. Home: 502 Plaza Rubio Santa Barbara CA 93103 Office: The Ednl Design Found PO Box 25 66 Old Coach Rd Norwich VT 05055

CARLSON, JANET FRANCES, psychologist, educator; b. Newport, R.I., Oct. 3, 1957; d. Robert Carl and Alice Marion (Orina) Carlson; m. Kurt Francis Geisinger, Sept. 22, 1984. BS summa cum laude, Union Coll., Schenectady, 1979; MA in Clin. Psychology, Fordham U., 1982, PhD in Clin. Psychology, 1987. Lic. psychologist NY, cert. sch psychologist NY. Clin. psychology intern Conn. Valley Hosp., Middletown, Conn., 1983-84; rsch. fellow Schering-Plough Found., Bronx, N.Y., 1984-85; psychologist I Creedmoor Psychiat. Ctr., Queens Village, N.Y., 1985-86; psychologist Hallen Sch., Mamaroneck, N.Y., 1986-88; asst. prof. psychology Fordham U., Bronx, N.Y., 1988-89; asst. prof. sch. and applied psychology Fairfield (Conn.) U., 1989-93, dir. sch. and applied psychology programs, 1989-90; from asst. prof. counseling and psychol. svcs. to prof. SUNY, Oswego, 1993—2002, assoc. dean Sch. Edn., 1998-2001; prof. psychology, head dept. gen. academics Tex. A&M U., Galveston, 2002—. Cons. N.Y.C. Bd. Edn. Office Rsch., Evaluation and Assessment, 1988—92; vis. asst. prof. psychol. LeMoyne Coll., Syracuse, NY, 1992—93; dir. Office Tchg. Resources in Psychol., 2001—. Recipient Sugarfree scholarship, 1984—85; grantee Sigma Xi, 1984—85. Fellow: APA; mem.: NASP, N.Y. Assn. Sch. Psychologists, Northeastern Ednl. Rsch. Assn. (ed newsletter 1988—91, bd dirs. 1990—93, pres. 1995—96), N.Y. State Psychol. Assn., Eastern Psychol. Assn., Am. Ednl. Rsch. Assn., Sigma Xi, Psi Chi, Phi Kappa Phi (pres. 1995—96). Avocations: wildlife preservation, conservation issues.

CARLSON, JENNIE PEASLACK, bank executive; b. Ft. Thomas, Ky., June 11, 1960; d. Roland A. and Shirley (Willen) Peaslack; m. Charles I. Michaels, Aug. 13, 1983 (div. May 1989); m. Richard A. Carlson, May 2, 1992. BA in English, Centre Coll., 1982; JD, Vanderbilt U., 1985. Bar: Ohio 1985. Atty. Taft, Stettinius & Hollister, Cin., 1985-91; sr. v.p., dep. gen. counsel Star Banc Corp., Cin., 1991—95; gen. counsel Star Bank Corp., Firstar Corp, 1995—2001; dep. gen. counsel U.S. Bancorp, 2001, exec. v.p., human resources, 2002—. Office: US Bancorp US Bancorp Ctr 800 Nicollet Mall Minneapolis MN 55402*

CARLSON, KAREN, actress; b. Shreveport, La., Mar. 2, 1950; Student, U. Ark., 1962—65. Actress ABC/CBS/NBC, Los Angeles, 1966—96; co-mgr. Oz Audio Recording Studio, Franklin, Tenn., 1993—96; owner Once Upon A Garden, Primm Springs, Tenn., 1998—2003. V.p. PTO, Fairview, Tenn., 2001. Recipient 1st Runner-up, Miss America, 1964. Mem.: Master Gardeners of Tenn., Am. Fedn. TV & Recording Artists, Screen Actors Guild. Office: Once Upon A Garden 7983 Shoals Branch Rd Primm Springs TN 38476 Office Phone: 615-799-4071. E-mail: kccan@bellsouth.net.

CARLSON, KATHLEEN BUSSART, law librarian; b. Charlotte, NC, June 25, 1956; d. Dean Allyn and Joan (Parlette) Bussart; m. Gerald Mark Carlson, Aug. 15, 1987. BA in Polit. Sci., Ohio State U., 1977; JD, Capital U., 1980; MA in Libr. and Info. Sci., U. Iowa, 1986. Bar: Ohio 1980. Editor Lawyers Coop. Pub. Co., Rochester, N.Y., 1980-83; asst. state law libr. State of Wyo., Cheyenne, 1987-88, state law libr., 1988—. Mem. Bd. Adjustment, City of Cheyenne, 2001--; 2d v.p., bd. dirs. Wyo. coun. Girl Scouts U.S., Casper, 1990-92, 1st v.p., bd. dirs., 1993-96. Mem. Am. Assn. Law Librs. (indexing legal periodical lit. adv. com. 1993-96, chair 1994-96, scholarship com. 1996-98, citation format com. 1998-2000, 2002-2003, fair bus. practices com. 2000-02, exec. bd. 2003—, edn. com. State Ct. and County Law Librs. sect. 1991-92, sec.-treas. 1992-95, chair grants com. 1997-98 nominating com. 1998-99, co-chair membership com., chair edn. com. 2000-01), Western Pacific Assn. Law Librs. (pres. 1996-97, 2003—), Wyo. Libr. Assn. (sec. acad. and spl. librs. sect. 1990-92, pres. 1994-95), Bibliog. Ctr. for Rsch. (trustee 1991-95), Zonta (pres. local club 2002-2003), Kappa Delta, Beta Phi Mu. Avocations: arts and crafts, baking, travel. Home: 911 E 18th St Cheyenne WY 82001-4722 Office: State Law Libr 2301 Capitol Ave Cheyenne WY 82002-0001 E-mail: kcarls@state.wy.us.

CARLSON, KAYE LILIEN, retired music educator; b. Mpls., Minn., July 23, 1947; d. Herbert Richard and Hilma Emma Hermann; m. Jerry Dale Carlson; children: Richard Dale, Sharon Kristine. BA, Augsburg Coll., Mpls., 1969; MusM, Mankato State U., 1980. Band dir. Anoka-Hennepin Ind. #11, Anoka, Minn., 1969—70, Fridley Mid. Sch., Fridley, Minn., 1970—, ret., 2003. Supr. student tchrs. Fridley (Minn.) Mid. Sch., 1970—, music dept. chairperson, 1987—94; chair, nat. rsch. com. Band Lit. List. Facilitator of after care groups St. Mary's Rehab. Ctr., Mpls., 1989—92; facilitator of student support groups Fridley Mid. Sch., Fridley, Minn., 1985—90. Mem.: NEA, Fridley Edn. Assn., Edn. Minn., Minn. Band Dirs. Assn., Music Educator's Nat. Conf., Am. Sch. Band Dirs. Assn. (past sec. of Minn. chpt., past state chair, panel moderator 1985). Avocations: reading, travel, activities with my family. Home: 1690 Canyon Ln New Brighton MN 55112 Personal E-mail: jerrykaye@hotmail.com.

CARLSON, P(ATRICIA) M(CELROY), writer; b. Guatemala City, Guatemala, Feb. 3, 1940; (parents Am. citizens); d. James Benjamin and Alene (Jones) McElroy; m. M.A. Carlson, Aug. 20, 1960; children: Geoffrey, Richard. BA, Cornell U., 1961; MA, Cornell, 1966, PhD, 1974. Instr., lectr. psychology and human development Cornell U., Ithaca, N.Y., 1973-78. Mem. bd. dirs. Bloomington Restorations, Inc., 1982-84. Author: (with M. Potts, R. Cocking and C. Copple), Structure and Development in Child Language, 1979, Audition for Murder, 1985, Murder is Academic, 1985, Murder is Pathological, 1986, (with Richard Darlington) Behavioral Statistics, 1987, Murder Unrenovated, 1988, Rehearsal for Murder, 1988, Murder in the Dog Days, 1991, Murder Misread, 1991, Bad Blood, 1991, Gravestone, 1993, Bloodstream, 1995, Renowned Be Thy Grave, 1998, Murder, They Wrote II, 1998, The First Lady Murders, 1999, Murder Most Celtic, 2001; fourteen short stories. Chair Ithaca Environ. Commn., 1975-78; bd. dirs. Historic Ithaca, 1976-77. Mem. Mystery Writers Am. (bd. dirs. 1990-92, editor Mystery Writers Ann. 1993-96, 98-2000), Sisters in Crime (internat. sec. 1990-91, v.p. 1991-92, pres. 1992-93). Address: Vicky Bijur Literary Agy 333 W End Ave New York NY 10023-8128*

CARLSON, SUZANNE OLIVE, architect; b. Worcester, Mass., Aug. 20, 1939; d. Sigfrid and Helga (Larson) C. BS, RI Sch. Design, 1963. Jr. ptnr. Dingnam-Fauteux & Ptnrs., Worcester, 1969-70; ptnr. Richard Lamoureux Assoc., Worcester, 1970-75, Herron & Carlson (AIA), Worcester, 1975-96; arch. Edgecomb, Maine, 1997—. Guest lectr. Holy Cross Coll., 1969-70. Chmn. Worcester Hist. Commn., 1976-88; trustee Worcester Heritage Soc., 1982-88, Park Spirit of Worcester Inc., 1987—; v.p. Lincoln County Hist. Assn., 2001--; trustee Worcester Girls Inc. of Worcester, pres. 1989-92, 95-2002, sec. 1994-95; trustee Performing Arts Sch. Worcester, 1977-86, v.p. 1980-85; trustee Cultural Assembly Greater Worcester, 1981-86, v.p., 1982-83; pres. Edgecomb Hist. Soc., 1997—. Recipient European Honors Program grant Rome, Italy, 1961-62; recipient AIA School medal for excellence, 1963. Mem. AIA (exec. bd. Ctrl. Mass. chpt. 1969-71, sec.-treas. 1970-71, v.p. 1971-72, pres. 1972-73), Mass. Soc. Archs. (exec. bd. 1972-74, v.p. 1975, pres. 1976), New Eng. Regional Coun. Archs. (pres. 1977), New Eng. Antiquities Rsch. Assn. (membership chair 1982-84, 90-94, resource devel. chair 1994—, graphics dir. jours. 1982—, publs. chair 1995—, trustee 1990—). Home and Office: Suzanne O Carlson Architect 94 Cross Point Rd Edgecomb ME 04556-3208

CARLSON ARONSON, MARILYN A. English language and education educator; b. Gothenburg, Nebr., July 24, 1938; d. Harold N. and Verma Elnora (Granlund) C.; m. Paul E. Carlson, July 31, 1959 (dec. Sept. 1988); 1 child, Andrea Joy; m. David L. Aronson, July 8, 1995. BS in Edn., English and Psychology, Sioux Falls Coll., 1960; MA in History, U. S.D., 1973, MA in English, 1992, EdD in Ednl. Adminstrn., 1997. Tchr. English and social scis. curriculum coord. Beresford (S.D.) Pub. Sch., 1960-78; tchr. English and social scis. Sioux Empire Coll., Hawarden, Iowa, 1979-85; instr. English and ESL, Midwest Inst. for Internat. Studies, Sioux Falls, S.D., 1985-89; asst. prof. English Augustana Coll., Sioux Falls, 1989-97, asst. prof. English and edn., 1997-2000; acad. affairs coord. acad. evaluation U. S.D., Vermillion, 2000—02; assoc. acad. dean Nat. Am. U., Sioux Falls, 2002—03, acad. dean, 2003—. Part time instr. psychology Northwestern Coll., 1985; part time instr. English and lit. Nat. Coll., 1985-88; part time instr. English and history Augustana Coll., 1986-89; presenter in field. Author: Visions of Light: Flannery O'Connor's Themes and Narrative Method, 1992, A Higher Education Perspective: Themes and Narrative Methods of Flannery O'Connor and Eudora Welty, 1997; Plains Goddesses: Heroines in Willa Cather's Prairie Novels, 1995; contbr. articles and revs. to profl. publs. including The Social Sci. Jour., others. Humanities Scholar evaluator Rainbow Project and Increasing Cultural Understanding Seminar, 2000; evaluator Profl. Devel. Conf. Native Am. Curriculum, Rapid City, S.Dak., 2001; mem. S.D. Humanities Coun., 2003—. Recipient Internat. Prof.'s Exch. award Sor Trondelag Coll., Trondheim, Norway, Jan. 1999; named Tchr. of Yr. Beresford (S.D.) Pub. Schs., 1976; S.D. Humanities scholar, 1993—; Bush mini-grantee, 1993, Internat. Studies grantee, 1994, 98, 99, S.D. Humanities Spkr.'s Bur. grantee, 1996—. Mem.: Delta Kappa Gamma. Home: 29615 469th Ave Beresford SD 57004-6457 Office: Nat Am U 2801 S Kiwanis Ave Sioux Falls SD 57105 Office Phone: 605-334-5430. E-mail: mcarlson@national.edu.

CARLTON, LISA, state legislator; b. Sarasota, Fla., May 7, 1964; d. Mabry C., Jr. BA in Sociology, Stetson U., 1986; JD, Mercer U., 1989. Co-owner, mgr. Mabry Carlton Ranch Inc.; legis. aide James M. Lombard, 1992, John McKay, 1993; mem. Fla. Ho. of Reps., Tallahassee, 1994-98; chair water and resource mgmt. com., 1998; mem. ecot. impact, govtl. svcs., procedural couns.; mem. Fla. State Senate, 1998—. Active United Way, Leadership Sarasota, Rep. Exec. Com., Sarasota County Environ. Pest

Mgmt. Bd., 1991-92, Sarasota Planning Commn., 1992-94; dir. 4-H Found.; charter class mem. Fla. Leadership program Agr. and Natural Resources Mem. Fla. Bar Assn., Georgia Bar Assn., Greater Sarasota C. of C., Venice Area C. of C., Alpha Chi Omega, Phi Alpha Delta. Baptist. Office: Fla Capitol 310 Senate Office Bldg 404 S Monroe Tallahassee FL 32399-6526 E-mail: carlton.lisa@leg.state.fl.us.

CARLTON, MAGGIE, state legislator; b. St. Louis, July 24, 1957; m. Merritt Carlton; children: M. Grace, Lucy. Mem. Nev. Senate, 1998—, mem. commerce and labor com.; mem. legis. affairs and operation com. Nev. State Senate, mem. natural resources com. Democrat. Home: 5540 Cartwright Ave Las Vegas NV 89110-3802 E-mail: mcarlton@sen.state.nv.us.

CARLTON, NEELY C. state legislator, lawyer; b. Greenville, Miss., July 13, 1970; Student, U. So. Miss., U. Miss. State senator Miss. State Senate, Jackson, 1996—. Vice chair conservation and water resources Miss. State Senate, mem. environtl. protection, conservation and water resources, agriculture, econ. devel., tourism and parks, edn., fin., judiciary, public health and welfare, state libr. coms. Mem. Washington County Anti-Drug Task Force. Mem. Greenville C. of C., Colonial Dames, DAR, Alice Bell Garden Club, Washington County Bar Assn., Miss. Bar Assn., Pi Beta Phi. Baptist. Democrat. Home: PO Box 451 Greenville MS 38702-0451 Office: State Capitol Bldg Rm 448 PO Box 1018 Jackson MS 39215-1018 E-mail: ncarlton@mail.senate.state.ms.us.

CARLUCCI, MARIE ANN, nursing administrator, consultant; b. N.Y.C., Apr. 22, 1953; d. Clarence Hugh and Anna Rebecca (Mills) McNamee; m. Paul Pasquale Carlucci, Aug. 18, 1973; children: Christine, Patricia. Diploma in nursing, Mt. Vernon Hosp. Sch. Nursing, N.Y., 1974; BS in Behavioral Sci. summa cum laude, Mercy Coll., 1991; MPH, N.Y. Med. Coll., 1997. Cert. emergency nurse; cert. nurse adminstr.; lic. healthcare risk mgr.; cert. legal cons. Staff nurse Mt. Vernon (N.Y.) Hosp., 1974-82, Lawrence Hosp., Bronxville, N.Y., 1982-84, No. Westchester Hosp., Mt. Kisco, N.Y., 1984-91, asst. dir. nursing, mem. nurse mgmt. and ethics coms., 1991-94; asst. DON svcs. Ferncliff Manor, Yonkers, N.Y., 1994-95, dir. nursing svcs., 1995-97; dir. nursing svcs. Taylor Care Ctr., Westchester, N.Y., 1997-2000; dir. residential svcs. Hillsborough (Fla.) Assn. for Retarded Citizens, 2000; dir. nursing Am. Retirement Corp., Sun City Center, Fla., 2000—01; med.-legal nurse cons., 2001—. Religious edn. tchr. St. John and St. Mary's Ch., Chappagua, N.Y., 1984-99; campaign mgr. Com. to Elect Paul P. Carlucci, Chappagua, 1990; mem. Surrogate Decision Making Com., N.Y. Commn. Quality Care for Mentally Disabled; mem. bd. trustees Field Home-Holy Comforter, 1995-99; guardian ad litem 13th Judical Cir., Tampa, Fla., 2000 ; bd. adv. Hillsborough County Children's Svcs., 2002-. Mem.: Phi Gamma Mu, Psi Chi. Roman Catholic. Home: 3916 Appletree Dr Valrico FL 33594-4315

CARMACK, MILDRED JEAN, retired lawyer; b. Folsom, Calif., Sept. 3, 1938; d. Kermit Leroy Brown and Elsie Imogene (Johnston) Walker; m. Allan W. Carmack, 1957 (div. 1979); 1 child, Kerry Jean Carmack Garrett. Student, Linfield Coll., 1955-58; BA, U. Oreg., 1967, JD, 1969. Bar: Oreg. 1969, U.S. Dist. Ct. Oreg. 1980, U.S. Ct. Appeals (9th and fed. cirs.) 1980, U. S. Claims Ct. 1987. Law clk. to Hon. William McAllister Oreg. Supreme Ct., Salem, 1969-73, asst. to ct., 1976-80; asst. prof. U. Oreg. Law Sch., Eugene, 1973-76, assoc. Schwabe, Williamson & Wyatt, Portland, Oreg. 1980-83, ptnr., 1984-96, ret., 1996. Writer, lectr., legal educator, Oreg., 1969—; mem. exec. bd. Appellate sect. Oreg. State Bar, 1993-95. Contbr. articles to Oreg. Law Rev., 1967-70. Mem. citizen adv. com. State Coastal Planning Commn., Oreg., 1974-76, State Senate Judiciary Com., Oreg., 1984; mem. bd. visitors Law Sch. U. Oreg., 1992-95; mem. Oreg. Law Commn. Working Group on Conflict of Laws, 2000. Mem. Oreg. State Bar Assn., Order of Coif.

CARMAN, JOANNE G. consultant; d. Patricia Mary and Joseph Anthony Genova; m. Richard Daniel Carman, June 19, 1993. BA, Hartwick Coll., Oneonta, NY, 1986—90; MA, U. Albany, Rockefeller Coll., 1990—94, PhD, 1995—. Data analyst Philliber Rsch. Associates, Accord, NY, 1992—96; sr. rsch. assoc. Rockefeller Inst., Albany, NY, 1996—98; rsch. asst. Ctr. for Policy Rsch., Albany, NY, 1998—; cons. Carman & Miller Consulting, Albany, NY, 1999—. Author: Nonprofit Mgmt. & Leadership, (book) New Directions for Evaluation. Mem.: Assn. for Rsch. on Nonprofit Organizations and Voluntary Action, Am. Evaluation Assn. Home: 44 Corlear St Albany NY 12209 Personal E-mail: carmanj@nycap.rr.com.

CARMAN, MARY ANN, retired special education educator; b. Kerrville, Tex., July 12, 1941; d. William Earl and Virginia (Tracy) Gregg; m. Douglas Gary Carman, July 20, 1968; 1 child, Christina Tracy. BA in Psychology, So. Meth. U., 1959-63; MS in Spl. Edn., E. Tex. State U., 1971. Cert. spl. edn. tchr., Iowa; teaching credential, Tex. Salesperson James K. Wilson Clothing Store, Dallas, 1963; sec. psychology dept. So. Meth. U., Dallas, 1964; EEG technician Dr. Paul Levin, Neurologist, Dallas, 1965-68; sec. geography dept. E. Tex. State U., Commerce, 1968-70; tchr. pilot program early childhood edn. Farmers Br. (Tex.) Sch. Dist., 1971; chair dept. spl. edn. U. Dubuque, Iowa, 1972-75; tchr.'s aide Crockett Elem. Sch., San Marcos, Tex., 1978, 79; spl. edn. tchr. Travis Elem. Sch., San Marcos, 1980—2000, ropes course facilitator campus improvemnt team, 1994-95, tchr. class-within-a-class 2d and 3d gr. levels, presenter project math 2d gr. campus improvement team, ropes course facilitator, 1995-96. Mem. dist. ednl. improvement coun. San Marcos Consol. Ind. Sch. Dist., 1991, participant strategic planning workshop, 1991, learning styles tng. course, 1992, chmn. sight based mgmt. team, 1991; facilitator ROPES course, 1993. Winant vol. Episcopal Ch., E. India Dock, London, 1963; coach state meet Spl. Olympics team San Marcos Consol. Ind. Sch. Dist., 1981, ofcl. at state games, 1988; facilitator exptl. edn. TRUST (Teamwork, Responsibility, Understanding for Students and Tchrs.), 1993. Recipient 1st place Bill Gray award Tex. Assn. Bus., The Spl. Kid's Co., 1991, Teaching Excellence award Lions Club San Marcos, 1991. Mem. ASCD, Phi Delta Kappa. Home: 817 Willow Creek Cir San Marcos TX 78666-5061

CARMAN, SUSAN HUFERT, nurse coordinator; b. Detroit, Oct. 2, 1940; d. Theodore Louis and Margaret L. (O'Connor) Hufert; children: Amy E., Holly C., John T. BSN, Johns Hopkins U., 1964; MEd, Northeastern U., 1975; MS in Health Care Adminstrn., Simmons Coll., 1988. Instr. psychiat. nursing Salem (Mass.) Hosp. Sch. Nursing, 1975-78, Curry Coll., Milton, Mass., 1978-80; editor Beacon Comm. Corp., Acton, Mass., 1980-84; writer health promotion Honeywell Inc., Waltham, Mass., 1984-85; mgr. mental health unit Heritage Hosp., Somerville, Mass., 1986-87; specialist adult psychiatry Mass. Dept. Mental Health, Boston, 1987-93; clinician intensive clin. svcs. MHMA, Boston, 1994-96; dir. Arbour Counseling Svcs. Boston, 1996—. With SHC Assocs., Boston, 1993—; bd. dirs. Com. to End Elder Homelessness, Boston, Mass., 1993-99; bd. dirs. Dept. Social Svcs., Lowell, sec., 1982-92. Chair health planning com. Jamaica Plain (Mass.) Tree of Life/Arbol da Vida, 1994—2003; docent Arnold Arboretum, Boston, 1989—2000; founding mem. Boston Coalition for Promotion of Child and Adolescent Mental Health, 2000—; bd. dirs. First Steps/Health Families, Jamaica Plain, 1998—2002, Match-Up Interfaith, Boston, 2001—; chmn. Jamaic Plain Domestic Violence Provider Network, 2001. Mem. ANA. Avocations: travel, reading, walking, classical music.

CARMEN MARIA, LOPEZ, sales executive; b. Havana, Cuba, Apr. 30, 1959; came to U.S., 1960; d. Roberto Diego and Milagros Antonia (Gonzalez) L. BS in Psychology, Georgetown U., 1981; MBA in Internat. Bus., George Washington U., 1986. Group mgr. C&P Telephone Co., Washington, 1981-84; asst. staff mgr. AT&T, Fairfax, Va., 1984-87, product mgr. Fairfax, Va. and Basking Ridge, N.J., 1987-89, quality mgr. Silver Spring, Md., 1989-92, dist. mgr. Pleasanton, Calif., 1992-93, gen. mgr. tech. svc. orgn. Denver, 1993-95; gen. sales mgr. New England Lucent Technologies, Waltham, Mass., 1995-97, v.p. area svs. Miramar, Fla., 1997—2001; v.p. tech. svs. Avaya, Inc., Miramar, Ill., 2002—03, v.p. centralized ops. and regional support, 2003—. First co-chmn. Republican Nat. Hispanic Assembly, Washington, 1990-92; founding mem. N.Y. Relay Svc. Adv. Bd., 1988-89; chmn. HISPA Leadership Forum, 1993-98. Mem. Hispanic Assn. AT&T Employees (pres. nation's capital chpt. 1991-92, Eagle award winner 2001). Home: 2333 NE 8th St Fort Lauderdale FL 33304-3507 Office: Avaya Inc 3130 Miramar Pkwy Hollywood FL 33025

CARMICHAEL, JUDY LEA, record industry executive, concert jazz pianist; b. Lynwood, Calif., Nov. 27, 1952; d. John Alvin and Jeanne Pauline (Boock) Hohenstein. Student, Calif. State U., Long Beach, 1970-73, Calif. State U., Fullerton. Owner C&D Prodns., N.Y.C., 1989—. Chmn. jazz fellowships com. NEA, Washington, 1990-91; featured on Nat. Pub. Radio, Marian McPartland's Piano Jazz, 1990, Morning Edition Nat. Pub. Radio, also TV programs Entertainment Tonight, CBS, Sunday Morning with Charles Kuralt, 1993. Performed as pianist at Breda Jazz Festival, The Netherlands, 1986, Carnegie Hall, N.Y.C., 1988, 89, Rio de Janeiro, 1989, Peggy Guggenheim Mus., Venice, Italy, 1990, Am. Acad., Rome, 1990, 91, USIA Tour, Portugal, 1991, Spain, 1991, India, 1988, China, 1992, Singapore, 1994, S. Am., 1996, major U.S. tours 1993-95, also L.A., Zurich, Switzerland, Paris, Cannes, France; performer Stanford Symphony Pops with Skitch Henderson, 1997; author (music) Judy Carmichael's Complete Book of Stride Piano, 1987, You Can Play Stride Piano, 1996; prodr., artist (LP's) Jazz Piano, 1983, Two Handed Stride, 1980, (CD's) Trio, 1989, Old Friends, 1991, Pearls, 1985, ...And Basie Called Her Stride, 1993, Judy, 1994, Chops, 1995, PianoDisc, 1995, QRS piano rolls, 1996, (CD and player piano formats) High on Fats and Other Stuff, 1997; featured on CBS Sunday Morning with Charles Osgood, Entertainment Tonight, Prairie Home Companion, Nat. Pub. Radio's Morning Edit.; jazz editor Sheet Music mag., 1989-90; host, creator, prodr. Judy Carmichael's Jazz Inspired, Nat. Pub. Radio, 2000—, Pub. Radio Internat. on Sirius Satellite Network; stage show with Steve Ross 2000-2003 aboard QEII and throughout Europe and U.S., and QEII, Canary Islands, Lisbon, Atlantic crossing; tour of Australia and New Zealand, 2004; contbr. numerous articles to profl. jours. NEA fellow, grantee; Grammy award nominee, 1980; chosen to be Steinway artist, 1986; nominated for Mac award Manhattan Assn. Cabarets and Clubs for Stage Show with Steve Ross, 1996. Avocations: golf, softball, tennis, skiing. Office Phone: 631-725-3603. Personal E-mail: judy@judycarmichael.com.

CARMICHAEL, MARY ALICE, artist, genealogist; b. Colon, Panama, Nov. 28, 1936; arrived in U.S., 1937; d. Donald Croom and Mary Alice (Gatling) Beatty; m. James Donald Carmichael, Oct. 28, 1961; children: James Donald Jr., Beatty Payseur, Daniel Troy. BA, Howard Coll., 1960. Contbr. articles to profl. jours. Organizing mem. Ala. Men's Hall of Fame, 1988—, chair, 2002—; mem. Women's Com. of 100 of Birmingham, pres. 1989-91; steering com. Reynold's Hist. Soc., 1988—. Named one of Outstanding Young Women of Am., 1972-73. Mem. DAR (Outstanding Jr. Mem. award 1968, Most Outstanding Hist. Paper award 1988), Soc. Mayflower Descendants Ala. (gov. 1990-94, registrar 1985-94), Rotary (sec., helped initiate 1st heart pacemaker bank for the indigent in Bolivia). Presbyterian. Avocations: art, genealogy, photography, travel. Home: 2857 Canterbury Rd Birmingham AL 35223-1201

CARMICHAEL, ROBERTA KAY, writer; b. Daytona Beach, Fla., [illegible] 11, 1956; d. James Lawton and Barbara Kent Coward; m. Del Carmichael, July 5, 1974; 1 child, Joseph. Grad. H.S., Crescent City, Fla.; Breaking into Print Diploma, Long Ridge Writers Group, West Redding, Conn., 2000. Tchr. Kiddie Korner Nursery Sch., Crescent City, 1972—77; freelance writer Homosassa, Fla., 2000—. Contbr. articles to publs. Phys. therapy vol. Citrus Meml. Hosp., Inverness, Fla., 1992—93. Mem.: Pisgah Camping Club. Avocations: writing, reading, woodcarving, hiking, horseback riding. Home: 3610 S Springbreeze Way Homosassa FL 34448

CARMODY, CAROL J. government agency professional; BA, U.of Oklahoma; M in Public Administration, American U. Aviation staff member Senate Commerce Comm., 1988—94; U.S. rep. to the Council Internat. Civil Aviation Org., Montreal, 1994—99; acting chmn. Nat. Transportation and Safety Bd., 2002—03. Office: NTSB 490 L'Enfant Plaza SW Washington DC 20594

CARNAHAN, DORIS JEAN, budget analyst; b. Altoona, Pa., Jan. 18, 1942; d. Ray Alvin Smith and Phyllis Marie (Linn) Bolton; m. Ronald James Carnahan, Apr. 2, 1961; children: Tamy Jean Carnahan Jones, Tina Marie Carnahan Wilson, Randy James. Grad. H.S., Altoona. Clk. typist U.S. Govt.-Pentagon, Washington, 1959-60; editl. clk. U.S. Govt.-Indsl. Coll. of the Armed Forces, Washington, 1960-61; mail and file clk. U.S. Govt.-Pentagon, Washington, 1962-66; budget analyst U.S. Govt., Ft. Bragg, N.C., 1976—. Mem., sec. bd. dirs. N.C. Ballet Co., Fayetteville, 1980-83; mem., ch. sec. Golfview Bapt. Ch., Hope Mills, N.C., 1993—. Mem. Am. Soc. Notaries, Women of the Moose Lodge. Democrat. Baptist. Avocations: crafts, computers. Office: Tng Support Brigade Bragg Fort Bragg NC 28307-5000 Home: 8612 Ardenwood Ct Trinity FL 34655-5337

CARNAHAN, JEAN, former senator; m. Mel Carnahan (former governor) (dec. 2000); children: Randy(dec.), Russ, Robin, Tom. BA in Bus. and Pub. Admin., George Washington U. First lady of Mo., 1993—2000; U.S. senator, 2001—02. Mem. armed svcs. com, small bus. and entrepreneurship com., gov. affairs com., commerce, sci. and transportation com., special com. aging, State of Mo.; co-founder Children in the Workplace; spkr. for domestic violence, cancer, osteoporosis, mental health, drug problems. Author: If Walls Could Talk, 1998, Christmas at the Mansion: Its Memories and Menus, 1999, Don't Let the Fire Go Out, 2004; contbr.: Vital Speeches of the Day, 1999, Will You Say a Few Words, 2000. Recipient Robert C. Goshorn award for pub. svc., State of Mo. Martin Luther King, Jr. Special Achievement award, Child Adv. of Yr. award, Boys' and Girls' Town Mo., 1995, Citizen of Yr., March of Dimes, 1997, Woman of Yr., St. Louis Zonta Clubs Internat., 1999. Bd. mem. William Woods U. Democrat. Achievements include representing her husband's posthumously won seat in the U.S. Senate from 2001 to 2002 after he and their son, Randy, tragically died in a plane crash.

CARNES, COLLEEN KENNEDY, writer, retired military officer; b. Washington, Feb. 8, 1954; d. George Grant Kennedy and Valera Kennedy Keene; m. Paul Carnes, Jan. 17, 1998. Diploma in nursing, Ga. Bapt. Hosp., Atlanta, 1975; BSN, Auburn U., 1985; MA, Webster U., 1993. Staff nurse USAF Hosp. Pease, Portsmouth, 1977—80; staff nurse, hosp. supr., nurse mgr. USAF Hosp. Maxwell, Montgomery, Ala., 1980—83; nurse mgr. USAF Hosp. Moody, Valdosta, Ga., 1985—86; chief nurse recruiting 3549 USAF Recruiting Squadron, Oklahoma City, 1986—89; chief health professions recruiting group 3904th USAF Recruiting Group, San Antonio, 1989—91; nurse mgr. 59th Med. Group, San Antonio, 1991—94; chief nurse USAF Hosp. Holloman, Alamogordo, N.Mex., 1994—98; writer, 1998—. Rep. to Field Officers' Conf. for Better Understandings Moody AFB, 1986; mem. air combat command quality evaluation team, augment mem. Air Combat Command, Langely AFB, Va.; dir. joint commn. on accreditation of hosps. bd. of experts, dir. human resource devel., group edn. and tng., chmn. nursing quality improvement coun. USAF Hosp. Holloman, Alamogordo, 1991—94, sr. staff quality improvement advisor, 1992—94; res. nurse liason USAF Hosp. Maxwell, Montgomery, 1981—82. Children's choir dir. Cmty. United Meth. Ch., High Rolls /Mountain Park, N.Mex., 2001—02; bd. dirs. Mil. Officers Assn. Am., Alamogordo, 2000—02. Lt. col. USAF, 1977—98. Decorated Air Force Commendation medal USAF, Meritorious Svc. medal, Air Force Achievement medal, Meritorious Svc. medal; named Big Sister of Yr., Big Bros./Big Sisters of Am., Portsmouth, 1980, Top Nurse Specialist Recruiting Team (Leader) in the nation, Air Force Recruiting Svc., 1987, Top Health Professions Recruiting Team (Leader) in the nation, USAF Recruiting Svc., 1991, Air Combat Command Field Grade Nurse of the Yr., Air Combat Command, 1995, Air Combat Field Grade Nurse of the Yr., 1995; scholar scholarship, Air Force Inst. of Tech., 1993—95. Mem.: S.W. Writers, Lanoche Women's Club (pres. 2002—03), P.E.O. (assoc.; gaurd 2000—01, chaplain 2001). Achievements include development of USAF recruiting service flow trend analysis. Home: 2608 Oaktree Ct Alamogordo NM 88310

CARNES, JULIE ELIZABETH, judge; b. Atlanta, Oct. 31, 1950; m. Stephen S. Cowen. AB summa cum laude, U. Ga., 1972, JD magna cum laude, 1975. Bar: Ga. 1975. Law clk. to Hon. Lewis R. Morgan U.S. Ct. Appeals (5th cir.), 1975-77; spl. counsel U.S. Sentencing Commn., 1989, commr., 1990-96; asst. U.S. Atty. U.S. Dist. Ct. (no. dist.) Ga., Atlanta, 1978-90, judge, 1992—. Office: US Courthouse 75 Spring St SW Ste 2167 Atlanta GA 30303-3309

CARNES, LA ZETTA, elementary school educator; b. Dallas, Dec. 1, 1933; d. Clint Leo and Jimmie Lee Rosser C. BA, U. Dallas, 1969; MEd, East Tex. State U., 1978; postgrad., Richmond Coll., London, 1984, Tex. A&M U., 2000. Tchr. Mineral Wells (Tex.) Ind. Sch. Dist., 1969-71, St. Mary's, Sherman, Tex., 1972-73, Grayson County Jr. Coll., Sherman, Tex., 1986, Whitewright (Tex.) Ind. Sch. Dist., 1973-80, Bells (Tex.) Ind. Sch. Dist., 1973-95, Sherman Ind. Sch. Dist., 1998—. Author of poems. Mem. AAUW, United Daus. Confederacy, Tex. Ret. Assn., Grayson County Retired Sch. Personnel. Home: 1508 N Highland Ave Sherman TX 75092-3500

CARNESOLTAS, ANA-MARIA, lawyer; b. Havana, Cuba, Feb. 9, 1948; came to U.S., 1962; d. Manuel Ramon and Zenaida de las Mercedes C.; 1 child, Caroline. BA, U. Calif., Santa Barbara, 1970; JD, Loyola U., L.A., 1978. Bar: Calif. 1978, Fla. 1979. Dep probation officer Probation Dept., Santa Barbara, Calif., 1970-73; personnel analyst Dept. Personnel, L.A., 1973-77; dep. dist. atty. Dist. Atty.'s Office, L.A., 1978-80; asst. U.S. atty. U.S. Atty.'s Office, Miami, Fla., 1980-82; pvt. practice law, Miami, 1982-83, Coral Gables, Fla., 1985-89; asst. city atty. City Atty.'s Office, Miami, 1983-85; judge Dade (Fla.) County Ct., 1989-93; pvt. practice, 1993—; lectr. YMCA, Miami, 1983-89; adj. prof. Fla. Internat. U.; prof. Miami-Dade C.C., 1989-92; hearing officer Dade County Pub. Schs., Miami, 1985-89; legal commentator Sta. TeleMiami, Fla., 1997—; legal commenrator WCMQ, Miami, 1993-97. Bd. dirs. Am. Heart Assn., M iami, 1983-86, YWCA, 1985-89, Alzheimer's Disease and Related Disorders Assn., 1987. Named Disting. Advocate, Loyola Law Sch., 1978. Mem. Nat. Assn. Women Judges (outreach com., task force on minority concerns, internat. community outreach com.), Conf. County Ct. Judges (edn. com., small claims com., civic proc. rules com.), Calif. Probation Parole and Corrections Assn. (v.p. 1972-73), Cuban Am. Attys. Council (sec. 1979-80), Cuban Am. Bar Assn. (dir. 1983, 88, sec. 1984), Dade County Bar Assn., ABA, Fla. Assn. Women Lawyers, Assn. Trial Lawyers Am., Fed. Bar Assn., Latin Bus. and Profl. Women's Club (pres. 1984-85, v.p.), Cuban Women's Club. Republican. Roman Catholic. Office: 1900 S Bayshore Dr Miami FL E-mail: amc4/aw@aol.com.

CARNEY, JEAN KATHRYN, psychologist; b. Ft. Dodge, Iowa, Nov. 10, 1948; d. Eugene James and Lucy (Devlin) C.; m. Mark Krupnick, Jan. 1, 1977 (dec. Mar. 2003); 1 child, Joseph Carney Krupnick. BA, Marquette U., Milw., 1970; MA, U. Chgo., Chgo., 1984; PhD, U. Chgo., 1986. Registered Clin. Psychologist, Ill. Reporter Milw. Jour., 1971-76, editorial writer, 1976-79; asst. prof. psychology St. Xavier Coll., Chgo., 1985-86; dir. Lincoln Park Clinic, Chgo., 1986-87; pvt. practice psychotherapist Chgo., 1987—. Sci. staff Michael Reese Hosp. Med. Ctr., Chgo., 1987-2002; instr. Northwestern U. Med. Sch., 1991-95; clin. asst. prof. U. Ill. Coll. Medicine, 1993—. Editor: Self-Regulation: Issues of Attention and Attachment, Psychoanalytic Inquiry, Vol. 22, No. 3. Recipient Best Series Articles, 1975, Best Editorial, 1978, Milw. Press Club, William Allen White Nat. Award for Editorial Writing, 1978, Robert Kahn Meml. Award for Research on Aging, Univ. Chgo., 1985. Mem. APA, Ill. Psychol. Assn., Chgo. Assn. Psychoanalytic Psychology. Office: 55 E Washington St Chicago IL 60602-2115

CARNEY, MARGARET E. administrative assistant, small business owner; b. Herkimer, N.Y., Apr. 2, 1938; d. Donald Francis and Helen Mary (McLaughlin) Kane; m. John J. Carney Jr., July 18, 1959; children: John III, Caralee, Julie, Christy. BS, Geneseo Coll., 1960. Co-owner, book dealer Carney Books, Oneonta, N.Y., 1978—; sec. United U. Professions, Albany, N.Y., 1983—. Election inspector City of Oneonta, 1980—; vol. Planned Parenthood. Mem. NOW, Comm. Workers Am. Democrat. Avocations: reading, walking, swimming. Home: 44 Elm St Oneonta NY 13820-1834 Office: United Univ Professions State Univ Coll Oneonta NY 13820

CARNEY, PATRICIA, Canadian government official; b. Shanghai, May 26, 1935; d. John James and Dora (Sanders) C.; m. Paul S. White, Sept. 5, 1998; two children. BA in Econs. and Polit. Sci., U. B.C., Can., 1960, MA in Cmty. and Regional Planning, 1977, LLD, 1990, 91. Econ. journalist various publs., 1955-70; owner, cons. Gemini North Ltd., Vancouver, B.C., Can., 1970-80, Yellowknife, Canada, 1971, 1971; mem. Can. Ho. of Commons, Ottawa, Ont., 1980-88, opposition critic for energy, mines and resources, 1980-84, minister of energy, mines and resources, 1984, minister for internat. trade, 1986-88; pres. Treasury Bd., 1988; apptd. to senate Can., 1990. Mem. Planning and Priorities com., Fgn. Def. Cabinet com., Past Chair Standing Senate com. on energy, the environment and natural resources; adj. prof. U. B.C. Sch. Cmty. and Regional Planning, 1989—97. Author: Trade Secrets: A Memoir, 2000. Founding mem. Arthritis Rsch. Ctr. Can., Vancouver; bd. mem. Can. Arthritis Network, 2004—. Recipient Can. Women's Press award, 1968, 3 MacMillan Bloedel Ltd. awards Mem.: Senate Aboriginal Peoples Com., Senate Fgn. Affairs Com., Assn. Profl. Economists B.C., Royal Architects Inst. Can. (hon.).*

CARNEY, RITA J. educational administrator; b. Hoboken, N.J., July 17, 1941; BA, Beaver Coll., Glenside, Pa., 1962; MA, Seton Hall U., South Orange, N.J., 1965; EdD, Columbia U., 1977; MA, Princeton Theol. Sem., 1980. Tchr. Latin and English, Phillipsburg (N.J.) Pub. Schs., 1962-65; guidance counselor Jefferson Twp. Pub. Schs., Oak Ridge, NJ, 1965-67; admin. asst. Supt./H.S. prin. Madison Twp. Pub. Schs., Old Bridge, NJ, 1967—70; program devel. N.J. Dept. Edn., Trenton, 1970—75; county supt. schs. Middlesex County, NJ, 1975—80; N.J. asst. commr. for rsch., planning and evaluation; assoc. v.p. for acad. adminstrn. Temple U., Phila.; asst. to pres., v.p. for acad. and student affairs Georgian Ct. Coll., Lakewood, NJ, 1990—2001. Lectr, presenter profl and ch related orgns; consult planning and orgn analysis. Pres. Diocesan Pastoral Coun., Trenton, Blessed Sacrament Parish Coun., Trenton, NJ, Hiltonia Civic Assn., Trenton; chmn. exec. com. Mercy Higher Edn. Colloquium, 1994—2000. Mem.: Soc Col and Univ Planning (state rep 1996—2000). Home: 32 N Avon Dr Jackson NJ 08527-3975 E-mail: ritacarney@care2.com.

CARO, LUISA, lawyer; BA in French Lit., BS in Econ. cum laude, U. Pa., 1992; JD cum laude, Georgetown U., 1997. Bar: Md. 1997, D.C. 1998. Asst. investment officer World Bank group Internat. Fin. Corp., Washington, 1992-94; clk. to Hon. Emmet G. Sullivern, U.S. Dist. Ct. for D.C., Washington, 1997-98; assoc. Sidley & Austin, Washington, 1998—. Exec. editor Georgetown Law Jour. Office: Sidley & Austin 1722 I St NW Fl 7 Washington DC 20006-3705 Fax: 202-736-8177. E-mail: lcaro@sidley.com.

CAROFF, PHYLLIS M. social work educator; b. Bklyn., Feb. 22, 1924; d. Harry and Irene (Lesser) Friedman; m. Joseph Caroff, May 16, 1943; children[00bf] Michael, Peter. BA, Douglass Coll., 1944; MSW, N.Y. Sch. Social Work, 1947; DSW, Columbia U., 1969; DHL (hon.), Hunter Coll, CUNY, 1995. Caseworker ARC, 1944-45; caseworker, student supr. Community Service Soc., N.Y.C., 1956-61; from [illegible] Hunter Coll. Sch. Social Work, N.Y.C., 1961-76, prof., 1976-87; dir. Postmasters Program in Advanced Clin. Social Work, 1977-87; pvt. practice psychotherapy N.Y.C., 1964—. Cons. VA Hosp., N.Y.C., 1977-85, USPHS Hosp., S.I., 1974—; mem. adv. bd. Found. Thanatology, 1976—; mem. profl. adv. com. Grad. Program in Social Work, Inst. Health Professions, Mass. Gen. Hosp., 1980-86. Author: (with others) Before Addiction, 1973; editorial bd. Clin. Social Work Jour., 1972[00bf], Jour. Gerontol. Social Work, 1978[00bf] ; editor: (with others) Social Work in Health Services: An Academic Practice Partnership, 1980, A New Model in Academic/Practice Partnership, 1985, Psychosocial Advances in Clinical Social Work, 1985. Mem. exec. com. of bd. Planned Parenthood N.Y.C., 1974-79, chmn. rsch. and evaluation com., 1974-77, bd. dirs., 1971-86. Named Disting. Practitioner, Nat. Acad. Practice in Social Work, 1983; NIMH fellow, 1964-65; various grants. Fellow Am. Orthopsychiat. Assn., N.Y. Acad. Medicine; mem. AAUP, Nat. Assn. Social Workers (chmn. clin. council 1981-84, mem. peer rev. adv. com. 1982-84), N.Y. State Soc. Clin. Social Work Psychotherapists, The Douglass Soc. Home: 15 W 81st St New York NY 10024-6022

CAROL, JOY HAUPT, writer, educator, cultural organization administrator; b. Lincoln, Nebr., Apr. 28, 1938; d. Wilson J. and Alma J. (Weilage) Haupt. BA in Edn., Nebr. Wesleyan U., 1959; postgrad., Scarritt U., 1960-61; MA in Counseling Psychology, U. Md., 1968; postgrad., NYU, 1974-75; MA in Spirituality, Gen. Theol. Sem., 1998; LHD (hon.), Nebr. Wesleyan U., 1994. Tchr., dir. Project Head Start various pub. schs., 1959-60, 64-68; project dir. Meth. Ch. Edn. Sys., Karachi, Pakistan, 1961-63; psychol. counselor pub. and pvt. schs., 1969-73; founder, dir. Union Ctr. for Women, Bklyn., 1973-76; assoc. exec. dir. YWCA Bklyn., 1978; mem. staff UN Devel. Program, Suva, Fiji, 1979-80; program officer Ford Found., N.Y.C., 1980-82; program devel. officer Cultural Info. Svcs., N.Y.C., 1983-84; dir. Asia/Pacific region Save the Children, Westport, Conn., 1984-93; dir. internat. programs Christian Children's Fund, Richmond, Va., 1993-95; dir. devel. Internat. Women's Tribune Ctr., N.Y.C., 1996-97. Cons. UN/World Coun. Chs., N.Y. and Asia, 1976-77, 84, women's orgns., Oslo, 1974, Trauma Response Assistance for Children, 2002-03. Author: You Don't Have to be Rich to Own a Brownstone, 1971, (Women in Devel. publ.) But We're Not Afraid to Speak Anymore, 1976, (booklet) Already I Feel the Change, 1989, Towers of Hope, 2002, Finding Courage, 2002, Journeys of Courage, 2004; author ofcl. report on end of Internat. Women's Decade, UN Devel. Program, 1985; contbr. numerous articles to mags. Bd. dirs. Vietnamese Meml. Assn., Ctrl. Europe Inst., 1990—, United Meth. Ch.; mem. nat. adv. coun., bd. dirs. Nebr. Wesleyan U., 1992—; co-founder self-help cmty. ctr. CHIPS, Bklyn., 1972-75; nat. convernor U.S. Forum on Vietnam, Cambodia, Laos, N.Y., 1990-95; co-founder, vol. Project Reach Youth, N.Y.C., 1965-68; vol. support groups for brain tumor patients at area hosps., Richmond, 1992-94, vol. chaplain Bellevue Hosp., 1997-98, hospice vol., 1994-98, spiritual dir., 1997-98; vol. chaplain Am. Red Cross, 2001-04; vol. Ctrl. Pk. Conservancy, 2002-04. Named one of Outstanding Women of Am., 1966; named Outstanding Educator in U.S., U.S. Jaycees, Colo., 1966, Outstanding Woman, Bklyn. City Coun., 1970. Mem. AAUW, NOW, Women's Internat. League for Peace and Freedom, Soc. for Internat. Devel. Avocations: writing, reading, hiking, music, gardening. Home: 549 W 123rd St Apt 13H New York NY 10027-5040

CAROOMPAS, CAROLE JEAN, artist, educator; b. Oregon City, Oreg., Nov. 14, 1946; d. John Thomas and Dorothy Lietta (Dirks) C. BA, Calif. State U., Fullerton, 1968; MFA in Painting, U. So. Calif., 1971. Instr. El Camino Coll., Torrance, Calif., 1971—72; vis. artist Calif. State U., Northridge, 1972—75; instr. Immaculate Heart Coll., L.A., 1973—76; vis. artist Calif. State U., Fullerton, 1976—78; instr. U. Calif., Irvine, 1976—80, Claremont (Calif.) Grad. Sch., 1976—79, Art Ctr. Coll. of Design, Pasadena, 1978—86, UCLA Extension, L.A., 1984—93; prof. fine arts Otis Coll. Art and Design, L.A., 1981—. Vis. artist Anderson Ranch Art Ctr., Aspen, Colo., 1996, 98. One-woman shows include Jan Baum Art Gallery, L.A., 1978-82, Karl Bornstein Gallery, L.A., 1985, L.A. Contemporary Exhbns., 1989, U. Calif., Irvine, 1990, Sue Spaid Fine Art, L.A., 1992, 94, P.P.O.W., N.Y.C., 1994, Otis Coll. of Art and Design Art Gallery, 1997-98, Mark Moore Gallery, Santa Monica, 1997, 99, 2000, Western Project, Culver City, Calif., 2004; exhibited in group shows at Pasadena Mus. Art, 1972, Whitney Mus. of Art, 1978, Mus. Modern Art, N.Y.C., 1976, L.A. County Mus., 1982, Corcoran Gallery of Art, 43rd Biennial Exhbn. of Contemporary Am. Painting, Washington, 1993, Under Contstrn. Armory Ctr. for Arts, Pasadena, 1995, UCLA Hammer Mus. of Art, L.A., 1996, Los Angeles County Mus. Art, 1996, Beaver Coll., 1996, L.A. Mcpl. Art Gallery, 1997, UCLA Hammer Mus. Art, 2000, Calif. State U., Fullerton, 2001, San Jose Mus., 2002, Rosamund Felson Gallery, Santa Monica, Calif., 2003, Lewis and Clark Coll., Portland, Oreg., 2003, San Luis Obispo Art Ctr., 2003; also a vocalist; recs. include 2 individual albums and inclusion in The Record: 13 Vocal Artists; contbr. articles to Paris Rev., Dreamworks, Whitewalls. Fellow Guggenheim Meml. fellow, 1995, Individual Artist's fellow, City of L.A. Cultural Affairs Dept., 2000; grantee NEA grantee, 1987, 1993, Faculty Devel. grantee, New Sch. Social Rsch., 1989, Support grantee, Esther and Adolph Gottlieb Found., 1993. Office: Otis Coll Art and Design 9045 Lincoln Blvd Los Angeles CA 90045-3505

CARPENTER, ANGIE M. county legislator, small business owner, editor; b. Bay Shore, N.Y., Sept. 30, 1943; d. Joseph and Ida (Gullo) Linarello; m. Joe David Carpenter, Apr. 13, 1964; children: Richard, Robert. Student, Nassau C.C., 1962-63. Office mgr., graphic designer, typographer Merrick (N.Y.) Typographers and Maverick Pubs., 1966-76; founder, v.p. AC Typesetters and Printing, Inc., West Islip, N.Y., 1976-93. Editor, pub., co-founder West Islip Record, 1986-91; columnist The Graphic, The Beacon, 1985-87. Chmn. publicity com., trustee Babylon/West Islip Windmill Com., Inc., Babylon, N.Y., 1986—, ASK US, 1987-98; trustee West Islip After-Sch.-Care program, 1987-97, Our Lady of Consolation Geriatric Care Ctr.; vice chmn. West Islip Youth Enrichment Svcs., 1986-87; mem. govt. action coun. L.I. Assn., 1987; mem. recycling panel Town of Islip, 1987; chairperson TOI Blue Ribbon Com. on Recycling, 1987-88; trustee Suffolk County Vanderbilt Mus., 1990-93; vice chair Suffolk County Salvation Army Adv. Bd.; mem. Suffolk County Legislature, 1993—, dep. presiding officer, chmn. pub. safety com. Mem. West Islip C. of C. (v.p., mchts. dir. 1982-84, pres. 1985, 86, 87, 88). Republican. Roman Catholic. Office: Office County Legislature 4 Udall Rd West Islip NY 11795-2341 E-mail: www.acarpent@suffolk.lib.ny.us.

CARPENTER, BETTY O. writer; b. Montreal, June 1, 1926; d. Harry and Dorothy (Schacher) Shmerling; m. David G. Ostroff, Apr. 6, 1946 (div. 1972); children: Jack Ostroff, Lucy Ostroff Harrow; m. Russell William Carpenter, Jr., Oct. 2, 1976 (dec.); stepchildren: Annette Marie Carpenter Freedman, Cynthia Carpenter Jefferson, Lori Carpenter Bembry. BA in Edn., Bklyn. Coll., 1947, MA in Edn., 1953; PhD in Adminstrn., NYU, 1973. Cert. sch. supt., prin., N.J., guidance counselor, elem. tchr., N.Y. Tchr. elem. grades N.Y.C. Pub. Schs. 54 and 139, Bklyn., 1946-54, 62; asst. prin. Pub. Sch. 139, Bklyn., 1962-67; pres. asst. prin. assoc. Ctrl. Office Bd. of Edn., N.Y.C., 1967-68, v.p. coun. suprs. and adminstrs., 1968-69, adminstrv. asst. pers., 1968-70; asst. supt. Plainfield (N.J.) Pub. Schs., 1970-74; supt. schs. Glen Rock (N.J.) Pub. Schs., 1974-84; ret. Author: Curriculum Handbook for Parents and Teachers, 1991, Tutoring for Pay, 1991, Musing, 1994, (book of poetry) The Brosh (Bionic Replacement of Species Humanoid), 1998, Lady of the Lake, 1999, Inherit the Rainbow, 2000, Art and Craftiness, 2001, Crystal Slopes, 2002, A Style of Their Own, 2002, Make Way for Pugsley, 2002. Trustee Glen Rock Libr. Bd., 1974-80, United Fund Bd., Glen Rock, 1975-77; vice chmn. Iredell County Bd. of Adjustment N.C., 1990-95; fellow mem. Lake Owners Gathered in Concern, N.C., 1985-88. Recipient Founders Day award NYU, 1973, Adminstry Leader, [illegible], 1984. Mem. Soc. Children's Book Writers and Illustrators, Romance Writers Am., Nat. Writers Assn., Bergen County Supts. Assn. (pres.-elect), Nat. Scrabble Assn., Am. Contract Bridge League. Avocations: sculpture, golf, water aerobics, computers, bridge. Home: 11730 N 91 Pl Scottsdale AZ 85260-6866 E-mail: bcbcarp@aol.com.

CARPENTER, CANDICE, writer, former media executive; m. Peter Olson, 2001; children: Michaela, Ellie. BS in Biology, Stanford U.; MBA, Harvard U. V.p. consumer mktg. Am. Express Co., N.Y.C.; pres. Time Life Video & Television (Time Warner), N.Y.C., 1989-93, QVC, Inc. (Q2 shopping channel), 1993-94; co-founder, CEO iVillage, N.Y.C., 1995—2000, chair, 2000—01. Author: Chapters: Create a Life of Exhilaration and Accomplishment in the Face of Change, 2001. Dir. Breakthrough Found. E-mail: candicec123@aol.com.*

CARPENTER, CAROL SETTLE, communications executive; b. Schenectady, N.Y., Oct. 22, 1953; d. Carl Oscar and Ursula Elsen (McEldowney) Settle; m. R. Jay Carpenter, May 4, 1985; children: Reilly, Evie. BBA, Rochester Inst. Tech., 1975; postgrad., Inst. Children's Lit., 1988-91. Mgmt. trainee Lincoln First Bank, Rochester, N.Y., 1976-77; investment sec. Blyth Eastman Dillon, Scottsdale, Ariz., 1977-79; stock-broker E.F. Hutton, Scottsdale, 1979, Rauscher Pierce Refsnes, Scottsdale, 1979-81; exec. v.p. RL Kotrozo Inc., Scottsdale, 1981-85; asst. v.p. United Bank Ariz., Phoenix, 1985-88; asst. v.p. investments Citibank, Phoenix, 1988-91; freelance greeting card designer Phoenix, 1991; v.p. Warning Comm., Inc., Phoenix, 1992—. Staff vol. Crisis Nursery, Phoenix, 1987; co-pres. parent coun. Khalsa Sch., 1994—95, mem. mid. sch. com., 1999—; mem. Brophy Mothers' Guild, 2002—; mem. staff support com. Shepherd of the Valley Luth. Ch., 2000—; bd. dirs. Khalsa Montessori Elem. Schs., 1995—2001, v.p., 2001—; career adv. network Rochester Inst. Tech., 1999—2001. Named Khalsa Sch. Parent of Yr., 1994-2000. Mem. Phoenix Country Club, Phi Gamma Nu. Republican. Lutheran. Avocations: music, art, writing for children. Home: 374 E Verde Ln Phoenix AZ 85012-3012 E-mail: carol@1-800-phoneword.com.

CARPENTER, DEE, publishing executive; Grad., Roanoke Coll. Pres. & pub. Virginian-Pilot, 2000—. Bd. dirs. Multiple Sclerosis Soc. of Hampton Roads. Mem. Va. Beach C. of C. Office: Virginian-Pilot 150 W Brambleton Ave Norfolk VA 23510

CARPENTER, DOROTHY FULTON, retired state legislator; b. Ismay, Mont., Mar. 13, 1933; d. Daniel A. and Mary Ann (George) Fulton; m. Thomas W. Carpenter, June 12, 1955; children: Mary Ione, James Thomas. BA, Grinnell Coll., 1955. Elem. tchr., Houston and Iowa City, 1955-58; mem. Iowa Ho. of Reps., 1980-94, asst. minority fl. leader, 1982-88, chair ethics and state govt. coms., 1992-94; ret., 1994. Bd. dirs. Planned Parenthood Fedn. of Am., 1977—80; pres. Planned Parenthood of Iowa, 1970; active West Des Moines Human Rights Commn., 1999—; fin. chair Episcopal Diocese, Iowa, 1979—80. Recipient Grinnell Coll. Alumni award, 1980; named Citizen of Yr., West Des Moines C. of C., 1999.

CARPENTER, FLORENCE ERIKA, retired human services administrator; b. Rochester, N.Y., July 28, 1913; d. William Rice and Alice Leah (Harman) Foster; m. Lawrence Edmund Carpenter, Oct. 30, 1937 (dec. June 1968); children: Luke, Susan, Michael, Patricia Carpenter-Light. BA, U. Rochester, 1935. Cert. nursing home adminstr., cert. case worker, N.Y. With rsch. dept. Eastman Kodak Co., Rochester, 1936-42; social worker Monroe County Dept. Social Svcs., Rochester, N.Y., 1960-62; med. social worker Strong Meml. Hosp., Rochester, 1966-71, Organized Home Care, 1962-64; exec. dir. Regional Coun. on Aging (now Life Span), Rochester, 1971-79; administv. svcs. Wayne, Ontario, Seneca and Yates counties Soc. for Prevention Cruelty to Children, Rochester, 1979-80; interim dir. Monroe County Mental Health Assn., Rochester, 1980; adminstr. Home and Family Svcs., Rochester, 1980-88, ret., 1988. Bd. dirs. Monroe County Dept. Health, 1988-94, Family Svcs., Rochester; pres., bd. dirs. Monroe County Mental Health Chpt., 1993-95, Rushville (N.Y.) Health Ctr., 1980-97; chmn. Liberal Party Monroe County, 1966; bd. dirs. Unitarian-Universalist Ch. Canandaigua, 1991-94. Recipient plaque Monroe County Mental Health Chpt., 1985, Monroe County Dept. Health, 1989. Mem. Am. Assn. Ret. Persons (N.Y.S. vote coord. 1988-92, mem. nat. legis. com. 1992-93), LWV (treas., bd. mem. 1948-97). Home: 5050 County Road 11 Rushville NY 14544-9704

CARPENTER, JANELLA ANN, retired librarian; b. Knoxville, Tenn., Sept. 20, 1936; d. J. Beecher Carpenter, M. Janella Hooper. BS, U. Tenn., 1958; MA, George Peabody Coll. Tchrs., 1963. Cert. tchg. cert. N.C., 1958. Libr. Elizabeth Elem. Sch., Charlotte, NC, 1958—63, Merry Oaks Elem. Sch., Charlotte, NC, 1963—64; libr., media specialist Rama Rd. Elem. Sch., Charlotte, NC, 1964—88; ret., 1988. Sch. area rep., tchrs. adv. coun. Charlotte-Mecklenburg Schs., Charlotte, NC, 1983—88. Bd. dirs. Newport/Cocke County Mus., Newport; mem. Newport Regional Planning Commn., Newport, 1995—, Newport/Cocke County Tourism Coun., Newport, 1995—2002; mem. coordinating com. for growth planing Newport/Cocke County, Newport, 1998—2002; newsletter editor Dead Pigeon River Coun., Newport, 1989—93. Named Carpenter Ctr., Rama Rd. Elem. Sch., 1988. Mem.: ALA, DAR, Classroom Tchrs. Assn. (pres. 1975—76), Profl. Educators N.C. (life; 1st pres. 1979—82), Newport Garden Club, Alpha Omicron Pi, Beta Sigma Phi, Delta Kappa Gamma. Republican. Baptist. Avocations: amateur desktop printing, painting, genealogy, gardening.

CARPENTER, LIZ (ELIZABETH SUTHERLAND CARPENTER), journalist, writer, equal rights leader, lecturer; b. Salado, Tex., Sept. 1, 1920; d. Thomas Shelton and Mary Elizabeth (Robertson) Sutherland; m. Leslie Carpenter, June 17, 1944 (dec.); children: Scott Sutherland, Christy. BJ, U. Tex., 1942; PhD (hon.), Mt. Vernon Coll., Austin Coll. Reporter UP, Phila., 1944-45; propr. with husband of news bur. representing nat. newspapers Washington, 1945-61; exec. asst. to V.P. Lyndon B. Johnson, 1961-63; pres. sec., staff dir. to Mrs. Johnson, 1963-69; v.p. Hill & Knowlton, Inc., Washington, 1972-76; cons. LBJ Library, Austin, Tex.; asst. sec. Dept. Edn., 1980-81; with White House Com. on Aging, 1998—. Co-chmn. ER-America, 1976-81; dir. Nat. Wildflower Rsch. Ctr. Author: Ruffles and Flourishes, 1970, Getting Better All the Time, 1987, Unplanned Parenthood, 1994, Start with a Laugh. An Insider's Guide To Making Speeches, Roasts, and Eulogies, 2000; co-author (with George Arnold) Growing Up Simple: An Irreverent Look at Kids in the 1950s, 2003. Recipient Woman Year award in field of politics and pub. affairs Ladies Home Jour., 1977, Disting. Alumnae award U. Tex., 1974-75; named to Tex. Women's Hall Fame, 1985. Mem. Nat. Women's Polit. Caucus (founding mem. 1971), Women's Nat. Press (pres. 1954-55), Alpha Phi, Theta Sigma Phi (Nat. Headliners award 1962), Press Club (Washington), Headliners Club (Headliner award), Univ. Club (Austin).*

CARPENTER, MARGARET S. (MOLLY CARPENTER), artist; b. Wilmington, Del., Jan. 21, 1960; d. Richard Paulett and Margaret Marvel Sanger; m. Samuel Preston Carpenter, Oct. 4, 1981; children: Benjamin Sanger, Margaret Paulett. Student, Pa. Acad. Fine Arts, Phila., 1978—79, Frudakis Acad. Fine Arts, 1978—81. Apprentice Charles Cropper Parks, Wilmington, 1977-80; sculptor, Salem, 1981—. One-woman shows include Gallery 50, Bridgeton, N.J., 1983, 86, 92, Gloucester C.C., 1988, Vineland Pub. Libr., 1988; exhibited in group shows, including Wilmington Christmas Shop Artists' Gallery, 1981-2000, Glassboro State Coll., 1989, Longwood Gardens, Kennett Square, Pa., 1993, Rockfeller Ctr., 1996, Indepen dence Seaport Mus., Phila., 1996, The Coliseum, N.Y.C., 1996, Ronald McDonald House, [illegible] Sculpture Soc., 1997, Catherine Lorillard Wolfe Art Club, Nat. Arts Club, N.Y.C, 1999, Del. Art Mus., 1999, Olympic Regional Devel. Assn., Mus., 2000, Goodwill Games Mus., 2000; represented in permanent collections Independence Seaport Mus., Du Pont Children's Hosp., Wilmington, 1989; commns. include Constl. Compass Rose, Del. Heritage Commn. for U.S. Constn. Bicentennial, Legis. Hall, Dover, 1987, bas relief sculpture to honor Judge Samuel Desimone, Bar Assns. Cumberland, Salem and Gloucester Counties, N.J., 2000; portrait sculptures include Vince Gioaya, Robert Kasey, Dr. Martin Luther King Jr.; designer rooms class Phila. Flower Show, 1990-2001. Bd. dirs. Salem County Arts Alliance, 1997—, v.p., 2000—; mem. arts com. Salem County Cultural and Heritage Commn., 1998—; bd. dirs. Salem County Cultural and Heritage, 1998—. Recipient numerous best of show awards, award sculpture AIDS Del., 1998; creator of Achievement Award in Sculpture, Creative Grandparenting Del., 2000. Mem. Nat. Sculpture Soc. Home: 465 Kings Hwy Salem NJ 08079 E-mail: sculptor@mollycarpenter.com.

CARPENTER, MARY CHAPIN, singer, songwriter; b. Princeton, N.J., 1958; d. Chapin and Mary Bowie. BA, Brown U., 1981, D (hon.), 1996. Owner GETAREALJOB Music and Why Walk Music. Albums Hometown Girl, 1987, State of the Heart, 1989, Shooting Straight in the Dark, 1990, Come On Come On, 1992, Stones in the Road, 1994, A Place in the World, 1996, Party Doll and Other Favorites, 1999, recs. CBS, 1987—. Named Top Female Vocalist by Country Music Assn., 1992, 1993, Acad. of Country Music Awards Top New Female Vocalist, 1990, Top Female Vocalist, 1993; recipient Grammy award for Best Female Country Vocal Performance for four consecutive years, 1992, 93, 94, 95, Country Album of the Yr., "Stones in the Road", 1995. Mem.: ASCAP. Office: Sony Music Entertainment Corp AGF Mgmt Ltd Clarysage 550 Madison Ave Fl 6 New York NY 10022-3211

CARPENTER, NANCY J. health science association administrator; Assoc. dir. H.A. Chapman Inst. Med. Genetics, Tulsa, Okla.; pres. Am. Bd. Med. Genetics, 2001—. Adj. prof. biochemistry Okla. State U. Office: H A Chapman Inst Med Genetics 4502 E 41st St Tulsa OK 74135-2553 Business E-Mail: ncarpenter@hillcrest.com.*

CARPENTER, REBECCA LEE, secondary school educator, music educator; b. Mankato, Minn., May 28, 1964; d. Phillip Edward and Darlene Ruth Lee; m. Paul A. Carpenter; children: Laura, Eric. BA, St. Olaf Coll., 1986; MS, Minn. State U., 1992. Tchr. instrumental and choral Mounts View Pub. Schs., New Brighton, Minn., 1986—87; tchr. music Minnesota Lake Pub. Sch., 1987—89; tchr. instrumental music Maple River Ind. Sch. Dist., Mapleton, 1989—. Mem.: Music Assn. Minn. State High Sch. League, Music Educators Nat. Conf., Minn. Band Dirs. Assn. Office: Maple River High Sch 101 6th Ave NE Mapleton MN 56065 Office Phone: 507-524-3930.

CARPENTER, SHARON QUIGLEY, municipal official; Tchr. history St. Louis Pub Schs.; elected recorder of deeds City of St. Louis, 1980—. Mem. Mo. Reapportionment Commn. Dem. Committeewoman 23rd ward St. Louis, 1964—; chair Dem. Ctrl. Com. St. Louis; founding mem, 1st chair, bd. dirs. Maria Droste Residence, St. Louis; mem. Mo. Commn. on Intergovernmental Rels, 1996—, adv. bd. Cath. Youth Coun., St. Louis., 1997—. Mem. Recorders' Assn. Mo. (past pres.). Office: City of St Louis Office Recorder of Deeds Market & Tucker Aves Rm 126 Saint Louis MO 63103

CARPENTER, SHEILA JANE, lawyer; b. Kyoto, Oct. 16, 1950; d. Chester Elwin and Betty (Boulger) C.; m. William Joseph McCarthy, May 26, 1973; 1 child, Diana Elizabeth. BA, Purdue U., 1972; JD, Yale U., 1975. Bar: Md. 1975, U.S. Dist. Ct. Md. 1976, D.C. 1977, U.S. Dist. Ct. D.C. 1978, U.S. Supreme Ct. 1980, U.S. Dist. Ct. (no. dist.) Ohio 1980, U.S. Claims Ct. 1982, U.S. Ct. Appeals (D.C. cir.) 1983, U.S. Ct. Appeals (4th and Fed. cirs.) 1984, U.S. Ct. Appeals (8th cir.) 2000. Assoc. Weinberg & Green, Balt., 1975-77, Sutherland, Asbill & Brennan, Washington, 1977-82, ptnr., 1982-96, Jorden Burt LLP, Washington, 1996—. Pub. svc. com. Sutherland, Asbill & Brennan, 1990-94, chair, 1990-92, chair litigation group Washington office, 1991-93; Web chair life, health and disability com. Def. Rsch. Inst., 2000—. Contbr. articles to profl. jours. Mem. ABA (mem. excess surplus lines and reins. com. TIPS sect., vice chmn. 1992-94, chair elect 1994-95, chair 1995-96, vice chair pub. regulation ins. commn. TIPS sect. 1995-2000), Am. Arbitration Assn. (arbitrator large complex case panel), Md. Bar Assn., Phi Beta Kappa. Office: Jorden Burt LLP Ste 400E 1025 Thomas Jefferson St NW Washington DC 20007-5208 E-mail: sjc@jordenusa.com.

CARPENTER, SUSAN KAREN, defender; b. New Orleans, May 6, 1951; d. Donald Jack and Elise Ann (Diehl) C. BA magna cum laude with honors in English, Smith Coll., 1973; JD, Ind. U., 1976. Bar: Ind. 1976. Dep. pub. defender of Ind. State of Ind., Indpls., 1976-81, pub. defender of Ind., 1981—; chief pub. defender Wayne County, Richmond, Ind., 1981. Bd. dirs. Ind. Pub. Defender Coun., Indpls., 1981—; Ind. Lawyers Comm., Indpls., 1984-89; trustee Ind. Criminal Justice Inst., Indpls., 1983—. Mem. Criminal Code Study Commn., Indpls., 1981—, Supreme Ct. Records Mgmt. Com., Indpls., 1983—, Ind. Pub. Defender Commn., 1989—, Ind. Supreme Ct. Commn. on Race and Gender Fairness, 2000—. Mem. Ind. State Bar Assn. (criminal justice sect.), Nat. Legal Aid and Defender Assn., Nat. Assn. Defense Lawyers, Phi Beta Kappa. E-mail: scarpenter@iquest.net.

CARPENTER, TERRI RUDD, music educator; b. Lake Charles, La., Dec. 30, 1958; d. John Pierce and Barbara Yocum Rudd; m. David Karl Carpenter, June 14, 1980; children: Aaron Kyle, Allison Kaye, Allen Keith. MusB in Edn., N.W. State U., 1980, MusM, 1989, EdS, 2003. Tchr. Oberlin (La.) Elem., La., 1980—82, Winnfield (La.) Mid. Sch., 1982—83; dir. music Pineville (La.) Jr. HS, 1984—2004; instrnl. tech. facilitator Rapides Parish Sch. Bd., La., 2004—. Pianist Pinehurst Bapt. Ch., Ball, La., 1988—. Mem.: La. Music Educators Assn. (state bd. 1980—), Am. Choral Dirs. Assn. Avocations: computer technology, singing, piano, gardening, family. Home: 726 Ates Rd Pineville LA 71360

CARPENTER-MASON, BEVERLY NADINE, quality assurance professional, medical/surgical nurse; b. Pitts., May 23, 1933; d. Frank Carpenter and Thelma Deresa (Williams) Carpenter Smith; m. Sherman Robert Robinson Jr., Dec. 26, 1953 (div. Jan. 1959); 1 child, Keith Michael Robinson ; m. David Solomon Mason Jr., Sept. 10, 1960; 1 child, Tamara Nadina Mason. Grad., Shadyside Hosp. Sch. Nursing, Pitts.; BS, St. Joseph's Coll., North Windham, Maine, 1979; MS, So. Ill. U., 1981; PhD, Columbia Pacific U., 1995. RN Pa., DC, Fla., cert. PNP; state ombusman long term care North Pinellas Pasco County Long Term Care Ombudsman Coun., parish nurse 2004, lay spkr. 1999, lay del. Fla. Conf. United Meth. Ch., 1998. Staff nurse med. surgery, ob-gyn neonatology and pediat., Pa., N.Y., Wyo., Colo. and Washington, 1954-68; mgr. clinician dermatol. svcs. Malcolm Grow Med. Ctr., Camp Spring, Md., 1968-71; PNP Dept. Human Resources, Washington, 1971-73; asst. DON Glenn Dale Hosp., Md., 1973-81; nursing coord. medicaid divsn. Forest Haven Ctr., Laurel, Md., 1981-83, spl. asst. to supr. for med. svcs., 1983-84; spl. asst. to supt. for quality assurance Bur. Habilitation Svcs., Laurel, 1984-89; exec. asst. quality assurance coord. Mental Retardation Devel. Disabilities Adminstrn., Washington, 1989-91, also bd. dirs.; owner, prin. BCM Assocs., 1992—; coord. quality assurance health svcs. divsn. UPARC, Clearwater, Fla., 1993-94. Mem. exec. com. Am. Found. Edn. Healthcare Quality, 1995—97;

bd. dirs. Dist. V, Fla. Dept. HHS, 1997—2002; cons.; lectr. in field. Author: (book) Quality Assurance: Toward a Paradigm of Universality, 1995; mem. editl. bd., case study editor: Am. Jour. Quality Assurance, 1985—; contbr. articles to profl. jours. Mem., star donor ARC Blood Dr., Washington, 1975—91; mem. health and human svcs. bd. Fla. Dept. Children and Families, 1997—2000, cons. Dist. XI, 1998; bd. dirs. Pinellas County (Fla.) Coun., Pinellas County WAGES Coalition, 1999; lay del. United Meth. Ch. Fla. Conf., 1998—; bd. dirs. North Pinellas divsn. Am. Cancer Soc., 2002—04; bd. trustees, dir. Upper Pinellas Assn. Retarded Citizens Bd./Found., 2002—; chair nominations com. Prince Georges Nat. Coun. Negro Women, Md., 1984—85; exec. sec. Pipers Meadow Home Owners Assn., 1993—2001; mem. Long Term Care Fla. State Ombudsman Coun., 2000—. Named Woman of the Yr., 1990—96; recipient awards, Dept. Air Force and DC Govt., 1966—92, Della Robbia Gold medallion, Am. Acad. Pediat., 1972, John P. Lamb Jr. Meml. Lectureship award, E. Tenn. State U., 1988, Outstanding Svc. award, U.S. Congress Adv. Bd. Svc., 1991. Fellow: Am. Coll. Med. Quality (case study editor, mem. jour. editl. bd. 1985—, chmn. publs. com. 1987—2003, asst. treas. 1988—93, Svc. award 1999); mem.: NAFE, Internat. Platform Assn., Healthcare Quality Inst., Assn. Retarded Citizens, Am. Bd. Quality Assurance and Utilization Rev. Physicians (asst. treas. 1988—94, chair exam. com. 1990—93, chief proctor exam. com. 1995—97, Chmn. of the Yr. award 1992, presdl. citation, Calvin R. Openshaw Svc. award 1993), Am. Assn. Mental Retardation (conf. lectr. 1988), Top Ladies Distinction (1st v.p. 1986—91), Soroptimists Internat. (sec. Pinellas chpt. 1999, Achievement in Healthcare award 1997), Order Ea. Star (Achievement award Deborah chpt. 1991). Democrat. Avocations: studying languages, travel, reading, writing, collecting antiques.

CARPER, FERN GAYLE, small business owner, writer; b. Pitts., Jan. 28, 1934, d. Phillip Jack and Jean Edith (Epstein) Whitman; m. Robert S. Carper, Aug. 3, 1958; children: Pamela Hope, Bruce Alan. Diploma, Taylor Alderdice HS, 1952. Exe. sec. J.J. Gumbrg & Co., Pitts., 1952—58; author, owner Pete The Toad Enterprises, Potomac, Md., 2000—. Author: Pete The Toad and Friends, 2002. Democrat. Achievements include development of line of Pete The Toad stuffed animals and tee shirts. Avocations: oil and acrylic artist, still life painting, singing. Home: 9203 Gatewater Terr Potomac MD 20854 Office: Pete The Toad Enterprises 9203 Gatewater Terr Potomac MD 20854

CARPER, GERTRUDE ESTHER, artist, marina owner; b. Jamestown, N.Y., Apr. 13, 1921; d. Zenas Mills and Virgie (Lytton) Hanks; m. J. Dennis Carper, Apr. 5, 1942; children: David Hanks, John Michael Dennis, Michelle Kristen. Student violinist, Nat. Acad. Mus., 1931-41; diploma fine arts, Md. Inst. of Art, 1950; voice student, Frazier Gange, Peabody Inst. Music, 1952-55. Interior decorator O'Neill's (Importers), Balt., 1942-44; auditor Citizens Nat. Bank, Covington, Va., 1945-46; owner, developer Essex Yacht Harbour Marina, Balt., 1955—, owner, developer St. Michael's Sanctuary wildlife preserve, 1965—. Jewelry designer, 1987—; portrait artist, 1947—; exhibited one-woman shows Ferdinand Roten Gallery, Balt., 1963, Highfield Salon, Balt., 1967, Le Salon des Nations a Paris, 1985, Ducks and Geese of North Am., 1986, Series of Lighthouses, 1991; exhibited group shows Md. Inst. Alumni Show, 1964, Essex Libr., 1981, Hist. Preservation of Am., Hall of Fame, 1989, others; works included in collections including Prestige de la Peinture d'Aujourd'hui dans le Monde, 1990, Artists and Masters of the Twentieth Century, 1991; author: Expressions for Children, 1985, Fidere, 1993, Mentation, 1993; contbr. articles and poetry to ch. publs. and newspapers. Vol. tchr. of retarded persons, 1942—; leader Women's Circle at local Presbyn. chs., 1952-87, mem. 40 yrs. of choir svc. Mem. Md. Inst. Art Alumni Assn. (life), Grand Coun. World Parliament of Chivalry (Nobless of Humanity citation), Nat. Mus. Women in the Arts (charter, Washington). Avocations: raising orchids, reading, writing essays and poetry. Office: Essex Yacht Harbour Marina 500 Sandalwood Rd Baltimore MD 21221-5830

CARPI, JANICE E. lawyer; b. Whittier, Calif., June 15, 1952; d. Leonard William and Elizabeth Louise (Severns) Carpi; m. Garland M. Harwood III, July 3, 1993; 1 child, Sarah Elizabeth. BA in Internat. Affairs, George Washington U., 1975; JD, So. Meth. U., 1978. Bar: Nev. 1978, Tex. 1979, Va. 1994. Assoc. Wesner Wylie & Pleasant, Dallas, 1979—80; underwriting atty. Chgo. Title Ins. Corp., Dallas, 1980—83; underwriting counsel Lawyers Title Ins. Co., Dallas, 1983—86, v.p., sr. underwriting counsel Richmond, Va., 1986—98, Land Am. Fin., Richmond, 1998—. Spkr. Practicing Law Inst., N.Y.C., 1998—. Contbr. chpts. in books. Vol. Jr. League Dallas, 1983—85, Habitat for Humanity, Richmond, 1996—; eucharistic min. St. Martin's Episc. Ch., Richmond, 2001—. Fellow: Am. Coll. Real Estate Lawyers (chair meetings com. 2001—); mem.: ABA (chair Title Ins. com. 2001—), Coll. of State Bar Tex., Phi Delta Phi. Avocation: travel. Office: Land America Fin Group 101 Gateway Centre Pkwy Richmond VA 23235*

CARR, ANNE ELIZABETH, theology educator; b. Chgo., Nov. 11, 1934; d. Frank James and Dorothy Margaret (Graber) C. AB, Mundelein Coll., 1956; AM, Marquette U., 1963, U. Chgo., 1968, PhD, 1971. Instr. Mundelein Coll., Chgo., 1963-66, asst. prof., 1966-71, Ind. U., Bloomington, 1972-74; asst. prof., asst. dean U. Chgo. Divinity Sch., 1975-78, assoc. prof., assoc. dean, 1978-88, prof., 1988—. Donnelan vis. prof. Trinity Coll., Dublin, Ireland, 1983. Author: Theological Method of K. Rahner, 1977, Transforming Grace, 1988, Search for Wisdom and Spirit, 1988; editor: (with E.S. Florenza) Women, Work and Poverty, 1987, Motherhood: Experience, Institution, Theologu, 1989, Women's Special Nature?, 1991; bd. cons. Jour. of Religion, 1975-86, co-editor, 1987-94; assoc. editor Horizons, 1974—; editorial bd. Concilium, 1985-91. Trustee Mundelein Coll., Chgo., 1977-91. Postdoctoral fellow Harvard Divinity Sch., 1983-84. Mem. Am. Acad. Religion (program com. 1978-80), Cath. Theol. Soc. Am., Coll. Theology Soc. Roman Catholic. Office: U Chgo Divinity Sch 1025 E 58th St Chicago IL 60637-1509

CARR, BESSIE, retired middle school educator; b. Nathalie, Va., Oct. 10, 1920; d. Henry C. and Sirlena (Ewell) C. BS, Elizabeth City Coll., N.C., 1942; MA, Columbia U. Tchrs. Coll., 1948, PhD, 1950, EdD, 1952. Cert. adminstr., supr., tchr. Prin. pub. sch., Halifax, Va., 1942-47, Nathalie-Halifax County, Va., 1947-51; prof. edn. So. U., Baton Rouge, 1952-53; supr. schs. Lackland Schs., Cin., 1953-54; prof. edn. Wilberforce U., Ohio, 1954-55; tchr. Leland Sch., Pittsfield, Mass., 1956-60; chair math. dept., tchr. Lakeland Mid. Sch., N.Y., 1961-83. Founder, organizer, sponsor 1st Math Bowl and Math Forum in area, 1970-76; founder Dr. Bessie Carr award Halifax County Sr. High Sch., 1962. Mem. Nat. Women's Hall of Fame. Mem. AAUW (auditor 1970-85), Delta Kappa Gamma (auditor internat. 1970-76), Assn. Suprs. of Math. (chair coordinating council 1976-80), Ret. Tchrs. Assn., Black Women Bus. and Profl. Assn. (charter mem. Senegal, Africa chpt.). Democrat. Avocations: travel, photography, souvenirs.

CARR, CAROLYN KINDER, deputy director and chief curator; b. Providence, R.I. BA in Art History, Smith Coll.; MA in Art History, Oberlin Coll.; PhD in Art History, Case Western Reserve U. Instr. art history Kent (Ohio) State Univ., 1963-65, 67-68; art critic Akron (Ohio) Beacon Jour., 1968-73; chief curator Akron Art Mus., 1978=83; asst. dir. for collections Nat. Portrait Gallery, Washington, 1984-90, dep. dir., chief curator, 1991—. Vis. lectr. Akron U., Spring 1975, '76; organizer numerous art exhibitions Akron Art Mus., 1978-83, Nat. Portrait Gallery, 1984—. Contbr. articles to art publs. including Nat. Portrait Gallery, The Dictionary of Art, Am. Art, The Am. Art Jour., Dialogue, Currier Gallery of Art Bull.; author: art catalogs for exhibitions at Akron Art Mus., Chrysler Mus. of Art, Nat. Portrait Gallery and Smithsonian Instn. Office: Nat Portrait Ballery 750 9th St NW Box 37012 Washington DC 20013-7012 Office Phone: 202-275-1867. E-mail: carrc@npg.si.edu.

CARR, CASSANDRA COLVIN, communications company executive; b. Champaign, Ill., Nov. 14, 1944; d. A.B. and Irene Colvin; m. Edward M. Carr, Nov. 27, 1970. BA, Vanderbilt U., 1966; MA, U. Tex., 1973. Div. mgr. revenue requirements Southwestern Bell Telephone Co., Austin, Tex., 1985, div. mgr. congl. asst. program Washington, 1986; dir. govt. rels. Southwestern Bell Corp., St. Louis, 1986-87, mng. dir. govt. rels., 1987-88, v.p. fin., treas., 1988, sr. v.p. fin., treas., 1988-90, v.p. revenues and pub. affairs Austin, Tex., 1990—, sr. v.p. human resources San Antonio, Tex., sr. exec. v.p. external affairs. Commr. St. Louis Regional Conv. and Sports Complex Authority; bd. dirs. The Arch Funds, Inc., St. Louis, The Conf. Bd., N.Y.C., Found. Women's Resources, Austin. Recipient YWCA Leader award YWCA of St. Louis, 1988. Mem. Fin. Execs. Inst., Nat. Assn. Corp. Treasurers, St. Louis Club, Forest Hills Country Club. Office: SBC Communications Inc PO Box 2933 175 E Houston 6th Fl San Antonio TX 78299-2933 Home: 4400 River Garden Trl Austin TX 78746-2916

CARR, CLAUDIA, art gallery director, owner, artist; b. N.Y.C., June 7, 1948; d. Charles Robert and Geraldine Carr; m. Jacques Marcel Levy, Apr. 27, 1980; children: Maya, Julien. BA, Adelphi U., 1970; MA, SUNY, Buffalo, 1976. Artist, curator 22 Wooster Art Gallery, N.Y.C., 1977-84; assoc. dir. Sindin Gallery, N.Y.C., 1991-92; instr. art history Colgate U., Hamilton, N.Y., 1992-93, 94-95, asst. curator collections Picker Art Gallery, 1993-94; owner, dir. Claudia Carr Gallery, N.Y.C., 1996—; curator Jenny Okun at Show Walls, the Durst Orgn., 2002. Curator "Architectonics" The Durst Orgn., 2002. Painting exhbns. include 22 Wooster Gallery, 1978, 80, Provincetown Art Assn., 1984; author: (essay) Towards Abstraction, 1975, (catalogues) Harold Wallin: Anchorage Mus., 1999, Jason Stewart Spirals, 1999. Pres. Shuttleworth Artists Corp., N.Y., 1978-81. Recipient Regents award N.Y. State, 1966, 5 Towns Music and Art Sculpture award 5 Towns L.I., 1968. Mem. Soho Alliance. Office: Claudia Carr Gallery 478 W Broadway New York NY 10012-3168 E-mail: claudiacarr@nyc.rr.com.

CARR, GLADYS JUSTIN, publishing company executive, consultant, editor, writer; b. N.Y.C. d. Jack and Mollie (Marmor) Carr. BA, MA, Smith Coll.; postgrad., Cornell U. Sr. editor Prentice-Hall, Inc., Englewood Cliffs, N.J., 1969; exec. editor Cowles Comm., Inc., N.Y.C., 1969-71; editl. dir., editor-in-chief Am. Heritage Press, N.Y.C., 1971-75; sr. editor McGraw-Hill, Inc., N.Y.C., 1975-81, editor in chief, editorial dir., chmn. editorial bd., 1981-89, v.p., pub., 1988-89, HarperCollins Pubs., Inc., N.Y.C., 1989-2000; mng. dir. GJ Carr Assocs., N.Y.C., 2000—. Contbr. articles to literary and profl. jours. Marjorie Hope Nicholson trustee fellow Smith Coll.; vis. Ford Found. fellow, Walter Francis Wilcox fellow Cornell U. Mem. PEN Am. Ctr., Women's Media Group, Acad. Am. Poets, Poetry Soc. Am., Nat. Arts Club, Exec. and Chemists Club, Smith Coll. Club (N.Y.C.), Phi Beta Kappa. Home and Office: 920 Park Ave New York NY 10028-0208 also: 1 Boulder Ln East Hampton NY 11937-1047

CARR, IRIS CONSTANTINE, artist, writer; b. Smyrna, Turkey, Aug. 4, 1922; d. John and Julia Kyrides Constantine (parents Greek citizens); m. Herman Edgar Carr Jr., 1947; 3 children. Diploma in dental nursing, Boston Sch. Dental Nursing, 1942; BA, Simmons Coll., 1970, postgrad., 1990-91, DeCordova Mus. Sch., 1986—. Anesthetist for oral surgeon, Boston, 1942-43; exec. med. sec. Boston Evening Clinic, 1943-44, lab. tech. dir. Boston Dispensary, 1944-45, Children's Hosp., Boston, 1944-47; editl. asst. Internat. Rsch. and Publs., 1947—; developed improved interlibr. loan svc. Wellesley Coll. Libr., 1964. Demonstrator watercolor technique Needham (Mass.) Arts Festival, 1996. One woman show at Needham Village Gallery, 1991, Needham Travel Svc. Bur., 1998-99; group shows include Mass. Med. Soc., 1999, Needham and Wellesley Art Assn., 1999, Needham Libr., 1999, Mass. Med. Soc. Alliance (Best in Show award); contbr. articles to profl. jours.; contbg. editor Mass. Med. Soc. Alliance. Recipient over 14 awards for pastel, watercolor and oil paintings. Mem. Mass. Med. Soc. Alliance (pub. rels. com. 1985-94, contbg. editor 1995—), Dedham Art Assn. (featured artist), Wellesley Soc. Artists (bd. dirs., registration com. 1994—), Needham Art Assn. (bd. dirs., publicity com., pres. 1989-90, co-inaugurated 1st art gallery 1990), Nat. Mus. Women in Arts, Mus. Fine Arts, Boston. Democrat. Home: 14 Ingleside Rd Needham MA 02492-4239

CARR, MARGARET, elementary school educator; b. St. Louis, Mar. 13, 1947; d. John William Henry and Dorothy Eugene Ryan Long; m. Douglas A. Ries Jr., June 7, 1969 (div. July 1979); children: Colleen Margaret, Kathryn Anne; m. Daniel Francis Carr, Sept. 25, 1982. AB cum laude, St. Louis U., 1969; MA in Tchg., Webster U., 1979. Life cert. tchr., Mo. Tchr. St. Timothy's, St. Louis, 1970-71, St. Peter's, St. Charles, 1972-73, Immocolata, St. Louis, 1971-72, 76-77; tchr., home tutor Spl. Sch. Dist., St. Louis, 1977-80; tchr. Our Lady of Sorrow Sch., St. Louis, 1980-84, United Ch. of Christ Sch., St. Louis, 1984-86, Mary Queen of Peace Sch., Webster Groves, Mo., 1987—. Author: Fort San Carlos, May 26, 1780, 1997, History of Mary Queen of Peace School, 1999. Recipient award and medal Am. citizenship VFW, 1998; named Tchr. of Yr., VFW, 2001. Mem. Mo. State Soc. U.S. Daus. of 1812 (state pres. 1998—, pres. St. Louis pioneer chpt. 1995-98), DAR Mo., Continental Soc. Daus. of Indian Wars (gov. Mo. soc. 1994-98, hon. gov. 1998—), New Eng. Women (state pres. 199—), Colonial Dames of the 17th Century (vice regen Margaret Allyn Wyatt chpt.), Colonial Dames of Am., Descs. of the Founders of Hartford, Sons and Daus. of the Pilgrims, Daus. of Union Vets., Delta Kappa Gamma (Beta Theta chpt. 1996—). Avocations: collection sewing tapes, antique costume jewelry, angels. Home: 17 S Maple Ave Webster Groves MO 63119-3021 Office: Mary Queen of Peace Sch 680 W Lockwood Ave Webster Groves MO 63119-3598

CARR, MARIE PINAK, book distribution company executive; b. Buffalo, June 17, 1954; d. Henry and Hildegard (Poech) Pinak; m. Richard Wallace Carr, Oct. 18, 1980; children: Katharine Marie, Ann Louise, Elizabeth Ashby. BS, Syracuse U., 1976. Cancer microbiologist Nat. Cancer Inst., Rockville, Md., 1976-78; mktg. specialist Precision Sci., Washington, 1978-80; art importer Dicmar Trading Co., Inc., Washington, 1981-83, book dist. Silver Spring, Md., 1983—. Bd. dir. CARE. Co-author: The Willard Hotel, 1986. Bd. dirs. Salvation Army Women's Aux., Washington, 1982—, pres., 1990-91; bd. dirs. Am. Cancer Soc., Washington, 1988-90; co-chmn. Nat. Cancer Ball, 1989, 90; active Jr. League Washington, 1987-90; bd. dirs. Achievement Rewards for College Students, 2000—; mem. exec. bd. CARE USA. Mem. Washington Club. Republican. Roman Catholic. Avocations: gardening, collecting textiles, tennis, travel. Office: Dicmar Trading Co Inc 4057 Highwood Ct NW Washington DC 20007-2131

CARR, MARSHA HAMBLEN, elementary school principal; b. Dunlap, Tenn., Nov. 28, 1961; d. Jackie Robert and Molly Ann (Johnson) Hamblen; m. Lonnie Gerron Carr, Feb. 26, 1980; 1 child, Gerra Sheree. BS in Spl. Edn. magna cum laude, Tenn. Tech. U., 1989, MA in Supervision of Instrn., 1992, ednl. specialist degree Edn. Leadership, 1997. Resource tchr. Sequatchie County Bd. Edn., Dunlap, 1989-90; early childhood spl. edn. tchr. Project CHILD Sequatchie County Bd. Edn., Dunlap, 1990-91, coord., 1991-97; principal Griffith Elem. Sch., Dunlap, Tenn., 1997—. Presenter Tenn. Young Children Assn., Chattanooga, 1992—; mem. adv. bd. Tenn. Early Intervention System, Chattanooga, 1990—; behavior mgmt. cons., Dunlap, 1990—; presenter Am. Edn. Rsch. Assn., San Diego. Active First Bapt. Ch. of Dunlap; Title I Sch. Support Svc. Facilitator. Mem. NEA, Tenn. Edn. Assn., Sequatchie County Edn. Assn., Assn. Supervision and Curriculum, Internat. Plastform Assn., Phi Kappa Phi, Delta Kappa Gamma (1st v.p., Internat. Xi state mem. chair), Pi Lambda Theta, Kappa Delta Pi. Democrat. Baptist. Avocations: reading, oil painting, travel, old movies. Home: 1043 Tram Trl Dunlap TN 37327-4446 Office: Griffith Elem Sch PO Box 819 Dunlap TN 37327-0819 Fax: (423) 949-6872.

CARR, PATRICIA WARREN, adult education educator; b. Mobile, Ala., Mar. 24, 1947; d. Bedford Forrest and Mary Catherine (Warren) Slaughter; m. John Lyle Carr, Sept. 26, 1970; children: Caroline Elise, Joshua Bedford. BS in Edn., Auburn U., 1968, MEd, 1971. Tchr. DeKalb County Schs., Atlanta, 1969-70; counselor Dept. Defense Schs., Okinawa, Japan, 1972-75; tchr. Jefferson County Schs., Jefferson, Ga., 1975-76; counselor Clarke County Schs., Athens, Ga., 1976-78; tchr. Fairfax County Schs., Adult and Community Edn., Fairfax, Va., 1980—. Instrnl. supr. Vol. Learning Program; coord. Enrichment for Srs. Program Fairfax Area Agy. on Aging and Adult and Cmty. Edn., 1985-89; cons. State Va. Dept. Edn., 1984—, Va. Assn. Adult and Cmty. Edn., 1987, Commn. on Adult Basic Edn., 1988; instr. George Mason U., Fairfax, 1985. Tchr. Met. Meml. United Meth. Ch., Washington, 1981—; co-leader McClean, Va. troop Girl Scouts U.S., 1985-88. Mem. Am. Assn. Adult and Community Edn., Smithsonian Nat. Assocs., No. Va. Assn. Vol. Adminstrs., Va. Assn. Adult and Community Edn., Greater Washington Reading Coun. Methodist. Avocations: tennis, horseback riding. Office: Fairfax County Adult & Community Edn Woodson Adult Ctr 9525 Main St Fairfax VA 22031-4006 E-mail: M4573@EROLS.com.

CARR, RUTH MARGARET, plastic surgeon; b. Waco, Tex., July 2, 1951; MD, U. Okla., 1977. Intern U. Okla. Med. Sch., Oklahoma City, 1977-78; resident U. Okla. Health Sci. Ctr., Oklahoma City, 1978-81, UCLA, 1981-83; plastic surgeon St. John's Hosp., 1989—, Santa Monica (Calif.) Hosp., 1989—. Clin. asst. prof. UCLA, 1983—. Office: 1301 20th St Ste 470 Santa Monica CA 90404-2082 E-mail: rcarr@ucla.edu.

CARRAHER, MARY LOU CARTER, art educator; b. Cin., Mar. 9, 1927; d. John Paul and Martha Leona (Williams) Carter; m. Emmett Carraher, Nov. 6, 1943 (div. July 1970); children: Candace Lou Holsenbeck-Smith, Michael Emmett, Cathleen C. Kruska. Student, U. Cin., 1946-48, Calif. State U., 1973-74. Lifetime credential in adult edn.: art, ceramics, crafts, Calif. Substitute tchr. Cobb County Schs., Smyrna, Ga., 1961-63; art tchr. pvt. lessons Canyon Country, Calif., 1968-72; adult edn. art tchr. Wm. S. Hart H.S. Dist., Santa Clarita, Calif., 1973-97; children's art and calligraphy cmty. svcs. Coll. of the Canyons, Santa Clarita, Calif., 1976-96. Fine arts coord. Santa Clarita Sr. Ctr., 1990—, founder, bd. dirs. Santa Clarita Art Guild, 1972-80; art dir. European tours Continental Club, Canyon Country, 1977-81; art tour guide and travel cons. Northridge (Calif.) Travel, 1981-91; vol. art tchr. stroke patients Henry Newhall Meml. Hosp., Valencia, Calif., 1993-96; craft tchr. for respite care program, Newhall, Calif., 1995-96, Respite Care Ctr., Santa Clarita Valley Sr. Ctr., 1995-96; art tour guide, Andulusia, Spain, 1997, 99. Artist, author History of Moreland School District, San Jose, California, 1965; prin. works include Paintings for each season of Church Year, 1970's, Baptismal painting, 1988, Sr. Ctr. Watercolors Ctr. Scenes, 1993, Watercolors of Christmas Charity Home Tour, 1993, Henry Mayo Newhall Meml. Hosp., 1997, 1999, 2001, 2002, 2003, murals painted for Christian Ch. and Sr. Ctr., 1997—99, mall st. painting for charity, 2000. Tchr., mem. Santa Clarita United Meth. Ch., 1966-96; judge for art contests and exhibits, Santa Clarita, 1973-96; mem. Santa Clarita Valley Hist. Soc., 1989-96; mem. Alumni Assn., Norwood (Ohio) City Schs., 1993-96; leader art tours to Spain, 1997, 99, 2002, Italy, 2001, Portugal, 2002, Australia, New Zealand and Fiji, 2003; designer certs. with scenes of Sr. Ctr., Cir. of Friends certs. Recipient Bravo award nomination for Outstanding Achievement in Art, 1995, Sr. of Yr. Santa Clarita Valley Sr Ctr. and Svc. Newspaper "The Signal", 1995, Christian Svc. award Santa Clarita United Meth. Ch., 1988; invited by Citizen Amb. Program of People to People Internat. to join U.S. del. to assess bus. and trade opportunities of the craft industry in China. Mem. Santa Clarita Valley Arts Coun., Hosp. Home Tour League, Nat. Women in the Arts (charter, Washington). Republican. Methodist. Avocations: travel, art related crafts, reading.

CARRANZA, JOVITA, delivery service executive; b. Chgo., June 29, 1949; m. Joel Roque; 1 child, Klaudene. Undergraduate, U. Miami, Calif. State U., LA; MBA for exec., U. Miami. Night-shift hub clerk UPS, 1967; supr. UPS, Metro LA Hub Oper., 1976—79; human resources supr. UPS, Metro LA, 1979—85, workforce planning mgr., 1985—87, bus. mgr., 1987; dist. human resources mgr. UPS, Cent. Tex., 1987—90, UPS, Ill., 1990—91, divsn. mgr. hub, packer, and feeder opers., 1991—96, 1996—99, mgr. Am. regions (including Mexico, PR, Dominican Rep., Virgin Islands), 1999—2000, region mgr. internat. opers., 2000—03, v.p. air opers. Louisville, 2003—. Vol. Habitat for Humanity; bd. mem. Libr. Found., Louisville. Named Woman Yr., Hispanic Bus. Mag., 2004. Mem.: Nat. Coun. La Raza. Achievements include first female internat. region pres. in UPS history; highest ranking Hispanic female at UPS; expanded UPS in Latin Am. Office: UPS 2245 Hikes Ln Louisville KY 40218 Office Phone: 502-459-8788.*

CARREL, MARIANNE EILEEN, music educator; b. Greenville, Pa., Aug. 28, 1957; d. Francis Raymond Cremi, Betty Hutton Cremi; m. Marion Lee Carrel. Student, Clarion U. Pa., 1975—76; BS, Edinboro U., 1979, MEd, 1985. Cert. elem. tchr. Ohio. Substitute tchr. Greenville and Reynolds Sch. Dists., Greenville, Pa., 1979—80; tchr. music Webster County Schs., Cowen, W.Va., 1980—84; grad. asst. Edinboro U., Edinboro, Pa., 1984—85; tchr. music Madison Local Schs., Madison, Ohio, 1985—86; tchr. music Geneva Area City Schs., Geneva, Ohio, 1986—. Sec. All-Am. Judges Assn., Ohio, 1989—. Named Assoc. of Yr., Am. Bus. Women's Assn., 2000-2001. Mem.: NEA, Internat. Double Reed Soc., Music Educators Nat. Conf., Ohio Edn. Assn., Kappa Delta Pi, Sigma Alpha Iota (life). Home: 4850 Boughner Rd Rock Creek OH 44084 Office: Geneva Area Schs 839 Sherman St Geneva OH 44041 Personal E-mail: mandmcarrel@direcway.com.

CARRICK, KATHLEEN MICHELE, law librarian; b. Cleve., June 11, 1950; d. Michael James and Genevieve (Wenger) C. BA, Duquesne U., Pitts., 1972; MLS, U. Pitts., 1973; JD, Cleve.-Marshall U., 1977. Bar: Ohio 1977, U.S. Ct. Internat. Trade 1983. Rsch. asst. The Plain Dealer, Cleve., 1973-75; head reference SUNY, Buffalo, 1977-78, assoc. dir., 1978-80, dir., asst. prof., 1980-83; dir., assoc. prof. law Case Western Res. U., Cleve., 1983—. Cons. Mead Data Central, Dayton, Ohio, 1987-91. Author: Lexis: A Research Manual, 1989; contbr. articles to profl. jours. Fellow Am. Bar Found.; mem. ABA, Am. Law Inst., Am. Assn. Law Librs., Assn. Am. Law Schs., Scribes. Home: 1317 Burlington Rd Cleveland OH 44118-1212 Office: Case Western Res U 11075 East Blvd Cleveland OH 44106-5409

CARRIER, LYNNE THOMSON, journalist; b. Mar. 7, 1945; BA in Internat. Affairs, George Washington U., 1967. Reporter San Diego Tribune, 1977-86, dep. editor editl. page, 1987-91; politics and govt. writer San Diego Daily Transcript, 1992-96; contbg. editor San Diego Met. Mag., 1998—. Office: 211 Orange Ave Coronado CA 92118-1410 E-mail: lcarrier@cts.com.

CARRIER, RACHEL ESTHER, music educator, director; b. Dayton, Ohio, Dec. 22, 1949; d. Robert Richard Folkerth and Amber Mae Spitler; m. Harold Gene Carrier, Jan. 27, 1968; children: Bryan Patrick, Alan Brent. BA in Performing Arts, Wittenberg Univ., 1975; student, Sinclair Coll., 1986—87, Wright State U., 1987—90; studied with, Douglas MacCash, 1964—84, D. Maddafore, 1968—73, Joan Swank. Cert. dental asst. nat., 1980. Orthodontic asst. Drs. King, Mayerson, Pope, Dayton, 1968—73; dental forensic asst. Wm. Bernard Weaver, D.M.D, Dayton, 1978—93; vocal instr. Northmont H.S., Clayton, Ohio, 1994—. Music cons. Bel Canto Young Singers Music Club, Dayton, 1997—; dir. children's drama and show choir Miami-Montage Children's Theater, Vandalia, Ohio, 1996—98;

dir. children's choir Concord United Meth. Ch., Englewood, Ohio, 1973—74, asst. dir. music, youth dir., 1977—92; youth choir dir. Englewood (Ohio) United Meth. Ch., 1989—91; dir. music Vandalia (Ohio) United Meth. Ch., 1993—98; dir. music ministries and drama and Christian edn. Shiloh Ch., Dayton, 1998—2001; vocal judge Regional Star Search, Cincinnati-Dayton, Ohio, 2004. Singer: George Washington [illegible] Dayton (Ohio) [illegible] Dayton (Ohio) Performing Arts Programs, 1998—2003. Named Woman of the Yr., Am. Biog. Assoc., 2001. Mem.: Dayton Music Club (corr.; cons. to the jr. music club 1998—2003), The Fellowship/Music and Worship Arts (corr.), Ohio Fedn. of Music Clubs (state festival chmn. 1998—), Ohio Ea. Star (past matron 1979—80, State of Ohio Vocalist 1978, 1979, 1980, 1982, 1984). Republican. Protestant. Avocations: breeding english springer spaniels, swimming, acting, gardening, directing handbells. Home: 4339 Gorman Ave Englewood OH 45322 Office: Shiloh Church UCC 5300 Philadelphia Dr Dayton OH 45415 Office Phone: 937-277-8953. Personal E-mail: rachcar898@aol.com. E-mail: rachelcarrier@shiloh.org.

CARRIERE, MARGARET E. energy executive; BS, Georgetown U., 1973; JD, So. Meth. U., 1979. With legal dept. Halliburton, Houston, v.p. legal and assoc. gen. counsel, v.p. human resources, regional chief counsel for Europe and Africa, 1986—88, 1994—98, v.p. and sec., legal, 2002—. Mem.: Am. Soc. Corp. Secs., Am. Corp. Counsel Assn., Tex. State Bar Assn., La. State Bar Assn. Office: Halliburton Ste 2400 PO Box 42807 5 Houston Ctr 1401 McKinney Houston TX 77242-2807*

CARRILLO, JUANITA, gerontological services consultant; b. Passaic, N.J., June 5, 1937; d. William and Channie (Fortney) Pitts; m. Manuel Carrillo, Jan. 1, 1961 (div. Sept. 1992); children: Manuel Jr., Karen. BMusEd magna cum laude, Howard U., 1959; MSW, Fordham U., 1977, PhD of Social Work, 2002. LCSW N.Y. Dept. Edn., 1978. Caseworker, supr. Bur. Pub. Assistance N.Y.C. Human Resources Adminstrn., 1961—80, dir. programs for homeless individuals and families Crisis Intervention Svcs., 1980—86, supr. profl. social workers Medicaid/Disability Rev. Divsn., 1986—90, dir. through Regional Adminstr. Home Care Svcs. Program, 1990—2001; cons. gerontology Fordham U., N.Y.C., 2002—. Consortium mem. through project coord. Pilot Program for Professionalism in Elder Care Forham U., N.Y.C., 2002—. Pub. policy com. mem. N.Y. State Soc. on Aging, Albany, 2002—; bd. dirs. SonRise CDC First Bapt. Ch., Englewood, NJ. Mem.: NASW, AAUW (co-v.p. Northern Valley chpt. 2003—), Nat. Assn. Black Social Workers, Gerontol. Soc. Am., Alpha Kappa Alpha Sorority (life). Avocations: music, home decorating.*

CARRILLO, LAURIE YVETTE, aerospace engineer; b. San Antonio, Feb. 4, 1976; d. Pedro and Amalia Lujan Carrillo. BS in Materials Sci. and Engring., BA in Math. and Computational and Applied Math., Rice U., 1998; Master of Engring. in Space Ops., U. Colo., Colorado Springs, 2002. EIT, cert. ascent analyst. Engr. mission ops. mission control team NASA-JSC, Houston, 1998—2000, mgr. advanced curation lab. for future extraterrestrial samples, 2000—03, engr. advanced propulsion plasma rocket team, 2003—. Author: Space Operations: Past, Present, Future, and Beyond, 2002. Mem.: Mex. Am. Engr. and Scientists (pres., nat. bd. dirs., co-chair internat. symposium). Roman Catholic. Avocations: flying, dance, star-gazing, writing, volunteering. Office: NASA-JSC 2101 NASA Rd 1-MC: ST Houston TX 77058

CARRINGTON, MARIAN DENISE, university administrator, counselor, motivational speaker; b. Smithfield, N.C., Aug. 12, 1960; d. James A. Stevens and Marian Louise (Revels) Whitley; children: Wynnona Alexis, Crystal Elizabeth. BS, Old Dominion U., 1982; MA, Hampton U., 1991; doctoral student in Am. Studies, Coll. William and Mary. Coord. cooperative edn. and internships Hampton (Va.) U., 1982-90; corporate recruitment coord. Christopher Newport U., Newport News, Va., 1990-91, dir. multicultural student affairs, 1991—. Grantwriter The Lighthouse Found., Bethel Temple, Hampton, Va., 2000—; founder MARVEL M. Presentations, Hampton, 1990—, The Coun. for Humanity, Urban Renewal and Cmty. Wholeness, 1994—; founder, dir. New Beginnings for God's Women, Hampton, 1994—; cons. U. Ala., Tuscaloosa, 1985. Mem. exec. bd. YWCA Phyllis Wheatley Br., Newport News, 1992—, Hampton Coalition for Youth, Hampton, 1993—, Machen Elem. Sch. PTA, Hampton, 1994-95, Colonial Coast Girl Scout Coun., Norfolk, Va., 1994; bd. mem. Menchville House Ministries, Inc., 1998—. Grantee U.S. Dept. Edn., 1983-90, State Coun. Higher Edn., 1990-94, 93-96. Mem. Va. Assn. Black Faculty and Adminstrs., Va. Counselor's Assn., Vocat. Edn. Adv. Coun. Avocations: singing, volleyball, reading suspense novels, writing poetry. Office: The Lighthouse Found 1705 Todds Ln Hampton VA 23666-3122 Home: PO Box 9736 Hampton VA 23670-0736

CARRINGTON, VIRGINIA GAIL (VEE CARRINGTON), marketing professional, consultant; b. Dodge City, Kans., Apr. 20, 1949; d. Virgel Troy and Betty Lou (Rynerson) Fakes; Lynn Nugent Friesner, Aug. 4, 1971 (div. Feb. 1985); m. Paul Henry Carrington, Apr. 4, 1987. BA, Kans. Wesleyan, 1971; MS, U. Ill., 1972; MA, Kans. State U., 1978. Sci. cataloger Kans. State U. Libr., Manhattan, 1972-74, humanities bibliographer, 1974-78; dir. libr. devel. State Libr. Kans., Topeka, 1978-84; libr. network dir. Kans. Libr. Network, Topeka, 1982-84; edn. officer Pub. Libr. Assn. ALA, Chgo., 1984-86; pres. Carrington Cons., Waterbury, Conn., 1986-97; promotion coord. Assn. Coll. and Rsch. Librs. ALA, Middletown, Conn., 1997-01; pres. Carrington Cons. Assocs., Waterbury, Conn., 2001—. Mgr. mem. svcs. Mattatuck Mus., Waterbury, 1992-97. Asst. editor: Guide to Reference Books, 11th ed., 1994; asst. to editor: Guide to Reference Books Supplement to 10th ed., 1990; contr. article: How Small businesses Can Save Money on Mailing, 2002 Mem. ALA (Continuing Libr. Edn. Network and Exch. Roundtable, Ind. Librs. Exch. Roundtable), Am. Mktg. Assn., Mountain Plains Libr. Assn., New Haven Postal Customer coun. (exec. bd., 2002-). Democrat. Methodist. Avocations: travel, reading. Home: 130 Melbourne Ter Waterbury CT 06704-1843 Office: Carrington Co PO Box 392 Southington CT 06489 E-mail: veegeecee@yahoo.com.

CARROLL, ADORNA OCCHIALINI, real estate executive; b. New Britain, Conn., Aug. 24, 1952; d. Antonio and Mary Ida (Reney) Occhialini; m. Christopher P. Buchas, Sept. 7, 1974 (div. Nov. 1982); 1 child, Jenna Rebecca; m. John Francis Carroll, Oct. 15, 1983; children: Jordan Ashley, Sean William. BA in Philosophy, Cen. Conn. State U., 1975; grad., Realtors Inst., 1989. Lic. real estate broker; accredited buyer rep. Dir. therapeutic recreation program Ridgeview Rest Home, Cromwell, Conn., 1974, Meadows Convalescent Home, Manchester, Conn., 1975, Andrew House Health Care, New Britain, 1976; owner, mgr. Liquor Locker, Newington, Conn., 1977-87; owner, broker A.O. Carroll & Co., Newington, 1985-93, A. O. Carroll & Agostini Co., Kensington, Conn., 1994-99; ptnr. Realty 3 Carroll & Agostini, 1999—. Ptnr. Marco Realty & Devel. Co., Newington, 1978-97, Dynamic Directions, Inc., ednl. and sales tng. cons., 1997—. Mem. Nat. Assn. Realtors (dir. 1995-2001, multiple listing policy forum 1993, legis./polit. forum 1993, mem. svcs. com. 1994, 96, 97, recruitment and retention forum 1994, state fiscal affairs com. 1995, personal asst. working group 1995, vice chair membership devel. and promotion forum 1996, 97, edn. forum 1995, cons. and meetings com. 1996-97, vice chmn. mktg. forum 1998, chmn. mktg. forum 1999, mem. lic. law com. 1999, regional v.p. region I 2001), Liaison Assn. Leadership Group Info. Commn. and Edn., Conn. Assn. Realtors (pres.-elect 1996, state pres. 1997, v.p.-at-large 1992-94, vice-chair legislation 1991, mem. legis. policy & RPAC coms. 1991, conv. com. 1990, polit. affairs com. 1988, 89, chair state MLS task force 1994, chair agy. task force 1994, 95, chair personal assts. 1995, chair comms./tech. com. 1995, Educator of Yr. 1999), Greater New Britain Assn. Realtors (local dir. 1991, 92, chair legislation and nominating coms. 1991-92, pres. 1990, 93, 96, chair bylaws com. and state conv. 1990, pres.-elect 1989, chair programs and polit. affairs & AM HM WK 1988, spkr. 1989—, Realtor of Yr. 1991, state dir. 1995), Nat. Package Store Assn., Conn. Package Store Assn. (legis. lobbyist 1984-88, pres. 1986-88, Disting. Svc. award 1985), Greater Hartford Package Store Assn. (pres. 1981-82), Marchegian Soc. New Britain (pres. 1992, corr. sec. and chair budget 1991), Newington C. of C. (bd. dirs. 1987-88, chmn. legis. 1988). Avocations: [illegible] softball, golf. Home: 23 Occhialini Ct Newington CT 06111-4754 Office: 1201 Farmington Ave Berlin CT 06037 E-mail: Adorna@Adorna.com.

CARROLL, BARBARA, musician, composer, singer; b. Worcester, Mass., Jan. 25, 1925; d. David Louis and Lillian Rose (Lavine) Coppersmith; m. Joseph Shulman, Sept. 20, 1954 (dec. Aug. 2, 1957); m. Bertram Joseph Block, Oct. 7, 1960 (dec. July 9, 1986); 1 child, Suzanne Elizabeth. Student, New Eng. Conservatory of Music, 1943-44; D in Music (hon.), Pine Manor Coll., 1980. Leader Barbara Carroll Trio, 1951-60. Appearances for 3 months Bemelmans Bar, The Carlyle, N.Y.C., spring and fall; Broadway appearances in Me and Juliet; TV appearances include All My Children, 1983, Today Show, Tonight Show, CBS Sunday Morning, 1995; (albums) Have You Met Miss Carroll, It's a Wonderful World, (CDs) Live At the Carlyle, This Heart of Mine, Everything I Love, Old Friends. Bd. mem. Duke Ellington Meml. Fund. Mem. ASCAP, Songwriter's Guild, Friars Club. Avocations: gardening, entertaining, cooking.

CARROLL, DIAHANN, actress, singer; b. N.Y.C., July 17, 1935; d. John and Mabel (Faulk) Johnson; m. Monte Kay (div.); m. Fredde Glusman (div.); m. Robert DeLean, 1975 (dec. 1977); m. Vic Damone, 1987. Student, N.Y. U. Began career as model; actress: motion pictures, including Claudine (Nominated for Acad. award as best actress by the Acad. Motion Picture Arts and Scis. 1974), Carmen Jones, Porgy and Bess, Hurry Sundown, Paris Blues, The Split. The Five Heartbeats, 1991, Eve's Bayou, 1997; on Broadway in No Strings, House of Flowers; appeared in: play Same Time, Next Year; TV series Julia, Dynasty, 1984-87, Lonesome Dove, 1994; TV movies Death Scream, 1975, I Know Why the Caged Bird Sings, 1979, Sister, Sister, 1982, Murder in Black and White, 1990, A Perry Mason Mystery: The Case of the Lethal Lifestyle, 1994, The Sweetest Gift, 1998, Motown 40: The Music is Forever, 1998, Having Our Say: The Delany Sisters' First 100 Years, 1999; TV miniseries Motown 40: The Music is Forever, 1998, Jackie's Back!, 1999, The Courage to Love, 2000, Sally Hemmings: An American Scandal, 2000. Address: William Morris Agy Inc care Peter Levine 151 S El Camino Dr Beverly Hills CA 90212-2704

CARROLL, DONNA M. academic administrator; MA, U. Cin., 1977, PhD in Edn., 1981. Program dir. U. Cin.; dean of students Fairleigh Dickenson U., Madison, NJ, Mt. Vernon Coll., Washington, v.p. devel.; sec. Fordham U., 1991—94, exec. sec. Bd. Trustees, 1991—94; pres. Dominican U., River Forest, Ill., 1994—. Office: Dominican U 7900 W Division River Forest IL 60305*

CARROLL, E JEAN, columnist, writer; b. Dec. 1943; Advice columnist Ask E. Jean, Elle; co-founder & advice columnist greatboyfriends.com and ejeanlive.com. Contbg. editor Esquire; written articles for Rolling Stone, Outside and New York Magazine. Author: Female Difficulties: Sorority Sisters, Rodeo Queens, Frigid Women, Smut Stars and Other Modern Girls, 1985, Hunter: The Strange Savage Life of Hunter S. Thompson Plume, A Dog in Heat Is a Hot Dog and Other Rules to Live By, 1997, Mr. Right, Right Now!: How a Smart Women Can Land Her Dream Man in 6 Weeks, 2003. Achievements include nominated for an Emmy for her writing for Saturday Night Life.*

CARROLL, ELLEN A. judge, lawyer; b. San Francisco, Feb. 6, 1947; BA, Mundelein Coll., 1970; JD with honors, U. San Francisco, 1980. Bar: Calif. 1980. Law clk. to Hon. Lloyd King No. Dist. Calif., 1981; partner Bronson, Bronson & McKinnon, San Francisco, 1988-93; counsel Murphy, Weir & Butler, San Francisco, 1993-98; judge U.S. Bankruptcy Ct., L.A., 1998-. Com. lawyer reps. of U.S. Bankruptcy Ct. No. Dist. Calif., 1988-90. Mem. ABA (bus. bankruptcy com., uniform comml. code com., bus. law sect. 1990—), State Bar Calif. (mem. uniform comml. code com. 1985-88), Bar Assn. San Francisco (bd. dirs. 1992—, chair 1989, comml. law and bankruptcy sect.), Bay Area Bankruptcy Forum (bd. dirs. 1991-92). Address: US Bankruptcy Ct Cent Calif 1634 Roybal Fed Bldg & US Ct House 255 E Temple St Los Angeles CA 90012-3332

CARROLL, FRANCES LAVERNE, librarian, educator; b. Scammon, Kans., Dec. 6, 1925; d. Robert Allen and Truda Hilda (Flanagan) C. BS in Ed., Kans. State Tchrs. Coll., 1948; MA in Libr. Sci., U. Denver, 1956; postgrad., Western Res. U., 1957; PhD in Edn., U. Okla., 1970. Bookkeeper Baxter Springs Bank, Kans., 1944; tchr. English and journalism high sch. Caney, Kans., 1947-49; libr. Field Kindley Meml. HS, Coffeyville, Kans., 1949-54; librarian Coffeyville Jr. Coll., 1954-62; supr. elem. sch. libraries Coffeyville, 1957-62; asst. prof. library sci. U. Okla., Norman, 1962-67, assoc. prof., 1972-75, acting dir. sch. library sci., 1974-75, prof., 1975-86, emeritus, 1986—. Head library studies Nedlands Coll. Advanced Edn. (formerly Western Australian Secondary Tchrs. Coll.), Perth, 1977-81; guest lectr. Drexel Inst. Tech., Phila., 1964, U. London, 1972, Pahlavi U., Shiraz, Iran, 1976, Beijing Fgn. Studies U., 1992; dir. US Office Edn. Inst., 1966, 67, 69. Author: (with Mary Meacham) The Library at Mount Vernon, 1977, Exciting, Funny, Scary, Short, Different and Sad Books Kids Like, 1984, More Exciting, Funny, Scary, Short, Different and Sad Books Kids Like, 1992, (with Pat Beilke) Guidelines for the Planning and Organization of Sch. Libr. Media Ctr., 1979, Guidelines for Planning and Organization of Library Media Centers, 1990, Arabic translation, 1995, Recent Advances in Sch. Librarianship, 1981, (with John Harvey) Internationalizing Libr. Ed., 1987; nat. series editor: Reading for Young People, 1979-85; editor: (with Philip Schwartz) Biog. Directory of Nat. Librarians, 1989, Destination Discovery! Activities and Resources for Studying Columbus and Other Explorers, 1994, (with Susan Houck) Internat. Biog. Directory of Nat. Archivists, Documentalists and Librarians, 1996, (with John Harvey and Susan Houck) Internat. Librarianship, 2001; contbr. articles to profl. jour. US Office Edn. grantee, 1969 Mem. AAUW, AAUP, ALA, Okla. Student Libr. Assn. (state sponsor 1963-84), Okla. Libr. Assn., Internat. Rels. Round Table (chmn. membership 1970-74), Internat. Fedn. Libr. Assn. (chmn. sect. sch. libr. 1973-77), Delta Kappa Gamma, Phi Delta Kappa, Beta Phi Mu. Office: Sch Library & Info Studies 401 W Brooks St Norman OK 73019-6032

CARROLL, JANE HAMMOND, artist, writer, poet; b. Greenville, S.C., May 15, 1946; d. Charles Kirby and Margaret (Cooper) Hammond; m. Robert Lindsay Carroll Jr., Feb. 3, 1968; children: Jane-Gower, Robert Lindsay III. BA, U. S.C., 1968. Tchr. A.C. Flora High Sch., Columbia, S.C., 1968-70; exec. field dir. N.E. Ga. Girl Scout Coun., Athens, 1970-71; asst. dir. AID-Vol. Greenville, 1971-73; author, artist Winston Derek Pubs., Nashville, 1985—. CEO Leader Pub., Atlanta. Author, artist: Grace, 1987 (Gov.'s Collection 1988), Intimate Moments, 1987 (Gov.'s Collection), (art book) Dayspring, 1989; one-person shows include Williams Salon, Atlanta, 1989, 92, 93, 94, 95, 99, 2000, Galerie Timothy Tew, Jenny Pruitt Realty, 1989, Ariel Gallery, Atlanta, 1996, 2002, Revis Lewis Gallery, Greenville, SC, 2002; group shows include Fine Art Mus. of the South, Mobile, Beyond the Wall, 1990, Mus. Archives, Washington, 1992, Internat. Pastel Show, Ga., 1991, 95, Savannah Nat. (1st pl. award in drawing), Telfare Mus. Savannah, 1995, 2000, 02, Telfare Art Fair, Ariel Gallery, 1995-99, Calloway Garden, 1998, Art Forms Exhbn. Cathedral of St. Philips, Atlanta, 2000, 13th, 16th, and 17th Nat. Art Exhbn. South Cobb Alliance, 2000, 02, 03, Ga. Nat. Fair, Perry, (Drawing prize and Merit award); permanent collections represented Greenville Meml. Hosp., S.C., Embassy Suites, Ill., Macan Motor Cars, Ga., Jenny Pruitt Reality, Ga.,Leader Publs. and others; commns. include Landscape, Portraits, family, others; pub. and pvt. collections; author: (art) book Orchard; contbr. poetry to anthologies; request of guest applications of mentorships, Atlanta Coll. Art, High Mus, woodruff Art Complex. Bd. mgr. Greenville Jr. League, 1971-73; artist for fundraiser Rehab. Edn. for Handicapped Adults and Children, Atlanta, 1992-95, vol. artist Arts in the Atlanta Project, 1993, Symphony of Greenville [illegible] 2002. Mem. Nat. League Am. Pen Women (chair art's program 1984-2000, Achievement award 198 7, 89, 93, 94, 95, 96, 97, 98), Atlanta Artist Club (v.p. 1984-85, Merit mem.). Presbyterian. Avocations: travel, reading, outdoor activities, yoga. Home and Office: 2979 Majestic Cir Avondale Estates GA 30002-1611 E-mail: janescapeltd@cs.com.

CARROLL, KAREN COLLEEN, physician, infectious disease educator, medical microbiologist; b. Balt., Nov. 7, 1953; d. Charles Edward and Ida May (Simms) C.; m. Bruce Cameron Marshall, Feb. 13, 1982; children: Kevin Charles Marshall, Brian Thomas Marshall. BA, Coll. Notre Dame of Md., 1975; MD, U. Md., 1979. Diplomate Am. Bd. Internal Medicine, Am. Bd. Infectious Diseases, Am. Bd. Pathology. Intern U. Md., 1979-80, U. Rochester, AHP, 1980-82, chief med. resident in internal medicine, 1982-83; fellow infectious diseases U. Mass., 1984-86; fellow med. microbiology Health Scis. Ctr. U. Utah, 1989-90; asst. prof. pathology U. Utah Med. Ctr., Salt Lake City, 1990-97, adj. asst. prof. infectious diseases, 1990-97, assoc. prof. pathology, adj. assoc. prof. infectious disease, 1997—; dir. microbiology lab. Associated Regional and Univ. Pathologists, Inc., Salt Lake City, 1990—. Contbr. articles to profl. jours. Fellow Am. Acad. Microbiology, Coll. Am. Pathologists; mem. Am. Soc. for Microbiology, Infectious Diseases Soc. Am. Avocations: skiing, hiking, reading. Office: U Utah Med Ctr Dept Pathology 50 N Medical Dr Salt Lake City UT 84132-0001 E-mail: carrolkc@aruplab.com.

CARROLL, KIM MARIE, nurse; b. Ottawa, Ill., Feb. 13, 1958; d. John J. and Charin E. (Reilley) Marmion; m. Thomas Christopher Carroll, Aug. 25, 1979; children: Christopher John, Meaghan Elizabeth, Sean Reilley. BSN, U. Denver, 1983; diploma, Copley Meml. Hosp. Sch. Nursing, Aurora, Ill., 1979. RN, Ill., Ind., Colo., NY, Pa., Calif.; critical care practitioner. Staff nurse Penrose Hosp., Colorado Springs, Colo., 1979-83, asst. head nurse cardiac floor, 1983-84; asst. dir. nurses Big Meadows Nursing Home, Savanna, Ill., 1985-86, dir. nurses, 1986-88; clin. dir. Ind. Heart Physicians, Inc., Beech Grove, Ind., 1989-95; ambulatory care adminstr. The Gates Clinic, Denver, 1995-98; clin. mgr. Aurora Denver Cardiology Assoc., 1998—2002; triage nurse McKesson Health Solutions, Englewood, Colo., 2002—04; clin. mgr. nursing program CC Denver-Ctr. Health Svcs.-Lowry, 2004—. Mem. Beta Sigma Phi (chpt. pres. 1988-89, rec. sec. 1991-92, treas. 1996-97), Sigma Theta Tau. Roman Catholic. Avocation: skiing. Home: 5293 S Cathay Way Centennial CO 80015-4859 Office: Community Coll of Denver Ctr for Health Sciences-Lowry 1070 Alton Way, Bldg #849 Denver CO 80230

CARROLL, LUCY ELLEN, choral director, music coordinator, educator; b. NYC, Oct. 11; d. Edward Joseph and Lucy Sophie (Czapszys) C. B in Music Edn., Temple U., 1968; MA, Trenton State Coll., 1973; D in Musical Arts, Combs Coll. Music, Phila., 1982. Cert. tchr. music, N.J., Pa., Nat. Cert., 1991. Tchr. music Log Coll. Jr. High Sch., Pa., 1968-72, Ind. (Pa.) High Sch., 1972-73, William Tennent High Sch., Warminster, Pa., 1973-98, dir. mus. theater, 1973-98; choir dir. St. John Bosco Parish Choir, 1999—2001; organist, dir. Carmelite Monastery, Phila., 1996—. Music coord. Centennial Schs., 1991-98; founder, dir. Madrigal Singers, Warminster, Pa., 1971-98; choral dir. Cabrini Coll., Radnor, Pa., 1974-77, First Day Singers, Phila., 1979-83, Combs Coll. Music, Phila., 1981-84, 87-88; choral adjudicator various Music festivals, 1973-98; theatre dir., Villa Joseph Marie (Holland), 1998-99; del. Internat. Arts Conf., Cambridge, Eng., 1992; adj. assoc. prof. Westminster Choir Coll., Princeton, 2002—; lectr. in field. Singer (operas Ambler Festival) Street Scene, 1970, Death of Bishop of Brindisi (premiere); (Robin Hood Dell) La Boheme; dir. (jazz theater piece N.Y.C.) Murder of Agamemnon, 1980, (drama) Power of Love (1705), 1986, (outdoor music theater) Vorspiel (Pa. Historic Commn. 1989); editor The Monastery Hymnal, 2002, Music of the Ephrata Cloister, 2003; columnist Polyphony mag., Adoremus Bulletin, 2002—; creator Churchmouse Squeaks cartoons, Monastery Mice cartoons; author The Music of EPHRATA, 2003, The Bastet Worry-Stone and Other Tales, 2004; contbr. articles to profl. jours. and mags. Dir. Monastery Choir, Phila., 2001—. Recipient awards Writers of Future, 1985, 87, Andrew Ferraro award Combs Coll. Music, 1989, plaque for svc. to music Bucks County Commr., 1991, Disting. Citizen medal Southampton Twp., 1994, Harmony award Country Gentlemen Nat. Soc. for Preservation and Encouragement Barbershop Quartet Singing in Am., 1994; Scholar-In-Residence, Pa. Hist. and Museum Commn.; named Humanities Spkr. for 2000, Pa. Humanities Coun. Mem. Am. Choral Dirs. Assn., Sci. Fiction Fantasy Writers of Am., Am. Musicol. Soc., Am. Guild Organists, Organ Hist. Soc., Latin Liturgy Assn., Del. Valley Composers (choral cons. 1988-90), Hist. Soc. Pa., Smithsonian Assocs., Musical Fund Soc. of Phila., The Soc. for Am. Music, Pa. Music Educators Assn. (adv. bd. 1986-87, contbg. writer Spotlight on Tchg. Chorus 2003), Nat. Assn. State Tchrs. of the Yr., Ephrata Cloister Assocs., Sigma Alpha Iota. Republican. Roman Catholic. Avocation: travel. Home: 712 High Ave Hatboro PA 19040-2418 E-mail: LucyCarroll@att.net.

CARROLL, M(ARGARET) LIZBETH CARR, art educator, graphics designer, photographer; b. Washington, Feb. 9, 1936; d. J. Franklin and Dorothy Mae (Colborn) Carr; m. Eugene R. Carroll, Jr., June 2, 1979 (div. May 2000); children: Kyung Soo Kim, Whan Kim. BFA in Studio Art, U. D.C., 1979; MFA in Visual Comm. & Photography, George Washington U., 1984. Visual info. specialist U.S. Fed. Govt., Washington, 1966—84; sr. graphics designer Office of the Comptr. of the Currency, Dept. of the Treasury, Washington, 1984—99; adj. assoc. prof. fine arts U. D.C., Washington, 1989—; adj. prof. lectr. in art George Washington U., Washington, 2001—. Adv. for Native Am. artists/pvt. cons. ArtDirections, Washington, 1994—. Author, photographer: Native Peoples Mag., 1995, Piecework Mag., 1998, Am. Rivers, Pres.'s Coun. Environ. Quality, U.S. Congl. Record, Friends of the Earth, U.S. Nat. Pk. Svc., Nat. Pks. Conservation Assn., Sierra Club, Wilderness Soc. in Support of Conservation and Wilderness Legis.; Represented in permanent collections U.S. Dept. Interior, Grand Canyon Nat. Pk., exhibitions include Gallery 42, U. D.C., 2003, exhibited in group shows at Martin Luther King, Jr. Libr., Washington, 2003, U. D.C., 1976—79, Cath U. Am., 1979; others. Home: 3313 Runnymede Pl NW Washington DC 20015-2415 Office: Univ DC Dept Mass Media Visual & Performing Arts 4200 Connecticut Ave NW Washington DC 20008

CARROLL, MARY PATRICIA, writer; b. Chgo., June 28, 1938; d. Anthony Bernard Carroll and Marie Cecilia Delaney. Student in writing, Columbia Coll., U. Fla.; BS in Humanities magna cum laude, Loyola U., Chgo., 1961, MSW, 1965; DSW, Smith Coll., 1970. Caseworker II Cook County Dept. Pub. Assistance, Chgo., 1961-64; sr. psychiat. social svc. worker Chgo. Bd. Health, Lower North Cmty. Mental Health Ctr., 1964—66; sch. social worker Sch. Dist. #81, Schiller Park, Ill., 1966—68; dist. dir. Family Svc. Assn. Greater Boston, 1970-73; program rep. United Cerebral Palsy Assns., N.Y.C., 1973-75; assoc. prof. George Williams Coll., 1975—77, Ind. U.-Purdue U., Indpls., 1977-81; assoc. prof., chmn. social work dept. U. Alaska, Anchorage, 1981-85; writer Mary P. Caroll Enterprises, 1985—. Contbr. articles, essays, short stories, poems to profl. and lit. publs. Recipient Hon. Mention award for fiction Writers Digest, 1987, for poetry, 1999, 2003; fellow VA Pub. Health, 1963-65, NIMH, 1968-70. Mem. Poetry Soc. of Va., Live Poets Soc., Amnesty Internat., Am. Acad. Poets, Nat. Com. to Preserve Social Security and Medicare. Democrat. Roman Catholic. Avocation: outdoor activities. E-mail: wnm4444@aol.com.

CARROZZA, ANN-MARGARET E. state legislator, lawyer; BS, SUNY, Albany; JD, Hofstra U. Mem. 26th Dist. N.Y. State Assembly, Albany, 1996—, mem. aging com., mem. election law and govtl. employees com., mem. ins. and vets. affairs com.; ct. atty. Civil Cir. Ct. Judge Peter O'Donoghue; clin. intern Queens County Dist. Attys. Office. Advocate for Disabled Am. Vets. Mem. N.Y. State Bar Assn. (elder law com.), Queens County Women's Bar Assn. Office: 33-17 Francis Lewis Blvd Bayside NY 11358

CARRUTHERS, CATHARINE, federal judge; b. 1954; BA, U. N.C., 1975; JD, Wake Forest U., 1980. Bar: N.C. 1980. Assoc. Billings Burns & Wells, Winston-Salem, 1982-84; ptnr. Allman Spry Leggett & Crumpler, Winston-Salem, 1985-95; law clk. to Hon. Rufus W. Reynolds, U.S. Bankruptcy Ct. for Mid. Dist. N.C., Winston-Salem, 1980-81, bankruptcy judge, 1995—. Office: US Bankruptcy Ct 226 S Liberty St Winston Salem NC 27101-5211

CARSEY, MARCIA LEE PETERSON, television producer; b. South Weymouth, Mass., Nov. 21, 1944; d. John Edwin and Rebecca White (Simonds) Peterson; m. John Jay Carsey, Apr. 12, 1969; children: Rebecca Peterson, John Peterson. BA in English Lit., U. N.H., 1966. Exec. story editor Tomorrow Entertainment, L.A., 1971-74; sr. v.p. prime time series ABC-TV, L.A., 1978-81; founder Carsey Prodns., L.A., 1981; co-owner Carsey-Werner Co., 1982—; co-exec. producer TV series Oh Madeline, 1983; exec. producer The Cosby Show, 1984-92, A Different World, 1987-93, Roseanne, 1988-92, Chicken Soup, 1989-90, Grand, 1990, Davis Rules, 1991, You Bet Your Life, 1992-93, Frannie's Turn, 1992, Grace Under Fire, 1993, Cybill, 1995-97, 3rd Rock From The Sun, 1996—, Cosby, 1996—, Men Behaving Badly, 1996-97, Townies, 1996. Office: Carsey-Werner Prodns 4024 Radford Ave Bldg 3 Studio City CA 91604-2101

CARSON, CYNTHIA LEE, physician's assistant; b. Pitts., Oct. 10, 1956; d. Charles Raymond and Mary Arlene (Parry) C. B.Med. Sci. summa cum laude, Alderson Broaddus Coll., 1978. Cert. physician's asst., Conn. Physician's asst. surg. resident Norwalk Hosp./Yale U., 1978-79, clin. coord./instr., 1995-98; staff physician's asst. in surgery Norwalk (Conn.) Hosp., 1978-98; physician asst. in plastic and reconstructive surgery Kaiser Permanente, San Diego, 1998—. Staff physician asst. rep. operating rm. com. Hahnemann U. Physician Asst. Program, 1984-98, clin. asst. instr., 1981-98; adj. asst. prof. health care scis. George Washington U., 1991-98. Contbr. articles to profl. jours. Recipient Yoichi Katsube Meml. award Pa. Surg. Residency, 1979, Frank J. Scallon Med. Writing award, 1984, 86. Mem. Am. Acad. Physician's Assts., Conn. Acad. Physician's Assts. Avocations: biking, cross-country skiing, hiking, stamp collecting, sailing. Home: 3043 W Canyon Ave San Diego CA 92123-5422 Office: Kaiser Permanente Dept Plastic and Reconstructive Surgery 3250 Fordham St San Diego CA 92110-5397

CARSON, DORA A. secondary school educator; b. Dayton, Ohio, Nov. 3, 1945; d. Neely C. and Mary A. (Whitelow) Sampson; m. Alfred N. Carson, Mar. 18, 1967; 1 child, Tyra Lynne. BS, Wright State U., 1972, MS, 1978. English tchr., curriculum specialist Meadowdale High Sch., Dayton, Ohio, 1969-95; asst. prin. Colonel White H.S. for the Arts, Dayton, 1995—. NFL Teacher of the Year, 1992. Mem. Dayton Edn. Assn., Ohio Edn. Assn., NEA, NCTE. Home: 1733 Sunnyview Ave Dayton OH 45406-1927 Office: Colonel White HS for the Arts 501 Niagara Ave Dayton OH 45405-3743

CARSON, JANINE MARIE, marketing professional; b. Denver, May 14, 1979; d. Clarence Jackson Carson and Lucy Ann Barros. BA in Comm., U. Colo., Denver, 2001; Spanish Certification, Universitas Castellae, Valladolid, Spain, 2001. Comm. and mktg. coord. Am. Water Works Assn., Denver, 2000; pub. rels. intern Sun Microsystems, Broomfield, Colo., 2000—01; mktg. specialist Vectra Bank Colo., Denver, 2002—. Mem.: Am. Mktg. Assn. (v.p. internal comm. 2002—03, bd. dirs. Colo. chpt. 2002—03), Golden Key Nat. Honor Soc., Alpha Kappa Alpha Sorority, Inc (grad. advisor Epsilon Nu Omega chpt. 2002—03). Office: Vectra Bank Colorado 2000 S Colorado Blvd Ste 2-1200 Denver CO 80222

CARSON, JULIA M. congresswoman; b. Louisville, July 8, 1938; 2 children. Ed., Ind. U., 1960-62, St. Mary of the Woods, 1976-78. Mem. Ind. Ho. of Reps., Indpls., 1972-76, Ind. Senate, 1976-90, U.S. Congress from 7th Ind. dist. (formerly 10th), 1997—. Mem. fin. svcs. com., 1997—, Vets. Affairs com., 1997—. V.p. Greater Indpls. Prog. Com.; nat. Dem. committeewoman; trustee YMCA; bd. didrs. Pub. Svc. Acad. Recipient Woman of Yr. Ind. award, 1974, Outstanding Leadership award AKA, Humanitarian award Christian Theol. Sem. Mem. NAACP, Urban League, Nat. Coun. Negro Women. Democrat. Baptist. Office: 1535 Longworth HOB Washington DC 20515-1410*

CARSON, MARGARET, human services administrator; d. Chief and Lena Mae Carson. Cert. dietian cooking Vigo County Health Dept., Ind., nurses tng. Vigo County Health Dept., Ind., CPR Vigo County Health Dept., Ind., home health Vigo County Health Dept., Ind.; RN Vigo County Sch. of Nursing, 1965. Home health nurse numerous; organizer variuos cmty. svc. projects with the sole purpose of ending hunger and poverty. Mem. regional bd. Los Angeles County Food Bank, Calif., 1998—2003; music dir., mem. choir 54th St. Seventh Day Adventist Ch., L.A., 1999—2002, dir. cmty. svcs. program. Recipient Cmty. Services Dir. of the Yr., L.A. City Cmty. Svc. Dept., 2001, Excellence in Serving Your Cmty., L.A. City Mayor's Office, 2002. Democrat. Seventh-Day. Avocations: serving her community, singing, fundrasing, interior decorating, catering for the less fortunate. Office: SDA Ch Cmty Svcs 1973 W 54th Street Los Angeles CA 90062-2610 Office Phone: 323-292-2762. Business E-Mail: office@54thstreetsda.org.

CARSON, MARLENE ANN, artist; d. Casper S. and Ruth S. Cramer; m. James W. Carson, Mar. 17, 1963; 1 child, Christine Marie Willson. BS, Ill. State U., 1960—63. Cert. Tchr. Ill., 1963. Co-owner Creative Stained Glass Studio, Steamboat Springs, Colo., 1983—87; owner Stained Glass Treasures, Chadron, Nebr., 1987—90, Inspirations In Glass, Delta, Colo., 1990—. Cons. Inspirations In Glass, Delta, Colo., 1990—. Stained glass restoration, Historical Restoration (Colo. Preservation Inc, Statewide Honor award, 1996). Chmn. City of Delta Pub. Arts Com., Delta, Colo., 1998—2001; mem. City of Delta Mural Com., Delta, Colo., 1998—2003; pres. The Juniper Tree, Delta, Colo., 1991—92; sec. Bd. of Trustees, Delta United Meth. Ch., Delta, Colo., 1994—2003; chair Stained Glass Restoration Com., Delta, Colo., 1993—96. Mem.: Stained Glass Assoc of Am., Partners for Sacred Places. Home: 521 Cypress Wood Lane Delta CO 81416 Personal E-mail: jcarson940@aol.com.

CARSON, MARY SMITH, marketing and communications consultant; b. Evansville, Ind., Oct. 15, 1939; d. Richard and Edith (Miller) Smith; m. Roger Warren Carson, Feb. 1, 1958; children: John Brett, Richard Charles, Cheryl Lee. BA, Mary Washington Coll., 1971; MBA, Marymount U., 1990. Dir. United Way, Fredericksburg, Va., 1971-75; dir. alumni Mary Washington Coll., Fredericksburg, Va., 1976-81; assoc. dir. Am. Gas Assn., Arlington, Va., 1981-94; v.p. WE & Assocs., Ltd., Arlington, Va., 1995—2000, Roger Carson Enterprises, 2000—. V.p. WE & Assocs., Ltd.; program dir. Vent-Free Gas Products Alliance GAMA, 1995—/ Small bus. coord. Bob Dole for Pres., Washington, 1988; ethnic campaign coord. Reagan for Pres., Washington, 1979, head Washington office, 1980; bd. dirs. Habitat for Humanity Women's Guild, 2003—. Inducted into Hall of Honor Am. Gas Assn., 1993; recipient Alumni Appreciation award Marymount U., 2002. Mem. Nat. Coun. Housing Industry (co-chair 1994), Marymount U. Alumni Assn. (bd. dirs. 1993—). Republican. Roman Catholic. Avocations: reading, skiing, scuba, swimming, decorating. Home: 8225 Madrillon Estates Dr Vienna VA 22182-3778 Office: WE & Assocs Ltd 2107 Wilson Blvd Ste 800 Arlington VA 22201-3052

CARSON, REGINA E. healthcare administrator, geriatric specialist, pharmacist, educator; b. Washington; BS in Pharmacy, Howard U.; MBA in Mktg., MBA in Health Care Adminstrn., Loyola Coll., Balt., 1987. Asst. prof., asst. dir. pharmacy U. Md., Balt., 1986-88; asst. prof., coord. profl. practice Howard U., Washington, 1988-95; prin. Marrell Cons., Randallstown, Md., prin., mng. ptnr., 1993—; exec. dir. Sunrise Assisted Living, Fairfax, Va., 1997-99. Drug utilization rev. cons. Md. Pharmacy Assn., Balt., 1986—90; cons. pharmacist Baltimore county Adv. Coun. Drug Abuse, Towson, Md., 1984—86; edn. cons. ADWHE, Accra, Ghana, 1999; program evaluator Train Pharm., UMF-Cluj, Romania, 1999—2002. Bd. dirs. N.W. Hosp. Ctr. Aux., Randallstown, Joshua Johnson Coun., Balt. Mus. Art, Alzheimers Assn. Ctrl. Md.; trustee C.C. of Baltimore County, 1997—. Named Outstanding Alumni, Howard U. Coll. Pharmacy, 1992; recipient Gregor T. Popa medal, UMF-Iasi, Romania, 2000. Fellow: Am. Soc. Cons. Pharmacists; mem.: Nat. Assn. Retail Druggists (adv. com., long-term care com.), Nat. Pharm. Assn. (life, Outstanding Women in Pharmacy 1984), Am. Assn. Colls. Pharmacy, Nat. Assn. Health Svc. Execs. Avocations: pharmacognosy, gardening, American art.

CARSTAIRS, SHARON, legislator; b. Halifax, N.S., Can., Apr. 26, 1942; d. Vivian and Harold Connolly; m. John Esdale Carstairs, 1966; children: Catherine, Jennifer. BA in Polit. Sci. and History, Dalhousie U., 1962; MA in Tchg. of History, Smith Coll., 1963; postgrad., Georgetown U., 1964, U. Calgary, 1968; LLD (hon.), Brandon U., 2003. Tchr. Dana Hall Sch. for Girls, Wellesley, Mass., 1963-65, Calgary (Alta.) Separate Sch. Bd., 1965-71; chmn. bd. referees Unemployment Ins. Commn., 1973-77; tchr. St. John's Ravenscourt Sch., Winnipeg, Man., 1978-81, St. Norbert (Man.) Collegiate, 1982-84; elected leader Liberal Party in Man., 1984; elected mem. Man. Legis. Assembly, River Heights, 1986—, elected leader Ofcl. Opposition, 1988-90; apptd. to Senate, 1994—; apptd. dep. leader of the govt. in the Senate, 1997-99; leader of the govt. in the Senate, 2001—03; minister with spl. responsibility for palliative care, 2001—03. Scriptwriter, narrator Calgary and Region Ednl. TV, 1967-69. Brownie leader, Halifax and Winnipeg; mem. Parks and Recreation Bd., City of Calgary; fund-raiser Manitoba Heart Found.; canvasser Can. Cancer Soc., Alta., Man., Alta. Soc. for the Mentally Retarded; vol. Man. Mus. of Man and Nature; bd. mem. Women and the Arts, Nursing Coun. Man.; campaign worker provincial elections, Nova Scotia, 1948, 52, 56, 60; exec. positions Dalhousie U. Liberal Club, Nova Scotia, 1958-62; nat. exec. Univ. Liberals, Nova Scotia, 1960-62, others; poll capt. Fed. elections, Alta. 1965, 68, 72, 74; exec. Alta. Women's Liberal Assn., 1965-68; sec. Liberal Party, Alta., 1968-70, v.p., 1972-74, pres., 1975-77, nat. exec. 1975-77; Calgary Regional v.p., Liberal Party Alta., 1970-72; mem. Fed. Campaign com., Alta. 1972, 74, Man. 1983—; candidate Provincial Liberal, Alta. 1975; poll worker Ft. Rouge Provincial constituency, Man., 1977, Ft. Garry Fed. constituency, Man., 1979-80; office mgr, Tuxedo Provincial constituency, Man., 1981; exec., River Heights Provincial constituency, Man., 1983—; mem. Man. Legislative Assembly 1986—; elected leader Official Opposition, Man., 1988-90. Recipient Dalhousie U. Entrance scholarship, Dalhousie U. scholarship, Smith Coll. Grad. fellowship. Mem. Winnipeg C. of C. Liberal Party Can.

CARSTEN, ARLENE DESMET, financial executive; b. Paterson, N.J., Dec. 3, 1937; d. Albert F. and Ann (Greutert) Desmet; m. Alfred John Carsten, Feb. 11, 1956; children: Christopher Dale, Jonathan Glenn. Student, Alfred U., 1955-56. Exec. dir. Inst. Burn Medicine, San Diego, 1972-81, adv. bd. mem., 1981-92; founding trustee Nat. Burn Fedn., 1975-83; CFO A.J. Carsten Co., Inc., San Diego, 1981-91, Powell River, Canada, 1992-97, dir., cons., 1997—2003; CFO A.J. Carsten Co., Ltd., Powell River, Canada. Pres. Raven View Holdings, Ltd. Contbr. articles to profl. jours. Organizer, mem. numerous cmty. groups; chmn. San Diego County Mental Health Adv. Bd., 1972-74, mem., 1971-75; chmn. cmty. rels. subcom., mem. exec. com. Emergency Med. Care Com., San Diego, Riverside and Imperial Counties, 1973-75; pub. mem. psychology exam. com. Calif. State Bd. Med. Quality Assurance, 1976-80, chmn., 1977; mem. rep. to Health Svcs. Agy. San Diego County Govt., 1980; mem. Calif. Dem. Ctrl. Com., 1968-74, exec. com., 1971-72, 73-74; treas. San Diego Dem. County Ctrl. Com., 1972-74; chmn. edn. legis. com. women's divsn. So. Calif. Dem. Com., 1972; dir. Muskie for Pres. Campaign, San Diego, 1972; organizer, dir. numerous local campaigns; chair Rep. for Casady for Mayor San Diego, 1981; councilwoman City of Del Mar, Calif., 1982-86, mayor, 1985-86; bd. dirs. Gentry-Watts Planned Indsl. Devel. Assn., 1986-90, pres., 1987-90; v.p. Okeover Rate Payers Assn., 1996-97, pres., 1997-2003, bd. dirs., 1996—; sec. Powell River Hosp. Found. Millenium Celebration Com., 1998-99; chair Alliance for Responsible Shellfish Farming, 2000—; mem. adv. bd. Malaspina Complex Integrated Action Plan, 2002—; commencement spkr. Alfred U., 1984. Recipient Key Woman award Dem. Party, 1968, 72, 1st Ann. Cmty. award Belles for Mental Health, Mental Health Assn., San Diego, 1974, citation Alfred U. Alumni Assn., 1979. Home: RR 2 Malaspina Rd C-68 Powell River BC Canada V8A 4Z3

CARSTENS, JANE ELLEN, retired library science educator; b. New Iberia, La., Apr. 19, 1922; d. Charles John and Marie Claudia (Blanchet) C. BA in Elem. Edn., U. Southwestern La., 1942; BS in LS, La. State U., 1945; MS in LS, Columbia U., 1955, DLS, 1975. Asst. libr. Hamilton Lab. sch. and instr. libr. sci. U. Southwestern La., Lafayette, 1942-54, asst. prof., 1954-65, assoc. prof., 1965-75; children's librarian/storyteller N.Y. Pub. Libr., N.Y.C., 1947, 48-49; vis. lectr. U. Minn., Mpls., 1955-56, summer 59, La. State U., Baton Rouge, summer 1958, State Coll. Iowa, Cedar Falls, summer 1963; prof. libr. sci. U. Southwestern La., Lafayette, 1975-94. Vis. lectr. Syracuse U., summers 1962, 64, U. Tex., Austin, summers 1976-86, 89. Trustee Our Lady of Wisdom Cath. Ch., 1995-2004. Named Tchr. of Yr., Amoco, 1982, Outstanding Alumna, U. Southwestern La., 1986; recipient Essae Culver Disting. Svc. award La. Libr. Assn., 1987, Alumni Faculty Excellence award Blue Key, 1990, Faculty Advisor of Yr. award U. Southwestern La. Student Govt. Assn., 1992, Point of Excellence award Kappa Delta Pi, 1992, Outstanding Tchr. award USL Found., 1994; Blue Key Faculty/Student Staff Directory dedicated to her, 1994-95. Mem. ALA, Assn. Libr. and Info. Sci. Edn., Assn. Libr. Svc. to Children (mem. Newbery award com. 1989-90), Am. Assn. Sch. Librs., La. Libr. Assn. (pres. 1959-60), Young Adult Libr. Svc. Assn., Lafayette Pub. Libr. Found., Univ. Women's Club, Phi Kappa Phi (pres. USL chpt. 1984-85), Delta Kappa Gamma (pres. Alpha chpt. 1988-90). Roman Catholic. Home: 214 Saint Joseph St Lafayette LA 70506-4535 also: ULL La Lafayette PO Box 40298 Lafayette LA 70504-0001

CARSTENSEN, LAURA LEE, gerontology educator; b. Phila., Nov. 2, 1953; d. Edwin Lorenz Carstensen and Pam. McDonald; m. Ian H. Gotlib, Aug. 27, 1995; 1 child, David Joseph Pagano. BS, U. Rochester, 1978; MA, W.Va. U., 1980, PhD, 1983. Asst. prof. Ind. U., Bloomington, 1983-87, Stanford (Calif.) U., 1987-94, assoc. prof., 1995—. Sci. cons. Max Planck Inst. Human Devel. & Edn., Berlin, 1992—; assoc. dir. Terman gifted project Stanford U., 1994—. Author book chpt.; co-author Psychology: The Study of Human Experience, 1991; co-editor: Handbook of Clinical Gerontology, 1987. Recipient First Investigator award Nat. Inst. Aging, 1987. Fellow Gerontol. Soc. Am. (mem.-at-large 1994—, Kalish Innovative Publication award 1993); mem. APA, Am. Psychol. Soc. Office: Stanford U Dept Psychology Bldg 420 Jordan Hall Stanford CA 94305-2130

CARSWELL, JANE TRIPLETT, retired family physician; b. Raeford, N.C., Feb. 26, 1932; d. Arthur Dula and Madeline Mapp (Warburton) C. Student, Flora Macdonald Coll., 1950-52; AB in Chemistry, U. N.C., 1954; MD, Med. Coll. Va., 1958. Diplomate Am. Bd. Family Practice. Resident Med. Coll. Va., Richmond, 1958-61; practice medicine specializing in family medicine Harlan, Ky., 1961-62, Lenoir, N.C., 1962—. Chmn. Lenoir Human Relations Com., N.C., 1962-64; vice-chmn. Caldwell County Council Status of Women, Lenoir, 1976-78 Mem. Caldwell County Med. Soc. (pres. 1965), N.C. Acad. Family Physicians (N.C. Family Physician of Yr. award 1983), N.C. Med. Soc., Am. Acad. Family Practice (Nat. Family Dr. of Yr. award 1984) Presbyterian. Avocations: wildflowers; hiking; backpacking; skiing; photography.

CARSWELL, LOIS MALAKOFF, botanical gardens executive, consultant; b. N.Y.C., Mar. 2, 1932; d. Arthur and Dora (Krechevsky) Malakoff; m. Donald Carswell, Oct. 12, 1957; children: Anne Carswell Tang, Alexander, Robert Ian. AB magna cum laude, Radcliffe Coll., 1953; cert. in bus. adminstrn., Harvard U. and Radcliffe Coll., 1954. Editor Dell Pub. Co., N.Y.C., 1954-56; publicist Ruth E. Pepper Co., N.Y.C., 1957-58; vol. Bklyn. Botanic Garden, 1964—, co-chmn. plant sales, 1967—, co-chmn. capital campaign, 1984-88, chmn. bd. dirs., 1989-98, chmn. emeritus, 1998—. Chmn. Coalition Living Mus. N.Y. State, N.Y.C., 1980—; cons. N.Y. State Natural Heritage Trust, 1982—. Office: Bklyn Botanic Garden 1000 Washington Ave Brooklyn NY 11225-1008 Office Phone: 718-623-7225. E-mail: loiscarswell@bbg.org.

CARTAINO, CAROL ANN, editor; b. N.Y.C., Dec. 7, 1944; d. Pietro Michael and Ann Wanda (Scotch) C.; 1 child, Clayton Collier-Cartaino. BA, Rutgers U., 1966; postgrad., NYU, 1967-68. Cert. English tchr., N.J. Prodn. editor trade book Prentice-Hall, Inc., Englewood Cliffs, N.J., 1966-68, from asst. to assoc. editor trade book, 1968-72, edit. trade book, 1972-77; editor-in-chief Writer's Digest Books, Cin., 1978-86, freelance editor and collaborator, 1986—; editl. dir. Don Aslett, Inc., Pocatello, Idaho, 1987-93, Marsh Creek Press, Pocatello, Idaho, 1993—; assoc. Collier Assoc. Literary Agy., Seaman, Ohio, 1987-94; proprietor freelance editing and book cons. svc. White Oak Edits., 1987—; proprietor Carol Cartaino, Lit. Agt., 1994—. Speaker in field; instr. in writing So. State C.C., Hillsboro and Wilmington, Ohio, 1989—. Author: Keeping Work Simple, 1997, Get Organized, Get Published!, 2001. Vol. nurses aide Hackensack (N.J.) Hosp. State of N.J. scholar, 1962-66, Emerson (N.J.) PTA scholar, 1962. Roman Catholic. Avocations: hiking, photography, gardening, nature study. Home and Office: 2000 Flat Run Rd Seaman OH 45679-9412 E-mail: cartaino@aol.com.

CARTER, ANNA DEAN, volunteer; b. Lafayette, Tenn., June 21, 1935; d. Virgil Heston and Elsie Irene (Law) King; m. Billy Wilson Carter, Nov. 3, 1954; children: Billy Jr., Gerald, Debra. Grad. high sch., Lafayette, Tenn. Waitress Walgreen Drug, Lafayette, Tenn., 1951-54; factory Formfit Rogers, Lafayette, Tenn., 1955-56; substitute tchr. Macon County Schs., Lafayette, Tenn., 1958-59; factory True Loom Mfg. Co., Lafayette, Tenn., 1959-67; sch. sec. Macon County Schs., Lafayette, Tenn., 1968; bookkeeper Macon-Trousdale Coop., Lafayette, Tenn., 1968-98; retired, 1998. County commn. Macon County Govt., 1990—; E911 bd. dirs. Macon County, 1994—; mem. Tenn. Rural Health, Cookeville, 1998; sec. Macon County Health Coun., 1996—2001; v.p. Upper Culberland Health, 1998—2000, mem. Macon County Fair Bd., 1996—; active Macon County Job Svc., 1997—2002; mem. Macon Edn. Found., 1997—; bd. dirs. Tenn. Families First, 1998—, Cordell Hull Echomanic Opportunity Cooperation, 1998—2003. Named to, Board-Macon County Sports Hall of Fame, 2000. Mem.: Am. Assn. Retired People, Macon Sch. Health Advisory Bd., Macon County C. of C. (bd. dirs. 1998—2001, pres. 1999—2000), Sr. Citizens Orgn. (bd. dirs. 1999—), Historic Preservation Soc. (pres. 1996—). Baptist. Avocations: reading, needlework, photography, writing, walking. Home: 209 Donoho Ave Lafayette TN 37083-1404 E-mail: adcarter@nctc.com.

CARTER, ANNETTE WHEELER, state legislator; b. May 24, 1941; divorced. Grad., Ala. State Coll. Mem. Conn. Ho. of Reps., Hartford, 1988—, mem. pub. safety, cmty. and exportation coms., vice chmn. appropriations com., asst. majority leader, mem. black caucus; housing advisor Capitol Region Conf. Chs. Recipient Outstanding Accomplishments award Hope SDA Ch., 1990, Crispus A. Tucks award, 1991, Conn. State Black Dem. award, 1992. Mem. NAACP (award 1993), Greater Hartford Black Dem. Club. Democrat. Episcopalian. Home: 207 Branford St Hartford CT 06112-1406 Office: Conn Ho of Reps Legislative Office Bldg Hartford CT 06106

CARTER, BARBARA DALE, pianist, piano teacher, clinical counselor; b. Boulder, Colo., Jan. 15, 1932; m. Frank Pierce Carter, Aug. 25, 1952; children: Frank Pierce Jr., Roseann Marie, Michael Gene. AA, Stephens Coll., 1952, BA, 1989; MA, Washington U., 1995, postgrad., 1993—. Nat. cert. in piano, theory, music therapy. Performer concerts and piano presentations, 1936-99; ind. piano tchr., 1948-99. Participant Van Cliburn Piano Competition, 1984; owner pvt. counseling svc., 1990-99. Den mother coach Boy Scouts Am., 1958; mem. Calif. bd. Campfire Girls Am., 1968; pres. Children's Theatre, Savannah, Ga., 1963; dir. Mental Health Assn., Savannah, 1964-65, Mental Health Assn., San Bernardino, Calif., 1969; creator Design for Living program. Recipient Most Outstanding Air Force Wife cert. Hunter AFB, 1966. Mem. Nat. Music Tchrs. Assn., Am. Assn. Women Deans, Am. Pen Women (poetry awards 1984), Ill. State Music Tchrs. Assn. (chair music therapy 1980-81, mem. state bd. certification 1981), Metro-East Music Tchrs. Assn. (pres. 1979-81). Avocations: raising old english sheepdogs, collectibles, fashion. E-mail: fpcarter3@netscape.net.

CARTER, BARBARA POSSIS, elementary school educator; b. St. Paul, Oct. 29, 1951; d. Thomas Stanley Possis and Lillian Romaine Franke; m. John Michael Carter, Mar. 7, 1998. BS, U. Minn., 1973. Cert. elem. edn. 3d & 4th grade tchr. Buffalo (Minn.) Sch. Dist., 1973—75, 1st grade tchr., 1975—. Recipient Tchg. award, Asland Oil, 1994. Mem.: Social Studies Com., Am. Fedn. Tchrs. Home: 7995 Everest Ln N Maple Grove MN 55311 Office: Tatanka Elem Sch 703 8th St NE Buffalo MN 55313 Office Phone: 763-682-8609.

CARTER, BETSY L. magazine editor; b. N.Y.C., June 9, 1945; d. Rudy and Gerda Cohn; m. Gary Hoenig. BA, U. Mich., 1967. Editorial asst. McGraw Hill, 1967—68; editor co. mag. Am. Security and Trust Co., 1968—69; editorial asst. Atlantic Monthly, 1969—70; researcher Newsweek, N.Y.C., 1971—73, asst. editor, 1973—75, assoc. editor, 1975—80; sr. editor Esquire Mag., N.Y.C., 1980—81, exec. editor, 1981—82, sr. exec. editor, 1982—83, editorial dir., 1983—85; creator, editor-in-chief New York Woman, N.Y.C., 1988; now editor-in-chief New Woman mag., N.Y.C. Freelance contbr. to Atlantic, Washington Post, Family Weekly, Glamour, Food and Wine. Bd. dirs. Nat. Alliance of Breast Cancer Orgns. Mem.: Am. Soc. Mag. Editors (exec. com. 1988—91, v.p. 1997—).

CARTER, CAROLYN HOUCHIN, advertising agency executive; b. Louisville, Nov. 2, 1952; d. Paul Clayton and Georgia (Houchin) C.; m. Jeffrey Starr, Dec. 8, 1988. BS in Journalism, Northwestern U., 1974, MS in Journalism, 1975. Asst. account exec. SSC&B Advt., Inc., N.Y.C., 1975-76, account exec., 1976-77, Grey Advt., Inc., N.Y.C., 1977-79, account supr., 1979-82, v.p., 1981-82, v.p., mgmt. supr., 1982-87, v.p., group mgmt. supr., 1985-87, sr. v.p., 1987-92, exec. v.p., 1992—2000; pres. Grey Worldwide Europe, Mid. East and Africa, 2000—02, Grey Global Group Europe, Mid. East, Africa, 2002—. Mem. Nat. Advt. Rev. Bd., 1983-87; mem. adv. bd. advt. history Smithsonian Nat. Mus. Am. History, 1988-94. Chmn. media advt. coun. March of Dimes, 1981-86; mem. U.S. coun. World Comm. Yr., 1983; active YMCA Acad. Women Achievers, 1992. Recipient Clairol Mentor award Clairol, Inc., 1991. Mem. Women in Comm. (pres. N.Y. chpt. 1982-83, N.Y. Matrix award in advt. 1988, Nat. Headliner award 1991), Internat. Women's Forum (bd. dirs. N.Y. chpt. 1994), Advt. Women N.Y. (bd. dirs. 1987-88). Office: Grey Global Group 777 3d Ave New York NY 10017-1401

CARTER, CATHERINE LOUISE, elementary school educator; b. Oakland, Calif., Mar. 31, 1947; d. Robert Collidge and Mae (Riedy) C. BA, Ohio Wesleyan U., 1969. Tchr. Barclay Elem. Sch., Cherry Hill, N.J., 1969-72, Malberg Elem. Sch., Cherry Hill, 1972-80, Beck Mid. Sch., Cherry Hill, 1980-89, 94-95, Carusi Jr. H.S., Cherry Hill, 1989—94, 1995—2002. Coord. Nat. Women's History [illegible] Cherry Hill Jr. Schs., 1993-2002. Advisor Mother Earth and Friends Environ. Club, 1989-2000; mem. dist. Recycling Program Cherry Hill Pub. Schs., 1990-94, Womyn and Religion Unitarian Universalist Ch. Cherry Hill, Nat. Women's History Mus., Nat. Mus. Women Arts, Women's Philharm.; sponser Childreach. Mem. Nat. Ret. Tchr. Educators Assn., N.J. Ret. Tchr. Edn. Assn., Camden County Ret. Tchr. Edn. Assn., Cherry Hill Ret. Tchr. Edn. Assn., NOW, World Wildlife Fedn., Global Fund for Women, Planned Parenthood, Alice Paul Centenial Found., Seeking Edn. Equity and Diversity (study group 1994), Freedom from Hunger, Population Comms. Internat. Avocations: foreign travel, foreign films, arts, nature, jazz. Home: 10 Brookwood Dr Voorhees NJ 08043-4757

CARTER, CHARLENE ANN, psychologist; b. Marshall, Mich., Apr. 7, 1941; d. Charles V. F. and Eva L. (Hesling) Hampton.; m. Ross E. Carter, Jan. 15, 1966; children: Laura, Paul. BA in Psychology and Sociology, Albion Coll., 1962; MA in Clin. Psychology, Mich. State U., 1964, PhD in Clin. Psychology, 1968. Lic. psychologist, Wis. Clin. intern VA Hosp., Battle Creek, Mich., 1963-65, Psychol. Clinic, Mich. State U., East Lansing, 1965-66, Counseling Ctr., Mich. State U., East Lansing, 1966-68, asst. prof., 1968-69; clin. assoc. prof. dept. psychiatry and mental health sci. Med. Coll. Wis., Milw., 1983—; clin. asst. prof. dept. psychology U. Wis., Milw., 1993—; pvt. practice Bangor, Maine, 1971, Media, Pa., 1974-75, Milw., 1988—. Dir. clin. tng. Wis. Sch. for Girls, Oregon, Wis., 1969—70; staff psychologist The Counseling Ctr., Cmty. Mental Health Ctr., Bangor, Maine, 1971; mem. staff Aurora Psychiat. Hosp., 1989—, Waukesha Meml. Hosp., Waukesha, Wis., 1992—, Rogers Hosp., 2001—; psychologist cons. Office of Hearing and Appeals, Social Security Adminstrn., Milw., 1986—91; lectr. in field. Contbr. articles to profl. jours. USPHS fellow, 1962, 65, 66. Mem. APA. Office: Mayfair North Tower 2600 N Mayfair Rd Ste 320 Milwaukee WI 53226-1313

CARTER, DIXIE, actress; b. McLemoresville, Tenn. m. Hal Holbrook, May 27, 1984. Student, U. Tenn., Southwestern U., Memphis; B in English, Memphis State U. Actress: The Winter's Tale, Oklahoma!, Kiss Me Kate, Carousel, The King and I; broadway: Sextet, 1974, Pal Joey, 1976, The Master Class, 1997, Thoroughly Modern Millie, 2004; off broadway Fathers and Sons, (Drama Desk nomination), Jesse and the Bandit Queen (Theatre World award), A Coupla White Chicks Sitting Around Talking, Buried Inside Extra (TV series) One Life to Live, 1974, The Edge of Night, 1974-76, On Our Own, 1977-78, Out of the Blue, 1979, Filthy Rich, 1982-83, Diff'rent Strokes, 1984-85, Designing Women, 1986-93, Ladies Man, 1999, Family Law, 1999-2002; (films) The Killing of Randy Webster, (TV films) Gambler V: Playing for Keeps, 1994, Dazzle, 1994, Judith Krantz's Dazzle, 1995, Gone in the Night, 1996, Comfort and Joy, 2003; (instructional video) Dixie Carter's Unworkout, 1993; author: Trying to get to Heaven: Opinions of a Tennessee Talker, 1996. Avocations: family, singing. Office: ICM c/o Sam Cohen 8942 Wilshire Blvd Beverly Hills CA 90211-1934*

CARTER, EDITH HOUSTON, statistician, educator; b. Charlotte, N.C., Oct. 12, 1936; d. Z. and Ellie (Hartsell) Houston; m. Fletcher F. Carter, Apr. 2, 1961. BS, Appalachian State U., 1959, MA, 1960; PhD, Va. Poly. Inst. and State U., 1976. Transcript analyst Fla. Dept. Edn., Tallahassee, 1961-65; instr. Radford U., 1969-70, 91-94, asst. prof., 1994—. Prof. New River C.C., Dublin, Va., 1970-83, dir. instl. research, 1974-78, asst. dean Coll. Arts and Scis., 1978-79, statistician, 1979-83. Editor Community Coll. Jour. Research and Planning, 1981-93, Am. Assn. Community Colls. Jour. (rsch. review editor 1991-95), Newsletter Southeastern Assn. C.C. Research, 1972—; mem. editorial bd. C.C. Rev., 1990-93. Violist New River Valley Symphony, Va. Poly. Inst. and State U. Orch., Radford U. Orch., S.W. Va. Opera Soc. Orch., summer mus. Enterprise ORch., 1999—; sec./treas. Radford New River Valley chpt. Am. Sewing Guild, 1991-94, pres., 1994-96. Mem. Am. Ednl. Rsch. Assn., State and Regional Ednl. Rsch. Assn. (sec./treas. 1989-93, pres. 1993-95, svc. chmn. 1995-97, database chair 2003—, Leadership award 1995, 2002-03), Assn. Instl. Rsch. (exec. bd. 1976-78), Southeastern Assn. C.C. Rsch. (exec. bd. 1976-78, Outstanding Svc. award, Disting. Svc. award 1981, Edith Carter Svc. award 1998), Nat. Coun. Rsch. and Planning (Outstanding Svc. award 1992, James R. Montgomery Svc. award, 2001), Coll. Music Soc., Am. String Tchrs. Assn., Va. Ednl. Rsch. Assn. (pres. 1997, corr. sec. 2002-04), Va. Fedn. Women's Clubs (dir. 1968-70), Va. Tech. U. Alumni (pres. New River Valley chpt. 1982-83), So. Assn. for Instnl. Rsch., Radford Jr. Woman's Club (pres. 1967-68), Phi Delta Kappa (pres. New River Valley chpt. 1997-99, newsletter editor, 2003-04). Presbyterian. Home: 6924 Radford Univ Radford VA 24142 Office: Radford U Peters Hall Radford VA 24142 E-mail: ecarter@radford.edu.

CARTER, ELEANOR ELIZABETH, business manager; b. Durham, N.C., July 16, 1954; d. Joseph William Jr. and Sheila Dale (Swartz) C. BS in Social Work, N.C. State U., 1977. Field worker family planning Wake County Health Dept., Raleigh, N.C., 1975-76; sales rep. Bristol-Myers Products, N.C., 1977-80, regional adminstn. asst., 1980, regional trainer Washington, N.C., Va., 1980, sales adminstrn. mgr. corp. hdqrs. N.Y.C., 1980-81, dist. supr. Cin., 1981-82; account rep. Fuji Photo Film U.S.A., Inc., Cin., 1982-83, spl. account mgr. Chgo., 1983-90; nat. account mgr. Fuji Photo Film U.S.A., Itasca, Ill., 1991-97, v.p. nat. accounts, 1997—. Mem. NAFE, Alpha Kappa Delta. Presbyterian. Avocations: jogging, horseback riding, travel, dance. Office: 850 Central Ave Hanover Park IL 60133-5422 Office Phone: 800-869-8600 x5807. Business E-Mail: lcarter@fujifilm.com.

CARTER, EMILY ANN, physical chemist, researcher, educator; b. Los Gatos, Calif., Nov. 28, 1960; d. David and Rebecca (Blumberg) C.; m. Bruce E. Koel, 1994; 1 child, Adam. BS in Chemistry, U. Calif., Berkeley, 1982; PhD in Chemistry, Calif. Inst. Tech., 1987. Postdoctoral rsch. assoc. U. Colo., Boulder, 1987-88; asst. prof., physical chemistry UCLA, 1988-92, assoc. prof., 1992-94, prof., 1994—2002, prof. chemistry and materials sci. and engring., 2002—. Mem. Def. Sci. Study Group, 1996-97; vis. scholar in physics Harvard U., 1999; cons. Inst. for Def. Analysis, 1998-, Los Alamos Nat. Lab., 2000-, mem. theoretical divsn. rev. com., 2000-; vis. scholar in aeronautics Calif. Inst. Tech., 2001; UCLA dir. modeling and simulation Calif. Nano Systems Inst.; McDowell lectr. U. B.C., 2002. Mem. editl. bd. Jour. Phys. Chemistry, 1995-2000, Surface Sci., 1994-99, Ency. Chem. Physics and Phys. Chemistry 1996-2001, Chem. Phys. Letters, 1998-2003, Phys. Chem. Comm., 1998-2002, Chem. Phys. Chem., 2000-, Jour. Chem. Phys., 2000-02, Modeling and Simulation in Materials Sci. and Engring., 2001—, SIAM jour., 2001-; guest editor Jour. Phys. Chem., 1999-2000; contbr. numerous articles to tech. jours; given over 225 invited lectures. Recipient rsch. innovation recognition awards Union Carbide Co., 1990, 91, New Faculty award Camille and Henry Dreyfus Found., 1988, Hanson-Dow award for excellence in tchg., 1998, others; NSF Presdl. Young Investigator award, 1988, Dreyfus Tchr. Scholar award, 1992, Alfred P. Sloan fellow, 1993, Internat. Acad. of Quantum Molecular Sci. medal, 1993, Exxon faculty fellow, 1993, Glen T. Seaborg Rsch. award, 1993, Herbert Newby McCoy Rsch. award, 1993, Peter Mark Meml. award Am Vacuum Soc., 1995, Dr. Lee vis. rsch. fellow Oxford U., 1996, UCLA Hanson-Dow award, 1998, UCLA Dean's Recognition award for rsch., 2002. Fellow AAAS, Am. Vacuum Soc., Am. Phys. Soc., Inst. of Physics; mem. Am. Chem. Soc., Material Rsch. Soc., Sigma Xi, Phi Beta Kappa. Democrat. Jewish. Avocations: theater, films, cooking, reading, tennis. Office: U California Dept Chem Box 951569 Los Angeles CA 90095-1569 E-mail: eac@chem.ucla.edu.

CARTER, ENITA JOY, conductor; b. Dallas, Tex., Nov. 18, 1950; d. Clyde Heflin, Vera Birdie Heflin; m. Ambrose Wayne Carter; children: Christopher, Terri, Melissa Betts. BMus, Henderson State U., 1973. Cert. tchr. K-12 choral music 1988, Orff Level III 1992, Kodaly Level I 2000, Perform Max Personality Profile 1990, music tchr. Nat. Bd., 2003. Choral dir. Picayune Jr. H.S., Picayune, Miss., 1999—; mktg. team leader Sam's Club, Tupelo, Miss., 1993—98; choral dir. Lee County Sch., Saltillo, Miss., 1988—93; owner, instr. Joy Carter Sch. Fine Arts, Russellville, Ala., 1980—86; analyst work mgmt. Blue Cross of La., Baton Rouge, 1978—80, analyst nat. performance stds., 1976—78. Choral dir. Saltillo Sch. Sys., Saltillo, Miss., 1986—93. Dir.: Established and grew a music program, 1986; composer (songs for children and Orff instruments): Songs of the Psalms, 1991. Children's choir specialist Miss. Bapt. Conv., Jackson, 1980—92; sponsor Tri M Music Honor Soc., Picayune, 1999—; dir. handbells New Palestine Bapt. Ch., Picayune, 1998—. dir. children's choir, 1999—2001; mem. grant funding com. United Way, Tupelo, 1995—97; com. mem. Lee County Improvement Task Force, Tupelo, 1995—96. Nominee Internat. Musician of Yr., 2004; named Oustanding Young Women Am., 1982. Mem.: Picayune Fedn. Tchrs., Miss. Music Educator's Assn. Baptist. Avocations: swimming, sewing, boating, gardening, travel. Office: Picayune Junior High School 702 Goodyear Blvd Picayune MS 39466 Office Phone: 601-749-7998. Business E-Mail: spufmusik@yahoo.com.

CARTER, FRANCES TUNNELL (FRAN CARTER), fraternal organization administrator; b. Springville, Miss. d. David Atmond and Mary Annie (McCutcheon) Tunnell; m. John T. Carter; children: Wayne, Neil Branum. BS, U. So. Miss., 1946; MS, U. Tenn., 1948; EdD, U. Ill., 1954. Elem. sch. tchr., Thaxton, Miss., 1942-43, Cumberland, Miss., 1943-44; tchr. high sch. home econs. Randolph, Miss., 1944-45, Maben, Miss., 1946-47; instr. Wood Coll., Mathiston, Miss., 1948, East Central Jr. Coll., Decatur, Miss., 1948-49; prof. home econs. Clarke Coll., Newton, Miss., 1950-56; prof. Samford U., Birmingham, Ala., 1956-84; editor, children and youth products and resources Woman's Missionary Union, Birmingham, 1983-85; pres. CarterCraft, Inc., Birmingham, 1985-89; nat. exec. dir. Kappa Delta Epsilon, Birmingham, 1987—. Vis. prof. Hong Kong Bapt. U., 1965-66, Anhui Normal U., People's Republic of China, 1987; tchr. workshops in China, 1988, 90, 92, 95, 97, 2000; tchr. workshops in Indonesia, 1993; lectr. in symposium at invitation of Russian Edn. Ministry, Moscow, 1994, U. Nanjing, People's Republic of China, 1997; curriculum writer Bapt. Brotherhood Commn., 1986-90; writer N.Am. Mission Bd., 1995-98. Author: Sammy in the Country, 1960, Tween-Age Ambassador, 1970, Ching Fu and Jim, 1978; co-author: Sharing Times Seven, 1977, also short stories, articles; feature writer: Crusader Mag., 1986-95, The Current, 1987—; editor 103 Rosie Stories, 2001. Tchr. Sunday sch. Bapt. Ch., Birmingham, 1980—; mem., lt. col. CAP, 1968—, bd. dirs. Aerospace Edn. Ala. Wing, 1991-94, dir. pub. affairs regional S.E., 1994-95; v.p. Women's Civic Club of Birmingham, 1997—; placement officer ESL Sch., 1995-98, pres., 1982-83, Test of English as a Fgn. Lang. tchr., 1998--. Recipient Career Achievement award Profl. Fraternity Assn., 1988, Outstanding Alumnae award Wood Coll., 1992, Outstanding award Kappa Delta Pi, 1992, Brewer award for Aerospace Edn. Southeast region CAP, 1994, Vol. of Yr. award Nat. Profl. Fraternity Assn., 1999; elected Birmingham's Woman of Yr., 1977, Birmingham's Vol. of Yr., 1980, Silver rep. Dist. 6 Ala. Nat. Silver Haired Congress, 1996—; named Ala. Silver Haired Legislator Dist. 55 Jefferson County, 1994-97, cert. Rosie the Riveter reunion, Little White House, Warm Springs, Ga.., 1997. Mem. AARP (local pres. 1988-89, asst. state dir. 1989-93, Nat. Cmty. award 1992), Birmingham's Women C. of C. (pres. 1975-76), Nat. League of Am. Pen Women (3rd v.p. 1988-90, nat. pres. 1994-96), Ala. League of Pen Women (pres. 1970-72), Birmingham League of Am. Pen Women (pres. 1968-70, 76-78), Ala. Writers Conclave (pres. 1978-79), Ala. State Poetry Soc. (pres. 1979-82), Ala. Federated Women's Clubs (dist. dir. 1988-90, Outstanding Woman of Ala. Club award 1988), Freedoms Found. Valley Forge (pres. Birmingham Area chpt. 1990-91), Nat. Fellowship Bapt. Educators (sec. 1987-93), Birmingham Bus. and Profl. Club (pres. 1986-87), Am. Rosie the Riveter Assn. Inc. (founder, pres. 1998—), Kappa Delta Epsilon (nat. pres. 1980-85, co-dir. ESL Sch. 1994-98), Alpha Delta Kappa, Delta Kappa Gamma, Phi Delta Kappa (Nat. Profl. Fraternity Assn. award 1999, cert. emeritus 2000). Home and Office: 2561 Rocky Ridge Rd Birmingham AL 35243-4442 E-mail: fran.carter@juno.com.

CARTER, HARRIET RODES, language educator; b. St. Louis, Mo., Dec. 4, 1928; d. Boyle Owsley Rodes and Harriet Hall Moore; m. William H. Carter, 1969 (dec. Aug. 17, 1999); m. Wallace Meigs, 1950 (div. 1968); children: Joe V., Rebecca W., Stephen R., Sarah P., Thomas M. BA English, Clark Univ., Worchester, Mass., 1970; MEd, Worcester State Coll., Worcester, Mass. Cert. tchr. English 7-12. Tchr. Maj. Edwards Sch., West Boylston, Mass., 1970—71; English/lang. arts tchr. Harrington Way Jr. H.S., Worcester, Mass., 1971—78; English/lang. arts Quinisigamond C.C., Worcester, Mass., 1999—2003. Book reviewer Sunday Telegram and Gazette, 1973—77. Author: (essays) numerous (many awards). Faculty advisor Student Writing, mid. sch. spelling bee. Mem.: Princeton Hist. Soc., Worcester County Tchrs. Assn., Nat. Edn. Assn. (life), Friends of Princeton Libr., Princeton Art Soc., Wachusett Garden Club, Creative Wrting Club, Forest Grove Mid. Sch. Drama Club. Independent. Protestant. Avocations: gardening, landscape architect, tutor.

CARTER, JAINE M(ARIE), human resources specialist, director; b. Chgo., Oct. 29, 1946; d. Bruno and Louise Kucinski; m. James Dudley Carter, Apr. 8, 1970; children: Paul, Todd. BS, Northwestern U., 1968; PhD, Walden U., 1988. Mgmt. cons. to bus., 1964—69; chmn. bd. Pers. Devel., Inc., Palatine, Ill., 1969—; dir. women's divsn. Lake Forest (Ill.) Coll. Advanced Mgmt. Inst., 1970—. Writer, lectr., tchr., cons. mgmt. devel. programs; faculty AMA; speaker weekly cable TV series Life Skills; pres. bd. dirs. Family Renewal Inst., 1991—96. Author: (book) How to Train for Supervisors, 1969, Career Planning Workshop for Women, 1975, Training Techniques That Bring About Positive Behavioral Change, 1976, Assertive Management Role Plays, 1976, Understanding the Female Employee, 1976, Rx for Women in Business, 1976, New Directions Needed in Management Training Programs, 1980, The Burnout of Retirement, 1983, Successfully Working with People, 1984, Assertiveness Training for Supervisors, 1985, Successfully Managing People, 1986, The New Success, 1986, Employee Assistance Program Handbook, 1988, Stay Out of Your Own Way-And Get the Job You Want, 1989, He Works/She Works-Successful Strategies for Working Couples, 1996; columnist: Scripps- Howard News Svc., Balancing Work and Family, 1996—; moderator, content expert (TV spl.) Commitment to Quality, Nat. Tech. U., 1989; author: (TV series) Executive Communications, 1988 prodr.: (TV series) Relationships, 1992; creator, prodr., host (TV series) Choices, 1992, 1993, host (radio talk show), 1992—96, columnist Scripps-Howard News Svc. He Works/She Works, 1996—, co-host (radio talk show) Your Own Business!, 1993—97. Mem.: Pres.'s Forum (exec.dir.), SAG, Am. Mgmt. Assn., AGVA, AFTRA.

CARTER, JANE FOSTER, agriculture industry executive; b. Stockton, Calif., Jan. 14, 1927; d. Chester William and Bertha Emily Foster; m. Robert Buffington Carter, Feb. 25, 1952 (dec. Dec. 1994); children: Ann Claire Carter Palmer, Benjamin Foster; m. Frank Anthony Bauman, Aug. 15, 1998 (div. Aug. 2003). BA, Stanford U., 1948; MS, NYU, 1949. Pres. Colusa (Calif.) Properties, Inc., 1953—; owner Carter Land and Livestock, Colusa, 1965—; pres. Sartain Mut. Water Co., Inc., 1992—2003, Carter Mut. Water Co. Inc., 2003—, J&B Rice Farms, Inc., Colusa, 1996—. Sec./treas. Carter Farms, Inc., Colusa, 1975—94, pres., 1994—2002; bd. dirs. Colusa Bean Growers, Inc., 1996—2002, sec., 1998—2002. Author: If the Walls Could Talk, Colusa's Architectural Heritage, 1988; author, editor: Colusa County Survey and Plan for the Arts, 1981, 82, 83, Implementing the Colusa County Arts Plan, 1984, 85, 86. Adv. mem. Calif. Gov.'s [illegible] Sacramento, 1979—82, Calif. Rep. Ctrl. Com., 1976—94; trustee Calif. Hist. Soc., 1979—89, regional v.p., 1984—89; mem. Calif. Reclamation Bd., 1982—96, sec., 1986—96; mem. Calif. Hist. Resources Commn., 1994—2001, vice chair, 1996—97, chair, 1997—99; mem. Colusa Heritage Preservation Com., 1976—2000, chmn., 1977—83, vice chmn., 1983—91, sec., 1997—2000; bd. dirs. Colusa Cmty. Theatre Found., 1980—99; trustee Calif. Preservation Found., 1989—95; del. Rep. Nat. Conv., Kans. City, Mo., 1976, Detroit, 1980, Dallas, 1984; bd. dirs. The English-Spkg. Union of the U.S., N.Y.C., 1995—2001, English-Spkg. Union, San Francisco, 1992—, pres., 1993—95, v.p., 1995—; bd. dirs. Leland Stanford Mansion Found., Sacramento, 1992—; bd. dirs. Colusa County br. Am. Cancer Soc., 1960—86, chmn., 1964—86. Recipient award of Merit for Hist. Preservation Calif. Hist. Soc., 1989, Design award Calif. Preservation Found., 1990, Pres.'s award, 2001, Citizens award English-Speaking Union U.S., 2002, Congrl. Order of Merit, Nat. Rep. Congl. Com., 2003. Mem. Sacramento River Water Contractors Assn. (sec. 1992-2003, exec. com. 1974-2003), Francisca Club, Kappa Alpha Theta. Episcopalian. Avocations: travel, the arts, historic preservation. Home and Office: 4746 River Rd Colusa CA 95932-4200

CARTER, JANICE JOENE, telecommunications executive; b. Portland, Oreg., Apr. 17, 1948; d. William George and Charline Betty (Gilbert) P. Student, U. Calif., Berkeley, 1964, U. Portland, 1966-67, U. Colo., Boulder, 1967-68; BA in Math, U. Guam, 1970; MBA, Golden Gate U., 1998. Computer programmer Ga.-Pacific Co., Portland, 1972-74; systems analyst ProData, Seattle, 1974-79; systems analyst, mgr. Pacific Northwest Bell, Seattle, 1979-80; data ctr. mgr. Austin Co., Renton, Wash., 1980-83; in bus. devel. Wright-Runstad, Seattle, 1983-84; system adminstr. Hewlett-Packard, Bellevue, Wash., 1984; corp. telecomms. dir. Nordstrom, Inc., Seattle, 1984-96; global telecomm. mgr. Hewlett-Packard Co., Palo Alto, Calif., 1996-98; dir. info. tech. 20th Century Fox, L.A., 1998-2000; regional sales dir. AT&T, L.A., 2000—02; prin. cons. Carter Comms., Marina del Ray, Calif., 2000—. Ski instr. Alpental, Snoqualmie Pass, Wash., 1984-87; bd. dirs. Educationally Gifted Children, Mercer Island, Wash., 1978-80; mem. curriculum com. Mercer Island Sch. Bd., 1992-95; adult literacy tutor. Mem.: Century City C. of C. Avocations: roller blading, french, travel, opera theater, dancing and singing. Office: 4314 Marina City Dr #726C Marina Del Rey CA 90292

CARTER, JEAN GORDON, lawyer; b. Fort Belvoir, Va., July 30, 1955; d. Thomas Laney and Cleone (Hunter) Gordon; m. Michael L. Carter, Sept. 17, 1977; children: Christina Jean, William Gordon. BS magna cum laude with honors in Accountancy, Wake Forest U., 1977; JD with high honors, Duke U., 1983. Bar: N.C. 1983; CPA; bd. cert. specialist in estates. Acct. Arthur Andersen & Co., Charlotte, N.C., 1977-80; atty. Moore & Van Allen, Raleigh, N.C., 1983-90; ptnr. Hunton & Williams, Raleigh, N.C., 1990—. Mem. Am. Coll. Trusts and Estates Coun., N.C. Bar Assn., Wake County Estate Coun. (pres. 1991-92), Order of Coif, Phi Beta Kappa. Democrat. Presbyterian. Avocation: reading. Home: 3913 Stratford Ct Raleigh NC 27609-6351 Office: Hunton & Williams 1 Hannover Sq Ste 1400 Raleigh NC 27601-2947 E-mail: jcarter@hunton.com.

CARTER, JENNIFER LEIGH, special education educator; b. Athens, Ga., Nov. 26, 1973; d. Gary Fred and Gail Overton Carter. BA, Kennesaw (Ga.) State U., 1999; MA, U. South Fla., 2002. Cert. spl. edn. tchr. grades K-12 Fla. Dept. Edn., 2003, art tchr. grades K-12 Fla. Dept. Edn., 2000. Spl. edn. tchr. Pinellas County Sch. Sys., Largo, Fla., 1999—. Docent Mus. Fine Arts, St. Petersburg, Fla., 2003—, chair ednl. outreach com., 2003—04. Grantee in field, 2002—03; Classroom Funding grantee, Wal-Mart, 2002. Mem.: Coun. for Exceptional Children (v.p. 2003—, publicity chair 2002—03, finalist for Rookie Tchr. of the Yr. 2003), St. Petersburg Mus. Fine Arts, Tampa Theater. Methodist. Avocations: travel, literature, boating. Home: 225 Turtle Creek Cir Oldsmar FL 34677 Office: Morgan Fitzgerald Middle School 6410 118th Ave Largo FL 33773 Personal E-mail: cjennif1@hotmail.com.

CARTER, JOAN PAULINE, investment company executive; b. Pitts., July 2, 1943; d. Paul Joseph and Hazel Elizabeth (Hykes) C.; m. John Aglialoro, 1979; children: Mark David Henderson, Liesl Ann Henderson. BA, Coll. of Wooster, 1965. V.p. United Med. Corp., Haddonfield, N.J., 1973-85, pres., 1985—. Bd. dirs. UM Holdings, Ltd., Haddonfield, N.J., Phila. Fed. Reserve Bd., Premier Rsch. Worldwide, Phila., Cybex Internat. Bd. trustees N.J. State Aquarium, Camden, 1995, Coll. Wooster, 1986—; mem. World Affairs Coun., Phila., 1982—. Mem. Drug Info. Assn., Union League (Phila.), N.Y. Women's Econ. Forum, CATO Inst. Republican. Office: UM Holdings Ltd 56 N Haddon Ave Haddonfield NJ 08033-2422

CARTER, JULIA MARIE, secondary school educator; b. Topeka, May 2, 1958; d. Jack Earnest and Bonita Aileen (Hatfield) Estes; m. Dan W. Carter; children: John-Thomas, Jessica Raye. BA, Ouachita Bapt. U., 1982; MBA, U. Phoenix, 2003. Cert. tchr. K-12, Ark., Fla., Md., Va., Pa., Mich., Ohio, Iowa. Tchr. French Dunbar Jr. High, Little Rock, 1989-91; tchr. Mt. Vernon (Ark.) Schs., 1991; tchr. French Cathedral Sch., Little Rock, 1991-92; tchr. St. Mark's Episcopal Sch., Oakland Park, Fla., 1992-93; tchr. French Miramar (Fla.) High Sch., 1993-96, Benjamin Franklin Sch., 1996—98, West Village Acad., 1999—2000, Detroit Public Sch., 2000—01, Bettendorf (Iowa) Pub. Schs., 2001—, Davenport (Iowa) Pub. Schs., 2003—. Owner Carter's Ednl. Svcs.; author, presenter in field. Vol. Chicot Elem., Little Rock, 1989-90, Silver Lake Mid. Sch., North Lauderdale, Fla., 1992-93, Miramar High Sch., 1993-95; mem. Ednl. Materials Equality Com., Little Rock, 1990-91. Fullbright scholar, 1989. Mem. Am. Assn. Tchrs. French (Prof. du Laureat 1989, 92), Am. Fedn. Tchrs. Democrat. Methodist. Avocations: traveling, historic research, writing. Home: 3946 Madison St Dearborn Heights MI 48125-2156

CARTER, KIMBERLY FERREN, nursing educator; b. Wheeling, W.Va., July 15, 1963; d. Donald Ray and Nan Shaw Ferren; m. Gregory Lawrence Carter; children: Leanna, Brandon. Diploma, Ohio Valley Gen. Hosp. Sch. Nursing, Wheeling, 1984; BSN, Radford U., 1986; MSN, U. Va., 1987, PhD, 1997. Cert. breast health facilitator Am. Cancer Soc.; RN; cert. 2nd Degree Reiki practitioner. Pub. health nurse educator Ctrl. Shenandoah Health Dist., Staunton, Va., 1987—88; nursing edn. specialist edn. and health promotion Kennestone Regional Health Care Sys., Marietta, Ga., 1988—90; asst. prof. nursing West Ga. Coll., Carrollton, Ga., 1990—92; from instr. to assoc. prof. Radford U., Va., 1992—. Bd. dir. Salem Rsch. Inst.; bd. rev. Advances in Nursing Sci., Fredericksburg, 1999—; rsch. cons. VA Med. Ctr., Salem, 1997—2002; mem. adv. bd. Radford U. Environ. Health Ctr. of Excellence, 2004—. Co-author: (profl. stds. document) Essentials of Baccalaureate Nursing Ed. for Entry Level Cmty./Pub. Health Nursing (C/PHN), 2000, Carter Skin Lesion Assessment Tree, 2003—04; author: (book) Documenting Health Assessment Findings: an Applications Module, 1995, Instructor's Guide and Test Bank for Sims, 1995; bd. rev. Jou. Advanced Nursing, 2004—. Mem. Roanoke Valley Task Force on Homelessness, Roanoke, 1996—; mem. Radford U. IRB, 2002—. Recipient Am. Cancer Soc. award for Outstanding Svc. and Commitment to Breast Cancer Detection, 1999; fellow in Acad. Leadership, Am. Acad. Colls. Nursing, 2004—; Curriculum Devel. grantee, Helene Fuld Health Trust, 2001—03, Faculty Seed grantee, Radford U., 1999, Faculty Rsch. grantee, 1997, Tobacco Control grantee, Am. Cancer Soc., 2003, Faculty-Student Collaborative grantee, 2003. Mem.: Phi Kappa Phi, Sigma Theta Tau (corr. sec. 1996—2000, 2002—). Office: Radford U Box 6964 Radford VA 24142 Business E-Mail: kcarter@radford.edu.

CARTER, LA RAE DUNN, music educator; b. Salt Lake City, Oct. 17, 1932; d. Charles Oscar Dunn and Gretta Smith Haslam-Dunn; m. Ronald G. Carter, Aug. 7, 1956; children: Gary, Eric, Thomas, Jeffrey, John, Kristen, Karen, Shannon, Joseph. BA, Brigham Young U., 1954, MA, 1955; D in Musical Arts, Claremont U., 1996; cert. in tchr. edn., Boise State U., 1982. Music tchr. Boise Sch. Dist., 1954—56; vocal instr. Brigham Young U., Provo, Utah, 1956—57; music tchr. Nebo Sch. Dist., Springville, Utah, 1982—86; choral instr. Claremont (Calif.) Sch. Dist., 1987—99, chair fine arts depts., 1989—98; dir. choral activities Park City (Utah) H.S., 1999—, chair fine arts dept., 2001—. Dist. music team leader Park City Sch. Dist., 2001—03. Recipient Bravo award for the Arts, L.A. Music Ctr., 1996—97. Mem.: Utah Music Educators Assn., Music Educators Nat. Conf., Am. Choral Dirs. Assn., Utah Sch. Activities Assn. (region choral chmn. 1999—). Republican. Mem. Lds Church. Office: Park City High Sch 1750 Kearus Blvd Park City UT 84060 E-mail: rcarter@parkcityus.com.

CARTER, LAURA LEE, academic librarian, psychotherapist; b. Iowa City, Apr. 9, 1955; d. Jack L. and Martha Ann (Shelton) C.; m. William Douglas Rolfe, Oct. 1, 1994 (div. 2001). BA in East Asia Studies magna cum laude, U. Colo., 1977; M of Librarianship, U. Washington, 1979; grad. FALCON program, Cornell U., 1983; tng. in Chinese lang., Stanford Ctr., Taipei, Taiwan, 1983-84; MA in Third World History, U. Colo., 1988; MA in Transpersonal Counseling Psychol., Naropa Inst., Boulder, Colo., 1995. Internat. documents libr., asst. libr. Documents Divsn. Marriott Libr., U. Utah, Salt Lake City, 1979-82; original cataloger Norlin Libr., U. Colo., Boulder, 1986-89; internat. documents libr., asst. prof. Govt. Publs. Libr., U. Colo., Boulder, 1989-94; documents libr., asst. prof. Colo. State U., Ft. Collins, 1995-98; gen. ref. libr. Regis U., Denver, 1998—2004. Part-time instr. Chinese and Japanese history dept history U. No. Colo., Greeley, 1987; invited participant/libr. collection devel. tour S.E. Asia, China and Japan, 1982; judge Most Notable Documents sect. Libr. Jour., 1994; organizer programs and confs.; lectr. and presenter in field. Contbr. book revs. to profl. publs., articles to periodicals. Participant Boulder County Big Sisters Program, 1992. Co-recipient READEX/GODORT/ALA Catherine Reynolds award, 1991, Univ. Colo. Program grant, 1990-91; Japan Found. Libr. Support grantee U. Utah, 1980-81; Nat. Resource fellow for Chinese lang. study Cornell U., 1982-83; tuition scholar Inter-Univ. Program for Advanced Chinese Lang. Studies, 1983-84. Mem. ALA (coord. internat. documents task force 1992-93, program chmn. internat. documents task force 1991). Avocations: gardening, hiking, biking, cooking, remodeling. Home: 920 Deborah Dr Loveland CO 80537 E-mail: lcarter@regis.edu.

CARTER, LYNDA, actress, entertainer; b. Phoenix; m. Robert Altman. Student, U. Ariz. Beauty and fashion dir. Maybelline Cosmetics. Toured with the Garfin Gathering; appeared 5 movies for TV, The New, Original Wonder Woman, 1975, A Master of Wife...and Death, 1976, The Last Song, 1980, Rita Hayworth-Love Goddess, 1983; 5 TV variety spls.; star of television series Wonder Woman, 1976-77, The New Adventures of Wonder Woman, 1977-79; star of TV movie Stillwatch, 1986; recording artist: album Portraits. Hon. crusade chmn. Am. Cancer Soc., 1985-86; hon. chairperson Exceptional Children Found., 1987-88. Named Miss World-USA, 1973; recipient Hispanic Woman of Yr. award, 1983, Golden Eagle award, 1986. Achievements include being a profl. performer since age 15. Office: William Morris Agy 151 S El Camino Dr Beverly Hills CA 90212-2775

CARTER, MAE RIEDY, retired academic official, consultant; b. Berkeley, Calif., May 20, 1921; d. Carl Joseph and Avis Blanche (Rodehaver) Riedy; m. Robert C. Carter, Aug. 19, 1944; children: Catherine, Christin Ann. BS, U. Calif., Berkeley, 1943. Ednl. adviser, then program specialist div. continuing edn. U. Del., Newark, 1968-78; asst. provost women's affairs, exec. dir. status of women Office Women's Affairs, U. Del., 1978-86; mem. adv. bd. Rockefeller Family Grant Project, 1979-83. Regional v.p. Del. PTA, 1960-62; pres. Friends Newark Free Library, 1968-69; mem. fiscal planning com. Newark Spl. Sch. Dist., 1972. Author: Research on Seeing and Evaluating People, 1982, (with Geis and Butler) Seeing and Evaluating People, 1982, revised, 1986, (with Haslett and Geis) The Organizational Woman: Power and Paradox, 1992, also papers and reports in field. Recipient Outstanding Svc. award Women's Coordinating Coun., 1977, 79, Spl. Recognition award Nat. U. Extension Assn., 1977, award for credit programs, 1971, Creative Programming award, 1971, medal of distinction U. Del., 1998; AAUW grantee, 1968; Fulbright grantee, 1976; annual award named for returning Adult Students, 1988—, named to Del. Women Hall of Fame, 1995, professorship named for, in Women's Studies, 2003. Mem. AAUW (past br. pres.), LWV, NOW, Women's Legal Def. Fund, Nat. Women's Polit. Caucus, Global Fund Women, Planned Parenthood, Freedom From Hunger, Population Comm. Internat. Democrat. Home: 604 Dallam Rd Newark DE 19711-3110

CARTER, MANDY, professional organization administrator; Nat. field dir. Nat. Black Gay and Lesbian Leadership Forum, Washington, also bd. dirs., liaison to human rights campaign. Pub. policy advocate Human Rights Campaign staff, 1992; active D.C. Coalition of Black Lesbians; founder N.C. Mobilization, 1996. Office: NBLGLF 1755 Broadway Fl 15 Oakland CA 94612-2155

CARTER, MARJORIE JACKSON, special education educator, consultant; b. Moulton, Ala., Dec. 2, 1946; d. Johnnie Henry Stover and Marie Edith McDaniel; m. Youncy Pippin Carter, June 27; 1 child, Coreen Marie Diaz. BS in Edn., Slippery Rock (Pa.) U., 1968; MEd in Spl. Edn., U. Pitts., 1974. Cert. tchr. Pa., tchr. spl. edn., social studies, learning disabilities, mental retardation Fla. Spl. edn. tchr. Pitts. Bd. Edn., 1974—79; program specialist Fla. Atlantic U., Boca Raton, 1981—82; program dir. Ann Storck Ctr. for the Disabled, Ft. Lauderdale, Fla., 1982—83; tchr. spl. edn. Broward County Schs., Ft. Lauderdale, 1982—. Mem. com. Cmty. Action Plan, Ft. Lauderdale, 2000—; bd. dirs. Wiggins-Henry Found., Pembroke Pines, Fla., 2001—. Democrat. Baptist. Avocations: real estate investment, tutoring, aerobics. Office: Dillard HS 2501 NW 11th St Fort Lauderdale FL 33311

CARTER, MARY ANDREWS, paralegal; b. Greenville, S.C., Sept. 27, 1958; d. Harold M. Andrews and Mary Nancy Dollar; m. Donald P. Carter, Aug. 1, 1982 (div. Sept. 27, 1986); children: Christina Marie, Jason Paul. Diploma in paralegal, Greenville Tech., 1988. Paralegal Alan. O Campbell, P.E., Inc., Sullivan's Island, SC, 1995—99; pvt. practice, 1999—2001; paralegal Campbell, Schneider & Assocs., John's Island, SC, 2001—. Mem. adv. coun. Clark Acad., Charleston, 1998—2000; guardian, litem State of S.C., Charleston, 1999—2001. Office: Campbell Schneider and Assocs 3690 Bohicket Rd Ste 1D Johns Island SC 29455

CARTER, MELINDA, municipal official; b. Springfield, Ohio; BA in English lit., Ohio U., 1986; JD, Capital U., 1989. Assoc. Beatty and Roseboro, Columbus, Ohio; spl. counsel Ohio Atty. Gen. Columbus; exec. dir. New Salem Cmty. Reinvestment Corp., Columbus; exec. asst. to the dir. Equal Bus. Opportunity Commn., City of Columbus, exec. dir., 1996—. Mem. New Salem Missionary Bapt. Ch. Mem. Ohio U. Alumni Assn., Nat. Coalition 100 Black Women, Network Black Women for Justice, Alpha Kappa Alpha. Office: Equal Bus Opportunity Commn City of Columbus 109 N Front St Fl 4 Columbus OH 43215-2806

CARTER, NANETTE CAROLYN, artist; b. Columbus, Ohio, Jan. 30, 1954; d. Matthew Gameliel and Frances (Hill) C. BA, Oberlin Coll., 1976; MFA, Pratt Inst. of Art, 1978. Tchr. art Dwight Englewood Prep Sch., Englewood, NJ, 1978-87; profl. artist, 1987-92, CCNY, 1992-93; vis. lectr., one woman shows Pratt Inst. of Art, Bklyn., 2001—. Artist-in-residence Triangle Workshop, Pine Plains, NYC, 1991. One-woman shows include Ericson Gallery, NYC, 1983, G.R. N'Namdi Gallery, Detroit, 1984, 86, 92-2002, Birmingham, Mich., 1989, 92, 96, 99, Chgo., 1999-2002, Cinque Gallery, NYC, 1985, Montclair (NJ) Art Mus., 1988, Jersey City (NJ) Mus., 1990, June Kelly Gallery, NYC, 1990, 94, 97, 2000, Southampton (NY) Coll., 1991, Franklin Marshall Coll., Lancaster, Pa., 1992, Kebede Fine Arts, LA, 1992, Sande Webster Gallery, Phila., 1993, 95, 97, 99, Alitash Kebete, LA, 1995, Hodges-Taylor Gallery, Charlotte, NC, 1997; exhibited in group shows at Bklyn. Mus., 1981, Newark Mus., 1985, Pa. Acad. Fine Arts, Phila., 1986, Clocktower Gallery, NYC, 1986, Associated Am. Artists Gallery, NYC, 1986, Wennigger Gallery Boston, 1987, Kenkelaba Gallery, NYC, 1987, Fashion Moda Gallery, Bronx, NY, 1988, Studio Mus. in Harlem, NY, 1988, Louisa McIntosh Gallery, Atlanta, 1990, Sande Webster Gallery, 1990, East Hampton Ctr. for Contemporary Art, NY, 1990, Space Gallery, Cleve., 1991, Mary Ryan Gallery, NYC, 1991, New Visions Gallery, Ithaca, NY, 1991, Bennington (Vt.) Coll., 1991, The Rifle Gallery, Columbus, Ohio, 1991, Bristol-Myers Squibb Co., Princeton, NJ, 1992, The Nat. Mus. of Woman in the Arts, Washington, 1992, The Paine Webber Art Gallery, NYC, 1993, Mus. Art, R.I. Sch. of Design, Providence, 1994, 98, Pratt's Inst.'s Manhattan Ctr., NYC, 1995, Skoto Gallery, NYC, 1995, Phila. Mus. Art, 1996, Wayne State U., Detroit, 1996, Pitts. Ctr. for Arts, 1996, W.Va. Wesleyan Coll., Buckhannon, 1996, Yale U. Art Gallery, New Haven, 1996, Spelman Coll. Mus. Fine Art, Atlanta, 1996, Rush Art, NYC, 1997, The Schomburg Ctr., NYC, 1998, Louis Ross Gallery, NYC, 1998, Nabisco, East Hanover, NJ, 1998, The Parish Art Mus., Southampton, NY, 1998, Elise Goodheart Gallery, Sea Harbor, NY, 1998, RI Sch. Design, Providence, 1998, Arlene Bujese Gallery, East Hampton, NY, 1999, Nat. Arts Club, NYC, 1999, Concordia Coll., Ann Arbor, Mich., 2000, Ark. Arts Ctr., Little Rock, 2000, and numerous others; represented in permanent collections Planned Parenthood, NYC, Jane Zimmerli Art Mus., Rutgers U., New Brunswick, NJ, Jersey City Mus., Libr. of Congress, Washington, ARCO, Phila., Reader's Digest, Pleasantville, NY, Schomburg Libr., NYC, Salomon Bros., NYC, Newark Mus., Herbert Johnson Mu., Art, Cornell U., Ithaca, NY, Studio Mus. Harlem, NY, MCI Telecomm., Chgo., Times Mirror, NYC, AT&T, NJ, IBM, Stamford, Conn., Lang Comm., Randolph, Vt., Merck Pharm. Co., Phila., Johnson & Johnson, Inc., New Brunswick, Pepsi-Cola, NYC, Motown Corp., L.P., LA, Am. Express, Mpls., Mus. Art RI Sch. Design, Providence, Yale Gallery of Art, New Haven, Conn., USA Assurance, San Antonio, Tex., Nextel Corp., LA, GE, Fairfield, Conn., Cochran Found., La Grange, Ga., Rutgers Grad. Sch. Mgmt., Newark, ARCO, Phila., Magic Johnson Enterprises, LA, Nissho Iwai Am. Corp., NYC, Pa. Acad. Fine Arts, Phila., Lucent Tech., Basking Ridge, NJ, Butler Inst. Am. Art, Youngstown, Ohio, Conkling Gallery, Minn. State Univ., Mankato, MN, 2002; Group shows: Jacktilton Gallery, NYC, Exhibit A Gallery, NYC; Pfizer Incorp., NYC, 2002; and numerous others. Grantee Nat. Endowment for Arts, 1981, The Jerome Found., 1981, NJ Coun. on Arts, 1985, NY Found. for Arts, 1990, The Pollock-Krasner Found., 1994, Wheeler Found., NYC, 1996, Fellowship, Lower East Side Printshop, NYC, 1997, Fellowship, Brandywine Workshop, Philadelphia, 1999

CARTER, PAMELA LYNN, former state attorney general; b. South Haven, Mich., Aug. 20, 1949; d. Roscoe Hollis and Dorothy Elizabeth (Hadley) Fanning; m. Michael Anthony Carter, Aug. 26, 1971; children: Michael Anthony Jr., Marcya Alicia. BA cum laude, U. Detroit, 1971; MSW, U. Mich., 1973; JD, Ind. U., 1984. Bar: Ind. 1984, U.S. Dist. Ct. (no. dist.) Ind. 1984, U.S. Dist. Ct. (so. dist.) Ind. 1984. Rsch. analyst, treatment dir. U. Mich. Sch. Pub. Health and UAW, Detroit, 1973—75; exec. dir. Mental Health Ctr. for Women and Children, Detroit, 1975—77; consumer litigation atty. UAW-Gen. Motors Legal Svcs., Indpls., 1983—87; securities atty. Sec. of State, Indpls., 1987—89; Gov.'s exec. asst. for health and human svcs. Gov.'s Office, Indpls., 1989—91, dep. chief of staff to Gov., 1991—92; with Baker & Daniels, 1992—93; atty. gen. State of Ind., Indpls., 1993—96; ptnr. Johnson & Smith, 1996—97; v.p., gen. mgr. Europe, Mid. East & Africa Cummins Engine Co., Inc., Columbus, Ind., 1998—. Author (numerous poems). Active Jr. League, Indpls., Dem. Precinct, Indpls., Cath. Social Svcs., Indpls. Named Breakthrough Woman of the Year, 1989; named one of Outstanding Young Woman of America, 1977; recipient Outstanding Svc. award, Ind. Perinatal Assn., 1991, Cmty. Svc. Coun. Ctrl. Ind., 1991, Non-profl. Healthcare award, Family Health Conf. Bd. Dirs., 1991, award for excellence, Women of the Rainbow, 1991. Mem.: Ind. Bar Assn., Nat. Bar Assn., Coalition of 100 Black Women. Democrat. Avocations: gardening, hiking, travel, reading. Office: VP, Global Sales & Marketing Cummins Engine Co Inc 500 Jackson St Columbus IN 47201*

CARTER, PAULA J. state legislator; LLD, Lincoln U., 1999. Mem. Mo. Ho. of Reps from 61st dist., Jefferson City, 1986-2000, Mo. Senate from 5th dist., Jefferson City, 2000—. Vice chmn. Mo. State Dem. Party; pres. Mo. Legis. Blafk Caucus Found. Home: 5936 Summit Pl Saint Louis MO 63147-1119 Office: Mo Ho of Reps State Capitol Building Jefferson City MO 65101-1556

CARTER, ROBERTA ECCLESTON, therapist, counselor; b. Pitts. d. Robert E. and Emily B. (Bucar) Carter; divorced; children: David Michael Kiewlich, Daniel Michael Kiewlich. Student, Edinboro State U., 1962-63; BS, California State U. Pa., 1966; MEd, U. Pitts., 1969; MA, Rosebridge Grad. Sch., 1987. Tchr. Bethel Park Sch. Dist., Pa., 1966-69; writer, media asst. Field Ednl. Pub., San Francisco, 1969-70; educator, counselor, specialist Alameda Unified Sch. Dist., Calif., 1970—. Master trainer Calif. State Dept. Edn., Sacramento, 1984—; personal growth cons., Alameda, 1983—. Author: People, Places and Products, 1970, Teaching/Learning Units, 1969; co-author: Teacher's Manual Let's Read, 1968. Mem. AAUW, NEA, Calif. Fedn. Bus. and Profl. Women (legis. chair Alameda br. 1984-85, membership chair 1985), Calif. Edn. Assn., Alameda Edn. Assn., Charter Planetary Soc., Oakland Mus., Exploratorium, Big Bros of East Bay, Alameda C. of C. (svc. awsard 1985). Avocations: aerobics, gardening, travel. Home: 1516 Eastshore Dr Alameda CA 94501-3118

CARTER, ROSALYNN SMITH, former First Lady of the United States; b. Plains, Ga., Aug. 18, 1927; d. Edgar and Allie (Murray) Smith; m. James Earl Carter, Jr., July 7, 1946; children: John William, James Earl III, Donnel Jeffrey, Amy Lynn. Grad., Ga. Southwestern Coll.; DHL (hon.), Morehouse Coll., 1980; LLD (hon.), U. Notre Dame, 1987. First Lady of U.S., Washington, 1977—81; Disting. fellow dept. women's studies Emory U., Atlanta, 1990—. Vice chair, bd. trustees The Carter Ctr., chair Mental Health Task Force Carter Ctr.; pres., bd. dirs. Rosalynn Carter Inst. of Ga. Southwestern State U.; co-founder Every Child by Two Campaign for Early Immunization. Author: First Lady from Plains, 1984, (with Jimmy Carter) Everything to Gain: Making the Most of the Rest of Your Life, 1987, Helping Yourself Help Others: A Book for Caregivers, 1994, Helping Someone With Mental Illness: A Compassionate Guide for Family, Friends and Caregivers, 1998. Bd. advisors Habitat for Humanity; mem. Ga. Gov.'s Commn. to Improve Svcs. Mentally and Emotionally Handicapped, 1971; hon. chmn. Pres.'s Commn. Mental Health, 1977-78. Recipient Presdl. Citation APA, 1982, Nathan S. Kline medal of merit Internat. Com. Against Mental Illness, 1984, Disting. Alumnus award Am. Assn. State Colls. and Univs., 1987, Dorothea Dix award Mental Illness Found., 1988, Dean's award Columbia U. Coll. Physicians and Surgeons, 1991, Notre Dame award for internat. humanitarian svc., 1992, Eleanor Roosevelt Living World award Peace Links, 1992, Nat. Caring award, The Caring Inst., 1995, Kiwanis World Svc. medal, Kiwanis Internat. Found., 1995, Jefferson award Am. Inst. for Pub. Svc., 1996, Into the Light award Nat. Mental Health Assn., 1997, Presdl. Medal of Freedom, 1999; named to Nat. Women's Hall of Fame, 2001. Fellow: Am. Psychiat. Assn. (hon.). Democrat. Office Phone: 404-331-3900.*

CARTER, RUTH B. (MRS. JOSEPH C. CARTER), foundation administrator; b. Charlotte, Vt. d. Ira E. and Sadie M. (Congdon) Burroughs; m. Joseph C. Carter, June 28, 1935. PhB, U. Vt., 1931. Prin. Newton Acad., Shoreham, Vt., 1931-35; substitute tchr. Spaulding High Sch., Barre, Vt., 1931-35, Woodbury (Vt.) High Sch., 1935-36; tchr. Craftsbury Acad., Craftsbury Common, Vt., 1936-38; sales mgr., buyer Vt. Music Co., Barre, 1939-44; statistician Syracuse U., 1944-46; instr. English Temple U., Phila., 1946-47; records clk. sec. Phila., 1947-56; tchr. English Cen. High Sch., Phila., 1957, Springfield Twp. Sr. High Sch., Montgomery County, Pa., 1964-65; exec. dir. White-Williams Found., 1966-82, trustee, 1982-95. Author: (with Joseph C. Carter) Anchors Aweigh Around the World with Ernest Vail Burroughs, 1960, Pilgrimage to the Lovely Lands of our Ancestors, 1984. Recipient Humanitarian award Chapel of Four Chaplains, 1981, city coun. citation City of Phila., 1982, citation White-Williams Found., 1994. Mem.: DAR (regent Germantown chpt. 1983—86, pub. rels. chmn. from 1986, regent Germantown chpt. 1989—92, treas. 1992—95, registrar 1995—2001, chmn. membership from 2001, historian from 2001, treas., com. chmn., budget dir.), AAUW (admissions chmn. Phila. chpt. 1959—61, sec. 1961—64, treas. 1965—67), Vt. Hist. Soc., Women for Greater Phila., The English Speaking Union, Geneal. Soc. Vt., New Eng. Hist. Geneal. Soc., Soc. Mayflower Descs. (bd. dirs. 1983—84, sec. 1985—91), Regent's Club (Phila. chaplain 1986—88), Temple U. Women's Club, Temple U. Faculty Wives Club (rec. sec. 1983—86, sec. 1997—2000, pres. Old York group). Republican. Methodist. Home: Williston, Vt. Deceased.

CARTER, SARALEE LESSMAN, immunologist, microbiologist; b. Chgo., Feb. 19, 1951; d. Julius A. and Ida (Oiring) Lessman; B.A., National Coll., 1971; m. John B. Carter, Oct. 7, 1979; children: Robert Oiring, Mollie. Supr. lab. immunology Weiss Meml. Hosp., Chgo., 1973-80; lab. immunology supr. Henrotin Hosp., Chgo., 1980-84; tech. dir. Lexington Med. Labs., West Columbia, S.C., 1984—; mem. nat. workshop faculty Am. Soc. Clin. Pathologists; clin. instr. faculty Med. U. S.C. Mem. Am. Soc. Clin. Pathologists (subspecialty cert. in microbiology and immunology, cert. med. technologist). Researcher Legionnaires Disease and mycoplasma pneumonia World Soc. Pathologists, Jerusalem, Israel, 1980. Contbr. articles to profl. jours.; Mem. Rep. Senoritorial Inner Circle, co-chmn. S.C. Young Profls. for George Bush. Office: 110 Medical Ln E Ste 100 West Columbia SC 29169-4817

CARTER, SYLVIA, journalist; b. Keokuk, Iowa; d. Charles Sylvester and Frances Elizabeth (Smith) C. B of Journalism, U. Mo., 1968. Intern Quincy (Ill.) Herald-Whig, 1966, Detroit Free Press, 1967; reporter The N.Y. Daily News, 1968-70; successively gen. assignment reporter, edn. reporter, food writer, restaurant critic, food columnist Newsday, Melville, N.Y., 1970—; food writer, restaurant critic N.Y. Newsday, N.Y.C., 1985-95; founder, editor Kidsday Newsday, Melville. Author: Eats: The Best Little Restaurants in New York, 1988, Eats N.Y.C.: A Guide to the Best, Cheapest, Most Interesting Restaurants in Brooklyn, Queens and Manhattan, 1995; contbr. to Family Circle and other publs. Trustee Anne O'Hare McCormick Scholarship Fund, N.Y.C., 1988—. Recipient Feature Writing award U. Mo., 2000; nominee James Beard Journalism awards, 2001. Mem. Newswomen's Club N.Y. (pres. 1990-92, bd. dirs., Front Page award 1982). Democrat. Presbyterian. Avocations: reading, collectibles, hiking, music, cooking. Home: 111 Waverly Pl New York NY 10011-9142 also: 46 Crescent Bow Ridge NY 11961-2915 Office: Newsday 235 Pinelawn Rd Melville NY 11747-4250 E-mail: sylvia.carter@newsday.com.

CARTER, VALERIE, food products executive; d. John and Katherine Daniels. BA in Bus. Adminstrn., Lincoln U., 1978; Masters Degree, Cardinal Stritch Coll., 1982. Mgmt. trainee Firstar Bank (formerly First Wis. Nat. Bank), 1978; auditor MGIC Investment Corp., 1981; co-founder V&J Foods, 1984, CEO. Recipient Sacajawea award for creativity, 1997, named Entrepreneur of Yr., Ernst & Young and Merrill Lynch, 1994. Mem. Milw. World Festival Inc. (pres. bd.). Office: 6933 W Brown Deer Rd Milwaukee WI 53223-2103

CARTER, YVONNE JOHNSON, writer, editor, English educator; d. John Miller and Lorraine Johnson; m. Vernon L. Carter, Jr.. BA cum laude, St. Paul's Coll., 1971; MA, U. Md., 1979; PhD, Howard U., 1994. Contract specialist Dept. Def., Richmond, Va., 1972-75; edn. reporter Washington Afro-Am. Newspaper, 1980-82; writer-editor U.S. Army Engr. Sch., 1982-83, U.S. Dept. Army, Alexandria, Va., 1983-84; sr. editor Nat. Def. U., Washington, 1984-85; writer-editor USIA, Washington, 1985-91; lectr. Bowie (Md.) State U., 1994-96; writer-editor U.S. EEOC, Washington, 1995—. Mem. Fed. Commn. Network, Washington, 1997—. Editor: The United States and the World Economy, 1984; editor (periodical) The Civil Rights Movement and the Legacy of Dr. King, 1989, (periodical) Two Cultures, Shared Values: Nigeria and the U.S., 1990; author (periodical) EEOC Mission, 1995—. Mem. Habitat for Humanity, Atlanta, 1999, Corcoran Gallery Art, Washington, 1999, Nat. Hist. Preservation Soc., Washington, 1999, Smithsonian, Washington, 1999, Libr. of Congress Assocs., 1999, Fed. Comms. Network, Washington, 1999. Fellow U. Md., 1978; Ivan Earle Taylor scholar Howard U., 1992. Mem. AAUP, AAUW, Alpha Kappa Alpha. Democrat. Baptist. Office: EEOC 1801 L St NW Washington DC 20036-3811

CARTER-MILLER, JOCELYN, retail executive; BSc in Acctg., U. Ill., Urbana-Champaign; MBA in Mktg. and Fin., U. Chgo. CPA. Various sr. level positions Mattel, Inc., 1984—93; corp. v.p., chief mktg. officer Motorola, Inc., 1993—2002; exec. v.p. Office Depot, Inc., Delray Beach, Fla., 2002—, chief mktg. officer, 2002—. Author (with Melissa Giovagnoli): Networlding: Building Relationships and Opportunities for Success. Office: Office Depot Inc 2200 Old Germantown Rd Delray Beach FL 33445

CARTMAN, SHIRLEY ELEISE, retired music educator; b. Chgo., June 27, 1931; d. Johnny Theophilus Cartman and Hattie Lee Marshall. BS in Music Edn., U. Ill., 1950—53; M in Bus. Mgmt. and Supervision, Ctrl. Mich. U., 1977—78. Cert. tchg. cert. Wash., 1960, provisional tchg. cert. Gary Cmty. Sch. Corp., 1966, life tchg. cert. Ga. Dept. Edn., 1987. 4th grade tchr. Clover Park Sch. Dist., Tacoma, 1960—64; strings tchr. Gary (Wash.) Cmty. Sch. Co-op., 1965—70; music tchr. Prince Georges C.C., Camp Springs, Md., 1973—74; orch. tchr. Dekalb County Bd. of Edn., Decatur, Ga., 1989—91; string ensemble prof. Spelman Coll., Atlanta, 1998—99; music conservatory directress Chapel Hill Harvester Ch., Decatur, Ga., 1992—96; strings instr. New Birth Missionary Bap. Ch. Faith Acad. Sc., Decatur, Ga., 1997—2000. Talent coord. for talented Youth of Gary, Ind., 1968—70; cons. "Jackson Five" Steel Town Record C., Gary, 1967—68; mgr. New Generation Band, New Experience Bank, Decatur, 1985—87; first lady of gospel violin various churches throughout Atlanta area, 2000—01; pt. time strings instr. DeKalb County (Ga.) Bd. Edn., 2000—01; creator, designer The Cartman Fun Music Curriculum Greenforest McCalep Early Learning Ctr., Decatur, Ga. Musician (profl. entertainer): Shelia Carr, 1970; musician: (songwriter) (songs) Lonely Heart, 1968 (Sung by the Jackson Five, 1972); author: (children's short story collection) Stolen Key, 1974, A Teacher Remembers the Jacksons, 1987, 4 children's music books; designer and creator (songs books and teaching aids) The Cartman Fun Music Method, 2002; author: tiny-tot music books for children. SP4 U.S. Army, 1974—75, Fort Mead, Md. Mem.: NAACP (life; ACT-SO chairperson 2000—02, Plaque for Svc. as ACT-SO chairperson 2000—01). Democrat. Avocation: travel. Home: 3945 Johns Hopkins Ct Decatur GA 30034 Office: Cartman Music Studio 3945 Johns Hopkins Ct Decatur GA 30034

CARTON, CRISTINA SILVA-BENTO, elementary school educator; b. Santiago, Beira Alta, Portugal, Jan. 23, 1928; came to U.S. Jan. 4, 1936; d. Mario Antunes and Alice (Silva) Bento; m. Jorge Luis Rodriguez; children:

A. James DeCosta, Robert J. DeCosta, Wanda Rodriguez. BA, Queens Coll., 1968, MS, 1973; MA, SUNY, Stony Brook, 1983. Cert. elem. tchr. N.Y., Fla., ESOL tchr. Fla. Tchr. Our Lady of Loretto, Hempstead, N.Y., 1961-66, Hempstead Pub. Schs., Hempstead, 1968-70, Cen. Islip (N.Y.) Pub. Schs., 1970-87, Broward County Pub. Schs., Ft. Lauderdale, Fla., 1988—2000; drop out prevention coord., lead tchr. Pines Mid. Sch., 1990—92, tchr. ESL coord., 1992—96; drop out prevention 6th grade tchr. Silver Trail Mid. Sch., 1996-98, 6th grade health and sci. tchr., 1998—99, tchr., 1999—2000; ret., 2000. Instr. philosophy Barry U., Miami, 1989-90. Mem. Nat. Cancer Assn., Stony Brook, N.Y., 1971-73; internat. chairperson AAUW, Stony Brook, 1970-73; fund raiser Dem. Party, Selden, N.Y., 1976. Recipient Fellowship for Study Abroad Gulbenkian Found., 1967. Mem. Nat. Edn. Assn., N.Y. State Tchrs. Assn., Cen. Islip Tchrs. Assn., Parent Tchrs. Assn. (membership chair 1970-75), Kappa Delta Pi, Phi Delta Kappa. Democrat. Avocations: travel, painting, reading, opera, ballet. Home: 410 NE 45th St Fort Lauderdale FL 33334-2314

CARTON, LONNIE CAMING, educational psychologist; b. Balt. d. Daniel and Shirley (Cooper) Caming; m. Edwin B. Carton; children: Evan, Deborah, Paula. BS, Johns Hopkins U.; MS, U. Md.; PhD, Pa. State U. Tchr. Laurel (Md.) H.S.; instr. Pa. State U., State College, Temple U., Phila.; newspaper columnist Delaware County Times, Chester, Pa.; instr., then asst. prof. Tufts U., Medford, Mass., 1964-80; learning sys. cons. Tufts New Eng. Med. Ctr., Boston, 1968-73. Broadcast journalist CBS Radio, N.Y.C., 1974—; family support sys. cons. Boston Ptnrs. in Edn., 1985—; ind. cons., lectr., workshop leader in field; guest appearances of various radio and TV shows; family lit. cons. Mass. Dept. Edn., 2001—; cons., dir. teen and family resources Warm 2 Kids, Inc., 2003—. Author: Mommies, 1960, Daddies, 1963, Raise Your Kids Right, 1980, No is a Love Word, 1992, (cassette tapes) Parenting Preschoolers from the Park Bench, 1999; sr. editor Edn. Today, Boston, 1992-98; broadcast journalist Voice of Am., 1995-98; contbr. articles to profl. publs. Grantee Gannet Found., U.S. Dept. Edn., Mass. Dept. Edn., U.S. Dept. Hwy. Safety, Mass. Gov.'s Alliance Against Drugs; recipient Nat. Media award APA, 1978, 80, San Francisco State Broadcast Media award, 1983, Contbn. to Lives of Children award UNICEF, Margaret Sanger Soc. award Planned Parenthood, 1985, Don Bosco Friend of Youth award Salesian Soc., awards from Mass. Psychol. Assn., Nat. Commn. Against Drunk Driving, Gabriel Broadcaster's and Allied Communicators, Mass. Soc. Against Cruelty to Children, 1988; named to One Hundred Most Remarkable Women in Mass., Boston Woman's Mag., 1989, Freedoms Found., George Washington medal for pub. comms., 1998. Avocations: tennis, spectator football, reading. Office: The Learning Ctr PO Box 204 New Town MA 02456-0204 E-mail: ebclcc@aol.com.

CARTWRIGHT, CAROL ANN, university president; b. Sioux City, Iowa, June 19, 1941; d. Carl Anton and Kathryn Marie (Weishapple) Becker; m. G. Phillip Cartwright, June 11, 1966; children: Catherine E., Stephen R., Susan D. BS in Early Childhood Edn., U. Wis., Whitewater, 1962; MEd in Spl. Edn., U. Pitts., 1965, PhD in Spl. Edn., Ednl. Rsch., 1968. From instr. to assoc. prof. Coll. Edn. Pa. State U., University Park, 1968-72, from assoc. prof. to prof., 1972-79, dean acad. affairs, 1981-84, dean undergrad. program, vice provost, 1984-88; vice chancellor acad. affairs U. Calif., Davis, 1988-91, prof. human devel., 1988-91; pres. Kent (Ohio) State U., 1991—. Bd. dirs. First Energy Corp. (formerly Ohio Edison), Akron, 1992—, KeyCorp., Cleve., PolyOne Corp., The Davey Tree Expert Co., Kent; exec. bd. Nat. Coun. for Accreditation Tchr. Edn., 2002—; chair NCAA Exec. Com.; mem. N.E. Ohio Coun. Higher Edn., Knight Commn. Intercollegiate Athletics, 2000. Editorial bd. Topics in Early Childhood Special Education, 1982-88, Exceptional Education Quarterly, 1982-88. Pres., bd. dirs. Child Devel. Coun. of Center County, Title XX Day Care Contractor, 1977-80; bd. dirs. Center County United Way, State College, Pa., 1984-88, Urban League of Greater Cleve., 1997—; bd. mem. Davis (Calif.) Art Ctr., 1988-91, Davis Sci. Ctr., 1989-91; bd. dirs. Ohio divsn. Am. Cancer Soc., 1993-2000, nat. bd. dirs., 1993—; mem. nat. bd. First Ladies Libr.; bd. trustees Woodrow Wilson Internat. Ctr. for Scholars, 1999—; bd. dirs. Ctr. for Rsch. Librs., 2002—. Named to Ohio Women's Hall of Fame; recipient Disting. Alumni award, U. Wis.-Whitewater, U. Pittsburgh Sch. Edn., Clairol Mentor award, Women of Achievement award, YWCA of Greater Cleve., Franklin Delano Roosevelt award for Excellence, March of Dimes. Mem. AAUW, Am. Coun. Edn. (Commn. on Women in Higher Edn., 2003-), Am. Ednl. Rsch. Assn., Am. Assn. for Higher Edn., Nat. Assn. State Univs. and Land-Grant Colls., Coun. for Exceptional Children, the Greater Akron Chamber, Cleve. Tomorrow. Roman Catholic. Avocations: walking, reading, traveling. Home: 1703 Woodway Rd Kent OH 44240-5917 Office: Kent State U Office of the President PO Box 5190 Kent OH 44242-0001 E-mail: carol.cartwright@kent.edu.*

CARTWRIGHT, NANCY, actress, television producer; b. Kettering, Ohio, Oct. 25, 1957; d. Frank and Miriam Cartwright; m. Warren Murphy, Dec. 24, 1988; children: Lucy Mae, Jackson. Student, Ohio U., 1976—77; BA in theatre, UCLA, 1981. Founder Cartwright Entertainment Inc. Author: (biography) My Life as a 10-Year-Old Boy, 2000; prodr.: (animated internet series) The Kellys, 2001—; actor(voice): (TV series) The Richie Rich/Scooby-Doo Hour, 1980, Richie Rich, 1981, Monchichis, 1983, Saturday Supercade, 1983, Alvin & the Chipmunks, 1983, The Shirt Tales, 1983—85, The Snorks, 1984, Galaxy High School, 1986, My Little Pony and Friends, 1986, Pound Puppies, 1986, Popeye and Son, 1987, (voice of Bart Simpson) The Tracy Ullman Show, 1987—89, (voice) Fantastic Max, 1988, (voice, Bart Simpson/Nelson/Todd Flanders/Ralph Wiggum/others) The Simpsons, 1989— (Emmy award outstanding voice-over performance, 1992), (voice) Dink, the Little Dinosaur, 1989, Goof Troop, 1992, Raw Toonage, 1992, Bonkers, 1993, Animaniacs, 1993 (Daytime Emmy awards honors for contbg., 1996), Problem Child, 1993, The Pink Panther, 1993, Aladdin, 1993, 2 Stupid Dogs, 1993, The Critic, 1994, Timon and Pumbaa, 1995, The Twisted Adventures of Felix the Cat, 1995, Toonsylvania, 1998, Pinky, Elmyra & the Brian, 1998 (Daytime Emmy awards honors for contbg., 1999), Mike, Lu & Og, 1999, Big Guy and Rusty the Boy Robot, 1999—, God, the Devil and Bob, 2000, (voice of Chuckie) Rugrats, 2001—04, (voice of Rufus) Kim Possible, 2002, (voice of Chuckie) All Grown Up, 2003, (voice): (videos) The Land Before Time VI: The Secret of Saurus Rock, 1998, Wakko's Wish, 1999, Timberwolf, 2002, Kim Possible: The Secret Files, 2003; (TV films) Kim Possible: A Stitch in Time, 2003; (films) The Chipmunk Adventure, 1987, The Little Mermaid, 1989, Petal to the Metal, 1992, Rugrats Go Wild!, 2003, : (TV films) Marian Rose White, 1982, The Rules of Marriage, 1982, Deadly Lessons, 1983, Not My Kid, 1985, Yellow Pages, 1988, On Hollywood Blvd., 1988, Precious Victims, 1993, Vows of Deception, 1996, Suddenly, 1996; (films) Twilight Zone: The Movie, 1983, Flesh & Blood, 1985, Godzilla, 1998; (plays) The Transgressor, 1980, Guys and Dolls, 1984, Coming Attractions, 1985, In Search of Fellini, 1995 (DramaLogue award best performance one-person show, 1996), Cat's Meow, 1998. Co-founder Neko Tech Learning Ctr., Ghana, W. Africa, 2000; mem., commr. Citizens Commn. on Human Rights, 1996—; active with Famous Fone Friends, The World Literacy Crusade, Make A Wish Foundation, The Way to Happiness Internat. Recipient Am. Libr. Assn. award, 1992, Elizabeth Andersch award, 1992, County of LA Pub. Libr. award, 1994, Annie award for outstanding individual achievement for voice acting field of animation, Internat. Animated Soc., 1995, PMA Star Power award, 2000. Mem.: Screen Actors Guild. Office: Cartwright Entertainment Inc 9420 Reseda Blvd #572 Northridge CA 91324*

CARTY, MARY ELLEN, psychologist; b. N.Y.C., Aug. 7, 1958; d. Walter Vincent and Sally Rita (Clarke) C. BA, Coll. of New Rochelle, 1980, MS, 1991; PsychD, Yeshiva U., 1997. Cert. sch. psychologist, N.Y.; lic. psychologist., N.Y. Grad. asst. Coll. of New Rochelle, N.Y., 1989-90, rsch. asst., 1990-91; sch. psychologist intern Pawling (N.Y.) Ctrl. Sch. Dist., 1990-91; sch. psychologist Pawling Jr./Sr. H.S., 1991-93, Clarkstown H.S. South, West Nyack, N.Y., 1993-94; behavior specialist, psychologist Esperanza Ctr., N.Y.C., 1993-96; clin. psychology intern, postdoctoral fellow Ctr. Preventive Psychiatry, 1996-98; program psychologist So. Westchester Bd. Coop. Ednl. Svcs., Harrison, 1998—2002; sch. psychologist Rye Neck Middle/H.S., Mamaroneck, NY, 2002—; sch. counselor Iona Coll., New Rochelle, N.Y., 1990-94, 96-97. Vol. English tchr. Immaculate Conception H.S., Jamaica, 1983—85, 1983—85; mem. grad. sch. adv. bd. Coll. of New Rochelle, 1999—2001; co-pres. alumni assn. Ferkaut Grad. Sch. Psychology, Yeshiva U., 2000—03; dir. Alumni Assn. Coll. of New Rochelle, 2001—; trustee, mem. ch. coun. St. Pius X Ch., Jamaica, 1983—85. Recipient Ursula Laurus citation, 2000; Empire Challenger fellow N.Y. State Edn. Dept., 1988-89. Mem.: APA, NY Assn. Sch. Psychologists (Ted Bernstein award 1996), Psi Chi. Democrat. Roman Catholic. Avocations: cycling, meditation, travel. Home: 434 N High St Mount Vernon NY 10552-3103 Office: Rye Neck Union Free Sch Dist 300 Hornridge Rd Mamaroneck NY 10543 E-mail: carty434@netscape.net.

CARTY, RITA MARY, dean, nurse; b. Pitts., Dec. 23, 1937; d. Ignatius and Frances (Brisini) Cardillo; m. Wayne Lee Carty, Aug. 20, 1966; 1 child, Gina Marie. Diploma in Nursing, Ohio Valley Gen. Hosp., McKees Rocks, Pa., 1958; BSN, Duquesne U., 1965, PhD (hon.), 1995; MSN, Cath. U., 1966, DNSc, 1977. Sch. nurse South Fayette Twp. Sch. Dist., McDonald, Pa., 1958-60; charge nurse Ohio Valley Gen. Hosp., McKees Rocks, Pa., 1960-62, instr., 1962-65; asst. prof. Cath. U., Washington, 1966-72, lectr., 1972-74; dir. nursing div. univ. affiliated program Georgetown U., Washington, 1978-81; assoc. prof., grad. program coordinator George Mason U., Fairfax, Va., 1981-85, chmn. dept. nursing, 1985-93, dean and prof. sch. nursing, 1993—, dean, prof. Coll. Nursing and Health Sci., 1993—; dir. Inst. of Post. Grad. Health Sci., 1991—. Dir. WHO Collaborating Ctr., 1991—. Contbr. articles to profl. jours. Mem. Luxmanor Citizens Assn., Rockville, Md., 1985—. Recipient Bice Lectureship award, sch. nursing U. Va., Charlottesville, 1984, Progress of Excellence award region III Nat. U. Continuing Edn., 1985, Chief Nurse Officer award, 1992. Fellow Am. Acad. Nursing; mem. ANA, Va. Soc. Profl. Nursing (bd. dirs. 1985-87), Am. Assn. Coll. Nursing (bd. dirs. 1987-90, pres. 1990-92), Nat. League Nursing (exec. com. 1987-89), Cath. U. Nurses Alumnae (pres. 1979-81), Golden Key Soc. (hon.), Sigma Theta Tau (1st v.p. 1970-73). Roman Catholic. Avocations: horse back riding, painting, drawing. Office: George Mason U Coll Nursing & Health Sci 4400 University Dr Fairfax VA 22030-4444

CARUANA, LAURA E. special education educator; b. Buffalo, July 23, 1976; d. Joseph A. and Christine M. Caruana; m. Mark D. Bechtel, June 8, 2002. BA U. Buffalo; MS Magna Cum Laude, Daemen Coll. Cert. EMT NY, 2000; spl. edn. tchr. N.Y., Ga. Presch. tchr. Page 1 Presch., Amherst, NY, 1999; tchr. asst. United Cerebral Palsy NY, Cheektowaga, 1999; spl. edn. tchr. Cantalician Ctr. for Learning, Buffalo, 2000—01, Northwestern Mid. Sch., Alpharetta, Ga., 2001—. Youth group dir. Our Lady of Peace Ch., Clarence, NY, 2000—01. Campaign mem. Elect Bill Paxon for Congress, Buffalo, 1994. Recipient Presdl. scholarship, Niagara U., 1994, achievement award, Clarence Fire Dept., N.Y., 1999. Mem.: Coun. for Exceptional Children, Clarence Fire Dept. Assn. (v.p. 1998—99). Republican. Roman Catholic. Avocation: travel, softball. Home: 911 Bradford Creek Trail Duluth GA 30096

CARUNCHIO, FLORENCE REGINA, financial planner; b. Jersey City, July 30, 1952; d. Alfred Peter and Florence Concetta (Pirozzi) Carunchio. BA summa cum laude, Montclair State U., 1975. CFP; lic. ins. provider N.J., N.Y., Va., Fla.; tchr. psychology and social studies K-12 N.J. Tchr. social studies St. Michael's Acad., Palisades Park, NJ, 1975—79; coord. film libr. and youth programs World Vision, Midland Park, NJ, 1981—82; owner Gifts of the Magi, Westwood, NJ, 1982—84; exec. asst. to CEO, Biomatrix, Inc., Ridgefield, NJ, 1985—94; assets mgr. Balden Assocs., Ridgefield, NJ, 1985—94; advanced advisor Am. Express Fin. Advisors, Paramus, NJ, 1996—2002, sr. fin. advisor, 1999—2002. Advisor of record pension plan, I.U.O.E. Am. Express Fin. Advisors, Paramus, 2000—04; spkr. in field. Avocations: music, literature, Bible translation and distribution. Office: Am Express Fin Advisors 140 Rt 17N Ste 316 Paramus NJ 07652

CARUSO, AILEEN SMITH, managed care consultant; b. Albany, N.Y., July 25, 1949; d. Robert Vincent and Mary (Prince) Smith; 1 child, Patrick Michael. AAS in nursing, Russell Sage Jr. Coll., Albany, 1970; BSBA cum laude, Coll. St. Rose, 1994. Cert. case mgr., adminstr. Physician Practice Mgmt. (CAPPM); RN N.Y. Staff nurse neuro and thoracic surgery units VA Hosp., 1970-71; staff nurse family practice Milton F. Gipstein, MD, Schenctady, N.Y., 1971-74; psychiat. nurse Peter F. Andrus, MD, Albany, 1977-81; coll. health nurse Siena Coll., Loudonville, N.Y., 1978-81; health nurse State U. N.Y., Albany, 1979-82; orthopedic staff nurse Rosa Road Orthopedics, Schenectady, 1980-82; coll. health nurse Union Coll., Schenectady, 1982-87; customer svc. rep. Empire Blue Cross, Albany, 1987-88; fin. planner N.Y. Life Ins., Albany, 1988-89; sr. mgr. Corp. Health Demensions, Troy, N.Y., 1989-94, dir. implementation and tng., 1994-96, dir. implementation and corp. case mgmt., 1996, v.p. implementation, 1997, v.p. ops., 1998-99; dir. clin. ops. U.S. Oncology Network, 1999—. Mem. adv. bd. Amgen, MGI Pharma; advisor Gen. Elec. Corp. R&D Safety Com., Schenectady, 1992-94; chmn. profl. devel. Northeast N.Y. Health Promotion, Albany, 1994-99; com. chair Schenectady Health Coalition, 1993-95; edn. and by laws com., com. chair govt. affairs Am. Occupational Health Nurses, Albany, 1994-99; cert. adminstr. physician practice mgmt.; cons. for healthcare for bus., 2003—. Co-author: Occupational Health Services Administrative/Patient Management Manual. Pres. Ch. Women, St. George's Episcopal Ch., 1994-97, mem. exec. bd. dirs., 1989-97, sr. vestryman, mem. exec. search com., 1998-99, also lector; chmn. worksite program N.E. N.Y. Tobacco-Free Coalition, 1993-94; co-mgr. The Bookshop at St. Georges, 1993-95; mem. Futures Charity Golf Tournament; mem. USON Exec. Leadership/Clin. Leadership Coun., mem. exec. bd., 2002-; co-chair Cancer Survivors Day, 2001-02; mem. reimbursement com. Uson Clin. Leadership Coun.; mem. Nat. Patient Advocate Found.; co-chair N.Y. state task force Patient Advocate Found.; mem. Am. Cancer Soc. Making Strides Work. Recipient Rector's Recognition award St. George's Ch., 1991, U.S. Oncology Excellence award, 2004. Mem. Am. Assn. Occupl. Health Nurses (chair govtl. affairs com.), Capital Dist. Occupl. Health Nurses (nominating com.), Schenectady County Health Promotion Consortium, Health Promotion Coun. of N.E. N.Y., Oncology Nurses Soc., Schenectady County Bus. and Profl. Women, Capital Dist. Case Mgmt. Assn. (nominating com.), Am. Acad. Physician Practice Mgmt., Alpha Sigma Lambda. Avocations: racquetball, boating, reading, golf. Home: 1156 Spearhead Dr Scotia NY 12302-3122 Office: US Oncology/Hematology 1003 Loudon Rd Latham NY 12110

CARUSO, ANN S. fashion editor, stylist; b. Worcester, Mass., Feb. 6, 1966; d. John Stephen and Helene Patricia Caruso. BS, Bentley Coll., 1989. Design asst. Ralph Lauren, N.Y.C., 1989-91; Vogue fashion editor Vogue Mag. Conde Nast, N.Y.C., 1991-96; fashion editor Quest Mag., N.Y.C., 1999-2001; contbg. fashion editor Tatler Mag., London, 2001—. Stylist for VH1 Fashion Awards show, 1996; stylist for advt. campaigns, including Nautica, St. Regis Hotel, Weight Watchers, Am. Express, Neiman Marcus, London Fog, Susan Lazar, Douglas Hannant, Tommy Hilfiger, Ralph Lauren, among others; freelance cons. various mags., including Tatler, Vanity Fair, InStyle, Marie Claire, Esquire, N.Y. Mag., others. Chmn. Kids N' U Found., N.Y.C., 1993-98; mem. Bot. Gardens, 1998-2001, Nat. Hist. Mus., 1992-2000, Henry St. Settlement, 1999-2000, N.Y. Acad. Art, 1994-98, Group for the South Fork, 1997-2000, Chances for Children, 1999, Parrish Art Mus., 2001, ASPCA, 2000, 01. Home: 69 5th Ave Apt 10A New York NY 10003-3008

CARVAJAL, VICTORIA LAVONE, customer service administrator; d. John and Millie Rice; m. Frank Carvajal, Dec. 25, 1994. AS in Computer Info. Sci., Connors State Coll., 1991; BS in Mgmt. Info. Sci., Northeastern State U., 1998. Lic.: Dept. Vets. Affairs (mediator). Owner/mgr. R&L Ranch/Hilltop Farms, Ft. Gibson, Okla., 1987—91; clk. Dept. Vets. Affairs, Muskogee, Okla., 1991—94, adjudicator, 1994—2001, rating vets. svc. rep., 2001—. CPR instr. Am. Heart Assn., Muskogee, 1995—. Mem.: NAFE, Promoting Animal Welfare Soc. Avocations: animal rescue, animal training, genealogy. Home and Office: Krystle Kennel Club PO Box 1932 Muskogee OK 74402-1932

CARVALHO, JULIE ANN, psychologist; b. Washington, Apr. 11, 1940; d. Daniel Henry and Elizabeth Cecilia (Gardiner) Schmidt; children: Alan R., Dennis M., Melanie D., Celeste A., Joshua E. BA with high honors, U. Md., 1962, postgrad., 1962-63, 68-73; MA, George Washington U., 1966; postgrad., Va. Poly. Inst., 1979-88; doctoral studies in curriculum and instrn., Argosy U., 2003—. Social sci. rsch. analyst Mental Health Study Ctr., NIMH, Adelphi, Md., 1963-67; edn. and tng. analyst Computer Applications, Inc., Silver Spring, Md., 1967-68; edn. program specialist, program analyst Nat. Ctr. for Ednl. R&D, U.S. Office of Edn., Washington, 1969-73; equal opportunity specialist Office of Sec., HEW, Washington, 1973-77; legis. program, civil rights analyst Office for Civil Rights Dept. Health and Human Svcs., Washington, 1977-85; ind. cons. Adj. lectr. No. Va. C.C., George Mason U., Montgomery Coll., Strayer U., Park U., Shepherd Coll., Germanna Coll., U. Md. U. Coll., Va. Internat. U., Prince William Hosp., Fairfax County Pub. Schs., Fairfax County Dept. Social Svcs., all Washington area, 1986—; proposal evaluator HUD, HHS, 1989—. Contbr. articles to profl. jours. Bd. dirs. Child Care Ctrs., 1970—76, HEW Employees Assn., 1973—78, D.C.-Balt. Region Unitarian Universalists for Social Justice, 2003—; mem. steering com. Alliance for Child Care, 1975—80; tchr. seminars for single-parent and spiritual groups. Mem.: ASPA (condr. panels 1975, 1991), APA (panel condr. 1969—75, editor Bull. of Peace Psychology 1991—97, divsn. 48), Unitarian Universalists for Social Justice (Balt.-Washington region) (bd. mem. 2003—), Federally Employed Women (nat. editor 1975—79), Psychologists Soc. Responsibility (cons.), Capitol Area Social Psychologists Assn. (conf. chmn. 1985, 1993), Fairfax County Assn. for the Gifted (pres. 1980), Phi Alpha Theta, Psi Chi, Alpha Sigma Lambda (hon.). Home and Office: PO Box 11500 Alexandria VA 22312-0500 E-mail: visionaries@pocketmail.com.

CARVER, DOROTHY LEE ESKEW (MRS. JOHN JAMES CARVER), retired secondary school educator; b. Brady, Tex., July 10, 1926; d. Clyde Albert and A. Maurine (Meadows) Eskew; m. John James Carver, Feb. 26, 1944; children: John James, Sheila Carver Bentley, Chuck, David. Student, So. Oreg. Coll., 1942-43, Coll. Eastern Utah, 1965-67; BA, U. Utah, Hayward, 1968; MA, Cal. State Coll. at Hayward, 1970; postgrad., Mills Col., 1971. Instr. Rutherford Bus. Coll., Dallas, 1944-45; sec. Adolph Coors Co., Golden, Colo., 1945-47; instr. English Coll. Eastern Utah, Price, 1968-69; instr. speech Modesto (Calif.) Jr. Coll., 1970-71; instr. personal devel. men and women Heald Bus. Colls., Oakland, Calif., 1972-74, dean curricula Walnut Creek, Calif., 1974-86; instr. Diablo Valley Coll., Pleasant Hill, Calif., 1986-87, Contra Costa Christian H.S., 50 1992; ret., 1992. Communications cons. Oakland Army Base, Crocker Bank, U.S. Steel, I. Magnin, Artec Internat.; presenter in field. Author: Developing Listening Skills. Mem. Gov.'s Conf. on Higher Edn. in Utah, 1968; mem. finance com. Coll. Eastern Utah, 1967-69; active various cmty. drives; bd. dirs. Opportunity Ctr., Symphony of the Mountain;; pres. adv. bd. Walnut Creek Srs., 1998—. Mem. AAUW, Bus. and Profl. Womens Club, Nat. Assn. Deans and Women Adminstrs., Delta Kappa Gamma. Episcopalian (supt. Sunday Sch. 1967-69). Clubs: Soroptimist Internat. (pres. Walnut Creek 1979-80, sec., founder region 1978-80); Order Eastern Star. Home: 20 Coronado Ct Walnut Creek CA 94596-5801

CARVER, JUANITA ASH, plastic company executive; b. Apr. 8, 1929; d. Willard H. and Golda M. Ashe; children: Daniel Charles, Robin Lewis, Scott Alan. Student, Ariz. State U., 1948, 72, Mira Mar Coll., 1994. Pres. Carver Corp., Phoenix, 1977—. Author series of children's stories. Bd. dirs. Scottsdale Meml. Hosp. Aux., 1964-65, now assoc. Republican. Methodist. Achievements include patents for latch hook Yarner; Pressure Lift.

CARVER, RITA, fundraising consultant; b. Minden, Nebr. d. Jess Albert and Marguerite Florence Ford; m. Rodney A. Carver, July 9, 1971 (div. June 1999); children: David Christopher, Heather Michelle. BS in Comm., Dallas Bapt. U., 1976; MA in human scis., Our Lady of the Lake, 2000. Freelance writer, 1976—82; account exec. Walvoord, Killian, McCabe, Dallas, 1982—86; sr. v.p. Resource Devel., Inc., Plano, Tex., 1986—2001; pres. R-Designs Inc., Plano, 2001—. Instr. Resource Inst., Springfield, Mo., 1986-99. Creative dir.: Portraits of Hope, 1996; editor: He Leadeth Me, 1999. Vol. Collin County Children's Adv. Ctr., Plano, 1999—. Named Outstanding Young Women of Am., 1980, Most Stressed Out Bus. Traveler, Rosewood Hotel and Resorts, 1994. Mem. AAUW, NAFE, Sierra Club, Plano C. of C. Methodist. Avocations: scuba diving, writing, dance, traveling. Office: R-Designs Inc 752 Nicklaus Dr Plano TX 75025

CARVER, ROBIN CAMPBELL, business software educator; b. Orlando, Fla., Jan. 13, 1962; d. Herman Lee and Pauline Lucille Campbell; m. Vernon Charles Carver. AA, Valencia C.C., Orlando, Fla. Cert. master instr. Microsoft. Payroll tax asst., computer project specialist Harcourt Brace Jovanovich, Orlando, 1984—92; PC coord. Fed. Home Life Ins. subs. of Harcourt Brace Jovanovich, Orlando, 1990—92; bus. tech. instr. Orange County Pub. Schs., Orlando, 1992—. Bingo caller Fairways Country Club, Orlando, 2003. Republican. Baptist. Achievements include development of State of Florida Frameworks for PC Support Services Program. Avocations: golf, fishing, assisting senior citizens with computer challenges. Office: Winter Park Tech 901 Webster Ave Winter Park FL 32789 E-mail: carverr@ocps.net.

CARVEY, JULIE AMBER, behavior specialist, educational consultant; d. Craig Lewis and Nikki Gatz Carvey; life ptnr. Charles Anthony Cohara, Jan. 3, 2004. BA in Psychology and Comm., Miami U., Oxford, Ohio, 2001, postgrad. in Curriculum, 2002—. Cert. case mgmt. Ohio Dept. Mental Retardation/Developmentally Disabled, 2003. Lead trainer Interfaith Ctr. for Peace, Columbus, 1993—2001; trainer Ctr. for Peace Edn., Cin., 2001—03; behavior specialist Butler County Bd. Mental Retardation/Developmentally Disabled, Hamilton, Ohio, 2001—. Curriculum devel. vol. Vineyard Cmty. Ch., Cin., 2003—03. Finalist, Harry S. Truman Found., 2000; recipient Leadership for a Lifetime award, Leadership Worthington, 1995, Cmty. Svc. award, The Columbus Dispatch, 1997. Mem.: Assn. for Conflict Resolution. Avocations: Tae Kwon Do, backpacking, culinary arts, skydiving, genealogy. Home: 48 Ridgeway Rd Cincinnati OH 45216 Personal E-mail: julieamber@fuse.net.

CARWELL, HATTIE VIRGINIA, health physicist; b. Bklyn., July 17, 1948; d. George and Fannie (Tunstall) C. BS in Chemistry/Biology, Bennett Coll., 1970; MS in Radiation Sci., Rutgers U., 1971; postgrad., U. Calif., Berkeley, 1973-75. Rsch. asst. Thomas Jefferson U. Hosp., Phila., 1970-72; health physicist AEC, Upton, N.Y., 1972-73, Energy Rsch. Adminstrn., Oakland, Calif., 1973-80; internat. nuclear safeguards insp. and group leader Internat. Atomic Energy Agy., Vienna, Austria, 1980-85; health physicist U.S. Dept. Energy, Oakland, Calif., 1985-90, program mgr. for high energy and nuclear programs, 1990-91, program mgr. Berkeley, Calif., 1991-93, ops. br. chief, 1993-94, ops. team head, 1994—. Asst. environ. survey team leader Dept. Energy, Washington, 1987; lectr. U. Calif.-Berkeley, Stanford U., Cabrillo Coll., Can. Coll., Tougaloo Coll; dir. Mus. African Am. Tech. Sci. Village. Author: Blacks In Science: Astrophysicist to Zoologist, 1977, In Pursuit of Excellence: Dr. Warren Henry - World

Class Scientist, 1998, Solar Cooker Design Training Guide, 1996; contbr. sci. articles to profl. jours. Co-founder, chmn. Devel. Fund for Black Students in Sci. and Tech., Washington, 1983—; dir., co-founder Mus. African Am. Tech. Sci. Village, 2000—; bd. dirs. Nat. Inventors Hall of Fame Found., 2001—03; treas. Nat. Coun. Black Scientists and Engrs., 2001—03; regional dir., mem. Nat. Tech. Assn., Washington, 1977—80. Named inductee, Black Coll. Hall of Fame, 1991, included in exhibit, The African Am. Presence in Physics, 1999; recipient Fed. Cmty. Svc. award, 1977, Elijah McCoy award, 1989, vol. recognition, Dept. Energy, 1990, Disting. Alumni award, 1992, Image award, Bennett Coll., 1997, Inspiring Scientist award, Jr. Arts and Sci. Ctr. of Oakland, 2002. Mem.: NAACP (life), No. Calif. Coun. Black Profl. Engrs. (pres. 1986, 1987, sec. 1988, pres. 1994, 1995, sec. 1996—99, pres. 2000—04), Inst. Materials Mgmt. (treas. Vienna chpt. 1985), Nat. Health Physics Soc., Nat. Tech. Assn. (James C. Jones Humanitarian award 2000). Avocations: writing, travel. Home: 4622 Meldon Ave Oakland CA 94619-2646

CARY, ALICE SHEPARD, retired physician; b. Gaziantep, Turkey, June 2, 1920; (parents Am. citizens); d. Lorrin Andrews and Virginia (Moffat) Shepard; m. Otis Cary, Dec. 9, 1944; children: Beth D., Ann B., Frank B., Ellen Cary Bearn. BA, Wellesley Coll., 1942; MD, Yale U., 1945. Intern, resident New Haven Hosp., 1945-47; physician Doshisha U. Health Ctr., Kyoto, Japan, 1947-50, Japan Bapt. Hosp., Kyoto, 1955-95; dir. Aoibashi Family Clinic Counseling Ctr., Kyoto, 1981-91; ret., 1996. Assoc. missionary United Ch. Bd. World Ministries, N.Y.C., 1947-96. Mem. adv. com. on women's issues UN Women's Decade, Prime Min.'s Office, Tokyo, 1970-75. Recipient 40th Anniversary award Coll. Women's Assn. Japan, 1989, internat. contbn. award City of Kyoto, 1992. Democrat. Mem. United Ch. of Christ. Home: 33 Linda Ave Apt 1601 Oakland CA 94611-4817

CASADESUS, PENELOPE ANN, advertising executive, film producer; b. Calcutta, India, Sept. 20, 1940; came to U.S., 1980; d. Francis John and Betty (Walker) Copeland; m. Jean-Claude Casadesus, Jan. 20, 1960; children: Caroline, Sebastian. Gen. Cert. of Edn., Godolphin Sch., Eng. Head of prodn. S.S.C.B. Lintas, Paris, 1975—78, Grey-France, Paris, 1978—80, Grey Worldwide, N.Y.C., 1980, exec. producer Internat. Health and Beauty divsn., 1991—, sr. v.p., group prodr. Ind. film producer, 1984—. Author, producer (screenplays) Transvaal Episode, The Cuckoo.

CASADY, ANE, realtor; b. Baytown, Tex., Dec. 26, 1947; d. Curtis Alfred and Shirley Ann Baker; m. Michael Kelly Casady, Aug. 11, 1973 (div. Dec. 16, 1998); 1 child, Navette. AA, Kilgore Coll., 1968; BA, U. Tex., 1970; MLA, So. Meth. U., 1973. Police officer Dallas (Tex.) Police, 1972—82; realtor Keller Williams, Frisco, Tex., 1999—. Mem. coun. Town of Prosper, 2003—; mem. sch. bd. Prosper (Tex.) Sch., 1985—2001. Avocations: travel, reading, crossword puzzles. Home: PO Box 726 Prosper TX 75078-0726 Office: Keller Williams Realty PO Box 726 Prosper TX 75078-0726

CASALS, ROSEMARY, retired professional tennis player; b. San Francisco, Sept. 16, 1948; Profl. tennis player, 1968—; nat. championships and major tournaments include U.S. Open singles (finalist), 1970, 71, U.S. Open doubles, 1967, 71, 74, 82, U.S. Open mixed doubles, 1975, Wimbledon doubles, 1967, 68, 70, 71, 73, Wimbledon mixed doubles, 1971, 73, finalist with Dick Stockton, 1970, Italian doubles, 1967, 70, Family Circle Cup (winner), 1973, Wightman Cup, 1967, 76-81, Bridgeston doubles championships (finalist), 1975, Spalding mixed doubles, 1976, 77, U.S. Tennis Assn. Atlanta doubles, 1976, Fedn. Cup, 1967, 76-81; winner 1st Virginia Slims tournament, 1970; 3d place Virginia Slims Championships, 1976, 4th place, 1977, 78; winner Murjani-WTA championship, 1980; Fla. Fed. Open doubles, 1980; pres. sports promotion co. Sportswoman, Inc., Sausalito, Calif., 1981—; Virginia Slims Legends Tour, 1995—. Mem. Los Angeles Strings team, World Team Tennis, 1975-77; founder Women's Sports Legends Inc. Virginia Slims Event tennis winner, 1986, doubles winner (with Martina Navratilova), 1988, 89; inducted in to Internat. Tennis Hall of Fame, Newport, R.I., 1996. Mem. Women's Internat. Tennis Assn. (bd. dirs.). Office: Sportswonn Inc PO Box 537 Sausalito CA 94966-0537 E-mail: sportswonn@aol.com.

CASAS, LAURIE ANN, plastic surgeon; b. May 26, 1956; married; 2 children. BS, BA, U. Ill., Champaign/Urbana, 1974—78; MD, Northwestern U. Med. Sch., Chgo., 1978—82. Diplomate Am. Bd. Plastic Surgery. Resident, gen. surgery Northwestern U. Med. Ctr., Chgo., 1982—85, resident, plastic surgery, 1985—88; microsurgery rsch. fellow So. Ill. U., Springfield, 1988; aesthetic plastic surgery fellow NYU, N.Y.C., 1989; breast reconstruction fellow St. Joseph Hosp., Atlanta, 1989; clin. instr., surgery Northwestern U. Med. Sch., Chgo., 1987—88, asst. prof., surgery, 1990—2001, assoc. prof., surgery, 2001—; adj. staff, asst. attending in plastic/reconstructive surgery Evanston Hosp., Ill., 1990, assoc. attending in plastic/reconstructive surgery, 1992, attending in plastic/reconstructive surgery, 1996; co-dir., ctr. for plastic and aesthetic surgery Glenbrook Hosp., Glenview, Ill., 1990—95, adj. staff, asst. attending in plastic/reconstructive surgery, 1990, assoc. attending in plastic/reconstructive surgery, 1992, attending in plastic/reconstructive surgery, 1996; acting head, divsn. plastic surgery Evanston Hosp. Corp., Ill., 1993—96; head, divsn. plastic surgery Evanston Northwestern Healthcare, Glenbrook Hosp., Glenview, Ill., 1996—. Mem. editl. bd. Plastic Surgery Today, 2000, Guide to Aesthetic Plastic Surgery, 2000, Your Image, 2002—03, editor-in-chief Aesthetic Soc. News, 2000—. Fellow: Am. Coll. Surgeons; mem.: AMA, Ill. Med. Soc., Plastic Surgery Rsch. Coun., Internat. Soc. Aesthetic Plastic Surgery, Midwestern Assn. Plastic Surgeons, The Rhinoplasty Soc., Chgo. Med. Soc., Chgo. Plastic Surgery Soc., Am. Soc. Plastic Surgery, Am. Soc. Aesthetic Plastic Surgery. Office: 2050 Pfingsten Ste 270 Glenview IL 60025

CASBON, MONICA LYNN, accountant; b. Michigan City, Ind., Aug. 10, 1955; d. Frank John and Mary Frances (Ray) K.; m. Robert D. Casbon, Sept. 30, 2000; 1 child, Katie Frances. BS in Bus., Ind. U. N.W., Gary, 1991, MBA, 1994. Cons. Hair Master, Chesterton, Ind., 1977-94; acct. SB Assocs., Valparaiso, Ind., 1994—; auditor State Bd. Accounts, 1998—2001; acct. McDonough Assocs., Chgo., 2000—03. Precinct com. person Porter County, Ind., 1989-91; fin. chmn. St. Patricks Festival, Chesterton, 1993, 94; vol. Spring Valley Homeless Shelter, Valparaiso, 1993—, Hilltop Neighborhood House, Valparaiso, 1997—. Mem. NAFE, Inst. Mgmt. Accts. Republican. Roman Catholic. Avocations: golf, reading, running, volunteer work. Home: 560 S 400 W Hebron IN 46341

CASCIO, TONI ANGELA, social worker, educator; b. Balt., Sept. 18, 1965; d. Anthony Vincent and Marilyn Jean Cascio. BA, Johns Hopkins U., 1987; MSW, U. Md., 1990; PhD, U. Pa., 1996. LCSW Md. Asst. prof. U. S.C., Columbia, 1996—99, U. Md., Balt., 1999—2002, assoc. prof., 2002—. Cons. Ctr. for Capital Litigation, Columbia, 1998—99; bd. dirs. Md. chpt. Crohn's and Colitis Found. Am., Balt., 2000—02. Co-editor: Religious Organizations in Community Service: A Social Work Perspective, 2003. Avocations: writing, baking. Office: Univ Md Sch Social Work 525 W Redwood St Baltimore MD 21201

CASE, DONNI MARIE, investment company executive; b. Chgo., Feb. 20, 1948; d. Donald Milton and Felecia Virginia (Krantz) Schuette; m. Lawrence Lee Hewitt, Apr. 20, 1996. BA in Econs., U. Ill., 1970. Pres. FRB/Weber Shandwick, Chgo., 1972—. Bd. dirs. Inst. Bus. and Profl. Ethics Depaul U. Mem.: Chicago Network, TEC Internat. Home: 2417 N Geneva Ter Chicago IL 60614-5914 Office: FRB/Weber Shandwick 676 N St Clair 13th Fl Chicago IL 60611-1803

CASE, KAREN ANN, lawyer; b. Milw., Apr. 7, 1944; d. Alfred F. and Hilda M. (Tomich) Case. BS, Marquette U., 1963, JD, 1966; LLM, NYU, 1973. Bar: Wis. 1966, U.S. Ct. Claims 1973, U.S. Tax Ct. 1973. Ptnr. Meldman, Case & Weine, Milw., 1973-85, Meldman, Case & Weine divsn. Mulcahy & Wherry, S.C., 1985-87; Sec. of Revenue State of Wis., 1987-88; ptnr. Case & Drinka, S.C., Milw., 1989-91, Case, Drinka & Diel, S.C., Milw., 1991-97, CoVac, 1997—. Lectr. U. Wis., Milw., 1974-78; guest lectr. Marquette U. Law Sch., 1975-78; dir. WBBC, 1998—. Contbr. articles to legal jours. Mem. gov.'s Commn. on Taliesin, 1988, gov.'s Econ. Adv. Commn., 1989-91, pres.'s coun. Alverno Coll., 1988-94, nat. coun., 1998-2000; bd. dirs. WBCC, 1998—. Fellow Wis. Bar Found. (dir. 1977-90, treas. 1980-90); mem. ABA, Milw. Assn. Women Lawyers (founding mem., bd. dirs. 1975-78, 81-82), Milw. Bar Assn. (bd. dirs. 1985-87, law office mgmt. chair 1992-93), State Bar Wis. (bd. govs. 1981-85, 87-90, dir. taxation sect. 1981-87, vice chmn. 1986-87, 90-91, chmn. 1991-92), Am. Acad. Matrimonial Lawyers (bd. dirs. 1988-90), Nat. Assn. Women Lawyers (Wis. del. 1982-83), Milw. Rose Soc. (pres. 1981, dir. 1981-83), Friends of Boerner Bot. Gardens (founding mem., pres. 1984-90), Profl. Dimensions Club (dir. 1985-87), Tempo Club (sec. 1984-85). Home: 2212 Harbour Ct Longboat Key FL 34228-4174 Office: CoVac 9803 W Meadow Park Dr Hales Corners WI 53130-2261 Office Phone: 414-425-5672.

CASE, MARGARET A. state legislator; b. Albany, N.Y., Feb. 15, 1938; d. Kosta Stefan and Mary Collins K.; m. Frank G. Case; children: Martin, Matthew. Student, Boston U.; BS, U. N.H., 1976. N.H. state rep. Dist. 6, Rockingham County, 1982-86, Dist. Rockingham 2, 1994—; mem. health, human svc., and elderly affairs coms. N.H. Ho. of Reps. Devel. tester. Mem. N.H. Assn. Realtors, Rockingham Woman's Coun. Realtors (v.p. 1993, pres. 1994), N.H. Womens' Coun. Realtors (sec. 1993-94, pres.-elect 1994-95). Address: 44 Beach Head Rd 22 Lake Shore Dr Nottingham NH 03290-4927

CASE, ROSALIND See AVRETT, ROZ

CASE, TAMMY, bank executive; BBA magna cum laude, Upsala Coll., 1995; grad. with honors, U. Del., 1998. Platform asst. to asst. br. mgr. Nat. Bank Sussex County, 1977—81, adminstrv. asst. to asst. cashier, 1981—86, asst. v.p., compliance officer, 1986—89, v.p., 1989—93; sr. loan officer Newton (NJ) Trust Co., 1993—, sr. v.p. bus. banking svcs., 2001—. Chair Sussex County C. of C., past chair govt. legis. com.; past chair ARC; trustee Patriots Path Boy Scout Coun., Ct. Appointed Spl. Advocates; past chair found. bd. SCARD; mem. interfaith hosp. network Sparta Presbyn. Ch.; bd. dirs. Sussex County Econ. Devel. Ptnrship. Named one of 25 Women to Watch, US Banker Mag., 2003; recipient Vol. of Yr. award, Sussex County C. of C., 2001, Women of Yr. award, Patriot's Path Boy Scout Coun., 2001. Office: Newton Trust Co 29 Trinity St Newton NJ 07860*

CASEBIER, LINDY, state legislator; b. Dec. 27, 1960; BMEd, ME, U. Louisville. Rep. dist. 29 Ky. State Ho. of Reps., 1987-92; senator dist. 7 Ky. State Senate, 1993—. Del. Rep. Nat. Conv., 1984; chmn. Jefferson County Rep. Party, 1991. Mem. Am. Cancer Soc. (former bd. dirs.), Ky. Edn. Assn., Jefferson County Tchrs. Assn., Valley Optimist Club. Baptist. Address: 9116 Wooddale Dr Louisville KY 40272-2755 Office: Ky State Senate State Capitol Frankfort KY 40601

CASEI, NEDDA, mezzo-soprano; b. Balt. d. Howard Thomas and Lyda Marie (Graupman) Casey; m. John A. Wiles, Jr., 1971 (div. 1979); m. Samuel Strasbourger, 1983 (dec. 1987). Cert., Mozarteum, Salzburg, Austria, 1959; B in Performing Arts Adminstrn. magna cum laude, Fordham U., 1982; studied voice with, William P. Herman, N.Y.C., Vittorio Piccinini, Milan, Italy, Loretta Corelli, N.Y.C., also student piano, langs., modern dance, ballet. Tchr. master classes, lectr. univs. and festivals. Judge vocal competitions for Met. Opera, Fulbright Scholarship, Rosa Ponselle Internat. Competition, Savannah Festival, George London Found. Competition, First Internat. Vocal Competition, Baku, Azerbaijan, and others; vis. prof. Aichi Prefectural U. Fine Arts and Music, Nagoya, Japan; guest prof. Flaine Festival/Paris Conservatory, Haut Savoie, France, Mannes Coll. Music, New Sch. Social Rsch., N.Y.C., Internat. Vocal Arts Inst., Tel Aviv; pvt. tchr. Operatic debut Theatre Royal de la Monnaie, Brussels, 1960, with La Scala, Milan, Met. Opera, N.Y.C., 1964, Theatre Royal de la Monnaie, Brussels (with La Scala); operatic performances at Met. Opera, 1964-86, Basel Stadttheater, Gran Liceo, Barcelona, Teatro Carlo Fenice, Genova, San Remo Festival, Trieste Opera, Opera du Rhin, Strasbourg, Salzburg Festspielhaus, Teatro San Carlo, Naples, Chgo. Lyric Opera, Bogota Opera, Caracas Opera, Pitts. Opera, Vancouver Opera, Cape Town Opera, Brno Opera, Bratislava Opera, Kosice Opera, Prague Opera, Miami Opera, Houston Opera, San Diego Opera, Hartford Opera, Phila. Opera, Toledo Opera, Dayton Opera, Memphis Opera, Mobile Opera, Los Angeles Opera, Boston Opera, N.J. Opera, Taipei Opera, Opera of Mexico City; performances in numerous mus. festivals, concerts, recitals and operatic guest appearances in Europe, South Africa, Cen. Am., S.Am., Can., U.S., Far East, Middle East and Australia, including Detroit Symphony, Cin. Orch., Toronto Symphony. Liepzig Gewandhaus, Philharm. Bruxelles, Phila. Orch., NY Philharm.; performed on radio and TV in Holland, Belgium, Leipzig, Japan, U.S., German Dem. Republic, Fed. Republic of Germany, Hong Kong, Singapore; performed at White House, Washington; made various recs. Supraphon, Everest, Nonesuch, Concert Hall, Vanguard, CETRA, VAI, others; contbr. articles to profl. jours.; guest editor Opera Quar. Coord. mus. events and benefits for Internat. Ctr. for Disabled, Morningside Home, Aging in Am. Gerontol. Acad.; mem. adv. bd. Fordham U at Lincoln Ctr., 1984—; bd. dirs. Theatre for a New Audience, Am. Coun. for Arts, Nat. Cultural Alliance, Songs of Love; mem. Career Transition for Dancers Nat. Adv. Bd. Recipient Outstanding Young Singers award, 1959, Martha Baird Rockefeller Found. award, 1962, 1964, Woman of Achievement award, 1969, Cmty. Leaders and Noteworthy Americans, 1975—76, Outstanding Achievement award on behalf of Arts and Edn., Opera Music Theater Internat. and Children's Emergency Med. Fund, 2000, Outstanding Lifetime Achievement award, Licia Albanese/Puccini Found., 2001, Extraordinary Women award, 2000, honors at, 100 Year Verdi Celebration by Met. Opera. Mem. AFTRA, Actors Equity, Am. Guild Mus. Artists (nat. pres. 1983-93. chmn. Emergency Relief Fund 1983-94), Nat. Assn. Tchrs. Singing (bd. govs.), N.Y. Singing Tchrs. Assn., Assn. Music Tchrs. League, The Players, James Beard Found. E-mail: neddanewyork@nyc.rr.com., neddanagoya@guitar.ocn.ne.jp.

CASEIRAS, JO ANN STRIGA, artist, educator; b. Bklyn., Dec. 17, 1950; d. Michael Striga and Stella Mary Lango; m. Frank Caseiras, May 21, 1983; children: Michael Allen, Kevin Frank, Amanda Beth, Robert Anthony. BFA, St. John's U., Jamaica, N.Y., 1972; MFA, SUNY, New Paltz, 1975. Tchr. continuing edn. SUNY, New Paltz, 1974-75, prof. Buffalo, 1976-78; tchr. Marlboro (N.Y.) Elem. Continuing Edn., 1980-82; parent advocate Rondout Valley Ctrl. Sch. Dist., Accord, N.Y., 1992-97, tchr. program for the handicapped, 1999—. Exhibited in shows at Reavin Gallery, New Paltz, N.Y., 1976, Benjamin's Works of Art, Buffalo, 1977, Art Zone 208, New Paltz, 1979, Mamaroneck Artists Guild, White Plains, N.Y., 1979, Womanart Gallery, N.Y.C., Schenectady (N.Y.) Mus., 1980, New Rochelle (N.Y.) Art Assn., 1994, Heritage Art Gallery, Poughkeepsie, N.Y., 1995, St. John's U., Jamaica, N.Y., 1996, Heritage Gallery, Rhinebeck, N.Y., 1997, Highland (N.Y.) Cultural Art Ctr., 1996-98, Coffey Gallery, Kingston, N.Y., 1998, Woodstock (N.Y.) Art Assn., 1995—, First Union Bank, New Paltz, 2000, Marbletown Arts Assn., 2002, Marbletown Tricentennial Exhbn., 2003. Recipient Mortimer L. Medrich Meml. award, 1979. Mem. Woodstock Art Assn., Art Soc. Kingston, Downs Syndrome Assn. Democrat. Roman Catholic. Avocations: sports, swimming, piano, photography. E-mail: jstrigacaseiras@aol.com.

CASELLA, MARGARET MARY, artist; b. Bklyn. d. John August and Ann Elizabeth (Krajci) Butkovsky; m. Anthony Joseph Casella, Nov. 23, 1961; children: Paul Joseph, David John, Gregory Anthony. Cert. in Merchandising, Tobe-Coburn Sch., N.Y.C., 1961; BFA, L.I. U., 1982, MFA, 1984. Lectr. in field. Photographer: (book) Garbage or Art?, 1990 (Gold award Photo Design Mag. 1990); exhibited in solo exhbns. Midtown Y Photography Gallery, N.Y.C., 1991, Grand Ctrl. Terminal, N.Y.C., 1991, Ctr. for Photography at Woodstock, N.Y., 2000, Hort. Soc. N.Y./Webster Gallery, 2000, Elaine Benson Gallery, Bridgehampton, N.Y., others; group shows include U. Tex. at Arlington, Deutser Art Gallery, Houston, Heckscher Mus., Huntington, N.Y., Konica Plz., Tokyo, Firehouse Gallery, Garden City, N.Y., The Visual Club, N.Y.C., Hillwood Art Mus., Greenvale, N.Y.; works in permanent collections of Mus. for Photography, Branschweig, Germany, Yergeau Musee Internat. d'Art, Montreal, Fine Art Mus. of L.I., Hempstead, N.Y., Houston fotofest Permanent Archives, Houston. Founder, dir. Art Upstairs Gallery, East Williston, 1983-91; mem. adv. bd. C.W. Post Campus Sch. of Visual and Performing Arts. Named to Women's Roll of Honor, Town of North Hempstead, NY, 2003. Avocation: gardening. Studio: Casella Photography 889 Broadway New York NY 10003-1212 E-mail: nyctwoonetwo@aol.com.

CASE-SCHMIDT, MARY E. pathologist, educator; b. Jefferson City, Mo., Feb. 27, 1943; BA, U. Mo., 1965; MD, St. Louis U. Sch. Medicine, 1969. Resident in pathology St. Louis U. Sch. Medicine, St. Louis, 1969—71, asst. in pathology, 1969—73; postdoctoral fellow Nat. Inst. Neurol. Disease and Stroke, St. Louis, 1971—72; resident in neuropathology St. Louis U. Sch. Medicine, 1972—73, instr. in pathology, 1973—75; vis. asst. prof. neuropathology U. Mo., Sch. Medicine, Columbia, Mo., 1975—77; asst. prof. pathology St. Louis U. Sch. Medicine, 1975—81; cons. neuropathology St. Luke's Hosp., East and West, 1973—77; asst. med. examiner St. Louis County, 1975—88, City of St. Louis, 1977—80; assoc. prof. pathology St. Louis U. Sch. Medicine, 1981—99; dep. chief med. examiner City of St. Louis, 1980—85; cons. neuropathology St. John's Mercy Hosp., St. Louis, 1973—88; spl. projects, divsn. forensic and environ. pathology St. Louis U. Sch. Medicine, 1985—; chief med. examiner St. Charles County, 1986—, St. Louis County, 1988—, Jefferson County, 1992—, Franklin County, 1993—; prof. pathology St. Louis U. Health Scis. Ctr., 1999—, co-dir., divsn. forensic pathology, 1996—. Dean's adv. bd. St. Louis U., 2000—; bd. dirs. Greater St. Louis Region Critical Incident Stress Mgmt. Team, 1995—; mem. Nat. Medicolegal Rev. Panel for Devel. Guidelines for Death Invest. for Nat. Inst. Justice, 1996—. Recipient Spl. Leadership award for Professions, Meto. St. Louis YWCA, 1990, Norman Westbrook "Hall of Fame" award, Mo. Police Juvenile Officers Assn., 1992, Recognition award "Teen Drinking and Driving", St. Louis Metro. Med. Soc., 2001, Spl. Recognition award, St. Charles Crime Stoppers, 2002. Fellow: Am. Acad. Forensic Sci. (ethics com. 2001—), Am. Soc. Clin. Pathology, Coll. Am. Pathologists; mem.: AMA, Nat. Assn. Med. Examiner (bd. dir. 2000—, exec. com. 2001—), Am. Assn. Neuropathologists, Internat. Acad. Pathology, St. Louis Path. Soc., St. Louis Metro. Med. Soc., Am. Profl. Soc. on Abuse of Children, Mo. State Med. Assn., Mo. Network of Cert. Pathologists for Child Death Autopsies (chmn. 1996—), Am. Journal Forensic Medicine and Pathology. Office: St Louis U Sch Medicine Dept Pathology 1402 S Grand Saint Louis MO 63104-1004

CASEY, BARBARA A. PEREA, state legislator, school superintendent; b. Las Vegas, N.Mex., [illegible] 1951; d. [illegible] and Julia A. (Aguilo) Perea, m. Frank J. Casey, Aug. 5, 1978. BA, N.Mex. U., 1972; MA, Highland U., Las Vegas, N.Mex., 1973. Instr. N.Mex. Highlands U., Las Vegas, 1972-74; tchr. Roswell Ind. Schs., Roswell, N.Mex., 1974-96; supt. Hondo Valley Pub. Schs., N.Mex.; mem. N.Mex. Ho. of Reps., 1984—; supt. Hondo (N.Mex.) Valley Pub. Schs., 1996—2000, West Las Vegas (N.Mex.) Schs., Las Vegas, 2000—. Instr. N.Mex. Mil. Inst., Roswell, 1977-82, Roswell Police Acad., 1984. N.Mex. advisor Nat. Trust for Hist. Preservation. Mem. NEA (Adv. of of Yr.), AAUW, Am. Bus. Women's Assn., N.Mex. Endowment for Humanities. Democrat. Roman Catholic. Avocations: hunting, reading, writing, poetry. Home: 509 Raynolds Ave Las Vegas NM 87701-4323

CASEY, BARBARA JEANNE, marketing professional; b. Glen Cove, N.Y., Mar. 6, 1970; d. William Royal DeMeo and Barbara Louise (Anderson) Terry; m. John Edward Casey, Sept. 12, 1998. BA, U. So. Calif., 1992; MBA, Columbia U., 1998. Client svcs. rep. Christie's Inc., N.Y.C., 1992-93, adminstr., 1993-94, overseas liaison, 1994-96; assoc. mktg. mgr. Time Inc., N.Y.C., 1998-99; dir. mktg. Onview.com., N.Y.C., 1999—2001; v.p. client rels. Chilton Investment Co., Inc., 2001—. Mem. jr. com. Search and Care, Inc., 1993—. Mem. N.Y.C. Alumni Club (v.p. 1996-98, co-pres. 1998-2002), Doubles Club (assocs. com. 1993—), Delta Gamma (v.p. programming alumni club 1994-95). Avocations: dogs, tennis, golf, skiing, arts and entertainment. Home: 945 Fifth Ave Apt 3D New York NY 10021-2655 Office: Onview dot com 300 Park Ave 19th Fl New York NY 10022

CASEY, BONNIE MAE, artist, educator; b. Chgo., Ill., Aug. 1, 1932; d. Edward Frances Kusch, Bessie Elaine (Moulding) Kusch; m. George Daniel Casey, Feb. 21, 1953; children: Cheryl Ann, Stuart Evan, Charles Alan. Student, Am. Acad. Art, Chgo., Harper Jr. Coll., Schamburg, Ill. Instr. Village Art Sch., Skokie, Ill., 1965—80, Art Barn, Elk Grove Village, Ill., 1978—83, Mountain Artists Guild, Prescott, Ariz., 1985—2000, Pima Coll., Green Valley, Ariz. Bd. dirs. Southwestern Artists Assn.; mem. visual arts com. Prescott Fine Arts Assn., 1995—2003; bd. dirs. Prescott Arts and Humanities, 1986—99; tchr. Vaison la Romaine, France, San Mignel del Allende, Mexico; instr. in field; organizer, arts curator Open Space Alliance, 2001. Contbr. articles to Fine Art Collector mag. ., Wine and Dine mag.; prin. works include painting 9-11-01, 2001, logo design, Arts and Humanities Coun., Prescott, Town of Chino Valley, Ariz., mural design, History of Chino Valley, one-woman shows include Mitchell Mus., Trinidad, Colo., 1992, 50 Yr. Art Retrospective, 2003, exhibited in group shows at Phippen Mus. Named Curator of Yr., Prescott Fine Arts Assn.; recipient Grumbacher Gold medal, 1992, 1996, Gov.'s award nominee, Ariz. Commn. on Arts; featured artist 50 Yrs. of Art Retrospective, Prescott Fine Arts Gallery, 2003. Mem.: Southwestern Artists Assn., Western Acad. Women Artists (historian), Oil Painters Am., Phippen Western Art Mus., Prescott Art Docents (docent auditor 1996—2003). Avocation: travel. Home: 3380 N Yuma Dr Chino Valley AZ 86323

CASEY, DARLA DIANN, elementary school educator; b. West Linn, Oreg., Mar. 21, 1940; d. Karl F. and Lucille Iona (Wilson) Lettenmaier; m. Charles Emerson Casey, July 30, 1965; children: John, Michael, Kim. BSEd, U. Wis., Milw., 1965; MEd, postgrad., Oreg. State U., U. Oreg., West State, Port State. Cert. tchr. grades K-9, basic art grades 1-12. Tchr., grade 3, swimming instr., grades 4-6 Lakeside (Oreg.) Elem.; tchr., readiness rm. K-1 Siuslaw Elem., Florence, Oreg.; tchr., grades K and 1st, spl. reading, art Washington Elem., Canon City, Colo.; tchr., grade 1 Sam Case Elem. Sch., Lincoln County Sch. Dist., Newport, Oreg. Mentor tchr. N.W. Sci. Survey Com.; aerospace sci. tchr. 3d through 5th and 4H Young Astronauts 3d through 5th NASA's Space Down to Earth Program, 1998; speaker in field. Contbr. articles to profl. jours. Named Oreg. Elem. Sci. Tchr. of Yr. Am. Electronics Assn. and Dept. Edn., 1989; NASA scholar (Nasa edn. workshop for elem. sci. tchrs. program), 1992, 95, Oreg. Cadre for All tchrs. of Sci. scholar, 1993, NASA Flight Opportunities for Sci. Tchr. Enrichment Project scholar, 1995, Am. Astron. Soc. Tchr. Resource Agt., 1996, ASTRA scholar U. Tex. and McDonald Observatory, 1996. Mem. Oreg. Sci. Tchrs. Assn., Oreg. Reading Assn., Oreg. Seacoast Reading Coun. (past pres.), Oreg. Math. Tchrs. Assn., Phi Delta Kappa. E-mail: dasey1@harborside.com.

CASEY, HEATHER ANNE KENYON, education educator; b. Edison, N.J., Dec. 7, 1973; d. John Robert and Joan Kenyon; m. James Smith Casey, July 3, 1998; 1 child, Ryan James. BA in English and Secondary Edn. with highest honors, Rutgers U., New Brunswick, N.J., 1995; EdM in Reading, Rutgers U., 2000, postgrad. Cert. tchr. secondary English, elem. edn., reading N.J. Lang. arts tchr. Manalapan Englishtown Mid. Sch., Englishtown, NJ, 1995—2002; tchg. asst. Rutgers U., New Brunswick, 2000—02, instr., 2003—. Cons. Ednl. Testing Svc., Princeton, NJ, 2003—. Contbr. articlels to profl. jours., chpts. to books. Fellow Edward Fry fellow, Rutgers U., 2001. Mem.: N.J. Reading Assn., Nat. Coun. Tchrs. English, Internat. Reading Assn. (mem. subcom. on poetry and prose award 2003—). Democrat. Dutch Ref. Ch. Avocations: reading, running, bicycling. Home: 51 Lench Ave Edison NJ 08820 Office: Rutgers Univ 10 Seminary Pl New Brunswick NJ

CASEY, KAREN ANNE, banker; b. Bklyn., Oct. 5, 1955; d. Stanley Joseph and Helen Katherine (Kosowski) Mozeleski; m. Dennis Joseph Casey, May 14, 1977; children: Christopher Sean, Erin Michelle. BBA, Baruch Coll., CUNY, 1977. CPA, N.Y., CFP. Jr. acct. Coopers & Lybrand, N.Y.C., 1977-78, sr. acct., 1978-79, supr., 1979-81; asst. fin. contr. Gulf Internat. Bank, N.Y.C., 1981-82, fin. contr., 1982; v.p., fin. contr. Allied Irish Banks plc, N.Y.C., 1982-87, sr. v.p., fin. contr., 1988-89, sr. v.p. mgmt. support svcs., 1989-92, sr. v.p., CFO, 1992-94, sr. v.p., head pvt. fin. svcs., 1994-2001, sr. v.p., head retail and bus. banking, 2001—. Bank rep. to Inst. Cert. Fin. Planners, 1991—. Mem. AICPA. Roman Catholic. Avocations: gardening, golf, tennis, reading. Office: Allied Irish Banks Plc 405 Park Ave New York NY 10022-4405 Personal E-mail: kcasey55@aol.com.

CASEY, LYNN M. public relations executive; b. Bismark, N.D., June 18, 1955; BA, U. N.C., 1976; MA, U. Minn., 1979; MBA, Coll. St. Thomas. Comms. specialist Burlington Northern, 1979-80, asst. editor employee comms., 1980-81, asst. mgr. mktg. comms., 1981-82, mgr. mktg./comms., 1982-83; with Brum & Anderson, 1983-87; v.p. Padilla Speer, 1987-91; COO Padilla Speer Beardsley, 1991—. Mem. Pub. Rels. Soc. Am., Phi Beta Kappa. Office: Padilla Speer Beardsley 224 W Franklin Ave Minneapolis MN 55404-2394

CASEY, MARY A. telecommunications company executive; Dir. operator svcs. Call Am., 1988-91; dir. customer svc. WCT, 1991-93; co-founder, sec. STAR Telcom., Inc., Santa Barbara, Calif., 1993—; pres. STAR Telecom., Inc., Santa Barbara, Calif., 1996—. Office: STAR Telecom Inc 223 E De La Guerra St Santa Barbara CA 93101-2206

CASEY, NANCY J. women's healthcare company executive; BA in English, San Diego State U. Owner, mgr. Nancy Casey Pub. Rels., 1985-97; dir. pub. rels. WestCom Group, 1987-90; sales asst. Dale Fitzmorris, 1990-92; co-founder, co-CEO, As We Change, LLC, 1995-98; v.p. catalog ops. Women First HealthCare, Inc., San Diego, 1998-99, v.p. pub. rels., 1999—. Office: Women First HealthCare Inc 23330 El Camino Real Ste 400 San Diego CA 92130 Fax: 619-509-1353.

CASEY, PAULA JEAN, former prosecutor; b. Charleston, Ark., Feb. 16, 1951; d. Arthur Clinton and Mildred Aleene (Underwood) C.; m. Gilbert Louis Glover II, Mar. 13, 1981. BA, Ea. Cen. (Okla.) U., 1973; JD, U. Ark., 1977. Staff atty. Ctrl. Ark. Legal Services, Hot Springs, Ark., 1977-79; dep. pub. defender 6th Jud. Dist. Pub. Defender, Little Rock, 1979; clinic supr. U. Ark. at Little Rock Law Sch., 1979-81, asst. prof., 1981-84, assoc. prof., 1984-92, prof., 1992-93, assoc. dean, 1986-90; legis. dir., chief counsel U.S. Senator Dale Bumpers, 1990-92; lobbyist Ark. Bar Assn., 1993; U.S. atty. Ea. Dist. Ark., 1993—2001; prof. law U. Ark. at Little Rock Law Sch., 2001—. Cons. for juvenile affairs 6th Jud. Dist. Judges, Ark., 1987. Author, editor: Poverty Law Practice Manual, 1985. Sec. Pulaski County Dem. Com., Little Rock, 1984-89; mem. Ark. Dem. Com., 1984-89; mem. Juvenile Adv. Group, Little Rock, 1985-89; mem. Gov.'s Task Force on Juvenile Cts., Ark., 1987; chmn. Ark. Dem. Jud. Com., 1987; bd. dirs. Ctrl. Ark. Legal Svcs., Little Rock, 1986-89. Named One of Top 100 Women in Ark., Ark. Bus. Pubs., 1996, 98, 99; recipient Gale Pettus Pontz award U. Ark.-Fayetteville Law Sch. Women Students Assn., 1994, award of merit Organized Crime Drug Enforcement Task Force, 1997. Fellow Ark. Bar Found. (bd. dirs.); mem. Ark. Bar Assn. (del. 1986-90), Am. Inns Ct., Overton Am. Inns of Ct., 8th Cir. Ct. Appeals (fed. adv. comm. 2001-05). Democrat. Office: U Ark at Little Rock Sch Law 1201 McMath Blvd Little Rock AR 72202 E-mail: pjcasey@ualr.edu.

CASEY, SUE (SUZANNE MARGUERITE PHILIPS), actress, real estate broker; b. L.A., Apr. 8, 1926; d. Burke Dewey and Mildred Louise (Hansen) Philips; children: Colleen O'Shaughnessy, John Joseph Durant III, Christopher Kent Durant, Diane M. Kelly; m. Jack Hoffmann (div.); stepchildren: Joy Hoffmann Molloy, Kristen Hoffmann Blutman. Student, UCLA Extension, 1972-75. Lic. real estate broker and saleswoman, Calif. With Coldwell Banker, Beverly Hills, Calif. Appeared in numerous movies, including swimming in 5 Esther Williams films, singing and dancing in over 20 films, Goldwyn Girl, 1945-47; Star Is Born, Surf Terror, 1965, Catalina Caper, 1967, Happy Ending, Secrets of Monte Carlo, The Family Jewels, Marriage Young Stockbroker, The Big Circus, The Errand Boy, Two Weeks in Another Town, Paint Your Wagon, Camelot, Evil Speak, 1981, Swamp Country, Ladies Man, Lucky Lady, Annie Get Your Gun, Show Boat, Carpetbaggers, Rear Window, Breakfast at Tiffany's, The Scarf, Main Event, Brady Bunch Sequel, 1996, American Beauty, 1999; appeared in TV shows, including Hunter, Hotel, Hart to Hart, White Shadow, Sunny Valley, Lucy, Gunsmoke, Arnie, Marcus Welby, Sky Terror, Dallas, Days of Our Lives, Unsolved Mysteries, Rosie O'Neill, Haggerty, Emergency, California Fever, I Love Lucy, Farmer's Daughter, Beverly Hillbillies, Delta House, Bodies of Evidence, The Faculty, Divorce Court, Colgate Comedy Shows, Carol Burnett Shows, Red Skelton Show, Roy Bolger Show, All Star Revues, Bob Hope Specials, Ann Southern Show, Family Medical Center, Red Shoe Diaries, What Love Sees, Boy Meets World, 1997, Diagnosis Murder, 1999; has appeared in over 200 TV commls.; stage appearances include Picnic, Goodnight Ladies. Ball chmn. The Footlighters, Inc., 1971-73, 93-94, press chmn., 1972-73, pres., 1982-83, 98-99, parliamentarian, 1983-94, 99-00,02-03, hospitality chmn., 1992-93. Named Ms. Sr. Am. of L.A., 1993. Mem. AFTRA, SAG, Actors Equity Assn. Office: Coldwell Banker 301 N Canon Dr Beverly Hills CA 90210-4722 Office Phone: 310-777-6344. E-mail: suecaseyla@yahoo.com.

CASH, DEANNA GAIL, retired nursing educator; b. Coatesville, Pa., Nov. 28, 1940; Diploma, Jackson Meml. Hosp., 1961; BS, Fla. State U., 1964; MN, UCLA, 1968; EdD, Nova U., Ft. Lauderdale, Fla., 1983. Staff and relief charge nurse Naples (Fla.) Comty. Hosp., 1961-62; staff nurse Glendale (Calif.) Comty. Hosp., 1964-65; instr. Knapp Coll. Nursing, Santa Barbara, Calif., 1965-66; staff nurse, team leader Kaiser Found. Hosp., Bellflower, Calif., 1968-69; prof. nursing El Camino Coll., Torrance, Calif., 1969-96, ret., 1996. Coord., instr. Internat. RN Rev. course, L.A., 1974-76; mentor statewide nursing program, Long Beach, Calif., 1981-88; clin. performance in nursing exam. evaluator Western Performance Assessment Ctr., Long Beach, 1981-96. Mem. ANA.

CASH, LAVERNE (CYNTHIA CASH), physicist; b. Statesville, N.C., Oct. 7, 1956; d. William J. and Martha Lee (Stroud) C. BS, Appalachian State U., 1979; MS, Clemson U., 1982; AA, Mitchell C.C., 1976; PhD, Johns Hopkins U., 1999. Physicist U.S. Army Material Systems Analysis Activity, Aberdeen Proving Ground, Md., 1984-88; rsch. physicist U.S. Army Edgewood Rsch., Devel. and Engrng. Ctr., Aberdeen Proving Ground, 1988—. Contbr. articles to profl. publs. Mem. Oak Grove Bapt. Ch, Bel Air, Md., singer in choir, sound engr., numerous others. Mem. Am. Phys. Soc., Sigma Phi Sigma, Pi Mu Epsilon, Phi Theta Kappa, Gamma Beta Phi. Baptist. Home: 100 Drexel Dr Bel Air MD 21014-2002 Office Phone: 410-436-1763. E-mail: lavernecash@yahoo.com.

CASH, MARY FRANCES, minister, retired civilian military employee; d. Hugh Lester and Myrtle Victoria (Byrd) Flucas; m. William Hadley Cash, May 7, 1966; children: Aleta Grace Pearson, William Anthony, Antonio Hadley. Diploma, Atlantic Bus. Coll., 1961; Assoc. in Religious Edn., Washington Saturday Coll., 1996; Masters Degree in religious edn., Bethel Bible Coll./Seminary, 2003. Ordained elder African Meth. Episcopal Ch., 1999. Sec., stenographer Dept. Human Resources, Washington, 1964—77; adminstr. Flu-Bea Enterprises, Landover, Md., 1977—80; substitute tchr. Pineview Elem. Sch., Valdosta, Ga., 1980—81; sec. Moody AFB, Valdosta, 1981—82, Andrews AFB, Camp Spring, Md., 1982—92, Dept. Def., Va., 1992—94; pastor Cmty. African Meth. Episcopal Ch., Whitehall, Ark., 1995. Leader, trainer Girl Scout Coun. Am., Washington, 1971—79, Valdosta, Ga., 1980—82, Washington, 1982—96; mem. adv. bd. Duke Ellington Sch. Art, Washington, 1986; instr. Summer Tchg. Program for Children, Jonesboro, 1996—2000; dir. Saturday Sch. Brown Meml. African Meth. Episcopal Ch., Washington, 1990—96. Named Mother of the Yr., Brown Meml. African Meth. Episcopal Ch., 1988; recipient Spl. Svc. award, Girl Scout Coun. Nations Capitol, 1994, Superior award, Young and Adult Missionary Soc., 1996. Mem.: East No. Ark. Annual Conf. of the 12th Episcopal Dist. (Sec. 2002—). Office: Cmty AME Ch 12th Episcopal Dist 1995 Poff Ln Jonesboro AR 72401

CASH, ROSANNE, country singer, songwriter; b. Memphis, May 24, 1955; b. May 1955; d. John R. Cash and Vivian (Liberto) Distin; m. Rodnay J. Crowell, Apr. 7, 1979 (div. 1992); children: Caitlin Rivers, Chelsea Jane, Carrie Kathleen. Student, Vol. State C.C., 1974, Vanderbilt U., 1976, Lee Strasberg Theatre Inst., 1977. Rec. artist Ariola Records, Europe, 1978-84, CBS Records, worldwide, 1979—. Songwriter Blue Moon with Heartache, 1979, Seven Year Ache, 1980 (Gold Record award Rec. Industry Assn. Am. 1981), I Don't Know Why You Don't Want Me, 1984, (Grammy award 1985), Hold On (Robert J. Burton award 1987), others; Albums: Right Or Wrong, The Wheel, Seven Year Ache, 1980, Somewhere in the Stars, Rythym & Romance, 1985, King's Record Shop, 1987, Hits 1979-89, 1989, Interiors, 1990, 10 Song Demo, 1996, Retrospective, 1997. Bd. advisors Nashvillians for Nuclear Arms Freeze, 1987-90. Mem. AFTRA, Nat. Acad. Rec. Arts and Scis. (Grammy award 1985), Am. Fedn. Musicians, Screen Actors Guild, Broadcast Music, Inc. (Spl. Achievement awards), Nashville Songwriters Assn. Internat. Democrat. Home: 131 Mercer St Apt 5A New York NY 10012-3888

CASHION, ANN, food service executive; b. Jackson, Miss. B, Harvard U., 1976; postgrad., Stanford U., 1976—78. With Oh-la-la!, San Francisco, 1982; chef Restaurant Nora, Washington, Dakota; head chef Austin Grill, Washington, 1988; exec. chef Jaleo, Washington, 1993—95; chef, owner Cashion's Eat Pl., Washington, 1995—; ptnr. Johnny's Half Shell, 1999—. Named Chef of the Yr., Restaurant Assn. Met. Washington, 1997. Mem.: Coun. Ind. Restaurateurs Am., Internat. Assn. Women Chefs and Restaurateurs, Les Dames d'Escoffier. Office: Cahions Eat Pl 1819 Columbia Rd NW Washington DC 20009-2005

CASHION, PATRICIA SUE, minister; b. Amarillo, Tex., Dec. 12, 1947; d. John Clifford and Mary Jane Cashion; m. Charles Richard Johnson, Sept. 8, 1967 (div. July 1985); children: Carrie Lee Patten, Jennifer Anne Johnson. BA in Art, Mercer U., 1980; MDiv, Columbia Theol. Sem., 1994, D of Ministry, 2004. Ordained min. 1994. Substitute tchr. Oviedo (Fla.) H.S., 1984—85, part-time tchr., 1985; dir. market support Baxter-Travenol, Orlando, Fla., 1985—88; dir. comm. First Presbyn. Ch., Orlando, 1988—92, min. Ozark, Ark., 1994—97, min. of the laity Fremont, Ohio, 1997—2001, min., head of staff Lawton, Okla., 2001—. Bd. dirs. New Beginning Ministries, Oviedo, Cameron Campus Ministries, Lawton; presenter in field; U.S. rep. PC (USA) and Coun. of Chs., 1994. Author: A New Beginning, 2000. Cons., counselor County Teen Crisis Ctr., Lawton, 2003—. Avocations: art, gardening, quilting, writing, travel. Office: First Presbyn Ch 1302 SW A Ave Lawton OK 73501

CASIANO, KIMBERLY, publishing executive; b. NY; m. Juan Woodroffe; children: Natalia, Juan Antonio. BA in politics and Latin Am. studies magna cum laude, Princeton U.; MBA, Harvard. Founded Caribbean Mktg. Overseas Corp., Wash., DC, 1981—88; v.p. Casiano Comm., 1988—94, pres., CEO, 1994—. Bd. mem. Ford Motor Co., 2003—, mem. fin. bd. com., mem. nom. com., mem. corp. governance com., mem. environ. and pub. policy com. Bd. trustees Hispanic Coll. Fund; mem. bd. dirs. Young Pres. Orgn. (YPO) PR chpt. Named one of Elite Women, Hispanic Bus. mag., 2004. Achievements include apptd. to US Savings Bond Nat. Com. by US Treas. Sec. Office: Casiano Comm 1700 Ave Fernandex Juncos San Juan PR 00909-2938 Office Phone: 787-728-3000. Office Fax: 787-268-1001.*

CASILLAS, OFELIA MARIE, journalist; d. Fernando Sabino and Ofelia Rita Casillas. B in Journalism and English, U. Fla., 2000. Staff writer L.A. Times, 2000—01, Chgo. Tribune, 2001—. Mem.: Nat. Assn. Hispanic Journalists (assoc.). Home: 1544 N Oakley Blvd #2 Chicago IL 60622-1849

CASINI, JANE SLOAN, wholesale distribution executive; b. Richmond, Va., Sept. 22, 1947; d. James Turner and Jane Patrick (Coleman) Sloan; m. Mauro Casini (div.). Student, Villa Mercede, Florence, Italy. Owner, Richmond and Washington; retailer; leather salesman. Bd. dirs. Va. Home for Boys, Richmond, 1991. Home: 5621 Cary St Rd Richmond VA 23226 Office: Jane Casini 5407 Lakeside Ave Richmond VA 23228

CASKEY, CAROLINE, lab administrator; MBA, Rice U., Houston, 1993. Founder, pres., CEO Identigene Corp., Houston, 1993—. Office: Identigene Corp 5615 Kirby Ste 800 Houston TX 77005

CASKIE, JUDITH MAUREEN, physical therapist; b. Redding, Calif., Nov. 4, 1949; d. Robert Alexander and Anne Marie Caskie. AA in Psychology, Shasta Jr. Coll., Redding, 1969; BS in Phys. Therapy, U. Calif., San Francisco, 1971. Lic. phys. therapist Calif. Staff phys. therapist Oroville (Calif.) Hosp.; asst. dir., sr. phys. therapist Redding Med. Ctr.; staff phys. therapist Redding Med. Home Care, Addus Health Care, Redding. Tutor Laubad Literacy League, Redding, 1995—2000. Mem.: World Wildlife Fund, So. Poverty Law Ctr., Nature Conservancy. Avocations: fly fishing, camping, travel, gardening. Office: Addus Health Care 1957 Pine St Redding CA 96001

CASO, DAWN MARIE, lawyer, consultant, law educator; b. Boynton Beach, Fla., Sept. 4, 1967; AA in Psychology, Palm Beach (Fla.) C.C., 1992; BA, Barry U., 1994; JD, Nova Southeastern U., 2000. Cert.: (notary pub.) 1998. Novelist, Rome and other cities, Italy, 1992—93; asst. editor The National Enquirer, Lantana, Fla., 1993—96; editor self employed, Boca Raton, Fla., 1996—98; jud. asst. to judges Palm Beach County, West Palm Beach, Fla., 1998—99; law clk., legal rschr. Legal Help, West Palm Beach, Fla., 1999—2000; legal instr., asst. prof. law Coll. for Profl. Studies, Paralegal Program, Boca Raton, Fla., 2000—01. Legal cons., provider free legal aid, educator Caso, Inc., Deerfield Beach, Fla., 2001—. Author: (Numerous Books and Study Guides) Every Major Legal Subject- Torts, Contracts, Mediation, etc., 2001 (Specialty Publication acknowlegement, 2001), numerous books and study guides, 2001—. Supporter Families Against Mandatory Minimum Sentences, 1998—; contbr., supporter Broward Outreach Ctr., Hollywood, Fla., 2000—; pro choice advocate NOW, Washington, 1993—; active polit. advocate for women's rights West Palm Beach, 1985—. Mem.: ABA, Broward County Bar Assn., Nat. Assn. Pub. Interest Law, Fla. Assn. Women Lawyers (assoc.), Broward County Bar Association (Featured in Journal), National Association of Public Interest Law, Florida Association of Women Lawyers. Liberal. Home and Office: 441 NE 20th Ave # 205 Deerfield Beach FL 33441 E-mail: dawncaso@yahoo.com.

CASON, MARILYNN JEAN, technological institute official, lawyer; b. Denver, May 18, 1943; d. Eugene Martin and Evelyn Lucille (Clark) C.; married. BA in Polit. Sci., Stanford U., 1965; JD, U. Mich., 1969; MBA, Roosevelt U., 1977. Bar: Colo. 1969, Ill. 1973. Assoc. Dawson, Nagel, Sherman & Howard, Denver, 1969-73; atty. Kraft, Inc., Glenview, Ill., 1973-75; corp. counsel Johnson Products Co., Inc., Chgo., 1975-86, v.p., 1977-86, mng. dir. Lagos, Nigeria, 1980-83, v.p. internat. Chgo., 1986-88; v.p., gen. counsel DeVry, Inc., Chgo., 1989-96, sr. v.p. gen. counsel, corp. sec., 1996—. Trustee Arthritis Found., Atlanta, 1993—96, Chgo. Symphony Orch., 1997—2003; bd. dirs. Ill. chpt. Arthritis Found., Chgo., 1979—, chmn., 1991—93; bd. dirs. Internat. House, Chgo., 1986—92, Interfaith House, Chgo., 1996—2002, Ill. Humanities Coun., Chgo., 1987—96, chmn., 1993—96; bd. dirs. Lit. for All of Us, 1997—, chmn., 2002—. Mem. ABA, Nat. Bar Assn., Cook County Bar Assn. (pres. cmty. law project 1986-88), Stanford Club (Chgo., pres. 1985-87). Home: 3108 Colfax St Evanston IL 60201-1842 Office: DeVry Inc 1 Tower Ln Ste 1000 Oakbrook Terrace IL 60181-4663 Office Phone: 630-574-1901. E-mail: mcason@devry.com.

CASPER, MARIE LENORE, middle school educator; b. Honesdale, Pa., Mar. 26, 1954; d. Frank J. and Ellenore L. (Austin) Shedlock; m. Gerald Joseph Casper, Oct. 9, 1976 (dec. Oct. 1998); children: Julia Anne, Jennifer Marie. BA, Marywood Coll., 1976; masters equivalency cert., State of Pa., 1982. Cert. elem. and secondary social studies tchr., Pa. Substitute tchr. Western Wayne Sch. Dist., South Canaan, Pa., 1976-81, secondary and elem. tchr., 1981-86, chpt. 1 math. specialist, 1986-90, middle sch. social studies tchr., 1990—; social studies tchr. Wallenpaupack Area Sch. Dist., Hawley, Pa., 1980-81. Coord. Western Wayne Middle Sch., WWII commemorative com. Contbr. articles to profl. jours. Active PTA Wilson Sch., Western Wayne Mid. Sch. Mem. NEA, Pa. State Edn. Assn., Pa. Mid. Sch. Assn., Waymart Hist. Soc., Western Wayne Edn. Assn., Wayne County Hist. Soc., Smithsonian Instn., Audubon Soc., Nat. Geog. Soc., Platform Assn., Am. Legion Aux. (life). Republican. Roman Catholic. Avocations: piano and vocal music, needlecraft, reading, antiques, genealogy. Home: PO Box 31 Lake Quinn Rd South Canaan PA 18459-0031 Office: Western Wayne Mid Sch RR 8 Box 8170 Lake Ariel PA 18436-9802

CASS, MARY LOUISE, librarian; b. Jersey City, May 27, 1956; d. Eugene Louis and Catherine (Reynolds) Cass; m. Edward John Skillin, Dec. 2, 2000. BA in History, Rutgers U., 1978, MLS, 1979. Cataloguer Fairleigh Dickinson U., Madison, NJ, 1979-81; mgr. Montclair Pub. Libr., 1982-96, br. dir., 1996—. Bibliographer: (book) Suicide, 1991. Treas. Upper Mountain Gardens Bd., Montclair, 1998-2003. Mem. ALA (pres. cmty. info. sect. 1991-92). Democrat. Roman Cath. Home: 29 Upper Mountain Ave Montclair NJ 07042-1919 Office: Montclair Pub Libr 185 Bellevue Ave Upper Montclair NJ 07043 Office Phone: 973-744-2468.

CASSEL, CHRISTINE KAREN, physician; b. Mpls., Sept. 14, 1945; d. Charles Moore and Virginia Julia (Anderson) Cassel. AB, U. Chgo., 1967; MD, U. Mass., 1976. Diplomate Am. Bd. Internal Medicine (chmn. 1998-99). Intern, resident in internal medicine Children's Hosp., San Francisco, 1976—78; fellow in bioethics Inst. Health Policy Studies, U. Calif., San Francisco, 1978—79; fellow geriatrics Portland (Oreg.) VA Hosp., 1979—81; asst. prof. medicine and public health U. Oreg. Health Scis. U., 1981—83; asst. prof. geriatrics and medicine Mt. Sinai Med. Ctr., N.Y.C., 1983—85; prof. medicine, prof. pub. policy U. Chgo., 1985—95, chief gen. internal medicine, 1985—95; chmn. and prof. geriatrics and medicine Mt. Sinai, 1995—2001; dean sch. of medicine Oreg. Heatlh and Sci. U., 2001—02. Author: Ethical Dimensions in the Health Professions, 1981, Geriatric Medicine: Principles and Practice, 1984, 1990, Nuclear Weapons and Nuclear War: A Sourcebook for Health Professionals, 1984. Bd. dirs., chmn. Greenwall Found. Fellow Hastings Ctr. fellow, 1991—92, Ctr. Advanced Study in Behavioral Sci. fellow, 1991—92; scholar Henry J. Kaiser Family Found. faculty scholar, 1982—85. Fellow: ACP (regent 1989—97, pres. 1997—98), Am. Geriatrics Soc.; mem.: Am. .Soc. Law and Medicine (bd. dirs.), Soc. Health and Human Values (pres. 1986), Physicians for Social Responsibility (dir. 1983—, pres. 1988—), Inst. of Medicine of NAS. Office: ABIM Found 510 Walnut St Philadelphia PA 19105 E-mail: casselc@abim.org.

CASSELS, MARTHA BEASLEY, realtor, developer; b. Greenwood, S.C., Oct. 22, 1932; d. Hugh Alton and Ora Faith (Mitchell) Beasley; m. Marion Carlyle Crenshaw, Jr., June 25, 1953 (div. 1979); children: Marion Carlyle III, William Frank, Hugh Charles, Faith Byrd; m. Samuel Jones Cassels, III, Oct. 6, 1979 (div. 1999). BA, Converse Coll., 1953. Cert. residential specialist Realtors Nat. Mktg. Inst., 1979. Tchr. Carr Jr. H.S., Durham, N.C., 1953-55, 1st Congl. Pre Sch., Branford, Conn., 1964-66; dir. Barfield Kindergarten, Durham, 1966-68, Duke Meml. Pre Sch., Durham, 1968-74; sec. corp. Bob Gunter Realty, Inc., Durham, 1972-77; owner Crenshaw Co., Inc., Durham, 1977-79, Cassels Real Estate, Montgomery, Ala., 1980—. Pres. Hampton Killingsworth, Inc. 1990—, Montgomery Area Bd. Realtors, Ala. Bd. Realtors, 1979—, Nat. Bd. Realtors, Chgo., 1974—. Mem. County Bd. Edn., Durham, 1972—79; patron theatre dept. Ala. State U., Montgomery, 1994—; active Montgomery Zoo; bd. dirs. Scott and Zelda Fitzgerald Mus., Montgomery, 1986—, sponsor statewide lit. contest for high schs. and colls. Named Top Prodr., Montgomery Area Bd. Realtors, 1981; recipient Top Residential award Montgomery Area Bd. Realtors, 1982, 10 Consecutive Yrs. of Multi Millions award Montgomery Area Bd. Realtors, 1990. Mem.: YMCA, AAUW, Greater Montgomery Home Builder Assn., Prattville C. of C., Montgomery Area C. of C., C.E.O. Roundtable, Jr. Twentieth Century Club, Mobile Yacht Club. Episcopalian. Avocations: reading, swimming, sailing. Office: Cassels Real Estate 623 S Perry St Montgomery AL 36104-5890 E-mail: sales@casselsrealestate.com.

CASSETTA, RHONDDA KING, statistician; b. Trumansburg, N.Y. d. Frederick Anthony and Genevieve (Davies) King; m. James Vincent Cassetta, July 6, 1940; children: James Vincent, Stephen King. AB summa cum laude, Elmira Coll., 1933; student, Cornell U., 1937—39. Tchr. math & econs., 1933—35; asst. in prices & stats. Cornell U., 1935—41; statistician mental health rsch. unit N.Y. State Dept. Mental Hygiene, 1957—67; assoc. instl. rsch. coll. environ. sci. and forestry State U., Syracuse, NY, 1967—81. Contbr. articles to profl. jours. Mem.: AAUW (life), Phi Beta Kappa, Delta Sigma Rho. Home: 2420 NW Marshall St Apt 103 Portland OR 97210-2975

CASSIAN, NINA, poet, composer; b. Galati, Romania, Nov. 27, 1924; arrived in U.S., 1985; d. Joseph and Jana Cassian; m. Alexandru Iancu Stefanescu, June 26, 1948 (dec.); m. Maurice Edwards, Mar. 12, 1999. Vis. prof. NYU, N.Y.C., 1985. Author: You're Terrific--I'm Leaving You, 1971, Fictitious Confessions, 1974, Parlor Games, 1984; poet: On the Scale of One to One, 1947, Our Soul, 1949, The Measures of the Year, 1957, Time Devouring: Selected Poems, 1969, Spectacle in the Open-air: Selected Love Poems, 1974, One Hundred Poems, 1975, For Mercy, 1981, Blue Apple, 1981, Lady of Miracles, 1982, Count Down, 1983, Call Yourself Alive, 1988, Cheerleader for a Funeral, 1992, Life Sentence, 1992, Take My Word For It, 1998, numerous others, Something Old, Something New, 2002, translator various works; composer: Tutorial Fascinations, 1980, Vivarium, 1981, Variation Perpetua, 1984, The Magic Clarinet, 1985.

CASSIDY, CATHERINE, editor-in-chief; Exec. editor Prevention Mag., N.Y.C., 1997—2001, editor-in-chief, 2001—. Office: Prevention Mag 733 3d Ave New York NY 10017

CASSIDY, ESTHER CHRISTMAS, retired government official; b. Upper Marlboro, Md., Aug. 5, 1933; d. Donelson and Esther Christmas; divorced; children: William Keeling, Carroll Cassidy Drewyer, Daniel Clark. BA, Manhattanville Coll., 1955. Phys. scientist, R&D Nat. Bur. Standards, Gaithersburg, Md., 1955-73; sci. advisor U.S. Congressman Teno Roncalio, Washington, 1973-74; asst. dir. congl. affairs Energy R&D Adminstrn. Dept. Energy, Washington, 1974-78; dir. congl. and legis. affairs Nat. Inst. Stds. and Tech., Gaithersburg, 1978-98; ret., 1998. Contbr. articles to profl. jours. Mem. IEEE (sr.). Avocations: horse racing, golf.

CASSON MADDEN, CHRIS, entrepreneur, interior designer; m. J. Kevin Madden; children: Patrick, Nick. Student, Fashion Inst. Tech. Founder, CEO Chris Madden, Inc., Rye, NY, 1995—; photographer Sports Illustrated; with Random House, G.P. Putnam & Sons, Farrar, Straus & Giroux. Design expert Today Show, Good Morning Am., Oprah, CBS Sunday Morning, CNN; nat. spokesperson JC Penny Home Collection, 2003—. Author: The Complete Lemon, 1979, The Summer House Cookbook, 1979, Baby Hints Handbook, 1982, Baby's First Helpings: Super-Healthy Meals for Super-Healthy Kids, 1984, Kitchens: Information and Inspiration for Making the Kitchen the Heart of the Home, 1993, Bathrooms: Inspiring Ideas and Practical Solutions for Creating a Beautiful Bathroom, 1996, Chris Madden's Guide to Personalizing Your Home: Simple, Beautiful Ideas for Every Room, 1997, A Room of Her Own: Women's Personal Spaces, Clarkson Potter, 1997, Getaways: Carefree Retreats for All Seasons, 2000, Bedrooms: Creating the Stylish Comfortable Room of Your Dreams, 2001, Chris Casson Madden's New American Living Rooms, 2003; co-author: Interior Visions: Great American Designers and the Showcase House, 1988, Rooms With a View: Two Decades of Outstanding American Interior Design from the Kips Bay Decorator Show Houses, 1995, Interior Details: The Designers' Style, 1996; columnist: Interiors by Design; host (TV series) Interiors By Design, HGTV, 1995—. Office: Chris Madden Inc 35 Purchase St Rye NY 10580*

CASSOTTO, MARY LOU GRACE, language educator; b. Winsted, Conn., Feb. 12, 1949; d. Vito Anthony Cassotto and Grace Lucy Paxcia; m. Donald J. McCarthy, Jr., Oct. 17, 1977 (div. May 2001); 1 child, Gabriella McCarthy. BA in English, Coll. New Rochelle, 1974; JD, Seton Hall U., 1974; MEd, Trinity U., 1981; cert. in art, Ctrl. Conn. State U., 1991; cert. ednl. adminstr., U. Conn., 1993. Assoc. Athanson & Webber, Hartford, Conn., 1974—81; tchr. Art and English East Cath., Manchester, Conn., 1981—93; counselor, legal rsch. Cath. Family Svcs., Hartford, 1995—97; tchr., counselor Gastonbury/Middletown Sch. Sys., Windsor, Middletown, Conn., 1997—. Prof. Traxis C.C., Farmington, Conn., Manchester C.C., Conn., East C.C., Willimantic, Conn., Hartford Coll. Mem.: AAUW, Nat. Coun. Tchrs. English, Phi Delta Gamma. Republican. Roman Catholic. Home: 422 Founders Rd Glastonbury CT 06033*

CAST, ANITA HURSH, small business owner; b. Columbus, Ohio, July 11, 1939; d. Charles Walter and Hulda Marie (Ramsey) Hursh; m. William R. Cast, Apr. 1, 1961; children: Jennifer, Carter, Meghan. BA, DePauw U., 1961. Ptnr. Cast Hursh and Assocs., Ft. Wayne, Ind., 1982—; pianist Words and Music, Ft. Wayne, 198[illegible]—; owner Anita Cast's Wearable Art, Ft. Wayne, 1986—. Bd. dirs. Fort Wayne Philharm., Indpls. Internat. Violin Competition; mem. exec. com. Arts United; past pres. exec. com. Ind. U. Friends of Music; pres. Ind. Endowment for the Arts. Bd. dirs., pres. Am. Symphony Orch. League, vol., v.p., 1985—86; commr. Ind. Gov.'s Mansion Commn., 1987, Ind. Arts Commn., 1979—87; bd. dirs. Ft. Wayne Philharm., pres., 1977—79; mem. Mayor's Bicentennial Exec. Bd., 1989—94, Ind. Cultural Congress Hon. Com.; active Ft. Wayne's Celebrate 2000 Com.; bd. dirs. WBNI Nat. Pub. Radio, Ft. Wayne; chmn. bd. dirs. Fine Arts Found., Ft. Wayne, 1988; pres. bd. dirs. Ind. Endowment Arts; chmn. bd. dirs. Arts United Greater Ft. Wayne, 1988—90; bd. dirs. Arts United; pres., bd. dirs. Ind. U. Friends Music, 1995—97, past pres. exec. com.; v.p. adv. bd. Leadership Ft. Wayne; pres. Met. YMCA, Ft. Wayne, 1986—. Lily Endowment Leadership fellow; named Miss Indiana. Mem.: Duodecimo Club, Quest Club. Republican. Episcopalian. Avocations: music, cooking, golf, hiking, reading. Home and Office: Anita Cast Wearable Art 4401 Taylor St Fort Wayne IN 46804-1913

CASTAGNA, VANESSA, retail executive; b. Muncie, Ind. m. Neil Castagna. BS in Psychology and Speech Comm., Purdue U. Sr. v.p., gen. merchandise mgr. Marshall's Stores, Mass.; sr. v.p., gen. mgr. Wal-Mart Stores Divsn., Bentonville, Ark., 1994-99; exec. v.p. and COO J.C. Penney Co., Inc., Plano, TX. Office: JC Penney Co Inc PO Box 10001 Dallas TX 75301-0001

CASTEEL, CAMILLE, school system administrator; EdD, Nova Southeastern U. Fischler Grad. Sch. of Edn. and Human Svcs., 1991. 1st grade tchr. to supt. Chandler (Ariz.) Unified Sch. Dist., 1971—91, supt., 1991—. Named Ariz. Nat. Supt. of Yr., 2002; recipient Excellence award, Ariz. Sch. Pub. Rels. Assn., Achievement award, Ariz. Year Round Edn. Assn. Office: Chandler Unified Sch Dist 1525 W Frey Rd Chandler AZ 85224*

CASTEEL, STEVEN W. federal agency administrator; b. Ill. Degree in Zoology, Degree in Chemistry, So. Ill. U. Dep. sheriff Ill. Sheriffs Dept., 1971—72; spl. agt. U.S. Dept. Justice-Bur. Narcotics and Dangerous Drugs (now Drug Enforcement Adminstrn.), 1972; exec. asst. to the career bd. Drug Enforcement Adminstrn., Washington, exec. asst. to dep. adminstr., sr. exec. svc., head Office Inspections, 1994—96, assoc. spl. agt. in charge Houston field divsn., 1996—98, spl. agt. in charge Seattle field divsn., 1998—99, asst. adminstr. for intelligence Alexandria, Va., 1999—. Office: Drug Enforcement Adminstrn Washington DC 20537

CASTELGRANT, ELIZABETH ANN SAYLOR, physical education educator, consultant; b. Neshanic Station, N.J., Jan. 9, 1951; d. Clement Joseph and Dorothy Ann (Wargo) Saylor; m. Daniel Peter Castelgrant, Apr. 20, 1991. BS, East Stroudsburg U., 1972. Phys. edn. tchr. West Amwell Sch., Lambertville, N.J., 1972-87, Lebanon (N.J.) Borough Sch., 1978-88, Flemington (N.J.) Raritan Schs., 1987—. Steering com. Juvenile Task Force, Flemington, 1980-83; mem. task force Sch. Health and Edn. Resource Ctr., Flemington, 1983-85; cons. North Hunterdon In-Svc. Day, Clinton, N.J., 1983; mem. EIC Tchr. Adv. Bd., Morristown, 1983-86; training cons. N.J. Edn. Assn., 1993—; in-svc. cons. Hunterdan County, 1999. Editor: Hunterdon County Edn. Assn. Bulletin, 1976-97. Publicity chair Hunterdon County Spl. Olympics, 1973-77; chair Camp Isabel Internat. Food Festival, Flemington, 1979, Tchrs. to Re-elect Meyner, Florio, McConnel, Foran, Weidel, 1976-90, South County Sr. Citizen's Program, Hunterdon County, 1978-82; vol. LVW, Hunterdon County, 1980-85, local bicentennial com., Lambertville, 1976, Deborah Hosp. Fund Drive, Flemington, 1984-86, Big Bros./Sisters, Flemington, 1983-86; mem. Flemington Tenants' Orgn., 1984-86, Hunterdon/Somerset Bus. and Edn. Partnership Adv. Coun., 1990—, Hunterdon County Dental Health Commn., 1989—, chair, 1995—; steering com. Hunterdon County Staff Devel. Coop., 1996—, paradigm pioneer com., 1993—; decision making com. Flemington Raritan Participatory, 1996—. Mem. AAUW, NEA, AAHPERD, N.J. Edn. Assn. (mem.'s rights com. 1972—, chair 1975—, chair Be Heard Campaign, 1980, mem. fair play com. 1983—, del. assembly 1978-83, 90-92, 98—), Hunterdon County Edn. Assn. (pres. 1978-82, 90-92, v.p. 1992—), Flemington-Raritan Edn. Assn. (v.p.-at-large 1987—, shared decision making com. 1993—), Hunterdon-Somerset County Bus. and Edn. Partnership (adv. bd., steering com. 2001/SCANS project 1991-97), Delta Kappa Gamma (1st v.p. Rho chpt.), Alpha Omicron Pi. Avocations: helping others, reading, quiet times. Home: 223 Longview Rd Bridgewater NJ 08807-2091 Office: Desmares Sch 16 Old Clinton Rd Flemington NJ 08822-5700 also: NJEA Region 13 47 E Main St Flemington NJ 08822-1216

CASTELLANO, CHRISTINE MARIE, lawyer; b. Jacksonville, Fla., Jan. 10, 1966; d. James Todd and Constance Marie (Wallis) Drylie; m. Ralph Castellano, Sept. 15, 1997. BA summa cum laude, U. Colo., 1987; JD cum laude, U. Mich., 1990. Bar: Colo. 1990, Ill. 1991, U.S. Dist. Ct. Colo. 1991, U.S. Dist. Ct. (no. dist.) Ill. 1991, U.S. Dist. Ct. (ctrl. dist.) Ill. 1994, U.S. Ct. Appeals (10th cir.) 1991, U.S. Ct. Appeals (7th cir.) 1993, U.S. Supreme Ct. 1995. Clk. to chief judge Sherman G. Finesilver U.S. Dist. Ct. Colo., Denver, 1990-91; income ptnr. McDermott, Will & Emery, Chgo., 1991-96; ops. atty. Corn Products divsn. of CPC Internat. Inc., Summit-Argo, Ill., 1996-97; atty. Corn Products Internat., Inc., 1998—2002, counsel, U.S. and Can., 2002—. Adminstr. Family Law Project, Ann Arbor, Mich., 1988-91; judge Julius H. Miner Moot Ct., Northwestern U. Sch. Law, 1993-95, Northwestern U. Sch. Law Negotiation Competition, 1992-94. Writer newspaper The Res Gestae, 1987-90; editor yearbook The Quadrangle, 1988-90; contbg. editor Jour. of Law Reform, 1988-90. Vol. Lincoln Park Homeless Shelter, Chgo., 1991-92, Chgo. Cares, 1993-96; co. coord. Youth Motivation Program, 1991-96. Recipient Negligence Sect. award Mich. Bar Assn., 1990; Carl B. Gussin Meml. prize U. Mich., 1991; scholar Elk's, 1983-84, faculty U. Colo., 1983-84; U. Colo. grantee, 1987. Mem. ABA, Colo. Bar Assn., Ill. Bar Assn., Denver Bar Assn. (vol. teen ct. 1991), Chgo. Bar Assn., Chgo. Coun. Laywers, Women Law Students Assn., U. Colo. Alumni Assn., U. Mich. Alumni Assn., Moot Ct., Mortar Bd., Phi Beta Kappa, Pi Sigma Alpha. Avocations: photography, ice skating, camping, hiking. Office: Corn Products Internat 5 Westbrook Corporate Ctr Westchester IL 60154

CASTELLANO, JOSEPHINE MASSARO, medical records specialist; d. Ignazio and Maria Massaro Castellano. BS in Med. Tech., Fla. State U., 1952; tchrs. cert., U. Tampa, 1955; MA, Columbia U., 1961. Med. technologist St. Joseph's Hosp., Tampa, Fla., 1952—55; tchr. Hillsborough County Sch. Bd., Tampa, 1955—85; med. records specialist Robert Martinez, M.D., Tampa, 1985—95, David L. Castellano, DDS, Tampa, 1996—, Domenic M. Castellano, DDS, Tampa, 1996—. Mem.: AAUW (mem. adv. bd. 1999—2002), Christian Med. Found. (mem. adv. bd. 1996—2003), Kappa Delta Pi (mem. adv. bd. 2000—02). Roman Catholic. Avocations: reading, horseback riding, tennis, gardening, bowling. Home: 305 N Hesperides St Tampa FL 33609-2020 Office: David L and Domenic M Castellano DDS 8365 W Hillsborough Ave Tampa FL 33615-3899

CASTELLANOS, MARIA LUISA A. architect, general contractor; b. Havana, Cuba, May 31, 1953; came to U.S., 1961; d. Armando I. and Maria Luisa (de la Torriente) C.; m. Eduardo Escobar, Feb. 1, 1985 (div. 1991); 1 child, Edward. BS, Ga. Inst. Tech., 1974, MArch, 1976. Registered architect, Fla.; cert. gen. contractor. Arch. intern Saez & Pacetti, Miami, Fla., 1976—77; arch. Greenleaf/Telesca, Miami, 1977—78, Urban Archs., Miami, 1978—82; pvt. practice arch. Coral Gables, Fla., 1982—84; arch. Lemuel Ramos & Assocs., Miami, 1984; arch., pres., gen. contractor Alligator Constrn. Corp., Miami, Fla., 1985—90; arch., pres. United Archs., Inc., Miami, 1990—. Active Coalition of Hispanic Am. Women, 1983-86. Recipient Appreciation cert. Dade County (Fla.) Sch. Bd., 1986. Mem.: Nat. Assn. Women Bus. Owners, Coconut Grove C. of C. Democrat. Avocations: reading, writing. Office: United Archs Inc Ste 207 1385 Coral Way Coral Gables FL 33145

CASTELLON, CHRISTINE NEW, information systems specialist, real estate agent; b. Pittsfield, Mass., June 22, 1957; d. Edward Francis Jr. and Helen Patricia (Cordes) New; m. John Arthur Castellon, Oct. 1, 1988. BS in Elec. and Computer Engring., U. Mass., 1979; MBA, Northea. U., 1986. Engr. microwave radio system design New England Tel. Co., Framingham, Mass., 1979-82, mgr. minicomputer support group Dorchester, Mass., 1982-85; mgr. current sys. planning/network svcs. NYNEX Svc. Co., Boston, 1985-87; mem. tech. staff computing environs. Bellcore, Piscataway, N.J., 1987-90; assoc. dir. info. sys. provisioning NYNEX Telesector Resources Group, N.Y.C., 1990-93; sales assoc. Weidel Realtors, Flemington, N.J., 1994—. Spkr. Careers-In-Engring. program New England Tel., 1980-82. Leader 2nd violin sect. Ctrl. Jersey Symphony Orch., Raritan Valley C.C., N.J., 1988—; prin. 1st violinist New England Conservatory Extension Divsn., Boston, 1979-87; violinist Civic Symphony Orch., Boston, 1982-87; active coll./industry adv. com. U. Mass. Named Monument Mountain H.S. valedictorian, 1975; recipient Arion Music award Monument Mountain H.S., 1975, cert. Applied Music and Theory Pittsfield Cmty. Music Sch., 1975. Mem. N.E. U. MBA Alumni Assn. Roman Catholic. Home: 622 Old York Rd Neshanic Station NJ 08853-3600

CASTIGLIA, PATRICIA ANNE THORSON, dean, nursing educator; b. Johnson City, N.Y. d. Theodore William and Isabelle Alice (Lane) Thorson; children: Karen, Patricia, Joseph. Diploma in Nursing, St. Vincent's Hosp., N.Y.C., 1955; BSN, U. Buffalo, 1962; MSN, SUNY, Buffalo, 1965; PhD, SUNY, 1976. RN, N.Y.; cert. sch. nurse tchr., N.Y. Staff nurse Our Lady of Lourdes Hosp., Binghamton, NY, 1955-56; asst. head nurse Hosp. of the Good Shepherd, Syracuse, NY, 1956; sch. nurse tchr. North Collins Cen. Sch., North Collins, NY, 1956-62; clin. instr. SUNY, Buffalo, 1965-73; asst. prof. Niagara U., NY, 1976-77; from asst. prof. dir. ind. study to assoc. prof. SUNY, Buffalo, 1977-89, assoc. dean, 1983-89; acting dean, assoc. prof. SUNY at Buffalo Coll. Nursing, 1989; dean, prof. Coll. Nursing and Health Scis. U. Tex., El Paso, 1990—2002, asst. to pres. for health affairs, 2001—02, prof. emeritus, 2002—, SUNY, Buffalo, 1991—, cons. for higher edn. issues; interim assoc. dean U. Tex. Med. Br., San Antonio, 2004. Stockholder, treas. Profl. Nurse Consultants P.C., Buffalo; pediatric nurse practitioner Erie County Health Dept., Buffalo, 1982-89; vis. prof. SUNY Buffalo, 2003; dean emeritus Am. Assn. Colls. Nursing, 2003; interim assoc. dean acad. affairs SON, WTMB, 2004-. Author chpts. to books; chair book of yr. awards Pediatric Nursing, 1986-88; manuscript reviewer Pediatric Nursing, Clin. Nurse Specialist, 1985—; editor: Jour. of Pediatric Health Care; co-editor: Child Health Care: Process and Practice, 1992; contbr. articles to MCN, Pediatric Nursing, Jour. Pediatric Health Care. Recipient Reach award YWCA, 1995, Charles and Shirley Leavell Endowed chair; named Nurse of Yr., Tex. Nurse Assn. 1996, Woman of the Yr. in Edn., El Paso Commn. for Women, 1996; grantee P.I. Kellogg Cmty. Partnership; SUNY Faculty Exch. scholar, Albany, 1985. Fellow Am. Acad. Nursing; mem. NAPNAP, N.Y. State Nurses Assn., Coalition of Nurse Practitioners, U. Buffalo Alumni Assn., St. Vincent's Alumni Assn., Rotary Internat., Sigma Theta Tau. Roman Catholic. Avocations: travel, piano, theatre, reading, knitting. E-mail: pcastiglia@adelphia.net.

CASTIGLIONE, ANITA, pianist, music educator; b. Long Branch, N.J. m. Dennis Spyros (dec.). BM, U. Miami, Fla.; MS in Piano Performance, Juilliard Sch.; DMA in Accompanying/Chamber Music, U. Miami, Fla., 2002. Cert. music educator K-12 N.J. Choral dir. Mt. Pleasant Jr. H.S., Livingston, NJ, 1979—89; choral dir., music theory tchr. Livingston (N.J.) H.S., 1989—. Freelance pianist, accompanist. Recipient Alumni Award in Piano, Juilliard Sch., Provost award, U. Miami Sch. Music, 1999, 2000. Mem.: Music Tchrs. Nat. Assn., Music Educators Nat. Conf. Home: 65 Hawthorne Pl #E1 Montclair NJ 07042

CASTILLO, CARMEN, staffing company executive; b. Mallorca, Spain; Founder, pres., CEO Superior Design Internat., 1992—. Bd. mem. Fla. Regional Minority Bus. Coun. Named Minority Supplier Yr. (for Superior Design Internat.), Nat. Minority Supplier Devel. Coun. (NMSDC), 2002, 34th Largest Hispanic Bus. in US, Hispanic Fortune mag., 2002, Class III Supplier Yr., Ga. Minority Supplier Devel. Coun., 2002, NY/NJ Minority Purchasing Coun., 2002; named to Top 200 Fla. Pvt. Co., Fla. Trend, 2000; recipient Corporate Plus award, Nat. Minority Supplier Devel. Coun. (NMSDC), 1997. Achievements include featured in Women's Enterprise mag., 2003. Office: 6365 NW 6th Way Ste 360 Fort Lauderdale FL 33309 Office Phone: 954-938-5400. Office Fax: 953-772-5061.*

CASTILLO, SUSAN, school system administrator; b. L.A., Aug. 14, 1951; m. Paul Machu. BA, Oreg. State U., 1981. Mem. staff Oreg. Pub. Broadcasting Radio, 1979-82; journalist, reporter legis. sessions Sta. KVAL-TV, Salem, 1991, 93, 95, journalist, reporter Eugene, 1982-97; mem. Oreg. State Senate, Salem, 1997—2002, vice chair edn. com., mem. health and human svcs. com., mem. transp. com., asst. Dem. leader legis. sessions, 1999, 2001, supt. pub. instrn., 2003—. Leader Oreg. Women's Health & Wellness Alliance. Mem. Gov.'s Task Force on DUII, 1997, Gov.'s Task Force on Cmty. Right to Know; bd. dirs. Oreg. Commn. on Hispanic Affairs, 1997, Birth to Three, Oreg. Environ. Coun.; mem. adv. com. Oreg. Passenger Rail Adv. Coun.; mem. Labor Comm.'s Adv. Com. on Agrl. Labor; vice-chair Farm Worker Housing Task Force. Democrat. Achievements include being the first Hispanic woman to serve in Oregon legislature. Office: Oregon Dept Education 255 Capitol St NE Salem OR 97301-0203

CASTLE, JANINE, psychologist; d. John Charles and Eileen Marie Castle; m. Brian Jay Young, June 9, 2001. MS, PhD, Syracuse U., N.Y., 2001. Lic. psychologist Pa., 2002. Psychologist in tng. SUNY Upstate Med. U., Syracuse, NY, 2000—01, Life Span Psychol. Svcs., Lancaster, Pa., 2001—02; psychologist Lancaster Gen. Hosp., Pa., 2002—. Group facilitator Mental Health Assn., Lancaster, Pa., 2001—02. Contbr. articles to profl. jours. Mem. Feminist Majority Found., Syracuse, NY, 1998—99. Recipient Rsch. Experience for Undergraduates award, NSF, 1992; fellow, Syracuse U. fellow, 1994; scholar Women Studies scholar, Syracuse U., 2000, Syracuse U. grad. assistantship, 1995—99, Tchrs. Asst. Program scholar, U. of Del., 1992—93. Mem.: APA (Student Rsch. award 2000), Lancaster Lebanon Psychol. Assn., Phi Kappa Phi, Psi Chi, Mortar Bd. Achievements include research in women with a history of sexual assault.

CASTLE, NANCY MARGARET TIMMA, accountant, banker; b. Seattle, June 16, 1945; d. Guy Church and Nancy L. (Fraser) B.; m. George L. Wittenburg (div. May 1972); 1 child, Guy Charles; m. Geoffrey Baird Castle, Dec. 12, 1992. Student, Stephens Coll., 1963-64. Legal adminstr. Mullen, McCaughey & Henzell, Santa Barbara, Calif., 1965-67; trust adminstr. First Interstate Bank of Calif., Santa Barbara, 1974-84; pres., owner, acct. N.T.B. Profl. Bus. Svc., Santa Barbara, 1984—. Owner Castle Enterprises, Ltd., Castle Catering Co., 1992—; mem. Continuing Edn. Bar. Mem. Am. Inst. Banking, Nat. Assn. Female Execs, Nat. Fedn. Ind. Bus. Clubs: Santa Barbara Assocs., University (Santa Barbara), Santa Barbara Yacht Club, Cottage Assocs., Santa Barbara Cottage Hosp. Republican. Episcopalian. Avocation: tennis.

CASTLE-HUGHES, KEISHA, actress; b. Donnybrook, WA, Australia, Mar. 24, 1990; d. Tim Castle and Desrae Hughes. Actor: (films) Whale Rider, 2002 (New Zealand Film and TV award for best actress, 2003, Acad. award nomination for best actress, 2004). Mailing: Creative Artists Agy c/o Kim Hodgert 9830 Wilshire Blvd Beverly Hills CA 90212-1825

CASTNER, CATHERINE S. information technology administrator; b. L.A., Apr. 14, 1968; d. Stanley Vernon Castner and Ursula Philomena McCaffrey. BS, Calif. Poly. State U., 1991; MBA, Belmont U., 2000. Participant svc. rep. Bankers Trust, L.A., 1992-94, interactive voice response analyst Nashville, 1994-97; tech. project mgr., dir. MetLife, Nashville, 1998-2000; tech. project mgr. Coval Bus. Solutions, Nashville, 2000—. Avocations: international travel, mystery novels, counted cross stitch, photography, cooking. Home: 3500 Glenfalls Dr Hermitage TN 37076-4446

CASTNER, DEBORAH A. librarian; b. Kingston, Pa., Jan. 15, 1957; d. Robert D. and Dorothy F. O'Malley; children: Jennifer, Kyle. BS in Elem. Edn., Coll. Misericordia, Dallas, Pa., 1978; MEd in Classroom Tech., Wilkes U., Wilkes-Barre, Pa., 2002. Tchr. 6th to 8th grade Holy Child Sch., Plymouth, Pa., 1988—2000; libr. Wyoming Valley West, Plymouth, Pa., 2000—; bookseller Barnes & Noble, Wilkes-Barre, Pa., 1999—. Mem.: NEA, Pa. State Edn. Assn. Home: 13 Willow St Plymouth PA 18651

CASTOR, BETTY, academic administrator; BA, Glassboro State Coll., 1963; MEd, U. Miami, 1968. Commr. edn. State of Fla., Tampa, 1986—93; pres. U. South Fla., 1994—99, Nat. Bd. Profl. Tchg. Stds., San Antonio, 2000—.

CASTORINO, SUE, communications executive; b. Columbus, Ohio, May 5, 1953; m. Randy Minkoff, Oct. 23, 1983. BS in Speech, Northwestern U., Evanston, Ill., 1975. Grad. fellow Ohio Gov.'s Sch., Columbus, 1975; producer, community affairs Sta. WBBM-TV, Chgo., 1975; news anchor, reporter Sta. WBBM, Chgo., 1981-86; news reporter Sta. WHTH-AM/FM, Newark, Ohio, 1975; news anchor, reporter Sta. WERE, Cleve., 1975-78, Sta. WWWE, Cleve., 1978-81; founder, pres. Sue Castorino: The Speaking Specialists, Chgo., 1986—. Pvt. voice coach; active internat. exec. comm. tng. in media, crisis and issue mgmt.; presenter, lectr. in field. Author: North Shore Mag., 1987—92. Recipient Golden Gavel award, Chgo. Soc. Assn. Execs., 1991, various news reporting awards, AP, UPI, Chgo., 1981—86. Avocations: sports, film, accomplished pianist. Office: The Speaking Specialists Ste 2602 435 N Michigan Ave Fl 2602 Chicago IL 60611-4001 Office Phone: 312-527-2252.

CASTORO, ROSEMARIE, sculptor; b. Bklyn., Mar. 1, 1939; d. Michael Peter and Camille C. Student in painting, Mus. Modern Art, N.Y.C., 1955-56; BFA cum laude, Pratt Inst., Bklyn., 1963. Tchr. Sch. Visual Arts, N.Y.C., 1971, Hunter Coll., N.Y.C., 1972, Calif. State U., Fresno, 1973, Syracuse (N.Y.) U., 1975, U. Colo., Boulder, 1977, Stockton State U., N.J., 1983, Boston Mus. Sch., 1983, Am. U., Corciano, Italy, 2000. Lectr. art Boston Mus. Sch. Art, 1971, 80, New Sch. Social Rsch., N.Y.C., 1972, 73, Phila. Coll. Art, 1974, Atlanta Coll. Art, 1974, Rome Art Assn., N.Y. State, 1975, Syracuse (N.Y.) U., 1975, U. Calif., Berkeley, 1976, Suzuki-Walker, Sausalito, Calif., 1976, Art Inst. Sch., Chgo., 1980, Pratt Inst., N.Y.C., 1982, 95, C.W. Post, L.I., N.Y., 1984, San Jose (Calif.) U., 1984, 85, N.J. Ctr. for Visual Arts, Summit, 1989, Ecole Nat. Superieure des Beaux-Arts, Paris, 1995. Solo shows include Tibor de Nagy Gallery, N.Y.C., 1971, 72, 73, 75, 76, 78, 81, 83, 85, 89, Hal Bromm Gallery, N.Y.C., 1976, 78, 79, 80, 83, 87, 91-92, 97, 2002, Julian Pretto, N.Y.C., 1978, 79, Marion Deson, Chgo., 1981, Am. Ctr., Paris, 1983, Eaton/Shoen Gallery, San Francisco, 1984, 86, Newark Mus., 1991, Arnaud Lefebvre Gallery, Paris, 1993, 95, 97, 98, 99, 2003, Stella R Graphics, Paris, 1993, Eaton Fine Arts, West Palm Beach, Fla., 2000, 04; group shows include Bklyn. Mus., 1963, Tibor de Nagy Gallery, 1966, Stable Gallery, 1966, Dwan Gallery, N.Y.C., 1968, 69, Richard Feigen Gallery, N.Y.C., 1968, Paula Cooper Gallery, N.Y.C., 1969, 71, Vancouver (B.C., Can.) Art Gallery, 1970, Stadtische Kunsthalle, Dusseldorf, Germany, 1970, Allen Art Mus., Oberlin, Ohio, 1970, Hundred Acres Gallery, N.Y.C., 1970, 112 Greene St Gallery, N.Y.C., 1971, 72, Richard Gray Gallery, Chgo., 1972, Storm King Art Gallery, Mountainville, N.Y., 1972, 74, 75, Grapestake Gallery, San Francisco, 1975, 76, Moore Coll. Art, Phila., 1977, John Weber Gallery, N.Y.C., 1977, Hal Bromm Gallery, 1977, 81, 82, 85, 86, 87, Indpls. Mus. Art, 1978, Whitney Mus. Am. Art, N.Y.C., 1978, Nancy Lurie Gallery, Chgo., 1978, Smithsonian Instn., Washington, 1980, Hunter Mus. Art, Chatanooga, Tenn., 1980, Banco Gallery, Brescia, Italy, 1980, Hirshhorn Mus. and Sculpture Garden, Washington, 1981, Pratt Inst. Art Gallery, Bklyn., 1981, Eaton/Shoen Gallery, 1982, 2003, Maier Mus. Art, Lynchburg, Va., 1983, 90, Laguna Gloria Art Mus., Austin, Tex., 1985, Mus. Modern Art, N.Y.C., 1985,

Newark Mus., 1987, Marvin Seline Gallery, Houston, 1990, Jan Baum Gallery, L.A., 1990, Stellar Graphics, Paris, 1992, Galerie Arnaud Lefebvre, Paris, 1993, 95-96, 2001, 2003, Henry St. Settlement, N.Y.C., 1993, Athenaeum Music & Arts Libr., La Jolla, Calif., 1995, Beaumanoir, Le Leslay, France, 1995, and many, many others; commns. include Battery Park City, N.Y.C., 1978, GSA, Topeka, Kans., 1979, Am. Ctr., Paris, 1983, Athena Found., L.I., N.Y., 1986, Woodstock '94, Saurgerties, N.Y., 1994, and others; permanent collections include Allen Art Mus., Oberlin, Ohio, Boca Raton (Fla.) Mus., Bank of Am., Calif., Chase Manhattan Bank, N.A., GSA, Washington, Mus. Modern Art, N.Y.C., Newark Mus., SNAF, Nat. Collection, France, Univ. Art Mus., U. Calif., Berkeley, U. Mass., Woodward Found., Washington, and others. Treas. HIV-Arts, N.Y.C., 1994-2004. Guggenheim fellow, 1971; grantee Woodward Found., 1970, CAPS, 1972, 74, NEA, 1974-75, 84-85, Tiffany Found., 1977, Pollock-Krasner Found., 1989-90, 97-98. Home: 151 Spring St # 6 New York NY 10012-3850 E-mail: rcastoro@earthlink.net.

CASTRO, BERNADETTE, state official; b. N.Y. Commr. N.Y. Parks, Recreation and Hist. Preservation Office, Albany, 1995—. Office: 1 Empire State Plz Albany NY 12238-0001 Fax: (518) 474-1365.

CASTRO, IDA L. state official, former federal official; d. Ezequiel and Aurora Castro; 1 child, Isamar. BA, U. P.R., 1972; MA, Rutgers U., 1978, JD, 1982; PhD (hon.), St. Joseph's Coll., West Hartford, Conn., 2000. Assoc. prof. Rutgers Inst. Mgmt. & Labor Relations, 1976—83; asst. dep. pub. advocate State of NJ, 1986—87; dir. of labor relations C.U.N.Y., 1988—90; with New York Health and Hospitals Corp., 1990—94; acting dep. solicitor Nat. Ops.; dep. asst. sec. workers' comp. Employment Stds. Adminstrn. U.S. Dept. Labor, Washington, 1994—98, acting dir. Women's Bur., 1996-98; chair, CEO, gen. coun. Equal Employment Opportunity Commn., Washington, 1998—2001; comm. NJ Dept. of Personnel, Trenton, NJ, 2002. Tchr. labor law Rutgers U., N.J.; dir. job tng. and job devel. programs, P.R. and N.J.; union rep. as labor lawyer; active Hostos C.C., South Bronx; active numerous labor, women's and Hispanic orgns. Mem., dir. manpower mayor's cabinet Municipality of Carolina, P.R.; founder, co-chair Hispanic Women's Com. of N.J.; dep. campaign mgr. Mayor Dinkins campaign, N.Y.C.; sen. adv. & dir. Dem. Nat. Comm. Women Vote Ctr., 2001-2002. Democrat. Mailing: NJ Dept Personnel PO Box 317 Trenton NJ 08625 Office: 44 S Clinton Ave Trenton NJ 08625

CASTRO, JAN GARDEN, writer, arts consultant, educator; b. St. Louis, June 8, 1945; d. Harold and Estelle (Fischer) Garden; 1 child, Jomo Jemal. Student, Cornell U., 1963-65; BA, U. Wis., 1967; pub. cert., Radcliffe Coll., 1967; MA in Tchg., Washington U., St. Louis, 1974, MA, 1994. Life cert. tchr. secondary English, speech, drama and social studies, Mo. Tchr., writer, St. Louis, 1970—; dir. Big River Assn., St. Louis, 1975-85; adj. prof. humanities Lindenwood Coll., 1980—. Co-founder, dir. Duff's Poetry Series, St. Louis, 1975-81; founder, dir. River Styx P.M. Series, St. Louis, 1981-83; arts cons. Harris-Stowe State Coll., 1986-87; vis. scholar Am. Acad. in Rome, summer 2000. Contbg. author: rev. books San Francisco Rev. Books, 1982—85, Am. Book Rev., 1990—93, Mo. Rev., 1991, New Letters, 1993, 1996, Tampa Rev., 1994—2000, The Nation, Am. Poetry Rev., Sculpture Mag., 1997—; author: (poetry) Mandala of the Five Senses, 1975, The Art and Life of Georgia O'Keeffe, 1985, 1995, Memories and Memoirs...Contemporary Missouri Authors, 2000, (poetry) The Last Frontier, 2001—, Sonia DeLaunay: La Moderne, 2002—; editor: (jours.) River Styx mag., 1975—86; co-editor: (essays) Margaret Atwood: Vision and Forms, 1988; co-prodr.(TV host, co-prodr.): (shows) The Writers Cir., Double Helix, 1987—89; contbg. editor: (jours.) Sculpture Mag. Seeking St. Louis, Voices from a River City, 1670—2000. Mem. University City Arts and Letters Commn., Mo., 1983-84. NEH fellow UCLA, 1988, Johns Hopkins U., 1991, Camargo Found. fellow (Cassis, France), 1996; recipient Arts and Letters award St. Louis Mag., 1985, Editor's award and editor during G.E. Younger Writers award to River Styx Mag., Coord. Coun. for Lit. Mags., 1986, Arts award Mandrake Soc. Charity Ball, 1988, Leadership award YWCA St. Louis, 1988. Mem. MLA, CAA, PEN Am. Ctr., Nat. Coalition Ind. Scholars, Margaret Atwood Soc. (founder). Home: 7420 Cornell Ave Saint Louis MO 63130-2914 Office: LCIE Coll Lindenwood U Saint Charles MO 63301 E-mail: jan_g_castro@mail.com.

CASTRO, JUDITH ANA, social worker; b. Stamford, Conn., Oct. 22, 1976; d. Frank Castro and Ana Serafina Recio; m. James L. Trasport, Jr., June 21, 2001. BA in Polit. Sci., Anthropology, Fla. Atlantic U., Boca Raton, 1999, MA in Women's Studies, 2003. Coord. incentive program Carver Estates Youth Program, Delray Beach, Fla., 1997—2002; grad. asst. women's studies Fla. Atlantic U., Boca Raton, 2001—02; coord. resident svcs. St. Vincent de Paul, Eugene, Oreg., 2002—. Spkr. in field. Pres. Student NOW, Boca Raton, Fla., 1999—2001; mem. South Fla. Global Justice Group, Boca Raton, Fla., 1999; pres., founding mother Cmty. Action Responsible for Empowerment, Boca Raton, Fla., 2000—02. Finalist Kenneth R. Williams Leadership award, Fla. Atlantic U., 2000; recipient Laura S. Myers award, 2000, Annette von Have award, 2001, 2003. Avocations: ceramics, sewing, singing, dance, gardening.

CASTRO, MARIA GRACIELA, medical educator, geneticist, researcher; b. Buenos Aires, Mar. 2, 1955; d. Nestor Antonio Castro and Maria Esther Rodriquez; m. Pedro Ricardo Lowenstein, Jan. 12, 1988; 1 child, Elijah David Lowenstein. BSc 1st class in Chemistry, Nat. U. La Plata, Argentina, 1979, MSc in Biochemistry, 1981, PhD in Biochemistry, 1986. Fogarty postdoctoral fellow Lab. Neurochem. & Neuroimmunol. Nat. Inst. Child Health and Human Devel. NIH, Bethesda, Md., 1986-88; sr. rsch. fellow Lab. Molecular Endocrinology Dept. Biochemistry and Physiology U. Reading, England, 1988-90; lectr. dept. molecular and life scis. U. Abertay, Dundee, Scotland, 1991-92; lectr. in neurosci., dept. physiology U. Wales Coll. Cardiff, 1991-95; sr. lectr. medicine Sch. Medicine U. Manchester, England, 1995-98, prof. molecular medicine, 1998—, dir. molecular medicine and gene therapy unit, 1996—. Expert Women in Sci. Tech., Sheffield, England, 1996—; neurosci. panel Wellcome Trust, England, 1999—; co-dir. dept. molecular medicine Cedar-Sinai Med. Ctr., 2001—; co-dir. bd. govs. Gene Therapeutics Rsch. Inst., Cedars Sinai Med. Ctr., 2001—; prof. medicine UCLA, 2002—. Mem. editl. bd.: Jour. Endocrinology, Jour. Molecular Endocrinology, Current Gene Therapy, Gene Therapy, Pituitary, 2000, Neuro Molecular Medicine, 2001—; contbr. articles to profl. jours. Rsch. grantee, Brit. Heart Found., 1997, Med. Rsch. Coun., 1998, Biotechnology and Biol. Rsch. Coun., 1999—2000, Wellcome Trust, 1999, NIH, 2003—. Mem.: NIH, Nat. Inst. Neurol. Disorders and Stroke (mem. study sect., grant award), Internat. Soc. Nerovirology (founding mem.), Soc. Neuroscience, Endocrine Soc., Am. Gene Therapy Assn. Achievements include patents in field; research in program development of gene therapy for chronic neurological diseases and brain cancer. E-mail: castromg@cshs.org.

CASTRO, SANDRA IVETTE, special education educator; b. Ponce, Puerto Rico, May 6, 1962; d. Sixto Castro and Aida Mercedes Busanet; m. Sandra Ivette Santana, Aug. 6, 1996; 1 child, Marlenie Barada. AA, Fiorello H. Laguardia C.c., 1985—88; B in profl. studies of human svc., Coll. Of Human Svc./Audrey Cohen Coll. Sch. For Human Svc., 1989—91; MS in edn., City Coll., The Sch. Of Edn., 1993—98. NYC Pub. Sch. Bilingual Common Branches Spanish NYC Dept. Of Edn., 1996, Pub. Sch. Tchr. Cert. U. Of The State Of NY Edn. Dept., 1998, Tchr. Of Spl. Edn. NYC Dept. Of Edn., 2000. Bilingual spl. educator Pub. Sch. 112, NYC, 2001—; bilingual spl. educator, resource tchr. and cons. educator Pub. Sch. 155, NYC, 2000—01; spl. edn. educator East Bronx NAACP Day Care Ctr., Bronx, NY, 1991—2000; montessori tchr. West Chealse Montessori Ctr., NYC, 1987—91. Achievements include research in 2nd grade math currricculum.

CASTRO, STEPHANIE L. business management educator; b. San Antonio, Mar. 8, 1968; d. Reuben Riley and Mary Jaquelyn Loeffler; m. Erik Ricardo Castro, Aug. 21, 1993; children: Cole Anthony, Erika Jewel. BBA, Fla. Internat. U., 1993; PhD, U. Miami, 1998. Asst. prof. La. State U., Baton Rouge, 1998—2000; vis. asst. prof. U. Miami, 2000—02; asst. prof. Fla. Atlantic U., 2002—. Mem.: APA, Acad. Mgmt., Soc. Indsl. Orgnl. Psychologists. Home: 17411 SW 61st Ct Fort Lauderdale FL 33331-1715

CASTRO-KLAREN, SARA, Latin American literature educator; b. Arequipa, Sabandia, Peru, June 9, 1942; d. José Andrés and Zoila Rosa (Rivas) Castro-Valdivia; m. Peter F. Klaren, Sept. 3, 1962; 1 child, Alexandra. BA, UCLA, 1962, MA, 1965, PhD, 1968. Asst. prof. Dartmouth Coll., No. Hampshire, N.H., 1970-84; chief Hispanic div. Lib. of Congress Fed. Govt., Washington, 1984-86; prof. Latin Am. lit. Johns Hopkins U., Balt., 1986—. Dir. program Latin Am. Studies, JHU. Author: El Mundo Magico de J.M. Arquedas, Lima, 1973, Mario Vargas Llosa, Analisis Introductorio, Lima, 1988, Escritura Sujeto y Transgresión, Mexico, 1989, Understanding Mario Vargas Llosa, U. S.C., 1990, Women's Writing in Latin America, 1991, Latin American Women's Narrative: Practices and Theoretical Perspectives, 2003. Fellow Woodrow Wilson Ctr. for Scholars, Washington, 1977-78. Mem. MLA, AAUP, Latin Am. Studies Assn., Ibero-americana, Soc. Hispanists, Am. Assn. Colls. and Univs. Avocation: gardening. Home: 9438 Rabbit Hill Road Great Falls VA 22066

CASTRONOVO, BERNADINE MARRO, music educator; b. Peekskill, NY, Oct. 17, 1949; d. Joseph A. and Mary L. Marro; m. Charles Castronovo, Aug. 14, 1982. BS in Music Edn., We. Conn. U., 1971, MS in Music Edn., 1975. Music tchr./chorus dir. Austin Rd. Elem., Mahopac, NY, 1971—75, Mahopac H.S., Mahopac, 1975—86, Mahopac Falls Elem., Mahopac, 1975—77, Lakeview Elem., Mahopac, 1977—80, Mahopac Jr. H.S., Mahopac, 1980—86, Mahopac Mid. Sch., Mahopac, 1986—92, Lakeview Elem., Mahopac, 1992—. Choral dir./Mahopac H.S. in performance at Carnegie Hall, N.Y.C., 1982. Recipient Ruth DeVilla Franca Music award, We. Conn. U., 1971, Cert. Recognition award, Nat. Assn. Music Edn. Mem.: Nat. Assn. Music Edn., We. Conn. Univ. Alumni Assn., N.Y. State Sch. Music Assn., N.Y. State United Tchrs., Music Educators Nat. Conf. Avocation: animals, swimming, cooking, singing. Home: 453 Austin Rd Mahopac NY 10541 Office: Lakeview Elem Lakeview Drive Mahopac NY 10541

CASTRO-POZO, TALIA, dancer, educator; b. Lima, Peru, Oct. 2, 1975; came to U.S., 1995; d. Jose and Renée Castro. Profl. degree in Ballet and Modern Dance, Nat. Ballet Sch., Lima, Peru, 1992; studied with Sergei Radchenko, Mabel Silvera Studio, Buenos Aires, 1992; student, Sch. Am. Ballet, 1995-96. Soloist Nat. Ballet, 1992-95; supr. Stepping Out Studios performing, tchr. ballroom dancing, 1999—. Rep. Internat. Ballet Competition, U.S.A., 1994, World Ballet Competition, Osaka, Japan, 1995, 30th Course of Ballet and Modern, Varna, Bulgaria. Dancer in classical, contemporary, modern pieces including Don Quixote, Spring Waters, Spartacus, A Solas; featured dancer in film Summer of Sam; choreographer in ind. film Angela, 1999. Dancer/choreographer Korean Army Festivities, Lima, 1992; dancer First Festival for Children's Rights, Lima, 1995. Recipient 1st Place award Latin Am. competition, 1989; Best Dancer of Yr. award Peruvian Press, 1991. Mem. Nat. Assn. Writers and Artists. Home: 228 W 18th St Apt 27 New York NY 10011-4530

CASWELL, DOROTHY ANN COTTRELL, visual artist, arts administrator; b. N.Y.C., Dec. 18, 1938; d. Donald Peery and Eleanor Hildaborg (Westberg) Cottrell; m. Allen Edward Caswell, Oct. 24, 1959; children: David Alan, Bruce Leland. Student, Carleton Coll., Northfield, MN, 1956-59; AB in Psych., George Wash. U., 1960-61; postgrad. in vocal performance, SUNY, Oneonta, 1971-76. Sec. U.S. Fgn. Service, Tunis, Tunisia, 1959-61; mng. dir. Glimmerglass Opera, Inc., Cooperstown, N.Y., 1975-78; exec. dir. Upper Catskill Community Council on the Arts, Oneonta, N.Y., 1978-80; devel. officer Catskill Arts Consortium, Oneonta, 1981-83; devel. cons. Otsego Urban Rural Self-Devel. Assocs., Inc., Oneonta, 1982-83; co-founder, pres. Catskill Choral Soc., 1970-76, 81-84; assoc. producer Orpheus Theatre, Inc., Oneonta, 1984-91; voice tchr. Oneonta, 1984—; ptnr., co-owner OnStage Prodn. Svcs., 1991—. Cons., arts adminstrv. Dorothy Caswell Assocs., Oneonta, 1981—; past pres., mem. sub-area coun. Health Sys. Agy. NE, NY, mem. planning adv. group, rev. adv. Actor(film series Susquehanna Stories): WSKG-TV Pub. TV, 1990—. Mem. chorus Glimmerglass Opera, Cooperstown, 1974—; mem. mil. acad. selection com. Congressman Sherwood Boehlert, NY, 1993—; mem. Otsego County Health Planning Adv. Coun. Otsego Publ Health Partnership; bd. dirs. Otsego County Tourism Bur., 1987—90, Oneonta Downtown Coalition, 1982—84. Recipient Honored for Outstanding Performance and Svcs. to Cmty., SUNY, 1975. Democrat. Avocations: painting, performing arts, gardening, swimming.

CASWELL, FRANCES PRATT, retired English language educator; b. Brunswick, Maine, June 25, 1929; m. Forrest Wilbur Caswell, June 30, 1956; children: Lucy Caswell Hilburn, Helen Caswell Watts, Harold F. BA, U. Maine, 1951; MA, U. Mich., 1955. Tchr. English, Bridgton (Maine) High Sch., 1951-54, Grosse Point (Mich.) High Sch., 1955-56; instr. South Maine Tech. Coll., South Portland, 1968-84, chmn. dept., 1984-93. Bd. dirs. Maine Vocat. Region 10, 1993-2003. Author: Growing Through Faith, A History of the Brunswick United Methodist Church, 1821-1996, 1996; contbg. author: Brunswick, Maine, 250 Years A Town, 1989. Pres. United Pejepscot Housing Inc., Brunswick, 1987-93. Mem. AAUW, Casco Bay Art League. Methodist. Avocations: painting, gardening.

CATALANO, JANE DONNA, lawyer; b. Schenectady, N.Y., Feb. 21, 1957; d. Alfred and Joan (Futscher) Martini; m. Peter Catalano, June 18, 1988. BA, SUNY, Plattsburgh, 1979; JD, Albany Law Sch., 1982. Bar: N.Y. 1983, U.S. Dist. Ct. 1983. Atty. Pentak, Brown & Tobin, Albany, N.Y., 1982-87, Niagara Mohawk Power Corp., Albany, 1987—. Mem. N.Y. State Bar Assn., Albany County Bar Assn. Home: 7 Blackburn Way Latham NY 12110-1943 Office: Niagara Mohawk Power Corp A National Grid Co 1125 Broadway Albany NY 12204

CATALFO, BETTY MARIE, health service executive, nutritionist; b. N.Y.C., Nov. 2, 1942; d. Lawrence Santo and Gemma (Patrone) Lorefice; children— Anthony, Lawrence, Donna Marie. Grad. Newtown High Sch., Elmhurst, N.Y., 1958. Sec., clk. ABC-TV, N.Y.C., 1957-60; founder, lectr., nutritionist Weight Watchers, Manhasset, N.Y., 1964-75; founder, pres. Every-Bodys Diet, Inc. dba Stay Slim, Queens, N.Y., 1976—; dir. in-home program N.Y. State Dept. Health, N.Y.C., 1985—; founder, pres. Delitegul Diet Foods, Inc., 1988—; lectr. in field. Author: 101 Stay-Slim Recipes, 1983, Get Slim and Stay Slim Diet Cook Book, rev. ed., 1987, Diet Revolution, 1991, Holiday Cookbook, 1992, Fat Counts in Fast Food Spots, 1992, Choose to Loose!, 1993, You Are Not Alone, 1993, Eating Out, 1994, Change or Select, 1994, Calories Do Count!, 1994, Fat Free Receipes, 1994; author, dir., producer: (video) Dancersize for Overweight, 1986, Get Slim and Stay Slim Diet Cook Book, Eating Right for Your Life, Hello It's Me and I'm Slim, (videos) Stay Slim Line Dancing, 1989, Stay Slim Food Facts, 1989, Help Me Before I Give In, 1990, A New Year A New You!, 1991, Relax and Meditate, 1991, Come Shop with Me, 1991, Change or Accept, 1993, The Bag Lady, 1993, Sneak Eater, 1993, Sins That Every Dieter Makes, 1994, Stay Slim from Start to Finish, 1994, Here's Some Helpful Diet Tips, 1994, What Every Smart Dieter Knows, 1994, Mirror Mirror on the Wall, 1994, Weight Management Techniques, 1995; author, editor: (video) Eating Right For Life, 1985, Isometric Techniques for Weight Reduction, Dance Your Calories A-Weigh; author, producer: (video) Eating Habits, 1986—; (video) Isometric Techniques for Weight Reduction, 1986, Patience Is a Virtue When Weight Loss is the Goal, 1986, Slow Down you Eat to Fast, 1994, Always Giving Never Receiving, 1994, Relax and Don't You Worry, 1994; producer, dir.: (video) Positive and Negative Diet Forces, 1987, (video) Hello It's Me and I'm Thin, 1987, (video) Dance Your Calories A-Weigh, 1987, (video) Positive and Negative Diet Forces, 1987. Sponsor, lectr. St. Pauls Ctr., Bklyn., 1981—, Throgs Neck Assn. Retarded Children, Bronx, 1985, active ARC, LWV, Am. Italian Assn., United Way Greenwich, Council Chs. and Synagogues, Heart Assn., N.Y. Meals on Wheels, 1985—, Health Assn. Fairfield County, Food Svcs. for Homeless People, 1993, 94, 95; chairperson, sponsor Battered Women, 1994—. Named Woman of Yr., Bayside Womens Club, N.Y., 1983, O, PK Woman of Yr., 1986—, Woman of Yr. Richmond Boys Club, 1987, Woman of Yr. Bronx Press Club Assn., 1987; recipient Merit award for Svc. Cath. Archdiocese of Bklyn., 1985, Merit award Svcs. Cath. Archdioces of Bklyn. and Queens, 1992, 93, 94, Community Service award Sr. Citizens Sacred Heart League Bklyn./Queens Archdiocese. N.Y. State Nutritional Guidance for Children Nat. Assn. Scis. Mem. Nat. C. of C. for Women (Woman of Yr. 1987, 90), Pres.'s Coun. on Nutrition, Roundtable for Women in Food Service, Bus. and Profl. Women's Club, Pres. Council for Phys. Fitness, Nat. Assn. Female Execs., Assn. for Fitness in Bus. Inc., Nat. Assn. Female Bus. Owners. Democrat. Roman Catholic. Club: Mothers Sacred Heart Sch. (chairperson 1979-82). Avocations: reading; travel, golf, family. Home: 21422 27th Ave Flushing NY 11360-2608 also: 58 Riverview Ct Greenwich CT 06831-4127 Office: 10005 101st Ave Ozone Park NY 11416-2601

CATALLO, HEATHER, newscaster; b. Mich. Graduate, S.I. Newhouse Sch. of Pub. Comm., Syracuse, N.Y. Reporter WTVH-TV, Syracuse, NY; police beat reporter KREM-TV, Spokane, Wash.; investigative reporter WXYZ-TV, Detroit, 1999—, anchor Sunday morning and noon shows, 1999—. Recipient Hearst Nat. TV award Excellence, 1998. Office: WXYZ-TV 20777 W Ten Mile Rd Southfield MI 48037

CATCHINGS, KELLY SUZANNE, photographer; b. Houston, Tex., May 15, 1964; d. Billy and Fran Catchings. Applied photography, Art Inst. Houston; student, Calumet Inst. Techs., Md. State U., 1998. Photographer, photography asst. Advanced Photographic Direction, N.Y.C., 1991—94; photography asst. Herb Ritts Photography, L.A., 1996—2002; photographer Raw Talent Photo, Santa Barbara, Calif., 2001—; owner, photographer Kelly Catchings Studio, Houston, 2003—. Contbr. photographs Photographs Forum Book, 1999; editor, photographer: Houston Headline Newspaper, 1995—96; works appeared in publs. including, Vanity Fair, Rolling Stone, GQ, Alternative Press, others, exhibitions include Checkered Past, Rosenberg, Tex., 2002—03, Rosebud's Emporium, 2003—. Mem. ACLU, L.A., 1999—2002; photographer Picture This, L.A., 2001. Recipient scholarship, Md. State U., 1998, KINSA award 1st pl., Houston Chronicle and Kodak, 1992. Mem.: Watercolor Art Soc., Women in the Arts-Womens Mus., Am. Assn. Mus., Advt. Photographers of Am. Avocations: nature activities, art, travel, dogs. Office: Kelly Catchings Photography 807 W 19th St Houston TX 77008 E-mail: kelly@kellycatchings.com.

CATCHINGS, TAMIKA, professional basketball player; b. Stratford, N.J., July 21, 1979; d. Harvey Catchings. Grad., U. Tenn., 2001. Profl. basketball player Ind. Fever, 2001—. Mem. USA Basketball Jr. World Championship Team, 1997. Named Nat. Rookie of Yr., Sporting News, 1998, Naismith All-Am., Atlanta Tip-Off Club, 1999, Naismith Player of Yr., 2000, Nat. Player of Yr., Associated Press, U.S. Basketball Writers Assn. (USBWA), Kodak/WBCA, 2000, Coll. Player of the Yr., Espy Awards, 2000, WNBA Rookie of the Yr., 2002; named to Kodak All-Am. 4 Times; recipient Gold medal, FIBA Jr. World Championship, 1997, R. William Jones Cup, 1998, All-Am., Sports Illustrated, Sporting News, 1999, 2000. Office: 125 S Pennsylvania St Indianapolis IN 46204

CATCHPOLE, JUDY, state official; m. Glenn Catchpole; children: Glenda, Fred, Katie. BA in Edn., U. Wyo. Former state supt. pub. instrn. State Dept. Edn., Cheyenne, Wyo.; mem. Wyo. Higher Edn. Assistance Authority, 2002—. Exec. dir. Wyoming Rep. Party; mem. Wyoming Land and Investment bd., CCSSO Bd. Dirs., U. Wyo. Bd. Trustees, Edn. Commn. of States Commr., STARBASE Bd. Dirs., pres. Mem. Wyo. Sch. Bds. Assn. (past vice chmn.), Wyo. Early Childhood Assn. (past pres.). Office: Wyo Dept Edn 2300 Capitol Ave Fl 2 Cheyenne WY 82002-0050

CATES, JO ANN, library administrator, writer; b. Ft. Worth, June 25, 1958; d. Charles Kimbrough and Lydia Joe (Sachse) C.; m. Joseph Daniel Frank, Oct. 28, 1989; children: Jacob Abraham Frank, Dec. 9, 1993, Mabel Rose Frank, Sept. 2, 1996. BS in Journalism, Boston U., 1980; MLS, Simmons Coll., 1984. Advt. asst. Boston Phoenix, 1978-79; med. serials asst. Mass. Gen. Hosp., Boston, 1979-80; editorial asst. Exceptional Parent Mag., Boston, 1980-81; libr. reference asst. Lesley Coll., Cambridge, Mass., 1981-84; head reference libr. Lamont Libr., Harvard U., Cambridge, Mass., 1984-85; chief libr. Poynter Inst. for Media Studies, St. Petersburg, Fla., 1985-91; head transp. libr. Northwestern U., Evanston, Ill., 1991-94; regional rsch. mgr. Ctr. for Bus. Knowledge Ernst & Young, 1997—2001; libr. dir. Columbia Coll., Chicago, Ill., 2001—. Tchr. News Libr. and Newsroom Seminars Poynter Inst., 1990-91; mem. Harvard Com. on Instrn. Libr. Use, 1984, mem. adv. com. on book and serial budgets, 1991-94; cons. journalism orgns. Calif., Fla., Mass., 1984—; book reviewer Libr. Jour., Choice, 1985-2000, Am. Reference Book Annual, 1993—; knowledge mgmt. column editor B&F Divsn. Bull., 1999-2000. Author: Journalism: A Guide to the Reference Literature, 1990, 2d edit., 1997; editor Transp. Divsn. Bull., 1992-94; mem. editorial bd. Footnotes, 1991-94; contbr. articles to profl. jours. Mem. Transp. Rsch. Bd. Info. Svcs. Com., 1991-94; media intern Dem. Nat. Com., Boston, 1979-80. Scholar Women in Comm., 1976-78; Trustee scholar Boston U., 1978-80; Simmons Coll. grantee, 1982-84. Mem. Spl. Librs. Assn., Assn. for Edn. in Journalism and Mass Comm., Suncoast Info. Specialists (pres. 1990-91). Am. Libr. Assoc. Avocations: gourmet cooking, collecting books. Home: 540 Hinman Ave Apt 4 Evanston IL 60202-3081

CATES, SUE SADLER, educational diagnostician; b. Ft. Worth, Aug. 7, 1947; d. Randall and Mary Jo (Merkt) Sadler; m. Dennis Lynn Cates, Aug. 9, 1975. BA, Baylor U., 1970; MEd, Sul Ross State U., 1977. Cert. tchr., counselor, ednl. diagnostician, Tex. Tchr. spl. edn. Eagle Pass (Tex.) Ind. Sch. Dist., 1974-76, Beeville (Tex.) Ind. Sch. Dist., 1976-80; supr., ednl. diagnostician Sinton (Tex.) Ind. Sch. Dist., 1980-81; counselor, diagnostician Snyder (Tex.) Ind. Sch. Dist., 1981-86; ednl. diagnostician Pampa (Tex.) Ind. Sch. Dist., 1987-89; elem. counselor Richland County Sch. Dist., Columbia, S.C., 1989-95; ednl. diagnostician Wichita Falls (Tex.) Ind. Sch. Dist., 1995-97, Graham (Tex.) Ind. Sch. Dist., 1997-98, Carrollton-Farmers Branch (Tex.) Ind. Sch. Dist., 1998-2000, Cedar Hill Ind. Sch. Dist., 2000-01, Arlington (Tex.) Ind. Sch. Dist., 2001—02, Ft. Worth (Tex.) Can! Acad. Charter Sch., 2002—, Ft. Worth Can! Acad. Charter Sch., 2002, Van Zandt/Rains County SSA-Edgewood ISD, 2003—. Bd. dirs. Scurry County Sheltered Workshop, 1981-85, Tex. Assn. Children with Learning Disabilities, 1976-77, 81-83; coach Tex. Spl. Olympics, Beeville, amd Sinton, 1978-81; mem. sanctuary choir Floral Heights United Meth. Ch., Wichita Falls, 1995-98, Stephen min., 1992-2003; tchr. Sunday sch., youth coordinator, various other positions. Mem. Tex. Ednl. Diagnosticians' Assn., Council Exceptional Children, Council Ednl. Diagnosticians, Assn. Supervision and Devel., Nat. Assn. Workshop Dirs., NEA, Tex. State Tchrs. Assn., Tex. Classroom Tchrs. Assn., Am. Assn. Counseling and Devel., Tex. Assn. Counseling and Devel., Tex. Ednl. Diagnosticians Assn., AAUW, Phi Delta Kappa, Zeta Phi Eta. Avocations: swimming, coin collecting, travel, singing, jewelry. Home: 4402 York St Wichita Falls TX 76309-4014 Office: Edgewood Ind Sch Dist Van Zandt/Rains County SSA PO Box 727 Edgewood TX 75117

CATHCART, JANE WILSON, recreational therapist, social worker, psychotherapist; b. Jackson Heights, N.Y., Oct. 18, 1946; d. Frank Robert and Antoinette Dyczko Wilson; m. Conrad W. Cathcart, Sept. 9, 1989; m.

Keith J. Jurosko, Sept. 23, 1967 (div. Sept. 1969); m. Patrick H. Downes, Dec. 24, 1970 (div. May 1984). BA, Adelphi Univ., 1967; MSW, N.Y.U., 1996. LCSW Cert. Social Worker NYS Edn. Dept., 1997; cert. Acad. of Registered Dance Therapists Am. Dance Therapy Assn., 1976, Movement Analyst Labam/Bartenieff Inst., 1979. Dance movement therapist Manhattan State Hosp., N.Y.C., 1970—71; dir. dance therapy programs Manhattan Children's Psychiatr. Ctr., N.Y.C., 1971—91; faculty Wesleyan Univ. GLSP, Middletown, Conn., 1985—2002; dance therapist/social worker Little Meadows Early Childhood Ctr., Fresh Meadows, NY, 1988—; psychotherapist Pvt. Practice, N.Y.C., 1976—. Artist in res. CUNY, N.Y.C., 1981; producer/oxberry stand J. Freeman Assocs., N.Y.C., 1984—86; prodn. asst. for prodn. of Mother Teresa, Petrie Prodns., N.Y.C., 1984; trustee, sec. Marian Chace Found., 1996—. Contbg. author: Movement & Growth: Dance Therapy for The Special Child, 1980, The Choreography of Object Rels., 1982; Movement Therapy (educational films) Dance Therapy: The Power of Movement, 1982. Mem. bd. dir. Laban/Bartenieff Inst., N.Y.C., 1983—85, Red Peonies Performance Project, N.Y.C., 1986—88; bd. dir. 327 4 St CO-OP, N.Y.C., 1990—. Recipient PSC-CUNY Rschr. award_, The City Univ. of N.Y. - Hunter Coll., 1987—88. Mem.: Am. Dance Therapy Assn., Nat. Assn. of Social Work. Democrat. Avocations: collage, calligraphy, jewelry making, cooking, musicology. Office: Jane Wilson Cathcart ADTR CMA CSW 80 East 11th Street Suite 307 New York NY 10003

CATHCART, MARY R. state legislator; m. Jeam Dearman; 3 children. BA in English with distinction, Rhodes Coll., 1963; postgrad. in English, Vanderbilt U., 1964-65. Project dir., steering com. Spruce Run Assn., Bangor, Maine, 1977-83, cmty. edn. coord., 1983-88; mem. Maine Ho. of Reps., Augusta, 1988-94; chair U.S. Commn. on Child and Family Welfare, 1995-96; mem. Dist. 7 Maine Senate, Augusta, 1997—. Mem. appropriations and fin. affairs com. Maine State Senate, joint standing com. on human resources, 1989-90, Blue Ribbon Task Force to Promote Equality of Opportunity for Women in Pub. Sch. Sys., 1989-90, joint standing com. on judiciary, 1991-94, juvenile corrections task force, 1993, Healthy Start task force, 1993, joint standing com. on aging, retirement and vets., 1993-94, joint standing com. on edn. and cultural affairs, chair joint select com. on R&D, chair joint standing com. on labor. Mem. Maine Commn. for Women, 1985-89, chair, 1986-87; mem. planning bd. Town of Orono, 1986-93; mem. adv. bd. Maine Family Law Project, 1990-93; mem. steering com. Communities United for Reproductive Safety, 1994—; bd. dirs. Maine Women's Fund, 1995-98; mem. Orono Econ. Devel. Commn., 1998—; vice chair Maine del. New Eng. Bd. Higher Edn., 1997—; chair Commn. to Study Providing Educators with More Authority to Remove Violent Students from Ednl. Settings, 1998. Democrat. Home: 120 Main St Orono ME 04473-3800 Office: Maine State Senate 3 State House Sta Augusta ME 04333-0003 E-mail: maryorono@aol.com, SenMary.Cathcart@State.Me.us.

CATHEY, MARY ELLEN JACKSON, religious studies educator; b. Florence, S.C., Jan. 12, 1926; d. John William and Mary Ellen (Heinrich) Jackson; m. Henry Marcellus Cathey, May 31, 1958; children: Mary Emily Cathey Ewell, Henry Marcellus Jr. AB, Winthrop Coll., 1947; MRE, Presbyn. Sch. Christian Edn., Richmond, Va., 1953. Cert. Christian educator. Tchr. English, drama Jenkins Jr. High Sch., Spartanburg, S.C., 1947-51; dir. Christian edn. First Presbyn. Ch., Anderson, S.C., 1953-56, Bethesda (Md.) Presbyn. Ch., 1956-59; organizer, dir. Co-op Nursery Sch., Bethesda Presbyn. Ch., 1967-70, dir. Christian edn. Potomac Presbyn. Ch., Potomac, Md., 1977-83, Bethesda Presbyn. Ch., 1983-85, Nat. Presbyn. Ch., Washington, 1985-88; freelance cons. and educator Nat. Capital Presbytery, Washington, 1988—. Edn. cons. Covenant Presbyn. Ch., Arlington, Va., 1987, First Presbyn. Ch., Arlington, 1989-91, Lewinsville Presbyn. Ch., McLean, 1990; elder Nat. Presbyn. Ch., 1990—; elder commr. Gen. Assy., Presbyn. Ch., Milw., 1992. Author hymn text: God Almighty, God Eternal, 1956, others, numerous poems; co-author: Confirmation Guidebook, 1988, The Circle of Wholeness, 1991. Mem. Nat. Leadership Ctr., Washington, 1999—2000; mem. pres.;s adv. coun. Union Sem.-Presbyn. Sch. Christian Edn., Richmond, Va.; pub. trustee Washington Theol. Consortium; elder Presbyn. Ch. USA, copmmr. gen. assembly, 1992. Recipient Sparkler Award Presbyn. Sch. of Christian Edn. Alumni/ae Coun., 1991. Mem. Hymn Soc. U.S. and Can., Presbyn. Writers' Guild, Presbyn. Assn. Musicians, Assn. Presbyn. Ch. Educators, Nat. Capital Presbytery Educators. Avocations: travel, theatre, music, dance, writing. Home and Office: 1817 Bart Dr Silver Spring MD 20905-4418

CATHEY, PATRICE ANTOINETTE, secondary school educator, director; b. Buffalo, Oct. 13, 1954; d. Eulis Merle and Ruth Houston Cathey; children: Jonathan Eulis Barr, Patrick Jason Barr, Stephan James Barr. BA, Canisius Coll., 1995—98, EdM, 2000—02; PhD, Walden U., 2002—. Cert. of Interior Design J.R. Powers Sch., 1982. Founder/dir. Poetically Speaking Poetry Workshops For Children, Buffalo, 1995—, Ethics and Etiquette, Buffalo, 1996—; writers in edn. instr. Just Buffalo Llt. Ctr., 1996—2000; tchr. St. John Christian Acad., Buffalo, 1997—2000; academic coord. Upward Bound of Buffalo State Coll., 2000—01; dir. Liberty Partnerships Program, Buffalo, 2001—. Comm. coord. B.E.A.M. Buffalo-Area Engring. Awareness for Minorities, 1996—; founder/pub. Onya Pub., Buffalo, 1998—; dir. of mentoring/tutoring Liberty Partnerships Program, Buffalo, 2001—. Actor: (performance poetry) A Woman of Her Words; author: (cd) Perhaps Virginia, When Poems Take Wings...Life Poems, 2003, numerous poems. Mem. Cmty. Sch. #53, Buffalo, 2001—02; vol. Darwin Martin Ho., Buffalo, 2002, Albright Knox Art Gallery, Buffalo. Recipient Distinguished Alumni Award, The Buffalo Sem., 2002, Uncrowned Queens, African Am. Women Cmty. Builders of Western N.Y., 2001; scholar Academic Scholarship, Women's Bus. Soc. of Amherst, 1997. Mem.: Internat. Soc. of Poets (award 2000), Poetry Soc. of Am., The Acad. of Am. Poets, Women in Higher Edn., Nat. Assn. of U. Women, Nat. Assn. of Black Sch. Educators, AEEE, The Jr. League of Buffalo, Alpha Kappa Alpha Sorority. Office: Liberty Partnerships Program 1300 Elmwood Avenue-CLL-E103 Buffalo NY 14222 Personal E-mail: patricecathey@yahoo.com. E-mail: catheypc@buffalostate.edu.

CATHOU, RENATA EGONE, chemist, consultant; b. Milan, June 21, 1935; d. Egon and Stella Mary Egone; m. Pierre-Yves Cathou, June 21, 1959. BS, MIT, 1957, PhD, 1963. Fellow, rsch. assoc. in chemistry MIT, Cambridge, 1962-65; rsch. assoc. Harvard U. Med. Sch., Cambridge, 1965-69, instr., 1969-70; rsch. assoc. Mass. Gen. Hosp., 1965-69, instr., 1969-70; asst. prof. dept. biochemistry Sch. Medicine, Tufts U., 1970-73, assoc. prof., 1973-78, prof., 1978-81; pres. Tech. Evaluations, Lexington, Mass., 1983-2000; sr. cons. SRC Assocs., Park Ridge, N.J., 1984-93. Sr. investigator Arthritis Found., 1970-75; vis. prof. dept. chemistry UCLA, 1976-77; mem. adv. panel NSF, 1974-75; mem. bd. sci. counselors Nat. Cancer Inst., 1979-83; ind. cons. and writer. Mem. editl. bd. Immunochemistry, 1972-75; contbr. chpts. to books and articles to profl. jours. MIT Company Founders citation, 1989; NIH predoctoral fellow, 1958-62; grantee Am. Heart Assn., 1969-81, USPHS, 1970-81. Mem. AAAS, Am. Soc. for Biochemistry and Molecular Biology, Am. Assn. Immunologists, U.S. Power Squadron (past dist. lt. comdr.), Charles River Squadron (past comdr.), Circumnavigators Club. Avocations: photography, opera, fine arts.

CATLEY-CARLSON, MARGARET, not-for-profit executive; b. Nelson, B.C., Oct. 6, 1942; d. George Lorne and Helen Margaret Catley; m. Stanley F. Carlson, Oct. 30, 1970. BA with honors, U. B.C., 1966; postgrad., Inst. Internat. Rels., U. W.I., St. Augustine, Trinidad and Tobago, 1970; LLD (hon.), U. Regina, 1985; LittD (hon.), St. Mary's U., 1985; LLD (hon.), Concordia U., 1989, Mt. St. Vincent U., 1990, Carleton U., 1994, U. Calgary, 1994, U. B.C., 1994. Joined Dept. External Affairs, Canada, 1966, with, 1970-74, asst. under-sec., 1981-82; 2d sec. Can. High Commn., Colombo, Sri Lanka, 1968, econ. counsellor London, 1975-77; v.p. Can. Internat. Devel. Agy., 1978, sr. v.p., acting pres., 1979-80, pres., 1983-89; asst. sec. gen. UN; dep. exec. dir. ops. UNICEF, 1981—83; fellow Ryerson Poly. U., 1986; dep. min. Health and Welfare Country Can., 1989-92; pres. Population Coun., N.Y.C., 1993-99. Chmn. Global Water Partnership; chmn. water resource adv. com. Group Suez, Paris; chmn. change devel. and mgmt. team CGIAR, Washington, 2001; vice-chair Internat. Devel. Rsch. Ctr., Ottawa; chmn. Ctr. Agr. Rsch. Dry Areas, Syria; mem. 2020 vision policy global food policy Internat. Food Policy Rsch. Inst., Washington; with Libr. Alexandria, Egypt, Inter-Am. Dialogue, Washington; clin. prof. Tulane U., New Orleans. Home: 249 E 48th St Apt 8A New York NY 10017

CATO, GLORIA MAXINE, retired secondary education educator, school program administrator; b. Covington, La., Mar. 22, 1942; d. Dan and Roxieana (Washington) Smith; widowed; 1 child, Mark. BS, Southern U., 1965; MS, Pepperdine U., 1974. Tchr. Los Angeles Unified Sch. Dist., 1965-81, counselor, magnet program coordinator, 1981—, PUSH for Excellence program coordinator, 1978-80, student activities coordinator, 1982-84, coll. advisor, 1984-85, personnel specialist, tchr. advisor, 1986-87, asst. prin., 1992—99; ret., 1999. Edn./counselor cons. L.A. Unified Sch. Dist. Trustee L.A. Ednl. Allance Restructuring Now. Recipient Community-Sch. Service award City of Los Angeles, 1978; named to Top Ladies of Distinction, 1992. Charter mem. NEA, Nat. Assn. Biology Tchrs. (finalist Tchrs. award 1978), Magnet Coordinator Assn., Los Angeles Counselors Assn.; mem. United Tchrs. Los Angeles, Associated Adminstrs. L.A., Assn. Calif. Sch. Adminstrs., Asst. Prin. Secondary Counseling Svcs. Orgn., Phi Delta Kappa, Alpha Kappa Alpha (Mu Beta Omega chpt.). Democrat. Baptist. Home: 3661 Kensley Dr Inglewood CA 90305-2230

CATOE, BETTE LORRINA, pediatrician, educator; b. Apr. 7, 1926; d. John Booker and Laura Beola (Adams) C.; m. Warren J. Strudwick, Sept. 17, 1949; children: Laura Christina, Warren J., William J. BS cum laude, Howard U., 1948, MD, 1951. Intern Freedmen's Hosp., Washington, 1951-52; pediat. resident Howard U./Freedman's Hosp., 1952-55, practice medicine specializing in pediatrics, 1956—2003, ret., 2003; instr. bacteriology Howard U., 1955-57; mem. staff Providence Hosp., Columbia Hosp., Howard U. Hosp., Wash., Hosp. Ctr.; sch. health officer Dept. Health, Washington, 1960-64; clin. instr. Howard U., 1956-58; health cons., 2003—. Mem. D.C. Health Planning Adv. Coun., 1967-77, chmn. 1973-77; chmn. D.C. Devel. Disabilities Adv. Coun., 1970-74; mem. D.C. Mayor's Commn. on Food and Nutrition, 1971-72, Mayor's Commn. on Maternal and Child Health, 1978-84, appt. vice chmn. Pub. Benefit Corp., 1997-2001; mem. D.C. Commn. Jud. Tenure and Disabilities, 1977-2001, chmn. Bd. Public Benefit Corp. of D.C., 1998-2001; bd. govs. St. Alban's Sch., 1978-84; bd. dirs. D.C. Health and Welfare Coun., 1968-73, pres., 1973-74; del. Democratic Nat. Conv., 1976; bd. dirs. Met. Washington Health and Welfare Coun., 1970-72, Parent Coun. of Washington, 1974-75, Met. Med. Founds., Inc., Silver Spring YMCA, 1977-80, Kingsburg Ctr., 1997-99; mem., chair emergency med. com. Mayor's Health Policy Coun., 1998-2001. Mem.: NAACP, AMA, Women's Aux. Medico-Chirurg. Soc., Assn. Comprehensive Health Planners (dir. 1975—77), Urban League, Am. Med. Women's Assn., Nat. Med. Assn. (chmn. pediat. sect. 1981—83), D.C. Chirurg. Soc. (trustee 1996—99, nominating com. 2000—03, jud. legis. com. 2001—03), Women's Nat. Dem., Jack and Jill Am., Carrousels Club (nat. v.p. 1986—88, nat. pres. 1988—90), Links Club, Century Club of Nat. Assn. Negro Bus. and Profl. Women's Clubs (pres. 1985—89), Alpha Kappa Alpha. Home and Office: 1748 Sycamore St NW Washington DC 20012-1031

CATOLINE-ACKERMAN, PAULINE DESSIE, small business owner; b. Ft. Worth, Dec. 17, 1937; d. Byron Hillis and Dessie Elizabeth (Plumlee) Doggett; children: Sherry Lou, Brenda Lynn; m. Donald Ralph Ackerman, Feb. 19, 1993. BA in Bus. Mgmt. (labor rels. specialty), Hiram Coll., 1989. Sec. Gen. Am. Life Ins. Co., Ft. Worth, 1956-57, Kelly Girl Svcs., Youngstown, Ohio, 1965-69; legal sec. Burgstaller, Schwartz & Moore, Youngstown, 1962-65, Green, Schiavoni, Murphy & Haines, Youngstown, 1969-71, Flask & Policy, Youngstown, 1971-83; sec. Western Res. Care System, Youngstown, 1983-87, exec. sec., 1987-90; owner, mgr. Pauline's Place, Youngstown, 1993—; legal sec. Henderson, Covington, Stein, Donchess & Messenger Law Firm, 1993-94; exec. adminstrv. asst. to pres. CEO, sr. v.p. Internat. Renaissance Developers, Youngstown, 1994-96; adminstrv. asst. to v.p. and client svc. mgr. Bank One Investment Mgmt. & Trust Group, Youngstown, 1996—2000; admin. assoc. regional divsn. Am. Heart Assn., Youngstown, 2000—01; owner, mgr. Paulines Pl., 2001—; staff Kelly Svcs., Youngstown, Ohio, 2001—. Pres. PTA, Cottage Hills, Ill., 1968-69, brownie and scout leader, 1968-69. Mem. Mahoning County Legal Secs. Assn. (v.p. 1973-74, editor monthly booklet 1974-75), Exec. Link, Missionary Group Club. Democrat. Methodist. Avocations: oil painting, reading poetry, tennis, swimming, horseback riding. Home: 3961 Cannon Rd Youngstown OH 44515-4604

CATTANEO, JACQUELYN ANNETTE KAMMERER, artist, educator; b. Gallup, N.Mex., June 1, 1944; d. Ralph John and Gladys Agnes (O'Sullivan) Kammer; m. John Leo Cattaneo, Apr. 25, 1964; children: John Auro, Paul Anthony. Student, Tex. Woman's U., 1962-64. Portrait artist, tchr., Gallup, N.Mex., 1972. Coord. Works Progress Adminstrn. art project renovation McKinley County, Gallup, Octavia Fellin Performing Arts wing dedication, Gallup Pub. Libr.; formation com. mem. Multi-Modal/Multi-Cultural Ctr. for Gallup; exch. with Soviet Women's Com. USSR Women Artists del., Moscow, Kiev, Leningrad, 1990; Women Artists del. and exch., Jerusalem, Tel Aviv, Cairo, Israel; mem. Artists Del. to Prague, Vienna and Budapest; mem. Women Artists Del. to Egypt, Israel and Italy, 1992, artist del., Brazil, 1994, Greece, Crete, Turkey, Spain, 1996, N.S. and Ont., N.B., PEI, Can., 2000. One-woman shows include Gallup Pub. Libr., 1963, 66, 77, 78, 81, 87, Gallup Lovelace Med. Clinic, Santa Fe Sta. Open House, 1981, Gallery 20, Farmington, N.Mex., 1985—, Red Mesa Art Gallery, 1989, Soviet Retrospect Carol's Art & Antiques Gallery, Liverpool, N.Y., 1992, 97, N.Mex. State Capitol Bldg., Santa Fe, 1992, Lt. Govt. Casey Luna-Office Complex, Women Artists N.Mex. Mus. Fine Arts, Carlsbad, 1992, Rio Rancho Country Club, N.Mex., 1995; exhibited in group shows including Navajo Nation Libr. Invitational, 1978, Santa Fe Festival of the Arts Invitational, 1979, N.Mex. State Fair, 1978, 79, 80, Catharine Lorrilard Wolfe, N.Y.C., 1980, 81, 84, 85, 86, 87, 88, 89, 90, 91, 92, 4th ann. exhbn. Salmagundi Club, 1984, 90, 98, 3d ann. Palm Beach Internat., New Orleans, 1984, Fine Arts Ctr., Taos, 1984, The Best and the Brightest O'Brien's Art Emporium, Scottsdale, Ariz., 1986, Gov.'s Gallery, 1989, N.Mex. State Capitol, Santa Fe, 1987, Pastel Soc. West Coast Ann. Exhbn., Sacramento Ctr. for Arts, Calif., 1986-90, gov.'s invitational Magnifico Fest. of the Arts, Albuquerque, 1991, Assn. pour la Promotion du Patrimone Artistique Française, Paris Nat. Mus. of the Arts for Women, Washington, 1991, Artists of N.Mex., Internat. Nexus '92 Fine Art Exhbn., Trammell Corw Pavillion, Dallas, Carlsbad (N.Mex.) Mus. Fine Art; represented in permanent collections Zuni Arts and Crafts Ednl. Bldg., U. N.Mex., C.J. Wiemar Collection, McKinley Manor, Gov.'s Office, State Capitol Bldg., Santa Fe, Hist. El Rancho Hotel, Gallup, Sunwest Bank, Fine Arts Ctr., Taos, Armand Hammer Pvt. Collection, Wilcox Canyon Collections, Sadona, Ariz., Galaria Impi, Netherlands, Woods Art and Antiques, Liverpool, N.Y., Stewarts Fine Art, Taos, N.Mex., Rehoboth McKinley Christian Hosp. & Sacred Heart Cathedral, Gallup, NM. Mem. Dora Cox del. to Soviet Union-U.S. Exch., 1990. Recipient Cert. of Recognition for Contbn. and Participation Assn. pour la Patrimone du Artistique Français, 1991, N.Mex. State Senate 14th Legislature Session Meml. # 101 for Artistic Achievements award, 1992, Award of Merit, Pastel Soc. West Coast Ann. Membership Exhbn., 1998, award N.Mex. State Ho. Reps. for Artistic Achievement, 2001, Holbein award for excellence in painting Pastel Soc. West Coast Internat. Juried Exhbn.; honored for preservation of WPA Dept. Edn. N.Mex. State Ho. of Reps., 2001. Mem. Internat. Fine Arts Guild, Am. Portrait Soc. (cert.), Oil Painters of Am., Pastel Soc. Am. (signature), Pastel Soc. of West Coast (cert., signature, Hobein award, award of excellence mem.'s show 1999), Mus. N.Mex. Found., N.Mex. Archtl. Found., Mus. Women in the Arts, Fechin Inst., Artists' Co-op (co-chair), Gallup C. of C., Gallup Area Arts and Crafts Coun. (nat. and internat. artist of distinction award 1997), Catharine Lorillard Wolfe Art Club of N.Y.C. (oil and pastel juried membership), Oil Painters of Am., Pastel Soc. N.Mex., Soroptomists (Internat. Woman of Distinction 1990), Salmagundi Art Club. Address: 210 E Green St Gallup NM 87301-6130 E-mail: cattaneo@cnetco.com.

CATTELL, HEATHER BIRKETT, psychologist; b. Carlisle, eng., Dec. 16, 1936; came to U.S., 1958; d. Wilfred B. and Anne Birkett; m. Russel B. Shields, June 10, 1958 (div. 1968); children: Vaughn, Gary, Heather Luanne; m. Raymond B. Cattell, May 9, 1981. BA, U. Hawaii, 1974, MA, 1977, PhD, 1979. Lic. clin. psychologist, Hawaii. Dir. rsch. Salvation Army, Honolulu, 1979-81; pvt. practice Honolulu, 1981—. Lectr., workshop leader, U.S., Australia, Can., and United Kingdom, 1989—. Author: The 16PF: Personality in Depth, 1989, The Cattell Comprehensive Personality Inventory, 1998. Mem. Phi Beta Kappa.

CATTERLIN, CINDY LOU, English educator; b. Linton, Ind., Nov. 20, 1958; d. Ralph Lloyd and Betty Lou Miller; m. Davey Lee Catterlin Jr., July 3, 1982; children: Davey Lee III, Melissa Joy. BS summa cum laude, Ind. State U., 1980, MS, 1981. Cert. advanced profl. tchr. Music tchr. Kossouth St. Bapt. Sch., Lafayette, Ind., 1981-82; pvt. instrumental music instr. Beckley, W.Va., 1986-94; bd. dir. Raleigh County Bd. Edn., Beckley, 1994-95; tchr. English Heritage Christian Acad., Englewood, Fla., 1997—, also bd. dirs., choir dir. Pianist Calvary Bapt. Ch., Englewood, 1995—, boys and girls Awana dir., 1995—. Mem. Am. Assn. Christian Schs. Avocations: sewing, music. Home: 620 N Elm St Englewood FL 34223-2753 Office: Heritage Christian Acad 75 Pine St Englewood FL 34223-3925

CATTERTON, MARIANNE ROSE, occupational therapist; b. St. Paul, Feb. 3, 1922; d. Melvin Joseph and Katherine Marion (Bole) Maas; m. Elmer John Wood, Jan. 16, 1943 (dec.); m. Robert Lee Catterton, Nov. 20, 1951 (div. 1981); children: Jenifer Ann Dawson, Cynthia Lea Uthus. Student, Carleton Coll., 1939-41, U. Md., 1941-42; BA in English, U. Wis., 1944; MA in Counseling Psychology, Bowie State Coll., 1980; postgrad., No. Ariz. U., 1987-91. Registered occupl. therapist, Occupl. Therapy Cert. Bd. Occupl. therapist VA, N.Y.C., 1946-50; cons. occupl. therapist Fondo del Seguro del Estado, PR, 1950-51; dir. rehab. therapies Spring Grove State Hosp., Catonsville, Md., 1953-56; occupl. therapist Anne Arundel County Health Dept., Annapolis, Md., 1967-78; dir. occupl. therapy Ea. Shore Hosp. Ctr., Cambridge, Md., 1979-85; cons. occupl. therapist Kachina Point Health Ctr., Sedona, Ariz., 1986. Regional chmn. Conf. on revising Psychiat. Occupl. Therapy Edn., 1958-59; instr. report writing Anne Arundel C.C., Annapolis, 1974-78. Editor: Am. Jour. Occupl. Therapy, 1962—67. Active Md. Mental Health Assn., 1959—60; mem. task force on occupl. therapy edn. Md. Dept. Health, 1971—72; chmn. Anne Arundel Gov. Com. on Employment of Handicapped, 1959—63; gov.'s com. to study vocat. rehab. Md., 1960; com. mem. Annapolis Youth Ctr., 1976—78; curator Dorchester County Heritage Mus., Cambridge, 1982—83; citizen interviewer Sedona Acad. Forum, 1993, 1994; vol. Respite Care, 1994—98, Verde Valley Caregivers, 1993—; ministerial search com. Unitarian Ch. Anne Arundel County, 1962; v.p., officer Unitarian-Universalist Fellowship Flagstaff, 1988—93, v.p., 1993—97; co-moderator, founder Unitarian Universalist Fellowship Sedona, 1994—96, pres., 1997—98, co-pres., 2001—03. Mem.: Dorchester County Mental Health Assn. (pres. 1981—84), Md. Occupl. Therapy Assn. (del. 1953—59), Am. Occupl. Therapy Assn. (chmn. history com. 1958—61), P.R. Occupl. Therapy Assn. (co-founder 1950), Sedona Muses, Nature Conservancy, Zero Population Growth, Ret. Officers Assn., Pathfinder Internat., Air Force Assn. (Barry Goldwater chpt., sec. 1991—92, 1994—), Newcomers (Sedona, pres. 1986), Severn Town Club (treas. 1965, sec. 1971—72, 1994—95), Toastmasters, Internat. Club (Annapolis, publicity chmn. 1966), Delta Delta Delta. Republican. Home: 415 Windsong Dr Sedona AZ 86336-3745

CATTRALL, KIM, actress; b. Liverpool, Eng., Aug. 21, 1956; Student, London Acad. Music and Dramatic Art, Banff Sch. Fine Arts, Alta., Can.; grad., Am. Acad. Dramatic Arts, N.Y.C. Actor: (films) Rosebud, 1975, Tribute, 1980, Ticket to Heaven, 1981, Porky's, 1982, Police Academy, 1984, Turk 182!, 1985, City Limits, 1985, Hold-Up, 1985, Big Trouble in Little China, 1986, Mannequin, 1987, Masquerade, 1988, Palais Royale, 1988, Midnight Crossing, 1988, The Return of the Musketeers, 1989, La Famiglia Buonanotte, 1989, Honeymoon Academy, 1990, Bonfire of the Vanities, 1990, Star Trek VI: The Undiscovered Country, 1991, Split Second, 1992, Breaking Point, 1993, Live Nude Girls, 1995, Above Suspicion, 1995, Where Truth Lies, 1996, Unforgettable, 1996, Exception to the Rule, 1997, Modern Vampires, 1998, Baby Geniuses, 1999, The Devil and Daniel Webster, 2001, 15 Minutes, 2001, Crossroads, 2002, others; (TV films) Sins of the Past, 1984, Miracle in the Wilderness, 1992, Double Vision, 1992, Two Golden Balls, 1994, Running Delilah, 1994, OP Center, 1995, The Heidi Chronicles, 1995, Every Woman's Dream, 1996, Invasion, 1997, Creature, 1998, 36 Hours to Die, 1999, Sex and the Matrix, 2000; (TV series) Angel Falls, 1993, Sex and the City, 1998—2004 (SAG award, 2001, Golden Globe award, 2002, Women in Film Lucy award, 1999); (TV miniseries) Wild Palms, 1993, (various TV guest appearances); co-author (with Mark Levinson): Satisfaction, 2002. Office: c/o Jeffrey Witjas William Morris Agy 151 El Camino Dr Beverly Hills CA 90212*

CATULLO, DORIS JANE, sculptor; b. Phila., Aug. 17, 1929; d. Charles J. and Jane M. (Karsner) Corrigan; m. Albert Catullo, May 18, 1949 (dec. Sept. 6, 1993); 1 child, Jayne-Leslie; m. Frank Riggenbach, May 20, 1995. Student, No. Va. C.C., Mary Washington Coll., Corcoran Sch. Art, Washington, Art League Sch., Alexandria, Va., 1986-87, Biani and Cacia Art Foundry, Pietrasanta, Italy, 1988, Bruno Cacciatori Marble Studio, 1988, Scottsdale (Ariz.) Artist Sch., 1989-90, Loveland Acad. Fine Arts, Loveland, Colo., 1996. Sculptor, 1986—. Sculptor: (bronze bas relief) Aaron Burr (at site of birth) Newark, N.J., 1997, (5 foot bronze ballerina) Attitude (lobby Concert Hall) George Mason U., 1993, (bust) Gen. Lewis B. Hershey (Selective Svc. hdqts.) Washington, William Ford Bldg., William Ford NPWA, Alexandria Park, Alexandria, Va., Norman Hamilton Bldg., Washington, Md.; exhbns. include Arts Club of Washington, 1988, Art League Gallery, Alexandria, Va., 1988, 89, Allied Artists of Am. 78th ann. exhibit, Nat. Arts Club, .Y.C., 1991, Nat. Acad. Design, N.Y., 1994, Nat. Sculpture Soc. "Making Faces", Americas Tower, N.Y.C., 1996; solo show Campbell House, Southern Pines, N.C., 2000. Recipient Elaine and Albert Ominsky award for Portraiture Knickerbocker Artists N.Y., 1992, Traditional Sculpture Catherine Lorrilard Wolfe award, 1993, Elected Signature Artist award Knickerbocker Artist Internat., 1993, Award of Excellence Art League, Alexandria, Va., 1988, 89. Mem. Nat. Sculpture Soc., Knickerbocker Artist Internat., Pen and Brush N.Y. Home: 7 Piney Pt Whispering Pines NC 28327-9475

CATULLO, LAURA A. psychotherapist, artist; b. Youngstown, Ohio, June 26, 1957; d. Joseph Francis and Susan Katherine Catullo; children: Lisa, Tiffany. BFA, Kent State U., 1979; MS in Edn., SUNY, Buffalo, 1987; MA in Counseling Psychology, Antioch New Eng., 1992; postgrad., Nova Southeastern, 2001—. Tchr., Lusaka, Zambia, 1980—83; tchr. art, art edn. program adminstr., instrnl. spkr. Lansing Ctrl. Schs., NY, 1983—87; psychotherapist, counselor, expressive arts therapy pvt. practice, Albany, 1992—2000; grants chair, writer Averill Park Ctrl. Sch. Dist., 1998—, coord. Title IX, 1998—. Mem.: Oakroom Artists. Avocations: art, writing, poetry, cooking. Home: 3 N Schodack Rd East Greenbush NY 12061 Office: Averill Park Ctrl Schs Averill Park NY

CAUDELL, JOAN EDWARDS, critical care nurse, consultant; b. Wabash, Ind., Sept. 28, 1927; d. Roy U. Edwards and Mary Elizabeth Davenport; m. Alan C. Claudell, June 27, 1945 (dissolved Jan. 1969); children: Alan J., Paul M. BS, Ind. U., 1979. RN Ind., 1948, cert. operating room nurse, Assn. Operating Nurses. Staff nurse US Ve. Hosp., Indpls., 1948—51; pvt. nurse Bur. Profl. Nurses, Indpls., 1951—70; [illegible] Hosp., Indpls., 1964—69; critical care nurse, oper. rm. nurse Winnona Hosp., Indpls., 1969—79; dir. surgery Parkview Hosp., Pueblo, Colo., 1981—83; asst. dir. surgery Children's Hosp., Denver, 1983—85; dir. ambulatory surgery Vanderbilt U. Med. Ctr., Nashville, 1985—94; cons. State Ind., Indpls., 1994—2003. Roman Catholic. Avocations: reading, gardening, travel. Office: State of Ind 420 W Washington St Indianapolis IN 46207

CAUFFIELD, CHRISTINE ANNE, psychologist; BS in Comm. magna cum laude, U. Ctrl. Fla., 1974; MS in Counseling Psychology summa cum laude, Ga. State U., 1987; MS in Clin. Psychology, Fla. Inst. Tech., 1995, Doctor of Psychology, 1997. Cert. clin. psychologist Fla. Mgr. dept. inflight svc. Delta Airlines, Atlanta, 1974—85, Miami, Fla., 1974—85; dir. tng. and intervention svcs. Human Affairs Internat., N.Y.C., 1985—89; nat. dir. tng. and clin. svcs. Mediplex, Inc., N.Y.C., 1989—91; pres. Cauffield & Assoc., Windemere, Fla., 1991—93; dir. Geriatric Inst. Nova Southeastern U., Ft. Lauderdale, Fla., 1998—99; pres. and CEO Coastal Behavioral Healthcare, Inc., Sarasota, Fla., 1999—. Com. chair Workplace and Bus. Cmty. Task Group, 1999—; bd. dirs. Fla. Coun. Cmty. Mental Health, Tallahassee. Contbg. author: Optimal Aging: Your Guide from Experts in Medicine, Law, and Finance, 2003; contbr. articles to profl. jours. Named Alumnus of Yr., Sch. Psychology Fla. Inst. Tech., 2003. Mem.: APA, Fla. Juvenile Justice Assn. (bd. dirs. 1999—), Fla. Alcohol and Drug Assn. (bd. dirs. 2002—), Human Svcs. Planning Assn. (com. chair 1999—), Fla. Psychol. Assn., Leadership Fla. (mem. class XXII), Jr. League (mem. adv. bd. 2002—03). Avocations: reading, travel, water sports. Office: Coastal Behavioral Healthcare Inc 1565 State St Sarasota FL 34236

CAULFIELD, JOAN, director, educator; b. St. Joseph, Mo., July 17, 1943; d. Joseph A. and Jane (Lisenby) Caulfield; m. Alan Warne, Sept. 7, 1996. BS in Edn. cum laude, U. Mo., 1963, MA in Spanish, 1965, PhD, 1978; postgrad. (Mexican Govt. scholar), Nat. U. Mexico, 1962-63. TV tchr. Spanish Kansas City (Mo.) pub. schs., 1963-68; tchr. Spanish, French Bingham Jr. High Schs., Kansas City, 1968-78; asst. prin. S.E. High Sch., Kansas City, 1984; prin. Nowlin Jr. High Sch., Independence, Mo., 1984-86, Lincoln Coll. Preparatory Acad., Kansas City, Mo., 1986-88; asst. supt. Kansas City, 1988-89; part-time instr. U. Mo.-Kansas City; dir. English Inst. Rockhurst Coll., summers 1972-75; coord. sch. coll. rels. Rockhurst U., 1989-2001, chmn. edn. dept.; adj. prof. St. Louis U.; pres., CEO The Brain Inc., 2001—. Mem. nat. steering com. Brain-Based Learning Network, facilitator; assessor dept. elem. and secondary edn. State Mo.; mem. women's coun. bd. U. Mo.-Kansas City, 1994-98, pres. 1998-; pres., CEO The Brain Inc.; vis. social scientist Midwest Rsch. Inst. Contbr. articles to profl. jours. Co-Author: Inciting Learning: a Guide to Brain Compatible Instr. Active Sister City Commn., Kansas City, 1980—, Kans.' Quality Performance Assessment Team, Metro-Vision Task Force; ofcl. translator to mayor on trip to Seville, Spain, 1969; bd. dirs. Kansas City chpt. NCCJ, Expo '92 World's Fair, Seville, transl., 1992, St. Theresa's Acad., 1991-94, Kansas City Acad. of Learning; selected leadership training Greater Mo.; trainer Harmony in a World of Difference, 1989-93; task force C. of C. bd. dirs.; edn. alumni bd. U. Mo., Kansas City; del. leader Spain People to People Internat., 1997; trustee Kansas City Pub. Libr. mem. mayor's commn. on race, Kansas City; mem. adv. bd. NCCJ, 2002—. Named Outstanding Secondary Educator, 1973. Mem.: MLA (contbr. jour.), ASCD, Mo. Mid. Sch. Assn. (contbr. jour.), Am. Assn. Tchrs. Spanish and Portuguese, Nat. Assn. Secondary Sch. Prins., Magnet Schs. Am. (contbr. jour.), Friends of Art, Friends of Seville, Sigma Delta Pi, Phi Kappa Phi, Delta Kappa Gamma (state scholar 1977—78, contbr. jour. Bull.), Phi Delta Kappa, Phi Sigma Iota, Kappa Delta Pi. Presbyterian. Home: 431 W 70th St Kansas City MO 64113-2022 E-mail: joancaulfield@prodigy.net.

CAULFIELD, KATHLEEN MARIE, medical association administrator, medical/surgical nurse; b. Albany, N.Y., Aug. 4, 1956; d. Frederick A. Caulfield and Mary G. Graver; 1 child, Jean Marie. BS in Med. Record Adminstrn., SUNY Coll. of Tech., Utica. Registered HIA AHIMA Chgo., Il., 1983; RN N.Y., 1976. RN St. Clare's Hosp., Schenectady, NY, 1976—79, New Eng. Deaconess Hosp., Boston, 1979—81, Teresian Ho., Albany, NY, 1981—83; nursing supr. Oneida City Hosp., NY, 1983—87; dir. of med. records N.Y. State Dept. of Corrections, Albany, 1987—2001; supervising med. record adminstr. Bronx Psychiat. Facility, NY, 2002—. Roman Catholic. Avocations: exercise, bicycling, quilting, feng shui cons., dog grooming.

CAUSEY, CARLEY CLAIRE, art educator, consultant, art therapist, researcher; b. Meridian, Miss., Nov. 26, 1962; d. Bill Watkins Causey, Sr. and Charlotte Rose Causey. PhD, Fla. State U., 1998. Asst. prof. Miss. Coll., Clinton, Miss., 1996—2000; art tchr./art therapist Madison County Alternative Sch., Canton, Miss., 2000—02. Mem.: APA, Am. Art Therapy Assn., Inc. (assoc.). Achievements include first to understand the kinds of cognitions and the role of emotion in creating works of art for the purpose of self expression using protocol analysis as the psychological research methodology. Avocations: art study in Europe, golf, writing, tennis. Home: 319 Monterey Dr Clinton MS 39056 Office Phone: 601-573-4122.

CAUSEY, RHONDA MARIE, elementary school educator; b. St. Augustine, Fla., Nov. 2, 1941; d. Edward Washington Causey and Mildred Electa Bailey; m. Neil Wallace Sederberg, June 27, 1967 (div. Mar. 1993); children: Karyn, Janie. Student, Brenau Coll., Gainesville, Ga., 1959—61; BS in Edn., Fla. State U., 1963; postgrad., Marquette U., 1965, St. Johns River Jr. Coll., Palatka, Fla., 1967. Tchr. Bay Vista Elem., St. Petersburg, Fla., 1963—64, Wauwatosa (Wis.) Elem., 1964—66; tchr. summer sch. Atwater Elem., Shorewood, Wis., 1964—66; tchr. RB Hunt Elem., St. Augustine, Fla., 1966—67, Lincoln Elem., Hartford, Wis., 1967—68, Centreville (Va.) Day Sch., 1981—87; tchr. learning disabled White Oaks Elem., Fairfax, Va., 1987; tchr. Jermantown Elem., Fairfax, 1987—93, Kelley Smith Elem., Palatka, Fla., 1994—2001, Webster Elem., St. Augustine, 2001—. Co-leader Brownies, Fairfax, Va., 1980—84; vol. Med. Libr. Commonwealth Hosp., 1982—84. Tchr. Quest grantee, U. Fla. Rsch. Ctr., 2000. Mem.: Nat. Edn. Assn., Delta Kappa Gamma, Zeta Tau Alpha. Avocations: gardening, tennis, reading, swimming. Home: 335 Palos Ct Saint Augustine FL 32086 Office: Webster Elem 420 Orange St Saint Augustine FL 32084

CAUTHEN, CARMEN WIMBERLEY, legislative staff member, jewelry designer; b. Raleigh, N.C., Aug. 4, 1959; d. William Peele and Cliffornia (Grady) Wimberley; m. Ricky Leon Cauthen, May 26, 1990; 1 child, Kena Elizabeth. Student, Ga. Inst. Tech., 1977-78; BA in Polit. Sci., N.C. State U., Raleigh, 1986. Asst. sgt.-at-arms N.C. Ho. of Reps., Raleigh, 1981, 82, computer calendar clk.; owner, jewelry designer Accessories and Things, Raleigh, 1984—; sec. Coll. Humanities/Social Sci. N.C. State U., Raleigh, 1989-91; owner bookkeeping/typing svc. CTYPE, Raleigh, 1990—; jour. clk. N.C. Ho. of Reps., Raleigh, 1992-94, adminstrv. clk., 1992—. Mem. Am. Soc. Legis. Clks. and Secs. Democrat. Christian. Avocations: reading, furniture refinishing, cross-stitch, sewing. Home: 703 Latta St Raleigh NC 27607-7203 Office: NC Gen Assembly House Prin Clks Office Legis Bldg Jones St Raleigh NC 27603-5924

CAUTHEN, FLORENCE M. protective services official; married; 2 children. B, So. Meth. U., 1976; JD, U. Ala. Assoc. Rushton, Stakely, Johnston & Garrett, Montgomery, Ala.; U.S. marshal U.S. Marshal's Svc., Montgomery, Ala., 1995—. Part-time instr. Jones Law Sch., Montgomery. Office: US Marshals Svc Frank M Johnson Fed Bldg 15 Lee St Ste 224 Montgomery AL 36104-4055

CAUTHRON, KATHLEEN DOWNIE, protective services official; b. Richmond, Va., Feb. 25, 1948; d. John Forbes and Agnes Lewis (Fox) Downie; m. Richard Mason Cauthorn, Aug. 16, 1969; children: Todd Ashley, Kristin Elizabeth. BA, Roanoke Coll., 1970. Sec., teller Security Nat. Bank, Roanoke, Va., 1970—72; case mgr. Roanoke County Welfare Dept., 1972—75; substitute tchr. St. Paul Elem. Sch., 1977—81; coord., probation officer U.S. Ct. Cmty. Corrections, St. Paul, 1985—. Dir. Christian edn. 1st Presbyn. Ch., Covington, Va., 1982—84. Recipient Meritorious Svc. award, Girl Scouts Am., 1983, Outstanding Cmty. Leadership award, 1991. Mem.: Roanoke Area Substance Abuse Coalition, Chi Omega (v.p. 1968—70). Office: Ct Cmty Correction Alleghany County Courthouse 266 W Main St Covington VA 24426

CAUTHRON, ROBIN J. federal judge; b. Edmond, Okla., July 14, 1950; d. Austin W. and Mary Louise (Adamson) Johnson. BA, U. Okla., 1970, JD, 1977; MEd, Cen. State U., Edmond, Okla., 1974. Bar: Okla. 1977. Law clk to Hon. Ralph G. Thompson U.S. Dist. Ct. (we. dist.) Okla., 1977-81; staff atty. Legal Svcs. Ea. Okla., 1981-82; pvt. practice law, 1982-83; spl. judge 17th Jud. Dist. State Okla., 1983-86; magistrate U.S. Dist. Ct. (we. dist.) Okla., Oklahoma City, 1986-91, judge, 1991—. Editor Okla. Law Rev. Bd. dirs. Juvenile Diabetes Found. Internat., 1989-92; mem. nominating com. Frontier Coun. Boy Scouts Am., 1987, Edmond Ednl. Endowment; trustee, sec. First United Meth. Ch., 1988-90. Mem. ABA, Okla. Bar Assn., Okla. County Bar Assn. (bd. dirs. 1990— bench and bar com.), McCurtain County Bar Assn. (pres. 1986), Am. Judicature Soc., Nat. Assn. Women Judges, Fed. Bar Assn., Nat. Coun. Women Magistrates (bd. dirs. 1990-91), Okla. Jud. Conf. (v.p. 1985), Am. Inns of Ct. (pres. 1991-92), Order of Coif, Phi Delta Phi. Office: US Courthouse 200 NW 4th St Ste 3108 Oklahoma City OK 73102-3029

CAVALLERO, ANN FREANEY, literature educator; b. Bradford, Pa., May 14, 1939; d. Laurence James and Marian Barry Freaney; m. Richard Joseph Cavallero; children: Dominic Francis, Robin Marie Ackerman, Susan Sundahl Teribery, Nancy Sundahl Billman, Richard Joseph. BS, Ind. U. of PA, Indiana, PA, 1961; MS, St. Bonaventure U., Saint Bonaventure, NY. Tchr. Bradford Area Sch. Dist., Bradford, Pa., 1961—2002; art tchr. Limestone Union Sch. Dist., Limestone, NY, 1968—72; title I reading specialist Beacon Light Behavioral Health, Custer City, Pa., 1987—. Bookkeeper Wee World Nursery Sch., Bradford, Pa., 1970—; sec. Friends of the Libr., Bradford, Pa., 1999—2001. Recipient Woman of the Yr. Award, AAUW, 1991. Mem.: Bradford Area Edn. Assn., PA State Edn. Assn., Delta Kappa Gamma Internat. (rec. sec. 1998—), AAUW (program vice-president 1999—2002). Roman Catholic. Avocations: reading, walking, scrapbooking, bridge. Home: 26 Chamberlain Avenue Bradford PA 16701 Office: Beacon Light Behavioral Health Systems 945 South Avenue Custer City PA 16725

CAVALLO, JO ANN, Italian language educator; b. Summit, N.J., May 21, 1959; d. Joseph Anthony and Jacqueline Amelia (Toth) C.; children: Maria Cristina, Alberto Joseph. Student, U. Florence, Italy, 1979-80, U. Valencia, Spain, 1980; BA, Rutgers U., 1981; student, Inst. French Studies, Avignon, 1982; MA, Yale U., 1984, PhD, 1987. Instr. dept. Italian Yale U., New Haven, 1983-86, instr. dept. Spanish, 1986-87, instr. Sch. Music, 1986-87; asst. prof. U. Wash., Seattle, 1987-88; assoc. prof. of Italian Columbia U., N.Y.C., 1988—. Mem. sci. com. Boiardo Quincentennial Celebration, Italy, 1993-94; founder and program dir. Columbia U. Summer Program in Scandiano, Italy, 1995—. Author: Boiardo's Orlando Innamorato: An Ethics of Desire, 1993; co-editor: Fortune and Romance: Boiardo in America, 1998; adapter: Orlando Innamorato for young readers, 2001; author: Il Maggio Epico Emiliano: ricordi, riflessioni, brani, 2003, The Romance Epics of Boiardo, Aristo, and Tasso: From Public Duty to Private Pleasure, 2004. Recipient scholarship Nat. Italian Am. Found., Washington, 1986, fellowship grant Columbia U. Coun. for Rsch. in the Humanities, 1989, 90. Mem. Am. Assn. for Tchrs. of Italian, Am. Assn. of Italian Studies, Renaissance Soc. Am., Am Folklore Soc., Phi Beta Kappa. Roman Catholic. Home: 733 Buchanan St Toms River NJ 08753-7207 Office: Columbia Univ Italian Dept 1130 Amsterdam Ave Hamilton Hall Rm 514 New York NY 10027 Business E-Mail: jac3@columbia.edu.

CAVANAUGH, JANIS LYNN, protective services official, educator; b. Montebello, Calif., Feb. 15, 1952; d. William Franklin Cavanaugh and Anne Mildred Dederick; life ptnr. Jeanne Lynn Renner, Aug. 14, 1992. AS in Police Sci., Rio Hondo Coll., Whittier, Calif., 1973; BS in Criminal Justice, Calif. State U., L.A., 1995; MPA, U. of La Verne, Calif., 2000. Police officer El Monte Police Dept., Calif., 1972—77, Amtrak RR Police, L.A., 1977—84; asst. rangemaster Rio Hondo Police Acad., Whittier, Calif., 1977—96; prof. adminstrn. of justice and forensic sci. Rio Hondo C.C., Whittier, Calif., 1996—; coord. forensic sci. program & acad. La Puente Valley Regional Occupl. Program, 2003—, pub. safety coord., 1992—2000, instr., 2002—, supr./supply coord., 2000—. Cons. Tri-Cities Regional Occupl. Program, Whittier, 2000—, East San Gabriel Valley Regional Occupl. Program, West Covina, Calif., 2002—03, SE Regional Occupl. Program, Cerritos, Calif., 1995. Mem. Whittier Conservancy, Calif., 1984—2003; vol. ARC, Whittier, Calif., 1984—2003. Recipient Women of the Yr. award, Soroptomist Orgn., 1996; grantee Vocat. Ednl. Equipment grantee, State of Calif., 2001, Vocat. Ednl. grantee, 2003. Mem.: Crim. Justice Educators, Forensic Sci. Club (advisor 2000—), Nat. Assn. of Pub. Adminstrn. (assoc.), Rio Hondo Faculty Assn. (assoc.; sec. 1996—98), Calif. Assn. Criminal Justice Educators Kiwanis Greater Whittier (assoc.; sec. 1994—96), Internat. Assn. of Identification (assoc.), So. Calif. Assn. of Fingerprint Officers (assoc.), NRA (life), Kiwanis, Calif. Police Pistol Assn. (life), Alpha Gamma Sigma (assoc.; advisor 1996—2003, v.p. 2002—03). Presbyterian. Achievements include patents pending for forensic identification logo; forensic science curriculum. Avocations: combat shooting, hiking, photography. Home: 11743 North Circle Dr Whittier CA 90601 Office: Rio Hondo Cmty Coll 3600 Workman Mill Rd Whittier CA 90601 Office Phone: 626-810-3300 x233. Personal E-mail: cavarenn@aol.com. E-mail: msforensics@janiscavanaugh.com.

CAVANAUGH, LUCILLE J. oil industry executive; b. Phila. Bachelor's, Immaculata Coll. With Exxon Mobil Corp., 1977—, gen. mgr. supply and engring., pres. credit corp., gen. mgr. west coast refining and mktg., v.p. global supply and distbn., v.p. human resources, 2002—. Office: Exxon Mobil Corp 5959 Las Colinas Blvd Irving TX 75039-2298*

CAVANAUGH, MARGARET ANNE, chemist; b. Dayton, Ohio, July 17, 1947; m. Joseph C. Cavanaugh. BS in Chemistry, U. Pitts., 1968; PhD in Phys. Inorganic Chemistry, Cath. U. Am., 1973. Asst. prof. chemistry and physics St. Mary's Coll., Notre Dame, Ind., 1975-79, assoc. prof., 1979-86, prof., chair, 1981-82, 85-89, acting dept. chair, 1981-82, 85-86; program officer chemistry divsn. NSF, Arlington, Va., 1989-91, program dir. chemistry divsn., 1991-2000, staff assoc. for env., Office of Dir., 2000—. Vis. asst. prof., rsch. assoc. chemistry U. New Orleans, 1973-75; vis. scientist UOP, Inc., 1983; test devel. com. for advanced placement exam. in chemistry The Coll. Bd., 1988-91; lectr. Am. U., 1991, George Wash. U., 1990-92. Trustee U. Dayton, 1990-99. Fellow Am. Inst. Chemists; mem. Am. Chem. Soc. (councilor 1984-90, women chemists com. 1982-88, chair 1988, meetings and expositions com. 1985-87, nominations and elections com. 1988-90, soc. com. on edn. assn. 1991-95, coun. com. pub. rels. chair 1994-96, com. on sci. 1997—, chair 2002—, C&EN adv. bd. 1998—, award for encouraging women into careers in chem. scis. 1995), Internat. Union Pure and Applied Chemistry, Sigma Xi, Iota Sigma Pi (editor 1981-87, v.p. 1987-90, pres. 1990-93, immediate past pres. 1993-96). Achievements include research in synthesis and reactions of transition metal compounds, particularly those containing metal clusters, unusual oxidation states, [illegible] proton interactions. Office: NSF Directors Office Rm 1205 Arlington VA 22230-0001 E-mail: mcavanau@nsf.gov.

CAVAZOS, ANA A. librarian; b. L.A., Mar. 30, 1963; d. Alfonso and Lidia Gloria Aguirre; m. Fred Cavazos, May 22, 1982; children: Cassandra Lee, Melissa Lizzette. BA, U. Tex., Brownsville, 1995, cert. in elem. early childhood edn., cert. in elem. self contained grades 1-8, cert. in elem. English grades 1-8, U. Tex., Brownsville, 1996, learning resources endorsement, 1999. Libr. asst. San Benito (Tex.) Ctrl. Ind. Sch. Dist., 1987—92, computer lab. mgr., 1992—94, tchr. grade 2, 1994—2003, libr., 1997—. Tech. rep. elem. and middle sch., 1997—. Author poetry. Sponsor Girl Scout, 1999—2000. Avocations: reading, writing, walking. Home: 26762 Kornegay Rd San Benito TX 78586 Office: San Benito CISD 2901 Shafer Rd San Benito TX 78586

CAVENDISH, KIM L. MAHER, museum administrator; b. Washington, Feb. 25, 1946; d. Joseph Wilson and Helen Elizabeth (Bell) Leverton; m. William Fredrick Maher, June 12, 1965 (div. 1980); 1 child, Lauren Robinson; m. Daryl Kent Cavendish, Feb. 26, 2000. Student, Duke U., 1963-65, George Washington U., 1966; BA in English, U. Fla., 1969. Social worker Fla. Health and Rehab. Svc., Gainesville, 1969-71, Delray Beach, 1972-74, fraud unit supr. West Palm Beach, 1974-76, direct svc. supr., 1977-78; ctr. dir. Palm Beach County Employment and Tng. Adminstrn., West Palm Beach, 1979-81; exec. dir. Discovery Ctyr., Inc., Ft. Lauderdale, Fla., 1981-92, Mus. Discovery & Sci., Ft. Lauderdale, 1992-94; CEO Va. Air and Space Ctr., Hampton, 1995-99; pres. Orlando Sci. Ctr., 2000—02, Mus. Discovery & Sci., Ft. Lauderdale, 2002—. Bd. dirs. Singing Pines Mus., Boca Raton, Fla., 1984-88, Broward Art Guild, Ft. Lauderdale, 1985-91, Va. space grant consortium Va. Aerospace Bus. Roundtable, Hampton, 1995—, Assn. Sci./Tech. Ctrs., 2002—; mem. Leaderhip Broward II, Ft. Lauderdale, 1983-84; mem. faculty Inst. New Sci. Ctrs., 1992. Recipient Cultural Arts award Broward Cultural Arts Found., 1985, Woman of Yr. award Women in Comm., 1990, Woman of Distinction award So. Fla. Mag., 1993; namedOutstanding Fundraiser, Fla. Assn. Nonprofit Orgns., 1994. Mem. Am. Assn. Mus., Assn. Sci. and Tech. Ctrs., Southeastern Mus. Conf., Va. Assn. Mus. (bd. dirs. 1999—), Fla. Sci. Tchrs. Assn. (bd. dirs.), Fla. Assn. Mus. (bd. dirs. 1989—, pres. 1993-95), Leadership Broward Alumnae (curriculum com. 1984—), Ft. Lauderdale Downtown Coun. (bd. dirs. 1992—), Women's Exec. Club, Phi Kappa Phi. Republican. Methodist. Avocations: scuba diving, piano, creative writing, collecting art and antiques, painting. Office: Mus Discovery & Sci 401 SW 2nd St Fort Lauderdale FL 33311

CAVILEER, SHARON E. writer, public relations executive, consultant; b. Washington, Apr. 27, 1949; d. Douglas Richards and Grace Elizabeth Cavileer; m. Peter L. D'Alessandro; children: Jessica Flaherty, Rachel Pullen. BA in English, Kent State U., 1970, postgrad., George Mason U. Account exec. E.G. White & Assocs., Vienna, Va., 1983—85, Stackig, McLean, Va., 1985—88; pres. Cavileer & Co., Clifton, Va., 1987—; pub. rels. mgr. Prince William County Park Authority, Manassas, Va., 1992—99. Press officer The Freedom Mus., Manassas, 1999—; media relations staff Spotlight on the Arts, Fairfax, 1992; dir. Fairfax City Auto Dealers Assn., 1992—; lectr. in field. Author: Virginia Curiosities, 2002; contbr. stories to mags. and newspapers including Destinations, Home & Away, So. Living, Mid-Atlantic Travel, Washington Flyer, The Boston Herald, Cleveland Mag., others, articles to profl. jours. Mem.: Greater Manassas C. of C., Ctrl. Fairfax C. of C., Soc. Am. Travel Writers (Phoenix com. 2001—). Republican. Presbyterian. Office: Cavileer & Co 12950 Clifton Creek Dr Clifton VA 20124

CAVIN, KRISTINE SMITH, lawyer; b. Decatur, Ga., Mar. 26, 1969; d. Richard Theodore and Sherri (Nash) Smith; m. James Michael Cavin, May 13, 1995. BA, Furman U., 1991; JD, Calif. Western Sch. Law, 1995. Bar: Ga. 1995. Legal asst. Smith & Jenkins, P.C., Atlanta, 1991-92; intern child abuse and domestic violence unit San Diego City Atty.'s Office, 1995; assoc. Smith, Ronick & Corbin, L.L.C., Atlanta, 1995—. Mem. ABA, Nat. Assn. Women Lawyers, Nat. Assn. Profl. Mortgage Women, Mortgage Bankers Assn. (assoc.), Ga. Bar Assn., Ga. Assn. for Women Lawyers, Ga. Real Estate Closing Attys. Assn. (sec. 1997-2004, v.p. 2004—), Atlanta Bar Assn. Avocations: gourmet cooking, wine, gardening. Office: Smith Ronick & Corbin LLC 750 Hammond Dr NE Bldg 11 Atlanta GA 30328-5532 E-mail: kristinecavin@closingattorney.com.

CAVINS, JACQUELINE LOU, education educator, adult nurse practitioner; d. James Garfield and Margaret Elizabeth Watts; m. Timothy Cavins, May 28, 1985; m. Donald R. Hinkle, Mar. 4, 1972 (div.); 1 child, Donald James. BS, Morehead (Ky.) State U., 2002. Registered Ashland (Ky.) CC, 1986. Instr. Ashland (Ky.) Cmty. and Tech. Coll.; registered nurse Kings Daughters Med. Ctr., Ashland, Ky., Highlands Regional Med. Ctr., Prestonburg, Ky.; health scis. dir. Ky. Tech. Area Tech. Ctr., Inez, 1994—96. Adv. bd. mem. health scis. program Ky. Tech. Martin County, Inez, 1997—. Office: Vocational Health Tchr Ky Tech Coll 4818 Roberts Dr Ashland KY 41102

CAWLEY, JUANITA SANDGREN, director; BS, SUNY, Cortland, 1972; MS, U. of Okla., Norman, 1973; cert. advanced study, Old Dominion U., Norfolk, VA, 1987—90. Cert. post grad. profl. Va., 2001. Dir. of spl. programs West Point (Va.) Pub. Schools, 1998—; dir. of spl. edn. Hampton City Schools, 1993—98. Sec. Rotary Club of West Point, Va., 1998—2003.

CAWLEY, PATRICIA BLONTS, secondary school educator; d. Edward Conrad and Donna Branch Blonts; m. Daniel Joseph Cawley, Mar. 12, 1994; 1 child, Seamus Patrick. BA, Old Dominion U., Norfolk, Va., 1993, MS, 2003. English tchr. Chesapeake (Va.) Pub. Sch. Communication dir. Women's Polit. Caucus, Norfolk, Va., 1992—99. Mem.: NEA (assoc.), Chesapeake Edn. Assn. (assoc.; comm. dir. 1997—99), Va. Edn. Assn. (assoc.), Va. Reading Coun. (assoc.), Southeastern Va. Assn. of Tchr. of English (assoc.), Va. Assn. of Tchr. of English (assoc.), Nat. Coun. of Tchr. of English (assoc.), Phi Kappa Phi. Democrat-Npl. Episc. Avocations: family, travel, literature.

CAWS, MARY ANN, French language and comparative literature educator, critic; b. Wilmington, NC, Sept. 10, 1933; d. Harmon Chadbourn and Margaret Devereux (Lippitt) Rorison; m. Peter Caws, June 2, 1956 (div. 1987); children: Hilary, Matthew. BA, Bryn Mawr Coll., 1954; MA, Yale U., 1956; PhD, U. Kans., 1962; D.Humane Letters, Union Coll., 1983. Asst. instr. Romance Langs. U. Kans., Lawrence, 1957-62, asst. editor Univ. press, 1957-58, vis. asst. prof., spring 1963; lectr. Barnard Coll. Columbia U., NYC, 1962-63; mem. faculty Sarah Lawrence Coll., Bronxville, NY, 1963-64, Hunter Coll. CUNY, NYC, 1966-88; prof. Grad. Sch. CUNY, NYC, 1969-88, exec. officer comparative lit. program Grad. Sch., 1977-79, exec. officer French program Grad. Sch., 1979-86, Disting. prof. French and comparative lit. Grad. Sch., 1983—, prof. English, 1985—, Disting. prof. French, comparative lit., English Grad. Sch., 1987—. Phi Beta Kappa vis. scholar, 1982-83; dir. NIH summer seminars for coll. tchrs., 1978, 85; mem. faculty Sch. of Criticism and Theory, Dartmouth U., 1988, Sch. Visual Arts, 1993; professeur associé Université de Paris VII, 1993-94; co-chair Henri Peyre Inst. for the Humanities, 1980-1996, French Inst., 1997-2002; lectr. NY Coun. for Humanities, 1992-96. Author: Surrealism and the Literary Imagination, 1966, The Poetry of Dada and Surrealism, 1970, The Inner Theatre of Recent French Poetry, 1972, The Presence of René Char, 1976,

René Char, 1977, The Surrealist Voice of Robert Desnos, 1977, La Main de Pierre Reverdy, 1979, The Eye in the Text, Essays on Perception, Mannerist to Modern, 1981, André Breton, 1982, 96, The Metapoetics of the Passage, Architextures in Surrealism and After, 1982, Yves Bonnefoy, 1984, Reading Frames in Modern Fiction, 1988, Edmond Jabès, 1988, The Art of Interference: Stressed Readings in Visual and Verbal Texts, 1989, Women of Bloomsbury, 1991, Robert Motherwell: What Art Holds, 1996, Carrington and Lytton: Alone Together, 1996, The Surrealist Look: An Erotics of Encounter, 1997, Picasso's Weeping Woman: The Life and Art of Dora Maar, 2000, Virginia Woolf: Illustrated Life, 2002, Robert Motherwell with Pen and Brush, 2003, Marcel Proust: Illustrated Life, 2003, To the Boathouse: A Memoir, 2004; co-author: Bloomsbury and France: Art and Friends, 1999; editor: Dada-Surrealism, 1972, co-editor, 1980-2002, Le Siècle éclaté, 1974-78, About French Poetry from Dada to Tel Quel, 1974, Selected Poetry Prose of Stéphane Mallarmé, 1982, Selected Poems of St.-John Perse, 1983, Writing in a Modern Temper, 1984, Textual Analysis, 1986, Perspectives on Perception: Philosophy, Art, and Literature, 1989, City Images, 1992, Joseph Cornell's Theater of the Mind: Selected Diaries, Letters and Files, 1994, Manifesto: A Century of Isms, 2001, Mallarme in Prose, 2001, Surrealist Painters and Poets, 2001, Surrealist Love Poems, 2002, Vita Sackville-West: Selected Writings, 2002, Surrealism, 2004; co-editor: Selected Poems of René Char, 1992, Contre-Courants: Les femmes s'écrivent à travers les siècles, 1994, Écritures de femmes: Nouvelles Cartographies, 1996; translator: Poems of René Char, 1976, Approximate Man and other Writings of Tristan Tzara, 1975, Mad Love, 1987, The Secret Art of Antonin Artaud, 1998, Ostinato, 2002; co-translator: Poems of André Breton, 1984, Communicating Vessels, 1990, Break of Day, 1999; chief editor Harper Collins World Reader, 1994, Manifesto: A Century of isms, 2001, Surrealist Painters and Poets, 2001, Mallarmé in Prose, 2001, Yale Anthology of Twentieth Century French Poetry, 2004; contbr. articles to profl. jours. Decorated officier Palmes Académiques, France; fellow Guggenheim Found., 1972-73 NEH, 1979-80, Fulbright traveling fellow, 1972-73, Rockefeller Found. fellow, 1994; Getty scholar, 1990. Mem. MLA (exec. coun. 1973-77, v.p. 1982-83, pres. 1983-84), Am. Assn. Tchrs. French, Assn. for Study Dada and Surrealism (pres. 1982-86), Internat. Assn. Philosophy and Lit. (exec. bd. 1982—, chmn. 1984), Acad. Lit. Studies (pres. 1985), Am. Comparative Lit. Assn. (exec. com. 1981, v.p. 1986—, pres. 1989-91). Home: 140 E 81st St New York NY 10028-1805 Office: CUNY Grad Ctr 365 Fifth Ave New York NY 10016 Office Phone: 212-817-8371.

CAYCE, KAY C. accountant; b. Hopkinsville, Ky., Sept. 13, 1950; d. Ralph and Dot Cochran; m. Ken O. Cayce, Aug. 15, 1969 (div. Feb. 1994); children: Ken IV, Chris. BBA in Acctg., Austin Peay State U., 1982. CPA, Ky. Mem. AICPA, Ky. Soc. CPAs. Home: 912 Burning Springs Cir Louisville KY 40223-3610

CAYWOOD, BARBARA MAY, artist, educator; b. Long Beach, Calif., July 24, 1921; d. Herbert Abram and Juliette (Bagby) Shutt; m. Phillip Kinnie Caywood, Oct. 21, 1940 (div. Feb. 1974); children: Wayne, Nancy, Darryl, Juliette, David. Student, Cuesta Coll., 1974-76. Cert. pre-sch.-kindergarten edn. Meth. Ch. Bd. Edn.; cert. Inst. Children's Lit. Lab. tchr. Meth. Ch. Bd. Edn., L.A., 1965-69; artist various locations, 1975-80, 1987-89, 1981-89; artist, tchr. Morgan City (La.) Housing Authority, 1980—; sec. South Bay Artist's Guild, Lahi, 1970-72; tchr. Laubach Literacy Act, Los Osos, Calif., 1988-89; tchr., artist Morgan City Goal #2000 Sch. Bd., 1991-97. Author: (children's books) Teaching Creativity, 1993, Andy's Day; exhibited in group shows South Bay Artists Guild, 1971, 72, Los Angeles County Mus., 1972, Cambria, Calif., 1976, San Luis Obispo, Calif., 1974-76, Siracusa, Sicily, 1982, Los Osos, Calif., 1982-83, Morgan City, La., 1993, 94, 95, 96, 97, others. Charter mem. Friends of Morgan City Pub. Libr., 1993; bd. dirs. Morgan City Visions, 1993-97. Tchg. grantee Morgan City, 1994. Mem. Artists Guild United (children's show chmn. 1991), Nat. Mus. Women in Arts (charter), La. Watercolor Soc., Sierra Club, Wilderness Soc. Avocations: hiking, sailing. Home: 109 El Bosque Dr San Jose CA 95134-1607

CAZALAS, MARY REBECCA WILLIAMS, lawyer, nurse; b. Atlanta, Nov. 11, 1927; d. George Edgar and Mary Annie (Slappey) Williams; m. Albert Joseph Cazalas (dec.). BS in Pre-medicine, Oglethorpe U., Atlanta, 1954; MS in Anatomy, Emory U., 1960; JD, Loyola U., 1967, Loyola U., New Orleans, 1967. RN, Ga.; Bar: La. 1967, U.S. Dist. Ct. (ea. dist.) La. 1967, U.S. Ct. Appeals (5th cir.) 1972, U.S. Supreme Ct. 1975, U.S. Ct. Appeals (fed. cir.) 1999. Gen. duty nurse, 1948-68; instr. maternity nursing St. Josephs Infirmary Sch. Nursing, Atlanta, 1954-59; med. rschr. in urology Tulane U. Sch. Medicine, New Orleans, 1961-65; legal rschr. for presiding judge La. Ct. Appeals (4th cir.), New Orleans, 1965-71; pvt. practice New Orleans, 1967-71; asst. U.S. atty., 1971-79; sr. trial atty. Equal Employment Opportunity Commn., New Orleans, 1979-84; owner Cazalas Apts., New Orleans, 1962—. Lectr. in field. Contbr. articles to profl. jours. Bd. advisors Loyola U. Sch. Law, New Orleans, 1974, v.p. adv. bd., 1975; active New Orleans Drug Abuse Adv. Com., 1976-80; task force Area Agy. on Aging, 1976-80, pres. coun. Loyola U., 1978—; adv. bd. Odyssey House, Inc., New Orleans, 1973; chmn. womens com. Fed. Exec. Bd., 1974; bd. dirs. Bethlehem House of Bread, 1975-79. Named Hon. La. State Senator, 1974; recipient Superior Performance award U.S. Dept. Justice, 1974, Cert. Appreciation Fed. Exec. Bd., 1975-78, Rev. E.A. Doyle award, 1976, Commendation for tchg. Guam Legislature, 1977, Career Achievement award Mt. de Sales Acad., 1995. Mem. Am. Judicature Soc., La. Sate Bar Assn., Fed. Bus. Assn. (v.p. 1976—, pres. 1976-78, bd. dirs. 1972-75), Fed. Bar Assn. (1st v.p. 1973, pres. New Orleans chpt. 1974-75, nat. coun. 1974-79), Assn. Women Lawyers, Nat. Health Lawyers Assn., DAR, Bus. and Profl. Womens Club, Am. Heart Assn., Emory Alumni Assn., Oglethorpe U. Alumni Assn., Loyola U. Alumni Assn. (bd. dirs. 1974-75, 77, v.p. 1976), Jefferson Parish Hist. Soc., Sierra Club, Zonta, Leconte Hon. Sci. Soc., Phi Delta Delta (merged with Phi Alpha Delta pres. 1970-72, bd. dirs., vice justice 1974-75), Alpha Epsilon Delta, Phi Sigma. Democrat.

CAZDEN, COURTNEY B(ORDEN), education educator; b. Chgo., Nov. 30, 1925; d. John and Courtney (Letts) Borden; m. Norman Cazden (div. 1971); children: Elizabeth, Joanna. BA, Radcliffe Coll., 1946; MEd, U. Ill., 1953; EdD, Harvard U., 1965. Elem. tchr. pub. schs., N.Y., Conn., Calif., 1947-49, 54-61, 74-75; asst. prof. edn. Harvard U., Cambridge, Mass., 1965-68, assoc. prof., 1968-71, prof., 1971-95, Charles William Eliot prof. emerita, 1996—. Vis. prof. U. N.Mex. summer 1980, U. Alaska, Fairbanks, summer 1982, U. Auckland, N.Z., spring 1983, Bread Loaf Sch. of English, Vt., 1986—; chairperson bd. trustees Ctr. Applied Linguistics, Washington, 1981-85. Author: Child Language and Education, 1972, Classroom Discourse: The Language of Teaching and Learning, 2d edit., 2001, Whole Language plus Essays on Literacy in the US and New Zealand, 1992; co-editor: Functions of Language in the Classroom, 1972, English Plus: Issues in Bilingual Education, 1990; editor: Language in Early Childhood Education, rev. edit., 1981. Trustee Highland Ednl. and Rsch. Ctr., New Market, Tenn., 1982-84; bd. dirs. Feminist Press, Old Westbury, N.Y., 1982-84; clk. New Eng. regional office Am. Friends Svc. Com., Cambridge, 1989-92. Recipient Alumna Recognition award Radcliffe Coll., 1988; fellow Ctr. Advanced Study in Behavioral Scis., Stanford, Calif., 1978-79; Fulbright research fellow, New Zealand, 1987. Mem. Nat. Acad. Edn., Coun. on Anthropology and Edn. (pres. 1981, George & Louise Spindler award 1994), Am. Assn. Applied Linguistics (pres. 1985), Nat. Conf. on Rsch. in English (pres. 1993-94), Am. Ednl. Rsch. Assn. (exec. com. 1981-84, award for disting. contbns. to ednl. rsch. 1986). Mem. Soc. Of Friends. Office: Harvard U Grad Sch Edn Appian Way Cambridge MA 02138

CAZEAUX, ISABELLE ANNE MARIE, retired musicology educator; b. N.Y.C., Feb. 24, 1926; d. François and Marie-Anne (Fort) C. BA magna cum laude, Hunter Coll., 1945; MA in Musicology, Smith Coll., 1946; MS in Libr. Sci., Columbia U., 1959, PhD in Musicology, 1961. Licence d'Enseignement, Ecole Normale de Musique, Paris, 1950; Première Médaille, Conservatoire Nat. de Musique, Paris, 1950. Sr. music cataloguer, head sect. music and phonorecords cataloguing N.Y. Pub. Libr., N.Y.C., 1957-63; mem. faculty Manhattan Sch. Music, N.Y.C., 1969-82, Bryn Mawr Coll., Pa., 1963-92, chmn. dept., 1978-92, prof., 1972-92, Alice Carter Dickerman prof. emeritus music, 1992—. Vis. prof. Douglass Coll. Rutgers U., New Brunswick, N.J., 1978. Author: French Music in the 15th and 16th Centuries, 1975; editor: The Chansons of Claudin de Sermisy, 1974; translator: The Memoirs of Philippe de Commynes, 1969, 2d vol., 1973; contbr. articles to profl. jours. Recipient Libby van Arsdale prize Hunter Coll., 1945; fellow Smith Coll., 1945-46, Inst. Internat. Edn., 1948-50; Martha Baird Rockefeller Fund grantee, 1971-72, Herman Goldman Found. grantee, 1980. Mem. Am. Musicol. Soc. (coun. 1968-70, com. on status of women 1974-76), Music Libr. Assn., Soc. Française de Musicologie, Internat. Musicol. Soc. Roman Catholic. Avocations: opera, concerts. Home: 415 E 72nd St New York NY 10021-4412

CEBALLOS, JACQUI MICHOT, feminist activist, organizer, administrator; b. Mamou, La., Sept. 8, 1925; d. Louis Joseph Michot and Marie Adele Domás; m. Alvaro Ceballos, Jan. 3, 1951; children: Douglas, Denis, Michele, Janine. BA in Edn.-Music, U. La., 1946. Founder, pres. Teatro de la Opera, Bogota, Colombia, 1960—64; pres. NOW, N.Y.C., 1971—72, v.p. east region, 1972—73; co-founder Nat. Women's Polit. Caucus, 1973—74; pres. Ceballos Phillips Corp., N.Y.C., 1973—75; co-founder, exec. dir. Women's Forum, N.Y.C., 1992—; founder, pres. Vet. Feminists Am., N.Y.C., 1992—, New Feminist Talent, A Spkrs. Bur., 1972—. Founder, pres. Acadiana Women's Polit. Caucus, 1967—71; co-founder La. Women's Polit. Caucus, 1997—. Prodr. New Feminist Theatre, N.Y.C., 1968—70; pres. New Yorkers for Women in Pub. Office, 1972—. Democrat. Avocations: opera, concerts, art, reading. Office: Vet Feminists Am #225D 220 Doucet Rd Lafayette LA 70503-3471

CECIL, BONNIE SUSAN, elementary school educator; b. Louisville, Sept. 29, 1951; d. Robert Lawrence and Mary Hedwig (Kluesner) C. BA in Edn., U. Ky., 1973; MS in Edn., Ind. U., 1978; postgrad., U. Louisville, 1988—. Tchr. grades 1-4 Roosevelt Cmty. Sch., Jefferson County, Ky., 1972-80; tchr. ages 6 and 7 Wandle Primary Sch., London, 1980-81; tchr. 1st grade Foster Elem. Sch., Jefferson County, 1981-82; tchr. ages 5-8 Brown Sch. Primary, Jefferson County, 1982—. Co-dir., instr. writing process for tchrs. Ky. Writing Insts. I and II, Boone County, 1986-88; instr. writing process insvc. Jefferson County Pub. Schs., 1988-89, workshop presenter on environ. edn., 1990, 92, supr. student tchrs., 1989-90, 92, 94, 95, 97; instr. lang. arts U. Louisville, 1990-91; participant Fulbright Tchr. Exch. Program, London, 1980-81, Brown Sch. Dream Team, 1992; presenter ann. conf. Ky. Assn. Edn. Young Children-Louisville Assn. for Children Under Seven, 1990; presenter Cmty. Learning Resource Conf., 1992; participant Louisville Writing Project, 1984-85, premier class Leadership Edn., 1986-87. Tchr. rep. J. Graham Brown Sch. PTSA, 1983-90, 92-97; tchr. rep. site-based decision making coun., 1996—; bd. dirs. Roosevelt Cmty. Sch., Inc., 1973-76; creator, dir. summer reading and writing program Portland Mus., Louisville, 1985, treas. Louisville Homefront Performances, Inc., 1986-87, sec., 1988-90, bd. dirs. 1984-96; state bd. dirs. Cmty. Farm Alliance, 2001-2002, v.p. Henry County chpt., 2001-. Recipient Golden Apple Achievement award Ashland Oil Co., 1990, Individual Tchr. Achievement award, 1992, Nat. Educator award Milken Family Found., 1994, ExCel award WHAS-TV and PNC Bank, 1995; named Jefferson County Elem. Tchr. of Yr., 1992, Ky. Elem. Tchr. of Yr., 1993, Ky. Tchr. of Yr., 1993, Milken Family Nat. Educator Project Mentor, 1998; grantee Ky. Arts Coun., 1986-87, Jefferson County Pub. Schs.-U. Louisville, 1989-91, U. Louisville, 1991, Rosenbaum Found., 1998; named Milken Virtual Workspace Mentor, 1998; inducted into The Commonwealth Inst. for Tchrs., 1998. Mem. ASCD, NEA, Assn. Childhood Edn. Internat., Nat. Coun. Tchrs. English (conf. presenter 1988, chmn., presenter nat. conf. 1992), Ky. Edn. Assn., Jefferson County Tchrs. Assn., Leadership Edn. Alumni Assn. Avocations: music, gardening, pets. Office: J Graham Brown Sch 546 S 1st St Louisville KY 40202-1816 E-mail: bcecil2@jefferson.K12.ky.us.

CEDARBAUM, MIRIAM GOLDMAN, federal judge; b. N.Y.C., 1929; d. Louis Albert and Sarah (Shapiro) Goldman; married; 2 children. BA, Barnard Coll., 1950; LLB, Columbia U., 1953. Bar: N.Y. 1954, U.S. Dist. Ct. (so. dist.) N.Y. 1956, U.S. Ct. Appeals (2d cir.) 1956, U.S. Ct. Claims 1958, U.S. Supreme Ct. 1958, U.S. Dist. Ct. (ea. dist.) N.Y. 1980, U.S. Ct. Appeals (5th and 11th cirs.) 1981. Law clk. to judge Edward Jordan Dimock U.S. Dist. Ct. (so. dist.) N.Y., 1953-54, asst. U.S. atty., 1954-57; atty. Dept. Justice, Washington, 1958-59; part-time cons. to law firms in litig. matters, 1959-62; 1st asst. counsel N.Y. State Moreland Act Commn., 1963-64; assoc. counsel Mus. Modern Art, N.Y.C., 1965-79; assoc. litig. dept. Davis, Polk & Wardwell, N.Y.C., 1979-83, sr. atty., 1983-86; acting village justice Village of Scarsdale, NY, 1978—82, village justice, 1982-86; judge U.S. Dist. Ct. (so. dist.) N.Y., 1986-98, sr. judge, 1998—. Trustee Barnard Coll.; mem. com. defender svcs. Jud. Conf. U.S., 1993—99; mem. emerita bd. visitors Columbia Law Sch.; chmn. N.Y. State Selection Com. for Rhodes Scholarship, 2003. Contbr. articles to profl. jours. Recipient Medal of Distinction Barnard Coll., 1991; James Kent scholar. Mem. ABA (chmn. com. on pictorial graphic sculptural and choreographic works 1979-81, copyright com. fed. practice and procedure 1983-84), Am. Law Inst., N.Y. State Bar Assn. (chmn. com. on fed. legis. 1978-80, com. on dist., city, village, and town cts. 1983-84), Assn. of Bar of City of N.Y. (com. on copyright and lit. property 1982-84, com. on the Bicentennial 1988-92), Fed. Bar Coun., Copyright Soc. U.S.A. (trustee, exec. com. 1979-82), Supreme Ct. Hist. Soc. Jewish. Office: US Dist Ct US Courthouse 500 Pearl St Rm 1330 New York NY 10007-1312

CEDERBURG, BARBARA M. printing company executive; b. St. Paul, Sept. 22, 1953; BA in Chemistry and Biology, Macalester Coll.; MS in Chemistry, U. Minn. Wilver Halide Emulsion trainee Minn. 3M Rsch. Ltd., Harlow, Eng., 1979; tech. mgr. Color Proofing Lab., 1986; mgr. graphic rsch. lab. 3M, St. Paul, 1986-90, lab. mgr., tech. dir. Dry Imaging Tech. Ctr., 1991-93, tech. dir. printing and pub. sys. divsn., 1994; bus. dir. printing and pub. sys. Imation/3M, St. Paul, 1994-97; gen. mgr. printing and proofing bus. Imation Enterprises, St. Paul, 1997-98; pres. product techs., v.p. Imation Corp., St. Paul, 1998—. Active St. Paul Civic Symphony. Mem. Am. Chem. Soc., Graphic Arts Tech. Found., Soc. Imaging Sci. and Tech. Achievements include co-inventor of Matchprint II Negative. Office: Imation Corp Jason Thunstrom Pub Rels 1 Imation Pl Oakdale MN 55128-3414

CEDERING, SIV, poet, writer; b. Overkalix, Sweden, Feb. 5, 1939; came to U.S., 1953, naturalized, 1958; d. Hilding and Elvy (Wikstrom) C.; children: Lisa, Lora, David. Artist Elaine Benson Gallery, Bridgehampton, NY, 1991—98, Loveland Mus., Loveland, Colo., 1992, East End Arts Coun. Gallery, Riverhead, NY, 1992, Clayton-Liberatori Gallery, Bridgehampton, NY, 1991, Guild Hall Mus., East Hampton, NY, 2001, Hutchin Gallery, Green Vale, NY, 1993, Peconic Gallery, Riverheard, NY, 1993, East. New Mex. Univ., Portales, N.Mex., 1992, Nordic History Mus., 1998. Lectr. U. Mass., Amherst, 1973; cons. Coordinating Council Lit. Mags., 1972-75 Author: (poems and photographs) Cup of Cold Water, 1973, Letters from the Island, 1973; (poems) Letters from Helge, 1974, Two Swedish Poets, Gost Friberg and Goran Palm (transl. from Swedish), 1974, Mother Is, 1975, The Juggler, 1977, How to Eat a Fortune Cookie, 1977, Color Poems, 1978, Letters From the Floating World: New and Selected Poems, 1984, The Blue Horse, 1979; (children's poems) Leken i Grishuset, 1980 (books transl. into Japanese, Swedish); Oxen, 1981, Letters From an Observatory, 1998, Poetry Paintings, 2003, Adirondack Notebook, 2004; editor, translator: Det Blommande Trädet (The Flowering Tree, collection Am. Indian and Eskimo lyrics), 1973, You and I and the World, Poems by Werner Aspenström, 1980, Letters From The Observatory New and Selected Poem 1973-1998, 1998, Painting Poems, 2003, Adirondack Notebook, 2004; poems and prose published in several periodicals, including, Harper's, New Republic, Partisan Rev., Paris Rev., Quar. Rev. Lit., others, exhibited photography, Modernage Galleries, NYC, 1973. Recipient William Marion Reedy award Poetry Soc. Am., 1970, John Masefield Narrative Poetry award, 1969; Annapolis Fine Arts Festival poetry prize Md. Fine Arts Council, 1968; Photography prize Sat. Rev., 1970; Borestone Mountain Poetry award, 1974; Pushcart prize, 1977; Emily Dickinson award, 1978; NY State Council on Arts fellow, 1974; Swedish Writers Union stipend, 1979; grantee Swedish Writers Found., 1995-2000. Mem. Poetry Soc. Am. Home: PO Box 89 Sagaponack NY 11962-0089

CEHELSKA, OLGA M. music educator, flight instructor; b. Austria, Apr. 6, 1946; d. George Michael and Veronica Bronislava (Drozdowska) C. BMus magna cum laude, Temple U., 1968; MusM, U. Miami, 1978; MSc, Am. Coll. Holistic Health, 1995; PhD holistic nutrition, Clayton Coll. Natural Health, 1999. Cert. Music Educator, N.J.; Cert. Flight Instr., FAA; Cert. Music Therapist Nat. Assn. Music Therapy. Tchr. music Phila. Pub. Sch. System, 1967-71; flight instr. Tamiami Airport, Homestead Airport, Homestead, Fla., 1973-74, Fulton County Airport, Atlanta, Ga., 1974-75; intern activity therapy Ga. Mental Health Inst., Atlanta, 1974; dir. activity therapy Met. Psychiat. Ctr., Atlanta, 1974-75; coord. adult psychiat. day treatment North Dekalb Cmty. Mental Health Ctr., 1975-80; piano instr., 1980—; CEO Cehelska Piano Studio, 1991—; flight instr. Norfolk Airport, Va., 2000—. Musician Young Audiences of Va., Norfolk, 1990-95, cons. Dekalb County Day Program, 1975-80, Nutritional Wellness, Va. Beach, 2000—. Contbr. articles to profl. jours. Mem. Ukrainian Women's League of Am., Ukrainian Scouting, Ukrainian Dancers of Miami, Ukrainian Am. Club of Miami, Nat. Assn. Music Therapy, Aircraft Owners and Pilots Assn., Nat. Assn. Flight Instr., Sigma Alpha Iota Alumni, Tidewater Music Tchrs. Forum, Music Tchrs. Nat. Assn., Va. Music Tchrs. Assn. Ukrainian Catholic. Avocation: traditional ukrainian music on bandura. Office: Cehelska Piano Studio/Nutr Wellness 2313 Beach Haven Dr Unit 103 Virginia Beach VA 23451-1263 E-mail: omcstudio@msn.com.

CEIPS, CATHERINE C. state representative; b. Berkeley County, S.C., Feb. 16, 1955; d. Sidney and Virginia Black Crawford; m. Richard N. Ceips, May 17, 1986. BS, U. S.C., 1976. Fed. rep. field dir. Congressman Joe Wilson, Congressman Floyd Spence; tchr. Beaufort and Berkeley County Schs.; owner Sea Island Ophthalmology; state rep. dist. 124 S.C. Legis., 2003—, mem. med., mil., pub. and mcpl. affairs com. Commn. svc. dir. Med. U. S.C.; mem. Beaufort Hist. Found., Open Land Trust, Beaufort Little Theatre, Beaufort County GOP. Mem.. Women in the Outdoors, Beaufort County Rep. Women's Club. Republican. Lutheran. Office: State Capitol 326A Blatt Bldg Columbia SC 29211 Home: 1207 Bay St 29902 E-mail. CeipsC@scstatehouse.net.

CELELLA, KAREN ANN, music teacher, author; b. Altoona, Pa., Aug. 16, 1954; d. Alfred Richard and Anna Irene (Harpster) Gerhard; m. Philip Gregory Celella, Sept. 6, 1976 (div.); m. Kelly Ann, Philip Richard. AA, Nassau C.C., Uniondale, N.Y., 1972-74; BA, L.I. U., Brookville, N.Y., 1974-76. Nat. cert. musician. Sales Brandells, Garden City, N.Y., 1972-74, Wordsworth Books, Garden City, 1974-77; ind. music tchr. piano, organ, keyboard, theory, Suffolk County, N.Y., 1972—; tchr. Carol Piano Studio, Coram, 1976-79, Frank & Camille's Studio, Port Jefferson, N.Y., 1982-84, K.C. Studio, Coram, 1979—. Adjudicator Music Educators Nat. Conf., 1993—, Am. Coll. Musicians, Nat. Guild Piano Tchrs., 1998—. Author: KAC Music Assignment Journal, 1995—, also articles; presenter workshops. With USCG auxilliary. Named to Piano Guild Hall of Fame, 2001, Nat. Honor Roll, Nat. Piano Playing Auditions, 1988—. Mem. Suffolk Piano Tchrs. Forum (treas. 1990-96, pres. 1996—2000, v.p. 2000—02, bd. dir., 2002—), Am. Coll. Musicians (cert. tchr.), Music Educators Nat. Conf., Music Tchrs. Nat. Assn., Suffolk County Music Educators Assn., Aircraft Owners and Pilots Assn., U.S. Coast Guard Aux. Avocations: art (cut mat board designs), flying, computers. Home: 20 Summercress Ln Coram NY 11727-2617 Office: KC Studio 20 Summercress Ln Coram NY 11727-2617 E-mail: KCelella2@aol.com.

CELENTANO, SUZANNE, theater educator, dance educator; b. Pitts., Nov. 4, 1967; d. Patrick Earl and Dixie Lea Carmack; m. Ronald Joseph Celentano, June 19, 1993; children: Christopher, Brandon, Sophia. BA in Comm. Arts and Theater cum laude, Allegheny Coll., 1989; MFA in Theater, U. Ala. and Ala. Shakespeare Festival, 1991. Cert. group fitness, yoga instr. Aerobic and Fitness Assn. Am. Actor, dir., choreographer, 1992—; group fitness and Pilates instr., 1998—; professorial lectr. dept. performing arts Am. U., Washington, 2003. Adj. instr. theater Coll. Charleston, Charleston, SC, 1992—95, St. Louis U., 1996—99; bd. dirs. Lorton (Va.) Arts Found., 2002—; arts mgmt. cons., 1992—; spkr., presenter in field, 1992—. Co-author: (book) Theatre Management: A Successful Guide to Producing Plays on Commercial and Nonprofit Stages, 1998; actor: (films) April Is My Religion, 2001; dancer Am. Coll. Dance Festival Nat. Gala and Southeastern Gala, 1990; profl. actor, dancer : (film, TV, and theater, including) Kathy Harty Gray Dance Theatre, Wilma Theatre, Ala. Shakespeare Festival, Walt Disney World; playwright Phoenix Theatre, D.C. 1st v.p. Lorton Sta. Elem. Sch. PTA, 2003—04; theater coord. Piccolo Spoleto Festival, Charleston, 1994. Recipient Nat. scholarship, Internat. Thespian Soc., 1985. Mem.: Southeastern Theatre Conf., Pilates Method Alliance, Officers Wives Clubs (scholarship coord. 1984—95), Officers Spouses Club (pres. 2001—02). Democrat. Roman Catholic. Avocations: director and choreographer, personal trainer, distance running, community activist, yoga. Home: 9109 Stonegarden Dr Lorton VA 22079

CELESTINO-ARGUINZONI, WILMA, academic administrator; b. Bklyn., Aug. 3, 1952; d. Ramon and Julia Arguinzoni; children: Myriam Berrios, Angelisse Pepin. AS, Bunker Hill C.C., Boston, 1989; BA, Suffolk U., 1991, MEd, 1998. Asst. dir. multicultural affairs Suffolk U., Boston, 1990—. Notary pub., Boston; justice peace, Chelsea, Mass. Recipient Hispanic Heritage award Gov. Michael Dukakis, 1984, Yes You Can award Nat. Puerta Rican Forum, 1997; Truman scholar Harry S. Truman Found., 1989. Mem. Justice Peace Assn., Nat. Puerto Rican Coalition, Centro Latino (bd. dirs., v.p., 1998). Office: Suffolk U 8 Ashburton Pl Boston MA 02108-2770

CELL, GILLIAN TOWNSEND, historian, educator; b. Birkenhead, Cheshire, Eng., June 5, 1937; came to U.S., 1962; d. Thomas Edmund and Doris Abigail (Clark) Townsend; m. John Whitson Cell, Oct. 19, 1962 (dec.); children: Thomas K., Katherine A., John D. BA, U. Liverpool, Eng., 1959, PhD, 1964. Instr. U. N.C., Chapel Hill, 1965-66, asst. prof., 1966-70, assoc. prof., 1970-78, prof., 1978-91, affirmative action officer, 1981-83, chmn. dept. history, 1983-85, dean Coll. Arts and Scis., 1985-91; provost Lafayette Coll., 1991-93, Coll. of William and Mary, 1993—2004; ret., 2004. Author: English Enterprise in Newfoundland: 1577-1660, 1969; editor: Newfoundland Discovered, 1982.

CELLER, ADELINE (LYNN) MARIE, art educator; b. Sydney, Australia; m. George K. Celler; children: Mark Stefan, Catherine Sylvia. BA with honors, U. of Sydney, 1973; MA, Purdue U., 1976. Art tchr./dept. head New Providence Sch. Dist., New Providence, NJ, 1992—; art tchr. NJ. Ctr. for the Visual Arts, Summit, 1990—. Exhibitions include Diversity Education (NJ. Dept. of Edn. P.R.I.D.E. award, 1999), exhibited in group shows, Sydney, Watson-Crick Gallery, Purdue U., 1995, Lafayette Art Ctr., 1996, Mercer County C.C., Princeton, NJ, 1997, Ctr. for Visual Arts, Summit,

1998—2004. Advisor Nat. Art Honor Soc., New Providence, NJ, 1999—2003. Chefs-in-the-Schools grant, New Providence PTSA, 2002—03. Mem.: NJEA. Office: New Providence HS 35 Pioneer Dr New Providence NJ 07974

CELMINS, VIJA, artist; b. Riga, Latvia, 1939; U.S. Student Yale U. [illegible] UCLA, 1965. One-woman shows include Whitney Mus. Am. Art, N.Y.C., 1993, Represented in permanent collections Sheldon Meml. Art Gallery and Sculpture Garden, U. Nebr., Lincoln, F.M. Hall Collection. Office: 745 5th Ave Fl 4 New York NY 10151-0099

CENSKY, ELLEN JOAN, curator, biologist; b. Milw., Sept. 20, 1955; d. Schubert Charles and Rosemary Alma (Gleuckstein) C. BS in Zoology, U. Wis., Milw., 1979; PhD, U. Pitts., 1994. Rsch. asst. U. Wis., Milw., 1977-79; technician Milw. Pub. Mus., 1978-79; preparator Carnegie Mus. Natural History, Pitts., 1979-80, curatorial asst., 1980-85, collection mgr., 1985-93, acting head amphibians and reptiles, 1993, curator amphibians and reptiles, 1994; dir. Conn. St. Museum of Nat. History (U Conn.), Storrs, Conn. Cons. Govt. Anguilla, Ministry Edn. and Environ., 1992-93, environ. edn. program Govt. Anguilla UN Devel. Program, 1992-94. Editor geog. distbn. sect. Herpetological Rev., 1983-87; contbr. articles to profl. jours. Nat. Geographic Soc. grantee, 1990. Mem. Herpetologists' League (publs. sec. 1994—, mem. long range planning and fin. com. 1987-93, chmn. 1990-93), Soc. for Study Amphibians and Reptiles (sect. editor 1983-87), Am. Soc. Icthyologists and Herpetologists, Soc. Preservation Natural History Collections (fin. com. 1988-92), Assn. Systematics Collections, Biol. Soc. Washington, Fla. Acad. Scis., Pa. Biol. Survey (amphibian and reptile tech. com. 1994—), Sigma Xi (assoc.). Address: Conn St Museum of Nat Hist Univ Conn U-23 Storrs Mansfield CT 06269-3023

CENTAFONT, LUCY ANN ALEXANDER, occupational therapy consultant; b. Anchorage, Alaska, Apr. 6, 1953; d. Robert C. and Lucy Ann (Morgan) Alexander; m. Richard A. Centafont, May 13, 1978; children: Ryan Alan, Jeffrey Richard, Lauren Ann. BS in Occupational Therapy, Temple U., 1977, MS, 1987; BS in Health Edn., Slippery Rock U., 1975. Occupational therapy cons. Bucks County Assn. for Retarded Citizens, Doylestown, Pa.; dir. occupational therapy Community Found. for Human Devel., Sellersville, Pa.; chief occupational therapy Rolling Hill Hosp., Elkins Park, Pa.; pvt. practice occupational therapy cons. Southampton, Pa. Mem. Am. Occupational Therapy Assn., Pa. Occupational Therapy Assn. (developmental disabilities spl. interest group, adminstrv. spl. interest group).

CENTENO-DAINTY, SONIA MARGARITA, artist; b. Arecibo, P.R., Mar. 4, 1948; arrived in U.S., 1960; d. Eugenio Centeno Faria and Carmen Maria Valencia Franco; m. James Albert Dainty, Jan. 17, 1970; 1 child, James William Dainty. Student journalism and art schs. Educator Boys & Girls Club, N.Y.C.; real estate realtor N.Y.C.; owner constrn. co. Produced portraits and landscapes for pvt. collections. Republican. Roman Catholic. Avocations: gardening, travel, sewing, photography. Home: 348 Old Dutch Hollow Rd Monroe NY 10950

CENTRELLO, GINA, publishing executive; Joined as copy editor Pocket Books, Simon & Schuster, 1981, exec. v.p. pub., 1993—94, pres. pub., 1994—99, Ballantine Books, 1999—2003, Random House Ballantine Book Group, 2003—. Office: Random House Inc 1745 Broadway New York NY 10019*

CEPIELIK, ELIZABETH LINDBERG, elementary school educator; b. Syracuse, N.Y., Sept. 18, 1941; d. Herman Elroy and Kathryn Emily (Karl) Lindberg; m. Michael A. Zemel, Apr. 22, 1967 (div. Jan. 1973); 1 child, Molly; m. Martin Joseph Cepielik, Mar. 10, 1973; children: Jeffrey, Kristina, Julie. AA, Stephens Coll., Columbia, Mo., 1961; BA, San Jose State Coll., 1963; postgrad., Calif. State U., L.A., 1963-67. Tchr. Humphreys Ave. Sch., L.A., 1963-71; math. specialist Non-Pub. Schs. Program, L.A., 1971-84; tchr. Sheridan Street Sch., L.A., 1984—2003; receptionist Weight Watchers, Arcadia, Calif., 1987—. Editor News of Polonia. Vol. Sta. KPCC, Pasadena, Calif., 1988-94. Mem.: DAR (sec 2004—), Swedish Am. Ctrl. Assn. (auditor 1987—90, sec. 1989—), Polish Nat. Alliance (sec. lodge 1980—, sec. coun. 1983—93, treas. Woman's divsn. 1992—93), Polish Am. Congress (sec. 1990—93, auditor, bd. dirs. 2001—), Skandia (auditor, sec. Pasadena lodge 1983—), Stephens Coll. Alumnae Club (pres. Pasadena chpt. 1967—68), Swedish Am. Women's Club (sec. 2004—). Republican. Presbyterian. Address: Ste 104 2245 E Colorado Blvd Pasadena CA 91107-3651 E-mail: polishnews@earthlink.net.

CEREZO, CARMEN CONSUELO, federal judge; b. 1940; BA, U. P.R., 1963, LLB, 1966. Pvt. practice, 1966-67; law clk. U.S. Dist. Ct., San Juan, 1967-72; judge Superior Ct., P.R., 1972-76, Ct. Intermediate Appeals, 1976-80, U.S. Dist. Ct., P.R., 1980-93, chief judge, 1993—; dist. judge. Office: Federico Degetau Fed Bldg Rm CH-131 150 Carlos Chardon Ave Hato Rey PR 00918-1761

CERNIGLIA, ALICE MAY, museum program director, consultant; b. Bklyn., N.Y., June 10, 1949; d. Stephen Cerniglia and Josephine Fiore; m. Henry Nuwer (div. Mar. 1979); 1 child, H. Christian. BA, New Mex. Highlands U., 1970—72; MS, Eastern Mich. U., 1985—86. Asst. curator Sierra Nev. Mus. of Art, Reno, 1979—85; program coord. Henry Ford Estate, U. Mich., 1987—91, facilities dir., 1991—92; interim exec. dir. Ella Sharp Mus., 1993, dir. edn., 1992—94; exhbn. coord. U. of Mich. Med. Ctr., 1995—99; exec. dir. Washtenaw Coun. for the Arts, 1996—99; coord., vol. and ednl. develop. Walter P. Chrysler Mus., 1999—2001; ind. cons., 1994—2003. Cons. Nev. Art Mus., Dearborn, Mich., 1985, St. Albert Sch., Reno, Washtenaw Cmty. Coll.; sub. tchr. Ann Arbor Pub. Schools, 2002—03; rsch. cons. Edison Inst., Henry Ford Mus., 1986; bd. dir. Washtenaw Hist. Soc. Christmas ornament selected and displayed at the White House, 1994. Chair Profl. Vol. Corp., Ann Arbor, Mich., 1998; vol. Leukemia Soc., 2001; mem. U. Choral Union, 1986—99; pres. Grad. Student Body, Reno, 1975; mktg. tour and conv. com. Dearborn C. of C., 1988—92. Recipient Rocky Mountain Press award, 1976, Gannett Press Citation for excellence in mus. installations, 1983; Grad. assistantship, Ea. Mich. U., 1986—87. Democrat. Avocations: singing, walking, running. Home: P O Box 7503 Ann Arbor MI 48107

CERNOSEK, KITTY, interior decorator; b. Dallas, Aug. 9, 1938; d. G.V. and Martha M. (Watkins) Whitefield; m. Larry A. Cernosek, June 17, 1979; children: Melinda A. Morris, Curt Robbins, Katrina Burgess. Student, Abilene Christian U., 1954-57; cert. in floral design, Lamar U., 1982. Floral designer, area floral trainer Safeway Stores, Inc., Port Arthur, Tex., 1982-86; display designer, saleswoman Teters Floral Co., Irving, Tex., 1986-88; owner, designer, bd. dirs., cons. Decorating Den, Austin, Tex., 1988-95; owner Accessories by Kitty, Taylor, Tex., 1995—. Freelance interior decorator, 1985-88; seminar dir. Balcones Woods Women's Assn., Austin, 1989; chmn. Tex. Home Owners Show Sale, Austin, 1988, 89 Vol. Blue Santa, Austin, 1988-89, ARC, Austin, 1988; founding mem. Austin Lyric Opera Chorus, Austin Choral Union; vol. receptionist Taylor C. of C., 1996—. Mem. Nat. Home Furnishing Assn., Austin C. of C. Avocations: singing, reading, travel. Home and Office: Accessories by Kitty 912 James St Taylor TX 76574-2654

CERNY, CHARLENE ANN, director; b. Jamaica, N.Y., Jan. 12, 1947; d. Albert Joseph and Charlotte Ann (Novy) Cerny; children: Elizabeth Brett Cerny-Chipman, Kathryn Rose Cerny-Chipman. BA, SUNY, Binghamton, 1969. Curator Latin-Am. folk art Mus. Internat. Folk Art, Santa Fe, 1972-84, mus. dir., 1984-99; dir. instnl. advancement Santa Fe Prep. Sch., 1999—. Adv. bd. C.G. Jung Inst., Santa Fe, 1990-98. Mem. Mayor's Commn. on Children and Youth, Santa Fe, 1990-93, adv. bd. Recipient Exemplary Performance award State of N.Mex., 1982, Internat. Ptnr. Among Mus. award, Mayor's Recognition award, 1999, Mus. N.Mex. Regents award, 1999; Smithsonian Instn. travel grantee, 1976; Florence Dibell Bartlett Meml. scholar, 1979, 91; Kellogg fellow, 1983. Mem. Am. Assn. Mus. Internat. [illegible] (bd. dirs. 1991[illegible], exec. bd. 1991-95), Am. Folklore Soc., Mountain-Plains Mus. Assn., N.Mex. Assn. Mus. (chair membership com. 1975-77). Office: 1301 Camino De Cruz Blanca Santa Fe NM 87505-0349

CERVANTEZ, MICHELLE, marketing professional; b. 1965; Intern J. Walter Thompson; customer rels. rep. Ford Motor Co., 1988—92; group leader, supr. Ford Customer Assistance Ctr., 1992—94; Asia Pacific product planner Ford Motor Co., 1994—95, mktg. comm. specialist, Lincoln Mercury, 1997—2000, brand devel. mgr. Lincoln Mercury, 1997—2000, v.p. N. Am. mktg. Jaguar, 2000—03; v.p. mktg. Mercedes-Benz, Montvale, NJ, 2003—. Office: Mercedes Benz USA LLC 3 Paragon Dr Montvale NJ 07645*

CERVEN, LAURA KAY, language educator, translator, music educator; b. Lansing, Mich., Sept. 18, 1954; d. Robert Randal Pollock and Ellen Janice Allen; m. John Thomas Cerven, July 11, 1992; m. Thomas Lloyd Buller, Jan. 8, 1977 (div. Mar. 21, 1991); children: John Robert, Jason Andrew Buller, Stephen Gregory Buller. BA in French and Music summa cum laude, Albion Coll., 1976; MA in French, U. Ill., 1979. Cert. profl. edn. Mich., 1976, Wash., 1979, N.H., 1982. Music tchr. Grand Ledge (Mich.) Pub. Schs., 1976—76, The Annie Wright Sch., Tacoma, 1979—80; music instr. Lebanon (N.H.) C.C., 1981—82; music libr. Dartmouth Coll., Hanover, NH, 1983—85; French tchr. Island Christian Sch., Vashon, Wash., 1990—91; French, music, and English tchr. John Sedgwick Jr. H.S., Port Orchard, Wash., 1991—96; French tchr. and translator Laura Cerven Enterprises, Vashon, 1976—. Choir dir. First United Meth. Ch., Vashon, 1998—2002. Translator: La Traductière, 2000, Song a Name for Life, 2000. Musician numerous sacred and secular groups, Vashon, 1986—2003; treas. Vashon-Maury Co-op Preschool, 1987—88. Mem.: Cercle Français de Tacoma, Vrais Voisins de Vashon (founder and pres. 1998).

CERVILLA, CONSTANCE MARLENE, marketing consultant; b. Lafayette, Ind., Dec. 28, 1951; d. Norman Cimmino and Marilyn Jane (Stonebraker) C. AB, Harvard U., 1974, postgrad., 1974-75. Mktg. asst. Gen. Mills, Inc., Mpls., 1975-76; product dir. Pillsbury Co., Mpls., 1976-78; asst. v.p. Citicorp, N.A., Rochester, N.Y., 1978-80; cons. Bain & Co., Boston, 1980-81; owner, pres., CEO Core Group Mktg., Inc., Mpls., 1981—; co-founder, v.p. Mil. Communications Ctr., Inc., Mpls., 1983-89; co-founder Gift Certificate Ctrs., Inc., 1990—. Speaker to bank mktg. orgns. Patentee in field. Mem. Bank Mktg. Assn., Harvard/Radcliffe Club Minn., Mpls. Inst. Arts, Woman's Club Mpls., Wilderness Soc., Nat. Rowing Assn., Harvard Club (N.Y.C.). Avocations: rowing, swimming, business development. Office: Core Group Mktg Inc 7171 Shady Oak Rd Eden Prairie MN 55344-3516

CESARINI, DANIELLE KRISTIN, psychologist; b. Flushing, N.Y., Nov. 5, 1973; d. John Peter and Elvesia Cesarini. BA, Siena Coll., 1995; MS, L.I. U., 1997, D in Psychology, 2001. Lic. clin. psychologist N.Y. Psychology intern Kings County Hosp., Bklyn., 1998—99; psychology asst. Forensic Mental Health Svcs., N.Y.C., 1999—2001; assoc. psychologist Office Mental Health-Bedford Hills (N.Y.) Correctional Facility, 2001—, lic. psychologist, 2002—; pvt. practice Pleasantville, NY, 2003—. Mem.: APA, N.Y. State Psychol. Assn. Avocations: travel, reading, theater, literature. Office: Ste 210 57 Wheeler Ave Pleasantville NY 10570

CESSNA, JANICE LYNN, systems administrator, information technology manager; d. Alexander Carl and Camilla Dorothy Wagenfohr; 1 child, Christopher Alexander. AS data processing, Pasco-Hernando C.C., New Port Richey, Fla., 1982—84, AA, 1995—97; BS in Computer Info. Systems, St. Leo U., St. Leo, Fla., 1998—2000; MS computer info. tech., Regis U., Denver, Colo., 2001—03. Info. processing mgr. Pasco-Hernando C.C., New Port Richey, Fla., 1985—90, programmer/analyst, 1990—96, systems mgr., 1996—98, dir. mgmt. info. services, 1998—. Chair/mem., tech. adv. Fla. Cmty. Coll. Computer Consortium, Pensacola, Fla., 1994—; mem., MISATFOR Fla. Cmty .Coll. Sys., Tallahassee, 1998—; mem. - CIO com. Fla. Cmty. Coll. Sys., Tallahassee, 1998—. Mem.: N.Am. UNISYS User Assn. (assoc.), The Fla. Assn. Ednl. Data Systems (assoc.). Independent Thinkers. Luth. Avocations: fitness, travel, gardening, cooking, reading. Office: Pasco-Hernando Cmity Coll 10230 Ridge Road New Port Richey FL 34654 E-mail: cessnaj@phcc.edu.

CESSNA, KATRINA J. music educator, composer; b. L.A., Apr. 4, 1962; d. Donald and Rose Cessna. B magna cum laude in Music Edn., N.E. Mo. State U., 1985; M in Music Composition, Ind. U., 1991. Cert. tchr. Ill. State Bd. Edn., 1997. Music educator Urbana (Ill.) Mid. Sch., 1996—97; orch. dir. Herscher (Ill.) H.S., 1999—. Staff composer Herscher H.S., 1997—; assoc. percussion instr. Olivet Nazarene U., Bourbonnais, Ill., 2001—; sub. condr. Kankakee Valley Youth Symphony, Kankakee, Ill., 2002—. Composer: (jazz ensemble) Hearts and Flowers, 1989, (mixed chorus and organ) Psalm 126, 1991, (brass quartet and organ) Variations on Victimae paschali laudes, 1992; composer, arranger (marching band shows), 1995—. John J. Pershing scholar, N.E. Mo. State U., 1980—85. Mem.: Am. String Tchrs. Assn., Ill. Music Educators Assn. Home: PO Box 573 Herscher IL 60941 Office: Herscher High Sch Herscher IL 60941

CEYER, SYLVIA T. chemistry educator; Grad. summa cum laude, Hope Coll., Holland, Mich.; PhD, U. Calif., Berkeley. Postdoctoral fellow Nat. Bur. Standards; faculty mem. dept. chemistry MIT, Cambridge, Mass., 1981—, J.C. Sheehan prof. chemistry. Recipient Recognition award for young scholars AAUW Ednl. Found., 1988, Nobel Laureate Signature awd. for Graduate Education in Chemistry, Am. Chemical Soc., 1993. Fellow AAAS, NAS (chmn. chemistry sect.), Am. Phys. Soc., Am. Acad. Arts and Scis. Office: MIT 6-217 Dept Chemistry 77 Mass Ave Dept Cambridge MA 02139-4307

CHA, GRACE SEUNGYUN, financial company executive; b. Seoul, Korea, Nov. 21, 1966; came to U.S., 1988; d. Dang Ho and Kyung Ok (Byun) Cha; m. Edward H. Kim, July 31, 1988 (div. Dec. 1991); 1 child, Christina S. BA in Econs., U. Calif., San Diego, 1994. Fin. svcs. rep. San Diego Trust and Savs. Bank, 1992-94; sr. collateral examiner First Interstate Bank of Calif., L.A., 1994-96; CFO Millenium Fin. Corp., Diamond Bar, Calif., 1996—. Mem. Nat. Notary Assn. Home: 150 Cottonwood Cove Dr Diamond Bar CA 91765-1513

CHABRIAN, PEGGY, air transportation executive; Pres., founder Women in Aviation Internat., 1990—; acad. dean, assoc. v.p. Parks Coll.; dean acad. support Embry-Riddle Aero. U., Prescott, Ariz.; chair dept. aviation Ga. State U., Atlanta. Bd. dirs. Ctr. Excellence Aviation/Space Edn., Daytona Beach, Fla., U.S. Air and Trade Show; spkr. in field. Publisher: Aviation for Women; contbr. articles to profl. jours. Named to Crown Circle of Nat. Congress on Aviation and Space Edn., 1998; recipient Adminstrs. award, FAA, Civic award, AIAA. Mem.: U. Aviation Assn. (past pres., bd. dirs.), Exptl. Aircraft Assn. Aviation Found. (bd. dirs.). Office: Women in Aviation Internat 101 Corsair Dr Ste 101 Daytona Beach FL 32114

CHACON, MARI B. counseling administrator; b. Conway, Ark., Sept. 21, 1962; d. Robert J. and Elizabeth M. Peterson; m. Edward F. Chacon, Jan. 2, 1987; children: Zachary E., Aryne M. BS in Psychology, U. Wis., LaCrosse, 1984; MS, Ft. Hays State U., Hays, Kan., 1997. Lic. sch. counselor, clin. profl. counselor, cert. vocat. evaluator. Vocat. evaluator Arrowhead West, Inc., Dodge City, Kans., 1986—94; case mgr. Area Mental Health Ctr., Dodge City, Kans., 1994—2001; counselor Cuba H.S., N.Mex., St. Michaels H.S., Santa Fe, 2002—. Adv. PTA, Santa Fe, 2002—. Mem.: Nat. Rehab. Assn., Rocky Mountain Counselor Assn. Office: St Michaels H S 100 Siringo Rd Santa Fe NM 87505

CHADWICK, LAURIE L. secondary school educator; b. Centralia, Wash., July 2, 1962; d. Theron Thorton Ticknor Jr. and Linda Lee Ticknor; m. Ronald J. Chadwick, July 11, 1998; stepchildren: Melissa, Sarah, Emily. BA in English Edn., Ea. Wash. Univ., 1984; MA in Organizational Leadership, Gonzaga Univ., 1990. Cert. Fifth Yr. Continuing Tchr. Edn. Ea. Wash. Univ., 1987, Adminstrn. cert. Gozaga Univ., 1994. Tchr. Lincoln Mid. Sch., Clarkston, Wash., 1984—85, Mead HS, Spokane, Wash., 1985—87, Ctrl. Kitsap Jr. HS, Silverdale, Wash., 1987—88; adminstrn. asst. Cmty. Coll. Spokane (Wash.) Athletic Dept., 1988—89; tchr. Med. Lake (Wash.) HS, 1989—2001, Mead HS, Spokane, Wash., 2001—. Coach USGF. Bd. mem. Spokane Sports Unlimited, 1989—98; big sister Big Bros. & Big Sisters, Spokane, Wash., 1994—99. Recipient 3A/2A Gymnastic Coach of the Yr., Wash. State Gymnastics Coaches, 2002, Sectional Coach of the Yr., Nat. HS Coaches, 2002, Nat. Coach of the Yr., Nat. Fdn. HS Coaches. Mem.: Inland N.W. Track & Field - Masters Rep., U.S. Track & Field, Nat. Assn. Women's Gymnastics Judges, U.S. Gymnastics Fdn., Nat. Fdn. HS Coaches, Wash. State Coaches Assn. Avocations: reading, running, antiques. Office: Mead HS W 302 Hastings Spokane WA 99218 Office Phone: 509-465-7000.

CHAFEE, INGRID ROBERTA HOOVER COLEMAN, French language educator; b. Evanston, Ill., Dec. 12, 1934; d. Richard Thomas and Ingrid (Krogvig) Hoover; m. Samuel Henry Coleman III, Sept. 10, 1958 (wid. Oct. 1974); children: Robert D., Charles E.; m. Nathaniel Chafee, July 8, 1989. AB, Western Coll. of Miami, Oxford, 1956; MA, U. Va., 1959; PhD, Emory U., 1980. Part-time instr. Ga. State U., Atlanta, 1976-81; asst. prof. Morehouse Coll., Atlanta, 1981-83, 1990-95, assoc. prof., 1995—, acting chair dept. modern fgn. langs., 2000. Tech. writer, trainer Am. Software, Inc., Atlanta, 1984-90; coord. European Program, Morehouse Ctr. for Internat. Studies, Atlanta, 1994-96; jour. referee Jour. of Assn. for W. Ga. Coll., 1996—. Contbr. articles to profl. jours. Coord. prisoner of conscience coms., Amnesty Internat., Atlanta, 1983-87. Mem. MLA, South Atlantic Modern Lang. Assn., Am. Assn. Tchrs. of French, Phi Beta Kappa. Democrat. Avocations: writing, listening to music, history, film, theatre, swimming, sailing. Home: 476 Princeton Way NE Atlanta GA 30307-1131 Office: Morehouse Coll Dept Modern Fgn Langs 830 Westview Dr SW Atlanta GA 30314-3773 E-mail: ingridcc@aol.com., Ichafee@morehouse.edu.

CHAFEL, JUDITH ANN, education educator; b. Rochester, N.Y., Apr. 8, 1945; d. James Arthur and Florence Joan (Santangelo) C. AB, Vassar Coll., 1967; MSEd, Wheelock Coll, 1971; PhD, U. Ill., 1979. Cert. elem. tchr., Mass., N.J., N.Y. Tchr. Spruce St. Sch., Lakewood, N.J., 1972-74, Sodus (N.Y.) Primary Sch., 1974-76; grad. research and teaching asst. U. Ill., Urbana, 1976-79; vis. asst. prof. U. Tex., Austin, 1979-80; asst. prof. dept. curriculum and instrn. Ind. U., Bloomington, 1980-86, assoc. prof., 1986—2001, prof., 2001—; mem. profl. staff U.S. Ho. Reps., Washington, 1989-90. Adj. assoc. prof. philanthropic studies Ctr. on Philanthropy, 1991-2001; reviewer Hist. Publs. and Records Commn., Nat. Archives, Washington, 1979, Little, Brown and Co., Boston, 1982-84, Office for Ednl. Rsch. and Improvement, U.S. Dept. Edn., 1991, 93. Mem. editorial adv. bd. Early Child Devel. and Care, 1985—, Youth and Soc., 1995—, Jour. of Poverty: Innovations on Social, Political and Economic Inequalities, 1998—; cons. editor Early Childhood Rsch. Quar., 1988-91, 92-95; contbr. editor Am. Jour. of Orthopsychiatry, 2000—; reviewer and contbr. articles to profl. jours. Proffitt Endowment grantee, Ind. U., 1982, 88, 1998, Ctr. on Philanthropy grantee, 1991, Spencer Found. grantee, 1985, 98; Congl. Sci. fellow Soc. Rsch. in Child Devel., 1989. Mem. Soc. Rsch. in Child Devel. (program com. 1986, 92), Am. Ednl. Rsch. Assn. (program com. 1984, 86, 87, 91, 92, 94, 96-99, 2002, nominations com. 1986, 88, chair 1993-95, mem.-at-large spl. interest group on early edn. and child devel. 1991-93), Nat. Assn. Edn. Young Children (reviewer 1980—), Assn. Childhood Edn. Internat. (pub. com. 1982-84, bull. and pamphlets rev. editor jour. 1982-84, rsch. com. 1984-88). Office: Ind U Sch Edn 3214 Education Bldg Bloomington IN 47405

CHAFFIN, VIRGINIA LOUISE, licensed practical nurse; b. Miami, Ariz., Dec. 29, 1936; d. Angelita Cutbirth; m. Patrick R. Chaffin, July 21, 1956; children: Denise M., Mary Therese, Diana M., Gina Lee, Cecilia R. Real estate broker, Western Coll., 1984; LPN, Gateway C.C., 1992. Real estate broker Ariz. Dept. Real Estate, Phoenix, 1983—96; LPN Ariz. State Bd. Nursing, Phoenix, 1992—. Contbr. articles to newspapers. Girl Scouts U.S.A., Phoenix, 1965-70; active Cath. Women's Groups, Phoenix, 1965-73, Hear My Voice, Ann Arbor, Mich., 1995—, Greater Phoenix Child Abuse Prevention Coun., 1996—, comty vol., 1995— Avocations: writing, gardening, genealogy, photography, hiking.

CHAFKIN, RITA M. dermatologist; b. N.Y.C., Apr. 11, 1929; d. Joseph and Dora (Winslow) Melnick; m. Samuel Chafkin, June 29, 1952; children: Elise Ceil Perkins, Marc David Chafkin (dec.). BA, NYU, 1949; MD, NYU Med. Sch., 1953; cert. in dermatology, NYU Postgrad. Med. Sch., 1957. Diplomate Am. Acad. Dermatology, 1959. Intern in internal medicine Kings County Hosp., Bklyn., 1953-54; dermatology resident Bellevue Hosp., N.Y.C., 1954-55; postgrad. trainee NYU Postgrad. Med. Sch., 1955-56, fellow in dermatology, 1956-57; precepteeship with Dr. Marion Sulzberger; pvt. practice dermatology, 1958-94; assoc. clin. prof. dermatology U. Calif., Davis, 1975-97. Clinic dir. dermatology Stanislavs County Med. Ctr., Modesto, 1958-97. Artist in mixed media. Bd. dirs. Stanislaus County Med. Ctr. Found., 1982-97, pres. 1984-85. Recipient Tchr. of the Yr. award Stanislaus County Med. Ctr., Modesto, 1988, Founder's Dinner honoree, 1992. Fellow Am. Acad. Dermatology; mem. AMA, Calif. Med. Soc., San Francisco Dermatology Soc., Stanislaus County Med. Soc. (pres. 1983-84), Pacific Dermatology Assn. (fin. com. 1959—). Jewish.

CHAGNON, LUCILLE TESSIER, workforce development and literacy specialist; b. Gardner, Mass., June 1, 1936; d. Fred G. Tessier and Alfreda C. (Ross) Noel; m. Richard J. Chagnon, Sept. 16, 1978; children: Daniel, David. BMus, Rivier Coll., Nashua, N.H.; cert. in human resource mgmt. and cmty. devel., Inst. Cultural Affairs, Chgo., 1969; MEd, Boston Coll., 1972. Educator, N.H., 1960-73; internat. cons. Inst. Cultural Affairs, Chgo., 1973-79; staff tng. dir. CO-MHAR, Inc., Phila., 1979-81; pres., owner Chagnon Assocs., Collingswood, N.J., 1981-86; prin. Sacred Heart Sch., Camden, N.J., 1986-87; founder, dir. Lifeline Literacy Project, 1988-94; literacy and developmental learning specialist Rutgers U., Camden, 1989-99; coord. work readiness, Workforce Devel. Inst. Drexel U., Phila., 1999-2000. Adj. grad. faculty dept. counseling psychology Temple U. Sch. Edn., Phila., 1985—90; sr. project staff Right Assocs., Phila., 1982—91, 2001—. Author (with Richard J. Chagnon): The Best is Yet to Be: A Pre-Retirement Program, 1985; author: Easy Reader, Learner, Writer, 1994, Voice Hidden, Voice Heard: A Reading and Writing Anthology, 1998, You, Yes YOU, Can Teach Someone to Read, 2004. Bd. dirs. Camden County Literacy Vols. of Am., 1987—91, Handicapped Advocates for Ind. Living, 1987—; mem. Collingswood (N.J.) Bd. Edn., 1985—89. Mem.: ASCD, Internat. Reading Assn., Internat. Alliance for Learning, Inst. Cultural Affairs, Brain-Based Edn. Network, Nat. Learning Found. (adv. bd. 1997—). Home and Office: 408 River Rd Wilmington DE 19809-2731 E-mail: chagnon@comcast.net.

CHAGNONI, KATHLEEN, energy executive; BA with honors, Stanford U., 1981; JD, Columbia U., 1985. Assoc. O'Melveny & Myers, Washington, 1985—89, Hogan & Harlson, Balt., 1989—94; asst. v.p., assoc. group counsel USF&G Corp., 1996—98; v.p., corp. group gen. counsel St. Paul Cos., Inc., 1999—2003; v.p., gen. counsel, corp. sec. Constellation Energy, Balt., 2002—. Office: Constellation Energy Group 750 E Pratt St Baltimore MD 21202

CHAIRSELL, CHRISTINE, academic administrator; children: T., Tyler. EdD, MA in polit. sci., BA in polit. sci., U. Nev. Las Vegas. Acting pres. Nev. State Coll., 2002; assoc. vice chancellor U. & CC Sys. Nev.; assoc. vice pres. Computing Svc.; dean spl. programs CC So. Nev.; dir. environ. edn. U. Nev. Las Vegas, faculty polit. sci. dept. Pres. Aqua Vision, 1992—94; mem. Leadership Las Vegas Class, 1993. Recipient women of achievement edn., Las Vegas Chamber Commerce, 1993. Office: NV State Coll 1125 Dawson Ave Henderson NV 89015

CHAIT, ANDREA MELINDA, school psychologist; b. Buffalo, May 7, 1970; d. Marvin and Rochelle (Benatovich) C. BS in Health Edn., Ithaca (N.Y.) Coll., 1992; MEd in Spl. Edn., U. Fla., 1995, MA in Edn., 2001, PhD in Sch. Psychology, 2002. Nat. cert. sch. psychologist. Substitute tchr. Cortland (N.Y.) H.S., 1992; tchrs. aid, substitute Stanley G. Falk, Cheektowaga, N.Y., 1993; pvt. spl. edn. tutor Buffalo and Gainesville, 1992—99; behavioral disorders tchr. Paul D. West Middle Sch., East Point, Ga., 1995-96; chair discipline com. spl. edn. dept. Paul P. West Middle Sch., East Point, Ga., 1995—; grad. tchg. asst. U. Fla., 1998-99; sch. psychologist internal sub. Browar Co. Pub. Schs., 2001—02. Adj. mem. faculty Santa Fe C.C., 2000—; clin. coord. LEAP program Kennedy Krieger Inst., 2002—. Vol. Task Force for Battered Women, Ithaca, 1991, Human Rights Orgn., Gainesville, 1993-94. Mem. APA, Nat. Assn. Sch. Psychologists, Pi Lambda Theta, Kappa Delta Pi, Phi Kappa Phi. Jewish. Avocations: reading, drawing. Home: 1600 Trebor Ct Lutherville MD 21093

CHAIT, FAY KLEIN, health administrator; b. Chgo., Jan. 12, 1929; d. Victor and Rose (Begun) Magid; m. Jerome G. Klein, June 27, 1948 (div. 1970); children: Leslie Susan Janik, Debra Lynne Maslov; m. Manuel Chait, Aug. 28, 1994. BA in English, UCLA, 1961; MA in Pub. Adminstrn., U. So. Calif., 1971. Cert. health adminstrn. Supr. social workers L.A. County, 1961-65; program specialist Econ. and Youth Opportunity Agy., L.A., 1965-69; sr. health planner Model Cities, L.A., 1971-72; dir. prepaid health plan Westland Health Svcs., L.A., 1972-74; exec. dir. Coastal Region Health Consortium, L.A., 1974-76; grants and legis. cons. Jewish Fed. Council of L.A., 1976-79; planning coun. Jewish Fed. Coun. of So. Fla., Palm Beach to Miami, 1979-82; adminstrv. dir. program in kidney diseases Dept. Medicine UCLA, 1982-84; exec. dir. west coast Israel Cancer Rsch. Fund, L.A., 1984-94; cons. to non-profit orgns. Santa Monica, 1994—. Cons. Arthritis Found., L.A., 1984, Bus. Action Ctr., L.A., 1982, Vis. Nurses Assn., L.A., 1982. Charter mem. L.A. County Mus. of Art, Mus. of Contemporary Art; cons. L.A. Mcpl. Art Gallery, 1979; mem. UCLA/Armand Hammer Mus. Fellow U.S. Pub. Health, U. So. Calif., 1970-71. Mem. APHA, UCLA Alumni Assn. (life), U. So. Calif. Alumni Assn. (life).

CHAITMAN, HELEN DAVIS, lawyer; b. NYC, July 5, 1941; d. Philip and Miriam (Pfeffer) D.; m. Edmund Chaitman, Feb. 29, 1964 (div. 1978); children: Jennifer, Alison; m. George B. Gelman, Oct. 21, 1979. AB cum laude, Bryn Mawr Coll., 1963; JD, Rutgers U., 1976. Bar: N.J., 1976, N.Y. 1978, U.S. Dist. Ct. N.J. 1976, U.S. Dist. Ct. (so. and ea. dists.) 1978, U.S. Supreme Ct. 1981, Ct. Fed. Claims 2001, U.S. Ct. Appeals (8th cir.) 2002. Assoc. Paul, Weiss, Rifkind, Wharton & Garrison, N.Y.C., 1977-82, ptnr. Wilentz, Goldman & Spitzer, Woodbridge, N.J., 1983-87, Ross & Hardies, Somerset, N.J., 1987-99, Wolf Haldenstein Adler Freeman & Herz LLP, N.Y.C., 1999—2002, Phillips Nizer LLP, NYC, 2002—. Author: The Law of Lender Liability, 1990; contbg. author: Commercial Damages, 1985; editor Emerging Theories of Lender Liability, 1985-87. Mem.: ABA (chmn. comml. fin. svcs. com. 1994—97, sect. bus. law), Pub. Law Inst., Am. Law Inst. (sustaining mem. 1992—2004). Home: The Farm 115 Fairview Rd Frenchtown NJ 08825-3013 Office: Phillips Nizer LLP 666 Fifth Ave New York NY 10103-0084 also: 45 Essex St Hackensack NJ 07601 Office Phone: 212-841-1320. E-mail: hchaitman@phillipsnizer.com.

CHALCRAFT, ELENA MARIE, actress, singer; b. Bklyn., Oct. 14, 1959; d. James Abdou and Vivian (Trovato) Edwards; m. Rory Charles Chalcraft, Aug. 1, 1992; 1 child, Christopher Aston. BA in Speech, English and Theater Arts, Shippensburg State Coll., 1981; MFA in Acting, Va. Commonwealth U., 1984. Human resources analyst APA, Washington, 1985-98; music dir. Our Lady Queen of Peace Ch., Arlington, Va., 1992-98; soprano Philomusica Chamber Choir, 1999—; ind. kitchen cons. The Pampered Chef, 1999—; soprano St. Bartholomew Choir, 2000—01. Actor, singer (plays): Man of La Mancha, 1988, Ben, 1989-90, Maryland Renaissance Festival, 1987-91, Ziggy, 1992, The Snow Queen, 1994; actor: (play) Broadway Bound, 1993, (tng. film) GAO, 1990; dramaturg (play) Ballets Russes and Drood, 1993. Mem. liturgy com. Our Lady Queen of Peace Ch., 1995-98. Roman Catholic. Avocations: reading, writing children's books, piano, cross-stitch, crosswords. E-mail: emcrcc@worldnet.att.net.

CHALERMVONGSENEE, MAYTHEENEE, air freight administrator, consultant; b. Bangkok, Dec. 23, 1976; d. Piseth and Chantipar Chalermvongsenee; life ptnr. Christopher Mirasol. BS in Internat. Bus., San Francisco State U., 2002. Inbond team asst. Fritz Companies, Inc., Boston, 1996—98, Apple computer team asst. South San Francisco, Calif., 1998—2000; air freight coord. Mitsubishi Logistics Am. Corp., Burlingame, 2000—. Mem.: Golden Key Honor Soc. Office: Mitsubishi Logistics Am Corp 1799 Bayshore Hwy Ste 129 Burlingame CA 94010

CHALFANT-ALLEN, LINDA KAY, retired Spanish language educator; b. New Kensington, Pa., Oct. 9, 1943; d. Fred and Evelyn V. (Peters) C.; m. Charles V. Utley, Sr., Jan. 26, 1963 (div.); children: Charles V. Utley, Yvette Melissa Utley; m. Simon Allen, Feb. 13, 1998. BA in Child Study, Vassar Coll., 1965; MS in Spanish and Linguistics, Georgetown U., 1971. Cert. tchr., N.Y., D.C. Bilingual rsch. asst. Georgetown U., Washington, 1966-71; curriculum writer D.C. Pub. Schs., 1969-70, 91; asst. prof., rsch. assoc. U. D.C., 1982-85; asst. to dir. Latin for Modern Sch., McLean, Va., 1968-94; tchr. D.C. Pub. Schs., 1965-95, ret., 1995; freelance cons., editor, 1961—; bilingual legal sec. Wilkinson, Barker, Knauer & Quinn, Washington, 1996-97; legal sec. Thelen Reid & Priest, 1998-2000. Proposal review panelist Nat. Endowment for Humanities, Washington, 1984, 87, 89, U.S. Dept. Edn., Washington, 1986. Founder, 1st pres. Fgn. Lang. Action Group, Washington, 1978-79; Sunday sch. tchr., Washington, 1972-93. Recipient Grad. Study fellowship King Juan Carlos Found., Spain, 1994, Travel grant Spain '92 Found., 1994. Roman Catholic. Avocations: travel, reading, bowling, baking, exercise, crochet. E-mail: lchalfantallen@cfl.rr.com.

CHALIFOUX, THELMA, Canadian senator; b. Calgary, AB, Can., Feb. 8, 1929; children: Robert, Scott, Clifford, Deborah, Orleane(dec.), Sharon, Paul. Student, Chgo. Sch. Interior Design, So. Alta. Inst. Tech., Lethbridge C.C. Field staff cmty. devel. Co. Young Can., 1973—75; land claims negotiator, 1979—82, 1996—98; panel mem. Alta. Family and Social Svcs., 1989—98; senator The Senate of Can., Ottawa, 1997—. Cons. Chalifoux & Assocs., 1996—98; cons., senator Metis Nation of Alta. Assn., 1990—95. Recipient Nat. Aboriginal Achievement award, 1995. Liberal. Office: 808 Victoria Bldg The Senate of Canada Ottawa ON Canada K1A 0A4

CHALK, ROSEMARY ANNE, federal agency administrator; b. Cin., May 25, 1948; d. John Henry and Virginia R. (Kamphaus) Chalk; m. Michael Anthony Stoto, June 28, 1986; children: Anna Murilius, Benjamin John. BA, U. Cin., 1970; postgrad., George Washington U., 1970-72. Policy analyst Libr. of Congress, Washington, 1972-75; rsch. fellow MIT, Cambridge, Mass., 1982-83; program dir. AAAS, Washington, 1976-86; cons. Harvard Sch. Pub. Health, Boston, 1986-87; study dir. Inst. of Medicine, Washington, 1987-89, Nat. Acad. Sci., Washington, 1989—. Cons. The Field Found., N.Y.C., 1986-87, The Acadia Inst., Bar Harbor, Maine, 1988-91; adv. com. on ethics and values studies NSF, 1984-87. Editor: Science, Technology and Society: Emerging Relationships, 1988; contbr. articles to profl. jours. Fellow AAAS (coun. and section officer 1987—), Fedn. Am. Scientists (coun. mem. 1982-90), Student Pugwash USA (bd. dirs. 1988—). Roman Catholic. Office: Inst Medicine NAS 500 Fifth Street NW Washington DC 20001*

CHALKLEY, JACQUELINE ANN, retail company executive; b. Benson, Minn., Jan. 3, 1946; d. Vincent Otto and Dorothy Mildred (Alsaker) Kaehler; m. C. Wayne Callaway. BA in Art History cum laude, Brown U., 1967; MA, Columbia U., 1968; postgrad. in Contemporary Art, New Sch. for Social Rsch., N.Y.C., 1968-70; postgrad. in Ceramics, U. Md., 1970-72. Art tchr. Summit (N.J.) High Sch., 1968-70, Rockville (Md.) High Sch., 1970-74; adj. prof. ceramics Montgomery Coll., Rockville, 1974-78; owner Jackie Chalkley at Foxhall Square, Washington, 1978-99, Jackie Chalkley at Willard Collection, Washington, 1986-99, Jackie Chalkley at Chevy Chase Plz., Washington, 1989-99; retail and product devel. cons., 1999—. Juror Rhinebeck Craft Fair, 1981, New Eng. Buyers Market, Boston, 1982, Craft Art '82, Richmond, Va. Craft Show, 1983, Smithsonian Crafts Exhbn. '83, Smithsonian Instn. Women's Com. Craft Show, 1984, Annie Albers fashion show at Renwick Gallery, 1984, Morristown Craft Fair, 1984, Washington Craft Show, 1986, Potomac Craftsmen's Guild Show, 1987, Harrisburg Arts Festival, 1987, Ceramic Guild Washington, 1987, Washington Guild Goldsmiths, 1987, 18th Bienniel Exhbn. Creative Crafts Coun., 1988, Art Balt., 2003, others; appointee screening com. Piedmont Craftsman's Guild, Winston-Salem, N.C., 1983-86, D.C. Commn. Arts, 1983-85; mem. hon. com. Brandeis Art Exhbn., 1984; mem. hon. com. various exhbns. and fundraisers Textile Mus., 1984-86. Featured in Ceramics Monthly, 1994, Women's Wear Daily, 1995. Mem. hon. com. 2d Ann. 34th St. Art Fair, John Eaton Sch., 1985; mem. benefit com. Washington Charitable Fund, 1989; hon. bd. trustees D.C. chpt. Design Industries Found. for AIDS, 1989, 90; mem. auction ann. benefit com. Washington Project for Arts, 1989, 90, benefit com. Source Theater, 1993, benefit com. Corcoran Mus. Jazz Evening, 1993, hon. com. Lab Sch. Wash., 1992, hon. benefit com. Arena Stage Living Theater, 1997, 98; sponsor Wearable Art Fashion Show, Renwick Mus., 1993; juried Smithsonian Craft Show, 1994; hon. chmn. Friends of the Corcoran Mus. Benefit, 1999-2000, mem. exec. com., 2001-02; mem. benefit com. Living Stage & Arena Theatre, 1997, 98, 99; chmn. Craft Leaders Caucus Day 2000; mem. nat. resource bd. James Renwick Alliance of Renwick Mus., 2000-03, gala exec, com. Rincones Dance Theater, 2001-; mem. Hon. Com. Aid to Artisans D.C., Cambodian Embassy, 2003. Appeared on cover of Forecast Mag., 1978; recipient Best Taste in Washington award Washingtonian Mag., 1982, 1st Ann. Outstanding Accessories Merchandising award Accessories Mag., 1985; named one of 23 People to Watch in 1983, Washingtonian Mag., 1982; her apt. chosen as Residential Interior of Yr., Am. Soc. Interior Designers, 1985, 92; her store named 1986 Comml. Interior of Yr., Am. Soc. Interior Designers; nat. award for logo design Am. Corp. Identity, 1988, 91 Mem. Am. Craft Coun., Washington Fashion Group, James Renwick Craft Leaders Caucus, Friends of the Corcoran Gallery of Art, Washington Performing Arts Soc. (Impresario coun. 2001-). Avocations: travel, food, modern dance, visual arts, swimming. Office: Jackie Chalkley 2130 Cathedral Ave NW Washington DC 20008-1302

CHALOULT, NANCY MARIE, nursing administrator; d. Clifford Joseph and Mary Mae Chaloult. BSN, U. So. Maine, 1982; M of Mgmt., Troy State U., 1993. RN. Commd. 2d lt. USAF, 1982, advanced through grades to lt. col.; staff nurse Patrick AFB, Cocoa Beach, Fla., 1983—85; staff nurse, surg. nurse MadDill AFB, Tampa, Fla., 1988—91; night shift charge nurse Riyadh, Saudi Arabia, 1991; night nursing supr. South Bay Hosp., Sun City Center, Fla., 1991—93; adminstrv. supr. Holmes Regional Med. Ctr., Melbourne, 1993—99, nursing dir., 1999—. Deacon Presbyn. Ch. Good Shepherd, Melbourne, 2002—. Decorated Meritorious Svc. medal, Commendation medal. Mem.: Res. Officer Assn., Assn. Nurses Endorsing Transp., Fla. Orgn. Nurse Execs., Am. Orgn. Nurse Execs. Avocations: bicycling, running, movies, dance. Home: 1185 White Oak Cir Melbourne FL 32934 Office: Holmes Regional Med Ctr 1350 S Hickory St Melbourne FL 32901 E-mail: nmchaloult@aol.com.

CHAMBERLAIN, BARBARA KAYE, small business owner, communications executive; b. Lewiston, Idaho, Nov. 6, 1962; d. William Arthur and Gladys Marie (Humphrey) Greene; m. Dean Andrew Chamberlain, Sept. 13, 1986 (div.); children: Kathleen Marie, Laura Kaye; m. Daniel Eric Pocklington, Apr. 11, 1998. BA in English cum laude, BA in Linguistics cum laude, Wash. State U., 1984; MPA, Ea. Wash. U., 2002. Temp. sec. various svcs., Spokane, Wash., 1984-86; office mgr. Futurepast, Spokane, 1986-87; dir. mktg. and prodn. Futurepast: The History Co., Melior Publs., Spokane, 1987-88, v.p., 1988-89; founder, owner PageWorksInk, 1989—; mem. dist. 2 Idaho State Ho. of Reps., 1990-92; mem. Idaho State Senate, 1992-94; dir. comm. and pub. affairs Wash. State U., Spokane, 1998—. Adj. faculty North Idaho Coll., 1995, trustee, 1996-2001, bd. chair, 1999-2001. Author North Idaho's Centennial, 1990; editor Washington Songs and Lore, 1988. Bd. dirs. Mus. North Idaho Coeur d'Alene, 1990-91, Ct. Apptd. Spl. advocates, 1993-96; bd. dirs. Spokane Pub. Rels. Coun., 1999—, pres., 2002-03. Named Child Advocate Legislator of Yr., Idaho Alliance for Children, Youth and Families, 1993. Democrat. Office: 534 E Trent Ave Spokane WA 99210-1495

CHAMBERLAIN, CARA LEE, literature educator, writer; b. Salt Lake City, Utah, Oct. 11, 1959; d. Thomas Marvin Chamberlain and Barbara Helen Tripp; m. Bernard William Quetchenbach, Mar. 17, 1984; 1 child, Thomas Glenn Quetchenbach. BA magna cum laude, U. of Utah, 1978—81; M.A., Purdue U., 1986—88. Instr./lectr. Purdue U., West Lafayette, Ind., 1988—90; instr. NW Coll., Powell, Wyo., 1991—95; curatorial asst. Buffalo Bill Hist. Ctr., Cody, Wyo., 1993—94; instr. (professeure) Université de Moncton a Edmundston, Edmundston, Canada, 1996—97; instr. U. of Maine at Ft. Kent, 1997—99, Fla. So. Coll., 2001—. Editl. asst. Sycamore Rev., West Lafayette, Ind., 1989—89. Author: (poetry) published 115 poems in 75 journals including The Southern Review, Virginia Quarterly Review, others; contbr. short stories; contbg. editor: (journal) Common Ground, 2000—02, The River Rev./La Revue Riviere, 1997—2000. Vol. McKeel Acad. of Tech., Lakeland, Fla., 1999—2000; sec. Sycamore Chpt./Nat. Audubon Soc., Lafayette; mem. MoveOn.org, 2002—. Recipient Whetstone prize, Whetstone Mag., 1988, Pushcart Prize nomination, 1988, Puschcart Prize nomination, 1995, Pushcart prize nomination, 2003; Rsch. grant, U. of Denver, 1985. Mem.: Phi Beta Kappa. Green Party. Avocations: gardening, birdwatching, classical guitar.

CHAMBERLAIN, ELIZABETH SIMMONS, retired English language educator; b. St. Louis, June 15, 1929; d. George Edwin and Myrtle Coline (Smith) Simmons; m. Barnwell Rhett Chamberlain Jr., Aug. 11, 1956; 1 child, Edwin Rhett. AB, Wellesley Coll., Mass., 1951; AM, U. Mich., 1955; PhD, U. N.C., Chapel Hill, 1979. Tchr. English and Bible history, adminstr. Kingswood Sch. Cranbrook, Bloomfield Hills, Mich., 1951-55, Ashley Hall, Charleston, S.C., 1955-56; tchr. English and social studies Charlotte (N.C.) Country Day Sch., 1956-58; instr. English Meredith Coll., Raleigh, N.C., 1962-68; asst. prof. English N.C. Ctrl. U., Durham, 1981-95. Editor: Bancombe Democrat, 2003—. Mem. Human Rels. Com., Durham, 1983-88, 91-94, chair, 1986-88, 93-94; mem. Civic Ctr. Authority, Durham, 1988-91, mem. merger com. City and County Planning Depts., Durham, 1983-84, Nursing Home Adv. Com., Durham, 1982-85, exec. com. Dem. Party N.C., 2000—; chmn. Bancombe County Dem. Party, 2003—. Mem. Common Cause (mem. dist. bd. 1996-2002), Nat. Soc. DAR, Today's Book Club (sec. 1996-98, v.p. 1999-2001). Democrat. United Methodist. Avocations: politics, reading. Home: 340 Blackberry Inn Rd Weaverville NC 28787-9766

CHAMBERLAIN, FRANCES W. writer; b. Olney, Ill., Sept. 23, 1951; d. Paul Gerald Waite and Harriet Norman; m. Timothy Plyler, May 14, 2002; children from previous marriage: Brangwyn Chamberlain Gonzalez, Nicole C. Chanberlain, Alexandra C. BA, Shimer Coll.; MLS, Wesleyan U. Journalist N.Y. Times, N.Y.C., 1990—. Tchr. Internat. Coll. Hispitality Mgmt., Washington, 1995—2003. Author of poems. Judge Conn. Pietry Soc. Mem.: Toastmasters (sec. 2002—03, award 2003). Home: PO Box 1287 Washington CT 06793

CHAMBERLAIN, KATHRYN BURNS BROWNING, retired career officer; b. Rapid City, S.D., Jan. 17, 1951; d. George Alfred III and Mildred Doty Browning; m. Thomas Richard Masker, Apr. 19, 1975 (widowed Sept. 1978); m. Guy Caldwell Chamberlain III, Mar. 25, 1980 (div. Oct. 1988); children: Burns Doty, Anne Caldwell. BA, La. Tech. U., 1973; postgrad., Naval Postgrad. Sch., Monteray, Calif., 1978-79; MA, Auburn U., 1984; postgrad., U. Ill., 1994-96, Govs. State U., 1995-96. Ensign USN, 1974, lt. jg., 1976, lt., 1978, advanced through grades to comdr., 1983, surface warfare designation, 1980, joint staff officer, 1986, comdg. officer Mil. Sealift Command Office, 1986-88; comdr., exec. officer USNAVFAC, 1991-94; planner City of Montgomery, 1998—. Mem. Am. Inst. Cert. Planners, Am. Planning Assn., Urban and Regional Info. Sys. Assn. Home and Office: 364 Felder Ave Montgomery AL 36104-5616 E-mail: kchamberlai1@earthlink.net.

CHAMBERLAIN, PATRICIA ANN, writer, farmer, retired environmental manager, land use planner; b. Tex. d. James Franklin and Roberta Marie; m. Herbert F. Chamberlain, July 20, 1962 (div. Oct. 1967); children: Norma, Catherine; m. Clayton C. Wright, Mar. 5, 1994 (dec. May 2000). AA, Odessa (Tex.) Jr. Coll., 1970; BS in Secondary Edn., Tex. Tech. U., 1971, PhD in Land Use Planning, Mgmt. & Design, 1984. Cert. wildlife biologist. Lab. and x-ray tech. Med. Ctr. Hosp. and Drs. offices, Odessa, 1964-68; supr. urban wildlife program Tex. Rodent & Predatory Animal Control Svc., San Antonio, 1972-80; rsch. wildlife biologist USDA U.S. Forest Svc., Lubbock, Tex., 1981-84; community planner USAF San Antonio Real Property Maintenance Agy., 1985-87; environ. engr. USAF SARPMA, San Antonio, 1987-88; br. chief USAF Environ. Br., Brooks AFB, Tex., 1988-91; community planner USAF Ctr. Environ. Excellence, San Antonio, Brooks AFB, 1991-94, natural resources specialist, 1994-98; freelance writer, farmer, 1998—. Mem. USAF Graphics Working Group, Washington, 1987-91. Mem. Target '90 Goals for San Antonio, 1986-87. With U.S. Army, 1960-62. Caesar Kleberg Wildlife Rsch. Found. grantee, 1980-84; named to San Antonio Women's Hall of Fame, 1992. Mem. Am. Planning Assn. (regional treas. 1986-87), Soc. Am. Mil. Engrs., Wildlife Soc. (nat. urban wildlife and regional planning com. 1980-82), Phi Kappa Phi, Sigma Tau Delta, Beta Beta Beta. Avocations: photography, art (oils and acrylics), fishing, hunting.

CHAMBERLAIN HAYMAN, SUSAN DENISE, psychotherapist, pain management therapist; b. Platte, S.D., Feb. 18, 1954; d. Oran Lee and Lola Marion Chamberlain; m. Paul William Hayman, Dec. 17, 1984; children: Tiffany Cheré, Prairie Rose. BS, Black Hills State U., 1983; MS, S.D. State U., 1997. Lic. profl. counselor, S.D. Bd.; owner Life Without Boundaries, Rapid City, S.D.; pain mgmt. therapist Rapid City Regional Hosp.; mental health therapist Luth. Social Svcs., Rapid City. Mem. Polit. Incident Stress Debriefing Team Katharsis, Rapid City, 1999—. Advisor, Parent Alliance Concerning Teen Support, Rapid City, 1998. E-4, U.S. Army. Mem. AAUW, Am. Counseling Assn., Am. Rehab. Counselors Assn., S.D. Counseling Assn. Avocation: bassist. Home: 3405 Leland Ln Rapid City SD 57702 Office: Life Without Boundaries 3202 W Main St Rapid City SD 57702 E-mail: hayman@rapidnet.com.

CHAMBERLIN, MARJORIE RUTH, elementary school educator; b. Easton, Pa., Mar. 1, 1949; d. William Hermon and Ruth Elizabeth (King) Werner; m. Kermit Jay Chamberlin, Nov. 27, 1974; 1 child, Jay William. BA, Glassboro (N.J.) State U., 1971; MEd, Pa. State U., 1979. Cert. tchr., N.J., Pa. Tchr. Warren County Vo-Tech., Washington, N.J., 1971-83; supr. Monroe County Vo-Tech., Bartonsville, Pa., 1987-88; substitute tchr. East Stroudsburg (Pa.) Sch. Dist., 1995—99, tchr., 1999—2001. Adj. Northampton County C.C., Bethlehem, Pa., 1986-87; cons. N.J. Dept. Edn., Trenton, 1979. Bd. dirs. Fine Arts Discovery Series, Reeders, Pa., 1993-96. Mem. LWV (Monroe county treas. 1991-93, pres. 1993-95), United Meth. Women (treas. 1990-91). Avocations: spinning, weaving, water activities, travel. Home: PO Box 88 Delaware Water Gap PA 18327-0088

CHAMBERS, ANNE COX, newspaper executive, former diplomat; b. Dayton, Ohio; Student, Finch Coll., N.Y.C.; D in Pub. Svc. (hon.), Wesleyan Coll., 1982; DHL (hon.), Spelman Coll., 1983; LLD (hon.), Oglethorpe U., 1983; DHL (hon.), Brenau Coll., 1989; LLD (hon.), Clark Atlanta U., 1989. Chmn. bd. Atlanta Jour.-Constn.; Am. amb. to Belgium, 1977-81. Bd. dirs. Cox Enterprises, Inc. Bd. dirs. Atlanta Arts Alliance, High Mus. Art, Cmtys. in Schs., MacDowell Colony, Forward Arts Found., Emory Mus. Art and Archaeology, N.Y. Bot. Garden, Coun. Am. Ambs., Chmn.'s Coun., Met. Mus. Art, Fr.-Am. Found.; trustee Mus. Modern Art, Carter Ctr.; mem. internat. coun. Mus. Modern Art; mem. nat. com. Whitney Mus. Am. Art. Decorated Legion of Hon. (France). Mem. Coun. Fgn. Rels. Office: 6205 Peachtree Dunwoody Rd Atlanta GA 30328

CHAMBERS, CAROLYN SILVA, communications company executive; b. Portland, Oreg., Sept. 15, 1931; d. Julio and Elizabeth (McDonnell) Silva; widowed; children: William, Scott, Elizabeth, Silva, Clark. BBA, U. Oreg. V.p., treas. Liberty Comm., Inc., Eugene, Oreg., 1960-83; pres. Chambers Comm. Corp., Eugene, 1983-95, chmn., 1996—; chmn., CEO, bd. dirs. Chambers Constrn. Co., 1986—. Bd. dirs., dep. chair bd. Fed. Res. Bank, San Francisco, 1982-92; bd. dirs. Portland Gen. Corp.; bd. dirs. U.S. Bancorp. Mem. Sacred Heart Med. Found., 1980—, Sacred Heart Gov. Bd., 1987-92, Sacred Heart Health Svcs. Bd., 1993-95, PeaceHealth Bd., 1995—; mem. U. Oreg. Found., 1980—, pres., 1992-93; chair U. Oreg. Found., The Campaign for Oreg., 1988-89; pres., bd. dirs. Eugene Arts Found.; bd. dirs., treas., dir. search com. Eugene Symphony; mem. adv. bd. Eugene Hearing and Speech Ctr., Alton Baker Park Commn., Pleasant Hill Sch. Bd.; chmn., pres., treas. Civic Theatre, Very Little Theatre; negotiator, treas., bd. dirs., mem. thrift shop Jr. League of Oreg. Recipient Webfoot award U. Oreg., 1986, U. Oreg. Pres.'s medal, 1991, Disting. Svc. award, 1992, Pioneer award, 1983, Woman Who Made a Difference award Internat. Women's Forum, 1989, U. Oreg. Found. Disting. Alumni award, 1995, Tom McCall awrd Oreg. Assn. Broadcasters, 1995, Disting. Alumni award U. Oreg., 1995, Outstanding Philanthropist award Oreg. chpt. Nat. Soc. Fund Raising Execs., 1994. Mem. Nat. Cable TV Assn. (mem. fin. com., chmn. election and by-laws com., chmn. awards com., bd. dirs. 1987-89, Vanguard award for Leadership 1982), Pacific Northwest Cable Comm. Assn. (conv. chmn., pres.), Oreg. Cable TV Assn. (v.p., pres., chmn. edn. com., conv. chmn., Pres.'s award 1986), Calif. Cable TV Assn. (bd. dirs., conv. chmn., conv. panelist), Women in Cable (charter mem., treas., v.p., pres., recipient star of cable recognition), Wash. State Cable Comm. Assn., Idaho Cable TV Assn., Community Antenna TV Assn., Cable TV Pioneers, Eugene C. of C. (first citizen award, 1985). Home: PO Box 640 Pleasant Hill OR 97455-0640 Office: Chambers Comm Corp PO Box 7009 Eugene OR 97401-0009

CHAMBERS, CLARICE LORRAINE, clergy, educational consultant; b. Ossining, N.Y., Oct. 7, 1938; d. Willie and Louise (McDonald) Cross (dec.); m. Albert W. Chambers, June 9, 1962; children: Albert W., Cheryl L. Fultz.

Diploma, Manna Bible Inst., Phila.; BS in Bibl. Studies, Trinity Coll. of Bible, Newburgh, Ind., 1983; MA in Bibl. Theology, Internat. Bible Inst. and Sem., Orlando, Fla., 1986. Ordained to ministry Pentecostal Ch., 1977. Master data specialist Naval Supply Dept., Phila., 1957-65; dir. tng., tchr. Opportunities Indsl. Ctr., Harrisburg, Pa., 1969-72; pub. info. asst. Pa. Dept. Revenue, Harrisburg, 1972-79; pastor Antioch Tabernacle United Holy Ch. of Am., Harrisburg, 1979—. Fin. sec. United Holy Ch. of Am., Greensboro, N.C., 1978-92, treas. no. dist., Linden, N.J., 1992-96; screening team La. Dept. Edn., Baton Rouge, 1995. Mem. Harrisburg Sch. Bd., 1975-2001; pres. Pa. Sch. Bds. Assn., New Cumberland, 1992; bd. dirs. Nat. Sch. Bds. Assn., Alexandria, Va., 1993-2002, pres., 2000; trustee Shippensburg (Pa.) U., 1989-96. Recipient Cmty. Sv. award Ctrl. Pa. chpt. Nat. Assn. Black Accts., 1984, Harrisburg chpt. Black United Fund. Pa., 1989, Outstanding Leadership award Greater Harrisburg NAACP, 1987, Svc. award Coun. of Pub. Edn., 1995. Democrat. Avocations: singing, reading. Home: 140 Sylvan Ter Harrisburg PA 17104-1079 Office: Antioch Tabernacle UHC Am 1920 North St Harrisburg PA 17103-1631 E-mail: pastor.c@att.net.

CHAMBERS, CLYTIA MONTLLOR, public relations consultant; b. Rochester, N.Y., Oct. 23, 1922; d. Anthony and Marie (Bambace) Capraro; m. Joseph John Montllor, July 2, 1941 (div. 1958); children: Michele, Thomas, Clytia; m. Robert Chambers, May 28, 1965. BA, Barnard Coll., N.Y.C., 1942; Licence en droit, Faculte de Droit, U. Lyon, France, 1948; MA, Howard U., Washington, 1958. Assoc. dir. dept. rsch. Coun. for Fin. Aid to Edn., N.Y.C., 1958-60; asst. to v.p. indsl. rels. Sinclair Oil Corp., N.Y.C., 1961-65; writer pub. rels. dept. Am. Oil Co., Chgo., 1965-67; dir. editorial svcs., v.p. Hill & Knowlton Inc., N.Y.C., 1967-77, sr. v.p., dir. spl. svcs. L.A., 1977-90, sr. cons., 1990—. Cons. and trustee Children's Inst. Internat., L.A., 1988-93. Co-author: The News Twisters, 1971; editor: Critical Issues in Public Relations, 1975. Mem.: Calif. Rare Fruit Growers (editor Fruit Gardener 1979—2000, editor emerita 2000—). Home: 11439 Laurelcrest Dr Studio City CA 91604-3872 E-mail: clytia@sbcglobal.net.

CHAMBERS, ELENORA STRASEL, artist; b. Strassel, Oreg. d. Augustine George and Frieda Rose (Westermann) Strasel; m. Edward Lucas Chambers, Oct. 9, 1954; children: Robert, Margaret L. BA, Marylhurst (Oreg.) Univ., 1942; student, Portland Art Mus. Sch., U. Miami, Fla., Fla. Internat. U. One person shows include Mirell Gallery, Coconut grove, Fla., 1961, Miami Mus. Modern Art, 1965, 80 Washington Sq. E., N.Y.C., 1983; Kendall Campus Art Gall., Miami, 1992, group exhbns. include Ringling Mus. Sarasota, Fla., 1956, Norton Gallery, West Palm Beach, 1956, Lowe Art Mus., Miami (award winner), 1957, 1976, Soc. of Four Arts, Palm Beach, 1958, 61, 62, 65, 67, 72, 74, 77, 81, Ft. Lauderdale Mus. Arts (award winner), 1964, 65, Profl. Women Artists, Lowe Art Mus., Miami, 1976, Mus. of Arts and Scis., Daytona Beach, Fla., 1979, Met. Dade County Coun. of Arts and scis., Miami, 1979, Lowe Levinson Gallery, Miami Beach, 1981, North Miami Mus. and Art Ctr., 1987, Metro-Dade Cultural Ctr., Miami, 1990, Mus. Contemporary Art, 1995, House Art Gallery, N.Y., 1996, Ambrosino Gallery, Miami, 1997, Ambrosino Gallery, Miami, 1998, Robert Hittel, Ft. Lauderdale, 1998, Dorsch Gallery, Miami, 1999, Kendall Campus Art Gallery, Miami, 2000, Snitzer Gallery, Miami, 2002; works in permanent collections Miami Mus. Modern Art, Hopkins-Easton Assocs., Omni Internat., many pvt. collections. Recipient Beaux Art award Lowe Art Mus., 1957, Hortt Meml. award Ft. Lauderdale Mus. Arts, 1964, Atwater Kent award 29th Ann. Exhbn. Contemporary Am. Paintings, Soc. Four Arts, 1967, 39th Ann. exhbn., 1977. Home: 5790 SW 51st Ter Miami FL 33155-6324

CHAMBERS, IMOGENE KLUTTS, school system administrator, financial consultant; b. Paden, Okla., Aug. 6, 1928; d. Odes and Lillie (Southard) Klutts; m. Richard Lee Chambers, May 27, 1949. BA, East Ctrl. State U., 1948; MS, Okla. State U., 1974, EdD, 1980. High sch. math. tchr. Marlow (Okla.) Sch. Dist., 1948-49; with Bartlesville (Okla.) Sch. Dist., 1950-94; asst. supt. bus. affairs, treas. Ind. Sch. Dist. 30, 1977-87, treas., 1985-94; fin. acctg. cons. Okla. State Dept. Edn., 1987-92; dir. Plz. Bank, Bartlesville, 1984-93. Adv. dir. Bank Okla., 1994-96. Treas. Okla. Schs. Ins. Assn., 1982—97, adminstr., 1993—97; bd. dirs. Mutual Girls Club, 1981—. Mem. Okla. Assn. Sch. Bus. Ofcls., Assn. Sch. Bus. Ofcls. Internat., Okla. Ret. Educators Assn., Washington County Ret. Educators Assn., Okla. State U. Alumni Assn., East Ctrl. U. Alumni Assn. (bd. dirs. 1994-96). Democrat. Methodist. Home: 911 SE Greystone Pl Bartlesville OK 74006-5141 E-mail: ikcgene@bartnet.net.

CHAMBERS, JOAN LOUISE, retired librarian, retired dean; b. Denver, Mar. 22, 1937; d. Joseph Harvey and Clara Elizabeth (Carleton) Baker; m. Donald Ray Chambers, Aug. 17, 1958 BA in English Lit., U. No. Colo., Greeley, 1958; MS in L.S., U. Calif.-Berkeley, 1970; MS in Systems Mgmt., U. So. Calif., 1985; cert., Coll. for Fin. Planning, 1989. Libr. U. Nev., Reno, 1970-79; asst. univ. libr. U. Calif., San Diego, 1979-81, univ. libr. Riverside, 1981-85; dean librs., prof. Colo. State U., Ft. Collins, 1985-97, emeritus dean and prof., 1997—. Mgmt. intern Duke U. Libr., Durham, N.C., 1978-79; sr. fellow UCLA Summer, 1982; cons. tng. program Assn. of Rsch. Libraries, Washington, 1981; libr. cons. Calif. State U., Sacramento, 1982-83, U. Wyo., 1985-86, 94-95, U. Nebr., 1991-92, Calif. State U. System, 1993-94, Univ. No. Ariz., 1994-95. Contbr. articles to profl. jours., chpts. to books. Bd. dirs. Consumers Union, 1996—. U. Calif. instl. improvement grantee, 1980-81; State of Nev. grantee, 1976, ARL grantee, 1983-84. Mem.: PEO, Colo. Mountain Club, Phi Kappa Phi, Kappa Delta Phi, Phi Lambda Theta, Beta Phi Mu. Avocations: hiking, snow shoeing, skiing, cycling, tennis. Home and Office: PO Box 1477 Edwards CO 81632-1477 E-mail: chambers@vail.net.

CHAMBERS, JOHNNIE LOIS (TUCKER CHAMBERS), elementary school educator, rancher; b. Crockett County, Tex., Sept. 28, 1929; d. Robert Leo and Lois K. (Slaughter) Tucker; m. R. Boyd Chambers; children: Theresa A., Glyn Robert, Boyd James, John Trox. BEd, Sul Ross State U., Alpine, Tex., 1971. Tchr. 1st and 2d grades Candelaria (Tex.) Elem. Sch., 1971-73; head tchr. K-8 Ruidosa (Tex.) Elem. Sch., 1973-77, Presidio Ind. Sch. Dist. at Candelaria Elem. Sch., 1977-91, tchr. 2d and 3d grades, 1991-93, tchr. pre-kindergarten, kindergarten and 1st grade, 1993-98; acting prin. Candelaria Elem. and Jr. High, 1995-98, head tchr. pre-K to 8th grades, 1996-98, tchr. pre-K, kindergarten, 1st and 2d grades, 1996—99, ret., 1999; tchr. Redford (Tex.) Elem. Sch., 2001—, tchr. pre-K-6, 2001—01. Mem. sight-base decision making, Presidio, 1991-94; mem. Chihuahuan Desert Rsch. Inst., Alpine, 1982-94. Leader Boy Scouts Am., Ruidosa and Candelaria, 1973-91, Cub Scout leader, 1973-91; chpt. mem. Sheriffs Assn. Tex., Austin, 1980; bd. dirs. Big Bend Regional Hosp. Dist., 2001—; mem. Ctr. for Big Bend Studies. Recipient awards Boy Scouts Am., 1969, 83, winner Litter Gitter award, 1994-95. Mem. Tex. State Tchrs. Assn., Tex. Fedn. Rep. Women, The Archaeol. Conservancy, Phi Alpha Theta. Avocations: hiking, camping, anthropologic digs, cave exploring, cooking. Home: 99 Retirement Cir Marfa TX 79843 E-mail: johnnieltc@yahoo.com.

CHAMBERS, LINDA DIANNE THOMPSON, social worker; b. Mexia, Tex., Apr. 21, 1953; d. Lee and Essie Mae (Hopes) Thompson; m. George Edward Chambers, Nov. 30, 1978; 1 child, Brandon. AS cum laude, Navarro Coll., 1974; B in Social Work magna cum laude, Tex. Women's U., 1976; cert. gerontology and Human Svcs. Mgmt., Sam Houston U., 1982; M in Social Work, U. Tex., Arlington, 1990. Lic. marriage and family therapist, social worker-advanced practitioner; cert family life educator; registered sex offender treatment provider. Mem. social work staff Dept. Human Res., Ft. Worth, 1975, Children's Med. Ctr., Dallas, 1976, Mexia State Sch., Tex., 1976-93, Methodist Home, Waco, Tex., 1993-96, Tex. Dept. Health, Waco, Tex., 1996—, Parkview Regional Hosp., 1996—; mem. social work staff geripsychiatric program Limestone Med. Ctr., 2001—. Pres. Raven Exquisites, Mexia, 1983-84, sec.-treas., 1984-85; pres., bd. dirs., Limestone County Child Welfare Bd., Hospice, Inc., Limestone County unit Am. Cancer Soc. Bd. dirs. Gibbs Meml. Libr., Teen Pregnancy Prevention Coun., Childcare Mgmt. Svcs.; vol. McLennan County Pub. Health Dist. AIDS Clinic, Ctr. for Action Against Sexual Assault, Family Abuse Ctr.; coord. founder Limestone County Teen Parent Program, co-founder Limestone County Parenting Coalition; mem. Limestone County Youth Adv. Com, Limestone County Parenting Coalition (co-founder); PTO sec. Ctrl. Tex. Literacy Coalition, 1992—; mem. Tex. Hist. Found., Nat. Mus. Women in the Arts, 1985—. Recipient numerous awards for scholarship and profl. excellence. Fellow Internat. Biog. Assn. (dep. bd. gov., life); mem. NAFE, AAUW, Am. Sociol. Soc. (sec. 1975-76), Tex. Dem. Women, Univ. Women's Assn., Am. Childhood Edn. Internat., Nat. Assn. Social Workers, Am. Assn. Mental Retardation, Nat. Assn. Future Women, Am. Soc. Profl. and Exec. Women, Nat. Assn. Negro Bus. and Profl. Women's Clubs, Tex. Woman's U. Nat. Alumni Assn., Mortar Bd. Honor Soc. (sec.-treas. 1975-76), Tex. Soc. Clin. Social Workers, Internat. Platform Assn., Internat. Assn. Bus. and Profl. Women, Am. Biog. Assn. (dep. bd. govs.), Nat. Mus. Women Arts, Los Amigos, Phi Theta Kappa, Alpha Kappa Delta, Alpha Delta Mu, Young Dems. Avocations: reading, gardening, gourmet cooking. Home: 102 Harding Mexia TX 76667

CHAMBERS, MARGARET-ANNE, art educator, muralist; d. Newland Wilson Phillips and Mary Louise Craft; m. William Hartsworth McAuley, Junior, Aug. 11, 1973 (div. Apr. 0, 1984); children: Justin Hartsworth McAuley, Meghan Elizabeth McAuley. AA, Sandhills C.C., So. Pines, N.C., 1969; BA in Arts Edn., K-12th, East Carolina U., Greenville, N.C., 1972. Cert. tchr. N.C., 1967. Viaual arts educator Winston-Salem/Forsyth County Sch., Winston-Salem, NC, 1972—79; visual arts educator Episcopal Day Sch., So. Pines, NC, 1984—85, Moore County Sch., Carthage, NC, 1985—. Arts camp dir./instr. Moore County Arts Coun., So. Pines, NC, 1992—94; visual arts instr. Camp Cherokee, Ga., 1989. Mural painting, Mission of the Apostles, Responcible Acting Student Tree, Donor Tree, Toni's Beachscape. Mem. Carthage Garden Club, NC, 1991, Carthage Hist. Com., NC, 1995; sec. Pines USABDA, So. Pines, NC, 2002. Grantee Grassroots Grant, Moore County Arts Coun., 2003. Mem.: N.C. Art Educators Assn. (assoc.). Christian. Avocations: ballroom dancing, landscaping, weaving, drawing and painting, clothing construction. Office: Moore County Sch hwy # 15/501 S Carthage NC 28327 Personal E-mail: dance19492001@yahoo.com.

CHAMBERS, MARJORIE BELL, historian; b. N.Y.C., Mar. 11, 1923; d. Kenneth Carter and Katherine (Totman) Bell; m. William Hyland Chambers, Aug. 8, 1945; children: Lee Chambers-Schiller, William Bell, Leslie Chambers Trujillo, Kenneth Carter. AB cum laude, Mt. Holyoke Coll., South Hadley, Mass., 1943; MA, Cornell U., 1948; PhD, U. N.Mex., 1974; LLD honoris causa, Ctrl. Mich. U., 1977; LHD (hon.), Wilson Coll., 1980, Northern Michigan U., 1982. Staff asst. Am. Assn. UN, League of Nations Assn., N.Y.C., 1944-45; program specialist dept. rural sociology Cornell U., Ithaca, N.Y., 1945-46, rsch. asst. dept. speech and drama, 1946-48; substitute tchr. Los Alamos (N.Mex.) Pub. Schs., 1962-65; project historian U.S. AEC, Los Alamos, 1965-69; adj. prof. U. N.Mex., Los Alamos, 1970-76, 84-85; pres. Colo. Women's Coll., Denver, 1976-78; dean Union Inst. and U. Grad. Sch. Interdisciplinary Arts and Scis., Cin., 1979—82, mem. core faculty Grad. Sch., 1979—; interim pres. Colby-Sawyer Coll., New London, N.H., 1985-86. Vis. prof. Cameron U., Lawton, Okla., 1974; commr., vice-chair N.Mex. Commn. on Higher Edn., Santa Fe, 1987-91; dir. N.Mex. Endowment for Humanities, 1995-2002, sec.-treas. 2001-2002; mem. bd. dirs. Coun. Ind. Colls. and Univs., Santa Fe, 1991-2001; rep. Los Alamos County Labor Mgmt. Bd.; lectr. U. N.Mex., Albuquerque, 1986. Contbr. articles to profl. jours. Coun. treas. Sangre de Cristo Girl Scouts Am., 2002; chair Los Alamos County Coun., 1976, councilor, 1975-76, 79; Rep.candidate N.Mex. 3d Congl. Dist., 1982, lt. gov. N.Mex., 1986; chair Sec. of Navy's Advisor Bd. on Edn. and Tng., Washington and Pensacola, Fla., 1981-89; chair Citizen Bd. of U.S. Army Command and Gen. Staff Coll., Fort Leavenworth, Kans., 1989-1992; acting chair, vice-chair adminstrn. Pres. Carter's Com. for Women, Washington, 1977-80; chair Pres. Ford's Nat. Adv. Bd. on Women's Ednl. Programs, Washington, Los Alamos County Pers. Bd., 1985-90, mem. bd., 1983-90; mem. nat. adv. coun . U.S. SBA, 1990-92; mem. Los Alamos and N.Mex. Rep. Ctrl. com., 1982—; trustee Colby-Sawyer Coll., New London, N.H., 1980-89; pub. mem. U.S. Dept. State Fgn. Svc. selection bd., 1978; mem. U.S. del. UN Conf. Women, Copenhagen, 1980; bd. dirs. N.Mex. Endowment for the Humanities, 1997—. Recipient Teresa d'Avila award Coll. St. Teresa, Winona, Minn., 1978, Disting. Woman award U. N.Mex. Alumni Assn., Albuquerque, 1990, N.Mex. Disting. Pub. Svc. award Gov. and Awards Coun., Albuquerque, 1991, Zia award U. N.Mex. Alumni Assn., 2001; named Outstanding N.Mex. Woman Gov. and Com. on Status of Women, Albuquerque, 1988, 89, Lifetime Achievement award, 2003. Mem. AAUW (life, U.S. rep. coun. 1973-75, nat. pres. 1975-79, pres. Edn. Found.), DAR, Bus. and Profl. Women (Los Alamos parliamentarian and dist. parliamentarian 1991-93), Nat. Women's Polit. Caucus (gov. bd. conv., keynoter, vice-chair Rep. caucus 1971-89), Internat. Women's Forum (founding mem. Colo. forum), N.Mex. Hist. Soc. (pres.), Los Alamos Hist. Soc. (pres., Sangre de Cristo Girl Scouts "Woman of Distinction" 1996). Presbyterian. Avocations: figure skating, skiing, swimming, painting, public speaking.

CHAMBERS, RUTH COE, writer; d. Walter Homer Coe and Ruth Lucille Johnson; m. Jack Allen Chambers, Aug. 24, 1957; children: Melissa Ann, Wendy Colleen. BA, Calif. State U., 1981. Coord. of info. services projects U. of Pitts., Pittsburgh, Pa., 1986—89; grad. coord. biol. sci. U. of Md., Baltimore, Md., 1989—91; adminstrv. asst. Fla. C.C., Jacksonville, Fla., 1991—2001. Editl. readers bd. Kalliope A Jour. of Women's Lit. and Art, Jacksonville, Fla., 1994—; planning com. Fla. First Coast Writers' Festival, Jacksonville, Fla., 2001—. Author: (novel) The Chinaberry Album, (short story) Uncle Henry, Friends; contbr. articles to profl. jours. Mem.: Phi Kappa Phi. Democrat-Npl. Home: 2028 Marye Brant Loop N Neptune Beach FL 32266 Personal E-mail: ruthcchambers@aol.com.

CHAMBERS, SARA LYNN, music educator; b. Fort Dodge, Iowa, Jan. 7, 1974; d. Roland Eugene and LaVonne Frances Beneke; m. Sean William Chambers, Oct. 21, 2000; children: Julianna Nicole Sorenson, Logan Paul. BA in Music, Truman State U., 1995; MusM in Edn., Wichita State U., 2002. Music educator k-12 Wichita (Kans.) Pub. Schs., 1998—. Pvt. music instr., Wichita, Kans., 1991—. Music min., ch. pianist Risen Savior Luth. Ch., Wichita, Kans., 2000. Mem.: Sigma Alpha Iota (life; v.p. of ritual 2000—01, Rose of Honor 1995). Lutheran. Avocation: outdoor activities with family. Home: 6725 Kerman Dr Park City KS 67219 Office: Wichita Public Schs 201 N Water Wichita KS 67201 Personal E-mail: texbeneke@cox.net.

CHAMBERS-MANGUM, FRANSENNA ETHEL, special education educator; b. Meridian, Miss., June 27, 1957; d. Forrest S. and Betty (Wade) Chambers; 1 child, Richard Jomar Sullivan. BS, Jackson State U., 1979, MA, 1980, EdS, 1986. Cert. tchr., Miss., secondary adminstr., Miss. Chpt. tchr. Meridian Pub. Schs., 1979; tchr. spl. edn. Magee (Miss.) Pub. Sch., 1980-84; speech pathologist Heritage Sch. Learning Disability, Jackson, Miss., 1984-85, Canton (Miss.) Pub. Schs., 1985-86, spl. edn. tchr., 1986-88, pre-sch. coord., 1988-89; tchr. spl. edn. lang. delayed Jackson (Miss.) Pub. Schs., 1989-90, tchr. spl. edn., 1990—, mid. sch. reading tchr., 1993—. Miss. Writing Project cons. tchr., 1989—, Adult Edn. tchr. (ages 16-65). Writer and editor poems. Mem. Miss. Registrar Voters Com., Jackson, 1975—, Vista/Peace Corps, Jackson, 1980, NAACP, Jackson, 1982-85; bd. dirs., sec. and coord. Roshea Recovery Ctr., 1993—; tchr. Sunday sch., Jackson, 1992. Named Miss Miss. Elks, 1972-74, Miss Miss. Congeniality, Jaycees, 1972; Black Women's Assn. partial scholar, 1975. Mem. Miss. Writers of Am., Miss. Assn. Colls. and Evaluator Univs., Miss. Assn. Tchrs. (evaluator 1986—, Educator of Yr.), Learning Disabled Assn. Miss., Miss. Assn. Edn., Eastern Star, Daus. of Isis. Democrat. Avocations: writing poetry, public relations. Home: 1772 Casteel Dr Jackson MS 39204-3508

CHAMBERS-MCCARTY, LORRAINE, painter, educator; b. Detroit, Aug. 17, 1920; Student, Detroit Art Acad., 1938, Stephens Coll., 1940, Wayne State U., 1942; studied with, Glen Michaels, Emil Weddidge, Robert Wilbert, Guy Palazzola, Ray Fleming, Edgar Yaeger, Hughie Lee Smith, Bertold Schweitz, Thomas Hart Benton, Carol Wald, Adolph Dehn. Mem. faculty Flint Inst. Arts, Mich., 1970-85, Grosse Point (Mich.) War Meml., 1972-90; pvt. tchr. art Royal Oak, Mich.; mem. faculty Muskegon (Mich.) Inst. Arts, 1978-80, Flint Inst. Arts, 1978—; artist in residence Stephens Coll., Columbia, Mo., 1981; now juror, critic, lectr., tchr. pvt. profl. students. Advisor, designer Internat. Women's Air & Space Mus., Ohio, 1986-00, Okla., juror, critic in field, lectr.in field; ofcl. artist USAF, 1981-99; instr. Birmingham Bloomfield (Mich.) Art Assn., Islanders of St. Loud-Workshop Retreats in No. Mich., 1979-94, Paint Creek Ctr. for Arts, Rochester, Mich., Mt. Clemens Ctr. for Arts, Mich., Flint Inst. Arts,, Muskegon Mus. of Art, Jesse Besser Mus., Alpena, Ella Sharpe Mus., Jackson, Mich, Ctr. for Creative Studies, Detroit, Art League, Marco Island, Fla., Blue Water Art Assn., Stephens Coll., Mo., Milford Fine Arts Assn., Mich., 1990-00, Sanibel-Captiva Art Assn., Fla. others; cons. Greenfield Village Mus., 1991-00; mentor U. Mich., 1992, Cranbrook Art Acad.; trustee, designer Internat. Women's Air and Space Mus., Cleve., 1997—. Numerous one woman shows including Midland Arts Coun., 1978, Dayton Art Inst., 1978, Flint Inst. Arts, 1980, Nat. Acad. Arts and Letters, 1980, Stephens Coll., 1981; numerous group shows including Women '71, DeKalb, Ill., Butler Mus. Am. Art, Youngstown, Ohio, Detroit Inst. Arts, 1980, Ohio Arts Coun. Nat. Traveling Show, 1982; represented in permanent collections including Smithsonian Nat. Air and Space Mus., Muskegon Mus. Art, Butler Mus. Am. Art, Dow Chem. Co., Midland, Mich., No. Ill. U., DeKalb, K Mart Internat. Hdqrs., Troy, Mich., Capital City Airport, Lansing, R.L. Polk Co., Detroit, Bohn Aluminum and Brass, Southfield, Mich., Jug Pilots P047s, N.Y.C., Am. Natural Resources Hdq., Beech Aircraft, Wichita, Cessna Aircraft Corp., Dennos Mus., Federal Aviation Admintsrn., Flint Inst. Arts, Internat. Women's Air and Space Mus., Mich. Dept. Aviation, Renaissance Ctr.; commns. include murals for Gen. Dynamics Landsystems 1 Mich., Alpena Light & Power Co., art works for Lear Siegler Seating Co., Mich., 4 H Hdqrs., Washington, Trusswall Internat., Mich., R.L Polk Co., Mich., Capitol City Airport, Mich., Gerald Behaylo, Mich., Upjohn Pharm. Hdqs., Mich., Dow Chem. Co., Mich., Internat. Women's Air and Space Mus., Hi-Lex Corp., Mich. and Japan; producer TV series The Artist in You; inventor, designer Artist's Eye: Visual Aid for Artists. Mem. exec. com. Oakland County Cultural Coun. Recipient numerous awards including Purchase prize Butler Mus. Am. Art, 1969, Grand Jury award 16th Ann. Mid-Mich., Best Painting by a Woman award Detroit Inst. Arts, 1971, Disting. Alumnae award Stephens Coll., 1982, 1st place award Nat. Fedn. Local Cable Programmers, 1984; recipient grant Lester Hereward Cooke Found., 1984, Ossabaw Island Project, 1965, 67, 72; named creative artist, Mich. Coun. Arts, 1983, master to apprentice, Mich. Coun. Arts, 1983, artists consultancy, Mich. Coun. Arts, 1983. Mem. Detroit Soc. Women Painters and Sculptors, All Women Transcontinental Air Race Assn., Mich. Watercolor Soc., Artists Equity Assn., Mich. Acad. Arts Sci. Letters. Home: 1112 Pinehurst Ave Royal Oak MI 48073-3370

CHAMBLISS, LINDA R. obstetrician, gynecologist, consultant; b. Summit, N.J., Feb. 13, 1951; d. Robert E. and Alice (Dunne) C. BSN, Duke U., 1973; MD, Mich. State U., 1980. Diplomate Am. Bd. Ob-Gyn. Pediat. intern U. Chgo., 1980—81; resident in ob-gyn. Cook County Hosp., Chgo., 1981—85; fellow in maternal-fetal medicine U. So. Calif.-L.A. County Hosp., 1988—90; chief obstetrics Indian Health Svcs., Tuba City, Ariz., 1985-88; dir. obstetrics Maricopa Med. Ctr., Phoenix, 1990—; clin. prof. ob-gyn. U. Ariz., 2001—, clin. prof. family and cmty. medicine. Comdr. USPHS, 1985—. Recipient Alumna Excellence award Mich. State U., 1996, Nat. Faculty Excellence award Coun. on Resident Edn. in Ob-Gyn., 1995. Fellow ACOG; ; mem. AMA (cons.), AAUW, Soc. for Maternal Fetal Medicine, Am. Women's Med. Assn. Democrat. Office: Maricopa Med Ctr Dept Obstetrics 2601 E Roosevelt St Phoenix AZ 85008-4973

CHAMLEE, ANN COMBEST, music educator; b. Waco, Tex., Jan. 5, 1934; d. Otis Carter Ray and Hazel Meharg; children: Ann Alisabeth Chamlee, Margaret Carter Chamlee Zabcik. BM, Baylor U., 1969, MM, 1987; postgrad., Sam Houston State U., 1978-82. Exec. sec. Rocketdyne, McGregory, Tex., 1953-56; legal sec. Brown Assocs., Temple, Tex., 1977-80; fashion salesperson The Rosebud, Temple, Tex., 1980-85; choir master, organist Covenant Luth. Ch., Temple, Tex., 1984-89; piano tchr. Temple, Tex., 1964-87; music educator Temple Coll., 1988—. Artist in schs. Cultural Activities Ctr., Temple, 1980—. Author: Music Fundamentals Workbook, 1989, Two Halves Make a Whole, 1985. Performer with Linda Kowalski Cmty. Concert Tour, Ind., 1978; music dir. Gatesville/Milam County Tex.; bd. dirs. City Fedn. Womens Club, Temple, Temple Civic Theatre, 1998—. Recipient Outstanding Cmty. Vol. award City Fedn. of Womens Club, 1991, U2 award Child Help, Inc., 1991, Musician of Yr. award Wildflower Guild, 1994. Mem. Nat. Music Tchrs. Assn., Tex. Coalition for Quality in Arts Edn. (bd. dirs. 1995—), Music Club of Temple (past pres. 1968-89), Ctrl. Tex. Music Tchrs. Assn. (past pres. 1970-72, 94-96), Tex. Music Tchrs. Assn. (conv. presenter 1993, 97), Nat. Piano Guild (judge 1980-97), Lions (bd. dirs. 1993-95, Hon. Lion or Yr. 1970, Lion of Yr. 1993). Office: Temple Coll 2600 S 1st St Temple TX 76504-7435

CHAMPAGNE, MARY T. dean; BSN, San Jose State Coll., 1968; MSN, U. Tex., Austin, 1975, PhD, 1981. Prof. U. Nebr. Med. Ctr., 1977-82, U. N.C., Chapel Hill, 1982-90; prof. sch. Nursing Duke U., Durham, N.C., 1991—, dean Sch. Nursing. Cons. Ctr. Minority Health, 1993—. Mem. editl. rev. bd. Diabetes Spectrum, 1987-90; manuscript reviewer Rsch. in Nursing and Health, 1989, Jour. Gerontology: Med. Scis., 1989, Jour. Profl. Nursing; co-editor: Key Aspects of Comfort: Management of Pain, Fatigue, and Nausea, 1989, Key Aspects of Caring for the Chronically Ill: Hospital to Home, 1993, Key Aspects of Caring for the Acutely Ill: Technological Aspects, Patient Education and Quality of Life, 1995; contbr. articles to profl. jours. Office: Duke U Med Ctr PO Box 3322 Durham NC 27710-0001

CHAMPE, PAMELA CHAMBERS, biochemistry educator, writer; b. Oakland, Calif., Aug. 29, 1945; d. Robert Leroy and Leah June (Musser) Chambers; m. Sewell Preston Champe, June 28, 1969 (dec.); stepchildren: Mark Adrian, Sewell Peter. BA, Stanford U., 1967; MS, Purdue U., 1969; PhD, Rutgers U., 1974. Instr. Rutgers Med. Sch., Piscataway, N.J., 1974-76; asst. prof. Robert Wood Johnson Med. Sch. U. Medicine and Dentistry N.J., Piscataway, 1977-84, assoc. prof. Robert Wood Johnson Med. Sch., 1984-96; prof. emeritus Robert Wood Johnson Med. Sch., 1996—. Lectr. several med. schs. and tng. programs. Co-editor: Gene Families of Collagen and Other Proteins, 1980; co-author: Biochemistry (Lippincott's Illus. Revs.), 1987, 3d edit., 2004; co-author, co-editor: Pharmacology (Lippincott's Illus. Revs.), 2d edit., 1997, Microbiology (Lippincott's Illus. Revs.), 2001. Health and Human Svcs. grantee, 1988-94; recipient Nat. award Basic Sci. Educator of the Yr., 1995. Mem. AAAS, Assn. Am. Med. Colls., N.Y. Acad. Scis., Alpha Omega Alpha. Avocation: malacology. Office: U Medicine and Dentistry NJ Robert Wood Johnson Med Sch 675 Hoes Ln Piscataway NJ 08854-5627

CHAMPEY, ELAINE, science and technology research coordinator; b. Amityville, N.Y., Sept. 1, 1950; d. Chris Strum-Arden and Celia Strum; m. Michael Champey, June 20, 1976; children: Christine Anne, Michael Edward, Lauren Marie. BA in Polit. Sci., St. John's U., 1971, postgrad., 1974-76; M in Liberal Scis., SUNY, Stony Brook, 1993. Permanent cert. in chemistry, biology, gen. sci. Rsch. technician dept. pharmacology SUNY, Stonybrook, 1977-80; pvt. piano instr. Smithtown, N.Y., 1980-96; substitute tchr. St. Anthony's H.S. Smithtown Sch. Dist., 1991-96, tchr., 1996—; adj. prof SUNY, Albany, 1999—. Cons. Dept. Edn. Grant, 1999; technician tissue culture Procs. of NAS, 1978, technician biochem. assays, 1980; mentor finalists Siemens-Westinghouse Sci. Competition, 1999, 2000, 02. Named Tchr. of Merit, Intel Sci. Talent Search, 1998-2002; recipient Commendation for finalist Internat. Sci. and Engring. Fair, 2000, Recognition award N.Y. Sci. Talent Search, 1998, 99, 2000, 2001, 2002; First Robotic Advisor, 2001-2003; Recognition award Jr. Scis. and Humanities Symposium, 2001. Mem. N.Y. State Tchr. Union, Smithtown Parent Tchr. Assn., Smithtown Sch. Dist. Tchr. Ctr. (vice chair 1996-2001, mini-grantee 1998), Smithtown H.S. Industry Adv. Bd. (exec. bd., com. chair 1996-2003), Suffolk County Sci. Tchrs. Assn. (historian 1999-2000). Avocations: playing piano, singing. E-mail: echampey@juno.com.

CHAMPION, KIM PANETSKI, psychologist; b. Rochester, N.Y., Mar. 17, 1968; d. Charles Edward Panetski, Jr. and Carl Hughes Panetski; m. Christopher William Champion, Aug. 25, 1990; children: Malachi Christopher, Rachael Marie. BA summa cum laude, U. Detroit, 1990; MA, U. Del., 1995, PhD, 1998. Lic. psychologist Del. Supervising aux. officer U. Detroit Pub. Safety, 1987—90; child rehab. specialist Mary Cariola Children's Ctr., Rochester, NY, 1987—90; infant/toddler tchr. Gretchen's House, Ann Arbor, Mich., 1990—91; psychologist Pike Creek Psychol. Ctr., Newark, 1995—; psychology intern Devereux Found., Malvern, Pa., 1997—98. Pres. Wellspring Svcs., Inc., Newark, 2003—. Author, designer: child abuse prevention program and manual Mastering Assertiveness and Personal Safety, 2000. Scholar, U. Detroit, 1986—90; Child Abuse Prevention grantee, Del. Children's Trust Fund, 2000—03. Mem.: APA, Christian Assn. for Psychol. Studies. Avocations: reading, hiking, camping, travel. Office: Pike Creek Psychol Ctr 8 Polly Drummond Hill Rd Newark DE 19711

CHAMPION, NORMA JEAN, communications educator, state legislator; b. Oklahoma City, Jan. 21, 1933; d. Aubra Dell (dec.) and Beuleah Beatrice (Flanagan) Black; m. Richard Gordon Champion, Oct. 3, 1953 (dec.); children: Jeffrey Bruce, Ashley Brooke. BA in Religious Edn., Cen. Bible Coll., Springfield, Mo., 1971; MA in Comm., S.W. Mo. State U., 1978; PhD in Tech., U. Okla., 1986. Producer, hostess The Children's Hour, Sta. KYTV-TV, NBC, Springfield, 1957-86; asst. prof. Cen. Bible Coll., 1968-84; prof. broadcasting Evangel U., Springfield, 1978—; mem. Springfield City Coun., 1987-92, Mo. Ho. of Reps., Jefferson City, 1993—2002, Mo. Senate, 2003—. Adj. faculty Assemblies of God Theol. Sem., Springfield, 1987—, pres. coun.; bd. dirs. Global U.; mem. Commn. on Higher Edn., Assemblies of God, 1998—, Mo. Film Commn., Mo. Pain Mgmt. Bd.; Mo. Film Commn., 2003-; spkr. Internat. Pentecostal Press Assn. World Conf., Singapore, 1989. Mem. bd Mo. Access to Higher Edn. Trust, 2003-, pain mgmt. bd., 2004-, Boys & Girls Town of Mo.; adv. coun. pain mgmt. Mo. Film Commn.; judge Springfield (Mo.) City Schs. Recipient commendation resolution Mo. Ho. of Reps., 1988; numerous award for The Children's Hour; Aunt Norma Day named in her honor City of Springfield, 1976. Mem. Nat. Broadcast Edn. Assn., Mo. Broadcast Edn. Assn., Nat. League Cities, Mo. Mcpl. League (human resource com. 1989, intergovtl. rels. com. 1990), Nat. Assn. Telecom. Officers and Advisors, PTA (life). Republican. Mem. Assemblies of God Ch. Avocations: gardening, reading, interior decoration. Home: 3609 S Broadway Ave Springfield MO 65807-4505 Office: Evangel Univ 1111 N Glenstone Ave Springfield MO 65802-2125 Business E-Mail: mchampion@senate.state.mo.us.

CHAMPION, SARA STEWART, lawyer; b. Boston, Apr. 1, 1942; d. William Julius Champion and Mary Stewart Cunningham; m. Wayne L. Kinsey, Dec. 12, 1964 (div. Feb. 1971); m. John Q. Adams, Apr. 25, 1998 (div. Oct. 2000). BA, Duke U., 1963; MA, U. Calif., Davis, 1974; JD cum laude, N.Y. Law Sch., 1992. Bar: N.Y. 1992, Conn. 1992. Rsch. analyst Nat. Security Agy., Ft. Meade, Md., 1963-65; instr. Russian Def. Lang. Inst., Monterey, Calif., 1970-72; claims rep. Social Security Adminstrn., San Francisco, 1974-78, claims rep., ops. supr. N.Y.C., 1978-87; office adminstr. Bachelder Law Offices, N.Y.C., 1987-97, assoc., 1992-97, ptnr., 1997—2002; ptnr., shareholder, head NY exec. compensation practice Vedder, Price, Kaufman and Kammholz, N.Y.C., 2002—. Mem.: DAR, Colonial Dames Am., Soc. Mayflower Descs., New Eng. Soc., Silver Spring Country Club (Ridgefield, Conn.), Univ. Club, Wianno Yacht Club (Osterville, Mass.). Avocation: genealogy. Office: Vedder Price Kaufman & Kammholz 805 3d Ave New York NY 10022 E-mail: schampion@vedderprice.com.

CHAMPLIN, DEBORAH LOUISE, medical/surgical nurse, consultant; b. Brabanta, Congo, Oct. 26, 1957; arrived in U.S., 1963; d. G. Darrell and Louise May (Grings) Champlin. Cert. of completion, Lancaster (Pa.) Bible Coll., 1976; diploma, Jameson Meml. Hosp. Sch. Nursing, 1979; Christian workers diploma magna cum laude, Piedmont Bible Coll., Winston-Salem, N.C., 1982; diploma BLET, Guildford Tech. C.C., Greensboro, N.C., 1986. RN Ariz., Calif., Pa., Tex. Staff nurse pediat. Mansfield (Ohio) Gen. Hosp., 1979—80; sch. nurse Piedmont Bible Coll., Winston Salem, 1980—82; pvt. duty nurse various temp. agys. Winston Salem, 1982—85; IV therapy nurse Wesley Long Cmty. Hosp., Greensboro, 1985—86, operating rm. nurse, 1986—87; ind. contract travel RN various agys., 1987—; interim mgmt. specialist, cons. RN, 1987—. Pres., owner Tygger Too, Inc., Greensboro, 1987—2000. Mem.: Assn. Oper. Rm. Nurses. Republican. Avocations: swimming, horseback riding, reading, motorcycling, nature exploring. Home: 2405 Lourance Blvd Greensboro NC 27407-6030

CHAN, JANET, publishing executive; children: Jack, Laura. Sr. editor Glamour Mag.; exec. dir. Good Housekeeping, Redbook; v.p., editor Parenting Mag., 1996—. Editl. dir. Time Inc.'s Parenting Group including Baby Talk, Family Life and Healthy Pregnancy. Office: The Parenting Group Inc 530 Fifth Ave 4th Fl New York NY 10036

CHAN, SIU-WAI, materials science educator; b. Hong Kong, Feb. 27, 1958; m. Kung Yip Cheung, July 6, 1984; children: L.Y., K.Y. BS, Columbia U., 1980; ScD, MIT, 1985. Summer instr. IBM, Fishkill, N.Y., 1979, 80; rsch. assoc. MIT, Cambridge, 1980-85, tchg. asst., 1981; mem. tech. staff Bellcore, Murray Hill, N.J., 1985-86, Red Bank, N.J., 1986-90; assoc. prof. materials sci. Columbia U., N.Y., 1990—. Edn. coord. Chinese Sch. of CCC N.J., 1991-93. Presdl. Faculty fellow Nat. Sci. Found., 1993. Office: Columbia U Sch Engring & Applied Sci 510 Mudd Bldg, MC 4714 500 W 120th St New York NY 10027-8031

CHAN, WILMA, county official; b. Boston; married; 2 children. BA, Wellesley Coll.; M in Policy Analysis and Adminstrn., Stanford U. Mem. Oakland (Calif.) Bd. Edn., 1990-94, pres., 1991-93; supr. dist. 3, then v.p. Alameda County Bd. Suprs., Oakland, 1994—; mem. Calif. Ho. of Reps., 2001—. Chair legis. com. and health com. Alameda County Bd. Suprs., chmn. budget tech. com., bd. rep. to Alameda Reuse and Redevel. Authority, San Francisco Bay Conservation Devel. Commn., Local Agy. Formation Commn.; past program coord. Effective Parenting Info. for Children. Office: Alameda County Bd Suprs 1221 Oak St Ste 536 Oakland CA 94612-4224 also: PO Box 942849 Sacramento CA 94249

CHANATRY-HOWELL, LORRAINE MARIE, artist, designer, educator; b. Utica, N.Y., Aug. 6, 1934; d. Elias and Catherine (Esso) Chanatry; m. James Burt Howell, III, Feb. 18, 1995. BFA, Syracuse U., 1955; MA, Cath. U. Am., 1958; postgrad., Temple U., 1963, U. San Francisco-Guadalajara, Mex., 1965; EdD, U. South Fla., 1966; postgrad., U. Valencia, Spain, 1966, Am. U. Beirut, 1968. Cert. art tchr. Art supr./tchr. New Hartford (N.Y.) Ctrl. Sch., 1955-56; guidance counselor Washington-Lee H.S., Arlington, Va., 1959-60; interior designer B. Altman & Co., N.Y.C., 1960-61; chmn. art depts. Maitland (Fla.) Jr. H.S., 1962-64; chmn. art dept. Mid-Fla. Tech. Inst., Orlando, 1964-70, Liverpool (N.Y.) H.S., 1970-72; owner, dir. Lorraine Marie Art Ctr., Liverpool, 1972-73, Utica, N.Y., 1973-94; freelance artist and designer, cons., 1994—. Cultural amb., Egypt, Syria, Lebanon, Jordan, 1961; adj. prof. fine arts Mohawk Valley C.C., Utica, 1988-94, Utica Coll., 1976-77. Bd. govs. Cath. U. Am., Washington, 1995—. Mem. Syracuse U. Alumni Assn. (pres. 1964-70, sec. 1980-88, class '55 revision com.), Alpha Omicron Pi (charter 2d Century Soc., v.p. alumni chpt. Orlando 1966-69, pres. Syracuse 1970-72, found. amb., 2000—). Greek Melchite Catholic. Avocations: travel, gardening, sewing. Home: 23 Shadow Brook Dr Bridgeton NJ 08302-3616 also: 429 San Jose Dr Winter Haven FL 33884-1742

CHANCE, JANE, English literature educator; b. Neosho, Mo., Oct. 26, 1945; d. Donald William and Julia (Mile) C.; m. Dennis Carl Nitzsche, June, 1966 (div. Mar. 1969); 1 child, Therese; m. Paolo Passaro, Apr. 30, 1981,(div. May 2002); children: Antony Damian, Joseph Sebastian. BA in English with honors and highest distinction, Purdue U., 1967; AM in English, U. Ill., 1968, PhD in English, 1971. Lectr. U. Saskatchewan, Can., 1971-72, asst. prof., 1972-73; asst. prof. English, Rice U., Houston, 1973-77, assoc. prof., 1977-80, prof., 1980—; hon. rsch. fellow U. Coll. U. London, 1977-78. Sec., Scientia, 1982-83, acting dir., 1983-84; dir. NEH Summer Seminar for Coll. Tchrs. on Chaucer and Mythography, 1985, NEH Inst. for Coll. Tchrs. on Medieval Women, 1997; pres., founder TEAMS, 1986-89; founding dir. med. studies program Rice U., 1986-92; founding mem. Rice U. Commn. on Women, 1986-88; resident Rockefeller Found., Bellagio, Italy, 1988; mem. Sch. Hist. Studies Inst. for Advanced Study, Princeton U., 1988-89; vis. rsch. fellow Inst. for Advanced Studies in Humanities, U. Edinburgh, summer, 1994; Eccles fellow Humanities Ctr., U. Utah, 1994-95; spkr. in field; lectr. in field. Author: The Genius Figure in Antiquity and the Mid. Ages, 1975, Tolkien's Art: A Mythology for Eng., 1979, Woman as Hero in Old English Lit., 1986, The Lord of the Rings: The Mythology of Power, 1992; : rev. edit., 2001, Japanese trans., 2003, Medieval Mythography: From Roman North Africa to the Sch. of Chártres, AD 433-1177 (South Ctrl. MLA book prize, 1994), The Mythographic Chaucer: The Fabulation of Sexual Politics, 1995, Medieval Mythography, vol. 2: From the Sch. of Chártres to the Ct. at Avignon, 1177-1350, 2000; translator: Christine de Pizan's Letter of Othea to Hector, 1990; editor: The Mythographic Art: Classical Fable and the Rise of the Vernacular in Early France and Eng., 1990, Medievalism in the Twentieth Century, Studies in Medievalism, vol. 2:2, 1983, The Inklings and Others, vol. 3:3, 1990, Gender and Text in the Later Mid. Ages, 1986, rpt. pb., 2003, The Assembly of Gods, 1999, Tolkien the Medievalist, 2002, Tolkien and the Invention of Myth: A Reader, 2004, Women Medievalists and the Academy, 2004; co-editor: Mapping the Cosmos, 1985, Approaches to Tchg. Sir Gawain, 1986; gen. editor: Focus Libr. of Medieval Women, 1988—, Boydell & Brewer Libr. of Medieval Women, 1997—, series editor: Greenwood Guides to Hist. Events in the Medieval World, 2001—, Praeger Series on the Mid. Ages, 2003—, mem. editl. bd.: Coll. Lit., 2002—. Bd. dirs. Rice U. Press, 1981-88. NEH fellow, 1977-78, Guggenheim fellow, 1980-81, ACLS Travel grantee, 1982, Mellon leave Rice U., 1988, Disting. Faculty Tchg. fellow, 1995, Ctr. for Study Cultures fellow, 1998, NEH Fellow, St. Louis Univ. Ctr. for Med. Studies, 2003, Mellon Fellow, Pope Pius Vatican Film Libr., 2003; recipient Women's Ctr. IMPACT award Rice U., 1998. Mem. AAUP (Rice U. chpt. sec., treas. 1975-76), MLA, Scientia (acting dir. 1983-84, sec. 1982-00), Internat. Soc. Classical Tradition, Internat. Neo-Latin Soc., Internat. Chaucer Soc. (internat. adv. bd.), Tex. Faculty Assn. (mem. exec. com., 1995-99, v.p., 1998-2000, Achievement award 1998). Avocations: book collecting, photography, travel. Office: Rice U Dept English MS 30 PO Box 1892 Houston TX 77251-1892 Office Phone: 713-348-2625. Business E-Mail: jchance@rice.edu.

CHANCE, M. SUE, psychiatrist, author, publisher; b. Paris, Tex., Apr. 27, 1942; d. John Bruce and Sally (McDaniel) Scott; m. Thomas E. Chance, Jr., Jan. 1, 1976 (div. Apr. 1989); m. Arthur J. Overgaag, July 18, 1992; 1 child, Jim Scott (dec.). BA, Angelo State U., San Angelo, Tex., 1971; MD, U. Tex., Galveston, 1978. Diplomate Am. Bd. Psychiatry and Neurology. Intern U. Okla. Health Sci. Ctr., Oklahoma City, 1978-79; resident in psychiatry Menninger's Clinic, Topeka, 1980-81, 82-83; pvt. practice, Houston, 1983-86, Tyler, Tex., 1986-87, Dallas, 1987-92; med. dir. adult psychiatry Mainland Ctr. Hosp., Texas City, Tex., 1984-86; unit chief adult chem. dependency unit Willowbrook Hosp., Waxahachie, Tex., 1987-90; med. dir. adult svcs. The Cedars Hosp., De Soto, Tex., 1990-91; dir. geriatric cons. svc. Chestnut Hill Hosp., Travelers Rest, S.C., 1995-96; sr. psychiatrist Pickens (S.C.) MHC, 2002—. Author: Stronger Than Death: When Suicide Touches Your Life, 1992 (Menninger Popular Press award 1993), A Voice of My Own: A Verbal Box of Chocolates, 1993, (novel) Stoneflowers, 1994; columnist Bonne Chance, Psychiat. Times, 1986-96. Recipient Esther Haar award Am. Acad. Psychoanalysis, 9195, award for cover design Nat. Assn. Ind. Pubs., 1994. Fellow Am. Psychiat. Assn.

CHANDLER, ALICE, higher education consultant, university president; b. Bklyn., May 29, 1931; d. Samuel and Jenny (Meller) Kogan; m. Horace Chandler, June 10, 1954; children: Seth, Donald, Barnard C. AB, Columbia U., 1951, MA, 1953, PhD, 1960; LHD, Kean U., 1997, Ramapo Coll., 2001. Instr. Skidmore Coll., 1953-54; lectr. Columbia U. Barnard Coll., 1954-55, Hunter Coll., CUNY, 1956-57; from instr. to prof. CCNY, 1961-76, v.p. instl. advancement, 1974-76, v.p. acad. affairs, 1974-76, provost, 1976-79, acting pres., 1979-80; pres. SUNY Coll., New Paltz, 1980-96; interim pres. Ramapo Coll., 2000-2001. Cons. in higher edn., 1996—; bd. dirs. Mohonk Mountain House, N.J. Coun. Humanities. Author: The Prose Spectrum: A Rhetoric and Reader, 1968, The Theme of War, 1969, A Dream of Order, 1970, The Rationale of Rhetoric, 1970, The Rationale of the Essay, 1971, From Smollett to James, 1980, Foreign Student Policy: England, France, and West Germany, 1985, Obligation or Opportunity: Foreign Student Policy in Six Major Receiving Countries, 1989, Access, Inclusion and Equity: Imperatives for America's Campuses, 1997, Public Higher Education and the Public Good: Public Policy at the Crossroads, 1998, Paying the Bill for International Education: Programs, Purposes, and Possibilities at the Millenium, 1999. Lizette Fisher fellow. Mem. Lotos, Phi Beta Kappa.

CHANDLER, ESTELLE T. artist; b. Redlands, Calif., Feb. 22, 1961; Exhibited in group shows at The Paper Crane, Half Moon Bay, Calif., 2000, Moondance Gallery, Stony Creek, Conn., 2000, Gallery Alexander, La Jolla, Calif., 2001, Papierie Landolt-Arbenz, Zurich, Switzerland, 2001, Boston (Mass.) Symphony, 2001, many others, Nat. Broadcasting Co., NBC, The Rikki Lake Show, The Nat. Cardiology Soc., Rand McNally, Inc., Thomas Nelson Gifts, Ltd., The Walt Disney Co., exhibited in group shows at Boston Symphony, 2001, Papierie Landolt-Arbenz, Zurich, Switzerland, 2001, Gallery Alexander, 2001. Office: 2002 W Chicago Ave 172 Chicago IL 60622

CHANDLER, FAY MARTIN, artist; b. Norfolk, Va., Sept. 15, 1922; d. Howard Gresham and Alpine Douglas (Gatling) Martin; m. Alfred Dupont Chandler Jr., Jan. 8, 1944; children: Alpine C. Bird, Mary C. Watt, Alfred D. III, Howard Martin. BA, Sweetbriar Coll., 1943; MFA, Md. Inst. Coll. Art, Balt., 1967. Coord., dir. Fell's Point Gallery Md. Inst. Coll. Art, 1968-73; fellow Va. Ctr. Creative Arts, Sweetbriar, 1993. Bd. dirs. Md. Inst. Alumni Coun., Nantucket Island Sch. Design and Arts, Mass., Boston Ctr. for the Arts; hon. bd. dirs. Mass. Vol. Lawyers for the Arts; founder, bd. dirs. The Art Connection, Boston; arts in edn. adv. coun. Harvard Grad. Sch. Edn.; mem. Coun. for the Arts at MIT. One-woman shows include Kenneth Taylor Little Gallery, Nantucket, 1973, 76, Fells Point Gallery, Balt., 1974, 76, Mills Gallery, Boston, 1974-88, Main St. Gallery, Nantucket, 1977, Ensign-Sibley Gallery, Nantucket, 1978, Sibley Gallery, Nantucket, 1980-85, Billiard Room Gallery, Cambridge, Mass., 1980, Helen Shlien Gallery, Boston, 1980, Bodley Gallery, N.Y.C., 1980, St. Botolph Club, Boston, 1982, Stebbins Gallery, Cambridge, Mass., 1987, Bentley Coll., Waltham, Mass., 1987, Columbia (Md.) Ctr. for the Arts, 1987, Babcock Gallery Sweet Briar Coll., Va., 1993, Wenham (Mass.) Mus., 1993, Nantucket Island Sch. Design Gallery, 1994, Boston Ctr. For the Arts, 1995, Children's Mus., Boston, 1996, Decker Gallery/Md. Inst. Art, 1997, Stenbaum Krauss Gallery, N.Y.C., 1997, Sacramento St. Gallery, Cambridge, Mass., 2002, Revolving Mus., Lowell, Mass.; exhibited in group shows. Bd. dirs. Friends of Art-Sweetbriar Coll., 2001—. Papers and slides chosen to be preserved Schlesinger Libr., Radcliffe Coll., Cambridge, Mass. Mem. Cambridge Art Assn. (bd. dirs.). Avocations: train trips, mystery books, philosophy. Home: 1010 Memorial Dr Apt 17E Cambridge MA 02138-4857 Studio: Engine House Studios 444 Western Ave Boston MA 02135-1016 E-mail: fay@dougwatt.com.

CHANDLER, HARRIETTE LEVY, state legislator, management consultant, educator; b. Balt., Dec. 20, 1937; d. S. Lester and Reba K. Levy; m. Burton Chandler, July 12, 1959; children: Frank Levy, Victoria Jane, Edward Lee. BA, Wellesley Coll., 1959; MA, Clark U., 1963, PhD, 1973; MBA, Simmons Coll., 1983; PhD in Pub. Adminstrn. (hon.), Worcester State Coll., 1998. High sch. history tchr. Worcester (Mass.) Pub. Schs., 1959-61; polit. sci. prof. Clark U., Worcester, 1973-77; prof. polit. sci. Tufts U., Medford, Mass., 1977-78; exec. dir. nat women's com. Brandeis U., Waltham, Mass., 1978-81; cons. Prime Computer, Natick, Mass., 1983-84; mgr. documentation tng. Adelie Corp., Cambridge, Mass., 1984-85, mgr. mktg. svcs., 1985-87, prin., 1987-89; dir. communication Open Software Found., Cambridge, 1989; mgmt. cons. Chandler Assocs., 1990—. Author: U.S. Soviet Relations During World War II, 1982. Chmn. com. on shareholder responsibility Clark U., 1982—86; com. mem. Worcester Sch., 1992—94, vice-chmn., 1994, Mass. Comm. on Common Core of Learning, 1994; chmn. bd. trustees Worcester Meml. Auditorium, 1987—89; founding mem. Worcester Women's Polit. Caucus, 1985, Worcester Com. Fgn. Rels.; incorporator YWCA, Greater Worcester Cmty. Found., Worcester Art Mus.; past pres. Jewish Healthcare Ctr.; state rep. 13th Worcester Dist., Mass. Legislature, 1995—2000, chair joint com. on health care, 1996—2000, state sen., 2001—, chair fed. fin. asst., 2001; vice chair health care Assembly on Fed. Issues, Nat. Coun. State Legislatures, 1998—99; mem. Dem. State Com., 1999—; co-chair Ctrl. Mass. Legis. Caucus, 2001—02, chair joint com. on pub. svc., 2002, chair joint com. on housing and urban devel., 2003—, vice-chair transp., 2003, joint com. on health care, long term debt, pub. safety, energy, and counties, 2003—; steering com. Reforming States Group. Mem.: Worcester Econs. Club. Jewish. Avocations: walking, swimming, knitting, reading. Home: 97 Aylesbury Rd Worcester MA 01609-1314 Office: Rm 518 State House Boston MA 02133

CHANDLER, JULIETTE ANNE, writer, communications executive; b. Denver, Jan. 10, 1959; d. Peter James Bissell and Ruby Louise (Chandler) Racine; m. Gregory Lanigan, May 9, 1992 (div. July 1996); 1 child, Brendan; m. Roy Boggie, Oct. 18, 1997. BA in Journalism, U. Md., 1981; cert. in writing, U. Calif., San Diego, 1990, cert. in hatha yoga, 1994. Tech. writer, trainer Computer Scis. Corp., San Diego, 1982-85; documentation mgr. Mantech Math. Corp., San Diego, 1985-88; bus. owner, writer, CFO, sec. Chandler Comms., Inc., Ventura, Calif., 1988—. Pub. rels. writer Westroots Bus. Writing, La Jolla, Calif., 1990; journalist; spkr. in field. Contbr. articles, columns to newspapers. Vol. 12-step recovery programs, Calif., 1987-97. Mem. Ventura County Writer's Club. Home: 654 Bellefontaine St Pasadena CA 91105-2441 Office: Chandler Comms Inc 1349 E Santa Clara St Apt 207 Ventura CA 93001-3248

CHANDLER, KATHLEEN, retired executive secretary; b. Clayton, Wis., Oct. 13, 1927; d. William Henry and Evelyn Jean (Vassau) Olson; m. Calvin Hewitt Chandler, Dec. 21, 1954; children: Sarah Kay, Blake Hewitt. BA in Bus./Psychology summa cum laude, Briar Cliff Coll., Sioux City, Iowa, 1991. Lic. realtor, Mass. Sec. to pres. Union State Bank, Amery, Wis., 1948-51; sec. to mgr. Social Security Adminstrn., Mpls., 1951-52; sec. to asst. contr. N.W. Banco, Mpls., 1952-54; sec. to v.p. Celanese Corp., Charlotte, N.C., 1954-55, Monsanto Chem. Co., St. Louis, 1955-58; exec. sec. AC Rochester divsn. Gen. Motors Corp., Sioux City, 1981-92. Editor GM plant newspaper Throttle Body Lines, 1982-92. Mem Welcom Wagon Club of Sun City West, Ariz., pres., 1997—. Mem. AAUW, PEO Sisterhood (treas. DQ chpt. 1995—), Sun City West Iowa Club (pres. 1995—). Presbyterian. Avocations: bridge, reading, art.

CHANDLER, KIMBERLEY LYNN, educational administrator; b. Waynesboro, Va., Sept. 28, 1961; d. Alden Hugh and Cecille Frances (Brooks) C. BA in Elem. Edn., Coll. William and Mary, 1984, MA in Edn./Gifted Edn., 1992, postgrad. Lic. educator, Va. Tchr. Fredericksburg (Va.) Pub. Schs., 1984-87, Henrico County Pub. Schs., Richmond, Va., 1987-98; gifted edn. resource specialist Hanover County Pub. Schs., Richmond, Va., 1998-2000; supr. enrichment programs, coord. of sci. K-12 Amherst County Pub. Schs., Va., 2000—03; cert. curriculum cons. Ctr. for Gifted Edn., 2002—; panel reviewer Jacob K. Javits Grant Program, U.S. Dept. Edn., 2002; postdoctoral fellow, curriculum coord. Ctr. for Gifted Edn. Coll. of William and Mary, Williamsburg, Va., 2003—. Summer sch. coord. Henrico County Pub. Schs., 1996, 97, staff devel. presenter, 1996, 97; curriculum cons. Coll. of William and Mary, Williamsburg, Va., 1996; presenter in field.; mem. gifted edn. staff devel. talent bank, mem. tchr. stds. com. Va. Dept. Edn.; mem. peer coaching program, Prin.'s Acad.; sch. renewal planning team facilitator Hanover County Pub. Schs.; mem. adj. faculty U. Va. Sch. Continuing and Profl. Studies, 2001—; instr. Casenex, Inc.; participant David L. Clark Grad. Student Seminar, 2003. Author: (curriculum unit) Literary Reflections, 1992; author: (with others) Aiming for Excellence-Gifted Program Standards: Annotations to the NAGC Pre-K-Grade 12 Gifted Program Standards, ERIC Research Report, 2002, (book review) Gifted and Talented International; editor (newsletter): Va. Assn. for the Gifted, 1999—. Vol. Hanover Humane Soc., 1994—, Habitat for Humanity Global Village Program, Nicaragua Disaster Relief Mission Team, 1999, Brazil VBS Mission Team, 2000; mem. Habitat for Humanity Global Village Team to South Africa, 2001. Recipient Doctoral Student award Nat. Assn. for Gifted Children, 2002, Hollingworth Rsch. award, 2003; grantee Henrico Edn. Found., 1997, Henrico Gifted Adv. Coun., 1997, Pntrs. in Arts grantee Richmond Arts Coun., 1996, Hanover Edn. Found., 1999, Coll. William and Mary, 2003; postdoctoral fellow Ctr. Gifted Edn., Coll. William and Mary, 2003—. Mem.: Va. Assn. for the Gifted (ex officio bd. dirs.), Va. Soc. for Tech. in Edn., Hanover County Prins. Acad., Nat. Assn. for Gifted Children (sec./treas. technol. divsn. 1997—99, sec./treas. profl. devel. divsn. 1997—99, chair profl. devel. divsn. 2003—, Harry Passow Classroom Tchr. scholarship 1997, Outstanding Curriculum award 2000, Doctoral Student award 2002, Hollingworth award 2003), Delta Kappa Gamma, Kappa Delta Pi (chpt. sec.). Home: 11444 New Farrington Ct Glen Allen VA 23059-1629 Office: Coll William and Mary Ctr for Gifted Edn PO Box 8795 Williamsburg VA 23187-8795 E-mail: kchan11444@aol.com.

CHANDLER, MARCIA SHAW BARNARD, farmer; b. Arlington, Mass., Aug. 22, 1934; d. John Alden and Grace Winifred (Copeland) Barnard; m. Samuel Butler Chandler, Aug. 31, 1952 (dec. 1986); children: Shawn Chandler Seddinger, Mark Thurmond, Matthew Butler. BA, Francis Marion Univ., Florence, S.C., 1976; MEd, U. S.C., 1985. Resource person United Cerebral Palsy of S.C., Dillon, 1976-79; instr. English Horry-Georgetown Tech. Coll., Conway, S.C., 1980-81; farm owner, mgr. Dillon; drama critic Dillon (S.C.) Herald, 1986—. Author: (with others) Best of Old Farmer's Almanac, First 200 Years, 1991, A Primer for the New Millennium, 1999; cover artist So. Bell Telephone Directory, 1988; artist Dillon County Lib., 1998. Bd. dirs., publicist, artist Dillon County Theatre, Inc., 1985—; publicist, bd. dirs., artist MacArthur Ave. Players, Dillon, 1990—; bd. dirs. Friends of Francis Marion U., 1985-95; pres. Dillon Area Arts Coun.,

1980-85, Jr. Charity League of Dillon, 1960-75; nat. poetry judge DAR, 1982; Dunbar libr. com., Dillon County, 1999. Recipient Honorable Commendation for civic involvement S.C. Ho. Reps., Mar. 22, 1990. Mem. Cousteau Soc., Ctr. Environ. Edn., Internat. Fund Animal Welfare, World Wildlife Fund, Nature Conservancy, Sea Shepherd Conservation Soc., Humane Soc. U.S., Ocean Conservancy. [illegible] animal welfare activities, theater, travel. Home: 309 E Reaves Ave Dillon SC 29536-1919 E-mail: marciacani@aol.com.

CHANDLER, MARGUERITE NELLA, real estate corporation executive; b. New Brunswick, N.J., May 16, 1943; d. Edward A. and Marguerite (Moore) C.; m. Ronald Wilson, May 30, 1964 (div. Nov. 1973); children: Mark, Adam; m. Richmond Shreve, Nov. 22, 1979; 1 child, Laura. BS in Acctg., Syracuse U., 1964; MS in Polit. Mgmt., George Washington U., 1988. Tax acct. Peat Marwick Mitchell, Providence, 1964; grant adminstr., psychology dept. Brown U., Providence, 1965; intern in devel. cons. Washington, 1973-75; prin., tng. cons. M. Chandler Assocs., 1975-76; mgmt. cons. Edmar Corp., Bound Brook, N.J., 1976-78, pres., chief exec. officer, 1978-90, pres., 1991—. Peace Corps vol., 1966-68; established Food Bank Network of Somerset County, 1982, pres., 1982-85; established Worldworks Found., Inc., 1983; founder PeopleCare Ctr., 1984, pres., 1984-86; bd. dirs. N.J. Coun. for Arts, 1986-87; pres. bd. trustees N.J. Coun. of Chs., 1985-90; bd. dirs. United Way Somerset Valley, 1984-91, gen. campaign chmn., 1985-86; recorder Blue Ribbon Com. on Ending Hunger in N.J., 1984-86; vol. Somerset Community Action Program, 1969-71, Missionaries of Charity, Calcutta, India, 1981; treas. Somerset County Day Care Assn., 1969-71; mem. N.J. Gov.'s Task Force on Pub./Pvt. Sector Initiatives, 1986-91; Dem. candidate for U.S. Congress Dist. 12, 1990; mem. adv. bd. US-USSR Youth Exch., Ptnrs. in Peacemaking, The Giraffe Project; mem. Gov.'s Adv. Coun. on Solid Waste Mgmt., 1991-92; chairperson numerous fund-raising events to combat world hunger; established Heritage Trail Assn. of Somerset County, pres. 1994—97; chmn. bd. dirs. Friends Retirement Inc., 1996—02. Named Woman of Yr., Women's Resource Ctr. Somerset County, 1983, Citizen of Yr., Somerset County C. of C., 1985, N.J. Chpt. Nat. Assn. Soc. Workers, 1986, Bus. and Profl. Women's Club, 1987, Person of Decade, Courier-News, 1989, Bus. Person of Yr., Bus. for Ctrl. N.J. mag., 1993; recipient People's Champion award Somerset Family Planning Svc., 1985, Disting. Svc. award N.J. Speech-Lang.-Hearing Assn., 1986, N.J. Women of Achievement award Douglass Coll. and N.J. Fedn. Women's Clubs, 1986, Brotherhood award Cen. Jersey chpt. Nat. Conf. Christians and Jews, 1986, Presdl. End Hunger award, 1987, Somerset Alliance for the Future Quality of Life award, 1996. Mem. Assn. N.J. Recyclers (pres. 1991-93), Somerset C. of C. (chmn. bd. 1989-90, chmn. strategic planning cultural and heritage com., tourism coun.), World Bus. Acad. (bd. dirs. 1988-89), Rotary (pres. Bound Brook-Middlesex club 1993-94), Regional Plan Assn. (bd. dirs. 1994-96), Heritage Trail Assn. Somerset County (founder, pres. 1994-99), Crossroads of the Am. Revolution Assn. (pres. 2001-). Mem. Soc. Of Friends. Avocation: quilting. Home: PO Box 250 Cape May Point NJ 08212 Office: PO Box 710 Bound Brook NJ 08805-0710

CHANDLER, MARSHA, academic administrator, educator; BA, CCNY, 1965; PhD, UNC Chapel Hill, 1972. Prof. political econ. Univ. Toronto, 1977-96, dean arts and sci., 1990-97; sr. vice chancellor U. Calif., San Diego, MA, 1996—. Vis. scholar Harvard U., Boston, 1995-96. Co-author: Trade and Transmissions, 1990, The Political Economy of Business Bailouts, 2 vols., 1986, The Politics of Canadian Public Policy, 1983, Public Policy and Provincial Politics, 1979, Adjusting to Trade: A Comparative Perspective, 1988; contbr. articles to profl. jours. Fellow, Royal Soc. of Canada, mem., Dept. of Political Sci., Faculty of Law, bd. dirs. San Diego Opera, Mingei Mus. of Internatl. Folk Art, UCSD Found. Bd. and the Charter 100, adv. com. on Fed. Judicial Appts., bd. of Canadian Inst. for Adv. Rsch.; trustee, Art Gall. of Ontario, Mt. SInai Hosp., Huntsman Marine Sci. Ctr., Ontario Lightwave, Laser Rsch. Ctr. Office: U Calif 9500 Gilman Dr La Jolla CA 92093-5004

CHANDLER, MELANIE LYNN, surgical technologist, paralegal; b. Hammond, Ind., Oct. 11, 1967; d. Michael Edward and Mary Josephine Simkins; children: Courtney, Brian, Lindsey. Student paralegal studies, Calumet Coll. St. Joseph, 2001. Cert. surgical technologist. Cert. nurses aide Resthaven Christian Svs., South Holland, Ill., 1996—98; gastrointestinal lab technician Adv. Trinity Hosp., Chicago, Ill., 1998—2000, cert. surg. technologist, 1997—; paralegal Barry Sherman & Assocs., Hammond, Ind., 2002—. Latex allergy liason Adv. Trinity Hosp., Chgo., 1999—. Mem.: Calumet Coll. Paralegal Club (sec., treas. 2002). Office: Barry Sherman & Assocs 6920 Hohman Ave Hammond IN 46320 Personal E-mail: melaniechandler@aol.com.

CHANDLER, PATRICIA ANN, retired special education educator; b. Stow, Maine, May 25, 1929; d. Herbert Raymond and Tressia May (Walker) Harmon; m. Robert Leslie Chandler, Mar. 25, 1949 (dec. June 1991); children: Rose Ann Chandler Savage, Alexander Michael. BS, U. Maine, Portland, 1965; MEd, U. So. Maine, 1978. Tchg. prin. Annie Heald Sch., Lovell, Maine, 1954—70, New Suncook Sch., Lovell, Maine, 1970, Sadie Adams Sch., North Fryeburg, Maine, New Suncook Sch., Lovell, Maine; ret., 1983. Contbr. articles to profl. jours. Mem.: Oxford County Ret. Tchrs. Assn., Maine Assn. of Retirees, Inc. (licentiate). Republican. United Ch. Of Christ Congl. Avocations: cooking, travel, writing, painting. Mailing: 75 State St Apt 432 Portland ME 04101-3714

CHANDRA, DEVAKI, researcher in economics, analyst; b. N.Y.C., May 24, 1963; d. Harish and Lalitha Chandra; m. John Kuriyan, Jan. 16, 1987. PhD, CUNY, 1996. Adj. instr. Baruch Coll., CUNY, N.Y.C., 1996; sr. analyst AT&T, Basking Ridge, N.J., 1996-2001; economist Legg Mason, Emeryville, Calif., 2001—. Recipient Emily award AT&T Consumer Fin. Orgn., 1999, 2000. Mem. Eastern Econs. Assn. Avocation: music. Home: 936 Oxford St Berkeley CA 94707-2435

CHANEY, ETHEL SCOTLAND, English language educator; b. Cleve., Mar. 16, 1914; d. Bayard Scott and Beatrice Louise (Homan) Scotland; m. William Stanton Chaney, Oct. 8, 1939 (div. Mar. 1988), remarried Jan. 10, 2001; children: Scott Clay, Karen Marie Kauffman, Norma Chaney Shear, Ruth Margot Walker. BS, U. Ill., 1935; MA, Roosevelt U., 1966. Tchr. various levels various schs., Joliet, Ill., 1936-80; tchr. English Gulf H.S., New Port Richey, Fla., 1980, Pasco C.C., New Port Richey, Fla., 1981, Rutledge Jr. Coll., Raleigh, N.C., 1987, Huntington Learning Ctr., Raleigh, 1988; substitute tchr. Wake County Sch., Raleigh, 1988-98. Docent N.C. Mus. Art, Dickens Soc., Jane Austen Soc., Crime Writers Soc. Mem. Univ. Women (life), U. Ill. Alumni (life), Roosevelt U. Alumni (life), Pi Beta Phi (life). Democrat. Unitarian-Universalist. Home: 2406 Wesvill Ct Apt F Raleigh NC 27607-2911

CHANG, BARBARA KAREN, medical educator; b. Milltown, Ind., Jan. 6, 1946; m. M.F. Joseph Chang-Wai-Ling, Oct. 6, 1967; children: Carla Marie Yvonnette, Nolanne Arlette. BA, Ind. U., 1968; MA, Brandeis U., 1970; MD, Albert Einstein Coll. Medicine, 1973. Diplomate Am. Bd. Internal Medicine, Am. Bd. Med. Oncology, Am. Bd. Hematology. Resident in internal medicine Montefiore Med. Ctr., Bronx, N.Y., 1973-75; fellow in hematology/oncology Duke U. Med. Ctr., Durham, N.C., 1975-78; staff physician VA Med. Ctr., Augusta, Ga., 1978-95, chief hematology/oncology, 1980-89, assoc. chief of staff edn., 1990-95; prof. medicine Med. Coll. Ga., Augusta, 1978-95; chief of staff, chief med. officer VA Med. Ctr., Albuquerque, 1995—2002; assoc. dean U. N.Mex. Sch. Medicine, Albuquerque, 1995—2002, prof. medicine, 1995—; cons. Capital Assets Realignment for Enhanced Svcs. Program VA Ctrl. Office, Washington, 2002—03, dir. program evaluation Office Academic Affiliations, 2003—. Mem. Sci. Adv. Bd., Washington, 1983-88; mem. expert panels computer applications Dept. Vets. Affairs, Washington, 1988-95; prof. Med. Sch. U. N.Mex., 1995—. Contbr. numerous articles on cancer rsch. to profl. jours. Youth coord. Am. Hemerocallis Soc., Augusta, 1993-95, pres. local chpt. 1997, Albuquerque, garden judge 1997—, region 6 youth liaison, 2000—01, exhbn. judge 2001. [illegible] Am. Cancer Soc., 1978-93; David M. Worthen award Acad. Excellence Dept. Vet. Affairs, 2000. Fellow ACP, Am. Soc. Clin. Oncology, Bioelectromagnetic Soc. (bd. dirs. 1983-86). Office: Dept Vets Affairs Med Ctr 1501 San Pedro Dr SE Albuquerque NM 87108-5153 E-mail: barbara.chang@med.va.gov.

CHANG, DEBBIE I-JU, health services director; BS in Chem. Engring., MIT, 1984; MPH, U. Mich., 1987. Presdl. mgmt. intern Health Care Fin. Adminstrn. Office Legislation and Policy, 1987-89; sr. health policy advisor Senator Donald W. Riegle Jr., 1989-94; dir. office legis. and intergovt. affairs Health Care Fin. Adminstrn., Washington, 1994-98; co-chair steering com. on state children's health ins. prog. Health Care Fin. Adminstrn., Dept. HHS, Washington, 1997-99; dir. divsn. Medicaid coverage benefits and payments Health Care Fin. Adminstrn., Washington, 1998; dep. sec. for health care financing Medicaid, Balt., 1999—. Contbr. articles to profl. jours. Office: Health Care Financing Md Dept Hlth/Mental Hygiene 201 W Preston St Baltimore MD 21201-2323

CHANG, HELEN CHUNG-HUNG HSIANG, music educator; b. Shanghai, July 20, 1937; d. Shou-Tsu Edward and Chen-Tze Kiang Hsiang; m. Nai Lin Chang; children: Tai Deborah, Huan Justina, Lan Samantha, Ling Patricia. BA cum laude, Mt. Mercy Coll., Cedar Rapids, Iowa, 1960; BMus cum laude, Lawrence U., 1980; postgrad. in pedagogical study, Am. Suzuki Inst., Stevens Point, Wis., 1972, 83, 88-89. Cert. tchr. Music Tchrs. Nat. Assn., Wis. Music Tchr. Assn., Suzuki Assn. of the Ams. Co-chair Fox Valley Keyboard Tchrs., Appleton, Wis., 1981-82, chair, 1982-83, treas., 1996-97; recital chair Suzuki Edn. Assn. of the Fox Valley, Appleton, 1984-96. Judge regional competitions Wis. Music Tchrs. Assn., 1988-97, state competition, 1994, 95, others, coach numerous students. Mem. Northeast Wis. Chinese Assn. (Chinese lang. instr. 1972-76), Wis. Music Tchrs. Assn. (award of excellence 1981, 94, 99, 2003), Music Tchr. Nat. Assn., Suzuki Assn. of the Ams., Suzuki Assn. of Wis.

CHANG, JANICE MAY, lawyer, naturopathic doctor, psychologist; b. Loma Linda, Calif., May 24, 1970; d. Belden Shiu-Wah (dec.) and Sylvia (Tan) C. BA, cert. paralegal studies, Calif. State U., San Bernardino, 1990, cert. creative writing, 1991; JD, LaSalle U., 1993; D in Naturopathy, Clayton Sch. Natural Healing, 1993; DFA in Creative Writing: Poetry, Am. Internat. U., 1999; MD in Alternative Medicines, Open Internat. U., 2001; D of Psychology, Calif. Coast U., 2002; LLM in Taxation, Wash. Sch. of Law, 2004. Bd. cert. alternative med. practitioner; notary pub. Calif., cert. loan signing agt. Victim/witness contact clk.-paralegal Dist. Atty.'s Office Victim/Witness Assistance Program, San Bernardino, Calif., 1990; gen. counsel JMC Enterprises, Inc., Riverside, Calif., 1993—; law prof. LaSalle U., Mandeville, La., 1994-97; corp. counsel, CFO JDS Assocs., Inc., Loma Linda, 1998-99, DJS, L.P., Loma Linda, 1998-99; trust officer/trust svcs. Southeastern Calif. Conf. Seventh-Day Adventists, Riverside, 1998—; CFO/mgr. Stanberden Properties, 2001—. Spkr. graduation ceremony/conv. Internat. U., Las Vegas, 1998. Contbr. poetry to anthologies, including Am. Poetry Anthology, 1987-90, The Pacific Rev., 1991, The Piquant, 1991, River of Dreams, 1994, Reflections of Light, 1994, Musings, 1994 (Honorable Mention award 1994), Treasured Poems of America, 1994, Windows of the Soul, 1995, Best Poems of 1995 (Celebrating Excellence award 1995, Inspirations award 1995), Am. Poetry Annual, 1996, 99, Best New Poems of 1996, Interludes, 1996, Meditations, 1996, Perspectives, 1996 (Honorable Mention award 1996), Keepsakes, 1997 (Honorable Mention award 1997), Best Poems of 1997, Poetic Voices of America, 1997, The Isle of View, 1997, The Other Side of Midnight, 1997, Treasures, 1998, Best Poems of 1998, Writingscapes: Insights & Approaches to Creative Writing, 1998, Mirrors, 1999 (Pres.'s Lit. Excellence award), Pieces of the Heart, 2000, The Silence Within, 2001, Nature's Echoes, 2001, The Best Poems and Poets of 2001, The Best Poems and Poets of 2002; contbr. to Internat. Libr. Photography: Tapestry of Dreams, 1999, Mystical Seasons, 1999, Candid Captures, 2001, The Mirror's Reflection, 2003. Vol. Health Fair Expo La Sierra U., 1988, 1989, Path of the Just Tree Project, 1998; vol. first aid, CPR, other classes ARC, 1994—; sponsor Student Employment Recognition Banquet La Sierra U., Riverside, Calif., 1999—2003. Recipient Poet of Merit award, Am. Poetry Assn., San Francisco, 1989, Golden Poet award, World of Poetry, Washington, 1989, Publisher's Choice award, Watermark Press, 1990, Editor's Choice award, The Nat. Libr. Poetry, 1990—97, Pres.'s award for lit. excellence, Iliad Press, 1995—99, Editor's Choice award, Poetry.com, 2002. Fellow Am. Coll. Internat. Physicians; mem. ABA, ATLA, Nat. Bar Assn., Am. Coll. Legal Medicine, Nat. Notary Assn., Brit. Guild Drugless Practitioners (life). Republican. Seventh-Day Adventist. Avocations: poetry writing, photography, music, drama, literature, coin collecting/numismatics. Home: 1025 Crestbrook Dr Riverside CA 92506-5662 Office: Southeastern Calif Conf 7th-Day Adventists PO Box 8050 11330 Pierce St Riverside CA 92515-8050 E-mail: changjm@secc-sda.org.

CHANG, JEANNETTE, publishing executive; BS, CCNY. Advt. sales rep. Cosmopolitan mag. Hearst Mags., N.Y.C., 1973-77, fashion advt. mgr., 1977-79; dir. fashion mktg. Bazaar mag. Hearst Mags., N.Y.C., 1979-84; assoc. pub. Harper's Bazaar mag. Hearst Mags., N.Y.C., 1984-94, v.p., 1992-94, v.p., pub., 1994—2000; sr. v.p., internat. pub. dir. Hearst Mags., Intl., 2000—. Spkr. in field. Active City Meals on Wheels, Meml. Sloan Kettering Found., Susan G. Komen Breast Cancer Found. Named to YWCA Acad. of Women Achievers, 1992. Mem. Fashion Group Internat. (bd. dirs., chair cosmetic exec. women's com.). Office: Mearst Mags Intl 959 8th Ave Rm 306 New York NY 10019-3737

CHANG, LENG KAR, interior designer; b. Ipoh, Perak, Malaysia, Aug. 31, 1973; arrived in U.S., 1997; MA, Savannah Coll. Art and Design, 1999; cert., Visionary Designing, 2001. Interior designer Innervision Design Cons., Kuala Lumpur, Malaysia, 1994—96, Winsonart Design and Contracts, Paya Lebah, Singapore, 1997—98, Ai Group, Atlanta, 2000—. Contbr. (design) Residential Product and Interior Design, Home Max, 1997. Named Monroe Curus Propes fellow, Savannah Coll. Art and Design, 1998, Internat. and Regional winner, Interior Design Educators Coun. Student Design Competition, 1999; scholar, Savannah Coll. Art and Design, 1998. Home: PO Box 190802 Atlanta GA 31119-0802 Office: Ai Group 3424 Peachtree Rd NE Ste 1600 Atlanta GA 30326 Personal E-mail: lengkar@hotmail.com. Business E-Mail: lchang@aigroupdesign.com.

CHANG, LING WEI, consulting services executive; b. Taiwan, China, July 27, 1960; arrived in U.S., 1976; d. Thomas T.P. and Hou Hsin (Wang) C. BE, Cooper Union, 1982; MS, Syracuse U., 1989. Engr. Data Systems div. IBM Corp., Poughkeepsie, N.Y., 1982-85, sys. engr. U.S. mktg. and svcs. N.Y.C., 1985-90; adv. mktg. rep. N.Y. gov. br. IBM U.S., N.Y.C., 1991-92; acct. mgr. N.Y. Pub. Svcs. IBM N.Am., N.Y.C., 1993-94; br. mgr. LEXIS-NEXIS, N.Y.C., 1994-95; nat. account mgr. Computer Assocs. Internat. Inc., N.Y.C., 1996-99; acct. prin. Compaq Profl. Svcs., N.Y.C., 1999-2000, dir. N.Y./N.J. area, 2000—01; client prin. Hewlett-Packard Svcs., 2002—. Vol. City Hosp. Ctr. at Elmhurst, N.Y., 1978; jr. judge Nat. Energy Found., 1979-82; bd. mgrs. Queens Ctr. Pla. Condominium, 1990-92. Mem.: Exec. Women's Golf Assn. (pres Big Apple chpt.), Eta Kappa Nu, Tau Beta Pi. Avocations: piano, golf, skiing. Home: 87-08 Justice Ave Apt 10D Elmhurst NY 11373-4580 Office: Hewlett-Packard Co 2 Penn Plz Fl 8 New York NY 10121-0899 Office Phone: 212-856-2364. E-mail: ling.chang@hp.com.

CHANG, LYDIA LIANG-HWA, social worker, educator; b. Wuhan, Hubei, China, Sept. 25, 1929; came to U.S., 1960; d. Shu-Tze Yu-Rou and Jian-Bung (Young) C.; m. Norman Stock, Aug. 20, 1998; children: Elizabeth Shu-Mei L. Ip, George Shu-Ang Lee. Diploma in Spanish and [illegible], Paris, 1959, MSW, NYU, 1963; cert. in advanced social work, Columbia U., N.Y.C., 1977, PhD in Social Work, 1980. Cert. social worker, cert. sch. bilingual social worker, N.Y. Supr. Cath. Charities, N.Y.C., 1969-71; dir. mental health cons. ctr. Univ. Settlement, N.Y.C., 1971-73; psychotherapist Luth. Med. Ctr., Bklyn., 1974-78; assoc. prof. U. Cin., 1978-80; asst. prof. Borough of Manhattan C.C., N.Y.C., 1983-86; bilingual sch. social worker N.Y.C. Bd. Edn., 1987-98, instr. for staff devel. program, 1991-98; psychotherapist Western Queens (N.Y.) Consultation Ctr., 1998—. Govt. ofcl.; cmem. mty. sch. bd. Dist. 30 N.Y.C. Bd. Edn., 1999—; cons. Cath. Social Svc. Bur., Cin., 1978-80; faculty advisor Borough of Manhattan C.C., 1983-86. Author: numerous poems; contbr. articles to profl. jours. Adv. bd. Pub. Sys. of Schs., Cin., 1978-80, Orange County Asian Am. orgn., Goshen, NY, 1980-82; treas. US-China Ednl. Fund, NY, 1994—; founder of the Shu-Tze Chang and Jian-Bung Young Chang Ednl. scholarship fund, China, 1996. Mem. NASW, Nat. Assn. Sch. Social Workers, Columbia Alumni Assn., Nankai Alumni Assn. (v.p. 1991-94), Am. Voters Assn., Asian-Am. Dem. Assn. Episcopalian. Avocations: flute, tai-chi-chuang, swimming, reading. Home: 77-11 35th Ave Apt 2P Jackson Heights NY 11372

CHANG, MARIAN S. filmmaker, composer; b. Atlanta, Aug. 19, 1958; d. C. H. Joseph and C. S. (Chun) Chang. MusB, Harvard U., 1981; MFA in Filmmaking, Columbia U., 1994. Composer, dir., choreographer Exptl. Theatre, Dance, Boston, 1981-88; composer for modern dance co. Performing Arts Ensemble, Boston, 1986-88; co-dir., choreographer, performer Theatre S., Boston, 1987-88; prodr., dir., writer, sound designer, composer N.Y.C., 1991—. Founder, prodr. Shy Artists Prodns., Boston, N.Y.C., 1988—94. Recipient 1st prize, Kansas City Music Scholarship Competition, 1976, Nino Cerruti Film award, 1995; grantee Fellowship Program Finalist award in choreography, Mass. Artists, 1987, N.Y. Coun. Humanities, 1998; Fellowship Program Finalist award in music composition, Mass. Artists, 1988. Home: 220 E 27th St Apt 7 New York NY 10016-9234

CHANG, PATTI, foundation administrator; b. Hawaii; BA in Internat. Rels., JD, Stanford U. Pres., CEO Women's Found., San Francisco, 1993—2003, Women's Found. Calif., San Francisco, 2003—. Past commr. San Francisco Commn. on the Environment. Mem.: Women's Inst. for Leadership Devel. for Human Rights (mem. adv. bd.), San Francisco Commn. on the Status of Women (past pres.), Nat. Com. for Responsible Philanthropy (nat. adv. bd.), GenderPAC (nat. adv. bd.), Women's Leadership Alliance, Asian Pacific Am. Women's Leadership Inst. (bd. mem.), Women's Funding network (chair bd. dirs., bd. mem.). Office: Womens Found Calif Ste 302 340 Pine St San Francisco CA 94014*

CHANG, SHIRLEY LIN (HSIU-CHU CHANG), librarian, educator; b. Chia-yi, Taiwan, June 22, 1937; came to U.S., 1962; naturalized, 1977. d. Tzu-kun and Ying (Chang) Lin; m. Parris H. Chang, Aug. 3, 1963; children: Yvette Y., Elaine Y., Bohdan P. BA, Nat. Taiwan U., Taipei, 1960; postgrad., U. Wasn., 1962-63; MLS, Columbia U., 1967; MA, Pa. State U., 1988. Libr. asst. Yale U., New Haven, 1964-67; asst. ref. libr. Pa. State U., University Park, 1971-75; cataloguer Australian Nat. U., Canberra, 1978; catalog/ref. libr. Lock Haven U., 1979—, asst. prof., 1982-88, assoc. prof., 1988—. Catalog/reference libr., reference desk coord. Lock Haven U., Pa. Author: Taiwan's Brain Drain and Its Reversal, 1999. Mem. ALA, Chinese-Am. Librs. Assn. (chmn. awards com. 1982-83), Asian/Pacific Am. Librs. Assn., Assn. for Asian Studies, Pa. Libr. Assn., Phi Beta Delta Honor Soc. Home: 1221 Edwards St State College PA 16801 Office: Lock Haven U Stevenson Libr Lock Haven PA 17745 E-mail: schang@lhup.edu.

CHANG, SUN-YUNG ALICE, mathematics educator; b. Ci-an, China, Mar. 24, 1948; came to U.S., 1970; d. Fann Chang and Li-Ching Chen; m. Paul Chien-Ping Yang, Mar. 24, 1973; children: Ray Yang, Lusann Yang. BS, Nat. Taiwan U., 1970; PhD, U. Calif., Berkeley, 1974. Asst. prof. math. U. Md., College Park, 1977-79; prof. UCLA, 1981—, Princeton U., 1998—. Speaker Internat. Congress of Math., 1986, 2002. Sloan Found. fellow, 1977, 78; Guggenheim fellow, 1999. Mem. Am. Math. Soc. (v.p. 1989, 90, Ruth Lyttle Satter prize 1995), Am. Women in Math. Office: Princeton Univ/Dept Math Fine Hall Washington Rd Princeton NJ 08544-1000 Business E-Mail: chang@math.princeton.edu.

CHANG, SYLVIA TAN, health facility administrator, educator; b. Bandung, Indonesia, Dec. 18, 1940; came to U.S., 1963; d. Philip Harry and Lydia Shui-Yu (Ou) Tan; m. Belden Shiu-Wah Chang, Aug. 30, 1964 (dec. Aug. 1997); children: Donald Steven, Janice May. Diploma in nursing, Rumah Sakit Advent, Indonesia, 1960; BS, Philippine Union Coll., 1962; MS, Loma Linda (Calif.) U., 1967; PhD, Columbia Pacific U., 1987. Cert. RN, PHN, ACLS, BLS instr., cmty. first aid instr., IV, TPN, blood withdrawal. Head nurse Rumah Sakit Advent, Bandung, Indonesia, 1960-61; critical care, spl. duty and medicine nurse, team leader White Meml. Med. Ctr., L.A., 1963-64; nursing coord. Loma Linda U. Med. Ctr., 1964-66; team leader, critical care nurse, relief head nurse Pomona (Calif.) Valley Hosp. Med. Ctr., 1966-67; evening supr. Loma Linda U. Med. Ctr., 1967-69, night supr., 1969-79, adminstrv. supr., 1979-94; sr. faculty Columbia Pacific U., San Rafael, Calif., 1986-94; dir. health svc. La Sierra U., Riverside, Calif., 1988—. Site coord. Health Fair Expo La Sierra U., 1988-89; adv. coun. Family Planning Clinic, Riverside, 1988-94; blood and bone marrow drive coord. La Sierra U., 1988—. Counselor Pathfinder Club Campus Hill Ch., Loma Linda, 1979-85, crafts instr., 1979-85, music dir., 1979-85; asst. organist U. Ch., 1982-88. Named one of Women of Achievement YWCA, Greater Riverside C. of C., The Press Enterprise, 1991, 2000, Safety Coord. of Yr. La Sierra U., 1995. Mem. Am. Coll. Health Assn., Pacific Coast Coll. Health Assn., Adventist Student Pers. Assn., Sigma Theta Tau. Republican. Seventh-day Adventist. Avocations: music, travel, collecting coins, shells and jade carvings. Home: 1025 Crestbrook Dr Riverside CA 92506-5662 Office: 4700 Pierce St Riverside CA 92515-8247 Office Phone: 909-785-2200. Business E-Mail: schang@lasierra.edu. E-mail: schang@lasierra.edu.

CHANIN, LEAH FARB, law library administrator, lawyer, consultant, law educator; b. Glaveston, Tex., Nov. 29, 1929; d. A.C. and Celia (Rubenstein) Farb; m. Louis Chanin, Feb. 4, 1951 (dec. 1991); children: Scott, Leonard, Johanna, Rebecca. BA, So. Meth. U., 1950; LLB, Mercer U., 1954. Bar: Ga. 1954, U.S. Dist. Ct. (mid. dist.) Ga. 1954. Practice, Macon, Ga., 1959-63; mem. Kenmore & Culpepper, 1959-63; mem. faculty Walter F. George Sch. Law, Mercer U., 1964-92, ast. prof. law, 1969-72, assoc. prof., 1972-77, prof., 1977-92, dir. law libr., 1964-92, dean pro tem, 1986-87; disting. prof., dir. libr. U. D.C. Sch. Law, 1992-96; head pub. svcs. Howard U. Law Libr., Washington, 1997—2001. Mem. Fed. Merit Rev. Com., 1979-81; bd. visitors Mercer Law Sch., 1992-98. Author: Specialized Legal Research, 1987, Georgie Legal Research, 1990, Legal Research in D.C., Maryland and Virginia, 1995, 2d edit., 1999; contbr. articles to profl. jours. Mem. State Bar Ga. (adv. ethics opinions bd., pres. author's ct. 1985-86). Democrat. Jewish. Home: 3001 Veazey Ter NW Apt 1027 Washington DC 20008-5416 E-mail: leahfchanin@aol.com.

CHANNING, CAROL, actress; b. Seattle, Jan. 31, 1921; d. George Channing and Adelaide (Glaser) C.; m. Charles F. Lowe, Sept. 5, 1956 (div.); 1 son, Channing George. Student, Bennington Coll. Actress: (Broadway prodns.) No for an Answer, 1941, Let's Face It, 1941, Proof Through the Night, 1942, So Proudly We Hail, Lend an Ear, 1948 (Theatre World award, Critic's Circle award), Gentlemen Prefer Blondes, 1949, 51-53, Wonderful Town, 1953, Pygmalian, 1953, The Vamp, 1955, Show Business, 1959, Show Girl, 1961, George Burns-Carol Channing Musical Revue,

1962, The Millionairess, 1963, Hello Dolly, 1964-67, also 3 revivals (Tony award for Best Actress, N.Y. Drama Critics Cir. award for Best Actress), Carol Channing and Her Ten Stout-Hearted Men, 1970 (London Critics award), Four on a Garden, 1971, In Cabarets, 1972, Festival at Ford's, 1972, Carol Channing and Her Gentlemen Who Prefer Blondes Revue, 1972, Jerry's Girls, 1984-85, Legends, 1986, (theatre tours) Lorelei, 1973-75, Carol's Broadway Revue; (films) First Travelling Saleslady, 1956, Thoroughly Modern Millie, 1967 (Golden Globe award as Best Supporting Actress 1967), Skidoo, 1968, Shinbone Alley (voice), 1971, Sgt. Peppers Lonely Hearts Club Band, 1978, Happily Ever After (voice), 1990, Hans Christian Andersen's Thumbelina (voice), 1994, The Line King: Al Hirschfeld, 1996, others; (TV prodns.) Svengali and the Blonde, Three Men on a Horse, Crescendo; (TV appearences) The Love Boat, 1977, Alice in Wonderland, 1985, Where's Waldo? (voice), 1991, Addams Family (voice), 1992, The Magic School Bus (voice), 1994, Homo Heights, 1998; autobiography: Just Lucky I Guess, 2002 Recipient Best Night Club Act award, 1957, 64, Spl. Tony award, 1968, Theatre World award for Bronze medallion City of N.Y., 1978, Lifetime Achievement Tony award, 1995. Christian Scientist. Office: William Morris Agy 1 William Morris Pl Beverly Hills CA 90212

CHANNING, STOCKARD (SUSAN STOCKARD), actress; b. N.Y.C., Feb. 13, 1944; d. Lester Napier and Mary Alice Stockard; m. Walter Channing, Jr., 1963 (div. 1967); m. Paul Schmidt, 1970 (div. 1975); m. David Debin, 1976 (div. 1980); m. David Rawle, 1982 (div. 1988). BA cum laude, Harvard U. Actress movies include The Fortune, 1975, The Big Bus, 1976, Sweet Revenge, 1977, The Cheap Detective, 1978, Grease, 1978, The Fish That Saved Pittsburgh, 1979, Safari 3000, 1982, Without a Trace, 1983, The Men's Club, 1986, Heartburn, 1986, A Time of Destiny, 1988, Staying Together, 1989, Meet the Applegates, 1990, Lunes de Fiel, 1992, Six Degrees of Separation (Acad. award nomination Best Actress), 1993, Married to It, 1993, To Wong Foo, Thanks for Everything, Julie Newmar, 1995, Smoke, 1995, Edie and Pen, 1996, The First Wives Club, 1996, Up Close and Personal, 1996, Moll Flanders, 1996, Twilight, 1998, Lulu on the Bridge (voice), 1998, Practical magic, 1998, The Red Door, 1999, Other Voices, 1999, Isn't She Great, 1999, The Venice Project, 1999, Where the Heart Is, 2000, Life or Something Like It, 2002, Le Divorce, 2003, Anything Else, 2003; tv movies include Girl Most Likely to..., 1973, Lucan, 1977, Silent Victory: The Kitty O'Neill Story, 1979, Not My Kid, 1985, The Room Upstairs, 1987, Echoes in the Darkness, 1987, Tidy Endings, 1988, Perfect Witness, 1989, Lincoln, 1992, David's Mother, 1994, Mr. Willowby's Christmas Tree, 1995, An Unexpected Family, 1996, Lily Dale, 1996, The Prosecutors, 1996, An Unexpected Life, 1998, The Baby Dance, 1998, tv series include Road to Avonlea, King of the Hill (voice), Batman Beyond, 1999, The West Wing (Emmy Outstanding Supporting Actress in a Drama Series 2002), 1999-, The Matthew Shepard Story (Emmy Outstanding Supporting Actress in a Miniseries or a Movie), 2002, Hitler: The Rise of Evil, 2003; actress (play) A Day in the Death of Joe Egg (Tony Actress in a Play), 1985. Office: ICM c/o Andrea Eastman 40 W 57th St Fl 16 New York NY 10019-4098*

CHANOS, ADRIANA ESCOBAR, state agency administrator; BA, U. Nev.; JD, Calif. W. Sch. Law. Assoc. Dunbar & Dunbar, San Diego; dep. city atty. City of San Diego; founding ptnr. Chanos Escobar Chanos, P.C.; mem. Nev. Taxicab Authority, 1997—2001; commr. Pub. Utilities Commn., Carson City, Nev., 2001—. Prodr.: (TV series) Spanish Lang. TV programs for drug abuse prevention. Active Nev. Assn. Handicapped, bd. dir. Latin C. of C. Recipient Profl. of Yr. award, Latin C. of C. Office: Nevada PUC 1150 E William St Carson City NV 89701

CHAO, ELAINE L. secretary of labor; d. James S.C. and Ruth M.L. (Chu) C.; m. Mitch McConnell, 1993. AB, Mt. Holyoke Coll., 1975; MBA, Harvard U., 1979; LLD (hon.), Villanova U., 1989, St. John's U., 1991, Sacred Heart U., 1991; DHL (hon.), Niagara U., 1992, Goucher Coll., 1996, U. Louisville, 1996; DHum (hon.), Drexel U., 1992, Thomas More Coll., 1994; DHL (hon.), Bellarmine Coll., 1995, U. Toledo, 1995; LLD (hon.), U. Notre Dame, 1998; DHum (hon.), Ky. Wesleyan Coll., 1998; DHL (hon.), U. S.C., 2001; D Arts and Letters (hon.), Miami-Dade C.C., 2001; DPA (hon.), Campbellsville U., 2002; D Pub. Svcs. (hon.), DePauw U., 2002; LLD (hon.), St. Marys Coll., 2002; D in Orgnl. Leadership (hon.), Regent U., 2003; DHL (hon.), No. Ala. U., 2003, Centre Coll., 2003; LLD (hon.), Fu-Jen Cath. U., 2003. Assoc. Gulf Oil Corp., Pitts., summer 1978; sr. lending officer Citicorp, NA, N.Y.C., 1979-83; v.p. capital markets group BankAmerica, San Francisco, 1984-86; dep. maritime adminstr. U.S. Dept. Transp., Washington, 1986-88; chmn. Fed. Maritime Commn., Washington, 1988; dep. sec. U.S. Dept. Transp., Washington, 1989-91; pres. United Way Am., Alexandria, Va., 1992-96; sr. editor, disting. fellow The Heritage Found., Washington; sec. U.S. Dept. Labor, Washington, 2001—. White House fellow, 1983-84; adj. asst. prof. Grad. Sch. Bus. Adminstrn., St. John's U., 1984. Recipient Young Achiever award Nat. Coun. Women U.S., Inc., 1986; Eisenhower Fellow Assn. fellow, 1984; named. one of 10 Outstanding Women of Am., 1988. Mem. Coun. on Fgn. Rels., Inc., Am. Coun. Young Polit. Leaders (bd. dirs. 1989), Harvard Bus. Sch. (vis. com. 1989, Outstanding Alumni award 1993), Harvard Club. Republican. Office: Dept Labor Office of Sec 200 Constitution Ave NW Washington DC 20210*

CHAO, YU CHEN, musician, cellist, educator; b. Fengshan, Taiwan, Feb. 26, 1961; came to U.S., 1987; d. Kun-Ho and Kuei-Lan (Ma) C. BA, Taung-Hai U., Taichung, Taiwan, 1985; MMus in Performance, Manahttan Sch. Music, 1990, MMus in Orch. Performance, 1994. Assoc. prin. N.Y. Chamber Sinfonia, N.Y.C., 1992-94; substitute Albany (N.Y.) Symphony Orch., 1995; assoc. prin. N.Y. Asiana Orch., N.Y.C., 1995-97. Solo recitalist St. Peter's Ch., N.Y.C., 1998, Riverside Ch., N.Y.C., 1998, Carnegie Hall/Weill Recital Hall, N.Y.C., 1998; music dir. Cello Allegro, Inc., N.Y.C., 1996—; founder, tchr. Harlem Cello Sch. Program, N.Y.C., 1999. Recipient Laura R. Conover Pedagogy award Cecilian Music Club, 1998, Schlarship award Elan Internat. Music Festival, 1998; winner Artist Internat. Competition, 1998, Alumni winner, 1999; Victoria Summer Festival scholar, 1992, Waterloo Summer Festival fellow, 1990; participating hon. 104th Congress at the White House, 1995. Avocations: gardening, photography, travel, checkers, charity works. Home: 302 W 107th St Apt 3B New York NY 10025-2716

CHAPEL, TENNILLE MARIA, speech pathology/audiology services professional; b. Charleston, Ill., Nov. 6, 1976; d. Kim Lee Bushur and Debbie Dale Smith; m. Robert Dean Chapel, June 22, 2001. BS, Northern Ill. Univ., Dekalb, Ill., 1998; MA, Univ. N.C., Greensboro, N.C., 2000. Cert. CCC-SLP/L EI. PreK-5th grade speech lang. pathologist Archer Elem., Greensboro, NC, 2000—02; jr. high speech lang. pathologist New Lenox Sch. Dist. 122, New Lenox, Ill., 2002—03; early intervention speech lang. pathologist Kid Talk, New Lenox, Ill., 2003—. Cheer leading coach Liberty Jr. High, New Lenox, Ill., 2002—03; specialist co-chair Archer Elem., Greensboro, NC, 2001—02. Contbr. poster presetation. Grantee Adolescent Lang. Grant, Univ. N.C., 1999. Mem.: Ill. Speech Hearing Assn., Am. Speech Lang. Hearing Assn. Avocations: yoga, gardening, cooking, dance, family. Home: 20453 S Acorn Ridge Dr Frankfort IL 60423

CHAPELLE, SUZANNE ELLERY GREENE, history educator; b. Phila., Sept. 21, 1942; d. John Channing and Jessie Horn (Myers) Ellery; m. Michael Thomas Greene, Sept. 15, 1972 (dec. 1973); 1 child, Jennifer; m. Francis Oberlin Chapelle, Apr. 14, 1984 (dec. 1999). BA, Harvard U., 1964; MA, Johns Hopkins U., 1966, PhD, 1970. Asst. prof. Am. history Towson State U., Balt., 1969-71; assoc. prof. Am. history Morgan State U., Balt., 1971-75, prof., 1975—. Author: Books for Pleasure, 1976, Baltimore: An Illustrated History, 1980, 2d rev. edit., 2000; sr. author: Maryland: A History of its People, 1986; revisions author: A Child's History of the World, 1994, African American Leaders of Maryland, 2000, The Maryland Adventure, 2001; mem. publs. bd. Md. Hist. Soc. Bd. dirs. Md. Interfaith Coalition for the Environment, 1997-2001, v.p., 1999-2001; bd. dirs. Md. Conservation Coun., 1999-2000, Irvine Nature Ctr., 2001—. Mem. Am. Hist. Assn., Am. Studies Assn. (mem. exec. bd. Chesapeake chpt. 1988-90), Popular Culture Assn. (bd. dirs. 1980-82), Orgn. Am. Historians, Md. Hist. Soc. (publs. com. 1998—), Mid-Atlantic Popular Culture Assn. (pres. 1977-80), Balt. County League Environ. Voters (exec. bd. 1992-96), Episcopal Diocese of Md. Com. on the Environ. (sec. 1994-2003), Ruxton-Riderwood Assn. (bd. govs. 1987-91), The Johns Hopkins Club, The Harvard-Radcliffe Club Md. Episcopalian. Home: 6021 Lakeview Rd Baltimore MD 21210-1033 Office: Morgan State U Hist Dept Baltimore MD 21251-0001 Office Phone: 443-885-3190. E-mail: schapelle@moac.morgan.edu., suechapelle@hotmail.com.

CHAPIN, MARY Q. television personality, arbitrator, mediator, writer, performing artist; b. Shepherdstown, W.VA., May 5, 1933; d. Guy Estil and Anne Mildred (Jones) Quisenberry; m. Edward John Chapin Jr.; children: John Edward, Susan Q. (dec.). SUNY Regent's Degree, 1985; AAS, SUNY, Binghamton, BS, 1991. Pers. adminstr. Mohawk Valley Psychiatric Ctr., Utica, N.Y., 1976-89; arbitrator Am. Arbitration Assn., N.Y.C., 1989-99; pres. Dispute Resolution Internat., New Hartford, N.Y., 1993—; neutral chair NYSDOL Office of Labor Mgmt., Albany, N.Y., 1993—. Mem. adv. coun. on safety and security in N.Y. State schs. N.Y. State Dept. Edn., Albany, 1995-97; founder, mem., bd. dirs. Forum on Conflict and Concensus, 1993-941 chair Mohawk Valley Women's History Project, 1998—; host weekly TV show, Mohawk Valley Srs., Sta. WUTR, 2002—. Author: Woman's Suffrage: A Dream of Full Citizenship; author, performer An Afternoon with Susan B. Anthony. Pres. Utica/Rome Metro League of Women Voters, 1992-97; coord. Com. on Met. Orgn., 1995-97; coord. of multicultural commn. League of Women Voters Edn. Fund, 1997; trustee amerita Mohawk Valley Cmty. Coll., 1996-2002; Utica C. of C., 1995-98. Recipient Found. award The Found. of SUNY at Binghamton, 1992, Recognition award NYS League of Women Voters, 1995, 97, Recognition award U.S. LWV Edn. Fund, 1998, Labor Mgmt. award Office of Mental Health, 1988, Conservator of Women's History award NOW, 2002. Mem. AAUW, Central N.Y. Futurist, Bd. Neighborhood Ctr. Home and Office: 56 Woodbrooke Rd New Hartford NY 13413-4805

CHAPKIS, WENDY LYNN, women's studies educator; b. Pasadena, Calif., Sept. 2, 1954; d. Robert Lynn and Marjorie Jean (King) C.; m. Gabriel Demaine, Oct. 1989. BA, U. Calif., 1977, MA, 1989, PhD, 1995. Project dir. Transnat. Inst., Amsterdam, The Netherlands, 1979-86; lectr. U. Calif., Santa Cruz, 1989-95; asst. prof. U. Southern Maine, Portland, 1995-99, assoc. prof., 1999—. Resource development Santa Cruz AIDS project, 1986-90, WomenCare Cancer Advocacy, Santa Cruz, 1994. Author: Beauty Secrets: The Politics of Appearance, 1986, Live Sex Acts: Women Performing Erotic Labor, 1996; editor: Loaded Questions, 1981, Of Common Cloth, 1983. Fulbright Found. fellow, 1993-94. Mem. Am. Sociol. Assn., Soc. for Study of Social Problems, Nat. Lesbian and Gay Task Force. Office: U Southern Maine 94 Bedford St Portland ME 04102-2801

CHAPLIN, PEGGY LOUIE, lawyer; b. Guantanamo Bay Naval Base, Cuba, Nov. 22, 1940; d. Raymond Gerard Fannon and Joan Marie (Carguil) Boyce. BS, Johns Hopkins U., 1971; JD, U. Md., 1973; LLM in Internat. Comml. Law, Georgetown U., 1983. Bar: Md. 1973, U.S. Dist. Ct. Md. 1973, U.S. Ct. Internat. Trade 1975, U.S. Ct. Appeals (fed. cir.) 1986, (D.C. cir.) 1988, U.S. Supreme Ct. 2002. V.p. Vanguard Shipping & Import, Balt., 1972-77, F.W. Myers & Co., Inc., Balt., 1977-84; assoc. Ober, Kaler, Grimes & Shriver, Balt., 1984-91, ptnr., 1992-97, Sandler, Travis & Rosenberg, P.A., Balt., 1997—. Chair Johns Hopkins U. Inst. of Policy Studies com. Logistics and the Economy, 1996-99. Contbr. articles to bar jours. Mem. Gov.'s Commn. World Trade Efforts, 1984, Balt. City Wage Commn., 1986-90, Md. Trade Policy Com., 1986; chair 2d Ann. Md. Internat. Trade Conf.; chair air cargo devel. com. BWI Econ. Devel. Coun., 1993-96. Mem.: NAFTA (chpt. 19 roster), Assn. Transp. Law, Logistics and Policy (newsletter editor Import/Export Regulation), Am. Assn. Exporters and Importers, Am. Arbitration Assn. (panelist), Md. Internat. Trade Assn. (pres. 1984—86), Women's Bar Assn. Md. (pres. 1977—78), Md. State Bar Assn. (chair internat. comml. law sect. 1991—92), Md. C. of C. (chmn. internat. trade com. 1984—97). Office: Sandler Travis & Rosenberg PA 111 S Calvert St Ste 2700 Baltimore MD 21202-6143 E-mail: pchaplin@strtrade.com.

CHAPMAN, ALISON BEATON, music educator; b. Suffolk, Va., Jan. 10, 1959; d. Leland Farley and Betty Page (Delk) Beaton; m. Joseph O. Jr., Sept. 25, 1982; children: Courtney Mae, Matthew Joseph. MusB, Va. Commonwealth U., 1980. Pvt. music instr., Smithfield, Va., 1984—88; music tchr. Smithfield Bapt. Presch., 1994—98, Peninsula Christian Sch., Smithfield, 1998—2000, Hardy Elem. Sch., Smithfield, 2000—. Ch. organist Whitehead's Grove Bapt. Ch., Smithfield, 1972—77, 1982—98, Smithfield Bapt. Ch., 1998—. Mem.: Nat. Assn. for Music Edn. Avocation: community theater.

CHAPMAN, CAROLYN, broadcasting director; b. Portsmouth, Ohio, Feb. 4, 1933; d. Roger Donald and Flowery Alice (Callaway) Carr; diploma Portsmouth Interstate Bus. Coll., 1954, S. Ohio Manpower Tng. Ctr., 1965; m. Edward J. Chapman, May 13, 1966; children— Cheryl, Roger, Lisa, Mark, Edmond, Sean. Dep. probation officer Scioto County Juvenile Ct., Portsmouth, 1960-63: coder II, Aid for Aged, Ohio Dept. Pub. Welfare, Columbus, 1964; clk. typist II, Bur. Vital Stats., Dept. Health, Columbus, 1964, clk.-stenographer II, CD Div., 1966; clk.-stenographer ABC, Los Angeles, 1967, ops. coordinator, 1968-72, assoc. dir., on-air dir., 1972— ; cons. in video tape and TV prodn.; mem. negotiating com. Teamsters Union, Los Angeles, 1970. Ch. sec. Findlay St. Meth. Ch., Portsmouth, 1959-63, chmn. women's day program, 1962, chmn. commn. on missions, 1959-62, del. ann. conf., Cleve., 1963, sec. ofcl. bd., 1959-62; pres. local chpt. Ohio Republican Council, 1959-62, mem. state bd., 1962, del. from Scioto County to State Rep. Conv., Ohio, 1962; mem. film editing com. Social Health and Hygiene Assn., 1961-62; tribute com. for Tribute to Dorothy Arzner, 1975; Los Angeles Jr. C. of C., 1977. Mem. ABC Employees Assn. (pres. Hollywood branch, 1971-73), Dirs. Guild Am. (council 1981-83). Address: PO Box 43025 Los Angeles CA 90043-0025

CHAPMAN, DELINDA (ANN), retired state official; b. Decatur, Ill., Apr. 25, 1947; d. Roy Wesley and Margere Jane (Daunt) C.; m. Lewis Steven Shelton, June 21, 1969 (div. May 1974); m. John Edward Erickson, Aug. 31, 1979; stepchildren: Linda Dumich, Debra Schoonover, Pamela Sitch, Scott, Paula Martin. BA, Ill. Coll., 1969; MA, Sangamon State U., Springfield, Ill., '974; EdD, U. Ill., 1979. Cert K-9 tchr., supt.'s endorsement, gen. adminstrv., Ill. Tchr., asst. prin., acting prin. Sch. Dist. 186, Springfield, 1969-76; rsch. asst. U. Ill. Coll. Edn., Champaign, 1976-78; supr. elem. edn. Charles County Bd. Edn., La Plata, Md., 1978-80; vis. prof. U. Guam, Mangilao, 1980-81; regional coord., adminstr. field svc., assoc. dept. Ill. Dept. Children and Family Svcs., Springfield, 1982-86, mgr., 1991-92; dir. data processing Office Sec. State, State of Ill., Springfield, 1986-91; assoc. dir. Ill. Liquor Control Commn., Springfield, 1992-93; spl. asst. to dir. Ill. Dept. Pub. Aid, Springfield, 1993—2002, ret., 2002. Mem. textbook selection com. State of Ill., Springfield, 1973-74; coord. Charles County Afro Am. Heritage Exhibit, Pomonkey, 1979-80; mem., sec. sch. attendance adv. com. Chgo. Pub. Schs., 1985-86; presenter in field. Chmn. Ill. Commn. for Celebration 75th Anniversary of 19th Amendment, Springfield, 1994-95; mem. coun. Inter-Civic Club, 1994-96; organizer Springfield Edn. Advocacy Coalition, 1995-96; vice chmn., sec. So. div. March of Dimes, 1989-96. Recipient cert. of appreciation Afro Am. Heritage Soc., Charles County, 1980, gov.'s cert. of appreciation State of Ill., 1995, Elizabeth Cady Stanton award Springield (Ill.) Women's Polit. Caucus, 1998; named Vol. of Yr., Greater Ill. chpt. March of Dimes, 1993. Mem. AAUW (pres. Springfield br. 1994-96, Ill. dir. planning and devel. 1995-98, pres. Ill. 1998—, Great Lakes regional dir., 2001—, Agt. of Change award 1997), Ill. Coll. Alumni Assn. (pres. 1997-99, trustee 2000—). Avocations: tennis, golf, book clubs. Home: 77 Cottage Grv Springfield IL 62707-8933 Office: Ill Dept Pub Aid 100 S Grand Ave E Springfield IL 62704-3802

CHAPMAN, FAY L. lawyer; b. San Jose, Calif., Dec. 17, 1946; BA, UCLA, 1968; JD, NYU, 1972. Bar: N.Y. 1973, Wash. 1975. Atty. Foster Pepper & Shefelman, Seattle, 1979—97; exec. v.p., gen. counsel Washington Mutual, Inc., Seattle, 1997—99; sr. exec. v.p., gen. counsel Washington Mutual Inc, Seattle, 1999—. Mem. Amer Bar Assn., Wash. Bankers Assn., Wash. Savs. League. Office: Washington Mutual Inc 1201 3rd Ave Ste 1601 Seattle WA 98101-3033

CHAPMAN, LINDA LEE, computer company executive, consultant; b. Omaha, Apr. 27, 1965; d. Olin Parks Chapman and Phyllis May Chapman-Wakefield; m. Chris Barkley; children: Lea Lee Noell, Phillip Wayne Noell, Cameron David Barkley, Jasmine Lauren Barkley. Grad., Centennial H.S., Utica, Nebr., 1983. MCSE, MCP Microsoft, cert. product specialist NT 4.0 Enterprise Microsoft, product Ssecialist NT 4.0 Workstation Microsoft, product specialist NT 4.0 Server Microsoft, cert. product specialist IIS 3.0 and Index Server Microsoft. LAN mgr. and programmer Wiig-Codr Underwriters, Omaha, 1986—93; sr. IT engr. MCI Consumer Markets, Austin, Tex., 1993—94; sr. migration cons. Levi-Strauss & Co., San Fransisco, 1994—95, Advanced Micro Devices (AMD), Austin, 1995—96; sr. migration cons., tech. project mgr. Continental Airlines, Houston, 1996—97; sr. migration cons., global arch. Dell Computer Corp., Round Rock, Tex., 1997—99, sr. product mgr., 1999—2000; pres., CEO, founder Migration Specialists Inc., Round Rock, 2001—. Recipient Outstanding Tech. Article award, 2000. E-mail: linda.chapman@migrationspecialistsinc.com.

CHAPMAN, ROBYN LEMON, music educator; b. Ogden, Utah, Jan. 17, 1974; d. Kent Lowell Lemon and Joanette Avonne Emery, Steven George Piccoli (Stepfather) and Cathy S. Lemon(Stepmother), Rick Alden Emery (Stepfather); m. Christopher Carl Chapman, Apr. 8, 2001. MusB, U. of Nev., Las Vegas, 1992—98. License for Educational Personnel Nev., 1998, Professional Education Certificate Wash. Supt. of Pub. Instrn., 2002. Long term substitute Mike O'Callaghan Mid. Sch., Las Vegas, 1998, band dir., 1998—2001, Theron Swainston Mid. Sch., North Las Vegas, 2001—02; music specialist Totem Falls Elem. Sch., Snohomish, Wash., 2002—. Camp adminstr. U. of Nev., Las Vegas Bands, 1993—2002; mid. sch. honor band chair Clark County Sch. Dist., Las Vegas, 2000—02. Recipient New Tchr. of the Yr., Clark County Sch. Dist., 1998—99. Mem.: Women Band Dirs. Internat., Wash. Music Educators Assn., Nat. Band Assn., Music Educators Nat. Conf. D-Conservative. Church Of Jesus Christ Of Latter-Day Saints. Avocations: reading, bicycling, bowling. Personal E-mail: gabynomel@aol.com.

CHAPMAN, ROSALYN M. federal judge; b. Chgo., May 16, 1943; BA cum laude, U. Mich., 1964; JD, Boalt Hall, 1967. Adminstrv. law judge Office of Adminstrv. Hearings State of Calif., 1977-95; apptd. magistrate judge cen. dist. U.S. Dist. Ct. Calif., 1995. Arbitrator Fed. Mediation and Conciliation Svc. and Am. Arbitration Assn., assoc. dir. Western Ctr. on Law and Poverty; lectr. UCLA Sch. Law. Office: US Courthouse 312 N Spring St Los Angeles CA 90012-4701 Fax: 213-894-4949.

CHAPMAN, SHELLEY C. lawyer; AB with distinction, Cornell U., 1978; JD cum laude, Harvard U., 1981. Bar: Ill., U.S. Dist. Ct. (no. dist.) Ill. 1982, N.Y., U.S. Dist. Ct. (so. and ea. dists.) 1984. Ptnr. Sidley & Austin, N.Y.C. Adj. prof. Bklyn. Law Sch., 1985-86. Editor Harvard Civil Rights-Civil Liberties Law Rev., 1980-81. Office: Sidley & Austin 875 3d Ave New York NY 10022 Fax: 212-906-2021. E-mail: schapman@sidley.com.

CHAPPELL, ANNETTE M. higher education consultant, minister; b. Washington, Oct. 31, 1939; d. Joseph John and Annette B. (Harley) C.; m. Brian Thomas Flower, Sept. 3, 1960 (div. Mar. 1983); m. Frank Joseph Sanders, Apr. 8, 1985 (dec. Dec. 1995). BA in English, U. Md., 1962, MA, 1964, PhD, 1970; MDiv, Gen. Theol. Sem., 2003. Lectr. European div. U. Md., Eng., 1965-66, instr. English, 1966-69; asst. prof. English Towson (Md.) U., 1969-72, assoc. prof., 1972-79, prof., 1979—99, spl. asst. to pres., affirmative action officer, 1974-77; dean humanistic, social and managerial studies Towson (Md.) State U., 1977-82, dean Coll. Liberal Arts, 1982-95, assoc. v.p. acad. affairs, 1995-99; ind. cons., 1999—; rector Ch. of the Redemption, Balt., 2003—. Contbr. articles to profl. jours. and book revs. to Ms Mag., Balt. Sun. Lay reader, chalicist All Saints Episcopal Ch., Reisterstown, Md., 1973-2003; pres. Baltimore County Commn. for Women, 1977-79; bd. dirs. Baltimore County Sexual Assault and Domestic Violence Center, 1978-83, pres., 1980-82. Mem. AAUP, MLA, Am. Assn. Higher Edn., Council Colls. Arts and Scis. (bd. dirs. 1984-86), Exec. Women's Council Md. (1st v.p. 1980, pres. 1981) E-mail: achappell@towson.edu.

CHAPPELL, ANNIE-DEAR, retired information technology company official; b. Riverside, Calif., Oct. 24, 1947; BSBA, Kensington U., 1985. Bus. mgr. Santa Clara Valley Ear, Nose and Throat Clinic, Sunnyvale, Calif., 1983-93; dir. adminstrv. svcs. NCA Computer Products, Sunnyvale, Calif., 1994-96; mgr. adminstrn. Datatools/BMC Software, Sunnyvale, Calif., 1996-97; br. adminstr. Bay Alarm Co., Santa Clara, 1997-99; tech. mgr. IBM bus. unit Analysts Internat., San Jose, Calif., 1999—2001; owner A.C.T., 2001—. Vol. Cherokee Nat. Hist. Soc., H.O.B.Y. Mem. NAFE. Avocation: women's self defense. Home: 22200 E Lolo Pass Rd Zigzag OR 97049-8756

CHAPPELL, BARBARA KELLY, child welfare consultant; b. Oct. 17, 1940; d. Arthur Lee and Katherine (Martin) Kelly; 1 child, Kelly Katherine. BA in English and Edn., U. S.C., 1962, MSW, 1974. Tchr. English Dept. Edn., Honolulu, 1962-65, Alamo Heights H.S., San Antonio, 1965-67; caseworker Dept. Social Svcs., Columbia, S.C., 1969-70; supr. Juvenile Placement and Aftercare, Columbia, 1970-72; child welfare cons. Edna McConnell Clark Found., N.Y.C., 1974-75; dir. Children's Foster Care Rev. Bd. Sys., Columbia, 1975-85, child welfare cons., 1985-89; adminstr. Dept. Human Resources and Juvenile Svcs., Balt., 1989-92; exec. dir. New Pathways, Inc., Balt., 1992-97; accreditation coord./social worker IV Dept. Mental Health, Columbia, 1997—. Lectr. in field. Contbr. articles to profl. jours. Coord. Child's Rights to Parents, Columbia, 1970-75. Episcopalian. Home and Office: 3215 Girardeau Ave Columbia SC 29204-3314

CHAPPELL, ELIZABETH IRENE, special education educator; b. Macon, Ga., Nov. 11, 1973; d. Rodney Lewis and Colleen Nova Chappell. BS in spl. edn., Bob Jones U., Greenville, S.C., 1995; MA in curriculum and instrn., Nat. Louis U., Evanston, Ill., 2001. Cert. tchr. in mental disabilities, emotional disorders, learning disabilities Ill. Mid. sch. spl. edn. instr. Kankakee Spl. Edn. Coop., Manteno, Ill., 1995—96; HS spl. Edn. instr. Plainfield Sch. Dist. 202, Plainfield, Ill., 1996—2001; alternative HS spl. edn. instr. Indian Prairie Sch. Dist. 204, Naperville, Ill., 2001—02, HS spl. edn. instr., 2002—. Activities coord. Greenville (S.C.) County Spl. Olympics, 1995; athlete asst. Spl. Olympics, Chgo., 2000—. Pub. rels. Shadow Lakes Assn., Wilmington, Ill., 2000—01; organist Phelan Acres Bible Ch., Wilmington, Ill., 1988—, bible sch., Sunday sch. tchr., 1991—. Grantee Academic Scholarship, Lion's Club, 1991—95. Mem.: NEA (union rep. 1997—2001), Coun. for Exceptional Children. Mem. Independent Bible Ch. Avocations: swimming, reading, exercise, softball, volleyball. Home: 177 Smallmouth Ln Wilmington IL 60481

CHAPPELLE, LOU JO, physical therapist assistant; b. Watertown, N.Y., Mar. 7, 1952; d. Harold Joseph and Alice Jean (Marcellus) Getman; m. Richard George Tobey, Aug. 14, 1982 (div.); m. Gerald E. Chappelle, Sept. 14, 1996; stepson, Scott C. AA, Hudson Valley Community Coll., 1972; BSE, State U. Coll., Cortland, N.Y., 1974; AAS, St. Philips Coll., 1981. Cert. elem. and secondary tchr., N.Y. Educator [illegible] ville (N.Y.) Central Sch., 1974-79, 1000 Islands Jr.-Sr. High Sch., Sand Bay-Clayton, N.Y., 1980-82; phys. therapist asst. II N.Y. State Veteran's Home, Oxford, 1982-91; phys. therapy asst. F.F. Thompson Health Sys., Inc., Canandaigua, N.Y., 1992-98, SunDance Rehab Corp, Ontario County Health Facility, 1998, Finger Lakes Vis. Nurse Svc., 1999—. EMT Gilbertsville (N.Y.) Emergency Squad, 1983-89. Capt. USAR, 1977-96. Decorated Army Achievement medal. Home: 4313 Deep Run Cv Canandaigua NY 14424-9777

CHAPSON, LOIS JESTER, interior designer; b. Plumas County, Calif., May 18, 1922; d. Lewis and Agda Edwards (Olsson) Jester; m. Elmer Donald Chapson, Nov. 7, 1959. AB, U. Calif., Berkeley, 1954; BS, San Jose State U., 1977. Pvt. practice interior designer, Los Gatos, Calif., 1978—. Planning commr. Town Los Gatos, Calif., 1978-84. Mem. Am. Soc. Interior Designers (allied mem.), Calif. Coun. of the Blind. Democrat. Home and Office: 323 Pennsylvania Ave Los Gatos CA 95030-5830

CHAR, PATRICIA HELEN, lawyer; b. Honolulu, Mar. 23, 1952; d. Lincoln S. and Daisy Char; m. Thomas W. Bingham, Mar. 20, 1982; children: Matthew Thomas Bingham, James Nathan Bingham. BA, Northwestern U., 1974; JD, Georgetown U., 1977. Bar: Wash. 1977, U.S. Dist. Ct. (we. dist.) Wash. 1977, U.S. Dist. Ct. (ea. dist.) Wash. 1982, U.S. Ct. Appeals (9th cir.) 1981, U.S. Supreme Ct. 1984. Assoc. Bogle & Gates, Seattle, 1977-84; ptnr., mem. Bogle & Gates PLLC, Seattle, 1984-99; of counsel Garvey, Schubert & Barer, Seattle, 1999-2000; ptnr. Preston Gates & Ellis LLP, Seattle, 2000—. Author: Ownership By a Fiduciary, 1997. Trustee YWCA, Seattle-King County-Snohomish County, United Way King County; vol. King County Big Sisters, United Way of King County, Seattle, 1987-90, Guardian Ad Litem Program, Seattle, 1987-93. Fellow Am. Coll. Trust and Estate Counsel; mem. ABA, Wash. State Bar Assn. (co-author chpts. 3 and 4 Wash. Civil Procedure Deskbook 1992). Office: Preston Gates & Ellis LLP 925 4th Ave #2900 Seattle WA 98104-1158 Office Phone: 206-623-7580. E-mail: pchar@prestongates.com.

CHARBONNET, GABRIELLE, writer; b. New Orleans, July 24, 1961; d. J. Arthur and Grace (Raffalovich) C.; m. Barry John Varela, May 5, 1991. BA, Loyola U., 1985. Prodn. asst. Random House, N.Y.C., 1987-88; assoc. editor Daniel Weiss Assocs., Inc., N.Y.C., 1988-89, mng. editor, 1989-93; writer, 1993—. Author: Snakes Are Nothing to Sneeze At, 1990, (adapter) Else-Marie and Her Seven Little Daddies, 1991, Boodil, My Dog, 1992, Tutu Much Ballet, 1994, Competition Fever, 1996, And Sleepy Makes Seven, 1998, The Divine Miss Ariel, 1999, Good-Bye Jasmine?, 1999, The Gum Race, 1999. Mem. DES Action Network. Avocations: gardening, sewing, travel, cooking, collecting antique children's books. Office: Henry Holt & Co care Susan Barry 115 W 18th St Fl 6 New York NY 10011-4113

CHARDAVOYNE, LARA J. social worker; b. Norwalk, Conn., Sept. 7, 1967; d. Arthur Duggan Norton and Barbara Marie Lindsley; m. Peter Lee Chardavoyne, May 23, 1999; children: Peter William, Carly Ann. BA in Psychology, Denison U., 1989; MS, Case Western Res. U., 2002. Asst. camp dir. YWCA, Greenwich, Conn.; med. social worker Mount Sinai Med. Ctr., Cleve.; case supr. Exchange Club Ctr. Prevention Child Abuse, Stanford, Conn., asst. dir., field instr. Mem.: NASW, Denison Alumni Recruiting Team. Republican. Roman Catholic.

CHARETTE, CECILE M. music educator; b. Lowell, Mass., Oct. 15, 1920; d. Arthur Joseph and Eva Marie (Croteau) C. MusB, U. Montreal, 1956, MusM, 1962; postgrad., Boston U., 1965-67. Joined Order of Holy Cross, 1939. Prof. music Basile Moreau Coll., St. Laurent, Canada, 1946—62, Notre Dame Coll., Manchester, NH, 1962—2002; pvt. music instr. Goffstown, NH. Choir dir., dir. operas, 1974-78. Mem. Nat. Assn. Tchrs. Singing (N.H. gov. 1978-84), Metro. Opera Guild, Nat. Music Tchrs. Roman Catholic. E-mail: cecilecha@aol.com.

CHARETTE, SHARON JULIETTE, library administrator; b. Woonsocket, RI, Apr. 24, 1956; d. Roland Alfred Lionel and Juliette Cecile (Lavoie) C. BA in French and English, R.I. Coll., 1978; MLS, U. R.I., 1981; cert. in computer info. systems, Bryant Coll., 1989; student, RISD, 1989-91. Asst. serials Wheaton Coll., Norton, Mass., 1978—79, catalog asst., 1979—82, libr. acquisitions, 1982—86; dir. libr. and instnl. rsch. New Eng. Inst. Tech., Warwick, RI, 1986—. Seamstress, designer, craftsman, 1976—. Chair Franco Am. com. R.I. Heritage Commn., Providence, 1987-90, treas., 1982-87; costume designer Kaleidoscope Theatre, 2003—. Mem. ALA, New England Libr. Assn., R.I. Libr. Assn., No. R.I. Coun. of Arts, Theatre Works (costume designer 2001—, web mgr. 2002—), Mensa, TechACCESS of R.I. (bd. dirs., corr. sec. 1992-98, 2003—, chair 1998-2003, web mgr. 2002—). Avocations: jewelry design, historical costume reproduction, computers, music, theatre. Home: 147 Greenville Rd North Smithfield RI 02896-7422 Office: New Eng Inst Tech 2500 Post Rd Warwick RI 02886-2244 E-mail: scharette3@cox.net.

CHARIS, BARBARA, nutritionist, consultant, health researcher; b. Pitts., Feb. 26, 1934; d. Robert Edward and Clara L. Wakefield; m. Roger S. Markle, May 19, 1956 (div. July 1980); children: Mitchell, Tarri, Heidi, David. Student, Pa. State U., 1951-53, U. Pitts., 1954, Harbor Coll., Wilmington, Calif., 1966; M. in Holistic Health Sci., Columbia Pacific U., San Rafael, Calif., 1982. Dir., cons. Charis Holistic Ctr., North Hollywood, Calif., 1982—. Host (radio show) The Health Beat, L.A., 1988-89; producer (TV show) Sharing from the Heart, L.A., 1996-97; author: Sharing from the Heart, 1995. Mem. Nat. Health Fedn., Vegetarian Soc. (v.p. 1982-83), Book Publicists So. Calif. Avocations: poetry, songwriting, lecturing, spiritual counseling, running (L.A. Marathon 1994, 99, 2004). Home and Office: Charis Holistic Ctr 6227 Morse Ave North Hollywood CA 91606-2948

CHARLES, BLANCHE, retired elementary education educator; b. Spartanburg, S.C., Aug. 7, 1912; d. Franklin Grady and Alice Floride (Hatchette) C. BA, Humboldt State U., 1934. Tchr. Mt. Signal and El Centro schs., 1934—48, Calexico (Calif.) Unified Sch. Dist., 1958-94; libr. Calexico Pub. Lib., 1948—59; ret., 1994. Elem. sch. named in her honor, 1987. Mem. NEA, ACT, Calif. Tchrs. Assn., DAR, Nat. Soc. Daus. of Confederacy, Delta Kappa Gamma. Avocations: gardening, reading. Home: 37133 Hwy 94 Space 3 Boulevard CA 91905-9524

CHARLES, CATHERINE ELAINE, music educator; b. Charlotte, N.C., Jan. 31, 1962; d. Andrew Jackson and Vivian Brinkley Charles. MusB, U. N.C., Greensboro, 1987. Cert. educator N.C. Organist and choirmaster St. Thomas Episcopal Ch., Ahoskie, NC, 1988—2002; dir. choral music Hertford County Mid. Sch., Murfeesboro, 1988—96, Hertford County HS, Asnokie, 1996—2002; dir. music Holy Trinity Episcopal Ch., Hampstead, 2002—; music educator New Hanover County Schs., Wilmington, NC, 2002—. Musical dir. Gallery Theatre, Ahoskie, 1990—97; staff accompanist Chowan Coll. Music, Murfeesboro, 1992—96; arts chair Hertford County HS, Ahoskie, 1999—2002. Bd. mem. Gallery Theatre, Ahoskie, 1997—2002. Recipient Tchr. of Yr., Students of Hertford HS, 2002. Mem.: Am. Guild Organists, N.C. Assn. of Educators, Music Educators Nat. Conf. Democrat. Episcopalian. Achievements include development of music curricula for mid. sch. and HS. Avocations: canoeing, gardening, horseback riding, reading. Home: 506 N 21st St Wilmington NC 28405 Office: New Hanover County Schs 6410 Carolina Beach Rd Wilmington NC 28412

CHARLES, CORY ANNE, television guest booking director; b. Bklyn., Oct. 3, 1965; d. John Thomas and Anne Jane Azumbrado; m. Nick Charles, Oct. 4, 1997; 1 stepchild, Katie. BA in Comms. cum laude, L.I. U., 1987; MA in Polit. Sci., U. Calif., Santa Barbara, 1988. Asst. dir. rsch. McLaughlin Group, Washington, 1989-90; rschr., editl. prodr. CNN, Atlanta, 1990-98; dir. [illegible] guest booking CNN, Atlanta, 1998—, copy person N.Y. Daily News, 1986. Participant BMW-Quandt Fedn. Transatlantic forum. Fellow German Marshall Fund, 2001. Mem. Coun. on Fgn. Rels. Avocations: travel, reading, cooking, photography, animals. Office: CNN 1 CNN Center Atlanta GA 30303 E-mail: Cory.Charles@turner.com.

CHARLES, ISABEL, university administrator; b. Bklyn., Mar. 10, 1926; d. James Patrick and Isabel (Roney) C. BA, Manhattan Coll., 1954; MA, U. Notre Dame, 1960, PhD, 1965; postgrad., U. Mich., 1968-69. Chmn. dept. English Bishop Watterson High Sch., Columbus, Ohio, 1954-59, St. Mary of the Springs Acad., Columbus, 1959-62; asst. prof. English Ohio Dominican Coll., Columbus, 1965-68, acad. dean, exec. v.p., 1969-73; asst. dean Coll. Arts and Letters, U. Notre Dame, 1973-75, acting dean, 1975, dean, 1976-82, asst. provost, 1982-87, assoc. provost, 1987-95; assoc. provost emerita U. Notre Dame, 1995—. Contbr. articles to profl. jours. Mem. MLA, Assn. Am. Colls. Home: 1802 Stonehedge Ln South Bend IN 46614-6341

CHARLES, SALLY ALLEN, financial analyst; b. Atlanta, Jan. 9, 1950; d. Thomas Roach Jr. and Lucille (Blake) Allen; m. Darrell Charles, Dec. 28, 1974; children: Carey Robert, Jane Allen. BA in Speech Comm., Auburn U., 1972; MBA, Kennesaw State U., 1989; cert. in small bus. mgmt., U. Ga., 1995. Cons. Small Bus. Devel. Ctr. Kennesaw (Ga.) State U., 1990-96, dir. Small Bus. Inst., 1992-96; purchasing agt. Portal Tech., CD Rom Tng. Voice Overs, Mgmt. Com., 1997—99; exec. asst., v.p. fin. Johnson Controls, 2000—02; registered bus. analyst Am. Acad. Fin. Mgmt., 2004—. Mem. adj. faculty dept. mgmt. and entrepreneurship Kennesaw State U., 1991-94; mem. small bus. adv. coun. Apple Computers, Napa Valley, Calif., 1994. Contbr. cover quote, reviewer: Market Planning Guide (Andy Bangs), 1998. Press credentials chair Woodstock (Ga.) Welcome for Pres. and Mrs. George Bush, 1992; instr. annual tng. Ga. Soc. CPA's, Atlanta, 1993; advisor facilities Kappa Alpha Theta, Emory U., Atlanta, 1994-2003. Recipient Outstanding Young Citizen award, Woodstock (Ga.) Jaycees, 1985; recipient Small Bus. Inst. Cases of the Yr. award Ga.-U.S. Small Bus. Adminstrn., Atlanta, 1992, 93, 95; Small Bus. Inst. grantee U.S. Small Bus. Adminstrn., Washington and Atlanta, 1991-95. Mem. Small Bus. Inst. Dirs. Assn. (mem. adv. com. 1994-96, reviewer 1996-99, newsletter editor 1995-97, track chair 1998, coord. new dir. tng. 1995, v.p. 1996, Showcase award 1994); Ansley Terrace Condo Assn., (bd. dirs., 2004-). Republican. Baptist. Home: 175 15th St 117 Atlanta GA 30309-2311 Office: State of Ga Road and Tollway Authority 101 Marietta St 2500 Atlanta GA 30303

CHARLETON, MARGARET ANN, child care administrator, consultant; b. Orange, Calif., Aug. 3, 1947; d. Arthur Mitchell and Isabelle Margaret (Esser) C.; (div. Sept. 1985). AA in Liberal Arts, Orange Coast Coll., 1968; BA in Psychology, Chapman U., 1984. Head tchr. Presbyn. Ch. of the Master, Mission Viejo, Calif., 1977-81; child care program adminstr. Crystal Stairs, Inc., L.A., 1981—2001. Mem. adv. bd. Children's Home Soc., Santa Ana, Calif., 1982-83; cons. Calif. Sch. Age Consortium, Costa Mesa, 1987, Calif. State Dept. of Edn., 1988; trainer preschool edn. program Sesame Street PBS, 1994-96; lectr. in field; presenter Western Regional Child Care Food Program Conf., San Francisco, 1997, Save the Children Conf., Atlanta, Ga., 1998, 10th Ann. Child Care Food Program Sponsor's Conf., 2001. Contbr. articles to profl. jours. Mem. South Orange County Community Svc., Mission Viejo, 1983—; liaison Family Svcs.-Marine Base, El Toro, Calif., 1989—; mem. adv. bd. Dept. Social Svc., 1997—. Recipient Plaque of Recognition, Vietnamese Community of Orange County, 1984. Mem. NAFE. Roman Catholic. Avocations: sailing, skiing, traveling, wine. Office: Child Nutrition Program So Calif 7777 Alvarado Rd Ste 700 La Mesa CA 91941

CHARLTON, SHIRLEY MARIE, educational consultant; b. Nashville, Nov. 20, 1934; d. Ottis Ruby and Irene Lenoir (Cabler) C.; children: David Matthew Christian Sironen, Charlton Gwynn Cabler Sironen. BS, George Peabody Coll. Tchrs., 1954; MA in Ednl. Adminstrn. and Supervision, U. Tenn., Chattanooga, 1970. Cert. supr., Tenn. Classroom tchr. Albany (Ga.) Pub. Schs., 1954-55, 56-57, Orlando (Fla.) Pub. Schs., 1960-61, Grand Forks (N.D.) Pub. Schs., 1962-65; TV and resource tchr. Chattanooga Publ Schs., 1965-67, supr., 1967-97; cons., 1997-99. Mem. NEA, Tenn. Edn. Assn., Chattanooga Edn. Assn. (charter mem. negotiating team 1979-81), Alpha Delta Kappa (v.p. 1981-83). Episcopalian. Avocations: history, genealogy, acting, art, music.

CHARNIN, JADE HOBSON, magazine executive; b. NYC, Mar. 12, 1945; d. John Louis Campo and Elizabeth (Anne) Stanton); m. David Alan Hobson,Dec. 30 (div. 1972); m. Martin Charnin, Dec. 18, 1984. BA, NYU, 1967. Asst. editor Glamour mag., N.Y.C., 1970; accessory editor Vogue mag., N.Y.C., 1970-78, fashion editor, 1978-81, fashion dir., 1981-86, creative dir. fashion, 1987-88; v.p., dir. creative svcs for fashion and design group Revlon Inc., 1988; exec. creative dir. Mirabella Mag., 1988-94; fashion dir. N.Y. Mag., 1994-98; freelance journalist, 1999—. Pres. Growing things (landscape design co.), 2002—; cons. editor Self mag., N.Y.C., 1979—81. Costume coord. for off-Broadways shows Upstairs at Oneals, 1981, Laughing Matters, 1989, Martin Charnin, the Hits and the M.S.'s, 1990. Mem.: ASPCA, Hort. Soc. N.Y. (bd. dirs.), Am. Hort. Soc., Assn. Profl. Landscape Designers, Humane Soc. N.Y. (bd. dirs.), Wilton Garden Club (bd. dirs.). Avocations: gardening, opera, ballet, theater, skiing. Office Phone: 203-762-9666. Personal E-mail: jadehobson@aol.com.

CHARO, ROBIN ALTA, law educator; b. Bklyn., June 6, 1958; d. Jon and Ethel (Munach) C. BA, Harvard U., 1979; JD, Columbia U., 1982. Bar: N.Y. 1983. Assoc. dir. Legis. Drafting Rsch. Fund, N.Y.C., 1982-85; lectr. Columbia Law Sch., N.Y.C., 1983-85, U. Paris, Paris, 1985-86; legal analyst Congl. Office of Tech. Assessment, Washington, 1986-88; fellow U.S. Agy. for Internat. Devel., Washington, 1988-89; assoc. prof. law U. Wis., Madison, 1989-98, prof. law, 1998—. Cons. Congl. Office of Tech. Assessment, 1988-92, U.S. AID, 1989-91, Can. Law Reform Commn., Ottawa, Can., 1989-90, NAS, 1989—. Contbr. articles to profl. jours. Active U. Wis. Human Subjects Com., Madison, U. Wis. Hosp. Ethics Com., Madison, Abortion Strategy Group, Madison; cons. Rural South Cen. Wis. Perinatal Substance Abuse Project, 1989—. Fulbright grantee, 1985-86. Fellow AAAS; mem. Internat. Bioethics Assn., Am. Soc. Law and Medicine. Democrat. Jewish. Avocations: travel, folk music, foreign languages. Office: U Wis Law Sch 975 Bascom Mall Madison WI 53706-1399

CHAROENWONGSE, CHINDARAT, pianist, music educator; b. Bangkok, Aug. 18, 1968; d. Vivat and Yuwadee Charoenwongse; m. George Grover Shaw, Sept. 25, 1999. BFA, Chulalongkorn U., Bangkok, 1989; M of Music Edn., U. Rochester, 1993; D of Musical Arts in Piano Performance, and Pedagogy, U. Okla., 1998. Instr. piano Chulalongkorn U., Bangkok, 1989-90; instr, lectr. piano Kasetsart U., Bangkok, 1990-91; exec. sec., adminstrv. asst. Johnson Electric Indsl. (Thailand) ltd., Bangkok, 1989-91; dir. piano dept. Chintakarn Music Inst., Bangkok, 1997-98; pianist, instr., dir. In Tune Music Co. Inc., Oklahoma City, 1999—; asst. prof. piano U. Ctrl. Okla., 2000—. Clinician, workshop presenter and cons., Alfred Publs., Bangkok, 1998, Chintakarn Music Inst., 1993, 97-98, 2000—, Hal Leonard Publs., Bangkok, 2000—; guest lectr. Chulalongkorn U., Bangkok, 1998, 2000—, Srinakharinwirot U., Prasanmitr Campus, 2000. Contbr. articles to profl. jours. Pianist Outreach Mission Com., Norman, Okla., 1996-97, 1999, St. John's Episcopal Ch., Norman, 1996-97. Fulbright scholar, 1991-93, Marjorie Martin Caylor scholar, U. Okla., Norman, 1994-96, Martha Boucher scholar, U. Okla., Norman, 1996-97; rsch. grantee U. Okla., Norman, 1997. Mem. Music Tchrs. Nat. Assn., Okla. Music Tchrs. Assn., Ctrl. Okla. Music tchrs. Assn. (co-chmn. notification com. 1998-2003), Phi Kappa Phi, Sigma Alpha Iota (sec. corr. com 1996-97). Episcopalian. Avocations: travel, reading, musical performances, theater, opera. Office: U Ctrl Okla Sch Music 100 N U [illegible] Dr Edmond OK 73034

CHARON, RITA, medical educator; b. Providence, 1949; BA in Biology and Child Edn., Fordham U., 1970; MD, Harvard U., 1978; MA in English, Columbia U., 1990, MPhil in English with distinction, 1992, PhD in English, 1999. Resident Montefiore Hosp. and Med. Ctr., Bronx, NY; instr. in medicine Coll. of Physicians and Surgeons, Columbia U., 1983—88, asst. prof. medicine, 1983—88, asst. prof. clinical medicine, 1988—93, assoc. prof. clinical medicine, 1993—2001; asst. attending physician Presbyn. Hosp., N.Y.C., NY, 1982—93, assoc. attending physician, 1993—; prof. clinical medicine Coll. Physicians and Surgeons Columbia U., 2001—, dir. program in narrative medicine and clinical skills assessment program, 1996—. Editor-in-chief: Lit. and Medicine jour.; co-editor: (anthology) Stories Matter: The Role of Narrative in Medical Ethics, 2002. Named Outstanding Woman Physician of Yr., 1996; recipient Nat. award for innovation in med. edn., Soc. Gen. Internal Medicine, 1997; grantee Guggenheim fellowship, 2002; 1st recipient of Virginia Kneeland Frantz award for Outstanding Woman Dr. of Yr., 1987. Achievements include development of innovative new teaching method called the parallel chart systems which brings together literature and medicine. Office: Presbyn Hosp 9 E 105 Gen Medicine 622 W 168th St New York NY 10032*

CHARRIERE, SUZANNE, architectural firm executive; Mng. ptnr. Corgan Assocs., Dallas. Rep. for firm Dallas (Tex.) Citizen's Coun. Pres. Friends of Dallas (Tex.) Police Assn.; adv. bd. Women's Mus., Dallas; bd. dir. Goodwill Industries, Dallas, Dallas (Tex.) Pks. and Trees Found. Mem.: Nat. Assn. Women Bus. Owners (Louise Razzio Pathfinder award 2004), Internat. Women's Forum (v.p.), Greater Dallas (Tex.) C. of C. (bd. dir.). Office: Corgan Associates Inc 501 Elm St Dallas TX 75202

CHARTERS, ANN, biographer, editor, educator; b. Bridgeport, Conn., Nov. 10, 1936; d. Nathan and Kate Danberg; m. Samuel B. Charters, Mar. 14, 1959; children: Mallay, Nora Lili. AB, U. Calif.-Berkeley, 1957; MA, Columbia U., 1960, PhD, 1965. Mem. faculty Colby Jr. Coll., New London, NH, 1961—63; lectr. Columbia U., 1965—66; asst. prof. Am. lit. N.Y.C. Community Coll., 1967-70; assoc. dean of the coll. Brown U., 1989-90; prof. Am. lit. U. Conn., Storrs, 1974—. Author: Nobody—Life and Times of Bert Williams, 1967, Kerouac, 1973, 2d edit., 1986, I Love—Story of Vladimir Mayakovsky and Lili Brik, 1979, The Story and Its Writer, 6th edit., 2002, The Beats: Literary Bohemians in Post-War America, 1983, Beats and Company: A Portrait of a Literary Generation, 1986, The Viking Portable Beat Reader, 1992, Major Writers of Short Fiction, 1993, The Viking Portable Jack Kerouac Reader, 1995, Selected Letters of Jack Kerouac, 1995, (with Samuel Charters) Literature and Its Writers, 1997; author intro. Penguin Classic edit. Three Lives and Q.E.D. (Gertrude Stein), On the Road (Jack Kerouac), Selected Letters of Jack Kerouac, vol. 2, 1999, The American Short Story and Its Writer, 1999, (with Samuel Charters) Blues Faces, 2000, Beat Down to Your Soul, 2000, The Portable Sixties Reader, 2003. Office: U Conn Dept English PO Box U-25 Storrs Mansfield CT 06269-0001 E-mail: acharters@uconn.edu.

CHARTERS, KAREN ANN ELLIOTT, critical care nurse, health facility administrator; b. Chelsea, Mass., Apr. 3, 1946; d. Albert Charles and Hazelle Marie (Kraus) Elliott; m. Byron James Charters, Feb. 4, 1972. Diploma, Grace New Haven Sch. Nursing, New Haven, Conn., 1967; student, So. Conn. State Coll., 1968, U. New Haven, 1974; BS in Healthcare Adminstrn., St. Leo Coll., 1999. CCRN. Asst. head nurse Yale New Haven (Conn.) Hosp., 1972-76; staff nurse critical care unit Hosp. Corp. Am., 1982—; relief clin. coord. Cmty. Hosp. of New Port Richey, Fla., 1987—, nursing supr., 1997—. Mem. AACN (bd. dirs. Gulf Coast chpt. 1990-91, 96-97, treas. 1991-93), Am. Heart Assn. (past bd. dirs.). Home: 7519 Clanton Trail Hudson FL 34667 Office: Cmty Hosp New Port Richey 5637 Marine Pkwy New Port Richey FL 34652

CHASANOW, DEBORAH K. federal judge; b. 1948; BA, Rutgers U., 1970; JD, Stanford U., 1973. Pvt. practice atty. COle & Groner, Washington, 1975; asst. atty. gen. State of Md., 1975-79; chief criminal appeals divsn. Md. Atty. Gen.'s Office, 1979-87; U.S. magistrate judge U.S. Dist. Ct. Md., 1987-93, dist. judge, 1993—. Instr. law schs. U. Balt., U. Md., 1978-84. Mem. Fed. Magistrate Judges Assn., Md. Bar Assn., Prince George's County Bar Assn., Women's Bar Assn., Marlborough Am. Inn. Ct. (pres. 1988-90), Phi Beta Kappa. Office: US Courthouse 6500 Cherrywood Ln Rm 465A Greenbelt MD 20770-1249

CHASE, ALYSSA ANN, editor; b. New Orleans, Dec. 23, 1965; d. John Churchill and Alexandra Andra (de Monsabert) C.; m. Robert Brian Rebein, July 1, 1995; children: Alexandra Maria Rebein, Rowen Jakob Rebein. BA in Lit. in English, U. Kans., 1988; BA in Studio Art magna cum laude, SUNY, Buffalo, 1994. Asst. editor Dial Books for Young Readers, N.Y.C., 1989-90; assoc. editor Holiday House, Inc., N.Y.C., 1990-92, Buffalo (N.Y.) Spree Mag., Buffalo, N.Y., 1992-95; copy editor, writer The Riverfront Times and St. Louis Mag., St. Louis, Mo., 1995-97; mng. editor St. Louis Mag., 1997-98; editor RCI Premier Mag., Indpls., 1998—. Freelance copy writer, proofreader, copy editor and/or rschr. Harper Collins Children's Books, N.Y.C., 1990-92, Morrow Jr. Books, N.Y.C., 1990-92, Tambourine Books, N.Y.C., 1990-92, Lothrop, Lee & Shepherd Books, N.Y.C., 1990-92, Dorling Kindersley, Inc., N.Y.C., 1990-92, The Humanist: Prometheus Books, 1993, Printing Prep, Buffalo, 1994, Georgette Hasiotis, Buffalo, 1994, August Tavern Creek Developers, St. Louis, 1996; tchg. artist, docent coord., tour guide The Arts in Edn. Inst. of Western N.Y., Cheektowaga, N.Y., 1995. Mem. Phi Beta Kappa. Avocations: painting, writing childrens books, travel, gardening, running. Home: 306 N Ridgeview Dr Indianapolis IN 46219-6127

CHASE, DORIS TOTTEN, sculptor, educator, filmmaker; b. Seattle, 1923; d. William Phelps and Helen (Feeney) Totten; m. Elmo Chase, Oct. 20, 1943 (div. 1972); children: Gregary Totten, Randall Jarvis Totten. Student, U. Wash., 1941-43. Lectr. tours for USIA in S.Am., 1975, Europe, 1978, India, 1972, Australia, 1986, Eastern Europe, 1987, Ireland, England, France; vis. lectr., presenter U. Colo., Boulder, Mary Mount Coll., N.Y., the Kitchen Ctr. for Film & Video, Nat. Film Bd. of Can., Toronto, N.Y. Grad. Sch.; artist-in-residence Pilchuck Glass Sch., 1999. One-woman shows include Ruth White Gallery, N.Y.C., 1967, 69, 70, Fountain Gallery, Portland, Oreg., 1970, U. Wash. Henry Gallery, 1971, 77, 98, Wadsworth Athenum, Hartford, Conn., 1973, Hirshhorn Mus., Washington, 1974, 77, Anthology Film Archives, N.Y.C., 1975, 80, 83, Donnell Libr., N.Y.C., 1976, 79, 83, 92, Performing Arts Mus. at Lincoln Ctr., 1976, Mus. Modern Art, N.Y.C., 1978, 80, 87, 93, 98, High Mus., Atlanta, 1978, Herbert Johnson Mus., 1982, A.I.R. Gallery, N.Y.C., 1983-85, Art in Embassies, USIS, 1984-88, Inst. Contemporary Art, London, 1989, Woodside/Braseth Gallery, 1990, 92, 94, John F. Kennedy Ctr., 1990, Seattle Arts Mus., 1990, 92, 95, 99, 2002, Mus. N.W. Art La Conner Wash., 1995; circulating exhibit Western Mus. Assn., 1970-71, Am. Inst. Archs., Seattle, 1994, Friesen Gallery, Seattle, 1997, 98, 99, 2001; represented in permanent collections Finch Coll. Mus., N.Y.C., Mus. Modern Art, N.Y.C., Seattle Art Mus., Ashai Shimbum, Tokyo, Georges Pompidou Ctr., Paris, Battelle Inst., Mus. Fine Arts Boston, Milw. Art Inst., Art Inst. Chgo., Mus. Fine Arts Houston, Frye Art Mus., Seattle, Nat. Collection Fine Arts, Smithsonian Instn., Washington, Wadsworth Athenum, N.C. Mus. Art, Raleigh, Mus. Modern Art, Kobe, Japan, Pa. Acad. Art, Phila., Portland Art Mus., Vancouver (B.C.) Art Gallery, Montgomery (Ala.) Mus. Fine Art, Hudson River Mus., N.Y.C., Tacoma Art Mus.; works represented in archival collections Ctr. for Film and Theatre Rsch., U. Wis., Madison, U. Wash., Seattle, UCLA Film Archives, Lincoln Ctr. Performing Arts Libr., N.Y.C., Pompideau, Paris, Archieves of Am. Art Smithsonian Instn., Washington; executed monumental kinetic sculpture Kerry Park, Seattle, Lake Park, 1976, Anderson, Ind., Expo '70, Osaka, Japan, Sculpture Park, Atlanta, Met. Mus. Art, N.Y.C., Montgomery Mus. Fine Arts, monumental bronze sculpture installed, Seattle Ctr., 1999; multi-media sculpture for 4 ballets, Opera Assn. Seattle; included in Sculpture in Park program N.Y.C., Playground of Tomorrow ABC-TV, L.A.; prodr., dir. (film and video) Doris Chase Dance Series, 1971-80, Concept Series, 1980-85, By Herself Series: Table for One (with Geraldine Page), 1985; prodr. (with Jennie Ventris) Glass Curtain, 1984(with Anne Jackson) Dear Papa, 1986, (with Luise Rainer) A Dancer, 1987, (with Priscilla Pointer) Still Frame, 1988, (with Joan Plowright) Sophie, 1989, The Chelsea, 1994, Danse de colour, 2002. Recipient honors and awards at numerous festivals in U.S. and fgn. countries; grantee Nat. Endowment for Arts, Am. Film Inst., 1988, N.Y. State Coun. for Arts, Mich. Arts Coun., Seattle Art Commn., 1992, Jerusalem Film Festival, 1987, Berlin Film Festival, 1985, 87, Athens Film Festival 1995, London Film Festival, 1986, Am. Film Inst. Festival, 1987, 94, Retirement Rsch. Found., 1994, Lockwood Found., Herzman Family Found., Seattle Center Found., NEA, N.Y. State Coun. for Arts; subject of documentary Doris Chase: Portrait of the Artist, PBS, 1985; subject of book and video: Artist in Motion, 1993; subject of documentary Doris Chase: Circle at the Center, PBS, 1999; Doris Chase Day proclaimed by Mayor and City Coun. Seattle; recipient Wash. Gov.'s Art award, 1992; honored at N.Y. Pub. Libr. and N.Y. Film Video Coun., 2003. Mem. Actors Studio (writer, dirs. wing 1986). Achievements include all work in film and video being in collection and archives of Mus. Modern Art, N.Y.C.; established Doris Totten Chase scholarship fund U. Washington, 2002.

CHASE, KAREN SUSAN, English literature educator; b. St. Louis, Oct. 16, 1952; d. Stanley Martin and Judith C.; m. Michael H. Levenson, Dec. 30, 1984; children: Alexander Nathan, Sarah Sophie. BA, UCLA, 1974; MA, Stanford U., 1977, PhD, 1980. Asst. prof. U. Va., Charlottesville, 1979-85, assoc. prof., 1985-91, prof., 1992—. Author: Eros and Psyche, 1984, George Eliot's Middlemarch, 1990; co-author: The Spectacle of Intimacy: A Public Life For The Victorian Family, 2000 Office: Univ of Va English Department 219 Bryan Hall Charlottesville VA 22903

CHASE, MARILYN, journalist; b. L.A. AB in English, Stanford U., 1971; MA in Journalism, U. Calif., Berkeley, 1973. Reporter Wall St. Jour., San Francisco, 1978—94, health columnist, 1994—99, sr. spl. writer health and medicine, 1999—. Author: (book) The Barbary Plague: The Black Death in Victorian San Francisco, 2003. Office: Wall St Jour 201 California St Ste 1350 San Francisco CA 94111-5022

CHASE, NORAH CAROL, English language educator; b. Bklyn., Dec. 18, 1942; d. Homer Bates Chase and Dorothy (Teitelbaum) Weiner; m. M. Alan Ettlinger, Dec. 31, 1970 (div. Nov. 1985), 1 child, Gabrielle Ettlinger. Attended, Rutgers U., New Brunswick, N.J., 1966-75; MA in Comparative Lit., U. Minn., Mpls., 1969; PhD in Women's Studies, The Union Inst., Cin., 1995. Prof. Kingsborough Cmty. Coll., Bklyn., 1968—; prof. ext. program Queen's Coll., N.Y.C., 1992—97. Mem. exec. com. and grievance counselor Profl. Staff Congress, N.Y.C., 1994—; co-facilitator Women Writing Women's Lives Seminar. Recipient Rsch. grantee CUNY, 1984, 86, 06, The Ford Found. 1985-87 Mem. NOW. Office: English Dept Kingsborough CC Oriental Blvd Brooklyn NY 11235

CHASE, PATRICIA M. management consultant; d. Walter H. and Amy D. Wiehe; m. Lewis R. Chase, Mar. 4, 1983; children: Scott, Ronald, Eric. Regional practice administr. HCA Physician Svcs., Tampa Bay, Fla., 1983—2003; pres., owner Med. Mgmt. Consulting, Spring Hill, Fla., 2003—. Mem.: NAFE, Profl. Assn. Health Care Office Mgrs. (cert. med. mgr. 1997), Am. Acad. Profl. Corder (cert. procedural coder 2002). Home: 14234 Van Ct Spring Hill FL 34610 Office Phone: 727-857-2474. Personal E-mail: patchase@tampabay.rr.com.

CHASE, SANDRA LEE, clinical pharmacist, consultant; b. Oak Park, Ill., July 31, 1959; d. William Warren and Charlene Lois (Johnson) Chase; m. Christopher Paul Bloch, Sept. 8, 1984; children: Kyle Thaddeus Bloch, Matthew William Bloch. Student, Mich. State U., 1977-80; BS in Pharmacy, U. Mich., 1983, PharmD, 1984. Lic. pharmacist Del., Mich., Pa.; cert. leader arthritis health. YMCA Aquatic Program. Rsch. asst. U. Mich., Ann Arbor, 1980-81; pharmacy intern Three Rivers (Mich.) Hosp., 1981, Cmty. Pharmacy, Ann Arbor, 1980-83; pharmacy intern, grad. intern St. Francis Hosp., Wilmington, Del., 1982-83; resident in hosp. pharmacy Thomas Jefferson U. Hosp., Phila., 1984-85, clin. pharmacist in cardiopulmonary medicine, 1985-89; sr. med. info. coord. ICI Pharms. Group, Wilmington, Del., 1989-92; clin. pharmacist Thomas Jefferson U. Hosp., Phila., 1989-93, clin. pharmacist drug use policy and clin. svcs., 1993-98; clin. pharmacy specialist Spectrum Health, Grand Rapids, Mich., 1999—. Adj. assoc. prof. clin. pharmacy Temple U. Coll. Pharmacy, 1990—98, Ferris State U. Coll. Pharmacy, 1999—; clin. instr. in pharmacy practice Phila. Coll. Pharmacy and Sci., 1985—87, clin. asst. prof., 1987—88, clin. assoc. prof., 1988—98; instr. clin. care cardiopulmonary medicine in nursing Episcopal Hosp., Phila., 1986—88, Thomas Jefferson U. Hosp., Phila., 1985—91, Our Lady of Lourdes Med. Ctr., Camden, NJ, 1988—91; coord., prof. pharmacology and drug therapeutic for advanced nursing practice course Nursing Ctr. Profl. Devel., U. Pa., Phila., 1994—2001; mem. Pa. Osteoporosis Soc. Bd., 1996—98; presenter in field. Mem. editl. bd. : RN, referee; contbg. editor; mem. editl. bd. : Med. Econs., referee: AHFS Drug Info., Am. Druggist, Am. Jour. Hosp. Pharmacy, Nursing 96 Drug Handbook, Nursing 97 Drug Handbook, Pharmacotherapy, Annals of Pharmacotherapy, U. Hosp. Consortium Monographs; contbr. articles to profl. jours. Mem. adv. bd. Nursing Mothers Network; cert. leader aquatic program Arthritis Found. YMCA, 2000—; chmn. Coll. Pharmacy Alumni Soc., 2000—; mem. women's heart advantage steering com. Spectrum Health, 2003—; mem. alumni bd. govs. U. Mich. Coll. Pharmacy, 1991—97, 1998—, chair bd. govs., 2000—03; mem. Heartbeat Gala com. Am. Heart Assn., 2004—; mem. State of Mich. Task Force for Cardiovasc. Health, 2002—03; bd. dirs. Coll. Pharmacy Alumni Soc., 1991—97, 1999—; Corey Lake Assn., 2003—. Fellow, Mich. Pharmacists Assn., 2001. Mem.: Am. Heart Assn., Aerobics and Fitness Assn. Am., Western Mich. Soc. Health-Sys. Pharmacists (bd. dirs. 1998—2000), Pediat. and Adult Asthma Network West Mich., Mich. Soc. Health Sys. Pharmacists (chair adv. com 2000—), Mich. Pharm. Assn. (mem. exec. bd. 2002—), Del. Pharm. Soc. (conv. com 1990—94, ACPE com. 1990—94), Nat. Headache Found., Am. Diabetes Assn., Am. Pharm. Assn., Am. Soc. Health Sys. Pharmacists, Am. Coll. Clin. Pharmacy, Rho Chi Pharm. Soc. Republican. Lutheran. Avocations: aerobics, waterskiing, cross-country skiing, gardening. Office: Spectrum Health Dept Pharmacy 100 Michigan St NE Grand Rapids MI 49503-2560 E-mail: Sandra.Chase@spectrum-health.org.

CHASEK, ARLENE SHATSKY, academic director; b. Newark, N.J., June 1, 1934; d. Herman and Rose (Sporn) Shatsky; m. Marvin B. Chasek, Apr. 10, 1960; children: Pamela S., Laura N., Daniel J. BA, Cornell U., 1956; MA, Columbia U., 1957; postgrad. U. ND., 1972-74, Rutgers U., 1981-91. Tchr. English and journalism Elizabeth (N.J.) Pub. Schs., 1978-80, Summit (N.J.) Pub. Schs., 1978-80; coord. MA program Fairleigh Dickinson U., Teaneck, N.J., 1979-81; editor AT&T, Murray Hill, N.J., 1980-81; project coord. Consortium for Ednl. Equity, Rutgers U., New Brunswick, N.J., 1981-85, project dir., 1985-88, dir. spl. projects, 1988-93, dir. family involvement programs in math., sci. and tech., 1993-95, dir. Ctr. for Family Involvement in Schs., 1995—. Mem. steering com., N.J. coord. Am. Goes Back to Sch. initiative U.S. Dept. Edn., 1997. Author, editor: Rutgers Family Tools and Technology, 1994, Rutgers Family Science, 1993, Mathematics in Art/Art in Mathematics, 1986 (U.S. Dept. Edn. award

1987), From Jumping Genes to Red Giants: A Guide to High School Science Research; author: The Recruitment and Retention Challenge, 1982, Futures Unlimited, 1985 (Curriculum award am. Ednl. Rsch. Assn. 1986). Recipient Golden Apple award for Family Involvement Programs, Working Mother mag., U.S. Dept. Edn., and Tchrs. Coll. Columbia U., 1996. Mem. AAUW, LWV, NSTA, Nat. Assn. Equity Educators, Coop. Learning Assn. Internat. Tech. Edn. Assn., Assn. Math. Tchrs. N.J. Home: 9 Schindler Pl New Providence NJ 07974-1738 Office: Rutgers Univ Center for Math, Science, and Computer Busch Campus, SERC New Brunswick NJ 08903 E-mail: aschasek@aol.com.

CHASEY, JACQUELINE, lawyer; Bar: N.J. 1983, N.Y. 1984. Formerly counsel Bertelsmann, Inc.; sr. counsel Bertelsman, Inc., 1990-93, v.p. legal affairs, 1994—2002, sr. v.p. legal affairs, 2002—. Office: Bertelsmann Inc 1540 Broadway New York NY 10036-4039

CHAST, ROZ, cartoonist; b. Bklyn., Nov. 26, 1954; d. George and Elizabeth (Buchman) C.; m. William Franzen, Sept. 22, 1984; children: Ian, Nina. BFA, RISD, 1977. Contract artist The New Yorker Mag., N.Y.C., 1979—; cartoonist The Scis. Mag. Author: (cartoon collections) Unscientific Americans, 1982, Parallel Universes, 1984, Mondo Boxo: Cartoon Stories, 1987, The Four Elements, 1988, Proof of Life on Earth, 1991, The Party, After You Left : Collected Cartoons 1995-2003, 2004; illustrator of various books including The Joy of Being Single, 1992, Meet My Staff, 1998, Now I Will Never Leave the Dinner Table, 1999, Rationalizations to Live By, 2000, The New Yorker Book of Kids Cartoons, 2001, Weird and Wonderful Words, 2002, You're an Animal, Viskovitz!, 2003; work has been featured in Scientific American, N.Y. Times Mag., Rolling Stone, Nat. Lampoon. Office: care New Yorker Cartoonists Career Concepts 25 W 43rd St New York NY 10036-7406*

CHASTAIN, BRANDI DENISE, professional soccer player; b. San Jose, Calif., July 21, 1968; m. Jerry Smith; 1 stepchild. Student, U. Calif., Berkeley, 1986—88; BA in TV Comm., Santa Clara U., 1991. Mem. U.S. Women's Soccer Team, 1996—; asst. coach women's soccer team Santa Clara U.; profl. soccer player San Jose CyberRays, 2001—03. Mem. Shiroke Serena, Japan, 1993. Named World Cup Champion, 1999; recipient Gold medal, Olympic Games, 1996, Silver medal, Sydney Olympic Games, 2000. Achievements include mem. championship team U.S. Olympic Festival; CONCACAF Championship, N.Y., 1993. Office: c/o Santa Clara U Athletics Dept 500 El Camino Real Santa Clara CA 95050-4345 also: US Soccer Fedn 1801 S Prairie Ave # 1811 Chicago IL 60616-1319

CHATER, SHIRLEY SEARS, health educator; d. Norman and Edna Sears; m. Norman Chater, Dec. 5, 1959 (dec. Dec. 1993); children: Cris, Geoffrey. BS, U. Pa., 1956; MS, U. Calif., San Francisco, 1960; PhD, U. Calif., Berkeley, 1964. Asst., assoc., prof. dept. social and behavioral scis. Sch. Nursing U. Calif.-San Francisco, Sch. Edn.-Berkeley, 1964—86; asst. vice chancellor acad. affairs U. Calif., San Francisco, 1974—77, vice chancellor acad. affairs, 1977—82; council assoc. Am. Council Edn., Washington, 1982—84; sr. assoc. Presdl. Search Consultation Svc. Assn. Governing Bds., Washington, 1984—86; pres Tex. Woman's U., Denton, 1986—93; chair Gov's health policy task force State of Texas, 1992; commr. Social Security Administrn., Washington, 1993—97; Regent's prof. hist. for Health and Aging U. Calif. San Francisco, 1997, 99 Vis. prof. Inst. Health & Aging U. Calif., San Francisco, 1998—. Mem. commn. on women Am. Coun. on Edn.; bd. dirs. Carnegie Found. for Advancement Tchg., United Educators Ins. Risk Retention Group, Denton United Way, 1986—93. Mem.: Nat. Acad. Nursing, Nat. Acad. Social Ins., Nat. Acad. Pub. Administrn., Internat. Alliance, San Francisco Women's Forum West, Inst. Medicine NAS. Office: Inst Health and Aging 3333 California St Ste 340 San Francisco CA 94118-1944

CHATFIELD, MARY VAN ABSHOVEN, librarian; b. Bay Shore, N.Y. d. Cornelius and Elma Elizabeth (Sumner) van Abshoven; m. Robert W. Chatfield, June 22, 1963 (div. 1981); 1 child, Robert Warner Jr.; m. Alexander Watts, Jan. 6, 1996 (div. 2000). AB, Radcliffe Coll., 1958; SM, Columbia U., 1961; MBA, Harvard U., 1972. With library system Harvard U., Cambridge, Mass., 1961-92, librarian Bus. Sch., 1963-78, head libr., 1978-92; acting head libr. Countway Libr. Harvard Med. Sch., 1988-89; head libr. Angelo State U., San Angelo, Tex., 1992-95; collections care mgr. Fosterfields, Morristown, N.J., 1996-97; mgr. libr. svcs. Montclair (N.J.) Art Mus., 1997; exec. dir. Mendham (N.J.) Free Pub. Libr., 1997-99; coord. tech. svcs. Tom Green County Libr., San Angelo, Tex., 1999—. Mem. Daughters of Brit. Empire. Democrat. Episcopalian. Avocations: reading, embroidery, collecting, museum studies, market value. Home: 115 N Jackson St San Angelo TX 76901-3215 Business E-Mail: marychat@wcc.net.

CHATFIELD-TAYLOR, ADELE, historic preservationist; b. Jan. 29, 1945; d. Hobart and Mary Owen (Lyon) C-T; m. John Guare, May 20, 1981. BA, Manhattanville Coll., 1966; MS in Hist. Preservation, Columbia U., 1974; postgrad., Harvard U., 1978-79, ArtsD (hon.), Lake Forest Coll., 1995. Archtl. historian Hist. Am. Bldg. Survey, Washington, 1967; co-founder, dir. Urban Deadline Archs., Inc., 1968-73; with N.Y.C. Landmarks Preservation Commn., 1973-80; founder, exec. dir. N.Y. Landmarks Preservation Found., 1980-84; dir. design arts program Nat. Endowment for Arts, 1984-88; pres. Am. Acad. in Rome, N.Y.C., 1988—. Adj. prof. hist. preservation program Grad. Sch. Arch. and Planning, Columbia U., 1976-84; guest lectr. Harvard U., MIT, Columbia U., NYU, U. Va. Editor: articles to profl. jours. Mem. Thomas Jefferson Found. for Monticello, 2001—; bd. dirs. Preservation ACTION, 1976—84; trustee Ctr. for Bldg. Conservation, 1978—84; mem. U.S. del. to China Women in Arch., 1977, 1980, Hist. Preservationists, 1982; mem. exec. com. U.S./Internat. Coun. on Monuments and Sites, 1979—84, vice chmn. design arts policy panel, 1978—82; trustee Tiber Island History Mus., 1983—; bd. dirs. Internat. Design Conf., Aspen, 1986—90, Nat. Bldg. Mus., 1989—95; mem. commn. Fine Arts, 1990—94; trustee Nat. Trust for Hist. Preservation, 1999—; mem. restoration com. South St. Seaport Mus., 1975—84; mem. adv. bd. Jeffersonian Restoration, 1989—; bd. dirs. Greenwich Village Trust for Hist. Preservation, 1983—84; mem. lawn adv. bd. U. Va., 1982—86. Recipient Rome prize Am. Acad. in Rome, 1983-84, Merit award AIA N.Y. chpt., 2003; Loeb fellow Harvard U., 1978-79; named to Grand Office Ordine al Meito Pres. Italian Republic, 2002; archtl. fellow Ednl. Facilities Lab. Acad. Ednl. Devel., 1982-83, fellow N.Y. Inst. Humanities, 1983-89. Fellow Am. Acad Arts & Scis.; mem. Nat. Trust Hist. Preservation, Friends of Cast Iron Arch., Met. Mus. Art, Century Assn., Pug Dog Club of Greater N.Y. Office: Am Acad in Rome 7 E 60th St New York NY 10022-1001 E-mail: a.chatfield-taylor@aarome.org

CHATLEN, MARTHA CAHILL, middle school counselor; b. Dearborn, Mich., Feb. 1, 1962; d. Daniel J. Cahill, Sr. and Mary E. Cahill; m. Stanley L. Chatlen, June 9, 1990; children: Sarah, Emily, John. BS in Bus., Ferris State U., 1984; MS in Edn., L.I. U., 1990. Cert. tchr. K-12 N.Y., Ga. Salesperson Pan Am. Airlines, Detroit, 1984—87; sales mgr. Continental Airlines, 1977—90; sch. counselor Pt. Jefferson (N.Y.) Sch., 1993—97, The Davis Acad., Atlanta, 1998—2002, transition coord., mid. sch. counselor, 2002—. Tchr. religious edn. St. Bridget Cath. Ch., Alpharetta, Ga., 2002, Alpharetta, 03, Alpharetta, 04. Bd. dirs. Tourette Syndrome Assn. Ga. and SC, 2003—. Recipient ednl. scholarship to visit Israel, The Davis Acad., 2003. Mem.: ACA, Prejudice Awareness Summit (Summit winner 2002, Summit award 2003), Tourettes Support Group of North Atlanta (leader 2003—), Tourettes Assn. Ga. Avocations: yoga, reading, walking. Home: 3300 Sundew Ct Alpharetta GA 30005 Office: The Davis Acad 8105 Roberts Dr Atlanta GA 30350 E-mail: mchatlen@hotmail.com.

CHATTERJI, ANGANA P. anthropologist; b. Calcutta, India, Nov. 17, 1966; d. Bhola and Anubha (Sengupta) C.; m. Richard Murray Shapiro, May 10, 1998. MA, U. Delhi, 1989; PhD, Calif. Inst. Integral Studies, San Francisco, 1999. Cons. Planning Com. India, New Delhi, 1990-92; dir. rsch. Asia forest network program Ctr. South Asia Studies U. Calif., Berkeley, 1992—. Asst. adj. prof. Calif. Inst. Integral Studies, 1997—; cons. Swed Forest Internat., Stockholm, 1997—; cons. in field Author: In Search of Reality, 1984. Ford Found. grantee, 1993. Mem. Am. Anthropol. Assn. Avocations: gliding, reading, computers, travel, symphony.

CHAU, MAY YING, librarian, educator; b. Hong Kong, Feb. 16, 1952; d. Zea Wan Chau and Yok Mei Chen. BFA, BS, Brigham Young U., 1984, MS, 1987; MSLS, Wayne State U., 1990. Rsch. asst. Wayne State U., Detroit, 1987—89; rsch. technician Strohtech Inc., Detroit, 1989—90; plant sci. libr., asst. prof. Colo. State U., Ft. Collins, Colo., 1991—94; agrl. sci. libr., assoc. prof. Oreg. State U., Corvallis, Oreg., 1994, agrl. sci. libr., 1994—. Co-chmn. pres. commn. Oreg. State U., 2000—01. Contbr. articles to profl. jours. Mem.: ALA (racial & ethnic diversity com. 1997—98), Oreg. Libr. Assn. (honor, award & scholarship com. 1999—). Office: Oregon State University 121 The Valley Library Corvallis OR 97330-4551 Business E-Mail: may.chau@orst.edu.

CHAU, PIN PIN, bank executive; b. Hong Kong; d. Waihing Wong; m. Raymond Chau; 1 child, Christine. B.A, Coe Coll., 1965; MA in Asian hist., Yale U., 1967; grad., Stonier Grad. Sch. of Banking, Rutgers U. With Nat. Westminster Bank (now Fleet), 1970—87; chief lending officer United Orient Bank, N.Y.C., 1987—88, COO, 1988—89, pres., CEO, 1989—93, The Summit Nat. Bank, Atlanta, 1993—; CEO Summit Bank Corp., Atlanta, 1999—. Bd. dirs. Consumer Credit Counseling Service; exec. com. Ga. Dept. Industry, Trade and Tourism, 1999—. Bd. dirs. Atlanta Coll. Arts; bd. councilors Carter Ctr. Mem.: Internat. Women's Forum, Soc. Internat. Bus. Fellows (assoc.). Avocation: painting. Office: Summit Bank Corp 4360 Chamblee-Dunwoody Rd Atlanta GA 30341*

CHAUDERLOT, FABIENNE-SOPHIE, foreign language educator; b. Marseilles, France, Aug. 11, 1960; came to U.S., 1985; d. Michel Hubert and Georgia Kalafatides. Maitrise English Lit., U. Scis. Humaines, Aix-en-Provence, France, 1982; MBA in Internat. Adminstrn., Puyricard, France, 1985, PhD, U. Calif., San Diego, 1995. Lectr. U. Calif., Riverside, 1995-96; asst. prof. U. P.R., Mayaguez, 1996-97, Wayne State U., Detroit, 1997-2000; with Veritas Software Internat. Strategies, 2000—. V.p. Alliance Francaise, San Diego, 1990-93; founder, pres. Femmes Francaises du Sud Calif., San Diego, 1989-93. Rsch. grantee Humanities Ctr., Detroit, 1997-98. Avocations: painting, piano, cats, aerobics, photography. Office: Wayne State U 487 Manoogian Hall Detroit MI 48202 E-mail: f.chauderlot@Wayne.cdu.

CHAUDHRY, MARIE-LAURENCE, elementary education educator, administrator; b. France, July 18, 1947; came to U.S., 1963; d. Gerard Leopold and Gisèle Delienne Dominique; children: Aisha Khan, Daud, Sara, Sadia. Student, Northwestern U., 1964-68; M of Applied Tchg. in Reading, Northeastern Ill. U., 1975; Cert. of Advanced Studies in Ednl. Leadership and Administrn., Nat. Louis U., 1993. Lab. technician Evanston (Ill.) Hosp., 1968-69; chemist libr. Velsicol Chem., Chgo., 1969-70; tech. libr. C-E Refractories, Chgo., 1970; tchr. Chgo. Pub. Schs.-Schiller Sch., 1970-80, Hilel Sch., Chgo., 1980-82; tchr. elem. edn. Hammond Sch., Chgo., 1982—; staff devel. facilitator, 1990; administr Melrose Pk. Sch. Dist. 89, Chgo., 2000. Owner, mgr. apt. bldgs., Melrose Park, Ill., 1994—; several shopping centers and malls; ins. profit., 1998—; pres. MLC Enterprises, Inc. Organizer Ednl. Confs. for Hammond Schs., 1991-99; regional pres. ladies aux. Ahmadiyya Movement in Islam, 1990-93, pres. local chpt., 1988-93; regional sec. Children's Aux. Orgn., 2001—; vol. DuPage Convalescent Ctr., Wheaton, 1993-95; spkr. Women in Islam, various univs. Moslem. Office: PO Box 1062 Melrose Park IL 60161-1062

CHAUDOIR, JEAN HAMILTON (JEAN HAMILTON), secondary school educator; b. Lake Charles, La., July 31, 1945; d. John Gardiner and Nora (Alford) Hamilton; divorced; 1 child, Elizabeth Jean. BS, La. State U., 1967, MEd, 1986, postgrad., 2002. Tchr. 3d grade St. Pius X Sch., Baton Rouge, 1967-69; tchr. 2d grade St. Francis Cabrini Sch., Alexandria, La., 1969-75; tchr. 3d grade St. Theresa Sch., Shreveport, La., 1975-76; tchr. 4th grade Sacred Heart Sch., Baton Rouge, 1976-79, West Baton Rouge Parish, Brusly, La., 1979-80; tutor Ed-U-Care, Baton Rouge, 1987-88; with summer program East Baton Rouge Parish, Baton Rouge, 1990-91, tchr. Chpt. 1 summer sch., 1993, 94; part time tchr. Modern Curriculum Press, Baton Rouge, 1995—; tchr. for instrnl. support Lanier Elem. Sch., Baton Rouge, 1997—2002, chair improvement team. Chair Adopt-A-Sch. at Park Forest Elem., Baton Rouge, 1986-94; chair mktg. com. Park Forest Elem. Sch., Baton Rouge, La., 1986-94, mem. adv. coun., 1993-94, chair monitoring com., 1993-94; mem. Title 1 Sch. Wide Com., 1995. Sustaining mem. Jr. League Baton Rouge, 1985—2001. Mem.: Delta Kappa Gamma (pres.). E-mail: jchaudoir@ebrpss.k12.la.us.

CHAVE, CAROLYN MARGARET, arbitrator, retired lawyer; b. Chgo., Jan. 30, 1948; d. Grant Carruthers and Priscilla Morrison (Shaw) C.; m. Robert Edmund Hand; children: Joshua, Chloe, Robert, Grant. BA, U. Chgo., 1970; MAT, Oakland U., 1971; JD, Loyola U., Chgo., 1976. Bar: Ill. 1976, N.Y. 1980. Tchr. corps intern Pontiac (Mich.) Pub. Schs., 1970-71; sec., receptionist Grad. Sch. Bus., U. Chgo., 1971; counselor Sonia Shankman Orthogenic Sch., Chgo., 1972; pvt. practice Chgo., 1976-78; asst. v.p., assoc. counsel Bank of Tokyo, N.Y.C., 1978-85; substitute tchr. N.Y.C. Pub. Schs., 1986-88; with Breckenridge Law Offices, 1986-88; sr. v.p., counsel, mgr. human resources Tokai Bank, N.Y.C., 1988-97; dir., counsel Deutsche Bank, N.Y.C., 1997-99. Arbitrator Am. Arbitration Assn., N.Y.C., 1986—. Vol. lawyer Chgo. Vol. Legal Svcs., 1977-78; designer playground PS 41 Parent Assn., Greenwich Village, N.Y., 1987. Avocations: weaving, dance, patchwork quilting.

CHAVERS, BLANCHE MARIE, pediatrician, educator, researcher; b. Clarksdale, Miss., Aug. 2, 1949; d. Andrew and Mildred Louise C.; m. Gubare Mpambara, May 21, 1982; 1 child, Kaita. BS in Zoology, U. Wash., 1971, MD, 1975. Diplomate Am. Bd. Pediats. Intern U. Wash., Seattle, 1975-76, resident in pediatrics, 1976-78; instr. U. Minn., Mpls., 1982, asst. prof. pediatrics, 1983-90, assoc. prof. pediatrics, 1990-99, prof. pediatrics, 1999—. Attending physician dept. pediatrics, U. Minn. Sch. Medicine, Mpls., 1982. Co-editor: Am. Jour. Kidney Diseases, 2001—; contbr. articles to profl. jours. Recipient Clin. Investigator award NIH, 1982; Pediatric Nephrology fellow U. Minn., 1978-81. Mem. Am. Soc. Nephrology, Am. Soc. Pediatric Nephrology, Internat. Soc. Nephrology, Internat. Soc. Pediatric Nephrology, Am. Soc. Transplantation. Democrat. Methodist. Avocations: tennis, reading, collecting african artifacts, art. Office: Univ Minn MMC 491 420 Delaware St SE Minneapolis MN 55455-0348

CHAVEZ, JEANETTE, editor; m. Leo Chavez; children: Laura, Stephanie. BS in Journalism with honors, U. Colo., 1973. Mem. staff Office of U.S. Rep. Spark Matsunga, Washington; reporter Colorado Springs (Colo.) Sun; reporter, copy desk chief, city editor, news editor Ft. Collins (Colo.) Coloradoan; copy editor Daily Herald, Arlington Heights, Ill., 1981—82; copy editor, then news editor bus. sect. Chgo. Sun Times, 1982—84; dep. news editor Denver Post, 1984—91, assoc. editor features, 1991—97, mng. editor, 1997—, mng. editor ops., 2000—. Office: Denver Post 1560 Broadway Denver CO 80202-1577*

CHAVEZ, LINDA, civil rights organization executive; b. Albuquerque, June 17, 1947; m. Christopher Gersten Chavez; 3 children. BA, U. Colo., 1970; postgrad., UCLA, 1970-72, U. Md., 1974-75. Mem. staff House

Judiciary Subcom. on Civil and Constl. Rights, Washington, 1972-74; asst. dir. legis. Am. Fedn. Tchrs., 1975—77; cons. civil rights sect. Office Mgmt. and Budget, Washington, 1977; editor Am. Educator mag., 1977-83; asst. to pres. Am. Fedn. Teachers, 1982—83; staff dir. U.S. Commn. on Civil Rights, 1983-85; dep. asst. to pres. and dir. Office Pub. Liaison Exec. Office of Pres., 1985-86; US Senate candidate Md., 1986; chmn. Nat. Commn. Migrant Edn., 1988—92; mem. UN Subcommission on prevention of discrimination and protection of minorities, 1992—96; founder, pres. Ctr. for Equal Opportunity, Washington, 1995—, Stop Union Polit. Abuse, 2001—; founder, chmn. Rep. Issues Campaign, 2003—. Bd. dirs. ABM Industries, Inc.; polit. analyst FOX News Channel; Pres. George Bush's nominee for Sec. Labor until she withdrew her name from consideration, 2001. Author: Out of the Barrio: Toward a New Politics of Hispanic Assimilation, 1991, An Unlikely Conservative: The Transformation of an Ex-Liberal, 2002; syndicated weekly columnist Chgo. Tribune; freelance columnist Wall St. Jour., Washington Post, The New Republic, Commentary, Crisis; appeared on To the Contrary, CNN & Co., Equal Time, The McNeil-Lehrer News Hour; host (radio show) Linda Chavez Show. Bd. dirs. Campaign to Prevent Teen Pregnancy. Recipient Living Legend award, Libr. of Congress, 2000. Mem.: Coun. Fgn. Rels. (co-chair com. on diversity 1998—2000). Office: Ctr for Equal Opportunity 815 15th St NW Ste 928 Washington DC 20005-2253*

CHAVEZ, MARY ANN, osteopathic family physician; b. York, Pa., Dec. 6, 1942; d. Henry David Gross and Mary Ellen (Ness) Rhoads; m. Richard L. Ziegler, Dec. 24, 1965 (div. Jan. 1983); children: Richard L. Ziegler Jr., Mara L. Tammaro, Brian L. Ziegler. BS, Alvernia Coll., 1983; DO, Coll. Osteo. Medicine, Phila., 1992. Legal sec. Louis Sager, Esquire, Pottstown, Pa., 1962-67; homemaker, tailor in pvt. practice Pottstown, 1967-85; intern Riverside Hosp., Wilmington, Del., 1992-93, resident in family practice, 1993-95; pvt. practice Spring Grove, Pa., 1995-97, Lancaster, Pa., 1997-999, Chillicothe, Ohio, 1999-2000, Sullivan, Ind., 2001—. Pell grantee, Beog grantee Alvernia Coll., 1979-83. Mem. AMA, Am. Osteo. Assn., Am. Coll. Osteo. Family Physicians, Am. Acad. Osteopathy, Pa. Osteo. Med. Assn., York County Osteo. Med. Assn, Nat. Osteo. Women's Physicians Assn., Ohio Osteo. Medicine, Ohio State Med. Soc., Ind. State Med. Assn., Sullivan Rotary Club, Sullivan Bus. and Profl. Women's Club. Avocations: oil painting, piano, tailoring, gardening. Home: 204 W Giles St PO Box 450 Sullivan IN 47882-0450 Office: Sullivan Med Clinic 222 W Beech St Sullivan IN 47882 E-mail: maryann.chavez@verizon.net.

CHAVEZ, MARY LYNN, pharmacy educator; b. Detroit, May 8, 1950; d. Gilbert E. and Dorothea J. (Munro) Van Sickle; m. Pedro I. Chavez, May 12, 1973; children: Pedro C., Stephen J. BS in Pharmacy, U. Tex., 1973; PharmD, Purdue U., 1985. Instr. Coll. Pharmacy U. P.R., San Juan, 1983-84, 87-88, asst. prof. pharmacy practice, 1988-92, clin. pharmacy specialist Med. Sch.-Pediat. Oncology Group, 1990-93, assoc. prof. pharmacy, 1990-93; assoc. prof. dept. pharmacy practice Chgo. Coll. Pharmacy, Midwestern U., Downers Grove, Ill., 1993-98, acting asst. chmn. clin. edn., 1997-98; dir. didactic edn. Midwestern U. Coll. Pharmacy, Glendale, Ariz., 1998—; dir. complementary therapies Rsch. Ctr. Advancement Pharmacy Practice, Glendale, 1998—, prof. pharmacy practice, 1999—. Writer pharmacy exam. CAT-NAPLEX/NABPLEX Licensure, Park Ridge, Ill., 1996; reviewer posters and presentations Am. Assn. Health Sys. Pharmacies, Bethesda, Md., 1996—; reviewer manuscripts Annals of Pharmacotherapy, Cin. Therapeutics, Am. Jour. Pharm. Edn., Jour. Pharmacy Tech., Am. Jour. Health Sys. Pharmacy, 1995—. Mem. editl. bd. Jour. Am. Pharmacy Assn., Prima Pub., Jour. Herbal Pharmacotherapy; contbg. editor Hosp. Pharmacy. Asst. to cub pack leader area coun. Boy Scouts Am., Naperville, Ill., 1995, 96. Mem. Am. Pharm. Assn., Am. Assn. Colls. of Pharmacy, Am. Soc. Hosp. Pharmacists, Am. Coll. Clin. Pharmacists, Sigma Xi, Rho Chi. Office: Midwestern U Coll Pharmacy Glendale AZ 85308

CHAVEZ, NELBA R. state agency administrator, former federal agency administrator; b. Mar. 9, 1940; BA in Sociology and Psychology, U. Ariz.; MSW, UCLA; PhD in Philosophy, U. Denver; student sr. exec. program in state and local govt., Harvard U. From therapist to exec. dir., CEO, COO La Frontera Ctr., Tuscon, 1971-89; prin. Chavez and Assocs., 1989-91; dir. juvenile probation svcs. City and County of San Francisco, 1991-94; adminstr. Substance Abuse and Mental Health Svcs. Adminstrn., U.S. Dept. Health and Human Svcs., Washington, 1994-2000; dep. dir. Ariz Dept. Econ. Security, 2003—. Bd. dirs. nat. coalition of Hispanic Health and Human Svc. Organs,; mem. U.S. Senate Hispanic Adv. Com., Pres. Nat. Coun. on Handicapped, White House Prevention Com. on Drug-Free Am. Mem. Tuscon Mayor's Task Force on Children. Recipient Outstanding Leadership award Ariz. State U., 1985, Dedication and Commitment award Tenth Ann. Chicano Conf., 1989, Disting. Svc. award Nat. Assn. Profl. Asian Am. Women, 1995, Mujer 95 award League United L.Am. Citizens, 1995, Rafael Tavares, MD, Meml. award Assn. Hispanic Mental Health Profls., 1995, Nat. Health Leadership award Nat. Coalition Hispanic Health and Human Svcs., 1997, Leadership award Fedn. Families for Children's Mental Health, 1997, Nat. Coun. on Aging award for Leadership in Health Promotion, 2000; named to Honor Roll Latino Behavioral Health Inst., 1998. Office: Ariz Dept Econ Security PO Box 6123 Phoenix AZ 85005

CHAVEZ-THOMPSON, LINDA, labor union administrator; b. Lubbock, Tex., Aug. 3, 1944; m. Robert Thompson (dec.); 2 children. Union sec. Am. Fedn. State, County & Mcpl. Employees, 1967-71, internat. rep., 1971-73, asst. bus. mgr., bus. mgr., exec. dir. local 2399, 1973-95, exec. dir. coun. 42, 1977-95, nat. v.p. labor coun. L.Am. Advancement, 1986-96, internat. v.p., 1988-96, exec. dir. Tex. Coun. 42, 1977-95; v.p. AFL-CIO, Washington, 1993-95, exec. v.p., 1995—. Office: AFL-CIO 815 16th St NW Washington DC 20006-4145

CHAVIS, KATHERINE (KITTY CHAVIS), disability consultant, artist; b. Bklyn., Dec. 4, 1938; d. Allen Joseph Holmes and Doris Viola (Hobson) Holmes Osborne; m. Herbert Chavis, Dec. 16, 1956 (dec. Feb. 1972); m. Johnnie Jones Jr., Apr. 24, 1977 (dec. Oct. 1988). IBM coder Met. Life Ins. Co., N.Y.C., 1955-62; receptionist Assemblyman Mills Calif. State Legis., San Diego, 1963-65; traffic coord. Air Products & Chems., Inc., N.Y.C., 1965-67; exec. sec. Dept. Water, Gas and Electricity, N.Y.C., 1967-68; statis. typist Haryou Act Inc., N.Y.C., 1968-70; typist Worker's Compensation Bd., N.Y.C., 1970-82; police adminstrv. aide N.Y.C. Police Dept., 1982-91; assoc. dir. Inst. disability Advocacy, Bklyn., 1992—; pres. Kandi Creations, Bklyn., 1995—. Participant: (book) American Negro Art, 1959; solo exhbns. include Fournier's Studio, Greenwish Village, N.Y., 1966, Madau Gallery, Bklyn., 1967-70; group shows include Soul Gallery, N.Y.C., 1961, Manor Gallery, Bklyn., 1962, Atelier d'Arts Gallery, N.Y.C., 1967, Bklyn. Mus., 1968, Design Masters Gallery, N.Y.C., 1988, Creative Concerns Gallery, Bklyn., 1989, ACCAA Gallery, Bklyn., 1990-91, Ctr. of Arts Gallery, Bklyn., 1992, 94; work represented in several permanent collections, including Met. Opera House, N.Y.C., UNESCO, Brussels, Bklyn. chs. Sec. S.E. San Diego Cmty. Guild, 1963-65, Classon/Franklin/Greene Aves. Block Assn., Inc., Bklyn., 1988; 2d v.p. young adult coun. NAACP, 1967; trustee N.Y.C. Guardian Assn., Inc., 1986; acting chmn. BedStuy Cmty. Citizens Action Taskforce, Pub. Advocates Office, N.Y., 1995; co-editor BedStuy Interag. Coun. of Aging, 1995—. Recipient Tillman award Pub. Sch. 167 Bd. of Edn., Bklyn., 1952, 1st prize Wall St. Art Assn. U.S. Trust Co., 1962, 2d prize Hunter Coll. Irish Feis, 1961, 62. Mem. N.E. Assn. Women Police (life), African Peoples Christian Orgn., Nat. Conf. Artists (asst. newsletter 1989—), Ancient Order of Foresters (chief ranger 1981-82). Office: Kandi Creations PO Box 22517 Brooklyn NY 11202-2517

CHAVOOSHIAN, MARGE, artist, educator; b. NYC, Jan. 8, 1925; d. Harry Mesrob and Anna (Tashjian) Kurkjian; m. Barkev Budd Chavooshian, Aug. 11, 1946; children: J. Dean, Nora Ann. Student, Art Students League, 1943, Reginald Marsh, N.Y.C., 1943, Mario Cooper, 1977. Designer Needlework Arts Co., N.Y.C., 1943-44; illustrator John David Men's Store, N.Y.C., 1944-45; illustrator, layout artist Fawcett Publs., N.Y.C., 1945-47; designer, illustrator Pa. State U., University Park, 1947-49; art tchr. Trenton Pub. Sch., N.J., 1958-68, art cons. Title One Program, 1968-74; painting instr. Princeton Art Assn., N.J., 1974-77, 96, Jewish Cmty. Ctr., Ewing, N.J., 1974-85, Comtemporary Club, Trenton, 1974-85, YMCA, YWCA, Trent Ctr., Trenton, 1974—, various watercolor workshops, N.J., 1990—. Artist-at-large Alliance For Arts Edn., NJ, 1979—80; adj. asst. prof. art instr. Mercer County Coll., West Windsor, NJ, 1985—93; tchr. watercolor workshops Chalfonte, 2001, Cape May, NJ, H. Leeche Studio, Sarasota, Fla., 1998, Sarasota, 99, Art Ctr., Sarasota, 2001, Sarasota, 02. One-woman shows include Rider U., 1974, 2000, Rider Coll., 2002, Jersey City Mus., 1980, N.J. State Mus., 1981, 2001, Trenton City Mus., 1984, 1987, Arts Club, Washington, 1991, Magnolia Rm., Cape May, 1993—2003, Coryell Gallery, Lambertville, N.J., 1993, Chalfonte Cape May, 1993—96, 2001—03, Louisa Melrose Gallery, 2002, exhibited in group shows at Douglas Coll., N.J., 1977, Bergen Mus., Paramus, NJ, 1980—82, Hunterdon Art Ctr., Clinton, N.J., 1982, 1995, Morris Mus., Morristown, N.J., 1984, Allied Artists of Am., 1984, 1986, 1989, 1991—99, Salmagundi Club, N.Y.C., 1988, 1991—92, 1994—99, German Mus., 1995—96, Barron Art Ctr., Woodbridge, NJ, Ridgewood (N.J.) Art Inst., Art Works of Princeton and Trenton, 1995, Hunterdon County Cultural and Heritage Commn. Show, Clinton, N.J., 1995, Trenton City Mus., 2001; actor: others; Represented in permanent collections Mercer County Cultural and Heritage Commn., Arts Club of Washington, N.J. State Mus., Jersey City Mus., Trenton City Mus., Morris Mus., Rider U., Art Mus. San Lazarre, Italy, Bristol Myers Squibb, Johnson and Johnson, Schering Plough Corp., Pub. Svc. Electric and Gas Co., U.S. Trust, N.J. Blue Cross and Blue Shield, Eden Inst., Princeton, N.J., others. Recipient numerous awards Union Coll., E. Jane Given Meml. award, 1996, Pres. award, 1996, Rockport Pubs. Mass. Pub. Inclusion: Best of Watercolor, 1995, Watercolor Places, 1996, Graphic-Sha Pub. Co., The Best of Watercolor, Tokyo, 1996, Landscape Inspirations, 1997, Best of Sketching & Painting, 1998, The Artistic Touch 3, Creative Art Press, 1999, Mercer County Cultural and Heritage Commn. purchase award, 1999, Phillips Mill, Walter E. Martin Meml. award 1992, Patrons award for watercolor 1994, Am. Watercolor Soc., Phila Watercolor Club, Ligorno and Solansky award Hunterdon County Cultural and Heritage Commn., 1991, Cynthia Goodgal Meml. award, Moshe Bahire award Ridgewood Art Inst., 1992, 99, Ruth Ratay award Cmty. Arts Assn. Mid Atlantic Show, 1994, Elliot Liskin Meml. award Salmagundi Open Show, 1995, Thomas Moran Meml. award Salmagundi Open Show, 1999, Mus. award Trenton City Mus., 2000, D. Rodney and DaVinci Paint award Garden State Watercolor Soc., 2000, Dale Meyers medal, Salmagundi Club, NY, 2002, Niece Lumber award, Coryell Gallery, Lambertville, 2003; named Woman of Month Woman's Newspaper of Princeton, 1984, NJ State Coun. Arts fellow, 1979. Fellow Am. Artists Profl. League (Am. Arts Clon award 1973, Winsor Newton award 1980, Gold medal, Barron Art Ctr. award 1991, 93, Merit award 1993, Am. Artists Profl. League award 1994, Best in Show award, Best in Watercolor award 1995, others, representational painting award 1995); mem. Nat. Assn. Women Artists (two yr. nat. travel award 1985, Jeffrey Childs Willis Meml. award, Natl. Assn. Women Artists award 1999), S. Winston Meml. award 1988, (two yr. travel award 1996—), Catherine Lorillard Wolfe Art Club (Bee Paper Co. award 1977, Anna Hyatt Huntington bronze medal, 2000, Cynthia Goodgall Meml. award 1995), Allied Artists Am. (elected mem., Henry Gasser Meml. award 1992), N.J. Watercolor Soc. (Newton Art Ctr. award 1972, Helen K. Bermel award 1984, Howard Savs. Bank award 1986-87, Forbes Mag. award 1997, Lambertville Hist. Soc. award Coryell Gallery, 1995, 2001), Painters and Sculptors Soc. (Medal of Honor, Digby Chandle medal, others), Garden State Watercolor Soc. (Triangle Art Ctr. award 1976, 89, 94, Grumbacher Silver medal 1981, Merit award 1982, Trust Co. award 1987, Triangle award 1994, Art Express award, 1995, Rider U. Gallery award 1995, Cranbury Sta. Art Gallery award 1997, Daler Rowney and Da Vinci paint award 2000), Midwest Watercolor Soc., Nat. Arts Club (John Elliott award 1988), Phila. Watercolor Club (Village Art award 1991), Nat. Watercolor Soc. (signature), Am. Watercolor Soc. (signature). Democrat. Mem. Apostolic Ch. Armenia. Home: 222 Morningside Dr Trenton NJ 08618-4914

CHAWNER, LUCIA MARTHA, English educator; b. Ithaca, N.Y., Dec. 2, 1933; d. Lowell Jenkins and Lucia Mary (Soule) C.; m. Movses Guichen Andreassian, Mar. 18, 1967 (div. June 1971). Student, Earlham Coll., 1951-53; BA, U. Colo., 1956; MA, So. Meth. U., 1975. Provisional cert. elem., secondary and talented and gifted, Tex.; profl. cert. reading specialist, Tex. Tchr. grade 7 lang. arts and social studies Stonewall Jackson, Dallas Ind. Sch. Dist., 1959-63; reading clinician Reinhardt, Dallas Ind. Sch. Dist., 1963-66; Reading Resource Pilot Project Lakewood, Dallas Ind. Sch. Dist., 1972-74; devel. curriculum specialist El Centro Coll., Dallas County C.C. Dist., Dallas, 1977-78; English tchr. Health Magnet, Dallas Ind. Sch. Dist., 1979-95; univ. supervising tchr. U. Tex. Dallas, Richardson, 1996—. Part-time instr. El Centro & Richland Colls., Dallas, 1978-88, Brookhaven Coll., Farmers Branch, Tex., 1996-98; mem. English lit. textbook adoption com. Dallas Ind. Sch. Dist., 1988-89; chmn. English dept. Health Magnet, Dallas Ind. Sch. Dist., 1989-94, mgr. innovative grant, 1994-95. Co-leader child and youth study U. Md., Dallas, 1967-69; pres. English-Speaking Union-Dallas Br., 1992-96; mem. Leadership Arts, Dallas Bus. Com. Arts, 1994-95, World Affairs Coun. Greater Dallas; region 7 chmn., nat. bd. mem. English-Speaking Union of USA, 1996-2000. Recipient Instrnl. grant Richland Coll., 1980; Advanced Study grantee Dallas Ind. Sch. Dist., 1973; Named Tchr. of the Yr., Health Magnet, 1991, Rotary Tchr. of the Yr., Health Magnet, 1993, nat. Merit award, English-Speaking Union of USA, 2000. Mem. Dallas Mus. Art League (bd. dirs. 1997-2004), New Conservatory of Dallas (bd. mem. 1999—, sec. 2002—), Friends SMU Librs. (bd. dirs. 1995-98), Assemblage (pres. 1987-88), Brit. Am. Commerce Assn., Dau. Brit. Empire (sec. 2003—), Soc. Mayflower Descs., Dallas Knife and Fork Club, Inc. (Bd. Dirs. 2003—), Delta Delta Delta, Phi Delta Kappa, Pi Lambda Theta (Alpha Sigma chpt. pres. 2002—). Avocations: sculpture, needlepoint, fitness exercise, travel. Office: PO Box 141179 Dallas TX 75214-1179

CHEADLE, LOUISE, concert pianist, educator; b. Donora, Pa., July 4, 1935; d. Max Raphael and Helen Louise Busto; m. William George Cheadle, Feb. 12, 1959 (dec. Dec. 1993); children: William Robert, Amy Louise Fleming. BMusic, The Juilliard Sch., 1959. Founder, dir. Westminster Conservatory of Music/Rider U., Princeton, NJ, 1972—82; head piano dept. Amherst Summer Music Ctr., Raymond, Maine, 1971—72; adj. instr. music Bucks County C.C., Newtown, Pa., 1982-85; nationwide concert tours and workshops, various mgmts. and agys., throughout U.S., 1980s; nat. adjudicator Nat. Guild Piano Tchrs., Austin, Tex., 1999—; freelance recitals, workshops and pvt. tchg. includes Lincoln Ctr., Carnegie Hall, N.Y.C., 1980—. Debut recital with Pitts. Concert Soc., 1954; contbg. author: Teaching Piano, 1981; CD release Virtuoso Piano Music by Cecile Chaminate and Fanny Mendelssohn-Hensel, 2002. Bd. dirs., chair Cmty. Outreach. Juilliard Sch. scholar, 1956-59. Mem. Music Tchrs. Nat. Assn., N.J. Music Educators Assn. (bd. dirs., v.p.), N.J. Music Tchrs. Assn. (chair Young Artist Competition 1999, 2000, chair Master Class Competition 1999, 2000), Rossmoor (N.J.) Music Assn. (bd. dirs.), Piano Tchrs. Congress N.Y., Music Club of Princeton. Avocations: writing, reading, cooking, cultural events. Office: PO Box 7792 Princeton NJ 08543-7792 E-mail: chealou@aol.com.

CHEATHAM, BELZORA, writer; b. Lodi, Tex., Mar. 13, 1932; d. Calvin and Hattie Geneva Brown; m. Andy Cheatham, Sept. 9, 1950 (dec. Jan. 1979); children: Jacqueline, Russell E., David R. Divsn. head Sears Roebuck & Co., Chgo., 1970-93. Author: Whittaker Cemetery Index, 1995, The History of Whittaker Memorial Cemetery, 1996 (Tex. Hist. Marker award 1996), Slaves and Slave Owners of Bowie County, Tex., 1850, 1996. Mem. Afro-Am. Geneal. and Hist. Soc. Chgo. (treas. 1992-97, pres. 1999-2001). Methodist. Avocation: genealogy. E-mail: mscheats@aol.com.

CHEATHAM, WANDA M. music educator; b. Memphis, June 29, 1952; d. Roy Bennett Cheatham, Billie Jewel Cheatham. BS in Music Edn., U. Memphis, 1974, MEd in Music, 1983; student fgn. study program, Univ. of So. Miss., Vienna, Austria, 1991, Glasgow (Scotland) U., 1995; student, Univ. of Miss., 1997. Elem. music tchr. Memphis City Schs., 1975—81; h.s. choral dir. Evangelical Christian Sch., Cordova, Tenn., 1981—. Audition and rehearsal pianist Theatre Memphis, 1998, 2001. Organist Ctrl. Ch., Memphis, 1972—83, First Evangelical Ch., Memphis, 1984—2001; organist/music dir. St. Andrews Presbyn. Ch., Cordova, 2001—. Named a Outstanding Young Woman of Am., 1983; recipient, 1985, Outstanding Tchr. award, Tenn. Gov.'s Sch. for Arts, 1993, 1997, 1999. Mem.: Tenn. Music Educators Assn., Music Educators Nat. Conf., Am. Choral Dir. Assn. Presbyterian. Avocations: antiques, travel, reading, walking, gardening. Office: Evangelical Christian PO Box 1030 7600 Macon Rd Cordova TN 38088 Office Phone: 901-754-7217. Office Fax: 901-754-8123. E-mail: wcheatham@ecseagles.net.

CHECCONE, IOLE CARLESIMO, foreign language educator; b. Frosinone, Lazio, Italy, Dec. 7, 1943; d. Alfredo Tullio and Caterina (Morelli) Carlesimo; m. Albert Checcone, June 14, 1969; children: Emidio Albert, Mark Anthony, Anne Marie. BA, Marygrove Coll., Detroit, 1965; MA, Wayne State U., 1968; PhD in French Lit., U. Pitts., 1995. Cert. tchr., Mich., Ohio. Grad. tchg. asst. Wayne State U., Detroit, 1965-67; French tchr. Oak Park (Mich.) Local Schs., 1966-68, Grosse Pointe (Mich.) Local Schs., 1968-70; tchg. fellow U. Pitts., 1987-90; asst. prof. French lit. Youngstown (Ohio) State U., 1999—. Mem. adv. com. for gifted children Canfield (Ohio) Local Schs., 1979. Democrat. Roman Catholic. Avocations: singing, reading, sewing, quilting. Office: Youngstown State U Dept Fgn Langs One University Plz Youngstown OH 44555-3461

CHEDID, LISA LEASURE, food scientist; b. Phila., Aug. 3, 1962; d. James and Ann (DeHaven) Leasure; m. Pierre Chedid, June 5, 1988; children: Amanda, Thomas, James. BS in Chem. Engring., Rutgers U., 1985, MS in Food Sci./Engring., 1989. From chemist to sr. chemist Nabisco Foods Group, East Hanover, N.J., 1988-94; project supr. Nat. Starch & Chem., Bridgewater, N.J., 1994-96; sr. food scientist Church & Dwight Co. Inc., Princeton, N.J., 1996—. Patentee in field. Mem. Am. Chem. Soc., Am. Assn. Cereal Chemists, Inst. Food Technologists. Office: Church & Dwight Co Inc 469 N Harrison St Princeton NJ 08540-3510

CHEE, ANN-PING, music educator; b. July 26; came to U.S., 1964; d. To-Khiem Thi and Thanh-Phuc Dong; m. Anthony N.C. Chee, Dec. 27, 1969; children: Andrew, Lawrence. BA in Music cum laude, Conn. Coll., 1970. Tchr. piano, music theory, Houston, 1972—. Named to Piano Guild Hall of Fame, Austin, Tex., 1997. Mem. Nat. Guild Piano Tchrs. (cert.), Music Tchrs. Nat. Assn. (cert.), Tex. Music Tchrs. Assn., Houston Music Tchrs. Assn., Houston Fedn. Music Clubs, Forum Music Tchrs. Assn., Associated Bd. Royal Schs. Music London.

CHEE, GLORIA Y.M. secondary school educator; b. Honolulu, Hawaii, July 5, 1949; d. Thomas P.L. and Agnes Y.K. Chee. B in Edn., U. Hawaii, 1971. Cert. tchr. Hawaii, 1972. ESL instr. Pacific Internat. Lang. Sch., Honolulu, 1990—91; instr. Hawaii Bus. Coll., 1991—94; tchr. McKinley Cmty. Sch. for Adults, 1993—, U. Hawaii, Manoa, 1995—. Co-chair retention com. Hawaii Bus. Coll., 1993—94, advisor Nat. Vocat. Tech. Honor Soc., 1994; standards based com. mem. McKinley Sch. Adults, 2000—. Mailing: McKinley Cmty Sch Adults 634 Pensacola St Rm 216 Honolulu HI 96814

CHEEK, BARBARA LEE, college reading program director, educator; b. Springfield, Mo., Oct. 25, 1935; d. Curtis Earl and Gertrude Helen (Ahonen) Nelson; m. Lee Roy Clyde, June 16, 1961; children: Michael, Paul, Daniel. BA in Edn. cum laude, Pacific Luth. U., 1957; postgrad., U. Wash., Seattle, 1961-62; MA in Elem. Reading Edn., Boise (Idaho) State U., 1982; postgrad., Ea. Oreg. U., 1983, Seattle U., 1989. Cert. elem. and secondary edn. tchr., Wash. Sec. engring. dept. Boeing Aircraft Co., Seattle, 1957; instr. Edmonds (Wash.) Sch. Dist., 1957-61, Clover Pk. Sch. Dist., Tacoma, 1961-62, Payette (Idaho) Sch. Dist., 1970-74; bookkeeper Cheek Dairy Supply, Payette, 1970-71; instr. Ontario (Oreg.) Sch. Dist., 1975-79; prof. Treasure Valley C.C., Ontario, 1979-89, Pierce Coll., Tacoma, 1989-2001, dir. reading dept., 1989-96; dir. Alternative Learning Ctr. at Pierce Coll., Puyallup, Wash., 1996—2001; mem. faculty emeritus Pierce Coll., Puyallup, Wash., 2001—; instr. Profl. Excellence Program Tacoma (Wash.) Sch. Dist., 1994; pvt. reading tutor and cons., 2001—; leader Stephen Ministries Luth. Ch., 2003—. Sec. Malheur Reading Coun., Ont., 1986—87; faculty exec. bd. Treasure Valley C.C. Faculty, Ont., 1986—88; mem. Peer Evaluation Oreg. Devel. Edn., Ont., 1986; cons. Tacoma Sch. Dist. Profl. Excellence Program, 1993—; exec. Pharmanex/Nu-Skin Enterprises, 1994—; rep. Avon Cosmetics, 2003—. Moderator Ont. candidate's fair AAUW, 1985, state sec., Payette, 1972-74, sec. N.W. region, 1974, br. pres., 1970-72, 75-77; bd. dirs. Boy Scouts Am., Oregon, Idaho, 1971-84; deacon, v.p. Luth. Ch., 1986; mem. basic literacy steering com. Tacoma, 1992; mem. Pierce County Literacy Coalition, Tacoma, Scandinavian Cultural Ctr., Pacific Luth. U.; asst. min. Luth. Ch., 1984—, Stephen Min. Leader, 2003-, Stephen Min., 2002-. Recipient Faculty Devel. award Higher Edn. State of Wash., 1990-91. Mem. AAUW (chpt. pres. 1970-72), ASCD, Western Coll. Reading Assn., Wash. State C.C., Faculty Devel. (state com.), Wash. Devel. Edn. Assn., Am. Assn. Women in Comty. and Jr. Colls., Wash. Fedn. of Tchrs. (faculty exec. bd.), Coll. Reading and Learning Assn. (pres-elect Washington, Idaho 1998-99, pres. N.W. region 1999-2001), Tchr. English to Spkrs. of Other Langs., Sweet Adelines (pres. Tacoma chpt. 2001-02), Internat., Alpha Delta Kappa (v.p. 1986), N.W. Coll. Reading and Learning Assn. (pres. 1999-2000). Republican. Avocations: handbell choir, soloist, reading, golf, skiing. E-mail: tracinda@worldnet.att.net.

CHEEK, CHERYL A. language educator; b. Flagstaff, Ariz., Feb. 22, 1947; d. Charles L. and Betty P. Osterberg; m. Lawrence L. Cheek, Sept. 4, 1971; children: Alan L., Erin M. BA, Oreg. State U., 1969; MEd, U. Mont., 1998. Cert. English, French and libr. media tchr. Mont. Personnel adminstrn. Bechtel Power Corp., Norwalk, Calif., 1971—77, Western Forge Corp., Colorado Springs, Colo., 1977—79; co-editor, pub. Tobacco Valley News, Eureka, Mont., 1980—92; tchr. English, French Eureka Pub. Schs., 1988—. Bd. dirs. Lincoln County Librs., Libby, Mont.; tour dir. Edn. First, France, Switzerland, Italy and Gt. Britain, 1998—, internat. exch. coord., Boston, 2001—. Mem.: Mont. Edn. Assn., Nat. Coun. Tchrs. of English. Avocations: gardening, photography, reading, travel, hiking/camping. Home: PO Box 1430 Eureka MT 59917 Office: Lincoln County HS PO Box 2000 Eureka MT 59917

CHEEK, NORMA JEAN, retired educator; b. Ada, Okla., Feb. 7, 1928; d. John Herbert and Jewell Esther (Hobbs) Winters; m. George A. Cheek, Dec. 5, 1947; children: George Allen III, Michael Kirby. AA, Conners Jr. Coll., 1948; BS, Ctrl. State Coll., Edmond, Okla., 1961, MEd, 1964. Tchr. Mid-Del Schs., Midwest City, Okla., 1961-89, coach, 1978-87. Salesman vol. YMCA, 1970—; bldg. rep. Midwest City Assn. Classroom Tchrs., 1980. Mem. AAUW, Alpha Delta Kappa (various positions including v.p. 1980). Democrat. Baptist. Home: 604 Traub Pl Midwest City OK 73110-2738 Office Phone: 405-412-8659.

CHEEVES, AMATINE CONNELLY, realtor; b. Sherman, Tex., Mar. 19, 1916; d. Ernest F. and Sallie Isabel Mercer; m. Tom Sylvester Connelly (dec. 1961); children: Mary Louise Connelly, Jack Joseph Connelly, Sylvia Ann Connelly; m. Ray Cheeves (dec.). Degree, Abilene Christian Coll., 1934. Cert. realtor. Realtor Connelly Realty, Dallas, 1952—. Named Tex. Woman Realtor of the Yr., 1972. Mem.: Tex. Women Coun. of Realtors (pres. 1972). Home: 1911 Newport Dallas TX 75224 Office: Connelly Realty 2743 S Hampton Rd Dallas TX 75224

CHEIFETZ, LORNA GALE, psychologist; b. Phoenix, Mar. 22, 1953; d. Walter and Ruth Cheifetz. BS, Chapman Coll., Orange, Calif., 1975; D of Psychology, Ill. Sch. Profl. Psychology, 1981. Psychology intern Cook County Hosp., Chgo., 1979-80; clin. psychologist City of Chgo., 1980-84, Phoenix Inst. for Psychotherapy, 1984-87; pvt. practice Phoenix, 1987—. Cons. to judges, attys., cts., 1984—; adj. faculty Met. U., Phoenix, 1984-88, Ill. Sch. Profl. Psychology, 1982-86. Contbr. chpt. to book Listening and Interpreting, 1984; contbg. editor Internat. Jour. Communicative Psychoanalysis and Psychotherapy, 1991-93. Cons., vol. Ariz. Bar Assn. Vol. Lawyer Program, 1985—; co-coord. Psychology Info. Referral Svc., Maricopa County, Ariz., 1984-96. Named Psychologist of Yr. Ariz. Bar Assn., 1987, 95, 99. Mem. APA (activist 1989—), Nat. Register Health Svc. Providers in Psychology. Avocation: parenting. Office: 3930 E Camelback Rd Ste 207 Phoenix AZ 85018-2634

CHELETTE, TAMARA LYNNE, biomedical engineer; b. Morgantown, W.Va., July 11, 1962; d. Charles Caruthers and Nancy Ruth (Williams) Cook; m. Murry René Chelette, June 1, 1985; children: Murry René Jr., Andrew John. BS in Engring., Boston U., 1984; PhD of Biomed. Scis., Wright State U., 1994. Registered profl. engr., Ohio. Intern clin. engring. Mass. Eye and Ear Infirmary, Boston, 1983-84; biomed. engr. VA, Little Rock, 1984-86, Dayton, Ohio, 1986-87; biomed. sys. engr. Krug Internat., Dayton, 1987-89; biomed. engr. human effectiveness directorate Air Force Rsch. Lab., Wright-Patterson AFB, Ohio, 1989—. Adj. prof. Wright State U., Dayton, 1994—. Patentee in field; contbr. articles to profl. jours. Treas. Wright-Patt Young Heroes Assn., Dayton, 1992—. Recipient Outstanding Achievement award Soc. Women Engrs., 1982, Arthur Flemming award, Washington JayCees, 1995, Dayton English and Sci. Found. outstanding engr. of Miami Valley award, 2000. Fellow Aerospace Human Factors Assn.; mem. IEEE (Fritz Russ award in biomedical engring. 2000) Aerospace Med. Assn. (assoc. fellow, Innovative Rsch. award 1994, pres. life scis. br. 1996, Eric Liljencrantz award 1997, Paul Bert award 1998), Engring. in Medicine and Biology Soc., SAFE Assn. (v.p. Wright Bros. chpt. 1994-95, pres. 1998-99). Avocation: gardening. Office: Air Force Rsch Lab Bldg 824 Rm 206 2800 Q St Wright Patterson Afb OH 45433-7008

CHELL, BEVERLY C. lawyer, media company executive; b. Phila., Aug 12, 1942; d. Max M. and Cecelia (Portney) C.; m. Robert M. Chell, June 21, 1964. BA, U. Pa., 1964; JD, N.Y. Law Sch., 1967; LLM, NYU, 1973. Bar: N.Y. 1967. Assoc. Polur & Polur, N.Y.C., 1967-68, Thomas V. Kingham Esq., N.Y.C., 1968-69; v.p., sec., asst. gen. counsel, dir. Athlone Industries Inc., Parsippany, N.J., 1969-81; asst. v.p., asst. sec., assoc. gen. counsel Macmillan Inc., N.Y.C., 1981-85, v.p., assoc. gen. counsel, 1985-90; vice chmn., gen. counsel K-III Holdings, N.Y.C., 1990-92; vice chmn., gen. counsel, sec. Primedia Inc. (formerly K-III Comm. Corp.), N.Y.C., 1992—. Mem. Assn. of Bar of City of N.Y., Am. Soc. Corp. Secs. Home: 1050 5th Ave New York NY 10028-0110 Office: Primedia Inc 745 5th Ave Fl 23 New York NY 10151-0099

CHELSTROM, MARILYN ANN, political education consultant; b. Mpls., Dec. 5; d. Arthur Rudolph and Signe (Johnson) C. BA, U. Minn., 1950; LHD, Oklahoma City U., 1981. Staff asst. Mpls. Citizens Com. Public Edn., 1950-57; coord. policies and procedures Lithium Corp. Am., Inc., Mpls., N.Y.C., 1957-62; exec. dir. The Robert A. Taft Inst. Govt., N.Y.C., 1962-77, exec. v.p., 1977-78, pres., 1978-89, pres. emeritus, 1990—; polit. edn. cons., 1990—; pres. Chelstrom Connection, 1992—. Home: 9600 Portland Ave Minneapolis MN 55420-4564 Office: 155 E 38th St New York NY 10016-2660

CHEMBERLIN, PEG, clergy, religious organization administrator; Ordained deacon Moravian Ch. of Am., 1982, consecrated presbyter, 1986. BA cum laude, U. Wis., Parkside; grad., United Theol. Sem. Twin Cities, 1982. Formerly dir. campus ministries, tchr., youth min.; also outreach min., parish intern pastor; exec. dir. Minn. Coun. Chs., 1995—. Former pres., former program chmn. Nat. Assn. Ecumenical and Interfaith Staff, 1992, 97. Recipient Women of Excellence award Minn. Gov., 1994, NOVA Peace and Justice award, 1985; Angel of Reconciliation award, 2003. Mem.: Nat. Coun. of Ch. (exec. bd. 2003). Office: Minn Coun Chs 122 W Franklin Ave Minneapolis MN 55404 2447

CHEN, CHING-CHIH, information science educator, consultant; b. Foochow, Fukien, China, Sept. 3, 1937; came to U.S, 1959; d. Han-chia and May-ying (Liu) Liu; m. Sow-Hsin Chen, Aug. 19, 1961; children: Anne, Catherine, John. BA, Nat. Taiwan U., Taipei, 1959; MLS, U. Mich., 1961; PhD, Case Western Res. U., 1974. Asst. Sch. Libr. Sci. U. Mich., Ann Arbor, 1960-61, svc. libr., 1961-62; sci. reference libr. McMaster U., Hamilton, Ont., Can., 1962-63, head sci. libr., 1963-64; sr. sci. libr. U. Waterloo, Ont., Can., 1964-65, head engring., math. and sci. libr., 1965-68; assoc. sci. libr. MIT, Cambridge, Mass., 1968-71; asst. prof. Grad. Sch. Libr. and Info. Sci. Simmons Coll., Boston, 1971-76, asst. dean for acad. affairs, 1977-79, assoc. dean, prof., 1979-96, prof., 1979—. Cons. Am. Soc. Info. Sci./Cath. U. Am., 1976-77, Chung-Shan Inst. Sci. Rsch., Taiwan, 1977-87, Abt Assocs., Inc., 1980-82, Sci. and Tech. Info. Ctr. Nat. Sci. Coun., Taiwan, 1973-77, S.E. Asia Region WHO, 1980, 81, Engring. Info. Inc., 1982, UNESCO, Paris, 1984, Nat. Geog. Soc., 1985, Norman Bethuen U. Med. Scis. Libr., 1986, Getty Trust, 1988, USIA, 1988, Ont. Coun. Gradual Studies, 1989, FID, 1989, World Bank, 1990, UNESCO, 1991, DataConsult, Mex., 1991, Soros Found., 1992-93, USIA, 1993-95, UN Devel. Program, 1997, Tsinghua U., Taiwan, 1997, Nat. Sci. Coun., Taiwan, 1998—2001; mem. US President's Info. Tech. Adv. Com., 1997—2001; guest prof. Tsinghua U., Beijing, 1999-2002. Author, editor 36 books including Biomedical, Scientific and Technical Book Reviewing, 1976, Sourcebook on Health Sciences Librarianship, 1977, Quantitative Measurement and Dynamic Library Service, 1978, Scientific & Technical Information Sources, 2nd edit., 1987, (with others) Numeric Databases, 1984, HyperSource on Hypermdia/Multimedia Technologies, 1989, HyperSource on Optical Technologies, 1989, Optical Technologies in Libraries; Use & Trends, 1991, Planning Global Information Infrastructure, 1995, Consortium of Electronic Resources, 1999, IT and Global Digital Library Development, 1999, Global Digital Library Development in the New Millennium, 2001; editor-in-chief: Microcomputers for Information Management, 1983-96; mem. editl. bd.: Electronic Library, 1990-; also editor numerous conf. procs.; contbr. over 150 articles to profl. jours. Barbour scholar U. Mich., 1959-61, Case Western Res. U. fellow, 1973-74, NATO fellow, 1975, AAAS fellow, 1985; Emily Hollowell Rsch. grantee, 1972—, Simmons Coll. Fund Rsch. grantee, 1972-81, co-principal investigator NSF US-China Million Book Digital Libr. Grant Project, 2001-; recipient Disting. Svc. award Chinese-Am. Librs. Assn., 1982, Cert. of Appreciation, Asian-Pacific-Am. Librs. Assn., 1983, Disting. Alumni award U. Mich., 1983, Outstanding Svc. award Nat. Cen. Libr., 1986, Disting. Svc. award Asian-Am. Libr. Assn, 1992, Cindy award Assn. Visual Comm., 1992, Grazella Shepherd Meml. award for Excellence in Edn., Case Western Reserve U. Educator's Forum, 1999, NSF Internat. Digital Libr. Program award Chinese Memory Net: U.S.-Sino Collaborative Rsch., 1999-2003, Global Memory Net, 2003-, Ernest A. Lynton award Am. Assn. Higher Edn., 2001. Fellow AAAS; mem. ALA (disting. svc. award 1989, Humphrey award 1996), AAUP, Am. Soc. Info. Sci. (best Info. Sci. Tchr. award 1983), Assn. Am. Libr. Schs., Assn. Coll. and Rsch. Librs., Libr. Info. Tech. Assn. (Gaylord Libr. and Info. Tech. Achievement award 1990, Outstanding Achievement Libr. Hi Tech. award 1994), New Eng. Libr. Assn. (Emerson Greenaway award 1994), Assn. Libr. and Info. Sci. Edn. (1st ALISE Pratt-Severn Nat. Faculty award 1997). Avocations: travel, stamp collecting. Home: 1400 Commonwealth Ave Newton MA 02465-2830 Office: Simmons Coll 300 Fenway Boston MA 02115-5820 Office Phone: 617-521-2804. E-mail: chen@simmons.edu.

CHEN, CONCORDIA CHAO, mathematician; b. Peiping, China; came to U.S., 1955, naturalized, 1969; d. Chun-fu and Kwie Hwa (Wong) Chao; BA in Bus. Adminstrn., Nat. Taiwan U., 1954; MS in Math., Marquette U., 1958; postgrad. Purdue U., 1958-60, M.I.T., 1961-62; m. Chin Chen, July 2, 1960; children: Marie Hui-mei, Albert Chao. Teaching asst. Purdue U., Lafayette, Ind., 1958-60; system analysis engr. electronic data processing div. Mpls.-Honeywell, Newton Highlands, Mass., 1960-63; mgmt. planning asst. Lederle Labs., Am. Cyanamid Co., Pearl River, N.Y., 1964, computer applications specialist, 1967, ops. analyst, 1967; staff programmer IBM, Sterling Forest, N.Y., 1968-73, adv. programmer Data Processing Mktg. Group, Poughkeepsie, 1973-80, mgr. systems programming and systems architecture, Princeton, N.J., 1980-82, sr. systems analyst, 1982-83, data processing mktg. cons., Beijing, 1983-88; sr. planner IBM DSD, Poughkeepsie, 1988-92; program mgr. Chiang Indsl. Charity Found Ltd., 1993-94; mgr. software engring. China Weal Bus. Machinery Co., Ltd., Hong Kong, 1995-99, exec. gen. mgr., 1999-2001; prof. South China U. Tech., 2003—. Chmn. edn. council Hudson region MIT. Mem. Am. Math. Soc., Soc. Indsl. and Applied Maths., MIT Club Hudson Valley (pres.). Home: 12 Mountain Pass Rd Hopewell Junction NY 12533-5331 Office: Flat E 32/F Tower 5 South Horizons Hong Kong

CHEN, JOIE, cable news anchor; B of Journalism, M of Journalism, Northwestern U. Reporter Sta. WCIV-TV, Charleston, S.C.; from reporter to anchor Sta. WXIA-TV, Atlanta; host CNNI World News, Atlanta; co-host CNN Saturday Morning News and CNN Sunday Morning News, Atlanta, 1994 96; co-anchor The World Today, CNN. Office: c/o CNN 1 CNN Ctr NW Atlanta GA 30303-2762

CHEN, JULIE, newscaster; b. N.Y.C., Jan. 6, 1970; B in Broadcast Journalism and English, U. of So. Calif., 1991. Prodn. asst. ABC News, LA, 1990—91; prodr. ABC News One, Dayton, 1991—95; reporter WDTN-TV, Dayton, 1995—97; reporter, anchor WCBS-TV, N.Y.C., 1997—99; news anchor, substitute anchor The Early Show, 1999—2002; anchor CBS Morning News, 2002—. Substitute anchor CBS Morning News, 1999, This Morning, 1999; host Big Brother, 2000—. Office: CBS News 524 W 57th St New York NY 10019

CHEN, LENA, broadcast executive; b. Taubate, Sao Paulo, Brazil, Dec. 13, 1970; d. Chi H. and Lu Chen. BS, NYU, 1992. Sr. account exec. Terra Chips, Bklyn., 1991—94; owner LC Concepts, N.Y.C., 1995—96; dir. billing USA Network/Sci Fi Channel, N.Y.C., 1998—2000; dir. programming, head network ops. TRIO Network/Universal TV, N.Y.C., 2001—. Voting mem. Brit. Acad. Film and TV Arts, N.Y.C., 2001—; assoc. bd. mem. Internat. Emmys, N.Y.C., 2002—. Supervising prodr. various concerts for T.V., (music video show) TRIO Pure Video, supervising prodr., dir. (music video) Sweet Thunder, Ode To Innocence- Aerial Version (Feat The Pendulum Flyers)- artist Sasha Lazard, writer, prodr., dir. (epk) various ind. artists; contbr. articles to publs. Vol. Survivors of the Shoah, N.Y.C., 1994—94, Food Allergy Initiative, N.Y.C., 2001—, Assn. to Benefit Children, N.Y.C., 1997—98, N.Y. Cares, N.Y.C., 2002—03. Office: TRIO Network/Universal Television 1230 Avenue of the Americas New York NY 10020

CH'EN, LI-LI, writer, Chinese language, literature and comparative literature educator; b. Beijing, Apr. 6, 1934; came to U.S., 1951, naturalized, 1963; d. Shujen and Yu-wu (Kuan) C. BA magna cum laude, Wilson Coll., 1957, Litt.D., 1980; MA, Radcliffe Coll., 1958; PhD (Harvard-Yenching Inst. fellow, Ford Found. fellow), Harvard U., 1969. Prof. Chinese lang., lit. and comparative lit., dir. Chinese program Tufts U., Medford, Mass., 1972—94, prof. emerita, 1994—. Translator: Master Tung's Western Chamber Romance, 1977 (Nat. Book Award for Transl.); Contbr. articles to profl. jours. Am. Council Learned Socs. grantee, 1976-77; MacDowell Colony fellow, 1980; Michael Karolyi Found. fellow, 1980; Recipient Nat. Mag. Award for Fiction, Criticism, and Belles Lettres for short story Peking! Peking!, 1977 Mem. Phi Beta Kappa. Home: 186 Upland Rd Cambridge MA 02140-3624 Office: Tufts U Olin Hall Medford MA 02155

CHEN, LIYA, chemist; b. Taishun, Zhejiang, China, Jan. 12, 1956; came to U.S., 1994; d. Jinde Chen and Cailian Pan; m. Ronghui Lin, Jan. 24, 1987; 1 child, Cindy (Xinyue) Lin. BS, Hangzhou (China) U., 1982, MS, 1986, So. Ill. U., 1997. Technician Taishun (China) Chem. Co., 1982-83; lectr. Zhejian Med. U., Hangzhou, 1986-93; rsch. assoc. So. Ill. U., Carbondale, 1995-97, Chiron Corp., Emeryville, Calif., 1997-98; chemist Merck & Co., Inc., Rahway, N.J., 1998—. Contbr. articles to profl. jours.; patentee in field. Recipient excellent paper award Zhejiang Soc. Sci. and Tech., 1991. Mem. Am. Chem. Soc. Avocations: cooking, sewing, dance, singing. Home: 23 Bearsley Dr East Brunswick NJ 08816-2041 Office: Merck & Co Inc PO Box 2000 RY 800-B309 Rahway NJ 07065-0900

CHEN, LU, figure skater; b. Changchun, Jilin, China, Nov. 24, 1976; Figure skater, China, 1981—. Mem. Chinese Nat. Figure Skating Team, 1988—. Recipient Bronze medal Olympic Games, Nagano, 1998, 7 time Chinese Nat. Champion and 2 time Olympic Bronze medalist. Avocations: reading, music, dance. Address: c/o Yuki Saegusa 22 E 71st New York NY 10021

CHEN, PING, physician; b. Kunming, Yunnan, China, Apr. 9, 1963; arrived in Can., 2000; d. Lian Wen Chen and Dong Xiu Bao; m. Min Chen, June 26, 1999; 1 child, Zanyu. MD, Kunming Med. Sch., China, 1984. Ophthalmologist Yunnan Red Crss Hosp., 1984—96; postdoctoral fellow Henry Ford Hosp., Detroit, 2000—. Contbr. articles. Mem.: Assn. Rsch. Vision and Ophthalmology. Avocations: reading, swimming, cooking, gardening, ping pong/table tennis. Home: 576 Caron Ave N9A 5B4 Windsor Canada Office: Henry Ford Hosp OFP 4D Detroit MI 48202

CHENAULT MINOT, MARILYN, legal executive; b. Mt. Vernon, Ill., Oct. 21, 1949; d. Nathan Bullock and Marguerite (Woodberry) Chenault; m. Tom Dee McFall, Aug. 29, 1969; children: Shannon, Nathan; m. Troy David Phillips, Aug. 14, 1981; stepchildren: Todd, Brittany; m. Winthrop Gardner Minot, June 6, 1998; stepchildren: Hilary, Amory, Constance. BS with honors, Okla. State U., 1970. Retail analyst Opticks, Inc. divsn. G. D. Searle, Dallas, 1977-78; dir. of adminstrn. Glast, Phillips and Murray, Dallas, 1978-81; exec. dir. Haynes and Boone L.L.P., Dallas, 1981-94; prin. Chenault and Co., 1994-95; exec. dir. Wolf, Greenfield & Sacks, P.C., 1995-96; COO Legalink Corp., 1997-98, Wolf, Greenfield & Sacks, P.C., Boston, 1999—2000, Hill & Barlow, 2000—01; founder, pres., CEO Disbursement Mgmt. Assocs., LLC, 2001—. Adj. prof. So. Meth. U. Sch. Law, Dallas, 1981-94; instr. paralegal program So. Meth. U., 1981-85; legal adv. coun. Wang Labs., 1985-91, Pitney Bowes, 1991-96; mem. Tech. Task Force, 1989-93; chair Practicing Law Profitability Conf., 1984, Large Law Firm Tech. Conf., 1990; co-chair Law Net Inc. Conf., 1988. Contbr. articles to Nat. Law Jour., PC Week. Lou Wentz scholar Coll. Bus., Okla. State U., Stillwater, 1969-70, also C.V. Richardson scholar, 1969-70; named Outstanding Coll. Bus. Grad., 1970. Mem. NAFE, State Bar Tex. (law office mgmt. com. 1991-94), Dallas Bar Assn. (strategic planning com. 1990-94, chair mktg. subcom.), Tex. Lawyer Law Tech. Planning Com. 1992, Nat. Assn. Legal Adminstrs. (dir. of adminstrn. sect. 1979-85, large firm adminstrn. sect. 1985-91, com. mem. 1986-88, vice-chmn. 1989-90, chmn., 1990-91, chair in-house tng. task force, 1990-91, communication/governance/structure issues task force 1988-89, instr. law office adminstrn. course 1984, 87, pres. Dallas chpt. 1985-86, prin. adminstrs. team 1992-96, nat. nominating com. 1992-93, nat. certification task force 1996-97, vice-chair intellectual property affinity group 2000—), Inst. Assoc. Devel. Home: 42 Nichols Rd Cohasset MA 02025-1166 E-mail: marilyn_minot@dmalaw.com .

CHENEY, LYNNE V. humanities educator, writer; b. Casper, Wyo., Aug. 14, 1941; d. Wayne and Edna (Lybyer) Vincent; m. Richard Bruce Cheney, Aug. 29, 1964; children: Elizabeth, Mary. BA, Colo. Coll., 1963; MA, U. Colo., 1964; PhD in 19th century Brit. lit., U. Wis., 1970. Freelance writer, 1970-83; lectr. George Washington U., Washington, 1972-77, U. Wyo., Casper, 1977-78; researcher, writer Md. Pub. Broadcasting, Owings Mills, 1982-83; sr. editor Washingtonian mag., Washington, 1983-86; chmn. NEH, Washington, 1986-93; W.J. Brady Jr. fellow Am. Enterprise Inst., Washington, 1993-95, sr. fellow, 1996—. Commr. U.S. Constitution Bicentennial Commn., Washington, 1985-87. Author: Executive Privilege, 1978, Sisters, 1981, Telling the Truth, 1995; (with others) Kings of the Hill, 1983, 96, The Body Politic, 1988, (report) American Memory: A Report on the Humanities in the Nation's Public Schools, 1988, (essay) Academic Freedom, 1992, America: A Patriotic Primer, 2002, A is for Abigail, 2003; contbr. articles to profl. jours. Mem. Women's Forum Washington. Mem. Congl. Club, Phi Beta Kappa, Kappa Alpha Theta. Republican. Methodist. Office: Am Enterprise Inst 1150 17th St NW Ste 1100 Washington DC 20036-4603*

CHENG, GRACE ZHENG-YING, music educator; arrived in U.S., 1982; d. Chang Cheng and Guan-Zhi Fang. B Music, Shanghai Conservatory Music, China, 1980; M Music, U. Nebr., 1985. Tchg. asst. Shanghai Conservatory Music, China, 1976—82, U. Nebr., Lincoln, 1983—85; piano tchr. Freehold (N.J.) Music Ctr., 1985—. Piano soloist Arts in the Aisles, Lincoln, Nebr., 1984, Cecilian Music Club, Monmouth County, NJ, 1986—92; pianist, NJ, 1985—. Recipient Laura R. Conover Pedagogy award Outstanding Tchg., Carnegie Hall, N.Y.C., 1998, 5th Yr. Tchr.'s award, Cecilian Music Club, 1997. Mem.: ASPCA, Nat. Guild Piano Tchrs. (piano adj. 1994—), N.J. Music Tchrs. Assn. (piano adj. 1998), Nat. Music Tchrs. Assn. (piano adj. 1993), Sierra Club. Avocations: internet, travel, photography, gardening. Home: 1 Swallow Ln Howell NJ 07731 Office: Freehold Music Ctr 3681 Unit 4 Rte 9 Freehold NJ 07728 Personal E-mail: gchennj@aol.com.

CHENG, MEI-FANG, psychobiology educator, neuroethology researcher, biologist, educator; b. Kee Lung, Taiwan, Republic of China, Nov. 24, 1938; came to U.S., 1959; d. Chao-Chin Hsieh and Ai Tsu; m. Wen-Kwei Cheng; m. June 7, 1963; children: Suzanne, Po-Yuan, Julie. BS summa cum laude, Nat. Taiwan U., Taipei, 1958; PhD, Bryn Mawr Coll., 1965. Postdoctoral fellow U. Pa., Phila., 1965-68; asst. rsch. prof. Inst. Animal Behavior Rutgers U., Newark, 1969-73, assoc. prof., 1973-79, prof., 1979, acting dir. Inst. Animal Behavior, 1989—91, dir., 1991-95. Cons. NIMH, mem. neurosci. study sect., 1991-95; cons., mem. behavioral neurobiology br. NSF; mem. NIH Reviewers Res., 1995—; cons. numerous granting agys. Author: Advance in the Study of Behavior, 1979; co-editor: Reproduction: A Behavioral and Neuroscientific Perspective, 1986; assoc. editor Hormones and Behavior, 1986-96; cons. Brain Rsch., Sci., others; contbr. articles to profl. jours. Fulbright scholar, 1959; recipient Rsch. Scientist Devel. award NIMH, 1974-79, 79-84, Johnson & Johnson Discovery award, 1989, Hoechst-Celanese Innovative award, 1993, award of excellence in rsch. Rutgers Bd. Trustees, 1998. Mem. Internat. Conf. Neuroethology, Neurosci. Achievements include discovery that a bird's own songs stimulate the endocrine changes; demonstration of the vocal-auditory-endocrine pathways involved in voice and sound mediation of endocrine change, and provide anatomical basis for emotion-sharing theory of vocal communication; discovery of cell loss can trigger neurogenesis in the adult brain and may be harnessed for brain repair and functional recovery. Office: Rutgers U Dept Psychology 101 Warren St Newark NJ 07102-1811

CHEN-HAFTECK, LILY, music educator; b. Hong Kong, China, July 20, 1965; arrived in US, 2001; d. Charles Chen and Wen-Ying Chin; m. Pierre Hafteck, Aug. 8, 1992; children: Claire Hafteck, Lucie Hafteck. BA in music with honors, U. Hong Kong, China, 1987; MA in music edn., U. Reading, England, 1990; PhD in music edn., U. Reading, 1996. Tchr. Creative Primary Sch., Hong Kong, 1987, St. Mary's Canossian Coll., Hong Kong, 1987—88; tchg. asst. U. Hong Kong, 1988—89; tchr. Parkview Internat. Preschool, Hong Kong, 1990—93, Maputo Internat. Sch., Mozambique, 1993—95; adj. prof. U. Pretoria, South Africa, 1997—98, 1999—2001; vis. scholar Hong Kong Bapt. U., China, 1998—99; asst. prof., mus edn. coord. Kean U., Union, NJ, 2001—. Reviewer Internat. Jour. of Music Edn., 1997—2001, editl. bd., 2001—; reviewer Asia-Pacific Jour. Tchr. Edn. Devel., 1998; post doctoral rsch. fellow Ctr. for Advanced Studies in Music, U. Surrey Roehampton, London, 1996—2001, U. Pretoria, 1997—2000. Contbr. articles various profl. jours., chapters to books The Phenonmenon of Singing, 1998, Music, Mind and Science, 1999. Recipient Young Rschr. award, European Soc. for the Cognitive Scis. of Music, 1997; Marden Found. scholarship, Marden Found., 1989, Rayson Huang scholarship, U. Hong Kong, 1990. Mem.: Internat. Sco. for Music Edn. (bd. dirs. 2002—, chair, Youth Focus Group 2002—, chair, Early Childhood Commn. 2000—02, commr., Early Childhood Comm. 1996—2000). Office: Kean U Dept Music 1000 Morris Ave Union NJ 07083 E-mail: lhafteck@kean.edu.

CHENHALLS, ANNE MARIE, nurse, educator; b. Detroit, May 26, 1929; d. Peter and Beatrice Mary (Elliston) McLeod; m. Horacio Chenhalls, 1953 (dec.); children: Mark, Anne Marie Chenhalls Delahanty. Student, Detroit Conservatory Music, 1946-47; grad., Grace Hosp. Sch. Nursing, 1951; B Vocat. Edn., Calif. State U., L.A., 1967; BS in Nursing, Calif. State U., 1968; MA, Calif. State U., Long Beach, 1985. RN, Calif. Nurse Grace Hosp., Detroit, 1951-52; pvt. duty nurse Mexico City, 1953-54; nurse St. Francis Hosp., Lynwood, Calif., 1957-63; assoc. prof. nursing Compton Coll., Calif., 1964-72; health educator, sch. nurse Santa Ana (Calif.) Unified Sch. Dist., 1972-76, 79—. Med. coord., internat. health cons. Agape Movement, San Bernardino, Calif., 1976-79; instr. community health, Uganda, 1982; med. evaluator Athletes in Action, 1979; pub. health nurse Orange County Health Dept., Calif., 1990-95. Assoc. staff mem. Campus Crusade for Christ; solo vocalist, Santa Ana, Orange, Seal Beach, Dinner Theater, Calif., Civic Light Opera, Buena park, Calif.; acting Master's Repertory Theater, 1990-94, Santa Ana. U.S. govt. grantee, 1968. Mem. Calif. Sch. Nurses Assn., Calif. Tchrs. Assn., Baxter, Fed. C. of C. Republican. Home: 2601 E Ocean Blvd 810 Long Beach CA 90803-2504 Office: Santa Ana Unified Sch Dist 1601 E Chestnut Ave Santa Ana CA 92701-6322 E-mail: annechenhalls@yahoo.com.

CHENOWETH, KRISTIN, actress; b. Tulsa, Okla., July 24, 1968; MA in Opera, Oklahoma City U. Actor: (Broadway plays) Steel Pier, 1999 (Theatre World award), You're a Good Man, Charlie Brown, 1999 (Tony award Best Featured Actress, 1999, Drama Desk award, 1999, Clarence Derwent award, 1999, Outer Critics Circle award, 1999), Epic Proportions, 1999—2000, Funny Girl, 2002, Wicked, 2003— (Tony award nominee, Best Actress in a Musical, 2004); (plays) A New Brain, Scapin, The Fantasticks, Dames at Sea, Strike Up the Band, 1998; (TV series) LateLine, 1998, Frasier, 1993, Kristin, 2001, Baby Bob, 2002, Sesame Street, 2003—; (TV miniseries) Paramour, 1999; (TV films) Annie, 1999, The Music Man, 2003; (films) Topa Topa Bluffs, 2002; guest soloist: West Side Story Suite of Dances; singer: (albums) Let Yourself Go, 2001. Metropolitan Opera award. Performed leading roles at Goodspeed Opera House, Guthrie Theatre, Paper Mill Playhouse, North Shore Music Theatre; guest soloist with National Symphony Orchestra, New York Philharmonic, London's Divas at Donmar series, Carnegie Hall, Lincoln Center and the Kennedy Center, and has performed with Placido Domingo, Paul Newman, Joshua Bell and Harvey Fierstein. Office: [illegible] New York NY 10017-7111*

CHENOWETH-HAGE, HELEN P. former congresswoman; b. Topeka, Kans., Jan. 27, 1938; 2 children. Attended, Whitworth Coll., 1975-79; cert. in law office mgmt., U. Minn., 1974; student, Rep. Nat. Com. Mgmt. Coll., 1977. Bus. mgr. Northside Med. Ctr., 1964-75; state exec. dir. Idaho Rep. Party, 1975-77; chief of staff Congressman Steve Symms, 1977-78; campaign mgr. Symms for Congress Campaign, 1978, Leroy for Gov., 1985-86; v.p. Consulting Assocs., Inc., 1978—; mem. U.S. Congress from Idaho, Washington, 1995-2001; chairwoman Nev. Live Stock Assn., Hawthorne, Nev., 2003—; property rights activist. Mem. agriculture, resources, vets. affairs coms., chmn. forest subcom.; bd. dirs. Ctr. Study of Market Alternatives, Mountain States Legal Found.; chmn. bd. America 21. Deacon Capitol Christian Ctr., Boise. Republican. Office: Nev Live Stock Assn PO Box 639 Hawthorne NV 89415*

CHER, (CHERILYN SARKISIAN), singer, actress; b. El Centro, Calif., May 20, 1946; d. Gilbert and Georgia LaPiere; m. Sonny Bono, Oct. 27, 1964 (div.); 1 child, Chastity; m. Gregg Allman, June 1975 (div.); 1 child, Elijah Blue. Student drama coach, Jeff Corey. Singer with husband as team, Sonny and Cher, 1964-74; star TV shows: Cher, 1975-76, The Sonny and Cher Show, 1976-77; concert appearances with husband, 1977, numerous recs., TV, concert and benefit appearances with Sonny Bono; TV appearances, ABC-TV, 1978, appearance with Sonny Bono in motion pictures, Good Times, 1966, Chastity, 1969; film appearances include Silkwood, 1983, Mask, 1985 (Best Actress, Cannes Internat. Film Festival), The Witches of Eastwick, 1987, Suspect, 1987, Moonstruck (Golden Globe award 1988, Acad. award for best actress 1988), 1987, Mermaids, 1990, The Player, 1992, Pret-a-Porter, 1994, Faithful, 1996, Tea With Mussolini, 1999; TV movies; If These Walls Could Talk, 1996, Happy Birthday Elizabeth: A Celebration of Life, 1997, AFI's 100 Years...100 Movies, 1998; helped form rock band, Black Rose, 1979; recorded albums include Black Rose, 1980, Cher, 1988, Heart of Stone, 1989 (Double Platinum and 3 Gold Singles), Love Hurts, 1991, It's A Man's World, 1996, The Casablanca Years, 1996, Believe, 1998 (Grammy award best dance recording 1999), Not Commercial, 2000, Living Proof, 2002; exec. prodr. Sonny & Me: Cher Remembers, 1998. Office: c/o ICM 8942 Wilshire Blvd Beverly Hills CA 90211-1934 also: Reprise Records 3000 Warner Blvd Burbank CA 19010-4694*

CHEREPANOV, ELENA, psychologist, educator; b. Moscow, Nov. 18, 1958; d. Yulia and Mihail Ianotovsky; 1 child, Peter. PhD, Moscow State U., 1988. Cert.Psychologist Ont., Can., 1997, LMHS Bd. of Allied Mental Health, Mass., 2001, Cert. Trauma Specialists Assn. of Trauma Specialists. Coord. trauma svcs. Child and Family Svc., West Springfield, Mass., 2000—; adj. prof. U. Toronto, Toronto, Canada, 1996—2000; mental health officer Doctors without Borders, Macedonia, 1999, peer support network trainer, 1998—; dir. mental health program Caritas, 1992; mental health officer Assoc. Traumatic Stress Specialists, Belarus, 1989—92. Assoc. prof. Moscow State Ped. U., 1988—95. E-mail: echer02@yahoo.com.

CHERMAYEFF, ALEXANDRA SASHA, artist; b. N.Y.C., Feb. 17, 1960; d. Ivan and Sara Anne (Duffy) C.; m. Philip W. Howie, May 10, 1992; children: Phineas Alexander, Olivia Isabel. BA, U. Vt., 1982; postgrad., N.Y. Studio Sch., 1983-86. Cert. appraiser N.Y. Univ. Sch. Appraisal Studies. Cons. Alexandra Chermayeff Artist Svcs., N.Y.C., 1987—91; asst. to chmn., bd. dirs. Andy Warhol Found., N.Y.C., 1991-93; collection mgr., curator Frederick Hughes, N.Y.C., 1991—2000; dir. exhbns. Thomas cole Hist. Site Gallery, 2001—. Exhibited in group shows Bowery Gallery, NY, 1992, Addison Gallery, Andover, Mass., 1993, Parrish Art Mus., NY, 1994 (award 1994), NY Studio Sch. Gallery, 1995, NY Studio Sch. Gallery, 1995, 96, 97, 98, Carrie Haddad Gallery, Hudson, NY, 2000, Global Art Source, Zurich, 2001, 02. Recipient Allied Artist award Nat. Arts Club, 1985; Ellen Battell Stoeckel fellow Yale U., 1985. Mem. Greene County Coun. on the Arts, Friends of the Hudson (Hudson riverkeeper). Avocations: art and antique collection, birdwatching, fossils. E-mail: philandsasha@surferz.net.

CHERNEY, ISABELLE DENISE, education educator, researcher; d. Jean-Claude Schindler and Denise Genevieve Chavaz; m. Michael Gerard Cherney, June 14, 1985; children: Sebastien Alexandre, Raphael Gerard. BA, Creighton U., 1996; MA, U. Nebr., 1999, PhD, 2001. Mktg. mgr. Digital Equipment Corp., Geneva, 1981—84; libr. mgr. Unix Europe, London, 1984—85; fin. analyst Apollo Computers, Geneva, 1985—86; interpreter/translator The Internat. Word, Omaha, 1990—94; adj. prof. U. Nebr., 1999—2000; asst. prof. Creighton U., Omaha, 2000. Asst. dir. of honors program Creighton U., Omaha, 2002. Recipient Dissertation Scholarship award, U. of Nebr., 2001, Outstanding Grad. Helen Hansen Student award, 1999, Leo R. Kennedy award, Creighton U., 1996; Academic Devel. and Tech. fellowship, 2002—03, Rhoden Grad. Thesis scholarship, U. of Nebr., 1999, Women in Sci. grant, Nebr. EPSCOR, 2002, Summer Faculty Rsch. grant, Creighton U., 2001, Presdl. Grad. fellowship, U. of Nebr., 1997—98, Rsch. Summer fellowship, Coun. of Undergraduate Rsch., 1995. Mem.: APA, Nebr. Acad. of Sci., Midwestern Psychol. Soc., Soc. for Rsch. in Child Devel., Am. Psychol. Soc., Cognitive Devel. Soc., Coun. of Undergraduate Rsch., Psi Chi. Catholic. Avocation: travel. Office: Creighton U 2500 California Plaza Omaha NE 68178 Personal E-mail: isabellecherney@hotmail.com.

CHERNOFF, DEBORAH SHELLEY, art educator; b. Phila., Jan. 10, 1951; d. Bernard and Helene Chernoff. AA, Atlantic Cape C.C., Mays Landing, N.J., 1973; BS, Moore Coll. Art and Design, 1974; MA, Rowan U., 1980. Cert. Nat. Bd. Profl. Tchg. Stds., Nat. Bd. Profl. Tchg. Standards 2002. Instr. art Atlantic City H.S., 1988—93; instr. comml. and fine arts Mainland Regional H.S., Linwood, NJ, 1975—. Mem. bd. edn. Jewish Fedn. Atlantic County; mem. So. Regional Inst. Stockton State Coll., Pomona, NJ, 2002—. Represented in permanent collections Congregation Beth Judah Sch., Atlantic Cape C.C., Haggadah Congregation Beth Judah's 75th Anniversary, illustrated, Haggadah, Congregation Beth Judah's 75th Ann. Bd. dirs. Atlantic City Concerts Assn. Mem.: NEA, Art Educator's N.J., Phila. Calligrapher's Soc., N.J. Edn. Assn., Nat. Art Edn. Assn. (presenter conv.), Shaloma Hadassah (life), Phi Delta Kappa. Home: 208 N Newark Ave Ventnor City NJ 08406 Office: Mainland Regional HS 1301 Oak Ave Linwood NJ 08221 Office Phone: 609-927-4151.*

CHERNOW, ANN LEVY, artist, art educator; b. NYC, Feb. 1, 1936; d. Edward P. and Mollie (Citrin) Levy; m. Philip Chenok, Aug. 11, 1957 (div. Jan. 1969); children: David Charles Chenok, Daniel Joshua Chenok; m. Burt Chernow, Dec. 11, 1970. MA, NYU, 1969. Instr. Mus. Modern Art, N.Y.C., 1966-71; prof., head art dept. Norwalk (Conn.) Cmty. Tech. Coll., 1974-96. Guest lectr., instr. studio and art history Silvermine Sch. Arts Silvermine Coll., 1968—80; vis. artist, lectr. Housatonic C.C., Conn., 1975—80; guest lectr. Am. Coll. in Paris, 1985, Salem State Coll., 1993, 94, Yale U., 1995, Westport Hist. Soc., 1994, Fairfield U., 1993; vis. artist CAP program Wesleyan U., 1979; coord. Bicentennial Exhbn. Norwalk C.C., 1976, Yale U. Art Gallery, 1996; master drawing class The Nat. Acad., N.Y.C., 2000—, N.Y.C., 2001; vis. artist and lectr. Bryn Mawr U., 2003, Ind. U., 2003; vis. artist Pa. Acad. Fine Arts, 2004. One-woman shows include Wesleyan U., Middleton, Conn., 1979, Beall/Lambremont Gallery, La., 1980—81, Gallery Suzanne Maag, Zurich, 1980, Douglass Gallery, Rutgers U., N.J., 1980, Queens Coll., N.Y.C., 1982, Alex Rosenberg Gallery, 1982, Mattatuck (Conn.) Mus., 1982, Munson Gallery, Conn., 1984, 1988—89, Snug Harbor Cultural Ctr., L.I., 1984, Stamford (Conn.) Mus., 1985, Conn. Fine Arts Mus., 1986, Katonah Gallery, N.Y., 1987, Fairfield U., Conn., 1988, U.F.O. Gallery, Princeton, N.J., 1988, Provincetown, Mass., 1990—91, 1994, Uptown Gallery, 1989, Uptown Galley, N.Y.C., 1995, Uptown Gallery, [illegible], Conn. Gallery, 1989, Lust Gallery, N.Y.C., 1992, Winfisky Gallery, Salem, 1993, Washington Art Assn., Conn., 1993, NCTC Gallery, Norwalk, Conn., 1994, New Rochelle Libr. Gallery, N.Y., 1995, Mcpl. Mus. of St. Paul de Vence, France, 1996, PMW Gallery, Stamford, Conn., 1997—98, Westchester C.C., 1997, Albert Merola, Provincetown, 1998, Stamford Mus., 1999, Queens Coll., N.Y.C., 2000, Erlich Gallery, Marblehead, Mass., 2002, Raclin Gallery Ind. U., 2003, Print Ctr., Phila., 2003, Dorothy Rogers Fine Art, Santa Fe, N.Mex., 2003, exhibited in group shows at Alex Rosenberg Gallery, 1980, Mus. Contemporary Art, Sao Paulo, Brazil, 1980, Aldrich Mus., Ridgefield, Conn., 1981, Silvermine Guild, 1982, Print Club, Phila., 1983, Artists Choice Mus., Marisa Del Re Gallery, N.Y.C., 1983, Morris Mus., Morristown, N.J., 1984, John Slade Ely House, New Haven, 1985, Munson Gallery, 1985, Stamford Mus., 1985—86, 1994—95, Katonah Gallery, 1986, Internat. Miniature Print Bienniale, New Canaan, 1987, Uptown Gallery, N.Y.C., 1994, Martin Sumers Gallery, 1994, Nat. Drawings Assn., 1994, SAGA Prints, 1994, Fairfield, Conn., 1994, Americas, 2000, S.D., 1994, Triton Mus., Santa Clara, Calif., 1994, Ctr. for Visual Arts, Oakland, Calif., 1994, Discovery Mus., Conn., 1995, Calif. Soc. Printmakers, San Francisco, 1995, Millennium Portfolio of Time and Place, 1999—2001, Bklyn. Mus., 2001, Nat. Acad., 2001, NY Soc. Etchers, 2002, Nat Arts Club, NYC, 2002, Mus. City of NY, 2002, Salle des Fetes, Paris, 2003, Trois Rivieres, Can., 2003, Jessedra Gallery, Sophia, Bulgaria, 2004, Black Ch. Gallery, Dublin, 2004, Westford Arts Ctr., Conn., 2004, Represented in permanent collections Met. Mus. Art, Rose Art Mus., Brandeis U., Nat. Mus. Women in Arts, Washington, William Benton Mus. Art, Storrs, Conn., Mus. of City of N.Y., UN, Westport, Achenbach Found., San Francisco, New Britain Mus. Am. Art, Conn., Neuberger Mus., Purchase, N.Y., Housatonic Mus. Art Yale U., Mattatauk Mus., Lehigh U. Art Collection, Pa., Utah Mus. Fine Arts, U. Ariz. Art Collection, Lyman Allyn Mus., Conn., Bruce Mus., Butler Inst. Am. Art, Ohio, Rutgers U., Hofstra U., Elvejhem Mus., Wis., N.Y. Pub. Libr., Duxbury Mus. Mass., USO of Met. N.Y., Amity Art Found., Conn., Reading (Pa.) Pub. Mus., Portland (Oreg.) Art Mus., De Cordova Mus., Lincoln, Mass., Yale U. Art Gallery, Utah Mus. Fine Arts, Ohio Wesleyan U., Worcester Mus. Art, Mass., Oakland Mus., Calif., U.S.O. Greater Met. N.Y., Reading Pub. Mus., Pa., Transit Mus., N.Y.C., others;, author numerous poems; contbr. articles to profl. jours. Named Conn. Woman of Decade in Arts, UN Assn., 1987, U.S.A. rep., Agart World Print Festival, Ljubljana, Slovenia, 1999, UN Artist of Yr., 2002; recipient Purchase award, Delta Internat. Prints, 1996, Etching award, L.A. Printmaking Soc., 1997, Painting award, Manhattan Arts Internat., 1997, Etching award, Audubon artists, 1997, Print Biennial Silvermine Guild of Art, Conn., 1998, Four winners award, Stamford Mus. & Nature Ctr., Conn., 1998, Eisner Found. award, 1998, Richard Florsheim award, 1998, Exhbn. award/Boston Printamkers and Delta Internat. awards, Print Club, 2001, Purchase award, Delta Internat. Prints, 2001, Trustees Merit award, Housantonic C.C., 2003, Legion of Honor award, Achenbach Found., San Francisco; fellow Yale Mellon, 1993—94; grantee Yale/Mellon, 1995. Mem.: N.Y. Etchers Soc., Print Club Albany, Print Club Phila., L.A. Print Soc., Boston Printmakers, Calif. Soc. Printmakers, Nat. Acad. Art, Nat. Acad. Art (elected Academician Graphics), Soc. Am. Graphic Artists (coun.). Studio: 2 Gorham Ave Westport CT 06880-2531 Office Phone: 203-227-8016. E-mail: finearts@rcn.com.

CHERRY, SANDRA WILSON, lawyer; b. Dec. 31, 1941; d. Berlin Alexander and Renna Glen (Barnes) Wilson; m. John Sandefur Cherry, Sept. 24, 1976; 1 child, Jane Wilson. BA, U. Ark., 1962, JD, 1975. Bar: Ark. 75, U.S. Dist. Ct. (ea. dist.) Ark. 79, U.S. Supreme Ct. 79, U.S. Ct. Appeals (8th cir.) 79. Tchr. social studies Little Rock Sch. Dist., 1966—70; chmn. social studies dept. Horace Mann Jr. H.S., Little Rock, 1970—72; asst. U.S. atty. Dept. Justice, Little Rock, 1975—81, 1983—, 1st asst. U.S. atty., 2002—; commr. Ark. Pub. Svc. Commn., Little Rock, 1981—83. Adj. instr. U. Ark. Sch. Law, Little Rock, 1980; mem. 8th cir. gender fairness task force, Ark. dist. ct. magistrate selection panel, 2001. Contbr. case note to Ark. Law Rev., 1975. Pres. bd. dirs. Gaines House, Inc.; pres. U. Ark. at Little Rock Law Sch. Assn., 1980—81, bd. dirs., 1982, Jr. League Little Rock, 1974, Ark. Cmty. Found., 1997—, Gov.'s Mansion Assn., 1998—. Recipient Gayle Pettus Pontz award, U. Ark. Law Sch. Women Lawyers Assn., 1990. Mem.: ABA, Little Rock C. of C., Ark. Bus. Assn. (com. on the status of women and minorities), Ark. Women Lawyers Assn., Pulaski County Bar Assn. (bd. dirs. 1989—90, 1991—92, pres.-elect 1993—94, pres. 1994—), Ark. Bar Assn. (Ho. of Del. 1984—86, sec.-treas. 1986—89, Ho. of Del. 1989—, tenured del. 1994, exec. coun. chair 1995—, pres. 2001—02, 8th cir. gender fairness task force, Golden Gavel award 1992), Phi Beta Phi. Republican. Presbyterian. Home: 4100 S Lookout St Little Rock AR 72205-2030 Office: US Atty's Office PO Box 1229 Little Rock AR 72203-1229

CHERVITZ, RANDI S, art gallery director, artist; b. Gary, Ind., Mar. 26, 1968; d. Judith and James Chervitz; m. Adam Lieberman, July 26, 1991 (div. Oct. 24, 2000). BFA, So. Ill. U. at Carbondale, 1989—91. Gallery dir. Craft Alliance, St. Louis, Mo., 1999—; owner, designer Uncommon Threads, LLC, St. Louis, Mo., 1991—. Juror Ohio State Fair, Columbus, Ohio, 2003; spkr. Can. Consulate, Chgo., 2000—02; instr., metalsmithing for kids and workshops for adult students Craft Alliance, St. Louis, 1999—. Mixed media wall art, Mixed Media Series. Bd. mem. St. Louis Gallery Assn., St. Louis, Mo., 2002—03. Mem.: Soc. of North Am. Goldsmiths (assoc.), Am. Craft Coun. (assoc.), Art St. Louis (assoc.). Office: Craft Alliance 6640 Delmar Blvd Saint Louis MO 63130 E-mail: gallerydirector@craftalliance.org.

CHESBRO, KAREN E. HENISE, registered nurse; b. York, Pa., Oct. 2, 1960; d. Lamar and Bonnie (Palmer) Henise; children: Ashley B., Samuel T. BSN, West Chester (Pa.) U., 1982. RN, Pa.; cert. CPR instr. Primary care staff nurse Phoenixville (Pa.) Hosp., 1982-84, Brandywine Hosp., Coatesville, Pa., 1984-89; telemetry nurse Community Hosp. of Lancaster, Pa., 1989-95; staff nurse Kimberly Quality Care of Lancaster (Pa.), 1990-92; charge nurse Dauphin County Nursing Home, 1992-94; staff nurse Pinnacle Health Home Care, 1995-2000; nursing supr. Masonic Homes Health Care Ctr., Elizabethtown, Pa., 2000—. Home: 9 Foxbury Dr Elizabethtown PA 17022-1760

CHESKY, EVELYN G. state legislator; Chmn. bd. Hoyoke Pub. Works, 1978; counsillor-at-large, 1985; state rep. dist. 5 Mass. Ho. of Reps., Boston, mem. energy com., pub. safety and sci. and tech. and human svcs. com. Mem., bd. dirs. Holyoke Boys and Girls Club. Recipient Polish Heritage Citizens award Holyoke Hosp. Aux. Democrat. Office: Mass Ho of Reps State House Rm 473-B Boston MA 02133 also: 3 Brenan St Holyoke MA 01040-1049

CHESLAK, MONICA LYNN, marketing professional, director; b. Knoxville, Nov. 24, 1969; d. Albert Joseph Cheslak and Ellen Jane Warne. BFA, George Mason U., 1992; MA, Am. U., 1994. Cert. Am. Arts Sotheby's Inst., 1997. Edn. coord. Allied Arts of Greater Chattanooga, 1994—95; asst. dir. Blues in the Schs., Charleston, SC, 1995—97, Scalamandré, N.Y.C., 1997—98, Sotheby's, N.Y.C., 1998—99; mktg. mgr. Waterworks, Danbury, Conn., 1999—2001; dir. mktg. D&D Bldg., N.Y.C., 2002—. Mng. pres. Big Cat Gallery, Westport, 2001—02, Big Cat Comm., Westport, Conn., 2002—. Mem.: MDMA, IFDA, Smithsonian Instn., The Beaux Arts Alliance, Victorian Soc., Am. Friends of the Ga. Group, Inst. Classial Architecture, Whitney Mus. Am. Art, Metropolitan Mus. Art, Colonial Williamsburg, Nat. Trust for Historic Preservation. Office: D&D Bldg 979 Third Ave Ste 1400 New York NY 10022

CHESLER, GAIL, arts organization development [illegible] May 22; d. Leon William and Sylvia (Spiegel) C.; m. Richard Allen Lippe (div. May 1989); children; Wendy Ann, David Allen. BA in History, Beaver Coll.; MA in Performing Arts Adminstrn., NYU, 1988. Outreach coord. North Shore Cmty. Arts Ctr., Gt. Neck, N.Y., 1976-79; pub. rels. cons. Gt. Neck, 1979-85; dir. of devel. and mktg. ART/New York, N.Y.C., 1987-88; exec. dir. Jennifer Muller/The Works, N.Y.C., 1989; dir. of devel. Temple Beth-El, Gt. Neck, 1989-92; nat. dir. planned giving and endowments Women's Am. ORT, N.Y.C., 1993-96; planned giving officer N.Y. Presbyn. Hosp./Weill Med. Coll. of Cornell U., N.Y.C., 1996-2000; dir. planned and spl. gifts The Met. Opera, N.Y.C., 2000—. Co-founder, bd. dirs. Teen to Teen, Carle Place, N.Y., 1985-88. Mem. Planned Giving Group of Greater N.Y. (past pres. 1999—, pres. 1998-99, v.p. 1997-98, treas. 1996-97). Avocations: opera, travel, theater. Home: 128 Central Park S # 3B New York NY 10019-1565 Office: The Metropolitan Opera Lincoln Ctr New York NY 10023

CHESNEY, MARGARET A. medical educator, medical researcher; BA in Psychology and Sociology, Whitman Coll., Walla Walla, Wash., 1971; MA in Psychology, Colo. State U., 1973, PhD in Psychology, 1975. Postdoctoral fellow dept. psychiatry Temple U., Phila., 1975—76; dir. and sr. health psychologist dept. behavioral medicine SRI Internat., 1976—87; assoc. prof. prevention scis. group, dept. epidemiology U. Calif., San Francisco, 1987—89, prof. prevention scis. group, 1989—, co-dir. Ctr. for AIDS Prevention Studies, 1994—; dir. behavioral core AIDS Clin. Trials Group San Francisco Gen. Hosp., 1994—. Sci. cons. behavioral medicine Stanford U. Med. Ctr., 1978—; chair working group on psychosocial factors in AIDS clin. trials and vaccine trials NIMH, 1993—; chair working group for women's health initiative clin. trial NIH, 1993—; co-chair recruitment, adherence, retention com. AIDS Clin. Trials Group, 1995—; mem. HIV vaccine working group NIAID, 1994—95; mem. data safety and monitoring bd. Women's Health Initiative NIH, 1993—; mem. panel on AIDS interventions and rsch. NAS, 1988—90; mem. AIDS adv. com. Nat. Heart, Lung and Blood Inst., 1987—93. Contbr. numerous articles to profl. jours.; co-author (with Ray Rosenman): Anger and Hostility in Cardiovascular and Behavioral Disorders. Mem.: APA (pres. health psychology divsn. 1990—91, Ann. Award for Outstanding Contbn. to Health Psychology 1982), Am. Psychosomatic Soc. (pres.-elect 1996, Ann. Award for Outstanding Contbn. to Health Psychology 1985), Inst. Medicine of NAS, Phi Beta Kappa, Sigma Xi. Office: Univ Calif AIDS Rsch Inst 74 New Montgomery Ste 600 San Francisco CA 94105

CHESNEY, MAXINE M. judge; b. 1942; BA, U. Calif., Berkeley, 1964, JD, 1967. Trial atty. Office Dist. Atty., San Francisco, 1968-69, sr. trial atty., 1969-71, prin. trial atty., 1971-76, head atty., 1976, asst. chief dep., 1976-79; judge San Francisco Mcpl. Ct., 1979-83, San Francisco Superior Ct., 1983-95, U.S. Dist. Ct. (no. dist.) Calif., San Francisco, 1995—. Bd. dirs. San Francisco Child Abuse Coun., 1976-79, Hosp. Audiences, 1978-81. Mem. Fed. Judges Assn., Nat. Assn. Women Judges, Edward J. McFetridge Am. Inn of Ct., U.S. Assn. Constl. Law, Queen's Bench, Ninth Jud. Cir. Hist. Soc. Office: US Dist Ct No Dist Calif PO Box 36060 450 Golden Gate Ave San Francisco CA 94102-3661

CHESNEY, SUSAN TALMADGE, writer, developer; b. N.Y.C., Aug. 12, 1943; d. Morton and Tillie (Talmadge) Chesney; m. Donald Lewis Freitas, Sept. 17, 1967 (div. May 1976); m. Robert Martin Rosenblatt, Apr. 9, 1980. AB, U. Calif., Berkeley, 1967. Placement interviewer U. Calif., Berkeley, 1972-74, program coord., 1974-79; pers. adminstr. Hewlett-Packard Co., Santa Rosa, Calif., 1982-84; pres. Mgmt. Resources, Santa Rosa, 1984-97; human resources mgr. BioBottoms Inc., Petaluna, Calif., 1990-91; human resources adminstr. Parker Compumotor, Rohnert Park, Calif., 1991-93; writer, developer The E-Myth Acad., Santa Rosa, 1997-98. Cons. Kensington Electronics Group, Healdsburg, Calif., 1984-85, Behavioral Medicine Assocs., Santa Rosa, 1985-86, M.C.A.I., Santa Rosa, 1986-87, Bowdon Designs, Santa Rosa, 1987-88, Bass & Ingram, Santa Rosa, 1988-96, Eason Tech., Inc., Healdsburg, 1995-96, Interim Svcs., Inc., Santa Rosa, 1995-98, Flex Products, Inc., Santa Rosa, 1996-97, Nev. Prodn. Co., 1998-99. Avocations: cooking, gardening, music.

CHESNUT, NONDIS LORINE, screenwriter, consultant, reading and language arts educator, instructor, counselor; b. South Daytona, Fla., June 29, 1941; d. Anthony Valentine and Myrtle Marie (Allen) Campbell; m. Raymond Otho Chesnut, Aug. 25, 1962; 1 child, Starlina Mintina Chesnut Kladler. BS in English and Speech, Concord Coll., 1962; postgrad., Frostburg U., 1967; MEd, Shippensburg U., 1972; postgrad., W.Va. U., 1973; Advanced Grad. Specialist Degree, U. Md., 1974; postgrad., Md. State Dept. Edn., 1976-95, Inst. Children's Lit., 1995-97, Screenwriters Unlimited, 1997; writing coursework, Charter Oak State Coll., 2000. Cert. adminstr., secondary prin., elem. prin., reading splist., tchr. English and speech, drama. Tchr. English and speech Harpers Ferry (W.Va.) H.S., 1962-64; with Sears Roebuck, summer 1965; libr. Great Mills (Md.) H.S., 1968-69; tchr. English and reading North Hagerstown H.S., Hagerstown, Md., 1964-73; tchr. South Hagerstown H.S., Hagerstown, 1974-77; reading resource tchr. Woodland Way Elem. Sch., Hagerstown, 1977-83; adj. instr. grad. sch. Hood Coll., Frederick, Md., 1982-83; reading specialist Fountain Rock Elem. Sch., Hagerstown, 1983-85; tchr. Williamsport (Md.) H.S., 1985-95. Reading and lang. arts cons., Md., 1973-95, Fla., 1996-2000; adj. reading instr. Daytona Comm. Coll., 1996-97, Galaxy Middle Sch., 1997-98, drama, lang. arts, reading tchr., 1997-98, key source, 1999; instr. English and writing Bethune-Cookman Coll., fall 2000, ajd. instr. reading, English, Daytona Beach C.C., 2001—; spkr., presenter local, nat. and internat. workshops, 1973-2000; speech and debate coach. Writer for radio programs and advertisements for reading, 1986—, TV programs, 1974-78, 90-91; appeared on TV programs, 1974-78; co-editor column Beckley Post Herald, 1957-59; contbr. articles to newspapers and mags., 1964—; appeared in film Guarding Tess, 1993; screenwriter Heaven on Planet Earth, 2000, Love From Heaven, 2000. Mem. debating team Concord Coll., 1961-62, mem. newspaper staff, 1959-61; mem. Washington County Network of Orgns., 1984-88; co-dir. Billy Bud, 1962; v.p. Women's Ind. Club, 1962, treas., 1961; sec.-treas. Fgn. lang. Club, 1961, Debate Club, 1961-62; treas. Meth. Youth Fellowship, 1961; pres. Tri-Hi-Y, 1959; legis. chairperson State of Md. Reading Coun., 1977-78; active Life in Spirit Group, Emmanuel Meth. Ch., White Sul, 1953-84, St. Ann's Roman Cath. Ch., 1994-95, Grace United Meth. Ch., 1984-95, Lady of Hope Cath. Ch., 1996—; mem. Fla. State Reading Coun., 1996-99. Recipient Pres.'s award State of Md. Reading Coun., 1981, Pres.'s award Washington County Reading Coun., 1981, Guidance Helping award, 1987, Voice of Democracy award VFW/Ladies Aux., 1992, Am. Heritage Writing award Williamsport Lions Club, 1995, numerous others; W.Va. Legislature scholar, 1959-62. Mem. AAUW (ednl. chairperson 1983-85, legis. v.p. 1986-87, cmty. chairperson 1987-89), NEA (publicity and scholarship coms., bldg. rep. 1989-95, del.), ASCD, VFW (chairperson Voice of Democracy 1989-95, VFW award 1989-95), Md. Dist. Am. Heritage Lions (Region II Lions award, Williamsport Am. Heritage Lions award 1995), State of Md. Internat. Reading Assn. Coun. (sec. 1975-79, v.p. elect 1979-80, v.p. 1980-81, pres. 1981-82, nominating chairperson 1982-83), Washington County Tchrs. Assn. (rep., scholarship chair, publicity), Internat. Reading Assn. (sec.-treas. sex differences in reading group 1976-77, 83-85, mem. gender differences in reading group 1985-86, mem. readability interest group, mastery learning interest group, del. convs., internat. rsch. com. 1976-77, 84-85, disabled learners interest group 1975-82), Washington County Reading Assn. (pres. 1981-82), Am. Legion (chairperson oratorial contest 1989-95, speech coach), Fla. Devel. Edn. Assn. (mem. com. registration 1996). Democrat. Avocations: writing, swimming, dance, travel, psychology. Home: 107 Old Sunbeam Dr Daytona Beach FL 32119

CHESNUTT, JANE, publishing executive; b. Kenedy, Tex., Oct. 10, 1950; m. W. Mallory Rintoul. BJ, U. Tex., 1973. Editorial asst. Am. Jour. Nursing, N.Y.C., 1975-78; asst. editor Woman's Day mag., N.Y.C., 1978-82, health editor, 1982-89, beauty, health, fashion editor, 1989-91, editor-in-chief, 1991—, sr. v.p., group editl. dir., 2002—. Sr. v.p. & group editl. dir. Transplant Am. Nat. Kidney Found. Mem. bus. adv. coun. Washington Irving H.S., N.Y.C. Named one of Editor of Yrl, Adweek, 1992, Top Players, Min Mag., 2000; recipient Editor of Yr., Adweek, 1992. Mem. Am. Soc. Mag. Editors, Women in Comms., Inc. (Clarion award 1985, Headliner award 1996), YWCA Acad. of Achievers. Office: Woman's Day Mag Hachette Filipacchi Mags Inc 1633 Broadway New York NY 10019-6708

CHESS, SONIA MARY, retired language educator; b. Ashton, Lancashire, Eng., Apr. 14, 1930; came to U.S., 1951, naturalized, 1963; d. Arthur and Sarah Ann (Hulme) Bradburn; m. Joseph Campbell Chess, Nov. 17, 1950; children: Denise Ann, Tanya Marie, Michele Elise, Luana Jo. BA in English Lit., U. Hawaii, Honolulu, 1970, MA, 1973, MA in Am. Studies, 1989, PhD in Am. Studies, 1996. Prof. English U. Hawaii/Honolulu Community Coll., 1971-93, chmn. English dept., 1980-84, div. chairperson lang. arts, 1989-91, ret. Tchr. cons. Hawaii Writing Project, Honolulu, 1983—; tchr. summer sch. Regent, Sandwich Isle chpt. Daus. of Brit. Empire, Honolulu, 1978-80. Recipient Excellence in Teaching medal, U. Hawaii Bd. Regents, 1983; Dickens fellow, Nat. Endowment for Humanities, 1985, Hawaii Writing Project fellow, U. Hawaii Found., 1983. Mem. Hawaii Council Tchrs. English, Assn. Women in Jr. Colls., Humanities Assn. Episcopalian. Avocations: writing, knitting, reading, swimming, travel, gardening.

CHESSER, JUDY LEE, municipal official; b. Albany, N.Y., May 27, 1948; d. Owen Francis (deceased) and Sylvia Alice (Tefft) C. BA, Syracuse U., 1970; JD cum laude, Boston Coll., 1977. Bar: D.C. 1977. Legis. asst. Urban Environment Council, Washington, 1973-74, Project on Budget Priorities, Washington, 1974-77; atty. SEC Gen. Counsel's Office, Washington, 1977-78; congl. liaison officer HUD, Washington, 1978-79; spl. asst. to asst. sec. for legislation Health and Human Svcs., Washington, 1979-80; legis. rep. City of N.Y. Washington Office, 1980-83, dir., 1983-94, dep. commr. for legis. Social Security Adminstrn. Congressional and Legis. Affairs, Washington, 1994-2001; dir. pub. policy, acting exec. dir. United Cerebral Palsy Assn., Washington, 2001—; dir. City of N.Y., Washington Office, 2002—. Coordinator Goodell Senate Campaign, N.Y., 1970, McGovern Presdl. Campaign, Pa., 1972. Mem. D.C. Bar. Democrat. Home: 3901 Alton Pl NW Washington DC 20016-2209 Office: City NY WA Office 1301 Penn Ave NW 350 Washington DC 20004 E-mail. jchesser@cityhall.nyc.gov.

CHESTER, LYNNE, foundation administrator, artist; b. Fargo, N.D., May 29, 1942; BA in Music, Hillsdale Coll., 1964; MA in Guidance Counseling, Mich. State U., 1965; PhD in Psychology, U. Mich., 1971. Tchr. Warren (Mich.) Consol. Schs., 1965-70; curriculum advisor Royal Oak (Mich.) Pub. Schs., 1974-75; co-founder, exec. dir. Peace Rsch. Found., Carmel, Calif., 1993-98. Assoc. Hillsdale Coll., 1989—; guest lectr. ceramics James Milliken U., Decatur, Ill., 1991; guest lectr. creative covergence Carl Cherry Ctr. for Art, Carmel, 1991, Compton lectr., Monterey, Calif., 1996—; mem. Nat. Assn. Fund Raising Execs., 1991-96; co-founder, bd. dirs. Monterey Peninsula Coll. Art Gallery, 1991—; guest juror Monterey County Essay Contest, 1997; cons. Monterey Mus. of Art; guest lectr. Hillsdale (Mich.) Coll., 1997; juror Monterey County Poetry Contest, 1993—; juror photographic show Beauty at the Heart of Things, Carl Cherry Ctr. for Arts, Carmel, 1999. Artist of multiple commd. sculptures for pvt. collections; also ceramics, sculpture and photographs in pvt. and corp. collections; represented in permanent collection at Krammert Art Mus., Champaign, Ill., Fresno (Calif.) Mus. Art; juried show Ctr. for Photographic Art, Carmel, Calif., 1996; art represented at Who's Who in Art, Monterey, 1989-96, Christmas Miniatures/Invitational Ctr. for Photographic Art, Carmel, 1996, Holiday Print Show Ctr. for Photographic Art, Carmel, 1996 (Dir.'s Choice 1996); author of poetry; juror essay contest Personal Heroes Monterey County K-12, 1997; juror poetry contest Monterey County 9-12 grades, Carl Cherry Ctr. for the Arts, 1993-2001; exhibited in photography show at Asilomer Conf. Ctr., Monterey Peninsula Airport, Pacific Grove Art Ctr., Carl Chevry Ctr., Seaside City Hall, Pacific Grove Mus. Natural History, 1995-98, Hillsdale Coll., 1997, Monterey Peninsula Airport, 1998, Calif. State U., Monterey Bay, 1998, Pacific Grove (Calif.) Art Ctr., 1998, Carl Cherry Ctr. for Arts, Carmel, Calif., 1998, Pacific Grove Mus. Nat. History, 1998, Salinas (Calif.) Courthouse, 1998, Asilomar Conf. Ctr., Pacific Grove, 1998, Prints Charming Gallery, Carmel, 1998, Triton Mus. Art, 1998, Pre-auction show KTEH, 1998, 2000, Triton Mus., 1998; one-woman show Prints Charming Gallery, Carmel, Calif., 2000; represented by Prints Charming Gallery and Carmel Express Internat. Co-founder Southfield (Mich.) Symphony, 1972, World Rhythms Festival, Carmel, 1994; mem. citizens adv. bd. City of Royal Oak, 1978-83; co-founder, bd. dirs. Monterey Bay Artists Day, Sta. KAZU-FM, 1987-89; pres., bd. dirs. Carl Cherry Ctr. for Arts, Carmel, 1988-94, 95, 97; bd. dirs. Monterey Peninsula Mus. Art, 1991-94, Carmel Pub. Libr. Found., 1991-94, Monterey Inst. for Rsch. in Astronomy, 1985-95, Cultural Coun. for Monterey County, 1993-98; fundraiser Student Art Gallery, Monterey Peninsula Coll., 1990-97, mem. mentors program Women Helping Women, 1998—. Recipient Citizens Adv. Coun. award City of Royal Oak, 1983, Best of Show award for monoprint Monterey Peninsula Coll., 1990, Poetry prizes Carl Cherry Ctr. for Arts, 1990-94, Benefactor of Arts award Monterey County Cultural Coun., 1992, 93, 94, Soccer Mgr./Coach of Yr. 1976-81, 1st pl. award photography contest Monterey Regional Park Dist. Celebration of Open Space, 1998; artist-in-residence Naubinway, Mich., 1997. Mem. AAUW, Internat. Platform Assn., Internat. Sculpture Ctr., Nat. Soc. Fund Raising Execs., Nat. Mus. Women in Art (charter mem.), Am. Crafts Coun., Sigma Alpha Iota (Ruby Sword of Honor 1963). Avocations: reading, playing piano, composing, hiking, photography. Home: 9645 Sandbur Pl Salinas CA 93907-1031

CHESTNUT, CYNTHIA MOORE, state legislator; b. Tallahassee, July 25, 1949; m. Charles S. Chestnut; 1 child, Christopher Moore. BS, Fla. A&M U., 1970; MS, Fla. State U., 1971; PhD, Nova U., 1981. Comnr. Gainesville City, 1987-90, mayor-comnr., 1989-90; state rep. dist. 23 Fla. Ho. of Reps., 1990—. Tchr.; dir. student affairs Alachua County Sch. Bd.; vice chmn. Dem. Caucus, edn. appropriations com., acad. excellence coun., com. on children and family, com. on edn. K-12, transp. com. Fla. Ho. of Reps. Mem. NAACP, LINKS (pres. 1989), Jr. League, Alpha Kappa Alpha. Democrat. Methodist. Office: 101 SE 2nd Pl Ste 108 Gainesville FL 32601-6591

CHESTON, SHEILA CAROL, lawyer; b. Washington, Nov. 5, 1958; d. Theodore C. and Gabrielle Joan (Hellings) C. BA, Dartmouth Coll., 1980; JD, Columbia U., 1984. Bar: N.Y. 1986, D.C. 1986, U.S. Dist. Ct. D.C. 1987, U.S. Ct. Appeals (D.C. cir.) 1987, U.S. Dist. Ct. (so. and ea. dists.) N.Y. 1989, U.S. Ct. Appeals (2d cir.), U.S. Supreme Ct. 1989. Law clk. to judge U.S. Ct. Appeals for 9th Cir., L.A., 1984-85; assoc. Wilmer, Cutler & Pickering, Washington, 1985-92, ptnr., 1992-93; gen. counsel Def. Base Closure and Realignment Commn., 1993; spl. assoc. counsel to Pres. of U.S., 1994; dep. gen. counsel Dept. Air Force, 1993-95, gen. counsel, 1995-98; ptnr. Wilmer, Cutler & Pickering, Washington, 1998—2002; sr. v.p., gen. counsel BAE Systems N.A., Rockville, Md., 2002—. Adj. prof. in internat. litig. Georgetown Law Sch., 1991—. Mem. ABA, D.C. Bar Assn., Women's Bar Assn., Am. Soc. Internat. Law. Democrat. Episcopalian. Office: BAE Systems NA 1601 Research Blvd Rockville MD 20850-3173 E-mail: sheila.cheston@baesystems.com.

CHETTA, HOLLY ANN, transportation executive; b. New Orleans, Aug. 18, 1945; d. Henry John and Ernestine Rose (Blaise) C. BS, Tulane U., 1967, MS, 1970, MPH, 1977. Assoc. realtor Latter & Blum, New Orleans, 1978-83; adminstr. loan svc. First Fin. Bank, New Orleans, 1981-83; adminstr. USDA, New Orleans, 1982-84; pers. evaluator U.S. Dept. Transp., USCG, New Orleans, 1984-91, regional maritime pers. examiner, 1991—. Author: (poems) Toward the Twenty-First Century, 1985, New Year's Eve, 1984. Mem. Internat. Platform Assn. Republican. Roman Catholic. Avocations: pet training, writing poetry. Home: 940 Emerald St New Orleans LA 70124-3523 Office: US Dept Transp US Coast Guard Exam Ctr 1615 Poydras St New Orleans LA 70112-1254

CHEVERS, WILDA ANITA YARDE, former state official and educator; b. N.Y.C. d. Wilsey Ivan and Herbert Lee (Perry) Yarde; m. Kenneth Chevers, May 14, 1950; 1 child, Pamela Anita. BA, CUNY, 1947; MSW, Columbia U., 1959, PhD, 1981. Probation officer, Office Probation for Cts., N.Y.C., 1947-55, supr. probation officer, 1955-65, br. chief, 1965-72, asst. dir. probation, 1972-77, dept. commr. dept. probation, 1978-86; prof. pub. adminstrn. John Jay Coll. Criminal Justice, CUNY, 1986-91. Conf. faculty mem. Nat. Council Juvenile and Family Ct. Judges; mem. faculty N.Y.C. Tech. Coll., Nat. Coll. Juvenile Justice; mem. adv. com. Family Ct., First Dept. Sec. Susan E. Wagner Adv. Bd., 1966—70; sec., bd. dirs. Allen Cmty. Day Care Ctr., 1971—75; mem. Las Vegas EMA Ryan White Title I Planning Coun., 1998—2000; chmn., bd. dirs. Allen Christian Sch., 1987—91; bd. dirs. Allen Sr. Citizens Housing, Queensboro Soc. for Prevention Cruelty to Children, Las Vegas LWV. Named to Hall of Fame, Hunter Coll., 1983. Mem. ABA (assoc.), ASPA (coun.), NASW, N.Y. Acad. Pub. Edn., Nat. Coun. on Crime and Delinquency, Acad. Cert. Soc. Workers, Mid. Atlantic States Conf. on Correction, Alumni Assn. Colmbia U. Sch. Social Work, NYU Alumni Assn., NAACP, Counselors, Las Vegas LWV (bd. dirs.), SNCCW (pres. 2002-03), Hansel and Gretel Club (pres. Queens, N.Y. 1967-69), Delta Sigma Theta. Home: 9012 Covered Wagon Ave Las Vegas NV 89117-7010

CHEWNING, LISA LEE, writer, educator; b. Pitts., Jan. 26, 1953; d. Aaron and Betty-Jo Krochmal; m. Charles W. Chewning, Oct. 17, 1947; children: Charles W., Geoffrey A. MFA, U. Pitts., 1993. Writer, Pitts., 1991—; writing instr. Pitts. Ctr. for Arts, U. Of Pitts., C.C. Allegheny County, 1996—2003. Home: 416 Noble St Pittsburgh PA 15232 Office: Write It Right 416 Noble St Pittsburgh PA 15232 Personal E-mail: llchewning@wildglobe.com. E-mail: llchewning@wildglobe.com.

CHEYNEY, WENDY, special education educator, researcher; b. Jamestown, N.Y., May 1, 1938; d. Horace and Dorothy Williams; m. Frazier Cheyney; children: Siri, Kim, Melissa, Kristi. BS, SUNY, Buffalo, 1961; MA, U. Buffalo, 1966; EdD, U. Miami, 1974. Cert. speech lang. pathology, reading/elem. edn. Speech/lang. pathologist Bd. Coop. Edn. Svcs. Erie County, Buffalo, 1961—66, spl. edn. tchr., 1966—72; prof. Fla. Internat. U. Coll. Edn., Miami, 1973—. Co investigator assessment intervention project Fla. Internat. U./Miami Dade Sch. Readiness Coalition; nat. tchr. trainer Wright Group and Scott Foresman Reading. Author: Focus on Phonics, 2001, (curriculum) Building Early Language and Literacy, 2003; sr. author: Scott Foresman Reading Program, 2001—. Mem.: ASCD, Coun. for Exceptional Children, Internat. Reading Assn. Home: 12341 SW 113 Ave Miami FL 33176 Office: Fla Internat Univ Mgmt and Rsch Ctr Rm 350 Miami FL 33199

CHI, HANNAH T. poet, writer; b. Vietnam, Nov. 18, 1973; arrived in U.S., 1984; d. Duong A. Chi and Nhu Thu Diec; m. Pasang Gelja Sherpa, June 17, 2003; 1 child, Tenzing Tharke Sherpa. BA, U. Wash., 1997; MFA, U. Mass. Amherst, 2002. Fulbright scholar in creative writing Fulbright Commn., 2001—02; instr. English U. Mass. Amherst, 2001; writer Renton, Wash., 2003—. Instr. Malpi Internat. Coll. U. Colo., Denver, 2003; instr. writing Sann Inst. Nursing Ea. Ky. U., 2003. Contbr. An Other Voice, 2001. Avocations: reading, writing, walking, music, puzzles. Home: 36 150PL NE Bellevue WA 98007*

CHI, LOIS WANG, retired biology educator, research scientist; b. Fuchow, China, May 12, 1921; came to U.S., 1941; d. Leland and Ada (Pang) Wang; m. Henry Chi; children: Lanie, David, Joycelyn. BS, Wheaton Coll., 1945; MS, U. So. Calif., 1947, PhD, 1954. Rsch. fellow Loma Linda (Calif.) U., 1954-57; instr. to assoc. prof. biology Immaculate Heart Coll., L.A., 1957-66; assoc. prof. to prof. biology Calif. State U., Dominguez Hills, 1966-91, rsch. dir., 1979-86, prof. emeritus. Mem. NIH Nat. Adv. Allergy and Infectious Disease Coun., 1973-74; dir. Minority Biomed. Rsch. Program Calif. State U., Dominguez Hills, 1979-86, Minority Honor Program, 1982-86. Contbr. more than 30 articles to profl. jours. Co-founder, pres. and v.p. Chinese Am. Faculty Assocs. So. Calif., Chinese Am. Engrs. and Scientists Assocs. So. Calif. Home: 2839 El Oeste Hermosa Beach CA 90254-2234

CHIARA, MARGARET MARY, United States attorney; BA, Fordham U.; MA Pace U.; JD, Rutgers U. Assoc. French and Lawrence, Cassopolis, Mich., 1979—82; prosecuting atty. Cass County Prosecutor's Office, 1982—96; adminstr. Trial Ct. Assessment Commn., 1997—98; policy and planning dir. Office of Chief Justice of Mich. Supreme Ct., 1999—2001; U.S. atty. We. Dist. Mich. U.S. Dept. Justice, 2001—. Office: PO Box 208 Grand Rapids MI 49501

CHIAVARIO, NANCY ANNE, business and community relations executive; b. Centralia, Ill., Aug. 17, 1947; d. Victor Jr. and Alma Maria (Arsenault) C. Asst. mgr. rent supplement B.C. Housing Mgmt. Commn., Vancouver, 1975-81, adminstrv. asst., 1981-84, mgr. tenants and ops. svc., 1985-86, adminstrv. asst., 1986-87; commr., vice chmn. Vancouver Park Bd., 1986-90, chair, 1991-93; trustee Vancouver Pub. Libr., 1987-93; city councillor Vancouver, 1993-99; dir. Greater Vancouver Regional Dist., 1996-99; v.p. Greater Vancouver Housing Corp., 1994-99; NAC vol. cons., 1986—. Bd. dirs. B.C. Recreation and Parks Assn., 1986-91, pres. 1989-90; exec. dir. B.C. Sport and Fitness Coun. for the Disabled, 1989-90; dir. B.C. Wheelchair Sports Assn., 1991-92, Tree Can. Found., 1995—; mem. Non-Partisan Assn., 1986-99; vice chair Lower Mainland (Aboriginal) Treaty Adv. Com., 1994-96, chair, 1997-99; bd. dirs. Can. Oceans Blue Found., 1996—2000 (treas.), pres. Brewery Creek Hist. Soc., 1993—, Vancouver Police Hist. Soc. and Mus., 2000-, Columbia Housing Adv. Assn., 2000-; housing mgr. Downtown Eastside Residents' Assn., 2000-2001; founder, candidate Vancouver Civic Action Team, 2002 (bd. dirs. 2003-), B.C. Non- Profit Housing Assn. (Vancouver bd. dirs. 2001-), exec. dir., West End Sr. Network, 2003-, founding bd. mem., Network of East Vancouver Cmty. Org., 2003-, Vancouver Olympics, Inner City Bid Com., 2001-2003. Mem. Inst. Housing Mgmt. (cert. adminstr. 1983, cert. finance 1985), West End Commn. Ctr. Assn. (pres. 1985-86), Mt. Pleasant Commn. Ctr. Assn. (pres. 1981-83, dir. 2000-), Stanley Park Ecology Soc. (life; founder). Democrat. Avocation: journalism. Home: 90 E 11th Ave #210 Vancouver BC Canada V5T 2B8

CHICAGO, JUDY, artist; b. Chgo., July 20, 1939; d. Arthur M. and May (Levenson) Cohen. BA, UCLA, 1962, MA, 1964; doctorate (hon.), Russell Sage Coll., 1992, Lehigh U., 2000, Smith Coll., 2000, Duke U., 2003. Co-founder Feminist Studio Workshop, L.A., 1973, Through the Flower Corp., 1977; vis. artist Ind. U., fall 1999, Duke U. fall 2000, U. N.C., fall 2000, Cal Poly Pomona, fall 2003. Author: Through the Flower: My Struggle as a Woman Artist, 1975, The Dinner Party: A Symbol of Our Heritage, 1979, Embroidering Our Heritage: The Dinner Party Needlework, 1980, The Birth Project, 1985, Holocaust Project: From Darkness Into Light, 1993, Beyond the Flower: The Autobiography of a Feminist Artist, 1996, The Dinner Party, 1996, Women and Art: Contested Territory, 1999; one-woman shows include, Pasadena (Calif.) Mus. Art, 1969, Jack Glenn Gallery, Corona del Mar, Calif., 1972, JPL Fine Arts, London, 1975, Quay Ceramics, San Francisco, 1976, San Francisco Mus. Modern Art, 1979, Bklyn. Mus., 1980, 2002, Parco Galleries, Japan, 1980, Fine Arts Gallery, Irvine, Calif., 1981, Musee d'Art Contemporain, Montreal, 1982, ACA Galleries, N.Y.C., 1984, 85, 86, Nat. Mus. of Women in the Arts, 2002; group exhbns. include Jewish Mus., N.Y.C., 1966, 67, Whitney Mus., 1972, Winnipeg Art Gallery, 1975; represented in permanent collections Bklyn. Mus., San Francisco Mus. Modern Art, Oakland Mus. Art, Pa. Acad. Fine Arts, L.A. County Mus. Art, also numerous pvt. collections. Office: 101 N 2nd St Belen NM 87002 E-mail: throughtheflower@compuserve.com.

CHICHILNISKY, GRACIELA, mathematician, educator, economist, writer; b. Buenos Aires, Mar. 27, 1946; arrived in U.S., 1968, naturalized, 1992; d. Salomon Chichilnisky and Raquel Gavensky; children: Eduardo Jose, Natasha Sable. Student, MIT, 1967—68; MA, U. Calif., Berkeley, 1970, PhD in Math., 1971, PhD in Econs., 1976. Postdoctoral fellow Harvard U., 1974, lectr. dept. econs., 1975-77, fellow Harvard Inst. Internat. Devel., 1978; assoc. prof. Columbia U., N.Y.C., 1977-80, prof., 1981—, dir. Program on Info. and Resources, 1994—, prof. stats., 1996—, dir. Columbia Ctr. for Risk Mgmt., 1998—, UNESCO prof. math. and econs., 1995—99. CEO Cross Border Exch. Corp., 1999-2003, chmn. 2003-; mem. presdl. cabinet Banco Ctrl. Republica Argentina, 1971-74; co-prin. investigator Urban Inst., Washington, 1975-77; vis. scholar Internat. Inst. Applied Sys, Analysis Laxenburg, Austria, 1975-77; prin. investigator U.S. Dept. Labor, 1977-78, Rockefeller Found. Project Internat. Rels., 1981-83; project dir. UN Inst. Tng. and Rsch., N.Y., 1979-83; chaired prof. econs. U. Essex, 1980-81; vis. prof. inst. math and its applications U. Minn., 1983-84, U. Siena, Italy, summers, 1991-93, 2002; vis. prof. Stanford Inst. Theoretical Econs., Stanford U., summers, 1991-93, dept. econs., Inst. Internat. Studies, 1993—, vis. prof. depts., econ. and ops. rsch. Stanford U., 1993-94; prof. missionaire U. des Antilles et de la Guyane, spring 1984-85; NSF prof. dept. math. U. Calif., Berkeley, 1985-86; CEO, chmn. FITEL Ltd., 1985-89; exec. dir. Sci. Internat. Ltd., 1989-90; vis. prof. U. Cath. Buenos Aires, Aug. 1993; cons. in field; UNESCO chair in math. and econs., Columbia U., 1995—; Salinbemi chair U. Siena, Italy, 1994-95; CEO Cross Border Exchange, NY, 1999-, chmn. 2003-. Co-author: Catastrophe or New Society? A Latin American World Model, 1976; author: (with G. Heal) The Evolving International Economy, 1986, Oil in the International Economy, 1991, Sustainability: Dynamics and Uncertainty, 1998, Mathematical Economics, 1998, Topology and Markets, 1998, Markets, Information and Uncertainty, 1998, Environmental Markets: Equity and Efficiency, 1999; assoc. editor Jour. Devel. Econs., 1976-86, Advances in Mathematics, 1985, Risk Decision and Policy; mem. various editl. bds.; contbr. articles to profl. jours. Bd. trustees Nat. Resources Def. Coun., N.Y., 1994—. Recipient Internat. Rels. award Rockefeller Found., 1983-84; named Most Disting. Woman Economist, Newcombe Found. and Omega Delta Epsilon, 1991, Leif Johansen award U. Oslo, Norway, 1995; grantee NSF, 1974—; fellow Ford Found., 1967-69, Banco Ctrl. Republica Argentina, 1972-74, spl. fellow UN Inst. Tng. and Rsch., 1977-76. Mem. Coun. Social Choice and Welfare Soc. Office: Columbia U 629 Mathematics New York NY 10027 Mailing: 335 Riverside Dr New York NY 10025

CHICK, LAURA, councilwoman; BA, UCLA; MSW, U. So. Calif. Chief field dept. 3rd dist., L.A.; city councilwoman City of L.A., 1993—, chair govtl. efficiency com., vice chair info. tech. and gen. svcs. com., former chair pub. safety com. Vice chair Pub. Works Commn. Office: Ste 1220 200 N Main St Los Angeles CA 90012-1196 E-mail: lchick@council.lacity.org

CHICKADONZ, GRACE HARLOW, dean; BSN, U. Kans., 1958; MS, U. Md., 1968, PhD, 1974; attended, Inst. Edn. Mgmt., Harvard U., 1985. Staff nurse U. Kans. Med. Ctr., Kansas City, 1958-59; instr. Enid (Okla.) Gen. Hosp. Sch. Nursing, 1959-61; staff nurse grants N.Mex. State Health Dept., 1961-63; staff nurse Arlington (Va.) County Health Dept., 1963-64; asst. prof. nursing Georgetown U., Washington, 1967-78; Robert Wood Johnson nurse faculty fellow in primary care U. Md., Balt., 1978-79, dir. nursing practice, psychophysiology clinic, dept. psychiatry, 1979-80; dean, prof. nursing Med. Coll. Ohio, Toledo, 1979-87, Syracuse (N.Y.) U., 1987—. Designer plan Ohio Commn. on Nursing Implementation Project, 1981-82; vice chancellor for health affairs' com. Deans and Dirs. of Baccalaureate Programs Rev. Com., 1981-86; pres. Ohio Coun. of Deans and Dirs. of Baccalaureate Programs and Grad. Programs, 1986-87; mem. N.Y. State Health Task Force, 1988; mem. statewide planning com. N.Y. State Legis. Nurse of Distinction Program, 1988-93; accreditation site visitor Calif. State U., Dominguez Hills, 1989; presenter in field. Contbr. articles to profl. jours. Mem. Cradle-to-Kindergarten Health Subcom., 1988-89, mem. task force and steering com., 1989-90; chair health care adv. com. Loretto Geriatric Ctr., 1989—, also mem. med. adv. com., bd. trustees; mem. long term care task force Ctrl. N.Y. Health Sys. Agy., 1989—, mem. capital investment com., 1989-92, mem. regional maternal and newborn svc. adv. com., 1990-92; mem. infant mortality coalition Women's Commn., Syracuse, 1990-94, mem. health task force, 1990-94; bd. dirs. Boys and Girl's Club of Syracuse, 1990—, mem. pers. com., 1991—, mem. pub. rels. com., 1991, mem. exec. dir. search, 1993, mem. devel. officer search, 1994; organizer, co-chair Ctrl. N.Y. Com. to Establish Nurse-Midwifery Ednl. Program, 1991—. Spl. Nurse fellow NIH, 1972-74; recipient Leadership award Ohio Nurses Assn., 1984, Program Excellence award Ohio Bd. Regents, 1986-87, Disting. Alumnus award U. Kans., 1990, Martha M. Borlick award U. Md., 1990. Fellow Am. Acad. Nursing; mem. ANA, Nat. League Nursing (mem. nat. rsch. com. 1981-83, accreditation visitor 1982-89, bd. rev. 1990-93), Am. Assn. Colls. Nursing (mem. membership com. 1980-81, mem. rsch. com. 1984-86, mem. edn. and credentialing com. 1989-91), N.Y. State Nurses' Assn. (chair coun. on nursing edn. 1992—, mem. ad hoc com. on recredentialing 1993—), N.Y. State Deans and Dirs. Colls. Nursing (treas. 1990-94), Sigma Theta Tau (mem. nat. rsch. com. 1979-83, Omicron chpt. 1987—). Home: 15 Arnold Park Rochester NY 14607-2001 Office: Syracuse U Coll Nursing 426 Ostrom Ave Syracuse NY 13210-2938

CHICOREL, MARIETTA EVA, publishing company executive, consultant; b. Vienna; came to U.S., 1939, naturalized, 1945; d. Paul and Margaret (Gross) Selby. AB, Wayne State U., 1951; MALS, U. Mich., 1961. Asst. chief libr. acquisitions divsn. U. Wash., Seattle, 1962-66; project dir. Macmillan Info. Scis., Inc., N.Y.C., 1968-69; pres. Chicorel Library Pub. Corp., N.Y.C., 1969-79, Am. Libr. Pub. Co., Inc., 1979—; pub. cons. Creative Solutions Co., 1986—. Asst. prof. dept. libr. sci. CUNY (Queens Coll.), 1986—; mem. edn. com. Gov.'s Commn. on Status of Women, Wash., 1963-65; instr. libr. scis. No. Ariz. U., Flagstaff, 1990; bd. dirs. Skills Devel. Tng. counseling; pub. cons. creative solutios. Chief editor: Ulrich's International Periodicals Directory, 1966-68; editor, pub.: Chicorel Indexes, 1969—; founding editor: Jour. Reading, Writing and Learning Disabilities International, 1985-90; contbr. chpt. on univs. to Library Statistics: A Handbook of Concepts, Definitions and Terminology, 1966. Mem. ALA (exec. bd. tech. svcs. divsn. 1965-68, chmn. libr. materials price index com. 1968-69, councilor 1969-73), Am. Assn. Profl. Cons., Am. Book Prodrs. Assn., Book League N.Y. (bd. govs. 1975-79), Am. Soc. for Info. Sci., Can. Libr. Assn., Pacific N.W. Libr. Assn., N.Y. Libr. Club, N.Y. Tech. Svcs. Librarians. Home and Office: PO Box 4272 Sedona AZ 86340-4272

CHIECHI, CAROLYN PHYLLIS, federal judge; b. Newark, Dec. 6, 1943; BS magna cum laude, Georgetown U., 1965, JD, 1969, LLM in Taxation, 1971, LLD honoris causa, 2000. Bar: DC 1969, U.S. Dist. Ct. DC, U.S. Ct. Fed. Claims, U.S. Tax Ct., U.S. Ct. Appeals (5th, 6th, 9th, DC, and fed. cirs.), U.S. Supreme Ct. Atty. advisor to Hon. Leo H. Irwin U.S. Tax Ct., Washington, 1969-71; assoc. Sutherland, Asbill & Brennan, Washington, 1971—76, ptnr., 1976—92; judge U.S. Tax Ct., Washington, 1992—. Mem. bd. regents Georgetown U., Washington, 1988—94, Washington,

1995—2001, mem. nat. law alumni bd., 1986—93; mem. bd. govs. Georgetown U. Alumni Assn., 1994—2000; bd. dirs. Stuart Stiller Meml. Found., 1986—99; prin. Coun. for Excellence in Govt., 1990—92. Dept. editor: Jour. Taxation, 1986—92; contbr. articles to profl. jours. Fellow: Am. Coll. Tax Counsel, Am. Bar Found., mem.: ABA, Am. Judicature Soc., Women's Bar Assn., DC Bar Assn., Fed. Bar Assn., Georgetown U. Law Alumni Assn. (Law Ctr. Alumnae Achievement award 1998, award 1994). Office: US Tax Ct 400 2nd St NW Washington DC 20217-0002

CHIEF EAGLE, JOAN, secondary school educator; b. Pine Ridge, June 27, 1952; d. Eugene J. Chief Eagle, Alice V. Weasel Bear/Chief Eagle; children: Leslee M. McMath, Joelle M., Lorena L., Danielle J. McCane. AA, Standing Rock Coll., Ft. Yales, N.D., 1989; BA, Minot State U., N.D., 1991. Native Am. artist Five Nations Arts, Mandan, ND, 1987—; tchg. asst. Ft. Yates Pub. Sch. #4, Ft. Yates, 1993—97, fgn. lang. tchr., 1998—. Cons. for Native Am. lang. and art Ft. Yates Pub. Sch. #4, 1994—. With U.S. Army, 1970—71. Avocations: reading, sewing, culinary arts. Home: 179 Box 500 Sioux Village Fort Yates ND 58538 Office: Fort Yates Public Sch #4 105 Agency Ave Fort Yates ND 58538

CHIEGER, KATHRYN JEAN, recreation company executive; b. Detroit, July 13, 1948; BA, Purdue U., 1970; MA, U. Mich., 1974; MBA, U. Denver, 1983. Libr. U. Mich., Ann Arbor, 1970-74; staff aide U.S. Sen. Gary Hart, Denver, 1974-79; dir. fin. rels. Petro-Lewis Corp., Denver, 1979-86; dir. investor rels. Kraft Inc., Glenview, Ill., 1987-89; v.p. corp. affairs Gaylor Container Corp., Deerfield, Ill., 1989-96; v.p. corp. and investor rels. Brunswick Corp., Lake Forest, Ill., 1996—. Mem. Nat. Investor Rels. Inst. (chpt. bd. dirs. 1979-84, v.p. mem. 1982-83, pres. 1983-84, nat. bd. dirs. 1984-88), Chgo. Execs. Club, Investor Rels. Assn., Sr. Investor Rels. Roundtable. Office: Brunswick Corp 1 N Field Ct Lake Forest IL 60045-4811 E-mail: kathryn.chieger@brunswick.com.

CHILD, ABIGAIL, filmmaker, educator; b. Newark, Jan. 1, 1949; d. Albert L. Natelson and Ruth (Robinson) Natelson Pollack; m. Jonathan Child, 1969 (div. 1977). B.A. in History and Lit. magna cum laude, Radcliffe Coll., 1968; M.F.A. in Graphics and Film with honors, Yale U., 1970. Vis. prof. film SUNY-Purchase, 1979; adj. prof. film NYU, N.Y.C., 1980-85; asst. prof. film Mass. Coll. Art, Boston, 1985— ; film programmer 80 Langton St., San Francisco, 1979; lectr. Inst. Policy Studies, Washington, 1981; judge Creative Artist Pub. Service Grants, N.Y.C., 1982; curator Corcoran Gallery, Washington, 1982. Filmmaker-dir., editor documentaries, including: Game, 1972; Between Times, 1976; filmmaker-dir. exptl. films, including: Mutiny, 1982-83; Prefaces, 1981, Covert Action, 1984. Author: From Solids, 1983; Climate Plus, 1985; also articles. Vice pres. 303 E. 8th St. Project, N.Y.C., 1982— . Recipient various awards for films; grantee Am. Film Inst., 1972, Creative Artist Pub. Service, 1980, MacDowell Colony, 1983, 86, N.Y. Cultural Found., 1985. Avocation: swimming.

CHILD, JULIA MCWILLIAMS (MRS. PAUL CHILD), cooking expert, television personality, author; b. Pasadena, Calif., Aug. 15, 1912; d. John and Julia Carolyn (Weston) McWilliams; m. Paul Child, Sept. 1, 1945 (dec.). BA, Smith Coll., 1934. With advt. dept. W.&J. Sloane, N.Y.C., 1939-40; with OSS, Washington, Ceylon, China, 1941-45. Co-founder Am. Inst. Wine & Food, 1982. Hostess (TV program) The French Chef, WGBH-TV, Boston, 1963—73, Julia Child & Co., 1978—79, Julia Child & More Co., 1980, Dinner at Julia's, PBS, 1983, Cooking with Master Chefs series, PBS, Baking with Julia, Julia and Jacques Cooking at Home, PBS, (occasional cooking segment) Good Morning Am., ABC-TV, 1980—, (video cassettes) The Way to Cook, 1982;, 1982; author (with Simone Beck and Louisette Bertholle): Mastering the Art of French Cooking, 1961, Mastering the Art of French Cooking, Vol. II, 1970, rev. edit., 1983; author: The French Chef Cookbook, 1968; author: (with Simone Beck) From Julia Child's Kitchen, 1975; author: Julia Child & Company, 1978, Julia Child & More Company, 1979, The Way to Cook, 1989, Julia and Jacques Cooking at Home, 1999; columnist McCall's mag., 1975—82, Parade mag., 1982—86, Julia's Kitchen Wisdom, 2000; voice Dr. Bleeb : (filmography) We're Back! A Dinosaur's Story, 1993. Recipient Peabody award, 1964, Emmy award, 1966, French Ordre de Merite Agricole, 1967, Ordre National de Merite, 1974, Ralph Lowell award, Corp. for Pub. Broadcasting, 1998, TV Cooking Show award James Beard Found., Emmy for Outstanding Svc. Show host, 1995-96, Daytime Emmy for Outstanding Svc. Show Host, 2000-01; French Legion of Honor, 2000. Office: 1406 Garden St #2 Santa Barbara CA 93101

CHILDEARS, LINDA, banker; b. Council Bluffs, Iowa, Jan. 25, 1950; d. Nolan Glen and Mary Lucile (Dunken) Jackson. Grad., U. Wis., Am. Inst. Banking; student, U. Colo., U. Denver. Various positions First Nat. Bank Bear Valley (formerly Norwest Bank Bear Valley), Colo., 1969-79; v.p. adminstrn. First Nat. Bancorp., 1979-83; pres., CEO, Equitable Bank of Littleton, 1983—; founder The Fin. Consortium; pres., CEO, Young Ams. Bank, Denver, 1987—, also vice-chmn. bd. dirs. Pres., CEO, vice chmn. Young Ams. Edn. Found. Contbr. articles to Time and Newsweek. Bd. dirs. Cherry Creek Art Festival, Denver, 1989-96, Jr. Achievement, Mile High United Way, Cherry Creek Bus. Improvement Dist., U. Denver Bridge Project; mem. adv. bd., nat. past pres. Camp Fire Coun. Colo. Named hon. life mem. Nat. CampFire, past chmn., numerous other awards Camp Fire Inc. Mem. Am. Bankers Assn. (past chmn. Edn. Found.), Found. Tchg. Econs. (trustee), Colo. Bankers Assn., Metro C. of C. Republican. Office: Young Ams Bank 311 Steele St Denver CO 80206-4414

CHILDERS, BRENDA SUE, medical/surgical nurse; b. Camp Lejeune, N.C., Oct. 9, 1960; d. Oral Sidney and Lueretta Ruth Childers. Nursing diploma, Burge Sch. Nursing, 1982. ACLS instr. Am. Heart Assn., BCLS instr. Am. Heart Assn., PALS provider Am. Heart Assn.; RN Mo., cert. emergency nurse, bd. cert. emergency nursing; BTLS advance provider BTLS Internat. Staff RN emergency rm. Lake Regional Health Sys., Osage Beach, Mo., 1982—; prehospital RN City of Osage Beach Ambulance, 1996—. Firefighter Osage Beach Fire Protection Dist., 1990—, med. coord., 1992—. Mem.: Firefighters Assn. Mo., Mo. Emergency Med. Svcs. Assn., Emergency Nurses Assn., Ladies Aux. VFW. Avocations: scuba diving, travel, home remodeling, gardening. Home: 1377 Dogwood Ln Osage Beach MO 65065

CHILDERS, CAROL LOUISE, elementary school educator, music educator, musician; b. Salem, Ohio, Jan. 31, 1957; d. William Edward McClaren and Lela Mae Graber; m. James Gregory Childers, June 16, 1990; m. Thomas Daniel Bolha, Aug. 12, 1978 (dec. Sept. 15, 1985); 1 child, Jonathan David Bolha. MusB, Youngstown State U., 1979; MLS, Kent State U., 1988. Cert. elem. music and media tchr. k-12 Ohio, 1979. Elem. music specialist Youngstown Bd. Edn., Ohio, 1986—; bassoon player W.D. Packard Band, Warren, 1987—. Free lance bassoon player, Youngstown, 1977—. Children's worker Hwy. Tabernacle, 1982—2003, musician, 1986—, libr., 1988—; youth and family com. Greater Youngstown Coalition of Christians, 1992—94. Music scholar, Youngstown State U., 1975—79, Salem Sr. Music Club, 1978—79. Mem.: Youngstown Edn. Assn., Internat. Double Reed Soc., Music Educators Nat. Conf. Assembly Of God. Avocations: bicycling, camping, canoeing.

CHILDERS, MARY ANN, newscaster; m. Jay Levine. BS in Speech, Northwestern U., Evanston, Ill. Assoc. prodr. Phil Donahue Show, Chgo.; with WAVE-TV, Louisville, WTHR-TV, Indpls.; anchor, med. editor and reporter WLS-TV, Chgo., 1980—94, WBBM-TV, Chgo., 1994—, co-anchor 11am and 4pm and med. editor. Hon. bd. mem. Y-Me, Nat. Kidney Found. of Ill., Nat. Spinal Cord Injury Assn.; mem. Chgo. Cancer Rsch. Found.; mem. nat. adv. coun. Northwestern U. Sch. of Speech; mem. Chgo. Network. Recipient 2 Emmys. Office: WBBM-TV 630 McClurg Ct Chicago IL 60601

CHILDERS, PAMELA BARNARD, secondary school educator; b. Mt. Holly, N.J., Oct. 11, 1943; d. George W. and Audrey (Clerihue) Barnard; m. Malcolm G. Childers, 1993. BA, Radford Coll., Radford, 1965; MS, Radford U., Radford, 1975; MA, Northeastern U., Boston, 1988; EdD, Nova Southeastern U., 1995. Poetry tchr./cons. Geraldine R. Dodge Found., Morristown, N.J., 1986—; coll. tchr. Woodrow Wilson Nat'l Fellowship Found., Princeton, N.J., 1987-88; Caldwell chair composition The McCallie Sch., Chattanooga, 1991—; English tchr. Red Bank Regional High Sch., Little Silver, N.J., 1966-91, McCallie Sch., Chattanooga, 1991—. Editor The Grapevine, Northeastern U. Writing Newsletter, Boston, 1986-90; mem. editorial bd. The Writing Ctr. Jour., 1987—, Computers and Composition, 1987-90; treas. Assembly of Computers in English; instr. Lesley U., Cambridge, Mass., 2003—; mem. assoc. exec. bd. Internat. Writing Ctrs. Author: Waking Dreams, 1989, The High School Writing Center, 1989, Nat. Directory of Writing Centers, 1992, Waking Dreams II, 1992Programs and Practices, 1994, Articulating: Teaching Writing in a Visual World, 1998. Mem. MLA, Nat. Coun. Tchrs. English (nat. bd. cons.), Internat. Writing Ctrs. Assn. (exec. bd.). Democrat. Presbyterian.

CHILDERS, SUSAN LYNN BOHN, special education educator, administrator, human resources and transition specialist, consultant; m. Lawrence J. Childers; 1 child. AA, Ohio U., 1978, BS in Edn. cum laude, 1982; MEd in Supervision, Ashland U., 1991. Profl. cert. 1-8 elem. tchr., K-12 edn. handicapped, permanent cert., ; spl. edn. tchr., Ohio. Educator learning disabilities, developmentally handicapped Maysville Local Sch. Dist., South Zanesville, Ohio, 1982-89; work-study coord. Holmes County Office Edn., Millersburg, Ohio, 1990, editor spl. edn. newsletter, 1990-93, cons., supervisor work-study programming, 1991-93; spl. edn. supr. Wayne County Bd. Edn., Wooster, Ohio, 1993-94; adminstr. severe behavior handicapped program, supr. special edn. Ashland-Wayne County Bd. Edn., Wooster, 1994-95; cons. Tri-County Ednl. Svc. Ctr., Wooster, 1996-99; supr. spl. edn., supr. instrn. support Zanesville City Sch., Ohio, 1999-2000; dir. spl. edn. Licking County Ednl. Svc. Ctr., Newark, Ohio, 2000-01; supr. spl. edn. Lancaster City Sch., Ohio, 2001—; pres. Ohio Assoc. Supr. and Coord. of Exceptional Students, 2003. Mem. Holmes County Spl. Edn. Adv. Coun., 1990—93, E. Holmes Local Sch. Dist. Strategic Planning Action Team Job/Life Skills, 1993; rep. Ohio Devel. Handicapped Issues Forum; mem. steering com. Ohio Speaks, 1991—94; mem. strategic planning com. Ashland-Wayne County Bd. Edn., 1994—95; mem. Chippewa Local Sch. Dist. Child Care Bd., 1995—96; chmn. Direct Student Svcs. Strategic Planning Com., 1995—96; mem. safety com. Ashland-Wayne Ednl. Svc. Ctr., 1994—96; mem. svc. coordination com. Wayne County Children and Family First Initiative, 1995, 96, Edn. Rep. Safety Com., Tri-County Ednl. Svc. Ctr., Wooster, 1997—99; mem. exec. com. Licking County Children and Family First Initiative, 2000—01; mem. Licking County Mental Health and Recovery Bd., Newark, 2001, Licking County Behavioral Health Assessment Team, 2000—01, Newark Cmty. Corps Adv. Com., 2001, Fairfield County Children and Family First Clin. Cluster, 2001—02; pres.-elect Ohio Assn. Suprs. and Coords. of Exceptional Students, 2002; spkr. in field. Editor Spl. Edn. Newsletter Holmes County Office Edn., 1990-93. Mem. adv. bd. Holmes County Job Placement, Holmes County Litter Prevention Cmty. Action Plan Com., 1993; vol. Ohio Buckeye Book Fair, 1991—93, 1999, Holmes County Spl. Olympics, 1990—93, chairperson vols., 1993; mem. jr. assembly Bethesda Hosp., 1970—78; mem. Beaux Arts Zanesville Art Ctr., 1972—78; mem. spl. needs adv. bd. Ashland-West Holmes Career Ctr., 1990—93; mem. Transition and Comm. Consortium on Learning Disabilities, Ohio U. Alumni Career Resource Network, Holmes County Abuse Prevention Cmty. Action Plan Com., 1993, Ohio Staff Devel. Coun., Wayne County Family and Children First Coun. (Clin. Cluster), 1994—96; co-chairperson fundraising com. Creating Connections Symposium, Akron, Ohio, 1994; mem. Ashland-Wayne-Holmes Counties Adv. Com. for Tech. and Tng. Subcom., Ohio, 1996—97; adv. com. for tech. 3-county rep. Ashland, Wayne, Holmes, Ohio, 1996—98; A-site tech. tng. com., 1996—97; mem., regional rep. School/Net Communities of Practice, 1996; mem. Licking County Behavioral Health Assessment Team, 2000—01, Licking County Spl. Edn. Collaborative Com., 2000—01, Cmty. Corps Adv. Com., Newark, Ohio, 2001, Licking County Mental Health and Recovery Bd, Newark, 2001, Licking County Fostercare Collaborative Coun., Newark, 2000—01; mem. asst. tech. com., chair speech-lang. dept. Lancaster City Sch., 2002—03; mem. Lancaster City Schs. Career Adv. Bd., 2003—. Recipient award Muskingum County Office Litter Prevention, 1988, Kids Care Project, 1989, Maysville Bd. Edn. commendation, 1989, Merit award Keep Ohio Beautiful program, 1991, Ohio Future Forum's Exemplary Transition from Sch.-to-Work Model award, 1993, Model Program designation Ohio's Employability Skills Project, 1987, Franklin B. Walter Outstanding Educator award, 1996, 98. Mem. ASCD, AAUW, Career Edn. Assn., Coun. Exceptional Children, Ohio Rural Edn. Assn., Ohio Sch. Supr. Assn., Ohio Assn. Vocat. Edn. Spl. Needs Pers., Wayne-Holmes Elem. Adminstr. Assn., Ohio Pupil Pers. Assn., Ohio Assn. Supervision and Coordination for Exceptional Students (regional pres. 2003), Ladies of Lancaster Red Hat Soc., Phi Delta Kappa. E-mail: s_childers@lancaster.k12.oh.us.

CHILD-OLMSTED, GISÈLE ALEXANDRA, language educator; b. Port-au-Prince, Haiti, Dec. 27, 1946; (parents Am. citizens); d. Daniel McGuire Child and Alice Dejean Child; m. Hans George Bickel, Sept. 1967 (div. Apr. 1984); children: Anna Kristina Villemez, Maia Selena Deubert; m. Jerauld Lockwood Olmsted, June 17, 1988. BA in French with honors, U. Md., 1970; MA in French, Johns Hopkins U., 1978, PhD in Romance Langs., 1981; cert. in translation, Georgetown U. Vis. instr. U. Md., College Park, 1980-81; instr. Johns Hopkins U., Balt., 1981-82; lang. instr. Holton-Arms Sch., Bethesda, Md., 1982-83; asst. prof. dept. modern langs. and lit. Loyola Coll., Balt., 1983-89, assoc. prof., 1989-98, chair dept. modern lang. langs. and lit., 1989-94, prof., 1998—2003. V.p. faculty coun. Loyola Coll., 1998-2000, mem. steering com. Ctr. for Humanities, 1989-94; organizer, dir. Colloquia on Lang., Lit. and Soc., Balt., 1990, 95, 99, 2002. Author: Jean Genet: Criminalité et Transcendance, 1987; contbr. articles to profl. jours. Faculty rsch. grantee Loyola Coll., 1984, 89, study grantee French Embassy, 1986, 89; Gillman Fellow, 1970-73, 79-80; visitor's scholar U. Cape Town, South Africa, 1995. Mem. MLA (del. Mid-Atlantic region 1992-94, 96-98), Am. Assn. Tchrs. French, Soc. Prof. Français et Francophones d'Amérique, Les Amis de Stendhal, Phi Beta Kappa. Avocations: painting, golf, antiques, classical music, flamenco dancing. Home: 7735 Arrowood Ct Bethesda MD 20817-2821 Office: Loyola Coll 4501 N Charles St Baltimore MD 21210-2601 E-mail: gchildolmsted@loyola.edu.

CHILDRESS, JANET LYNN, logistician; b. Knoxville, Tenn., July 24, 1954; d. Albert Lee and Cartha Lynn (Doyle) C. AA, U. Md., 1989; BS, Cameron U., 1996; postgrad., U. Okla., 1997, Embry-Riddle Aeronaut. U., 1998, Ctrl. Mich. U., 1999. Logistician Fed. Civil Svc., 1981—. Intern Fed. Civil Svc., 1997-99, facilitator quality mgmt. bd., 1995-97, writer orgn. self-assessment team, 1997; presenter in field. Contbr. articles to profl. jours. With U.S. Army, 1980-84. Mem. Leadership Lawton (Okla.), 1997, Okla. Comm. Status of Women, Oklahoma City, 1996-97; chair Mayor's Commn. Status of Women, Lawton, 1995-97. Mem. Am. Soc. Pub. Adminstrn., Women in Military Svc. for Am., Federally Employed Women, Phi Kappa Phi, LWV (v.p. 1995-97). Democrat. Avocations: volunteering, travel, movies, reading, golf. Office: 37376 Charter Oaks Blvd Clinton Township MI 48036 E-mail: childj@tacom.army.mil.

CHILDREY BARKSDALE, JOYCE, writer, social worker; b. Bronx, Oct. 9, 1950; d. George William and Margaret Thomas Odle; m. Woodrow Barksdale, May 6, 1977 (dec. Feb. 1992); 1 child, Rita Barksdale ; m. Joseph Childrey, Oct. 22, 1997. AD, Hudson Valley C.C., 1995. Human [illegible] Bronx, 1972—82, dir. social svcs., 1982—90, tng. specialist, 1990—98, adminstrv. liaison, 1998—99, housing cons., dir., 1999—2002, ret., 2002; freelance writer, poet, painter, 1970—. Author of poems, short stories. Housing cons. Northwest Bronx Coalition, 1977—79; sec., co-founder Better Sisters Soc., 2002—03. Recipient Poetry award, Anthology of H.S. Lit., 1966, Poetry-.com, 2001—02. Democrat. Avocations: painting, landscaping, corporate head hunting. Home: 1709 Treecrest Pkwy Decatur GA 30035-3571

CHILDS, LUCINDA, choreographer; b. New York, June 26, 1940; d. Edward Patterson and Lucinda Eustis (Corcoran) C. BA, Sarah Lawrence Coll., 1962. Choreographer, performer Judson Dance Theater, N.Y.C., 1963—73; owner, choreographer, performer Lucinda Childs Dance Co., N.Y.C., 1973—. Choreographer, dancer Judson Dance Theatre, N.Y.C., 1962-66, choreographer, dancer, artistic dir. Lucinda Childs Dance Co., N.Y.C., 1973—; choreographer, dancer: Einstein on the Beach, 1976 (Robert Wilson and Philip Glass) (Obie award 1978); actress I Was Sitting On My Patio This Guy Appeared I Thought I Was Hallucinating, 1977-78. Decorated officer Order Arts and Letters (France); Guggenheim Found. fellow, 1979, Nat. Endowment Arts fellow.

CHILDS, RHONDA LOUISE, motivational speaker; b. Albany, N.Y., Sept. 29, 1946; d. David Cornelius and Rhoda Louise (Rodeniser) Curley; m. Lindsay N. Childs, July 22, 1972; children: Ashley Louise, Nathan Shreeve David Curley, Justin David Curley. BA in Sociology and Anthropology, Cath. Convent Coll., Buffalo, 1966; cert. proficiency exam, McGill U., Montreal, Que., Can., 1968; student, Siena Coll., Loudonville, N.Y., Russell Sage Coll. Adminstrv. asst. Hypersonic Lab., McGill U., 1966-68; adminstrv. asst. dept. comparative religions Sir George Williams U., Montreal, 1966-68; with various cmty. svc. orgns., Europe, Can., Africa, 1968-71; rechr. N.Y. State Mental Hygiene Dept., Albany, 1971-72; non-teaching profl. SUNY, Albany, 1973-75; cmty. liaison Collins Bay Penitentiary, Kingston, Ont., Can., 1976-77; ct. monitor Family Ct., 1975-78; pres. Concerned Citizens Against Crossgates, Guilderland, N.Y., 1978-80; adminstrv. asst. St. Catherine's Ctr. for Children, Albany, 1980-85; dir. govt. and cmty. affairs Empire Blue Cross and Blue Shield, Albany, 1985-94; devel. counsel St. Peter's Hosp., Albany, 1994-96; prin. New Visions, A Childs Co., Slingerlands, N.Y. Cons. to numerous nonprofit orgns.; founder, coord. Family Agys. Committed to Svc., 1983-86; founder, pres. Corp. Vol. Coun.; lectr. numerous ednl. and exec. seminars; motivational spkr. in field. Author: My Own Telephone Book, 1988. Bd. dirs. Sr. Svc. Ctrs. Found.; grad. Capital Leadership, 1988-94; past pres. adv. bd. Ret. Sr. Vol. Programs; trustee, pres. St. Anne Inst. Recipient Outstanding Svc. award Family Agys. Committed to Svc., 1985, Community Svc. award Cystic Fibrosis Found., 1988, Tribute to Women award, YWCA, 1991, Franklin D. Roosevelt Vol. award March of Dimes, 1991, June A. Bonneau award Sr. Svc. Ctrs. Albany, Citizen of Yr. award Samaritans, 1994, Golden Rule award, 1994, Lifetime Achievement award Women of Excellence, 1994, Outstanding Svc. award St. Anne Inst., 1994. Mem. APHA, Nat. Soc. Fund Raising Execs., Albany-Colonie Regional C. of C. (numerous coms., guest lect.), Corp. Vol. Couns. Am., NAFE, SUNY Women's Club, Enterprising Women's Leadership Inst., Rotary (pres. Albany chpt., coms. Dist. 7190 Citizen of Yr. award 1990, Airport Citizen of Yr. award 1990, Paul Harris fellow 1990). Democrat. Roman Catholic. Office: New Visions A Childs Co 308 Quidor Ct Slingerlands NY 12159-9554 Office Phone: 518-346-5224. E-mail: r.childs1@nycap.rr.com., childs@global2000.net.

CHILDS, WENETTA GRYBAS, artist; b. Chgo. d. Joseph and Hattie Zilewicz Grybas; widowed; children: Carol, April Childs Kerr. Student, U. Chgo., 1933—35, Chgo. Art Inst., 1933—35. Exhibitions include paintings and sculptures San Diego County Fair and San Diego Mus. Contemporary Art (Best of Sculpture award San Diego County Fair, 1981), Represented in permanent collections created the Sun Sculpture at, Solana Beach Plaza, Calif. Lead numerous coms. to beautify Solana Beach, Calif., 1953—80; including redesign and landscape of Solana Beach Plaza, 1966—68; established landscaped median strips on Hwy. 101, 1974—75; established maintenance dists., 1974—75; created bike trail on Hwy. 101, 1974—75; mem. Solana Beach Civic & Hist. Soc., Calif., 1953—, chair billboard removal, 1955—65, pres., 1970—71; dir. Solana Beach C. of C., Calif., 1973—76, mem. Sun Festival, 1976; mem. citizens' com. rev. cultural arts ctr. feasibility Solana Beach, 1988—89. Co-recipient Hist. monument dedicated to her and Senator Bill Craven, Solana Beach Civic and Hist. Soc., 2003; named Solana Beach Citizen of Yr., Blade Tribune, Oceanside, Calif., 1977; named one of Outstanding Women of North County, Assn. Retarded Citizens, County of San Diego, 1984; recipient Grand prize, Holy Cross Luth. Ch. Festival, Claremont, Calif., 1968. Avocations: classical music, reading, travel.

CHILES, CAROL S. architectural firm executive; Assoc. prin. Tsoi/Kobus & Assoc. Inc., Cambridge, Mass., 1998—2002, prin., v.p., 2002—. Office: Tsoi/Kobus & Assoc Inc One Brattle Sq PO Box 9114 Cambridge MA 02238-9114

CHILES, MARY JANE, secondary school educator; b. Hampton, Iowa, Apr. 26, 1950; d. Thomas Donald and Grace Hermina (Bouvink) Stark; m. Stephen Eugene Chiles, July 8, 1972; 1 child, Samantha Kathryn Chiles Graef. BA, U. Iowa, 1972; postgrd., Morningside Coll., Sioux City, Iowa, 1974, Okla. State U., Stillwater, 1979-82. Tchr. 7th and 8th grade English Woodbury Ctrl. Sch., Moville, Iowa, 1974-75; tchr. 5-8th grade English Anderson Middle Sch., Sand Springs, Okla., 1979-80; tchr. 6th grade Anderson Elem. Sch., Sand Springs, 1980-81; tchr. 9th and 10th grade English Moore (Okla.) West Mid High, 1981-88; tchr. 9th grade English Moore West Jr. H.S., 1988—. Mem. Supt.'s Adv. Coun., Moore, 1997—, Supt.'s Patron Adv. Coun., Moore, 1997—, chair profl. devel. com., 1998-2000; field tester book Elements of Writing, 1993. 8 gallon donor Okla. Blood Inst., Oklahoma City, 1981—; mem. steering com. Educators of Moore PAC, 1983—90. Mem.: NEA (del. assembly 1985—, Western regional conf. 1990—), Moore Assn. Classroom Tchrs. (profl. negotiations team 1982—, exec. com. 1985—86, sec. 1986—88, exec. com. 1988—, chair constn. com. 1989—90, chair resolutions com. 1992—94, v.p. 1996—98, chair constn. com. 1998—99, treas. 1999—), Okla. Edn. Assn. (del. assembly 1983—, sec. resolutions com. 1984—97, standing rules com. 1997—98, sec. resolutions com. 1998—2002, bd. dirs. 2003—, ESP com. 2003—). Democrat. Avocations: travel, swimming. Home: 3201 Willow Lane Moore OK 73170-7912 Office: Moore West 9400 S Pennsylvania Ave Oklahoma City OK 73159-6903

CHILL, MYRTLE N. advertising copywriter, promoter; b. Indpls., Apr. 5, 1906; d. Henry and Mathilda (Kuhn) Newman; m. George F. Chill, June 28, 1932. BSJ, Northwestern U., Medill Sch. Journalism, 1927. Editor Armitage News, Chgo., 1927—28; mng. editor The Nor'wester, Chgo., 1928—29; asst. sales promotion editor Sears, Roebuck & Co., 1929—32; head copywriter Goldblatt Bros. Dept. Stores, Chgo., 1932—39; gen. mgr. Substantial Products Co., Chgo., 1939—65; part-time advt. work Edelstein-Nelson, Reich & Kahn; Chicago Bar and Restaurant Supply, Chgo., 1967—2001; promotion mgr. Barbara Newman Designs, Chgo., 2001—. Achievements include presently promoting a fused glass pin that with a necklace or cord becomes a pendant; updating her exentsive 1992 Newman family medical history that now includes the fifth living generation; with medical research and care so specialized, it is important to know the allergies inherited from our genes.

CHILMAN, CATHERINE EARLES STREET, social welfare educator, author; b. Cleve., Sept. 20, 1914; d. Elwood Vickers and Augusta (Jewitt) Street; m. C. William Chilman, Sept. 27, 1936 (dec. 1977); children: Margaret Chilman Carpenter, Jeanne Chilman Klovdahl, Catherine Chilman Brown. AB, Oberlin Coll., 1935; MA, U. Chgo., 1938; PhD, U. Syracuse, 1958. Caseworker United Charities Chgo., 1937-39, Family Svcs., Roanoke, Va., 1939-40; psychiat. cons. ARC, Syracuse, N.Y., 1943-44; tchr. dept. child devel., family rels. Syracuse U., 1947-49, instr., 1949-57, asst. prof., 1957-61; sr. social worker N.Y. State Mental Health Rsch. Unit, Syracuse, 1955-57; parent edn. specialist Children's Bur. HEW, Washington, 1961-64; rsch. adminstr. U.S. Welfare Adminstrn., 1964-69; dean faculty Hood Coll., Frederick, Md., 1969-71; curriculum dir. Internat. Population Planning and Social Work Edn. Project, U. Mich., Ann Arbor, 1971-72; prof. Sch. Social Welfare, U. Wis., Milw., 1972-86, prof. emerita, 1986—; pres. Nat. Groves Conf. on the Family, 1975-78. Speaker, cons. on rsch., family life, pub. policy to univs., fed. govt. and profl. orgns. Author: Your Child: 6 to 12, 1966, Moving into Adolescence, 1966, Growing Up Poor, 1967, Adolescent Sexuality in a Changing American Society, 1983, Families in Trouble, 5 vols., 1988, (with others) Mental Health Crisis and the Nation's Children, 1972, Programs and Policies of National Family Organizations, 1997; mem. editl. bd. Jour. Marriage and Family, 1963-69; contb. articles to profl. jours., chpts. to books. U.S. Office Edn. grantee, 1960-62; Wis. State grantee, 1973-75; Nat. Inst. Child Devel. grantee, 1976-77; recipient Hon. Alumni award Sch. Social Svcs. Adminstrn., U. Chgo., 1978, Honored Scholar award Groves Conf. Marriage and the Family, 1989. Fellow APA; mem. Nat. Coun. on Family Rels. (bd. dirs. 1991-93, sec. 1992-93), Groves Conf. on Marriage and Family (hon. life, bd. dirs., nat. workshop dir. 1992). Home: Cluster 3110 10450 Lottsford Rd Mitchellville MD 20721-2734

CHILOW, BARDARA GAIL, social worker; b. Grand Forks, ND, June 7, 1936; d. Alfred Thomas and Florence (Micken) Seeley; m. Steven Chilow, Aug. 15, 1987; children: John Mark Doss, Timothy Stephen Doss, Elizabeth De La Cruz, David Chilow. BS, UCLA, 1957; MSW, U. So. Calif., 1970; MPA, Calif. State U., Long Beach, 1985. Lic. social worker, Calif., Utah, marriage, family and child counselor, Calif. Social worker Dept. Pub. Welfare, San Diego, 1957, Dep. Pub. Assistance, Whitman, Mass., 1966-68; psychiat. social worker State of Calif., Pomona, 1971-73; clin. social worker Orange County Dept. Mental Health, Santa Ana, Calif., 1973-74, sr. clin. social worker, 1974-79; dep. dir. mental health Orange County Human Svcs. Agy., Santa Ana, 1979-80, dep. regional mgr., 1980-82, adminstrv. mgr. II, 1982-93; clin. coord. Brightway at St. George, Utah, 1993-2000; pvt. practice Newport Beach, Calif., 1977—93, Dessert Hills Therapeutic Svcs., 2002—. Chmn. So. Calif. Case Mgmt. Coun., 1987-89, Orange County Bd. and Care Quality Com., Santa Ana, 1984-89; owner, mgr. Desert Hills Therapeutic Svcs., Inc., St. George, 1998-. Pres. Winchester Hills Homeowners Assn., St. George, 1995-97; elected to Southwestern Spl. Svc. Dist. BD., 1997-, Leadership Dixie, 1998-99; trustee Music Hall Found.; gala bd. Cancer Soc., 2003-04. Mem. NASW, AAUW (v.p. 2002), DAR (Boston Tea Party chpt.), Alliance for Mentally Ill (pres. Orange County chpt. 1994-95), Phi Alpha Alpha, Gamma Phi Beta. Democrat. Presbyterian. Avocations: hiking, piano, reading, travel. Home: 1110 W 5830 N Saint George UT 84770-5944 Office: Desert Hills Therapeutic Svcs Troon Park Plz 1240 E 100 S Ste 18B Saint George UT 84790-3001

CHILTON, ELIZABETH EASLEY EARLY, newspaper executive; b. Williamson, W.Va., Dec. 9, 1928; d. Carl Brooks and Susie Mason (Easley) Early; m. William Edwin Chilton III, Apr. 5, 1952 (dec. Feb. 1987); 1 child, Susan Carroll Chilton Shumate. Student, Hollins Coll., Va., 1946-48; AA in Primary Edn., Marjorie Webster Coll., Washington, 1950. Pub. rels. staff The Charleston (W.Va.) Gazette, 1952-87; v.p., treas. Daily Gazette Co., Charleston, 1987-91, pres., 1991—, also dir., 1994—, chmn. bd. dirs. Mgmt. com. The Charleston Newspapers, 1991-99; adv. bd. Eberly Coll. Arts and Scis., 1996. Editl. bd. The Charleston Gazette, 1987—. Chmn. W.Va. Gov.'s Mansion Preservation Found., Charleston, 1989—; bd. trustees U. Charleston, 1989-98, Marshall U.-Yeager Scholars, Huntington, W.Va., 1990-96, W.Va. State Coll. Found., Inst., 1988-96, WSWP-TV Pub. Broadcasting, 1980-94, Faculty Merit Scholars, 1991—, W.Va. Humanities Coun., 1994-2000; bd. dirs. BIDCO, 1996-98, Advantage Valley, Charleston, 1996-98, Greater Kanawha Valley Found., 1980-86, adv. bd., 1986—; bd. dirs. Childrens Express, 1987—, Charleston Renaissance, 1995—, Washington, 1997—, Gunston Hall Plantation, 1977-92, pres., 1989-92; bd. dirs., exec. com. Worth Bingham Prize Found., 1987—; bd. dirs. Nat. Youth Sci. Found., 1998; trustee W.Va. U., 2000—, Sulgrave Manor Found., 2001; bd. dirs. Clay Ctr. for Arts and Scis., 1998—. Recipient John Marshall medal for civic responsibility, Marshall U., 1997, Pres. Disting. Svc. award, W.Va. U., 2000. Mem. So. Newspaper Pubs. (journalism edn. com. 1992-94, minority affairs com. 1994—), Nat. Soc. of Colonial Dames of W.Va. (pres.), Internat. Press Inst. (dir. Am. com. 1994—), Newspaper Assn. Am. (com. mem. 1987—), Nat. Trust for Historic Preservation, Garden Club of Am. (chmn. libr., bd. dirs. 1989-92), Jr. League of Charleston, Edgewood Country Club of Charleston, Yale Club of N.Y.C., Sulgrave Club of Washington, Briar Hills Garden Club, Kanawha Garden Club, Sea Pines Country Club of Hilton Head. Democrat. Presbyterian. Avocations: travel, reading, golf, gardening. Home: 806 Cedar Rd Charleston WV 25314-1206 Office: The Charleston Gazette 1001 Virginia St E Charleston WV 25301-2895

CHIN, CECILIA HUI-HSIN, librarian; b. Tientsin, China; came to U.S., 1961; d. Yu-lin and Ti-yu (Fan) C. BA, Nat. Taiwan U., Taipei, 1961; MSL.S., U. Ill., 1963. Cataloger, reference librarian Roosevelt U., Chgo., 1963; reference librarian, indexer Ryerson & Burnham Libraries, Art Inst. Chgo., 1963-70, head reference dept. indexer, 1970-75; acting dir. libraries Art Inst. Chgo., 1976-77, assoc. librarian, head reference dept., 1975-82; chief librarian Smithsonian Am. Art Mus. and Nat. Portrait Gallery, Smithsonian Inst., Washington, 1982—. Compiler: The Art Institute of Chicago Index to Art Periodicals, 1975 Recipient awards, Nat. Portrait Gallery, Smithsonian Instn., 1984, 1989, Smithsonian Instn. Libr., 2001. Mem. Art Librs. Soc., D.C. Libr. Assn., Washington Rare Book Group. Office: 750 9th St # 2100 Washington DC 20560-0975 Fax: 202-275-1929. E-mail: chinc@si.edu.

CHIN, JANET SAU-YING, data processing executive, consultant; b. Hong Kong, July 27, 1949; came to U.S., 1959; d. Arthur Quock-Ming and Jenny (Loo) C. BS in Math, U. Ill., Chgo., 1970; MS in Computer Sci., U. Ill., Urbana, 1973. Sys. programmer Lawrence Livermore (Calif.) Lab., 1972-79; sect. mgr. Tymshare Inc., Cupertino, Calif., 1979-83, Fortune Systems, Redwood City, Calif., 1983-85; div. mgr. Impell Corp, Berkeley, Calif., 1985; pres. Chin Assocs., Oakland, Calif., 1985-88; bus. devel. mgr. Sun Microsystems, Mountain View, Calif., 1988-92; engring. dir. Cadence Design Systems, San Jose, Calif., 1992-94; quality dir. Cadence Design Sys., San Jose, Calif., 1994-95; asst. to CEO, Avant! Corp., Fremont, Calif., 1995-99; provost World Inst. Tech., Fremont, Calif., 1996-98; cons. Second Resource, Oakland, 2000—. Vice-chmn. Am. Nat. Standards Inst. X3H3, N.Y.C., 1979-82, internat. rep. X3H3, 1982-88. Co-author: The Computer Graphics Interface, 1991; contbr. tech. papers to profl. publs. Mem. Assn. Computing Machinery, Sigma Xi. Avocations: Karate, iaido, taiko, science fiction/fantasy, piano. E-mail: barronchin@earthlink.net.

CHIN, JING-YI SYZ, chemist, educator; arrived in US, 1973; d. Chao-Ching and Nae-Quang Syz; m. Henry T. Chin, May 12, 1984. BS, City Coll. NY, 1978; MPhil, CUNY, 1984, PhD, 1993. Adj. instr. chemistry CUNY, NYC, 1984—89; from adj. instr. chemistry to assoc. prof. chemistry SUNY, Seldon, 1989—2000, assoc. prof. chemistry, 2000—. Mem.: Chem. Edn., Am. Chem. Soc. Avocations: stamp collecting/philately, travel. Office: Suffolk County Cmty Coll 533 College Rd Selden NY 11784

CHIN, KATHERINE MOY, nutritionist, consultant; b. Washington, Apr. 13; d. David Chee Nie and Mary Ng Jue Hie Moy; m. Calvin Chin, Oct. 7, 1951; 1 child, Stephanie Anne Chung. BS, U. Md., College Park, 1951. Registered dietitian Md., lic. nutritionist Md. Clin. dietitian Johns Hopkins Hosp., Balt., 1954; instr. nutrition, dietetics Sch. Nursing Johns Hopkins Hosp., Balt., 1955—68; owner Chinese Gourmet Restaurant, Balt., 1980—83; nutrition edn. and tng. specialist Balt. County Pub. Sch., Md., 1983—98; partnership specialist Bur. Census Dept. Commerce, Balt., 1999—2000. Bi-lingual interpreter for Cantonese speaking students Balt. County Pub. Schs., 1983—; commr. Asian-Pacific Am. Adv. Coun., Md., 1997—; instr. chinese cooking sch. The Internat. Gourmet Ctr., 1969—79. Coord., fundraiser Asian Cmty., Balt., 1960; lay reader ch. Mem.: Towson U. Asian Arts/Culture Ctr., Balt. Asian Trade Coun. (chairperson 1968—), Am. Dietetic Assn., AAUW, Md. Sch. Food Svc. Assn. (pres. 1984—86), Md. Dietetic Assn. (pres. 1968—70). Democrat. Episcopalian. Avocations: travel, reading, music, volunteering. Home: Unit 208 4100 N Charles St Baltimore MD 21218 Office: Balt Asian Trade Coun 4100 N Charles St Unit 208 Baltimore MD 21218

CHIN, SUE SOONE MARIAN (SUCHIN CHIN), conceptual artist, portraitist, photographer, community affairs activist; b. San Francisco; d. William W. and Soo-Up (Swebe) C. Grad., Calif. Coll. Art, Mpls. Arts Inst.; scholar, Schaeffer Design Ctr.; student, Yasuo Kuniyoshi, Louis Hamon, Rico LeBrun. Photojournalist All Together Now Show, 1973, East-West News, Third World Newscasting, 1975-78, Sta. KNBC Sunday Show, L.A., 1975, 76, Live on 4, 1981, Bay Area Scene, 1981. Chmn. Full Moon Products; pres., bd. dirs. Aumni Oracle Inc. Graphics printer, exhbns. include: Kaiser Ctr., Zellerbach Pla., Chinese Culture Ctr. Galleries, Capricorn Asunder Art Commn. Gallery (all San Francisco), Newspace Galleries, New Coll. of Calif., L.A. County Mus. Art, Peace Pla. Japan Ctr., Congress Arts Comm., Washington, 1989; SFWA Galleries, Inner Focus Show, 1989—, Calif. Mus. Sci. and Industry, Lucien Labaudt Gallery, Salon de Medici, Madrid, Salon Renacimiento, Madrid, 1995, Life is a Circus, SFWA Gallery, 1991, 94, UN/50 Exhibit, Bayfront Galleries, 1995, Somar Galleries, 1997, 2003 (Merit award 2003), Sacramento State Fair, 2000, Star Child, Women thru the Ages - Somarts Gallery, 2000, AFL-CIO Labor Studies Ctr., Washington, Asian Women Artists (1st prize for conceptual painting, 1st prize photography), 1978, Yerba Buena Arts Ctr. for the Arts Festival, 1994; represented in permanent collections L.A. County Fedn. Labor, Calif. Mus. Sci. and Industry, AFL-CIO Labor Studies Ctr., Australian Trades Coun., Hazeland and Co., also pvt. collections; author: (poetry) Yuri and Malcolm, The Desert Sun, 1994 (Editors Choice award 1993-94). Del. nat., state convs. Nat. Women's Polit. Caucus, 1977-83, San Francisco chpt. affirmative action chairperson, 1978-82, nat. conv. del., 1978-81, Calif. del., 1976-81. Recipient Honorarium AFL-CIO Labor Studies Ctr., Washington, 1975-76, Bicentennial award 1976; award Centro Studi Ricerche delle Nazioni, Italy, 1985; bd. advisors Psycho Neurology Found. Bicentennial award L.A. County Mus. Art, 1976, 77, 78, Mandolay Merit award Som Arts Gallery, 2003. Mem. Asian Women Artists (founding v.p., award 1978-79, 1st award in photography of Orient 1978-79, Merit award 2003), Calif. Chinese Artists (sec.-treas. 1978-81), Japanese Am. Art Coun. (chairperson 1978-84, dir.), San Francisco Women Artists, San Francisco Graphics Guild, Pacific/Asian Women Coalition Bay Area, Chinatown Coun. Performing and Visual Arts. Address: PO Box 421415 San Francisco CA 94142-1415

CHIN, SYLVIA FUNG, lawyer; b. N.Y.C., June 27, 1949; d. Thomas and Constance (Yao) Fung; m. Edward G.H. Chin, July 10, 1971; children: Arthur F., Benjamin F. BA, NYU, 1971; JD, Fordham U., 1977. Bar: N.Y. 1978, U.S. Dist. Ct. (so. and ea. dists.) N.Y. 1979, U.S. Supreme Ct. 1990. Law clk. to dist. judge U.S. Dist. Ct. (so. dist.), N.Y.C., 1977-79; assoc. White & Case, N.Y.C., 1979-86, ptnr., 1986—. Adj. assoc. prof. law Fordham U., N.Y.C., 1979-81. Mem. editl. bd.: Bus. Law Today, 1996—2002. Mem.: ABA, Am. Coll. Comml. Fin. Lawyers, Am. Coll. Investment Counsel (bd. dirs. 1999—, pres. 2002—03), Nat. Asian Pacific ABA (treas. 1997—98), Women's World Banking (bd. dirs.), Asian Am. Bar Assn. N.Y. (bd. dirs. 1991—97, pres. 1994—96), N.Y. County Lawyers Assn., Assn. Bar City N.Y., Asian Am. Bar Assn. N.Y. Found. (treas.), Fordham Law Alumni Assn. (bd. dirs.). Office: White & Case LLP 1155 Ave of Americas New York NY 10036-2711

CHINN, PEGGY LOIS, nursing educator, editor; b. Columbia, S.C., Feb. 25, 1941; d. Hubert R. and Margaret (Gasteiger) Tatum; m. Philip C. Chinn, June 15, 1964 (div. 1974); children: Kelleth Roger, Jonathan Mark (dec.). AA, Mars Hill Coll., 1960; BS, U. Hawaii, 1964; MS, U. Utah, 1970, PhD, 1971. From instr. to asst. prof. U. Utah, Salt Lake City, 1971-74; assoc. dir., prof. Tex. Woman's U., Denton, 1974-78; prof. Wright State U., Dayton, Ohio, 1978-81, SUNY, Buffalo, 1981-90, U. Colo., Denver, 1990-96. Founder, editor Advances in Nursing Sci., Rockville, Md., 1978—; cons., lectr. in field. Author: Child Health Maintenance, 1974, 2d edit., 1978, Theory in Nursing, 1983, 5th edit. 1999, Peace and Power, 5th edit., 2001; contbr. articles to profl. jours. Co-founder Cassandra: Radical Feminist Nurses Network, nationwide 1982, Margaret Daughters Inc., Buffalo, 1984. Fellow Am. Acad. Nursing (governing coun. 1987-90); mem. Am. Nurses Assn., Nat. League for Nursing, Sigma Theta Tau. Office: U Conn Nursing Health Sci Ctr 231 Glenbrook Rd Storrs Mansfield CT 06269-9005 E-mail: peggy.chinn@uconn.edu.

CHIORAZZI, MARY LORRAINE, psychiatrist; b. New York; BS, Marymount Manhattan Coll., 1966; MD, Georgetown U., 1970. Diplomate Am. Bd. Psychiatry. Pvt. practice child, adolescent, adult psychiatry, Englewood, N.J., 1975—. Office: 163 Engle St Englewood NJ 07631-2530

CHIOU-TAN, FAYE, physician, educator; b. Hsin-Chu, Taiwan, Mar. 27, 1964; d. George and Tricia Chiou; m. Filemon Tan, Jr.; children: Filemon III, Michelle. AB, Princeton U., 1985; MD, Baylor U., 1990. Diplomate Am. Bd. Electrodiagnostic Medicine, Am. Bd. Phys. Med. Rehab. Asst. prof. Baylor Coll. Medicine, Houston, 1995—2003, assoc. prof., 2003—. Contbr. articles to profl. jours. Chief svc. phys. medicine and rehab. Harris County Hosp. Dist., Houston, 2000—, dir. electrodiagnosis, 1995—, dir. Ctr. for Trauma Rehab. Rsch., 2000—. Recipient Excellence in Rsch. Writing award Assn. Acad. Physiatrists/Am. Jour. Phys. Medicine and Rehab., 1999, 2000, 2003; named one of Am's Top Physicians, Consumer's Rsch. Coun. Am., 2003. Mem.: Assn. Acad. Physiatrists (rsch. com.), Am. Assn. Electrodiagnostic Medicine (rsch. com.). Avocations: cooking, hiking, antiques. Office: Baylor Coll Medicine Dept PM&R 3601 N MacGregor Way Ste 240 Houston TX 77004

CHIPMAN, DEBRA DECKER, title insurance executive; b. Oneonta, N.Y., Sept. 21, 1959; d. Leon Hannibal and Patricia Elizabeth (Ainsworth) Decker; m. Michael A. Chipman, May 24, 1980 (div. Sept. 1990); 1 child, Amanda Michelle. Student, Robert Morris Coll., 1988-94. Sec., receptionist Power Engring. Corp., Binghamton, N.Y., 1977-78; accts. payable clk. Old Dominion U. Rsch. Found., Norfolk, Va., 1978-80; adminstrv. asst. U. Pitts., 1980-81; paralegal Papernick & Gefsky, Attys. at Law, Pitts., 1981-93; mgr. Preferred Settlement Svcs., Inc., Pitts., 1993-97; asst. v.p., agy. rep. First Am. Title Ins. Co., Pitts., 1997-2000, Fidelity Nat. Title Ins. Co. of N.Y., 2000—. Recipient award Otsego County Bankers Assn., 1977. Mem.: Pa. Land Title Assn. (western Pa. chpt. sec., chair 2002), Pa. Assn. Notaries, Pitts. Paralegal Assn. (co-chair fundraising com. 1990). Methodist. Avocations: golf, skiing. Home: 2593 Hunters Point Ct S Wexford PA 15090-7986 Office: Fidelity Nat Title Ins Co Grant Building Ste 1412 Pittsburgh PA 15219-2203 E-mail: dchipman@fnf.com.

CHIPMAN, SUSAN ELIZABETH, psychologist, researcher; b. St. Paul, Feb. 12, 1946; d. Robert Louis and Margaret Alice Fitzgerald; m. Eric George Chipman, Aug. 27, 1966. AB in Math., Harvard U., 1966, MBA, 1967, AM in Psychol., 1969, PhD in Exptl. Psychol., 1973. Asst. prof. U. Mich., Ann Arbor, 1974-75; assoc. Nat. Inst. Edn., Washington, 1976-78, asst. dir., 1979-84; sci. officer U.S. Office Naval Rsch., Arlington, Va., 1984-85, cognitive sci. program mgr., 1985—. Mem. adv. bd. James S. McDonnell Found., St. Louis, 1987-98. Editor, author: Thinking and Learning Skills, 1985, Women and Mathematics, 1985, Foundations of Knowledge Acquisition, 1993, Cognitively Diagnostic Assessment, 1995, Cognitive Task Analysis, 2000; contbr. articles to profl. jours. Fellow APA, APS. Avocation: photography. Home: 2606 S Joyce St Arlington VA 22202-2214 Office: Office Naval Rsch 342 800 N Quincy St Arlington VA 22217-5660

CHIRA, SUSAN, editor; BA in History and East Asian Studies, Harvard U., 1980. From trainee to fgn. editor The N.Y. Times, 1982—2004, fgn. editor, 2004—. Office: The New York Times 229 W 43rd St New York NY 10036-3959

CHISHOLM, MARGARET ELIZABETH, retired library education administrator; b. Grey Eagle, Minn., July 25, 1921; d. Henry D. and Alice (Thomas) Bergman; children: Nancy Diane, Janice Marie Lane. BA, U. Washington, 1957, MLS, 1958, PhD, 1966. Libr. Everett (Wash.) C.C., 1961-63; from asst. to assoc. prof. edn. U. Oreg., Eugene, 1963-67; assoc. prof. edn. U. N.Mex., Albuquerque, 1967-69; prof., dean U. Md. Coll. Libr. and Info. Svcs., College Park, 1969-75; v.p. univ. rels. and devel. U. Washington, Seattle, 1975-81; dir., prof. Grad. Sch. Libr. and Info. Sci., U. Wash., Seattle, 1981-92; ret., 1992. Adv. com. White House Conf. on Libr. and Info. Sci., 1989-91, Pub. Broadcasting Svc. Archive; commr. Western Interstate Commn. Higher Edn., Colo., 1981-85. Author: Information Technology: Design and Applications (with Nancy Lane), 1990. Mem. USIA del. to Mexican-Am. Commn. on Cultural Coop., 1990. Civilian aide U.S. Army, 1978-88. Recipient Ruth Worden award U. Wash., Seattle, 1957, Disting. Alumni award St. Cloud (Minn.) U., 1977, Disting. Alumni award U. Wash., 1979, John Brubaker award Cath. Libr. Assn., 1987, Pres.'s award Wash. Libr. Assn., 1991. Mem. ALA (exec. bd. 1989-90, pres. 1988-89, v.p. 1986-87), Assn. Pub. TV Stas. (trustee 1975-84, 87-93), White House Conf. on Libr. and Info. Svcs. (adv. com. 1989-91), U. Wash. Retirement Assn. (v.p. 1995-96, pres. 1996-98). Home: 20900 Big Basin Way Saratoga CA 95070-5750

CHISHOLM, SALLIE WATSON, biological oceanography educator, researcher; b. Marquette, Mich., Nov. 5, 1947; BA, Skidmore Coll., 1969; PhD, SUNY, 1974. Postdoctoral researcher biol. oceanography Scripps Instn. Oceanography, 1974-76; vis. scientist, biology dept. Woods Hole Oceanog. Instn., 1978—; prof., dept. civil and environ. engring. MIT, Cambridge, 1976—, prof. dept. biology, 1993—, Lee & Geraldine Martin prof. environ. studies, co-dir., Earth Sys. Initiative, 2002—, co-dir., Terrascope, 2003—. MIT dir. MIT-Woods Hole Joint Program in Oceanography, 1988-95; steering com. U.S. Joint Global Flux Study, 1989-92; mem. ocean studies bd. NRC, 1990-93. Assoc. editor Jour. Phycology, 1983-87; mem. editorial bd. Jour. Marine Molecular Biology and Biotech., 1991—, Marine Ecology Progress Series, 1992—; contbr. articles to profl. jours. Recipient Rosenstiel Award in Ocean Sciences, 1991; fellow, Am. Acad. of Arts and Sciences, 1992; Guggenheim fellow, 1997—98, Resident Scholar, Bellagio Ctr., Italy, 1998, elected, NAS, 2003. Mem.: Soc. of Analytical Cytology, AAAS, Ecological Soc. of Am., The Oceanography Soc., Am. Geophysical Union (fellow 1996), Phycological Soc. of Am., Am. Soc. Microbiology (fellow 1993), Am. Soc. Limnology and Oceanography, Sigma XI. Office: MIT 3 Cambridge Center, NE20 Cambridge MA 02139*

CHISHOLM, SHIRLEY ANITA ST. HILL, former congresswoman, educator, lecturer; b. Bklyn., Nov. 30, 1924; d. Charles Christopher and Ruby (Seale) St. Hill; m. Conrad Chisholm, Oct. 8, 1949 (div. Feb. 1977), m. Arthur Hardwick, Jr., Nov. 26, 1977. BA cum laude, Bklyn. Coll.; MA, Columbia U.; LL.D. (hon.), Talladega (Ala.) Coll., Hampton (Va.) Inst., LaSalle Coll., Phila., U. Maine, Portland, Capital U., William Patterson Coll., Pratt Inst., Coppin State Coll., N.C. Coll., Kenyon Coll., Wilmington (Ohio) Coll., Acquinas Coll., Grand Rapids, Mich., Reed Coll., Portland, Oreg., U. Cin., Smith Coll., Northampton, Mass. Former nursery sch. tchr., dir. nursery sch.; ednl. cons. Div. Day Care, Bur. Child Welfare, N.Y.C.; mem. N.Y. State Assembly, 1964-68, 91st-98th Congresses from 12th Dist. N.Y., 1969-83; Purington chair Mount Holyoke Coll., South Hadley, Mass., 1983-87. Lectr. Spellman Coll., Atlanta. Author: Unbought and Unbossed, 1970, The Good Fight, 1973. Hon. mem. bd. dirs. Cosmopolitan Young People's Symphony Orch., N.Y.C.; adv. bd. Fund. for Research and Edn. in Sickle Cell Disease; bd dirs. Bklyn. Home for Aged; mem. Central Bklyn. Coordinating Council; mem. nat. adv. council Inst. for Studies in Edn., Notre Dame; mem. adv. com. Washington Workshops; nat. bd. dirs. Ams. for Democratic Action; mem. adv. council NOW; hon. com. mem. United Negro Coll. Fund.; Presdl. candidate Dem. Party, 1972. Named Alumna of Year Bklyn. Coll. Alumni Bull., 1957; recipient award for outstanding work in field of child welfare Women's Council of Bklyn., 1957, Key Woman of Year award, 1963, Woman of Achievement award Key Women, Inc., 1965 Mem. Nat. Assn. Coll. Women, Bklyn. Coll. Alumni, LWV, Key Women, NAACP, Delta Sigma Theta. Methodist.

CHISWICK, NANCY ROSE, psychologist; b. East Orange, N.J., May 8, 1945; d. Haim Hershel and Beatrice May (Levinson) C.; m. Arthur Howard Patterson, Aug. 5, 1973; children: Michael Chiswick-Patterson, Emily Chiswick-Patterson. AB, Smith Coll., 1966; MA, U. Ill., Chgo., 1970, PhD, 1973. Lic. psychologist, Pa. Intern Northwestern U. Med. Sch., Chgo., 1973; mental retardation specialist The Counseling Svc., Bellefonte, Pa., 1973-75; clin. staff psychologist Pa. State U., 1975-80; pres., clin. psychologist Child, Adult and Family Psychol. Ctr., State College, Pa., 1980—. Adj. prof. human devel. Pa. State U., 1974—; mem. allied staff Ctr. Cmty. Hosp., State College, 1985—; staff Meadows Psychiat. Hosp., Centre Hall, Pa., 1985—. Creator, co-host pub. TV Series About Women, 1979-80. Del. White House Conf. Families, 1980, bd. dirs. Meadows Psychiat. Hosp., 1983-85, Jewish Cmty. Ctr., 1989-96. Named Guest in Residence W. Marlin Butts Com. Oberlin (Ohio) Coll., 1978. Fellow Ctrl. Pa. Psychol. Assn. (sec. 1987-89); mem. APA, Pa. Psychol. Assn. Home: 2443 Hickory Hill Dr State College PA 16803-3361 Office: Child Adult & Family Psychol Ctr 315 S Allen St Ste 218 State College PA 16801-4850

CHITTICK, ELIZABETH LANCASTER, women's rights activist; b. Bangor, Pa., Nov. 11, 1908; d. George and Flora Mae (Mann) Lancaster. Student, Columbia U., 1944-45, N.Y. Inst. Fin., 1950-51, Hunter Coll., 1952-56, Upper Iowa U., Fayette, 1976. Adminstrv. asst., chief clk U.S. Naval Air Stas., Seattle and Banana River, Fla., 1941-45; v.p. treas. W.A. Chittick & Co., MAnila, 1945-52; 31062Smith; real estate salesperson, 1949; registered rep. Bache & Co., N.Y. Stock Exch., N.Y.C., 1950-62, Shearson & Hamil, 1962-63; investment adviser, 1962-65; revenue officer IRS, N.Y.C., 1965-72; pres. Nat. Woman's Party, Washington, 1971-89, Woman's Party Corp., 1978-91; commr. Washington Commn. on Status of Women, 1982-86; pres., adminstr. Sewall-Belmont House. Bd. dirs. Wexita Corp., N.Y.C., Pan Am. Liason Com. of Women's Orgns. Inc.; 1st v.p., bd. dirs. Nat. Coun. Women U.S. Lectr., TV and radio commentator on Equal Rights Amendment; author: Answers to Questions About the Equal Rights Amendment, 1973, 76. Mem. Coalition for Women in Internat. Devel., Internat. Women's Yr. Continuing Com., 1978-81, Women's Campaign Fund, Washington, 1975-80, Women's Nat. Rep. Club, N.Y.C., Women Govt. Rels., Washington; mem. U.S. com. of cooperation to Inter-Am. Commn. of Women, OAS, 1974-80; del. U.S. World Conf. of Internat. Women's Yr., Mexico City, 1975; mem. women's history ctr. task force Am. Revolution Bicentennial Adminstrn., 1973-76; mem. adv. com. U.S. Ctr. for Internat. Women's Yr., 1973-76; vice convenor com. on law and status of women Internat. Coun. of Women; chmn. UN Drive for war orphans and widows, Manila, 1949 Mem. Greater Washington Soc. Assn. Execs.,

Internat. Coun. Women (Paris), Nat. Fedn. Bus. and Profl. Women's Clubs, Gen. Fedn. Women's Clubs, Women's Press Club (N.Y.C.), Am. Newswomen's Club, Nat. Press Club, Order Eastern Star. Home and Office: 4046 5th Ave Lake Worth FL 33462-2012

CHITTUM, LORETTA [illegible], [illegible] agency) administrator, b. Richmond, Va. m. Warren Chittum, June 2002. BS in crim. justice, polit. sci., sociology, Radford U. Dep. asst. sec. US Dept. Edn., Spec. Edn. and Rehab. Svcs., Wash., 2001—; dir., ctr. for elder rights Va. Dept. of Aging; chief dep. commr. Va. Dept. Rehab. Svcs.; leg. coord. Va. Sec. Health and Human Resources; staff Medicaid Agy., Va., Protection Advocacy Agy., Commonwealth Va. Alter. mem. Fed. Interagency Coord. Coun.; serves Access Bd.; apptd. Va. Devel. Disabilities Coun., Adult Edn., Literacy Coun. Office: US Dept Edn Spec Edn and Rehab Svcs 330 C St SW Mary E Switzer Bldg Rm 3006 Washington DC 20202

CHIU, BELLA CHAO, astrophysicist, writer; b. Beijing, May 24, 1931; came to U.S., 1938; d. Yuen Ren and Buwei (Yang) Chao; m. Hong-Yee Chiu, June 25, 1960 (div. 1966); 1 child, Lihu Mason Chiu. BA, U. Calif., Berkeley, 1953; MS, Cornell U., 1956. Rsch. staff MIT, Cambridge, 1971-81; tchr. ESL Ctrl. S. U. Tech., Changsha, China, 1982-83; fgn. expert Qinghua U., Beijing, 1986-87; writer Arlington, Mass., 1987-97; rschr., 1997—. English editor Nat. Assn. Chinese Ams., 1984-86. Grantee NSF, 1972, 75, 79. Mem. Am. Astron. Soc. (hist. divsn.), Archeol. Inst. Am., Women's Health Initiative.

CHIVERTON, PATRICIA ANN, nursing educator, dean; b. Rochester, N.Y., Nov. 21, 1947; d. Paul and Eleanor (Buyck) Gilmore; 1 child, Laura. BS, Ctrl. Mo. State U., 1970; MS, U. Rochester, 1980, EdD, 1990. Exec. dir. Alzheimer's Assn., Rochester, N.Y., 1987-89; clin. assoc. U. Rochester, 1987-89, clin. chief psychiat. mental health nursing, 1990-97, asst. prof. clin. nursing, 1994-95, interim chair health care sys. divsn., 1994-95, assoc. prof. clin. clin. nursing, 1996—99, CEO cmty. nursing ctr., 1996—, assoc. dean clin. affairs Sch. Nursing and Med. Ctr., 1998—99, interim dean Sch. Nursing and Med. Ctr., 1999—2000, dean Sch. Nursing and Med. Ctr., 2000. Judge Book of the Yr., Am. Jour. Nursing, 1999, reviewer, 1998—; cons. F.f. Thompson Continuing Care Facility, Canadaiguia, N.Y., 1997-99. Contbr. chpts. to books. in field. Rep. N.Y. State Alzheimer's Assn., 1985-88; bd. dirs. Health and Wellness Ctr., Livingston County, N.Y., Monroe County Long Term Care Agy., Rochester, 1997—. Mem. Am. Psychiat. Nurses Assn. (pres. Northwestern chpt. 1995-97, Excellence in Leadership award 1994), Ea. Nursing Rsch. Soc., Nat. Acads. Practice (Disting. Practitioner), Sigma Theta Tau. Office: U Rochester Sch Nursing 601 Elmwood Ave Rochester NY 14642-0001 E-mail: patricia_chiverton@urmc.rochester.edu.

CHLUDZINSKI, CAROL A. medical products executive; b. Bayonne, N.J., May 22, 1954; d. Henry Chludzinski and Margaret Waclawik. BA, Chestnut Hill Coll., 1976. Sales rep. Bristol Myers, Phila., 1977-78, dist. sales mgr., 1979-80, corp. trainer N.Y.C., 1978-79; med. sales rep. Baxter Travenol, Phila., 1980; regional sales mgr. Sharplan Lasers Inc., Allendale, N.J., 1981-86; dir. sales Living Tech., Inc., Warminster, Pa., 1986-88, Heraeus Inc., Milpitas, Calif., 1989-93; nat. sales mgr. Cybex Inc., Ronkonkoma, N.Y., 1993-95; v.p. sales and mktg. Vida Med Ltd., Menlo Park, Calif., 1995—. Advisor Healthcare Recruiters, Walnut Creek, Calif., 1994—. Congl. campaign worker N.J. 14th Dist., 1974, 76. Democrat. Roman Catholic.

CHO, ALINA, anchor; BA, Boston Coll.; MS in Journalism, Northwestern U. Reporter Chicagoland T.V.; Washington corr. Sta. KEZI-TV, Eugene, Oreg., Sta. KGNC-TV, Amarillo, Tex.; anchor, gen. assignment reporter Sta. WFTS-TV, Tampa, Fla.; MSNBC bur. anchor CNBC, Secaucus, N.J. Office: CNBC 1 Msnbc Blvd Secaucus NJ 07094-2419

CHO, MARGARET, comedienne, actress; b. San Francisco, Dec. 5, 1968; d. Sueng-Hoon Cho and Young-Hie. Comedian, 1991—. TV appearances include All-American Girl, 1994—. Named Best Female Comedian Am. Comedy Awards, 1993. Office: Abrams Artist Agy 9200 W Sunset Blvd Ste 1130 Los Angeles CA 90069-3606

CHOATE, JEAN MARIE, historian, humanities educator; b. Syracuse, N.Y., Dec. 17, 1935; d. Max and Betty (Black) Molyneux; m. Woodrow Choate; children: Anne, Mike, Ruth, Susan. BA, Alma Coll., 1958; MA, U. Wis., 1962; MS, St. Cloud State U., 1972; PhD, Iowa State U., 1992. Instr. Open Bible Coll., Des Moines, 1983-85, Des Moines Area Coll., 1985-97; asst. prof. No. Mich. U., Marquette, 1992-99; assoc. prof. Coastal Ga. C.C., Brunswick, 1999—. Chair women's commn. No. Mich. U., 1996-97. Author: Disputed Ground: Farm Groups that Opposed New Deal Agricultural Programs; book reviewer Jour. of the West, 1996-2000; contbr. articles to profl. jours. Grantee No. Mich. U., 1993, Iowa Found., 1994; Everett Dirksen grantee, 1995, Franklin and Eleanor Roosevelt grantee, 1996, Carl Albert Libr. grantee, 1998, White House Hist. Assn. grantee, 2002. Mem. AAUW (v.p. 1995-97), Agrl. History, Women Historians of Midwest, Orgn. Am. Historians, Am. Hist. Assn., Social Sci. History Assn. Office: Coastal Ga C C Brunswick GA 31520 E-mail: jchoate@bc9000.b.c.peachnet.edu.

CHOCK, RAELENE, school system administrator; Bachelors, U. Hawaii; Masters, Columbia U.; EdD, Brigham Young U. Tchr., 1966—86; vice prin. Kaimuki H.S., 1986—88, Washington Mid. Sch., 1988—90; prin. Kuhio Elem. Sch., 1990—95, Kaimuki H.S., 1995—99; dep. supt. Honolulu Sch. Dist., 1999—2000, acting dist. supt., 2000—. Office: Honolulu Sch Dist 4967 Kilauea Honolulu HI 96816*

CHODOROW, NANCY JULIA, psychoanalyst, psychotherapist, educator; b. N.Y.C., Jan. 20, 1944; d. Marvin and Leah (Turitz) C.; children: Rachel Esther Chodorow-Reich, Gabriel Issac Chodorow-Reich. BA, Radcliffe Coll., 1966; PhD, Brandeis U., 1975; grad., San Francisco Psychoanalytic, 1993, cert. in adult psychoanalysis, 2000. From lectr. to assoc. prof. U. Calif., Santa Cruz, 1974-86, from assoc. prof. sociology to prof. Berkeley, 1986—, clin. prof. dept. psychology, 1999—. Faculty San Francisco Psychoanalytic Inst., 1994—. Author: The Reproduction of Mothering, 1978 (Jessie Bernard award Sociologists for Women in Soc. 1979, named one of Ten Most Influential Books of Past 25 Years, Contemporary Sociology 1996), 2nd edit., 1999, Feminism and Psychoanalytic Theory, 1989, Femininities, Masculinities, Sexualities, 1994, The Power of Feelings: Personal Meaning in Psychoanalysis, Gender, and Culture, 1999 (L. Bryce Boyer prize Soc. for Psychol. Anthropology 2000); contbr. articles to profl. jours. Fellow Russell Sage Found., NEH, Ctr. Advanced Study Behavioral Scis., ACLS, Guggenheim Found., Radcliffe Inst. for Advanced Study; recipient Contbn. to Women and Psychoanalysis award APA, L. Bryce Boyer prize Soc. for Psychol. Anthropology, 2000. Mem. Internat. Psychoanalytic Assn., Am. Psychoanalytic Assn., San Francisco Psychoanalytic Soc. Office: 5305 College Ave Oakland CA 94618 Office Phone: 510-547-5423.

CHOHLIS, DANA MARIE, elementary school educator, theater director; b. San Francisco, Dec. 8, 1957; d. Francis P. and Irene Marion (Edwards) Severn; children: Alyssa Katrina, Christina Alexis. BA, Calif. State U., Hayward, 1992, MA, 2000. Cert. English tchr. Tchr. San Leandro (Calif.) Unified Sch. Dist., 1992—; instr. pub. spkg. Peralta C.C., Oakland, Calif., 2000—. Dir. A Midsummer Night's Dream, 1999, Bridge to Terabithia, 1998, Circus in the Wind, 1997, A Case for Two Detectives, 1996, Electra, 2001; performer: Cypress, Taming of the Shrew, Edinburgh Fringe Festival, 2002. Tech. grantee San Leandro Bus. Assn., 1997, 98, 99, 2004, Long's Drugs Adopt-a-Class grantee, 2001. Mem. San Leandro Tchrs. Assn. (sec.), No. Calif. Edn. Theatre Assn. (rep.. mem. English/lang. arts stds. com., master tchr., retention program coord.), Alameda YAcht Club (sec. exec. bd. 2002-2004). Avocations: sailing, yacht racing, acting, dance, hiking. Home: 1448 Church Ave San Leandro CA 94579-1523 E-mail: argumentationclass@yahoo.com.

CHOI, JAY LEE, women's apparel executive; Pres. By Design LLC, 1994—, CEO, 1995—. Office: By Design LLC 1411 Broadway 28th Fl New York NY 10018 Fax: (212) 302-4556.

CHOI, THERESA SUN, performing arts association administrator; b. Cheverly, Md., Apr. 24, 1975; d. Jason Sung Kul and Hai Sun Choi. BA in Art History, U. Va., Charlottesville, 1997. Asst. to the gen. mgr. Red Light Mgmt., Charlottesville, 1997—98; receptionist Charlottesville (Va.) Broadcasting Corp., 1999; asst. to the v.p., talent buyer Clear Channel Entertainment, N.Y.C., 2000—01; promotions dir. Irving Plz. Concerts, Inc., N.Y.C., 2000—02; devel. assoc. Manhattan Sch. of Music, N.Y.C., 2002—. Mem.: U. of Va. Alumni Assn.

CHOICE, PRISCILLA KATHRYN MEANS (PENNY CHOICE), educational director, international consultant; b. Rockford, Ill., Nov. 8, 1939; d. John Z. and Margaret A. (Haines) Means; m. Jack R. Choice, Nov. 14, 1964; children: William Kenneth, Margaret Meta. BA, U. Wis., 1963; MEd, Nat.-Louis U., 1990; MA, N.E. Ill. U., 1995. Field rsch. dir. Tatham-Laird and Kudner Advt., Chgo., 1964-69; drama specialist Children's Theatre Western Springs (Ill.), 1969-81; gifted teaching asst. Sch. Dist. 181, Hinsdale, Ill., 1980-84; tchr. Sch. Dist. 99, Cicero, Ill., 1984-85; gifted edn. program coord. Cmty. Consolidated Sch. Dist. 93, Carol Stream, Ill., 1985-99; coord. gifted edn. and fine arts Ednl. Svcs. Divsn., Lake County Regional Office Edn., Grayslake, Ill., 1999—. Drama specialist, cons. Choice Dramatics, Hinsdale and Clarendon Hills, Ill., 1976—; producing dir. Mirror Image Youth Theatre, Hinsdale, 1986-88; adj. prof. Coll. DuPage, Glen Ellyn, Ill., 1990-92, Nat.-Louis U., Evanston, Ill., 1991—, Aurora (Ill.) U., 1995—, Govs. State U., University Park, Ill., 1992-93; internat. cons. in gifted edn. and drama-in-edn., 1989—; co-chair advocacy com. Ill. Assn. Gifted Children, 2002—; trustee Friends of the Lake Co. Discovery Mus., 2003—; chair arts divsn. Nat. Assn. for Gifted Children, 2003—. Contbg. author Gifted/Arts Resource Guide, 1990; contbg. editor Ill. Theatre Assn., Followspot News, 1992-95. 96-2002. Mem. gifted adv. com. Ednl. Svc. Ctr., Wheaton, Ill., 1987—90, 1992—95, Regional Office of Edn., Wheaton, 1995—99, Northeastern Ill. U.1993-95, Chgo., 1993—95; bd. dirs. Ill. Theatre Assn., Chgo., 1983—87; chair Arts Divsn. Nat. Assn. for Gifted Children, 2003—; co-chair advocacy Com. Ill. Assn. for Gifted Children, 2002—. Recipient Ill. State Bd. Edn. gifted edn. fellowship, 1988, AAUW continuing edn. scholarship, 1986, 90, Excellence award Ill. Theatre Assn., 1991, Excellence award Ill. Math. and Sci. Acad., 1990, 98, Recognition of Excellence, No. Ill. Planning Commn. Gifted Edn., 1990, Award of Excellence Ill. and Math. Sci. Acad., 1998. Mem. ASCD, World Coun. on Gifted Edn., Nat. Assn. Gifted Children, Ill. Assn. Gifted Children (membership chmn. 1992-94, advocacy com. 1995—, co-chair advocacy com. 2002—), Ill. Coun. Gifted, Am. Assn. Theatre in Edn., Ill. Theatre Assn. (bd. dirs. 1983-87, Outstanding Achievement award 1991), Inst. for Global Ethics, Ill. Alliance Arts Edn., Theatre Western Springs, Phi Delta Kappa. Avocations: swimming, walking, reading. Home: 113 S Prospect Ave Clarendon Hills IL 60514-1422 Office: Lake County Ednl Svcs 19525 W Washington St Grayslake IL 60030-1152

CHOKSI, MARY, investment company executive; BA in French, U. Minn.; MA in Internat. Rels., John Hopkins U.; MPA, U. Minn. With pension devel. divsn. World Bank, sr. program officer South and S.E. Asia; mng. dir. Strategic Investment Ptnrs. Inc. and Emerging Markets Investors Corp., Arlington, Va., 1987—. Bd. mem. Emerging Markets South Asia Fund, Emerging Markets Quantitative Portfolio, HJ Heinz Co. Trustee Nat. Mus. Women in the Arts; bd. dirs. Beauvoir-The Nat. Cathedral Elem. Sch. Office: Strategic Investment Group 16th Fl 1001 19th St N Arlington VA 22209-1722*

CHOLDIN, MARIANNA TAX, librarian, educator; b. Chgo., Feb. 26, 1942; d. Sol and Gertrude (Katz) Tax; m. Harvey Myron Choldin, Aug. 28, 1962; children: Kate and Mary (twins). BA, U. Chgo., 1962, MA, 1967, PhD, 1979. Slavic bibliographer Mich. State U., East Lansing, 1967—69; Slavic bibliographer, instr. U. Ill., Urbana, 1969—73, Slavic bibliographer, asst. prof., 1973—76, Slavic bibliographer, assoc. prof., 1976—84, head Slavic and East European Libr., 1982—89, head, prof., 1984—2002, dir. Russian and East European Ctr., 1987—89, C. Walter and Gerda B. Mortenson Disting. prof., 1989—2002, dir. Mortenson Ctr. for Internat. Libr. Programs, 1991—2002, prof. emerita, 2003—. Author: Fence Around the Empire: Russian Censorship, 1985; editor: Red Pencil: Artists, Scholars and Censors in the USSR, 1989, Books, Libraries and Information in Slavic and East European Studies, 1986. Chair Soros Found. Network Libr. Program Bd., 1997—2000. Recipient Pushkin gold medal for contbns. to culture, Russian Presdl. Coun. on Culture, 2000. Mem. ALA, Am. Assn. for Advancement of Slavic Studies (pres. 1995), Internat. Fedn. Libr. Assns. and Instns., Phi Beta Kappa. Jewish. Home: 888 S Michigan Ave #403 Chicago IL 60605

CHONG, RACHELLE B. lawyer, federal communications commissioner; b. Stockton, Calif., June 22, 1959; m. Kirk E. Del Prete. BA in Journalism with high honors, U. Calif., Berkeley, 1981; JD, Hastings Coll. of Law, San Francisco, 1984. Bar: Calif. 1984, D.C. 1985. Assoc. Kadison, Pfaelzer, Woodard & Rossi, Washington and Palo Alto, Calif., 1984-87, Graham & James, San Francisco, 1987-92, ptnr., 1992-94; commr. FCC, Washington, 1994-97; ptnr. Coudert Bros., San Francisco, 1998-2000; gen. counsel, v.p. govt. affairs BroadBand Office Inc., San Mateo, Calif., 2000—. Commr. Legal Svc. Trust Fund Commn. of Calif. State Bar, San Francisco, 1992-94. Editor-in-chief Comm/Ent Law Jour., 1983-85. Finalist for 1994 Woman of Yr., Marketplace Channel 7 KGO-TV, San Francisco, 1994. Mem. ABA (mem. forum fed. comm. bar assn.), Women in Telecomm. (co-chair), Fed. Comm. Bar Assn. Republican. Methodist. Office: BroadBand Office Inc 951 Mariners Island Blvd San Mateo CA 94404-1561

CHOPP, REBECCA S. university president; m. Frederick H. Thibodeau; 3 children. BA, Kans. Wesleyan U., 1974; MDiv, St. Paul Sch. Theology, 1977; PhD, U. Chgo., 1983; DD (hon.), Lehigh U. Asst. prof. theology U. Chgo. Div. Sch., 1982—86; asst. prof. Candler Sch. and Grad. Divsn. Religion Emory U., Atlanta, 1986—89, assoc. faculty Inst. Liberal Arts, 1987, assoc. faculty Inst. for Women's Studies, 1987, dean of faculty and acad. affairs Candler Sch. of Theology, 1993—97, prof. theology Candler Sch. and Grad. Divsn. Religion, 1993, Charles Howard Candler prof. theology Grad. Divsn., 1996, interim provost, v.p. acad. affairs, 1997—98, provost, exec. v.p. for acad. affairs, 1998—2001, dir. grad. studies Inst. for Women's Studies; dean, Titus Street prof. theology and culture Yale U. Div. Sch., 2001—02; pres., prof. philosophy and religion Colgate U., 2002—. Bd. dirs. Scholars Press; trustee Carnegie Found. Author: The Praxis of Suffering: An Interpretation of Liberation and Political Theologies, 1986, The Power to Speak: Feminism, Language, God, 1989, Saving Work: Feminist Practices of Theological Education, 1995; Co-editor: Differing Horizons: Feminist Theory and Theology, 1997, Reconstructing Christian Theology, 1999; theology editor Religious Studies Rev., 1989-93; editor-at-large Christian Century, 1989-95; editor Quar. Rev., 1998-; editl. bd. Emory Theol. Studies, Religion and Ideology, Jour. of Religion, Word and World, Internat. Jour. of Practical Theology; contbr. articles to profl. publs. Recipient Alumna Achievement award Kans. Wesleyan U., 1990, Disting. Alumna award St. Paul Sch. of Theology, 1991, Founder's Day award Baker U., 1995, Alumna of Yr. award U. Chgo. Divinity Sch., 1997. Mem. Am. Acad. of Religion (pres. southeastern divsn.), Am. Theol. Soc. (chair women in leadership project). Office: Colgate U 13 Oak Dr Hamilton NY 13346*

CHORY, JOANNE, plant biologist; Rsch. scientist Salk Inst. for Biological Studies, San Diego, Calif., now assoc. prof. Recipient Initiatives in Rsch. NAS, 1994, Charles Albert Shull award Am. Soc. Plant Physiologists. Office: Salk Inst Biol Studies PO Box 85800 San Diego CA 92186-5800

CHOTIN, ELIZABETH ETTLINGER, research organization administrator; b. Chgo., Apr. 11, 1946; d. Ralph Jr. and Margery (Helm) Ettlinger; m. Arthur David Chotin, Apr. 5, 1970; children: Matthew, David. BA, Boston U., 1968. Mem. staff civil rights divsn. U.S. Dept. Justice, Washington, 1968-72; mem. nat. staff McGovern Presdl. Campaign, Washington, 1972; lexis supr. Mead Data Ctrl., N.Y.C., 1973-77; dir. Nat. Abortion Rights Action League Polit. Action Com., Washington, 1978-79; internat. affairs officer Carter Adminstrn., Washington, 1979-81; exec. dir. Fund for Integrative Biomed. Rsch., Washington, 1982-83; corp. and found. officer NAS, Washington, 1988-90; dir. devel. Washington Lawyers' Com. for Civil Rights, 1991-94; dir. Washington office Weizmann Inst. Sci., 1994—. Cons. infield, 1983-88. Campaign vol. Dem. Party; vol., officer Washington elem., jr. high and high schs.; active religious and polit. orgns., Washington. Democrat. Jewish. Avocation: sailing. Office: Am Com for Weizmann Inst Sci 1730 Rhode Island Ave NW Washington DC 20036-3101

CHOUDHURY, DIPA, mathematician, educator; b. Dhaka, Bangladesh, Feb. 1, 1953; d. Sisir and Monorama Sarkar; m. Japobrata Choudhury, July 18, 1972; children: Progga-Paromita, Atish-Dipankar. PhD, Johns Hopkins U., 1986. Asst. prof. Loyola Coll., Balt., 1986—94, assoc. prof., 1994—. Contbr. articles to profl. jours. Pres. Sanskriti, Washington, 1998—99. Mem.: Math. Assn. Am. (program chmn. Md./D.C./Va. sect. 2002—). Home: 13026 Broadmore Rd Silver Spring MD 20904 Office: Loyola Coll 4501 N Charles St Baltimore MD 21210 Personal E-mail: dsc@loyola.edu. Business E-Mail: dsc@loyola.edu.

CHOUKAS-BRADLEY, MELANIE, writer, photographer; b. Jacksonville, N.C., Aug. 20, 1952; d. Michael Jr. and Juanita May (Crosby) Choukas; m. James Richard Bradley, June 21, 1975; children: Sophia Crane, Jesse Elliott. BA in English, U. Vt., 1974; student, Pierce Coll., Athens, 1971; postgrad., U.S. Dept. Agr. Grad. Sch., Chevy Chase, Md., 1995—. From reporter to news dir. Radio Sta. WBRL, Berlin, N.H., 1975-77; rsch. asst. subcom. on oversight and investigations Commerce Com., U.S. Ho. of Reps., Washington, 1978; writer, 1978—. Earth Day chmn. Sugarloaf Citizens Assn., Barnesville, Md., 1990-92. Author: (Book) City of Trees, 1987, Sugarloaf: The Mountain's History, Geology and Natural Lore, 2003; contbr. articles to Washington Post, Audubon Naturalist News, others; author: An Illustrated Guide to Eastern Woodland Wildflowers and Trees, 2004. Grantee Am. Forest Inst., Nat. Forest Products Assn., Time Inc., Bendix, Union Camp Corp., 1978-81, naturalist lead field trips for Audubon Naturalist Soc., 2000—; grantee Sugarloaf Regional Trails, 1995, 2001. Mem. Authors Guild. Democrat. Achievements include member Capitol Steps adult synchronized skating team, participant National Championships 2001 and 2002; member Capital Classics synchronized skating team, 2003-04. Avocations: hiking, cross country skiing, syncronized figure skating, running, botany. E-mail: choukas@erols.com.

CHOW, AMY, gymnast, Olympic athlete; b. San Jose, Calif., May 15, 1978; Student, Stanford U. Mem. USA Team, Hamamatsu, Japan, 1993, World Championships Team, Dortmund, Germany, 1994, Pan Am. Games Team, Mar del Plata, Argentina, 1995, U.S. Olympic Team, Atlanta, 1996. Placed 1st vault U.S. Gymnastics Championships, Ohio, 1992, 1st all around, vault, uneven bars, balance beam, 2d floor exercise, Mex. Olympic Festival, 1992, 3rd all around, vault, 1st floor exercise, USA/Japan Competition, Hamamatsu, Japan, 1993, 3rd vault Coca-Cola Nat. Championships, Nashville, Tenn., 1994, 1st vault, 2d uneven bars, 3rd all around Pan Am. Games, Mar del Plata, Argentina, 1995; recipient Gold medal Women's Gymnastics Team competition and Silver medal uneven bars, Olympic Games, Atlanta, 1996. Mem., U.S. Olympic Team, Sydney, 2000. Address: Octagon 2 Union St #300 Portland ME 04101-4046

CHOW, RITA KATHLEEN, nursing consultant; b. San Francisco, Aug. 19, 1926; d. Peter and May (Chan) Chow. BS, nursing diploma, Stanford U., 1950; MS, Case Western Res. U., 1955; profl. diploma in nursing edn. adminstrn, Columbia U., 1961, EdD, 1968; B of Individualized Studies, George Mason U., 1983. Asst. in teaching Stanford U., Calif., 1951—52; instr., dir. student health Fresno (Calif.) Gen. Hosp. Sch. Nursing, 1952—54; instr. Wayne State U. Coll. Nursing, Detroit, 1957—58; rsch. assoc., project dir. cardiovasc. nursing rsch. Ohio State U., Columbus, 1965—68; commd. officer USPHS, 1968, advanced through grades to nurse dir. (capt.), 1974; spl. asst. to dep. dir. Nat. Ctr. Health Svcs. Rsch., Health Svcs. and Mental Health Adminstrn., HEW, Rockville, Md., 1969—73, dep. dir. manpower utilization br., 1970—73; dep. dir. Office Long Term Care; dep. chief nurse officer USPHS, Rockville, 1973—77; chief quality assurance br. div. long-term care Office Stds. and Certification, Health Standards and Quality Bur., Health Care Fin. Adminstrn., HHS, 1977—82; supervisory clin. nurse and spl. asst. to health systems adminstr. USPHS Indian Hosp., HRSA, HHS, Rosebud, SD, 1982—83; dir. patient edn., asst. dir. nursing G. W. Long Hansen's Disease Ctr., USPHS, Carville, La., 1984—89; dir. nursing Fed. Med. Ctr., Ft. Worth, 1989—95; pvt. cons., 1995—98; dir. Nat. Interfaith Coalition on Aging, Natl. Coun. on Aging, Washington, 1998—. Author: (book) Identifying Nursing Action with the Care of Cardiovascular Patients, 1967, Cardiosurgical Nursing Care: Understandings, Concepts and Principles for Practice, 1975; mem. editl. bd. Nursing and Health Care, 1983—95; contbr. articles to profl. jours. Served with Nurse Corps U.S. Army, 1954—57 USAR, 1957—68. Recipient Nursing Svc. award, Assn. Mil. Surgeons U.S., 1969, Commendation medal, USPHS, 1972, Meritorious Svc. medal, 1977, Disting. Svc. medal, 1987, citation for outstanding contbn. to cardiovascular nursing, Am. Heart Assn., 1972—79, award for disting. achievement in nusring rsch., Nursing Edn. Alumni Assn., Columbia U. Tchrs. Coll., 1973, Disting. Alumnus award, Case Western Res. U. Sch. Nursing, 1979, Women's Honors in Pub. Svcs. award, ANA, 1988, Commendable Svc. medal, U.S. Dept. Justice, Bur. Prisons, 1995, Holistic Nurse of the Yr. award, Am. Holistic Nurses Assn., 2001, Artist of Life First prize, Internat. Womens Writing Guild, 1987, Chief Nurse Officer award, USPHS, 2003; fellow Nat. League Nursing fellow, 1959—61; grantee, Sigma Theta Tau, 1966. Fellow: Am. Assn. of Integrative Medicine (diplomate Coll. of Nursing 2003).

CHOWNING, ORR-LYDA BROWN, dietician; b. Cottage Grove, Oreg., Nov. 30, 1920; d. Fred Harrison and Mary Ann (Bartels) Brown; m. Kenneth Bassett Williams, Oct. 23, 1944 (dec. Mar. 1945); m. Eldon Wayne Chowning, Dec. 31, 1959. BS, Oreg. State Coll., 1943; MA, Columbia U., 1950. Dietetic intern Scripps Metabolic Clinic, LaJolla, Calif., 1944; sr. asst. dietitian Providence Hosp., Portland, Oreg., 1945-49; contact dietitian St. Lukes Hosp., N.Y.C., summer 1949; cafeteria food svc. supr. Met. Life Ins. Co., N.Y.C., 1950-52; set up food svc. and head dietitian McKenzie-Willamette Meml. Hosp., Springfield, Oreg., 1955-59; foods dir. Erb Meml. Student Union, Eugene, Oreg., 1960-63; set up food svc. and head dietitian Cascade Manor Retirement Home, Eugene, 1967-68; owner, operator Veranda Kafe, Inc., Albany, Oreg., 1971-80; owner, operator, sec.-treas. Chownings Adult Foster Home, Albany, 1984-98. Contbr. articles to profl. jours. Lin County Women's chair Hatfield for Senator Spaghetti Rally, Albany H.S., 1966; food preparation chair Yi for You, Mae Yih for State Senate, Albany Lebanon, Sweet Home, 1982; Silver Clover Club sponsor Oreg. 4-H Found., Oreg. State U., Corvallis, 1994-96. Recipient coll. scholarship Nat. 4-H Food Preparation Contest, Chgo., 1939. Mem. Am. Dietetic Assn. (registered dietitian, gerontol. nutritionist dietetic practice group 1988—), Oreg. Dietetic Assn. (diet therapy chair, newsletter editor 1963-64), Willamette Dietetic Assn., Kappa Delta Pi (Kappa chpt.), Mu

Beta Beta. Republican. Mem. Christian Ch. (Disciples Of Christ). Avocations: gardening, genealogy, swimming, travel, pet therapy. Home and Office: 4440 Woods Rd NE Albany OR 97321-7353

CHOYKE, PHYLLIS MAY FORD (MRS. ARTHUR DAVIS CHOYKE JR.), management executive, editor, poet; b. Buffalo, Oct. 25, 1921; d. Thomas Cecil and Vera (Buchanan) Ford; m. Arthur Davis Choyke Jr., Aug. 18, 1945; children: Christopher Ford, Tyler Van. BS summa cum laude, Northwestern U., 1942. Reporter City News Bur., Chgo., 1942-43, Met. sect. Chgo. Tribune, Chgo., 1943-44; feature writer OWI, N.Y.C., 1944-45; sec. corp. Artcrest Products Co., Inc., Chgo., 1958-88, v.p., 1964-88; pres. The Partford Corp., Chgo., 1988-90. Founder, dir. Harper Sq. Press div., 1966-90. Author: (under name Phyllis Ford) (with others) (poetry) Apertures to Anywhere, 1979; editor: Gallery Series One, Poets, 1967, Gallery Series Two, Poets—Poems of the Inner World, 1968, Gallery Series Three Poets: Levitations and Observations, 1970, Gallery Series Four, Poets, I am Talking About Revolution, 1973, Gallery Series Five/Poets—To An Aging Nation (with occult overtones), 1977; (manuscripts and papers in Brown U. Library). Bonbright scholar, 1942. Mem. DAR (corr. sec. Gen. Henry Dearborn chpt. 1991-92, treas. 1992-2003, regent, 2003-04), Soc. Midland Authors (bd. dirs. 1987—, treas. 1988-93, pres. 1993-95, membership dir. 1997-98, corr. sec. 1999—), Mystery Writers Am. (assoc.), Chgo. Press Vets. Assn., Arts Club Chgo., John Evans Club (Northwestern U.), Poetry Soc. Am. (N.Y.C.), Acad. Am. Poets (N.Y.C.). Home: 23 Windsor Dr Elmhurst IL 60126-3971

CHRETIEN, CAROL ANN, chemical engineer; b. Biddeford, Maine, Oct. 1, 1967; d. Royal Raymond and Yvonne Deodati C. BS in Chem. Engring., cert. advanced study, U. Maine, 1990. Chem. engr. Brown and Root, Houston, 1990-93, 95-96, Internat. Tech., Houston, 1994-95, Asea Brown Boveri, Houston, 1997—99, Fluor Corp., 2001—. Pulp and Paper Found. scholar, 1986-90. Mem. AICHE, Technical Assn. Pulp and Paper Industry (treas. student sect. 1989). E-mail: Chret@hotmail.com., CChretien@aol.com.

CHRETIEN, JANE HENKEL, internist; b. Jersey City, Mar. 24, 1941; m. Paul B. Chretien, Apr. 11, 1970; children: Jean Paul, Yves. AB, Barnard Coll., 1962; MD, N.J. Coll. Medicine, 1966; MPH, Harvard U., 1970. Diplomate Am. Bd. Internal Medicine, Am. Bd. Infectious Disease. Intern Cornell U. Med. Divsn-Bellevue Hosp. Ctr., N.Y.C., 1966-67; resident Meml. Hosp. Sloan Kettering Inst. Med. Ctr., N.Y.C., 1967-69, fellow Georgetown U. Hosp., Washington, 1970-72, clin. instr., staff physician student health svc., 1972-75, asst. dir. student health svc., 1975-87, med. dir., 1987-94, clin. asst. prof., 1975-79, clin. assoc. prof., 1979-94; assoc. prof. George Washington U., 1994-98, clin. assoc. prof., 1998—. Fellow ACP; mem. Am. Pub. Health Assn., Infectious Diseases Soc. Am., Internat. Soc. Travel Medicine. Office Phone: 301-656-4010.

CHRETIEN, MARGARET CECILIA, public administrator; b. Tupper Lake, N.Y., Jan. 19, 1953; d. William Lawrence and Catherine Eileen (Dowdle) LaGasse; m. Thomas J. Chretien, Oct. 1, 1977. BA, Siena Coll., 1975; MPA, SUNY, Albany, 1983, postgrad., 1992—. Program coordinator Saratoga County Office for Aging, Ballston Spa, N.Y., 1977-80; crime prevention specialist N.Y. State Div. Criminal Justice Svcs., Albany, 1980-84, pub. info. officer, 1984-86, criminal justice program rep., 1986—2000, S.T.O.P. Violence Against Women program adminstr., 2000—01, sr policy analyst, 2001—. Publicity chair Nat. Mus. Dance, Saratoga Springs, N.Y., 1987-90; peer review panelist U.S. Dept. Justice, Office of Justice Programs. Mng. editor NYS Crime Prevention Update, 1980-84; mem. editorial rev. bd. Mng. N.Y. State, 1987-89. Bd. dirs. Vol. Ctr. Albany, 1988—, sec., 1992, pres., 1994-2000; fundraising vol. St. Cecilia's Orch., 1992; life mem. Saratoga Performing Arts Ctr. Mem. Women's Press Club N.Y. State, Inc. (v.p. 1984-86). Roman Catholic. Avocations: biking, golf, mountain climbing. Home: 8 Wagner Rd Saratoga Springs NY 12866-3744 Office: NY Div Criminal Justice Svc Executive Pk Albany NY 12203

CHRISMAN, NANCY CAROL, city manager, director, small business owner; b. Walnut Ridge, Ark., Mar. 22, 1943; d. Williford Ray and Syble Oleeta (Atkinson) Cooksey; m. Herbert Dale Chrisman, June 4, 1961; children: Stanley Ray, Eric Dale. Student, Ark. State U., 1963. Payroll clk. GE, Jonesboro, Ark., 1965-66, 68; sec., bookkeeper 1st Christian Ctr., Jonesboro, 1969-76; payroll clk. GE, Jonesboro, 1976-77; office mgr. Barrett, Wheatley, Smith and Deacon, Jonesboro, 1977-88; adminstrv. asst. Richard Stevenson, M.D., P.A., Jonesboro, 1988-89; adminstr. N.E. Ark. Women's Clinic, P.A., Jonesboro, 1989-98; exec. dir. Jonesboro Ctrl. Planning Assn., 1999—2003; co-owner La Boutique Panache, Jonesboro, 2003—. Dir. Mid South Bank, Jonesboro, 1995—; mem. Widowed Persons Adv. Bd., Jonesboro, 1990-98. Charter bd. dirs., past sec., past chmn. Crime Stoppers, Jonesboro, 1991-95; pres. Showtime divsn. Found. Arts, Jonesboro, 1992; chmn. leadership coun. Jonesboro Cmty. Oriented Policing, 1998-99; dir. Cmty. Policing Inst., Knoxville, 1999—. Recipient Good Neighbor Spotlight award Sta. KAIT-TV, 1993. Mem. Med. Group Mgmt. Assn., Univ. Rotary Club (Paul Harris fellow 1995, dir. 1998-01), Jonesboro C. of C. (dir. 1994-99, treas. 1997, chmn. 1997-98, Leadership Jonesboro 1993), Pi Omega Pi Democrat. Baptist. Avocations: needlepoint, reading. Office: Jonesboro Ctrl Planning Assn 407 Union St Jonesboro AR 72403-9246

CHRIST, CAROL TECLA, academic administrator; b. NYC, May 21, 1944; d. John George and Tecla (Bobrick) Christ; m. Larry Sklute, Aug. 15, 1975 (div. Dec. 1983); children— Jonathan, Elizabeth BA, Douglas Coll., 1966; M.Ph., Yale U., 1969, PhD, 1970. Asst. prof. English U. Calif., Berkeley, 1970-76, assoc. prof. English, 1976-83, prof. English, 1983—, dean dept. English, 1985-88, dean dept. humanities, 1988, acting provost, dean, 1989-90, provost, dean Coll. Letters and Sci., 1990-94, vice chancellor, provost, 1994-2000; pres. Smith Coll., Northampton, Mass., 2002—. Former dir. summer seminars for secondary and coll. tchrs. NEH; former tchr. Bread Loaf Sch. of English; invited lectr. Am. Assn. Univs., Am. Coun. Edn. Author: The Finer Optic: The Aesthetic of Particularity in Victorian Poetry, 1975, Victorian and Modern Poetics, 1984; mem. editl. bd. Victorian Literature, The Victorian Visual Imagination, The Norton Anthology of English Literature; contbr. articles to profl. jours. Mem. MLA Office: Smith Coll College Hall 20 Northampton MA 01063

CHRIST, ROXANNE E. lawyer; BA, UCLA, 1982; JD, Loyola Law Sch., 1985. Bar: Calif. 1985. With Paul, Hastings, Janofsky & Walker, Latham & Watkins, L.A., ptnr., 2001—. Office: Latham and Watkins LLC 633 W Fifth St Ste 4000 Los Angeles CA 90071*

CHRISTENBURY, LEILA, education educator; BA English, Hollins Coll., 1972; MA English, U. Va., 1973; EdD English Edn., Va. Tech., 1980. Tchr. English Roanoke Cath. High Sch., Va., 1973—75, William Fleming High Sch., 1975—78; asst. prof. dept. English lang. and lit. U. No. Iowa, Cedar Falls, 1979—80; asst. prof. English dept. James Madison U., Harrisonburg, Va., 1982—86; asst. prof., assoc. prof. Sch. Edn. Va. Commonwealth U., Richmond, 1968—95, prof. Sch. Edn., 1996—. Contbr. articles to profl. jours. Scholar, Va. Commonwealth U. Sch. Edn., 1993. Mem.: Va. Writers' Club, Va. Conf. English Educators, Va. Assn. Tchrs. English (treas., Frances Wimer award 2001), Assembly Women in Lit., Assembly Appalachian Lit., Assembly Lit. Adolescents, Nat. Conf. Rsch. Lang. and Lit., Nat. Coun. Tchrs. English (pres., Rewey Belle Inglis award Outstanding Women in English Edn. 1997), Omicron Delta Kappa, Phi Beta Kappa, Phi Kappa Phi, Phi Delta Kappa. Office: Va Commonwealth U Sch Edn PO Box 842020 Richmond VA 23284-2020

CHRISTENSEN, DONNA RADOVICH, needlecraft designer, consultant, educator; b. Midvale, Utah, Sept. 16, 1925; d. Daniel and Clara Ellen (Turley) Radovich; B.A., U. Utah, 1947; M.A. Columbia U., 1951; m. John Whittaker Christensen, Feb. 2, 1952; children: Carlyn M. Christensen Szalanski, John Chipman, Craig Whittaker. Tchr. and guidance counselor Jordan High Sch., Sandy, Utah, 1947-50; sec. Placement Bur. of Columbia U. Tchr.'s Coll., N.Y.C., 1950-51; free-lance designer of needlecrafts, 1970—; tchr. of needlecraft, 1965—; tchr. 18th Century painted finishes Isabel O'Neil Found. for Art of Painted Finish, N.Y.C., 1975-77; cons. in crafts, 1965—. V.p. Silvermine Guild of Artists, 1965-68, hospitality chmn., 1958-65. Recipient Service award Silvermine Guild, 1963, Journeyman's medallion O'Neil Studio, 1974. Mem. Embroider's Guild of Am., Needle and Bobbin Club (v.p. 1977-82, pres. 1982-89, bd. dirs. 1989-91), New Canaan Sewing Group (exec. bd. 1977-81), Phi Kappa Phi, Pi Lambda Theta, Kappa Delta Pi. Mormon. Club: New Canaan Garden (exec. bd. 1972-77, v.p. 1987-89, pres. 1989-91), Federated Garden of Conn. Inc. (asst. civic devel. chmn. 1991-93). Home: 788 Ponus Rdg New Canaan CT 06840-3412

CHRISTENSEN, IONE, Canadian senator; b. Oct. 10, 1933; m. Arthur Christensen; children: Paul, Philip. BSBA, Coll. San Mateo. With Govt. Yukon Territory, 1958—67; justice of peace, juvenile ct. judge, chair City of Whitehorse, 1971—75, mayor, 1975—79; commr. Yukon Territory, 1979; pres. Hospitality North Ltd., 1980—86; with Energy, Mines and Resources Can. office City of Whitehorse, 1984—89; chair adv. com. on waste mgmt. Govt. of Yukon, 1989—94; ptnr. Cameras North, 1994—99; senator The Senate of Can., Ottawa, 1999—. Chair Assn. Yukon Municipalities, 1975—79; bd. dirs. Fedn. Can. Muncipalities, Petro-Can., Panarctic Oil Ltd.; chair Yukon Placer Mining Guidelines Rev. Com., 1980—86; vice-chair Yukon Econ. Coun., 1984—89; exec. dir. Crossroads Alcohol and Drug Treatment Ctr., 1989—94; bd. dirs. Nat. Assn. Can. Land Surveyors. Office: 552-N Centre Block The Senate of Canada Ottawa ON Canada K1A 0A4

CHRISTENSEN, JOAN K. state legislator; children: Cara, David, Laura, Michael. Grad., Met. Bus. Coll., Chgo.; student, Syracuse U. Mem. Syracuse Common Coun., Syracuse Bd. Assessment Rev.; mem. 119th dist. N.Y. State Assembly, Syracuse, DeWitt, Onondaga, and Salina, 1990—, chair legis. women's caucus, chair task force on women's issues, chair adminstrv. regulations rev. commn., mem. aging, housing, higher edn., labor, real property taxation, and small bus. coms., hon. mem. Puerto Rican/Hispanic task force, mem. task force worker's compensation reform. Mem. local govt., cities, small bus., labor and aging coms.; hon. mem. N.Y. State Assembly P.R./Hispanic Task Force; served Assembly Task Force Workers' Compensation Reform; mem. Ho., higher Edn., Ins., Labor, Real Property Taxation and Small Bus. Com. Liaison Mayor's Syracuse Commn. Women; mem. City of Syracuse (N.Y.) Bd Assessment Rev., 1984, Syracuse Common Coun., chair fin., taxation and assessment com., Vets. Airport, Pub. Safety, Pub. Works and Transp. Coms.; bd. dirs. Am. Heart Assn., Meals on Wheels, Paul Robeson Performing Arts Co., Eric Trust Meml. Found.; bd. dirs., vice chair Neighborhood Watch Groups of Syracuse; hon. co-chair Pregnancy Hotline Task Force; active Thursday Morning Roundtable; sponsor, advocate Quality Child Care and Protection Act, 2000; chmn. Assembly's Task Force Women's Issues, 1995-2000, Assembly's Adminstrv. Regulation Commn. Recipient Svc. award Greater Eastwood C. of C., 1990, Valley Dem. of Yr. award, 1991, Onondaga County Dem. of Yr. award, 1992, Jeannette Rankin award Onondaga County Women's Polit. Caucus, 1992, Women Working Wonders award YWCA, 1997, Children's Champion award Coalition Child Care of Nassau County, Friend of Children award Child Care Coun. Onondaga County and Syracuse Assn. Edn. Young Children, 1998; named Feminist Legislator of Honor NOW (Ctrl. N.Y.) Mem. VFW Post 1955 Ladies Aux., South Side Bus. Assn., Urban League of Onondaga County, Inc., Women in Govt., Nat. Order of Women's Legislators, Everson Mus. Art Bd. Trustees, Vietnam Vets. Am. (hon., ctrl N.Y. chpt. #103), Met. Bus. and Profl. Women's Club Syracuse, South Side Bus. Assn., Korean War Vets Assn., VFW Post #1955 Ladies Aux., Delta Kappa Gamma. Democrat. Office: NY State Assembly Legislative Office Bldg Rm 502 Albany NY 12248-0001 also: 119th Assembly Dist (Part Onondaga County) 4317 E Genesee St Syracuse NY 13214 Office Phone: 518-455-5383. E-mail: christj@assembly.state.ny.us.

CHRISTENSEN, KAREN KAY, lawyer; b. Ann Arbor, Mich., Mar. 9, 1947; d. Jack Edward and Evangeline (Pitsch) Christensen; m. Kenneth Robert Kay, Sept. 2, 1977; children: Jeffrey Smithson Kay, Braden Kay, Bergen Kay. BS, U. Mich., 1969; JD, U. Denver, 1975. Bar: Colo. 1975, DC 1976, U.S. Supreme Ct. 1979. Atty., advisor office of dep. atty. gen. U.S. Dept. of Justice, Washington, 1975-76, trial atty. civil rights div., 1976-79; legis. counsel ACLU, Washington, 1979-80; staff atty. DC Pub. Defender Svc., Washington, 1980-85; asst. gen. counsel Nat. Pub. Radio, Washington, 1985-93; gen. counsel Nat. Endowment Arts, Washington, 1993-98, acting dep. chmn. for grants and partnership, 1997-98, dep. chmn. grants and awards, 1998—2001; arts cons., 2002—. Mem. DC Bd. Profl. Responsibility, 1990—98, chair, 1996—98. Bd. dirs. Corcoran Art Mus., 2001—03, Liz Lerman Dance Exch., 2002—. Mem.: NCA/ACLU (mem. exec. bd. 1986—93, chair 1993), DC Bar Assn., Phi Beta Kappa.

CHRISTENSEN, KATHLEEN ELIZABETH, foundation administrator; b. Madson, Wis., May 25, 1951; d. Norbert Martin and Janet Cull C.; m. John Joseph Murray III, May 25, 1990; children: Clare, Grace. BS summa cum laude, U. Wis., Green Bay, 1973; MS, Pa. State U., 1979, PhD, 1981. Policy analyst Urban Inst., Washington, 1973-75; from asst. prof. to prof. psychology CUNY, N.Y.C., 1981-91, prof., 1991-99; program dir. Alfred P. Sloan Found., N.Y.C., 1994—. Cons. in field. Author: Women & Home-based Work: The Unspoken Contract, 1988, Turbulence in the Workplace, 1990; editor: The New Era of Homebased Work, 1988, Contingent Work: American Employment Relations in Transition, 1998. Mem. adv. bd. Ctr. Work & Family Boston Coll., 1990-94. Humanities fellow NEH, 1977-79, Danforth fellow Danforth Found., 1979-81, Mellon fellow Aspen Inst., 1982. Mem. AAAS, Am. Sociol. Assn., Am. Anthropol. Assn. Office: Alfred P Sloan Found 630 Fifth Ave New York NY 10111 E-mail: christensen@sloan.org.

CHRISTENSEN, MARGARET ANNA, nurse, health management educator; b. Nov. 10, 1938; d. John Bernard and Catherine (Scott) Thielen; m. Robert Edwin Christensen, June 24, 1961; children: Marthe Elizabeth Christensen Groves, Katrina Marie Christensen Head, Andrea Susan Christensen Clark. BS, Wichita State U., 1978; EdM, U. Cen. Okla., 1984; EdD, Okla. State U., 1986. Staff devel. supr. St. Joseph Med. Ctr., Wichita, Kans., 1972-79; head nurse Bapt. Med. Ctr., Oklahoma City, 1979-80; clin. supr. Mercy Health Ctr., Oklahoma City, 1980-81, staff devel. coord., 1981-84; pres., sr. cons. Human Resource Cons., Inc., Edmond, Okla., 1982-90; dir. planning and devel. Allied Nursing Care, Inc., Oklahoma City, 1984-85; rehab. specialist LDH Cons., Oklahoma City, 1985-90; pres., CEO Christensen Mgmt. Co., Bella Vista, Ark., 1990—, sr. cons.; mktg. mgr. Holiday Retirement Corp., 2003—. Adj. faculty U. Cen. Okla., Edmond, 1986-90; assoc. prof. Ctrl. Mich. U., 2003—; asst. prof., coord. health scis. grad. programs Ohio U., 1990-94, coord. health sci. grad. program, 1994-96; coord. health care mgmt. program, assoc. prof. dept. bus. Shawnee State U., Portsmouth, 1996-2001; dir. Shawnee State Grad. Ctr., 1999-2001; author performance enhancement plans for long-term care employees, 1995, mgrs. and supr. Health Care, 1992; performance enhancement plans for profl., tech. workers in health care, 1992, performance enhancement plans for office/clerical svc. and maintenance workers Health Care, 1992. Author human resource devel. process, 1984, (booklet) Live-In Companion Guide, 1984, report on hosp. appraisal sys. impact, 1986. Bd. dirs. Ohio Presbyn. Retirement Svcs., Columbus. Mem. Am. Coll. Health Care Execs., Am. Coll. Health Care Adminstrs., Assn. Univ. Programs in Health Adminstrn., Alpha Chi, Kappa Delta Pi, Sigma Kappa, Phi Eta Sigma. Republican. Roman Catholic. Home: 33 Sherlock Dr Bella Vista AR 72715-4904 E-mail: rchris@cox-internet.com.

CHRISTENSEN, PAMELA KAREN, pediatric nurse; b. Mason City, Iowa, Aug. 5, 1957; d. Buford LeRoy and Violet Mae (Shepherd) C. AS, North Iowa Area Community Coll, Mason City, 1982. Cert. med. asst. Lakeland Med. Acad., Mpls., 1977. Staff nurse pediat. and med.-surg. unit Boone County Hosp., Boone, Iowa, 1982-84; traveling charge nurse, pediat. and adult Yuma (Ariz.) Med. Ctr., 1985-86, 89, 90-92, White Meml. Hosp., L.A., 1985, City of Faith Hosp., Tulsa, Okla., 1985, charge nurse pediat., staff nurse pediat. ICU, 1986-89; traveling nurse charge pediat. Chinle (Ariz.) Navajo Hosp., 1985; traveling charge nurse pediat. Dallas Children's Med. Ctr., 1989; traveling nurse in pediat. Havasu Samaritan Hosp., Lake Havasu City, Ariz., 1990, 93; traveling pediatric nurse Univ. Med. Ctr., Lubbock, Tex., 1990; traveling pediatric and adult nurse Vanderbilt U. Med. Ctr., Nashville, 1991-92; adult charge nurse and NICU Audubon Humana Hosp., Louisville, 1991-92; traveling pediatric nurse City of Hope Med. Ctr., Duarte, Calif., 1993; traveling pediatric charge nurse St. Vincent Meml. Hosp., Taylorville, Ill., 1993-94; traveling pediatric nurse Jersey Shore Med. Ctr., Neptune, N.J., 1994; traveling pediatric charge nurse Ark. Children's Hosp., Little Rock, 1994; traveling nurse in pediat. Phoenix Children's Hosp., 1995; staff nurse in pediats. ICU Mayo Eugenio Litta Children's Hosp., Rochester, Minn., 1995-98; ASK, Mayo Med. Ctr., 1998—. Spkr. pediat. ICU conf. Mem. Am. Assn. Med. Assts. (past local pres. and state sec.). Home: 329 Chestnut St Osage IA 50461-1920

CHRISTENSEN, PATRICIA ANNE WATKINS, lawyer; b. Corpus Christi, Tex., June 24, 1947; d. Owen Milton Jr. and Margaret (McFarland) Watkins; m. Steven Ray Christensen, May 28, 1977 (dec. 1985); children: Geoffrey Holland, Jeremy Ladd. BS, U. North Tex., 1971; JD, U. Houston, 1977. Bar: Utah 1977, Tex. 1977, U.S. Dist. Ct. Utah 1977, U.S. Ct. Appeals (10th cir.) 1977, U.S. Supreme Ct. 1990. Assoc. Berman & Giauque, Salt Lake City, 1977-80; ptnr. Parr, Waddoups, Brown, Gee & Loveless, Salt Lake City, 1980—, pres., 1991-93, 2002—03. Adj. prof. law U. Utah Law Sch., Salt Lake City, 1979-81; judge pro tem Third Dist. Ct., 1995—. Legis. asst. U.S. Senate, 1970-74; bd. dirs. Comml. Law Affiliate, 1997-2001, co-chair litigation sect.; trustee Rowland Hall St. Mark's Sch., chair devel. com., 1987-90; mem. steering com., comprehensive capital campaign U. Utah Sch. Nursing; mem. steering com. Utah Electronic Law Project. Named Utah Woman Lawyer of Yr., 1992. Mem. ABA, Utah State Bar (Dorothy Merrill Brothers award 1996), State Bar of Tex., Salt Lake County Bar Assn. (exec. com. 1979-87, author editor Utah Lawyers Practice Manual 1986), Women Lawyers Utah (pres. 1988-89, bd. dirs. 1987-90), Phi Delta Phi, Delta Gamma, Alpha Lambda Delta. Office: Parr Waddoups Brown Gee & Loveless 185 S State St Ste 1300 Salt Lake City UT 84111-1537 E-mail: pwc@pwlaw.com.

CHRISTENSON, EILEEN ESTHER, geriatrics nurse; b. Fosston, Minn., July 26, 1950; d. Arthur L. and Gertrude E. (Jaworsky) Maruska; m. Leonard Dale Christenson, Mar. 16, 1968; children: Kristy, Dale, Melissa, Alicia. Grad., Thief River Fall Tech. Inst., Minn., 1967. LPN, Ill., N.Mex., Minn. Staff nurse Beltram (Minn.) Nursing Home, 1990—, Clearwater County Meml. Hosp., Bagley, Minn. Troop leader Land O'Lakes coun. Girl Scouts U.S., 1974-89. 1st lt. USAF, 1968-76, Vietnam. Decorated Purple Heart, Silver Cross, Bronze Star with bronze oak leaf cluster. Mem. VFW, Am. Legion, Eagles 351. Home: 8161 Hillcrest Dr NE Bemidji MN 56601-8531

CHRISTENSON, LINDA, state legislator; m. Duane Christenson; 4 children. BA, MS, Minot State U. English tchr.; mem. N.D. Ho. of Reps. from 18th dist., Bismarck, 1994-98; mem. judicary, govt. and vet. affairs coms. N.D. Ho. of Reps., Bismarck; mem. N.D. Senate from 18th dist., Bismarck, 2000—. Bd. dirs. Firehall Cmty. Theater, United Health Svc. Named Martin Luther King Educator of Yr., N.D., 1991. Mem. Grand Forks Edn. Assn. Address: 3424 Cherry St Apt A5 Grand Forks ND 58201-7692

CHRISTIAN, BETTY JO, lawyer; b. Temple, Tex., July 27, 1936; d. Joe and Mattie Manor (Brown) Wiest; m. Ernest S. Christian, Jr., Dec. 24, 1960. BA summa cum laude, U. Tex., 1957, LL.B. summa cum laude, 1960. Bar: Tex. 1961, U.S. Supreme Ct. 1964, D.C. 1980. Law clk. Supreme Ct. Tex., 1960-61; atty. ICC, 1961-68, asst. gen. counsel, 1970-72, assoc. gen. counsel, 1972-76, commr., 1976-79; ptnr. Steptoe & Johnson, Washington, 1980—. Atty. Labor Dept., Dallas, 1968-70 Fellow Am. Bar Found., Tex. Bar Found.; mem. ABA, FBA (Younger Fed. Lawyer award 1964), Tex. Bar Assn., Am. Law Inst., Am. Acad Appellate Lawyers, Adminstrv. Conf. U.S., City Tavern Club. Office: 1330 Connecticut Ave NW Washington DC 20036-1704 E-mail: bchristi@steptoe.com.

CHRISTIAN, BRENDA JEAN, physician assistant, educator; b. Logan, W.Va., Nov. 6, 1948; d. Ronald Smith and Helen Louise Dingess; m. Thomas Lee Christian, Sept. 4, 1974; children: Kenneth Wade, Kevin Ward, Rikk Anthony Murray. BS, Hahnemann U., 1978; MEd, Antioch U., 1985. Physician asst. Jordan Glaser, MD, S.I., 1992—2000; staff Wagner Coll./SIUH physicians asst. Program, 1999—2000, clin. coord., 2000—01, academic coord., 2001—. Exec. dir. Healthy Living Orgn. Mem.: Am. Acad. Physician Assts. Personal E-mail: bjchristian69@msn.com.

CHRISTIAN, CHERYL LYNN, editor, writer; b. Richmond, Va., July 20, 1953; d. DeLos Horace and Veloa Montgomery Christian; m. Samuel Henderson, Sept. 29, 1990. BFA magna cum laude, Ithaca Coll., 1974; MA, U. Toronto, 1978; MEd, U. Vt., 1982; MA, U. Tex., 1990, PhD, 1995. Prof. Briam Inst., Madrid, 1976—77; tchr. Kennett H.S., Conway, NH, 1982—88; instr. U. Tex., Austin, Tex., 1988—92, St. Edwards U., Austin, 1992; sr. editor Holt, Rinehart & Winston, Austin, 1994—2003, Steck-Vaughn, Austin, Tex., 2003—04; owner Elkhorn Enterprises, 2004—. Bd. dirs. Winnow Press, Austin, Tex.; instr. Austin C.C., Austin, 1989, 91, St. Edwards U., Austin, 1992, Austin C.C., 1994. Contbg. editor: Historic Needlework Guild/Fine Lines, 1998—; contbr. articles to mags. and profl. jours. Mem. Nat. Coun. Tchrs. English, Ill., 1981—. Mem.: Internat. Reading Assn. Home and Office: 7912 Elkhorn Mountain Trail Austin TX 78729-6407

CHRISTIAN, MARY JO DINAN, educational administrator, educator; b. Denver, May 7, 1941; d. Joseph Timothy and Margaret Rose Dinan; m. Ralph Poinsett Christian, Aug. 27, 1966. BA, Loretto Heights Coll., Denver, 1964; MA, George Washington U., 1983. Cert. English educator, adminstrn. and supervision secondary edn. English tchr. Denver Pub. Schs., 1964-67, Prince George's County Pub. Sch., Md., 1967-81; vice-prin. Prince George's County High Sch., Md., 1981-97; program dir. Tchr. Equity Equals Achievement, 1997—99, tchr., mentor, 2002—. Presenter tchr. equity and student achievement Nat. Conf.; Generating Expectations for Student Achievement equity assurance coord. instrs. in-svc. and adminstrs., 1997—99; tchr. mentor, 2002; pres. Tchr. Equity Equals Student Achievement Inc.; owner Independence House Bed and Breakfast, Washington, 2000—. Columnist: WomenSpeak, 1981-91. Rep. Prince George's County Commn. Women UN Fourth World Conf. Women Forum, Beijing, 1995. Md. Ho. of Dels. recognition 1984. Mem. NAFE, ASCD, NEA (chair adminstrs. caucus 1991-93, adminstr.-at-large resolutions com. 1986-92, polit. action com. 1984-86, coord.-at-large women's caucus 1981-91, Creative Leadership award 1989), Md. State Tchrs. Assn. (state coord. Sen. Sarbane campaign 1982, state voter registration coord. 1984, issue coord. Tom McMillen campaign 1986, Women's Rights award 1988), Phi Delta Kappa, Alpha Delta Kappa. Home: 504 Independence Ave SE Washington DC 20003-1143

CHRISTIAN, MICHAELE CHAMBLEE, internist, oncologist; b. 1948; MD, Georgetown U., Washington, 1980. Diplomate Am. Bd. Internal Medicine. Assoc. dir. CTEP, NCI, Bethesda, Md. Mem.: Am. Assn. Cancer Rsch. (bd. dirs.). Office: National Cancer Inst Executive Plz N Rm 742 6130 Executive Blvd Bethesda MD 20892

CHRISTIAN, PEARL C, musician; b. N.Y.C., July 18, 1927; d. Joseph Obadiah and Clotilda Cecelia Clifton; m. Lloyd Micah Christian, Jan. 28, 1948; children: Peter Lloyd, Donna Laverne, Lawrence Micah. Piano instr. Queens Village Sch. of Music, N.Y., 1989—91, pvt. studio, N.Y., 1991—. Performer: (Concert) Bklyn. Queens Conservatory Music, 2000—04.

CHRISTIAN, SANDRA SVEC, retired state official; b. Evanston, Ill., Dec. 11, 1947; d. Joseph Francis and Martha Marjorie (Randau) Svec; m. Terry L. Yonker, June 28, 1969 (div. 1990); m. Bernard L. Christian, Aug. 20, 2001. BS in Meteorology, U. Wis., Madison, 1969. Sec., sales asst. Moore Bus. Forms Inc., Lansing, Mich., 1970-72; rsch. asst. Mich. Dept. Social Svcs., Lansing, 1972-74; adminstrv. analyst Mich. Pub. Svc. Commn., Lansing, 1974-79, supr. orgn. devel., 1980-84; program mgr. Gov.'s Energy Awareness Adv. Com., Lansing, 1979-80; labor rels. rep. Mich. Dept. Agr., Lansing, 1984-87, acting personnel dir., 1987-89, asst. to chief dep. dir., 1989-93, dir. EEO/affirmative action office, 1991-97, program mgr. human resources, 1997—2000; benefit analyst Human Resource Mgmt. Network, 1998—2002, ret., 2002. Bd. dirs. Lansing Area Advocates for Choice, 1991-93, Downtown Neighborhood Assn., Lansing, 1990—, v.p., 1992-95, sec., 1998-2000; vol. Radio Talking Book, East Lansing, Mich., 1974-93, Am. Cancer Soc. Relay for Life, 2003—; active Stratford (Ont., Can.), Shakespearean Festival, 1974—; Marshal vol. co-chair Oldsmobile Classic Ladies PGA event, East Lansing, 1993-96, Marshal vol., 1997-98, mdse. vol. co-team leader, 1999-2000; mem. Covenant Assn. United Ch. of Christ, Church and Ministry Com., 1992-96, chair, 1996. Mem.: Am. Bus. Women's Assn. (treas. Virgo chpt. 1998—2000, Woman of the Yr. award 1977), Friday Frolics. Avocations: golf, walking, community theater, conservation. Home: 1512 Settlers Hill Dr Lansing MI 48917-1284 E-mail: kangaroo333@comcast.net.

CHRISTIAN, SUZANNE HALL, financial planner; b. Hollywood, Calif., Apr. 28, 1935; d. Peirson M. and Gertrude (Engel) Hall; children: Colleen, Carolyn, Claudia, Cynthia. BA, UCLA, 1956; MA, Redlands U., 1979. CFP. Instr. L.A. City Schs., 1958-59, Claremont (Calif.) Unified Schs., 1972-84, dept. chair, 1981-84; fin. planner Waddell & Reed, Upland, Calif., 1982-96, sr. acct. exec., 1986; br. mgr. Hornor, Townsend & Kent, Claremont, 1996—2002, Linsco Pvt. Ledger Fin. Svcs., 2002—. Past corp. mem. Pilgrim Place Found., Claremont; lectr. in field. Author: Strands in Composition, 1979; TV cable host Money Talks with Suzanne Christian, 1993—. Legal and estate planning com. Am. Cancer Soc., 1988-95; profl. adv. com. YWCA-Inland Empire, 1987; treas. Fine Arts Scripps Coll., 1993-94; bd. dirs. Casa Colina Hosp., 1994-2003; past bd. dirs. Galelio Soc. Harvey Mudd Coll. Recipient Athena Internat. Businesswoman of Yr. award, 1997. Mem. Inst. CFPs, Fin. Planning Assn., Planned Giving Roundtable, Estate Planning Coun. Pomona Valley (pres. 2001-2002, bd. dirs.), Claremont C. of C. (pres., bd. dirs. 1994-95), Curtain Raisers Club Garrison (pres. 1972-75), Circle of Champions (pres.'s coun. 1994-95, Silver Crest award 1985-87, 94-95, HTK top ten leader 1996-2003), Harvey Mudd Coll. Galileo Soc. (bd. dirs. 1997-98), Kappa Kappa Gamma (pres. 1970-74). Avocations: tennis, gardening, archaeology. Home: PO Box 1237 Claremont CA 91711-1237 Office: Hornor Townsend & Kent 419 Yale Ave Claremont CA 91711-4340 Fax: 909-625-3661.

CHRISTIAN-CHRISTENSEN, DONNA MARIE, congresswoman; b. Teaneck, N.J., Sept. 19, 1945; d. Almeric L. Christian and Virginia Sterling; children: Rabiah Green, Karida Green; m. Chris Christensen; stepchildren: Lisa, Esther, Bryan, David. BS, St. Mary's Coll., Ind., 1966; MD, George Washington U., 1970; LLD (hon.), Moravian Coll. Pvt. medical practice, 1973—74; cmty. health physician U.S. V.I. Dept. Health; med. dir. Gov. Juan F. Luis Hosp., St. Croix; vice chairperson U.S. V.I. Dem. Territorial Com., 1980; mem. U.S. V.I. Bd. Edn., 1984; committeewoman Nat. Dem., 1984; apptd. U.S. V.I. Status Commn., 1988-92; del. Dem. Nat. Conv.; at large repr. from V.I. U.S. Ho. of Reps., 1997—; chair Congl. Black Caucus Health Braintrust, 1999—. Mem. Resources Com., Small Bus. Com.; mem. Select Com. Homeland Security; mem. Congl. Caucus Women's Issues; mem. Steering Com. Congl. Travel and Tourism Caucus; mem. Congl. Rural Caucus, Congl. Nat. Guard and Res. Caucus. Trustee, founding mem. Caribbean Youth Orgn. Recipient Disting. Alumni award, George Washington U., Disting. Svc. award, Howard U. Sch. Medicine. Mem. Nat. Med. Assn. (trustee), Caribbean Studies Assn., V.I. Med. Inst., V.I. Med. Soc. (pres., sec.), Women's Coalition St. Croix, St. Croix Environ. Assn. Democrat. Achievements include first to be the female delegate from U.S. Virgin Islands. Office: 1510 Longworth Ho Office Bldg Washington DC 20515-0001 E-mail: donna.christensen@mail.house.gov.*

CHRISTIANSEN, LAURI A. marketing professional; b. Huntington, N.Y., May 30, 1964; d. Jack H. and Gladys M. Christiansen. BS in Mktg.and English, Pa. State U., 1987; postgrad. in MBA program, Hofstra U., 2000—. Mktg. coord. and cons. Roux Assocs., Inc., Hauppauge, NY, 1991—95; mktg. specialist MSC Indsl. Direct Inc., Melville, NY, 1996—98, program mgr., 1998—2001; mgr. corp. devel. brand mktg. A.D.I., Melville, 2001—. Office: ADI 263 Old Country Rd Melville NY 11747 Home: 24 West Dr Kings Park NY 11754-3815

CHRISTIANSEN, PEGGY, principal; Prin. Sequoia Elem. Sch., Santa Rosa, Calif., Blinkley Elem. Sch., Santa Rosa, Calif., 1995—. Recipient Elem. Sch. Recognition award U.S. Dept. Edn., 1989-90. Office: Blinkley Elem Sch 4965 Canyon Dr Santa Rosa CA 95409-3204

CHRISTINA, SONJA (ALISA MORRIS), writer, poet; b. Dec. 21, 1925; m. Desmond Halton Morris, June 17, 1950; 1 child, Belinda. Owner La Esmeralda Club and Restaurant, London, 1947—50; owner art gallery Domani, N.Y.C., 1968. Model for painter Sir Augustus John, London, 1941-43; dancer Phillis Dixy Prodns., London, 1943-45. Author: (poetry) Emotions, 1973, If, 2002, The Secret to Her Heart, 2002, Ground Zero, 2002; prodr. (play) The Future Was Yesterday, 1952; poem displayed at Mus. of Tolerance. Recipient 10 Merit awards World of Poetry, Outstanding Poetry award Am. Poetry Assn., 1986, Golden Poet award World of Poetry, 1985, 86, 88, 90, 91, 1st prize in short story Globe Contest, 1984, Editors Choice award Internat. Libr. Poetry, 1999, Recognition award Famous Poets Soc., 1999, Poets Fantasy award, 2000, Outstanding Achivement award Drury's Publs., 2002; world record holder (for personal jours.-286) Guinness Book of World Records. Mem. Internat. Soc. Poets (hon. charter mem.). Home: PO Box 142 Lenox Hill New York NY 10021-0012

CHRISTISON, MURIEL BRANHAM, retired art museum director, fine arts educator; b. Mpls. d. Harold D. and Helen (Ferguson) Branham; children: Evelyn, Carolyn. BA, U. Minn., 1933, MA, 1940; diploma, U. Paris, 1936, U. Brussels, 1938. Grad. asst. Dept. Fine Arts U. Minn., Mpls., 1933-36; curatorial rsch. asst. Mpls. Inst. Arts, Mpls., 1936-42, head edn., 1944-47; assoc. dir. Va. Mus. Fine Arts, Richmond, 1948-61; oper. and assoc. dir. Krannert Art Mus. U. Ill., Champaign, 1962-74, dir. Krannert Art Mus., 1975-82; ret., 1982; interim dir. Muscarelle Mus. Coll. William and Mary, Williamsburg, Va., 1984-85, 94-96, mem. vis. com., 1982-96, vis. prof. fine arts, 1983-98. Head program mus. studies U. Ill., 1974—82; cons. U. Tex., Austin, Washington U. St. Louis, 1972—78; v.p. Midwest Mus. Conf. Am. Assn. Mus., regional rep., 1972—82; examiner S.C. Arts Coun., 1984, 86, Ohio Arts Coun., 1986. Carnegie scholar Inst. Internat. Edn., 1936; CRB fellow Beligan-Am. Edn. Found., 1938; recipient Disting. Svc. award Midwest Mus. Conf., 1982, hon. nominee Va. Mus. Libr. Fund, 2003. Mem.: Colonial Williamsburg Fund, William and Mary Found., Coun. Va. Mus. Fine Arts, Assn. Preservation Va. Antiquities, Am. Assn. Museums (regional rep. 1972—82, coun. 1972—82, surveyor, examiner 1982—), Assn. Art Mus. Dirs. (emerita 1982, hon. 1982—), Cosmopolitan Club (N.Y.C.). Home: 257 Littletown Quarter Williamsburg VA [illegible] E-mail: [illegible]@aol.com.

CHRISTMAN, JILL COREY, literature educator, writer; b. Miami, Fla., Aug. 16, 1969; d. Peter Sanford and Martha Ingraham Christman; m. Mark Allen Neely, Apr. 18, 2003. BA with honors, U. Oreg., 1992; MFA, U. Ala., Tuscaloosa, 1999. Rsch. asst. psychology dept. U. Oreg., Eugene, 1992—95; instr. English dept. U. Ala., Tuscaloosa, 1999—2001; coord. creative writing program English dept. U. Minn., Mpls., 2001—02; asst. prof. English dept. Ball State U., Muncie, Ind., 2002—. Author: (memoir) Darkroom: A Family Exposure (Associated Writing Programs Award for Creative Nonfiction, 2001). Mem.: Phi Beta Kappa. Office: English Dept Ball State Univ Muncie IN 47306-0460 Office Phone: 765-285-8534. E-mail: jcchristman@bsv.edu.

CHRISTMAN, JOLLEY BRUCE, educational research executive, educator; b. Greenville, S.C., Aug. 30, 1947; d. James McDuffie and Mamie (Jolley) Bruce; children: Andrew, Kate, Sarah. BA, Randolph-Macon Woman's Coll., 1969; MS in Edn., U. Pa., 1971, PhD, 1987. Cert. secondary English and social studies tchr., Pa.; cert. prin., Pa. Tchr. Phila. Sch. Dist., 1970-75; lectr., cons. Grad. Sch. Edn. U. Pa., Phila., 1975-84; rsch. assoc. Phila. Sch. Dist., 1985-90, cons., 1990-92; pres. Rsch. for Action, Phila., 1992—. Bd. dirs. Coun. on Anthropology and Edn. Author: Anthropology and Education Quarterly, 1987, (chpt.) Speaking the Language of Power, 1993. Bd. dirs. Community Edn. Ctr., Phila., 1993—, Grad. Sch. Edn. Alumni Assn., U. Pa., Phila., 1990—. Recipient Ethnographic Evaluation award Am. Anthrop. Assn., 1992. Democrat. Episcopalian. Office: Rsch for Action 3701 Chestnut St Philadelphia PA 19104

CHRISTOFFEL, KATHERINE KAUFER, pediatrician, epidemiologist, educator; b. N.Y.C., June 28, 1948; d. George and Sonya (Firstenberg) Kaufer; m. Tom Christoffel, 1970 (div. 1992); children: Kevin, Kimberly. BA, Radcliffe Coll., 1969; MD, Tufts U., 1973; MPH, Northwestern U., 1981. Diplomate Am. Bd. Pediat., Nat. Bd. Med. Examiners. Intern Columbus (Ohio) Children' Hosp., 1972-73; resident then fellow Children's Meml. Hosp., Chgo., 1973-76; asst. prof. Sch. Medicine U. Chgo., 1976-79; asst. prof., then assoc. prof. Northwestern U. Med. Sch., Chgo., 1979-91, prof., 1991—; dir. Nutrition Evaluation Clinic Children's Meml. Hosp., Chgo., 1982-2000; med. dir. violent injury prevention ctr. Children's Meml. Med. Ctr., Chgo., 1993—. Chmn. steering com. Handgun Epidemic Lowering Plan, Chgo., 1993—; dir. then assoc. dir. Pediatric Practice Rsch. Group, Chgo., 1984-97; dir. statis. scis. and epidemiology program Children's Meml. Inst. for Edn. and Rsch., 1994—. Contbr. numerous articles to med. jours. Recipient M. Fay Spencer Disting. Woman Physician Scientist award Nat. Bd. Hahnemann Med. Sch., 1997. Fellow Am. Acad. Pediatrics (spokesperson on firearms 1985—, injury com. 1985-93, coun. on pediatric rsch. 1996-2000, chair adolescent violence task force 1994, 1st Injury Control award 1992); mem. APHA (Disting. Career award 1991), Am. Coll. Epidemiology, Soc. for Pediatric Rsch., Ambulatory Pediatric Assn. (bd. mem. 2000—, Rsch. award 2000). Avocations: hiking, walking, creative writing, photography. Office: Childrens Meml Hosp 2300 N Childrens Plz # 208 Chicago IL 60614-3394

CHRISTOFOROUS, ALEXIS, reporter; b. N.Y.C., N.Y. BA in Journalism, BA in English, NYU. Reporter, anchor Bloomberg Bus. Report, Bloomberg Morning Show, Conn., CBS Marketwatch.com, 1999—. Hostess Educated Investor TV show, Various markets, 2000—. Office: CBS 524 W 57th St New York NY 10019

CHRISTOPH, FRANCES, painter; b. Bronxville, N.Y., Mar. 27, 1931; d. Charles DeGuire and Reba (Skipwith) Christoph; m. Charles Robert Salerno, Apr. 4, 1952; 1 stepchild, Franklin Robert Salerno; children: Lucia Salerno Lilien, Christoph Robert Salerno. Student, Art Students League, 1945-49, Adelphia Coll., 1948, Temple U., 1949-50, State U. Iowa, 1950-51, U. Paris Sorbonne, 1951-52, Acad. de la Grande Chaumiere, Paris, 1951-52. One-man show South Mainland Libr., Micco, Fla., 2003; exhibited in shows at Am. Students and Artists Ctr., Paris, Pietrantonio Galleries, N.Y.C., S.I. Mus., Richmond Art Gallery, S.I., Internat. Art Exhbn., Mojacar, Spain, others; writer, editor: Salerno Sculpture, 1965. Mem.: Royal Scottish Country Dance Soc., Nat. Mus. Women in the Arts (Fla. com.), Strawbridge Art League, Brevard Watercolor Soc., Archives Nat. Mus. Women in Arts, Art Students League (life). Democrat. Episcopalian. Avocation: gardening. Home: 5828 Lindsay Rd Micco FL 32976-2604 E-mail: fansale@aol.com.

CHRISTOPHER, DORIS K. consumer products company executive; m. Jay Christopher, 1967; children: Julie, Kelley. BS in Home Econs., U. Ill., 1967. Cert. in family and consumer svcs. H.S. home econs. tchr.; with U. Ill. Coop. Extension Svc.; founder, chmn. The Pampered Chef Ltd., Addison, Ill., 1980—. Appeared on various TV programs including Oprah Winfrey Show, NBC Weekend Today, CNBC, CNN. Author: Come to the Table: A Celebration of Family Life, 1999. Recipient Torch award Marketplace Ethics, Better Bus. Bureau, Chgo. & No. Ill., 1998. Mem.: Direct Selling Assn. (bd. dirs. 1992—, past chairperson), Am. Assn. Family and Consumer Scis., America's Second Harvest, Com. of 200. Office: The Pampered Chef 1 Pampered Chef Lane Addison IL 60101-5630*

CHRISTOPHER, IRENE, librarian, consultant; b. Greece, Nov. 17, 1922; came to U.S., 1923; d. George and Helen (Stephens) C. AB, Boston U., 1944; BLS, Simmons Coll., 1945. Gen. asst. Robbins Pub. Libr., Arlington, Mass., 1945-46, Boston U. Chenery Libr., 1946-47, head circulation dept., 1947-48, head reference dept., 1948-62; dir. libr. Emerson Coll., Boston, 1962-68; dir. Gordon McKay libr. Harvard U., Cambridge, Mass., 1968-70; chief libr. Boston U. Med. Ctr., 1970-92. Mem. AAUW, ALA (various coms. 1962-82, coun. 1970-74), Spl. Librs. Assn. (various coms. Boston chpt. 1952-75), Am. Soc. Info. Sci., Women's Nat. Book Assn., North Atlantic Health Scis. Librs., Med. Libr. Assn., New Eng. Online Users Group, Inc., Mass. Libr. Assn., Boston U. Women's Coun. Home: 790 Boylston St Apt 11C Boston MA 02199-7911

CHRISTOPHER, SHARON A. BROWN, bishop; b. Corpus Christi, Tex., July 24, 1944; d. Fred L. and Mavis Lorraine (Krueger) Brown; m. Charles Edmond Logsdon Christopher, June 17, 1973. BA, Southwestern U., Georgetown, Tex., 1966; MDiv, Perkins Sch. Theology, 1969; DD, Southwestern U., 1990; DST, McMurray Coll., 1996. Ordained to ministry United Meth. Ch., 1970; elected bishop 1988. Dir. Christian Edn. First United Meth. Ch., Appleton, Wis., 1969-70, assoc. pastor, 1970-72; pastor Butler United Meth. Ch., Butler, Wis., 1972-76, Calvary United Meth. Ch., Germantown, Wis., 1972-76, Aldersgate United Meth. Ch., Milw., 1976-80; dist. supt. Ea. Dist. Wis. Conf. United Meth. Ch., 1980-85; asst. to bishop Wis. Conf. Wis. Conf. United Meth. Ch., Sun Prairie, Wis., 1986-88; bishop North Cen. jurisdiction United Meth. Ch., Minn., 1988-96, bishop Ill. area, 1996—, resident bishop Ill. area Springfield, 1996—. Contbr. articles and papers to religious publs. Bd. dirs. Nat. Coun. Chs. of Christ, 1988—, United Meth. Ch. Bd. of Ch. & Soc., 1988-92, bd. discipleship, 1992—; trustee Hamline U., St. Paul, 1988-96; gen. and jurisdictional conf. del., 1976, 80, 84, 88; mem. N. Cen. Jurisdiction Com. on Episcopacy, 1984-88, Com. on Investigation, 1980-88, Gen. Bd. Global Ministries, 1980-88, chmn. Mission Pers. Resources Program Dept., 1984-88. Named one of Eighty for the Eighties, Milw. Jour., 1980.

CHRISTOPHERSON, ELIZABETH GOOD, broadcast executive; b. Cin. d. Walter R. and Jean S. Good; m. Paul C. Christopherson; 1 child, Katherine. BA, Wellesley Coll. Bd. dirs. N.J. State Coun. Arts, 1982—, chmn., CEO, 1989—91; exec. dir. N.J. Pub. TV and Radio, Trenton, 1991—; pres. NJN Found., 1994—. Bd. dirs. PNC Bank N.J., PBS, Liberty Sci. Ctr., Wellesley Coll. Bus. Leadership Coun. Pres., bd. dirs. Leadership Am. Assn., Alexandria, Va., 1991—92; bd. dirs. N.J. Tech. Coun. Mem.: Internat. Woman's Forum (past pres. N.J. chpt.). Office: NJ Network PO Box 777 Trenton NJ 08625-0777

CHRISTOPHERSON, KAREN MARIE, education educator; b. Huron, SD, May 5, 1953; d. Ardis Brammer and Kenneth Burnette Peterson; m. Martin Louis Christopherson, Dec. 28, 1974; children: Dustin Charles, Darby Marie, Danielle Rae. BS, No. State U., 1971—75. Vocal/instrumental dir. Woonsocket Pub. Schools, SD, 1975—80, Wolsey Pub. Schools, SD, 1980—88; vocal music dir. Wessington Springs Pub. Schools, SD, 1988. Recipient Disting. Svc. award, Wessington Springs H.S., 1998, Bronze Staff Recognition award, SD Music Ecucators Assn., 2000. Mem.: SD Choral Directors Assn., SD Music Educators Assn. (assoc.). Home: 202 Pershing Ave North Wessington Springs SD 57382 Office: Wessington Springs Sch Dist 301 Dakota North Wessington Springs SD 57382

CHRISTY, CINDY, telecommunications industry executive; m. Randy Christy; 4 children. BBA, Am. U. Joined AT&T Network Sys., 1988, various mgmt. positions in market rsch., market mgmt., sales, product planning, project mgmt. and product mgmt.; dir. CDMA/PCS Project Mgmt. Lucent Techs., Murray Hill, NJ, 1995—98, v.p. AMPS/PCS product mgmt. and mktg., 1998—2000, COO wireless networks group, 2001, COO mobility solutions group, 2002—03, pres. mobility solutions group, 2004—. Mem.: Cellular Telecom. Industry Assn. (bd. dirs., mem. exec. com.). Office: Lucent Techs 600 Mountain Ave Murray Hill NJ 07974

CHRISTY, CONNIE ANNETTE, music educator, webmaster; b. Richwood, W.Va., May 27, 1961; d. Alfred Lewis and Alberta Mae O'Brien; m. Robert Elliott Christy, Jan. 1, 1984; children: Jeremiah Luke, Denrey Hamilton. BA in Music Edn., West Liberty State Coll., West Liberty, W.Va., 1983; MA of Tech. in Edn., Lesley U., Boston, 2002. Cert. tchr. music edn. K-12 S.C., 1988, grant writing specialist SC., 1999. Music tchr. West Greene Sch. Dist., Graysville, Pa., 1983—88, Marion Sch. Dist. #2, Mullins, SC, 1988—94, Horry County Schs., Conway, SC, 1994—. Band dir. Blue Pan Jam Steel Band, Aynor, SC, 1998—; webmaster Aynor Elem. Sch., SC, 2000—, Myrtle Beach Elem. Sch., SC, 2002—; web servant Conway Ch. of Christ, Conway, 2001—. Dir.: (steel drum & african drum bands) Blue Pan Jam (Grammy Award for Excellence in Music Edn., 1992), D.R.U.M. Band. Area coord. Spl. Olympics, Aynor, 2002—03; bible study tchr. Conway Ch. of Christ, Conway, SC, 1994—2003. Named Tchr. of the Yr., Horry County Sch. Dist., 2003—, Aynor Elem. Sch., 2002—03, Wal-Mart (Conway, SC), 1997, Mullins Sch. Dist. #2, 1990; recipient, North Mullins Primary Sch., 1990, Golden Apple, WBTW TV Sta., 1996; grantee Target 2000 Arts in Edn. grantee, S.C. Dept. of Edn., 2000, Small Tchr. grantee, 1997. Mem.: Music Educators Nat. Conf. Church Of Christ. Avocations: musician, horseback riding, hot sauce creator, camping, gardening. Home: 1465 Butler Rd Galivants Ferry SC 29544 Office: Aynor Elem Sch 516 Jordanville Rd Galivants Ferry SC 29544 Office Phone: 843-358-3680 220. Personal E-mail: bobcon@sccoast.net. E-mail: cchrist@ae.hcs.k12.sc.us.

CHROMOW, SHERI P. lawyer; b. N.Y.C., Aug. 27, 1946; d. Abe and Sara L. Pinsky. BA, Barnard Coll., N.Y.C., 1968; JD, NYU, 1971. Ptnr. Shearman & Sterling, N.Y.C., 1979—2001, Katten, Muchin, Zavis Rosenman, N.Y.C., 2001—. Lectr. Practising Law Inst., N.Y. County Bar Assn., Urban Land Inst.; mem. exec. com. N.Y. dist. coun. U. L.I.; mem. adv. bd. Furman Real Estate Inst. N.Y.U. Law Sch. ; mem. adv. bd. Ticor Title Ins. Co; judge Real Estate Bd. N.Y. Bd. dirs. Bklyn. (N.Y.) Philharm. Orch. Recipient Most Ingenious Deal of Yr. award, Real Estate Bd. N.Y. Mem. Urban Land Inst. (gen. counsel), Assn. Fgn. Investors in Real Estate. Office: Katten Muchin Zavis Rosenman 575 Madison Ave New York NY 10022 Office Phone: 212-940-8529. Business E-Mail: sheri.chromow@kmzr.com.

CHRONISTER, ROCHELLE BEACH, former state legislator; b. Neodesha, Kans., Aug. 27, 1939; m. Bert Chronister, 1961; children: Pam, Phillip. AB, U. Kans. State rep. dist. 13 Kans. Ho. of Reps., until 1999; former asst. majority leader; sec. for social and rehab. svcs. Kans. Cabinet, 1995-99. Chmn. Kans. Rep. Party, 1989—. Named Woman of Yr., Neodesha C. of C. Mem. AMA (aux.), Bus. and Profl. Women. Methodist. Home: RR 2 Box 321 A Neodesha KS 66757-9562

CHRZANOWSKI, LEYE JEANNETTE, publisher; b. Aug. 28, 1946; Student, Ctrl. Tex. Coll., 1978-79, Enterprise State Jr. Coll., 1982-83. Pres., founder Excel Networking Group, Inc., Va., 1991-94; v.p., exec. editor EKA Comms., Md., 1993-97; pres. Disability News Svc., Chantilly, Va., 1997—2000, Disability Press Assn., 2000—. Mem. Soc. Profl. Journalists, Investigative Reporters and Editors, Soc. Disability Studies, Washington Ind. Writers. Office: 13703 Southernwood Ct Chantilly VA 20151-3345 E-mail: leyech@cox.net.

CHRZANOWSKI, ROSE-ANN CANNIZZO, art educator; b. Bklyn., Mar. 13, 1952; d. Francis Salvatore and Vincenza Pilaro Cannizzo; m. Raymond David Chrzanowski; 1 child, Karen Kuczenski. BA, CUNY, Bklyn., 1974; MS, Fordham U., 1977; postgrad., So. Conn. State U., 1990. Cert. in elem. edn. N.Y. Permanent Tchg. Cert., Conn. Profl. Tchg. Cert., in art Conn. Profl. Tchg. Cert., art EAYA. 3d grade tchr. St. Michael Sch., Bklyn., 1974—78; art tchr. Naugatuck Elem. Schs., Naugatuck, Conn., 1978—90; tchr. City Hill Mid. Sch., Naugatuck, 1990—2000, Naugatuck H.S., 2000—. Tchr., tutor supr. Naugatuck Youth Svcs., 1978—84; edn. program coord. Human Resources Devel. Agy., Naugatuck, 1985—87; adj. prof. Teikyo Post U., Waterbury, Conn., 1996; mem. adv. coun. Celebration Excellence, New Haven, 1998—. Contbg. author: Doing What's Right in the Middle, Promising Practices of Schools with Middle Grades, 1999. Chmn. Naugatuck Arts Commn., 1996—98; nat. tchr. forum rep. State Dept. Edn., 2001. Recipient Emeritus award, Celebration Excellence, 1999. Mem.: NEA, Conn. Art Edn. Assn., Nat. Art Edn. Assn., Phi Delta Kappa. Office: Naugatuck HS 543 Rubber Ave Naugatuck CT 06770 Personal E-mail: rayrochrz@earthlink.net.

CHU, DEH-YING, chemist, researcher; b. Shanghai, Nov. 13, 1944; came to the U.S., 1981; d. Han Chang Chu and Cai Di Xu; (div. 1995); children: Kevin S. Lu, Xiao Qin Lu. MS, U. Sci. & Tech., Beijing, 1981; PhD, U. Notre Dame, 1986. Asst. faculty fellow U. Notre Dame, South Bend, Ind., 1987-90; R&D chemist Calgon Corp., Pitts., 1990—2000. Symposium presenter Photochemistry and Photophysics, 1996. Contbr. articles to books. Mem. ACS (polymer divsn., analytical chemistry divsn.). Home: 385 Wells Ter West Chester PA 19380-2138 Office: Kensey Nash Corp 55 E Uwchlan Ave Exton PA 19341-1204

CHU, JUDY MAY, psychology educator, city official; b. L.A., July 7, 1955; d. Judson and May C.; m. Michael Eng, Aug. 8, 1978. BA in Math., UCLA, 1974; MA in Clin. Psychology, Calif. Sch. Profl. Psychology, 1977, PhD, 1979. Lectr. UCLA, 1980-86; assoc. prof. L.A. City Coll., 1981-88; prof. East L.A. Coll., Monterey Park, 1988—2001; mem. Calif. Ho. of Reps., 2001—. Author, editor: Linking Our Lives: Chinese American Women in Los Angeles, 1984; contbr. articles profl. jours. Mem. city coun. City of Monterey Park, 1988—, mayor, 1990-91, 94-95; bd. dirs. Garvey Sch. Dist., 1985-88; chair Commn. for Sex Equity, L.A. Unified Sch. Dist., 1984-85; bd. dirs. Rebuild L.A.; mem. adv. com. U.S. Census Bur., 1994—; Bd. dirs. Gabriel Valley chpt. ARC; bd. dirs. Asian Youth Ctr., San Gabriel

Valley United Way, West San Gabriel Valley Juvenile Deversion Project. Named One of 88 Leaders for 1988, L.A. Times, 1988, Dem. of Yr., 59th Assembly Dist. Dem. Com., 1989, Vol. of Yr. San Gabriel Valley chpt. United Way, 1989, L.A. Outstanding Founder, 1995; recipient Achievement award Asian Pacific Family Ctr., 1980, Pub. Svc. award Asian Pacific Legal Ctr., 1989, award for Excellence in Pub. Svc., UCLA Alumni, 1991, Leadership award West San Gabriel Valley chpt. ARC. Mem. Soroptimists. Office: PO Box 942849 Sacramento CA 94249

CHU, LILI, jewelry designer, consultant; b. Hong Kong, Aug. 14, 1960; d. Woon Charn and Wai (Sau) C.; 1 child, Cassandra Chu Currens. BFA in Illustration, Parsons Sch. Design, 1984. Jewelry designer Carvin French, Inc., N.Y.C., 1987-89; design dir. Omar Torres, Inc., N.Y.C., 1992-94; jewelry designer Avon Products, Inc., N.Y.C., 1994-96; design dir. Mikimoto, N.Y.C., 1996—. Designer of collection for Mikimoto Internat., Walt Disney Art Classics: Fantasia 2000, Burbank, Calif.; cons. for Avons Products, Smithsonian Instn. Product Devel., Washington, 1994-96. Recipient 26th ann. Internat. Pearl Design contest Japan Pearl Promotion Soc., 1998, Jewelry Hons. with Josie Natori Asia Soc., 1998. Avocations: tennis, bird watching, photography, painting, motherhood. Office: Mikimoto 40 W 57th St New York NY 10019-4001

CHU, MARGARET S. Y. federal agency administrator; b. Jan. 10, 1946; BS in Chemistry, Purdue U., 1967; PhD in Phys. Chemistry, U. Minn., 1973. Mem. tech. staff Sandia Nat. Labs., Albuquerque, 1980-86, disting. mem. tech. staff, 1986-91, tech. mgr., 1991-97, sr. mgr. nuclear waste mgmt., 1997-99, dir. nuclear waste mgmt., 1999—2002; Dir Civilian Radioactive Waste Mgt Dept Energy, Washington, 2002—. Contbr. numerous articles to sci. and profl. jours. Founding faculty mem. Albuquerque Chinese Sch., 1980. Mem. Am. Chem. Soc., N.M. Chinese Assn., Chinese Inst. Engrs. (bd. dirs., officer N.Mex. chpt. 1997-98). Office: Dept Energy Cicilian Radioactive Waste Mgt 1000 Independence Ave SW Washington DC 20585-0001

CHUGHTAI, RAANA LYNN, psychiatric nurse practitioner; d. Arshad Iqbal and Lynnette Janet Chughtai. BSN, U. Pitts., 2000. RN Pa., 2001. Crisis clinician Mercy Behavioral Health, Pitts., 2000—02, nurse/therapist Wexford, Pa., 2002—. Rsch. asst. U. Pitts., 1999—2000. Mem.: Grad. Nursing Student Orgn., Am. Psychiat. Nurses Assn., Three Rivers Rowing Assn., Golden Key.

CHULA, MARGARET JEAN, poet, writer; b. Brattleboro, Vt., Oct. 10, 1947; AS, Bay Path Coll., 1967. Engl. instr. Kyoto Seika Coll., 1982—92, Doshisha Women's Coll., Kyoto, 1983—92; instr. Artists in the Schs., Portland, Oreg., 1995—; editor, owner Katsura Press, Portland, 1992—. Author: Book of Haiku, Grinding My Ink, 1993 (Haiku Soc. of Am. Merit Book award, 1994); author: (with R. Youmans) Book of Haibum, Shadow Lines, 1999; author: Book of Tanka, Always Filling, Always Full, 2001, Book of Haiku, The Smell of Rust, 2003. Bd. dirs. Asian Arts Coun., Portland, 1993—2003, Internat. Assoc. Japanese Gardens, Portland, 1993—2000. Fellowship, Oreg. Lit. Arts, 1998, Project grant, Regional Arts and Culture Coun., 2001. Mem.: Acad. Am. Poets, Haiku Soc. Am., Poetry Soc. Japan. Home: 206 SW Carey Ln Portland OR 97219 Office: Katsura Press PO Box 275 Lake Oswego OR 97034 Office Phone: 503-699-9250. E-mail: daruma@aracnet.com.

CHUN, JACQUELINE CLIBBETT, artist, educator; d. Sydney H. and Hilda C. Moore; m. Edward W.C. Chun, Dec. 1967; children: Christine, Diana, David. Student, London Coll. Music, 1956—58; BA summa cum laude, U. Hawaii Manoa, 1992, MFA, 1997. Freelance musician, singer, songwriter, 1960—; pres. JCM Prodns., Honolulu, 1978—; lectr. painting Kapiolani C.C., Honolulu, 1999; faculty Kaimuki Cmty. Sch. Adults, Honolulu, 1988—; lectr. U. Hawaii Manoa, Honolulu, 1996—. Courtroom sketch artist KGMB TV, KHNL TV, Honolulu, 2000—. Editor: The Touch of God, 1999, The Science of Happiness, 2000. Band dir., choir dir. Girl Scout Coun. Pacific, Honolulu. Recipient Acquisition award, State Found. Culture and Arts. Mem.: ASCAP, Acad. Am. Poets, Portrait Soc. Am., Nat. Music Pub. Assn., Musician's Assn. Hawaii, Phi Beta Kappa. Avocations: swimming, gardening, travel. Office: JCM Prodns PO Box 8363 Honolulu HI 96830-0363

CHUN, SHINAE, federal agency administrator; Dir. Labor Dept., Chgo., 1998; dir. women's bur. U.S. Dept. Labor, Washington, 2001—. Office: US Dept Labor Women's Bur 200 Constitution Ave NW Washington DC 20210

CHUNG, AMY TERESA, lawyer, property manager; b. San Francisco, Sept. 1, 1953; d. Burk Him and Mary Angeline (Lin) C.; children: Adrian Thomas, Alison Nicole. AB in Psychology, U. Calif., Berkeley, 1975; JD, U. Calif., Hastings Coll. of Law, San Francisco, 1978. Bar: Calif. Legal counsel M & B Assocs., San Francisco, 1978—; v.p. Anza Parking Corp., Burlingame, Calif., 1993—. Mem. adv. com. U. Calif., San Francisco, 1992—; v.p. Castle Peak Homeowners Assn., West Hills, Calif., 1987-89; v.p. Chinatown Stockton St. Mchts. Assn., San Francisco, 1994-1999; chair Chinese Cmty. Housing Corp., San Francisco, 1991-1999; project area com. Mid-Market, San Francisco, 1996—. Mem. Calif. Bar Assn. Avocations: piano, singing, ballet, swimming. Office: M & B Assocs 835 Washington St San Francisco CA 94108-1211

CHUNG, CAROLINE, foreign service officer; b. Washington, Apr. 27, 1970; d. Jae Wan and Soojun Chung. BS, U. Wis., 1992; MBA, Vanderbilt U., 1997. Cert. Mad Dogg Spinning, Aerobics and Fitness Assn. Am. Mgr. ops. rsch. and statis. analysis Continental Airlines, 1997—99; mgr. product devel. USAirways, 1999—2001; ops. rsch. cons. Warden Assocs., 2001—02; fgn. svc. officer U.S. Dept. of State, 2002—. Roman Catholic. Avocations: professional aerobics instructor, travel, reading, world maps, music.

CHUNG, CONNIE (CONSTANCE YU-HWA CHUNG), broadcast journalist; b. Washington, Aug. 20, 1946; d. William Ling and Margaret Chung; m. Maurice Richard Povich. BS, U. Md., 1969; DJ (hon.) (hon.), Providence Coll., 1988; LHD (hon.), Brown U., 1987; LLD (hon.) (hon.), Wheaton Coll., 1989. News copyperson, writer, reporter Sta. WTTG-TV, Metromedia, Washington, 1969—71; corr. CBS News, Washington, 1971—76; TV news anchor Sta. KNXT-TV, CBS, L.A., 1976—83; anchor NBC News, NBC News at Sunrise, NBC Nightly News (Saturday), NBC News Digests, NBC News Mag. 1986, NBC News Spls., N.Y.C., 1983—89, Saturday Night with Connie Chung, CBS-TV, 1989—90, CBS Evening News (Sunday edit.), 1989—93, Face to Face, 1990—91, Eye to Eye, 1993—95; co-anchor CBS Evening News, 1993—95; anchor, corres. 20/20 ABC, N.Y.C., 1997—2002; anchor CNN, New York, NY, 2002—03. Recipient Achievement Cert. for series of broadcasts, U.S. Humane Soc., 1969, Metro Area Mass Media award, AAUW, 1971, Outstanding Young Women of Am. award, 1971, Atlanta chpt. Nat. Assn. Media Women award, 1973, Outstanding Excellence in News Reporting and Pub. Svc. award, Chinese-Am. Citizens Alliance, 1973, Hon. award for news reporting, Chinese YMCA, Boston, 1974, Woman of Distinction award, Golden Slipper Club, Phila., 1975, Best TV Reporting award, Sta. KNXT-TV and L.A. Press Club, 1977, Outstanding TV Broadcasting award, Valley Press Club, 1977, Golden Mike award for best documentary, 1978, Emmy award for individual achievement, L.A. chpt. NATAS, 1978, 1980, Mark Twain trophy, Calif. AP TV and Radio Assn., 1979, Best News Broadcast 4:30 p.m., 1980, Women in Comm. award, Calif. State U. at L.A., 1979, George Foster Peabody award for programs on environ., Md. Ctr. Pub. Broadcasting, 1980, Portraits of Excellence award, Pacific S.W. region B'nai B'rith, 1980, Newscaster of Yr. award, Temple Emanuel Brotherhood, 1981, First Amendment award, Anti-Defamation League of B'nai B'rith, 1981, Best Newscast 6:00 p.m. award, AP, 1981, Calif. AP TV and Radio Assn. award, 1981, Golden Mike award for best news broadcast, 1981, Disting. Contbns. in area of Comm. Media award, L.A. Basin Equal Opportunity League, 1983, Women in Bus. award, 1983, L.A. Press Club award for 4:30 p.m. boradcast, 1983, L.A. Press Club award for 6:00 p.m. broadcast, 1983, Emmy award, 1986, Emmy award for outstanding interview, 1989, 1990, Silver Gavel award, ABA, 1991, Ohio State of Achievement of Merit award, 1991, Nat. Headliner award, NCCJ, 1991, Clarion award, Women in Comm., 1991, Commendation award for AIDS and rape stories, Am. Women in Radio and TV, Commendation award for best implant stories, 1991, Godl Apple award, Nat. Media Network Film and Video Competition, 1999, Edward R. Murrow award for best news documentary, Nat. Assn. Radio and TV News Dirs., 1999, Cine Golden Eagle award, 1999, East Seals EDI award, 1999, Comm. award, Crystal award of Excellence, 1999, plaque award, Nat. Network for Youth, 2000, Gold Camera award, U.S. Internat. Film and Video Festival, 2000, 1999 award, Chgo. Internat. TV Competition, 2000, Media Spotlight award, Amnesty Internat., 2000, Salute to Excellence award, Nat. Assn. Black Journalists, 2000.*

CHUNG, CYNTHIA NORTON, communications specialist; b. Milton, Mass., Apr. 14, 1955; d. Ralph Arnold and Mary Elizabeth (McDonald) N.; m. Chinsoo Chung; children: Sara Jane, Steven Joonmok. BFA in Archtl. and Graphic Design, U. Mass., 1977. Graphic designer Garber Travel, Inc., Brookline, Mass., 1977-78; graphic and exhibit designer Rust Craft, Inc., Dedham, Mass., 1978-80; corp. advt. artist Morse, Inc., Canton, Mass., 1980-83; pvt. practice designer Boston, 1983-84; asst. art dir. Cahners Pub. Co., Newton, Mass., 1984-86, art dir., 1986-87, Knapp, Inc., Brockton, Mass., 1987-89; customer svc. rep. TWA, Boston, 1990; communications specialist Boston Fin., Quincy, Mass., 1992—. Designer graphs and charts for Vols. I and II State Budget Commonwealth of Mass., 1982; art dir. Mini Micro Systems, 1984-87. Mem. Kappa Kappa Gamma (Pres. 1975-76). Avocations: photography, real estate, travel. Home: 134 Samoset Ave Quincy MA 02169-2452 Office: Boston Financial 2000 Crown Colony Dr Quincy MA 02169

CHUN OAKLAND, SUZANNE NYUK JUN, state legislator; b. Honolulu, June 27, 1961; d. Philip Sing and Mei-Chih (Chung) Chun; m. Michael Sands Chun Oakland, June 11, 1994; children: Mailene Nohea Pua Oakland, Christopher Michael Sing Kamakaku Oakland, Lauren Suzanne LeRong Kemelenohea Oakland. BA in Psychology and Comms., U. Hawaii, 1983. Adminstrv. asst. Au's Plumbing and Metal Works, Hawaii, 1979-90; community svc. specialist Senator Anthony Chang, Hawaii, 1984; adminstrv. asst. Smolenski and Woodell, Hawaii, 1984-86; rsch. asst., office mgr. City Coun. Mem. Gary Gill, Hawaii, 1987-90; mem. Hawaii Ho. of Reps., 1990-96, Hawaii Senate, Dist. 14, Honolulu, 1996—; chair com. health and human svcs. Hawaii Senate, 1999—, co-chair com. human resources, 1997—; mem. coms. health and environ., consumer protection; commerce and info. tech., 1997—. Past chair, mem. several coms. Hawaii State Senate; mem. Sterile Needle Exch. Oversight Com., 1992—; apptd. pres. Kalihi-Palama Svc. Area Bd. on Mental Health and Substance Abuse, gov. Hawaii, 1985-89. Mem. adv. bd. Lanakila Multi-Purpose Sr. Ctr., 1991—, Sex Abuse Treatment Ctr., 1993—, Teen Line, 1993, Hawaii Cmty. Found. Children's Trust Fund, 1995—, Habitat for Humanity, 1998—; mem. Grow For It Program, 1996—, Hawaii Early Childhood Alliance, 1995-96, Families Together Initiative Core Team, 1993-95; coun. mem. Hawaii Even Start Family Literact Program, 1993-94; mem. coord. coun. Hawaii Early Intervention, 1993—, Early Childhood Edn. and Care, 1992-96, mem. adv. coun. Children's Trust Fund, 199[illegible]—; mem. [illegible] West Honolulu Pub. Health Nursing Sect., 1992—, Honolulu divsn. Casey Family Program, 1994—, Early Childhood Sys. Cost/Implementation, 1992-94; chair Liliha/Kalapama Neighborhood Bd., 1984-90; mem. project steering com. Hawaii Summit 2011, 1996—; mem. Healthy Mothers, Healthy Babies Coalition, 1992; convenor Elder Abuse and Neglect Task Force, 1995—; mem. task force Blueprint for Change, Child Protective Svcs., 1994-96, Hawaii Assistive Tech. Tng. and Svcs. Project Cmty., 1995—; mem. coun. Hawaii Kids Count, 1994—; bd. dirs. Honolulu Neighborhood Housing Svcs., 1986-88, 89—, pres., 1987-88, 92-93, 93-94; bd. dirs. McKinley H.S. Found, 1989—; Catholic Immigration Ctr., 1991-97, Hawaii Dem. Movement, 1991-97, Hawaii Cmty. Svcs. Coun., 1993-97, Hawaii Cmty. Edn. Assn., 1984-98, Hawaii Lawyers Care, 1994—, Susannah Wesley Cmty. Ctr., 1994—, Hawaii Housing Devel. Corp., 1993—, YWCA, 1994—, ARC, 1998—, Breakthroughs for Youth at Risk, 1998—, Providing Awareness Referrals Edn. Nurturing Therapy Support, 1999—; precinct pres. Hawaii Dem. Party, 1990. Named Legis. of Yr. Hawaii Long Term Care Assn., 1993, 98, Healthcare Assn. Hawaii, 1993, 95, Hawaii Psychiat. Med. Assn., 1994, Autism Soc. Hawaii, 1994, Mental Health Assn. Hawaii, 1996, Aloha State Assn. of Deaf, 1999; recipient cert. of appreciation YMCA, 1985, Hawaii Assn. for Edn. of Young Children, 1992, Winners at Work, 1993, Am. Box Car Racing Internat., 1996, Congress of Visayan Orgn., 1996, Pack 201 Boys Scouts Am., 1997, Partners in Policymaking Hawaii, 1998, Excellence award Honolulu Neighborhood Housing Svcs. Inc., 1988, mini internship program cert. Honolulu County Med. Soc., 1993, Friend of Social Workers award NASW, 1995, Outstanding Govt. Svc. award Hawaii Pacific Gerontol. Soc., 1996, Outstanding Legislator award Hawaii Med. Assn., 1996, Na Lima Kokua Ma Waema O Makua award Pacific Gerontol. Soc., 1996, Friend of the Family award Hawaii Assn. for Marriage and Family Therapy, 1998. Mem. Liliha/Palama Bus. Assn. (bd. dirs. 1994—), Hawaii Women's Legal Found., Good Beginnings Alliance, Kalihi-Palama Culture and Arts Soc., Chung Wah Chung Kung Hui, Hawaii Chinese Civic Assn., Hawaii State Youth Vol. Bd. (past pres.), Ma'ema'e Sch. SCBM, Legis. Women's Caucus, Small Bus. Caucus, Keiki Caucus (co-chair 1991—), Chinese C. of C., McKinley Alumni Assn. (bd. dirs. 1989—). Democrat. Episcopalian. Avocations: raising animals, gardening, swimming. Office: State Senate 415 S Beretania St Rm 228 Honolulu HI 96813-2407

CHURCH, BARBARA RYAN, organizational psychologist; b. Vallejo, Calif. d. William Russell and Geraldine Hall (Hatcher) Ryan; divorced; children: Gabrielle Church Russell, Elizabeth Broward McGhie. BA, U. Fla., 1974; MA in Psychology, West Ga. Coll., 1981; EdD in Applied Psychology and Adult Edn., U. Ga., 1985. Pub. svc. dir., news editor, anchorwoman WJKS-TV, Jacksonville, Fla., 1969-71; dir. cmty. rels. Atlanta Assn. Ret. Citizens, 1977-78; coord. pub. info. Mental Health Assn., Atlanta, 1978-80; edn./testing specialist Federal Law Enforcement Tng. Ctr., Glynco, Ga., 1984-86; dir. evening coll., asst. prof. psychology Brewton-Parker Coll., Mt. Vernon, Ga., 1986-88; tng. rsch. analyst Federal Law Enforcement Tng. Ctr., 1988-90; researcher, edn. specialist U.S. Dept. Justice, Immigration & Naturalization Svc., Glynco, 1990-98, chief rsch. and evaluation, 1998—. Tchr., cons. adult edn. courses Ga. State U., Atlanta, 1978, Brunswick (Ga.) Coll., 1993; adj. prof. orgnl. behavior and Leadership, MBA Program, Sch. Bus. Adminstrn., Brenau U., 1997—. Convenor, cons. Kettering Found., 1987-88; mem. adv. bd. HRD degree, dept. adult edn. U. Ga. Recipient award for best campaign of non-profit orgn. Am. Mktg. Assn., 1978, ann. award for innovative programming Ga. Adult Edn. Assn., 1983; named communicator of yr. United Way, 1980. Mem. U. Ga. Lifelong Learning Assn., Ga. Adult Edn. Assn. (bd. dirs. 1989-91), Soc. Police & Criminal Psychology, Commn. Profs. of Adult Edn. Episcopal. Avocations: writing non-fiction, painting, travel, photography. Home: 257 Charlemagne Cir Ponte Vedra Beach FL 32082-2907

CHURCH, GAIL GRAHAM, television producer, consultant; b. Providence, May 10, 1924; d. Harry Jackson and Gertrude (Conners) Graham; m. William Rice Gerber, Jan. 20, 1951 (div. Jan. 1971); children: Cheryl Ann Gerber, Linda Lee Gerber; m. Herbert Church Jr., July 6, 1974. BS, R.I. State Coll., 1945; M of Nursing, Yale U., 1948. Nurse, instr. Mary Hitchcock Hosp., Hanover, N.H., 1948-49; head nurse rooming-in unit Grace New Haven Hosp., 1949-51; nurse, instr. Home Health Agy., Chicopee, Mass., 1951; educator, pub. health nurse N.H. Divsn. Pub. Health, Concord, N.H., 1972-74; ednl. advisor communicable diseases N.H. Dept. Edn., Concord, 1980; founder, prodr. pub. affairs TV series Life: Living It and Loving It, Concord, 1985-89, 2001—. Advisor Hospice Adv. Com., Concord, 1985; pres. Life: Living It and Loving It, Inc., Concord, 1985—. Founder, pres. Concord Area Drug Action Com., 1968; initiator first HELP-Line in N.H., Concord, 1969; organizer Reps. for Clinton/Gore, N.H. Dem. Party, Concord, 1992; mem. Task Force Against Racism, Concord, 1997—; mem. adv. bd. Internat. Health Found., 1999—. Recipient Leadership award YMCA, 1969, Dedicated Svc. to N.H. award Gov. Walter Peterson, 1970, Vol. Svc. award Gov.'s Coun. on Volunteerism, 1987. Mem.: LWV, AAUW (membership chair Concord 1997, pres. Concord br. 1997—2000, co-pres. 1999—2000), Capital Area League Women Voters, UN Assn., N.H. Women's Lobby. Episcopalian. Avocations: painting, reading, walking, art, music, watercoloring, biking, reading, walking, art and music appreciation. Home: 1 Pleasant View Ave Concord NH 03301-2555

CHURCH, LILLIAN HAZEL See BROOKS, LILLIAN

CHURCH, MARTHA ELEANOR, retired academic administrator, scholar; b. Pitts., Nov. 17, 1930; d. Walter Seward and Eleanor (Boyer) Church. BA, Wellesley Coll., 1952; MA, U. Pitts., 1954; PhD, U. Chgo., 1960; DSc (hon.), Lake Erie Coll., 1975; LittD (hon.), Houghton Coll., 1980; LHD (hon.), Queens Coll., 1981, Ursinus Coll., 1981, St. Joseph Coll., 1982, Towson State U., 1983, Dickinson Coll., 1987, Coll. Notre Dame Md., 1995; LLD (hon.), Hood Coll., 1995; LHD (hon.), Ill. Coll., 2003. Instr. geography Mt. Holyoke Coll., South Hadley, Mass., 1953-57; lectr. geography Ind. U. Gary Ctr., 1958; instr., then asst. prof. geography Wellesley Coll., 1958—65; dean coll., prof. geography Wilson Coll., 1965-71; assoc. exec. sec. Commn. Higher Edn., Mid. States Assn. Coll. and Secondary Sch., 1971-75; pres. Hood Coll., Frederick, Md., 1975-95, pres. emerita, 1995—; sr. scholar Carnegie Found. for Advancement of Tchg., Princeton, 1995—97; interim pres. Ill. Coll., 2002—03. Bd. dirs. Farmers and Mechanics Nat. Bank, 1982—2000, dir. emerita, 2000—; cons. Choice: Books for Coll. Librs.; co-chmn. nat. adv. panel Nat. Ctr. for Rsch. to Improve Postsecondary Tchg. and Learning, U. Mich., 1985—90; mem. bd. visitors Def. Intelligence Coll., 1988—91; mem. adv. bd. dirs. Automobile Club Md., 1991—2002; bd. dirs. AAA Mid-Atlantic, 1997—2002; mem. adv. bd. The Boyer Ctr. Messiah Coll., Grantham, Pa., 1997—. Author: The Spatial Organization of Electric Power Territories in Massachusetts, 1960; Co-editor: A Basic Geographical Library: A Selected and Annotated Book List for Am. Colls, 1966; cons. editor, Change mag., 1980-2001. Bd. dirs. Coun. for Internat. Exch. of Scholars, 1979-80, Japan Internat. Christian U. Found., 1977-91, Nat. Ctr. for Higher Edn. Mgmt. Sys., 1980-83; bd. dirs. Am. Coun. on Edn., 1976-79, vice chmn., 1978-79, mem. nat. identification panel, 1977-95, Nat. Rsch. Com., 1993-96; bd. advisors Fund for Improvement of Postsecondary Edn., HEW, 1976-79; mem. Sec. of Navy's Adv. Bd. on Edn. and Tng., 1976-80; chmn. Md. Commn. on Civil Rights, 1981-82; trustee Bradford Coll., Mass., 1982-87, Peddie Sch., N.J., 1982-98, chair acad. affairs com., 1987, 96-97, adv. trustee, 1998—, trustee; trustee Carnegie Found. for the Advancement of Tchg., 1986-96, vice chair, 1990-92, chair, 1992-94, immediate past chair, 1994-96; trustee Nat. Geog. Soc., 1989—, mem. com. for rsch. and exploration, 1998—, chair audit rev. com., 1993-98, chair mission, membership, medals and awards com., 2000—, mem. exec., audit and compensation coms.; trustee Nat. Geog. Soc. Edn. Found., 1989-96, 99—; chmn. bd. dirs. Medici Found., Princeton, N.J., 1985—; trustee United Bd. for Christian Higher Edn. in Asia, 1995-2004, sec. bd. trustees, 1998-2003, chmn. com. on trustees, 1997-2004, chmn. East and Intra-Asia program subcom., 1996-97, exec. com., 1998-2004; mem. Md. Humanities Coun., 1985-86, Md. Jud. Disabilities Commn., 1985-94; commr. Edn. Commn. States, Md., 1981-99; exec. com. Campus Compact: Project for Pub. and Cmty. Svc., 1986-89—; trustee Internat. Partnership for Svc. Learning, 1999-2002. Mem. AAUW, Am. Assn. Advancement of Humanities (bd. dirs. 1979-81), Am. Assn. Higher Edn. (chmn. 1980-81, bd. dirs. 1979-83), Assn. Am. Geographers, Nat. Assn. Ind. Colls. and Univs. (bd. dirs. 1983-86), Md. Ind. Colls. and Univs. Assn. (pres. 1979-81, mem. exec. com. 1988-92), Assn. Am. Colls. and Univs. (mem. adv. com. project on status and edn. of women 1980-85), Women's Coll. Coalition (mem. exec. com. 1976-80, 87-89), Am. Conf. Acad. Deans (sec., editor 1969-71), Coun. Protestant Colls. and Univs. (bd. dirs. 1969-71), Soc. Coll. and Univ. Planning (mem. editl. bd. 1979-95), Cosmos Club (mem. jour. editl. bd. 1990-94), Inst. Ednl. Leadership (bd. dirs. 1982-87), Sigma Delta Epsilon, Delta Kappa Gamma (hon.). Home: 3124 Chartwell Crescent Ln Adamstown MD 21710-9643 Fax: 301-644-1701. E-mail: marthachurch@edurostream.com.

CHURCH, SONIA JANE SHUTTER, librarian; b. York, Pa., Dec. 15, 1940; d. Robert Benjamin and Eva Alverta (Horn) Shutter; m. Ernest Layton Church, May 20, 1966; children: Robert Bruce, Jennifer Grace. BS in Edn., Millersville Coll., 1962; MLS, U. Pitts., 1978. Playground supr. York City Sch. Dist., Pa., 1961; children's libr. Prunedale br. Monterey County Libr., Calif., 1978-79, youth svcs. coord., 1979-83, 85-88, head libr. Prunedale br., 1983-85; children's svc. mgr. Ventura (Calif.) County Libr., 1988-94; youth svcs. coord. Chattanooga Hamilton County Bicentennial Libr., 1994-95; head Children's Learning Ctr. Pub. Libr. Cin. and Hamilton County, 1995—. Writer Book Beat column for Fortnighter Newspaper, Salinas, 1983-85, Book Corner column, Warm 98 Family Mag., 1997—. Editor pamphlet: What Will We Do with the Baby?, A Collection of Nursery Rhymes and Finger Plays, 1977. Mem. Deferred Comp. Task Force, Monterey County, 1983-88, Mgmt. Coun., Monterey County, 1983-88; chmn. adminstrv. com. Social Svcs. Commn., Monterey County, 1983-85, chmn. ad hoc com., 1983-88; coord. com. Boy Scouts Am., Salinas, 1983-85; mem. Children's Svcs. Mgmt. Consortium, 1986-87; tchr. Sun Sch., Luth. Ch. Good Shepherd, Salinas, 1982-88; chmn. latchkey com. Child Care Task Force, Ventura County; chmn. children's com. Black Gold Libr. Sys., Calif., 1991; mem. children's coord. coun. Ventura County, 1993-94; asst. coord. S.W. chpt., Ohio Libr. Coun., 1998-99, coord., 1999-2000. Capt. USMC, 1962-66. Recipient Celebrate Literacy award Internat. Reading Assn., Margaret Lynch Exemplary Svc. award Calif. Reading Assn.; Sico scholar, 1958-62. Mem. ALA, Assn. Libr. Svc. to Children (liaison with nat. orgns. serving child com.), Calif. Libr. Assn. (pres. children's svcs. chpt. 1989-90, Beatty award com. 1990-92, chair Beatty com. 1993-95, children's svcs. mgmt. chpt., assembly 1991-95, planning com. 1992-95), Ohio Libr. Coun., Assn. Children's Librs. No. Calif., Sch. and Pub. Librs. Assn. Monterey Bay Area (pres. 1979-80, 85-86), Assn. Childhood Edn. Internat., Nat. Story League (co-founder Ventura County storytellers group), Calif. Reading Assn., Internat. Reading Assn. (pres. 1991-92), Ventura County Lit. Coun., So. Calif. Coun. Lit. for Children and Young People, Soc. Children's Book Writers, Am. Legion (comdr. 1984-85), Women's Internat. Bowling Congress, Women's Bowling Assn., U. Pitts. Alumni Assn., Millersville U. Alumni Assn., Beta Phi Mu, Beta Sigma Phi. Democrat. Lutheran. Office: Pub Library 800 Vine St Cincinnati OH 45202-2071 Address: 1428 Swanbrooke Dr Las Vegas NV 89144-1646 E-mail: childrenhead@plch.lib.oh.us.

CHURCHILL, KAREN LYNN, curator, educator; b. Ft. Worth, July 18, 1956; d. Richard Lionel and Yonova (Muncy) C. Student, Mills Coll., 1973-75; AB in British Lit., Colgate U., 1977; MA in Art History, Ariz. State U., 1986; MA in Arts Adminstrn., MBA, So. Meth. U., 1987; postgrad. in art history, Case Western Res. U., 1992—97. Coord. cultural programs So. Meth. U., Dallas, 1987-89; dir. Gray Gallery, Univ. Mus. East Carolina U., Greenville, N.C., 1989-90; faculty assoc. Ariz. State U., Tempe, 1991; asst. prof. Kent (Ohio) State U., 1993-94; photography rsch. asst. Cleve. Mus. Art, 1995—97; mng. editor Sharlot Hall Mus. Press, Prescott, Ariz., 1998—2001; adj. prof., grad. advisor Prescott Coll., Ariz., 1999—; adj.

prof. Yavapai Coll., Prescott, Ariz., 2001—04, Embry-Riddle Aero. U., Prescott, Ariz., 2003—04; area coord. No. Ariz. U. Yavapai, Prescott, 2004—. Mem. adv. bd. Scottsdale (Ariz.) Cultural Coun., 1991-93, Internat. Friends of Transformative Art, Paradise Valley, Ariz., 1991-93; gallery cons. Ind. State U., Terre Haute, 1994; exhibn. cons. J. Paul Getty Mus., Malibu, Calif., 1994-97; bd. dirs. Friends of Yavapai Coll. Art, Prescott, 2004—. Various (art exhibns.) Bo. Mich. U., 1987-89, E. Carolina U., 1989-91, Eco-Logic: Ariz. Artists as Environmental Activists, 1992, The Cleve. Mus. of Art, 1995-97. Commn. appointee Christopher Columbus Quincentary Commn., Dallas, 1987-89. N.C. Arts Commn. rsch. grantee, 1990; Case Western Res. U. scholar, 1992-97; Andrew Mellon fellowship, 1996. Mem. Am. Assn. Mus., Coll. Art Assn. Avocations: photography, cooking, biking, reading. Home: 723 Coronado Ave Prescott AZ 86303-3710 Office: No Ariz Univ 551 1st St Prescott AZ 86301 Office Phone: 928-445-5231.

CHURCHILL, MAIR ELISA ANNABELLE, medical educator; b. Liverpool, Eng., Nov. 28, 1959; BA in Chemistry, Swarthmore (Pa.) Coll., 1981; PhD in Chemistry, Johns Hopkins U., 1987. Lab. asst. Swarthmore Coll., 1979-81; teaching asst. Johns Hopkins U., Balt., 1981-83; non-clin. sci. staff grade I MRC Lab. Molecular Biology, Cambridge, Eng., 1987-93; asst. prof. biophysics U. Ill., Urbana, 1993-98; assoc. prof. biophysics U. Colo., Denver, 1998—. Contbr. numerous articles to profl. jours. Am. Cancer Soc. fellow, 1987-89, Cambridge U. fellow, 1988-91. Mem. Am. Chem. Soc., Sigma Xi (assoc.). Office: U Colo Health Scis Dept Pharm Campus Box C236 4200 E 9th Ave Denver CO 80220-3706

CHURGIN, AMY, publishing executive; Assoc. pub. Seventeen Mag., 1992—94; Pub. K III Mag. Corp. (now Primedia Corp.--N.Y. Mag.), N.Y.C., 1994—99; group pub., N.Y., Chgo. Automobile Mag., 1999; Pub. Archtl. Digest, Condé Nast, L.A., 1999—. Office: Architectural Digest Condé Nast 6300 Wilshire Blvd Ste 1100 Los Angeles CA 90048-9083

CHUTE, MARY L. federal agency administrator, library director; BA in art history, U. Mich.; MA in art history, Boston U.; MLS, Simmons Coll. With Mass. Libr. Sys.; pub. libr. cons. divsn. of devel. Md. State Dept. Edn., 1997—99; dir. and state libr. Del. Divsn. Libr./State Libr., 1999—2002; dep. dir. libr. svcs. Inst. of Mus. and Libr. Svcs., Washington. Office: Inst Mus and Libr Svcs Office Libr Svcs Rm 802 1100 Penn Ave NW Washington DC 20506*

CHWALEK, CONSTANCE, real estate broker, mortgage broker; b. N.Y.C., Nov. 1, 1928; d. Sylvester James Maguire and Justine Rita Nigra; m. Raymond McVey, Feb. 27, 1949 (div. Oct. 1959); 1 child, Deidre McVey; m. Frank Charles Chwalek, Aug. 15, 1975. Student, Empire State Coll. Bookkeeper/adminstr. various cos., N.Y.C., 1953-75; real estate broker, mortgage broker Century 21 Fortune Realty, N.Y.C., 1975—. Mem. L.I. Bd. Realtors, Howard Beach Civic Assn. Republican. Roman Catholic. Avocations: golf, tennis, skiing, art, dance. Home: 15535 Huron St Howard Beach NY 11414-2854

CHWAT, ANNE, recording industry executive; Student, NYU. Assoc. Clearly Gottlieb Steen & Hamilton, 1987—95; assoc. corp. counsel Joseph E. Seagram & Sons, Inc., 1995—2000; v.p. legal and bus. affairs BMG Entertainment, N.Y.C., 2000—03, co-gen. mgr., sr. v.p. legal and bus. affairs, 2003—, chief ethics and compliance officer. Office: BMG Entertainment 1540 Broadway New York NY 10036*

CHWATSKY, ANN, photographer, educator; b. Phila., Jan. 11, 1942; BS in Art Edn., Hofstra U., 1965, MS, 1971; postgrad., L.I. U., 1973-74. Cert. tchr. Photography editor L.I. Mag., 1976-80; instr. Internat. Ctr. Photography, N.Y.C., 1979-80, Parrish Art Mus., Southampton, N.Y., 1984—. Mem. art faculty NYU, 1991—. Author, photographer: The Man in the Street, 1989; photographer The Four Seasons of Shaker life; photographs featured in Time, Newsweek, Newsday, Manchete, N.Y. Times, MD Med. Times; one person shows include Lincoln Ctr., Buenos Aires, 1983, Photographers Gallery, London, 1985, shakers, Nassau County Mus. Fine Arts, 1987, Greater Lafayette (Ind.) Mus. Art, 1988, Bklyn. Coll., 1990, Kiev, USSR Exhbn. Hall, 1991, Bklyn. Coll., Carrie Haddad Gallery, Hudson, N.Y., 2001, N.Y. Faculty show, 2003, Digital Artist, Little Rock, 2004; group shows include The Other, Houston Ctr. Photography, 1988, L.I. Fine Arts Mus., 1984, Women's Interart Ctr., N.Y.C., 1976, 80, Parrish Art Mus., Southampton, 1979, Internat. Ctr. Photography, N.Y.C., 1980, 82, Nassau County Mus. Fine Arts, 1983, Soho 20 Gallery, N.Y.C., 1984, New Orleans World's Fair, 1984, Southampton Gallery, 1988, 89, Lizan Tops Gallery, L.I., 1994, Apex Art, N.Y.C., 1995, Am. Mus., Prague, 1997, First Seoul Internat. Tribunal, 1998; represented in permanent collections Bass Mus. Art, Fla., Forbes N.Y.C., Midtown YWCA, Nassau County Mus. Fine Arts, Susan Rothenberg, others. Recipient Estabrook Disting. Alumni award Hofstra U., 1984; Kodak Profl. Photographers award, 1984; Eastman Found. grantee, 1981-82, Poloroid grantee, 1980. Mem. Assn. Am. Mag. Profls., Picture Profls. Am., Profl. Women Photographers N.Y.C. Studio: 29 E 22nd St Apt 3N New York NY 10010-5305

CIAIO, LAURA ASHMORE, accountant; b. Laramie, Wyo. d. Glenn L. Ashmore and Angela L. (Edwards) Bennett; m. Andrew Charles Ciaio, aug. 5, 1989; children: Nathan Andrew, Benjamin James. BSBA, Rochester Inst. Tech., 1989. CPA, N.Y. Staff acct. Coopers & Lybrand, Rochester, N.Y., 1989-92; gen. acctg. mgr. Lewis Tree Svc., Inc., Rochester, 1992-95; mgr. fin. reporting Getinge USA Inc., Rochester, 1995—. Tutor, bd. dirs., treas., chmn. fin. com. Literacy Vols. Am.-Rochester, N.Y., Inc., 1989-97. Mem. ICP, Inst. Mgmt. Accts., N.Y. State Soc. CPA's. Office: Getinge/Castle Inc 1777 E Henrietta Rd Rochester NY 14623-3133

CIANCIO, MARILYN, television producer; b. Jamestown, NY, June 4, 1943; d. James S. and Casima M. (Lisciandro) Bonfiglio; m. Sebastian G. Ciancio, Nov. 16, 1963; children: Michele Ann, Sebastian James. BA, SUNY, Buffalo, 1973, MA, 1978. Cert. tchr. NY. Elem. tchr. St. Peter and Paul Sch, Jamestown, 1963—65, St. Benedict Sch., Buffalo, 1963—65; lectr. in leadership and volunteerism various local and nat. orgns., 1979—; alt. host Reggie Keaton Show Adelphia TV, Buffalo, 1984—94, prodr., host Artscope, 1994—, arts corr. Crossroads, 2001—. Mem. spkrs.' bur. World U. Games, Buffalo, 1993; mem. spl. studies faculty Chautauqua (NY) Instn., 1993; collaborative prodr. Video Arts Coun., Buffalo, 2003—04; adv. coun. Ctr. Arts U. Buffalo. Contbg. editor: handbook Here's Buffalo, 1984; co-editor: (theatrical cookbook) Women of Studio Arena Theatre - Edible Entertainment, 1985—87; prodr.: (documentary) Women's Pavilion PanAm, 2001. Bd. dirs. Arts Coun. Buffalo and Erie County, 1999—; bd. mgrs. Women's Pavilion PanAm 2001, Buffalo, 2000—02; mem. adv. bd. Cir. of Daus., Buffalo, 2002—; co-founder, bd. dirs. Chautauqua Dental Congress, 1980—; trustee, sec. Studio Arena Theatre, Buffalo, 1987—89; pres. Women's Dental Guild, 1974, Women of Studio Arena, 1985—87, U. Buffalo Women's Club, 1994. Recipient Citation of Excellence, Artvoice, Buffalo, 2001, Bronze Telly award, Nat. Telly Awards, Cin., 2003, Zodiaque Dance Co. Dir.'s award, U. Buffalo, 2003. Avocations: organ, needlepoint, travel, art, art advocacy.

CIANCIOLO-CARNEY, ROSSANA, investigative analyst; b. Knoxville, Tenn., July 4, 1964; d. Salvatore and Mariluz Cianciolo; m. Patrick Michael Carney, Jan. 8, 1961. B.A. in Polit. Sci./Fgn. Langs., Stephens Coll., 1986. Intelligence rsch. specialist Nat. Drug Intelligence Ctr., Johnstown, Pa., 1994-95; investigative analyst FBI, San Diego, Calif., 1995—. Informal resolution program counselor Nat. Drug Intelligence Ctr., Johnstown, 1995. Spkr. Cmty. Outreach, 1995—, participant/San Diego Elder Abuse Fraud Task Force, 1998—; wish grantor Make-a-Wish, San Diego, 1997—; bd. dirs. Women in Bus. Aiding the Cmty., 1996—. Republican. Roman Catholic. Avocations: running, swimming, reading, travel. Home: 369 Park Street NE Vienna VA 22180 Office: FBI 7799 Leesburg Pike Falls Church VA 22037

CIANI, JUDITH ELAINE, [illegible] Medford, Mass., July 24, 1943; d. A. Walter and Ruth Alice (Bowman) C.; m. Marion M. Smith, Sept. 29, 1982. Grad., Thayer Acad., Braintree, Mass., 1961; MA, Mt. Holyoke Coll., 1965; JD, Boston Coll., 1970. Bar: Calif. 1971, U.S. Dist. Ct. (no. dist.) Calif. 1971, U.S. Ct. Appeals (9th cir.) 1971. Aide/press sec. Rep. James A. Burke, Washington, 1965-67; atty. Pillsbury, Madison & Sutro, San Francisco, 1970-78, ptnr., 1978-90; ret., 1990. Del. Calif. Bar Conv., San Francisco, 1973-78, 83-85. Mem. San Francisco Police Commn., 1976-80, Juvenile Justice Task Force, San Francisco, 1981-83; bd. dirs. Bernard Osher Found., San Francisco, 1977—; pres. Common Fund for Legal Svcs., San Francisco, 1985—, Sinfonia San Francisco, 1985-86. Fellow Am. Bar Found.; mem. Bar Assn. San Francisco (bd. dirs., pres. Found. 1978—, bd. dirs. 1981-83, treas. 1987). Home: PO Box 960 Inverness CA 94937-0960 E-mail: jeciani@svn.net.

CIANNELLA, JOEEN MOORE, museum director; b. Warren, Ohio, Mar. 20, 1948; d. Joseph Alvie and Elizabeth Dorthea Moore; m. Christopher M. Ciannella, July 31, 1976 (div. Jan. 1987); children: Bryce C., Tara E. BA in French, Denison U., 1970. Profl. staff U.S. Senate Rep. Policy Com., Washington, 1971-75; owner Jo Moore-Sophisticated Country, Park Ridge, NJ, 1984—; dist. dir. Congresswoman Marge Roukema U.S. Ho. Reps., Ridgewood, NJ, 1985—2002; exec. dir. Hermitage Mus., Hohokus, NJ, 2003—. Mem. Nat. coun. Boy Scouts Am., 1995—98; trustee Greater Roles and Opportunities for Women N.J. GOP, 1997—2002; mem. Park Ridge Bd. Health, 1984—86; founding mem. Pioneer Women Bergen County, 1992—; mem. exec. bd. Bergen coun. Boy Scouts Am., 1991—98, co-chair Pascak Valley Dist. Lunchoree, 1991—92, chair spl. events fin., 1993—94, mem. exec. com., 1993—98, vice chmn. fin., 1995—98, mem. exec. bd. No. N.J. coun., 1999—, vice chair fin., 2000—02; mem. exec. bd. Ramapo Coll. Found., 1991—, theme chairperson fundraiser, 1991—94, disting. citizen dinner com., 1991—, mem. bus. network com., 1994—97, chmn. pub. rels. and mktg. com., 1996—2000, mem. exec. com., 1996—, chmn. mktg./instl. rels., 2000—; com. mem. N.J. Network Found. Gala, 2000—02; bd. dirs. Helen Hayes Theater Co., Nyack, NY, 2001—, mem. devel. com. spl. events, 2002—, Day in the Garden, 2003; chairperson spl. effects West Bergen Mental Health 40th Anniversary Ruby Ball, 2003; founding mem. W. Bergen Mental Health Found., 2003; active Bush for Pres. Campaign, 1988, 1992, Dole for Pres. Campaign, 1996; elected mem. Park Ridge County Com., 1983—, mcpl. chairperson, 1986—96; active Bergen County (N.J.) Rep. Com., 1983—, Park Ridge Rep. Orgn., 1983—, v.p., 1988—89; active N.E. Rep. Orgn. Dist. 39, NJ, 1984—, sec., 1990—91, treas., 1991—92, chairperson, 1992—93; ofcl. com. mem. N.J. GOP Conv., 1991; charter mem. Women Leadership Summit Rep. Network to Elect Women, 1996—97. Recipient Mission award, Ramapo Coll. Found., 1999, Silver Beaver award, Boy Scouts Am., 1999. Mem.: Jr. League Bergen County (com. mem. Festival of Trees 1988), Ridgewood Unit Rep. Women, Bergen County Women's Rep. Club, N.J. Fedn. Rep. Women, Rep. Women of 90's State N.J., Rotary (mem. com. annual auction Park Ridge chpt. 1990—, chairperson holiday party 1991—). Avocations: gardening, antiques, sports, travel. Home: 34 Spring Valley Rd Park Ridge NJ 07656-1860 Office: The Hermitage Mus 335 N Franklin Turnpike Ho Ho Kus NJ 07423 Office Phone: 201-445-8311. E-mail: jciannella@thehermitage.org.

CIARAMELLA, SUZANNE, psychologist; b. Islip, NY, Feb. 25, 1973; d. John Anthony and Elaine Ciaramella. BS, SUNY, Stonybrook, 1995; D in Psychology, U. Hartford, 2001. Clinical psychologist Natchany Hosp., Storrs, Conn., 2000—03. Office: Natchaug Hosp 189 Starrs Rd Mansfield Center CT 06250 E-mail: drsuec@hotmail.com.

CICCO, CECILIA VICTORIA, music educator; b. Andrews AFB, Md., May 17, 1974; d. Frank and Ebelena C. Klco. BS in Music Edn., Duquesne U., 1996. Instrumental instr. Pitts. Diocese, 1996—98; asst. dir. Thomas Jefferson H.S., Pitts., 1998—99; dir. of bands Thomas Jefferson HS., Pitts., 1999—2002; percussion tech. Gen. Butler Vagabonds, Pitts., 1999—2000; pit. capt. head Project Percussion, Pitts., 2002—; dir. of bands Deer Lakes H.S., Pitts., 2002—. Educators com. Pitts. Symphony Orch.; exec. bd. PIMBA. Mem.: ALE - KISKI Band Dlr. Assn. (v.p.), Percussive Arts Soc., The Nat. Assn. for Music Edn. Office: Deer Lakes HS 163 E Union Rd Russellton PA 15076 Office Phone: 724-265-5320.

CICCONE, AMY NAVRATIL, art librarian; b. Detroit, Sept. 19, 1950; d. Gerald R. and Ruth C. (Kauer) Navratil. BA, Wayne State U., 1972; AM in Library Sci., U. Mich., 1973. Rsch. libr. Norton Simon Mus., Pasadena, Calif., 1974-81; chief libr. Chrysler Mus., Norfolk, Va., 1981-88; head libr. Architecture and Fine Arts Libr. U. So. Calif., L.A., 1988-97, acting asst. univ. libr. pub. svcs., 1993-95, ref. libr., 1997—2004, assoc. coord. collection devel., 2004—. Contbr. articles to profl. jours.; cons. editor Art Reference Svcs., 1990-98. Mem. Art Libraries Soc. N.Am. (moderator Decorative Arts Roundtable, 1991-93, facilities standards com. 1986-91, chmn. strategic planning task force 1994-96, vice-chmn. So. Calif. chpt. 1989, chmn. 1990, chmn. 2001 conf.), Rsch. Librs. Group, Art & Architecture Group (steering com. 1992-94). Office: U So Calif Libr Los Angeles CA 90089-1823 Office Phone: 213-740-1958. Business E-Mail: aciccone@usc.edu.

CICCONE, MADONNA LOUISE VERONICA See MADONNA

CICERCHI, ELEANOR ANN TOMB, fundraising executive; b. Sayre, Pa., Dec. 11, 1944; d. William Horton and Brinton Elizabeth (Cauffiel) Tomb; m. Robert A. Weskerna, Nov. 19, 1966 (div. Feb. 1981); children: Amy Marie, Robert Campbell; m. Philip J. Cicerchi, July 1982. AB with great distinction, Mt. Holyoke Coll., 1966; MS, New Sch. Social Rsch., 1992. Cert. fundraising exec. Sr. mktg. rep. Group Health Plan, Guttenberg, N.J., 1976-79; dir. comty. rels. Burke Rehab. Ctr., White Plains, N.Y., 1979-84; exec. dir. Bergen comty. Coll. Fedn., Paramus, N.J., 1984-86; campaign counsel Brakeley John Price Jones, Inc., Stanford, Conn., 1986-88; v.p. instnl. advancement Marymount Coll., Tarrytown, N.Y., 1988-93; dir. maj. gifts Am. Found. for AIDS Rsch., N.Y.C., 1993-95, chief devel. officer, 1995-96; v.p. devel. and external affairs ORBIS Internat., Inc., N.Y.C., 1996-2000; assoc. v.p. devel. Save the Children, Westport, Conn., 2000—02; dir. devel. The Corning Mus. of Glass, 2002—. Faculty mem. Fundraising Sch., Ctr. Philanthropy, Ind. U., Indpls., 1989—; adj. grad. faculty mem. NYU, N.Y.C., 1990-97, New Sch. for Social Rsch., N.Y.C., 1995—, chmn. PR Group for Vision 2000: The Right to Sight, Geneva, 1998-99; bd. dirs. AMD Alliance, 1999-2001. Author: Raid!, 1978, Anonymous Giving, 1991; co-author: The Earth Shook and the Sky Was Red, 1976, The Flower of the Virginian, 1980; editor: The Architecture of Bergen County, 1991. Pres. Dem. Club, River Vale, N.J., 1978-81; bd. dirs., past chmn. Philharmonia Virtuosi, Dobbs Ferry, N.Y., 1985-2002; v.p. Orch. of the Finger Lakes, 2003—; bd. dirs., sec. Am. Anorexia-Bulimia Assn., N.Y.C., 1984-1999; bd. dirs. Planned Parenthood of the So. Finger Lakes, 2003—. Woodrow Wilson fellow, 1966; Sarah Williston scholar, 1964, Mt. Holyoke scholar, 1963. Mem. Nat. Soc. Fundraising Execs. (Greater N.Y. chpt. v.p. 1993-95, Finger Lakes chpt. bd. dirs. 2002—), Assn. for Rsch. on Nonprofit Orgns. and Voluntary Action, Phi Beta Kappa. Office: The Corning Museum of Glass One Museum Way Corning NY 14830 E-mail: ecicerchi@att.net.

CIELINSKI-KESSLER, AUDREY ANN, writer, publishing executive, small business owner; b. Cleve., Sept. 10, 1957; d. Joseph and Dorothy Antoinette (Hanna) Cielinski. BJ with high honors, U. Tex., 1979. Reporter, writer Med. World News mag., N.Y.C., 1979, asst. copy chief Houston, 1983-84; free-lance writer, editor, 1984—; editl. asst. Jour Health and Social Behavior, Houston, 1980-81; sec. dept. psychiatry Baylor Coll. Medicine, Houston, 1980-81; procedures analyst, tech. writer, tech. libr. Harris County Data Processing Dept., Houston, 1981-83; comm. specialist III, Wang systems adminstr. Office of planning and rsch. Houston Police Dept.; tchr. tech. writing class, 1985-89; tech. writer Chevron Exploration and Prodn. Svcs. Co., Houston, 1990-92; freelance tech. writer, 1992—; owner Write Hand Ohio, Kent, 1992—. Editor: (newsletter) At the Sigmmut, Signals, CEPS Synergy, PCLIBtm Letter, Insights, Steps & Specs., The Voter, LPC Portage County Leader; contbr. stories and articles to newspapers and mags. Vol. editor newsletters Greater Houston area Am. Cancer Soc., VGS, Inc., W. Knoll News; mem. bd. zoning appeals City of Kent, 1996—, vice chair, 1998, 2004, chair, 1999—2002, mem. shade tree commn., 1996—, chair, 1999—2002, mem. assessment equalization bd., 1998—, mem. fair housing bd., 1998—, mem. environ. commn., 1999; mem. transp. study citizen involvement com. Akron Met. Area, 1999—, vice chair, 2000, chair, 2001—02; mem. Leadership Portage County, 1999; bd. dirs. Keep Kent Beautiful, vice chair, 2002—03; vol. writer, graphic designer office religious edn. St. Ambrose Roman Cath. Ch., Houston, 1983—92; trustee Cath. Charities Portage County, v.p., 2002, pres., 2003—04. Recipient Commendation award, Chief of Police, Houston, Chief's Command Employee of Month award, 1989. Mem.: NAFE, Soc. Tech. Comm. (mgr. policies and procedures spl. interest group), Am. Med. Writers Assn., Nat. Assn. Desktop Pubs., Women in Comm., Soc. Children's Book Writers (assoc.), Kent Area C. of C., Women's Network, Alpha Lamda Delta, Phi Kappa Phi, Sigma Delta Chi. Home and Office: 1638 S Lincoln St Kent OH 44240-4449 Office Phone: 330-677-8598.

CIESZEWSKI, JOYCE CATHERINE, writer, educator; b. Cleve., Apr. 20, 1940; d. Chester L. and Cecilia (Laska) Cieszewski. BS, Ursuline Coll., Cleve., 1961; postgrad., John Carroll U., Cleve., 1962—64, Cuyahoga C.C., 1984—86, postgrad., 1995, Lakeland C.C., Kirtland, Ohio, 1998—; student, Sony Video Sch., L.A., 1994. Tech. editor/writer NASA Glenn Rsch. Ctr., Cleve., 1962—91, editl. br. chief, 1991—94, pubs. officer, 1994—95; tech. writer/editor Cortez III Svc. Corp., Cleve., 1995—99, Indyne, Inc., Cleve., 1999—2000; part-time faculty Lakeland C.C., Kirtland, Ohio, 1998—2003, Cuyahoga C.C., Cleve., 2001—03; freelance writer/bus. owner Edit Plus Tech., Walton Hills, Ohio, 1992—. Mem. Cleve. Nat. Engrs. Wk. Com., 1991—92; cons. Cortez III Svc. Corp., Cleve., 1995—96; team tutor Glendale Elem. Sch., Bedford, Ohio, 1999—2002. Co-author: (student handbook) Lakeland Community College Technical Communications Student Handbook, 2000—03. Recipient Disting. Svc. award, NASA, 1996, Special Act or Svc. award, NASA Glenn Rsch. Ctr., 1994, Quality award, 1988. Mem.: Soc. Tech. Comm., Cleve. Tech. Socs. (mem. coun. 1992—94), N.E. Ohio Soc. Women Engrs. (pres. 1992—93), Walton Hills Women's Club (pres., sec. 1992—), NASA Glenn Bus. and Profl. Women (pres. membership 1989—, newsletter editor). Avocations: reading, writing, skiing, photography. Home: 7015 Walton Rd Walton Hills OH 44146-4354

CIESZEWSKI, SANDRA JOSEPHINE, artist, retired manufacturing company manager; b. Cleve., June 7, 1941; d. Chester L. and Cecilia (Laska) C. BA in Chemistry, Ursuline Coll., 1962; BA in Art History, Cleve. State U., 1981; Exec. MBA, Baldwin Wallace Coll., 1989. Chemist Harshaw Chem. Co., Cleve., 1962-65, Union Carbide Corp., Parma, Ohio, 1965-79; project mgr. Gould, Inc., Eastlake, Ohio, 1979-91; product engrng. mgr.- lithium Duracell Global Bus. Mgmt. Group, Lexington, NC, 1992-2001; interim exhbns. coord. Davidson County C.C., 2003—. Mem. Soc. of Women Engrs. (N.E. Ohio sect.) Cleve. Garden Ctr., Cleve. Mus. Art. Mem.: Electrochem. Soc. (treas. 1980), Soc. Applied Spectroscopy, Am. Chem. Soc., Winston-Salem Cinema Soc. (programming chmn. 1997—98, bd. dirs. 1997—2004, treas. 1998—2002), Assoc. Artists of Winston-Salem (bd. dirs. 1998—, sec. 1999—2002, interim exec. dir. 2002, pres. 2002—03), Women's Club (sec. Walton Hills chpt. 1985, treas. 1991). Avocations: gardening, skiing, cycling. Home: 1494 Hickory Tree Rd Winston Salem NC 27127-9142 E-mail: scies@aol.com.

CIFALDI, ROSALIE, private investigator; Lic. pvt. detective Wis. Pvt. detective Rapid Results Investigations, Brookfield, Wis. Office: Rapid Results Investigations LLC PO Box 143 Brookfield WI 53008

CIJKA, MICHELE DAWN, minister; b. White Plains, N.Y., Aug. 29, 1966; d. Theodore Richard Plessner and Nancy Ann Parks; m. Stanley Michael Cijka, Sept. 6, 1998; children: David Pierce, Connor Gabriel. BS in Math., Defiance Coll., 1990; postgrad., U. Mass., 1992; MDiv, Lancaster Theol. Sem., 1995. Math. tchr. Eagle Hill Sch., Hardwick, Mass., 1990—91; interim min. Roscoe (N.Y.) United Ch., 1995—96; min. First Congl. Ch., United Ch. Christ, Hinsdale, Mass., 1997—. Organizer Com. to Help Welfare Reform, Pittsfield, Mass., 1998—99. Avocations: hiking, fine art, singing, quilting, cooking. Home: 412 Maple St Hinsdale MA 01235

CILELLA, MARY WINIFRED, director; b. Oak Park, Ill., Aug. 24, 1943; d. Charles William Sr. and Theresa Mary (Gilligan) Broucek; m. Salvatore G. Cilella Jr., Aug. 29, 1970; children: Salvatore George III, Peter Dominic. BA, Dominican U., 1965; MAT, U. Notre Dame, 1966; grad. The Prin.'s Inst., Harvard U., 1993; postgrad., U. S.C., 1994-97. Tchr. Miner Jr. H.S., Arlington Heights, Ill., 1966-67; sec. White House, Washington, 1969-70; devel. officer Textile Mus., Washington, 1982-83; dir. meetings and continuing edn. Am. Assn. Mus., Washington, 1983-87; interim lower sch. head, lower sch. head Heathwood Hall Episc. Sch., Columbia, S.C., 1989-94, dir. acad. adminstrn., 1994-95, dir. fin. and adminstrn., 1995-96, asst. head, 1996-98, assoc. head fin. and ops., 1998—2001; cons. Park Tudor Sch., Indpls., 2001—02, dir. Russel and Mary Williams Learning Project, 2002—. Mem. profl. edn. unit adv. com. U. S.C., 1996-2001; mem. U.S. Dept. of Edn.'s Blue Ribbon Schs. Planning Group, 1996; examiner Malcolm Baldrige Nat. Quality award bd. U.S. Dept. Commerce and Nat. Inst. Stds. and Tech., 1999, 2000. Mem. ASCD, Phi Delta Kappa. Roman Catholic. Avocations: gardening, collecting antiques, music, aerobics. Home: 905 Tamarack Cir S Dr Indianapolis IN 46260 Office: Park Tudor Sch 7200 North College Ave Indianapolis IN 46240 E-mail: mcilella@parktudor.org.

CIMA, CHERYL ANN, medical/surgical nurse; b. St. Charles, Mo., Jan. 29, 1965; d. Harry H. and Margaret Mary (Schuette) C. Diploma in nursing with honors, St. Luke's Sch. Nursing, St. Louis, 1986; BSN magna cum laude, U. Mo., St. Louis, 1988. RN, Mo. Staff nurse cardiothoracic stepdown unit Barnes Hosp., St. Louis, 1986-93, staff nurse interventional and vascular radiology, 1993-99; staff nurse, acute dialysis unit Barnes Jewish Hosp., 1999—2003; clin. rsch. nurse coord. Dept. Surgery Washington U., St. Louis, 2003—. John Sullivan Waggoner scholar, St. Luke's Merit scholar, Bridgeton Kiwanis scholar. Mem. U. Mo.-St. Louis Nursing Honor Soc., Sigma Theta Tau. Home: 12480 Larkwood Dr Saint Louis MO 63146-4634

CIMINO, ANN MARY, education educator; b. Easton, Pa. d. John and Melina (Castelluzzo) C. BS, Pa. State U., 1955, MEd, 1958; student cert., Lehigh U. Cert. reading specialist. Instr. Sonoma State U., Santa Rosa, Calif., 1958-59, U. Md., 1959-60; asst. prof. Muhlenberg Coll., Allentown, Pa., 1960-69, Towson (Md.) State U., 1967-68; assoc. prof. Kutztown (Pa.) U., 1996-2001; menter L.V. adv. bd. Pa. State U., 2001—. Bd. dirs. Alumni Coun., Coll. Edn.-Pa. State U., mem. Lehigh Valley adv. bd.

CINCA, SILVIA (ROBERTA KING), writer, producer; b. Bucharest, Romania; came to U.S., 1977; d. Stephan Niculescu and Alexandrina (Mosu) Niculescu; married, Feb. 19, 1968; children: Robert, Shelby. Grad., Inst. I.L. Caragiale, Inst. Dramatic Art & Cinema, 1960, Tex. U., 1978-79,

No. Va. C.C., 1979-80, Amb. Bible Coll., 1992. Editor, film critic, TV sect. Romanian Nat. Broadcasting Sys., 1960-73, Radio Free Europe/Radio Liberty, Washington, 1982-99. Author in Romanian lang.: The Cat and The Words, 1966, Destroy the Mirrors, 1969, The Non-Stop Express, 1971, The Unseen Snow, 1973, Scream, 1989, X Ray for Love, (Romfest award Can. 1992), 1992, The Ocean, 1992, X Ray for Success, 1993 (Contact Internat. award 1993), Himera: Leaves on Route 7, 1993, Gabriel Speaks, 1996, Gabriel Comes Back, 1997, Fascination of Misteries, 1998, Texas Hit, 1998, Forest of Angels, 1998, Messenger of Hope, 1999, The Change, The Stroke, 2000; author in Eng. lang.: The Night of the Rising Dead, 1985, Comrade Dracula (ARA award 1988), Homo Spiritus (ARA award 1988), 1988, Scream, Romania Ceausescu's Era, 1990, Hoot of the Owl, Forest of Angels, 1999, Lumina, Magical Journey of Life, Dreams, Success, 2002; Texas H4, 2003; contbr. articles to Romanian periodicals; founder Moonfall Press. Mem. Am. Romanian Acad., Pen Am. Writers Club (founder), LiterArt-XXI Internat. Assn. Romanian Writers and Artists, Owner Editura. Home: 202 N George Mason Dr #3 Arlington VA 22203 E-mail: cincaSilvia@aol.com.

CINELLI, BETHANN, school health educator; b. Norristown, Pa., Apr. 23, 1958; d. Anthony and Donna (George) C. BS, Ind. U. of Pa., 1980; MEd, Temple U., 1982; EdD, Pa. State U., 1986. Cert. health edn. specialist. Health edn. instr. Pa. State U., State College, 1982-86; asst. prof. health edn. West Chester (Pa.) U., 1987—. Pres. Healthcor Assoc., Exton, Pa., 1989—. Contbr. articles to profl. jours. Com. HIV/AIDS Edn. Pa. Acad. Profession of Teaching, Harrisburg, 1990, comprehensive sch. health Pa. Dept. Health, Harrisburg, 1990. Mem. Am. Sch. Health Assn. (bd. dirs. 1989-90), Pa. Sch. Health Assn. (pres. 1990). Office: West Chester U Dept Of Health West Chester PA 19383-0001

CINO, MARIA, political organization administrator, former federal agency administrator; b. Buffalo, Apr. 19, 1957; d. Richard J. and Lucy M. (Tripi) C. BA in Polit. Sci., St. John Fisher Coll. Project supr. Rep. Nat. Com., 1981-82, dir. local programs, 1983-84, exec. asst. field dir., 1985-86, dep. chmn. polit. and congl. rels., 2000—01, dep. chmn., 2003—; rsch. analyst Am. Viewpoint, Inc., 1986-88; adminstrv. asst. Rep. L. William Paxon, 1989-93; exec. dir. Nat. Rep. Congl. Com., 1993—97; sr. advisor Wiley, Rein & Fielding, 1997—99; nat. polit. dir. Bush for Pres., 1999—2000; asst. sec. and dir. general, U.S. comml. svc. U.S. Dept. Commerce, Washington, 2001—03. Mem. Ho. Adminstrv. Assts. Assn. Republican. Avocations: antiques, travel, golf. Office: Rep Nat Comt 310 First St SE Washington DC 20003

CIOCIOLA, CECILIA MARY, development specialist; b. Chester, Pa., Feb. 9, 1946; d. Donato Francis Pasqual and Mary Theresa (Dugan) C. BA, Immaculata Coll., 1975; MA, West Chester U., 1984. Tchr. Archdiocese of Phila., 1964-72, Harrisburg Diocese, Pa., 1972-74, Camden Diocese, NJ, 1974-76; tchr., elem. sci. chairperson Archdiocese of Phila., 1976-86; ednl. cons. Macmillan Pub. Co., Delran, NJ, 1986-88; program officer PATHS/PRISM, Phila., 1988-90; mgr. spl. programs minority engring., math., sci. program Prime, Inc., Phila., 1988-99; dir. partnership and cmty. devel. FOUNDATIONS, Inc., 1999-2001; grants adminstr. Chester Cmty. Charter Sch., Pa., 2001—. Tchr. cert. adv. com. U. the Scis., Phila.; cons. Delaware County Intermediate Unit, Media, Pa., chair elem. (grades 1 8), sci. com. Phila. Archdiocese, 1985-86; coord. Chester County Cath. Schs.: Computer Edn., Pa., 1982-84, Fed. Nutrition Program, St. Agnes Sch., West Chester, Pa., 1983-84, Justice Edn. Teaching Strategies, St. Agnes Sch., West Chester, 1983-84; mem. Mayor's Telecom. Policy Adv. Com., Phila., 1998-2000, Phila. 4-H Program Devel. Com., 1998-2000. Author, editor: (curriculum) Elementary Life and Earth Science, 1984. Mem. adv. com. environ. edn. program Fairmount Pk. Commn., 1998. NSF grantee Operation Primary Phys. Sci., La. State U., 1997—, Project GLOBE, 1997-2000. Mem. ASCD, Nat. Sci. Tchrs. Assn., Pa. Biotech. Assn. (edn. coun.), U. of the Scis. in Phila. (sci. edn. adv. com.), Pa. Sci. Tchrs. Assn. Avocations: poetry, country music, reading, photography, fitness. Office: 214 E 5th St Chester PA 19013-4510

CIPARICK, CARMEN BEAUCHAMP, judge; b. N.Y.C., 1942; Grad., Hunter Coll., 1963; JD, St. John's U., 1967. Staff atty. Legal Aid Soc., N.Y.C.; asst. counsel Office of Jud. Conf., 1969—72; chief law asst. N.Y.C. Criminal Ct., 1972—74, judge, 1978—82; counsel Office of N.Y.C. Adminstrv. Judge, 1974—78; judge N.Y. Supreme Ct, 1982—94; assoc. judge N.Y. State Ct. Appeals, N.Y.C., 1994—. Former mem. N.Y. State Commn. Jud. Conduct. Trustee Boricua Coll.; bd. dirs. St. John's U. Sch. of Law Alumni Assn. Named to Hunter Coll. Hall of Fame, 1991. Office: NY State Ct Appeals 122 E 42nd St New York NY 10168-0002*

CIPLIJAUSKAITE, BIRUTE, humanities educator; b. Kaunas, Lithuania, Apr. 11, 1929; came to U.S., 1957; d. Juozas and Elena (Stelmokaite) C. BA, Lycée Lithuanien Tubingen, 1947; MA, U. Montreal, 1956; PhD, Bryn Mawr Coll., 1960. Permanent mem. Inst. Rsch. in Humanities U. Wis., Madison, 1974, asst. prof., 1961-65, assoc. prof., 1965-68, prof., 1968-73, John Bascom prof., 1973—. Author: Solitude and Spanish Contemporary Poetry, 1962, Poetry and the Poet, 1966, Baroja, a style, 1972, Plentytude as Commitment: The Poetry of Jorge Guillén, 1973, The Generation of 1898 and History, 1981, The Unsatisfied Woman: Adultery in Realist Novel, 1984, Contemporary Women's Novel (1970-85), 1988, Literary Sketches, 1992, Of Signs and Significations. I: Games of the Avant-Garde, 1999, Carmen Martín Gaite, 2000, Guilleniana, 2002; editor: (Luis de Góngora), Complete Sonnets, 1969, 75, 79, 81, 85, 99, critical edit., 1989, Jorge Guillén, 1975, (with C. Maurer) The Will to Humanism. Homage to Juan Marichal, 1990, Novísimos, postnovísimos, clásicos: Poetry of the 80s in Spain, 1991; translator: (Juan Ramón Jiménez), Platero and I, 1982, (María Victoria Atencia), Trances of the Holy Virgin, 1989, Voices Within Silence: Contemporary Lithuanian Poetry, 1991, Birute Pukeleviciute, Lament, 1994, (with Nicole Laurent-Catrice) Twenty Lithuanian Poets of Today, 1997, (Vidmante Jasukaityte), The Miraculous Grass Along the Fence, 2002, (J. Degutytė and B. Pukelevičiute) Between the Sun and Dispossession, 2002, (Mercè Rodoreda) The Girl of the Doves, 2002, (Nijole Miliauskaitė) Forbidden Room, 2003, others. Guggenheim fellow, 1968 Mem. Assn. For Advancement Baltic Studies (v.p. 1981), Asociación Internacional de Hispanistas. Office: U Wis Inst Rsch in Humanities 1401 Observatory Dr Madison WI 53706-1209

CIRELLI, MARY M. state representative; b. Uniontown, Pa., July 4, 1939; married; 2 children. Grad., Canton (Ohio) City Sch. LPN Program; attended, Malone Coll. LPN; state rep. dist. 52 Ohio Ho. of Reps., Columbus, 2000—, ranking minority mem., vets. affairs subcom., mem. county and twp. govt., energy and environment, health, and human svcs. and aging coms., mem. regulatory reform subcom. Mem. Mayor's task force on pay equity, Canton, Ohio. Mem.: Red Cross Gray Ladies, Canton Friendship Ctr., Canton Preservation Soc. (bd. dirs.), Stark County Hunger Task Force, Canton McKinley Alumni, Dem. Womens Club. Democrat. Office: 77 S High St 10th fl Columbus OH 43215-6111

CIRILO, AMELIA MEDINA, educational consultant, supervisor; b. Parks, Tex., May 23, 1925; d. Constancio and Guadalupe (Guerra) Cirilo; m. Arturo Medina, May 31, 1953 (div. June 1979); children: Dennis Glenn, Keith Allen, Sheryl Amelia, Jacqueline Kim. BS in Chemistry, U. North Tex., 1950; MEd, U. Houston, 1954; PhD in Edn. and Nuc. Engring., Tex. A&M U., 1975; cert. in radioisotope tech., Tex. Woman's U., Denton, 1962; cert. in pub. speaking, Dale Carnegie, 1993. Cert. in supervision, bilingual Spanish Tex., permanent profl. tchr. Tex. Tchr. sci. dept. Starr County Schs., Rio Grande City, Tex., 1950—53; elem. tchr. San Benito-Brownsville, Tex., 1953—54, Kingsville (Tex.) Schs., 1954—56; tchr. sci. dept. head chem. physics LaJoya (Tex.) Pub. Schs., 1956—70; tchg. asst. Tex. A&M U., College Station, 1970—74; instr. fire chemistry Del Mar Jr. Coll., Corpus Christi, Tex., 1974—75; exec. dir. Hispanic Ednl. Rsch. Mgmt. Analysis Nat. Assn., Inc., Corpus Christi, 1975—79; head dept. chem. physics San Isidro (Tex.) HS, 1979—82; tchr. chemistry W.H. Adamson HS, Dallas, 1982—84; ednl. cons. Skyline HS, 1992—, tchr. high intensity lang. sci., 1984—86, chmn. faculty adv. com., 1983—84, chemistry tchr., 1986—92. Mem. core faculty Union Grad. Coll., Cin., P.R., Ft. Lauderdale and San Diego, 1975—79; mathematician Well Instrument Devel. Co., Houston, 1950—85; panelist, program evaluator Dept. of Edn., Washington, 1977—79; program evaluator, Robstown, Tex., 1975—79; tchr., trainer Edn. 20 and 2 Region Ctrs., Corpus Christi and San Antonio, 1975—79; rschr., writer Coll. Edn. and Urban Studies Harvard U., Cambridge, Mass., 1978—80; vis. prof. bilingual dept. East Tex. State Coll., Commerce, 1978; ednl. cons. and supr. Adult Basic Edn. Dallas Pub. Schs., 1994—99, kindergarten tchr., 1999—2000, tchr. elem. sci. and math., 2000—02, newcomers ESL tchr., 2002—; conf. presenter program evaluation, 1977—79. Author, rschr. Comparative Evaluation of Bilingual Programs, 1978 (named one of best US books), (poetry) Reflections, 1983; contbr. chapters to books. Mem. Srs. Active in Life adv. com. Dallas City Parks and Recreation; Brazos County advisor Tex. Constl. Revision Commn., 1973—74; sec. Goals for Corpus Christi Com. of 100; Corpus Christi rep. Southwestern Ednl. Authority, Edinburg, Tex., 1977—79; pres. Elem. PTA, 1972—75; mem. Women's Polit. Caucus, Mex. Am. Dems.; exec. bd. Nat. Com. Domestic Violence, 1978—80; bd. trustees Sci. Cluster Skyline HS, 1994—; bd. dirs. Meth. Home for Elderly, Weslaco, Tex., 1968, Am. Cancer Soc. fund drive, College Station, 1971—74; co-founder, bd. dirs. Women's Shelter, Corpus Christi, 1977—78. Named Educator of Yr., Literary Couns. of Greater Dallas, 1997—98; recipient Sr. Salute award for achievements in edn., City of Dallas and NYL Care, 1996; grantee, NSF, The Women's U., 1963—65. Mem.: AAUW, NEA, Metroplex Educators Sci. Assn., Rocky Mountain Sociol. Assn., So. Sociol. Assn., Chem. Soc., Tex. Assn. Bilingual Educators, Tex. Tchrs. Assn., League United Latin Am. Citizens (pres. College Station 1973—74, past dist. dir. Corpus Christi), Pan Am. Round Table, Fiesta Bilingual Toastmasters. Avocations: ballroom dancing, comedy. Home and Office: 5005 Oak Trl Dallas TX 75232-1643

CIRONA, JANE CALLAHAN, investment company executive; b. Detroit, Feb. 23, 1949; d. Earl J. and Madeline Katherine (Freihaut) Callahan; children from previous marriage: Christopher Randall, Elisabeth Anne; m. James M. Cirona, Aug. 29, 1992. BA, Albion Coll., 1970; postgrad., Aquinas Coll., 1989—. Asst. mgr. Nat. Bank of Detroit, 1971-75, program coord. Muskegon (Mich.) C.C., 1978-79; services coord. Muskegon (Mich.) County Cmty. Mental Health, 1979-81; supr. engring. services Teledyne Continental Motors, Muskegon; v.p. investment UBS PaineWebber Inc., Muskegon, 1982—. Dir. Muskegon Econ. Growth Alliance, 1987—, Every Woman's Place, Muskegon, 1979-86; mem. Albion Coll. Planned Giving Adv. Bd., 1989—; mem. Commn. on Growth and Devel. Episcopal Diocese of Western Mich., 1985-88, Consumers Power Citizen Adv. Panel, Muskegon, 1983-84; bd. dirs. Mercy Hosp., Muskegon. Mem.: Zonta Internat. Avocation: travel. Office: UBS PaineWebber Inc PO Box 959 Muskegon MI 49443-0959 E-mail: jane.cirona@ubs.com

CISAR, MARGARET, special education educator; b. Chgo., Oct. 13, 1951; d. William Miser and Winifred (Stevens) F.; m. Thomas Joseph Cisar, Jan. 14, 1977; children: Winifred Catherine, William George. BS in Edn., U. Ariz., 1973; postgrad., U. of the South, 1992-96; MA in Ednl. Leadership, Aurora U., 2001. Cert. tchr. Ill.; cert. in learning disabilities, behavior disorders, trainable mentally handicapped, educable mentally handicapped, exceptional needs, nat. bd. cert. tchr/exceptional needs specialist. Grad. asst. No. Ill. U., DeKalb, 1974-75; tchr. Project Adv., Aurora, Ill., 1975-78; Christian edn. dir. Grace Episcopal Ch., Hinsdale, Ill., 1990-96; tchg. asst. Hinsdale South High Sch., Darien, Ill., 1997; spl. edn. tchr. Waubonsie Valley High Sch., Aurora, Ill., 1997—, spl. edn. dept. liaison, 2001—. Co-chair social comms. com. Vocat. Alliance Autism Project, 2002—03. Vol. humane edn. Hinsdale Humane Soc., 1981—, vol. pet therapy, 1989-90; vol. coord. Lyons Twp. HS, LaGrange, Ill., 1997-98. Mem.: Coun. Exceptional Children (sec. Ill. divsn. on devel. disabilities), Assn. Supervision and Curriculum, Delta Delta Delta (1st v.p. 2003—). Office: Waubonsie Valley High Sch 2590 Ogden Ave Aurora IL 60504-5999

CISLER, THERESA ANN, osteopath; b. Tucson, Dec. 20, 1951; d. William George and Lucille (Seeber) Cisler; 1 child, Daniel Luttrell. BSN, U. Ariz., 1974; DO, Kirksville Coll. Osteopathy, 1983. Diplomate Am. Bd. Osteopathic Manipulative Medicine. Operating room technician St. Joseph's Hosp., Tucson, 1973-74, operating room nurse, 1974-78, operating room inservice coordinator, 1978-79; intern Tucson Gen. Hosp., 1983-84; family practice and manipulation Assoc. Jane J. Beregi, D.O., Tucson, 1984-87; practice medicine specializing in osteo. manipulation Tucson, 1987—. Active med. staff Tucson Gen. Hosp., 1984—91, med. records chmn., 1986—87; part-time med. staff Westcenter Drug & Rehab., Tucson, 1984—88; vol. med. staff St. Elizabeth Hungary Clinic, 1984—87; mem. substance abuse com. Westcenter-Tucson Gen. Hosp., 1986—88, mem. osteo. concepts com., osteo. manipulative cons., 1986—91. Roadrunner Civitan, 2000—01; chair Ariz.-S. Nev. Jr. Civitan, 2001—; eucharistic min. St. Pius X Ch., Tucson, 1984—86, eucharistic min. coord., 1087—1990. Mem.: Cranial Acad. (bd. dirs. 1997—2003, pres. 2003—), Ariz. Osteo. Med. Assn. (at-large ho. of dels. 1985—93), Am. Acad. Osteopathy (chair med. econs. com. 1994—99, bd. govs. 1997—), Am. Osteo. Assn., Kirksville Coll. Osteopathy-Century Club. Roman Catholic. Avocations: sewing, country dancing. Home and Office: 800 N Swan Rd Ste 128 Tucson AZ 85711-1276 Office Phone: 520-795-3772.

CISNEROS, EVELYN, dancer; b. Long Beach, Calif., 1958; Mem. San Francisco Ballet Co., 1977—99. Performances include Scherzo, Mozart's C Minor Mass, Romeo and Juliet, Medea, The Tempest, 1980, Stars and Stripes, In the Night, A Midsummer Nights Dream, Cinderella, A Song for Dead Warriors, 1984, Confidences, 1986, Sleeping Beauty, 1992, Swan Lake, 1993. Office: San Francisco Ballet 455 Franklin St San Francisco CA 94102-4471

CISNEROS, SANDRA, poet, short story writer, essayist; b. Chgo., Dec. 20, 1954; BA, Loyola U., 1976. College recruiter, counselor Loyala U., Chicago; literature dir. Guadalupe Cultural Arts Center, San Anto, Tex.; artist-in-residence Foundation Michael Karolyi, France. Guest prof. Calif. St. U., U. Calif., Berkeley, U. Mich., U. N.M. Author: (books) The House On Mango Street, 1984 (Am. Book award Columbus Found. 1985), Woman Hollering Creek and Other Stories, 1991, (children's) Hairs=Pelitos, 1994, (poetry) Bad Boys, 1980, The Rodrigo Poems, 1985, My Wicked, Wicked Ways, 1987, Loose Women, 1994, La Casa en Mango Street, 1994, El Arroyo de la Llorona, 1996, Caramelo, 2002. Fellow NEA, 1982, 87, MacArthur fellow, 1995; recipient Lannan Found. Lit. award, 1991. Home and Office: Susan Bergholz Literary SvcsAgy 17 W 10th St # 5 New York NY 10011-8746

CISSNA, SHARON, state representative; b. Seattle, Apr. 5, 1942; m. Stanley Robbins (dec.); 1 child, Robin Naughton. Student, U. Wash., 1964—67; BA, U. Alaska, Anchorage, 1972; MS, Alaska Pacific U., 1992. Owner publ. svc. bus., 1972—; legis. aide Sate of Alaska, 1971, 1973, 1995; owner Solutions, 1994—; mem. Alaska Ho. of Reps., 1998—. Bd. dirs. World Wide Desing, Inc. Chair Chugach State Park Ad Hoc Com., 1969—70; past pres. citizen adv. bd. Chugach State Park; co-chair PARC, Alaska Voters for Open Primary. Mem.: Alaska Press Women, Alaska Pacific U. Alumni Assn., U. Alaska Anchorage Alumni Assn., Toastmasters. Democrat. Office: Rm 420 State Capitol Juneau AK 99801-1182 Address: 716 W 4th Ste 610 Anchorage AK 99501-2133

CITRANO-CUMMISKEY, DEBRA MOIRA, chemist, network technician; b. Glen Cove, Ny, Feb. 23, 1957; d. Helen Marie and Roy Maurice Citrano; 1 child, Nikki Marie Cummiskey. A+ Certification Computer Career Ctr., 2002. Raw materials auditor Hi-Tech Pharm., Amityville, NY, 2003—; qc raw materials chemist Kos Pharmaceuticals, Edison, NJ, 2003—03. Corp. reference std. coord. DuPont Pharmaceuticals, Garden City, NY, 1978—2001. Mem.: Am. Chem. Soc. American Independent. Catholic. Avocations: dance, swimming. Office: Hi-Tech Pharmacal Co Inc 369 Bayview Avenue Amityville NY 11701 Personal E-mail: corporatewoman@msn.com.

CITRON, BEATRICE SALLY, law librarian, lawyer, educator; b. Phila., May 19, 1929; d. Morris Meyer and Frances (Teplitsky) Levinson; m. Joel P. Citron, Aug. 7, 1955 (dec. Sept. 1977); children: Deborah Ann, Victor Ephraim. BA in Econs. with honors, U. Pa., 1950; MLS, Our Lady of the Lake U., 1978; JD, U. Tex., 1984. Bar: Tex. 1985; cert. all-level sch. libr., secondary level tchr. Tex. Claims examiner Social Security Adminstrn., Pa., Fla. and N.C., 1951-59; head libr. St. Mary's Hall, San Antonio, 1979-80; media, reference and rare book libr., asst. and assoc. prof. St. Mary's U. Law Libr., San Antonio, 1984-89; asst. dir. St. Thomas U. Law Libr., Miami, Fla., 1989-96, assoc. dir./head pub. svc., 1996-99, acting dir., 1997-98. Law libr. cons., 2000—. Mem.: ABA, South Fla. Assn. Law Librs. (treas. 1992—94, v.p. 1994—95, pres. 1995—96), S.E. Assn. Law Librs. (newsletter, program and edn. coms. 1991—98), S.W. Assn. Law LIbrs. (continuing edn. com. 1986—88, chmn. local arrangements 1987—88), Am. Assn. Law Librs. (publs. com. 1987—88, com. on rels. with info. vendors 1991—93, bylaws com. 1994—96).

CIURCZAK, ALEXIS, librarian; b. Long Island, N.Y., Feb. 13, 1950; d. Alexander Daniel and Catherine Ann (Frangipane) C. BA Art History magna cum laude, U. Calif., L.A., 1971; MA Libr. Sci., San Jose State U., 1975; cert. tchr. ESL, U. Calif., Irvine, 1985. Intern IBM Rsch. Libr., San Jose, Calif., 1974-75; tech. asst. San Bernardino Valley Coll. Libr., Calif., 1975; tech. svcs. librarian Palomar Coll., San Marcos, Calif., 1975-78, pub. svcs. librarian, 1978-81, libr. dir., 1981-86, pub. svcs. librarian, 1987—, instr. Libr. Technology Cert. Program, 1975—; exchange librarian Fulham Pub. Libr., London, 1986-87; coord. San Diego C.C. Consortium Semester-in-London Am. Inst. Fgn. Study, 1988-89. Mem. ALA, San Diego Libr. Svcs. com., Calif. Libr. Media Educators Assn., Patronato por Niños, Kosciuszko Found., So. Calif. Tech. Processes Group, Pacific Coast Coun. Latin Am. Studies, Libros, Reforma, Libr. Assn. (British), Calif. Libr. Assn., Calif. Tchrs. Assn., Phi Beta Kappa, Beta Phi Mu. Office: Palomar CC 1140 W Mission Rd San Marcos CA 92069-1415 E-mail: aciurczak@palomar.edu.

CIVIELLO, MARY, correspondent; Bachelor, Master, U. Mo. Reporter L.A. Times, 1974-77; anchor, reporter Sta. WEAU-TV, Eau Claire, Wis.; reporter various stas., Sta. WNBC-TV, N.Y.C., 1982-98; corr. CNBC, Ft. Lee, N.J., 1998—; pres., chmn. Civiello Comm. Group, Bronxville, N.Y. Recipient 3 Emmy awards, N.Y. Press Club Byline award, Deadline Club Sigma Delta Chi award. Office: Civiello Comm Group 5 Woodland Ave Bronxville NY 10708

CIVISH, GAYLE ANN, psychologist; b. Lynnwood, Calif., Sept. 29, 1948; d. Leland and Arline (Frazer) Civish; children: Nathan Morrow, Shane Morrow. BA, U. Nev., Reno, 1970; MA, U. Colo., 1973, PhD, 1983; student, Iliff Sch. Theology, 2001—. Lic. psychologist, Colo., Pa.; cert. sch. psychologist, Colo. Sch. psychologist Jefferson County (Colo.) Schs., 1983-03, psychologist in pvt. practice Lakewood, Colo., 1983-99, Boulder, Colo., 1999—. Cons. charter schs. integrated spl. edn., 1998. Contbr. articles to profl. jours. and books. Mem. APA (editor newsletter regional divsn.), Colo. Psychol. Assn. (bd. dirs. 1990-93), Pa. Psychol. Assn., Colo. Women Psychologists (past external liaison), Am. Soc. Clin. Hypnosis, Feminist Therapy Inst. (steering com. 1994-99), Assn. for Women in Psychology, Phi Kappa Phi, Phi Delta Kappa. Democrat. Office: #8 2885 Aurora Ave Ste 14 Boulder CO 80303-2251

CLAES, GAYLA CHRISTINE, writer, editorial consultant; b. L.A., Oct. 17, 1946; d. Henry George and Glorya Desiree (Curran) Blasdel; m. Daniel John Claes, Jan. 19, 1974. AB magna cum laude, Harvard U., 1968; postgrad., Oxford (Eng.) U., 1971; MA, McGill U., Montreal, 1975. Adminstrv. asst. U. So. Calif., L.A., 1968-70; teaching asst. English lit. McGill U., Montreal, 1970-71; editorial dir. Internat. Cons. Group, L.A., 1972-78; v.p. Gaylee Corp., L.A., 1978-81, CEO, 1981-88; writer, cons. L.A. and Paris, 1988—. Dir. pub. rels. Ctr. Internat. for the Performing Arts, Paris and L.A., 1991—2000. Author: (play) Berta of Hungary, 1972, (novel) Christopher Derring, 1990; contbr. articles to lit. and sci. jours. Co-founder White Swan Awards, ann. benefit for Crippled Children's Soc. dba AbilityFirst, 1999. Mem. Harvard-Radcliffe Club of So. Calif., Royal Commonwealth Soc. (London).

CLAFLIN, TRACIE NADINE, private school educator; b. Rapid City, S.D., June 28, 1970; d. Ron H. Williams and Patricia Claflin; BFA, Ringling Sch. Art and Design, Sarasota, Fla., 1993. Freelance artist; art tchr., 1999—; tchr. Prew Acad., Sarasota, 1994—; field trip supt., art tchr. YMCA, Sarasota, 1994—; art tchr. Divine Mercy and Our Lady of Lourdes, Brevard County, Fla. Home: 221 Miami Ave Indialantic FL 32903-3518

CLAGETT, VIRGINIA PARKER, county official; b. Washington, July 18, 1943; d. William Merrick and Virginia (Lawrence) Parker; m. Brice McAdoo, Sept. 18, 1965; children: John Brice, Ann Broke. Student, U. Geneva, 1963-64; BA, Smith Coll., 1965. Asst. reporter Triangle Stas., Phila., 1966-68; county councilwoman County of Anne Arundel, Annapolis, Md., 1974-94, council chmn., 1984-91; mem. Md. Gen. Assembly Ho. of Dels., 1994—. Vice chmn. Balt. Regional Planning Coun., 1984—; trustee Hammond-Harwood Ho., 1978—, Chesapeake EPA, 1976—; mem. Alcohol and Drug Abuse Adv. Com., 1985—; mem. Anne Arundel County Agrl. Adv. Com., 1978—; bd. dirs. Historic Annapolis, Inc. Mem. Am. Bus. Womens Assn., Md. Assn. Counties (legis. com.). Democrat. Episcopalian. Avocations: tennis, gardening, horseback riding. Home: PO Box 1 West River MD 20778-0001 Office: Ho of Dels Md Gen Assembly 212 Lowe Office Bldg 84 College Ave Annapolis MD 21401

CLAIBORNE, LIZ (ELISABETH CLAIBORNE ORTENBERG), fashion designer; b. Brussels, Mar. 31, 1929; came to U.S., 1939; d. Omer Villere and Louise Carol (Fenner) C.; m. Arthur Ortenberg, July 5, 1954; 1 son by previous marriage, Alexander G. Schultz. Student, Art Sch., Brussels, 1948-49, Academie, Nice, France, 1950; DFA, R.I. Sch. Design, 1991. Asst. Tina Lesser, N.Y.C., 1951-52, Omar Khayam, Ben Reig, Inc., N.Y.C., 1953; designer Juniorite, N.Y.C., 1954-60, Dan Keller, N.Y.C., 1960-76, Youth Guild Inc., N.Y.C., 1976-89; designer, pres., chmn. Liz Claiborne Inc., N.Y.C., 1985-89, pres., 1976-89, chmn., chief oper. officer, until 1989; chmn. Liz Claiborne Cosmetics, 1985-89, cons. Guest lectr. Fashion Inst. Tech., Parsons Sch. Design; bd. dirs. Coun. of Am. Fashion Designers, Fire Island Lighthouse Restoration Com. Recipient Designer of Yr. award Palciode Hierro, Mexico City, 1976, Designer of Yr. award Dayton Co., Mpls., 1978, Ann. Disting. in Design award Marshall Field's, 1985, One Co. Makes a Difference award Fashion Inst. Tech., 1985, award Coun. Fashion Designers, 1986, Gordon Grand Fellowship award Yale U., 1989, Jr. Achievement award Nat. Bus. Hall of Fame, 1990, Frederick A.P. Barnard award Barnard Coll., 1991, Hon. Doctorate, R.I. Sch. of Design, 1991; named to Nat. Sales Hall of Fame, 1991. Mem. Fashion Group. Roman Catholic.

CLAMAR, APHRODITE J. psychologist; b. Hartford, Conn. d. James John and Georgia (Panas) Clamar; m. Richard Cohen, June 24, 1973. BA, CCNY, 1953; MA, Columbia U., 1955; PhD, NYU, 1978; student, S. Adler Conservatory Acting, 1987-91. Mgmt. cons., psychologist Milla Alihan

Assocs., N.Y.C., 1957-62; rsch. psychologist coord. Inst. Devel. Studies N.Y. Med. Coll., N.Y.C., 1964; intern psychologist Bellevue Psychiat. Hosp., N.Y.C., 1964-66; assoc. prof. Fashion Inst. Tech., N.Y.C., 1966-69; supervising psychologist Lifeline Ctr. Child Devel., N.Y.C., 1966-67; chief psychologist I Spy Health Program Beth Israel Med. Ctr., N.Y.C., 1967-70; dir. community-sch. mental health programs Soundview Community Svcs., Albert Einstein Coll. Medicine Yeshiva U., N.Y.C., 1970-73; dir. treatment program court-related children, dept. child psychiatry Harlem Hosp.; mem. faculty dept. psychiatry Coll. Physicians and Surgeons Columbia U., N.Y.C., 1973-76; pvt. practice psychotherapy, N.Y.C., 1976—; co-founder, pres. Richard Cohen Assocs. Pub. Rels. Agy., N.Y.C., 1979—99; prof. John Jay Coll., CUNY, 2000—. Cons. to pub. health and mental health agys., N.Y.C., 1976-91; mem. faculty Lenox Hill Hosp. Psychoanalytic Psychotherapy Tng. Program, 1982-88; theater producer, artistic dir. Tom Cat Cohen Prodns., Inc., 1990—. Author: (with Budd Hopkins) Missing Time, 1981; contbr. articles to profl. jours. Fellow AAAS; mem. APA, Dramatists Guild, Authors Guild. Democrat. Greek Orthodox. Home: 155 W 68th St Apt 1618 New York NY 10023-5829

CLANCY, CAROLYN, science foundation director, researcher, educator; Grad., Boston Coll., U. Mass. Fellow Henry Kaiser Family Found. U. Pa.; clin. assoc. prof. dept. health care scis. George Washington U. Sch. Medicine; asst. prof. dept. internal medicine Va. Commonwealth U./Med. Coll. Va.; dir. Ctr. Primary Rsch. Agy. Healthcare Rsch. and Quality, HHS, internist Ctr. Outcomes and Efffectiveness Rsch. (COER), 1997—, dir., 2002—. Rschr. in field. Sr. assoc. editor Health Svcs. Rsch. ; mem. editl. bd.: Am. Jour. Pub. Health ; Jour. Evaluation in Clin. Practice, Jour. Gen. Internal Medicine, Med. Care Rsch. and Rev. ; contbr. articles in peer-reviewed jours. Recipient award, APHA Women's Caucus . Mem.: Soc. Gen. Internal Medicine. Office: Agcy for Healthcare Research Quali 540 Gaither Rd Rockville MD 20850-6649

CLANCY, MARGUERITE ALINE (MEG CLANCY), librarian; b. Holyoke, Mass., July 8, 1961; d. Robert Elmer and Constance Aline (Hubert) Clancy; 1 child, Aaron Hubert Soule. AA, Holyoke C.C., 1981; BA, U. Mass., 1983; MLS, So. Conn. State U., 1994. Cert. libr. Mass., 1994. Adminstrv. asst. South Hadley Pub. Libr., Mass., 1986—96, youth svcs. libr., 1996—. Mem. statewide steering com. Mass. Summer Reading Program, 1998—2000. Sec. South Hadley Dem. Town Com., 1994—; register of voters, 1999—. Mem.: New Eng. Libr. Assn., Mass. Libr. Assn. (sec. exec. bd. 2002—03, mem. legis. com. 1989—2003, mem. youth svcs. sect. 1998—2003), Am. Libr. Assn. Office: South Hadley Pub Libr 27 Bardwell St South Hadley MA 01075 Office Phone: 413-538-5045.

CLANCY, PATRICIA, state representative; b. Cin., Aug. 10, 1952; BS, U. Cin. State rep. dist. 29 Ohio Ho. of Reps., Columbus, 1996—, mem. fin. and appropriations, rules and reference, and state govt. coms., mem. agr. and devel., and ethics and elections subcoms., majority fl. leader. Mem. Hamilton County Solid Waste Dist. Task Force, Colerain Ave. Task Force; past pres., trustee Colerain Twp. Mem.: Hamilton County Twp. Assn. (sec.-treas.), Colerain Twp. Hist. Soc., Colerain Twp. Rep. Club (sec.), Hamilton County Rep. Club. Republican. Office: 77 S High St 14th fl Columbus OH 43215-6111

CLAPP, LAURI, state representative; b. Denver, Dec. 1, 1962; m. Rolley Clapp; 3 children. State rep. dist. 37 Colo. Ho. of Reps., Denver, 1998—, vice chair joint com. on health, edn., welfare and instns. and HECF, chair health, environment, welfare and instns. com., mem. judiciary com. Mem.: VFW Women's Aux., Englewood Hist. Soc., Arapahoe County Rep. Men's Club, Englewood Women's Rep. Club, Cherry Creek Rep. Women's Club. Republican. Avocation: canning james, jellies and syrups. Office: State Capitol # 320 200 E Colfax Ave Denver CO 80203

CLAPP, MILLICENT EVANS, real estate broker; b. Enfield, N.H., Sept. 1, 1923; d. Walter Edgar and Georgianna M. (Bourdeau) Evans; m. Michael Sabal, Apr. 5, 1943; 1 child, Kerry Eileen. Student, Travelers Ins. Co. Group Agency, Hartford, Conn., 1941-43, Am. Inst. Banking, 1960, U. N.H., 1972, Vt. Real Estate Inst., 1973. Radio broadcaster Sta. WTSL, Hanover, N.H., 1952-55, Sta. WOTW, Nashua, N.H., 1952-55; dir. publicity and pub. rels. N.H. Children's Aid Soc., Nashua, 1956-57; asst. to execs. Soc. for Savs., Hartford, Conn., 1957-62; customer svc. rep. Hallmark Cards, Kansas City, Mo., 1966-68; make-up artist Max Factor, Hollywood, Calif., 1968; real estate broker Mass., N.H., Vt. and Fla., 1984—, Mackle Bros., Fla., 1969; with U.S. Census 2000 Bureau. Owner Milly's Antiques and Collectibles, 1990—. Vice chmn. Ellington (Conn.) Rep. Party, 1961-68; chmn. Enfield Bicentennial Com., 1975-77. Recipient Disting. Svc. award Deltona Corp., 1969. Mem. Nat. Assn. Realtors, Abenaki Nation of N.H. Lutheran. Avocations: traveling, antiques, photography, writing children's stories. Home: RR 1 Box 1186 Kingfield ME 04947-9801

CLAPPER, MARIE ANNE, magazine publisher; b. Chgo., Nov. 21, 1942; d. Chester William and Hazel Alice (Gilso) Reinke; m. William Neil Petersen, Aug. 17, 1963 (div. 1975); children: Elaine Myrtice Petersen, Edward William Petersen; m. Lyle N. Clapper, Jan. 1, 1980; children: Jeffrey Leland, Anne Reinke stepchildren: John Scott, Susan Louise Clapper Kashmier. Student, Augustana Coll., Rock Island, Ill., 1960-63; EdB, Northeastern U., 1964. Writer Pack-o-Fun mag., Park Ridge, Ill., 1976-77, editor Des Plaines, Ill., 1977-78, pub., 1990—; asst. to pub., circulation dir. Crafts 'n Things mag., Des Plaines, Ill., 1978-82, pub., 1982—, Decorative Arts Painting mag., Des Plaines, 1990—, The Cross Stitcher mag., Des Plaines, 1991—, 101 Bridal Ideas mag., Des Plaines, 1991—; pub., pres. Clapper pub. Host TV show The Crafts 'n Things Show, 1984-86, Crafting for the 90s, 1990-94; author: EveryDay Matters, 1996. Mem. TEC, Mag. Pubs. Am. (bd. dirs.), Hobby Industry Am. (bd. dirs., treas. 1998-99), Soc. Craft Designers. Office: Crafts 'n Things 2400 E Devon Ave Ste 375 Des Plaines IL 60018-4618

CLAREY, PATRICIA, association executive; BS, Union Coll.; M Pub. Adminstrn., Harvard U. John F. Kennedy Sch. of Govt. With Nat. Park Svc., Washington, Dept. of Interior, Washington; govt. affairs rep. Chevron Corp., San Francisco; dep. chief of staff Calif. Gov. Pete Wilson; v.p. public affairs Transamerica, San Francisco, 1999—. Pres. Transamerica Found., 1998—. Office: Transamerica Found 600 Montgomery St San Francisco CA 94111-2702

CLARIDGE, RHONDA L. writer, educator; b. Nassau, Bahamas, Aug. 2, 1967; d. William Hugh Claridge and Elizabeth Doreen Falloon; m. Sean P. McNamara, July 20, 1996. BA in Journalism and Classical Lit., NYU, 1989; MA in English Lit., U. Colo., Boulder, 1995. Contbg. writer Abaco Life, Raleigh, NC, 1991—, Writers on the Range, Paonia, Colo., 2002—; instr., fiction Ah Haa Sch. for the Arts, Telluride, Colo., 1995—; instr. Mesa State Coll., Montrose, Colo., 1999—2001; resident artist Colo. Young Audiences, Denver, 1999—; contbg. writer Mountain Gazette, Breckenridge, Colo., 2000—; ESL instr. Wright Stuff Found., Telluride, Colo., 2001—03; tchr. English and social studies Forest Heights Acad., Marsh Harbour, The Bahamas, 2002—03. Editor Streams of Conscience, stories by Telluride High School's Grade 11, Telluride, Colo., 1996, Valley Floor Anthology, Telluride, Colo., 2002—; panelist Colo. Coun. on the Arts Fiction/Nonfiction Fellowship Awards, Denver, 2001. Prodr.: Krapp's Last Tape, 1994; author: one-act play; contbr. fiction to lit. jours. and anthology (Colo. Coun. on the Arts Lit. fellow, 1999, Phoebe Fiction award, 1998, Philip Roth Writer-in-Residence, 1997, Transatlantic Rev. award, 1995, Jovanovitch Imaginative Writing award, 1995, Hon. Mention, Katherine Anne Porter prize, The Nimrod/Hardman awards, 2001, Highly Commended, Commonwealth Broadcasting Prize for Short Fiction, 2001, 3d prize Writers' Soc. of the Bahamas, 1996). Vol. staff EarthWatch/Ctr. for Whale Rsch., Friday Harbour, Wash., 1990; spokesperson Friends of the Environment, Marsh Harbour, 1991—2003, Sheep Mountain Alliance Environ. Orgn., Telluride, Colo., 1996—2003. Scholar, Squaw Valley Cmty. of Writers, 1993. Home and Office: P O Box 2083 Telluride CO 81435

CLARK, ALICIA GARCIA, political party official; b. Vera Cruz, Mex. came to U.S., 1970; d. Rafael Garcia Aully and Maria Luisa (Cobos) Garcia; m. Edward E. Clark, Oct. 20, 1970; 1 child, Edward E. MS in Chem. Engring., Nat. U. Mex., Mexico City, 1951. Chemist Celanese Mexicana, Mexico City, 1951-53, lab. mgr., 1951-53, sales promotion mgr., 1958-65, sales promotion and advt. mgr., 1965-70; nat. chmn. Libertarian Party, Houston, 1981-83, coord. coun. state chairs, 1987-95. Pres. San Marino (Calif.) Guild of Huntington Hosps., 1981-82, chmn. Celebrity Series, 1989-90, 90-91. Pres. bd. dirs. L.A. Opera League, 1990-96; founder, co-chair Hispanics for L.A. Opera, 1991-99; bd. dirs. Guild Opera Co., 1994-96, Club 100, 1996-99; mng. dir. L.A. Opera, 1995—; mem. opera panel Nat. Endowment for Arts, 1997. Recipient award La Mujer de Hoy mag., 1969, Heroes of L.A. award Hispanic Traditions and Heritage Coun., 1995, Star of Our Culture award Mex. Cultural Inst. L.A., 1998, Placido Domingo award, 2000. Mem. Fashion Group (treas. 1969-70, award 1970). Fax: 626 796-3485.

CLARK, ANN BLAKENEY, educational administrator; b. Greensboro, N.C., May 21, 1958; d. Blake Campbell and Nancy (Hamel) C. BA in English, Davidson (N.C.) Coll., 1980; MEd, U. Va., 1982; postgrad., U. N.C., 1985—. Spl. edn. tchr. Virginia Beach (Va.) Pub. Schs., 1982-83, Devonshire Elem. Sch., 1983-87; asst. prin. Montclare Elem. Sch., 1987-88; prin. Shamrock Gardens Elem. Sch., 1988-90, Alexander Graham Mid. Sch., Charlotte, N.C., 1990-96, Vans H.S., NC, 1996—2001; asst. supt. high schs. Charlotte-Mecklenburg Schs., Charlotte, NC, 2001—. Vice pres. Jr. League of Charlotte, 1988-89; mem. bd. mgrs. Johnston YMCA, Charlotte, 1987—; chmn. bd. A Child's Place, Charlotte, 1989—. Named Nat. Principal of Yr. 1994; named Tchr. of Yr., Devonshire Elem., 1987-88. Mem. ASCD, NAESP, Coun. for Exceptional Children, Coun. for Children, Phi Delta Kappa. Republican. Episcopalian. Avocations: golf, tennis. Home: 7920 Neal Rd Charlotte NC 28262-3226

CLARK, ANN D. marriage and family therapist; b. Frankfort, Ky., Feb. 22, 1939; d. Snyder Highfield Downs and Emma Ruth Sullivan Downs; children: Deanna Smith, Tandice Tinney. BA in english, U. of Ky., 1960, MS in guidance and counseling, MS in spl. edn., U. of Ky., 1964; PhD, U. of Wis., 1969; CME, U. New Mexico, 1979. Cert. Marriage, Family, and Child Counselor State of Calif., 1986, Employee Assistance Profl. State of Calif., 1988. Founder & CEO ACI, San Diego, 1983—; state dir. of rsch. Wis. State Dept. of Edn., 1966—67; asst. prof., program dir. U. of Wis., 1967—75; assoc. prof. Peabody Vanderbilt Coll. for Teachers, Nashville, 1975—77; spl. adv. to wife of gov. Bruce King, 1979; state dir. of child abuse services & dir. of edn. State of N.Mex, 1977—80; prof. of psychology and chem. dependency US Internat. U., San Diego, 1986—87. Author: (book) Surviving Your Boss: How to Cope with Office Politics and Get on With Your Job, Looking Good: Images of Sober Women, (collection of copyrighted columns) Words for Women, (booklet) Alone But Not Lonely; contbr. articles. Named one of San Diego's Women who Mean Business, 1998; recipient Bravo award, Nat. Assn. Women Bus. Owners, 2004; BEH Doctoral Fellowship Program, U. of Wis., 1966—68, A Consortium of UAF Spl. Educators, USOE, 1971—72, grant, 1978, UAF - Spl. Edn. in Mental Retardation grant, 1969—75, grant, 1976—77. Mem.: NAFE, Assn. of Labor Mgmt. Administrators and Consultants on Alcoholism, Nat. Counseling Assn., Calif. Women's Commn. on Alcohol and Drug Dependencies, Calif. Assn. of Marriage and Family Therapists, Employee Assistance Soc. of N.Am., Employee Assistance PA. Avocations: bicycling, travel, art, interior design. Office: ACI Ste 650 8910 University Ctr Ln San Diego CA 92122 Office Phone: 858-452-1254.

CLARK, ANNA M. minister, lobbyist; b. Nashville, Sept. 6, 1930; d. Willie Lee Wright and Carol Jackson Martin; m. Clifford Edward Clark Jr., Oct. 19, 1959; children: David, Clifford III; 1 child, Itsie. Minister Bible Ministries Inc., Tampa, Fla., 1986—. Adminstrv. asst. Medicaid, Pensacola, Fla., 1987—88; spkr. Vets. & Srs., 1959—; lobbyist Vets., Tampa, 1965—; reporter Metro News, Tampa, 2000—; pastor VA Hosp., Tampa, 1983—2001. Staff mem. Rep. Party, 1974—. Mem.: Vets. (dir. corm 1992—93, commdr. dava 1983—84). Avocations: reading, writing, music. Home: 8006 W Hiawatha St Tampa FL 33615 Office: The Investigative Reporter 8006 W Hiawatha St Tampa FL 33615 E-mail: rev.sam3@ij.net.

CLARK, BARBARA JUNE, elementary school educator; b. Leoti, Kans., May 29, 1934; d. Robert Carter and Adlee Belle (Wilson) C. BS in Edn., Ft. Hays State U., 1958, MS in Edn., 1967. 4th grade tchr. McKinley Elem., Liberal, Kans., 1954—56, Lincoln Elem., Liberal, 1958—61, 5th grade tchr., 1961—62, 4th grade tchr., 1962—2001. Mathfest chmn. Unified Sch. Dist. 480, Liberal, 1987-88, grade level chmn., 1988-89, social studies textbook selection com., 1990-92, intensive assistance team, 89-91, Lincoln Sch. site coun., 1993-94, Lincoln preassessment team, 1992-98, Lincoln strategic action com., 1994-98, reading textbook selection com., 1995-96, others; quality performance accreditation chmn. math team, 1998-2001; with Ft. Hay State U. travel study tours, Hawaii, 1960, Europe, 1962. Editor: Wilson History, 1970—; author Lincoln School History, 1978. Singer Meth. Chancel Choir; pres. Meth Wesleyan Svc. Guild, 1963-66, v.p. 1962-63, treas., 60-62, rec. sec. Meth Dodge City Dist., 1965-68; sponsor, bus. mgr. Meth Ctrl. Kans. Conf. Mission Edn. Tour, 1975-78; rec. sec. United Meth. Ch. Circle 9, 1986-88, v.p., 1996-99, Circle 8, 1999—; vol. Lincoln Elem., 2002-03. Recipient Representative Young Tchr. award Jr. C. of C., Liberal, 1962, PTA Life Membership, Lincoln Elem., Liberal, 1962, Morale Enhancement award, 2001, Elem. Tchr. of Yr., 2001. Mem. NEA, Kans. NEA, Liberal NEA (Master Tchr. award 1989), Bus. and Profl. Women's Club (pres. 1979-80, treas. 1989-90, 94—, v.p. 1991-94, fin. chair 1992—, Woman of Yr. award 1974), Beta Sigma Phi (Laureate Pi chpt. treas. 1981-91, pres. 1991—, Silver Circle award 1992, Order of Rose award 1974), Delta Kappa Gamma (Phi state conv. registration chmn. 1974, 95, rec. sec. 1986-88, music chmn. 1992-94, pres. 1999-2002, state mem. com. 2001-03, state rsch. com. 2003—), Santa Fe Trail Assn. (charter life). Avocations: geneology, history.

CLARK, BARBARA MARLENE, state legislator; b. Beckley, W.Va., June 12, 1939; m. Thomas Clark; children: Jan, Crystal, Thomas II, Brian. Mem. N.Y. State Assembly, Albany, 1986—. Past mem. assembly standing com. on aging, housing, small bus., and social svcs.; mem. standing com. on children and families, corps., authorities and commns. edn. and labor. V.p. Parents Assn.; mem. exec. bd., prin. consultative coun. Andrew Jackson H.S., Sprinfield Garden Jr. H.S., P.S. 176, Cambria Heights, N.Y.; mem. adv. coun. Teen Pregnancy Prevention Program; active NAACP, Nat. Coun. Negro Women. Democrat. Office: NY District Office 97-01 Springfield Blvd Queens Village NY 11429 also: NY State Assembly Legis Office Bldg Rm 538 State Capitol Albany NY 12248

CLARK, BEVERLY ANN, lawyer; b. Davenport, Iowa, Dec. 9, 1944; d. F. Henry and Arlene F. (Meyer) C.; m. Richard Floss; children: Amy and Barry (twins); stepchildren: Heather, Gretchan. Student, Mich. State U., 1963—65; BA, Calif. State U., Fullerton, 1967; MSW, U. Iowa, 1975, JD, 1980; grad., Iowa Massage Inst., 1999. Bar: Iowa 1980; lic. social worker, Iowa; nat. cert. lic. massage therapist. Probation officer County of San Bernardino, San Bernardino, Calif., 1968, County of Riverside, Riverside, Calif., 1968-69; social worker Skiff Hosp., Newton, Iowa, 1971-73, State of Iowa, Mitchellville, 1973-74, planner Des Moines, 1976-77, law clk., 1980-81; corp. counsel Pioneer Hi-Bred Internat., Inc., Des Moines, 1981-2000; atty. Jasper County Legal Aid, 2002—03; pvt. practice, 2000—. Instr. Des Moines Area C.C., Ankeny, Iowa, 1974—75, 2001—; adj. prof. Drake Law Sch., 1993—96, Buena Vista U., 2002—; pub. Sweet Annie Press; past owner Annie's Place, The B&B Connection Gift Catalog. Editor: Proceedings: Bicentennial Symposium on New Directions in Juvenile Justice, 1975; author monthly column; contbr. articles to prof. jours. Founder Mother of Twins Club, Newton, 1971; co-chmn. Juvenile Justice Symposium, Des Moines, 1974-75; mem. Juvenile Justice Com., Des Moines, 1974-75; mem. Nat. Offender Based State Corrections Info. Sys. Com., Iowa rep., 1976-78; incorporator, dir. Iowa Dance Theatre, Des Moines, 1981; mem. Pesticide User's Adv. Com., Fort Collins, Colo., 1981-88; co-developer Iowa Migrant Ombudsmen Project, Pioneer, Inc. and Proteus, Inc. Recipient Disting. Alumni award U. Iowa, 1990, Nat. award Ctr. for Pub. Resources. Mem.: DAR, ABA (termination-at-will subcom. 1982—2000, subcom. on devel. individual rights in work place, columnist), Jasper County Bar Assn., Iowa Bar Assn., Iowa Orgn. Women Attys. (bd. dirs., sec. 2001).

CLARK, CANDY, actress; b. Norman, Okla., June 20, 1947; d. Thomas Prest and Ella Lee C.; m. Marjoe Gortner (div.), 1978, Jeff Wald, 1987. Student public schs., Ft. Worth. Appeared in movies Fat City, 1971, American Graffiti, 1973 (nominated for best supporting actress), The Man Who Fell to Earth, 1975, I Will, I Will...for Now, 1976, Citizens Band, 1976, The Big Sleep, 1977, When Ya' Coming Back Red Ryder, 1978, More American Graffiti, 1978, Nobody's Perfeky, 1981, National Lampoon Goes to the Movies, 1981, Q, 1982, Blue Thunder, 1983, Amityville 3-D, 1983, Stephen King's Cat's Eye, 1984, Hambone and Hillie, 1984, At Close Range, 1986, The Blob, 1988, Blind Curve, 1988, Cool-As-Ice, 1991, Buffy the Vampire Slayer, 1992, Original Intent, 1992, Deuce Coupe, 1992, Radioland Murders, 1994, Niagara, Niagara, 1996, Cherry Falls, 1999, The Month of August, 2002, appeared in TV movies James Dean, 1976, Amateur Night at the Dixie Bar and Grill, 1978, Circus of the Stars #4, 1979, Where The Ladies Go, 1980, Rodeo Girl, 1980, Cocaine and Blue Eyes, 1983, Popeye Doyle, 1986, Plan of Attack, 1992; TV Appearances: Banacek, 1973, Faerie Tale Theatre, 1982, Magnum P.I., 1985, Simon & Simon, 1986, Starman, 1986, Hunter, 1986, The Hitchhiker, 1987, Matlock, 1987, St. Elsewhere, 1988, Father Dowling Mysteries, 1989, Baywatch Nights, 1995. appeared in off-Broadway show A Coupla White Chicks Sitting Around Talking, 1981, (play) It's Raining on Hope Street, 1988, Loose Lips, 1995.

CLARK, CAROLYN, performing company executive; Student, Rutgers U. Artistic dir. N.J. Ballet Co., Livingston, NJ, 1967—. Pres.'s coun. on arts John F. Kennedy Ctr.; adv. bd. Channel 13; bd. dir. ArtPride N.J. Dancer (Broadway plays) Music Man, Gay Life and Talent '60's; dir.: (TV series) Belle Telephone Hour; dancer (ballets) Met. Opera, Radio City, N.J. State Opera, N.J. Ballet. Recipient N.J. Pride award, N.J. Monthly Mag., 1995. Office: New Jersey Ballet Company 15 Microlab Rd Livingston NJ 07039*

CLARK, CAROLYN CHAMBERS, nurse, educator, publishing executive; b. Superior, Wis., Mar. 25, 1941; d. John and Phyllis (Olsen) Stark. BS, U. Wis., 1964; MS, Rutgers U., Newark, 1966; EdD, Columbia U., 1976. RN, Fla.; cert. advanced registered nurse practitioner, Fla.; diplomate Am. Bd. Forensic Nursing. Instr. Bergen C.C., Paramus, N.J., 1972-74; pvt. practice wellness nursing, 1972—. Found, dir. The Wellness Inst., Sloatsburg, 1979-84; assoc. prof. Pace U., Pleasantville, N.Y., 1983-84; prof., wellness coord. U. Tampa, Fla., 1984-85; cons. VA Med. Ctr., Bay Pines, Fla., 1988-89, provider continuing programs for nurses, 1990—; nurse practitioner/cons. Bay Area Psychol. Svcs., 1994—; dir. Women's Wellness Ctr. of the Resource Ctr. for Women, 1994—; mem. grad. faculty Walden U., 1999—, Schiller Internat. U., 1998—, mem. doctoral faculty, 1998—. Author: Nursing Concepts and Processes, 1977, The Nurse as Group Leader, 1977, 3rd edit., 1994 (also pub. in Swedish, German), Mental Health Aspects of Community Health Nursing, 1978, Classroom Skills for Nurse Educators, 1978, Assertive Skills for Nurses, 1978, Management in Nursing, 1979, The Nurse as Continuing Educator, 1979, Enhancing Wellness: A Guide for Self-Care, 1981, Wellness Nursing: Concepts, Theory, Research and Practice, 1986, Deadlier than Death, 1993, Dangerous Alibis, Cast Into The Fire, 1994, Wellness Practitioner, 1996, Creating a Climate for Power Learning, 1997, Integrating Complementary Procedure Into Practice, 2000; editor, pub. The Wellness Newsletter, 1980-94; editor Alternative Health Practitioner: The Jour. of Complimentary and Natural Care, 1995-99; pres. Wellness Resources, 1992—; editor-in-chief Ency. Complementary Health Practice, 1999; contbr. articles to profl. jours.; mem. editl. bd. Am. Jour. Holistic Nursing, 1985-88, Women's Health Care Internat., 1985—. Recipient award Fla. Free Lance Writers Assn., 1988, 92, comm. and media award Fla. Nurses Assn., 1997, Book of the Yr. awards, 1996, 99. Fellow Am. Acad. Nursing. Office: 1817 Bridge St Englewood FL 34223-1522

CLARK, CAROLYN COCHRAN, lawyer; b. Kansas City, Mo., Oct. 30, 1941; d. John Rogers and Betty Charleton (Holmes) Cochran; m. L. David Clark, Jr., Dec. 29, 1967; children: Gregory David, Timothy Rogers. BA, U. Mo., 1963; LLB, Harvard U., 1968. Bar: N.Y. 1968, Fla. 1979. Assoc. Milbank, Tweed, Hadley & McCloy, N.Y.C., 1968-76, ptnr., 1977—2001, cons. ptnr., 2002—. Mem. deferred giving com., former regional chmn. major gifts com. Harvard Law Sch. Fund; mem. vis. com. Harvard Law Sch., 1982-88; mem. com. on trust and estate gift plans Rockefeller U.; trustee Madison Ave. Presbyn. Ch., 1984-86, N.Y. Bot. Garden, 1993-96, Vis. Nurse Assn. N.Y. and Vis. Nurse Health Care, 1991-96, Riverdale Country Sch., 1994-98, Milbank Meml. Fund, 1996—, The Woodlawn Cemetery, 1999—; del. John D. Rockefeller Conf. Philanthropy in the 21st Century, N.Y., 1989; bd. advisors NYU program Philanthropy and the Law; chmn. program taxation exempt orgns. NYU Tax Inst. Recipient Disting. Alumna award U. Mo., 1989. Fellow Am. Coll. Trust and Estate Counsel (ind. regent, chmn. com. on charitable giving and exempt orgns.), N.Y. Bar Found., Am. Bar Found.; mem. ABA (chmn. subcom. income taxation of charitable trusts 1976-78, chmn. com. charitable instns. 1989-94), Assn. Bar City of N.Y. (chmn. com. on non-profit orgns. 1986-89, sec. com. philanthropic orgns. 1976-82, mem. com. trusts, estates and surrogates cts. 1977-80, 85-86), N.Y. State Bar Assn. (com. estate planning, trusts and estates sect. 1978-89), Am. Law Inst., Practising Law Inst. (lectr.), Harvard U. Law Sch., Assn. Greater N.Y. (trustee 1978-80, v.p. 1980-81, pres. 1981-82), NYU Tax Inst. (chmn. conf. tax planning charitable orgns. 1993-95), Nat. Harvard Law Sch. Alumni Assn. (exec. com. 1978-80, v.p. 1986-90, pres. 1990-92), Soc. Colonial Dames Am. in Mo., Maidstone Club. Home: 161 E 79th St New York NY 10021-0480 Office: Milbank Tweed Hadley Et Al 46th Fl 1 Chase Manhattan Plz New York NY 10005-1401 E-mail: cclark@milbank.com.

CLARK, CHRISTINE MAY, editor, author; b. Peoria, Ill., Apr. 25, 1957; d. Darrell Ronald and Alice Venita (Burkitt) French. BA, Judson Coll., 1978. Assoc. editor David C. Cook Pub., Elgin, Ill., 1978-80; editor Humpty Dumpty, 1980-94, Jack and Jill, 1983-86, Turtle mag., 1990—; editl. dir. Children's Better Health Inst., Indpls.; assoc. editor Highlights for Children, Honesdale, Pa., 1994-96, mng. editor, 1996—2001, v.p. editl., 1997—, editor, 2001—, also bd. dirs. Recipient Journalism award EDPRESS, 1986, 87, 88, 89, 90, 92, Outstanding Reporting award Soc. Profl. Journalists, 1990; Aurora Found. scholar, 1975. Mem. Am. Soc. Mag. Editors, Soc. Children's Book Writers and Illustrators, Ednl. Press Assn., Judson Coll. Alumni Assn. Reorganized Ch. of Jesus Christ of Latter-day Saints. Avocations: piano, travel. Office: Highlights for Children 803 Church St Honesdale PA 18431-1895*

CLARK, CLAUDIA ANN, business development manager; b. Sharon, Pa., Sept. 15, 1954; d. Harry Malin Shilling and Betty Ann Harper Shilling; m. Charles Irving Shaffer, Jan. 8, 1973 (div. Apr. 1979); 1 child, Clover Shaffer. BS in Environ. Sci., Westminster Coll., 1982; M in Environ. Pollution Control, Pa. State U., 1988. Sci. educator Bellefonte (Pa.) Sch. Dist., 1984,

Harrisburg (Pa.) Sch. Dist., 1985—86; account exec. Wadsworth/Alert, Canton, Ohio, 1986—88; regional sales mgr. Roy F. Weston, University Park, Ill., 1988—94; bus. devel. mgr. Paragon Analytics, Ft. Collins, Colo., 1994—. Mem.: Soc. Am. Mil. Engrs. Avocations: skiing, horseback riding. Office: Paragon Analytics Inc 225 Commerce Dr Fort Collins CO 80524

CLARK, CYNTHIA ZANG FACER, federal agency administrator; b. Sterling, Colo., Apr. 1, 1942; d. Joseph Elmer and Flora Burnell Zang; m. Glenn Willett Clark, Aug. 20, 1963; children: Randall, Drew, Ariel Silver, Allison, Timothy, Emily McDaniel. BA in Maths., Mills Coll., Oakland, Calif., 1963; MS in Maths., U. Denver, 1964; MS, Iowa State U., 1973, PhD in Statistics, 1977. Instr. dept. maths. U. Denver, 1963-66, Drake U., Des Moines, 1971-72; mathematical statistician Statistical Rsch. Divsn. Bur. Census, 1977-79; econ. statistician Office Fed. Statistical Policy and Standards Dept. Commerce, 1979-81; statistical policy analyst Statistical Policy Office Office Info. and Regulatory Affairs Office Mgmt. & Budget, 1981-83; asst. divsn. chief for rsch. & methodology Agriculture Divsn Bur. Census, 1983-90, dir. rsch. and applications divsn., 1990-92; dir. survey mgmt. divsn. Nat. Agrl. Statistics Svc. Dept. Agriculture, 1992-96; assoc. dir. methodology and standards Bur. Census Dept. Commerce, Washington, 1995—. Contbr. articles to profl. jours. Recipient Sr. Exec. Svc. bonus award, 1994, 1995, 1997—2003. Fellow Am. Statistical Assn. (mem. InterCASIC 1996 conf. planning com., past pres. sect. govt. statistics, bd. dir.); mem. Am. Assn. Pub. Opinion Rsch., Washington Statis. Soc. (pres.), Internat. Assn. Survey Statistics, Sr. Exec. Assn. (Dept. Agriculture chpt. pres. 1993-95), Caucus for Women in Statistics (past pres.), Natural Resource Conservation Svc. (blue ribbon panel on info. and data mgmt. 1996). Mem. Ch. of Jesus Christ of Latter Day Saints. Avocations: family history, geneaology, ice skating, cultural activities, travel. Office: Dept Commerce Bur Census Fed Office Bldg 3 Rm 2031 Washington DC 20233-0001 Home: 6628 Mclean Ct Mc Lean VA 22101-4001

CLARK, DEANNA DEE, civic leader and volunteer; b. Cedar Rapids, Iowa, June 1, 1944; d. Cyrus Dean and Isabelle Esther Thomas; m. Glen Edward Clark, July 16, 1966; children: Andrew Curtis, Carissa Jane. AA, Coll. of the Desert, 1964; BA, Coe Coll., 1966. Fund devel. chmn. Nat. Assistance League, 1992—94; resource devel. writer and trainer, 1992—2002; convenor U.S. Internat. Youth Exch. Initiative Cmty. Network, Utah, 1984—94; human svcs. subcom. child advocacy project, social justice and peacemaking min. unit Presbyn. Ch. U.S.A., 1992—93; pres. Provo-Jordan River Pkwy. Found., 1993—95; sustaining mem. Jr. League Salt Lake City, 1976—, Assistance League Salt Lake City, 1986—; bd. dirs. Friends of Libr., U. Utah, 1991—94; moderator, nominating com. Synod of the Rocky Mountains, 1999—2002; numerous civic coms. and found. Utah, 1992—; sec., vice-chmn. City of Holladay Interfaith Coun., 1999—; info practices com. Utah Legislature, 1990; exec. com. of Gen. Assembly Coun., Presbyn. Ch. (U.S.A.), 1993—97; elder Presbyn. Ch., 1983—; mem. coun. Presbytery of Utah, 1985—2001, moderator, 2000—01. Mem. LWV (Utah pres. 1981-83), P.E.O. (historian Utah chpt. 1992-95, chpt. H pres. 1995-97, Utah chmn. Gump & Agers Scholarship Com. 1998-99). Home: PO Box 711098 Salt Lake City UT 84171-1098

CLARK, DIANNE ELIZABETH, religious studies and reading educator; b. Vinton, Iowa, Apr. 20, 1951; d. Edward J. and Bernadine H. (Potthoff) Rhinehart; m. John T. Clark, Oct. 31, 1999; children: Daniel, Craig, Andrea Fullerton. BS/LTD, Concordia Tchr.'s Coll., 1972; MA, U. Iowa, 1986; specialist degree in Christian edn., Concordia Coll., Seward, Nebr., 1991. Cert. classroom tchr. K-9, reading clinician K-12. Dir. Christian edn. Peace Luth. Ch., Hastings, Nebr., 1991—; tchr., reading curriculum com. chair Columbus Community Schs., Columbus Junction, Iowa; tchr. Sylvan Learning Ctr., Coralville, Iowa; substitute tchr. Iowa City Public Schs., Iowa City. Ednl. adv. com. Iowa Wesleyan Coll.; mem. Our Redeemer Preschool Bd.; presenter in field. Mem. NEA, Internat. Reading Assn., Iowa Edn. Assn., Tri-area Reading Assn., Columbus Edn. Assn., Autism Soc. Am., Luth. Edn. Assn. Home: 69 Modern Way Iowa City IA 52240-3068

CLARK, ELIZABETH LAMB, art historian, researcher; b. Boston, Feb. 24, 1932; d. Charles Alexander and Mary Louise (Alguire) Lamb; m. Francis Goodell Barnum Jr., Sept. 1, 1951 (dec. July 1968); children: William Goodell Barnum, Elizabeth Goodell Barnum Rose; m. Grenville Clark Jr., Dec. 30, 1972 (dec. Dec. 1994). BA, Wellesley Coll., 1987; MA, Boston U., 1989; M in Philosophy, CUNY, 1997. Rsch. asst. lectr. Met. Mus., N.Y.C., 1993-95, rsch. asst., 1996—, Boston Athenaeum, 1994; rsch. curator Jewish Mus. N.Y.C., 1996-97. Co-author exhbn. catalogue: Boston Library Society 1794-1994: An Exhibition of Portraits, Views and Materials, 1994, Facing the New World: American Jews in Colonial and Federal Periods, 1996-97. Grad. intern Met. Mus., 1994. Mem. Coll. Art Assn. Avocations: travel, gardening, sailing, reading. Home: 85 Grove St Wellesley MA 02482-7812 Office: 35 W 90th St Apt 7J New York NY 10024-1507

CLARK, ELOISE ELIZABETH, biologist, educator; b. Grundy, Va., Jan. 20, 1931; d. J. Francis Emmett and Ava Clayton (Harris) C. BA, Mary Washington Coll., 1951; PhD in Zoology, U. N.C., 1958; DSc, King Coll., 1976; postdoctoral rsch., Washington U., St. Louis, 1957-58, U. Calif. at Berkeley, 1958-59. Rsch. asst., then instr. U. N.C., 1952-55; instr. physiology Marine Biol. Lab., Woods Hole, Mass., 1958-62; from instr. to asst. prof. Columbia U., 1959—65, assoc. prof. biol. sci., 1966-69; with NSF, Washington, 1969-83, head molecular biology, 1971-73, div. dir. biol. and med. scis., 1973-75, dep. asst. dir. biol., behavioral and social scis., 1975-76, asst. dir. biol., behavioral and social scis., 1976-83; v.p. acad. affairs Bowling Green State U., Ohio, 1983—96, prof. biol. sci. to trustee prof. emeritus, 1983—2002, trustee prof. emeritus, 2002—. Contbr. articles to profl. jours. and congl. hearings. Mem. alumnae bd. Mary Washington Coll., U. Va., 1967—70; bd. regents Nat. Libr. of Medicine, 1973—83; mem. policy group competitive grants program U.S. Dept. Agr.; mem. White House Interdepartmental Task Force on Women, 1978—80, Task Force for Conf. on Families, 1980, Com. on Health and Medicine, 1976—80; vice chmn. Com. on Food and Renewable Resources, 1977—80; mem. selective excellence task force Ohio Bd. Regents, 1984—85; mem. Ohio Adv. Coun., Coll. Prep. Edn., 1983—84, Ohio Inter-Univ. Coun. for Provosts, 1983—96, chmn., 1984—85, 1995—96; nat. adv. rsch. resources coun. NIH, 1987—89; mem. informal sci. edn. panel NSF, 1986—88, adv. com., social, behavioral and econ. scis., 1997—2000; program adv. coun. sci., tech. and pub. policy Harvard U., 1988—90, mem. editl. bd. Forum, 1997—2001; mem. governing bd. OhioLink, 1990—96, vice chair, 1992, chair, 1993—94. Named Disting. Alumnus Mary Washington Coll., 1975; Wilson scholar, 1956; E.C. Drew scholar, 1956; USPHS postdoctoral fellow, 1957-59; recipient Disting. Service award NSF, 1978 Mem. AAAS (coun. 1969-71, bd. dirs. 1978-82, pres.-elect, 1992, pres., 1993, chmn. bd. 1994), Soc. Gen. Physiology (sec. 1965-67, coun. 1969-71), Biophys. Soc. (coun. 1975-76), Am. Soc. Cell Biology (coun. 1972-75), Am. Inst. Biol. Scientists, Marine biol. Lab. (trustee 1993), NASULGC (higher edn. and tech. com. 1988-93, com. on info. tech. 1994-96), Consortium of Social Sci. Assn. (bd. dirs. 1993-96), Ohio Coun. rsch. and Econ. Devel., Assn. Women in Sci. (bd. dirs. 1998-2001), Phi Beta Kappa (com. on qualifications 1985—, chair 1998-2004, senate 1996—, exec. com. 1997-2003), Sigma Xi, Omicron Delta Kappa. Home: 1222 Brownwood Dr Bowling Green OH 43402-3503 Office: Bowling Green State U Dept Biol Scis Bowling Green OH 43403-0001 Office Phone: 419-372-9390.

CLARK, EVE VIVIENNE, linguistics educator; b. Camberley, U.K., July 26, 1942; came to U.S., 1967; d. Desmond Charles and Nancy (Aitken) Curme; m. Herbert H. Clark, July 21, 1967; 1 child, Damon Alistair. MA with honors, U. Edinburgh, Scotland, 1965, PhD, 1969. Rsch. assoc. Stanford (Calif.) U., 1969-71, from asst. prof. to assoc. prof., 1971-83, prof., 1983—. Author: Ontogenesis of Meaning, 1979, Acquisition of Romance, 1985, The Lexicon in Acquisition, 1993, First Language Acquisition, 2003; co-author: Psychology and Language, 1977. Fellow Ctr. for Advanced Study in the Behavioral Scis., 1979-80, Guggenheim Found., 1983-84. Mem. Dutch Acad. Scis. (fgn.).

CLARK, GLORIA A. music educator; b. Indpls., Ind., Feb. 7, 1937; d. Franklin T. and Jean Agnes Gamage; m. Robert A. Mead, Dec. 5, 1957 (div. Dec. 1959); 1 child, Allison M. Szabo ; m. William H. Clark, Jan. 25, 1981. BS in Sociology, Regents Coll., Albany, N.Y., 1989; MA in Philosophy, Calif. State U. Dominguez Hills, 1992. Svc. rep. United Telephone; prof. philosophy S. Fla. C.C.; tchr. Butte Ctrl. Cath. Schs. Performing musician; mural artist; choir dir. Gold Hill Luth. ch., Butte, Mont.; pvt. piano tchr., Butte. Virginia City (Mont.) Art Festival. Bd. dirs. Cmty. Concerts, Butte; vol. cellist Butte Symphony, 1991—2003; pianist Grant Kohrs Nat. Park. Recipient Butte City Artist award, Butte Silver Bow County, 1991—97; grantee Music Edn. grant, Cmty. Concerts, Butte, 1996—2004. Mem.: Nat. Accredited Music Tchrs. Assn. Avocations: crocheting, theater, walking, cribbage. Home: 311 W Quartz Butte MT 59701

CLARK, JANET EILEEN, political scientist, educator; b. Kansas City, Kans., June 5, 1940; d. Edward Francis and Mildred Lois (Mack) Morrissey; m. Caleb M. Clark, Sept. 28, 1968; children: Emily Claire, Grace Ellen, Evelyn Adair. AA, Kansas City Jr. Coll., 1960; AB, George Washington U., 1962, MA, 1964; PhD, U. Ill., 1973. Staff US Dept. Labor, Washington, 1962-64; instr. social sci. Kans. City Jr. Coll., Kans., 1964-67; instr. polit. sci. Parkland Coll., 1970-71; asst. prof. govt. N.Mex. State U., Las Cruces, 1971-77, assoc. prof., 1977-80; assoc. prof. polit. sci. U. Wyo., 1981-84, prof., 1984-94; prof. polit. sci., head dept. State U. West Ga., Carrollton, 1994—. Co-author: Women, Elections and Representation, 1987, The Equality State, 1988, Women in Taiwan Politics: Overcoming Barriers to Women's Participation in a Modernizing Society, 1990; editor Women and Politics, 1991-2000, contbr. articles to profl. jours. Wolcott fellow, 1963-64, NDEA Title IV fellow, 1967-69. Mem. Internat. Soc. Polit. Psychology (gov. coun., 1987-89), NEA (pres. chpt. 1978-79), Am. Polit. Sci. Assn., We. Polit. Sci. Assn. (exec. coun. 1984-87), Western Social Sci. Assn. (exec. coun. 1978-81, v.p. 1982, pres. 1985), Women's Caucus for Polit. Sci. (treas. 1982, pres. 1987), LWV (exec. bd. 1980-83, 2002-2003, treas. 1986-90, pres. 1991-93, 2004-06), Women's Polit. Caucus, Beta Sigma Phi (v.p. chpt. 1978-79, sec. 1987-88, treas. 1988-89, v.p. 1989-90, pres. 1990-91), Phi Beta Kappa Chi Omega (prize 1962), Phi Kappa Phi. Home: 2507 Waterford Rd Auburn AL 36832-4113 Office: State University of West Georgia Dept Polit Sci Carrollton GA 30118-0001

CLARK, JOYCE NAOMI JOHNSON, retired nurse, counselor; b. Corpus Christi, Tex., Oct. 4, 1936; d. Chester Fletcher and Ermal Olita (Bailey) Johnson; m. William Boyd Clark, Jan. 4, 1958; (div. 1967); 1 child, Sherene Joyce. Student, Corpus Christi State U., 1975-77. RN, CNOR, ACLS, TNCC; cert. instrument flight instr., cert. core trauma nurse. Staff nurse Van Nuys (Calif.) Cmty. Hosp., 1963-64, U.S. Naval Hosp., Corpus Christi, 1964-68; patient care coord. Spohn Meml. Hosp. (formerly Meml. Med. Ctr.), Corpus Christi, 1968—2002; counselor Christus Spohn Wellness Program, 1999—2002; ret., 2002. Leader Paisano Coun. Girl Scouts U.S.A., Corpus Christi, 1968-74; vol. transporting those in need; past comdr. 3rd group USAF Aux., CAP Air Search and Rescue, wing chief pilot, ret. lt. col. 1993. Recipient Charles A. Mella award Meml. Med. ctr., 1981, Paul E. Garbert award CAP, 1986, cert. of appreciation in recognition of Support Child Guard Missing Children Edn. Program Nat. Assn. Chiefs of Police, Washington, 1987, Charles E. Yeager Aerospace Edn. Achievement award, 1985, Grover Loenig Aerospace award, 1986, Cert. of World Leadership Internat. Biographical Ctr., Cambridge, Eng., 1987, Gill Robb Wilson award #1021, 1988, Merit award Drug Free Am. Through Enforcement, Edn., Intelligence Nat. Assn. Chiefs of Police, Sr. Mem. of Yr. USAF Aux., CAP Air Search and Rescue, 1986. Mem. USAF Aux., CAP Air Search and Rescue (past comdr. 3rd group, wing chief pilot, ret. lt. col., Sr. Mem. of Yr. 1986), Aircraft Owners and Pilots Assn. Avocation: flying. Home: 2802 Cimmaron Blvd Apt 221 Corpus Christi TX 78414-3455 E-mail: pangyau@grandecom.net.

CLARK, JOYCE T. piano teacher, church organist; d. Richard LeVake Tonk and Louise (Fambrough) Richards; m. Jon Perryman Clark, July 17, 1982. BS in Elem. Edn., U. Calif., Santa Barbara, 1961; BA in Music, U. So. Maine, 2001. Lic. elem. edn. tchr. Calif. Elem. sch. tchr. Hudson Sch. Dist., LaPuente, Calif., 1961—62, Glendale (Calif.) Unified Sch. Dist., 1962—69; church organist Christian Sci. Soc., Boothbay Harbor, Maine, 1974—76; adminstrv. asst. David Wendell Assocs., Edgecomb, Maine, 1981—94; pvt. practice piano tchr. Woolwich, Maine, 1974—; church organist First Ch. of Christ, Scientist, Brunswick, Maine, 1976—; piano tchr. Portland Conservatory of Music, 2002—. Freelance accompanist various soloists and choruses, Maine, 1970—. Mem.: Am. Guild of Organists-Portland, Maine Music Tchrs. Assn. (treas. 1994—95, 2002—). Avocations: kayaking, quilting, knitting, canoeing, snowshoeing. Home: 255 Montsweag Rd Woolwich ME 04579

CLARK, JUDY, newscaster; m. Tom Clark; 2 children. Grad., U. Wis., Eau Claire. Reporter, anchor WAXX-WAYY; noon anchor NewsCenter 13 WEAU-TV, Eau Claire, Wis., 1992—98, anchor at five and ten, 1998—. Avocations: reading, fishing, gardening. Office: WEAU-TV PO Box 47 Eau Claire WI 54702

CLARK, KAREN, state legislator; BS, Coll. St. Teresa, Winona, Minn.; MPA, Harvard U. Mem. Minn. Ho. of Reps., 1981—, mem. jobs and econ. devel. com., commerce com. Recipient Martin Luther King, Jr. award, 1987, Minn. Alliance Progressive Leadership award, 1991, Leadership award Nat. Gay & Lesbian Task Force. Office: Minn State House Office Bldg 100 Constitution Ave Saint Paul MN 55155-1232

CLARK, KAREN HEATH, lawyer; b. Pasadena, Calif., Dec. 17, 1944; d. Wesley Pelton and Lois (Ellenberger) Heath; m. Bruce Robert Clark,Dec. 30, 1967; children: Adam Heath, Andrea Pelton. Student, Pomona Coll., Claremont, Calif., 1962—64; BA, Stanford U., 1966; MA in History, U. Wash., 1968; JD, U. Mich., 1977. Bar: Calif. 1978. Instr. Henry Ford C.C., Dearborn, Mich., 1968-72; assoc. Gibson, Dunn & Crutcher LLP, Irvine, Calif., 1977-86, ptnr., 1986—2003, adv. ptnr., 2004—. Bd. dirs. Dem. Found. Orange County, 1989-91, 94—, Planned Parenthood Orange County, Santa Ana, Calif., 1979-82, New Directions for Women, Newport Beach, 1986-91, Human Options, 2001-03; bd. dirs. Women in Leadership, chair, 1995-99; trustee Newport Beach Pub. Libr., 2001—; mem. deans adv. coun. Sch. Humanities, U. Calif., Irvine. Recipient 1996 Choice award Planned Parenthood of Orange & San Bernardino Counties. Mem. Women in Leadership (founder 1993). Office: Gibson Dunn & Crutcher LLP 4 Park Plz Ste 1400 Irvine CA 92614-8557 E-mail: kclark@gibsondunn.com.

CLARK, KATHERINE KAREN, software company executive; b. Washington, Apr. 2, 1957; d. Austin Bryant Jackson and Barbara (McClenon) C.; m. Patrick H. McGettigan, Dec. 7, 1983 (div. Sept. 1992). MBA, George Mason U., 1993-95. From file clk. to sys. programmer Blue Cross/Blue Shield, Washington, 1975-83; co-founder, v.p., pres., CEO Landmark Sys. Corp., Vienna, Va., 1983—. Trustee Walter H. McClenon Fund, Washington, 1990—; vice chair No. Va. Tech. Coun., 1991; mem. exec. com. No. Va. Econ. Roundtable, 1994. Mem. Va. State C. of C. (vice-chair). Avocations: running, biking, sailing. Address: Landmark Systems Corp 12700 Sunrise Valley Dr Reston VA 20191-5801

CLARK, KATHLEEN MULHERN, foreign language and literature educator; b. Phila., Oct. 10, 1948; d. John Joseph Jr. and Rosalie (Callahan) Mulhern; m. Robert Lee Clark, Oct. 7, 1972; children: Matthew, Kelly. AB, Immaculata U., 1970; MA, Villanova U., 1981; postgrad., U. Laval, Que., Can., 1969, Ecole Francaise des Attachés de Presse, Paris, 1991. Cert. French tchr. French tchr. Great Valley H.S., Devault, Pa., 1971-72, Conestoga Sr. H.S., Berwyn, Pa., 1970-71, 72-78; lectr. fgn. lang. Immaculata (Pa.) U., 1973-89, prof. fgn. lang., lit., 1989—, dept. chmn., 1997—. Translator Burroughs Corp., Paoli, Pa., 1976-78; translator, cons. Smith, Kline Animal Health Products, West Chester, Pa., 1985; co-developer, designer Leadership Core Curriculum, Immaculata, 1990—. Class rep. Immaculata U. Alumnae Assn., 1970-98, bd. govs. 1996-2002. Recipient grant U. Laval, 1969, Pew Meml. Trust, 1990. Mem. AAUP, Pa. State MLA (exec. bd. dirs., 1999-2002), Am. Assn. Tchrs. French (v.p. Phila. chpt.), Am. Coun. on Tchg. of Fgn. Langs., Pa. Soc. Tchg. Scholars, Alliance Française, Pi Delta Phi, Lambda Iota Tau. Roman Catholic. Avocations: travel, music. Home: 65 Rossiter Ave Phoenixville PA 19460-2509

CLARK, KATHRYN, government agency administrator; m. Robert Ike. MA, PhD, U. Mich. Faculty dept. anatomy and cell biology U. Mich., 1993; dep. dir. NASA Comml. Space Ctr., 1996—98; space sta. chief scientist NASA Office Space Flight, Washington, 1998—. Grantee, NIH, Nat. Inst. Aging, Am. Fedn. for Aging Rsch., NSF, NASA. Mem.: Internat. Soc. Women Pilots, Internat. Soc. for Gravitational and Space Biology, Am. Soc. for Gravitational and Space Biology, Soc. for Neurosci., Am. Coll. Sports Medicine. Avocations: cycling, swimming, skiing. Office: NASA Hdqs Bldg HQ Rm 4022 Washington DC 20546-0001

CLARK, KELLY, Olympic athlete; b. Newport, R.I., July 26, 1983; Grad., Brattleboro (Vt.) Union H.S., 2002. Former mem. U.S. Women's Snowboarding Team. Named World Jr. halfpipe champion, 2000, U.S. halfpipe and snowboardcross champion, 2001; recipient Gold medal, 2002 Olympic Games, Salt Lake City. Address: US Ski and Snowboarding Assn Box 100 1500 Kearns Blvd Park City UT 84060

CLARK, LAVERNE HARRELL, writer; b. Smithville, Tex., June 6, 1929; d. James Boyce and Belle Bunte Harrell; m. L.D. Clark, Sept. 15, 1951. BA, Tex. Women's U., 1950; student, Columbia U., 1951-54; MA, U. Ariz., 1962, MFA, 1992. Reporter, libr., photographer Ft. Worth Press, 1950-51; with sales and advt. depts. Columbia U. Press, N.Y.C., 1951-53; asst. promotion-news Episcopal Diocese Bull., N.Y.C., 1958-59; founding dir. U. Ariz. Poetry Ctr., Tucson, 1962-66, photographer, 1966-99. Author, photographer: They Sang for Horses, 1966 (award U. Chgo. 1967), rev. edit., 2001, Revisiting the Plains Indian Country of Mari Sandoz, 1977, Focus 101, 1979, The Deadly Swarm and Other Stories, 1985, 87, Keepers of the Earth, 1997, 2d edit., 2002 (1st Novel award Western Writers of Am. 1998), Mari Sandoz's Native Nebraska, 2000; editor, photographer: The Face of Poetry, 1976, 2d edit., 1979. Recipient 19 awards Nat. League Am. Pen Women, 1967-96, Disting. Alumna award Tex. Woman's U., Denton, 1973; grantee Am. Philos. Soc., 1967, 69. Mem. PEN, Western Writers of Am., Westerners Internat., Women Writing the West, Sandoz Heritage Soc. (hon. mem. adv. bd. 1989-2002), Tex. Inst. Letters. Democrat. Episcopalian. Avocations: travel, bicycling, showing slides. Home: 604 Main St Smithville TX 78957 Office Phone: 512-237-2796. E-mail: lhldclark@aol.com.

CLARK, LETITIA Z. federal judge; b. 1945; BA, Rice U., 1967; MA, Rutgers U., 1970; JD, Syracuse U., 1973. Atty. EPA, Dallas, 1974-76; asst. U.S. atty. Southern District of Texas, 1982-85, bankruptcy judge, 1985—. Office: US Bankruptcy Ct Box 61010 515 Rusk St Houston TX 77002-2600

CLARK, LYNNETTE FAYE, music educator; b. Sioux Falls, S.D., Oct. 28, 1954; d. Ben and Ui Engbrecht; m. Rick W. Clark, May 25, 1974; children: Alecia, Nathan. BA in Music, Sioux Falls Coll., 1976. Music tchr., coach Parkston (S.D.) Schs., 1976—80; music tchr. Aberdeen (S.D.) Schs., 1980—81, Baltic (S.D.) Schs., 1982—92, West Cen. Schs., Hartford, SD, 1992—97, Lynd (Minn.) Sch., 1997—98, Marshall (Minn.) Pub. Schs., 1998—. Mem.: NEA, Music Educators Nat. Conf., Am. Choral Dirs. Assn. Avocations: singing, performing. Home: 81 Deer Path Trimont MN 56176 Office: Marshall Schs 421 S Saratoga Marshall MN 56258

CLARK, MARGARET ANN-CYNTHIA, television producer, writer; b. New Orleans, Aug. 20, 1964; d. Joseph Christian and Elizabeth Rose Muller; m. Samuel Varnell, Oct. 5, 1991 (div. Aug. 1997); m. Kenneth Clark, Sept. 12, 2000. Diploma, St. Mary's Dominican Coll., 1984; AS in Nursing, U. NY, 1990; BA in Journalism, 1999; postgrad., Harvard U., 2002. Pediatric, neonatal therapist Charity Hosp., New Orleans, 1984-86; therapist/nurse Touro Infirmary, New Orleans, 1986-91; therapist St. John's Mercy Hosp., St. Louis, 1991-92; nurse Grady Meml. Hosp., Atlanta, 1992-95; dir. pulmonary rehab. Touro Infirmary, 1995-98; writer prodr. WYES-TV, New Orleans, 1996-00; contbr. The Shakespeare Bulletin, Easton, Pa., 1996-01; corr. Advance News Mags., King of Prussia, Pa., 1990—; clin. coord. pulmonary medicine Boston U., 2001—; writer Ga. Med. Care Found., 2003. Author: Inspiration, 1998, Write for You, 2000, Dinner with Francis, 2001; editor: Medscape, 2001—; contbr. articles to profl. jours.; writer, producer (TV series) By Louisiana Hands, 1999, Steppin Out, 1996-99; 1st alto Jefferson Performing Arts Soc., 1996-98. Bd. dir. Shakespeare Festival, Tulane U., New Orleans, 1996—; pres. Officer's Wives Club, Ft. Gillen, Ga., 1993-95; mem. La. Cols., New Orleans, 1997—. Recipient Bird Lifetime Achievement award Am. Assn. Respiratory Care, 1996. Mem. Am. Assn. Respiratory Care, Am. Med. Writers Assn., Am. Coll. Chest Physicians, Nat. Acad. TV Arts & Sci. Roman Catholic. E-mail: maraisells@aol.com.

CLARK, MARIAN WILSON, writer; b. Hereford, Tex., Sept. 8, 1934; d. Robert Lee and Mabel Faulkner Wilson; m. Kenneth K. Clark, Dec. 29, 1963; children: Rebecca, Kevin. BS in Vocat. Home Econs. Edn., Tex. Tech. U., 1957. Home svc. advisor Tex. Elec., Ft. Worth, 1958—59; tchr. McCamey (Tex.) Pub. Schs., 1959—61, Odessa (Tex.) Pub. Schs., 1961—66. Spkr. various Rt. 66 groups, nationwide, 1993—; writer Rt. 66 Mag. and Rt. 66 Fedn. Newsletter, 1993—. Author: Southwestern Heritage, 1989, Route 66 Cookbook, 1993, 2000, Main Street of America, 1997, Hogs on 66: Best Food for Road Trips on Route 66, 2004. Pres., bd. dirs. Camp Fire Girls, Tulsa, Okla., 1981—82. Recipient Gulick award, Camp Fire Girls, Tulsa, 1983. Mem.: Green Country Home Economists (pres.), Mortar Bd., United Meth. Women (pres.), Salvation Army Aux. (United Way chair 1999—2002), Phi Upsilon Omicron. Methodist. Avocations: travel, aerobics. Home: 3019 S Madison Ave Tulsa OK 74114 E-mail: mclark66@sbcglobal.net.

CLARK, MARTHA FULLER, state legislator, architectural historian, preservation consultant; b. York, Maine, Mar. 14, 1942; m. Geoffrey Clark; 3 children. BA, Mills Coll., 1964; MA, Boston U., 1977. Mem. N.H. Ho. of Reps., Dist. 36; asst. Dem. leader N.H. Ho. of Reps., 1995—. Bd. dirs. Strawbery Banke, 1976-92, Strawbery Banke Overseas, 1994—; founder, pres. Inherit N.H., 1989-96; trustee Friends of Music Hall, 1989-96; bd. dirs. Preservation Action, 1988—, adv. bd., 1993—, Wiss Inst., 1995—; mem. Hist. Dist. Commn., 1977-80, Portsmouth Mus. Commn., 1985-89, Gov.'s Commn. on 21st Century Living Landscape Task Force, 1989-90; mem. state com. N.H. Dem. Party, 1995—. Mem. N.H. Hist. soc. (trustee 1992—), Leadership Seacoast, 1993, Leadership N.H., 1997. Demcrat. Avocations: sailing, gardening, skiing. Office: NH House of Reps State Capitol Concord NH 03301

CLARK, MARY CANNON, art educator; b. St. George, S.C., Nov. 20, 1919; d. Claude Claiborne and Anne Connelia (Johnston) Cannon; m. Arthur Watts Clark, Nov. 21, 1942; children: Arthur Watts Jr., Claiborne Marshall, Johnston Jewell. BS Charleston Coll., S.C., 1940; postgrad studies portrait painting under Mabel Pugh, Peace Coll., Raleigh, N.C., 1970—75. Art tchr. extended ednl. program Duke U., Durham, NC; art tchr.

Durham Art Guild, 1972—75; art tchr. pvt. practice Durham, 1965—; registered copyist Nat. Art Gallery, Washington, 1975—. Represented in permanent collections. Presbyterian. Avocations: line dancing, reading, swimming. Home: 3540 Rugby Rd Durham NC 27707

CLARK, MARY ETTA, science writing consultant; b. Wilmington, Del., Mar. 15, 1961; d. Albert Ridge and Mary E. (Bendler) C. BA, U. Del., 1983; M in Tech. and Sci. Comm., Miami U., Oxford, Ohio, 1984; PhD, N.C. State U., 1997. Tchg. asst. U. Del., Newark, 1982-83, Miami U., 1983-84; med. writer ICI Pharms., Wilmington, Del., 1984-89; sci. writing cons. Wilmington, N.C., 1995—. Part-time faculty mem. U. N.C., Wilmington, 1998—; editl. cons. U. Del., 1986-87; substitute instr. N.C. State U., Raleigh, 1992-94. Vol. Meals on Wheels, Raleigh, 1989-97, Kairos Prision Ministry, Raleigh, 1998—. Grad. fellow N.C. State U. Alumni Assn., 1989, rsch. fellow Smithsonian Instn., 1993; rsch. grantee Am. Mus. Natural History, 1991. Mem. Am. Med. Writers Assn., Am. soc. Limnology and Oceanography, Sierra Club (publicity chair Del. chpt. 1986-88). Achievements include publishing first study to telemeter agonistic activity in a free-ranging marine invertebrate. E-mail: m_clark@mediwriter.com.

CLARK, MARY HIGGINS, writer, communications executive; b. N.Y.C., Dec. 24, 1929; d. Luke J. and Nora C. (Durkin) Higgins; m. Warren Clark, Dec. 26, 1949 (dec. Sept. 1964); children: Marilyn, Warren, David, Carol, Patricia; m. John J. Coheeney, Nov. 3, 1996. BA, Fordham U., 1979; hon. doctorate, Villanova U., 1983, Rider Coll., 1986, Stonehill Coll., 1992, Marymount Manhattan Coll., 1992, Chestnut Hill, 1993, Manhattan Coll., 1993, St. Peter's Coll., 1993; 7 additional hon. doctorates. Advt. asst. Remington Rand, 1946; stewardess Pan Am., 1949-50; radio scriptwriter, prodr. Robert G. Jennings, 1965-70; v.p., ptnr., creative dir., prodr. radio programming Aerial Communications, N.Y.C., 1970-80; chmn. bd., creative dir. D. J. Clark Enterprises, N.Y.C., 1980—. Author: Silent Night, Aspire to the Heavens, A Biography of George Washington, 1969 (N.J. Author award 1969), Where Are the Children?, 1976 (N.J. Author award 1977), A Stranger Is Watching, 1978 (N.J. Author award 1978), The Cradle Will Fall, 1980, A Cry in the Night, 1982, Stillwatch, 1984, Weep No More, My Lady, 1987, While My Pretty One Sleeps, 1989, The Anastasia Syndrome and Other Stories, 1989, Loves Music, Loves to Dance, 1991, All Around the Town, 1992, I'll Be Seeing You, 1993, Remember Me, 1994, The Lottery Winner, 1994, Bad Behavior, 1995, Let Me Call You Sweetheart, 1995, Moonlight Becomes You, 1996, Pretend You Don't See Her, 1997, The Plot Thickens, 1997, You Belong to Me, 1998, All Through the Night, 1998, We'll Meet Again, 1999, Before I Say Good-Bye, 2000, Deck the Halls, 2000, Daddy's Little Girl, 2002, Silent Night/All Through the Night, 2002, On the Street Where You Live, 2002, Kitchen Privileges, 2002, The Second Time Around, 2003; (with Thomas Chastain and others) Murder in Manhattan, 1986; editor: Murder on the Aisle: The 1987 Mystery Writers Anthology, 1987. Recipient Grand Prix de Litterature Policiere, France, 1980, Horatio Alger Award, 1997, Gold Medal of Honor, Irish-American Historical Society, Spirit of Achievement Award, Albert Einstein Coll. of Med., Yoshiva University, Nat. Arts Club Gold Medal in Education. Mem. Mystery Writers Am. (pres. 1987, dir.), Authors League, Am. Soc. Journalists and Authors, Acad. Arts and Scis. Republican. Roman Catholic.*

CLARK, MAXINE, retail executive; b. Miami, Fla., Mar. 6, 1949; d. Kenneth and Anne (Lerch) Kasselman; m. Robert Fox, Sept. 1984. B.A. in Journalism, U. Ga., 1971. Exec. trainee Hecht Co., Washington, 1971, hosiery buyer, 1971-72, misses sportswear buyer, 1972-76; mgr. mdse. planning and research May Dept. Stores Co., St. Louis, 1976-78, dir. mdse. devel., 1978-80, v.p. mktg. and sales promotion Venture Stores div., 1980-81, sr. v.p. mktg. and sales promotion Venture Stores div., 1981-83, exec. v.p. mktg. and softlines, 1983-85; exec. v.p. apparel Famous-Barr, St. Louis, 1985-86; v.p. mdsing. Lerner Shops div. Limited Inc., N.Y.C., 1986-88; exec. v.p. Venture Stores, St. Louis, 1988-92; pres. Payless ShoeSource, Topeka, 1992-96; founder, CEO Smart Stuff, Inc. children's retail concept devel. firm and the Build-A-Bear Workshop, 1996—; bd. dirs. Earthgrains Co., Tandy Brands Accessories Co., Wave Techs., Inc., Dept. 56, J.C. Penney Co., Inc., 2003-. Sec., Lafayette Sq. Restoration Com., 1978-79; mem. Com. 200 Nat. Coun. Coll. Arts and Scis. Washington U., St. Louis; trustee U. Ga. Found., 1995—; mem. nat. adv. coun. Girl Scouts U.S.A., 1995-97. Office: Build A Bear Workshop 1960 Innerbelt Business Center Overland MO 63114-5760

CLARK, MIZZELL PHILLIPS (MITZI CLARK), school librarian; b. Kansas City, Mo., May 15, 1925; d. Mizzell and Genevieve Dugey Phillips; m. Champ Clark, Feb. 2, 1949; children: Genevieve, Jane Bennett, Champ, Julie. Student, Washington U., 1942—43, Kansas City Jr. Coll., 1944—45, Piedmont Va. C.C., Charlottesville, 1980—90. Reporter city desk Kansas City Star, 1944—50; pub. rels. dir. Glenview (Ill.) Elem. Schs., Glenview, 1970—74; radio reporter news Sta. WJMA, Orange, Va., 1976—82; pub. rels. dir. Orange Phys. Therapy, 1992—95; spl. collections rschr. Alderman Libr. U. Va., Charlottesville, 1998—. Mem. First Ladies' adv. com. Susan Allen, Wife of Former Va. Gov. George Allen, 1995—96; del. Rep. Nat. Conv., Dallas, 1984; regional vice chmn. # 7 Dist. Rep. Com., Va., 1997—2001. Avocations: hiking, singing, reading, sports, adult education. Home: 3392 Fredericksburg Rd Ruckersville VA 22968 Personal E-mail: mitziclark@aol.com.

CLARK, NANCY LUCINDA BROWN, retired music teacher; b. Akron, Ohio, Dec. 11, 1946; d. Gardner Lane Brown and Ruth Marie Thomas; m. Eugene Ernest Zielinski, Aug. 1968 (div. Mar. 1989); children: Ruth Karlotte Zielinski Hansen, Jennifer Jane Zielinski Webber; m. Douglas Napier Clark, Mar. 11, 1989. Student, Kent State U., 1964-66; BS in Mus. Edn., U. Ill., 1968; postgrad., Nazareth Coll., 1981-82. Music tchr. pre-kindergarten and kindergarten Diocese of Rochester, N.Y., 1970s; tchr., supr. Muzak Cranford (N.J.) Mid. Sch., 1982-87; asst. music dir. First Presbyn. Ch., Maplewood, N.J., 1984-89; music min. Salem Bapt. Ch., Lexington, Ga., 1990-96, ret., 1996. Author (book chpt.) Nantucket Postmarks to 1890, 1989, Philatelic Congress Book Maine Fancy Cancels, 2000; contbr. articles to profl. jours. Pres. Olymphilex 96, Atlanta, 1992—96; mem. Barnstable County Hist. Pres. Commn., 2001—; juror, team leader Juvalux 98, Luxembourg, 1998, 2000; chmn. 1st Nat. Youth in Philately Symposium, 2002; v.p. Barnstable County Hist. Pres. Commn., 2002—03, chair, 2003—; dir. edn. Stamp Camp USA, 2003—, co-chair, 2003—; bd. dirs. Oglethorpe County Libr., Lexington, 1989—98, Athens-Clarke County Regional Libr., 1992—98. Recipient Internat. Gold award ROCPEX Taipei, China, 1981, Polska, 1997, Grand Stamporee award, Palm Beach, Fla., 1996. Mem.: Aux. Markings Club (pres. 2003—), Cape Cod Area Philatelic Group (bd. dirs. 2001—03, pres. 2004—), Am. Assn. Philatelic Exhibitors, Boston Philatelic Group (sec.-treas. 2004—), Collectors Club N.Y., Am. Philatelic Soc.

CLARK, NOREEN MORRISON, behavioral science educator, researcher; b. Glasgow, Scotland, Jan. 12, 1943; came to U.S., 1948; d. Angus Watt and Anne (Murphy) Morrison; m. George Robert Pitt, Dec. 3, 1982; 1 child, Alexander Robert. BS, U. Utah, 1965; MA, Columbia U., 1972, MPhil, 1975, PhD, 1976. Rsch. coord. World Edn. Inc., N.Y.C., 1972-73; asst. prof. Sch. Pub. Health Columbia U., N.Y.C., 1973-80, assoc. prof., 1980-81, Sch. Pub. Health U. Mich., Ann Arbor, 1981-85, prof., chmn. dept. health behavior and health edn., 1985-95, Marshall H. Becker prof. of pub. health, 1995—, dean, 1995—. Adj. prof. health adminstrn. Sch. Pub. Health Columbia U., 1988—; prin. investigator NIH, 1977—; mem. adv. com. pulmonary diseases Nat. Heart, Lung & Blood Inst., Rockville, Md., 1983-87, mem. adv. com. for prevention, edn. and control, 1987-91, coordinating com. Nat. Asthma Edn. Program, 1991—; assoc. Synergos Inst., N.Y.C., 1987-99; nat. adv. environ. health scis. coun. NIH, 1999-2002; task force on preventive cmty. svc. CDC, 2002—. Co-author: Evaluation of Health Promotion, 1984; editor Health Edn. and Behavior, 1985-97; assoc. editor Ann. Rev. of Pub. Health, 2002—; mem. editl. bd. Women in Health, Advances in Health Edn. and Promotion, Home Health Care Services Quar.; contbr. articles to profl. jours. Bd. dirs./advisors Aaron Diamond Found., 1990 97, Family Care Internat., N.Y.C., 1987—, Internat. Asthma Coun., Am. Lung Assn., N.Y.C., 1988—, World Edn., Inc., The Healthtrak Found. Prize. Fellow Soc. Pub. Health Edn. (pres. 1985-86, Disting. Fellow award 1987); mem. APHA (chair health edn. sect. 1982-83, Derryberry award in behavioral sci. 1985, Disting. Career award 1994), Am. Thoracic Soc. (Health Edn. Rsch. award Nat. Asthma Edn. Program 1992, Healthtrak Edn. prize 1997), Internat. Union Health Edn., Soc. Behavioral Medicine, Coun. Fgn. Rels., Inst. Medicine of NAS, Pi Sigma Alpha. Office: U Mich Sch Pub Health 109 Observatory St Ann Arbor MI 48109-2029

CLARK, PATSY VEDDER, retired educator and staff developer; b. Forsyth, Ga., Mar. 28, 1944; d. Roland Roger and Nolia Ernestine (Piland) Vedder; m. James Edwin Clark, Aug. 10, 1965; children: Elizabeth Ellen, James Kenneth. BS in Edn., Tift Coll., 1966; MS in Edn., SUNY, Buffalo, 1976, degree in Specialist in Ednl. Adminstrn., 1989. Cert. elem. educator in social studies; cert. specialist in ednl. adminstrn. Tchr., adminstr. Niagara Falls (N.Y.) City Sch. Dist., 1966-99, staff developer, mentor tchr., 1985-87, asst. adminstr., 1990-92, 96-99. Ednl. cons. N.Y. State United Tchrs., Albany, 1988—. Mem. adv. bd. Friends of the Libr., Niagara Falls, 1999—; founder West Lincoln Cmty. Care, Smithville, Ont., Can., 1985; mem. Friends of Local History, Niagara Falls, 1999—. Mem. Nat. Coun. Tchrs. English (sec.), Delta Kappa Gamma (pres. 1988—, past v.p.), Phi Delta Kappa. Mennonite Brethren. Avocations: reading, travel. Home: PO Box 2750 Niagara Falls NY 14302

CLARK, PAULA IRENE, elementary school educator, consultant; d. Phillip and Julie Clark. BS in Elem. Edn., U. South Fla., 1993; MS in Reading Edn., Fla. State U., 1999; postgrad., Regent U., 2001—, cert. ednl. specialist, 2003. Cert. elem. tchr. Fla., primary tchr. Fla., in reading Fla. Tchr. Hernando County Sch. Dist., Brooksville, Fla., 1996—, reading specialist, 2001—; tng. evaluator Ednl. Testing Svc., Tampa, Fla., 2003—; mem. faculty online campus U. Poenix, 2004. Treas. Pine Grove Elem. PTA, Brooksville, 1996—2002. Named Golden Poet, 1992, Hernando County PTA Person of the Yr., Hernando County Coun., 2001; Doane scholar, U. South Fla., 1993. Mem.: ASCD, Hernando County Acad. Tchrs., Fla. Reading Assn., Internat. Reading Assn. (manuscript reviewer 2001—), Kappa Delta Pi, Phi Delta Kappa. Republican.

CLARK, PEGGY RILLANN, principal; d. Basil Anest and Velma Cornelia Berchekas; m. Clayton Wayne Clark, July 10, 1992; m. Claude Lee Stuart, Jr., July 18, 1970 (div. Mar. 24, 1984); children: Clayton Wayne Jr., Michelle Suzanne Everhart, Brenda Marie Van Arsdale, Claude Lee Stuart III, Bethann Anita Arlington, Chad Nicholas Stuart. MS, Ind. U., Indpls., 1975; BS, Purdue U., 1970. Cert. secondary sch. adminstrn. Ind., secondary tchr. math. Ind. Math. tchr. Griffith Sr. H.S., Indpls., 1978—83, Indpls. Pub. Schs., 1970—78, 1983—93, vice prin., 1993—2000; prin. Arsenal Tech. H.S., Indpls., 2000—. Recipient Stipher award, Arsenal Tech. H.S. Alumni Assn., 2003, Golden Apple award, Indpls. Power and Light, 1991, Disting. Alumni award, Arsenal Tech. H.S. Alumni Assn., 2001; scholar, Ind. U. Sch. Edn., 1988. Mem.: ASCD, Nat. Assn. of Secondary Sch. Prins., Ind. Assn. of Sch. Prins., Phi Delta Kappa, Alpha Omicron Pi. Methodist. Avocations: travel, reading.

CLARK, PHYLLIS YVETTE, marketing professional, consultant; b. L.A., Calif., July 19, 1958; d. Barbara J. and John H. Scott(Stepfather), Arthur L. Clark; m. Leonard R. Norris (div. Dec. 19, 1996); children: Nile L. Norris, Jarrett R. Norris. AAS in Arts Fashion Merchandising, L.A. Harbor Coll., Wilmington, Calif., 1979; BS in Bus. & Mgmt., U. Redlands, Calif., 2002. Cert. vocat. coll. instr. U. Calif., Riverside, 1989. Sales and mktg. Ernst Strauss Inc., L.A., 1981—84; nat. sales mgr. Gollas Am., N.Y.C., 1984—87, Kevan Hall Couture, L.A., 1987—89; image cons./personal shopper Nordstrom, Riverside, Calif., 1991—96, regional breast health awarness mgr. Costa Mesa, Calif., 1996—98; new account mgr. Bob Siemon Designs, Santa Ana, Calif., 1998—99, mktg., product devel., 1999—2001; new account rep. Blood Bank of San Bernardino & Riverside Counties, Calif., 2001—03, corp. ptnrs. & events coord., 2003—. Spkr. Women & Bus. Expo, Riverside, Calif., 1993—96, Nat. Business-women's Leadership Assn., Anaheim, Calif., 1993—93; prodr. Making the Most of Me, Nordstrom, Riverside, Calif., 1994—99; prodr. celebrate life Nat. Coun. Negro Women, Riverside, Calif., 1997; adv. bd. L.A. Trade Tech. Coll., 1983—87; fashion merchandising instr. Studio 7 Fashion Coll., West Covina, Calif., 1989—90; adv. bd. Mt. San Antonio Coll., Walnut, Calif., 1994—98; adj. faculty instr. Orange Coast Coll., Costa Mesa, Calif., 1996—98, Mt. San Antonio Coll., Walnut, Calif., 1996—98; cons., breast health awarness Desert Sierra Breast Cancer Partnership, Riverside, Calif., 1998—98. Recipient Sentinel Women of the Yr., L.A. Sentinel Newspaper, 1986, Women of the Yr. award, Am. Bus. Women Assn., 1987, Image Cons. of the Yr., Assn. of Image Cons. Internat., 1996, Yellow Rose award, Nat. Coun. of Negro Woman, 1997; scholar Woman's Re-Entry to Coll., Talbots, 1998. Mem.: Am. Image Cons. Internat. (pres. 1997—98), Calif. Inland Counties Am. Mktg. Assn. (program com., sec. 2003—), Art 2000. Christian. Avocations: God & family, swimming, travel, arts & crafts, self development. Home: PO Box 56404 Riverside CA 92517 Office: Blood Bank of San Bernardino & Riverside 384 Orange Show Rd San Bernardino CA 92408 Personal E-mail: pyclark@yahoo.com. E-mail: clarkph@bbsbrc.org.

CLARK, RANJANA B. bank executive; arrived in U.S., 1987; BA in Econs., MA in Mktg. and Sales. With Deutsche Bank, Bombay, 1982; joined Wachovia Bank as product mgr. capital markets divsn. Charlotte, NC, 1989; sr. v.p. - group exec. Treas. Svcs. Divsn., 1999—2001; exec. v.p., head Treas. Svcs. Divsn., 2001—. Named One of Most Powerful Women in Banking, U.S. Banker Mag., 2003. Office: Wachovia Bank 301 South College St Charlotte NC 28288-0570*

CLARK, REBECCA LEIGH, sociology educator; b. Danville, Va., Nov. 22, 1949; d. Clyde Odell and Lillian Evelyn (Turner) C.; 1 child, Jon Clark Sells. BA magna cum laude, Stratford Coll., 1972; MA, Ariz. State U., 1975, PhD, 1987. Cert. C.C. tchr., Ariz. Vis. staff mem. Maricopa County (Ariz.) C.C. Dist., 1974-89; Phoenix area field rschr. HRS, Inc., L.A., 1982; faculty assoc. dept. sociology Ariz. State U., Tempe, 1976, 79, 86-89, faculty rsch. assoc. adolescent and family devel. project, 1988-89; prof. sociology Averett U., Danville, Va., 1989—. Presenter in field; manuscript reviewer Harper Collins Pubs., 1989—; chmn. faculty coun. Averett U., 2000-02. Interviewed on local TV program; contbr. articles, book revs. to profl. jours. Chair conf., 1993-95; project dir. survey on quality of life Danville C. of C. 1991; project dir. on recreational needs for Danville Parks and Recreation, 1998. Recipient Leadership award Danville C. of C., 1992. Mem. Am. Assn. Collegiate Ind. Study, Popular Culture Assn. in the South, Alpha Kappa Delta. Home: 215 Montague St Danville VA 24541-2828 Office: Averett U 420 W Main St Danville VA 24541-3612

CLARK, ROSE ANN, chemist, educator; b. Akron, Ohio, Nov. 30, 1967; d. Allen Eugene and Abbie Jean Clark; m. Edward Paul Zovinka, May 28, 1994; children: Edward Alan Zovinka, Shane Paul Zovinka. BS in Chemistry, U. N.C., Wilmington, 1990; PhD in Chemistry, N.C. State U., 1995. NSF postdoctoral fellow Pa. State U., State College, 1995-97; assoc. prof. chemistry St. Francis U., Loretto, Pa., 1997—. Author (with others): (book) Electrochemistry in Neuronal Microenviroments, 1998; contbr. articles to profl. jours. Presenter Rural Outreach Chemistry for Kids, Loretto, 1997—2002. Fellow Electronic Materials, Dept. of Edn., 1992—95; grantee Tchg. Incentive, GE, 1990—91, Rsch., NSF, 1998, Soc. Analytical Chemists of Pitts., 2001, SACP, 2002. Mem.: AAAS, Coun. Undergrad. Rsch., Soc. Electroanalytical Chemists, Am. Chem. Soc., Sigma Xi. Avocations: golf, bicycling. Office: St Francis U PO Box 600 Loretto PA 15940-0600 Fax: 814-472-2773. Business E-Mail: rclark@francis.edu.

CLARK, ROSE SHARON, elementary school educator; b. Winslow, Ind., Oct. 31, 1942; d. William Noel Fettinger and Mary Emaline Jones; m. Charles Edgar Clark, June 2, 1968; children: Mary Elizabeth, Christopher Edgar. BS, Oakkland City (Ind.) U., 1964; MS, Ind. U., 1968. Elem. edn. tchr. Hendricks Twp. Sch., Shelbyville, Ind., 1964—67, Thomas A. Hendricks, Shelbyville, Ind., 1967—74, 1984—. Mem. bd. First Ch. of the Nazarene, Shelbyville, 1994—, First Ch. of God, Shelbyville, 1969—90; bd. dirs. Bright Star Pre-Sch., Shelbyville, 2001—. Mem.: AAUW (v.p.-treas. 1972—2000), Alpha Delta Kappa. Home: 2466 N Richard Dr Shelbyville IN 46176 Office: Thomas A Hendricks Sch 1111 St Joseph St Shelbyville IN 46176

CLARK, SANDRA MARIE, school administrator; b. Hanover, Pa., Feb. 17, 1942; d. Charles Raymond Clark and Mary Josephine (Snyder) Clark Wierman. BS in Elem. Edn., Chestnut Hill Coll., 1980; MS in Child Care Adminstrn., Nova U., 1985; MS in Ednl. Adminstrn., Western Md. Coll., 1992. Cert. elem. tchr., elem. prin., Pa. Tchr. various elem. schs., Pa., 1962-75; asst. vocation directress Mt. St. Joseph Motherhouse, Chestnut Hill, Pa., 1975-76; tchr. St. Catharine's Sch., Spring Lake, N.J., 1976-77; asst. mgr. Jim's Truck Stop, New Oxford, Pa., 1977-81; adminstr. Little People Day Care Sch., Hanover, 1981-88, sec., treas. bd. dirs., 1985-86; coord. regional resource Magic Yrs. Child Care & Learning Ctrs., Inc., Hanover, 1987-88; prin. St. Vincent de Paul Sch., Hanover, Pa., 1988—. Presenter Hanover Area Seminar for Day Care Employees, 1983-86. Coord. sch. safety patrols St. Vincent's Sch., Hanover, 1969-75, vice-chmn. bd., 1982-84; multi-media instr. first aid ARC, Hanover, 1983-86, bd. dirs., 1984-88; exec. sec. of bd. of dirs. ARC, Hanover, 1988; 1st v.p. Hanover Area Coun. of Chs., 1988, pres., 1989; validator accredidation program Nat. Acad. Early Childhood Programs, Washington, 1987—; bd. dirs. Life Skills Unltd. Handicapped Adults, 1988—; facilitator Harrisburg Diocesan Synod, Hanover, 1985-88, parish del., 1988. Pa. Dept. Pub. Welfare tng. grantee, 1986. Mem. NAFE, Nat. Cath. Ednl. Assn. Clubs: Internat. Assn. Turtles (London). Democrat. Roman Catholic. Avocations: swimming, reading, writing children's stories. Home: 348 Barberry Dr Hanover PA 17331-1302 Office: St Vincent De Paul Sch Hanover PA 17331 Office Phone: 717-637-5190.

CLARK, SHARON ANN, educational consultant, music educator; b. Lowell, Mass., Aug. 3, 1961; d. William K. and Dorothy A. (McNamara) Clark; m. Mortenson J. Eric, July 11, 1998. MusB, U. of Mass. at Lowell, Lowell, MA, 1983; MED, Fitchburg State Coll., Fitchburg, MA, 1988; EdD, Nova Southeastern U., Ft. Lauderdale, Florida, 2003. Cert. tchr. Mass., 1983. Ednl. cons. Edn. Performance Systems, Inc., Woburn, Mass., 2000; instrnl. specialist Lowell Pub. Schools, Mass., 2001—. Music specialist Lowell Pub. Schs., Mass., 1989—2000. Choir mem. St. Margaret Ch., Lowell, Mass., 1997—2003. Vis. scholar Comprehensive Sch. Reform grant, Mass. Dept. of Edn., 2002; Lighthouse Tech. grant, 1999, Jordan Fundamentals grant, Michael Jordan Found. - NIKE, 2001, Creative Schools grant, Mass. Cultural Coun., 2002. Mem.: Lowell Sch. Adminstrs. Assn., Am. Fedn. Tchrs., Music Educators Nat. Conf., Nat. Staff Devel. Coun. Avocations: biking, painting, travel. Home: 18 Crestwood Dr Hudson NH 03051 Office: BFButler Mid Sch Tech 1140 Gorham St Lowell MA 01852 Personal E-mail: shadotclark@earthlink.net. E-mail: sharonclark@lowell.k12.ma.us.

CLARK, SHARON JACKSON, private school administrator; b. Istanbul, Turkey, Feb. 3, 1939; d. John Warren and Maxine Jett (Brient) Jackson; m. Ronald Eugene Clark, June 6, 1959; children: Kristen Anne, Kevin Brooks, Jeffrey Kimball. BFA, Calif. Coll. Arts and Crafts, 1968; MS in Edn., Wheelock Coll., 1978; student, Moore Coll. Art. Co-founder Jowanio, Syracuse, NY, The Thoreau Sch., Salt Lake City, Glen Urquhart Sch., Beverly, Mass.; head, founder Clark Sch. for Creative Learning, Danvers, Mass. Mem. Gifted/Talented Educators North Shore (bd. dir.), Danvers Hist. Soc. (bd. dir.). Home: 487 Locust St Danvers MA 01923-1252

CLARK, SHELIA ROXANNE, sports association executive, legislative analyst; b. June 28, 1959; d. Milton Cornell and Mable Juanita (Grubb) C. BS in Polit. Sci., Radford U., 1983; MPA, James Madison U., Harrisonburg, Va., 1987. Dir. Black Teenage World Scholarship Program, Va., 1977-88; intern Field Found., New River Valley, Va., 1984-85, Rep. Rick Boucher, Washington, 1987; adminstrv. asst. OMB Watch, Washington, 1988; legis. asst. Nat. Community Action Found., Washington, 1988-93; exec. dir. Gary Clark's Sports Camp, 1990—; interim dir. talent search program Va. Tech. U., Blacksburg, 1997-98, athletic acad. advisor/lectr., 1998—, asst. coord.-student athletic Office of Acad. Enrichment, 1998—. Project coord. Student Coalition Against Tobacco, 1994-95; cons., asst. Nat. Children's Day Found., Washington, 1991-93; advisor Soc. of African Am. Scholars, Alpha Kappa Mu, Va. Tech. U., Blacksburg; cons. Profl. Athletes Svcs. Success, 2002-. Program dir. Project Unity, Va., 1984; bd. mem. VA Action, 1985, Grassroots Leadership Project, N.C., 1987; campaign worker Clinton Presdl. Campaign/Transition, Washington, 1992. Internship The Field Found., 1984-85, Congressman Rick Boucher, Washington, 1987. Mem. Nat. Coun. Negro Women. Office: Gary Clarks Sports Camp PO Box 202 Dublin VA 24084-0202 E-mail: clarkclark80@aol.com.

CLARK, SHIRLEY SUZANNE, music educator; b. Detroit, June 23, 1927; d. Nicolas Orlando and Mary Antoinette (Moseley) Ray; m. Harold Edward Clark, June 20, 1949; children: Teresa Clark Ellis, Steven Douglas, Michael David, Mark Anthony. MusB, Evansville Coll., 1949; BME; MA, Utah State U. Cert. tchr. Ind. Pvt. music educator, Evansville, Ind.; music educator Evansville Sch. Dist., substitute tchr., 1970—2003; leader string ensemble Evansville; tchr. Warrick Co., Mt. Vernon Sch. Corp. Prin. cellist Christian Fellowship Ch. Orch. Inspector at polls Rep. Party Highland Sch., 1991—2001; mem. Evansville Philharmonic Orch., 1941—81, Owensboro (Ky.) Symphony Orch., 1950—60; trustee Salem United Methodist Ch., 2003—. Mem.: Purdue Women in Song Vanderburgh County Choral Club, Bloomington Ind. Symphony, Nashville Local Musicians Union, Sinawik Club (pres. elect), Tri State Navy Mothers Club Am. (1st vice commdr. 2003—), Ind. State Navy Mothers Club (1st vice commdr. 2003—), Darnistadt-McCutchanville Kiwanis Club (past pres.), Kappa Kappa Iota, Sigma Alpha Iota (Rose of Honor, Sword of Honor), Phi Mu. Republican. Methodist. Avocations: camping, hiking, photography, boating, horseback riding, walking. Home: 9827 Darmstadt Rd Evansville IN 47710-5032

CLARK, SUSAN (NORA GOULDING), actress; b. Sarnia, Ont., Can., Mar. 8, 1940; d. George Raymond and Eleanor Almond (McNaughton) Clark; m. Alex Karra; 1 child, Katie Karras. Student, Toronto (Ont.) Children's Players, 1956-59; student (Acad. scholar), Royal Acad. Dramatic Art, London. Ptnr. Georgian Bay Prodns. Actor: (stage prodn.) Appearances to the Contrary, 2000, Glass Menagerie, 2002, Sisters Rosensweig, 2002, BiCoastal Woman, 2003; (TV series) Webster, 1983, Emily of New Moon, 1998; (films) Nobody's Perfekt, 1981, Porky's, 1981, Butterbox Babies, 1995; (TV films) Babe, 1975 (Emmy for oustanding lead actress in a drama, 1975), Sherlock Holmes: The Strange Case of Alice Faulkner, 1981, The Choice, 1981, Maid in America, 1982, Tonya & Nancy: The Inside Story, 1994, Snowbound: The Jim and Jennifer Stolpa Story, 1994, (stage prodn.) Dancing at Lughnasa, 2003. Mem. ACLU, Am. Film Inst. Office: care Georgian Bay Prodns 13400 Riverside Dr Ste 308 Sherman Oaks CA 91423-2541

CLARK, SUZANNE UNDERWOOD, writer; b. Nyack, New York, Oct. 4, 1950; d. Roger Leslie Underwood and Mary Lee Hester; m. Albert John Clark, June 17, 1978; children: Katy, Stephen, Emily. BS magna cum laude,

James Madison U., 1972; MA, Johns Hopkins U., 1975. Adj. prof. English King Coll., Bristol, Tenn., 1991—. Copy editor Comml. Appeal, Memphis, 1975—76; presenter workshops, seminars on writing Va. Highlands C.C., Abingdon, 1996, Chalcedon Christian Sch., Roswell, Ga., 1997; adj. prof. English East Tenn. State U., Johnson City, 1999, Va. Intermont Coll., Bristol, 2000; weekly columnist Kingsport Times News, Kingsport, Tenn., 2001. Author: Blackboard Blackmail, 1988, Weather of the House, 1994, Sketches of Home, 1998, What a Light Thing, This Stone, 1999, The Roar on the Other Side, 2000. Bd. dirs. Steele Creek Nature Ctr., Bristol, Tenn.; mem. adv. bd. Abortion Alternative & Crisis Pregnancy Ctr., Bristol, Tenn., 1982—. Recipient 1st prize in poetry, Va. Highlands Creative Writing Contest, 1995, Honorable Mention in Poetry, Now & Then Mag., 1998, Sow's Ear Review, 1996; fellow, Va. Ctr. for Creative Arts, 1992. Mem.: Appalachian Writers Assn., Appalachian Ctr. for Poets and Writers. Presbyterian. Avocations: birdwatching, hiking, shelling. Office: Mercy Med Airlift 4620 Haygood Rd Virginia Beach VA 23455

CLARK, TERESA WATKINS, psychotherapist, clinical counselor; b. Hobart, Okla., Dec. 18, 1953; d. Aaron Jack Watkins and Patricia Ann (Flurry) Greer and Ralph Gordon Greer; m. Philip Winston Clark, Dec. 29, 1979; children: Philip Aaron, Alisa Lauren. BA in Psychology, U. N.Mex., 1979, MA in Counseling and Family Studies, 1989. Lic. profl. clin. counselor, N.Mex.; nat. cert. counselor. Child care worker social svcs. divsn. Family Resource Ctr., Albuquerque, 1978-79; head tchr., asst. dir. Kinder Care Learning Ctr., Albuquerque, 1979-80; psychiat. asst. Vista Sandia Psychiat. Hosp., Albuquerque, 1980-87; psychotherapist outpatient clinic Bernalillo County Mental Health Ctr.-Heights, 1989-91; therapist adult and adolescent program Charter/Heights Behavioral Health Sys., Albuquerque, 1991-2000; therapist New Day Youth and Family Svcs., Albuquerque, 2001—. Vol. mental health svcs. disasters ARC. Mem. ACA, Am. Assn. Multicultural Counseling and Devel., Nat. Bd. Cert. Counselors, N.Mex. Health Counselors Assn. (former cen. regional rep., ethics chair, bd. dirs.), Mental Health Councelor's Assn., Billy The Kid Outlaw Gang Hist. Soc. Democrat. Avocations: music, camping, horseback riding, reading. Office: New Day Youth and Family Svcs 1330 San Pedro Ne Albuquerque NM 87110

CLARK, TERRI, singer; b. Montreal, Can., Aug. 5, 1968; d. Les Sauson and Linda Clark. Previous jobs include work at restaurants, Gilley's, the Wax Mus., Nashville. Albums: Terri Clark, 1995, Just the Same, 1996, How I Feel, 1998, Fearless, 2000, Pain to Kill, 2003. Named Top New Female Country Artist Billboard mag., 1995; recipient Album of Yr. award Country Music Assn., 1996, Song of Yr., 1996, Vista Rising Star award, 1996, Canadian County Music Assoc. best single, 2003. Office: Mercury Records 66 Music Sq W Nashville TN 37203-3208*

CLARK, TRUDY H. career officer; BA in sociology with honors, U. Md., 1972; student, Comm. Electronics Officer Sch., 1973—74; MS in guidance and counseling, Troy State U., 1987; disting. grad., Squadron Officer Sch., Maxwell AFB, 1980, Air Command and Staff Coll., 1987, Armed Forces Staff Coll., 1992, Air War Coll., Maxwell AFB, 1993. Second lt. USAF, 1973, first lt., 1975, cptn., 1977, major, 1985, lt. col., 1989, col., 1994, brigadier gen., 1999, maj. general, 2003; dir. command, control, comm. and computer sys. US Strategic Command, Offutt AFB, Nebr., 1999—2001; deputy dir. Defense Threat Reduction Agency (DTRA), Ft. Belvoir, Va., 2003—; chief tel. installations 392nd Comm. Group, Vandenberg AFB, Calif., 1974—76; chief programs mgmt. div. 2006th Comm. Group, Incirlik AFB, Turkey, 1976—79; chief comm. branch Joint Studies Group, Nellis AFB, Nev., 1979—81; chief threat analysis 4440th Tactical Fighter Training Group, Red Flag, Nellis AFB, Nev.; chief facilities operation branch 2146th Comm. Group, Osan AB, Republic of Korea, 1981—82; chief telecom. div. Langley AFB, Va., exec. officer, Hdqs. Tactical Comm. Div., 1982—84; comdr. 1880th Info. Systems Squadron, Tonopah Test Range, Nev., 1984—86; chief tactical command and control comm. sys. Hdqs. USAF, Washington, directorate, programs and evaluation, exec. officer for dep. dir. of programs and evaluation, 1987—89; comdr. staff support unit White House Comm. Agy., Washington, presdl. comm. officer, 1989—92; comdr. 60th comm. group Hdqs. 15th Air Force, Travis AFB, Calif., chief comm. div., 1993—94. Office: 8725 John J Kingman Rd MSC 6201 Fort Belvoir VA 22060-6201*

CLARKE, ALYCE GRIFFIN, state legislator; b. Yazoo City, Miss. m. L.W. Clarke Jr.; 1 child, DeMarquis Johntrell. BS, Alcorn State U.; MS, Tuskegee Inst.; postgrad., Jackson State U., Miss. Coll. Nutritionist; mem. Miss. Ho. of Reps., 1985—, vice chmn. interstate coop com., mem. various coms. Active Econ. Devel. Com., Exec. Dem. Commn., New Hope Found. Mem. Nat. Assn. Cmty. Health Ctrs., Pub. Health Assn., Jack & Jill Am., Alcorn Alumni, Alpha Kappa Alpha. Democrat. Baptist. Home: 1053 Arbor Vista Blvd Jackson MS 39209-7135 Office: Miss State Senate State Capitol Jackson MS 39201

CLARKE, BETTY ANN, librarian, minister; b. Townsend, Va., Nov. 9, 1947; d. Joshua Samuel and Queenie Victoria (Morris) Spady; m. Kenneth Clarke, June 30, 1972; 1 stepchild, Cynthia Clarke Rhinehart. BA in Polit. Sci., Norfolk State U., 1970; postgrad., N.J. Conf. Ministerial INst., 1979—84; MA, Rowan U., 1995. Cert. libr. N.J. Sr. libr. Atlantic County, Mays Landing, NJ, 1978—; pastor St. Mark African Meth. Episcopal Ch., Lindenwold, NJ, 1987—. Chaplain trauma unit Cooper Hosp., Camden, NJ, 1990—98. Recipient Jarena Lee award, Harrisburg Dist. African Meth. Episcopal Ch., 1992, African Am. Women's Network Bronze Star, Delaware Valley Humanity Field Health, 1996, Woman Making A Difference award, Bethel African Meth. Episcopal Ch., 2002. Democrat. Avocations: reading, travel, writing, bowling. Home: 14 Jefferson Ave Browns Mills NJ 08021 Office: St Mark AME Ch 929 Walnut & Taylor Aves Lindenwold NJ 08021 Office Phone: 609-625-2776 ext. 6328.

CLARKE, CHERYL CRIDER, music educator; b. Tuscaloosa, Ala., May 31, 1956; d. Byron and Gloria Hall Crider; m. John Eugene (Gene) Clarke, July 8, 1978; children: Amy Elizabeth, Emily Dyan. BS in music edn., U. Ala., 1974—77. Band dir. Wilson Hall Mid. Sch., Grove Hill, Ala., 1977—; choir dir. Grove Hill United Meth. Ch., 1990—. Team mem. Clarke County Edn. Tech., Grove Hill, 1981—; state spl. talent coord. Ala. Jr. Beta Club, Montgomery, 1998—. Named Tchr. of Yr., Walmart, 1995; named one of Outstanding Young Women in Am., 1988—89. Mem.: Ala. Edn. Assn., Ala. Bandmasters Assn. Republican. Meth. Avocations: computers, theater, travel, books. Home: 143 Foscue Ave Grove Hill AL 36451 Office: Wilson Hall Mid Sch 401 Carter Dr Grove Hill AL 36451

CLARKE, CORDELIA KAY KNIGHT MAZUY, management consultant, artist; b. Springfield, Mo., Nov. 22, 1938; d. William Horace and Charline (Bentley) Knight; m. Logan Clarke, Jr., July 22, 1978; children by previous marriage— Katharine Michelle Mazuy, Christopher Knight Mazuy. AB in English with honors, U. N.C., 1960; MS in Stats., N.C. State U., 1962. Statistician Research Triangle Inst., Durham, NC, 1960-63; statis. cons. Arthur D. Little, Inc., Cambridge, Mass., 1963-67; dir. mktg. planning and analysis Polaroid Corp., Cambridge, 1967-70; dir. mktg. and bus. planning Transaction Tech. Inc., Cambridge, 1970-72; pres. Mazuy Assos., Boston, 1972-73; v.p. Nat. Shawmut Bank, Boston, 1973-74; sr. v.p., dir. mktg. Shawmut Corp., 1974-78; sr. v.p., dir. retail banking Shawmut Bank, 1976-78; v.p. corp. devel. Arthur D. Little, Inc., 1978-79; v.p. Conn. Gen. Life Ins. Co., 1979-85; pres. CIGNA Securities, 1983-85; chmn. Templeton, Inc., 1985-92, 95—; exec. v.p. McGraw-Hill Inc., 1988-90; pres. micromarketing divsn. ADVO, 1990-95. Faculty Williams Sch. Banking; adv. com. Bur. of Census, 1978-84; bd. dirs. Guardian Life Ins. Co., Berkshire Life Ins., Providence Jour. Co.; tchr. Amos Tuck Grad. Sch. Bus., Dartmouth Coll., 1964-65, exec.-in-residence, 1978, 80; bd. overseers, 1979-85; exec.-in-residence Wheaton Coll., 1978; vis. prof. Simmons Grad. Sch. Mgmt., 1978; mem. schs. adv. coun. Bank Mktg. Assn., 1976-78; mem. corp. adv. bd. Hartford Nat. Bank & Trust Co., 1980-87. Columnist Am. Banker, 1976-78. Mem. Mass. Gov.'s Commn. on Status of Women, 1977-79; bd. corporators Babson Coll., 1977-80; adv. bd. Boston Mayor's Office Cultural Affairs, 1977-79; bd. dirs. McGraw-Hill, Inc., 1976-88, Blue Shield of Mass., 1976-79, Greater Hartford Arts Coun., 1979-93, Cybex Internat. Inc., 1996-2000; trustee Children's Mus. Hartford, 1980-82; corporator Inst. of Living, 1981-92; regent U. Hartford, 1982—; bd. dirs. Hartford Art Sch., 1982-94, Hartford Stage Co., 1985-99, Manhattan Theatre Club, 1988-91, Inst. for Future, 1988-92, N.Y. Internat. Festival of Arts, 1988-91, Goodspeed Opera, 1990—, Inst. Design, 1990-98, Aeroflex Found., 1972—. Mem. Artists Assn. Nantucket (elected), Lyme Art Assn. (assoc.), Essex Art Assn. (assoc.), Internat. Womens Forum, Power 10, Phi Beta Kappa, Phi Kappa Phi, Kappa Alpha Theta. Home and Office: 89 River Rd East Haddam CT 06423-1462 Office Phone: 860-526-3368.

CLARKE, EVELYN WOODMAN, volunteer; b. National City, Calif., May 24, 1917; d. William Irving and Lena Edah (Crouse) Woodman; m. George Samuel Clarke, May 25, 1935 (dec. Nov. 1974); children: Peter Brian, August William, George Woodman. Grad., Herbert Hoover H.S., San Diego, 1935; student, San Diego State Coll., 1935. Clk. U.S. Post Office, Grossmont, Calif., 1943-70. Del. 49th Congl. Dist. Calif. White House Conf. on Aging, 1995-96; mem. San Diego County Dem. Cen. Com., 1978-83; chair 78th Assembly Dist., 1985-86; alt. del. Dem. Nat. Conv., N.Y., 1980; commr. San Diego City Pub. Utilities Adv. Commn., 1992-2000, San Diego County Commn. on Status of Women, 1980-83; mem. program/budget rev. panel United Way, 1980-83; observer U.S. Nat. Conf. for Women, Houston, 1977, UN Internat. Women's Yr. Tribunal, Mexico City, 1975; mem. U.S. Dem. Congl. Campaign Com., U.S. Dem. Senatorial Campaign Com., Clinton/Gore '96 Campaign. Recipient Vol.'s commendation United Way, San Diego, 1983, Susan B. Anthony cert. NOW, San Diego, 1982, named Hon. Life Mem. Calif. Congress Parents and Tchrs., 1948. Mem. YWCA, Uptown Dem. Club, Emily's List, Nat. Women's Polit. Caucus (Spl. Recognition award 1993, Alice Paul award 1985), Older Women's League (Wonderful Older Woman's award 1985), San Diego Hist. Soc., San Diego Opera, San Diego Zool. Soc., UN Assn. Avocations: current events, photography. Home: 605 W Walnut Ave Apt A San Diego CA 92103-3987

CLARKE, JANE CAROL, academic administrator, director, principal; b. Shelby, Ohio, Mar. 20, 1940; d. Clyde Eugene and Hazel Ruth (Johnson) Smith; m. Edward Dean Clarke, July 15, 1971; children: Suzanne, Karla, Jeff, Ethan, Jeremy. Assoc. degree, Lansing C.C., 1977; BS, Ea. Mich. U., 1980, MA, 1982. Cert. dir. spl. edn., elem. adminstr., K-12 spl. edn. tchr. Dir. spl. edn., prin., dir. alt. edn. Stockbridge (Mich.) Schs., 1988—. Dir. Mich. Alt. Edn. Orgn., 1995-96; recommended to Dissertation Nat. Rsch. Conf.-Ednl. Rsch. Assn., 1995. Mem. AAUW, Mich. Adminstrs. of Spl. Edn., Mich. Elem. and Mid. Sch. Prins. Assn. Avocations: golf, reading. Office: Stockbridge Cmty Schs 303 W Elizabeth St Stockbridge MI 49285-9791 Home: 5317 Versailes Ave Brighton MI 48116-4709

CLARKE, JEAN ALDERMAN, orchestra director; b. Memphis, May 15, 1949; d. Allison M. and Ruth Edwards Alderman; m. William Trantham Clarke, Nov. 19, 1977; 1 child, William Alderman Trantham. AB magna cum laude, Duke U., 1971; MS in Music Edn., U. Ill., 1972. Cert. tchr. S.C., N.C. Orch. dir. Charleston (S.C.) Sch. Dist., 1972—74, Sch. Dist. of Greenville County, SC, 1974—89, 1996—97, Beech Springs Intermediate Sch., Duncan, SC, 1997—, Berry Shoals Internmediate Sch., Duncan, 2001—. Trustee bd. dirs. Greenville Symphony Assn., 1998—. Mem.: Music Educators Nat. Conf., Am. String Tchrs. Assn., Am. Viola Soc. (S.C. chpt. treas. 2001—), S.C. Music Educators Assn. (pres. orch. divsn. 1989—91, bd. dirs. 1987—93). Baptist. Avocations: running, tennis, sailing, swimming. Home: 9 Phillips Trl Greenville SC 29609-6421 Office: Berry Shoals Intermediate Sch 300 Shoals Rd Duncan SC 29334

CLARKE, JUDY, lawyer; b. Asheville, N.C., 1953; B in Psychology, Furman U., 1974; JD, U. S.C., 1977. Trial atty. Fed. Defenders San Diego, Inc., exec. dir.; pvt. practice, 1991-92; pub. defender Fed. Pub. Defender's Office, Spokane, Wash., 1992—. Mem. faculty Nat. Criminal Def. Coll., Macon, Ga., bd. regents, 1985—. Author: Federal Sentencing Manual; contbr. articles to profl. jours. Mem. NADCL (pres. 1996-97). Office: Fed Pub Defenders Office 10 N Post St Ste 700 Spokane WA 99201-0705

CLARKE, KATHLEEN BURTON, federal agency administrator; b. Utah; BA in in Political Science, Utah State U. From dir. constituent svcs. to exec. dir. Office of Congressman James V. Hansen, 1987—93; dep. dir. Utah Dept. Natural Resources, 1993—98, exec. dir., 1998—2001; dir. Bur. Land Mgmt. U.S. Dept. Interior, Washington, 2001—. Office: US Dept Interior Bur Land Mgmt 1849 C St NW Washington DC 20240

CLARKE, KIT HANSEN, radiologist; b. Louisville, May 24, 1944; d. Hans Peter and Katie (Bird) Hansen; m. John M. Clarke, Feb. 14, 1976; children: Brett Bonnett, Blair Hansen, Brandon Chamberlain; stepchildren: Gray Campbell, Jeffrey William John M. AB, Randolph-Macon Woman's Coll., 1966; MD, U. Louisville, 1969. Diplomate Am. Bd. Radiology. Intern Louisville Gen. Hosp., 1969-70; resident in internal medicine and radiology U. Tenn., Knoxville, 1970-73; resident in radiology U.S. Fla., Tampa, 1973-74; staff radiologist Palms of Pasadena, St. Petersburg, Fla., 1974—, chmn. radiology dept., 1992—. Active Fla. Competitive Swim Assn. of Amateur Athletics Union. Fellow Am. Coll. Radiology; mem. AMA, Fla. West Coast Radiology Soc., Radiol. Soc. N.Am., Fla. Med. Assn., Pinellas County Med. Soc., Fla. Radiology Soc., Am. Horse Show Assn. (hunter, jumber divsn.). Episcopalian. Home: 7171 9th St S Saint Petersburg FL 33705-6218 Office: 6550 1st Ave N Saint Petersburg FL 33710

CLARKE, LOUISE RIGDON, gifted student program administrator, principal; b. Kansas City, Mo., July 23, 1936; d. Raymond Harrison and Margret (Britt) Rigdon; children: Michael Terrell, Steven Harrison. BA, Agnes Scott Coll., 1954-58; postgrad., U. Va.; M in Adminstrn. and Supervision, Radford U., 1986; CAGS in Adminstrv. Leadership, Va. Tech., 1994. Cert. middle sch. supr., prin. Arborvirus serologist Ctr. for Disease Control, Atlanta, 1958-64; English tchr. Chinese Middle Sch., Taipei, Taiwan, 1965-67; dir. Navy Relief Soc. for Marine Base Camp LeJeune, Jacksonville, N.C., 1975-76; sci. tchr. jr. high sch., 1980-84; hons. resource tchr. jr. high programs for gifted, 1984-86; coord. programs for gifted, talented and highly motivated Roanoke (Va.) City Pub. Schs., 1986-99, supr. sci. K-8, 1986-99; prin. Ctrl. Elem. Sch., South Williamsport, Pa., 1999—. Adj. faculty Hollins (Va.) Coll., 1989-98; past pres. Roanoke Regional Coun. Edn. of the Gifted. Mem. ASCD, Va. Assn. Supervision and Curriculum Devel., Nat. Assn. Gifted Children (pres.), Va. Assn. for Edn. Gifted, Am. Ednl. Rsch. Assn., Phi Dela Kappa. Avocations: tennis, bird watching, hiking. Home: 1400 Watson St Williamsport PA 17701-2334 Office: South Williamsport Sch Dist 515 W Central Ave Williamsport PA 17702-7206

CLARKE, MARJORIE JANE, environmental educator, consultant, author, researcher; b. Miami, Fla., July 14, 1953; d. Garnet Winston Clarke and Janice Marie (Platt) Johnson. BA in Geology, Smith Coll., 1975; MA in Environ. Sci., Johns Hopkins U., 1978; MS in Energy Tech., NYU, 1982; MPhil, CUNY, 1996, PhD in Earth and Environ. Scis., 1999. Cert. qualified environ. profl., 1994—. Intern EPA, Washington, 1974-75, 76; phys. scientist U.S. EPA, N.Y.C., 1978; sr. economist Tri-State Regional Planning Commn., N.Y.C., 1979-81; policy coord. N.Y. Power Authority, N.Y.C., 1981-83; environ. scientist N.Y.C. Dept. Sanitation, 1984-88; dir. solid waste rsch. INFORM, Inc., N.Y.C., 1988-90; tech. rsch. cons. for four PBS Videos WNET-Channel 13, N.Y.C., 1990; environ. cons. Natural Resources Def. Coun., N.Y.C., 1990—; sr. solid waste cons. INFORM, 1990-94; cons. Air & Waste Mgmt. Assn./Solid Waste Mgmt., 1993-94; rsch. fellow Ctr. for Applied Studies of the Environment, CUNY, 1992—; instr. geography dept. Rutgers U., 1999—2000. Adj. asst. prof. Hunter Coll., 1996, 98, 99, 2001, 03—; adj. asst. prof. Lehman Coll., 2002—, scientist in residence, 2001—; cons. Hampshire County (Eng.), Coun., 1994-95; cons. to Commonwealth, 1996; cons., instr. Profl. Recyclers Pa., 2001—2002; mem. steering com. Citywide Recycling Adv. Bd., N.Y.C., 1991—, vice-chair, 2001-2003; mem. Camden County Environ. Tech. Adv. Com., 1993-95; mem. N.J. Dept. Environ. Protection and Energy, Mercury Emission Std.-Setting Task Force, 1992-95; mem. N.Y. State Adv. Bd. on Operating Requirements, Albany, 1988-92; examiner Qualified Environ. Profls. Program, 1995; peer reviewer Environ. Def. Fund, N.Y.C., 1988—, Nat. Resources Def. Coun., N.Y.C., 1988-90; mem. Manhattan Citizens' Solid Waste Adv. Bd., 1990—, chair, 1992-94, vice chair, 1994-96, 2001-2003, chair waste prevention com., 1991—; mem. steering com. N.Y.C. Waste Prevention Coalition, 2000—, vice chair 2001-. Co-author: Burning Garbage in the U.S., 1991, Waste Incineration and Public Health, 1999; contbr. articles to profl. confs. and jours., 1983—; webmaster. Mem. USEPA/Nat. Recycling Coaliton's Nat. Task Force to develop and promote a source reduction procurement strategy, 1996-98; mem. source reduction forum Nat. Recycling Coalition, 1998-2002; founder, pres. Riverside-Inwood Neighborhood Gardens, 1984—, newsletter editor, 1995-2002, webmaster, 1997—; mem. 9/11 Environ. Action Steering Com., 2002—. Recipient citation Dartmouth Coll., 1974, Roy F. Weston award Jour. Solid Waste Tech. and Mgmt., 1997, Cert. of Merit for Best Film by NGO category Environment India's 1998 Internat. Film Festival; featured on cover Money Mag., 1981; U.S. EPA grantee, 1991-95; Gilleece fellow CUNY, 1991-95. Mem. ASME (indsl. and mcpl. waste rsch. com. 1986—, operator cert. com. 1988-98), Nat. Acad. Scis. (nat. rsch. coun. com. health effects waste incineration 1995-99), Air and Waste Mgmt. Assn. (sec. 1988-89, session chair annual meeting 1988—, vice chair 1989-90, chmn. solid waste and thermal treatment com. 1990-92, vice chair solid waste intercom. task force 1992-94, chair integrated waste mgmt. com. 1994-2000, tech. dir. video 1993-94, vice chair mcpl. and med. waste mgmt. divsn. 2000-2003, fellow 2002, chair 2003-), Nat. Recycling Coalition, NRC Source Reduction Forum (steering com.), N.Y. Assn. for Reduction, Reuse and Recycling, N.Y. Cycle Club (ride leader 1982—). Democrat. Avocations: bicycling, photography, guitar, gardening. Home and Office: 1795 Riverside Dr Apt 5F New York NY 10034-5334 E-mail: mclarke@hunter.cuny.edu.

CLARKE, MARYANNA, theater director; d. Theresa Irizarry; m. Christopher Caldwell Clarke, Oct. 6, 1979; 1 child, Kate. BS in Speech and Theatre, Mid. Tenn. State U., 2001. Freelance actor/dir. various theatre cos., Nashville area, Tenn., 1989—2002; exec. dir., founder Tenn. Women's Theater Project, Nashville, 2002—. Mem. theatre comms. group Ctr. Nonprofit Mgmt. Recipient Best Actress award, The Tennessean, 1999. Achievements include Founder of the Tennessee Women's Theater Project, a professional, nonprofit, 501(c)(3) theater company dedicated to giving voice to women through theater arts. Avocations: singing, horseback riding, jogging. Business E-Mail: maryanna@twtp.org.

CLARKE, PAULA KATHERINE, anthropology educator, sociology educator; b. Berkeley, Gloucestershire, Eng., July 27, 1946; d. Percy George and Grace Anne C.; m. Warren Ted Hamilton. BA, U. Calif., Berkeley, 1982; PhD, U. Calif., San Francisco, 1991. Prof. anthropology and sociology Columbia Coll., Sonora, Calif., 1997—. Spkr. 3d Internat. Conf. on Gender and Equity, Bangkok, 2001. Contbr. articles (Nominated-Kathleen Gregory Klein Award by Women's Caucus/Popular and Am. Culture Assn. for best unpublished article on feminism and popular culture, 1999); contbr.: Men and Masculinities: A Social, Cultural, and Historical Encyclopedia, 2003; contbr. articles to ednl. jours. Creator Future Promise Award scholarship Columbia Coll., Sonora, 2001. Recipient Excellence in Tchg. award, Tuolumne County Bd. Edn., 2002. Office: Columbia Coll 11600 Columbia College Dr Sonora CA 95370 Office Phone: 209-588-5356. Business E-Mail: clarkep@yosemite.cc.ca.us.

CLARKE, VICTORIA, federal agency administrator; BA, George Washington U., 1982. Editl asst., photographer, graphics editor Washington Star newspaper, 1979—82; press asst. to Vice-Pres. George Bush, 1982; press sec. to Congressman, then Sen. John McCain; asst. U.S. trade rep. under Amb. Carla Hills Pub. Affairs and Pvt. Sector Liaison, 1989—92; press sec. for reelection campaign Pres. George Bush, 1992; v.p. for pub. affairs and strategic counsel Nat. Cable TV Assn., 1993—98; pres. Bozell Eskew Advt.; gen. mgr. Hill and Knowlton, Washington; asst. sec. def. for pub. affairs U.S. Dept. Def., Washington, 2001—03.

CLARK-JOHNSON, SUSAN, publishing executive; Pres., pub. Reno Gazette-Jour., 1985—2000; sr. group pres. Pacific Newspaper Group, Gannett, 1985—2000; chmn. & CEO Phoenix Newspapers, 2000—; publ. Arizona Republic, 2000 . Bd. dirs. Harrah's Entertainment, Inc.; bd. visitors John S. Knight Fellowships for Profl. Journalists, Stanford U. Office: Arizona Republic PO Box 1950 Phoenix AZ 85001*

CLARK-LANGAGER, SARAH ANN, curator, director, university official; b. Lynchburg, Va., May 14, 1943; m. Craig T. Langager, 1979. BA in Art History, Randolph-Macon Woman's Coll., 1965; postgrad., U. Md., 1968; MA in Art History, U. Wash., 1970; PhD in Art History, CUNY, 1988. Assoc. edn. dept., lectr. Yale U. Art Gallery, New Haven, 1965-67, Albright-Knox Art Gallery, Buffalo, 1967-68; asst. to dir. Richard White Gallery, Seattle, 1969-70; curatorial asst. to curators painting and sculpture San Francisco Mus. Modern Art, 1970; assoc. edn. dept., lectr. Seattle Art Mus., 1971-73, 74-75; asst. curator, and then assoc. curator modern art, lectr. Seatle Art Mus., 1975-79; curator 20th century art, lectr. Munson-Williams-Proctor Inst., Utica, NY, 1981-86; asst. prof. art history, dir. Univ. Art Gallery, U. North Tex., Denton, 1986-88; dir. Western Gallery, curator outdoor sculpture collection Western Wash. U., Bellingham, 1988—, mem. adj. faculty, 1988—. Lectr., cons. in edn. N.Y. Cultural Ctr., N.Y.C., 1973-74; editl. asst. October, MIT Press, N.Y.C., 1980; lectr. art history South Seattle C.C., 1975; lectr. 20th century art Cornish Inst. Fine Arts, Seattle, 1977-78; sole rep. for N.Y. State, Art Mus. Assn. Am., 1984-86; bd. mem. Wash. Art Consortium, 1988—, v.p., 1989-90, pres., 1990-93, acting pres., 1996, pres. 1990-93, 1999-2001, v.p. 1989-90, 2001-2003; cons. State of Wash. SOS (Save Outdoor Sculpture), 1994—, others. Contbr. articles to profl. jours.; curator exhbns., 1970—, including Rodney Ripps traveling exhbn., 1983, Sculpture Space: Recent Trends, 1984, Order and Enigma: American Art Between the Two Ward, 1984, Stars over Texas: Top of the Triangle, 1988, Master Works of American Art from the Munson-Williams-Proctor Institute, 1989, Public Art/Private Visions, 1989, Drawing Power, 1990, Audiophone Tour for Sculpture Collection-20 Interviews, 1991, Focus on Figure, 1992, Chairs: Embodied Objects, 1993, Northwest Native American and First Nations People's Art, 1993, New Acquisitions, 1995, Stars and Stripes: American Prints and Drawings, 1995, Photographs from America, 1996, (catalog introduction) Metalcrafts, 1998, Western Gallery; author: The Outdoor Sculpture Collection: The Development of Public Art at Western, 2000 The Italian Period in Susan Bennerstoom, 2000, Sculpture in Place: A Campus as Site, 2002, Isamu Noguchi: Beyond Red Square, 2004. Juror Arts in Pub. Places, Seattle Arts Commn., 1975, 78-79, Wash. State Arts Commn., 1976, 91, 92-93, King County Arts Commn., Seattle, 1979, Ctrl. N.Y. regional art exhbns., Syracuse, Utica, Rome, Potsdam, 1981-86, East Tex. State U., Commerce, 1987, Brookhaven C.C., Farmers Branch, Tex., 1988, Bellingham Mcpl. Arts Commn., 1989, 90; mem. adv. com. Steuben Park Fountain, Utica, 1985-86. Recipient Woman of Merit in Arts award Mohawk Valley C.C. and YWCA, Utica, 1985; Kress Found.

fellow U. Wash., 1970; Helena Rubenstein Found. scholar CUNY Grad. Ctr., 1980. Office: Western Wash U Western Gallery Fine Arts Complex Bellingham WA 98225-9068 Office Phone: 360-650-3963. E-mail: sarah.clarklangager@wwu.edu.

CLARKSON, ADRIENNE, former General of Canada, b. Hong Kong, 1939; m. John Ralston Saul. BA with honours, MA in English Lit., U. Toronto; postgrad., Sorbonne, Paris. Host, writer, prodr. CBC TV, 1965-82; first agt.-gen. for Ont. Paris, 1982-87; pres, pub. McClelland & Stewart, 1987-88; exec. prodr., host, writer Adrienne Clarkson's Summer Festival, Adrienne Clarkson Presents, 1988-98; gov. gen. Govt. of Can., 1999—. Chair, bd. trustees Can. Museum of Civilization, Hull, Que.; pres. exec. bd. IMZ, Vienna; active numerous arts and charitable orgns. Exec. prodr., host CBC TV program Something Special, others; writer, dir. several films, Can. Named Officer of the Order of Can., 1992, Chancellor and Prin. Companion of the Order of Can., 1999. Office: Rideau Hall 1 Sussex Dr Ottawa ON Canada K1A 0A1

CLARKSON, CHERYL LEE, healthcare executive; b. Chgo., Apr. 14, 1953; d. George Mendenhall and Carol Ann (Fertig) C.; m. Daniel J. Townsend; children: Drew Scott Clarkson-Townsend, Danielle Ann Clarkson-Townsend. BA in Sociology, Ariz. State U., 1975; MS in Mgmt., MIT, 1990. Sales rep. Am. Hosp. Supply, Inc., Phoenix, 1975-78, area sales mgr. Dallas, 1978-79, Edison, N.J., 1979-81, regional mgr. Boston, 1981-83, dir. sales Evanston, Ill., 1983-85; v.p. sales, mktg. Rudolph Beaver, Inc., Waltham, Mass., 1985-88; pres. Beaver Steriseal, Inc., Waltham, 1987-88, Clarkson and Assocs., 1988-90, Abiodent, Inc., Danvers, Mass., 1990-92; CEO, COO, bd. dirs. Peer Review Analysis, Inc., Boston, 1992-95; CEO, pres. SkinHealth, Inc., Wellesley, Mass., 1999—. Bd. overseers Boston U. Med. Ctr. Hosp., 1993—; bd. dirs. Visualization Tech., Inc., Andover, Mass., NMT Med. Inc., Boston. Trustee Kingsley Montessori Sch., Boston, 1996—; bd. mem. Northeastern U. Sch. of Bus., 1998—; bd. trustees Mass. Eye and Ear Infirmary, Boston, 1998—. Mem. Algonquin Club (Boston). Avocations: travel, golf, horseback riding. Office: SkinHealth Inc 251 Washington St Wellesley Hills MA 02481

CLARKSON, ELISABETH ANN HUDNUT, volunteer; b. Youngstown, Ohio, Apr. 20, 1925; d. Herbert Beecher and Edith (Schaaf) Hadnut; m. William M. E. Clarkson, Sept. 23, 1950; children: Alison H., David B., Andrew E. AB, Wilson Coll., 1947, LHD, 1985; MA, SUNY, 1973, postgrad. With J. L. Hudson Co., Detroit, 1947-50; writer Minute Parade daily Sta. WGR, Detroit, 1948-50. Author: (book) You Can Always Tell a Freshman, 1949, An Adirondack Archive: The Trail to Windover, 1993; contbr. articles to profl. jours. Trustee Wilson Coll., Chambersburg, Pa., 1970—83, chmn. bd. trustees, 1979—82; collector, curator Graphic Controls Corp. art collection, 1976—83; active N.Y. State Mus., 1985—90; past chmn. jr. group Albright Knox Art Gallery; mem. Buffalo Art Commn., 1983—, 1990—96; sustainer Jr. League, 1983—; mem. exec. bd. arts adv. coun. SUNY, Buffalo, 1995; mem. cmty. adv. panel Niagara Frontier Transp. Authority, 1991—94; trustee Clarkson Ctr. Human Svcs., 1995—2000, Irish Classical Theatre Co., 1998—; mem. Trinity Episcopal Ch., 1950—, Trinity Vestry, 1996—99, mem. cultural leadership group, 1994—96, 1998—2000; mem. racism commn. Episcopal Diocese of Western N.Y., 1989—92; mem. Companion of the Holy Cross, 1971—, companion-in-charge soc., 1985—90; bd. dirs. Buffalo Mus. Sci., 1972—87, 1990—96, Bischoff Clarkson Hudnut Corp., North Creek, NY, 1973—83, Windover Corp., 1997—, pres., 1998—2001; bd. dirs. N.Y. State Mus. Assn., Albany, 1985—90; adv. bd. dirs. North Creek R.R. Mus., 2003—. Recipient Trustee award for disting. svc., Wilson Coll., 1983, award in the arts, NCCJ, 1998. Mem.: Sloane Club (London), Buffalo Tennis and Squash Club, Garret Club (bd. dirs. 2000—03, pres. 2001—02). Home: 156 Bryant St Buffalo NY 14222-2003

CLARKSON, PATRICIA, actress; b. New Orleans, Dec. 29, 1959; d. Buzz and Jackie Clarkson. Student, La. State U.; B in Theatre Arts, Fordham U., 1982; MFA, Yale U. Actor: (films) The Untouchables, 1987, The Dead Pool, 1988, Rocket Gibraltar, 1988, Everybody's All-American, 1988, Tune in Tomorrow, 1990, Jumanji, 1995, Pharaoh's Army, 1995, High Art, 1998, Playing by Heart, 1998, Simply Irresistable, 1999, Wayward Son, 1999, The Green Mile, 1999, Joe Gould's Secret, 2000, Falling Like This, 2000, The Pledge, 2001, Wendigo, 2001, The Safety of Objects, 2001, Welcome to Collinwood, 2002, Far from Heaven, 2002, Heartbreak Hospital, 2002, The Baroness and the Pig, 2002, Pieces of April, 2003 (Acad. award nomination for best supporting actress, 2004), All the Real Girls, 2003, The Station Agent, 2003, Dogville, 2003, Miracle, 2004; (TV films) The Old Man and the Sea, 1990, Legacy of Lies, 1992, An American Story, 1992, Four Eyes and Six-Guns, 1992, Blind Man's Bluff, 1992, Caught in the Act, 1993, She Led Two Lives, 1994, London Suite, 1996, Wonderland, 2002, Carrie, 2002; (TV series) Davis Rules, 1991, Murder One, 1995—96; (TV miniseries) Queen, 1993, (TV guest appearance) Six Feed Under, 2001 (Emmy for outstanding guest actress in a drama series, 2002), Frasier, 2001. Mailing: Gersh Agy 120 W 42nd St New York NY 10036*

CLARNO, BEVERLY ANN, state legislator, farmer; b. Langlois, Oreg., Mar. 29, 1936; d. Howard William and Evelyn June (Young) Boice; m. Ray Clarno, July 15, 1983; children: Dan, Don, Randy, Cindi. B in Comm. and Mgmt., Marylhurst Coll., 1985; postgrad., Lewis & Clark Law Sch., 1985—87. Real estate broker Lake Realty and Hatfield & Skopil, Lake Oswego, Oreg., 1984-85; pres. T & H Hog Farms, Wasco, Oreg., 1973-76; securities examiner State of Oreg., Salem, 1981-83; circuit ct. clerk Deschutes County, Bend, Oreg., 1987-88; mem. Oreg. Ho. of Reps., Salem, 1988—2000, house majority leader, 1994—95, house spkr., 1995—2000; mem. Oreg. Senate from 27th dist., Salem, 2000—03, asst. majority leader, senate Rep. leader, 2002—03; regional rep. Region X U.S. Dept. Health and Human Svcs., Seattle, 2003—. Interim dir. Deschutes County Commn. on Children and Families, Bend, Oreg.; coord. Pub. Safety Coun., Bend; bd. mem. Ctrl. Oreg. Ind. Health Svcs., Bend. Recipient Cost Cutting award, Citizens for Cost Effective Govt., Portland, 1991. Mem. Boys & Girls Aid Soc., Kiwanis Club, Lions Club, High Desert Mus., Eastern Star. Republican. Methodist. Avocations: flying, trap shooting, cattle drives. Home: PO Box 7970 Bend OR 97708-7970

CLARY, ALEXIA BARBARA, purchasing agent; b. Waterbury, Conn., Sept. 17, 1954; d. John Joseph and Veza (Mandzik) Zurlis; 1 child, Jason Farrell. BBA, U. Miami, Coral Gables, Fla.; MBA, U. New Haven. Buyer Hewlett Packard, Cupeztino, Calif., 1981-83; purchase mgr. ICI, Redmond, Wash., 1983-84; commodity mgr. No. Telecom, St. Mountain, Ga., 1985-88; mfg. rep. Montgomery Mktg., Norcross, Ga., 1988-90; internat. purchasing agt. Sci. Atlanta, Norcross, Ga., 1990-91; sr. buyer Amphenol, Danbury, Conn., 1992-94; purchasing mgr. Danaher-Gulton Graphic, East Greenwich, R.I., 1994-96; materials control mgr. Amphenol Corp., Danbury, Conn., 1996-2000; materials mgmt. The Siemon Co., Watertown, Conn., 2000—; purchasing agt. Boehinger-Ingelheim Pharms., Inc., 2001—. Prof. econs.; internat. bus., logistics and mgmt. Teikyo Post U. U. Miami scholar, 1974-75. Mem. Women in Electronics (v.p. sponsors 1989-90, guest speaker 1989), NAFE, Nat. Assn. Purchasing Mgrs. Republican. Roman Catholic. Avocations: golf, tennis, swimming, reading, jogging. Home: 18 Cynthia St Waterbury CT 06708-2702 Office: Boehringher Ingelheim Purchasing Agt Ridgefield CT 06877

CLARY, INEZ HARRIS, music educator; b. Portsmouth, Va., June 3, 1918; d. Ambrose Edward and Annie Eula Harris; m. Salone Clary, Oct. 18, 1936; children: Salone T., Margaret Elizabeth Clary Gray. BS in Music Edn., Norfolk State U., 1962; MS in Music Edn., Va. State U., 1973. Organist, choir dir. Bank St. Bapt. Ch., Norfolk, 1945—84; instr. piano Norfolk State U., 1954—64; tchr. music Norfolk Pub. Schs., Va., 1962—82.

Mem.: Music Educators Nat. Conf., Order of Ea. Star (mem. Mt. Hermon chpt. #19), Alpha Kappa Alpha. Democrat. Baptist. Home: 2 Vaughn Ct Portsmouth VA 23701

CLARY, ROSALIE RHANDON CHILDRESS, timber farm executive, civic worker; b. Evanston, Ill., Aug. 3, 1928; d. Frederick Charles Hite-Smith and Rose Cecile (Liebich) Stanton; m. Virgil Vincent Clary, Oct. 17, 1959; children: Rosalie Marian Hawley, Frederick Stanton, Virgil Vincent, Katheleen Elizabeth. BS, Northwestern U., 1950, MA, 1954. Tchr. Chgo. Pub. Schs., 1951-61; faculty Loyola U., Chgo., 1963; v.p. Stanton Enterprises, Inc., Adams County, Miss., 1971-89; timber farmer, trustee Adams County, Miss., 1975—. Author Family History Record, genealogy record book, Kenilworth, Ill., 1977—. Lectr. Girl Scouts U.S., Winnetka, Ill., 1969-71, 78-86, Cub Scouts, 1972-77; badge counselor Boy Scouts Am., 1978-87; election judge Rep. Com., 1977—; vol. Winnetka Libr. Genealogy Projects Com., 1995—. Mem. Nat. Soc. DAR (Ill. rec. sec. 1979-81, nat, vice chmn. program com. 1980-83, state vice regent 1986-88, state regent 1989-91, rec. sec. gen. 1992-95, state parliamentarian 1999—); Am. Forestry Assn., Forest Farmers Assn., North Suburban Geneal. Soc. (governing bd. 1979-86, 99—, pres. 1997-99), WInnetka Hist. Soc. (governing bd. 1978-90, 95—), Internat. Platform Assn., Delta Gamma (mem. nat. cabinet 1985-89). Roman Catholic. Home: 509 Elder Ln Winnetka IL 60093-4122 Office: PO Box 401 Kenilworth IL 60043-0401

CLASTER, JILL NADELL, university administrator, history educator; d. Harry K. and Edith Lillian Nadell; m. Millard L. Midonick, May 24, 1979; 1 child from previous marriage, Elizabeth Claster (dec.). BA, NYU, 1952, MA, 1954; PhD, U. Pa., 1959. Instr. history U. Pa., 1956-58; instr. ancient and medieval history U. Ky., Lexington, 1959-61, asst. prof., 1961-64; adj. asst. prof. classics NYU, N.Y.C., 1964-65, asst. prof. history, 1965-68, assoc. prof., 1968-84, prof., 1984—, acting undergrad. chmn. history, 1972-73, dir. M.A. in liberal studies program, 1976-78; assoc. dean Washington Sq. and Univ. Coll., 1978, acting dean, 1978-79, dean, 1979-86; dir. Hagop Kevorkian Ctr. for Near Eastern Studies, NYU, 1991-96. Appointee N.Y.C. Commn. on Status of Women. Author: Athenian Democracy: Triumph or Travesty, 1967, The Medieval Experience, 1982; Contbr. articles to profl. jours. Danforth grantee, 1966-68; Fulbright grantee, 1958-59 Mem. Am. Hist. Assn., Medieval Acad. Am. Home: 161 W 15th St New York NY 10011-6720 Office: NYU Dept History 53 Washington Sq S Dept History New York NY 10012-1098 Office Phone: 212-998-8611. E-mail: jill.claster@nyu.edu.

CLATWORTHY, CATHERINE LYNN, educational trainer, graphics designer; b. Chatham, Ont., Can., June 10, 1963; d. John Ferguson Clatworthy and Patricia Anne (Maynard) Clatworthy. A.O.C.A., Ont. Coll. Art and Design, Toronto, 1985. Graphic designer Burton Kramer Assocs., Toronto, 1985—87; co-owner/mgr. The Allery, Toronto, 1997—98; tng. ctr. instr. Larson-Juhl Co., Atlanta, 1998—2003; v.p., mktg. mgr. Dakota Framing Specialties, Inc., Watertown, SD, 2000—02; propr., cons. Lily-Crest, Huron, SD, 2002. Com./facilitator Color Mktg. Group, Alexandria, Va., 2000—; mem. Visual Arts Ont., Toronto, 1985—; educator/lectr. Profl. Picture Framers assn., Jackson, Mich., 1996—; mem. Can. Conservation Inst., Ottawa, 1998—. Am. Inst. Conservation, Washington, 2002—. Author: The Art of Colour & Design for the Art and Framing Industry, 1999; contbr. mags., newspapers, and interviews in field. Mem.: Visual Arts Ont., Profl. Picture Framers Assn., Color Mktg. Group. Avocations: art, antiques, travel, photography, cooking. Office: LilyCrest PO Box 906 Huron SD 57350 E-mail: lilycrest@hur.midco.net.

CLAUSELL, DEBORAH DELORIS, artist; b. Mobile, Ala., July 16, 1951; d. Stephen Joseph and Estell Abney Clausell. BA in Sociology, U. Mobile, 1976; cert., Barbizon Modeling Sch., 1984. Movie extra Century Casting, Santa Monica, Calif., 1984—85; libr. Mobile Pub. Libr., 1996-97. Exhibited in group shows Greater Gulf State Fair, Mobile, 1990, 96 (3d, 2d and 1st prize ribbons), 97 (3rd prize ribbon), 99, Mercy Med. Gallery, Daphne, Ala., 1993, Mus. of City of Mobile, 1993, Fine Art Mus. of the South, Mobile, 1993, Spring Hill Art, Mobile, 1993, Greater Gulf State Fair Exhibit Fine Arts, 1999, Monticello-Thomas Jefferson Meml., 1993; pvt. collection The White House, Heritage Hall, 2000 and Art Auction, Energen Corp. Artpark Exbhn., 2001. Mem. Smithsonian Inst., 2001, USS Constn. Mus., 2002, U.S. Border Control, 2003. 2d lt. USAF, res. Recipient Gold Eagles and Stars Letters from U.S. President Bush, 2001. Mem. VFW, Internat. Platform Assn., Nat. D-Day Mus., U.S. Naval Inst., Libr. Congress Assn., Nat. Trust for Hist. Preservation, Civil War Trust, Mt. Vernon Ladies Assn., Navel League, Preservation Alliance. Democrat. Roman Catholic. Avocations: classic guitarist, harmonica, swimming, vocal singing, reading. Home: 5859 Reams Dr N Mobile AL 36608-3652

CLAUSING, ALICE, state legislator; b. June 7, 1944; BA, U. Wis., Oshkosh. Property mgr.; mem. from dist. 10 Wis. State Senate, Madison, 1992—, mem. child abuse and neglect prevention bd., mem. Minn.-Wis. boundary area com., mem. Miss. River Pkwy. com., mem. Wis. Assn. of Lakes, John Muir Sierra Club. Office: 1314 Wilson Ave Menomonie WI 54751-2927

CLAUSING, KIMBERLY ANNE, economics educator; b. Urbana, Ill. July 22, 1970; d. Arthur M. and Willa Louise (Spence) Clausing; m. Benjamin Richard Hufford; children: Holden Clausing-Hufford children: Ursula Clausing-Hufford. BA, U. Carleton Coll., 1991; PhD, Harvard U., 1996. Staff economist Coun. Econ. Advisers, Washington, 1994—95; assoc. prof. econs. Reed Coll., Portland, Oreg., 1996—; Fulbright rsch. scholar Ctr. for European Policy Studies, Brussels, 1999—2000. Contbr. articles to profl. jours., 2001. Recipient NSF Rsch. award, 2002—05; scholar Sr. rsch. scholar, Fulbright Assn., 1999—2000. Mem.: Am. Econ. Assn. Office: Reed Coll 3203 SE Woodstock Blvd Portland OR 97202-8199 Business E-Mail: clausing@reed.edu.

CLAUSSEN, EILEEN BARBARA, federal agency administrator; b. N.Y.C., June 9, 1945; d. Louis and Elsie (Young) Lerner; children: Hillary Anne, Geoffrey David. BA, George Washington U., 1966; MA, U. Va., 1967. Systems analyst USN, Washington, 1967-68; cons. Booz, Allen & Hamilton, Inc., Washington, 1968-69; asst. dir. ctr. for comml. devel. Boise Cascade Corp., Washington, 1969-72; various mgmt. positions Office of Solid Waste U.S. EPA, Washington, 1972-83, dir. characterization and assessment div., 1984-87, acting dep. asst. administr. air and radiation, 1988-89, dir. atmospheric and indoor air programs, 1987-93; spl. asst. to pres., sr. dir. global environ. affairs Nat. Security Coun., Washington, 1993—; asst. sec. Oceans, Intl. Enviromental & Sci. Affairs State Dept., Washington. Home: 4712 Chesapeake St NW Washington DC 20016-4466 Office: Dept of State Oceans Internat Environ Affairs 2201 C St NW Washington DC 20520-0001

CLAWSON, JUDITH LOUISE, middle school educator; b. Cleve., Nov. 24, 1938; d. Frank Anthony and Bettie (Cerny) Lisy; m. Robert Wayne Clawson, June 25, 1961; children: Deborah Marie, Gregory Scott. BS in Edn. magna cum laude, Bowling Green State U., 1960; postgrad., UCLA, 1961-65, Kent State U., 1976-80. Cert. secondary sch. math. tchr. Elem. tchr. Long Beach (Calif.) Unified Sch. Dist., 1960-61, L.A. Unified Sch. Dist., 1961-65, Stow (Ohio) City Schs., 1969-78, middle sch. math. tchr., 1978—97; ret. 1997. Cons. presenter in field. Recipient Cert. of Recognition, Martha Holden Jennings Foundn., 1987. Mem. ASCD, AAUW, NEA, LWV, Nat. Coun. Tchrs. of Math., Stow Tchrs. Assn., Ohio Edn. Assn., Ohio Coun. Tchrs. of Math., Delta Gamma (fin. advisor Kent State U. chpt. 1978-90, pres. alumnae chpt. 1987-89, 91-93, Pres.'s award 1987, housing

dir. at-large nat. coun. 1997-2001), Kappa Delta Pi. Republican. Methodist. Avocations: golf, tennis, skiing, scuba diving, reading. Home: 7336 Westview Rd Kent OH 44240 5912 Office: Kimpton Mid Sch 380 N River Rd Munroe Falls OH 44262 1331

CLAWSON, ROXANN ELOISE, college administrator, computer company executive; b. Dallas, Oct. 15, 1945; d. Robert Wellington Clawson and Jeannette Irene (Rodenhauser) Clawson Clayton. BFA, Mich. State U., 1968. Library asst. Cooper Union, N.Y.C., 1970-75, asst. librarian, 1976-82, assoc. to dean, 1985—; computer cons., 1986—. Acting appearance in The Dragon's Nest, La MaMa Theatre, 1989. Mem. NAFE, N.Y. Personal Computer Group. Democrat. Lutheran. Avocation: administration.

CLAXTON, HARRIETT MAROY JONES, retired language educator; b. Dublin, Ga., Aug. 27, 1930; d. Paul Jackson and Maroy Athalia (Chappell) Jones; m. Edward B. Claxton, Jr., May 27, 1953; children: E. B. III, Paula Jones. AA with honors, Bethel Woman's Coll., 1949; AB magna cum laude, Mercer U., 1951; MEd, Ga. Coll., 1965. Social worker Laurens County Welfare Bd., Dublin, 1951-56; HS tchr. Dublin, 1961-66; instr. Mid. Ga. Coll., Cochran, 1966-71, asst. prof. English, lit. and speech, 1971-85, assoc. prof., 1985-86, adj. prof., 1987—; rsch. tchr. Trinity Christian Sch., 1986, 92, sr. English tchr., 1986-87; ret., 1987. Instr. Ga. Coll., 1987, E. Ga. Coll. 1988—99; weekly columnist Dublin Courier Herald, 1995—. Author: (book) History of Laurens Superior Court; editor: Laurens County History, II, 1987; contbr. articles to profl. jours. Named Woman of the Yr., St. Patrick's Festival, Dublin, 1979, Most Popular Tchr., Dublin Ctr., 1985, Olympic Torch Bearer, 1996; recipient Outstanding Svc. award, Cancer Soc., Dublin, 1985, 1993, 1998, Outstanding Alumni award for cmty. svc., Ga. Coll., 1996. Mem.: UDC (chaplain 1999—), DAR (regent, vice regent, historian, state, dist., nat. awards), Dublin Assn. Fine Arts (pres. bd. 1974—76, 1982—84, 1990—98, 2001—03), Dublin Hist. Soc. (pres. 1976—78, 1995—98, bd. dirs. 1998—), Erin Garden Club (pres.), Woman's Study Club (pres.), U.S. Daus. of 1812, Daus. Am. Colonists (sec. 2004—), Daus. Colonial Wars (sec. 2004—), Delta Kappa Gamma, Chi Delta Phi (sec.), Phi Theta Kappa (treas.), Alpha Delta Pi (Middle Ga. alumni chpt. 1999—, scholarship plaque 1950), Sigma Mu. Democrat. Baptist. Home: 101 Rosewood Dr Dublin GA 31021-4129

CLAY, CAROL ANN, family nurse practitioner; b. South Hill, Va., Sept. 21, 1967; d. Arthur Lee and Helen Irene Bottoms; m. Edward Alan Clay, Oct. 1, 1996. BSN, Radford U., 1990; MSN, Old Dominion U., 1995. RN Va., cert. clin. specialist, Am. Nurse's Credentialing Ctr., family nurse practitioner, Am. Acad. Nurse Practitioners. RN charge nurse Southside Regional Med. Ctr., Petersburg, Va., 1990; RN staff nurse Culpeper (Va.) Meml. Hosp., 1990-91; RN charge nurse W.S. Hundley Annex, South Hill, Va., 1991; charge nurse, house supr. Brian's Ctr., Lawrenceville, Va., 1991-92; PN, NA instr. Southside Va. C.C., Alberta, 1991-95, 97-98; RN PRN pool Cmty. Meml. Health Ctr., South Hill, 1993-97, family nurse practitioner urgent care, 1997-98, family nurse practitioner occupl. health svcs., 1998—. Mem.: APHA, Am. Acad. Nurse Practitioners. Avocations: reading, rescuing abandoned animals. Home: 19491 Highway One Brodnax VA 23920-2247 Office: Cmty Meml Health Ctr 412 Bracey Ln South Hill VA 23970-1431

CLAY, LAREATHA H. commissioner; Mng. ptnr. Omni Bus. Enterprises, Inc.; mgr. AT&T; mgmt. cons. Primary Resource Mgmt., Inc., Dallas; commr. Tex. Hist. Commn., Austin, 2001—. Mem. City of Orlando (Fla.) Hist. Preservation Bd.; trustee Orlando Libr.; pres. Dallas Symphony Orch. League Innovators; bd. dirs. Downtown Orlando Partnership. Mem.: ASTD, Leadership Tex. Alumni Assn., Internat. Assn. Facilitators, Vis. Nurses Assn. (bd. dirs.), U. Tex. Ex-Students' Assn. (life). Office: PO Box 12276 Austin TX 78711-2276

CLAYPOOL, NANCY, social worker; b. Monterey, Calif., Aug. 6, 1957; d. Harold Herbert and Nancy Jeanne (Klohe) C.; 1 child, James Paul. BA in Social Welfare cum laude, San Francisco State U., 1980; M Social Work, U. Calif., Berkeley, 1985. Lic. ind. social worker. Program developer Women's Found., San Francisco, 1984-85; foster care coord., house supr. Charila Svcs. for Girls, San Francisco, 1985-87; therapist Sierra Clinic, San Francisco, 1987-88; clin. social worker Youth Homes, Inc., Walnut Creek, Calif., 1988-90; homebased early childhood devel. tchr. Thurgood Marshall Family Resource Ctr., Oakland, Calif., 1990-92; psychiat. social worker Eden Med. Ctr., Castro Valley, Calif., 1992-94; chief clinician, primary therapist Transitions Geropsychiatry Alameda (Calif.) Hosp., 1994-96; program dir. transitions geopsychiatry Alameda (Calif) Hosp., 1996-97; cons. to orgns. serving sr. citizens-clin. social workers Washington Twp. Hosp., Fremont, Calif., 1997-98; spl. edn. social worker and therapist Deming (N.Mex.) Pub. Schs., 1998—. Contbr. articles to profl. publs. Mem. Alameda County Mental Health Bd., 1992-95, chair, 1993-94, vice chair, 1994-95. Named Regional Clinician of Yr., Horizon Mental Health Svcs., 1994; Health-Social Networking grantee, 1984. Mem. Nat. Assn. Social Workers, Internat. Platform Assn. (appointee 1995). Home: 427 44th Ave San Francisco CA 94121-1410

CLAYTON, EVA M. retired congresswoman, former commissioner; b. Savannah, Ga., Sept. 16, 1934; m. Theaoseus T. Clayton; children: Theaoseus Jr., Martin, Reuben, Joanne. BS, Johnson C. Smith U., 1955; MS, NC Central U., 1965. Founder, pres. Tech. Resources Internat., NC, 1981—92; mem. U.S. Congress from 1st N.C. dist., Washington, 1993—2002; mem. agriculture com.; mem. com. on budget. Mem. Warren County NC Bd. Commrs., 1982—92, chair, 1982—90. Named Legislator of Yr., Am. Planning Assn., 2002. Democrat. Presbyterian.*

CLAYTON, PAMELA SANDERS, special education educator; b. Sulphur Springs, Tex., Feb. 8, 1952; d. Carl Louis Sanders, Jr. and Beatrice Coletha Sanders; children: Chad, Cicely. BS, E. Tex. State U., 1974, MEd, 1991. Kindergarten cert., mental retardation cert. Tchr. Saltillo ISD, 1976—77, resource specialist, tchr., 1977—80, Lamar Elem. Sch., Sulphur Springs, 1980—98, Sulphur Springs H.S., 1998—. Dir. student coun., uil prose & poetry dir., taas tutorial coach Sulphur Springs H.S., 1999—2002. Actor: (plays) A Christmas Carol, 1997 (Best Supporting Actress, 1998); singer: (concert) N.E. Tex. Choral Soc., 1998. Mem. allocation com. Hopkins County United Way, Sulphur Springs, 2000—01; bd. dirs. Lakes Regional MHMR, Terrell, Tex., 1997—, Sulphur Springs Pub. Libr., 1994—96. Mem.: Tex. Classroom Tchrs., Delta Kappa Gamma. Methodist. Avocations: poetry, rollercoaster riding, reading, piano. Home: 404 Lamar St Sulphur Springs TX 75482 Office: Sulphur Springs ISD 1200 Connally St Sulphur Springs TX 75482 Office Fax: (903)439-6116. Personal E-mail: pclayton@ssisd.net.

CLAYTON, VERNA LEWIS, retired state legislator; b. Hamden, Ohio, Feb. 28, 1937; d. Matthews L. and Yail (Miller) Lewis; m. Frank R. Clayton, Feb. 4, 1956; children: Valerie S., Barry L. Office mgr. Village of Buffalo Grove, Ill., 1972-78, village clk., 1971-79, village pres., 1979-91; mem. Ill. Ho. of Reps., Springfield, 1993-99. Bd. dirs. Savannah Lakes Property Owners Assn., 2000, pres., 2004. Mem. Lake County Solid Waste Planning Agy., chmn. tech. com., chmn. agy., Nat. League of Cities, chmn. transp. and comms. steering com. Recipient Disting. Svc. award Amvets, 1981; named Libr. Legislator of the Yr. 1997. Mem. N.W. Mcpl. Conf. (pres. 1983-84), Chgo. Area Transp. Study Coun. Mayors (vice chmn. 1981-83, chmn. 1985-91), Mcpl. Clks. Ill. (treas. 1978-79), Mcpl. Clks.

Lake County (pres. 1977-78), Ill. Mcpl. League (bd. dirs., v.p. 1985-90, pres. 1989-90), Buffalo Grove Rotary Club (hon. mem.), Buffalo Grove C. of C. (bd. dirs.). Republican. Methodist. Home: 11 Overlook Pt Mc Cormick SC 29835-2850 E-mail: frclayton9@wctel.net.

CLAYTON, XERNONA, media executive; b. Muskogee, Okla., Aug. 30, 1930; m. Paul L. Brady. BS with honors, Tenn. State U., 1952; postgrad., U. Chgo. Cert. tchr. Ill., Calif. Tchr. pub. schs., Chgo., Los Angeles; with So. Christian Leadership Conf., Atlanta; host Sta. WAGA-TV, Atlanta, 1967-79; with Sta. WTBS-TV, Atlanta, 1979—, host, producer, 1981-82, coordinator of minority affairs, 1982—, now corp. v.p. of urban affairs. Guest lectr. Harvard U.; appointed Motion Picture and TV Commn., Ga., commr. Bd. Review, Appellate Bd. of unemployment compensation. Author: (with Ed Clayton) The Peaceful Warrior. Coordinated Doctors' Com. for Implementation, Atlanta; bd. trustees Martin Luther King, Jr. Ctr.; bd. dirs Nat. Assn. Advancement Colored People, Multiple Sclerosis Soc., Sci. and Tech. Mus. Atlanta, Nat Assn Sickle Cell Disease; mem. Nat. Issues Forum of Jimmy Carter Presidential Library. U. Chgo. scholar; recipient numerous awards including Bronze Woman of the Year, 1969, President's award Nat. Conf. Mayors, 1983, Communications Woman of Achievement award Am. Women in Radio and TV, 1984-85, The Kizzy award, 1979, Humanitarian award, Hillside Internat. Truth Ctr., 1986, Acad. Women Achievers, YWCA, 1986, American Spirit award USAF Recruiting Service, 1987; Xernona Clayton Scholarship named in her honor by the Am. Intercultural Student Exchange, 1987-90; featured on cover of The New York Time Mag.; cited for her accomplishments by Ebony, Town & Country, Georgia Mags. Mem. Nat. Assn. Media Women (pres.), Alpha Kappa Alpha. Baptist. Office: Turner Broadcasting One CNN Center Atlanta GA 30303

CLEARY, BEVERLY ATLEE (MRS. CLARENCE T. CLEARY), writer; b. McMinnville, Oreg., Apr. 12, 1916; d. Chester Lloyd and Mable (Atlee) Bunn; m. Clarence T. Cleary, Oct. 6, 1940; children: Marianne Elisabeth, Malcolm James. BA, U. Calif., 1938; BA in Librarianship, U. Wash., 1939; LHD (hon.), Cornell Coll., 1993. Children's librarian Pub. Libr., Yakima, Wash., 1939-40; post librarian U.S. Army Regional Hosp., Oakland, Calif., 1942-45. Author: Henry Huggins, 1950, Ellen Tebbits, 1951, Henry and Beezus, 1952, Otis Spofford, 1953, Henry and Ribsy, 1954, Beezus and Ramona, 1955, Fifteen, 1956, Henry and the Paper Route, 1957, The Luckiest Girl, 1958, Jean and Johnny, 1959, The Real Hole, 1960, Hullabaloo ABC, 1960, 98, Two Dog Biscuits, 1961, Emily's Runaway Imagination, 1961, Henry and the Clubhouse, 1962, Sister of the Bride, 1963, Ribsy, 1964, The Mouse and the Motorcycle, 1965, Mitch and Amy, 1967, Ramona the Pest, 1968, Runaway Ralph, 1970, Socks, 1973, (play) The Sausage at the End of the Nose, 1974, Ramona the Brave, 1975, Ramona and Her Father, 1977 (Newbery Honor Book award ALA 1978), Ramona and Her Mother, 1979, Ramona Quimby, Age 8, 1981 (Newbery Honor Book award ALA 1982), Ralph S. Mouse, 1982, Dear Mr. Henshaw, 1983 (ALA Notable Book citation 1984, John Newbery medal 1984), Ramona Forever, 1984, Lucky Chuck, 1984, The Ramona Quimby Diary, 1984, Beezus and Ramona Diary, 1986, Janet's Thingamajigs, 1987, The Growing Up Feet, 1987, A Girl from Yamhill: A Memoir, 1988, Muggie Maggie, 1990, Strider, 1991, Petey's Bedtime Story, 1993, My Own Two Feet: A Memoir, 1995, Ramona's World, 1999. Recipient Disting. Alumna award U. Wash., 1975, Laura Ingalls Wilder award ALA, 1975, Regina medal Cath. Libr. Assn., 1980, De Grummond award U. Miss., 1982, U. So. Miss. medallion, 1982, Hans Christian Andersen medal nominee, 1984, Nat. Medal of the Arts, 2003. Mem. Authors Guild of Authors League Am. Office: c/o Harper Collins Children's Books 1350 Sixth Ave New York NY 10019-4702

CLEARY, MANON CATHERINE, artist, educator; b. St. Louis, Nov. 14, 1942; d. Frank and Crystal (Maret) C. BFA, Washington U., St. Louis, 1964; MFA, Tyler Sch. Art, Temple U., 1968. Instr. fine arts SUNY, Oswego, 1968-70; from instr. to assoc. prof. D.C. Tchrs. Coll., Washington, 1970-78; from assoc. prof. to prof. art U. D.C., Washington, 1978—2000, acting chmn. dept., 1985-86, 90-91, assoc. dean Coll. Liberal and Fine Arts, 1992-94, acting coord. art program, 1994—2000. One woman shows include Mus. Modern Art Gulbenkian Found., Lisbon, Portugal, 1985, Iolas/Jackson Gallery, N.Y.C., 1982, Osuna Gallery, Washington, 1974, 77, 80, 84, 89, Univ. D.C., 1987, Tyler Gallery SUNY at Oswego, 1987, J. Rosenthal Fine Arts, Washington, 1991, Addison/Ripley Gallery, Washington, 1994, 99, Md. Arts Pl., 1997, Kramer Book Afterwords, 1998, Pass Gallery, Washington, 2000, others; group exhibits include Art Inst. Chgo., Twentieth Century Am. Drawings: The Figure in Context, Traveled Nat. Acad. Design, 1984-85, Butler Inst. Am. Art, Youngstown, Ohio, 1987, Huntsville (Ala.) Mus., 1987, Boca Raton (Fla.) Mus. Art, 1987, Corcoran Gallery Art, Washington, 1987, 96, Dimock Gallery, Washington, 1987, Tretyakov Gallery, Moscow, 1990, Nohra Haime Gallery, 1994, Holter Mus., Helena, Mont., 1996, Gallery Stendahl, N.Y.C., 1996, Alt. Mus., N.Y.C., 1996, Kasteyev Mus., Almaty, Kazakstan, 1996, Alouan Gallery, Almaty, 1997, RAP, Rockville, Md., 2000-01, Nat. Mus. Women in the Arts, Washington, others. Artist-in-residence Herning Hojskole, Denmark, 1980, Ucross Found., Wyo., 1984, Bridge Assn., Creative Lab. Project, Almaty, 1996, 97. Recipient Faculty Rsch. award, U. D.C., 1984, 89, Mayor's 14th ann. award for excellence in an artistic discipline, 1998; individual artist grantee D.C. Commn. on the Arts, 2000-01. Mem. Coll. Art Assn., Pi Beta Phi. Democrat. Presbyterian. Home: 1736 Columbia Rd NW Washington DC 20009-2815 E-mail: manonart@aol.com.

CLEARY, PAMELA ANN, symphony executive; b. Omaha, Jan. 24, 1947; d. Carson Poe Jr. and Helen D. (Nelson) Dole; m. David O. Gilson, June 18, 1965 (div. 1977); children: Kevin D., Kyle, Kreg; m. John P. Cleary, Sept. 13, 1980; children: Shawn, Robert, Kevin M., Daniel, Charles, Colleen. BSBA, U. Nebr., 1977. Acct., bus. mgr. Northwestern Steel & Supply, Omaha, 1977-84; sr. dir. fin. and adminstrn. Omaha Symphony Assn., Omaha, 1984-93, exec. dir., 1992—. Mem. DAR, Oak Hills Country Club. Republican. Roman Catholic. Home: 5706 Oak Hills Dr Omaha NE 68137-3316 Office: Omaha Symphony Assn 1605 Howard St Omaha NE 68102-2705

CLEAVE, MARY L. environmental engineer, former astronaut; b. Southampton, N.Y., Feb. 5, 1947; BS in Biol. Scis., Colo. State U., 1969; MS in Microbiol. Ecology, Utah State U., 1975, PhD in Civil and Environ. Engring., 1979. Mem. rsch. staff Utah State U., 1971-80; astronaut NASA, Lyndon B. Johnson Space Ctr., Houston, 1980-90, mission specialist STS 61-B, 1985, mission specialist STS-30, 1989; now dep. project mgr. NASA Ocean Color Satellite Program, Greenbelt, Md. Mem. Tex. Soc. Profl. Engrs., Water Pollution Control Fedn., Sigma Xi, Tau Beta Pi. Office: NASA Headquarters 300 E St SW Washington DC 20024-3202*

CLEAVER, LYDIA RUTH, musician, educator; b. Detroit, Nov. 16, 1963; d. Robert Gregory and Blanche Edmonia Alexander; m. Gerald Whitney Cleaver, Aug. 19, 1983 (div. Mar. 15, 2000). MusB in Music Edn., U. Mich., 1991, MusM in Performance, 1992, cert. specialist in music, 1998. Harpist Birmingham (Mich.)/Bloomfield Symphony, 1994, Warren (Mich.) Symphony Orch., 1995—2002, Dearborn (Mich.) Symphony Orch., 1997—. Instr. Spring Arbor (Mich.) U., 2000—; tchr. Detroit Pub. Schs., 2000—; vis. prof. U. Mich., Ann Arbor, 2003. Musician: (albums) Fidan and Khuraman Kasimova, 1997, Requiem - Renaissance Voices, 1999, Joy To You, 2000. Mem. family selection com. Habitat for Humanity, Detroit, 2002—03. Recipient Martin Luther King, Jr. Spirit Award, U. Mich., 1998. Mem.: Am. Harp Soc., Fedn. Musicians Local 5, Detroit Fedn. Tchrs. (alt. bldg. rep. 2002—03). Avocations: travel, bicycling. Personal E-mail: lrc64@hotmail.com.

CLEGG, KAREN KOHLER, lawyer; b. Junction City, Kans., Jan. 7, 1949; d. John Emil and Delores Maxine (Letkeman) Kohler; m. Stephen J. Clegg Jr., Mar. 28, 1970. BS, Emporia State U., 1970; JD, U. Kans., 1975; MBA, Rockhurst Coll., 1989. Bar: Kans. 1975, U.S. Dist. Ct. Kans. 1975, Mo. 1977, U.S. Dist. Ct. (we. dist.) Mo. 1977. Asst. atty. gen. State of Kans., Topeka, 1975-77; atty. The Bendix Corp., Kansas City, Mo., 1977-81, sr. atty., 1981-84; counsel Allied Corp. (now Allied Signal, Inc.), Kansas City, 1984-90, v.p. adminstrn., 1990—; pres. Honeywell Fed. Mfg. and Technologies Honeywell Internat., 1999—. Mem. council human resources mgmt. adv. bd. Commerce Clearing House, Chgo., 1985-88. Sec. Assn. Greater Devel. Coll. Blvd., Shawnee Mission, Kans., 1986-87; bd. dirs. adv. council Avila Coll. Bus., Kansas City, 1984—, Dimension's Unltd., Kansas City, 1985-86. Mem. ABA, Mo. Bar Assn., Am. Soc. Personnel Adminstrn. (v.p., bd. dirs. EEO 1985, profl. services 1986-87), Greater Kansas City C. of C. (centurian leadership program). Avocations: music, theatre, art, reading, travel. Office: Honeywell 2000 E 95th St Kansas City MO 64131-3030 Home: 6909 Burnt Sienna Cir Naples FL 34109-7828

CLEHANE, DIANE CATHERINE, journalist, writer, communications executive; b. N.Y.C., Sept. 2, 1960; d. Charles and Rita (Morley) C. BA in Journalism and Sociology, U. Mass., 1982. Asst. buyer Macy's N.Y., N.Y.C., 1982-84; dir. pub. rels. Anne Klein II, N.Y.C., 1984-85; dir. publicity, pub. rels. Liz Claiborne, Inc., N.Y.C., 1985-87; dir. pub. rels. Danskin, N.Y.C., 1987-88; sr. promotion writer Vogue, N.Y.C., 1988; mktg. promotion mgr. Elle Mag., N.Y.C., 1989; pres., creative dir. Madeline Comms., N.Y.C., 1989—; contbg. editor TV Guide, 1996—; corr. People mag., 1999—. Author: Diana--The Secrets of Her Style, 1998; author: I Love You, Mom!, 2003; contbg. author: TV Guide Fifty Years of Television, 2002. Fundraiser, mktg. cons. Adopt-A-Dog, Greenwich, Conn., 1994-96; fundraiser, pub. rels. Montefiore Hosp., N.Y.C., 1994-96. Mem. Fashion Group Internat. (editor newsletter 1990-91, events com. 1994—), Women in Comm. (co-chmn. program com.) Cosmetic Exec. Women, Alpha Chi Omega. Office: Madeline Comms 700 Scarsdale Ave Apt 3H Scarsdale NY 10583-5129

CLELAND, GLADYS LEE, university administrator, adult education educator; b. Schenectady, Feb. 27, 1959; d. Anthony John and Anna Mae (Feight) Campana; m. Michael Joseph Cleland, Aug. 4, 1984. BA in Communications and Edn. cum laude, SUNY, Plattsburgh, 1981; MA summa cum laude, U. Fla., 1986; MS summa cum laude, Syracuse U., 1994. Asst. instr. communications SUNY, Plattsburgh, 1982-83, admissions/media rels. advisor, 1987-88; asst. instr. communications U. Fla., Gainesville, 1985-86; instr. English and communications Clinton Community Coll., Plattsburgh, 1986-87; news cons., acad. liaison Sta. WCFE-TV, Plattsburgh, 1987-88; pub. info. dir. Syracuse (N.Y.) U., 1989-93, pub. rels. coord., 1993-94; spl. projects mgr. SUNY Health Sci. Ctr., Syracuse, 1994-96. News. cons. Sta. WCFE-TV 57, Plattsburgh, 1987-88; producer, rschr. CVPH Med. Ctr., Plattsburgh, 1982-87; freelance talent Sta. WIXT-TV 9, Syracuse, 1988—; press steward Winter Olympic Games, lake Placid, N.Y., 1980; radio announcer, news reporter, sales rep. Sta. WIRY-AM, Plattsburgh, 1980-83; freelance producer, news reporter Sta. WPBT-TV, Miami, Fla., 1983-84. Author: Satellite News Gathering, 1986. Recipient broadcast awards N.Y. State Broadcast Assn., Plattsburgh, 1982-84, Outstanding Talent award Internat. TV Assn., Gainesville, 1986. Mem. Women in Comms. (Woman of Yr. award, 1994), Broadcast Educators Assn., Coll. Media Advisors, RTNDA, Pub. Rels. Soc. Am., Syracuse Press Club, Omicron Delta Kappa, Phi Kappa Chi. Roman Catholic. Avocations: gardening, boating, reading. Home: 4239 Mill Run Rd Liverpool NY 13090-1813 Office: SUNY 103 Charleton Hall Morrisville NY 13408

CLELAND, NORA TEMPLE, writer, editor; b. Longton, Kans., Feb. 1, 1929; d. Oakes Richard and Lela Alice (Millikan) Temple; m. William Miles Cleland, Mar. 10, 1951; children: Sara A., Linda A., Anita L., William Ross. BS in Journalism, U. Kans., 1949. News and feature writer Lawrence Jour.-World, Kans., 1949-53, agrl. news writer, 1954; pub. rels. writer U. Kans. Sch. Arch. & Engring., Lawrence, 1953-58; home town news editor Divsn. of U. Rels./U. Kans., Lawrence, 1974-80; Oread newsletter editor U. Kans., Lawrence, 1984-93, acting news divsn. coord., 1992-93; freelance news and feature writer Baldwin, Kans., 1993-96; agrl. news corr. Farm Talk, Parsons, Kans., 1996—; columnist Grass and Grain, Manhattan, Kans., 1996, 98. Youth Projects Dir. Nat. Fedn. of Press Women, Arlington, Va., 1992-2001; pres. Kans. Press Women, Inc., Topeka, 1988-90. Writer, editor: Vinland Telephone Company History, Kan. Com., 1982 (Nat. Fedn. Press Women Comms. Contest award 1983); editor: Hometowning Pub. Rels. Sys., 1977 (Dist. award Coun. Support of Edn.), others. Mem. AAUW, Kans. Press Women. Republican. Avocation: leading 4-h activities.

CLEM, HARRIET FRANCES, library director; b. Akron, Ohio, Nov. 8, 1940; d. Paul Milton and Mary Eva (Koppes) Miller; m. Ross Lynn Clem, June 23, 1979. BA cum laude, Kent State U., 1963, MLS, 1965. Teletype operator Babcock & Wilcox Co., Barberton, Ohio, 1958-59; bookmobile libr. Wadsworth (Ohio) Pub. Libr., 1963-64; head ext. dept. Rodman Pub. Libr., Alliance, Ohio, 1965-68, libr. dir., 1969—. Instr. children's lit. Mt. Union Coll., Alliance, 1970-71; instr. libr. sci. Kent (Ohio) State U., 1975-7 Trustee YMCA, Alliance, 1974-84; pres. ARC, Alliance, 1975-77; bd. dirs. Leadership Stark County, Canton, Ohio, 1997-2003. Named Boss of Yr., Assn. Secs., Alliance, 1982; honoree Stark County Bicentennial Wall of Fame, 2003. Mem. Ohio Libr. Coun. (founder acctg. divsn.), Alliance C. of C. (pres. 1983, 93, Athena award 1990), Greater Alliance Devel. Corp. (pres. 2000), Beatrix Potter Soc., C.S. Lewis Soc., Alliance Women's Club (pres. 1977), Alliance Country Club, Coterie, Sorosis, Beta Phi Mu (nat. coun. 1978-80). Episcopalian. Avocations: travel, cooking. Home: 13484 Louisville St NE Paris OH 44669-9713 Office: Rodman Pub Libr 215 E Broadway St Alliance OH 44601-2650

CLEMENS, DEB FISCHER, state legislator, nursing administrator; DON; mem. S.D. Ho. of Reps., Pierre, 1995—, mem. health and human svcs., local govt. coms., 1995—. Democrat. Office: Queen of Peace Hosp 525 N Foster St Mitchell SD 57301-2999

CLEMENT, CATHLEEN MCMULLIN, fundraiser; b. Inglewood, Calif., Dec. 14, 1946; d. Everett Kieth and Patricia (Gibson) McM.; children: Patrick Ian, Rachel Marie; m. Paul Wayne Clement, July 28, 1990; stepchildren: Paul Wayne Jr., Blake Jordan, Erika Dawn. BA, Pepperdine Coll., 1968; MA, Fuller Theol. Sem., 1977. Cmty. resources dir. Fuller Psychol. Ctr., Pasadena, Calif., 1984-87; assoc. dir. devel. Fuller Theol. Sem., Pasadena, Calif., 1987-88; dir. devel. Five Acres, Altadena, Calif., 1988—. Consulting mentor L.A. Unified Sch. Dist., 1993—. Pres. Pepperdine U. Alumni Bd., Malibu, Calif., 1981-82; vestry mem. All Saints Episcopal Ch., Pasadena, 1988-92, 2003—. Recipient Svc. award Pepperdine U., 1983. Mem. San Gabriel Valley Estate Planning Coun., Planned Giving Roundtable. Avocations: travel, skiing. Home: 750 Galaxy Heights Dr La Canada CA 91011-1831

CLEMENT, EDITH BROWN, federal judge; b. Birmingham, Ala., Apr. 29, 1948; d. Erskine John and Edith (Burrus) Brown; m. Rutledge Carter Clement Jr., Sept. 3, 1972; children: Rutledge Carter III, Catherine Lanier. BA, U. Ala., 1969; JD, Tulane U., 1972. Bar: La. 1973. Law clk. to Hon. Herbert W. Christenberry U.S. Dist. Ct., New Orleans, 1973-75; ptnr. Jones, Walker, Waechter, Poitevent, Carrere & Denegre, New Orleans, 1975-91; judge U.S. Dist. Ct. (ea. dist.) La., New Orleans, 1991—2001, U.S. Ct Appeals (5th cir.), New Orleans, 2001—. Fellow La. Bar Found. (life); mem. Am. Law Inst., La. Bar Assn., Federalist Soc. Advisory Bd. Louisiana Chpt., Maritime Law Assn. U.S., Fed. Bar Assn., Am Inn Ct., Com. Admin. Office of the Judicial Conference of the U.S., 5th Cir. Judicial Coun. Office: US Ct Appeals 5th Cir 600 Camp Street Rm 200 New Orleans LA 70130-3313*

CLEMENT, HOPE ELIZABETH ANNA, retired librarian; b. North Sydney, N.S., Can., Dec. 29, 1930; d. Harry Wells and Lana (Perkins) C. BA, U. of King's Coll., 1951; MA, Dalhousie U., 1953; BLS, U. Toronto, 1955; D of Civil Law (hon.), U. King's Coll., 1992. With Nat. Library of Can., Ottawa, Ont., 1955-92, chief nat. bibliography div., 1966-70, asst. dir. research and planning br., 1970-73, dir. research and planning br., 1973-77, assoc. nat. librarian, 1977-92. Editor: Canadiana, 1966-69. (Outstanding Svc. to Librarianship award 1992), Internat. Fedn. Libr. Assns. (medal 1991).

CLEMENTE, LILIA CALDERON, capital company executive; b. Manila, Philippines, Feb. 21, 1941; d. Jose Damocles and Belen-Dimatulac (Fabros) Calderon; m. Leopoldo Manalac Clemente, June 24, '964. BSBA, U. Philippines, 1960; MA, ABD in Econs., U. Chgo., 1962. Investment analyst, portfolio mgr. CNA Fin. Corp., Chgo., 1967-69; dir. of investments, rsch. and asst. treas. The Ford Found., N.Y.C., 1969-76; 1st v.p., chief investment officer, internat. investments Paine Webber Inc. Mitchell Hutchins Asset Mgmt., N.Y.C., 1983-86; chmn., chief exec. officer Clemente Capital Inc., N.Y.C., 1976—. Asian cons. Am. Can, Greenwich, Conn., 1982-83; cons. on Asian portfolio Eberstadt Internat. Fund; cons. on Japanese and Asian portfolio Capital Rsch., L.A., Geneva, 1976-78; cons. Montreal Investment Mgmt., Can., 1978, Vilas Fischer Assocs., 1978-82, Yasuda Trust Internat. Dept., 1978; mem. U.S. Export Devel. Mission to Japan, 1978; del. Fin. Analysts Fed., 1976-78; chmn. Philipine Am. Found. Bd. trustees Manhattan Coll., 1987—. Named Most Outstanding Overseas Filipino Presdl. award Rep. of the Philippines, 1990; recipient Excellence 2000 award U.S. and Asian C. of C., 1989, Outstanding Alumni, U. Philippines. Roman Catholic. Avocations: writing, poetry, gardening, painting. Office: Clemente Capital Inc 575 Madison Ave New York NY 10022

CLEMENT-FOUTS, SHIRLEY GEORGE, educational services executive; b. El Paso, Tex., Feb. 14, 1926; d. Claude Samuel and Elizabeth Estelle (Mattice) Gillett; m. Paul Vincent Clement, Mar. 23, 1946 (dec. 1997); children: Brian Frank, Robert Vincent, Carol Elizabeth, Rosemary Adele; m. Robert Warren Fouts, Sept. 4, 1998. BA in English, Tex. Western Coll., 1963; postgrad., U. Tex., El Paso, N.Mex. State U., 1988; MEd in Reading, Sul Ross State U., 1987; postgrad. in art history, Paris Am. Acad., 1994-98. Tchr. lang. arts Ysleta Ind. Schs., El Paso, 1960-62; tchr. adult edn., 1962-64; tchr. reading/lang. arts, 1964-77; owner, dir. Crestline Learning Sys., Inc., El Paso, 1980-90; dir. Crestline Internat. Schs., 1987-90; instr. Park Coll., Ft. Bliss, Tex., 1992—, U. Phoenix, 1995—. Dir. tutorial for sports teams U. Tex., El Paso, 1984; bd. dirs. S.W. Inst., pres., 1993; dir. continuing edn. program El Paso Cmty. Coll., 1985; mem. curriculum com. Ysleta Ind. Schs., El Paso, 1974; mem. Right to Read Task Force, 1975-77; mem. Bi-Centennial Steering Com., El Paso, 1975-76; presenter Poetry in the Arts, Austin, Tex., 1992, 97; judge student poetry contest, Austin, Tex., 1995; Poetry Soc. Tex. program presenter Mesilla Valley Writers, 1993-96, El Paso Writers, 1994-2001, Poetry Soc. Tex., 1993-2001; instr. writing Paris Am. Acad., summer 1994, 98; cons. Ysleta Schs., 1995; poetry critic, judge Writers Workshop, Albuquerque, 1999, 2002; lectr. on reading in 4 states; poetry judge E.P. Writers League contest. Author: Writers Organizer, 2000; (poems) Echoes Through the Pass, 1998; co-author: Beginning the Search for God-The Edgar Cayce Approach, 1979; contbr. articles to profl. jours.; contbr. poems to Behold Tex., 1983, Writers Mag., 2004; contbr. poems Arts Mag., 2004. Treas. El Paso Rep. Women, 1956; facilitator Goals for El Paso, Rep. Women, 1956; mem. hospitality com. Sun Carnival, 1974, Cotton Festival, 1975. Recipient 1st prize Sky Blue Waters Poetry Contest, 2000, 1st prize EP Writer's League Hist. Memories Contest, 2001. Mem. Internat. Reading Assn. (pres. El Paso County coun. 1973-74, presentor 1978-87), Assn. Children with Learning Disabilities (tchr. 1980), Poetry Soc. Tex. (Panhandle Penwomen's first place award 1981, David Atamian Meml. award 1991, judge 1995), Nat. Fedn. State Poetry Soc. (1st place award ann. contest 1988, 1st prize El Paso Hist. Essay contest 1991, 2nd prize 1995, honorable mention Writer's Digest Contest 1996), El Paso Writers' League (pres. 2003), Chi Omega Alumnae (pres. 1952-53). Home: 537 Spring Crest Dr El Paso TX 79912-4155 E-mail: clement@elp.rr.com.

CLEMENTS, JANICE, science educator; PhD, U. Md. Prof. Johns Hopkins U. Sch. Medicine, Balt. Contbr. articles to profl. jours. Achievements include research on molecular basis of viral diseases - SIV model for AIDS. Office: Johns Hopkins U Sch Medicine Traylor G-60 720 Rutland Ave Baltimore MD 21205-2109 Fax: 510-955-9823. E-mail: jclement@bs.jhmi.edu.

CLEMENTS, LINDA L. materials engineer, educator, journalist; b. Phoenix, Oct. 6, 1945; d. Howard Abner Clements and Louella Tooley; m. John Laurence Crowley; children: Timothy Crowley, Colin Crowley. BS, Stanford U., 1967; MS Engring., U. Pa., 1971; PhD, Stanford U., 1974. Engr. Lawrence Livermore Lab., Livermore, 1974—78, program mgr., 1977—78; project dir. Advanced Rsch. and Applications Corp., Sunnyvale, Calif., 1978—81, NASA-Ames Rsch. Ctr., Moffett Field, Calif.; assoc. prof., materials engring. San Jose State U., 1981—85, full prof., materials engring., 1985—91; dir. of materials R& D TFI Inc., Pacifica, Calif., 1989—98; adj. prof. U. of Nev., Reno, 1995—99; nat. adj. faculty ASM Internat., Materials Park, Ohio, 1984—2002; instr. Soc. for the Advancement of Material and Process Engring., Covina, Calif., 1995—; adj. faculty Western Nev. C.C., Carson City, Nev., 1999—2002; dir. of materials r & d 2Phase Technologies, Inc., Dayton, Nev., 1998—; pres. C & C Technologies, Dayton, 1991—. Faculty advisor student chpt. Soc. of Women Engineers San Jose State U., 1980—86, San Jose State U. SAMPE, 1985—91; reviewer ASM Internat., Materials Park, Ohio, 1983—99, Technomic Pub. Co., Lancaster, PA., 1999—2000; peer rev. bd. Jour. of Advanced Materials, Covina, 1999—; steering com. Composites Fabrication mag., Arlington, 2000—; reviewer NSF Grad. Fellowships, 1995, DOE Integrated Manufacturing Fellowships, 1997, Ford Found. Fellowships for Minorities, 2004. Mem. editl. bd.: SAMPE Jour., 2000—, correspondant: Advanced Composites Bull., 1999—2000, contbg. editor: High-Performance Composites Mag., 1998—2000, Composites Fabrication Mag., 2000—. Mem. engring. adv. bd. Western Nev. C.C., Carson City, 1998—, chair engring. adv. bd., 2001—03. Recipient Clements award, Western Nev. Cmty. Coll, 2004; Rsch. innovation grants (3), Northrop Corp., 1986—90, NSF Grad. fellow, 1995, DOE Integrated Mfg. fellow, 1997, Ford Found. fellow minorities, 2004, Clements award scholar, Western Nev. Cmty. Coll., 2004—. Mem.: ASTM (d-30 com. sec. 1976—78), Soc. of Plastics Engineers, Am. Chem. Soc., ASM Internat., Soc. for the Advancement of Materials and Process Engring. (internat. com. chmn. 1986—2003, chpt. dir. 1996—, internat. sec. 2003—, bd. dirs.), Dayton (Nev.) Hist. Soc. (bd. dirs. 2002—), Friends of the Dayton Valley Libr. (pres. 1995—2000, sec. 2000—02, bd. dirs. Do-Mor Dayton 2002—, Vol. of the Yr. 2002), Dayton (Nev.) Mus. Hist. Soc. (bd. dirs. 2003—), Phi Kappa Phi, Tau Beta Pi, Phi Beta Kappa. Avocation: genealogy, historic preservation, science fiction, camping, sewing. Office: C & C Technologies PO Box 1089 Dayton NV 89403 Business E-Mail: llclements@composites-training.com.

CLEMENTS, LYNNE FLEMING, marriage and family therapist, application developer; b. Bklyn., Aug. 8, 1945; d. Daniel Gillies and Dorothy Frances (Zitzmann) Fleming; m. Louis Myrick Clements, Feb. 19, 1972; children: Ryan Louis, Glenn Fleming. BA in Sociology, Bradley Univ., 1967; MSW, Fordham Univ., 1973; post grad. studies, Columbia Univ., 1970-71; cert. in family therapy, Inst. for Mental Health Edn., 1990. LCSW NJ, cert. social work mgr. Computer programmer Employer's Comml. Union Group Ins. Co., Boston, 1967-69, Harvard Bus. Sch., Cambridge, Mass., 1969-70, Volkswagon of Am., Englewood Cliffs, NJ, 1971; psychiat. social worker Associated Cath. Charities Family and Children's Svc., Paramus, NJ, 1973-74, Christian Health Ctr., Wyckoff, NJ, 1976; owner, mgr. Wicker Wagon, Bergenfield, NJ, 1977-85; psychotherapist The Psychotherapy Counseling Ctr., Bergenfield, NJ, 1982-89; programmer analyst Atlas Computing Svc., Secaucus, NJ, 1984-86; program coord., family therapist Divsn. Family Guidance, Hackensack, NJ, 1986-91; pres. Corp. Family Resources, Ridgewood, NJ, 1989—; family therapist cons. Family Recovery of Valley View, White Plains, NY, 1992-94, Furman Clinic, Fair [illegible] Inst. for Family Living, Englewood, NJ, 1996; cert. social work mgr., 1997—. Part time family therapist NJ Ctr. Psychotherapy Inc., Ridgefield Pk., NJ, 1990. Chmn. curriculum enhancement com. Bergen County Acad. Advancement Sci. and Tech., NJ, 1992—96; chmn. entertainment Bergen County Children's Festival, NJ, 1993; founder, chmn. Bergenfield Coun. of the Arts, NJ, 1993; chmn., designer Bergenfield Coun. Arts, NJ, 1993—99, chmn. author and poet program, 1996—2003, Bergenfield Coun. of the Arts, NJ, 1996—; mem. fundraising com., arts programming chmn. Bergenfield Cmty. Ctr., NJ, 2000—; sec. Mayor's Beautify Bergenfield Com., NJ, 1991—95; chmn. bd. cmty. play ctr. All Saints Ch., 1977—78, Sunday sch. tchr., 1982—89; mem. Twin Boro Youth Ministry Coun., 1989—; Sunday sch. tchr. All Saints Ch., 1994—. Recipient First and Second Pl. Awards, Bergenfield Art Contest, 1980, Best Practice Award for Author/Poet Program, N.J. Dept. Edn., 2003, Best Practice Award, State of N.J., 2003; grantee NIMH, 1973. Mem.: NASW, AAUW, N.J. Coalition Mental Health Profl., N.J. Soc. Clin. Social Workers (bd. dir., chmn. mktg. and vendor 1999—2003, membership chmn. 2003—), N.J. Commerce and Indsl. Assn. (child care com. 1990—, human resources com. 1990—), Fordham U. Alumni Assn., Am. Orthopsychiatric Assn., Acad. Cert. Social Workers, Gifted Child Soc. (parent workshop coord. 1989—, bd dir.), Women of Accomplishments (founder, pres. 1990—, chmn. women's coalition conf. 1993—), Zonta (Amelia Earhart chmn. 1987—88, chmn. status women com. 1993—94, lit. com. 1995—). Episcopalian. Avocations: walking, art, music, crafts, boating, acting. Home: 148 Harcourt Ave Bergenfield NJ 07621-1917 Office: Corp Family Resources 15 Godwin Ave Ste 1 Ridgewood NJ 07450-3739

CLEMENTS, MARY LOU, epidemiologist, educator; BA, Tex. Tech U., 1968; MD, U. Tex., 1972; DTMH, U. London, Eng., 1975; MPH, Johns Hopkins U., 1979. Diplomate Am. Bd. Internal Medicine, subspecialty of infectious diseases. Intern, resident in internal medicine Temple U. Hosp., Phila., 1972-75; spl. epidemiologist WHO, Uttar Pradesh, India, 1975-77; corrd. accreditation self-study Sch. Hygiene and Pub. Health Johns Hopkins U., Balt., 1978, asst. faculty mem. Sch. Medicine, 1979-81, assoc. prof. dept. internat. health Sch. Hygiene and Pub. Health, 1985-90, mem. med. staff Sch. Medicine, 1986—, dir. Ctr. Immunization Rsch., 1986—, prof., head divsn. vaccine scis. dept. internat. healthSch. Hygiene and Pub. Health, 1990—, prof., head dept. immunology and infectious diseases Sch. Hygiene and Pub. Health, 1991—; dir. home health care program, staff internist E. Balt. Med. Plan, 1978-79; mem. med. staff dept. medicine Johns Hopkins Hosp., Balt., 1979-81, 86—; asst. prof. dept. medicine, chief clin. studies sect. Ctr. Vaccine Devel. Sch. Medicine, U. Md., 1979-84, asst. prof. dept. epidemiology and preventative medicine, 1983-85, assoc. prof. dept. medicine, 1984-85; mem. med. staff Francis Scott Key Med. Ctr., 1986—. Mem. com. for AIDS Rsch. Johns Hopkins Med. Instns., 1990—; mem. adv. com. on immunization practices Ctrs. for Disease Control and Prevention, 1990—; mem. com. on The Children's Vaccine Initiative: Strategies towards full U.S. Participation, Inst. Medicine, 1991—; active U.S. AID/PHS Consultative Group on Vaccine Devel., 1991-93, Data and Safety Monitoring Bd. for Respiratory Syncytial Virus Immunoglobulin Treatment Trials, 1991—; med. cons. to numerous med. orgns. including WHO, APHA, NIH. Contbr. chpts. to books; contbr. articles to profl. med. jours. Fellow Am. Infectious Disease Soc. Am.; mem. Am. Soc. Microbiology. Am. Soc. Virology, Delta Omega (alpha chpt.). Office: Johns Hopkins U Ctr Immun Res Sch Pub Health 624 N Broadway Baltimore MD 21205-1900

CLEMETSON, CHERYL PRICE, minister, consultant; b. Des Moines, Wash, Aug. 31, 1958; d. Herman B. and Vivian P. Price; children: Alexander Sekou, Sierra Christiana. BA, Am. U., Washington, 1980; MDiv, Colgate Rochester Div. Sch., 1985; PhD, Sch. Theology, Claremont, Calif., 1992. Ordained to ministry Bapt. Ch., 1985. Dir. edn. and outreach Christ Luth. Ch., Rochester, NY, 1985-87; devel. coord. Inst. Religion & Wholeness, Claremont, 1987-88; cons. 2d Bapt. Ch., LA, 1988; dir. christian edn. and youth 1st United Meth. Ch., Ontario, Calif., 1988-89; nat. black pastors fellow AAAS & Congress Nat. Black Ch., Washington, 1989-90; mgr. tech. svc. and comm. Congress Nat. Black Ch., Washington, 1990-92; min. discipleship Met. Bapt. Ch., Washington, 1992-99; co-founder, christian edn. cons. New Cmty. Bapt. Ch., Washington, 1992-99; project mgr. Interaction Action Com., Capitol Heights, Md., 1999; asst. to pastor and min. of Christian Ed. Mt. Zion Bapt. Ch., Seattle, 2000—. Instr. Sch. Divinity Howard U., Washington, 1993, 99. Contbr. articles to profl. jour. Vol. Jewels Ann Pvt. Day Sch., Washington, 1996-97, Woodmore Elem. Sch., 1999; mem. Mayor's Com. Teeanage Pregnancy, Washington, 1997—. Mem. Am. Acad. Religion, Alpha Kappa Alpha. Avocations: reading, writing short stories, developing educational material, traveling, swimming.

CLEMONS, JANE ANDREA, state legislator; b. Poughkeepsie, N.Y., Apr. 2, 1946; d. Mary (Longendyke) Martin; m. Michael R. Clemons, Oct. 15, 1966; children: Bret, Nick, Benjamin. Student, Moore Gen. Hosp., Grasmere, N.H., 1966. Nurse various orgns., Nashua, N.H., 1967-89; accounts mgr. D & M Cleaning Co., Nashua, 1989-92; mem. N.H. Ho. of Reps., Dist. 31, Nashua, 1990—. Sponsor Sr. Citizen Computer Health Care Program, Nashua, 1983-84; ward chair Dem. City Com., Nashua, 1988; del. Dem. State Conv., Nashua, 1988; vol. Merrimack (N.H.) Friars Club, 1990-92; del. State Dem. Pary, 1993. Greek Orthodox. Avocations: gardening, reading, camping. Home: 177 Kinsley St Nashua NH 03060-3649 Office: NH House Reps State House Concord NH 03301

CLEMONS, JULIE PAYNE, telephone company manager; b. Attleboro, Mass., June 13, 1948; d. John Gordon and Claire (Paquin) P.; m. W. Richard Johnson, Oct. 10, 1970 (div. Oct. 1980); m. E.L. Clemons, Apr. 23, 1988; adopted son, Jason Corey. BS, U. R.I., 1995. Svc. rep. New England Telephone, East Greenwich, R.I., 1970-71, So. Bell, Jacksonville, Fla., 1971-73, bus. office supr., 1973-77, bus. office mgr., 1978-84, staff mgr. assessment, 1984-86, mgr. assessment ctr., 1987-89; dir. human resource assessment State of Fla., Jacksonville, Fla., 1987-89, Customer Svcs. Revenue Recovery Ctr., 1989-93, mgr. small bus. sales and svc., 1994-95, br. mgr. small bus. No. Fla., 1995-97; product support mgr. Small Bus. Mktg., 1997-98, sr. product support mgr., 1998-2000, project mgr. network and transport svcs., 2000-01, ISDN product mgr., 2001—02; ret., 2002. Subst. tchr. Gwinnett County Sch. Bd., 2003—04, Georgia Med. Inst., 2003—04; bus. mgr. Dr. Kenneth J. Sobel Internal Medicine. Vol. Learn to Read; bd. dirs. Duval Assn. Retarded Citizens, Jacksonville, 1981-86, treas., 1983-84; Boy Scouts den leader, Pack 569, 2002-; mem. Leadership Jacksonville, Class of '97; with Career Network Ctr. Admin. St. Lawrence Ch., 2003—. Mem. NAFE, Am. Mgmt. Assn., Pioneers of Am., Jacksonville C. of C. Roman Catholic. Avocations: gardening, water and snow skiing. Office Phone: 770-513-2072. E-mail: jpc@bellsouth.net.

CLERICI, SUSAN MARIE, psychotherapist; b. Walpole, Mass., Nov. 1, 1952; d. Camelio Anthony and Roberta May Roberts Clerici; m. Javier Marcos Flores, Apr. 19, 2003; 1 child, Adam Anthony Louis Litwin. BS in Psychology, Nova U., 1993; MS, NSU Sch. Social and Systematic Studies, Ft. Lauderdale, Fla., 1995. Lic. marriage and family therapist Fla., alcohol and other drug abuse counselor, clin. cert. forensic counselor, lic. clin. hypnotherapist. Owner SolutionPartners Psychotherapeutic, Life Strategy and Tng. Svcs., Inc., Plantation, Fla., 1995—. Mem.: Am. Assn. Marriage and Family Therapists. Democrat. Avocations: art, writing, hiking. Office: SolutionPartners Psychotherapeutic 7487 NW 4th St Plantation FL 33304 E-mail: psysusan@yahoo.com.

CLEVELAND, ASHLEY, musician; b. Knoxville, Tenn., Feb. 2, 1957; m. Kenny Greenberg. Rec. Big Town, 1991, Bus Named Desire, 1993, Lesson of Love, 1996 (Grammy award for Best Rock Gospel Album, 1996, Nashville Music award, 1996), You Are There, 1998 (Grammy award for Best Rock Gospel Album, 1999), [illegible] 2002, singer on over 200 albums, appearances (TV series) Austin City Limits, Saturday Night Live, TNN Country News, American Music Shop, 1991, CCM-TV, 1993, Gospel Music Assn. Dove Awards, 1994, 1996, 1998, The Road, 1994, Prime Time Country, 1996, Peace In The Valley, CeCe's Place, Stone Country: A Tribute To The Rolling Stones, 1997, Profiles in Praise, 1999. Named Big Town one of 1991's Ten Most Overlooked Albums, Billboard; recipient Dove award for Praise and Worship Album of Yr., 1994. Office: PO Box 50181 Nashville TN 37205

CLEVELAND, MARY LOUISE, librarian, media specialist; b. Clarksdale, Miss., Dec. 4, 1922; d. George Washington and Beatrice (Orange) Jones; m. Chester Lloyd Cleveland, June 5, 1950 (div. 1973); 1 child, Ann. BS, Ala. State U., 1947; MLS, Case-Western Res. U., 1957; EdD, East Tex. State Coll., 1991. Asst. prof. libr. edn. Ala. State U., Montgomery, 1957-65; head libr. Talladaga (Ala.) Coll., 1965-66; asst. prof. Atlanta U., 1966-71; head libr. Wiley Coll., Marshall, Tex., 1971-77; assoc. prof. Ala. A&M U., Huntsville, 1977-83; dir. libr. Tex. Coll., Tyler, 1985—. So. Edn. Found. fellow, 1963, East Tex. State U. fellow, 1982-83. Democrat. Methodist. Avocations: writing, preparation of audio-visual materials. Home: 2508 Fieldcrest Dr NW Huntsville AL 35810-2122 Office: Tex Coll 2404 N Grand Ave Tyler TX 75702-1962 E-mail: marylcleveland@dell.com.

CLEVELAND, PEGGY ROSE RICHEY, cytotechnologist; b. Cannelton, Ind., Dec. 9, 1929; d. "Pat" Clarence Francis and Alice Marie (Hall) Richey; m. Peter Leslie Cleveland, Nov. 25, 1948 (dec. 1973); children: Pamela Cleveland Litch, Paula Cleveland Bertloff, Peter L. Cert., U. Louisville, 1956, B in Health Sci., 1984. Cytotechnologist cancer survey project NIH, Louisville, 1956-59; chief cytotechnologist Parker Cytology Lab., Inc., Louisville, 1959-75; mgr. cytology dept. Am. Biomed. Corp., 1976-78, Nat. Health Labs., Inc., Louisville, 1978-89; with various hosps. and labs., 1990—. Leader cytotechnologist del. to China, 1986; clin. instr. cytology Sch. Allied Health, U. Louisville, 1989; ptnr. Sham Star Stable thoroughbred horse breeding and racing. Mem. Am. Soc. Clin. Pathologist (cert. cytotechnologist), Internat. Acad. Cytology (cert. cytotechnologist), Am. Soc. Cytology (del.-person to person cytology delegation, amb. USSR 1990), Kentuckiana Cytology Soc., Cytology Soc. Ind., Horseman's Benevolent and Protective Assn. Democrat. Roman Catholic. Home: 8774 Lieber Hausz Rd NE Lanesville IN 47136-8522

CLEVELAND, SUSAN ELIZABETH, library administrator, researcher; b. Plainfield, N.J., Mar. 14, 1946; d. Robert Astbury and Grace Ann (Long) Williamson; m. Stuart Craig Cleveland, Aug. 21, 1971; children: Heather Elizabeth, Catherine Elisa. BA, Douglass Coll., Rutgers U., 1968; MLS, Rutgers U., 1969. Acquisitions libr. Jefferson U., Phila., 1970-71; biomed. libr. VA Hosp., Hines, Ill., 1972; med. cataloger U. Ariz., Tucson, 1973-74; dir. U. Pa. Hosp. Libr., Phila., 1974-87; exec. dir. Cleveland, Lamb, Urban Assocs., 1987-89; libr. dir. Mt. Sinai Hosp., Phila., 1989, West Jersey Health System (now Virtua Health Sys.), Voorhees, NJ, 1990—2002, Our Lady of Lourdes Med. Ctr., Camden, NJ, 2002—. Cons. in field, Phila. USPHS fellow, Detroit, 1969-70; recipient Chapel of 4 Chaplains Legion of Honor. Mem. Med. Libr. Assn. (Phila. chpt.), Spl. Libr. Assn., Basic Health Sci. Libr. Consortium, So. N.J. Consortium for Health Info. Svcs., Health Scis. Libr. Assn. N.J., Acad. Health Info. Profls., Caravan Club. Home: 9 Sylvan Ct Laurel Springs NJ 08021 E-mail: clevelands@lourdesnet.org.

CLEVEN, CAROL CHAPMAN, state legislator; b. Hanover, Ill., Nov. 2, 1928; d. Edward William and Vivian (Strasser) Chapman; m. Walter Arnold Cleven; children: Kern W., Jeffrey P. BS, U. Ill., 1950, postgrad., 1950-56. Elem. sch. tchr. Derinda Ctr., Ill., 1946-47; with rsch. staff U. Ill., Urbana, 1950-56; exec. dir. Crittenton Hasting House, Brighton, Mass., 1975-86; mem. Mass. Ho. of Reps., Boston, 1987—. Mem. edn. com., mem. human svcs. com., mem. election laws com. Mass. Ho. Reps.; mem. Rep. Task Force on Pediatric AIDS, Mass. Caucus of Women Legislators, Gov.'s Adolescent Health Adv. Coun., Spl. Commn. on Pub. Assiatance, Spl. Com. on Women and the Criminal Justice System; co-chair Legis. Caucus on Older Citizens' Concerns, Dept. Social Svcs. Working Group; mem. steering com. Mass. Legis. Children's Caucus. Mem. Chelmsford (Mass.) Sch. Com., 1969-87, mem. elem. needs com., 1969-71, mem. sch. bldg. com., 1971-76; bd. dirs. Camp Paul for Exceptional Children, 1987—; past pres. Lowell (Mass.) YWCA, Lowell Coll. Club; mem. Merrimack River Watershed Coun., Mass. Coalition for Pregnant and Parenting Teens, Alliance for Young Families; treas. Boston Ctr. Blind Children; bd. dirs. Chelmsford Ednl. Found.; bd. dirs. Greater Lowell Alzheimers Assn., Ea. Mass. Alzheimers Assn.; mem. spl. adv. bd. Cmty. Teamwork, Inc. Mem. Mass. Assn. Sch. Coms. (life), Friends of the Library, Chelmsford Hist. Soc., Chelmsford LWV, Florence Crittenton League of Lowell, Phi Sigma, Sigma Delta Epsilon. Congregationalist. Home: 4 Arbutus Ave Chelmsford MA 01824-1113 Office: State House Rm 167 State Capitol Boston MA 02133

CLEVENGER, PENELOPE, international business consultant; b. Denver, Dec. 6, 1940; d. Harold Friedland and Charlotte (Glatt) Friedland Beskin; m. Willie K. Clevenger, Oct. 15, 1961 (div.). AA, Stephens Coll., 1960. Pers. mgr. Rolm/Midwest, Chgo., 1979-82; office mgr. Malcolm S. Gerald, Chgo., 1977-79; office adminstr. Nutech Engrs., Chgo., 1982-83; office mgr. Am. Acad. Orthop. Surgeons, Chgo., 1983-85; dir. adminstrn. Telecomm. Industry Assn. (formerly U.S. Telecomm. Suppliers), Chgo., 1985-88; pres. InterWorld Svcs., Ltd., Chgo., 1988—2002, Vosges Haut-Chocolat, 2001—. Bd. dirs. Ctr Tng. and Rehab. of Disabled, Chgo., 1981-84; vol. Northwestern Meml. Hosp., 1985-87, Christian Indsl. League, 1992-97. Mem. Meeting Profls. Internat., Chgo. Coun. on Fgn. Rels., U.S. China Friendship Assn. Democrat. Jewish. Home: 233 E Wacker Dr Apt 3910 Chicago IL 60601-5116 E-mail: clev104763@cs.com.

CLEVER, LINDA HAWES, physician; b. Seattle; d. Nathan Harrison and Evelyn Lorraine (Johnson) Hawes; m. James Alexander Clever, Aug. 20, 1960; 1 child, Sarah Lou. AB with distinction, Stanford U., 1962, MD, 1965. Diplomate Am. Bd. Internal Medicine, Am. Bd. Preventive Medicine in Occupl. Medicine. Intern Stanford U. Hosp., Palo Alto, Calif., 1965—66, resident, 1966—67, fellow in infectious disease, 1967—68; fellow in cmty. medicine U. Calif., San Francisco, 1968—69, resident, 1969—70; med. dir. Sister Mary Philippa Diagonostic and Treatment Ctr. St. Mary's Hosp., San Francisco, 1970—77; chmn. dept. occupl. health Calif. Pacific Med. Ctr., San Francisco, 1977—. Clin. prof. medicine U. Calif. Med. Sch., San Francisco; NIIH rsch. fellow Sch. Medicine, Stanford U., 1967—68; mem. nat. adv. panel Inst. Rsch. on Women and Gender, 1990—, chair panel, 1998—2000; mem. San Francisco Comprehensive Health Planning Coun., 1971—76; bd. dirs., mem. Calif.-OSHA Adv. Com. on Hazard Evaluation Sys. and Info. Svc., 1979—85, Calif. Statewide Profl. Stds. Rev. Coun., 1977—81, San Francisco Regional Commn. on White House Fellows, 1979—81, 1983—89, 1992, 95, chmn., 1977—81, 2001—02; bd. sci. counselors Nat. Inst. Occupl. Safety and Health, 1995—. Editor We. Jour. Medicine, 1990—98; contbr. articles to profl. jours. Trustee Stanford U., 1972—76, 1981—91, v.p., 1985—91; pres. RENEW, 2000—; bd. dirs. Sta. KQED, 1976—83, chmn., 1979—81; bd. dirs. Ind. Sector, 1980—86, vice chmn., 1985—86; bd. dirs. San Francisco U. H.S., 1983—90, chmn., 1987—88; active Womens Forum West, 1980—, bd. dirs., 1992—93; mem. Lucile Packard Children's Hosp. Bd., 1993—97, Lucile Packard Found. Children, 1997—99; mem. policy adv. com. U. Calif. Berkeley Sch. Pub. Health, 1995—, chair, 1995—2000; bd. dirs. The Redwoods Retirement Cmty., 1996—2001, Buck Inst. for Rsch. in Aging, 2000—; bd. govs. Stanford Med. Alumni Assn., 1997—2002, 2003—, pres., 2003—; bd. dirs. No. Calif. Presbyn. Homes and Svcs., 2000—. Master: ACP (agov. No. Calif. region 1984—89, chmn. bd. govs. 1989—90, regent 1990—96, vice chair bd. regents 1994—95); fellow: Am. Coll. Occupl. and Environ. Medicine; mem.: APHA, [illegible] Medicine Assn., Calif. Acad. Medicine, Calif. Med. Assn., Inst. Medicine NAS, Stanford U. Women's Club (bd. dirs. 1971—80), Chi Omega. Office: 2340 Clay St Ste 106 San Francisco CA 94115-1931

CLIFF, JOHNNIE MARIE, mathematics and chemistry educator; b. Lamkin, Miss., May 10, 1935; d. John and Modest Alma (Lewis) Walton; m. William Henry Cliff, Apr. 1, 1961 (dec. 1983); 1 child, Karen Marie. BA in Chemistry, Math., U. Indpls., 1956; postgrad., NSF Inst., Butler U., 1960; MA in Chemistry, Ind. U., 1964; MS in Math., U. Notre Dame, 1980; postgrad., Martin U., 2000. Cert. tchr., Ind. Rsch. chemist Ind. U. Med. Ctr., Indpls., 1956-59; tchr. sci. and math. Indpls. Pub. Schs., 1960-88; tchr. chemistry, math. Martin U., Indpls., 1989—, chmn. math. dept., 1990—, divsn. chmn. depts. sci. and math., 1993—. Adj. instr. math. U. Indpls., 1991, Ivy Tech State Coll., Indpls., 2002. Contbr. rsch. papers to sci. jours. Grantee NSF, 1961-64, 73-76, 78-79, Woodrow Wilson Found., 1987-88; scholarship U. Indpls., 1952-56, NSF Inst. Reed Coll., 1961, C. of C., 1963. Mem. AAUW, NAACP, NEA, Assn. Women in Sci., Urban League, N.Y. Acad. Scis., Am. Chem. Soc., Nat. Coun. Math. Tchrs., Am. Assn. Physics Tchrs., Nat. Sci. Tchrs. Assn., Am. Statis. Assn., Am. Assn. Ret. Persons, Neal-Marshall-Ind. U. Alumni Assn., U. Indpls. Alumni Assn., U. Notre Dame Alumni Assn., Ind. U. Chemist Assn., Notre Dame Club Indpls., Kappa Delta Pi, Delta Sigma Theta. Democrat. Baptist. Avocations: gardening, sewing. Home: 405 Golf Ln Indianapolis IN 46260-4108 Office: Martin U 2171 Avondale Pl Indianapolis IN 46218-3878

CLIFF, KARISSA, consumer researcher, recruiter; b. Lancaster, Calif., Dec. 15, 1965; d. John Oliver and Frances Kay (Spencer) Cliff; m. Kevin Kenneth Ross, Apr. 14, 1984 (div. June 1988); children: Kevin Kenneth Ross, II, Serenity Angeline Ross; m. Ira C. Baxter, 1998 (div. Feb. 2003); children: Madeline Elizabeth, Rosalyn Andrea Regina. BBA magna cum laude, Belmont U., 1995; MBA, Vanderbilt U., 1997. Mgr., liaison Mercantile Stores, Nashville, 1983-87; researcher Ericson Mktg. Comm., Nashville, 1994-95; marketer Armor All, Charleston, S.C., 1996; consumer rschr. Procter & Gamble, Nashville, 1997-2000; sr. analyst Clorox, Nashville, 2000—03. Cons. Am. Beauty Cosmetics, Gallatin, Tenn., 1995. Founder Homeless Day Labor, Nashville, 1996-97; chair 100% Owen Svc. Orgn., Nashville, 1996-97; vol. soup kitchen Union Rescue Mission, Nashville, 1995-97; vol. Refugee Relocation, Nashville, 1995-97. Wendell scholar for Mktg. Studies, Belmont U., 1994-95, Morris scholar Vanderbilt U., 1995-97. Fellow Ctr. for Transition and Orgnl. Design; mem. MENSA, Delta Gamma Beta. Democrat. Avocation: flute. Home: 211 Deerfield Ln Franklin TN 37069-6012 E-mail: karissacliff@yahoo.com.

CLIFFORD, CHERYL KUCHTA, Christian education administrator; b. Winsted, Conn., July 30, 1947; d. George Henry and Gertrude Marie (Weaving) Kuchta; m. Steven Dale Clifford, July 22, 1989; children: Ruth Marie, Paul Arthur, Heidi Lynn, Robert Steven (quadruplets). BS in Elem. Edn., U. Hartford, 1970; MS in Remedial Reading, Ctrl. Conn. State U., 1978; MDiv, Gordon-Conwell Theol. Sem., 1986. Ordained to ministry United Ch. of Christ, 1988; cert. tchr., Conn. Tchr. East Hartland (Conn.) Elem. Sch., 1970-81; assoc. pastor St. John's United Ch. of Christ, Massillon, Ohio, 1988-91; interim pastor Emmanual United Ch. of Christ, Akron, Ohio, 1992; dir. Christian edn. First United Ch. of Christ, Canton, Ohio, 1994—99; co-owner tax acctg. firm Clifford & Assocs., Canton, 1991—. Editor newsletter The Witness of Ohio, 1990-93. Recipient Cory Meml. Scholarship award for excellence in Christian edn. Scripture Press Ministries, 1986. Mem. Nat. Assn. Evangelicals. Republican. Avocations: downhill skiing, crafts, letterwriting. Office: Clifford & Associates 4150 Belden Village St NW Ste 601 44718 Office Phone: 330-493-1814.

CLIFFORD, GERALDINE JONCICH (MRS. WILLIAM F. CLIFFORD), education educator; b. San Pedro, Calif., Apr. 17, 1931; d. Marion and Geraldine Joncich; m. William F. Clifford, July 12, 1969 (dec. 1993). AB, UCLA, 1954, M.Ed., 1957; Ed.D., Columbia U., 1961. Tchr., San Lorenzo, Calif., 1954-56, Maracaibo, Venezuela, 1957-58; researcher Inst. Lang. Arts, Tchrs. Coll., Columbia, 1958-61; asst. prof. edn. U. Calif., Berkeley, 1962-67, asso. prof., 1967-74, prof., 1974-94, assoc. dean, 1976-78, chmn. dept. edn., 1978-81, acting dean Sch. Edn., 1980-81, 82-83, dir. edn. abroad program, 1988, 89, prof. grad. sch., 1994—. Author: The Sane Positivist: A Biography of Edward L. Thorndike, 1968, The Shape of American Education, 1975, Ed Sch: A Brief for Professional Education, 1988, Lone Voyagers: Academic Women in Coeducational Universities, 1870-1937, 1989, Equally in View: The University of California, Its Women, and The Schools, 1995. Macmillan fellow, 1958-59, Guggenheim fellow, 1965-66, Rockefeller fellow, 1977-78; recipient Willystine Goodsell award for Contbns. to Women in Edn. Mem. History Edn. Soc., Am. Ednl. Rsch. Assn., Phi Beta Kappa, Pi Lambda Theta. Home: Apt 733 1661 Pine St San Francisco CA 94109-0420

CLIFFORD, LISA MARY, marketing professional; b. Albany, N.Y., Nov. 23, 1969; d. John Rocco and Kathleen Mary Fedele; m. Timothy Stephen Clifford, Sept. 16, 1995; children: Christian Gerard, John Anthony. BS in Fin., St. John Fisher Coll., Rochester, N.Y., 1991. Pension consulting assoc. First Albany Corp., 1992—94; assoc. v.p. mktg. First Albany Asset Mgmt., 1994—2000; dir., mktg. and bus. devel. Curran Investment Mgmt. of Wachovia Securities, Albany, 2000—. Mem. women's adv. bd. Wachovia Securities, Albany, 2003; bd. dirs., mem. investment com. Wildwood Found., Albany, 2002; mem. Capital Leadership Class 2004 Albany-Colonie (N.Y.) C. of C., 2003. Mem.: Am. Mktg. Assn., Investment Mgmt. Consultants Assn. Office: Curran Investment Mgmt of Wachovia Securities 80 State St Albany NY 12207 E-mail: lisa.clifford@wachoviasec.com.

CLIFT, ELEANOR, magazine correspondent; b. Bklyn., July 7, 1940; d. Erk and Inna Roeloffs; m. Brooks Clift, 1964-1981; children: Edward, Woodbury, Robert; m. Tom Brazaitis, 1989. Student, Hofstra U., Hunter Coll. Former White House corr. now contbg. editor Newsweek. Commentator The McLaughlin Group, also Fox News Channel. Co-author: War Without Bloodshed: The Art of Politics, 1996, Madam President: Shattering the Last Glass Ceiling, 2000, Founding Sisters and the 19th Amendment, 2003. Office: Newsweek Washington Bur 1750 Pennsylvania Ave NW Washington DC 20006-4502 E-mail: eclift@newsweek.com., eclift@aol.com.

CLIFTON, ANNE RUTENBER, psychotherapist, educator; b. New Haven, Dec. 11, 1938; d. Ralph Dudley and Cleminette (Downing) Rutenber; 1 child, Dawn Anne. BA, Smith Coll., 1960, MSW, 1962. Lic. clin. social worker, Mass.; diplomate Clin. Social Work. Psychiat. case worker adult psychiatry unit Tufts-New Eng. Med. Ctr., Boston, 1962-68, supr. students, 1967-68; pvt. practice psychotherapy, Cambridge and Newton, Mass., 1966—. Supr. med. students, staff social workers out-patient psychiatry Tufts New Eng. Med. Ctr., 1973—, also mem. exec. bd. Women's Resource Ctr., interim co-dir., 1986-88; asst. clin. prof. psychiatry Tufts U. Med. Sch., 1974—, research dept. psychiatry, 1966-68, 73, 77—. Contbr. articles to profl. jours. Mem. NASW, Acad. Cert. Social Workers, Cambridge Tennis Club, Mt. Auburn Tennis Club, Phi Beta Kappa, Sigma Xi. Home: 126 Homer St Newton MA 02459-1518 Office: 59 Church St Ste 4 Cambridge MA 02138-3724 E-mail: annerclifton@aol.com.

CLIFTON, JUDY RAELENE, association administrator; b. Safford, Ariz., Nov. 8, 1946; d. Ralph Newton and Fayrene (Goodner) Johnson; married. Student, Biola Coll., 1964-65; BA in Christian Edn., Southwestern Coll., 1970. Editl. asst. Accent Publications, Denver, 1970-73; expediter Phelps

Dodge Corp., Douglas, Ariz., 1974-78; exec. asst. So. Ariz. Internat. Livestock Assn., Inc., Tucson, 1978-81; adminstrv. asst. Phelps Dodge Corp., 1981—. Sec. exec. bd. PAC, Phelps Dodge Corp., 1981—. Mem. adv. bd. Ariz. Lung Assn.; mem. Silver City Arts Coun., 1986-90; mem. Am. Security Council, 1979-85; leader 4-H, Douglas; mem. Rep. Nat. Com., 1978—, Conservative Caucus, 1979-85; del. Quadrennial N.Mex. State Rep. Con., 1988, 92. Recipient Am. Legion Good Citizen award, 1964, DAR award, 1964. Mem. NAFE, DAR, Nat. Assn. Evangelicals, U.S. Tennis Assn., Nat. Right to Life, So. Ariz. Internat. Livestock Assn., AAUW, Eagle Forum, Freedom Found., N.Mex. Eagle Forum, Mus. N.Mex. Found., Lordsburg/Hidalgo County C. of C. (1st v.p. bd. dirs. 1990-97), Concerned Women of Am., Sigma Lambda Delta. Clubs: Trunk & Tusk, Pima County Republican, Centre Ct., Westerners Internat., So. Ariz. Depression Glass, Tucson Tennis, Rep. Senatorial. Baptist. Home: Drawer M Playas NM 88009

CLIFTON, KAREN S. secondary school educator; b. Ft. Worth, Apr. 2, 1958; d. Calvin L. and Wanda L. Stoner; m. John D. Clifton, July 18, 1980; children: Travis John, Kari Leigh. BS, Tarleton State U., 1979, MEd, 1983. Tchr., coach Santo (Tex.) Ind. Sch. Dist., 1979—80; tchr. Ranger (Tex.) Ind. Sch. Dist., 1980—82, tchr., coach, 1983—; tchr. Strawn (Tex.) Ind. Sch. Dist., 1982—83. Nominee Tchr. of the Yr., Disney, 2002; named, C. of C., 1995. Mem.: Assn. Tex. Profl. Educators (pres. Ranger chpt.). Avocations: gardening, horseback riding, deep sea fishing, bicycling. Office: Ranger HS RR 3 Box 12 D Ranger TX 76470-9782

CLIFTON, LUCILLE THELMA, author; b. Depew, N.Y., June 27, 1936; d. Samuel Louis and Thelma (Moore) Sayles; m. Fred James Clifton, May 10, 1958 (dec. Nov. 1984); children[00bf] Sidney, Fredrica (dec. 2000), Channing (dec. 2004), Gillian, Graham, Alexia. Student, Howard U., 1953-55, Fredonia (N.Y.) State Tchrs. Coll., 1955. Prof. literature and creative writing U. Calif., Santa Cruz, 1985-90; dist. prof. humanities St. Mary's Coll. Md., 1990—, Hilda C. Landers endowed chair in liberal arts, 2000—. Poet-in-residence, Coppin State Coll., Balt., 1972-76, Jenny Moore vis. writer, George Washington U., 1982-83. Author: Good Times, 1969, Good News About The Earth, 1972, An Ordinary Woman, 1974, Generations, 1976, Two-Headed Woman, 1980, Sonora Beautiful, 1981, Next, 1987, Good Woman, 1987, Quilting, 1991, The Book of Light, 1993, Blessing the Boats, 2000 (Nat. Book award), Everett Anderson books and other books for children; co-author: Free to Be You and Me, 1974 (Emmy award), Free To Be A Family. Named Poet Laureate, State of Md., 1979; recipient Discovery award Poetry Center, 1969, winner Nat. Book Award, 2000; YMHA grantee, 1969; Nat. Endowment Arts grantee, 1970, 72 Fellow Am. Acad. Arts and Scis.; mem. Authors League, Author Guild, P.E.N., Acad. Am. Poets (chancellor), Poetry Soc. Am. (bd. dirs., Lila Wallace/Reader's Digest award 1999). Office: St Marys Coll of Maryland Divsn Arts and Letters Montgomery Hall 126 Saint Marys City MD 20686

CLIFTON, MELANIE FAIRLIGHT, bank executive; b. Harrison, Ark., Oct. 25; d. W. Lee and Dianne B. Clifton. BBA in Fin., Real Estate Fin., Orgnl. Behavior & Bus. Policy, So. Meth. U., Dallas, 2000. From banking specialist to personal banker III Bank of Am., Plano, Tex., 1994—98; human resources 7-11, Dallas, 1998; cons., comml. lending - large corp. & mid. market groups Bank One, Dallas, 1999; investment banking analyst, energy UBS Warburg, Dallas, 2000—01; co-founder, prodr. Forever Entertainment, Wylie, Tex., 2001—03; br. mgr. Cmty. Credit Union, Allen, Tex., 2002—. Prodr.: (films) Stationery Games, 2003. Master: SouthEastern Intercollegiate Sailing Assn. (corr.; grad. treas. 2000—03), Allen High Noon Lions Club (corr.; pres. 2003); mem.: COX Real Estate Soc. (assoc.). Avocations: sailing, horseback riding, acting, rock climbing. Office: Community Credit Union 321 E McDermott Allen TX 75002 Personal E-mail: melaniefairlight@yahoo.com. Business E-Mail: melanie.clifton@communitycu.org.

CLIFTON, NELIDA, social worker; b. Buenos Aires, Aug. 16, 1944; arrived in U.S., 1968; d. Juan Antonio and Zaira Elizabeth (Vera) Tovar; m. Mark Earl Jolls, Nov. 8, 1968 (div. July 1984); children: Patricia Elizabeth, Michael Thomas, Diana Marie Kathleen; m. Anthony Gene Clifton, June 19, 1993. BA in Bus. Adminstrn., Nat. Sch. Commerce, Tucuman, Argentina; BA in Psychology magna cum laude, Fairleigh Dickinson U., 1986; postgrad., William Paterson Coll., 1988-89. Cert. diplomate Am. Psychotherapy Assn.; lic. cert. social worker Bd. Social Work Examiners, N.J.; cert. bilingual. Social worker Bergen County Bd. Social Svcs., Rochelle Park, N.J., 1987—. Crisis intervention vol.; phone counselor; cmty. resources referral profl. Mem. APA, NASW, Am. Assn. Christian Counselors, Phi Zeta Kappa, Phi Omega Epsilon, Psi Chi Nat. Honor Socs. Republican. Avocations: reading, chess, tennis, gardening. Home and Office: PO Box 8581 Saddle Brook NJ 07663-8581

CLIFTON-SMITH, RHONDA DARLEEN, art educator, art center administrator; b. Dyersburg, Tenn., Mar. 19, 1954; d. Charles Burton Clifton and Mary Opal (Carter) Harris; m. Michael Frederick Smith, Feb. 14, 1980 (dec. Sept. 1981). BS in Art Edn., Columbus Coll., 1977; MA in Hist. Adminstrn., Eastern Ill. U., 1986. Asst. cataloging libr. Lawton (Okla.) Pub. Libr., 1978-79; registrar Mus. of the Great Plains, Lawton, 1979-82; curator Boot Hill Mus., Dodge City, Kans., 1982-94; exec. dir. Carnegie Ctr. for Arts, Dodge City, 1994—; drawing and painting instr. Dodge City H.S. Author: (booklet) Dodge City: The Early Years, 1985; co-author: (booklet) Cattle and Wheat: Agricultural Growth in 19th Century Dodge City, 1985. Mem. Am. Assn. Mus., Am. Assn. State & Local History (c-chair mem. com. 1990-92), Kan. Mus. Assn. (treas. 1989—, area rep. 1982-85), Mt. Plains Mus. Assn., Soroptimists Internat. Avocations: painting and drawing, theater. Office: Carnegie Ctr for Arts 701 2d Ave Dodge City KS 67801 E-mail: carnegie@dodgecity.net.

CLINE, ANN, artist, designer; b. Greensboro, N.C., Apr. 7, 1933; d. Grady Alton and Mae Josephine (Karsten) Merriman; scholar Cooper Union, N.Y.C., 1954, Fashion Inst. Tech., 1957, Arts Students League, 1961-62, Fine Arts Acad., 1962-63, Joachim Simon Atelier, Tel Aviv, 1962; A.B., N.E. La. U., Monroe, 1971; m. S.C. Johananoff, Mar. 9, 1959 (div. 1973); 1 child, Pamela; m. Francis X. Cline, Feb. 14, 1973. Asst. designer Adele Simpson Couture, 1959; pres. Johananoff Designs, 1967-70, Ann Cline Art Objects, Monroe, La., 1975— ; pres. 165 North Properties; artist; works exhibited in group shows Haifa Mus., 1961, Am. Watercolor Soc., 1962; one person shows include: Barzansky Gallery, 1962, La. Polytech. U. Art Gallery, 1967, Mittel's Art Gallery, 1969, N.E. La. U., 1973, 71, Am. Consulate, Tel Aviv, 1962, Contemporary Gallery, Dallas, 1970, Brooks Gallery, Memphis, 1971, 14th Ann. Delta Art Exhbn. Nat. Found. Arts, 1971, Jackson Arts Ctr. Ann. Exhbn., Miss., (prize award 1971), 22d Ann. Delta Exhbn., Ark. Arts Ctr., 1972, 79, Mayor's Show, Monroe, 1979, Wesley Found. Award Show, 1979, 80, 81, Roundtree Gallery, Monroe, 1985-87, others. Bd. dirs. La. Council Performing Arts, 1974; rep. Gov.'s Conf. Arts; bd. adjustments Monroe Zoning Commn.; trustee Masur Mus., 1974-75; bd. dirs. Little Theater of Monroe, 1975-76; bd. dirs. Women of the Ch., Episcopal Ch., 1977-78, mem. Daus. of the King, 1979-82, chmn. meml. com. Recipient Young Designer competition award Fontana of Rome, 1957, 1st prize Fashion Inst. Tech., 1957, Young Designer's award Women's Wear Daily, 1960, 1st prize, Arts Students League, 1961, 2d prize, 1963, 2d prize Fine Arts Acad., 1962, 1st prize, Woodstock Gallery, 1962, 1st prize, La. Folk Art Festival, 1966, 68, 72, prize awards Temple Emmanuel Ann., Dallas, 1969, 71, 74. Mem. Internat. Butler Soc., Bayou Desiard Country Club, Little Rock Country Club, Lotus Club. Illustrator: Jessie Strikes Louisiana Gold, 1969, Rhet, the Egret. Home and Office: The Herb Soc Am Ark Unit 1 Tree Tops Ln Apt 503 Little Rock AR 72202-1517

CLINE, JANET E. SAFFORD, school district administrator, desktop publisher; b. London, Aug. 28, 1945; came to U.S., 1946; d. Don F. and Elizabeth G. (Taylor) Safford; m. Raymond D. Cline, Aug. 23, 1966; children: Roger D., Martin A. BA, West Tex. State U., Canyon, 1967. Admissions clk. North Tex. State U., Denton, 1971-72; comms. dir. United Meth. Temple, Port Arthur, Tex., 1973-75; edn. and health reporter Port Arthur News, 1977-82; coord. sch./cmty. rels. Port Arthur Ind. Sch. Dist., 1982-97, dir. comms., 1997—. Owner Janet Cline Pub. Author, editor numerous PAISD Publs.; contbr. articles to profl. jours. Mem. Mayor's Com. on Edn., Port Arthur, 1994-96chmn. Port Arthur Centennial Activities Commn., 1996—; pres. Mid/South Jefferson County chpt. Am. Heart Assn., 1997—, Samaritan Counseling Ctr., Jefferson County, 1997—. Recipient Anson Jones award Tex. Med. Assn., 1983, Silver Star of Tex. award Tex. Hosp. Assn., 1983. Mem. Tex. Sch. Pub. Rels. Assn. (regional v.p. 1988-89, chair com. 1983-97, Bright Idea award 1997), North Port Arthur Rotary Club (v.p. 1997—). Methodist. Avocations: reading, bridge, cross stitch, travel.

CLINE, PAULINE M. educational administrator; b. Seattle, Aug. 25, 1947; d. Paul A. and Margaret R. Cline BA in Edn., Seattle U., 1969, MEd, 1975, EdD, 1983. Cert. tchr., prin., supt., Wash. Tchr. Marysville High Sch., Wash., 1969-70; tchr., adminstr. Blanchet High Sch., Seattle, 1970-78; asst. prin. Edmonds High Sch., Wash., 1978-84; prin. College Place Middle Sch., Edmonds, 1984-85, Mountlake Terrace High Sch., Wash., 1985-93; asst. supt. Mount Vernon Sch. Dist., 1993-2000, Bethel Sch. Dist., 2002—. Recipient Washington award for excellence in edn. Gov. and Supt. Pub. Instruction, 1992, IDEA Kettering fellow, 1984, 86-87, 90-95, 97. Mem. ASCD, Am. Assn. Sch. Adminstr., Rotary (charter mem., past pres. Alderwood club), Phi Delta Kappa. Roman Catholic. Avocations: skiing, kayaking, backpacking, golf. Office Phone: 253-683-6000.

CLINE, RUTH ELEANOR HARWOOD, translator, historian; b. Middletown, Conn., Oct. 31, 1946; d. Burton Henry and Eleanor May (Cash) Harwood; A.B., Smith Coll., 1968; M.A., Rutgers U., 1969; Ph.D., Georgetown U., 2000; cert. translation from French, Georgetown U., 1978; m. William R. Cline, June 10, 1967; children: Alison, Marian. Reviewer, U.S. Dept. State, Washington, 1979-94. Former v.p. Smith Coll. Class of 1968; rsch. assoc. dept. history Georgetown U., 2002--. Mem. Am. Translators Assn. (cert. in French, Spanish and Portuguese), MLA, Internat. Arthurian Soc. Episcopalian. Translator English verse: Yvain; or the Knight with the Lion (Chretien de Troyes), 1975; Perceval; or the Story of the Grail (Chretien de Troyes), 1983, Lancelot or the Knight of the Cart (Chretien de Troyes), 1990 (Lewis Galantiere Prize 1992), Erec and Enide (Chretien de Troyes), 2000, Cliges (Chretien de Troyes), 2000. Home: 5315 Oakland Rd Chevy Chase MD 20815-6638

CLINE, STARR, elementary school educator; b. Bklyn., Feb. 27, 1937; d. Albert and Amy (Barocas) Funess; B.A. magna cum laude, Molloy Coll., 1974; postgrad. Hofstra U., 1977; Ed.D., Columbia U., 1985; m. Jerome Z. Cline, Apr. 27, 1957; children— Adam, Larry. Tchr., Oceanside (N.Y.) Public Schls., 1974-81, tchr. gifted elem. program, Herricks Public Schs., 1981— ; coordinator Inst. on Gifted and Talented, Columbia U. for Three Village Sch. Dist., Setauket, L.I., 1978, asst. coordinator summer inst., 1978; field reader U.S. Dept. HEW, 1978; adj. instr. Molloy Coll., Hofstra U., C.W. Post Coll., Adelphi U.; regional coordinator Advocacy for Gifted and Talented Edn., 1984, state coordinator, 1985; leader delegation U.S. Amb. Program to Moscow and Siberia, 1991; lectr., cons. in field. Pres., Ocean Lea Civic Assn., 1977; adv. com. N.Y.C. Gifted Ed., 1979. Winner 1st, 2d prizes Creative Problem Solving Inst., Buffalo, 1979; Pub. Service TV Tri-State award, N.Y., N.J., Conn., 1980, others. Mem. Advocacy Gifted and Talented Edn. (dir., treas., pres.), World Council Gifted and Talented Children, Nat. Assn. Gifted Children, Nat. Alliance State Assns. for Gifted Edn. (chair 1993), L.I. Soc. Gifted and Talented, Assn. for Supervision and Curriculum Devel. Clubs: Kiwanettes (trustee 1982, pres. 1985). Author: Independent Study, 1980, Teaching for Talent, 1984, The Independent Learner, 1986, What Would Happen If I Said Yes?, 1989; contbr. articles to profl. jours. Home: 14 Saint James Pl Lynbrook NY 11563-2618

CLINE, STEPHANIE E. food service executive; 2 children. V.p. sys. devel. Jack in the Box Inc., San Diego, 1994—2000, v.p., chief info. officer, 2000—. Named IT Operator of Yr., Hospitality Tech. mag., 2001. Office: Jack in the Box Inc 9330 Balboa Ave San Diego CA 92123

CLINE, VIVIAN MELINDA, lawyer; b. Seneca, S.C., Oct. 6, 1953; d. Kenneth H. and Wanda F. (Simmons) Fuller; m. Terry S. Cline, June 15, 1974 (div. Oct. 1986); 1 child, Alicia C. BSBA, Calif. State U., Northridge, 1974; JD, Southwestern U., L.A., 1983. Bar: Calif. 1983, Tex., 1990. Paralegal Internat. House Pancakes, North Hollywood, Calif., 1976-78; assoc. Tuohey & Prasse, Santa Ana, Calif., 1983-85; paralegal Smith Internat., inc., Newport Beach, Calif., 1978-83, sr. corp. counsel Houston, 1985—. Bus. cons. Jr. Achievement, Houston, 1992—94, 1997—99. Mem. Exec. Women's Network (sec. 1993, pres. 1994, dir. programs 1995, sec. 1996, 2000, treas. 1998-2001), Am. Soc. Corp. Secs. Inc. (sec. Houston chpt. 1995-96, treas. 1996-97, v.p., program dir. 1997-98, pres. 1998-99). Republican. Presbyterian. Office: Smith Internat Inc 16740 Hardy Rd Houston TX 77032-1125 E-mail: vcline@smith.com.

CLINTON, BARBARA MARIE, university health services director, social worker; b. Bklyn., May 21, 1947; d. Lawrence Joseph and Kathleen Byrne C.; m. James Edward Selin, Sept. 12, 1981; children: Greta Maureen, Caitlin Carol. Auditor's cert., U. Tunis, Tunisia, 1968; BS, State U. Coll., Buffalo, 1971; student, SUNY, Buffalo, 1970-71; MSW, U. Ga., 1979. Child care worker Gateway United Meth. Youth Ctr., Williamsville, N.Y., 1970; caseworker Erie County Dept. Social Svcs., Buffalo, 1975-76; social worker Orchard Park (N.Y.) Nursing Home, 1976-77; group counselor Erie Med. Ctr., Buffalo, 1976-77; therapist Buffalo Children's Hosp., 1977-78; intern N.E. Ga. Community Mental Health Ctr., Athens, 1980-81; assoc. dir. ctr. health svcs. Vanderbilt U., Nashville, 1981-87, acting dir. ctr. health svcs., 1987-88, dir. ctr. health svcs., 1988—. Lectr. sch. medicine SUNY, Buffalo, 1977-78; gov.'s intern State of Ga., 1978, 79; dir. Maternal Infant Health Outreach Worker Project, 1982-90; adj. lectr. community health sch. nursing Vanderbilt U., 1986—; expert panelist Nat. Resource Ctr. Children Poverty Columbia U., 1987-89, Save The Children Fedn., Westport, Conn., 1992-93, cons.; evaluation advisor Tenn. Commn. Aging, 1991-92; mem. adv. bd. Vanderbilt U. Women's Ctr., 1992-94; presenter in field. Author: (with Mary Porter) Postnatal Home Visit Guide: The Second Year of Life, 1986, (with Toby Barnett) The Emotional Development of Infants: A Discussion Guide for Outreach Workers, 1987; contbr. articles to profl. jours. Active Bring Urban Recycling Nashville Today, Woodbine Community Orgn.; mem. steering com. S.E. Women's Employment Coalition, Lexington, Ky., 1988-91, bd. dirs., 1989-91; bd. dirs. Tenn. Coalition Def. Battered Women, 1990—, Vanderbilt Women's Ctr., 1992—, U. Ky. Coalition on Cancer, Lexington, 1992—. Regents scholar State of N.Y., 1965, 66, 68, 69; grantee Ford Found., 1982-88, J.C. Penny Found., 1983, Robert Wood Johnson Found., 1983-89, van Leer Found., 1986-93, Pub. Welfare Found., 1989-93, Unitarian Universalist Veatch Fund, 1988-93. Mem. APHA, NASW, Nat. Women's Health Network, Internat. Childbirth Edn. Assn., Tenn. Primary Care Assn., Acad. Cert. Social Workers. Home: 313 Peachtree St Nashville TN 37210-4925 Office: Vanderbilt U Ctr Health Svcs Sta 17 Nashville TN 37232-0001

CLINTON, HILLARY RODHAM, senator, lawyer, former First Lady of United States; b. Chgo., Oct. 26, 1947; d. Hugh Ellsworth and Dorothy (Howell) Rodham; m. William J. Clinton, Oct. 11, 1975; 1 child. BA with high honors, Wellesley Coll., 1969; JD, Yale U., 1973; LLD (hon.), U. Ark., Little Rock, 1985, Ark. Coll., 1988, Hendrix Coll., 1992, U. Sunderland, 1993, U. Pa., 1993, U. Mich., 1993, U. Ill., 1994, U. Minn., 1995, San Francisco State U., 1995; D Pub. Svc. (hon.), George Washington U., 1994, U. Md., College Park, 1996; DHL (hon.), Drew U., 1996, Ohio U., 1997. Bar: Ark. 1973, U.S. Dist. Ct. (ea. and we. dists.) Ark. 1973, U.S. Ct. Appeals (8th cir.) 1973, U.S. Supreme Ct. 1975. Atty. Children's Def. Fund, Cambridge, Mass. and Washington, 1973-74; legal cons. Carnegie Coun. on Children, New Haven, 1973-74; counsel, impeachment inquiry staff Judiciary Com. U.S. Ho. of Reps., Washington, 1974; asst. prof. law, dir. Legal Aid Clinic U. Ark. Sch. Law, Fayetteville, 1974-77, asst. prof. law Little Rock, 1979-80; ptnr. Rose Law Firm, Little Rock, 1977-92; First Lady of the U.S., 1993—2001; chair Presdl. Task Force on Nat. Health Care Reform, 1993; mem. U.S. Senate from N.Y., 2001—. Author: Handbook on Legal Rights for Arkansas Women, 1977, 87, It Takes a Village: And Other Lessons Children Teach Us, 1996, Living History, 2003; syndicated columnist Talking It Over, 1995—; contbr. articles to profl. jours. Bd. dirs. Childrens Def. Fund, Washington, 1976-92, chair, 1986-91, Legal Svcs. Corp., Washington, 1977-81, chair, 1978-80; founder, pres., bd. dirs. Ark. Advs. for Children and Families, 1977-84; bd. dirs. Child Care Action Campaign, 1986-92, Nat. Ctr. on Edn. and the Economy, 1987-92, Ark. Children's Hosp., 1988-92, Franklin and Eleanor Roosevelt Inst., 1988-92, Children's TV Workshop, 1989-92, Pub./Pvt. Ventures, 1990-92; chmn. Ark. Edn. Stds. Com., 1983-84; mem. commn. on quality edn. So. Regional Edn. Bd., 1984-92; chair ABA Commn. on Women in the Profession, 1987-91; former hon. pres. Girl Scouts of Am.; mem. adv. bd. HIPPY, 1988-92, bd. dirs.; former hon. chair Pres.' Com. on the Arts and Humanities, U.S. Del., UN Fourth World Conf. on Women, 1995; hon. mem. The Pen and Brush, 1996—. Named Outstanding Layman of Yr. Phi Delta Kappa, 1984, Health Educator of Yr., Ryan White Found., 1995; recipient Lewis Hine award Nat. Child Labor Law Com., 1993, Albert Schweitzer Leadership award Hugh O'Brian Youth Found., 1993, Iris Cantor Humanitarian award UCLA Med. Ctr., 1993, Friend of Family award Am. Home Econs. Assn., 1993, Charles Wilson Lee Citizen Svc. award Com. for Edn. Funding, 1993, Claude D. Pepper award Nat. Assn. for Home Care, 1993, Commitment to Life award AIDS Project L.A., 1994, Disting. Svc., Health Edn. and Prevention award Nat. Ctr. for Health Edn., 1994, First Ann. Eleanor Roosevelt Freedom Fighter award, 1994, Brandeis award U. Louisville Sch. of Law, 1994, Social Justice award United Auto Workers, 1994, Ernie Banks Positivism trophy Emil Verban Meml. Soc., 1994, Humanitarian award Alzheimer's Assn., 1994, Elie Wiesel Found., 1994, Internat. Broadcasting award Hollywood Radio and TV Soc., 1994, Ellen Browning Scripps medal Scripps Coll., 1994, Disting. Pro Bono Svc. award San Diego Vol. Lawyer Program, 1994, HIPPY U.S.A. award, 1994, C. Everett Koop medal Am. Diabetes Assn., 1994, Women's Legal Def. Fund award, 1994, Martin Luther King, Jr. award Progressive Nat. Bapt. Conv., 1994, 30th Anniversary Women at Work award in Pub. Policy, Nat. Commn. on Working Women, 1994, Greater Washington Urban League award, 1995, Servant of Justice award N.Y. Legal Aid Soc., 1995, Presdl. award Bklyn. Coll., 1995, Outstanding Mother award Nat. Mother's Day Com., 1995, Dedication, Annual Survey Am. Law, NYU, 1995, Nat. Breast Cancer Coalition Leadership award, 1995, Faith in Humanity award Nat. Coun. Jewish Women, 1996, NICHE Humanitarian award, 1996, Nat. Assn. Elem. Sch. Prins. Dist. Svc. award, 1996, Grammy award, 1997, Bully Pulpit award Nat. Coun. for Adoption, 1997, Nat. Family Advocate award Parents' Plus Newspaper, 1997, Disting. Svc. to Edn. award Coll. Bd., 1997, Disting. Svc. award Columbia U. Ctr. of Addiction and Substance Abuse, 1997, Commitment to Children award The Elizabeth Glaser Pediat. AIDS Found., 1997, Eleanor Roosevelt Living World award Peace Links, 1997; Paul Harris fellow Rotary Found., 1996. Fellow Am. Bar Found., mem. Ark. Bar Assn., Ark. Trial Lawyers Assn., Ark. Women Lawyers Assn., Am. Trial Lawyers Assn., Pulaski County Bar Assn. Democrat. First First Lady elected to the U.S. Senate and the first woman elected statewide in N.Y. Office: 476 Russell Senate Office Bldg Washington DC 20510*

CLINTON, LOTTIE DRY EDWARDS, retired state agency administrator; b. Wilmington, N.C., July 26, 1937; d. King Solomon Dry and Bessie Theresa Mouzon; m. Edmund Russell Edwards III, Aug. 30, 1954 (dec. Aug. 29, 1969); children: Desireé, Vickie, Edmonia, Cheryl, Michele, Kevin; m. Robert Clinton, June 24, 1993. AAS in Bus. Adminstrn., Cape Fear Cmty. Coll., 1972; student, U. N.C., Wilmington, 1974—75, Ctrl. Piedmont Coll., 1984. Cert. Notary Pub. N.C. From acctg. clk. to supr. shipping and receiving N.C. State Port Authority, Wilmington, 1976—80, supr. open dock, 1980, adminstrv. supr., 1980—83, 1985—98, adminstr. supr. Charlotte Intermodal Terminal, 1983—85; ret., 1998. Apptd. 1898 Wilimgton Race Riot commn. State of N.C., 2002—. Chmn. Svc. to Disabled, Wilmington, 1970—80, Com. on African Am. History, Wilmington, 1980—90; bd. dirs. New Hanover Cmty. Health Ctr., Wilmington, 1997—. Named Woman of Yr. N.C. liberty light chpt., ABWA, 1979; named an Outstanding Citizen, Winston-Salem Alumni Assn., 1995. Democrat. African Methodist Episcopal Zionite. Achievements include appointed mem. of 1898 Wilmington Race Riot Commn. State of NC. Avocations: reading, sewing, gardening, music, beach. Home: 127 Blount Dr Wilmington NC 28411 Personal E-mail: loddec@aol.com.

CLINTON, MARIANN HANCOCK, educational association administrator; b. Dyersburg, Tenn., Dec. 7, 1933; d. John Bowen and Nell Maurine (Johnson) Hancock; m. Harry Everett Clinton, Aug. 25, 1956; children—Carol, John Everett. BMus, Cin. Conservatory Music, 1956; BS, U. Cin., 1956; MMus, Miami U., Oxford, Ohio, 1971. Tchr. music public schs., Hamilton County, Ohio, 1956-57; tchr. voice and piano Butler County, Ohio, 1964—; instr. music Miami U., 1972-75; exec. dir. Music Tchrs. Nat. Assn., Cin., 1977-86. Mng. dir. Am. Music Tchr., 1977-86. Mem. adminstrv. bd. Middletown (Ohio) 1st United Methodist Ch., 1968-72; bd. dirs. Friends of the Sorg Opera House; concert presenter Friends of Music of Charlotte County (Fla.). Mem. Music Educators Nat. Conf., Am. Ednl. Research Assn., Am. Soc. Assn. Execs., Nat. Fedn. Music Clubs, Pi Kappa Lambda, Kappa Delta Pi, Mu Phi Epsilon, Phi Mu. Republican. Home: 714 Macedonia Dr Punta Gorda FL 33950-8013

CLIPSHAM, JACQUELINE ANN, artist; b. Hertfordshire, Eng., July 27, 1936; (parents Am. citizens), July 27, 1936; d. George Frederick and Helene Lucille (Lees) C. BA, Carleton Coll., 1958; postgrad., Universita per Stranieri, Perugia, Italy, 1959; MA, Western Res. U., 1962. Mem. Clay Art Center, Port Chester, N.Y., 1963-66; dir. ceramics program and art workshop CORE Community Center, Sumter, S.C., 1965; mem. faculty Bklyn. Mus. Art Sch., 1968-79, Essex. County Coll., Newark, 1979-80. Mem. Atlantic Gallery, N.Y.C., 1974-83; mem. crafts task force Nat. Endowment for Arts, 1980; Culpeper Found. project coordinator, dept. community edn. Met. Mus. Art, N.Y.C., 1981-82; mem. grants panel for crafts N.J. State Council Arts, 1982; visiting artist, Dayton Hudson, 1987; instr. Carleton Coll., N. Field, Minn., 1987. One-woman show: Willoughby (Ohio) Fine Arts Ctr., 1982, Hunterdon Mus. Art, 2001; works exhibited: Mid-Atlantic States Arts Found., 1987, Schwab Rehabilitation Inst., Chgo., 1987, Cleve. Mus., Bklyn. Mus., Mus. Contemporary Crafts, N.Y.C., Butler Inst. Art, Youngstown, Ohio, Hunterdon Mus. Art, Clinton, N.J., Greenwich House Pottery, N.Y.C., Pratt Inst., Bklyn., Atlantic Gallery, N.Y.C., 1980, Webster Coll., St. Louis, 1981, Clay Art Ctr., Sound Shore Gallery, Port Chester, N.Y., 1983, Gemans Van Eck Gallery, N.Y.C., 1983, Thorpe Intermedia Gallery, Sparkill, N.Y., 1984, N.Y. Pub. Library, 1984; work loaned to Dept. Acad. Affairs, Met. Mus. Art, 1978; cons. dept. Am. art Met. Mus. Art, N.Y.C.; represented in permanent collections: Cleve. Mus. Art, Johnson & Johnson Corp. Collection, New Brunswick, N.J., Mus. Modern Art., N.Y.C., N.Y., Carnegie Mus., Pitts., Pa., N.J. State Mus., Trenton, N.J., Zimmerli Mus., Rutgers U., New Brunswick, N.J., Newark (N.J.) Pub. Libr., Hunterdon Mus., Clinton, N.J., Noyes Mus., Oceanville, N.J., Dance Libr. Rutgers U., Newark, N.J., Alexander Libr., Rutgers U., New Brunswick, N.J. Featured in Women Artists' Book, Women's Caucus for Art Exhbn., 1982, Artists' Books, From the Traditional to the Avant Garde, 1982, also govt. publ. on employment of disabled; reviewer NEA accessibility guidelines; artist in residence Balt. (Md.) Clayworks. Recipient awards for ceramics and sculpture Butler Inst. Am. Art, 1963, 64, 65, nat. merit award for ceramics Mus. Contemporary Crafts, 1966; N.Y. State Council Arts grantee, 1982-83. Mem. Coll. Art Assn., Am. Crafts Council, Women's Caucus for Art (chair panel Nat. Conf.), Images of Disabled People in Western Art), Alumni Assn. Cleve. Inst. Art. Home and Studio: PO Box 387 Califon NJ 07830-0387

CLONTZ, KAREN LYNN, social worker; b. Chapel Hill, NC, Dec. 12, 1975; d. Timothy Clontz and Wendelin Jones McBride. BA in Internat. Studies, U. N.C., Chapel Hill, 1998; MSW, U. Md., Balt., 2001. LCSW Md., Washington. Case worker Bread for the City/Zacchaeus Free Clinic, Washington, 1998—99; social worker intern Yorkwood Health Ctr., Balt., 1999—2000; rsch. asst. Family Connections U Md., Balt., 2000—01; social work intern Adoptions Together, Silver Spring, Md., 2000—01, contract social worker, 2001—; clin. case mgr. PSI Family Svcs., Lanham, Md., 2001—02; social worker Child and Family Svcs. Agy., Washington, 2002—. Recipient Ruth H. Young Endowment award for excellence in child welfare, U. Md., Balt., 2001. Mem.: Nat. Assn. Social Workers. Democrat. Mem. United Ch. Of Christ. Avocations: reading, singing, crafts. Office: Child and Family Svcs Agy 400 6th St SW Washington DC 20024

CLOPINE, MARJORIE SHOWERS, librarian; b. N.Y.C., June 25, 1914; d. Ralph Walter and Angelina (Jackson) Showers; m. John Junior Clopine, June 19, 1948 (div.); m. Frank Mason Storck, Sept. 14, 1985. BA, Pa. State U., 1935; MS, Drexel U., 1936; MS, Columbia U., 1949. Gen. asst. Libr., Drexel U., Phila., 1937-42; asst. libr. Gen. Chem. Div., Allied Chem. Corp., Morristown, N.J., 1943-46; bibliographer U.S. Office Tech. Svcs., Washington, 1946; med. libr. VA Hosp., Washington, 1946-49; asst. libr. U.S. Naval Obs., Washington, 1949-52, libr., 1952-63; assoc. libr. Bethany (W.Va.) Coll., 1967-69. Alice B. Kroeger Meml. scholar Drexel U., 1935-36. Mem. AAUW, LWV, Inst. Retired Execs. and Profls., Women's Resource Ctr. of Sarasota, Friends of the Arts and Scis., Spl. Libraries Assn., Beta Phi Mu. Contbr. articles to profl. jours. Home and Office: 8400 Vamo Rd Apt 540 Sarasota FL 34231-7816

CLOPTON, KAREN VALENTIA, lawyer, president civil services commission; BA with hons., Vassar Coll., 1980; JD, Antioch U., 1983. Bar: Calif. Maguire fellow internat. and comparative labor studies, London, 1984; trial atty NLRB, Washington, San Francisco; counsel Leland, Parachini, Steinberg, Matzger & Melnick LLP, San Francisco, 1998—. Lectr. mgmt. tng. programs emphasizing preventive labor rels.; mem. faculty San Francisco State U. Coll. Extended Learning. Past mem. L.A. Dist. Atty.'s Office Youth Adv. Bd; pres. San Francisco City and County Civil Service Commn. Mem. Lawyers Club of San Francisco (bd. govs.), Calif. Young Lawyers Assn. (Jack Berman Individual award of achievement 1994). Office: Leland Parachini et al 333 Market St Ste 2700 San Francisco CA 94105-2128

CLOSE, BETSY L. state representative; b. Shelton, Wash., May 4, 1950; m. Chris Close; 4 children. BA, Wash. State U., 1972, Ctrl. Wash. U., 1974; MS, Oreg. State U., 1978. Tchr. Wash. State Pub. Schs., 1974—76; grad. tchg. asst. Oreg. State U., Corvallis, 1976—78; instr., job devel. Benton County, 1978—79; tchr. Albany Pub. Schs., 1979—81; mem. Oreg. Ho. of Reps., 1998—. Chair Benton County Rep. Party, 1996—98; bd. dirs. Palestine Rural Fire, 1997—. Republican. Office: 900 Court St North East H-493 Salem OR 97301

CLOSE, ELIZABETH SCHEU, retired architect; b. Vienna, June 4, 1912; came to U.S., 1932, naturalized, 1938; d. Gustav and Helene (Riesz) Scheu; m. Winston A. Close, 1938; children: Anne Miriam Close Ulmer, Roy Michel, Robert Arthur. Student, Technische Hochschule, Vienna, 1931-32; B.Arch., MIT, 1934, M.Arch., 1935; LHD (hon.), U Minn. Coll. of Arch., 2003. Draftsman Oscar Stonorov, Architect, Phila., 1935-36; designer Magney & Tusler, Mpls., 1936-38; ptnr., architect Elizabeth and Winston Close (changed to Close Assos., Inc., 1969), Mpls., 1938-92. Instr. Mpls. Sch. Art, 1936-37; instr. design U. Minn. Sch. Architecture, 1938-39 Prin. works include Garden City Devel, Brooklyn Center, Minn., 1957, Duff House, variety structures Met. Med. Center Complex, 1960-75, Golden Age Homes, 1960, Peavey Tech. Center, Chaska, Minn., 1970, Gray Freshwater Biol. Inst., Orono, Minn., 1974, U. Minn. Music Bldg., Mpls., 1985, Internat. Sch. Minn., Eden Prairie, 1988. Bd. dirs. Civic Orch. Mpls., 1951-68; bd. dirs. Minn. Opera Co.; past pres. New Friends Chamber Music; mem. Commn. on Minn.'s Future. Recipient Honor award Pub. Housing Adminstrn., 1964; hon. mention F.D. Roosevelt Meml. competition, 1960, 25 Yr. award MSAIA, 1988; named Outstanding Woman of Yr., YWCA, 1983, Gold Medal for Lifetime Achievement award Minn. chpt. Am. Inst. of Arch., 2002. Fellow AIA (dir. Mpls. chpt. 1964-69, jury of Fellows 1986-87, recipient Gold medal Minn. chpt., 2002); mem. Minn. Soc. Architects (pres., Honor award 1975), Minn. Hist. Soc. (jury bldg. competition 1986). Home: 1588 Fulham Ave Saint Paul MN 55108-1312

CLOSE, GLENN, actress; b. Greenwich, Conn., Mar. 19, 1947; d. William and Bettine Close; m. Cabot Wade (div.); m. James Marlas, 1984 (div.); 1 child, Annie Maude Starke BA, Coll. William and Mary, 1974. Profl. actress; also accomplished mus. performer (lyric soprano). Co-owner The Leaf and Bean Coffee House, Bozeman, Montana, 1993-94 Joined New Phoenix Repertory Co., 1974; made Broadway debut in Love for Love; other Broadway appearences include The Rules of the Game, The Member of the Wedding, 1974-75, Rex, Barnum, 1980-81 (Tony award nominee), The Real Thing, 1984-85 (Tony award for Best Actress in Drama), Benefactors, 1986, Wine Untouched, Death and the Maiden, 1992 (Drama League N.Y. Distinguished Performance award, 1992, Tony award for Best Actress in Drama, 1992), Sunset Boulevard, 1994-95 (Tony award Lead Actress in a Musical, 1995); other theatre appearences include Uncommon Women and Others, The Singular Life of Albert Nobbs, 1982 (Obie award), Childhood, 1985, one performance oratorio Joan of Arc at the Stake, 1985, Sunset Boulevard (L.A.), 1993-94, The Vagina Monologues, 1998 and other repertory and regional theatres; films include The World According to Garp, 1982 (Acad. award nominee), The Big Chill, 1983 (Acad. award nominee), The Natural, 1984 (Acad. award nominee), Greystoke: The Legend of Tarzan, Lord of the Apes (voice), 1984, The Stone Boy, 1984, Maxie, 1985, Jagged Edge, 1985, Fatal Attraction, 1987, Light Years (voice), 1988, Dangerous Liaisons, 1988, Immediate Family, 1989, Reversal of Fortune, 1990, Hamlet, 1990, Hook (cameo), 1991, Meeting Venus, 1991, The House of the Spirits, 1994, The Paper, 1994, 101 Dalmations, Mars Attacks!, 1996, Air Force One, 1997, Paradise Road, 1997, Cookie's Fortune, 1999, Things You Can Tell Just by Looking at Her, 2000, 102 Dalmatians, 2000, The Safety of Objects, 2001, Pinocchio (voice), 2002, Le Divorce, 2003; TV films include Too Far To Go, 1979, Orphan Train, 1979, The Elephant Man, 1982, Something about Amelia, 1984 (Emmy award nominee), The Elephant's Child (host), 1987, The Emperor's New Clothes (host), 1987, The Legend of Sleepy Hollow (narrator), 1988, Stones for Ibarra, 1988, (also exec. prodr.) Sarah, Plain and Tall, 1991, Skylark, 1993 (Emmy award nomine for Lead Actress in a Miniseries, 1993), Serving in Silence: The Margarethe Cammermeyer Story, 1995 (Emmy award), In the Gloaming, 1997, Sarah, Plain and Tall: Winter's End, 1999, The Ballad of Lucy Whipple, 2001, South Pacific, 2001, The Girl in Hyacinth Blue, 2002, The Lion in Winter, 2003. Recipient Woman of Yr. award Hasty Pudding Theatricals, 1990, Dartmouth Film Soc. award, 1990. Mem. Phi Beta Kappa Office: Creative Artists Agy 9830 Wilshire Blvd Beverly Hills CA 90212-1804*

CLOSSON, HELGA C. councilwoman; b. Oneida, N.Y., July 13, 1945; d. Kurt Adolf and Viola May (Merthiew) Rissman; m. Arthur E. Closson, Jr., Aug. 20, 1963; children: Christine, Tammy, Arthur III, Kurt. Cert. tchrs. aide. Councilwoman City of Oneida, 1991—. Mem. ways and means com. City of Oneida, 1991—96, mem. cable com., 1991—96, mem. fin. com., 1991—96, liaison city water bd.; mem. Woman Polit. Caucus, Nelson, NY, 1992—96. Author poems. Co-founder, chairwoman United Neighbors Orgn., Oneida, 1989—96; vol. Kaffet Civic Ctr., Oneida, 1993—; mem. Dem. Com. Oneida and Madison Counties, 1991—; liaison city water bd.; bd. dirs. City of Oneida Housing Authority; pers. mgmt. course Utica Sch. Commerce, planning and land mgmt. [illegible] Mem. Atlantic States Orgn. Lutheran. Avocations: poetry, reading, teacher's aide, travel, home school teacher. Home: 512 Fitch St Oneida NY 13421-1516

CLOUD, GARY LYNN, food and nutrition services administrator; b. Knoxville, Tenn., July 14, 1945; d. Henry Kelso Cloud. BS in Home Econs., Food and Nutrition, U. Tenn., 1966; MPH, U. N.C., 1972; postgrad., SUNY, Albany, 1988—. Lic. dietitian and pub. health nutritionist, Tenn.; registered Am. Dietetic Assn. Dietetic technician Fort Sander's Presbyn. Hosp., Knoxville, Tenn., 1966; dietetic internship N.Y. State Dept. Mental Hygiene Hudson River State Hosp., Poughkeepsie, N.Y., 1966-67; svc. systems corp. Del Monte, Inc., Bennington, Vt., 1967-70; sr. nutritionist, apprentice nutrition svc. cons. to nutrition svcs. cons. N.Y. State Dept. Health, 1970-73; assoc. nutritionist N.Y. State Bd. Social Welfare, Albany, 1973-76; playground supr. Knox County Dept. Recreation, Knoxville, 1980; chief clin. dietitian II, asst. dietary dept. dir. N.C. Dept. Human Resources, O'Berry Ctr., Goldsboro, N.C., 1980-82; nursing asst. Hillcrest North Nursing Home, Knox County, Tenn., 1988; libr. asst. U. Tenn. Libr.-Reserve Book Rm., 1990; shared facility registered dietitian Hillhaven Corp., Loudon Health Care, Tenn., 1990; auditor RQA Inc. Nat. Retail Quality Evaluators, Darion, Ill., 1994—. Regional supervising dietitian Svc. Sys. Corp., Del Monte Inc., 1967-70; dir. Bur. Nutrition Svcs. Mem. Am. Dietetic Assn., Tenn. Dietetic Assn., Knoxville Dist. Dietetic Assn., Knoxville Nutrition Coun. Home: General Delivery Albany NY 12201-9999

CLOUD, LINDA BEAL, retired secondary school educator; b. Jay, Fla., Dec. 4, 1937; d. Charles Rockwood and Agnes (Diamond) Beal; m. Robert Vincent Cloud, Aug. 15, 1959 (dec. 1985). BA, Miss. Coll., 1959; MEd, U. So. Fla., 1976; EdS, Nova U., 1982; postgrad., Walden U., 1983. Cert. tchr. Fla. Tchr. Ft. Meade (Fla.) Jr.-Sr. HS, 1959-67, 80-89, Lake Wales (Fla.) H.S., 1967—80, drama coach vocal music dir., conversational Spanish composition, creative writing, English lit.; pres. Cloud Aero Svcs., Inc., Babson Park, Fla., 1992—; owner Diamond Firefox Peruvians. Part-time tchr. Spanish, English Polk County Adult Schs., 1960—76; cons. Fla. Assn. Student Couns. Workshops, 1968—81; instr. Spanish Warner So. Coll., Lake Wales, 1974; instr. vocal music, drama, composition Webber Coll., Babson Park; pvt. tutor in field; writer, dir. numerous pageants for schs.; judge beauty pageants, theatre casting; cons. theatre workshops; guest reader local schs., 2002—03. Contbr. articles to profl. jours. and equine publs., poetry to The Color of Thought. Dir. Imogene Theatre, Milton, Fla., 2001; judge various beauty pageants and talent shows; soloist Babson Park Cmty. Ch., 1970—99, First Bapt. Ch., Jay, 1999—; charter mem., bd. dirs. Lake Wales Little Theatre, Inc., 1976; dir. Four Sq. swing choir; entertainer various orgns.; ring announcer Peruvian and Paso Fino Horse Shows, Naples, Fla. State Fair, 1987—88; mem. Defenders Crooked Lake; vol., dir. candy stripers Lakes Wales Hosp., 1973—79. Recipient Best Actress award, Lakes Wales Little Theatre, Inc., 1978—79. Mem.: AAUW, Fla. Ret. Tchrs. Assn., Fla./Santa Rosa County Ret. Educators Assn., Polk Fgn. Lang. Assn., Polk Coun. Tchrs. English, Fla. Coun. Tchrs. English, Nat. Coun. Tchrs. English, Jay Mural Soc. (bd. dirs.), Jay Hist. Soc., Sassy Singers, Babson Park Womans Club, Southeastern Peruvian Horse Club (life). Republican. Avocations: singing, acting, costume design, horseback riding, Peruvian horse exhibitions and parades. Home: Diamond Firefox Peruvians 4405 Spring St Jay FL 32565

CLOUTIER, CATHERINE A. state legislator; Dist. mgr. M & M Assocs.; mem. Del. Ho. of Reps., Dover, 1999-2000, Del. Senate from 5th Dist., Dover, 2001—. Office: PO Box 1401 Dover DE 19903 also: Carvel State Office Bldg 820 N French St Wilmington DE 19801

CLOWNEY, MARY L. educational media specialist, librarian; b. Spartanburg, S.C., Aug. 20; d. Albert Clyde and Louise (Farr) Goode; m. Morris E. Clowney; children: Treva Marie, Shaun Edward. BS in LS, S.C. State U., Orangeburg, 1966; MA in Edn., Seton Hall U., 1987. Cert. pub. libr., sch. libr. Libr. Charleston St. Elem. Sch. Libr., Newark, 1966-67; children's libr. Newark Pub. Libr., 1967-68; libr. Peshine Ave. Sch., Newark, 1968-71, George Washington Carver Sch., Newark, 1971-91, East Side H.S., Newark, 1991-93; head libr. Malcolm X Shabazz H.S., Newark, 1993—. Mem. deaconess bd. Greater Abyssinian Bapt. Ch., also sec.; mem. Christian Advocates for Pub. Edn. Mem. Newark Sch. Libr. Assn. (pres.), Order Eastern Star, Tau Gamma Delta. Democrat. Baptist. Home: 1725 Cedarwood Dr Piscataway NJ 08854-2020 Office: Malcolm X Shabazz HS 80 Johnson Ave Newark NJ 07108-2729

CLOYD, HELEN MARY, accountant, educator; b. Austria-Hungary, 1918; came to U.S., 1922, naturalized, 1928; d. Valentine and Elizabeth (Kretschmar von Kienbusch) Yuhasz; m. George S. Smith, Mar. 4, 1939 (dec.); children: George, Nora; m. Chester L. Cloyd, Apr. 16, 1960 (dec.). BS, Eastern Mich. U., 1953; MA, Wayne State U., 1956; PhD, Mich. State U., 1963. CPA, Mich., Ind., W.Va. Pub. acct. Haskins & Sells, Detroit, 1945-53; tchr. Marine City (Mich.) H.S., 1954-59; instr. acctg. Ctrl. Mich. U., Mt. Pleasant, 1959-60; asst. prof. Wayne State U., Detroit, 1960-61; tchr. Grosse Pointe (Mich.) H.S., 1961-64; assoc. prof. acctg. Ball State U., Muncie, Ind., 1964-71; prof. Shepherd Coll., Shepherdstown, W.Va., 1971-76; assoc. prof. George Mason U., Fairfax, Va. Contbr. numerous articles to publs. Recipient McClintock Writing award CPA, Mich., Ind. W.Va. Mem. AICPA, AAAS, Am. Acctg. Assn., Am. Econs. Assn., Assn. Sch. Bus. Ofcls., Delta Pi Epsilon, Pi Omega Pi, Pi Gamma Mu, Order Eastern Star, White Shrine. Home: PO Box 186 Inwood WV 25428-0186

CLUGSTON, ANGELA M. medical technician; b. Dekalb, Ill., Oct. 22, 1970; AA, El Paso Cmty. Coll., 1993. Cert. ARRT 1993, RDMS 1995, registered sonographer. Staff sonographer SW Ultrasound, El Paso, 1994—96; sr. staff sonographer HealthSouth, Colorado Springs, 1996—. Office: Healthsouth Premier Diagnostics 3920 N Union #130 Colorado Springs CO 80907

CLUNN, PATRICIA ANN, nursing educator, writer; b. Phila. children: Steven, Jeffrey. BSN, U. Pa., 1964, EdD, 1975; MA, Columbia U., 1975. Cert. clin. specialist in child and adolescent mental health psychiat. nursing ANCC. Dir. psychiat. mental health nursing divsn. ANA, Kansas City, Mo., 1979-80; prof. nursing U. Miami, Fla., 1983-98; ret. Author: (with D. Payne) Psychiatric Mental Health Nursing (transl. into Polish 1980), (textbook) Child Mental Health Nursing, 1991. Grantee HHRS, U. Miami, 1985-90, HHRS, 1993-96. Mem. ANA (coun. psychiat. mental health nurses, award for contbn. to direct practice 1979), Sigma Theta Tau. Home: 2406 Tamarind Dr Fort Pierce FL 34949-1508

CLUTTER, MARY ELIZABETH, federal official; b. Charleroi, Pa.; BS, Allegheny Coll., 1953, DSc., 1986, MS, U. Pitts., 1957, PhD in Botany, 1960; Rsch. assoc. Yale U., 1961-73, lectr. biology, 1965-78, sr. rsch. assoc., 1973-78; program dir. NSF, Washington, 1976-81, sect. head, 1981-84, div. dir., 1984-85, 87-88, sr. sci. advisor, 1985-87, asst. dir., 1989—. Mem. AAAS (bd. dirs. 1986-90), Human Frontiers Sci. Program (trustee), Internat. Soc. Plant Molecular Biology, Am. Soc. Cell Biology, Am. Soc. Plant Physiologists, Soc. Devel. Biology, Assn. Women in Sci. Office: Nat Sci Found Biological Sciences 4201 Wilson Blvd Arlington VA 22203-1859

CLYBURN, MIGNON L. commissioner; b. Charleston, S.C., Mar. 22, 1962; BS Banking Fin. & Econs., U. S.C., 1984. Newspaper editor, gen. mgr., publisher Coastal Times, Inc., 1984—; elected Pub. Svc. Commn. S.C., 1998—, Mem.: Nat. Assn. Regulatory Utility Commr., Southeastern [illegible] Regulatory Utility Commrs., Southeastern Publishers Assn., Black Women Entrepreneurs, S.C. Assn. Black Journalists. Office: PO Drawer 11649 Columbia SC 29211

CLYNES, CAROLANN ELIZABETH, realtor; b. Hoboken, N.J., June 30, 1944; d. Merwin Cecil and Marie Dolores Beck; m. Patrick Robert Clynes, June 10, 1967 (div. Oct. 1986); m. Robert Bradford Bourne, Oct. 8, 1988; stepchildren: Jonathan Bourne, Christopher Bourne, Mark Bourne, Sarah Bourne, Susan Bourne, Molly Bourne. Student, Seton Hall U., 1964; BA in History and French, Georgian Ct. Coll., 1965; student, The Sorbonne, Paris, 1966; student in real estate courses, NYU Adult Edn., 1984; student, Inst. Residential Mktg., 1990. Cert. appraiser Nat. Realtors Appraisal Inst., 1987. Sales assoc. Helen Fisher Realty, 1970—72, Peter Farley Realtor, 1972—76; broker, sales assoc. Burgdorff Realtors, 1976—88; dir. sales Lois Schneider Realtor, 1988—94, Murray Hill Farm, 1988—94; broker Burgdorff Realtors, Summit, NJ, 1994—, broker, mgr., v.p. Summit office, 1994—96, v.p. corp. bus. develop., 1996—. Mem. Summit Hist. Preservation Commn., 1995—2003; mem. planning com. Summit Downtown, Inc., 1994—96; mem. capital cabinet Nat. Interfaith Hospitality Network, 1997—. Recipient award, Jr. League of Summit, N.J., 1997, appointment to N.J. Historic Trust, Gov. McGreevey, 2002. Mem.: Real Estate Brokerage Mgrs. Coun. (cert. 1995), N.J. Assn. Realtors Disting. Sales Club (Dist. Sales Club 1991). Democrat. Episcopalian. Avocations: antiques, reading, choral music and opera, French, historic preservation. Home: 130 Pine Grove Ave Summit NJ 07901 Office: Burgdorff Realtors 401 Springfield Ave Summit NJ 07901 Office Phone: 908-522-3003. E-mail: carolann-clynes@burgdorff.com.

CMAR, JANICE BUTKO, home economics educator; b. Pitts., Nov. 10, 1954; d. Edward Michael and Ruth Lillian (Pickard) Butko; m. Dennis Paul Cmar, children: Michael, Nicole. BS, Mansfield U., 1976; MS, Duquesne U., 1990. Home econ. tchr. Duquesne (Pa.) Sch. Dist., 1978-83; special edn. tchr. Allegheny Intermediate Unit, Pitts., 1985-95; home econs. tchr. Peters Twp. Sch. Dist., McMurray, Pa., 1995—. Sponsor Duquesne High Sch., Y-Teens and Future Homemakers Am., 1979-83, Pathfinder Student Coun., Bethel Park, Pa., Mon-Valley Secondary Sch. Yearbook and Prom, Jefferson, Pa. Vol. Allegheny County Dept. Cmty. Svcs., Pitts., 1986—97; mem. com. Allegheny County Dem. Orgn.; elected Borough Jefferson Hills Coun., 1997, 2001—, coun. v.p., 2000, 2002; mem. cmty. adv. panel Hercules Corp., 2000; bd. dirs. South Hills Coun. Govts., 2000. Mem. Am. Fedn. Tchrs., Am. Assn. Family and Consumer Scis., State Assn. Family and Consumer Scis., Allegheny County Assn. Family and Consumer Scis. (pres. 1991-92), Phi Delta Kappa, Alpha Sigma Tau. Democrat. Home: 918 Old Hickory Ln Jefferson Hills PA 15025-3437 Office: 625 E Mcmurray Rd Mc Murray PA 15317-3497

COADY, NICOLE, food service executive; b. W.Va. Student, W.Va.; degree in Baking and Pastry Arts, degree in Culinary Arts, Johnson & Wales U., 1993. Worked with Norman Love and David Robbins Ritz Carlton, Buckhead; chef Finale, Boston. Named One of Industry's Hot New Chefs, Newsweek. Mem.: Nat. Restaurant Assn., U.S. Pastry Alliance, Profl. Pastry Guild New England. Office: Finale 1 Columbus Ave Boston MA 02116

COAKLEY, DEIRDRE, writer; b. Detroit, Aug. 10, 1927; d. Cecil Francis and Elizabeth Kearney Coakley. Grad., Hollywood (Calif.) H.S., 1944. Mem. editl. staff L.A. Examiner, 1943-46; mem. editl. staff various other newspapers L.A., to 1954; advt. exec., mag. editor Las Vegas (Nev.) Sun, 1954-66, Sunday mag. editor, 1977-85; freelance advt. and pub. rels. exec. Las Vegas, 1966-68; pub. rels. exec. Jimmy Snyder Info. Unltd. Tropicana Hotel, Las Vegas, 1968-74; pub. rels. dir. Desert Springs Hosp., Las Vegas, 1974-77; writer, columnist Gadsden (Ala.) Times, 1985—. Editor: The Way it Was: Diary of a Pioneer Woman, 1979-80; author: The MGM Grand Hotel Fire, 1982, Portrait of a City: An Informal History of Gadsden, Alabama 1846-1996, 1996; writer, curator Voices and Images of World War II. Publicist United Way of Etowah County, Gadsden, 1994—; bd. dirs. Metro. Arts Coun., 1988-95, Gadsden Symphony Orch., 1990-96; mem. Gadsden Ctr. Cultural Arts. Mem. Gadsden Art Assn., Etowah Hist. Soc. Democrat. Roman Catholic. Avocation: genealogy. Home: 739 Church Rd Gadsden AL 35904-3143

COAN, PATRICIA A. magistrate judge; b. N.Y.C., July 21, 1945; 2 children. BSN, Georgetown U., 1967; JD, U. Denver, 1981. Bar: Colo. 1982; RN N.Y., Conn., Mont. Pvt. practice, Denver, Colo., 1982-96; magistrate judge U.S. Dist. Ct. for Dist. Colo., Denver, 1996—. Bd. dirs. Colo. Lawyers Health Program. Mem. FBA, Women's Bar Assn., Am. Soc. Law and Medicine, Colo. Bar Assn., Denver Bar Assn., Sigma Theta Tau, Alpha Sigma Nu. Office: 901 19th St Denver CO 80294-1929

COARD, STEPHANIE IRBY, psychologist, researcher; b. Washington, July 20, 1967; d. Robert Leroy and Betty Anne Irby; m. Richard Livingston Coard, Sept. 24, 1994; children: Naya Simone, Aiyana Joi, Skyler Chayton. BA in bus. mgmt., BA in psychology, NC State U., 1985—89; MSEd, U. of Pa., 1990—91; PhD, Columbia U., 1991—97. Clin. staff assoc. Columbia U., NY State Psychiat. Inst., New York, NY, 1994—96; pediatric clin. pre-doctoral intern Divsn. of Behavioral and Devel. Pediat., U. of Md. Med. Ctr., Baltimore, Md., 1996—97; postdoctoral fellow Divsn. of Adolescent Medicine, U. of Md. Med. Ctr., Baltimore, Md., 1997—98; asst. prof. of psychiatry NY U. Sch. of Medicine, New York, NY, 1998—2002; rsch. scholar Duke U., Ctr. for Child and Family Policy, Durham, NC, 2002—. Dir. Cultural Strategies for Parenting Project: Black Parenting Strengths and Strategies (BPSS) Program, focuses on the transl., implementation and testing of clinically efficacious interventions into cmty. settings, Durham, NC, 2000—. Contbr. articles to profl. jours. Scientist Devel. award, Nat. Inst. for Mental Health, 2000—. Mem.: APA, Soc. for Prevention Rsch., Black Child Devel. Institute, Soc. for Rsch. in Adolecence, Soc. for Rsch. in Child Devel., Assn. of Black Psychologists, Jack and Jill of Am., Inc., Alpha Kappa Alpha Sorority, Inc. Avocations: travel, community and church service. Office: Duke University 2024 W Main St Room C223 Box 90545 Durham NC 27708-0545 E-mail: coard@duke.edu.

COATES, DIANNE KAY, social worker; b. Adrian, Mich., Jan. 4, 1945; Student, Jackson Bus. U., 1962-63; AA with honors, Macomb C.C., Warren, Mich., 1977; BA with high distinction, Madonna Coll., 1979; MSW, Wayne State U., 1982; postgrad., Internat. Grad. Sch., 1984, Ea. Mich. U., 1989. Cert. social worker, Mich. Nat. svc. officer Mil. Order of the Purple Heart, Detroit, 1973-80; psychology technician VA Med. Ctr., Allen Park, Mich., 1980-84; clin. cons. HOMEBASE, Detroit, 1983-85; clin. social worker Cmty. Counseling Assocs., Adrian, 1983, Roseville, Mich., 1983-87, Ypsilanti (Mich.) Regional Psychiat. Hosp., 1987-90, Southgate (Mich.) Regional Ctr. for the Developmentally Disabled, 1990-92, 92-96, Lafayette Clinic, 1992; from intake/admissions/discharge coord. to dir. social work svcs. Southgate Ctr., 1996—2001; clin. social worker Northville Psychiat. Hosp., 2001—02, acting dir. social svcs., 2002—03; clin. social work mgr. Walter Reuther Psychiat. Hosp., 2003—. Group counselor Survivors of Homicide, Detroit, 1981-82; vol. HAVEN, Pontiac, Mich., 1986-87; internat. exch. counselor Edn. Found. Fgn. Study, 1987-92; field instr. Wayne State U., 1988—; ind. contract therapist Renaissance West Cmty. Mental Health Svcs. Clinic, Detroit, 1988-89, Caknipe-Kovach Assocs., 1988-92; area rep. Ednl. Resource Devel. Trust, 1991-94 Recipient Ann. Disting. Svc. award LA MOPH Dept. of Mich., 1992. Mem. NASW (bd. cert. diplomate), Acad. Cert. Social Workers, Assn. State Employed MSW's (v.p. 1991-93), Mich. Mental Health Assn., Mich. Assn. Mental Health Profls., Social Work Assn. Madonna Coll. (co-founder), Wayne State U. Alumni Assn., Bus. and

Profl. Women, VietnamVets. Am. (hon. life assoc. mem.), Met. Svc. Officers Assn. (pres. 1990-92), Ladies Aux. Mil. Order of Purple Heart (region 2 v.p. 1985-86, nat. membership officer 1995-96), Ladies Aux. VFW, DAV Aux. Home: 1502 Elias St Westland MI 48186-4919 Office: Walter Reuther Psychiatric Hosp 30901 Palmer Westland MI 48186

COATES, VERONA AGNES, secondary school educator; b. Boyd, Oreg., June 21, 1916; d. Willard Eli and Agnes Viola (Hastings) Adkisson; m. William Stanley Coates, June 29, 1941; children: William, Anne Olson, Jane Ormiston, David. AA, Sacramento Jr. Coll., Sacramento, Calif., 1936; BS, Oreg. State Univ., 1940, MS, 1942. Cert. tchr. Oreg., Calif. Extension asst. Oregon State Univ., Corvallis, 1944-45; adult edn. tchr. Hayward (Calif.) Sch. Dist., 1950-59; jr. high tchr. Mt. Eden Sch. Dist., Hayward, 1960-63, Union Sch. Dist., San Jose, Calif., 1963-69, Petaluma (Calif.) Sch. Dist., 1969—; vocational edn. tchr. Sonoma County, Santa Rosa, Calif., 1977-82; fashion merchandising tchr. Santa Rosa Jr. Coll., 1978-80; sub. tchr. Sonoma County, Santa Rosa, Calif. Active Self Help for Heard of Hearing, Napa, Calif., 1990—. Recipient Dist. Woman of Yr., Calif. State Leg., 1991. Mem. Am. Assn. Univ. Women, Am. Home Econs. Assn., Calif. Tchrs. Assn., Nat. Edn. Assn. Democrat. Protestant. Avocations: flower arranging, quiltmaking. Home: 203 Nicole Way Napa CA 94558-1668

COBB, CLARA JO, pre-school special education educator; b. Decatur, Ala., Aug. 26, 1969; d. Clarence Handley and Sydney Louise Bolte; m. Charles Beverley Cobb, July 19, 1997; children: Sydney Elizabeth, Beverly Jo. BS, Auburn U., 1991; MS in Edn. Behavioral Disorders, Armstrong Atlantic, Savannah, Ga., 1996. Mem.: Coun. for Children with Comm. Disorders, Coun. for Children with Behavioral Disorders, Coun. for Exceptional Children, AASU Alumni Assn., Auburn Alumni Assn. Baptist. Office: Pulaski Elem Sch 5330 Montgomery St Savannah GA 31405 E-mail: ccb3cobbs@bellsouth.net.

COBB, KAY BEEVERS, state supreme court justice, former state senator; m. Larry Cobb; children: Barbara Cobb Murphy, Elizabeth Cobb DeBusk. BS, Miss. U. Women; JD, U. Miss. Former spl. asst. atty. gen. North Miss.; assoc. justice Miss. Supreme Ct. Mem. Nat. Alliance/Model State Drug Laws, Vets. Aux., C. of C. Baptist. Office: Miss Supreme Ct PO Box 117 450 High St Jackson MS 39205 Home: PO Box 604 Oxford MS 38655-0604

COBB, ROWENA NOELANI BLAKE, real estate broker; b. Kauai, Hawaii, May 1, 1939; d. Bernard K. Blake and Hattie Kanui Yuen; m. James Jackson Cobb, Dec. 22, 1962; children: Shelly Ranelle Noelani, Bret Kimo Jackson. BS in Edn., Bob Jones U., 1961; broker's lic., Vitousek Sch. Real Estate, Honolulu, 1981. Lic. real estate broker, Honolulu; cert. residential specialist, 1995-. Med. supr. Hawaii Med. Svc. Assn., 1964-65, 66-68; bus. mgr. Micronesian Occupl. Ctr., Koror Palau, 1968-70; prin. broker Cobb Realty, Lihue, Hawaii, 1983—; sec. Neighbor Island MLS Svc., Honolulu, 1985-87, vice chmn., 1987-88; chmn. MLS Hawaii, Inc., Honolulu, 1988-90. Assoc. editor Jour. Entymology, 1965-66. Sec. Koloa Cmty. Assn., 1981-98, pres., 1989, bd. dirs. 2002—; mem. Hoi'Ke Pub. TV, 1998—, treas., 1999, v.p., 2002, pres. 2000-2002, 2003; vice chair Kauai Schs. Adv. Coun., 1995-98, pres., 2000; mem. adv. bd. KKCR Radio, 2000; bd. dirs. Kekahu Found, 1999-2001, Kauai United Way, 2003; chmn. Kauai Ctr. Arts, Edn. and Tech., 2003. Mem. Nat. Assn. Realtors (grad. Realtors Inst., cert. residential specialist), Hawaii Assn. Realtors (cert. tchr., state bd. dirs. 1984, v.p. 1985, dir. 1995-96), Kauai Bd. Realtors (v.p. 1984, pres. 1985, bd. dirs. 1995-97, treas. 1999, Realtor Assoc. of Yr. award 1983, Realtor of Yr. award 1986), Kauai C. of C., Soroptomists (bd. dirs. Lihue chpt. 1986-89, treas. 1989). Avocations: reading, music, travel. Office: PO Box 157 Koloa HI 96756-0157 E-mail: ro@jrcobb.net.

COBB, RUTH, artist; b. Boston, Feb. 20, 1914; d. Charles Edward and Bessie (Cohen) C.; m. Lawrence Kupferman, Apr. 29, 1937; children: Nancy Rose, David. Diploma, Mass. Coll. Art, 1935. One-woman shows include Shore Galery, Boston, 1958, 60, 63, 65, 70, DeCordova Mus., Lincoln, Mass., 1955, Art Unlimited Gallery, San Francisco, 1961, Cober Gallery, N.Y.C., 1962, 65, 67, McNay Mus., San Antonio, 1966, Phila. Art Alliance, 1962, Galerie Moos, Montreal, Que., Can., 1969, Witte Mus., San Antonio, 1967, Harold Ernst Gallery, Boston, 1974, 75, 76, Midtown Gallery, N.Y.C., 1981, 82, Foster Harmon Gallery, Sarasota, 1984, Francesca Anderson Gallery, Boston, 1984, 87, Cen. Pl. Galleries, Bangor, Maine, 1988, Thayer Acad., Braintree, Mass., 1994, Cataumet (Mass.) Art Ctr., 1997, A.R.A. Gallery, Hamilton, Mass., 1999, Women Studies Rsch. Ctr. Brandeis U.; featured in exhbn. Boston's Honored Artists, Danforth Mus., Framingham, Mass., 1995; represented in permanent collections Boston Mus. Fine Arts, Brandeis U., Butler Inst. Am. Art, Munson-Williams-Proctor Inst., Addison Gallery Am. Art, Va. Mus. Fine Arts, DeCordova Mus., Tufts U.; featured in TV program Artist At Work, 1981; work featured in Am. Artist mag., 1979, Newton mag., 2004. Recipient awards Pa. Acad. Fine Arts, 1967, awards Allied Artists N.Y.C., 1966 Mem. Am. Watercolor Soc. (award), New Eng. Watercolor Soc., Allied Artists Am. (award), NAD (award)

COBB, SHIRLEY ANN DODSON, public relations consultant, journalist; b. Oklahoma City, Jan. 1, 1936; d. William Ray and Irene Dodson; m. Roy Lampkin Cobb, Jr., June 21, 1958; children: Kendra Leigh, Cary William, Paul Alan. BA in Journalism with distinction, U. Okla., 1958, postgrad., 1972, Jacksonville U., 1962. Info. specialist Pacific Missile Test Ctr., Point Mugu, Calif., 1975-76; reporter, sptly. editor Religion and Fashion News Chronicle, 1977-81; cons. pub. rels., cable tv, telecomm. Camarillo, Calif., 1977—; media mgr. pub. info. cable TV and telecom. City of Thousand Oaks, Calif., 1983-99. Contbr. articles to profl. jours. Pres. Point Mugu Officers' Wives Club, 1975-76; trustee Ocean View Sch. Bd., 1976-79; bd. dirs. Camarillo Hospice, 1983-85, Long Term Care of Ventura County, Inc., 2001-03; sec. Ednl. TV for Conejo, 1997-98, pres., 1998-2000, bd. dirs., 1997-2002; vice chair Greater Thousand Oaks Telecmty., 1999-2000; treas. Thousand Oaks Rep. Women Federated, 2001-03, pres., 2004; with Ventura County Leadership Acad., 1999-2002; bd. dirs. LWV Ventura County, 1999-2003, comms. dir., 2002-03. Recipient Spot News award San Fernando Valley Press Club, 1979, First Pl. spl. program Calif. Assn. Pub. Info. Ofcls., 1985, Helen Putnam award League of Calif. Cities, 1989, Telecom. Proj. award, League of Calif. Cities Telecom., 1998, 1st place award Best Practice award Govt., Bus., Edn. Tech Expo '98. Mem. Pub. Rels. Soc. Am. (L.A. chpt. liaison 1991), Calif. Assn. Pub. Info. Ofcls. (pres. 1989-90, Paul Clark Lifetime Achievement award 1993), Conejo Valley Hist. Soc. (sec. 1993-96, co-chmn. oral history com. 2001-, chair 2003-, bd. dirs. 2003-), Las Posas Country Club, Spanish Hills Country Club, Town Hall of Calif. Club, Phi Beta Kappa, Chi Omega (v.p. 1957-58). Republican. Home and Office: 2481 Brookhill Dr Camarillo CA 93010-2112 E-mail: cobbweb@aol.com.

COBB, SUE MCCOURT, lawyer, educator; b. Los Angeles, Aug. 18, 1937; d. Benjamin Arnold and Ruth (Griffin) McCourt; m. Charles E. Cobb, Jr., Feb. 28, 1959; children: Christian McCourt, Tobin Templeton. BA, Stanford U., 1959; JD, U. Miami, 1978. Bar: Fla. 1978, U.S. Dist. Ct. (so. dist.) Fla. 1980, D.C. 1989. Tchr., Crystal Springs Sch. for Girls, Hillsborough, Calif., 1960-68; assoc. Greenberg, Traurig, Hoffman, Lipoff, Rosen & Quentel, P.A., Miami, Fla., 1978-83, ptnr., 1983—; Martindale Hubbard a/v rating; chmn. bd. Fed. Res. Bank Atlanta, Miami br., 1984, 86, 88. Chmn., Dade County Super Bowl Authority, 1982-87; bd. dirs. Ransom-Everglades Sch., 1976-86; dir. United Way Dade County. Mem. ABA, Dade County Bar Assn., Nat. Assn. Bond Lawyers, Boca Raton Club, Ocean Reef Club, Grove Isle Club, Deering Bay Club. Republican.

COBB-HUNTER, GILDA, state representative, social worker; b. Grifford, Fla., Nov. 5, 1952; d. Selvin Cobb Sr. and Nina (Walker) Cobb; m. Terry Keith Hunter, July 30, 1975. BS, Fla. A&M U., 1973; MA, Fla. State U., 1978. LCSW S.C., 1990. Social work adminstr.; state rep. dist. 66 S.C. Legis., 1992—, mem. ways and means com. Bd. dirs. Planned Parenthood S.c.; mem. develop. adv. com. Fed. Res. Fifth Dist. Commn.; mem. Dem. Legis. Campaign Com., Orangeburg County Dem. Party; nat. com. woman Dem. Nat. Com. Mem.: NAACP, Nat. Assn. Social Workers, S.C. Am. Civil Liberties Union. Democrat. Baptist. Office: State Capitol 309C Blatt Bldg Columbia SC 29211 Home: 112 Estate Ct Orangeburg SC 29115 E-mail: gch@scstatehouse.net.

COBERLY, MARGARET, psychologist, educator; d. Charles Wheeler Coberly and Elizabeth Chandler Stephens; m. Harry Martin Eichelberger, III, Sept. 9, 1968 (div. 1981); children: Ariana Eichelberger, Ian Eichelberger. RN, St. Francis Sch. Nursing, San Francisco, 1965; BS, SUNY, Albany, 1989; MA, U. Hawaii, 1992, PhD, 1996. RN Calif., Hawaii. Staff and charge nurse Met. Hosp. Trauma Ctr., N.Y.C., 1978—81, Calif. Hosp. Med. Ctr., L.A., 1981—84; case mgr. Hospice Hawaii, Honolulu, 1989—93, dir. rsch., 1997—2001; dir. nurses, v.p., co-owner Respite Care Hawaii, Honolulu, 1993—96; faulty U. Phoenix, Honolulu, 1998—2000; psychology prof. U. Hawaii Windward, Kaneohe, 1999—. Bd. dirs. Jamyang Found., Honolulu; cons., tchr. in field. Author: Sacred Passage: How to Provide Fearless, Compassionate Care for the Dying, 2002, 2003; contbr. chapters to books, articles to profl. jours. Sec.-treas. Internat. Found. Transpersonal Studies, Honolulu, 1998—. Mem.: APA, Sakyadhita Assn. Buddhist Women (treas. 1991—). Achievements include development of unique system of tracking the stages of dying by using the ancient Tibetan Buddhist teachings about death. Avocation: writing. Office: Univ Hawaii Windward 45-720 Kea ahala Rd Kaneohe HI 96744

COBLE, WILMA LORETTA, real estate investor, property management; b. McCaskill, Ark., Jan. 14, 1934; d. Willis and Jodie Olla (Stuart) Goff; m. Clyde Thomas Coble, Aug. 11, 1956; 1 child, Clyde Craig. BS, U. Md., 1972. Bookkeeper Singer Sewing Machine Co., Washington, 1951-56; sec. Nat. Security Agy., Fort George G. Meade, Md., 1956-68; sch. tchr. D.C. Pub. Schs., Washington, 1971-76; real estate sales profl. Douglas Realty, Inc., Washington, 1976-81; pvt. practice real estate investment and property mgmt. Washington, 1976—. Tchr. adv. bd. D.C. Pub. Schs., 1974-76. Vol. campaign worker Ted Kennedy Presdl. Campaign, Washington, 1980; pres. Property Owners Assn. of Arundel-on-the-Bay, Annapolis, Md., 1981-84, chmn. bd. dirs., 1986-88; vol. The White House, Washington, 1993—. Democrat. Avocations: horseback riding, reading, gardening, traveling, shopping. Home: 9016 Levelle Dr Chevy Chase MD 20815-5608

COBURN, MARJORIE FOSTER, psychologist, educator; b. Salt Lake City, Feb. 28, 1939; d. Harlan A. and Alma (Ballinger) Polk; m. Robert Byron Coburn, July 2, 1977; children: Polly Klea Foster, Matthew Ryan Foster, Robert Scott Coburn, Kelly Anne Coburn. B.A. in Sociology, UCLA, 1960; Montessori Internat. Diploma honor grad. Washington Montessori Inst., 1968, M.A. in Psychology, U. No. Colo., 1979; Ph.D. in Counseling Psychology, U. Denver, 1983. Licensed clin. psychologist. Probation officer Alameda County (Calif.), Oakland, 1960-62, Contra Costa County (Calif.), El Cerrito, 1966, Fairfax County (Va.), Fairfax, 1967; dir. Friendship Club, Orlando, Fla., 1963-65; tchr. Va. Montessori Sch., Fairfax, 1968-70; spl. edn. tchr. Leary Sch., Falls Church, Va., 1970-72, sch. adminstr., 1973-76, [illegible] San Diego, 1976-77, Coburn Montessori Sch., Colorado Springs, Colo., 1977-79; pvt. practice psychotherapy, Colorado Springs, 1979-82, San Diego, 1982— ; cons. spl. edn., agoraphobia, women in transition. Mem. Am. Psychol. Assn., Am. Orthopsychiat. Assn., Phobia Soc., Council Exceptional Children, Calif. Psychol. Assn., San Diego Psychological Assn., The Charter 100, Mensa. Episcopalian. Lodge: Rotary. Contbr. articles to profl. jours.; author: (with R.C. Orem) Montessori: Prescription for Children with Learning Disabilities, 1977. Office: 836 Prospect St Ste 101 La Jolla CA 92037-4206 E-mail: mcoburn@san.rr.com.

COCAIN HASTLER, CYNTHIA LUCILLE, artist, graphic designer; b. Akron, Ohio, Aug. 18, 1956; d. Harry William Vincent and Sally Lucille (Houghland) Cocain; m. Ronald Ernest Hastler, Oct. 9, 1979. BFA in Drawing, U. Akron, 1983. Coord. display design Lighthouse Pools, Cuyahoga Falls, Ohio, 1975-77; 3-D casting drafter Indsl. Artcraft, Akron, Ohio, 1977-80; freelance graphicist, potrait artist R.C.H. Studios, Akron, 1980—. Art dir. Shrine Circus, Tadmor Temple, Akron, 1993-98; cons., advisor home restoration Ohio Hist. Soc., Columbus, 1980, Summit County Hist. Soc., Akron, 1980; cons. Harvey Whitehill Painting, Sonoma, Calif., 1991—; pvt. chef gourmet cooking, 1999—. Contbr. articles to popular mags.; artist logos for small bus. Assoc. fellow Bee Sharp Prodns., 1995—. Avocations: gardening, restoring antiques. Office: R C H Studios 294 Grove St Akron OH 44302-1625

COCCHIARELLA, VICKI MARSHALL, state legislator; b. Livingston, Mont., Dec. 19, 1949; d. James and Ruth E. (Officer) Marshall; m. Larry Ray Cocchiarella, 1973; children: Cara Jo, Michael James. BA, U. Mont., 1978, MA, 1985. Property mgr., 1975—; teaching asst. U. Mont., 1979-80, adminstrv. clk., 1981-89; mem. Mont. Ho. of Reps., 1989-98, mem. interim com. state employee compensation; mem. Environ. Qual. Council, 1993-, Mont. Senate, Dist. 32, Helena, 1998—. Bd. dirs. Child & Family Resource Coun. Mem. Mont. Pub. Employees Assn. (former bd. dirs., former 1st v.p., pres. 1987—). Democrat. Office: Mont State Senate State Capitol Helena MT 59620

COCCHIARELLI, MARIA, artist, educator; b. Bklyn., Apr. 10, 1956; d. Joseph Paul and Mary Jannace Cocchiarelli. BA in Art History, Syracuse U., 1978; BA in Art, CUNY, N.Y.C., 1983, MS in Art Edn., 1985, postgrad., 2002—. Lic. art tchr. grades K-12, N.Y. Instr., curator Queens (N.Y.) Coll. Ctr. for Improvement of Edn., 1983-84, 88-89; instr. Museum's Collaborative and N.Y.C. Youth Bur., Queens, 1984-85; mus. educator The Queens Mus., 1985-87; journalist Cover Arts Jour., N.Y.C., 1986-88; curator Mission Graphics Support Gallery, N.Y.C., 1987-88; artist, tchr. Inst. for Contemporary Arts/P.S.1 Mus., L.I. City, N.Y., 1989-91; artist in residence Children's Mus. Manhattan, N.Y.C., 1989-93, N.Y. Found. for Arts, N.Y.C., 1989-93; edn. dir. Socrates Sculpture Park, L.I. City, N.Y., 1991-93; curator edn. U. Wyo. Art Mus., Laramie, 1993-96; dir. edn. Kemper Mus. Contemporary Art & Design, Kansas City, Mo., 1996-97; programs dir. Grand Arts, Kansas City, Mo., 1997-98; watercolor instr. summer H.S. residency program Kansas City Art Inst., 1999—2002; residence Mo. Arts Coun., 1999—2001; garden artist, project developer Gem Theater and Linwood YWCA Youth Arts Garden, Kansas City, 1999—2002; K-5 and H.S. art tchr. Kansas City (Mo.) Sch. Dist., 2000—, exhbn. planner, 2001; artist in residence P.S. #6 Manhattan, 2003—. Pub. arts commns. for N.Y.C. Pub. Sch. Commn./One Percent for the Arts, Science City/Union Sta., Kans. City. Nebr. Arts Coun., numerous others, Omaha, Assn. Queens Artists, 1994, one-woman shows include The Skyline, L.I. City, 1987, Nancy Bratton Gallery, N.Y.C., 1989, YWCA, Bklyn., 1993, Coal Creek, Laramie, Wyo., 1996, Prospero, Kansas City, 1999, Blue Bird, 1999, Commerce Bankshares, 1999, Muddy's, 1999, First Bank, Warrenton, Mo., 1999, State of the Art, 2000, Kansas City, Mo., 2000, exhibited in group shows at Clocktower Mus., N.Y.C., 1991, Gallery 72, Omaha, 1991—96, Tribeca 148 Gallery, N.Y.C., 1993, Wyo. Arts Coun. Traveling Exhibi, 1994—95, U. Wyo. Art Mus., Laramie, 1994, Urban Ctr. Mcpl. Art Soc., N.Y.C., 1994, Yale U. Art Gallery, New Haven, 1995, Bennington (Vt.) Ctr. for the Arts, 1995, Nicyolaysen Art Mus., Casper, Wyo., 1996, Late Show Gallery, Kansas City, 1998, Manelyst, Oslo, 1999, Leedy Volkos Art Ctr., Kansas City, 1999, State of the Arts, 1999—2000, Museo Internazionale dell'Immagine Postale, Comune di Belvedere Ostrense, Italy, 2001, Coll. of Art, Seoul, 2001, permanent collections, Hallmark Cards Inc., Kansas City, Wyo. State Mus., Cheyenne, Omaha Children's Mus. . Exhbn. planner UN World Habitat, N.Y.C., 1988; instr., organizer Environ. Arts, Laramie, Wyo., 1996; lectr., cons. J. Paul Getty Conf., Omaha, 1996; mem. steering com. Cmty. Anti-Violence Initiative, Kansas City, Mo., 1996-2001. Mem. NOW, Am. Assn. Mus., Nat. Orgn. Italian-Am. Women. Avocations: swimming, writing, singin. Studio: 184-36 Avon R Jamaica NY 11432

COCCO, JACQUELINE M. state legislator; b. Bridgeport, Conn. Grad., St. Vincent's Sch. Nursing. Mem. Conn. Ho. of Reps., Hartford, 1987—, chmn. family and workplace com., mem. labor and pub. employees com., pub. health com., asst. majority leader. Mem. Charter Rev. Com., 1988-89; vis. nurse. Mem. Dem. Town Com., 1984—; mem. Bd. Humane Affairs, 1986-90. Home: 93 Heppenstall Dr Bridgeport CT 06604-1007 Office: Conn Ho of Reps Legislative Office Bldg Hartford CT 06106

COCHRAN, BETH, gifted and talented educator; b. New Orleans, La., Nov. 2, 1951; d. Hugh Greene Smith, Kathryn Ann Smith; m. Cole Cochran; children: Michael, Steven. B in Music Edn., Ctrl. Mo. State U., 1973; MEd, U. Kans., 1999. Cert. Vocal Music Edn., K-12 1973, Gifted Edn. 2001. Tchr. vocal music Lexington Sch. Dist., Lexigton, Mo., 1973—75; tchr. elem. music North Kansas City Schs., Kansas City, Mo., 1975—77; dir. edn. Tokyo Bapt. Ch., Tokyo, 1984—90; dir. choral music Piper Sch. Dist., Kansas City, Kans., 1990—2000; tchr. vocal music Appleton City Schools, Appleton City, Mo., 2000—02; gifted resource tchr. Appleton City Schs., Appleton City, Mo., 2001—02, Butler Schs., Butler, Mo., 2002—. Min. music First Bapt. Ch., Adrian, Mo., 2001—. Mem.: Gifted Assn. Mo. Baptist. Home: 503 N High St Butler MO 64730 Office: Butler R-5 Schs 4 South High St Butler MO 64730 E-mail: cbcochran@osagevalley.net.

COCHRAN, CAROLYN, library director; b. Tyler, Tex., July 13, 1934; d. Sidney Allen and Eudelle (Frazier) C.; m. Guy Milford Eley, June 1, 1963 (div.). BA, Beaver Coll., 1956; MA, U. Tex., 1960; MLS, Tex. Woman's U., 1970. Libr. Canadian (Tex.) High Sch., 1970-71; rep. United Food Co., Amarillo, Tex., 1971-72; libr. Bishop Coll., Dallas, Tex., 1975-76, St. Mary's Dominican, New Orleans, 1976-77, DeVry Inst. Tech., Irving, Tex., 1978-98, libr. dir. emeritus, 1998—. With Database Searching Handicapped Individuals, Irving, 1983—; vol. bibliographer Assn. Individuals with Disabilities, Dallas, 1982-85. Mem. Am. Coalition of Citizens with Disabilities, 1982-85, Assn. Individuals with Disabilities, 1982-86, Vols. in Tech. Assistance, 1985—, Radio Amateur Satellite Corp., 1985-86; sponsor 500, Inc., 1988-95. Reviewer Libr. Jour., 1974, Dallas Morning News, 1972-74, Amarillo Globe-News, 1970-71. Mem. Dallas regional adv. com. Tex. Commn. for the Blind, 2001. HEW fellow, 1967; honored Black History Collection, Dallas Morning News, Bishop Coll., Dallas, 1973. Mem. ALA, Spl. Libr. Assn., Am. Coun. of Blind (sec. Dallas chpt. 1997-99), Toastmistress Club (pres. 1982-83) (Irving). E-mail: carolyn_cochran@sbcglobal.net.

COCHRAN, GLORIA GRIMES, retired pediatrician; b. Washington, June 24, 1924; d. Paul DeWitt and Muriel Ann (Quackenbush) Grimes; m. Winston Earle Cochran, June 10, 1950 (dec. June 19, 2003); children: Edith Ann, Winston Earle, Jr., Donald Lee, Robert Edward. BS in Zoology, Duke U., 1945; MD, 1949; MPH, Johns Hopkins Sch. Hygiene, Balt., 1979. Diplomate Nat. Bd. Med. Examiners, 1950, Am. Bd. Pediatrics, 1958. Asst. resident Pathology Boston Children's Hosp., Boston, 1949—50, asst. resident Pediatrics, 1950—51; chief resident Pediatrics Charlotte Memorial Hosp, Charlotte, NC, 1952—53; clinic pediatrician, sch. med. advisor health dept. Montgomery County, 1955-65; fellow in pediat. habilitation St. Christopher Hosp. for Children, Phila., 1965-66; assoc. dir. Child Development Clinic Baylor Med. Sch., Tex. Children's Hosp., 1966-72; dir. Northern Va. Child Devel. Field Svcs. Bur. Child Health State Health Dept. Commonwealth Va., 1972-76; coord. Handicapped Svcs. Children's Hosp. Nat. Med. Ctr., Washington, 1976-78; acting chief Divsn. of Svcs. to Children with Spl. Needs Bur. Sch. Health Svcs., Washington, 1982-89; retired, 1989. Cons. Head Start Program, Md., Va., Tex., Pa., D.C., 1965-89; bd. mem. Ctrs. for Handicapped, Silver Spring, Md., 1982-89; Child Health com. Med. Soc. D.C., Washington, 1976-91. Producer, editor: (teaching film) Challenge for Habilitation: The Child with Congenital Rubella Syndrome, 1976. Steering com. Rock Days Inter-Church Camp, Washington, 1978-82; bd. mem. Open Door Cmty. Ctr., Columbus, Ga., 1993-94; co-chair curriculum com. Columbus Coll. Acad. of Life Long Learning, Columbus, 1994. Mem. Am. Assn. Mental Retardation, Am. Med. Women's Assn., Assn. for Retarded Citizens, Am. Acad. Cerebral Palsy, Am. Acad. Pediatrics, Phi Beta Kappa, Delta Omega. Democrat. Methodist. Avocations: travel, gardening. Home: 800 Canadian Trails Dr Apt 346 Norman OK 73072-7658

COCHRAN, JACQUELINE LOUISE, management executive; b. Franklin, Ind., Mar. 12, 1953; d. Charles Morris and Marjorie Elizabeth (Rohrbaugh) C. BA, DePauw U., 1975; MBA, U. Chgo., 1977. Fin. analyst Pan Am World Airways, N.Y.C., 1977-79, Gen. Bus. Group W. R. Grace & Co., N.Y.C., 1979-80; sr. fin. analyst Gen. Bus. Group div. W. R. Grace & Co., N.Y.C., 1980-81, mgr. fin. analysis, 1981-82; dir. fin. planning and analysis Gen. Bus. Group div. W. R. Grace & Co., N.Y.C., 1982 85, v.p. fin. Am. Breeders Svc. div. DeForest, Wis., 1985-87, v.p. feed ops. Grace Animal Svc. div., 1987-89, gen. mgr., chief ops. officer SoftKat div. Chatsworth, Calif., 1990; pres. SoftKat div. W.R. Grace & Co., Chatsworth, Calif., 1990-92; vice-chmn., chief adminstrv. officer Baker & Taylor, Inc., Chatsworth, Calif., 1992, pres. SoftKat div., 1992. Exec. cons. Jacqueline Cochran Cons., Westlake Village, Calif., 1993, 94; gen. mgr. Attica Cybernetics, Inc., Chatsworth, Calif., 1995; pres., owner CorporateLinks, Westlake Village, Calif., 1996—. Bd. visitors DePauw U., 1993-96. Recipient Women of Distinction award Madison (Wis.) YWCA, 1987; named to Acad. Women Achievers YWCA N.Y., 1984. Mem. Omicron Delta Epsilon, Phi Beta Kappa, Alpha Lambda Delta, Delta Delta Delta (advisor scholarship com. Madison chpt. 1985-89, treas. 1986-89, ho. corp. bd. dirs. 1986-89, fin. advisor 1986-89). Republican. Methodist. Avocations: reading, golf.

COCHRAN, SUSAN MILLS, librarian; b. Grinnell, Iowa, Nov. 21, 1949; d. Lawrence Omen and Louise Jane (Morgan) Mills; m. Stephen E. Cochran, July 1, 1972; children: Bryan, Jeremy. Libr. Iowa Geneal. Soc., Des Moines, 1987-96; asst. to dir. Local History Ctr., Canon City (Colo.) Pub. Libr., 1997—. Editor: Mingo, Iowa 1884-1984, 1984; contbr. articles to profl. jours. Past bd. dirs. Jasper County Libr., Newton, Iowa; past mem. Jasper County Cemetery Commn., Newton; mem. Jasper County His. Soc. Mem. Iowa Geneal. Soc., Jasper County Geneal. Soc., State Assn. for the Preservation of Iowa Cemeteries (charter), Fremont County Geneal. Group (coord.), Colo. Coun. Geneal. Socs. Avocations: genealogy, history, birding. Office: Canon City Pub Libr 516 Macon Ave Canon City CO 81212-3310

COCHRANE, BETSY LANE, former state senator; b. Asheboro, N.C. d. William Jennings and Bobbie (Campbell) Lane; m. Joe Kenneth Cochrane, 1958; children: Lisa, Craig. BA cum laude, Meredith Coll., 1958. Tchr. for eleven yrs.; mem. N.C. Ho. of Reps., Raleigh, 1980-88, house minority leader, 1985-88; mem. N.C. Senate, Raleigh, 1988-2001, chmn. Commn. on Aging, 1989-99, vice chmn. higher edn. com., 1991-92, senate minority whip, 1993-94, senate minority leader, 1995-96, vice chmn. senate appropriations, 1995—2000, vice chmn. senate commerce comm., 1995—2000, ranking minority mem. senate agr., 1995—2000. Tchr. Winston-Salem Sch. System, Highland Presbyn. Ch. Sch; mem. Nat. Rep. Platform Com., Order of LongLeaf Pine, 1992, Joint Legis. Ethics Com., 1989—2000, So. Regional Edn. Bd., 1987—2001; chmn. Joint Legis. Ethics Com., 1989—90; mem. N.C. Parks Commn., 1989—96, Retail Merchants Adv. Bd., 1989—2000, Govtl. Ops., 1989—97, Select Com. on Redistricting, 1991, 92, Revenue Law, 1992—2000, Select Com. on Redistricting, 1994, Environ. Rev. Com., 1997—2001, Utility Rev. Com., 1997—2001, Gov.'s

Advocacy Coun. on Children and Youth, 1990—2001. Trustee Davie County Hosp.; bd. advisors Z. Smith Reynolds Found., 1996—99, Meredith Coll., chmn. pres.'s adv. coun., 1999—2001, govs. adv. budget com., 1989—93, pub. sch. forum, 1985—99; mem. Davie County Schs Task Force on Facilities, 2001—02, So. Regional Edn. Bd., 1987—2001; del. GOP Nat. Conv., 1976, 1988, [illegible] Bible Study fellow, discussion leader, 2003—; bd. dirs. Forks of the Yadkin Mus., 2002—, vice chmn., 2004. Named to N.C. GOP Hall of Fame, 2001, GOP Hall of Fame, Davie County, 2003; recipient Woman in Govt. award, N.C. Jaycees, 1985, One of 10 Outstanding Legislators in Nation, 1987, Disting. Citizen of Yr., N.C. Libr. Dirs., 1991, Legislator of Yr., N.C. Divsn. Aging, 1991, N.C. Assn. for Home Care, 1992, N.C. Health Facilities Assn., 1993, N.C. Wildlife Fedn., 1995, Autism Found., 1995, Myers-Honeycutt award for excellence in pub. svc., 1996, Disting. Alumnae of the Yr., Meredith Coll., 1996, Dr. Ewald W. Busse award, Aging Advocates of N.C., 1997, Women Achievement award, FWC N.C., 2002. Baptist. Home and Office: 122 Azalea Cir Advance NC 27006-9582 E-mail: betsyco@prodigy.net., betsyc@ncleg.net., jcochrane1@triad.rr.com.

COCKERHAM, KIMBERLY PEELE, ophthalmologist, educator; b. Bellevue, Wash., Apr. 10, 1961; d. Fred Arthur and Dorothy Anne (Cooper) Piontkowski; m. Glenn Cooper Cockerham, Feb. 22, 1997. BA in Biology, U. Calif., San Diego, 1983; MD, George Washington U., 1987. Commd. 2nd lt. U.S. Army, 1983, advanced through grades to maj.; surg. intern Letterman Army Ctr., San Francisco, 1987-88; chief emergency svcs. McDonald Army Hosp., Newport News, Va., 1988-89; neuro-opthalmology cons. Fitzsimons Army Med. Ctr., Denver, 1993-94; resident in ophthalmology Walter Reed Army Med. Ctr., Washington, 1989-92, neuro-ophthalmology fellow, 1992-93, mem. neuro-ophthlamology staff, 1993-94, 95—; orbital disease fellow Allegheny Gen. Hosp., Pitts., 1994-95; dir. orbital disease and oculoplastics Walter Reed Army Med. Ctr., Washington, 1995-98; ret., 1998; ophthalmologist Cockerham Eye Cons., Lock Haven, Pa., 1997—; dir. oculoplastics, orbital disease and reconstrn. Allegheny Gen. Hosp., Pitts., 1999—2002; dir. neuro-ophthalmology and orbital oncology Allegheny Cancer Ctr., Pitts., 2002—. Asst. clin. prof. Uniformed U. Health Scis., Bethesda, Md., 1992-98; instr. neuro-ophthalmology Harvard's Lancaster, U. Houston's Stanford basic ophthalmology courses, 1994—; asst. clin. prof. Drexel U. Sch. Medicine, 2000—; oral bd. examiner Acad. Ophthalmology, 1998—; cons. surg. neuro-ophthalmology U. Pitt. Med. Ctr.; bd. dirs. Vision Svcs.; team opthalmologist Pitts. Pirates baseball team. Author: Practical Diagnois & Management of Orbital Disease, 2001; assoc. editor Jour. of Allegheny Med. Soc.; contbr. articles to profl. jours., chpts. to books. Eye camp doctor Charitable Trust, New Delhi, India, 1996; mem. Surg. Eye Expedition Internat., 1997-99. Fellow ACS, Am. Acad. Ophthalmology, Am. Soc. Ophthalmic Plastic and Reconstructive Surgeons, Am. Soc. Oculofacial Plactics Reconstrn.; mem. N.Am. Soc. Neuro-Ophthalmology, Assn. Rsch. in Vision and Ophthalmology, Orbital Soc., Pa. Med. Soc. (alt. del.), Orbital Soc., Rotary Internat., Alpha Omega Alpha. Avocations: running, writing, tennis, gardening, cooking. Office: Allegheny Ophthalmic & Orbital Assocs 320 E North Ave Ste 116 Pittsburgh PA 15212-4756

COCKRILL, ANNETTE S. elementary school educator, music educator; b. Cartersville, Ga., Mar. 3, 1955; d. Arthur Webb and Margaret Bagwell Smith; m. Millard Dale Cockrill, Nov. 23, 1996. Assoc. in Music, Truett McConnell Coll., 1975; B of Music Edn., Shorter Coll., 1977; MEd, Columbus U., 1981. Cert. tchr. Ga. Music tchr. Pine Log and Adairsville (Ga.) Elem., 1977—78, Adairsville Elem. Sch., 1977—. Facilitator Student Support Team, Adairsville, 2000—. Mem.: Am. Orff-Schulwerk Assn., Music Educators Nat. Conf., Profl. Assn. Ga. Educators. Baptist. Avocations: reading, crocheting, knitting, home decorating, playing clarinet. Home: 110 Amberidge Dr NW Cartersville GA 30121 E-mail: www.musictchr1@aol.com.

CODERRE, ELAINE ANN, state representative; b. Providence, Oct. 11, 1947; d. Henry N. and Mary A. (McDonald) Daigneault; m. Raymond Russell Coderre, Feb. 3, 1967; children: Robert, Thomas, Karen. Student, U. R.I., 1965-68. Bank teller Pawtucket (R.I.) Inst. for Savs., 1970-82; pres. Dano USA, Pawtucket, 1982—99; rep. R.I. Ho. Reps., 1984—. Bd. dirs. Sr. Inn., Pawtucket, 1985—. Mem. Heart Fund Drive, Pawtucket, 1985, Pawtucket Tenants Affairs Bd., 1985—; sec. Child Support Enforcement Commn., 1985—. Named one of Outstanding Young Women in America, 1981. Mem. Vis. Nurses Assn. (bd. dirs. 1986—), VFW Aux. (sr. v.p. 1984-87, legisl. chair 1986-87), Jaycee Women. Democrat. Roman Catholic. Home: 18 Angle St Pawtucket RI 02860-3006 Office: State House 323 State House Providence RI 02903

CODERRE, NANCY ADELE, financial analyst; b. Cleve., Aug. 21, 1962; d. Richard Alfred and Julia (Viedt) C. BA, U. Colo., 1984; MBA with high honors, Babson Coll., 1986. Cert. mgmt. acct. Sr. cost acct. M/A Com., Omni Spectra, Waltham, Mass., 1987-88; fin. analyst Analogic Corp., Peabody, Mass., 1988-93, Carrier Corp., Syracuse, N.Y., 1994-95; product specialist SAS Inst., Cary, NC, 1995—. Mem. Inst. Mgmt. Accts., Beta Gamma Sigma. Avocations: swimming, chess. Home: 205 Livingstone Drive Cary NC 27513 E-mail: nancy.coderre@SAS.com.

CODO, CHRISTINA, securities executive; b. Evanston, Ill., Jan. 13, 1960; d. Norman Fredric and Charlotte Jean (Bailey) Codo; m. Patrick Joseph Maloney; children: Beatrice Grace Codo Maloney, Daniel Patrick Codo Maloney. BA in Econs., Northwestern U., 1980; MBA, Yale U., 1987. Exec. officer in lending Lloyds Bank Internat. Inc., Miami, Fla., 1982-85; exec. officer high yield capital markets Salomon Inc., N.Y.C., 1987-89; with instnl. sales Whitehill Capital Inc., N.Y.C., 1989, v.p. instnl. sales, 1989-91; mem. instnl. adv. staff Euromobiliare, SpA, Milan, 1991-92; assoc. fgn. securities group JP Morgan, N.Y.C., 1992-93, v.p. Emerging Markets, 1993-94, Chgo., 1994-98; assoc., controller's divsn. Continental Ill. Bank and Trust Co. Inc., 1999—. Fin. dir. Jr. League of Evanston-North Shore, Winnetka, 1999—2001, co-chmn. fundraising com., 1997—98; mem. exec. bd. Ronald Knox Montessori Sch., chair fundraising com., 2001—02, pres. bd. dirs., 2003—04; vice chair New Trier Township Youth Com., 2000—. Mem.: Chgo. Coun. Fgn. Rels. Avocations: opera, golf, tennis, internat. travel.

CODOGNI, IWONA M. scientific information analyst, chemist; b. Ketrzyn, Poland, May 26, 1959; came to U.S., 1991; d. Tadeusz and Marianna Wyzlic; m. Zdzislaw Antoni Codogni, Dec. 26, 1997; 1 child, Christopher Thadeusz. MSc in Chemistry, Nicolaus Copernicus U., Torun, Poland, 1982, PhD, 1991. Rsch. assoc. Nicolaus Copernicus U., 1983-91; postdoctoral fellow Ohio State U., Columbus, 1991-93, rsch. assoc., 1993-95; asst. sci. info. analyst Chem. Abstracts Svc., Columbus, 1995-98, assoc. sci. info. analyst, 1998—. Contbr. articles to profl. jours.; patentee in field. Mem. Am. Chem. Soc. Office: Chem Abstracts Svc 2540 Olentangy River Rd Columbus OH 43202-1505

CODY, ARLENE J. CLARK BRATTAIN, interior designer; b. Phila., July 27, 1938; d. Franklin Corning Clark and Nora May Robertson; children: Kathy, Kurt, Karen, David. Cert. in interior design, N.Y. Sch. Interior Design, 1975; BS, U. Minn., 1986. State cert. interior designer, Minn. Exec. United Way, Mpls., 1980; interior designer AB Interiors, Minnetonka, Minn., 1982—. Pvt. practice color analyst, Minnetonka, 1984—; cons. showroom Rollin B. Child Tile, Plymouth, Minn., 1985; interior designer Room & Bd. Stores, Minnetonka, 1985-86. Designer Window Fashions mag., 1988—, Am. Soc. Interior Designers Showcase Home, 1987, Showcase Home for March of Dimes, 1988, Showcase Vignette, 1989. Trainer dist. Camp Fire Girls, Minnetonka, 1967-78; trainer, leader Boy Scouts Am., Mpls., 1967-80; pres. PTA, Minnetonka, 1970; pres. Music Boosters, Minnetonka, 1976-84. Recipient Silver Fawn award Boy Scouts Am., 1973. Mem. Am. Soc. Interior Designers (profl.), Internat. Furnishings and Design Assn. (exec. 1988—), Nat. Trust for Hist. Preservation, Mensa. Business E-Mail: mary.boutiette@nhcc.mnscu.edu.

CODY, JUDITH, composer, writer. Student, U. Calif., [illegible] Foothill Coll., Los Altos Hills, Calif., 1972—75; pvt. student in Japanese culture and music, 1966—68. Editor: Resource Guide on Women in Music, 1981; author: Vivian Fine: A Bio-Bibliography, 2001; (poems) Eight Frames Eight, 2002; contbr. poems to lit. jours.; composer: Trio for flute, classical guitar and poem, 1974, Firelights: Variations for classical guitar, 1976-77, City and Country Themes in G, 1976, Dances, opus 8, 1977, Nocturne, opus 9, 1977, classical guitar Seven Concert Etudes, opus 7, 10, 11, 13, 14, 15 & 18, 1977, classical guitar, Christmas Theme, opus 17, 1977, Opus 16, flute & guitar, 1977, Trio, opus 21, two flutes and guitar, 1978, Three Songs of Middle English, opus 26, voice and guitar, 1978, Sonata, opus 22, flute and guitar, 1978, Theme and Variations, opus 27, piano, 1978, Three Patterns, opus 29, piano, 1978, Two Patterns, opus 30, piano, 1978, Flute Poems, opus 19, 1978, Meditation for Four Hands, duet, steel string and classical guitars, 1983, Rain on the Face of Buddha at Kamakura, classical guitar, 1984, Three Haiku Love Songs, piano and soprano, 1986, Danger Dance, piano and soprano, 1986, Whales' Song, piano, 1986, Swan River, piano, 1986, Looking Under Footprints, voice and classical guitar, 1986, Two Songs, piano, 1999, Heart-Blood-Heart, piano, 1999, Death of a Small Animal, piano, 1999, Earth of Ukraine, piano, 1999, Song Cycle: Updated History of the Universe, classical guitar, flute ensemble, voice, 2003. Founder steering com., mem. 1st Bay Area Congress on Women in Music, San Francisco State U., 1980—81. Recipient 1st Prize poem Amelia Mag., 1993, music composition winner New Times Concerts, La. State U., 1979, winner Atlantic Monthly Poetry Contest, 1973, Hon. Mention Emily Dickinson Poetry award, 2003; poetry placed in permanent collection Smithsonian Instn., Washington, 1978. Mem. PEN, Am. Music Ctr., Poets and Writers, Inc., Bay Area Congress on Women in Music (founding Steering Com. mem.). Achievements include First to discover and document composer's creative explosions in youth and old age, 2001; first woman engineering drafter in city and county of San Francisco Power and Utilities Engineering Bureau, 1963. Avocations: soprano in opera chorus, classical guitar. E-mail: jcpoetnow@yahoo.com.

COE, DIANA WARD (DINA COE), language educator, writer; b. Balt., Mar. 30, 1943; d. Ward Baldwin, Jr. and Diana Chittenden Coe; m. Gregory James McGrath, Feb. 14, 1998; m. David Keller, Sept. 1, 1981 (div. Nov. 5, 1990). BA, Hollins Coll., Va., 1965; MA in Creative Writing, C.C. CUNY, N.Y.C., 1989. Flight attendant Pan Am. World Airways, Jamaica, NY, 1965—85; adj. prof. CCNY, N.Y.C., 1989—95, Rider Coll., Lawrenceville, NJ, 1996—97. Dodge poet Geraldine R. Dodge Found., Madison, NJ, 1986—2002; poet in the schs. N.J. State Coun. on the Arts, Trenton, 1988—2002. Poet: published in numerous periodicals and anthologies. Recipient Grolier prize, Grolier Bookstore, Boston, 1984; Fellowship in Poetry, N.J. State Coun. on the Arts, 1981, 1987, 1994, Bread Loaf Scholar, Bread Loaf (Vt.) Writer's Conf., 1989. Democrat. Avocations: gardening, hiking, belly dancing, vegetarian cooking. Home: 742 Canns Neck Way Great Cacapon WV 25422

COE, JUDITH ANNE, music educator, composer, performer; b. Denver, June 11, 1955; d. James Arnold and Sonya Diane (Regnier) Hall; m. Loren R. Coe, June 14, 1975 (div. Dec. 1993); children: Jared, Joshua, Jessica. BM, Colo. State U., 1981, MM, 1983; DMA, U. Colo., 1991. Rsch. intern Denver Ctr. for Performing Arts Voice Lab., 1984-91; vis. artist Denver Sch. of Arts, 1991-92; vocal coach, vis. artist Denver Ctr. Theatre Co., 1991-92; instr. Front Range C.C., Ft. Collins, Colo., 1988-91; designer Vestige Pub. Co., Ft. Collins, 1994-96; asst. prof. dept. music Miss. U. for Women, Columbus, 1996-2001; asst. prof. music & entertainment industry studies U. Colo., Denver, 2001—. Adj. prof. Colo. State U., Ft. Collins, 1990-94. Author: Report on the Status of Women in College Music, 2000; assoc. editor: (ency.) Women Musicians in America, 2000; author/compiler: (webliography) Cyberspace Music Resources, 1999. Performing arts roster Miss. Arts Coun., 1999—; cmty. outreach affiliate Columbus Arts Coun., 1999—. Miss. U. for Women Faculty Devel. grantee, 1996, 97, 98, 99, 2000; Nat. Inst. for Deafness and Other Comm. Disorders grantee, 1990, 91, Columbus Arts Coun. grantee, 1999, 2000, Blas Internat. Sch. Traditional Irish Music and Dance grantee, 1999. Mem. AAUW (Leadership award 1999), NOW, Internat. Alliance for Women in Music (coord. of pub. advocacy 1999—, bd. dirs. 1996—), Am. Soc. Composers, Authors and Pubs., Coll. Music Soc. (co-chair com. on music, women and gender 1999—, profl. devel. com./ann. planning com. 1999—), Acad. and Rec. Industry Alliances (team organizer 2000), Nat. Assn. Tchrs. Singing (v.p., adjudications chair 1983-85), Southeastern Composers League, Internat. Assn. for Study of Popular Music. Democrat. Avocations: web design and development, photography, architecture, popular culture, travel. Office: U Colo Arts Bldg 288H Campus Box 162 PO Box 173364 Denver CO E-mail: judith.coe@cudenver.edu.

COE, JUDITH LYNN, retired automobile manufacturing company administrator; b. Washington, Oct. 4, 1945; d. Raymond G. and Lynn (Pulliam) Coe. BA in Math., Converse Coll., 1967; Exec. Sec. cert., Washington Sch. for Secs., 1968. Sec. to v.p. and sec. Nonprescription Drug Mfrs. Assn., Washington, 1968-72; sec. to regional mgr. Electro-Motive div. GM Corp., Atlanta, 1972-83; sec. to asst. zone mgrs. Pontiac div. GM Corp., Atlanta, 1983-87, zone mgr.'s sec. Washington, 1987-95; ret., 1995. Bd. dirs. Lynn Properties, Washington, 1989-99. Active Met. Meml. United Meth. Ch. Mem. Holton-Arms Sch. and Converse Coll. Alumnae Assn., The Washington Club (admissions com. 1998—, bd. govs. 1999-2002), Congl. Country Club. Republican. Home: 4802 Jamestown Rd Bethesda MD 20816-2711

COE, MARGARET LOUISE SHAW, community service volunteer; b. Cody, Wyo., Dec. 25, 1917; d. Ernest Francis and Effie Victoria (Abrahamson) Shaw; m. Henry Huttleston Rogers Coe, Oct. 8, 1943 (dec. Aug. 1966); children: Anne Rogers Hayes, Henry H.R., Jr., Robert Douglas II. AA, Stephens Coll., 1937; BA, U. Wyo., 1939. Asst. to editor The Cody Enterprise, 1939-42, editor, 1968-71. Bd. trustees Buffalo Bill Historical Ctr., 1966—, chmn., 1974-98, chmn. emeritus, 1998—; trustee emeritus Ctrl. City Opera House Assn., Millicent Rogers Found.; commr. Wyo. Centenniel Commn., Cheyenne, 1986-91. Recipient The Westerner award Old West Trails Found., 1980, Gold Medallion award Nat. Assn. Sec. of State, 1982, disting alumni award U. Wyo., 1984, exemplary alumni award, 1994, Gov.'s award for arts, 1988; inducted Nat. Cowgirl Hall of Fame, 1983. Mem. P.E.O., Delta Delta Delta. Republican. Episcopalian. Avocation: duplicate bridge. Home: 1400 11th St Cody WY 82414-4206

COELING, HARRIET VAN ESS, nursing educator, editor; b. Grand Rapids, Mich., Dec. 3, 1943; d. Louis and Helen Angeline (DeGraff) Van Ess; m. Kenneth J. Coeling, June 27, 1970; children: Valerie Coeling Nandor, Beverly Coeling Corder. BSN, U. Mich., 1966, MS, 1968; PhD, Bowling Green State U., 1987. RN, Ohio; clin. nurse specialist. Head nurse, clin. specialist Presbyn. Univ. Hosp., Pitts., 1968-70; instr. U. Pitts. Sch. Nursing, 1970-72; staff devel. instr. Braddock (Pa.) Hosp., 1976-78, Med. Coll. Ohio, Toledo, 1978-83; asst. prof. U. Mich. Sch. Nursing, Ann Arbor, 1987-88, Kent (Ohio) State U. Coll. Nursing, 1988-93, asoc. prof., 1994—. Editor, Online Jour. Issues in Nursing, ANA/Kent State U., 1998—; contbr. articles to profl. jours. Coord. St. Malachi Healthcare Clinic, Cleve., 1993-98. Tchr. and Nonsvc. fellow Bowling Green State U., 1983-87; Nursing Practice award, ANA. Mem. Nat. Assn. Clin. Specialists, Ohio Assn. Advanced Practice Nurses, Ohio Nurses Assn. (chair human rights com. 1998—2002), Greater Cleve. Nurses Assn., Midwest Nursing Rsch. Assn., Christian Assn. Psychol. Studies, Sigma Theta Tau (Excellence in Use of Tehc. award 1997). Christian. Avocations: travel, swimming. Office: Kent State U 1743 Settlers Reserve Westlake OH 44145 E-mail: hcoeling@kent.edu.

COEN, ADRI STECKLING See ADRI

COEN, MARY ELLEN, adult education educator, secondary school educator, chemist; b. Pueblo, Colo., Jan. 10, 1943; d. David Wesley Belvill and Lola Belle Crawford; m. Maurice G. Coen, May 19, 1984; m. Harry D. Williams, Sept. 1, 1960 (div. June 1, 1976); children: Jason Wesley Williams, Jeffrey David Williams. BA summa cum laude, Idaho State Univ., Pocatello, 1965, MST summa cum laude, 1976. Secondary tchr. #25 Sch. Dist., Pocatello, Idaho, 1965—71; rschr. T.A. Idaho State Univ., Pocatello, Idaho, 1973—76; secondary tchr. #70 Sch. Dist., Pueblo, Colo., 1977—78; chemist Environ. Test Lab, Pueblo, Colo., 1978—79, Colo. Inst. Gas, Pueblo, Colo., 1979—84; ptnr. Coen Birdseed and Farms, Towner, Colo., 1984—89; dir. fed. programs and staff devel. Bur. of Coop. Edn. Svc., Lamar, Colo., 1989—95. Evaluation team U.S. Dept. of Edn., Washington, 1995—96; bd. dirs. Colo. Endowment for Humanities, Denver; chair Co.-Govs. Awards for Excellence in Edn., Denver, 1993—95. Recipient Rsch. award, Ariz. Hydrology Soc., 1976, 1st pl. Rurtal Schs. Curriculum award, Colo. Drug Free Schs., 1995—96; Dr. of Arts fellow, Idaho State U., 1976—77. Mem.: Philanthropic, Ednl. Orgn., Orange Pk. Art Guild, Gen. Fedn. of Women's Clubs. Methodist. Avocations: painting, piano, reading.

COEYMAN, EMILY NOLLIE ROGERS, civic worker; b. Waynesboro, Miss., Jan. 10, 1921; d. Olin Deauward and Ethel Louise (Finkbohner) Rogers; m. William Henry Coeyman, Apr. 5, 1941 (div. June 1952); children: Louis Brooke Roger, Louise Edna Coeyman Thomas. Student, Tomlinson Vocat. Inst., St. Petersburg, Fla., 1951, LaSalle Ext. Law U., 1957-59, St. Petersburg Jr. Coll., 1970-75, 85. Sec. Shorthand Reporter-Ct. Reporter, Washington, D.C., 1939-40, Colonial Decorating Co., Washington, D.C., 1940-41; clk-typist fin. and transp. dept. War Dept., Washington, D.C., 1941-43; clk. carrier U.S. P.O., Washington, D.C., 1943-44, ry. and postal clk. ry. mail svc., 1944; mdse. control clk. Hecht Co. Dept. Store, Washington, 1945-46; transcribing machine oprtor, clk.-typist REA, Washington, 1946; clk.-stenographer Glenn Dale (Md.) TB Sanitorium, 1946-48; clk.-cashier, admitting clk. Mound Park Hosp., St. Petersburg, 1948-51; clk.-typist VA, Pass-A-Grille, Fla., 1951-52; med. sec. to chief physiatrist Gallinger Hosp. (name now D.C. Gen. Hosp., Washington, 1955-60; ret., 1960. First woman mail carrier, Washington, D.C. (WWII), 1944. Bd.-dirs.-at-large, mem. citizens adv. com. Met. Planning Orgn., Pinellas County, Fla., 1984—; St. Petersburg rep. Tampa Bay Regional Planning Coun. Area Agy. on Aging, Pinellas County, 1981-90; bd. dirs.-at-large, mem. citizens adv. com. Pinellas Suncoast Transit Authority, Pinellas County, 1988-94, Fast Speed and High Speed Monorail, Pinellas, Hillsborough Counties Joint Com.-Citizens Adv., 1993—; active participant numerous city and county govt. meetings, including Environ. Devel. Commn., Bd. Adjustment, Pinellas County Sch. Bd., Pinellas Suncoast Transit authority, Juvenile Welfare Bd., Com. Neighborhood Assn. Named to Hon. Sr. Hall of Fame, City of St. Petersburg, 1987, Sr. Hall of Fame, 1988; recipient hon. proclamation as a vol. Pinellas County Commrs., 1991, hon. proclamation Pinellas Sports Authority, 1992. Mem. Nat. Assn. Ret. Fed. Employees, Am. Assn. Ret. Persons, Pinellas Geneal. Soc., Sr. Citizens Sunshine Ctr. Club, St. Petersburg Stamp Club, Suncoast Tiger Bay Club, Women of Moose, St. Petersburg Rock, Gem and Mineral Soc., UDC (assoc.). Republican. Baptist. Avocations: stamp and rock collecting, genealogy, volunteering. Home: 6936 40th Ave N Saint Petersburg FL 33709-4610

COFFEE, VIRGINIA CLAIRE, civic worker, former mayor; b. Alliance, Nebr., Dec. 8, 1920; D. James Maddigan and Adelaide Mary (Forde) Kennedy; M. Bill Brown Coffee, June 21, 1942; children: Claire, Sara, Virginia Anne, Sue. BS, Chadron State Coll., 1942. Prin. Whitman (Nebr.) H.S., 1942; bookkeeper Coffee & Son, Inc., Harrison, Nebr., 1965—, officer, 1967, pres., 1987-97, v.p., 1998—; dir. Friends of Agate Fossil Beds, Inc., Harrison, 1988, v.p., 1988-2001. Chmn. compilation com. book Sioux County Memoirs of Its Pioneers, 1967; coord. Harrison sect. book Nebraska Our Towns, 1988. Mayor City of Harrison, 1978-80; leader Girl Scouts U.S.A., 1953-63; mem. Harrison Elem. Sch. Bd., 1958-64, liason com. Chadron State Coll., 1975, pub. rels. chmn. Nebr. Cowbelles, 1968; hon gov. Nebr. Centennial, 1967; sec. NW Stock Growers, 1971-73; corp. officer Ft. Robinson Centennial, 1973-88; officer Gov's Ft. Robinson Centennial Commn., 1973-75; chmn. Sioux County Bicentennial, 1973-77; trustee Nebr. State Hist. Soc. Found., 1975—, Village of Harrison, 1973-80; bd. dirs. Chadron State Coll. Found., 1996—, sec., 2003; bd. dirs. Harrison Cmty. Club, Inc., 1983-86, officer, 1984-86; apptd. Sioux County Vis. Com. 1989-2003, adm. Nebr. Navy, 1992; mem. com. for marker to honor Harrison Centennial 1985-86; mem. Sioux County History Book Com. 1985-86. Recipient Disting. Svc. award Chadron State Coll., 1994. Mem. Nebr. State Hist. Soc. (life, dir. 1979-85, 2d v.p. 1982-84, 1st v.p. 1984-85), Wyo. State Hist. Soc., Sioux County Hist. Soc. (life, bd. dirs. 1975-81, 83-84, 87-90, 97-2003, pres. 1988-90, co-pres., 2d v.p.), Nebr. Cattle Women, Harrison Cmty. Inc., Cardinal Key. Roman Catholic. Address: PO Box 336 Harrison NE 69346-0336

COFFEL, PATRICIA K. retired social worker; b. Bismarck, N.D., Sept. 14, 1934; m. Raymond A. Kobe, 1956; children: Anne, Elizabeth, Colleen, Denise, Tim, Heidi; m. Mitchel D. Coffel, 1983. Student, U. N.D., 1954-55; BA in Sociology, Coll. St. Benedict, 1956; MSW, Wayne State U., 1981. Diplomate in clin. social work; cert. social worker, Mich. Dir. social svcs. dept. Pontiac Nursing Ctr., 1978-84; dir. of med. social work dept. Advanced Profl. Home Health Care, Troy, Mich., 1985-86; med. social worker Visiting Nurses of Met. Detroit, 1987; family worker, therapist Camp Oakland Youth Svcs., Oxford, Mich., 1987-89; client svcs. case mgr. Macomb-Oakland Regional Ctr., Mt. Clemens, Mich., 1989-90; clin. social worker, case mgr. Oakdale Regional Ctr., Lapeer, Mich., 1990-91; clin. social worker Clinton Valley Ctr., Pontiac, Mich., 1991-96; retired, 1996. Counselor Suicide Prevention, Inc., St. Louis, 1971-72, Macomb County Crisis Ctr., Warren, Mich., 1973-74; geriatric counselor Beverly Enterprises, Pontiac and Novi, Mich., 1981-83; grief and loss counselor Hospice SE Mich., Southfield, 1982-83. Grad. profl. scholar Wayne State U. Sch. Social Work, 1980. Mem. NASW (qualified clin. social worker), Acad. Cert. Social Workers. Avocations: antique silver collecting, needlepoint, videotape collecting. Home: 645 Oakwood Rd Ortonville MI 48462-8589

COFFEY, JOANNE CHRISTINE, dietician; b. Cambridge, Mass., Aug. 18, 1942; d. Timothy Patrick and Helen (Stevens) C. BS in Nutrition, Simmons Coll., 1964, M in Libr. and Info. Sci., 1994; MPH, U. Calif., Berkeley, 1966. Registered dietitian. Dietitian, clin. sect. chief VA Med. Ctr., Manchester, N.H., 1978-80, chief dietetic svc. Altoona, Pa., 1980-82, Providence, 1982-89, asst. chief dietetic svc. Boston, 1989-96, supervisory dietitian, 1996-97. Mem. Nature Conservancy, Smithsonian. Mem. Am. Dietetic Assn. Democrat. Roman Catholic. Avocations: cooking, music, reading, walking.

COFFEY, KIMBERLY E. secondary school educator; d. Jeffrey J. and Edith M. Morelock; m. Robert G. Coffey. BA in Math., Hartwick Coll., Oneonta, N.Y., 1995; MA in Math. Edn., Columbia U., 1997; postgrad., N.Y. Inst. Tech. Cert. permanent cert. in secondary math. N.Y. Tchr. math. Clarkstown Ctrl. Sch. Dist., New City, NY, 1997—. Pvt. tutor math., 1997—; curriculum devel. com. Felix Festa Mid. Sch., West Nyack, NY, 1997—. Mem.: Assn. of Math. Tchrs. of N.Y. State (Mem. Scholarship award 1998—), Nat. Coun. Tchrs. Math., Kappa Delta Pi. Office: Felix festa Mid Sch 30 Parot Rd West Nyack NY 10994

COFFEY, MARGARET TOBIN, education educator, county official; b. Binghamton, N.Y., Mar. 30, 1940; d. Henry L. and Mary Margaret (Keenan) Tobin; m. Joseph M. Coffey, Aug. 20, 1968; children: Timothy, Erin, David, Tobin. BA, Manhatten Coll. Sacred Heart, 1962; Cert. Edn., SUNY, Cortland, 1967. Cert. tchr., N.Y. Tchr. Binghamton Sch., 1963-69; early childhood coord. Broome Community Coll., Binghamton, 1971-72; staff caseworker U.S. Rep. Matthew F. McHugh, Washington and Binghamton, 1974-79; dir. Bur. of Census, Binghamton, 1979-80; tchr. adult edn. PROBE Local CBO, Binghamton, 1980-81; tchr. Binghamton City Sch. Dist., 1981-86, coord. VEA, 1986-90, prog. mgr. BCSD adult edn. programs, 1990—. Bd. dirs. Inner City Nursery Sch., Local Devel. Corp., Binghamton; bd. pres. Broome County Coun. Alcoholism, 1986-90; del. N.Y. Dem. Com., Albany, 1970-74; legislator Broome County, 1982—; mem. Children Youth Svcs. Coun., Youth Bur. Bd. Mem. Am. Vocat. Assn., Adult Continuing Edn. Assn., Phi Delta Kappa. Roman Catholic. Home: 30 Davis St Binghamton NY 13905-4318 Office: Binghamton City Sch Dist Columbus Sch Cite PO Box 2126 Binghamton NY 13902-2126

COFFEY, MARILYN JUNE, writer, educator; b. Alma, Nebr., July 22, 1937; d. June Thomas and Zelma Theola Coffey; m. John Raymond Powell, III (div.); m. Tom Henshaw (div.); 1 child, Ian Michael Henshaw. BA in Journalism, U. Nebr., 1959; MFA in Creative Writing, Bklyn. Coll., 1981. Journalist Lincoln (Nebr.) Evening Jour., 1959—60, Good Housekeeping, N.Y.C., 1960—61, Home Furnishings Daily, N.Y.C., 1964—66; asst. prof. Boston U., 1969—71; tenured prof. Pratt Inst., Bklyn., 1966—69, 1973—90; comm. instr. St. Mary's Coll., Lincoln, 1990—92; prof. creative writing Ft. Hays State U., Hays, Kans., 1992—2000; ret., 2000. Literature artist Kans. Arts Commn., Topeka, 1990—92, Nebr. Arts Coun., Lincoln, 1990—91; creative writer-in-residence Lawrence (Kans.) Arts Ctr., 1991. Author: Marcella, 1973, 1976, (book-length poem) A Cretan Cycle: Fragments Unearthed from Knossos, 1991. Named Listed Writer, Poets and Writers, 1973—2004, Admiral Nebr. Navy, Nebr. gov., 1977, Marilyn Coffey collection, U. Nebr. Librs. Archives, 1987—; recipient Pushcart prize, Pushcart Press, 1976; grantee rsch. grantee, Ludwig Vogelstein Found., 1985—87, Mellon Funds through Pratt Inst., 1987—88. Mem.: Charlotte Writers Club. Avocations: Hatha yoga, walking, music, confabulating, computer games. Home: 1646-6 Chippendale Rd Charlotte NC 28205 E-mail: mcoffey65@hotmail.com.

COFFEY, NANCY ANN, real estate broker; b. Palm Springs, Calif. d. Arthur Johnson and Joan (Hunter) Coffey. BA, Stanford U., 1967, MS in Engring., 1977. Indsl. real estate broker Coldwell Banker, Houston, 1977-79, comml. broker San Francisco, 1980-87, Cushman & Wakefield, N.Y.C., 1987-90; model Gilla Roos, N.Y.C., 1991-96; real estate broker, 1990-96; comml. real estate broker The Rolfe Group, N.Y.C., 1997 98, Cushman & Wakefield, Inc., N.Y.C., 1998-2000, Halstead Property, NYC, 2001—. Active Jr. League, San Francisco, 1981—87, N.Y.C., 1987—2000, sustainer, 1999—2000, Palo Alto Jr. League, 2000—01, N.Y. Jr. League, 2001—; mem. exec. com. spl. projects bd. Meml. Sloan Kettering Cancer Ctr., N.Y.C.; vice chair membership com. Soc. Meml. Sloan Kettering, 1999—2000, mem. adminstrv. bd., 2002—; v.p. Class of 1967 Stanford U.; parish life com. mem. St. James Ch., 1997—2000. Mem.: River Club NY, Rockaway Hunting Club. Home: Smoke Tree Ranch Palm Springs CA 92264

COFFEY, SUSANNA JEAN, art educator; b. New London, Conn. d. Edwin Raymond and Magel C. (Willingham) C. BFA magna cum laude, U. Conn., 1977; MFA, Yale U., 1982. Tchg. asst. Yale U., 1982; prof. painting Sch. of the Art Inst. of Chgo., 1982—, 1985—. Vis. artist various schs., 1983—; adj. assoc. prof. U. Ill, 1983; vis. critic Royal Coll. Art, London, 1995, Vt. Studio Ctr., 1994; panel mem. Harvard Ctr. for Religious Studies, 2001. Illustrator: The H Hymn to Demeter, 1989, Monovassia (Eleni Fourtouni), 1979; one-woman shows include The Cultural Ctr. of the Chgo. Pub. Libr., 1986, Weatherspoon Gallery, Greensboro, N.C., 1993, Alpha Gallery, 1995, Galeria Alejandro Sales, Barcelona, 1995, Tibor De Nagy Gallery, 1996-97, 2001, 2003, others; represented in permanent collections Northwestern U., Evanston, Ill., Art Inst. Chgo., Mpls. Mus. Art, Bryn Mawr (Pa.) Coll., Boston Mus. Fine Arts, Weatherspoon Gallery, and pvt. collections. Individual Artists grant Conn. Commn. on the Arts, 1980, Residency grant Ragdale Found., Lake Forest, Ill., 1984, Faculty Enrichment grant SAIC, 1987, 90-91, Chgo. Artists Abroad grant, 1990, Ill./Arts Coun. grant, 1985, 92, Studio Program grant Marie Walsh Sharpe Found., 1992, Nat. Endowment for the Arts grant, 1993; Guggenheim fellow, 1996; recipient Louis Comfort Tiffany Found. award, 1993, Acad. award in art Am. Acad. of Arts and Letters, 1995; named to Nat. Acad. Design, 2001. Office: Sch of the Art Inst of Chgo 37 S Wabash Ave Chicago IL 60603-3002

COFFIELD, SHIRLEY ANN, lawyer, educator; b. Portland, Oreg., Mar. 31, 1945; BA, Willamette U., 1967; MA, U. Wisc.-Madison, 1969; JD, George Washington U., 1974. Bar. D.C. 1975. Clk. Stitt, Hemmendinger and Kennedy, Washington, 1973-74; asst. gen. counsel Office U.S. Trade Rep., Washington, 1975-79; ptnr. Reaves & Coffield, Washington, 1979-82; sr. counsel to dep. asst. sect. textiles and apparel U.S. Dept. Commerce, Washington, 1982-85; spl. counsel Skadden, Arps, Slate, Meagher and Flom, Washington, 1985-87; ptnr. Piper & Marbury, Washington and Balt., 1987-90, Baker & Hostetler, Washington, 1990-94, Keller and Heckman, L.L.P., Washington, 1994-98, Duane, Morris & Heckscher, 1998-2000, Coffield Law, Washington, 2000—. Adj. prof. internat. econ. law Georgetown U. Law Sch., 1982—. Mem. Fed. Bar Assn., Am. Soc. Internat. Law, D.C. Bar, Pi Gamma Mu, Phi Delta Phi. Office: Coffield Law Ste 315 666 11th St NW Washington DC 20001-4530 E-mail: coffieldlaw@yahoo.com.

COFFILL, MARJORIE LOUISE, civic leader; b. Sonora, Calif., June 11, 1917; d. Eric J. and Pearl (Needham) Segerstrom; m. William Charles Coffill, Jan. 25, 1948 (dec.); children: William James, Eric John. AB in Social Sci. with distinction, Stanford U., 1938, MA in Edn., 1941. Asst. mgr. Sonora Abstract & Title Co., Calif., 1938—39; dean of women's staff Stanford U., 1939—41; instr. psychology, social dir. women's campus Pomona Coll., 1941—43; asst. to field dir. ARC, Lee Moore AFB, Calif., 1944—46; ptnr. Riverbank (Calif.) Water Co., 1950—68. Mem. Tuolumne County Mental Health Adv. Com., 1963—70; central adv. coun. Supplementary Edn. Ctr., Stockton, Calif., 1966—70; adv. com. Columbia Jr. Coll., 1972—89, pres., 1980—. Pres. Columbia Found., 1972—74, bd. dirs., 1974—77; active Tuolumne County Bicentennial Com., 1974—, PTA, ARC; trustee Sonora Union HS, 1969—73, Salvation Army Tuolumne County, 1973—; active Tuolumne County Rep. Women, 1952—; assoc. mem. Calif. Rep. Central Com., 1950; vestry mem. Episcopal Ch., 1968, 1975; bd. dirs. Lung Assn. Valley Lode Counties, 1974—. Named Outstanding Citizen, C. of C., 1974, Citizen of Yr., 1987, Alumnus of Yr., Sonora Union HS, 1994; named to Columbia Coll. Hall of Fame, 1990; recipient Pi Lambda Theta award, 1940, Woman of Distinction award, Soroptimist Internat., 1993. Mem.: AAUW (charter Tuolumne County br., pres. Sonora br. 1965—66). Episcopalian. Home: 376 Summit Ave Sonora CA 95370-5728

COFFIN, ANNE GAGNEBIN, art association administrator, editor; b. Neptune, N.J., Aug. 2, 1939; d. Albert Paul and Genevieve (Hope) G.; m. John Devereux Coffin, Apr. 7, 1962; children: Samuel Devereux, Thomas Huguenin. BA, Smith Coll., 1961. Asst. editor, feature writer Look mag., N.Y.C., 1961-71; N.Y. rep., newsletter editor Villa I Tatti, Harvard U. Ctr. for Italian Renaissance Studies, Florence, 1984-92; dir. Internat. Print Ctr., N.Y.C., 2000—. Curator, exhbn. organizer Am. Art: The Last 4 Decades, London, 1977. Bd. dirs N.Y. Landmarks Conservancy, N.Y.C., 1981—; bd. dirs. Chamber Music Soc. Lincoln Ctr., N.Y.C., 1984—, Leopold Schepp Found., 1991—, Brit.-Am. Arts Assn., 1985—; co-chmn. Contemporary Arts Coun., Mus. of Modern Art, N.Y.C.; mem. Art Table, Villa I Tatti Coun., 1992—. Mem.: Cosmopolitan Club. Office: 526 W 26th St Rm 824 New York NY 10001

COFFIN, BERTHA LOUISE, telephone company executive; b. Atlanta, Aug. 19, 1919; d. William Wesley and Bertha Louise (Marsh) Mendenhall; m. J. Donald Coffin, Feb. 14, 1943 (dec. Sept. 1978). BA, U. Kans., 1940. Med. technologist Midwest Rsch. Lab., Emporia, Kans., 1940—43; ins. agt. Coffin Ins. Agy., Council Grove, Kans., 1943—99, sole owner, mgr., 1978—82; treas. Council Grove Tel. Co., 1947—50, sec.-treas., 1950—78, pres., chmn. bd., 1978—98, gen. mgr., 1978—99. Del. legis. confs. Nat. Tel. Coop. Assn., 1986, 88, 91-92, 94, 97, comem. comml. co. com., 1987-91, mem. govt. affairs com., 1991-98, exec. com., 1996-98; founder, pres., chmn. bd. Kans. Personal Comm. Svcs. Ltd., 1995—; officer Cities Unltd., Inc., 1999—. Copy preparation for book The Story of the Santa Fe Trail, 1982; author: History of Council Grove Telephone Company, 1991; ann. civic sects. tel. directory. Pres. various lit. clubs, Council Grove, 1945-72; speaker various civic, polit. and religious groups, 1962—; mem. adv. coun. Manhattan Christian Coll., 1983-86, trustee, 1986-92, 93-99, 2000—, chmn., 1991-92. Mem. Kans. Telecomm. Assn. (bd. dirs. 1992-95), Ind. Tel. Pioneers (dir. 1984-92). Avocations: travel, church related activities, speaking.

COFFIN, JUDY SUE, lawyer; b. Beaumont, Tex., Aug. 17, 1953; d. Richard Wilson and Genie (Mouton) C.; m. Gary P. Scholick, Nov. 10, 1983; children: Jennie Sue, Kate Frances. BA, U. Tex., 1974; JD, So. Meth. U., 1976. Bar: Tex. 1977, Calif. 1982. Atty. NLRB, Tex., 1977-80; shareholder Littler Mendelson, San Francisco, 1980-99, also bd. dirs.; sr. counsel, employment and labor law Cath. Healthcare West, San Francisco, Calif., 2000—. Office: Catholic Healthcare West Legal Dept 1700 Montgomery St Ste 300 San Francisco CA 94111-1024 E-mail: jcoffin@chw.edu.

COFFINAS, ELENI, lawyer; b. Bklyn., Jan. 12, 1961; BA, Bklyn. Coll., 1982, JD, 1985. BAr: N.Y. 1985. Assoc. Sullivan & Liapakis, P.C., N.Y.C., 1986-93; ptnr. Sullivan, Papain, Block, McGrath & Cannavo, N.Y.C., 1993—, ptnr., supr. med. malpractice dept., 1994—. Mem. ATLA, Assn. Bar City N.Y. (med. malpractice com. 1996—), N.Y. State Trial Lawyers Assn. (bd. dirs. 1997—). Greek Orthodox. Home: 9423 Shore Rd Brooklyn NY 11209-7259 Office: Sullivan Papain Block McGrath & Cannavo PC 120 Broadway New York NY 10271-0002

COFFINGER, MARALIN KATHARYNE, retired career officer, consultant; b. Ogden, Iowa, July 5, 1935; d. Cleo Russell and Katharyne Frances (McGovern) Morse. BA, Ariz. State U., 1957, MA, 1962; diploma, Armed Forces Staff Coll., 1972, Nat. War Coll., 1977; postgrad., Inst. for Higher Def. Studies, 1985. Commd. 2d lt. USAF, 1963, advanced through grades to brig. gen., 1985; base comdr., dep. base comdr. Elmendorf AFB, Anchorage, Alaska, 1977-79; base comdr. Norton AFB, San Bernardino, Calif., 1979-82; chmn. spl. and incentive pays Office of Sec. Def., Pentagon, Washington, 1982-83; dep. dir. pers. programs USAF Hdqrs., Pentagon, Washington, 1983-85; command dir. NORAD, Combat Ops., Cheyenne Mountain Complex, Colo., 1985-86; dir. pers. plans USAF Hdqrs., Pentagon, Washington, 1986-89; ret. USAF, 1989; dir. software products ops. Walsh America, 1992-94. Mem. Phoenix Symphony Orch., 1954—63; prin. flutist Sonoran Wind Quartet, Scottsdale Cmty. Orch. Band, Scottsdale Concert Band, Ariz.; mem. adv. bd. Joe Foss Inst., keynote spkr., mem. dedication ceremonies Vietnam Meml. Com., Phoenix, 1990. Decorated Air Force D.S.M., Def. Superior Svc. medal, Legion of Merit, Bronze Star.; recipient Nat. Medal of Merit. Mem. NAFE, Air Force Assn. (vet./retiree coun., pres. Sky Harbor chpt. 1990), Nat. Officers Assn., Ret. Officers Assn., Maricopa County Sheriff's Exec. Posse, Ariz. State U. Alumni Assn. (Profl. Excellence award 1981), Nat. Assn. Uniformed Svcs., Recording for the Blind and Dyslexic. Roman Catholic. Home: 8059 E Maria Dr Scottsdale AZ 85255-5418 E-mail: mcoffinger@att.net.

COFFMAN, BARBARA LEANN, environmentalist; b. Conrad, Mont., Nov. 21, 1968; d. Walter Lloyd and Loretta Louise (Tomsha) C. AS in Agrl. Tech., Mont. State U.-No., 1990, AS in Environ. Health, 1991, BS in Water Quality and Chemistry, 1993, MS in Gen. Sci. Edn., 2001. Cert. backflow assembly tester and proctor. Indsl. waste technician No. Mont. Coll., City of Havre (Mont.), Burlington No., 1990; rsch. technician No. Mont. Coll., Mont. Salinity Control Assn., 1990-93; EPA grant asst., tng. asst. No. Mont. Coll. (now Mont. State U.-No.), 1989-93, lab. technician, 1991-93, lab. tchg. asst., 1992; hydrotechnician, rsch. asst. Mont. Bur. Mines and Geology, Butte, 1993-94; tng. specialist Mont. Environ. Tng. Ctr., Gt. Falls, 1994-2000; Mont. class I wastewater treatment plant operator City of Havre, Mont., 2000—. Mem. continuing edn. credit rev. com. for Mont. water and wastewater cert., 1996-2000; adv. bd. Mont. State U. No. Sci., 1997-2000. Bd. dirs. Collins (Mont.) Cmty. Hall, 1994-2000. Recipient Earth Team Vol. award Soil Conservation Svc., Havre, 1989, cert. of achievement Dept. Energy, Richland, Wash., 1991. Mem. Am. Water Works Assn. (sec.-treas. Mont. sect. 1999-2003, exec. sec. Mont. sect. 2003—), Am. Backflow Prevention Assn. (cert. tester and proctor), Water Environment Fedn. Avocations: family farming, stamp and rock collecting, fly fishing, horseback riding, playing basketball. Office: City of Havre PO Box 231 Havre MT 59501

COFFMAN, JENNIFER BURCHAM, judge; b. 1948; BA, U. Ky., 1969, MA, 1971, JD, 1978. Ref. libr. Newport News (Va.) Pub. Libr., 1972-74, U. Ky. Libr., 1974-76; atty. Law Offices Arthur L. Brooks., Lexington, Ky., 1978-82; ptnr. Brooks, Coffman and Fitzpatrick, Lexington, 1982-92, Newberry, Hargrove & Rambicure, Lexington, 1992-93; judge U.S. Dist. Ct. (ea. dist. and we. dist.) Ky., 1993—. Adj. prof. Coll. Law, U. Ky., 1979-81. Elder Second Presbyn. Ch., 1993—96; bd. dirs. YWCA Lexington, 1986—92, Shepherd Ctr., 2000—. Mem. Ky. Bar Assn., Fayette County Bar Assn., U. Ky. Law Sch. Alumni Assn. Office: 306 US Courthouse 101 Barr St Lexington KY 40507-1313

COFFMAN, LUCINDA HARRISON, writer; b. Shelbyville, Ky., Feb. 21, 1940; d. Charles W. and Virginia Stone Hedden; m. James F. Coffman, Feb. 14, 1969; children: Peter, Gabrielle. BA in English, Eastern Ky. U., 1969; MA in Creative Writing, U. Wis., Milw., 1975; MFA in Playwriting, Ohio U., Athens, 1990. Contbr. short stories to lit. jours. Home and Office: 1481 Rockbridge Rd Shelbyville KY 40065

COFFMAN, ORENE BURTON, hotel executive; b. Fluvanna, Va., Mar. 13, 1938; d. John C. and Adele (Melton) Burton; m. John H. Emerson, Aug. 5, 1955 (div. 1972); 1 child, Norman Jay; m. Mack H. Coffman, Oct. 26, 1986. Degree in hotel and motel mgmt., Michigan State U., 1966-70. Cert. hotel mgr., Mich. State U., 1970. Telephone operator Colonial Williamsburg (Va.) Hotel, 1962-64, room clk., mgr. front office, 1968-83; asst. mgr. Williamsburg Inn, 1983—. Pres. Colonial Williamsburg Employees Fed. Credit Union, 1980-85; owner Scavengers Paradise, Inc., 1995—. Mem. Am. Hotel Motel Assn. (nat. acctg. award 1970). Democrat. Baptist. Office: Williamsburg Inn PO Box 392 Williamsburg VA 23187-0392

COFFMAN, TERESA SUSAN, music educator; d. Walter Eugene and Mary Maxine Scroggs; m. William Loren Coffman, Dec. 18, 1982. B in Music Edn., U. Ctrl. Ark., 1984; MA in Choral Music, Ea. Mich. U., 1987; Mus D in Conducting, U. Houston, 1997. Adj. instr. music Iowa Western C.C., Council Bluffs, 1988—90, Peru (Nebr.) State Coll., 1988—90; choral dir. First United Meth. Ch., Ft. Smith, Ark., 1991—93; asst. prof. music U. S.D., Vermillion, 1997—98. Adj. instr. music U. Houston, 1996—99; assoc. prof. music RI Coll., Providence, 1999—; site visitor RI State Coun. Arts, Providence, 2001, grant rev. panelist, 02; condr. RI Sr. All-State Choir, 2003, Am. Festival Arts, Houston, 2003. Mem.: Coll. Music Soc., Nat. Assn. Tchrs. Singing, Am. Choral Dirs. Assn., Pi Kappa Lambda, Phi Kappa Phi, Sigma Alpha Iota (Sword of Honor 1984). Avocations: gardening, reading, west highland white terriers, pilates. Office: RI Coll Dept Music Theatre Dance 600 Mt Pleasant Ave Providence RI 02908

COGAN, MARY HART, community activist, educator; b. Hyannis, Mass., Aug. 2, 1928; d. Walter Vincent and Marie Margaret (Welch) Hart; m. John F. Cogan, Jr., May 1, 1951 (div. Mar. 1989); children: Peter, Pamela, Jonathan, Gregory. BS in Edn., Bridgewater State Coll., 1951, D in Pub. Svc. (hon.), 1999. Tchr. Lexington (Mass.) Pub. Schs., 1951-58; health ins. cons. Mass. Businessman's Assn., Braintree, Mass., 1980-85. Elderly vote coord. Sen. Paul Tsongas, Mass., 1972; del. Dem. Nat. Conv., N.Y.C., 1974, 78; field dir. Mass. Carter Campaign, 1980; mem. fin. com. Dem. Nat. Com., 1988-92; pres. Boston U. Hops. Aux., 1985, Brigham and Women's Hosp. Aux., Boston, 1990; bd. dirs. Friends Monomoy Theater, Chatham, Mass., 1995-98, Acad. Performing Arts, Orleans, Mass., 1997—; trustee Boston Ballet, 1994—, Bridgewater Coll. Found., 1994—, Bridgewater State Coll., 1999—, Cape Mus. Fine Arts, 2000—, Heritage Gardens and Mus., 2004—. Mem. Stage Harbor Yacht Club, Bridgewater State Coll. Alumni Assn. (exec. bd. 1999—). Avocations: figure skating, biking, tennis, choral music, watercolor/pastel painting. Home: 77 Tisquantum Rd Chatham MA 02633-2573

COGGAN, PATRICIA CONNER, elementary school educator; d. Leslie Lynn and Grace Hartnell Conner; m. Leland Latrill Coggan, Jr., July 26, 1958; children: Robert Leslie, Sharon Coggan McBride. BS, U. Okla., 1958; M in Humanities, U. Dallas, 1983. Life tchg. cert. Tex., std. tchg. cert. Okla. 1st grade tchr. Dallas Ind. Sch., 1958—60; elem. tchr. The Hockaday Sch., Dallas, 1976—. Devel. tester Gesell Inst., New Haven, 1978—; trained tchr. Met. Opera-Creating Original Opera, N.Y.C., 1996—; trained evaluator All Kinds of Minds, Raleigh, NC, 1999—. Dallas host com. Rep. Conv., 1984; Presbyn. Women pres. Highland Pk. Presbyn. Ch., 1974; pres. Kappa Alpha Theta Alumnae, Dallas, 1970—71. Named hon. life mem., Presbyn. Women, 1974, hon. alumnae, Hockaday Alumnae Assn., 2003; Curriculum Writing grantee, Hockaday Bd. Trustees, 2002. Mem.: Nat. Coun. for Social Studies, Ela Hockaday Cum Laude Soc. (past pres. 1976—), Michael Stoner DAR (charter), Dallas Craft Guild, Tex. Old Missions and Forts Restoration Assn. Avocations: gardening, book binding, book reviewer. Office: The Hockaday Sch 11600 Welch Rd Dallas TX 75229

COGGINS, RUTHANNE L. GABLE, music educator; d. Richard Bennett and Jean Frost Gable, Mary Savage Gable; m. Warren Earl Coggins, Feb. 7, 1985; children: Jeffrey, Carleton. BA, Furman U., 1977; M of Ch. Music, Southwestern Bapt. Theol. Sem., 1983. Tchr. 4th grade Anderson Sch. Dist 5, Belton, SC, 1977—79; owner, music tchr. Kindermusik of Ft. Worth, 1988—94; music tchr. Arlington (Tex.) Ind. Sch. Dist., 1994—98, Greenville (S.C.) County Schs., 1998—. Chair fall festival Ft. Worth Music Tchrs. Assn., 1995, 96, author music Creative Arts Camp, 2000, 01. Named Arts Educator of Yr., Cen. Carolina Bank, 2001; recipient Arts Curricular grant, S.C. State Dept. Edn., 2001. Mem.: Music Tchrs. Nat. Assn., Early Childhood Music and Movement Assn. (nat. conf. com. 1996), Am. Orff Schulwerk Assn. (pres. Foothills chpt. 2002—04, 1998—2002). Avocation: gardening.

COGGINS, SUZANNE BRIDGES, music educator; b. Greenville, SC, May 31, 1957; d. Charles Perry and Mary Ellen Dorr Bridges; m. Jack O'Neal Coggins, Aug. 15, 1981. BM in Music Edn., Vocal Performance, Converse Coll., Spartanburg, S.C., 1979; MA in Early Childhood Edn., Furman U., Greenville, S.C., 1982, MA in Elem. Edn., 1990. Cert. early and mid. childhood music SC, 2002. 2d, 3d and 4th grade tchr. Sch. Dist. of Greenville County, SC. Pianist, vocal soloist various chs., SC, 1970—; interim music dir. Buncombe Rd. Bapt. Ch., Greenville, SC, 1978—79; ladies' ensemble dir. Greer First Bapt. Ch., SC, pianist; piano accompanist Rotary Club Spring Sing, Greenville, SC; vocal soloist in "The Creation", Greenville Civic Chorale, SC, 1984. Grantee, Met. Arts Coun., Greenville, S.C., 2001-2002; Quickstart grant, S.C. Arts Commn., 2000-2001, Residency-Plus grant, 2001-2002. Mem.: Orff-Schulwerk Assn. (S.C. Foothills chpt.), SC. Music Educators Assn., Music Educators Nat. Conf. Southern Baptist. Achievements include Vocal Scholarship, Brevard Music Center, Brevard, North Carolina, 1975; Voice and Piano Recital, Fine Arts Center, Greenville, South Carolina, 1975; Vocal Junior Recital, Converse College, Spartanburg, South Carolina, 1978; Vocal Senior Recital, Converse College, Spartanburg, South Carolina, 1979; Daniel Music Scholar, Converse College, Spartanburg, South Carolina, 1975-1979; President, Converse College Chorale, Spartanburg, South Carolina; Preliminary Talent Winner and Second Runner-Up, Miss Greenville Pageant, Greenville, South Carolina, 1978; First Runner-Up, Miss Spartanburg Pageant, Spartanburg, South Carolina, 1979; First Place, South Carolina National Association of Teachers of Singing, 1979; Vocal Soloist in Dido and Aeneas, Converse College, 1977; Vocal Soloist in Game of Chance, Converse College, 1978; Vocal Soloist, Converse College Chorale, Spartanburg, South Carolina, 1977-1979. Avocations: singing, playing the piano, attending plays, musicals, and concerts, cooking, traveling.

COGLE, MONICA R. social worker; b. Winchester, Va., June 17, 1974; d. Linda C. and Donald M. Cogle(Stepfather), Victor L. and Amy D. Cogle(Stepmother); life ptnr. Lewis E. Jones, Jr.. BSW, Shepherd Coll., 1997; MSW, W.Va. U., Martinsburg, 2003. Lic. social worker W.Va. Bd. Social Work, 1997. Child protective services WVDHHR, Martinsburg, W.Va., 1997—2001; svc. coord. Ea. Panhandle Tng. Ctr., Martinsburg, 2001—01; case mgr. Big Bros. Big Sisters Ea. Panhandle, Martinsburg, 2001—. Custody evaluator Family Ct. Berkeley, Morgan, and Jefferson County, Martinsburg, 2002—. Recipient Ride A Long Vol. Appreciation award, Martinsburg City Police, 2002, 2003. Mem.: NASW. Democrat. Methodist. Office: Big Brothers Big Sisters 630 Winchester Ave Martinsburg WV 25401 Personal E-mail: soclwkr97@adelphia.net. E-mail: bbbs@intrepid.net.

COHANE, HEATHER CHRISTINA, magazine publisher, editor; b. Camberley, Surrey, Eng. came to U.S., 1982; d. William Willoughby and Naomi Mary (Winder) Fausset; m. John Philip Cohane, May 13, 1961 (dec. Dec. 1981); children: Alexander, Candida, Ondine; m. Ossian Kare Berga, Nov. 2, 1985. (dec. Oct. 2000). Student pvt. schs., Isle of Wight, Eng. and Neuchatel, Switzerland. Founding editor, pub. Quest mag., N.Y.C., 1987—; exec. v.p. Gotham Mag., N.Y.C., 1999—2001; editor-at-large Avenue Mag., 2002—. Office: Avenue Mag 63 W 38th #206 New York NY 10018

COHEN, ABBY JOSEPH, investment strategist; b. N.Y.C., Feb. 29, 1952; d. Raymond and Shirley (Silverstein) Joseph; m. David M. Cohen. AB in Econs., Cornell U., 1973; MA in Econs., George Washington U., Washington, 1976. CFA. Economist Fed. Res. Bd., Washington, 1973-76; economist/analyst T. Rowe Price Assocs., Balt., 1976-83; investment strategist Drexel Burnham Lambert, N.Y.C., 1983-90, Goldman, Sachs & Co., N.Y.C., 1990—, mng. ptnr., 1998—. Trustee/fellow Cornell U.; bd. overseers Cornell Med. Sch. Recipient Woman Achiever (Woman of Yr.) award YWCA, N.Y.C., 1989; named to top 50 in Global Fin., 1996, Wall St. Week Hall of Fame, 1997. Mem. Nat. Assn. Bus. Economists, Inst. Chartered Fin. Analysts (chair), N.Y. Soc. Security Analysts (mem. bd. govs.), Nat. Economists Club (bd. govs.), Assn. for Investment Mgmt. and Rsch. (chair bd. govs. 1997-98). Office: Goldman Sachs & Co 85 Broad St New York NY 10004-2456*

COHEN, ADELE, state legislator, lawyer, elementary school educator; BA, Brooklyn Coll.; MA in Edn., Long Island U. Office mgr., benefits dir. Internat. Ladies Garment Workers Union; atty. Dist. Coun. 37 Legal Svcs., 1988—98. Mem. Shorefront Democratic Club; com. mem. Com. to Preserve Brighton Beach and Manhattan Beach; former N.Y. pres. Nat. Womens Political Caucus. Mem.: Brooklyn Womens Bar Assn., U. Jewish Bus. and Profl. Womens Club of Bay Ridge. Office: 2823 W 12th St Ste 1F Brooklyn NY 11224

COHEN, BARBARA ANN, artist; b. Milw., Feb. 18, 1953; d. Joseph and Irene Marion (Brown) C. BS in Art, U. Wis., 1975. One-woman shows include 1st Wis. Nat. Bank, 1981; exhibited in group shows at San Francisco State, 1975-76, Comprehensive Employment Tng. Act, Milw., 1979, San Dieguito Art Guild, 1981, Imperial Valley Art Show, 1982, La Jolla Light Photo Contest, 1986, Clairemont Art Guild, 1989-95. Recipient 1st place award for oil painting Imperial Valley Art Show. Democrat. Jewish. Home: 8627 Via Mallorca Apt D La Jolla CA 92037-9021

COHEN, BETH DIANE, law educator; b. N.Y.C., June 22, 1959; d. Gerald Cohen and Lynn Carla; children: Nora Emily Mitnick, Ian Samuel Mitnick. BA in Polit. Sci., SUNY at Stony Brook, 1981; JD cum laude, Suffolk U., Boston, 1984; Advanced Internat. Legal Studies Diploma, U. of the Pacific, Calif., 1984. Admission: Supreme Jud. Ct. of Mass. 1985, U.S. Dist. Ct. 1986. Law clk. U.S. Dist. Ct., Springfield, Mass., 1987—89; legal rsch. and writing instr. Western New Eng. Coll. Sch. of Law, Springfield, Mass., 1990—99, asst. prof. of law and dir., legal rsch. and writing program, 1999—. Mem.: ABA, Internat. Alliance of Holistic Lawyers, Legal Writing Inst., Assn. of Legal Writing Dirs. Office: Western New England Coll Sch of Law 1215 Wilbraham Rd Springfield MA 01119-2684

COHEN, BETSY Z. bank executive; m. Edward C. Cohen; children: Daniel, Jonathan, Abigail. BA cum laude, Bryn Mawr Coll.; JD cum laude, U. Pa. Law clk. hon. John Biggs chief judge U.S. Ct. Appeals 3rd Cir.; law prof. Rutgers U. Law Sch.; co-founder Spector, Cohen, Gadon & Rosen, Phila.; founder, chmn., CEO Jefferson Bank, Downingtown, Pa., 1974—; founder Jefferson Bank N.J., 1992; chmn., CEO JeffBanks, Inc., 1993—; founder Resource Asset Investment Trust; chmn. Financialmuse.com, Phila. Bd. dirs. Aetna US Healthcare, The Opera Co. Phila., WHYY-TV; trustee Phila. Mus. Art, Jewish Theol. Sem.; vice chair Bryn Mawr Coll., chair fin. com.; chair Phila. Mus. Art Corp. Ptnrs. Article editor The Law Rev. Recipient Paradigm award Greater Phila. C. of C., 1997, Elizabeth Dole Glass Ceiling award Southeastern Pa. ARC, 1998; named Delaware Valley Master Entrepreneur of the Yr., 1994, one to Top 50 Bus. Women in Commonwealth of Pa., 1996, one of 50 Leading Female Entrepreneurs of the World, Nat. Found. for Women Bus. Owners, 1997, A Woman of Distinction, Cmty. Women's Edn. Project, 1998; ranked 103 Working Woman Mags. Top 500 Bus. Women, 1998. Mem. Order of the Coif. Office: Fl 28 1818 Market St Philadelphia PA 19103-3629 E-mail: bcohen@jeffbanks.com.

COHEN, CAROLYN ALTA, healthcare educator; b. Boston, Aug. 25, 1943; d. Haskell Mark and Sarah (Siegal) Cohen. BS, Boston U., 1965; postgrad., Boston State Coll., U. Mass., 1978, Boston Leadership Acad., 1989, Boston Leadership Inst., 1997. Health and phys. edn. tchr., coach, girls athletic coord. Roslindale H.S., Boston, 1965—76; health and phys. edn. tchr., coach, athletic coord. West Roxbury H.S., Boston, 1976—87; asst. dir. health phys. edn. athletics Madison Park Campus, Boston, 1979—87; health educator dept. phys. edn./athletics West Roxbury H.S., Boston, 1989—90, 1990—, lead tchr., 1995—2000; commr. girls' basketball Boston Pub. Schs., 1979—. Cheerleading judge various orgns., 1963, 64, 65, 70, 74, 80, 69-74; coach recreational programs N.E. Deaconess Hosp. Sch. Nursing, 1962-64, Beth Israel Hosp. Sch. Nursing, 1961-64; basketball ofcl. Bay State League, Pvt. Sch. League, Cath. H.S., 1961-80; coach phys. edn. dept. Boston U., 1962-65, 65-68; ofcl. Boston Park and Recreation Dept., 1962-75, summer playgrounds instr., 1961-65; instr. garening, athletic specialist agr. dept. Boston Schs., 1965-76. Trustee Adaptic Environ. Ctr., Boston, 1986—, treas., mem. exec. bd., 1990—; trustee Friends of Boston Harbor Islands, Inc.; instr. ARC, 1965—; rep. Office Children-Area IV, Roslindale, Boston, 1974—76; liaison West Roxbury H.S. and Cmty. Sch. New Move Unlimited Theatre, Boston, 1981—84; liaison spl. arts project West Roxbury H.S., 1993—94. Named to Boston U. Scarlet Key Soc., 1998, N.E. New Agenda Hall of Fame, 2003; recipient Spl. Citation, Boston U. Sargent Coll. Alumni Assn., 1980, Cert. of Appreciation, ARC Mass. Bay, 1986, New Agenda award, Boston Salute to Women in Sport, 1993, Disting. Svc. to Alma Mater award, Boston U., 1994, Citation, Mass. Celebration Women in Sports Day, 2002, citation, Mil. Order of World Wars, 2002, Youth Patriotic & Leadership, 2002. Mem.: Sargent Coll. Alumni Assn. (class sec., editor class newsletter 1965—, Spl. Citation 1980, Black Gold award 1995), Boston U. Nat. Alumni Coun., Boston U. Alumni Assn. (v.p. 1980—82, 1987—89, v.p. cmty. 1995—97, sec. 1997—), Mass. Assn. Health, Phys. Edn., Recreation and Dance (state and exec. com. 1969—74, treas. 1981—94, coord. registration ann. state conv. 1975—94, Honor award recognition 1978, Presdl. Citation 1988, Joseph McKenney award 2002), AAHPERD (bud. mgr. nat. conv. 1988—89), Boston U. Women's Grad. Club (v.p. for scholarship 1981—83, 1985—). Home: 100 Corey St West Roxbury MA 02132-2330 Office Phone: 617-635-8917.

COHEN, CLAIRE GORHAM, investors service company executive; b. St. Johnsbury, Vt., May 9, 1934; d. John David and Muriel (Somers) Gorham; m. Richard D. Cohen, Nov. 26, 1959; 1 son, James H. BA, Radcliffe Coll., 1956; student, U. Vt., 1953-54. Proofreader Dun & Bradstreet, Inc., 1956, mcpl. bond analyst, 1957-64, sr. state analyst, 1965-66, sr. analyst, 1970-71, Moody's Investors Svc. Inc., N.Y.C., 1971-75; v.p., assoc. dir. rsch. Mcpl. Bond Rsch. Divsn., N.Y.C., 1975-86, v.p. mng. dir. state ratings, 1986-89; exec. mng. dir. govtl. fin. Fitch Investors Svc., Inc., N.Y.C., 1989-91, exec. v.p., 1991-94, vice chmn., 1994-97, Fitch IBCA, 1997—. Mem. Govt. Acctg. Stds. Adv. Bd., 1999-2002; adv. bd. Fed. Acctg. Stds., 2002-. Mem. Task Force on N.Y. State Pub. Authorities, 1974-75. Mem. N.Y. Harvard-Radcliffe Schs. Com.; 1952 class agt. St. Johnsbury Acad., 1981-86; 1956 class agt. Radcliffe Coll., 1981-86. Recipient Disting. Svc. award State Debt Mgmt. Network, 1999. Mem. Mcpl. Forum N.Y. (Career Svc. award 2002), Mcpl. Analysts Group N.Y. (treas. 1983-84, chmn. 1984-85), Nat. Fedn. Mcpl. Analysts (bd. govs. 1984-86, chmn. awards com. 1984-85, Career Achievement award 1991), Soc. Mcpl. Analysts, India House Club (bd. govs. 2003—). Office: Fitch IBCA One State St Plz New York NY 10004-2614

COHEN, CLAUDIA, journalist, television personality; b. Englewood, N.J., Dec. 16, 1950; d. Robert B. and Harriet (Brandwein) C.; 1 child, Samantha. BA, U. Pa., 1972. Mng. editor The Daily Pennsylvanian; with More Mag., N.Y.C., 1973-76; mng. editor, 1976-77; reporter N.Y. Post, N.Y.C., 1977-78; editor, author Page Six column, 1978-80; daily columnist I, Claudia N.Y. Daily News, N.Y.C., 1980-81; tv entertainment reporter Live with Regis and Kathie Lee, 1983—; reporter Eyewitness News WABC, 1984—89. Bd. overseers Sch. Arts and Scis. U. Pa.; mem. adv. bd. N.Y. Hosp. Cornell Med. Ctr. Honoree Sarah Herzog Meml. Hosp. Centennial, 1995, Rita Hayworth Gala Benefit for Alzheimers, 2000. Office: Sta WABC 7 Lincoln Sq New York NY 10023-5900

COHEN, CORA, artist; b. N.Y.C., Oct. 19, 1943; d. George and Anne (Lenarsky) C. BA, Bennington Coll., 1964, MA, 1972. Vis. artist U. Pa., 1969-70, U. Chgo., 1983-95, Art Inst. Sch. Chgo., 1983-85, 97, Boston Mus. Sch. Fine Arts, 1994-95, U. Minn., 1996, Kunsthögskolan, Stockholm, 1996, Washington U., St. Louis, Mo., 2003; vis. prof. Art Inst. Sch. Chgo., 1992-93; adj. faculty NYU, 1990-2000, State U. N.J., Newark, 2004; assoc. prof. art, U. N.C., Greensboro, 1998-2003, Vt. Studio Ctr., 1999-2002; nat. focus artist Emory and Henry Coll., Emory, Va., 2003-04. One-person shows include Everson Mus. Art, Syracuse, N.Y., 1974, Max Hutchinson Gallery, N.Y.C., 1979-80, 84, Wolff Gallery, 1988, Holly Solomon Gallery, 1990, New Arts Program, Kutztown, Pa., 1993, Jason McCoy Gallery, N.Y.C., 1993-94, David Beitzel Gallery, N.Y.C., 1994, Sarah Moody Gallery Art, Tuscaloosa, Ala., 1996, Joslyn Art Mus., Omaha, 1996, Hering Raum, Bonn, Germany, 1997-98, Rena Bransten Gallery, San Francisco, 1997, Jason McCoy Gallery, N.Y.C., 1997, Belvedere Strasse, 1999, Bentley Gallery, Scottsdale, Ariz., 1999, 2002, Stefanie Hering, Berlin, 2000, McCoy Chelsea, 2001, Emory (Va.) and Henry Coll., 2003-04; exhibited in group shows at Baxter Art Gallery, Pasadena, Calif., 1985, Am. Acad. and Inst. Arts and Letters, N.Y.C., 1987, Barbara Krakow Gallery, Boston, 1987, Pamela Auchincloss Gallery, Contemporary Surfaces, N.Y.C., 1992, A/C Project Room, An Esemplastic Shift, N.Y.C., 1992, Sandra Gering Gallery, 1992, Piccolo Spoleto Festival, Charleston, S.C., 1992, The Fetish of Knowledge, A/C Project Room, N.Y.C., 1992, Daniel Weinberg Gallery, L.A., 1989, Wolff Gallery, N.Y.C., 1991, Feigen Gallery, 1991, Sytsema Galleries, Baarn, Holland, 1992, Jason McCoy Gallery, N.Y.C., 1993, The Painting Ctr., N.Y.C., 1993, White Columns, N.Y.C., 1993, Bill Maynes Contemporary Art, N.Y.C., 1994, Penine Hart Gallery, N.Y., 1994, Trans Hudson Gallery, Jersey City, Out of the Blue Gallery, Edinburgh, Scotland, 1994, Cepa Gallery, Buffalo, 1995, 2000, the Smart Fair, Stockholm, 1995, NYU, N.Y.C., 1995, Newhouse Ctr. Contemporary Art, S.I., N.Y., 1997, Galleri Mariann Ahnlund Umea, Sweden, 1996, Accrochage, Hering Raum, Bonn, 1996, Galerie Brigitte Schenk, Köln, Germany, Köln Art Fair, 1997, Cepa Gallery, Buffalo, Galleri Mariann Ahnlund, Stockholm, Stalke Out of Space, Copenhagen, Barbara Davis Gallery, Houston, 1998, Oppenhoff & Rädler, Leipzig, Stockholm Art Fair, Hunter Coll., Times Square Gallery, N.Y., The Art Fair, The 69th Regiment Armory, N.Y., 1999, 2002, 04, McCoy, Kansas City, 2000, Open Studio to Benefit the Coalition for the Homeless, N.Y., 2000, U. Ariz. Mus. Art, Tucson, 2001, The Five and Dime Series, Jan Vande Donk, NY, 2001, Cynthia Broan Gallery, N.Y., 2002, Painting Painting N3 Project Space, Williamsburg, Brooklyn, N.Y., 2003, Sheldon Art Galleries, St. Louis, 2003; photgrapher: Cohen, Cora: The Record, The Death, The Surprise, 1999. Recipient N.Y. Found. Arts Gottlieb Found. award, 1990, Pollock Krasner award, 1998, Kohler Fund award U. N.C., 1999; Painting fellow Nat. Endowment for the Arts, 1987; Yaddo Residence grantee, 1982, 95, New Faculty grantee U. N.C., 1999. Mem. Simon Wiesenthal Ctr., Coll. Art Assn. Jewish. Home: 287 Broadway New York NY 10007-2004 E-mail: ccohen287@earthlink.net.

COHEN, CYNTHIA MARYLYN, lawyer; b. Bklyn., Sept. 5, 1945; AB, Cornell U., 1967; JD cum laude, NYU, 1970. Bar: N.Y. 1971, U.S. Ct. Appeals (2nd cir.) 1972, U.S. Dist. Ct. (so. and ea. dists.) N.Y. 1972, U.S. Supreme Ct. 1975, U.S. Dist. Ct. (ctrl. and no. dists.) Calif. 1980, U.S. Ct. Appeals (9th cir.) 1980, U.S. Dist. Ct. (so. dist.) Calif. 1981, U.S. Dist. Ct. (ea. dist.) Calif. 1986. With Paul, Hastings, Janofsky & Walker, LLP, L.A., N.Y.C. Lawyer del. 9th Cir. Jud. Conf. Bd. dirs. N.Y. chpt. Am. Cancer Soc., 1977-80; active Pres.'s Coun. Cornell Women; lawyer del. Ninth Cir. Jud. Conf. Recipient Am. Jurisprudence award for evidence, torts and legal instns., 1968-69; John Norton Pomeroy scholar NYU, 1968-70, Founders Day Cert., 1969. Mem. ABA, Assn. Bar City N.Y. (trade regulation com. 1976-79), Assn. Bus. Trial Lawyers, Fin. Lawyers Conf., N.Y. State Bar Assn. (chmn. class-action com. 1979), State Bar Calif., Los Angeles County Bar Assn., Order of Coif, Delta Gamma. Avocations: tennis, bridge, rare books, wines. Home: 4531 Dundee Dr Los Angeles CA 90027-1213 Office: Paul Hastings Janofsky & Walker LLP 515 S Flower St 25th Fl Los Angeles CA 90071 Office Phone: 213-683-6000. E-mail: cynthiacohen@paulhastings.com.

COHEN, D. ASHLEY, clinical neuropsychologist; b. Omaha, Oct. 2, 1952; d. Cenek and Dorothy A. (Bilek) Hrabik; m. Donald I. Cohen, 1968 (div. 1976); m. Lyn J. Mangiameli, June 12, 1985. BA in Psychology, U. Nebr., Omaha, 1975, MA in Psychology, 1979; PhD in Clin. Psychology, Calif. Coast U., 1988; PhD in Neuropsychology, Pacific Grad. Sch., 2000. Lic. psychologist, Calif.; lic. marriage and family therapist, Nev. Family specialist Ea. Nebr. Human Svcs. Agy. Consultation & Edn., 1979-80; psychotherapist Washoe Tribe, Gardnerville, Nev., 1980; therapist Family Counseling Svc., Carson City, Nev., 1980-93; mental health dir. Alpine County Mental Health, Markleeville, Calif., 1981—93, dir., 1990-93; psychologist Golden Gate Med. Examiners, San Francisco, San Jose, Calif., 1993-97; prin., owner CogniMetrix, San Jose, Calif., 1997—. Conf. presenter and spkr. in field; presenter rsch. findings 7th European Conf. Personality, Madrid, 1994, Oxford (Eng.) U. ISSID Conf., 1991; site coord. nat. standardization Kaufmann brief intelligence test A.G.S., 1988-90, nat. standardization WISC-IV, WPPSI-III Bayley Scales of Infant Development. Vol. EMT, Alpine County, 1983-93. Recipient Svc. to Youth award Office Edn., 1991. Mem. Internat. Soc. Study Individual Differences, Nat. Acad. Neuropsychology. Avocations: astronomy, adventure travel, dog training. Office: 320 S 3d St # 201 San Jose CA 95112

COHEN, DIANA LOUISE, psychology, educator, psychotherapist, consultant; b. Phila., Apr. 8, 1942; d. Nathan and Dorothy (Rubin) Blasberg; 1 child, Jennifer. BA, Temple U., 1964, MEd, 1969, PhD, 1996. Lic. psychologist, Pa., N.J.; lic. profl. counselor, N.J.; cert. mental health counselor. Caseworker Phila. Gen. Hosp., 1964-69, staff psychologist, 1969-70, Atlantic Mental Health Ctr., McKee City, N.J., 1970-80, unit dir., 1980-87, v.p. profl. svcs., 1987-91; pvt. practice Pa., N.J., 1991—. Adj. faculty Glassboro (N.J.) State Coll., 1988—; cmty. and family mediator Cmty. Justice Inst., Atlantic County, N.J., 1990—. Com. chmn. Atlantic County Commn. for Missing and Abused Children, 1984—89; co-project dir. Employee Assistance Program, 1994—. Grantee N.J. Dept. Edn., 1988-89, N.J. Job Tng. Partnership Act, 1990. Mem. APA (assoc.), N.J. Counseling Assn., N.J. Mental Health Counselors Assn. (pres.-elect 1996, pres. 1997), South Shore Region Mental Health Counselors Assn. (sec. 1994-97). Avocations: painting, tennis, cross-country skiing. Home: 2 Dee Dr Linwood NJ 08221-1910 Office: 2106 New Rd Ste E1 Linwood NJ 08221-1052 Office Phone: 609-926-8777.

COHEN, DIANE A. rabbi; b. Boston, Dec. 1, 1945; d. Louis Hyman and Mary Aronson; m. Roy Cohen, June 18, 1967 (div. July 18, 1990); children: Scott David, Joshua Daniel, Charles Lawrence. BA in English, UCLA, 1967; MA in Edn., B of Hebrew Letters, U. of Judaism, L.A., 1989. Ordained rabbi Jewish Theol. Sem. of Am., 1993. Rabbi Temple Ohev Shalom, Colonia, NJ, 1995—2003, Temple Bnai Israel, Willimantic, Conn.; adj. rabbi Congregation Neve Shalom, Metuchen, NJ, 2003—. Author: (book chpt.) Women's Bible Commentary; contbr. articles to profl. jours. Mem. Middlesex County Human Rels. Commn., Middlesex County, NJ, 1997—2000; sec. Woodbridge (N.J.) Interfaith Clergy Coun. Recipient Woman of Excellence award, Middlesex County Comm. on the Status of Women, 1999. Mem.: Rabbinical Assembly N.J. Region (v.p., treas. 1999—2003), Rabbinical Assembly. Jewish. Avocations: reading, cooking, photography, grandchildren. Home: 234 Temple Way Colonia NJ 07067 Personal E-mail: ravdina@aol.com.

COHEN, ELAINE HELENA, pediatrician, cardiologist, educator; b. Boston, Oct. 14, 1941; d. Samuel Clive and Lillian (Stocklan) C.; m. Marvin Leon Gale, May 7, 1972; 1 child, Pamela Beth Gale. AB, Conn. Coll., 1963; postgrad., Tufts U., 1963—64; MD, Woman's Med. Coll. Pa., 1969. Diplomate Am. Bd. Pediat. Intern in pediat. Children's Hosp. of L.A., 1969-70, resident in pediat., 1970-71; fellow in pediat. cardiology UCLA Ctr. Health Scis., 1971-72, L.A. County/U. So. Calif. Med. Ctr., LA, 1972-74; pediatrician Children's Med. Group of South Bay, Chula Vista, Calif., 1974—. Clin. instr. dept. pediat. UCLA Sch. Medicine, 1971-72, U. So. Calif., L.A., 1972-74; asst. clin. prof. dept. pediat. U. Calif., Calif. Sch. Medicine, San Diego, 1974-98, preceptor dept. pediat., 1992—, assoc. clin. prof. dept. pediat., 1998—. Fellow Am. Acad. Pediat.; mem. Calif. Med. Assn., San Diego County Med. Soc. Avocations: sketching, design. Office: Children's Med Group South Bay 280 E St Chula Vista CA 91910-2945 Office Phone: 619-425-3951.

COHEN, ELANA UNGAR, psychotherapist, researcher, consultant; b. Atlanta, Ga., Apr. 1, 1966; d. Rabbi Robert and Sura D. Ungar; m. Allan G. Cohen, Sept. 24, 2002; m. Steven E. Rauch, June 29, 1986 (div. 1990); 1 child, Jeremy N. Rauch. AA, Yeshiva U., NYC, 1985, BA, 1986; MA, Ferkauf Grad. Sch. Psychology, YU, Bronx, NY, 1988; PhD, Union Grad. Sch., Cin., Ohio, 1998. Internship Bellevue Psychiat. Hosp., New York, NY, 1985—86; social worker Fairview Nursing Home, Forest Hills, NY, 1986—87; rschr. on substance abuse Ferkauf Grad. Sch. of Psychol., New York, NY, 1987—88; clinician, emergency rm. psychol. St. Barnabas Hosp., Bronx, NY, 1988—90; psychotherapist Pvt. Practice, Long Is., NY, 1992—95; psychotherapist, supr. New Hope Guild Ctr., Far Rockaway, NY, 1990—95; dir. psychol. svc. New Horizon Counseling Ctr., Far Rockaway, NY, 1995—2002. Instr. workshops, 1994—2002; spkr., lectr., cons. in field. Author: (book) Improved Treatment for the Chronic Schizophrenic, 1998, (poem) A Celebration of Poets, 1998, A Pleasant Reverie, 1998. Recipient Suma Cum Laude, Yeshiva Univ./NY, NY; scholar Roth Scholar, Albert Einstein Coll. of Medicine/NY, NY. Mem.: New York State Psychol. Assn. (mem. 1997—), Am. Psychol. Assn. (mem. 1994—). Democrat. Jewish. Achievements include research in early warning signs of patients' decompensation, techniques for interdisciplinary teamwork treating the psychiatric population, schizophrenic symptoms and treatments, depression vs. anxiety; psychotropics for psychologists, crisis intervention techniques. Avocations: poetry, music, medicine, motherhood, psychol., suicide and schizophrenism. Home: 240 Central Ave #3K Lawrence NY 11559

COHEN, ELIZABETH G. education and sociology educator, researcher; b. Worcester, Mass., May 1, 1931; d. Jacob and Anita (Asher) Ginsburg; m. Bernard P. Cohen, Sept. 20, 1953; children: Anita Cohen Williams, Lewis Samuel. BA, Clark U., Worcester, 1953; MA, Harvard U., 1955, PhD, 1958. Lectr. sociology Boston U., 1957-58; lectr. sociology and edu. Stanford U., 1962-66, asst. prof., 1966-69, assoc. prof., 1969-75, prof., 1975—99, dir. Environ. for Teaching, 1970-76, chmn. social sci. in edu., 1970-93, dir. program for complex instruction, 1982—99, prof. emeritus, 1999—. Author: A New Approach to Applied Research, 1968, Designing Groupwork: Strategies for Heterogeneous Classrooms, 2d edit., 1994; contbr. chpts. in books and articles in field to profl. jours. Trustee Clark U., 1986-03. Woodrow Wilson fellow, 1954-55; AAUW fellow, 1956-57; Fulbright fellow, 1972 Mem. Pacific Sociol. Assn. (v.p. 1981-82), Sociology of Edn. Assn. (v.p. 1982-83), Am. Sociol. Assn. (sect. chmn. 1979-80), Am. Ednl. Research Assn., Sociol. Research Assn. Democrat. Jewish. Home: 851 Sonoma Ter Palo Alto CA 94305-1024 Office: Stanford Univ Sch Of Edn Stanford CA 94305

COHEN, GLORIA ERNESTINE, elementary education educator; b. Bklyn., July 6, 1942; d. Victor George and Marion Theodosia (Roberts) C. BS in Edn., Wilberforce U., 1965; MA in Elem. Edn., Adelphi U., 1975; Profl. Diploma in Ednl. Adminstrn., L.I. U., 1984; MS in Edn., Bklyn. Coll., 1986. Tchr. Bd. Edn., Bklyn., 1965—; case worker Dept. Welfare, Bklyn., 1965—. Mem. comprehensive sch. improvement program Pub. Sch. 149, 1990—91, mem. open corridor planning com., 1990—91, mem. consultation com., 1990—; tchr. in charge of after sch. reading and math. tutorial program, 1995—96; dean grades 4-6, 1996—98; supr. Sat. Acad.; tchr. in charge of Read Extended Day program, 1997—98; cons. tchr. for 4th grade class, 1999; tchr. in charge of food and nutrition distbn. Maxwell H.S., Bklyn., 1999, P.S. 64 Dist. 27, Queens, 2000; tutorial tchr. Pub. Sch. 149, 2001—02; tchr. in charge of food and nutrition distbn. P.S. 174 Dist. 19, Bklyn., 2001—03; tutorial reading tchr. P.S. 149, Bklyn., 2004. Mem.: U.S. Profl. Tennis Registry, U.S. Tennis Assn., Hempstead Lake Tennis Club, Rockville Racqhet Club, Kappa Delta Pi, Zeta Phi Beta. Democrat. Roman Catholic. Avocations: tennis, skiing, swimming. Office: Bd Edn PS 149 700 Sutter Ave Brooklyn NY 11207-4224

COHEN, HELEN HERZ, camp owner, director; b. N.Y.C., Oct. 29, 1912; d. Fred W. and Florence (Hirsch) H.; m. Albert F. Schliefer, Sept. 22, 1933 (dec. Nov. 1941); m. Edwin S. Cohen, Aug. 31, 1944: children: Edwin C., Roger, Wendy. PhB, Brown U., 1933; MA, Columbia U., 1934; postgrad., NYU, Columbia. Counselor Camp Walden, Denmark, Maine, 1930-38, owner, 1939—; tchr. social studies Alcuin Prep. Sch., 1935; office mgr. Lewis P. Weil Importer, 1935-40; pres. The Main Idea, 1968—. Founder, pres. Main Idea, Inc., 1969—. Author: Choosing a Camp for Your Child, Getting Ready for Camp; co-author: Fabulous Foods for Fifty, 1970; contbr. articles to instrnl. booklets, mags. Active alumni coun. Pembroke Coll., 1960; chmn. camp divns. Bridgton (Maine) Hosp. Fund, 1962—; trustee Fund for Advancement Camping, 1980-90. Recipient Gold Key award Columbia Scholastic Press, 1972, award Fund for Advancement of Camping Patron, 1982. Mem. Am. Camping Assn. (regional bd. dirs. 1947-50, 52-55, 56-59, 60-63, standards visitor 1957-93, chmn. pvt. camps 1961, bd. dirs. 1963—, v.p. N.Y. 1963-75, Va. sect. 1975), Pioneers of Camping, Maine Camp Dirs. Assn. (legis. com. 1960-63, bd. dirs. 1963—, Halsey Gulick award 1991), Pembroke Coll. Club (co-founder), Cosmopolitan Club, Cornell Club, Farmington Country Club, Boar's Head Sports Club. Home: Ednam Forest 104 Stuart Pl Charlottesville VA 22903-4740 Office: Camp Walden PO Box 3427 Charlottesville VA 22903-0427 E-mail: waldenherz@aol.com.

COHEN, IDA BOGIN (MRS. SAVIN COHEN), import and export executive; b. Bklyn. d. Joseph and Yetta (Harris) Bogin; m. Barnet Gaster, June 26, 1941 (div. May 1955); m. 2d Savin Cohen, Aug. 30, 1964. Student, St. John's U.; BS, NYU. Sec.-treas. J. Gerber & Co., Inc., N.Y.C., 1942-54, v.p., dir., 1954-73. Pres., dir. Austracan U.S.A., Inc., N.Y.C., 1960-73; v.p. Parts Warehouse, Inc., Woodside, N.Y., 1970-72, sec.-treas., 1972-83; also engaged in pvt. investments. Contbr. articles to South African Outspan, newspapers. Home: 12 Shorewood Dr Sands Point NY 11050-1909

COHEN, JUDITH W. academic administrator; b. N.Y.C., May 14, 1937; d. Meyer F. and Edith Beatrice (Elman) Wiles; BA, Bklyn. Coll., 1957, MA, 1960; cert. advanced studies Hofstra U., 1978; MA Columbia U., 1986, postgrad. 1986—. m. Joseph Cohen, Oct. 19, 1957; children: Amy Beth (dec.), Lisa Carrie, Adam Scott Frank, Elyssa Lily. Tchr. N.Y.C. Pub. Schs., Bklyn., 1957-60; tchr. Mid. Country Sch. Dist., Centereach, N.Y., 1970-93, retired 1993; prof. psychology 5 Towns Coll., Dix Hills, N.Y., 1994—. prof. edn. Dowling Coll., Oakdale, N.Y., Title IX compliance officer, 1980-86, team leader 1987-91; dir. Long Island U. Summer Adventure Program, 1994—. Bus. adv. Women's Equal Rights Congress, Suffolk County Human Rights; chmn. bd. edn., Temple Beth David, trustee, 1975-79; pres. CHUMS, 1979-82; Tchr. of Gifted Post-L.I. U. Saturday Program, 1985—; L.I. Writing Project fellow, Dowling Coll., 1979— ; cert. sch. dist. adminstr., supr., adminstr., N.Y. State; adj. prof. Five Towns Coll., 1994—; adj. prof. edn. Dowling Coll., Oakdale, N.Y., 1997—. Mem. Nassau Suffolk Coun. Adminstrv. Women in Edn. (prds. 1979-81), Assn. for Supervision and Curriculum Devel., Assn. Gifted/Talented Edn., Women's Equal Rights Congress Com. (exec. bd.), Suffolk County Coordinating Council Gifted and Talented, Phi Delta Kappa, Delta Kappa Pi. Author: Arts in Education Curriculum in Social Studies and Language Arts, 1981. Home: 35 Gaymor Ln Commack NY 11725-1305

COHEN, LITA INDZEL, state legislator; m. Stanley S. Cohen; children: Reuven, Shoshana. AB in Polit. Sci. cum laude, U. Pa., 1962, postgrad., JD, 1965. Bar: Pa. 1965. Clk. Henderson, Wetherill & O'Hey, Norristown, 1964, Levi, Mandel & Miller, Phila., 1965; asst. regional counsel HUD, 1966-67; asst. counsel Sch. Dist. Phila., 1967-71; pvt. practice Merion, Pa., 1971-76; exec. v.p., gen. counsel, COO Ind. Broadcasting Co., Inc. and

Banks Broadcasting Co., 1976-82; pres. Orange Prodns., Inc.-Nat. Radio Syndication Co., 1983-87, Lita Cohen Radio Svcs., Merion, Pa., 1987-93; mem. Ho. of Reps., Conshohocken, Pa., 1992—. Bd. dirs. Merion Civic Assn.; mem. citizens fire prevention com. Phila. Fire Dept.; active Lower Merion/Narberth Watershed Assn., Lower Merion Twp. Police Pension Assn., Har Zion Temple; v.p. bd. dirs. Phila. Child Guidance Ctr.; Lower Merion Twp. commr., 1986-93; capt. Heart Fund Block; mem. women's adv. com. Montemery County C.C.; hon. pres. Golda Meir Profl. Women's Hadassah; past bd. dirs. Kaiserman JYC, Atwater Kent Mus. Mem. Pa. Bar Assn., Phila. Bar Assn., Montgomery County Bar Assn. Office: Pa Ho of Reps PO Box 202020 Harrisburg PA 17120-2020 also: 117 E 4th Ave Conshohocken PA 19428-1979

COHEN, MARCIA FRIEDLANDER, writer, editor-in-chief, journalist; b. Spring Valley, Pa. d. Morris and Belle Podolin Friedlander; m. Laurance Resnick Cohen, Jan. 10, 1953; children: Elizabeth Marion, Jesse Laurance. BA cum laude, Harvard U., 1952. Reporter/editor Sun-Bull., Binghamton, NY, 1968—72; exec. editor Hearst, N.Y.C., 1975—77; reporter/editor N.Y. Daily News, 1979—83; sr. corr. Earth Summit Times, N.Y.C., 1990; founding editor-in-chief Her N.Y., 1993. Author: The Sisterhood, 1988; co-author: The Parents' Pediatric Companion; contbr. articles to numerous mags. and newspapers. Dir. N.Mex. com. Nat. Mus. of Women in the Arts, Santa Fe; mem. Santa Fe Coun. on Internat. Rels.; mem., facilitator Nat. Urban League, Binghamton. Mem.: PEN Internat., Authors Guild, Vet. Feminists Am. Avocations: painting, travel, hiking, gardening. Home: 3 Conchas Pl Santa Fe NM 87508-8807 E-mail: cohennyc3@aol.com.

COHEN, MARCY SHARON, lawyer; b. N.Y.C., Apr. 29, 1954; d. Morton Gilbert and Sue Cohen. AB, Lehman Coll., 1975; JD, N.Y. Law Sch., 1978. Bar: N.Y. 1979, U.S. Dist. Ct. (ea. and so. dists.) N.Y. 1979, U.S. Supreme Ct. 1982. Assoc. Marcus & Marcus, N.Y.C., 1978-80; v.p., assoc. gen. counsel Bank Leumi Trust Co. N.Y., N.Y.C., 1980-84; sr. v.p., gen. counsel Atlantic Bank N.Y., N.Y.C., 1984-93; 1st v.p., dep. gen. counsel Republic Nat. Bank N.Y., N.Y.C., 1993-99; counsel for N.Am., Westdeutsche Landesbank Girozentrale, 1999—. Mem. faculty Am. Inst. Banking, N.Y.C., 1984-88. Mem. ABA (mem. corp. bankig and bus. law com.), Assn. of Bar of City of N.Y. (mem. banking law com.), N.Y. State Bar Assn. (chair corp. counsel sect.), Assn. Comml. Fin. Attys. Avocations: photography, art history, english and french literature. Office: Westdeutsche Landesbank Girozentrale 1211 Ave of Americas New York NY 10036-8701

COHEN, MARLENE LOIS, pharmacologist; b. New Haven, May 5, 1945; d. Abraham David and Jeanette (Bader) C.; m. Jerome H. Fleisch, Aug. 11, 1976; children: Abby, Sheryl. BS, U. Conn., 1968; PhD, U. Calif., San Francisco, 1973. Registered pharmacist, Calif., Conn. Postdoctoral fellow Roche Inst. of Molecular Biology, Nutley, N.J., 1973-75; sr. pharmacologist Eli Lilly & Co., Indpls., 1975-80, rsch. scientist, 1980-85, sr. rsch. scientist, 1985-89, rsch. advisor, 1989-94, Lilly Rsch. fellow, 1994—. Adj. asst. prof. dept. pharmacology and toxicology Ind. U. Sch. Medicine, Indpls., 1976-82, adj. assoc. prof., 1982-86, adj. prof., 1987—; rsch. asst. Pfizer Labs., Groton, Conn., 1967; cons. Drug Dependence Inst., Yale U., New Haven, 1974. Mem. editorial bd. Jour. Clin. and Exptl. Hypertension, 1978—, Proceedings of the Soc. for Exptl. Biology and Medicine, 1979-84, Life Sci., 1984—, Jour. Pharmacology and Exptl. Therapeutics, 1987—, Current Drugs: Serotonin, 1999—, Current Topics in Pharmacology, 1994—; ad hoc reviewer for profl. jours.; author: (with others) Principles of Medicinal Chemistry, 1974, 3d edit., 1989, New Antihypertensive Drugs, 1976, The Serotonin Receptors, 1988, The Peripheral Actions of 5-Hydroxytryptamine, 1989, Central and Peripheral 5-HT3 Receptors, 1992; contbr. articles to profl. jours. Mem. Soc. for Exptl. Biology and Medicine, Am. Soc. for Pharmacology and Exptl. Therapeutics (chairperson subcom. on women in pharmacology 1984-89, chairperson nominating com. 1984, com. on profl. affairs 1984-89, membership com. 1989-92, bd. publs. trustees 1989—), Serotonin Club (councilor 1987-90, nomenclature com. 1988—), Alpha Lambda Delta, Phi Kappa Phi, Rho Chi. Office: Lilly Rsch Labs Lilly Corp Ctr Indianapolis IN 46285-0001

COHEN, MARY ANN, judge; b. Albuquerque, July 16, 1943; d. Gus R. and Mary Carolyn (Avriette) C. BS, UCLA, 1964; JD, U. So. Calif., 1967. Bar: Calif. 1967. Ptnr. Abbott & Cohen, P.C. and predecessors, L.A., 1967-82; judge U.S. Tax Ct., Washington, 1982—, chief judge, 1996-2000. Mem. ABA (sect. taxation), Legion Lex. Republican. Office: US Tax Ct 400 2nd St NW Washington DC 20217-0002

COHEN, MARYJO R. manufacturing executive; BS in Bus. Adminstrn., U. Mich., 1973, JD, 1976. Bar: Mich. 1976. Assoc. resident counsel Nat. Presto Industries, 1976-82, asst. to treas., 1982-83, treas., 1983-86, v.p., 1986-89, pres., 1989—, CEO, 1995—, COO, CFO. V.p. subsidiaries and divsns. Canton Sales & Storage Co., Century Leasing & Liquidating, Inc., Jackson Sales and Storage Co., Nat. Def. Corp., Nat. Holding Investment Co., Presto Export Ltd., Presto Mfg. Co., Presto Products Mfg. Co. Office: Nat Presto Industries 3925 N Hastings Way Eau Claire WI 54703

COHEN, MELANIE ROVNER, lawyer; b. Chgo., Aug. 9, 1944; d. Millard Jack and Sheila (Fox) Rovner; m. Arthur Wieber Cohen, Feb. 17, 1968; children: Mitchell Jay, Stephanie Tomasky, Jennifer Sue, Jason Canel. AB, Brandeis U., 1965; JD, DePaul U., 1977. Bar: Ill. 1977, U.S. Dist. Ct. (no. dist.) Ill., U.S. Ct. Appeals (7th cir.). Law clk. to Justice F.J. Hertz U.S. Bankruptcy Ct., 1976-77; ptnr. Antonow & Fink, Chgo., 1977-89, Altheimer & Gray, Chgo., 1989—2003, Quarles & Brady, Chgo., 2003—. Mem. Supreme Ct. of Ill. Atty. Registration and Disciplinary Commn. Inquiry Bd., 1982-86, hearing bd., 1986-94; instr. secured and consumer transactions creditor-debtor law DePaul U., Chgo., 1980-90; bd. dirs. Bankruptcy Arbitration and Mediation Svcs., 1994-96; instr. real estate and bankruptcy law John Marshall Law Sch., Chgo., 1996-98. Contbr. articles to profl. jours. Panelist, spkr., bd. dirs., v.p. Brandeis U. Nat. Alumni Assn., 1981-90; life mem. Brandeis Nat. Women's Com., 1975—, pres. Chgo. chpt., 1975-82; mem. Glencoe (Ill.) Caucus, 1977-80; chair lawyers com. Ravinia Festival, 1990-91, chmn. sustaining com., 1991, mem. annual fund, 1991—. Brandeis U. fellow. Fellow: Am. Coll. Bankruptcy; mem.: ABA (co-chair com. on enforcement of creditors' rights and bankruptcy), Internat. Women's Insolvency and Restructuring Confederation, Internat. Fedn. Insolvency Profls., Internat. Insolvency Inst., Turnaround Mgmt. Assn. (pres. Chgo./midwest chpt. 1990—92, internat. bd. dirs. 1990—2004, mem. mgmt. com. 1995—2003, pres. internat. bd. dirs. 1999—2000, chmn. internat. bd. dirs. 2000—01), Comml. Fin. Assn. Edn. Found. (bd. govs.), Ill. Trial Lawyers Assn., Comml. Law League, Chgo. Bar Assn. (chmn. bankruptcy reorgn. com. 1983—85), Ill. State Bar Assn. Home: 167 Park Ave Glencoe IL 60022-1351 Office: Quarles & Brady 500 W Madison Ave Ste 3700 Chicago IL 60661 Office Phone: 312-715-5050. E-mail: mcohen@quarles.com.

COHEN, RACHEL RUTSTEIN, financial planner; b. Phila., June 10, 1968; d. Charles Lawrence and Ronna (Newman) Rutstein(Stepmother), Susan Ellen (Yokel) Sansweet; m. Kipp B. Cohen, Nov. 22, 1995; children: Brandon Erik, Ryan Cameron. BS in Bus. Adminstrn., Pa. State U., 1990; student, U. Tel Aviv, 1989; MBA in Fin., Temple U., 1997. CFP; cert. wealth mgmt. advisor. V.p. Merrill Lynch, Bala Cynwyd, Pa., 1990—. V.p. bd. dirs. Phila. chpt. Shaare Zedek Hosp.Charity, 1992-96, co-chair Phone-A-Thon, 1993. Mem.: Phila. Fin. Assn. (co-chair dinner com.), Pa. State U. Alumni Assn., Phila. C. of C. (diplomate 1991—95, nursery sch. com. 2003—), Green Valley Country Club. Republican. Avocations: golf, tennis, travel, language (spanish), reading. Office: Merrill Lynch 2 Bala Plz Bala Cynwyd PA 19004 Office Phone: 610-668-6170. E-mail: rachel_cohen@ml.com.

COHEN, RACHELLE SHARON, journalist; b. Phila., Oct. 21, 1946; d. Hyman and Diane Doris (Schultz) Goldberg; m. Stanley Martin Cohen, June 22, 1968; 1 dau., Avril Heather. BS, Temple U., 1968. Editor, Somerville Jour. (Mass.), 1968-70; reporter Lowell Sun (Mass.), 1970-72, AP, Boston, 1972-79; state house bur. chief Boston Herald Am., 1979-80, editorial page editor, 1980-82; editorial page editor, columnist Boston Herald, 1982— . Mem. Mass. Bar Assn. (bench, bar, press com.), Mass. Assn. Mental Health (bd. dirs. 1993—). Office: Boston Herald 1 Herald St Boston MA 02118-2200

COHEN, ROBERTA JANE, government executive; b. N.Y.C., Feb. 5, 1940; d. George H. and Ethel (Israel) Cohen; m. David A. Korn, Apr. 8, 1981; stepchildren: Marie Korn, David Korn, Philip Korn, Stephen Korn. BA, Barnard Coll., 1960; MA, Johns Hopkins U., 1963. Exec. dir. Internat. League for Human Rights, N.Y.C., 1971-78; sr. adviser to U.S. del. to UN and human rights officer Dept. of State, Washington, 1978-80, dep. asst. sec. state for human rights, 1980-81; head pub. affairs office U.S. Embassy, Addis Ababa, 1982-85; hon. sec. Parliamentary Human Rights Group, London, 1985-86; sr. adviser to refugee policy group Washington, 1989-96; sr. advisor NAS Com. on Human Rights, Washington, 1991-95; sr. advisor on internally displaced to rep. UN Sec.-Gen., 1994—; co-dir. project on internal. displacement Brookings Instn., Washington, 1994—, sr. fellow, 2001—. Cons. World Bank, various govt. and non-govt. orgns., 1991—94; chmn. task force on human rights UN Assn., Washington, 1993—94; chair task force on China Internat. Human Rights Law Group, Washington, 1997—99, vice chair, 1992—96; bd. dirs. Jacob Blaustein Inst. for Advancement Human Rights; mem. adv. com. Human Rights Watch/Africa, RFK Meml. on Human Rights, Internat. League Human Rights, Acad. on Human Rights & Humanitarian Law, Am. U. & Wash. Coll. Law, Trinity Coll. Human Rights Program; mem. Coun. Fgn. Rels., Women's Fgn. Policy Group, Fund for Peace, Human Rights Bus. Roundtable; commr. Women's Commn. on Refugee Women & Children. Author: People's Republic of China: The Human Rights Exception, 1987; co-author: Masses in Flight: The Global Crisis of Internal Displacement, 1998; co-editor: The Forsaken People, 1998, Compliance of the Law of the South Caucusus with the Guiding Principles on Internal Displacment: Georgia, Armenia & Azerbaijan, 2003. Pub. mem. U.S. del. UN Commn. on Human Rights, 1998, Orgn. for Security and Cooperation in Europe, 2003. Recipient Superior Honor award, U.S. Info. Agy., Addis Abada, 1985, Human Rights award, UN Assn., 1994, Fiftieth Ann. award for Exemplary Writing on Fgn. Affairs and Diplomacy, Diplomats and Consular Officers Ret., 2002. Mem.: Cosmos Club.

COHEN, SARAH, reporter; BA, U. N.C.; M in Pub. Affairs Reporting, U. Md. Reporter Tampa Tribune, St. Petersburg Times, Investigative Reporters and Editors; database editor Washington Post, 1999—. Office: Washington Post 1150 15th St NW Washington DC 20071

COHEN, SASHA (ALEXANDRA PAULINE COHEN), ice skater; b. Westwood, Calif., Oct. 26, 1984; d. Roger and Galina Cohen. Winner Junior Grand Prix, Stockholm, 1999; 2nd place U.S. Championships, 2000; winner Pacific Coast Sectional, 2000; 3rd place Trophée Lalique, 2001; Silver medalist U.S. Nats. Championship, 2001—02; 2nd place U.S. Championships, 2002; 4th place World Championships, 2002, Olympic Winter Games, 2002; 2nd place Hersheys Kisses Challenge, 2002; 4th place Campbells Classic, 2002; 1st place Skate Can., 2002, Trophee Lalique, 2002; 2nd place Cup of Russia, 2002; 1st place Crest White Strips Challenge, 2002; bronze medalist Nats., 2003; 4th place Worlds, 2003; champion Grand Prix Finals, 2003; 1st place Trophy Lalique, 2004, Skate CAn., 2004, Skate Am., 2004, Campbells Soup, 2004; silver medalist World Championships, 2004. Recipient Gardena Winter Trophy, 1999, Finlandia Trophy, 2001. Avocations: art, jewelry making, reading, designing costumes. Office: 9 Journey c/o Ice Palace Aliso Viejo CA 92656*

COHEN, SELMA, reference librarian, researcher; b. N.Y.C., Mar. 14, 1930; d. George and Rose (Cohen) Unger; m. Irwin H. Cohen, Nov. 19, 1950; children: Barbara Katzeff, Joel. Grad. high sch., William Howard Taft High Sch., 1948. Asst. bookkeeper acctg. dept. Severud, Perrone et al, N.Y.C., 1970-75, Russell Reynolds Assocs., Inc., N.Y.C., 1976-77, rsch. asst., 1977—, reference libr., 1985—. Chairwoman Scott Tower Charity Com., Bronx, 1976-84, Scott Tower Property Improvement Com., Bronx, 1983-84. Home: 3400C Paul Ave # 10H Bronx NY 10468-1042 Office: Russell Reynolds Assocs 200 Park Ave New York NY 10166-0005 Office Phone: 212-351-2032.

COHEN, SHARLEEN COOPER, interior designer, writer; b. L.A., June 11, 1940; d. Sam and Claretta (Ellis) White; m. R. Gary Cooper, Dec. 18, 1960 (dec. Feb., 1971); m. Martin L. Cohen, M.D., Aug. 27, 1972; children: Cami Gordon, Dalisa Cooper Cohen. Student, U. Calif., Berkeley, 1957-58, UCLA, 1958-60, L.A. Valley Film Sch., 1976-78. Owner, mgr. Designs on You, L.A., 1965-77; writer L.A., 1977—. Prodr. Jewish Repertory Theatre, N.Y.C., 1996. Author: The Day After Tomorrow, 1979, Regina's Song, 1980, The Ladies of Beverly Hills, 1983, Marital Affairs, 1985, Love, Sex and Money, 1988, Lives of Value, 1991, Innocent Gestures, 1994, (play) Solomon and Sheba, 1990, (musical) Sheba, 1996; assoc. prodr. : Broadway Street Corner Symphony; prodr.: Cookin' At The Cookery, The Best of Times; assoc. prodr. : Duet; writer: Stormy Weather, 1999, Blackout, 2000. Mem. exec. com. Women of Distinction United Jewish Appeal, 1990-95; chair L.A. chpt. Nat. Gaucher Found., 1991-95; bd. dirs., mem. com. chair Calif. Coun. for the Humanities, San Francisco, 1992-98; bd. dirs. Amas Mus. Theatre; mem. acquisitions com. Modern Contemporary Art Coun., L.A. County Mus. Art. Recipient Hon. Mention, Santa Barbara Writers Conf., 1978, Writer's Digest Writing Competition, 2000. Mem.: PEN, League of Profl. Theatre Women, The Drama League, Theatre Guild, Dramatists Guild, Writers Guild Am. E-mail: SccInc1@aol.com.

COHEN, SHIRLEY MASON, retired secondary school educator, volunteer; b. Jersey City, June 24, 1924; d. Herman and Esther (Vinik) Mason; m. Herbert Leonard Cohen, June 24, 1951; children: Bruce Mason, Annette Pauline, Carol Elyse, Debra Tamara. BA, Rutgers U., 1945; MA, Columbia U., 1946; postgrad., U. Calif., Berkeley, 1946-51. Instr. U. Calif., Berkeley, 1946-51, Am. River Coll., Sacramento, 1962; tchr. various H.S., Sacramento, 1975-92. Mentor tchr. Sacramento City Unified Sch. Dist., 1987-88. Author: Yearning to Breathe Free: The Story of the Vinik, Mason, and Gatkin Families, 1997. Bd. dirs. Sacramento Cmty. Concerts, 1965—. Mem. Phi Beta Kappa. Avocations: theatre, music, tennis, writing, literature.

COHEN, SUSAN LOIS, writer; b. Chgo., Mar. 27, 1938; d. Martin and Ida Handler; m. Daniel E. Cohen, Feb. 2, 1958; 1 child, Theodora (dec.). BA, New Sch. for Social Rsch., 1960; MA in Social Work, Adelphi U., 1962. Social worker, N.Y.C., 1962-67; various social work positions in N.Y.C., 1962-68. Author: The Liberated Couple, 1969, reassued under title Liberated Marriage, 1973; (under name Elizabeth St. Clair) Stonehaven, 1974, The Singing Harp, 1975, Secret of the Locket, 1975, Provenance House, 1976, Mansion in Miniature, 1977, Dewitt Manor, 1977, The Jeweled Secret, 1978, Murder in the Act, 1978, Sandcastle Murder, 1979, Trek or Treat, 1980, Sealed with a Kiss, 1981; (with Daniel Cohen) The Kids' Guide to Home Computers, 1983, The Kids' Guide to Home Video, 1984, Teenage Stress, 1984, Screen Goddesses, 1984, Rock Video Superstars, 1985, Wrestling Superstars, Vol. 1, 1985, Vol. 2, 1986, Hollywood Hunks and Heroes, 1985, Heroes of the Challenger, 1986, A Six-Pack and a Fake ID, 1986, The Encyclopedia of Movie Stars, 1986, A History of the Oscars, 1986, Teenage Competition: A Survival Guide, 1987, Young and Famous: Hollywood's Newest Superstars, 1987, Going for the Gold, 1987, What You Can Believe about Drugs, 1988, What Kind of Dog is That, 1989, When Someone You Know Is Gay, 1989, Zoo Superstars, 1989, Zoos, 1992, Where to Find Dinosaurs Today, 1992, Going for the Gold: Medal Hopefuls for Winter '92, 1992, Gold Medal Glow: The Story of America's Women's Gymnastic Team, 1996, Pan Am 103, 2000, rev. edit. 2001, Hauntings and Horrors, 2002. Mem. Wodehouse Soc. (pres.), Watson's Erroneous Deductions, Chapter One, The Capers of Sherlock Holmes, Clumber Spaniel Club of Am. Avocation: cats. Address: 877 W Hand Ave Cape May Court House NJ 08210-1865 E-mail: blndgscast@aol.com.

COHEN, VALERIE A. entertainment company executive; b. 1956; BA, Middlebury Coll.; JD, Harvard U. Law clerk NJ Supreme Court; ptnr. Leisure Newton & Irvine, Dewey Ballentine; sr. v.p. bus. devel. Walt Disney Co., Burbank, Calif., assistant general counsel, corp. sr. v.p., 1995—. Office: Walt Disney Co 500 S Buena Vista St Burbank CA 91521-0006*

COHEN-DEMARCO, GALE MAUREEN, pharmaceutical executive; b. Rochester, N.Y., June 4, 1947; d. Maurice Cohen and Florence Michaels; m. David Earl McCarty, June 16, 1975 (div. Nov. 1979); 1 child, Brock Adam; m. Peter Francis DeMarco, Aug. 3, 1984. BA, U. Rochester, 1969; MA, SUNY, Buffalo, 1971. Various pharm. cos.; hosp. rep., dirs. mgr., med. liason Glaxo Pharms., 1987—97; regional bus. mgr. Axcan Pharma, 1997—2003, sr. regional account mgr., 2003—. Grantee, NIH, 1969; scholar, N.Y. State Regents, 1964. Democrat. Jewish. Avocations: environmental activities, charity organizations. Home: 27621 W Lakeview Dr N Wauconda IL 60084-2362 Office: Axcan Pharma 22 Inverness Ctr Pkwy Ste 310 Birmingham AL 35242 Office Phone: 800-950-8085. Personal E-mail: jap19472002@yahoo.com.

COHEN-STRONG, ELAYNE BARBARA, social services administrator, educator; b. Detroit, Jan. 29, 1952; d. Lawrence Cohen and Rae Sarah Saulles; m. Leroy Strong, Jr., May 16, 1987; 1 child, Kacie Leah Strong. BA, Mich. State U., 1974; student, Oakland C.C., Farmington Hills, Mich., 1969—71, Calif. State U., Long Beach, 1995. Cert. assistive tech. applications Calif. State U. Northridge, multi-subject tchg. credential Calif., Clear credential in spl. edn.-visually handicapped Calif. Med. technician Henry Ford Hosp., Detroit, 1975—85; adminstrv. asst. Hosp. Homecare of Orange County, Santa Ana, Calif., 1985—87; pvt. billing office asst. Doctors and Nurses, Newport Beach, Calif., 1987—91; dir. youth outreach dept. and tech., tchr. for the visually impaired Blind Children's Learning Ctr., Santa Ana, 1991—. Contbr. mag. Individuals with Disabilities News, newspaper In Focus, L.A. Times. Named Tchr. of the Yr., Wal-Mart, 1996. Mem.: PTA (assoc.; historian 2002—03), CEC (assoc.), Assn. for the Edn. and Rehab. of the Visually Impaired (assoc.), Calif. Transcribers and Educators of the Visually Impaired (assoc.). Avocations: swimming, travel, ceramics. Home: 6478 New Gate Way Yorba Linda CA 92886 Office: Blind Children's Learning Ctr 18542-B Vanderlip Santa Ana CA 92705 Personal E-mail: teachem45@aol.com. E-mail: elayne.strong@blindkids.org.

COHEN-VADER, CHERYL DENISE, municipal official; b. Ft. Bragg, N.C., Mar. 23, 1955, BA, Princeton U., 1977; MBA, Columbia U., 1983. Treas. internat. divsn. commodity import-export financing Bank of N.Y., N.Y.C., 1977-81; v.p. Citicorp Securities Markets, Inc. Citicorp, N.Y.C., 1983-90; v.p. Weldon, Sullivan, Carmichael & Co., 1990-92; asst. v.p. Kirkpatrick Pattis, 1993-95; mgr. revenue dept. City of Denver, 1996—. Mem. Mcpl. Securities Rulemaking Bd., 1998-2001. Bd. dirs. Mile High chpt. ARC, Colo. Episcopal Found. Recipient Consortium of Grad. Mgmt. Edn. fellowship, 1981-83, Recognition of Achievement award Five Points Bus. Assn., Inc., 1995, Leadership Denver award Denver C. of C., 1994; honored in Living Portraits of African-Am. Women Nat. Coun. Negro Women, 1997. Mem. Govt. Finance Officers Assn. Office: City Denver Revenue Dept McNichols Bldg Rm 300 144 W Colfax Ave Denver CO 80202-5391

COHN, JANE SHAPIRO, public relations executive; b. N.Y.C., May 19, 1935; d. Harry I. and Ann (Safanie) Shapiro; m. Albert M. Cohn, June 30, 1957 (div. 1972); children: Theodore David, William Alan. BA, Brandeis U., 1956; postgrad., Coll. of New Rochelle, 1974-76; student, Harvard U., 1985. Dir. pub. rels. Hudson River Mus., Yonkers, N.Y., 1976-79; account exec. Dudley-Anderson Yutzy Pub. Rels. Agy. subs. Ogilvy Mather, N.Y.C., 1979-81; dir. communications Haines Lundberg Waehler, N.Y.C., 1981-91; prin. Jane Cohn Pub. Rels., Sherman, Conn., 1991—. Cons. to various firms in architecture, engring., and constrn. industry, 1983; spkr., mktg. promotion strategies conf., 1989, AIA N.Y. Chpt., panelist So. New England Chpt.; organizer, co-spkr.Interplan Conv.; organizer and moderator Soc. Mktg. Profl. Svcs. N.Y. Chpt., 1996; spkr. Soc. Mktg. Profl. Svcs. Nat. Conf., 1997; panelist AIA Nat. Conv., 1998. Contbr. articles to profl. jours., chpts. to books. Fellow Soc. Mktg. Profl. Svcs. (cert.; bd. dirs. N.Y. chpt. 1988-89, 92-95, spkr. ann. convs., Gold Medal award 1994); mem. AIA (assoc. 1988, 98, panelist nat. conv. 1998, spkr. ann. conv.), Am. Mktg. Assn. (panelist ann. conv. 1987, moderator profl. services sect. ann. conv. 1988, exec. mem.), Practice Mgmt. Assn. (spkr. promotion strategies conf. 1989) Democrat. Jewish. Avocations: art, sculpture, gardening. Office: Jane Cohn Pub Rels 31 Spring Lake Rd Sherman CT 06784-1201

COHN, KATHLEEN MANDRY, writer; b. Utica, N.Y., Feb. 22, 1944; d. Alphonse Valentine and Helen Cudilo Mandry; m. Martin Cohn, Dec. 29, 1972; 1 child, Aaron. BA in English Lit., Harpur Coll., 1965. Copywriter Benton & Bowles Advt., N.Y.C., 1965—71; copywriter, v.p. creative McCaffrey & McCall Advt., N.Y.C., 1972—78; freelance writer N.Y.C., 1978—80; assoc. creative dir. Foote Cone Belding, San Francisco, 1980—82; v.p. creative Dancer Fitzgerald Sample, San Francisco, 1982—84. Creative cons., San Francisco, 1983—86. Author: How to Make Elephant Bread, 1971, The Cat & The Mouse & The Mouse & The Cat, 1972, How Does it Feel to Live Next Door to a Giraffe?, 1973, (plays) I Don't Want to be Like My Father, 1973, How to Grow a Jelly Glass Farm, 1974, The World on My Windowsill, 1975, (adult non-fiction) First American Peanut Growing Book, 1976, (children's TV) ABC's Schoolhouse Rock, 1976; lyricist Rufus Xavier Sarsaparilla. Vol., parent bd., chair sch. events French Am. Internat. Sch.; vol. The Urban Sch. Avocations: growing lavender, hiking, swimming, yoga, reading. Home: 1524 Willard St San Francisco CA 94117

COHN, MARIANNE WINTER MILLER, civic activist; b. Denver, Jan. 15, 1928; d. Henry Abraham II and Esther (Sheflan) Winter; m. Benjamin K. Miller, Dec. 29, 1948 (dec. Dec. 1972); children: Judy Ellen, Philip Henry (dec. 1996); m. Isidore Cohn Jr., Jan. 3, 1976; stepchildren: Ian Jeffrey Cohn, Lauren Kerry Cohn Fouros. Student, Colo. U., 1946-47. Women's bd. dirs. Nat. Jewish Hosp. at Denver, 1951—60, pres. women's divsn., 1960—61, mem., sec. gov. bd., 1972—76; mem. nat. bd. Nat. Jewish Ctr., 1976—; mem. exec. bd. Greater New Orleans Tourist and Conv. Commn., 1985; chmn. spouse program arrangements Am. Coll. Surgons, La., 1985; mem. exec. bd. NCCJ, New Orleans, 1987—96, sec., 1991—92, treas., 1993—94, nat. bd. dirs., 1993; bd. dirs. Jewish Endowment Found., New Orleans, 1987—88, La. ArtWorks of Arts Coun. of New Orleans, 2000; mem. Arts Coun. of New Orleans, 1988—, v.p. devel., 1991—92, v.p. grants, exec. bd., 1995—96, pres., 1997—98, chmn. bd., 1999, v.p. grants, 2001; chmn. Exhibit Sunking, Louis XIV La. State Mus., 1984, bd. dirs., 1994—2001, mem. governing bd., 1992—; pres. La. Mus. Found., 1989—90; bd. dirs. New Orleans Symphony Aux., 1980; chmn. Odyssey Ball of New Orleans Mus. Art, 1992; bd. dirs. La. Coun. for Music and Performing Arts, 1991—92; regional vice chmn. Nat. Jewish Ctr., 1999—; mem. Sisterhood of Temple Emanuel Denver, pres., 1957—60. Recipient Edgar L. Feinberg Meml. award James D. Rives Surg. Soc., 1988, Woman of Fashion award Men of Fashion, 1989, Humanitarian award Nat. Jewish Ctr. Immunology and Respiratory Medicine, 1995, role model award Young Leadership Coun. New Orleans, 1998—, Nat. Jewish Ctr. Chmn.'s award, 1999. Republican. Avocations: travel, cooking.

COHN, MARJORIE BENEDICT, curator, art historian, educator; b. N.Y.C., Jan. 10, 1939; d. Manson and Marjorie (Allen) Benedict; m. Martin Cohn, Dec. 19, 1960. BA, Mt. Holyoke Coll., 1960; AM, Radcliffe Coll., 1961; DFA, Mt. Holyoke Coll., 1996. Conservator works of art on paper Art Mus. Harvard U., Cambridge, Mass., 1963-89, lectr. fine arts, 1974-77, sr. [illegible], prin. curator, 1983[illegible], acting dir., 1990-91, 2002—. Vis. lectr. Boston U., 1972, 73, Wellesley (Mass.) Coll., 1973; vis. asst. prof. Brown U., Providence, 1975. Author: Wash & Gouache, 1977, A Noble Collection: The Spencer Albums of Old Master Prints, 1992, (with S.L. Siegfried) Works by J.A.D. Ingres in Collection of the Fogg Art Museum, 1980, Francis Calley Gray and Art Collecting for America, 1986, Lois Orswell, David Smith and Modern Art, 2002. Sec. Arlington (Mass.) Hist. Commn., 1972-85. Mem. Am. Acad. Arts and Scis., Print Coun. Am. Democrat. Office: Harvard U Fogg Art Mus 32 Quincy St Cambridge MA 02138-3845 E-mail: cohn@fas.harvard.edu.

COHN, MILDRED, biochemist, educator; b. N.Y.C., July 12, 1913; d. Isidore M. and Bertha (Klein) Cohn; m. Henry Primakoff, May 30, 1938; children: Nina, Paul, Laura. BA, Hunter Coll., 1931, DSc (hon.), 1984; MA, Columbia U., 1932, PhD, 1938; DSc (hon.), Women's Med. Coll., 1975, Radcliffe Coll., 1978, Washington U., St. Louis, 1981, Brandeis U., 1984, U. Pa., Phila., 1984, U. N.C., 1985; PhD (hon.), Weizmann Inst. Sci., 1988; DSc (hon.), U. Miami, 1990. Rsch. asst. biochemistry George Washington U. Sch. Medicine, 1937—38; rsch. assoc. Cornell Med. Coll., 1938—46, Washington U. Sch. Medicine, 1946—58; assoc. prof. biol. chemistry Washington U., 1958—60; assoc. prof. biophysics and phys. biochemistry U. Pa. Med. Sch., 1960—61, prof., 1961—71, prof. biochemistry and biophysics, 1971—82, Benjamin Rush prof. physiol. chemistry, 1978—82, prof. emerita, 1982—; sr. mem. Inst. Cancer Rsch., Phila., 1982—85; chancellor's vis. prof. biophysics U. Calif., Berkeley, 1982; vis. prof. biol. chemistry Johns Hopkins U. Med. Sch., 1985—91. Rsch. assoc. Harvard U. Med. Sch., 1950—51; established investigator Am. Heart Assn., 1953—59; career investigator, 1964—78; vis. prof. chemistry Yale U., 1973. Mem. editl. bd. Jour. Biol. Chemistry, 1958—63, 1967—72. Recipient Hall of Fame award, Hunter Coll., 1973, Disting. Alumni award, 1975, Cresson medal, Franklin Inst., award, Internat. Assn. Women Biochemists, 1979, Humboldt award, Germany, 1980, 1982, Nat. Medal Sci., 1983, award, Am. Acad. Achievement, 1984, Chandler medal, Columbia U., 1986, Women in Sci. award, N.Y. Acad. Sci., 1992, Gov.'s award for excellence in sci., Pa., 1993, Founders medal, Magnetic Resonance in Biology, 1994, Stein-Moore award, Protein Soc., 1997. Mem.: NAS, Inst. de Biologie Physico-Chimique, Coll. Physicians of Phila. (Disting. Svc. award 1987), Am. Biophys. Soc., Am. Soc. Biochemistry and Molecular Biology (pres. 1978—79), Harvey Soc., Am. Chem. Soc. (chmn. divsn. biol. chemistry 1975—76, Garvan medal 1963, Remsen award Md. sect. 1988, Cinn. sect. Oesper award 2000), Am. Philos. Soc. (v.p. 1994—2000), Am. Acad. Arts and Scis., Iota Sigma Pi (hon. nat. mem. 1988), Sigma Xi, Phi Beta Kappa. Office: U Pa Med Sch 242 Anat Chem Bldg Dept Biochemistry & Biophys Philadelphia PA 19104-6059 Office Phone: 215-898-8404.

COHN, REBECCA, state representative; b. Vallejo, Calif., Mar. 30, 1954; m. Ron Cohn; 1 child, Andrew. BS, U. Tex., Galveston, 1975, degree in Physical Therapy, 1976. Physical therapist, 1976—91; sr. cons. Bus. Design Assocs., 1991—2000; mem. Calif. Assembly, 2000—. Mem. diversity task force, Joint Venture Silicon Valley, 1989—90, Santa Clara County Domestic Violence Coun., County Domestic Violence Coun., 1998—2000, Silicon Valley Dem. Forum, 1997—2000; bd. dirs. Support Network Battered Women, 1987—2000; bd. dirs., sec. Calif. Indsl. Med. Coun., 1991—96. Mem.: Emily's List, Century Club. Democrat. Jewish. Office: PO Box 942849 Rm 3173 Sacramento CA 94249 Address: 901 Campisi Way Ste 300 Campbell CA 95008

COIN, SHEILA REGAN, organization and management development consultant; b. Columbus, Ohio, Feb. 17, 1942; d. James Daniel and Jean Cook (Hodgson) Regan; m. Tasso H. Coin, Sept. 17, 1967 (div.); 1 child, Tasso ; 1 child, Alison Regan. BS, U. Iowa, 1964. RN staff nurse VA Hosp., Boston, 1964-66; field rep. ARC, Chgo., 1966-67, chief nurse, 1967; asst. divsn. dir. Am. Hosp. Assn., sec. Am. Soc. Hosp. Dirs. Nursing, Chgo., 1967-69; owner Coin & Assocs., 1975-77; ptnr., orgn. devel. and performance mgmt. sr. cons. Coin, Newell & Assocs., 1976-96, Buck Cons., Inc., Washington, 1996-2000; pres. Coin Alisso Group, 2000—03; sr. organizational effectiveness cons. Potomac Elec. Power Co., Washington, 2003—. Instr. dept. continuing edn. Loyola U., Chgo., 1975—77, Rock Valley Coll. Mgmt. Inst., Rockford, 1978—80, Ill. Ctrl. Coll. Inst. Personal and Profl. Devel., Peoria, 1979—85, Triton Coll. Continuing Edn., River Grove, 1983—86, No. Ill. U. Continuing Edn., DeKalb, 1983—86; mem. editl. bd. Tng. Today mag., 1992—94, assoc. editor, 1994—96. Vol. Art Inst., Chgo., 1968—69; mem. Chgo. Beautiful Com., 1968—73; mem. jr. governing bd. Chgo. Symphony Orch., 1971—81; chmn. Mayor Daley's Chgo. Beautiful Awards Project, 1972; mem. jr. bd. Girl Scouts Assn., 1975—76; pres. Chgo. Symphony Orch., 1977—78; governing mem. Orchestral Assn., 1977—81; bd. dirs. Mid Am. chpt. ARC, 1979—81, bd. dirs. Chgo. dist., 1981—89; dir. com. Thalossemia Chgo. Bd., 1981—82; mem. Women's bd. Nat. Com. Prevention Child Abuse, 1981—82; chmn. fin. devel. com. Mid Am. chpt. ARC, 1982—85, vice chmn. dist. bd., 1986—89; mem. State Ill. Disabled Persons Adv. Coun., 1988—97; bd. dirs., mem. Survive Alive House Found., 1989—96; bd. dirs. Ill. chpt. Lupus Found. Am., Chgo., 1991—93; bd. dirs. Mid Am. chpt. ARC, 1991—94, mem. planning and evaluation subcom., 1991—96, chmn. quality mgmt. steering com., 1992—94; acad. specialist mgmt. devel. US Info. Agy., 1994. Mem.: Soc. for Human Resource Mgmt., Washington Human Resources Leadership Forum, OD Network, Ill. State Soc., Christ Child Soc., ASTD (exec. com. mgmt. devel. prof. practice area 1992—95). Office: Pepco 701 9th St NW Washington DC 20068 Office Phone: 202-872-3005.

COKER, CHARLOTTE NOEL, political activist; b. New Orleans, Dec. 28, 1930; d. Cecil Eugene and Esta Reed (Williams) Mahaffey; m. Rainey Morris Coker, Nov. 17, 1950; children: Patricia A. Coker Ross, Carol J. Coker goebel, Teresa J., Robert M. Student X-ray technician tng., St. Mary's Hosp., Port Arthur, Tex., 1947-48; X-ray therapy, Emory U., 1949. Precinct committeewoman Spokane County Dem. Com., Spokane, Wash., 1970—, 6th legis. dist. leader, 1973-74, 77-78; Wash. State rep. to Dem. Nat. Com., Washington, 2000—. State committeewoman Spokane County Dem. Ctrl. Com., 1975-76, 79-80, 81-82, 95—; vice chmn. Wash. State Dem. Com., Seattle, 1981; region 6 dir. Wash. State Fedn. Dem. Women's Clubs, 1979-80, state dir., 1981-85; mem. Dem. Nat. Com., 1992—, mem. exec. com., 1995-97, pres. Nat. Fedn. Dem. Women, 1995-97; tour guide Wash. Ho. of Reps., Olympia, 1975; aide Office of Gov. Dixy Lee Ray, Spokane, 1978-80; presdl. elector for Wash. State, 2000—; chair Wash. State Electoral Coll., 2000. Mem. Spokane Quality of Life Coun., 1975-77, Spokane Task Force for Cmty. Devel. Funds, 1978, Human Rights Commn. Wash. State, 1998—, chair, 2003—. Mem.: Spokane Fedn. Women's Orgns. (pres. 1985—87), Nat. Fedn. Dem. Women (pres. 1995—97), Nat. Assn. Parliamentarians, Jane Jefferson Dem. Club (v.p. 1979). Avocations: plate collecting, bridge, public affairs. Home: 2215 E 45th Ave Spokane WA 99223-6466 Fax: 509 448-8091.

COKER, MELINDA LOUISE, counselor; b. Springfield, Mo., Apr. 28, 1946; d. Joe H. and Margaret L. (Owens) Bull; m. Richard H. Coker, Aug. 12, 1967; children: Shay, Candace, Logan. BA, Baylor U., 1968; MS, East Tex. State U., 1994. Nat. cert. counselor Nat. Bd. Counselor Cert.; lic. profl. counselor, Tex. Tchr. Houston Ind. Sch. Dist., 1968-71; owner, mgr. Greenleaves, Tyler, Tex., 1978-84; realtor Coldwell Banker, Tyler, 1989-91; counselor intern Hunt County Mental Health Mental Retardation, Greenville, Tex., 1993, Andrews Ctr., Tyler, 1994; career counselor intern Tyler (Tex.) Jr. Coll., 1994-95, spl. populations counselor, 1995-97, dir. career planning and placement svcs., 1997—2003; cons. Splash, 2003—. Recipient Counselor of Yr. award, Piney Woods Counseling Assn., 2004. Mem. ACA, Nat. Career Devel. Assn., Chi Sigma Iota. Avocations: tennis, swimming. Home: 6701 Lacosta Dr Tyler TX 75703-5753

COKER, SALLY JO (BOZEMAN), sociology educator; b. Springfield, Ill., Aug. 24, 1956; d. Charles D. and Barbara J. (Bailey) Bozeman; m. Joel Dwain Coker, Nov. 7, 1974; 1 child, Corey Alan. BS, U. Houston, 1992, MA, 1995. Rsch. asst. to prof. psychology U. Houston, 1991; student asst. to dean adminstrn. Lee Coll., Baytown, Tex., 1992; instr. sociology, Am. minorities, social problems, marriage and family, San Jacinto C.C., Pasadena, Tex., 1995—; instr. sociology, Am. minorities, social problems, marriage and family Alvin (Tex.) C.C., 1995-97; instr. sociology, Am. minorities, social problems, orgnl. behavior Lee Coll., 1992—; instr. deviance, social inequality, prins. of sociology Am. minorities U. Houston, 1999—. Human resource mgmt. spkr. H.B. Zachry, Houston, 1995; tng. cons. H.B. Zachry Co., 1999; human resources cons. Mem. AAUP, Am. Sociol. Assn., Tex. C.C. Tchr.'s Assn., Phi Kappa Phi. Democrat. Home: 3607 Trailwood Dr Baytown TX 77521-4835 Office: U Houston Downtown One Main Houston TX 77002 E-mail: sallycoker@cs.com.

COKER, SYBIL JANE THOMAS, counseling administrator; b. Elizabeth, La., Aug. 16; d. Andrew J. and Lillye M. Thomas; m. Charles Mitchell Dolo Coker (dec. Apr. 13, 1983). AA, L.A. City Coll., 1952; BA, Calif. State U., L.A., 1955, Pepperdine U., 1957; MS, Mt. St. Mary's Coll., 1980. Tchr. Barton Hill Sch., 1957—58, 96th St. Sch., 1958—63; tng. tchr., reading specialist Hooper Ave. Sch., 1963—65, tng. tchr., 1980—87; reading specialist dept. chair Vermont Ave. Sch., 1965—68; head start tchr. L.A. Urban League, 1966—68; tng. tchr., tchr. of gifted clusters, grades 4,5,6 Angeles Mesa Sch., 1970—87; Eng. tchr., speech coach Horace Mann Jr. High Mid. Sch., 1987—88, speech coach, 1988—90, bilingual coord./ESL, career, coll. and chap. 1 counselor, 1988—92, 8th grade counselor, career counselor, 1992—94, counselor 8th grade ctr., 1994; counselor David Starr Jordan HS, L.A., 1995—. Pres., founder Charles Dolo Coker Jazz Scholarship Found., Inc., L.A., 1983—; freelance wedding coord., cons., 1960—; freelance writer, 1983—; sponsor Motivating Our Students Through Experience Horace Mann Jr. High Mid. Sch., sponsor Young Black Profls., sponsor USC Med Core, UCLA Partnership. Contbr. columns in newspapers. Founder, dir. 2d Bapt. Ch. Drama Guild, 1957—67. Named Media Woman of Yr., 1977; recipient Unsung Heroine in Edn. award, Top Ladies of Distinction, 1992, Dist. Svc. award, 2d Bapt. Ch., 1991, Trailblazer award for outstanding contbns. in field of music, Delta Mothers and Sponsors Club, 2002. Mem.: NEA, PTA (life), NAACP (life; subscribing Golden Heritage mem., past bd. mem. L.A. br.), The Soc., Inc., Internat. Assn. Jazz Educators, Counselor's Assn., Black Women's Forum, L.A. Press Club, Soc. Profl. Journalists, Top Ladies of Distinction (L.A. chap., area VI, pub. rels. chair), Nat. Assn. Media Women (nat. recording sec., charter mem. Beverly Hills/Hollywood chap., past pres.), Pol. Action Com. of Educators, United Tchrs. of L.A., Nat. Coun. Negro Women (life), Santa Barbara Jazz Soc., L.A. Jazz Soc., Internat. Assn. Jazz Appreciation, Emanon Birthday and Social Club (charter mem., past pres.), New Frontier Dem. Club, Order of the Ea. Star, Phi Delta Kappa, Delta Sigma Theta (life; Century City alumnae chap., L.A. alumnae chap., Delta Choraliers). Democrat. Baptist. Avocations: creative writing, knitting, singing with the Delta Choraliers, studying piano. Home and Office: 5336 Highlight Pl Los Angeles CA 90016

COKUSLU, LYNDA ELIZABETH MCCORD, medical assistant; b. Atlanta, June 11, 1956; d. Joseph Adair and Yvonne (Champagne) McCord; m. Fethi Cokuslu, Aug. 24, 1985; children: Sasha, Sedef, Samantha. Cert. med. asst., Bryman Sch., 1975. Casualty/liability claims processor Continental Ins./UAC, Atlanta, 1978—82; nutrition asst. Fayette County Edn., Peachtree City, Ga., 2001—03. Host benefit Hapeville (Ga.) Hist. Soc., 1988; officer PTA, Hapeville, 1997; catechist Youth/Adult Sch. Religion, Hapeville, 1996—2002, Fayetteville, 2003—04. Mem.: Am. Sch. Food Svc. Assn., Am. Med. Asst. Assn., Travelers Protective Assn., Learning Disorder Assn., Midtown Bus. Assn., Internat. Poet Soc. Roman Catholic. Avocations: travel, collector, gardening, guitar, archaeology. Home: 105 Buckeye Ln Fayetteville GA 30214 Office: Audvi Elecs 140 A Robinson Dr Fayetteville GA 30214

COLAGE, BEATRICE ELVIRA, education educator; b. Cleveland, Ohio, Aug. 13, 1958; BSEdn., Bowling Green State U., 1980; M of Curriculum, Cleveland State U., 1985. Spanish tchr. Cleveland (Ohio) City Schs., 1980—84, Mayfield (Ohio) City Schs., 1984—85, Solon (Ohio) City Schs., 1985—86, Orange (Ohio) City Schs., 1986—; adult edn. tchr. Mayfield (Ohio) City Schs. Lectr. Italian, Spanish and English. Author: book of 101 poems, 2003. Humanitarian and supporter of arts, civic, social and cultural instns. Mem.: NEA, Il Cenacolo Cleve., Ohio Fgn. Lang. Assoc., Ohio Edn. Assn., Am. Assn. Tchrs. of Spanish and Portuguese.

COLAMARINO, KATRIN BELENKY, lawyer; b. N.Y.C., Apr. 29, 1951; d. Allen Abram and Selma (Burwasser) Belenky Lang; ; m. Barry E. Brenner, June 1, 1974 (div. June 1979); 1 child, Rachel Erin; m. Leonard J. Colamarino, Mar. 20, 1982 BA, Vassar Coll., 1972; JD, U. Richmond, 1976. Bar: Ohio 1976, U.S. Ct. Appeals (fed. cir.) 1982. Staff atty. AM Internat., Inc., Cleve., 1977-79; atty. Lipkowitz & Plaut, N.Y.C., 1980-81, Docutel Olivetti Corp., Tarrytown, N.Y., 1981-84, NYNEX Bus. Info. Sys., White Plains, N.Y., 1984-85; corp. counsel, sec. Logica Data Architects, Inc., N.Y.C., 1986-90; corp. counsel SEER Technologies, Inc., N.Y.C., 1990-91; v.p. chief tech. counsel global relationship bank Citibank N.A., N.Y.C., 1991-97; v.p. asst. gen. counsel, mgr. technology and supplier contracts group JPMorgan Chase Bank, N.Y.C., 1997—. Lectr. CLE Computer Law Assn., Cyberspace Camp Conf., San Jose, Calif., 1997, Milbank Tweed Law Firm Global Tech. Transactions Conf., N.Y.C., 1999, Consumer Bankers Assn., 2000, N.Y. County Lawyers Assn., 2001; lectr. in field. Exec. bd. Ethical Fieldston Sch. Alumni Assn., 1980—90, 1992—95, v.p., 1987—90; alumnae coun. rep. Vassar Coll., 1982—86, class corr. Vassar Quar., 1992—97, mem. Alumni/Alumnae of Vassar Coll. fund adv. bd., 1997—2000, dir.-at-large Alumni/Alumnae of Vassar Coll. Bd., 2000—04; bd. dirs. U. Richmond Law Sch. Alumni Assn., 1999—2002. Mem.: Computer Law Assn., Assn. Bar City N.Y. Office: JP Morgan Chase Bank 1 Chase Manhattan Plz Fl 25 New York NY 10081-0001

COLANDER, PATRICIA MARIE, newspaper editor; b. Chgo., Oct. 25, 1952; d. Charles L. Colander and Mary Elizabeth Connors; m. Paul Michael Ansell, Aug. 18, 1980 (div. Jan. 1993); children: Charles Thomas, Ida Kay Ansell; m. Jeffery A. Kumorek, Dec. 12, 1997. BJ, U. Ill., 1973. Staff writer Chgo. Tribune, 1973-77, Chgo. Reader, 1977-81; adj. prof. Medill Sch. Journalism Northwestern U., 1982-87; editor Copley Newspapers, Chgo. suburbs, No. Ill., 1987-92; asst. mng. editor The Times, 1992-93, pub. Ill. edits., 1993-96, mng. editor, 1996—. Exec. devel. program Am. Press Inst., Reston, Va., 1994. Author: Thin Air: The Life and Mysterious Disappearance of Helen Brach, 1982, Hugh Hefner's First Funeral and Other True Tales of Love and Death in Chicago, 1985. Recipient awards AP, 1987, 88, 89, Suburban Newspapers Am., 1988. Mem. Inland Press Assn. (award 1991), Hoosier State Press, Tavern Club Chgo. Office: The Times 601 45th Ave Munster IN 46321-2819

COLANDER-RICHARDSON, LATASHA, Olympic athlete; b. Portsmouth, Va., Aug. 23, 1976; Degree in comms., U. N.C., 1998. Winner Gold Medal 4x400 meter relay U.S.A. Track and Field Team, Sydney, 2000. Office: USA Track and Field Team One RCA Dome Ste 140 Indianapolis IN 46225

COLBERT-CORMIER, PATRICIA A. secondary school educator; b. Lake Charles, La., Nov. 12, 1943; 4 children. BS in Biology, U. La., 1965, MS in Microbiology, 1975. Edn. specialist cert. in reading 1978. Tchr. biology dept. Lafayette (La.) H.S., 1975—. Mem. editl. adv. panel Cold Spring Harbor Labs. [illegible] DuPont fellow, 1994, Albert Einstein fellow, NASA, Washington, 2000—01, Disney Ch. Am. Tchr. and Tandy Tech. scholar, 1996. Office: Lafayette HS Biology Dept 3000 W Congress St Lafayette LA 70506

COLBORN, NANCY WOOTTON, school librarian; b. Emporia, Kans., Aug. 29, 1959; d. Calvin Richard and Linda Jean Wootton; m. James Randall Colborn; children: Elizabeth Milhander, Tyler. BS, Kans. State U., 1981; MLIS, Ind. U., 1993. Asst. libr. ref. Franklin D. Schurz Libr., Ind. U. South Bend, Ind., 1994—98, assoc. libr. ref., coord. pub. rels. and staff develop., 1998—2002, assoc. libr., coord. libr. instr. and staff devel., 2002—. Contbr. articles to profl. jours. Mem.: ALA (mem. machine-assisted ref. sect. of user access svc. com. 1998—2002, chair machine-assisted ref. sect. of user access svc. com. 1999—2000, occasional papers subcom. 2002—), Assn. Coll. Rsch. Librs., Ind. Acad. Libr. Assn. (exec. bd. mem. 1997—, sec./treas. 2001—, vice chmn. 2002—03, chmn. 2003—), Ind. Libr. Fedn., Beta Phi Mu (Chi chpt. exec. bd. 1999—2000). Office: Franklin D Schurz Library IUSB 1700 Mishawaka Ave PO Box 7111 South Bend IN 46634 Business E-Mail: ncolborn@iusb.edu.

COLBURN, JENNIFER CHRISTINE, business analyst; b. Putnam, Conn., Oct. 24, 1973; d. Edward Dennis and Patricia Claire Colburn; m. Curtis Randal Ladig, Aug. 8, 2003. BA, Hollins U., 1996, MA in Liberal Studies, 2003. Office mgr. Northwestern Mut. Life, Roanoke, Va., 1996—99; provider rels. liaison Delta Dental Plan Va., 1999—2003; bus. analyst New Age Tech., Louisville, 2004—. Bd. dirs. March of Dimes Birth Defects Found., Ohio Valley Div., 2004—; active Jr. League Roanoke Valley, 1998—2001. Scholar, Hollins U., 1991, 1992, 1994, 1995. Mem.: Louisville Women in Tech. Home: 5103 Magdalen Sq Louisville KY 40241 Office: New Age Tech 819 W Main St Louisville KY 40202

COLBURN, NANCY DOUGLAS, social worker, educator; d. Cleaveland Fisher Colburn and Virginia Colburn Bahrs. BA, Rutgers U., 1963; MSW, U. Ill., Chgo., 1971; MDiv, McCormick Theol. Sem., 1971; MPA, San Diego State U., 1997. LCSW Calif.; Ordained to ministry Vineyard Christian Fellowship 1990, cert. tchr./adminstr. child devel. programs Calif. Social worker Dept. Social Svcs. County of San Diego, 1979—92; social worker Family Advocacy, USN, San Diego, 1992—97. Scholar, State of N.J.

COLBY, JOY HAKANSON, critic; b. Detroit; d. Alva Hilliard and Eleanor (Radtke) Hakanson; m. Raymond L. Colby, Apr. 11, 1953; children: Sarah, Katherine, Lisa. Student, Detroit Soc. Arts and Crafts, 1945; BFA, Wayne State U., 1946; DFA (hon.), Coll. for Creative Studies, 1998. Art critic Detroit News, 1947—; originator exhibit Arts and Crafts in Detroit, 1906-1976; with Detroit Inst. Arts, 1976. Author: (book) Art and A City, 1956; contbr. articles to art periodicals. Mem. visual arts adv. panel Mich. Coun. Arts, 1974—79; mayor's appointment Detroit Inst. Arts, 1974; mem. Bloomfield Hills Arts Coun., 1974. Recipient Alumni award, Wayne State U., 1967, Art Achievement award, 1983, Headliner award, 1984, award arts reporting, Detroit Press Club, 1984, Art Leadership award, Coll. for Creative Studies, 1989. Office: 615 W Lafayette Blvd Detroit MI 48226-3124 Office Phone: 313-222-2276. Business E-Mail: jcolby@detnews.com.

COLBY, KAREN LYNN See WEINER, KAREN

COLBY-HALL, ALICE MARY, Romance studies educator; b. Portland, Maine, Feb. 25, 1932; d. Frederick Eugene and Angie Fraser (Drown) C.; m. Robert A. Hall, Jr., May 8, 1976 (dec. 1997); stepchildren: Philip, Diana Hall Goodall, Carol Hall Erickson. BA, Colby Coll., 1953; MA, Middlebury Coll., 1954; PhD, Columbia U., 1962. Tchr. French, Latin Orono (Maine) H.S., 1954-55; tchr. French Gould Acad., Bethel, Maine, 1955-57; lectr. French Columbia U., 1959-60; instr. Romance lit. Cornell U., Ithaca, N.Y., 1962-63, asst. prof., 1963-66, assoc. prof., 1966-75, prof. Romance studies, 1975-97, prof. emerita, 1997—, chmn. Romance studies, 1990-96. Author: The Portrait in Twelfth Century French Literature: An Example of the Stylistic Originality of Chrétien de Troyes, 1965; mem. editl. bd. Speculum, 1976-79, Olifant, 1974—. Fulbright grantee, 1953-54; NEH fellow, 1984-85; recipient Médaille des Amis d'Orange, 1985; decorated chevalier de l'Ordre des Arts et Lettres, 1997. Mem. Modern Lang. Assn., Medieval Acad. Am. (councillor 1983-86), Internat. Arthurian Soc., Société Rencesvals, Académie de Vaucluse, Phi Beta Kappa. Republican. Congregationalist. Home: 308 Cayuga Heights Rd Ithaca NY 14850-2107 Office: Cornell U Dept Romance Studies Ithaca NY 14853 E-mail: amc12@cornell.edu.

COLE, ANN HARRIET, psychologist, consultant; b. Phila., Feb. 27, 1949; d. Albert and Deborah (Mann) Brawerman; m. Stephen Cole, June 4, 1969 (div. June 18, 1987); children: Richard David, Robert Walter; m. Allan J. Besbris, Aug. 4, 1998. BA, SUNY, Stony Brook, 1971, MA, 1975. Dir. field rsch. Opinion Rsch. Assocs., 1974-76; v.p. Social Data Analysts, Inc., 1976-86; rsch. assoc. Jay Schulman, Inc., N.Y.C., 1986-87; cons. Litigation Scis., Inc., N.Y.C., 1988-90, Stanley S. Arkin, P.C., N.Y.C., 1990; cons.. Chadbourne & Parke, N.Y.C., 1990-91; pres. Ann Cole Opinion Rsch. and Analysis, N.Y.C., 1991—. CBS news cons., 1994-95. Mem. Am. Soc. Trial Cons. (bd. dirs. 1994-99, v.p. 1996-97, pres. 1997-99), Nat. Coalition to Abolish the Death Penalty, Qualitative Rsch. Cons. Am. Office: Ann Cole Opinion Rsch and Analysis 1560 Broadway Ste 813 New York NY 10036-1518 Home: PO Box 60577 Saint Petersburg FL 33784-0577 E-mail: ahcole@acoraweb.com.

COLE, BARBARA TODD, bookseller; b. Evanston, Ill., Dec. 26, 1912; d. Charles Cameron and Mary Barkley (Miller) Todd; m. John Allen Cole, Oct. 9, 1943 (dec.); children: Charles Allen, Susan Hale Cole Oliver. Grad., Park Sch., Buffalo; student, Chgo. Art Inst. Decorator Carson Pirie Scott, Chgo., 1930-32; bookseller E.P. Judd Bookseller, New Haven, 1933-39; with acquisition dept. Yale U. Libr., New Haven, 1939-42; dir. Chgo. office Army Map Svc., Washington, 1942-45; bookseller, owner John Cole's Book Shop, La Jolla, Calif., 1946—. Bd. dirs. La Jolla Mus. Art, La Jolla Hist. Soc., Friends of the Libr., U. Calif. San Diego, Athenaeum, La Jolla. Mem. Am. Booksellers Assn., San Diego Booksellers Assn., So. Calif. Booksellers Assn., Athenaeum Art and Music Libr., San Diego Mus. Contemporary Art, San Diego Mus., numerous others. Congregationalist. Avocations: traveling, sailing. Office: John Coles Book Shop 780 Prospect St La Jolla CA 92037-4228

COLE, C. SUZANNE, librarian; b. Bryn Mawr, Pa., Oct. 2, 1967; d. Taylor Whitney and Mary Ann Cole; m. Daniel Conroy Bigelow, Aug. 15, 1992; children: Warren Andrew Bigelow, Margaret Frances Bigelow. BA, Bowdoin Coll., 1989; MA in Sociology, U. Pa., 1992; MS in Libr. and Info. Sci., Drexel U., 1995. Ref. intern Van Pelt Libr., U. Pa., Phila., 1994-95; info. svcs. libr. Lehigh U., Bethlehem, Pa., 1995-96, team leader, 1996-97; pres. Emerac Info. Svcs., Doylestown, Pa., 1997; libr. The Pew Charitable Trusts, Phila., 1997-99, chief libr., 2000—. Bd. dirs. Words in Time, Inc., Takoma Park, Md. Contbr. articles to profl. jours. Ruling elder Collenbrook United Ch., Drexel Hill, Pa., 1994-95. Mem. Spl. Librs. Assn., Consortium of Found. Librs. (chair 2000-02), Phi Beta Kappa, Beta Phi Mu. Democrat. Office: The Pew Charitable Trusts 2005 Market St Ste 1700 Philadelphia PA 19103 E-mail: scole@pewtrusts.com.

COLE, CAROLYN, photojournalist; b. Boulder, Colo., Apr. 24, 1961; BA in photojournalism, U. Tex., 1993. Staff photographer El Paso Herald Post, 1986—88, San Francisco Examiner, 1988—90; freelance photographer Mexico City, 1990—92; staff photographer Sacramento Bee, 1992—94, LA Times, 1994—. Contbr. (photographs) Holy Lands, Life Books, Time Inc., The American Spirit, Life--The Year in Pictures, 2002. Recipient Pictures of the Year, newspaper portrait/personality award of excellence, U. Mo., 1986, first place, photojournalism for "Third World Street Girls", Tex. Associated Press, 1987, first place, feature pictures story for "Cadet McKeag: Wentworth Academy's Only Female", Calif. Press Photographers Assn., 1993, Mark Twain Award, first place picture story for "Haiti: Crisis in the Caribbean", AP News Execs. Coun., 1994, best spot news photo or photographic series for "Haiti: Crisis in the Caribbean", LA Times Editl. Award, 1994, best feature photo or photographic series for "Health Crisis in Russia", LA Time Editl. Award, 1995, first place, newspaper feature picture & newspaper feature story award of excellence, Pictures of the Year, U. Mo., 1994, issue reporting picture story award of excellence for "California's Fragile Future", 1996, third place issue reporting, 1998, Journalist of the Year Award, Times Mirror Corp., 1998, Pulitzer Prize, breaking news for LA Times team coverage of the North Hollywood shootout, 1998, newspaper feature story, second place for "In the Shadow of War", Pictures of the Year, U. Mo., 1999, global news picture story, award of excellence for "No Winners in War, 1999, general news picture award of excellence for "Face of Conviction", 2000, newspaper photographer of the year, Nat. Press Photographers Assn., 2002, Mark Twain Award for best of show, AP News Execs. Coun., 2002, first place, people in the news for "Church of the Nativity", World Press Photo, 2003, first place, mag. news story editing & second place, feature picture story for "Church of the Nativity", Pictures of the Year, U. Mo., 2003, Robert Capa Award for courage in photography for covering the siege at the Church of the Nativity, Bethlehem, Overseas Press Club, 2003, Pulitzer Prize for feature photography, 2004. Office: LA Times 202 W First St Los Angeles CA 90012

COLE, CAROLYN JO, brokerage company executive; b. Carmel, Calif. d. Joseph Michael Jr. and Dorothea Wagner (James) C. AB, Vassar Coll., 1965. Sr. v.p. UBS Painewebber, Inc., N.Y.C., 1975—95; exec. v.p. Tucker Anthony, Inc., Boston, 1995—97; chmn. Inst. Econ. & Fin., Inc., N.Y.C., 1997—98; mng. dir. Citigroup, N.Y.C., 1998—. Guest lectr. Harvard U. Bus. Sch.; lectr. Securities Industry Inst., Wharton Sch. U. Pa.; past chmn. bd. dirs. N.Y. Women's Bldg.; bd. dirs. Women's Venture Fund. Named to YWCA Acad. Women Achievers. Mem. NOW, DAR, N.Y. Soc. Security Analysts (past bd. dirs.), Assn. Investment Mgmt. and Rsch., Soc. Fgn. Analysts, Aspen Inst. Humanistic Studies, Fin. Women's Assn., Women's Econ. Roundtable, Econ. Club N.Y., Women in Need (past bd. dirs.), Vassar Club. Democrat. Office. Citigroup Alternative Investments 388 Greenwich St New York NY 10013-2339 E-mail: cali.cole@citigroup.com.

COLE, DIANE JOYCE, writer; b. Balt., July 11, 1952; d. Alfred J. and Roselda (Katz) C.; m. Peter Baida, Aug. 7, 1977; 1 child, Edward Aaron. AB, Radcliffe Coll., 1974; MA, Johns Hopkins U., 1975. Author: After Great Pain, 1992, Hunting the Headhunters, 1988; co-author: Is It You, Or Is It Me?, 1998. Home: 305 E 86th St New York NY 10028-4702

COLE, ELMA PHILLIPSON (MRS. JOHN STRICKLER COLE), social welfare executive; b. Piqua, Ohio, Aug. 9, 1909; d. Brice Leroy and Mabel (Gale) Phillipson; m. John Strickler Cole, Oct. 3, 1959. AB, Berea Coll., 1930; MA, U. Chgo., 1938. Social work staff, 1930-42; dir. dept. social svc. Children's Hosp. D.C., Washington, 1942-49; cons. pub. coop. Midcentury White House Conf. on Children and Youth, Washington, 1949-51; exec. sec. Nat. Midcentury Com. on Children and Youth, N.Y.C., 1951-53; cons. recruitment Am. Assn. Med. Social Workers, 1953; assoc. dir. Nat. Legal Aid and Defender Assn., 1953-56; exec. sec. Marshall Field Awards, Inc., 1956-57; dir. assoc. orgns. Nat. Assembly Social Policy and Devel., 1957-73; assoc. exec. dir. Nat. Assembly Nat. Vol. Health and Social Welfare Orgns., 1974; dir. edn. parenthood project Salvation Army, 1974-76, asst. sec. dept. women's and children's social svcs., 1976-78, dir. rsch. project devel. bur., 1978-92, ind. cons., 1993—. Mem. Manhattan adv. bd., 1975—, sec., 1984—; cons. nat. orgns. Golden Anniversary White House Conf. on Children and Youth, 1959-60; mem. adv. coun. pub. svc. Nat. Assn. Life Underwriters and Inst. Life Ins.; judges com. Louis I. Dublin Pub. Svc. awards, 1961-74; v.p. Blue Ridge Inst. So. Cmty. Svc. Execs., 1977-79, exec. com., 1979-81; mem. awards jury Girls Clubs Am., 1981-93; adv. bd. Nat. Family Life Edn. Network, 1982-97. Com. pub. rels. and fundraising Am. Found. for Blind Commn. on Accreditation, 1964-67; task force on vol. accreditation Coun. Nat. Orgns. for Adult Edn., 1974-78; adv. bd. sexuality edn. project Ctr. for Population Options, 1977-86; bd. dirs., sec. James Lenox House, 1985-89, pres., 1989-94, treas., 1994-98; bd. dirs., sec. James Lenox House Assn., 1985-89, pres., 1989-94, sec., 1994-98; bd. dirs. Values and Human Sexuality Inst., 1980-85, Presbyterian Sr. Svcs., N.Y., 1998, Sexuality Info. and Edn. Coun. of U.S., 1993, exec. com. Mem. Pub. Rels. Soc. Am. (cert.), Nat. Assn. Social Workers (cert.), Nat. Conf. Social Welfare (mem. pub. rels. com. 1961-66, 69-82, chair adminstrn. sect. 1966-67), Soc. Sci. Study Sexuality, Jr. League N.Y., Women's Club of N.Y., Pi Gamma Mu, Phi Kappa Phi. Home: 30 Rockefeller Plz Ste 4340 New York NY 10112-4399

COLE, ELSA KIRCHER, lawyer; b. Dec. 5, 1949; d. Paul and Hester Marie (Pellegrom) Kircher; m. Roland J. Cole, Aug. 16, 1975; children: Isabel Ashley, Madeline Aldis. AB in History with distinction, Stanford U., 1971; JD, Boston U., 1974. Bar: Wash. 1974, U.S. Supreme Ct. 1980, Mich. 1989, Kans. 1997, Ind. 1999. Asst. atty gen., rep. dept. motor vehicles State of Wash., Seattle, 1974-75, asst. atty. gen., rep. dept. social and health svcs., 1975-76, asst. atty. gen., rep. U. Wash., 1976-89; gen. counsel U. Mich., Ann Arbor, 1989-97, NCAA, Indpls., 1997—. Presenter ednl. issues various confs. and workshops. Contbr. articles to profl. jours. Fellow: Nat. Assn. Coll. and Univs. Attys. (mem. nominations com., mem. site selection com. 1987—88, co-chair student affairs sect. 1987—88, program 1988—89, mem. fin. com., articles com., by-laws com. 1988—89, co-chair student affairs sect. 1988—89, bd. dirs. 1988—91, program 1989—90, chair profl. devel. com. 1990—91, program 1991—92, honors and awards, ethics com. 1991—92, program 1992—93, bd. ops. 1992—93, mem. nominations com., mem. site selection com. 1995—96, CLE com. 1995—96, program 1995—96, CLE com. 1996—97, pub. com. 1996—97, CLE com. 2000—02, honors and awards com. 2002—03, named NACUA fellow 1998); mem.: Nat. Sports Law Inst. (bd. advisors 2001—), Sports Lawyers Assn. (bd. dirs. 2001—), Indpls. Bar Assn. (sports and entertainment sect. bd. dirs. 2001—), Seattle-King County Bar Assn., Wash. Women Lawyers (pres. Seattle-King County chpt. 1986, state chair candidate endorsement com. 1987, v.p. membership, state bd. dirs. 1987—88, state chair candidate endorsement com. 1988), Wash. State Bar Assn. (chair law sch. liaison com. 1988—89). Office: NCAA PO 6222 Indianapolis IN 46206-6222 E-mail: ecole@ncaa.org.

COLE, HARRIETT, writer, media consultant; m. Chinese George Cole. BA summa cum laude, Howard U. Asst. editor Contemporary Living, Essence mag., 1986—90; editor, Lifestyle section and fashion dir. Essence mag., 1990—95; pres. and creative dir. Profudities, Inc., New York, 1999—. Mem. adv. bd. TheKnot.com; author, "Signature Style" column NiaOnline. Author: Jumping the Broom: The African-American Wedding Planner, 1993, Jumping the Broom Wedding Workbook, 1996, How to Be: Contemporary Etiquette for African Americans, 1999, Choosing Truth: Living an Authentic Life, 2003, Vows: The African-American Couples' Guide to Designing a Sacred Cermony, 2004. Mem.: Fashion Outreach, Delta Sigma Theta Sorority (mem. Nat. Commn. on Arts and Letters). Office: Profundities Inc 10 W 15th St New York NY 10011*

COLE, HEATHER ELLEN, librarian; b. Rochester, N.Y., Nov. 7, 1942; d. Donald M. and Muriel Agnes (Kimball) C.; m. Stratis Haviaras; 1 child, Elektra Maria Muriel BA, Cornell U., 1964; MS, Simmons Coll., 1973. Mgr. Brentano's, Boston, 1968-70; intern Harvard Coll. Libr., Cambridge, Mass., 1970-73, reference libr., 1973-77, libr., 1977—, Hilles and Lamont Librs., 1977—. Mem. AAUW, ALA, Am. Soc. Info. Sci. (New England chpt.), Assn. Coll. Rsch. Librs. Democrat. Episcopalian. Avocation: gardening. Home: 19 Clinton St Cambridge MA 02139-2303 Office: Harvard Coll Lamont Library Cambridge MA 02138

COLE, JEAN ANNE, artist; b. Greeley, Colo., Jan. 30, 1947; d. Philip Owen and Rose Margaret (Maser) Dahl; m. Nelson Bruce Cole, June 22, 1968; children: Ashley Paige, Travis Allyn. BA in Interior Design, U. Calif., Berkeley, 1968. Interior designer K.S. Wilshire Design, L.A., 1969-70, Milton Swimmer Planning & Design, Beverly Hills, Calif., 1970-73, Denver, 1973-75. Tchr. watercolor workshops, 1991—. Exhibited in numerous shows at Foothills Art Ctr., Golden, Colo., 1989, 91, 93, 94, 96, 98, 99, 2002, Brea (Calif.) Civic and Cultural Ctr., 1989, 90, Nevile Pub. Mus., Green Bay, Wis., 1990, 93, Nat. Watercolor Soc., 1991, Denver Mus. Natural History, 1991, Pikes Peak Ctr. Performing Arts, Colorado Springs, Colo., 1992, Colo. History Mus., 1992-98, Kneeland Gallery, Las Vegas, Nev., 1993, 94, 95, 97, Salmagundi Club, N.Y.C., 1994, 97, 99, Met. State Coll. Ctr. for Visual Arts, Denver, 1994, U. So. Colo., 1997, Wichita Art Mus., 1997, Colorado Springs Fine Art Ctr., 1998, Acad. of Art Gallery, San Francisco, Onewest Art Ctr., Ft. Collins, Colo., Wyo. Brennial, Wash. State Conv. and Trade Ctr., N.W. Watercolor Soc., Seattle, Arvada Ctr. Arts Humanities, 2002; work represented in various publs.; contbr. articles to mags.; artist greetings cards Leanin'Tree. Recipient 2d pl. watercolor award Art Zone Regional Show, 1988, 1st pl. watercolor award Colo. ARtists Convention, 1989, 1st pl., hon. mention People's Choice awards Denver Allied Artists, 1989, Best of Show award Pikes Peak Watercolor Invitational, 1992, Quaintance award Rocky Mountain Nat. Watermedia Exhibit, 1993, Paul Schwartz Meml. award Am. Watercolor Soc., 1994, Founder's award Watercolor West XXVI Ann. Nat. Transparent Watercolor Exhbn., Calif., 1994. Mem. Nat. Watercolor Soc., Colo. Watercolor Soc. (pres., treas., award of merit 1993). Republican. Avocations: hiking, skiing, gardening, photography, horseback riding.

COLE, JOAN CAROL, music educator; b. Beaufort, S.C., May 7, 1961; d. Howard Arthur Cole and Phyllis Cole Norris. MusB in Edn., Valdosta (Ga.) State U., 1984, MusM in Edn., 1994. Dir. bands Louisville (Ga.) HS, 1984—88; asst. dir. bands Washington-Wilkes HS, Washington, 1989—97; dir. bands Washington-Wilkes Mid. Sch., Washington, 1989—97, Elbert County Mid. Sch., Elberton, Ga., 1997—98; music coord. Talia Ferro County Bd. Edn., Crawfordville, Ga., 2000—, dir. bands, 2000—. Golf instr. Golf Augusta (Ga.) Pro Shops, 2000; chef Reynolds Plantation Ritz Carlton, Greensboro, Ga., 1998—2000; cons. Talio Ferro County Sch., 2000. Mem. vestry Ch. of the Mediator, Washington, 2000—03. Recipient John Philip Sousa award. Mem.: MENC, Ga. Music Educators Assn., Women Band Dirs. Internat. Episc. Avocations: golf, cooking, travel. Home: 203 N Alexander Ave Washington GA 30673-1523

COLE, JOAN (ELLEN) BLYLER, financial executive; b. Phila., Sept. 27, 1946; d. Charles Frederick and Ellen Elizabeth (Leavitt) Blyler; m. Charles Chatfield Cole Jr., Jan. 27, 1968; children: Charles Chatfield III, Christopher Andrew. BA, Rosemont (Pa.) Coll., 1968; BS, Kutztown (Pa.) U., 1984; MBA, Lehigh U., 1996. Cert. mgmt. acct. (CMA), Inst. Mgmt. Accts., 1987, treasury profl. (CIP), Assn. Fin. Profl., 1998. With Lehigh Portland Cement Co., Allentown, Pa., 1984—, various fin. positions, treas. Mem. Inst. of Mgmt. Accts. (pres. Lehigh Valley chpt. 1992-93), Assn. Fin. Profls. Home: 4300 Rosewood Ln Allentown PA 18103-9646 Office: Lehigh Cement Co 7660 Imperial Way Allentown PA 18195-1040

COLE, JOHNNETTA BETSCH, academic administrator, educator; b. Jacksonville, Fla., Oct. 19, 1936; d. John Thomas and Mary Frances (Lewis) Betsch; m. Robert Eugene Cole (div. 1982); children: David, Aaron, Ethan; m. Arthur J. Robinson, Jr. (div. 2002). Student, Fisk U., 1953; BA in Sociology, Oberlin Coll., 1957; MA in Anthropology, Northwestern U., Evanston, Ill., 1959, PhD, 1967. Instr. UCLA, 1964; dir. black studies Wash. State U., Pullman, 1969-70; prof. anthropology U. Mass., Amherst, 1970-83, assoc. provost undergrad. edn., 1981-83; vis. prof. Hunter Coll., N.Y.C., 1983-84, prof. anthropology, 1983-87, dir. Inter-Am. Affairs Program, 1984-87; pres. Spelman Coll., Atlanta, 1987-97, pres. emeritus, 1997—; pres. Bennett Coll. for Women, Greensboro, NC, 2002—. Corp. bd. dirs. Merck & Co., Inc., Atlanta Falcons; presdl. disting. prof. anthropology, women's studies and Afro-Am. studies Emory U., 1998-2001. Author, editor: Anthropology for the Eighties, 1982, All American Women, 1986, Anthropology for the Nineties, 1988, Conversations: Straight Talk with America's Sister President, 1993, Dream the Boldest Dreams, 1998; author: (with Beverly Guy-Sheftall) Gender Talk: The Struggle for Women's Equality in African American Communicies, 2003; mem. editl. bd. The Black Scholar. Recipient numerous hon. degrees. Fellow Am. Anthrop. Assn.; mem. Am. Acad. Arts and Scis., Assn. Black Anthropologists (past pres.). United Methodist. Office: Bennett Coll for Women 900 E Washington St Greensboro NC 27401 E-mail: jcole@bennett.edu.

COLE, KAREN JEAN, music educator; b. Streator, Ill., Apr. 10, 1972; d. John Victor Cole and Joy Lynn Summers. BME, Ill. State U., 1995. Cert. tchr. Ind., Ill. Band dir. Thomson Cmty. Schs., Ill., 1995—96; band and gen. music tchr. Creve Coeur Cmty. Schs., Ill., 1996—98; mid. sch. band dir. and asst. H.S. band dir. Wa-Nee Cmty. Schs., Nappanee, Ind., 1998—2001; mid. sch. band dir. Met. Sch. Dist. Lawrence Twp., Indpls., 2001—. Percussion instr. marching band Normal Cmty. W. H.S., Ill., 1996—98, Ill. State U., Normal, 1997, Lawrence N. H.S., Indpls., 2001—. Mem.: Am. Fedn. Musicians U.S. and Canada, Percussive Arts Soc. Office: Craig Mid Sch Met Sch Dist Lawrence Twp 6501 Sunnyside Rd Indianapolis IN 46236

COLE, KATHLEEN ANN, advertising agency executive, retired social worker; b. Nov. 22, 1946; d. James Scott and Kathryn Gertrude (Borisch) Cole; m. Brian Brandt, Mar. 21, 1970. BA, Miami U., 1968; MSW, U. Mich., 1972; MM, Northwestern U., 1978. Social worker Hamilton County Welfare Dept., Cin., 1969—70, Lucas County Children Svcs. Bd., Toledo, 1970—74, East Maine Sch. Dist., Niles, Ill., 1974—77; account supr. Leo Burnett Advt. Agy., Chgo., 1978—93; primary therapist Lifeline, Chgo., 1994—95; acct. dir. GreenHouse Comm., 1995—2001; sr. program specialist N. Shore Sr. Ctr., 2004—. Field instr. Loyola U., Chgo., 1976—77. Mem. North Shore United Meth. Congregation. Mem.: NASW (chair pub. rels. task force), Kellogg Alumni Assn., Northwestern U. Prof. Women's Assn., Miami U. Alumni Assn. (dir. 1976—), Acad. Cert. Social Workers. Home: 414 Kelling Ln Glencoe IL 60022-1113 E-mail: colemarketing@comcast.net.

COLE, KIRSTEN, reporter; b. Newington, Conn. married. BA in Comm. Journalism, Loyola U., Chgo., 1995. Anchor/reporter WINY-TV, 1995—97; anchor/reporter WSYX-TV, WTTE-TV, Columbus, Ohio, 1997—99, WPIX-TV, N.Y.C., 2000—01; reporter CBS2, 2001—. Recipient Numerous awards, Various City Press Assns., 1996—. Office: CBS 2 524 W 57th Sr New York NY 10019

COLE, MAX, artist; b. Hodgeman County, Kans., Feb. 14, 1937; d. Jack Delmont C. and Bertha (Law) Fakes; m. Richard Cole, Sept. 4, 1955 (dec. April 1958); children: Douglas, Janet, Cindy. BA, Fort Hays State U., 1961; MFA, U. Ariz., 1964. One-man shows include Louver Gallery, L.A., 1978, 80, Sidney Janis Gallery, N.Y.C., 1977, 80, Zabriskie Gallery, N.Y., 1987, Haines Gallery, San Francisco, 1988, 93, 96, 98, Galerie Schlegl, Zurich, 1990, 96, 99, 2000, Mus. Folkwang, Essen, Germany, 1993, Kunstraum Kassel (Germany), 1992, Roswell (N.Mex.) Mus. and Art Ctr., 1996, Stark Gallery, N.Y., Galerie Michael Strum, Stuttgart, 1997, 99, Mus. Modern Art, Otterndorf, Germany, 1998, Haus Konstructive und Konkrete Junst, Zurich, 2001, Walter Storms Gallery, Munich, 2002, Kunstverein, Aschaffenberg, Germany, 2002, Diozesan Museum, Cologne, 2004; exhibited in group shows including L.A. County Mus. Art, 1976, Corcoran Gallery Art, Washington, 1977, La Jolla Mus., 1980, Santa Barbara Mus., 1980, Mus. Fine Arts of N.Mex., 1984, Neuberger Mus., Purchase, N.Y., 1984, Marilyn Pearl Gallery, N.Y.C., 1985, Pratt Manhattan Ctr. Gallery, 1985, UCLA, 1988, Nat. Gallery Modern Art, New Delhi, 1988, Panza Found., Verese, Italy, 1995, Aagauer Kunsthaus, Aarau, Switzerland, 1995, Trento (Italy) Mus., 1996, Galerie Schlegl, Zurich, 1996, Manif, 1997, Internat. Art Forum, Seoul, 1997, Mus. Modern Art, Otterndorf, Germany, 1998, Haines Gallery, San Francisco, 1998; represented in permanent collections L.A. County Mus. Art, Newport Harbor Mus. Art, La Jolla Mus. Contemporary Art, Mus. N.Mex., Dallas Mus. Art, Santa Barbara Mus., Everson Mus., Tel Aviv Mus., La. Mus., Van Der Heyt Mus., Wuppertal, Germany, Denmark, Panza Collection, Italy, Diozesan Mus., Cologne, Chiat Found., N.Y., Panza Collection, Italy, Lembach Haus, Munich, Ingolstaadt Mus., Germany. Address: PO Box 56 Ruby NY 12475*

COLE, NANCY STOOKSBERRY, educational research executive; b. Brenham, Tex., Nov. 29, 1942; d. Joe Brady and Grace Darling (Pyburn) S.; m. James W.L. Cole, June 4, 1966; 1 child, David Leverett. BA, Rice U., 1964; MA, U. N.C., 1967, PhD, 1968. Rsch. psychologist Am. Coll. Testing Program, Iowa City, 1968-71, dir. test devel., 1971-73, asst. v.p., 1973-74; from assoc. prof. to prof. U. Pitts., 1975-85; prof., dean edn. U. Ill., Champaign, 1985-89; exec. v.p. Ednl. Testing Svc., Princeton, N.J., 1989-93; pres., 1994-2000; sr. advisor, 2000—04; ret., 2004. Contbr. articles on ednl. testing to profl. jours. Fellow Am. Psychol. Assn.; mem. Nat. Acad. Edn., Nat. Coun. on Measurement in Edn. (pres. 1983-84), Am. Ednl. Rsch. Assn. (pres. 1988-89).

COLE, NATALIE MARIA, singer; b. L.A., Feb. 6, 1950; d. Nathaniel Adam and Maria (Hawkins) C.; m. Marvin J. Yancy, July 30, 1976 (div.); 1 child, Robbie; m. Andre Fisher (div.); m. Rev. Kenneth Dupress, 2001 (sep. 2004). BA in Psychology, U. Mass., 1972. Rec. singles and albums, 1975—; albums include Dangerous, 1985, Everlasting, 1987, The Natalie Cole Collection, 1987, Inseparable, Thankful, Good To Be Back, 1989, Unforgettable, 1991 (4 grammys, 3 grammys 1992), Too Much Weekend, 1992, I'm Ready, 1992, I've Got Love On My Mind, 1992, Take A Look, 1993 (Grammy award nominee best jazz vocal 1994), Holly and Ivy, 1994, Stardust (2 Grammy awards), Magic of Christmas, 1999, Snowfall on the Sahara, 1999, Greatest Hits, 2000, Ask a Woman Who Knows, 2002; television appearances include Lily in Winter, 1994; appeared in TV movies Always Outnumbered, 1998, Freak City, 1999; co-author: Angel on My Shoulder, 2000. Recipient Grammy award for best new artist, best Rhythm and Blues female vocalist 1975, 76; recipient 1 gold single, 3 gold albums; recipient 2 Image awards NAACP 1976, 77; Am. Music award 1978, other awards. Mem. AFTRA, Nat. Assn. Rec. Arts and Scis., Delta Sigma Delta. Baptist. Office: care Jennifer Allen 8500 Wilshire Blvd Ste 700 Beverly Hills CA 90211*

COLE, PATRICIA A. federal agency administrator; BS, Wilson Coll.; JD, U. Md. Trial atty. litigation adn legal advice staff Immigration and Naturalization Svc., Houston, appellate counsel, assoc. gen. counsel for gen. law sect., asst. gen. counsel; sr. policy analyst U.S. Commn. Immigration Reform; mem. bd. immigration appeals Exec. Office Immigration Rev. Dept. Justice, Falls Church, Va., 1995—. Office: Dept Justice Exec Office Immigration Rev 5107 Leesburg Pike Ste 2400 Falls Church VA 22041-3234

COLE, PAULA, pop singer, songwriter; b. Rockport, Mass. Student, Berklee Sch. Music, Boston. Back-up singer Melissa Etheridge, Sarah McLachlan, Peter Gabriel; rec. artist Imago Records, 1992; rec. artist Harbinger, 1992, This Fire, 1996, Amen, 2000, I Believe in Love, 2003. Office: Warner Bros Records Inc 3300 Warner Blvd Burbank CA 91505-4694

COLE, RACHEL P. science educator; b. McKenney, Va., Sept. 24, 1942; d. Alex Luther and Fannie Wynn Parham; m. Moses Cole, Sept. 20, 1969; 1 child, Marsha Lynn. BS in Biology, Va. State U., Petersburg, 1964; BA in Biology, NYU, 2002. CLU; ChFC. Sci. tchr. Franklin City Schs., Va., 1964—66; pension cons. Equitable Life, N.Y.C., 1966—91; sub. tchr. Bd. of Edn., N.Y.C., 1992—98; tchr. Aux. Svc. High Schs., N.Y.C., 1998—. Pres. Black Tchrs. Who Care, N.Y.C., 2000—; chairperson Scholarship Commn., N.Y.C., NY, 1993—. Mem.: Nat. Assn. Univ. Women. Democrat. Baptist. Avocations: reading, watching basketball, tennis.

COLE, SALLY J. (SARAH JEWELL COLE), archaeologist, researcher; b. Murfreesboro, Tenn., Apr. 8, 1942; d. John Jennnings and Sarah Hays Jewell; m. Charles Robert Cole, June 13, 1964. BA, Vanderbilt U., 1964, Mesa State Coll., 1981; MA, Norwich U., 1989. Ind. profl. photographer, various locations, 1968-82; ind. profl. archaeologist, 1981—. Profl. archaeologist-researcher Utah Mus. Natural History, U. Utah, Salt Lake City, 1992—; cons. Mesa Verde Nat. Park, Colo., 1996—, U.S. Bur. Land Mgmt., Ariz., Colo., Utah; adj. prof. anthropology Ft. Lewis Coll., Colo. Author: Legacy on Stone: Rock Art of the Colorado Plateau and Four Corners Region, 1990, Katsina Iconography in Homol'ovi Rock Art, Middle Little Colorado River, Arizona, 1992; contbr. articles to profl. jours. Trustee Mus. Western Colo., Grand Junction, 1986-92. Grantee rsch. and publ. grantee, Colo. Endowment for the Humanities, 1988—89, 2000—01, field rsch. grantee, Ctr. for Field Rsch.-Earthwatch, 1993—2001, rsch. grantee, Colo. Hist. Soc., 1996—97, Colo. Hist. Soc. and Mesa Verde Nat. Pk. Mus. Assn., 1999—, Colo. Hist. Soc. and Ft. Lewis Coll., 2002—. Mem. Soc. for Am. Archaeology, Am. Anthropol. Assn., Colo. Archaeol. Soc. (adv. bd. mem. 1986-92), Colo. Coun. Profl. Archaeologists (sec. 1985-86). Avocations: backpacking, hiking, wildlife watching, rafting, canoeing. Office: Utah Mus Natural History Univ Utah Pres Cir Salt Lake City UT 84112

COLE, SUSAN A. university president, English language educator; m. David Cole, two children. BA in English and Am. Lit., Columbia U., 1962; MA in English and Am. Lit., Brandeis U., 1964, PhD in English and Am. Lit., 1972. Tchg. asst. Clark U., 1964-65; assoc. prof. CCUNY-N.Y.C. Tech. Coll., 1968-77; assoc. dean for acad. affairs Antioch U., 1977-80; v.p. for univ. adminstrn. and pers. Rutgers U., New Brunswick, N.J., 1980-92; pres., prof. English Met. State U., Mpls. and St. Paul, 1993-98; pres. Montclair State U., Upper Montclair, N.J., 1998—. Guest adj. assoc. prof. Pace U., fall 1977; vis. sr. fellow in acad. adminstrn. Office Acad. Affairs, CUNY, 1991-93; bd. dirs. Western State Bank; presenter in field. Contbr. articles to profl. jours. Chmn. edn. resolutions sessions, coord. edn. panels N.Y. State meeting Internat. Women's Year, Albany, 1977; agy. mem. N.J. Gov.'s Mgmt. Improvement Program, 1982; v.p., bd. dirs. Bklyn. Ecumenical Coops., 1988-90; mem. cmty. health care policy task force Robert Wood Johnson Univ. Hosp., New Brunswick, 1991; mem. blue ribon task force Mpls. Pub. Libr., 1994-95; mem. steering com. Greater St. Paul Tomorrow, 1994—; trustee Twin Cities Pub. TV, 1994—, Sci. Mus. Minn., 1994; bd. dirs., mem. exec. com. St. Paul Riverfront Corp., 1994—; v.p., founding bd. dirs. St. Paul Pub. Schs. Found., 1995—; bd. dirs. St. Paul Found., 1995—. Mem. Am. Assn. State Colls. and Univs. (urban and met. steering com. 1993—), Am. Coun. on Edn. (Commn. on Women in Higher Edn. 1993—), Greater Mpls. C. of C. (enterprise devel. task force 1994—). Office: Montclair State U Ofc of Pres 1 Normal Ave Montclair NJ 07043-1624

COLE, SUSAN STOCKBRIDGE, theatre educator; b. San Francisco, Jan. 26, 1939; d. Elmer Leroy Stockbridge and Martha Louise Rosenauer; m. John Michael Day, June 28, 1965 (div. May 1968); m. Willie Robert Cole, June 12, 1976. AB, Stanford (Calif.) U., 1960, MA, 1961; PhD, U. Oreg., 1972. Asst. prof. theatre Bakersfield (Calif.) Coll., 1962-69; grad. tchg fellow U. Oreg., Eugene, 1969-72; asst. prof. theatre Keuka Coll., Keuka Park, N.Y., 1972-75; prof. Appalachian State U., Boone, N.C., 1975—, dept. chair theatre and dance, 1989—. Cons. Dept. Pub. Instrn., Raleigh, N.C., 1980—, N.C. Arts Coun., Raleigh, 1989-93. Author: American National Biography, 1999, Notable Women in American Theatre, 1990; designer more than 100 play prodns., 1962—; dir. more than 60 play prodns. Mem.: Nat. Assn. of Schs. of Theatre, Am. Soc. for Theatre Rsch., Assn. for Theatre in Higher Edn., N.C. Theatre Conf. (pres. 1991—92, Svc. award 1997), Southeastern Theatre Conf. (pres. 1998—99, Suzanne Davis award 2002), Lions Club Internat. (dist. officer 1997—2003, treas. 1999—2004, past pres.), Alpha Psi Omega (pres. 1997—2002). Democrat. Episcopalian. Avocation: reading. Home: PO Box 220 Todd NC 28684-0220 Office: Dept of Theatre and Dance Appalachian State U Boone NC 28608-2123 Office Phone: 828-262-3028.

COLE, SUSIE CLEORA, retired government employee relations official; b. Bloomsburg, Pa. d. Harry E. and Chloe Ann (McKinstry) Cole; m. Richard Edward Miller, July 31, 1959 (div. Aug. 1977); 1 child, Terri Lee Miller; m. Gerald Edward Nelson, Feb. 18, 1978 (div. June 1982). Student, No. Va. C.C., 1982. With Dept. of Navy, Washington, 1957-74; clk., technician U.S. Dept. Navy, Washington, 1957-62, navy mil. pay regulations specialist, 1962-71, mgr. error detection/reduction program mil. pay, 1967-71, fiscal acct., 1971-74; fiscal clk. Dept. State, Washington, 1975-77, sr. retirement claims examiner, 1977-83, employee rels. officer, 1983-94, also mgr. fed. health benefits program, 1983-94, mgr. fed. life ins. program, 1983-94, ret., 1994. Active Citizen's Band Radio Club, Fairfax, Va., 1974-82, Retarded Children's Ctr., Fairfax, 1981-82. Recipient various govt. awards including Sustained Exceptional Achievement award Dept. State, 1983-93. Democrat. Avocations: reading, travel, writing, history, music, art. Home: 4910 N Arnold Dr Apt 3 Prescott Valley AZ 86314-6160

COLE, TERRI LYNN, organization administrator; b. Tucson, Dec. 28, 1951; m. James R. Cole II. Student, U. N.Mex., 1975-80; cert., Inst. Orgn. Mgmt., 1985. Cert. chamber exec. With SunWest Bank, Albuquerque, 1971-74, employment adminstr., 1974-76, communications dir., 1976-78; pub. info. dir. Albuquerque C. of C., 1978-81, gen. mgr., 1981-83, pres., 1983—. Pres. N.Mex. C. of C. Execs. Assn., 1986-87, bd. dirs., 1980—; bd. regents Inst. for Orgn. Mgmt., Stanford U., 1988—, vice chmn., 1990-91, chmn., 1991; bd. dirs. Hosp. Home Health, Inc. Recipient Bus. Devel. award Expn. Mgmt. Inc., 1985, Women on Move award YWCA, 1986; named one of Outstanding Women of Am., 1984. Mem. Am. C. of C. Execs. Assn. (chmn. elect bd. 1992—). Republican. Avocations: skiing, cycling, gardening. Office: Greater Albuquerque C of C PO Box 25100 Albuquerque NM 87125-0100

COLEMAN, ARLENE FLORENCE, retired pediatrics nurse; b. Braham, Minn., Apr. 8, 1926; d. William and Christine (Judin) C.; m. John Dunkerken, May 30, 1987. Diploma in nursing, U. Minn., 1947, BS, 1953; MPH, Loma Linda U., 1974. RN, Calif. Operating room scrub nurse Calif. Luth. Hosp., L.A., 1947-48; indsl. staff nurse Good Samaritan Hosp., L.A., 1948-49; staff nurse Passavant Hosp., Chgo., 1950-51; student health nurse Moody Bible Inst., Chgo., 1950-51; staff nurse St. Andrews Hosp., Mpls., 1951-53; pub. health nurse Bapt. Gen. Conf. Bd. of World Missions, Ethiopia, Africa, 1954-66; staff pub. health nurse County of San Bernadino, Calif., 1966-68, sr. pub. health nurse, 1968-73, pediatric nurse practitioner, 1973—. Contbr. articles to profl. jours. Mem. bd. dist. missions Bapt. Gen. Conf., Calif., 1978-84; mem. adv. coun. Kaiser Hosp., Fontana, Calif., 1969-85, Bethel Sem. West, San Diego, 1987—; bd. dirs. Casa Verdugo Retirement Home, Hemet, Calif., 1985—; active Calvary Bapt. Ch., Redlands, Calif., 1974—; mem. S.W. Bapt. Conf. Social Ministries, 1993—. With Cadet Nurse Corps USPHS, 1944-47. Calif. State Dept. Health grantee, 1973. Fellow Nat. Assn. Pediatric Nurse Assocs. and Practitioners; mem. Calif. Nurses Assn. (state nursing coun. 1974-76). Democrat. Avocations: gardening, travel, reading. Home: 622 Esther Way Redlands CA 92373-5822

COLEMAN, BARBARA MCREYNOLDS, artist; b. Omaha, Neb., May 5, 1956; d. Zachariah Aycock and Mary Barbara (McCulloh) McR.; m. Stephen Dale Dent, Mar. 12, 1983 (div. Dec. 20, 1992); children: Madeleine Victoria, Matthew Stephen; m. Ross Coleman, Oct. 16, 1993; 1 child, Mia Jeanne Coleman. Student. U. N.Mex., 1979, MA in Cmty. and Regional Planning, 1984. Lectr. U. N.Mex. Sch. Arch., Albuquerque, 1979-82, 91—; assoc. planner, urban designer planning divsn. City of Albuquerque, 1982-84, city planner, urban designer N.Mex. redevel. divsn., 1984-88; v.p. Hydra Aquatic, Inc., Albuquerque, 1997—. Cons. City of Albuquerque Redevel. Dept., 1987-88; urban design cons. Southwest Land Rsch., Albuquerque, 1991, instr. at Ctr. for Action and Contemplation, Albuquerque, NM, 1999-present. Columnist for Kids and Art, 1990-92; author: Coors Corridor Plan (The Albuquerque Conservation Assn. Urban Design award 1984), Electric Facilities Plan, Downtown Core Revitalization Strategy and Sector Development Plan; contbg. author: Anasazi Architecture and American Design, 1994; contbr. articles to profl. jour.; exhibited in shows and solo exhibitions at Dartmouth St. Gallery, Albuquerque, 2000, Chimayo (N.Mex.) Trade and Mercantile, JoAnne Chappel Gallery, San Francisco, Southwest Arts Festival, Albuquerque, Act I Gallery, Taos, N.Mex., Nat. Arts Club, NYC, Hermitage Mus., Norfolk, Va., Schimmel Ctr. for the Arts, Pace U., NYC, Musée Granet, Aix-en-Provence, France, Fine Arts Gallery, Albuquerque, 1999 (1st pl.). Vol. art tchr. A. Montoya Elem. Sch., Roosevelt Mid. Sch., Albuquerque, 1989-97. Recipient First Pl. for pastels N.Mex. Art League, 1991, Merit award Pastel Soc. of S.W., 1989, 1st pl. award N.Mex. State Fair Fine Arts Gallery, Albuquerque, 1999; finalist Nat. Cath. Reporter Jesus 2000 contest. Mem. Pastel Soc. of Am. (signature mem.), Pastel Soc. N.Mex. (pres. 1991-92, Best of Show 1990 award, 4th pl. Am. Artist Mag. award 1999). Democrat. Episc. Avocations: hiking, skiing, running. Office: U NMex Sch Architecture Albuquerque NM 87131-0001

COLEMAN, BONNIE WATSON, assemblywoman; m. William E. Coleman; 1 child, William stepchildren: Troy, Jared. BA, Thomas Edison State Coll.; PhD (hon.), Richard Stockton State Coll. Cert. pub. mgr. Asst. commr. N.J. Dept. of Cmty. Affairs, 1980; assemblywoman N.J. Gen. Assembly, 1998—, chair appropriations com., 2002—, mem. assembly budget com. Bd. trustees Richard Stockton Coll., 1981—98, chair, 1990—91; mem. N.J. Governing Bds. Assn. of State Colls., 1987—98, pres., 1991—93; chair N.J. State Coll. of Governing Bds., 1991; mem. Ewing Twp. Planning Bd., 1996—97; chair Dem. State Com., 2002—. Field rep. N.J. Divsn. on Civil Rights; chief Bur. of Housing and Pub. Accommodations; establisher, dir. State Dept. of Transp. first office of Civil Rights, Contract Compliance and Affirmative Action, 1974—80; mem. exec. com. Assn. of State Dem. Chairs, 2002; mem., deaconess Shiloh Bapt. Ch., Trenton, NJ. Mem.: Nat. Polit. Congress of Black Women, Nat. Assn. for Advancement of Colored People to Met. Trenton (life), Alpha Kappa Alpha Sorority, Inc. Democrat. Office: 226 W State St Trenton NJ 08608 E-mail: AswWatsonColeman@njleg.org.

COLEMAN, CAROLYN, state legislator; b. Oklahoma City, Oct. 15, 1952; d. Irwin Arthur and Beulah Wyatt; m. Richard E. Coleman; children: Mary Rachel, Sarah Elizabeth. Student, Rose State Coll., Southwestern Bible Coll. Mem. Okla. Ho. of Reps., Oklahoma City, 1990—. Mem. Metro South Crisis Ctr., Okla. Fedn. Rep. Women. Home: 1608 E Main St Moore OK 73160-8120 Office: Okla Ho of Reps Rm 505 2300 N Lincoln Blvd Oklahoma City OK 73105

COLEMAN, CAROLYN QUILLOIN, association executive; b. Savannah, Ga. 1 child. BS in History, Savannah State Coll.; MS in Adult Edn. and C.C. Adminstrn., N.C. A&T State U. Nat. staff mem. NAACP, N.C. state exec. dir., so. voter edn. dir., dir. voter registration/voter edn./voter turnout campaign in the South, 1989—92, coord. voter registration, 1990, 1991, mem. nat. bd. dirs.; dir. James B. Hunt Jr. campaign for gov., 1992; spl. asst. for cmty. affairs to Gov. James B. Hunt Jr., 1993—. Mem.: Nat. Assn. Negro Bus. and Profl. Women, Greensboro Br. NAACP, Wildacres Leadership Initiative, Women's Polit. Forum, Delta Sigma Theta (Greensboro Alumnae chpt.). Baptist. Office: NAACP 4805 Mt Hope Dr Baltimore MD 21215*

COLEMAN, CATHERINE G. astronaut; b. Charleston, S.C., Dec. 14, 1960; d. James J. Coleman and Ann L. Doty; m. Josh Simpson. BS in Chemistry, MIT, 1983; D in Polymer Sci. and Engring., U. Mass., 1991. Commd. 2nd lt. USAF, 1983, advanced through grades to lt. col.; rsch. chemist materials directorate Wright Lab., Wright Patterson AFB; astronaut NASA Johnson Space Ctr., Houston, 1992—, with astronaut office mission support br., spl. asst. to ctr. dir., with astronaut office payloads and habitability br., mission specialist on STS-73, 1995, mission specialist on STS-83, lead mission specialist on STS-93, 1999. Surface analysis cons. for Long Duration Exposure Facility; vol. test subject centrifuge program Crew Sys. Directorate Armstrong Aeromedical Lab. Mem. ACS, AAUW, Soc. Photo-Optical Instrumentation Engrs., Internat. Womens' Air and space Mus. Avocations: flying, scuba diving, sports, music. Office: NASA Lyndon B Johnson Space Ctr Houston TX 77058

COLEMAN, CLAIRE KOHN, public relations executive; b. New Castle, Pa., Nov. 19, 1924; d. Louis and Florence (Frank) Kohn; m. Frederick H. Coleman, Mar. 10, 1957; children: Franklin, Elliot. BA, Pa. State U., 1945. Market editor Fairchild Publs., N.Y.C., 1945-48; asst. home editor N.Y. Times, 1949-50; pub. rels. dir. United Wallpaper, Chgo., 1950-53, Assoc. Am. Artists, N.Y.C., 1953-54; dir. Wallpaper Info. Bur., N.Y.C., 1954; dept. head Roy Bernard, Inc., N.Y.C., 1955-58; pub. rels. dir. Siesel Co., N.Y.C., 1972—, sr. v.p., 1988; pres. Tisch Trask Comm. Resources Pub. Rels. Group, 1988-89; sr. v.p. Anthony M. Franco, N.Y.C., 1989-90; pres. Coleman Comm., N.Y.C., 1990—. Ctrl. steering com. Sch. Dist. Critical Assessments, New Rochelle, NY, 1969—71; active Mayor's Adv. Coun. on Aging, 1966, Mayor's Adv. Coun. on Bd. Edn. Appts., 1969; v.p. Coun. of PTAs, 1969—70; chmn. women's divsn. United Jewish Appeal, New Rochelle, 1971; v.p. Found. Women Execs. Pub. Rels., 1992—93, pres., 1993—94, bd. dirs., 1998—; bd. dirs., v.p. Beechmont Assn., 1969—74, adv. bd., 1990—. Fellow: Internat. Furnishings and Design Assn. (founder 1947, exec. chmn. 1947, pres. 1947, v.p. 1948—50, nat. treas. 1977—78, nat. pres. 1980—81, N.Y. chpt. v.p. 1994, nat. v.p. mktg. 1998—2000, formerly Nat. Home Fashions League, v.p. Chgo. chpt. 1950—53, Cir. of Excellence award 1994, Internat. Hon. Recognition award 1998); mem.: Women Execs. Pub. Rels. (bd. dirs. 1983—84, sec. 1986—87, pres.-elect 1994—95, pres. 1996—97). Fax: 914-576-6885. Office Phone: 914-633-6914. E-mail: ckcpr@aol.com.

COLEMAN, DEBORAH ANN, electronics company executive; b. Central Falls, R.I., Jan. 22, 1953; d. John Austin and Joan Mary Coleman. BA, Brown U., 1974; MBA, Stanford U., 1978; PhD in Engring. (hon.), Worcester (Mass.) Poly., 1987. Mfg. supr. Tex. Instruments, Attleboro, Mass., 1974; with fin. mgmt. tng. program Gen. Electric, Providence, 1975-76; with fin. mgmt. Hewlett-Packard, Cupertino, Calif., 1978-81; contr. Macintosh/Apple 32 group Apple Computer, Cupertino, 1981-84, dir. ops., 1984-85, v.p. worldwide mfg., 1985-87, CFO, 1987-89, CIO, 1990-92; v.p. materials ops. Tektronix Inc., Wilsonville, OR, 1992-94; chmn., CEO Merix Corp., Forest Grove, OR, 1994—; CIO Apple Computer, Cupertino, 1990-92; v.p. materials ops. Tektronix Inc., Wilsonville, Oreg., 1992-94; chmn., CEO, pres. Merix Corp., Forest Grove, Oreg., 1994—. Mem. U.S. Dept. Def. Mfg. Sci. Tech. Bd., 1988-91; bd. dirs. VMX, Inc., Software Pub Corp., Octel. Mem. adv. coun. Stanford Inst. Mfg. Automation, 1985-87; mem. Harvard U. Bus. Sch. Vis. Com., 1987—, Com. of 200, 1987—; trustee San Jose/Cleve. Ballet, 1989-92, Brown U., 1994—. Mem. Internat. Women's Forum. Democrat. Roman Catholic. Office: Merix Corp 1521 Poplar Ln Forest Grove OR 97116-0300

COLEMAN, ELIZABETH, college president; b. N.Y.C., Nov. 23, 1937; d. Lewis and Sophie (Brantman) Ginsburg; m. Aaron Coleman, June 14, 1959; children: Daniel, David. BA, U. Chgo., 1958; MA, Cornell U., 1959; PhD, Columbia U., 1965; Doctorate (hon.), Hofstra U.; LLD (hon.), U. Vt. Instr. humanities SUNY, N.Y.C., 1960-65; assoc. dean faculty New Sch. Social Research, N.Y.C., 1966-76, dean Coll. Arts and Scis., 1977-84, prof. literature and humanities, 1984-87; pres. Bennington (Vt.) Coll., 1987—. Vis. lectr. Hebrew U., 1972, SUNY-Stony Brook, 1975; curriculum cons. Howard U., 1973; chmn. outside evaluating com. CUNY, 1976 Contbr. articles to profl. pubs. Mem. nat. adv. coun. Woodrow Wilson Found., 1990; bd. dirs. Ctrl. Vt. Pub. Svc. Corp., 1990-96; bd. trustees Inst. Ecosystem Studies, 1994. Fellow Ford Found., 1954-58; Woodrow Wilson fellow, 1958-59; F.J.E. Woodbridge fellow Columbia U., 1963-64; Pres.'s fellow Columbia U., 1964-65 Mem. MLA, Am. Assn. Colls. Home and Office: Bennington Coll Office of Pres Rte 67A Bennington VT 05201

COLEMAN, FRAN NATIVIDAD, state representative; b. Denver, July 5, 1945; m. Ben H. Coleman; stepchildren: Pam DiMarco, Steve, Craig, Wayne; children: Matt Lopez, Mitch Lopez. BA in Bus. Adminstrn., Loretto Heights Coll., 1987; MS in Telecomm., Denver U., 1992; cert. govt. contracting, U. Phoenix, Denver, 1995. State rep., dist. 1 Colo. House Rep., Denver, 1998—, mem. joint com. on legis. audit, mem. bus. affairs and labor, and local govt. coms. Mem. Bus. Affairs and Labor Com., Joint Com. on Legis. Audit, Local Govt. Com. Adv. bd. LARASA, Ft. Logan Citizens; apptd. Denver Corrections Bd., 1992—97. Mem.: Nat. Alliance for Mentally Ill, Women in Govt. Democrat. Roman Catholic. Avocations: reading, golf, gardening, exercise. Office: State Capitol #357 200 E Colfax Ave Denver CO 80203

COLEMAN, JEAN BLACK, nurse, physician assistant; b. Sharon, Pa., Jan. 11, 1925; d. Charles B. and Sue E. (Dougherty) Black; m. Donald A. Coleman, July 3, 1946; children: Sue Ann Lopez, Donald Ashley. Grad., Spencer Hosp. Sch. Nursing, Meadville, Pa., 1945; student, Vanderbilt U., 1952-54. RN, Ga. Nurse, dir. nursing Bulloch Meml. Hosp., Statesboro, Ga, 1948-51, nurse supr. surgery, 1954-67, dir. nursing, 1967-71; physician's asst., nurse anesthetist Office Dr. Robert H. Swint, Statesboro, 1971-96; physician asst. Office Dr. Earl L. Alderman, Statesboro, 1996-98, Dr. Swaroop Reddy, Statesboro, 1998—. Mem. physician's asst. adv. com. Ga. Med. Bd., 1989-97; mem. physician assts. adv. com. Ga. Bd. Med. Examiners, 1987-97, ex-officio mem., 1994-95. Recipient Dean Day Smith Svc. to Mankind award, 1995; named Woman of Yr. in med. field Bus. and Profl. Women, 1980; Paul Harris fellow Rotary Club. Mem. ANA, Am. Acad. Physician Assts., Ga. Nurses Assn., Ga. Assn. Physician Assts. (bd. dirs. 1975-79, v.p. 1979-80, pres. 1980-81). Republican. Roman Catholic.

COLEMAN, K(ATHERINE) ANN, behavioral psychology educator; b. Plattsburg, N.Y. d. John and Anna C. BS, Elms Coll., 1963; MS, Springfield Coll., 1964; PhD, Boston Coll., 1971; MPH, Harvard U., 1978. Psychologist Exec. Office of the Pres., Washington, 1964-66; rsch. assoc. Harvard U., Cambridge, Mass., 1970-71; asst. prof. SUNY, Stony Brook, 1971-75, assoc. prof., 1975-78, Boston U., 1978—. Owner, pres. La Di Da Properties, Cambridge, 1986—. Co-author: Behavioral Statistics: The Core, 1994, Fundamentals of Behavioral Statistics, 9th edit., 2000; contbr. articles to profl. jours. Fellow APA, Am. Psychol. Soc.; mem. New Eng. Ednl. Rsch. Orgn. (bd. dirs. 1974-86, v.p. 1985-86, pres. 1986-87), Ea. Ednl. Rsch. Orgn. (chmn. 1979-91, bd. dirs. 1985-91). Home: 44 Concord Ave Cambridge MA 02138-2380 Office: Boston U Dept Psychology 64 Cummington St Boston MA 02215-2407 E-mail: kaycole@bu.edu.

COLEMAN, LINDA, state legislator; BA, U. Miss.; JD, Miss. Coll. State rep., vice chairwoman penitentiary com., mem. appropriations com., judiciary com., fees and salaries pub. officers com. Miss. Ho. of Reps., Jackson. Mem. Nat. Bar Assn., Magnolia Bar Assn. Democrat. Baptist. Office: Miss Ho of Reps State Capitol PO Box 1018 Jackson MS 39215-1018

COLEMAN, MARY H. state legislator; b. Noxapater, Miss., July 25, 1946; m. Cayle Coleman, children Marcus, Crystal, Arqullas. Student, L.A. Trade-Tech. Coll., Tougaloo Coll. Mem. Miss. Ho. of Reps., 1987—; mem. edn., ins., pub. bldgs., pub. health coms.; mem. ways and means com. Exec. asst. to State Auditor, 1987-92; pres. Nat. Black Caucus of St. Legislators. Mem. NAACP, NOW, SCLC, Women in Govt., Alpha Kappa Alpha (Beta Delta Omega chpt.). Democrat. Baptist. Home: 308 Lynwood Ln Jackson MS 39206-3931 Office: State Capitol Bldg PO Box 1018 Jackson MS 39215-1018*

COLEMAN, MARY STALLINGS, retired chief justice; b. Forney, Tex. d. Leslie C. and Agnes B. (Huther) Stallings; m. Creighton R. Coleman, June 24, 1939 (dec.); children: Leslie Ann Hagan, Carol Coleman-Sheenson. BA, U. Md., 1935; JD, George Washington U., 1939; LL.D., Eastern Mich. U., 1974, Western Mich. U., 1974; L.H.D., Nazareth Coll., 1973; LL.D., Alma Coll., 1973, Olivet Coll., 1973, Detroit Coll. Law, 1975, Adrian Coll., 1976, U. Md., 1978, Saginaw Valley State Coll., 1979, Ferris State U., 1981, Hope Coll., 1981, N.Y. Law Sch., 1982; D.P.A., Albion Coll., 1982, U. Detroit, 1983, Grand Valley State Coll., 1984. Bar: D.C. 1940, Mich. 1950. Practiced in, Washington, 1940-46; ptnr. Wunsch & Coleman, Battle Creek, Mich., 1950-61; probate and juvenile ct. judge Calhoun County, Mich., 1961-73; justice Mich. Supreme Ct., 1973-83. Dir. K Mart Internat., Nat. Bank Detroit and NBD Bancorp, Biggs/Gilmore. Contbr. articles to profl. pubs. Hon. trustee Albion Coll.; mem. Nat. Commn. for Observance of Internat. Women's Year, 1975-76. Recipient Disting. Alumna award Law Sch., George Washington U., 1973, Alumni Disting. Career Achievement award, 1983, Disting. Alumni award U. Md., 1973, Disting. Mem. award Phi Kappa Phi, 1973, award Calhoun County Bd. Edn., 1964, award NAACP Young Adults, 1969, George award Enquirer & News, 1969, Internat. Wyman award Alpha Omicron Pi, 1975, Disting. Woman award Mich. Bus. and Profl. Women's Club, 1973, Religious Heritage of Am. award, 1974, Disting. Citizen award Mich. State U., 1977, joint resolution of commendation Mich. Legis., 1977, 82, DAR medal of honor, 1978, Disting. Svc. award Mich. Juvenile Detention Assn., 1980, award of Merit Am. Judges Assn., 1980, Disting. Vol. Leadership award March of Dimes, 1981, Disting. Jurist award Miss. State U. Pre-Law Soc., 1988; named Woman of Yr. Mich. Assn. Professions, 1976, U. Md. Hall of Fame, 1995, 1 of 10 Top Michigians of Yr., 1980, Disting. Woman Northwood U., 1981, Mich. Women's Hall of Fame, 1983, Legal Milerton of State Bar Mich., 1999. Fellow Mich. Bar Found. (founder); mem. PEO, Mich. Bar Assn. (Champion of Justice award 1993), Mich. Assn. Woman Lawyers, Bus. and Profl. Women's Club, Jr. League (hon.), Big Sisters-Big Bros. (hon.), Altrusa Internat. (hon .), Gainesville Golf and Country Club, Beta Sigma Phi, Delta Kappa Gamma, Alpha Delta Kappa, Alpha Omicron Pi. Address: 8011 NW 27th Blvd Apt D214 Gainesville FL 32606-8615

COLEMAN, MARY SUE, academic administrator; b. Richmond, Ky, Oct. 2, 1943; m. Kenneth Coleman; 1 child, Jonathan. BA, Grinnell Coll., 1965; PhD, U. N.C., 1969. NIH postdoctoral fellow U. N.C., Chapel Hill, 1969—70, U. Ky., 1971—72, instr., rsch. assoc. depts. biochemistry and medicine, 1972—75, asst. prof. dept. biochemistry, 1975—80, assoc. prof. dept. biochemistry, 1980—85, prof. dept. biochemistry, 1985—90; prof. dept. biochemistry and biophysics U. N.C., Chapel Hill, 1990—93; provost, v.p. for academic affairs, prof. biochemistry U. N.Mex., 1993—95; pres., prof. biochemistry, prof. biol. scis. U. Iowa, Iowa City, 1995—2002; pres. U. Mich., 2002—. Pres. Iowa Health Sys., 1995—2002; vice chancellor grad students and rsch. U. N.C., 1992—93, assoc. provost, dean rsch., 1990—92; trustee U. Ky., 1987—90, assoc. dir. rsch. L.P. Markey Cancer Ctr., 1983—90, dir. grad. studies biochem., 1984—87; acting dir. basir rsch. U. Ky. Cancer Ctr., 1980—83; NSF summer trainee Grinnell Coll., 1962; scientific cons. Abbott Labs., 1981—85, Collaborative Rsch., 1983—88, Life Techs., Inc., 1992; bd. trustees Univs. Rsch. Assn., 1998—; mem. rsch. accountability task force Am. Assn. Univs., 2000—, chair undergrad. edn. com., 1997—, mem. exec. com., 2001—; mem. task force on tchrs. edn. Am. Coun. Edn., 1998—; bd. dirs. Meredith Corp., Am. Coun. Edn.; mem. Big Ten Coun. Pres.'s, 1995—2002; mem. stds. success adv. bd. Am. Assn. Univs. and he Pew Charitable Trusts, 2000—; co-chair Inst. Medicine Com. on Consequences of Uninsurance, 2000—; mem. Gov.'s Strategic Planning Coun., 1998—2000, Imagining Am. Pres.'s Coun., 1999—, Bus.-Higher Edn. Froum, 1999—, Knight Commn., 2000—01; presenter in field. Mem. editl. bd.: Jour. Biol. Chemistry, 1989—93; contbr. articles to profl. jours. Trustee Crinnell Coll., 1996—; mem. bd. govs. Warren G. Magnuson Clin. Ctr., NIH, 1996—2000, State of Iowa Gov.'s ACCESS Edn. Commn., 1997; bd. dirs. United Way, Albuquerque, 1995. Fellow postdoctiral fellow, Clayton Found. Biochem. Inst., U. Tex., 1970—71. Fellow: AAAS, Am. Acad. Arts and Scis.; mem.: Nat. Coll. Athletic Assn. (bd. dirs. 2002—), Nat. Assn. State Univs. ans Land Grant Colls. Coun. Cchief Acad. Officers (exec. com. 1993—95), Am. Soc. Biochem. and Molecular Biology, Am. Assn. Cancer Rsch.

COLEMAN, VERONICA FREEMAN, prosecutor; U.S. atty. We. Dist. Tenn., U.S. Dept. Justice, Memphis, 1993—. Office: US Attys Office 800 Federal Office Bldg 167 N Main St Memphis TN 38103-1816

COLEMAN, WINIFRED ELLEN, academic administrator; b. Syracuse, N.Y., Oct. 3, 1932; d. Peter Andrew and Josephine (Fahey) C. BA, Le Moyne Coll., Syracuse, N.Y., 1954; MA, Marquette U., 1956; DHL (hon.), Le Moyne Coll., 1993. Dean of students Cazenovia (N.Y.) Coll., 1957-70, Trinity Coll., Washington, 1970-80; exec. dir. Nat. Coun. Catholic Women, Washington, 1980-85; pres. Cashel House, Ltd., Syracuse, NY, 1985—, St. Joseph Coll., West Hartford, Conn., 1991—. Trustee LeMoyne Coll., Syracuse, 1995—, The Mark Twain House, Hartford; trustee emerita Loretto Geriatric Ctr., Syracuse, N.Y.; pres. Assn. Mercy Coll. Presidents, 1993-97, Hartford Consortium for Higher Edn., 1993-97; bd. dirs. Conn. Higher Edn. Student Loan Adminstrn., Hartford Mutual Funds. Bd. dirs. St. Francis Hosp. and Med. Ctr. Hon. membership Trinity Coll. Alumnae, Washington, 1978, Cazenovia (N.Y.) Coll. Alumnae, 1961, Naming of Winifred E. Coleman Student Union, Cazenovia Coll., 1963; recipient Chantal Award, Catholic Woman of the Yr., 1965. Mem.: Nat. Jesuit Honor Soc. for Women, Gamma Pi Epsilon. Roman Catholic. Avocations: reading, composing lyrics. Home: 27 Buckingham Ln West Hartford CT 06117-2758 Office: St Joseph Coll 1678 Asylum Ave West Hartford CT 06117-2764

COLEMAN-PERKINS, CAROLYN, medical/surgical nurse; b. Kansas City, Kans., Nov. 15, 1947; d. Samuel Coleman and Theorist Vernice Osborne-Coleman; m. Carl Edward Mitchell, June 1968 (div. Oct. 1973); 1 child, Vicki Lynn Mitchell ; m. Charles Talmadge Perkins, July 20, 1977; 1 child, Cynthia Perkins. Diploma in nursing, 1966. Sales clk. J.C. Penney Dept. Store, Kansas City, Mo., 1964—65; nurse Bapt. Meml. Hosp., 1966—68, San Francisco Blood Bank, 1968—71, Kaiser Permanente Med. Ctr., 1972—. V.p. Local 250 Health Care Workers Union, Oakland, Calif., 1988—. Democrat. Baptist. Avocations: football, walking. Home: 2208 89th Ave Oakland CA 94605-3928 Office: SEIU Local 250 560 20th St Oakland CA 94612 Office Phone: 415-833-3224.

COLES, ANNA LOUISE BAILEY, retired dean, nurse; b. Kansas City, Kans., Jan. 16, 1925; d. Gordon Alonzo and Lillie Mai (Buchanan) Bailey; children: Margot, Michelle, Gina. Diploma, Freedmen's Hosp. Sch. Nursing, 1948; BSN, Avila Coll., Kansas City, Mo., 1958; MSN, Cath. U. Am., 1960, PhD in Higher Edn., 1967. Instr. VA Hosp., Topeka, 1950—52, supr.

Kansas City, Mo., 1952—58; asst. dir. in-service edn. Freedmen's Hosp., Washington, 1960—61, adminstrv. asst. to dir. nursing, 1961—66, assoc. dir. nursing services, 1966—67, dir. nursing, 1967—69; dean Howard U. Coll. Nursing, Washington, 1968—86, dean emeritus, 1986—; cons. pvt. practice, Kansas City, Kans.; dir. minority devel. U. Kans., 1991—95. Pres. Nurses Examining Bd., 1967—68; cons. Gen. Rsch. Support Program, NIH, 1972—76; mem. Inst. Medicine, NAS, 1974—; cons. VA Ctrl. Office continuing edn. com., 1976—; mem. D.C. Health Planning Adv. Com., 1967—68, Tri-State Regional Planning Com. for Nursing Edn., 1969, Health Adv. Coun., Nat. Urban Coalition, 1971—73; bd. dirs. Hilton Grand Vacation CLub Seaworkd Internat. Ctr. Contbr. articles to profl. jours. Trustee Cmty. Group Health Found., 1976—77, cons., 1977—; bd. regents State Univ. Sys. Fla., 1977; adv. bd. Am. Assn. Med. Vols., 1970—72; bd. dirs. Iona Whipper Home for Unwed Mothers, 1970—72, Nursing Edn. Opportunities, 1970—72. Recipient Sustained Superior Performance award, HEW, 1962, Meritorious Pub. Svc. award, Govt. of D.C., 1968, medal of honor, Avila Coll., 1969, Disting. Alumni award, Howard U. Nat. Assn. for Equal Opportunity in Higher Edn., 1990, Cmty. Svc. award, Black Profl. Nurses Kansas City, 1991, Lifetime Achievement award, Assn. Black Nursing Faculty in Higher Edn., 1993, Svc. award, Midwest Regional Conf. on Black Families and Children, 1994. Mem.: ANA, Am. Assn. Colls. Nursing (sec. 1975—76), Am. Congress Rehab. Medicine, Nat. League Nursing, Societas Docta (charter, pres. 1996—99), Freedmen's Hosp. Nursing Alumni Assn., Alpha Kappa Alpha, Sigma Theta Tau. Home: 15107 Interlachen Dr Apt 205 Silver Spring MD 20906-5627

COLES, DIANNA ROBYN, benefits compensation analyst; b. Buffalo, Jan. 18, 1970; d. Robert A and Chyrel E Coles. BS, State U. Coll. at Buffalo, 1990—94. Cert. Domestic Violence and Rape Counseling Crisis Services, 1998. Admissions counselor Brylin Hospitals, Buffalo, 1991—94; network mgr. CMG Health, Owings Mills, Md., 1994—95; sr. profl. rels. rep Excellus, Buffalo, 1995—98; specialist network devel. Blue Cross and Blue Shield of WNY, Buffalo, 1998—2000; asst. dir., govt. programs and compliance HIP Health Plan of Greater NY, NYC, 2000—. Cons. Nexus Consulting, NYC, 1998—. Author: (book of poetry) Petals. Bd. mem. Old Bridge Libr., NJ, 2003; vol. United Way, NYC, 2000—03; cmty. educator AIDS Cmty. Svc., Buffalo, 1994—99. Adminstrv. Residency, St. Vincent's Hosp. Physician Hosp. Orgn., 1998. Mem.: Nat. Assn. for U. Women (assoc.), Nat. Assn. for Female Executives (assoc.; sec. 1998—99), Nat. Assn. of Women in the Arts (assoc.). Democrat-Npl. Avocations: reading, travel, art, theater. Office: HIP Health Plan of Greater New York 7 West 34th St New York NY 10001 Personal E-mail: drcoles1520@yahoo.com. E-mail: dcoles@hipusa.com.

COLES, LORI JANE, secondary school educator; b. Elkhart, Kans., Mar. 5, 1963; d. Lawrence R. and Elma Ruth Smith; m. Lyn Mark Coles, June 30, 1984; children: Jamie, Jason. Student, Emporia State U., 1981—84; BS, Cameron U., 1985; MS, Pittsburg State U., 1996. Cert. tchr. Kans. Sci. instr. Cherokee (Kans.) Unified Sch. Dist. 247, 1989—97, Plains (Kans.)-Kismet Unified Sch. Dist. 483, 1997—99, Meade (Kans.) Unified Sch. Dist. 226, 1999—. Mem. sch. improvement com. Cherokee USD 247, 1992—97, Meade USD 226, 1999—; presenter in field. Vol. Boy Scouts Am., Cherokee, Meade, 1991—. Grantee Students in Free Enterprise grant, Pittsburg State U., 1995, 1996, Excellence in Edn. grant, Wolf Creek Nuc. Corp., Burlington, Kans., 1998, 2000. Mem.: Kans. Assn. Tchrs. Sci., Nat. Sci. Tchr. Assn. Avocations: needlecrafts, reading, crafts, camping. Office: [illegible] 400 Meade [illegible]

COLESANTI, ROSEANN, medical/surgical nurse, consultant; m. Charles J. Colesanti, Nov. 19, 1966; children: Jeanmarie, Michelle. Degree in nursing, Ocean County Coll., N.J., 1982. Cert. cast mgr. 1993, gerontological nurse 1997. Head nurse Cmty. Meml. Hosp., Toms River, NJ; dir. nursing Forum Group, Deerfield Beach, Fla.; dir. nurses Courtat Palm Aire, Pompano Beach, Fla.; clin. resource dir. Avante Group, Hollywood, Fla.; dir. profl. svcs. Staff Builders HOme Healthcare, Miami Lakes, Fla.; pres. Info. Inst. Inc., Coral Springs, Fla. Mem.: Acad. Cert. Case Mgrs., Lions (v.p. 2003). Office: Info Inst Inc 10984 NW 21st St Coral Springs FL 33071 E-mail: ccolesanti@aol.com.

COLE-SCHIRALDI, MARILYN BUSH, occupational therapy educator; b. N.Y.C., Jan. 29, 1945; d. George Lyman and Theis (Maurer) Bush; m. Carl E. Cole, Aug. 31, 1968 (div. June 1981); children: Charlot E. Sleeper, Bradley Eric Cole; m. Martin M. Schiraldi Sr., July 3, 1982. BA, U. Conn., 1966; grad. cert., U. Pa., 1969; MS, U. Bridgeport, 1982. Registered occupl. therapist, Conn. Staff occupational therapy Ea. Pa. Psychiat. Inst., Phila., 1968-69; dir. occupational therapy Middlesex Meml. Hosp., Middletown, Conn., 1973-76; supervising occupational therapist Lawrence & Meml. Hosps. Day Treatment Ctr., New London, Conn., 1976-79; staff occupational therapist Newington Children's Hosp., Newington, Conn., 1980-82; asst. prof. occupational therapy Quinnipiac Coll., Hamden, Conn., 1982-95, assoc. prof., tenured, 1995—. Vis. faculty fellow Yale U., 1999-2001; cons. psychiat. svcs. VA Med. Ctr., West Haven, Conn., 1983-91; cons. Fairfield Hills Hosp., Newtown, Conn., 1989-91. Author: (textbook) Group Dynamics in Occupational Therapy, 1993, 3d edit., 2004; co-author Structured Group Experiences, 1982; contbr. chpts. to books, articles to profl. jours. Grantee Quinnipiac Coll, 1986; recipient Best Seller award Slack, Inc., 1999. Fellow: Am. Occupl. Therapy Assn. (Comms. award 1976, Svc. awards 1998, cert.); mem.: AAUW (cultural chair 1972, publicity chair 1973—76, edn. chair 1989—91, nominations 1993—96, membership treas. 1998—2001), Ctr. Study Sensory Integrative Dysfunction (cert. 1979), World Fedn. Occupl. Therapists, Conn. Occupl. Therapy Assn. (sec. 1978, nominations chair 1982—89, state mental health chair spl. interest sect. 1999—), U.S. Sailing Assn., U.S. Power Squadron, Sigma Xi. Republican. Episcopalian. Office: Quinnipiac U Dept Occupl Therapy 275 Mount Carmel Ave Hamden CT 06518-1961 Office Phone: 203-582-8518. E-mail: marilyn.cole@quinnipiac.edu.

COLEY, BARBARA YVONNE, computer software consultant; b. Albany, Ga., July 20, 1949; d. Leonard Earl and Hazel (Brady) C. BS in Math., U. Ga., 1971, MS in Stats., 1974. Statistician U.S. Forest Service, Athens, Ga., 1973-76; systems analyst Energy Mgmt. Assocs., Atlanta, 1976-78, product mgr., 1978-84; prin. cons. New Energy Assocs., Atlanta, 1984—. Pvt. practice cons., Atlanta, 1979—. Mem. Am. Mgmt. Assn., Phi Beta Kappa. Avocations: classical music, historical novels. Office: New Energy Assocs Ste 1400 400 Interstate North Pkwy SE Atlanta GA 30339-5029

COLEY, BRENDA ANN, elementary school educator; b. Indpls., Sept. 17, 1958; d. Jack Louis Mullis and Margaret Ann (Crites) Farris; m. Keith Alan Coley, Feb. 17, 1978; children: Amy Michelle, Jared Wesley, Adam Jacob. B Music Edn., Ind. U., 1981; MS in Music Edn., Ind. State U., 1987. Tchr. music Clay Community Sch. Corp., Staunton, Ind., 1981-84; choral dir. Spencer (Ind.)-Owen Community Sch. Corp., 1984-90, tchr. music, 1990—2000; asst. prin. McCormick's Creek Elem. Sch., Spencer, Ind., 2000—. Composer children's musical: Up! Up to the Moon!!, 1992; composer gospel music., founder "Jubilation in Christ", gospel singing group, 1997-. Choir dir. 1st Christian Ch., Spencer. Mem. NEA, Music Educators Nat. Conf., Ind. Music Educators Assn., Spencer-Owen Edn. Assn., Order Ea. Star, Kappa Kappa Kappa, Pi Lambda Theta, Delta Theta Tau. Democrat. Avocations: singing, sports, bowling. Home: 40 Mozart Ln Spencer IN 47460-9344 Office: McCormick's Creek Elem Sch 1601 Flatwoods Rd Spencer IN 47460-1499

COLEY, JOAN DEVELIN, education educator, academic administrator; b. Phila., Nov. 12, 1944; d. Paul Kennedy Develin and Lillian Marian Stiles; 1 child, David Kennedy. AB, Albright Coll., Reading, Pa., 1966; MEd, U. Md., 1970, PhD, 1973. Reading specialist Prince George's County (Md.), 1966-70, dir. secondary sch. vol. program, 1970-71; adj. prof. Univ. Coll., U. Md., College Park, 1971-73; prof., chair edn. dept., dean grad. programs, provost McDaniel Coll. (formerly Western Md. Coll.), Westminster, 1973—2000, pres., 2001—. Reading cons. Simon & Schuster Pub., 1986—. Editor: Reading: Issues and Practices, 1984-88; editorial adv. bd. Reading Rsch. and Instrn., 1977-81; author programmed reading vocabulary for tchrs. Mem. Internat. Reading Assn. (pres. Carroll County 1979-81, Tchr. Educator of Yr. 1989, Outstanding Educator in Reading 1982), Coll. Reading Assn. (bd. dirs. 1980-83), Nat. Reading Conf., Md. Higher Edn. Reading Assn. (pres. 1975-76). Home: 2 College Hill Westminster MD 21157-4450 E-mail: jcoley@mcdaniel.edu.

COLEY, LINDA MARIE, retired secondary school educator; b. Albany, Ga., Apr. 19, 1945; d. Leonard Earl and Hazel (Brady) C. BS in Math., Piedmont Coll., 1966; MS in Math., U. Ga., 1972, postgrad. Cert. tchr., Ga.; certed gifted tchr. Tchr. Toccoa (Ga.) Pub. Schs., 1966-67, Hall County Sch. Dist., Gainesville, Ga., 1967-68, Clarke County Sch. Dist., Athens, Ga., 1968—2001. Sec., 1st v.p. Clarke County Dem. Com., Athens, 1981—, Gov.'s Club. Mem. NEA, Ga. Edn. Assn., Clarke County Assn. Educators (treas., sec.), Alpha Delta Kappa (treas., sec., pres., dist. treas.), Phi Delta Kappa. Democrat. Baptist. Home: 135 Ravenwood Pl Athens GA 30605-3344

COLFER, CAROL JEAN PIERCE, anthropologist, researcher; b. Melrose Park, Ill., Aug. 27, 1945; d. Joe Eugene Pierce and Gwendolyn Marie Harris Pierce; m. Richard George Dudley, Feb. 2, 1985. MA, U. Wash., 1969, PhD, 1974; MPH, U. Hawaii, 1979. Field rschr. Abt Assocs., Quilcene, Wash., 1972—77; exec. dir. PACT: Social Analysts, Seattle, 1976—77; field rschr. Man and Biosphere Program, Long Segar, Indonesia, 1979—80; women in devel. asst. specialist U. Hawaii, Honolulu, 1980—82, farming systems assoc. rschr. Sitiung, Indonesia, 1992—96; assoc. prof. Sultan Qaboos U., Al Khodh, Oman, 1988—90; cmty. specialist Asian Wetlands Bur., Danau Sentarum Wildlife Res., Indonesia, 1992—93; prin. scientist Ctr. Internat. Forestry Rsch., Bogor, Indonesia, 1996—98, 2003—, program leader, 1998—2002; vis. fellow Cornell U., Ithaca, NY, 2002—03. Cons. Ctr. Internat. Forestry Rsch., Bogor, Indonesia, 1994—, FAO, Portland, Oreg., 1990—91. Author: (book) Toward Sustainable Agriculture in the Humid Tropics, 1991, Shifting Cultivators of Indonesia, 1993, Beyond Slash and Burn, 1997; editor: People Managing Forests, 2001, Which Way Forward?, 2002; contbr. articles to profl. jours. Named William S. Main Disting. Visitor, U. Calif. Berkeley, 1991, Profl. Affiliate Award, East-West Ctr., 1979; recipient Invitation to give Plenary Address, Internat. Union Forestry Rsch. Orgns., 2000, Appointment to Adv. Group, Ctr. Social Forestry, Mulawarman U., E. Kalimantan, Indonesia, 1999, Participant award for productivity, stability, sustainability and the small-scale Farmer, East-West Ctr., 1985, Profl. Affiliate award, 1977, Cert. of Outstanding Contbn./Rural Edn., Rural/Regional Ednl. Assn., 1976; fellow Fellow on population info., edn. and comm., East-West Ctr., 1975, Fulbright-Hayes Predoctoral fellow/Iran, Fulbright Hayes/U.S. Govt., 1972, fellow to study langs., NDEA, 1964—67; grantee to study interactions between people and forests in E. Kalimantan, U.S. Man and Biosphere program, 1979—80. Fellow: Internat. Union Forestry Rsch. Orgns. (vice chair 2001), Soc. Applied Anthropology, Med. Anthropology Soc., Am. Anthrop. Assn.; mem.: Soc. Study of Common Property. Liberal. Avocations: reading, beading, swimming, canoeing, travel. Home: 14845 SW Murray Scholls Dr Ste 110 Beaverton OR 97007-9237 Office: Ctr Internat Forestry Rsch PO Box 6596 JKPWB Jakarta 10065 Indonesia Office Fax: 62-21-622100. E-mail: c.colfer@[illegible]

COLFORD, ANN M. freelance/self-employed writer; b. Reading, Mass., June 24, 1958; d. Alfred Edward Colford and Helen Kathryn Bennett. BS in Acctg., U. Mass., Lowell, 1980; MA in Am. and New Eng. Studies, U. So. Maine, Portland, 1998. Acct. So. Meth. U., Dallas, 1981—82, U. N.H., Durham, 1982—85; acctg. mgr. Prototech Co., Newton, Mass., 1985—88; computer specialist U. N.H., Durham, 1988—91; MIS mgr. Spokane County Cmty. Svcs., Spokane, Wash., 1991—94; acct. (part-time) East Wash. State Hist. Soc., Spokane, 1995; acct. / rsch. assoc. Barba Architecture and Preservation, Portland, Maine, 1997—99; mus. asst. East Wash. State Hist. Soc., Spokane, 1999—2002; freelance writer Spokane, Wash., 1999—. Dir. YWCA of Spokane, Wash., 1992—94; contbg. writer Spokane Pub. Radio, Wash., 1999—2003; centennial com. St. Ann's Cath. Ch., Spokane, Wash., 2001—02; writer-at-large, editl. bd. The Pacific NW Inlander, Spokane, Wash., 2002—. Author (co-producer): (weekly radio series) Art A La Carte (First Pl., weekly series, Pub. Radio News Directors Internat., 2000); curator (exhibition) Audrey Jackson Soule: A Flair For Color; contbr. articles to mags. and profl. jours. including Spokane Home and Life S. Core team mem. Spokane Alliance, Wash., 2000—03. Named Vol. of the Yr. - Prodn., Spokane Pub. Radio, 2000; recipient 2d place radio commentary, Soc. of Profl. Journalists, Inland NW Chpt., 2000, 2d place weekly series, Pub. Radio News Dirs. Internat., 2001. Mem.: Pacific NW Am. Studies Assn., Am. Studies Assn., Nat. Trust for Hist. Preservation. Catholic. Avocations: music ministry, automobile travel, photography, cooking. Home and Office: 1220 W 6th Ave Apt B Spokane WA 99204 Office Phone: 509-747-2364. E-mail: colford@earthlink.net.

COLGATE, DORIS ELEANOR, sailing school owner and administrator; b. Washington, May 12, 1941; d. Bernard Leonard and Frances Lillian (Goldstein) Horecker; m. Richard G. Buchanan, Sept. 6, 1959 (div. Aug. 1967); m. Stephen Colgate, Dec. 17, 1969. Student, Antioch Coll., 1958-60, NYU, 1960-62. Rsch. supr. Geyer Moyer Ballard, N.Y.C., 1962-64; administrv. asst. Yachting Mag., N.Y.C., 1964-68; v.p. Offshore Sailing Sch. Ltd., Inc., N.Y.C., 1968-78, pres. Ft. Myers, Fla., 1978—2001; pres., CEO On and Offshore, Inc., Ft. Myers, 1984-2001; v.p. Offshore Travel, Inc., City Island, 1978-88; pres., CEO Offshore Sailing Sch. Ltd., Inc., Ft. Myers, 2001—. Pres. bd. dirs. Women's Sailing Found., 1998-2000, chmn. 2000-02, adv. coun., 2002—; mem. exec. com. Internat. Sailing Summit, 2000—. Author: The Bareboat Gourmet, 1983, Sailing: A Woman's Guide, 1999; contbr. articles to profl. jours. Bd. dirs. Fla. Repertory Theatre. Recipient Betty Cook Meml. Lifetime Achievement award, 1994, Sail Industry Leadership award, 1996, Southam award, 2000, Timothea Larr award US Sailing, 2003. Mem. Royal Ocean Racing Club (London chpt.), Nat. Women's Sailing Assn. (founder, chair nat. women's adv. bd. 1990-94, pres. 1994-2000, chair 2000-02, Leadership in Women's Sailing award, 2004), Am. Women's Econ. Devel. Corp. (adv. bd. 1980-86), Boat U.S. (nat. adv. coun. 1995—), Sail Am. (bd. dirs. 2000—), Internat. Sailing Summit (exec. com. 2000-). Avocations: piano, sailing, photography, writing, cooking. Home: 15400 Catalpa Cove Ln Fort Myers FL 33908 Office: Offshore Inc 16731 McGregor Blvd Fort Myers FL 33908-3843 Office Phone: 239-985-7511. E-mail: doris@offshore-saling.com.

COLISH, MARCIA LILLIAN, history educator; b. Bklyn., July 27, 1937; d. Samuel and Daisy (Kartch) C. BA magna cum laude, Smith Coll., 1958; MA, Yale U., 1959, PhD, 1965; DHL (hon.), Grinnell Coll., 1999. Instr. history Skidmore Coll., Saratoga Springs, NY, 1962-63; instr. Oberlin (Ohio) Coll., 1963-65, asst. prof., 1965-69, assoc. prof., 1969-75, prof. history, 1975-2001, Frederick B. Artz prof. history, 1985-2001, chmn. dept. history, 1973-74, 78-81, 85-86; vis. fellow Yale U., 2001—. Vis. prof. history and religious studies Yale U., 2002-03, vis. scholar Am. Acad. Rome, 1968-69; lectr. history Case Western Res. U., Cleve., 1966-67; editl. cons. W.W. Norton & Co., 1973, John Wiley & Sons, Inc., 1981, SUNY Press, 1983, 85, U. Chgo. Press, 1988, U. Calif. Press, 1988, Princeton U. Press, 1988, 96, 98, U. Notre Dame Press, 1991, 92, 94, U. Ill. Press, 1995, U. Pa. Press, 1995, 97, 99, Yale U. Press, 1997, 98, Oxford U. Press, 1998, 2001, Blackwell's, 1998, Liturgical Press, 1999, Cambridge U. Press, 2002, E.J. Brill, 2003; cons. dept. history Grinnell Coll., 1974, Knox Coll., 1981, St. John's U., 1981, Whitman Coll., 1982, Hope Coll., 1995, Kenyon Coll., 1996; mem. exec. bd. Ohio Program Humanities, 1976-81, exec. bd., 1978-81, vice chmn., 1979-81; writing residency, Villa Serbelloni, Bellagio, 1995; mem. Sch. Hist. Studies, Inst. for Advanced Study, Princeton, 1986-87 Author: The Mirror of Language: A Study in the Medieval Theory of Knowledge, 2d rev. edit., 1983, The Stoic Tradition from Antiquity to the Early Middle Ages, 1985, enlarged paperback edit., 1990, Peter Lombard, 1994, Medieval Foundations of the Western Intellectual Tradition, 400-1400, 1997, 2d printing, 1998, paperback edit., 1999, (Italian transl.) La Cultura del Medioevo, 2001. Mem. exec. bd. Oberlin ACLU, 1970-74, chmn., 1972-74, rec. sec., 1976-77, vice chmn., 1979-80; mem. exec. bd. Oberlin YWCA, 1966-70. Recipient Wilbur Cross medal Yale Grad. Sch. Alumni Assn., 1993, Marianist award U. Dayton, 2000; Etienne Gilson lectr. Pontifical Inst. of Mediaeval Studies, Toronto, 2000; Samuel S. Fels fellow Yale U., 1961-62, Younger Scholar fellow Inst. for Rsch. in Humanities, U. Wis., 1974-75, Nat. Humanities Ctr. fellow, 1981-82, Guggenheim fellow, 1989-90, Woodrow Wilson Ctr. fellow, 1994-95, NEH fellow, 1968-69, 81-82; NEH summer grantee U. Calif., 1993. Fellow Medieval Acad. Am. (coun. 1987-89, 2d v.p. 1989-90, 1st v.p. 1990-91, pres. 1991-92, Haskins medal 1998); mem. Am. Hist. Assn., Medieval Assn. Midwest (coun. 1978-81), Midwest Medieval Conf. (pres. 1978-79), Renaissance Soc. Am., Ctrl. Renaissance Conf., Soc. Internat. pour Etude Philosophie Medievale, Internat. Soc. for Classical Tradition, Internat. Soc. Intellectual History, Phi Beta Kappa. Home: 80 Seaview Terr #29 Guilford CT 06437 E-mail: marcia.colish@yale.edu.

COLLAS-DEAN, ANGELA G. former state commissioner, small business owner; b. Manila, Oct. 20, 1933; arrived in U.S., 1960; d. Juan Damocles Collas and Soledad Martinez Garduño; m. Bruce Goring Dean, Aug. 8, 1961; children: Heather Frances Dean, Jennifer Ashton Dean. BA in English Lit. and Humanities, U. of the Philippines, Diliman, Quezon City, 1955; MA in Drama, Baylor U., 1962. Owner Philippine Party Foods, Eugene, Oreg., 1984-96; dir., pres. Philippine Am. C. of C., Oreg., 1996-97. Instr. U. Philippines, Quezon City, 1963—65, Baylor U., Waco, 1965—68. Mem. Lane County Arts Adv. Com., Oreg., 1972—76, Affirmative Action Adv. Com., Lane County, Oreg., 1980—81; bd. dirs. Sign Code Bd. Appeals, Eugene, 1985—87; city commr. Human Rights Commn., Eugene, 1985—87, Cultural Arts Commn., Eugene, 1989—93; com. mem. Joint Soc. Svc. Fund, Lane County, Eugene, Springfield, 1986—88; bd. advisors U. Oreg. Ctr. Asian Pacific Studies, 1998—2000. Fulbright/Smith-Mundt grantee, U.S. Dept. Edn., Manila, 1959, Fulbright grantee, 1960. Mem.: Coun. Filipino Am. Assns. Oreg. (incorporator, trustee 2000—), Asian Am. Found. (founding mem., officer Eugene 1993—), Asian Coun. (founding mem., officer Eugene and Springfield 1985—), Philippine Am. Assn. (founding mem., officer Eugene 1983—). Office: Philippine Trading Co Inc 2092 Roland Way Eugene OR 97401-2061 E-mail: deancollas@aol.com.

COLLEDGE, DEBORAH GAIL, gifted and talented elementary educator; b. Altoona, Pa., Aug. 9, 1956; d. Charles E. Sr. and Shirley J. (Bragonier) C. BS, Clarion (Pa.) State, 1977; MEd, Pa. State U., 1981, EdD, 1993; prins. cert., 1983. Cert. elem. and middle sch. tchr., prin., adminstr., reading specialist, tchr. gifted. Elem. tchr. gifted Altoona Area Sch. Dist., 1978-85; tchr. Tuscarora Intermediate 11, McVeytown, Pa., 1983—85; tchr. gifted grades 3-6 Mesa (Ariz.) Pub. Schs., 1985—. Numerous grants. Mem. Assn. for Supervision and Curriculum Devel., Nat. Assn. for Gifted Children, Phi Delta Kappa, Kappa Delta Pi. Home: 2212 17th Ave Altoona PA 16601 Office: Mesa Pub Schs 549 N Stapley Dr Mesa AZ 85203-7203

COLLETTE, FRANCES MADELYN, retired tax specialist, lawyer, ombudsman, advocate; b. Yonkers, N.Y., Aug. 5, 1947; d. Morris Aaron and Esther (Gang) Volbert; m. Roger Warren Collette, Dec. 25, 1971; children: Darren Roger, Bonnie Frances. BEd summa cum laude, SUNY, Buffalo, 1969; JD cum laude, U. Miami, 1980. Bar: Fla. 1980. Employment counselor Fla. Bur. Employment Security, Miami, Fla., 1969-73; unemployment claims adjudicator Fla. Bur. Unemployment, Miami, 1973-77; owner Unemployment Svcs. Fla., Inc., Miami, 1977-93. Cons. Fla. unemployment tax and personnel; lectr. in field. Ad hoc comm. students with Asperger's Syndrome Dade County Pub. Schs., 1998-2000; vol. child advocate Exceptional Student Edn., 1993-; 1st v.p. BBB South Fla., 1980-81, bd. govs., 2d vice chair, 1990-91; mem. Supt.'s Dist. Adv. Panel for Exceptional Student Edn., Miami-Dade County Pub. Schs., 2003-. Jewish.

COLLETTI, ROSEANNE, reporter; b. Tex. married; 1 child. BA in Comm., U. Houston. Reporter KFDM-TV, Beaumont, Tex.; anchor WNGE-TV, Nashville, KSLA, Shreveport, La.; gen. assignment reporter WCBS, N.Y.C., 1978—86, investigative reporter Troubleshooter unit, 1986—95, reporter Steals and Deals, 1995—97; consumer reporter NewsChannel4 NBC, N.Y.C., 1997—. Recipient Best Documentary award, Assoc. Press Broadcasters. Office: NBC 30 rockefeller Plz New York NY 10112

COLLETTI, TERESA ANN, polymer chemist; b. Balt., Aug. 26, 1967; d. John Bruce and Elizabeth Grace (Schmidt) Schott; m. Ronald Francis Colletti, Sept. 23, 1989; 1 child, Christopher Robert. BS, U. So. Miss., 1989. Chemist, microscopist Monsanto, Pensacola, Fla., 1990-92, process engr., 1992-93, new product engr., 1993-94, process tech. team leader Greenwood, S.C., 1994-96; sr. mktg. tech. svc. specialist Solutia, St. Louis, 1996-99, sr. credit analyst, 1999—. Presenter in field. Contbr. articles to sci. jours. Mem. Am. Chem. Soc. (mem. women chemist com. 1993-94, 95-01, treas. Pensacola sect. 1991-93), Soc. of Plastics Engrs. Home: 257 Harbour Pointe Dr Wildwood MO 63040-1956

COLLEY, KAREN J. medical educator, medical researcher; b. Nov. 3, 1958; BS in Chemistry, Duke U., 1981; PhD in Molecular Biology, Washington U., St. Louis, 1987. Postdoctoral fellow dept. biol. chemistry UCLA, 1987—91; postdoctoral fellow NIH, 1990; asst. prof. dept. biochemistry U. Ill., Chgo., 1991—97, assoc. prof., 1997—. Mem. med. adv. bd. Leukemia Rsch. Found., 1994—, reviewer study sect., 1994—; outside reviewer NSF Grants, 1995—, VA Rsch. Grants, 1995—; mem. pathiobiochemistry study sect. NIH, 1998—. Reviewer: Jour. Biol. Chemistry, Jour. Cell Biology, Molecular and Chem. Neuropathology, Jour. Cell Sci., Devel. Biology; contbr. articles to profl. jours.; patentee in field. Recipient Established Investigator award, Am. Heart Assn., 1996; fellow (sr.), Am. Cancer Soc., 1991; grantee, 1992, U. Ill., 1992, 1996, Leukemia Rsch. Found., Inc., 1993. Mem.: AAAS, Soc. Glycobiology, Am. Soc. Biochemistry and Molecular Biology, Am. Soc. Cell Biology, Sigma Xi. Office: U Ill Dept Biochemistry and Molecular Biology 1819 W Polk St Chicago IL 60612-7331

COLLIE, PAULA RENEA, secondary school educator; b. Gonzales, Tex., Dec. 23, 1971; d. Paul Jr. and Kathy (Maulding) C. BA in Geography and Polit. Sci., SW Tex. State U., 1994. Clk. City of Gonzales, 1989-90; salesperson Laurel Ridge Antiques, Gonzales, 1990; subs. tchr. Gonzales Ind. Sch. Dist., 1990—94; with Gonzales County Archives, Gonzales Hist. Commn., 1993-94; geography tchr. Luling (Tex.) H.S., 1994—, social studies dept. head, 1995—, student coun. sponsor, 1996—, summer sch. tchr., 2000—. Participant All State Tex. Alliance Conf., Clear Lake, 1994, Nat. Conf. for Geographic Edn., Lexington, Ky., 1994. Mem. Nat. Geographic Soc., Nat. Coun. for Geographic Edn., Tex. Alliance for Geographic Edn., NEA, Tex. Student Edn. Assn. Avocations: genealogy, fishing. Home: 1611 Gardien St Gonzales TX 78629-4318 Office: Luling Ind Sch Dist 218 E Travis Luling TX 78648

COLLIER, COURTNEY CAROLE, mathematics educator; b. Miami, Sept. 15, 1966; d. Otis and Hazel Williams Collier. Bachelors, Fla. A&M U., 1991. Student tchr. Cobb Mid. Sch., Tallahassee, 1991; math. educator Deerklake Mid. Sch., Tallahassee, 1991—99, Hammocks Mid. Sch., Tallahassee, 1999—. Adj. prof. Tallahassee C.C., 1998—99. Vol. NAACP-ACTSO Program, Tallahassee, 1994—95, Spl. Olympics, Tallahassee, 1991—95. Recipient Ida S. Baker Minority Tchr. of Yr., Deerlake Mid.

Sch., 1995. Mem.: United Tchrs. Dade. Democrat. Ame Ch. Avocations: traveling, reading. Office: Hammocks Mid Sch 9889 Hammocks Blvd Miami FL 33196 Business E-Mail: collierc@hammocks.dadeschools.net.

COLLIER-EVANS, DEMETRA FRANCES, veterans benefits counselor; [illegible] (Williams) Collier-Sheffield; m. George Perry Evans, Dec. 21, 1966; 1 child, Richard Edward. AA in Social Sci., Solano C.C., Suisun City, Calif., 1974; BA in Social Sci., Chapman Coll., Orange, Calif., 1981. Cert. tchr., Calif. Specialist placement, case responsible person employment devel. dept. City of San Diego, 1975-82; vocat. tchr. San Diego Community Coll., 1982-83; specialist placement N.J. Job Service, Camden, 1984-86, mgr. job bank, 1985; specialist placement Abilities Ctr., Westville, N.J., 1987-88; veteran's benifits counselor VA, Phila. 1988-2000, ret., 2000; mem. bd. dirs. Welfare Rights; cons. Bumble Bee Canning Co., San Diego, 1982; developer women's seminar Women's Opportunity Week, City of San Diego, 1982, network seminar Fed. Women's Week, City of Phila., 1986. Bd. dirs. Welfare Rights Orgn., San Diego, 1982; mem. Internat. YWCA. Served with USAF, 1956-59. Recipient Excellence cert. San Diego Employer Adv. Bd., 1981, Leadership cert. Nat. U., San Diego, 1981. Mem. AAUW, NAACP (life, rec. sec. San Diego 1982), Black Advs. State Svc. (charter, corr. sec. San Diego Chpt. 1981-82), Nat. Assn. Female Execs., Am. Fedn. Govt. Employees (officer of yr. award 1999), Bonton Club (svc. award 1998), Chapman Coll. Alumni Assn., Alpha Gamma Sigma. Democrat. Avocation: calligraphy. Office: PO Box 5015 Cherry Hill NJ 08034-0391

COLLINA, KATHLEEN ALICE, corrugated box company executive; b. N.Y.C., Oct. 24, 1938; d. Louis Orville and Evelyn Dorothy (Cosgrove) Seawood; m. Nido Edward Collina, Sept. 14, 1957; children: Susan B. Collina Schulte, Gary E., Jill A. Collina Labar, Douglas J., Steven J. Grad. high sch., Easton, Pa. Svc. rep. Bell Telephone Co. of Pa., Easton, 1956-59, Stanley Home Products, Westfield, Mass., 1962-78; exec. asst. MA 500, Inc., Nazareth, Pa., 1973-86, Century Packaging Inc., Whitehall, Pa., 1987—. Capt. leadership team capital campaign Notre Dame High Sch., Easton, 1991-92. Mem. Ladies Ancient Order of Hibernians (pres. 1993-96, treas. 97—, Anna Malia Ruddy award 1997). Office: Century Packaging Inc 5217 Kemmerer St Whitehall PA 18052-1848 Home: 3800 Tiffany Dr Easton PA 18045-3047

COLLINE, MARGUERITE RICHNAVSKY, maternal, women's health and pediatrics nurse; b. Bayonne, N.J., Nov. 30, 1953; d. John P. and Margaret M. (Conaghan) Richnavsky; m. Richard L. Colline, Oct. 8, 1977; children: Jennifer, Nicole, Danielle, James Michael. Diploma in practical nurse, Union County Tech. Inst., Scotch Plains, N.J., 1973; BSN, Seton Hall U., 1978. RN, N.J., Md. Practical nurse oncology unit John E. Runnell's Hosp., Berkley Heights, N.J.; staff nurse infant unit Johns Hopkins Hosp., Balt.; staff nurse neonatal unit Overlook Hosp., Summit, N.J.; parish nurse Somerville, NJ. Mem. Nat. Assn. Neonatal Nurses, Sigma Theta Tau.

COLLINS, ALMA JONES, English educator, writer; d. Walter Melville Jones and Anne Teresa Harrington; m. Daniel Francis Collins, Apr. 9, 1994. BA, Conn. Coll., 1943; MA, Trinity Coll., 1952, U. Conn., 1962. Tchr., counselor W. Hartford (Conn.) Bd. Edn., 1947-72; pres. Arts Universal Rsch. Assocs., 1978—. Interviewed Salvador Dali (CD located in archives Wadsworth Atheneum Mus. Art), 1978, 79; cons. for corp. product devel.; rep. for artists. Contbr. articles and monographs in nat. and internat. publs. Mem. Phi Beta Kappa, Delta Kappa Gamma Internat. Avocation: writing poetry and fiction. Home and Office: 275 Steele Rd A318 West Hartford CT 06117-2763

COLLINS, ANGELO, science educator; b. Chgo., June 15, 1944; d. James Joseph and Mary (Burke) C. BS, Marian Coll., 1966; MS, Mich. State U., 1973; PhD, U. Wis., 1986; hon. degree, Edgewood Coll. High sch. biology tchr. various schs., Wis., 1966-81; rsch. asst. U. Wis., Madison, 1981-86; asst. prof. Kans. State U., Manhattan, 1986-87, Stanford (Calif.) U., 1988-90, Rutgers U., New Brunswick, N.J., 1990-91; assoc. prof. Fla. State U., Tallahassee, 1991-95; prof. Vanderbilt U., 1995—2000; exec. dir. Knowles Sci. Tchg. Found., 2000—. Mem. Working Group on Sci. Stds., Washington, 1992, dir. 1993—; sci. com. Nat. Bd. Profl. Tchg. Stds., Washington, 1991—; chmn. adv. bd. BioQuest, Beloit, Wis., 1988—; bd. dirs. Jour. for Rsch. in Sci. Tchg. Editor Tchr. Edn. Quarterly, 1991; reviewer several books; contbr. articles to profl. jours. Henry Rutgers fellow Rutgers U., 1990; recipient Devel. Scholar award Fla. State U., 1993-94. Fellow AAAS; mem. Nat. Assn. Biology Tchrs. (Outstandng Biology Tchr. Wis. 1977), Nat. Assn. Rsch. Sci. Tchg., Assn. Edn. Tchrs. Sci., Am. Ednl. Rsch. Assn., Sch. Sci. and Math., Assn. Tchr. Educators, Sigma Xi, Phi Delta Kappa. Office: KSTF 20 E Radman Ave Haddonfield NJ 08033 E-mail: angelo.collins@kstf.org.

COLLINS, ANITA MARGUERITE, research geneticist; b. Allentown, Pa., Nov. 8, 1947; d. Edmund III and Virginia (Hunsicker) C. BSc in Zoology, Pa. State U., 1969; MSc in Genetics, Ohio State U., 1972, PhD in Genetics, 1976. Instr. biology Mercyhurst Coll., Erie, Pa., 1975-76; rsch. geneticist Honey Bee Breeding Lab. Agrl. Rsch. Svc., USDA, Baton Rouge, 1976-88, rsch. leader Honey Bee Rsch. Lab. Weslaco, Tex., 1988-95, rsch. geneticist Bee Rsch. Lab. Beltsville, Md., 1995—. Co-author: Bee Genetics & Breeding, 1986; contbr. articles to profl. jours. Mem.: Soc. for Cryobiology, Internat. Union for Study of Social Insects, Am. Genetics Assn., Am. Beekeeping Fedn. (rsch. com. 1990, 1992—94), Assn. for Women in Sci. (pres. Baton Rouge chpt. 1982), Entomol. Soc. Am. (chair sect. C 1997), Internat. Embryo Transfer Soc., Sigma Xi. Office: USDA ARS Bee Rsch Bldg 476 BARC-East Beltsville MD 20705 E-mail: collinsa@ba.ars.usda.gov.

COLLINS, ANNAZETTE R. state representative; b. Chgo., Apr. 28, 1962; m. Keith Langston; 1 child, Angelique. BS in Sociology, No. Ill. U.; MS in Criminal Justice, Chgo. State U., 1983. Social worker Ada S. McKinley Interventions, 1982—83; correctional officer Fed. Bur. Prisons, 1983—86; social worker Cook County Social Svcs., 1986—90; adminstr. Dept. Children Family Svcs., 1990—2000, Chgo. Pub. Schs., 2000; mem. Ill. Ho. of Reps., 2000—. Mem. St. Joseph Sch. Bd., 1992—95; v.p. pres.'s club Cosmopolitan Cmty. Ch., 2001. Democrat. Baptist. Office: 252-W Stratton Office Bldg Springfield IL 62706 Address: 110 N Pulaski Rd Chicago IL 60624

COLLINS, ARLENE, secondary school educator; b. Mandan, N.D., Sept. 7, 1940; d. John Marcellus and Cecelia Magdalena (Schaaf) Weber; m. Abdul Rahman Rana (dec.); children: Fazale Rahman, Habeeb Rahman; m. Freddie L. Collins. BS in math., N.D. State U., 1962; postgrad., W.Va. Inst. Tech., 1974; M in Edn. Adminstrn., WVCOGS, 1988. Cert. mid. sch. tchr., W.Va. Tchr. physics, math. Montgomery (W.Va.) H.S., 1970; tchr. math., sci. Spencer (W.Va.) Jr. H.S., 1974-80; sci. tchr. Poca (W.Va.) Mid. Sch., 1980—, team leader, 1983-96. W.Va. textbook adoption com., W.Va. Bd. Edn., 1984-90. Leader Girl Scouts U.S.A., Montgomery, 1966-70, 99—, Boy Scouts Am., Montgomery, 1966; bd. dirs. Violet Twp. Womens League, 2002-. Fellow: African Am. Law Enforcement Agts. Assn., Inc.; mem.: NOW (bd. dirs. 1986), Am. Fedn. Tchrs., Laurel Soc., Am. Legion Aux. (sec. 2002—), Buckeye Sertoma, Soroptimists Internat. Home: 7292 Fox Den Ct Pickerington OH 43147-9019 E-mail: ac0907@aol.com.

COLLINS, AUDREY B. judge; b. 1945; BA, Howard U., 1967; MA, Am. U., 1969; JD, UCLA, 1977. Asst. atty. Legal Aid Found. L.A., 1977-78; with Office L.A. County Dist. Atty., 1978-94, dept. dist. atty., 1978-94, asst. dir. burs. ctrl. ops. and spl. ops., 1988-92, asst. dir. atty., 1992-94; judge. U.S. Dist. Ct. (Ctrl. Dist.) Calif., 1994—. Dep. gen. counsel Office Spl. Acad. scholar Howard U.; named Lawyer of Yr., Langston Bar Assn., 1988; honoree Howard U. Alumni Club So. Calif., 1989; recipient Profl. Achievement award UCLA Alumni Assn., 1997, Ernestine Stahlhut award, Women Lawyers Assn., 1999. Mem. FBA, Nat. Assn. Women Judges, Nat. Bar Assn. (life), State Bar Calif. (com. bar examiners, chmn. subcom. on moral [illegible]), Los Angeles County Bar Assn. (exec. com. litig. sect. 1999-2002, task force on criminal justice sys. 2002-03), Assn. Los Angeles County Dist. Attys. (pres. 1983), Black Women Lawyers Los Angeles County, Women Lawyers L.A. (life, Ernestine Stahlhut award 1999), Calif. Women Lawyers (life), Order of Coif, Phi Beta Kappa. Office: US Dist Ct Edward R Roybal Fed Bldg 255 E Temple St Ste 670 Los Angeles CA 90012-3334

COLLINS, BARBARA LOUISE, retired elementary school educator; b. Pasadena, Nov. 6, 1934; d. Harry Carl and Grace Eleanor (Varnum) Wallerman; m. Wayne G. Collins, July 6, 1961; children: Lisa, Garth. BA in Elem. Edn., Calif. State U., LA, 1956; postgrad., U. Vienna, Austria, 1960; Cert. Art Specialist, Clarke Coll., Dubuque, Iowa, 1980. Tchr. Mt. Diablo Sch., Concord, Calif., 1957—60; prin. asst. Regina Pub. Sch., Canada, 1961—62; tchr. adult basic edn. Dubuque, Iowa, 1966—67; substitute tchr. K-12 Dubuque Pub. Schs., 1967—, substitute art specialist. Tutor trainer Laubach Literacy, Dubuque, Iowa, 1970—90; tchr. pottery, painting, weaving Dubuque Mus. Art, 1985—98; artist-in-residence Cedar Falls (Iowa) Schs., 2000—01. Clay sculpture, pottery, water color paintings, color pencil drawings, exhibitions include Clarke Coll. Gallery, 1985, Dubuque Mus. Art Old Jail Gallery, 1987. Bd. dirs. Dubuque Mus. Art, 1994—97, chair Friends of DUMA, 1995—97. Recipient Best of Show, Grant Wood Art Fest, 1994. United Ch. Of Christ. Avocations: sewing, travel, camping, cooking. Home: 11092 Mound View Rd Dubuque IA 52003

COLLINS, CARDISS, retired congresswoman; b. St. Louis, Sept. 24, 1931; m. George W. Collins (dec.); 1 child, Kevin. Ed., Northwestern U.; hon. degree, Winston-Salem State U., Spelman Coll., John Marshall Law Sch., Rosary Coll., Forest Inst. Profl. Psychology. Barber Scotia Coll.; mem. 93d-104th Congresses from 7th Ill. Dist., 1973-97; ret., 1997. Ranking minority mem. govt. reform & oversight com.; former chair. govt. activity and transp. subcom.; former chair commerce, consumer protection and competition subcom.; former majority whip-at-large; former asst. regional whip; former chair Congl. Black Caucus, sec.; dir. emeritus, former chair Congl. Black Caucus Found.; former chair Mems. Congress for Peace through Law. Recipient award Roosevelt U., Loyola U. Mem. NAACP, Nat. Coun. Negro Women (past v.p.), Chgo. Urban League, Black Women's Agenda, The Chgo. Network, The Links, Dem. Nat. Com., Alpha Kappa Alpha. Democrat. Baptist. Home: 1110 Roundhouse Ln Alexandria VA 22314-5934

COLLINS, CINDY ELAINE, property manager; b. LA, Oct. 7, 1957; d. Shirley Rose Hughes; life ptnr. Angela Cornwell; 1 child, James. VISTA vol. Evansville (Ind.) Housing-Sponsor, 1989—94; property mgr. Evansville Housing Authority, 1994—. Pres. Fulton Resident Council, Evansville, Ind., 1990—98; exec. dir. Resident Mgmt. Corp., Evansville, 1992—94; mem. Citizens Adv. Coun. Evansville Mayor's Com., Evansville, 1993; v.p. Cedar Hall Neighborhood Assn., Evansville, 1996—98; pres. City Wide Resident Coun., Evansville, 1998—. Recipient Vol. award, Substance Abuse Coun., 1999; grantee Cmty. Devel. grant, Housing and Urban Devel., 1992, Cmty. Devel. Block grant, City of Evansville, 1994. Avocations: basketball, camping, fishing, bargain hunting. Office: Evansville Housing Authority 500 Court St Evansville IN 47708 Personal E-mail: tabby1957@yahoo.com. Business E-Mail: cindycollins@evansvillehousing.org.

COLLINS, CYNTHIA JANE, marriage and family therapist, priestess; b. Florence, Ala., Oct. 21, 1950; d. William Lee and Johnie Glenn (Lutts) Collins; m. Christopher Martin Waldeck, Oct. 2, 1996 (dec. Mar. 1998); m. Harry Blaise Spirito, July 31, 1999; children: Stephanie Kim Collins Newburger Bush, Samuel Collins Newburger, Allan Lee Collins Sylvester. BA in Fine Arts and Philosophy (mark of distinction), Franklin Coll., 1985; MDiv cum laude, Christian Theol. Sem., Indpls., 1989; MS in counseling, U. Evansville, 1991. Lic. marriage and family therapist Ind.; ordained high priestess Cir. of Silver Cauldron. Domina Re:Creations, 1968—; career counselor, 1974-78; counselor, tchr., 1978-86; pastor, counselor South Ind. Conf. hdqs. United Meth. Ch., Indpls., 1986-91; marriage and family therapist Collins Counseling Svcs., 1991—. Bd. dirs. Maine Pagan Clergy, 2001—, chair ordination and licensure com., 2001—. Author: Building a Magical Relationship: The Five Points of Love, 2002—; author, workshop leader: Women in the History of the Church, 1987, Vacation Pagan Sch. First, Second and Third, 1998—; one-woman shows include Ceres St., Portsmouth, N.H., 2001—, 100-piece exhbn., Abrams Gallery Exhbn., 1981; prodr., dir. (radio program) CTS Today, 1986—87; mental health columnist: Our Maine, 2000—. Bd. dirs. Hist. Cannelton, Ind., 1990, 93, Leadership Perry County, 1993, 94; advisor Perry County Devel. Corp., 1994; elder, founding mem., Domina Cir. of the Silver Cauldron, 1994—. Recipient Svc. award Mental Health Assn., 1995. Mem. Am. Assn. for Marriage and Family Therapy (clin. mem.), Mental Health Assn. Spencer County (pres. 1992-94), Perry County Meth. Clergy Assn. (v.p. 1989-91), Kiwanis Internat. (pres. 1992-93, 93-94), Mensa (Officially Overworked Vol. 1998, 99), Phi Kappa Phi. Wiccan. Office: Re Creations 86 High St Saco ME 04072 E-mail: thea@loa.com.

COLLINS, DELORIS WILLIAMS, secondary school educator; b. Jackson, Miss., Oct. 24, 1959; d. Eddie (Stepfather) and Mary Louise Lewis; m. Bobby Collins, July 18, 1981; children: Garrian V., Bryan L. AA, Hinds Jr. Coll., Jackson, Miss., 1987; BBA in Office Adminstrn., Jackson State U., 2000. Circulation clk. Eudora Welty Libr., Jackson, Miss., 1989—91; tech. specialist/libr. circulation clk. H.T. Sampson Libr. Jackson State U., 1991—93; libr. media tech. specialist Canton Pub. Schs. Dist., 1993—96; with U.S. Postal Svc., Jackson, 1999—2000; substitute tchr. Jackson Pub. Schs. Dist., Jackson, 2000—. Cert. facilitator Family Connections, Jackson, 1999; seminar and workshop condr. Author: They Are Throwing Rocks, 1997, Chasing After the Wind, 1998, Anointed Hyms-Poems, 1999, Treasured Recipes, 1999, Marriage in Yesterday and Today Society: There is Hope, Its All in the Lord, 2000, The Talking Partridge, 2003. Nominee Poet of the Yr., 2003; named to Wall of Tolerance, Civil Rights Meml. Ctr., 2003; recipient Editors Choice award, 2003. Mem.: Internat. Soc. of Poets (hon.). Avocations: reading, cooking. Home: 403 Stillwood Dr Jackson MS 39206

COLLINS, DOROTHY CRAIG, retired educational administrator; b. Evansville, Ind., Oct. 11, 1912; d. Edmund Lawrence and Mable Irene (Ross) Craig; m. Ralph Leonard Collins, June 13, 1940; 1 child, David Harrington. BA cum laude, Western Coll. for Women, 1934; MA, U. Chgo., 1937. Rsch. asst. Kinsey Inst., Ind. U., Bloomington, 1951-56; asst. dir. Instnl. Rsch., Ind. U., Bloomington, 1963-64; rsch. asst. Office of Pres., Ind. U., Bloomington, 1965-69; rsch. and editl. assoc. Office of Univ. Chancellor, Ind. U., Bloomington, 1969-92; ret., 1992. Co-author: Pictorial History of Indiana University, 1992. V.p. United Way of Monroe County, Bloomington, 1974; pres. bd. dirs. Bloomington Hosp., 1963; pres. Monroe County Comprehensive Health Planning, Bloomington, 1971-73. Mem. Univ. Women's Club (pres.), Consumers Health Task Force, Theatre Circle (pres.), Friends of Lilly Libr. (bd.), Office of Women's Affairs (adv. bd.), Collins Living-Learning Ctr. (adv. bd.). Democrat. Avocations: reading, travel, theatre attendance, art appreciation. Home: 919 Juniper Pl Bloomington IN 47408-1285

COLLINS, EILEEN MARIE, astronaut; b. Elmira, N.Y., Nov. 19, 1956; d. James Edward and Rose Marie (O'Hara) C.; m. James Patrick Youngs, Aug. 1, 1987. AS in Math., Sci., Corning C.C., 1976; BA in Math., Econs., Syracuse U., 1978; grad., USAF Undergrad. Pilot Tng., Vance AFB, Okla., 1979, USAF Test Pilot Sch., Edwards AFB, Calif., 1990; MS in Ops. Rsch., Stanford U., 1986; MA in Space Systems Mgmt., Webster U., 1989. Commd. 2d lt. USAF, 1979, [illegible] through grades to col., [illegible], instr. pilot 71st flight tng. wing, 1979-82, aircraft comdr. 86th mil. airlift squadron Travis AFB, Calif., 1983-85; asst. prof. math. USAF Acad., Colorado Springs, Colo., 1986-89; astronaut Johnson Space Ctr. NASA, Houston, 1990—. Second in command, space shuttle Discovery, 1995, space shuttle Atlantis, 1997; comdr. space shuttle, Columbia, 1999. Decorated Air Force Commendation medal with one oak leaf cluster, Meritorious svc. medal with one oak leaf cluster, Air Force Expeditionary medal, Def. Meritorious Svc. medal, French Legion Honor Disting. Flying Cross; 1st woman pilot of the Space Shuttle; 1st woman comdr.*

COLLINS, GAIL, editor; BA in Journalism, Marquette U., 1967; MA in Govt., U. Mass., 1971. Founder Conn. State News Bur., 1972—77; freelance writer, 1977—79; sr. editor Conn. Mag.; columnist Conn. Bus. Jour., 1977—79; host pub. affairs program Conn. Pub. TV, 1977—79; instr. journalism So. Conn. State Coll., 1977—79; fin. reporter UPI, N.Y.C., 1982—85; columnist N.Y. Daily News, N.Y.C., 1985—91, N.Y. Newsday, N.Y.C., 1991—95; mem. editl. bd. The N.Y. Times, N.Y.C., 1995—, host This Week Close-Up cable news program, 1997—, columnist op-ed page, 2000—01, editl. page editor, 2001—. Author (with Dan Collins): The Millennium Book, 1991; author: Scorpion Tongues, 1998, America's Women: Four Hundred Years of Dolls, Drudges, Helpmates and Heroines, 2003. Recipient Meyer Berger award, Columbia U., 1987, Matrix award, Women in Comm, 1989, award for commentary, AP, 1994; Bagehot fellow, Columbia U., 1981—82. Office: The NY Times 229 W 43d St New York NY 10036*

COLLINS, GWENDOLYN BETH, health administrator; b. Akron, Ohio; d. Emmert Samuel and Lillice Elizabeth (Matthews) Shaffer; 1 child, Holly Marie. BA, Case Western Res. U. Exec. dir. Canton Area Regional Health Edn. Network, 1981-88; project dir. Region VII Cancer Registry, Canton, Ohio, 1984-88; program dir. Diabetes Mgmt. Ctr., St. Petersburg, Fla., 1988-89, 92-94, Pasadena Sr. Health Ctr., St. Petersburg, 1995-96; health mgmt. and mktg. cons. Largo, Fla., 1986-88, 95—; practice adminstr. Santiago Morales, MD, P.A., Largo, Fla., 2000—02, Diagnostic and Consultative Cardiology, Brandon, Fla., 2003—. Mem. continuing med. edn. com. Aultman Hosp., 1983-88; planner and evaluator Directions for Mental Health, Inc., Clearwater, Fla., 1990-92. Mem. adv. com. Camp Y-Noah, 1985-86. HHS grantee, Canton, 1986-88. Mem. Cancer Control Consortium Ohio (mem. cancer incidence mgmt. com. 1986-87). Republican. Avocations: reading, music, walking. Home and Office: 9508 Cavendish Dr Tampa FL 33626

COLLINS, IRMA HELEN, music educator, consultant; b. Horatio, Ark., May 15, 1930; d. Roy DeWitt Hopkins and Irma Virginia Morgan; m. Walter Ray Collins, Aug. 27, 1960 (div. Feb. 15, 1976). BA, Ouachita Coll., 1952; BS in Music, Southwestern Sem., 1954; MusM, George Peabody Coll., 1958; D in Musical Arts, Temple U., 1979. Instr. Mars Hill (N.C.) Coll., 1954—57; assoc. prof. W.Va. Wesleyan Coll., Buckhannon, 1958—65; tchr., adminstr. Bd. Edn., Pitts., 1965—68; chair dept. music Ea. Coll., St. Davids, Pa., 1968—72; prof. music Murray (Ky.) State U., 1976—93; adj. prof. music Shenandoah U. Conservatory, Winchester, W.Va., 1998—. Arts cons.; founder Jour. Music Tchr. Edn.; rschr., writer standards of learning Commonwealth Va., 2001. Contbr. articles to profl. jours.; author: (songs) I Call to Thee, In the Eyes of a Child; reviewer (jours.) including Southeastern Music Edn. Jour. Violinist Ark. State Symphony, Carnegie-Mellon Symphony, Nashville Symphony, Paducah Symphony; soloist Temple Sinai Synagogue, Pitts. Mem.: Ky. Music Educators Assn. (Tchr. of Yr. award), Soc. Music Tchr. Edn. (nat. chairperson), Sigma Alpha Iota (Outstanding Mem. award).

COLLINS, JACKIE, writer; b. London, Oct. 4, 1941; m. Oscar Lerman. Author: The World Is Full of Married Men, 1968, The Stud, 1969, Sunday Simmons and Charlie Brick, 1971 (pub. as The Hollywood Zoo, 1975), Lovehead, 1974 (pub. as The Love Killers, 1977), The World Is Full of Divorced Women, 1975, Lovers and Gamblers, 1977, The Bitch, 1979, Chances, 1981, Hollywood Wives, 1983, Sinners, 1984, Lucky, 1985, Hollywood Husbands, 1986, Rock Star, 1987, Lady Boss, 1989, American Star, 1993, Hollywood Kids, 1994, Vendetta: Lucky's Revenge, 1997, Thrill, 1998, L.A. Connections, 1998, Dangerous Kiss, 1999, Lethal Seduction, 2000, Hollywood Wives: The New Generation, 2001, Deadly Embrace, 2002. Office: c/o Simon & Schuster 1230 Ave of Amer New York NY 10020*

COLLINS, JACQUELINE Y, state senator; b. McComb, Miss., Dec. 10; Grad. journalism, Northwestern Univ.; MA, Harvard's John F. Kennedy Sch. of Gov.; MA Human Svc. Admin., Spertus Coll.; MA Theol. Studies, Harvard Divinity Sch., 2003. State Senator US Senate, Dist. 16, 2003—; min. of Comm. St. Sabina Cath. Ch., Chgo.; journalist in print, radio and TV; press sec. Congressman Gus Savage. Mem. Appropriations I, Environ. and Energy, Revenue (VC), Revenue Subcommittee on Spl. Issues. Recipient Emmy Award - nominated news editor, CBS-TV/ Chgo.; fellow Legislative Fellow with US Senator Hillary Rodham Clinton. Democrat. Catholic. Office: Capitol Bldg M-108 Springfield IL 62706 also: 1155 W 79th St Chicago IL 60620

COLLINS, JEAN KATHERINE, English educator; b. Norfolk, Va., June 14, 1928; d. Elwood Brantley and Katherine Belle (Lambertson) C. BA in Liberal Arts, James Madison U., Harrisonburg, Va., 1945-49; MA in English, U. Richmond, 1950-51; edn. credits, U. Va., Eastern Shore of Va., 1950, 60; art edn. credits, Millersville State Tchrs. Coll, summer 1970. Continuity writer Radio Station WLEE, Richmond, Va., 1949; English, critic tchr. Farmville H.S., Longwood Coll., Va., 1951-53; English tchr., art tchr. Hermitage H.S., Richmond, Va., 1953-55; prin., art tchr. Cape Charles (Va.) H.S., 1957-59; head English dept., tchr. Northampton H.S., Eastville, Va., 1960-63; art tchr. Pvt. Studio, Cape Charles, Va., 1964-90. Pres. Lambda chpt. Delta Kappa Gamma Soc., Eastern Shore of Va., 1966-68; recording sec. Iota State Delta Kappa Gamma Soc., Headqtrs., Richmond, Va., 1967-69; adv. bd. Eastern Shore Pub. Libr., Accomac, Va., 1981-89; bd. dirs. Eastern Shore of Va. Hist. Soc., Onancock, Va., 1957-60. Author: (poetry) Madison Quarterly, 1948, 49; author, illustrator: An Eastern Shore Sampler, 1975; author: History of Trinity United Methodist Church, 1993. Named Woman of Yr. Young WOmen's Club of Cape Charles, Va., 1958. Mem. Eastern Shore of Va. Hist. Soc., Cape Charles Hist. Soc., Trinity United Meth. Ch., Delta Kappa Gamma Soc.. Republican. Methodist. Avocations: painting, needlework, history, theater, dance, writing.

COLLINS, JENNY LYNN, music educator; d. Jerry Wayne and Shelby Jean Collins. MusB in Edn., Morehead State U., Ky., 1993—98; MusM in Edn., Wichita State U., Kans., 2001—02. Instrumental Music K-12 Ky. and S.C., 2003. Band dir. Whitley County HS, Williamsburg, Ky., 1998—2001; grad. tchg. asst. Wichita State U., Kans., 2001—02; band dir. Berkeley HS, Moncks Corner, SC, 2002—. Band chair, dist. 10 Ky. Music Educators Assn., Williamsburg, Ky., 2000—01; treas. Bluegrass All-Region Band, Middlesborough, Ky., 2001—01. Mem.: Women Band Directors Internat. Assn., S.C. Band Directors Assn., Music Educators Nat. Conf., Gamma Beta Phi, Tau Beta Sigma, Sigma Alpha Iota (music dir., v.p. of ritual 1996—98). Avocations: canoeing, travel, reading. Office: Berkeley High School Bands 406 West Main Street Moncks Corner SC 29461

COLLINS, JOAN HENRIETTA, actress; b. London, May 23, 1933; came to U.S., 1938; d. Joseph William and Elsa (Bessant) C.; m. Maxwell Reed (div.); m. Anthony Newley (div.); children: Tara, Sacha; m. Ronald S. Kass, Mar., 1972 (div.); 1 child, Katy; m. Peter Holm (div.); m. Percy Gibson, 2002. Ed., Francis Holland Sch., London; student, Royal Acad. of Dramatic Art. Actor: (films) Cosh Boy, Our Girl Friday, I Believe in You, Girl in the Red Velvet Swing, Sea Wife, Rally Round the Flag Boys, Island in the Sun, Seven Thieves, Road to Hong Kong, Sunburn, The Stud, Game for Vultures, The Bitch, The Big Sleep, The Good Die Young, Land of the Pharoahs, The Bravados, Esther and the King, Warning Shot, The Executioner, Subterfuge, Revenge, Quest for Love, Tales From the Crypt, The Bawdy Adventures of Tom Jones, The Opposite Sex, The Virgin Queen, Quest for Love, Decadence, 1994, In the Bleak Mid-Winter, 1995, The Clandestine Marriage, 1998, The Flintstones-Viva Rock Vegas, 1999, Joseph and His Technicolor Dreamcoat, 1999, Ozzie, 2001, (theater appearances) Jassey, Claudia, The Skin of Our Teeth, The Praying Mantis, The Last of Mrs. Cheyney, The 7th Veil, A Doll's House, Private Lives, 1990, Love Letters, 2000, Over the Moon, 2001; (TV films) Drive Hard, Drive Fast, 1973, The Man Who Came to Dinner, Paper Dolls, 1982, The Wild Women of Chastity Gulch, 1982, The Cartier Affair, The Making of a Male Model, 1983, Her Life as a Man, 1984; (TV miniseries) The Moneychangers, 1976, Sins, 1986, Monte Carlo, 1986, Tonight at 8:30, 1991, Dynasty: The Reunion, 1992; star (TV series) Dynasty, 1981—89; actor: (TV appearance) Faerie Tale Theater (Showtime TV), 1982, Roseanne (ABC), 1993, Mama's Back spl., 1993, Will and Grace, 2000, (TV movie) Annie: A Royal Adventure, 1995, Hart to Hart spl., 1995, Sweet Deception, 1998, These Old Broads, 2000; (TV series) Pacific Palisades, 1997, Guiding Light, 2002, (video spl.) Secrets of Fitness and Beauty, 1994; author: (autobiography) Past Imperfect, 1978, Katy, A Fight for Life, Joan Collins Beauty Book, 1980, (autobiography) Second Act, 1996, (novels) Prime Time, 1988, Love and Desire and Hate, 1991, My Secrets, 1994, Too Damn Famous, 1995, My Friends Secrets, 1999, Star Quality, 2002, Joan's Way, 2002. Decorated Order of Brit. Empire; recipient Emmy nomination, Golden Globe award, Ace award, People's Choice award; named to Order Brit. Empire. Avocations: travel, 18th century art. E-mail: pkeylock@aol.com.

COLLINS, JOE LENA, retired secondary school educator; b. Mt. Pleasant, Tenn., Nov. 18, 1922; d. Morton Daniel and Rosetta Francis C. BS in English, Tenn. Tech., 1949; MA in English, George Peabody, 1968, EdS in English, 1975. Cert. profl. tchr. Sec. to Dr. G.C. English and Dr. C.D. Walton, Mt. Pleasant, Tenn., 1942-46; tchr. Maury Co. Schs., Mt. Pleasant, Tenn., 1949-51, Tenn. Tech., Cookeville, Tenn., 1951; acct. Cookeville Prodn. Credit, Tenn., 1951-52; tchr. Metro Nashville Schs., 1952-88. Lectr. Ret. Learning Vanderbilt U., 2000—. Mem. Shepherd's Ctr. West End Book Club, 1989—2002, Metro Retired Tchrs. Assn., 1988—, chmn. Shepherd's Ctr. West Book Club; com. work Dem. Party, 1980—2003. Mem. AAUW (pres.), Tenn. Art League, Tenn. Writers Alliance, Tenn. Hist. Soc., Women in the Arts, United Meth. Women (Woman of Purpose award). Avocations: reading, writing, painting, sports. Home: 6212 Henry Ford Dr Nashville TN 37209-1738

COLLINS, JUDITH ANN, literature educator; d. Marshall and Lucille Irene Bottoms; m. Roger M. Collins, Sept. 21, 1969 (div. June 3, 1986); 1 child, Ellen Wallace. MA English, creative writing, Western Washington Univ., Bellingham, Wash., 1993; PhD English, Rhetoric, Arizona State Univ., Tempe, Ariz., 2000. English instr. Western Washington Univ., Bellingham, Wash., 1994—96, Ariz. State Univ., Tempe, Ariz., 1996—2001; asst. prof. Kans. State Univ.-Salina, Salina, Kans., 2001—. Author: (book) Squall Line, 1995, (article) Strategies for Tchg. First Year Composition, 2001, (jour.) Seattle Rev., 2003. Presenter Conf. on Info. Tech., Milwaukee, Wis., 2003, Am. Soc. of Engring. Educators, Midwest sect., Rollo, Mo., 2003. Mem.: Kans. Assn. of Tchr. of English, Nat. Coun. of Tchr. of English. Avocations: wilderness advocate, hiking, photography. Home: 630 West Iron Ave Salina KS 67401 Office: Kansas State Univ Salina 2310 Centennial Ave Salina KS 67401

COLLINS, JUDY MARJORIE, singer, songwriter; b. Seattle, May 1, 1939; d. Charles T. and Marjorie (Byrd) Collins; m. Peter A. Taylor, Apr. 1958 (div.); 1 child, Clark Taylor (dec.). Pvt. study piano, 1953-56. Debut as profl. folk singer, Boulder, Colo., 1959; has since appeared in numerous clubs, U.S. and around world; performer concerts including Newport Folk Festival, maj. concert halls and summer theatres, throughout U.S. and Europe; also appeared radio and TV, including HBO TV spl. Judy Collins: From the Heart, 1989; recording artist, Elektra; profl. acting debut as Solveig in N.Y. Shakespeare Festival prodn. of Peer Gynt, 1969; producer, dir. documentary movie Antonia: A Portrait of the Woman, 1974; composer songs including Albatross, 1967, Since You've Asked, 1967, My Father, 1968, Secret Gardens, 1972, Born to the Breed, 1975; albums include Bread & Roses, Colors of the Day, So Early in the Spring/The First Fifteen Years, 1977, Hard Times for Lovers, 1979, Running for My Life, 1980, Trust Your Heart, 1987, Sanity and Grace, 1989, Recollections, Fires of Eden, 1990, Judy Sings Dylan: Just Like a Woman, 1993; author: (autobiography) Trust Your Heart, 1987, Sanity and Grace, A Journey of Suicide, Survival and Strength, 2003. Recipient Grammy award, 1968, 6 Gold LP's., Silver medal Atlanta Film Festival, Blue Ribbon award Am. Film Festival, NYC, Christopher award. Office: care Charles Rothschild Prodns 330 E 48th St New York NY 10017-1766 also: Mesa/Blueman Records 209 E Alameda Ave Ste 101 Burbank CA 91502-2673*

COLLINS, JULIE, healthcare organization executive; Chief adminstrv. officer Sun Healthcare Group, Inc., Albuquerque, 1998—. Office: Sun Healthcare Group Inc 101 Sun Ave NE Albuquerque NM 87109-4373

COLLINS, KAREN JEANNE, music educator; b. Washington, Oct. 5, 1951; d. John Albert and Bessie Arlene Miller; m. William Arthur Collins, July 21, 1973; 1 child, William Bradford. B in Music Edn., Carson-Newman Coll., 1973. Music tchr. Montgomery County Pub. Schs., Rockville, Md., 1973—. Mem. steering com. Music Curriculum Task Force, Rockville, 1985—87. Lobbyist Concerned Women for Am., Washington, 1975—80. Arts grantee, Washington Post Newspaper, 1990. Mem.: Arts Coun. Co-op, Christian Educators Assn. Internat., Montgomery County Music Edn. Assn. (advisor 1975—), Md. Music Educators Assn., Nat. Right to Life Com., Olney (Md.) Womens Rep. Club. Baptist. Avocations: hiking, swimming, music. Home: 3412 Dartmoor Ln Olney MD 20832 Office: Germantown Elem Sch 19110 Liberty Mill Rd Germantown MD 20874

COLLINS, KATHLEEN ANNE, artistic director; b. Elmira, N.Y., Dec. 20, 1951; d. James G. and Joyce (Balmer) C.; m. Andrew Stephon Elston, May 28, 1977; children: Megan, Kate. BA, SUNY, Albany, 1974; MA in Theatre, U. Wash., 1976, MFA in Theatre, 1979. Dir. edn. Seattle Children's Theatre, 1975-78; instr. drama Lakeside Sch., Seattle, 1978-79; artistic dir. Honolulu Theatre for Youth, 1979-83, Fulton Opera House, Lancaster, Pa., 1983-98; prof. Cornish Coll. of Arts, Seattle, 1999—. Guest lectr. U. Hawaii, Honolulu, 1981, U. Wash., Seattle, 2002—03; guest dir. Seattle Children's Theatre, 2002—03; adj. faculty Lesley U., 2000—. Contbg. author: Drama With Children, 1979. Bd. dirs. PTO, Lancaster, 1990-98. Mem. Am. Assn. Theatre Educators, Assn. and Soc. for Theatre and Children. Democrat. Roman Catholic. E-mail: kalcollins@comcast.net.

COLLINS, LAURA JANE, music educator, singer, accompanist; b. Mauston, Wis., Mar. 25, 1957; d. Horace Rexford and Mary Jean Collins; m. Thomas Henry Buchholz, Dec. 30, 1977 (div. Dec. 19, 1982); 1 child, Erik M. Assoc., Viterbo Coll., LaCrosse, Wis., 1977; BA, Cameron U., Lawton, Okla., 1979. Cert. music educator K-12 Okla., 1979, Yamaha Music Sch. Tchr. Yamaha Internat. Corp., 1980. Yamaha music sch. tchr. Keynote Music Co., Tulsa, Okla., 1980—82; vocal, gen. music educator Tulsa (Okla.) Pub. Schs., 1981—. Instr. Tulsa Opera Childrens Workshop, 1986—87; chapel accompanist All Souls Unitarian Ch., 1993—96, choir accompanist, 1995—96; chapel organist Hillcrest Hosp., Tulsa, 2000—; vocalist, performer Vocal Jazz Ensemble with Rick Fortner, 2003—; vocal jazz performer R.F. Singers, 2003—. Cast mem. Tulsa, Gilbert and Sullivan Operetta Soc., 1988—89. Mem. Tulsa Opera Guild, 2003; co-mgr. office Anderson for Pres., Tulsa, 1980; vol. Orza for Gov., Tulsa, 2002; liason Democratic Tulsa Pub. Sch. Tchrs.; mem. children's advocacy team All Souls Unitarian Ch., Tulsa, 1993. Mem.: NEA (del. 2003), Am. Assn. Univ. Women, Music Edn. Nat. Assn., Okla. Music Edn. Assn., Music Tchr. Nat. Assn. (accredited in voice and piano 1982), Okla. Edn. Assn. (del. 2003), Tulsa Classroom Tchrs. Assn. Democrat. Unitarian. Avocations: gardening, reading, walking, composing, politics. Home: 3903 S Rockford Ave Tulsa OK 74105 Office: Hoover Elementary Sch 2327 S Darlington Tulsa OK 74114 E-mail: collila@tulsaschools.org.

COLLINS, MARGERY LOUISE, elementary school educator; b. Manilla, Iowa, Nov. 12, 1932; d. Edward Henry and Theresa Caroline (Nickelsen) Theobald; m. Thomas Joseph Collins, Mar. 11, 1955; 1 child, Ann. BS in Elem. Edn., Butler U., 1964; MA in Early Childhood Edn., San Jose State U., 1975, MA in Adminstrv. Svcs., 1977. Cert. elem. tchr., adminstrv. svcs., early childhood edn., reading specialist, jr. coll. tchr., Calif., Ind. Tchr. Mapleton Iowa) Pub. Schs., 1952-54, Hammond (Ind.) Pub. Schs., 1954-55, Met. Schs. of Lawrence Twp., Indpls., 1964-65; tchr., team leader Palo Alto (Calif.) Unified Schs., 1965—, mentor tchr., 1992-94, literacy mentor, literacy trainer, 1996—. Resident tchr. San Jose State U., San Francisco State U., 1970-80; mentor, mem. rev. team Calif. State Dept. Edn., Sacramento, 1976-78; instr. DeAnza Coll., Cupertino, Calif., 1977—, U. San Diego Ext., 1997—; workshop leader, presenter, spkr. in field, 1977—; grant writer Palo Alto Schs., 1980-97 Co-creator, co-chair Internat. Visitors Ctr., Palo Alto, 1986-92; mem. Sister Cities Internat./Neighbors Abroad, 1973— (pres. 1986-87); mem. adv. bd. Gamble Garden, 1996-98. Lucille Nixon scholar, 1974; grantee Whitney Found., Hewlett-Packard, Palo Alto Found.; recipient Tall Tree award for outstanding profl. Palo Alto C. of C., 1994. Mem. AAUW (pres. 1992-93, mem. state nominating com. 1994), NEA, Calif. Tchr. Assn., Palo Alto Edn. Assn., Calif. Reading Assn., Santa Clara County Reading Assn., ASCD, UN Assn. (bd. dirs. 1994-96), Phi Delta Kappa, Phi Kappa Phi. Democrat. Roman Catholic. Avocations: reading, hiking, travel, gardening. Home: 3950 Duncan Pl Palo Alto CA 94306-4550

COLLINS, MARIBETH WILSON, foundation president; b. Portland, Oreg., Oct. 27, 1918; d. Clarence True and Maude (Akin) Wilson; m. Truman Wesley Collins, Mar. 12, 1943; children: Timothy Wilson and Terry Stanton (twins), Cherida Smith, Truman Wesley Jr. BA, U. Oreg., 1940. Pres. Collins Found., Portland, 1964—. Dir. Collins Pine Co., Collins Holding Co., Ostrander Resource Co. Life trustee Willamette U., Salem, Oreg., also mem. campus religious life. Mem. Univ. Club, Gamma Phi Beta. Republican. Methodist. Home: 2275 SW Mayfield Ave Portland OR 97225-4400 Office: Collins Found 1618 SW 1st Ave Ste 505 Portland OR 97201-5708

COLLINS, MARTHA, English language educator, writer; b. Omaha, Nov. 25, 1940; d. William E. and Katheryn (Essick) C.; m. Theodore M. Space, Apr. 1991. AB, Stanford U., 1962; MA, U. Iowa, 1965, PhD, 1971. Asst. prof. N.E. Mo. U., Kirksville, 1965-66, from instr. to prof. English U. Mass., Boston, 1966—2002, co-dir. creative writing, 1979—2000; Pauline Delaney prof., co-dir. creative writing Oberlin (Ohio) Coll., 1997—. Author (poetry): The Catastrophe of Rainbows, 1985, The Arrangement of Space, 1991, A History of Small Life on a Windy Planet, 1993, Some Things Words Can Do, 1998; translator: The Women Carry River Water, 1997. Fellow Bunting Inst., 1982-83, Ingram Merrill Found., 1988, NEA, 1990; grantee Witter Bynner/Santa Fe Art Inst., 2001, Lannon Found. Residency, 2003; recipient Pushcart prize, 1985, 96, 98, Di Castagnola award, 1990, Lannan residency, 2003. Mem. Poetry Soc. Am., Assoc. Writing Programs. Democrat. Office: Oberlin Coll Rice Hall Oberlin OH 44074

COLLINS, MARTHA LAYNE, college president, former governor; b. Shelby County, Ky., Dec. 7, 1936; d. Everett Larkin and Mary Lorena (Taylor) Hall; m. Bill Collins, July 3, 1959; children: Stephen Louis, Marla Ann. Student, Lindenwood Coll.; BS, U. Ky., 1959. Former tchr. Fairdale High Sch., Louisville, Seneca High Sch., Louisville, Woodford County Jr. High Sch., Versailles; lt. gov. State of Ky., 1979-83, gov., 1983-87; exec. in residence U. Louisville Sch. of Bus., from 1988; pres. St. Catherine Coll., St. Catherine, Ky., 1990—. Pres. Martha Layne Collins & Assocs., Lexington, 1988—; sec. Ky. Edn. and Humanities Cabinet, 1984-87; chmn. Nat. Conf. Lt. Govs., 1982-83, So. Growth Policies Bd., 1986-87, So. Regional Edn. Bd., 1986, Nat. Gov.'s Task Force on Drug ans Substance Abuse, 1987, So. Growth Policies Bd., 1986; bd. dirs. Eastman-Kodak Co., Inc., Rochester, N.Y., R.R. Donnelley & Sons, Chgo., Bank of Louisville. Mem. Woodford County (Ky.) Democratic Exec. Com.; mem. Dem. Nat. Com., 1972-76; chmn. Dem. Nat. Conv., San Francisco, 1984; former coordinator Women's Activities for State Dem. Hdqrs.; del. Dem. Nat. Conv., Miami, 1972, Mid-term charter Conf., Kansas City, 1974; mem. credentials com. Dem. Nat. Com. Vice Presdl. Selection Process Commn., co-chair credentials com. Dem. Nat. Conv., Atlanta, 1988; Ky. chairwoman 51.3 Com. for Carter, 1976; mem. Ky. Dem. Central Exec. Com.; sec. Ky. Dem. Party; elected clk. Ct. of Appeals, 1975; clk. Supreme Ct. Ky., 1975; past tchr. Sunday sch.; mem. Ky. Commn. on Women; exec. dir. Ky. Friendship Force; mem. Dem. Nat. Com. Policy Commn. and Fairness Commn.; hon. chmn. bd. USO of Ky. Inc.; hon. co-chmn. Parents Against Child Exploitation; mem. adv. bd. Lexington Child Abuse Council; bd. govs. Dream Factory; organized first Woodford County Jr. Miss Pageant. Fellow Harvard U. Inst.; mem. So. Gov.'s Assn. (chmn. 1987), Woodford County Jaycee-ettes (past pres.), U. Ky. Alumni Assn., Women's Missionary Union (past pres.), Nat. Conf. Appellate Ct. Clks., Leukemia Soc. Am. (hon. chairperson), Young Writer's Contest Found. (hon. bd. advs.), Ky. Alliance for Arts Edn. (hon. bd. dirs.), Leadership Ky. (bd. dirs.) Japan Am. Soc. Ky., Internat. Women's Forum, Hope for Drug-Free Am. (statesmen com.), Psi Omega Dental Aux. (past pres.). Clubs: Bus. and Profl. Women's, Order Eastern Star. Baptist. Office: St Catherine Coll Office of the President Saint Catharine KY 40061

COLLINS, MARY, health science association administrator, retired legislator; b. Vancouver, B.C., Can., Sept. 26, 1940; d. Fredrick Claude and Isabel Margaret (Copp) Wilkins; children: David, Robert, Sarah. Student, U. B.C., Queen's U., Kingston, Ont., Can.; LLD (hon.), Royal Rds. Mil. Coll., 1994. Mem. Can. Ho. of Commons, 1984-93; pres., CEO B.C. Health Assn., 1994-97; pres. Amarok Holdings, Ltd.; health care policy advisor WHO, Moscow. Mem. fed. cabinet Can., assoc. min. nat. def., 1989-92, min. Western econ. diversification, 1993, min. state environ., 1993, min. responsible for status of women, 1990-93, min. of health, 1993. Mem. Internat. Womens Forum. Office: WHO Russia 28 Ostozhenka 119034 Moscow Russia E-mail: mcollins@who.org.ru

COLLINS, MARY, writer, educator; b. Hartford, Ct., June 24, 1961; BS cum laude, Gettysburg Coll., 1983; MA, U. Va., 1986. Editor Nat. Geographic Soc., Washington, 1999—2002; prof. grad writing program Johns Hopkins U., 1996—; editor, writer Smithsonian Instn., Washington, 2002—. Author: The Essential Daughter: Changing Expectations for Girls at Home, 2002. Home: 513 Robinson Ct Alexandria VA 22302

COLLINS, MARY ALICE, psychiatric social worker, educator; b. Everett, Wash., Apr. 20, 1937; d. Harry Edward and Mary (Yates) Caton; BA in Sociology, Seattle Pacific Coll., 1959; MSW, U. Mich., 1966; PhD, Mich. State U., 1974; m. Gerald C. Brocker, Mar. 24, 1980. Diplomate Am. Bd. Social Workers. Dir. teenage, adult and counseling depts. YWCA, Flint, Mich., 1959-64, 66-68; social worker Catholic Social Services, Flint, 1969-71, Ingham Med. Mental Health Center, Lansing, Mich., 1971-73; clin. social worker Genesee Psychiat. Center, Flint, 1974-82, Psychol. Evaluation and Treatment Ctr., East Lansing, Mich., 1982-84; pvt. practice, East Lansing, 1984—; instr. social work Lansing C.C.; lectr. Mich. State U., 1974, 87-93, part-time adj. asst. prof., 1993—; vis. prof. Hurley Med. Center, 1979-84; v.p. Brief Psychotherapy Coalition, 1994; cons. Ingham County Dept. Social Services, 1971-73. Advisor human relations Youth League, Flint Council Chs., 1964-65; sec. Genesee County Young Democrats, 1960-61, pres. Round Lake Improvement Assn., 1984-87. Mem. NASW, Acad. Cert. Social Workers, Phi Kappa Phi, Alpha Kappa Sigma. Contbr. articles to profl. jours. Home: 5945 Round Lake Rd Laingsburg MI 48848-9454

COLLINS, MARY ALISE, music educator, non-commissioned officer; d. Robert Leon and Brenda Ann Collins. EdB, Hannibal La-Grange Coll., Hannibal, Mo., 1997—2002. Band instr. Hot Springs Sch. Dist., Hot Springs, SD, 2002—03; motor transport operator US Army Res., Hannibal, Mo., 1997—. Mem. Dakota Choral Union, Rapid City, SD, 2003. Sgt. USAR, 1997—2003, Hannibal, Mo. Mem.: Music Educators Nat. Conf. So. Bapt. Avocations: hiking, travel, singing, writing. Home: 315 S River St Apt 4 Hot Springs SD 57747 E-mail: mary.collins@hssd.k12.sd.us.

COLLINS, MERLE, English and comparative literature educator; b. Oranjestaad, Aruba, Sept. 29, 1950; d. John and Dorothy Helena Collins Grenada. BA, U. West Indies, 1972; MA, Georgetown U., 1981; PhD, U. London, 1990. Cert. in translation. Sr. lectr. Caribbean Studies U. North London, Eng., 1990-94; prof. English and Comparative Lit. U. Md., College Park, 1995—. Dir. U. Md. Study in Mexico City, 1997; vis. prof. St. George's U., Grenada, 1998; cons. editor Jour. of Caribbean Women Writers, Miami, 1998 . Author: Angel, 1987, Rain Darling, 1990, Rotten Pomerack, 1992; co-editor: Watchers and Seekers, 1987 Grantee U. Md., 1996. Mem. Assn. of Caribbean Women Writers and Scholars, Caribbean Studies Assn. Office: U Md Dept English 3101 Susquehanna Hall College Park MD 20742-8800 E-mail: merle_collins@umail.umd.edu.

COLLINS, MOIRA ANN, graphics and communications company executive, calligrapher; b. Dec. 16, 1942; d. Peter William and Louise (Carroll) Collins; m. Andrew Joseph Griffin, Aug. 21, 1965; children: Andrew Fitzgerald, Timothy Collins. BA, U. Toronto, Ont., Can., 1964; MA in Tchg., Northwestern U., 1965; MEd in Urban Studies, Northeastern U., Chgo., 1968; studied with profl. calligraphers, Haystack Mountain Sch., Deer Isle, Maine, 1973, U. Calif., Santa Cruz, 1973-74. Tchr. Chgo. Bd. Edn., 1965-68; freelance calligrapher, 1974-78; mem. publicity and promotional staff Swallow Press, Chgo., 1978-79; owner Letters, Chgo., 1979—. Pres. Astrogram, Chgo. 1986-99, Kiddygram, 2000-; intern Gestalt Inst. of Toronto & Oasis Ctr, Chgo., 1986-87. HEW fellow Northeastern U., 1967-68. Author, contbr.: Celebration: Anais Nin, 1975; contbr. to Goodfellow Rev. of Crafts, 1979; calligrapher: Erotica, 1976, Chgo. Rev., 1978. Chmn. fund raising Van Gorder Walden Sch., Chgo., 1979-80. Mem. Chgo. Calligraphy Collective (co-founder, chmn. 1976-77, pres. 1978-79, hon. mem.), Soc. Scribes N.Y., Soc. Scribes and Illuminators (Eng.), Friends Calligraphy Calif. Democrat. Roman Catholic. Home: 3920 N Lake Shore Dr Apt 9N Chicago IL 60613-3465 Office: 533 Lake Front Dr Beverly Shores IN 46301 E-mail: mac@moiracollins.com.

COLLINS, MONICA ANN, journalist; b. Rockville Center, N.Y. d. Louis Andrew and Eileen Ann Collins. BA, Vassar Coll. Writer, editor The Real Paper, Cambridge, Mass., 1975-79; TV critic Boston Herald Am., 1979-83, USA Today, Arlington, Va., 1983-89; columnist Boston Mag., 1983-85, TV Guide, 1989-93; TV critic, editl. page columnist Boston Herald, 1989—. Roman Catholic. Office: The Boston Herald 1 Herald St Boston MA 02118-2200 E-mail: mcollins@bostonherald.com.

COLLINS, NANCY LEE, mathematician, educator; b. St. Louis, May 17, 1925; d. Charles Alonzo and Leno Rosie (Squires) Roberts; m. Major Charles Brown Sr., Dec. 23, 1946 (dec. Feb. 1984); children: Major Charles Brown Jr., Victor Ivy Brown; m. James Pickett Collins, Nov. 29, 1986. BA, Harris Stowe State Coll., 1947; MEd, St. Louis U., 1955; MA in Counseling, Washington U., St. Louis, 1968. Cert. elem. and secondary counselor, Mo. Elem. tchr. St. Louis Bd. Edn., 1947-87, adult basic edn. tchr., 1967-72, secondary counselor, 1967-87; supr. computer math. lab. Meramec C.C., St. Louis, 1989—90. Counselor seven up program Villa Duschesne, Ladue, Mo., summer, 1970; tutor continuing edn. program. Univ. City, Mo., 1972-74. Author: Potpourri and Remembrances, 2003; co-editor: Profiles and Silhouettes: The Contribution of Black Women in Missouri, 1979; contbr. poetry to publ. Nat. Libr. of Poetry, 1997; artist compact disc For God and Country, 2004. Spl. advocate vol. Juvenile Ct., St. Louis, 1989 95; mem. exec. bd. Women's Missionary Soc., St. James A.M.E. Ch.; vol peer counselor Older Adult Svcs. Info. Sys. Parsons Blewett scholar St. Louis Bd. Edn., 1977; NSF fellow, 1963; recipient Top Teens Thrust award Top Ladies of Distinction, Inc., St. Louis, 1993, Black History in Mo. Appreciation award AAUW, 1994, Cert. Appreciation Ct. Appointed Spl. Advocates, 1994, Editor's Choice award Outstanding Achievement in Poetry, 2001, Internat. Libr. Poetry, 2003; honoree St. James Ch., 1997. Mem. Mo. Conf. Womens Missionary Soc. (membership, recruitment chair 1995), Mo. Conf. Lay Orgn. (local pres. 1993-95, now 3d v.p.), Internat. Soc. Poets (life), Order Eastern Star (worthy matron), Delta Sigma Theta (choir mem. 1986-95, 50 Yr. Mem. award 1995, Cert. Appreciation award 1993), Am. Assn. U. Women, Nat. Assn. U. Women, Mo. State Tchrs. Assn., Retired Sch. Employees of St. Louis. Democrat. African Methodist Episcopalian. Avocations: mathematics, reading, piano, aerobics, Scrabble. Home: 955 Jeanerette Dr University City MO 63130-2719 Office: Meramec CC 11333 Big Bend Rd Kirkwood MO 63122-5720

COLLINS, PATRICIA A. lawyer, judge; b. Camp Lejeune, N.C., Mar. 12, 1954; d. Thomas and Margaret (Parrish) C. BA, U. Va., 1976; JD, Gonzaga U., 1982. Bar: Alaska 1982, U.S. Dist. Ct. Alaska, U.S. Ct. Appeals (9th cir.) 1982. Assoc. Guess & Rudd, Anchorage and Juneau, 1982-84, 85-87; asst. pub. defender Alaska Pub. Defender's Office, Ketchikan, 1984-85; prin. Collins Law Office, Juneau, 1987-95; judge Alaska Dist. Ct., Ketchikan, 1995-1999, Juno Superior Ct., Alaska, 1999—. Part time fed. magistrate judge U.S. Cts., Juneau, 1988-95, Kitchikan, 1996—; adj. prof. U. Alaska, Juneau, 1991-95. Mem. Alaska Bar Assn., Ketchikan Sailing Club. Office: Alaska Superior Ct 114100 Juneau AK 99811-4100

COLLINS, ROSE ANN, minister; b. Pittsburgh, Pennsylvania, July 5, 1935; d. Joseph and Rochelle (McCrary) Covington; m. Frank Collins, June 30, 1960 (div. 1978); children: Gar Andre, Guy Tracy. BA, Ctrl. Bible Coll., Springfield, Mo., 1987; MDiv, Assemblies of God Theol. Sem., Springfield, Mo., 1989. Ordained to min., 1990. Assoc. min. Deliverance Temple World Outreach Ministries, Springfield, Mo., 1988-90, evangelist Springfield and Pitts., 1991-93; chaplain Western Ctr., Canonsburg, Pa., 1993-96; min. New Jerusalem Holiness Ch., Pitts., 2002—. Trustee Northside Ch. of God in Christ, Pitts., 1982-87, bd. dir., 1983-87. Vol., Ctr. for Victims Violent Crime; vol. mentor Lydia's Pl., Pitts., Pa., 2003—. Mem. Soc. Chaplains (Western chpt.), Pa. Coun. Chs., Ret. Enlished Assn. (hon., Steel City chpt. 72 chaplain 1994-96). Avocations: reading, walking. Home: 6290 Auburn St Apt 622 Pittsburgh PA 15206-3136

COLLINS, SALLY DUKE, forest service manager; b. Ames, Iowa, Nov. 17, 1951; d. Frederick Robert and June Marie (Morgan) Duke; m. John Leopold Collins, June 11, 1977; 1 child, Catherine Duke. BS in Recreation, U. Colo., 1977; MPA, U. Wyo., 1978. Environ. planner Bur. Lang Mgmt., Denver, 1978-83; land use planner Sinslaw Nat. Forest, Corvallis, Oreg.,

1983-87; mem. lands and minerals staff Deschutes Nat. Forest, Bend, Oreg., 1987-90, dep. forest supr., 1990-93, forest supr., 1993—. Trustee High Desert Mus., Bend, 1994; bd. dirs. United Way-Deschutes, Bend, 1994, Dollars for Scholars, Bend, 1993. Avocations: canoeing, hiking, skiing. Office: Deschutes Nat Forest 1645 NE Highway 20 Bend OR 97701-4868

COLLINS, SANDRA ANN, librarian; b. Bethelehm, Pa., July 10, 1951; d. Robert J. and Doris (Hottle) C. BS, Kutztown State Coll., 1973; MLS, U. Pitts., 1975; MPA, U. Utah, 1993. Children's libr. Bethlehem Pub. Libr., 1976-82, br. libr., 1982-87; children's libr. Weber County Libr., Ogden, Utah, 1982-87, tech. svcs., 1987-96, assoc. dir., 1989-96, asst. dir., 1996-98; dir. Northland Pub. Libr., Pitts., 1998—. Chair intellectual freedom com. Assn. of Libr. Svc. to Children, 1989; catloging needs of pub. librs. Pub. Libr. Assn., 1990-97. Mem. ALA, LWV (bd. dirs. 1982), Am. soc. Pub. Adminstrn., Internat. Pers. Mgmt. Assn., Utah Libr. Assn. (conf. co-chair ann. conf. 1994), Mountain Plains Libr. Assn., Pa. Libr. Assn., Soroptomist Internat. (sec., v.p. 1992-1998), No. Boroughs Rotary, (pres. 2004-2005). Democrat. Home: 9252 Highland Rd Pittsburgh PA 15237-4532 Office: Northland Public Library 300 Cumberland Rd Pittsburgh PA 15237-5410

COLLINS, SHERRI SMITH, music educator; b. Winston-Salem, N.C., Apr. 5, 1954; d. Roland Wilson and Foye Cook Smith; m. Paul Steven Collins, Dec. 29, 1979; children: Daniel Joseph, Carrie Elizabeth. BS in Instrumental Music, Western Carolina U., 1976; M in Music Edn., U. N.C.G., 1990. Legal sec. Smith Atty. At Law, Pilot Mountain, NC, 1973; salesperson Southwestern Book Co., Nashville, 1974—76; band dir. East Surry H.S., Pilot Mountain, 1976—88; music specialist Surry County Schs., Dobson, NC, 1990—. Sec. Pilot Mountain Auditorium Restoration, 2000—; pianist, organist First Presbyn. Ch., Pilot Mountain, 1976—, mem. pulpit com., 1977, elder on session, 1993—96. Grantee, Altrusa of Mountain Arry. N.C., 1997—98. Mem.: N.C. Music Educators, N.C. Assn. Educators. Republican. Presbyterian. Avocations: clogging, tennis. Home: 109 Westfield Td Pilot Mountain NC 27041 E-mail: sherrijo54@surry.net.

COLLINS, SUSAN M. senator; b. Caribou, Maine, Dec. 7, 1952; BA in Govt. magna cum laude, St. Lawrence U., 1975. Prin. advisor bus. affairs U.S. Senator Bill Cohen; commr. Maine Dept. Profl. and Fin. Regulation; dir. New England ops. U.S. Small Bus. Adminstrn.; exec. dir. Ctr. Family Bus., Husson Coll., Bangor, Maine; U.S. senator from Maine, 1997—. Staff dir. Senate Subcom. on Oversight Govt. Mgmt., 1981-87; chair Cabinet Coun. on Health Care Policy, State of Maine; mem. U.S. Senate com. health, edn., labor and pensions, 1997—, subcom. on children and families, 1997—, subcom. on pub. health and safety, 1997—, com. on govtl. affairs, 1997—; chmn. permanent subcom. on investigations, 1997—; mem. spl. com. on aging. Rep. candidate for Gov., State of Maine, 1994. Recipient Outstanding Alumni award St. Lawrence U., 1992. Mem. Bangor Rotary Club, Phi Beta Kappa. Republican. Roman Catholic. Office: 172 Russell Sen Office Bldg Washington DC 20510*

COLLINS-BROWN, E. DORLEE (E. DORLEE WOODYARD), systems support specialist; b. Crown City, Ohio, July 10, 1954; d. Walter Woodyard and Ruth Evelyn Simmons; m. Jeffrey Lynn Brown, Feb. 14, 2004; 1 child, Brian Scott Brown ; children from previous marriage: Angela Nycole Collins, Tiara Dorlee Elizabeth Collins. AA, We. Wyo. Coll., 1986; BS in Women's Studies, U. Utah, 1991, BS in Psychology, 1994. Cert. hypnotherapist, child protection svcs./youth and family, adult protection; cert. bus. counselor. Rsch. asst. U. Utah, Salt Lake City, 1988-91; sales mgr. Life and Safety, Sandy, Utah, 1992-94; edn. specialist ITT Tech. Inst., 1994-95; br. mgr. SOS Staff Svcs., Inc., Jackson Hole, Wyo. br., Salt Lake City, 1995-96; social worker Wyo. Dept. Family Svcs., Rock Springs, 1991—99; bus. counselor Small Bus. Devel. Ctr., U. Wyo., Rock Springs, 2000—01; faculty Inst. for Social Rsch. U. Mich., Ann Arbor, 2002—; employment trainer Affiliated Computer Svcs., 2004—. Mem. Nat. Inst. Survey Rsch. U. Mich., Ann Arbor, 2002. Named Miss Regal USA, Amarillo, Tex., 1981, Ms. Wyo. USA, 1997. Mem. AAUW, LWV, Psi Chi. Mem. Lds Ch. Avocations: reading, skiing.

COLLINSON, VIVIENNE RUTH, education educator, researcher, consultant; b. Kitchener, Ont., Can., July 30, 1949; d. Earl Stanley and Mary Magdalena (Sauder) Feick; m. Charles L. Collinson, May 21, 1983. BA, Wilfrid Laurier U., Waterloo, Ont., 1974; EdM, U. Windsor, Ont., 1989; PhD, Ohio State U., 1993. Cert. adminstr. Tchr. Waterloo County Bd. Edn., 1969-84, Windsor Bd. Edn., 1984-89; vis. asst. prof. U. Windsor, 1989-90, U. Md., College Park, 1993-94, asst. prof. edn., 1994-98; assoc. prof. Mich. State U., 1999—. Author: Teachers As Learners, 1994, Reaching Students, 1996. Charter mem. Eleanor Roosevelt Found., 1989—; benefactor Stratford (Ont.) Shakespearean Festival Found. Recipient Ont. Silver medal for piano U. We. Ont. Conservatory of Music, 1965, McGraw-Hill awrd, 1969; Ont. scholar, 1968; Wilfrid Laurier U. grad. scholar. Mem. AAUW, Am. Ednl. Rsch. Assn., Fedn. Women Tchrs. Assn. Ont. (provincial resource leader 1988-94), Nat. Soc. for Study of Edn., Delta Kappa Gamma (Doctoral Dissertation award 1994), Phi Kappa Phi. Avocations: music, theatre, travel. Office Phone: 517-353-5091., 517-353-5091. Fax: 313-824-2949.

COLLINS-PRAVEL, PAULA MARIE, marketing professional; d. Edward Joseph Rupinski and Stephanie Cecelia Chylinski; m. Michael John Collins, Sept. 27, 1969 (div.); children: Patrick Michael Collins, Jessica Stephanie Collins Stephens; m. John Paul Pravel, Aug. 5, 2001. Student, Schenectady County C.C. Adminstrv. asst. Knous Atomic Power Lab., Schenectady, 1968—72; program mgr. Joseph E. Mastrianni Inc., Schenectady, 1978—91; sales coord. Glen Sanders Mansion, Scotia, NY, 1991—93; mktg. and sales staff Delmar Thomson Learning, Albany, NY, 1993—2000; mktg. project mgr. Newkirk Products Inc., Albany, 2000—. Sec., membership chair Aux. Alplaus (N.Y.) Fire Co., 1982—85; polit. campaign vol. Schenectady County Dem. Party, 1976—; liturgy cons., parish coun. sec., pres. PTA Ch. of St. Adalbert, Schenectady, 1970—85. Mem.: Capital Region Chpt. Am. Mktg. Assn. (v.p. members svcs. 2002—03). Avocations: running, Tae Bo, reading, gardening, interior decorating.

COLLYER, ESTHER RITZ, volunteer, educator; b. Crothersville, Ind., Feb. 25, 1907; d. Volna Ernest and Mamie Audrey (Gallion) Ritz; m. George Stanley Collyer; 1 child, George Stanley Jr. BS in Music, DePaw U., 1928. Tchr. music, art Knightstown (Ind.) Pub. Schs., 1928-31; dir. music, art Allen County Schs., Ft. Wayne, Ind., 1946-63; tchr. Butler U. Sch. Music, Indpls., summer, 1953, Ind. U. Sch. Music, Bloomington, summer, 1954. Editor: The Libretto. Chair Fine Arts Festival, Arts United, Ft. Wayne; asst. dir. Ft. Wayne Mus. Art, interim dir., bd. dirs.; pres., bd. dirs. Ft. Wayne Philharmonic Orch., bd. adv. docent prog. IU Art Mus. Esther Ritz Collyer Award for Lifetime Achievement, Arts United Fort Wayne. Avocations: sculpture, painting, dance, reading, travel. Home: 1049 Sassafras Cir Bloomington IN 47408-1281

COLMAN, WENDY See ERSKINE, KALI

COLOM, VILMA, alderman; b. San Juan, P.R., June 7, 1954; d. Andres and Niza (Miranda) C.; divorced; 1 child, Omar Otero. BA, Northeastern U., 1978; MA, U. Ill., 1980. Mem. U.S. Sen. Task Force, Washington, 1983-90; chmn. Nat. Puerto Rican Forum, N.Y.C., 1986-89; pres. Colom Internat. & Assocs., 1986-88; bilingual educator Richard Yate Pub. Sch., 1993-95; alderman, committeeman 35th ward City of Chgo., 1995—. With nat. Hispanic affairs Allstate Ins., 1983-90. Asst. dir. U. Ill., Chgo., 1990-93; mem. adv. bd. LeadershipAm., 1994—; bd. dirs. Nat. Network Latino Women, 1995—; chmn. Chgo. office Nat. Puerto Rican Forum, N.Y.C., 1986-89, mem. adv. bd. nat. hqrs.; mem. aux. bd. Golden Apple Found., fundraising chmn., 1995—; mem. corp. nat. bd. Nat. Svc. Jobs for Progress. Recipient Signature award Leadership Am., 1994, Hispanic State Law Enforcement award, 1996, Law Enforcement award Hispanic Inst., 1996, Internat. award Logan Sq. Lions Club, 1996; named Hispanic of Yr., 1996. Mem. Nat. Women's C. of C. [illegible] Omega Sigma Alpha [illegible] 3510 N Ridgeway Ave #1 Chicago IL 60647-1118

COLOMB, MARJORIE MONROE, investor, volunteer; b. New Orleans, Sept. 9, 1929; d. Joseph Percy and Mary Velma Monroe; m. Charles McConvill Hardie, June 6, 1953 (div. Nov. 1972); m. John Joseph Colomb, Jr., Sept. 28, 1983 (dec.). BA Art History, La. State U., New Orleans, 1973; BS Bus., U. New Orleans, 1982. Adv.. coun. fanfare/columbia U. SE La., Hammond; adv. bd. dirs. New Orleans Mus.; bd. dirs. Easter Seals La., New Orleans; trustee J.Edgar Monroe Found., New Orleans. Fellow: New Orleans Mus. Art; mem.: Raintree Svcs. (hon. bd. dirs.). Republican. Roman Catholic. Home: 302 Glorias Pl Mandeville LA 70471-1612

COLOMER, VERONICA, medical educator, researcher; b. Mexico City, Mex., Nov. 9, 1957; married. BS, U. Mexico City, Mex., 1983; PhD, NYU, 1990. Postdoctoral fellow in lab. dept. cell biology NYU Med. Ctr., 1990-94; instr. lab. dept. cell biology Cornell Med. Coll., 1995; instr. in lab. dept. psychiatry Johns Hopkins U. Sch. Medicine, 1996—. Guest investigator in lab. dept. cellular physiology and immunology Rockefeller U., 1982-84. Contbr. articles to profl. jours. Recipient Minority Scientist Devel. award Am. Heart Assn., 1996, Career award MSDA Am. Heart Assn., 1996—; Undergrad. Student fellowship Consejo Nacional de Ciencia y Tecnologia, 1981-82, Grad. Student fellowship, 1984-87, Ella Fitzgerald fellow Am. Heart Assn., 1991, Postdoctoral Participating Lab. award fellowship Am. Heart Assn., 1991-94. Mem. Am. Soc. Cell Biology, Royal Soc. Tropical Medicine and Hygiene, N.Y. Acad. Scis., Mex. Soc. Biochemistry, Mex. Soc. Immunology. Office: Johns Hopkins U Sch Medicine Dept Psychology 720 Rutland Ave # 618 Baltimore MD 21205-2109

COLON, EUGENIA VALINDA, development executive; b. N.Y.C., Nov. 24, 1955; d. Israel H.D. and Inez Genevieve (Cavallaro) C. BA in Medieval English Lit., SUNY, Purchase, 1978; MPA, George Washington U., 1996. Cert. fund raising exec. Spl. asst. to asst. chancellor NYU, N.Y.C., 1985-87; ESL tchr. CES Sch., N.Y.C., 1984-88; spl. asst. to v.p. acad. affairs George Washington U., Washington, 1989-93, spl. asst. to dean Sch. Bus. and Pub. Mgmt., 1993-94; devel. cons. in pvt. practice, Vienna, Va., 1990-97; nat. dir. corp. devel. United Negro Coll. Fund, Farifax, Va., 1997-2001; v.p. devel. AFP Found. Philanthropy, 2001—02; pres., CEO Colon & Assocs., LLC, Devel. Cons., 2002—. Freelance writer, ind. cons., 1978—. Author: (collected poems) Volume I: Collected Poems, 1989; author short story and play. Vol. cons. Literacy Vols. of Am., Washington. Mem. Assn. Fundraising Profls. Democrat. Christian. Avocations: creative writing, reading, dance, painting, music. Office: Colon & Assocs LLC 2914 Cashel Ln Vienna VA 22181 E-mail: ginacolon@hotmail.com.

COLONA, JANE B. transplant nurse coordinator; b. Corry, Pa., May 14, 1958; d. James H. and Rose M. (Larson) Bennett; m. Jorge L. Colona, June 8, 1979 (div. Sept. 1988); children: Jorge Luis Christopher, Jaclyn Nicole. Diploma, Jackson Meml. Hosp. Sch.; AS, Miami Dade C.C., 1980. RN, Fla.; cert. CCRN; cert. clin. transplant coord.; cert. ACLS, PALS, pediatric ACLS instr. Staff nurse progressive care unit Palmetto Gen. Hosp., Hialeah, Fla., 1980-82, assoc. head nurse, 1982-84; pvt. duty nurse Jackson Meml. Hosp., Miami, Fla., 1984-86, nurse II pediatric ICU, 1986-92; transplant coord. U. Miami, 1992—. Mem. Transplant Found. South Fla.; facilitator Greater Miami Transplant Network Support Group. Mem. PTA Madie Ives Elem., North Miami Beach Sr. H.S. Recipient Svc. award Transplant Found. of South Fla., 1993, Outstanding Svc. award Nat. Kidney Found., 1994, Vol. of Yr. award Transplant Found. South Fla., 1997. Mem. AACN, Am. Assn. Kidney Patients (nat. bd. dirs. 1999—), N.Am. Transplant Nurse Orgn., Am. Heart Assn. (cardiovas. nursing coun.), Internat. Transplant Nurse Soc., Zool. Soc. Fla. Republican. Lutheran. Avocations: golf, swimming, bicycling, skiing, music, travel. Home: 20618 NE 6th Ct Miami FL 33179-2416 Office: U Miami Transplant Program 1150 NW 14th St Ste 605 Miami FL 33136-2117 Fax: (305) 243-7602. E-mail: jcolona@med.miami.edi.

COLONY, PAMELA CAMERON, medical researcher, educator; b. Boston, Apr. 18, 1947; d. Donald Gifford Colony and Priscilla (Adams) Pratley; m. E. Paul Cokely Jr., Apr. 26, 1986 (div. 2000); children: Daniel Patrick Cokely, John Travis Cokely; m. Richard M. Sparling, June 1, 2003. BA, Wellesley (Mass.) Coll., 1969; PhD, Boston U., 1976. Rsch. asst. sch. medicine Boston U., 1969-71, U. Hosp., 1971-73, Peter Bent Brigham Hosp., Boston, 1973-75; instr. dept. anatomy Harvard Med. Sch., 1975-77; assoc. staff in medicine Peter Bent Brigham Hosp., Boston, 1976-79; sr. fellow, instr. Harvard Med. Sch., Boston, 1979-81; asst. prof. anatomy and medicine Pa. State Coll. Medicine, Hershey, Pa., 1981-88; assoc. prof. rsch., pre-health advisor Franklin and Marshall Coll., Lancaster, 1988-91; adj. assoc. prof. of surgery Pa. State Coll. Medicine, Hershey, 1988-91, sr. rsch. assoc. dept. surgery, 1991-95; asst. prof. SUNY, Cobleskill, 1995-97, assoc. prof., 1997-99, program dir. histotech., 1995—, prof. biology, 1999—, co-dir. Women in Sci., 1996—. Bd. dirs. N.Y. State Histotechnol. Soc.; ind. assessor Nat. Health and Med. Rsch. Coun., Australia, 1985—; ad-hoc reviewer NIH, Nat. Cancer Inst., Bethesda, Md., 1986; lectr., adj. instr. Harrisburg Area Cmty. Coll., 1991—95. Contbr. articles to profl. jours. Fellow Nat. Found. Ileitis and Colitis, 1979-81; grantee Fed. Republic Germany, 1978, Cancer Rsch. Ctr., 1982-83, NIH, 1982-91. Mem.: Nat. Soc. for Histotech., N.Y. Histotechnol. Soc. (bd. dirs. 2001—), Am. Soc. Clin. Pathology. Avocations: endurance and competitive trail riding, breeding and showing horses. Office: SUNY Cobleskill Dept Natural Scis Main St Cobleskill NY 12043 E-mail: colonyp@cobleskill.edu.

COLOSIMO, LISA MARIE, software engineer; b. Buffalo, N.Y., Apr. 15, 1969; d. Donald Domenico and Donna Louise (Glinski) C. BS in Applied Math./Computer Sci., Carnegie Mellon U., 1991; MSE in Computer and Info. Sci., U. Pa., 1993. Systems engr. GE Aerospace, Valley Forge, Pa., 1991-93; software engr. Mars Electronics Internat., West Chester, Pa., 1993-94; cons. First Consulting Group, Wayne, Pa., 1994—2002; tech. arch. CIBER Inc., Wayne, Pa., 2002; sys. analyst Siemens Med. Solutions, Malvern, Pa., 2002—. Mem. IEEE, Soc. Women Engrs. (career guidance chairperson 1993-96, sec. Phila. sect. 1996-98, spl. projects chmn., 1999, pres., 2002-03), Chi Omega. Roman Catholic. Office: Seimens Medical solutions 51 Valley Stream Pkwy Malvern PA 19355

COLPITTS, GAIL ELIZABETH, artist, educator; b. Chgo., Nov. 26, 1954; d. Robert Moore and Mary Lee (Means) C. BA, Greenville Coll., 1976; MA, No. Ill. U., 1984, MFA, 1990. Grad. tchg. asst. No. Ill. U., DeKalb, Ill., 1982-83, tchg. intern, 1990, instr. Office Campus Recreation, 1989-90; artist-tchr. MFA program Vt. Coll., Montpelier, 1993; instr. Harold Washington Coll., Chgo., 1993, Columbia Coll., Chgo., 1995; artist, lectr. Judson Coll., Elgin, Ill., 1995, asst. prof. art, 1996—2000, assoc. prof. art and design, 2000—, chair dept. art and design, 2001—. One-woman shows include No. Ill. U., DeKalb, 1990, Bethel Coll., Arden Hills, Minn., 1995, Greenville (Ill.) Coll., 1993, Wheaton (Ill.) Coll., 1996, Trinity Christian Coll., Palos Heights, 1998, Cliff Dwellers, Chgo., 1999, Northwestern Coll., St. Paul, Minn., 2000, Judson Coll., Elgin, Ill., 2003; assoc. editor: Shoal Dance, 1995-96, contbr. revs. and news; contbr. poetry to mags.; included in Best of New Ceramic Arts, 1997, Making Visible the Invisible, 2003. Dir. Christians in the Visual Arts, 2003. Grad. sch. fellow No. Ill. U., 1987-88. Mem. Coll. Art Assn., Christians in Visual Arts, Chgo. Artists Coalition, Ill. Higher Edn. Art Assn. (bd. dirs.). Wesleyan. Avocations: genealogical research, reading, travel. Office: Art Dept Judson Coll 1151 N State St Elgin IL 60123-1404

COLSON, ELIZABETH FLORENCE, anthropologist; b. Hewitt, Minn., June 15, 1917; d. Louis H. and Metta (Damon) C. BA, U. Minn., 1938, MA, 1940, Radcliffe Coll., 1941, PhD, 1945; D of Sociology, Brown U., 1979; D.Sc., U. Rochester, 1985, U. Zambia, 1992. Asst. social sci. analyst War [illegible] Authority, 1942-43, research asst. Harvard, 1944-45; research officer Rhodes-Livingstone Inst., 1946-47, dir., 1948-51; sr. lectr. Manchester U., 1951-53; assoc. prof. Goucher Coll., 1954-55; research assoc., assoc. prof. African Research Program, Boston U., 1955-59, part-time, 1959-63; prof. anthropology Brandeis U., 1959-63, U. Calif.-Berkeley, 1964-84, prof. emeritus, 1984—; vis. prof. U. Zambia, 1987. Lewis Henry Morgan lectr. U. Rochester, 1973; vis. rsch. assoc. Refugee Studies Program Queen Elizabeth House, Oxford, 1988-89. Author: The Makah, 1953, Marriage and the Family Among The Plateau Tonga, 1958, Social Organization of the Gwembe Tonga, 1960, The Plateau Tonga, 1962, The Social Consequences of Resettlement, 1971, Tradition and Contract, 1974, A History of Nampeyo, 1992; jr. author Secondary Education and the Formation of an Elite, 1980, Voluntary Efforts in Decentralized Management, 1983, sr. author For Prayer and Profit, 1988, The History of Nampeyo, 1991; sr. editor: Seven Tribes of British Central Africa, 1951; jr. editor People in Upheaval, 1987. AAUW travelling fellow, 1941-42, fellow Ctr. Advanced Study Behavioral Scis., 1967-68, Fairchild fellow Calif. Inst. Tech., 1975-76. Fellow Am. Anthrop. Assn., Assn. Social Anthropologists of the Commonwealth, Royal Anthrop. Inst. (hon.); mem. Nat. Acad. Sci., Am. Acad. Arts and Scis., Am. Assn. African Studies (Disting. Africanist award 1988), Soc. Applied Anthropology, Soc. Woman Geographers, Phi Beta Kappa. Avocations: walking, opera, reading. Office: U Calif Dept Anthropology Berkeley CA 94720-0001 E-mail: gwembe@uclink.berkeley.ed.

COLSON, JUDY C. music educator; b. Leavenworth, Kans., Nov. 4, 1951; d. Robert A. and Doris D. Lange; m. Ed L. Colson, Aug. 7, 1982; children: Amanda L. Zinn, Ed R. MusB in Edn., Baker U., 1974, MLA, 1988. Cert. tchr. Kans. State Dept. of Edn., 1974, Mo. Dept. of Edn., 1974. Band dir., Olathe, Kans., 1980—. Founding com. mem. John Philip Sousa Kans. Jr. Honors Band, Lawrence, Kans., 2002. Recipient elem. tchr. of yr., N.E. Kans. Educators Assn., 2003—04. Mem.: Women Band Dirs. Internat., Kans. Music Educators (assoc.; dist. one sec. 1982—84), Kans. Bandmasters Assn. (assoc.), Internat. Assn. Jazz Educators (assoc.), Music Educators Nat. Conf. (assoc.). Home: 13283 S Kimberly Circle Olathe KS 66061 Office: Olathe Northwest High Sch 21300 College Blvd Olathe KS 66061 E-mail: jcolsononw@olatheschools.com.

COLTON, BONNIE MYERS, writer, folklorist; b. Oswegatchie, N.Y., Dec. 7, 1931; m. Donald M. Colton, Jan. 4, 1952; children: Cherie Binns, Tricia Kennison, Jean Balch, Roger, Ben, Lin Sawyer, Neil. Student, Newspaper Inst. of Am., N.Y.C., 1961, Dale Carnegie Inst., Watertown, N.Y., 1978, Jefferson C.C., Lowville, N.Y., 1985. Record keeper, tax acct. Homewood Farm, Boonville, N.Y., 1958-89; cons./oral history interviewer Tug Hill Commn., Watertown, 1988-91; freelance writer/columnist, photographer Lowville, 1981—; newsletter editor, program coord. THRIFT newsletter, Lowville, 1991-94; newsletter editor, 2003—; ind. oral history interviewer, folklorist, 1991—; co-owner North Country Environ. Cons., 1999—. Writer weekly col. Jour. and Republican, Lowville, 1990-2002. Contbr. numerous articles to profl. jours.; author/editor/pub.: Christmas Treasures, 1995. Vol. newsletter editor First Presbyn. Ch., Lowville, 1990-93; vol. critic Nat. Writers Club, Aurora, Colo., 1988—; mem. legis. adv. com. Chloe Ann O'Neil, N.Y. State Assemblywoman, 1995—; pub. poetry readings at Lewis County Hist. Soc., Ogdensburg Libr., Lowville Libr., 1993-95; pres. Tug Hill Resources Investment For Tomorrow, 1997-99, N.Y. Forest Owners Assn., 1983-87. Mem. Lewis County Hist. Assn. (life, videotape and hist. programs), N.Y. Forest Owners Assn. (Heiburg Award for svc. to forestry 1992), Adirondack Mus. Avocations: museums, creating woodgrain art plaques, grandchildren, poetry, songwriting. Home and Office: 5595 Trinity Ave Lowville NY 13367-1416

COLTON, ELIZABETH WISHART, government agency administrator; b. Rockville Centre, N.Y., June 25, 1929; d. Ronald Sinclair Wishart and Elizabeth Lathrop Phillips. BA cum laude, We. Coll. for Women, 1951; postgrad., Am. U., 1951—52, Bowie State Coll., 1989—90. Jr. mgmt. asst. U.S. C.S.C., Washington, 1954, test developer, 1954—55, civil svc. insp., 1955—58, stds. developer and writer of qualification and classification stds., 1958—59, developer and implementer nationwide evauation plans of maj. fed. depts., 1958—62; developed and implemented bureauwide pers. mgmt. improvement programs Bur. of Reclamation Dept. of Interior, Washington, 1962—65, asst. dir. of pers. for nat. pk. svc., 1965—70, staff specialist dir. equal opportunity Office of Equal Employment Opportunity Programs, 1970; dep. dir. of pers. for pers. mgmt. evaluation and asst. to dep. dir. for classification and pay Dept. of Treasury, Washington, 1970—78; dir. divsn. pers. sys. imrprovement Office Asst. Sec. Health and Human Svcs., Washington, 1978—85. Real estate broker, Annapolis, Md., 1985—2003; antique dealer, Annapolis, 1985—2003. Job counselor displaced homemakers YWCA, Annapolis, 1985—92, active, 1985—92; ct. -apptd. spl. advocate for a foster child; developer and leader inner-city boys cooking class N.Y. Ave. Presbyn. Ch., Washington, 1960—69. Mem.: We. Coll. Alumnae Assn. Miami U. (bd. trustees), Victoria Walk Unit Owners Assn. (sec. treas. 2003). Presbyterian. Avocations: ancient history, gardening, traveling, genealogy. Home: 402-B Goldsborough St Easton MD 21601 E-mail: bcolton@goeaston.net.

COLTON, ZANNE BEAUFORT, performing company executive; Studied with Ron Colton; graduate, Balanchine's Sch. Am. Ballet. Mem. touring ensemble Atlanta (Ga.) Ballet; artistic dir. Augusta (Ga.) Ballet, 1995—. Tchr. ballet; panelist Artists-in-Schools, Ga. Coun. Arts. Dancer (ballets) Charleston (S.C.) Ballet Co., Atlanta (Ga.) Ballet. Scholar, Ford Found. Office: Augusta Ballet PO Box 3828 Augusta GA 30914*

COLTON SKOLNICK, JUDITH A. artist; b. Washington, Jan. 31, 1947; d. Bernard and Helen (Glick) Colton; 2 children. Student, Corcoran Sch. Art, 1964, student, 1993—94; BA in Art and Art History with honors, U. Md., 1972; postgrad., Montgomery Coll., 1990—91. Tchr. faux painting workshop The Artful Framer, 1991, Craft Country, Olney, Md., 1991; artist guest lectr. Radford U., spring 1996; supr. painting Paint Out Aids Ea. Market, Washington, 1992; asst. to art cons. Capitol Arts, Washington, 1992-96; tech. illustrator Vitro Corp., 1981-86; artist assoc. Mary Anne Reilly, 1995; founder Unity in Diversity Women's Exhibn. Group; interviewer, active Va. Juvenile Detention Ctr., 1993; spkr., presenter in field. One-woman shows include Beltone Hearing Aid, Washington, 1963, New Trends, Springfield, Va., 1971, Artful Framer, Olney, Md., 1991, Kurz, Koch, Doland and Dembling, Washington, 1992, Heartland Cafe, 1992, "R" St. Gallery Jackson Sch., 1993, Franklin Ct. Gallery, 1994, Parish Gallery, 1995, Flossie Martin Gallery Radford U., Blacksburg, Va., 1996, Sunrise Gallery, Kilmarnock, Va., 1997, Nat. Press Club Bldg., Washington, 1997—98, Art Mine Agora Gallery, N.Y.C., 1998—2001, Very Spl. Arts Online Gallery, Washington, 1998—2001, Articulate Gallery, 1999, exhibited in group shows at The Artful Framer, 1991, Glen Echo (Md.) Park, 1991, The Montpelier Cultural Arts Ctr., Laurel, Md., 1991, 1994, Md. Arts Pl., Rockville, 1992, Emerson Art Gallery, McLean,Va., 1992, Mus. Latin and Hispanic Art, Miami, Fla., 1992, Willow St. Gallery, Washington, 1992—93, SODARCO, Montreal, 1993, Howard C.C., Columbia, Md., 1993, Feminist Expo, Balt., 2000, N.Y.C., 1993—94, Art Expo N.Y., 2000, Fresno (Calif.) Mus. Art, 1993, Agora Galleries, N.Y.C., 1992—2001, Santa Barbara (Calif.) Mus. Art, 1993, U. Md., Albin O. Kuhn Libr. and Gallery U. Md., Balt., 1994, Owen Patrick Gallery, Phila., 1994, D.C. Arts Ctr., 1994, Mus. Ams., Washington, 1994, Mus. Nacional Palacio Bellas Artes, Havana, Cuba, 1995, French Emb., Washington, 1995, Very Spl. Arts Gallery, 1996, Venable Neslage, Washington, 1996, Nat. Mus. Women in Arts, 1995, 1998, B'nai B'rith Klutznick Nat. Jewish Mus., Washington, 1997, Corcoran Mus. Art, 1999, King St. Stephen Mus., Hungary, 2000,

Jemison-Carnegie Heritage Hall Mus., Ala., 2001, Attleboro (Mass.) Mus., 2001, The Music, Comune de Imola, Italy, 1999, Castel S. Pietro Terme, 1999—2003, Maison Francois de Bologne, Sung Kyun Kwan U., Seoul, Korea, CIA, McLean, Va., 1998, Amsterdam Whitney Gallery, NYC, 2002—03, Nat. Assn. Women Artists, 2002—03, Poughkeepsie (NY) Art Mus., 2004, others; (command murals, faux painting); contbr. to profl. mags. and pubs. Mem. Nat. Assn. Women Artists Inc., Nat. Mus. Women in Arts, Corcoran Sch. Art Alumni Assn. (presenter). Republican. Jewish. Avocations: poetry, reading, walking, boating. Home: 2301 E St NW A1115 Washington DC 20037

COLUCCI, JACQUELINE STRUPP, insurance agent, small business administration specialist, sculptor, special project coordinator; b. Montevideo, Uruguay, July 24, 1963; d. Gunther and Silvia (Klemens) S.; children: Matias Camprubi-Soms, Mercedes Camprubi-Soms; m. John Michael Colucci, Sept. 6, 1997. BA with hons. cum laude, NYU, 1986. AFLAC rep. Customer svc. mgr. Games Mag./Mail Order, N.Y.C., 1984-86; treas., property mgr., asst. to chief exec. officer Hudson Properties, Lyndhurst, N.J., 1986-90; sales assoc. Bloomingdale's, Palm Beach Gardens, Fla., 1990-91, staff tng. supr. and pers. asst., 1991-92; legal asst., bookkeeper Gov.'s Bank and Bruce W. Keihner, Palm Beach, Fla., 1993; asst. Ideas & Things, 1994-97; freelance bus. mgr., 1993—; personal and bus. coach, 1993-97; bus. mgr. MCR/Michael Colucci Race Engring., Inc., Jupiter, Fla., 1997—; special coord. AFLAC. Office: MCR/Michael Colucci Race Engineering Inc 1092 Jupiter Park Ln Ste 270 Jupiter FL 33458-6024

COLUMBUS, SHANNA S. advertising executive; With Price Weber Mktg. Comm. Inc., Louisville, Ky., 1979—, pres., CEO, chmn., 1988—. Office: Price Weber Mktg Comms Inc 2101 Production Dr Louisville KY 40299-2111

COLVIN, SHAWN, recording artist, songwriter; b. Vermillion, S.D., Jan. 10, 1956; Past mem., founder Shawn Colvin Band, Carbondale, Ill.; past mem. Dixie Diesels, Austin, Tex. Albums include Live Tape, 1988, Steady On, 1989, Fat City, 1992, Cover Girl, 1994, Round of Blues, 1995, Live '88, 1995, Few Small Repairs, 1996, (single Grammy award Record of the Year for Sonny Came Home, 1998), Holiday Songs and Lullabies, 1998, (single) I Don't Know Why, 1992, (extended play single) Every Little Thing, 1994; background vocals, arranger I Know, 1987; background vocals Solitude Standing, 1987, Ghosts Upon the Road, 1989, Ben & Jerry's Newport Folk, 1989, Festival, 1989, State of the Heart, 1989, Long Road, 1990, Days of Open Hand, 1990, Stages, 1991, Come on Come on, 1992, Life is Messy, 1992, Stones in the Road, 1994, House on Fire, 1995, Strangers World, 1995, Down in There, 1996, Last Tango, 1996; vocals, guitar Samp, 1988, Bob Dylan's 30th Anniversary, 1993, Concert, 1993, Columbia Records Radio Hour (vol. 1), 1994, Best of Columbia Records Radio Hour, 1996; vocals Standing Eight, 1989, Time Was, 1995; harmony vocals Land of the Bottom Line, 1992, Road to Ensenada, 1996; vocals, prodr., Tin Cup, 1996; prodr. Tide, 1994; vocals, background vocals Shooting Straight in the Dark, 1990, others; appearances include (off-broadway) Pump Boys and Dinettes, Diamond Studs, Lie of the Mind, (film) It Could Happen to You, Grace of My Heart, (TV) TNN's presentation of The Players, 1999, An All Star Tribute to Joni Mitchell, 2000. Recipient Grammy award Song of the Year, 1998. Office: care Sony Music 550 Madison Ave New York NY 10022-3211

COLWELL, RITA ROSSI, microbiologist, former federal agency administrator, medical educator; b. Nov. 23, 1934; BS in Bacteriology with distinction, Purdue U., 1956, MS in Genetics, 1958; PhD, U. Wash., 1961; DSc, Heriot-Watt U., Edinburgh, Scotland, 1987, Hood Coll., 1991, Purdue U., 1993, U. Surrey, Eng., 1995, U. Bergen, Norway, 1999, Coastal Carolina U., 1999, U. Md. Balt. County, 1999, St. Mary's Coll., 1999, Mich. State U., 2000, Washington Coll., 2000, U. Conn., 2000, Williams Coll., 2000, SUNY, Albany, 2000, U. Ancona, Italy, 2001, George Washington U., 2001, Mount Holyoke, 2001, Washington U., St. Louis, 2001, Calif. Poly. Inst., San Luis Obispo, 2001, Renssalaer Poly. Inst., 2001, U. Newcastle, U.K., 2001, Mercy Coll., 2002, U. Queensland, Australia, 2002, U. Glasgow, 2002, Weizmann Inst. Sci., Israel, 2002, Tuskegee Inst., 2003, U. Ill., 2003, Dartmouth Coll., 2003; LLD, U. Nebr., 2003, Notre Dame Coll., 1994; DHL (hon.), U. Ala., 2001. Rsch. asst. genetics lab. Purdue U., West Lafayette, Ind., 1956—57; rsch. asst. U. Wash., Seattle, 1957—58, predoctoral assoc., 1959—60, asst. rsch. prof., 1961—64; asst. prof. biology Georgetown U., Washington, 1964—66, assoc. prof. biology, 1966—72; prof. microbiology U. Md., 1972—98, v.p. for acad. affairs, 1983—87; dir. Ctr. Marine Biotech., 1987—91; founder, pres. Md. Biotech. Inst. U. Md., 1991—98; dir. NSF, Arlington, Va., 1998—2004; chmn. Canon US Life Scis., Inc., 2004—; Disting. Univ. prof. U. Md., College Park, 2004—, Johns Hopkins Bloomberg Sch. Pub. Health, 2004—. Hon. prof. U. Queensland, Brisbane, Australia, 1988; mem. ocean scis. bd. NAS, 1977—80; hon. prof. Quindao U., China, 1995; cons. Washington area comms. media, congressman, legislators, 1978—; external examiner various univs. abroad, 1964—; vice chmn. polar rsch. bd. NAS, 1990—94; mem. Nat. Sci. Bd., 1984—90; mem. sci. adv. bd. Oak Ridge Nat. Labs., 1988—90, 1993—96; adv. com. FDA, 1991—92, food adv. com., 1993—96, sci. bd., 1996—; Koch lectr., Berlin, 2000. Author (manual numerical taxonomy): Collecting the Data, 1970; author: (with M. Zambruski) Rodina-Methods in Aquatic Microbiology, 1972; author: (with L.H. Stevenson) Estuarine Microbial Ecology, 1973; author: (with R.Y. Morita) Effect of the Ocean Environment on Microbial Ecology, 1973; author: (with A. Sinsky and N. Pariser) Marine Biotechnology, 1983; author: Vibrios in the Environment, 1985, Nucleic Acid Sequence Data, 1988; author: (with others) Marine Biotechnology, 1995; Microbial Diversity, 1996; author: Viable But Nonculturable Microorganisms in the Environment, 2000, others; mem. editl. bd.: Microbial Ecology, 1972—91, Applied and Environ. Microbiology, 1969—81, Oil and Petrochemical Pollution, 1980—91, Jour. Washington Acad. Scis., 1981—87, Johns Hopkins U. Oceanographic Series, 1981—84, Revue de la Fondation Oceanographique Ricard, 1981—, Estuaries, 1983—89, Zentralblatt fur Bacteriologie, 1985—, Jour. Aquatic Living Resources, 1987—, Sys. Applied Microbiology, 1985—2000, World Jour. Microbiology and Biotech.., 1988—95, Environ. Microbiology, 2001—; contbr. articles to profl. jours.; (Koch lecture) Anatomy Lesson, Amsterdam, 2002. Named Prof. Extraordinairo, U. Catolica Valparaiso, Chile, 1976, Scholar of Yr., Phi Kappa Phi, 1992; recipient Gold medal, Internat. Biotech. Inst., 1990, Purkinje Gold medal for achievment in sci., Czechoslavakian Acad. Sci., 1991, Civic award, Gov. Md., 1990, Woman of the Yr. award, Women Legis. of Md., 1996, Cert. of Recognition, NASA, 1984, Alice Evans award, Am. Soc. Microbiol., 1988, Andrew White medal, Loyola Coll., 1994, medal of distinction, Barnard Coll./Columbia U., 1996, Gold medal, Charles U., Prague, 2000, Gold medals, UCLA, 2000, Alumna Summa Laude Dignata award, U. Wash., 2000, Achievement award, AAUW, 2001, Carey award, Am. Assn. Adv. Sci., 2001, Thomas award, Explorer's Club Lowell, 2000. Fellow: AAAS (chmn. sect. biol. scis. 1993—94, pres. 1995, chmn. bd. 1996, Carey award 2001), Marine Tech. Soc. (exec. com. 1982—88), Washington Acad. Scis. (bd. mgrs. 1976—79, pres. 1996—98), Am. Acad. Microbiology (chmn. bd. govs. 1989—99), Grad. Women. Sci., Can. Coll. Microbiologists; mem.: NAS, Royal Swedish Acad. Sci., Soc. Gen. Microbiology, Internat. Coun. Sci. Unions, Am. Soc. Limnology and Oceanography, World Fedn. Culture Collections, Classification Rsch. Group Eng. (charter), Am. Soc. Microbiology (hon.; various sci. coms. 1961—, pres. 1985, chmn. program com. REGEM-1 1988, Fisher award 1985), U.K. Soc. Applied Microbiology (hon.), Bangladesh Soc. Microbiology (hon.; fgn.), French Soc. Microbiology (hon.), Israeli Soc. Microbiology (hon.), Australian Soc. Microbiology (hon.), Soc. Indsl Microbiology (bd. govs. 1976—79, Charles Thom award 1998), U.S. Fedn. Culture Collections (governing bd. 1978—88), Internat. Coun. Sci. Unions (exec. bd. 1993—96, gen. com.), Am. Inst. Biol. Scis. (bd. govs. 1976—82), Internat. Union Microbiol. Soc. (v.p. 1986—90, pres. 1990—94), World Fedn. Culture Collections, Royal Soc. Can., Explorers Club (Lowell Thomas award 2000), Omicron Delta Kappa, Phi Beta Kappa, Sigma Delta Epsilon, Sigma Xi (nat. pres. 1991, Ann. Achievement award 1981, Rsch. award 1984), Delta Gamma (Delta Gamma Rose award 1989). Achievements include research in marine biotechnology; marine and estuarine microbial ecology; survival of pathogens in aquatic environments; ecology of Vibrio cholerae and related organisms; microbial systematics; marine microbiology; antibiotic resistance; environmental aspects of Vibrio cholerae in transmission of cholera; in global climate and cholera transmission.

COLWELL-SNYDER, LUCY FAY, music educator; b. Southbridge, Mass., Jan. 14, 1965; d. Charles Frederick and Carolyn Fay Colwell; m. Kevin Michael Snyder, July 26, 2002; 1 child, Abram Charles Colwell. MusB in Performance, Shenandoah Conservatory of Music, Winchester, Va., 1987; Artists Diploma, Hartt Sch. Music, Hartford, Conn., 1994; MA in Tchg., Coll. of Our Lady of the Elms, Chicopee, Mass., 2003. Cert. tchr. Mass. Dept. of Edn., 2003. Music tchr. Tantasqua Regional Sch. Dist., Sturbridge, Mass., 1996—; French horn instr. Joy of Music Program, Worcester, Mass., 2001—; adj. faculty Coll. of Our Lady of the Elms, Chicopee, Mass., 2000—03; French horn instr. Anna Maria Coll., Paxton, Mass., 2001—02; instrumental instr. Wales (Mass.) Elem. Sch., 1998—2003. Prin. French horn Thayer Symphony Orch., Fitchburg, Mass., 1995—. Mem. pastor parish rels. com. Charlton City United Meth. Ch., Charlton, Mass., 1996—99. Mem.: Am. Fedn. Musicians Local 173, Mass. Tchrs. Assn., Sigma Alpha Iota (life). Methodist. Avocations: camping, entertaining, family. Home: 143 Bemis Rd West Brookfield MA 01585 Office: Tantasqua Jr High Sch Brookfield Rd Fiskdale MA 01518 Personal E-mail: luab3@aol.com.

COLY, LISETTE, foundation executive; b. N.Y.C., Apr. 6, 1950; d. Robert Raymond and Eileen (Lyttle-Garrett) C.; children: George Robert Damalas, Anastasia Eileen Damalas. BA cum laude, Hunter Coll., 1973. Sec. Parapsychology Found., Inc., N.Y.C., 1972-75, assoc. editor, 1975—, v.p., 1978—, exec. dir., 1999—. Assoc. editor Parapsychology Rev. and Procs. Ann. Internat. Parapsychology Found. Confs., 1978—; editor, conf. coord. Procs. Ann. Internat. Confs., 1989—; editor-in-chief Internat. Jour. Parapsychology. Office: Parapsychology Found Inc PO Box 1562 New York NY 10021-0043 E-mail: lisettecoly@parapsychology.org.

COMAR, MARY ALICE, art educator, farmer; b. Adrian, Mich., Mar. 2, 1945; d. Rae Jack and Pauline Isabelle Comar; children: Jack Michael Findley, J. Brent Findley. MA in Humanities, Ctrl. Mich. U., 1993; BS, Siena Heights U., 1967. Teaching Cert. State of Mich., 1967. K-12 art tchr. Benton County Cmty. Schools, Oxford, Ind., 1967—68; sr. high art instr. Lafayette Diocese, Lafayette, Ind., 1968—71; instr. speech comm. Alpena C.C., Oscoda, Mich., 1979; instr. secondary art and English Alpena Pub. Schools, Mich., 1974—. Set dir./play dir. sch. musicals Lafayette Diocese, Lafayette, Ind., 1969—70; practicing artist, photographer, videographer, Ossineke, Mich.; yearbook advisor/drama club advisor/play dir. Alpena H.S., 1985—99; secondary curriculum revision com. mem.; designed course Film as Lit. Alpena Pub. Schools; mem. sch. improvement team Alpena H.S. Oil painting, Vatican Two (Grand Prize Greater Lafayette Art Festival, 1968), (Indpls. 500 Festival of Arts, Second Most Meritorious Work Amateur Divsn., 1968), oil painiting, Pax (Detroit Inst. of Arts Rental Gallery); dir.: (advisor to student produced yearbook) Anamakee (Am. Scholastic Press Assn. First Pl. Award); 9' x 6' commissioned oil painting, Jesus Loving the Little Children, 24' x 10' commissioned mural design, Mountain Scene;, author story, poetry, editorials published. Mem., sec. and vice chairperson Alpena Twp. Planning and Zoning Commn., 1980—88; vol. prop artist Alpena Civic Theatre and Thunder Bay Theatre, 1972—84; program com. Very Spl. Arts Festival Mich. Coun. for Very Spl. Arts, Alpena, 1980—80; vol. docent Jesse Besser Mus., Alpena, 1978; 4-H youth leader Mich. State County Ext. 4H Program, Alpena, 1978; vol. demonstrator artist Mich. Art Train Mich. Coun. for Arts, Alpena, 1978; vol. art work contbr. Jesse Besser Mus. Art Auction Fund Raiser, Alpena, 1980; adv. for those too young, old, sick, or unborn toward clean air and a healthy environment Citizen and registered voter of Mich. and the USA, Alpena, Mich., 1972—2003; bd. mem., sec., spkrs. bur., com. co-chairperson toxic and hazardous waste study com., chairperson ERA study com. Alpena County LWV, 1977—80; religious edn. tchr. St. John the Bapt. Cath. Parish, Alpena, 1999; lectr. and eucharistic min. St. Bernards Cath. Ch., Alpena, 1983—85; initiated a ch. youth group St. Bernard's Parish, Alpena, 1983—85. Recipient Classrooms of Tomorrow Tchr., Mich. Gov. Blanchard, 1990. Mem.: NEA, So. Poverty Law Ctr. (charter mem., leadership coun.), Siena Heights U. Alumni Assn., Mich. Edn. Assn., Alpena Edn. Assn. (exec. com. bldg. rep. 1991—92), Nat. Mus. of Women in Arts (corr.). Democrat. Roman Catholic. Avocations: horse training, swimming, dance, golf.

COMBS, ANN L. federal agency administrator; BA, U. Notre Dame, 1978; JD, George Washington U., 1981. Prin. William M. Mercer Cons.; deputy asst. sec. labor, 1987—2001; asst. sec. pensions and welfare benefits adminstrn. U.S. Dept. Labor, Washington, 2001—. Office: US Dept Labor 200 Constitution Ave NW Washington DC 20210

COMBS, DIANE LOUISE, elementary school educator, music educator; b. Amittyville, NY, Feb. 8, 1952; d. Earl Foster and Eloise Mae Jones; m. Gary Stephen Combs, June 30, 1979; children: Steven Richard, Jason. BS, Jacksonville U., 1974, MA in Tchg., 1977. Phys. edn. tchr. Clay County Schs., Green Cove Springs, Fla., 1974—79; phys. edn./music tchr. Seminole County Schs., Sanford, Fla., 1979—83; music tchr. Clay County Schs., Green Cove Springs, Fla., 1983—. Dir. music, organist Ortega Presbyn., Jacksonville, 1968—69, Trinity Luth., Jacksonville, 1978—79, Ch. of the Messiah, Winter Garden, Fla., 1979—83, Orange Pk. (Fla.) Presbyn., 1983—97; organist, asst. dir. Orange Pk. United Meth. Ch., 1997—; organist, dir. Lakewood Presbyn., Jacksonville, 1970—78; organist Riverside Pk. United Meth., Jacksonville, 1978. Chair Clay County Elem. Music Festival, Orange Park, 1994—; scholarship chairperson Concert on the Green, Orange Park, 2002—03; design team mem. Southeastern Conf. of Meth. Musicians, Nashville, 2003—; chair Sch. Adv. Com., Middleburg, Fla., 2003—. Mem.: Meth. Conferece The Fellowship (assoc.; design team mem. 2003—), Fla. Music Educator's Assn. (assoc.). Methodist. Avocations: swimming, reading, guitar, piano, organ. Home: 2559 Brockview Pointe Orange Park FL 32073 Office: Tynes Elementary School 1550 Tynes Blvd Middleburg FL 32068

COMBS, HOLLY MARIE, actress; b. San Diego, Dec. 3, 1973; m. Bryan Smith, 1993 (div. 1997); m. David W. Donoho, 2004. Actor: (films) Walls of Glass, 1985, Sweet Hearts Dance, 1988, New York Stories, 1989, Born on the Fourth of July, 1989, Simple Men, 1992, Dr. Giggles, 1992, Chain of Desire, 1993, A Reason to Believe, 1995; (TV films) A Perfect Stranger, 1994, Sins of Silence, 1996, Love's Deadly Triangle: The Texas Cadet Murder, 1997, Daughters, 1997, See Jane Date, 2003; (TV series) Picket Fences, 1992—96 (best young actress in a new TV series Young Artist award, 1993), Charmed, 1998—; prodr., 2000—. Office: c/o SFM 1122 S Robertson Blvd #15 Los Angeles CA 90035*

COMBS, JUDY DIANE, elementary school educator, civic association administrator; b. Adams County, Iowa, Aug. 6, 1939; d. Carlton Matthew and Faye Maxine Stewart; m. Donald Dean Combs, June 24, 1956; children: Jeffery Dean, Victor Lee. BS in Elem. Edn. summa cum laude, N.W. Mo. State U., 1965, MS in Elem. Adminstrn., 1970; MS in Elem. Tchg., U. Mo., 1969. Cert. tchr. Iowa. Elem. tchr. North Nodaway Sch., Hopkins, Mo., 1965—66, South Page Cmty. Sch., College Springs, Iowa, 1966—73; instr. dept. elem. edn. N.W. Mo. State U., Maryville, 1973—75; mid. sch. tchr. Fox Valley Cmty. Sch., Milton, Iowa, 1975—77; gifted edn. coord., tchr. Davis County Cmty. Sch., Bloomfield, Iowa, 1977—98; ret. program dir. Bloomfield Main St., 1998—2002. Mem. gifted edn. and history day adv. com. So. Prairie Edn. Agy., Ottumwa, Iowa, 1983—98. Sec. Bloomfield Hist. Preservation Commn., 1994—; bd. dirs. Bloomfield Main St. Named Iowa History Day Tchr. of Yr., State Hist. Soc. Iowa, 1998; recipient Gov.'s Vol. award in econ. devel., State of Iowa, 2001. Mem.: NEA (life), Iowa Reading Assn. (local v.p., pres., state com. chmn. 1966—98, Iowa Reading Tchr. of Yr. 1982), Nat. Reading Assn., Nat. Trust for Hist. Preservation, Order of Ea. Star, Delta Kappa Gamma (local v.p., pres.). Republican. Methodist. Avocations: quilting, environmental restoration, gardening, antiques, reading. Office: Bloomfield Main Street 101 E Franklin Bloomfield IA 52537

COMBS, LINDA MORRISON, federal agency administrator; b. Lenoir, N.C., June 29, 1946; d. Robert Hugh and Vera Ludema (Bryant) Morrison; m. David Michael Combs, June 20, 1970. AA, Gardner Webb Coll., 1966, PhD (hon.), 1985; BS, Appalachian State U., 1968, MA, 1978; EdD, Va. Poly. Inst. and State U., 1985. Tchr., adminstr. Winston-Salem (N.C.)/Forsyth County Schs., 1968-79, sch. bd. mem., 1980-82; exec. sec., dep. U.S. Dept. Edn., Washington, 1982-84, dep. under-sec., 1984-86; pub. edn. advisor State of N.C., Raleigh, 1986-87; owner Combs Group Cons., Winston-Salem, 1987; acting asst. for mgmt. U.S. Dept. Vet. Affairs, Washington, 1987-89; asst. sec. for mgmt. U.S. Dept. Treasury, Washington, 1989—; chief financial officer EPA, Washington, 2002—. Gov.'s advocate Com. for Children and Youth, Winston-Salem, 1974-75; treas. Michael Britt for N.C. Senate, Forsyth County, 1976; v.p. Forsyth County Young Reps. Club, 1980-81. Recipient Honor and Outstanding Svc. award Combined Fed. Campaign, Washington, 1983, Alumnus of Yr. award Gardner Webb Coll., Boiling Springs, N.C., 1987, Disting. Alumnus of Yr. Appalachian State U., Boone, N.C., 1986. Mem. Forsyth County Rep. Womens Club, Pres.'s Coun. on Mgmt. Improvement (vice chair, Outstanding Leadership award 1989), Phi Delta Kappa, Delta Kappa Gamma. Republican. Baptist. Avocations: running, cooking, tennis. Office: EPA Off of the Chief Financial Officer 1200 Pennsylvania Ave NW Washington DC 20460

COMBS, SUSAN, commissioner of agriculture; married; 3 children. Grad., Vassar Coll.; JD, U. Tex. Formerly asst. dist. atty., Dallas; mem. Tex. Legislature, 1993-96; owner, operator ranch in West Tex.; commr. of agr. State of Tex., 1999—. Named Outstanding Legis. Crimefighter, Greater Dallas Crime Commn., 1993. Mem. Tex. Wildlife Assn. (bd. dirs., Tex. and Southwestern Cattle Raisers Assn. (bd. dirs.). Office: Tex Dept Agr PO Box 12847 Austin TX 78711-2847 E-mail: scommissioner@agr.state.tx.us.

COMEAU, CAROL SMITH, school system administrator; b. Berkeley, Calif., Sept. 4, 1941; d. Floyd Franklin and Bessie Caroline (Campbell) Smith; m. Dennis Rene Comeau, Dec. 27, 1962; children: Christopher, Michael, Karen. BS in Edn., U. Oreg., 1963; M in Pub. Sch. Adminstrn., U. Alaska, 1985. Third grade tchr., Springfield, Oreg., 1963-64; elem. sch. tchr. Ocean View Elem. Sch., Anchorage, 1975-84, 2d-6th grade tchr.; 6th grade tchr. Spring Hill Elem. Sch., Anchorage, 1985-86; adminstrv. intern Tudor Elem. Sch., Anchorage, 1986-87; prin. Orion Elem. Sch., Anchorage, 1987-89; prin. Spring Hill Elem. Sch., 1989-90; exec. dir. elem. edn. Anchorage Sch. Dist., 1990-93; asst. supt. instrn., 1993-2000; supt., 2000—; community activist ednl. issues. Chair Alaska PTA Edn. Commn., 1987-88; sec. bd. Frontier (Alaska) State Credit Union, 1987-91; vice-chair Anchorage United Way, 2002--, bd. dirs. KAKM pub. TV, 1990-92, Alaska Ctr. Performing Arts. Named Tchr. of Yr., Anchorage Sch. Dist. PTA Coun., 1976, Top 25 Most Powerful Alaskans, 2002, Alaska Supt. of Yr., 2003. Mem. NEA, Nat. Assn. Elem. Sch. Prins., Alaska Assn. Elem. Sch. Prins., Anchorage Edn. Assn. (Tchr. of Yr. 1986), Phi Delta Kappa, Kappa Delta Pi. Democrat. Home: 13632 Jarvi Dr Anchorage AK 99515-3934 Office: Anchorage Sch Dist Adminstrn Bldg 4600 Debarr Rd Anchorage AK 99519-6614

COMEAU, LORENE ANITA EMERSON, real estate developer; b. Haverhill, Mass., Sept. 6, 1952; d. Russell Paul and Jeannette (La Course) Emerson; m. Peter Robert Comeau, May 6, 1950; children: Stephen David, Michelle Patricia. BA with honors, Northeastern U., 1975; MBA with high honors, Simmons Coll., 2002. Lic. real estate broker. Housing rep., pub. liaison U.S. Dept. HUD, Boston, 1975-78; devel. mgr. John M. Corcoran & Co., Milton, Mass., 1978-84, v.p., 1984-94; ptnr. Corcoran Realty Assocs., Milton, 1994-2000; co-owner, treas. Refrigeration Engring. & Contracting Co., Inc., 1995—. Bd. dirs. Stoneham Coop. Bank, bd. affairs com., 1992-93, security com., 1993—, chair bldg. com., 1997—; v.p. Merrimack Valley Housing Partnership, Lowell, Mass., 1986-89. Active Fessenden Sch. Parent's Orgn., 1995—97, Shady Hill Sch. Parents Coun., 1998—99; bd. dirs. Merrimack Valley YMCA, 1982—92, vice chair, 1988—90, chair, 1990—92; mem. Andover Fair Housing Com., 1982—87, Andover Housing Partnership Com., 1990—2001, vice-chair, 2000—01; mem. Andover Planning Bd., 1993—96, Andover Master Plan Com., 1982—84, chair com. housing component and master plan, 1989—90; assoc. mem. Andover Zoning Bd. Appeals, 1984—87; fin. com., cor. bd. Merrimack Valley YMCA, Lawrence, Mass., 1984—86, 1991—94, treas. corp. fin. com., 1992—94; low income housing subcom. corp. bd., 1992—99; vice-chair adv. bd. Caritas Cmtys., 1994—97, chair adv. bd., 1998—2000; treas. Merrimack Valley YMCA, Andover, Mass., 1986—88. Mem. LWV (fin. chair Andover chpt. 1981-83, budget chair 1983-84, 86-87), New England Women in Real Estate (seminars com. 1992, cmty. rels. com. 1992-97, program com. 1996-2000, chair 1998-2000, steering com. 1997-2001, spl. events com. 1999-2000, awards com. 1999-, v.p. 1999-2000, pres. 2000-01), Nat. Assn. Indsl. and Office Properties (pub. affairs com. 1992—, vice-chair land use com. 1999), past mem. Nat. Pvt. Developers Coun., Svc. Club of Andover, Sanborn Sch. PTO (curriculum enrichment com. 1988-95) West Mid. Sch. PAC (curriculum enrichment com., women's history month 1993-95). Republican. Episcopalian. Home: PO Box 4108 Andover MA 01810-0812 Office: RECCO 39 Commercial St Medford MA 02155 E-mail: lori_comeau@yahoo.com.

COMEAUX, KATHARINE JEANNE, realtor; b. Richland, Wash., Jan. 18, 1949; d. Warren William and Ruth Irma (Remington) Gonder; m. Jack Goldwasser, May 25, 1992; children: Thelma Morrow, Aaron Warren Jacob. AA, West Valley Coll., 1970; student, San Jose State U., 1970-71. Cert. realtor. Realtor Value Realty, Cupertino, Calif., 1975-79, Valley of Calif., Cupertino, 1979-81, Coldwell Banker, Cupertino, 1981-82, Fox & Carskadon, Saratoga, Calif., 1984-90. With Los Gatos-Saratoga Bd. Realtors Polit. Action, 1984-89; v.p. Hospice of Valley Svc. League, Saratoga, 1984-89; Big Sister Big Bros./Big Sisters, San Jose, Calif., 1976-90; bd. dirs. Mountain Energy Inc., Energia Natural, Honduras, Boys and Girls Club, 1996-98, United Way of Josephine Co., 1995-98. Avocations: reading, drawing, writing, needlepoint, photography. Home: 4330 Fish Hatchery Rd Grants Pass OR 97527-9547 E-mail: catharine@hydropwr.com.

COMER, BRENDA WARMEE, elementary school educator, real estate company officer; b. Lakewood, Ohio, May 14, 1938; d. Walter Byron and Annabelle (Broderick) Warmee; m. Gerald Edmund Comer, June 30, 1962; children: Brian, James, David, Kristen. BS, Kent State U., 1961; postgrad., Bowling Green State U., 1981, 82, 83-84; reading cert., Baldwin Wallace Coll., 1987. Elem. tchr. Lorain (Ohio) Bd. Edn., 1961-63, tchr. aux. svcs. remedial reading and math., 1979-87, tchr. Chpt. I reading program, 1987—. V.p. Warmee, Inc., real estate. Vice pres. Lakeland Woman's Club, Loraine, 1972, scholarship chmn., 1973-76. Mem. NEA, Ohio Edn. Assn., Loraine Edn. Assn., Internat. Reading Assn., Daniel T. Gardner Reading Coun., AAUW (v.p. Lorain 1981-82, scholarship chmn. 1986-90). Home: 1075 Archwood Ave Lorain OH 44052-1248

COMFORT, PRISCILLA MARIA, retired college official, human resources professional; b. Ft Dix, NJ, Feb. 20, 1947; d. Jennie Rita (Manes) McGuire; children: James, Aimee. BS, Montclair State Coll., 1969; MEd,

Trenton State Coll., 1980. Cert. tchr., guidance counselor, NJ. Tchr. Burlington Twp. and City Sch., NJ, 1969-72; employment svc. interviewer NJ Dept. Labor and Industry, 1972-74; career devel. specialist, pers. tech. princ. NJ Dept. Civil Svc., Trenton, 1974—79; dir., asst., assoc. v.p. Human Resources Richard Stockton Coll. NJ, Pomona, 1979—2003, spl. asst. to pres., 2003—. Bd. govs. Bacharach Inst. for Rehab. [illegible] Assn. for Human Resources (life), C. of C. of South Jersey. Roman Catholic. Avocations: reading, travel, collecting bells, books, candles. Office: Richard Stockton Coll NJ Jim Leeds Rd Pomona NJ 08240

COMFREY, KATHLEEN MARIE, lawyer; b. Boston, July 9, 1951; d. George A. and Mary E. (Burke) C.; m. Peter Joseph McCabe, Aug. 23, 1975; children: Peter Joseph, Michael George. BA, Duquesne U., 1973; JD, U. Notre Dame, 1976. Bar: N.Y. 1977, U.S. Dist. Ct. (so. and ea. dists.) N.Y. 1977, U.S. Ct. Appeals (2nd cir.) 1988, U.S. Supreme Ct. 1991, U.S. Dist. Ct. (we. dist.) N.Y. 1994. Assoc. Shearman & Sterling, N.Y.C., 1976-84, ptnr., 1985—. Mem. ABA, Assn. Bar City of N.Y., Women's Bar Assn. State of N.Y.

COMINI, ALESSANDRA, art historian, educator; b. Winona, Minn., Nov. 24, 1934; d. Raiberto and Megan (Laird) C. BA, Barnard Coll., 1956; MA, U. Calif., Berkeley, 1964; PhD with distinction, Columbia U., 1969. Tchg. asst. U. Calif., Berkeley, 1964, vis. instr., 1967; preceptor Columbia U., 1965-66, 67-68, instr., 1968-69, asst. prof., 1969-74; vis. asst. prof. So. Methodist U., summers 1970, 72, assoc. prof. art history, 1974-75, prof., 1975—, univ. disting. prof., 1983—. Alfred Hodder resident humanist Princeton U., 1972-73; disting. vis. lectr. Oxford U., 1996; vis. asst. prof. Yale U., 1973; vis. humanist various univs.; lectr. in English, German and Italian; keynote spkr. Gewandhaus Symposia, Leipzig, Germany, 1983, 85, 87, 89, Mahler Internat Congress, Amsterdam, 1988, 95, Hamburg, 1989, Oxford, 1996, Montpellier, 1996, Internat. Mahler Fest, Boulder, Colo., 1998; featured spkr. Purchase, N.Y., 1989, Leningrad, 1990, Stockholm, 1991, Berlin, 1993, Bethoven Extravaganza, Milw., 1994, Schiele Symposium, Indpls., 1994, Helsinki, 1996, Schubertiads at Curtis Inst., Phila., Reed Coll., Oreg. and So. Meth. U., 1997, Santa Fe Opera, 1997, 98, 99, 2000, 01, 02, Mozart Internat. Symposium U. Dublin, Ireland, 1999, San Diego Mus., 1999, 2000, 01, 02, 03; panelist NEH Mus. and Pub. Programs, 1978—; vis. scholar Kalamazoo Coll., 1999. Author: Schiele in Prison, 1973, Egon Schiele's Portraits, 1974 (Nat. Book award nominee 1975, reissued 1990, Charles Rufus Morey Book award 1975), Gustav Klimt, 1975, reissued 1986, 90, 93, also German, French and Dutch edit., Egon Schiele, 1976, reissued 1986, 94, also German, French and Dutch edits., The Fantastic Art of Vienna, 1978, The Changing Image of Beethoven, 1987, Egon Schiele: Nudes, 1995, In Passionate Pursuit: A Memoir, 2004; contbg. author: World Impressionism, 1990, Käthe Kollwitz, 1992, Egon Schiele, 1994, Violetta and her Sisters, 1994, Salome, 1996, By a Finnish Fireside: An Evening with Akseli Gallen-Kallela and Gustav Mahler, 1997, The Visual Wagner, 1997, Irony and Gustav Mahler, 2000, Toys in Friend's Attic, 2001, Beethoven and His World, 2000, In Passionate Pursuit: A Memoir, 2004; contbr. numerous articles to Stagebill, Arts Mag., English Nat. Opera, Chgo. Lyric Opera; also author various catalogue and book introductions, also book revs. for N.Y. Times, Women's Art Jour. Awarded Grand Decoration of Honor for svcs. to Republic of Austria, 1990; recipient Charles Rufus Morey Book award Coll. Art Assn. Am., 1976, Laural award AAUW, 1979; named Outstanding Prof., 1977, 79, 83, 85, 86, 87, 88, 90, 98, 99, 2000, 01, 02, 03, 04, Laurence Perrine prize Phi Beta Kappa Gamma of Tex., 2003; AAUW travel fellow, 1966-87; NEH grantee, 1975; named Meadows Disting. Tchg. Prof., 1986-87, Tchr./Scholar of Yr., United Meth. Ch., 1996. Mem. ASCAP, Nat. Mus. for Women in the Arts (nat. bd. 1997—), Coll. Art Assn. Am. (bd. dirs. 1980-84), Women's Caucus for Art (bd. dirs. 1974-78, Life Achievement award 1995, Tex. Women's Hall of Fame 2002), Tex. Inst. Letters. Democrat. Home: 2900 McFarlin Blvd Dallas TX 75205-1920 Office: So Meth U Divsn Art History Dallas TX 75275 E-mail: acomini@mail.smu.edu.

COMISKEY, ANGELA PICARIELLO, accountant; b. Alexandria, Va., Oct. 4, 1971; d. Ralph C. Picariello and Martha Eileen Garretson-Worley; m. John J. Comiskey, Sept. 9, 2000. Student, George Mason U., Fairfax, Va., 1989-91; B Acctg., George Washington U., Washington, 1993. CPA, Va.; registered investment advisor, securities lic., life and health ins. lic. Fin. mgr. Linnhoff March, Houston, 1989-93; acct. Rosenblum, et. al., Rockville, Md., 1993-95; fin. cons. Merrill Lynch, Vienna, Va., 1995-96; acct. Regardie, Brooks, et. al., Bethesda, Md., 1996—. Treas. R.P. Tools, Inc., Falmouth, Va. Mem. AICPA, Va. Soc. CPAs (com. mem. 1995—), Beta Gamm Signa. Repubican. Roman Catholic. Avocations: painting, home renovating, crafts, dogs and cats. Office: Regardie Brooks & Lewis 7101 Wisconsin Ave Ste 1012 Bethesda MD 20814-4876 Home: 12839 Old Bridge Ln Woodbridge VA 22192-5044 E-mail: arp@rblcpa.com.

COMISKEY, NANCY, newspaper editor; Mng. editor features The Indpls. News; dep. mng. editor features and readership The Star & The News, Indpls., 1998—. Office: The Indpls News PO Box 145 Indianapolis IN 46206-0145

COMISKY, HOPE A. lawyer; b. Phila., Apr. 23, 1953; married; three children. BA with distinction, Cornell U., 1974; JD, U. Pa., 1977. Bar: Pa. 1977, U.S. Dist. Ct. (ea. dist.) Pa. 1978, D.C. 1979, U.S. Ct. Appeals (3d cir.) 1979, U.S. Supreme Ct. 1987, U.S. Dist. Ct. (mid. dist.) Pa. 1991, N.Y. 1993. Law clerk ea dist. U.S. Dist. Ct., Pa., 1977-78; assoc. Dilworth, Paxson, Kalish & Kauffman, Phila., 1978-84, ptnr., 1985-91, Anderson Kill & Olick, P.C., Phila., 1992-98, mng. ptnr. Phila. office, 1995-98; ptnr. labor & employment dept. Office of Pepper Hamilton, Phila., 1998—. Spkr. in field. Contbr. articles to profl. jours. Bd. dirs. Phila. Sch., 1989-2003, pres. 2001—, Fedn. Day Care Svcs., 1991-97, mem. exec. com., chmn. pers. practices com., 1985-91, Ctr. for Literacy, 1996—, chmn. pers. com. 2000—, dir. Women's Law Project, 1998—, Fedn. Early Learning Svcs., 2003—; mem. Phila. Regional Employment Adv. Com. Am. Arbitration Assn., 1996. Mem. Am. Arbitration Assn. (comml. and employment arbitrator), Phi Beta Kappa, Mortar Bd. Office: Pepper Hamilton LLP 3000 Two Logan Sq 18th & Arch Sts Philadelphia PA 19103-2799

COMMIRE, ANNE, playwright, writer, editor; b. Wyandotte, Mich., Aug. 11, 1939; BS, Eastern Mich. U., 1961; postgrad., Wayne State U., NYU. Author: (plays) Shay, 1973, Transatlantic Bridge, 1977, Put Them All Together, 1978, Sunday's Red, 1982, Melody Sisters, 1983, Starting Monday, 1988; author: (with Mariette Hartley) (book) Breaking the Silence, 1990; editor: Something About the Author, 1970—90, Yesterday's Authors of Books for Children, 1977—78, Historic World Leaders, 1994, Women in World History: A Biographical Encyclopedia, 1999—2002 (Dartmouth medal, 2002). Recipient Eugene O'Neill Theatre award, 1973, 1978, 1988; grantee, Creative Artists Program, 1975; playwriting grant, Rockefeller Found., 1979. Mem.: PEN, Writers Guild Am., Dramatists Guild, Authors Guild. Home: 11 Stanton St Waterford CT 06385-1400

COMOLA, JACQUELINE PETERMANN, management consultant; b. Yazoo City, Miss., Aug. 8, 1937; d. John Winfred and Flo (Pearce) Petermann; divorced; children: James Paul Comola II, Jon Ronald Comola. BA in Polit. Sci., U. Tex., 1969, MA in Urban Inst., 1975, postgrad. in Orgn. Behaviour. Dir. tng. U.S. Dept. Energy, Dallas, Tex., 1973-74; project dir. U.S. Office Pers. Mgmt., Dallas, 1974-79, Am. Productivity and Quality Ctr., Houston, 1979-82, 85-86, v.p. White Collar Improvement, 1986-90, sr. v.p. Adv. Svc. and Rsch., 1990-91, dir. Internat. Svcs. Practice, 1991-93; exec. v.p. Psychol. Cons., Inc., Houston, 1982-83; pres. Collaborative Resources, Inc., Houston, 1993—. Rev. panel U.S. Dept. Edn., Washington, 1990-93; task force Gov.'s Task Force on Productivity Improvement, Austin, Tex., 1989; bd. dirs. Internat. Coaching Lab., Coach Lab Interant., Bradmark Techs., Am. Productivity and Quality Ctr., Gulf Coast Newcomers Assn.; exec. bd. Bradmark Tech. Co-author: Improving Productivity in Healthcare, 1988, Educating for Excellence, 1991; contbg. author: Handbook of Management Audits, 1993; contbr. articles to profl. jours. Bd. dirs. City Planning and Zoning Bd., Euless, Tex., City Libr., Bedford, Tex.; pres. PTA, Bedford. Mem.: Am. Mgmt. Assn., ASQC, Inst. Noetic Sci., World Future Soc., Mus. of Art, Coast C. of C., Ctr. for Photography, Founders Bus. Club. Episcopalian. Avocations: art collecting, promoting and painting, travel, family history rsch.

COMOSS, PATRICIA B. cardiac rehabilitation nurse, consultant; b. Shamokin, Pa., Apr. 20, 1947; d. William J. and Lucille M. (Shipulski) McCall; m. Eugene J. Comoss, Nov. 25, 1970. Diploma, St. Joseph's Hosp., Reading, Pa., 1968; BS in Health Care Mgmt., Pa. State U., Harrisburg, 1982. CCU staff nurse Polyclinic Med. Ctr., Harrisburg; head nurse, cardiac rehab. Rehab. Hosp., Mechanicsburg, Pa.; dir. edn. AMSCO/Rehab., Mechanicsburg; founder, pres. Nursing Enrichment Consultants, Harrisburg. Co-author: Cardiac Rehabilitation: A Comprehensive Nursing Approach, 1979; co-editor: Cardiac Rehabilitation: A Guide to Practice in the 21st Century, 1999; contbr. articles to profl. jours. Fellow Am. Assn. Cardiovascular and Pulmonary Rehab. (bd. dirs. 1986-88, v.p. 1988-90, pres.-elect 1990-91, pres. 1992, chair fed. project on clin. practice guidelines on cardiac rehab. 1992-95); mem. ANA, AACCN, Am. Coll. Sports Medicine, Am. Heart Assn. Home: 4100 Elmerton Ave Harrisburg PA 17109-1327

COMPSTON, MARION F. small business owner; b. San Francisco, June 5, 1928; d. Stephen James Gilbert and Lorene Alice Schenkel; m. James Compston, Nov. 13, 1948; children: Linda, Kathryn, Mary, Garey, Nancy, Sharon. Attended, San Jose State, 1946-48. Cert. tchr. Diocese of Reno Dept. Relious Edn. Kindergarten tchr. Nev. Dept. Edn., Carson City, 1969-73; owner, bookkeeper Wellington (Nev.) Sta. Resort, 1969—. Dir. religious edn. St. John's Cath. Ch., Wellington, 1972—; mem. (life) Nev. PTA, pres., 1972; active, sec.-treas. parish coun., 1990—; active, treas. Smith Valley Cmty. Hall Bd., Wellington, 1973-98; active, v.p. Lyon County Br. Libr. Bd., Wellington, 1990-98; active, treas. Lyon Co. Park and Recreation Bd., 1988-90; leader 4-H, 1960-85. Mem. Beta Sigma Phi Internat. Republican. Avocations: gardening, stamp collecting, antiques. Home: PO Box 36 Wellington NV 89444-0036 Office: Wellington Station Resort 2855 State Route 208 Wellington NV 89444-9701

COMPTON, DORIS MARTHA, lay worker; b. Eudora, Kans., July 9, 1927; d. Roscoe John and Mabel Ann Robinson; 1 child, Christine Lee Compton-Smith. BA, Ft. Hays State U., Hays, Kans., 1949; MA, U. Ark., Fayetteville, 1951; Cert. Lay Pastor, Sterling (Kans.) Coll., 2000. Commissioned Lay Pastor Presbytery of No. Kans./Kans., 2000; life credential tchr. Dept. of Edn./Kans., 1951. Tchr. of English, speech, journalism, drama, and Latin Kans. Pub. Schs., Winfield, Ashland, Marysville, Washington, 1951—71; English instr. Am. U. Cairo, 1972—74; founder and dir. Colegio Internacional Miguel Otero Silva, Ciudad Guayana, Venezuela, 1975—80; speech and linguistics U. P.R./Interamerican U., Rio Piedras, PR, 1982—84; temp. English instr. Kans. State U., Manhattan, 1987—89; chmn. English dept. Ramses Coll. for Girls, Cairo, 1989—93; stated supply pastor Little Blue River Parish, Narka, Kans., 1993—97; commd. lay pastor Faith United Ch. Presbyn., Clifton, Kans., 2000—. English instr. for an immersion sch. for ESL Fordham U., San Juan, PR, 1982; completed evaluation for Commonwealth HS, Rio Pedro, P.R. Mid. States Assn., Phila., 1981—82, mem. evaluation team for St. Dunstan's Sch., St. Croix, U.S. Virgin Islands, 1982. Author: (book of poetry) Whisper In The Pines (awards for individual poems); contbr. poems to lit. jours. ($1000 by Am. Poetry Assn., San Francisco, 1985, $200 by Internat. Soc. Poets, Washington, D.C., 1996, First Pl. by Kans. Author's Club, 2000); singer: (solo vocal concerts) Egypt, Venezuela, Am.; performer: (47 dramatic prodns.) Egypt, Venezuela, P.R., Am. Spkr. Presbyn. Ch., 81 cities in Kans., Nebr., Iowa, Mo., Ill.; author of VBS curriculum Presbyn. Ch., Clifton, Kans., 2001—03; display of art and antiquities for schools pub. schs., 5 cities in Kans., 1996—2003. Recipient numerous scholarships for internat. peacemaking, Presbyn. Ch., 1994—. Mem.: Synod of Mid Am. (assoc.; commr. of higher edn. 2001—03), Presbytery of No. Kans. (assoc.), Clifton (Kans.) C. of C. (assoc.). Presbyn. Avocations: music, collecting art and antiquities, writing poetry, travel, caring for two grandchildren. Home: 207 East Bartlett Clifton KS 66937 Office: Faith United Ch Presbyterian 200 West Hwy Clifton KS 66937

COMPTON, MARY BEATRICE BROWN (MRS. RALPH THEODORE COMPTON), public relations executive, writer; b. Washington, May 25, 1923; d. Robert James and Abia Eliza (Stone) Brown; m. Ralph Theodore Compton, Mar. 18, 1961. Grad. Thayer Acad., Chandler Sch., Leland Powers Sch. Radio, TV and Theatre, Boston, 1942. Radio program dir. Converse Co., Malden, Mass., 1942-45; head radio continuity dept. Sta. WAAB, Yankee Network, Worcester, Mass., 1945-46; asst. dir. radio Leland Powers Sch. Radio, TV and Theatre, Boston, 1946-49, dir., 1949-51; program asst. Sta. KNBH, Hollywood, Calif., 1951-52; v.p. Acorn Film Co., Boston, 1953-54; dir. women's communications, editor Program Notes, radio interviewer NAM, N.Y.C., 1954-61. Celebrities pub. rels. Nat. Citizens for Nixon, 1968, Kennedy Ctr. Pub. Info., 1985-89, Washington Nat. Cathedral Visitor's Svcs., 1989—2001. Mem. Soc. Old Plymouth Colony Descs., Magna Carta Dames, Congl. Country Club (Bethesda, Md.), White House Hist. Assn. Home: 15300 Wallbrook Ct Apt 3F Silver Spring MD 20906-1455

COMPTON, NORMA HAYNES, retired university dean, artist; b. Washington, Nov. 16, 1924; d. Thomas N. and Lillian (Laffin) Haynes; m. William Randall Compton, Mar. 27, 1946; children: William Randall, Anne Elizabeth. AB, George Washington U., 1950; MS, U. Md., 1957, PhD, 1962; D of Letters, Purdue U., 1996. Rschr. Julius Garfinckel & Co., Washington, 1955; tchr. Montgomery Blair High Sch., Silver Spring, Md., 1955-57; instr. U. Md., 1957-60, teaching and rsch. fellow Inst. Child Study, 1960-61, assoc. prof., 1962-63; psychology extern St. Elizabeths Hosp., Washington, 1962-63; assoc. prof. Utah State U., 1963-64, prof., 1964-68, head dept. clothing and textiles, 1963-68, dir. Inst. for Rsch. on Man and His Personal Environment, 1967-68; dean Sch. Home Econs. Auburn (Ala.) U., 1968-73; dean Sch. Consumer and Family Scis. Purdue U., 1973-87, prof. family studies, 1987-90; faculty The Edn. Ctr., Longboat Key, Fla., 1991-2000, mem. ednl. adv. bd., 1995-98. Cons. Burgess Pub. Co., Mpls., 1975-81, Nat. Advt. Rev. Bd., N.Y.C., 1978-82; bd. dirs. Armour & Co., Phoenix, 1976-82, Home Hosp., Lafayette, Ind., 1983-89; adv. com. Women's Resource Ctr. of Sarasota, Fla., 1992-96; chair Adv. Commn. Status Women, Sarasota, 1993-96; mem. advocates coun. Family Law Network Sarasota, 1994—; exec. bd. Sarasota-Manatee Phi Beta Kappa Assn., 1996-99; bd. trustees Plymouth Harbor, Inc., 2003—. Author: (with Olive Hall) Foundations of Home Economics Research, 1972, (with John Touliatos) Approaches to Child Study, 1983, Research Methods in Human Ecology/Home Economics, 1988; contbr. articles to profl. jours. Mem. exec. coun. Plymouth Harbor Residents Assn., Sarasota, 2001—, bd. trustees, 2003—. Recipient Woman of Impact Lifetime Achievement award, 1997. Mem.: PEO, AAUW, APA, Nat. League Am. Pen Women (v.p. Sarasota br.), Am. Assn. Family and Consumer Sci., Sigma Xi, Phi Beta Kappa, Psi Chi, Omicron Nu, Phi Kappa Phi. Congregational United Ch. Christ. E-mail: normahc@aol.com.

COMRIE, SANDRA MELTON, human resource executive; b. Plant City, Fla., Sept. 15, 1940; d. Finis and Estelle (Black) Melton; m. Allan Crecelius; children: Shannon Melissa, Colleen Megan. BA, UCLA, 1962, grad. exec. program, 1984. Div. mgr. City of L.A., 1973-77, asst. pers. dir., 1977-84; v.p. Transam. Life Cos., L.A., 1984-89; chief operating officer Treacy & Rhodes Consultants, Solana Beach, Calif., 1989-92; exec. dir. Reward Strategy Group, Inc., Del Mar, Calif., 1992-98. Bd. dirs. Found. for Employment and Disability, Sacramento, Clif.; mem. Asian Pacific Employment Task Force, Los Angeles, 1986-89. Bd. dirs. L.A. Urban League, 1985-92, Vols. of Am.-L.A., 1985-89; active United Way Downtown Bus. Consortium, Child Care Task Force, L.A., 1985-86; mem. adv. bd. L.A. City Child Com., 1987-89. Recipient [illegible] Woman of Achievement award Soroptimists of Los Angeles, 1979. Mem. Internat. Pers. Mgmt. Assn. (mem. assessment coun., co-chair program com. for 1982 nat. conf., chair human rights com. 1983, pres. 1985), So. Calif. Pers. Mgmt. Assn., Planning Forum, Human Resource Planning Soc., Soc. for Human Resource Mgmt., Am. Compensation Assn., Am. Mgmt. Assn., L.A. C. of C. (human resources com. 1986-89). Democrat. Avocation: travel. Office: Reward Strategy Group Inc 9276 Scranton Rd Ste 120 San Diego CA 92121

COMSTOCK, AMY L. social services administrator; BA, Bard Coll.; JD, U. Michigan. Attorney U.S. Dept. of Education, 1988—93; asst. gen. counsel for ethics Dept. of Education, 1993—98; assoc. counsel to the Pres. White House, 1998—2000; dir. U.S. Office of Govt. Ethics, 2000—03; exec. dir. Parkinson's Action Network, Washington, 2003—. Office: Parkinsons Action Network Ste 900 1000 Vermont Ave NW Washington DC 20005

COMSTOCK, ELIZABETH J. marketing executive; married; 2 children. BA, Coll. of William and Mary. Program dir. Nat. Cable TV Assn., Washington, Arlington (Va.) Cmty. TV; publicist, media mgr. NBC, Washington, 1986, corp. comm. mgr. N.Y.C.; publicity dir. media rels. Turner Broadcasting, N.Y.C., 1990-92; dir. entertainment publicity CBS/Broadcast Group, N.Y.C., 1992-93; v.p. news media rels. NBC, N.Y.C., 1993-96, sr. v.p. corp. comm. and media rels., 1996—98; v.p., corp. communications GE Corp., N.Y.C., 1998—2003, corp v.p. mktg., chief mktg. officer, 2003—. Named Mktg. Executive of the Year, BtoB mag., 2003, PR Professional of the Year, PR Week mag., 2004; recipient Clarion award Women in Comm., 1995. Office: GE Corp 3135 Easton Turnpike Fairfield CT 06828

COMSTOCK, REBECCA ANN, lawyer; b. Mpls., Mar. 13, 1950; d. Clark Franklin and Ruth Carolyn (Sundt) C. Student, Conn. Coll., 1968—70; BA summa cum laude, U. Minn., 1973; JD Order of St. Ives, U. Denver, 1977; MBA, Northwestern U., 2002. Bar: Minn. 1978, U.S. Dist. Ct. Minn., U.S. Ct. Appeals (8th cir.). Atty. Dorsey & Whitney LLP, Mpls., 1982—. Bd. dirs. St. Paul Chamber Orch., 1996-2001, Big Bros./Big Sisters Greater Twin Cities, 2003—. Mem. ABA, Minn. Bar Assn., Hennepin County Bar Assn., Legal Aid Soc. Mpls. (bd. dirs. 1988-93), Nat. Assn. Women Bus. Owners, Licensing Exec. Soc. (USA and Can.), Environ. Law Inst. Avocations: skiing, biking, golf, music, theatre. Office: Dorsey & Whitney LLP 50 S 6th St Minneapolis MN 55402-1498 E-mail: comstock.becky@dorsey.com.

CONANT, TARA PATRICIA, photographer; b. Boston, July 13, 1964; d. Ronald and Patricia C. (Madsen) Conant. BA, Westfield State, 1987; MFA, Bard Coll., 1996. Owner TC Photography, Westfield, Mass., 1994—. Adj. faculty Westfield State Coll., Holyoke C.C. Author, photographer "Murder Sites of Twenty Women", 1995; one-woman shows include Marcuse Gallery, N.Y., Westfield State Coll., Mass.; exhbns. include Danforth Mus. Art, MAss., Soho Photo Gallery, NYC, Orange County Ctr. Contemporary Art, Calif. Bard fellow, 1993-95. Mem. Kodak Profl. Photographers Assn., Ilforo Photographers Assn. Avocations: mountain biking, tennis, gardening. Home: 13 Heritage Ln Westfield MA 01085-3404

CONAWAY, JANE ELLEN, elementary school educator; b. Fostoria, Ohio, July 9, 1941; d. Robert and Virginia C.. BA in Elem. Edn., Mary Manse Coll., Toledo, Ohio, 1966—67; MEd in Elem. Edn., U. Ariz., 1969; postgrad. in reading, U. Toledo, 1975—77; postgrad., U. Wis., 1987—. Cert. reading specialist in diagnostic and remedial reading Wis. Tchr. Sandusky pub. schs., Ohio, 1969—70; coord. 1st grade small group instrn. program St. Mary's Grade Sch., Sandusky, 1970—71; tchr. Chpt. I remedial reading Eastwood Local schs., Pemberville, Ohio, 1971—87; dist. dir. Right to Read program; reading specialist Middleton-Cross Plains (Wis.) Area Sch. Dist., 1987—. Mem.: Madison Area Reading Coun., Middleton Edn. Assn., Wis. Edn. Assn., NEA. Home: 1302 Wexford Dr Waunakee WI 53597-1842 Office: Middleton Cross Plains Sch Dist Sauk Trail Sch 2205 Branch St Middleton WI 53562-2840 Office Phone: 608-829-9190.

CONAWAY, MARGARET GRIMES (PEGGY CONAWAY), library administrator; b. Minot, N.D., June 6, 1944; d. John Francis and Veronica Ann (McCarthy) Grimes; m. Steven L. Conaway, July 15, 1967 (div. July 1991); 1 child, Anne Marie. BS in Edn., Minot State Coll., 1966; MA in English, San Jose State U., 1978, MLS, 1988. Cert. secondary tchr., Calif.; cert. c.c. tchr., Calif. Instr. Boise (Idaho) Ind. H.S., 1966-67, Santa Maria (Calif.) Joint Union H.S. Dist., 1967-72; libr. asst. San Jose (Calif.) Pub. Libr., 1984-86, libr., 1986-89, sr. libr., 1989-97, divsn. mgr., 1997—2000; libr. dir. Los Gatos (Calif.) Pub. Libr., 2000—. Oper. design project mgr. San Jose Pub. Libr./San Jose State U. Joint Libr., 1998—2000; vice chmn. adminstrv. coun. Silicon Valley Libr. Sys., 2001—02, chmn. adminstrv. coun., 2002—03. Author: (Ency. of Lib.and Info.Sci.) Shared Libraries, 2003, (libr. jour.) One Reference Service for Everyone?, 2000. Recipient Helen Putnam award for excellence League of Calif. Cities, 1997. Mem. ALA, Calif. Libr. Assn., Pub. Libr. Assn., Libr. Adminstrn. and Mgmt. Assn. Avocations: writing, history, travel. Office: Los Gatos Pub Libr 110 E Main St Los Gatos CA 95030 Office Phone: 408-354-6895.

CONDIE, CAROL JOY, anthropologist, research facility administrator; b. Provo, Utah, Dec. 28, 1931; d. LeRoy and Thelma (Graff) Condie; m. M. Kent Stout, June 18, 1954 (div. Jan. 2003); children: Carle Ann, Erik Roy, Paula Jane. BA in Anthropology, U. Utah, 1953; MEd in Elem. Edn., Cornell U., 1954; PhD in Anthropology, U. N.Mex., 1973. Edn. coordinator Maxwell Mus. Anthropology, U. N.Mex., Albuquerque, 1973, interpretation dir., 1974-77; asst. prof. anthropology U. N.Mex., 1975-77; cons. anthropologist, 1977-78; pres. Quivira Research Ctr., Albuquerque, 1978—. Cons. anthropologist U.S. Congl. Office Tech. Assessment, chair Archeol. Resources Planning Adv. Com., Albuquerque, 1985-86; leader field seminars Crow Canyon Archeol. Ctr., 1986—; appointee Albuquerque dist. adv. coun., bur. land mgmt. U.S. Dept. Interior, 1989; study leader Smithsonian Instn. Tours, 1991; mem. Albuquerque Heritage Conservation Adv. Com., 1992. Author: The Nighthawk Site: A Pithouse Site on Sandia Pueblo Land, Bernalillo County, New Mexico, 1982, Five Sites on the Pecos River Road, 1985, Data Recovery at Eight Archeological Sites on the Rio Nutritas, 1992, Data Recovery at Eight Archeological Sites on Cabresto Road Near Questa, 1992, Archeological Survey in the Rough and Ready Hills/Picacho Mountain Area, Dona Ana County, New Mexico, 1993, Archeological Survey on the Canadian River, Quay County, New Mexico, 1994, Archeological Testing at LA 103387, Nizhoni Extension, Gallup, McKinley County, New Mexico, 1995, Two Archeological Sites on San Felipe Pueblo Land, New Mexico, 1996, Four Archeological Sites at La Cienega, Santa Fe County, New Mexico, 1996, A Brief History of Berino, Berino Siding, and Early Mesilla Valley Agriculture, Dona Ana County, New Mexico, 1997; (with M. Kent Stout) Historical and Architectural Study of the Old Peralta Elementary School, Valencia County, New Mexico, 1997, Archeological Survey of 720 Acres on Ball Ranch, Sandoval County, New Mexico, 1998; (with H. H. Franklin and P. J. McKenna) Results of Testing at Three Sites on Tesuque Pueblo Land, Santa Fe County, New Mexico, 1999, Cultural Resources Investigations at the Old Roswell Airport for the Proposed Cielo Grande Recreation Area, Chaves County, New Mexico, 2000, Archeological Survey in Las Lomas de la Bolsa, Santa Fe County, N.Mex., 2001, A Plethora of Walls...the Vigil Properties, Old Town Albuquerque, 2002, (with Susan DeWitt for the City of Albuquerque) Doves Along the Ditchbank, La Orilla de la Acequia Historic District (Albuquerque), 2003; co-editor: Anthropology in the Desert West, 1986. Mem. Downtown Core Area Schs. Com.,

Albuquerque, 1982. Ford Found. fellow, 1953-54; recipient Am. Planning Assn. award, 1985-86, Gov.'s award, 1986, Archaeol. Achievement award Archaeol. Soc. N.Mex., 1998. Fellow Am. Anthrop. Assn.; mem. Soc. Am. Archeology (chmn. native Am. rels. com. 1983-85), Archeol. Soc. N.Mex. (bd. dirs. 2001--), N.Mex. Archeol. Coun. (pres. 1982-83, hist. preservation award 1988), Albuquerque Archeol. Soc. (pres. 1992), Maxwell Mus. Assn. (bd. dirs. 1980-83), Las Arañas Spinners and Weavers Guild (pres. 1972), N.Mex. Heritage Preservation Alliance, Archeol. Conservancy (bd. dirs.), 2003-. Democrat. Avocations: spinning, weaving, gardening. Home and Office: Quivira Research Ctr 1809 Notre Dame Dr NE Albuquerque NM 87106-1011

CONDIT, LINDA FAULKNER, economist; b. Denver, May 30, 1947; d. Claude Winston and Nancy Isobel (McCallum) Faulkner; m. John Michael Condit, Dec. 20, 1970; 1 child, David Devin. BA, U. Ark., 1969; MA, U. Wis., 1970; postgrad., U. Minn., 1974-77. Rsch. asst. U. Wis., Madison, 1969—70; economist St. Louis Fed. Res. Bank, 1971—73; ops. analyst No. States Power co., Mpls., 1973-76; energy economist, 1976—78; from ecomonist to v.p. Pennzoil Co., Houston, 1978—95, v.p., 1995—98; v.p., corp. sec. Pennzoil-Quaker State Co., Houston, 1998—2002. Econ. cons. Jr. Achievement, 1983. Recipient Alumni award U. Ark., 1969. Mem. Internat. Assn. Energy Economists (pres., v.p., treas.), Nat. Assn. Bus. Economists, Internat. Bus. Coun. (v.p.), Am. Econ. Assn., N.Am. Soc. Corp. Planners, Am. Soc. Corp. Secs. (membership chmn.), Hits Theatre (bd. dirs.), Corp. Alliance To Eliminate Ptnr. Violence (bd. dirs.), Leadership Am., Harvard Discussion Group Indsl. Economists, Forst Club, River Oaks Women's Breakfast Club (v.p., pres.), Mortar Bd., Phi Beta Kappa, Kappa Alpha Theta. Home: 11822 Village Park Cir Houston TX 77024-4418

CONDITT, MARGARET KAREN, research scientist, policy analyst; b. Mobile, Ala., Aug. 7, 1953; m. David Joseph Bruno, Feb. 13, 1988; 2 stepchildren: Josh, Holly. BS in Chemistry, U. Ala., Tuscaloosa, 1975; PhD in Chemistry, U. Colo., 1984. Field hydrologist U.S. Geol. Survey, Tuscaloosa, 1975; sci. aide II Geol. Survey Ala., Tuscaloosa, 1975-77; tchg. asst. U. Ala., Tuscaloosa, 1977-79; rsch. asst. U. Colo., Boulder, 1979-84; sr. scientist Procter & Gamble, Cin., 1984—. Reviewer sci. edn. grant proposals NSF, Washington, 1988; mem. water sci. and tech. bd. com. Nat. Acad. Scis., Washington, 1989-91. Author: (chpt.) Advanced Techniques in Synthetic Fuels Analysis, 1983; contbr. articles to profl. jours. Intern Colo. Gov.'s Sci. and Tech. Adv. Coun., 1981—83; appointee Liberty Twp. Bd. Zoning Appeal, 1994—97; elected trustee Liberty Twp., 1998—2001. Recipient fellowship Mining and Mineral Resources and Rsch. Inst., 1980, Rsch. fellowship U. Colo. Grad. Sch., 1981, Browns-Rickett grant AAUW, 1982. Mem. Am. Chem. Soc. Roman Catholic. Avocations: collecting antiques, boy scouts. Home: 6959 Rock Springs Dr Liberty Township OH 45011-9376

CONDON, ANN BLUNT, psychotherapist; b. Brockton, Mass., Sept. 25, 1938; d. Hugh Francis and Ann Collins Blunt; m. John Weston Condon, Jan. 2, 1965 (div. Feb. 1966); 1 child, Pamela Condon Porter. BA, Newton Coll. Sacred Heart, 1960; MSW, Boston U., 1981. LCSW Mass. Pvt. practice psychotherapy, Centerville, Mass., 1982—; pvt. career and edn. cons., 1998—; pvt. writing coach, 2000—. Seminar leader Landmark Edn., Quincy, Mass., 1986—92; workshop leader Greening Prodns., Centerville, 1988—. V.p. Svc. Employees Internat. Union, Boston, 1965—69; town meeting mem. Town of Barnstable, 1973—75; mem. bd. trustees Cape Cod Cmty. Coll., 1973—81. Mem. AAUW (AAUW, diplomate), Altrusa Club Cape Cod (founding mem., 1st pres.). Democrat. Roman Catholic. Avocations: gardening, writing, cooking, baseball. Office: PO Box 58 7 Woodvale Ln Centerville MA 02632

CONDOS, BARBARA SEALE, real estate broker, developer, investor; b. Kenedy, Tex., Feb. 24, 1925; d. John Edgar and Bess Rochelle (Ainsworth) Seale; m. George James Condos, Dec. 24, 1955 (dec.); 1 child, James Alexander. MusB magna cum laude, U. Incarnate Word, San Antonio, 1946. Lic. real estate broker, Tex. Ptnr., CEO Mountain Top-V.I. Devel. Properties, V.I., 1977-85; pres. Investment Realty Co., L.C., San Antonio, 1978—. Choreographer, dancer San Antonio Symphony's Youth Concerts and Opera Festival; actress San Antonio Little Theatre-Patio-Players 1948—. Trustee San Antonio Little Theatre, 1953-76; trustee Incarnate Word Coll., 1977-89, vice chair, 1980-82, trustee emerita, 1989—; mem. coun. McNay Mus., 1986—, chmn. coun., 1987—, chair coun., 1988—, trustee, 1989-97, trustee emerita, 1997—; bd. dirs. San Antonio Performing Arts Assn., 1978—; mng. trustee Russell Hill Rogers Fund for Arts. Mem. Internat. Real Estate Fedn., Internat. Real Estate Inst., Nat. Assn. Realtors, Tex. Assn. Realtors, San Antonio Bd. Realtors, Tex. Watercolor Soc. (signature mem.), The Argyle Club. Avocation: painting. Home: 217 Geneseo Rd San Antonio TX 78209-5913 Office: Investment Realty Co 1635 NE Loop 410 San Antonio TX 78209-1625 E-mail: bsc@investmentrealty.com.

CONDRAN, CYNTHIA MARIE, gospel musician; b. Avon Park, Fla., Apr. 29, 1953; d. Kenneth Dale and Ruth Mae (Garber) Grubb; m. Lee Light Condran, July 3, 1971. Student, Lebanon Valley Coll., 1970—72. Piano tchr., Sebring, Fla., 1968-70, Annville, Pa., 1971—; gospel musician, writer, arranger Condran Music Co., Annville, Pa., 1972—, also recording engr. Writer comml. jingles. Sang by spl. invitation at Elipse of The White House, 1982; composer The Only Thing Holding You Back, 1977, Just A Few More Rivers, 1975, The Patchwork Quilt, 1978, Freedom, 1976, The Little Things, 1980, We're America, Heavens Fiesta, He's the Lord of Everyday, 1989, I've Never Known Such Love, 1990, I Just Want To Talk To You, 1990, Sweep Our Sins, 1990, Eternal Friends, 1991, The Precious Jewels At Christmas Time, 1992, Lost On My Way Back Home, 1993, I Believe in the Power of Love, 1993, To Speak Your Name, 1994, Forever, 1994, We Praise You Lord, 1994, R.D. #11, Heaven, 1996, Surprise, 1997, Patience, 1998, His Healing Blood, 1999, Back Door Blessings, 2000. Recipient Contemporary Country Artists of Yr. award Internat. Country Gospel Music Assn., 1995, Internat. Star Music award, 1997, Contemporary Country Duo of Yr. award, 1999, Entertainer of Yr. Silver Heart award, 1999, Female Vocalist of Yr. northeast region, 1999, Golden Heart award for the Nat. Female Vocalist of Yr., 1999; named Female Vocalist of the Yr., Country Gospel Music Assn., 1999, Reciter of the Yr., Country Gospel Music Assn., 2000, 2002. Mem. Gospel Music Assn., Broadcast Music Inc., Christian Bus. and Prof. Women (music chmn.), So. Gospel Music Guild. Republican. Avocations: skiing, golf, swimming, tennis, racquetball. Home: 935 N Route 934 Annville PA 17003-9803 Office Phone: 717-867-4567. Personal E-mail: leecindyco@aol.com.

CONDREA, LYDIA, linguist, educator, researcher; b. Chisinau, Moldova, May 26, 1949; came to U.S., 1988; d. Vladislav and Ecaterina (Rusu-Ciobanu) Chiricenco; m. Arcady Condrea, June 8, 1980 (dec.); children: Gabriela, Daniel. MA in French Philology, BA in Edn., Chisnau State U., 1977; MA in Romance Linguistics, U. Wash., 1990, PhC, 1993. Cert. tchr., Wash. Tchr. English, Italian, French, Spanish, Russian, Romanian various schs., Moldova, Ukraine, 1977-78; lectr. French, English Art Inst., Chisinau, 1978-80; tchr. French U. Wash., Seattle, 1988-93; interpreter French, Romanian, Russian Seattle Mcpl. Ct. & Berlitz, 1989—; adj. faculty mem. Wash. Acad. Langs. and Seattle Pacific U., 1993—. Dir. French studies Canoe French Camp, San Juan Islands, Wash., 1995, West Seattle H.S., 1997—. Avocations: weaving, painting, playing piano. Home: 12563 B Densmore Ave N Seattle WA 98133-7730

CONDRILL, JO ELLARESA, freelance/self-employed small business owner, writer, consultant; b. Hull, Tex., Oct. 25, 1935; d. Freddie (dec.) and Ida (Donatto) Founteno; m. Edwin Leon Ellis, Jan. 9, 1955 (div. 1979); children: Michael Edwin, James Alcia, Resa Ann, Thomas Matthew; m. Donald Richard Condrill, Sept. 21, 1980 (div. 1985). BSBA, Our Lady of the Lake U., 1982; MS in Pub. Adminstrn., Ctrl. Mich. U., 1987; grad., U.S. Army War Coll., 1993. Editorial asst. Airman Mag., San Antonio, 1978; mgmt. analyst San Antonio Air Logistics Ctr., San Antonio, 1979-82; inventory mgr. ground fuels Detachment 29, Alexandria, Va., 1982-83; logistics plans officer Mil. Dist. Washington, 1983-85, chief logistics plans ops. and mgmt., 1985-88; chief integration br. Office of the Dep. Chief of Staff for Logistics, 1990-95; deputy chief logistics plans and ops. div. Hdqs. U.S. Army, The Pentagon, 1995-97; owner Seminars by Jo, Alexandria, Va., 1984-86, GoalMinds, Beverly Hills, Calif., 1997—. Author: Leadership: From Vision to Victory in Six Powerful Steps, 1996, 101 Ways to Improve Your Communication Skills Instantly, 1998, A Millennium Primer: Take Charge of Your Life, 1999, From Book Signing to Best Seller: An Insider's Guide to a Successful Low-Cost Booksigning Tour, 2001 (Best Writer's Ref. Guide, Bay Area Ind. Pubs. Assn. 2001-2002), Take Charge of Your Life: Dare to Pursue Your Dreams, 2003. Civilian v.p. student coun. Army War Coll., Carlisle, Pa. Recipient decoration for Exceptional Civilian Svc., U.S. Army, 1997; Best Speaker award Def. Logistics Agy. Mem. NAFE, Nat. Spkrs. Assn., Rotary Internat., Toastmasters Internat. (dist. 27 gov. 1991-92, internat. dir. 1994-96, top ranking dist. gov. in internat. orgn. 1991-92, Internat. Pres. Disting. Dist. award 1991-92). Roman Catholic. Avocations: travel, dance, reading. Office: Goal Minds 11301 W Olympic # 345 Los Angeles CA 90064 E-mail: info@jocondrill.com.

CONDRON, BARBARA O'GUINN, metaphysics educator, school administrator, publisher; b. New Orleans, May 1, 1953; d. Bill Gene O'Guinn and Marie Gladys (Newbill) Jackson; m. Daniel Ralph Condron, Feb. 29, 1992; 1 child, Hezekiah Daniel. BJ, U. Mo., 1973; MA, Coll. Metaphysics, Springfield, Mo., 1977, DD, D in Metaphysics, 1979. Cert. counselor; ordained min. Interfaith Ch. Metaphysics. Field rep. Sch. Metaphysics, New Orleans, 1978-80; dir. Interfaith Ch. Metaphysics, 1884-89; pres. Nat. Hdqs., Sch. Metaphysics, Windyville, Mo., 1980-84, prof., 1989—, chmn. bd. dirs., 1991-98, mem. coun. elders, bd. govs. internat. edn., 1998—; CEO SOM Pub., Windyville, 1989-98. Guest lectr., instr. Wichita (Kans.) State U., 1977, U. New Orleans, 1979, La. State U., 1981, Am. Bus. Womens Assn., 1982, U. Mo., Kansas City, 1984, Unity Village, 1985, Kans. Dept. Social Svcs. Conf., Topeka, 1986, U. Mo., Columbia and St. Louis, 1986, Mo. Tchrs. Conf., St. Louis, 1991, U. Okla., Norman, 1988—89, Parliament of World's Religions, Chgo., 1993, Mo. Writers Guild Conf., 2001, many others; creator Sch. Metaphysics Assocs., 1992; initiator Universal Hour Peace, 1995; initiator, internat. coord. Nat. Dream Hotline, 1988—; radio and TV guest, 1977—; creator Maker's Dozen-Visionary Schs. Recognition, 1999, Taraka Yoga Psi Counseling Program; initiator Spiritual Focus Sessions, 1997—; internat. coord. Peace Dome dedication and One Voice Initiative, 2003, Soc. for Intuitive Rsch., 2003—. Author: What will I do Tomorrow?, Probing Depression, 1977, Search for a Satisfying Relationship, 1980, Strangers in My Dreams, 1987, Total Recall: An Introduction to Past Life & Health Readings, 1991, Kundalini Rising, 1992, Dreamers Dictionary, 1994, The Work of the Soul: Past Life Recall & Spiritual Enlightenment, 1996, Uncommon Knowledge, 1996, First Opinion: 21st Century Wholistic Health Care, 1997, Spiritual Renaissance Elevating Your Conciousness for the Common Good, 1999, The Bible Interpreted in Dream Symbols, 2000, Every Dream is About the Dreamer, 2001, Remembering Atlantis: The History of the World Vol. 1, 2002, How to Raise an Indigo Child, 2002, Peacemaking: 9 Lessons for Changing Yourself, Your Relationships and Your World, 2003, The Invitation: A Play and Film in Four Acts, Satyagraha: A Play Based on the Life of Mohandas K. Gandhi; author series When All Else Fails; editor-in-chief Thresholds Jour., 1990-2001; editor Wholistic Health and Healing Guide, 1992-2000; dir. (film) Peace is Reel, 2003; also numerous poems. Mem. Internat. Platform Assn., Am. Bus. Women's Assn., Interfaith Ministries, Kundalini Rsch. Network, Planetary Soc., Heritage Found., Mo. Writers Guild, Sigma Delta Chi. Office: Sch Metaphysics World Hdqs Windyville MO 65783

CONE, CAROL LYNN, public relations executive; b. N.Y.C., June 7, 1950; d. William Addison Cone and Harriet (Gurney) Brown. BA, Brandeis U., 1972; MS, Boston U., 1978. Account exec. Newsome and Co., Boston, 1977-80; pres., CEO Cone Comm. Inc., Boston, 1980—. Mem. Gov.'s Entrepreneurial Adv. Council, Boston, 1982, Dukakis for Pres. campaign nat. fin. com., Boston, 1987. Named Outstanding Female Entrepreneur La Salle Jr. Coll., Newton, Mass., 1986, YWCA Achievement Entrepreneur, Boston, 1986, Entrepreneur of Yr. Arthur Young/Venture Mag., 1988; recipient Golden Quill award Internat. Assn. Bus. Communicators, 1987. Mem. Counselor's Acad. of Pub. Relations Soc. Am., Pub. Relations Soc. Am. (Silver anvil 1987), Am. Mktg. Assn. Avocations: skiing, windsurfing, walking. Office: Cone Inc 90 Canal St Boston MA 02114-2018

CONE, FRANCES MCFADDEN, data processing consultant; b. Columbia, S.C., Oct. 20, 1938; d. Joseph Means and Francis (Graham) McFadden: m. Charles Cone Jr., May 1962 (div. Sept. 1964); 1 child, Deborah Ann Cone Craytor. BS, U. S.C., 1960, MEd, 1973, M Math., 1977. Systems svc. rep. IBM, 1960-62; programmer/analyst Ga. Power Co., Atlanta, 1964-68, S.C. Fin. and Data Processing, Columbia, 1968-69; instr., head dept. Midlands Tech. Coll., Columbia, 1969-75; tng. coord. S.C. Nat. Bank, Columbia, 1975-79; systems analyst S.C. Dept. Health and Environ. Control, Columbia, 1979-80; project analyst So. Co. Svcs., Atlanta, 1980-89; cons. George Martin Assocs., Atlanta, 1989-93; sr. sys. developer Emory U., Atlanta, 1993-97; sys. analyst Southland Life Ins. Co., Atlanta, 1997-99; team leader ING-Life of Ga., Atlanta, 1999—2002; ret., 2002. Adj. prof. Golden Gate U., Sumter, S.C., 1976-80. Vol. Ga. Wildlife Found., Save the Manatee Club, Names Project, Ellijay Wildlife Rehab. Sanctuary, 2000—02, Shepherd Spinal Ctr., 2000—01, Alpha Delta Pi 150-Yr. Conv., 2001; chair Silver Polishing Daughters of the King Cathedral of St. Philip. Mem. Nat. Mgmt. Assn. (sec., treas., awards comn. 1981-89). Episcopalian. Avocations: reading, embroidery. E-mail: fcone@mindspring.com.

CONE-SKELTON, ANNETTE, artist, museum director; Student, LaGrange Coll., 1960—62; BFA, Atlanta Coll. Art, 1968. Dir. Heath Gallery, Inc., Atlanta, 1978—87; pres. Annette Cone-Skelton, Inc., Atlanta, 1987—2000; co-founder, dir. Mus. Contemporary Art of Ga., Atlanta, 2000—. Fine arts instr. Atlanta Coll. Art, Oglethorpe U., Atlanta. Mng. editor: Contemporary Art Southeast, 1977—79; one-woman shows include Chattahoochee Valley Art Assn., LaGrange, Ga., 1968, Image South Gallery, Atlanta, 1974, 1975, Dick Jemison Gallery, Birmingham, Ala., 1974, DeKalb Cmty. Coll., Clarkston, Ga., 1976, Heath Gallery, 1977, 1979, 1980, 1982, 1984, LaGrange Coll., 1979, Auburn U., Ala., 1980, Piedmont Coll., Demorest, Ga., 1995, City Gallery of Chastain, Atlanta, 1996, Kiang Gallery, 1998, 2001, 2002, exhibitions include Emory Mus. Art and Archeology, Emory U., 1967, 1986, 1989, Hunter Mus. Art, Chattanooga, Tenn., 1967, 1970, 1976, 1977, Arts Festival of Atlanta, 1969, 1972, 1977, Mus. Arts and Scis., Macon, Ga., 1971, 1972, 1974, 1978, Image South Gallery, Atlanta, 1972, 1973, 1974, 1975, 1976, de la Penha Gallery, Ft. Lauderdale, Fla., 1973, U. Ga., Athens, 1973, Chiaha Second Annual, Rome, Ga., 1974, Dick Jemison Gallery, Birmingham, Ala., 1974, High Mus. Art, Atlanta, 1975, 1976, 1979, 1988, Galleries Internat., Winter Park, Fla., 1975, Ga. State U., Atlanta, 1975, Gallery Contemporanea, Jacksonville, Fla., 1976, Colony Sq., Atlanta, 1976, Berry Coll., Rome, Ga., 1976, Heath Gallery, 1976, 1977, 1978, 1979, 1986, 1988, 1992, 1995, 1996, Birmingham Mus. Art, 1977, Greenville (S.C.) County Mus. Art, 1977, Nexus Contemporary Art Ctr., Atlanta, 1977, 1980, 1987, 1988, 1998, Southeastern Ctr. Contemporary Art, Winston-Salem, N.C., 1978, 1988, Atlanta Coll. Art, 1979, 1980, 1981, 1984, We. Carolina U., Cullowhee, N.C., 1979, Auinlan Art Ctr., Gainesville, Ga., 1980, James Madison U., Harrisonburg, Va., 1980, U. W. Fla., Pensacola, 1980, Loyola U., New Orleans, 1980, Chattahoochee Valley Art Assn., LaGrange, 1980, 1997, Lamar Dodd Art Ctr., LaGrange Coll., 1982, Two Nine One Gallery, Atlanta, 1986, Madison (Ga.) Morgan Cultural Ctr., 1987, Contemporary Art Ctr., New Orleans, 1988, TULA Found. Gallery, Atlanta, 1990, TULA Women's Gallery, Feminist Women's Health Ctr., 1994, Atlanta History Ctr., 1996, Nat. Mus. Women in Arts, Washington, 1996, Spelman Coll. Mus. Fine Art, Atlanta, 1997, Kiang Gallery, 1998, Michael C. Carlos Mus., Emory U., 1998, Agnes Scott Coll., Atlanta, 1999, New Orleans Mus. Art, 2001, U. Ala., Huntsville, 2002, Weatherspoon Art Mus., Greensboro, N.C., 2002, Santa Barbara Contemporary Arts Forum, 2003—04, Represented in permanent collections Am. Tele. and Telegraph Co., N.Y.C., J.B. Speed Mus., Louisville, Ky., High Mus. Art, Kenneth of N.Y., N.Y.C., Omni Internat. Hotel, Miami, Fla., St. Joseph's Hosp., Atlanta, Herbert F. Johnson Mus. Art, Cornell U., and others. Recipient Purchase award, 15th Hunter Mus. Ann., 1976, Individual Artists award, Fulton County Arts Coun., Atlanta, 1995—96, Ga. Women in Visual Arts Achievement award, Ga. Commn. on Women, 1997, Critics' Choice Best Visual Artist award, Creative Loafing, 1998; fellow, Hambridge Ctr., Rabun Gap, Ga., 1991, 1993, 1995, 1998; grantee, CGR Advisors Artist Initiatvie, Atlanta, 1996; scholar, Ford Found., Atlanta Coll. Art, 1964—68, CGR Advisors, Hambridge Ctr., 1995. Office: Mus Comtemporary Art GA 1447 Peachtree St NE Atlanta GA 30309

CONETTA, TAMI FOLEY, lawyer; b. Akron, Ohio, Aug. 29, 1965; d. Charles David and Roxanne (Onyett) Foley; m. Anthony Joseph Conetta, July 29, 1989 (div.); 1 child, Emory Elizabeth Conetta; m. Barry Frank Spivey, June 8, 2002. BA in Polit. Sci., Furman U., 1987; JD with honors, U. Fla., 1990. Bar: Fla. 1991; bd. cert. estates, trusts and wills Fla. Bar Bd. Legal Specialization. Ptnr. Gassman & Conetta, PA, Clearwater, Fla., 1990-98, Ruden, McClosky, Smith, Schuster & Russell, PA, Sarasota, Fla., 1998—. Contbr. articles to profl. jours. Mem. planned giving com. All Children's Hosp. Found.; bd. dirs. Literacy Coun. of Sarasota, Sch. Readiness Coalition of Sarasota County. Recipient Am. Jurisprudence awards in Estate Planning and Taxation of Gratuitous Transfers, 1990. Mem. Am. Bus. Womens Assn. (pres. Sunrise chpt. 2002-03, Woman of Yr. 2003), Sarasota County Bar Assn. (chair probate and estate planning sect. 2000-01), Clearwater Bar Probate Com. (chair 1996-98), Southwest Fla. Estate Planning Coun., Fla. Bar Assn. (chair probate rules com. 2003-2004, rules jud. adminstrn. com.). Avocations: golf, reading. Office: Ruden McClosky Smith Schuster & Russell PA 1549 Ringling Blvd Ste 600 Sarasota FL 34236-6772 also: PO Box 49017 Sarasota FL 34230-6017 E-mail: tami.conetta@ruden.com.

CONEY, STEPHNÉ RENIA, communications and telecommunications educator; b. Camden, N.J., Oct. 29, 1963; d. Douglas Tyrone and Bette Louise Coney; 1 child, Sescily Reneé. BA, Johnson C. Smith U., Charlotte, N.C., 1986; MA, Tex. So. U., Houston, 1988; postgrad., U. Santa Barbara. Prof. edn. Hargest Coll., Houston, 1988-90; tax examiner IRS, Phila., 1990-96; founder, exec. dir. Nat. Stop the Violence Alliance, Inc., Camden, 1991—. Founder, exec. dir. Camden County Internat. Nat. Festival, 1994—, Actors, Artists and Athletes Against Violence, 1995—, Facing Attitudes Concerning Ednl. Spirits, 1996, Peace Troopers: A Youth Partnership with Law Enforcement, 1998. Recipient Stop the Violence award Assembly of N.J./Camden City Coun., 1995. Mem. Delta Sigma Theta. Democrat. African Methodist Episcopal. Avocations: directing, acting, singing, reading, writing. Office: Nat Stop the Violence PO Box 1293 Camden NJ 08105-0293

CONGALTON, SUSAN TICHENOR, lawyer; b. Mt. Vernon, N.Y., July 12, 1946; d. Arthur George and M. Marjorie Tichenor; m. Christopher William Congalton, May 29, 1971. BA summa cum laude, Loretto Heights Coll., 1968; JD, Georgetown U., 1971. Bar: N.Y. 1972, Ill. 1986, Colo. 1990. Assoc. Reavis & McGrath (now Fulbright & Jaworski), N.Y.C., 1971-78, ptnr., 1978-85; v.p., gen. counsel, sec. Carson Pirie Scott & Co., Chgo., 1985-87, sr. v.p. fin. and law, 1987-89; mng. dir. Lupine LLC (formerly known as Lupine Ptnrs.), Chgo., 1989—; chmn., CEO Calif. Amforge Corp., 2002—. Bd. dirs. Harris Fin. Corp., Harris Bankcorp, Inc.; chmn. Cmty. Reinvestment Act Com., 1990-97, chmn. audit com., 1997—; bd. dirs. Pulitzer Inc., St. Louis; chmn. bd., CEO, Calif. Amforge Corp., 2002—. Mem. editorial staff Georgetown U. Law Jour., 1969-70, editor, 1970-71. Mem. bd. overseers Ill. Inst. Tech., Chgo., Chgo. Kent Coll. Law, 1985-89; mem. bus. adv. coun. Bus. Sch., U. Ill., Chgo., 1987-90; mem. planning com. Ann. Corp. Counsel Inst., 1986-89; bd. dirs. Ill. Inst. Continuing Legal Edn., 1992-95; mem. Chgo. Workforce Bd., 1995-98; chmn. Strategic Planning Task force, 1995-96, chmn. Performance Rev. Com., 1996-98. Mem. ABA, Nat. Assn. Corp. Dirs. (bd. dirs. Chgo. chpt. 2001—), Econ. Club Chgo., Chgo. Club (bd. dirs. 1996—2004, treas. 1999-02, sec. 2002—04). Office: Lupine LLC 1520 Kensington Rd Ste 112 Oak Brook IL 60523-2140 E-mail: lupineLLC@aol.com.

CONGER, CYNTHIA LYNNE, financial planner; b. Omaha, Dec. 8, 1948; d. Bob Bruce Ashton and Cleo (Artz) Ashton Taplin; m. Terry H. Conger, Dec. 21, 1969 (div. June 1989); children: Cynthia T., Scott A. BA in Acctg., U. Ark., Little Rock, 1980, MBA in Fin. and Econ., 1983. CPA, Ark.; cert. fin. planner. Staff acct. Leaseway Ark., Inc., Little Rock, 1981-83; rsch. asst. Indls. Rsch. and Econ. Com., Little Rock, 1983; agt. Conn. Mutual Life, Little Rock, 1983-84; v.p., fin. planner Ark. Fin. Group, Inc., Little Rock, 1984-94, pres., 1995—, Cynthia L. Conger, CPA, PA, Little Rock, 1989—. Mem. found. bd. U. Ark., 2002—. Mem. LWV (adv bd. 1997—), Registry Fin. Planning Practitioners, Internat. Assn. Fin. Planning (Ark. chpt., v.p. 1986—87, pres. 1987—89, nat. bd. dirs. 1994—98). Methodist. Avocations: reading, travel, cooking. Office: Ark Fin Group Inc 225 E Markham St Ste 275 Little Rock AR 72201-1634 Office Phone: 501-376-9051. E-mail: cindyc@arfinancial.com.

CONIGILARO, PHYLLIS ANN, retired elementary education educator; b. Ilion, N.Y., Nov. 27, 1932; d. Gus Carl and Jennie Margaret (Marine) Denapole; m. Paul Anthony Conigilaro, July 16, 1983. BS cum laude, SUNY, Cortland, 1955; MA in Edn., Psychology, Cornell U., 1961. Cert. tchr., N.Y. Elem. classroom tchr. Mohawk (N.Y.) Central Sch., 1955-88. Contbr. articles to profl. jours. Bd. dirs. United Fund of Ilion, Herkimer, Mohawk and Frankfort, 1984-86, pres., 1986; pres. bd. edn. St. Mary's Parochial Sch., 1978; mem. Herkimer County Hist. Soc., 1988—, trustee, 1994-97; bd. dirs. local Federal Emergency Mgmt. Agy., 1987-96. Recipient Outstanding Elem. Tchrs. of Am. award, Outstanding Elem. Tchrs. of Am. Wash. D.C., 1974. Mem. N.Y. State United Tchrs., Mohawk Tchrs. Assn. (past pres.), AUW (pres. Herkimer chpt. 1981-82), N.Y. State Ret. Tchrs. Assn. (past legis. chmn. Herkimer County chpt.), Rep. Women's Club, Kappa Delta Pi. Republican. Roman Catholic. Avocations: golf, travel, reading, music. Home: 137 7th Ave Frankfort NY 13340-3612 E-mail: pconigil@twcny.rr.com.

CONKLIN, MARA LORAINE, public relations executive; b. Vallejo, Calif., July 28, 1962; d. Kenneth J. and Laura T. (Siegrist) Cichosz; m. Rex D. Conklin, Sept. 6, 1986; children: Elisabeth, Emily, Margaret. BA, Marquette U., 1984. Nat. news editl. staff Nat. Safety Coun., Chgo., 1984-85; corp. comm. specialist Household Internat., Prospect Hgts., Ill., 1985-86; acct. supr. Posner McGrath Ltd., Lincolnshire, Ill., 1986-90, v.p., 1990-92, sr. v.p., 1992-94, exec. v.p., 1994-97, pres., 1997-98, Clarus Comms. Ltd., Libertyville, Ill., 1998—. Recipient Spectra award Internat. Assn. Bus. Communicators, 1992, 94, Silver Trumpet award Publicity Club Chgo., 1993. Mem. Marquette Club Chgo. (chair alumni com. 1986-94, pres. 1994-96). Office: Clarus Comms Ltd 620 Mullady Pkwy Libertyville IL 60048-3729

CONKLIN, SUSAN JOAN, psychotherapist, educator, corporate staff developer, TV talk show host; b. Bklyn., Feb. 7, 1950; d. Joseph Thomas Hallek and Stella Joan Kuceluk; m. John Lariviere Conklin, July 25, 1981; children: Genevieve Therese, Michelle Therese. BA, CCNY, 1972; MSW, CUNY, 1975. Lic. ind. clin. social worker; bd. cert. diplomat. Shop counselor Assn. for Help of Retarded Citizens, N.Y.C., 1971-75; dir. social svcs., acting exec. dir. North Berkshire Assn. for Retarded Citizens, North

Adams, Mass., 1975-77; project dir. Title XX tng. grant State of Mass., North Adams, 1978-79; pvt. practice psychotherapy, Williamstown, Mass., 1979—. Adj. asst. prof. Mass. Coll. Liberal Art, 1977—2000, Berkshire C.C., Pittsfield, Mass., 1985—86, Pittsfield, 1995; docent Clark Art Inst., 1995—2003; Therapeutic Touch practitioner, 1978—; talk show host Pub [illegible] Channel 17, 1999—2003, vol. Salvation Army. WTC Disaster Relief Family Assistance Ctr., 2001, 9/11 United Svcs. Group, 2002; adj. faculty Springfield Coll. Sch. Social Work, 2002. Pres. Williamstown PTO, 1989-91; bd. dirs., edn. com., spl. events coord. Hospice No. Berkshire, Inc., 1989—. Named Berkshire County Social Worker of Yr., 1999, Mass. Social Worker of Yr., 2002; recipient Cmty. Svc. award, Salvation Army, North Berkshire, Mass., 2004. Mem. NASW (bd. dirs. 1981-83, regional coun. mem. 1980-83, 93-2003), LWV, Nurse Healers-Profl. Assn., Inc. (trustee 1981-83, rec. sec., editor-in-chief Coop. Connection newsletter 1983-88), Women of Vision Action. Democrat. Episcopalian. Office: 85 Hawthorne Rd Williamstown MA 01267-2700 Home: 5 Fallingwater Dr Linwood NJ 08221

CONLAY, LYDIA, physician, health sciences administrator; b. Natchitoches, La., June 30, 1952; d. Floyd R. and Lou Althea (Roberts) Conlay. BS, Northwestern State U., Natchitoches, 1972; MD, La. State U., Shreveport, 1976; PhD in Neurochemistry, MIT, 1983; MBA with high honors, Boston U., 1995. Intern Johns Hopkins Hosp., Balt., 1976-77; residnet in anesthesia Mass. Gen. Hosp., Boston, 1977-79; asst. prof. anesthesia Harvard Med. Sch., Boston, 1984-89, assoc. prof. anesthesia, 1989-97; lectr. brain and cognitive scis. MIT, Cambridge, Mass., 1986-88; dir. ambulatory recovery svcs. Mass. Gen. Hosp.-Harvard Med. Sch., Boston, 1996-97; prof., chair dept. anesthesiology Temple U. Sch. Medicine, Phila., 1997—. Mem. practice plan bd. Temple U. Practice, Phila., 1977—. Assoc. editor Survey in Anesthesiology, 1996—; contbr. articles to Sci., Nature, Jour. AMA, Prcs. Nat. Acad. Scis., others. Chair Ether Monument Restoration Group, Boston Pub. Garden. Grantee NIH, Glaxo-Welcome Pharms., Marion-Merrell Dow. Mem. Soc. for Ambulatory Anesthesia (bd. dirs. 1996—, treas. 2000—, pres.-elect 2001—), Assn. Univ. Anesthesiologists (mem. coun. 1999—, treas. 2000), Coll. Phys. Phila., Union Club of Boston, Alpha Omega Alpha. Office: Temple U Sch Medicine Dept Anesthesia 3401 N Broad St Philadelphia PA 19140-5103

CONLEY, CHRISTINE, music educator; b. Lawrenceberg, Ind., Nov. 9, 1963; d. Philip Howard and Sarah Ann Conley. MusB, Northwestern U., 1986; MusM, U. Miami, 1988, New Eng. Conservatory of Music, 1992. Tchr. Ayer (Mass.) H.S. and Mid. Sch. Ayer Pub. Schs., 1994—98; tchr. Bartlett H.S. Webster (Mass.) Pub. Schs., 1998—99; tchr. Needham B. Broughton H.S. Wake County Pub. Sch. Sys., Raleigh, NC, 2000—. Dir. music Lexington (Mass.) United Meth. Ch., 1994—98; soloist Old South Ch., Boston, 1990—92; mem. chorus Greater Miami (Fla.) Opera, 1986—88. Mem.: Music Educators Nat. Conf., Profl. Educators of N.C., Pi Kappa Lambda. Avocations: hiking, backpacking, cooking, reading. Office: Needham Broughton HS 723 St Mary's St Raleigh NC 27605 E-mail: cconley@wcpss.net.

CONLEY, DARLENE ANN, actress; b. Chgo. d. Raymond and Melba (Manthey) C.; m. William Woodson, Oct. 1959 (div. 1966); 1 child, Raymond. Actress Broadway prodns. including: The Baker's Wife, The Night of the Iguana Actress feature films including: Tough Guys, Faces, Minnie and Moscowitz, Play it As it Lays, Lady Sings the Blues, Valley of the Dolls, The Birds; TV movies include: I Want to Live, The Fighter, The Choice, Return Engagement, The President's Plane is Missing; TV episodes include: Get Christie Love, Scarecrow and Mrs. King, Highway to Heaven, Murder She Wrote, Bill Cosby Show, Little House on the Prairie; continuing role on The Young and The Restless, 1980-88, The Bold and The Beautiful, 1989—. Emmy nominee for Outstanding Supporting Actress, 1991, 92; statue made for Madame Tussaud's Wax Mus., 1998. Office: Bell-Phillip TV Prodns Inc 7800 Beverly Blvd # 3371 Los Angeles CA 90036-2112

CONLEY, RUTH IRENE, poet; b. Seattle, Jan. 26, 1920; d. Irving Birch Anderson and Gertrude Evelyn Unsworth Edwins; m. Samuel Glenn Conley, June 12, 1946 (div. Nov. 1963); children: Joan Evelyn, Mary Jacquelyn, James Harper. BA in Gen. Studies, U. Wash., 1964, BA in English, 1965, MA in English, 1966, MA in Comparative Lit., 1970; studied with Theodore Roethke. Editor publs. office U. Wash., Seattle, 1965—66, acctg. asst., 1973—86. Author numerous poems; author: (poet) (chapbooks) Time of Apple Harvest, Icicle River, and Short Poems from the Japanese. Democrat. Avocation: gardening.

CONLEY, SARAH ANN, health facility administrator; b. Richmond, Ind., Sept. 14, 1942; d. Harry Herbert and Mary Janet Kercheval; m. Philip Howard Conley, Apr. 5, 1963 (dec.); children: Christine L., Philip Douglas. BS, Purdue U., 1964; postgrad., U. Cin., 1965. Elem. tchr. Southwest Local Schs., Harrison, Ohio, 1964-66; svc. office mgr. Renault of Dayton (Ohio), 1970-73; mgr. Office of Charlotte Ames, Xenia, Ohio, 1974-77; bus. mgr. Radiol. Physicians, Inc., Dayton, 1977-79, Nat. Tractor Pullers Assn., Columbus, Ohio, 1979-85; HMO adminstr. Cen. Benefits Mutual Ins. Co., Columbus, 1985-90; adminstr. Orthopedic and Neurol. Cons., Columbus, 1990-97, Peripheral Vascular Surgery, Columbus, 1997-99; owner Conley Mgmt. Svc., Westerville, Ohio. Mem. Am. Coll. Med. Practice Execs. (cert.), Ohio Med. Group Mgmt. Assn. (pres. 1993-94), MidOhio Med. Mgmt. Assn., Med. Group Mgmt. Assn., Licking County Bus. and Profl. Women (pres. 1989-91). Democrat. Methodist. Avocations: piano, organ, church choir, teaching sunday school. E-mail: conleyserv.@cs.com.

CONLIN, KATHLEEN F. dean, theater director; b. Youngstown, Ohio, Aug. 2, 1949; d. George Joseph Fallat and Agnes Frances Gonda; m. William James Conlin, Aug. 26, 1971; 1 child, Matthew. BA, Youngstown State U., 1971; MA, U. Pitts., 1974; PhD, U. Mich., 1984. From asst. prof. to assoc. prof. U. Tex., Austin, 1978—87; dir. sch. of theatre Ohio U., Athens, 1987—92; chair theatre dept. Ohio State U., Columbus, 1992—96; assoc. artistic dir. Utah Shakespearean Festival, Cedar City, 1990—; dean Coll. Fine Arts and Applied Arts U. Ill., Urbana, 1996—. Freelance theatre dir. Dir.: (plays) Shakespeare and Am. Classics, 1978—. Chair campus charitable fund dr. U. Ill., 2000—01. Recipient Tchg. Excellence award, U. Tex., 1980; Endowed Faculty fellow, 1980. Mem.: Soc. Stage Dirs. and Choreographers, Nat. Assn. Schs. of Theatre, Nat. Theatre Conf. (pres.). Avocations: films, literature. Home: 2502 Lakewood Dr Champaign IL 61822 Office: Univ Ill Coll Fine Arts and Applied Arts 608 Lorado Taft Dr Urbana IL 61820

CONLIN, LINDA MYSLIWY, federal agency administrator; b. Springfield, Mass. m. Joseph F. Conlin Jr.. Pres. Park-Main Travel Agy.; protocol visits officer U.S. Dept. State; from corp. liaison officer for US/USSR intiatives to assoc. dir. Office of Pvt. Sector Coms. U.S. Info. Agy.; asst. sec. commerce for mktg. U.S. Travel and Tourism Adminstrn., 1989—93; dir. Office Travel and Tourism N.J. Commerce Dept., 1994—98; exec. dir. Office Travel and Tourism N.J. Commerce and Econ. Growth Commn., 0998—1999; dep. to program chmn. 2000 Rep. Nat. Conv.; sr. campaign coord. Bush/Cheney 2000-Southeastern Pa. Region; asst. sec. trade devel. Dept. Commerce, Washington, 2001—. Republican. Office: Dept Commerce Trade Devel 14th & Constution Ave Nw Washington DC 20230

CONLIN, ROXANNE BARTON, lawyer; b. Huron, SD, June 30, 1944; d. Marion William and Alyce Muraine (Madden) Barton; m. James Clyde Conlin, Mar. 21, 1964; children: Jacalyn Rae, James Barton, Deborah Ann, Douglas Benton BA, Drake U., 1964, JD, 1966, MPA, 1979; LLD (hon.), U. Dubuque, 1975. Bar: Iowa 1966. Assoc. Davis, Huebner, Johnson & Burt, Des Moines, 1966-67; dep. indsl. commr. State of Iowa, 1967-68, asst. atty. gen., 1969-76; U.S. atty. So. Dist. Iowa, 1977-81; ptnr. Conlin, P.C., Des Moines, 1983—. Adj. prof. law U. Iowa, 1977-79; chmn. Iowa Women's Polit. Caucus, 1973-75, del. nat. steering com., 1973-77; cons. U.S. Commn. on Internat. Women's Year, 1976-77; gen. counsel NOW Legal Def. and Edn. Fund, 1985-88, pres., 1986-88; lectr. in field. Co-editor: ATLA's Litigating Tort Cases, 6 vols., 2003; contbr. articles to profl. jours. Nat. committeewoman Iowa Young Dems.; pres. Polk County Young Dems., 1965-66; del. Iowa Presdl. Conv., 1972; Dem. candidate for gov. of Iowa, 1982; bd. dirs. Riverhills Day Care Ctr., YWCA; chmn. Drake U. Law Sch. Endowment Trust, 1985-86; bd. counselors Drake U., 1982-86; pres.. founder Civil Justice Found., 1986-88; pres. Roscoe Pound Found., 1994-97; chair Iowa Dem. Party, 1998-99. Named scholarship in her honor, Kansas City Women Lawyers; named one of Top Ten Litigators, Nat. Law Jour, 1989, 100 Most Influential Attys., 1991, 50 Most Powerful Women Attys., Nat. Law Jour., 1998, 10 Most Influential Women Attys., 2002; recipient award, Iowa ACLU, 1974, Alumnus of Yr. award, Drake U. Law Sch., 1989, ann. award, Young Women's Resource Ctr., 1989, Verne Lawyer award as Outstanding Mem., Iowa Trial Lawyers Assn., 1994, Rosalie Wahl award, Minn. Women Lawyers, 1998, Marie Lambert award, 2000, Mary Louise Smith award, YWCA, 2001, Lifetime Achievement award, Des Moines Human Rights Commn., 2003, Ruth Bader Ginsberg award, 2004; scholar Reader's Digest scholar, 1963—64, Fishcher Found., 1965—66. Mem.: ATLA (chmn. consumer and victims coalition com. 1985—87, chmn. edn. dept 1987—88, parliamentarian 1988—89, sec. 1989—90, v.p. 1990—91, pres.-elect 1991—92, pres. 1992—93, Lifetime Achievement award 2003), ABA, NOW, Trial Lawyers Care (bd. dirs.), Inner Circle of Advocates, Higher Edn. Commn. Iowa (co-chmn. 1988—90), Iowa Acad. Trial Lawyers, Internat. Acad. Trial Lawyers, Assn. Trial Lawyers Iowa (bd. dirs.), Iowa Bar Assn., Chi Omega, Alpha Lambda Delta, Phi Beta Kappa. Office: Griffin Bldg 319 7th St Ste 600 Des Moines IA 50309-3826

CONLON, PEGGY EILEEN, publisher; b. Santa Monica, Calif., Mar. 2, 1951; d. Daniel Francis and Mary Eileen (Garrity) C.; m. Robert J. Reale, May 21, 1993. AA, Victor Valley Jr. Coll., Apple Valley, Calif.; BA, Calif. State U., Fullerton; MA, U. So. Calif.-Annenberg, L.A. Account exec. Dozier Eastman, Santa Ana, Calif., 1973-75; advt. and pub. rels. mgr. ITT Marine Divsn., Costa Mesa, Calif., 1975-80, EECO, Santa Ana, 1980-82; group pub. CMP Publs., Manhasset, N.Y., 1982-92; pub. Broadcasting & Cable, N.Y.C., 1992—. Lt. USNR, 1974-81. Mem. Internat. Radio and TV Soc. (bd. dirs. 1993-96). Office: Broadcasting & Cable 245 W 17th St New York NY 10011-5300

CONLON, SUZANNE B. federal judge; b. 1939; AB, Mundelein Coll., 1963; JD, Loyola U., Chgo., 1968; postgrad., U. London, 1971. Law clk. to judge U.S. Dist. Ct. (no. dist.) Ill., 1968-71; assoc. Pattishall, McAuliffe & Hostetter, 1972-73, Schiff Hardin & Waite, 1973-75; asst. U.S. atty. U.S. Dist. Ct. (no. dist.) Ill., 1976-77, 82-86, U.S. Dist. Ct. (cen. dist.) Calif., 1978-82; exec. dir. U.S. Sentencing Commn., 1986-88; spl. counsel to assoc. atty. gen., 1988; judge U.S. Dist. Ct. (no. dist.) Ill., 1988—. Asst. prof. law De Paul U., Chgo., 1972-73, lectr., 1973-75; adj. prof. Northwestern U. Sch. Law, 1991-95; vice chmn. Chgo. Bar Assn. Internat. Inst., 1993—; vis. com. U. Chgo. Harris Grad. Sch. Pub. Policy, 1997—. Mem. ABA, FBA, Am. Judicature Soc., Internat. Bar Assn. Judges Forum, Lawyers Club Chgo. (pres. 1996-97). Office: US Dist Ct No Dist Everett McKinley Dirksen Bldg 219 S Dearborn St Ste 2356 Chicago IL 60604-1878

CONLY, DIANE CARROLL, dentist; b. Miami, Fla., July 8, 1966; d. Patrick Edward and Patricia Novak (Wallace) C. BS, U. So. Calif., 1988; MS, Calif. State U., Long Beach, 1990; DDS, U. So. Calif., 1994. Lic. dentist, Calif. Rsch. scientist Calif. State U., 1988-90; dental anesthesiologist U. So. Calif., L.A., 1992-94; resident in gen. practice UCLA West L.A. VA Hosp., Westwood, 1994-95; pvt. practice dentistry Whittier, Calif., 1995—. Tchr. U. So. Calif. Dental Sch., L.A., 1991—. Dentist Whittier Assistance League, 1995—. Mem. ADA, Acad. Gen. Dentistry (Garrett Newkirk award 1994), Omicron Kappa Upsilon, Whittier C. of C. Office: Diane C Conly DDS 5702 Magnolia Ave Whittier CA 90601-2976

CONN, REBECCA DARLENE, psychologist; d. John Harrison Jones and Sherry Darlene Moses; m. Lester Conn, July 29, 1978; children: Aimee Michelle, Amber Lianne. ADN, Cumberland Coll., 1980, BS, 1993; MS, Murray State U., 1996. Lic. psychol. assoc. Ky. RN Bapt. Regional Med. Ctr., 1981—87; psychol. assoc. Cumberland River Comprehensive Care Ctr., Williamsburg, Ky., 1996—. Contbr. articles to profl. jours. Bd. dirs. Multidisciplinary Task Force on Child Sexual Assault, 1997—; mem. Family Violence Prevention Bd., 1997—. Mem.: Ky. Assn. Sexual Assault Programs (child sexual assault counselor 1997—), Psi Chi. Avocation: antiques. Office: Cumberland River Comprehensive Care Ctr Cemetary Rd Williamsburg KY 40769

CONNELL, KATHLEEN, state official; PhD, UCLA. Holder 6 lics. SEC. Instr. UCLA Bus. Sch., U. Calif. Bus. Sch., Berkeley; owner, mgr. investment banking firm, until 1994; contr. State of Calif., Sacramento, 1994—. Chmn. Franchise Tax Bd. Named One of 10 Rising Stars of Dem. Party, Time mag., 1996. Office: State Calif Office Contr 300 Capitol Mall Ste 1850 Sacramento CA 95814-4341

CONNELL, KINNY, state representative; b. Phila., Nov. 3, 1951; 2 children. BA, U. Pa., 1973; postgrad., Yale U. State rep. State of Vt., 2001—. Past mem. Warren Sch. Bd.; past chair Warren Libr. Commn., Vt. Festival of Arts, Warren PTO; pres. Friends of Mad River; mem. Warren Selectboard; mem. steering com. Mad River Valley Planning Dist. Democrat. Office: PO Box 76A 141 Brook Rd Warren VT 05674

CONNELL, MARY ELLEN, diplomat; b. Laconia, N.H., Jan. 20, 1943; d. Howard Benjamin and Jessie Louise Smith Naylor; m. O. J. Connell III, Nov. 4, 1969 (div. Aug. 1988); 1 child, Piers Andrew. BA, Smith Coll., Northampton, Mass., 1964; MPhil, U. Kans., 1969; MS, Nat. War Coll., 1992. Info. ctr. dir. U.S. Fgn. Svc., Nairobi, Kenya, 1978-80, pub. affairs officer Bujumbura, Burundi, 1980-82; officer African affairs USIA, Washington, 1982-85, exec. asst. to assoc. dir. for policy, 1985-86; counselor pub. affairs U.S. Fgn. Svc., Copenhagen, 1986-90; vis. scholar St. Deiniol's Wales, 1991; exec. sec. USIA, Washington, 1992-95; pub. affairs advisor U.S. Mission to NATO, Brussels, 1995-97; spl. asst. to asst. sec. defense for pub. affairs Washington, 1997-99; mem. policy planning staff Dept. of State, Washington, 1999—. Mem. Internat. Inst. Strategic Studies, Am. Fgn. Svc. Assn., Atlantic Coun., Army and Navy Club. Episcopalian. Office: Dept of State S P Rm 7313 Washington DC 20520-0001 E-mail: connellme@aol.com.

CONNELL, S. CLARE, minister; b. Traverse City, Mich., May 5, 1949; d. Chester Cox and Garie McComb Green; m. Christopher Thomas Connell, Sept. 14, 1974; children: Garie Elizabeth, Adam Christopher Martin. BA, Bethany Coll., W.Va., 1971; MDiv, Episc. Div. Sch., Cambridge, Mass., 1975. Ordained priest Episc. Ch., 1990. Asst. chaplain St. Michael's Chapel, Rutgers U., New Brunswick, NJ, 1975—78; assoc. deacon St. Mark's Ch., Hammonton, NJ, 1979—82, St. Raphael's Ch., Brick, NJ, 1983—90; hospice chaplain Cmty. Med. Ctr., Toms River, NJ, 1990—97; vicar Trinity Ch., Vincentown, NJ, 1998—99; interim priest St. Mark the Evangelist, North Bellmore, NY, 2000—. 1st superior Sisters of St. Gregory. Avocation: reading. Office: St Mark the Evangelist Episc Ch 1692 Bellmore Ave North Bellmore NY 11710

CONNELL, SANDRA BENNETT, school librarian; b. Nashville, Ga., Apr. 12, 1943; d. Walter David and Brunelle Ernestine Bennett; m. Edward Lamar Connell, Jr., Aug. 24, 1963. AB in English, Valdosta State U., Ga., 1964; MEd in Libr. Sci., U. Ga., Athens, 1976. Cert. tchr. Ga. Libr. South Ga. Regional Libr., Valdosta, 1964—65, Lowndes County Bd. Edn., Valdosta, Ga., 1967—74, Valdosta Bd. Edn., Ga., 1975—98, Valwood Sch., Valdosta, Ga., 1999—2003. Editor (newsletter): Cherokee Rose, 1982; compiler (cookbook): Sharing Our Best, columnist: newspaper column, 1999—2003. Mem.: Ga. Ret. Tchrs. Assn., Lit. Guild (sec. 1998—2000), Delta Kappa Gamma (monthly chmn. 2001). Republican. Methodist. Avocations: writing, gourmet cooking, ceramics, storytelling. Home: Rt 1 Box 650 Stockton GA 31649 Office: Valwood Sch 4380 Old US Hwy 41 N Hahira GA 31632

CONNELL, SHIRLEY HUDGINS, public relations professional; b. Washington, Oct. 5, 1946; d. Orville Thomas and Mary (Beran) H.; m. David Day Connell, Dec. 13, 1980 (div. 1985). BA, U. R.I., 1968, MA, 1970. Lic. property, casualty broker, N.Y. Clk., editor MGM Studios, Culver City, Calif., 1970-72; scriptor, talent Monarch Records, Studio City, 1972-73; communications specialist U. So. Calif., L.A., 1973-81; dir. pub. rels. Six Flags Movieland, Buena Park, Calif., 1981-82, Donald J. Fager & Assocs., N.Y.C., 1982-93, dir. policy holder/pub. rels., 1993-99, asst. v.p., 1999—. Cons. Children's TV Workshop, N.Y.C., 1978; ind. beauty cons. Mary Kay Cosmetics, 1991—; instr. Princeton Rev., 1990-91. Editor: Coastal Ocean Space Utilization III, 1995; contbr. articles to profl. jours.; contbg. editor Greater N.Y. Doctor's Shopper mag., 1987—. Pres. bd. trustees Oaks at North Brunswick Condominium Assn., 1987-2000; founding mem. Mcpl. Svcs. Com., North Brunswick; mgr. Animal Rescue Force, 1988—; chair environ. com. Twp. of North Brunswick, 1990-2001, vice chair, 2001—; snuggler pediat. and neonatal units St. Peter's Hosp.; Blue Belt Tiger Schulmann's Karate, 1997; founding mem., trustee, bd. dirs. Lawrence Brook Watershed Partnership, 1998—. Mem. NAFE, Marine Tech. Soc. (vice chmn. 1980-81), Mensa (pub. rels. adv. com. 1989—, pub. rels. coord. Ctrl. N.J. chpt. 1992—, bd. dirs. 1992—), Oceanic Soc. (bd. dirs. 1979-81), Stony Brook Millstone Watershed Assn. (water qualification monitor 1994—), Ctrl. N.J. Mensa (trustee, chair pub. rels. 1990—). Avocations: photography, reading, swimming, wood finishing, writing. E-mail: sconnell@mlmic.com.

CONNELL-ALLEN, ELIZABETH ANN, elementary school educator; b. Portsmouth, Va., Sept. 21, 1949; d. Robert Joseph and Juanita Georgia (Harrill) C.; m. Larry Allen. BS in Edn., Old Dominion U., Norfolk, Va., 1971; MA in Reading Edn., U. No. Colo., Greeley, 1975; PhD in Edn., Lit. and Curriculum, U. Colo., Boulder, 1991. Cert. elem. edn. K-6, reading edn. K-12, K-12 adminstrn. Tchr. 6th grade Norfolk Pub. Schs., 1971-74; tchr. Littleton (Colo.) Pub. Schs., 1975—. Tchg. assoc. U. Colo., Boulder, 1988-90; instr. U. Colo., Denver, 1994; lit. com. When Author Meets Author, Colo. Coun. of Internat. Reading Assn., Denver; judge children's writing contest Friends of the Libr., Littleton, 1992-96. Author: A Community of Learners Selecting and Developing Writing Topics, 1991, Eternal Portraits, 2003. Recipient Outstanding Tchr. award Assn. for Childhood Edn. Internat., Denver, 1992; multicultural grantee Summit CHART: Pub. Edn. Coalition, Denver, 1994. Mem. ASCD, NEA, Internat. Reading Assn., Colo. Edn. Assn., Littleton Edn. Assn., Phi Delta Kappa. Avocations: reading, singing, playing piano. Office: Littleton Pub Schs Franklin Elem Littleton CO 80209

CONNELLY, AMY REECE, career planning administrator, consultant; b. Savannah, Ga., June 13, 1963; d. Charles David and Judith Boswell Reece; m. Kevin S. Connelly, Apr. 27, 1991; children: Kristine S., Kara S. BS, Ball State U., Muncie, Ind., 1985, MA, 1986. Cert. tng. cons. Ball State Sch. of Continuing Edn., 1994. Dir. of student activities Converse Coll., Spartanburg, SC, 1986—88; asst. dir., career ctr. Ind. State U., Terre Haute, Ind., 1988—91; assoc. dir., career services Butler U., Indpls., 1991—95; exec. recruiter/rsch. mgr. Johnson Brown Assoc., Inc., Indpls., 1995—99; cons. self-employed, Indpls., 1997—. Cons./project employee Right Mgmt. Cons., Indpls., 2002—; cons./mgr., career svcs. ACA, Alexandria, Va., 2002—. Grad. Richard G. Lugar Excellence in Pub. Svc. Series, Indpls., 1998; pres. Pike Twp. GOP Club, Indpls., 2000—01; vice precinct committeeman Marion County Rep. Party, Indpls., 1995—2002; mem. Bethel United Meth. Ch., Indpls.; pres. Eagles Landing Homeowners Assn., Indpls., 2001—02. Recipient Outstanding Young Alumnus, Ball State Alumni Assn., 1994, Benny Award, 1992; scholar Emens Scholarship, Ball State U., 1981-85, Ball State Presdl. Scholarship, 1981-1985. Mem.: ACA, Nat. Career Devel. Assn. Republican. Meth. Avocations: vocal performance, gardening, church and family activities. Personal E-mail: a613research@aol.com.

CONNELLY, BARBARA CATHERINE, organization administrator; b. Somerville, Mass., Sept. 15, 1940; d. Sebastiano and Mary (Igo) DeFilippo; m. James Patrick Connelly, Oct. 19, 1961 (dec. Feb. 1987); children: Kathleen, James (murdered), Patricia, Barbara, Terence. Student, Empire State Coll. Cert. bereavement therapist, cmty. crisis interventar crisis response team. Sec. Brookhaven Hosp. Home Care, Patch, NY, 1987-89; sec. dept. rehab. St. Charles Hosp., Port Jefferson, N.Y., 1990-92; exec. dir. Outreach program for the secondary victim Parents of Murdered Children, Shirley, N.Y., 1996—. Exec. dir. Children Have Feelings Too, 1990—; sec. L.I. chpt. Parents of Murdered Children, 1981-86, treas., 1987-96, pres., 1991-96, state coord., 1996-98. Recipient Leadership award L.I. Newsday, 1992; named Point of Light for volunteerism George Busch, 1992. Mem. NAFE. Democrat. Roman Catholic. Avocation: sewing.

CONNELLY, DIANE, elementary educator; b. Logan, Utah, Sept. 27, 1952; d. Melvin Abraham and Grace Huppi; m. Alvin Lee Connelly, July 14, 1990. BS, Utah State U., 1973, MEd, 1988. Elem. tchr. Uinta County Sch. Dist., Evanston, Wyo., 1975—. Presenter in field. Tchr. Cmty. Edn., 1977-78; student body vol. dir. Student Svcs., Logan, Utah, 1972-73; pres. Uinta County Reading Coun., 1988, 98; bd. dirs. Girl's Youth Volleyball, Evanston; rep. youth com. Evanston Parks and Recreation. Named Vol. of Yr. Utah State Student Svcs., 1973, Elem. Tchr. Qtr. Tchrs. Assn. Mem. NEA, Wyo. Edn. Assn., Evanston Edn. Assn., Internat. Reading Assn., Delta Kappa Gamma. Avocations: reading, family, pets, friends, working with youth. Office: Uinta Meadows Elem Sch PO Box 6002 Evanston WY 82931-6002

CONNELLY, ELIZABETH ANN, retired state legislator; b. N.Y.C. d. John Walter and Alice Marie (Mallon) Keresey; m. Robert Vincent Connelly; children: Alice, Robert, Margaret, Therese. Grad. H.S., Bronx; LLD (hon.), Wagner Coll., 1996. Telephone sales Pan Am. World Airways, N.Y.C., 1946-54; mem. N.Y. State Assembly, Albany, 1973-2000, chair com. on mental health, retardation/devel. disabilities, 1977-92, chair com. on standing coms., 1993-95, speaker pro tem, 1995-2000, chair intern com., 1995-2000; ret., 2000. Chair Legis. Women's Caucus, N.Y. State, 1993-95. Recipient over 350 awards and honors including S.I. Hosp. Vol. of Yr. award, 1972-73, Cert. Appreciation Willowbrook chpt. Benevolent Soc. Retarded Children, 1978, Legislator of Yr. award N.Y. State Coun. on Alcoholism, 1983, Woman of Yr. award Epilepsy Ctr., 1984, Disting. Humanitarian of Yr. award S.I. Ctr. Ind. Living, 1987, Alliance for Mentally Ill of N.Y. State award, 1988, Thomas G. Gilbert Meml. award N.Y. State Mental Health Soc., 1989, Nat. Barrier Awareness Found., 1990, Irish Am. Heritage Mus., 1991, N.Y. State Head Injury Assn. Pub. Policy award, 1994, N.Y. State Cath. Conf. Pub. Policy award 1996, St. John's U. Pres.' medal, 1998, Pres.' medal CUNY Coll. of S.I. Mem. Am.-Irish Legislators' Soc. (pres. 1999—). Democrat.

CONNELLY, JENNIFER, actress; b. New York, NY, Dec. 12, 1970; m. Paul Bettany, 2003. Actress: appeared in Italian, Canadian, British, Argentinian, and U.S. films: Once Upon a Time in America, 1984, Phenomena, 1985, The Valley, 1985, Labyrinth, 1986, Seven Minutes in Heaven, 1986, Some Girls, 1988, Etoile, 1988, The Hot Spot, 1990, Career Opportunities, 1991, The Rocketeer, 1991, Higher Learning, 1994, Far Harbor, 1996, Mulholland Falls, 1996, Of Love and Shadows, 1996, Dark City, 1997, Inventing the Abbots, 1997, Waking the Dead, 2000, Requiem for a Dream, 2000, Pollock, 2000, A Beautiful Mind, 2001 (Best Supporting Actress Acad. award 2001, Golden Globe, 2001, Am. Film Inst. award, Brit. Acad. award, Golden Satellite award, KCFCC award, OFCS award, SEFCA award and BFCA award 2001-2002, nominee Best Actress SAG award 2001, Featured Actor of Yr. Female Movies AFI Film award 2002), The Hulk, 2003, House of Sand and Fog, 2003; TV movies: The Heart of Justice, 1993; TV series: The Street, 2000. Office: Internat Creative Mgmt 8942 Wilshire Blvd Beverly Hills CA 90211-1934*

CONNELLY, JOAN BRETON, archaeologist; BA, Princeton U., 1976, MA, 1979; PhD, Bryn Mawr Coll., 1984. Asst. dean undergrad. coll., lectr. in classical and Near Eastern archaedology Bryn Mawr Coll., 1984—86; assoc. prof. fine arts NYU, 1986—, Lillian Vernon chair for tchg. excellence, 2002—, dir. Yeronisos Island Excavations, 1990—. Mem. French Archaeol. Mission to Failaka, Kuwait U. de Lyon, 1985—; mem. Pres.'s Cultural Property Adv. Com. U.S. Dept. State, 2003—. Author: Votive Sculpture of Hellenistic Cyprus, 1988. Named hon. citizen, Republic of Cyprus, Municipality of Peyia, 2000; recipient MacArthur Genius award, 1996; Classical fellow and Norbert Schimmel fellow, Met. Mus. Art, 1982—84, Oxford U. vis. fellow, All Souls Coll., 1994—95, New Coll., 1997, Magdalen Coll., 1998, John D. and Catherine T. MacArthur Found. fellow, 1996—2001, Radcliffe Inst. for Advanced Study, Harvard U., 2000, vis. scholar, Phi Beta Kappa Soc., 2000—01. Fellow: Explorers Club, Royal Geog. Soc., Soc. Antiquaries of London; mem.: Soc. for Preservation of the Greek Heritage (trustee), Soc. Women Geographers. Office: NYU Dept Fine Arts 303 Main Bldg 100 Washington Sq E New York NY 10003-6688 E-mail: joan.connelly@nyu.edu.

CONNELLY, MARY CREEDON, insurance company executive; b. Niagara Falls, N.Y., Apr. 1, 1950; d. Daniel Francis and Anne Walle (Moynihan) C. BA, Coll. New Rochelle, 1972. Dir. divsn. ins. Fed. Savs. and Loan Ins. Corp., Washington, 1984-86, dep. exec. dir., 1987-88, exec. dir., 1989; assoc. dir. FDIC, Washington, 1989-91; COO Farm Credit Sys. Ins. Co., McLean, Va., 1991—. Mem. Women in Housing and Fin. Avocation: watercolors. Home: 4315 31st St N Arlington VA 22207-4115 Office: Farm Credit Sys Ins Corp 1501 Farm Credit Dr Mc Lean VA 22102-5004

CONNELLY, SHARON RUDOLPH, lawyer; b. Kingwood, W.Va. d. John E. and Lorene E. Rudolph; 1 child, John. BS, W.Va. State U., 1966; MBA, Ind. U., 1968; JD, Cath. Univ., 1976; LLM in Taxation, Georgetown U., 1995. Bar: Va. 1977. Mgr. IRS, Washington, 1969-76, asst. contr. Mfrs. Hanover, N.Y.C., 1976-77; compliance chief D.C. Dept. Labor, Washington, 1977-79; dir. compliance U.S. Dept. Commerce, Washington, 1979-82; asst. insp. gen. NASA, Washington, 1982-84; dir. insp. office Nuc. Regulatory Commn., Washington, 1984-89, spl. asst. internal controls, 1989-98. Owner, fin., investment and mgmt. companies, 1998—. Contbr. articles to profl. jours.

CONNER, EUNICE EILEEN, city official; b. Germantown, Ohio, Sept. 13, 1929; d. George Washington and Mable Marguerite (Hoyt) Crickmore; m. Francis Herbert Simonson, June 4, 1949 (div. Mar. 1974); m. Charles Richard Conner, Dec. 20, 1975. Student, Miami Jacobs Bus. Coll., 1960, Ohio U., 1964-66; cert. of grad., Citizens Police Acad., 1993. Notary pub., Ohio; cert. of tng. Career Devel. in Pub. Sector, State of Ohio; cert. of tng. Enforcement Reporting and Procedure Standardization, State of Ohio; cert. of tng. Liquor Law Enforcement, State of Ohio. Sec. LWV, Dayton, Ohio, 1962-64; string reporter Dayton Tribune, 1966-67; exec. sec. Ohio Dept. Liquor Control, Columbus, 1972-82. Mem. bd. electors Yavapai Regional Med., Prescott, Ariz., 1989-91; rep. transit 4 County Conf./Devel. Dis., Prescott, 1994-95; rep. Nat. Assn. Coun. Govt., Flagstaff, Ariz., 1994—. Author: (cookbook) Peaches, Pine and Wine, 1971, (book) Star Buck, 1982; contbr. numerous poems and articles to mags. and newspapers. Sec. Mont. County Dem. Women, Dayton, 1969-70; pres. Prescott Valley Pub. Libr., 1987-88, v.p. bd., 1988-89; sec. Prescott Valley Art Guild, 1987; pres. Friends of Prescott Valley Pub. Libr., 1987-88; v.p. Prescott Valley Hist. Soc., 1996-97. Recipient Presdl. citation Am. Amateur Press, 1971, Cert. of Achievement, Am. Mgmt. Assn., 1982, Grand Prize for poetry Prescott Valley Art Guild, 1987, Cert. of Appreciation, Coun. of Electors, 1989-90, Local Elected Ofcl. award White House Conf. on Libr. and Info. Svcs. Task Force, 1993. Mem. DAR (v.p. 1996-97, mus. docents, state officers and chairperson of DAR Vets.-Patient Svc. VA Hosp., Cert. of Excellence in Comty. Svc. 1996), NAFE, Internat. Platform Assn., Am. Assn. Ret. Persons (charter mem. Prescott Valley chpt.), Ariz. Women in Mcpl. Govt., Toastmasters Internat., Prescott Valley C. of C., Mountain View Garden Club. Avocations: rock hounding, fishing, gardening, writing, sewing own clothing. Home: 7480 E Las Flores Ave Prescott Valley AZ 86314-5535

CONNERLEY, MARY L. psychologist, educator; b. Iowa; BS, Iowa State U., 1987, MS, 1988; PhD, U. Iowa, 1993. Assoc. prof. Va. Tech., Blacksburg, 2000—, asst. prof., 1993—2000. Mem.: Am. Psychol. Soc., Soc. for Human Resource Mgmt., Soc. for Indsl. and Orgnl. Psychologists, Acad. Mgmt. Office: Virginia Tech 2007 Pamplin Hall Blacksburg VA 24061 Business E-Mail: maryc@vt.edu.

CONNERLY, DIANNA JEAN, business official; b. Urbana, Ill., June 7, 1947; d. Ellsworth Wayne and Imogene (Sundermeyer) C. Student, Ill. Comml. Coll., 1967. Bookkeeper Jerry Earl Pontiac, 1968-72; office mgr. Jack Nicklaus Pontiac, 1972-76, Simon Motors Inc., Palm Springs, Calif., 1977-83, bus. mgr., 1983—. Vol. counselor How Found., 1992. Mem. Am. Bus. Women's Assn. (dir. pub. rels. Trendsetter chpt. 1983-85). Office: 78-611 Hwy 111 La Quinta CA 92253

CONNOLLY, ELMA TROUTMAN, artist, contractor, designer; b. Middleburg, Pa., May 10, 1931; d. Benjamin F. and Eva Ellen (DeLong) Hollenback; m. Kenneth R. Troutman, Aug. 15, 1950; children: Kenneth, Linda, Robert, Terri; m. Jerome P. Connolly, Apr. 15, 1973. Student, Lock Haven State Tchrs. Coll., 1949. Profl. dancer, 1949—51; instr.; cons. for exceptions unit Pa. Tax Bur., Harrisburg; owner, founder, pres. Arts ETC Co., Sunbury, Pa.; owner Art Gallery, 1976-93. Bus. cons. Cohen, Danville, 1970-72; art restoration work, 1955-2004; art instr., Pa., Fla. and Idaho, 1959-2004. Murals (with Jerome Connolly): Nature Ctr., Winston Salem, N.C., 1974, South Am. Hall-Smithsonian Nat. History Mus., Washington, 1975, George Page Mus. of La Brea Discoveries, L.A., 1976, Makah Mus., Neah Bay, Wash., 1978, Woolly Mammoth Background, Frozen Delta Diorama Provincial Mus. B.C., Can., 1979, The African Hall Springfield (Mass.) Sci. Mus., 1980, Big Cypress Nature Ctr., Naples, Fla., 1982, Indian Hall Ill. State Mus., 1984, Edn. Ctr. Taipei, Taiwan, 1987, African Water Hole, American Kudu, Carnagie Mus. Nat. History, Pa., 1992, 21K Diorama, 1974, Alaskan Brown Bear, Carnagie Mus. Natural History, Pitts., 1994; sculpture, murals George Page Mus., Provincial Mus., Springfield Sci. Mus., Big Cypress Nature Ctr. Fla., Pa. State Univ., 2000, Pa. Messiah Coll. Oak Mus., 2001-02, entire Page Mus.; sculpture The Foregrounds for Mass. Mus., Nature Ctr. Fla.; restoration of painting, design jewelry and costume La Brea Women. Pres. Susquehanna Art League, 1999. Named Woman of Yr., ABI, 1991; recipient Am. Women's award. Mem. NAFE, Sunbury Mchts. Coun. (pres.), C. of C. (govt. affairs com.), Susquehanna Art Soc. (pres.), Internat. Platform Assn. Republican. Avocations: sculpture, writing, civic affairs, art, bldg. contractor. Home: RR 2 Box 176n3 Selinsgrove PA 17870-9657 Office Phone: 570-743-7008. Personal E-mail: murals051031@aol.com.

CONNOLLY, JANET ELIZABETH, retired sociologist and criminal justice educator; b. New Rochelle, N.Y., June 28, 1929; d. Michael A. and Vincentia (Bonitatibus) Dandry; m. Edward C. Connolly, June 7, 1952; children: Michael, Matthew, Christopher, Benedict, Andrew. BA, Chestnut Hill Coll., Phila., 1951; MA, Temple U., Phila., 1970, PHD, 1975; hon. degree, Rilski Neofit U., Blagoevgrad, Bulgaria, 1992. Intelligence clk. CIA, Washington, 1951-52; tchr. Prince George's County Bd. Edn., Hyattsville, Md., 1952-53; rsch. assoc. Pa. Prison Soc., Phila., 1974-76; field dir. rsch. Georgetown U. Law Sch., Washington, 1976-77; rsch. dir. Phila. Commn. for Effective Criminal Justice, 1977-78; mem. faculty dept. criminal justice Temple U., Phila., 1980-91; mem. faculty dept. sociology Am. U. in Bulgaria, Blagoevgrad, 1991-96; guest lectr. Sch. Law Kiril E Metodi Univerzitet, Skopje, Macedonia, 1993. Cons. Bucks County Correctional Facility, Doylestown, Pa., 1987-91; evaluator Phila. Prison System, 1973. Campaign chairperson, Doylestown, Pa., 1980, 82, 84, 86, 90; pres. Bucks County Assn. for Corrections and Rehab., Doylestown, 1988-91; trustee Bucks County Community Coll., Newtown, Pa., 1989-91; bd. dirs. ARC, Bucks County chpt., Doylestown, 1980-82; mem. New Hope (Pa.) Civil Svc. Commn., 1986-91; bd. dirs. Planned Parenthood, 1986-88. U.S. Justice Dept. dissertation grantee, Washington, 1972. Mem. ACLU, LWV, Law and Soc. Assn., Am. Correctional Assn., Balkan Ednl. and Sci. Assn. (mem. sci. senate). Democrat. Avocations: gardening, embroidery, oil painting. Home: 762 Fairview Ave Apt C Annapolis MD 21403-2962 E-mail: zdravete@aol.com.

CONNOLLY, VIOLETTE M. small business owner; b. N.Y.C., Nov. 25, 1918; d. Gysbert Martens and Marie Therese dePont; m. Joseph Vincent Connolly Jr., Feb. 27, 1957 (dec.). BA, Hunter Coll., 1940; Ms, Columbia U., 1941. Accredited Pub. Rels. Soc. Am. Analyst The Payne Fund, N.Y.C., 1941-53; ptnr. Elser & Assocs., N.Y.C., 1954-56, The J.V. Connolly Co., N.Y.C., 1957-64; cons. on pub. rels., radio and TV Assn. of the Jr. Leagues of Am., N.Y.C., 1964-72; asst. dir. N.Y. Assn. for Brain Injured Children, N.Y.C., 1973-74; circulation mgr. Plants and Gardens Bklyn. Botanic Garden, N.Y.C., 1974-82; adminstr. Nat. Broadcasting Co., N.Y.C., 1983-86; owner, mgr. The White House, Block Island, R.I., 1986—; clk. Town of New Shoreham, Block Island, 1986—. Bd. mem., publicist The Village Art Ctr., N.Y.C., 1944-54; pres. Washington Sq. Bus. and Profl. Women's Club, N.Y.C., 1953-55; founder, chair House and Garden Tours Com., Block Island Hist. Soc., 1971-96; pres. Block Island Gardeners, 1986-97. Capt. First Assembly Dist., Rep. Club, N.Y.C., 1945-57; mem. Bishop's com. St. Ann's Ch., 1995—. Republican. Avocations: oriental gardens, antique collecting, traveling. Home: The White House PO Box 447 Block Island RI 02807-0447

CONNOR, CAROL J. library director; BA in History, Molloy Coll., 1964; MA in History, Georgetown U., 1970; MS in Libr. Sci., Drexel U., 1972. Various adminstrv. positions in ednl. fields, various U.S. Cities, 1964-72; spl. asst. tech. processes divsn. Lincoln (Nebr.) City Librs., 1972-73, coord. tech. processes divsn., 1973-76, asst. dir., 1976-78, dir., 1978—. Mem. Mayor's Com. for Internat. Friendship, Lincoln, 1973—; adv. com. U. Nebr., search for dean of librs., 1984-85; del. to cmty. retreat, Star Venture, 1986, edn. task force, 1987-88, vocat. edn. task force, 1988-89, downtown child care task force, 1988-89; mem. cmty. adv. com. Lincoln Pub. Schs. Search for English Cons., 1991, Search for Media Dir., 1992; mem. Nebr. Ctr. for Book Bd., 1990-95, Nebr. Libr. Commn. state adv. coun. 1985-86, Nebr. Lit. Festival Com., 1990-92; bd. dirs. Postsecondary Ednl. Librs. and Resource Ctrs. of Nebr. 1991-94, chair 1992; mem. edn. com. Am. Cancer Soc., Lancaster County, Nebr., 1989-91, Family Svcs. Bd., 1991—, vice chair chair elect 1992, chair, 1994; leadership Lincoln VI 1990-91; mem. Lincoln Cancer Ctr. adv. bd., 1988-94, vice chair 1991-94. Mem. ALA, (bylaws com., membership com., LITA/LAMA conf. com. 1996-97), Mountain Plains Libr. Assn. (chair continuing edn. com. 1984-85; membership devel. com. 1986-87, vice chair and chair of pub. libr. sect. 1975-77, v.p./ pres. elect 1996-97, pres. 1997-98), Nebr. Libr. Assn. (chair intellectual freedom com. 1975-76, state rep. to Mountain Plains Libr. Assn., 1984-86, vice chair and chair of pub. libr. sect. 1987-89), Urban Librs. Coun. (leadership programs 1994-95), Capitol Bus. and Profl. Women (v.p. 1983), Downtown Lincoln Assn. (mktg. com. 1988-89). Office: Lincoln City Librs 136 S 14th St Lincoln NE 68508-1899

CONNOR, CATHERINE BROOKS, educational media specialist; b. Dothan, Ala., Oct. 29, 1955; d. James Bolling and Margaret Elizabeth (Jones) Brooks; m. Joseph Yauger Whealdon, Jr., June 12, 1983 (div. Aug. 1990); 1 child, Joseph Yauger III; m. William Christopher Connor, Dec. 28, 1991. BS, Fla. State U., 1980, MS in Libr. Sci., 1990. Cert. profl. media specialist, Fla., nat. cert. libr. media specialist. 2002. Asst. br. mgr. City Fed. Savs. and Loan, Birmingham, Ala., 1976-77; elem. tchr. Louise S. McGehee Sch., New Orleans, 1981-85; kindergarten tchr. Lafayette Elem. Sch., New Orleans, 1986; grad. asst. Fla. State U. Sch. Libr. Sci., Tallahassee, 1990; media specialist Lely H.S., Naples, Fla., 1990-91, Frank M. Golson Elem. Sch., Marianna, Fla., 1991—, chmn. sch. adv. coun., 1995-98, leadership team, 1994—. Bd. dirs. Jackson County Pub. Libr.-Friends of Libr., Marianna, 1992-94, mem. adv. bd. 1998—, sec. 1998—; bd. dirs. Jackson County unit Am. Cancer Soc., 1998-2000, chair nominating com., 1998-99; charter mem. Libr. of Congress, Washington, 1994—; mem. Panhandle Pub. Libr. Coop. Sys. Bd., 1998—, mem. pers. com., 2000—. Mem. DAR (libr. 2000—), Colonial Dames, Descs. of Knights of the Garter. Democrat. Episcopalian. Avocations: geneology, travel, sculling. Home: PO Box 507 Marianna FL 32447-0507 Office: Frank M Golson Elem Sch 4258 2d Ave Marianna FL 32446-1905

CONNOR, DORINDA A. state legislator; BS, West Chester State Coll. Mem. Dist. 12 Del. Senate, Dover, 1997—. Mem. adminstrv. svcs. com. Del. State Senate, bond bill com., children, youth and families com., labor and indsl. rels. com., natural resources and environ. control com. Republican. Home: 18 Crippen Dr New Castle DE 19720-3243 Office: Delaware State Senate PO Box 1401 Dover DE 19903-1401

CONNOR, NANCY L. foundation executive; b. Chgo., Sept. 7, 1960; d. Edward Joseph and Bernadette Marie Cider; m. Martin David Connor, June 16, 1984 (div. Nov. 1987). BS, Towson State U., 1982. Sys. adminstr. Ballistics Rsch. Lab., Aberdeen, Md., 1982-84; programmer, documentation specialist Symbolics, Inc., Boston, 1984-86; pres., chmn. FTP Software, Inc., Boston, 1986-93; pres. Ringing Rocks Found., Phila., 1995—. Co-chmn. discretionary fund Women's Way, Phila., 1995-2001. Mem. Internat. Soc. Study Subtle Energy and Energy Mgmt., Inst. Noetic Scis., James Smithson Soc. of Smithsonian Instn. Avocations: gardening, pottery, gliding. Office: Ringing Rocks Found PO Box 22656 Philadelphia PA 19110-2656

CONNOR, WILDA, government health agency administrator; b. Pleasantville, N.J., Apr. 9, 1947; d. Herman Smith and Rubina (Miraglilo) Cooney; m. James J. Connor Jr., Nov. 5, 1966; 1 child, James J. III. BSBA cum laude, Rowan U., 1985; MS, U. Pa., 1995. Employee services coord. Turning Point Drug Outpatient Program, Collingswood, NJ, 1976-78; mgmt. specialist Camden County Ctr. Addictive Diseases, Lakeland, NJ, 1978-87; adminstr. Family Practice Ctrs. Camden (N.J.) County Health Dept., 1988—; fiscal analyst Camden County Dept. Health & Human Svcs., Lakeland, NJ, 1995—2002; COO Med. One, Inc., Mays Landing, NJ, 2002—. Com. fund raiser Camden County Dem. Congl. Campaign, Stratford, N.J., 1986; mem. Solid Waste Adv. Coun., Camden County; mem. Coastal Resources Adv. Commn. Dept. Environ. Protection. Mem. N.J. Assn. Alcoholism Counselors, N.J. Substance Abuse Cert. Bd. (cert. 1987, 89 MSA), LWV, Solid Waste Adv. Council. Roman Catholic. Avocations: jogging, aerobics, skiing, travel. Home: 228 Vasey Ave Lindenwold NJ 08021-2249 Office: Medical One Inc 4622 Black Horse Pike Mays Landing NJ 08330 E-mail: wconnor@docisp.com.

CONNORS, DORSEY, television and radio commentator, newspaper columnist; b. Chgo. d. William J. and Sarah (MacLain) C.; m. John E. Forbes; 1 dau., Stephanie. BA cum laude, U. Ill. Fl. reporter WGN-TV Rep. Nat. Conv., Chgo., Dem. Nat. Conv., L.A., 1960. Conducted: Personality Profiles, WGN-TV, Chgo., 1948-49, Dorsey Connors Show, WMAQ-TV, Chgo., 1949-58, 61-63, Armchair Travels, WMAQ-TV, 1952-55, Homeshow, NBC,1954-57, NBC Today Show, Dorsey Connors program, WGN, 1958-61, Tempo Nine, WGN-TV, 1961, Society in Chgo, WMAQ-TV, 1964; writer: column Hi! I'm Dorsey Connors, Chgo. Sun Times, 1965—; Author: Gadgets Galore, 1953, Save Time, Save Money, Save Yourself, 1972, Helpful Hints for Hurried Homemakers, 1988. Founder Ill. Epilepsy League; mem. woman's bd. Children's Home and Aid Soc., mem. women's bd. USO. Named one of Am.'s Outstanding Irish Am. Women, World of Hibernia mag., 1995. Mem. AFTRA, NATAS (Silver Cir. award 1995), SAG, Mus. Broadcast Comm. (founding mem.), Soc. Midland Authors, Chgo. Hist. Soc. (guild com., costume com.), Chi Omega. Roman Catholic. Office: Chgo Sun Times 401 N Wabash Ave Chicago IL 60611-5642

CONNORS, MICHELE PERROTT, wholesale beverage company executive; b. Ft. Lauderdale, Fla., June 28, 1952; d. Samuel R. and Mariette (Larouche) Perrott; m. Robert Gary Connors, Apr. 14, 1973; children: Eva Marie, Colleen Elizabeth. AA, Daytona Beach Community Coll., Fla., 1972. Legal sec. Richard Krause, Ormond Beach, Fla., 1972-74; sec. S.R. Perrott, Inc., Ormond Beach, 1974-79, v.p., ops. mgr., 1979-83, pres., chief exec. officer, 1983—. Prin., pres. Michele & Group Modeling Talent Agy., 1989—. Bd. dirs. Daytona Beach Easter Seals Soc., 1985—, chmn. fundraising, 1983-86; bd. dirs. Am. Cancer Soc., 1989—; tennis dir., coach Father Lopez H.S., 1995—. Mem. Beer Industry Fla., Nat. Beer Wholesalers, Ormond Beach C. of C. (pres. 1984), Oceanside Country Club, Trails Racquet Club. Republican. Roman Catholic. Office: S R Perrott Inc PO Box 836 Ormond Beach FL 32175-0836

CONOLLY, KATHARINE FARNAM, editor; b. Rochester, N.Y., Dec. 2, 1969; d. Henry W. III and Bonnie Lou (Ewell) Farnam; m. Christopher Jason Conolly, Oct. 10, 1998. BA in Psychology and English Lit. summa cum laude, St. John Fisher Coll., Rochester, 1998. Cert. in publishing/editing U. Calif. Berkeley. Exec. asst. Chase Manhattan Bank, Rochester, 1992-98; editor New World Libr., Novato, Calif., 1999—. Presenter N.Y. State English conf. Recipient Sholastic Gold Key award in photography. Mem. Sigma Tau Delta (pres. Coll. chpt. 1997-98), Psi Chi, Delta Epsilon Sigma, Alpha Xi Delta. Avocations: hiking, outdoor activities, reading, writing, photography. Office: New World Library 14 Pamaron Way Novato CA 94949-6215 Home: 2550 Gibson Rd Alpine NY 14805-9800 Fax: 415-884-2199. E-mail: katie@nwlib.com.

CONOVER, MONA LEE, retired adult education educator; b. Lincoln, Nebr., Nov. 9, 1929; d. William Cyril and Susan Ferne (Floyd) C.; m. Elmer Kenneth Johnson, June 14, 1953 (div. 1975); children: Michael David, Susan Amy, Sharon Ann, Jennifer Lynne. AB, Nebr. Wesleyan U., 1952; student, Ariz. State U., 1973-75; MA in Edn., No. Ariz. U., 1985. Cert. tchr., Colo., Ariz. Tchr. Jefferson County R-1 Sch., Wheat Ridge, Colo., 1952-56, Glendale (Ariz.) Elem. Sch. 40, 1972-92; dir. Glendale Adult Edn., 1987-92; ret., 1992. Author: ABC's of Naturalization, 1989. Mem. FOGG, Garden of Gods volunterr Information Ctr.,, NIA (Nat. Assn for Interpretation) NEA Ret. Life, Heard Mus., Cheyenne Mountain Zoo, Order of Ea. Star. Republican. Methodist. Avocations: music, travel, photography, history.

CONOVER, NANCY ANDERSON, retired secondary school counselor; b. Manhattan, Kans., July 8, 1943; d. Howard Julius and Wilma June (Katz) Anderson; m. Gary Hites Conover, Aug. 10, 1968; children: Chad Anderson, Cary Hites. BS in Edn., Kans. State U., 1965; MEd, Wichita State U., 1991. Cert. sch. counselor, tchr., Kans.; lic. profl. counselor, Kans. Tchr. Flint (Mich.) Sch. Dist., 1965-66, Unified Sch. Dist. 259, Wichita, Kans., 1967-68, Overland Park (Kans.) Sch. Dist., 1968-70; bus. mgr., sec.-treas. Gary Conover, D.D.S., Wichita, 1985-94; sch. counselor Unified Sch. Dist. 259, Wichita, 1991-94; secondary sch. counselor Unified Sch. Dist. 385, Andover, Kans., 1994—2002; ret., 2002. Mem. Am. Counselors Assn., Kans. Sch. Counselors Assn., Kans. Assn. Counselors, Mental Health Counselors Assn., Kans. Dental Aux. (sec. 1970-74), Wichita Dist. Dental Aux. (pres. 1970-75), Jr. League Wichita (adminstrv. v.p. 1978-82), Gamma Phi Beta, Phi Kappa Phi. Republican. Lutheran. Avocations: golf, reading. E-mail: gcon810000@sbcglobal.net.

CONOVER, NELLIE COBURN, retail furniture company executive; b. Lebanon, Ohio, Dec. 21, 1921; d. Frank C. and Isabel (Murphy) Coburn; student public schs.; m. Lawrence E. Conover, Jan. 11, 1941; children—Lawrence R., Carol, David C., Constance, Christina. Co-founder, 1949, since exec. sec.-treas. Larry Conover Furniture & Appliance, Inc., and predecessor, Milford, Ohio, also trustee co. pension fund. Mem. Milford C. of C., Cin. Hist. Soc., Milford Hist. Soc., DAR. Democrat. Roman Catholic. Home: 438 Main St Milford OH 45150-1128

CONOVER, PAMELA C. cruise line executive; married. Cashier Wells Fargo Bank, London, with NYC, 1979—81; asst. treas. US Line, 1981—85; various positions in mng. dir. N. Am. ship financing divsn. Citicorp, 1985—94; pres. Epirotiki Cruises, Carnival Corp., 1994; v.p. strategic planning Carnival Corp., 1994—98; COO Cunard Line Ltd., Carnival Corp., 1998—, pres., 2001—. Achievements include only female pres. major cruise line; Cunard Line Ltd. launched Queen Mary II in 2004, largest transatlantic cruise ship to date. Office: Cunard Line Ltd 6100 Blue Lagoon Dr Ste 400 Miami FL 33126*

CONOVER-CARSON, ANNE, writer; d. George Richards and A. Louise (Pinkerton) Conover; m. Thomas N. Ambrose, June 22, 1959 (div. Oct. 1967); 1 child, Natalie Anne Ambrose ; m. Thomas B. Carson, Nov. 14, 1970 (dec. June 2002). BA, Stanford U., 1959, MA, 1966. Editor Curtis Pub. Co., Phila., 1959—61, Johns Hopkins Press, Balt., 1966—68; editor, writer Libr. Congress, Washington, 1968—76, U.S. Info. Agy., 1976—90; editor-in-chief Anne Carson Assocs., 1990—. Author: Caresse Crosby: From Black Sun to Roccasinibalda, 1990, Ezra Pound and the Cadsby Continental Editions, 1993; author: (with Julia Montgomery Walsh) Risk and Rewards: A Memoir, 1998; author: Ezra Pound and Olga Rudge: What Thou Lovest Well, 2001, Olga Rudge: Pound's Muse and the Circe of the Cantos in Ezra Pound: Nature and Myth, 2003. Mem. Women's Nat. Dem. Club, U.S. Capitol Hist. Soc. Nominee Best Scholarly Biography of Yr., Yale Press, 2001. Mem.: MLA, Author's Guild, Am. Acad. Poets, Nat. Coalition Ind. Scholars, Knickerbocker Club (N.Y.C.), Met. Club (Washington). Democrat. Episcopalian. Avocations: chamber and early music, Chinese brush painting, travel.

CONRAD, CHERYL DIANE, behavioral neuroscientist; b. West Los Angeles, Mar. 18, 1963; d. Dale DeVere and Anita Clarice (Hudgin) C.; m. Curtis James Condon, Sept. 14, 1985 (div. July 1993); m. Stuart Greenstein, Aug. 23, 1996; 1 child. BS in Chemistry, BS in Biology, U. Calif., Irvine, 1986; PhD in Neurosci., U. Ill., 1994. Technician U. Calif., Irvine, 1986-87; postdoctoral fellow Rockefeller U., N.Y.C., 1994-97; asst. prof. psychology Ariz. State U., Tempe, 1997—2003, assoc. prof. psychology, 2003—. Contbr. articles to profl. jours. Recipient Doolen Scholarship for the Study of Aging, U. Ill., 1991-92. Mem. Am. Psychol. Soc., Soc. for Neurosci., Phi Kappa Phi. Democrat. Protestant. Avocations: weightlifting, softball, antiques, travel. Office: Ariz State U Dept Psychology Box 871104 Tempe AZ 85287-1104

CONRAD, KAREN M. music educator, musician; b. Jersey City, N.J., Oct. 18, 1951; d. Marinus L. and Dorothy Hoogerhyde; m. David W. Conrad, May 27, 1977; children: Kristen E., Paul C. BA Music Edn., Montclair State U., 1973; MusM Cello Performance, New Eng. Conservatory Boston, 1977. String tchr. (grades 3-9) Rockaway Twp. Schools, NJ, 1973—74; tchr. strings, band, orch. South Orange-Maplewood Sch. Dist., Maplewood, NJ, 1974—75; instr. instrumental music Montclair Magnet Sch. for Gifted and Talented, NJ, 1977—78; dir. strings and orch. South Orange-Maplewood Sch. Dist., 1978—98; dir. strings, orch. (grades 9-12) Millburn Twp. Schs., Millburn, NJ, 1998—. Freelance profl. cellist N.J. State Opera, Performing Arts Ctr., NJ, 1977—, Paper Mill Playhouse, Millburn, 1978—; pvt. cello tchr., NJ, 1968—98; organizing chair of region 1 orch. festivals NJSMA, Region 1 Orch. Festivals, 1998—; dir. orch. prep divsn. Montclair State U., 1984—86. Leader Girl Scouts of Essex/Hudson County, Maplewood, 1997—2000; choir mem. Prospect Presbyn. Ch., Maplewood. Mem.: Local 16, 204-373, Music Educators Nat. Conf., SAI (life). Achievements include Conducted in Munich, Germany 1985 World Youth Music Festival Conductor, Region 1 Orch., Master Tchrs. Collaboration, 2004. Avocations: reading, bicycling, cooking. Office: Millburn High School 462 Millburn Ave Millburn NJ 07041

CONRAD-ENGLAND, ROBERTA LEE, pathologist; b. Meriden, Conn., Aug. 25, 1950; d. Hans and Emma Ann (Bort) Conrad; m. Gary Thomas England, June 6, 1976; children: Eric Bryan, Christopher Ryan. BS in Microbiology, U. Ky., 1972, MD, 1976. Diplomate Nat. Bd. Med. Examiners, Bd. Am. Pathologists. Resident anatomic and clin. pathology Emory U. Affiliated Hosps., Atlanta, 1976-80; pathologist Western Bapt. Hosp., Paducah, Ky., 1980—. Cons. Marshall County Hosp., Benton, Ky., 1985—, chair infection control com., 1985—. Mem., com. chairperson PTA, Poducah, Ky., 1993-94; mother's asst. Boy Scouts Am., Poducah, 1991-94. Fellow Coll. Am. Pathologists, Am. Soc. Clin. Pathologists; mem. Ky. Med. Assn., Ky. Soc. Pathologists, Ky. Women Mentors in Sci., Alpha Omega Alpha, Phi Beta Kappa. Avocations: swimming, snorkeling, interior decorating.

CONRADER, CONSTANCE RUTH, artist, writer, librarian; b. Vandalia, Mo., Apr. 13, 1919; d. Gilbert Fordyce and Elizabeth Florence (Cleghorn) Stone; m. Jay Merten Conrader, Nov. 29, 1941 (dec. 1996). Student, Carroll Coll., 1938-40, North Park Coll., 1940-41. Cert. pub. libr. Artist, author, Oconomowoc, Wis., 1940—. Libr. Oconomowoc Pub. Libr., 1947-82, vol. 1982—; illustrator Turtox classroom charts Gen. Biol. Supply House, Chgo., 1940-60; manuscript critique Baha'i Pub. Trust, Wilmette, Ill., 1970-89, editor, 1988. Author, illustrator: Blue Wampum, 1958; co-editor: Tokens From the Writings of Baha'u'llah, 1973, Baha'i newsletter, 1997—; illustrator: Northwoods Wildlife Region, 1983; co-author, illustrator articles to profl. jours.; co-editor regional Baha'i Newsletter, 1997—. Chair UN Day, Oconomowoc, 1976-86. Avocations: gardening, music, reading, cooking. Home: 738 E Washington St Oconomowoc WI 53066-3110

CONRADT, JODY, basketball coach; b. Goldthwaite, Tex., May 13, 1941; BS in Phys. Edn., Baylor U., 1963, MS in Phys. Edn., 1969. Women's basketball, volleyball and track head coach Sam Houston State U., Huntsville, Tex., 1969—73; women's basketball, volleyball and softball head coach U. Tex., Arlington, 1973—76, head women's basketball coach Austin, 1976—, women's athletic dir., 1992—2001. Mem. Coaches vs. Cancer/Am. Cancer Soc.; hon. chair Susan B. Komen Race for the Cure fundraising walk/run, Austin, 2003; vol. annual walk Austin's SafePlace. Named one of Top 50 Women's Sports Execs. in the nation, Street & Smith's Sports Bus. Jour., 1998; named to Internat. Women's Sports Hall of Fame, N.Y.C., 1995, Naismith Meml. Basketball Hall of Fame, 1998, Women's Basketball Hall of Fame, 1999, Internat. Scholar-Athlete Hall of Fame, 2003, Tex. Women's Hall of Fame, 1986, Tex. Sports Hall of Fame, 1998, U. Tex. Women's Athletics Hall of Honor, 2000; recipient John and Nellie Wooden Nat. Coach of the Yr. award, 1996—97, Nat. Coach of the Yr. award, ESPN.com, 2002—03, Harvey Penick award for Excellence in the Game of Life, Caritas, Austin, 2003, Carol Eckman award, Women's Basketball Coach's Assn., 1987, Nat. Award for outstanding commitment to women's athletics, Nat. Assn. for Girls and Women in Sports, 1991, award for contbn. to sports, NCAA, 1992. Office: Univ of Texas Athletics Office PO Box 7399 Austin TX 78713*

CONROY, FRANCES, actress; b. Macon, Ga., 1953; m. Jan Munroe, 1992. Student, The Neighborhood Playhouse Sch. of the Theatre, New York, Dickinson Coll., Carlisle, Penn.; Degree in Drama, Juilliard Sch., New York. Actor: (films) Manhattan, 1979, Othello, 1979, Falling in Love, 1984, Amazing Grace and Chuck, 1987, In the Hands of the Enemy, 1987, Rocket Gibraltor, 1988, Another Woman, 1988, Dirty Rotten Scoundrels, 1988, Hostile Witness, 1988, Crimes and Misdemeanors, 1989, Billy Bathgate, 1991, Scent of a Woman, 1992, Sleepless in Seattle, 1993, The Adventures of Huck Finn, 1993, Angela, 1995, The Neon Bible, 1995, Developing, 1995, The Crucible, 1996, Maid in Manhattan, 2002, Die, Mommie, Die, 2003; (plays, stage debut) Measure for Measure, 1978; (Broadway plays) The Lady from Dubuque, 1980, The Secret Rapture, 1990 (Drama Desk Award, 1990), The Ride Down Mt. Morgan, 2000 (Tony Award nom., Outer Critics Circle Award, 2000); (TV series) Six Feet Under, 2001— (Emmy Award nom., 2002, Golden Globe award for best actress in a dramatic series, 2004, Screen Actors Guild Award for best actress in a drama series, 2004); (TV films) Carl Sandburg: Echoes and Silences, 1982, The Royal Romance of Charles and Diana, 1982, Kennedy, 1983, LBJ: The Early Years, 1987, Terrorist on Trial: The United States vs. Salim Ajami, 1988, Our Town, 1989, One More Mountain, 1994, Journey, 1995, Innocent Victims, 1996, Thicker Than Blood, 1998, Murder in a Small Town, 1999; (TV miniseries) Queen, 1993. Office: HBO 1100 6th Ave New York NY 10036*

CONROY, MARY A. state legislator; Mem. Md. Ho. of Dels., Annapolis, 1987—. Mem. ways and means com., joint com. on health care cost containment. Democrat. Office: Md Ho of Dels 208 Lowe House Office Bldg 84 College Ave Annapolis MD 21401-1991

CONROY, SARAH BOOTH, columnist, writer, educator; b. Valdosta, Ga., Feb. 16, 1927; d. Weston Anthony and Ruth (Proctor) Booth; m. Richard Timothy Conroy, Dec. 31, 1949; children: Camille Booth, Sarah Claire. BS, U. Tenn., 1950. Continuity writer Sta. WNOX, 1945-48; commentator, writer Sta. WATO, 1948-49; reporter, architecture columnist Knoxville News Sentinel, 1949-56; assoc. editor The Diplomat mag., 1956-58; columnist Washington Post, 1957-58, design editor, columnist, editor in chief Living in Style, 1970-82, feature writer, columnist, 1982-94, Chronicles columnist, 1986—; reporter, art critic Washington Daily News, 1968-70; regular contbr. N.Y. Times, 1968-70. Mem. adv. bd. Horizon mag., 1978-85 Author: Refinements of Love A Novel about Clover and Henry Adams, 1993. Recipient Raven award Mystery Writers Am., 1990, U. Tenn. Disting. Alumni award, 1995, Mortar Bd. award, 1997. Mem.: AIA (hon. first recipient Glenn Brown award 2000). Home: 5016 16th St NW Washington DC 20011-3842

CONSAGRA, SOPHIE CHANDLER, academic administrator; b. Radnor, Pa., Apr. 28, 1927; d. Alfred D. and Carol (Ramsay) Chandler; children: Maria, Pierluigi, Francesca, George. BA, Smith Coll., 1949; MA, Cambridge (Eng.) U., 1952. Exec. dir. Del. Arts Council, 1972-78; dir. visual arts and architecture N.Y. State Council Arts, 1978-80; dir. Am. Acad. in Rome, 1980-84, pres., 1984-88, pres. emerita, vice chmn./spl. projects, 1988-90. Cons. Nat. Endowment Arts. Recipient Smith Coll. award, 1986, Centennial medal Am. Acad. in Rome, 1995. Address: 955 Lexington Ave New York NY 10021-5128

CONSIDINE, JILL, banker; m. Martin Rettinger; 1 child, Danielle. BS in Biology, St. John's U., 1965, LLD (hon.), 1986; postgrad. in biochemistry, Bryn Mawr Coll., 1965-67; MS, Grad. Sch. Bus., Columbia U., 1980. V.p. Chase Manhattan Bank, N.Y.C., 1971-81, Bankers Trust, N.Y.C., 1981-83; pres., chief exec. officer The First Women's Bank, N.Y.C., 1983-85; supt. banks N.Y. State Banking Dept., N.Y.C., 1985-91; mng. dir., chief admin. officer American Express Bank Ltd., 1991—93; pres. New York Clearing House Assn., N.Y.C., 1993-99; chmn., CEO The Depository Trust Co., N.Y.C., 1999—. Dir., cons. Ambac Fin. Corp., Atlantic Mut. Ins. Comps., Fed. Res. Bank N.Y. Mem. Coun. Fgn. Rels., Japan Soc., Group of 30 Steering Com., N.Y.C. Partnership, Securities Industry Found. Econ. Devel.; dir., cons. Sept. 11 Fund, Alliance Downtown N.Y. Named equities achiever of the yr., Equities Mag., 2000. Office: Depository Trust Co 55 Water St New York NY 10041-0001*

CONSILIO, BARBARA ANN, legal administrator, management consultant; b. Cleve., June 22, 1938; d. Joseph B. and Anna E. (Ford) C. BS, Kent State U., 1962; MA, U. Detroit, 1973. Cert. social worker, Mich. Tchr. Chagrin Falls (Ohio) High Sch., 1962-64; probation officer Macomb County Juvenile Ct., Mt. Clemens, Mich., 1965-68, casework supr., 1968-74, dir. children's svcs., 1974-79; mgr. foster care and instns. Oakland County Juvenile Ct., Pontiac, Mich., 1979-83; ct. adminstr. Oakland County Probate Ct., Pontiac, 1983-93, ret., 1993. Bd. dirs. Children's Charter Cts. of Mich., Lansing, Statewide Adv. Bd. on Sexual Abuse, Lansing, Havenwyck Hosp., Auburn Hills, Orchards Children's Svcs., Southfield, Oakland County Coun. Children at Risk, Pontiac; mem. Nat. Women's Polit. Caucus, N.Y.C.; bd. dirs. Care House, Pontiac. Mem. Nat. Coun. Juvenile and Family Ct. Adminstrs. Group, Mich. Probate and Juvenile Register's Assn., Mich. Juvenile Ct. Adminstrs. Assn., Nat. Assn. Ct. Mgrs., Supreme Ct. Task Force on Racial and Ethnic Bias, Office of Children and Youth Svcs. (state foster care system rev. com.), Nat. Coun. Juvenile and Family Ct. Judges (Outstanding Ct. Adminstr. award, 1993). Avocations: music, sports, sports cars. Home: 3000 Carefree Blvd M-4 Fort Myers FL 33917

CONSOLO, FAITH HOPE, real estate broker; b. Ohio; BFA, NYU; MFA, Parsons Sch. Design; AA in Real Estate Studies, NYU. Owner internat. promotional modeling agy.; owner interior design studio; small stores real estate broker; joined Garret-Aug Assocs. Store Leasing Inc., N.Y.C., 1985, sr. mng. dir., vice chmn., 1999—; founder, vice chmn. Garrick-Aug Worldwide. Apptd. cons. The 42nd St. Redevel. Corp., N.Y.C., Penn Sta. Redevel., N.Y.C., The Downtown Alliance, N.Y.C.; lectr. Assn. Women on Econ. Devel., Nat. Assn. Women Bus. Owners, The Women's Econ. Roundtable, Inst. Internat. Rsch., Nat. Assn. Appraisers & Planners, Women Inc.; bd. dirs. The Real Estate Bd. N.Y., Internat. Coun. Shopping Ctrs., Nat. Broker's Network; advisor Mayor's Coun. on the Aging Related Issues; instr. NYU Parsons Sch. Design, The Wharton Bus. Sch.; lectr. in field. Author: (internet newsletter) The Faith Report; contbr. N.Y. Post, The N.Y. Times, Crain's N.Y. Bus., Real Estate Weekly, N.Y. Real Estate Jour., Real Estate N.Y., others. Named Woman of Yr., Associated Builders and Owners of Greater N.Y., 1999, Woman of Outstanding Achievement, Assn. Real Estate Women, 2003, Woman of Valor, Capuchin Food Pantries of St. John the Bapt. Friary, 2003; named one of N.Y. Most Influential Women in Bus., Crain's N.Y. Bus., 1996, 1999. Mem.: Young Men's/Women's Real Estate Assn., Assn. Real Estate Women (past pres., creator The Founder's award). Office: Garrick-Aug 360 Lexington Ave 4th Fl New York NY 10017*

CONSTANT, ANITA AURELIA, publisher; b. Youngstown, Ohio, Jan. 5, 1945; d. Sandu Nicholas and Erie Marie (Tecau) C. BA, Ind. U., 1967; postgrad., Northwestern U., Evanston, Ill., 1991. Sales rep. Economy Fin. Inc., St. Louis, 1967-69; recruiter Case Western U. Hosp., Cleve., 1969-70; sales rep. Internat. Playtex Inc., Chgo., 1970-71, John Wiley & Sons, Inc., Chgo., 1971-77; sr. product mgr. CBS Pub. Inc., The Dryden Press, Chog., 1977-80; exec. editor Dearborn Fin. Pub., Inc., Chgo., 1980-81, v.p., 1981-89, sr. v.p., prin., 1989-97; cons. to pub. industry, 1997-98; prin. Ea. European investment venture EUROTEC, 1997-99; sr. v.p., editor-in-chief Southwestern Coll. Pub. divsn. ITP Inc., 1988-94; sr. v.p. new bus. devel. South-Western/Thomson Learning, 2000—; v.p. devel. and contract mgmt. Riverside Pub. Divsn. Houghton Mifflin, 1995—. Bd. dirs. Romanian Heritage Ctr., Detroit, 1988—, Orthodox Brotherhood of Am., Detroit, 1985—. Mem.: Nat. Assn. Women Bus. Owners, Chgo. Book Clinic (bd. dirs. 1987—88, v.p. 1988—90, pres. 1990—91, past pres. 1991—92, Mary Alexander award 1995), Internat. Assn. Fin. Planners, Real Estate Educators Assn., Chgo. Women in Pub. Eastern Orthodox. Avocations: property development and renovation, hiking, bicycling. Office: 425 Springlake Dr Itasca IL 60143 E-mail: anita_constant@hmco.com.

CONSTANTINE, JAN FRIEDMAN, lawyer; b. N.Y.C., Jan. 22, 1948; d. Howard J. and Elayne (Sercus) Friedman; m. Lawrence Levien, Oct. 11, 1970 (div. Sept. 1974); m. Lloyd E. Constantine, June 22, 1975; children: Isaac, Sarah, Elizabeth. BA, Smith Coll., Northampton, Mass., 1970; JD, George Washington U., 1973. Bar: N.Y. 1974, U.S. Dist. Ct. (so. and ea. dists.) N.Y. 1975, U.S. Ct. Appeals (2d cir.) 1975. Staff atty. div. spl. projects FTC, Washington, 1973-75, staff atty. N.Y. office N.Y.C., 1975-77; asst. atty. U.S. Dist. Ct. (ea. dist.) N.Y., Bklyn., 1977-82; litigation counsel Macmillan, Inc., N.Y.C., 1982-84, assoc. gen. counsel, 1985-90, dep. gen. counsel, 1990-91; exec. v.p. and dep. gen. counsel News Am. Inc., N.Y.C., 1992—; sr. gen. counsel News Am. Mktg. and Pub. Groups, N.Y.C.; sr. v.p. The News Corp. Ltd., N.Y.C., 1996—. Vis. asst. prof. George Washington U. Law Sch., Washington, 1974; bd. mem. The Feminist Press. Mem. Assn. of Bar of City of N.Y. (mem. consumer protection com. 1981-84, corp. law com. 1987-90, media law com. 1991-94, women in the law com. 1994-96, comm. and media law com. 1996—, chair 1999-2001). Avocations: tap dancing, tennis. Home: 10 W 66th St New York NY 10023-6206 Office: The News Corp Ltd Ste 300 1211 Avenue Of The Americas New York NY 10036-8795

CONSTANTINE, MARGARET L(OUISE) (PEGGY CONSTANTINE), newspaper reporter, freelance writer; b. Racine, Wis. d. Charles Ezra and Margaret (Moore) C. BA, Duke U., 1952; MSJ, Northwestern U., 1954. Biography editor World Book Ency., Chgo., 1957-60; reporter, book columnist, copy editor Chgo. Sun-Times, 1960-87. Contbr. book revs. to N.Y. Times, 1990—. Rockefeller Found. fellow for tng. music critics, 1967. Episcopalian. Avocation: golf. Home: 1225 S Main St Racine WI 53403-1928

CONSTANTINI, JOANN M. small business owner, consultant; b. Danbury, Conn., July 30, 1948; d. William J. and Mathilda J. (Ressler) C. BA, Coll. White Plains, N.Y., 1970; postgrad., Ctrl. Conn. State Coll., 1977-78, U. Hartford, 1985-88, U. Jacksonville, 1991; MS, Nova Southeastern U., 1996. Cert. records mgr., 1987; lic. realtor, N.C. Psychiat. social worker N.Y. State Dept. Mental Hygiene, Wassaic, 1970-73; with N.E. Utilities, Hartford, Conn., 1973-88, methods analyst, 1979-82, records and procedures mgmt. adminstr., 1982-88; document contr., mgr. Ralph M. Parsons Co., Fairfield, Ohio, 1990-91, St. Johns River Power Park, Jacksonville, 1991—2001; dir. Jacksonville Elec. Authority, 2001—03; owner Contantini & Assocs., 1998—, Family Threads, 1997—. Mem. faculty Ctrl. Piedmont C.C., 1989-90, Fla. C.C., Jacksonville, 1993-95. Bd. dirs. Meriden YWCA, Conn., 1978-79; vol. Queen City Friends, Charlotte, 1988-89, Cath. Charities AIDS Ministries, Jacksonville, 1996-99; mem. Greater Charlotte Bd. Realtors, 1989-91, First Coast Chorus, 1998-2002; mem. adv. coun. Greater Hartford C.C., 1986, Clermont Coll., Cin., 1990-91, Jacksonville C.C., 1991-94; mem. com. St. Augustine Diocesan Task Force Alternative Ministries, 1997—2003. Mem.: NACDLGM (nat. v.p. 1999—2001, bd. dirs. 1999—, mem. human rights campaign 1999—, bd. dirs. Riverwoods HOA 2000—02, nat. pres. 2002—03), AAUW, Jacksonville Small Bus. Network, Am. Platform Assn., Inst. Cert. Records Mgrs., Nat. Trust for Hist. Preservation, Coll. White Plains Alumnae Assn., Electric Coun. New Eng. (chair records mgmt. com. 1985—87), Assn. Configuration Data Mgmt., Women Bus. Owners, Assn. Image and Info. Mgmt. (dir. 1984—86), Assn. Record Mgmt. and Adminstrs. (sec. 1984—85, bd. dirs. 1984—86, chair industry action com. for pub. utilities 1986—89, internat. chair industry [illegible] profl. issues com. 1997—99), N.E. Utilities Women's Forum Club (treas. 1983—88), Beta Sigma Phi. Democrat. Roman Catholic. Avocations: antiques, online auctions, travel, investing. Home: 11538 Jonathan Rd Jacksonville FL 32225-1314 E-mail: novaleo@yahoo.com.

CONSTANTINO, BECKY, political organization administrator; State chmn. Wyo. Rep. State Ctrl. Com., 1999—. Mem. Rep. Nat. Com. Western State Chmn. Assn., 1999—. Office: 400 E 1st St Ste 314 Casper WY 82601-2561 also: PO Box 241 Casper WY 82601

CONSTANTINO, YAMILA, journalist, media executive; Anchorperson Negocios Bloomberg; mgr. Spanish language TV and radio Bloomberg LP. Finalist Noche de Triunfos award, Nat. Assn. Hispanic Journalists (NAHJ), 2002; recipient Best in Bus. award for Negocios Bloomberg, NY Press Club, 2000. Office: 499 Park Ave New York NY 10022 Office Phone: 212-318-2000. Office Fax: 917-369-5000.*

CONSTANTINO-BANA, ROSE EVA, nursing educator, researcher, lawyer; b. Labangan Zamboanga delSur, Philippines, Dec. 25, 1940; came to U.S., 1964; naturalized, 1982; d. Norberto C. and Rosalia (Torres) Bana; m. Abraham Antonio Constantino, Jr., Dec. 13, 1964; children: Charles Edward, Kenneth Richard, Abraham Anthony III. BS in Nursing, Philippine Union Coll., Manila, 1962; MNursing, U. Pitts., 1971, PhD, 1979; JD, Duquesne U., Pitts., 1984. Lic. clin. specialist in psychiatric-mental health nursing; RN. Instr. Philippine Union Co., 1963-65, Spring Grove State Hosp., Balt., 1965-67, Montefiore Sch. Nursing, Pitts., 1967-70, U. Pitts., 1971-74, asst. prof., 1974-83, assoc. prof., 1983—, chmn. Senate Athletic Com., 1985-86, 89-90, sec. univ. senate, 1991-92, v.p., 1993-95. Project dir. grant divsn. of nursing HHS, Washington, 1983-85; bd. dirs. Am. Jour. Nursing; prin. investigator NIH NINR, 1991-94; bd. dirs. Internat. Coun. on Women's Health Issues, 1986—. Author: (with others) Principles and Practice of Psychiatric Nursing, 1982; contbr. chpts. to books and articles to profl. jours. Mem. Presdl. Task Force, Washington, 1980, Rep. Senatorial Com., Washington, 1980. Fellow Am. Acad. Nursing, Am. Coll. Forensic Examiners; mem. ABA, ATLA, Allegheny County Bar Assn. (bd. cert. forensic examiner), Pa. Bar Assn., Women's Bar Assn., Am. Assn. Nurse Attys., Am. Nurses Assn., Pa. Nurses Assn. (sec. 1994-98), Nat. League Nursing, Pa. League Nursing (chairperson area 6), So. Poverty Law, Allegheny County Bar Assn., U. Pitts. Sch. Nursing Alumni Assn., U. Duquesne Law Alumni Assn., So. Powerty Law Ctr., Sigma Theta Tau, Phi Alpha Delta. Mem. Seventh Day Adventist Ch. Avocations: cooking, piano. Home: 6 Carmel Ct Pittsburgh PA 15221-3618 Office: U Pitts Sch Nursing 4500 Victoria St Rm 415 Pittsburgh PA 15261-0001 Office Phone: 412-624-2063. E-mail: rco100@pitt.edu.

CONSTANTINOPLE, ALEXANDRA, communications executive; d. Nicholas and Donna Constantinople; m. Jordan Hoffner, Oct. 2, 1999; 1 child, Nicholas. BA in English lit., Dennison U. Sr. publicist Larry King Live, CNN, Wash., DC, 1991—93; sr. publicist news info. Today Show and Meet the Press, NBC, NYC, 1993; dir. corp. media rels. NBC, NYC, 1997—98, v.p. news comm., 1998—2002; gen. mgr. corp. and mktg. comm. Gen. Electric, 2002—. Mem.: NY Women in Comm. Office: Gen Electric 3135 Easton Turnpike Easton CT 06431*

CONTE, ANDREA, retail executive, healthcare consultant, advocate; b. Great Barrington, Mass., Feb. 13, 1941; d. Louis William and Rosalie (Salvini) C.; m. Philip Norman Bredesen, Nov. 22, 1974; 1 child, Benjamin Conte. BS in Nursing, U. Wash., 1968; MBA, Tenn. State U., 1983. RN. Nurse various hosps. and med. ctrs., Mass. and Calif., 1961-68, Vis. Nurse Service, Boston, 1968-70; clin. coordinator Reg. Med. Program, Boston City Hosp., 1970-72; trainer computer systems Searle Medidata, Lexington, Mass., 1973-75; dir. nursing mgmt. services Hosp. Corp. Am., Nashville, 1975-78; cons. various health care cos., Nashville, 1978-81; mgr. Ernst and Whinney, Nashville, 1981-83; pres. Conte Philips, Nashville, 1983—; founder, pres. You Have The Power, Inc., 1993—. Mem. Commn. on Future of Tenn. Jud. Sys., Juvenile Justice Reform Commn., 1998; chmn. You Have the Power Com.; bd. dirs. Family and Children's Svc., 1988—91, Cumberland Sci. Mus., 1988—93, Shepherd's Ctr. of West End, 1989—91, Tenn. Performing Arts Ctr., 1989—97, NCCJ, 1991—94, St. Thomas Hosp., 1994—99, Fisk U., 1995—2001, First Ctr. Visual Arts, 1998—. Avocations: cooking, gardening, skiing, herbs, hiking.

CONTI, ANNALEE COUSART, minister, writer; b. Phila., Pa., Dec. 2, 1945; d. Robert Edward and AnnaMae Personeus Cousart; m. Robert James Conti, June 10, 1967; 1 child, Robert Benjamin. BA in music & elem. edn., U. of Alaska, 1964—67; MA in bibl. lit., Assemblies of God Theol. Sem., 1986—90. Ordination Gen. Coun. of the Assemblies of God, 1983, cert. Professional Teaching Assn. of Christian Schools Internat., 1995; Teacher State of Mo. Bd. of Edn., 1973, Adult Education U. of the State of NY Edn. Dept., 1998. Editl. asst. Assemblies of God Hdqs., Springfield, Mo., 1973—77; min. of Christian edn. Glove Cities Assembly of God, Gloversville, NY, 1977—86; min. of Christian edn. and music Huntington Assembly of God, Huntington Station, NY, 1986—92; tchr. Berean Bible Inst., New York City, 1991—93, Faith Christian Acad., Poughkeepsie, NY, 1993—96; adult basic edn. and gen. edn. diploma tchr. Bd. of Coop. Edn. Services, Beacon, NY, 1997—; min. of Christian edn. Mercy Tabernacle Assemblies of God, Hopewell Junction, NY, 1997—; gen. edn. diploma tchr. Wappingers Ctrl. Sch. Dist. Continuing Edn., NY, 1998—; SAT preparation tchr. Wappingers Ctrl. Sch. Dist., NY, 1999—; Global U. Berean Study Ctr. tchr. Mercy Tabernacle Assemblies of God, Hopewell Junction, NY, Faith Assembly of God, Poughkeepsie. Curriculum writer Gospel Pub. Ho., Springfield, Mo., 1975—2000; Christian edn. com. NY Dist. Assemblies of God, Syracuse, NY, 1978—86, women's ministries com., 1989—93. Author: (book) Frontiers of Faith. So. Dutchess treatment ctr. bd. mem. Dutchess County Dept. of Mental Hygiene, Hopewell Junction, NY, 2001—. Recipient Outstanding Woman Student Coll. of Arts and Letters, Associated Woman Students, U. of Alaska, 1966. R-Conservative. Assemblies Of God. Avocations: arts and crafts, reading. Home: 6F Winthrop Court Wappingers Falls NY 12590 Office: Mercy Tabernacle Assemblies of God 1254 Corporate Park Dr Hopewell Junction NY 12533 Personal E-mail: frontiersoffaith@annaleeconti.com.

CONTI, ISABELLA, psychologist, consultant; b. Torino, Italy, Jan. 1, 1942; came to U.S., 1964; d. Giuseppe and Zaira (Melis) Ferro; m. ugo Conti, Sept. 5, 1964; 1 child, Maurice. JD, U. Rome, 1966; PhD in psychology, U. Calif., Berkeley, 1975. Lic. psychologist. Sr. analyst Rsch. Inst. for Study of Man, Berkeley, Calif., 1967-68; postgrad. rsch. psychologist Personality Assessment and Rsch. Inst./U. Calif., Berkeley, 1968-71; intern U. Calif. - Berkeley and VA Hosp., San Francisco, 1969-75; asst. prof. St. Mary's Coll., Moraga, Calif., 1978-84. Cons. psychologist Conti Resources, Berkeley, Calif., 1977-85; v.p. Barnes & Conti Assocs., Inc., Berkeley, 1985-90; pres. Lisardco, El Cerrito, Calif., 1989—; bd. dirs. ElectroMagnetic Instruments, Inc., El Cerrito, Calif., 1985—. Author: (with Alfonso Montuori) From Power to Partnership, 1993; contbr. articles on creativity and mgmt. cons. to profl. jours. Trustee Monterey Inst. Internat. Studies, 1996-98. Regents fellow U. Calif.-Berkeley, 1972; NIMH predoctoral rsch. fellow, 1972-73. Mem. APA. Office: Lisardco 1318 Brewster Dr El Cerrito CA 94530-2526

CONTI, JOY FLOWERS, judge; b. Kane, Pa., Dec. 7, 1948; d. Bernard A. Flowers and Elizabeth (Tingley) Rodgers; m. Anthony T. Conti, Jan. 16, 1971; children: Andrew, Michael, Gregory. BA, Duquesne U., 1970, JD summa cum laude, 1973. Bar: Pa. 1973, U.S. Dist. Ct. (we. dist.) Pa. 1973, U.S. Ct. Appeals (3d cir.) 1976, U.S. Supreme Ct. 1993. Law clk. Supreme Ct. Pa., Monessen, 1973-74; assoc. Kirkpatrick & Lockhart, Pitts., 1974-76, 82-83, ptnr., 1983-96; shareholder Buchanan, Ingersoll, P.C., Pitts., 1996—2002; dist. judge U.S. Dist. Ct.(we. dist.) Pa., Pitts., 2002—. Prof. law Duquesne U., Pitts., 1976-82; hearing examiner Pa. Dept. State, Bur. Profl. Occupation and Affairs, 1978-82; chairperson search com. for judge U.S. Bankruptcy Ct. (we. dist.) Pa., 1987, 95; active Pa. Futures Commn. on Justice in 21st Century, 1995-97. Contbr. articles to profl. jours. Mem. disciplinary hearing com. Supreme Ct. Pa., 1982-88; v.p. Com. for Justice Edn., Pitts., 1983-84; mem. Leadership Pitts., 1987-88. Named One of Ten Outstanding Young Women in Am., 1981. Fellow Am. Bar Found. (Pa. state chair 1991-97); mem. ABA (ho. of dels. 1980-86, 91-97), Am. Law Inst., Am. Coll. Bankruptcy, Pa. Bar Assn. (gov. 1993-95, ho. of dels. 1978—, corp. banking and bus. law sect. coun. 1983-89, treas. 1991-93, v.p. 1993-95, chair-elect 1995-97, chmn. 1997-99, chmn. commn. comml. law 1990-93, co-chair 1995-2002, chair civil rights and responsibilities com. 1986-89, Achievement award 1982, 87, 99, Anne X. Alpern award 1995), Nat. Conf. Bar Pres. (exec. coun. 1993-96), Am. Inns of Ct., Allegheny County Bar Assn. (adminstrv. v.p. 1984-86, 90, chairperson corp. banking and bus. law sect. 1987-89, treas. 1988-90, gov. 1991, pres.-elect 1992, pres. 1993), Internat. Women's Insolvency and Restructuring Confedn. (chair Tri-State Network 1996), Pa. Bar Inst. (dir. 1991-97), Duquesne Club. Roman Catholic. Office: US Dist Judge 936 US Courthouse 7th & Grant Sts Pittsburgh PA 15219

CONTI, LEE ANN, lawyer; b. Astoria, Oreg. BA with honors, So. Ill. U., 1970; JD summa cum laude, De Paul U., 1976. Bar: Ill. 1976, U.S. Dist. Ct. (no. dist.) Ill. 1976. Ptnr. Mayer, Brown & Platt, Chgo., 1983-94; assoc. gen. counsel Citizens Comm. Co., Stamford, 1994—2002. Contbr. articles to profl. jours. Mem. Bd. Edn. Cmty. Consol. Sch. Dist. 89, Du Page County, 1987-93. Recipient Am. Jurisprudence awards in Torts, Remedies. Mem. ABA, Am. Corp. Counsel Assn., Ill. State Bar Assn., Du Page County Bar Assn., Chgo. Bar Assn., Phi Kappa Phi, Pi Sigma Alpha, Phi Lambda Pi. Office: 635 S Park Blvd Glen Ellyn IL 60137-6977

CONTRERAS, DEE (DOROTHEA CONTRERAS), municipal official, educator; b. Kansas City, Mo., Nov. 13, 1945; d. Robert MacGregor Hubsch and Dorothea Ann (Bauer) Wilson; m. Michael Raul Contreras, May 1969 (div. Nov. 1979); 1 child, Jason Michael Raul. BA in Anthropology, UCLA, 1967; JD with honors, Western State U., 1979. Bar: Calif. 1979. Sr. social worker San Diego County, 1968-80; sr. field rep. Svc. Employees Internat. Union Local 535, San Diego, 1980 88; bus. rep. Stationary Engrs. Local 39, Sacramento, 1988-90; sr. employee rels. rep. City of Sacramento, 1990-95, dir. labor rels., 1995—. Mem. exec. bd. San Diego Imperial County Labor Coun., 1985-88; tchr. labor history U. Calif. Davis Ext., Sacramento, 1989—. Recipient Bread and Roses award Coalition of Labor Union Women, San Diego, 1981, Outstanding Tchr. award U. Calif. Davis Extension, 1993. Mem. Indsl. Rels. Assn. No. Calif. (exec. bd. 1988-94, pres. exec. bd. 1994-96). Democrat. Avocations: reading, writing. Office: City of Sacramento Ste 601 921 10th St Sacramento CA 95814-2711

CONVERSE, ELIZABETH, artist, writer; b. Springfield, Ill., Jan. 17, 1946; d. Frank Thomas and Frances Converse (Deal) Sheets; m. Daniel B. A. Richter, Apr. 12, 1979 (div. Mar. 1996); children: William, Joan Clair; m. Eddie Truman, June 2002. BA in Anthropology, Lake Forest Coll., 1964-67; student Writing Ctr., Sarah Lawrence Coll., N.Y.C., 1991; MA in Human Devel., Pacific Oaks Coll., 1999. Cert. multiple-subject tchr., Calif. Tchr., enrichment program Washington Accelerated Sch. Anthropol. field worker, interviewer NIMH, Chgo., 1967-70; v.p., creative dir. Prodn. Sys., Inc., N.Y.C., 1984-89; with The Light/Bright Project at youth activity ctrs.; exec. dir. Calif. Living Histories, 1999-2002; mem. We 7 Collaborative. Performer Absolute Reality Theatre, N.Y.C., The Bridge Collective, N.Y.C., The Performance Group, N.Y.C., 1971-78; dir. Whitney Counterweight, N.Y.C., 1971-78; dir. Uto Theatrical Experiment, N.Y.C., 1971-78; writer, dir., actor: (short film) Mercy, 1971-78; prodr., writer, actor: (ind. film) Alexyx, 1978-83; works included in publs. Artweek, Visions, Pasadena Weekly, L.A. Reader, mus. and galleries; author: (fiction) The Pursuit of Happiness, The Clearing, Imbroglio, Wild Thing, Dust and Gold, The Citadel, Stories for Our Times, Our Dream; exhibited in group shows Pierce Coll., Sierra Madre Libr., SouthBay Contemporary Mus., Restaurant Lozano, The Armory, Pasadena; commns. include Susan Chen, Above the Rest, Jim Grancich, Carol Tannenbaum, Judy Webb-Martin, Little Stuga, Eddie Truman, City of Sierra Madre, Dopkins Chapel, Lozano Restaurant; mural project for Mayor Riordan's Office, L.A., 2000. Chair Gooden Sch. Silent Auction, Sierra Madre, Calif., 1992, Harvest Ball Silent Auction, Greenwich, Conn., 1987. Avocations: bicycling, gardening, horse racing, traveling. Home: 823 Canyon Crest Dr Sierra Madre CA 91024-1313

CONVERSE, SANDRA, city finance director, financial planner; b. Galion, Ohio, July 23, 1949; d. Mervin E. Harper and Phyllis R. Bowden (dec.); m. Robert W. Marsh, Aug. 19, 2000; children: Kimberly Spencer, Kelly Converse. BS, Grambling State U., 1969. Payroll clk. Neighborhood Youth Corps., Mansfield, Ohio, 1977-78; asst. fin. dir. Mansfield City, 1978-93, fin. dir., 1993—. Charter commn. mem. City of Mansfield, 1988. Mem. NAFE, La. Edn. Assn., Govt. Fin. Officers Assn. U.S. and Can., Mcpl. Treas. Assn. U.S. and Can., Nat. Assn. Tax Preparers, Ohio Govt. Fin. Officers Assn., Mcpl. Fin. Officers Assn. Ohio (at-large bd. mem.), Mansfield C. of C., Kappa Delta Pi, Alpha Kappa Alpha, Delta Psi Kappa. Democrat. Pentecostal. Avocations: reading, learning, sewing, painting. Office: City of Mansfield 30 N Diamond St Mansfield OH 44902-1738 Home: 155 W Prospect St Mansfield OH 44907-1305 E-mail: sconverse@CI.mansfield.oh.us.

CONWAY, ANNE CALLAGHAN, federal judge; b. Cleve., July 30, 1950; AB, John Carroll U., 1972; JD, U. Fla., 1975. Bar: Fla. 1975, U.S. Ct. Appeals (5th and 11th cirs.), U.S. Dist. Ct. (mid., no. and so. dists.) Fla., U.S. Supreme Ct. 1981. Law clk. to justice U.S. Dist. Ct., Orlando, Fla., 1975-77; from assoc. to ptnr. Wells, Gattis & Hallowes, Orlando, 1978-81; assoc. Carlton, Fields, Ward, Emmanuel, Smith & Cutler, P.A., Orlando, 1982-85, ptnr., 1985-91; judge U.S. Dist. (Mid. Dist.) Fla., Orlando, 1991—. Mem. adv. com. on local rules U.S. Dist. Ct., Orlando, 1990-91, grievance com. Orlando divsn., mid. dist., 1986-91. Bd. dirs. So. Ballet Theatre, Winter Park, Fla., 1985-89, adv. bd., 1985-89; bd. dirs. Greater Orlando Area Legal Svcs., 1978-85. Mem. ABA, Orange County Bar Assn. (chairperson state and fed. trial practice com. 1989-90). Office: US Courthouse 80 N Hughey Ave Rm 646 Orlando FL 32801-2231

CONWAY, CONNIE ANNE See HELLYER, CONSTANCE

CONWAY, DOROTHY JEAN WILLIAMS, economist; b. Elizaville, Ky., Apr. 13, 1927; d. John Downing and Maud (Knight) Williams; m. Gene Farris Conway, Sept. 1, 1950; children: Lisa Ann Conway Allen, Janet Lee Conway Fleenor, Linda Knight Conway Hensley. Student, Ky. Wesleyan Coll., Winchester, 1945-46; BS, U. Ky., Lexington, 1949; student, Drexel Inst. Tech., Phila., 1952. Extension svc. agt. U. Ky., Maysville, 1949-52; tchr. home econ. Dayton (Ky.) H.S., 1952; therapeutic dietitian Doctor's Hosp., Phila., 1952-53; R&D lab. asst. Pillsbury Ballard, Louisville, Ky., 1953-54; home svc. adv. Indpls. Power and Light, 1954, The Gas Svc. Co., Topeka, Kans., 1954-56; lectr. home mgmt. U. Cin., 1963. Bd. mem. Mary P. Shelton Pub. Libr., Georgetown, Ohio, 1979-93; bd. United Way. Allocations Com. Cin., 1985-94; bd. mem., chmn. Georgetown United Meth. Ch., 1981-87; mem., pres., sec. U. Cin. Women's Club, 1958-98. Mem. DAR, Am. Home Econ. Assn., Brown County Gen. Hosp. Aux., Cin. Women's Club, Phi Epsilon Omicron. Methodist. Home: 315 E State St Georgetown OH 45121-1416

CONWAY, ELAINE WINGATE, state agency administrator; b. Elizabeth, N.J. d. John Williams and Isabel Barnun Wingate; m. E. Virgil Conway, June 28, 1969; children: William Wingate Gay, John Lawrence Gay. Grad., N.Y. Sch. Interior Design; DHL (hon.), SUNY, Buffalo, 1997, Marymount Coll., 1998. Decorator Elaine Wingate Conway Interiors, Bronxville, NY, 1965—; chmn. Friends of Thirteen, N.Y.C., 1982—94; dir. N.Y. State Divsn. for Women, N.Y.C., 1995—2003. Bd. dirs. N.Y. Sch. Interior Design, 2001—; appt. life trustee WNET Bd. of Public Broadcasting. Vice chmn. NY Transit museum conservation bd. Parks and Recreation of Westchester County, 1983—; gov., vice chmn. Lawrence Hosp., Bronxville, 1981—; mem. adv. bd. Mus. Natural History; active Girl Scout Coun. of Greater N.Y., 2002—; chmn. coun. Purchase Coll.; N.Y. state del. Rep. Conv., 1984—88; bd. dirs. N.Y. State Coun. on the Arts, 2003—. Named to Acad. Women Achievers, YWCA N.Y.C., 1996; recipient Disting. Svc. award, Bklyn. Bur. Cmty. Svc., 1995, Family of Yr. award, Family Svc. of Westchester, 1996. Mem.: Women's Forum, N.Y.C. Coun. on the Arts, Women's Govt. Rep. Club. Avocations: gardening, cooking, decorating. Home: 9 Rittenhouse Rd Bronxville NY 10708 E-mail: elainewconway@aol.com.

CONWAY, EVELYN ATKINSON, accountant, financial analyst; b. Goose Creek, Tex., Aug. 14, 1921; d. George Henry and Sadie Ray (Bouldin) Atkinson; m. Lucian Gideon Conway, Nov. 2, 1945; children: Lucian Gideon Conway Jr., Karen Elizabeth Conway, Rebecca Annette Conway, Terri Ruth Conway, Jerry Andrew Conway, Priscilla Janice Conway. BS in Acctg., La. Tech. U., 1943; postgrad., New Orleans Bapt. Theol. Sem., 1949—51. Sr. acct. McGuire & Mazur CPAs, Houston, 1943—45; math. tchr. Enterprise Sch., Summit, Miss., 1953—54; sr. ptnr. Conley & Conway, Coushatta, La., 1955—56; office mgr. Annuity Bd. Rep. SBC, Alexandria, La., 1959—83; regional mgr., pers. fin. analyst Primerica Life & PFS Investments, Inc., Alexandria, La., 1984—. Auditor The Bapt. Message, Alexandria, 1962—64. Emergency evacuation officer Civil Def., Coushatta, 1955—57; treas. Dist. 8 La. Bapt. Missions, Coushatta, 1955—56. Named Hometown All Am., Alexandria Daily Town Talk, 1995. Republican. Baptist. Avocations: sewing, music. Home: 118 Pearce Rd Pineville LA 71360

CONWAY, JOAN CARTER, state legislator; b. Balt., Apr. 5, 1951; married; 1 child. AA in Human Svcs., C.C. Balt., 1987; BA in Sociology, U. Balt., 1988. Gen. tax practitioner, co-owner CIG Profl. Tax Svcs. Inc.; mem. Dist. 43 Md. Senate, Annapolis, 1997—. Mem. econ. and environ. affairs com. Md. State Senate, joint com. on adminstrv., exec. and legis. review, joint com. on children, youth and families; program dir. S.U.R.E. Program, The Jentry McDonald Corp., 1994-95; HUB dir./mayor's rep. Housing and Cmty. Devel., Human Svcs. Divsn., Balt., 1993-94; various positions Urban Svcs. Agy., Balt., 1976-93, sec., planning asst., cmty. developer Model Cities Program, Balt., 1970-76. Sec. Md. Legis. Black Caucus; city councilwoman 3d Councilmanic Dist., Balt., 1995-97. Recipient Cmty. Svc. Day award, 1993, Cmty. Svcs. award Woodbourne Ctr., 1993. Democrat. Office: Md State Senate James Senate Office Bldg 110 College Ave Rm 305 Annapolis MD 21401-8012 Fax: 410-841-3135. E-mail: joancarterconway@senate.state.md.us.

CONWAY, LOIS LORRAINE, piano teacher; b. Caldwell, Idaho, Oct. 20, 1913; d. William Henry and Auttie Arrola (Bierd) Crawford; m. Edward Owen Conway, June 23, 1934; children: Michael David, Judith Ann, Steven Edward, Kathleen Jean. Degree, Albertson Coll. of Idaho, 1960's; student, Shorwood Music Sch., Chgo., Coll. of Notre Dame, San Francisco. Pvt. piano tchr., Ontario, Oreg., 1940-74, Pendleton, Oreg., 19774-92; ret., 1992. Nat. Guild Piano Tchrs. adjudicator spring auditions Am. Coll. Musicians, Austin, Tex., 1972-96. Author: (poetry) Pacifica-The Voice Within (Semi-finalist 1995). Chmn. Nat. Guild Auditions, Ontario, Oreg., 1959-72, Pendleton, Oreg., 1972-80; v.p., publicity Community Concerts Assn., Ontario, 1960-72, membership work, 1972-75. Democrat. Avocations: gardening, playing piano, bridge, duplicate bridge, motor home travel. Home: 114 Shamrock Cir Santa Rosa CA 95403-1156

CONWAY, LYNN, computer scientist, electrical engineer, educator; b. Mt. Vernon, N.Y., Jan. 2, 1938; BS, Columbia U., 1962, MSEE, 1963; D (hon.), Trinity Coll., 1997. Rsch. staff IBM Corp., Yorktown Heights, N.Y., 1964-68; sr. staff engr. Memorex Corp., Santa Clara, Calif., 1969-73; rsch. staff Xerox Corp., Palo Alto, Calif., 1973-78, rsch. fellow, mgr. VLSI systems area, 1978-82, rsch. fellow, mgr. knowledge systems area, 1982-83; asst. dir. for strategic computing Def. Advanced Research Projects Agy., Arlington, Va., 1983-85; prof. elec. engrng. and computer sci., assoc. dean U. Mich. Coll. Engring., Ann Arbor, Mich., 1985—. Vis. assoc. prof. elec. engrng. and computer sci. MIT, Cambridge, Mass., 1978-79; sci. adv. bd. USAF, 1987-90. Co-author: textbook Introduction to VLSI Systems, 1980; contbr. articles to profl. jours.; patentee in field. Mem. coun. Govt.-Univ.-Industry Rsch. Roundtable, 1993-98; mem. corp. Charles Stark Draper Lab., 1993—; mem. bd. visitors USAF Acad., 1996-2000, presdl. appt.; mem. Air Force Sci. and Tech. Bd., Nat. Acads., 2000—. Recipient Ann. Achievement award Electronics mag., 1981, Harold Pender award U. Pa., 1984, Wetherill Medal Franklin Inst., 1985, Sec. of Def. Meritorious Civilian Svc. award, 1985. Fellow IEEE; mem. NAE, AAAS, Soc. Women Engrs. (Ann. Achievement award 1990), Assn. Computing Machinery. Avocations: motocross racing, whitewater canoeing, natural landscaping. Office: U Mich 152 ATL Bldg Ann Arbor MI 48109-2110 E-mail: conway@engin.umich.edu.

CONWAY, NANCY ANN, newspaper editor; b. Foxboro, Mass., Oct. 15, 1941; d. Leo T. and Alma (Goodwin) C.; children: Ana Lucia DaSilva, Kara Ann Martin. Cert. in med. tech., Carnegie Inst., 1962; BA in English, U. Mass., 1976, cert. in secondary edn., 1978. Tchr. Brazil-Am. Inst., Rio de Janeiro, 1963-68; freelance writer, editor Amherst, Mass., 1972-76; staff writer Daily Hampshire Gazette, North Hampton, Mass., 1976-77; editor Amherst Bull., 1977-80, Amherst Record, 1980-83; features editor Holyoke (Mass.) Transcript/Telegram, 1983-84; gen. mgr. Monday-Thursday Newspapers, Boca Raton, Fla., 1984-87; dir. editorial South Fla. Newspaper Network, Deerfield Beach, 1987-90; pub., editor York (Pa.) Newspapers, Inc., 1990-95; metro editor Denver Post, 1995-96; exec. editor, v.p. Alameda Newspaper Group Oakland (Calif.) Tribune, 1996—2003; editor The Salt Lake (Utah) Tribune, 2003—. Bd. dirs. Math.: Opportunities in Engring., Sci. and Tech.-Pa. State, York, 1991-95. Recipient writing awards, state newspaper assns. Mem. Am. Soc. Newspaper Editors, Soc. Profl. Journalists. Avocations: literature, photography, communication, gardening. Office: Editor Salt Lake Tribune 143 S Main St Salt Lake City UT 84111 E-mail: nconway@angnewspapers.com.

CONWAY-GERVAIS, KATHLEEN MARIE, reading specialist, educational consultant; b. Bklyn., Apr. 18, 1942; d. John Joseph and Mary Josephine Conway; m. Stephen Paul Gervais, July 10, 1976; 1 child, John Joseph. BA, Coll. Mt. St. Vincent, 1970; MS, Hunter Coll. of N.Y.C., 1973, Reading Specialization, 1974. Cert. reading and social studies tchr., nursery and elem. ecuator, N.Y., N.J. Elem. tchr. Archdiocese of N.Y., N.Y.C., 1963-74; reading specialist Malverne (N.Y.) Union Free Sch. Dist., 1974-86, dist. reading, testing coord., 1986-91, reading specialist, 1992-95, East Meadow (N.Y.) Union Free Sch. Dist., 1995-96; reading cons., tchr. trainer, staff devel. team Uniondale (N.Y.) Union Free Sch. Dist., 1996—2003. Adv. bd. mem. Newsday in Edn., Melville, 1982—; adj. prof. Nassau C.C., Garden City, N.Y., 1995—, L.I. U. Grad. Sch., 2003—. Active Getting Out the vote presdl. election, N.Y., 1992. Recipient Ambassador in Edn. award Newsday, Melville, 1982, Congruence Model Project award N.Y. State Dept. Edn., Albany, 1988, Elizabeth Ann Seton award Office of Cathechesis and Worship, Long Island, 1991. Mem. ASCD, Internat. Reading Assn., N.Y. State Reading Assn. (del. L.I.), Orton Dyslexia Soc. (del.), Nassau Reading Coun. (bd. dirs., pres., exec. bd.). Democrat. Roman Catholic. Avocations: travel, reading, theater, swimming, computer. Home and Office: 174 Nassau Blvd West Hempstead NY 11552-2218 E-mail: watcher@optonline.net.

CONWAY-WELCH, COLLEEN, dean, nurse midwife; b. Monticello, Iowa, Apr. 26, 1944; d. John Andrew and Lorraine (Digman) Conway; m. Ted Houston Welch, Mar. 31, 1985. BSN, Georgetown U., 1965; CNM, Catholic Maternity Inst., 1969; MSN, Catholic U., Washington, 1969; PhD, NYU, 1973. Staff nurse Georgetown U. Hosp., Washington, 1965; staff nurse labor & delivery Queens Med. Ctr., Honolulu, 1966; nurse cons. U. So. Calif. Med. Ctr., L.A., 1967; staff assoc. Nat. League Nursing, N.Y.C., 1969-70; asst. prof. Downstate Med. Ctr., Bklyn., 1970-74, Georgetown U., 1974-76, assoc. dean, 1975-76; assoc. prof. George Mason U., Fairfax, Va., 1976-78, Calif. State U., Long Beach, 1978-80; prof. nursing U. Colo., Denver, 1980-84; dean Vanderbilt Sch. Nursing, Nashville, 1984—. Mem. Presdl. Commn. on HIV Epidemic, Washington, 1988, adv. coun. NIH Nat. Ctr. Nursing Rsch., Washington, 1989-93, bd. trust Healthcare Leadership Coun., Washington, 1990; chair nursing leadership coun. Inst. Healthcare Improvement, 1992; bd. dirs. Diversicare, Franklin, Tenn., Nat. League Nursing Community Health Accreditation, N.Y.C., Commonwealth Fund Nurse Exch. Fellowship Program, N.Y.C. Contbr. articles to profl. jours. Bd. govs. United Way, Middle, Tenn., 1989; active Mayor's Task Force for Substance Abuse, 1990, JFK Adv. Com. on Arts, Washington, 1991, Jr. League, 1973—. Recipient Dempsey Humanitarism award St. Clare's Hosp. AIDS Ctr., 1989; commencement speaker, Columbia Sch. Nursing, 1991. Fellow Am. Acad. Nursing; mem. Soc. Advancement Women's Health Rsch. (bd. dirs. 1991—), Rotary Club, Cosmos Club, Sigma Theta Tau (bd. dirs. 1968—). Avocations: snow skiing, scuba diving, hiking, reading. Home: 109 Lynnwood Ter Nashville TN 37205-2911 Office: Vanderbilt U Sch Nursing 111 Godchaux 461 21st Ave S Nashville TN 37240-1104

CONWELL, ESTHER MARLY, physicist, researcher; b. N.Y.C., May 23, 1922; d. Charles and Ida (Korn) C.; m. Abraham A. Rothberg, Sept. 30, 1945; 1 son, Lewis J. BA, Bklyn. Coll., 1942, DSc, 1992; MS, U. Rochester, N.Y., 1945; PhD, U. Chgo., 1948. Lectr. Bklyn. Coll., 1946-51; mem. tech. staff Bell Tel. Labs., 1951-52; physicist GTE Labs., Bayside, NY, 1952-61, mgr. physics dept., 1961-72; vis. prof. U. Paris, 1962-63; Abby Rockefeller Mauze prof. MIT, Cambridge, 1972; prin. scientist Xerox Corp., Webster, NY, 1972-80, rsch. fellow, 1981-98. Adj. prof. U. Rochester, 1990—2001, prof., 2001—; cons., mem. adv. com. engring. NSF, 1978—81. Author: High Field Transport in Semiconductors, 1967, also rsch. papers; mem. editl. bd. Jour. Applied Physics; Proc. of IEEE; patentee in field. Fellow IEEE (Edison medal 1997), Am. Phys. Soc. (sec.-treas. divsn. condensed matter physics 1977-82); mem. AAAS, NAS, NAE, Soc. Women Engrs. (Achievement award 1960). Office: U Rochester Dept Chemistry Rochester NY 14627 Business E-Mail: conwell@chem.rochester.edu.

CONYERS, JEAN LOUISE, chamber of commerce executive; b. Memphis, Nov. 10, 1932; d. Marshall Daniel and Jeffie (Ledbetter) Farris; m. Julius D. Conyers, June 1, 1956 (div.); children: Judith, James Jr., Jennifer. BA, LeMoyne Coll., 1956; MBA, Atlanta U., 1967. Exec. sec. Dept. Zoology, Wash. State U., Pullman, 1958-62, Sch. Bus., Atlanta U., 1965-68; dep. dir., planner Community Action Agy, Terre Haute, Ind., 1968-78, exec. dir., 1978-79; sr. assoc. exec. United Way of Genesee/Lapeer, Flint, Mich., 1980-82; pres., chief exec. officer Conyers & Assocs., Flint, 1982-86, Met. C. of C., Flint, 1986—, Ultimate Learning Systems, Inc., Flint, 1990—. Program coord. Greater Flint OIC, 1983-85. Bd. dirs. Urban Coalition, Flint, 1988—, Dort-Oak-Pk. Neighborhood Ho., Flint, 1982—. Recipient Cmty. Svc. award Negro Bus. and Profl. Women, Terre Haute, 1977, Supportive Svcs. award Top Ladies of Distinction, Flint, 1989, Black Caucus Found. of Mich.'s Cmty. Svc. award, 1994, Nat. Negro Bus. and Profl. Women's Club Sojourner Truth award, 1994; named Woman of Distinction for contbns. to minority bus. U. Mich., Flint, Mott Coll., Mayor of Flint, Mich. legis., Mich. Dept. of Labor, 1992; enshrined Zeta Phi Beta Hall of Fame, Flint, 1988. Mem. Kiwanis, Zonta Club of Flint II, Alpha Kappa Alpha (Outstanding Grad. Soror of Great Lakes Region 1992). Avocations: reading, travel. Office: 400 N Saginaw St Ste 101A Flint MI 48502-2045 E-mail: metro@tir.com.

COOCH, NANCY DUPONT (MRS. EDWARD W. COOCH JR.), sculptor; b. Greenville, Del., Dec. 28, 1919; d. Eugene Eleuthere and Catherine Dulcinea (Moxham) duPont; m. William Glasgow Reynolds, May 18, 1940 (dec. Jan. 1987); children: Katherine Glasgow Reynolds, William Bradford Reynolds, Mary Parminter Reynolds Savage, Cynthia duPont Reynolds Farris.; m. Edward W. Cooch, Jr., Sept. 6, 2003. Student, Goldey-Beacom Coll., Wilmington, Del., 1938. One-woman shows include Caldwell Inc., 1975, Nat. Museum of Women in Arts, 1998; exhibited in group shows at Corcoran Gallery, Washington, 1943, Soc. Fine Arts, Wilmington, 1937-38, 40-41, 48, 50, 62, 65, Rehoboth (Del.) Art League, 1963, NAD, N.Y.C., 1964, Pa. Mil. Coll., Chester, 1966, Del. Art Ctr., 1967, Del. Art Mus., Wilmington, Wilmington Art Mus., 1976, Met. Mus. Art, N.Y.C., 1977, Lever House, N.Y.C., 1979, Nat. Mus. Women in the Arts, Washington, 1998; represented in permanent collections Wilmington Trust Co., E.I. duPont de Nemours & Co., Children's Home, Inc., Claymont, Del., Children's Bur., Wilmington, Stephenson Sci. Ctr., Vanderbilt U., Nashville, Lutheran Towers Bldg., Travelers Aid and Family Soc. Bldg., Wilmington, bronze fountain head Longwood Gardens, Kennett Square, Pa., bronze statue Brookgreen Gardens, Murrells Inlet, S.C., bronze sculpture "Veiled Lady", Nat. Mus. Women in Arts, Washington, 1998, bronze sculpture U. Del., Newark, 2001, bronze sculpture Biggs Mus., Dover, Del., 2002; contbr. articles to profl. jours. Organizer vol. svc. Del. chpt. ARC, 1938-39; chmn. Com. for Revision Del. Child Adoption Law, 1950-52; pres., bd. dirs. Children Bur. Del.; pres., trustee Children's Home, Inc.; del., past regent Gunston Hall Plantation, Lorton, Va.; mem. adv. com. Longwood Gardens, Kennett Sq., Pa.; garden and grounds com. Winterthur (Del.) Mus.; mem. rsch. staff Henry Francis DuPont Winterthur Mus., 1955-63; mem. archtl. com. U. Del., Newark. Recipient Confrerie des Chevaliers du Tastevin Clos de Vougeot-Bourgogne France, 1960; Hort. award Garden Club Am., 1964, medal of Merit, 1976, Dorothy Platt award Garden Club of Phila., 1980, Alumni medal of merit Westover Sch., Middlebury, Conn., Medal of Distinction, U. Del., 1999. Mem. Pa. Hort. Soc., Wilmington Soc. Fine Arts, Mayflower Descs., Del. Hist. Soc., Colonial Dames, League Am. Pen Women, Nat. Trust Hist. Preservation. Garden Club of Wilmington (past pres.), Garden Club of Am. (past asst. zone 4 chmn.), Vicmead Hunt Club, Greenville Country Club, Chevy Chase Club (Washington), Colony Club (N.Y.C.). Episcopalian. Address: PO Box 3919 Greenville DE 19807-0919

COOGAN, MELINDA ANN STRANK, chemistry and biology educator; b. Davenport, Iowa, Mar. 29, 1955; d. Gale Benjamin and Margie Delene (Admire) Strank; children: James Benjamin, Jessica Ann. AA, Stephens Coll., Columbia, Mo., 1975; BS, E. Carolina U., Greenville, N.C., 1978. Biology and phys. sci. educator York (Pa.) Catholic H.S., 1989-90; sci. advisor Bettendorf (Iowa) Children's Mus., 1993; gifted, chemistry and physics educator St. Katherine' Coll. Prep. Sch., Bettendorf, 1994; biology educator Lewisville (Tex.) H.S., 1996-99, chemistry educator, 1996-99; ALS rsch. asst. U. Tex. Southwestern Med. Ctr., Dallas, 1998; chemistry, biology and human anatomy educator Milford HS, Ill., 2000—. Violinist Augustana Symphony Orch., Rock Island, Ill., 1993-94; pres. bd. dirs. Flower Mound (Tex.) Cmty. Orch., 1994-95; founder, instr. Northlakes Violin Acad., Flower Mound, 1994-99; violinist Waterforde Women's

String Ensemble, Lewisville, 1995-98, Clinton Symphony, 1999-2001, Country Theater, Cissna Park, Ill., 2002—; bd. dirs. Family Mus. Art and Sci., Bettendorf, 2000-01. student mentor, Earthwatch Prog., We. Ill. U. 2003— . Student mentor Earthwatch, 2003. Mem. Roanoke Art Mus. (docent 1983-86), Jr. Bd. of Quad City Symphony (chair promotion [illegible] League Moline (Ill.) (chair [illegible] 1987-88), Jr. League of York (Pa.) (chair thrift shop spl. sales 1989-92), Jr. League of Quad Cities (nom./placement 1993-94), Jr. League of Dallas (sustaining 1995-96), Gamma Beta Phi, Chi Beta Phi, Phi Kappa Phi. Democrat. Roman Catholic. Home: 2167 E 1170 N Rd Milford IL 60953

COOK, ANN HARRIS SHACKLETON, gifted and talented educator, psychotherapist; b. Joliet, Ill, Aug. 27, 1943; d. Allen Roy Shackleton and Rachel Hutchinson Harris; children: Kimberly Neely, Lauren O'Donnell, Jody. BA English, Northwestern U., Evanston, Ill., 1965; MS in Counseling, Shippensburg (Pa.) U., 1985. Cert. English Teacher 1975, PIAA Swimming & Diving Official 1990, Gifted Program Specialist 1980. Gifted students tchr. Carlisle Area Sch. Dist., Carlisle, Pa., 1979—. Psychotherapist Pvt. Practice, Carlisle, Pa., 1990—. Contbr. articles on coll. application Student Publs., 2001. Security vol. 1996 Olympics; Bd. pres. Carlisle (Pa.) YWCA, 1982—87; bd. dirs. United Way of Greater Carlisle Area, 1982—88, Carlisle YMCA; bd. dirs. Junior League of Harrisburg, 1984—88; bd. sec. Carlisle Theatre, 1999—2002; bd. pres. CONTACT Harrisburg, Pa., 1989—90; lay leader, lay speaker Allison United Meth. Ch., Carlisle, 1996—99, disciple bible study tchr., 1997—2001; swim coach Carlisle YMCA, 1984—94. Recipient United Way Svc award, United Way of Greater Carlisle Area, 1986, 1987, 1988, Youth Svc. award, Carlisle YMCA, 1989, Kermit Kane Aquatics award, Carlisle YMCA Aquatics Assn., 1990. Mem.: NEA, Carlisle Area Edn. Assn., Pa. State Edn. Assn., Pa. Interscholastic Athletic Assn. (swimming & diving official 1988—2002), Amnesty Internat. (faculty advisor 2001—02), Marine Conservation Assn., World Wildlife Fund, Nature Conservancy, PEO Sisterhood (pres. 1999—2001). Methodist. Avocations: swimming, travel, writing. Home: 1234 White Birch Ln Carlisle PA 17013 Office: Carlisle Area Sch Dist 623 West Penn St Carlisle PA 17013 Personal E-mail: cookie1@pa.net. Business E-Mail: cooka@carlisleschools.org.

COOK, ANN JENNALIE, English language educator; b. Wewoka, Okla., Oct. 19, 1934; d. Arthur Holly and Bertha Mable (Stafford) C.; children: Lee Ann Merrick, Amy Ceil Leonard; m. Gerald George Calhoun, Apr. 1994. BA, U. Okla., 1956, MA, 1959; PhD, Vanderbilt U., 1972. Instr. English U. Okla., 1956-57; tchr. English N.C. and Conn., 1958-61; instr. So. Conn. State Coll., 1962-64; asst. prof. U. S.C., 1972-74; adj. asst. prof. Vanderbilt U., Nashville, 1977-82, assoc. prof., 1982-89, prof., 1990-98, prof. emeritus, 1999—. Exec. sec. Shakespeare Assn. Am., 1975-87; chmn. Internat. Shakespeare Assn., 1988-96, v.p. 1996—. Author: Privileged Playgoers of Shakespeare's London, 1981, Making a Match: Courtship in Shakespeare and His Society, 1991; assoc. editor Shakespeare Studies, 1973-80; contbr. articles to profl. jours. Trustee Folger Shakespeare Libr., 1985—90, Shakespeare Birthplace Trust (life); bd. mem. Friends of the Shakespeare Birthplace Trust, 2000—, patron, Nashville Symphony, 2000—, U. Sch. Nashvillle, 2000—04, Nashville Opera Guild, 2000—03, Nashville Shakespeare Festival, 2002—, Shakespeare on the Cumberland; pres. English-Speaking Union, 2003—. Recipient Letseizer award, 1956, Nat. Leadership award Delta Delta Delta, 1956; Danforth fellow, 1968-72, Folger summer fellow, 1973, Donelson fellow, 1974-75, fellow Rockefeller Found., 1984, Guggenheim Found., 1984-85; grantee Folger seminar NEH, 1992-93. Mem. Shakespeare Assn. Am., MLA, AAUP, Shakespeare Inst., Deutsche Shakespeare Gesellschaft, Renaissance Soc. Am. (bd. dirs.), Phi Beta Kappa. Episcopalian. Home: 114 Prospect Hl Nashville TN 37205-4721 Office: Vanderbilt U Dept English Nashville TN 37235

COOK, BETH MARIE, volunteer, poet; b. Electra, Tex., Jan. 4, 1933; d. Charles Bolivar Allen and Ida Marie (Nelson) Burton; m. William H. Cook, May 30, 1955 (div. Nov. 1981); children: David M., Dianne M. Gleason. Student, Rockmont Coll., 1951-54; BA, Antioch U. West, 1981. County coord. office econ. opportunity Upper Arkansas Coun., Salida, Colo., 1974-76; dir. area agy. on aging Upper Arkansas Coun./Dept. Social Svcs., State of Colo., 1976-80; specialist community devel. Mountain Plains Congress Sr. Orgns., Denver, 1980-82; sr. adminstrv. asst. Digital Rsch. Inc., Monterey, Calif., 1983-85, asst. to pres., 1985-87, retail rep., 1987-88; co-owner, ptnr. Scotia Gallery, Monterey, 1983-86; COO MiniSoft, Inc., Phoenix, 1988-89; property mgr. Parklane Arms Apts., 1989-92; exec. asst. Ft. Collins (Colo.) Housing Authority, 1989-92, occupancy specialist, 1992-95; vol. Peace Corps, Kingdom of Tonga, 1995-97, U.S. Dept. Commerce Census Bur., 1998-2000, 2002—. Hostess Sr. Sound-Off show, Sta. KVRH-AM/FM, Salida, 1978-80; cons. Devel. Assocs. Inc., Denver, 1982. Author: (poem) Jessie, 1989-90. Coord. crisis intervention line Chaffee County Comty. Crisis Ctr., Salida, 1976-80; committeewoman Chaffee County Dem. Ctrl. Com., Salida, 1979-80; speaker, program com. Colo. Gov.'s Conf on Aging, Denver, 1980; docent Lincoln Ctr.; vol. food distbn. SHARE; youth Bible tchr., deacon Westminster Presbyn. Ch.; mem. bd. dirs. Fort Collins Housing Corp., Neighbor to Neighbor. Recipient Human Devel. Svc. award HHS, 1980, Golden Poet award, 1989; named Woman of Yr. Chaffee County Bus. and Profl. Women's Club, 1978. Mem. Am. Assn. Ret. Persons, Nat. Mus. Women in Arts. Presbyterian. Avocations: art, study of ancient mexican civilizations, travel.

COOK, BEVERLY, federal agency administrator; b. Wash. BA in Metallurgical Engrng., U. Wash. Contractor Dept. Energy, various positions Office Nuc. Energy, prin. dep. dir., dir. Office Idaho Ops., 1999, asst. sec. environment, safety, and health, 2001—. Office: Dept Energy Environment, Safety, and Health 1000 Independence Ave SW Washington DC 20585-0001

COOK, BLANCHE WIESEN, history educator, journalist; b. N.Y.C., Apr. 20, 1941; d. David Theodore and Sadonia (Ecker) Wiesen. BA, Hunter Coll., 1962; MA, Johns Hopkins U., 1964, PhD, 1970; DHL (hon.), Russell Sage Coll., 1998. Instr. Hampton Inst., Va., 1963; instr. Stern Coll. for Women, Yeshiva U., N.Y.C., 1964-67; prof. history John Jay Coll., Grad. Faculty CUNY, 1968—; disting. prof., 1995—. Prodr., broadcaster program stas. WBAI and WKPFK Radio Pacifica, N.Y.C. and L.A., 1978—; vis. prof. UCLA, 1982-83; syndicated journalist; bd. dirs. Women's Fgn. Policy Adv. Coun., v.p., co-chair Fund for Open Info. and Accountability; mem. freedom to write com. PEN; elected univ.-wide union officer PSC-CUNY, 2000. Author: Crystal Eastman on Women and Revolution, 1978, Declassified Eisenhower, 1981 (N.Y. Times Notable Book), Biography of Eleanor Roosevelt, vol. 1, 1992 (L.A. Times Book award, N.Y. Times Notable Book), vol. 2, 1999, ER I, ER II (Best Books), Christian Sci. Monitor, 1999 (Notable Book award 1999); sr. editor: The Garland Library of War and Peace, 360 vols., 1970-80, Bella Abzug in Jewish Women's Encyclopedia, 1997; contbr. articles to various publs. Appointed to com. on documents for fgn. rels. U.S. Dept. State, 1986-90. Named Scholar of the Yr. N.Y. Coun. Humanities, 1996, Alumna of Yr. Hunter Coll. Hall of Fame, 1999; recipient Breakthrough award Women, Men and Media, 1992, Feminist of Yr. award Feminist Majority Found., 1992, Lambda Lit. Prize, 1992; faculty fellow CUNY, 1978, 84, 91. Mem. Orgn. Am. Historians (co-chair freedom of info. com.), Am. Hist. Assn. (v.p. for rsch. 1991-94), Coordinating Com., Women in Hist. Profession (pres. N.Y.C. chpt. 1969-71), Berkshire Women Historians, Soc. Historians Am. Fgn. Rels., Conf. on Peace Rsch. in History (bd. dirs., v.p.), Peace History Soc. Women's Internat. League for Peace and Freedom, Pi Sigma Alpha, Phi Alpha Theta. Office: CUNY John Jay Coll Dept History 445 W 59th St New York NY 10019-1104

COOK, CAMILLE WRIGHT, retired law educator; b. Tuscaloosa, Ala. d. Reuben Hall and Camille Tunstall (Searcy) Wright; children: Sydney, Reuben, Cade, Camille. AB, U. Ala., 1945, JD, 1948. Bar: Ala. 1948. Asst. prof. law, Law Sch. Auburn (Ala.) U., 1968; mem. faculty Sch. Law U. Ala., 1968-93, assoc. dean, dir. continuing legal edn., prof. law, Law Sch., 1975-93, asst. acad. v.p., 1984-85; prof. emeritus, 1993—. Bd. dirs. U. Ala. Law Sch. Found., Am/South. Mem. Smithsonian Coun., Washington, 1972-78, Ala. Air Pollution Commn., 1971-81; [illegible] Recipient outstanding commitment to tchg. award U. Ala., 1990, disting. alumni award, 1996, Algernon Sydney Sullivan award, 1999. Fellow Am. Bar Found., Ala. Bar Assn. (award merit 1973); mem. ABA (Rawles Spl. Merit award 1983), Farrah Law Soc. (trustee 1972—, disting. alumnae award 1992), Am. law Inst. (coun., Rawles Spl. Merit award 1983). Episcopalian. Home: 32 Ridgeland Tuscaloosa AL 35406-1607 Office: PO Box 870382 Tuscaloosa AL 35487-0001 E-mail: cwcook1@dbtech.net.

COOK, CATHARINE, library director; b. Anthony, Kans., Jan. 6, 1945; MA in Librarianship, U. Denver, 1972. Libr. cons. Kans. State U., Topeka, 1972—75, State Libr. Fla., Tallahassee, 1975—78, Okla. Dept. Librs., Oklahoma City, 1978—90; dir. Pub. Libr. of Enid (Okla.)/Garfield County, 1990—96; ctrl. mgr. Ft. Worth Pub. Librs., Ft. Worth; dir. Chickasha (Okla.) Pub. Libr., 1999—. Mem.: ALA, Okla. Libr. Assn., Mensa. Home: 1911 S 13th St Chickasha OK 73018 Office: Chickasha Pub Libr 527 Iowa Chickasha OK 73018 Office Fax: 405-222-6072. Business E-Mail: cathcook@chickasha.lib.ok.us.

COOK, CATHERINE WELLES, state legislator; b. New London, Conn., Jan. 24, 1950; BA, Conn. Coll. Mem. Dist. 18 Conn. Senate, Hartford, 1993—. Chief dep. minority leader; mem. commerce and com.; ranking mem. appropriations com., human svcs. com.; mem. subcoms. on conservation and devel.; gov.'s appointee Conn. Bd. of Protection and Advocacy for Persons with Disabilities; mem. Pres.'s Commn. of Nat. Acad. of Mental retardation. Republican. Office: Conn State Senate State Capitol Rm 3400 Hartford CT 06106

COOK, DEBBIE, lawyer, councilman; m. John Fisher; 1 child. BS, Calif. State U.-Long Beach; JD, Western State Coll. Law, 1994. Bar: Calif. Mayor City of Huntington Beach, Calif., 2000—01; mem. Huntington Beach (Calif.) City Coun., 2001—. Mem. Southern Calif. Assn. of Govt.'s Energy & Environ. Com., League of Cities' Admin. Policies Com., League Local Self Govt.'s Ethics Project Adv. Com.; dir. Orange County Sanitation Dist. Office: City Coun 2000 Main St Huntington Beach CA 92648 E-mail: hbdac@hotmail.com.

COOK, DEBORAH L. judge, former state supreme court justice; b. Pittsburgh, Feb. 8, 1952; BA in English, U. Akron, 1974, JD, 1978, LLD (hon.), 1996. Ptnr. Roderick & Linton, Akron, 1976-91; judge 9th dist. Ohio Ct. Appeals, 1991-94; justice Ohio Supreme Ct., 1995—2003; judge U.S. Court of Appeals, 6th cir., Cincinnati, Ohio, 2003—. Bd. trustees Summit County United Way, Vol. Ctr., Stan Hywet Hall and Gardens, Akron Sch. Law, Coll. Scholars, Inc.; bd. dirs. Women's Network; vol. Mobile Meals, Safe Landing Shelter. Named Woman of Yr., Women's Network, 1991. Fellow Am. Bar Found.; mem. Omicron Delta Kappa, Delta Gamma (pres., Nat. Shield award). Office: 532 Potter Stewart US Courthouse 100 E Fifth St Cincinnati OH 45202-3988

COOK, DORIS ADELE, artist; b. Ligonier, Pa., Apr. 16, 1930; d. William Issac and Adele Henrietta (Siebert) Routch; m. David Glen Eckholm, Feb. 14, 1956 (div. 1969); 1 child, Melissa Marie Schoenberg; m. George E. Cook, Apr. 13, 1973 (dec. 1992). AB, U. Houston. Sec. to dean of men Clarion (Pa.) State Tchr. Coll., 1948-49; sec. dean of edn. U. Houston, 1951-57; sec., v.p. Napko Corp., Houston, 1959-62; adminstrv. sec. Ben Taub Hosp., Houston, 1968-73; victim/witness coord Cherokee County Dist. Atty., Rusk, Tex., 1992—99; cmty. edn. coord. Hospice of Ea. Tex., 2000—. Bd. child advocacy ctr. Crisis Ctr., Cherokee, Jacksonville, 1996—; lay rep., libr. Rusk Libr., 1994—; east Tex. handweaver guild, Nacogdocher, Tex., 1985-92; coord. Anderson County Hospice of East Tex., 2002—. With USAF, 1949-51. Mem. Tyler Art League, Nat. Women's Mus., Cherokee County Art League (pres., sec., treas.). Home: RR 1 Box 221 Rusk TX 75785-9742 Office: Cherokee County 502 N Main St Rusk TX 75785-1337

COOK, DORIS MARIE, retired accountant, educator; b. Fayetteville, Ark., June 11, 1924; d. Ira and Mettie Jewel (Dorman) C. BSBA, U. Ark., 1946, MS, 1949; PhD, U. Tex., 1968. CPA, Okla., Ark. Jr. acct. Haskins & Sells, Tulsa, 1946-47; instr. acctg. U. Ark., Fayetteville, 1947-52, asst. prof., 1952-62, assoc. prof., 1962-69, prof., 1969-88, Univ. prof. and Nolan E. Williams lectr. in acctg., 1988-97, emeritus disting. prof., 1997—. Mem. Ark. State Bd. Pub. Accountancy, 1987-92, treas., 1989-91, vice chmn. 1991-92; mem. Nat. Assn. State Bds. of Accountancy, 1987-92; appointed Nolan E. Williams lectureship in acctg., 1988-97; Doris M. Cook chair in acctg. U. Ark., Fayetteville, 2000. Mem. rev. bd. Ark. Bus. Rev., Jour. Managerial Issues; contbr. articles to profl. jours. Recipient Bus. Faculty of Month award Alpha Kappa Psi, 1997, Outstanding Faculty award Ark. Tchg. Acad., 1997, Charles and Nadine Baum Outstanding Tchr. award, 1997, Outstanding Leadership and Svc. award from several women's orgns. for Women's History Month, 1999, AAUW, others. Mem. AICPA, Ark. Bus. Assn. (editor newsletter 1982-85), Am. Acctg. Assn. (chmn. nat. membership 1982-83, Arthur Carter scholarship com. 1984-85, membership Ark. 1985-87), Am. Women's Soc. CPAs., Ark. Soc. CPA's (life, v.p. 1975-76, pres. N.W. Ark. chpt. 1980-81, sec. Student Loan Found. 1981-84, treas. 1984-92, pres. 1992-97, chmn. pub. rels. 1984-88, 93-95, Outstanding Acctg. Educator award 1991, Outstanding Com. Svc. award 1995, Student Loan Found. Bd. award 2001, 21 Yrs. Outstanding Svc. award 2001), Acad. Acctg. Historians (life, trustee 1985-87, rev. bd. of Working Papers Series 1984-92, sec. 1992-95, pres.-elect 1995, pres. 1996), Ark. Fedn. Bus. and Profl. Women's Clubs (treas. 1979-80), Fayetteville Bus. and Profl. Women's Clubs (pres. 1973-74, 75-76, Woman of Yr. award 1977) Mortar Bd., Beta Gamma Sigma, Beta Alpha Psi (editor nat. newsletter 1973-77, nat. pres. 1977-78, Outstanding Alumni in Edn. Iota chpt. 1999, Outstanding Svc. award 1999), Phi Gamma Nu, Alpha Lambda Delta, Delta Kappa Gamma (sec. 1976-78, pres. 1978-80, treas. 1989-2000), Phi Kappa Phi. Home: 1655 Amy Ave Glendale Heights IL 60139

COOK, FRANCES D. international business consultant; b. Charleston, W.Va., Sept. 7, 1945; d. Nash and Vivian Cook. BA, Mary Washington Coll. of U. Va., 1967; MPA, Harvard U., 1978; LLD, Shenandoah U., 1998. Certificats d'Etudes, Université d'Aix-Marseille (France), 1966. Commd. fgn. svc. officer Dept. State, 1967; spl. asst. to R.S. Shriver amb. to France, Paris, 1968-69; mem. U.S. Del. Paris Peace Talks on Viet-Nam, 1970-71; cultural affairs officer, consul Am. Consul Gen., Sydney, Australia, 1971-73; cultural affairs officer, first sec. Am. Embassy, Dakar, Senegal, 1973-75; personnel officer for Africa USIA, Washington, 1975-77; dir. office public affairs African Bur. Dept. State, Washington, 1978-80, amb. to Republic of Burundi Bujumbura, 1980-83, consul gen. Alexandria, Egypt, 1983-86, dep. asst. sec. of state for refugees Washington, 1986-87, dir. Office of West African Affairs, 1987-89, amb. to Cameroon Yaoundé, 1989-93, U.S. coord. for Sudan, 1993; dep. asst. sec. of state for political-military affairs Dept. of State, Washington, 1993-95, amb. to Oman Muscat, 1996-99; founder The Ballard Group, LLC, 2002. Bd. dirs. ATK, Pegasus. Recipient various honor awards Dept. State. Mem. AAUW, Am. Fgn. Svc. Assn., Coun. of Fgn. Rels., Harvard Club of N.Y.C., Army-Navy Club/Washington, Phi Beta Kappa (alumni). Home: PO Box 40882 Washington DC 20016-0882

COOK, JANICE ELEANOR NOLAN, retired elementary school educator; b. Middletown, Ohio, Nov. 22, 1936; d. Lloyd and Eleanor Lee (Caudill) Nolan; m. Kenneth J. Cook, May 16, 1980 (dec.); children: Gerald W. Fultz Jr., Jana Linn Perkins, Jennylee Heard. BSEd, Miami U., 1971; MEd, reading specialist cert., Xavier U., 1982, rank 1 cert., 1987, spl. edn. cert., 1988. Tchr. pre-sch. and elem. Middletown (Ohio) Pub. Schs., 1957-58, 71-80; tchr. Boone County Schs., Florence, Ky., 1980-99; ret., 1999. Resource tchr. Ky. Internship Program, 1985—95; substitute tchr. Lebanon City Schs. Fellow ABI Rsch. Assn. (life); mem. NEA, Nat. Assn. [illegible] Young Children, Internat. Reading Assn., Nat. Coun. Tchrs. English, Ky. Edn. Assn., Boone County Edn. Assn., Assn. Childhood Edn. Internat., Nat. Coun. Tchrs. Math. Home: 926 Pineneedle Pl Maineville OH 45039-7019

COOK, JENIK ESTERM (JENIK ESTERM COOK SIMONIAN), artist, educator; b. Rezaieh, Iran, July 7, 1940; came to U.S., 1964; d. Sameual Amijon and Nanajan (Amreh Sarkissian) Simonian; m. Carrol Ross Cook, Sept. 28, 1961; children: Fiona Gitana Cook Anderson, Herold H. Studied with Hossein Delrish, Iran, 1968-70; studied with Barbara Lae, Scotland, 1970-78; studied with Chalita Robinson, 1981-87, studied with Jake Lee, 1987-90, studied with Dr. Alex Vilumsons, 1988-94. Tchr. art. Resident artist Orlando Gallery, L.A.; art tchr. U. Judaism, Bel Air. One-woman shows include Pacific Design Ctr., L.A., 1996, Orlando Gallery, 1997, 98, Bakery Digital Post Prodn. Ctr., L.A., West Wood Fed. Bldg., L.A., 1999, Hilton Hotel, L.A., 1999; exhibited in groups shows at Orlando Gallery, 1998, L.A. Conv. Ctr., 1998. Rheinfelden (Germany) Town Hall, 1998, Gallery Merkel, Grenzack, Germany, 1998, L.A. Art Expo, 1998, MGM Conf. Ctr., 1999, Long Beach Conv. Ctr., 1999, Art 21, Las Vegas MGM Conv. Ctr., 1999, Art Expo, N.Y., 2000; set designer, scenic artist North Hollywood Ch. of Religious Sci., 1999. Office: Everywomans Village 5650 Sepulveda Blvd Van Nuys CA 91411-2981 Home: 5643 Norwich Ave Van Nuys CA 91411-3233

COOK, JOAN, Canadian senator; b. English Harbor West, Newfoundland, Can., Oct. 6, 1934; children: Diane, Jean. V.p. Automobile Dealership; mgr. CJON Radio-TV; with Robert Simpson Ea. Ltd., Halifax; senator The Senate of Can., Ottawa, 1998—. Liberal. Office: 253 East Block The Senate of Canada Ottawa ON Canada K1A 0A4

COOK, KATHY H. elementary school educator, conductor, composer; b. Sarasota, Fla., Sept. 24, 1953; d. Robert W. Hatch and Anna May Vollet; m. Samuel Cook, Feb. 10, 1973; children: Stacy, Robert, Kevin. AA, Manatee Jr. Coll., Bradeuton, Fla., 1974; BA, Univ. S. Fla., Tampa, Fla., 1989; MEd, Nat. Louis Univ., Tampa, Fla., 1995. Orch. dir. Lincoln Mid. Sch., Fla., 1989—2000, Palmetto H.S., Fla., 1989—, Lee Margaret Mid. Sch., Bradenton, Fla., 2000—. Guest condr. March Jubliee, Fla. Orch. Assn, 1993—2003; contbr. articles for profl. jour. Bd. dirs. Performing Arts Downtown, Bradeuton, Fla. Recipient Tchr. of the Yr., Manatee County Sch., 1995. Mem.: Music Educators Nat. Conf., Fla. Music Educators Assn., Fla. Orch. Assn. (pres.), Golden Key Nat. Avocations: reading, camping, family.

COOK, MARCELLA KAY, retired theater educator; b. Albuquerque, Dec. 22, 1949; d. Joseph Raymond and Vivian Francis (Mullinax) Murdick; m. James Rogers Cook, Mar. 25, 1975 (dec. Aug. 1991); 1 child, Amanda Kay. BA, U. Albuquerque, 1971; MA, Eastern N.Mex. U., 1973. Prof. theatre, speech Vernon (Tex.) Coll., 1973—2002; co-owner, publicity dir. Umpire Entertainment and Enterprise Records, 1998—2001; dir. 112 plays Vernon Regional Coll., 1973—2002. Fine arts chair Vernon Regional Jr. Coll., 1982—87, 1997—2001; stage mgr. Columbia Cmty. Concert Series, 1976—91; actress, dir. Bill Fegan Attractions, Raton, N.Mex., 1974; costume designer Ea. N.Mex. U., Portales, 1972—73; head wardrobe mistress Cinegai Films, Rome, 1971, Paramount Studios, 1971. Writer, dir. : (plays) Waggoner Ranch's Entry Tex. Ranch Roundup, 1987, 1988, 1989. Named Outstanding Young Women Am., 1978; recipient Humanitarian Svc. award, Tex. Army N.G., 1979, Am. Coll. Theater Festival awards Excellence in Directing, 1987, 1997, Friends of Arts award, 2002; grantee, Stokes Found., Tex. Commn. Arts. Mem.: S.W. Theatre Assn., Tex. Ednl. Theatre Assn., Delta Psi Omega, Alpha Psi Omega, Phi Theta Kappa. Avocations: sculpting, travel, collecting classic cars, collecting classic rock and roll music. Home: 6309 Vista Montano NW Albuquerque NM 87120

COOK, MARGARET MOYER, special education educator; b. Odessa, Tex., Mar. 26, 1948; d. A.D Oscar and Georgina Swan Moyer; m. John Michael Cook, Dec. 12, 1970; children: Tina Marie, Dana Louise. MA in Edn., Tex. Woman's U., Denton, 1997. Cert. tchr. Tex., 1988, provisional HS home econs. Tex., 1988, provisional emotionally disturbed Tex., 1988, provisional lang./learning disabilities Tex., 1988. Learning disability tutor Highland HS, Medina, Ohio, 1985—87; resource English tchr. Brewer Mid. Sch., White Settlement, Tex., 1987—90, Brewer HS, White Settlement, Tex., 1990—94, content mastery tchr., 1993—94, vocat. adjustment coord., 1994—97, spl. edn. coord., 1997—2001, transition specialist, 2001—02, vocat. adjustment coord., 2002—. Mem. First Bapt. Ch. of Hurst, Hurst, Tex., 1986—2003. Mem.: Tex. Assn. Vocat. Adjustment Coords. (regional rep. 1999—2001, 2d v.p. 2001—03, editor), Internat. Reading Assn. Republican. Baptist. Avocations: bicycling, motorcycling, quilting, swimming, running. Home: 705 W Pleasantview Hurst TX 76054 Office: Brewer High Sch 1000 S Cherry Lane White Settlement TX 76108 Personal E-mail: mmcook31@msn.com. E-mail: mcook@wsisd.net.

COOK, MARY MARGARET, steamfitter, educator; b. Royal Oak, Mich., Apr. 28, 1944; d. John Patrick and Agnes Hannah (Anderson) McMahon; m. Barney Albert Cahill, Aug. 19, 1967 (div. Apr. 1971); m. Frank Melvin Cook, Jan. 26, 1974. BA in Elem. Edn., Ariz. State U., 1971; cert. United Assn. instr., Mich. State U., 1990; Cert., Ariz. C.C. Cert. elem. tchr., Ohio, Ariz.; mech. lic. journeyman and steamfitter. Tchr. St. Agnes Elem. Sch., Phoenix, 1967-71, Bevis Elem. Sch., Cin., 1971-73; GED instr. Scottsdale, Ariz., 1975-78; steamfitter United Assn. Local 469, Phoenix, 1978—. Instr. apprentices Rio Salado C.C., Phoenix, 1984-90; math. cons. Ariz. Dept. Edn., 1988-90; state dir. AFL-CIO Apprenticeship Awareness Program, 1990-92. Chair State Con. Emerging Careers for Women, 1992—98; mem. Apprenticeship Adv. Coun., 1990—97, chair, 1995—97; staff dept. commerce Workforce Devel. Coun., 1997—; mem. Gov.'s Commn. on Nontraditional Employment for Women; state dir. Project Nontraditional Assistance and Info. Link, 1992—99; extended staff Gov.'s Workforce Devel. Policy, 1997—; state dir. Ensuring Opportunity Coalition; cons. Pro Max, 1999—; apprenticeship and tng. rep. Ariz. Dept. Commerce, 2000—. Mem.: Ariz. State U. Alumni Assn. (life), Toastmasters Internat. (Advanced Toastmaster bronze). Avocations: computers, reading, weight lifting. Home: 22452 N 80th Ln Peoria AZ 85383-2149

COOK, SISTER M(ARY) MERCEDES, secondary school educator, principal; b. Hagerstown, Md., Dec. 18, 1939; d. Garland and Anita Rideoutt (Willis) C. Student, Fordham U.; BA, Ea. Conn. State U., 1974, MS, 1983; grad., Norwich Diocesan Prins. Acad., Conn., 1991. Joined Sistes of Charity of Our Lady of Mother of the Ch., Roman Cath. Ch.; cert. tchr., Conn. Tchr., prin. St. Joseph Sch., Baltic, Conn., 1959-61; tchr. Sacred Heart Sch., Byram, Conn., 1961-63, Bloomfield, Conn., 1963-66, Taftville, Conn., 1966-67, Acad. of Holy Family, Baltic, 1967-84; tchr., vice prin. Assumption Sch., Manchester, 1984—; vice-prin., tchr., chair dept. English, guide counselor Acad. of the Holy Family, Baltic, Conn., 1990—2003; dir. Sacred Heart Ednl. Ctr., Baltic, 2003—. Mem.: Nat. Cath. Ednl. Assn., Math. Assn. Am., Nat. Coun. Tchrs. English. Republican. Avocations: reading, writing, painting, cooking, interior decorating.

COOK, MARY PHELPS, chemistry educator; b. Memphis, Tenn., Sept. 21, 1960; d. James Burnette Phelps and Mary Margaret Botteron Jorgensen; m. Stephen D. Cook, Aug. 7, 1982; children: Daniel, Amy, Paul. BS, Christian Brothers Coll., 1982; PhD, Memphis State U., 1990. Grad. asst. U. Memphis, 1983-90; adj. prof. S.W. Tenn. C.C., Memphis, 1990-93, asst. prof., 1993-98, assoc. prof., 1998—. Mem. adv. bd. dept. chemistry

Christian Bros. Coll., Memphis, 1996-97. Author: in-house lab. manual; contbr. article to profl. jour. Com. chmn. troop 255 Boy Scouts Am., Bartlett, Tenn., 1997—, mem. staff N.E. dist. Cub Scout roundtable, 1998-99, dir. day camp, 1999, asst. den leader pack 255, 1999—; mem. Girl Scouts USA, Bartlett, 1995—. Van Fleet fellow Van Fleet Found., 1987-89. Mem. Am. Chem. Soc., Assn. Career and Tech. Edn. Office: SW Tenn CC 5983 Macon Cv Memphis TN 38134-7642 E-mail: mcook@stim.tec.tn.us.

COOK, MELANIE K. lawyer; b. Salt Lake City, June 3, 1953; BS, UCLA, 1974, JD, 1978. Assoc. Bloom Hergott Cook Diemer & Klein, Beverly Hills, Calif., 1987—92, ptnr., 1992—2002; of counsel Ziffren, Brittenham, Branca, Fischer, Gilbert-Lurie, & Stiffelman LLP, L.A., 2002—. Office: 1801 Century Park W Los Angeles CA 90067-6406

COOK, NANCY W. state legislator; b. May 11, 1936. Ed. U. Del. Mem. Del. Senate from 15th Dist.; mem. Kent County Dem. Com. Democrat. Home: PO Box 127 Kenton DE 19955-0127 Office: Del State Senate Legislative Hall PO Box 1401 Dover DE 19903-1401

COOK, REBECCA MCDOWELL, former state official; m. John Larkin Cook; children: Hunter, and Morgan. BA in Polit. sci., U. Mo., 1972, JD, 1975; D (hon.), Mo. We. State Coll., 1997. Former clk., assoc., ptnr. Limbaugh, Limbaugh, and Russell Law Firm, Cape Girardeau, Mo.; v.p. Oliver, Oliver, Waltz, and Cook Law Firm, 1979-92; del. to Mo. State Dem. Conv., 1980; mem. Mo. State Bd. Elem. and Sec. Edn., 1990-94; sec. of state State of Mo., 1994—2001. Mem. Future of South Commn., Dem. Nat. Com., 1995—. Recipient Order of Barristers Award., 1992, Woman of Achievement Award., Cape Girardeau Zonta Club, 1994, James C. Kirkpatrick Excellence in Governance Award; Henry Toll fellow. Mem. S.E. Mo. State U. Found., S.E. Mo. Hosp. Found., Nat. Assn. Secretaries of State (dir., exec. com.), Coun. Econ. Edn., Mo. K-16 Coalition, Lift Mo., Inc. Democrat. Presbyterian.*

COOK, SHARLA J. career officer; BS in Edn. with honors, Brigham Young U., 1971; disting. grad., Officer Tng. Sch., 1972; aircraft maintenance officer course, Chanute AFB, Ill., 1973; M in Logistics Mgmt., Air Force Inst. of Tech., 1977; grad., Air Command and Staff Coll., 1985; disting. grad., Indsl. Coll. of Armed Forces, 1993. Commd. 2d lt. USAF, 1972, advanced through grades to brigadier gen., 1998; wing job control officer U-Tapao Air Base, Thailand, 1975-76; aide-de-camp air logistics ctr. comdr. Sacramento Air Logistics Ctr., McClellan AFB, Calif., 1981-82, dep. br. chief inventory and scheduling br., 1982-84; comdr. 374th Orgnl. Maintenance Squadron, Clark Air Base, The Philippines, 1985-87; maintenance ops. officer 58th Tactical Tng. Wing, Luke AFB, Ariz., 1988-90, asst. dep. comdr. for maintenance, 1990-91; dep. comdr. 58th Support Group, Luke AFB, 1991-92; comdr. 8th Logistics Group, Kunsan Air Base, South Korea, 1993-94; chief maintenance engring. Hdqs. Pacific Air Forces, Hickam AFB, Hawaii, 1994-95, asst. dir. logistics, 1995-96; dir. aircraft directorate Ogden Air Logistics Ctr., Hill AFB, Utah, 1996-97; dir. logistics Hdqs. Air Edn. and Tng. Command, Randolph AFB, Tex., 1997—; comdr. 82d tng. wing Air Edn. and Tng. Command, Sheppards AFB, Tex., 1999—. Decorated Legion of Merit, Meritorious Svc. medal with 4 oak leaf clusters. Address: 82 TRW/CC Sheppard AFB TX 76311

COOK, SUSAN FARWELL, associate director planned giving; b. Boston, Apr. 28, 1953; d. Benjamin and Beverly (Brooks) Conant; m. James Samuel Cook Jr., Aug. 17, 1985; children: Emily Farwell, David McKendree. AB, Colby Coll., 1975; MBA, Thomas Coll., 2002. Bank teller Boston 5 Cent Savs. Bank, 1975-76; asst. technician plan cost John Hancock Mut. Life Ins. Co., Boston, 1976-77, technician plan cost, 1977 78, sr. technician plan cost, 1978-79, asst. mgr. group pension plan cost, 1979-81; assoc. dir. alumni rels. Colby Coll., Waterville, Maine, 1981-86, dir. alumni rels., 1986-97, assoc. dir. planned giving, 1997—. Co-dir. adv. bd. women's studies Colby Coll., 1987-89, adv. women's group, 1987-89; bd. dirs. Maine Planned Giving Coun., 2001—, treas., 2002--. Bd. dirs., newsletter sec. Literacy Vols. Am., Waterville, 1986—89, 1991—92, v.p., 1995—97, pres., 1997—99; treas. Pitcher Pond Improvement Assn., 1988—95, Gagnon/100 Campaign, 1996, 1998; coach Waterville Area Youth Hockey Assn., 1997—2001; bd. dirs. Youth Hockey Assn., 2001—; treas. Gagnon for Senate, 2000, 2002; trustee Universalist-Unitarian Ch., Waterville, 2001—, v.p., 2003—; bd. dirs. Congress Lake Assns., Yarmouth, Maine, 1988—92, Waterville Youth Soccer Assn., 2001—, Kennebec Montessori Sch., 1999—2001; pres. Waterville Youth Soccer Assn., 2002—. Mem. AAUW (sec. Waterville br. 1989-91, pres. 1991-93, co-pres. 1993-95), Coun. Advancement and Support of Edn., CASE Dist. I (exec. bd. dirs. 1994-97, sec. 1996-97, nominating com. 1997-99). Avocations: skiing, sewing, golf. Home: 6 Pray Ave Waterville ME 04901-5339 Office: Colby Coll 4372 Mayflower Hl Waterville ME 04901-8843

COOK, TRACI, sports association executive; BA in History, English and Polit. Sci., U. Miss., 1987. With Nat. Dem. Inst., Malawi, Central African Republic; staff mem. Sr. Christopher Dodd (Conn.), 1992; mktg., bus. devel. exec. Physicians' Online; v.p. mktg. comm. Shepardson, Stern and Kaminsky; sr. dir. strategic and corp. rels. Women's Nat. Basketball Assn., N.Y.C., 2001—. Office: Women's Nat Basketball Assn Olympic Tower 645 Fifth Ave New York NE 10022*

COOK, VIVIAN, state legislator; b. Rock Hill, S.C., May 23, 1937; d. McDonald Eaves and Eva Phillips; m. John Cook; 1 child, Reginald. Grad., DeFrans Bus. Inst. Mem. N.Y. State Assembly, Dist. 32, Albany; mem. alcoholism and drug abuse, commerce, industry and econ. devel., corps., authorities and commns., housing, ins., majority steering coms. N.Y. State Assembly, Albany, 1991—. Dist. leader Queens County; founder Cmty. Edn. Resource Ctr.; chairwoman Queens County Dem. Com.; mem. Dem. Nat. Com., Queens County Exec. Com.; del. Dem. Nat. Conv., 1988, 92; founder, exec. Allied Regular Dem. Club, Inc. Recipient Sojourner Truth award Nat. Assn. Negro Bus. and Profl. Women's Club, Inc., Sr. Citizens award 113th Precinct, Cmty. Svc. award 103 and 113th Precincts, Sutphin Blvd. Civic Assn. award, Cmty. Svc. award Citizens for Jenkins, 10-Yr. Cmty. Bd. Svc. award City of N.Y., Cmty. Svc. award Neighborhood Coun., Mother's Day award Springfield Gardens, Commn. Svc. & Leadership award NYS Martin Luther King, Jr. Inst., Polit. Action Com. award P.E.F., Little League award Rochdal Village. Mem.South Ozone Park Women's Assn. (founder, chmn. bd. dirs.). Office: 142-15 Rockaway Blvd South Ozone Park NY 11436-1420 also: NY State Assembly State Capitol Albany NY 12224

COOKE, BECKY JILL BERG, principal; b. Spokane, Wash., Sept. 27, 1962; d. Alan Loyd and Dolores Jean Berg; 1 child, Abigail Castle. BE, Ea. Wash. U., 1984; MEd, Western Wash. U., 1989; EdD, Tchrs. Coll. Columbia U., 2000. Cert. profl. adminstr. Supt. of Pub. Instrn., Wash. State, 1989. Mid. sch. prin. and assoc. prin. Bainbridge Island (Wash.) Sch. Dist., 1991—94; asst. prin. Mead Sch. (Wash.) Dist., 1994—96, prin., 1996—. Adj. prof. Wash. State U., Pullman, Wash., 2003—03; adj. instr. Ea. Wash. U., Cheney, Wash., 1999—99; manuscript reviewer Corwin Press, Thousand Oaks, Calif., 2003—. Mem. Ea. Wash. U. Profl. Edn. Adv. Bd., Cheney, Wash., 1994—. Mem.: Internat. Assn. Supr. and Curriculum Devel. (mem. leadership coun. 2003—), Wash. State Assn. Supr. and Curriculum Devel. (pres. 2001—02). Democrat. Office: Evergreen Elementary School 215 WEddy Spokane WA 99208 Office Phone: 509-465-6400.

COOKE, BETTE LOUISE, retired library director; b. Emporia, Kans., Oct. 26, 1929; d. Oscar Oliver and Ada Luella (Williams) C. Student, Grinnell (Iowa) Coll., 1947-49; BS in Edn., U. Mo., 1951; MA in Libr. Sci., Vanderbilt U., 1964; EdD, Ind. U., 1971. Tchr. pub. schs., Mo. & ILl., 1951-63; instr. in libr. sci. N.E. Mo. State U., Kirksville, 1964-66; asst. prof. libr. sci. Western Ill. U., Macomb, 1966-72; assoc. prof., chair dept. libr. sci. and instructional tech. Cen. Mo. State U., Warrenburg, 1972-80; prof. libr. sci., dir. libr. St. Mary of the Plains Coll., Dodge City, 1983—92; ret., 1994. Cons. sch. librs., Ill. and Mo., 1971-79; judge S.W. Kans. Project Fair Project, Dodge City, 1987—; grant evaluator Nat. Endowment for the Humanites, 1979; chair Dodge City Libr. Consortium, Dodge City, 1985. Mem. Dodge City Friends of Pub. Libr., 1987—; bd. dirs. Homeowners Assn., Dodge City, 1989k—. Ind. U. scholar, 1971; NEH/ACRL grantee, 1987. Mem. ALA, Kans. Libr. Assn., Kans. Coll. and Rsch. Librs. (program com.), Kans. Pvt. Acad. Librs., AAUW. Republican. Presbyterian. Avocations: gardening, health foods, health activities. Home: 916 Lakewood Dr Monett MO 65708-9354

COOKE, CHANTELLE ANNE, writer; b. Denver, Apr. 9, 1971; d. Frederick Blaize and Claire Gail (Jones) C. Student, Collin County C.C., Plano, Tex., 1989-93. Author: (poetry chapbook) Songs From Stars, 1995, (poetry chapbook) Wild Irises on God's Mountainside, 1999, (poetry cassette tape) Visions, 1997; contbg. editor tech. articles for computer industry, 1994-96; freelance writer articles and poems. Recipient Star of Loyalty, Paralyzed Vets. Am., 1996. Mem. Internat. Soc. Poets, Acad. Am. Poets, Poetry Connection, Magic Cir. Democrat. Roman Catholic. Avocations: mosaic art, home interior decorating, pistol target shooting, needlepoint.

COOKE, HONORE GUILBEAU, artist, educator; b. Baton Rouge, Feb. 11, 1907; d. Braxton Honoré Guilbeau and Mary Bangs Magruder; m. Edmund Vance Cooke Jr., Oct. 1930 (dec. Oct. 1978); children: Jennifer Gail, Jeremy Vance. Student, So. Meth. U.; grad., Sch. Art Inst. Chgo., 1926-29. Instr. Art Sch. Akron (Ohio) Art Inst.; artist, tchr. Nat. Mus. Women in the Arts, Washington. Works exhibited at The Cleve. Mus. Art, Phila. Mus. Art, Whitney Mus. Am. Art, N.Y., Cleve. Artist's Show in Miami Beach, Fla., Syracuse (N.Y.) Nat. Ceramic Exhbn., Massillon (Ohio) Mus., Instituto de Rels. Cultural, Mexico City, 1969, Sylvia Ullman Am. Crafts Gallery, Cleve., N.E. Ohio Mus. Art, Cleve., Akron Art Mus., 1995, N.Y. Art Assn. Nat., Cooperstown, 1995, 96, Fla. Pastel Assn., 1995, 96, Coopers Town Art Assn., 2001; author, illustrator: Mrs. Magpie's Invention, 1971; illustrator: The Adventures of Hajji Baba of Ispahan, 1947, A Connecticut Yankee in King Arthur's Court, 1948, Shaving Shagpat, 1955, I Know a Farm, 1960, The Birthday Tree, 1961, Who Goes There in My Garden?, 1963, Hundreds and Hundreds of Strawberries, 1969, Treemendous Gifts (Buck Cooke), 2000. Avocations: gardening, walking. Home: 1996 Major Rd Peninsula OH 44264-9681 also: 3605 E Shore Rd Miramar FL 33023-4953

COOKE, LYNNE CATHERINE, curator; b. Geelong, Victoria, Australia; arrived in U.S., 1989; d. Allan Stewart and Beryl Edith (Agg) C. BA with honors, U. Melbourne, Victoria, 1974, MA, London U., 1979; PhD, U. London, 1987. Lectr. dept. art history London U., 1979-88; co-curator Mus. Art Carnegie Internat./Carnegie Mus. of Art, Pitts., 1991; curator Dia Ctr. for Arts, N.Y.C., 1991—; artistic dir. Biennale of Sydney, Australia, 1995-96. Mus./exhbn. panelist Nat. Endowment for Arts, Washington, 1996. Mem. editl. bd. Burlington Mag., London, 1990—; contbr. articles, essays to mags., numerous exhbn. catalogues. Recipient award Gt. Britain-Sasakawa Found., 1987; Smithsonian fellow Hirshhorn Mus./Smithsonian Inst., 1989. Avocation: cinema. Office: Dia Art Found 535 W 22nd St New York NY 10011-1108

COOKE, SARA MULLIN GRAFF, daycare provider, kindergarten educator, medical assistant; b. Phila., Dec. 29, 1935; d. Charles Henry and Elizabeth (Mullin) Brandt Graff; m. Peter Fischer Cooke, June 29, 1963 (div. July 1994); children: Anna Cooke Smith, Peter Fischer Jr., Elizabeth Cooke Haskins, Sara Cooke Lowe; m. Laina Cooke Driscoll, Dec. 18, 1999. AA, Bennett Coll., 1955; BE in Child Edn., Westchester State Tchrs. Coll., 1956. Asst. to tchr. 1st grade The Woodlyn Sch., 1956-58; tchr. Sara Bircher's Kindergarten, Germantown, Pa., 1958-62, Chestnut Hill (Pa.) Acad., 1962-63, Tarleton Sch., Devon, Pa., 1963-64; with F.C.I. Mktg. Co-ordinators Inc., N.Y.C., New Canaan, Conn., 1980-86; fundraiser Children's Hosp., Phila., 1989-92, pres. women's com., 1987-88; coord., master of ednl. ceremonies Phila. Soc. for Preservation Landmarks, 1991-93; coord. Elderhostel Program Landmarks Soc., 1992-93. Pvt. day caretaker Spl. Care, Inc., 1988—; pvt. daycare and doctor's asst., 1994—. Bd. aux. Children's Hosp. Phila., 1970-76, women's bd., 1977—, pres., 1987-88; commonwealth bd. Med. Coll. Pa., 1984-99, Gimbel award com., 1994; alt. del. Rep. Nat. Conv., 1992; co-chmn. benefit St. Martin in the Field, London, 1997; vol. with parents of very sick children Connelly Family Resource Ctr./Children's Hosp. of Phila., 1999—, chmn., 2003; vol. Rep. Nat. Conv., 2000; press vol. Polit. Fest in Laura Bush Libr., 2000. Recipient Silver Cup award, Children's Hosp. Phila., 2002. Mem. Pa. Assn. Hosp. Auxs. (health rep.) Nat. Soc. Colonial Dames (garden com. 1988—), Ch. Women's Assn. (past pres.), Alumnae Assn. Madeira Sch. (class sec., class agt., Vol. Svc. award 1997), Phila. Cricket Club, Jr. League Garden Club (co-chmn. Daisy Day Children's Hosp. 2001). Republican. Episcopalian. Home and Office: 3421 Warden Dr Philadelphia PA 19129-1417

COOKE, WALTA PIPPEN, automobile dealership owner; b. Shreveport, La., Oct. 18, 1940; d. Billy Burt and Eula (Heaton) Pippen; m. John William Cooke II, Dec. 20, 1958; children: Cheryl Cooke Williams, John William III. BA, Baylor U., 1963. Co-owner, sec.-treas. Pippen Motor Co., Carthage, Tex., 1972-80, owner, sec.-treas., 1980—. Bd. dirs. Sabine River Authority of Tex., 1993-99, pres. bd., 1996-97; past dir. Toledo Bend Joint Project; chmn. lower basin project com. Sabine River Authority Tex., 1999, mem. by-laws com., chmn. 50th ann. com., 1999. Pianist for sanctuary choir Ctrl. Bapt. Ch., Carthage, 1986—; chmn. 50th anniversary celebration com. Sabine River Authority of Tex., 1999; bd. dir. Panola Co. Heritage Found., 2000—, patron mem., mem. ednl. found. steering com., 2002—; mem. task force Groundwater Conservation, East Tex. Area.; founding dir. Carthage Ind. Sch. Dist. Edn. Found. Mem. Carthage 32 Club, Carthage Book Club (rec. sec. 1995-97), The Carthage Club. Avocations: reading, gardening, travel, music. Home: 200 Timberlane Dr Carthage TX 75633-2231 Office: Pippen Motor Co 1300 W Panola St Carthage TX 75633-2346

COOKS, PAMALA ANIECE, insurance agent; b. Harvey, Ill., Dec. 31, 1973; d. Anthony T. Washington and Deloris Townsend; m. Paul Anthony Cooks, Dec. 8, 2002; 1 child, Olivia Janai Washington. BA, Govenors State U., 2001. Lic. prodr. Ill., 2000. Sales assoc. Aetna Inc., Chgo., 1996—. Evangelism ministry St. Mark Missionary Bapt. Ch., Harvey, 2002—03. Mem.: Nat. Campaign for Tolerance (assoc. Wall of Tolerance award 2002, 2003). Office Phone: 847-619-5590., 708-880-0436. Office Fax: 847-619-4936. Personal E-mail: pamalawashington@msn.com.

COOL, KIM PATMORE, retail executive, needlework consultant; b. Cleve., Feb. 1, 1940; d. Herman Chester Earl and Eva (Geneau) Patmore; m. Kenneth Adams Cool Jr., Mar. 12, 1963; 1 child, Heidi Adams. BA in Econs., Sweet Briar Coll., 1962; postgrad., Case Western Reserve U., 1962-63. Test adminstr. Pradco, Cleve., 1962-63; pvt. needlework cons. Cleve., 1970-72; retail v.p., treas., custom designer And Sew On, Inc., Cleve., 1973-92, exec. v.p., treas., 1982-92; v.p. Shure Stiches Inc., 1991-92; owner Shure Stitches, Inc., Cleve., 1992-93, The Hare Necessities, Venice, Fla., Germany, 1994—, Hare Necessities Craft & Needlework Mfg., Venice, Fla. Lectr. bus. seminars Nat. Needlework Assn.; tchr. Wellesley Coll. Continuing Edn. Program, 1986; pub. Fredericktown Press, Md.; designer and mktg. assoc. Kappie OriginalsLtd., 1988-93. Collector quality custom hand-painted canvases; co-author: How to Market Needlepoint-The Definitive Manual, 1988, Easy Macrame, 1990, Basic Macrame, 1990, Wearable Macrame, 1990, Playmate Dolls to Stitch, 1991, Pillows and Purses to Stitch, 1991, Needlepoint from Start to Finish, 1992, Pathway to Profit in the Needlework Industry, 1995, Ghost Stories of Venice, 2002, Ghost Stories of Sarasota, 2003, Circus Days in Sarasota & Venice, 2004; homes corr.: Venice (Fla.) Gondolier, 1995—, bus. editor:, 1998—, features editor: Venice Gondolier Sun. Rep. committeeman Cuyahoga County, Shaker Heights, Ohio, 1964-72. Recipient 1st pl. environ. writing, 3d pl. headline, Fla. Press Assn., 2002, 1st pl. spl. sect. and newspaper promotion, 2003. Mem.: Sweet Briar Coll. Alumnae Assn. (nat. bd. dirs., upper Midwest region 1965—66, class sec. 1988—92), S.E. Yarncrafters Guild (condr. merchandising seminars 1989—), Embroiderers Guild of Cleve. (bd. dirs. 1980—82), Am. Profl. Needlework Retailers, Nat. Needlework Assn. (lectr. seminar on mktg. needlepoint, seminars on buying and merchandising 1988—, charter assoc. retail), U.S. Figure Skating Assn. (gold test judge 1967—, competitions com., ea. vice chair precision, judges edn. tng. com., nat. vice chair for precision, nat. precision judge, sr. competiton judge), Fla. Curling Club (charter), Mayfield Country Club, Cleve. Skating Club. Mem. United Ch. of Christ. Avocations: skating, curling (attended 1st Women's Olympic Tng. Camp for Curlers, Regional champion 1987-88). Home and Office: Hist Venice Press 312 Shore Rd Venice FL 34285-3725

COOL, MARY L. education specialist; b. Buffalo, Dec. 7, 1954; d. Paul G. and Dorothy R. (O'Brien) Wailand; m. Ronald J. Cool, June 23, 1979; children: Logan Elizabeth, Colin Jeffery. BS in Elem. Edn. cum laude, SUNY, Fredonia, 1976; MS in Ednl. Leadership, Nova Southeastern U., 1996. Cert. tchr., N.Y., Fla. Tchr. grade 1, Buffalo, N.Y., 1976-77; tchr. grade 5 Orange County, Orlando, Fla., 1979-85; tchr. grade 1, ESEA Title I head tchr. Manatee County, Myakka City, Fla., 1977-79; tchr. grade 5, media specialist Volusia County, Osteen, Fla., 1985-89; intermediate resource tchr. S.W. Volusia County, Fla., 1989-91; dist. elem. resource tchr., elem. tchr. specialist Volusia County Schs., Fla., 1991-97, staff devel. specialist, 1997-98, elem. and sch. improvement coord., 1998—2002; sch. improvement coord. initiative implementation Charter Sch. Dist., 2002—, elem. edn. coord., 2003 . Grade level chair, sci. chair, reading chair, facilitative leader, coop. learning trainer, tchr. coach, tech. edn. coach, tchr. asst. coord., student success team coord., tchr. induction coord. Volusia County Schs.; ednl. cons. Scholastic, Inc., Sports Illus. for Kids, Kids Discover, Marvel Comics, Time for Kids, UNICEF, Miami Mus. Arts and Scis. Mem. ASCD, AAUW, Nat. Coalition for Sex Equity in Edn., Nat. Staff Devel. Coun., Fla. Coun. Elem. Edn., Kappa Delta Pi. Home: 1566 Gregory Dr Deltona FL 32738-6159 Office: PO Box 2410 Daytona Beach FL 32115-2410

COOLEY, FANNIE RICHARDSON, counselor, educator; b. Tunnel Springs, Ala., July 4, 1924; d. Willie C. Richardson and Emma Jean (McCorvey) Stallworth. BS, Tuskegee (Ala.) Inst., 1947, MS, 1951; PhD, U. Wis., 1969. Cert. counselor. Asst. inst. Tuskegee Inst., 1947-48, prof. counseling, 1969-2000, prof. emeritus, 2000—. Instr. Alcorn A&M Coll., Lorman, Miss., 1948-51; asst. prof. Ala. A&M Coll., Normal, 1951-62, assoc. prof., 1964-65; grad. fellow Purdue U., West Lafayette, Ind., 1962-64; house fellow U. Wis., Madison, 1965-69; cons. VA Med. Ctr. Tuskegee, 1969— . Mem. AAUW, AAUP, ASCD (bd. dirs., Disting. Svc. award 1985), Ala. Assn. Counseling and Devel. (pres. 1976-77, Svc. award 1978-79), Ala. Assn. for Counselor Edn. (pres. 1985-86), Aassn. Specialists in Group Work (pres. 1989-90, Career award 1998), Internat. Platford Assn., Chi Sigma Iota. Episcopalian. Home: 802-C Avenue A Tuskegee Institute AL 36088-2402 Office: Tuskegee Inst Dept Counseling and Student Devel Thrasher Hall Tuskegee Institute AL 36088

COOLEY, HILARY ELIZABETH, county official; b. Leesburg, Va., May 8, 1953; d. Thomas McIntyre and Helen Strong (Stringham) C. BA in Econs., U. Pitts., 1976; postgrad. in bus. adminstrn., Hood Coll., Frederick, Md., 1985-90. Mgr. Montgomery Ward, Frederick, 1976-80, merchandiser, 1980-82; asst. bus. mgr. Arundel Comm., Leesburg, 1982-84; bus. mgr. Loudoun Country Day Sch., Leesburg, 1984-85, bd. trustees, 1989-93, sec. bd. trustees, 1989-90, v.p., 1990-92; contr. Foxcroft Sch., Middleburg, Va., 1984-86, 91-92; corr. Loudoun Times Mirror, Leesburg, 1985-87; estate mgr. Delta Farm Inc., Middleburg, Va., 1988-98; cmty. ctr. mgr. County of Loudoun, 1998—. Area chmn. Keep Loudoun Beautiful, Middleburg, 1983-90, pres., bd. dirs. 1993-96; pres. Waterford (Va.) Citizens' Assn., 1985-86, Waterford Players, 1986-88; bd. dirs. Waterford Found., Inc., 1992-95, pres. 1995-98; bd. dirs. Loudoun Hist. Soc., Leesburg, 1987, Mt. Zion Ch. Preservation Assn., 1996-99; treas. Amendment 1 Inc., 1997-99, pres., 1999—. mem.bd.Loudoun County Arbor Day Commn. 2003- Mem. Penn Hall Alumnae Ann. (pres. 1987-92). Democrat. Episcopalian. Avocations: photography, music, drama, tennis. Home and Office: 171 Blue Ridge Acres Harpers Ferry WV 25425-9309

COOLEY, LISA, television news anchor; b. Washington, D.C., 1964; BS, U of Virginia, 1986. With WTVR, Richmond Va.; evening and weekend anchor WBTV Live at Five, Charlotte, N.C., 1990-95, anchor, 1995-97; weekend anchor, weekday gen. assignment reporter WCBS-TV, N.Y.C., 1997—. Office: WCBS-TV/CBS Corp 524 W 57th St New York NY 10019-2924

COOLEY, LORALEE COLEMAN, professional storyteller; b. Charleston, Ill., Jan. 17, 1943; d. Leland Henry and Lorene Madge (Carpenter) C.; m. Edwin Mark Cooley, July 1, 1967; foster children: Jenni, Gail, Bridgette, Carla, Shannon, Diana. BA, Ea. Ill. U., 1965; postgrad., So. Bapt. Theol. Sem., Ky., 1965-67, Ariz. State U., 1972-74; MA, Antioch U., 1994. Piano, music tchr. various schs., 1967-69; women's program dir. Sta. WDXB-AM, Chattanooga, 1969-70; tutoring svcs. coord. Newton Cmty. Ctr., Chattanooga, 1969-71; asst. editor New Age mag., Washington, 1971-72; publicity coord. Firebird Lake/Watersports World, Phoenix, 1975; asst. libr. Casa Grande (Ariz.) Pub. Libr., 1975-77; profl. storyteller Casa Grande, 1977-78, Richmond, Va., 1978-79, Atlanta, 1979-88, Anderson, S.C., 1988-94, Pampa, Tex., 1994—. Publicity dir. Callanwolde Fine Arts Ctr., Atlanta, 1987; toured Republic of Ga., Newly-Ind. States, started rsch. project on Georgian Folklore, 1989. Author: (juvenile novel) Huckle, Buckle, Beanstalk, 2000. Co-chmn. Casa Grande Bicentennial Com., 1974-76; bd. dirs. Genesis House, Pampa,1995-99, M.K. Brown Mcpl. Auditorium, Pampa, 1995-99, 2001—, chmn. bd. 1998-99, trustee, 1995-98; advisor Tribute to Woody Guthrie Ctr., Pampa, 2001, v.p., 2001—; mem. Panhandle Tourism and Mktg. Coun., 1998-2000. Named Miss Louisville, 1966 (preliminary to Miss Am. pageant). Mem. AAUW, Nat. Storytelling Network, So. Order Storytellers (founder 1982), Pampa Fine Arts Assn. (bd., pres. 1996-97, coord. Artrain tour to Tex. Panhandle 1998), Tex. Women's Forum/Amarillo, DAR, Pampa C. of C. (com. on tourism 1999—). Democrat. Presbyterian. Avocations: travel, walking, cooking, reading. Home: 410 Buckler Ave Pampa TX 79065-6207 E-mail: lcooleystoryspinning@hotmail.com.

COOLIDGE, MARTHA, film director; b. New Haven, Aug. 17, 1946; MFA, RISD, 1968; ed., Columbia U.; MA, NYU, 1971. Dir.: (films) David: Off and On, 1972, Old-Fashioned Woman, 1974, More Than a School, 1974, (also prodr.) Not a Pretty Picture, 1975, Employment Discrimination: The Troubleshooters, 1976, Bimbo, 1978, Valley Girl, 1983, City Girl, 1984, Joy of Sex, 1984, Real Genius, 1985, Plain Clothes, 1988, Rambling Rose, 1991, Lost in Yonkers, 1992, Angie, 1994, Three Wishes, 1995, Out to Sea, 1997, Introducing Dorothy Dandridge, 1999, If These Walls Could Talk II, 2000, The Prince & Me, 2004; (TV films) Trenchcoat in Paradise, 1989, Bare Essentials, 1991, Crazy in Love, 1992, Flaming Rising, 2001, The Ponder Heart, 2001; (documentaries) David; On and Off, 1972 (Am. Film Festival award), More Than A School, 1973 (Am. Film Festival award), Old Fashioned Woman, 1974 (Am. Film Festival award), Not A Pretty Picture, 1975 (Am. Film Festival award); (TV series) Winners, 1978, The Twilight Zone, 1985, Sledge Hammer, 1986, Sex and the City, 1998, Leap Years, 2001; exec. prodr.: (TV films) Rip Girls, 2000. Recipient Best

Dir. and Picture Rambling Rose, Independent Sprint Awards, nomination for If These Walls Could Talk II, Emmy awards. Mem.: Dir. Guild of Am. (pres. 2002—03). Office: Lee Rae Leaver 11800 Osborne St Lake View Terrace CA 91342

COOMBE, CAROL G., ... of Education Progr. 15, 1915, MONH, McGill U. Social worker; senator The Senate of Canada, Ottawa, 1984—. Liberal. Office: 178-F Centre Block The Senate of Canada Ottawa ON Canada K1A 0A4

COOMER, DONNA R. communications executive; b. Wise, Va., June 21, 1957; d. Martin B. and Anna L. (Noe) C. BA in English and Advt. summa cum laude, Tex. Tech U., 1983. Local sales mgr. KTVT-TV, Gaylord Broadcasting, Dallas, Ft. Worth; account exec. KXAS-TV, Ft. Worth; nat. sales mgr. KTVT Gaylord Broadcasting, Dallas, Ft. Worth; gen. mgr. MMT Sales Cox Comms., Dallas/Ft. Worth. Mem. NAFE, Am. Women in Radio & TV, Phi Beta Kappa. Address: 8022 Fair Oaks Ave Dallas TX 75231-4719

COON, PENNY K. human services administrator; b. Penn Yan, N.Y., May 21, 1959; d. Wilfred Orval and Marilyn Estelle (Wells) Knapp; m. Thomas Allen Gray, Aug. 30, 1980 (div. July 1990); m. David Charles Coon, May 23, 1992; 1 child, Rachel Mariah. BSW, Keuka Coll., 1980. Residence counselor Cath. Charities Residential Program, Penn Yan, 1981-82, residence mgr., 1982-92, residential supr., 1992-2001, quality and compliance dir., 2001—. Bd. dirs. Yates County (N.Y.) ARC, Penn Yan, 1993-98, Rushville Health Ctr., N.Y., 1985-1991; mem. incident rev., 1989-2001; co-chmn. Keuka Lake Conf. Com., Rochester, N.Y., 1986—; mem. Yates County Rep. Com.; mem. parent adv. coun. and bldg. level team Dundee (N.Y.) Ctrl. Sch., 1991—, N.Y. State Surrogate Decision Making Com., 2001-. Election insp. Yates County Bd. Elections, 1996—; mem. Yates County Rep. Com., Yates County Women's Rep. Club, Women of the Moose. Recipient Direct Care award N.Y. State Assn. Cmty. Residence Administrs. Mem. DAR, Daus. Am. Colonists. Avocations: reading, pets, camping. Home: 2599 Knapp Rd Dundee NY 14837-9730 Office: Cath Charities Community Services 1945 Ridge Rd E Ste 24 Rochester NY 14622 Office Phone: 585-339-9800 378.

COON, SAUNDRA KAY, home health nurse, small business owner; b. San Francisco, Oct. 31, 1943; d. Earl and Peggy Leona (Trippe) Raby; m. Robert T. Burns, Dec. 19, 1981 (div. Nov. 1987); 1 child, Gagen A. Coon. Student, U. Kansas City, Mo., 1961-62, Penn Valley C., 1963-64, 91-94, Coll. of Redwoods, 1973-87, U. Mo., Kansas City, 1994-95. Exec. sec. Kansas City Coll. Osteopathy and Surgery, 1963-66; office mgr. pvt. practice med. office, Mendocino and Ft. Bragg, Calif., 1973-88; med. office cons. Mendocino, 1977-88; owner Sound Explosion, Jamaica, W.I., 1987-89, Village Imports, Kansas City, 1988—; med. sec. pvt. practice med. office, Kansas City, 1990-92. Co-op mem. It's A Beautiful Day. Contbr. poetry to Nat. Libr. of Poetry: Best Poems of 1994, 95, also to profl. jours.; photographs exhibited in group show Kaw Valley Arts and Humanities, 1991; photography televised on KQED, 1994. Chair membership Congress of Racial Equality, Kansas City, 1963-66; mem. So. Poverty Law Ctr., Montgomery, Ala., 1986, Mendocino Environ. Ctr., Ukiah, Calif., 1990; mem. Nat. Abortion Rights Action League, 1989, Greenpeace, Women in the Arts, chair, bd. dirs. Ptnrs. U.S.A./Para Brazil, Rainforest Alliance Network; bd. dirs. Global and Multicultural Edn. Ctr., 1993—, chair, 1994. Mem. Internat. Platform Assn., Planned Parenthood of Greater Kansas City, Amnesty Internat., Habitat for Humanity, Sierra Club, Greater Kansas City Greens Club, Deer Creek Golf Club. Democrat. Humanist. Avocations: photography, writing poetry, yoga, study of eastern religions. Mailing: 7777 Holmes Rd #531 Kansas City MO 64131

COONEY, JOAN GANZ, broadcast executive, director; b. Phoenix, Nov. 30, 1929; d. Sylvan C. and Pauline (Reardan) Ganz; m. Timothy J. Cooney, 1964 (div. 1975); m. Peter G. Peterson, 1980. BA, U. Ariz., 1951; degrees (hon.), Boston Coll., 1970, Hofstra U., Oberlin Coll., Ohio Wesleyan U., 1971, Princeton U., 1973, Russell Sage Coll., 1974, Harvard U., 1975, Allegheny Coll., 1976, Georgetown U., 1978, U. Notre Dame, 1982, Smith Coll., 1986, Brown U., 1987, Columbia U., 1991, NYU, 1991. Reporter Ariz. Republic, Phoenix, 1953—54; publicist NBC, 1954—55, U.S. Steel Hour, 1955—62; prodr. Sta. WNET, Channel 13, pub. affairs documentaries, 1962—67; TV cons. Carnegie Corp. N.Y., N.Y.C., 1967—68; exec. dir. Children's TV Workshop (producers Sesame Street, Electric Company, others) (name changed to Sesame Workshop 2000), N.Y.C., 1968—70, pres., trustee, CEO, 1970—88, chmn., CEO, 1988—90, chmn. exec. com., 1990—. Bd. dirs. Johnson & Johnson; bd. dirs. Met. Life Ins. Co. Mem. Pres.'s Commn. on Marijuana and Drug Abuse, 1971—73, Nat. News Coun., 1973—81, Pres.'s Commn. for Agenda for 80's, 1980—81, Adv. Com. for Trade Negotiations, 1978—80, Carnegie Found. Nat. Panel on High Sch., 1980—82, Gov.'s Commn. on Internat. Yr. of the Child, 1979; Mus. TV and Radio; bd. dirs. Edison Schs.; trustee N.Y. Presbyn. Med. Ctr. Named to Hall of Fame, Acad. TV Arts and Scis., 1990; recipient numerous awards for Sesame Street and other TV programs including Nat. Sch. Pub. Rels. Assn. Gold Key, 1971, Disting. Svc. medal, Columbia Tchrs. Coll., 1971, Soc. Family Man award, 1971, Nat. Inst. Social Scis. Gold medal, 1971, Frederick Douglass award, N.Y. Urban League, 1972, Silver Satellite award, Am. Women in Radio and TV, Woman of Yr. in Edn. award, Ladies Home Jour., 1975, NAEB Disting. Svc. award, NEA Friends of Edn. award, Kiwanis Decency award, 5th Women's Achiever award, Girl Scouts U.S.A., Stephen S. Wise award, 1981, Harris Found. award, 1982, Ednl. Achievement award, AAUW, 1984, Disting. Svc. to Children award, Nat. Assn. Elem. Sch. Prins., 1985, DeWitt Carter Reddick award, Coll. Comm., U. Tex.-Austin, 1986, Emmy Lifetime Achievement award, Acad. TV Arts and Scis., 1989, Presdl. medal of Freedom, 1995, Nat. Humanities Medal, 2003. Mem.: NATAS, Am. Women in Radio and TV, Internat. Radio and TV Soc., Nat. Inst. Social Scis. Office: Children's TV Workshop 1 Lincoln Plz New York NY 10023-7129*

COONEY, PATRICIA RUTH, civic worker; b. Englewood, N.J. d. Charles Aloysius and Ruth Jeannette (Foster) McEwen; m. J. Gordon Cooney, June 8, 1957; 1 child, J. Gordon, Jr. Student, Fordham U., 1950-51; DHL honoris causa, Phila. Theol. Sem. St. Charles Boromeo, 1991. Blood bank chmn. Strafford Village Civic Assn., 1968-69, sec., 1970-71; vice chmn. Spl. Gifts Com. Cath. Charities Appeal of Archdiocese of Phila., 1980—, chmn., 1985. Mem. Coun. of Mgrs. Archdiocese of Phila., 1982-88, sec., exec. com., 1983-88; bd. dirs. Cath. Charities of Archdiocese of Phila., sec., exec. com., 1988-90, v.p., exec. com., 1991—; bd. dirs. Village of Divine Providence, Phila., sec., 1983-85, v.p. exec. com., 1990—; bd. dirs. St. Edmond's Home for Crippled Children, Phila., v.p. exec. com., 1990—; bd. dirs. Don Guanella Village of Archdiocese of Phila., v.p. exec. com., 1990—; v.p. exec. com., 1990—; bd. dirs. St. Francis Homes for Boys, 2000—, St. Joseph House for Boys, 2000-, St. Vincent Svcs. for Women and Children, 2000—, St. Joseph Cath. Home for Children, 2000—, St. Gabriel's Sys., 2000—, St. Vincent's Home, Tacony, 2003; mem. Archdiocesan Adv. Com. on Renewal, 1991-2000; Women's Com. Wills Eye Hosp., 1973—, mem.-at-large, 1st v.p.; mem. Women's Aux. St. Francis Country House, Darby, Pa., 1976—, treas., 1978-82; bd. dirs. United Way of Southeastern Pa., 1984-90, sec., 1986-88; bd. dirs. Chapel of Four Chaplains, 1984-89, Phila. Criminal Justice Task Force, 1989-90. Decorated Cross Pro Ecclesia et Pontifice, 1982, Lady Order St. Gregory the Gt., 1998. Republican. Avocations: reading, tennis, sailing. Home: 320 Gatcombe Ln Bryn Mawr PA 19010-3628

COONS, BARBARA LYNN, public relations executive, librarian; b. Peoria, Ill., June 1, 1948; d. Harold Leroy and Norma (Bauer) C. BA, Stephens Coll., Columbia, Mo., 1970; MA, U. N.C., 1972; MLS, Cath. U., 1982. Rsch. asst. Am. Revolution Bicentennical Office Libr. of Congress,

Washington, 1974-76, editl. asst., office of the Asst. Librarian, 1976-78; ednl. liaison specialist Libr. of Congress, Washington, 1978-82; dir. rsch. svc. Gray and Co., Washington, 1982-85, v.p., 1985-86; from v.p., dir. rsch. svcs. to sr. mng. dir. Hill and Knowlton Pub. Affairs Worldwide, Washington, 1986—2003; U.S. dir. rsch. svcs. Hill and Knowlton USA 2003—. Pres. Library of Congress Profl. Assn., 1982. Mem. Spl. Libraries Assn., Stephens Coll. Alumnae Club of Greater Washington (pres. 1987). Lutheran. Home: 709 Arch Hall Ln Alexandria VA 22314-6208 Office: Hill & Knowlton Pub Affairs Worldwide 600 New Hampshire Ave NW Washington DC 20037-2403 Office Phone: 202-333-7400. E-mail: bcoons@hillandknowlton.com.

COOPER, ALMETA E. lawyer, medical association administrator; Gen. counsel Ohio State Med. Assn., Hilliard, Ohio. Mem.: Am. Health Lawyers Assn. (pres.-elect, chair programs com., chair nominating com.). Office: Ohio State Med Assn 3401 Mill Run Dr Hilliard OH 43026 Business E-Mail: aecooper@osma.org.

COOPER, ANNETTE LYN, music educator; b. Marquette, Mich., Dec. 21, 1963; d. James Alexander and Anna Lorraine Cooper. B in Music Edn., U. Mich., 1986; MS in Music Edn., U. Ill., 1992. Band dir. Music Edn. Svcs., Elmhurst, Ill., 1988—91, Abilene (Tex.) H.S., 1992—96, Indian Prairie Sch. Dist., Aurora, Ill., 1996—. Musician, vocalist Abilene Classical Chorus, 1993—96; musician, clarinetist Naperville (Ill.) Mcpl. Band, 1996—2001, Fox Valley Concert Band, St. Charles, Ill., 1996—, bd. mem., 2001—. Vis. Artist grantee, Indian Prairie Edn. Found., 1999. Mem.: NEA, Ill. Grade Sch. Music Assn., Music Educators Nat. Conf. Avocations: reading, cross stitch. Home: 1007 S Fourth Aurora IL 60505 Office: F Granger Middle Sch 2721 Stonebridge Blvd Aurora IL 60504 Office Phone: 630-375-3880.

COOPER, APRIL HELEN, family nurse practitioner; b. Evergreen Park, Ill., Dec. 24, 1951; d. Frank and Anne (Mirocha) Stevens; m. Michael Dennis, June 20, 1970; children: Christine Michelle, Brian Michael, Jeannette Michelle. AAS, Ohio U., 1981, BSN, 1996; MS, Wright State U., 2000. RN Ohio; cert. family nurse practitioner, ANCC. Supr. home health care Med. Pers. Pool, Cambridge, Ohio, 1989-91; primary nurse pediat. home care Primary Care Nursing Svcs., Dublin, Ohio, 1989-91; case mgr. Buckeye Home Health Svc., Zanesville, Ohio, 1990-91; with home health svcs. Genesis Home Care, Zanesville, 1981-98; family practice nurse practitioner Bucyrus Cmty. Hosp., 2001—. Mem. ANA, Golden Key. Phi Kappa Phi, Sigma Theta Tau, Gamma Pi Delta. Republican. Methodist. Avocations: reading professional journals, travel. Home: 3172 Oak Dr Bucyrus OH 44820-9654

COOPER, CAROL DIANE, publishing company executive; b. Williamsport, Pa., Aug. 14, 1953; d. Ray Calvin and Norma Jane (Stiger) Cooper. BA, Colgate U., 1975; cert. in pub., Radcliffe Coll., 1975; MA, Syracuse (N.Y.) U., 1977. Editl. and promotion asst. St. Martin's Press, N.Y.C., 1977—78, sales rep., 1978—79; dir. sales, v.p. Clearwater Pub. Co., Inc., N.Y.C., 1979—80, dir. mktg., 1980—81, v.p., 1980—83; exec. v.p. K.G. Saur Inc., N.Y.C., 1983—87; v.p., pub. R.R. Bowker Co., N.Y.C., 1987—90; v.p. internat. pub. ops. Bowker, Martindale Hubbell, N.Y.C., 1990—92, Reed Reference Pub., New Providence, NJ, 1992—96, also bd. dirs., 1996; sr. v.p. pub. Martindale-Hubbell, New Providence, 1996—. Office: Martindale Hubbell 121 Chanlon Rd New Providence NJ 07974-1544

COOPER, CAROLYN SUE, translator, educator; b. Kansas City, Mo., July 19, 1949; d. Albert D. and Lois (Gay) C. BA, U. Mo., Kansas City, 1971, MA, 1979; PhD, U. Kans., 1984; MA in Philology and Translation, St. Petersburg (Russia) State U., 2003. Cert.elem. and spl. edn. tchr., sch. psychometrist, Mo. Tchr. North Kansas City Pub. Schs., 1971-80; project dir., insvc. tchr. trainer East Ctrl. Coop. in Edn., Baldwin City, Kans., 1982-84; postdoctoral fellow U. Kans., Lawrence, 1984-85; coord. spl. projects Western Carolina Ctr., Morganton, N.C., 1985-87; prof. spl. edn. Ea. Ill. U., Charleston, 1987—2002, assoc. dean grad. sch., dir. internat. programs, 1998—2000; rsch. assoc. Russian-E. European Ctr. U. Ill. Champaign-Urbana, 2002—. Instr. English, Herzen Pedagogical U., St. Petersburg, Russia, 1986-87, Fulbright lectr., fall 1994; cons. Ill. Bd. Edn., Springfield, 1987—; assoc. prof. translation, St. Petersburg (Russia) State U., 2002—. Contbg. author: The Second Handbook on Parent Educatin: Contemporary Perspectives, 1989; contbr. articles to profl. jours. Chmn. Birth-Five Coordinating Coun., Charleston, 1993-94; asst. leader del. Citizen Amb. Program, Prague, Czech Republic, Moscow and St. Petersburg, 1995. Pers. preparation grantee U.S. Office Edn., 1985-96, rsch. grantee Am. Coun. for Tchrs. Russian, Russia, 1996-97. Mem. Coun. for Exceptional Children, Internat. Soc. on Early Intervention. Avocations: reading, travel, studying russian, crocheting. Home: 2519 Woodlawn Dr Charleston IL 61920-4254

COOPER, CORINNE, communications consultant, lawyer; b. Albuquerque, July 12, 1952; d. David D. and Martha Lucille (Rosenblum) C. BA magna cum laude, U. Ariz., 1975, JD summa cum laude, 1978. Bar: Ariz. 1978, U.S. Dist. Ct. Ariz. 1978, Mo. 1985. Assoc. Streich, Lang, Weeks & Cardon, Phoenix, 1978-82; asst. prof. U. Mo.-, Kansas City, 1982-86, assoc. prof., 1986-94, prof., 1994-2000, prof. emerita, 2000—; pres. Profl. Presence, Conns., Tucson and Kansas City, Mo., 2001—. Vis. prof. U. Wis., Madison, 1985, 91, U. Pa., Phila., 1988, U. Ariz., 1993, U. Colo., 1994. Author: (with Bruce Meyerson) A Drafter's Guide to Alternative Dispute Resolution, 1991; editor: The Portable UCC, 1993, 3d edit., 2001, Getting Graphic I and II, 1993, 94, The New Article 9, 1999, 2d edit., 2000; editor in chief Bus. Law Today, 1995-97; mem. editl. bd. ABA Jour., 1999—; contbr. articles to profl. jours., chpts. to books. Legal counsel Mo. for Hart campaign, 1984; dir. issues Goddard for Gov. campaign, 1990; bd. dirs. Com. for County Progress, Kansas City, 1985-95. Mem. ABA (mem. coun. bus. sect. 1992-96, uniform comml. code com., chmn. bus. sect. membership com. 1992-94, editl. bd. Bus. Law Today, 1991-97, sect. of bus. law pubs. 1998-2002, standing com. on strategic comm. 2001—, coun. gen. practice sect. 2003—), Am. Law Inst., Am. Assn. Law Schs. (comml. law 1982-2000), Ariz. Bar Assn., Mo. Bar Assn. (comml. law com.), Order of Coif, Phi Beta Kappa, Phi Kappa Phi. Democrat. Jewish. Office: Profl Presence 4558 N 1st Ave Tucson AZ 85718

COOPER, CYNTHIA, professional baseball player; b. Chgo., Apr. 14, 1963; Degree in phys. edn., U. So. Calif., 1986. Basketball player Segovia, Spain, 1986—87, Parma, Italy, 1987—94, 1996—97, Alcamo, Italy, 1994—96, Houston Comets, 1997—2000, 2003—; head coach Phoenix Mercury, 2001—02. Mem. U.S. Goodwill Games, 1986, 90, World Championships, 1986, 90, Pan Am. Games, 1987. Named MVP, Women's NBA Championship, 1997, 1998; recipient Gold medal, Pan Am Games, 1987, U.S. Olympic Basketball, 1988, Bronze medal, 1992; mem. WNBA champion, Houston Comets, 1997, 1998, 1999. Achievements include Won two NCAA championships with USC, 1983-1984. Office: c/o Houston Comets Two Greenway Plz Ste 400 Houston TX 77046-3865*

COOPER, DORIS JEAN, market research executive; b. N.Y.C., Dec. 17, 1934; d. James N. and Georgina N. (Cassidy) Breslin; m. S. James Cooper, June 17, 1956; 1 son, David Austin. Student, Sch. of Commerce, NYU, 1953-55, Hunter Coll., 1956-57. Asst. coding supr. Crossley S-D Surveys, N.Y.C., 1955-57; asst. field supr. Trendex, Inc., N.Y.C., 1957-59; coding dir. J. Walter Thompson Co., N.Y.C., 1960-63, Audits & Surveys, N.Y.C., 1964-65; pvt. practice cons. N.Y.C., 1965-73; pres. Cooper Svcs., Hastings-on-Hudson, N.Y., 1973—; pres., CEO Cooper tabulation and data manipulation Doris J Cooper Assocs., Hastings-on-Hudson 1989—. Cons. market rsch. Mem. Am. Mktg. Assn. (N.Y. chpt.), nat. Bus. Women Owners

Assn., Am. Assn. Pub. Opinion Researchers (N.Y. chpt.), Acad. Health Svcs. Mktg., Hastings C. of C. Republican. Episcopalian. Office: Doris J Cooper Assocs Ltd 447 Warburton Ave Hastings On Hudson NY 10706-1542 Office Phone: 914-478-0444.

COOPER, EDYTHE E.D. political organization administrator; married; 4 children. Regent Nat. Fed. Rep. Women, Alexandria, Va., mem. exec. com. Mem.-at-large, immediate past pres. Wis. Fed. Rep. Women; officer Rep. Women of Waukesha County; mem. exec. com. Waukesha County Rep. Com., 1977, exec. dir., 1998—; 2nd vice chmn. Rep. Com. of Wis. Worker all Presdl. campaigns, Sen. Robert Kasten Campaign, Gov. Tommy Thompson Campaign, Congressman Mark Neumann Campaign for U.S. Senate. Avocations: decorating, gardening, entertaining. Office: Nat Fedn Rep Women 124 N Alfred St Alexandria VA 22314-3011 Fax: 703-548-9836.

COOPER, ELVA JUNE, artist; b. Wilmore, Ky., Mar. 18, 1933; d. Scott Combs and Rhoda Mae (Hundley) Bishop; m. Lowell Howard Cooper, Nov. 29, 1952; children: Lowell Scott, Linda Janet, Candace Lea, Connie Lynn, June Roxanne. Student, Georgetown Coll., 1952-53, Southwestern Jr. Coll., 1961, U. West Fla., 1994, Pensacola Jr. Coll., 1998. Owner June Bug Art and Gifts, Pensacola, Fla., 1973—2003, The Studio, Pensacola, Fla., 1986—. Cons. editor Church Recreation, 1993-95; contbr. articles to mags. Drama writer, dir. Myrtle Grove Bapt. Ch., Pensacola, Fla., 1977-96, artist in residence, 1973-96, discipleship tng. dir., 1973-79, 88-97; sec. Lillian (Ala.) First Bapt. Ch., 1984-95; writer Bapt. Sunday Sch. Bd., Nashville, Tenn., 1987-98; state recreation counselor Fla. Bapt. Conv., Jacksonville, 1994—; discipleship tng. dir. Pensacola Bay Bapt. Assn., 1994-96. Three time winner of Peggy award Popular Ceramics Mag., 1970; numerous other awards in art shows; inducted into Internat. Soc. Poetry as Disting. Mem. Mem. Quayside Art Gallery (asst. publicity, 1984), Art Study Club. Baptist. Avocations: porcelain doll making, sewing, flower arranging, stained glass artist.

COOPER, GINNIE, library director; b. Worthington, Minn., 1945; d. Lawrence D. and Ione C.; m. Richard Bauman, Dec. 1995; 1 child, Daniel Jay. Student, Coll. St. Thomas, U. Wis., Parkside; BA, S.D. State U.; MA in Libr. Sci., U. Minn. Tchr. Flandreau (S.D.) Indian Sch., 1967-68, St. Paul Pub. Schs., 1968-69; br. libr. Wash. County Libr., Lake Elmo, Minn., 1970-71, asst. dir., 1971-75; assoc. adminstr., libr. U. Minn. Med. Sch., Mpls., 1975-77; dir. Kenosha (Wis.) Pub. Libr., 1977-81; county libr. Alameda County (Calif.) Libr., 1981-90; dir. librs. Multnomah County Libr., Portland, Oreg., 1990—. Chair County Mgr. Assn.; county adminstr. Mayor's Exec. Roundtable. Mem. ALA (mem. LAMA, PLA and RASD coms., elected to coun. 1987, 91, mem. legislation com. 1986-90, mem. orgn. com. 1990—), Calif. Libr. Assn. (pres. CIL, 1985, elected to coun. 1986, pres. Calif. County Librs. 1986), Oreg. Libr. Assn., Pub. Libr. Assn. (pres. 1997-98). Office: Multnomah County Libr 205 NE Russell St Portland OR 97212-3708

COOPER, GLORIA, editor, press critic; b. Oak Park, Ill., Jan. 8, 1931; c. Sam and Madelyn (Brandt) Glaser; m. Wallace J. Cooper, June 3, 1950; children— Alison, Julie BA summa cum laude, Briarcliff Coll., 1970; MA, Columbia U., 1974. From asst. editor to mng. editor to dep. exec. editor Columbia Journalism Rev., N.Y.C., 1974—. Editor: Squad Helps Dog Bite Victim, 1980, Red Tape Holds Up New Bridge, 1987; contbr. articles, revs., editorials to Columbia Journalism Rev., 1974— Mem. Soc. Prof. Journalists, Princeton Club (N.Y.C.). Home: 91 Long Hill Rd E Briarcliff Manor NY 10510-2611 Office: Columbia U Columbia Journalism Rev 207 Journalism Bldg New York NY 10027 E-mail: gc15@columbia.edu.

COOPER, ILENE LINDA, magazine editor, author; b. Chgo., Mar. 10, 1948; d. Morris and Lillian (Friedman) C.; m. Robert Seid, May 28, 1972 (div. 1995). BJ, U. Mo., 1969; MLS, Rosary Coll., 1973. Head of children's svcs. Winnetka (Ill.) Libr. Dist., 1974-80; editor children's books Booklist Mag., ALA, Chgo., 1981—. Author: Susan B. Anthony, 1983, Choosing Sides, 1990 (Internat. Reading Assn.-Children's Book Coun. choice 1990), Mean Streak, 1991, (series) Frances in the Fourth Grade, 1991, The Dead Sea Scrolls, 1997, numerous others. Mem. Soc. Midland Authors, Soc. Children's Book Writers, Children's Reading Roundtable. Jewish. Office: Booklist Mag 50 E Huron St Chicago IL 60611-5295

COOPER, IVA JEAN, special education educator; b. Newark, Mar. 6, 1950; d. William Brady McClintock and Aleata Margaret Locke-McClintock; m. Jeffrey Lamont Cooper, Oct. 18, 1986; children: Brianna, Jasmine. BS Comms., Howard U., 1973; MA Comms., Mich. State U., 1976. Intern Crippled Children's Soc., Hollywood, Calif., 1979—80; speech & lang. therapist pediats. Sierra Permanente Med. Grp., Fontana, Calif., 1980—81; supr. speech & lang. pathology Head Start Devel. Coun., Stockton, Calif., 1981; spl. edn. educator Manteca Unified Sch. Dist., Calif., 1981—. Mem.: Internat. Soc. Poets, AAUW, Am. Speech Hearing & Lang. Assn. Home: 1928 W Bristol Ave Stockton CA 95204

COOPER, JACQUELINE GERSON, lawyer; BA summa cum laude, U. Wash., 1987; JD with honors, U. Chgo., 1990. Bar: Calif. 1993, D.C. 1994. Law clk. to Hon. Alex Kozinski, U.S. Ct. Appeals for 9th Cir., 1990-91; law clk. to Assoc. Justice Anthony M. Kennedy, U.S. Supreme Ct., Washington, 1991-92; ptnr. Sidley & Austin, Washington. Articles editor U. Chgo. Law Rev., 1989-90. John M. Olin fellow in law and econs., Harry S. Truman scholar U. Chgo. Mem. Order of Coif. Office: Sidley & Austin 1722 E St NW Washington DC 20006 Fax: 202-736-8711. E-mail: jcooper@Sidley.com.

COOPER, JAMIE LEE, writer; d. Ralph Francis Cooper and Esther Allene Kellner, Lee Frederick Kellner (Stepfather). Grad., Fairfax Hall, Waynesboro, Va., 1947. Radio comml. writer Sta. WKBV, Richmond, Ind., 1947—49; profl. writer, novelist, short stories, essays, libretti various pubs., N.Y.C., Paris, 1955—; creative writing tchr. Ind. U., Bloomington, 1964—88, Ball State U., Muncie, Ind., 1964—88, Evansville (Ind.) U., 1964—88. Liaison, mentoring, judging novel scholarships, nat. competitions Ind. U., Ball State U., Evansville U., judging competitions for several out of state univs., Ind., 1963—88. Author: The Horn in the Forest, 1963 (Most Disting. Fiction of Midwest, 1964), Shadow of a Star, 1965 (Most Disting. Fiction of Midwest, 1966), Rapaho, 1967 (Most Disting. Fiction of Midwest, 1968), The Castaways, 1970 (Most Disting. Fiction of Midwest, 1971), The Great Dandelion, 1972 (Most Disting. Fiction of Midwest, 1973), Grasshopper Summer, 1974 (Most Disting. Fiction of Midwest, 1975); librettist: chorale Song of Mankind, 1970 (Friends of Am. Writers award, 1971), We, the Dreamers, 1975 (Friends of Am. Writers award, 1976), Bad That Woman, 1976 (Friends of Am. Writers award, 1977). Grantee, NEA, 1976. Mem.: PEN, Nat. Writers' Union, Authors Guild. Avocations: playing the sitar, cooking, gardening.

COOPER, JANE TODD (J. C. TODD), poet, writer, educator; b. Bklyn., Dec. 24, 1943; d. John Curtis and Margaret E. (Johnston) C.; m. William Hudson Shoff; children: Donald Charles Taylor, Eamon Robert Shoff, Savannah Elizabeth Cooper-Ramsey. BA in Liberal Arts, Duquesne U., 1965; MFA in Creative Writing, Warren Wilson Coll., 1990. Instr. H.S., Pitts., 1967-73; ednl. dir. drug and alcohol treatment facility Pa. Dept. Corrections, Camp Hill, 1974-78; project mgr. domiciliary care, boarding home provider tng. Pa. State Coll. Medicine, Hershey, 1979-80, 82; dir. primary health care project Elizabethtown Hosp., Pa., 1980-81; instr. creative writing Coll. N.J., 1993-94; instr. creative writing Bryn Mawr Coll., 1999—2003; instr. creative writing Kutztown (Pa.) U., 2003—. Cons. Pa. Coun. on Arts, 1979-91; creative writing instr. Coll. N.J., 1992-94; instr. creative writing, Kutztown U., 2003; bd. dirs. Poetry Ctr., Phila., 1990-97, dir., 1994-97; artist in residence N.J. State Arts Coun., Pa. Coun. on the

Arts, 1982—. Author: Entering Pisces, 1985, Nightshade, 1995; contbg. editor: The Drunken Boat. Recipient Pa. Coun. on Arts Fellowship in Poetry award, 1998, Disting. Tchg. Artist award, N.J. State Arts Coun., 1999—2001, N.J. Gov.'s award for arts edn., 1999, Disting. Artist award, NEA, 1999—2000, Leeway Found. award, 2001, 2004; fellow fellow poetry, Va. Ctr. Creative Arts, 1997; lit. fellow, Geraldine R. Dodge Found., 1987—, Carroll scholar, 1964—65, Warner Lambert/Nat. Merit scholar, 1961—65, fellow poetry, Hambidge Ctr., 1991—93, VCCA Internat. exch. fellow, Schloss Wiepersdorf, Germany, 2002, Pa. Coun. on Arts Profl. Devel. grantee, 1999, 2000, 2002, 2004. Mem. Acad. Am. Poets, Poets and Writers, Poetry Soc. Am., Friends of Writers. Studio: 119 Herr St # A Harrisburg PA 17102-3303 Fax: 215-629-3656. E-mail: JCTODD66@aol.com.

COOPER, JANELLE LUNETTE, neurologist, educator; b. Ann Arbor, Mich., Dec. 11, 1955; d. Robert Marion and Madelyn (Leonard) C.; children: Lena Christine, Nicholas Dominic. BA in Chemistry, Reed Coll., 1978; MD, Vanderbilt U., 1986. Diplomate Nat. Bd. Med. Examiners; diplomate in neurology Am. Bd. Psychiatry and Neurology; registered med. technologist Am. Soc. Clin. Pathologists. Med. technologist Swedish Hosp. Med. Ctr., Seattle, 1978-80, U. Wash. Clin. Chemistry, Seattle, 1980-82, Vanderbilt U. Hosp., Nashville, 1983-84; intern medicine Vanderbilt U. Med. Ctr., Nashville, 1986-87, resident neurology, 1987-90; instr. neurology Med. Coll. Pa., Phila., 1990-91, asst. prof., clerkship dir., 1991—, mem. curriculum com., 1990-91, vis. asst. prof., 1991-95; neurologist Greater Ann Arbor Neurology Assocs., 1991-93; dir. neurol. svcs., med. dir. Indsl. Rehab. Program St. Francis Hosp., Escanaba, Mich., 1993-98; founder, dir. No. Neuroscis., Escanaba, 1993-98; pres. HolderLady, Ltd., 1996—; chmn. dept. medicine St. Francis Hosp., Escanaba, Mich., 1998-99; dir. Affinity Health Sys., Oshkosh, Wis., 1998—; med. dir. Memory Clinic of the Upper Peninsula, Escanaba, Mich., 1998—. Neurologist Affinity Med. Group, Oshkosh, Wis., 1998—; physician MCP Neurology Assocs., Phila., 1990-91; emergency rm. physician Tenn. Christian Med. Ctr., 1989-90. Contbr. articles to Annals of Ophthalmology, Ophthalmic Surgery. Vol. Rape and Sexual Abuse Ctr., Nashville, 1988-90; mem. adminstrv. bd. Edgehill United Meth. Ch., Nashville, 1989-90; mem. editorial bd. Nashville Women's Alliance, 1989-90; bd. dirs. Upper Peninsula Physicians Network, 1995-98; mem. adv. bd. Perspective Adult Daycare Ctr., 1996-99; founding dir. Memory Clinic of Upper Peninsula, 1998-00; profl. adv. com. NE Wis. Alzheimer's Assn., 1999—. Recipient Svc. award for outstanding contbns. Rape and Sexual Abuse Ctr., 1990; epilepsy minifellow Bowman Gray U., 1995. Mem. AMA (physician's Recognition award 1989—), AAAS, Am. Med. Women's Assn., Am. Acad. Neurology, Am. Psychol. Soc., Wis. State Med. Soc., N.Y. Acad. Scis., Upper Peninsula Neuro Assn. (v.p. 1998-99, trustee 1998-99), Upper Peninsula Physician Network (bd. dirs. 1995-98), Aircraft Owners and Pilots Assn., Women in Aviation Internat. (charter), Air Force Assn. (life patron). Methodist. Achievements include first synthesis of Difluoromethanedisulfonic Acid; research on neurobehavioral disorders; on neuroendocrinology of sexual development, identity and orientation; on the history of women in medicine on effects of dietary lipids on the etiology of Alzheimer's disease; clinical investigation trials for new medications for dementias and epilepsy. Home: 108 Country Club Ln Oshkosh WI 54902-7459 Office: Affinity Med Group Dept Neurology 2725 Jackson St Oshkosh WI 54901-1513 E-mail: jcooper@affinityhealth.org.

COOPER, JEAN SARALEE, judge; b. Huntington, N.Y., Mar. 7, 1946; d. Ralph and Henrietta (Halbreich) Cooper; stepchildren: Mitzi Concklin Prochnow, John Todd Concklin. BA, Sophie Newcomb Coll. of Tulane U., 1968; JD, Emory U., 1970. Bar: La. 1970, Ga. 1970, U.S. Dist. Ct. (ea. dist.) La. 1970, U.S. Ct. Appeals (5th cir.) 1972, U.S. Ct. Appeals (2d cir.) 1976, U.S. Ct. Appeals (4th cir.) 1977, U.S. Ct. Appeals (fed. cir.), U.S. Supreme Ct. 1974. Trial atty. Office of Solicitor, U.S. Dept. Labor, Washington, 1970-73, spl. projects asst., 1973, sr. trial atty., 1973-77; adminstrv. judge Bd. Contract Appeals, HUD, Washington, 1977—2003, acting chmn. and chief judge, 1980-81, vice chmn., 1983—2003; bd. mem. Coalition for Free Trade, 2003—. Cons.; lectr. Contbr. articles to profl. jours. Recipient Moot Ct. award, Tulane Law Sch., 1968. Fellow: ABA (life; jud. divsn. 1979—, standing com. on jud. selection, tenure and compensation. 1992—95, vice chair debarment and suspension com. pub. contracts sect. 1992—97, sec. Nat. Conf. Adminstrv. Law Judges 1996—97, vice chmn. 1997—98, chair-elect 1998—99, standing com. on fed. jud. improvements 2000—01, adminstrn. law sect, chair 1999—2000), Am. Bar Found. (life); mem.: Nat. Conf. Bd. Contract Appeals Mems., Contract Appeals Judges Assn., Nat. Assn. Women Judges (founder), BCA Bar Assn., Am. Judicature Soc., Prettyman-Leventhal Am. Inn of Ct. (past pres., master of bench), Am. Inns of Ct. Found. (trustee 1992—98, leadership com. 1998—), Am. Law Inst., Fed. Bar Assn. (jud. divsn. leadership coun.), La. Bar Assn. Republican. Home: 2800 Flagmaker Dr Falls Church VA 22042-2200 E-mail: jeansaralee@cs.com.

COOPER, JO MARIE, elementary school principal; b. L.A., Oct. 13, 1947; d. Joseph M. Langham and Christina (Burton) Lister; m. Leonard Cooper Jr., May 13, 1967; children: Leonard Joseph, Jo-Lynne Louise, Layton Bishop. Grad., Chgo. State Coll., 1967; MA, Governor State U., University Park, Ill., 1975; MA in Ednl. Adminstrn., Gov. State U., University Park, Ill., 1997. Postal worker, mail handler Chgo. Post Office, 1966-67; tchr. Chgo. Bd. Edn., 1968-75, resource tchr., 1975-93, instrnl. adminstrv. asst., 1993—, dean of girls; interim prin. Oglesby Elem. Sch., 1998, prin., 1998—. Advisor Homewood (Ill.) Full Gospel Ch., 1992-94, Homewood Christian Acad., 1994—. Pres. South Ctrl. Women's Aglow, Chgo., 1983-85; chair women's ministries Homewood Full Gospel Ch., 1990-94; South Chicago area leader Marriage Ministries Internat., University Park, 1994—; advisor Human Rels. Commn., University Park, 1987-89. Mem. ASCD. Pentecostal. Avocations: reading, walking, hooklatching, bowling. Office: Oglesby Elem Sch 7646 S Green St Chicago IL 60620-2854

COOPER, JOSEPHINE SMITH, trade association and public affairs executive; b. Raleigh, N.C., Aug. 2, 1945; d. Joseph W. and Marie (Peele) S. BA in Bus. and Econs., Meredith Coll., Raleigh, 1967; MS in Mgmt., Duke U., 1977. Program analyst Office of Air & Quality Planning and Stds. EPA, Rsch., Triangle Park, NC, 1968-78; environ. protection specialist Office of Rsch. and Devel., Washington, 1978-80; mem. profl. staff majority leader Howard H. Baker, Jr., U.S. Senate Com. on Environ. and Pub. Works, Washington, 1980-83; asst. adminstr. for external affairs EPA, Washington, 1983-85; asst. v.p. for environ. and health program Am. Paper Inst., Washington, 1985-86; sr. v.p. for policy Synthetic Organic Chem. Mfrs. Assn., Washington, 1986-88; sr. v.p., dir. environ. policy Hill & Knowlton, Inc., Washington, 1988-91; founder, dir. Capitoline Internat. Group, Ltd., Washington, 1991-92; v.p. environ. and regulatory affairs Am. Forest & Paper Assn., 1992-99; pres., CEO Alliance of Automobile Mfrs., Washington, 1999—2004; group v.p. for govt. and industry affairs Toyota Motor N.Am., 2004—. Treas. RTP Fed. Credit Union, 1969—72, pres., CEO, 1975; pres. Women's Coun. on Energy and Environment, 1986—88, Nat. Coun. on Clean Indoor Air, 1988—96; mem. nat. adv. environ. health scis. coun. NIH, 1990—94; mem. adv. com. EPA Clean Air Act, 1994—98; liaison mem. trade and environ. policy adv. com. USTR, 1994—2002; chmn. Nat. Urban Air Toxic Rsch. Ctr., 2003—. Bd. visitors Duke U. Nicholas Sch. Environ., 1994-2002, Duke U. Fuqua Sch. Bus., 2004-; bd. dirs. Leland Nat. Urban Air Toxics Rsch. Ctr., Washington First Bank, 2004-. Congl. fellow, 1979-80. Mem.: NAM (coun. bd. dirs. 2000—), Orgn. of Internat. Auto Assn. (pres.), Orgn. d'Internationale Constructeurs d'Automobiles (chmn. 2003—04), Am. Soc. Assn. Execs. (bd. dirs. 2000—03), U.S. C. of C. (Com. of 100 2000—04), Women in Govt. Rels., Federally Employed Women (pres. 1972—77, treas.). Mem. Christian Ch. (Disciples Of Christ). Office Phone: 202-463-6830.

COOPER, JUDITH KASE, retired theater educator, playwright; b. Wilmington, Del., Dec. 13, 1932; d. Charles Robert and Elizabeth Edna (Baker) Kase; stepchildren: James, Elizabeth, John, Katherine, Ann, Patty, Doreen, Jeff. BA, U. Del., 1955; MA, Case Western Res. U., 1956. Tchr., dir. children's theatre Agnes Scott Coll., 1956, U. Tenn., 1957, U. Md., Germany, 1958-60, Denver Civic Theatre, Denver U., Kent Sch., 1960-61; dir. children's theatre U. N.H., Durham, 1962-69; dir. theatre resources for youth Somersworth, N.H., 1966-69; assoc. prof. theatre U. South Fla., Tampa, 1969-74, assoc. prof. edn., 1975-83, prof., 1984—99, artistic dir. ednl. theatre, 1976—99, ret., 1999. Project dir. Hillsborough County Artists-in-Schs. Evaluation and Inservice Project, 1980-82; dir. Internat. Ctr. for Studies in Theatre Edn.; mem. Nat. Theatre Conf., Coll. Fellows Am. Theatre. Author: The Creative Drama Book: Three Approaches, other books; editor: Creative Drama in a Developmental Context; Children's Theatre, Creative Drama and Learning, Drama as a Meaning Maker, Introduction to Drama Teacher Resource Guide, Interconnecting Pathways to Human Experience, Teaching the Arts Across the Disciplines; contbr. articles to profl. jours.; pub. (plays) Snow White and The Seven Dwarfs, 1960, The Emperor's New Clothes, 1966, Southern Fried Cracker Tales, 1995. Bd. dirs. Fla. Alliance for Arts Edn., sec., 1976-77, vice-chmn., 1979-82, chmn., 1982-84; chmn. Wingspread Conf. on Theatre Edn., 1977; drama adjudicator Nat. Arts Festival, Ministry of Edn., Bahamas, 1975, 76, 79, 80; regional chmn. Alliance for Arts Edn., chmn. nat. adv. coun., mem. edn. adv. com., 1986—; trustee Children's Theatre Found.; bd. dirs. Coll. Fellows Am. Theatre of J.F. Kennedy Ctr. for Performing Arts, 1991-93, Fla. Assoc. Theatre Ed., exec. dir. 1995-99, Coll. Bus., 1993—; cons. S.E. Ctr. for Edn. in Theatre, 1995, Fla. Dept. Edn., 1994-96; cons. theatre edn. and prodn.; steering com. Arts for a Complete Edn., 1991-92; mem. curriculum writing com. Fla. Dept. Edn., 1994-96. Recipient Disting. Book of Yr. award, 1989, Arts Recognition award Arts Coun. Hillsborough County, 1995. Mem. Children's Theatre Assn. Am. (pres.-elect 1975-77, pres. 1977-79, chmn. symposia 1981-85, spl. recognition citation 1984), Am. Theatre Assn. (chief divsn. pres.'s coordinating coun. 1977-78, commn. on theatre edn. 1982—, elected), Am. Alliance for Theatre and Edn. (dir. & project dir. theatre literacy collaborative study Internat. Ctr. for Studies in Theatre Edn., Presdl. award 1992), Speech Comm. Assn. (membership dir. 1961), Southeastern Theatre Confs. (Sara Spencer award 1980), Fla. Theatre Confs. (Disting. Career award), Nat. Theatre Conf., Internat. Assn. Theatres for Children and Youth, Internat. Amateur Theatre Assn. (N.Am. bd. dirs.), Fla. Assn. for Theater Edn. (Theatre Edn. of Yr. award 1986, exec. dir. 1994-99), Children's Theatre Found. Am.(bd. trustees 1977-), Tampa Mus. Republican. Episcopalian.

COOPER, KATHLEEN BELL, federal agency administrator; b. Dallas, Feb. 3, 1945; d. Patrick Joseph and Ferne Elizabeth (McDougle) Bell; m. Ronald James Cooper, Feb. 6, 1965; children: Michael, Christopher. BA in Math. with honors, U. Tex., Arlington, 1970, MA in Econs, 1971; PhD in Econs, U. Colo., 1980. Research asst. econs. dept. U. Tex., Arlington, 1970-71, corp. economist United Banks of Colo., Denver, 1971-79, chief economist, 1980-81; v.p., sr. fin. economist Security Pacific Nat. Bank, Los Angeles, 1981-83, 1st v.p., sr. economist, 1983-85, sr. v.p., economist, 1985-86, sr. v.p., chief economist, 1986-87, exec. v.p., chief economist, 1988-90; chief economist Exxon Corp., Irving, Tex., 1990-99; chief economist, mgr. econs. & energy divsn. corp. planning Exxon Mobil Corp., 1999-2001; under sec. for econ. affairs U.S. Dept. Commerce, Washington, 2001—, Trustee Scripps Coll., 1987-2001, Com. for Econ. Devel.1993-2001; mem. Coun. on Fgn. Rels., Internat. Women's Forum. Mem. Nat. Assn. Bus. Economists (past pres. Denver and L.A. chpts.; bd. dirs. 1975-78, pres. 1985-86), Nat. Bur. Econ. Rsch. (bd. dirs. 1987-2001, exec. com., vice-chair 1999-2001), Am. Bankers Assn. (econ. adv. com. 1979-81, 86-90, chmn. 1989-90), U.S. Assn. Energy Econs. (pres. 1996), Am. Econ. Assn., Conf. Bus. Economists (tech. cons. to bus. coun. 1993-94). Office: US Dept Commerce Rm 4848 14th and Constitution NW Washington DC 20230

COOPER, LORRAINE W. special education educator; b. Milford, Del., Nov. 2, 1956; d. Albert John and Laura Lee Wildberger; m. Wayne Douglas Cooper, June 6, 1981; 1 child, Adam Jeremiah ; 1 child, Elliott Seth. BS in Edn., Kutztown State Coll., 1978. Tchr. visually impaired Manassas (Va.) Sch. Dist., 1979—81; tchr. deaf/blind unit Indian River Sch. Dist. Ennis Sch., Georgetown, Del., 1981—84; tchr. spl. edn. Frankford (Del.) Elem., 1984—86, Georgetown Elem., 1986—96, North Georgetown Elem., 1996—. Vol. Annual Thanksgiving Dinner for Needy, Georgetown, 1998—2003; supt., chair edn. Wesley United Meth. Ch., Georgetown, 1980—89, mem. mission com., 2002—03, co-chair caring com., 2003. Recipient various grants. Mem.: Coun. Exceptional Children, Assn. Am. Educators. Republican. Home: 22317 Deep Branch Rd Georgetown DE 19947 Office: North Georgetown Elem Sch 664 N Bedford St Georgetown DE 19947

COOPER, MARGARET LESLIE, lawyer; b. Geneva, N.Y., Apr. 13, 1950; d. Jack Frederick and Barbara Ann (Hitchings) C. BA in Math., Rollins Coll., 1972; JD, Mercer U., 1976. Bar: Fla. 1976, U.S. Dist. Ct. (so. dist.) Fla. 1977, U.S. Dist. Ct. (mid. dist.) Fla. 2001, U.S. Ct. Appeals (5th cir.) 1977, U.S. Ct. Appeals (11th cir.) 1981, U.S. Supreme Ct. 03, bd. cert. civil trial advocacy: Nat. Bd. Trial Advocacy 2002; bd. cert. civil litigation and bus. litigation Fla. Bar Assn. Assoc. Jones, Foster, Johnston & Stubbs, PA, West Palm Beach, Fla., 1976-81, ptnr., 1981—. Assoc. prof. Palm Beach Jr. Coll., West Palm Beach, 1985-86. Pres. Young People's Pres.'s Coun., Norton Gallery Art, West Palm Beach, 1982—84; bd. trustees Norton Sculpture Gardens; chmn. campaign Lou Frey for Gov., Palm Beach County, 1986; bd. dirs. Planned Parenthood of Palm Beach. Named to Sports Hall Fame, Rollins Coll., 1986, Winter Park H.S. Sports Hall of Fame, 1998. Fellow: Am. Bar Found. (Best Lawyers in Am. 2003); mem.: Fla. Bar (chmn. grievance com. 15th Jud. Cir., mem. client security fund com.), Fla. Tennis Assn. (treas. 1992—98, pres.-elect. 1999), U.S. Tennis Assn. (vice chair grievance com., capt. Maria Bueno Cup Team, fin. com., adult sn. competitive com.), Women's Internat. Tennis Assn. (disciplinary rev. bd. 1985), Palm Beach Jr. League, Exec. Women Palm Beach, Palm Beach County Bar Assn., The Beach Club. Republican. Avocations: tennis, snow skiing. Home: 2121 S Flagler Dr West Palm Beach FL 33401-8005 Office: Jones Foster Johnston & Stubbs PA PO Box 3475 West Palm Beach FL 33402-3475

COOPER, MARY BERRY, retired legal assistant, association executive; b. McDonough, Ga., July 27, 1923; d. Wilson Ray and Annie Vernis (Morgan) Berry; m. Raiford Wilson Cooper Sr, Feb. 18, 1944; children: Raiford Wilson Jr., Jack Glenn. Grad. H.S., Atlanta. Legal asst. Farris, Warfield, Kanaday Law Firm, Nashville, 1962-94; ret., 1994; exec. dir. Tenn. Feed and Grain Assn., Nashville, 1962—. Pres. Tenn. Assn. Legal Assts., Nashville, 1978-80. Chmn., bd. dirs. Miriam's Promise, Nashville, 1992—; organizer Serindipity House, 1970-98, Boone Youth Villagers, Memphis, 1998—; active Davidson County Dem. Exec. Com., Nashville, 1966-74; bd. mem. ARC, Nashville, 1970—; commr. Davidson County Human Rels., Nashville, 1975-85; chair adminstrv. bd. Glendale Meth. Ch., Nashville, 1982-92, chair fin. com., 1992-95; pres. Meth. Women, 1994—, treas., 1995—. Recipient Mary Catherine Strobel award Serindipity House, Nashville, 1985. Mem. Nat. Assn. Legal Assts. (charter, chair 1982 workshop, state bar liaison 1982-86), Tenn. Paralegal Assn. (organizer, dir. 1981-84), Order Ea. Star. Home: 626 General George Patton Rd Nashville TN 37221-2458

COOPER, MARY CAMPBELL, information services executive; b. Meadville, Pa., Aug. 14, 1940; d. Paul F. and Margaret (Webb) Campbell; m. James Nicoll Cooper, June 8, 1963; children: Alix, Jenny. BA, Mt. Holyoke Coll., 1961; MLS, Simmons Coll., 1963; MEd, Harvard U., 1965. Cert. museum adminstrn. With Harvard U. Libr., Cambridge, Mass., 1961-63, Carleton U. Libr., Ottawa, Can., 1965-85; archive cons. U.S., Can., 1985-86; info. mgr. Haley & Aldrich Inc., Cambridge, 1986-88, Tsoi/Kobus & Assocs., Cambridge, 1988-90; pres., founder Cooper Info., Cambridge, 1990—. Bd. dirs. Mass. Com. for Preservation of Archtl. Records, Boston. Author: Records in Architectural Offices, 1992, Records and Information Management: Meeting the Challenge, 1994, Records and Information Management: Order Out of Chaos, 1996. Bd. dirs. Berkshire Hist. Soc., Pitts., Mass. Travel grantee Nat. Hist. Pub. Records Commn., 1991. Mem. Spl. Librs. Assn., Am. Mus. Assn., Assn. Ind. Info. Profls., Assn. Moving Image Archivists, Assn. Records Mgrs. and Adminstrs. (nat. com. 1991—). Avocations: travel, tennis, swimming. Home and Office: 5 Ellery Pl Cambridge MA 02138-4200

COOPER, MARY LITTLE, federal judge, former banking commissioner; b. Fond du Lac, Wis., Aug. 13, 1946; d. Ashley Jewell and Gertrude (McCoy) Little. AB in Polit. Sci. cum laude, Bryn Mawr Coll., 1968; JD, Villanova U., 1972; LLD (hon.), Georgian Ct. Coll., 1987. Bar. N.J. 1972. Assoc. McCarter & English, Newark, 1972-80, ptnr., 1980-84; commr. N.J. Dept. Banking, Trenton, 1984-90; assoc. gen. counsel Prudential Property & Casualty Ins. Co., Holmdel, N.J., 1991-92; judge U.S. Dist. Ct. N.J., 1992—. Chmn. bd. Pinelands Devel. Credt Bank. Bd. trustees Exec. Commn. Ethical Standards, Trenton, 1984-90, Corp. Bus. Assistance, Trenton, 1984-91, N.J. Housing & Mortgage Fin. Agy., Trenton, 1984-90, N.J. Cemetery Bd. Assn., 1984-90, N.J. Hist. Soc., 1976-79., YMCA of Greater Newark, 1973-76; mem. Supreme Ct. N.J. Civil Practice Com., 1982-84, Supreme Ct. N.J. Dist. Ethics Com., 1982-84. Fellow Am. Bar Found.; mem. ABA, N.J. Bar Assn., Princeton Bar Assn., John J. Gibbons Am. Inn of Ct. Office: US Courthouse 402 E State St Ste 5000 Trenton NJ 08608-1507

COOPER, NANNIE COLES, education educator, consultant; b. Washington, Oct. 25, 1930; d. Harry Willie and Lucy Jackson Coles; m. Clement Theodore Cooper; children: Patricia, Karen, Stephanie, Bridgette, Stacy. BS, D.C. Tchrs. Coll., 1964; M in Art of Tchg., Trinity Coll., Washington, 1973. Cert. nat. tchrs. exam. Elem. sch. tchr. D.C. Pub. Schs., 1964—77; reading and SAT preparation specialist Cromwell Acad., Washington, 1978—82; adj. prof. U. D.C., 1984—87; magnet sch. substitute tchr. Montgomery County (Md.) Pub. Schs., 1988—96; adj. prof. reading Am. English Lang. Program Montgomery Coll., Takoma Park, Md., 1986—2002; cons. prescriptive and diagnostic testing Washington, 2002—. Curriculum developer D.C. Pub. Schs., 1980—84, instr. SAT rev., 1984—86; instr. SAT preparation U. D.C., 1984—87. Vol. Ward 4 Dem. race, Washington, 1996, Dem. Women, Washington, 1998—99; mem. choir Trinity Episcopal Ch., 1984—88. Named Outstanding Parent, Parent Tchrs. of Parochial Schs., Washington, 1985—87, Reading is Fundamental honoree, 1986. Mem.: Alpha Wives of D.C., Alpha Kappa Alpha. Avocations: reading, travel, writing. Home: 728 Dahlia St NW Washington DC 20012-1844

COOPER, PAULA, art dealer; b. Mass., Mar. 14, 1938; Student, Pierce Coll., Athens, Greece, Sorbonne, Paris, Goucher Coll., Inst. Fine Arts, NYU; DFA (hon.), R.I. Sch. Design, 1995. Asst. World House Galleries, N.Y.C., 1959-61; pvt. dealer, 1962-63; with Paula Johnson Gallery, N.Y.C., 1964-65; dir. Park Place Gallery, N.Y.C., 1965-67, Paula Cooper Gallery, N.Y.C., 1968—. Chmn. bd. dirs. Kitchen Ctr., N.Y.C., 1985-95. Named honoree, N.Y. Studio Sch., 2001; recipient Art Table award for disting. svc. to the visual arts, 2001. Mem.: Art Dealers Assn. Am. (bd. dirs. 1982—86, 1988—90, 1997—2000, v.p. bd. dirs. 1997—2000), Art Students League. Office: Paula Cooper Gallery 534 W 21st St New York NY 10011-2812

COOPER, REBECCA, art dealer; b. Phila., July 11, 1947; d. Frank N. Cooper and Bernice Silverstein; m. Michael J. Waldman, June 27, 1982. BA, MA, NYU; postgrad. Cert. appraiser. Owner Gallery Rebecca Cooper, Washington; pres. Rebecca Cooper Fine Art, N.Y.C., 1980s-90s. Hon. chairperson N.Y. Women Bus. Owners Art Roundtable, 1981; lectr. Resources Coun., 1983, N.Y. Mayor's com. on interior design and furnishings, 1983; sec. bd. assocs. Am. Craft Mus., lectr. Collectors Circle; nat. patron Am. Fed. Art., Ind. Curators Inc. Patron, Mus. Modern Art; benefactor New Mus. Dirs. Forum; exhbn. mem. dirs. coun. Whitney Mus.; art tours, cons. Mem. Am. Appraisers Assn. (assoc.), Dame de la Chaine des Rotisseurs, Women's 008 Investment Club, Pvt. Art Dealers Assn., Nat. Arts Club, Lotos Club, Guggenheim Mus. (internat. cir.).

COOPER, ROBERTA, mayor; b. Mar. 18, 1937; m. Jerrel Cooper. BA, MA. Ret. secondary sch. tchr.; mem. Hayward (Calif.) City Coun., 1988-92; mayor City of Hayward, 1994—. Former mem. Gen. Plan Revision Task Force, dir. League of Calif. Cities. Active Eden (Calif.) Youth Ctr., Literacy Plus, Hayward Edn. Assn. Democrat. Avocations: reading mysteries, gardening. Office: Mayors Office 777 B St Hayward CA 94541-5007

COOPER, ROSE MARIE, composer; b. Cairo, Ill., Feb. 21, 1937; d. Allen Britten and Janie May Cooper; m. William H. Jordan, Oct. 29, 1960; children: Bailey, Beth. MusB, Okla. Bapt. U., 1959; MA, Columbia U., 1960; PhD, U. NC, Greensboro, 1976. Composer: The Purple Dress, 1985, The Composer's Suite; contbr. musical works to profl. publs. Mem. exec. coun. U. Caroliniana Soc., U. SC, Columbia, 2000—04. Recipient more than 20 Standard awards, ASCAP. Mem.: DAR (vice-regent local chpt. 1999—2002, regent local chpt. 2002—). Home: 303 N Main ST Greer SC 29650

COOPER, SHARON MARSHA, marketing, advertising executive; m. Steven Jon Cooper; children: Robin Eve, Erik Scott. BA, Northeastern Ill. U., Chgo., 1974; MEd, Loyola U., Chgo., 1977. Adj. asst. prof. Chgo. Med. Sch., North Chicago, Ill., 1974-79; edn./media coord. Humana Hosp., Aurora, Colo., 1980-82; v.p. Healthcare Mktg. Corp., Denver, 1982-84; pres. Sharon Cooper Assocs., Ltd., Englewood, Colo., 1984—. Cons./speaker Jason Pharms., Balt., 1988—; cons. Am. Soc. Bariatric Physicians; lectr. in field; guest lectr. U. Denver, 1988—; pres. The Food Bank of Rockies Guild 2003—. Illustrator: A Manual of Radiographic Positioning, 1973; contbr. articles to profl. jours. Bd. dirs., v.p. The Barre Assn./Colo. Ballet, Denver, 1989—; bd. dirs. Am. Diabetes Assn., Denver, 1983—, Am. Cancer Soc., Denver, 1988—, Hospice of St. John, Denver, 1986-90; mem. adv. bd. U. Colo. Denver Sch. of the Arts, 1997—; pres. Colo. Angels, 2001-03, Food Bank of the Rockies Guild, 2003—. Named Co-Woman of the Yr., Lerner Newspapers, Chgo., 1973, Silver Microphone award, 1988, Golden Leaflet award, Colo. Hosp. Assn., 1981, 84. Mem. Am. Hosp. Assn., Assn. Healthcare Pub. Rels. and Mktg. (reg. rep. 1987—), Colo. Soc. Health Care Pub. Rels., Pub. Rels. Soc. Am., Zonta, Toastmasters (sec. 1972-84). Avocations: writing, art, aerobics. Office: Sharon Cooper Assocs Ltd Ste E-200 16 Inverness Pl E Englewood CO 80112-5612

COOPER, SIGNE SKOTT, retired nursing educator; b. Clinton County, Iowa, Jan. 29, 1921; d. Hans Edward and Clara Belle (Steen) Skott. BS, U. Wis., 1948; MEd, U. Minn., 1955. Head nurse U. Wis. Hosp., Madison, 1946-48; instr. U. Wis. Sch. Nursing, Madison, 1948-51, asst. prof., 1952-57, assoc. prof., 1957-62, prof., assoc. dean, 1948-83, prof. emeritus, 1983—. Prof. U. Wis. Extension, 1955-83. Contbg. author: American Nursing: A Biographical Dictionary, Vol. 1, 1988, Vol. 2, 1992, Vol. 3, 2000; contbr. articles to profl. jours. 1st Lt. U.S. Army Nurse Corps, 1943-46. Recipient NLN Linda Richards award, ANA Honorary Recognition award, Adult Edn. Assn. Pioneer award; named to Nursing Hall of Fame, 2000. Fellow Am. Acad. Nursing (named Living Legend 2003); mem. Am. Assn. for History Nursing (Pres.'s award 2003), Wis. Nurses Assn. (pres.).

COOPER, SUSAN LEE GENSEL, institutional advancement administrator; b. May 2, 1941; d. John Pershing and Doris Olive (Tonk) Oder; m. William E. Gensel, Mar. 30, 1961 (div. Dec. 1981); children: Douglas, Robert; m. Robert E. Cooper, Sept. 21, 1985. BA, U. Calif. Riverside, 1964; MLS, U. So. Calif., 1971. Head serials tech. processing and automation U. Calif. Riverside, 1964-70, [illegible] Harbor (N.Y.) Lab., 1972-77, dir. mktg. and libraries, 1978-87, dir. pub. affairs, info. svcs., 1988-94, dir. pub. affairs, devel. and libraries, 1994-97; dir. instl. advancement Trudeau Inst., Saranac Lake, NY, 1997—, v.p., 2003—. Personal asst. Harry Chapin, folk-singer and composer, 1976-81; library cons. Performing Arts Found. L.I., 1975-80, sec. to bd. trustees, 1975-80; library cons. Otisville, Inc., N.Y., 1983-84. Compiler: Cell Index, 1978; reviewer Med. Ref. Series Quar., 1982; spl. asst. Nobelist B. McClintock, 1983-92. Mem. State Task Force on Planning Libr. Devel. on L.I., 1976—78; del. Gov.'s Conf. on Librs., 1978; campaign chmn. Rep. for Sammis, Huntington, NY, 1983; mem. vestry St. Luke's Episcopal Ch., 2000—, sr. warden, 2004; bd. dirs. Sound Adirondack Growth Alliance, 1998—, Huntington Twp. Chamber Found., 1992—97. Mem. ALA, Spl. Libraries Assn. (chpt. pres. 1976-77, divsn. pres. elect 1978-79), Med. Theatre N.Y. (dir. 1975-77), Suffolk County Libr. Assn., Nassau Libr. Assn., L.I. Libr. Resources Coun. (pres. 1975-77), Rotary Club Saranac Lake (bd. dirs., pres. 2003—), Beta Phi Mu. Home: 31 View St Saranac Lake NY 12983-2203 Office: Trudeau Inst Inc PO Box 59 Saranac Lake NY 12983-0059 Business E-Mail: scooper@trudeauinstitute.org.

COOPER, VALERIE GAIL, minister; b. Houston, May 30, 1962; d. Rev. M.C. and Mildred Chappel Cooper. BS in Pre-Medicine, Paul Quinn Coll., 1985; MDiv, Interdenominational Theol. Ctr. Sem., 1998; poastdoctoral, Immauel Sch. Bible, 2003—. Elder Full Gospel Bapt. Ch., 2001. Pastor Vistors Chapel African Meth. Episc. Ch., El Paso, Tex., 1998—2000; assoc. pastor Morning Star Full Gospel Bapt. Ch., Houston, 2001—. Mem.: Sigma Gamma Rho. Home: 3805 Brill St Houston TX 77026 Office: Morning Star FGB Church 5110 Crane St Houston TX 77026 Personal E-mail: vallevonettecooper@yahoo.com. E-mail: morninstarfgbc@aol.com.

COOPER-GONZALEZ, ANGELA, counseling administrator; arrived in U.S., 1970; d. Lorenzo and Ana Caona González; m. Lynwood Cooper, Nov. 14, 1977; children: Yolanda Cooper, Lance Cooper. Student, Lehman Coll., 1977, student, 1991, CCNY, 1979, Columbia U., 1985. Bilingual tchr. N.Y.C. Bd. Edn., 1977, asst. to dir. pupil pers. svcs., 1982—92, guidance counselor Bronx, 1992—. Translator Cmty. Sch. Bd. 9, Bronx, 1999—. Mem.: Bronx Health Link. Democrat. Roman Catholic. Avocations: reading, angels.

COOTS, LAURIE, advertising executive; 1 child, Christopher. Student, Colorado State U. Joined Chiat/Day as sec. on Apple Computer bus., 1984; named new bus. coord., 1986; dir. new bus. and adminstrn., 1989; COO LA office, 1993—97; (Chiat/Day merges with TBWA, 1995); chief mktg. officer N. Am. TBWA/Chiat/Day, LA, 1997—2001, chief mktg. officer worldwide, 2001—. Office: TBWA Chiat/Day LA 5353 Grosvenor Blvd Los Angeles CA 90066

COOVER, DORIS DIMOCK, artist; b. Beaverdam, Wis., Aug. 8, 1917; d. Almon Crowe and Alma Josephine (Johnson) Dimock; m. Francis Merle Coover, Apr. 11, 1945; children: Cheryl, Danelle. Student in Fashion and Design, Woodbury U., 1937. One-woman shows include Chappqua (N.Y.) Pub. Libr., 1964-79, Katonah (N.Y.) Gallery, 1967-72, Briarcliff (N.Y.) Coll., 1969, Silvermine (Conn.) Guild of Artists, 1965-81, Am. Can Corp., Greenwich, Conn., 1971—, Village Gallery at Gallmofry, Croton, N.Y., 1974-81, Manhattan Savs. Bank N.Y.C.-White Plains, 1963-68; gallery artist Virginia Barrett, Chappqua, 1964-98; exhibited in groups shows at Okla. Art Ctr., Oklahoma City, 1959, Tex. Oil Industry, Dallas, 1958, Delgado Mus., New Orleans, 1958, Dallas Mus. art, 1958-59, Westchester Art Soc., White Plaine, N.Y., 1962-74, Silvermine Guild Artists, 1970-81, Crocker Art Mus. Art Auction, 1981-98, Neuberger Mus., Purchase, N.Y., 1985, Sacramento Fine Arts, 1985 and many others; cover artist Sci. and Tech. Mag., 1966; work included in Am. Refs., 1978, Who's Who in Am. Art, 1996-97, Rockport Pubs.-Painting Color, 1997, 98, Sketching and Drawing, 1998. Mem., historian Officers Club, L.A., 1940-45; artist judge No. Westchester chpt. Cancreare, Bedford Village, N.J., 1958. Recipient numerous awards for art, including Helbein award Western Colo. Watercolor Soc. Mem. Nat. Watercolor Soc. (assoc.), Am. Watercolor Soc. (assoc.), Nat. Mus. Woman in Arts (charter), Crocker Art Mem. Republican. Avocations: visiting galleries with friends, reading mysteries, experimenting with art.

COPE, CAROLINE BANCROFT, special education educator; b. Richmond, Ind., May 12, 1950; d. Eric George and Esther Gillett Curtis; m. Edward Cope; children: Joshua Bancroft, Richenda Marie. BA, Swarthmore Coll., 1973; MS in Edn., U. Pa., 1974; C.A.S., SUNY, 1993. Cert. adminstrn., spl. edn. tchr., elem. tchr., cert. reading tchr., cmty. coll. tchr. Spl. edn. dept. head DeWitt Mid. Sch., Ithaca City Sch. Dist., Ithaca, NY, 1982—, spl. edn. tchr., 1978—; acting dir. of spl. edn. Ithaca City Sch. Dist., Ithaca, NY. Mem. of corp. Haverford Coll., Pa., 2003; trustee Kendal at Ithaca, 1997—; mem. bd. SchoolWorks, Ithaca, NY, 2003; founding mem. Explicit Reading Instrn. Network, Ithaca, NY, 2001. Mem.: Coun. Exceptional Children, Internat. Dyslexia Assn., Delta Kappa Gamma. D-Liberal. Quaker. Avocation: travel. Office: DeWitt Mid Sch 560 Warren Rd Ithaca NY 14850

COPE, ESTHER OWENS, genealogical researcher; b. Ellenton, S.C., Apr. 5, 1942; d. Harry Hastings Owens and Alice Evelyn Hair; m. Winfred Dennis Cope, Nov. 28, 1963; children: Darlene Cope Williams, Bruce Kevin. Grad., Aiken H.S., S.C., 1960. Recorder gen. mil. svc. awards United Daus. of Confederacy, 1998—2000; state pres. Colonial Dames XVII Century, Aiken, SC, 2003—. Author: (cookbook) What's Cooking: History of Green Pond Baptist Church, children's stories; dir.: rsch. tours (Order of the Palmetto, 2001). Hist. rschr. Augusta Geneal. Soc., Ga., 1980—2003. Recipient Winnie Davis award, United Daus. of Confederacy, 1994, Order of the Palmetto, S.C. Gov., 2001. Mem.: Daughters of 1812 (state curator 2003—), DAR (dist. dir. 2000—03), United Daus. of Confederacy (recorder gen. mil. svc. awards 1998—2000), Soc. Colonial Dames XVII Century (state pres. 2003—). Baptist. Avocations: photography, reading, bowling, camping, drawing/painting. Home: 2756 Silver Bluff Rd Aiken SC 29803 Office: B & D Enterprises 2756 Silver Bluff Rd Aiken SC 29803 Personal E-mail: eocope@scescape.net.

COPE, JEANNETTE NAYLOR, executive search consultant; b. Corpus Christi, Tex., Feb. 9, 1956; d. Glen R. and Jeannine (Withington) N.; m. John R. Cope, May 22, 1993. BA in Psychology and Sociology, Trinity U., 1978. Asst. fin. dir. Jim Baker for Atty. Gen. Campaign, Houston, 1978; fin. dir. Rep. Party of Tex., Austin, 1979-81; regional Eagle rep. Rep. Nat. Com., Washington, 1981-83; devel. officer Nat. Endowment for the Arts, Washington, 1983-87; sr. project mgr. Internat. Skye Assocs., Washington, 1988; spl. asst. to Pres. of U.S. The White House, 1989-90, dep. asst. to Pres. of U.S., dep. dir. of presdl. pers., 1990-93; pres. J. Naylor Cope Co., Washington, 1994—. NEA liaison Pres.' Com. on Arts and Humanites, Washington, 1985-87; dir. Internat. Skye Advisor, Washington, 1988; bd. dirs. Bush/Quayle Alumni Assn., TransTech. Corp.; mem. Officer Pers. Mgmt.'s Task Force on Exec. and Mgmt. Devel., Washington, 1990; bd. dirs. Washington First Bank. Mem. Pres.'s Com. on the Arts and Humanities, 2001—; chmn. alumni admissions coun. Trinity U., Washington, 1986—87; mem. Bush Cheney Transition Team, 2001; vestrywoman St. John's Episcopal Ch., Washington, 1990—94, co-chmn. outreach com., 1991—94, chmn. search com. for 14th rector, jr. warden, 1994—97, sr. warden, 1998—2001; bd. dirs. The Compass Rose Soc. of the Anglican Communion, 1999—, exec. com., 2000—; bd. dirs. Coop. Urban Ministry Ctr., Washington, 1987—89, Pennsylvania Ave. Devel. Corp., 1993—96, Decatur House, Washington, 1998—, exec. com., 2000—, vice-chmn., bd. dirs., 2001—03, chmn. bd. dirs., 2004—; bd. visitors Kanuga Confs., 2001—. Tex. Coun. of Ch. Related Colls. scholar, 1974. Mem. Am. Soc. Assn. Execs. (exec. recruiter), [illegible] membership com. 1981), Nat. Trust for Hist. Preservation, Smithsonian Instn., Am. Film Inst., Mcpl. Art Soc. (N.Y.C.), 1925 F Street Club (chmn. mems. com.), Pres.'s Club, Columbia Country Club (Chevy Chase, Md.), Tex. Breakfast Club, Blue Key (sec. 1976-78), City Tavern Club, Chi Beta Epsilon (v.p. San Antonio coun. 1976). Republican. Episcopalian. Office: J Naylor Cope Co PO Box 40069 Washington DC 20016-0069 Business E-Mail: jnc@jnaylorcopecompany.com.

COPE, KATHLEEN ADELAIDE, critical care nurse, parish nurse, educator; b. Bethlehem, Pa., Sept. 12, 1926; d. Harry Raymond and Mabel Eva (Newhard) Stine; m. Robert Clayton Cope, Aug. 9, 1951; children: Debra Kathleen Howard, Terry Faye Cicero. BA in Psychology summa cum laude, Bellevue (Nebr.) Coll., 1972; diploma, St. Luke's Hosp., Bethlehem, 1951; student, Whitworth Coll., Spokane, 1989, Wash. State U., 1989. RN, Pa., Wash.; cert. nutrition support nurse; cert. critical care nurse, quality improvement, health promotion specialist. Pvt. duty nurse Exeter (N.H.) Hosp., 1957-60; nurse Red Cross Blood Mobile, Portsmouth area, N.H., 1961-65; staff nurse Clarkson Hosp., Omaha, 1966, asst. head nurse, 1966-67, head nurse, 1967-68, supr., organizer coronary care ctr., 1968-70; staff nurse ICU/critical care Sacred Heart Med. ctr., Spokane, 1973—; founder, dir. nutritional risk/identification network Health Improvement Partnership, Spokane, Wash., 1997—. Mem. adv. coun. edn. com. Nutrition Screening Initiative, Washington, 1992—, Nutrition Inst. La., New Orleans, 1993—; apptd. del. by U.S. Senate to White House Conf. on Aging, 1995; developer Body Mass Index awareness cmty. action project through Leadership Spokane Class, 1999; presenter Spokane's body mass index project U.S. Surgeon Gen.'s Inaugural Session on Obesity, 2001. Author: (manual) Malnutrition in the Elderly: A National Crisis, (resolution) Ensuring the Future of the Medicare Program presented to White House and Congress; contbr. articles to profl. jours. Apptd. Silver Senator by U.S. Senate for Wash. in Nat. Silver Haired Congress, 1997. Recipient Cmty. Leadership Recognition award, YWCA, Spokane, 1993, commendation for developing a model for nation from former U.S. Surgeon Gen., 1999, Spl. Recognition award for contrbn. to malnutrition awareness, U.S. Adminstrn. on Aging, 2000. Mem. ANA, Wash. State Nursing Assn., Nat. Coun. on Aging, Am. Soc. for Critical Care Nursing (founding), Am. Soc. for Parenteral and Enteral Nutrition, U.S. apptd. Silver Senator for Wash. State in Nat. Silver Haired Congress, Sigma Theta Tau. Avocations: reading, walking, hiking, bicycling, cooking, crafts. Home: 8315 N Lucia Ct Spokane WA 99208-9654 Fax: (509) 468-1026. E-mail: kcope@mindspring.com.

COPE, MELBA DARLENE, volunteer, photographer; b. Des Moines, Iowa, Feb. 16, 1944; d. Murray J. and Mary Lorena Van Hemert; m. Harvey J. Helgeland, 1964 (dissolved 1971); 1 child, Ingrid ; m. Thom K. Cope, Nov. 8, 1980. Student, Nebr. Wesleyan U., Lincoln, 1975—76; BA in Women's Studies with highest distinction, U. Nebr., 1996. Bus. mgr. Williamson Olds/Honda, Lincoln, 1982—88; Granny Smith Washington Apple Commn., Wenatchee, Wash., 1999—2000; photographer Images by Melba, Tucson, 2002—. Photographer Habitat for Humanity Bldg. Project, Lincoln, Nebr., 1998. Contbr. chapters to books. Mentor Women in Trades program YWCA, Lincoln, 1999; mem. Older Women's League, 1998—2002; big sister Heartland Big Bros./Big Sisters Orgn., 2001—02; bd. dirs., sec., v.p. Rape Spouse Abuse Crisis Ctr., 1993—2002; bd. dirs. YWCA, 2001; com. mem. Girls and Women in Sports and Fitness, 2001—02; mem. com. Women in Transition, 1999; commr., mem. exec. bd., v.p. Lincoln Lancaster Women's Commn., 1997—2001; bd. dirs. Coll. Arts and Scis. Alumni Assn. U. Nebr., 1997—2000; mem. Bd. Friends Commn., 2000—01; mem. comms. com. Sunflower Cmty. Assn., Tucson, 2002—. Recipient Elizabeth Kurtz Vol. award, Rape Spouse Abuse Crisis Ctr., Lincoln, Nebr., 2000, Outstanding Vol. award, United Way, Lincoln, 2000, Alice Paul award, Lincoln/Lancaster Women's Commn., Lincoln, 2001. Mem.: Sigma Alpha Iota (Sword of Honor award 1994), Phi Beta Kappa. Avocations: photography, hiking, reading, music, travel.

COPELAND, CAROLYN ABIGAIL, retired dean; b. White Plains, N.Y., May 5, 1931; d. Robert Erford and Mary Terwillinger; m. William E. Copeland, Aug. 16, 1964; children: Rob Cameron, Diana Elizabeth Bosworth. BA, U. Mich., 1973, MA, 1979, postgrad., 1992—. With dean's office Coll. Lit., Sci. and Arts U. Mich, Ann Arbor, 1967-91, asst. dean, 1980-84, assoc. dean, 1984-91. Rschr. in Buddhist art history. Author: Tankas from the Koelz Collection, 1980. CEW scholar, Rackham grad. student scholar. Mem. Phi Beta Kappa (mortar bd., v.p. Alpha chpt. 1984-86, pres. Alpha chpt. 1986-88). Home: 1867 Morley St Simi Valley CA 93065 Office: U Mich Ann Arbor MI 48109 E-mail: cabby1867@aol.com.

COPELAND, CHARLENE CAROLE, lawyer; b. Gloversville, N.Y., July 22; d. Joseph Frank and Marion (Dye) Born; children: Christopher, Todd, Tiffani. BS in Polit Sci., Lamar U.; JD, John Marshall U. Bar: Ill. 1991, U.S. Dist. Ct. (no. dist.) Ill. 1991, U.S. Ct. Appeals (7th cir.) 1993, Fed. Trial Bar, 1993. Assoc. Brenner, Mavrias & Alm, New Lenox, Ill., 1992-96; assoc. civil divsn. Will County State's Attys. Office, Joliet, Ill., 1997-1999; with Lehrer, Flaherty & Canavan, Wheaton, Ill., 2000—02; asst. atty. gen. Ill. Atty. Gen.'s office Indsl. Commn. Bur., 2002—. Mem. Will County Pro Bono Project; pres. Jaycettes, Port Authur, Tex., 1970-71; fin. chmn. League of Women Voters, 1971, pres. Joliet Region, 1979-81; area capt. March of Dimes Mothers' March, 1971; day chmn. George Bush for Senate Campaign, 1970; mem. Village of Shorewood Ad Hoc Com. on Ordinances, 1975, Fin. Com., 1976-78; pres. United Meth. Women of Grace Meth. Ch., 1980-81; crusade chmn. Shorewood Residential Cancer Crusade, 1982. Named Outstanding Pro Bono Vol., 1995. Mem. Ill. State Bar Assn., Will County Bar Assn., Will County Arbitration Panel, Will County Women's Bar Assn. (chmn. 1999), John Marshall Law Sch. Reunion Com. Home: 516 Ca Crest Dr Shorewood IL 60431-9729

COPELAND, JACQUELINE TURNER, music educator; b. Birmingham, Ala., Mar. 22, 1939; d. Charles Smith and Julia (Northrop) Turner; m. William Edward Copeland, Apr. 20, 1962; children: Denise Arlene, Dawn Alane. B in Music Edn., Birmingham-So. Coll., 1960; M in Music Edn., Wichita State U., 1977. Cert. music tchr. grades K-12, Ala., Ga., Kans., La., Va. Music tchr. Jefferson County Bd. Edn., Birmingham, 1960-62, 63-64, DeKalb County Bd. Edn., Decatur, Ga., 1965-68; choral music tchr. Fairfax (Va.) County Bd. Edn., 1968-69, Derby (Kans.) Unified Sch. Dist. #260, 1977-80, Maize (Kans.) Unified Sch. Dist. #266, 1980-84; music tchr. Montgomery (Ala.) County Pub. Schs., 1984-85; instr. voice and piano Acad. Performing Arts, Montgomery, 1985-95, Studio of Jacqueline T. Copeland, Montgomery, 1995—. Accompanist County-Wide Music Festivals, Birmingham, 1960-65; sect. leader Dekalb Cmty. Chorus, Decatur, Ga., 1965-68; sect. leader, exec. bd. New Orleans Concert Choir, 1970-74; asst. dir., dir. chorale Wichita Choral Soc., 1974-84; dir. opening ceremony Bicentennial Fair, Wichita, 1976; mem. Montgomery (Ala.) Civic Chorale, 1984-87; musical dir. for theatre depts. Performing Arts Jr. High, Performing Arts H.S., Faulkner U., 1986—. Author: Music Teacher Handbook, 1967; editor, contbg. author: Teacher Advisement Handbook, 1980. Secret svc. wife White House Wives, Washington, 1968-70; leader, trainer, area chmn. Camp Fire Girls, New Orleans, 1970-74; leader, membership com., exec. bd. Camp Fire Girls, Wichita, 1974-82; elected ofcl. Citizens Participation Orgn., Wichita, 1984; area chmn. Am. Heart Assn., Montgomery, 1988-94; vol. DA Election, Montgomery, 1994. Recipient Groovey Tchr. award WQXI Radio, Atlanta, 1967, Gov.'s commendation Revolutionary Bicentennial Com., Wichita, 1976; named Outstanding Young Women of Am., New Orleans, 1971. Mem. NOW, AAUW, Music Tchrs. Nat. Assn., Ala. Music Tchrs. Assn., Montgomery Music Tchrs. Forum, Alpha Chi Omega (Montgomery chpt. treas. 1995-99, pres. 1999—), Alpha Chi Omega Alumnae (del. to 4 nat. convs., pres., v.p.), [illegible] Avocation: searching for collectibles for country decor. Home: 6121 Bell Road Mnr Montgomery AL 36117-4362

COPELAND, SUZANNE JOHNSON, real estate executive; b. Chgo., Aug. 01; d. John Berger and Eleanor (Dreger) Johnson; m. John Robert Copeland, Aug. 1, 1971 (div. June 1976). Assoc. French Lang. and Culture, Richland Coll., Dallas, 1974; BFA, Ill. Wesleyan U., Bloomington, 1965. Commercial artist Barney Donley Studio, Inc., Chgo., 1966-69; art dir. Levines Dept. Store, Dallas, 1970-74; creative dir. Titche-Goettinger, Inc., Dallas, 1974-78; catering mgr. Dunfey Hotel, Dallas, 1978-82; regional dir. corp. sales Rayburn Country Resort, Austin, Tex., 1982-84; real estate sales assoc. Henry S. Miller, Dallas, 1984-86; v.p. Exclusive Properties Internat., Inc., Dallas, 1986—. Cons. North Tex. Commn., Dallas, 1988. Acquisitions editor: Unser, An American Family Portrait, 1988. Mem. The Rep. Forum, Dallas, 1983-94; vol. Star for Children, Dallas, 1988, Soc. for Prevention of Cruelty to Animals, Dallas, 1973-92, Preservation of Animal World Soc., 1986-92, Sedona Acad., 1996—, Sedona Humane Soc., 1996—, Sedona Women, 2001—; charter mem. P.M. League Dallas Mus. Art.; mem. Keep Sedona Beautiful, 1999—. Mem. Nat. Assn. Realtors, Tex. Assn. Realtors, Greater Dallas Assn. Realtors (com. chmn., Summit award 1984, 85), North Tex. Arabian Horse Club (bd. dirs. 1975-76, Pres.'s award 1978), Dallas Zool. Soc., Humane Soc. Dallas County (v.p. 1973-74), Humane Soc. U.S./Gulf States Humane Edn. Assn. (bd. dirs. 1990-91), Am. Montessori Soc., VASA Order of Am. (Red Rock chpt., bd. dirs. 2004-), Delta Phi Delta, Phi Theta Kappa. Lutheran. Avocations: arabian and thoroughbred horses, scuba diving, equitation instr. Office: Exclusive Properties PO Box 1973 Sedona AZ 86339 E-mail: azmtnlion@aol.com.

COPENHAVER, KIRSTEN JEANNETTE, health facility administrator, consultant; b. Helena, Mont., Nov. 28, 1969; d. Doris Elizabeth and Terry Lee Copenhaver. BS, U. Mont., Missoula, 1993, MS, 2000. Clinic asst. Intermountain Planned Parenthood, Missoula, Mont., 1997—98, clinic mgr., 2001—02; office mgr. Full Care Dental Practice, Missoula, Mont., 1998—99; adminstrv. asst. Ptnrs. in Home Care, Missoula, Mont., 1999—2001; clinic dir. Seattle Med. and Wellness Clinic, Seattle, 2003—. Actor: (comedy improv group) Public Privates. Bd. dirs. The Bra Show, Seattle, 2003, Intermountain Planned Parenthood, Missoula, Mont., 2000—01.

COPENHAVER, MARION LAMSON, former state legislator; b. Andover, Vt., Sept. 26, 1925; d. Joseph Fenwick and Christine (Forbes) Lamson; m. John H. Copenhaver, June 30, 1946; children: John III, Margaret, Christine, Eric, Lisa. Student, U. Vt., 1945-46. Mem. N.H. Ho. of Reps., Concord, ranking Dem. health and human svcs. com., 1973-2000, mem. adminstrv. rules com., 1982-2000, mem. health and human svcs. oversight, 1990-2000; ret., 2000. Chair Grafton County Dems., 1986-91; assoc. supr. Grafton County Soil Conservation Dist., 1980-2002, supr., 2002—; supr. Hanover (N.H.) Dem. Town Com., 1992; mem.-at-large Dem. State Com., Concord, 1992; bd. dirs. Dartmouth Hitchcock Found., Hanover, 1991—; bd. incorporators Dartmouth Hitchcock Med. Ctr., Lebanon, N.H., 1984—; bd. dirs. Grafton County Sr. Citizens Coun., Inc., 1995-96, 2001, vice chair, Outreach House, an Assisted Living Facility, 2001—, Hanover, Friends of Norris Cotton Cancer Ctr., Women's Policy Inst. N.H. Named N.H. Legislator of Yr. N.H. Nurses Assn., 1989; recipient Meritorious award N.H. Women's Lobby, 1996, James A. Hamilton award N.H. Hosp. Assn., 1997. Mem. NOW, Bus. and Profl. Women's Club (Outstanding Mem. award 1990). Democrat. Unitarian Universalist. Avocations: golf, skiing. Home: 14 Woodcock Ln Etna NH 03750-4402

COPLEY, CYNTHIA SUE LOVE, insurance adjuster; b. Defiance, Ohio, Oct. 26, 1957; d. Thomas Lee and Pauline Ann (Brandt) Love, Jr.; m. James Earl Copley, Jr., Oct. 19, 1985. B in Criminal Justice, Ohio U., 1981, A in Law Enforcement, 1979, A in Fire and Safety Tech., 1982. Cert. profl. ins. woman. With Spangler Candy Co., Bryan, Ohio, 1976-77; guard Juvenile Detention Ctr., Chillicothe, Ohio, 1978; security officer J.C. Penney Corp., Inc., Chillicothe, Ohio, 1979, Rink's Bargain City, Chillicothe, Ohio, 1979; with Rubbermaid Sales Corp., Chillicothe, Ohio, 1980; asst. dept. sec. and computer lab asst. Ohio U., Chillicothe, 1977-81; supr. collections and investigation Bur. of Support, Ross County, Chillicothe, 1981-82; asst. mgr. Tecumseh Claims Svc., Chillicothe, 1982—; owner Copley Adjusting, Chillicothe, 1982—. Part-time employee Ross County Bd. Elections, 1998-2003. Poll worker Rep. Party, Chillicothe, 1983-98; mem. Rep. Women Ross County, sec., 2000-2004. Mem. So. Ohio Claims Assn., Ohio Assn. Ind. Ins. Adjusters (sec.-treas. 1994, v.p. 1995, pres. 1996), Ohio Assn. Mut. Ins. Cos., Nat. Soc. Profl. Ins. Investigators. Lutheran. Avocations: golf, cooking, weekend trips. Home and Office: Tecumseh Claims Svc PO Box 15 Chillicothe OH 45601-0015

COPPENBARGER, CECELIA MARIE, special education educator; b. Kansas City, Mo., Nov. 3, 1961; d. Theodore Francis Bowman, Jr., Betty Marie Bowman; m. Charles Loren Coppenbarger, Jr.; children: Charles Loren Coppenbarger, III, Craig James, Cliff Robert, Joshua Richard, Elena Marie. A in Liberal Arts, Longview C.C., 1983; BA in Secondary Edn., BA in Eng., U. Missouri, 1998; postgrad., Ctrl. Mo. State U. Cert. cross categorical spl. edn. tchr. K-12, secondary Eng.tchr. 9-12. Cross-categorical spl. edn. tchr. Raytown C-2 Sch. Dist., Raytown, Mo., 1998—. Sponsor Raytown Chpt. Mo. State Tchrs. Assn.-Future Tchrs. Am., 2000—. Active James Lewis Elem. PTA, 2002—; mem. Plaza Heights Bapt. Ch. Choir, Blue Springs, 1998—; tchr. Plaza Heights Bapt. Ch. Sunday Sch. and Spl. Needs Ministry, Blue Springs, 1999—; mem. Lucy Franklin Elem. Sch. PTA, Blue Springs, 1998—2001, Blue Springs H.S. Parent Tchr. Student Assn., 1998—2001, 2003—, Brittany Hills Mid. Sch. Parent Tchr. Student Assn., 1998—2003; educator Raytown South H.S. Parent Tchr. Student Assn., Raytown, 1998—. Recipient Outstanding Scholastic Achievment and Excellence award, Golden Key Nat. Honor Soc., 1997, Outstanding Omer award, Odyssey of the Mind Program, 1997; scholar, U. Mo., Kansas City, 1997—98. Mem.: Mo. State Tchrs. Assn., Raytown Cmty. Tchrs. Assn., Coun. Exceptional Children, Pi Lambda Theta. Baptist. Home: 2114 NE 3rd St Blue Springs MO 64014 Office: Raytown South High Sch 8211 Sterling Raytown MO 64138 Office Phone: 816-268-7330. Personal E-mail: coppen@discoverynet.com. Business E-Mail: coppenbargerc@mail.raytown.k12.mo.us.

COPPENS, LAURA KATHRYN, special education educator; b. Hoddesdon, England, Jan. 12, 1948; d. Tomas Adriaan and Sylvia Helen Coppens; m. G. Lawrence McQueen (div. 1985); children: Isaac David, Sean Little Hawk. BA in Edn., John F. Kennedy Coll., Wahoo, Nebr., 1970; MEd in Spl. Edn., William Paterson U., 1976. Spl. edn. tchr. Bellmar (N.J.) Schs., 1970—71, N.J. Commn. for Blind, Teaneck, 1972—76; dir. Randolph County Learning Ctr., Roanoke, Ala., 1976—80; spl. edn. tchr. Lineville (Ala.) H.S., 1980—89, BOCES Alternative Program, Apalachin, NY, 1989—93, Owego (N.Y.) Apalachin Middle Sch., 1993—98, Owego Free Acad., 1998—. Dir. Youth Group, Owego, 2000—; co-coord. Inst. of Arts in Edn., Owego, 1996—; mentor tchr. Owego Apalachin Ctrl. Schs., 1999—. Pres. Randolph County Assn. for Retarded Citizens, Roanoke, 1980—83; lay reader St. Paul's Episc. Ch., Owego, 1998—. Recipient Outstanding Tchr. award, So. Tier Inst. of Arts, Binghamton, N.Y., 1998. Mem.: Broome Tioga Autism Soc. Am., Owego Apalachin Tchrs. Assn. (sec. 1998—), Coun. for Exceptional Children. Episcopalian. Achievements include creation of school for the handicapped in Roanoke; creation of first high school program for the multihandicapped in Lineville. Avocations:

tenor recorder, reading, singing in church choir. Home: 412 Forest Hill Rd Apalachin NY 13732 Office: Owego Apalachin Ctrl Schs Talcott St Owego NY 13827 E-mail: lcoppens@oagw.stier.org.

COPPERSMITH, SUSAN NAN, physicist; b. Johnstown, Pa., Mar. 18, 1957; d. Wallace Louis and Bernice Barbara (Evans) C.; m. Robert Daniel Blank, Dec. 20, 1981. BS in Physics, MIT, 1978; postgrad., Cambridge U., 1979; MS in Physics, Cornell U., 1981, PhD in Physics, 1983. Rsch. assoc. Brookhaven Nat. Labs., 1983-85; postdoctoral mem. tech. staff AT&T Bell Labs., Murray Hill, N.J., 1985-86, mem. tech. staff, 1987-90, disting. mem. tech. staff, 1990-95; prof. physics U. Chgo., 1995—. Vis. lectr. Princeton U., 1986-87; vis. professorship for women NSF, 1986-87; gen. mem. Aspen Ctr. for Physics, 1991—; chancellor's disting. lectr. U. Calif., Irvine, 1991. Trustee Aspen Ctr. for Physics, 1993-96. Winston Churchill scholar, 1978-79, Bell Labs. GRPW fellow, 1979-83. Fellow Am. Phys. Soc. Home: 1826 Camelot Dr Madison WI 53705-1008

COPPOCK, JANET ELAINE, mental health nurse; b. Tipton, Ind., June 2, 1954; d. Jack Donavon and Bonnie Ruth (Luse) Weismiller; divorced; children: Jonathan Andrew, Daniel Jason. Student, Ball State U., 1972-73; ASN, Ind. U., Kokomo, 1977. RN, Ind., Mich.; cert. psychiat./mental health nurse ANCC. RN charge staff and med.-surg. Tipton County Meml. Hosp., Ind., 1977-79; RN psychiat. staff Howard Cmty. Hosp., Kokomo, 1987-89; pvt. nurse Kokomo, 1989-95; RN psychiat. and addiction treatment, instr. Koala Hosp. & Counseling Ctr. Behavioral Healthcare Corp., Kokomo, 1995-98; RN psychiat. and addiction treatment Lafayette (Ind.) Behavioral Health System, 1998-99; RN psychiat. staff, patient care coord. Home Hosp. of Greater Lafayette Health Svcs., Inc., Lafayette, 1999—. Instr. parenting edn. Kinsey Youth Ctr., Kokomo, 1995-96; co-developer Koala Halfway House, Behavioral Healthcare Corp., Kokomo, 1996, house mgr., 1996-98. Author: Poetic Reflections, Expressions and Inspirations, 1986, Faithful Resolutions, 1993, Coming to Terms, 1998. Recipient Golden Poet award World Poetry Orgn., 1987, 88. Mem. Ind. State Nurses Assn., Internat. Platform Assn., Nurses Svc. Orgn., Writers' Ctr. Indpls., Ind. U. Alumni Assn. (life). Avocations: musical instruments, art, movies, basketball. Home: 2711 President Ln Kokomo IN 46902-3066

COPPOCK, KRISTEN ANNE K. newswriter, editor; d. Earl Hamilton and Anita Marie Coppock. Bachelor's, Rowan U., 1997. News clk. The Record, Hackensack, NJ, 1996—98; freelance writer, 1997—; staff writer and teen editor Burlington County Times, Willingboro, NJ, 1998—. Sales assoc. Macy's, Cherry Hill, NJ, 2001—. Vol. Bergen County Girl Scouts, NJ, 2003; advisor for explorers Burlington County Boy Scouts, Willingboro, 1998—99; vol. Rep. Nat. Conv., Phila., 2000. Mem.: Celine Sprue Assn., N.J. Press Assn. (2d Pl. award for best features portfolio 1999). Office: Burlington County Times 4284 Rte 130 Willingboro NJ 08046

COPPOLA, SARAH JANE, special education educator; b. Alton, Ill., Apr. 20, 1957; d. Howard Earl and Dorothy Elizabeth (Eads) Cox; m. Daniel Joseph Coppola Jr., June 26, 1977; children: Daniel Joseph III, Shawn Marie. BS, Trenton State Coll., 1979; M Counseling Edn., Kean Coll. of N.J., 1995. Cert. guidance counselor, substance abuse counselor, N.J., early childhood cert., CIE coop. coord. cert. 1998, WECEP cert. Substitute tchr. Dunellen (N.J.) Bd. Edn., 1979-87, Greenbrook (N.J.) Bd. Edn., 1979-87, Middlesex (N.J.) Bd. Edn., 1979-87, Bound Brook (N.J.) Bd. Edn., 1983-84; tchr. of handicapped Piscataway (N.J.) Bd. Edn., 1987—, prin. adv. bd., 1990-91, editl. yearbook advisor, 1998—. Youth group advisor Trinity Reformed Ch., North Plainfield, N.J., 1983-91, deacon, 1985-87, 2001—, elder, 1997-2001, head Christian Edn., 1997—, v.p. consistory, 2000. Mem. NEA, N.J. Edn. Assn., Piscataway Edn. Assn., Kean Coll. Alumni Assn. (vol. Fish Hospitality program). Avocations: reading, needlework, church choir. Home: 200 Barclay Ct Piscataway NJ 08854 Office: Piscataway Bd Edn 100 Behmer Rd Piscataway NJ 08854-4161 Office Phone: 732-981-0700 7130. E-mail: sarahjcoppola@yahoo.com.

COPPOLA, SOFIA CARMINA, film director, scriptwriter, actress; b. N.Y.C., May 1971; d. Francis Ford and Eleanor Coppola; m. Spike Jonze, 1999. Intern with Karl Lagerfield Chanel; designer Milk Fed. Actor: (films) The Godfather, 1972, The Godfather: Part II, 1974, The Outsiders, 1983, Rumble Fish, 1983, The Cotton Club, 1984, Frankenweenie, 1984, Peggy Sue Got Married, 1986, Anna, 1987, The Godfather: Part III, 1990, Inside Monkey Zetterland, 1992, Star Wars: Episode I-The Phantom Menace, 1999, CQ, 2001; dir., prodr., screenwriter (films) Lick the Star, 1998, Lost in Translation, 2003 (Golden Athena, Athens Intl. Film Festival, 2003, Boston Soc. of Film Critics award for best dir., 2003, Nat. Bd. of Review award for special achievement, 2003, NY Film Critics Circle award for best dir., 2003, Toronto Film Critics Assoc. award for best screenplay, 2003, Golden Globe for best screenplay, 2004, Academy award for best screenplay, 2004), dir., screenwriter The Virgin Suicides, 1999, host (TV series) Hi-Octane, 1994, segment writer N.Y. Stories, 1989, costume designer, 1989, series creator Platinum, 2003, writer, 2003; exec. prodr.: (TV series) Platinum, 2003; costume designer (plays) The Spirit of '76, 1990. Office: c/o William Morris Agy 1325 Avenue of the Americas New York NY 10019*

COPPS, SHEILA, former Canadian government official; b. Hamilton, Ont., Can., Nov. 27, 1952; d. Victor Kennedy and Geraldine (Guthro) C.; m. Austin Thorne; 1 child, Danelle. BA in French, English with hons., U. Western Ont., London; postgrad., U. Rouen, France, McMaster U., Hamilton. Reporter Ottawa Citizen, 1974-76, Hamilton Spectator, 1977; asst. to Ont. Liberal leader Stuart Smith, Hamilton, 1977-81; mem. Legis. Assembly Ont., Toronto, 1981-84, House of Commons, Ottawa, 1984-97; apptd. dep. leader Liberal Party Can., Ottawa, Ont., 1990—; dep. prime min. Govt. of Can., Ottawa, 1993-97, min. environ., 1993-96, min. of Can. heritage, 1996—2003. Author: Nobody's Baby, 1986. Mem. Liberal Party. Office: House of Commons Rm 509-S Ottawa ON Canada K1A 0A6 also: 275 Queenston Rd L8K 1G9 Hamilton ON Canada

CORAZA, MARY CATHERINE, psychologist; b. Newton, N.J. d. Alfred J. and Alice (Reynolds) C. Student, Lehigh U., 1970. Psychologist Pa. Hosp., Phila., 1980—; asst. prof. Univ. Pa. Med. Sch., Phila., 1991—. Cons. Phila. Dept. of Welfare and Human Svcs. Bd. dirs. Fitler Square Improvement Assn., Phila., 1987—; vol. Phila. Mus. of Art. Mem. APA, Pa. Psychol. Assn., Phila. Soc. Clin. Psychologists (bd. dirs. 1997—), Phila. Soc. of Clin. Psychologist (bd. dirs.), Psi Chi. Home: 2031 Locust St Apt 502 Philadelphia PA 19103-5693

CORBATO, EMILY S. photographer, researcher, musician; b. Brooklyn, NY, July 2, 1941; d. Sidney Joshua Gluck and Selma Epstein Abraham (deceased), Irving Abraham (deceased) (Stepfather); m. Fernando J. Corbato, Dec. 6, 1975; stepchildren: Carolyn Suzanne, Nancy Patricia; m. Herbert Gish, Sept. 6, 1961 (div. 1973); children: David Lawrence Gish, Jason Charles Gish. MusB, Syracuse U., Syracuse, New York, 1958—62; MusM performance, New Eng. Conservatory of Music, Boston, Mass., 1963—65. Tchr. of piano ind., Boston, 1962—95, concert pianist throughout USA, Boston based, Mass., 1970—, photographer Boston, 1996—; women's studies rsch. ctr., scholar Brandeis U., Waltham, Mass., 2001—. Pres., v.p., bd. mem. Am. Women Composers, Boston, 1985—95; v.p. Ernst Bacon Soc., Boston, 1995—; bd. mem. Firehouse Ctr. for the Arts, Newburyport, Mass., 1998—2001. Musician (pianist): (solo recitals - works by women) Concert Performance; exhibits, Black And White Photography. Grantee Rsch. Grant, Hadassah Internat. Rsch. Inst. on Women at Brandeis U., 2001. Avocation: tennis. Home: 88 Temple Street West Newton MA 02465 Office: Women's Studies Rsch Ctr Brandeis Univ Mailstop 079 Waltham MA 02454

CORBET, KATHLEEN A. diversified financial services company executive; b. Feb. 22, 1960; BS in mktg. and computer sci., Boston Coll.; MBA in fin., NYU. Chief investment opers. and global trading Alliance Capital, 1997—99, chmn., 1998—2000, 1998—2000; CEO Alliance Capital Ltd., London, 1998—2000; CEO fixed income divsn. Alliance Capital Mgmt., 2000—04; pres. Standard & Poor's, 2004—. Mem. bd. trustees Boston Coll. Mem.: Coun. Fgn. Rels. Office: Standard & Poor's 55 Water St New York NY 10041*

CORBETT, ALICE CATHERINE, investor; d. Marshal Richard and Coralyn Estelle Reckard; BS, U. Oreg., 1943. Tchr. Portland (Oreg.) Dept. Edn., 1944—47; mem. Oreg. Senate, Salem, 1950—58; commr. Multnomah County, Portland, 1964—68; investor Portland, 1964—. Mem.: Multnomah Club. Home: 1509 NE 24th Ave Portland OR 97232

CORBETT, CHANDA CARMELA, psychologist; b. Phila., Dec. 11, 1970; d. James Edward and Elizabeth Corbett. BA in Psychology, Lincoln U., 1992; MEd in Human Svcs., Lehigh U., 1994; PhD in Counseling Psychology, Temple U., 1998. Lic. psychologist N.H., 2000. Intern U. Memphis, 1997—98; behavioral specialist Phila. (Pa.) Mental Health Ctr., 1999, Devereaux, Phila., 1999; staff psychologist U. N.H., Durham, NH, 1999—; prin., owner Restoration Empowering Svcs. PLLC, Durham, 2001—. Resident dir. Semester at Sea, Pitts., 1998, religion coord., 98. Contbr. articles to profl. jours. Recipient Rising Star award, Lincoln U., 1999. Mem.: Am. Psychol. Assn., Am. Coll. Personnel Assn. (chmn. membership com.). Avocations: travel, crafts, bargain shopping. Office: University of New Hampshire 8 Garrison Durham NH 03824 Office Phone: 603-862-2090. Business E-Mail: chanda-corbett@hotmail.com.

CORBETT, ELLEN M. mayor; BS in Polit. Sci., U. Calif., Davis; JD McGeorge Law Sch., U. Pacific. Mem. San Leandro (Calif.) City Coun., 1990-94; mayor City of San Leandro, 1994—98; mem. Calif. Ho. of Reps., 1999—. Co-chair U.S. Conf. Mayors Police Policy Bd.; bd. dirs. Alameda County Econ. Devel. Adv. Bd. Co-chair San Leandro Partnership for Youth Safety. Office: PO Box 942849 Sacramento CA 94249

CORBETT, HELEN A. chemist, chemical engineer; b. Berkeley Springs, W.Va., Jan. 28, 1972; d. Harry Ralph and Florence Louise Barker; m. James Jay Corbett, Nov. 6, 1996. BS, Towson U., 1995. Lab. tech. State Hwy. Adminstrn., Hancock, Md., 1990-96; R&D chemist Garden State Tanning, Inc., Williamsport, Md., 1996-99; plant process engr. Rust-Oleum Corp., Hagerstown, Md., 1999—. Mem. Am. Chem. Soc., Fedn. Socs. for Coatings Tech. Episcopalian. Avocations: reading, walking. Home: 1051 Lindsay Ln Hagerstown MD 21742-4612 Office: Rust-Oleum Corp PO Box 1008 Hagerstown MD 21741-1008

CORBETT, LENORA MEADE, mathematician, community college educator; b. Reidsville, N.C., Aug. 1, 1950; children: Kenneth Russell Johnson, Ralph Nathaniel Brown. AAS in Electromechanics, Tech. Coll. of Alamance, 1985, AAS in Electronics, 1986; BS in Indsl. Tech., Electronics, N.C. A&T State U., 1996. Cloth insp. Burlington (N.C.) Industries, 1971-74; electrician's helper Williams Electric, Greensboro, NC, 1978, Nobility Mobile Homes, Reidsville, NC, 1979; instr. math. and physics Alamance C.C., Graham, NC, 1985—2002, chmn. learning resources, 1993. Contbr. poems to profl. publs. (Golden Poet award 1991, Merit award 1990, 92). Mem. ch. choir Jones Cross Rd. Ch., Reidsville, 1988-94, pastor's aide mem., 1988-90, jr. Sunday sch. tchr., 1989-91, asst. choir sec., 1988-94; bd. dirs. Nu Generation Enrichment Program; mem. bd. Nu Generation Enrichment Ctr., Teach Tolerance Nat. Campaign Tolerance, 2002, 03. Recipient Famous Poet, 1996, 2000, Editor's Choice Award, 1997, Famous Poets So. Recognition award, 1998. Mem. AAUP, AAUW, Alamance C.C. Alumni Assn., Golden Key, N.C. A&T State U. Alumni Assn. Baptist. Avocations: cooking, reading, writing poetry, drawing, singing.

CORBETT, SIOBHAN AIDEN, surgeon; b. Aug. 11, 1959; Diplomate Am. Bd. Surgery. Postdoctoral fellow Princeton (N.J.) U.; asst. prof. surg. scis. Robert Wood Johnson Med. Sch., New Brunswick, N.J., 1997—. Recipient Clin. Sci. award Am. Heart Assn., 1995-96. Address: Clin Acad Bldg 125 Paterson St New Brunswick NJ 08901-1962 Office: 1 Robert Wood Johnson Pl New Brunswick NJ 08901-1928

CORBETT, SUZANNE ELAINE, food writer, marketing executive, food historian; b. St. Louis, Jan. 23, 1953; d. George Edward and Opal Laverne (Duncan) Traxel; m. James Joseph Corbett, Jr., July 17, 1970 (div. 2000); 1 child, James J. III. BA, Webster U., 1994, MA in Media Comm., 1995. Cert. culinary profl., Internat. Assn. Culinary Profls. Tchr. Inst. Continuing Edn. St. Louis C.C., 1976—; tchr. cmty. edn. Lindbergh Sch. Dist. Pub. Schs., St. Louis, 1983-89; confectioner/caterer Suzanne Corbett Seasonal Confections, St. Louis, 1977-84; test baker Fleishman's Yeast, St. Louis, 1983; food stylist St. Louis, 1980—; rsch. cons./food mktg. and rsch. food/product history, 1994; rsch. cons. media prodn. PanCor Prodns., 1994—. Food historian, folklorist Jefferson Nat. Parks Assn., St. Louis County Parks and Recreation, Mo. Hist. Soc., St. Louis Art Mus., Colonial Dames of Am.; food media trainer Internat. Assn. Culinary Profls., 1990; ALFHM lectr. in field. Author: Cowpuncher's Provision, 1988, River Fare, 1990, Pharoh's Pheast-Food from the Nile, 1991, Tips from Missouri Win Country, 1993, Pushcarts & Stalls: The Souland Market History Cookbook, 1999; food writer, cookbook editor St. Louis Bugle food editor, 1991-96, columnist, 1991-96; columnist Sr. Circuit Newspaper; food writer, columnist News Weekly, Connoisseur; contbg. food editor St. Louis Home & Lifestyles, Achieve Mag. Bd. dirs. St. Louis South sect. Am. Heart Assn., Historyonics Theatre Co.; mem. Mo. Grape and Wine Adv. Bd. Recipient Folklife Greentree grant award Ralston Purina, 1989, grant award Commerce Bank, 1990, grant award Wetterau Foods, 1991. Mem. Women in Communications (pres. St. Louis chpt. 1996, Communication awards 1989, 90, 91, 92, 93, 94, 95, 96, 97, 98, 99), Nat. Fedn. Press Women (v.p. Mo. chpt.), Mo. Press Women (past pres., Communication award 1989, 96, 97, Communicator of Yr. 1993), Victorian Soc. Am. (past pres. St. Louis chpt.), James Beard Found. (charter), Am. Inst. Wine and Food, Internat. Assn. Culinary Profls. (cert., culinary historian Boston and Ann Arbor, internat. conf. com. 1990), Assn. Ind. Video and Filmmakers, St. Louis Press Club (former co-editor Courier, interim dir., Pres.' award, Press Club Charitable Fund pres. 1993-94), Nat. Fedn. Press Women (Communication and Writing awards), Nat. Trust for Hist. Preservation, St. Louis Culinary Soc. (sec., bd. dirs.), Order Eastern Star. Roman Catholic. Avocations: folklife crafts, gardening, travel, historic preservation. Home and Office: Apt B 12150 Queens Charter Ct Saint Louis MO 63146-5250 E-mail: corbettsuzanne@aol.com.

CORBI, LANA, communications executive; Sr. v.p. network distbn. Fox Broadcasting Co., 1994—95, exec. v.p. network distbn., 1996—97, pres. network distbn., 1997—99; pres., COO Blackstar, L.L.C., 1995—96; COO Odyssey Holdings, 1999—2000; exec. v.p., COO Crown Media Holdings, 2000—01; CEO Hallmark Channel, Coral Gables, Fla., 2001—. Office: Hallmark Channel 260 Crandon Blvd #32-77 Miami FL 33149-1536

CORBIERE, MARY LOUISE SAMBATARO, music educator, musician; b. Lawrence, Mass., Dec. 12, 1942; d. Louis John Sambataro and Geneva Mary Cascone; m. Paul Arthur Corbiere, Nov. 9, 1963 (div. July 7, 1995); children: Paul, Arthur, Geneva, Jacqueline. MusB, U. of Miami, Coral Gables, FL, 1960—65, MA iin Music Edn., 1982—85. Cert. tchr. Fla., 1965. Music tchr. Pine Ridge Elem. Sch., Fort Lauderdale, Fla., 1965—70, Sungate Acad., Hollywood, Fla., 1973—76, Cooper City (Fla.) Elem. Sch., 1976—90; music tchr. and magnet coord. Bethune Performing Arts Magnet, Hollywood, 1990—98; music tchr. Fox Trail Elem. Sch., Davie, 1998—2001, Pembroke Pines Charter H.S., 2001—. Dir. of music St. Bernadette Cath. Ch., Davie, 1977—89; parish dir. of music St. Mark Cath. Ch., S.W. Ranches, Fla., 1990—. Recipient Tchr. of Yr., Cooper City Elem. Sch., 1982, Bethune Elem. Performing Arts Magnet, 1985, Fox Trail Elem. Sch., 2000, Master Tchr. award, State of Fla., 1985. Mem.: Music Educators Nat. Conf., Fla. Music Educators Assn., Broward County Elem. Music Tchrs. Assn., St. Mark Women's Club. Roman Catholic. Avocations: children and grandchildren, entertaining, visiting, baking, sports. Office: Pembroke Pines Charter HS 17189 Sheridan Street Pembroke Pines FL 33331 E-mail: mcorbiere@pinescharter.com.

CORBIN, ROSEMARY MACGOWAN, former mayor; b. Santa Cruz, Calif., Apr. 3, 1940; d. Frederick Patrick and Lorena Maude (Parr) MacGowan; m. Douglas Tenny Corbin, Apr. 6, 1968; children: Jeffrey, Diana. BA, San Francisco State U., 1961; MLS, U. Calif., Berkeley, 1966. Libr. Stanford (Calif.) U., 1966-68, Richmond (Calif.) Pub. Libr., 1968-69, Kaiser Found. Health Plan, Oakland, Calif., 1976-81, San Francisco Pub. Libr., 1981-82, U. Calif., Berkeley, 1982-83; mem. coun. City of Richmond, 1985-93, vice mayor, 1986-87, mayor, 1993—2001. Mem. Solid Waste Mgmt. Authority, 1985-2001, Contra Costa Hazardous Materials Commn., Martinez, Calif., 1987-2001, San Francisco Bay Conservation and Devel. Commn., 1987-2001; mem. League of Calif. Cities Environ. Affairs Com., 1994-2001; mem. energy and environ. com. U.S. Conf. Mayors and Nat. League of Cities, 1993-2001. Contbr. articles to profl. publs. Mem. Rosie the Riveter Trust Bd., San Francisco Bay Trail Bd. Mem. LWV, NOW, Nat. Women's Polit. Caucus, Calif. Libr. Assn., Sierra Club, Inst. Local Self Govt. (pres.). Democrat. Avocations: reading, hiking, golf, quilting, gardening. Home: 114 Crest Ave Richmond CA 94801-4031

CORBINE ESPINOSA, JUANITA GRACE, cultural association administrator; b. Pine Ridge, S.D., Sept. 27, 1956; d. Melvin William and Philomene (Peltier) Corbine; m. Edward Paul Espinosa, Jan. 14, 1978 (div. 1979), children: Adonijah Edward Espinosa, Demetrius Paul Espinosa, Wastewin Margareta Patrice Gonzalez, Wakinyan Adelita Sandoval. AA, Mpls. C.C., 1985. Dir. Native Arts Ctr.; program dir. Native Am. Cultural Arts Program, COMPAS, Inc.; organizer People of Phillips, Mpls.; team leader Career Assessment Ctr., Heart of the Earth Survival Sch.; cmty. educator N.Am. Water Office, cooperative organizer, office mgr. Womanswork Diversified Arts; cons. Alliance Cultural Democracy, 1988-89, Lerner Pubs., 1990, Minn. Hist. Soc., 1992. Interim editor The Cir., co-prodr. Honor the Grandmothers, 1993. Bd. dirs. Mpls. Am. Indian Ctr., 1983—, Alley Newspaper, 1989-93, Alliance Cultural Democracy, 1992-97; adv. mem. McKnight Neighborhood Self Help Initiatives Program Found., 1987-92; pres. In the City Arts, 1990—; mem. grants com. Headwater Fund, 1992-94; pres., 2d circle bd. dirs. Atlah, 1996. Recipient McKnight Human Svc. award, 1985; Jerome Travel grantee, 1992. Avocations: beading, sewing, community radio voice work. Office: Native Arts Circle 3121 Elliot Ave Minneapolis MN 55407-1507 Office Phone: 612-879-1780.

CORBIN WALKER, KAROL, lawyer; b. Jersey City, Oct. 11, 1958; BA cum laude, N.J. City U., 1980; JD, Seton Hall U., 1986. Bar: N.J. 1986, N.Y. 1991, U.S. Dist. Ct. N.J. 1986, U.S. Dist. Ct. (so. and ea. dists.) N.Y. 1987, U.S. Dist. Ct. (no. dist.) N.Y. 1994, U.S. Ct. Appeals (3d cir.) 1991, U.S. Supreme Ct. 1993. Jud. law clk. to Hon. Davis S. Baime, Superior Ct. N.J., Appellate Divsn., 1986—87; adj. prof. law Seton Hall U. Sch. Law, 1988—90; atty. St. John & Wayne, LLC, Newark. Mem. adv. bd. Salvation Army Morristown Corps; active United Way of Essex and West Hudson. Mem.: ABA, Assn. Fed. Bar of State of N.J., Nat. Bar Assn. (treas. 1994—96, sec. divsn. ptnrs. in majority law firms 1999—2002, sec. 1998—99, 2d vice chair 1999—2002, comml. law sect. 1st vice chair 2002—), Garden State Bar Assn. (trustee 1989—91, pres. 1991—93), Essex County Bar Assn. (Young Lawyers divsn. exec. bd. 1990—92, chair minorities in profession com. 1991—93, chair continuing legal edn. com. 1993—97, trustee 1994—97), Morris County Bar Assn., N.J. State Bar Assn. (Young Lawyers divsn. exec. bd. 1990—93, chair minorities in profession com. 1991—93, trustee 1995—99, chair diversity com. 1997—98, chair jud. and prosecutorial appointments com. 1998—99, sec. 1999—2000, treas. 2000—01, 2d v.p. 2001—02, 1st v.p. 2002, pres.-elect 2002—03), Phi Alpha Delta. Office: St John and Wayne LLC 2 Penn Plz E Newark NJ 07105-2249

CORBITT, ANN MARIE, municipal official; b. Jersey City, N.J., Nov. 28, 1966; d. Andrew M. and Maria Gisondi; m. Frederick William Corbitt, Sept. 18, 1988; children: Frederick Francis, Benjamin Brandon. Cert. Tax Collector, Rutgers U., 1988. Cert. fire fighter. Work study program in tax office Twp. of Parsippany, N.J., 1983-84, acct. clk. tax office, 1984-87, sr. acct. clk., 1987-88, dep. tax collector, 1988-94; tax collector Twp. Morris, N.J., 1994-99, City of East Orange, N.J., 1999—. Vol. Denville Fire Dept., 1992—, firefighter, 1997—. Mem. Essex County Tax Collectors Assn., Tax Collectors and Treasurers N.J. Republican. Roman Catholic. Avocations: camping, fishing, outdoor activities. Office: 44 City Hall Plz East Orange NJ 07017-4104

CORBITT, EUMILLER MATTIE, elementary and secondary education educator, special education educator; b. Detroit, Jan. 07; d. Harrison and Arnetha (Tatum) Jones; m. Luther Corbitt (div. Dec. 1976); children: Tonya, Stephen. BS, Wayne State U., 1969, MEd, 1976, EdS, 1995. Cert. elem. and secondary sch. tchr., cert. tchr. spl. edn. emotionally and mentally impaired, grades K-12, elem. secondary sch. and central office administration. Tchr. mentally impaired Detroit Pub. Schs., 1969-72, tchr. emotionally impaired, 1972-75, spl. edn. tchr. cons., 1975—, Title I tchr. math. and sci., summers 1993-96; mediator Spl. Edn. Mediation Svcs., Lansing, Mich., 1986-96, Spl. Edn. Mediation Svcs. State Project PL 94-142, Lansing, Mich., 1985—; spl. edn. hearing officer Mich. Dept. Edn., Lansing, 1985—. Developer at-risk program for emotionally impaired, socially maladjusted and ADHD students 12-17 yrs. Wolverine Human Svcs., Detroit, Mich. 1998—; mem. U.S. del. educators and attys. to South Africa for evaluation of schs. and govtl. agys. under leadership of Nelson Mandella Citizen Amb. program People to People, Spokane, Wash., 1996; mem. citizens alliance to uphold spl. edn. study adv. com. Emotionally Impaired Children in Mich./Lansing, 1986; mem. North Ctrl. Assn. accreditation com. Grand Rapids (Mich.) Pub. Schs., 1981; presenter profl. devel. conf. Detroit Fedn. Tchrs. and Det. Pub. Sch. Adminstrs., 1996. Chairperson Met. Detroit chpt. March of Dimes, 1987; chairperson Women Who Dare to Care com. United Negro Coll. Fund, Detroit, 1987-89; gen. coord. Mus. African Am. History, Detroit, 1987; tutor, usher, chairperson Hartford Meml. Bapt. Ch., Detroit, 1979—. Recipient Mayor's award of merit for Cmty. Svc., City of Detroit, 1987, plaque and cert. March of Dimes, 1987; recognized as outstanding educator Detroit Tchr., Detroit Fedn. Tchrs., 1987, 94. Mem. Coun. for Exceptional Children (presenter nat. conv. 1983, cert. 1983), Soc. Profls. in Dispute Resolution, Wayne State U. Alumni Assn., Delta Sigma Theta (chairperson 1965—), Phi Delta Kappa (chairperson). Avocations: golf, writing poetry, racquetball, painting, reading. Home: 1249 Navarre Pl Detroit MI 48207-3014 Office: Martin Luther King Jr Sr HS 3200 E Lafayette Detroit MI 48207 E-mail: eumillercorbitt@aol.com.

CORCORAN, BARBARA, real estate company executive; b. Edgewater, N.J. m. Dale Barlow, 1979 (div.); m. Bill Higgins, 1988; 1 child, Thomas. BA in English and Theology, St. Thomas Aquinas Coll.; Doctorate (hon.), Marymount Coll. Founder Corcoran Group, N.Y.C., 1973—80, founder, chmn., 1980—; founder Corcoran Wexler Healthcare Properties, Corcoran Comml. Investments, Corcoran Group Mktg. Instr. NYI. Author: If You Don't Have Big Breasts, Put Ribbons in Your Pigtails, 2003, Use What You've Got: And Other Business Lessons I Learned From Mom, 2003, (newsletter) Corcoran Report, 1981—. Former chair N.Y. chpt. Young Pres. Orgn.; former bd. govs. Real Estate Bd. N.Y. Office: Corcoran Group 660 Madison Ave New York NY 10021

CORCORAN, DENISE MARIE (LACEY), music educator; b. Sayre, Pa., May 26, 1976; d. John Earl and Diane Marie (Vergason) Lacey; m. Jeremy Michael Corcoran, Aug. 19, 2000. MusB in Music Edn., Ithaca Coll., N.Y., 1998; MS in Music Edn., Syracuse U., N.Y., 2000. Cert. music tchr. N.Y. Musician, 1994—; saxophone tchr., 1994—; music tchr. Vestal Mid. Sch., NY, 2000— [illegible] Music Educators Assn., Music Educator's Nat. Conf., N.Y. State Sch. Music Assn., N.Y. State Mid. Sch. Assn., Phi Kappa Phi. Methodist. Avocations: genealogy, cross country skiing.

CORCORAN, JANET PATRICIA, elementary school educator; b. St. Louis, Feb. 9, 1949; d. Oliver Albert Schuh and Eleanor Louise Schottel; m. Gregory Edward Corcoran, Aug. 29, 1970; children: Kelly, Bryan, Terence, Jason. BS in Secondary Edn., U. Ill., 1971; MA in Specific Learning Disabilities, Marycrest Coll., 1983. Nat. bd. cert. tchr. Tchr. Antioch (Ill.) Schs., 1971—72, Belvidere (Ill.) Schs., 1974—75, Davenport (Iowa) Schs., 1980—. Bd. dirs., sec. Scott County Hist. Preservation Soc., Davenport, 1995—2003; del. Nat. Dem. Conv., N.Y.C., 1992. Mem.: AAUW (scholarship chmn. 1993—2001), NEA (conv. del. 1990—2003), Davenport Edn. Assn. (local rep. 1983—2003). Democrat. Roman Catholic. Home: 4407 N Linwood Davenport IA 52806 Office: JB Young Mid Sch Davenport IA 52806

CORCORAN, MAUREEN ELIZABETH, lawyer; b. Iowa City, Feb. 4, 1944; d. Joseph and Velma (Tobin) C. BA in English with honors, U. Iowa, 1966, MA in English, 1967; JD, Hastings Coll. of Law, San Francisco, 1979. Bar: Calif. 1979, D.C. 1988, U.S. Ct. Appeals (9th cir.), 1979, U.S. Dist. Ct. (no. dist.) Calif., 1979, U.S. Dist. Ct. (cen. dist.) Calif., 1979, U.S. Ct. Appeals (D.C. cir.) 1983. Assoc. Hassard Bonnington Rogers & Huber, San Francisco, 1979-81; spl. asst. to gen. counsel HHS, Washington, 1981-83; assoc. Weissburg & Aronson, San Francisco, 1983-84; gen. counsel U.S. Dept. Edn., Washington, 1984-86; ptnr. Pillsbury Winthrop LLP (and predecessor firms), San Francisco, 1987-; bd. dirs. Hastings Coll. Law U. Calif., San Francisco, 1993—, chmn., 1998-2000. Chmn. Managed Health Care Conf., 1989; mem. AIDS adv. com. Ctrs. for Disease Control, 1989-91; spkr. health law mtgs. Author: (book) Managed Care Contracting: Advising the Managed Care Organization, 1996; contbr. articles on health law to profl. jours. Mem. U.S. delegation to 1985 World Conf. to Review and Appraise Achievements of UN Decade for Women, Nairobi, Kenya, 1985; mem. Adminstrv. Conf. U.S., Washington, 1985. Mem. ABA (sect. health law), Calif. State Bar Assn., Am. Health Lawyers Assn. Office: Pillsbury Winthrop LLP Ste 1004 50 Fremont St San Francisco CA 94105

CORCORAN, NANCY HELEN, minister; b. Portsmouth, N.H., Dec. 19, 1944; d. Maurice Richard and Helen Clare (Warren) C. BA in govt., Regis Coll., Weston, Mass., 1966; M Theol. Studies, Harvard U., 1991. Tchr. St. Joseph's Sch., Waipahu, Hawaii, 1966-69, St. Agnes Sch., St. Louis, 1969-70, Holy Name Elem. Sch., St. Louis, 1971-77; tchr. art and sculpture Broome County (N.Y.) Cath. Schs., 1977-79; dir. ancillary svcs. Nazareth Home, St. Louis, 1979-82; dir. literacy ctr. Lowndes County Cath. Ctr., Hayneville, Ala., 1982-88, Excel, Okalona, Miss., 1988-89; campus min. Regina Dominican, Wilmette, Ill., 1991-97, Regis Coll., 1997—98; founding dir. grassroots Women's Spirituality Cttr., Newton, Mass., 1998—. Cons. anti-racism workshops; facilitator cultural diversity workshops; facilitator and presenter feminist spirituality/preaching retreats. Contbr. articles to profl. jours. Literacy trainer Laubach Literacy, 1986; leader Alternative Spring Break, Ozarks, 1995—. Mem. Am. Acad. of Religion. Roman Catholic. Avocations: retreat directing, preaching. Office: Grass Roots Womens Spirituality Ctr PO Box 67511 Newton MA 02467 Office Phone: 617-969-2720.

CORDEIRO, ELIZABETH DALEIN, law enforcement training educator; b. New Bedford, Mass., Oct. 18, 1958; children: Vincent, Lisa. AS in Criminal Justice, Bristol C.C., 1979; BS in Adminstrn. of Criminal Justice, Roger Williams Coll., 1982. Court transp. officer New Bedford 3rd Dist. Ct., 1980-81; police officer U.S. Dept. Defense Police, Mass. and R.I., 1981-86; corrections officer S.E. Correctional Ctr., Bridgewater, Mass., 1986-87; police instr. Police Survival Def. Tactics Tng., New Bedford, 1987—. Specialized training include Training Rsch. Validation, 1989, Use of Force Reporting Systems, 1989, Monadnock PR-24 Police Baton instr., 1988, Court Room Survival, 1989, Edges Weapon Defense, 1989, Street Survival, 1982-87 and others. Author: Who's Who in Law Enforcement Collecting and Police Trainers, 1988; editor, pub.: Who's Who in Law Enforcement Institutes and Schools, Trainers, and Training Organizations, 1995, 2d edit., 1999—, Who's Who in Law Enforcement Trainers, 2d edit., 1999-2000. Office: Police Survival Def Tactics PO Box 6454 New Bedford MA 02742-6454

CORDELL, BEULAH FAYE, special education educator; b. Clifty, Ark., Mar. 5, 1939; m. Jack Cordell; children: Dennis, Kevin. B in English and Social Studies, U. Ark., 1987, M in Spl. Edn. and Reading, 1994. Cert. tchr. K-12, Ark. Tchr. Benton County Alternative Sch., Rogers, Ark., 1988-90, Job Tng. Partnership Act at Fayetteville, Ark., 1990-91; reading and study skills tchr. N.W. Ark. C.C., Rogers, 1991-94; dir. spl. edn. tutoring The One-Room Sch., Springdale, 1993—; kindergarten tchr. Springdale, 1994-96; tchr. ESL and GED N.W. Tech. Inst., 1996—. Contbg. writer The Mailbox Mag., 1999—; author & illus. Pinky's Family, 2001, The Christmas Coloring Book, Pinky's Coloring Book, The Artist's Coloring Book, 2001. Bd. dirs. Ozark Literacy, Inc., Fayetteville, 1984-90; contbg. mem. Beaver Lake Lit., Inc., Rogers, 1994—. Recipient Tchg. Excellence award Gamma Beta Phi, 1993, Outstanding Achievement cert. Internat. Biog. Inst., Cambridge, Eng., 1998. Mem. Coun. for Exceptional Children, Am. Assn. Mentally Retarded, Poets and Writers Assn., Am. Biog. Inst. (rsch. bd. of advisors 1999). Avocations: oil painting, writing poetry and children's fiction. Home: 1100 N Monitor Rd Springdale AR 72764-9024 Office: 807 C Bailey St Springdale AR 72764-4247

CORDELL, JOANN MEREDITH, music educator; b. Memphis, Tenn., Jan. 16, 1952; d. Lena Clark Hurd; m. Ronald Eugene Cordell, Sept. 24, 1976; children: David Chadwick, Andrea Kristin. BS, U. Memphis, 1975; BA in Vocal Performance, U. Charleston, 1998. Cert. Orff Music Level 1 U. Memphis, 1998, Kodaly Level 1 Colorada Coll., 1997, Kindermusik Kindermusik Internat., 1996, tchr.spl. edn. Nat. Tchr. Assn. Spl. edn. tchr. Memphis City Sch. Sys., Memphis, 1975—81; children's music dir. St. Matthew's Episcopal Ch., Charleston, W.Va., 1993—96, St. Anthony Cath. Sch., Charleston, W.Va., 1997—2001, Christ Ch. United Meth., Charleston, W.Va., 1997—2000; Kindermusik instr. Bapt. Temple Ch., Charleston, W.Va., 1999—; founder/artistic dir. WomanSong Chorale, Charleston, W.Va., 1997—; assoc. dir. Appalachian Children's Chorus, Charleston, W.Va., 2000—; music instr. leap program Kanawha County Schs., Charleston, W.Va., 2000—02; coord. of soothing sounds music program for pregnant women and high risk teens Charleston Area Med. Ctr., Charleston, W.Va., 2001—. Creator Cantus Early Childhood Music Edn. Program Appalachian Children's Chorus, Charleston, W.Va., 2000—; music clinician arts camp Charleston Stage Co., Charleston, W.Va., 1999—; music clinician for Camp William U. of Charleston, Charleston, W.Va., 2003—. Dir.(artistic director): (choral performance) Kennedy Ctr. Performing Arts (womanSong Chorale chosen by jury to represent W.Va. at the nation's capitol for WV day, 2001). Campaign mgr. Com. to elect Nancy Kessel, Charleston, W.Va., 1993—97; state legis. chairperson W.Va. State Med. Alliance, W.Va., 1993—95; dir. of program to fundraise for W.Va. chpt. Susan G. Komen Assn. WomanSong, Charleston, W.Va., 2002; dir. of choral program to raise funds for Ronald McDonald Ho. of So. W.Va. WomanSong and Ronald McDonald Charities of So. W.Va., Charleston, W.Va., 2003; creator of children's early childhood music program Christ Ch. United Meth., Charleston, W.Va., 1990—2000; v.p. Jr. League of Charleston, Charleston, W.Va., 1990—91; mem. Cantori Montani Choral Ensemble, Charleston, W.Va., 1993—98. Grantee, W.Va. Humanities Found. and W.Va. Fund for the Arts, 2003. Mem.: Am. Guild Organists (bd. dirs. 2002—03), Music Educators Nat. Coun., Am. Orgn. Kodaly Educators, Am. Choral Dirs. Assn. (stds. and repertoir chmn. for women's choirs, W.Va. divsn. 2003—), W.Va. Orff Schulwerk Assn. [illegible] Democrat. United Methodist. Avocations: creating English gardens, reading, playing piano/autoharp, cooking, scuba diving.

CORDER, JAN BUSBY, nursing educator, university dean; BSN, U. La., Monroe, 1964; MSN, U. Miss., 1977; DSN, U. Ala., Birmingham, 1992. Asst. instr., then instr. Meth. Hosp. Sch. Nursing, Memphis, 1965-67, chmn. maternal-child nursing dept., 1967-70; coord., instr. dept. maternal-child nursing High Point (N.C.) Meml. Hosp., 1970; mgr. ob-gyn. dept. Bethesda Hosp., Cin., 1970-72; instr. nursing Northeast La. U., Monroe, 1972-76, asst. prof., 1984-90, assoc. prof., 1990-95, prof., 1996, assoc. dir. Sch. Nurisng, 1996, dir. sch. nursing, 1997-99, dean Coll. Nursing, 2000—. Pvt. practice childbirth educator, Monroe, 1977-80; part-time staff nurse Glenwood Regional Med. Ctr., West Monroe, La., 1986-87, St. Francis Med. Ctr., Monroe, 1988-89, North Monroe Cmty. Hosp., 1993; state edn. coord. Internat. Childbirth Edn. Assn., 1978, 89, 80; cons. for edn. Nursing Home Dirs. Assn., 1993. Contbr. articles to profl. jours. Mem. ANA, So. Nursing Rsch. Soc., La. State Nurses Assn., Monroe Dist. Nurses Assn., Monroe C. of C. (leadership coun. 1996-97), Am. Heart Assn., Northeast La. U. Nursing Honor Soc., Sigma Theta Tau (judge rsch. poster contest 1994-99). Office: U La 700 University Ave Monroe LA 71209-9000

CORDERO, MERCEDES PAULA, director, consultant; d. Juan Jose Gonzalez and Maria Teresa Vazquez; m. Ivan Francisco Gonzalez, Feb. 22, 1982; children: Teresa Mercedes, Luis Ivan. AA in Pre-Latin Am. Studies summa cum laude, Miami Dade C.C., Fla., 1978; BA in Internat. Rels. magna cum laude, Fla. Internat. U., 1980, MS in Tchg. English to Spkrs. of Other Lang., 1992; postgrad., Barry U., Miami Shores, Fla., 1996; EdS, Barry U., 1995, postgrad. instrl. tech. leadership. Cert. tchr. Fla., 1989. Comml. bank officer Consol. Bank NA, Hialeah, Fla., 1980—88; tchr. Miami-Dade Pub. Schs., Miami, Fla., 1988—97; site dir. Bolt, Beranek & Newman, Fla., 1997—98; site dir. Broward County Co-nect, Inc., Pembroke, Fla., 1998—2000, projects and partnership specialist, 2000—01, area mgr. S.E. Pembroke Pines, Fla., 2001—02, regional dir., south, 2002—. Author: (curriculum writing) Miami-Dade County Public Schools, ESOL Competency Based (CBC) Elementary Curriculum, Florida International University, Project FLASH (Family Literacy at School and Home Elementary Curriculum, Unit 8 Off Line Curriculum, Words on Wings, Jostens Learning. Named Tchr. of the Yr., Palm Springs North Elem. Sch., 1992; recipient Outstanding Alums award, Barry U., 1996. R-Consevative. Roman Catholic. Avocations: travel, creative writing, reading, home decorating, entertaining. Home: 18155 Sw 5 Ct Pembroke Pines FL 33029 Office: Co-nect Inc 625 Mt Auburn St Cambridge MA 02138 Office Phone: 954-663-9850. Personal E-mail: mcordero@aol.com. E-mail: mcordero@co-nect.net.

CORDES, LOVERNE CHRISTIAN, interior designer; b. Cleve., Feb. 13, 1927; d. Frank Andrew and Loverne Louise (Brown) Christian; m. William Peter Cordes, Nov. 14, 1959; children: Christian Peter, Carey Pomeroy. BS, Purdue U., 1949. Owner, mgr. Loverne Christian Cordes, Chagrin Falls, Ohio, 1967—. Tchr. John Carroll U., Cleve., 1976-77 Interior designer, Fred Epple Co., Cleve., 1949-67. Fellow AIA, Am. Soc. Interior Designers, Nat. Home Fashion League (past pres. Ohio chpt.), Am. Inst. Interior Designers (past pres. Ohio chpt., nat. bd. dirs. 1969-75, nat. v.p. East Central region 1972-75, nat. exec. bd. 1972-75, recipient 1st Presdl. citation 1973, 74, 75); mem. Soc. Collectors Dunham Tavern Mus. (bd. dirs. 1961-62), Dunham Dames (past pres.), Western Res. Hist. Soc., Cleve. Mus. Art, Cleve. Garden Center, Chagrin Falls Hist. Soc., Nat. Trust for Hist. Preservation, Internat. Platform Assn., Am. Furniture Collectors (bd. dirs. 1998—, decorative arts trust v.p. 1998), Audobon Soc., Confrérie de la Chaine des Rôtisseurs, Decorative Arts Trust Cleve. Cir.(pres. 2001-02), Wallkill Golf Club, Chagrin Valley Country Club, Dogwood Garden Club, Intown Club, Arcadian, Kappa Kappa Gamma. Republican. Congregationalist. Avocations: golf, cross country skiing, wine maker, calligraphy. Address: 60 S Franklin St Chagrin Falls OH 44022-3235

CORDOBA TAIT, ALICIA ROSE, music educator; b. Melrose Park, Ill., Dec. 15, 1962; d. John Leon and Virginia Rose Cordoba; m. Thomas Jeffrey Tait, Aug. 1, 1992 (div. Dec. 2000); 1 child, Mary Alicia Tait. MusB, U. Ill., 1985, MusM, 1986; D in Musical Arts, Julliard Sch., 1990. Freelance tchr., Chgo., 1992—; oboist Arbitrio, Lisle, Ill., 1999—; chair dept. fine and performing arts Benedictine U., Lisle, 2000—; prin. oboe Sinfonia Da Camera, Urbana, Ill., 2002—. Mem.: Coll. Music Soc., Music Educators Nat. Conf., Am. Fedn. Musicians, Internat. Double Reed Soc., Sigma Alpha Iota. Republican. Roman Catholic. Office: Benedictine U 5700 Coll Rd Lisle IL 60532

CORDOBES, DOROTHY ESKEW, art educator; b. Atlanta, Dec. 9, 1949; d. John Hardin and Dorothy Cortez McGarity Eskew; m. Richard Jonathan Cordobes, Oct. 15, 1989; 1 child, Briana Marie Dennis. BFA in Graphic Design, U. Ga., 1973. Cert. art edn. K-12 Ga. Graphic designer, office mgr. Crown Printing Co., Forest Park, Ga., 1973—98; art tchr. Henry County Bd. Edn., McDonough, Ga., 1998—. Mem.: Profl. Assn. Ga. Educators, Ga. Art Edn. Assn., Nat. Art Edn. Assn. Avocations: writing, poetry, drawing, painting, photography. Office: Pleasant Grove Elem Sch 150 Reagan Rd Stockbridge GA 30296

CORDOVA, MARIA ASUNCION, dentist; b. Punta Arenas, Magallanes, Chile, May 14, 1941; came to U.S., 1972; d. Miguel Cordova and Maria Asuncion Requena; m. Carlos F. Salinas, July 27, 1963; children: Carlos M., Claudio A., Lola. DDS, U. Chile, Santiago, 1965; DMD, Med. U. S.C., 1986. From instr. to assoc. prof. physiology U. Chile, Valparaiso, 1965—72; postdoctoral fellow Johns Hopkins U., Balt., 1972-75; from instr. to asst. prof. dept. physiology Med. U. S.C., Charleston, 1975—86; pvt. practice Charleston, 1986—. Vis. scientist N.Y. Med. Coll., 1975. Contbr. articles to profl. jours. V.p. Circulo Hispanic Charleston; country specialist Amnesty Internat. U.S.A., Spoleto, Charleston, mem. outreach com.; bd. dirs. YWCA, Trident Urban League, Robert Ivey Ballet, S.C. Humanities Coun., 1996—2002. Mem. Charleston Women's Network (pres. 1989-90). Roman Catholic. Office: 159 Wentworth St Charleston SC 29401-1731 Office Phone: 843-577-2898.

CORDY, JANE, Canadian senator; b. Sydney, Nova Scotia, Can., July 2, 1950; Tchg. cert., Nova Scotia Tchrs. Coll.; BEd, Mount Saint Vincent U. Tchr. Sydney Sch. Bd., Halifax County Sch. Bd., New Glasgow Sch. Bd., Halifax Regional Sch. Bd.; senator The Senate of Can., Ottawa, 2000—. Vice-chair Halifax-Dartmouth Port Devel. Commn.; chair bd. referees Halifax Region of Human Resources Devel. Can.; bd. dirs. Phoenix House; mem. judging com. Dartmouth Book Awards, 1993—95, 1999—2000; mem. strategic planning com. Colby Village Elem. Sch.; vol. religious edn. program St. Clement's Ch., Dartmouth. Liberal. Office: 314 Victoria Bldg The Senate of Canada Ottawa ON Canada K1A 0A4

CORE, MARY CAROLYN W. PARSONS, health facility administrator; b. Valpariso, Fla., Dec. 8, 1949; d. Levi and Mary Etta (Elliott) Willey; m. Joel Kent Core, Aug. 3, 1979; 1 child, Candace W. Parsons. Student, Peninsula Gen. Hosp. Sch. Radiologic Tech., Salisbury, Md., 1969; student, U. Del., 1969-73, Del. Tech. C.C., 1973-79, St. Joseph's Coll., 1983-86, BSBA, 1987; M in Gen. Adminstrn., U. Md., 1995. Cert. profl. in healthcare info. and mgmt. sys. Technologist Peninsula Gen. Hosp., Salisbury, 1967-72; tech. dir. edn. Sch. Radiologic Tech., Salisbury, 1973-75; technologist Johns Hopkins Hosp., Salisbury, 1972-73, Nanticoke Meml. Hosp., Seaford, Del., 1975-79; adminstrv. chief technologist, imaging depts. Shady Grove Adventist Hosp., Rockville, Md., 1979-81; dir. dept. radiol. scis. Anne Arundel Diagnostics, Inc., Annapolis, Md., 1981-92; COO Anne Arundel MRI (Magnetic Resonance Imaging), Annapolis, Md., 1985-92; CEO [illegible] Diagnostics, Inc. and Anne Arundel MRI, Annapolis, Md., 1987-92; v.p. corp. svcs. Anne Arundel Healthcare Systems, Inc., 1992-2001, v.p. strategic planning, 2001—04; v.p. corp. svcs. Civista Health, Inc., 2004—. Mem. Coun. Girl Scouts Am., Pres.'s award svc. team, 1989; bd. mem. Anne Arundel Trade Coun., 1996—98; adv. bd. YWCA; bd. dirs. Providence Ctr., 2001—, 2001—. Recipient twin award YWCA, 1988. Mem. NAFE, Md. Soc. Radiologic Technologists (pres. 1980-81, sr. bd. mem. 1982-83, various awards including 1st Pl. Essay awards 1974, 76, 84, 87), Am. Hosp. Radiology Adminstrs. (v.p. 1984-85, chmn. by-laws com. 1984-85, statis. resources com. 1985-86), Am. Mgmt. Assn., Radiology Bus. Mgrs. Assn., Ea. Shore Dist. Radiologic Technologists (pres. 1976-78), Md. Assn. Healthcare Execs., Project Mgrs. Inst., Leadership Anne Arundel, 1998—, Anne Arundel Trade Cncl., 1996-97, YWCA Careers, 1994-97, Phi Kappa Phi. Republican. Methodist. Home: 1013 Canterbury Lane La Plata MD 20646-2103 Office: 701 East Charles St PO Box 1070 La Plata MD 20646 E-mail: carolyn.core@civista.org.

CORELL, MARCELLA ANNE, community worker, retired educator; b. Denver, Mar. 2, 1919; d. Berton Wilson and Marcella Jacobs; m. Allen Lawrence Corell, Sept. 25, 1950 (dec. June 1996); children: Michele Anne, Lawrence Robert. AA, Colo. Woman's Coll., 1939; BA, Denver U., 1948. Tchr. Kiowa Sch. Dist., Colo., 1939-40, Jefferson Co. Sch. Dist., Arvada, Colo., 1941-49, Dept. Edn. Hawaii, Spreckelsville, 1949-50, substitute tchr. Kihei, Wailuku, Kahului, 1962-72. Mem. adv. bd. Maui Cmty. Mental Health Ctr., Wailuku, 1968-72; coord. Crisis Phoneline, 1971-81; founder Mental Health Assn. Maui, 1972, pres., 1972-75, bd. dirs., 1975-81, chmn. membership com. 1978-99, edn. com. 1985—, hon. mem. bd. 1991. Recipient 1st Lady's Outstanding Vols. award Vols. in Paradise, Hawaii, 1974, 76, 84, vol. award Maui United Way, 1975, Golden Rule award J.C. Penney, Honolulu, 1994, 98, Jefferson award Honolulu Advertiser, 1987. Avocation: organic gardening. Home: 357 Auhana Rd Kihei HI 96753-8519

COREY, KAY JANIS, business owner, designer, nurse; b. Detroit, Aug. 22, 1942; d. Alexander Michael Corey and Lillian Emiline (Stanley) Kilborn; divorced; children: Tonya Kay, William James, Jason Ronald. Student, C.S. Mott Community Coll., 1960-62, Mich. State U., 1962-64; AA, AS in Nursing, St. Petersburg Jr. Coll., 1978; student, U. South Fla., 1985-86. RN; cert. perioperative nurse; cert. varitypist. Mgr. display Lerner Shops, Flint, Mich., 1960-62; layout artist Abdulla Advt., Flint, 1966-67; varitypist, artist City Hall Print Shop, Flint, 1967-70; nurse Suncoast Hosp., Largo, Fla., 1976-78; nurse, coord. plastic surgery svc., perioperative staff nurse Largo Med. Ctr. Hosp., 1978-81, 84-90; assoc. dir. nursing Roberts Home Health Svc., Pinellas Park, Fla., 1982-84; co-owner Sand Castle Resort, White Bay, Jost Van Dyke, Brit. Virgin Island, 1990-95; perioperative nurse HCA Gulf Coast Surgery Ctr., 1995-99; perioperative nurse, surg. nurse Blake Med. Ctr. Hosp., 2000—. Designer, artist K.J. Originals clothing line, 1990-95, The Magic Needle clothing line, 1998; insvc. edn. instr., dir. video edn., team leader oncology dept. Largo Med. Ctr. Hosp., 1980-81; designer, mfr. Haelan Jewelers--Fine Custom Jewelry, 1999. Editor, illustrator: (book) Some Questions and Answers About Chemotherapy, 1981, Thoughts for Today, 1981; illustrator (cookbooks) Spices and Spoons, 1982, Yom Tov Essen n' Fressen, 1983; various brochures and catalogues; art work in permanent collection of C.S. Mott Jr. Coll., Flint, 1962; artist, designer of casual and hand painted clothing for children and adults. Historian Am. Businesswomen's Assn., Flint, 1968-73 (scholarship 1976); outreach chmn. Temple B'nai Israel, Clearwater, Fla., 1981-85; regional outreach coord. Union of Am. Hebrew Congregations, N.Y.C., 1983-85. Mem. Assn. of Oper. Rm. Nurses, Phi Theta Kappa. Republican. Jewish. Avocations: sailing, scuba diving, tennis, original teddy bear making, golf. Address: 4080 Kingsfield Dr Parrish FL 34219 E-mail: bubbekay@msn.com.

CORK, HOLLY A. former state legislator; b. Savannah, Ga., Mar. 8, 1966; d. William Neville Cork II and Helen Cork. BA, U. S.C., 1988, JD, 1999. Legis. asst. to Rep. Arthur Ravenel Jr., 1988-89; mem. S.C. Ho. Reps., dist. 123, 1989-92, S.C. Senate Dist 46, 1992-99. Republican. Methodist. Office: PO Box 155 Bluffton SC 29910

CORK, LINDA KATHERINE, veterinary pathologist, educator; b. Texarkana, Tex., Dec. 14, 1936; d. Albert James and Martine Sessions (Buntyn) Collins; m. P.S. Cork Jr., Mar. 1955 (div. 1965); children: Robin E., Jerald W. BS, Tex. A&M U., 1969, DVM, 1970; PhD, Wash. State U., 1974. Diplomate Am. Coll. Vet. Pathologists. Fellow Wash. State U., Pullman, 1970-74; asst. prof. U. Ga., Athens, 1974-76, Johns Hopkins U., Balt., 1976-82, assoc. prof., 1982-88, assoc. dir. rsch. Alzheimer's Disease Rsch. Ctr., 1985-93, prof., 1988-93; prof., chmn. Dept. Comparative Medicine Stanford U., 1994—. Coun. mem. NIH div. Rsch. Resources, Bethesda, Md., 1985-89; adv. bd. Registry Comparative Pathology, Bethesda. Grantee Nat. Inst. on Aging, 1985-89, Nat. Inst. Health, 1986-91, 86-93, 87-92. Mem. Inst. Medicine, Am. Assn. Neuropathologists (chmn. June 1988), Am. Assn. Pathology, U.S.-Can. Acad. Pathology. Methodist. Avocation: music. Office: Stanford Univ Dept Comparative Medicine MSOB Bldg Stanford CA 94305-5415

CORKRAN, VIRGINIA B. retired real estate agent; b. N.Y.C., Feb. 13, 1924; d. Stuart H. and Bessie (Moses) Bowman; m. Sewell H. Corkran, Jr., June 15, 1946; children: Sewell H. III, Leslie C. Price. BA, Conn. Coll., 1945. Tchr. Low-Heywood Sch., Stamford, Conn., 1946-47; editor North Shore Calendar, Winnetka, Ill., 1955-59; real estate assoc. Lodge McKee Realty Inc., Naples, Fla., 1969-2001; ret., 2001. Elected Naples City Coun., 1974-78; pres. Old Naples Assn., 1995-97; past bd. dirs. Big Cypress Nature Ctr., Naples, The Conservancy, Inc., Collier County LWV, Southwest Heritage, Inc., Naples; active Naples Garden Club (legis chmn.), Collier Co. Audubon; bd. mem. S.W. Heritage, Inc., Naples (hon. bd. mem., 2002). Recipient Guy Bradley award Collier County Audubon, ONA award Old Naples Assn., 1998.

CORLEY, FLORENCE FLEMING, retired history educator; b. Augusta, Ga., Jan. 6, 1933; d. William Cornelius and Sarah Virginia (Sibley) Fleming; m. James Weaver Corley, Jr., Dec. 29, 1955; children: Florence Hart Corley Johnson, James Weaver Corley III, Mary Anne Corley Herbert, Sarah Virginia Corley, William Thomas Corley. BA, Agnes Scott Coll., 1954; MA, Emory U., 1955; PhD, Ga. State U., 1985. Cert. tchr., T-5, Ga. Alumnae rep. Agnes Scott Coll., Decatur, Ga., 1955; history tchr. The Westminster Schs., Atlanta, 1968-88, The Walker Sch., Marietta, Ga., 1989; history instr. Kennesaw State U., Marietta, Ga., 1989-91, asst. prof. history, 1991-98, ret., 1998. U.S. history cons. The Coll. Bd., N.Y.C., 1978—; reader, table leader Ednl. Testing Svc., Princeton, N.J., 1975—. Assoc. editor: American Presbyterians, Phila., 1984—, Ga. Jour. of So. Legal History, Atlanta, 1989; editor: The Landmarker, 1978-79; author: Confederate City: Augusta, Georgia 1860-65, 1960, 74, 95; contbr. articles to hist. jours.; compiler (slides/tape) Where Were the Women? 1979. Sixth grade and adult tchr. First Presbyn. Ch., Marietta, 1960—, elder, 1990—; active U.S. history contest DAR, Marietta, 1991—; cons. Girls club of Cobb/Marietta 1981; mem. Ga. Nat. Registry Rev. Bd., 1994—, chmn. 1996-97; mem. Marietta Town Com. Woodrow Wilson fellow Emory U., 1954-55; recipient fellowship in women's history NEH, Stanford U., Palo Alto, Calif., 1978-79, scholarship in classical studies, Vergilian Soc., Cumae, Italy, 1982, scholarships in medieval Eng. and Eng. today, English Speaking Union, U.K., 1979, 80. Mem. Nat. Soc. Colonial Dames of Am., Cobb Landmarks and Hist. Soc. (charter bd. dirs., co-pres. 1985-86, 87-88), Atlanta Hist. Soc., Atlanta Civil War Round Table, Soc. Civil War Historians, Ga. Assn. Historians, Ga. Hist. Soc., So. Assn. Women Historians, So. Hist. Assn., So. Garden History Soc., Richmond County Hist. Assn., Presbyn. Hist. Soc., Phi Beta Kappa, Phi Alpha Theta. Democrat. Avocations: researching family and local history, oral history taping/interviewing, world travel, lecturing. Home: 285 Kennesaw Ave Marietta GA 30060-1671

CORLEY, GINGER ELAINE, secondary school educator; b. Marietta, Ga., Oct. 7, 1969; d. Jimmy Ray and Sonja (Matthews) Corley. BS in Edn., Jacksonville State U., 1991, M in Music Edn., 1994; edn. specialist, Ga. State U., 2000. K-5 music tchr. Gordon County Schs., Calhoun, Ga., 1991—92; middle grades music tchr. South Paulding Middle Sch., Dallas, Ga., 1992—96; choral music dir. Paulding County H.S., Dallas, Ga., 1996—. Mem.: Profl. Assn. Ga. Educators, Ga. Music Educators Assn. Baptist. Home: 107 Overlook Way Carrollton GA 30117 Office: Paulding County High Sch 1297 Villa Rica Hwy Dallas GA 30157

CORLEY, JENNY LYND WERTHEIM, elementary school educator; b. Lincoln, Ill., June 18, 1937; d. Robert Glenn and Nancy Lynd (Hoblit) Wertheim; m. William Gene Corley, Aug. 9, 1959; children: Anne Lynd Corley Baum, Robert William, Scott Elson. BS in Music Edn., U. Ill., 1959, MS in Music Edn., 1961; postgrad., U. Ill., Loyola U., 1985—2003. Tchr. choral music Mahomet (Ill.)/Seymour K-12, 1959-61; supr. music Fairfax County (Va.), 1961-63; tchr. music Highland Park (Ill.) 107, 1969, dir. gifted edn., 1969-70; tchr. music Glenview (Ill.) 34, 1981—2003, Corley Studio, 1959—. V.p. Corley Agroleum Properties, 1993—; water safety instr./trainer ARC; lifeguard instr./trainer Cmty. First Aid & Safety, 1995. Dir. mid-Am. bd. ARC, Chgo., 1980-86; mem. Chgo. Symhony Orch. Chorus, 1965-75. Recipient Heart of Gold United Way, 1992, Cmty. Svc. award Ill. Park & Recreation Assn./Ill. Assn. Park Dists., 1994, Disting. Svc. award Boys and Girls Swimming Ofcl., Ill. High Sch. Assn., 1994, also 25 yr. recognition as swimming ofcl. Mem. Music Edn. Nat. Conf., North Shore Music Tchrs. Assn. (treas. 1987-90), Jr. League Chgo. (treas. 1978-81), Sigma Alpha Iota, Phi Delta Kappa (found. chmn. 1994—), U. Ill. Music Alumnae (pres. bd. dirs. 1995-97). Presbyterian. Home: 744 Glenayre Dr Glenview IL 60025-4411 E-mail: corley@corleywg.com.

CORLEY, ROSE ANN MCAFEE, government official; b. Lawton, Okla., Aug. 21, 1952; d. Claude James and Mary Margaret (Holman) McAfee; m Gary Michael Griffin, Feb. 14, 1973 (div. Oct. 1984); m. Terry Joe Corley, July 31, 1988 (div. Oct. 2002); stepson Troy Justin Corley. BS, Cameron U., Lawton, Okla., 1970; diploma, Army Command and Staff Coll., Ft. Leavenworth, Kans., 1989; MCJA, Oklahoma City U., 1990; cert., Army Mgmt. Staff Coll., Ft. Belvoir, Va., 1991. Cert. in Distbn. Mgt. Supply clk. Dept. of Army, Ft. Sill, Okla., 1972-80, supply mgmt. asst., 1980-82, supply systems analyst Ft. Lee, Va., 1982, supply tech. Ft. Sill, Okla., 1982-83, supr. inventory mgmt. specialist, 1983-86, manprint program mgr., 1986-91; weapon system advisor Def. Logistics Agy., San Antonio, 1991-96, customer svc. rep. Robins AFB, Ga., 1996-98; dir. supply mgmt. NIH, Rockville, Md., 1998—2002, dir. divsn. logistics serviced, 2002—. Equal employment counselor USA Field Artillery Sch., Ft. Sill, Okla., 1976-82; mentor Fed. Women's Program, Kelly AFB, Tex., 1991-96. Active Md. Citizen Foster Care Rev. Bd., 1999—. Recipient Cert. of Appreciation, Sec. of Def., Washington, 1984, Cert. of Appreciation, Directorate of Engring. and Housing, Ft. Sill, 1986; decorated Order of St. Barbara, U.S. Army Arty. Sch., Ft. Sill, 1991. Mem. Fed. Women's Program, Soc. Logistics Engrs., Fed. Mgrs. Assn., Kelly Mgmt. Assn., World Affairs Coun. of San Antonio, Internat. City Mgmt. Assn., Tex. Corvette Assn. Avocations: autocrossing, reading, golf, crafts. Office: NIH Office Logistics Mgmt 6011 Executive Blvd Rockville MD 20852-3804 Home: 204 Park Ave Apt 305 Gaithersburg MD 20877-2944 Office Phone: 301-402-3512. Business E-Mail: corleyr@od.nih.gov.

CORMAN, LINDA WILSON, librarian; b. Washington, Nov. 25, 1944; d. Earl and Elsie (Bex) Wilson; m. Brian Corman, Sept. 2, 1967; 1 child, Sarah Wilson Corman. AB magna cum laude, Vassar Coll., 1966; MA, U. Chgo., 1969; MLS, U. Toronto, Ont., Can., 1974. Libr. Ont. Inst. for Studies in Edn., Toronto, Can., 1974-80; head libr. U. Toronto Trinity Coll., Ont., Can., 1980—. Author, compiler: Community Education in Canada, 1975 (best of eric award 1975); contbr. articles to profl. jours.; mem. edit. bd. Papers of the Bibliographical Soc. of Can., 1986-90; consulting editor: Jour. of Religious and Theological Info., 1990—. Mem. exec. com. Friends of the Osborne Collection, Toronto, 1979-85; bd. dir. Churchill Soc. Advancement Parliamentary Democracy, 1996—; mem. commn. accreditation Assn. Theol. Schs. U.S. and Can., 2000—. Recipient Nat. Merit scholarship, 1962-66, Academic Librarianship award Ontario (Can.) Confederation U. Faculty Assocs., 2000; Ont. Libr. Assn. prize, 1974; Brit. Coun. grant, 1988. Mem. Am. Theological Libr. Assn. (bd. dirs. 1991—, pres. 1995-96), Can. Libr. Assn. (chair pubs. com. 1987-88), Bibliographical Soc. Can., Phi Beta Kappa, Beta Phi Mu. Home: 94 Mayfield Ave Toronto ON Canada M6S 1K8 Office: Trinity Coll 6 Hoskin Ave Toronto ON Canada M5S 1H8

CORMIER, PATRICIA PICARD, academic executive; AS, Univ. Bridgeport, 1958; BS, Boston Univ., 1964; MEd, Univ. Va., 1969, EdD, 1975. Pvt. practive, 1958-64; instr. Northeastern Univ., Boston, 1964-68; instr. social dentistry Tufts Univ., Boston, 1964-68; instr. pediatrics Univ. Va., Charlottesville, 1968-72, rsch. assoc., 1969-72; asst. dean. dental auxiliary Univ. Pa., Phila., 1975-79, assoc. dean acad. affairs, assoc. prof. dental care, 1979-82; spl. asst. to pres. Wilson Coll., Chambersburg, Pa., 1982-83, acting dean, 1983-84, v.p., dean of coll., 1984-88; v.p. devel. and alumnae rels. Medical Coll. Pa., Phila., 1989-93; v.p. acad. affairs, prof. ednl. leadership Winthrop Univ., Rock Hill, S.C., 1993-96; pres., prof. edn. Longwood Coll., Historic Farmville, Va., 1996—. Regional v.p. devel. Allegheny Health, Edn. and Rsch. Found., 1991-93; exec. dir. Am. Diabetes Assn., Phila., 1988-89. Named Outstanding Young Women of Am., 1969. Fellow Coll. Physicians of Phila., Am. Coun. on Edn.; mem. Sigma Phi Alpha, Phi Delta Kappa. Home: 1403 Johnston Dr Farmville VA 23901-2807 Office: Longwood Coll 201 High St Farmville VA 23909-1800

CORNELL, ANNIE AIKO, nurse, administrator, retired military officer; b. L.A., Sept. 23, 1954; d. George and Fumiko (Iwai) Okubo; m. Max A. Cornell, Dec. 10, 1990. BSN, U. Md., 1976. RN, Calif. Enlisted U.S. Army, 1972, advanced through grades to maj., clin. staff nurse surg. ICU, clin. head nurse ICU Seoul, Korea, clin. head nurse gen. medicine ward Ft. Ord, Calif., chief nursing adminstrn., ret., 1992; nursing supr. Home Health Plus; dir. patient svcs. Hollister Vis. Nurses Assn., Calif.; asst. dir. patient svcs. Monterey Vis. Nurses Assn., Calif.; case mgr. supr. Cmty. Hosp. Home Health Svcs., Monterey, asst. mgr. Recipient Walter Reed Army Inst. nursing scholarship. Mem. Sigma Theta Tau. Home: 199 Linde Cir Marina CA 93933-2206

CORNELL, CAROLE ANNE WALCUTT, nurse; b. Paris, Ky., Apr. 29, 1957; d. Hardin Owsley and Cecele Christine (Smith) Walcutt; m. Richard Wood Arnold, Feb. 22, 1976 (dec. Apr. 1993); children: Richard Wood Jr., John Walcutt; m. Duane F. Cornell; stepchildren: Robert F., Joseph E. ADN, Midway Coll., 1975; BSN summa cum laude, St. Joseph's Coll., 1992. RN; cert. family genealogist. Staff nurse, evening supr. U. Ky. Med. Ctr., Lexington, 1976-77; office mgr. Arnold M.D., Cynthiana, Ky., 1977—; obstetric nurse Humana Corp., Lexington, 1983—; nurse, BSN Bapt. Hosp. East, Louisville; RN Twinbrook Rehab. Ctr. Dir. Woman's Missionary Union, 1982-87, Cynthiana Bapt. Ch., 1982-89, tchr. Sunday sch., 1978-92, mem. choir, 1978-92; mem. Harrison County Fine Arts Coun., 1980-92; mem. Ky. Heritage Woman's Mus., Inc. Recipient Woman of Achievement award YMCA, 1982; named to hon. order Ky. Cols., 1986-87; fellow U. Ky. Mem. ANA, Ky. Nurse's Assn., Ky. Hist. Soc., Blue Grass Trust, The Hereditary Register of the U.S., Daus. of 1812 (rec. sec. River Raisin chpt. 1989—, 1st v.p. 1988-90, 2d v.p. 1990-92, rec. sec.), Sovereign Soc., DAR (1st vice regent Lexington chpt., state program chmn. 1987-89, state corr. sec. 1989-92, state jr. mem. chmn. 1992-95, nat. vice chmn. scholarships 1992—, Good Citizenship award 1975, Outstanding Young Woman, 1st alt. nat. conv. 1980, Ky. State Page 1987-89, Nat. Congl. Page 1987-89, Nat. Personl Page to Pres. Gen. 1990, state mem. chmn. 1995—, state chaplain 1998-2001, mem. John Marshall chpt., nat. chmn. guest hospitality NSDAR), Harrison County Women's Club (fine arts chmn. 1978-80, 1st v.p. 1981-83), Colonial Dames 17th Century (hon. pres., 1st v.p. Sarah Morgan Boone chpts., Nat. Outstanding Young Woman of Yr. 1990-91, nat. chmn. jr. membership, state officer Ky., state corr. sec. 1990-92, historian, state libr., state nat. def. chair, chmn. membership com. 1988—, state first v.p., state pres. 2001--), Manikin Huquenot Soc. (past state rec. sec.), Family of Bruce Soc. Am., Owsley Family Soc. Am. (recipient merit award 1987), Sovereign Colonial Soc., Ams. Royal Descent, Harrison Hosp. Aux. (pres. 1979-80), Daus. Colonial Wars (W.Va. Soc.), Order St. Andrew of Jerusalem, Magna Charta Dames, Colonial Order of Crown in Am., Soc. Washington's Army Valley Forge, Jr. League Louisville, Colonial Dames Am. (chpt. 7), Pendennis Club Louisville, Spindle Top Club Lexington, Cornell Club N.Y., Woman's Club Louisville, The Chatauqua Womens Club, Midway Coll. Alumni Assn. (named Miss Midway Coll. 1975, Disting. Alumnae award 1989), Woman's Club Louisville, Pendennis Club, Cornell Club, Phi Theta Kappa, others.

CORNELL, HELEN W. manufacturing company executive; b. 1959; V.p. compressor ops., sec. Gardner Denver, Inc., Quincy, Ill. Office: 1800 Gardner Expy Quincy IL 62305-9364 Fax: 217-228-8247.

CORNING, JOY COLE, retired state official; b. Bridgewater, Iowa, Sept. 7, 1932; d. Perry Aaron and Ethel Marie (Sullivan) Cole; m. Burton Eugene Corning, June 19, 1955; children: Carol, Claudia, Ann. BA, U. No. Iowa, 1954; hon. degree, Allen Coll. Nursing. Cert. elem. tchr., Iowa. Tchr. elem. sch. Greenfield (Iowa) Sch. Dist., 1951-53, Waterloo (Iowa) Cmty. Sch. Dist., 1954-55; mem. Iowa Senate, Des Moines, 1984-90, asst. Rep. leader, 1989-90; lt. gov. State of Iowa, Des Moines, 1991-99. Past chmn. Nat. Conf. Lt. Govs. Bd. dirs. Inst. for Character Devel.; mem. policy bd. Performing Arts Ctr., U. No. Iowa, also trustee UNI Found.; bd. dirs. Nat. Conf. Cmty. and Justice, Des Moines Symphony, Planned Parenthood of Greater Iowa. Named Citizen of Yr., Cedar Falls C. of C., 1984; recipient ITAG Disting. Svc. to Iowa's Gifted and Talented Students award, 1991, Pub. Svc. award Iowa Home Econs. Assn., 1994, Friend of Math. award Iowa Coun. Tchrs. of Math., 1995, Iowa State Edn. Assn. Human Rights award, 1996, Govs. Affirmative Action award, Spl. Recognition award Nat. Foster Parent Assoc., Des Moines Human Rights Commn. award, Pub. Svc. award Coalition for Family and Children's Svcs in Iowa, Friends of Iowa Civil Rights, Inc. award, Martin Luther King Jr. Lifetime Svc. award, 1999, Svc. award Des Moines Area Religious Coun., 2002, NCCJ Brotherhood-Sisterhood award, 2003, Senator Barry Goldwater award Planned Parenthood Fedn. Am., 2003; recognized for Extraordinary Advocacy for Children of Iowa chpt. Nat. Com. for Child Abuse, award for leadership Early Care and Edn. Congress, Alumni Achievement award U. No. Iowa; named among YWCA Women of Achievement, 2000, Woman of Influence, Bus. Record, 2003; Nat. Conf. for Cmty. and Justice honoree, 2003. Mem. AAUW, LWV, PEO, Nat. Assn. for Gifted Children (mem. adv. bd. 1991-99), Rotary Club, Delta Kappa Gamma, Alpha Delta Kappa. Republican. Mem. United Ch. Of Christ. Home: 4323 Grand Ave No 324 Des Moines IA 50312-2443 E-mail: corningj@aol.com.

CORNISH, ELIZABETH TURVERET, stockbroker; b. Ionia, N.Y., Dec. 31, 1919; d. Clifford Dwight and Mildred Althea (Spicer) T.; m. Louis Joseph Cornish, June 21, 1941 (div. June 1955); 1 child, Carol Cornish Reeves. BS, Cornell U., 1941. Lic. stockbroker N.Y. Stock Exch., Prin. Reg. Options Prin., Commodity prin., Insur. prin. Teletype operator, sec. to mgr. Carl M. Loeb Rhoades & Co., Ithaca, N.Y., 1955-65, reg. rep., 1962-75; br. mgr. Loeb, Rhoades & Co., Ithaca, 1975-82; registered rep. Shearson Loeb Rhoades, Shearson Am. Express, Ithaca, 1982-86, Hutton, Shearson, Ithaca, 1986-88, First Albany Corp., Ithaca, 1988-91; registered rep., br. office mgr. A.G. Edwards & Sons, Inc., Ithaca, 1991-97, investment broker, 1998—. Charter mem. Nuveen Adv. Coun., 1984, 85, 86; instr. stock market and various br. office jobs for coll. interns; bd. dirs. McGraw House, 1996—. Mem. Planning Com. Downtown Mall, Ithaca, N.Y., 1972-75; chmn. campaign United Way Tompkins County, Ithaca, 1983, dir., 1983-89; bd. dirs. Ithaca Neighborhood Housing, Leadership Tompkins, 1986-88; pres. Friends of Ithaca Coll., 1985-86; mem. adv. coun. Ithaca Coll., 1986—; comdr. Ithaca Squadron of U.S. Power Squadron, 2003—. Mem. Downtown Bus. Women (pres. 1971-72), Tompkins County C. of C. (bd. dirs. 1974-77, 83-86, v.p. 1980-81, pres.-elect 1989, pres. 1990, ambs. coun. 1997—), Ithaca Yacht Club (bd. dirs. 1988-90). Republican. Episcopalian. Avocations: boating, reading, letter writing, coach of cornell women's rifle team, 1942-55. Office: A G Edwards & Sons Inc 2 Graham Rd W Ithaca NY 14850-1055 Office Phone: 607-266-8200.

CORNISH, KELLEY A. lawyer; BA in English summa cum laude, Pa. State U., 1980; JD magna cum laude, Northwestern U., 1983. Bar: N.Y. 1984, U.S. Dist. Ct. (so. and ea. dists.) N.Y. 1985, U.S. Dist. Ct. (we. dist.) N.Y. 1986. Ptnr. Sidley & Austin, N.Y.C. Mem. N.Y. State Bar, Bar Assn. City N.Y. (com. on profl. ethics), Order of Coif. Office: Sidley & Austin 875 3d Ave New York NY 10022 Fax: 212-906-2021. E-mail: kcornish@sidley.com.

CORNO, DONNA A. retired public relations executive, consultant; b. St. Louis, Feb. 9, 1942; d. Charles F. and Cecelia J. Zorumski; children from previous marriage: Vincent, Suzanne, Lisa. B in Polit. Sci., U. Mo., St. Louis; AA Summa Cum Laude, St. Louis C.C. Cert. pub. rels. 2003. Cmty. rels. dir. Ferguson-Florissant Sch. Dist., Florissant, Mo.; reporter various St. Louis Jour. newspapers; cons. in pub. rels., crisis mgmt., strategic comm., 2003—. Dir. North County, Inc. Bd. dirs. North County, Inc., Florissant Valley C. of C. Recipient numerous awards in writing field. Mem.: Mo. Sch. Pub. Rels. Assn. (pres., v.p. 1983—2001, numerous state and nat. awards), Nat. Sch. Pub. Rels. Assn. (numerous awards). Avocation: tennis, biking, skiing. Home: 223 Kehrs Mill Trail Ballwin MO 63011

CORNWALL, DEBORAH JOYCE, consulting firm executive, management consultant; b. Wilmington, Del., Dec. 9, 1946; d. Samuel and Norma (Bram) Handloff; m. Barry Newland Cornwall, June 22, 1968; 1 child, Deborah Leigh. BA, Mount Holyoke, 1968; MBA, Boston U., 1975. Editor Houghton Mifflin Co., Boston, 1967-69, Harbridge House, Inc., Boston, 1969-73, cons., 1973-74, assoc., 1974-75, sr. assoc., 1975-77, prin., 1977-79, v.p., 1979-81, v.p., divsn. mgr., 1981-83, sr. v.p., divsn. mgr., 1983-90; founder and mng. v.p. Korn/Ferry Orgnl. Cons., Boston, 1991-96; founder and mng. dir. The Corlund Group, L.L.C., Boston, 1996—. Mem. mid. mgmt. excellence com. City of Boston, 1986. Bd. dirs. Mass. divsn. Am. Cancer Soc., 1994-97. Mem. Phi Beta Kappa, Beta Gamma Sigma. Office: The Corlund Group LLC 101 Federal St Boston MA 02110-1817

CORNWELL, ILENE JONES, writer, editor; b. Spartanburg, S.C., Sept. 27, 1942; d. Thurmond G. and Elizabeth (Furber) Jones; m. James H. Cornwell, Mar. 2, 1963 (div. 1977); children: James David, Robert Grant. Student, U. Tenn., 1975, Tenn. State U., 1987-88, Cumberland U., 1990—, Nashville Travel Inst., 1991. Pub. info. officer Tenn. Hist. Commn., Nashville, 1974-78; publs. editor, pub. info. officer Vanderbilt U. Med. Ctr., Nashville, 1978-81; writer, editor, owner So. Resources Unlimited, Nashville, 1981-92; copy editor, editorial cartoonist West Nashville Digest, 1993-94; contbg. editor and ptnr. New South Archtl. Press, Richmond, Va., 1993-98; gen. editor, writer Serviceberry Press, Memphis, 1993—98; adminstrv. asst. tchr. edn. and Pew retention program Fisk U., Nashville, 1995-97; pubs. designer and typesetter Typography 2000, Nashville, 1995—; webmaster, HTML writer WebText 2000, 1995—2002; webmaster, exec. dir. West Nashville Founders' Mus., Nashville, 2002—; gen. editor, writer Serviceberry Press, 2002—. Speaker, panelist Women in Media Com., Saginaw State U., Mich., 1990; speaker, workshop leader Elderhostel, 1990, Austin Peay State U., 1990; asst. to coord. cmty. edn. Cohn Adult Learning Ctr., Nashville, 1992-93, program co-chair statewide women's history conf. Shaping A State: The Legacy of Tenn. Women, Nashville, 1995; planning com. The Perfect 36 Exhibit Fisk U.; compiler spl. exhibit on 4 black suffragists; founder Tenn. Womens Network, 1997, webmaster; spkr. in field. Author: Footsteps Along the Harpeth, 1970, 76, Travel Guide to the Natchez Trace Parkway, 1984; Biographical Directory of the Tennessee General Assembly, 1987-91, Ruskin!, 1972; (with Jim Leeson) The Old Trace in Tennessee, 1972; (screenplays) Early Travels on the Natchez Trace, 1974, Natchez Trace: Pathway to Parkway, 1986 (nominated Nashville's Emmy 1988); compiler: (selected bibliography) The Legacy of Tenn. Women, 1995; editor: The Perfect 36: Tennessee Delivers Woman Suffrage, 1998, The Essence of Mertie Buckman, 1998; editor Nat. Assn. Coll. Deans, Registrars, and Admission Officers News, 1998-99; collections include Ilene Jones-Cornwell Collection of Paul Adams' photographs, Great Smoky Mts. Regional Project Hodges Libr. U. Tenn., Knoxville, 2000; contbr. articles to profl. jours. Charter mem. West Nashville Founders' Mus., Nashville, 1987, bd. dirs., 1989-99; founding chmn. Richland Creek Campaign, West Nashville Community Coun., 1989-90; founder Bellevue-Harpeth Hist. Soc., 1970, 3-term pres.; Natchez Trace program presenter Internat. Conf. on Pkwys., Riverways, and Greenways Asheville, N.C., 1989; chair Natchez Trace Adv. Com., Tenn., 1990-2000; activist Natchez Trace Pky.: Doomed to Become an Interstate Hwy.?, 1990-2000; state judge Voice of Democracy student essay and scholarship contest, VFW, 1992, Tenn. Dept. Edn., Pencil student essay contest, 1994, history essay Tenn. students Tenn. Hist. Commn., 1989-2000; program co-chair Tenn. women's history symposium com. Vanderbilt U. Women's Ctr., 1993-95; mem. Mayor Bill Purcell's Neighborhood Hist. Preservation Com., 1999—. Recipient Vintage award Internat. Assn. Bus. Communicators, 1980, MacEachern award Am. Hosp. Assn., 1981, Pres. award Natchez Trace Pkwy. Assn., 1989, Outstanding Svc. and Leadership award West Nashville Cmty. Coun., 1989, Cert. of Merit, Unsung Am. Woman Essay competition Nat. Women's History Project, 1994, 1st pl. publs. Nat. Fedn. of Press Women Comm. Contest, 1999; named Tenn. Outstanding Young Woman, 1975; Lawlor scholar Cumberland U., 1990-91. Mem. Nat. League of Am. Pen Women (Nashville br., former pres., v.p., state conv. chair), Tenn. Woman's Press and Authors Club (affiliate of Nat. Fedn. of Press Women, pres. 1978, past v.p. and chair state conv.), White Bridge Neighborhood Assn. (charter, bd. dirs.), Tenn. Environ. Coun., Am. Biog. Inst. Rsch. Assn. (selected assoc. and mem. adv. bd. 1990), Friends of Richland Creek (charter), Nat. Women's History Project, Nat. Mus. of Women in the Arts (charter), Tenn. Native Plant Soc., Hypertext Markup Lang. (HTML) Writers Guild, U. S. Caroliniana Soc., Piedmont Hist. Soc., Old Pendleton Dist. Soc. Home: 5632 Meadowcrest Ln Nashville TN 37209-4631

CORNWELL, NANCY DUNN, secondary school educator; b. Franklin, Va., May 19, 1950; d. Robert James Dunn, Jr. and Catherine Edwards Dunn; m. Ronald Boothe Cornwell, Nov. 18, 1972; children: Matthew(dec.), Christopher, Ashley. BS, Longwood Coll., 1972; cert. in Tech., U. Va., Charlottesville, 2000, cert. in Gifted and Talented, 2004. Cert. collegiate profl. Va., 1972. HS art tchr. Sussex County Pub. Schs., Sussex, Va., 1972—77; K-12 art tchr. Southampton Acad., Courtland, Va., 1977—88; middle sch. and HS art tchr. Ctrl. State Hosp., Adolescent Edn. Dept., Petersburg, Va., 1988—98; middle sch. and HS art and social studies tchr. Merrimac Juvenile Detention Ctr., Williamsburg, Va., 1998—; tchr. Gov.'s Sch. for Gifted and Talented (Sci. and Tech.), Windsor (Va.) HS, 2003. Mem. character edn. com. Williamsburg/James City County Schs., Williamsburg, Va., 2002—03; presenter Va. Character Edn. Program, Richmond, Va., 2000—03; Stop Violence in Classroom com. Va. Dept. Edn., Richmond, Va., 1998—2003. Sunday Sch. tchr. Millfield Bapt. Ch., Ivor, Va. Mem.: Va. Art Edn. Assn.

CORNWELL, PATRICIA DANIELS, writer; b. Miami, Florida, June 9, 1956; Grad., Davidson Coll. Police reporter Charlotte (N.C.) Observer, 1979-81; computer analyst Office Chief Med. Examiner, Richmond, Va., from 1985. Author: A Time for Remembering: The Story of Ruth Bell Graham, 1983, Life's Little Fable, 1999, Food to Die For, 2001, Portrait of a Killer: Jack the Ripper, Case Closed, 2002, (novels) Postmortem, 1990, Body of Evidence, 1991, All That Remains, 1992, Cruel and Unusual, 1993, The Body Farm, 1994, From Potter's Field, 1995, Cause of Death, 1996, Hornet's Nest, 1997, Unnatural Exposure, 1997, Point of Origin, 1998, Southern Cross, 1998, Scarpetta's Winter Table, 1998, Black Notice, 1999, The Last Precinct, 2000, Isle of Dogs, 2001, Blow Fly, 2003. Vol. police officer. Address: ICM 40 W 57th St Fl 16 New York NY 10019-4001 also: Cornwell Enterprises PO Box 5235 Greenwich CT 06831-0504*

CORPREW, HELEN BARBARA, mental health services professional; b. N.Y.C., Sept. 20, 1928; d. Charles August Shipley and Florence Lillian Musgrave-Shipley; m. Gerald Wilson Corprew, June 3, 1953 (div. May 1974); 1 child, Gerald Wilson Jr. BSW, Temple U., Phila., 1971; MSW, Temple U., 1980. LCSW. Tng. supr. Bell Telephone of N.Y., N.Y.C., 1947—70; dir. girls' day care Wissahickon Boys/Girls Social Programs Cmty. Club, Phila., 1970—73; dir. juvenile justice spl. svcs. programs Phila. Family Ct., 1973—; SCOH program supr. Sleighton Sch., Lima, Pa., 1991—; clin. therapist Harmony Mental Health, Phila., 1989—. Cons. home assignment Sleighton Sch., Phila., 1995—. Mem. cmty. recourse devel. com. Summit Presbyn. Ch., Phila., 1990—93, bd. deacons, 1972—78, bd. mem. elders session, 1979—87; cmty. coord. resources Wissahickon Boys and Girls Club, Phila., 1972—75. Recipient Disting. Outstanding Svc. award, Ct. Judges, Phila., 1986. Mem.: NASW, Acad. of Clin. Social Workers. Presbyterian. Avocations: travel, camping, dance, reading, swimming. Mailing: 6701 Wissahickon Ave Philadelphia PA 19119

CORRADINI, DEEDEE, real estate company executive, former mayor; Student, Drew U., 1961—63; BS, U. Utah, 1965, MS, 1967. Adminstrv. asst. for pub. info. Utah State Office Rehab. Svcs., 1967-69; cons. Utah State Dept. Cmty. Affairs, 1971-72; media dir., press sec. Wayne Owens for Congress Campaign, 1972; press sec. Rep. Wayne Owens, 1973-74; spl. asst. to N.Y. Congl. Rep. Richard Ottinger, 1975; asst. to pres., dir. cmty. rels. Snowbird Corp., 1975-77; exec. v.p. Bonneville Assocs., Inc., Salt Lake City, 1977-80, pres., 1980-89, chmn., CEO, 1989-91; mayor Salt Lake City, 1992—2000; prin. Corradini & Co., Salt Lake City, 2000—; sr. v.p. Prudential Utah Real Estate, 2004—. Pres. U.S. Conf. of Mayors, 1998—, mem. unfunded fed. mandates task force, mem. crime and violence task force; chair Mayor's Gang Task Force; mem. intergovtl. policy adv. com. U.S. Trade Rep., 1993-94, 99—; mem. transp. and comm. com. Nat. League of Cities, 1993-94. Bd. trustees Intermountain Health Care, 1980-92; bd. dirs., exec. com. Utah Symphony, 1983-92, vice chmn., 1985-88, chmn., 1988-92; dir. Utah chpt. Nat. Conf. Christians and Jews, Inc., 1988; bd. dirs. Salt Lake Olympic Bid Com., 1989—; chmn. image com. Utah Partnership for Edn. and Econ. Devel., 1989-92; co-chair United Way Success by 6 Program; pres. Shelter of the Homeless Com.; active Sundance Inst. Utah Com., 1990-92; disting. bd. fellow So. Utah U., 1991; v.p. Internat. Women's Forum, co-chair program com.; trustee Am. Comm. Sch., Beirut; vice-chair 2012 Bid Selection Com., U.S. Olympic Com.; active numerous other civic orgns. and coms. Fellow Disting. sr. fellow in Urban Studies, Richard Riley Inst. Govt., Politics and Pub. Adminstrn., Furman U., 2000—. Mem. Salt Lake Area C. of C. (bd. govs. 1979-81, chmn. City/County/Govt. com. 1976-86). Democrat. Office: 2539 Fairway Village Dr Park City UT 84060 Office Phone: 435-649-7171.

CORREA, NEREIDA, women's health physician; b. P.R., 1946; married. AAS, Bronx C.C., 1966; BS, L.I. U., 1977; MA in Nursing Edn., NYU, 1979; MD in Psychopharmacology, Albert Einstein Sch. Medicine, 1985.

Numerous positions as staff nurse, nurse educator and adminstr.; nurse educator Manpower and Career Devel. Agy., N.Y.C., 1968—71; instr., counselor L.I. Physician's Asst. Program, 1971—78; asst. prof. maternal-child health nursing Medgar Evers Coll., 1978—82; resident in family practice Montefiore Med. Ctr., 1985—88, resident in ob-gyn, 1990—93 [illegible] Health Outreach, Kosovo, HIV/AIDS care and women's health problems, N.Y.C.; mem. women's, infants' and children's nat. adv. com. Dept. Agr. and Women's Health Steering Com., Health Resources and Svcs. Adminstr., U.S. Dept. Health and Human Svcs. Selected as part of, NIH's "Changing the Face of Medicine" exhbn., 2003. Fellow: Am. Coll. Ob-Gyn.; mem.: Nat. Hispanic Med. Assn. (adv. com.), N.Y. State Acad. Family Practice (chairperson leadership commn.). Office: Lincoln Hosp 234 E 149th St Bronx NY 10451*

CORREDOR, MARY B. language educator, consultant, translator; b. Fairbury, Ill. d. Agnes K. Runyon; 1 child, Erik. MA, Ill. State U., 1976; MA TESOL, Am. U., Washington, 1996. Lectr. Spanish, ESL, and pedagogy Sul Ross State U., Alpine, Tex., 1996-98; dept. chair ESL Austin (Tex.) C.C., 1998—. Freelance translator, Austin, 1999—. Mem. TESOL, Austin Translators and Interpreters Assn., Am. Assn. Tchrs. of Spanish and Portuguese. Office: Austin CC-Rio Grande Campus 1212 Rio Grande Austin TX 78701 Home: 2702 Deeringhill Dr Austin TX 78745-5112 E-mail: mcorredo@austin.cc.tx.

CORREU, SANDRA KAY, special education educator; b. Crowley, La., Aug. 24, 1938; d. Edward Dorsey and Elizabeth Mays (Wiggins) Peckham; m. Donald Audrey Correu, Sept. 5, 1959; children: Lisa G., Donald Andrew. BS in Edn., Mo. Western State Coll., 1976; postgrad., N.W. Mo. State Coll., 1980-86. Cert. in learning disabilities, behavior disordered, educable mentally handicapped, trainable mentally handicapped. Tchr. Autistic children Helen Davis State Sch., St. Joseph, Mo., 1976-78; tchr. behavior disordered St. Joseph (Mo.) Sch. Dist., 1978—. Pres., v.p., mem. Assn. for Retarded Citizens, St. Joseph, 1976-86; bd. mem. United Cerebral Palsy, St. Joseph, 1980-86; devel. dir. summer program for MRDD youth in cooperation with Mo. Western State Coll.; presenter in field. Elder Presbyn. Ch. Mem. Nat. Dem., Coun. for Exceptional Citizens, Assn. for Retarded Citizens, Mo. State Tchrs. Assn., Greenpeace, Gorilla Found., World Wildlife Fund, Humane Soc. U.S., Common Cause, People for Ethical Treatment of Animals, Habitat for Humanity, Assn. Handicapped Artists. Avocations: reading, sewing, crafts. Home: 500 NE 44th St Kansas City MO 64116 Office: St Joseph Sch Dist 10th and Edmond Saint Joseph MO 64507 E-mail: skcorreu@aol.com.

CORRIGAN, FAITH, journalist, educator, historian; b. Cleve., Oct. 16, 1926; d. William John and Marjorie (Wilson) C.; m. Sigvald Matias Refsnes, Sept. 18, 1957 (dec. Feb. 1994); children: Marjorie Refsnes, Sunniva Collins, Stephen Refsnes. BA, Ohio State U., 1948; MAT, Kent State U., 1987. Cert. tchr. English, reading, Ohio. Staff writer women's news N.Y. Times, N.Y.C., 1953-57; investigative reporter Cleve. Plain Dealer, 1962-66; dir. pub. info. Cuyahoga County Bd. Commrs., Cleve., 1966-69; dir. news, publs. Huron Rd. Hosp., East Cleveland, Ohio, 1970-73; lectr. II U. Akron, Ohio, 1990-91; adj. prof. Kent State U., North Canton, Ohio, 1996-97, Kent State U., Ashtabula br., Geauga/Twinsburg, Ohio, 1999—. Lectr. Fordham U., N.Y.C., 1956; expert witness U.S. Senate Medicare Hearings, Cleve., 1965; mgr. Cuyahoga County Welfare Levy Campaign, Cleve., 1966. Author: First Generation, 2002, Bread Glass and History, 2003; contbr. articles to newspapers. TESOL, Lit. Vols. Am.; mem. bd. mgrs. Eleanor B. Rainey Meml. Inst., Cleve., 1966-78; officer, trustee Lake County Cmty. Svcs. Coun., 1984-90; mem. adv. bd. Lake Geauga Legal Aid Soc., Painesville, Lake County, 1984-87; chair Initiative Petition Campaign on Environ. Waste Plant Issue, Willoughby, Ohio, 1991; officer, founder Ohio State U. chpt. Am. Newspaper Guild, 1947-48; del. rep. assembly N.Y. Newspaper Guild, 1954-57; poll judge Lake County Bd. Elections, 1984-2004; field rep. U.S. Census Bur., 1989—; recruiter, crew leader U.S. Census 2000. Recipient award of achievement Press Club of Cleve., 1964, Pulitzer nominee Cleve. Plain Dealer, 1964, 1st in state Ohio Newspaper Women's Assn., 1964, 1st in state Pub. Contest of Am. Heart Assn., 1972, 1st pl. publs. award Internat. Assn. Bus. Communicators, 1971-72. Mem. VFW (Ladies Aux.), Willoughby Hist. Soc. (trustee, v.p. 1997-2002, Heritage chmn. 2003-), Ohio Bicentennial Hist. Markers Rsch., Early Am. Pattern Glass Soc. Democrat. Roman Catholic. Avocations: expert on American china, glass, american labor history. Home: 37550 Euclid Ave Willoughby OH 44094-5622

CORRIGAN, HELEN GONZALEZ, retired cytologist; b. San Diego, Tex., Sept. 30, 1922; d. Rodrigo Simon and Eva Ruby (Corrigan) Gonzalez. BS, Our Lady of Lake, San Antonio, 1943. Registered cytologist Internat. Acad. Cytology. Tchr. San Diego H.S., 1943-45; microbiologist Nix Hosp. Profl. Lab., San Antonio, 1952-59; med. technologist Tucson Med. Ctr., 1959-60; cytologist in charge Jackson-Todd Cancer Detection Ctr., San Antonio, 1961-64; cytologist in charge cytology sect. Pathology Lab. 4th and 5th U.S. Army Ref. Area Lab., Fort Sam Houston, Tex., 1964-78; instr. trouble shooters, quality control analyst cytology sect. Brooks Med. Ctr., Fort Sam Houston, 1978-81; owner Corrigan Enterprises, San Diego, 1981-91; ret., 1997. Cytologist Waco (Tex. Med. Lab. Svc., 1988-89, Nat. Health Lab., San Antonio, 1989-90, Internat. Cancer Screening Lab., San Antonio, 1990-91; head cytologist Dr. R. Garza & Assocs., Weslaco, Tex., 1992—. Adv. bd. mem. EEO, Ft. Sam Houston, 1972-74. Mem. NAFE, Am. Soc. Clin. Pathologists (registered cytologist, registered med. technologist, assoc.), Greater San Antonio Women's C. of C. Republican. Roman Catholic. Avocations: fishing, hunting, tennis, skiing, dance. Home: 149 Perry Ct San Antonio TX 78209-6211

CORRIGAN, JANET M. health services association executive; MBA, M in Cmty. Health, U. Rochester; M in Indsl. Engring., U. M in Indsl. Engring., PhD in Health Svcs. Orgn. and Policy, U. Mich. V.p. planning and devel. Nat. Com. for Quality Assurance, 1991-95; prin. rschr. Ctr. for Studying Health Sys. Change Robert Wood Johnson Found., 1995; exec. dir. consumer protection and quality in health care industry Pres.'s Advisory Commn., 1998; dir. Health Care Svcs. Bd. Inst. Medicine of Nat. Academies, 1998—. Office: Inst Medicine Nat Acad Scis Health Care Svcs 500 5th St, NW, Rm 760 Washington DC 20418-0007 Fax: 202-334-1463. E-mail: jcorriga@nas.edu.

CORRIGAN, MAURA DENISE, judge; b. Cleve., June 14, 1948; d. Peter James and Mae Ardell (McCrone) Corrigan; m. Joseph Dante Grano, July 11, 1976 (dec.). BA with honors, Marygrove Coll., 1969; JD with honors, U. Detroit, 1973; LLD (hon.), No. Mich. U., 1999, Mich. State U., 2003; JD (hon.), Mercy Law Sch., 2002. Bar: Mich. 1974. Jud. clk. Mich. Ct. Appeals, Detroit, 1973-74; asst. prosecutor Wayne County, Detroit, 1974-79, asst. U.S. atty., 1979-89, chief appellate divsn., 1979-86, chief asst. U.S. Atty., 1986-89; ptnr. Plunkett & Cooney PC, Detroit, 1989-92; judge Mich. Ct. Appeals, 1992-98, chief judge, 1997-98; justice Mich. Supreme Ct., Detroit, 1999-2001, chief justice, 2001—. Vice chmn. Mich. Com. to formulate Rules of Criminal Procedure, Mich. Supreme Ct., 1982-89; mem. Mich. Law Revision Commn., 1991-98; mem. com. on standard jury instrns., State Bar Mich., 1978-82; lectr. Mich. Jud. Inst., Sixth cir. Jud. Workshop, Inst. CLE, ABA-Cin. Bar Litigation Sects., Dept. Justice Advocacy Inst.; v.p. Conf. Chief Justices, 2003-04. Contbr. chpt. to book, articles to legal revs. Vice chmn. Project Transition, Detroit, 1976-92; mem. citizens Adv. Coun. Lafayette Clinic, Detroit, 1979-87; bd. dirs. Detroit Wayne County Criminal Advocacy Program, 1983-86; pres., bd. dirs. Rep. Women's Bus. and Profl. Forum, 1991; mem. Pew Commn. on Children in Foster Care, 2003—. Recipient award of merit Detroit Commn. on Human Rels., 1974, Dir.'s award Dept. Justice, 1985, Outstanding Practitioner of Criminal Law award Fed. Bar Assn., 1989, award Mich. Women's Commn., 1998, Grano award, 2001, U.S. Dept. HHS award for child support, 2002; named Disting. Alumna, U. Detroit Mercy Law Sch., 2003, Marygrove Coll., 2003. Mem. Mich. Bar Assn., Detroit Bar Assn., Fed. Bar Assn. (pres. Detroit chpt. 1990-91), Inc. Soc. Irish Am. Lawyers (pres. 1991-92, Achievment award 2001), Federalist Soc. (Mich. chpt.). Office: Mich Supreme Ct [illegible]

CORRIGAN, PAULA ANN, career officer, internist; b. Cheyenne, Wyo., Feb. 17, 1961; d. Patrick Joseph and Eleanor Marie (Kasun) C. BS, U. Notre Dame, 1983; MD, U. N.Mex., 1987; M in Pub. Health in Tropical Medicine, Tulane Sch. Pub. Health, 1999. Diplomate Am. Bd. Internal Medicine, Am. Soc. Tropical Medicine and Hygiene, Am. Bd. Preventive Medicine, in Aerospace and Preventive Medicine Am. Bd. Preventive Medicine. Advanced through ranks to lt. col. USAF, chief internal medicine clinic, 1990-93, flight surgeon Hosp. 48 RQS, 1993-94, flight comdr. 18 AMDS/SGPF Kadena AB, Japan, 1996-98; res., Aerospace Med. Brooks AFB, 1999—2001. Mem. exchange assignment RAAF Aviation Medicine Policy, Canberra, Australia, 2001—. Mem.: AMA, ACP, Aviation Medicine Soc. Australia/New Zealand, Soc. USAF Flight Surgeons, N.Mex. Med. Soc., Aerospace Med. Assn., Am. Soc. Tropical Medicine and Hygiene, Am. Heart Assn. (mem. coun. 1992—93). Roman Catholic. Avocation: scuba diving. Office: Psc 277 Box 204 Apo AP 96549-0200 E-mail: pacorrigan@hotmail.com.

CORRIGAN-SYROCKI, PATRICIA ANN, art educator; b. Syracuse, NY, Dec. 13, 1964; d. Owen Joseph and Roseanne Katherine Corrigan; m. Paul Gerard Syrocki, Aug. 9, 1997. AAS in Advt. Design, Cazenovia (NY) Coll., 1985; BS in Art Edn., SUNY, Buffalo, 1987; MS in Art Edn., SUNY, Oswego, 1993. Tchr. art North Syracuse Sch. Dist., 1987—. Tchr. art summer sch. Onondago C.C., Syracuse, 1999—2003. Cazenovia Coll. scholar, 1983. Mem.: NY State Art Edn. Assn., Nat. Art Edn. Assn., Beaver Lake Nature Photography (sec., editor 2001—), Lions, Delta Kappa Gamma. Avocations: photography, skiing, swimming, hiking, drawing. Home: 4754 Howlett Hill Rd Marcellus NY 13108

CORRIHER, SHIRLEY, food writer; b. Atlanta, Feb. 23, 1935; d. A.J. and Clide (Mann) Ogletree; m. Theodore Hecht, 1958 (div. 1970); children: Terron Jan, Sherron Ann, Theodore Jr. BA in Chemistry cum laude, Vanderbilt U., 1956. Cert. culinaryn profl. Rsch. biochemist Vanderbilt Med. Sch., Nashville, 1956-58; co-founder, tchr. Brandon Hall, 1959, food svc. mgr., 1959-69; a founder First Montessori, 1963; traveling tchr., writer and cons., 1975—. Cons. DK's Desserts, Fine Cooking, Cook's Illus., others. Regular columnist, contbg. editor Fine Cooking, 1994—; author: CookWise, 1998; contbr. articles to Food and Wine, Ladies Home Jour., Fine Cooking, Martha Stewart Living, The Phoenix, Jour. Biol. Chemistry, others. Trustee Cooking Advancement, Rsch. and Edn. Found., 1984, chair, 1985. Recipient Best Reference Book of Yr. award, James Beard Awards, 1998, Best Tchr. of Yr. award, Bon Apetit's Food and Entertaining Awards, 2001. Mem. Internat. Assn. Cooking Profls. (bd. dirs. 1982, 83-84), Les Dames d'Escoffier, Inst. Food Technologists, Am. Inst. Wine and Food, Am. Assn. Cereal Chemists Home: 3152 Andrews Dr NW Atlanta GA 30305-2013

CORROTHERS, HELEN GLADYS, criminal justice official; b. Montrose, Ark., Mar. 19, 1937; d. Thomas and Christene (Farley) Curl; m. Edward Corrothers, Dec. 17, 1968 (div. Sept. 1983); 1 child, Michael Edward. AA in Liberal Arts magna cum laude, Ark. Bapt. Coll., 1955; BS in Bus. Adminstrn. Mgmt., Roosevelt U., 1965; grad. officer leadership sch., WAC Sch., 1965; grad, Inst. Criminal Justice, Exec. Ctr. Continuing Edn., U. Chgo., 1973; postgrad., Calif. Coast U., 1981—. Enlisted U.S. Army, 1956, advanced through grades to capt., 1969, chief mil. pers., 1965-67; dir. for housing Giessen Support Ctr., Germany, 1967-69; resigned, 1969; social interviewer Ark. Dept. Corrections, Grady, 1970-71, supt. women's unit Pine Bluff, 1971-83; commr. U.S. Parole Commn., Burlingame, Calif., 1983-85, U.S. Sentencing Commn., Washington, 1985-91; fellow U.S. Dept. Justice, Washington, 1992-95; criminal justice cons., 1996—. Instr. women & crime U. Md., College Park, 1994; instr. corrections U. Ark.-Pine Bluff, 1976-79; mem. bd. visitation Jefferson County Juvenile Ct., Pine Bluff, 1978-81; bd. dirs. Vols. in Cts., 1979-83, Vols. Am., 1985-94; mem. Am./Can. study team Mex. penal system Am. Correctional Assn., Islas Marias, Mex., 1981; mem. Ark. Commn. Crimes and Law Enforcement, 1975-78; mem. U.S. Atty. Gen.'s Correctional Policy Study Team, 1987. Mem. Ark. Commn. on Status of Women, 1976-78; bd. dirs. Com. Against Spouse Abuse, 1982-83; mem. nat. adv. bd. dept. criminal justice Xavier U., Cin., 1993-97; bd. dirs. Bapt. Mission Found. of Md./Del., Columbia, Md., 1993-98. Recipient Ark, Woman of Achievement award Ark. Press Women's Assn., 1980, Human Rels. award Ark. Edn. Assn., 1980, Outstanding Woman of Achievement award Sta. KATV-TV, Little Rock, 1981, Correctional Svc. award Vols. Am., 1984, William H. Hastie award Nat. Assn. Blacks in Criminal Justice, 1986, Outstanding Victim Advocacy award Nat. Victim Ctr., 1991, Appreciation cert. Dept. Justice Office for Victims of Crime, 1994; recipient testimonial for svc. to fed. judiciary Adminstrv. Office of Cts., 1991. Mem.: NAFE, Am. Soc. Criminology, Nat. Coun. on Crime and Delinquency, Ark. Law Enforcement Assn., N.Am. Assn. Wardens and Supts., Am. Correctional Assn. (treas. 1980—86, v.p. 1986—88, pres.-elect 1988—90, pres. 1990—92, mem. Del. Assembly 1993—, chmn. rsch. coun. 1997—2000, chmn. Correctional awards com. 2001—, E.R. Cass Correctional Achievement award 1993), Ark. Sheriff's Assn. (hon.), Delta Sigma Theta (local sec. 1976—79, local parliamentarian 1983). Baptist. Avocations: reading, music. Office: Am Correctional Assn 4380 Forbes Blvd Lanham Seabrook MD 20706-4863

CORRY, DALILA BOUDJELLAL, internist, educator; b. El-Arrouch, Algeria, July 7, 1943; came to U.S., 1981; MD, U. Algiers, 1974. Diplomate in internal medicine and nephrology Am. Bd. Internal Medicine. Intern Hosp. Mustapha Algiers, 1972-73; resident Hosp. Tenon, Paris, 1975-79; fellow in nephrology UCLA, 1981-83; chief renal divsn. Olive View-UCLA Med. Ctr., Sylmar, Calif., 1983—; from asst. prof. to prof. clin. medicine UCLA, 1993, prof. clin. medicine. Assoc. prof. clin. medicine UCLA. Fellow Am. Heart Assn. Office: Olive View-UCLA Med Ctr Dept Medicine 2B182 14445 Olive View Dr Sylmar CA 91342-1437

CORSAW, ARDITH, geriatrics nurse, administrator; b. Decatur, Ill., Sept. 10, 1950; d. Everette Eugene and Norma L. (Swarm) Kirkman; m. David Corsaw, Dec. 19, 1971; children: Adam, Tara, Karen. Diploma, Decatur Meml. Hosp., 1971. RN. Pvt. duty nursing, charge nurse med.-surg. unit Graham Hosp., Canton, Ill., 1972-82; nurse Hooper-Holmes Port-A-Medic, Peoria, Ill., 1982-83; office nurse family practice physician's office, Cuba, Ill., 1982-87; factory first-aid sta. relief nurse Caterpillar, Inc., Mapleton, Ill., 1986-88; nursing supr., insvc. dir. Heartland of Canton, Health Care and Retirement Corp., 1988-91, DON, 1991-92, quality assurance coord., rehab. coord., 1992; DON Sprucewood Health Care, Macomb, Ill., 1992-96, Ill. River Correctional Ctr., Canton, 1996—. Supr. nursing, clin. support br. chief ambulatory svcs. McDill AFB, 1991. Ill. Air N.G. Nurse Exec., 1971-95, comdr. med. squadron, 1995-96. Mem.: Assn. Air N.G. Nurses. Home: 8442 E Beaver Pass Rd Smithfield IL 61477-9427

CORSELLO, LILY JOANN, minister, counselor, educator; b. Newark, Mar. 30, 1953; d. Joseph DiFalco and Antonietta (Gandolfo) C. BA, Fla. State U., 1974; MEd, Fla. Atlantic U., 1977; MA, Southwestern Bapt. Theol. Sem., 1987; D of Ministry, Luther Rice Sem., 2003. Lic. profl. counselor, Tex.; lic. mental health counselor, Fla., 1999. Lang. arts tchr. Broward County (Fla.) Pub. Schs., 1974-80, guidance counselor, 1980-85; min. of single adults Park Pl. Bapt Ch., Houston, 1985-87; founder, exec. dir. SinglePlus, Inc., Flower Mound, Tex., 1989-96; guidance counselor Palm Beach and Broward County Pub. Schs., 1996-99; pastor Maranatha Ch., Pompano Beach, Fla., 2000—01; lic. counselor mental health In Spirit and In Truth Counseling Svs., Pompano Beach, 1999—. Writer, lectr. singles ministry and Christian Single mag. So. Bapt. Conv., Nashville, 1979-89. Mem.: Tex. Christian Counselors Assn., Nat. Assn. Single Adult Leaders, Am. Assn. Christian Counselors, Women's Club of Flower Mound (pres. 1989—90), Pilot Club of [illegible] (chaplain 1982—83), Phi Delta Kappa, Lambda Iota Tau. Democrat. Home and Office: PO Box 811 Pompano Beach FL 33061-0811

CORSON, MARY LOUISE, special education educator; d. Herbert E. and Dorothy Edna Jones; children: Elizabeth Ann Dietz, Eric Anthony. BA, Mich. State U., 1983; MA, U. Detroit, 1994. Tchr. learning disabilities Detroit Pub. Schs., 1987—. Trustee bd. edn. Lincoln Park (Mich.) Schs., 2002—. Mem.: ASCD (assoc.), Coun. for Exceptional Children. Avocations: reading, gardening, sewing, crafts.

CORTES, CAROL SOLIS, school system administrator; b. N.Y.C., N.Y., Aug. 16, 1944; d. Jesus and Dora Solis; m. Fernando Miranda, June 25, 1964 (div. Apr. 1978); children: Christopher, Christina Guerra; m. Jose Cortes (div. Nov. 1, 1983). BEd with hon., U. Miami, 1970; MSc, Fla. Internat. U., 1974. Cert. in Social Sci. & Adminstrn. Supr. From tchr. to dep. supt. Miami-Dade County Pub. Sch., Miami, Fla., 1970—96, dep. supt., 1996—. Exec. bd. Gender Equity Network. Exec. bd. Women's C. of C., Miami, Fla., 2000—01. Recipient Hispanic Educator award, Nova U., 1999, Cervantes Outstanding Educator award, 1999, Educator of Yr. award, 1999. Mem.: Phi Delta Kappa. Avocations: travel, dominoes. Home: 2105 SW 123rd Court Miami FL 33175 Office: Miami Dade Pub Schs 1450 NE 2nd Ave Miami FL 33132-1308

CORTESE, JULIA F. retired elementary school educator; b. Reading, Pa., Mar. 2, 1922; d. Frederick Hagman and Elizabeth Hartman Dechant; m. Sam Saunders Fitzsimmons, June 16, 1946 (dec. Aug. 1959); children: Samuel, Elizabeth Barclay, Carol Sargent, Sarah; m. Joseph Robert Cortese, June 20, 1964. BA, Lake Erie Coll., 1943; MEd, Western Res. U., 1961. Cert. tchr. comprehensive sci., Ohio. Rsch. chemist Hercules Powder Co., Wilminton, Del., 1943-44; rsch. biochemist Rockefeller Inst. for Med. Rsch., N.Y.C., 1944-46; rsch. asst. Maclean Hosp. Harvard Med. Sch., Boston, 1946-49; sci. tchr. Monticello Jr. High, Cleveland Heights, Ohio, 1959-64; sci. tchr., dept. chair Hathaway Brown Sch., Shaker Heights, Ohio, 1966-83; sci. tchr. U. Sch., Shaker Heights, 1985-96; ret. Bd. mem., trustee Ind. Schs. Assn. Ctrl. States, Downers Grove, Ill., 1976-79, Nat. Assn. Ind. Schs., Washington, 1980-83; bd. mem. Andrews Sch. for Girls, Willoughby, Ohio, 1984—, chmn., 1995—. Bd. dirs. Global Issues Resource Ctr., Cleve., 1988—; docent Cleve. Mus. Natural History, 1996—, Great Lakes Sci. Ctr., Cleve., 1996—. Recipient Disting. Tchg. award Ind. Schs. Assn. Ctrl. States, Downers Grove, 1974. Mem. ACLU, Nat. Assn. Biology Tchrs., Nat. Sci. Tchrs. Assn., Sierra Club, Common Cause. Democrat. Episcopalian. Avocations: reading, sewing, family activities. Home: 3911 Lander Rd # 2 Chagrin Falls OH 44022-1328

CORTEZ, MARTI, marketing professional; d. Carlos and Martha Cortez; m. Richard Geiser, Mar. 26, 1994; children: Nicholas Geiser, Gabriela Geiser. BA in Mktg., Webster U. Incentive travel sales rep. McDonnell Douglas, St. Louis, 1983—87; travel account exec. Maritz Travel, St. Louis, 1987—92; project mgr. Maritz Performance Improvement, St. Louis, 1992—96, events and comm. mgr., 1996—98; dir. mktg. ops. Maritz Rsch., St. Louis, 1998—2002; dir. brand mktg. Maritz Inc., St. Louis, 2002—. Host to fgn. dignitaries McDonnell, St. Louis, 1983—87. Mem. steering com. United Way Fund Raising - Maritz, St. Louis, 1999—2000; mem. Accion Social Comunitaria, St. Louis, 1994—95. Recipient 1st pl. Innovator award, 1998, Cost Savs. award, 2001. Mem.: Am. Mktg. Assn. Avocations: music, reading, jewelry making.

CORTI, LILLIAN ZELL, humanities educator, writer; b. Clinton, Okla., Dec. 18, 1942; d. Samuel Gordon Somers and Susie Mae Mote; children: Anna, Miriam, Paul. PhD in Comparative Lit., CUNY, 1984. Asst. prof. French and comparative drama Tulsa (Okla.) U., 1984—89; assoc. prof. English, world lit. and women's studies U. Alaska, Fairbanks, 1991—, prof., 2002—. Chair vis. spkrs. program U. of Alaska Statewide Women's Rsch. Consortium, Fairbanks, 2001—02. Translator: (book) The Fire of Origins (translation of Le Feu des Origines by Emmanuel Dongala, 2001; author: The Myth of Medea and the Murder of Children, 1998; contbr. anthology of essays Disorderly Eaters, 1992, articles to profl. jours. Faculty advisor student br. Amnesty Internat., Fairbanks, 1999—2002. Recipient Fulbright Tchg./Rsch. award, Coun. for Internat. Exch. of Scholars, Brazzaville, The Congo, 1990, associateship, Five Coll. Women's Studies Rsch. Ctr., 2000; grantee Summer Inst. on Homer and Oral Traditions, U of Ariz., Tuscon, NEH, 1994. Mem.: MLA. Avocations: travel, gardening, cycling, swimming. Office: U Alaska PO Box 755720 Fairbanks AK 99775 E-mail: fflzc@uaf.edu.

CORTINA, BETTY, magazine editor; B in journalism, U. Fla., 1992. City hall reporter Miami Herald; LA staff corr. People Weekly, 1995—96; assoc. editor People En Espanol, 1996—99; sr. writer Entertainment Weekly, 1999; founding news editor O, the Oprah mag., 1999—2001; editl. dir. Latina mag., 2001—. Adv. coun. Journalism Dept., U. Fla. Office: Latina Mag 1500 Broadway Ste 700 New York NY 10036*

CORTO, DIANA MARIA, lyric-coloratura, producer, educator; b. N.Y. d. Samuel and Margaret C.; 1 child, Christian Miles Stomsvik. BA, CUNY, 1977, MA, 1984; studied drama, Am. Place Theatre; studied voice with Maria Kurenko, studied ballet with Maria Nevelska, Bolshoi Theatre, Moscow. Founder, dir. Am. Opera Musical Theatre Co., Inc., 1995—. Prof. drama for musical theatre Pace U., N.Y.C.; mem. voice faculty Calif. State U., L.A., also stage dir. opera program; founder, dir. Am. Opera/Mus. Theatre Co.; appearance with Nat. Symphony Orch. of Cuba, 2004. Starred as Maria in West Side Story in numerous opera houses in Spain, Germany, Switzerland, Austria, 1984; appeared on Broadway in Her First Roman, Status Quo Vadis, Thirteen Daughters, West Side Story Revival, Stop the World, I Want To Get Off; concert tours in U.S., S.Am., Moscow, 1989-91; lead singer City of Angels Opera, Met. Studio; lyric-coloraturist in operas in U.S. and Europe; road tours include King and I, Man of La Mancha, Kismet; prodr. (N.Y. debut performance) The Jewel Box by Mozart/Griffiths; co-prodr. The Jewel Box with N.J. State Opera, Dmitiri Shostakovich concert with Fedn. of Russia, La Bohéme, and others; prodr., dir. Am. premiere of La Molinara by Paisiello at Town Hall, La Boheme; prodr.: Iolanta by Tchaikowski at Town Hall, Embassy of Russian Fedn., La Boheme, Rigoletto, Nat. Performing Arts Ctr. Taiwan. E-mail: corto@mindspring.com.

CORUJO, MARLENE, urologic surgeon; b. Bronx, N.Y., June 23, 1966; d. Norma Corujo. BA summa cum laude, CUNY, 1988; MD, Yale U., 1992. Diplomate Am. Bd. Urology. Resident in surgery Yale-New Haven Hosp., 1992-94, resident in urology, 1994-97; fellow in neuro-urology L.I. Jewish Med. Ctr., New Hyde Park, N.Y., 1997-98; asst. prof. urology Beth Israel Med. Ctr., N.Y.C., 1998—. Contbr. articles to profl. jours. Salk scholar, 1988, William and Charlotte Cadbury scholar, 1992. Mem. AMA, Am. Urologic Assn., Women in Urology, Soc. Urodynamics and Female Urology, Phi Beta Kappa. Avocations: writing poetry, music. Office: Beth Israel Med Ctr 10 Union Squaare E New York NY 10003

CORWELL, ANN ELIZABETH, public relations executive; b. Battle Creek, Mich. d. James Albert Corwell and Marion Elizabeth (Petersen) Shertzer. BA, Mich. State U., 1971, MBA, 1981; cert. fin., Wharton Sch., 1986. Sr. publicist City of Dearborn, Mich., 1972-76; sr. assoc. GM, Detroit, 1976-77, media coord. N.Y.C., 1977, mgr. cmty. rels. Pontiac, Mich., 1977-81, mgr. internal comm., 1981-82; dir. pub. rels. Pillsbury Co., Mpls., 1982-85, Avon Products Inc., N.Y.C., 1985-87; exec. v.p. MECA

Internat., Flat Rock, Mich., 1987-95; v.p. coll. rels. William Tyndale Coll., Farmington Hills, Mich., 1995—. Dir. Mich. State U. Nat. Alumni Bd. Mem. Pub. Rels. Soc. Am., Women In Comm., Oakland County C. of C. (dir. 1988-91), Dearborn C. of C. (dir. 1989-91). Office: William Tyndale College 35700 W 12 Mile Rd Farmington Hills MI 48331-3149 E-mail: acorwell@williamtyndale.edu.

CORWIN, AMBER, figure skater; b. Harbor City, Calif., Dec. 21, 1978; Placed 6th in World Jr. U.S. Team Selections, 1997, 5th place Nat. Sr., 1997, 10th place NHK Trophy, 1996, 3rd place Vienna Cup, 1996, 7th place World Jr. Selections Competition, 1997, 6th place Nat. Sr., 1996, 3rd place Pacific Coast Sr., 1996, 2d place Southwest Pacific Sr., 1996, 2nd place ISU Jr. Grand Prix Finals, 1998, 6th place U.S. Championships, 1998, 6th place World Jr. Selection Competition, 1998, 1st place Pacific Coast Sr., 1998, 8th place Cup of Russia, 1998, 2nd place Vienna Cup, 1998, 5th place Skate Canada, 1998, 2nd place Four Continents Championships, 1999, 6th place U.S. Championships, 1999, 4th place Skate Canada, 1999, 4th place Nebelhorn Trophy, 1999, 7th place NHK Trophy, 1999, 13th place U.S. Championships, 2000. Avocations: rollerblading, boogie boarding, movies, friends. Office: USFSA 20 1st St Colorado Springs CO 80906-3624

CORWIN, ELIZABETH A. foreign service officer; b. Newark, N.J., Nov. 22, 1961; d. Edward Stanley and Patricia Goldman C. BA, Johns Hopkins U., Balt., 1983; attended, Columbia U., N.Y.C., 1985. Jr. officer U.S. Consulate Gen., Munich, 1986-87; asst. cultural attache Am. Embassy, Warsaw, 1988-92; country affairs officer U.S. Information Agy., Washington, D.C., 1992-94; cultural attache Am. Embassy, Athens, 1995—99, press attache New Delhi, 1999—2000; officer pub. affairs Am. Consulate Bombay, 2000—03; press attache Am. Embassy, Athens, 2003—. Mem. bd. dirs. Hellenic Am. Union, Athens, 1995-99; exec. sec. Fulbright Program, Warsaw, 1990-92, dep. treas., Athens, 1995-99, pres. attache Am. embassy, New Delhi, 1999-2000. Office: Am Embassy 108 Box 48 Apo AE 09842-0001

CORWIN, JOYCE ELIZABETH STEDMAN, construction company executive; b. Chgo. d. Cresswell Edward and Elizabeth Josephine (Kimbell) Stedman; m. William Corwin, May 1, 1965; children: Robert Edmund Newman, Jillanne Elizabeth McInnis. Pres. Am. Properties, Inc., Miami, Fla., 1966-72; v.p. Stedman Constrn. Co., Miami, 1971—. Owner Joy-Win Horses, Gray lady ARC, 1969-70. Guidance worker Youth Hall, 1969-70; sponsor Para Med. Group of Coral Park H.S., 1969-70; hostess, Rep. presdl. campaign, 1968; aide Rep. Nat. Conv., 1972. Mem. Dade County Med. Aux. (chmn. directory com. 1970), Marion County Med. Aux., Fla. Psychiat. Soc. Aux., Fla. Morgan Horse Assn., Fla. Thoroughbred Breeders Assn., Coral Gables Jr. Women's Club (chmn. casework com.), Royal Dames of Ocala. Home: Windrift Farm 8500 NW 120th St Reddick FL 32686-4513

CORWIN, VERA-ANNE VERSFELT, small business owner, consultant; b. Glen Ridge, NJ, Nov. 12, 1932; d. Porter LaRoy and Vera Anna (Price) Versfelt; m. John M. Corwin, Apr. 9, 1955; children: Gail Elizabeth Corwin Bayne, Gregory John, Lynn B. Corwin Byers. BS, Upsala Coll., 1954; MEd, Wayne State U., 1972, PhD, 1977. Instr. Wayne (N.J.) Sch. Dist., 1954-55; engr., spec., analyst Chrysler Corp., Highland Park, Mich., 1955-56, 78-85; instr. Royal Oak (Mich.) Sch. Dist., 1968-78; sr. systems engr. Electronic Data Systems, Troy, Mich., 1985-87; owner, pres. Unique Solutions, Inc., Royal Oak, 1987—. Adj. prof. U. Mich., Dearborn, 1989, Wayne State U., 1989; expert cons. Teltech, Inc., Mpls., 1990—. Author: (tng. manuals) Statistical Process Control Philosophies and Tools, 1988, Design of Experiments Philosophies and Tools, 1989. Pres. Arlington Pk. Homeowners Assn., Royal Oak, 1984—85, rd. commr., 1984—90; sec. bd. dirs. Cmty. Concert Assn. Troy, 1996—99, 3rd v.p. bd. dirs., 1999—2002, 2d v.p. bd. dirs., 2002—; vol. Oakland County Mobile Meals, 1996—; trustee First Presbyn. Ch. Royal Oak, 1990—93, 2004—, sec., 1993, Presbies sec., 1994, choir, 1958—72, 1997—, ch. children's computer lab. cons., instr., 1997—, Christian edn. com., 2000—, adult computers instr., 2001—. N.J. scholar, 1950-51. Fellow Am. Soc. for Quality (standing rev. bd. 1996—); mem. Soc. Automotive Engrs. (trainer 1991—), Automotive Industry Action Group (chmn. design expts. subgroup 1988-94), Soc. Mfg. Engrs. (sr., trainer 1987-91), Am. Statis. Assn. Avocations: skiing, piano, travel. Office: Unique Solutions Inc PO Box 1711 Royal Oak MI 48068-1711 E-mail: corwinvj@aol.com.

COSMAN, FRANCENE JEN, former government official; b. Windsor, Ont., Can., Jan. 14, 1941; d. John Douglas and Dorothy Mae (Machel) McCarthy; m. David Killam Cosman, July 25, 1964 (div.); children: Lara Machel, Andrea Leigh; m. Aza Avramovitch, June 27, 1998 (dec.). Diploma in Nursing, St. John Gen. Hosp., N.B., 1962; postgrad. diploma, Margaret Hague Hosp., Jersey City, 1963. RN Can. Various nursing positions, 1963-68; county councillor County of Halifax, N.S., 1976-79; mayor Town of Bedford, N.S., 1979-82; pres. Adv. Coun. on Status of Women, N.S., 1982-86; exec. dir. N.S. Liberal Party, 1989-93; mem. Legis. Assembly, House of Assembly of N.S., Halifax, 1993-99, dep. spkr., min. comty. svcs., 1995-99; ret. Chair Sr. Citizens Secretariat, 1997-99; min. responsible adminstrn. Adv. Coun. Status Women Act, 1997-99; min. Cmty. Svcs., 1997-99; min. responsible Disabled Persons Commn. Act, 1997-99; mem. Healing Touch Ministry, 2000—. Contbr. numerous reports, brief, documents to provincial and fed. levels of govt.; opinion col. writer Chronicle Herald Newspaper, 1987-88. Liberal. Mem. United Ch. Avocations: artist, writing poetry, swimming, healing touch practitioner. E-mail: fjc@eastlink.ca.

COSSA, JOANNE, performing company executive; b. Fernwood, N.Y. m. Frank Cossa. Student in Theater, Syracuse U.; student in Music, CUNY. Musician Chamber Music Soc. Lincoln Ctr., N.Y., 1973—81, exec. dir., 1981—88; exec. v.p. Symphony Space, N.Y.C., 1989—2002; gen. dir. Glimmerglass Opera, Cooperstown, NY, 2003—. Office: Glimmerglass Opera PO Box 191 Cooperstown NY 13326*

COSTA, JERALITA, state legislator; b. San Diego, Sept. 18, 1959; Student, Everett C.C., Highline C.C. Cons., nat. trainer on criminal justice and victim svcs.; mem. customer svc. staffg Alaska Airlines, 1984-94; exec. dir. Families and Friends of Missing Persons and Violent Crimes, 1989-93; asst. dir. edn. and tng. Nat. Victim Ctr., 1993-94; mem. Wash. Senate, Dist. 38, Olympia, 1994—; mem. health and long-term care com. Wash. Legislature, Olympia, vice chair human svcs. and corrections com., mem. jud. com., mem. rules com., mem. transp. com., mem. sentencing guidelines commn. Mem. Crime Victims Compensation Bd.; exec. bd. dirs. Possession Sound Dem. Soc., Jail Industries Bd. State Wash.; mem. election adminstrn. and cert. bd. Wash. State Office Sec. State; mem. Everett C.C. Coll. Found. Bd. Recipient Outstanding Programs award Nat. Orgn. Victim Assistance, 1990, Cert. Merit for Exemplary Programs to Families and Friends of Mission Persons and Violent Crime Victims Nat. Victim's Ctr., 1992, Golden Hand award Deaconess Children Svcs., 1995, 99. Mem. Wash. Coalition Crime Victim Advocates, Learning Disabilities Assn. Wash., Marysville Bus. and Profl. Women, Mothers Against Violence in Am., Lions. Democrat. Office: 405 John Cherberg Bldg Olympia WA 98504-0001

COSTANTINI, MARY ANN C. writer, editor, retired elementary educator; b. Steubenville, Ohio, June 13, 1955; d. Thomas and Anna M. (Slabdorf) Colsh; m. William J. Costantini; children: Thomas Kyle, Susan Michelle. BS in Elem. Spl. Edn., U. Steubenville, 1977; MS in Sch. Counseling, U. Dayton, Steubenville, 1986; MS in Multihandicapped Edn., Ohio U., St. Clairsville, 1991. Cert. K-8 spl. edn., elem. tchr., Ohio. Substitute tchr. St. John's Elem. Sch., Wellsburgh, W.Va., 1977-78; mid. sch. tchr. All Saints Consol. Elem. Sch., Steubenville, 1979-80; elem. tchr., tchr. spl. edn. Steubenville City Sch. System, 1978-79; pvt. tutor, counselor, 1976-79; elem. tchr., tchr. spl. edn. Edison Local Sch. Dist., Hammondsville, Ohio, 1985-90; freelance writer and editor Steubenville, Ohio, 1995—. Coach Spl. Olympics, 1977, 79; instr. ARC; mem. Girl Scouts USA. With USMC, 1981-82. Mem. Epilepsy Found. Am., Nat. Writers Assn, Internat. Soc. Poetry, Am. Acad. Poetry.

COSTANZO, NANCI JOY, art educator; b. New Britain, Conn., June 2, 1947; d. Edward Francis and Vivian Evelyn (Allen) Sarisley; m. Joseph Paul Costanzo, Apr. 10, 1974; 1 child, Ashley Allen Bailey. BA, Cen. Conn. State U., New Britain, 1973; MAE, R.I. Sch. Design, 1979; cert. advanced grad. study in Expressive Art Therapy, European Grad. Sch., Leuk, Switzerland, 1999. Assoc. prof. art Elms Coll., Chicopee, Mass., 1985—, also chair dept. visual arts. Exhibited at Western New Eng. Coll., 1977, Springfield Art League Show, 1978, Zone Gallery, 1981, Westfield State Coll., 1985, Valley Women Arts Show, 1980, 83, 85-89, New Britain Mus. Am. Art, 1987-90, Borgia Gallery Elms Coll., 1989-92, Hampden Gallery at U. Mass., 1990, Sino-Am. Women's Conf., Beijing, People's Republic of China, 1990, Monson Arts Coun., 1995, Elms Coll., 1997, European Grad. Sch., Switzerland, 1998-99, Dane Gallery, 2001-02, NY Am. Mus. Illustrators, 2002, Yorktown Mus., NY, 2002, others; one woman shows include Thronja Art Gallery, 1979-80, Elms Coll., 1992, 2002, Dane Gallery, 2001-02; represented in pvt. collections in Mass., RI, Wash., NY, Italy, corp. collections in RI and Conn.; creator Cmty. Art Exhibit for 9-11; contbr. articles to profl. jours.; lectr. Greece, Mex. and China. Recipient Outstanding Arts Educator in Mass. award Mass. Alliance for Arts Edn., 1985, New Britain Mus. Am. Art, 1987, 88; Nat. Endowment for Humanities grantee, 1987, 88; Faculty Devel. grantee, Beijing, 1989, 90. Mem. Nat. Art Edn. Assn., Valley Women Artists, Mass. Art Edn. Assn. (mem. coun. 1984-86, v.p. 1986-88), Nat. Mus. of Women in the Arts, Coll. Art Assn., Nat. Women's Studies Assn., Internat. Soc. for Edn. through Art, Women's Caucus for Art. Avocations: painting, reading, gardening, skiing, sailing. Office: Elms Coll 291 Springfield St Chicopee MA 01013-2837

COSTELLO, ARLENE M. elementary school educator; arrived in U.S., 1983; d. Arturo A. and Rosa A. Morado; m. Frank J. Costello; 1 child, Patrick. BS in Edn., Bicol State U., Legazpi City, The Philippines, 1970; MA in Edn., Mich. State U., 1985. Cert. profl. edn., elem. edn., gifted edn. Fla. Dept. Edn. Tchr. St. Thomas More Sch., Pensacola, Fla., 1983—86; tchr.-in-charge program for Academically Talented Students Ctr. Escambia County Sch. Bd., Pensacola, 2001—. Mem. Unit Accreditation Bd.; coun. mem. Nat. Coun. for Accreditation Tchr. Edn. Co-author: Technology for Diverse Learners, 1995. Finalist Fla. Tchr. of Yr. for Gifted, Fla. Assn. for the Gifted, 1992; recipient Nat. Christa McAuliffe award, Nat. Found. for Improvement Edn., 1994. Mem.: Escambia Edn. Assn. (pres., bd. dirs., govt. rels. mem.), Fla. LWV (edn. com. 2002—03), Phi Delta Kappa (pres. N.W. Fla.). Office: Escambia County Pub Schs Program for Acad Talented Students 201 E Hancock Ln Pensacola FL 32503 Office Phone: 850-494-5640 260.

COSTELLO, DEBRA SMITH, interior designer; b. Kansas City, Mo., June 27, 1954; d. Eugene Danford and Clara Edith (Callahan) Smith. BFA, U. Kans., 1977. Designer Scott-Rice, Tulsa, 1977-80; designer, dir. McCune Ptnrs. Inc., Tulsa, 1980-84; designer, assoc. A.S.D., Tampa, Fla., 1984-89, v.p., 1989—. Mem. Tampa C. of C. Office: ASD 707 N Franklin St Tampa FL 33602-4419

COSTELLO, SHERI ANN, primary school educator; b. Grand Rapids, Mich., Nov. 14, 1967; d. Gary Allen and Ellen Hedderman Robbins; m. James Cloyd Costello, June 29, 1991. AA, Grand Rapids Jr. Coll., Mich., 1987; BA, Mich. State U., BS in Edn., Athens State U., Ala., 1999; MEd, Ala. A&M U., 2002. Social worker Dept. Human Resources, Camden, Ark., 1992—94; counselor/supr. Three Springs, Courtland, Ala., 1995—2000; tchr. kindergarten Decatur City Schs., Ala., 2002—. Mem.: Internat. Reading Assn. Lutheran. Home: 222 County Rd 337 Moulton AL 35650 Office: Decatur City Schs Somerville Rd Elem Sch 910 Somerville Rd Decatur AL 35601

COSTIGAN, CONSTANCE FRANCES, artist, educator; b. Hoboken, N.J., July 3, 1935; d. Charles Francis and Joan Aletta (Visser) C.; m. John Francis Christian, June 6, 1959 (div. 1972); m. Michael Krausz, May 14, 1976. BS, Simmons Coll. and Boston Mus. Sch. Fine Arts, 1957; MA, Am. U., 1965; postgrad., U. Calif.-Berkeley, 1971, U. Va.-Fairfax, 1968-69, U. D.C., 1972-73. Cert. tchr. Va. Designer Smithsonian Instn., Washington, 1957-59, mus. svcs. staff mem., 1962-68, drawing and design instr., 1971-76; art and crafts instr. Arlington County (Va.) Pub. Schs., 1970-75; prof. fine arts George Washington U., Washington, 1976—2002, prof. fine arts emeritus, 2003—; curator Arlington Art Ctr., Va., 1980; disting. vis. prof. Am. U. in Cairo, 1980-81; vis. prof. in drawing Haystack Mt. Sch. Crafts, Deer Isle, Maine, 1990. Jurist and judge art show D.C. area, 1975, 76, 90, 82, area show Del. Ctr. for Contemporary Arts, 1985; judge art show Sussex County Arts Coun. Mems. Show, 1991; mem. adv. bd. So. Del. Ctr. for the Arts and Humanities, 2003—; panelist Del. Divsn. of the Arts, 2004—. Author: Leonardo, 1982, Elements of Art: Line, 1980; one-woman shows Visual Arts Gallery, Habitat Ctr. for the Arts, Dehli India, 2003, Lavinia Ctr., Milton, Del., 2003, Soho 20 Gallery, N.Y.C., 1997, Hampshire Coll. Gallery Hampshire Coll., Amherst, Mass., 1996, Dimock Gallery, George Washington U., 1987, Franz Bader Gallery, Washington, 1985, 90, No. Va. C.C., Alexandria, 1983, Barbara Fiedler Gallery, Washington, 1979, 82, Phillips Collection, Washington, 1977, Gulbenkian Gallery, U. Kent, Canterbury, Eng., 1975, Talbot Rice Arts Ctr., Edinburgh, Scotland, 1974, Design Ctr. Gallery, Cleve., 1974, Annenburg Arts Ctr., Phila., 1973; represented pub. collections Hirschhorn Mus. and Sculpture Garden, Washington, Phillips Collection, Washington, U. Iowa Mus., Iowa City, Dimock Gallery, George Washington U., Del. Mus. Art, others; included in numerous pvt. collections USA and abroad. Sec. steering com. Del. chpt. Nat. Mus. for Women in the Arts, Newark, 1997—01. Named to Nat. Mus. for Women in Arts to represent Del., 1998; fellow, Macdowell Colony, 1977, Ossabaw Island project, 1980; grantee, Lester Hereward Cooke Found., 1978—79, GSAS Facilitating Fund, 1990. Fellow Royal Soc. Arts; mem. Am. Craft Coun., Coll. Art Assn. Home: 210 NE Market St Lewes DE 19958-1574 Office: 210 NE Market ST Lewes DE 20037-2515

COSTIN, REA-SILVIA, civil engineer; b. Salonika, Greece, Oct. 24, 1946; d. Stefan and Steliana Costin. MS in Civil Engring., Faculty of Hydrotech. Constrn., Bucharest, 1969; postgrad., U. Fla., 1985. Registered profl. engr., Fla. Design engr. Inst. of Mining, Bucharest, Romania, 1969—75; project engr. Machine Constrn., Bucharest, 1975—80; engr. III Fla. Dept. Environ. Regulation, Jacksonville, 1981—83; design engr. Aikenhead Engring., Jacksonville, 1983—88; project engr. Smith & Gilespie Engrs., Jacksonville, 1988—90; project mgr. City of Jacksonville, 1990—. Author: Short Stories: The Story of a Refugee, 1997; contbr. poetry to poetry.com web site, poetry to Noble House--Theater of the Mind, 2003. Named Poet Laureate, The Internat. Libr. Poetry, 2002; recipient Editors Choice award, Poetry.com, 2001, 2002, Pres'. award for Lit. Excellence, Nat. Authors Registry, 2003. Mem.: NSPE, Am. Pub. Works Assn., Fla. Engring. Soc. Avocations: reading, writing, running, weightlifting, skiing. Home: 1645 Flagler Ave Jacksonville FL 32207-3119

COSTON, BRENDA MARIA BONE, language arts educator; b. Pensacola, Fla., Sept. 25, 1961; d. Marvin Ralph and Irmgard Maria (Minna) Bone; m. Glen Howard Coston, Dec. 21, 1994. AA in Tchr. Edn., Pensacola Jr. Coll., Fla., 1981; BA in English and Comm. Arts, U. West Fla., 1983, MA in English, 1984; MS in Counseling and Human Devel., Troy State U., Pensacola, 1994. Cert. K-12 counseling, tchr. 6-12 English, tchr. 5-9 social sci. Tchr. 8th grade English Warrington Middle Sch., Pensacola, Fla., 1992—93; adj. instr. English Pensacola Jr. Coll., 1995—. Recipient Tchg. Excellence (Golden Apple) award, Pensacola Jr. Coll., 1999—2000, Award of Support for Student Support Svcs., 2002. Mem.: Phi Theta Kappa. Avocations: reading, writing, poetry, feeding wild animals. Home: 3022 N 14th Ave Milton FL 32583-5885

COSTON, SUZANNE, television producer; m. Harold Coston; 2 children. Pres. de Passe Entertainment, L.A., 1992—. Co-prodr.: (TV specials) Motown Returns to the Apollo, 1985 (Emmy award for outstanding variety, music or comedy program, 1985); prodr.: (TV films) Buffalo Girls, 1995; exec. prodr.: (TV specials) Motown 40: The Music is Forever, 1998; (TV films) Someone Else's Child, 1994, Zenon: Girl of the 21st Century, 1999, The Loretta Claiborne Story, 2000, Cheaters, 2000, Zenon: The Zequel, 2001; (TV miniseries) The Temptations, 1998; (TV series) Sister, Sister, 1994—99, Smart Guy, 1997—99; music supervisor (TV films) Happy Endings, 1983, Bridesmaids, 1989, (films) The Last Dragon, 1985. Office: care DePasse Entertainment 5750 Wilshire Blvd Ste 640 Los Angeles CA 90036-3685

COTÉ, DEBRA NAN, surgical nurse; b. White Plains, N.Y., Apr. 16, 1960; d. Morton and Sheila (Pshedesky) Schwam; children: Matthew Jonathan, Eric Martin. AAS, Rockland Community Coll., Suffern, N.Y., 1981. Staff nurse neurol./nuerosurg. flr. Columbia Presbyn. Med. Ctr., N.Y.C., 1981-84, staff nurse neurol. ICU, 1984-87, rsch. nurse clinician neurosurg. dept., 1987—; mgr. pharmacology unit Health and Scis. Rsch. Inc., Englewood, N.J.; clin. rsch. assoc. Regeneron Pharms., Tarrytown, N.Y., 1991-94, med. safety officer, 1994-96; dir. clin. coordination Mt. Sinai, N.Y.C., 1996-97; cons. Regions Ltd., 1997—99, Noven Pharm., 1999—2001; sr. cons. Ivax Rsch., Miami, Fla., 2001—03; project mgr. oncology PPD Devel., Wilmington, NC, 2003—. Instr. Am. Cancer Soc., N.Y.C., 1989-90; cons. in field. EMT, Spring Hill Ambulance Corps, Spring Valley, N.Y., 1978-81. Mem. Am. Assn. Neurosci. Nurses, Oncology Nurses Assn., Am. Clin. Pharmacology. Home: 3104 Joe Wheeler Dr Wilmington NC 28409

COTE, DENISE LOUISE, federal judge; b. St. Cloud, Minn., Oct. 13, 1946; d. Donald Edward and Dorothy (Garberson) C.; m. Howard F. Maltby, Dec. 24, 1987. BA, St. Mary's Coll., 1968; MA, Columbia U., 1969, JD, 1975. Bar: N.Y. 1976, U.S. Dist. Ct. (so. and ea. dist.) N.Y. 1976, U.S. Ct. Appeals (2d cir.) 1984. Law clk. to Hon. Jack B. Weinstein U.S. Dist. Ct. (ea. dist.) N.Y., 1975-76; assoc. Curtis Mallet-Prevost, N.Y.C., 1976-77; asst. U.S. Attys. Office (so. dist.), N.Y.C., 1977-85; dep. chief criminal divsn. so. dist. U.S. Attys. Office, N.Y.C., 1983-85, chief criminal divsn. so. dist., 1991-94; atty. Kaye Scholer Fierman Hays & Handler, N.Y.C., 1985-88, ptnr., 1988-91; judge U.S. Dist. Ct. (so. dist.) N.Y., 1994—. Mem. Assn. of Bar of City of N.Y. Office: 1040 US District Court 500 Pearl St New York NY 10007-1316

COTÉ, KATHRYN MARIE, psychotherapist, stress management educator; b. Oceanside, Calif., May 31, 1953; d. Richard Alfred Kauth and Carole Maxine Brue Potter; m. Dennis Malcolm Coté, Dec. 23, 1983; children: Claire Marie, Simone Gloria, Jesse Patrick. BA, St. Norbert Coll., DePere, Wis., 1975; MSSW, U. Wis., 1977. Lic. clin. social worker, Calif.; cert. clin. social worker, N.H. Psychiat. social worker Napa (Calif.) State Hosp., 1977-79, team leader, 1979-80; supr. adolescent clin. svcs. Solano County Mental Health, Vallejo, Calif., 1980-83; sect. head of residential svcs. for children and adolescents London Borough of Camden, 1983-84; mental health program mgr. Solano County Mental Health, Fairfield, Calif., 1985-87; clin. social worker, county liaison West Ctrl. Cmty. Svc. Ctr., Montevideo, Minn., 1987-90; pvt. practice as psychotherapist and stress mgmt. educator Berlin, N.H., 1990—; outpatient therapist N.E. Kingdom Human Svcs., St. Johnsbury, Vt., 2000—. Profl. cons. North Bay Suicide Prevention and Stressline, Napa, 1985-87. Bd. dirs. Coos County Family Health, Berlin, 1990—. Recipient Cert. of Appreciation, Solano County Mental Health Adv. Bd., 1987. Democrat. Roman Catholic. Avocations: hiking, travel, bicycling, cooking, reading. Office Phone: 802-748-1700.

COTE, LOUISE ROSEANNE, art director; b. Quincy, Mass., Sept. 16, 1959; d. John Anthony and Theresa Janet (Oriola) Burke; m. Robert Andrew Cote, Aug. 6, 1983. BA, Bridgewater State Coll., 1981. Advt. asst. Dunnington Super Drug, Brockton, Mass., 1978-81; bus. forms and graphic design artist Shawmut Bank of Boston, N.A., 1981-86; artist AlliedSignal Inc., East Providence, R.I., 1986-92, adminstr. creative svcs., 1992-94, supr. creative svcs., 1992-94, supr. computer graphics svcs., 1994-95; owner, design dir. Katmandu Studio, North Attleborough, Mass., 1995—. Active Town of North Attleborough Charter Commn., 2002—04. Mem.: Southeastern Regional Alumni Assn. (vice-pres.), Downtown Assocs. North Attleborough (pres. 2003), North Attleborough and Plainville C. of C. (bd. dirs. 1997—2004, chmn. 2000). Roman Catholic. Avocations: knitting, music, crafts. Office: Katmandu Studio PO Box 3064 North Attleboro MA 02761-3064

COTE, PATRICIA L. state legislator; b. Lynnfield Center, Mass., Apr. 20, 1926; m. Alfred J. Cote; 4 children. Grad. high sch., Wakefield, Mass. Mem. dist. 9 N.H. Ho. of Reps.; past mem. labor, industry and rehabilitative svcs. coms.; mem. mcpl. and county govt. com. Mem. bd. selectman, Danville, Mass., 1979—, chmn. 1985-89; past owner, attendant ambulance. PTA (past treas., pres.), 4-H. Home: 11 Cote Dr Danville NH 03819-3226 Office: State House 107 N Main St Concord NH 03301-4951

COTE-BEAUPRE, CAMILLE YVETTE, artist, educator; b. Worcester, Mass., May 21, 1926; d. Harvey and Blanche (Trahan) Cote. BA cum laude, Am. Internat. Coll., 1949; cert. in fine arts, Walker Studio Group, 1952; MS, U. Bridgeport, 1967. Dir. arts and crafts South End Cmty. Ctr., Springfield, Mass., 1955-58; art tchr. YWCA, Springfield, 1958-61; dir. workshops Hall Neighborhood House, Bridgeport, Conn., 1961-64, Jewish Cmty. Ctr., Bridgeport, 1964-69; tchr., chmn. art dept. Notre Dame H.S., Fairfield, Conn., 1970-95; chmn. art dept. Kolbe Cathedral H.S., 1995-98, Discovery Mus., 1998—. One-woman shows: Bridgeport Cath. Center, 1978, Creative Mind Gallery, Stratford, Conn., 1978, Burroughs Library, Bridgeport, 1979, Trumbull (Conn.) Library, 1981, St. Vincent's Hosp., Bridgeport, 1981, St. Joseph Manor, Trumbull, 1981, Kellogg Environ. Ctr., Derby, Conn., 1999, Derby Environ. Ctr., 2001; group shows include: Stamford (Conn.) Mus., 1977, Slade Mus., Norwich, Conn., 1975, Mus. Sci. and Industry, Bridgeport, 1974, Sacred Heart U., Bridgeport, 1979, Fairfield (Conn.) U., 1979, 56th Grand Nat. Am. Artists Profl. League, Ho. of Reps., Washington, 1993, Nat. Arts Club, 1996, Creative Graphics Internat. Competition, 1997, others; represented in permanent collections: Eastern Conn. State Coll., Trumbull Libr. Assn., St. Vincent's Hosp., St. Joseph's Manor. Mem. Am. Artists Profl. League, Conn. Classic Arts, Am. Portrait Soc., Acad. Artists Assn., Nat. Arts Club, Conn. Pastel Soc. Home: 12 Melon Patch Ln Monroe CT 06468-1120

COTHRAN, ANNE JENNETTE, educational administrator; b. Buffalo, Nov. 28, 1952; d. Raymond John and Thelma Lorraine C. BA in English, Gordon Coll., 1975; MBA in Specialization Mktg., U. Chgo., 1989; MEd, Loyola U., Chgo., 2000. Mgr. 1776 House, Salem, Mass., 1974-75; dept. mgr. Goldblatt's Dept. Store, Chgo., 1975-77; sales rep. Sta. WWMM, Arlington Heights, Ill., 1977-79, Sta. WYEN, Des Plaines, Ill., 1979-81; coop. mgr. Southtown Economist Newspapers, Chgo., 1981-83, div. sales mgr., 1983-88; retail advt. mgr. Lansing (Mich.) State Jour., 1988-90; advt. & mktg. dir. Herald-Bulletin Newspapers, Anderson, Ind., 1990-92; mgr. Dealer Network Advt. Sys. Newspaper Assn. of Am., Chgo., 1993-94; pub. dir. Standard Rate and Data Svc., Chgo., 1994—95; exec. dir. Sylvan Learning Systems, Contract Svcs. Divsn., Balt., 1996-98; tchr. Chgo. Pub. Schs., 1998-2000; dean J. Sterling Morton H.S. Dist. 201, 2000—02; sys. dir. Sch. Dist. 201, 2002—. Bd. dirs. Cabrini Green Legal Aid Clinic, Chgo., 1981-83. Mem. U. Chgo. Women's Bus. Group (bd. dirs. chpt.

devel., chair 1987), Am. Mktg. Assn. (exec.), Rotary (v.p. Anderson suburban chpt. 1992-93), Ikebana Internat., Nat. Mid. Sch. assn., ASCD, Internat. Reading Assn. Avocations: theater, ikebana, gardening.

COTOGNO, DENISE LETO, music educator, assistant principal; b. New Orleans, June 5, 1955; children: Brett, Brandi, Brittany. B in Music Edn., Southeastern La. U., 1975; cert. in elem. edn., Holy Cross Coll., 1975. Tchr. kindergarten & 2d grade St. Louise De Marillac, Arabi, La., 1975—78; gen. music & band tchr. Sebastian Roy Elem. Sch., 1978—79; band, choral dir. P.G.T. Beauregard H.S., 1979; band dir. Trist Mid. Sch., Chalmette, La.; 5th grade tchr. C.F. Rowley Elem., Chalmette, gen. music tchr., 1999—2002, asst. prin., 2002—03. Roman Catholic. Home: 3917 Kings Dr Chalmette LA 70043

COTTEN, ANNIE LAURA, psychologist, educator; b. Oxford, N.C., Nov. 18, 1923; d. Leonard F. and Laura Estelle (Spencer) Cotten; children: Hollis W., Rebecca Ann, Laura Cotten. Diploma, Hardbarger Bus. Coll., 1944; AB, Duke U., 1945; MEd, U. Hartford, 1965; PhD, The Union Inst., 1979. Diplomate Am. Bd. Sexology, lic. Am. Assn. Marriage & Family Therapists, 87. Asst. to pres. So. Meth. U., 1953; rsch. asst. Duke U., 1947-49; exec. sec. Ohio Wesleyan U., 1955-56, Conn. Coun. Chs., 1958-60; adj. prof. U. Hartford, 1976-78, 1976-78; clin. pastoral counselor Hartford Hosp., 1962-65; asst., then assoc. dir. social svcs. Hartford Conf. Chs., 1965-67; tchg. fellow U. N.C., 1970-71; assoc. prof. Ctrl. Conn. State U., New Britain, 1967-93, adj. prof., 1994—2002. Adj. prof. St. Joseph Coll., 1986-96; clin. intern Montefiore Med. Ctr., 1995; dir. elderhostel programs Ctrl. Conn. State U., 1989-93, organizer ctr. adult learners, 1991-93; cons. Somers Correctional Ctr., Conn., 1980-81, instr./rschr., 1980-81; cons. Conn. Life Ins. Mktg. Rsch., 1981-1982; amb. to China, spring, 1986; presenter 3d Internat. Interdisciplinary Cong. on Women, 1987; vis. prof., scholar Duke U., 1989; adj. prof. health and human svcs. Ctrl. Ch. St. U., 1995-2002; vis. prof. Conn. Coll., New London, 1990; mem. clin. faculty, Am. Bd. Sexology, 1994; land developer N.C. Triangle, 1995—. Cons. editor: Jour. Feminist Family Therapy, 2000—, reviewer: Contemporary Sexuality, 2003; author: Comparisons of Gender Differences in Sexuality 1970s/1990s. Fellow: Am. Acad. Clin. Sexologists (clin. faculty 1994—, founder), Nat. Coun. Family Rels.; mem.: APA (chair divsn. 1987—91), AAUW, Soc. Sci. Study of Sexuality (presenter ann. mtg. 2003), Am. Assn. Sex Educators, Counselors and Therapists, Conn. Assn. Marital & Family Therapists (bd. dirs. 2000—02), Sex Info. & Edn. Coun. of Conn. (bd. dirs. 1994—2002, human sexuality leader of yr. 1997), Conn. Psychol. Assn., Am. Assn. Sex Educators Counselors & Therapists (cert. outstanding svc. 1996, disting. svc. award 1998), Am. Assn. Marriage & Family Therapists, Hartford Women's Network.

COTTER, EMILY REXANN, social worker, marriage and family therapist; b. Ft. Sill, Okla., Aug. 31, 1974; d. Richard and Mary Frances Enevoldsen; m. Robert Edward Cotter, Sept. 2, 2000; 1 child, Matthew Dylan. BA in Psychology, Rockhurst Coll., 1997; MS in Counseling Psychology, Calif. Bapt. U., 2000. Therapist CBU Counseling Ctr., Riverside, Calif., 1999—2000; social worker Angelica Foster Family Agy., Perris, Calif., 2000; sr. social worker Inland Empire Residential Ctr., Redlands, Calif., 2000—01; social worker Internat. Foster Family Agy., Moreno Valley, Calif., 2001, Walden Family Svcs., Riverside, Calif., 2001—03, ABC Foster Family Agency, San Bernardino, Calif., 2004. Mem.: Am. Psychol. Assn., Calif. Assn. Marriage and Family Therapists. Avocations: son, movies, reading.

COTTER, KA, real estate company executive; Founding mem. The Staubach Co., Addison, Tex., 1979, exec. v.p., S.W. regional mgr., 1987—92, vice chmn., mem. exec. com. and bd. dirs. Office: The Staubach Co Ste 400 15601 Dallas Pkwy Addison TX 75001

COTTER, PATRICIA O'BRIEN, state supreme court justice; b. South Bend, Ind., 1950; m. Michael W. Cotter, 1979; 2 children. BS in Polit. Sci. and History with honors, We. Mich. U, 1972; JD, Notre Dame, 1977. Pvt. practice, South Bend, 1977—83, Great Falls, Mont., 1984; ptnr. Cotter & Cotter, Great Falls, 1985—2000; justice Mont. Supreme Ct., 2001—. Office: Rm 323 PO Box 203003 Helena MT 59620

COTTINGHAM, JENNIFER JANE, city official; b. Salt Lake City, July 10, 1961; d. Miles Dixon and Ruth Eugenia (Skeen) Cottingham; m. Richard Frame Cavenaugh, July 23, 1983 (div. Apr. 1989); 1 child, John Douglas. BS in Civil Engring., So. Meth. U., 1984; MBA, U. Dallas, 2001. Lic. profl. engr., Tex. Estimator Avery Mays Constrn., Dallas, 1981-83, project engr., 1984; owner, gen. contr. Dallas, 1985-89; asst. project mgr. Austin Comml., Dallas, 1989; ct. appointed receiver 14th Dist. Ct., State of Tex., Dallas, 1990-91; engr. asst. Dallas Water Utilities, 1990—2002, project mgr., program mgr. capital improvements, 1991—2002. Dir. CBC Investors, L.P., Dallas. Goodwill ambassador City of Dallas Water Utilities, 1990-92, 95-96, fin. strength com., 1991. Mem. CBC Investments (founding pres.), Dallas Symphony Orch. League, DAR (pres. jr. group 1989-92), Cotillion Book Club (founding mem.). Republican. Episcopalian. Avocations: creative writing, aerobic dance, reading, travel. Office: City of Dallas Water Utilities 2121 Main St Ste 300 Dallas TX 75201-4336

COTTINGHAM, MARTHA MAXFIELD, journalist, volunteer; b. Dallas, Sept. 1, 1952; d. Jack G.S. and Louise Maxfield; m. Lon Worth Cottingham, Apr. 7, 1979; children: Lara Elizabeth, Sara Worth. BFA, So. Meth. U., 1974. Adminstrv. asst. sci. com. U.S. Ho. Reps., Washington, 1975-76; flight attendant Am. Airlines, N.Y.C., 1976-79; contbg. writer Observer-Sun Newspapers, Kingwood, Tex., 1996-97, staff reporter, 1997-98; editor Humble Observer and Sun, 1998-99, sr. writer, 1999-2000; freelance writer, 2000—. Mem. cmty. adv. bd. Childhood Decides at North Harris Coll. Participant class II, Leadership North Houston, 1996-97. Recipient Best Original News Story, Tex. Cmty. Newspaper Assn., 1998, Cmty. Svc. award Tex. Cmty. Newspaper Assn., 1999, award of merit Med. Journalism Awards, Harris County Med. Soc., 2000, 3d Pl. award for Print Journalist of Yr., Houston Press Club, 2000. Mem. Leadership North Houston Alumni Assn. (v.p. 1997-98, sec.-treas. 1998-99, 99-2000), Assn. Jr. Leagues (state pub. affairs com., sec. 1994-95, resolutions com. 1998-2000), Jr. League North Harris County, chair pub. affairs com. 1993-94, treas. 1994-95, fin. v.p. 1995-96, sustaining adv. to fin. com. 1996-97), So. Meth. U. Alumni Assn. (life), Zeta Tau Alpha Alumnae Chpt. (treas. 1991-92, 92-93, historian/reporter 1993-94, 94-95, 95-96, 96-97, 99, corr. sec. 1994-95, 95-96, nominating com. chair 1994-95, pres. 1997-98, 98-99, Alumnae Cert. of Merit 1994).

COTTINGHAM, MARY PATRICIA, vocational rehabilitation counselor; b. Seattle, May 9, 1930; d. Carl Frank and Frances Mary (Keon) Fox; m. Ken Cottingham, Sept. 15, 1951 (div. Sept. 1982); children: Cathy Ann, David Carl, Susan Mary, Keith Bryan, Patricia Frances. BA, U. Wash., 1974, MEd in Psychology, 1977. Diplomate Am. Bd. Vocat. Experts; cert. mental health counselor, Wash.; cert. vocat. rehab. counselor. Counselor Mental Health North, Seattle, 1974-77; vocat. rehab. counselor Counseling Svcs. Northwest, Lynnwood, Wash., 1977-79; owner, cons. People Systems Inc., Seattle, 1979—. Bd. dirs. King County Mental Health Bd., Seattle, 1982-84; guardian ad litem King County Juvenile Ct., Seattle, 1981-84. Mem. AACD, Am. Mental Health Counselors Assn., Nat. Rehab. Assn., Pvt. Rehab. Orgns. Wash. (sec. 1986-89), Wash. Mental Health Counselors Assn. (sec. 1983-85). Office: People Systems Inc 155 NE 100th St Ste 406 Seattle WA 98125-8010 Address: PO Box 123 Lakewood WA 98259-0123

COTTLE, GAIL ANN, retail executive; b. Yakima, Wash. Student, U. Wash. With Nordstrom, Inc., 1969—, corp. mdse. mgr. Brass Plum Jr. Women's Apparel, 1982-92, v.p., officer Jr. Women's Apparel divsn., 1985-92, exec. v.p. product devel., 1992-2000; pres. Nordstrom Product Group, Seattle, 2000—. Trustee P.N. Ballet. Ford Found. grantee. Mem. Columbia Tower Club, Fashion Group Internat., Broadmoor Golf Club, Thunderbird Golf Club. Office: Nordstrom Inc 1617 6th Ave Seattle WA 98101-1742

COTTLE, KAREN OLSON, lawyer; b. Aug. 14, 1949; m. Robert Cottle. BA, Pomona Coll., Claremont, Calif., 1971; JD, U. Calif., Berkeley, 1976. Bar: Calif., Utah. Law clk. to Judge Spencer Williams U.S. Dist. Ct. (no. dist.) Calif., San Francisco, 1976-78; assoc., ptnr. Farella, Braun & Martel, San Francisco, 1978-86; corp. counsel Raychem Corp., Menlo Park, Calif., 1986-96, gen. counsel, 1996—99; v.p., gen. counsel Vitria Technology Inc., 2000—02; sr. v.p., gen. counsel, corp. sec. Adobe Systems Inc., San Jose, 2002—. Office: Adobe Systems Inc 345 Park Ave San Jose CA 95110-2704*

COTTLE, KIMBERLY LYNN, municipal official; b. Waynesburg, Pa., Oct. 30, 1963; d. Dale Anderson Pushey and Martha Joyce (Boord) Chambola; m. Eric Douglas Cottle, May 28, 1988; 1 child, Emily Lauren. BS Acctg., California U. Pa., 1987. Tax acct., supr. 84 Lumber Co., Eighty Four, Pa., 1987—91; pharmacy tech. Giant Eagle Pharmacy, Waynesburg, 1991—98; sec./treas. Jefferson Twp., Rices Landing, Pa., 1998. Office: Jefferson Twp 173 Goslin Rd Rices Landing PA 15357

COTTON, BARBARA JEAN, systems analyst; b. Cleve., Feb. 10, 1965; d. Eugene and Mamie Wilson; m. Robert Eugene Hunter, Feb. 19, 1991 (div. May 1993); 1 child, Robert Eugene Hunter,Jr. ; m. David Cotton, Nov. 27, 1997. AAB in Computer Studies, Cuyahoga C.C., Cleve., 1995; postgrad., Cleve. State U., 1995—96; Diploma, Capital U., Cleve., 2003. Sec. Analex Corp., Brookpark, Ohio, 1984—89; data modeler NASA Tech. Mgmt., Brookpark, 1989—97; documentation specialist NASA Software Engring., Brookpark, 1992—, data systems analyst, 1994—. Motivational spkr. NASA Spkrs.'s Bur., Cleve., 1989—. Author: (book) Eugene - A Biography of a Sad Lonely Boy Growing Up in the South, 1997. Sec. Women's Adv. Group, Cleve., 2000—02. Recipient Cmty. award, Bus. Profl. Women of Cleve., 2001, Fed. Women Exec. award, Women's Adv. Group Cleve., 2001, Spl. Recognition, High Speed Rsch., Cleve., 1997, Cert. of Appreciation, Spkr.'s Bur., numerous certs. of appreciation various orgns. Mem.: Nat. Tech. Assn. (career awareness coord. 1989—). Jehovah'S Witness. Avocations: dance, golf, writing. Office: NASA Glenn Research Ctr 21000 Brookpark Rd Brookpark OH 44135 E-mail: barbara@barbarajwilson.com.

COTTON, CORNELIA, photographer, art dealer; b. Berlin, Oct. 9, 1927; d. Leonhard Grebe and Hildegard Margarethe Grottewitz; m. William Cotton, Oct. 8, 1949 (dec. July 1992); children: Amy, Eve, Margaret. B, Humbold U., 1948; BA in social sci., Georgia State Coll. for Women, 1949; grad studies, New Sch. for Soc. Rsch. Staff mem. Buck's Rock Work Camp, New Milford, Conn., 1949—50, 1971—72; staff mem., co-dir. Shaker Village Work Group, New Lebanon, NY, 1951—70; photographer Self-Employed, 1970—85; art dealer, dir. Village Gallery, Croton-on-Hudson, NY, 1973—74; owner, dir. Cornelia Cotton Gallery, Croton-on-Hudson, NY, 1978—; writer Self-Employed, 1984—. Lectr. in field, 1970—; dir. Village Gallery, 1972—73; pvt. dealer, Croton, 1973—78; dir. Silo Gallery, Croton, 1978—80; lectr. in field.; organizer of the ann. exhbn. of photographers of No. Westchester, 1977—2001; curator of several mus. exhibitions. Contbr. reviews on art and music; author: (booklet) They Lived in Croton, 1998; Represented in permanent collections Marcuse Pfeifer Gallery, Exchange Nat. Bank, Chgo., Met. Mus. of Art, one-woman shows include Temple Israel of Northern Westchester, 1971, Parents Mag. Gallery, NYC, 1972, Garrison Art Ctr., Garrison's Landing, NY, 1972, Chappaqua Libr. Gallery. Mem. Croton Housing Task Force, 1987—89; art adv. Croton Coun. on the Arts, 1990—; founder, bd. mem. Croton Housing Network, 1989—; bd. mem. Friends of the Old Croton Aqueduct, Dobbs Ferry, NY, 1989—; founder, bd. mem. Croton Coun. on the Arts, 1974—. Recipient hon. mention, Life Magazine, 1970. Mem.: Proust Soc. of Am. Avocations: reading, gardening. Home: 209 Hessian Hills Rd Croton On Hudson NY 10520 Office: Cornelia Cotton Gallery 111 Grand St Croton On Hudson NY 10520

COTTRELL, JANET ANN, controller; b. Berea, Ohio, Dec. 2, 1943; d. Carmen and Hazel (French) Volpe; m. Melvin M. Cottrell, Mar. 2, 1963; children: Lori A., Gregory C. Student, Los Angeles State Coll., 1961-63. Lic. ins. agt., Calif. Loan processing Eastern Lenders, Covina, 1962-64; asst. bookkeeper Golden Rule Discount Stores, Rosemead, Calif., 1964-66; acctg. supr. Walter Carpet Mills, Industry, Calif., 1967-69; co-owner Motorcycle Specialties Co., Industry, 1969-78, Covina (Calif.) Kawasaki, 1978-84; v.p., contr. M.C. Specialties Inc., Covina, 1984—, Aviation Communications Inc., Covina, 1992—. Active various coms. relating to promotion, safety and advancement of the recreational vehicle and auto industry, So. Calif., 1981—. Mem. com. Miss Covina Pageant, 1986—, presdl. task force, nat., 1982—, Rep. nat. com., 1986—. Mem. Covina C. of C., Calif. Motorcycle Dealers Assn., Nat. Auto Dealers Assn., Internat. Jet Ski Boating Assn. Republican. Avocations: traveling, gourmet cooking. Office: Aviation Comm Inc 1025 W San Bernardino Rd Covina CA 91722-4106

COTTRELL, JEANNETTE ELIZABETH, retired librarian; b. Buffalo, Dec. 10, 1923; d. Benjamin Birch and Mary Jeannette (Ashdown) Milnes; m. William Barber Cottrell, Jan. 21, 1944 (dec.); children: Karen Jean, Susan Marie, William Milnes, Scott Barber, Stephen Ashdown. BA in Sociology, U. Tenn., 1970, MS, 1976; student, Alfred U., 1940-43. Cert. tchr. libr., Tenn. Nursery sch. tchr. Concord Meth. Ch., Knoxville, Tenn., 1964-65; libr. City Sch. Sys., Knoxville, Tenn., 1971-84, ret., 1984. Author: (with husband) An American Family in the 20th Century, 1987; recorder textbooks for the blind, 1983—. Libr. Concord United Meth. Ch., Knoxville, 1975—, curriculum chair spl. studies class, 1989—, reading chair Suzanna Wesley Circle. Mem. Phi Kappa Phi, Beta Phi Mu. Republican. Methodist. Avocations: singing, bridge, cooking, travel, reading. Home: 308 Camelot Ct Knoxville TN 37922-2076

COTTRELL, MARY-PATRICIA TROSS, bank executive; b. Seattle, Apr. 24, 1934; d. Alfred Carl and Alice-Grace (O'Neal) Tross; m. Richard Smith Cottrell, May 17, 1969 (dec. 1995). BBA, U. Wash., 1955. Sys. svc. rep. IBM, Seattle, Endicott, NY, 1955-58, customer edn. instr. Endicott, 1958—65; cons. data processing Stamford, Conn., 1965-66; asst. treas. Union Trust Co., Stamford, 1967-68, asst. v.p., 1969-76, v.p., 1976-78, v.p., head corp. svcs., 1978-83; v.p. corp. fin. svcs. Citytrust, Bridgeport, Conn., 1983-90, sr. v.p. cash mgmt. svcs., 1990-91; v.p. cash mgmt. Chase Manhattan Bank Conn., N.A., 1991-92, Centerbank, New Haven, 1992-95; v.p. corp. svcs. Lafayette Am. Bank, Bridgeport, 1995-97; sr. v.p. corp. svcs. Union Savs. Bank, Danbury, Conn., 1997—. Chmn. Family and Children's Agy., 1986—87, bd. dirs., 1982—; vice chmn. Gaylord Hosp., 1991, chmn. devel. com., 1992—, New Eng. Network, Inc., Bank Mktg. Assn., 1988—91; bd. trustees Norwalk Seaport Assn., 1997—2001; bd. dirs. Danbury Vis. Nurse Assn., 2003, Bridgeport Housing Svcs., 1985—91, Stamford Rehab. Ctr., 1996—; chmn. Stamford Rehab., 2003; bd. dirs. Gaylord Hosp., 1986—92, 1999—, Danbury Cemetery Assn., 2002—. Mem.: New Eng. Automated Clearing House Assn. (bd. dirs. 1995—97), Danbury Vis. Nurses Assn. (bd. dirs. 2003—), Fairfield County Bankers Assn. (dir., pres. 1984—85), Electronic Funds Transfer Assn. (vice chmn., bd. dirs., chmn. bd. dirs. 1983—84), Phi Beta Kappa, Beta Gamma Sigma. Republican. Roman Catholic.

COUGHLIN, CAROLINE MARY, librarian, educator, director; b. Bronx, N.Y., Dec. 6, 1944; d. Daniel Anthony and Antoinette (Aponte) C.; m. William Martin Weinberg, Oct. 3, 1981; 1 child, Nora Harie Weinberg. BA, Mercy Coll., 1966; MLS, Emory U., 1967; PhD, Rutgers U., 1976. Reference libr. First Nat. City Bank, N.Y.C., 1967-68; instr. Emory U., Atlanta, 1968-71; teaching asst. Rutgers U., New Brunswick, N.J., 1971-74; children's libr. Phillipsburg (N.J.) Pub. Libr., 1972-73; asst. prof. libr. sci. Simmons Coll., Boston, 1974-78; asst. dir. libr. Drew U., Madison, N.J., 1978-86, dir., 1986-94, assoc. prof. bibliography and rsch., 1986-94. Vis. lectr. Further Edn. Cen., Tampere, Finland, 1994, 96, Tallin, Estonia, 2000; cons. to librs., 1974—; team membership for site visits Mid. State Assn., 1979-94; chair libr. dir.'s group Assn. Ind. Colls. and Univs. of N.J., 1987-92; bd. dirs. Ctr. for Rsch. Librs., Chgo., 1987-92; vis. faculty mem. Rutgers U., 1988, 90, 93—2003; vis. prof. Internat. Libr. Sch. U. Coll. Wales, 1992; evaluator HEA Office of Edn. and IMLR, 1987-2000. Co-author: Lyle's Administration of College Library Text Bd. dirs. Womens Project of N.J., 1984—. Recipient Outstanding Alumnae award Mercy Coll., 2001. Mem. ALA (councillor 1977-81), Assn. Libr. and Info. Sci. Edn. (various coms.), Archons of Colophon, N.J. Libr. Assn. (pres. coll. and univs. librs. sect. 1974-75, Disting. Svc. award 1993, Rsch. award 1993), Soc. for History of Authorship, Reading and Publ. (treas. 1994-96), Beta Phi Mu. Democrat. Avocations: reading, rug making, travel. Home: 304 Grant Ave Highland Park NJ 08904-1828

COUGHLIN, JEANNINE M. music educator; b. Midland, Mich., May 30, 1969; d. Jeremiah Thomas and Marciann Coughlin. BA in Music Edn., Saginaw Valley State U., 1992, postgrad., 1996, postgrad., 2003. Instrumental music tchr. Saginaw (Mich.) Pub. Schs., 1993—. Tennis coach Saginaw H.S., 1988—2000, softball coach, 2001—; dir. Herter Band Camp, 1995—, Mich. H.S. All Star Band, 2001—; cons., presenter Reading and Writing in the Arts, Bay City, Mich., 2001, Success of Baldridge in the Classroom, Saginaw, Bay City, 2001—03. Co-author: (anthology) Reflections: Threads-Words that Bind Us, 2001. Leader Arenac County 4-H Club, Standish, Mich., 1999—. Named Saginaw Valley Tchr. of the Yr., Mich. H.S. Athletic Assn., 2000; recipient Excellence in Edn. award, Mich. Edn. Assn., 1996. Democrat. Roman Catholic. Avocations: reading, writing, sports, music. Home: 2640 Midland Rd Saginaw MI 48603 Office: Saginaw High Sch 3100 Webber St Saginaw MI 48601

COUGHRAN, JANE NORA, writer, editor, researcher; b. Visalia, Calif., Feb. 3, 1939; d. Tom Bristol and Florence Pogue (Montgomery) Coughran. AB, Stanford U., 1960. Exhibit mgr. Olivetti Corp. Am., N.Y.C., 1966-72; rschr. Time-Life Books, N.Y.C., 1973-76; editor Time-Life Inc., Alexandria, Va., 1976-98, cons., freelance writer, 1998—. Author: The Cabins of Mineral King, 1998; picture editor 55 books for 10 series of Time-Life Books, 1977-97. Bd. dirs. Mineral King Dist. Assn., Tulare County, Calif., 1999—. Mem. Am. Soc. Picture Profls. Avocations: travel, theatre, ballet. E-mail: CoughranJN@aol.com.

COULSON, ELIZABETH ANNE, physical therapy educator, state representative; b. Hastings, Nebr., Sept. 8, 1954; d. Alexander and Marilyn (Marvel) Shafernich; m. William Coulson, Feb. 14, 1986. Student, Wellesley Coll., 1972-73; BS in Edn., U. Kans., 1976; cert. in phys. therapy, Northwestern U., Chgo., 1977; MBA, Keller Grad. Sch. Mgmt., 1985; postgrad., U. Ill., 1991. Lic. phys. therapist, Ill. Assoc. prof. dept. phys. therapy Chgo. Med. Sch., North Chicago, Ill., chmn. dept. phys. therapy, 1993-96. Contbr. articles to profl. jours. Trustee Northfield Twp., Ill., 1993-97; Ill. state rep. 17th dist., 1997—. Mem. APHA, Am. Phys. Therapy Assn. (Ill. del. 1986-93, chief del. 1991-93), Ill. Phys. Therapy Assn. (chmn. jud. com. 1989-91). Home: 1701 Sequoia Trl Glenview IL 60025-2022

COULSON, ZOE ELIZABETH, retired consumer marketing executive; b. Sullivan, Ind., Sept. 22, 1932; d. Marion Allan and Mary Anne (Thompson) C. BS, Purdue U., 1954; AMP, Harvard U., 1983. Asst. dir. home econs. Am. Meat Inst., Chgo., 1954-57; acct. exec. J. Walter Thompson Co., Chgo., 1957-60; creative consumer dir. Leo Burnett Co., Chgo., 1960-64; mag. editor-in-chief Donnelley-Dun & Bradstreet, N.Y.C., 1964-68; food editor Good Housekeeping, N.Y.C., 1968-75; dir. G H Inst., 1975-81; corp. v.p. Campbell Soup Co., Camden, N.J., 1981-91. Mktg. cons. Internat. Exec. Svc. Corp., Russia, 1998-99. Author: Good Housekeeping Cookbook, 1972, Good Housekeeping Illustrated Cookbook, 1981. Trustee Cooper Hosp./Univ. Med. Ctr., 1982-91; elder Old Pine Presbyn. Ch., 1992-96; vol. exec. Internat. Exec. Svcs. Corp., 1998—. Named Disting. Alumni Purdue U., 1971. Mem. Women's Econ. Bus. Alliance (bd. govs. 1987-91), Food and Drug Law Inst. (food bd. dirs. 1979-81), Harvard Bus. Sch. Club (Phila. v.p. budget 1994-95, chmn. program com. 2003-04, bd. dirs. 2001-2004), Purdue Club Phila. (pres. 1999—), Harvard Bus. Sch. Club (mem. com., chmn. 2003-2004), Friends of Old Pine (sec. 1995—), Kappa Alpha Theta (pres. house corp. Beta Eta chpt. 1991-2000). Republican. Avocation: Meso-Am. archaeology. Home: 220 Locust St Apt 18B Philadelphia PA 19106-3931 Fax: (215) 922-4233. E-mail: zcoulson@aol.com.

COULTER, ANN, lawyer, author; b. New Caanan, Conn. Grad. with honors, Cornell U. Sch. Arts & Scis., 1985; JD, U. Mich. Law Sch. Clerked for Hon. Pasco Bowman II, US Ct. Appeals Eighth Cir., Kansas City, 1989; atty. Dept. Justice Honors Program for outstanding law sch. grads.; corp. lawyer, pvt. practice NYC; handled crime and immigration issues for Senator Spencer Abraham Senate Judiciary Com., Mich., 1994—96; polit. commentator MSNBC, 1996; litigator Ctr. Individual Rights, Wash., DC; legal affairs corr. Human Events. Writer syndicated column, Universal Press Syndicate; guest appearances Politically Incorrect, Larry King Live, Hannity and Colmes, The O'Reilly Factor, Am. Morning with Paula Zahn, Crossfire, "This Week", ABC, Good Morning Am., The Leeza Show. Author: High Crimes and Misdemeanors: The Case Against Bill, 1998, Slander: Liberal Lies About the American Right, 2002, Treason: Liberal Treachery from the Cold War to the War on Terrorism, 2003; editor: The Mich. Law Review. Office: Human Events One Mass Ave NW Washington DC 20001*

COULTER, BEVERLY NORTON, singer, pianist, opera director; b. Dallas, Feb. 27, 1953; d. George Melville Norton and Dorothy May Morrison; m. Fred P. Coulter, Apr. 24, 1981. BFA, Fla. Atlantic U., 1975; MusM, U. Miami, 1977, D of Mus. Arts, 1985. Grad. asst. U. Miami, Coral Gables, Fla., 1976—80; founder, artistic dir. Riuniti Opera, Inc., Miami, 1999—; prof. music. Miami-Dade C.C., 1981—2002, prodr. cmty. outreach program, 1992—; Stanley Sutnick endowed tchg. chair Miami-Dde C.C., 1994—97; prof. music, dir. opera and musical theatre Barry U., Miami Shores, Fla., 2002—. Adjudicator Silver Knight award Miami Herald, 2001. Prodr., dir. numerous operas, musical and shows. Musician Ctrl. Presbyn. Ch., Miami, 1992—2001, Christ the King Luth. Ch., Miami, 2002, Temple Judea, Miami, 2002. Mem.: Miami Music Tchrs. Assn. (rec. sec. 2000—01), Music Tchrs. Nat. Assn., Nat. Assn. Tchrs. of Singing. Democrat. Avocations: running, caring for homeless animals, collecting ethnic sculptures, collecting historical manuscripts. Home: 7345 SW 108 Ter Miami FL 33156 Office: Barry U 11300 NE 2d Ave Miami FL 33161-6695

COULTER, CYNTHIA JEAN, artist, educator; b. Lincoln, Nebr., Jan. 16, 1951; d. George Wallace and Arlene Jean (Winzenburg) C. Student, U. Tex., 1971; BFA in Sculpture, U. Colo., 1975; postgrad., U. Iowa, 1976-77; MFA in Sculpture, U. Okla., 1980. Instr. Arts Annex, Oklahoma City, 1977-78, Firehouse Art Ctr., Norman, Okla., 1979-80, U. Chgo. Lab. Sch., 1984—85, Francis Parker Sch., Chgo., 1986-87, Express-Ways Children's Mus. Art, Chgo., 1987, Wai Sch., Hong Kong, 1987, Field Mus. Natural History, Chgo., 1987-88, Oklahoma City Pub. Schs., 1988-90, Fine Arts Inst. of Edmond, Okla., 1990-91, U. Okla. Mus. Art, 1991, Okla. Sch. Sci. and Math., Oklahoma City, 1992, St. Michael's Presch., Amagansett, L.I.,

1994—, Country Sch., Amagansett, 1994—, Guild Hall, East Hampton, N.Y., 1994—. Instr. SPARK Program for Inner City Children, Oklahoma City, 1989; instr., artist-in-residence State Arts Coun., Oklahoma City, 1989-92, City Arts Coun., Oklahoma City, 1977, 89-92, State Arts Coun. Colo., Denver, 1990-95, BOCES Program, Suffolk County, N.Y., 1994-2003; art dir. Hampton Day Sch. Summer Camp, Bridgehampton, N.Y., 1993; set designer Okla. Children's Theater, 1992; instr. adult art edn. City Coll., Chgo., 1982-84; vis. artist Sch. of Art Inst. Chgo., 1980; instr. art fundamentals program U. Okla., 1979-80; NYFA grantee Children's Art Workshop, Libr., Livingston, N.Y., 1999. One-woman shows include Ctrl. Innovative Gallery, Oklahoma City, 1979, Alternative Space, Norman, Okla., 1979, U. Nev. Sheppard Fine Arts Gallery, Reno, 1981, Lenore Gray Gallery, Providence, 1981, Sch. of Art Inst. Chgo. Sculpture Gallery, 1981, ABC No Rio, N.Y.C., 1984, Gas Sta./Performance Space, N.Y.C., 1987, 1997 Gallery with Alvin Gallery, Hong Kong, 1988, Kirkpatrick Ctr., Mus., Oklahoma City, 1989, Helio Gallery, N.Y.C., 1989, Okla. State U. Gardiner Art Gallery, Stillwater, 1990, Oklahoma City Art Mus., 1991, City Arts Ctr., Oklahoma City, 1992, Brickhouse Gallery, Tulsa, 1992, Conscience Point Yacht Club, Southampton, N.Y., 1993, Ashawagh Hall, East Hampton, N.Y., 1994, TSL Warehouse, Hudson, N.Y., 1996, Leslie Urbach Gallery, 1998, Albright Coll., 1999, Upstate Art, Phoenicia, N.Y., 2001, Saratoga (N.Y.) Arts Ctr., 2004, others; exhibited in group shows at M.A. Doran Gallery, Tulsa, 1991, Individual Artists of Okla. Gallery, Oklahoma City, 1992 (award), U. Ctrl. Okla. Mus. Art, Edmond, 1989-93, Brickhouse Gallery, Tulsa, 1992, Ea. N.Mex. U., Portales, 1992 (award 1992), Spazi Fine Art, Housatonic, Mass., 1992-95, Ashawagh Hall, 1994-95, Gallery North, Setauket, N.Y., 1994 (award), Danette Koke Fine Art/Ramscale Art Assocs., N.Y.C., 1995, Kendall Art & Design, Hudson, N.Y., 1998, Albany (N.Y.) Ctr. Galleries, 1998, N.Y. State Mus., Albany, 1998, Rentschler/Law Gallery, Hudson, N.Y., 1998-1999, Schenectady Mus., 1998, Kendall Art & Design, Hudson, 1999, Upstate Art, 1999, SUNY Albany Art Mus., 2000, Firehouse Gallery, Bainbridge, Ga., 2000, Upstate Art, 2000, Carrie Haddad Gallery, Hudson, 2000-2001, Albany Inst. History and Art, 2002, Arts Ctr. Capital Region, Troy, N.Y., 2002, Upstate Art, Phoenicia, NY, 2003, Columbia Country Coun. Arts, Hudson, NY, 2003, BCB ARt, Hudson, N.Y., 2003, others; represented in permanent collections at Oklahoma City Art Mus., U. Okla. Mus. Art, also pvt. collections; represented in catalog Exhibition by Artists of the Mohawk/Hudson Region, 2002. Bd. dirs. Renaissance Arts Found., Oklahoma City, 1977. Grantee Inst. for Art and Urban Resources, N.Y.C., 1980-81, Ill. Arts Coun., Chgo., 1983-84, Artists Space Exhbn., N.Y.C., 1987, Columbia Coll., Chgo., 1988, Okla. Visual Arts Coalition, 1990, Pollack-Krasner Found., Inc., 1991, Eben Demarest Trust, 1995, N.Y. Found. for the Arts, N.Y.C., 1998, 2003, N.Y. Found. Arts, 2003.

COULTER, ELIZABETH JACKSON, biostatistician, educator; b. Balt., Nov. 2, 1919; d. Waddie Pennington and Bessie (Gills) Jackson; m. Norman Arthur Coulter Jr., June 23, 1951, 1 child, Robert Jackson. AB, Swarthmore Coll., 1941; A.M., Radcliffe Coll., 1946, PhD, 1948. Asst. dir. health study Bur. Labor Stats., San Juan, P.R., 1946; research asst. Milbank Meml. Fund, N.Y.C., 1948-51; economist Office Def. Prodn., 1951-52; research analyst Children's Bur.-HEW, 1952-53; from statistician to chief statistician Ohio Dept. Health, 1954-65; lectr. econs., then clin. asst. prof. preventive medicine Ohio State U., 1954-65; asst. clin. prof. biostats. U. Pitts. Sch. Pub. Health, 1958-62; assoc. prof. biostats. U. N.C., Chapel Hill, 1965-72, assoc. prof. econs., 1965-78, biostats. prof., 1972-90; adj. assoc. prof., hosp. adminstr. Duke U., 1972-79; assoc. dean undergrad. pub. health studies U. N.C., Chapel Hill, 1979-86, prof. biostats. emerita, 1990—. Contbr. articles to profl. jours. Mem. AAAS, AAUP, APHA (governing coun. 1970-72), Am. Econ. Assn., Am. Statis. Assn., Am. Acad. Polit. and Social Sci., Biometric Soc., Am. Evaluation Assn., Assn. for Health Svcs. Rsch., Sigma Xi, Delta Omega. Methodist. Home: 1825 N Lakeshore Dr Chapel Hill NC 27514-6734

COUPEY, SUSAN MCGUIRE, pediatrician, educator; b. Montreal, Que., Can., June 29, 1942; came to U.S., 1978; d. Clarence Herbert and Paulette (Lefevre) McGuire; m. Pierre M.L. Coupey, July 1964 (div. 1981); children: Marc M.R., Ariane S.; m. James R. English III, Nov. 23, 1988. BA, Queen's U., Kingston, Ont., Can., 1962; postgrad., McGill U., Montreal, 1962-63; MD, U. B.C., Vancouver, Can., 1975. Diplomate Am. Bd. Pediatrics, subboard in adolescent medicine. Devel. chemist Merck, Sharp & Dohme, Ltd., Montreal, 1963-64; rotating intern Montreal Gen. Hosp., 1975-76; resident in pediatrics Montreal Children's Hosp., 1976-78; fellow in adolescent medicine Montefiore Med. Ctr., Bronx, N.Y., 1978-79, attending pediatrician, 1980—; rsch. asst. Cancer Rsch. Ctr., U. B.C., 1967-72; instr., asst. prof. pediatrics Albert Einstein Coll. Medicine, Bronx, 1979-85, assoc. prof., 1985-93, prof., 1993—, assoc. dir. div. adolescent medicine, 1984—2001, course dir. introduction to clin. medicine, 1989—, mem. faculty senate, 1983-84, 88-90, chief adolescent medicine, 2002—. Attending pediatrician North Ctrl. Bronx Hosp., 1979-97; cons. in adolescent medicine Flushing (N.Y.) Hosp. and Med. Ctr., 1982-96; Maricopa-Pima vis. prof. U. Ariz., 1989; vis. prof. Children's Hosp. Ea. Ont., U. Ottawa and Ea. Can. chpt. Soc. for Adolescent Medicine, 1990; vis. prof. Philippine Children's Med. Ctr., U. Philippines Coll. of Medicine, 1997; chmn. health svcs. adv. com. Children's Aid Soc., 1985—, bd. trustees, 1993—; mem. adv. bd. Office Substance Abuse Ministry, Archdiocese of N.Y., 1983-85; spkr. Hosp. Italiano, Buenos Aires, Argentina, 1999, Israeli Soc. Adolescent Medicine, Jeruseleum, Israel, 2000, Greek Soc. Adolescent Med., Athens, Greece, 2000. Editor: Primary Care of Adolescent Girls, 2000; assoc. editor Adolescent Medicine: State of the Art Revs., 1990—; assoc. editor Jour. Devel. & Behavioral Pediatrics, 1992-96, editl. bd., 1996—2000; assoc. editor Jour. Pediat. & Adolescent Gynecology, 1992-98, editl. bd. 1998—; editl. bd. Jour. of Youth and Adolescence, 1998—; contbr. articles to med. jours., also chpts. to books and monographs. Fellow Am. Acad. Pediatrics (exec. com. sect. on adolescent health 1993-96); mem. Soc. for Adolescent Medicine (nominations com. 1984-85, chmn. jour. adv. com. 1987-97, program com. 1991-93, awards com. 1992-95, bd. dirs. 1997-2000), Am. Pediat. Soc. (abstract review com. 1999—2001), Soc. for Behavioral Pediatrics, N.Am. Soc. Pediat. and Adolescent Gynecology (bd. dirs. 1993-96, sec. 1996-2001, chair publs. com. 1996—, pres.-elect 2001-2002, pres. 2002-03), Ea. Soc. Pediat. Rsch., Soc. Rsch. in Adolescence, Sex Info. and Edn. Coun. U.S., Am. Acad. Physicians and Patients, Albert Einstein Coll. Medicine Alumni Assn. (v.p. pediatrics 1983-84, pres. 1984-85). Office: Albert Einstein Coll Medicine Montefiore Med Ctr 111 E 210th St Bronx NY 10467-2401 E-mail: coupey@aecom.yu.edu.

COUPLAND, JENNIFER CHANG, finance educator; b. San Diego, June 5, 1971; d. Howard Hai-Yain and Tao-Tao Chang; m. John Neil Coupland, May 19, 2002. BS, U. Calif., Berkeley, 1993; MS, PhD, Northwestern U., 1993—98. Asst. prof. mktg. Pa. State U., University Park, 1998—2003, tchg. prof. mktg., 2003—. Contbr. BBC documentary Buyology: The Science of Shopping, articles to profl. jours. Scholar, Northwestern U. Kellogg Sch., 1993—96; faculty fellow, Advt. Ednl. Found., 1999. Mem.: Assn. for Consumer Rsch. Office: Penn State University 701 Business Administration Bldg University Park PA 16802 E-mail: jxc75@psu.edu.

COURIC, KATIE (KATHERINE ANNE COURIC), broadcast journalist; b. Arlington, Va., Jan. 7, 1957; d. John and Elinor; m. John Paul (Jay) Monahan III, 1989 (dec. 1998); children: Elinor Tully Monahan, Caroline Couric Monahan. Grad. in Am. Studies, U. Va., 1979. Desk asst. ABC News, Wash., 1979; prodr. news show CNN, Atlanta, 1980; reporter, WTVJ NBC, Miami, 1984—86, reporter, WRC-TV Washington, 1987—89, Pentagon reporter, 1989, nat. corr., Today, 1990—91, co-anchor, Today, 1991—. Contbg. anchor Dateline NBC; co-host Macy's Thanksgiving Day Parade, 1991—, Summer Olympics, Barcelona, 1992. Anchor : (documentaries) Everybody's Business: America's Children, 1995; author: The Brand New Kid, 2000. Co-founder Nat. Colorectal Cancer Rsch. Alliance (NCCRA), 1999. Named News Person Yr., TV Guide, 2001; named one of 25 Most Intriguing People, People mag., 2001; recipient six Emmys, Associated Press award, Nat. Headliner award, Sigma Delta Chi award, Nat. Soc. Profl. Journalists, Matrix award, Gracie Allen award, Peabody award, 2001, Julius B. Richmond award, Harvard Sch. Pub. Health, 2003. Address: NBC TV Today Show 30 Rockefeller Plz Fl 2 New York NY 10112-0002*

COURSON, MARNA B.P. public relations executive; b. Waynesboro, Pa., Feb. 22, 1951; d. Eugene Perry ( ) and Charlotte Mae (Sherman) Roschli; m. Sydney E. Courson, May 24, 1982 (dec. 1999); 1 child, Sydney Alexandra ; m. David W. Bowen, Oct. 14, 2001. BA, Franklin and Marshall Coll., 1973; postgrad., U. Kans., Kansas City. Reporter Beach Haven Times/The Beacon, Manahawkin, N.J., 1973-74, Dailey Observer Newspaper, Toms River, N.J., 1974-76; comm. mgr. Frick India Ltd., New Delhi, 1976-77; reporter, dictationist UPI, Washington, 1978-80, reporter Richmond, Va.; reporter, editor AP, Balt., 1980-84; comm. coord. St. Luke's Hosp. Found., Kansas City, Mo., 1986-88; exec. v.p. pub. rels. Spaw and Assocs., Inc., Overland Park, Kans., 1988-89; exec. v.p. CCI Pub. Rels. & Mktg. Comm., Inc., Shawnee Mission, Kans., 1990-92, pres. Kansas City, Mo., 1992—. Former bd. dirs. Wonderscope Children's Mus., Ctr. for Mgmt. Assistance; active Kansas City Downtown Coun.; bd. mem. Notre Dame de Sion; former bd. dirs. and former exec. com. Mid Am. Youth Aviation Assn.; bd. mem. Miracle League, Kansas City. Recipient Prism award for fund raising, numerous awards and honors for reporting, 1973-80; also pub. rels. awards, 1988-2003. Mem.: Nat. Assn. Women Bus. Owners, Pub. Rels. Soc. Am. (Pres.'s award with GKC), Internat. Assn. Bus. Communicators, World Futurists Soc., Miracle League Kans. City, Greater Kans. City C. of C., Sertoma. Office: Ste 800 934 Wyandotte Kansas City MO 64105 Office Phone: 816-471-2900. Business E-Mail: marna@cci-pr.com.

COURT GIPSON, YVETTE KRISTINA, marketing professional; b. Indianapolis, Ind., Feb. 25, 1969; d. James Arthur Court, Linda Lou and Brice Alden Tressler(Stepfather); m. Steven Wayne Gipson; stepchildren: Nathan, Morgan. BA in Mktg., Ball State U., Muncie, Ind., 1991; Honors Coll., Ball State U., 1991. Lic. Life & Health Ins. Ind., 1995; cert. Series 6-Investment Co.Products & Variable Contracts Ind., 1999, Series 63-Uniform Securities Law Ind., 1999. Mktg. asst. catalogs S. R. Jacobs & Associates, Indpls., 1991—92; operator, supr., rep. Sharp brand Innovation Mktg., Indianapolis, 1992—94; asst. mktg. rep. North Star Mktg., Indianapolis, 1994—99; v.p. mktg. Tressler Fin. Group, New Palestine, Ind., 1999—. Producer, editor Tressler Fin. Group Monthly Newsletter, New Palestine, Ind., 1999—2002. Roman Catholic. Avocations: horseback riding, reading, travel, studying German lang., dog lover. Office: Tressler Fin Group 3609 S Southway Drive New Palestine IN 46163 Office Fax: 317-861-0678.

COURTNEY, ANN M. lawyer; b. 1951; BA, Bridgewater State Coll.; JD, Western New Eng. Coll. Bar: Maine 1989. Pvt. practice, Portland, Maine; asst. V.P. & Litigation counsel Unumprovident Corp. Mem. ABA, Maine State Bar Assn. (pres. 1999). Office: 517 Summit St Portland ME 04103 also: Unumprovident Corp 2211 Congress St Portland ME 04102

COURTNEY, CAROLYN ANN, school librarian; b. Plainview, Tex., Aug. 1, 1937; d. John Blanton and Geneva Louise (Stovall) Ross; m. Moyland Henry Courtney, Aug. 17, 1957; 1 child, Constance Elaine. BA summa cum laude, Wayland Bapt. Coll., 1969; MEd, W. Tex. State Coll., 1976; MLS, U. North Tex., 1990. Cert. elem., secondary, libr. tchr. 5th grade tchr. Hale Ctr. (Tex.) Ind. Sch. Dist., 1970-77, libr., 1977—. Bd. dirs. Plainvierw Cmty. Concerts, 2000—. Mem. LWV (bd. dirs. 1970-75), DAR (Good Citizen chair 1981-85), Tex. State Tchs. Assn. (life), Tex. Classroom Tchrs. Assn. (sec. 1983-85), Tex. Libr. Assn., Delta Kappa Gamma (rsch. chair 1975-77, publs. chair 1984-86, pres. 2002--, scholarship 1975). Methodist. Avocations: genealogy, travel. Home: 209 S Floydada St Plainview TX 79072-6665 Office: Hale Center Ind Sch Dist PO Box 1210 Hale Center TX 79041 E-mail: ccourtlibr@hotmail.com.

COUTO, NANCY VIEIRA, poet, literary consultant; b. New Bedford, Mass., June 11, 1942; d. Edward and Angelina (Vieira) C.; m. Joseph Anthony Martin, Aug. 13, 1988. BS in Edn., Bridgewater State Coll., 1964; MFA, Cornell U., 1980. Secondary rights asst. Cornell U. Press, Ithaca, N.Y., 1981-82, subsidiary rights mgr., 1982-94; cons., proprietor Leatherstocking Literary Svcs., Ithaca, 1994—. Juror literature fellowship program Pa. Coun. Arts, Harrisburg, 1994; mem. selection com. fellowships Am. Antiquarian Soc., Worcester, Mass., 1995. Author: The Face in the Water, 1990 (award), various poems; assoc. editor Epoch, 1979-82, The Laurel Review, 1992-2000; poetry editor Epoch, 2000—. Artist ptnr. Cmty. Arts Partnership of Tompkins County. Creative Artists Pub. Svc. fellow N.Y. State, 1982-83, NEA fellow, 1987, 99, Creative Performing Artists and Writers fellow Am. Antiquarian Soc., 1995; Constance Saltonstall Found. for the Arts grantee, 1998; recipient Gettysburg Review award, 1994. Mem. Associated Writing Programs. Democrat.

COUTRET, KAY ELIZABETH, financial analyst; b. Garden Grove, Calif., Aug. 15, 1962; d. Alex Griffin Coutret and Betty Sue Franklin. BA, Baylor U., Waco, Tex., 2000. Cost analyst L-3 Comm. (formerly Raytheon Sys., Inc), Waco, Tex., 1989—. Bd. dirs. Waco Hippodrome Theater, 1996—99. Mem.: Sierra Club (Lone Star chpt.), VFW Ladies Aux. (Hewitt post 6008). Republican. Methodist. Avocations: equestrian, water sports, auto racing.

COUTURE, DIANE RHEA, sister, artist, educator; b. Hartford, Conn., Jan. 8, 1952; d. Rheal Paul Couture and Mary O'Shea. BA, Flagler Coll., 1979; student, U. North Fla., 1979—80; student in Pastoral Studies, Baptist Hosp., 1981—82; student in Spiritual Direction, San Pedro Ctr., 1989—92; student in Painted Glass, Klopfenstein Studios, 1995—98; student in Glass Painting, Millard Studio, 2002—03. Sister St. Joseph of St. Augustine, Fla., 1973. With Pine Hills Bike & Mower Shop, Orlando, Fla., 1968—72, Senco of Fla., Orlando, Fla., 1972—73; psych. counselor Flagler Hosp., St. Augustine, Fla., 1975—76; pastoral asst. St. Catherine Labouere Manor, Jacksonville, Fla., 1979—83; counselor Oncology Unit Mercy Hosp., Miami, Fla., 1983—87; youth minister St. Agnes Cath. Ch., Key Biscayne, Fla., 1987—89; dir. social svcs. Fla. Manor Nursing Home, Orlando, 1989—94; dir. Sisters of St. Joseph Archl. Stained Glass Studio, Orlando, 1992—99, Sisters of St. Joseph Stained Glass Studio, Orlando, 2000—. Prin. works include Meml. Window for 9/11 Victims, N.Y., Meml. Window, St. Francis of Assisi Nat. Shrine. Recipient Nat. Leadership award, Pres. U.S., 2003. Mem.: Stained Glass Assn. Am. Roman Catholic. Avocations: fishing, hiking. Office: SSJ Stained Glass 2745 Industry Ctr Rd 6 Saint Augustine FL 32084

COVALT, EDNA IRENE, retired medical/surgical nurse; b. May 3, 1935; married; 5 children. Grad., Sch. Nursing, Blackwell, Okla., 1957; AS in Nursing, Grayson State U., 1971; BSN, Wichita State U., 1979. Charge nurse Blackwell Gen. Hosp., 1957—71, Madill (Okla.) Hosp., 1957—71; dir. nursing Christ Villa Nursing Home, 1974—79, Seneca Manor, 1979—83; contract nurse Nebr., Kans., Tex., Okla., 1983—98; ret. Nurse med. pers. pool, 1974—79. Sec. First Christian Ch., Lamont, Okla., 1998-99. Home: PO Box 213 302 S Walnut Lamont OK 74643 E-mail: Landpub@yahoo.com.

COVELL, RUTH MARIE, medical educator, medical school administrator; b. San Francisco, Aug. 12, 1936; d. John Joseph and Mary Carolyn (Coles) Collins; m. James Wachob Covell, 1963 (div. 1972); 1 child, Stephen; m. Harold Joachim Simon, Jan. 4, 1973; 1 child, David. Student, U. Vienna, Austria, 1955-56; BA, Stanford U., 1958; MD, U. Chgo., 1962. Clin. prof. and assoc. dean sch. medicine U. Calif. San Diego, La Jolla, 1969—; dir. Acad. Geriatric Resource Ctr. Bd. dirs. Calif. Coun. Geriatrics and Gerontology, Beverly Found., Pasadena, Alzheimer's Family Ctr., San Diego, San Diego Epilepsy Soc., Devel. Svcs. Inc., San Ysidro Health Ctr., NIH SBIR Study Sect. Geriatrics; cons. Agy. Health Care Po licy and Rsch.; chair Calif. Ctr. Access to Care Adv. Bd. Contbr. articles on health planning and quality of med. care to profl. jours. Mem. AMA (sect. on med. schs. governing coun.), Am. Health Svcs. Rsch., Assn. Tchrs. Preventive Medicine, Am. Pub. Health Assn., Assn. Am. Med. Colls. Group on Instl. Planning (chair 1973-74, sec. 1983-84), Phi Beta Kappa, Alpha Omega Alpha. Home: 1604 El Camino Del Teatro La Jolla CA 92037-6338 Office: U Calif San Diego Sch Medicine La Jolla CA 92093-0602

COVER, KATHI A. lawyer; BSEE, Rice U., 1992; JD, U. Tex., 1995. Bar: Tex. 1995, U.S. Dist. Ct. (no. dist.) Tex. 1995, U.S. Patent and Trademark Office 1995, U.S. Dist. Ct. (ea. dist.) Tex. 1996, U.S. Ct. Appeals (fed. cir.) 1996. Various positions Tex. Instruments[;] assoc. Sidley & Austin, Dallas. Mem. ABA, Dallas-Ft. Worth Intellectual Property Law Assn. Office: Sidley & Austin 717 N Harwood St Ste 3400 Dallas TX 75201-6534 Fax: 214-981-3400. E-mail: kcover@sidley.com.

COVEY, JOY D. finance and administration executive; BSBA summa cum laude, Calif. State U., Fresno; MBA, JD magna cum laude, Harvard U. CPA, Calif. CPA Arthur Young & Co. (now Ernst & Young); mergers and acquisitions assoc. Wasserstein Perella & Co.; CFO Digidesign, 1991-95; v.p. bus. devel., v.p. ops. broadcast divsn. Avid Tech.; CFO, v.p. fin. and adminstrn. Amazon.com, Seattle, 1996—. Office: Amazon dot Com PO Box 81226 Seattle WA 98108-1300

COVEY, SUSAN COWLES, director; b. Watsonville, Calif., Nov. 30, 1947; d. Omar Horace and Betty Lou Cowles; children: Sarah Cowles, Joshua Stephen. BA, U. Calif., Santa Barbara, 1969. Cert. fundraising exec. Mem. faculty San Jose State U. Non-Profit Devel. Ctr., San Jose, 1997—99; bd. dir. Silicon Valley Planned Giving Coun., Silicon Valley, Calif., Am. Red Cross, San Jose. Precinct walker Dem. Party, San Jose, 1992—2000, active phone-a-thon, 1992—2000. Recipient Outstanding Profl. Fund Raising Exec. award, Nat. Soc. Fund Raising Execs., 2000. Democrat. Avocations: sky diving, scuba diving, tap dancing. Home: 2073 Wente Way San Jose CA 95125 Office: Cmty Found Silicon Valley San Jose CA 95113

COVILLE, ANDREA, public relations executive; BA in English Lit. and Journalism, U. N.H. With Franson & Assocs.; joined Infocom, 1984, Brodeur Worldwide, Boston, 1987, mng. ptnr., gen. mgr., pres., C.E.O., founding ptnr. Began career in New England Newspapers and magazines. Mem. Brodeur Worldwide Global Bd. Avocations: family activities, outdoor activities. Office: Brodeur Worldwide 855 Boylston St Boston MA 02116-2622*

COVINGTON, ANN K. lawyer, former state supreme court justice; b. Fairmont, W.Va., Mar. 5, 1942; d. James R. and Elizabeth Ann (Hornor) Kettering; m. James E. Waddell, Aug. 17, 1963 (div. Aug. 1976); children: Mary Elizabeth Waddell, Paul Kettering Waddell; m. Joe E. Covington, May 14, 1977. BA, Duke U., 1963; JD, U. Mo., 1977. Bar: Mo. 1977, U.S. Dist. Ct. (we. dist.) Mo. 1977. Asst. atty. gen. State of Mo., Jefferson City, 1977-79; ptnr. Covington & Maier, Columbia, Mo., 1979-81, Butcher, Cline, Mallory & Covington, Columbia, Mo., 1981-87; justice Mo. Ct. Appeals (we. dist.), Kansas City, 1987-89, Mo. Supreme Ct., 1989—2001, chief justice, 1993-95; ptnr. Bryan Cave, St. Louis, 2001—. Bd. dirs. Mid Mo. Legal Services Corp., Columbia, 1983-87; chmn. Juvenile Justice Adv. Bd., Columbia, 1984-87. Bd. dirs. Ellis Fischel State Cancer Hosp., Columbia, 1982-83, Nat. Ctr. for State Cts., 1998—; chmn. Columbia Indsl. Revenue Bond Authority, 1984-87; trustee United Meth. Ch., Columbia, 1983-86, Am. Law Inst., 1998—. Recipient Citation of Merit, U. Mo. Law Sch., 1993, Faculty-Alumni award U. Mo., 1993; Coun. of State Govt. Toll fellow, 1988. Fellow Am. Bar Found.; mem. ABA (jud. adminstrv. divsn., mem. adv. com. on Evidence Rules, U.S. Cts.), Mo. Bar Assn., Boone County Bar Assn. (sec. 1981-82), Am. Law Inst., Acad. Mo. Squires, Order of Coif (hon.), Mortar Bd. (hon.), Phi Alpha Delta, Kappa Kappa Gamma. Office: Bryan Cave One Metropolitan Sq 211 N Broadway Ste 3600 Saint Louis MO 63102-2750*

COVINGTON, EILEEN QUEEN, secondary school educator; b. Washington, May 25, 1946; d. Louis Edward and Evelyn (Travers) Q.; m. Norman Francis Covington; children: Norman, Marina, Deanna, Trena. BS, D.C. Tchrs. Coll., 1971; postgrad., George Washington U., 1978-81. Tchr., coach Evan Jr. High Sch., D.C. Pub. Schs., Washington, 1971, Woodrow Wilson H.S., Washington, 1971-95, chmn. phys. edn. dept., 1971-75, 77-81, 1984-87, athletic dir., 1988-95, Anacostia Sr. H.S., Washington, 1995—, chmn. dept. health and phys. edn., tchr. health/phys. edn., 1995—, swim coach, 1996, softball coach, 1996—, student activities dir., 1995. Cons. Coaches Assn., Washington, 1973-76; athletic dir. Woodrow Wilson H.S., 1988-95; pres. DCAA Athletic Dir. Assn., 1997—; sports chmn. in field. Named Coach of Yr., Ea. Bd. Ofcls., 1977, Nat. Coaches Assn. 2d Region, 1982, 86, Nat. Fedn. State H.S. Assns., 2000, Winningest Coach Washington Coaches Assn., 1982, Coach of Yr. U.S., 1986, Coach of Yr. Washington Post, 1987, Athletic Dir. of Yr., 1989, Volleyball All-Interhigh Coach, 1989; recipient Billie Jean King award Women Sports and Am. Fedn. Coaches, 1980-81, Disting. Women award D.C. Polit. Women Com., 1996, D.C. Women's Bd. Affiliated Chs., 1996; inducted into Nat. High Sch. Athletic Coaches Assn. Hall of Fame, 2000. Mem. NAFE, Nat. High Sch. Athletic Coaches Assn. (bd. dirs., named to Hall of Fame 2000, regional dir. region II), D.C. Coaches Assn. (3rd v.p., v.p. volleyball 1981-83, softball coach 1990, Athletic Dir. of Yr. 1992, pres. 1993-96, chmn. crew coun. 1994, Regional Softball Coach of the Yr. 1993, Coach of the Yr. in Volleyball and Softball 1993, Softball Coach of Yr. 1994, 95, Coach/Athletic Dir. of Yr. 1988), NIAAA and D.C. Coaches Assn. (named Athletic Dir. of Yr. 1998, mem. dir.), Assn. Health, Phys. Edn. Athletics, D.C. High Sch. Coaches Club, Women's Sports Found., DCIAA (pres. athletic dir. 1997—). Home: 7601 Ingrid Pl Landover MD 20785-4624 Office: Anacostia Sr HS 16 & R Sts SE Washington DC 20020 Office Phone: 202-698-2173.

COVINGTON, GERMAINE WARD, municipal agency administrator; BS in Social Work, Ind. State U., 1966; MA in Urban Studies, Occidental Coll., 1972; postgrad., Harvard U., 1998. Budget analyst City of Seattle, Office Mgmt. and Budget, 1978-87; cmty. affairs mgr. City of Seattle, Engring. Dept., 1987-90, property and ct. svcs. mgr., 1990-91, dir. exec. mgmt., 1993-94, acting dir. drainage and wastewater utility, 1993-94; dep. chief staff City of Seattle, Mayor's Office, 1991-93; dir. office for civil rights City of Seattle, 1994—. Office: Seattle Office for Civil Rights 700 3rd Ave Ste 250 Seattle WA 98104-1827 E-mail: germaine.covington@seattle.gov.

COVINGTON, PATRICIA ANN, university administrator; b. Mt. Vernon, Ill., June 21, 1946; d. Charles J. and Lois Ellen (Combs) C.; m. Burl Vance Beene, Aug. 10, 1968 (div. 1981). BA, U. N.Mex., 1968; MS in Ed., So. Ill. U., 1974, PhD, 1981. Prof. art, asst. dir. Sch. Art So. Ill. U., Carbondale, 1974-88, asst. dir. in admissions and records, 1988-95, assoc. dir. in admissions and records, 1995—2003, emerita assoc. dir., 2003—; cons. records/registration & academic affairs, 2003—04; land developer, 2004—. Mem. Am. Coun. on Edn., Nat. Com. for Army, Registry Transcript, AARTS SMART (Sailor, Marines Registry Transcript); mem. tech. com. Ill. Articulation Initiative, Ill. Bd. Higher Edn.; vis. curator Mitchell Mus., Mt. Vernon, 1977-83, judge dept. conservation; mem. panel Ill. Arts Coun., Chgo., 1982; faculty advisor European Bus. Seminar, London, 1983; edn. cons. Ill. Dept. Aging, Springfield, 1978-81, Apple Computer, Cupertino, Calif., 1982-83; mem. adminstrv. profl. coun. Soc. Ill. U., 1989-93;

presenter in field. Exhibited papercastings in nat. and internat. shows in Chgo., Fla., Calif., Tenn., N.Y. and others, 1974—; author: Diary of a Workshop, 1979, History of the School of Art at Southern Illinois University at Carbondale, 1981, Guidelines of Transcripts & Records, 2003; co-author: Transcript and Reel Guide, AACRAO Transcript and Record [illegible] National Mayfield Pub., Random House, William C. Brown, Holt, Reinhart & Winston. Bd. dirs. Humanities Couns. John A. Logan Coll., Carterville, Ill., 1982-88; mem. Ill. Higher Edn. Art Assn., chmn. bd. dirs., 1978-88; mem. Post-Doctoral Acad., 1981-95; sec. adminstrv. profl. coun., 1989-90; del. Girl Scouts USA, 1992-93, 97—, bd. dirs., mgmt. com., fin. com., bldg. com., devel. com., nominating com., Shagbark Coun., treas., 2003, chair assessment com., 2003—. Grantee Kresge Found., 1978, Nat. Endowment for the Arts, 1977, 81, Ill. Bd. Higher Edn. HECA grantee, 1994, 95; named Outstanding Young Woman of Yr. for Ill., 1981, Woman of Distinction Girl Scouts U.S.A., Thanks Badge, 2004, Pride of Shagbark, 2003. Fellow Ill. Ozarks Craft Guild (bd. dirs. 1976-83); mem. Am. Assn. Coll. Registrars and Admissions Officers (task force on transcript guidelines 2001-03), Ill. Assn. Coll. Registrars and Admissions Officers (chair so. dist., exec. com. 1992-93, nominating com. 1993-94), Spinx (hon.), Rhen Soc., Chancellor's Coun., Phi Kappa Phi. Presbyterian. Home: 389 Lake Dr Murphysboro IL 62966-5955 Office: So Ill U Carbondale IL 62901 E-mail: mmouse@siu.edu.

COVINGTON, STEPHANIE STEWART, psychotherapist, writer, educator; b. Whittier, Calif., Nov. 5, 1942; d. William and Bette (Robertson) Stewart; children: Richard, Kim. BA cum laude, U. So. Calif., 1963; MSW, Columbia U., 1970; PhD, Union Inst., 1982. Diplomate Am. Bd. Sexology, Am. Bd. Med. Psychotherapists. Pvt. practice Inst. for Relational Devel., La Jolla, Calif., 1981—; co-dir. Ctr. for Gender and Justice, La Jolla, Calif., 1981—. Instr. U. Calif., San Diego, 1981—, Calif. Sch. Profl. Psychology, San Diego, 1982-88, San Diego State U., 1982-84, Southwestern Sch. Behavioral Health Studies, 1982-84, Profl. Sch. Humanistic Psychology, San Diego, 1983-84, U.S. Internat. U., San Diego, 1983-84, UCLA, 1983-84, U. So. Calif., L.A., 1983-84, U. Utah, Salt Lake City, 1983-84; co-dir. Inst. Relational Devel.; cons. L.A. County Sch. Dist., N.C. Dept. Mental Health, Nat. Ctrs. Substance Abuse Treatment and Prevention, Nat. Inst. Corrections, others; designer women's treatment, cons. Betty Ford Ctr.; presenter and lectr. in field; addiction cons. criminal justice sys. Author: Leaving the Enchanted Forest: The Path from Relationship Addiction to Intimacy, 1988, Awakening Your Sexuality: A Guide for Recovering Women, 2000, A Woman's Way Through the Twelve Steps, 1994, Helping Women Recover: A Program for Treating Addiction (with spl. edit. for criminal justice sys.), 1999, A Womans Way Through the Twelve Steps Workbook, 2000, Beyond Trauma: A Healing Journey for Women, 2003; contbr. articles to profl. jours. Mem. NASW (diplomate), Am. Assn. Sex Educators, Counselors and Therapists, Am. Pub. Health Assn., Am. Assn. Marriage and Family Therapy, Assn. Women in Psychology, Calif. Women's Commn. on Alcoholism (Achievement award), Am. Soc. Criminology, Western Soc. Criminology, Internat. Coun. on Alcoholism and Addictions (past chair women's com.), Kettil Brun Soc. (Finland), San Diego Soc. Sex Therapy and Edn., Soc. for Study of Addiction (Eng.). Avocations: reading, theater, raising orchids. Office: 7946 Ivanhoe Ave Ste 201B La Jolla CA 92037-4517 Office Phone: 858-454-8528. Personal E-mail: sscird@aol.com.

COVINGTON, VERONICA PRO, librarian, educator; b. Laredo, Tex., Nov. 14, 1949; d. Gilberto and Herminia (Esquivel) Pro; m. Billy C. Covington, Jan. 3, 1980; children: Christina, Jennifer, Elizabeth. BS in Edn., Tex. A&I U., 1971; MEd, Sam Houston State U., 1986; PhD in Curriculum and Instruction, Tex. A&M U., 1996. English tchr. Martin H.S., Laredo, Tex., 1970-73; English tchr., chair Dunbar H.S., Lubbock, Tex., 1973-75; asst. dir. Upward Bound Tex. Tech. U., Lubbock, 1975-77; English tchr. Matthews Jr. High, Lubbock, 1977-80; English tchr., chair Mance Park Jr. High, Huntsville, Tex., 1980-90; head libr. Huntsville H.S., 1990-95; coord., testing and program evaluation Huntsville Ind. Sch. Dist., 1995-98; libr. Austin Ind. Sch. Dist., 1998—2003. Cert. translator Tex. Dept. Criminal Justice, Huntsville, 1989—; adj. prof. children's lit. U. Tex., Austin, 2000-. Contbr. articles to profl. jours. Active Huntsville Leadership Inst., 1996-97; ambassador Huntsville-Walker County C. of C., 1997-98; mentor at-risk students Huntsville Ind. Sch. Dist., 1985-97. Elected del. The White House Conf. on Libr. and Info. Svcs., Washington, 1991. Mem. Nat. Assn. for Bilingual Edn., Tex. Assn. for Bilingual Edn., Tex. Assn. of Sch. Adminstrs., Coun. for Exceptional Children, Nat. Assn. for Gifted Children, Tex. State Tchrs. Assn. (pres. 1986-89), Delta Kappa Gamma (bd. dirs. com. chair 1985). Avocations: reading, travel, writing. Office: Sch Info Univ Tex Austin TX 78739-5501

COWAL, SALLY GROOMS, diplomat, association administrator; b. Oak Park, Ill., Aug. 24, 1944; d. James Joseph and Virginia Richmond (Colborn) Smerz; m. Thomas B. Grooms, Aug. 26, 1967 (div. Jan. 1979); m. Anthony Charles Cowal, Nov. 26, 1987 (dec. May 1995); stepchildren: Gregory, J. Kirsten, Alexandra. BA, De Pauw U., 1966; MA, George Washington U., 1969. Fgn. svc. U.S. Info. Agy. and State Dept., Washington, 1966-71; spl. asst. USIS, New Delhi, 1971-73; dir. Centro Colombo Americano, Bogota, Colombia, 1973-78; cultural attache U.S. Embassy, Tel Aviv, 1978-82; dir. internat. youth exchange USIS, Washington, 1982-83; polit. counselor U.S. Mission-UN, N.Y., 1983-85; min.-counselor U.S. Embassy, Mexico City, 1985-89; dep. asst. sec. State Dept., Washington, 1989-91; amb. U.S. Embassy, Port of Spain, Trinidad and Tobago, 1991-94; dir. external rels. Jointed UN Programme on HIV/AIDS, 1995-99; pres. Youth for Understanding Internat. Exch., Washington, 1999—. Mem. Coun. on Fgn. Rels., Phi Beta Kappa. Avocations: swimming, art collecting. Home: 3223 Garfield St NW Washington DC 20008-3514 Office: 3501 Newark St NW Washington DC 20016-3100

COWAN, MARIE JEANETTE, nurse, pathology and cardiology educator; b. Albuquerque, July 20, 1938; d. Adrian Joseph and Leila Bernice (Finley) Johnson; m. Samuel Joseph Cowan, Aug. 14, 1961; children: Samuel Joseph, Kathryn Anne, Michelle Dionne. Diploma, Mary's Help Coll., 1961; BS, U. Wash., 1964, MS, 1972, PhD, 1979. Charge nurse Herrick Meml. Hosp., Berkeley, Calif., 1961-62; staff nurse ICU Univ. Hosp., Seattle, 1966-68; asst. prof. Seattle U., 1972-75; from asst. prof. to prof. nursing U. Wash., Seattle, 1979-97, assoc. dean rsch., 1985-96; dean UCLA Sch. Nursing, 1997—. Rsch. grant reviewer Am. Heart Assn. Wash., Seattle, 1977-82, divsn. rsch. grants reviewer nursing study sect., 1987-90; chair CVN AHA, 1989-91. Mem. editl. bd. Ann. Rev. Nursing Rsch., Rsch. in Nursing and Health, Nursing Rsch.; contbr. articles to profl. jours. NIH grantee, 1977, 81, 84, 85, 91, 96, 2000. Fellow Am. Acad. Nursing; mem. ANA, AACN, Wash. State Nurses Assn., Calif. State Nurses Assn. Roman Catholic. Office: UCLA Sch Nursing PO Box 951702 Los Angeles CA 90095-1702

COWEN, JEAN, employee benefits consultant; b. Winthrop, Mass., Jan. 9, 1965; d. George Milton and Barbara Jean Cowen; m. Michael David Violet, Oct. 15, 1994; children: William Michael Violet, Caitlin Elizabeth Violet, Caitlin Elizabeth Violet. BS in Psychology, BA in Econs., U. Mass., 1988; MBA, Clark U., 1994. Cert. profl. ins. woman; cert. ins. svc. rep. Multiple employeer trust coord. Home Life, Wellesley Hills, Mass., 1988-91; agt. svc. rep. Consol. Group, Framingham, Mass., 1991-92; sr. account exec. Roblin Ins. Agy., Needham, Mass., 1992-94; account mgr. William Gallager Assocs., Boston, 1994-95; prodr. Van Gilder Ins. Corp., Colorado Springs, Colo., 1996-99; sr. account exec. McLean (Va.) Ins. Agy., 2001—. Mem. citizens goals Leadership Pikes Peak, 1988; active Jr. League, Colorado Springs; mem. nominating and fin. com. Wagon Wheel coun. Girl Scouts U.S., 1988—; vol. Women's Resource Ctr., Colorado Springs, 1996-98; sponsor Air Force Cadet Sponsor Program, 1995-97. Mem. Nat. Assn. Health Underwriters (pres.'s coun. 1988), Ins. Women Colorado Springs (pres. 1997-99, dir. 1996-97, Ins. Profl. of Yr. award 1995—), So. Colo. Assn. Health Underwriters, Colo. U. Exec. Club, Clark U. Alumni Assn., U. Mass. Alumni Assn., Soc. Cert. Ins. Svc. Reps., So. Colo. Ins. Profls., Soc. Cert. Resume Writers. Avocations: scuba, Tae Kwon Do, running, downhill skiing. Home: 313 W [illegible] Sterling VA 20164-1145

COWEN, LENORE JENNIFER, mathematician, educator, computer scientist; b. N.Y. C., Apr. 10, 1967; d. Robert H. and Ilsa R. Cowen; m. William J. Bogstad, July 5, 1997. BA, Yale U., 1987; PhD, MIT, 1993. Postdoctoral fellow U. Minn., Mpls., 1993, Rutgers U., Piscataway, NJ, 1994; from asst. to assoc. prof. Johns Hopkins U., Balt., 1994—2001; sci. fellow Radcliffe inst. for advanced study Harvard U., Cambridge, Mass., 1999—2000; assoc. prof. Tufts U., Medford, Mass., 2001—. Recipient Young Investigator award, Office of Naval Rsch., 1996—99. Office: Tufts University Halligan Hall 161 College Ave Medford MA 02155 E-mail: cowen@eecs.tufts.edu.

COWGILL, URSULA MOSER, biologist, educator, environmental consultant; b. Bern, Switzerland, Nov. 9, 1927; came to U.S., 1943, naturalized, 1945; d. John W. and Mara (Siegrist) Moser. AB, Hunter Coll., 1948; MS, Kans. State U., 1952; PhD, Iowa State U., 1956. Staff MIT, Lincoln Lab., Lexington, Mass., 1957-58; field work Doherty Found., Guatemala, 1958-60; research assoc. dept. biology Yale U., New Haven, 1960-68; prof. biology and anthropology U. Pitts., 1968-81; environ. scientist Dow Chem. Co., Midland, Mich., 1981-84, assoc. environ. cons., 1984-91; environ. cons., 1991—. Mem. environ. measurements adv. com. Sci. Adv. Bd. EPA, 1976-80; Internat. Joint Commn., 1984-89. Contbr. numerous articles on ecology, biology and minerology to sci. publs. Trustee Carnegie Mus., Pitts., 1971-75. Grantee NSF 1960-78, Wenner Gren Found., 1965-66, Penrose fund Am. Philos. Soc., 1978; Sigma Xi grant-in-aid, 1965-66 Mem. AAAS, Am. Soc. Limnology and Oceanography, Internat. Soc. Theoretical and Applied Limnology. Home and Office: PO Box 1329 Carbondale CO 81623-1329

COWIN, ANNA P. state legislator, educator; b. Bklyn., May 23, 1946; m. John A. Cowin; children: David, Lynda, Scott. BA, Coll. New Rochelle (N.Y.), 1968; MS, Fordham U. Prof., counselor; mem. Fla. State Senate, Tallahassee, 1996—. Vice chmn. Children, Families and Seniors Com.; mem. Edn. Com., Natural Resources Com., Transp. Com., Subcom. B. Edn. Ways and Means Com.; field underwriter; researcher in field. Pres. Com. for Fair Utility Prices; mem. Lake County Rept. Exec. Com., 1982—; precinct committeewoman; mem., chmn. Lake County Sch. Bd., 1982-90; chmn. Lake and Sumter Counties United Way Campaign; v.p., charter mem. Leadership Lake County; pres., charter mem. Altrusa Internat. Lake County; pres., founder Edn. Found. Lake County; mem. Hospice Ethics Bd., Lake Sumter C. C. Found. Recipient Cmty. Svc. award, Leadership award City of Leesburg. Mem. Fla. Sch. Bds. Assn., Leesburg Area C. of C., Leesburg Federated Rep. Women's Club (former pres.), Leesburg Federated Republican Club, Beta Beta Beta, Sigma Xi. Roman Catholic. Home: 716 W Magnolia St Leesburg FL 34748-5893 Office: Fla Capitol Senate Office Bldg 404 S Monroe St Rm 240 Tallahassee FL 32399-6526 also: PO Box 490238 Leesburg FL 34749-0238 E-mail: cowin.anna.web@leg.state.fl.us.

COWIN, JUDITH A. state supreme court judge; m. William; 3 children. Grad., Wellesley Coll., Harvard U. Prosecutor, Norfolk County; judge Mass. Superior Ct.; assoc. justice Mass. Supreme Judicial Ct., Boston, 1999—. Office: Mass Supreme Judicial Ct 1300 New Courthouse Pemberton Sq Boston MA 02108

COWLES, ELIZABETH HALL, program consultant; b. Wichita Falls, Tex., Aug. 27, 1936; d. Eugene DeWitt and Lorena (Perry) Hall; m. James Edgar Cowles, Dec. 26, 1957 (div. Jan. 1989); children: Gary Randall, Jan Alison Cowles Sendker, Richard Scott. BS in Edn., North Tex. State U., Denton, 1958; MAIS, U. Tex., Dallas, 1994. Elem. tchr. Long Beach (Calif.) Ind. Sch. Dist., 1958—59; tchr. 6th grade Austin (Tex.) Ind. Sch. Dist., 1960—62; statewide project dir. Rainbow Days, Inc., Dallas, 1989—90; LIFESPAN exec. dir. Dallas County Hosp. Dist., Dallas, 1990—94; Dallas Healthy Start exec. dir. Fed. Initiative Dallas County Hosp. Dist., Dallas, 1994—98; nat. cons. cmty. collaboration, program devel., resource devel., 1999—. State pres. Tex. Coalition for Juvenile Justice, Dallas, 1983-84; mem. adv. com. Tex. Juvenile Probation Commn., Austin, 1987-88. Author: Early Influences on Development of English Language, 1994; initiated Listener Project, 1981. Pres. bd. dirs. Lone Star coun. Camp Fire, Dallas, 1986-87; mem. nat. steering com. Camp Fire, Inc., Kansas City, Kans., 1989; bd. dirs. United Way of Met. Dallas, 1988-89; pres. bd. dirs. Women's Coun. Dallas County, 1988-89; mem. pub. affairs com. Mental Health Assn.; mem. cmty. leaders forum Ctr. for Non-Profit Mgmt., 1996-97; mem. cmty. action com. Dallas Coun. on Alcohol and Drug Abuse, 1996-97; chair adminstrv. bd. Lovers Lane United Meth. Ch., 1997; dir. Juvenile Justice. Recipient Cmty. Advocacy award Dallas County Juvenile Dept., 1985, Gulick award for cmty. svc. Camp Fire, Inc., 1989, Women Helping Women award Women's Ctr. of Dallas County, 1995, Susan B. Anthony award United Meth. Ch., 1997, Award for Ednl. Excellence in Programming Planned Parenthood of Dallas, 1998. Mem. LWV (bd. dirs. 1982-85), Nat. Assn. Healthy Start (founding mem. bd. dirs. 1998). Avocations: travel, reading, swimming, tennis, family.

COWLES, LOIS ANNE FORT, social worker, educator; b. Providence, Dec. 26, 1933; d. Charles M. and Rebecca Parker (Latham) Fort. AB in Philosophy, Ind. U., 1955, MA in Sociology, 1964; MSW, Ind. U., Indpls., 1966; PhD, U. Wis., 1990. Social worker Meth. Hosp., Indpls., 1963-67, Community Svc. Coun., Indpls., 1967-69, Indpls. Pub. Schs., 1969-74, Middleton (Wis.) Pub. Schs., 1974-75; rsch. asst. Wis. HHS, Madison, 1976-77, 80-81; rsch. assoc. U. Wis., 1981-83, tchg. asst., 1983; ind. rschr., 1983-89; asst. prof. social work Ind. State U., Terre Haute, 1989-93; assoc. prof. social work Idaho State U., Pocatello, 1993—2003, prof. emerita, 2003—; social worker St. Thomas Free Clinic, Franklin, Ind., 2003—; instr. Sch. Social Work Ind. U., 2003—. Author: Social Work in the Health Field: A Care Perspective, 2000, 2d edit., 2003; contbr. articles to profl. jours., poetry to anthologies. Mem. NASW, ACSW, Am. Pub. Health Assn., Coun. on Social Work Edn., Soc. Social Work Leadership in Health Care, Phi Kappa Phi. E-mail: cowllois@isu.edu.

COWLISHAW, MARY LOU, government educator; b. Rockford, Ill., Feb. 20, 1932; d. Donald George and Mildred Corinne (Hayes) Miller; m. Wayne Arnold Cowlishaw, July 24, 1954; children: Beth Cowlishaw McDaniel, John, Paula Cowlishaw Rader. BS in Journalism, U. Ill., 1954; DHL, North Ctrl. Coll., 1999; DHL (hon.), Benedictine U., 2000. Mem. editorial staff Naperville (Ill.) Sun newspaper, 1977-83; mem. Ill. Ho. of Reps., Springfield, 1983—2003, chmn. elem. and secondary edn. com., 1995—97, vice-chmn. pub. utilities com., 1995—2003, mem. joint Ho.-Senate edn. reform oversight com., 1985—97; assoc. Ctr. for Govtl. Studies No. Ill. U., 2003—; adj. prof. North Ctrl. Coll., Naperville, Ill., 2003—. Mem. Ill. Task Force on Sch. Fin., 1990-96; vice chmn. Ho. Rep. Campaign Com., 1990—; co-chair Ho. Rep. Policy Com., 1991-2003; chmn. edn. com. Nat. Conf. State Legislatures, 1993-97; mem. Joint Com. Adminstrv. Rules, 1992-2003; commr. Edn. Commn. of the States, 1995-2002; chair, Ill. Women's Agenda Task Force, 1994—; mem. Nat. Edn. Goals Panel, 1996—, bd. govs. Lincoln Series for Excellence in Pub. Svc., 1996—. Author: This Band's Been Here Quite a Spell, 1983; columnist Ill. Press Assn., 2003—. Mem. Naperville Dist. 203 Bd. Edn., 1972-83; co-chmn. Ill. Citizens Coun. on Sch. Problems, Springfield, 1985-2003. Recipient 1st pl. award Ill. Press Assn., 1981, commendation Naperville Jaycees, 1986, Golden Apple award Ill. Assn. Sch. Bds., 1988, 90, 92, 94, Outstanding Women Leaders of DuPage County award West Suburban YWCA, 1990, Activator award Ill. Farm Bur., 1996, 1998, Bd. of Dirs. award Little Friends, Inc., 1998, Honor award Ill. Math. and Sci. Acad., 2002, Pub. Svc. award West Suburban Higher Edn. Consortium, 2002; named Best Legislator, Ill. Citizens for Better Care, 1985, Woman of Yr., Naperville AAUW, 1987, Best Legislator, Ill. Assn. Fire Chiefs, 1994, Outstanding Edn. Adv. Indian Prairie Sch. Dist. 204, 1994, [illegible] of Yr., Ill. Assn. Pk. Dists., 1995; commr. Edn. Commn. of the States, 1994-2002; Mary Lou Cowlishaw Elem. Sch. named in her honor, 1997, Legislator of Yr., Ill. Assn. Mus., 1998. Mem. Am. Legis. Exch. Coun., Conf. Women Legislators, Nat. Fedn. Rep. Women, DAR, Naperville Rep. Women's Club (pres. 1994—), Jr. League of Greater DuKane (cmty. adv. bd. 1997—). Methodist. Avocation: the violin. Home: 924 Merrimac Cir Naperville IL 60540-7107 Office: North Central Coll 30 N Brainard St Naperville IL 60540-4690 Office Phone: 630-637-5579.

COX, ALMA TENNEY, retired English language and science educator; b. Sand Run, W.Va., Apr. 6, 1919; d. Albert Law and Viola Columbia (Gooden) Tenney; m. James Carl Cox Jr., Sept. 8, 1945; children: James Carl III, Joseph Merrils II, Alma Lee, Elizabeth Susan, Albert John. BA, W.Va. Wesleyan Coll., 1946; MEd, West Tex. State U., 1975. Elem. sch. tchr. Floyd (Va.) County Schs., 1940-42, Nicholas County Schs., Summersville, W.Va., 1942-43; high sch. English tchr. Harrison County Schs., Lewisburg, W.Va., 1943-45; English tchr. am. Embassy, Baghdad, 1956-58; high sch. English and Sci. tchr. Tulsa Sch. System, 1965-68, Plainview (Tex.) Ind. Sch. System, 1969-86, ret., 1986. Author: Birds in Plainview, 1998. Pres. Plainview Federated Women's Club, 1988-90, Hale County Retired Tchrs., 1990-91, Hale County Hist. Com., 1985-91, United Meth. Women; sec. Disable Am. Vet. Aux., 1990. Named Woman of Yr. Plainview Federated Women's Club, 1991, Hale County Retired Tchrs., 1990-91, Disable Am. Vet. Aux., 1991, Hale County Hist. Com., 1991; recipient Woman of Distinction AAUW, 1997, disting. youth educator award, Coprock Dist. Federated Womens Club & Texas State Federated womens club, 1997, Delta Kappa Gamma Soc. Internat. Pres. Achievement award, 2000. Mem. Delta Kappa Gamma (pres. Gamma Iota chpt. 1990-92, pres. Epsilon Alpha chpt. 1998-2001). Republican. Avocations: oil painting, reading, travel, tatting, crochetting, flower gardening. Home: 5105 Stacey Ave Fort Worth TX 76132-1628

COX, BRENDA LYNN, information technology manager; b. Toledo, Ohio, Dec. 18, 1962; d. Harry A. and Lorena R. Taylor; m. Thomas Stuart Cox, June 17, 1962; children: Jonathan Thomas, Richard William. BS Adminstrv. Svcs., U. Toledo, 1998; MS in Project Mgmt., George Washington U., 2004. Project mgmt. profl., cert. project mgr. Project Mgmt. Leadership Group, 2002. Project mgr. Holcim (US), Dundee, Mich., 1996—2002. Mem.: Project Mgmt. Inst. (assoc.). Home: 309 Meadow Ln Walbridge OH 43465 Personal E-mail: tcox5@woh.rr.com.

COX, CAROL THAYER, art therapist, educator; b. East Orange, N.J., Apr. 5, 1946; d. John Alden Thayer and Sylvia Jessen Ott; m. William Jerome Cox, Feb. 3, 1968; children: Christopher Lawrence, Kimberly Thayer. BA, Mary Washington Coll., 1968; postgrad., George Washington U., 1979-80, MA, 1984. Registered art therapist; lic. profl. art therapist. Co-owner The Limited Edition Art Gallery, Fredericksburg, Va., 1975-78; art therapy cons. Prince William (Va.) County Cmty. Health Ctr., 1981-84; art therapist Accotink Acad., Springfield, Va., 1984-88; art therapy cons. Md. Inst. for Individual and Family Therapy, College Park, 1984-92; asst. prof. George Washington U., Washington, 1994—98. Adj. prof. George Washington U., 1988-93; adj. faculty summer sch. grad. art therapy program Vt. Coll. Norwich U., Montpelier, 1992-96; faculty Ea. Regional Conf. on Abuse, Trauma, and Dissociation, Alexandria, Va., 1989-96; advanced internship child and adolescent svc. dept. psychiatry Walter Reed Army Med. Ctr., Washington, 1982-83. Co-author: Telling Without Talking: Art As a Window Into Multiple Personality, 1995; contbr. articles to profl. jours. and chpts. to book. Recipient Diagnostic Drawing Series Rsch. award, 1991. Mem. Am. Art Therapy Assn. (nominating com. chair 1995-96, mem. editl. bd. Art Therapy: The Jour. of the Am. Art Assn. 1990-2000), Assn. for Tchrs. of Mandala Assessment (co-founder, dir., treas. 1990—), Va. Art Therapy Assn. (co-founder, treas. 1986-88), Va. Coalition of Arts Therapy Assns. (treas. 1987-93). Democrat. Avocations: writing poetry, painting, photography, reading, collecting trivets. Home: 130 Springwood Dr Fredericksburg VA 22401-7026 Office: Washington Art Therapy Studio 2067 Connecticut Ave NW Washington DC 20008

COX, CATHY, state official; b. Bainbridge, Ga. A.Agr., Abraham Baldwin Agrl. Coll., 1978; BJ summa cum laude, U. Ga., 1980; JD magna cum laude, Mercer U., 1986. Newspaper reporter The Times, Gainesville, 1980-82, Post-Searchlight, Bainbridge, 1982-83; atty. Hansell & Post, Atlanta, 1986-88, Lambert, Floyd & Conger, Bainbridge, Ga., 1988-95; mem. Dist. 160 Ga. Gen. Assembly, 1993-96; asst. sec. of state State of Ga., Atlanta, 1996-98, sec. of state, 1999—. Editor Mercer U. Law Rev. Named Conservation Legislator of the Yr., Ga. Wildlife Fedn., 1994, Woman of Courage award Woman's Policy Group, 1995, Woman of Yr., Ga. Commn. on Women, 2000. Democrat. Methodist. Office: Office of Sec of State 214 State Capitol SW Atlanta GA 30334-1600 E-mail: sosweb@sos.state.ga.us.*

COX, CYNTHIA A. art education specialist; b. Cleve., Mar. 29, 1957; d. Jerry L. and Lynn (Hargrove) C. BFA, Kent State U., 1979; MSEd with all honors, Lake Erie Coll., 1996. Cert. visual arts K-12, edn. specialist, Ohio. Art edn. specialist East Cleveland Schs., 1980-86, Kenston Schs., Chagrin Falls, Ohio, 1987—. Instr. profl. devel. grad. program Lake Erie Coll., Painesville, Ohio, 1996, in-svc. spkr. Kenston Schs., Chagrin Falls, Ohio, 1993, East Cleveland Schs., 1981; spkr. U.S. Joint Conf. on Edn., Beijing, 1992; vis. tchr. J.F.K. Schule, Berlin; Am. spkr. 1994 Commemorative Ceremony for Tearing Down Berlin Wall, 1994; apptd. del. leader People to People, Japan, 1999. Author, designer: Building Bridges: An International Approach to the Fine Arts, 1996; author: A Social, Cultural and Political Comparison Study of Children's Art Work from China, Germany, Bosnia and the United States, 1996. Elder Lake Shore Christian Ch., 1986-93. Mem. Ohio Art Edn. Assn., Ohio Edn. Assn., Internat. Assn. Edn. Through Art, Dwight D. Eisenhower Citizen Ambassador Program, Am. Acad. Disting. Students, Internat. Assn. of Asian Studies (presenter conf. 2000). Office: Kenston Schs 9421 Bainbridge Rd Chagrin Falls OH 44023-2703

COX, DAWN EVERLINA, paralegal; d. Donald Lewis and Everlina Cox. AS in Criminal Justice Magna Cum Laude, Johnson Wales U., 1997, BS in Criminal Justice Magna Cum Laude, 1999, MA in Tchg., 2001. Lic.: N.Y. State Licensed Security Officer, cert.: RI Pistol Revolver Cert.; Am. Red Cross. Govt. intern Office Pub. Defender, Providence, 1997—98; intern Mayer Buddy Cianci Providence Police Dept., 1997; tchg. asst., special needs tutor Johnson Wales U., 1995—99; edn. outreach specialist Cmty. Care Svcs. Inc., Attleboro, Mass., 2000—01; court adv. Riker's Island Prison Women's Prison Assn., N.Y.C., 2001; clinician heroin addiction Cmty. Substance Abuse Clinic, Fall River, Mass., 2001. Organizer, writer NAACP, Bklyn. Recipient Most Studious award, Johnson Wales U., 1997, Tutor award, 1997. Mem.: Amnesty Internat. (charter mem.), Silver Key Honor Soc., Delta Theta Phi. Democrat. Roman Catholic. Avocation: travel. Home: 438 Kosciusko St Brooklyn NY 11221 Office: Home Office 60 Radcliffe Ave Providence RI 02908 E-mail: dawn_everlinacox@hotmail.com.

COX, DONNA (BOZARD), music educator; d. Alvin Donald and Rose Caldwell Bozard; m. William Donald Cox, Jr., June 2, 1984; children: Celeste Rose, Brittany Rachel. BA, Columbia Coll., Columbia, SC, 1974—77; MMEd, U. of Ga., Athens, Ga., 1978—79. Cert. tchr. SC, 1978. Music tchr. Irmo Elem. Sch., Irmo, SC, 1979—80; spl. edn. teacher (TMD) Sedgefield Mid. Sch., Goose Creek, SC, 1980—82; tupperware mgr. Tupperware Internat., Charleston, SC, 1982—88; spl. edn. teacher (PMD) Mt. Herman Exceptional Child Ctr., Jacksonville, Fla., 1988—92; music educator Holly Hill Mid. Sch., Holly Hill, SC, 1992—93; spl. edn. teacher (EMD) Knightsville Elem. Sch., Summerville, SC, 1993—99; spl. edn. tchr. (autism) H.E. Corley Elem. Sch., Irmo, SC, 1999—2001; music educator Claude A. Taylor Elem. Sch., Cayce, SC, 2001—. Pvt. piano instr. Cox Music Instrn., Columbia, SC, 1993—; wee deliver coord. Knightsville Elem. Sch., Summerville, SC, 1993—99, grade level chairperson, 1994—96, com. chairperson, 1996—97. Concession stand vol. at football games Dutch Fork HS Band Boosters, Irmo, SC, 2002, grocery coupon coord., 2002; chaperone Riverland Hills Bapt. Ch., Columbia, SC, 2003—03; children's choir coord./dir. Hillcrest Bapt. Ch., Jacksonville, Fla., 1990—92, Crossroads Cmty. Ch., Summerville, SC, 1993—95; keyboardist for praise/worship team Summerbrook Cmty. Ch., Summerville, SC, 1997—99; pianist/children's choir coord. Grace United Meth. Ch., Columbia, SC, 2000—02; keyboardist for praise/worship team Riverland Hills Bapt. Ch., Columbia, SC, 2001—, children's choir dir., 2002—. Scholar Civitan Spl. Educator of the Yr., Civitan Club, Jacksonville, FL, 1996. Mem.: Music Educators Nat. Conf. (licentiate), Delta Omicron (life). Home: 149 Weed Drive Columbia SC 29212 Office: Claude A Taylor Elementary 103 Ann Lane Cayce SC 29033 E-mail: dcox@lex2.org.

COX, JANE, writer; b. Hackensack, N.J., Oct. 29, 1917; d. Herbert Newton and Antoinette (Vogeley) C.; m. Max Schober, Apr. 7, 1945 (div. 1971); children: Bonni Schober, Brian Schober. Student, Columbia U., 1950s, Union Theol. Sem., 1960s, Cir. in Sq. Theater, N.Y.C., 1960s. Dir., actress Chancel Players, Bloomfield, N.J., 1959-64; dir., actress, technician Probe Theatre Inc., 1965-83; dir. N.J. Regional Theatre, 1960s and 1970s; tchr. theater arts Oak Knoll Sch., Summit, N.J., 1972-79; tchr. creative drama Student Devel. Programs, Livingston and Montclair, N.J., 1960s, Manhasset (N.Y.) After Sch. Program, 1980s; freelance writer, editor N.Y.C. N.J. state drama judge Fed. Women's Clubs for Edn. Tuition, 1960s and 1970s. Actress: (film series) Face Facts, 1992, (video), 1995— Mt. Sinai Hospital Observation Theatre; contbr. essays to popular publs. including N.Y. Times, Exec. Female, The Lobby, Prime of Life. Mem. Newspaper Inst. Am. (cert.). Avocations: ice skating, reading, music. Home: 464 Main St Apt 202 Port Washington NY 11050-3138

COX, JOY DEAN, small business owner; b. Oklahoma City, Sept. 13, 1940; d. Wordy John Neely and Ethel (Russell) Neely Biggs; m. Sidney Lee Johnson, Sept. 10, 1958 (div. 1963); m. Ronald Gene Cox, Sept. 22, 1964; children: Beverly Kay, Jeffrey Wilson; 1 stepchild, Ronald D. Student pub. schs., Oklahoma City. Long-distance operator S.W. Bell Tel. Co., Oklahoma City, 1958-59, L.A., 1959-60; clk. John Pilling Shoes, Oklahoma City, 1960-62; cashier Dial Fin. Co., Houston, 1966; file clk., typist N.Am. Ins. Co., Oklahoma City, 1966-67, bookkeeper, co-owner farm and ranch ops. Dewey County, Okla., 1968—78, Panola, Okla., 1977-2001; bookkeeper, co-owner farm and ranch ops., co-op R&J Farms-Ranch, Dewey County, 1991—. Co-owner, operator Apco Svc. Sta. and Bulk Fuel Plant, Taloga, Okla., 1972-76, D&R Svc. & Supply Co., Panola, 1979-89, Eufaula, Okla., 1989-95, Taloga, 1993—; co-owner, operator Panola Store, 1980-85; dealer, co-owner Cox Chevrolet, Wilburton, Okla., 1985. Contbr. articles to newspapers and jours. Pres. Taloga Ext. Homemakers, 1971-73, sec.-treas. 1973-75; entertainer Dewey County Rest Homes, 1969-78, Latimer County Rest Homes, Wilburton, 1978-88, County of McIntosh, Eufaula, 1990-93; leader, contbr. funds to drug abuse program Latimer County 4-H, Wilburton, 1979-89; fund raiser ARC, Am. Heart Assn., Girl Scouts U.S., Panola PTA, Drug Abuse Program, Panola 4-H, Latimer County, 1979-89, Salvation Army Donations, Pittsburg County, 1977-91, Am. Cancer Soc., Taloga, 1968-78, Panola, 1978-88, McIntosh Co., Eufaula, 1988-92, Nat. Help Hospitalized Vets., 1978-90; contbr. funds to drug abuse program Wilburton, Quinton and Okla. Police Dept., McIntosh County 4H; bd. dirs. Latimer County Pick-A-Star, 1985, Clown for Eufaula and Stigler Christmas Parade, Okla., 1989-93; clown, singer McIntosh Rest Homes, 1989-93; participant Paradeentry Desert Storm Support Day, 1991; singer Eufaula Arts and Crafts Festival, 1991-93, entertainer, 1991-92; clown, singer 4th July Parade and Arts Festival, Eufaula, 1992-93; fundraiser Dewey County Hist. Jail House Mus., 1993-2000, pres., 2000; singer Pittsburg County Ann. Masons Widows Banquet, 1993. Recipient Leadership award Latimer County 4-H, 1983, Citizen of Yr. award Com. to Keep and Bear Arms, 1986. Mem. Lake Eufaula Assn. (bd. dirs. 1990-91, entertainer ann. fund raiser 1989, Friendly Lake Eufaula Area Supporters (entertainer ann. fleas Christmas parties and talent show 1991-92), Lake Eufaula Area Flying Coun. (pub. rels. rep.), Taloga Kiwanis Club (v.p. 1999-2000, pres. 2000-01). Republican. Avocations: biking, sewing, swimming, walking, reading.

COX, JULIA DIAMOND, lawyer; b. Winfield, Ill., Mar. 1, 1971; d. Darrough Blain and Linda Mann Diamond; m. John Francis Cox, Jan. 7, 1995. BS, U. Ill., 1992; JD, U. Chgo., 1995. Bar: Ill. 1995, Ohio 1996, Fla. 1996. Assoc. McDermott, Will & Emery, Chgo., 1995-99, of counsel, 1999-2000, ptnr., 2001—. Mem. Phi Beta Kappa. Office: McDermott Will & Emery 227 W Monroe St Ste 3100 Chicago IL 60606-5096

COX, KATHLEEN, broadcast executive, lawyer; BS, U. Va.; JD, U. Chgo., 1979; M of Pub. Policy, Georgetown U., 1996. Atty., Washington, LA; intellectual property counsel Bell Atlantic Corp., Washington; assoc. gen. counsel Corp. Pub. Broadcasting, 1997, gen. counsel, 1998, sr. v.p., gen. counsel and corp. sec., 1999—2002, exec. v.p. and COO, 2002—. Office: Corp Pub Broadcasting 901 E St NW Washington DC 20004-2037*

COX, KATHRYN CULLEN, laboratory executive; b. Sedalia, Mo., June 29, 1943; d. Bernard Joseph and Ann (Matthews) Cullen; m. Paul John Cox, Oct. 3, 1964 (div. Sept. 1980); children: Donna, Eric. Diploma, St. John's Mercy Med. Ctr., 1964; BS, Coll. St. Francis, 1986. Staff RN Bapt. Med. Ctr., Kansas City, Mo., 1969-80, staff RN surgery, 1980-84; oper. rm. supr. Ctr. Eye Surgery, Kansas City, 1984-86; dir. nursing Hunkeler Eye Clinic, Kansas City, 1986-93; staff nurse Glendale (Calif.) Eye Med. Group, 1993-94; mgr. consumer affairs Alcon Labs., Irvine, Calif., 1994—. Cons. ophthalmology, 1988—. Mem. Am. Soc. Ophthalmic Registered Nurses (pres. local chpt. 1984-86), Assn. Oper. Rm. Nurses, Am. Soc. Cataract & Refractive Surgery. Avocations: reading, antique restoration, exercise. Office: Alcon Labs 15800 Alton Pkwy Irvine CA 92618-3818 Home: 2322 Hedgegate Court Orlando FL 32828

COX, KATHY, education commissioner; m. John Hamilton Cox Jr.; children: John, Alex. BA in polit. sci., MA in Polit. Sci., Emory U., Atlanta. Tchr. social studies McIntosh H.S., Fayette County Bd. Edn., Atlanta, 1987—2002; rep Ga. Ho. of Reps., Atlanta, 1998—2002; sch. superintendent State of Ga., Atlanta, 2002—. Supporter Boy Scouts Am. Cub Scout Pack 201, Boy Scout Troop 275. Mem.: Kiwanis, Phi Beta Kappa. Meth. Office: Ga Dept Edn Jesse Hill Dr SE Atlanta GA 30334

COX, KEVIN, state representative; b. Oklahoma City, Okla., Dec. 1, 1949; d. Frank B. and Martina (Creuzot) Cox; m. Carless Ann Washington; 1 child, Kenny. BS in Polit. Sci., Fla.A&M U., 1972; MPA, U. Ga., 1974. With State of Okla., Okla. City, 1974—78; rep. Ho. Reps., State of Okla., Okla. City, 1981—. Chmn. ins. com. Okla. Ho. Reps., Okla. City, 1981—, mem. common edn, energy and utilities regulation, pub, health, rules, and small bus. and entrepreneurship coms., 1981. Recipient Outstanding Svc. award, Eastside YNCA, Prince Hall Masons, Prince Hall Shriners, Urban League, Sigma Gamma Rho, Delta Sigma Theta, Alpha Kappa Alpha, Zeta Phi Beta sororities, Langston U., Millwood Pub. Schs. Dist., Mary Mahoney Health Ctr., Alpha Phi Alpha Fraternity. Mem.: NAACP (life), Fla A&M Alumni Assn. (life), Langston U. Alumni Assn. (life), Shriner, Masons (33d Degree). Democrat. Avocation: cert. fooball and basketball official. Office: 2300 N Lincoln Blvd Rm 537A Oklahoma City OK 73105 Home and Office: 5300 N Lottie Oklahoma City OK 73111 E-mail: coxke@lsb.state.ok.us.

COX, LINDA SUSAN, allergist, immunologist; b. Oakland, Calif., Aug. 17, 1955; d. James Lee Dolan and Nancy Jane (Christie) C.; m. Robert Louis Wolfgram Jr.; children: Mary Elizabeth Cox, Christopher Alexander Cox-Wolfgram. BA cum laude, Boston U., 1978; postgrad., Harvard U., 1978-79, Hahnemann Med. Coll., 1979-80; MD, Northwestern U., 1985. Diplomate Am. Bd. Internal Medicine, Am. Bd. Allergy and Immunology. Intern in internal medicine Jackson Meml. Hosp., U. Miami, Fla., 1985-88; emergency room physician North Ridge Med. Ctr., Ft. Lauderdale, Fla., 1988-89; fellow in allergy and immunology Nat. Jewish Hosp., Denver, 1989-91; pvt. practice Allergy, Asthma and Clin. Immunology Ctr., Miami, Fla., 1991-92, Adult and Pediat. Allergy and Immunology, Ft. Lauderdale, 1992—; emergency rm. physician Imperial Point Med. Ctr., 1997—. Part-time emergency room physician Fitzsimmons Med. Ctr., Aurora, Colo., 1989-91, Palmetto Gen. Hosp., 1992—; rschr. U. Miami Sch. Medicine Dept. Clin. Immunology, 1987, U. Colo. Sch. Medicine Dept. Allergy and Clin. Immunology, 1990-91; asst. clin. prof. medicine U. Miami Sch. Medicine, 1996—, also bd. dirs.; asst. clin. prof. medicine Nova Southeastern U. Ortho. Sch. Medicine. Fellow Am. Coll. Allergy and Immunology, ACP; mem. Am. Acad. Allergy and Immunology, Am. Coll. Chest Physicians, Fla. Allergy and Immunology Soc. (mem. exec. com. 1998—, sec. practice std. com., mem. edn. com.), Broward County Med. Assn. (bd. dirs. 1996—). Episcopalian. Avocations: ballet, skiing. Home: 5802 Poinsettia Ave West Palm Beach FL 33407-2536 Office: 5333 N Dixie Hwy Ste 210 Fort Lauderdale FL 33334-3454

COX, MARGARET STEWART, photographer; b. Indpls., Jan. 9, 1948; d. Douglass Falconer and Margaret Geraldine (Gates) Stewart; m. Herbert Leo Cox Jr., Dec. 21, 1977 (dec. Nov. 1985); 1 child, Matthew Michael. Student, Butler U., 1965-67, Rollins Coll., 1990—93. Real estate agt. Don Asher & Assocs., Orlando, Fla., 1972-80; real estate agt., appraiser Mary P. Logvin Real Estate, Orlando, 1987-90; freelance photographer Orlando, 1990—. Exhibited photographs in group shows at Marie Selby Bot. Gardens, 1993, 94, 98 (Merit awards), 1999 Exhibit, Orlando Artists Biennial Exhbn., 1992 (Merit award), Mt. Dora Ctr. for the Arts, 1994 (Merit award), others. Bd. dirs. Adult Literacy League, Inc., Orlando, 1987-95, pres., 1994; active Fla. Literacy Coalition, 1988-96; vice chair Orange City Devel. Adv. Bd., Orlando, 1991-95, active United Way Spkrs. Bur., 1994, 95; judge Chertok Nature Photo Contest, 1993, chairperson, 1995, 96, 98; mem. Lake County Dem. Exec. Com., 1997-2001. Recipient Spl. Mission Recognition award United Meth. Women, 1985. Mem. High Country Art and Craft Guild, Nat. Audubon Soc., Fla. Audubon Soc. (bd. dirs. 1998-99), Audobon Fla. (bd. dirs. 2003-), Orange Audubon Soc. (bd. dirs. 1993-96, 97—, 98-99, rec. sec. 1996, bd. pres. 1998—2002, conservation chmn. 2002-). Democrat. Avocations: reading, travel, wildlife art, birdwatching, gardening. Office: 9410 Oak Island Ln Clermont FL 34711-7304 Office Phone: 352-429-1042.

COX, MARJORIE MILHAM, marketing manager; b. Hamlet, N.C., June 11, 1960; d. Seth Thomas and Claudia Ann (Milham) C. BS in Psychology, Duke U., 1981; MBA in Mktg., Vanderbilt U., 1985. Adminstr. Stanley H. Kaplan Edn. Ctr., Nashville, 1984-85; brand mgr. Procter & Gamble, Cin., 1985-87, Planters Lifesavers, Winston-Salem, NC, 1987-90; promotions mgr. Holly Farms, Wilkesboro, NC, 1990; product mgr. Oscar Mayer, Madison, Wis., 1990-92; mktg. mgr. Hanes Hosiery Div. of Sara Lee Corp., Winston-Salem, 1992-93; brand marketer British Am. Tobacco, Ho Chi Minh City, 1994—2003; founder, pres. Dimarxx Consulting, 2003—. Democrat. Episcopalian. Avocations: water-skiing, reading, travel, water skiing, gardening. Address: Luzicka 6 Prague 12000 Czech Republic Office: Vinohradska 90 Prague 13000 Czech Republic

COX, TERI P. public relations executive; b. Pitts., May 21, 1952; d. Meyer and Faye Helen (Tischler) Polack; m. William R. Cox, Jan. 1, 1982. BA, U. Pitts., 1974; MBA in Mktg., NYU, 1989. Info. dir. United Mental Health; prodr., host weekly PA radio program; pub. rels. dir. Atlanta Merchandise Mart; mktg. rsch., pub. rels. cons. Pfizer Inc., NYU Stern Sch. Bus.; acct. supr. Burson-Marsteller; mng. ptnr. Cox Comms. Ptnrs., Lawrenceville, N.J., 1992-98, sr. mng. ptnr., 1998—. Bd. dirs. ea. divsn. Am. Cancer Soc.; chmn. bd. devel. workgroup N.J. Cancer Coun.; chair Bd. Devel. Workgroup; mem. Advocacy Leadership Team. Recipient Capitol Dome award Nat. Am. Cancer Soc., 1997. Mem.: NAFE, Women Execs. in Pub. Rels., Healthcare Businesswomen's Assn. (past pres., adv. bd.), Pub. Rels. Soc. Am. Office: Cox Communications Partners 2 Roseberry Ct Lawrenceville NJ 08648-1058 Office Phone: 609-896-3250. Personal E-mail: coxcomptnr@aol.com.

COX ARQUETTE, COURTENEY, actress; b. Birmingham, Ala., June 15, 1964; d. Richard Lewis and Courteney (Bass-Copland) C.; m. David Arquette, June 12, 1999. Appearances include (music video) Bruce Springsteen's Dancing in the Dark, 1984, The Rembrandts I'll Be There For You, 1995; (TV Series) Murder, She Wrote, 1984, Misfits of Science, 1985-86, Family Ties, 1987-88, Dream On, 1990, Seinfeld, 1990, The Larry Sanders Show, 1992, The Trouble with Larry, 1993, Friends, 1994-2004; (TV Pilots) Sylvan in Paradise, 1986; (TV Movies) If It's Tuesday, It Still Must Be Belgium, 1987, A Rockport Christmas, 1988, Roxanne: The Prize Pulitzer, 1989, Judith Krantz's Till We Meet Again, 1989, Curiosity Kills, 1990, Morton and Hays, 1991, Topper, 1992, Sketch Artist II: Hands That See, 1995; (films) Down Twisted, 1986, Masters of the Universe, 1987, Cocoon: The Return, 1988, Mr. Destiny, 1990, Blue Desert, 1990, Shaking the Tree, 1992, The Opposite Sex (and How to Live with Them), 1993, Ace Ventura, Pet Detective, 1994, Scream, 1996, Commandments, 1996, Scream 2, 1997, The Runner, 1999, Scream 3, 2000, 3000 Miles to Graceland, 2001, The Shrink Is In, 2001 (also exec. prodr.), Get Well Soon, 2001, Alien Love Triangle, 2002, November, 2004; exec. prodr. TV Series Mix It Up, 2003. Office: Brillstein Grey Entertainment 9150 Wilshire Blvd Beverly Hills CA 90212*

COX-BEAIRD, DIAN SANDERS, middle school educator; b. Murchison, Tex., Dec. 18, 1946; d. Jessie Jackson and Lola Mae (Burton) Sanders; m. Richard Lewis Cox, May 24, 1969 (div. Nov. 1993); 1 child, Stuart Scott; m. Charles A. Beaird, Dec. 1994. AA, Kilgore Jr. Coll., 1967; BA, Stephen F. Austin State U., 1969, MEd, 1983. Cert. provisional gen. elem. edn., provisional h.s. history, govt. and polit. sci. Tchr. 8th grade Am. history and 7th grade Tex. history Chapel Hill Ind. Sch. Dist., Tyler, Tex., 1970-79; tchr. 6th-7th grade regular, advanced, remedial reading Sabine Ind. Sch. Dist., Gladewater, Tex., 1981—. Mem., tutor East Tex. Literacy Coun., Longview, 1992—; sec. Sabine Jr. High PTO, Gladewater, 1990-91; faculty sponsor cheerleaders Chapel Hill Ind. Sch. Dist., Tyler, 1970-73, rep. curriculum com., 1976, historian PTO, 1974; mem. anthology com. N.J. Writing Project in Tex., Kilgore, 1991; selected hostess Internat. Reading Conf., Tucson, 1992. Presenter: The Toothpaste Millionaire, 1992; contbr.: (short story) Vocies from the Heart, 1991. Leader Girl Scouts Am., Tyler, 1973; counselor Camp Natowa-Campfire Girls, Big Sandy, Tex., 1970; dir. Bible Sch., 1st Meth. Ch., Overton, Tex., 1980; sec. Young Dems., Kilgore, 1965-67; actress Gallery Theater, Jefferson, Tex.; mem. Opera House Theater and Galley Theater, 1992—, bd. dirs., 1996—; bd. dirs. Opera House, 1996. Named Outstanding Tchr. in Tex., Macmillan/McGraw Hill, 1991; Free Enterprise Forum scholar East Tex. Bapt. U., 1991. Mem. Internat. Reading Assn. (presenter 1992), Tex. Mid. Sch. Assn., Piney Woods Reading Coun., Tex. State Tchrs. Assn. (campus rep. 1990—, sec. Chapel Hill Ind. Sch. Dist. 1971-72), Laubach Literacy Action, Delta Kappa Gamma. Avocations: reading, travel, camping, acting. Home: PO Box 1146 Hallsville TX 75650-1146 Office: Sabine Jr H S RR 1 Box 189 Gladewater TX 75647-9723

COXE, TRUDY, museum administrator, former state official; DSc (hon.), Mass. Maritime Acad.; LLD (hon.), U. R.I. Exec. dir. R.I. Save the Bay; sec. Mass. Environ. Affairs, Boston, 1993-98; chief exec. ofcr. The Preservation Soc., Newport, R.I. Named Woman of Yr. R.I. Bus. and Profl. Women. Office: Preservation Soc of Newport Cnty Newport Mansions 424 Bellevue Ave Newport RI 02840

COX-HAYLEY, DEON MELAYNE, geriatrics services professional; b. Trenton, NJ, 1960; MD, U. Health Scis., Coll. Osteopathic Medicine, 1986. Cert. internal medicine 1990, geriatric medicine 1992, internal medicine 2000, geriatric medicine 2002. Intern Riverside Hosp., Wichita, Kans., 1986—87; resident U. Kans. Sch. Medicine, Wichita, 1987—90; fellowship U. Chgo. Hosps., Chgo., 1990—92; assoc. prof., medicine U. Chgo. Pritzker Sch. Med., Dept. Medicine, Divsn. Biological Scis.; med. dir. Windermere Sr. Health Ctr., Chgo. Office: 5841 S Md Ave MC 6098 Chicago IL 60637 Address: Windermere Sr Health Ctr and Dental Assoc 5549 S Cornell Ave Chicago IL 60615

COY, DORIS RHEA, counselor, educator; b. Portsmouth, Ohio, Sept. 7, 1938; d. Haldor Ellsworth and Dorothy Evelyn (Weese) Rhea. BS, U. Rio Grande, Ohio, 1963; MA, Ohio State U., 1966, PhD, 1996. Nat. cert. counselor, nat. cert. career counselor, nat. cert. sch. counselor; lic. prof. counselor; cert. elem. prin., supr., pupil pers., sch. counselor, elem. tchr., Ohio. Sales clk. Morris 5&10, Jackson, Ohio, 1954-58; tchr. Jackson County Schs., Jackson, 1958-59, Whitehall (Ohio) City Schs., 1959-66, sch. counselor, 1966-92, chair dept., 1982-92; pres. Am. Sch. Counselor Assn., Alexandria, Va., 1989-90, ACA, Alexandria, 1994-95; pvt. practice Doris Rhea Coy & Assocs., Pickerington, Ohio, 1979—; lectr. U. North Tex., Denton, 1996-97, asst. prof. counselor edn., 1997—. Co-dir. ERIC/CASS Ctr. for Sch. Counseling, 1998—. Editor: Toward the Transformation of Secondary School Counseling; author booklet, articles and book chpts.; author conflict mgmt. and crisis mgmt. programs. Recipient numerous awards, honors and grants. Mem. ASCD, ACA, Am. Sch. Counselor Assn., Ohio Counseling Assn. (pres. 1992-93), Ohio Sch. Counselor Assn. (pres. 1984-85), Tex. Counseling Assn. (chair profl. devel. com. 1997—), Tex. Career Guidnce assn. (sec./newsletter editor 1997-98, pres.-elect 1998—), Tex. Sch. Counselor Assn., Tex. Assn. for Counselor Educators and Suprs., League for Profl. Women, AAUW, Nat. Career Devel. Assn., Assn. for Counselor Educators and Suprs., Delta Kappa Gamma, others. Office: U North Tex Dept Counseling PO Box 311337 Denton TX 76203-1337

COYE, MOLLY JOEL, state agency administrator; b. Bennington, Vt., May 11, 1947; d. Robert Dudley Coye and Janet (Loper) Coye Nelson; m. Daniel Noah Lindheim, Sept. 22, 1974 (div. 1980); m. Mark Douglas Smith, Feb. 22, 1980; 1 child, Langston Matthew Coye. BA, U. Calif., Berkeley, 1968; MA, Stanford U., 1972; MPH, MD, Johns Hopkins U., 1977. Diplomate Am. Bd. Preventive Medicine. Chief of occupational health clinic U. San Francisco, 1979-84; med. officer Nat. Inst. for Occupational Safety & Health, 1980-85; advisor health and environment Gov.'s Office of Policy & Planning, Trenton, N.J., 1985-86; dep. commr. N.J. Dept. Health, Trenton, 1986-87; v.p. strategic devel. Health Desk Corp., Berkely, Calif., 1988-98; sr. v.p. The Lewin Group, San Francisco, 1998—. Chair adv. com. graduate program in pub. health U. Medicine and Dentistry of N.J., Newark, 1986—; mem. tech. bd. Milbank Meml. Fund, N.Y.C., 1986-88; mem. com. role of primary care physician in occupational/environ. medicine Nat. Acad. Scis, Inst. Medicine, Washington, 1986-88; mem. adv. com. AIDS U.S. Pub. Health Svc., Washington, 1989; mem. adv. coun. Nat. Inst. for Environ. Health Scis., Betheseda, Md., 1989. Co-author, editor: China: Inside the People's Republic, 1972, co-editor: China Yesterday and Today. Contbr. peer review articles to profl. jours. Founding bd. dirs. The Calif. Endowment. Recipient Virginia Apgar award March of Dimes, Plainsboro, N.J., 1988, Woman of the Yr. award Jersey Woman mag., 1989. Mem. AMA, Am. Coll. Preventive Medicine, Am. Pub. Health Assn. (chair exec. bd. 1988), Assn. for Health Svcs. Rsch., Assn. State and Territorial Health Officers (chair exec. bd. 1988—, mem. AIDS com. 1988—), Soc. for Occupational and Environ. Health (mem. governing coun. 1988—). Avocations: murder mysteries, cooking. Office: The Lewin Group 455 Market St Ste 14 San Francisco CA 94105-2450

COYKENDALL, ABBY LYNN, literature educator; b. Tucson, Jan. 21, 1971; d. Joe Garret and Sandra Coykendall. BA, U. Ariz., 1992; Ma, SUNY, Buffalo, 1997, PhD, 2002. Grad. instr. SUNY, Buffalo, 1993—99, adj. lectr., 1998—2002; assoc. instr. Daemon Coll., Buffalo, 2002; asst. prof. Ea. Mich. U., Ypsilanti, 2002—. Regents scholar, U. Ariz., 1989—93. Mem.: MLA (Florence Howe award 2001), Am. Soc. for 18th Century Studies, Aphra Behn Soc. Office: Ea Mich U Dept English Lang and Lit 612 Pray Harrold Hall Ypsilanti MI 48197

COYLE, DIANE R. artist, educator; b. Seattle, Jan. 25, 1933; d. Raymond E. and Dorothy H. (Larson) Manning; m. Jack G. Coyle, Feb. 7, 1953; children: Michael Gordon, Patrick Colin, William Scott, Linda Diane. Comml. art tech., Sinclair C.C., 1980. Instr. mixed media Riverbend Art Ctr., Dayton, Ohio, 1983-87; instr. watercolor Sinclair C.C., Dayton, Ohio, 1984—, Kettering Adult Sch., Ohio, 1986-93, Centerville Adult Sch., Ohio, 1988-92. Chmn. Dayton Fine Art Expo, 1986, 89, 95, Art in the Park, Dayton, 1984; pres. Tri Art Club, Dayton, 1986-88; juror of awards Ohio Arts and Crafts Guild, 1997; tchr. summer classes, 1992—, watercolor on cruiseline, 2004. One-woman shows include Children's Med. Ctr. and Miami Valley Hosp., 1990-95, Gallery Ten, 1993, Benham's Grove, Centerville, 1994, 95, Thum'prints Gallery, Sea Pines Ctr., Hilton Head Island, S.C., 1994, 98, Miami Valley Gallery, 1996, Lumpkins Gallery, Centerville, 1996, Preble County Art Ctr., Eaton, Ohio, 1996, numerous others; exhibited in group shows at Ohio State U., Columbus, 1991, Middletown Fine Arts Ctr., 1992, Jade Gallery, Centerville, Ohio, 1997—, numerous others; represented in permanent collections Kettering Meml. Hosp., Miami Valley Hosp., Children's Med. Ctr., WHIO Radio/TV, Four Seasons Country Club, Sunrise Fed. Savs. and Loan, Pridgen Jewelers, Mattec Corp., Hospice of Dayton, Dayton Soc. Painters & Sculptors. Mem. Ohio Watercolor Soc. (assoc.), Western Ohio Watercolor Soc., Dayton Soc. Painters & Sculptors (pres. 1986-88). Republican. Roman Catholic. Studio: Coyle Studio 1610 Ambridge Rd Centerville OH 45459-5104

COYLE, MARIE BRIDGET, retired microbiologist, retired lab administrator; b. Chgo., May 13, 1935; d. John and Bridget Veronica (Fitzpatrick) Coyle; m. Zheng Chen, Oct. 30, 1995 (div. Aug. 2000). BA, Mundelein Coll., 1957; MS, St. Louis U., 1963; PhD, Kans. State U., 1965. Diplomate Am. Bd. Med. Microbiology. Sci. instr. Sch. Nursing Columbus Hosp., Chgo., 1957-59; research assoc. U. Chgo., 1967-70; instr. U. Ill., Chgo., 1970-71; asst. prof. microbiology U. Wash., Seattle, 1973-80, assoc. prof., 1980-94, prof., 1994-2000; ret., 2000. Assoc. dir. Univ. Hosp., Seattle, 1973—76; dir. microbiology labs Harborview Med. Ctr. U. Wash., Seattle, 1976—, co-dir. postdoctoral tng. clinic microbiology, 1978—96, dir. postdoctoral tng. clinic microbiology, 1996—2000. Contbr. articles to profl. jours. Recipient Pasteur award, Ill. Soc. Microbiology, 1997, Profl. Recognition awards, Am. Bd. Med. Microbiology, Am. Bd. Med. Lab. Immunology, 2000. Fellow: Am. Acad. Microbiology; mem.: Am. Soc. Microbiology (chmn. clin. microbiology divsn. 1984—85, mem. coun. policy com. 1996—99, bd. govs. 2000—, bioMerieux Vitek Sonnenwirth Meml. award 1994), Acad. Clin. Lab. Physicians and Scientists (sec.-treas. 1980—83, mem. exec. com. 1985—90), Kappa Gamma Pi. Avocations: hiking, skiing, bicycling. Business E-Mail: mbcoyle@u.washington.edu.

COYNE, JUDITH, editor; With Glamour mag., 1986—98, sr. editor articles dept., 1989—92, exec. editor, 1992—98; editor-in-chief New Woman, 1998—2000; v.p./editor-in-chief Women.com networks, 2000—01; exec. dir. Good Housekeeping, 2001—. Office: Good Housekeeping 959 Eighth Ave New York NY 10019*

COYNE, NANCY CAROL, advertising executive; b. Washington, Mar. 14, 1946; d. John David and Gloria Louise (Davie) Druckenbrod; 1 child, Kathleen Louise. BS, NYU, 1968. Dir. visitor svcs. Lincoln Ctr., N.Y.C., 1968-71; dir. advt. Sta. WRVR Radio, N.Y.C., 1971-74; creative dir. Blaine Thompson Inc., N.Y.C., 1974-77; chief exec. officer Serino, Coyne Inc., N.Y.C., 1977— [illegible] Yale U., New Haven, Conn., 1980—; bd. dirs. Actors Fund, Williamstown Theatre Festival. Office: Serino Coyne Inc 1515 Broadway Fl 36 New York NY 10036-8901

COZZENS, MIMI, actress, director; b. Bklyn. d. Milton L. Cozzens and Dorothy Pitt. Student, Emerson Coll., 1952—54; BA in Drama Speech, Hofstra Coll., 1956. Co-chmn. intern program Actors Alley, N. Hollywood, Calif., 1997—99; tchr., dir. The Va. Ave. Project, LA, 1991—92; v.p. Co. of Angels, LA, 1977—78. Actor: (TV series) It's Not About Me, The Practice, Will & Grace, Providence, 3rd Rock From The Sun, Seinfeld, Chgo. Hope, Seventh Heaven, The Drew Carey Show, Diagnosis Murder, Star Trek; (TV films) The Pandora Project, Perfect Prey, Tell Me No Secrets, Liz: The Elizabeth Taylor Story, Livewire, Daddy, Night Of The Cyclone, Spring Break; (Broadway plays) I Ought To Be In Pictures, Children Of A Lesser God, Same Time Next Year; (plays) The Dining Room, Mornings At Seven, Same Time Next Year, Prisoner Of Second Ave, Fallen Angels, Tribute, numerious regional prodns. Rep. Valley Theatre League, North Hollywood, Calif., 1992—94. Mem.: Women In Film (co-chmn. dirs. workshop 1990—96), Acad. TV Arts and Scis. Achievements include John Powers model since age 2 1/2; former champion water skier, 14 trophies in the 1950's. Avocations: water-skiing, scuba diving, sculpting.

CRABB, BARBARA BRANDRIFF, federal judge; b. Green Bay, Wis., Mar. 17, 1939; d. Charles Edward and Mary (Forrest) Brandriff; m. Theodore E. Crabb, Jr., Aug. 29, 1959; children: Julia Forrest, Philip Elliott. AB, U. Wis., 1960, JD, 1962. Bar: Wis. 1963. Assoc. Roberts, Boardman, Suhr and Curry, Madison, Wis., 1962-64; legal rschr. Sch. Law, U. Wis., 1968-70, Am. Bar Assn., Madison, 1970-71; U.S. magistrate Madison, 1971-79; judge U.S. Dist. Ct. (we. dist.) Wis., Madison, 1979—, chief judge, 1980-96, dist. judge, 1996—. Mem. Gov. Wis. Task Force Prison Reform, 1971-73 Membership chmn., v.p. Milw. LWV, 1966-68; mem. Milw. Jr. League, 1967-68. Mem. ABA, Nat. Assn. Women Judges, State Bar Wis., Dane County Bar Assn., U. Wis. Law Alumni Assn. Office: US Dist Ct PO Box 591 120 N Henry St Madison WI 53701-0591

CRABB, VIRGINIA GEANY RUTH, librarian; b. Whittier, Calif., Dec. 30, 1951; d. Lawrence Guerro and Nellie Aguilar Gutierrez; m. Rod D. Crabb, Sept. 8, 1973; 1 child, Adam Matthew. AA in Fgn. Lang., Calif. State U., Fullerton, 1973. Children's librarian-sr. libr. asst. Orange County Libr., La Palma, Calif., 1975—76, Brea, Calif., 1976—81, sr. libr. asst. Mission Viejo, Calif., 1981—83, Orange County Libr.-University Park, Irvine, Calif., 1982—83, Orange County Libr., San Juan Capistrano, Calif., 1983—96; libr. - part time in absence of regular libr. Laguna Beach Sch. of Arts, Laguna Beach, Calif., 1988—88; sr. libr. asst. Orange County Libr., Garden Grove, Calif., 1996—98, Orange County Library-Costa Mesa, Costa Mesa, 1998—2001; children's librarian Orangewood Children's Home Libr., Orange, Calif., 2001—. Art asst. vol. Irvine Fine Arts, Irvine, Calif., 1985—85. Recipient Perspectives Study Program Cert., U. S. Ctr. for World Mission, 2003. Avocation: art travel.

CRABTREE, BEVERLY JUNE, retired dean; b. Lincoln, Nebr., June 22, 1937; d. Wayne Uniack and Frances Margaret (Wibbels) Deles Dernier; m. Robert Jewell Crabtree, June 1, 1958; children: Gregory, Karen. BS in Edn., U. Mo., 1959, MEd, 1962; PhD, Iowa State U., 1965. Tchr. home econs. area pub. schs., Pierce City and Sarcoxie, Mo., 1959-61; mem. faculty home econs. Mich. State U., East Lansing, 1964-67; assoc. prof. U. Mo., Columbia, 1967-72, coord. home econs. edn., 1967-73, prof., 1972-73, assoc. dean home econs., dir. home econs. extension programs, 1973-75; dean Coll. Home Econs. Okla. State U., Stillwater, 1975-87; dean Coll. Family and Consumer Scis. Iowa State U., Ames, 1987-97, ret., 1997. Mem. faculty Family Impact Seminar Inst. Ednl. Leadership, George Washington U., 1976-82, Cath. U. Am., 1982-87; mem. nat. panel cons. for Vocat. Ednl. Pers. Devel., 1969-70; mem. nat. com. on future of coop. extension USDA and Nat. Assn. State Univs. and Land Grant Colls., 1982; mem. joint coun. on food and agrl. scis., 1987-91. Contbr. articles in field to profl. jours. Gen. Foods fellow, 1963-64; recipient Centennial Alumni award Coll. Home Econs. Iowa State U., 1971, Alumni Citation of Merit, Coll. Home Econs. U. Mo., 1976, Profl. Achievement award Iow State U., 1983. Mem. Am. Home Econs. Assn. (pres. 1977-78, chmn. adv. coun. Ctr. for Family 1982-83, mem. coun. profl. devel. 1980-83, a leader to commemorate 75th anniversary 1984, pres. found. 1987-88, chair Coun. for Certification 1991-92, chair Coun. for Accreditation 1997-98, Disting. Svc. award 1993), Okla. Home Econs. Assn. (Profl. Achievement award 1983), Nat. Assn. State Univs. and Land Grant Colls. (mem. commn. home econs. 1981-84), Assn. Tchr. Educators, Home Econs. Edn. Assn., Nat. Coun. of Adminstrs. of Home Econs., Am. Ednl. Rsch. Assn., Am. Assn. Higher Edn., Nat. Assn. Tchr. Educators for Home Econs. (pres. 1969), Nat. Coun. on Family Relations, Mortar Bd., Golden Key, Omicron Nu, Phi Upsilon Omicron, Phi Delta Kappa, Omicron Delta Kappa, Pi Lambda Theta, Phi Kappa Phi, Gamma Sigma Delta. Methodist. Home: 3113 Rosewood Cir Ames IA 50014-4589

CRABTREE, DAVIDA FOY, minister; b. Waterbury, Conn., June 7, 1944; Alfred and Davida (Blakeslee) Foy; m. David T. Hindinger Jr., Aug. 28, 1982; stepchildren: Elizabeth Anne, David Todd. BS, Marietta Coll., 1967; MDiv, Andover Newton Theol. Sch., 1972; D of Ministry, Hartford Sem., 1989. Ordained to ministry United Ch. of Christ, 1972. Founder, exec. dir. Prudence Crandall Ctr. for Women, New Britain, Conn., 1973-76; min., dir. Greater Hartford (Conn.) Campus Ministry, 1976-80; sr. min. Colchester (Conn.) Federated Ch., 1980-91; bd. dirs. Conn. Conf. United Ch. of Christ, Hartford, 1982-90; conf. min. So. Calif. Conf., United Ch. of Christ, Pasadena, 1991-96, Conn. Conf., United Ch. of Christ, Hartford, 1996—. Rsch. assoc. Harvard Div. Sch., Cambridge, Mass., 1975-76. Author: The Empowering Church, 1989 (named one of Top Ten Books of Yr. 1990); editorial advisor Alban Inst., 1990-98. Bd. dirs. Hartford region YWCA, 1979-82, Christian Conf. of Conn., 1997—; trustee Cragin Meml. Libr., Colchester, 1980-91, Hartford Sem., 1983-91, Sch. of Theology at Claremont, 1993-96, Andover Newton Theol. Sch., 1997—; founder Youth Svcs. Bur., Colchester, 1984-89; pres. Creative Devel. for Colchester Inc., 1989-91; coun. Religious Leaders of L.A., 1991-96; v.p. Hope in Youth Campaign, 1992-96; dir. UCC Ins. bd., 1993-2000; bd. dirs. Amistad America, 1998—; trustee UCC Cornerstone Fund, 2000—; chair Coun. of Conf. Mins., United Ch. of Christ, 2004—. Named one of Outstanding Conn. Women, UN Assn., 1987; recipient Antoinette Brown award, Gen. Synod, United Ch. of Christ, 1977, Conf. Preacher award, Conn. Conf. United Ch. of Christ, 1982, Woman in Leadership award, Hartford region YWCA, 1987, Pres.'s award, Conn. Coalition Against Domestic Violence, 1997, Somos Uno award, United Neighborhood Orgn., 1995. Mem. Nat. Coun. Chs. (bd. dirs. 1969-81), Christians for Justice Action (exec. com. 1981-91). Mem. United Ch. Of Christ. E-mail: dfc@ctucc.org.

CRABTREE, VALLERI JAYNE, real estate executive, lawyer; b. Columbus, Ohio, Feb. 22, 1957; d. Ralph Dale and Ida Mae (Call) C. BS in Bus. Adminstrn., Ohio State U., 1979; JD, Capitol U., 1983. Bar: Ohio 1983; lic. real estate broker, Ohio, Fla.; CLU; FLMI. Various mgmt. positions Nationwide Life Ins. Co., Columbus, 1980-87, dir. group annuity underwriting, adminstr., 1987-91; pvt. practice Columbus, 1991-95, 99—; real estate salesperson Metro II Realty, Henderson Realty, Columbus, 1991-94; pres., broker Onyx Real Estate Svcs., Inc., Columbus, 1994—2003, Condos to Castles Realty, Inc., 2003—; atty., owner Crabtree & Assocs., Attys. at Law, Columbus, 1995-99; owner Crabtree Jocularities, 2002—, Quixtar IBO, 2003—. Mem. adj. faculty Columbus State C.C., 1995-2002; instr. IFREC, 2003—; mem. equal opportunity com. Columbus Bd. Realtors, 1996-98, 2000-2002. Chair various coms. Welsh Hills Sch. Parent Orgn., 2000—02; asst. leader Brownie Girl Scout Troop 72, 2002—03; pres. Royal Ballet Parents Orgn., 2002—; trustee Unity Ch. Christianity, Columbus, 1991—94, 1999—2000 [illegible] 1998—99, vol. bus. mgr. Light in the Woods Ch., 2000—03; bd. dirs. Royal Celebration Ballet, Inc., 2003—. Mem. AAUW, ACLU, Nat. Assn. Realtors, Ohio Assn. Realtors, Columbus Bd. Realtors, Osceola County Assn. Realtors, Fla. Assn. Realtors, Rotary. Democrat. Avocation: toy collecting. Office: Condos to Castles Realty Inc 215 Celebration Pl Ste 500 Celebration FL 34747 Office Phone: 321-246-0361.

CRACKETT, DELORES, womens bureau administrator; B in Psychology, Spelman Coll.; M in Guidance and Counseling, Atlanta U. Comm. and employment mgr. Avon Products, Inc.; dep. dir. Women's Bur., Dept. of Labor, Washington, 1993-96, field ops. mgr., regional adminstr. Region IV, Atlanta, acting dir. Washington. Office: Dept Labor 61 Forsyth St Rm 7t45 Atlanta GA 30303-2219

CRADDOCK, CATHERINE TODD, accountant; b. Dallas, June 28, 1948; d. Milton Whaley and Margaret Mary Todd; m. John Parker Craddock, May 21, 1970; children: Cliff, Ashley, J. Forrest. BA, Austin Coll., Sherman, Tex., 1970. CPA, Tex. Med. technologist M.D. Anderson Hosp., Houston, 1972-74; acct. Price Waterhouse, Sydney, Australia, 1981, Greenstein Logan & Co., Houston, 1982-86; pvt. practice acctg., Houston, 1986—. Elder, mem. session St. Thomas Presbyn. Ch., Houston, 1990—; mem. steering com. Robert E. Lee H.S., Houston, 1994-98, treas. PTO, 1994-97, pres., 1997-98, mem. adv. com. for Houston Ind. Sch. Dist., 1997-98. Mem. Tex. Soc. CPA's, Houston Estate and Fin. Forum. Avocations: reading, cooking. Office: PO Box 5829 Leander TX 78645-0028

CRADDOCK, MARY SPENCER JACK, volunteer; b. Greensboro, Ala., Dec. 12, 1912; d. Theodore Henley Jack and Alice Searcy Ashley; m. George Barksdale Craddock, Feb. 1, 1941 (dec. Dec. 11, 1985); children: George B. Jr., Theodore J., Alice (Craddock) Massey. BA, Emory U., 1933. Pres. Lynchburg (Va.) Jr. League, 1944—45; founder, bd. dirs. Seven Hills Sch., Lynchburg, 1959—70; pres. Family Svc., Lynchburg; Va. regent Gunston Hall Plantation, Commonwealth Va., 1980—92. Pres. Hillside Garden Club of Va., 1959—61; founder, bd. dirs. Lynchburg Mus. Sys., 1975—79; bd. dirs. Meals on Wheels, Lynchburg, 1993—96, Lynchburg Bicentennial Commn., 1973—76, Greater Lynchburg Cmty. Trust, 1991—99. Mem.: Nat. Soc. Col. Dames of Am. (Roll of Honor 1992—93), Boonsboro Country Club, Phi Beta Kappa. Episcopalian. Avocations: travel, bridge, reading, historic preservation. Home: 3249 Landon St Lynchburg VA 24503

CRAFT, BARBARA J. state representative; b. Junction City, Kans., Nov. 23, 1942; m. Rod Craft; children: David, Christine. BA, U. Kans., 1964. Medtech, dir. blood bank Irwin Army Hosp., 1966—70; owner, mgr. Craft's Pharmacy, 1993—99; mem. Kans. Ho. of Reps., 2003—. Leader, trainer Girl Scouts, 1973—86; bd. edn. USO 475, 1987—; elder, deacon, tchr. First Presbyn. Ch.; bd. dirs. Food Pantry Geary County, 1990—93, Kans. for Strong Ft. Riley, 1999—. Republican. Office: 181-W State Capital 300 SW 10th Ave Topeka KS 66612

CRAFT, CAROLYN M. English literature educator, priest, religion educator; b. Boston, Mass., Aug. 8, 1942; d. James Pressley Jr. and Carolyn M. Craft BA, Agnes Scott Coll., 1964; MA, U. Pa., 1965, PhD, 1973. Ordained priest. Asst. prof. English Longwood Coll., Farmville, Va., 1968-73, assoc. prof. English, 1973-80, prof. English, 1980—; priest-in-charge St. James' Emporia and St. James' Warfield, Va., 1989-92; vicar, 1993-96; assoc. rector Christ Ch., Emmanuel, and St. James Cure, 1998—2002, rector, 2003—. Vis. scholar U. Va., Charlottesville, spring 1977. Mem. editl. bd., reviewer Cross Currents, 1977—; reviewer Cross Currents, 1977—; reviewer Libr. Jour., 1978—, christianity & Lit.; religion columnist Libr. Jour., 1990-95, (chpt.) A Companion to Old and Middle English Literature. Varied Episcopal Ch. & ecumenical, Farmville, Va., 1980—2003. Postdoctoral fellow Yale U., 1974-75. Mem. MLA, South Atlantic MLA, AAUP, Medieval Acad. Am., Am. Acad. Religion, Phi Kappa Phi. Episcopalian. Office: Longwood U Farmville VA 23909-0001 Office Phone: 434-395-2162.

CRAFT, CHERYL MAE, neurobiologist, anatomist, researcher; b. Lynch, Ky., Apr. 15, 1947; d. Cecil Berton and Lillian Lovelle C.; m. Laney K. Cormney, Oct. 14, 1967 (div. Sept. 1980); children: Tyler Craft Cormney, Ryan Berton Cormney (dec.); m. Richard N. Lolley (dec.). BS in Biology, Chemistry and Math., Valdosta State Coll., 1969; cert. in Tchg. Biology and Math., Ea. Ky. U., 1971; PhD in Human Anatomy and Neurosci., U. Tex., San Antonio, 1984. Undergrad. rsch. asst. Ea. Ky. U., Richmond, 1965-67; tchg. asst. dept. cell-structural biology U. Tex. Health Sci. Ctr., San Antonio, 1979-84; postdoctoral fellowship lab. devel. neurobiology NICHD and LMDB/NEI, Bethesda, Md., 1984-86; instr. dept. psychiatry U. Tex. Southwestern Med. Ctr., Dallas, 1986-87, asst. prof., 1987-91; dir. lab. Molecular Neurogenetics Schizophrenia Rsch. Ctr., VA Med. Ctr., Dallas, 1988-94; dir. Lab. Molecular Neurogenetics Mental Health Clinic Rsch. Ctr., U. Tex. Southwestern Med. Ctr., 1990-94; assoc. prof. U. Tex. Southwestern Med. Ctr., 1991-94; Mary D. Allen chair Doheny Eye Inst. U. So. Calif. Keck Sch. Medicine, L.A., Calif., 1994—, chmn. dept. cell and neurobiology, 1994—2004. Ad hoc reviewer NEI/NIH, Bethesda, 1993—; reviewer Molecular Biology, NSPB Fight for Sight Grants, 1991-94; STAR-sci. adv. bd. U. So. Calif./Bravo Magnet H.S., L.A., 1995—. Contbr. author: Melatonin: Biosynthesis, Physiological Effects, 1993; exec. editor Exptl. Eye Rsch. jour., 1993—; editor Molecular Vision. Recipient Merit award for rsch. VA Med. Ctr., 1992, 93, 94, nomination for Women in Sci. and Engring. award Dallas VA, 1992, 93; NEI fellow, 1986, NICHD/NIH fellow, 1986. Mem. AAAS, AAUW, Assn. for Rsch. in Vision and Ophthalmology (chair program planning com. 1991-94), Am. Soc. for Neurochemistry (Jordi Folch Pi Outstanding Young Investigator 1992), Sigma Xi (sec./treas. 1986-93, pres. 1993-94). Avocations: reading, travel. Office: U So Calif Keck Sch Medicine 1355 San Pablo St Rm 405 DVRC Los Angeles CA 90033 E-mail: ccraft@usc.edu.

CRAFTON-MASTERSON, ADRIENNE, real estate company executive; b. Providence, Mar. 6, 1926; d. John Harold and Adrienne (Fitzgerald) Crafton; m. Francis T. Masterson, May 31, 1947 (div. Jan. 1977); children: Mary Victoria Masterson Bush, Kathleen Joan, John Andrew, Barbara Lynn Harrison Student, No. Va. C.C., 1971-74; A in Biblical Studies, Christ to World Bible Inst., Jacksonville, Fla., 1992; A in Pastoral Leadership, Calvary Bible Inst., Jacksonville, Fla., 1993. Mem. staff Senator T.F. Green of R.I., Washington, 1944-47, 54-60, with U.S. Senate Com. on Campaign Expenditures, 1944-45; asst. chief clk. Ho. Govt. Ops. Com., 1948-49; clk. Ho. Campaign Expenditures Com., 1950; asst. appointment sec. Office of Pres., 1951-53; with Hubbard Realty, Alexandria, Va., 1962-67; owner, mgr. Adrienne C. Masterson Real Estate, Alexandria, 1968-82; pres. Adrienne Investment Real Estate (AIRE) Ltd., Alexandria, 1982-91; devel. staff writer Calvary Internat., Jacksonville, Fla., 1992-93; Adrienne Crafton-Masterson Real Estate, Winchester, Va., 1993-94, owner, prin., broker Haymarket, Va., 1994—. Pres. AIRE-Merkli developers, 1988-92; founder AIHRE USA, Inc., 1993—. Mem. adv. panel Fairfax County (Va.) Coun. on Arts, 1987-88; founder, pres. Mt. Vernon/Lee Cultural Ctr. Found., Inc. 1984-92; mem. Haymarket (Va.) Hist. Commn., 1994-95, 97-2001, chmn., 1999-2001. Fellow Internat. Biog. Ctr. (dep. dir. gen.); mem. Internat. Orgn. Real Estate Appraisers (sr.), Nat. Assn. Realtors, No. Va. Assn. Realtors (chmn. comml. and indsl. com. 1982-83, cmty. revitalization com. 1983-84, pres. land comml. indsl. mems. 1985, v.p. land comml. and indsl. mems. 1989), Fairfax Affordable Housing Inc. (sec. 1990-91), Haymarket-Gainesville (Va.) Busl. and Profl. Assn. (bd. dirs. 1996-99, sec. 1998-99), Alexandria C. of C., Mt. Vernon/Lee C. of C., Friends of Kennedy Ctr. (founder), Optimist Club Gainesville-Haymarket (charter, bd. dirs. 1997-99). Office: Haymarket Profl Ctr PO Box 305 6611 Jefferson St Ste H Haymarket VA 20168-0305 [illegible] Office Phone: 703-754-1166. E-mail: aihrecraft@earthlink.net.

CRAGIN, MAUREEN PATRICIA, aerospace transportation executive, former federal agency administrator; BS, U.S. Naval Acad., Annapolis, Md., 1985. Pub. affairs advisor, spokesperson Women's Bur. and Glass Ceiling Commn. U.S. Dept. Labor, 1992—95; dir. comms. Com. Armed Svcs. U.S. Ho. Reps., Washington, 1995—2001; dir. congl. rels. Raytheon Co., 2001; asst. sec. pub. and intergovtl. affairs Dept. Vet. Affairs, Washington, 2001—02; v.p., comm. The Boeing Co., Washington, 2002—. Dir. vol. adminstrn. 1992 Rep. Nat. Conv., Houston; bd. trustees Am. Folklife Ctr. Libr. Congress, Washington, 2001—, dir. Vets. History Project. Served USN, comdr. USNR, pub. affairs officer USNR, 1992—. Mem.: Pub. Rels. Soc. Am., Disabled Am. Vets., Naval Res. Assn., Res. Officers Assn. Office: The Boeing Co 1200 Wilson Blvd Arlington VA 22209 Office Phone: 703-465-3252. Office Fax: 703-465-3616.

CRAGLE, DONNA LYNNE, university administrator, researcher; b. Ft Knox, Ky., Oct. 14, 1953; BA in Biol. Scis., Ind. U., 1974; MS in Human Genetics, Med. Coll. Va., 1978; PhD in Environ. Epidemiology, U. N.C., 1984. Med. lab. technologist Blood Bank, N.C. Meml. Hosp., Chapel Hill, 1977-81; tchr. asst. dept. epidemiology U. N.C., Chapel Hill, 1979-80; epidemiologist Ctr. Epidemiol. Rsch., Oak Ridge Assoc. Univs., 1981082, epidmiology rsch. sect. leader, 1983-85, epidemiology rsch. sect. leader, dep. dir., 1986-91, epidemiology rsch. leder, dir., 1991—; dir. basic and applied rsch. Oak Ridge Assocs. Univs., 1998—. Tchr. gen. genetics Pellissippi State Tech. C.C., 1993-96; cons. in field. Contbr. articles to profl. jours. Office: Oak Ridge Assoc Univs Oak Ridge Inst Sci and Edn PO Box 117 Oak Ridge TN 37831-0117

CRAGNOLIN, KAREN ZAMBELLA, real estate developer, lawyer; b. Boston, May 19, 1949; d. John T. Zambella and Corrine M. (Feeney) Zenga; m. Robert Louis Cragnolin, Sept. 8, 1974; 1 child, Nikki Josephine. BA, Georgian Ct. Coll., 1971; JD, New Eng. Sch. Law, 1974. Bar: N.Y. 1974, D.C. 1981. Sr. tax editor Prentice-Hall, Englewood Cliffs, N.J., 1974-76; dir. pub. affairs Am.-Arab Affairs Coun., Washington, 1981-83; founder, dir. Am. Bus. Coun., Dubai, United Arab Emirates, 1983-86; dir. River Link, Inc., Asheville, N.C., 1987—. Bd. trustees Clean Water Mgmt. Trust Fund, WNC Tommorrow. Pres. Young Dems., Georgian Court, N.J., 1970-71; chair Greenway Commn., Asheville, N.C., 1990—; pres., bd. dirs. Leadership Asheville, 1993—, Asheville Area C. of C., 1992-96; bd. dirs. Hand Made Am., Asheville, 1994—, Handi-Skills, Asheville, 1986-90, chmn., 1986-88. Recipient Downtown Hero award Asheville Downtown Assn., 1991, Cir. Excellence Leadership Asheville, 1995, Friend of River award Land Regional Coun., 1995, Athena award Asheville C. of C., 1999. Mem. D.C. Bar Assn., N.Y. Bar Assn. Avocations: gardening, cooking, paddling. Home: 7 Cedarcliff Rd Asheville NC 28803-2905 Office: RiverLink Inc PO Box 15488 Asheville NC 28813-0488 E-mail: Karen@riverlink.org.

CRAHALLA, JACQUELINE R. state representative; b. Phila., Oct. 8, 1940; m. Benjamin R. Crahalla; children: Benny, Richie(dec.). BA in English (magna cum laude), Gwynedd-Mercy Coll. Supr. Lower Providence Twp.; twp. liaison Lower Providence Sewer Authority; Pa. state rep., 2002—. Mgr. corp. contbn. AstraZeneca; human health divsn. Merck & Co., Inc. Feature writer, weekly corr. (newspaper) Today's Post. Republican. Lutheran. Office: 164B East Wing Harrisburg PA 17120-2020

CRAIG, BARBARA KINKSON, academic administrator; BA in Psychology with honors, U. Maine, 1964; MPA, U. Conn., 1979, DPhil in Polit. Sci., 1982. Instr. polit. sci. U. Conn., Storrs, 1979-80; asst. prof. govt. Wesleyan U., Middletown, Conn., 1982-88, assoc. prof. govt., 1989-95, prof. govt., 1995—, chair, 1997—. Vis. prof. U. Conn., 1996; spkr, presenter in field. Contbr. articles to profl. jours. Chair, co-founder Andover Fair Govt. party, campaign mgr., 1989; commr. Housing and Neighborhood Devel. Bd., New HAven, Conn., 1982-84; treas. Cold Spring, Inc., New Haven, 1980-84; apptf. mem. New Haven Redist. Commn., 1976, mayoral appointments commn., 1976-77, Greater New Haven transit study adv. com., 1974-76; chair state conv. Conn. LWV, 1976, co-pres., 1975-76, mem. exec. bd., 1968-76; mem. exec. bd. Planned Parenthood New Haven, 1974, christian Cmty. Action, 1975, Jr. League New Haven, 1971-76; chair 18th ward, mem. New HAven Rep. Town Com., 1969-70. Recipient Bosworth award, 1978, U. Conn. Rsch. Found. Doctoral Dissertatin award, 1980-81, Silver Gavel award ABA, 1989; Wesleyan Project grantee, 1985-86, 87-88, 95, 96; AAUW Palmer fellow, 1988-89, vis. fellow Washington Ctr. Study Am. Govt., Johns Hopkins U., 1994-95. Mem. Am. Soc. Pub. Adminstrn. (bd. dirs. Conn. chpt. 1981-84), Am. Polit. Sci. Assn., New England Polit. Sci. Assn. (bd. dirs. 1985-88, 94—, pres. 1996-97, pres. elect 1995-96, v.p. 1994-95, program chair ann. conf. 1987, 88), Assn. Pub. policy Analysis and Mgmt., Phi Beta Kappa, Phi Kappa Phi. Office: Wesleyan U Dept Govt 213 Pub Affairs Ctr Middletown CT 06459-0001 E-mail: bcraig@wesleyan.edu.

CRAIG, CAROL MILLS, marriage, family and child counselor; b. Berkeley, Calif. BA in Psychology (hon.), U. Calif., Santa Cruz, 1974; MA in Counseling Psychology, John F. Kennedy U., 1980; doctoral student, Calif. Sch. Profl. Psychology, Berkeley, 1980-87, Columbia Pacific U., San Rafael, Calif., 1987—. Psychology intern Fed. Correction Inst., Pleasanton, Calif., 1979-81, Letterman Army Med. Ctr., San Francisco, 1980-82, VA Mental Hygiene Clinic, Oakland, Calif., 1981-82; instr. Martinez Adult Sch., 1983, Piedmont Adult Edn., Oakland, 1986; biofeedback and stress mgmt. cons. Oakland, 1986—; child counselor Buddies-A Nonprofit, Counseling Svc. for Persons in the Arts, Lafayette, Calif., 1993—; founder Chesley Sch., 1994, Healing with Music for People and All Animals, 1996, Music Therapy for animals, 1998—. Rsch. asst. Irvington Pubs., N.Y.C., 1979, Little, Brown and Co., Boston, 1983; music therapist for people and animals, 1998—. Mem. Calif. Scholarship Fedn. (life). Avocations: music-guitar, violin, folk and opera singing, song writing, art.

CRAIG, CHAUNA JANENE, language educator; b. Great Falls, Mont., May 3, 1970; d. Robert Lowell and Necha Connolly Craig; m. Peter Hugh Egan, Aug. 17, 1991 (div. Feb. 9, 1995). BA, Mont. State, Bozeman, 1992; MA, Ariz. State, Tempe, 1995; PhD, U. Nebr., Lincoln, 1999. Asst. prof. English U. Ark., Monticello, Ark., 1998—2000; asst. prof. creative writing Ind. U. Pa., 2000—. Dir. writing ctr. U. Ark., Monticello, 2000; summer faculty Ligonier Writers Conf., Ft. Ligonier, Pa., 2001. Author (short stories): Sudden Stories: An Anthology, 2003, Green Mountains Review, 2002 (Pushcart Prize nomination, 2002); author: (essay) Calyx: A Journal of Women's Art, 2003. Mem. women's studies curriculum com. Ind. U. Pa., 2002—03. Recipient Mari Sanooz Fiction prize, Prairie Schooner Mag., 1996, Fiction Writing residency, Ragdale Found., 2003; Arts fellowship, Va. Ctr. for Creative Arts, 2003. Mem.: Nat. Coun. Tchrs. English, Associated Writing Programs. Avocations: reading, hiking. Home: 1354 Trim Tree Rd Indiana PA 15701 Office: Ind Univ Pa Dept English 421 N Walk Leonard 110 Indiana PA 15705

CRAIG, CYNTHIA MAE, mathematics educator; b. Brownsville, Tex., Jan. 22, 1951; d. Richard Virgil and Mae Margaret (Phillips) Cole; m. Daniel Baxter Craig, Jan. 15, 1971; children: Tammy Michelle Craig Black, Heather Elizabeth Craig Rios. BA, Augusta (Ga.) Coll., 1985, MEd, 1989, specialist in edn., 1993. Cert. devel. specialist; cert. tchr., Ga. Tchr. 5th-6th grade tchr. Blessed Sacrament Sch., El Paso, Tex., 1981-82; tchr. 4-8th grade honors math. St. Mary on the hill Cath. Sch., Augusta, Ga., 1985-87; tchr. Aquinas H.S., Augusta, 1987-88; asst. prof. of math. in learning support Augusta State U., 1989—, assoc. chair dept. learning support, 1998—. Presenter at profl. confs. in field. Contbr. articles to profl. jours. Mem. ASCD, Ga. Assn. of Devel. Educators, Nat. Assn. for Devel. Edn., Phi Delta Kappa (newsletter editor 1990-93, v.p. membership 1993-94, newsletter editor 1989-92, 94-96, 97-98, found. rep. 1996-97, newsletter editor 1997-98, rsch. rep. 1998—). Avocations: reading, educational research, travel. Office: Augusta State U Learning Support 2500 Walton Way Augusta GA 30904-4562 E-mail: ccraig@aug.edu.

CRAIG, JENNY, weight management executive; b. New Orleans; d. James Yoric Guidroz and Gertrude Acosta; m. Sid Craig, 1979; children: Denise, Michele. Worked for Silhouette/Am. Health gym; owner Healthetic gym; from mgr. to nat. dir. ops. Body Contour, Inc.; co-founder Jenny Craig Inc., Australia, 1983—, entered US marketplace in LA, 1985, sold company, 2002. Achievements include providing a comprehensive weight mgmt. prog. designed by registered dietitians, psychologists and a med. adv. bd. to grow into one of the largest weight mgmt. cos. in the world; only weight mgmt. co. listed on N.Y. Stock Exch.

CRAIG, JOAN CARMEN, secondary school educator, performing arts educator; b. Sacramento, Calif., July 13, 1932; d. Frank Hurtado and Enid Pearl (Hogan) Alcalde; m. Elmer Lee Craig, Aug. 14, 1955 (dec. Jan. 1981); children: Shelley, Wendy, Cathleen, Scott; m. Donald E. Peterson, 1997. BA, San Jose State U., 1954, gen. secondary cert., 1955; postgrad. studies, various univs., 1956—. Cert. tchr. (life), Calif. Drama tchr. Willow Glen High Sch. San Jose (Calif.) Unified Sch. Dist., 1955-58, Kennedy Jr. High Sch. Cupertino (Calif.) Sch. Dist., 1968-93. Cons. Cupertino Unified Sch. Dist., 1990—; coord. program activiy Growth Leadership Ctr., Mountain View, Calif., 1993; presenter Computer Use in Edn., 1990-93. Author, coord.: Drama Curriculum, 1971-93, Musical Comedy Curriculum, 1985-93, (Golden Bell, Calif. 1992). Dir. Nat. Multiple Sclerosis Soc., Santa Clara County, 1983-86. Recipient Spl. Svc. award Nat. Multiple Sclerosis Soc., Santa Clara, Calif., 1986, Hon. Membership award Nat. Jr. Honor Soc., 1990, Hon. Svc. award Calif. Congress Parents, Tchrs. and Students, Inc., 1992; named Tchr. of Year, Kennedy Jr. High, Cupertino Union Sch. Dist., 1993. Mem. AAUW, NEA, Calif. Tchrs. Assn., Cupertino Edn. Assn. (rep. 1982). Avocations: theater, hiking, biking, writing, swimming. Home: 3381 Brower Ave Mountain View CA 94040-4512

CRAIG, JOANNA BURBANK, historic site director; b. N.Y.C., Feb. 21, 1942; d. Robert DuBose and Jane (Maroney) Burbank; m. Douglas Wheelock Craig, Oct. 30, 1965 (div.); 1 child, Megan Southard. AA in Liberal Arts, Bennett Jr. Coll., Millbrook, N.Y., 1962; BA in Psychology, U. S.C., 1982. Asst. to pub. rels. dir. The New Yorker Mag., N.Y.C., 1963-68; co-owner The Corner Bookstore, Camden, S.C., 1975-80; mng. editor Sporting Classics Mag., Camden, S.C., 1982-87; pres. Craig & Vartorella, Inc., Camden, S.C., 1987—; dir. Hist. Camden Revolutionary War Site, Camden, S.C., 1989—. Editor: The Decorative Arts of Camden and Kershaw County, 1988 (Gold Addy 1988, Mead Top 60 award 1988). Commn. City of Camden Planning Comm., 1992—, Olde English Dist., Chester, S.C., 1993; bd. dirs. Kershaw County Accomodation Tax Comm., Camden, 1992-95, Camden Main St., 1991-95; mem. Kershaw County LWV, Camden, 1994-97; bd. mem., past pres. Kershaw County Hist. Soc., 1980—. Mem. Am. Assn. Mus., Am. Assn. State and Local History, S.E. Mus. Conf., Rotary. Avocations: swimming, walking, touring historical sites, global travel, volunteering. Office: Hist Camden Rev War Site PO Box 710 Camden SC 29020-0710 E-mail: hiscamden@camden.net.

CRAIG, JUDITH, bishop; b. Lexington, Mo., June 5, 1937; d. Raymond Luther and Edna Amelia (Forsha) C. BA, William Jewell Coll., 1959; MA in Christian Edn., Eden Theol. Sem., 1961; MDiv, Union Theol. Sem., 1968; DD, Baldwin Wallace Coll., 1981; DHL, Adrian Coll., 1985, Otterbein Coll., 1993, Lebanon Valley Coll., Baldwin Wallace Coll. Youth dir. Bellefontaine United Meth. Ch., St. Louis, 1959-61; intern children's work Nat. Coun. of Chs. of Christ, N.Y.C., 1961-62; dir. Christian edn. 1st United Meth. Ch., Stamford, Ct., 1962-66; inst. adult basic edn. N.Y.C. Schs., 1967; dir. Christian edn. Epworth Euclid United Meth. Ch., Cleve., 1969-72, assoc. pastor, 1972-76; pastor Pleasant Hills United Meth. Ch., Middleburg Heights, Ohio, 1976-80; conf. council dir. East Ohio Conf. United Meth. Ch., Canton, 1980-84; bishop United Meth. Ch., Mich. area, 1984-92, West Ohio area, 1992-2000; ret. Mem. United Meth. Gen. Coun. Mins., 1976-80, 88-92, United Meth. Commn. Status Role Women, 1984-88; gen. conf. del., 1980, 84; mem. United Meth. Publ. House Bd., 1992—; bd. dirs. U.S. Health Corp.; frequent lectr. and preacher; bd. trustees 27 institutions in West Ohio. Contbr. articles to ministry mags. Bd. dirs. YWCA, Middleburg Heights, 1976-80. Recipient Citation of Achievement William Jewell Coll., 1985, Woman of Achievement award YWCA, 1995.

CRAIG, KARA LYNN, children's home administrator; b. Portland, Oreg., Nov. 29, 1962; d. Raymond L. and Donna J. (Telford) Spencer. BA in Communication, Boise State U., 1985; MA in Psychology, Pepperdine U., 1990. Office mgr. Ustick Chiropractic Clinic, Boise, Idaho, 1983-85; comm. asst. First Interstate Bank Idaho, Boise, 1985-87; dir. Golden Gate U., Irvine, Calif., 1988-91, adj. prof., 1990-91; case mgr. Big Bros./Big Sisters of S.W. Idaho, Boise, 1992-94; CEO Children's Home Soc. of Idaho, Boise, 1994—. Adj. prof. Boise State U., 1992—2000. Pub. rels. com. Sounds of Music (cmty. choir), Boise, 1987—88; mem. Leadership Boise, 1996—97, S.W. Idaho Planned Giving Coun. Mem.: MENSA, Downtown Boise Rotary Club (Gov.'s 2020 Blue Ribbon Task Force 2002—03, named Rotarian of Yr. 2003, Rotarian of the Yr. 2003), Psi Chi. Avocations: playing piano and flute, ballroom dancing. Home: 12345 W Mercedes St Boise ID 83713-0501 Office: Children's Home Soc Idaho 740 Warm Springs Ave Boise ID 83712-6420 E-mail: kcraig@childrenshomesociety.com.

CRAIG, KAREN LYNN, accountant, controller; b. Detroit, Mar. 17, 1959; d. John and Corinne (Legel) C.; m. Robert A. Steshetz, May 3, 1986; children: Kamden, Kara. AS in Commerce, Henry Ford C.C., 1980; BS in Bus. and Acctg., Wayne State U., 1982. CPA, Mich., Calif. Cost and staff acct. Wilson Dairy Co., Detroit, 1982-83; sr. acct. Coopers & Lybrand, Detroit, 1984-86, supr. acct. Newport Beach, Calif., 1987-89; corp. contr. J.F. Shea Co., Inc., Walnut, Calif., 1989-99, AccentCare, 1999—. Mem. Mich. Assn. CPAs, Calif. Soc. CPAs. Avocations: music, hockey, photography, baseball. Office: 135 Technology Ste 150 Irvine CA 92618 Office Phone: 949-623-1500. E-mail: kcraig@accentcare.com.

CRAIG, LINDA (TERI) CAROL, science educator; b. Susanville, Calif., Nov. 3, 1947; d. Wayne and Hazel Marie Craig. AA, Fresno (Calif.) City Coll., 1969; BA, Fresno (Calif.) U., 1972; MSc, Jacksonville (Ala.) U., 1979. Resource tchr. Clay County Bd. Edn., Ashland, Ala., 1977—, dir. alternative sch. Lineville, Ala. Chmn. Spl. Olympics, Ashland, 1982—90; pres. Clay County Animal Welfare, Ala., chmn. bd. dirs. 2d lt. U.S. Army, 1977—83. Mem.: Ala. Edn. Assn., Women's Army Corp. Vets. Assn. Avocations: hiking, animals. Home: 69348 Hwy 49 Lineville AL 36266 Office Phone: 256-396-2870.

CRAIG, MARY LAURI, accountant; b. Helena, Mont., Jan. 19, 1936; d. Henry and Hilma (Newman) Lauri; m. William Craig (div. 1982); children: Nona Marie, Lauri Sue. BS cum laude, Rocky Mtn. Coll., 1973. CPA. Acct. various firms, Billings, Mont.; sole practice CPA Billings, 1973-78; dir. Mont. Dept. Revenue, Helena, 1979-81; sole practice CPA Helena, 1982—. Commr.'s adv. group IRS, Washington, 1994-96; exec. com. Multi-State Tax Commn., Denver. Co-author: Adventure Bound in Montana. Mem. Am. Soc. Women Accts. (pres. chpt. 100 1976), Mont. Soc. CPAs. Avocations: fly fishing, gold mining, woodworking, watercolors, music. Home and Office: 408 Washington Dr Helena MT 59601-3911

CRAIG, SUSAN LYONS, library director; b. Barksdale Air Force Base, La., Feb. 23, 1948; BA, Trinity Coll., Washington, 1971; MSLS, Fla. State U., 1976; MBA, Rosary Coll., 1989. Pub. svcs. libr. St. Mary's Coll., Moraga, Calif., 1976-79; head pub. svcs. Hood Coll., Frederick, Md., 1979-85, Dominican U. (formerly Rosary Coll.), River Forest, Ill., 1985-87; dir. libr. Aurora (Ill.) U., 1987-97; dir. libr. and acad. info. svcs. Trinity Coll. Libr., Washington, 1997—. Adj. assoc. prof Rosary Coll. Grad. Sch. Libr. and Info. Sci., 1990-97. Mem. ALA, Assn. Coll. and Rsch. Librs. (nat. adv. com., rep. Ill. chpt. 1991-95), Pvt. Acad. Librs. of Ill. (pres. 1994-96), Ill. Libr. Assn. (del. pre-White House Conf., Chgo., 1989-90), Beta Phi Mu, Phi Eta Sigma (hon.). Office: Trinity Coll Libr 125 Michigan Ave NE Washington DC 20017-1091 Office Phone: 202-844-9351. E-mail: Susancraig23@yahoo.com.

CRAIG, TERRI L. social worker; b. Louisville, Mar. 17, 1961; d. Richard Wilburn and Joella Hall Willett. BS, U. Louisville, 1983; MSW, Kent Sch. Social Wk., Louisville, 1986. LCSW N.C.; cert. clin. case mgr., HIV/AIDS educator. Clin. social worker U.S. Army, Ft. Knox, Ky., 1986—87, Bindlach, Germany, 1987—89, Ft. Hood, Tex., 1989—91, Ft. Bragg, NC, 1991—96, Ft. Meade, Md., 1996—97, VA, Balt., 1997—99, U.S. Navy, Bethesda, Md., 1999—. Dir. Dogwood HIV/AIDS Consortium, Fayetteville, NC, 1993—96; com. mem. NNMC Civilian Working Group, Bethesda, 1999—. Bd. dirs. Lambda Assn. of Fayetteville, 1993—96. Mem.: AFGE, NASW, Altrusa. Avocation: scuba diving.

CRAIN, MARY ANN, elementary school educator; b. Dallas, Sept. 5, 1951; d. Robert Lee and Mary Ann (T.) Crain. MusB in Edn., Fla. State U., 1973; MusM, Ohio State U., 1974; EdS, U. Ga., 1998. Cert. tchr. T-6, music, early childhood edn., mid. grades, ednl. leadership Ga. First clarinet Vienna Kursalon Orch., Vienna, 1975—77; band dir. Sch. Bd. of Broward County, Ft. Lauderdale, Fla., 1977—78; teller Fla. Coast Bank, Coral Springs, Fla., 1978—79; strings tchr., grades 6-7 DeKalb County Bd. of Edn., Decatur, Ga., 1979—82, band tchr., grades 6-7, 1982—86, classroom tchr., grades 4-7, 1986—96, math. specialist, grades 2-5, 1996—2000, early intervention math. and reading specialist, grades 2-5, 2000—02; math. specialist, grades 1-5 Bethesda Elem. Sch., Lawrenceville, Ga., 2002—. Office: Bethesda Elem Sch 525 Bethesda Sch Rd NW Lawrenceville GA 30044

CRAIN, TERRI L. music educator, director; d. Gary and Cheryl Crain. BA in Music, MusB in Edn., No. Ill. U., 1987. Music educator Mt. Morris (Ill.) Sch. Dist., 1989—95, Oreg. (Ill.) Sch. Dist., 1995—2003; dir. of choirs Sycamore (Ill.) HS, 2003—. Sec. Autumn on Parade, Oreg., 2000—02; pres. Performing Arts Guild, Mount Morris. Grantee, Met. Opera, 1991. Mem.: Music Educators Nat. Conf. (dist. choral rep. 1998—2003), Ill. Edn. Assn. (local pres. 1999—2003, NEA Nat. Conv. Del. 2000—02), Internat. Thespian Soc. (life; sec. 1981—82, Honor Thespian 1982), Sigma Alpha Iota (life; sec. 1984—86). Avocations: singing, acting, reading, travel. Office: Sycamore High School Spartan Trail Sycamore IL 60178 Personal E-mail: choirtchr@aol.com.

CRAMER, BETTY F. life insurance company executive; b. Indpls., Dec. 9, 1920; d. Frank E. and Ethelyn L. (Jackson) C. BA, Butler U., 1943. Sec. to head pers. dept., payroll acct. Am. United Life Ins. Co., 1943-51; Sec. to v.p. and treas. Indpls. Life Ins. Co., 1951-69, supr. bond and stock acctg., 1969-75, accounting mgr., 1976-81, asst. treas., 1981-89, ret., 1989. Advisor Jr. Achievement, Indpls., 1959-60; campaign chmn. United Way, 1980 Mem. Nat. Assn. Corp. Treas., Life Ins. Women's Assn. Indpls. (past v.p., pres.) Republican. Roman Catholic. Avocations: swimming, reading, traveling. Home: 5158 N Central Ave Indianapolis IN 46205-1060

CRAMER, PHEBE, psychologist; b. San Francisco, Dec. 30, 1935; children: Mara, Julia. BA, U. Calif., Berkeley, 1957; PhD, NYU, 1962. Clin. psychologist Malmonides Hosp., Bklyn., 1962-63; asst. prof. Psychology Barnard Coll., N.Y.C., 1963-65; vis. asst. prof. Psychology U. Calif., Berkeley, 1965-70; assoc. prof. Psychology Williams Coll., Williamstown, Mass., 1970-73, prof. Psychology, 1973—. Pvt. practice in clin. psychology, Williamstown, 1970—; chief psychologist Berkshire Mental Health Ctr., Pittsfield, Mass., 1978-86. Author: (books) Word Association, 1968, Understanding Intellectual Development, 1972, The Development of Defense Mechanisms, 1991, Story-telling, Narrative, and the Thematic Apperception Test, 1996; mem. editl. bd. Jour. of Personality, 1987-96, assoc. editor, 1991-96; mem. editl. bd. Jour. of Personality Assessment, 1989—, European Jour. Personality, 2000—, Jour. Rsch. Personality, 2003—. Judge U.S. Figure Skating Assn., 1989—. Mem.: APA, Soc. Personality and Social Psychology, Soc. for Personality Assessment. Office: Williams Coll Dept Psychology Bronfman Sci Ctr Williamstown MA 01267 Home: 20 Forest Rd Williamstown MA 01267-2029 E-mail: phebe.cramer@williams.edu.

CRANDALL, ELIZABETH WALBERT, home economics educator; b. Columbus, Kans., Jan. 18, 1914; d. Stanley Giltner and Edna Maude (Daniel) Walbert; m. Robert Dalton Crandall, Aug. 3, 1946 (dec. Sept. 1999). BS, Kans. State Coll., 1935, MS, 1939; EdD, Boston U., 1962. Tchr. Cedar Point (Kans.) H.S., 1935-36, Ellsworth (Kans.) H.S., 1936-38; instr., asst. prof. home econs. Mich. State Coll., East Lansing, 1939-46; instr., asst. prof., assoc. prof. home econs. R.I. State Coll., Kingston, 1946-62; prof. home econs., dept. chair U. R.I., Kingston, 1962-73, acting dean, Coll. Home Econs., 1973-76, dean, Coll. Home Econs., 1976-77, prof. emerita, 1977—. Vice chair R.I. Consumer Adv. Com., Office Price Stabilization, Providence, 1952-53; mem. adv. com. R.I. Office Vocat. Rehab., Providence, 1962-64, Cmty. Homemaker Svcs. R.I., Inc., Providence, 1965-79; mem. various coms., U. R.I., 1961-77. Co-author (coll. textbooks): Home Management in Theory and Practice, 1946, Management for Modern Families, 1st edit., 1954, 2d edit., 1963, 3d edit., 1973, 4th edit., 1980. Mem. So. Poverty Law Ctr., Montgomery, Ala., 1974—, Equal Rights for Maine Coalition, Augusta, 1984; citizen lobbyist, Maine Women's Lobby and Women's Devel. Inst., Hallowell, 1989—; legis. chair Maine Home Econs. Assn., rep. Women's Legis. Agenda Coalition, Augusta, 1984-93, rep. Maine Choice Coalition, Augusta, 1990-93; mem. campaign com. for Hon. Sophia Pfeiffer's election to Maine Ho. of Reps., 1990; adv. com. Bath-Brunswick Child Care Svcs., Inc., 1994-95; various other civic activities. Recipient Presdl. award for courage, svc. and integrity, Maine Lesbian/Gay Polit. Alliance, Augusta, 1987; recipient Maine Women's Hall of Fame award Maine Fedn. Bus. & Profl. Women's Clubs and U. Maine, 1996. Mem. AAUW (hon. life mem.; pres. R.I. divsn. 1977-79, rep. New England Energy Task Force 1978-79, 79-81, mem. exec. bd. 1982-90, 92-95, chair legis. program 1984-86, chair women's issues com. 1986-88, chair legal advocacy fund 1992-95; Elizabeth "Liz" W. Crandall Rsch. & Projects Endowment, AAUW of Maine, 1996), LWV (exec. bd. Brunswick, Maine league 1981-93, pres. 1983-85), NOW, Family Planning Assn. Maine, Phi Kappa Phi, Phi Upsilon Omicron, Omicron Nu (nat. editor 1953-55, nat. pres. 1957-59). Democrat. Episcopalian. Avocations: philanthropy, feminism, physical fitness, social action, wildflowers. Home: 34 Belmont St Brunswick ME 04011-3051

CRANDALL, KAREN, government agency administrator; Bus. officer High Speed Rsch. Propulsion Project Office NASA, Cleve. Active Girl Scouts U.S.; vol. Animals' Disaster Team, Cleve. Avocation: Avocations: camping, hiking, sea kayaking. Office: NASA Glenn Rsch Ctr MS 60-2 Cleveland OH 44135

CRANDALL, NANCY LEE, mayor; b. Gary, Ind., Sept. 28, 1940; d. Lawson E. and Lela A. (Bartley) Cox; m. Donald K. Crandall; children: D. Kenneth, Keith A., Bradley D. BS in Nursing, Ind. U., 1961; M in Pub. Adminstrn., Western Mich. U., 1997. RN. Nurse Univ. Hosp., Ann Arbor, Mich., 1961—62; instr. psychiat. nursing Mercywood Hosp., 1962—63; cmty. rels. Hackley Hosp., 1985—88; mem. Mich. Ho. of Reps., 1988—90; dir. Office Svcs. to the Aging, Lansing, Mich., 1991—93; mayor Norton Shores, 1993—, City of Norton Shores, 1993—. Mem. state officer's compensation commn., 1994-98; mem. claims review bd., Norton Shores, Mich., 1998—; bd. dirs. West Mich. Planned Parenthood Assn., Child and Family Svcs., Muskegon Econ. Growth Alliance; bd. trustees Mich. Health Edn. Found. Past pres. Mich. State Med. Soc. Aux., Muskegon County Med. Soc. Aux.; commr. West Mich. Regional Shoreline Com., Muskegon, 1983-86, 93—; mem. Mich. Export Devel. Authority, Lansing, 1987-89; vol. S.W. Outward Bound Sch., 1980, Earthwatch Rsch. Team, 1985, Muskegon Community Leadership Acad.; mem. Norton Shores (Mich.) City Coun., 1981-86; mem. Muskegon County Rep. Exec. Com., 1986—; mem. adminstrv. bd. Cen. United Meth. Ch.; bd. dirs. Muskegon YFCA; mem. Every Woman's Place, Mich. Health Coun., Muskegon County Landfill Authority, others. Mem. AAUW, PEO, LWV, NAACP, League of Women Voters, Mich. State Med. Soc. Auxiliary (past pres.), Urban League. Avocations: skiing, tennis, golf, running.

CRANDELL, SUSAN, magazine editor; b. Troy, N.Y., July 31, 1951; d. Irwin Norton and Grace (Thompson) C.; m. Stephan Wilkinson, June 24, 1978; 1 child, Brook Crandell. BA in History cum laude, Middlebury Coll., 1973. Mng. editor Flying Mag., N.Y.C., 1973-79; editor-in-chief Direct Mag., N.Y.C., 1982-84; editor publ. devel. Comp-U-Card Internat., Stamford, Conn., 1985-86; editor custom media group Am. Express Publs., N.Y.C., 1986-90; exec. editor Travel & Leisure, N.Y.C., 1990-93; cons. editor Smart Money, N.Y.C., 1995, In Style, N.Y.C., 1993-95; exec. editor Ladies' Home Jour., N.Y.C., 1995-2000, MORE mag., N.Y.C., 1998—2000, editor, 2000—02, editor-in-chief, 2002—. Office: More 125 Park Ave New York NY 10017-5529

CRANE, BARBARA BACHMANN, photographer, educator; b. Chgo., Mar. 19, 1928; d. Burton Stanley and Della (Kreeger) Bachmann; children: Elizabeth, Jennifer, Bruce. Student, Mills Coll., 1945-48; BA in Art History, NYU, 1950; MS in Photography, Inst. Design, Ill. Inst. Tech., 1966. Prof. photography Sch. Art Inst. Chgo., 1967-93, prof. emeritus, 1993—; vis. prof. Phila. Coll. Art (now Univ. of the Arts), 1977, Sch. Mus. Fine Arts, Boston, 1979, Cornell U., Ithaca, N.Y., 1983; represented by Revolution Gallery, Ferndale, Mich., Troyer Gallery, Washington, N.C.E. Photographie Contemporaine, Paris, Stephen Daiter Gallery, Chgo., Flatfile Photography Gallery, Chgo. Vis. prof. Bezalel Acad. Art and Design, Jerusalem, 1987. Author: (retrospective monograph) Barbara Crane: 1948-80, (exhibn. catalog) Barbara Crane: The Evolution of a Vision, 1983, Barbara Crane: Chicago Loop, 2002, Barbara Crane Urban Anomalies: Chicago, 2002. Fellow Photography fellow, NEA, 1975, 1988, Guggenheim Meml. fellow in photography, 1979—80; grantee, Polaroid Corp., 1979—95, Ill. Arts Coun., 1985, 2001. Mem.: Friends of Photography (Carmel, Calif.), Soc. Photog. Edn. (Nat. Honored Educator award 1993). Studio: 1015 W Jackson Blvd Chicago IL 60607-2918

CRANE, CHARLOTTE, law educator; b. Hanover, N.H., Aug. 30, 1951; d. Henry D. and Emily (Townsend) C.; m. Eric R. Fox, July 5, 1975; children: Hillary, Teresa. AB, Harvard U., 1973; JD, U. Mich., 1976. Bar: N.H. 1976, Ill. 1978. Law clk. to presiding judge U.S. Ct. Appeals (6th cir.), Detroit, 1976-77; law clk. to presiding justice U.S. Supreme Ct., Washington, 1977-78; assoc. Hopkins & Sutter, Chgo., 1978-82; asst. prof. Northwestern U., Chgo., 1982-86, assoc. prof., 1986-90, prof., 1990—. Contbr. articles to profl. jours. Mem. U.S. Women's Nat. Crew Team, 1976. Mem. ABA, Chgo. Tax Forum. Office: Northwestern U Sch Law 357 E Chicago Ave Chicago IL 60611-3059

CRANE, DARLINE C. real estate broker; d. Monta Sarver and Helen Christina Howlett; m. Walter Howard Crane; m. Lawrence Francis Harrington (dec.); children: Natalie Lynn, Edward John Harrington, Mitchell Howlett, Margaret Ann Harrington. AA in sci. and bus. adminstr., NH. Tech. Inst., 1980—85. Lic. Real Estate Broker NH. Real Estate Commn., 1989. Real estate broker/owner Crane & Assoc. Real Estate, Hillsboro, NH, 1991—. Mem. Hillsboro C. of C., NH, 1992—2002. Recipient Omega Tau Rho Frat., Nat. Assn. of Realtors, 2001, REALTOR of the Yr., Contoocook Valley Bd. of REALTORS, 1997. Mem.: Nat. Assn. of Realtors. Office: Crane & Assoc Real Estate 205 Bear Hill Rd P O Box 2153 Hillsboro NH 03244 E-mail: darline@hillsboronhrealestate.com.

CRANE, LAURA JANE, research chemist; b. Middletown, Ohio, Nov. 2, 1941; d. David R. and Frances T. (Watkins) Scott; m. Robert K. Crane, Apr. 13, 1972. BS, Carnegie Inst. Tech., 1963; MS, Harvard U., 1964; PhD, Rutgers U., 1972. Postdoctoral fellow Roche Inst. Molecular Biology, 1972-74, rsch. assoc., 1974-75; analytical chemist Eastman Kodak Co., Rochester, N.Y., 1962; asst. scientist Warner-Lambert Co., Morris Plains, N.J., 1965, 67-68; English tchr. Am. Sch., Manila, 1966; assoc. scientist W.R. Grace & Co., Clarksville, Md., 1969; sr. scientist diagnostic enzymology Warner-Lambert Co., 1975, group leader coagulation rsch., 1976-79; mgr. lab. products rsch. J.T. Baker Inc., Phillipsburg, N.J., 1979, asst. dir. R&D, 1980-85, dir. R&D, 1986-92; sr. dir. new product innovation Schering-Plough Health Products, Inc., Memphis, 1992-93, sr. dir. adv. products rsch. and new product innovation, 1993—2003, rsch. fellow, 2003—. Mem. faculty Seton Hall U., 1979; participant profl. symposia; mem. R&D coun. N.J., state sci. adv. coun. Rutgers U. Contbr., editor sci. articles and books. US Dregsage Federation Bronze Medalist, 2003m, Armco Corp. scholar, 1959-63; Women's Dormitory Coun. scholar; William Connelly scholar: nat. Merit scholar; NSF fellow; DuPont fellow; NDEA fellow, 1969-72, others. Mem. AAAS, Am. Chem. Soc., U.S. Dressage Fedn., Arabian Horse Registry Assn., Al Khamsa Arabian Horse Breeders Assn. (pres.). Home: 7155 Highway 194 Williston TN 38076-3511 Office: Schering-Plough Health Products Inc 3030 Jackson Ave Memphis TN 38112-2020 E-mail: laura.crane@spcorp.com.

CRANE, PATRICIA SUE, probation services administrator, social worker; b. Rockway, N.Y., Jan. 17, 1948; d. Herbert Milton and Miriam (Rosenblum) Brager; m. Marvin J. Crane, May 2, 1971; 1 child, Elizabeth A. BA, U. Wis., 1969; MS in Criminal Justice with honors, Wayne State U., 1984. Cert. social worker. Dir. probation svcs. 52d dist. ct. 1st divsn. State of Mich., Novi, 1979—. Jewish. Avocations: marathon runner, athlete. Home: 5042 Meadowbrook Dr West Bloomfield MI 48322-1570 Office: 52nd Dist Ct 1st Divsn 48150 Grand River Ave Novi MI 48374-1222 E-mail: trissiec@aol.com.

CRANER, WANDA DIETZ, clergywoman, therapist; b. Columbia, Pa., Nov. 28, 1953; d. Ronald Nelson and June Faye (Kline) Dietz; m. Steven Michael Craner, Dec. 9, 1978. BS in Biology, Millersville (Pa.) U., 1975; MDiv, Lancaster Theol. Sem., 1986; postgrad., Lancaster Gen. Hosp., 1986. Ordained to ministry United Ch. of Christ, 1988; cert. group leader's program Shalem Inst. Spiritual Formation. Tchr. life sci. and phys. sci. Spring-Ford Sch. Dist., Royersford, Pa., 1975-81; assoc. pastor, min. of wholeness Shenkel United Ch. of Christ, Pottstown, Pa., 1987-96; min. spiritual nurture Pa. S.E. Conf., United Ch. of Christ, Collegeville, Pa., 1996—. Night mgr. Gateway Pharmacy, Phoenixville, Pa., 1977-78; gestalt pastoral care tng., S.I., N.Y., 1985-95; retreat leader, workshop and seminar leader United Ch. of Christ, Pa., 1985—, gestalt pastoral care therapist and spiritual dir., 1986—. Contbr. articles to religion publs. Bd. dirs. Prayer House Cmty., 1990—, sec., 1990-95; chmn. Ecumenical Adventure in Healing, 1990-95. Mem. Assn. Christian Therapists, N.E. Region Disciplined Order of Christ, Order St. Luke the Physician. Avocations: reading, birdwatching, hiking. Home: 67 Valley Brook Rd Boyertown PA 19512-7547

CRANNA, CHRISTINA M. social services specialist; b. Poughkeepsie, N.Y., May 27, 1975; d. Charles Francis and Mary M. Lauria. BS in Psychology, St. Thomas Aquinas Coll., 1997; MSW, Adelphi U., 2001. Mental health worker Rockland County Dept. Mental Health, Pomona, NY, 1997—98; svc. coord. Ulster-Green ARC, Kingston, NY, 1998—; social worker Foster Home for Children, 2000—. Mem.: NASW. Roman Catholic. Avocations: crafts, crocheting, swimming, traveling, history. Home: 2 Woods Rd Tivoli NY 12583-5429

CRANNEY, MARILYN KANREK, lawyer; b. Bklyn., June 18, 1949; d. Sidney Paul and Aurelia (Valice) Kanrek; m. John William Cranney, Jan. 22, 1970 (div. June 1975); 1 child, David Julian. BA, Brandeis U., 1970; MA in History, Brigham Young U., 1975; JD, U. Utah, 1979; LLM in Tax Law, NYU, 1984. Bar: N.Y. 1980, U.S. Dist. Ct. (so. and ea. dists.) N.Y. 1992. Assoc. Cravath Swaine & Moore, N.Y.C., 1979-81; 1st v.p., asst. gen. counsel Morgan Stanley Investment Advisors Inc., N.Y.C., 1981—. Mem. Order of the Coif. Democrat. Jewish. Avocations: travel, reading. Office: Morgan Stanley Investment Advisors Inc 22nd Fl 1221 Ave of the Americas New York NY 10020 Office Phone: 212-762-5294. E-mail: marilyn.cranney@morganstanley.com.

CRANSTON, PAMELA LEE, priest, writer; b. N.Y.C., Oct. 21, 1950; d. Day Lee and Nancy Mills; m. Edward Eugene Cranston, Aug. 18, 1984. BA, San Francisco State U., 1984; MDiv with distinction, Ch. Divinity Sch. of the Pacific, Berkeley, Calif., 1988. Nun Cmty. of St. Francis, San Francisco, 1974—78; adminstr., counselor Alcoholism Programs, Dept. of Pub. Health, San Francisco, 1978—85; spiritual dir. Oakland, 1982—; pastoral asst. Grace Cathedral, San Francisco, 1988—90; assoc. rector St. Timothy's Episcopal Ch., Danville, Calif., 1990—94, All Souls Episcopal Ch., Berkeley, 1995—98; assoc. priest St. Cuthberts Episcopal Ch., Oakland, 1998—; chaplain Hope Hospice, Dublin, Calif., 1998—, St. Paul's Towers, Oakland, Calif., 2001—. Pub., founder St. Huberts Press, 2002. Author: The Madonna Murders, Clergy Wellness and Mutual Ministry; contbr. fiction, poetry, essays, and revs. to profl. publs. Chair Clergy Wellness Commn. Diocese of Calif., San Francisco, 1992—. Liberal. Episcopalian.

CRAVEN, BETTY, educational association administrator; b. Petersburg, Va., July 10, 1955; d. Richard Wilson and Helen Rose (Ellington) Cheely; m. Thomas Leake Millner, June 5, 1976 (div. Feb. 1987); m. Erle Bulla Craven, IV, Apr. 29, 1989; children: Hannah Elizabeth, Erle Bulla V. Student, Randolph-Macon Coll., Ashland, Va., 1973-74, 74-75. Pres., dir. exercise leader Fitness Motivations, Greensboro, N.C., 1986-89; cultural arts, reflections chmn. Cash Elem. Sch., Kernersville, N.C., 1999—, PTA pres., 1998-99; mem. Zone 2 adv. bd. Winston-Salem/Forsyth County PTA Coun., N.C., 1998-00; vice dir. Dist. 16 N.C. State PTA, Raleigh, 1999-00, reflections chair, 1998—. Pres., dir. Eclectic Creations, Kernersville, 1985—. Recipient Outstanding Vol. award Cash Elem. PTA, 1997-98, 98-99, 99-00. Democrat. Presbyterian. Avocations: gardening, reading novels, drawing, music, piano. Home: 109 Croyden Dr Kernersville NC 27284-8399

CRAVEN, CHARMAROSE LANELLE, technology coordinator; b. Lucas, Kans., June 2, 1954; d. Charles James and Annabel Lee Shiroky; m. Robert Dean Craven, July 7, 1993; children: Jennifer, Warren. Assoc. degree, Barton County C.C., 1974; BS, Pittsburg (Kans.) State U., 1976; Master's degree, Ft. Hays State U., 1978. CNE Novell. Tchr. gifted edn. Unified Sch. Dist. #262, Valley Center, 1990—95; dist. tech. coord. Unified Sch. Dist. #407, Russell, Kans., 1997—. Contbr. revs. to mags. Mem. City Coun. City of Luray, 2002—; mem. Luray Hist. Soc., 2001—. Mem.: Kans. Nat. Edn. Assn., Kans. Tech. Coord.'s Network. Avocation: local historical research. Office: Unified Sch Dist #407 802 Main St Russell KS 67665

CRAVEN, DEBORAH, performing arts educator; b. Birmingham, Ala., Mar. 17, 1950; d. Jesse Auborn Adams and Jimmie Louise Myers; m. T. Judson Revelle; 1 child, Myer Brookins Craven. BS in Edn., Samford U., 1970; MA, PhD, Trinity U. Tchr. Birmingham Pub. Schs., 1970-73; newspaper columnist The Daily Herald, Houston, 1974-76; accompanist Suzuki Acad., Mt. Prospect, Ill., 1977-79; tchr., dir., CEO Craven Acad., Lake Forest, 1991—. Dir. CATSS Internat. Mus. Touring Co., Grayslake, Ill., 1996—. Author: Miss Debbie Series, 1996, Miss Debbie Coloring Books, 1996, Adagio Pedagogy, 1998, Andante Pedagogy, 1997, Allegro Pedagogy, 1998. Active People to People Amb. Program. Mem. Music Educators Nat. Conf., Internat. Soc. for Musical Edn., Nat. Assn. for Music Edn., Nat. Guild Piano Tchrs., Am. Coll. Musicians, Music Tchrs. Nat. Assn., Ill. State Music Tchrs. Assn., North Suburban Music Tchrs. Assn., Downtown Assn., Grayslake C. of C., Kiwanis, Exch. Club. Office: The Craven Acad Performing Arts 408 Center St Grayslake IL 60030-1626

CRAVEN, ELIZABETH, pediatrician; b. Mar. 9, 1936; BA Douglass Coll., 1957; MD, N.Y. Med. Coll., 1961. Emeritus clin. prof. pediat. Jefferson Med. Coll., Phila.

CRAVEY, CLARA, dancer, performing arts association administrator; From dancer to prin. Harkness Youth Dancers, 1968; mem. faculty Houston Ballet Acad., Houston, 1978—87, asst. prin., 1987—91, prin., 1991—. pres. Mem. artistic coun. Ballet Fla., U. Okla. Mem.: Nat. Assn. Sch. Dance (v.p.). Office: National Assn Schs of Dance 11250 Roger Bacon Drive Ste 21 Reston VA 20190-5248

CRAVEY, PAMELA J. librarian; b. Washington, Mar. 6, 1945; d. Jack M. and Marjorie M.W. Bristow; m. G. Randall Cravey; 1 child, Christopher B. BA, Baldwin Wallace Coll., 1967; MS, Fla. State U., 1968; PhD, Ga. State U., 1989. Libr., instr. Fla. State U., Tallahassee, 1968-69, U. Ga., Athens, 1969-72; asst. then assoc. libr. U. Ctrl. Fla., Orlando, 1973-75; asst. then assoc. prof., libr. Ga. State U., Atlanta, 1975-2000; pvt. practice $D, Decatur, 2000—. Author: Protecting Library Staff, Users, Collections, and Facilities, 2001; contbr. articles to profl. jours. and books. Libr. Svc. Enhancement Program grantee Coun. Libr. Resources; personal grantee Coun. Libr. Resources. Mem. ALA, Assn. Coll. Rsch. Librs. Home: 2413 Harrington Dr Decatur GA 30033-4903 Office: #308 2103 N Decatur Rd Decatur GA 30033-5305 E-mail: pamelajcravey@mindspring.com.

CRAWFORD, CAROL TALLMAN, law educator; b. Mt. Holly, NJ, Feb. 25, 1943; m. Ronald Crawford; children: Timothy, Jeffrey, Richard. BA, Mt. Holyoke Coll., 1965; JD magna cum laude, Washington Coll. Law, Am. U., 1978. Bar: Va. 1978, DC 1979. Legis. asst. to Senator Bob Packwood, Washington, 1969-75; assoc. firm Collier, Shannon, Rill & Scott, Washington, 1979-81; exec. asst. to chmn. FTC, Washington, 1981-83, dir. bur. consumer protection, 1983-85; assoc. dir. Office of Mgmt. & Budget, Washington, 1985-89; asst. atty. gen. legis. affairs U.S. Dept. Justice, Washington, 1989-90; commr. U.S. Internat. Trade Commn., 1991-2000; disting. vis. prof. law George Mason U., Arlington, Va., 2000-01. Bd. dirs. European Inst., Ind. Women's Forum, Smithfield Foods, Inc. Trustee Barry Goldwater Chair of Am. Instns., Ariz. State U., Phoenix, 1983—; chair internat. trade and investment subcom. Federalist Soc., 1998—99, chair internat. and nat. security sect., 1999—2003; mem. adv. com. NAFTA Labor Agreement, 2002—. Republican.

CRAWFORD, CINDY (CYNTHIA ANN CRAWFORD), model, actress; b. Dekalb, Ill., Feb. 20, 1966; d. Dan Crawford and Jennifer Moluf; m. Richard Gere, Dec. 12, 1991 (div. 1995); m. Rande Gerber, May 29, 1998; children: Presley Walker, Kaya Jordan. Student, Northwestern U. Model for Victor Skrebneski, 1984-86; signed with Elite Modeling Agy., 1986; spokesperson Revlon, 1989—, JH Collectibles, Pepsi Cola, Kay Jewelers, Blockbuster Video, others; host MTV's House of Style, 1989-95. Released Cindy Crawford Fragrance, 2003. First featured on cover Vogue, 1986; has appeared on covers of W, People, Harper's Bazaar, ELLE, Allure, many others; Actor: (films) Fair Game, 1995, 54, 1998, The Simian Line, 2000; (exercise videos): Cindy Crawford's Shape Your Body Workout, 1992, The Next Challenge Workout, 1993. Host: (TV specials) Sex With Cindy Crawford, 1998. Supporter breast cancer rsch.; active Leukemia Soc. of Am. Office: Wolf-Kasteler 132 S Rodeo Dr Ste 300 Beverly Hills CA 90212-2414

CRAWFORD, DEBRA P. women's healthcare company executive; BSBA in Acctg., San Diego State U. CPA, Calif. Dir. fin., mfg. contr. Advanced Cardiovasc. Sys., Inc., 1992-94; v.p. fin. and adminstrn., treas., asst. sec. IVAC Corp., 1994; CFO, v.p., CFO, treas., sec. IVAC Med. Sys., Inc., 1995-96; CFO, treas. IVAC Holdings, Inc., 1996; ind. fin. cons., acting CFO or corp. devel. fin. cons., 1997-98; v.p., CFO, treas. Women First HealthCare, Inc., San Diego, 1998—, asst. sec., 1998-99, sec., 1999—. Office: Women First HealthCare Inc 12220 El Camino Real Ste 400 San Diego CA 92130-2091 Fax: 619-509-1353.

CRAWFORD, HELENE HOPE, elementary school principal; b. N.Y.C. d. Jerome I. and Ethel Emily Lipson; m. Jon Kent, May 6, 1973 (div. Feb. 1984); m. John Larry Crawford, July 11, 1987. BA, Hunter Coll.; MS in Edn., CUNY, 1971; MS in Spl. Edn., Coll. of New Rochelle, 1978. Cert. sch. adminstr., supr., N.Y.; cert. intermediate supr., Conn. Tchr. I.S. 162, Bronx, N.Y., 1971-73, I.S. 183, Bronx, 1973-86; spl. edn. supr. Cmty. Sch. Dist. 7, 1986-95; asst. prin. P.S. 31X, Bronx, 1995-97; prin. P.S. 5X, Bronx, 1997—. Mem. ASCD, Nat. Trust for Historic Preservation, Orton Dyslexia Soc., Phi Delta Kappa. Avocations: reading, walking, movies, cooking.

CRAWFORD, JEAN ANDRE, clinical therapist; b. Chgo., Apr. 12, 1941; d. William Moses and Geneva Mae (Lacy) Jones; m. John N. Crawford Jr., June 28, 1969. Student, Shimer coll., 1959-60; BA, Carthage Coll., 1966; MEd, Loyola U., Chgo., 1971; postgrad., Nat. Coll. Edn., Evanston, Ill., 1971-77, Northwestern U., 1976-83. Lic. profl. counselor, Mich., Ill.; cert. sch. counselor Nat. Bd. Cert. Counselors, elem. edn., spl. edn. and pupil personnel svcs., Ill. Med. technologist, Chgo., 1960-62; primary and spl. edn. tchr. Chgo. Pub. Schs., 1966-71, counselor maladjusted children and families, 1971-88, counselor juvenile first offenders, 1968-88, post-secondary vocat. counselor, 1988-93; tchr. transition coord. Cook County Dept. Corrections Alternative H.S., Chgo., 1993-94; clin. therapist St. Mary of Nazareth Hosp. Ctr., Adolescent Partial Hosp., Chgo., 1994—. Vol. Sta. WTTW-TV; vol. counselor deaf/hearing impaired children and their families; vol., mem. cmty. devel. bd. New City YMCA, 1987-92; mem. scholarship com. Chgo. Urban League. Mem.: AACD, Coun. Exceptional Children, Ill. Mental Health Counselors Assn., Am. Mental Health Counselors Assn., Ill. Sch. Counselors Assn., Ill. Assn. Counseling and Devel., Am. Sch. Counselors Assn., Shimer Coll. Alumni Assn. (sec. 1982—84), Coord. Coun. Handicapped Children, Phi Delta Kappa. Home: 601 E 32d St Apt 1200 Chicago IL 60616-4205 Office: 2233 W Division St Chicago IL 60622-3043 E-mail: j412@webtv.net.

CRAWFORD, JENNY LYNN SLUDER, medical/surgical nurse, educator; b. Asheville, NC, Oct. 14, 1952; d. Fletcher Sumpter and M. Orva (Yost) Sluder; m. Thomas Rodney Crawford, Jan. 21, 1984; children: Orva Marie, Sara Lynn. AA, Stephens Coll., 1972; BSN, Baylor U., 1974; MSN, U. N.C., Charlotte, 1998. RN, Ola.; cert. med.-surg. nurse ANA. Staff nurse Comanche County Hosp., Lawton, Okla., 1974, VA Hosp., Asheville, 1975-77, VA Med. Ctr., Durham, N.C., 1977-84, Presbyn. Hosp., Charlotte, N.C., 1984-95; health occupations instr. Garinger H.S., Charlotte, 1995—2002; health occupations inst. Independence H.S., Charlotte, 2002—. Nursing instr. Presbyn. Hosp., Charlotte, 1989-95; instr. basic life support and CPR Am. Heart Assn., others. Mem.: ANA, Sigma Theta Tau. Avocations: camping, swimming, crosstitch, needlepoint, reading. Home: 8941 Dartmoor Pl Charlotte NC 28227-8983

CRAWFORD, KIM, computer company executive; BA in Polit. Sci., MS in Indsl. Enigring., Stanford U.; MBA, Harvard U. Former ptnr. Bain & Co.; v.p., gen. mgr. networking Dell Computer Corp., Round Rock, Tex. Office: Dell Computer Corp 1 Dell Way Round Rock TX 78682

CRAWFORD, LELA BURCH, school nurse; b. Fostoria, Ohio, Aug. 27, 1936; d. Jethro and Dorothy Leona (Brown) Burch; m. Roger A. Crawford Sr., Sept. 12, 1959 (dec. Oct. 1996); children: Regina Denise Crawford Kemp, Roger Alexander Jr. RN, St. Vincent's Sch. Nursing, 1957; BA in Elem. Edn., Mary Mause Coll., 1965; EdM in Guidance and Counseling, U. Toledo, 1976, Edn. Specialist Degree, 1977, M in Health Edn., 1982. Nurse St. Vincent's Hosp., St. Vincent's Med. Ctr., Toledo, 1957-60, St. Charles Hosp., Toledo, 1960-62, St. Teresa's Elem. Sch., Cath. Bd. Edn., Toledo, 1962-65; part-time staff nurse St. Luke's Hosp., Toledo, 1965-66; staff nurse, supr. Parkview Hosp., Toledo, 1966; sch. nurse Toledo Bd. Edn., 1966—2001; ret., 2001. Summer camp nurse Jewish Cmty. Ctr., Toledo, 1973; summer and part-time worker Toledo Hosp., 1974-76, Marigarde Nursing Home, Sylvania, Ohio, 1976-79; summer migrate workers program staff Toledo-Fed. Program, 1979-83; part-time instr. modeling Barbizon Modeling Sch., 1979-82. Mem. Dem. Bus. and Profl. Women's Club Lucas County, Toledo, 1996. Scholar St. Vincent Nursing Sch.-Grey Nuns, Toledo, 1954. Mem. Phi Kappa Phi. Baptist.

CRAWFORD, LINDA SIBERY, lawyer, educator; b. Ann Arbor, Mich., Apr. 27, 1947; d. Donald Eugene and Verla Lillian (Schenck) Sibery; m. Leland Allardice Crawford, Apr. 4, 1970; children: Christina, Lillian, Leland. Student, Keele U., 1969; BA, U. Mich., 1969; postgrad., SUNY, Potsdam, 1971; JD, U. Maine, 1977. Bar: Maine 1977, U.S. Dist. Ct. Maine 1982, U.S. Ct. Appeals (1st cir.) 1983. Tchr. Pub. Sch., Tupper Lake, N.Y., 1970-71; asst. dist. atty. State of Maine, Farmington, 1977-79, asst. atty. gen. Augusta, Maine, 1979-95; prin. Litigation Consulting Firm, N.Y.C., 1986—, Linda Crawford and Assoc. Law Firm, Cambridge, Mass., 1995-2000. Legal adv. U. Maine, Farmington, 1975; legal counsel Fire Marshall's Office, Maine, 1980-83, Warden Svc., Maine, 1981-83, Dept. Mental Health, 1983-90, litigation divsn. 1990-95; mem. tchg. team trial advocacy Law Sch., Harvard U., 1987—; lectr. Sch. Medicine Harvard U., 1991; counsel to Bd. of Registration in Medicine, 1994-95; chmn. editl. bd. Mental and Physical Disability Law Reporter, 1993-95; arbitrator Am. Arbitration Assn., 1995—; facilitator Nat. Constrn. Task Force, St. Louis, 1995. Contbg. editor: Med. Malpractice Law and Strategy, 1997—, Managed Care Law Strategist, 1999—2002. Bd. dirs. Diocesan Human Rels. Coun., Maine, 1977-78, Arthritis Found., Maine, 1983-88; atty. expert commn. experts UN War Crime Investigation in the former Yugoslavia, 1994. Named one of Outstanding Young Women of Yr. Jaycees, 1981. Mem. ABA (com. on disability 1992-95), Nat. Assn. State Mental Health Attys. (treas. 1984-86, vice chmn. 1987-89, chmn. 1989-91), Nat. Health Lawyers Assn. Home and Office: 1643 Cambridge #77 Cambridge MA 02138 also: 45 Rockefeller Plz Fl 20 New York NY 10111-2099 E-mail: lcandassociates@aol.com.

CRAWFORD, M. HOLLY, artist, writer, educator; b. San Buenaventura, Calif., Feb. 25, 1949; d. William Clyde Jr. and Audrey Eleanor (Bechtol) Shissler; m. R. George Crawford, May 17, 1980; 1 stepchild, Katherine Barnes Crawford. BA in Econs., UCLA, 1971, MS in Behavioral Sci., 1976, MA in Econs., 1978. Art lectr. UCLA, 1993—. Artist, author: (installations) Road: The Century Freeway, 1991, Water? Water$ Water!, 1992, Offering, 1993; poetry: Dog Days, 1994, Hollow Dog, 1995, The Bone, 1997. NIMH fellow, 1975; Notaro Internat. artist residency grantee, Poland, 1991. Mem. Coll. Art Assn. Address: Ste 243 236 Stanford Shopping Ctr Palo Alto CA 94304-1412 Office: Dept Art Dickson Hall UCLA Los Angeles CA 90024

CRAWFORD, MARIA LUISA BUSE, geology educator; b. Beverly, Mass., July 18, 1939; d. William Theodore Buse and Barbara (Kidder) Aldana; m. William A. Crawford, Aug. 29, 1963. BA, Bryn Mawr Coll., 1960; postgrad., U. Oslo, 1960-61; PhD, U. Calif., 1965. Asst. prof. Bryn Mawr (Pa.) Coll., 1965-70, assoc. prof., 1970-75, prof., 1975-92, prof. environ. studies and sci., 1992—, William R. Kenan Jr. prof., 1985-92, chmn. dept. geology, 1976-88, 98—; mem. U.S. Nat. Com. Geology, 1994-97. Chmn. women geoscientists com. Am. Geol. Inst., 1976-77; mem. U.S. Nat. Com. Geochemistry, 1980-82; organizing com. 28th Internat. Geol. Cong., 1987-89. MacArthur fellow, 1993-98; grantee NASA, 1973-76, NSF, 1967—. Fellow Geol. Soc. Am. (councillor 1982-85), Mineral Soc. Am. (councillor 1989-92);mem. Mineral Assn. Can. (councilor 1985-87), Am. Geophys. Union, Norwegian Geol. Soc., Phila. Geol. Soc., Assn. Women in Sci. Office: Bryn Mawr Coll Dept Geology Bryn Mawr PA 19010 E-mail: mcrawfor@brynmawr.edu.

CRAWFORD, MARY ELLEN, secondary school educator; b. Bklyn., Mar. 16, 1940; d. Robert P. and Kathryn C. (Guzzi) Graciano; m. Wheeler C. Crawford; children: Robert, Kathryn, Susan, Michael. BS, Marymount Manhattan Coll., N.Y.C., 1961; MA, Georgetown U., Washington, 1963. Tchr. math. Jr. H.S. 278, Bklyn., 1963-65; adj. instr. North Harris Coll., Houston, 1988—. Mem. Madame Alexander Doll Club, First Houston Doll Club (sec.), Alpha Chi. Roman Catholic. Avocations: collectibles, swimming, traveling. Home: 3007 Grand Elm Cir Houston TX 77068-2124

CRAWFORD, MARY LOUISE PERRI, career officer; b. Grand Haven, Mich., Nov. 26, 1949; d. Louis and Helen Marie (Buckley) Perri; m. Keith Eugene Crawford, Feb. 23, 1974 (dec. Oct. 1986); children: Matthew Perri, Michael Kirk. AA, Muskegon County C.C., 1969; BA, U. Mich., 1971. Commd. ensign U.S. Navy, 1972, advanced through grades to capt., 1993; pub. affairs officer Naval Air Sta., Key West, Fla., 1974-77, adminstrv., personnel officer Naval Air Res. Detachment, Patuxent River, Md., 1977-78, adminstrn. br. head Strike Aircraft Test Directorate, Naval Air Test Ctr., Patuxent River, 1978-80, ops. watch officer Command Ctr., Comdr.-in-Chief Naval Forces Europe Staff, London, 1980-84, officer-in-charge Personnel Support Activity Detachment, Patuxent River, 1984-86; engring. officer Chief Test and Evaluation Div., Strategic C3 Systems Directorate, Ctr. for Command, Control, and Communications, Def. Communications Agy., Washington, 1986-89; mgr. ultra high frequency Joint Satellite Communications Ctr., Joints Chiefs Staff, Pentagon, Washington, 1989-91; comdr. N.Y. Mil. Entrance Processing Sta., 1991-94; dir. personal, family & cmy support divsn. Bur. Navy Pers., Washington, 1994-95; head surveillance & navigations programs Office of Chief Naval Ops., Washington, 1996—. Mem. AAUW, Armed Forces Comm. & Electronics Assn., Women's Overseas Svc. League, U. Mich. Alumni Assn. Roman Catholic. Avocations: painting, ballet. Office: Office of CNO-N633 2000 Navy Pentagon Washington DC 20350-2000

CRAWFORD, MELINDA HEATHER, music educator, musician; b. Pitts., Oct. 14, 1978; d. Kenneth Edward and Gay Elena (Eger) Crawford. BS in Music Edn., Duquesne Univ., Pitts., 2000. Strings coach Three Rivers Young Peoples Orch., Pitts., 1997—2000; strings/orch. tchr. Calvert County Pub. Sch., Prince Fedrick, Md., 2000—01, Fairfax County Pub. Sch., Va., 2001—. Fiddler and co-founder Loch'd Oot (fiddle band), Falls Ch., Va., 2001—; dir. Robinson Sec. Fiddle Club, Fairfax, Va., 2001—; prin. violist McLean Symphony Orch., McLean, Va., 2002—. Composer Scottish fiddle music, (Scottish Air) Lament for Mr. P.J. Ross., 2003. Vol. health aid Fairfax County Health Agy., Fairfax, Va., 2003—. Recipient U.S. Nat. Scottish Fiddling Champion, Allegheny Mountain Fiddling Champion; Vira Heinz Travel/Study Scholarship, Vira Heinz Found., 1999. Mem.: Scottish Fiddling Revival, Am. String Tchrs. Assn., Music Educators Nat. Conf., Potomac Valley Scottish Fiddle Club (bd. mem., fiddling champion). Avocations: jewerly making, composing, travel. Home: 2810 W Glen Dr APt #14 Falls Church VA 22046 Office: 365 Foster Rd North Versailles PA 15137

CRAWFORD, MURIEL LAURA, lawyer, author, educator; d. Mason Leland and Pauline Marie (DesIlets) Henderson; m. Barrett Matson Crawford, May 10, 1959; children: Laura Joanne, Janet Muriel, Barbara Elizabeth. BA with honors, U. Ill., 1973; JD with honors, Ill. Inst. Tech., 1977; cert. employee benefit splst., U. Pa., 1989. Bar: Ill. 1977, Calif. 1991, U.S. Dist. Ct. (no. dist.) Ill. 1977, U.S. Dist. Ct. (no. dist.) Calif. 1991, U.S. Ct. Appeals (7th cir.) 1977, U.S. Ct. Appeals (9th cir.) 1991; CLU; chartered fin. cons. Atty. Washington Nat. Ins. Co., Evanston, Ill., 1977-80; sr. atty., 1980-81; asst. counsel, 1982-83; asst. gen. counsel, 1984-87; assoc. gen. counsel, sec., 1987-89; cons. employee benefit splst., 1989-91; assoc. Hancock, Rothert & Bushoft, San Francisco, 1991-92. Author: (with Beadles) Law and the Life Insurance Contract, 1989, (sole author) 7th edit., 1994, Life and Health Insurance Law, 8th edit., 1998; co-author: Legal Aspects of AIDS, 1990; contbr. articles to profl. jours. Recipient Am. Jurisprudence award Lawyer's Coop. Pub. Co., 1975, 2nd prize Internat. LeTourneau Student Med.-Legal Article Contest, 1976, LOMA FLMI Ins. Edn. award, 1999. Fellow Life Mgmt. Inst.; mem. Ill. Inst. Tech./Chgo.-Kent Alumni Assn. (bd. dirs. 1983-89, Bar and Gavel Soc. award 1977). Democrat.

CRAWFORD, NATALIE WILSON, applied mathematician; b. Evansville, Ind., June 24, 1939; d. John Moore and Edna Dorothea (Huthsteiner) Wilson; m. Robert Charles Crawford, Mar. 1, 1969. BA in Math., UCLA, 1961, postgrad., 1964-67. Programmer analyst N.Am. Aviation Corp., El Segundo, Calif., 1961-64; mem. tech. staff RAND Corp., Santa Monica, Calif., 1964—, project leader, engring. tech., theater conflict and force employment programs, 1975—; dir. Theater Forces Program, Santa Monica, 1988-90, Theater Force Employment Program, Santa Monica, 1990-92, Force Structure and Force Modernization Program, Santa Monica, 1992-93, Force Modernization and Employment Program, Santa Monica, 1993-95; assoc. dir. Project Air Force, Santa Monica, 1995-97, v.p.rand, dir. project, 1995-97; co-chair, USAF scientific advisory bd. Dept. of the Air Force, Washington, 1996—. Mem. Air Force Sci. Adv. Bd., 1988—, vice-chair, 1990-91, co-chair, 1996—; cons., joint tech. coordinating group munition effectiveness. Recipient Women's Bus. Coun. award Santa Monica C. of C., 1997, Clarence L. Kelly Johnson Meml. Lockheed Skunk Works award, 1999; named YWCA Woman of Yr., 1983; inducted into Santa Monica H.S. Hall of Fame, 1995. Mem. NDIA, USAF Assn. Republican. Home: 20940 Big Rock Dr Malibu CA 90265-5316 Office: Dept of the Air Force 1180 Air Force Pentagon Washington DC 20330-1180

CRAWFORD, RANDI, women's healthcare company executive; d. Edward F. Calesa. BA in Liberal Arts, Villanova U. Cons. on creation and prodn. children's programming Fox TV, Lifetime TV, DIC Entertainment, Saban Entertainment, 1991-95; rsch. analyst Calesa Assocs., 1995-97; co-founder, v.p. mktg. rsch., sec. Women First HealthCare, Inc., San Diego, 1997-98, v.p. ednl. program devel., 1998—. Office: Women First HealthCare Inc 12220 El Camino Real Ste 400 San Diego CA 92130-2091 Fax: 619-509-1353.

CRAWFORD, ROBIN YVETTE, county caseworker; b. Buffalo, N.Y., Sept. 13, 1954; d. Robert Lee and Sylvia Caroline Crawford. A in Specialized Tech., Art Inst. Pitts., 1986; BA, Carlow Coll., 2001; Diploma, Harty Bible Sch., 2001. Campus min. Coalition for Christian Outreach, Pitts., 1986—94; assistance dir. Covenant Ch. Pitts., 1994—95; infant care baby holder The Childrens Home Pitts., 1997—98; dir. program Bethany Bapt. Ch., Pitts., 1999; residential counselor Three Rivers Youth, Pitts., 1999—2002; vol. outpatient group Western Psychiat. Inst. and Clinic, Pitts., 1999—2002; county caseworker Allegheny County Children and Youth Svc., Pitts., 2002—. Creator (with others) Nat. Tribute Quilt documenting September 11, 2001. Adv. com. Pitts. Action Against Rape, 2002—03; bd.

dirs. Carlow Coll. Alumnae Assn., 2002—03. Recipient Aliquippa Embraces Art award, 2003; grantee, Pa. Coun. on Arts, Pitts., 1999, Multi-Cultural Arts Initiative, Pitts., 2001. Mem.: Quilt Co. East Quilter's Guild, Nat. Quilting Assn., Nat. Assn. Negro Bus. and Profl. Women. Baptist. Avocations: travel, jazz, performing arts, museums. Home: 1027 North Negley Ave # 11 Pittsburgh PA 15206

CRAWFORD, SARAH CARTER (SALLY CARTER CRAWFORD), broadcast executive; b. Glen Ridge, N.J., Oct. 3, 1938; d. Raymond Hitchings and Katherine Latta (Gribbel) Carter; m. Joseph Paul Crawford III, Sept. 10, 1960 (dec. 1966). BA, Smith Coll., 1960. Media dir. Kampmann & Bright, Phila., 1961-64; sr. media buyer Foote, Cone & Belding, N.Y.C., 1964-69; assoc. media dir. Grey Advt., L.A., 1969-75; account exec., research dir. Sta. KHJ-TV, L.A., 1975-76; mgr. local sales Sta. KCOP-TV, L.A., 1977-82; gen. sales mgr. Sta. KTVF-TV, Fairbanks, Alaska, 1982-96; nat. sales mgr. KTVF, KTVA, Fairbanks, 1996-97; gen. sales mgr. Sta. KYES-FM, Anchorage, 1997-2000; sta. and gen. sales mgr. mgr. Sta. KATN, Fairbanks, 2000—03; owner Crawford Commns. of Ala., 2003—; acct. rep. GCI, Fairbanks, 2003—. Mem. adv. com. Golden Valley Electric Corp., Fairbanks, 1984-86; mem. coun. UAF Tanana County Campus, 1989-96, 2000-01. Chmn. Fairbanks Health and Social Svc. Commn., 1986—93; vice chmn. Fairbanks North Star Borough Health and Social Svc. Commn., 1993—96; pres. Fairbanks Meml. Hosp. Aux., 1988—90, creator trust fund, 1990—94, chmn. fin. com., 1990—94; mem. Fairbanks Health Ctr. Coalition; mem. search com. UAF Tanana Valley Campus Dir.; mem. Tesoro (Alaska) Citiznes Adv. Coun., 1999; pub. rels. chair Kids Vote Anchorage; mem., chmn. mktg. com. Gov.'s Coun. on Youth Substance Abuse Prevention, 1999—2003; mem. Fairbanks Chamber Membership Com., 2000—; bd. dirs. Breast Cancer Detection Ctr., 2002—; mem. Intercollegiate Athletic Coun., 2002—; promotions com. Fairbanks Downtown Assn., 2000—; mem. sports commn. FCVB, 2003—; mktg. coord. World Eskimo Indian Olympics, 2003; mem. Fairbanks Sports Commn., 2003—; founder scholarship found. FKS Meml. Hosp. Aux., 1990; bd. dirs. Interior Regional Health Corp., 1992—97. Recipient Vol. of Yr. award, Fairbanks Downtown Assn., 2002, Flag and Citation, U.S. Senator Stevens, Cmty. Svc. award, Arctic Alliance for People, 2003. Mem.: Alaska Broadcasters Assn. (bd. dirs. 1995—, pres. 2001—02, founder scholarship found. 2001, Broadcaster of the Yr. 2001). Avocations: weight-lifting, stock and real estate investments, running, motorcycling. Home: 107 Maple Dr Fairbanks AK 99709-2956

CRAWFORD, SHEILA JANE, elementary education librarian, reading consultant; b. Beckley, W.Va., Mar. 1, 1943; d. Roger and Ruth (Ashworth) Crawford; m. Lloyd E. Johnston, June 4, 1966 (dec.); 1 child, Jacqueline ; m. Troy Thomason, June 28, 2000. BA, Tenn. Tech. U., 1963; MA in Christian Edn., Seabury Western Theol. Sem., 1965; MS in Curriculum and Instrn., U. Tenn., Martin, 1989; EdD in Instrn. and Curriculum Leadership, U. Memphis, 1994; postgrad., San Jose State U., U. Calif., Berkeley, U. Utah, Tex. Woman's U. Cert. tchr. Tenn. Dir. Christian edn. St. Luke's Episcopal Ch., Rochester, Minn., 1965-66; elem. tchr. Santa Catalina Sch. Girls, 1967-69, Rowland-Hall St. Mark's Sch., Salt Lake City, 1968-69, Union City (Tenn.) Christian Sch., 1984-87; libr. Dept. Edn. U. Tenn. at Martin, 1987-89; rsch. asst. U. Memphis, 1989-92, adj. prof., 1996; prof., edn. dept. chair Lane Coll., Jackson, Tenn., 1992-94; reading tchr., drama club sponsor Ashland (Miss.) Mid. Sch., 1994-95; workshop presenter Jackson, Tenn., 1989-96; ednl. cons. Delta Faucet of Tenn. div. Masco Corp., Jackson, 1995—; homebound tchr. Jackson-Madison County Schs., 1996-97; instr., libr. LaGrange-Moscow (Tenn.) Sch., 1997-99; libr. Lauderdale Sch., Memphis. Mem. campus All Stars, Honda, Jackson, Tenn., 1992—93; cons. in field. Contbr. articles to profl. jours. Mem. story telling conf. IASC, Dublin, 1999, 2004. Mem. AAUW, DAR, Nat. Libr. Assn., Ch. and Synagogue Libr. Assn., Order Eastern Star (worthy matron 1980-81), Sch. Libr. Assn., Sigma Tau Delta, Kappa Delta Pi. Anglican. Achievements include research in the effect of chess on predicting and summarizing skills; Participation in the International Association of School Librarians Storytelling Convention in Dublin. Home: 3207 Thirteen Colony Mall Apt 1 Memphis TN 38115-2972 E-mail: sheil101@cs.com.

CRAWFORD, SUSAN, library director, educator, writer; b. Vancouver, B.C., Can. d. James Y. and S. Young; m. James Weldon Crawford, July 5, 1955; 1 son, Robert James. BA, U. B.C., 1948; MA, U. Toronto, 1950, U. Chgo., 1954, PhD, 1970. With bur. libr. and indexing svc. ADA, 1954-56; with office exec. v.p. AMA, Chgo., 1956-60, dir. divsn. libr. and archival svcs., 1960-81; assoc. prof. Sch. Libr. Sci., Columbia U., N.Y.C., 1972-75; prof., dir. Sch. Medicine Libr. and Biomed. Comm. Ctr. Washington U., 1981-92; adj. prof. U. Ill., Chgo., 1994—. Author over 160 books and articles; mem. editl. bd. Med. Socioecon. Rsch. Sources, Index to Sci. Revs., Jour. Am. Soc. Info. Sci., Med. Libr. Assn. News, Health and Info. Librs., Budapest, Health Librs. Rev., London, Health Info. and Librs. Jour., Oxford, Eng., 2003—; assoc. editor Jour. Am. Soc. Info Sci., 1979-82; editor Med. Info. Sys., 1988-90; editor-in-chief Jour. Med. Libr. Assn., 1982-88, 91-92. Bd. regents Nat. Libr. Medicine, NIH, 1971-75; mem. bd. overseers for univ. librs. Tufts U., 1988-89. Janet Doe hon. lectr., 1983; recipient Disting. Alumni award U. Toronto, 1987, Grad. medal U. Toronto, 1989. Fellow AAAS (chmn. coms.), Med. Libr. Assn. (life, Eliot award 1976, chmn. com. on surveys and stats. 1966-75, publs. panel 1977-80, chmn. consulting editors panel 1981-88, 91-92, spl. award to editor of bull. 1988, Noyes award 1992, Pres.'s award 1992, Centennial award), Med. Libr. Assn. (100 Most Notable 1998); mem. ALA, Soc. Social Studies of Sci. Assn., Am. Soc. Info. Sci. (chmn. med. info. sys. 1987-88, outstanding splty. group award 1988, 89, bd. and program chair Chgo. chpt. 1993-95), Am. Med. Informatics Assn., Acad. Health Info. Profls. (disting. mem.), European Assn. Health and Info. Librs. (U.S. rep. 1989-94), Sigma Xi (chmn. coms.). Home: 2418 Lincoln St Evanston IL 60201-2151 E-mail: sjcrawf@aol.com.

CRAWFORD, SUSAN JEAN, federal judge; b. Pitts., Apr. 22, 1947; d. William Elmer Jr. and Joan Ruth (Bielau) C.; m. Roger W. Higgins; 1 child, Kelley S. BA, Bucknell U., 1969; JD, New Eng. Sch. Law, 1977. Bar: Md. 1977, D.C. 1980, U.S. Ct. Appeals for Armed Forces 1985, U.S. Supreme Ct. 1993. Tchr. history, coach Radnor (Pa.) H.S., 1969-74; assoc. Burnett & Eiswert, Oakland, Md., 1977-79; ptnr. Burnett, Eiswert and Crawford, Oakland, 1979-81; prin. dep. gen. counsel U.S. Dept. Army, Washington, 1981-83, gen. counsel, 1983-89; insp. gen. U.S. Dept. Def., Arlington, Va., 1989-91; judge U.S. Ct. Appeals for the Armed Forces, Washington, 1991-99, chief judge, 1999—. Asst. states atty. Garrett County, Md., 1978-79; instr. Garrett County C.C., 1979-81. Del. Md. Forestry Adv. Commn., Garrett County, 1978-81, Md. Commn. for Women, Garrett County, 1980-83; chair Rep. State Cen. Com., Garrett County, 1978-81; trustee Bucknell U., 1988—, chair bd. trustees, 2003—; trustee New Eng. Sch. Law, 1989—. Mem. FBA, Md. Bar Assn., D.C. Bar Assn., Edward Bennett Williams Am. Inn of Ct. Presbyterian. Office: US Ct Appeals Armed Forces 450 E St NW Washington DC 20442-0001

CRAWFORD-DICKERSON, CARRIE CAE, art gallery director; b. Pittsburg, Kans., May 14, 1976; d. Carl Oliver Crawford and Judith Lynn (Kunshek) Crawford; m. Brian S. Dickerson, Oct. 6, 2001. BFA, Pitts. State U., 1994—98, MSc in edn., 1999—2000. Cert. Vol. Mgr. Vol. Mgmt. Inst., 2003. Tour programs asst. Nelson-Atkins Mus. of Art, Kans. City, Mo., 2000—02; membership coord. Forum for Contemporary Art, St. Louis, 1999—2000; asst. dir. of devel. Kans. City Art Inst., 2002—. Acknowledgements chairwoman Susan G. Komen Breast Cancer Found., Kans. City Affiliate, 2002—; cmty. ball and cotillion chairwoman Jr. League of Wyandotte and Johnson Counties in Kans., 2004—. Mem.: Vol. Coordinators Coun., Arts and Humanities Assn. of Johnson County, Alpha Sigma Alpha Kans. City Alumna. R-Liberal. Methodist. Avocations: knitting, boating, painting, reading.

CRAWFORD-LARSON, KRIS, minister; b. Port Lavaca, Tex., July 17, 1957; d. Fred Morris Thedford and Wanda Qualls; m. Stanley A. Larson, May 5, 2001; children: John Patrick Crawford, Carly Crawford, Tara Shea Crawford. BS in Home Econs., Tex. Tech. U., 1980; MDiv, Austin Presbytery Theol. Seminary, 1994. Ordained min. Mission Presbytery P.C., 1995. Assoc. pastor Grace Presbyn. Ch., Victoria, Tex., 1995—2001; pastor First Presbyn. Ch. P.C., Morrilton, Ark., 2001—. Leader Mission Trip to Kenya, 2001; mem. com. on ministry P.C. Presbytery Ark., 2002—03. Chair founding bd. dirs. Conway County Christian Clinic, Morrilton, Ark., 2003. Mem.: Rotary Internat. Avocations: scrapbooks, reading, walking. Office: First Presbyn Ch 105 W Church St Morrilton AR 72110

CRAWFORD-MASON, CLARE WOOTTEN, television producer, journalist; b. Durham, N.C., July 22, 1936; d. Charles Thomas and Clare (Erly) Wootten; m. Robert Watts Mason; children: Victor Lawrence Crawford Jr., Charlene Elizabeth Crawford; stepchildren: John Mason, Robert Mason 3d. BA, U. Md., 1958. Reporter, columnist Washington Daily News, 1961-72; columnist Washington Star News, 1972-74; Washington bur. chief People mag., 1974-82; reporter, sr. prodr. NBC-TV, 1969-80; pres. CC-M Prodns. Inc., Washington, 1981—, managementwisdom.com. Prodr. 1st network documentary on spouse abuse NBC-TV, 1975 (blue ribbon San Francisco Film Festival), 1st network documentary on child sexual abuse NBC, TV, 1977, People of the Year (CBS), 1982, If Japan Can, Why Can't We, 1980 (Dupont award Columbia U. Sch. Journalism), It's Up to the Women, 1984, The Issues Hit Home, 1986, Windows on Women, 1986, How To Fix Up a Little Old American Town, 1987, Work Worth Doing, 1987 (Golden Eagle award Coun. on Internat. Non-theatrical Events), The Deming Library: Vols. I-27, Implementing Deming, vols. 1-4; co-author: Thinking About Quality, Progress, Wisdom and the Deming Revolution, 1995; prodr., dir. documentary series Quality of Else, 1991, W. Edwards Deming: The Prophet of Quality, 1994; co-author: Quality or Else: The Revolution in World Business, 1991; prodr. How Everyone Wins: Joy, Meaning and Profit in the Workplace, 1997, The Enneagram Nine Paths to a Productive and Fulfilling Life, 1999. Recipient Bill Pryor Meml. award, 1st prize Washington Newspaper Guild, 1966; Disting. Pub. Affairs Reporting award Am. Polit. Sci. Assn., 1967; Nat. Assn. Broadcasters award, 1971, 2 Emmy awards Nat. Acad. TV Arts and Scis., 1972, award for broadcast investigative reporting AAUW, 1972, award for investigative reporting Chesapeake Press Assn., 1971, Douglas Southall Freeman award for pub. service Va. Assn. Press Broadcasters, 1972; Washington Newspaper Guild award, 1974, Blue Ribbon Am. Film Festival, 1977, 1st place award Nat. Edn. Film Festival, 1985, documentary award Am. Women in Radio and TV, 1986, Golden Eagle award, 1986, 87, Award of Excellence Soc. Tech. Communication, 1988. Mem. AFTRA, SAG. Democrat. Roman Catholic. Office: 7755 16th St NW Washington DC 20012-1460 Office Phone: 202-882-7430. E-mail: cc-m@cc-m.com.

CRAYBAS, JILL, professional tennis player; b. Providence, July 4, 1974; d. Norbert and Camille. Degree in telecom., U. Fla., 1996. Profl. tennis player, 1996—. Recipient Ranked #8 in U.S. 18s, 1992, NCAA Champion, 1996, Ranked #97, WTA, Ranked #14 Among U.S. Players, Highest Season Ending Singles Rank #57, 2002, 1WTA Tour Singles Title, Japan, 2002, 1 WTA Tour Doubles Title, Madrid, 2003, 2 ITF Women's Circuit Tour Titles. Office: WTA Tour Corporate Headquarters One Progress Plz Ste 1500 Saint Petersburg FL 33701*

CREAMER, KATHY JAYNE, writer; b. Logansport, Ind., Dec. 10, 1960; d. James Hensley and Evelyn Lois (Good) Logan; m. Randall Wayne Creamer, Oct. 15, 1983; children: Jennifer Lois, Krysta Elizabeth. Lic., Beer Sch. Real Estate, 1987. Lic. real estate agt. Ind. Agt. Era Real Estate Co., Warsaw, Ind., 1987—88; referral agt. various real estate cos., Warsaw, 1988—89; freelance writer, 1992—. Author: (children's book) Case of the Missing Books, 1993, (novels) Shadows Dark, 1995. Vol. Am. Party, Ind., 1978; treas. sr. class Lakeland Christian Acad., Winona Lake, Ind., 1977—78. Republican. Baptist. Avocations: photography, quilting, reading, crafts, book collecting. Home: PO Box 184 Atwood IN 46502

CREAMER-FRANKE, SHANNON, graphic design company executive; b. Weisbaden, Germany, Mar. 22, 1969; (parents Am. citizens); d. Peter W. and Joette (Haley) C.; m. Eric M. Franke; children: Asia Marcellus, Ruby Mattox. Student, Moore Coll. Art and Design, Phila., 1988—89, Temple U., 1989—93. Pres., creative dir./owner Odd Graphic Co., Collingswood, NJ, 1994—. Avocations: sculpture, painting, drawing. Office: 1033 Park Ave Collingswood NJ 08108-3236 Office Phone: 856-833-0616.

CREANY, CATHLEEN ANNETTE, television station executive; b. Johnstown, Pa., Jan. 14, 1950; d. Eugene Anthony and Winifred Nell (Sheridan) C. BA in Communication Arts, U. Notre Dame, 1972. Ptnr. Technivision, Inc., N.Y.C., 1972-75; prodr. commls. Innervision Prodns., St. Louis, 1975-76; film editor Sta. KPHO-TV, Phoenix, 1976-77, promotion asst., 1977-78, comml. and documentary photographer and prodr., 1978-80; news photographer Sta. WTVH-TV, Syracuse, N.Y., 1980-81; field dir. PM Mag. show, Syracuse, N.Y., 1981-82, exec. prodr., 1982-83, program dir., 1983-86; v.p., gen. mgr. Sta. WTVH-TV, Syracuse, N.Y., 1986-92, Sta. WFAA-TV, Dallas, 1993-94, pres., gen. mgr., 1994-97; sr. v.p. TV sta. group Belo Corp., Dallas, 1997-99, Broadcast Divsn., Dallas, 2000. Bd. dirs. The Family Place, 1993—, Children's Med. Ctr. Dallas, Children's Med. Found. Dallas, Better Bus. Bur. Dallas; adv. bd., Jr. League, Dallas; mem. Charter 100 of Dallas. Recipient Excellence in Photography award for PM Mag. show, 1982, Excellence in Story Producing award, 1983. Mem. Nat. Assn. TV Program Execs., Nat. Assn. Broadcasters, Am. Women in Radio and TV, Inc., ABC TV Affiliates Assn. (vice chair bd. govs.). Avocations: running, skiing, boating, gardening. Office: Belo Corp 400 S Record St Fl 14 Dallas TX 75202-4841

CREASAP, SUSAN DIANE, music educator, conductor; b. Marion, Ohio, Feb. 19, 1951; d. John William Creasap and Barbara Ann Brinkman; m. John C. Hennen, Jr., June 9, 2001. BS, Indiana U. Pa., 1973; MA, U. Minn., 1982; DA, Ball State U., 1996. Tchr., band dir. Crawford County Schs., Meadville, Pa., 1973—80; band dir. Memphis City Schs., 1980—92; dir. of bands Clarion (Pa.) U. of Pa., 1992—93; assoc. dir. bands Morehead (Ky.) State U., 1996—. Guest condr. various honor bands, 1996—; adjudicator various concert and marching bands, 1996—. Rsch. assoc.: book Teaching Music Through Performance in Band, vol. 1-4, 1998—2003; contbr. articles to profl. jours. Mem.: Ky. Music Educators Assn. (dist. 8 pres.-elect 2003—, Ky. col. dist. 8 2003), Coll. Band Dirs. Nat. Assn. (Ky. chair 2003—), Women Band Dirs. Internat. (pres. 2000—02, Silver Baton award 1996), Pi Kappa Lambda. Democrat. Methodist. Avocations: travel, reading. Office: Morehead State Univ 202 Baird Music Hall Morehead KY 40351

CREASIA, JOAN CATHERINE, dean, nursing educator; b. Burlington, Vt., Aug. 14, 1941; d. Ramon J. and Marjorie E. (Rising) LaBelle; m. Donald A. Creasia, June 29, 1963; children: Karen, Tracey. BSN, U. Vt., 1964; MSN, U. Tenn., 1978; PhD, U. Md., 1987. Staff nurse psychiat. unit Mass. Mental Health Ctr., Boston, 1964-65; instr. D'Youville Sch. Nursing, Cambridge, Mass., 1965-66; staff nurse Boston Lying-In Hosp., 1966-67; staff nurse med. surg. units Norwood (Mass.) Hosp., 1967-70; staff nurse, nursing supr. Oak Ridge (Tenn.) Hosp., 1971-74; staff nurse, supr. Frederick (Md.) Meml. Hosp., 1977-78, 86-92; instr. in nursing U. Tenn., Knoxville, 1974-77; rsch. asst. U. Md., Balt., 1980-83; instr., coord., asst. prof. med. surg. nursing Frederick (Md.) C.C., 1978-80, 81-83; asst. prof., coord. RN-BSN program U. Md. Sch. Nursing, Balt., 1983-90, assoc. prof., chair RN-BSN/MS programs, 1990-94, dir. statewide programs, 1991-94; assoc. dean for acad. programs and interim dean Med. U. of S.C. Coll. Nursing, Charleston, 1994-95; dean, Coll. Nursing, U. Tenn., Knoxville, 1995—. Cons. in field. Author: Conceptual Foundations of Professional Nursing Practice, 1991, 96 (Book of Yr. award Am. Jour. Nursing 1992), Conceptual Foundations: The Bridge to Professional Nursing Practice, 2001; contbr. articles to profl. jours. and books. Recipient Outstanding Achievement in Indirect Nursing Rsch. award, 1987, Nat. Rsch. Svc. award, 1982, 83, Profl. Nurse Traineeship award, 1981, Outstanding Leadership award Md. Nurses Assn., 1990. Mem. ANA, Nat. League for Nursing, Sigma Theta Tau, Phi Kappa Phi. Home: 605 Scotswood Cir Knoxville TN 37919-7457 Personal E-mail: dcreasia@aol.com. Business E-Mail: jcreasia@utk.edu.

CREBO, MARY ELIZABETH, state agency official, assessor; b. Chgo., Oct. 30, 1939; d. George Henry Browne and Nellace Marie Kamman; m. Frank S. Crebo, Jan. 11, 1958; children: Tracey E., Jeanne M., Frank Andrew, Daniel J. Student, Sauk Valley Cmty. Coll. State appraiser State of Ill., 1993-99; assessing officer State Ill., Dept. of Revenue, 1983-99; adminstr., assessor Coloma Twp., Ill.; owner Mary Crebo, Appraisals, 1986-99. Mem. Rock Falls (Ill.) Sch. Bd., 1972-74. Mem. Whiteside County Assessors Assn. (sec. 1998-99, acting pres. 1985-86, v.p. 1984-85). Avocations: painting, writing, camping, travel, photography. Home: 1307 Riverdale Rd Rock Falls IL 61071-2433 Office: 1200 Prophetstown Rd Rock Falls IL 61071-1064

CRECCA, PAMELA MICHELLE, small business owner; b. Richmond, Va., July 26, 1969; d. Everett Ellis and Adele Fortune; m. Thomas Walter Crecca, June 24, 2000. BS cum laude in speech lang. pathology, Old Dominion U., 1991, MS Magna cum laude in edn. speech lang. pathology, 1996. Lic. speech lang. pathology NC. Lead speech lang. pathologist Ballard Therapy Svcs., Inc., New Bern, NC, 1997—2000; owner Speech Therapy Works, New Bern, 2000—. Best Practices in Spl. Edn., 2002. Sunday sch. tchr. First Bapt. Ch., New Bern, 2000—. Mem.: NC Speech - Lang. and Hearing Assn., Am. Speech Lang. Hearing Assn., Nat. Assn. Female Exe., Phi Kappa Phi Nat. Bapt. Avocations: weightlifting, reading, running, painting, writing poetry. Office: Speech Therapy Works PO Box 12063 New Bern NC 28561

CREDEUR, CATHERINE, social worker; d. Gilbert Joseph and Sally Stafford Credeur; m. Mark Edward White, Mar. 22, 2003. BS, La. Coll., 1993; MSW, La. State U., 1996. Lic. social worker La. Social worker Charter Behavioral Health Sys., DeRidder and Shreveport, La., 1996—98, Willis-Knighton Med. Sys., Shreveport, 1998—2002; patient adv. Am. Cancer Soc., Shreveport, 2002—04. Mem. adv. coun. Bossier Coun. on Aging, Bossier City, La., 2002—03. Co-orgainer Social Justice Ay of the Cross Pax Christi, Shreveport, 2000—03. Mem.: NASW, Assn. Oncology Social Workers. Republican. Roman Catholic. Avocations: gardening, travel. Office: Christus Schumpert Health Sys One St Mary Pl Shreveport LA 71101

CREECH, SHARON, children's author; b. South Euclid, Ohio; d. Arvel and Ann Creech; m. Lyle Rigg; children: Rob, Karin. BA, Hiram Coll.; MA, George Mason U. Editl. asst., indexer Congl. Quarterly, Washington; rschr. Libr. Congress. Author: Recital, Nickel Malley, Walk Two Moons, 1994 (School Library Journal Best Book of 1994, ALA Notable Children's Book Award, 1995, John Newbery medal 1995), Absolutely Normal Chaos, 1995, Pleasing The Ghost, 1996, Chasing Redbird, 1997, Bloomability, 1999, The Wanderer, 2000 (Newbery honor), Fishing in the Air, 2000, A Fine, Fine School, 2001, Love That Dog, 2001, Ruby Holler, 2002. Office: care HarperCollins Children's Bks c/o Author Mail 1350 Ave of the Americas New York NY 10019

CREEDON, GERALDINE, state legislator; b. Springfield, Mass., Sept. 26, 1945; m. Robert Stanton Creedon Jr.; children: Jennifer, Robert S. BA, Emmanuel Coll., 1967. Mem. Dist. 11 Mass. Ho. of Reps., Boston, 1995—, mem. post audit and oversight com., mem. house ways and means com., mem. human svcs. and elderly affairs com. Mem. Brockton (Mass.) City Coun., 1992-95, pres., 1995; bd. dirs. Charity Guild, 1990-97; mem. Dem. City Com. Roman Catholic. Office: Mass State Legis Rm 146 State House Boston MA 02133

CREEL, SUE CLOER, secondary school educator; b. Columbus, Miss., July 4, 1943; d. Cornelius Ducler Cloer and Sarah Verna (Shackelford) Cloer Mackie; children: Ricky (dec.), Ronny. BA, Harding U., 1982, MEd, 1986; grad., Jackson State U., 1996. Nat. bd. cert. Adolescent and Young Adult English Lang. Arts, 2000. Tchr. 8th grade English Alfh Jr. H.S., Searcy, Ark., 1982-87; part-time editor, writer for neurosurgery Miss. Med. Ctr., Jackson, 1987-89; adminstrv. asst. to dean of nursing U. Miss. Med. Ctr., Jackson, 1988-89; tchr. advanced placement English and creative writing Jackson Pub. Schs., 1990—; adj. instr. world lit. and Brit. lit. Holmes C.C. Adj. prof. Holmes C.C., 1999-2000; adj. instr. English Hinds C.C., Raymond, Miss., 1987-89; cons. Nat. Writing Project, 1995, Univ. Ctrl. Ark., Conway, Ark., Nat. Writing Project; session chair Writing-Across-the-Curriculum K-12, Charleston, S.C., 1997; tchr. long distance learning interactive video ETV, 1998-99, 2000-2001; presenter Nat. Coun. Tchrs. English, 2001. Contbg. poet: Moments in the Garden, 1998, Miss. Musings, Miss. Poetry Soc., 1997, The Drifting Sands, 1999. With USN, 1962—63. Grantee Entergy, Jackson, 1994-96; fellowship Jackson (Miss.) State U., 1996; recipient 3 Editor's Choice awards, Beyond Call of Duty award JPSD, 1999; named tchr. excellence Calloway H.S., 2000. Mem. Nat. Coun. Tchrs. of English, Miss. Poetry Soc. (v.p. ctrl. br. 2002-), The Poetry Guild (poetry included Best Poems of the 90s, 1998), Phi Kappa Phi, Beta Sigma Phi (v.p. XI chpt. 2002—, pres. 2003, Valentine Ball Queen 2003, mem. Internat. Queen's Ct. 2003), Alpha Chi, Kappa Delta Pi, Sigma Tau Delta, Phi Alpha Theta. Mem. Ch. Of Christ. Avocations: reading, writing, theater, gardening, competitions. Home: 625 Choctaw Rd Jackson MS 39206-5325

CREEM, CYNTHIA STONE, state legislator, lawyer; BSBA, JD, Boston U. Mem. Mass. Senate, Boston, 1998—. Mem. criminal justice Mass. State Senate, election laws com., fed. fin. assistance com., local affairs com. Mem. Newton Bd. Aldermen, Gov.'s Coun. Fellow Women's Bar Assn.; mem. Mass. Bar Assn. Democrat. Office: Mass State Senate State House Rm 416B Boston MA 02133 E-mail: ccreem@senate.state.ma.us.

CREENAN, KATHERINE HERAS, lawyer; b. Elizabeth, N.J., Oct. 7, 1945; d. Victor Joseph and Katherine Regina (Lederer) Petervary; m. Edward James Creenan; 1 child, David Heras. BA, Kean Univ., 1968; JD, Rutgers U., 1984. Bar: N.J. 1984, Maine, 1996, U.S. Dist. Ct. N.J. 1984, U.S. Ct. Appeals (3d cir.), 1998. Various tchg. positions including, Union and Stanhope, N.J., 1968-81; law clk. to presiding judge Superior Ct. of N.J. Appellate Div., Newark, 1984-85; assoc. Lowenstein, Sandler, Kohl, Fisher & Boylan, Roseland, N.J., 1985-88, Kirsten, Simon, Friedman, Allen, Cherin & Linken, Newark, 1988-89, Whitman & Ranson, Newark, 1989-93; sr. atty. Whitman Breed Abbott & Morgan LLP, Newark, 1993-99; assoc. Skadden, Arps, Slate, Meagher & Flom LLP, Newark, 1999—. Mem. ABA, N.J. State Bar Assn. Office: Skadden Arps Slate Meaghar & Flom LLP 1 Newark Ctr Newark NJ 07102-5297 Office Phone: 732-639-6832. E-mail: kcreenan@skadden.com.

CREIGHTON, JOANNE VANISH, academic administrator; b. Marinette, Wis., Feb. 21, 1942; d. William J. and Bernice Vanish; m. Thomas F. Creighton, Nov. 9, 1968; 1 child, William. BA with honors, U. Wis., 1964; MA, Harvard U., 1965; PhD, U. Mich., 1969. From instr. to prof. English Wayne State U., Detroit, 1968—85, assoc. dean liberal arts, 1983—85; dean arts and scis., prof. English U. N.C., Greensboro, 1985—90; v.p. acad. affairs, provost, prof. English Wesleyan U., Middletown, Conn., 1990—94, interim pres., 1994—95; prof. English, pres. Mt. Holyoke Coll., South Hadley, Mass., 1995—. Author: William Faulkner's Craft of Revision, 1977, Joyce Carol Oates, 1979, Margaret Dabble, 1985, Joyce Carol Oates:

Novels of the Middle Years, 1992. Grantee, Am. Coun. Learned Socs. Mem.: Phi Kappa Phi, Phi Beta Kappa. Home: 45 College St South Hadley MA 01075-1403 Office: Mount Holyoke Coll Office of Pres 50 College St South Hadley MA 01075-1423*

CREMEANS, SHARON LU, medical/surgical nurse; b. Warren, Ohio, Jan. 28, 1952; d. Jero Carl and Lucille Rita Salva; m. Charles Monroe Cremeans, Sept. 17, 1977 (div. Sept. 1990); 1 child, Charles Monroe Jr. Grad. in vocat. nurse, Choffin Sch. Practical Nursing, Youngstown, Ohio, 1975; AAS, Youngstown State U., 1985. RN Ohio, 1985, sexual assault nurse examiner, Ohio, 2003. Nurse float St. Joseph Hosp., Warren, Ohio, 1975—85, charge nurse, 1985—86, nurse ICU/CCU, 1986—92, nurse float, 1992—95; auxiliary dep. sheriff Mahoning County Sheriff's Dept., Youngstown, Ohio, 1988—92; part time pokice officer Newton Twp. Pokice Depts., Newton Falls, Ohio, 1989—98; behavioral nurse St. Joseph Health Ctr., Warren, Ohio, 1995—; nurse Trumbull County Correctional Instn., Leavitsburg, Ohio, 2001—02; sexual assault nurse examiner St. Elizabeth Health Ctr., Youngstown, Ohio, 2002—. Trustee Fraternal Order Police, Newton Falls, Ohio, 1990—92; rape crisis team Trumbull County, Inc., Warren, Ohio, 1990—. Recipient law and Order award, Am. Legion, 1995. Mem.: Nat. Assn. Female Execs., Midwest Gang Investigators Assn., Ohio Crime Prevention Assn. Democrat. Roman Catholic. Avocations: reading, music, photography. Office: St Joseph Ctr 667 Eastland Ave Warren OH 44484

CREMIN, SUSAN ELIZABETH, lawyer; b. Chgo., July 2, 1947; d. William Amberg and Rosemary (Brennan) C. AB cum laude, Vassar Coll., 1969; JD, Northwestern U., Chgo., 1976. Bar: Ill. 1977. Assoc. Winston & Strawn, Chgo., 1976-83, ptnr., 1983-93, capital ptnr., 1993—. Co-author: Registration and Reporting Under the Exchange Act, 1995, 2nd edit., 1996. Trustee The Shedd Aquarium, Chgo., The Masters Sch., Dobbs Ferry, N.Y. Office: Winston & Strawn 35 W Wacker Dr Ste 4200 Chicago IL 60601-1695

CRENSHAW, CAROL, charitable organization administrator; b. Chgo., July 3, 1956; BS in Acctg., Fin., No. Ill. U., 1978. CPA, Ill. Auditor CPMG Peat Marwick, Chgo., 1978-83, asst. contr., 1983, contr., 1983-94; CFO The Chgo. Cmty. Trust, 1994—. Mem. fin. acting practice com. Com. for the Found. Sector, 1997—. Office: The Chicago Community Trust 222 N Lasalle St Ste 1400 Chicago IL 60601-1088

CRENSHAW, MARTHA, political science educator; PhD, U. Va., 1973. John E. Andrus prof. govt. Weslyan U., Middletown, Conn., 1974—; rschr. Congressional Rsch. Svc. Author: (book) Terrorism and International Cooperation, Revolutionary Terrorism: The FLN in Algeria, 1954-1962; editor: Terrorism, Legitimacy and Power, Terrorism in Context, 1995. Recipient rsch. grants from Nat. Endowment Humanities, Harry Frank Guggenheim Found., Ford Found., Pew Faculty Fellowship Program, U.S. Inst. Peace. Mem. Internat. Soc. Political Psychology (pres. 1997-98). Office: Wesleyan U 238 Church St Middletown CT 06459-3139 Fax: 860-685-2781.

CRENSHAW, PATRICIA SHRYACK, sales executive, consultant; b. Kansas City, Mo., Oct. 7, 1941; d. George Randolf and Velma Irene (Carroll) Shryack; m. Paul Burton, Mar. 24, 1961 (div. 1971); m. Peter Frederick Schmidt, Jan. 21, 1989. Student, William Jewell Coll., 1959-60, S.W. Mo. State U., 1960-61; BEd, U. Mo., 1967; postgrad., Cen. Mo. State U., 1971-73. Cert. tchr. secondary edn. and history, Mo. Tchr. Lillis H.S., Kansas City, 1967—69, Park Hill H.S., Kansas City, 1969-73; terr. mgr. Hollister, Inc., Kansas City, 1973-75, field trainer, 1974-75, sales edn. mgr. Chgo., 1975; dist. sales mgr. Detroit Mich., 1976-81; regional sales mgr. Chgo., 1981-84; dir. contract sales Chgo. Serta, Inc., 1984-86, nat. dir. contract sales divsn., 1987-89, v.p. nat. contract sales, 1989-90; area v.p. B G Industries, Northridge, Calif., 1990-91, v.p. sales, 1992-95, v.p. internat. sales, 1995-97, v.p. clin. svcs., 1998—2002; ret., 2002. Mem. women's com. Young Reps., Kansas City, 1962. Mem. NOW, U.S. Golf Assn., Lake Barrington Shores (Ill.) Golf Club. Republican. Avocations: golfing, skiing, scuba diving, racquetball, reading, gardening. Home: 101 E Ocean Dr Key Colony Beach FL 33051

CRENSHAW, TENA LULA, librarian; b. Coleman, Fla., Dec. 15, 1930; d. Herbert Joseph Crenshaw and Nellie (Wicker) Cox. BS, Fla. So. Coll., 1951; postgrad., U. Fla., 1952-55; MLS (Univ. scholar), U. Okla., 1960. Tchr. pub. schs., Coleman, Fla., 1952-55, St. Petersburg, Fla., 1955-57, Houston, 1957-59; tech. libr. Army Rocket & Guided Missile Agy., Redstone Arsenal, Huntsville, Ala., 1960-61; acquisitions libr. Martin Marietta Corp., Orlando, Fla., 1961-64; reader svcs. libr. John F. Kennedy Space Ctr., NASA, Fla., 1964-66; rsch. info. analyst, specialist Lockheed Missiles and Space Co., Palo Alto, Calif., 1966-68; head svcs. to pub. A.W. Calhoun Med. Libr. Emory U., Atlanta, 1969-78; dep. dir. Louis Calder Meml. Libr. U. Miami (Fla.) Sch. Medicine, 1979-80; head edn. libr. U. Fla., Gainesville, 1980-84; libr. Westinghouse Electric Corp., Orlando, 1984-86; chief libr. tech. info. ctr. U. Ctrl. Fla., Orlando, 1986-87, libr. contracts and grants, 1987-88; libr. cons. Coleman, Fla., 1988-89; sch. libr., 1989-90; libr. Kennedy Space Ctr., Fla., 1990-91, Patrick Air Force Base, Fla., 1992-94, Coleman Pub. Libr., 1995—. Chmn. Fla. State Adv. Coun. on Librs. Mem. Spl. Librs. Assn. (treas. S. Atlantic chpt. 1970-72, chmn. membership com. 1973, v.p. 1973-74, pres. 1974-75, mem. resolutions com. 1975-76, nominating com. biol. scis. divsn. 1974-75, chmn. 1977-78), Med. Libr. Assn. (mem. conf. planning com. So. regional group 1973-74, membership com. 1977-79, by laws rev. com. 1979-80), Southeastern (mem. new directions com. 1972-74, chmn. spl. librs. sect. 1974), Ga. (careers in librarianship com. 1974-77), Fla. Libr. Assn., DAR, Alpha Delta Pi, Kappa Delta Pi. Democrat. Methodist. Office Phone: 352-748-4598. E-mail: Colemanlibrary@cfl.rr.com.

CREPPEL, CLAIRE BINET, hotel owner; b. New Orleans, Nov. 30, 1936; d. Albert Leo and Leocadie (Dominique) Binet; m. Jacques Jules Creppel, Feb. 2, 1957; children: Ingrid, Foster, Collette and Gregg (twins), Lisa, Morgan. BA in English, U. Southwestern La., 1971; MEd in Guidance/Counseling Psychology, Loyola U., New Orleans, 1975; post-grad. adminstrn., mgmt., supervision, Tulane U., New Orleans, 1978. Instr. English and Spanish Booker T. Washington Sr. High Sch., 1972-74, instr. English and reading, 1974-76, guidance counselor, 1976-77; intervention counselor Sophie B. Wright Middle Sch., 1977-79; owner, gen. mgr. Columns Hotel, New Orleans, 1980—; owner Woodland Plantation, 1997—. New Orleans regional dir. La. Coun. on Child Abuse, 1985—87; v.p. bd. Barataria Tereelsone Estuary Found. (Save the Wetlands), 2000—02; mem. adv. bd. Le Petite Thetre du Vieux Carre, 2000—; mem. citizens adv. bd. Jo Ellen Smith Hosp.; mem. task force Ct. Appointed Spl. Advocate; bd. dirs. So. Repertory Theatre of New Orleans, Odyssey House, Bravo, Arts Coun., Overture to the Cultural Season, pres., 1997—98. Named one of Top Exec. Women New Orleans, 1990, one of Top Women New Orleans Bus. Owners, 1997. Mem. Am. Pers. and Guidance Assn., AAUW, La. Pers. and Guidance Assn., Orleans Sch. Counselors Assn., St. Charles Ave. Bus. Assn., Street Car Inns, Fgn. Rels. Assn. New Orleans, Kappa Delta Pi, Sigma Delta Pi. Republican. Roman Catholic. Avocations: preservation projects, real estate market, scuba diving, snow and water skiing, travel. Home: 7927 St Charles Ave New Orleans LA 70118-2724 Office: Columns Hotel 3811 Saint Charles Ave New Orleans LA 70115-4681 E-mail: clairecreppel@aol.com.

CREQUE, LINDA ANN, non-profit educational and research executive, former education commissioner; b. N.Y.C. d. Noel and Enid Louise (Schloss) DePass; m. Leonard J. Creque, July 29, 1967; children: Leah Michelle, Michael Gregory. BS, CUNY-Queens, 1963, MS, 1969; PhD, U. Ill., 1986. Tchr. 2d grade Bd. Edn., N.Y.C., 1963, tchr. demonstrations, team tchr., 1964-65, master tchr., 1965-66; elem. tchr. P.S. 69, Jackson Hgts., N.Y., 1963-67; tchr. English Cath. U., Ponce, P.R., 1967; cmty. exch. elem. tchr. grades K-6 Ponce, 1966-67; tchr. 4th grade Dept. Edn., V.I., 1967-69, tchr. remedial reading, master tchr., 1968-69, program coord. Project HeadStart, V.I., 1969-73, coord. Inst. Developmental Studies, 1970-71, acting dir., 1972-73; prin. Thomas Jefferson Annex Primary Sch., St. Thomas, V.I., 1973-80, Joseph Sibilly Elem. Sch., St. Thomas, 1980-87; commr. edn. Dept. Edn., St. Thomas, 1987-94; founder, pres. V.I. Inst. for Tchg. and Learning, St. Thomas, 1995—. Cons. Edn. Devel. Ctr., Mass. Nat. SSI Project, 1992-93, Coll. V.I., 1978; mem. exec. com., bd. overseers Regional Lab. Ednl. Improvement NE and Islands, Andover, Mass., 1988-92; bd. dirs. V.I. Pub. TV; mem. exec. bd. Leadership in Edn. Adminstrv. Devel., V.I., 1989—; presenter, keynote spkr. confs. in field. Contbr. articles to profl. publs. Trustee U. V.I., 1989—; mem. V.I. Residential Task Force for Human Svcs., 1989-94, V.I. Labor Coun.; bd. dirs. Nat. Urban Alliance for Effective Edn. Tchrs. Coll. Columbia U., N.Y.C., 1993—, Cultural Inst. V.I., 1989-94; mem. cultural endowment bd., V.I., 1989-94; mem. governing bd. East End Health Ctr., 1979-80; mem. Gov.'s Conf. Librs., 1978. Grantee V.I. Coun. on Arts Ceramics for Primary Children, 1974-78, Comprehensive Employment and Tng. Act, 1977, NSF, 1989-93, Carnegie Found., 1988-90; recipient award NASA, award St. Thomas-St. John Counselors Assn., 1988, Ednl. Excellence award Harvard U. Prins. Ctr., Ill. Edn. Svc. Ctr., 1975, Outstanding Leadership award FEMA, 1990, Disting. Svc. award Edn. Commn. of U.S., 1991, Outstanding Svc. award Coun. of Chief State Sch. Officers, 1995. Mem. LWV, St. Thomas Reading Coun., Nat. Assn. Tchrs. Math., Edn. Commn. of States (commr. 1987-93, steering com. 1988-92, internal audit com. 1988, policies priority com. 1991, exec. com. 1992, alt. steering com. 1991-94), Coun. Chief of State Sch. Officers (chair extra jurisdictions com., bd. dirs., task force early childhood edn., ednl. equity com., restructuring edn. com.), Phi Kappa Phi, Kappa Delta Pi, Phi Delta Kappa. Office: VI Inst for Tchg and Learning PO Box 301954 St Thomas VI 00803-1954

CRESCENZ, VALERIE J. music educator; b. Bethlehem, Pa., Mar. 8, 1956; d. George Henry and Florence Showers; m. Joseph Martin Crescenz, July 26, 1980; children: Monica Lynn, Melanie Jane. BS in Music Edn., West Chester (Pa.) State Coll., 1978, MusM in Piano Performance, 1980. Music instr. West Chester State Coll., 1979—80, Delaware County C.C., Media, Pa., 1990—95; composer Hinshaw Music, Inc., Chapel Hill, NC, 1994—; music tchr., dir. Downingtown (Pa.) Sch. Dist., 1995—. Composer (choral music): various titles, including 3 written with composer James Green of Durham, N.C. ; composer: (commd. works) Durham Sch. Arts, 2002. Mem.: Music Educators Nat. Conf., ASCAP, NEA, Pa. State Edn. Assn., Pa. Music Educators Assn. (commn. 2001, 2002). Home: 10 Juniata Dr Coatesville PA 19320 Office: West Bradford Elem Sch 1475 Broad Run Rd Downingtown PA 19335

CRESS, CECILE COLLEEN, retired librarian; b. Colorado Springs, Colo., Feb. 26, 1914; d. John Leo and Elizabeth Veronica (Rouse) Haley; m. Arthur Henry Cress, May 8, 1937 (div. 1960); children: Ronnie Lou Kordick, Dan, Elaine. BA, Adams State Coll., 1936; MA in English, Colo. Coll., 1964; MLS, Denver U., 1970. 5th grade tchr. Westcliffe (Colo.) Elem., 1953-56; English tchr. Penrose (Colo.) H.S., 1956-59; English-social studies tchr. Excelsior Jr. H.S. Dist. 70, Pueblo, Colo., 1959-64; libr. Pueblo County H.S. Dist. 70, Pueblo, 1964-80, Nat. Coll./Pueblo Br., 1980-91; cataloger in libr. Pueblo C.C., 1992-95. Tutor adult literacy program South Cen. Bd. Coop. Svcs., 1991. Recipient Ace of Clubs award Am. Contract Bridge League, 1988, 89. Mem. Pueblo Ret. Sch. Employees (v.p. 1990-92, pres. 1982-84, state bd. 1982-86, sec. 1995-97), Colo. Libr. Assn., Unit 367 Am. Contract Bridge Assn., Irish Club Pueblo (pres. 1995-96), Welsh Terrier Club Colo., Alpha Delta Kappa (Pueblo chpt., pres. 1976-78, state historian 1980-82, state bd. 1980-82, rec. sec. 1994-98), Am. Contract Bridge League (v.p. unit 367 1998-2000). Democrat. Roman Catholic. Avocations: duplicate bridge, welsh terriers, travel. Home: 901 Jackson St Pueblo CO 81004-2425 E-mail: cccress@cs.com.

CRESWELL, DOROTHY ANNE, computer consultant; b. Burlington, Iowa, Feb. 6, 1943; d. Robert Emerson and Agnes Imogene (Gardner) Mefford; m. John Lewis Creswell, Aug. 28, 1965. AA, Burlington C.C., 1963; BA in Math., U. Iowa, 1965; MS in Math., Western Ill. U., 1970; postgrad., Iowa State U., 1974—. Computer programmer Mason & Hanger, Silas Mason Co., Inc., Burlington, 1965-74; systems programmer Contractor's Hotline, Ft. Dodge, Iowa, 1974; dir. data processing Iowa Cen. C.C., Ft. Dodge, 1975-80; systems programming mgr. Norand Corp., Cedar Rapids, Iowa, 1980-82; spl. svcs. mgr. Pioneer Hi-Bred Internat., Inc., Cedar Rapids, 1982-87; owner, pres. D.C. Cons., Inc., Ankeny, Iowa, 1987—2003. Computers-in-edn. del. to China, People to People Internat., Kansas City, Mo., 1987. Contbr. articles, papers to profl. publs. Mem. Data Processing Mgmt. Assn. (bd. dirs. 1986-87, v.p. 1988, 91-93, pres. 1993-94), Adminstrv. Mgmt. Soc. (sec. 1985-86, v.p. 1986-90, Merit award 1987), Assn. Computing Machinery, Hawkeye Pers. Computer Users, DEC Users Group (v.p. Ea. Iowa chpt. 1981-82), Ind. Computer Cons. Assn. (mem. editl. bd. 1989-96, chpt. pres.-at-large 1993-95). Democrat. Methodist. Avocations: jogging, travel.

CREWS, DENISE M. educational association administrator; b. Calif., Feb. 20, 1964; d. Eddie Marshall and Bernice Stockton; m. Kenneth Eugene Crews, Nov. 7, 1988; 1 child, Anna Clare stepchildren: Jake, Josh. BS, So. Ill. U., 1991, MS, 1997; EdD, U. Ill., 2002. Cert. tchg. certs. Ill. Spl. educator Massac County Sch. Dist., Metropolis, Ill., 1992—96; term faculty John A. Logan Coll., Carterville, Ill., 1998—; dir. John A. Logan Coll., Devel. Ednl. Programming, 1997—. Named to Oxford Round Table, Oxford U., 2002. Office: John A Logan Coll 700 Logan Coll Rd Carterville IL 62918 E-mail: denisecrews@jalc.edu.

CREWS, JANET M. elementary school educator; b. St. Louis, Mo., Oct. 31, 1967; d. James E. and Jeanne B. Crews. BS in Edn., S.W. Mo. State U., 1990; MAT, Webster U., 1995. Cert. elem. edn. Mo., mid. sch. edn. Mo., sci. edn. Mo. Tchg. intern Captain Sch Clayton (Mo.) Sch. Dist., 1990—91; tchr. 6th grade Wohlwend Elem. Mehlville Sch. Dist., St. Louis, 1991—92, tchr. 6th grade Trautwein Elem., 1992—94, tchr. 6th grade Hagemann Elem., 1994—99; tchr. 6th grade sci. Wydown Mid. Sch. Clayton Sch. Dist., 1999—2003; select tchr. as Regional Resource Dept. Elem. and Secondary Edn. and Clayton Sch. Dist., St. Louis, 2003—. Chair governing bd. Regional Profl. Devel. Ctr., St. Louis, 1998—2001; presenter workshops in field, 1999—; mentor, coop. tchr. for student tchrs. Recycling coord. Clayton Sch. Dist., 1999—; stream team sponsor Mo. Conservation Dept., St. Louis, 1995—; Environ. Club sponsor Leadership in Environ. Action Projects, St. Louis, 1996—. Named Mo. Conservation Educator of Yr., Dept. Conservation Fedn., 1998, Recycling Educator of Yr., Reynolds Aluminum, 1996; recipient Environ. Excellence award, Choose Environ. Excellence, 2002. Mem.: Sci. Tchrs. of Mo., Nat. Sci. Tchrs. Assn., Mo. Environ. Edn. Assn. (exec. bd. 2000—03), Mo. State Tchr.'s Assn. (exec. bd. 2000—04), Delta Kappa Gamma (corr. sec. 1999—). Avocations: reading, travel, cooking, music. Home: 310 Wildberry Ln Saint Charles MO 63304 Office: Clayton Sch Dist-Wydown 6500 Wydown Blvd Saint Louis MO 63105 E-mail: janet_crews@clayton.k12.mo.us.

CREWS, JUDITH YOUNG, career planning administrator; b. Pitts., Sept. 21, 1942; d. Alvin Mayro Young and Clara Loretta Lehnerd; m. Roderick Brian Crews (div.); 1 child, Kaelie Elizabeth. BA in art, Mercyhurst Coll., 1964; MS in art edn., Fla. State U., 1977. Cert. profl. educator Fla. Art tchr. Monongahela Jr. High, Sewell, NJ, 1964—67, Godby HS, Tallahassee, 1967—97; admin. asst. LeMoyne Art Found., Tallahassee, 1997—98; staff devel. Leon County Schs., Tallahassee, 1998—2000; guidance career specialist Leon HS, Tallahassee, 2000—. Southeastern secondary dir. Nat. Art Edn. Assoc., 1983—85, nat. secondary dir., 1985—87. Mem.: Fla. Art Edn. Assoc., Nat. Art Edn. Assoc., Phi Delta Kappa.

CRIBBS, MAUREEN ANN, artist, educator; b. Marinette, Wis., Feb. 17, 1927; d. Roy Cecil Hubbard and Lillian Worner (Hubbard) Yeoman; m. James Milton Cribbs, Apr. 22, 1950; children: Cynthia, Valerie. BA, DePauw U., 1949; student, Sch. of Art Inst., Chgo., 1971-72, 79-81; MA, Govs. State U., 1973. Cert. secondary sch. tchr., Ill. Tchr. art Sch. Dist. 163, Park Forest, Ill., 1960-78; instr. humanities Sch. Dist. 227, Park Forest, Ill., 1978-79; artist, painter, printmaker Park Forest, 1979—; instr. painting Village Artists, Flossmoor, Ill., 1980-87. Lectr. Chgo. State U., 1980—81; chair study group Homewood-Flossmoor cmty. assocs. of woman's bd. Art Inst. Chgo., 1989—95, sec., 1995—96; adj. prof. Govs. State U., University Park, 1995; artist-in-residence Ox Bow Sch. of Art, 1993; outreach presenter Art Insights, Art Inst. of Chgo., 1995—; docent Nathan Manilow Sculpture Park, Govs. State U., 1996—2004; instr. art, art history Robert Morris Coll., Orland Park, Ill., 1996—2001; woodcut printing and presenter Sr. Celebrations, Art Inst. Chgo., 1998—2002; participant printmaking Santa Reparata Graphic Art Ctr., Florence, Italy, 1999; mem. faculty Tall Grass Arts Assn. Sch., Park Forest, Ill., 2000, Tall Grass Arts Assn., 2001—. Exhibitions include Union St. Gallery, Chicago Heights, 2001, Recent Work South Suburban C.C., Thornton, Ill., 2001, Farnsworth House Gallery, Plano, Ill., 2001—03, Art de Chgo. Gallery, Highland Park, Ill., 2001, Union St. Gallery, Chicago Heights, 2002, Creative Experience Gallery, Frankfort, Ill., 2002—, Mid Am. Print Coun., Denver (Colo.) Airport, 2002, Ox Bow Benefits, 2002, 2003, A Portrait of Music, Ill. Philharm. Orch., 2003, exhibitions include watercolor Ill. Theatre Ctr., 2003, exhibitions include numerous others, one-woman shows include S. Suburban Coll., 2001, Moraine Valley Cmty. Coll., 2001, Tall Grass Arts Assn. Gallery, Park Forest, 2002, Prairie State Coll., 2002, No. Ind. Arts Assn., 2002, Denver Internat. Airport, 2002, Lessedra Gallery, Sofia, Bulgaria, 2003, World Art Print Ann., Palace of Culture, watercolor exhibit, Ill. Theater Ctr., Park Forest, Ill., 2003—, Represented in permanent collections Amity Found., Woodbridge, Conn., Lessedra Gallery. Bd. dirs. Ill. Philharm. Orch., Park Forest, 1981-83, Grace Migrant Day Care, Park Forest, 1981-85, LWV, Park Forest chpt., 2003-; adminstrv. chair Grace United Protestant Ch., Park Forest, 1984-94, v.p. Women's Christian Assn., 1999-2003, pres. 2004-; lay mem. No. Ill. Ann. Conf. of United Meth. Ch., 1996—, mem. commn. on christian unity and interreligious concerns, 1996—. Monetary grantee to produce 15 works Freedom Hall, 1982, Ill. Arts Coun. and Park Forest Cmty. Arts Coun.; Artist-in-Residence Cmty. Arts Coun. Park Forest, 1983, Sch. of Art Inst. of Chgo. at Ox Bow, 1993; recipient Russia Peace ribbon, 1987—. Mem. LWV, Mid-Am. Print Coun., Am. Print Alliance, Chgo. Artists Coalition, Chgo. Southland Visual Arts Coalition. Methodist. Avocations: reiki master, studying herbs & wildflowers, reading, travel, swimming. Home: 74 Blackhawk Dr Park Forest IL 60466-2146 Studio: 266 Somonauk St Park Forest IL 60466-2241 Office Phone: 708-748-5883.

CRINO, MARJANNE HELEN, anesthesiologist; b. Rochester, N.Y., Aug. 18, 1933; d. Michael Jay and Helen Barbara (Kennedy) C.; m. Michael Anthony La Iuppa, Nov. 12, 1960 (dec. Feb. 1996); children: James Michael, Barbara Helen, John Christopher. BS, Coll. St. Teresa, 1955; MD, Med. Coll. Wis., 1959; MA in Theology, St. Bernard's Inst., 1991. Diplomate Nat. Bd. Med. Examiners. House staff Genesee Hosp., Rochester, 1959-61; perinatal mortality rsch., resident in anesthesiology Jackson Meml Hosp.-U. Miami, 1962-65; attending staff in anesthesiology Genesee Hosp., Rochester, N.Y., 1969-2000; mem. exec. com., med. staff sec., 1980, 82; acting chmn. dept. anesthesiology Genesee Hosp., Rochester, N.Y., 1989, 91, chmn. pain control com., 1989-95; clin. instr. anesthesiology U. Rochester Sch. Medicine, 1983—. Cons. anesthesiology Rochester Psychiat. Ctr., 1975-85; instr. anesthesiology U. Miami Sch. medicine, 1966, 67; attending staff anesthesiology Jackson Meml. Hosp., Miami, 1966, 67. Mem. adv. bd. Isaiah House Hosp., 1994-2000, com. Pittsford (N.Y.) Rep. Party, 1970's-80's; vol. chaplain Genesee Hosp. Mem. N.Y. State Soc. Anesthesiologists (bd. dirs., vice spkr. 1983-86, del. 1971-82, 87-2002), Am. Soc. Anesthesiologists (del. 1979-86, 97), AMA, N.Y. State Med. Soc., Med. Soc. County of Monroe, Rochester Acad. Medicine, Cath. Physicians Guild Rochester (bd.dirs., pres. 1988-89), Margaret Roper Guild (pres. 1975-76), Cath. Women's Club (Diocese of Rochester). Roman Catholic. Avocations: reading, gardening, music.

CRISMAN, MARY FRANCES BORDEN, librarian; b. Tacoma, Nov. 23, 1919; d. Lindon A. and Mary Cecelia (Donnelly) Borden; m. Fredric Lee Crisman, Apr. 12, 1975 (dec. Dec. 1975). BA in History, U. Wash., 1943, BA in Librarianship, 1944. Asst. br. libr. in charge work with children Mottet br. Tacoma Pub. Libr., 1944-45, br. libr., 1945-49, br. libr. Moore br., 1950-55, asst. dir., 1955-70, dir., 1970-74, dir. emeritus, 1975—; mgr. corp. libr. Frank Russell Co., 1985-96, ret., 1997. Chmn. Wash. Cmty. Libr. Coun., 1970-72. Hostess program Your Libr. and You, Sta. KTPS-TV, 1969-71. Mem. Highland Homeowners League, Tacoma, 1980—, incorporating dir. 1980, sec., registered agt., 1980-82; mem. Denham West Condominium Assn., Sun City, Ariz., 1995—, chair by laws com., 1999, sec., 2002, 2003. Mem. ALA (chmn. mem. com. Wash. 1957-60, mem. nat. libr. week com. 1965, chmn. libr. adminstrn. divsn. nominating com. 1971, mem. ins. for librs. com. 1970-74, vice chmn. libr. adminstrn. divsn. personnel adminstrn. sect. 1972-73, chmn. 1973-74, mem. com. policy implementation 1973-74, mem. libr. orgn. and mgmt. sect. budgeting acctg. and costs com. 1974-75), Am. Libr. Trustee Assn. (legis. com. 1975-78, conf. program com. 1978-80, action devel. com. 1978-80), Pacific N.W. (trustee divsn. nominating com 1976-77), Wash. Libr. Assn. (exec. bd. 1957-59, state exec., dir. Nat. Libr. Week 1965, treas., exec. bd. 1969-71, 71-73), Urban Librs. Coun. (editl. sec. Newsletter 1972-73, exec. com. 1974-75), Ladies Aux. to United Transp. Union (past pres. Tacoma), Friends Tacoma Pub. Libr. (registered agt. 1975-83, sec. 1975-78, pres. 1978-80, bd. dirs. 1980-83), Smithsonian Assocs., Nat. Railway Hist. Soc., U. Wash. Alumni Assn., U. Wash. Sch. Librarianship Alumni Assn. Clubs: Quota Internat. (sec. 1957-58, 1st v.p. 1960-61, pres. 1961-62, treas. 1975-76, pres. 1979-80) (Tacoma). Home: 6501 N Burning Tree Ln Tacoma WA 98406-2108 also: 9054 N 109th Ave Sun City AZ 85351-4676

CRISMOND, LINDA FRY, public relations executive; b. Burbank, Calif., Mar. 1, 1943; d. Billy Chapin and Lois (Harding) Fry; m. Donald Burleigh Crismond, 1965 (dec.). BS, U. Calif.-Santa Barbara, 1964; M.L.S., U. Calif.-Berkeley, 1965. Cert. county libr., Calif., assn. exec. Reference libr., EDP coordinator San Francisco Pub. Library, 1965—72; head acquisition San Francisco Pub. Libr., 1972-74; asst. univ. libr. U. So. Calif., L.A., 1974-80; chief dep. county libr. L.A. County Pub. Libr., L.A., 1980-81, county libr. Downey, 1981-89; exec. dir ALA, Chgo., 1989-92; v.p. public rels. Profl. Media Svc. Corp., Chgo., 1992-98; v.p. pub. rels. Follett Media Distbn., Crystal Lake, Ill., 1999—2003; nat. media cons. BWI, Lexington, Ky., 2003—. Western rep. quality control council Ohio Coll. Libr. Ctr., Columbus, 1977-80; mem. Am. Nat. Standards Inst., N.Y.C., 1978-80; bd. councillors U. So. Calif. Sch. Libr. and Info. Mgmt., 1980-83; adv. bd. mem. UCLA Libr. Sch., 1981-89; chmn. bd. dirs. L.A. County Pub. Libr. Found., 1982-85; mem. OCLC Users Coun., 1988-89; mem. exec. com. L.A. County Mgmt. Coun., 1986-88, pres., 1988; cons. libr. Trinity Coll., 1995-99; prin. The Charleston Group, Inc., 1996—. Author: Directory of San Francisco Bay Area, 1968, Against All Odds, 1994; editor: Urban Librs. Coun. Exch., 1994—, The Charleston Report, 1996-99. Bd. dirs. So. Meth. U. Libr., 1992-98. Named Staff Mem. of Year San Francisco Pub. Libr., 1968 Mem. ALA, Calif. Libr. Assn. (council 1980-82), Calif. County Libr. Assn. (pres. 1984), L.A. County Mgmt. Assn. (pres. 1988). Home: 303 Mariner Dr Tarpon Springs FL 34689-5840

CRISP, SANDRA SUE, procurement analyst; b. Jefferson City, Sept. 13, 1941; d. William Frederick and Marguerite Walter (Wilson) Meyer; m. Samuel Henry White, Sept. 20, 1965 (div. Feb. 1982); 1 child, Janelle Lynn; m. Richard Leslie Crisp, Apr. 26, 1982. BSBA, Lincoln U., 1963; MS in Mgmt., Naval Postgrad. Sch., 1996. Missile components buyer McDonnell/Douglas Corp., St. Louis, 1977-78; contract specialist U.S. Army Aviation R&D Command, St. Louis, 1978-80; contracting officer U.S. Army Aviation Materiel Command, St. Louis, 1980-82; chief facilities and materials br. U.S. Army-Europe, Frankfort, Germany, 1982-83, chief host nations br., 1983-85; spl. tech. asst. to dir. comml. activities Asst. Sec. of Army for Installations, Logistics & Environ., Arlington, Va., 1985-87; spl. tech. asst. to U.S. Army Competition Adv. Gen. Asst. Sec. of Army for Rsch., Devel. and Acquisition, Arlington, 1987-92; dep. chief of staff for procurement, prin. asst. contracting U.S. Army Depot Sys. Command, Chambersberg, Pa., 1992-95; chief ammunition procurement divsn. U.S. Army Indsl. Ops. Command, Rock Island, Ill., 1995-98; chief acquisitions policy divsn. U.S. Army Ops. Support Command, Rock Island, Ill., 1999—2001, command ombudsman, competition advocate, 2002—. Mem. Nat. Contract Mgmt. Assn. (pres. Monterey chpt. 1995-96, edn. chair Quad City chpt. 1997-99), Nat. Def. Indsl. Assn. (bd. dirs. 1996—), U.S. Army Acquisition Corp. (sect. Army award for Professionalism in Contracting 1998), Women in Def. (founder, 1st pres. Ill.-Iowa chpt. 2001—). Avocations: volksmarching, needlework, gardening, reading, golf. Home: 228 Longview Ct Geneseo IL 61254-9270 E-mail: rcrisp@geneseo.net.

CRISPELL, MARILYN B. jazz musician; b. Phila., Mar. 30, 1947; d. Milton Amber and Frances (Mall) Braune; m. Gareth Crispell, June 14, 1967 (div. 1972). BMus, New Eng. Conservatory, Boston, 1968. Tchr. improvisation workshops; lectr. in field; performing artist New Eng. Found. Arts Touring Program, 1991-92. Pianist in collaboration with Anthony Braxton, 1978—, with his Quartet, 1983—, Creative Music Orch.; mem. Reggie Workman Ensemble, 1986—; featured performer N.Y.C. Opera in Anthony Davis's opera "X"; soloist London Jazz Composers Orch.; numerous appearances as soloist London Jazz Composers Orch.; recorder: (with Reggie Workman and Doug James) Gaia, 1987, (with others) Circles, 1991, (with Reggie Workman and Gerry Hemingway) Marilyn Crispell Trio, 1993, Stellar Pulsations/Three Composers, 1993, (with others) Santuerio, 1993, For Coltrane, 1993, Solo Concert '95/Mills College, Oakland, Calif., 1995, Contrasts, 1995, The Woodstock Concert, 1995; collaborator: (piano duo with Irene Schweizer) Overlapping Hands, 1991, (duo with Eddie Prevost) Band on the Wall, 1994, (with Fred Anderson and Hamid Drake) Destiny, 1994, (with Anders Jormin and Raymond Strid) Spring Tour, 1995, (with Barry Guy and Gerry Hemingway) Cascades, 1995, (with Peter Brotzmann and Hamid Drake) Hyperion, 1995, (duo with Tim Berne) Inference, 1995, (duo with Francois Houle) Any Terrain Tumultuous, 1995, (Greetje Bijma Trio with Marilyn Crispell and Mark Dresser) Barefoot, 1993, (with Bobby Zankel Trio) Human Flowers, 1996, (with Gary Peacock and Paul Motian) Nothing Ever Was, Anyway. Music of Annette Peacock, 1997, (with Joseph Jarman) Connecting Spirits, 1997, (with Evan Parker, Barry Guy and Paul Lytton) Natives and Aliens, 1997, (with Steve Lacy) Five Facings, 1997, (with Gary Peacock and Paul Motian) Amaryllis, 2001, (with Mark Helias and Paul Motian) Storyteller, 2003. N.Y. Found. for the Arts fellow, 1988-89, 94-95; recipient Mary Flagler Cary Charitable Trust composition commn., 1988-89.

CRISSEY, REBECCA LYNN, special education educator; b. Denver, Mar. 9, 1977; d. James Edward and Timber Smith Crissey. EdB, Auburn U., 1999; EdM, Vanderbilt U., 2000. Cert. early childhood spl. edn. State of Va., class B early childhood spl. edn. State of Ala. With E. Ala. Friends of Life, Auburn, 1997—99; ednl. asst. Blakemore Children's Ctr., Nashville, 1999; pvt. therapist, tutor Nashville, 1999—2000; spl. edn. tchr. Stafford County Pub. Schs., Fredericksburg, Va., 2000—02; presch. autism tchr. Fairfax County Pub. Schs., Va., 2002—. Early interventionist, therapist Chesapeake Ctr., Inc., Springfield, Va., 2002—; spl. edn. dance asst. Dance Abilities, Inc., Fairfax, 2002—03. Spl. needs vol. Fairfax County Pk. Auth., 2002—. Early Intervention grant, Vanderbilt U., 1999—2000. Mem.: Coun. Exceptional Children (mem. divsn. early childhood), Alpha Chi Omega, Golden Key Nat. Honor Soc. Order Omega, Gamma Sigma Alpha, Phi Eta Sigma, Lambda Sigma, Omicron Delta Kappa, Phi Kappa Phi (mem. mortar bd.). Republican. Lutheran. Avocations: dance, swimming. Home: 4462 Oakdale Crescent Ct #1232 Fairfax VA 22030 Office: William Halley Elem Sch 8850 Cross Chase Cir Fairfax Station VA 22039 E-mail: rlcrissey@hotmail.com.

CRISSMAN, PENNY M. state legislator; b. Nov. 20, 1943; m. Charles; children: Mitzi, Mark. Student, Ea. Mich. U., Oakland U. Mayor, Rochester, Mich., 1989-92; rep. Mich. Dist. 45, 1993-98; mem. Rochester City Coun., 1999—. Mem. Rochester City Coun., 1985-92; asst. Rep. whip Mich. Ho. Reps., 1993—, co-chair com. on civil rights & women's issues, edn. com., higher edn. com., local govt. coms., pub. health coms. Recipient disting. citizenship award Rochester Elks, 1992. Mem. Rochester C. of C., Optimists, Oakland U. Press Club. Office: 400 6th St Rochester MI 48307-1400

CRIST, CHRISTINE MYERS, consulting executive; b. Harrisburg, Pa., Feb. 5, 1924; d. John Eyster and Eunice Horton (Ingham) Myers; m. Robert Grant Crist, June 25, 1949; children: Catherine Ingham Crist Marcson, Jessica Rogers Crist, Robert Jeffrey Myers Crist. BA, Dickinson Coll., 1946. Reporter The Patriot, Harrisburg, Pa., 1946-49; editor West Shore Times, Lemoyne, Pa., 1964-65; adminstr. arts in edn. Pa. Dept. Edn., Harrisburg, 1974-77, dir. leadership in arts edn., 1977-79; press sec. gov.'s office Pa. Commn. for Women, Harrisburg, 1980-83, dir. Gov.'s Commn. for Women, 1983-87; exec. dir. com. for women Evang. Luth. Ch. in Am., Chgo., 1987-90; ptnr. Crist and Crist, Cons., Camp Hill, Pa., 1990—. Mem. State Employees Retirement Bd., 1986-88; state coord. We the People Edn. Program. Editor: Song As A Measure of Man, 1975 (excellent pub. 1975). Mem. Camp Hill (Pa.) Sch. Bd., 1967-73, Capital Area Intermediate Bd., Lemoyne, Pa., 1970-73; pres. Camp Hill (Pa.) Civic Club, 1970-72, women's orgn. Trinity Lutheran Ch., 1999; chair Ch. in Society, Lower Susquehanna Synod, Evang. Lutheran Ch. in Am.; mem. coun. Trinity Congregation, 1991-94; mem. Harrisburg Choral Soc., Dickinson Alumni Coun., 1992—; bd. dirs. Women's Polit. Network Pa., Camp Hill Cmty. Found., 1996—; mem. candidacy bd. Luth. Ch., 1992—; Pa. bd. Common Cause, 1997—; mem. Envision Capital Region Task Force, 2000-02; mem. Nat. Assn. Comms. for Women, 1987. Recipient Women in Comms. Freedom of Info. award, 1982, Great Commicators award, 1985, Pa. Women's History award, Pa. Com. for Women, 2003. Mem. Monday Club, Cumberland County Fedn. Women's Clubs (pres. 1996—). Lutheran. Home and Office: Crist and Crist 1915 Walnut St Camp Hill PA 17011-3854

CRIST, GERTRUDE H. civic worker; b. Barnard, S.D. d. Jacob H. and Lillian Belle (Freeman) Hartman; m. Howard Grafton Crist, Jr., Nov. 2, 1940; children: Howard Grafton III, Douglas Freeman. Student, S.D. State Coll., 1936-38. Owner, ptnr. Farm and Home Svc. Chmn. Westmoreland County chpt. ARC, 1946, sec., 1943-45, chmn. vol. spl. svcs., 1944-45; dist. chmn. Cancer drive Howard County; mem. Howard County Bd. Edn., 1953-70, pres., 1963-65; bd. dirs. Howard County Tb Assn.; adv. coun. Catonsville C.C., 1962-70; chmn. Emergency Civil Def. Hosp. Howard County, 1961-62; sec. Cmty. Action Coun. Howard County, 1965, dir., 1966; bd. dirs. Girl Scout Coun. Ctrl. Md., 1967-68; mem. Md. Coun. Higher Edn., 1968-76, State Bd. for C.Cs., 1968-77; trustee Howard C.C., 1966-71, v.p., 1969-70; bd. dirs. Howard County chpt. ARC, 1973-77, v.p., 1976-77; mem. Md. Bd. for Higher Edn., 1977-86, Howard County Commn. on Arts, 1975-77; v.p. Farm and Home Svc., Inc., 1968-78. Mem. LWV (county sec. 1957-59, dir. 1960-62, pres. 1959), Nat. Sch. Bds. Assn. (dir. 1968-71), Nat. Congress Parents and Tchrs. (hon. life mem.), Md. Congress Parents and Tchrs. (life), Md. Assn. Bds. Edn. (pres. 1966, 67), W. Friendship PTA (sec. 1949-51), Delta Kappa Gamma (hon. Alpha Beta State and Lambda chpts.), Cattail River Garden Club. Episcopalian (vestryman, chmn. parish day sch. bd. 1970-73). Home: Fairhaven C-87 7200 Third Ave Sykesville MD 21784

CRIST, JUDITH, film and drama critic; b. N.Y.C., May 22, 1922; d. Solomon and Helen (Schoenberg) Klein; m. William B. Crist, July 3, 1947 (dec. Apr. 1993); 1 son, Steven Gordon. AB, Hunter Coll., 1941; tchg. fellow, State Coll. Wash., 1942-43; MSc in Journalism, Columbia, 1945; DHL (hon.), SUNY, New Paltz, 1994. Civilian instr. 3081st Army AFB Unit, 1943-44; reporter N.Y. Herald Tribune, 1945-60, editor arts, 1960-63, assoc. theater critic, 1957-63, film critic, 1963-66; film, theater critic NBC-TV Today Show, 1963-73; film critic World Jour. Tribune, 1966-67; critic-at-large Ladies Home Jour., 1966-67; contbg. editor and film critic TV Guide, 1966-88; founding film critic N.Y. mag., 1968-75; film critic The Washingtonian, 1970-72, Palm Springs Life, 1971-75; contbg. editor, film critic Saturday Rev., 1975-77, 80-84, N.Y. Post, 1977-78, MD/Mrs., 1977—, 50 Plus, 1978-83, L'Officiel/USA, 1979-80; arts critic Sta. WWOR-TV, 1981-87; critical columnist for Coming Attractions, 1985-93; cons. editor Hollywood Mag., 1985-93; contbg. editor Columbia Mag., 1993-95. Instr. journalism Hunter Coll., 1947, Sarah Lawrence Coll., 1958-59; assoc. journalism Columbia Grad. Sch. Journalism, 1958-62, lectr. journalism, 1962-64, adj. prof., 1964—. Author: The Private Eye, The Cowboy and the Very Naked Girl, 1968, Judith Crist's TV Guide to the Movies, 1974, Take 22: Moviemakers on Moviemaking, 1984, rev. edit., 1991; contbr. articles to nat. mags. Trustee Anne O'Hare McCormick Scholarship Fund. Named to 50th Anniversary Honors List, Columbia Grad. Sch. Journalism, 1963, Hunter Alumni Hall of Fame, Hunter Coll., 1973; recipient Page One award, N.Y. Newspaper Guild, 1955, George Polk award, 1950, Newswomen's Club of N.Y. award, 1955, 1959, 1963, 1965, 1967, Edn. Writers Assn. award, 1952, Alumni award, Columbia Grad. Sch. Journalism, 1961, Centennial Pres.'s medal, Hunter Coll., 1970, Hall of Fame award for outstanding profl. achievement, 2003, Grad. Sch. Journalism's Faculty and Alumni award, Columbia U., 1998, Univ. Alumni Fedn. medal for conspicuous svc., 2003. Mem.: Soc. of the Silurians, Columbia Journalism Alumni Exec. Com. (pres. 1967—70), Sigma Tau Delta. Office: 180 Riverside Dr New York NY 10024-1048

CRISWELL, KIMBERLY ANN, executive coach, communications consultant, performing artist; b. L.A., Dec. 6, 1957; d. Robert Burton and Carolyn Joyce (Semko) C. BA with honors, U. Calif., Santa Cruz, 1980; postgrad., Stanford U., 1993-94, Coaches Tng. Inst., 2000. Cert. profl. co-active coach. Instr. English Lang. Svcs., Oakland, Calif., 1980-81; freelance writer Verbum mag., San Diego, 1986, Gambit mag., New Orleans, 1981; instr. Tulane U., New Orleans, 1981; instr., editor Haitian-English Lang. Program, New Orleans, 1981-82; instr. Delgado Coll., New Orleans, 1982-83; instr., program coord. Vietnamese Youth Ctr., San Francisco, 1984; dancer Khadra Internat. Folk Ballet, San Francisco, 1984-89; dir. mktg. comm. Centram Sys. West, Inc., Berkeley, Calif., 1984-87; comm. coord. Safeway Stores, Inc., Oakland, 1985; dir. corp. comm. TOPS divsn. Sun Microsystems, Inc., 1987-88; pres. Criswell Comm., 1988—. Dir. corp. comm. CyberGold, Inc., Berkeley, 1996-97; co-founder, v.p. Conferenza, Inc., 1998-99. Vol. coord. Friends of Haitians, 1981, editor, writer newsletter, 1981; dancer Komenka Ethnic Dance Ensemble, New Orleans, 1983; mem. Contemp. Art Ctr.'s Krewe of Clones, New Orleans, 1983, Americans for Nonsmokers Rights, Berkeley, 1985. Mem. Mem Gai Meets the Arts Soc. (founding). Democrat. Avocations: visual arts, travel, creative writing.

CRITELLI, NANCY BARBARA, music educator, cellist; b. Billings, Mont., Dec. 4, 1927; d. Frank S. and Inez Estell (MacDonald) C. MusB, Mont. State U., 1950, MusM, 1963; D of Mus. Arts, U. Mich., 1976. Orch. dir., tchr. Flathead County H.S., Kalispell, Mont., 1950-52; string instr. El Paso (Tex.) Pub. Schs., 1952-55; instrumental instr. Lansing (Mich.) Pub. Schs., 1957-62; instr. theory, cello, bass Wis. State U., Eau Claire, 1965-66; asst. prof. orch., chamber music theory, appreciation Rocky Mountain Coll., Billings, 1967-69; asst. prof. Western Ill. U. Lydian Quartet, Macomb, 1972-73; asst. prof. cello, bass, chamber music, theory Appalachian State U., Boone, N.C., 1974-80; instr., adj. prof. Ea. Mont. Coll., Billings, 1987; adj. prof. Rocky Mountain Coll., Billings, 1988—. Clinician N.W. Music Edn. Conv., Boise; workshop leader 7th Ann. Coulee region Festival of Arts, LaCrosse, Wis., 1966; organizer Solo and Small Ensemble Festival, Boone, N.C., 1977-78; adjudicator Orch. Contest Festival, Winston-Salem, N.C., 1978, Mont. Music Tchrs. Dist. Festival, Billings, 1982, NE Wyo. Music Festival, Sheridan, 1997, 98; dir., founder Flathead County Symphony, Kalispell, 1951-52, Lansing Jr. Symphony, 1959, Red Lodge (Mont.) Music Festival, 1964-73; cellist Mont. Suzuki Inst., 1980-90, mem. faculty, 1985-95. Performed as cellist with U. Mont. Orch., Western Ill. Symphony, Appalachian State U. Symphony, Billings Symphony; also numerous recitals, Mont., Wis., Mich., N.C. Mem. Nat. Music Tchrs. Assn. (cert.), Music Educators Nat. Assn., Am. String Tchrs. Assn., Yellowstone Chamber Music Players, Suzuki Assn., Billings Music Tchrs. Assn. Avocations: birding, outings with sierra club, instrument repair.

CRITTENDEN, ANTOINETTE, marketing professional; b. Cleveland, Miss., Jan. 7, 1962; d. William Lamar Nail Jr., Barbara Lee (Windham) Nail; m. Larry Allen Crittenden, July 31, 1982; 1 child, Philip Blake. BS, Miss. State U., 1983. Mgr. reins. Lamar Life, Jackson, Miss.; mktg. specialist Conseco Life, Jackson, 1996—97; dir. mktg. The L Group, Ridgeland, Miss., 1997—. Named State Ins. Woman of Yr., Nat. Assn. Ins. Women, 1998. Mem.: Ins. Women of Jackson (parliamentarian 2001—02, bd. dirs., pres., 1st v.p., 2d v.p., sec., treas., asst. treas., Ins. Woman of Yr. 1998—99). Republican. Baptist. Avocation: Avocations: camping, reading, quilting, antiquing. Home: 105 E Cynthia St Clinton MS 39056 Office: The L Group 107 Business Park Dr Ridgeland MS 39157

CRITTENDEN, FLORA DAVIS, state legislator; b. Bklyn., Aug. 10, 1924; m. Raymond Celester Crittenden Jr.; children: Raumond C. III, Thursa C. Thomas, Alonzo L. BS, Va. State Coll., 1945; MS, Ind. U., 1959. Mem. Va. State Legis., 1993—, mem. edn. com., mem. transp. com., mem. counties cities & towns com., mem. Chesapeake and its tributaries com. Democrat. Baptist. Office: Gen Assembly Bldg PO Box 406 Richmond VA 23218-0406

CRITTENDEN, MARTHA A. disability specialist; b. Georgiana, Ala., Nov. 2, 1957; d. Walter Ray and Martha Pugh C. AA, Lomax - Hannon Jr. Coll., Greenville, Ala., 1978; BS, Troy State U., 1987, MS, 1993. Cert. counselor Am. Counseling Assn./Ala. Alochol and Drug Abuse Assn.; cert. instr. HIV & AIDS, ARC; cert. criminal justice addiction profl., Ala. Patient care asst. Jackson Hosp., Montgomery, Ala., 1978-89, psychiat. tech., 1989-90; drug program specialist Bullock County Correctional, Union Spring, Ala., 1990-95; drug treatment counselor Montgomery Cmty. Based Facility, Mt. Meigs, Ala., 1995-99, Ala. Dept. Corrections, Birmingham, 1999-2000; disability specialist Ala. Dept. Edn. Birmingham Disability Determination Svcs., 2000—. Vol. Neighbors Who Care, 1999; tchr. Bethel Full Gospel Ch., Montgomery, 1986—, Faith Chapel Christian Ctr. Ch.., 1986—. Recipient Supr. of Yr. award Ala. Dept. Corrections, 1994. Mem. Ala. Alcohol and Drug Abuse Assn., Ala. Dept. Corrections (supr. 1990-95, Supr. of Yr. 1994), Addiction and Offender Counselors, Gamma Beta Phi. Avocations: reading, church, friends, walking or jogging, school. Office: Birmingham Disability Determination Svcs PO Box 830300 Birmingham AL 35283 also: Faith Chapel Christian Ctr 800 Quebec St Birmingham AL 35224-1571 Home: 140 Shady Acres Rd Alabaster AL 35007-4631

CRITTENDEN, SOPHIE MARIE, communications executive; b. Mansfield, Ohio, Apr. 14, 1926; d. Joseph S. and Mary Ellen (Hagerman) Wojcik; m. Robert Eugene Crittenden, Aug. 24, 1946 (dec. 1987); children: Robert J., Mark A., Christopher E., Laura Ann. Student, Coll. St. Francis, 1944-45, Ohio U., 1945-46, North Central Tech. Coll., 1976-78. Substitute tchr. Mansfield City Schs., 1956-62; lab. technician The Ohio Brass Co., Mansfield, 1962-68, draftsman, 1968, mgr. internal publs., 1969-78, mgr. advt., 1978-83, mgr. comm., 1983-88; cons. comm. EFE N.Am., Inc., Mansfield, 1989-90; account coord. D & S Creative Advt., Inc., Mansfield, 1990—2001; ret., 2001. Creator and shower of quilts. Com. chmn. United Way Campaign, Mansfield and Richland, Ohio, 1978; pub. relations chmn. Tribute to Women and Industry Project, Mansfield, 1986 (award 1985). Named Mrs. Mansfield/Mrs. Am. Contest, 1961. Mem. Altrusa (pres. 1976, internat. chmn. mktg. and pub. rels. 1991-93). Republican. Roman Catholic. Avocations: fiber arts, antiques, quilting. Home: 84 Briarwood Rd Mansfield OH 44907 E-mail: sophiec@att.net.

CRITTENDON, DONNA ELIZABETH, customer service administrator; b. San Diego, Aug. 3, 1954; d. Clayton Thomas and Bessie Mae Foster; m. Paul Gregory Crittendon, Mar. 14, 1955; children: Orin, Michelle. AA, Sacramento City Coll., 1975; BS in Bus. Adminstrn., U. Phoenix, Sacramento, 1999. Tchr. asst. Sutter County Schs., Yuba City, Calif., 1976, media clk. Comprehensive Employment Training Act program, 1977—79; svc. rep. Pacific Gas and Electric, Marysville, Calif., 1979—, safety coord., 1998—, Cordaptix trainer, 2002. United Way chairperson Pacific Gas and Electric Co., Marysville, 1998—; voter registration vol. Sutter County, Yuba City, Calif., 2000; corp. sec., treas., bookkeeper, media person Christ Temple Cmty. Ch., 1976—; vol. Women's Ministry at Convelesant Home, 1999—. Mem.: Calif. Dist. Coun. (sec./treas. 2001—, dist. #5 2001—03). Apostolic. Avocations: creating media, sewing, bookkeeping, gardening, cooking.

CRITZER, SUSAN L. health products company executive; BSME, Gen. Motors Inst.; MBA, U. Mich. Mgmt., info. sys., quality assurance and engring. positions GM, until 1986; various mgr. engring. and quality assurance positions Becton-Dickinson Corp., 1986-89; various mgmt. positions Davis and Geck divsn. Am. Cyanamid Corp., 1989-95, dir. engring. endosurgery divsn., until 1995; v.p. ops. Integ Inc., St. Paul, 1995-99, pres., CEO, 1999—. Office: Ingeg Inc 2800 Patton Rd Saint Paul MN 55113-1100 Fax: 651-639-9042.

CRIVELLI-KOVACH, ANDREA, public health and nutrition consultant, educator; b. Drexel Hill, Pa., Sept. 27, 1947; d. Albert Francis and Philomena Maria Crivelli; m. Gerald Charles Scullin, Apr. 24, 1971 (div. 1980); m. Edward Raphael Kovach, Aug. 6, 1982. BA in Biology, Immaculata Coll., 1969, MA in Nutrition Edn., 1988; PhD in Cmty. Health, Temple U., 1995. Cert. health edn. specialist. Info. specialist E.I. DuPont de Nemours & Co., Wilmington, 1969-83, contract info. specialist, 1987-91; nutrition cons. Health Choices Unltd., Media, Pa., 1988—; asst. prof., cmty. health coord. Phila. Coll. Osteopathic Medicine, 1994-96; rsch. evaluation cons. Crivelli Assocs., Media, Pa., 1996—; asst. prof., dir. cmty. health programs Arcadia U., Glenside, Pa., 1996—. Adj. prof. women's studies U. Pa., Phila., 1996-2002. Contbr. articles to profl. jours. including Jour. of Human Lactation, Birth, Jour. Korean Acad. Nursing, Jour. Osteo. Medicine. Chair Media Bd. of Health, 1997—; dep. health officer Media Borough, 1994—97; mem. nutrition adv. bd. Nursing Mothers Network, Springfield, Pa.; mem. profl. adv. bd. Breastfeeding Ctr. Mont. County, Women's Health and Environ. Network. Mem. Am. Dietetic Assn., Am. Pub. Health Assn., Soc. of Pub. Health Educators, Soc. of Nutrition Edn. (Del. Valley chpt.), Kappa Omicron Nu. Democrat. Achievements include research in cross-cultural international breastfeeding; development of measurement instrument to evaluate hospital breastfeeding policies based on the UNICEF/WHO baby-friendly hospital initiative; research in role of community lay health advocates in empowering low income pregnant women. Avocations: biking, swimming, boating, gardening, hiking, cross country skiing. Office: Arcadia U 450 S Easton Rd Glenside PA 19038-3215

CRNKOVIC, ANISE ELAINE, marriage and family therapist; b. Alamogordo, N.Mex., Dec. 18, 1970; d. Vernon Eugene Sr. and Gloria Elaine (Hairston) C. AA, BA, N.Mex. State U., 1993, MS, 1995, PhD, 1998. Lic. marriage and family therapist. Marriage and family therapist Mesilla Valley Hosp., Las Cruces, N.Mex., 1994—2002, intensive outpatient program dir., 1995—2002, dir. clin. svcs., 1999—2002, dir. outpatient svcs., 1999—, asst. adminstr., 2003—; tchg. asst., rsch asst. N.Mex. State U., Las Cruces, 1993-95, doctoral fellow, 1995-98, treatment foster care program dir., 1998—2002, instr. marriage and family therapy program, 1998—; cmty. counselor Cmty. Svcs., Oro Grande, High Rolls, N.Mex., 1986—2002; marriage and family therapist Assocs. for Marriage and Family Therapy, Las Cruces, 1997—2000. Ptnr., profl. clown Somer, Sault & Co., Las Cruces, 1990—98. Counselor, dir. Vacation Bible Sch. Oro Grande, High Rolls, 1987—2002. Mem.: N.Mex. Assn. for Marriage and Family Therapy (pres.-elect 2002), Am. Assn. for Marriage and Family Therapy. Republican. Baptist. Avocations: piano, writing, teaching. Home: Ste 158 2001 E Lohman Ave 110 Las Cruces NM 88001-3167 Office: Mesilla Valley Hosp 3751 Del Rey Blvd Las Cruces NM 88012-8526

CROCE, ANNE LALLY, nurse, commissioner; b. Staten Island, N.Y., Mar. 7, 1926; d. Austin and Anne (McStravick) Lally; m. James P. Croce Jr., June 9, 1951; children: Patricia L. Balcom, James Peter III, Kathleen Kampmann. Diploma, Bayonne Hosp. Sch. Nursing, 1949; postgrad., Polyclinic Med. Sch. and Hosp., 1950, Osaka (Japan) U., 1951. Sch. nurse Friends Acad., Long Island, N.Y.; pub. sch. nurse, day care nurse Roslyn Pub. Schs., L.I.; sch., camp nurse Doug Pierce/Price County Day Sch., L.I.; commr., ombudsman Town of North Hempstead, Manhasset, N.Y., 1989—. Pub. educator on blood pressure, CPR, diet; featured on local TV and in local newspaper. Bd. dirs. Roslyn Little League (Women of the Year award), Community Mammography and Breast Cancer Screening, Local Emergencies Planning Com., SARA III Program, Community Plus Program for Srs., Free Flu Shots Program; liason Town North Hempstead Civic Assn., Martin Luther King Edn., L.I. Heart Coun. (Gold Madalion award). Recipient Women of the Year award Roslyn Rotary Club., Roslyn Kiwanis Club. Mem. N.A.A.C.P. Office: Town North Hempstead 220 Plandome Rd Manhasset NY 11030-2399

CROCE, ARLENE LOUISE, critic; b. Providence, May 5, 1934; d. Michael Daniel and Louise Natalie (Pensa) C. Student, Women's Coll., U. N.C., 1951-53; BA, Barnard Coll., 1955. Founder, editor Ballet Rev., 1965-78; dance critic New Yorker mag., 1973-98. Dance panelist Nat. Endowment for Arts, 1977-80. Author: The Fred Astaire & Ginger Rogers Book, 1972, Afterimages, 1977, Going to the Dance, 1982, Sight Lines, 1987, Writing in the Dark, Dancing in the New Yorker, 2000. Recipient AAAL award 1979, award of Honor for Arts and Culture Mayor N.Y.C., 1979, Janeway prize Barnard Coll., 1955; Hodder fellow Princeton U., 1971; Guggenheim fellow, 1972, 86, NEH fellow 1992, Nat. Arts Journalism Program sr. fellow, 1999. Office: New Yorker Mag 4 Times Sq New York NY 10036-6561

CROCKER, BARBARA JEAN, clinical nurse specialist; b. Worcester, Mass., Oct. 13, 1942; d. Roy A. and Mildred E. (Ewing) Benson; m. David L. Crocker, Aug. 29, 1964; children: Beth, Mark, Matthew. Diploma, Henry Heywood Meml. Hosp., Gardner, Mass., 1963; BS, Anna Maria Coll., Paxton, Mass., 1982, MS in Nursing, 1985. Cert. infection control nurse. Staff nurse Worcester Hahnemann Hosp., 1965-72, nursing supr., 1972-81, infection surveillance nurse, 1981-85; nurse epidemiologist The Med. Ctr.-Hahnemann, Worcester, 1985-92; infection control practitioner U. Mass. Meml. Health Care, Worcester, Mass., 1992—2002, clin. nurse specialist, 2002—. Mem. Assn. Profls. in Infection Control and Epidemiology, Inc., Henry Heywood Meml. Hosp. Alumnae Assn.

CROCKER, JANE LOPES, library director; b. Mass., Sept. 19, 1946; d. Joseph Barros and Mary (Faria) Lopes; m. Lowell Steven Crocker, Feb. 14, 1976; children: Susan J., Jennifer L., Jacqueline M. BA in English, Bridgewater State Coll., 1968; MS in Libr. Sci., Simmons Coll., 1971. Cert. libr., Mass.; cert. secondary edn. tchr., Mass. Libr. New Bedford (Mass.) Pub. Libr., 1968-71; [illegible] libr. Simmons Coll. Libr., Boston, 1971-73, head libr. Boston City Hosp., 1973-76; libr. dir. Gloucester County Coll., Deptford, N.J., 1976—. Pres. Libr. Network Rev. Bd., 1994-95, vice-chmn., 1996-97; assoc. prof. Gloucester County Coll., 1995—. Editor Bay State Libr., 1974-76; contbg. author: Reference and Information Service, 1978, N.J. Libraries, 1984, 89-90, 94, Vocat. and Tech. Resources for C.C. Librs., Laun, Mary Ann Assn. of Coll. and Rsch. Librs., ALA. Vice chair Gloucester County Coll. Acad. Assembly, 1996-98, co-chair Tech. Roundtable, 2000—; sec. Internat. Union of Electronic, Elec., CWA Local #442, 1996—; mem. exec. com. VALE, 2000—; chmn. VALE ref. svcs. com., 2001-; pres. GCCEA, dir.'s group, 2002-. Recipient Ray Murray award N.J. Assn. Libr. Assts., 1991. Mem. ALA (mem. chpt. rels. coun. 1995—, chpt. councilor 1997—), N.J. Libr. Assn. (pres.-elect 1991-92, pres. 1992-93, vice-chair pub. policy com. 1996-97, exec. bd. 1997—), South Jersey Regional Libr. Coop. (pres. 1988-90, exec. bd. 1985—, Resolution of Appreciation award 1990, Pres.'s award 1993). Roman Catholic. Office: Gloucester County Coll 1400 Tanyard Rd Sewell NJ 08080-4222 E-mail: Jcrocker@gccnj.edu.

CROCKER, JEAN HAZELTON, retired educator, environmental volunteer; b. Hyannis, Mass., Nov. 7, 1930; d. James Barnard and Helene Snow (Cahoon) Hazelton; m. Merle McDonald Crocker, Sept. 13, 1952; children: Carolyn, James Lauchlan. BS, U. Mass., 1952; MSEd, SUNY, New Paltz, 1978; postgrad., Fitchburg (Mass.) State Coll., 1981, Troy State U., Montgomery, Ala., 1970. Cert. tchr., N.Y., Mass. Kindergarten - 6th grade tchr. Dept. Def., Heilbronn, Germany, 1953-54; tchr. 6th grade Fred Lynn Mid. Sch., Woodbridge, Va., 1965-68, curriculum resource dir., 1968-69; tchr. 6th grade Dept. Def. Edn. Overseas, Heidelberg, Germany, 1960-61, tchr., supr., asst. prin. Frankfurt, Germany, 1974-75, tchr. 4th grade Boeblingen, Germany, 1972-73; tchr. 7th and 8th grades, reading specialist N.Y. Mil. Acad., Cornwall-on-Hudson, N.Y., 1977-78; tchr. Mt. Watchusett C.C., Watchusett, Mass., 1979-80, Lowell Jr. Coll., Ft. Devens, Mass., 1980-81; tchr. ESL Manter Hall Sch., Osterville, Mass., 1981-83, Barnstable Cmty. Sch., Hyannis, 1982; tchr. Cape Cod C.C., West Barnstable, Mass., 1984-90. Author: (poetry) Songs of Psychosis, Camp Edwards: Seasons, Environs, Issues, Seaside Garden of Verses, A Cape Cod Pilgrim Sings, In Memoriam, A Cape Cod Pilgrim Grieves; writer articles, curricula, poetry. Co-founder and chair Save The Reservation and Our Nat. Guard, 1998-2002; mem. Otis Civilian Adv. Coun.; mem. citizen adv. bd. Internat. Ctr. for Clubhouse Devel. Recipient Pres. award, Nat. Guard AMA, 2001, George Washington Honor medal, Freedoms Found. at Valley Forge, 2002, Appreciation citation, Mass. Army Nat. guard, 2002. Mem.: VFW, DAV, AAUW, Nat. Alliance for the Mentally Ill, Patriots Advocating Camp Edwards Restoration and Survival, Friends of Mass. Mil. Reservation, Kappa Kappa Gamma (Cape Cod Alumnae chpt.). Methodist. Avocations: walking, biking, flower arranging, crafting. Home: 40 Tracy Rd Cotuit MA 02635-3417 E-mail: jhccotuit@comcast.com., jeancrocker@hotmail.com.

CROCKER, JOY LAKSMI, concert pianist and organist, composer; b. San Antonio, June 12, 1928; d. Hugo Peoples and Anna Kathryn (Ball) Rush; m. Richard Lincoln Crocker, July 24, 1948 (div. July 1977); children: Nathaniel Homer, Martha Wells Sandino, David Laramie. MusB, Yale U., 1950; MS, Yale U., Berkeley, Calif., 1956; postgrad., Grad. Theol. Sem., 1978-81. Min. music First Congl. Ch., Branford, Conn., 1949-62; dir. music therapy West Haven (Conn.) VA Hosp.; min. music St. Stephen's Episcopal Ch./Sch., Orinda, Calif., 1963, First Bapt. Ch., Oakland, Calif., 1964-66, Greek Orthodox Cathedral, Oakland, 1969, San Quentin (Calif.) Protestant Chapel, 1976-78, Plymouth United Ch. of Christ, Oakland, 1977-84; pianist, assoc. dir. First Bapt. Ch., Managua, Nicaragua, 1984-94; organist, pianist Mills Grove Christian Ch., 1995—96; organist St. Andrews Presbyn. Ch., Pleasant Hill, Calif., 1996—2001; dir. music ministries Trinity Meth. Ch., Berkeley, 2001—. Prof. organ San Francisco Conservatory Music, 1962-69; chmn. piano dept. Nicaraguan Nat. Conservatory Music, 1984-93; founder-dir., prof. Bapt. Conservatory of Music, Managua, 1989—; instr. Yogalayam Yoga Ashram; creator, dir. diverse low-budget innovative music edn. programs, 1969—; mem. adjudicator Nat. Guild Piano Tchrs., Music Tchrs. Assn. Calif.; invited lectr. 3d Encuentro Iberoamericano de Profesores y Estudiantes de Musica, Cuba, 1999; piano concert and master class tours, Cen. and South Am., 1995. Pianist, Internat. Symposium of Universal Articulate Understanding of Sci., 1999; concert/presentation World Parliament of Religions South Africa, 1999; pianist Balboa Park Pause for Peace Millennial Concert, 1999-2000, World Bank Counter Summit, Prague, UN 55th Anniversary Global Peace Walk Vigil, 2000. Civic and legislation coord. Ch. Women United, Oakland unit and state unit, 1996—, chair for global concerns; bd. dirs. Quantum Leap 2000, 1999—; pianist, organist Ch. Women United State Unit; San Francisco Bay area coord. for Hague Appeal for Peace; commr. World Summit on Peace and Time, Costa Rica, 1999, del./concert pianist World Social Forum, Brazil, 2001; pianist World Coun. Ch. Ann. Conv., Oakland, Calif., 2002, Forgiveness First Internat. Conv., Kamloops B.C., 2002. Named Woman of Yr., Bus. and Profl. Women's Club, Inc., 1995; recipient prizes for compositions, San Francisco Concerto Orch., 1997, Music Tchrs. Assn. Calif., 1998, 2000, 2001. Mem. Am. Guild Organists, Am. Coll. Musicians, Music Tchrs. Assn. Mem. United Ch. of Christ. Avocations: traveling, political activism. Home: 3065 Monterey Blvd Oakland CA 94602-3559 E-mail: jcrocker@rcn.com.

CROCKER, MARGARET SUYDAM SMITH, art association executive director, art historian; b. Binghamton, N.Y., Mar. 21, 1936; d. George Percy and Margaret Suydam (Fritts) Smith; m. Daniel Gano Ray, Mar. 21, 1956 (dec. May 1958); children: Margaret Suydam Ray, Danielle Gano Ray; m. David Weeks Crocker, Oct. 15, 1960; children: Andrew Fritts Crocker, Heidi Weeks Crocker. BA in Art History, SUNY, Binghamton, 1986; postgrad., Binghamton U. Gift shop mgr. Peter Altmann Jewelry, Binghamton, 1973-78; vol. coord. Roberson Ctr. for Arts & Scis., Binghamton, 1978-84, asst. dir. edn., 1984-86; exec. dir. Tioga County Coun. on the Arts, 1986-89, Discovery Ctr. of the Southern Tier, Binghamton, 1989—. Coord. exhibits Roberson Ctr., 1982, 83, 84, 85, curator faculty exhibits, 1983-85; curator Artspace Exhbns., Tioga County Coun. on Arts, 1986-89, Owego Nat. Bank Exhibits, 1986-89, Binghamton Savs. Bank Exhibits, 1986-89, Ahwagah Family Physicians Exhibits, Owego, 1986-89. Bd. dirs. Roberson Ctr., 1973-78, docent, 1958-78, ann. fund drive co-chmn. 1973; bd. dirs. YMCA, 1974-77, Southern Tier Civic Ballet, 1970-72, WSKG Pub. TV, 1975-79, Tri-Cities Opera, 1986-88, Southern Tier Inst. Arts in Edn., 1987-88, Discovery Ctr. Southern Tier, 1987-88; chmn. bd. deacons First Presbyn. Ch., chmn. coun. Christian edn., Sunday sch. tchr., 1978-78, bd. of session, 1984-87; vol. Jr. League of Binghamton, 1956-76. Recipient Watrous Bowl, Jr. League, 1976, Woman of Achievement award Broome County Status of Women Coun., 1989, Kennedy Ctr. Alliance award for disting. svc. to arts, 1991. Office: Discovery Ctr of Southern Tier 60 Morgan Rd Binghamton NY 13903-3667

CROCKER, PATRICIA CONWAY, former state legislator; b. N.Y.C., Feb. 17, 1949; m. David L. Crocker; 1 child. BS, Fordham U., 1979; MPA, U. Vt., 1999. State rep. Vt. Ho. of Reps., 1993-96. Mem. transporation and commerce coms. Chair Woodstock Dem. Com.; sec. Women's Legis. Caucus. Mem. Vt. Public Transp. Assn. (exec. dir.). Address: 49 River St Woodstock VT 05091-1228

CROCKER, SAONE BARON, lawyer; b. Bulawayo, Zimbabwe, Jan. 11, 1943; came to U.S., 1963; d. Benjamin and Rachel (Joffe) Baron; m. Chester Arthur Crocker, Dec. 18, 1965; children: Bathsheba Nell, Karena Wynne, Rebecca Masten. BA, U. Cape Town, 1961, BA with honors, 1962; MA, Johns Hopkins U., 1966; JD cum laude, Georgetown U., 1983. Bar: D.C. 1983, U.S. Ct. Appeals (D.C. cir.) 1985, U.S. Dist. Ct. D.C. 1990, U.S. Supreme Ct. 1990, U.S. Ct. Appeals (7th cir.) 1991, U.S. Ct. Appeals (4th cir.) 1998. Adminstr. Guinea program African Am. Inst., Washington, 1965-66, author Africa Report, 1966; writer [illegible], Washington, 1967-68; freelance writer Washington, 1968-80; atty. firm Wilmer, Cutler & Pickering, Washington, 1983-84; clk. to judge U.S. Ct. Appeals for D.C. Circuit, 1984-85; atty. firm O'Melveny & Myers, Washington, 1985-90, Beveridge & Diamond, Washington, 1990-92, Wright & Talisman, P.C., Washington, 1992-2001; pvt. practice Washington, 2001—. Contbg. author: Zambia Handbook, 1967. AAUW fellow, 1963-65; Fulbright fellow, 1963; Johns Hopkins U. fellow, 1964-65; recipient Lawyers Coop. Pub. Co. awards, 1980. Mem. ABA, AAUW (state pres. 1992-94), Fulbright Assn. Office Phone: 202-256-4777. E-mail: saonec@comcast.net.

CROCKER, VALERIE MARIAN, mechanical engineer; b. Annapolis, Md., July 21, 1962; d. Ernest O. and Virginia G. (Gleason) Crocker; m. Mark A. Young, May 18, 1991 (div. Apr. 1997); m. Christopher J. Day, Sept. 22, 2001. BS in Engring./Bioengring., U. Vt., 1984; MS in Biomed. Engring., Duke U., 1986; MBA, San Diego State U., 2002. Rehab. engr. Tufts U./New Eng. Med. Ctr., Boston, 1983; rsch. engr. Harvard Med. Sch., Southborough, Mass., 1987-88; project engr. surg. devices ETHICON Inc., Somerville, N.J., 1988-90; sr. mech. project engr. Abbott Labs., San Diego, 1990-92, supr. disposables mfg., 1992-94, mgr. mech. engring., R&D, 1994-2001; sr. program mgr. Gen-Probe, Inc., San Diego, 2001—. Contbr. articles to profl. jours. Avocations: triathlons, ocean swimming, marathons, bicycling, skiing. Home: 3624 Torrey View Ct San Diego CA 92130 Office: Gen-Probe Inc 10210 Genetic Ctr Dr San Diego CA 92121 E-mail: valerieday@gen-probe.com.

CROCKETT, DELORES, federal agency administrator; Asst. dir. U.S. Dept. Labor, Washington, 1989—; dir. U.S. Dept. of Labor: Women Bur., Atlanta, 1997—. Office: Atlanta Fed Ctr 61 Forsyth St SW Ste 7795 Atlanta GA 30303-8931

CROCKETT, DODEE FROST, brokerage firm executive; b. Oklahoma City, Oct. 19, 1956; d. Carl S. Frost and Mikki (Matheny) Marcus; m. Billy Crockett. M in Theol. Studies, So. Meth. U., 2003. 1st v.p., wealth mgmt. advisor Merrill Lynch Pvt. Client, Dallas, 1980—. Bd. dirs. North Dallas Shared Ministries, 1988-91, Ronald McDonald House of Dallas, 1992—, Dallas Social Venture Ptnrs., 2003-; trustee Dallas Opera, 1991—; mem. investment com. Dallas Women's Found., 1991-94; exec. bd. Perkins Sch. Theology, So. Meth. U., Dallas, 2003-, Dallas Found.; pres. Cir. Shared Housing Ctr., Dallas. Mem. Nat. Assn. Securities Dealers (gen. securities prin., mcpl. securities rulemaking bd. prin., registered options prin., bd. arbitrators), NYSE (com. mem.), Merrill Lynch Dirs. Cir., Park Cities Exch. Club (charter). Office: Merrill Lynch Pierce Fenner and Smith 2000 Premier Pl 5910 N Central Expy Ste 2000 Dallas TX 75206-5152

CROCKETT, JOAN M. human resources executive;, John Carroll Univ., 1972. Sr. v.p. human resources Allstate Ins. Co. Bd. dirs. INROADS; adv. bd. Univ. Ill. Chgo. Internat. Student Exchange Program; ptnr., bd. dirs. Ctr. for Human Resource Mgmt. Univ. Ill., gov. coun. Good Shepherd Hosp., Barrington, Ill. Named Human Resource Exec. of Yr., Human Resource Exec. mag., 1997. Office: Allstate 2775 Sanders Rd Northbrook IL 60062-6127

CROFT, CANDACE ANN, psychology educator, academic administrator; b. Lancaster, Wis., Jan. 14, 1957; d. Wilford Stanley and Myrna Viola Croft. BA, St. Olaf Coll., 1979; MS, U. Ariz., 1980; PhD, Pa. State U., 1984. Psychotherapist Forrester Clinic, Chgo., 1984-86; dir. rsch. on child and adolescent health Am. Acad. Ped., Elk Grove Village, Ill., 1986-92; dir. rsch. and sci. affairs Am. Acad. Orthop. Surgeons, Rosemont, Ill., 1992-94; sr. program assoc. Aon Found., Chgo., 1994-95; dir. Strong Spirit Wellness Ctr., Chgo., 1995-96; adj. prof. DePaul U., Chgo., 1993-96; assoc. prof. psychology, chmn. dept. psychology Clarke Coll., Dubuque, Iowa, 1996—2003, chair instl. rev. bd., 2000—03; dean Health & Human Svc. Occupations, SW Tech. Coll., Fennimore, Wis., 2003—. Textbook reviewer McGraw-Hill, 1998-2003; media contact Nat. Coun. Family Rels., St. Paul, 1998—, Clarke Coll.-Fox-40, Dubuque, Iowa, KWWL Channel 7, Dubuque, Iowa; adv. Clarke Coll. Author: Annalia's Simply Splendid, 2003; contbr. articles to sci. and profl. jour.; exec. producer film Heart of the Matter, 1991 (bronze award Houston Internat. Film Festival 1991); contbr. column to on-line pub., Living With Heart, 2002—. Mem. liturg. ministry St. Mary's Ch., Platteville, Wis., 1999—2001. Mem. Nat. Coun. Family Rels. (cert. family life educator, sect. religion and the family, sect. on family and health), Assn. Humanistic Psychology, Inst. Noetic Scis., Assn. for Transpersonal Psychology, Nat. Coalition for Campus Children's Ctrs., Nat. Assn. for the Edn. of Young Children, Phi Kappa Phi, Omicron Nu. Avocations: writing, music, aerobics, swimming, photography. Home: 119 North Monroe Lancaster WI 53813 Office: SW Tech Coll 1800 Bronson Blvd Fennimore WI 53809 Office Phone: 608-822-3262. Personal E-mail: cacroft@pcii.net.

CROFT, KATHRYN DELAINE, business executive, consultant; b. Eastover, S.C., Jan. 13, 1944; d. Randolph and Ethel (Williams) Lloyd; m. Daniel Marranzini, June 26, 1987. BS, Wilberforce U., 1965; MS, Columbia U., 1982, New Sch. for Social Rsch., 1988. Cert. social worker, N.Y. Exec. dir. Family Dynamics, Inc., N.Y.C., 1987-92; asst. provost Columbia U., N.Y.C., 1992-94; commr. N.Y.C. Child Welfare Adminstrn., N.Y.C., 1994-96; dir. ops. Just One Break, Inc., N.Y.C., 1997-2000, exec. dir., 2000—02; chief program officer ARC Greater N.Y.C., 2002—. Cons. various nonprofit orgns., N.Y.C., 1996—. Bd. dirs. Artsgenesis, N.Y.C., 1993—, chmn., 1996-99; bd. dirs. Ackerman Inst., N.Y.C., 1997-2000. Recipient scholarships New Sch. for Social Rsch., 1985-88, Columbia U., 1978-82. Mem. NAFE, Assn. Black Women in Higher Edn. Avocations: travel, reading, photography.

CROMLEY, JANE MEADORS, music educator; b. Spartanburg, S.C. d. Marshall L. Meadors, Jr. and Hannah Campbell Meadors; m. George P. Cromley, Mar. 18, 1978; children: Hannah Ann, Mary Florence, Parker Jr. BA in Music Edn., Columbia Coll., 1977; MEd, U. S.C., 1990. Cert. music edn. and early childhood edn. Music tchr. K-6 Kensington Elem., Georgetown, SC, 1977—81; owner, oper. Gosling Children's Shop, Murrells Inlet, SC, 1981—83; tchr. pre-kindergarten All Saints Episcopal Ch., Pawleys Island, RI, 1986—89; music tchr. Waccamaw Elem., Pawleys Island, 1989—. Asst. United Meth. Youth Conf. Choir, SC, 2001—02; mem. adv. bd. SC Early Childhood Assn., SC, 1989—94; mem., singer Coastal Chorale, Murrells Inlet, 1997—2003; children's choir dir. Belin United Meth. Ch., Murrells Inlet, 1989—92. Mem. conf. coun. of worship United Meth. Ch., Columbia, 1995—2002. Mem.: Music Educators Nat. Conf. United Methodist. Avocations: sewing, interior decorating, gardening, sailing, reading. Home: 225 Emerson Loop Pawleys Island SC 29585

CROMWELL, ADELAIDE M. sociology educator; b. Washington, Nov. 27, 1919; d. John Wesley, Jr. and Yetta Elizabeth (Mavritte) C.; 1 son, Anthony C. Hill. AB, Smith Coll., 1940, MA, U. Pa., 1941; cert. in Social Work, Bryn Mawr Coll., 1943; PhD, Radcliffe Coll., 1952; LHD (hon.), U. Southwestern Mass., 1972, George Washington U., 1989, Boston U., 1995. Mem. faculty Hunter Coll., 1942—44, Smith Coll., 1945—46, Boston U., 1951—85, prof. sociology, 1971—85, dir. Afro-Am. studies, 1969—88, prof. emerita sociology, 1985—; mem. faculty Harvard U. Ext., 1965—66. Mem. adv. com. vol. fgn. aid AID, 1964-80; mem. NEH, 1968-70; adv. com. corrections Commonwealth Mass., 1955-68; mem. commn. instns. higher edn., 1973-74; adv. com. to dir. IRS, 1970-71, to dir. census, 1972-75. Bd. dirs. Wheelock Coll., 1971-74, Nat. Ctr. Afro-Am. Artists, 1971-80, African Am. Scholars Coun., 1971—, Nat. Fellowship Fund, 1974-75, Mass. Hist. Commn., 1993; bd. dirs. Sci. and Tech. for Internat. Devel., 1984-86; mem. exec. com. Am. Soc. African Culture, 1967. Mem. [illegible] African Studies Assn. (bd. dir. 1966-68), Am. Acad. of Arts and Scis., Am. Sociol. Assn., Coun. on Fgn. Affairs (bd. fgn. scholarships 1980-84), Mass. Hist. Soc., Phi Beta Kappa. Home: 51 Addington Rd Brookline MA 02445-4519

CROMWELL, AMANDA CARYL, former soccer player, coach; b. Washington, June 15, 1970; BS in Biology, U. Va., 1992. Head women's soccer coach U. Md.; head coach U. Ctrl. Fla. Mem. U.S. Women's Nat. Soccer Team, 1991—, U.S. Team CONCAFCAF Qualifying Tournament, Haiti, 1991, Montreal, Canada, 94; mem. silver medal U.S. Team 1993 World Univ. Games, Buffalo; alternate gold medal U.S. Olympic Team; mem. 3d place U.S. Team, 1995 FIFA Women's World Cup, Sweden; mem. Hammarby Soccer Club, Stockholm, 1994, SA United Soccer Club of Fairfax, Va., 1997. Named NSCAA All-Am. (twice), Soccer Am. Freshman of Yr., H.S. Rookie of Yr., 1990. Office: US Soccer Fedn 1801-1811 S Prairie Ave Chicago IL 60616

CROMWELL, FLORENCE STEVENS, occupational therapist; b. Lewistown, Pa., May 14, 1922; d. William Andrew and Florence (Stevens) Cromwell. BS in Edn., Miami U., Oxford, Ohio, 1943; BS in Occupl. Therapy, Washington U., St. Louis, 1949; MA, U. So. Calif., 1952; cert. in health facility adminstrn., UCLA, 1978. Mem. staff, then supervising therapist Los Angeles County Gen. Hosp., 1949—53; occupl. therapist Goodwill Industries, L.A., 1954—55; staff therapist Vis. Nurse Assn., Phila., 1955—56; rsch. therapist United Cerebral Palsy Assn., L.A., 1956—60; dir. occupl. therapy Orthopaedic Hosp., L.A., 1961—67; coord. occupl. therapy Rsch. and Tng. Ctr. U. So. Calif. Med. Sch., L.A., 1967—70; assoc. prof. U. So. Calif., L.A., 1970—76, acting chmn. dept. occupl. therapy, 1973—76, mem. adv. bd. project SEARCH, Sch. Medicine, 1969—72; founding editor Occupl. Therapy in Health Care jour., 1984—88, editor emerita, 1988—. Assoc. dir. L.A. Job Corps Ctr., 1977—78; cons. in edn. and program devel., 1976—95; freelance editor, 1986—. Author: Manual for Basic Skills Assessment, 1960; contbr. articles to profl. jours. Mem. scholarship com. L.A. March of Dimes, 1963—70; mentor U. Tex.-Galveston Class 1990 Occupl. Therapy; bd. dirs. Am. Occupl. Therapy Found., 1965—69, v.p., 1966—69; bd. dirs. Nat. Health Coun., 1975—78. Served to lt. (j.g.) WAVES USNR, 1943—46. Recipient Disting. Alumni award, Washington U., 1978, Disting. Lectr., Calif. Occupl. Therapy Found., 1986. Fellow: Am. Occupl. Therapy Assn. (pres. 1967—73, Pres.'s WLWest commendation AOTA-AOTF 1999); mem.: Assn. Schs. Allied Health Professions (dir. 1973—74), Coalition Ind. Health Professions (chmn. 1973—74), So. Calif. Occupl. Therapy Assn. (pres. 1950—51, 1975—76), Inst. Medicine NAS (emerita 2002), Cwen, Kappa Kappa Gamma, Kappa Delta Pi, Mortar Bd.

CRONACHER, KAREN JAN, playwright, educator; b. Glen Cove, N.Y., Aug. 30, 1963; d. Warren William Cronacher and Lola Ann Lee; m. Joshua Hunter Thurman, Sept. 17, 1989. BA summa cum laude, Cornell U., 1985; MA, Brown U., 1988; PhD, U. Wash., 1993. Playwright Nat. Pub. Radio, Boston, 1993—94; performer Seattle Fringe Festival, Seattle, 1990—97; playwright Salvage Vanguard Theatre, Seattle, N.Y.C., 1980—2001; screenwriter If I Were You, Seattle, 2001—. Prof. Bellevue C.C., Wash., 2001—; evaluator Nat. Endowment Arts, Washington, 1992; judge playwriting contest Clauder Competition, Boston, 1990, Ruth Eckerd Hall, Clearwater, Fla., 2002—. Contbr. articles to profl. jours.; author: (plays) Unspeakable Pleasures, 1986, Scavengers, 1989. Mem.: AAUW (grantee 1992—93), Dramatist Guild, Assn. for Theatre in Higher Edn. (adjudicated debut panel in literary theory 1990). Avocations: gardening, travel, dance, reading.*

CRONE, PENNY, reporter; b. N.Y.C. married; 1 child. Reporter Hearst Newspaper, Balt.; writer, producer WJZ-TV; reporter KMOX-TV, St. Louis, WABC-TV, WOR-TV, N.Y.C., KHOU-TV, Houston, WNYW-TV, N.Y.C., 1988—2002, CBS 2, N.Y.C., 2002—. Recipient award, Internat. Film and TV Festival, 1979, 1980, Emmy Outstanding Crime Reporting, 1993, Emmy Outstanding Multi-Part News Feature, 1995, Emmy On Camera Achievement, 1996. Office: CBS 524 W 57th St New York NY 10012

CRONENWETT, LINDA HOUK, dean; BSN, PhD in nursing, U. Mich.; MSN in maternal-child nursing, U. Washington. Dir. profl. nursing, dir. nursing rsch. and edn. Mary Hitchcock Meml. Hosp., Lebanon, N.H., Dartmouth-Hitchcock Med. Ctr., Lebanon; mem. faculty U. Mich., U. N.H., Dartmouth U.; with U. N.C., Chapel Hill, 1998—, dean Sch. Nursing, 1999—. Mem. editl. bd. Jour. Nursing Measurement. With USN. Recipient Disting. Profl. Svc. award Assn. Women's Health, Obstetric and Neonatal Nurses, 1993, Disting. Scholar Nursing award NYU, 1997. Fellow Am. Acad. Nursing. Office: U NC Sch Nursing CB 7640 Carrington Hl Chapel Hill NC 27599-0001

CRONIN, BONNIE KATHRYN LAMB, museum director; b. Mpls., Mar. 11, 1941; d. Edwin Rector and Maude Kathryn (MacPherson) Lamb; m. Barry Jay Cronin, Jan. 23, 1963 (div. Feb. 1972); 1 son, Philip Scott. BA, U. Mo., 1963, BS, 1964; MS, Ill. State U., 1970. Copywriter Neds & Wardlow Advt., Columbia, Mo., 1962-64; tchr. Columbia Sch. System, 1964-68, Normal (Ill.) Sch. Sys., 1968-69; asst. gen. mgr. Sta. WGLT, Normal, 1969-70; dir. devel. Radio Sta. WBUR, Boston, 1970-71, program dir., 1971-75, gen. mgr., 1975-78; dir. pub. rels. Joy of Movement Ctr., 1978-80; dep. scheduler Anderson for Pres., 1980; scheduler Spaulding for Gov., 1980-81; dir. scheduling John Kerry Campaign, 1982; dir. of scheduling Mass. Lt. Gov.'s Office, dir. ops., 1983-84; dep. campaign mgr. Kerry for Senate Com., 1984; dir. ops. Senator John Kerry, Washington, 1985-86, dir. constituency outreach Boston, 1986-92, exec. asst., 1992-95; chief staff to Senator John Kerry Boston, 1995-97; dir. devel. and pub. affairs Working Capital, 1997-2001; dir. found. rels. USS Constn. Mus., 2001—. Chair Mass. Micro Enterprise Coalition, 2000-01. Active Melrose Econ. Devel. Coun., 2000—. Mem.: Mass. Broadcasters Assn. (dir. 1973—78, chairperson scholarship com., pub. svc. com., advminstrv. oversight com.), Polymnia Choral Soc. (pres. 2002—), Nat. Pub. Radio (dir. 1974—77, chairperson devel. com.). Office: Box 1812 Boston MA 02129 E-mail: bonniemelrose@aol.com.

CRONIN, PATTI ADRIENNE WRIGHT, state agency administrator; b. Chgo., May 25, 1943; d. Rodney Adrian and Dorothy Louise (Thiele) Wright; m. Kevin Brian Cronin, May 1, 1971; 1 child, Kevin. BA, Beloit (Wis.) Coll., 1965; JD with honors, U. Wis., 1983. Vol. Peace Corps, Turkey, 1965-67, recruiter, 1967-68; tchr. English Kamehameha III Sch., Lahaina, Hawaii, 1968-70, Evansville (Wis.) High Sch., 1972-77; tchr. math. and history Killian Sch., Hartford, Wis., 1977-78; tchr. English Kaiser High Sch., Honolulu, 1979-80; intern Wis. Ct. Appeals, Madison, 1983; exec. dir. Wis. Waste Facility Siting Bd., Madison, 1983—. Founder, v.p., bd. dirs. Justice Ctr. Honolulu, 1979-82; sec., treas. Cronin Constrn. Co., Inc., Madison, 1986—. Editor: Internat. Law Jour., 1982. Bd. dirs. Neighborhood Bd., Honolulu, 1979-82; chmn. United Way, 1989—; active Parent Citizens Adv. Coun. Recipient Mayor's award of outstanding achievement, City of Honolulu, 1980. Mem. Soc. Profls. in Dispute Resolution, ABA, State Bar Wis. Avocations: family, real estate, travel. Office: Waste Facility Siting Bd 201 W Washington Ave Madison WI 53703-2760 E-mail: patti.cronin@wfs.state.wi.us.

CRONSON, CAROLINE MARY, financial executive; b. Cosford, Eng. came to U.S., 1987; d. Charles Francis and Barbara Joan (Thompson) Milnes; m. Paul Christopher Cronson, Aug. 2l, 1986; one son, Christopher Charles. BA with honours, Oxford U., 1984; MBA, Columbia U., 1989.

Grad. trainee, exec. Charterhouse Bank, London, 1984-86; analyst Samuel Montagu, London, 1986-87; assoc. Shearson Lehman Hutton, Inc., N.Y.C., 1989-93; v.p. Lehman Bros., N.Y.C., 1993-95; assoc. dir. Larkspur Capital Corp., New York, 1995-97; CFO MetaStat Inc., New York, 1997—. Bd. dirs. Planned Parenthood of N.Y.C., Sch. of Am. Ballet. Mem. Colony Club, Edgartown Yacht Club. Roman Catholic. Avocations: performing arts, riding, sailing. Home: 111 E 80th St Apt 5A New York NY 10021-0350 Office: MetaStat Inc 545 Madison Ave Fl 11 New York NY 10022-4219 E-mail: ccronson@msn.com.

CROOG, ROSLYN ZEPORAH, chief systems engineer; b. New Haven, July 14, 1942; d. Herbert Bernard and Belle (Brown) Croog; children: Bradley Jordan Paul, Katie Miriam Paul. AS, Quinnipiac Coll., 1962; BS, Fla. Internat. U., 1982. Analyst, programmer DBA Systems, Inc., Melbourne, Fla., 1982-84, sys. mgr. Fairfax, Va., 1984-86; mem. tech. staff MRJ, Inc., Fairfax, Va., 1986-98; chief sys. engr. AverStar, Inc., Vienna, Va., 1998—2000. Avocations: photography, sailing, cross-country skiing.

CROOK, PENNY LORAINE, investment broker; b. Gettysburg, S.D., Feb. 20, 1968; d. Paul E. and Phyllis J. (Clark) Daneau; m. Marshall Keith Crook, Sept. 6, 1986; 1 child, Zachary Patrick. AS, Pensacola Jr. Coll., 1991; degree, Am. Inst. of Banking, 1993; student, U. West Fla., 1993—. Lic. ins. rep., lic. investment broker. Bank teller AmSouth Bank, Pensacola, 1991, sr. teller, 1991-92, customer svc. rep., 1992-93, fin. svcs. rep., 1994-95, br. mgr., 1995-97, asst. v.p., 1996—; investment broker AmSouth Investment Svcs., Pensacola, 1997-99, v.p., 1999—. Rep. Mary Kay Cosmetics. Mem. fund raising com. Sacred Heart Children's Hosp., Pensacola, 1995—; sec. facilities com. Milestone HomeOwners Assn., Pensacola, 1996—; vol. Emerald Coast Classic Golf Tournament, Pensacola, 1994—. Mem. Nat. Assn. Female Execs., Kiwanis. Avocations: scuba diving, softball, watersports, bargain shopping, computers. Home: 728 Rockland St Cantonment FL 32533-6561

CROOK, WENDY P. management consultant, educator; b. Trenton, N.J., May 28, 1952; B. Psychology, Trenton State Coll., 1979; MSW, Rutgers U., 1986, PhD, 1996. Rsch. asst. Princeton (N.J.) U., 1977-79; shelter mgr. Womanspace, Inc., Trenton, 1980-82; asst. exec. dir. Mercer unit N.J. Assn. Retarded Citizens, Inc., Trenton, 1982-87; acting exec. dir. United Cerebral Palsy Assns. of N.J., Inc., Trenton, 1988; exec. dir. United Cerebral Palsy of Mercer County, Inc., Hamilton, N.J., 1987-93; mgmt. cons. DWC Enterprises, 1993—. Adj. prof. Columbia U., N.Y.C., 1993-96, Temple U., Phila., 1993-96, Rutgers U., 1993-96, Monmouth Coll., 1993-96, Ocean County Coll., 1993-96; field cons. Sch. Social Work, Rutgers U., 1993-96, rsch. asst., 1993-96; asst. prof. Fla. State U., Tallahassee, 1996—. Author: (manual) Accessary and ECHO Housing, 1994. Team leader Stand Down for Homeless Vets., 1994; chmn. Mercer County Disabilities Coalition, 1991-93; peer mentor UCPA Regional Adminstrs. Coun., chmn. N.E. region, 1988-93; mem. contracting task force N.J. Dept. Human Svcs., 1992-93; mem. steering com., vice chmn. Mercer County Human Svcs. Coalition, 1986-89; mem. N.J. Ctrl. Region Human Rights Com., 1986-88; mem. United Way Spkrs. Bur., mem. allocations com., Princeton area, Ocean County, Delaware Valley, 1985-93; mem. Mayor Holland's Task Force on Emergency Housing, Trenton, 1981; steering com. Mercer County Food Coalition, 1980-81; pres. bd. dirs., chmn. pers. com. Womanspace, Inc., 1983-84; bd. pres. Tallahassee Coalition for the Homeless, 1998-99. Mem. NASW (conf. chmn., co-chair Ctr. for Social Policy Campaign), N.J. Assn. Cmty. Providers (bd. trustees 1983-93, past v.p.). Avocations: sailing, scuba diving, travel. Home: 277 Starmount Dr Tallahassee FL 32303-4218 Office: Fla State U UCC 2511 Tallahassee FL 32306-2570

CROOKE, ROSANNE M. pharmacologist; b. Pittsfield, Mass., Oct. 30, 1955; d. Myron Michael and Marian Geneva (Russell) Muzyka; m. Stanley T. Crooke, Sept. 5, 1986. BA, Williams Coll., 1978; PhD, U. Pa., 1986. Rsch. asst. endocrine sec. dept. medicine U. Pa., Phila., 1978-81; fellow Wistar Inst. Anatomy and Biology, Phila., 1986-89; prog. leader cardiovasc. disease, dir. antisense drug discovery ISIS Pharms., Carlsbad, Calif., 1989—. Contbr. articles to profl. jours. Mem. AAAS, Soc. Toxicology. Avocations: hiking, gourmet cooking, bicycling. Home: 3211 Piragua St Carlsbad CA 92009-7840 Office: ISIS Pharms 2280 Faraday Ave Carlsbad CA 92008-7208

CROOKER, BARBARA ANN, writer, educator; b. Cold Spring, NY, Nov. 21, 1945; d. Emil Vincent and Isabelle Charlotte Poti; m. Michael James Gilmartin, 1967 (div. 1973); 1 child, Stacey Erin Gilmartin Krastek ; m. Richard McMaster Crooker, 1975; children: Rebecca Cameron Ceartas, David MacKenzie. BA, Rutgers U., 1967; MSEd, Elmira Coll., 1975. Adj. instr. English Elmira (NY) Coll., 1975, Corning (NY) CC, 1974—76, Tompkins Cortland CC, Dryden, NY, 1975—76, County Coll. Morris, Randolph, NJ, 1978—79; instr. cmty. svcs. Leigh County CC, Schnecksville, Pa., 1980, 1993; adj. asst. prof. Northampton (Pa.) Area CC, 1980—82; instr. women's ctr. Cedar Crest Coll., Allentown, Pa., 1982—85, adj. prof., 1999—. Contbr. (poetry) lit. mags., anthologies, textbooks, online mags.; author: Writing Home, 1983, Starting From Zero, 1987, Looking for the Comet Halley, 1987, Obbligato, 1992, The Lost Children, 1989, In the Late Summer Garden, 1998, The White Poems, 2001, Ordinary Life, 2002, Paris, 2002, Greatest Hits, 1980—2003, Impressionism, 2004. Nominee Pushcart prize, 1978, 1989, 1998, 1999, 2001, 2002, 2003; named winner, Passages North and NEA Emerging Writers Competition, 1987, Poet Laureate, Riverside Festival of Arts, Easton, Pa., 2000, winner Thomas Merton Poetry of the Sacred award, 2003, winner April is the Cruelest Month award, winner Public Poetry Project, 2004, winner Chapbook Competition, Grayson Books, 2004; recipient Phillips award, Stone Country, 1988, 1st prize, Karamu poetry contest, 1997, 3d pl., Kinloch Rivers Chapbook Competition, 1998, Internat. Merit award, Atlanta Review, 1999, 1st pl. Y2K writing prize, New Millenium Writings, 2000, Grand prize, Dancing Poetry Contest, 2000, 1st Pl., Byline Chapbook Competition, 2001; fellow lit., Pa. Coun. Arts, 1985, 1989, 1993, Va. Ctr. for Creative Arts, 1990, 1992, 1994, 1995, 1995, 1997, 1998, 2000, 2001, 2003. Mem.: Am. Acad. Poets. Avocations: gardening, camping, cross country skiing. Home: 7928 Woodsbluff Run Fogelsville PA 18051 Office Phone: 610-395-5845. Personal E-mail: bcrooker@ix.netcom.com.

CROOKER, DIANE KAY, accountant; b. Elmira, N.Y., Nov. 19, 1945; d. John Woodrow and Katharine Eloise (Saunders) Wilson; m. Dennis H. Canfield, Mar. 25, 1963 (div. June 1970); children: Douglas Arthur, Dennis John; m. Walter E. Crooker, Apr. 17, 1988. AAS in Computer Sci., Elmira Coll., 1987, BS in Acctg. summa cum laude, 1992. Assembler Westinghouse Elec. Corp., Horseheads, N.Y., 1979-81, traceability coord., 1981-87; buyer Imaging & Sensing Tech. Corp., Horseheads, 1987-89, acct., 1989-95, Corning (N.Y.) Credit Union, 1995-98; supr. fixed asset and tax acctg. Toshiba Display Devices, Horseheads, 1998—2003; man. gen. acctg. Emhart Glass Inc., Elmira, NY, 2003—. Bd. dirs. Spalding Found. for Injured Drivers, Owego, N.Y., 1988—. Recipient Scholastic Achievement award N.Y. State CPA Soc., 1992. Mem. Inst. Mgmt. Accts. (v.p. membership 1994), Alpha Sigma Lambda (sec. 1993-94, treas. 1994—). Avocations: boating, cocker spaniels.

CROOKS, LISA ZAHN, elementary school educator; b. Kansas City, Mo., Oct. 1, 1958; d. F. George and Sue (Scott) Z.; children: Whitney, Rebecca. BA, Kansas City U., 1980; MS, U. Kans., 1982. Mid. sch. tchr. Kans. State Sch. for Deaf, Olathe, 1981-88, tchr., 1983-88; 4th grade tchr. Briarwood Elem. Sch., Olathe, 1988—97, Black Bob Elem. Sch., 1998—. Portfolio cons. Emporia State U., 1994—; instr. U. Kans., 1992-94; ednl. cons. Soc. Devel. Edn., 2000—. Author: Coloring Your World With Learning, 1995, The Best of Good Apple, 1995, Munchable Math, 2000, Connecting Math and Literature, 2002; contbr. articles to profl. jours. Bd. dirs. Paul Mesner Puppets, Kansas City, Mo., 1993—, com. chmn., exec. com. BOTAR, Kansas City, 1980—; chmn. Am. Royal BBQ Contest; bd. dirs. Midwest Ear Inst., Kansas City, 1988—. Recipient Presdl. award for Excellence in Tchg. Math. Office of Pres. U.S., 1994, Excellence in Tchg. Math. award Kans. Med. Soc., 1993; Christa McAuliffe fellow, 2002; named to Nat. Tchr. Hall of Fame, 2002, Mid-Am. Edn. Hall of Fame, 2003. Mem. NSTA, Nat. Supervisors of Tchrs. of Math., Nat. Coun. of Tchrs. of Math., Soc. Presdl. Awardees, Coun. Presdl. Awards for Math., Delta Kappa. Presbyterian. Avocations: cycling, hiking, needlepoint, backpacking. Home: 5213 W 84th Ter Shawnee Mission KS 66207-1716

CROPP, LINDA W. city official; m. Dwight S. Cropp; children: Allison, Christopher. BA, MA, Howard U. Past pub. sch. tchr. and guidance counselor; city councilwoman at large, 1990-98; chmn. city councilwomen, 1999—. Past chair human svcs. com., past mem. regional authorities, pub. svc. and youth affairs, govt. ops. and self-determination coms. Rep. Ward 4 Bd. Edn., 1979, past v.p., pres.; past mem. Washington Met. Area Transit Authority; active Rock Creek Civic Assn., Travelers Aid Soc., Girl Scouts Nation's Capital, Jr. Achievement; mem. adv. bd. United Negro Coll. Fund. Office: Council DC 1350 Penn Ave NW Washington DC 20004

CROPPER, SUSAN PEGGY, veterinarian; b. N.Y.C., Feb. 11, 1941; d. Eli and Ruth (Rader) Abrahams; divorced; 1 child, Tracy Lynn. BS, Kans. State U., 1962, DVM, 1964. Assoc. veterinarian Asbury Park (N.J.) Animal Hosp., 1964-65; instr. in Vet. Sci. Kans. State U., Manhattan, 1965-66; owner, veterinarian Markle (Ind.) Vet. Clinic, 1966-71, Meisels Animal Hosp. Clinic, Elmwood Park, N.J., 1971-73, Ridgewood (N.J.) Animal Hosp., 1973-75, Cropper House Call Practice, Wyckoff, N.J., 1975—. Editor Nat. Assn. Women Vets., 1966-68; mem. Audibon Soc. Mus. Natural History. Co-author: Loving and Losing a Pet; editor WJMA Jour., 1973; photographer: Best Diving Spots in Western Hemisphere, 1987. Leader Brownie troop Girl Scouts U.S., Glen Rock, N.J., 1976-77, Wyckoff, 1977-83; chairperson No. Jersey Tridents, Ridgefield, N.J., 1985-86. Mem. AVMA, Soc. Aquatic Vet. Medicine (treas.), No. N.J. Vet. Med. Assn. (pres. 1972-73), Met. Vet. Med. Assn., N.Y. Zool. Soc., Van Saun Zool. Soc., N.J. Acad., Ski and Scuba Club of Westwood, North Jersey Tridents Club (Ridgefield, chair 1985-86, Millennial Cert. for philanthropic recognition). Avocations: scuba diving, underwater photography, travel, racquetball, markmanship practice. Office: 310 Newtown Rd Wyckoff NJ 07481-2608 Office Phone: 201-444-6254. E-mail: dvm2go@optonline.net.

CRORY, ELIZABETH L. former state legislator; b. Gardner, Mass., Sept. 12, 1932; d. James Quaiel and Mary (Reilly) Lupien; m. Frederick E. Crory, Aug. 21, 1954; children: Thomas, David, Ellen, Ann, Edward, Stephen. AB, U. Mass., 1954; MALS, Dartmouth Coll., 1975. Tchr. Amherst (Mass.) Schs., 1954, Lyme (N.H.) Schs., 1972-76; mem. N.H. Ho. of Reps., 1977-87, 92-96, mem. commerce/consumer affairs com., 1977-87, 93-96, mem. spl. com. on med. malpractice, 1984; exec. dir. Children's Ctr. of Upper Valley, 1986-90. Bd. dirs. Mascoma Savs. Bank. Mem. character and fitness com. N.H. Supreme Ct., 1998-2002; chair N.H. Health Svcs. Planning and Rev. Bd., 1999—; bd. dirs. Kendal at Hanover, 2001—. Roman Catholic. Home: 40 Rip Rd Hanover NH 03755-1614 Fax: 603-643-4025.

CRORY, MARY, town official; b. Concord, Mass., Sept. 27, 1932; d. Lennart William and Mary Susan (Sullivan) Fougstedt; m. Arthur Donald Crory, Jan. 31, 1953; children: Michael, Patricia, Joanne, Paul, Mary Susan, Mark. Tax collector Town of Littleton, Mass., 1962-00, town clk., 1976—2003. Sec., St. Anne Sodality, 1960-76. Democrat. Roman Catholic. Avocations: golf, needlepoint. Home: P O Box 216 Littleton MA 01460-0216

CROSBY, DEBORAH BERRY, artist; b. Gulfport, Miss., Oct. 9, 1930; d. Thomas Davis and Deborah Bennett (Hewes) Berry; m. Charles E. McHale Jr., Nov. 23, 1950 (div. 1952); 1 child Deborah Bennett McHale; m. Hueston T. Fortner, Jr., Mar. 17, 1957 (div. 1963); 1 child, Hueston G. Fortner; m. Richard Louis Crosby, Dec. 27, 1981. BA, Sophie Newcomb Coll., 1951; MA, Ind. State U., 1968; postgrad., Utah State U., 1969, Tulane U., 1979; BA (hon.), U. New Orleans, 1984. Educator Wesleyan Coll., Rocky Mt., N.C., 1969-70; prof. Spanish, Bay de Noc Coll., Escanaba, Mich., 1970-72; instr. yoga, Spanish, U. So. Miss.-Gulf Park Campus, Long Beach, 1972-78, Miss. Gulf Coast Jr. Coll. Dist., Keesler AFB Ctr., 1972-78; instr. reading, English, Miss. Gulf Coast Jr. Coll. Dist.-Jefferson Davis Campus, Keesler AFB Ctr., 1972-78; freelance artist Metairie, La., 1988—. One-woman shows include Dixie Art Co., Jefferson, La., 1990, World Trade Ctr., New Orleans, 1993—2001, Reginelli's Eating Gallery, 1994, Marceline Bonorden Fine Arts Gallery, 1998, 1999, Agora Gallery, New Soho, N.Y.C., 2000, Movie Pitchers, 2000—01, Ambassador Hotel, New Orleans, 2002—, exhibited in group shows at Artists Showroom Gallery, 1993—95, Rivertown Art Gallery, Kenner, La., Slidell Cultural Ctr., La. State Archives, Baton Rouge, La., Martin Hall, U. of Mobile, Ala., George E. Ohr Arts and Cultural Ctr., Biloxi, Miss., Stamford (Conn.) Mus., Havre de Grace (Mich.) Mus., West Wind Gallery, Casper, Wyo., Jefferson SQ, Klamath Falls, Oreg., Destrehan (La.) Plantation, Lexington (Ky.) Mus., Falls River Mills, Calif., Our Lady of the Rosary Gallery, NOLA Pitot Historic Ho., New Orleans, La., Marceline Bonorden Fine Arts Gallery, Agora Gallery, Soho, N.Y.C., The Purple Mullet Gallery, Ala., Serenity Gallery, The Artisan Mkt., Riverview Gallery, Zigler Art Mus., Jennings La., New Orleans Mus. Art, Amsterdam Whitney Internat. Fine Arts Gallery, Inc., N.Y.C., 2002—, New Orleans Art Assn. Fine Arts Festival (1st place), St. Charles Art Assn. Fall Show (1st place), Metairie Art Guild Summer Show, 1996 (1st place), Oil Met. Art Guild (1st place), Grumbacher Fall Show (1st, 2d and 3d place, 2002), Represented in permanent collections World Trade Ctr., commission, Juvenile Diabetes Assn., 2001, month long themed group Christmas exhibit, WTC, New Orleans, 1995—2001; designer, executor (cover chess book) The Art of Bisguier, 2003. Chmn. auction Heart Ambs., 1995; mem. Ladies Leukemia League, 1994-, program chmn., 1996; mem. Goodwill Industries VS, 1995-2002, BRAVO Ballet; fiesta hostess Napoleon's Home, Spring Fiesta Assn., 2002—; bd. dirs. Profl. Women's Adv. ABI, Inc., 2003; mem. Contemproary Arts Ctr. NOLA; mem. New Orleans Arts Coun., 2003—. Named Sweetheart, Local Br. Am. Heart Assn. Heart Ambs., 2001; recipient Spl. Painting award, Winsor-Newton, 1994, Great Lady award, New Orleans Met. area by East Jefferson Hosp. Aux., 2000. Mem. Nat. League Am. Pen Women (chaplain 1996—, v.p. 1998-2000), New Orleans Art Assn. (v.p. 1995-98), Le Petit Art Guild (program chair 1995-97, Le Grand chairperson, 1995—, officer 1995-97), St. Charles Art Assn. (pres. 1994-95, Artist of Yr. award 1991-92), Nat. Mus. Women in the Arts. Avocations: yoga, community activist, foreign languages study, travel, songwriting. Home: 5600 Kawanee Ave Metairie LA 70003-1414

CROSBY, JACQUELINE GARTON, newspaper editor, journalist; b. Jacksonville, Fla., May 13, 1961; d. James Ellis and Marianne (Garton) Crosby. ABJ, U. Ga., 1983; MBA, U. Cen. Fla., 1987. Staff writer Macon Telegraph & News, Ga., 1983-84; copy editor Orlando Sentinel, Fla., 1984-85; dir. spl. projects Ivanhoe Communications, Inc., Orlando, Fla., 1987-89; producer spl. projects Sta. KSTP-TV, Mpls., 1989-94; asst. news editor Star Tribune Online, Mpls., 1994—. Recipient award for best sports story Ga. Press Assn., 1982; award for best series of yr. AP, 1985, Pulitzer prize, 1985 Mem. Quill Avocations: competing in triathlons, playing electric bass, tutoring, reading. Home: 5348 Drew Ave S Minneapolis MN 55410-2006 Office: Star Tribune Online 425 Portland Ave Minneapolis MN 55488-0001

CROSBY, JANET MARIE, gifted and talented educator, writer; b. Joliet, Ill., Apr. 25, 1945; d. William Jarvis Crosby and Alice Bonner; m. Janet Marie Fears, Dec. 7, 2002. A in Sociology, Joliet Jr. Coll., 1976. Tchr. asst. physically handicapped dept. Joliet Twp. H.S., Ill., 1972—. Author poems. Pres. Grace & Glory Ministry, Joliet, 1995—2003. Avocations: writing, aerobics, dance, reading, helping organizations for the homeless. Home: 350 N Ottawa St#2 Joliet IL 60432 Office: Joliet Township High Schs 204 E Jefferson St Joliet IL 60432 Home Fax: None. Personal E-mail: crosjanet1@aol.com.

CROSBY, KATHRYN GRANDSTAFF (GRANT CROSBY), actress; b. Houston, Nov. 25, 1933; d. Delbert Emery and Olive Catherine (Stokely) Grandstaff; m. Harry L. (Bing) Crosby, Jr., Oct. 24, 1957 (dec. Oct. 1977); children: Harry Lillis III, Mary Frances, Nathaniel Patrick. BFA, U. Tex., 1955; RN, Queens of Angles Sch. Nursing, Los Angeles, 1964; attended, UCLA; teaching credential, Immaculate Heart Coll., L.A., 1965. Actress: in plays including Sunday in New York, 1963, Pygmalion, Sabrina Fair, 1964, Peter Pan, 1965, Arms and the Man, 1965, Mary, Mary, 1966, The Guardsman, 1967, The Prime of Miss Jean Brodie, 1969, Same Time Next Year, 1977-78; films include Rear Window, Unchained, Reprisal, Operation Mad Ball, 1958, others; hostess daily TV talk show, Sta. KPIX, San Francisco; TV appearances Bing Crosby Christmas Specials, Suspense Theater, Ben Casey; Author: Bing and Other Things, 1967, My Life With Bing, 1983; also column Texas Gal in Hollywood, 1952-54. Mem. advisory com. arts State Dept.; Co-chmn. bd. trustees Immaculate Heart Coll.; trustee Eisenhower Med. Center. Named Distinguised Alumae U. Tex., 1969, Rodeo Queen Houston Fatstock Show, 1950 Mem. Am. Conservatory Theatre. Roman Catholic.

CROSBY, LAVON KEHOE STUART, state legislator, civic leader; b. Hastings, Nebr., Apr. 25, 1924; d. Charles William and Kathryn Marie (Farrell) Kehoe; m. Lester Stuart, Oct. 9, 1948 (dec. 1970); children: Mary Stuart Bolin, Michael, Timothy, Frederick Stuart; m. Robert B. Crosby, May 22, 1971. BA, U. Nebr., 1987. Asst. to pres. Hastings Tribune Corp., Nebr., 1941-68; mem. staff U.S. Senator Roman Hruska, Washington, 1968-71; mem. Nebr. State Legislature, 1988—, Appropriations Com., 1988—, Nebr. Retirement Systems com., 1992—, chmn. com. on coms., 1994—. Civic leader; b. Hastings, Nebr., Apr. 25, 1924; d. Charles William and Kathryn Marie (Farrell) Kehoe; m. Lester Stuart, Oct. 9, 1948 (dec. 1970); children— Mary Stuart Bolin, Michael, Timothy, Frederick Stuart; m. Robert B. Crosby, May 22, 1971. BA, U. Nebr., 1987. Asst. to pres. Hastings Tribune Corp., Nebr., 1941-68; mem. staff U.S. Senator Roman Hruska, Washington, 1968-71; mem. Nebr. State Legislature, 1988—; mem. Appropriations Com., 1988—, mem. Nebr. Retirement Systems com., 1992—, chmn. com. on coms., 1994—. Chmn. music com. Cathedral of Risen Christ Choir, Lincoln, Nebr.; pres. Lincoln Community Playhouse Guild; bd. dirs., chmn. membership com. Lincoln Community Playhouse; v.p., bd. dirs. Lincoln Symphony Guild; bd. dirs. Lincoln Symphony Orch. Assn., 1972-82; founder Nebr. Found. for Humanities; mem. Lincoln Symphony Found. Bd., 1984—; bd. dirs. Friends of Ctr. for Great Plains Studies, 1984—; vice chmn. Nebr. Arts Council, 1981-82, chmn., 1982-85; past mem. and sec. Pershing Auditorium Bd.; pres. Nebr. Legis. Ladies League, 1977-78; adv. bd. Cath. social Services Bur.; budget chmn. Nebr. Mother's Assn., chmn. legis. affairs Diocesan Council Cath. Women; v.p. Heritage League, Lincoln, 1985—; pres. Cornhusker Republican Women, 1974-75. Recipient Mayor's Arts award, Lincoln, 1985, Gov.'s Arts award, Nebr., 1986, YWCA Tribute to Women award, 1993. Mem. Nebr. Club (Lincoln). Chmn. music com. Cathedral of Risen Christ Choir, Lincoln, Nebr.; pres. Lincoln Community Playhouse Guild, bd. dirs., chmn. membership com. Lincoln Community Playhouse; v.p., bd. dirs. Lincoln Symphony Guild; bd. dirs. Lincoln Symphony Orch. Assn., 1972-82; founder Nebr. Found. for Humanities; mem. Lincoln Symphony Found. Bd., 1984—; bd. dirs. Friends of Ctr. for Great Plains Studies, 1984—; vice chmn. Nebr. Arts Council, 1981-82, chmn., 1982-85; past mem. and sec. Pershing Auditorium Bd.; pres. Nebr. Legis. Ladies League, 1977-78; adv. bd. Cath. social Services Bur.; budget chmn. Nebr. Mother's Assn.; chmn. legis. affairs Diocesan Council Cath. Women; v.p. Heritage League, Lincoln, 1985—; pres. Cornhusker Republican Women, 1974-75. Recipient Mayor's Arts award, Lincoln, 1985, Gov.'s Arts award, Nebr., 1986, YWCA Tribute to Women award, 1993. Mem. Nebr. Club (Lincoln). Office: State Legislature Rm 1010 State Capital Lincoln NE 68509

CROSBY, MARENA LIENHARD, retired college administrator; b. Shreveport, La., Mar. 2, 1948; d. John Joseph and Clara Curtis (Lawton) L.; m. H.W. Patrick Obrien, Sept. 23, 1977; m. John L. Crosby, Nov. 23, 1997. MEd, U. New Orleans; JD, Loyola U., New Orleans. Bar: La. 1971; lic. profl. counselor, La.; diplomate Am. Coll. Profl. Mental Health Practitioners. Instr. Delgado C.C., New Orleans, 1973-80, counselor, 1980-86, coord. testing, 1986-88, dir. admissions, 1988-90, dir. counseling and mktg., 1990-93, dir. degree audit program, 1993-97, asst. to v.p. student affairs, 1997-98, ret., 1998. Mem. DAR, FBA, ACA, Internat. Assn. for New Sci., Assn. for Rsch. and Enlightenment, Am. Psychotherapy Assn., Inst. Noetic Scis., Theosophical Soc. Am., Family Mediation Coun., La. Bar Assn., La. Notary Assn., La. Assn. Spiritual and Religious Values in Counseling, Assn. for Spiritual, Ethical and Religious Values in Counseling, New Orleans Bar Assn., New Orleans Womens Opera Guild, New Orleans Mus. Art, Colonial Dames, Magna Charta Dames. Republican. Avocations: reading, piano. E-mail: cmloc18@aol.com.

CROSBY, TONI M. state legislator; b. San Francisco, Oct. 9, 1957; m. Herbert W. Crosby; 3 children. Student, Fresno City Coll., U. N.H. Asst. mgr. bookstore, Concord, N.H.; mem. dist. 20 N.H. Ho. of Reps. Mem. small bus., consumer affairs and econ. devel. coms. N.H. Ho. of Reps. Leader svc. team Girl Scouts Am., 1986-94; bd. dirs., chair organizing and fundraising Nat. Abortion Rights Action League, N.H., 1990-93; bd. dirs., vol. coord. Conant (N.H.) Sch. PTO, 1993-94; mem. learning steering com. N.H. Dept. Edn., 1994—. Democrat. Address: 36 Wood Ave Concord NH 03301-2731

CROSKERY, BEVERLY ANN, education consultant; b. Oklahoma City, Okla., Oct. 19, 1934; d. Clarence Glenn and Mildred Estelle (Bell) Fulkerson; m. Robert William Croskery, Aug. 14, 1954; children: Richard W., Robert F., Kathryn Croskery Jones, Virginia. BA, U. Wichita, 1963; MEd, U. Toledo, 1973, PhD, 1978. Cert. provisional supt., elem. prin. Elem. tchr. Hamden (Conn.) Hall Country Day Sch., 1955-56; ROMPER ROOM tchr. Sta. KAKE-TV, Wichita, Kans., 1960-65; elem. tchr. Kenosha (Wis.) Unified Sch., 1966-68, Toledo (Ohio) Pub. Schs., 1969-75, adminstr., 1975-76; instr. U. Toledo, 1977; intermediate supr. N.W. Local Schs., Cin., 1977-79, elem. prin., 1979-84, dir. elem. edn., 1984-95. Trainer, multiple intelligences, 1993—; adj. prof. Wright State U., Dayton, Ohio, 1990—, Coll. of Mount St. Joseph, Cin., 1984—86, Miami U., Oxford, Ohio, 1979, Oxford, 98; writer, cons. WCPO-TV, Cin., 1977—79. Exec. producer (videotape) Children, Community, Challenge, 1994, (writer, producer) The Gifted Child, 1980 (motion picture) Everyone is Special: The Story of the Toledo Public Schools, 1971; author: Attitudes...Toward Death Education, 1979, Shamir the White Elephant: A Rain Forest Adventure, 1997. Mem. Ohio Dept. Edn. Missing Child Task Force, 1988—89; chmn. com., author book on religious curriculum Westwood First Presbyn. CH., Cin., 1994; mem. adv. bd. Classics for Kids Classics for Kids; mem. Supts. Adv. Com., 1982—84. Recipient Award of Honor Am. Cancer Soc., 1994. Mem. Ohio Community Edn. Assn. (pres. 1983-84), Ohio Assn. of Supervision and Curriculum Devel. (bd. dirs. 1980-83), Nat. Staff Devel. Assn. (Ohio affiliate 1992—), Ohio Valley Elem. Prins. Assn. (sec. 1982-83). Avocations: tennis, storytelling. Home: 5300 Hamilton Ave Ste 1000 Cincinnati OH 45224-3153 Office: 5300 Hamilton Ave Ste 1001 Cincinnati OH 45224-3153

CROSS, CHARLOTTE LORD, retired social worker, artist; b. Andalusia, Ala., Dec. 1, 1941; d. Roy Olice and Laura Emily (Smith) Lord; m. Jack Allen Cross, May 5, 1960; children: Jack Allen III, James Duane, Jeffrey Miles. BA in English, Auburn U., Montgomery, Ala., 1979, MS in

Psychology, 1980, MS in Secondary Edn./English, 1993. Social worker dept. human resources State of Ala., Andalusia, 1980—2002, ret., 2002. Tchr. in English conversation to Nat. Cancer Inst. rsch. scientists, Tokyo, 1965-66; adj. instr. psychology Lurleen B. Wallace State Jr. Coll, 1988-98, Troy State U., Fort Rucker, 1991; owner Capriccio's Coffee Shop and Gifts; portrait artist. Recipient [illegible] award, 1989. Mem.: Am. Soc. Portrait Artists. Baptist. Home: PO Box 1364 Andalusia AL 36420-1364

CROSS, DOLORES EVELYN, former university administrator, educator; b. Newark, Aug. 29, 1938; d. Charles and Ozie (Johnson) Tucker; children: Thomas E., Jane E. BA in Elem. Edn., Seton Hall U., 1963; MS, Hofstra U., 1968; PhD in Higher Edn. Adminstrn., U. Mich., 1971; hon. doctorates, Marymount Coll., Skidmore Coll., Hofstra U., Elmhurst Coll. Asst. prof. edn. Northwestern U., Evanston, Ill., 1971-74; assoc. prof. Claremont Grad. Sch., Calif., 1974-78; vice chancellor CUNY, 1978-81; prof. Bklyn. Coll., 1978-81; pres. N.Y. State Higher Edn. Svc. Corp., Albany, 1981-88; assoc. provost, assoc. v.p. acad. affairs U. Minn., Mpls., 1988-90; pres. Chgo. State U., 1990—97, Gen. Electric Fund, 1996-99, Morris Brown Coll., Atlanta, 1999—2002. Pres. Gen. Electric Fund, 1996-99; bd. dirs. Coll. Bd., Campus Compact, 1997—, Assn. Black Women in Higher Edn., No. Trust Co.; sr. cons. South Africa's Historically Black Colls.; bd. dirs. Inst. Internat. Edn., No. Trust Corp. Editor: Teaching in a Multicultural Society, 1978. Bd. dirs. Field Mus., Chgo. Urban League, Leadership for Quality Edn., Chgo. Area Fulbright Scholars Program. Recipient Tosney award Am. Assn. of Univ. Adminstrs., 1995. Mem. NAACP (life), Am. Edn. Rsch. Assn., Am. Assn. Higher Edn. (chair-elect 1997—), Am. Coun. on Edn. (bd. dirs.) Women Execs. in State Govt. (adv. bd.), Comml. Club (Chgo.). Avocations: running, hiking, bicycling, theatre, writing. Office: IIE Bd of Dirs 155 N Wacker Dr Chicago IL 60606-1787

CROSS, DOROTHY ABIGAIL, retired librarian; b. Bangor, Mich., Sept. 9, 1924; d. John Laird and Alice Estelle (Wilcox) C. BA, Wayne State U., 1956; MA in Libr. Sci., U. Mich., 1957. Jr. libr. Detroit Pub. Libr., 1957-59; adminstrv. libr. U.S. Army, Braconne, France, 1959-61, Poitiers, France, 1961-63, area libr. supr., 1963, asst. commd. libr. Kaiserslautern, Germany, 1963-67, acquisitions libr. Aschaffenburg, Germany, 1967, Munich, Germany, 1967-69, sr. staff libr. specialist, 1969-72, commd. libr. Stuttgart, Germany, 1972-75, dep. staff libr. Heidelberg, Germany, 1975-77; chief libr. 18th Airborne Corps and Ft. Bragg, N.C., 1977-79; chief ADP sect. Pentagon Libr., Washington, 1979-80, chief readers svcs. br., 1980-83, dir., 1983-91. Mem. ALA, U. Mich. Alumni Assn., Delta Omicron. Methodist. Home: 6511 Delia Dr Alexandria VA 22310-2609 E-mail: dacross@starpower.net.

CROSS, ELIZABETH, apparel manufacturing company executive; b. 1959; married; 3 children. Grad., U. Colo.; MBA, Stanford U., 1988. Cons. Bain and Co.; co-founder, co-pres. Ariat Internat., Inc., San Carlos, Calif., 1990—. Office: Ariat Internat Inc 3242 Whipple Rd Union City CA 94587-1217

CROSS, EUNICE D. elementary school educator; b. Foley, Minn, May 28, 1932; d. William Joseph and Elizabeth Agnes Latterell; m. Alan Viking Cross; children: Carol, Michael, Mari, Elizabeth, Jon, Catherine. BS, St. Cloud State U., 1956, MS, 1964. Rural sch. tchr. Dist. Common Sch. 51, North Benton, Minn., 1958-59; tchr. 4th grade Ind. Dist. 51, Foley, 1960-64, tchr. 1st grade, 1964-66, tchr. 6th grade, 1966-85, Chpt. I tchr., 1985-96, chairperson Chpt. 1 dept., 1986—98. Sec. Benton unit Am. Cancer Soc., 1985—89, pres., 1989—2004, daffodil chairperson, 1986—2004; mem. Foley Pub. Sch. Bd., 1999—2004, treas., 2001—04; mem. Foley Connection Team, 1987—99, Foley Found., 2003—04. Recipient Leadership in Edn. Excellence award Ctrl. Minn. Edn. Rsch., 1996. Mem.: Minn. Sch. Bd. Assn. (del. to assembly 2003—04), Ret. Tchr. Assn. Ctrl. Minn. (v.p. 1998—2003), Foley Edn. Assn. (pres. 1970—85, Tchr. of Yr. 1971). Democrat. Roman Catholic. Home: 50 6th Ave Foley MN 56329 E-mail: alanv@cloudnet.com.

CROSS, GOLDIE K. telecommunications engineer; b. Grosse Pointe, Mich., Aug. 4, 1955; d. William Issac Fowler and Garnet Christine Potter; m. Jamie John Cross, June 30, 1983 (div. May 1991). AAS in Electronics Engring. Tech., Macomb C.C., Warren, Mich., 1985; BAS in Electronics Engring. Tech., Sienna Heights Coll., 1992. Sec. Alexander & Alexander, Detroit, 1973-74; stage technician Detroit Pub. Schs., 1974-78, audio-visual technician, 1978-82, tchr. electronics and telecomm., 1982-87; telecomm. specialist Mich. Bell-Ameritech, Dearborn, 1987-96; network engr. I and II Bakersfield (Calif.) Cellular, 1996-98; network engr. III Bell South Mobility, Birmingham, Ala., 1998—. Chair tech. ops. com. Mich. Emergency Patrol-REACT, Detroit, 1979-84; past mem. Mich. Woman's Missionary Union, state rec. sec., 1995-97, Calif. Woman's Missionary Union, Calif. Girls in Action Cons., 1997-98. Recipient letter of commendation FBI, Bakersfield, 1998. Mem. Ala. Woman's Missionary Union (missions edn. vol.). Republican. Baptist. Avocations: scuba diving, bowling, travel, flying.

CROSS, KATHRYN PATRICIA, education educator; b. Normal, Ill., Mar. 17, 1926; d. Clarence L. and Katherine (Dague) C. BS, Ill. State U., 1948; MA, U. Ill., 1951, PhD, 1958; LLD (hon.), SUNY, 1988; DS (hon.), Loyola U., 1980, Northeastern U., 1975; DHL (hon.), De Paul U., 1986, Open U., The Netherlands, 1989. Math. tchr. Harvard (Ill.) Community High Sch., 1948-49; rsch. asst. dept. psychology U. Ill., Urbana, 1949-53, asst. dean of women, 1953-59; dean of women then dean of students Cornell U., Ithaca, N.Y., 1959-63; dir. coll. and univ. programs Ednl. Testing Svc., Princeton, N.J., 1963-66; rsch. educator Ctr. R&D in Higher Edn. U. Calif., Berkeley, 1966-77; rsch. scientist, sr. rsch. psychologist, dir. univ. programs Ednl. Testing Svc., Berkeley, 1966-80; prof. edn., chair dept. adminstrn., planning & social policy Harvard U., Cambridge, Mass., 1980-88; Elizabeth and Edward Conner prof. edn. U. Calif., Berkeley, 1988-94, David Pierpont Gardner prof. higher edn., 1994-96. Mem. sec. adv. com. on automated personal data sys. Dept. HEW, 1972-73; del. to Soviet Union, Seminar on Problems in Higher Edn., 1975; vis. prof. U. Nebr., 1975-76; vis. scholar Miami-Dade C.C., 1987; trustee Carnegie Found., 1999—, Berkeley Pub. Libr., 1998—; spkr., cons. in field; bd. dirs. Elderhostel. Author: Beyond the Open Door: New Students to Higher Education, 1971, (with S. B. Gould) Explorations in Non-Traditional Study, 1972, (with J. R. Valley and Assocs.) Planning Non-Traditional Programs: An Analysis of the Issues for Postsecondary Education, 1974, Accent on Learning, 1976, Adults as Learners, 1981, (with Thomas A. Angelo) Classroom Assessment Techniques, 1993, (with Mimi Harris Steadman) Classroom Research, 1996; contbr. articles, monographs to profl. publs., chpts. to books; mem. editl. bd. to several ednl. jours.; cons. editor ednl. mag. Change, 1980—. Active Nat. Acad. Edn., 1975—, Coun. for Advancement of Exptl. Learning, 1982-85; trustee Bradford Coll., Mass., 1986-88, Antioch Coll., Yellow Springs, Ohio, 1976-78; mem. nat. adv. bd. Nat. Ctr. of Study of Adult Learning, Empire State Coll.; mem. nat. adv. bd. Okla. Bd. Regents; mem. higher edn. rsch. program Pew Charitable Trusts; mem. vis. com. Harvard Grad. Sch. Edn., 1998—; bd. dirs. Elderhostel, 1999—; trustee Berkeley Pub. Libr., 1999—, Carnegie Found., 1999—. Mem. Am. Assn. Higher Edn. (bd. dirs. 1987—, pres. 1975, chair 1989-90), Am. Assn. Comty. and Jr. Colls. (vice chair commn. of future comty. colls.), Carnegie Found. Advancement of Tchg. (adv. com. on classification of colls. and univs.), Nat. Ctr. for Devel. Edn. (adv. bd.), New Eng. Assn. Schs. and Colls. (commn. on instns. higher edn. 1982-86), Am. Coun. Edn. (commn. on higher edn. and adult learner 1986-88). E-mail: patcross@socrates.berkeley.edu.

CROSS, MARY S. photojournalist; b. Louisville, Ky., Mar. 26, 1936; d. William Arthur Stoll and Dorothy Linthicum Smith; m. Lawrence Askew Warner, June 22, 1957 (div. Jan. 0, 1974); m. Theodore Lamont Cross, Nov. 30, 1974; children: Stuart Warner, Polly Warner, Ann Anderson. Student, Sweet Briar (Va.) Coll., Sweet Briar, VA, 1953—55, U. Sorbonne, Paris, 1955—56; B.A., Hollins Coll., Roanoke, VA, 1957—57. Mem. Adv. Coun., Dept.Comparative Lit., Princeton (N.J.)U., 1986—, Adv. Coun., Inst. for the Transregional Study of the Contemporary Mid. East, N[illegible] Asia, Princeton U., Princeton, NJ, 1995—, Internat. Adv. Coun. of the Nr. East Found., N.Y.C., 1996—, Adv. Bd., Am. U. in Cairo Press, Egypt, 2001—, Presdl. Search Com., Am. U. in Cairo, Cairo, 2002—03; chairperson Facilities Com., Am. U. in Cairo, Cairo, 1998—2000; mem. Academic Affairs Com., Am. U. in Cairo, Cairo. Co-author (book) Behind the Great Wall - A Photographic Essay on China, photographer (exhibition) Two by Mary Cross: Photographs of Egypt and Morocco (Arthur Ross Gallery of the University of Pennsylvania, Faces of Egypt (Phoebe Hearst Museum of Anthropology of the University of California at Berkeley), Vietnam (The Council on Foreign Relations, New York, NY), Vietnam (Meridian International Center, Washington, D.C.), author/photographer (book) Egypt, Morocco: Sahara to the Sea (Maroc du Sahara a La Mer (French edition), photographer/captions Vietnam: Spirits of the Earth, photographer (journal article) The Ontario Review, Photographs of Vietnam in the Smithsonian Magazine, (exhibition) Behind the Great Wall (The Los Angeles County Museum of Natural History), Egypt (Woodrow Wilson School, Princeton University sponsored by the Program of Near Eastern Studies), Egypt: Faces from the Deserts and Valleys (Houston Museum of Natural Science). Trustee Am. Sch. Tangier, Morocco, 1993—, Am. U. in Cairo, Egypt, 1993—; mem. NAACP Legal Def. & Ednl. Fund, Princeton, NJ, 1984—90, Adv. Bd., NAACP Legal Def. & Edicational Fund, Princeton, NJ, 1991—2003, The Century Assn., N.Y.C., 2003—; del. Mid. East Econ. Summit, Casablanca, Morocco, 1994—94; mem. Coun. on Fgn. Rels., New York, NY, 2003—. Mem.: The Cosmopolitan Club of NY. D-Liberal. Home: 1 Campbelton Cir Princeton NJ 08540 Office: Mary S Cross 200 West 57th St New York NY 10019

CROSSER, CARMEN LYNN, marriage and family therapist, social worker, consultant; b. Iowa Falls, Iowa, Jan. 17, 1970; d. Gary Laverne Sr. and Karen Dorothy (Ulrich) C. AA, Ellsworth C.C., 1990; BS, Iowa State U., 1993; MSW, U. Iowa, 1995; postgrad., U. Chgo., 1998—. Lic. clin. social worker, marriage and family thrapist, Ill.; cert. brief therapist, ACSW. Grad. teaching asst. U. Iowa, Iowa City, 1994-95; mental health therapy intern Mid-Eastern Cmty. Mental Health Ctr., Iowa City, 1994-95; clin. social worker Sinnissippi Ctrs., Inc., Dixon, Ill., 1995-97; family therapist Ctr. for Counseling, DeKalb, Ill., 1997—. Cons. sexual abuse svcs. Sinnissippi Ctrs. Inc., 1997—98; rsch. asst. U. Chgo., 1998—2000, tchg. asst., 1999—2001; revs. asst. Jour. of Marital and Family Therapy, 1999—2000; adj. prof. Dominican U., River Forest, Ill., 2002—. Mem. Dekalb Area Women's Ctr., 1997—2000; mem. instnl. rev. bd. No. Ill. U., DeKalb, 1997—2000. All-Am. scholar, 1995. Mem. ACA, NASW, NOW, Am. Soc. Prevention Cruelty Animals (voting mem.), Am. Assn. Marriage and Family Therapy (clin. mem.), Am. Coll. Counselors, Internat. Assn. Marriage and Family Counselors, Ill. Soc. Clin. Social Work, Assn. Play Therapy, Nat. Fedn. Socs. for Clin. Social Work, Golden Key, Phi Kappa Phi, Phi Alpha. Office: Ctr for Counseling 14 Health Svcs Dr Dekalb IL 60115 E-mail: c-crosser@uchicago.edu.

CROSSLEY, ANN COOK, writer; b. Tampa, Fla., June 16, 1939; d. James Hugh and Anna Margaret (Frierson) Caldwell; m. Ross William Crossley, Jun. 7, 1960; 1 child, Georgia Dunagan. BSHE, U. Ga., 1962. Editor ABI Press, Sarasota, Fla., 1989—. Author: The Army Wife Handbook, 1990, 2d edit. 1994, The Air Force Wife Handbook, 1992. Recipient Cert. of Appreciation for Patriotic Civilian Svc., Dept. of Army, 1988. Mem. Phi Kappa Phi. Home: 4094 Columns Dr SE Marietta GA 30067-5199

CROSSLEY, HELEN MARTHA, public opinion analyst, research consultant; b. Phila., Sept. 8, 1921; d. Archibald Maddock and Dorothy (Fox) C. BA in Govt. cum laude, Harvard U., 1942; MA in Social Sci. and Pub. Opinion, U. Denver, 1948; postgrad., Heidelberg U., Germany, Am. U., Washington, George Washington U., Yonsei U., Korea. Jr. info. analyst Office War Info., Washington, 1942-43; rsch. specialist, bus. analyst War Food Adminstrn., Washington, 1943-45; data analyst, field supr. Crossley Inc., N.Y.C., 1945-47; from grad. rsch. asst. to sr. analyst Opinion Rsch. Ctr. U. Denver, 1947-49; from study dir. to chief attitude rsch. br. Dept. Def., Heidelberg, Germany, 1950-53; sec., treas., v.p., pres., project dir. Arch-Cross Assocs., Inc., Princeton, N.J., 1954-85; survey specialist U.S. Info. Agy., Washington, 1955-60, rsch. specialist, 1979-92, ret., 1992; tng. evaluation officer Internat. Coop. Admin., Seoul, 1960-63; ind. cons. Princeton, 1964-78. Trustee Gallup Internat. Inst., Princeton, 1995-99; co-organizer Korean Soc. for Social Sci. Rsch., 1961-62; technical dir. Nat. Coun. on Pub. Polls, 1969-71; rsch. couns., 1993—. Author: Highlights of Population Shifts, 1944, Evaluation Survey of Korea/U.S. Participant Training Program, 1955-60, 1963; co-author: (with Don Cahalan and Ira Cisin) American Drinking Practices, 1970; contbr. articles to profl. jours. Sec., treas., pres. Penzance Players, Woods Hole, Mass., 1939-45. Recipient Ann Radcliffe scholarship Radcliffe Coll., 1938, cert. of appreciation Korean Ministry of Pub. Info., 1962, cert. of merit Nat. Safety Coun., 1965. Mem. AAUW, AARP, NOW, Am. Assn. Pub. Opinion Rsch. (pres. Washington chpt. 1956, 77-78, councillor-at-large 1970-72, sec., treas. 1973-75, mem. conf. com. 1994-95), World Assn. Pub. Opinion Rsch. (sec., treas. v.p., conf. chmn., pres. 1960-62, historian 1993—), Princeton PC Users Group, USIA Alumni Assn., Harvard Club of Princeton Harvard Club of Wash., Women's Coll. Club (scholarship prize 1938), Woods Hole Yacht Club, Nassau Club Avocations: travel, photography, music, sailing, history. Home and Office: 21 Battle Rd Princeton NJ 08540-4901

CROSSWHITE, JEANETTE ELVIRA, art educator; b. Halifax County, Va., Nov. 2, 1941; d. Miles Emory Elder and Elise Elizabeth Guthrie; m. Dean Harlow Crosswhite, Dec. 27, 1968. B in Music Edn., Longwood Coll., Farmville, Va., 1964; B in Ch. Music, So. Bapt. Theol. Sem., Louisville, 1966, M in Ch. Music, 1967; PhD in Music Edn., U. N.C., Greensboro, 1996. Assoc. prof. music Milligan Coll., Milligan College, Tenn., 1967—93, chair music dept., 1983—91; music cons. Tenn. Dept. Edn., Nashville, 1994—99, dir. arts edn., 2000—. Dean Tenn. Arts Acad., Nashville, 2000—; liaison to Tenn. Art Edn. Assn., 2000—, Tenn. Music Edn. Assn.; facilitator Arts Suprs. of Tenn., 2000—; bd. dirs. Tenn. Performing Arts Ctr., Nashville; evaluator Tenn. Bd. Examiners, 1999—; columnist Tenn. Musician, 1994—. Vol. Reach to Recovery, Am. Cancer Soc., Nashville, 1998—. Mem.: Nat. Ednl. Theatre Assn., Nat. Art Edn. Assn., Music Educators Nat. Conf. (local chair for nat. conf. 2002), Sigma Alpha Iota. Avocations: walking, crocheting, knitting, cooking. Office: Tenn Dept Edn Andrew Johnson Tower 5th fl 710 James Robertson Pkwy Nashville TN 37243

CROTEAU, MAUREEN ELIZABETH, journalism educator; b. Hartford, Conn., Feb. 1, 1949; d. Maurice Joseph and Muriel Lucille (Follert) C.; m. Wayne Worcester. BA, U. Conn., 1971; MS, Columbia U., 1973. Reporter Hartford (Conn.) Times, 1971-72; editor Hartford (Conn.) Courant, 1973-76; reporter, editor Providence (R.I.) Jour., 1976-83; freelance journalist, 1983—; dept. head, prof. journalism dept. Univ. Conn., Storrs, 1983—. Bd. dirs. Conn. Found. for Open Govt., Hartford, The New London Day newspaper. Co-author: Shipwrecked in the Tunnel of Love, 1983, The Essential Researcher, 1993. Mem. Assn. for Edn. in Journalism & Mass Communications, Soc. Profl. Journalists, Investigative Reporters and Editors. Office: Journalism Dept 337 Mansfield Rd Storrs Mansfield CT 06269-9015

CROTTO, DENICE, elementary school educator; b. Bell, Calif., Sept. 15, 1946; d. James Maurice Johnson and Eunice Elaine Brown; m. James Nicholas Crotto, Dec. 21, 1963; children: James Bradley Crotto, Denein Elaine Cusack. BS Elem. Edn. cum laude, S. Oregon U., 1986; MA in Counseling and Guidance, Pacific Lutheran U., 1994. Tchr. Franklin Pierce Sch. Dist., Tacoma, 1987-2000. Mem. AAUW, Humane Soc., Audubon, Kappa Delta Pi, Phi Kappa Phi. Democrat. Roman Catholic. Home: 9218 Milton Ave Gig Harbor WA 98332-1085 Office: Franklin Pierce Sch Dist [illegible] Tacoma WA 98444-3099

CROTTY, LADONNA DEANE, librarian; b. Williamson, W.Va., July 22, 1939; d. Kenneth B. and M. Virginia (Parcell) Crockett; m. Robert E. Crotty, Nov. 25, 1959; 4 children. BA, Marshall U., 1960. English instr. Northwest HS, McDermott, Ohio, 1976—79; media specialist, libr. Valley Mid. Sch., Lucasville, Ohio, 1979—. Mem.: NEA, Valley Tchrs. Assn., Ohio Edn. Assn. Home: 228 Pleasant Dr Lucasville OH 45648-9008 Office: Valley Mid Sch 393 Indian Dr Lucasville OH 45648

CROTTY, M. MAGGIE, state senator; b. Chgo., Ill., Oct. 16, 1948; m. Larry Crotty; 1 child, Kevin ; children: Keith, Mark. Dip., Mercy HS. State Senator US Senate, Dist. 19, 2002—; worker Spl. Ed. Rep. House of Rep., Ill., 1996—2002; mem. Exec. Appt., Health & Human Svc.; vice chair person Licensed Activities. Recipient Recognition Award, Women of Oak Forest Make a Dif., 1995, Outstanding Sch. Bd. Pres. of Ill., Nominee, Sch. Bd. of Ill., Theresa Roedl Meml. Award for Volunteerism, Theresa Roedl, 1988. Mem.: Oak Forest Civil Svc. Commn., Sch. Dist. #145 Bd. (pres.), Sch. Dist. #228 Ed. Found. (chmn.), Sch. Bd., 15 yr. (pres. 8 yr.), Kiwanis Club of Oak Forest (past pres.). Democrat. Office: Capitol 311 Capitol Bldg Springfield IL 62706 also: Dist 15028 So Cicero, Unit A Oak Forest IL 60452

CROUCHET, KATHLEEN HUNT, elementary educator, reading educator; b. Dec. 30, 1946; d. Abram Davis Sr. and May (Botsay) Hunt; m. Courtland Adam Crouchet, Sr., Feb. 5, 1966; children: Chantelle C. McInerney, Courtland Adam. BS in Elem. Edn., Our Lady of Holy Cross, New Orleans, 1983; MEd in Curriculum and Instrn., U. New Orleans, 1990, PhD in Curriculum and Instrn., 1998. Cert. reading specialist, supr. student tchg., parish and city sch. supervision of instrn. tchr. asessment, elem. and secondary prin., La. Tchr. Archdiocesan Schs., Arabi, La., 1965-84, Orleans Parish Schs., New Orleans, 1984-94, St. Bernard Parish Schs., Chalmette, La., 1994-97; reading instr. Nunez C.C., Chalmette, 1996—. Lectr., cons. Our Lady of Holy Cross Coll., New Orleans; adj. asst. prof. U. New Orleans; participant Model Career Option program State of La., New Orleans, 1991-92; tchr. assesor State of La., St. Bernard, 1994—; curriculum writer St. Bernard Parish Schs., 1997; cooperating tchr. U. New Orleans, 1989-90, 94; insvc. lectr. Co-author: Teacher Professionalism and Leadership in Louisiana, 1992. Moderator, 4-H Cleanest Parish Competition, St. Bernard, 1995. Mem. ASCD, Internat. Reading Assn., Nat. Coun. Tchrs. English, La. Middle Sch. Assn., Phi Delta Kappa, Kappa Delta Pi (historian, sec.). Avocations: reading, travel, gardening. Home: 4429 Colony Dr Meraux LA 70075-2286 Office: Nunez CC 3700 La Fontaine St Chalmette LA 70043-1249

CROUGH, MAUREEN M. lawyer; AB magna cum laude, Princeton U., 1983; JD cum laude, U. Mich., 1986. Bar: Ill. 1986, N.Y. 1995. Ptnr. Sidley & Austin, N.Y.C. Spkr. numerous confs., incluidng U.S. Energy Assn. Regional Environ. Auditing and Info. Sys. Workshop for Ctrl. Countries, Bratislava, Slovakia, 1995. Contbr. numerous articles to profl. publs. Mem. ABA (steering com. N.Y.C. met. area network of sect. natural resources, energy and environ. law). Office: Sidley & Austin 875 3d Ave New York NY 10022 Fax: 212-906-2021. E-mail: mcrough@sidley.com.

CROUSE, LINDSAY, actress; b. N.Y.C., May 12, 1948; d. Russel and Anna (Erskine) C. BA, Radcliffe Coll., 1970. Appearances include: (films) All the President's Men, 1976, Between the Lines, 1977, Slapshot, 1977, Prince of the City, 1981, The Verdict, 1982, Daniel, 1983, Iceman, 1984, Places in the Heart, 1984 (Acad. award nomination 1985), House of Games, 1987, Communion, 1989, Desperate Hours, 1990, Being Human, 1993, Bye Bye Love, 1995, Indian in the Cupboard, 1995, The Juror, 1996, The Arrival, 1996, Prefontaine, 1997, The Progeny, 1999, Man of the People, 1999, Stranger in My House, 1999, The Insider, 1999; (TV movies) Eleanor and Franklin, 1976, Eleanor and Franklin: The White House Years, 1977, Reunion, 1980, Paul's Case, 1980, Summer Solstice, 1981, Lemon Sky, 1987, Chantilly Lace, 1993, Final Appeal, 1993, Parallel Lives, 1994, Out of Darkness, 1994, Between Mother and Daughter, 1995 (Emmy award nomination), Norma Jean and Marilyn, 1996, If These Walls Could Talk, 1996, Beyond the Prairie: The True Story of Laura Ingalls Wilder, 1999; (TV series) Hill Street Blues, Murder She Wrote, Columbo, Law and Order, Lifestories, The Equalizer, Civil Wars, L.A. Law, Traps, ER, NYPD Blue, Millenium, Brimstone, Batman: The Animated Series, Buffy the Vampire Slayer, 1999-2000, Providence, The Division, Arliss, Fraiser, 2002. Recipient Obie award for Reunion, 1980, Theater World award for The Homecoming, 1992.

CROUSHLER, SARAH ISABELLA, dance and movement therapist; b. Phila., Mar. 7, 1973; d. Hayes Bates Croushore and Karen Ann Forbes; m. Patrick David Dishler, July 1, 2000. BA in Dance and Psychology, Goucher Coll., 1995; MA in Dance Therapy, Antioch Grad. Sch., 2000. Registered dance therapist Am. Dance Therapy Assn. Dance and movement therapist Regional Inst. Children and Adolescents, Balt., 2000—. Mem.: Am. Dance Therapy Assn. (pub. rels. 2001—03). Avocations: yoga, paper making. Office: Regional Inst Children and Adolescents 650 S Chapel Gate Ln Baltimore MD 21229

CROW, DOLORES J. state representative; b. Clovis, N.Mex. m. Wayne Crow; 6 children. Attended, Henager's Bus. Coll. Legal sec.; businesswoman; state rep. dist. 13A Idaho Ho. of Reps., Boise, 1996—, chair, revenue and taxation com., mem. commerce and human resources com. Republican. Baptist. Office: State Capitol PO Box 83720 Boise ID 83720-0038

CROW, ELIZABETH SMITH, editor; b. N.Y.C. d. Harrison Venture and Marlis (deGreve) Smith; children: Samuel Harrison, Rachel Venture, Sarah Gibson. BA, Mills Coll.; postgrad., Brown U. Exec. editor New York mag., N.Y.C.; editor-in-chief Parents mag., N.Y.C., 1978—83; pres., editl. dir., CEO Gruner & Jahr USA Pub.; editor-in-chief Mademoiselle Mag., N.Y.C., 1993-99; free-lance book reviewer N.Y. Times Book Rev.; pres. N.Y. Women in Comm., 1999-2000; v.p., editl. dir. Rodale Pub., N.Y.C., 2001—02; exec. v.p., editl. dir. Primedia Consumer Mag. and Media Group, 2002—03; v.p., editl. dir. Consumers Union, 2004—. Judge Nat. Mag. awards; bd. trustees Alan Guttmacher Inst. Bd. trustees March of Dimes; pres. N.Y. Women Comm. Found., 1999—2000. Recipient Nat. Mag. award for gen. excellence, 1988. Mem.: Am. Soc. Mag Editors, Century Assn., Cosmopolitan Club. Democrat.

CROW, LYNNE CAMPBELL SMITH, insurance company representative; b. Buffalo, Oct. 13, 1942; d. Stephen Smith and Jean Campbell (Ruggles) Hall; m. William David Crow II, Apr. 16, 1966 (div. Dec. 1989); children: William David III, Alexander Fairbairn, Margaret Campbell. BA, Sweet Briar (Va.) Coll., 1964; postgrad., Am. Coll., 1986. CLU; ChFC. Claims rep. Liberty Mut. Ins. Co., Bklyn. and N.Y.C., 1964-66; with McGraw-Hill Corp., N.Y.C., 1966-67; claims rep. Liberty Mut. Ins. Co., East Orange, N.J., 1967-68; sales assoc. Realty World/Allsopp Realtors, Millburn, N.J., 1981-82; field rep. Guardian Life Ins. Co., 1982—. Bd. dirs. Jr. League Oranges and Short Hills, Millburn, 1979-80, 95-96, Millburn LWV, 1979-80; campaign chair, bus. chair, bd. dirs. United Way Millburn/Short Hills, 1981-88, 90-96, sec., 1990-91; adult planning chair Cora Hartshorn Arboretum, 2000-03, bd. dirs., trustee, 2000—, sec., 2003-04. Named Life Underwriter of Yr., 1996. Mem. Nat. Assn. Ins. and Fin. Advisors (com. on nominations 2003-04, Nat. Quality award 1988, 91,

95, Nat. Health Achievement award 1988, 90), Nat. Assn. Health Underwriters, Am. Soc. Fin. Svc. Profls. (bd. dirs. 1994-99), N.J. Assn. Ins. and Fin. Advisors (dir. region II 1993-95, health chair 1995—, sec. 1998-99, 2d v.p. 1999-2000, 1st v.p. 2000-01, pres. 2001-02), Newark Assn. Life Underwriters (bd. dirs. 1986-94, sec. 1987-88, treas. 1988-89, 3d v.p. 1989-90, 2d v.p. 1990, pres.-elect 1991-92, pres. 1992-93, health chair 1995-98, Life Underwriter of Yr. 1986), Women in Fin. Svcs., Leader's Recognition Soc., Million Dollar Round Table (qualifying and life, capt. focus session on non-core products and investments 1999-2000, chair spl. events 2000-01), Million Dollar Round Table Found. (bd. trustees 2002, diamond knight, trusteeship com. 2003—), Assn. Health Ins. Advisors, Nat. Assn. Security Dealers, Chatham (Mass.) Beach and Tennis Club. Republican. Episcopalian. Avocations: travel, sailing, reading, hiking, photography. Home: 22 Winding Way Short Hills NJ 07078-2530 Office: 1150 Raritan Rd Cranford NJ 07016-3369 Office Phone: 908-709-0020 118. E-mail: lscrow22ww@aol.com.

CROW, MARTHA ELLEN, lawyer; b. Bryan, Tex., Dec. 7, 1944; d. Elvin Earl and Walteen (Daly) Burnett; m. Michael Paine Crow, Apr. 20, 1968; children: Jennifer Johanna, Emily Jeanne, Bryan Jacob. BA, Baker U., 1966; JD magna cum laude, Washburn U., 1992. Bar: Kans. 1993. Tchr., jr. high Shawnee Mission Schs., Johnson County, Kans., 1966-68; legal intern Speaker's Office Kans. Legis., Topeka, 1991; law clk. Freilich, Leitner, Shortlidge and Carlisle, Kansas City, Mo., 1992-93; planning cons. Kans. Dept. Health and Environment, Topeka, 1993-95; ptnr. Crow, Clothier & Bates, Leavenworth, Kans., 1995—. Comments editor: Washburn Law Jour., Vol. 31, 1991-92. Mem. Kans. Ho. of Reps., 41st dist., 1996—, Kans. Continuing Legal Edn. Commn., 1993—, chmn., 1997—; bd. dirs., founding mem. Leadership Leavenworth, 1988-90; chmn., vice chmn. Leavenworth City Planning Commn., 1978-90, 94-96; v.p. to pres. Leavenworth Bd. Edn., 1983-96; chmn. Leavenworth Bd. Zoning Appeals, 1979-89, 94-96; pres. Downtown Leavenworth Revitalization, Inc., 1988-90, Leadership Kans. Class of 1986; bd. dirs. YWCA, 1974-82, pres., 1977-79; bd. dirs. Leavenworth C. of C., women's divsn., 1980-86, Baker U. Alumni Assn., 1978-80, Mother to Mother Ministry, 1996—, Northeast Kans. Mental Health and Guidance Ctr., 1997—; co-chmn. residential divsn. United Way Drive, 1977, 78, numerous others. Recipient Michaud, Cordry, Michaud, Hutton scholarship, Wichita, Kans., 1991, scholarship Washburn Law Sch., 1991. Mem. ABA, Kans. Bar Assn., Kans. Trial Lawyers Assn., Washburn Sch. of Law (women's legal forum), Phi Kappa Phi, Phi Delta Phi, Phi Gamma Mu, Delta Delta Delta, PEO. Democrat. Methodist. Home: 1200 S Broadway St Leavenworth KS 66048-3118 Office: Crow Clothier & Bates PO Box 707 302 Shawnee St Leavenworth KS 66048-2063

CROW, SHERYL, singer, songwriter, musician; b. Kennett, Mo., 1963; Degree in classical piano, U. Mo., 1984. Backup singer Bad tour Michael Jackson, 1987; backup singer The End of the Innocence tour Don Henley, 1989; also backup singer George Harrison, Joe Cocker, Stevie Wonder, Rod Stewart; singer, songwriter Tuesday Night Music Club, 1992—. Albums Tuesday Night Music Club, 1993, Sheryl Crow, 1996, The Globe Sessions, 1998, C'mon, C'mon, 2002 (Grammy award best female rock vocal performance, 2003), singles Leaving Las Vegas, All I Wanna Do (Grammy awards for Record of Year and Female Pop Vocal, 1995), Strong Enough, Flesh & Blood, 2002, participant Lilith Fair, 1998, 1999. Recipient Grammy award for Best New Artist, 1995. Address: A&M Records Inc 70 Universal City Plz Universal City CA 91608-1011*

CROWDER, BONNIE WALTON, small business owner, composer; b. Lafayette, Tenn., Apr. 14, 1916; d. Edward Samuel Bailey and Nannie Elizabeth (Goad) Walton; m. Reggie Ray Crowder, Nov. 19, 1936; 1 child, Rita Faye. Grad., Nashville Beauty Coll. Owner, operator Bonnie's Beauty Salon, Tampa, Fla. Composer: A Man of Faith, 1988, This Miracle, 1988; (with Willard E. Walton) God Bless Our President, 1988, Awake, Arise America, 1989, Touching My Jesus, 1990, (with W.E. Walton) Muscle Jerky Boogie, 1992. Active ch. choir, Tampa; mem. Bus. and Profl. Women's Chorus, 1960-70's, U. South Fla. Cmty. Chorus, 1973-81. Mem. Beta Sigma Phi. Home: 266 Oak Knob Rd Lafayette TN 37083-4137

CROWDER, CAROLYN, educational association administrator, educator; m. Terry Crowder. Grad. cum laude, So. Nazarene U.; M in Elem. Edn., U. Ctrl. Okla. Artist-in-residence Okla. City Pub. Schs.; vocal, music tchr. Mustang Pub. Sch., Okla.; pres. Okla. Edn. Assn., Oklahoma City, 1997—. Chair Okla. Edn. Coalition, 1999—2000; workshop presenter Okla. State Reading Coun., Encyclopedia. Mem. Leadership Okla. Recipient award, Okla. Econ. Assn.; grantee, Okla. Reading Coun. Mem.: Okla. Edn. Assn. (pres., del., negotiator, bd. dirs., Political Activist award 1996), Delta Kappa Gamma. Office: Okla Edn Assn PO Box 18485 Oklahoma City OK 73154

CROWDER, DOROTHY SHOLES, nursing educator; b. Colonial Heights, Va., June 15, 1926; d. Wilbur Irwin and Dorothy (Townsend) Sholes; m. George Willard Crowder, Nov. 2, 1949; 1 child, Carol Elizabeth Crowder Johnson. BSN, Va. Commonwealth U., Richmond, 1974; MS, Va. Commonwealth U. Med. Sch. Nursing, Richmond, 1976. RN Va.; cert. childbirth educator Va. Night supr. Petersburg (Va.) Gen. Hosp., 1946—49; office nurse Dr. Thomas B. Pope, Petersburg, 1950—60; staff nurse Petersburg Gen. Hosp., 1960—64; instr. Petersburg Gen. Hosp. Sch. of Nursing, 1964—72; asst. prof. nursing Med. Coll. Va. Sch. of Nursing, Richmond, 1976—78, assoc. prof. nursing, 1978—93, assoc. prof. nursing emeritus, 1994—. Author Workbook on Electrolyte Balance; contbr. articles to mursing jours. Ward capt. Civic Assn., Petersburg, Va., 1952—60; Sunday Sch. tchr.; Ch. health and welfare nurse; Bd. dirs. Am. Cancer Soc., Richmond, 1999—, March of Dimes, Richmond, 1999—. Mem.: ANA, Med. Coll. Va. Nursing Alumni Assn., Assn. Women's Health, Obstetric and Neo-natal Nurses (chpt. pres. 1984—86), Va. Nurses Assn. (dist. pres. 1978—92, Maternal and Child Nurse of Yr. 1984), Sigma Tau. Methodist. Avocations: jogging, travel, reading, biking. Home: 205 Honeycreek Ct Colonial Heights VA 23834

CROWDER, ELIZABETH See WADDINGTON, BETTE

CROWDER, JANE NELSON, middle school educator; b. Denver, Aug. 14, 1936; d. Arthur S. and Mildred E. Nelson; m. Paul A. Crowder, Dec. 27, 1956; children: Jennifer, Steffanie, Paul N., Douglas. BA in Chemistry, Biology, Edn., U. Colo., 1958; postgrad., Cornell U., 1960; MA in Sci. Edn., U. Wash., 1979; postgrad., Western Wash. U., 1981, U. Oreg., 1985. Tchr. sci. Pine Lake Mid. Sch., Issaquah, 1979—. Curriculum developer U.S. Geol. Survey, K-12 Water Resources Sourcebook; adv. bd. Coalition for Earth Sci. Edn.; manuscript rev. panel Science Scope, 1991-94; creator, tchr. earth sci. workshops for tchrs. Co-author: Seismic Sleuths (tchr. and classroom manual), 1994, Earth: The Water Planet (tchr. classroom modules), 1989; author: The Quaternary Geology of the Issaquah Area, or How the Last Ice Sheet Shaped Our Land, 1987, Water Matters, vol. II, 1997. Recipient Issaquah Supts. Award for Excellence, 1988, Golden Acorn award Pine Lake Parent-Tchr.-Student Assn., 1995; named Issaquah Tchr. of the Yr., 1988, Eastside Educator of the Yr., Bellevue, 1989; Issaquah Schs. Found. grantee, 1988-89. Mem. Nat. Sci. Tchrs. Assn. (bd. dirs., exec. com. 1993-95), Soc. for Mining, Metallurgy and Exploration (mem. edn. steering com.), Am. Geol. Inst. (adv. bd. 1989-91, adv. panels for earth sci. sourcebooks project), Wash. Sci. Tchrs. Assn. (Middle Level Tchr. of Yr. 1993).

CROWDER, LENA BELLE, retired special education educator; b. Winston-Salem, N.C., Apr. 4, 1931; d. Henry Lee and Janie (Woods) Thomas; m. Raymond Crowder, June 12, 1954; 1 child, Rayonette Janease. BS in Edn., Winston Salem State U., 1952; MS in Edn., Agrl. and Tech. Coll., 1959. Cert. elem. edn. tchr., N.C. Tchr. 1st grade Early County Sch. Sys., Blakely, Ga., 1953-56; tchr. kindergarten Thomas-Anderson Kindergarten, Winston-Salem, 1956-57, 58-60, 61-62; tchr. 1st grade Beaufort (S.C.) County Schs., 1957-58; tchr. Chapel Hill (N.C.) City Sch. System, 1960-61, Forsyth County Sch. System, Winston-Salem, 1961-62, 1962-67, Winston-Salem/Forsyth County Schs., 1967-93, ret., 1993. Precinct election recorder Winston-Salem/Forsyth County Election Bd., 1961; fin. sec. Mt. Zion Bapt. Ch. Sunday Sch., Winston Salem, 1977—; supporter Crisis Control Ministry, Winston-Salem, 1982—; participant neighborhood watch system Winston-Salem Police Dept.; chair sch. involvement projects ARC, 1991-92. Mem. NEA, Nat. Assn. Univ. Women, Coun. Exceptional Children, Nat. Women of Achievement (rec. sec. S.E. region 2000—, S.E. bd. dirs., Winston-Salem bd. dirs.), Assn. Classroom Tchrs. Democrat. Home: 1140 Rich Ave Winston Salem NC 27101-3432 Fax: 336-725-6181.

CROWDER, LILLIE MAE BROWN, retired architectural engineer; b. Georgetown, S.C., May 31, 1936; d. Moses and Maude (Session) Brown; m. Charles Lamar Crowder, Apr. 15, 1960 (div. Feb. 1972); children: Barney, Frederick. BS in Archtl. Engring., S.C. State U., 1958; postgrad., Tuskegee Inst., 1960, Inst. Design and Constrn., 1961, 63; diploma in archtl. drafting, CUNY, 1971; MA in Urban Edn., L.I. U., 1981. Rated aero. engr./jr. archtl. engr. U.S. Civil Svc. Commn. Draftperson David Byrd Assoc., Washington, 1958-59; tchr. Choppee H.S., Georgetown, 1958-60; draftsperson Big 6 Press, N.Y.C., 1960-62; sr. warrant officer N.Y. Telephone Co., N.Y.C., 1963-64; chief draftsperson Wilbur Smith & Assoc. C.E., Manhattan, N.Y., 1964-67; asst. architect sch. planning and rsch. Bklyn. Bd. Edn., 1967-71, edn. facility coord. facilities planning divsn., 1971-84, archtl. faculty coord. divsn. spl. edn., 1984-90, sr. project liaison divsn. sch. facilities, 1990-98. Jr. engr. N.Y.C. Resignalization Study, 1959-60; organized 1st mech. drawing dept. at Choppee H.S. Spkr: Women History Month, 1998, Bus. and Profl. Women, N.Y.C.; Author: Essence of a Dream (featured in Sotheby's 8th Annual exhbn. of art by N.Y.C. pub. sch. tchrs. and students, 1998, contbr. poems to profl. publs. Trustee Salem United Meth. Ch., N.Y.C., 1972; bd. dirs. Lewis H. Latimer Fund, Inc., Flushing, N.Y., 1982—, Human Resource Ctr./St. Albans, Queens, N.Y., 1984; mem. adv. com. Black Am. Heritage Found. Music History Arch. York Coll., 1995—; women's com. Local 375, Architects and Engrs.; borough pres. Bklyn. Citation Achievement Field Edn. & Arch., Queens Black History Month-Mary McLeod Bethune Celebration; guest spkr. Women History Program, 1998, fed. women's com. Social Security Adminstrn. Recipient Disting Alumni award S.C. State U., 1981, Nat. Assn. Equal Oppty. Higher Edn., 1982, Quarter Century award Black Am. Heritage Found., 1993, Positive Image award Key Women of Am.; L.B. Crowder Day proclaimed borough pres., city coun., Queens, 1993 (cited in Jet Magazine and Congl. Record 1993, 94), award Borough Pres. of Queens; 1st woman in N.Y.C. to receive archl. drafting license; architecture achievement citation Borough Pres. of Brooklyn, N.Y.; Black history month citation Borough Pres., Queens. Mem. New Yorkers for Inclusive Edn. Curriculum, United Fedn. Tchrs., S.C. State U. Club (exec. bd., sec. 1976-81), Delta Sigma Theta Sorority, Inc. Democrat. Avocations: painting, piano, poetry, composing, writing lyrics. Home: PO Box 401 PO Box 635-91 W B Middle Island NY 11953-0401

CROWDER, MARJORIE BRIGGS, lawyer; b. Shreveport, La., Mar. 26, 1946; d. Rowland Edmund and Marjorie Ernestine (Biles) Crowder; m. Ronald J. Briggs, July 11, 1970 (div. Nov. 2000); children: Sarah Briggs, Andrew Briggs. BA, Carson-Newman Coll., 1968; MA, Ohio State U., 1969, JD, 1975. Bar: Ohio 1975, U.S. Ct. Appeals (6th cir.) 1983, U.S. Ct. Claims 1992, U.S. Supreme Ct. 2001. Asst. dean of women Albion Coll., Mich., 1969-70; dir. residence hall Ohio State U., Columbus, 1970-71, acad. counselor, 1971-72; assoc. Porter, Wright, Morris, Arthur, Columbus, 1975—83, ptnr., 1983-2000; AmeriCorps atty. Southeastern Ohio Legal Svs., Portsmouth, Ohio, 2000—02, staff atty., 2002—03; domestic violence team leader Legal Aid Soc. Columbus, 2003—. Legal aide Cmty. Law Office, Columbus, 1973—74. Co-author: (book) Going to Trial, A Step-By-Step Guide to Trial Practice and Procedure, 1989. Trustee, pres. Epilepsy Assn. Ctrl. Ohio, Columbus, 1977—84; bd. dirs. Scioto County Domestic Violence Task Force, v.p., 2001—; bd. dirs. Action Ohio Coalition Battered Women, 2002—, Columbus Speech & Hearing, 1977—82. Fellow: Columbus Bar Found. (trustee 1993—95); mem.: Scioto County Bar Assn., Columbus Bar Assn. (com. chmn. 1979—83, docket control task force 1989—91, editor 1981—83), ABA (mem. gavel awards com. 1989—96, gen. practice sect. 1983—, chair litig. com. 1987—89, mem. exec. coun. 1989—93, dir. bus. com. group 1990—91, chair program com. 1991—93, torts and ins. practice sect. 1993—, vice chair health ins. law com. 1993—96), Ohio Bar Assn. (mem. joint task force gender fairness 1991—93), Scioto County Bar Assn. Home: 2106 Summit St Portsmouth OH 45662 Office: Legal Aid Soc Columbus 40 W Gay St Columbus OH 43215 E-mail: mcrowder@columbuslegalaid.org.

CROWDER, MARY ELLEN, art educator, real estate agent; b. Mt. Clemens, Mich., Oct. 17, 1942; d. Thomas Lyman and Verda Mary Telford; m. C. J. Crowder Jr., Apr. 15, 1972; stepchildren: Kathy Kaye, Nancy Jean; 1 child, Wallace William Kenmuir Jr. Student, Det. Bus. Coll., 1962, Oakland Coll., 1975, Long Beach City Coll., 1980, St. Mary's Coll., San Francisco, 1980. Sales Godin Properties, Lakewood, Calif., 1989—; instr. art Fine Art Express, Costa Mesa, 2000—02, Long Beach Pks. and Recreation, Calif., 2000—. Treas., v.p., and pres. Long Beach Traders, Calif., 1980—85. Recipient 1st Pl. awards, Cerritos Art Guild, Cypress Art Guild, Los Alamitos Art Guild. Mem.: Lakewood Art Guild (v.p. 2002—, 1st Pl. award).

CROWDER, REBECCA BYRUM, music educator, elementary school educator; b. Suffolk, Va., Apr. 27, 1951; d. Joseph Etheridge and Jane Carroll Byrum; m. Melvin Linnwood Crowder, July 19, 1997. BS in Music Edn., Radford U., 1973, MS in Music Edn., 1976. Cert. music tchr. grades K-12, tchr. grades 4-7. Profl. musician, 1973—; music tchr. East Salem Elem., Salem, Va., 1973—78; music dir. Colonial Ave. Bapt., Roanoke, Va., 1973—79; music tchr. Andrew Lewis Jr. High, Salem, 1979—83, Salem High and Glenvar High, Salem, 1983—84, Glenvar High, Salem, 1984—90, Oak Grove Elem., Roanoke, 1990—. Music tchr. Hollins U., Roanoke, 2000; pianist, accompanist Colonial Ave. Bapt., Roanoke, 1963—79, Shady Grove Bapt., Thaxton, 1979—92, First Bapt., Roanoke, 1992—97, Salem Ch. of Christ, 1997—. Mem.: Music Educators Nat. Conf., Va. Congress Parents and Tchrs., Phi Kappa Phi. Avocations: ballroom dancing, reading, playing piano, crossword puzzles, singing. Home: 1606 Mountain Hgts Dr Salem VA 24153

CROWE, JENNIFER, newspaper reporter; b. L.A., Apr. 17, 1973; d. Timothy James and Beverly Jean Crowe. BA in Print Journalism and Polit. Sci., U. Nev., Reno, 1995. Intern Reno Gazette-Jour., Gannett Newspapers, 1993-95, feature writer, 1995-96, police reporter, 1996-98, edn. reporter, 1998—2000, legis. reporter, 2000—01, asst. opinion editor, 2001—02; congl. fellow Am. Polit. Sci. Assn., 2002—03; with Office of Sen. Maria Cantwell, Washington, 2003—. Reporting fellow Knight Ctr. for Journalists, College Park, Md., 1998. Vol., Salvation Army, Reno, 1997; Career Day spkr. Washoe County Schs., Nev., 1997—; coord. Make Time for Kids Vols., 1999—. Recipient Best Spot News Story award Nev. Press Assn., 1998, Best of Gannett 2d pl. award Gannett Newspapers Inc., 1996, Well Done news series award, 1996, Well Done news enterprise Gannett, 1999. Mem.: Soroptimists Internat. Avocations: downhill skiing, snowboarding, hiking, fishing. Office: Reno Gazette-Jour 955 Kuenzli St Reno NV 89502-1160

CROWELL, ROSEMARY ELAINE, criminal justice professional; b. Monroe, N.C., Sept. 14, 1942; d. Frederick Perry and Berthenia (Alexander) C. AA, Clinton Jr. Coll., 1961. Mem. staff Betty Bacharach Home Afflicted Children, Atlantic City, 1964-66, Murdoch Ctr., Butner, N.C., 1964-66; cottage parent N.C. Dept. Human Resources, Butner, 1966-68, cottage parent, then cottage mgr. C.A. Dillon Sch. div. youth svcs., 1968-82, asst. unit adminstr., 1982—98. Del. to Dem. Nat. Conv., Atlanta, 1988; Dem. precinct chmn., Butner, 1989; active Dem. presdl. candidate campaigns, 1988; mem. Dem. Leadership Coun., 1990; mem. Granville County Dem. Steering Com. for N.C. Gov., 1996; mem. Granville County Steering Com. for Sen. John Edwards, 1998; com. mem. Granville County 2015 Task Force Comprehensive Land Devel. Plan, 2002. Mem. Nat. Abortion Rights Action League, Elks. Episcopalian. Avocations: reading, travel, politics. Home: PO Box 334 Butner NC 27509-2144

CROWLEY, CYNTHIA WETMORE, real estate broker; d. Robert James and Cynthia Johnson Crowley. BA, Princeton U., Princeton, N.J., 1982. Dir. of relocation Olshan Realty Inc., N.Y., 1984—. Founding dir. Manhattan Assn. of Realtors, N.Y., NY, 1999—, pres., 2004—. Com. mem. N.Y. Women's Found., NY, 2002—; del. N.Y. Assn. of Realtors, Albany, NY, 2003—. Achievements include 4 Time National Tae Kwon Do Champion. Avocations: athletics, travel, reading. Office: Olshan Realty Inc 641 Lexington Ave 22nd Flr New York NY 10022 Office Phone: 212-751-3300.

CROWLEY, JUDY B. state representative; b. Rutland, Vt., Apr. 5, 1936; m. John P. Crowley; 5 stepchildren ; m. John Bloomer (dec.); 4 children. Student, Rutland Bus. Coll., Children's Hosp. Sch. Nursing, Boston, 1958. Mem. senate, 1995—96; state rep. State of Vt., 2001—, chair house local govt. com., 2003—. Legis. trustee Vt. State Coll., 1996—2000; nursing adv. coun. Castleton Stae Coll. Bd. dirs. Open Door Mission, Rutland H.S. Found.; past mem. West Rutland Planning Commn., Health Policy Coun.; mem. West Rutland Rep. Com. Mem.: Order of Eastern Star, Rutland Regional Med. Ctr. Auziliary, Am. Legion. Office: PO Box 432 West Rutland VT 05777

CROWLEY, L. C. telecommunications company executive; b. Pitts., Feb. 21, 1949; d. David A. and Elsie M. (Stark) C.; m. Thomas G. Wilson, June 21, 1969 (div. Nov. 1972); m. James W. Wilson Jr., Mar. 20, 1987. Student, Lowell Inst., 1984-86, Loyola U., 1975, MIT, 1967-69, 72-74; MS in Mgmt., Purdue U., 1992. Prodn. mgr. High Performance Products Inc., Hingham, Mass., 1969-71; mfg. mgr. Quadex (Compugraphic), Cambridge, Mass., 1977-81; asst. gen. mgr. Commerce Handling Co., Boston, 1982-83; dir. EDP Inter Consult Inc., Cambridge, 1984-86; mgr. receivables systems Sprint, Dallas, 1987-97, mgr. billing, 1997—. Graphics editor. Corporate Electronic Publishing Systems, 1986. Head SMITF Garden Guild, Southlake, Tex., 1997—; mem. St. Martin-in-the-Fields Episcopal Choir, 1988—. Mem. Purdue Pres.' Coun. Republican. Avocations: genealogy, organic gardening, legends car racing, target shooting. Home: 410 Lakewood Dr Trophy Club TX 76262-5296 Office: Sprint 1510 Rochelle Blvd Irving TX 75039-4307

CROWLEY, LISKA ANNE, historian; b. Denver, Colo., Mar. 19, 1949; d. Churchill Clement Crowley and Bettie Marie Cooper-Crowley; m. Vern Hicks, Oct. 14, 1979; m. David W. Crawford, Aug. 25, 1971 (div. July 27, 1977). Assoc., Mesa Jr. Coll., Grand Junction, Colo., 1969; Bachelors, Adams State Coll., Alamosa, Colo., 1972. Freelance writer, Washington, NJ, 1972—76; society editor Farmington Daily News, N.Mex., 1976—77; news dir. Kenn Radio Sta., Farmington, N.Mex., 1977—78; employment counselor State of N.Mex., Farmington, 1979—80; mental health aide Col. Gorge Ctr., Hood River, Oreg., 1980—81; group home counselor Taylor St. House, Hood River, Oreg., 1982—83; owner, mgr. River Spirit Trading Post, Klickitat, Wash., 1983—. Tourism promotion Columbia Gorge, Oreg., 1986—; living history cons. Port of Cascade Locks, Oreg., 1986—, Dalles Libr., Oreg., 1999—. A Celebration of Poets, 1998 (1st prize, 1998). Co-founder Farmington Women's Svc. Ctr. Recipient 3d prize, Midwest Poetry Review, 1996, Editor's Challenge award, Internat. Soc. Writers and Authors, 1998, Good Buddy award, Vernonia Muzzleloaders, 2001. Mem.: San Juan County Non Writers Assn. (founder), Mt. Adams C. of C. Democrat. Avocations: dog owner, gardening, cooking, friends.

CROWN, NANCY ELIZABETH, lawyer; b. Bronx, N.Y., Mar. 27, 1955; d. Paul and Joanne Barbara (Newman) C.; children: Rebecca, Adam. BA, Barnard Coll., 1977, MA, 1978; MEd, Columbia U., 1983; JD cum laude, Nova Law Sch., 1992. Cert. tchr.; Bar: Fla. 1992. Tchr. Sachem Sch. Dist., Holbrook, N.Y., 1978-82; v.p. mail order dept. Haber-Klein, Inc., Hicksville, N.Y., 1984-88; mgr. mdse., dir. ops. Sure Card Inc., Pompano Beach, Fla., 1988-89; legal intern Office U.S. Trustee/Dept. Justice, 1992; assoc. John T. Kinsey, P.A., Boca Raton, Fla., 1993-95; pvt. practice Nancy E. Crown, P.A., Boca Raton, Fla., 1995—; owner Crystal Title, Inc., 1999—. Recipient West Pub. award for acad. achievement, 1992. Mem. NOW, Fla. Bar Assn., South Palm Beach County Bar Assn., Bus. Partnership Coun., Phi Alpha Delta. Democrat. Jewish. Avocations: theatre, walking, reading, jazz. E-mail: necrownpa@aol.com.

CROYLE, BARBARA ANN, health care management executive; b. Knoxville, Tenn., Oct. 22, 1949; d. Charles Evans and Myrtle Elizabeth (Kellam) C. BA cum laude in Sociology, Coll. William and Mary, 1971; cert. corp. tax and securities law, Inst. Paralegal Tng., 1971; JD, U. Colo., 1975; cert. program mgmt. devel., Colo. Women's Coll., 1980; MBA, U. Denver, 1983. Bar: Colo. 1976. Paralegal Holland & Hart, Denver, 1972-73; law clk. Colo. Ct. Appeals, Denver, summer 1976; assoc. firm Shaw Spangler & Roth, Denver, 1976-77; mgr. acquisitions/lands Petro-Lewis Corp., Denver, 1977-85; mgr. strategic planning Westinghouse, Transp. Divsn., Denver, 1985-87; mng. dir. Benefit Resource Mgmt. Group (subs. Blue Cross We. Pa.), 1987-92; COO, v.p. D.T. Watson Rehab. Hosp., 1992-93; v.p. ambulatory care svcs., compliance officer Franciscan Med. Ctr., Dayton campus, Ohio, 1994-2000; exec. dir. Swedish Am. Ctr. for Complementary Medicine, Rockford, Ill., 2000—02; legal advisor Peninsula United Meth. Homes, Inc., Hockessin, Del., 2003—. Tchr. oil and gas law Colo. Paralegal Inst., 1978, 79; arbitrator Am. Arbitration Assn.; mediator Dayton Mediation Ctr. Mem. ABA, Del. Bar Assn., Inst. Noetic Scis., Am. Coll. Healthcare Execs. Home: 150 Mercer Mill Rd Landenberg PA 19350 Office: Peninsula United Meth Home 726 Loveville Rd Hockessin DE 19807 E-mail: bcroyle@earthlink.net.

CROZIER, PRUDENCE SLITOR, economist; b. Boston, Oct. 27, 1940; d. Richard Eaton and Louise (Bean) S.; m. William Marshall, June 20, 1964; children: Matthew Eaton, Abigail Parsons, Patience Wells. BA with honors, Wellesley Coll., 1962; MA in Econs., Yale U., 1963; PhD in Econs., Harvard U., 1971. Rsch. asst. Fed. Res. Bank, Boston, 1963-64; tchg. fellow, tutor Harvard U., Cambridge, Mass., 1966-69; instr. Wellesley Coll., Mass., 1969-70; sr. economist Data Resources Inc., Lexington, Mass., 1973-74; bd. dirs. Omega Fund, 1984-87, Mass. Ednl. Facilities Authority, 1985-93, Boston Pub. Libr. Found., 1994—, vice chmn., 1996—. Vis. com. Harvard Sch. Pub. Health, 1993—2000, Coll. des Conseillers French Libr. and Cultural Ctr., Boston, 1995—, trustee, 1996—2002. Contbr. articles to profl. jours. Trustee Newton Wellesley Hosp., Mass., 1978—90; overseer Ctr. Rsch. of Women, Wellesley, 1982—83, Mus. Fine Arts, Boston, 1999—; trustee Wellesley Coll., 1980—98, Nantucket Hist. Assn., 1997—2002, Nantucket Atheneum, 2001.

CRUDDEN, ADELE LOUISE, social work research educator; b. New Orleans, Sept. 25, 1957; d. Edwin Francis and Eunice Louise (Courtault) C.; m. Curtis Edward Alford; children: Abigail Louise Alford. BS, Miss. State U., Starkville, 1979; MEd, Miss. State U., 1980, PhD, 1997; MSW, La. State U., 1989. Lic. social worker, profl. counselor; cert. rehab. counselor, ins. rehab. specialist. Vocat. therapist Developmental Ctr., Decatur, Ala., 1981-82; supr. New Orleans Assn. Retarded Citizens, 1982-84; rehab. specialist Sullivan Rehab., New Orleans, 1984-90; social worker Nat. Med. Care, New Orleans, 1990-91; adminstr., dir. Vocat. Rehab. for Blind, Jackson, Miss., 1991-94; rsch. sci. Miss. State U., Starkville, 1994—, dir.

social work program. Counselor Children's Hosp., New Orleans, 1988, social work cons., 1989; social work cons. La. State U. Human Devel. Ctr., 1989. Active NOW, PTA, Coalition for Citizens with Disabilities, Miss., Parents for Pub. Schs., Starkville. Grantee Miss. Dept. Human Svcs., 1995-96, Nat. Inst. for Disability on Rehab. Rsch. Mem. NASW, Nat. Assn. [illegible] in Pvt. Sector, Assn. Edn. and Rehab. Blind and Visually Impaired. Office: Miss State U RRTC PO Box 6189 Mississippi State MS 39762-6189 Office Phone: 663-325-8859.

CRUDUP, PAMELA TRACY PARHAM, science educator, writer; m. Edward Wilson Crudup III (div. 1995); 1 child, Courtney Allison. Cert. cardiovasc. technologist, Shelby State Coll., 1996; BS in Biology, Crichton Coll., 2001; MS in Pub. Health, Walden U., 2004. Cardiovasc. technologist, cath lab. mgr. Meth. Hosp., Somierville, Tenn., 1995—96, radiology physician liaison Memphis, 1996—; author Memphis, 1986—; instr. sci. Memphis City Schs., 2001—. Instr. sci. Adult Program Memphis City Schs., 2001—; instr. anatomy/physiology Tenn. Sch. Massage, Memphis, 2001—. Author: The Hat Box, 2003, The Mist of Mineral Springs, 2004; editor: Morning Side of the Mountain, 2002, The Romance Writer, Memphis, 2002—. Mem.: NEA, Endometriosis Assn. (vol.), Assn. Pub. Health, Authors for Charity, Nat. Trust for Hist. Preservation. Republican. Baptist. Avocations: travel, antiques, tennis, walking, writing. Office: The Romance Writer PMB 348 6025 Stage Rd Ste 42 Bartlett TN 38134*

CRUIKSHANK, MARGARET LOUISE, humanities educator, writer; b. Duluth, Minn., Apr. 26, 1940; d. George Patrick and Louise Wimmer C. PhD, Loyola U., 1969; BA, Coll. St. Scholastica, Duluth, 1962; MA, San Francisco State U., 1992. Prof. City Coll., San Francisco, 1981-97; adj. prof. U. Maine, 1997—, U. So. Maine, 1999, 2003. Author: Thomas Babington Macaulay, 1978, The Gay and Lesbian Liberation Movement, 1992 (award Myers Ctr. for Human Rights, 1993); editor: The Lesbian Path, 1980, Lesbian Studies, 1982, New Lesbian Writing, 1984, Fierce with Reality (an anthology of literature about aging), 1995, Learning to be Old: gender, culture and aging, 2003. Affiliate scholar U. Calif., Berkeley, 1996-97, Stanford Ctr. for Rsch. on Women, 1981-88. Mem. Nat. Women's Studies Assn. Avocations: hiking, canoeing. Office Phone: 207-581-1228.

CRUMBLEY, ESTHER HELEN KENDRICK, retired real estate agent, retired secondary school educator, councilman; b. Okeechobee, Fla., Oct. 3, 1928; d. James A. and Corrine (Burney) Kendrick; m. Chandler Jackson, Oct. 24, 1949 (dec.); children: Pamela E., Chandler A., William J. BS in Math. Edn., Ga. So. Coll., 1966; M in Math., Jacksonville (Fla.) U., 1979. Cert. secondary edn. tchr., Ga. Secondary edn. tchr. Camden County Bd. Edn., St. Mary's, Ga., 1958-92, ret.; realtor Watson Realty, St. Mary's, 1985-98, ret., 1998. Dept. chairperson Camden H.S., St. Mary's, 1966-72. Reporter: for hometown newspaper. Councilwoman City of St. Mary's, 1979-86, mayor pro tem, 1981-86. Mem. Camden Ga. Assn. Educators (pres. 1976, sec.-treas. 1977-78, star tchr. 1972), PAGE (biog. com. rep. 1984-92, 1992 retired, named outstanding 8th dist. bldg. rep.), Camden Gen. Mcpl. Assn. (pres., sec.-treas. 1979-88), fin. and budget coms.), Math. Assn., Internat. Platform Assn. Internat. Dictionary Ctr., ABI. Republican. Baptist. Avocations: reading, art. Home: RR 3 Box 810 Folkston GA 31537-9729

CRUMP, CLAUDIA, geography educator; BS in Elem. Edn., Western Ky. State U., 1952; MS in Elem. Edn., Ind. U., 1957, EdD in Elem. Edn., 1952. Co-author: Teaching for Social Values in Social Studies, 1974, Indiana Map Studies, 1983, Indiana Yesterday and Today, 1985, Teaching History in the Elementary School, 1988, People in Time and Place: Indiana Hoosier Heritage, 1992. Home: 309 Whippoorwill Hts New Albany IN 47150-4255 Office: Ind U Southeast Divsn of Edn New Albany IN 47150 Office Phone: 812-948-8123. E-mail: ccrump700@cs.com.

CRUMP-CAINE, LYNN, food service executive; Mgmt. trainee McDonald's Corp., Oakbrook, Ill., 1975—77, various regional dept. head positions Norfolk, Nashville, S. Fla., 1977—85, head worldwide restaurant systems and U.S. restaurant systems, 1985—97, regional v.p. Atlanta region, 1997—2001, exec. v.p. worldwide ops. and systems, 2001—. Mem. adv. bd. Women Looking Ahead News Magazine; bd.dirs. Goodman Theater, Chgo. Recipient Outstanding Bus. and Profl. award, Dollars and Sense, 1991. Mem.: NAFE, McDonald's Black Employee Network. Office: McDonald's Corp McDonald's Plz Oak Brook IL 60523

CRUMPTON, EVELYN, psychologist, educator; b. Ashland, Ala., Dec. 23, 1924; d. Alpheus Leland and Bernice (Fordham) Crumpton. AB, Birmingham So. Coll., 1944; MA, UCLA, 1953, PhD in Psychology, 1955. Lic. psychologist, Calif.; diplomate Am. Bd. Profl. Psychology. Rsch. psychologist VA Hosp., Brentwood, L.A., 1955-77; asst. chief psychology svc., dir. clin. tng. VA Adminstrn. Med. Ctr. West Los Angeles, 1977-88; clin. prof. dept. psychology UCLA, assoc. rsch. psychologist dept. psychiatry, UCLA Sch. Med., 1957—; cons. chief of staff Brentwood div., VA Adminstrn. Med. Ctr. Contbr. numerous articles to profl. jours. Recipient Profl. Svc. award, Assn. Chief Psychologists VA, 1979. Fellow Soc. Personality Assessment; mem. APA, Western Psychol. Assn., Sigma Xi.

CRUVER, SUZANNE LEE, communications executive, writer; b. Indpls., Mar. 24, 1942; d. William Edward and Margaret Rosetta (McArtor) Ozzard; m. Donald Richard Cruver, June 9, 1963 (div. Feb. 1989); children: Donald Scott, Kimberly Sue, Brian Richard. BA in English, Rutgers U., 1964; postgrad., Rice U., 1990—. Asst. dir. pub. rels. dept. Upsala Coll., East Orange, N.J., 1964-65; asst. planner, pub. editor N.J. Divsn. State & Regional Planning, Trenton, 1967-68; realtor Vonnie Cobb Realtors, Houston, 1979-81; owner Sugar Land Comm., 1980-94; exec. v.p., mktg. mgr. Photoflight Aviation Corp., Sugar Land, Tex., 1982; exec. v.p., artist mgr. H. McMillan Orgn., Inc., Sugar Land, 1983-85; account exec. Mel Anderson Comm., Inc., Houston, 1986; exec. dir. Ft. Bend Arts Coun., Sugar Land, 1986-87; dir. resource devel., vol. svcs., pub. info. Richmond (Tex.) State Sch., Tex. Dept. Mental Health/Mental Retardation, 1987-93; dir. corp. and found. giving Meml. Found., Meml. Healthcare Sys., Houston, 1993-94; owner SLC Comms., Houston & Englewood, Fla., 1994-2000; mktg. coord., pub. info. officer Gulf Coast Workforce Bd. Houston-Galveston Area Coun., 2000—. Mem. adv. bd. Ft. Bend Regional Coun. on Alcoholism and Drug Abuse, Rosenburg, Tex., 1989—. Writer, editor: PATCH Handbook: A Parent to Parent Guide to Texas Children's Hospital, 1983, Ft. Bend mag., 1985-86; book editor, contbg. writer: Fort Bend County, Texas - A Pictorial History, 1996. Pres. Ft. Bend Arts Coun., Ft. Bend County, Tex., 1987-89; founding dir. PATCH, Tex. Children's Hosp., Houston, 1982; mem. adv. bd. Challenger Ctr. of Ft. Bend; committeeman Houston Livestock Show & Rodeo, 1996—; co-coord. 25th Anniversary of lunar landing celebration and internat. space expo, Houston, 1994; bd. dirs. United Way South Sarasota County. Mem. NAFE, Nat. Soc. Fundraising Execs., Women in Comm., Ft. Bend Profl. Women, Pub. Rels. Soc. Am., Houston World Trade Assn., Ft. Bend C. of C., Rosenberg/Rich C. of C., Leadership Tex. Alumni Assn., Exch. Club of Sugar Land, Ft. Bend Exch. Club (charter bd. mem.). Republican. Presbyterian. Avocations: travel, scuba diving, golf, dance, photography. E-mail: sue.cruver@theworksource.org.

CRUZ, PENELOPE, actress; b. Madrid, Apr. 28, 1974; d. Eduardo and Encarna Cruz. Studied classical ballet, Nat. Conservatory, Madrid. Actor: (films) El Laberinto griego, 1991; (TV films) Framed, 1992; (films) Belle époque, 1992, Jamón, jamón, 1992, La Ribelle, 1993, La Celestina, 1996, Más que amor, frenesí, 1996, Et Hjørne af paradis, 1997, Carne trémula, 1997, Abre los ojos, 1997, Don Juan, 1998, The Man with Rain in His Shoes, 1998, Talk of Angels, 1998, La Niña de tus ojos, 1998, The Hi-Lo Country, 1998, Todo sobre mi madre, 1999, Volavèrunt, 1999, Woman on Top, 2000, All the Pretty Horses, 2000, Blow, 2001, Captain Corelli's Mandolin, 2001, Sin noticias de Dios, 2001, Vanilla Sky, 2001, Waking Up in Reno, 2002, Masked and Anonymous, 2003, Fanfan la tulipe, 2003, Gothika, 2003. Address: William Morris Agy 151 E Camino Dr Beverly Hills CA 90212

CRUZ, ROBYN FLAUM, research scientist, clinician; b. Atlanta, July 13, 1954; d. Manning Herman and Jean Miller Flaum; m. Mario Cruz. BS, Vanderbilt U., 1975; MA, NYU, 1981; PhD, U. Ariz., 1995. Nat. cert. counselor. Rsch. specialist Nat. Ctr. for Neurogenic Comm. Disorders, U. Ariz., Tucson, 1994—99; dir. rsch. COPE Behavioral Svcs., Inc., Tucson, 1999—2002; dir. creative and expressive art therapy Western Psychiat. Inst. & Clinic, Pitts., 2002—. Co-Editor American Journal of Dance Therapy, American Dance Therapy Association, Columbia, MD, 1997—2001; adj. asst. prof. dept. ednl. psychology U. Ariz., 1997—2000; adj. faculty mem. grad. creative arts therapy program Pratt Inst. of Arts, N.Y.C., 2000—. Contbr. rsch. articles to profl. jours.; editor in chief: The Arts in Psychotherapy, 2002—. Mem.: APA, Am. Dance Therapy Assn. (cert., v.p. 2002—). Home: 5900 Jackson St Pittsburgh PA 15206 Office: Western Psychiat Inst & Clin Univ Pitts Med Ctr 3811 O'Hara St Pittsburgh PA 15213 E-mail: robyncruz@stargate.net., cruzrf@msx.upmc.edu.

CRUZ, ROSALINA SEDILLO, marriage and family therapist; b. Dumaguete City, The Philippines, Apr. 1, 1933; came to U.S., 1957; d. Dionisio Sedillo and Simplicia Raagas; m. Anatolio Benedicto Cruz Jr., Apr. 28, 1955; children: Raquel Regina, Anatolio Benedicto III, Anthony Bradley, Roselle Regina. BS in Edn., U. of the Philippines, Manila, 1955; MEd in Guidance Counseling, Trinity U., San Antonio, 1972; Specialist Degree Marriage/Family Therap, St. Mary's U., San Antonio, 1980. Cert. marriage and family therapist, Tex. Tchr. Roosevelt H.S., Manila, 1955-57, Holy Spirit Cath. Sch., San Antonio, 1968-70; counselor Holy Spirit Sch., San Antonio, 1972-75, part-time counselor, 1990—; pvt. practice marriage and family therapy San Antonio, 1980—. Adv. bd. Child Abuse Prevention Svcs., San Antonio, 1994—; chmn. family adv. bd. St. Mary's U., San Antonio, 1985-86. Named Vol. of Yr., Child Abuse Prevention Svcs., 1991. Mem. Am. Assn. Marriage and Family Therapy (clin.), Tex. Counseling Assn. (mem. lobbying-licensure com. 1980, ethics com. 1985—), San Antonio Marriage and Family Therapy (pres. 1985-86), South Tex. Assn. Marriage and Family Therapy, Lic. Profl. Counselors of Tex. (ethics com. 1995—). Roman Catholic. Avocations: tennis, reading, jogging, swimming, cooking. Home: 1118 Mount Eden Dr San Antonio TX 78213-2226 Office: 4402 Vance Jackson Rd San Antonio TX 78230-5336

CRUZ, TEOFILA PEREZ, nursing administrator; AS, U. Guam, 1970; BSN, St. Louis U., 1973; MS in Nursing Adminstrn., U. Hawaii, 1989. Founder 1st hemodialysis unit Guam Med. Hosp., Agana, Guam, 1974, hosp. nurse supr. II critical care units, 1978-85; with various hemodialysis units, 1974-77; emergency rm. dept. nurse III then headnurse Med. Ctr. Marianas, Guam, 1977; instr. Sch. Nursing U. Guam, 1978; nurse examiner adminstr. Dept. Pub. Health and Social Svcs., Guam, 1985-88, health profl. lic. adminstr., 1988-97, 98—; clin. svc. adminstr. Guam Meml. Hosp. Authority, 1997-98. —dminstr. Guam Bd. Nurse Examiners, Guam Bd. Med. Examiners, Guam Bd. Examiners for Pharmacy, Guam Bd. Examiners for Dentistry, Guam Bd. Examiners Optometry, Guam Bd. Allied Health Examiners, Commn. on Healing Arts of Guam, Bd. Cosmetology; mem. exam. com. computer adaptive test Nat. Coun. State Bds. Nursing, 1991-92, com. alt., 1993-98, mem. exam. com., 1998—; past mem. com. and chmn. Emergency Med. Svcs. Commn. Mem. Young Men's League of Guam Women's Aux., ROTC Parents Com., Sigma Theta Tau. Office: Guam Bd Nurse Examiners Dept Pub Health & Social Svcs 195 Asucena Ave Barrigada GU 96913-1241

CRUZ, WILHELMINA MANGAHAS, critical care physician, educator; b. Bulacan, Philippines, July 20, 1942; d. Rectorino Bernardo and Mercedes Correa (Mangahas) C.; m. Antonio I. Lee, May 28, 1977; children: Richard Anthony, Alexander Victor. AA, U. Santo Tomas, The Philippines, 1960, MD, 1965. Diplomate Am. Bd. Internal Medicine, Am. Bd. Nephrology (spl. qualifications in critical care medicine). Intern Meml. Hosp., Albany, N.Y., 1967-68; resident in internal medicine Coney Island Hosp., Bklyn., 1968-71; fellow in nephrology VA Hosp., Bronx, 1971-72, SUNY Downstate Med. Ctr., Bklyn., 1972-73; staff physician King's County Hosp. Ctr., Bklyn., 1973-76; coord. in medicine Kingsbrook Jewish Med. Ctr., Bklyn., 1976—. Assoc. med. dir. ICU Drs. Cmty. Hosp., Lanham, Md., 1977-99, med. dir. critical care svcs., 1999—; clin. asst. prof. SUNY Downstate Med. Ctr., 1977—. Mem. ACP, Med. and Chirurg. Soc. Md., Prince George's Med. Soc., Soc. Critical Care Medicine, Philippine Med. Assn. Washington. Roman Catholic. Office: 7700 Old Branch Ave Ste D205 Clinton MD 20735-1611

CRUZ, ZOE, investment company executive; m. Ernesto Cruz. With Morgan Stanley, 1982—, v.p., 1986—88, prin., fixed income, 1988—90, mng. dir., fixed income, 1990—93, co-chief, fgn. exch., 1993—2000, head of worldwide fixed income, fgn. exch. and commodities, 2000—. Office: Morgan Stanley 1585 Broadway New York NY 10036*

CRUZ-ROMO, GILDA, soprano; b. Guadalajara, Jalisco, Mexico; came to U.S., 1967; d. Feliciano and Maria del Rosario (Diaz) C.; m. Robert B. Romo, June 10, 1967. Grad., Coll. Nueva Galicia, Guadalajara, 1958; student, Nat. Conservatory of Music of Mexico, Mexico City, 1962-64. Tchr. voice U. Tex., Austin, 1990—. Assoc. prof., coach, voice tchr. U. Tex., Austin, 1990—. With, Nat. and Internat. Opera, Mexico City, 1962-67, toured, Australia, N.Z., S.Am., with, Dallas Civic Opera, 1966-68, N.Y.C. Opera, 1969-72, Lyric Opera Chgo., 1975, Met. Opera debut as Madama Butterfly, 1970, leading soprano, 1970—, appeared in U.S. and abroad including Covent Garden, La Scala, Vienna State Opera, Rome Opera, Paris Opera, Florence Opera, Torino Opera, Verona Opera, Portugal, Buenos Aires, others, concert appearances in U.S., Can., Mexico; U.S. rep. World-Wide Madama Butterfly Competition, Tokyo, 1970; La Scala rep. in: Aida, USSR, 1974; appeared on radio, TV; filmed and recorded: Aida, with Orange Festival, France, 1976; roles include Aida, Madama Butterfly, Suor Angelica, Tosca, Odabella in Attila; Manon Lescaut, Leonora in Il Trovatore; Norma; Maddelena in Andrea Chenier; Desdemona in Otello; Donna Anna in Don Giovanni; Santuzza in Cavalleria Rusticana; (title role) La Gioconda; Adriana Lecouvreur; Luisa Miller; Elisabetta in Don Carlo; Margherite in Faust; Venus in Tannhauser; Giorgetta in Il Tabarro; also roles in Macbeth, Turnadot, Norma, Medea; recipient Gold medal in Fine Arts, Mexico. Named Winner Met. Opera Nat. Auditions, 1970, Best Singer, 1976—77, honoree, Opera Guild of San Antonio, 2003; recipient Critics award, Union Mexicana de Cronistas de Teatro y Musica, 1973, Minerva al Arte award, Mexico, 1991, Silver Bird award, Govt. of Jalisco, Mexico, 1998, season Cronistas de Santiago de Chile, 1976, Baccarat 2001 award, The Licia Albanese-Puccini Found., 2001, Lifetime Achievement award, Nat. Opera Assn., 2003, Pedro Sarquis Messeure Found., 2004.

CRYER, GRETCHEN, playwright, lyricist, actress; b. Indpls., Oct. 17, 1935; d. Earl William and Louise Gerladine (Niven) Kiger; m. Donald David Cryer, June 7, 1958 (div. June 1970); children: Robin, Jon, Shelby. BA, DePauw U., 1957; MAT, Harvard U., 1960; ArtsD (hon.), Ea. Mich. U., 1986. Cert. tchr. Writer and lyricist, N.Y.C., 1967—; founder, owner The Extended Family, N.Y.C., 1991—. Founder, pres. The Extended Family. Writer, lyricist (with Nancy Ford) Off-Broadway and Broadway musicals Now Is the Time for All the Good Men, 1967, The Last Sweet Days of Isaac, 1970 (Obie award 1970), Shelter, 1973, Booth Is Back in Town, 1981, I'm Getting My Act Together and Taking it on the Road, 1978, Hang on to the Good Times, 1984, The American Girls Revue, 1998; (with Doug Dyer and Peter Link) The Wedding of Iphigenia and Iphigenia in Concert, 1971; theater appearances in Little Me, 1962, 110 In The Shade, 1963, Now is the Time For All Good Men, 1967, I'm Getting My Act Together and Taking it on the Road, 1978, A Circle of Sounds, 1978, Blue Plate Special, 1983, To Whom It May Concern, 1985-86, Alterations, 1986, The Fabulous Party, 1996, The American Clock [illegible], 1999; film appearances include Hiding Out, 1987; author, singer: (albums) Cryer and Ford, 1976, You Know My Music, 1977; author: (musical) Booth is Back in Town, 1981, Eleanor, 1984; playwright: The House That Goes On Forever, 1988. Recipient Ind. Arts award Gov. of Ind., 1982. Mem. Dramatists Guild (council), Actors Equity Assn., Screen Actors Guild. Democrat. Avocation: playing the piano. Home and Office: 885 W End Ave Apt 1A New York NY 10025-3512

CUBA, NAN BRINDLEY, small business owner, writer; b. Temple, Tex., Aug. 25, 1947; d. Hanes Hanby and Julia Martha (Barton) Brindley; m. Donald Lynn Cuba, July 10, 1967; children: Donald Lynn, Jr., Julia Nan. AA, Sullins Coll., Bristol, Va., 1965-67; BS, U. Tex., 1970; MFA, Warren Wilson Coll., 1989. Cert. tchr., Tex. Elem. sch. tchr. pub. and parochial schs., Dallas, San Antonio, 1970-81; freelance mag. writer San Antonio, 1982-87; fiction writer and poet, 1986—; host TV interview show Rogers Cablevision, San Antonio, 1984-88; writer in the schs. Tex. Commn. on Arts, San Antonio, 1986-91; faculty English dept. U. Tex, San Antonio, 1989-92; vis. writer Grad. dept. St. Mary's U., San Antonio, Spring 1992; founder readers' theater and alternative sch. Gemini Ink, San Antonio, 1992—. Co-creator and cons. Writers' Inst. at Our Lady of the Lake U., San Antonio, 1986-2003; vis. writer grad. dept., summer 1996; mem. Lit. Peer Rev. Panel, Tex. Commn. on the Arts, Austin, 1990-92, 2004—; adv. bd. Guadalupe Cultural Ctr. Lit., San Antonio, 1990-92; cons. Arts Teach Program San Antonio Arts and Cultural Affairs Dept., 1991; faculty advisor literary mag. U. Tex. at San Antonio, 1991-92. Author, poet: contbr. anthologies and literary revs., 1992— including poetry in Descant, Inheritance of Light, Poets of the Lake, Bloomsbury Rev. and others; works of fiction in Quar. West, Columbia, Crosscurrents, books revs. in Harvard Rev. and San Antonio Express-News; contbr. popular articles to regional magazines including San Antonio Mag., San Antonio Monthly, D. Magazine, Third Coast; cons. for Life, 1984; co-editor: (book) Writers at the Lake, 1997. Voting place official, Democrat, San Antonio, 1980's. Recipient 1st place fiction award San Antonio Writer's Guild, 1983, 1st place investigative article San Antonio chpt. Women in Comm., Inc., 1986; alt. Dobie Paisano fellowshp U. Tex. and Tex. Inst. Letters, 1989, 1st runner up Dobie Paisano, U. Tex., and Tex. Inst. Letters, 1991; honoree at Pen Party Friends of San Antonio Pub. Libr., 1984; Imagineer award Mind Sci. Found., 2000; Headliner in Edn. award Women in Comm., Inc., 2002. Episcopalian. Avocations: theater, opera, antiquing, roaming Tex. hill country. Office Phone: 210-826-7348. Personal E-mail: nacuba@aol.com.

CUBBERLEY, GAYLE SUSAN, band director; b. Trenton, N.J., Aug. 18, 1952; d. Carlton Burton Cubberley and Mary Elizabeth Tantum. BMus in Edn., U. Miami, 1974, MusM in Edn., 1975. Cert. tchr. Fla. Music tchr. Homestead (Fla.) Jr. H.S., Homestead, 1976—78, Campbell Jr. H.S., Florida City, 1978—79; band dir. Nautilus Jr. H.S., Miami Beach, Fla., 1979—80, West Miami Mid. Sch., Miami, 1980—2003, Lamar Louise Curry Mid. Sch., 2003—. Solo 1st chair clarinetist Greater Miami Symphonic Band, 1976—; clarinetist Klezmer Band, 2002—. Mem.: Dade County Music Educators Assn., Fla. Bandmasters Assn., Music Educators Nat. Conf. Avocations: tennis, sailing, scuba diving, skiing. Home: 11281 SW 88th St K-216 Miami FL 33176-1158 Office: Lamar Louise Curry Mid Sch 15750 SW 47th St Miami FL 33185

CUBBERLY, MARGARET THERESE, columnist, freelance writer; b. Troy, N.Y., Oct. 31, 1929; d. Joseph Francis and Alma Louise (Bechard) Cairns; m. Norman Graham Cubberly, Jan. 14, 1967; 1 child, Freya Morgan Cubberly. BA, U. R.I., 1951; MSLS, Cath. U., 1959. Head cataloguer Georgetown U., Washington, 1958-61; asst. libr. Calif. Acad. Scis., San Francisco, 1961-66; serials cataloguer U. Calif., Davis, 1966; head of serials Brown U., Providence, 1967-68; asst. head circulation U. Miami, Fla., 1969-72; head of circulation Fla. Internat. U., Miami, 1969-72; reporter, columnist York Town Crier, Yorktown, Va., 1978—; children's libr. Poquoson (Va.) Pub. Libr., 1990-92. Columnist (opinion column) York Town Crier (cert. merit Va. Press Assn. 1984), 1980—. Recipient Cert. of Merit Lifestyle, Va. Press Assn., 1982, Feature Story, 1983, Lifestyle writing 1989, I.D. Wilson award (reporting) Va. Vet. Medicine Assn., 1989. Mem. Friends of Tuva, Hampton Roads Sci. Fiction Assn. (co-founder). Democrat. Avocations: book collecting, victoriana, dance, pottery, tai chi. Home: 115 Marine Cir Grafton VA 23692-3420

CUBIN, BARBARA LYNN, congresswoman; b. Salinas, Calif., Nov. 30, 1946; d. Russell G. and Barbara Lee (Howard) Sage; m. Frederick William Cubin, Aug. 1; children: William Russell, Frederick William III. BS in Chemistry, Creighton U., 1969. Chemist Wyo. Machinery Co., Casper, Wyo., 1973-75; social worker State of Wyo.; office mgr. Casper, Wyo.; mem. Wyo. Ho. Reps., 1987-92, Wyo. Senate, 1993-94; pres. Spectrum Promotions and Mgmt., Casper, 1993-94; at-large repr. U.S. Ho. Reps. from Wyo., Washington, 1995—; mem. resources com., energy and commerce com. Mem. steering com. Exptl. Program to Stimulate Competitive Rsch. (EPSCOR); mem. Coun. of State Govts.; active Gov.'s Com. on Preventive Medicine, 1992; vice chmn. Cleer Bd. Energy Coun., Irving, Tex., 1993—; chmn. Wyo. Senate Rep. Conf., Casper, 1993—; mem. Wyo. Rep. Party Exec. Com., 1993; pres. Southridge Elem. Sch. PTO, Casper, Wyo. Toll fellow Coun. State Govts., 1990, Wyo. Legislator of Yr. award for energy and environ. issues Edison Electric Inst., 1994. Mem. Am. Legis. Exch. Coun., Rep. Women. Republican. Avocations: duplicate bridge, golfing, singing, reading, hunting. Office: US Ho Reps 1114 Longworth Ho Office Bldg Washington DC 20515-5001*

CUCCINELLO, DARLENE ANN, retirement home administrator, physical education educator; b. Flushing, N.Y., July 23, 1938; d. Anthony Francis and Clara Catherine Cuccinello. BS, NYU, 1960. Tchr. phys. edn. Oceanside (NY) H.S., 1960—64, Robinson H.S., Tampa, Fla., 1964—65, Notre Dame Acad., St. Petersburg, 1965—66; missionary Maryknoll Religious Order, Chile, 1966—84; coord. human rights Intercmty. Ctr., Manhattan, NY, 1980—91; recreational therapist College Point, 1991—96; activity dir. Rocky Creek Retirement Village, Tampa, 1996—2001; ret. Mem.: Exec. Women's Golf Assn. (pres. 2001—02). Democrat. Roman Catholic.

CUCCO, JUDITH ELENE, international marketing professional; b. Summit, N.J., Aug. 09; d. Louis John and Patricia T. (Procaccini) C. BS in Internat. Rels. and Spanish, Am. U., 1973; MBA, U. Md., 1983. Prof. English Universidad Nacional Autonoma de Mex., Mexico City, 1971-72; tchr. Spanish, ESL Montgomery (Md.) County Pub. Schs., 1973-81; acct. exec., industry cons. AT&T Comms., Parsippany, N.J., 1983-87; mgr. internat. mktg. support ctr. AT&T, Morristown, N.J., 1987-89, dir. market devel. internat. ops. divsn. Caracas, Venezuela, 1989-91, mgr. global product line Sch. Bus. Somerset, N.J., 1991-93, regional mgr. market mgmt. Latin Am., Network Wireless Systems Bus. Unit Whippany, N.J., 1994-95; bus. devel. dir. Asia/Pacific and Caribbean/L.Am. AT&T Global Bus. Multimedia Svcs., 1995-96; Ams. regional mgr. AT&T Internat. Product Mgmt., 1996-97; market analysis and bus. planning AT&T Internat. Traffic Mgmt., Morristown, N.J., 1997-2000; dir. bandwidth ops. Concert, Global Svcs. Direct, Morristown, 2000—02; data channel mgmt. AT&T Wholesale, Morristown, 2002; special products mgmt. AT&T, 2003—. Sponsor Child Reach, Warwick, R.I., 1984—, Friends of India, 1995—; mem. Small Faith Cmty., Bridgewater, 1992-98; vol. Interfaith Hospitality Network, Bridgewater, 1993—; mem. Womyn Included, 1994-2000. Mem. U. Md. Alumni Assn., Am. U. Alumni Assn., Pandora's Cir. Avocations: scuba diving, sailing, reading, traveling. Home: 308 Greenfield Rd Bridgewater NJ 08807-3714 Office: AT&T Rm N473 412 Mount Kemble Ave Morristown NJ 07960-6617

CUDAK, GAIL LINDA, lawyer; b. Bellville, Ill., July 13, 1952; d. Robert Joseph and Margaret Lucille C.; m. Thomas Edward Young, Sept. 15, 1979. BA, Kenyon Coll., 1974; JD, Case Western Res. U., 1977, MBA, 1991. Bar: Ohio 1977, U.S. Dist. Ct. (no. dist.) Ohio 1977, U.S. Ct. Appeals (6th cir.) 1977, U.S. Ct. Appeals (fed. cir.) 1989. Assoc. Fuerst, Leidner, Dougherty & Kasdan, Cleve., 1977-79; staff atty. The B.F. Goodrich Co., Akron, Ohio, 1979-84, sr. corp. counsel Independence, Ohio, 1985-89, divsn. counsel Brecksville, Ohio, 1990-98, group counsel, 1998-99; sr. attorney Eaton Corp., Cleve., 1999—. Trustee Great Lakes Theater Festival, 1996—, mem. exec. com.; fundraiser Ohio Found. Ind. Colls., 1993—. Mem.: ABA, Cleve. Internat. Lawyers Group, Cleve. Bar Assn. (chair corp. sect.), Ohio State Bar Assn. Home: 12520 Edgewater Dr Apt 1405 Lakewood OH 44107-1639 Office: Eaton Corp 1111 Superior Ave E Cleveland OH 44114-2507

CUDDIHY, JUNE TUCK, pediatrics nurse; b. Buffalo, June 15, 1936; d. John R. Sr. and Monica A. (Donahue) Tuck; m. Robert V. Cuddihy, Aug. 24, 1957; children: Robert V., Timothy, Kathleen. BSN, D'Youville Coll., Buffalo, 1957; MA, Seton Hall U., 1972, MSN, 1979. Cert. primary care nurse practitioner. Pub. health nurse Monroe County, Rochester, N.Y.; health coord. Early Childhood Learning Ctrs. N.J., Morristown; asst. prof. Seton Hall U., South Orange, N.J., 1977-81, William Paterson Coll., Wayne, N.J., 1981-94; clin. assoc. Coll. Nursing Ohio State U., 1994-97; cons. Berkeley BioMedical Group, Inc., 1991—; mem. faculty Western Mich. U., Kalamazoo, 1997—. Contbr. articles to profl. jours. Named Outstanding Grad. Student, Seton Hall U., 1979. Mem. ANA (vice chmn. bd. examiners for cmty. health nursing practice, chmn. sch. nurse practice subcom.), N.J. State Nurses Assn., Nat. Child Abuse Assn., Nat. Burn Victim Found., Pub. Health Assn., Sigma Theta Tau. Home: 20 Indian Run Watchung NJ 07069-5473 Office: Ohio State U Coll Nursing Dept Cmty Parent Child Psyc 1585 Neil Ave Columbus OH 43210-1216

CUEBAS IRIZARRY, ANA E. director; b. Mayaguez, P.R., Apr. 29, 1944; d. Francisco Cuebas and Isidora Irizarry. BA in Econ., Coll. Agr. & Mechanics Arts, Mayaguez, 1965; MLA, Pratt Inst., 1967; MPA, U. P.R., Rio Piedras, 1972; postgrad., U. P.R., San Germán, 2001—. Head reference collection Gen. Libr. U. P.R., Mayaguez, 1972—75, dir. pub. svcs., 1975—78, dir. documentation ctr. and cultural promotion, 1978—79, head purotorrican collector, 1978—80, head serials dept., 1980—86, project dir. title III Auguadilla, 1986—88, dir. continuing edn. and profl. studies, 1988—. Part-time prof. U. P.R., Mayaguez, 1972—82, mem. libr. personal com., Aguadilla, 1988—, coord. students deanship, 1990—, pres. continuing edn. dirs. com., Rio Piedras, PR, 1994—97; mem. consultive bd. Coun. Superior Edn., Rio Piedras, 1995; trustee Consorcio del Noroeste. Author: (book) Diccionario de siglas en uso en PR, 1979, En busca de una bibligrafía para Mayagüez, 1982; contbr. articles to profl. jours. Mem. Cultural: Eugenio María de Hostos, Mayaguez, 1985—94. Recipient Spl. recognition, Altrusa Internat. Mayaguez, 1996—98, plaque of Recognition, Sindrome Down Assn., 2002, Altrusa Internat. Ing. 14th Dist., 1992—94, cert. of Recognition, Coun. Superior Edn. P.R., 2002; grantee, 2002, P.R. Humanities Endowment, 1998, Consejo de Desarrollo Ocupacional y Recursos Humanos, 1998, Works Rights Adminstrn., 2000, Dept. Edn., Rincón Sch. Dist., 2002, Dept. Edn., P.R., 2002, San Sebastián Sch. Dist., P.R., 2002. Mem.: PR ASCD, ASCD, Puertorrican Assn. Continuing Edn., Asociación Puertorriqueña Educación Continua, Phi Delta Kappa. Avocations: cooking, reading, Three Kings collector. Home: 626 Yaurel ST Mayaguez PR 00682-6233 Office: U PR Bell St Aguadilla PR 00604-0160 Personal E-mail: a_cuebas@hotmail.com.

CULAN, KRISTIN LYNN, museum staff member; b. Pitts., Dec. 1, 1965; d. Michael George Culan, Verna Marie Culan. BS, Indiana U. Pa., 1989. Cert.: (paralegal); lic. cosmetologist 1998. Mgr. Body Shop, Pitts., 1997—2000; buyer, mgr. Historical Soc. Western Pa., Pitts., 2000—. Exhibited in group shows at Pitts. Art/Fashion, 1996. Active Humane Soc., World Wildlife Fund. Mem.: Museum Store Assn. Democrat. Avocations: travel, art, fashion, bicycling. Office: Historical Soc Western Pa 1212 Smallman St Pittsburgh PA 15222 Office Phone: 412.454.6374. Office Fax: 412.454.6026. Business E-Mail: klculan@hswp.org.

CULBERTSON, JANET LYNN, artist; b. Greensburg, Pa., Mar. 15, 1932; d. Joseph F. and Helen C. (Moore) Culbertson; m. Douglas I. Kaften, Sept. 30, 1964. BFA, Carnegie Inst. Tech., 1953; MA, NYU, 1963. Instr. art Pace Coll., N.Y.C., 1964-68, Pratt Art Inst., Bklyn., 1973; assoc. prof. Southampton Coll., 1976; drawing instr. Parrish Art Mus., 1979. Exhibited one-woman shows 20th Century West Gallery, N.Y.C., 1967, Molly Barnes Gallery, L.A., 1970, Midtown Gallery, Atlanta, 1971, Lerner-Misrachi Gallery, N.Y.C., 1971, Lerner-Heller Gallery, N.Y.C., 1973, 75, 77, Tower Gallery, Southampton, N.Y., 1976, Benson Gallery, Bridgehampton, N.Y., 1978, 81, 89, Interart Gallery, N.Y.C., 1979, Harriman Coll., N.Y., 1980, Nardin Gallery, N.Y.C., 1981, Aronson Gallery, Atlanta, 1982, Harrisburg State Mus. Pa., 1988, Women Artists Series Rutgers U., N.J., 1988, Carnegie Mellon U., Pitts., 1991, Acme Art Co., Columbus, Ohio, 1992, Islip (N.Y.) Mus., 1992, Suffolk Coll., Riverhead, N.Y., 1996, Stone Quarry Art Park, Cazenovia, N.Y., 1996, Wave Hill, Bronx, N.Y., 1997, Atelier A/E Gallery, N.Y.C., 1997, U. Alaska, Anchorage, 1997, Nat. Acad. Scis., Washington, 1998, Hoyt Mus., New Castle, Pa., 1998, U. Nebr., Omaha, 2002, Huntington Arts Coun. Gallery, N.Y., 2002-03, Cambridge Multicultural Arts Ctr., 2003, Nat. Mus. of Women in the Arts, Washington, 2004, Nassau County Mus., Hewlett-Woodmere Libr. Gallery, 2004; two-women shows Women's Art Ctr., San Francisco, 1975; four-women show Heckscher Mus., Huntington, N.Y., 1980; group exhbns. include Carnegie Mus., Pitts., 1953, ann. drawing Bucknell U., 1966-68, Palos Verdes (Calif.) Mus., 1970, 16th ann. all Calif. purchase L.A. Art Assn., 1969-70, nat. drawing ann. San Francisco Mus., 1970, Princeton Gallery Fine Arts, 1972, drawing show Fleisher Meml., Phila., 1974, Am. Acad. Arts and Letters, N.Y.C., 1975, Kingpitcher Gallery, Pitts, 1976, West Broadway Gallery, N.Y.C., 1976, Bronx Mus., 1976, Guild Hall, East Hampton, N.Y., 1976, 79, 82, 89, (invitational) 94 (Abstract award 1979, Mixed Media award 1992), Orgn. Ind. Artists, N.Y.C., 1978, Parrish Mus., Southampton, N.Y. Meml. Art Gallery, Rochester N.Y., 1979, Western Carolina U., Cullowhee, Phoenix Mus., Tucson Mus., 1980, The Arsenal, N.Y.C., 1981, 50 nat. women artists Edison Coll. Art Gallery, Ft. Myers, Fla., 1982, Norton Art Gallery, W. Palm Beach, Fla., 1985-86, Easthampton (N.Y.) Ctr. Contemporary Arts, 1988, Newport (R.I.) Art Mus., 1988, 91, Trabia Macafee Gallery, N.Y.C., 1988, Vered Gallery, Easthampton, 1989, 90, 92, Hillwood Mus., Brookville, N.Y., 1990, Islip Art Mus., N.Y., 1990, Ucross Wyo. (invitational), 1990, Women's Caucus for Art, Dallas, 1990, Wash., 1991, Benton Gallery, Southampton, N.Y., 1991, 92, 93, Ark. Arts Ctr. (invitational), Little Rock, 1991, Arlene Bujese Gallery, East Hampton, N.Y., 1994, Hillwood Art Mus., L.I. U., Brookville, N.Y., 1994, Hamilton Coll., Clinton, N.Y., 1995, Staller Mus., SUNY, Stony Brook, 1995, N.J. Ctr. Visual Arts, 2000, Censorship, Woman Made Gallery, Chgo., 2002, others; Babcock Gallery traveling exhibit, 1993-94, Art and the Law traveling exhbn., 1995-97, Anita Shapolsky Gallery, N.Y.C., 1995, Gerald Peters Gallery, 1996-97, ("Women Realists") Ringling Sch. Art and Design, Sarasota Fla., Nabi Gallery, Sag Harbor, 1997, Baruch Coll., N.Y.C., Telfair Mus. Art, Savannah, Ga., Seton Hall U., South Orange, N.J., U. Wyo., Laramie, C.W. Post U., N.Y., Staller Art Mus., SUNY, Stony Brook, Benson Gallery, 2001, Bridgehampton, N.Y., 1999, Parrish Art Mus., Southampton, N.Y., 2000, N.J. Ctr. Visual Arts, Summit, 2000, Toxic Landscapes, Puffin Found. traveling exhib., Morning, Noon and Night, The Long Island Mus. of Stony Brook, N.Y., Earth 2002, U. Miami Coral Gables, Denise Bibro Fine Art, N.Y.C., 2002, Soho Photo, N.Y.C., 2002, Savannah Coll. Art and Design, Ga., 2002, Long Beach Found. for Arts, NJ, 2002, others; contbr. collage to Attica Book, 1972; contbr. articles to profl. jours., prodr. and contbr. Heresies #13 mag. Creative Artists Pub. Svc. grantee, 1979. Recipient Shirk Meml. award for oil painting Nat. Assn. Women Artists, Inc., 1993, first place award Notorious L.I. exhibit Hillwood Art Mus., Brookville, N.Y., 1994, Purchase award Hoyt Art Inst., 1995, Purchase award Nassau County Mus. Art, 1997, Print Ctr. Excellence award, Phila., 2001; fellow Ossabaw Found., 1981, Dorland, 1983, Ucross Found., 1989, 99, Blue Mt. Found., 1991, 94, 96, 2000, 02, VCCA Ctr. Found., Ragdale Found., 1984, 2001; Ludwig Vogelstein grantee, 2004, Puffin grantee, 2004. Home: PO Box 455 Shelter Island Heights NY 11965

CULBERTSON, LESLIE S. computer company executive; Bachelor's, Lewis and Clark U., 1971. Cost mgr. British Petroleum/Standard Oil Ohio; acctg. mgr., controller Intel, Santa Clara, Calif., 1979—98, dir. corp. fin., 1997—, v.p., co-dir. materials orgn., 1998—2000, v.p., gen. mgr. sys. mfg., 2000—. Office: Intel 2200 Mission Coll Blvd Santa Clara CA 95052

CULLEENEY, MAUREEN ANN, information technology executive, educator; d. Robert P. and Marlene A. Culleeney. PhD, Loyola U. Chgo., 1996; EdM, U. Ill., 1992; MBA, DePaul U., 1983; BSW, U. Ill., 1976. Registered Social Worker State of Ill., 1982. Med. social worker St. Joseph Hosp., Elgin, Ill., 1977—81; co-founder and prin. Bus. Computer Edn., Inc., Chgo., 1981—84; regional mgr., tng. & product support ICC, Schaumburg, 1984—86; corp. trainer Ashton-Tate, Chgo., 1986—87; computer coord. Village of Schaumburg, Schaumburg, Ill., 1987—89; assoc. prof. Lewis U., Romeoville, Ill., 1989—. Author: (textbook published by prentice-hall, inc) WordStar Simplified: Mastering the Essentials on the IBM PC, WordStar Simplified: Mastering the Essentials; contbr. textbook published by prentice-hall Lotus 123: A Business Guide to Productivity; author: (textbook - french translation version) Utiliser WordStar.

CULLEN, MARY LYNNE, artist; b. Camden, N.J., Nov. 2, 1962; d. Philip Anthony and Elizabeth (Townsend) Chiusano; m. James Francis Cullen; children: Lynne Marie, Taylor Lynne, Christyn Maureen. Student, Santa Reparata Arts Studio, Florence, Italy, 1990; Cert., Pa. Acad. Fine Arts, 1992; BFA magna cum laude, U. Pa., 1993; MFA, Pa. Acad. Fine Arts, 1995. Artistic cons., adminstr. Chiusano, Inc., Marlton, N.J., 1985-93; shop asst. graphics dept. Pa. Acad. Fine Arts, Phila., 1991-96; owner, ptnr. Cullen and Howard Decorative Interior Finishes, Marlton, N.J., 1995-98. Residency, drawing instr. Inst. for Arts and Humanities Edn./Summer Arts Inst., Rider U., Lawrenceville, N.J., 1995; adj. prof. printmaking Rowan U., Glassboro, N.J., 1997-99. Exhibited in group shows at the Meyerson Gallery U. of Pa., Phila., 1998, Westby Hall Art Gallery, Rowan U., Glassboro, N.J., 1998, Maitland (Fla.) Art Ctr., 1995, West Chester (Pa.) U., 1995, Artist House Gallery, Phila., 1994, 96, 2001, Marketplace Design Ctr., Phila., 1993, Episcopal Acad., Merion, Pa., 1993, William Penn Charter Upper Sch., Phila., 1992, Art Ctr. Gallery, Westtown, Pa., 1992, The Plastic Club, Phila., 1993, The Painted Bride, Phila., 1995, Lincoln Gallery, Historic Yellow Springs, Pa., 1998, Lincoln Gallery, Historic Yellow Springs, Pa., 1998, Pa. Acad. Fine Arts, Phila., Revsin Gallery, 2000. Recipient Edna Pennypacker Stauffer Meml. prize, 1991, spl. notice Traditional Media Print prize, 1990, John R. Conner Meml. prize in printmaking, 1991, Morris Blackburn Print prize Fellow Pa. Acad. Fine Arts (Trust purchase award); mem. Phila. Print Club (prize 1990), Plastic Club Phila. (award 1992). Avocations: hiking, running, water skiing, gardening, reading. Home and Office: 305 Blueberry Ct Marlton NJ 08053-1015 E-mail: thecullens@netzero.com.

CULLEN, VALERIE ADELIA, secondary school educator; b. Northampton, Mass., May 28, 1948; d. Stanley Walter and Wanda Mary (Rup) Helstowski; m. Lawrence Joseph Cullen, June 26, 1982; 1 child, Shanna Valcric. BA, Westfield (Mass.) State Coll., 1970; MALS, SUNY, Stony Brook, 1975. Cert. secondary math. tchr., N.Y., Mass. Tchr. math. Brentwood (N.Y.) Pub. Schs., 1970-71, Center Moriches (N.Y.) Jr.-Sr. High Sch., 1971-88, BOCES I, Alternative High Sch. and Adolescent Pregnancy Program, Riverhead, N.Y., 1988-90, Ctr. Moriches (N.Y.) Jr.-Sr. High Sch., 1990—2002. Mem. Nat. Com. to Preserve Social Security and Medicare. Mem.: N.Y. State Ret. Tchrs., N.Y. Math. Tchrs. Assn., N.Y. State United Tchrs., Nat. Coun. Tchrs. Math., Smithsonian Assocs. Home: 4 Keswick Dr East Islip NY 11730-2808

CULLEN-RIVERA, AMY JANENE, management consultant; married. BS in Human Resource Mgmt. and Mgmt. Info. Systems, Oakland U., Rochester Hills, Mich., 1986; MA in Ednl. Psychology, U. Minn., 1991. Cert. profl. knowledge mgr. Knowledge Mgmt. Consortium Internat. Analyst programmer Cargill, Inc., Wayzata, Minn., 1986—87, systems analyst, 1987—91, human resources recruiter, 1991—92, human resources generalist, 1992—95, orgn. effectiveness cons., 1995—98, sr. orgn. effectiveness cons., 1998—. Recipient Excellence award, Human Resource Profls. of Minn., 1995. Mem.: SHRM, KM Pro, OD Network. Personal E-mail: amycullenrivera@earthlink.net.

CULLINAN, BERNICE E(LLINGER), education educator; b. Hamilton, Ohio, Oct. 12, 1926; d. Lee Alexander and Hazel (Berry) Dees; m. George W. Ellinger, June 5, 1948 (div. 1966); children: Susan Jane, James Webb; m. Paul Anthony Cullinan, June 9, 1967 (div. 1994); m. Kenneth Seeman Giniger, Apr. 13, 2002.. BS, Ohio State U., 1948, MA, 1951, PhD, 1964. Cert. elem. educator, Ohio, N.Y. Tchr. Maple Pk. Elem. Sch., Middletown, Ohio, 1944-46, Trotwood (Ohio) Elem. Sch., 1946-47, Columbus (Ohio) Pub. Schs., 1948-50, Upper Arlington (Ohio) Pub. Schs., 1950-52; instr. Ohio State U., Columbus, 1959-64, asst. prof., 1964-67, Ohio State U./Charlotte Huck prof. children's lit., 1997; assoc. prof. NYU, N.Y.C., 1967-72, prof. reading, 1972-97, prof. emeritus, 1998—; editor-in-chief Wordsong Books, Honesdale, Pa., 1990—. Adv. bd. The Reading Rainbow, 1979—, WGBH-TV, 1989—; chair selection com. Ezra Jack Keats New Writer award, 1984-2000; exec. sec. English Standards Project, 1993-94. Author (Lee Galda): Lit. and the Child, 1989, 5th edit., 2002; author: Children's Lit. in the Classroom: Weaving Charlotte's Web, 1989, 2nd edit., 1994, Read to Me: Raising Kids Who Love to Read, 1992, 2nd edit., 2000, Let's Read About: Finding Books They'll Love to Read, 1993; author: (with Brod Bagert) Helping Your Child Learn to Read, 1993; author: (with Dorothy Strickland and Lee Galda) Lang. Arts: Learning and Tchg., 2003; author: (with L. Galda and D. Strickland) Lang., Literacy and the Child, 1993; author:, 2002; author: (with Marilyn Scala and Virginia Schroder) Three Voices: Invitation to Poetry Across the Curriculum, 1995; author: 75 Authors and Illustrators Everyone Should Know, 1994; author: (with David Harrison) Poetry Lessons That Dazzle and Delight, 1999; editor: Children's Lit. in the Reading Program, 1987, Invitation to Read: More Children's Lit. in the Reading Program, 1992, Black Dialects and Reading, 1974, Fact and Fiction: Lit. Across the Curriculum, 1993, Children's Voices, 1993, Pen in Hand, 1993, A Jar of Tiny Stars, 1996; editor: (with Diane Person) The Continuum Ency. of Children's Lit., 2003; mem. editl. bd. The New Adv., 1987—99, mem. adv. bd. Ranger Rick Mag., 1992—; contbr. articles; author, editor: Books I Read When I Was Young, 1980, Lit. and Young Children, 1977, Children's Lit. in the Classroom: Extending Charlotte's Web, 1993. Editorial bd. Nat. Coun. Tchrs. English, Champaign, Ill., 1973-76; selection com. Caldecott Award Am. Libr. Assn., Chgo., 1982-83; trustee Highlights for Children Found., 1993—. Named Outstanding Educator in Lang. Arts, Nat. Coun. Tchrs. English, 2003; named to Ohio State U. Coll. Edn. Hall of Fame, 1995; recipient Ind. U. Citation for outstanding contbn. to literacy, 1995. Mem.: Reading Hall of Fame (pres. 1998—99, inducted 1989), Internat. Reading Found. (trustee 1984—91, Jeremiah Ludington award 1992), Internat. Reading Assn. (bd. dirs. 1979—84, chair Tchrs. Choices 1988—91, pres. 1984—85, Arbuthnot award for outstanding tchr. children's lit. 1989). Avocations: tennis, reading for pleasure, poetry. Home: 1045 Park Ave Apt 6A New York NY 10028 Office: 3 Tudor Ln Sands Point NY 11050-1104 E-mail: BerniceCullinan@Worldnet.att.net.

CULLINGFORD, HATICE SADAN, chemical engineer; b. Konya, Turkey, June 10, 1945; d. Ahmet and Emine Harmanci. Student, Mid. East Tech. U., 1962-66; BS in Chem. Engring. with high honors, Engring. Honors Cert., N.C. State U., 1969, PhD, 1974. Registered profl. engr., Tex.; cert. mgr. Statis. clk. Rsch. Triangle Inst., 1966; reactor engr. AEC, Washington, 1973-75; spl. asst. ERDA, Washington, 1975; mech. engr. U.S. Dept. Energy, Washington, 1975-78; staff mem. Los Alamos (N.Mex.) Nat. Lab., 1978-82; sci. cons. Houston, 1982-84; environ. control and life support systems test bed mgr. Johnson Space Ctr., NASA, Houston, 1984-85, sr. project engr. advanced tech. dept., 1985-86, sr. staff engr. divsn. solar system exploration, 1986-88, asst. divsn. advanced devel., 1988-90; sr. sys. engr. Exploration Programs Office NASA, Houston, 1990-92, mgmt. cons., 1992—. Founder Peace U., 1993; mem. internal adv. com. Ctr. for Nonlinear Studies Los Alamos Nat. Lab., 1981; organizer tech. confs., sessions at soc. meetings; lectr. in field; docent Mus. Fine Arts, Houston. Editor, author tech. reports; contbr. articles to profl. jours.; inventor and patentee in field. Mem. curriculum rev. com. U. N.Mex., Los Alamos, 1980. Recipient Woman's badge Tau Beta Pi, 1968, ERDA Spl. Achievement award, 1976, Inventor award Los Alamos Nat. Lab., 1982, Group Achievement award NASA Johnson Space Ctr., 1987, Outstanding Performance award NASA Johnson Space Ctr., 1987, 89, Superior Performance award NASA Johnson Space Ctr., 1987, 89, Cert. of Recognition for Inventions, NASA, 1988, 89, 90, 92, 93. Mem. AIAA (organizer, 1st chmn. human support com. Houston chpt. 1988-93), AIChE (organizer, 1st chmn. No. N.Mex. club 1980-81, organizer and chmn. low-pressure processes and tech. 1981-89), Am. Nuc. Soc. (sec.-treas. fusion energy divsn. 1982-84, vice chmn. South Tex. sect. 1984-86, local sects. com. 1986-88), Am. Chem. Soc., Soc. for Risk Analysis (organizer, sec. Lone Star chpt. 1986-88, chmn. soc. publicity 1990-93), No. N.Mex. Chem. Engrs. Club, Sierra Club, Houston Orienteering Club, Phi Kappa Phi, Pi Mu Epsilon.

CULLITON, BARBARA J. medical association administrator; b. Buffalo, May 2, 1943, Grad., Vassar Coll. Reporter, then news editor Science, 1972—91; dep. editor and head editl. ops. N.Am. Nature Pub., 1991—99; exec. editor sci. comm. and exec. editor GeneWire.com Celera Genomics, 1999—2001; v.p. for pub. The Inst. for Genomic Rsch., Rockville, Md., 2001—; editor-in-chief Genome News Network, Rockville, 2001—. Times Mirror vis. prof. and dir. Writing About Sci. The Writing Seminars, Johns Hopkins U., Balt., 1990—98; advisor Am. Bd. Internal Medicine; adv. com. Knight Journalism Fellows, MIT, Cambridge; journalism advisor Fulbright Scholars program; advisor Sound Print, the radio series; panelist Sci. Jour., a Pub. Broadcasting prodn. Bd. overseers Darmouth Med. Sch. Co-recipient George Polk award for journalism. Mem.: Coun. for Advancement of Sci. Writing (pres. 1985—89, bd. dirs.), Nat. Assn. Sci. Writers (pres. 1981—82), Inst. of Medicine of NAS (mem. governing coun.), Italian Soc. for Molecular Medicine (hon.), Sigma Xi (hon.). Episcopalian. Office: Genome News Network 9712 Medical Center Dr Rockville MD 20850

CULLUM, BONNIE BROOKS, theater producer, theater director, educator; b. San Antonio, Tex., Apr. 18, 1961; d. James Albert Cullum and Susan Estelle Kelso; m. Chad Michael Salvata, Sept. 14, 2002. BA in Theatre, U. Kans., 1983; MFA in Theatre, U. Tex., 89. Asst. beverage mgr. Hyatt Hotels, San Antonio, 1983—86; instr. U. Tex., Austin, Tex., 1986—89; producing artistic dir. Vortex Repertory Co., Austin, 1988—, v.p., 1988—; assoc. prodr. Pacific Vista Prodns., Petaluma, Calif., 1989—. Prodr.: (plays) over 200 shows, 1989—; dir. (plays) over 200 shows, 1989—. Panelist City of Austin, 1991; dem. caucus rep. Tex. State Conv., Houston, 1992. Recipient Best of Austin Best Dir. award, Austin (Tex.), 1996, 2000, B. Iden Payne award, Austin (Tex.) Cir. of Theatres, 2001, 2002. Mem.: Rat, Tejas Web, Reclaiming (spoke 2000—04). Democrat. Pagan. Avocations: swimming, photography, science fiction. Office: Vortex Repertory Co 2307 Manor Rd Austin TX 78722

CULLUM, LEE BROOKS, journalist; b. Dallas, Mar. 18, 1939; d. Charles Gillespie and Garland Chapman Cullum; m. James Howard Clark Jr., June 29, 1962 (div. June 1976); 1 child, James Howard Cullum Clark. Student, Sweet Briar Coll.; BA, So. Meth. U., 1961; DHL (hon.), Monterey Inst. Inter. Studies, 1997, U. Puget Sound, 2002. Reporter, then exec. prodr. and on-air moderator Newsroom Sta. KERA-TV, Dallas, 1970-76, v.p. program devel., 1976-81; account exec. Hill & Knowlton, Dallas, 1981-82; editor D Mag., Dallas, 1982-85; dir. client svcs. Hill & Knowlton, Dallas, 1985-86; editor editl. page Dallas Times Herald, Dallas, 1986-91; commentator Newshour with Jim Lehrer (formerly Macneil-Lehrer Newshour), Washington, 1988—; contbg. columnist Dallas Morning News, Dallas, 1992—. Bd. dirs. Coun. Fgn. Rels., N.Y., Pacific Coun. Internat. Policy, L.A. Author: Genius Came Early: Creativity in the Twentieth Century, 1999. Bd. dirs. S.W. Legal Found., Dallas, 1995-99, The Hockaday Sch., Dallas, 1997-2003; bd. visitors Internat. Programs Ctr., Okla. U., 1997—; mem. Am. Coun. on Germany; mem. Nat. Com. on U.S.-China Rels. Dallas Inst. for Humanities and Culture fellow; recipient Matrix award Women in Comms., 1977, 85, J. B. Marryatt award Dallas Press Club, 1996. Mem.: InterAm. Dialogue, Nat. Conf. Editl. Writers. Episcopalian. Avocations: the arts, traveling, books.

CULLY, MIKKI, artist; b. Boston, Feb. 18, 1963; d. James Spingle and Barbara (Berrio) Bertozzi; m. Christopher Patrick Cully, Feb. 8, 1994; children: Hannah, Noah. BFA, Swain Sch. Design, 1986; MFA, Cranbrook Acad. Arts, 1988. Textile designer and colorist Marcus Bros. Textile, N.Y.C., 1988—90; tchr. surface design Dartmouth Coll. Visual and Performing Arts U. Mass., New Bedford, Mass., 1994—97; textile designer and colorist Duro Textile Printers, Fall River, Mass., 1994—97; freelance artist Plymouth, Mass., 1997—. Recipient Gold Key award, Boston (Mass.) Globe, 1981; grantee, Swain Sch. Design, 1982—86, Cranbrook Acad. Art, 1986—88. Home: 36 Beach St Plymouth MA 02360

CULP, FAYE BERRY, state legislator; b. Kilmichael, Miss., Dec. 6, 1939; d. Otis Milton and Drapa (Clark) Berry; m. James H. Culp, Dec. 28, 1966; children: James Jr., David. BS in Bus. Edn., Miss. U. for Women, 1961; postgrad., Ga. State U., 1965-66; M, U. South Fla., Tampa, 1993. Tchr. Atlanta Pub. Schs., 1961-66; ednl. svcs. rep. IBM, San Francisco, 1966, Poughkeepsie, N.Y., 1967-68; real estate salesperson Yates Realty, Tampa, 1975-79; mem. sch. bd. Hillsborough County, Tampa, 1988-92; mem. Fla. Ho. of Reps., Tallahassee and Tampa, 1994—, majority whip, 1996-98. Chair Joint Ho. and Senate Com. for Legis. Info. Tech. Resources/Procedural Coun., mem. edn., appropriations, tourism coms.; mem. State Task Force for Tech. Fla. Sch. Bds. Assn.; chmn. legis. subcom. on spl. legislation, chmn. bylaws com. Fla. Sch. Bds. Assn.; mem. State Instrnl. Coun. Textbook Selection. Asst. dir. Theatre Atlanta prodns.; dir., prodr. musicals First United Meth. Ch., Tampa. Mem. Govs. Task Force for Prevention Teen-Age Suicides; del. Fla. Fedn. Rep. Women's Conv.; 1st pres. Child Abuse Coun. Aux.; pres. Hillsborough Women's Rep. Club, Tampa Realistic Artists, Inc., United Meth. Women, 1st United Meth. Ch., Tampa, Plant High Sch. Parent Student Tchrs. Assn.; v.p. various PTAs; area v.p. Hillsborough County Coun.; juvenile protection chmn. Hillsborough PTA County Coun.; youth coord., bd. trustees First United Meth. Ch.; bd. mem. Nat. Coun. Christians and Jews, Coun. Downtown Chs.; treas. West State Archaeol. Soc.; chmn. internat. affairs Tampa Civic Assn.; leader, den mother Cub Scouts; chmn. Just Friends Mentoring Program; bd. mem., officer Friends of Pub. Edn.; chmn. Masterpiece Morning. Named Woman of Distinction Girl Scouts Am., Tampa, Pacesetter in Ky. So. Women in Pub. Svc., 1997, Disting. Alumni of Yr. U. South Fla. Coll. Fine Arts, Tampa, 1997, Legislator of Yr. Internat. Coun. Shopping Ctrs., Orlando, Fla., 1997, 2003, One of Top 40 Legislators, Fla. C. of C., 1997, Legislator of Yr. Fla. Sch. Bds. Assn., 1997, Alliance Homeowners Assn., 2003; recipient over 150 awards in photography, 40 awards in painting, 3 awards in poetry, others. Mem. LWV, Nat. Order Women Legislators (stakeholder, regional dir. nat. conf., nat. pres. 2004—), Nat. Found. Women Legislators (chmn.), PEO (chpt. historian), Miss. U. for Women Alumni Assn. (pres. Suncoast chpt.), Fla. Ho. Reps. (vice chmn. gen. edn., children's svs.), Hillsborough County Pres. Roundtable, Greater Tampa C. of C. (mem. edn. coun.), South Tampa C. of C., Greater Town n' Country C. of C., Lamplighters, Red Cross Angels, Friends of the Arts, Fla. Orch. Guild, Port Tampa [illegible] Alpha. Republican. Methodist. Avocations: photography, painting, travel. E-mail: culp.faye@myfloridahouse.com.

CULP, KRISTINE ANN, dean, theology educator; B in Gen. Studies with distinction, U. Iowa, 1978; MDiv, Princeton Theol. Sem., 1982; PhD in Religion, U. Chgo., 1989. Vis. instr. theology St. Paul Sch. Theology, Kansas City, Mo., 1985-86, instr. theology, 1986-89, asst. prof. theology, 1990-91; dean Disciples Div. House U. Chgo., 1991—, sr. lectr. theology Div. Sch., 1991—. Contbr. articles to profl. jours. Office: U Chgo Disciples Divinity House 1156 E 57th St Chicago IL 60637-1536 also: The Divinity Sch-U Chgo Swift Hall S-406 1025 E 58th St Chicago IL 60637-1509

CULP, MILDRED LOUISE, corporate executive; b. Ft. Monroe, Va., Jan. 13, 1949; d. William W. and Winifred (Stilwell) C. BA in English, Knox Coll., 1971; AM in Religion and Literature, U. Chgo., 1974, PhD The Com. on History of Culture, 1976. Faculty, adminstr. Coll., 1976—81; dir. Exec. Résumés, Seattle, 1981—; pres. Exec. Directions Internat., Inc., Seattle, 1985—2000, Clive, Iowa, 2000—03, Crete, Ill., 2003—. MBA mgmt. skills adv. com. U. Wash. Sch. Bus. Adminstrn., 1993; spkr. in field; contract rschr. U.S. Army Recruiting Command, 1997. Author: Be WorkWise: Retooling Your Work for the 21st Century, 1994; columnist Seattle Daily Jour. Commerce, 1982-88; writer Singer Media Corp., 1991-98, Worldwide Media, 1999-2002, Globalvision, Inc., 2002—, WorkWise syndicated column, 1994—, Universal Press Syndicate, 1997-2001; WorkWise Internet audio program, 2000-03; WorkWise radio program, 2003-; featured on TV and radio; contbr. articles to profl. jours.; presenter WorkWise Report, Sta. KIRO, 1991-96. Admissions counselor U. Chgo., 1981—; mem. Nat. Alliance Mentally Ill, 1984—, adv. bd., 1988; mem. A.M.I. Hamilton County, 1984—; founding mem. People Against Telephone Terrorism and Harassment, 1990; co-sponsor WorkWise award, 1999-2000. Recipient Alumni Achievement award Knox Coll., 1990, 8 other awards; named Hon. Army Recruiter. Mem.: U. Chgo. Puget Sound Alumni Club (bd. dir. 1982—86), Knox Coll. Alumni Network.

CULPEPPER, MABEL CLAIRE, artist; b. St. Louis, June 20, 1936; d. John Raymond and Mabel Lorene (Hardy) Bondurant; m. James William Culpepper, Dec. 24, 1957; children: Julie Ann, James Jeffrey, John William. AA, Columbia Coll., 1956; BS in Edn., Mo. U., 1958, MEd, 1965. Represented by Artel Gallery, Emmitsburg, Md., 1987-88, Nob Hill Artisans, Albuquerque, 1993-94, Amapola Gallery, Albuquerque, 1995—. Art tchr. Twinbrook Bapt. Ch., Rockville, Md., 1972-75. One-woman shows include Artel Gallery, 1987, exhibited in group shows at Rockville (Md.) Art League, 1987, N.Mex. Watercolor Soc., 1989—2002, Nat. Watercolor Soc. Nat. Exhbn., Brea, Calif. Host parent, officer Am. Field Svc., Damascus, Md., 1978-80; program chmn. Albuquerque Newcomers, 1989-91; docent Albuquerque Mus., 1990-94; co-chair care com. Hope Evang. Free Ch., 2000—. Recipient First Prize Rockville Art League, 1987. Mem.: Frederick County Art Assn. (pres. 1988), N.Mex. Watercolor Soc. (pres. 1992—93, hosp. chair We. Fedn. Show 2002, 1st prize 1990, Best of Show 1993, 1st prize 1998, Best of Show 1999, Peter Walker award 2001, Collectors Guide award 2002, Village Framers award 2003), Nat. Watercolor Soc. (signature mem.) (western fedn. show hospitality chair 2002), Nat. League Am. Penwomen (pres. Yucca br. 1998—2000, editor newsletter 2001), Nat. Mus. Women in the Arts, Mortar Board, Delta Gamma. Avocations: hiking, singing in church choir, crafts, bible study, travel. Home: 3208 Casa Bonita Dr NE Albuquerque NM 87111-5610

CULPEPPER, MARY KAY, publishing executive; With Weight Watchers; exec. dir. Coastal Living, 2000—01; v.p. Cooking Light Mag., 2002—, editor, 2001—. Office: Cooking Light Magazine P O Box 62376 Tampa FL 33662

CULVERWELL, ROSEMARY JEAN, principal, elementary education educator; b. Chgo., Jan. 15, 1934; d. August John and Marie Josephine (Westermeyer) Flashing; m. Paul Jerome Culverwell, Apr. 26, 1958; children: Joanne, Mary Frances, Janet, Nancy, Amy. BEd, Chgo. State U., 1955, MEd in Libr. Sci., 1958; postgrad., DePaul U., 1973. Cert. supr., tchr. Tchr. Otis Sch., Chgo., 1955-59; tchr., libr. Yates Sch., Chgo., 1960-61, Nash Sch., Chgo., 1962-63, Boys Chgo. Parental, 1969-72, Edgebrook and Reilly Schs., Chgo., 1965-67; counselor, libr. Reilly Sch., Chgo., 1968, tchr., libr., asst. prin., 1973, prin., 1974—. Reviewer Ill. State Bd. Edn. Quality Review Team. Pres. Infant Jesus Guild, Park Ridge, Ill., 1969-70; troop leader Girl Scouts U.S., Park Ridge, 1967-69; sec. Home Sch. Assn., Park Ridge, 1969, v.p. spl. projects, 1970; mem. Ill. Svc. Ctr. Six Governing Bd., 1994; vol. Ctr. of Concern, Park Ridge, Ill., 1997; quality reviewer Ill. State Bd. Edn., 1998; mem. Ill. Quality Edn. Rev. Team, 1998; v.p. Renaissance Art Club, 1999—. Recipient Outstanding Prin. award Citizens Schs. Com., Chgo., 1987, For Character award, 1984-85, Whitman award for Excellence in Edn. Mgmt., 1990, Local Sch. Coun. award Ill. Bell Ameritech, 1991, Ill. Disting. Educator award Milken Family Found. Nat. Educators, 1991, Ill. Edn./Bus. Partnership award, 1994, 96. Mem. AAUW, LWV (chmn. speakers bur. 1969), Delta Kappa Gamma, Phi Delta Kappa. Avocations: acrylic painting, reading, swimming, making doll houses and furniture. Home: 1929 S Ashland Ave Park Ridge IL 60068-5460 Office: FW Reilly Sch 3650 W School St Chicago IL 60618-5358 E-mail: rosemary.culverwell@mciworldcom.net.

CUMMING, MARILEE, apparel company executive; b. Columbus, Nebr. m. Andrew Cumming; 1 child, Melissa. BA in Psychology, Rosemont Coll., 1969. Buyer trainee children's divsn. J.C. Penney, Inc., N.Y.C., 1975, asst. and assoc. buyer positions in children's and women's, 1975-82, catalog dress buyer, 1982-84, sr. buyer misses blouses, 1984-86, merchandise mgr. men's accessories and furnishings, 1986-87, merchandise mgr. women's, misses and updated apparel, 1987-90, dir. women's merchandise dept., 1990, dir. merchandising women's divsn., 1990-93, pres. home and leisure divsn., 1993-96, pres. women's apparel divsn., 1996-99; pres. merchandising J.C. Penney Stores and Catalog, 1999—. Co-chmn. nat. campaign March of Dimes, 1999—2000; bus. ethics com. J.C. Penney, supplier diversity com. Campaign vice chmn. Met. Dallas United Way Campaign, 1996; mem. NWCA N.Y., Acad. Women Achievers; adv. bd. Women's Ctr. U. Tex., 1999—2000; steering com. Dallas Mother of Yr. Luncheon. Avocations: health and fitness, family activities. Office: JC Penney Co Inc 6501 Legacy Dr Plano TX 75024-3698

CUMMING, PATRICIA A. writer; b. N.Y.C., Sept. 7, 1932; d. Egmont Arens and Camille Davied Rose; m. Edward Chandler Cumming, July 6, 1954 (dec. Feb. 6, 1960); children: Julie Emelyn, Susanna Arens. BA magna cum laude, Radcliffe/Harvard, 1954; MA, Middlebury U., 1956. Editl. assoc. Deadalus, Cambridge, Mass., 1966—69; assoc. prof. MIT, Cambridge, 1969—79. Mem. adv. bd. Sojourner, Cambridge, 1976—79; guest faculty Sarah Lawrence Coll., Bronxville, NY, 1988; vis. asst. prof. Wheaton Coll., Norton, Mass., 1988—96. Author: Afterwards, 1974, Letter from an Out-lying Province, 1976. Recipient grant-in-aid, St. Botolph Club Found., Cambridge, 1996. Mem.: Phi Beta Kappa. Home: PO Box 251 Adamsville RI 02801

CUMMINGS, ANDREA J. lawyer; b. 1967; BA in Polit. Sci., BS in Journalism, Boston U., 1990; JD, U. Va., 1995. Bar: Tex. 1995, Calif. 1999, Ill. 2000. With Locke Purnell Rain Harell, Tex., 1995—97, Weil, Gotshall Manges LLP, 1997—98, Nomura Asset Capital Corp., 1998—99, Gray Cary Uare Freidenrich, 1999—2000, Sidley Austin Brown & Wood LLP, Chgo., 2000—, ptnr., 2003—. Office: Sidley Austin Brown and Wood Bank One Plz 10 S Dearborn St Chicago IL 60603

CUMMINGS, ANN E. [illegible] m. Regis E. Cummings; children: Corin, Erica, Clancy, Megan. BA, Cardinal Cushing Coll., 1968; MSA, St. Michael's Coll., 1989. Social svc. worker Project Independence; owner Core Designs; mem., Wash. County Vt. Senate, Montpelier, 1997—. Bd. dirs. Woman Centered. Mem. USS Montpelier Assn., Vt. Craft Coun. Roman Catholic. Home: 24 Colonial Dr Montpelier VT 05602-3306

CUMMINGS, CANDACE S. apparel company executive; BA in Econs., Middlebury Coll., 1969; MD, U. Va., 1972. From assoc. to sr. bus. ptnr. Dechrt Price & Rhoads, Phila., 1972-94; v.p., gen. counsel VF Corp., Wyomissing, Pa., 1994-96, v.p. adminstrn. and gen. counsel, 1996—. Address: PO Box 21488 Greensboro NC 27420

CUMMINGS, ERIKA HELGA, business consultant; b. Offenbach, Germany; came to U.S., 1978; d. Erwin and Edith (Trunski) Maier; 1 child, Marisa Anne. BSBA, Calif. State U., Bakersfield; MBA in Internat. Mgmt., Am. Grad. Sch. Internat. Mgmt., Glendale, Ariz., 1983. Inflight supr. TWA, Paris; internat. ops. mgr. Cooper LaserSonics, Santa Clara, Calif., 1983-85; bus. cons. Suncoast Bus. Industries, Sarasota, Fla., 1985-89; cert. fin. planner Am. Express Fin. Advisors, Sarasota, 1989-94; Peace Corps. vol. City Adminstrn. of Vladimir, Russia, 1994-96; internat. cons. Solutions Internat., Sarasota, Fla., 1996—. Mem. Toastmasters, Beta Gamma Sigma. Avocations: travel, tennis, reading, langs. E-mail: ericum@aol.com.

CUMMINGS, JOAN E. health facility administrator, educator; BA, Trinity Coll., 1964; MD, Loyola U., 1968. Diplomate Am. Bd. Internal Medicine, Geriatric Medicine. Med. intern St. Vincent Hosp., Worcester, Mass., 1968-69; med. resident Hines VA Hosp., Hines, Ill., 1969-71, sr. resident in nephrology, 1971-72, ambulatory care svc. chief gen. med. sect., 1971-84, med. dir., hosp. based home care, 1972-87, chief, intermediate care svc., 1984-87, assoc. chief of staff, extended care and geriatrics, 1987-90, med. dir., extended care center, 1987-90, dir., 1990—; asst. prof. clin. medicine U. Ill., 1976-82, Loyola U., 1983-91, assoc. prof. clin. medicine, 1991—; network dir. Dept. Vet. Affairs, Hines, Ill. Mem. ad hoc com. on primary care U. Ill., 1980-82, coll. edn. policy com. U. Ill., 1980-82, State Ill. Emergency Med. Svc. Coun., 1981-83, Comprehensive Health Ins. Plan Bd. State Ill., 1990—, Med. Licensing Bd. State Ill., 1992—, exec. com. Chgo. Fed. Exec. Bd. State Ill., 1992—; program dir. Loyola/Hines Geriatric Fellowship Program, 1987-90. Contbr. to profl. mags. and jour. Recipient Disting. Svc. award Abraham Lincoln Sch. Med. Univ. Ill., 1979, 81, Leadership award VA, 1980, Certificate of Appreciation award VA, 1980, Laureate award Am. Coll. Physicians, 1990. Fellow ACP; mem. AMA (Ill. delegation 1985—, vice speaker ho. of dels. 1987-89), Chgo. Med. Soc. (pres. Hines-Loyola br. 1982-83), Ill. State Med. Soc. (trustee 1984—, chmn. com. on Ill. med., 1988—, spkr. ho. of dels. 1989-91, exec. com., 1989-91, policy com., 1989—), Chgo. Geriatric Soc., Am. Geriatric Soc. Office: Bldg 18 PO Box 5000 5th Ave & Roosevelt Rd Hines IL 60141-5000 Office Phone: 708-202-8400. E-mail: joan.cummings@med.va.gov.

CUMMINGS, JOSEPHINE ANNA, writer, consultant, advertising executive; b. Gainesville, Fla., July 12, 1949; d. Robert Jay and Marcella Dee (Mount) Cummings. ABJ./Design cum laude, U. Ga., Athens, 1971; MA, NYU, 1999. Copywriter William Cook, Jacksonville, Fla., 1971-73; creative dir. Leo Burnett, Chgo., 1973-76; sr. v.p., group creative dir. D. D. B. Needham, Chgo., 1976-84; sr. v.p., creative dir. Saatchi-Saatchi, N.Y.C., 1984; sr. v.p., sr. creative dir. Ted Bates, N.Y.C., 1984; exec. v.p., chief creative officer Tracy-Locke, Dallas, 1985-87; exec. v.p., exec. creative dir. Bozell, Chgo, 1989; exec. v.p., creative dir. Y&R, N.Y.C., 1990-92; pres. The Joey Co., N.Y.C., 1992—. Author: (play) Azaleas, 1988, (short story collection) Crimes of Passion, 1988, (childrens' book) The Hospital is a Funny Place, 1988, (short film) Night Magic, 1989. Named as creator One of Hundred Best TV Commls. Advt. Age, 1978-79, one of Advt. 100 Best Advt. Age, 1986, one of People to Watch Fortune mag., 1986, Ad Age one of Best and Brightest, N.Y. Mem. Amelia Earhard, Ninety Niners Club, N.Y. Women in Film. Avocations: reading, writing, juggling. Office: The Joey Co Ste 656S 55 Washington St Brooklyn NY 11201

CUMMINGS, KAREN SUE, retired corrections classification administrator; b. Ft. Wayne, Ind., July 15, 1939; d. Floyd Henry and Mary Emma (Wolfe) Kneller; m. Oswald Wade Cummings, Feb. 16, 1962; children: Ruth Marie Cummings Everett, John Phillip. BA, Bethal Coll., 1976; MA, Webster U., 1989; grad., Corrections Mgmt. Sch., La., 1991. Sub. tchr. various sch., Mishawaka, Ind., La., 1978-82; classification dir. Work Tng. Facility North La. Dept. Corrections, Pineville, La., 1978-82; eligibility worker Office of Family Security, Alexandria, La., 1982-84; classification officer Work Tng. Facility North La. Dept. Corrections, Pineville, 1984-92, classification dir. Work Tng. Facility North, 1992—, ret., 2002—. Big sister Big Bros./Big Sisters, Mishawaka, 1974-76, Pineville, 1990-91. With USAF, 1957-65. Mem. Am. Correctional Assn., So. States Corrections Assn. Republican. Baptist. Avocation: travel. Office: 1519 Dupree Rd Pineville LA 71360-8718

CUMMINGS, MARY VOIGT, counselor; b. Eagle Grove, Iowa, Sept. 23, 1937; d. Wilson Burns and Evelyn Louise (Allen) Voigt; m. William Grosvenor Cummings, Jr.; children: William Grosvenor III, Grace Ann, Mary Joan, Margaret Louise, Nancy Elizabeth. BS, Northwestern U., 1959; MA, U. South Fla., 1977. Counselor Pinellas Park H.S., Largo, Fla., 1977-84; guidance coord. Clearwater (Fla.) H.S., 1984—2000. Bd. dirs. Samaritan Counseling, Clearwater, 1984, Fla. Bot. Gardens, 2003-; bd. dirs., trustee MPM Health Systems, Clearwater, 1991-97; pres. Jr. League, Clearwater, 1975; altar guild, 2002-, Christcare leader, 2003-; active in PTAs, sch. adv. bds., etc. Named Outstanding Young Woman, Jr. Woman's Club, Clearwater, 1975, Beautiful Activist, Burdines, Clearwater, 1977, Master Tchr., State of Fla., 1986. Mem. Am. Counselors Assn., Fla. Counselors Assn., Suncoast Counselors Assn., Pinellas County Counselors, Phi Kappa Phi, Carlouel Yacht Club (oversight com.). Episcopalian.

CUMMINGS, MAXINE GIBSON, elementary school educator; b. Tupelo, Miss., Oct. 7, 1940; d. T. Ruben and Maggie (Ruff) Gibson; m. Willie B. Cummings, Aug. 15, 1964; 1 child, Stanley. BS, Barber-Scotia Coll., Concord, N.C., 1962; MA, Northeastern Ill. U., Chgo., 1974. Cert. tchr., N.C., Ill. Tchr. Walter Reed Elem. Sch., Chgo., 1963-75, reading tchr., 1975-82, social studies tchr., 1982-85; reading resource tchr. Arna Bontemps Sch., Chgo., 1985-91, ESEA lab. tchr., 1991—; Title I reading/math tchr. St. Sabina Acad., Chgo. Mentor tchr. Tchrs. for Chgo. Program, Arna W. Bontemps Sch. Site, 1996—; counselor Westside YWCA, Chgo., 1963-68; chmn. reading com. Bontemps Sch., 1986-92, chmn. activity com., 1992-93; mentor tchr. Bontemps Tchrs. for Chgo. Program; mem. staff devel. team Reading Tchrs. Acad. for Profl. Growth, Chgo. Bd. Edn.; Title I tchr., presenter in field. Contbr. articles to profl. jours. Mem. Vol. Edna White Century Garden; sec. S.W. Morgan Park Civic Assn., Chgo., 1990-92; block rep. Neighborhood Watch Program, Chgo., 1989-90; trustee Morgan Park Presbyn. Ch., peace and justice com., mem. choir; Great Books Discussion leader Walker Br. Libr., ordination elder Morgan Park Presbyn., 1999; race rels. com. Beverly/Morgan Park Neighborhood-Task Force; coord. garden site Metra Train Sta. Grantee Chgo.-Incentive, 1987, NEH, 1984, Northeastern Ill. U., 1980; recipient Regional Cmty. Gardening award, Morgan Park Neighborhood, Chgo., 1998, Mayor Daley's Landscape Improvement Program award, 1999, 2d place award City Scape Gardening Corner, Chgo., 1999. Mem. Minority Students of Chgo. Area (recruiter), Barber-Scotia Alumni Club (sec. 1989-92), Pi Lambda Theta. Avocations: biking, walking, reading, travel, gardening. Home: 11116 S Longwood Dr Chicago IL 60643-4043 Office: St Sabina Acad 7801 S Throop St Chicago IL 60620-

CUMMINGS, PEGGY ANN, counseling administrator; b. Plainfield, N.J., May 18, 1957; d. Peter James Cummings and Marjorie Ann Pope. MA in Student Pers. Svcs. summa cum laude, Rowan U., 1986, BA in Spl. Edn. summa cum laude, 1979; AS in Restaurant Mgmt., Restaurant Sch. Phila., 1989. Cert. Tchr. of Handicapped State of NJ., 1979, lic. Profl. Counselor State of NJ., Bd. of Marriage and Family Therapy Examiners, 2002, Nat. Cert. Counselor Nat. Bd. For Cert. Counselors, Inc. and Affiliates, NC, 2003, cert. Dietary Mgr. Dietary Mgrs. Assn., Ill., 1992, Food Mgr./Operator Cert. Chester County Health Dept., PA, 1993, cert. Student Pers. Svcs. Dept. of Edn., State of N.J., 1986. Sch. counselor Montgomery Twp. Sch. Dist., Skillman, NJ, 1999—, spl. edn. tchr., 1995—99; dist. mgr. Nutrition Mgmt. Svcs. Co., Kimberton, Pa., 1994—95, food svc. dir., 1990—94; spl. edn. tchr. Haddon Heights Sch. Dist., NJ, 1979—88; dir., camp Jotoni Somerset County Assn. for Retarded Citizens, Manville, NJ, 1979—82. Co-pres. MTEA Challenger Little League, Montgomery Twp., NJ, 2002—. Author (school guidance department member) school guidance curriculum, grades 3-4; contbr. workshop presentation Character Education Conference, Central NJ; co-author (character education committee member): (elementary character education curriculum) Montgomery Township Character Education Curriculum. Sch. rep. Rocky Hill/Montgomery Twp. Mcpl. Alliance, Belle Mead, NJ, 2002—03; donor membership Sharing Network Organ and Tissue Donation Svcs., Springfield, NJ, 2001—; vol. MTEA Challenger Little League, Belle Mead, 2001—; vol./contbr. Samaritan Interim Homeless Program, Somerville, NJ, 2001—. Mem.: PTA, NEA, ACA, N.J. Edn. Assn., N.J. Sch. Counselor Assn. (Somerset County Counselor of Yr. 2002—03), Am. Sch. Counselor Assn., Kappa Delta Pi, Gamma Tau Sigma, Mortar Bd. Achievements include development of Elementary School Peer Mediation Student Leader and Peer Partners Programs. Avocations: golf, swimming, hiking, gardening, bicycling. Home: 423 Jackson Ave Manville NJ 08835 Office: Montgomery Township School District 1014 Rte 601 Skillman NJ 08558 E-mail: pcummings@mtsd.k12.nj.us.

CUMMINGS ROCKWELL, PATRICIA GUILBAULT, psychiatric nurse; b. Ludlow, Mass., June 22, 1939; d. Lee Allen and Mavis Isabella (White) Guilbault; m. Philip W. Cummings, Oct. 23, 1960 (dec. Jan. 1978); children: Sharon Ellen Timmons, Geoffrey Scott Cummings, Susan Mavis Lornitzo, Lee Millett Cummings, Mary Rockwell Thon; m. William Leonard Rockwell Jr., Aug. 18, 1990. ADN, Vt. Coll., 1982; BSN, Norwich U., 1987. RN, Vt. Staff nurse Ctrl. Vt. Hosp. Nursing Home, Berlin, 1982-84, 87—; staff psychiat. nurse Va. Hosp. Ground East, White River Junction, Vt., 1987-94; owner Globe Travel, Bradford, Vt., 1988-94; rschr. Norwich U., Northfield, Vt., 1988—. Nurse-entrepeneur Globe Travel, 1988—. Tchr. adult edn. ARC, Bradford, Vt., 1988, 89; dir. Vt. Lakes and Pond Assn.; v.p. Vale Hospice Internat.; dir. Fedn. Vt. Lakes and Ponds Inc. Mem. ANA (nat. and Vt. chpts.), AAUW, New Eng. Hist. Geneal. Soc. Avocations: writing, traveling, medical genealogy. Home: 307 Godfrey Rd East Thetford VT 05043-9517 E-mail: patsy@together.net., patsy@valehospice.org.

CUMMINS, KATHLEEN K. retired elementary school educator; b. Fountain County, Ind., June 20, 1919; d. Homer Elston Krout and Edith Zerilda Allen; m. Robert E. Cummins, Oct. 4, 1940 (dec. Mar. 1984); 1 child, Robert E. Jr. BS in Edn., Ind. State U., 1952. Elem. tchr. East Allen Cmty. Schs., New Haven and Ft. Wayne, Ind., 1940—76; ret., 1976. Deaconess Trinity English Luth. Ch., Ft. Wayne, 1982—. Recipient Ret. Tchr. of Yr. award, Instant Copy, Ft. Wayne, 1993. Mem.: AAUW (grantee 1984), Allen County Ret. Educators Assn. (pres. 1986—88), Ft. Wayne Hist. Mus. (past pres. Barr St. Irregulars), Ft. Wayne Women's Club (bd. dirs. 1988—, chmn. fine arts dept.), Fortnightly Club (pres. 1994—96), Delta Kappa Gamma (chpt. pres. 1964—66). Democrat. Lutheran. Avocations: painting, reading, bridge, knitting, gardening. Home: 3808 Oak Park Dr Fort Wayne IN 46815

CUMMINS, MICHELLE MARIE, otolaryngologist, head and neck surgeon; b. Windsor, Ont., Can., July 14, 1959; came to U.S., 1994; d. James Thomas and Helen Mary (Weiler) C.; m. Jerry Dean Pilkington. BS, U. Waterloo, Can., 1982; MD, U. Toronto, 1987, MSc, 1994. Intern St. Joseph Health Ctr., Toronto, 1987-88; resident Santa Barbara (Calif.) Cottage Hosp., 1988-89, U. Toronto, 1989-92; otolaryngologist Dalhousie U., Nova Scotia, Can., 1992-94. Lectr. in field. Contbr. articles to profl. jours. Otolaryngology & Profl. Voice fellow Bowman Gray Sch. Medicine, Winston-Salem, N.C., 1994-96. Mem. AMA, Am. Acad. Sleep Disorders, Am. Acad. Otolaryngology Head & Neck Surgery, Am. Rhinological Soc., European Laryngological Soc., Can. Soc. Otolaryngology, Pan Am. Allergy Soc. Roman Catholic. Avocations: fitness walking, pottery, skiing, swimming, biking. Office: 1300 N Virginia St Ste 112 Port Lavaca TX 77979-2512

CUMMINS, NANCYELLEN HECKEROTH, electronics engineer; b. Long Beach, Calif., May 22, 1948; d. George and Ruth May (Anderson) Heckeroth; m. Weldon Jay Cummins, Sept. 15, 1987; children: Tracy Lynn, John Scott, Darren Elliott. Student, USMC, Memphis, 1966-67. From tech. publ. engr. to engring. instr. Missile and Space divsn. Lockheed Corp., Sunnyvale, Calif., 1973-77; test engr. Gen. Dynamics, Pomona, Calif., 1980-83; quality assurance test engr. Interstate Electronics Co., Anaheim, Calif., 1983-84; quality engr., certification engr. Rockwell Internat., Anaheim, 1985-86; sr. quality assurance programmer Point 4 Data, Tustin, Calif., 1986-87; software quality assurance specialist Lawrence Livermore Nat. Lab., Yucca Mountain Project, Livermore, Calif., 1987-89, software quality mgr., 1989-90; from sr. constrn. insp. to sr. quality assurance engr. EG&G Rocky Flats, Inc., Golden, Colo., 1990-91, engr. IV software quality assurance, 1991-92, instr., developer environ. law and compliance, 1992-93; software, computer cons. CRI, Dabois, Wyo., 1993-97; contractor Dept. of Energy, Golden, Colo., 1997-98; test mgr. Keane Inc., Lakewood, Colo., 1998, project officer, 1998—. Customer engr. IBM Gen. Sys., Orange, Calif., 1979; electronics engr. Exhibits divsn. LDS Ch., Salt Lake City, 1978; electronics repair specialist Weber State Coll., 1977-78. Author: Package Area Test Set, 6 vols., 1975, Software Quality Assurance Plan, 1989. Vol., instr. San Fernando (Calif.) Search and Rescue Team, 1967-70; instr. emergency preparedness and survival, Claremont, Calif., 1982-84, Modesto, Calif., 1989; mem. Lawrence Livermore nat. Lab. Employees Emergency Vols., 1987-90, EG&G Rocky Flats Bldg. Emergency Support Team, 1990-93, Dubois Search and Rescue, 1995-97. Mem. NAFE, NRA, Nat. Muzzle Loading Rifle Assn., Am. Soc. Quality, Job's Daus. (majority mem.), Ea. Starr. Republican. Avocations: history, weapons, camping, native American crafts. E-mail: whiltierna@fortinedsl.net.

CUMMIS SANDLAUFER, DEBORAH GWEN, lawyer; b. Orange, N.J., Nov. 6, 1959; d. Clive Sanford and Ann Estelle (Denburg) C. BA, Brandeis U., 1980; MA, NYU, 1988; JD, Seton Hall U., 1991. Bar: Calif. 1992, N.J. 1994, U.S. Ct. Appeals (9th cir.) 1994. Adminstrv. asst. Associated Press, 1981-83; mgr. olympic affiliate rels. ABC Radio Networks, 1983-84; cons. Free-Lance Radio, 1984-85; mgr., affiliate rels. MJI Broadcasting, 1985; dist. team asst. CBS Television Network, 1986-87; legal asst. Kaye Scholer Fierman Hays & Handler, 1987-88, Covenant House Inst. Youth Advocacy, 1989; law clerk Dickson Creighton & Lowenstein, 1989-90; summer assoc. Hannoch Weismen, 1990; law clk. Hayden Perle & Silber, 1990-91; pvt. practice, 1992-94; asst. prosecutor Domestic Violence Unit Union County (N.J.) Prosecutor's Office, 1994-98; assoc. Genova Burns & Vernoia, Livingston, NJ, 1998—99, Grotta, Glassman & Hoffman, Roseland, NJ, 1999—2002; dep. atty. gen. N.J. Dept. Law & Pub. Safety, Whippany, NJ,

2002—. Law Students Rights Found. fellow, 1989. Mem. ABA, AAUW (various exec. positions), Am. Assn. Univ. Women (pres., 1884-86, v,p, programming, 1988-91, dir., 1986-88), Am. Jewish Congress (bd. dirs., 2001-),N.J. Bar Assn., Essex County Bar Assn. Democrat. Jewish. Avocations: computers, women's literature, cooking, gardening. Office: Genova Burns & Vernoia 354 Eisenhower Pkwy Livingston NJ 07039-1022 Personal E-mail: dcummis@yahoo.com. Business E-Mail: sandlauferd@njdcj.org.

CUNEO, NGAIRE E. corporate development executive; b. Oct. 24, 1950; BA in Econs., Coll. New Rochelle, N.Y.; MBA, Iona Coll. Deputy dir. Metropolitan Transit Authority, N.Y.C., 1972-75; mem. staff Gen. Acctg. Office, 1975-86; sr. v.p. Gen. Electric Capital Corp., 1986-92; executive v.p. Conseco Inc., Carmel, Ind., 1992—. Bd. dirs. Bankers Life Holding Corp., Am. Life Holdings, Inc., Am. Life Holding Co., Duke Realty Investments, Inc., NAL Financial Group Inc. Office: Conseco Inc 11825 N Pennsylvania St Carmel IN 46032-4604

CUNHA, JANE, artist, consultant; d. John Lewis and Margaret Theresa (Nolan) Cumbo; m. Bruce Clifford Manly, Nov. 25, 1977; children: Alia, Philip, Evan. BFA magna cum laude, Maryland Inst. Coll. of Art, 1977; attended, U. Hartford, Conn., 1985—86, Lyme Art Acad., 2002. Artist, 1954—; designer Austin Kennedy Jewelers, 1977—87; gallery dir. Carriage House Gallery, 1987—94; cons. Jane Cunha Associates, 1994—. V.P. Madison Art Soc., Madison, Conn., 2000—. Author: (poetry) Into Blue Borders, 1994. Founder and chair-woman Shoreline High Sch. Art Exhbn., Madison, Conn., 2000—. Mem.: Glastonbury Art League, Guilford Art League. Achievements include numerous art awards. Avocations: reading, writing, yoga.

CUNNANE, PATRICIA S. medical facility administrator; b. Clinton, Iowa, Sept. 7, 1946; d. Cyril J. and Corinne Spain; m. Edward J. Cunnane, June 19, 1971. AA, Mt. St. Clare Coll., Clinton, Iowa, 1966. Mgr. Eye Med. Clinic of Santa Clara Valley, San Jose, Calif. Mem. Med. Adminstrs. Calif. Polit. Action Com., San Francisco, 1987. Mem.: NAFE, No. Calif. Med. Group Mgmt. (pres. 2002—03, treas. 2003—), Healthcare Human Resource Mgmt. Assn. Calif., Women Health Care Execs., Am. Soc. Ophthalmic Adminstrs., Profl. Secs. Internat. (sec. 1979—80), Exec. Women Internat. (v.p. 1986—87, pres. 1987—), Am. Coll. Med. Group Adminstrs. (nominee), Med. Group Mgmt. Assn., Nat. Notary Assn. Roman Catholic. Avocations: calligraphy, golf. Home: 232 Tolin Ct San Jose CA 95139-1445 Office: Eye Med Clinic Santa Clara Valley 220 Meridian Ave San Jose CA 95126-2903 E-mail: patricia.cunnane@gte.net.

CUNNIFF, SISTER GEORGETTE, religious organization administrator; b. Brookline, Mass., June 22, 1945; d. George Andrew Cunniff and Dorothy Anastasia Dwyer Cunniff. BA, Mt. Alvernia Coll., 1974; MA, St. Bonaventure U., 1980. Tchr. Immaculate Conception Sch., Augusta, Ga., 1967—68, St. Michael's Sch., Tybee Island, Ga., 1968—70, St. Cecilia Sch., Solvax, NY, 1970—79, Cathedral Day Sch., Savannah, Ga., 1979—83; diocesan dir. religious edn. Cath. Diocese of Savannah, 1983—94; parish dir. religious edn. Our Lady of Lourdes, Pt. Wentworth, Ga., 1996—. Rep. Nat. Conf. of Catectical Leadership, Washington, 1984—94; rep. for nat. conf. Holy Childhood Assn., Washington, 1988—89. Roman Catholic. Home: 1990 Hwy 21 S Springfield GA 31329 Office: Our Lady of Lourdes 501 S Coastal Hwy 25 Savannah GA 31407

CUNNIFF, SUZANNE, surgical technician; b. Detroit, Dec. 3, 1960; d. Louis Thomas and Joyce Lenore (Barkell) C. AA in Surgical Tech., Marygrove Coll., 1986; BS Med. Tech., Mich. State U., 1984. Cert. surgical technologist. Surg. technologist Botsford Gen. Hosp, Farmington Hills, Mich., 1986-88, St. Joseph Mercy Hosp., Pontiac, Mich., 1988-91; cardiothoracic surg. asst. Cardiothoracic Surgeons, Pontiac, 1991-97, Lynchburg, Va., 1997—. Mem. Assn. Surg. Technologists. Avocations: figure skating, volleyball, bowling, wool spinning. Office: 2015 Tate Springs Rd Lynchburg VA 24501

CUNNING, TONIA, newspaper managing editor; BS in Journalism, U. Nev. Soc. editor/feature writer-editor/asst. mng. editor Reno (Nev.) Gazette-Jour., 1971-92, mng. editor, then exec. editor, 1992—. Office: Reno Gazette Journal PO Box 22000 Reno NV 89520-2000

CUNNINGHAM, ANDREA LEE, public relations executive; b. Oak Park, Ill., Dec. 15, 1956; d. Ralph Edward and Barbara Ann C.; m. Rand Wyatt Siegfried, Sept. 24, 1983. BA, Northwestern U., 1979. Feature writer Irving-Cloud Pub. Co., Lincolnwood, Ill., 1979-81; account exec. Burson-Marsteller Inc., Chgo., 1981-83; group account mgr. Regis McKenna Inc., Palo Alto, Calif., 1983-85; founder, owner, pres. Cunningham Communication Inc., Santa Clara, Calif., 1985—. Mem. Am. Electronics Assn., U.S. C. of C., Young Pres.' Orgn., Software Pubs. Assn., Boston Computer Soc., Leadership Calif., U.S. Cambridge C. of C. Republican. Avocations: running, roller skating, aerobics, racquetball.

CUNNINGHAM, BETTY JEAN DE BOW, adult education educator; b. Venice, Ill., Apr. 11, 1942; d. John Wells and Anna DeBow; m. Langford Allen Cunningham, July 18, 1967 (div. Dec. 1976); 1 child, Langford Allen Jr. BS in Elem. Edn., So. Ill. U., 1967; M in Secondary Edn. and Adult Edn., U. Mo., St. Louis, 1991. Dir. Madison (Ill.) County Equal Opportunity Ctr., 1966—67; reading tchr. Venice-Lincoln Tech. Ctr., 1968—. Mem. Metro East Literacy Adv. Coun., East St. Louis, Ill., 1989—94. Vol. Des Peres Hosp., St. Louis, 1993—95. Recipient Steward of Records, Bethel A.M.E. Ch., 2003. Mem.: Ill. Adult and Continuing Educators Assn., Inc. (jr. dir. Region V 1996—97, sr. dir. Region V 1997—98). Office: Venice-Lincoln Tech Ctr 300 S Fourth St Venice IL 62090

CUNNINGHAM, JACQUELINE LEMMÉ, psychologist, educator, researcher; b. Biddeford, Maine, Apr. 22, 1941; d. S. James and Alice (Fréchette) Lemmé; m. Seymour Cunningham II, Dec. 16, 1960 (dec. 1987); children: Macklin Todd, Danielle, Alyssa. BA in Psychology cum laude, U. Maine, Orono, 1963; MS in Psychology, U. South Ala., 1983; PhD in Ednl. Psychology, U. Tex., 1994. Tchr. Mobile (Ala.) Pub. Schs., 1976-81; psychology intern Devereux Found., Devon, Pa., 1988-89; fellow in developmental disabilities Children's Hosp. Harvard Med. Sch., Boston, 1990; prof. U. S.D., Vermillion, 1994-95; fellow in pediat. neuropsychology Children's Nat. Med. Ctr., George Washington U. Med. Ctr., Washington, 1995—97; psychologist pvt. practice, Wilmington, Del., 1997—2000, Children's Hosp. of Phila., Phila., 2000—. Cons. in field. Contbr. articles to profl. jours., chapters to books. Mem. Am. Psychol. Assn. (outstanding dissertation of yr. award 1994), Internat. Neuropsychol. Soc., Nat. Acad. Neuropsychology, Soc. History Behavioral Scis., Phila. Neuropsychology Soc. (bd. dirs. 1998-2002), Phi Kappa Phi. Avocations: travel, writing. Office: Children's Hosp of Phila 34th St & Civic Ctr Blvd Philadelphia PA 19104

CUNNINGHAM, JUDY EVALYN, elementary school administrator, educator; b. Rockford, Ill., May 11, 1947; d. James William and June Evalyn (Davis) Geddes; m. Charles Edward Cunningham, June 21, 1969 (div. Oct. 1984); 1 child, Charles Arthur. BS in Edn., No. Ill. U., 1969, MS in Edn., 1972, EdD, 1997. Intervention specialist Rockford Office of Edn., 1985-86; counselor Belvidere (Ill.) Jr. H.S., 1986-90; prin., counselor Tibbets Elem. Sch., Elkhorn, Wis., 1990-92; prin., curriculum coord. Sch. Dist. of Beloit, Wis., 1992-95; therapist Janet Wattes Mental Health Ctr., 1996; counselor Rockford Pub. Schs., 1996—. Cons. Ill. 4-H program, Urbana, 1979-83; presenter regional edn. confs., 1987-90. Author: Colors of Leadership, 1981 (Alumni State award 1981). Youth leader First Free Ch., Rockford, 1985—; active Starlight Cmty. Theatre, Rockford, 1988—. Mem. Nat. Counselors Assn., Ill. Counselors Assn., Sports Car Club of Am. (past bd. dirs. local chpt.), Alpha Chi Omega, Pi Lambda Theta, Kappa Delta pi. Avocations: show horses, cattle, theater. Home: 10863 N Meriian Rd Rockton IL 61072-9797

CUNNINGHAM, JULIA WOOLFOLK, author; b. Spokane, Oct. 4, 1916; d. John George and Sue (Larabie) C. Grad., St. Anne's Sch., Charlottesville, Va., 1933. Author: (juveniles): The Vision of Francois the Fox, 1960, Dear Rat, 1961, Macaroon, 1962, Candle Tales, 1964, Dorp Dead, 1965 (Children's Spring Book Festival award), Violet, 1966, Onion Journey, 1967, Burnish Me Bright, 1970, Wings of the Morning, 1971, Far in the Day, 1972, The Treasure Is the Rose, 1973, Maybe, A Mole, 1974, Come to the Edge, 1977 (Christoper award 1978), Tuppenny, 1978, A Mouse called Junction, 1980, Flight of the Sparrow, 1980 (Commonwealth Club Calif. award, Honor Book award Boston Globe), The Silent Voice, 1981, Wolf Roland, 1983, Oaf, 1986, (with Betsy Hearne) Dorp Dead, 2002; (poetry) Shadow Heart, 1999, The Stable Rat and Other Christmas Poems, 2001, Cicada, 2001. Mem. Authors Guild. Home: Rancho Santa Barbara 333 Old Mill Rd Space 88 Santa Barbara CA 93110-4429

CUNNINGHAM, KATHLEEN ANN, human resources specialist, purchasing agent; b. St. Louis, May 1, 1952; d. Russell Martin Hagan and Helen Marie Hogan; children: Merrit Cunningham-Neptune, Clayton. LPN, Waukesha County Tech. Inst., 1976. Dep. property tax assessor New Trier Twp., Winnetka, Ill., 1988—89; trustee Northfield Twp., Glenview, Ill., 1984—90; v.p. Cunningham Fluid Power, Inc., Ocala, Fla., 1993—2003; staffing coord. Donbar Svc. Corp., Tampa, 2001—02; head human resources, purchasing specialist Odyssey Marine Exploration, Tampa, 2003—. Cons. John F. Kennedy Assassination Records Rev. Bd., Washington, 1993—98. Contbr. Killing the Truth, 1993, Killing Kennedy, 1995, Between the Signal and the Noise, 1995, Not In Your Lifetime, 1998, Assassination Science: Experts Speak Out on the Death of JFK, 1998; contbr. articles to profl. jours. Precinct capt. Northfield Twp. Rep. Orgn., Glenview, 1981—83, election judge, 1979—88, area chairperson, 1983—90; chmn. bd. dirs. Northshore Rehab. Fund, Northbrook, Ill., 1987—90; bd. dirs. Citizens for the Truth in the Kennedy Assassination, L.A., 1995—2001; bd. trustees Northfield Twp., Glenview, Ill., 1984—90. Achievements include donation of large collection of documents relating to John F. Kennedy's assassination to the Special Collections department at University of South Florida. Avocations: canoeing, reading, writing, historic research. Home: 18307 Aintree Ct Tampa FL 33647 Office: Odyssey Marine Exploration 3604 W Swann Tampa FL 33609

CUNNINGHAM, KIMA HICKS, minister, client services manager; b. Dayton, Ohio, July 2, 1960; d. Barbara Ann Brooks and Kermit Hicks; m. Michael Bernard Cunningham, Nov. 13, 1965; 1 child, Alan Michael. Bachelor, Ohio State U., Columbus, 1982; Master, Payne Theol. Sem., Wilberforce, Ohio, 2002. Mgr., client mgmt. svcs. Sankofa Corp., Dayton, Ohio, 1994—. Min. Mt. Enon Bapt. Ch., Dayton, Ohio, 1997—. Recipient Scholastic All-American, US Achievement Acad., 2002, Outstanding Sr. Sermon, Dr. Cutis O. Greenfield and Faculty, 2002, Academic Achievement, Payne Sem. Faculty, 2002, Nat. Scholarly Achievement Award, 2002. Home: 6 Mario Dr Trotwood OH 45426 Office: Sankofa Corp 220 Park Manor Dr 4th Fl Solarium Dayton OH 45410

CUNNINGHAM MILAMARI ANTOINELLA, anesthesiologist; b. Cody, Wyo., Oct. 4, 1949; d. Milo Leo and Mary Madeline (Haley) Olds; m. Michael Otis Webb, June 4, 1970 (div. Feb. 1971); m. James Kenneth Cunningham, June 14, 1975. BA with honors, U. Mo., 1971, MD, 1975. Diplomate Am. Bd. Anesthesiologists. Intern and resident U. Mo., Columbia, 1975-78; jr. ptnr. Anesthesiologist, Inc., 1979-82, ptnr., 1982-86; owner Cunningham Anesthesia, 1986—; dir. anesthesia dept. Ellis Fischel Cancer Ctr., 1991-92; acting chief anesthesia Harry S. Truman Meml. Vets. Hosp., 1994-95. Mem. med. staff Columbia Regional Hosp., U. Mo. Hosp. and Clinics, Columbia; mem. rev. com. Mo. Health Facilities, 2001—. Mem. editl. bd.: Mo. Medicine Jour., 2001. Active Mo. Med. Polit. Action Com., 1991-2000, Friends of Music, Friends of Libr., Boone County Fair, 1978-94, with ham breakfast divsn., 1978-85, with draft horse and mule show, 1986-88; bd. dirs. A Call to Serve Mo., 1996—. Fellowship Am. Coll. Anesthesiologists, 1977; named Lifetime Senator, World Nations Congress, 2003. Mem.: AMA (Physicians Recognition award 1978, 1985, 1987, 1991, 1995), Vis. Nurses Assn. (bd. dirs. 1982—89, chair 1984—86, adv. bd. 1989—93), Am. Soc. Anesthesiologists (alt. dir. dist. 17 2003, Mo. dist. dir. 2003—), Mo. State Med. Assn. (commn. econs. third party payors 1986—89, chair 1989, Mo. health facilities rev. com. 2001—), Boone County Med. Soc. (membership chair 1982—84, alt. del. 1986, del. 1987—89, sec.-treas. 1996, del. 1996, bd. dirs. 1996—99, del. 1997, pres. 1998, del. 1999—2000, 2004), Mo. Soc. Anesthesiologists (v.p. 1986—87, pres. elect 1987—88, pres. 1988—89, del. 1989—98, 2000, del 2000—02, alternate dist. 17 dir. 2003, Mo. dir. 2003—, spkr. ho. dels. 1992—2002), Am. Med. Women's Assn., Phi Beta Kappa. Home: 8202 S Bennett Dr Columbia MO 65201-9178 Office: PO Box 1301 Columbia MO 65205-1301 E-mail: mila@tranquility.net.

CUNNINGHAM, NANCY SCHIEFFELIN, business educator; b. Mobile, Ala., Sept. 14, 1951; d. William Orville and Burline (Livingston) Schieffelin; m. Donald Frank Cunningham, Aug. 18, 1975; children: Benjamin Grant, Paige Allison. BA magna cum laude, U. North Tex., 1975; MA, Ohio State U., 1982. Cert. Myers Briggs Type Indicator adminstr. Mem. English faculty Franklin U., Columbus, Ohio; English curriculum coord. Ctr. for Unique Learners, Rockville, Mo.; mem. English faculty McClennan C.C., Waco, Tex.; coord. bus. writing Baylor U., Waco. Contbr. articles to profl. jours.; created and administers a writing proficiency exam. for bus. students; sr. editor: The Perryman Report, 1991—, The Perryman Texas Letter, 1992—. Baylor U. summer rsch. grantee. Mem. MLA, Assn. for Bus. Communication (rep.), Nat. Coun. Tchrs. English, Soc. for Tech. Comm., Perryman Tex. Editors (editor newsletters). E-mail: nancysc@perrymangroup.com., ncunningham@perrymangroup.com.

CUNNINGHAM, PATRICIA ANN CAHOY, band director, musician; d. Arnold Stephan Cahoy and Carolyn Ann Thiry; m. Gregg A. Cunningham, July 30, 1988. MusB Edn., U. No. Iowa, Cedar Falls, Iowa, 1980; MusM, Boston U., Boston, Mass., 1997. Band dir. Allamakee Cmty. Sch., Waukon, Iowa, 1981—81, Ventura Cmty. Sch., Ventura, Iowa, 1981—83, Ctrl. City Cmty. Sch., Central City, Iowa, 1983—85, Merrimack Cmty. Sch., Merrimack, NH, 1986—. Prin. clarinetist N.H. Philharm. Orch., Manchester, NH, 1985—; clarinetist New Eng. Wind Symphony, Manchester, NH, 1985—, New Eng. Symphony Orch., North Conway, NH, 1998—, Granite State Symphony, Concord, NH, 2000—02, Gt. Waters Music Festival Orch., Wolfeboro, NH, 1999—, North End Marching Band, Boston, 2001—. Musician: (featured soloist) North Iowa Wind Ensemble, N.H. Philharmonic Orch. Music merit badge advisor Boy Scouts, Nashua, NH, 1990; sec. N.H. Philharm. Orch., Manchester, NH, 1987—95. Scholar Meritorious Performer, Boston U., 1996. Mem.: NEA (assoc.), Merrimack Teachers' Assn. (assoc.), N.H. Music Educators' Assn., Internat. Clarinet Assn. (assoc.), Nat. Band Assn. (assoc.), Iowa Bandmasters' Assn. (assoc.), Pi Kappa Lambda (assoc.). Achievements include Merrimack High School Band receives top ratings at competitions. Avocations: travel, gardening, tennis. Office: Merrimack H S 38 McElwain St Merrimack NH 03054 Personal E-mail: pcunningham@merrimack.k12.nh.us.

CUNNINGHAM, SARAH BAINTER, dean, educator; b. Pittsfield, Mass., Apr. 15, 1967; d. John Joseph and Belinda Cunningham. MA, Vanderbilt U., 1996; BA, Kenyon Coll., 1989. Dean of sch. The Oxbow Sch., Napa, Calif., 1999—; dir. of devel. The Verde Valley Sch., Sedona, Ariz., 1998—99; asst. prof. of philosophy U. Maine, Orono, Maine, 1997—98; fellow, ctr. for tchg. Vanderbilt U., Nashville, 1996—97. Contbr. multiple presentations in US / UK on Teaching / on Philosophy. Mem.: Am. Soc. Eighteenth Century Studies, Am. Soc. Aesthetics, Am. Philos. Assn., North Am. Kant Soc., Ultimate Players Assn. (team founder 2002—03). Democrat. Achievements include Helped to found The Oxbow School, a semester program in visual arts for high school juniors and seniors. Avocations: flute, writing. Home: 623 Third Street Napa CA 94559 Office: Am Acad Liberal Education 1710 Rhode Island Ave Washington DC 20036 Personal E-mail: sbcunning@yahoo.com. E-mail: scunning@oxbowschool.org., scunningham@aale.org.

CUPKA, NANCY IRVINE, artist, educator; b. Indpls., Oct. 9, 1942; d. Don E. and Marie Irvine; m. W. Roger Cupka, Apr. 8, 1961; children: Gregory, Thomas. Group shows include Am. Artists Profl. League Nat. Exhbn., N.Y.C., 2001, Lafayette Art Assn.,1997, Hoosier Salon, 1970, 89, 92, 93, 97, 98, 2001, 2002, Ind. Heritage Arts Exhbn. Contemporary Ind. Artists, 1991, 92, 93, 94, 97, 98, 99, 2000, 01, Southside Art League, Inc., 1992, 93, 94, 95-97, Ind. Artist's Club, Indpls., 1995, 98, 2000, 01, Brown County Art Gallery, Nashville, 1988-97, Renditions Fine Art Gallery, Indpls., 1998-2002, Honeysuckle Gallery, Nashville, 1998-2002; permanent collections include St. Elizabeth's Hosp., Lafayette, Ind., Ind. State Mus., Indpls., Franklin (Ind.) Coll. Past bd. dirs. Brown County Art Gallery, Nashville, Southside Art League, Indpls.; founder Eastview Women's Support Group for Women with Chronic Pain, Martinsville, Ind.; assoc. mem. So. Ind. Ctr. for the Arts, Brown County Art Gallery Hist. Assn. Recipient numerous awards. Mem. Am. Artists Profl. League (artist mem.), Allied Artists Am. (assoc.), Southside Art League, Hoosier Salon Patron's Assn., Ind. Heritage Arts (artist mem.), Brown County Art Guild (assoc.), Ind. Artists Club. Avocations: walking trails, photography. Home and Office: 272 Painted Hls Martinsville IN 46151-8677

CURETON, CLAUDETTE HAZEL CHAPMAN, biology educator; b. Greenville, S.C., May 3, 1932; d. John H. and Beatrice (Washington) Chapman, m. Stewart Cleveland, Dec. 27, 1954; children: Ruthye, Stewart II, S. Charles, Samuel. AB, Spelman Coll., 1951; MA, Fisk U., 1966; DHum (hon.), Morris Coll., Sumter, S.C., 1996. Tchr. North Warren High Sch., Wise, N.C., 1952-60; tchr. Sterling High Sch., Greenville, 1960-66, Wade Hampton High Sch., Greenville, 1967-73; instr. Greenville Tech. Coll., 1973-95, ret., 1995. Bd. dirs. State Heritage Trust, 1978-91; commr. Basic Skills Adv. Program, Columbia, 1990—; mem. adv. bd. Am. Fed. Bank, NCNB Bank, Greenville, 1991—. Mem. Greenville Urban League, NAACP, S.C. Curriculum Congress; v.p. Woman's Bapt. E.& M. Conv. of S.C.; mem. S.C. Commn. on Higher Edn. Com. for Selection of the 1995 Gov.'s Prof. of the Yr.; mem. Gov.'s Task Force on Juvenile Crime, S.C., Gov.'s Juvenile Justice Task Force, 1997, S.C., Gov.'s Juvenile Justice Youth Coun., S.C., 1996—, Best Chance Network Task Force of Am. Cancer Soc., 1995—; bd. dirs. Sisters Saving Sisters, Roper Mountain Sci. Ctr., 2003—. Recipient Presdl. award Morris Coll., 1987, 91, Svc. award S.C. Wildlife and Marine Dept., 1986, Outstanding Jack and Jill of Am. citation, 1986, Excellence in Tchg. award Nat. Inst. for Staff and Orgnl. Devel., U. Tex., Austin, 1992-93, Educator of Yr. award Greenville chpt. Am. Cancer Soc., 1994, Outstanding Svc. award Best Chance Network/Am. Cancer Soc., 1994, Citation S.C. House of Reps., 1995; named Unsung Hero of the Cmty. for Outstanding Svc. to Humankind Greenville Tech. Coll., 1999. Mem. AAAS, AAUW, Nat. Assn. Biology Tchrs., S.C. Curriculum Congress, Nat. Coun. Negro Women, Inc., Higher Edn. S.C. Com. for Selection Prof. of Yr. 1995, Delta Sigma Theta (past v.p. Greenville chpt. alumnae). Home: 501 Mary Knob Greenville SC 29607-5242

CURIEL, CAROLYN, ambassador; b. Hammond, Ind. BA in Radio-TV-Film, Purdue U., 1976. Chief Caribbean Divsn. UPI; editor Late Editions Fgn. Desk N.Y. Times, N.Y.C., Washington Post; writer, prodr. ABC News Nightline, 1992; spl. asst. to pres., sr. presdl. speechwriter White House, Washington; apptd. U.S. amb. to Belize Dept. State, 1997—. Office: 6710 Ohio Ave Hammond IN 46323-1914

CURL, LEIGH ANN, orthopedist, surgeon; b. 1963; d. Frank and Barabara Curl. Bachelors, U. Conn., 1985; MD, Johns Hopkins U., 1989. Intern, reisdent Johns Hopkins Hosp., Balt.; fellow in sports medicine and shoulder surgery Hosp. for Spl. Surgery, Cornell U., N.Y.C., 1994—95; asst. prof. orthop. surgery and sports medicine U. Md. Med. Sys.; head team physician U. Md. Terrapins, 1997—2002; Balt.asst. prof. orthop. surgery Johns Hopkins Hosp., Balt., 2002—; team orthop. surgeon Balt. Ravens (NFL), 2001—; orthopedic surgeon Johns Hopkins Bayview Med. Ctr., Balt. Vol. team physician USA Women's Basketball, USA Women's Rugby and Johns Hopkins U. Named GTE Acad. All-Am. (twice), Big East Scholar-Athlete of Yr. (twice); inducted into, GTE Acad. Hall of Fame, 1998. Fellow: Am. Acad. Orthop. Surgery. Office: Johns Hopkins Bayview Med Ctr 4940 Eastern Ave Baltimore MD 21224

CURLE, ROBIN LEA, computer software industry executive; b. Denver, Feb. 23, 1950; d. Fred Warren and Claudia Jean (Harding) C.; m. Lucien Ray Reed, Feb. 23, 1981 (div. Oct. 1984). BS in Bus. Comm., U. Ky., 1972. Systems analyst 1st Nat. Bank, Lexington, Ky., 1972-73, SW BancShares, Houston, 1973-77; sales rep. Software Internat., Houston, 1977-80; dist. mgr. UCCEL, Dallas, 1980-82; v.p. and gen. mgr. Southeastern region Info. Sci., Inc., Atlanta, 1982-83; v.p. sales and mktg. TesserAct, San Francisco, 1983-86, Foothill Rsch., San Francisco, 1986; pres., founder Curle Cons. Group, San Francisco, 1986-89; mgr. strategic mktg. MCC, Austin, Tex., 1989-90; founder, exec. v.p. Evolutionary Tech., Inc., Austin, 1991-99; pres., CEO Journée Software, Austin, 1999-2000; founder, mng. dir. CEO Partnerships, Austin, 2000—02; pres., CEO Zebra Imaging, 2002—. Bd. dirs. Evolutionary Techs. Internat., Austin Software Coun., Tex. Property and Casualty, Zebra Imaging, Govs. Bus. Coun.; adv. bd. 360 Summit; dir. adv. bd. U. Tex. Engrng. Sch. Recipient Ma Ferguson award Exec. Women Internat. 1997, Grad of Yr. award Nat. Bus. Incubator Assn. 1996, Profiles in Power award, 1999, Entrepreneur of Yr. award 360 Summit Adv. Bd.; feature in Forbes Mag., 1996, Entrepreneur Mag., 1997; named top 50 most prestigious people Digital South; profile documentary Entrepreneurial Revolution, 1997, Inc 500 List, 1997, 98. Mem. U. Ky. Alumni Assn., Women in Tech., Women of Austin, Software Exec. Com., Inc. 500 Cos., Austin C. of C. (bd. dirs.), Delta Gamma (pres. 1969). Republican. Avocations: scuba diving, running, skiing, cooking. Home: 7009 Quill Leaf Cv Austin TX 78750-8306 Office Phone: 512-251-5100. E-mail: rcurle@zebraimaging.com., rcurle@zebraimaging.com., rcurle@austin.rr.com.

CURLEY, NANCY PALMER, marriage and family therapist; b. Syracuse, N.Y., Mar. 2, 1940; d. Percival Peter Morgan and Mildred May Lansley; m. James Samuel Curley, July 28, 1962; children: Cynthia Lynne, Geoffrey Morgan. BA cum laude, Ea. U., 1962; MS, Villanova U., 1988. Cert. Nat. Bd. Cert. Counselors, 1990, lic. prof. counselor Pa., 2002. Child care caseworker Cecil County Bd. Assistance, Elkton, Md., 1962—63; caseworker Chester County (Pa.) Bd. Assistance, 1963—66; asst. libr. Chester County (Pa.) Libr. Sys., 1967—80; counselor adolescents, supr. social workers Downingtown (Pa.) Indsl. and Agr. Sch., 1988—89, supr. coll. sr. yr. interns, 1988—89; psychotherapist Comprehensive Psychol. Svcs., Havertown, Pa., 1989—91; pvt. practice West Chester, Pa., 1991—. Psychotherapist Cath. Social Svcs. Del. County, Springfield, Pa., 1989—92. Vol. Chester County (Pa.) Day, 1970—80. Mem.: Am. Assn. Marriage and Family Therapy, Nat. Bd. Cert. Counselors, Internat. Transactional Analysis Assn., Internat. Integrative Pscyhotherapy Assn., Pa. Assn. Marriage and Family Therapy (bd. dir. 2003—), Kappa Delta Pi. Episc. Avocations: reading, travel, conservation of natural resources.

CURNAN, SUSAN P. social policy and management educator; b. Hyde Park, N.Y., Mar. 7, 1949; d. Charles Agustus and Mildred (Kron) C. BA cum laude, Stony Brook U., 1971; MS, SUNY, New Paltz, 1972; MFS, Yale U., 1978. Cert. tchr. K-12. Rsch. assoc. Yale U., New Haven, 1976-78; dir. New England Non-Profit Corp., Vt., 1978-82; dep. dir., sr. rsch. assoc. Ctr. Human Resources Brandeis U., Waltham, Mass., 1989 94, dir. Ctr. Human Resources, assoc. prof. Heller Grad. Sch. Advanced Studies in Social Welfare, [illegible] prof. social policy and mgmt. Heller Sch., dir. Ctr. for Youth and Cmty. Co-founder, pres. ER's Kitchen Cabinet, spec. food co., 2001. Contbr. articles to profl. jours. Trustee Taconic Found., N.Y.C., 1987—93; co-founder, chmn. Inst. for Just Cmtys., 2001. Fellow Berkley Coll. Yale U., 1985, 88; Grad. fellow Yale U., 1976-78; recipient Key to City and Cert. Hon. Citizenship, New Orleans Mayor and City Council, 1991, Outstanding Young Woman in Am. award, 1982; Rsch. grantee Yale U., 1977-78. Mem. Am. Edn. and Rsch. Assn., Yale U. Sch. Forestry and Environ. Studies Alumni Assn. (class sec. 1988—), Assn. Yale Alumni (bd. govs. 1983-86). Home: 174 Boston Post Rd Sudbury MA 01776-3102 Office: Brandeis U 60 Turner St Waltham MA 02453-8923

CURNOW, KATHY, art historian, educator; BA in Art History magna cum laude, Pa. State U., 1974; MA in Art History, Ind. U., 1980, PhD in Art History, African Studies, 1983. Prin. lectr. dept. design Nigerian TV Coll., Jos Plateau State, 1983-85, head dept. gen. studies, sr. lectr., 1985-88; exec. asst. Am. Found. Negro Affairs, Nat. Edn. Rsch. Fund, Phila., 1988-89; vis. asst. prof. dept. art Cleve. State U., 1990-91, asst. prof., 1991-94, assoc. prof., 1995—. Grad. asst. Ind. U., Bloomington, 1978-80; adj. asst. prof. U. Pa., Phila., 1989-91; vis. asst. prof. dept. art Lincoln U., Pa., 1989-90, dept. humanities U. Arts, Phila., 1990; lectr. Met. Mus. Art, N.Y.C., 1990; vis. Fulbright assoc. prof. U. Benin, Benin City, Nigeria, 1997-98. Author: (chpt.) Communications Training and Practice in Nigeria, 1987, Kulte, Kunstler, Könige in Afrika, 1997; contbr. articles to profl. jours. Recipient Nigerian Learning Materials award, 1987, Nat. Merit award Nigerian Festival TV Programming, 1987; Westinghouse scholar, 1973; Ind. U. fellow, 1977-80; grantee Rsch. Challenge, 1992, Social Sci. Rsch. Coun., 1993, NEH, 1993-98, Fulbright award, 1997-98. Mem. African Studies Assn. (arts coun., textbook writing com. 1991-93, bd. dirs. 1993-97, chair book prize com. 1994-95, sec.-treas. 1995-97), African Studies Assn., Coll. Art Assn., Delta Studies Assn., Midwest Art Historians Assn., Sierra Leone Studies Assn. Avocation: writing fiction. Office: Cleve State U Art Dept 111 AB Cleveland OH 44115

CURNUTTE, MARY E. artist, restorer of painting, educator; b. Valera, Tex., Dec. 15, 1920; d. Robert Franklin and Mary Elizabeth (Walker) Line; m. James Richard Curnutte, Oct. 14, 1950 (dec. Feb. 1972); 1 child, Sandra Elizabeth Curnutte Ziter; m. Robert Frederick Furman, Apr. 27, 1985 (dec. Apr. 2003). Grad. h.s., 1936. Bookkeeper, sec. drug stores, 1942-49, NCO Club, Goodfellow AFB, San Angelo, Tex., 1949-51; bookkeeper Boyce Hardware and Fuel Oil, Portsmouth, Va., 1953; artist/logs/filing Christian Broadcasting Network, Portsmouth, 1972-73; tchr. art Frederick Mil. Acad., Portsmouth, 1978-82, Alliance Christian Sch., Portsmouth, 1981-85; artist and pvt. tchr. art and music, restorer of art Portsmouth, 1959-89; artist Winter Haven, Fla., 1989—. Recipient Silver Cup award Alliance Christian Sch., 1984. Mem. Nat. Mus. Women in the Arts (charter mem.), Women of the Moose, NARFE. Baptist. Avocations: photography, swimming, fishing, music, travel.

CUROL, HELEN RUTH, librarian, English language educator; b. Grayson, La., May 30, 1944; d. Alfred John and Ethel Lea (McDaniel) Broussard; m. Kenneth Arthur Curol, June 25, 1967 (div. 1988); children: Edward, Bryan. BA, McNeese State U., 1966; postgrad., L.I. U., 1969-70; MLS, La. State U., 1987. Tchr., libr. Cameron Parish Schs., Grand Lake, La., 1966-67; media specialist Brentwood (N.Y.) Sch. Dist., 1967-69; sch. libr. Patchogue (N.Y.) H.S., 1969-70, 1976-95; reference libr., mgr. circulation dept. McNeese State U., Lake Charles, La., 1976-96; test adminstr. Edn. Testing Svc., Princeton, N.J., 1987-95; asst. prof. McNeese U., 1989-95; owner Curol Consulting, Lake Charles, 1995—2002; head adult svcs. Laman Pub. Libr., North Little Rock, Ark., 1996; media libr., tech. rep. LaGrange H.S., Lake Charles, 1997—. Rschr. Boise Cascade, DeRidder, La., 1987-88, Vidtron, Dallas, 1990-92, Nat. Archives, Washington, 1989; cons. Cmty. Housing Resource Bd., Lake Charles, 1988-93, Boyce Internat. Engrs., Houston, 1988-89, La. Pub. Broadcasting, Baton Rouge, 1989; devel. cons. Calcasieu Women's Shelter, 1988-92; reference cons. Calcasieu Parish Pub. Libr., 1990-95; presenter at confs. Sr. arbitrator Better Bus. Bur., Lake Charles, 1986-95; local facilitator La. Com. for Fiscal Reform, Lake Charles, 1988; state bd. dirs. PTA, Baton Rouge, 1981-83, LWV La., Baton Rouge, 1983-85; chairperson budget panel com. United Way S.W. La., Lake Charles, 1992-94, bd. dirs., 1995-96; judge La. region IV Social Studies Fair, 1979-89; program spkr. region IV tng. conf. HUD, El Paso, 1992; rep. to Nat. Taxpayer Advocacy Panel, 2002-04, to La.'s Virtual Libr. Commn., 2000—. Named Citizen of the Day, Sta. KLOU, 1978; grantee La. Endowment for Humanities, 1987, La. Divsn. Arts, 1989, Fair Housing Initiative Program, 1990, HUD, 1992, La. Ctr. Women and Govt. of Nicholls State U., 1993. Mem. ALA (sec. coun. 1988-90, chairperson coun. 1990-91), AAUW (chairperson intellectual freedom com. 1988-89), La. Libr. Assn. (chairperson reference group 1988-90), La. Assn. Coll. and Rsch. Librs. (chairperson 1995-96), Ark. Libr. Assn., McNeese U. Alumni Assn., S.W. La. C. of C. (mem. legis. com. 1992), Krewe du Feteurs (Mardi Gras Ct. Duchess 1992), Beta Sigma Phi (pres. Lake Charles chpt. 1983-84), Beta Phi Mu. Republican. Lutheran. Office: La Grange Media Ctr 3420 Louisiana Ave Lake Charles LA 70607-1842 Address: 1005 Cherryhill St Lake Charles LA 70607-4911

CURPHEY, GERALDINE CASTERLINE, church musician, retired; b. Cleve., Jan. 6, 1921; d. Charles and Lyla Mae (Overmyer) Casterline; m. Clifford L. Curphey, Mar. 31, 1943 (div. Sept. 1971); children: Denis Hall, Devon Scott. Assoc. in Fine Arts, Assoc. in Music, Stephens Coll., 1940; MusB, Sherwood Music Sch., 1942; postgrad., Fla. State U., 1954, Acad. Music, Vienna, 1969-73. Pvt. tchr. piano and voice, 1942—; organist, dir. Holy Trinity Episcopal Ch., Chgo., 1945-48; min. of music First Bapt. Ch., Ft. Lauderdale, Fla., 1949-63; dir. of music Christ United Meth. Ch., Ft. Lauderdale, 1963-72; piano instr. Broward C.C., Ft. Lauderdale, 1969-95; organist, dir. St. Clement Cath. Ch., Ft. Lauderdale, 1972-75, St. Andrew's United Methodist, Ft. Lauderdale, 1978-89, ret., 1989. Founding conductor Ft. Lauderdale Symphony Chorus, 1951-56; pres. Soroptimist Club, 1952-54. Composer: Song Cycle, 1941, Suite for Orchestra, 1942, Choral: The Mother's Name Was Mary, 1942, Choral: The Lord of Glory is My Light, 1968. Recipient 1st pl. honors Am. Composer's Clinic, 1941. Mem. Am. Guild Organists (past dean Ft. Lauderdale chpt. 1963-64), Music Tchrs. Nat. Assn., Fla. State Music Tchrs. Assn., Broward County Music Tchrs. Assn. (pres. 1970-72), Morning Musicale Federated Music Club (pres. 1955-56), Nat. League Am. Pen Women (Fla. state first pl. award 1972). Home: 220 Thorn Apple Ct Royal Palm Beach FL 33411-1689

CURRAN, AUDREY HARWELL, psychologist, educator; b. Cleve., Dec. 12, 1943; d. Millard and Nora Maria Harwell; children: Robert Criste Jr., Michaelann, Aline, Audrey. BA magna cum laude, Seaton Hill Coll.; MA, Fielding Inst., 1984, PhD, 1986. Lic. clin. psychologist, Calif., Ohio, internat. forensic psychologist. H.S. tchr., counselor, Glendora, Calif.; pvt. practice clin. psychologist Beachwood, Ohio, 1986—; chair psychology dept. Notre Dame Coll., South Euclid, Ohio, 1989—. Adj. prof. psychology/grad. program John Carroll U., Ohio, 1994-98; cons. in field. Contbr. articles to newspapers and mags.; writer syndicated column, Curran Events, 1980-87, Headlines, 1980-87. Recipient Disting. Alumnae award Seton Hill Coll., 2000. Mem. APA, Am. Psychol. Assn., Ohio Psychol. Assn. Avocations: travel, snow and water skiing, snorkeling, horse riding, reading. Home: 27020 Cedar Rd alt109 Beachwood OH 44122-1163 E-mail: acurran@ndc.edu.

CURRAN, BARBARA ADELL, retired law foundation administrator, lawyer, writer; b. Washington, Oct. 21, 1928; d. John R. and Beda Curran. BA, U. Mass., 1950; LLB, U. Conn., 1953; LLM, Yale U., 1961. Bar: Conn. 1953. Atty. Conn. Gen. Life Ins. Co., 1953-61; mem. rsch. staff Am. Bar Found., Chgo., 1961-93, [illegible] dir., 1970-80, rsch. atty., 1986-93, rsch. fellow emeritus, 1993—. Vis. prof. U. Ill. Law Sch., 1965, Sch. Social Svc., U. Chgo., 1966-68, Ariz. State U., 1980; cons. in field. Author of eight books in field; contbr. articles to profl. jours. Mem. Ill. Gov.'s Consumer Credit Adv. Com., 1962-63; consumer credit adv. com. Nat. Conf. Commns. on Uniform State Laws, 1964-70; credit legis. subcom. Mayor Daley's Com. on New Residents, 1966-69; cons. Pres.'s Commn. on Consumer Interests, 1966-70, Ill. Commn. on Gender Bias in the Cts., 1987-92. Mem. ABA, Pi Beta Phi. Office: Am Bar Found 750 N Lake Shore Dr Chicago IL 60611-4403

CURRAN, COLLEEN A. editor, writer; b. Milw., Wis., July 31, 1974; d. John C. Curran and Marybeth Raff. BA, N.Y. U., N.Y., 1996; MFA, Va. Commonwealth U., Richmond, VA, 2001. Adj. instr. Va. Commonwealth U., Richmond, Va., 1998—2001; assoc. editor Richmond.com, 1427 W. Main St., Va., 2001—. Contbr. chapters to books The Dictionary of Failed Relationships, articles to pril. jour. Recipient Fiction Contest Winner, Jane Mag., 2002, Richmond Mag., 2003, Seth Barkas Prize for Best Short Story, N.Y. U., 1996. Office: Richmondcom 1427 W Main St Richmond VA 23220 E-mail: ccurran@richmond.com.

CURRAN, EMILY KATHERINE, museum director; b. Boston, Mar. 27, 1960; d. George Morton and Gloria Rose (Martino) C.; m. John Vincent Callahan, Oct. 8, 1989; 1 dau., Clara Huiru. AB in Fine Arts, Bard Coll., 1982; MS in Mus. Leadership, Bank Street Coll., 1992. Sr. developer The Children's Mus., Boston, 1982-88; dir. edn. The Old South Meeting House, Boston, 1988-92, exec. dir., 1992—. Vis. cmty. artist Great George's Project, Liverpool, Eng., 1983. Author: Science Sensations, 1989, An Architectural History of the Old South Meeting House, 1995. Bd. dirs. Freedom Trail Found., Boston, 1992-97; elected mem. Colonial Soc. Mass., 1996—; mem., exec. com. mem. cmty. adv. bd. WGBH, Boston, 1996-99, vice chair, 1998-99. Mus. edn. fellow Bank Street Coll., 1989-91. Mem. Am. Assn. Mus., Am. Assn. State and Local History, New Eng. Mus. Assn., Boston Mus. Educators' Roundtable (chair steering com. 1989-91). Office: Old South Meeting House 310 Washington St Boston MA 02108-4616

CURRAN, LEIGH, actress, playwright; b. Santa Barbara, Calif., Dec. 5, 1943; d. John Van Benschoten and Barbara (Hansl) Griggs; m. Edward Herrmann, Sept. 9, 1978. Grad., Am. Mus. and Dramatic Acad., 1964. Actress: (Broadway debut) How Now, Dow Jones, Lunt-Fontanne Theatre, 1968, (stage prodns.) The Lunch Girls, 1977 (also author), 'night, Mother, 1985, Stitchers and Starlight Talkers, 1986, Walking The Blonde, 1989 (also author), The 52nd Street Project, 1987-91, (feature films) I Never Promised You a Rose Garden, 1977, Reds, 1981, (TV series) Adam's Rib, 1974, St. Elsewhere, 1985, Another World, 1986, L.A. Law, 1991; author: (play) Alterations, Useful Trash, Zone 13 Hair, Michelle Hammer, Girl Detective, Destiny, Destiny, Destiny; (teleplays) The Paper Chase, St. Elsewhere; artistic dir. The Virginia Avenue Project, 1991—. Mem. AFTRA, Actors' Equity Assn., Screen Actors Guild, Writers Guild, Dramatists Guild, Women in Film. Office: 555 W 57th St # 1230 New York NY 10019-2925

CURRAN, MARY ANN, chemical engineer; b. Cin., Oct. 1, 1957; d. Ernst Carl and Marilyn W. Braun; m. Roger Wayne Curran, July 16, 1982 (div. May 1998); children: Amanda, Margo. BS in Chem. Engring., U. Cin., 1980; MSc, Lund (Sweden) U., 1996. Chem. engr. U.S. EPA, Cin., 1980—. Editor: Environmental Life Cycle Assessment, 1996. Mem. AIChE (chmn. 1989-90). Home: 5760 Willnean Dr Milford OH 45150-2032 Office: US EPA 26 W Ml King Dr Cincinnati OH 45268-0001 E-mail: curran.maryann@epa.gov.

CURRAN-SMITH, ANITA STILES, retired public health medicine educator, dean; b. Northampton, Mass., 1929; BA, U. Conn., 1951; MD, N.Y. Med. Coll., 1955; MPH, Col. U., 1974. Diplomate Am. Bd. Preventive Medicine (bd. dirs.). Intern Mountainside Hosp., Montclair, N.J., 1955-56; house officer Maryview Hosp., Portsmouth, Va., 1960-63; pediat. clinic physician Met. Hosp., N.Y.C., 1963-65; med. dir. Newark Presch. Coun., 1965-70; child health physician N.J. Dept. Health, 1965-73; resident in pub. health N.Y.C. Dept. Health, 1974-75, dir. lead poisoning control program, 1974-78, dep. com., 1976-78; com. health Westchester County (N.Y.) Health Dept., 1978-89; prof. clin., environ. and cmty. medicine U. Medicine and Dentistry N.J. R.W. Johnson Med. Sch., New Brunswick, 1989—, assoc. dean cmty. health, 1992-96. Mem. exec. com. Am. Bd. Med. Specialists, 1995-98; chair residency review com. coun. Accreditation Coun. for Grad. Med. Edn., 1992-94. Fellow Am. Coll. Preventive Medicine, N.Y. Acad. Medcine, N.Y. Acad. Scis.

CURRENCE, ANNA, publishing executive; Exec. B.Dalton Bookseller, Barnes & Noble; CEO Kitchen Bazaar; pres., COO Crown Books Corp., Landover, Md., 1998—. Office: Crown Books Corp 333 Thornall St Edison NJ 08837-2220

CURREY, MELODY ALENA, state legislator; b. Margaretsville, N.Y., Dec. 17, 1950; m. Donald Currey; children: Rebecca, Jeffrey, Matthew. Student, SUNY, Cobleskill. Tchr. St. Mary's Ch.; mem. from dist. 10 Conn. State Ho. of Reps., 1993—, dep. spkr. Mem. Dem. Town Com., Hartford, Conn., 1984—, mem. fin. com., 1988; mem. rules com. Hartford Town Conv., 1989, 90; chmn. 5th Dem. Dist. Com., 1988-92, also sec.; issues chmn. Com. to Elect John Larson, 1990; canvass chmn. Rosemary Moynihan for State Rep., 1990, mem. steering com., 1990; coord. Com. to Re-elect Congresswoman Barbara Kennelly, East Hartford, Conn., 1990; scheduling dir. DelPonte for Mayor Com., 1991; leader Girl Scouts U.S.; mem. Student at Risk Com., 1988. Mem. Nat. Sch. Vol. Am., Supts. Adv. Coun., Dem. Women's Club (former sec.), Sci. Ctr. Conn. (leadership coun.). Address: 14 Martin Cir East Hartford CT 06118-1119 Office: Conn Ho of Reps State Capitol Hartford CT 06106

CURRIE, BARBARA FLYNN, state legislator; b. LaCrosse, Wis., May 3, 1940; d. Frank T. And Elsie R. (Gobel) Flynn; m. David P. Currie, Dec. 29, 1959; children: Stephen Francis, Margaret Rose. AB cum laude, U. Chgo., 1968, AM, 1973. Asst. study dir. Nat. Opinion Rsch. Ctr., Chgo., 1973-77; part time instr. polit. sci. DePaul U., Chgo., 1973-74; mem. Ill. Ho. of Reps., 1979—, chmn. House Dem. Study Group, 1980-83, asst. majority leader, 1993, asst. minority leader, 1995, majority leader, 1997. V.p. Chgo. LWV, 1965-69; mem. Hyde Park-Kenwood Cmty. Conf., Ind. Voters of Ill., Ill. Conf. Women Legislators, Ind. Precinct Orgn., Hyde Park Coop. Soc., Ams. for Dem. Action., Women United for S. Shore. Named Best Legislator Ind. Voters of Ill., 1980, 82, 84, 86, 88, 90, 92, 94, 96, 98, Best Legislator Ill. Credit Union League, Outstanding Legislator Ill. Hosp. Assn., 1987; Legislator of Yr. Ill. Nurses Assn., 1984, Nat. Assn. Social Workers, 1984, Ill. Women's Substance Abuse Coalition, 1984; recipient Leon Despres award, 1991, Ill. Environ. Coun. award, Ill. Women's Polit. Caucus Lottie Holman O'Neill award, Susan B. Anthony award, honor award Nat. Trust Historic Preservation; awards Welfare Rights Coalition of Orgns., Ill. Pub. Action Coun., Chgo. Heart Assn., BEST BETS award Nat. Ctr. Policy Alternatives, 1988, Svc. award Nat. Ctr. for Freedom of Info. Studies, 1989, Beautiful Person award Chgo. Urban League, 1989, Friend of Labor award Ill. AFL-CIO, 1990, Ill. Maternal and Child Health Coalition award, 1990, Ill. Hunger Coalition award, 1991, Cert. of Appreciation SEIU Local 880, 1989, March of Dimes, 1988, Chgo. Tchrs. Union, Ill. Hosp. Assn., Ptnr. Vision award Families' and Children's AIDS Network, Woman of Vision award Womens' Bar Assn. Ill., 1997, Nat. Elected Pub. Offcl. award Nat. Assn. Social Workers, 1997, Outstanding Working Woman of Ill. award Ill. Fedn. Bus. and Profl. Women, Dist. Pub. Health Legislator award Am. Pub. Health Assn., 1999, Legis. award Ill. Primary Health Care Assn., 2002, others. Mem.: LWV, ACLU (bd. dirs. Ill.). Office: Ill Gen Assembly 300 State House Springfield IL [illegible]

CURRIE, CAMERON MCGOWAN, federal judge; b. 1948; BA, U. S.C., 1970; JD with honors, George Washington U., 1975. Tchr. Moultrie H.S., Mt. Pleasant; law intern to magistrate judge Hon. Arthur L. Burnett U.S. Dist. Ct. D.C., 1973-74; atty. Arent, Fox, Kintner, Plotkin & Kahn, Washington, 1975-78; asst. U.S. Atty. Office U.S. Atty., Washington, 1978-80, Columbia, S.C., 1980-84; magistrate judge U.S. Dist. Ct. S.C., Columbia, 1984-86; pvt. practice Columbia, 1986-89; chief dep. atty. gen. Office Atty. Gen., State of S.C., Columbia, 1989-94; judge U.S. Dist. Ct. S.C., Columbia, 1994—. Adj. prof. in trial advocacy Sch. Law U. S.C., 1986-89. Assoc. editor SEC No Action Letters Index, 1972-73. Bd. dirs. Wings, Inc., 1986-94, sec., 1992-94. Mem. S.C. Bar, D.C. Bar, S.C. Women Lawyers Assn., Fed. Judges Assn., John Belton O'Neall Inn of Ct. Office: US Dist Ct 901 Richland St Columbia SC 29201

CURRIE, JO ANNE, art educator; b. Wilson, N.C., Feb. 12, 1946; d. Samuel Gordon House, Jr. and Maude Boswell House; 1 child, Elizabeth Anne. BS, East Carolina U., 1968; M in Art Edn., RISD, 1989. Postgrad. profl. lic. Edn., 2003. Art instr. Raleigh (N.C.) City Schs., 1968—70, Highland Park (N.J.) Schs., 1974—75, Montgomery County Schools, Rockville, Md., 1976—81; mktg. rep. Nat. Energy Resources, Knoxville, Tenn., 1981—83; art educator Charlottesville (Va.) City Schs., 1983—; master tchr. U. Va., Charlottesville, 1986—. Mem.: Alpha Delta Kappa (assoc.; altruistic 2002—03). Avocations: photography, travel, swimming, painting, art. Home: 73 Georgetown Green Charlottesville VA 22901 Office: Charlottesville City Schools 1562 Dairy Rd Charlottesville VA 22903

CURRIE, NANCY JANE, astronaut; b. Wilmington, Del., Dec. 29, 1958; m. David W. Currie; 1 child. BA in Biol. Scis., Ohio State U., 1980; MS in Safety, U. So. Calif., 1985; D in Indsl. Engring., U. Houston, 1997. Neuropathology rsch. asst. Ohio State U. Coll. Medicine; commd. 2nd lt. U.S. Army, 1981, helicopter instr. pilot, sect. leader, platoon leader, brigade flight standardization officer, master army aviator; flight simulation engr. shuttle tng. aircraft NASA Johnson Space Ctr., Houston, 1987, astronaut, 1991, flight crew rep. for crew equipment, lead for remote manipulator sys., spacecraft communicator, flight engr. mission specialist on STS-57, 1993, flight engr. mission specialist on STS-70, 1995, flight engr. mission specialist on STS-88, 1998, flight engr. mission specialist on STS-109, 2002, chief asstronaut office robotics br. Mem. Army Aviation Assn. Am., Ohio State U. and ROTC Alumni Assns., Inst. Indsl. Engrs., Human Factors and Ergonomics Soc., Phi Kappa Phi. Avocations: weightlifting, running, swimming, scuba diving, skiing. Office: NASA Lyndon B Johnson Space Ctr Houston TX 77058*

CURRIER, RUTH, dancer, choreographer and educator; b. Ashland, Ohio, Jan. 4, 1926; d. Elmer MacDonald and Zada (Holliman) Miller. Student, Black Mountain Coll., 1942-44, NYU, 1944-45. Soloist José Limón Dance Co., N.Y.C., 1949-63, artistic dir., 1973-77; asst. to Doris Humphrey, 1950-58; prin. Ruth Currier and Dance Co., N.Y.C., 1957-68; asso. prof. dance, dir. Am. Dance in Repertory, Ohio State U., Columbus, 1968-73; freelance choreographer N.Y.C., 1978-81; dir. Ruth Currier Dance Studio, N.Y.C., 1981-90. Adj. mem. faculty Bennington Coll., 1958-63; guest tchr., choreographer numerous colls., dance cos. Choreographer over 50 mus. prodns.

CURRIN, LYNNE IRENE, art educator; b. Weehawken, N.J., Feb. 4, 1948; d. James and Irene Marion McSorley; m. John Stanley Hudson, Nov. 17, 1979 (div. Oct. 1989); 1 child, Courtney Lynne Hudson ; m. Gary Horton Currin, June 26, 1993. BA in Art History, U. S.C., 1976; MA, Winthrop U., 1999. Art tchr. Newberry County Schs., 1999—2001; tchr. art enrichment St. John Newmann Sch., Columbia, 2001—03. Contbr. S.C. Symphony/Philharm. Columbia, 2003, Sister Care Civic Orgn. Columbia, 2003, Sertoma Civic Organ. Columbia, 2003. Grantee, Columbia Student Loan Corp., 1999. Mem.: Nat. Assn. Art Educators, Pi Lambda Theta, Kappa Delta Pi. Achievements include a copyright for original art process depicting State of S.C. emblem-palmetto tree, U. S.C. symbol-gamecock. Avocations: sewing, yoga, crossword puzzles, interior design, researching collectibles. Home and Studio: 586 Coldstream Dr Columbia SC 29212*

CURRY, ANN, correspondent, anchor; b. Agana, Guam, Nov. 19, 1956; d. Robert Paul and Hiroe (Nagase) Curry; m. Brian Wilson Ross, Oct. 21, 1987; children: Anna McKenzie, William Walker. Student, U. Oreg., 1974—78. Reporter Sta. KTVL-TV, Medford, Oreg., 1978—81; reporter, weekend anchor Sta. KGW-TV, Portland, Oreg., 1981—84; reporter Sta. KCBS-TV, L.A., 1984—90; corr., anchor NBC News at Sunrise NBC News, N.Y.C., 1991—96; news anchor Today Show, 1997—. Nominee Emmy award, 1985, 1986, 1987, 1988; recipient Golden Mike award, RTNA, 1986, 1987, 1989, Cert. Excellence award, AP, 1987, 1988, Greater L.A. Press Club, 1987, Superior Reporting award, NAACP, 1989, Emmy award, Acad. TV Arts and Scis., 1987, 1989, Nat. award, AAJA, 2000, AmeriCares Humanitarian Medial award, 2002. Avocation: art history. Office: NBC News 30 Rockefeller Plz # 374E New York NY 10112-0002*

CURRY, CYNTHIA J. R. geneticist; b. Cleve., July 20, 1941; MD, Yale U., 1957. Diplomate Am. Bd. Med. Genetics; Am. Bd. Pediatrics. Intern U. Wash., Seattle, 1967-68, resident, 1968-69, U. Minn., Mpls., 1969-70; fellow med. genetics U. Calif., San Francisco, 1975-76; med. faculty UCSF, Fresno, Calif.; med. dir. genetics Valley Children's Hosp., Madera, Calif., 1976—. Contbr. 15 chpt. to books, numerous articles to profl. jours. Office: Valley Childrens Hosp Genetic Med FC21 9300 Valley Childrens Pl Madera CA 93638-8762

CURRY, DALE BLAIR, retired journalist; b. Memphis, May 30, 1941; d. Hamilton Minter and Doris (Terry) Blair; m. Douglas Hester Curry, Dec. 21, 1963; children: Jennifer, Elizabeth. BA, U. Miss., 1963. Reporter The Commerical-Appeal, Memphis, 1962-63, Atlanta Constn., 1963-65, The States-Item, New Orleans, 1969-72, The Morning Advocate, Baton Rouge, 1974-76, 82-84; food editor The Times-Picayune, New Orleans, 1984—2004; ret., 2004. Elder St. Charles Ave. Presbyn. Ch., New Orleans, 1984-87, 91-94. Recipient award AP, UPI, New Orleans Press Club; named among Top 50 alumni 50th Anniversary U. Miss. Sch. Journalism, 1998. Mem. Assn. Food Journalists (pres. 1994-96), Theta Sigma Phi (Alumni of Yr. U. Miss. chpt.). Office: The Times-Picayune 3800 Howard Ave New Orleans LA 70125-1429 Business E-Mail: dale.curry@timespicayune.com.

CURRY, DENISE, university women's basketball coach; BS, UCLA, 1982, MA in Humanities, 1985. Asst. coach Calif., San Jose Lasers, 1996; head coach Calif. State Fullerton, 1997—. Named to Naismith Meml. Basketball Hall of Fame, French Profl. Player of the Decade 1980's, Three-time Kodak All-Am.; recipient Olympic gold medal. Office: Women's Athletic Dept Calif State Fullerton PO Box 6810 Fullerton CA 92834-6810

CURRY, EMMA BEATRICE, elementary school educator; b. Commerce, Ga., July 7, 1927; d. John Henry and Annie Bell (Wilkins) Thomas; m. Harvey Curry, Aug. 4, 1946; children: Gloria Dawn, Harvey Nathaniel, Norbert. BA in Psychology, U. Hawaii, 1971; MEd, counseling degree, Boston U., 1973; postgrad., U. So. Calif., Heidelberg, 1981; postgrad. in fine arts, City Coll., Heidelberg, 1986; postgrad., U. Md., Woxton Coll., Eng., U. Calif., Berkeley. Cert. tchr. social studies, N.J., English, cosmetology, psychology, social studies, DOD. Substitute tchr. Waupahu (Hawaii) H.S. and Leilehua (Hawaii) H.S., 1961-67, DOD, Augsberg, Germany,

1967-69; tchr. Mannheim Am. H.S., Germany, 1971-73, 1977-99; substitute tchr. Pennsauken (N.J.) Ctrl. Elem. Sch., 2000—. Author: (poetry) Feelings: Contemporary Verse, 1999. Bd. dirs. PTA, Mannheim Am. H.S., 1985-86, multicultural chairperson, 1971-73, 77-99; choir condr., soloist Meth. Ch., Wahiwai, 1964, Augsberg, Germany, 1968-69; Sunday sch. tchr. arts and crafts ch., Dachau, Germany, 1955-59. Mem. Nick Virgilio Haiku Assn. Democrat. Methodist. Avocations: poet, artist, sculpturing, piano, guitar. Home: 4716 Temple Hills Rd Temple Hills MD 20748

CURRY, JANE LOUISE, writer; b. East Liverpool, Ohio, Sept. 24, 1932; d. William Jack and Helen Margaret (Willis) C. Student, Pa. State U., 1950-51; BS, Indiana U. of Pa., 1954; postgrad., UCLA, 1957-59; AM, Stanford U., 1962, PhD, 1969; student, U. London, 1961-62, 65-66. Tchr. art East Liverpool schs., 1955, L.A. schs., 1956-59; teaching asst. dept. English Stanford (Calif.) U., 1959-61, 64-65, acting instr., 1967-68, instr., 1983-84, lectr., 1987. Storyteller, 1962—. Author: Down from the Lonely Mountain, 1965, Beneath the Hill, 1967, The Sleepers, 1968, The Change-Child, 1969, The Daybreakers, 1970, Mindy's Mysterious Miniature, 1970, Over the Sea's Edge, 1971, The Ice Ghosts Mystery, 1972, The Lost Farm, 1974, Parsley Sage, Rosemary and Time, 1975, The Watchers, 1975, The Magical Cupboard, 1976, Poor Tom's Ghost, 1977, The Birdstones, 1977, The Bassumtyte Treasure, 1978, Ghost Lane, 1979, The Wolves of Aam, 1981, Shadow Dancers, 1983, The Great Flood Mystery, 1985, The Lotus Cup, 1986, Back in the Beforetime, 1987, Me, Myself and I, 1987, The Big Smith Snatch, 1989, Little Little Sister, 1989, What the Dickens?, 1991, The Great Smith House Hustle, 1993, The Christmas Knight, 1993, Robin Hood and his Merry Men, 1994, Robin Hood in the Greenwood, 1995, Moon Window, 1996, Dark Shade, 1998, Turtle Island, 1999, A Stolen Life, 1999, The Wonderful Sky Boat, 2001, The Egyptian Box, 2002, Hold Up the Sky, 2003, Brave Cloelia, 2004. Office: Simon & Schuster Children's Publ Divsn 1230 Ave of Ams New York NY 10020

CURRY, KATHLEEN BRIDGET, retired librarian; b. Parnell, Iowa, May 19, 1931; d. John Michael and Ellen Theresa (Clear) Curry. BSLS, Marycrest Coll., 1953. Head libr. Moline (Ill.) Sr. HS, 1953-90; ret., 1990. Part-time libr. Moline Pub. Hosp. Sch. Nursing, 1957—66; mem. sch. nursing libr. St. Anthony's Hosp., Rock Island, Ill., 1955; hist. libr. Rock Island Hist. Libr., Moline, 1956—59; libr. Black Hawk Coll., Moline, 1958—59. Guild mem. Quad City Symphony Orch., Davenport, 1972 ; bd. dirs. Quad City Arts Coun., Davenport, 1990, Miss Black Hawk Coll., Moline, 1986—; exec. bd. Miss Iowa Pageant, Davenport, 1987—. Recipient Disting. Svc. award, Moline HS PTA, 1983, Marycrest Coll., 1987. Mem.: AAUW, NEA, Iowa Libr. Assn., Moline Edn. Assn., Ill. Sch. Libr. Assn., Ill. Edn. Assn., Zonta Internat., Delta Kappa Gamma. Democrat. Roman Catholic. Avocations: playing the piano, cooking. Home: 3646 71st St Ct Moline IL 61265-1833 E-mail: gmedhus@aol.com.

CURRY, MARTHA ANN, music educator; b. Hattiesburg, Miss., Dec. 3, 1946; d. Edwin Marion and Ione Spinks Harris; m. Burnice Wesley Curry III, May 31, 1969; children: Burnice Wesley Curry IV, Martha Jane. B of Music Edn., U. So. Miss., 1969. Music tchr. Sacred Heart Sch., Hattiesburg, Miss., 1992—93, 2001—. Prodr., dir. : (plays, local theatre and schs.). Fin. chair Hattiesburg Jr. Aux., 1983—84, pres., 1984—85; bd. dirs., officer Thames Elem. Sch., Hattiesburg, Powan Jr. H.S., Hattiesburg, Hattiesburg H.S.; dir. childrens choir Trinity Episcopal Ch., Hattiesburg, 1980—86. Episcopalian. Office: Sacred Heart Sch 608 Southern Ave Hattiesburg MS 39401 E-mail: [illegible]@hotmail.com

CURRY, NANCY ELLEN, psychologist, psychoanalyst, educator; b. Brockway, Pa., Jan. 26, 1931; d. George R. and Mary F. (Covert) C. BA, Grove City Coll., 1952; MEd, U. Pitts., 1956, PhD, 1972; grad., Pitts. Psychoanalytic Inst., 1988, grad. child analytic program, 1992. Lic. psychologist, Pa. Tchr. public schs., East Brady and Oakmont, Pa., 1952-55; presch. demonstration tchr. Arsenal Family and Children's Center, U. Pitts., 1955-79, assoc. dir., 1971-79; from instr. in psychiatry to prof. child devel. Sch. Social Work, U. Pitts, 1957-93; prof. emeritus Sch. Social Work, U. Pitts.; also mem. faculty U. Pitts Sch. Medicine, Sch. Edn., Sch. Health Related Professions.; pvt. practice in psychanalysis and psychotherapy; ret., 2000. Supr., cons.; Fulbright exchange tchr. North Oxford Nursery Sch., Oxford, Eng., 1957-58; vis. prof. Oreg. State U., summer, 1964, Ariz. State U., summer, 1969; assoc. dir. early childhood project Edn. Professions Devel. Act, U.S. Office of Edn., 1970-74; cons. in field. Co-producer 12 films on children's play; co-author Beyond Self-esteem, 1990; editor The Feeling Child; author numerous articles on child devel. Mem. APA, Assn. Child Psychoanalysis, Am. Psychoanalyists Assn. Home: 149 Shadow Ridge Dr Pittsburgh PA 15238-2133 E-mail: NCU149@aol.com.

CURRY, SADYE BEATRYCE, gastroenterologist, educator; b. Reidsville, N.C., Oct. 17, 1941; BS cum laude, Johnson C. Smith U., 1963; MD, Howard U., 1967. Intern Duke U. Med. Ctr., Durham, N.C., 1967-68, fellow in gastroenterology, 1969-72; instr. dept. medicine Duke U., Durham, 1969-72; resident medicine VA Hosp., Washington, 1968-69; asst. prof. medicine divsn. gastroenterology Howard U. Coll. Medicine, Washington, 1972-78, assoc. prof. medicine divsn. gastroenterology, 1978—; asst. chief med. officer Howard U. Med. Svc., D.C. Gen. Hosp., Washington, 1973-74; asst. chief medicine in-charge of undergrad. med. edn. Howard U., Washington, 1974-77. Contbr. articles to profl. jours. Mem. bd. trustees Lake Land 'Or Property Owners Assn., Ladysmith, Va., 1989-90. Recipient Howard U. Coll. Medicine Student Coun. Faculty award for Teaching Excellence, 1975, Kaiser-Permanente Faculty award for excellence in teaching, Howard U. Coll. Medicine, 1978, Howard U. Coll. Med. Student/Am. Med. Women's Assn. woman of yr., 1990; named U.S. Friendship Force amb. to West Berlin, 1980. Mem. AAUW, AMA, Nat. Med. Assn., Am. Soc. Internal Medicine, Medico-Chirurgical Soc. D.C., Med. Soc. D.C., Am. Digestive Diseases Soc., Leonidas Berry Soc. for Digestive Diseases, Nat. Coun. of Negro Women, Alpha Kappa Alpha, Beta Kappa Chi, Alpha Kappa Mu. Office: Howard U Hosp 2041 Georgia Ave NW Washington DC 20060-0001

CURT, DENISE MORRIS, artist, limner, photographer; b. New Haven, Nov. 15, 1936; d. Bertrand and Anna Geraldine (Fiak) Rocheleau; m. John Morris, Oct. 4, 1954 (dec.); children: Tyler John, Cynthia Leigh Morris Bell; m. Albert A. Curt, 1973 (div. 1981). Student of Louis Crescenti, Orange, Conn., 1950-52; student, Whitney Sch. Art, New Haven, 1950, Luchetti Sch. Art, 1951, Paier Sch. Art, Hamden, Conn., 1951. Dir. Meet The Artists and Artisans, Milford, Conn., 1962—; interior designer State of Conn., Hartford, 1972-75. One-woman shows Gull Gallery, Provincetown, Mass., Chapelle Jean Cocteau, Villefranche Sur Mer, France, Garfield Galleries, Orange, Conn., Yale U., Stratford Gallery, Stevenson (Md.) Galleries, also others; represented in numerous pvt. and pub. collections throughout world. Lectr. to numerous civic orgns.; mem. Vis. Artists in Schs., 1970—; commr. Conn. Commn. on Arts, 1974-79; photography chmn. Milford Fine Arts Coun., New Haven Arts Coun.; bd. dirs. Milford Hosp. Aux.; mem. Literacy Vols., Milford. Recipient award Mystic Art Festival, 1969, Sterling House Art Show, 1985, Glastonbury Art Guild, 1988. Mem. Guilford Art League (bd. dirs. 1975-80), Nat. League Am. Pen Women (category painting, bd. dirs. Fairfield chpt., art chair), Conn. Classic Arts, Milford Hist. Soc., Yale U. Gallery, Met. Mus. Art. Republican. Congregationalist. Avocations: renaissance and baroque music, antiques, foreign travel. Home: 41 Green St Milford CT 06460-4709 E-mail: ctlimner@snet.net.

CURTAIN, HELENA HAMBUCH, foreign language specialist; b. Kassel, Germany, Oct. 9, 1946; came to U.S., 1952; d. John and Elisabeth (Bayer) Hambuch; m. Jerry Anderson, Nov. 24, 1973 (div. 1980); m. Tony Max Curtain, Feb. 23, 1985. BA in Spanish and German, Marquette U., 1969; MS in Curriculum and Instruction, U. Wis., 1978, postgrad., 1991. Tchr. German, Spanish, reading and lang. arts Peckham Jr. High Sch., 1969-73, tchr. ESL, 1973-77, resource tchr., program coord. multi-lang. sch., 1977-79; coord. ESL Milw. Pub. Schs., 1979-83, fgn. lang. curriculum specialist, 1979—. Cons. Lilly Endowment, Indpls., 1981, Ferndale, Mich., 1983, Lindbergh Sch. Dist., St. Louis, 1986, 87, West Hartford (Conn.) Pub. Schs., 1986-87, Kenosha (Wis.) Unified Sch. Dist., 1986-89, Brookline (Mass.) Pub. Schs., 1987, Ga. State Dept. of Edn., 1987-89, N.C. State Dept. Edn., 1987, 89, 90, Hinsdale (Ill.) Pub. Schs., Manila Internat. Sch., 1988, Hawaii State Dept. of Edn., 1989, Wilmette (Ill.) Pub. Schs., 1989, 90, 91, Savannah/Chatham County (Ga.) Pub. Schs., 1989, Green Bay (Wis.) Pub. Schs., 1989, Am. Schs. in Japan, Tokyo, 1990, Detroit Pub. Schs., 1991, Winnetka (Ill.) Pub. Schs., 1991, Dept. Def. Dependent Schs., Wiesbaden, Germany, 1991, numerous others; presenter numerous profl. confs., meetings, and workshops. Contbr. articles to profl. jours. Mem. ASCD, Am. Assn. Tchrs. of German, Am. Assn. Tchrs. of Spanish and Portuguese, Am. Coun. Teaching of Fgn. Langs. (exec. coun. 1988—), Tchr. of English to Speakers of Other Langs., Wis. Assn. Fgn. Lang. Tchrs. (pres. 1984-86, Cert. of Recognition 1989, Disting. Fgn. Lang. Educator award 1991), Wis. Tchrs. of English to Speakers of Other Langs. Assn. (exec. bd. 1978-79, v.p. 1980-82, adv. coun. rep. ESL bilingual edn. spl. interest group Detroit chpt. 1981), Phi Delta Kappa. Office: Milw Pub Schs PO Box 10K Milwaukee WI 53201-0010 Home: N72w14324 Good Hope Rd Menomonee Fls WI 53051-4636

CURTIN, JANE THERESE, actress, writer; b. Cambridge, Mass., Sept. 6, 1947; d. John Joseph and Mary Constance (Farrell) C.; m. Patrick F. Lynch, Apr. 31, 1975. AA, Elizabeth Seton Jr. Coll., 1967; student, Northeastern U., 1967-68. Appeared in plays The Proposition, Cambridge and N.Y.C., 1968-72, Last of the Red Hot Lovers touring co., 1973; Broadway debut in Candida, 1981; author, actress Off-Broadway mus. rev. Pretzels, 1974-75; star TV series NBC Saturday Night Live, 1975-79, Kate & Allie, 1984-88, Working It Out, 1990, 3rd Rock from the Sun, 1996-2001 (Golden Satellite for best actress 1996); appeared in films including Mr. Mike's Mondo Video, 1979, How to Beat the High Cost of Living, 1980, O.C. and Stiggs, 1987, Coneheads, 1993, Antz, 1998; TV films include Divorce Wars-A Love Story, 1982, Suspicion, 1988, Maybe Baby, 1988, Common Ground, 1990, Tad, 1995, Christmas in Washington, 1996, Catch a Falling Star, 2000; TV guest appearance Recess, 1997. Recipient Emmy nomination, 1977, 87; Emmy awards for outstanding actress in comedy series, 1984, 85 Mem. Screen Actors Guild, Actors Equity, AFTRA. Office: ICM care Boaty Boatwright 40 W 57th St Fl 16 New York NY 10019-4098

CURTIN, PHYLLIS, music educator, dean, vocalist; b. Clarksburg, W.Va. d. E. Vernon and Betty R. (Robinson) Smith; m. Eugene Cook, May 6, 1956 (dec.); 1 child, Claudia Madeleine. BA, Wellesley Coll., 1943. Prof. Yale Sch. Music, New Haven, 1974 83; master Branford Coll. Yale U., New Haven, 1979-83; dean Coll. Fine Arts, prof. music Boston U., 1983-91, prof. music, 1983—, dean emerita, prof. music, 1991—; artist-in-residence Tanglewood Music Ctr., Tanglewood, Lenox, Mass., 1965—. Former mem. Nat. Coun. on the Arts; named Amb. for the Arts; tchr. master classes U.S., Can., Beijing, Moscow. Made recital debut Town Hall, N.Y.C., 1950, opera debut, N.Y.C. Opera in U.S. premiere of The Trial, 1953, recitals throughout U.S. and fgn. countries; soprano soloist leading symphony orchestras; performer, tchr., Aspen Mus. Festival, 1953-57, appeared as Cressida in, Walton's Troilus and Cressida in, N.Y. premiere, 1955; title role in Floyd's: Susannah, world premiere Tallahassee, 1955; title role in; Darius Milhaud's Medea, U.S. premiere, Brandeis U., 1955, world premiere Floyd's opera Wuthering Heights, 1958, Floyd's Passion of Jonathan Wade, 1959, Flower and Hawk, 1971; U.S. Premier Peter Grimes, 1946; leading soprano: Vienna Staatsoper, 1960, 61; debut as Fiordiligi in Cosi Fan Tutte, Met. Opera Co., 1961; debut, La Scala Opera, Milan, 1962; U.S. premiere Benjamin Britten's War Requiem, with Boston Symphony, 1963; world premiere of Darius Milhaud's opera La Mére Coupable, Geneva, 1966; U.S. premiere Dimitri Shostakovitch's Symphony No. 14, with, Phila. Orch., 1971. Recipient Alumnae Achievement award Wellesley Coll., Nadia Boulanger Achievement award Longy Sch. Music, Letter of Distinction for Svc. to Am. Music, Am. Music Ctr. Home: 9 Seekonk Rd Great Barrington MA 01230-1558 E-mail: curtinphyllis@msn.com.

CURTIS, ANN B. utilities executive; Mgr., adminstr. Gibbs & Hill, Inc.; v.p. mgmt. and fin. svcs. Calpine Corp., 1984—92, sr. v.p., 1992—98, dir., 1996—, exec. v.p., sec., 1998—, vice chmn., 2002—. Office: Calpine 50 W San Fernando St 5th Fl San Jose CA 95113

CURTIS, BARBARA, consumer products company professional; b. Cleve., Nov. 4, 1953; d. Ralph Willis Sr. and Alice Pearl Kitzmiller; m. Marc David King (div.); 1 child, Justin Matthew; m. David Charles Curtis, Sept. 28, 1995. MA in Psychology, Shelbourne U.; postgrad., Andersonville Bapt. Sem. Cert. Langevin tng. mgr./dir., DDI facilitator, achieve global facilitator, Corey facilitator, William Bridges facilitator. Teller/operator C&P Tel. Co., Laurel, Md., 1972-76; transp. clk. Ryder Truck Rental, Houston, 1976-78; lease/rental mgr. Lawrence Marshall Chevrolet-Oldsmobile, Hempstead, Tex., 1978-80; contr./treas. Bluebonnet Sungs, Hempstead, 1980-84; br. mgr. Heights Savs., Hempstead, 1984-89; sr. performance and devel. specialist Cingular Wireless, Houston, 1990—. Trainer, facilitator A.J.R.S., Houston, 1995-98. Editor Ralston Meml. Pres. Ch., Houston, 1999. Mem. ASTD. Avocations: cooking, gardening, horseback riding. Home: 11205 Debra Rd Houston TX 77013-3319 Office: Cingular Wireless One West Loop South Houston TX 77027

CURTIS, CANDACE A. former state legislator; m. Michael Curtis; 1 child, Jameson. BA, Mich. State U., 1982. Environ. health Genesee County Health Dept. Mich.; dep. ct. clk. 67th Dist. Ct., Mich.; chair Genesee County Commrs.; rep. Mich. Dist. 51, 1993-98. Mem. Genesee County Dem. Com. Mem. Farm Bur., South End Dem. Club.

CURTIS, DOLORES ROGERS, writer; b. Columbus, Ohio, Apr. 16, 1929; d. Charles William and Lillian Beatrice Rogers. Student, Ctrl. State U., Xenia, Ohio, 1956—57; B.Elem.Edn., Ohio State U., 1963; attended, John Carroll U., 1980. Bookkeeper Spiegel's, Chgo., Kronfeld's, Manhattan, NY; libr. U.S. Govt. Facility, Columbus; sec. to traveling entertainer, 1949—54; tchr. Columbus Pub. Schs., 1963—68, Cleve. Bd. Edn., 1968—93. Author: Rhyming Pretzels, 2002. Avocations: reading, art, playing piano and organ, writing.

CURTIS, JAMIE LEE, actress; b. L.A., Nov. 22, 1958; d. Tony Curtis and Janet Leigh; m. Christopher Guest; 1 child. Student, U. of the Pacific. Actress: (films) Halloween, 1978, The Fog, 1980, Prom Night, 1980, Terror Train, 1980, Halloween II, 1981, Road Games, 1981, Love Letters, 1983, Trading Places, 1983, Grandview USA, 1984, Adventures of Buckaroo Banzai, 1984, Perfect, 1985, Amazing Grace and Chuck, 1987, Un Homme Amoreux, 1987, Dominick and Eugene, 1988, A Fish Called Wanda, 1988, Blue Steel, 1990, Queens Logic, 1991, My Girl, 1991, Forever Young, 1992, Mother's Boys, 1994, My Girl 2, 1994, True Lies, 1994 (Golden Globe award Best Actress - Musical or Comedy), House Arrest, 1996, Ellen's Energy Adventure, 1996, Fierce Creatures, 1996, Halloween H2O, 1998, Homegrown, 1998, Virus, 1999, Drowning Mona, 2000, The Tailor of Panama, 2001, Daddy and Them, 2001, Rudolf the Red-Nosed Reindeer and the Island of Misfit Toys (voice), 2001, Halloween: Resurrection, 2002, Freaky Friday, 2003; (TV pilots) Callahan, She's in the Army Now, 1981, Tall Tales, (TV series) Operation Petticoat, 1977-78, Anything but Love, 1990-93, (TV movies) Death of a Centerfold: The Dorothy Stratten Story, 1981, Money on the Side, 1982. As Summers Die, 1982, The Heidi Chronicles, 1995, Nicolas' Gift, 1997; author: When I Was Little, 1993; dir.: Anything But Love, 1989, Office: Creative Artists Agy care Rick Kurtzman 9830 Wilshire Blvd Beverly Hills CA 90212-1804

CURTIS, LISA A. accountant, administrator; b. Syracuse, N.Y. d. David William and Barbara Ann Barron; m. Douglas Garfield Curtis, June 27, 1998. BS in Mech. Engring., Ga. Inst. Tech., 1992. Engr. in tng. Lockwood Greene Engrs., Atlanta, 1992-96; acctg. mgr. No. Trust Retirement Cons. LLC, Atlanta, 1996—. Named Young Engr. of Yr. Ga. Soc. Profl. Engrs., 1994. Mem. ASME (chair). Avocations: stained glass design, walking. Office: Northern Trust & Retirement Cons LLC Ste 850 400 Perimeter Center Ter NE Atlanta GA 30346-1299

CURTIS, LORETTA O'ELLEN, retired construction executive; b. Washington, Pa., Apr. 5, 1937; d. Monroe and Mildred (Carr) Bogan; m. Joseph H. Dudley (div. Oct. 1964); children: Ronald S., Joseph T., Mildred M.; m. Wayne J. Curtis (dec. 12/98). AS, Franklin U., 1983, BS, 1989; Grad., Columbus Leadership Program, 1991; grad., Premier Sch. of Travel, 1996. With Bur. Employment Svcs., Columbus, Ohio, 1962-87, examiner, equal employment opportunity officer, 1983-87, ret., 1987; v.p. Aries Constrn., Inc., Columbus, 1988-91, pres., 1991-96; ret., 1996. Mediator small claims divsn. Franklin County; tour leader GLAMER; chmn. Sch. of Ushering ICUA (Interdenominational Church Ushers Assn.), Columbus, substitute tchg., Columbus Pub. Schs., 1999—. Mem. Interdenominational Ch. Ushers Assn. Columbus. Recipient Plaque ICUA of Dayton, 1989, ICUA of Columbus, 1991. Mem. NAFE, Nat. Assn. Parliamentarians (profl. registered parliamentarian), Nat. United Ch. Ushers Assn., Ohio Assn. Colored Women (treas. 1990-94), Ohio Assn. Parliamentarians (pres. 1989-90), ICUA of Columbus (pres. 1977-84), Mayme Moore Club (pres. 1990-93, cert. 1989). Avocations: cooking, reading, golf, volunteer work. Home: 2257 Century Dr Columbus OH 43211-1919

CURTIS, MARY E. (MARY CURTIS HOROWITZ), publishing company executive; d. Lloyd E. and Jean Curtis; m. Irving Louis Horowitz, Oct. 30, 1979 AB cum laude, Washington U., St. Louis, 1968. Editl. dir. Transaction Pubs., New Brunswick, N.J., 1968-74, exec. v.p., 1987-97, pres., 1997 , chmn. bd. dirs., 1994-97; editor in chief Praeger Pubs. subs. CBS Ednl. Pub., N.Y.C., 1974-79; v.p., pub. periodicals John Wiley and Sons, N.Y.C., 1979-87; v.p. Scripta Techica subs. John Wiley and Sons, Washington, 1984-87; mem. mgmt. bd. MIT Press, 1998—; vice chair, trustee Horowitz Found. for Social Policy, 1998—. Chair adv. com. Serials Industry Systems, 1985-88; dir. Transaction Pubs. (U.K.) Ltd.; lectr. in field. Contbr. articles to profl. jours. Mem. Soc. Scholarly Pubs. (bd. dirs. 1984-88), Assn. Am. Pubs. (Freedom to Read com.). Jewish. E-mail: mcurtis@transactionpub.com.

CURTIS, PAULA ANNETTE, elementary and secondary education educator; b. Natrona Heights, Pa., Apr. 16, 1953; d. Stephen John and Josephine Kathleen (Killian) C. BS In Edn., Geneva Coll., 1974; postgrad., U. Vt., 1975, Pa. State U., New Kensington, 1978. Cert. religious edn. tchr., Pitts. Diocese. Tchr. Transfiguration Sch., Russellton, Pa., 1979—, dir. religious edn., 1995-98; tchr. continuing edn. C.C. of Allegheny County, Pitts., 1992—, Pa. State U., New Kensington, 1988 ; tchr. O'Mara Driving Sch., Lower Burrell, Pa., 1976—, Lenape Votech., 1990—; CCD tchr. Transfiguration Sch., Russellton, 1995-97, head tchr., head fine arts dept., 1995-97. Chmn. vision and values in Pitts. Diocese, Transfiguration Sch., 1980-97; CCD tchr. St. Clement Parish, Tarentum, Pa., 1986-92, dir. religious edn., 1987-92; dir. religious edn. St. Joseph Parish, Natrona, Pa., 1992-93; product tester Nat. Family Opinion Poll, 1987—, model Van Enterprises, Cranberry, Pa., 1989-92; tchr. driver edn. Plum (Pa.) Sr. H.S., 1996-98; Act 48 presenter for Penn Hills Sch. Dist. and Pitts. Diocesan Schs., 2002—; freelance model, fashion Mag. 1998—; vol. Help Beautify the County with Art, Russellton. Mem. Nat. Cath. Educators Assn., Nat. English Tchrs. Assn. Democrat. Roman Catholic. Avocations: craft designs, needle work, collecting reptiles, collecting and breeding tropical birds, breeding shih-tzus. Home: 211 W 9th Ave Tarentum PA 15084-1241 Office: Transfiguration Sch CCD Office 100 Mckrell Rd Russellton PA 15076-1100

CURTIS, SUSAN M. lawyer; b. Nashville, 1956; BA, U. Tenn., Knoxville. Ptnr. Skadden, Arps, Slate, Meagher & Flom, N.Y.C. Office: Skadden Arps Slate Meagher & Flom 4 Times Sq Fl 24 New York NY 10036-6595

CURTIS, SUZANNE M. school system administrator, educator; b. Great Falls, Mont., June 24, 1947; d. Doreen M Swager and David George Curtis; 1 child, Miles Stanert Curtis-Philips. AA, GoldenWest Coll., 1978; BA, U. of Mont., 1989; MA, Middlebury (Vt.) Coll., 1995. Cert. tchr. Wash., 1996. Tchr. LaCrosse (Wash.) HS, 1989—96, Rainier (Wash.) HS, 1996—; asst. to on-site dir. Bread Loaf Sch. of English, Santa Fe, 2000—. Advisor student yearbook and newspaper LaCrosse (Wash.) HS, 1989—96, advisor honor soc., 1994—; v.p. Inland NW (Wash.) Coun. Tchrs. English, 1994—96. Editor: (newspaper) The Branding Iron (2nd Pl. spot layout award So. Calif. JACC, 1977). Wall of tolerance com. Nat. Campaign for Tolerance, 2002; pres. Barnes Lake Pk. Homeowners Assn., Tumwater, Wash., 1999—2002. Recipient First Pl. Newspaper award, Soc. for Profl. Journalists Assn., Wash., 1992; grantee Writing for the Pub. grant, Clemson U., 1991; scholar Rural English Tchr.'s scholarship, Middlebury (Vt.) Coll., 1991, Reginald and Juanita Cook scholarship, Bread Loaf Sch. of English, Middlebury Coll., 1993, Dulcie Scott Meml. scholarship, 1995. Mem.: Nat. Coun. of Tchrs. English (assoc.). Avocations: photography, health spas & retreats, travel, languages. Home: 1500 Lake Park Drive 63 Tumwater WA 98512 Office: Rainier High School PO Box 98 Rainier WA 98576 Office Phone: 360-446-2205. E-mail: curtiss@rainier.wednet.edu.

CURTISS, CAROL PERRY, healthcare consultant; b. Worcester, Mass., Dec. 9, 1946; d. Joseph Anthony and Marjorie Ruth (Riedle) Perry; m. Jack Daniel Curtiss, Feb. 8, 1970; children: Paul Daniel, Jennifer Perry. Diploma in nursing, Mass. Gen. Hosp. Sch. Nursing, Boston, 1967; BS, Am. Internat. Coll., Springfield, Mass., 1978; MSN, Yale U., 1981. RN Mass. Staff nurse Franklin Med. Ctr., Greenfield, Mass., 1970, Greenfield Ob-Gyn. Assocs., 1972-74, Greenfield Vis. Nurses, 1974-75; instr. Slim Living Program YMCA, Greenfield, 1977-78; instr. nursing Greenfield C.C., 1978; asst. prof. nursing Elms Coll., Chicopee, Mass., 1981-84; oncology program mgr. Franklin Med. Ctr, Greenfield, 1986-93; cancer care cons. Curtiss Cons., Greenfield, 1981—. Mem. faculty Greenfield C.C., 1985—87; vis. lectr., clin. instr. Fitchburg (Mass.) State Coll., 1985—86; vis. lectr. Elms Coll., Chicopee, Mass., 1984—85; mem. adj. faculty SUNY, 1987—90, U. Mass., Amherst, 1989—; peer reviewer Agy. for Health Care Policy and Rsch., Cancer Pain Gidelines, HHS, 1993; presenter in field, U.S. and abroad, 1981—; adj. faculty Sch. Nursing U. So. Ind. Co-author: Cancer Doesn't Have to Hurt, 1997; guest editor Oncology Nursing Forum, 1993; contbr. articles to profl. jours. Bd. dirs. Franklin County, Am. Cancer Soc., Greenfield, 1979-95, mem. nurse and social work scholarship com., 1988-96, nursing com. liaison, 1990-98; mem. steering com. Mass. Cancer Pain Initiative, 1988-90, 2002—, liaison, 1990-97, cons. chmn., 2002—; trustee Oncology Nursing Found., 1995-2000. Recipient Am. Alliance of Cancer Pain Initiatives award, Dahl Lectureship: Leadership in Systems Change. Mem.: Internat. Union Against Cancer, Oncology Nursing Soc., Am. Soc. Pain Mgmt. Nurses, Am. Pain Soc., Internat. Union Against Cancer (U.S. com. 1992—2000), Oncology Nursing Soc. (mem. numerous sub coms. 1987—, mem. numerous subcoms. 1987—, pres.-elect 1991—92, 1991—92, corp. adv. bd. 1991—93, corp. adv. bd. 1991—93, bd. dirs. 1991—, 1991—, nat. pres. 1992—93, Oncology Nursing Press pres. 1992—94, pres. Oncology Nursing Press 1992—94, pres. 1993—94, co-chair conf. on pain 1994, Disting. Svc. award 1999), Am. Soc. Pain Mgmt. Nurses, Am. Pain Soc., Sigma Theta Tau. Avocations: biking, skiing, tennis, carpentry. Home: 73 James St Greenfield MA 01301-3607 Office Phone: 413-774-5238. E-mail: carol.curtiss@verizon.net.

CURWICK, DEBORAH, realtor; d. James T. Curwick, Sr. and Beverly Nygren; life ptnr. Christopher Dunne; children: Andrea Milling, Brandon Milling. Degree, Realtor's Inst., 1998. Accredited buyers representative

Fla., 2001. Realtor Coldwell Banker, Palm Beach Gardens, Fla., 1997—98, Illus. Properties, Palm Beach Gardens, 1998—2003, RE/MAX No. Palm Beaches, Palm Beach Gardens, 2003—. Mem.: Real Estate Buyer's Agt. Coun., Nat. Assn. Realtors, Nat. Assn. Female Execs., Fla. Assn. Realtors, Women's Coun. Real Estate, Office: RE/MAX Northern Palm Beaches 11770 U.S. Hwy One, 503 North Palm Beach FL 33408 Personal E-mail: debbie@deborahcurwick.com. E-mail: debbie@deborahcurwick.com.

CURZON, SUSAN CAROL, university administrator; b. Poole, Eng., Dec. 11, 1947; came to U.S., 1952. d. Kenneth Nigel and Terry Marguerite (Morris) C. AB, U. Calif., Riverside, 1970; MLS, U. Wash., 1972; PhD, U. So. Calif., 1983. Spl. libr. Kennecott Exploration, San Diego, 1972-73; various positions L.A. County Pub. Libr., 1973-89; dir. libr. Glendale (Calif.) Pub. Libr., 1989-92; dean univ. libr. Calif. State U., Northridge, 1992—, 1992—. Cons. Grantsmanship Ctr., L.A., 1981-83; vis. lectr. Grad. Sch. Libr. and Info. Sci. UCLA, 1986-92. Author: Managing Change, Managing the Interview. Libr. of the Year, Libr. Jour., 1993. Mem. ALA, Calif. Libr. Assn. Democrat. Avocations: history, horseback riding. Office: Calif State U Libr Office of the Dean 18111 Nordhoff St Northridge CA 91330-8326

CUSACK, JOAN, actress; b. N.Y.C., Oct. 11, 1962; d. Richard and Nancy C.; m. Dick Burke; 2 children. BA, U. Wis., 1985. Stage appearances include Road, 1988, Brilliant Traces, 1989, Cymbeline, 1989; TV appearances include Saturday Night Live (regular 1985-86 season), The Mother, 1994, What About Joan, 2001, A Very Merry Muppet Christmas, 2002; film appearances include My Bodyguard, 1980, Class, 1983, Grandview USA, 1984, Sixteen Candles, 1984, The Allnighter, 1987, Broadcast News, 1987, Stars and Bars (aka An Englishman in New York), 1988, Married to the Mob, 1988, Working Girl, 1988 (Acad. award nominee best supporting actress 1989), Say Anything, 1989, Men Don't Leave, 1989, My Blue Heaven, 1990, The Cabinet of Dr. Ramirez, 1991, Hero, 1992, Toys, 1992 (also musician), Addams Family Values, 1993, Corrina, Corrina, 1994, Nine Months, 1995, Two Much, 1996, Mr. Wrong, 1996, A Smile Like Yours, 1997, In and Out, 1997, Grosse Pointe Blank, 1997, Arlington Road, 1999, Runaway Bride, 1999, Toy Story 2, 1999, Arlington Road, 1999, Cradle Will Rock, 1999, High Fidelity, 2000, Where the Heart Is, 2000, School of Rock, 2003, Looney Toons--Back in Action, 2003, Raising Helen, 2004. Office: United Talent Agy Inc 9560 Wilshire Blvd Fl 5 Beverly Hills CA 90212

CUSHING, SARA ELIZABETH, English language educator, writer; b. Richmond, Va., July 7, 1950; d. William Routledge and Sara Margie (Williams) C. BA, Duke U., 1972; MS, SUNY, Cortland, 1978. Cert. tchr. secondary English, N.Y. Adminstrv. asst. Duke Players/Duke U., Durham, N.C., 1970-72; substitute tchr. Maine-Endwell and Union Endicott Schs., Endicott and Endwell, N.Y., 1972-73; tchr. English and drama John F. Kennedy High Sch., Richmond, Va., 1973-75; project coord. Alekna Constrn., Endicott, 1975-77; tchr. English Vestal (N.Y.) Sr. High Sch., 1977-78, Greene (N.Y.) Jr.-Sr. High Sch., 1978-88; writer, editor, writing cons., 1981—; instr. English, computer lab. mgr., weekend coord. coll. Piedmont Tech. Coll., Greenwood, SC, 1988—2002; cons. Time to Celebrate, 2003. Rental agt. Drucker and Falk, Richmond, 1974-75; liaison/amb. to Lander Coll., Greenwood, 1990-91, co-chmn. Praxis Conf., 1990-91; team leader S.C Advanced Technol. Edn. Exemplary Faculty Team, 1995-98, Ad-hoc Workplace Rsch. Team Leader, 1996-97. Author: (textbook) You, Too, Can Write, 1990, 4th edit., 1998. Named Faculty Educator of Yr., Piedmont Tech. Coll., 2002; recipient summer seminar stipend, NEH, Atlanta, 1984. Mem. Ea. Regional Competency-Based Edn. Consortium (bd. dirs., conf. chair 1999-2000, treas. 2001—), Greene Tchrs. Assn. (pres. 1983-85, mem. negotiating team 1984-86), Educators Assn., Phi Theta Kappa (hon.). Avocations: writing, gardening, reading, dramatics, pets. Home: 119 Parkwood Rd Greenwood SC 29646-8535 Office: Piedmont Tech Coll PO Box 1467 Greenwood SC 29648-1467

CUSHMAN, HELEN MERLE BAKER, retired management consultant; b. Perth Amboy, N.J. d. Ivan F. and Lucile (Atkinson) Baker; m. Robert Arnold Cushman, June 2, 1945; children— Lucinda Ann, Robert Rorem. AB in History, Barnard Coll., 1942; postgrad., NYU, 1944. Route analyst intelligence divsn. Air Transport Command, Washington, 1943-44; personnel asst. Gen. Cable Corp., N.Y.C., 1944-45; sr. staff asst. to chmn. bd. Trans World Airlines, N.Y.C., 1945-50; pres. H.M. Baker Assocs., Westfield, N.J., 1958-93; ret., 1993. Past archivist-historian N.J. chpt. Am. Records Mgmt. Assn. Author: ARMA-New Jersey, The Founding Years, 1972, A History of Shreve, Crump and Low, 1974, Butterick and the Story of Sewing, 1975, The Anniversary Manual, 1976, Gears, Machines, Systems, 1978, Mountainside Chapel: Yesterday, Today, Tomorrow, 1981, Serving Westerly Since 1800, 1985, The Mill on the Third River, 1992, From Seed to Harvest, 1993, The Church at the Crossroads, 1999; editor, pub. Ministry Press, The Bus. History Letter; contbr. to Am. Archivist. Recipient Lit. award Am. Records Mgmt. Assn., 1972. Mem.: PEO Sisterhood (pres. chpt. AE., Princeton N.J.), various hist. socs., Newcomen Soc., Barnard Coll. Club North Ctrl. NJ (past pres.). Address: 321 Sharon Way Monroe Township NJ 08831-1561

CUSHMAN, KAREN LIPSKI, writer; b. Chgo. married; 1 child, Leah. BA in English/Greek, Stanford U., 1963; MA in Human Behavior, USIU, 1977; MA in Mus. Studies, JFK U., 1987. Faculty mus. studies dept. John F. Kennedy U., San Francisco. Author: Catherine, Called Birdy, 1994, The Midwife's Apprentice, 1995 (John Newberry award 1996), The Ballad of Lucy Whipple, 1996, Matilda Bone, 2000, Rodzina, 2003. Office: Clarion Books 215 Park Ave S New York NY 10003-1603

CUSHMAN, MARGARET JANE, home care executive, nurse; b. Pahokee, Fla., Nov. 17, 1948; d. Edmund Francis and Mary Margaret (Adams) C. Diploma in nursing, Johns Hopkins Hosp., 1969; BSN, U. Pa., 1972; MSN, Yale U., 1976; MA in Bot. Healing, TAI Sophia Inst., 2004. Asst. dir. nursing St. Joseph's Hosp., Phila., 1972-74; asst. dir. Regional Vis. Nurse Agy., North Haven, Conn., 1976-78; exec. dir. Waterbury (Conn.) Vis. Nurse Assn., 1978-82; exec. v.p VNA Health Care, Inc., Plainville, Conn., 1982-86; pres. Vis. Nurse And Home Care, Inc. (name changed to VNA Health Care, Inc.), Plainville, Conn., 1986-98; CEO Home Care U. Nat. Assn. for Home Care, Washington, 1998—2002; v.p. Nat. Assn. Home Care, Washington, 1999—2002; exec. dir. Home Healthcare Nurses Assn., Nat. Assn. for Home Care, 1999—2002; editor-in-chief Caring Mag., Nat. Assn. for Home Care, 1999—2002; editl. cons. Caring Mag., 2003; clin. herbalist and cons. Herbs and Health LLC, Freeport, Maine, 2004—. Asst. clin. prof. Yale U. Sch. Nursing, New Haven, 1978-99, assoc. clin. prof., 1999—; asst. clin. prof. U. Tex. Sch. Nursing, San Antonio, 1990-97; cons. U. S.C. Sch. Nursing, 1987-89, U. Tex. Sch. Nursing, San Antonio, 1989-90; corporator Am. Savs. Bank, 1993-98, Hartford Hosp., 1993—, Hosp. for Special Care, 1994-98. Contbg. author: Home Health Adminstration, 1988; mem. editl. adv. bd. Home Healthcare Nurse, 1988-95; co-editor Certification for Home Care/Hospice Execs. Study Guide; contbr. articles to profl. jours. Mem. Conn. Gov.'s Blue Ribbon Com. to Investigate Nursing Home Industry in Conn., Hartford, 1975-77; mem. nat. adv. com. Ctr. for Health Policy Rsch., Denver, 1989-94; mem. Conn. Award for Excellence Health Adv. Task Force, 1993-94; sec. Found. for Hospice and Home Care, 1989-95; mem. joint adv. coun. and pub. health adv. coun. Conn. Dept. Pub. Health and Addiction Svcs., 1994-95; bd. dirs. St. Mary's Hosp., Waterbury, Conn., 1996-98, Health Tech, 1997-98. Robert Wood Johnson/Nat. League for nursing fellow, 1975, fellow Found. for Hospice and Home Care, 1992; recipient Andrew Veckerelli prize Yale U. Sch. Nursing, 1976, Disting. Alumni award, 1986, Creative Thinking Assn. Tribute, 1990, Leadership award Conn. Assn. for Home Care, 1995. Fellow Am. Acad. Nursing; mem. ANA, Am. Herbalists Guild, Inst. of Noetic Scis., Creative Thinking Assn.,

Nat. League for Nursing (nat. adv. coun. home health outcome study 1989-93), Nat. Assn. Home Care (chmn. 1986-88, sec. 1984-86, 91-94, vice chair 1995-98, Mem. of Yr. award 1984, 97, Virginia Henderson award for excellence in nursing 1997), Conn. Assn. Home Care (sec. 1981-85), Greater Hartford C. of C. (women's activity com. 1990-91), Conn. Interagy. Health Group, Alumni Assn. Leadership Greater Hartford, Sigma Theta Tau. Avocation: herb gardening. Home: 75 Shore Dr Freeport ME 04032 Office Phone: 207-865-6444.

CUSICK REIMINK, RUTH ELIZABETH, community health nurse; b. Nunica, Mich., Oct. 26, 1929; d. Jacob A. Venema and Nellie K. Holtrop-Venema; m. Roger Duane Cusick, Sept. 26, 1953 (dec. Apr. 1994); children: Mary Kay, William Roger, Beth Ann; m. Harvey Reimink, June 28, 1997 (dec. Nov. 1997). BS, St. Joseph's Coll., North Windham, Maine, 1989; RN, Hackley Hosp. Sch. Nursing, Muskegon, Mich., 1951. Nurse mgr. Holland (Mich.) City Hosp., 1953—54; nurse North Ottowa Cmty. Hosp., Grand Haven, Mich., 1955—66, St. Mary's Hosp., Grand Rapids, Mich., 1982, Butterworth Hosp., Grand Rapids, Mich., 1982—84, Hackley Hosp., Muskegon, 1966—2002, Hackley Vis. Nurses, Muskegon, 2003—. Mem.: Assn. Women's Health Ob-Gyn. and Neonatal Nursing, Am. Nurses Assn. Office: Hackley Vis Nurses Terrace Plz Ste 150 Muskegon MI 49440

CUSMANO, J. JOYCE, public relations executive; b. Mich. BA, Eastern Mich. U.; MA, U. Md., 1972. Asst. dir. Detroit Youtheatre Detroit Inst. Arts; spl. events dir. Detroit Renaissance, 1979—84; v.p. Franco Pub. Rels. Group, Detroit, 1985-90, sr. v.p., 1991—98, dir., consumer group, 1991—98; pres. Sojourn Comm. Grp., Grosse Point Woods, Mich., 1998—. Mem. Women's Econ. Club. Office: Sojourn Comm Grp 19776 E Ida Ln Grosse Pointe Woods MI 48236

CUSSON-CAIL, KATHLEEN, consulting company executive; b. Manchester, N.H., Mar. 17, 1971; m. Alan Cail, Feb. 26, 2000. AS in Archtl. Engring. Tech., N.H. Tech. Inst., 1994; BS in Mgmt., Franklin Pierce Coll., 1995, MBA, 2000. Lic. securities, life, property, casualty. Personal fin. analyst Primerica Fin. Svcs., Nashua, NH, 1996—2003; instructor Introduction to Windows and Word Processing, Adult Comm. Education program Merrimack Sch. District, 2000—02; prin., owner Aggregate Bus. & Comm. Cons., Inc., Manchester, NH, 2002—, Collabresource, Manchester, 2002—, Ideal Instr., Manchester, 2002—. Vol. Vt. Adaptive Ski and Sport, 1996—98, Jerry Lewis Labor Day Telethon, 1998—2003, Riverfest, 1999. Recipient Good Citizenship award DAR, 1985. Avocations: volleyball, horseshoes, motorcycling, winter hiking. Office: Aggregate Business & Communication Cons Inc 1361 Elm Street Ste 208 Manchester NH 03101

CUSTURERI, MARY CATHERINE FOCA, literature educator; b. Jersey City, Dec. 28, 1929; d. Joseph and Rosa (Scala) Foca; m. Domenick Custureri, July 31, 1948; children: Frank, Richard. BS, Fla. Atlantic U., 1969, MEd, 1972, EdS, 1986, EdD, 1989. English lectr. Embry Riddle Aeronautical U., Daytona Beach, Fla.; lectr., coll. instr., 1999—. Tchr.-trainer learning strategies, speaker at confs. in field and at Internat. Reading Assn., Nat. Coun. of Tchrs. of English. Instructional Strategies: Helping all Students Succeed, 2004; contbr. articles to profl. jours. Grantee Palm Beach County Edn. Found., 1985, Fla. Atlantic U., 1980, Cardinal Newman H.S., Latner Found., Nat. Cath. Edn. Assn., Good Sam Wallmart. Mem. Internat. Reading Assn. (spkr. 1988), Nat. Cath. Edn. Assn., Fla. Reading Assn., Nat. Coun. Tchrs. English (spkr.), Fla. Writers Assn., Assn. for Supervision and Curriculum Devel. (spkr. various confs.), Fla. Devel. Assn. (spkr. 2003), Delta Kappa Gamma (North Palm Beach chpt., spkr.). Roman Catholic.

CUTHBERT, EMILIE ANN (EMILIE WINTHROP), interior designer; b. Denver, Apr. 13, 1932; d. Theodore Kostitch and Florence Engelbach; m. Robert Whiting Caulfield, Mar. 4, 1955 (dec. May 1961); 1 child, Emilie Florence ; m. William Kendal Cuthbert, June 7, 1968 (dec. Apr. 1994). Student, Pomona Coll., 1949—50; grad., Parson's Sch. Design, 1953; student, U. Calif., San Diego. Designer Guy Brink, Inc., Pasadena, Calif., 1954—55; sr. designer Gerald Jerome, Inc., La Jolla, 1960—65; owner, designer Emilie Winthrop, 1965—; entertainment editor San Diego Writers Monthly, 1998—; writer The News Chronicle Mag., Encinitas, 1994—95; writer, arts editor Calif. Women Mag., 1995—97; exec. editor San Diego Decor & Style, Solana Beach, 1998; editor Mt. LaJolla News, 1975—84. Bd. govs. Mt. La Jolla, 1973—75. Avocations: travel, gardening, genealogy, gemology. Home: 3207 La Costa Ave Carlsbad CA 92009

CUTLER, CATHY GORDON, women's health nurse practitioner; d. Allen R. and Ethel B. Gordon; m. James J. Cutler, Jr., Apr. 28, 1991; children: William, Katherine. BSN, Vanderbilt U., 1980; MEd, U.S.C., 1985; MSN, U. Fla., 1997. RN Fla., Ga., Calif., Md. Clin. nurse specialist Fla. Hosp., Orlando, 1998—. Gen. bd. mem. Healthy Start, Seminole County, Fla., 1999—; bd. mem., program chair Ctrl. Fla. Advanced Practice Nursing Coun., Orlando, Fla., 2002—. Capt. USAF, 1987—94. Mem.: Assn. Women's Health Neonatal Obstetric Nursing, Sigma Theta Tau.

CUTLER, LAUREL, advertising agency executive; b. N.Y.C., Dec. 8, 1926; d. A. Smith and Dorothy (Glaser) C.; m. Stanley Bernstein, July 3, 1952 (div. 1983); children— Jon Cutler, Amy Sarah, Seth Perry Ba, Wellesley Coll., 1946. Reporter Washington Post, 1946—; copywriter J. Walter Thompson, N.Y.C., 1947-50; copy chief Wesley Assocs., 1950-56; v.p. Fletcher, Richard, Calkins & Holden, N.Y.C., 1956-63; sr. v.p., creative dir. McCann Erickson, N.Y.C., 1963-72; sr. v.p. Leber Katz Ptnrs., N.Y.C., 1972-80, exec. v.p., dir. mktg. planning, 1980-84, vice chmn., 1984—, FCB/Leber Katz Ptnrs., N.Y.C., 1986—; v.p. consumer affairs Chrysler Corp., Highland Park, Mich., 1988-91; global dir. mktg. and planning Foote Cone & Belding Comms., Chgo., 1991-98; dir. Fallon McElligott, N.Y.C., 1998—. Spkr. to orgns. including Assn. Nat. Advertisers, Am. Mktg. Assn., Produce Mktg. Assn., Grocery Mfrs. Am., Conf. Bd.; bd. dirs. True North Comms., Inc., Hannaford Bros. Co., Quaker State Corp., Domino's Mktg. Adv. Bd. Recipient Matrix award Women in Comm., 1985, Achievement award Wellesley Alumni Assn., 1990; named Ladies Home Jour. One of Am.'s Fifty Most Powerful Women, 1990, Advt. Industry Man of Yr., 1995. Mem. Fashion Group (bd. dirs.), N.Y.C. Partnership, Com. of 200, Cosmopolitan Club, Womens' Forum Inc. Avocations: reading, antiques, art. Home: 180 E 79th St New York NY 10021-0437 also: 14 John St Sag Harbor NY 11963-2620 Office: Fallon McElligott 79 5th Ave New York NY 10003-3034

CUTLER, RONNIE, artist; b. N.Y.C. d. Leo and Sarah (Saks) C.; m. Mar. 1, 1951 (dec. May 1990). Student, Columbia U., 1955-56, Bklyn. Mus. Art, 1958, Art Students League, N.Y.C., 1959-60. Exhibited in group shows William Whipple Mus., Southwest State U. Minn., Internat. Works on Paper, Watercolor, 2003, Monique Goldstorm Gallery, N.Y.C., 2002, Whitney Mus. Am. Art, N.Y.C., 1954, am. Watercolor Soc. 132d Ann. Internat., 1999, 2000, 133d Ann. Internat., 2000, Delgado Mus. Art, New Orleans, 1955, Berkshire Mus. Art, Pittsfield, Mass., 1955, 56, Bklyn. Mus., 1956, 58, Riverside Mus. Art, N.Y.C., 1957, Springfield (Mass.) Mus. Art, 1957, Nat. Acad. Art, N.Y.C., 1958, Provincetown (Mass.) Art Assn. and Mus., 1993, 57th Ann. Audubon Artists, 1999; permanent coll., Southwest State U., oil landscape, 2003. Recipient Sherwood prize in oil, Silvermine Guild Artists, 1955, 1st prize, Riverside Mus. Art, 1957, alumni purchase award, Art Students League, 1960, 1st ptize in oil, So. Berkshire Assn., 1979, 1980, Painters and Sculptors Soc., 1955, Frederix/Tara prize, Audubon Artists 58th Ann., First Prize Oil Works on Canvas, Pen and Brush, N.Y.C., 2003, Thomas E. Picard award Oil Salmagundi. Mem. Am. Watercolor Soc. Internat., Salgamundi Club. Home: 175 W 12th St Apt 11J New York NY 10011-8206

CUTNAW, MARY-FRANCES, retired communications educator, writer, editor, publisher; b. Dickinson, N.D., June 15, 1931; d. Delbert A. and Edith (Calhoun-Pritchard) C. BS, U. Wis., 1953, MS, 1957 Life tchg. license in speech, English and French, Wis, Vol. tchr. Vocat. Sch. for World War II vets., U. Wis./ Baraboo Ft. McCoy (formerly Camp McCoy) ext., Milw., 1953-55; tchg. asst. dept. speech U. Wis., Madison, 1956-57, spl. asst. Sch. Edn., summer 1957; instr. speech U. Wis.-Stout, Menomonie, 1957-58, dean of women, 1958-59, asst. prof. speech, 1959-64, assoc. prof. speech, 1964-74, prof. emeritus, 1974—. Comm. and pers. cons., St. Paul, 1974—; writer, editor, pub. New Legal Press, 1995—. Author: How to Settle a Living Trust, 1996, 4th edit., 2003. Organizer, past advisor Young Dems., Menomonie, 1959—; founder Edith and Kent Cutnaw Scholarship, U. Wis., Stevens Point, 1960—; bd. dirs. Blaisdell Place, Mpls., 1980-85. Hon. scholar U. Wis., Madison, 1959-60, 67-68. Mem. ACLU, NOW, Internat. Platform Assn., Nat. Women's History Wis., Wis. Acad. Arts and Scis., Wis. Women's Network, Progressive Roundtable (Mpls.), Calhoun Beach Club (Mpls.), Amnesty Internat., World Jewish Congress (charter), U. Club St. Paul, Greenpeace, Dunn County Humane Soc., Sierra Club, Soc. for Prevention of Cruelty to Animals, Humane Soc. U.S., Gamma Phi Beta, Phi Beta, Sigma Tau Delta, Pi Lambda Theta. Roman Catholic. Avocations: ecology, civil rights, animal rights, consumer protection, health and wellness. Office: New Legal Press PO Box 282 Menomonie WI 54751-0282 E-mail: cutnawm@uwstout.edu.

CUTNEY, BARBARA ANN, philosophy educator; b. N.Y.C., Aug. 28, 1941; d. Andrew and Josephine (Gondar) C.; 1 child, Justine. BA cum laude, Queens Coll., 1963; MA, Boston U., 1970; PhD, NYU, 1974. Cert. philosophical counselor 1998. Assoc. prof. philosophy Coll. of New Rochelle, 1966—; dir. curriculum devel., 1994-95, asst. dean for acad. programs, 1995-96; pvt. practice N.Y.C., 1998; chairperson philosophy and religious studies divsn. Coll. of New Rochelle, 2003—. Conducted philosophical forums Barnes and Noble, N.Y.C., 2001—03. Author: Challenges and Pleasures: Living Ethically in a Competitive World, 1997; contbg. editor Dance Pages, 1987; contbr. numerous articles and book reviews to profl. jours.; choreographer St. John's Eve, N.Y.C., 1987, numerous other ensemble dances, cons. for John Cage Retrospective Concert, N.Y.C., 1992; acting roles in N.Y.C. incl. Maria in Twelfth Night, Mrs. Morehead in The Women, 3d old woman in Lysistrata. Bd. dirs. 782 W. End Ave. Coop., 1990-91, 94-96, 2003—; mem. Meml. Sloan Kettering's Inst. Animal Care and Use Com., 1998-99. NDEA fellow in philosophy of sci. Western Res., 1964, E. S. Brightman fellow Boston U., 1965-66, Walter A. Anderson fellow NYU, 1971-73; grantee NEH funds Coll. of New Rochelle, summers 1987, 89, 96 Mem. Am. Philos. Assn., Soc. for Women in Philosophy, Middle Atlantic States Philosophy Edn. Soc., Columbia U. Moral Edn. Seminar, Phi Beta Kappa. Avocations: dance, theatre, reading, sports, acting. Home: 782 W End Ave New York NY 10025-5446 Office: Coll of New Rochelle 29 Castle Pl New Rochelle NY 10805-2338

CUTONE, KATHALEEN KELLY, figure skater, former skating judge, athletic representative; Athletic rep. U.S. Figure Skating Assn., Colo. Springs, Colo., 1998—. Placed 16th Nat. Sr. competition, 1997, 2nd place Ea. Sr., 1997, New England Sr., 1997, 12th place Nat. Sr., 1996, 4th place Ea. Sr., 1996, 1st place New England Sr., 1996, 6th place World Univ. Games, 1995, 11th place Nat. Sr. competition, 1995, tie for 5th place Nat. Sr., 1995, 2d place Ea. Sr., 1995, 3rd place Ea. Sr., 1995, 1st place Nat. Collegiates, 1994, 12th place U.S. Olympic Festival, 1990, others. Mem. U.S. Figure Skating Assn. Office: USFSA 20 1st St Colorado Springs CO 80906-3624

CUTRIGHT, LORETTA ANN, special education educator; b. Washington, Jan. 8, 1953; d. Charles Anthony and Dorothy Dolores DeCesaris, Angelina Marie DeCesaris (Stepmother); m. Robert, Jr. Henry DeCesaris, May 28, 1972; children: Robert, III Henry, Angelina Marie Jonsson, Dorothy Dolores Bearden. BA in Elem. Edn., Bowie State U., Md., 1981; EdM, Bowie State U., Md., 1984; EdD, NOVA Southeastern U., North Miami Beach, Fla., 2002. Cert. advanced profl. edn. Md., sch. leaders lic. assessment Md., 2002. Cmty. referenced instrn. coord. Prince George's County Pub. Schools, Upper Marlboro, Md., 1992—2003; spl. edn. specialist Prince George's County Pub. Sch., Upper Marlboro, Md., 2003—. Crisis counselor Prince George's County Cmty. Crisis Ctr., Hyattsville, Md., 1988—; vol. counselor Sch. Based Resiliency Tng. Author: (support group curriculum) Resiliency Tng. Program. Mgmt. team Prince George's County Md. Spl. Oylmpics, Balt., 2001—03; bd. mem. Prince George's County Cmty. Crisis Ctr., Hyattsville, Md., 2003—03. Recipient Vol. of the Yr., Prince George's County Cmty. Crisis Ctr., 1995, 1999, 2000, 2002, Spl. Educator of the Yr., So. Prince George's Rotary, 1997-98, Noreen Webber Honor award, Nova Southeastern U., 2003; grantee Teen Support Group Implementation, Freddis Mac Found., 1999. Mem.: Coun. for Exceptional Childern (assoc.). Roman Catholic. Achievements include development of specialized teams for special olympians/ bocce teams; patents for school-based Resiliency Training curriculum for HS. Avocations: camping, gardening, reading. Home: 2809 Ridge Waldorf MD 20603 Office: Prince George's County Pub Sch School Lane Upper Marlboro MD 20772

CUTRONA, CHERYL F. mediator; b. Detroit, Mich., Aug. 15, 1952; d. Samuel Frank and Mayline Bova Cutrona; m. Neil Henry Kugelman, June 27, 1982; children: Rachel May Kugelman, Louis Samuel Kugelman. JD, Temple U., 2002; BA, Mich. State U., 1977; MLS, Wayne State U., 1979. Exec. dir. Good Shepherd Mediation Program, Phila., 1991—; sole propr. Eighteen East Consulting, Phila., 1985—90; editor Labor Rels. Press (now Axon Group), Horsham, Pa., 1979—85. Mem. editl. bd. Conflict Resolution Quar., 2001—; trainer mediator Tng. Workshops Good Shepherd Mediation Program, Phila.; presenter UN Conf. on Status of Women, 2004; participant, contbr. South Africa Cultural Exch. Project Linking Cmty. Peace and Safety with Peer Mediation U.S. Info. Agy., Johannesburg, 1996—97; participant, pilgrim Maison Mere du Bon Pasteur Sisters of Good Shepherd, Angers, Angers, 1999; bd. dirs. Pa. Coun. Mediators, 2002—; mediator Bur. Spl. Edn., Office for Dispute Resolution PA Dept. of Edn., Harrisburg, Pa., 1987—; mediator U.S. Equal Employment Opportunities Commn., Phila., 1998—, U.S. Postal Svc., Phila., 1999—; trainer Basic Mediation Tng. Good Shepherd Mediation Program, Phila., 1991—, trainer Mediating Disability Related Disputes, 2002—, trainer Comm. and Conflict Resolution Skills Workshops, 1991—. Chief indexer (encyclopedia) International Encyclopedia of Communications; author: (junior high textbook) The Department of Labor; contbr. articles to profl. jours. Recipient Take the Lead honoree for Bldg. Bridges through Comm., Girl Scouts of Southeastern Pa., 1996. Mem.: ABA, Nat. Assn. Cmty. Mediation, Assn. for Conflict Resolution (formerly Soc. for Profls. in Dispute Resolution) (publications chair 1989—93), PA Coun. Mediators (bd. of directors 2002—03). Office: Good Shepherd Mediation Program 5356 Chew Ave Philadelphia PA 19138 Personal E-mail: ccmed8r@aol.com.

CUTRONE, AGATHA MICHELE, information systems specialist; b. Flushing, N.Y., May 5, 1959; d. Victor N. and Elizabeth Ann (Colleary) C. AAS in Graphic Arts Tech., SUNY, Farmingdale, 1980. Tech. advisor Weber & Stevens Inc., Melville, N.Y., 1980-84; sys. applications mgr. CMP Media Inc., Manhasset, N.Y., 1984-93, editl. sys. support mgr., 1993-94, mgr. worksta. support, 1994-97, sr. mgr. worksta. support and tng., 1997-98; mgr. svc. desk and tng. Time Inc., N.Y.C., 1998-99, mgr. desktop engring. and support, 1999—. Democrat. Roman Catholic. Avocations: travel, music. Home: 2751 Orchard St North Bellmore NY 11710-2831 Office: Time Inc 1271 Avenue Of The Americas New York NY 10020-1300

CUTSHALL-HAYES, DIANE MARION, elementary school educator; b. Pitts., Jan. 15, 1954; d. William Edward and Irma Delores (Marion) Snowden; m. John Steven Baran, Jan. 11, 1975 (div. 1982); 1 child, Allison

Rae; m. Dean F. Cutshall, Dec. 17, 1989. BA, Eureka Coll., 1975; BS, Ind. U., Ft. Wayne, 1986. First grade tchr. Hoover Elem. Sch., Schaumburg, Ill., 1976-79, Indian Meadows Elem. Sch., Ft. Wayne, Ind., 1979-80, 82-86, Perry Hill Elem. Sch., Ft. Wayne, 1981-82; second grade tchr. Indian Meadows Elem. Sch., Ft. Wayne, 1986—. Tchr. rep. State Ill. Rsch. Adv. Coun., 1991; active ISTEP Blue Ribbon Commn., Ill., 1989, State Ill. Lang. Arts Adv. Commn., 1988, Project REAP Adv. Bd., 1988. Spl. events chair Greater Ft. Wayne (Ind.) Crime Stoppers, 1992-95; active YMCA Camp Potawotami, Ft. Wayne, 1993—, Eureka Coll. Alumni Assn., 1992—, pres., 1995—. Christa McAuliffe fellow State of Ind., 1987; recipient Excellence in Edn. award Inst. Copy Corp., 1988, Outstanding Young Alumna award Eureka Coll., 1990, Armstrong Tchr. Educator award, 1998; named Ind. State Elem. Tchr. of Yr., 1993. Mem. Nat. Coun. Tchrs. Math., Internat. Reading Assn., Tchrs. Applying Whole Langs. Lutheran. Avocations: inline skating, racquetball, reading, walking. Home: 5809 Eagle Creek Dr Fort Wayne IN 46814-3207 Office: Indian Meadows Elem Sch 4810 Homestead Rd Fort Wayne IN 46814-5461

CUTTING, MARY DOROTHEA, audio and audio-visual communications company executive; b. N.Y.C., Feb. 20, 1943; d. Elliotte Robinson and Mary Dorothea (Clarke) Little; m. James H. B. Cutting, July 18, 1964; children— Gwendolyn Louise, Laura Elizabeth. Student Whitman Coll., 1960-62; B.A. in English Lit., U. Wash., 1964. Tchr. English, Severna Park High Sch., Md., 1965-66; remedial reading substitute tchr. St. Patrick's Day Sch., Washington, 1976-77; v.p. mktg. The Cutting Corp., Washington, 1978—; bd. dirs. Potomac Talking Book Svcs, Inc., 1990—; Editor children's cassettes: Fisher-Price Toys Spellbinder Series, 1983 (Consumer Com. of Ams. for Democratic Action award for being one of nation's 6 best toys for under $5 1983). Vol. chmn., bd. dirs. Washington Assn. for TV and Children, 1977. Mem. Internat. Assn. Bus. Communicators, Jr. League Washington (bd. dirs. 1977). Republican. Episcopalian. Office: 4940 Hampden Ln Ste 300 Bethesda MD 20814-2945

CUTTLER, DONA LOU, music educator, writer; b. Washington, Sept. 27, 1961; d. Donald Arthur Cuttler and Louise Hebbard (Cuttler) Ehlers. BA, Coll. Charleston, 1983; MEd, U. S.C., 1986. Music educator North Myrtle Beach Elem. Sch., Little River, SC, 1984—2002. Dir. christmas pagent North Myrtle Beach Elem. Sch., Little River, 1984—99, dir. chorus, 1985—2000; chmn. Horry County Schools Festival of Circles, Conway, SC, 1986—92; coord. fine arts day North Myrtle Beach Elem. Sch., Little River, 1986—2002, fine arts dept. chair, 1990—93, fine arts chair so. accreditation of coll. and sch., 1991—92; cons. MIE sys. Horry County Schools, Conway, SC, 1991—92; dir. handbell choir North Myrtle Beach Elem. Sch., Little River, 1994—2002, internal coord. strategic planning, 1995—2002, co-chmn. Peace Circle, 1997—2002, techn. tutor for staff, 1997—2001; lectr. Montgomery County Hist. Soc. Genealogy Club, Rockville, 1999—2001; weekly sch. newsletter North Myrtle Beach Elem. Sch., Little River, 2000—, dir. World Music Drummers, 2000—02, dir. multi-cultural night, 2001—02. Author: The History of Comus, 1999, The History of Barnesville and Sellman, 1999, The Cemeteries of Hyattstown, 1999, The History of Dickerson, Mouth of Monocacy, Oakland Mills and Sugar Loaf Mountain, 1999, The Montgomery Circuit Records 1788-1988, 1999, The History of Poolesville, 2000, The Genealogical Companion to Rural Montgomery Cemeteries, 2000, The History of Clarksburg, King's Valley, Purdum, Browningsville and Lewisdale, 2001, One Man's Family, 2001, Paper Clips, 2002. Grantee Yamaha MIE 1 Keyboards grant, S.C. Target 2000 Arts, 1990—91, African Drums, Epuipment, Accesories and Instruction grant, S.C. Arts in Edn., 2000. Mem.: S.C. Music Educators Assn., Music Educators Nat. Conf., Montgomery County Hist. Soc. Mem. Seventh-Day Adventist. Avocations: genealogy, piano, organ, history.

CUTTNER, JANET, hematologist, educator; b. N.Y.C. d. William Robert and Ida Edith C. BA, NYU, 1953; MD, Med. Coll. of Pa., 1957. Diplomate Am. Bd. Internal Medicine, Am. Bd. Hematology. Intern, resident King's County Hosp., Bklyn., 1957-61; hematology fellow Mt. Sinai Med. Ctr., N.Y.C., 1961-63, rsch. assoc. hematology, 1963-65, asst. prof. medicine, 1965-72, assoc. prof. medicine, 1972-86, prof. medicine, 1986—. Recipient Jacobi Medallion Alumni Mt. Sinai Med. Ctr., 1999. Fellow N.Y. Acad. Scis.; mem. Am. Soc. Hematology, Am. Soc. Clin. Oncology, Am. Assn. for Cancer Rsch. Office: 1735 York Ave Ste P2 New York NY 10128

CYGANOWSKI, MELANIE L. bankruptcy judge; b. Chgo., June 8, 1952; d. Daniel F. and Sophia A. C.; married, 1989. AB in anthropology, Grinnell Coll., 1974; postgrad. in urban devel., Cornell U., 1975; JD magna cum laude, SUNY, Buffalo, 1981. Bar: N.Y. 1982, U.S. Supreme Ct., U.S. Ct. Appeals (2d cir.), U.S. Dist. Ct. (so., ea. and we. dists.) N.Y. Coord. program planning, planner, cons. dept. community devel. and human resources City of Buffalo, N.Y., 1974-78; dir. individual referral program Broadway-Filmore Area Coun., Inc., Buffalo, 1978-79; summer assoc. Hodgson, Russ, Andrews, Wood & Goodyear, Buffalo, 1980; law clk. to Hon. Charles L. Brieant U.S. Dist. Ct. (so. dist.) N.Y., 1981-82; litigation assoc. Sullivan & Cromwell, N.Y.C., 1982-89; sr. atty. Milbank, Tweed, Hadley & McCloy, 1989-93; judge U.S. Bankruptcy Ct. (ea. dist.) N.Y., Ctrl. Islip, 1993—. Adj. prof. law bankruptcy program St. John's U. Sch. Law. Contbr. articles to legal jours. Mem. Nat. Conf. Bankruptcy Judges, N.Y. State Bar Assn., N.Y.C. Bar Assn. Roman Catholic. Avocations: bicycling, gardening, fishing. Office: US Bankruptcy Ct The Long Island Fed Ct 290 Federal Plz Central Islip NY 11722

CYPRESS, KAREN LENETT, special education educator; b. Memphis, May 8, 1969; d. James Hugh and Ethel Mae Cypress. BSW, Freed-Hardeman U., Henderson, Tenn., 1991; MS, U. Memphis, 1995, EdD, 2003. Lic. tchr. Tenn., adminstr. Tenn., cosmetologist Tenn. Social worker Arlington Devel. Ctr., Tenn., 1991—94, program dir., 1994—96; tchr. Fayette County Schs., Somerville, Tenn., 1996—97, Memphis City Schs., 1997—98; asst. prof. spl. edn. Freed-Hardeman U., Henderson, 1998—. Ednl. cons. Fayette County Schs., 2002—. Recipient Cmty. award, Bell South, 1987, Outstanding Tchr. award, Freed-Hardeman U., 2000. Mem.: Coun. for Exceptional Children, Kappa Delta Pi, Phi Delta Kappa. Ch. Of Christ. Office: Freed Hardeman Univ 158 E Main St Henderson TN 38340-2398

CYR, ELAINE MARIE, special education educator; b. Edmundston, New Brunswick, Can., Feb. 26, 1952; d. Bertrand and Rita Collins; m. Philip Cyr; children: Scott, Erica. Bachelor's degree, U. Maine, Farmington, 1974. Cert. tchr. Maine. Tchr. secondary spl. edn. Maine Sch. Adminstrv. Dist. #33, St. Agatha, 1974—2002. Mem. tenure licensure com. Wisdom/Mid. H.S., St. Agatha, 1994—2003. Home: 165 Cleveland Rd Saint Agatha ME 04772 Office: Wisdom/Mid HS 368 Main St Saint Agatha ME 04772 Personal E-mail: pecyr@mfx.net.

CYR, KAREN D. lawyer; Gen. counsel Nuclear Regulatory Commn., Rockville, Md., 1994—. Office: Nuclear Regulatory Commn 11555 Rockville Pike Rockville MD 20852-2738

CZAJKOWSKI, EVA ANNA, aerospace engineer, educator; b. New Britain, Conn., Sept. 4, 1961; Student, Yale U., 1978; BS in Aero. Engring. cum laude, M in Aero. Engring., Rensselaer Poly. Inst., 1983; SM in Aeronautics and Astronautics, MIT, 1985; PhD in Aerospace Engring., Va. Poly. Inst. and State U., 1988. Registered profl engr, NY. Student trainee U.S. Govt., Washington, 1981-82; intern N.Y. State Assembly, Albany, 1983; teaching asst. Rensselaer Poly. Inst., Troy, N.Y., 1983, rsch. asst. U.S. Army Rsch. Office Ctr. Excellence, 1982-83; engring. analyst Pratt & Whitney Aircraft, West Palm Beach, Fla., 1984; rsch. asst. Gas Turbine and Plasma Dynamics Lab., Cambridge, 1984-85; rsch. asst., tchg. asst. dept. aerospace & ocean engring. Va. Poly. Inst. and State U., Blacksburg, 1985-88, aerospace engr., 1988-91, sr. aerospace engr., 1991-94, prin. aerospace engr., 1994-2001, aerospace engring. and tech. mgr., 2001—. Participant U.S. dels. to ten European nations, 1991—2003. Author: (book) Russian Aeronautical Test Facilities, 1994; contbr. scientific papers confs, articles profl jours and ency. Assoc mem Nat Air and Space Mus, Am Mus Natural History; vol. New Britain Gen Hosp, 1977—79. Named Dame Commandeur, Ordre Souverain et Militaire de la Milice du Saint Sepulcre, 1990, Dame, The World Order Sci.-Edn.-Culture, 2002; recipient Medal Hon. Sci. Award, Bausch & Lomb, 1978, Joseph B. Platt Award, 1997, Int. Sci. Medal, 2001, Internat. Woman of Yr., 1991—92, 1996—97, Scientist of Yr., 2001; fellow Amelia Earhart, Zonta Int., 1983—85, Prat Presdl. Eng. Program, 1985—88; scholar, Unico Nat., 1979—80, Am. Helicopter Soc. Vertical Flight Found., 1983. Mem.: NAFE, AIAA, London Diplomatic Acad, NY Acad Scis, Confederation Chivalry (dame, named Dame), Nat Space Soc, World Found Successful Women, Int Platform Asn, Planetary Soc, Polish Rotorcraft Asn, Am Helicopter Soc, Am Astronaut Soc, World Order Sci.-Edn.-Culture (dame, named Dame), Gamma Beta Phi, Phi Kappa Phi, Tau Beta Pi, Sigma Gamma Tau, Sigma Xi. Avocations: art, horseback riding, piano, flying private plane, sailing. Home: 170 Carlton St New Britain CT 06053-3106

CZAJKOWSKI-BARRETT, KAREN ANGELA, human resources specialist; b. Bklyn., Sept. 13, 1957; d. Frank Henry and Cecilia (Artowicz) Czajkowski; div. Mar. 1992; children: Jennifer Marie, Michael Joseph. BSBA, Fairfield U., 1979; MBA, Sacred Heart U., 1984. Office systems analyst Union Trust Co., Stamford, Conn., 1979-80, sr. office systems analyst, 1980-81; ops. analyst Homequity, Inc., Wilton, 1981-82, project leader human rels. dept., 1982-85, organization devel. cons., 1985-87; tng. and devel. cons. People's Bank, Bridgeport, Conn., 1987-90; mgr. human resource planning and devel. Pitney Bowes Mgmt. Svcs., Stamford, 1990-93, dir. human resources planning and devel., 1993-98; regional learning mgr. Hewitt Assocs. LLC, Rowayton, Conn., 1998—. Adj. instr. Sacred Heart U., Bridgeport, 1987. Sec. Cub Scouts Adv. Com., 1991-92, mem. regional bd. Conn. Fedn. Cath. Sch. Parents, 1993-94; treas. St. Theresa Sch.-Home Sch. Assn., 1994-96. Recipient award Nash Engring., 1979; named Bus. Advisor of Yr., INROADS/Fairfield-Westchester Counties, Inc., 1993. Mem. ASTD, Am. Mgmt. Assn., Human Resource Planning Soc.. Exec. Women's Golf Assn. Home: 28 Wendover Rd Trumbull CT 06611-1530 Office: Hewitt Assocs LLC 45 Glover Ave Norwalk CT 06850

CZARNEZKI, MARY ELAINE, media specialist; b. Milw., June 3, 1952; d. Gerald J. and Eleanor H. (Lietz) C. BS, U. Wis., Milw., 1973; MA, U. Wis., Madison, 1975; postgrad., U. Pitts., 1982. Cert. instructional library media specialist. Librarian for kindergarten through 8th grade Columbus (Wis.) Pub. Schs., 1976-90; media specialist Edgerton Elem. Sch., Hales Corners, Wis., 1990—. Mem. ALA, Am. Assn. Sch. Librarians (mem. pub. awareness com.), Wis. Libr. Assn., Wis. Assn. Sch. Librs., Milw. Met. Sch. Libr. Assn., Columbia County Libr. Assn. (past pres.), Beta Phi Mu, Kappa Delta Pi. Home: 12418 W Cleveland Ave New Berlin WI 53151-4002

CZERWINSKI, RENE D. counselor; b. Chgo., Dec. 6, 1969; d. Philip C. and Diane C. Wilson; m. Bruce W. Czerwinski, May 28, 1993; children: Bailey A., Elizabeth K. MA in Clin. Psychology, Roosevelt U., 1994. Lic. clin. profl. counselor State Ill.-Dept. Regulations, 2002, profl. counselor State Ill.-Dept. Regulations, 2000, cert. bereavement facilitator Acad. Bereavement, 2001; mediator St. Xavier U., 2001, nat. cert. counselor NBCC, 2000. Therapist Human Corps, Inc., Maywood, Ill., 1995—98; child welfare specialist Luth. Social Svcs. Ill., Oak Park, 1995—98, lead child welfare specialist, 1998—99, child welfare supr., 1999—2000; crisis intervention counselor The Bridge Youth and Family Svcs., Palatine, Ill., 2000—; crisis intake counselor Good Shepherd Hosp., Lake Barrington, Ill., 2002—. Mem.: ACA (assoc.). Democrat. Roman Catholic. Avocations: reading, swimming. Office: The Bridge Youth and Family Services 1585 N Rand Rd Palatine IL 60074 Personal E-mail: renecz93@hotmail.com.

CZIN, FELICIA TEDESCHI, Italian language and literature educator, small business owner; b. Vallata, Avellino, Italy, Jan. 20, 1950; came to U.S., 1958; d. Pasquale Aurelio and Maria (Branca) Tedeschi; m. Peter Czin, Oct. 19, 1972; children: Jonathan, Michael. BA, Douglass Coll., Rutgers U., 1972; MA, NYU, 1978, ABD, 1981, postgrad. Prodr. RAI Corp. Italian TV, N.Y.C., 1973-84; tchg. asst. dept. Italian NYU, 1977-79, adj. instr. dept. English, 1979-81; asst. prof. Vassar Coll., Poughkeepsie, N.Y., 1981-84; co-owner Czin Opticians, Teaneck, N.J., 1984—. Coord. Symposium on Italian Poetry, N.Y.C., 1978; adj. prof. SUNY at the Fashion Inst. Tech., N.Y.C., 2000—. Editor Out of London Press, N.Y.C., 1977-82, dir. pub. rels., 1977-82; editor jour. Yale Italian Studies, 1979-82; translator for jours. Avocations: hiking, swimming, knitting, cooking, sewing. Home and Office: 489 Cedar Ln Teaneck NJ 07666-1710

CZNARTY, DONNA MAE, secondary school educator; b. Bridgeport, Conn., Aug. 17, 1950; d. Richard W. and Dorothy Mae (Kosturko) Oefinger; m. Wiliam C. Cole, Jr., July 11, 1970; 1 child, Michael William Cole; m. Thomas Robert Cznarty, Apr. 29, 1983. BS in Edn., So. Conn. State U., 1973, MS in Edn., 1977. English and reading tchr. Shelton Bd. Edn., Conn., 1973-82; English tchr. Millbrook Bd. Edn., N.Y., 1985-86; sec., bd. dirs. Hopewell Precision Inc., Hopewell Junction, N.Y., 1986—, CEO, 1999—, 1999. Bd. dirs. Dutchess Arts Coun. Mem. NAFE. Republican. Avocations: interior design, antiques and collectibles, woodworking, boating. Home: Field Haven Stanfordville NY 12581 Office: Hopewell Precision Inc Ryan Rd Hopewell Junction NY 12533

DABBS RILEY, JEANNE KERNODLE, retired public relations executive; b. Corsicana, Tex., 1922; d. Robert and Anne (Forrest) McCluer; m. John David Kernodle, June 27, 1942 (div. 1968); 1 child, Elizabeth Kernodle Cabell; m. Jack Autrey Dabbs, Feb. 14, 1981 (dec. 1992); m. James J. Riley, Jr., June 28, 1997 (dec. 1999). BS in Sociology, Tex. Woman's U., 1970. Supr., writer pub. rels. St. Paul's Hosp., Dallas, 1974-76; dir., v.p. mktg. svcs. Fidelity Union Life Ins. Co., Dallas, 1976-81, ret., 1981. Pres. aux. Seton Med. Ctr., Austin, 1985—86; mem. Dallas Civic Chorus, Austin Choral Union. Recipient Editl. medal Freedoms Found. Valley Forge, 1973, Eddy award Internat. Assn. Bus. Communicators, 1974, 76, 79, Matrix award Women in Comm., Inc., 1975, Best of Show award Life Ins. Advts. Assn., 1980, Sr. Vol. award Retirees Coordinating Bd., 1989. Mem. Tex. Women's U. Alumnae Assn. (pres. Capital Area chpt. 1987-89), Tuesday Book Club Austin (pres. 1986), Austin Poetry Soc. Methodist. Avocations: book reviewer, singing. Home: 2211 W North Loop # 126 Austin TX 78756

DABINETT, DIANA FRANCES, visual artist; d. Leslie Frank and Ivy Annie May; m. Patrick Dabinett, Aug. 1969; children: Emily Thomas. BA in fine arts, U. Cape Town, 1963. H.S. art tchr., Zimbabwe, 1965-66; H.S. English tchr., 1967-69; asst. curator London (Ont.) Art Gallery, 1969-73. Visual arts advisor, adv. panel Fed.-Prov. Cultural Agreement, Newfoundland, Can., 1992-00; Can. artists rep. Newfoundland and Labrador, 1980-97; artist in residence Hopedale, Labrador, 1998-99, Gros Morne Park Newfoundland. One-woman shows include St. John's, 1989-92, Lunenberg, N.S., 1992, Christina Parker Fine Art St. John's, 1994, 98, 2000, 02, 04, Can. Embassy Tokyo, 2001, Can. Embassy Washington, 2003, Argyle Fine Art Gallery, Halifax, 2003; two-person exhbn. Pathways, 1997-99; exhibited in group shows at Discovery Travelling Maritimes, 1997; commd. works at Birthing Ctr. and Cancer Ctr., Cmty. Hosp. of the Monterey Peninsula, St. Lawrence Hosp. and Labrador Health Ctr., Newfoundland, N.S. Health and Welfare Dept. Halifax; illustrator: Icebergs-Castles in the Sea, 2000; collection HRH Queen Elizabeth II. Mem.: Canadian Soc. Water Colour Painters. Avocations: reading, snow shoeing, hiking. Address: Box 1005 Torbay NF Canada A1K 1K9 E-mail: dianadabinett@roadrunner.nf.net.

DABNEY, MICHELLE SHEILA, administrative assistant; b. Newark, Oct. 19, 1959; d. Charlie Louis and Agatha Cecelia Talley; m. James Charles Dabney, Oct. 3, 1981; children: Jameel Charles, Nadiyah Aliyah. Student, Del. State Coll., 1977-79, Union County Coll., 1979-83; certificate, Taylor Bus. Inst, Bridgewater, N.J., 1985; BS in Sociology, Kean Coll., 1997; postgrad., Rutgers U. Sec., adminstrv. asst. Newark Beth Israel Med. Ctr., 1978-85; sec. AT&T Info. Svcs., Piscataway, N.J., 1985-87; legal sec. Timins & Lesniak, Esq., Elizabeth, N.J., 1987; assoc. mgr. AT&T Communications, Bedminster, N.J., 1987—, AT&T, Bedminster, N.J., 1992—. Mem. NAACP, Plainfield Teen Parenting Program. Mem. IDE Alliance of Black Telecommunications Employees (co-chair profl. devel.), Plainfield Tsunami Track Club (dir.). Democrat. Avocations: cooking, jogging, knitting. Home: 30 Leland Ave Plainfield NJ 07062-1102 Office: AT&T Comm Rt 22/206 N Bedminster NJ 07921

DABROWSKA, DOROTA MARIA, statistician, educator; b. Warsaw, Dec. 10, 1954; arrived in U.S., 1981, naturalized, 1992; d. Emma Katalin Juhasz-Dabrowska and Cyryl Alfons Dabrowski. MA in Math., Warsaw U., 1978; PhD in Stats., U. Calif., Berkeley, 1984. Rsch. assoc. Polish Acad. Sci., Warsaw, 1978—81; asst. prof. Carnegie-Mellon U., Pitts., 1984—88, U. Calif., L.A., 1988—91, assoc. prof., 1991—96, prof., 1996—. Assoc. editor: Jour. Multivariate Analysis, 1999—, Lifetime Data Analysis, 2002—; contbr. articles to profl. jours. Recipient Evelyn Fix Meml. medal, U. Calif., 1984; grantee, NSF, 1989—2003, NIH, 1995—2003; Earl C. Anthony fellow, U. Calif., 1981—82, Regents fellow, 1982—83, UC Presdl. fellow, 1986—88. Fellow: Inst. Math. Stats.; mem.: Biometric Soc., Bernoulli Soc., Am. Statis. Assn. Roman Catholic. Avocations: music, travel, art. Office: Univ Calif LA Sch Pub Health/Biostatistics Los Angeles CA 90095-1772

D'ABRUZZO, STEPHANIE, actress; Grad., Northwestern U. Actor: (Broadway plays) Chess, 2003, Avenue Q, 2003 (Drama Desk nominee best actress, 2003, Tony nominee best actress in a musical, 2004); (TV series) The Wubbulous World of Dr. Seuss, 1996, Sesame Street, 1998—2001, (voice) Sheep in the Big City, 2000, The Book of Pooh, 2001, Oobi, 2003; (films) The Adventures of Elmo in Grouchland, 1999, Sesame Street 4D, 2003. Office: Golden Theater 252 W 45th St New York NY 10036*

DACBERT-FRIESE, SHARYN VARHELY, social worker, evangelist; b. Utica, N.Y., Dec. 10, 1947; d. Henry Alexander Varhely and Elouise Fulmore; m. Thomas Jewett Mitchell III, Oct. 20, 1968 (div. Dec. 1982); children: Sharyn Mitchell Wallace, James Bailey Mitchell, Jaclyn Ashley Mitchell; m. Guenther Roland Friese, Dec. 16, 1998. BA, U. Ala., 1968; MSW, Our Lady of the Lake U., San Antonio, Tex., 1991. Lic. master social worker Advanced Clin. Practitioner, 1991, cert. clin. supr. 1998, LCSW 2003. Entrepreneur, Laredo, Tex., 1972—85; founder, owner Jacob's Well, Laredo, Tex., 1980—87, corp. v.p. Dacbert Music Co., San Antonio, 1992—94; individual and family psychotherapist Fuller & Assocs., San Antonio, 1991—94; pvt. practice San Antonio, 1994—; sr. pastor, founder, pres., chmn. Sheepgate Fellowship, San Antonio, 1997—; dir., founder, pres., chmn. Christian Family Counseling Ctr., San Antonio, 1997—. Radio personality, counselor Sta. KSLR-AM, San Antonio, 1997—2001; individual and family psychotherapist Adult Parent Child, San Antonio, 1991—92. Contbr. articles to profl. jours. Mem.: NASW, Nat. Assn. Bus. and Profl. Women, Am. Assn. Christian Counselors, Play Therapy Assn., Tuesday Musical Club. Avocations: oil painting, camping, drawing, cooking, fishing. Office: Christian Family Counseling Ctr PO Box 460686 San Antonio TX 78246 E-mail: sdacbert1@aol.com.

DACEK, JOANNE CAROLE, psychologist; b. Oceanside, N.Y., July 26, 1963; d. Gerald S. and Teresa E. (Iusi) Martinis; m. Stephen T. Dacek, Jan. 17, 1988; children: Stephen Thomas, Mark Brendan, Megan Michelle, Phoebe Lauren, Benjamin Ryan. BA, Adelphi U., 1984; MS, Syracuse U., 1987; MA, Sem. of Immaculate Conception, 1995. Cert. sch. psychologist. Psychologist Greece (N.Y.) Ctrl. Schs., 1987-90, Bellmore (N.Y.) Union Free Sch. Dist., 1990-95; chair C.S.E., Bellmore (N.Y.) Unified Sch. Dist., 1995—98. Office: Bellmore Unified Sch Dist 2750 S Saint Marks Ave Bellmore NY 11710-5016

DACEY, EILEEN M. lawyer; b. NYC, Dec. 15, 1948; d. Gabriel A. and Mary (Breen) D.; m. Kinchen C. Bizzell, Jan. 1, 1984. BA in Sociology, SUNY, Stony Brook, 1970; JD, St. John's U., 1975. Assoc. Mendes & Mount, NYC, 1976-80, jr. ptnr., 1980-88; ptnr. Adams, Duque & Hazeltine, NYC, 1988-94, Morrison Mahoney & Miller, NYC, 1994-96, Querrey & Harrow, NYC, 1996-98. Mem. mediation program U.S. Dist. Ct. (so. dist.) N.Y. Vol. Lawyers for the Arts, Jewish Braille Inst.; mem. elderly project Vols. of Legal Svc. Recipient Candle of Understanding award, Jewish Braille Inst., 2001. Mem. ABA (tort and ins. practice sect.), N.Y. State Bar Assn., Assn. Bar City N.Y., Practicing Law Inst. (mem. ins. law adv. bd.), Assn. Profl. Ins. Women. Home: New York, NY. Died Oct. 7, 2002.

DACEY, KATHLEEN RYAN, lawyer, former federal judge; b. Boston; m. William A. Dacey (dec. Aug. 1986); 1 child, Mary Dacey White AB with honors, Emmanuel Coll., 1941; MS in L.S., Simmons Coll., 1942; JD, Northeastern U., 1945; postgrad., Boston U. Law Sch., 1945-46; LLD (hon.), Suffolk Law Sch., 1990, Emmanuel Coll., 1992. Bar: Mass. 1945, U.S. Supreme Ct. 1957. Law clk. to justices Mass. Supreme Jud. Ct., 1945-47; Practiced in Boston, 1947-75; asst. dist. atty. Suffolk County, Mass., 1971-72, 1971-72; auditor, master Commonwealth of Mass., Boston, 1972-75, Suffolk and Norfolk Counties, Mass., 1972-75; asst. atty. gen., chief civil bur. Mass. Dept. Atty. Gen., Boston, 1975-77; U.S. adminstrv. law judge Commonwealth of Mass., Boston, 1977-99; of counsel Cushing & Dolan P.C., Mass., 1999—; asst. dist. atty. Suffolk County, Mass., 1971-72. Mem. panel def. counsel for indigent persons U.S. Dist. Ct. Dist. Mass.; lectr., speaker in field Contbr. articles to profl. jours. Bd. dirs. Mission United Neighborhood Improvement Team, Boston; mem. Boston Sch. Com., 1945-46, chmn., 1946-47 Recipient Silver Shingle award Boston U. Sch. Law, 1980; named Alumnae Woman of Yr., Northeastern U. Law Sch. Assn., 1976 Mem. ABA (ho. of dels. 1982—, exec. com. conf. of adminstrv. law judges jud. adminstrn. divsn. 1987—), Internat. Bar Assn., Mass. Bar Assn., Boston Bar Assn., Norfolk Bar Lawyers Assn., Nat. Assn. Women Lawyers (pres.), Mass. Assn. Women Lawyers, Internat. Fedn. Women Lawyers, Boston U. Law Sch. Alumni Assn. (corr. sec. 1974-76), Boston U. Nat. Alumni Coun.

D'ADDARIO, EDITH, performing company executive; Dir. Joffrey Ballet Sch., N.Y.C., 1961—. Office: Joffrey Ballet Sch Am Ballet Ctr 434 Ave of the Ams New York NY 10011

DADLEY, ARLENE JEANNE, sleep technologist; b. Cleve., Sept. 13, 1941; d. Bernard and Bernice Anne (Selleck) Davis; m. Charles Dadley, Sept. 15, 1967 (div. Oct. 1977); children: Anitra, Charles. BA in Bus., Ursuline Coll., 1980; postgrad., Case Western Res. U., 1983-85, Stanford U., 1988. Registered polysomnographic technologist. Jr. fund acct. Am. U., Washington, 1967-70; htn and cancer rsch. asst. Case Western Res. U., Cleve., 1976-87, gastroent. rsch. assoc., 1984, sleep rsch. assoc., 1985-87; sr. clin. sleep technologist Metrohealth Med. Ctr., Cleve., 1987—2004, sleep diagnostics tchr., trainer, 1987—. Judge regional and state sci. fairs. Exhibited in group shows at Cleve. Mus. Art, Butler Inst. Art, Corcoran Gallery Art, Washington, Internat. Traveling Am. Artists Exhibit (Jury 1st award); contbr. articles to profl. jours. Recipient Presdl. Lit. Achievement citation, League Am. Pen Women, 1974, citation, ARC, 1991; scholar, Case Western Res. U., 1976—80, Yale U., 1982, Respironics, Inc., 1988; Pell grantee, 1976—80, Ohio Instl. grantee, 1976—80. Mem.: Assn. Polysomnographic Technologists, Internat. Platform Assn. Avocations: oil painting, sleep education, thoroughbred horses, gardening. Home: PO Box 894 Columbia Station OH 44028-0894 Office: Metrohealth Med Ctr 2500 Metrohealth Dr Cleveland OH 44109-1900

DADO, DIANE VALENTINA, plastic and reconstructive surgeon, pediatric plastic surgeon; b. Chgo., Feb. 14, 1952; d. Ralph N. and Violet M. Dado; 1 child, Joseph. BA, St. Xavier Coll., Chgo., 1973; MD, Loyola U., Maywood, Ill., 1976. Cert. Am. Bd. Plastic and Reconstructive Surgeery. Intern in surgery Loyola U. Med. Ctr., Maywood, 1976-77, resident in surgery, 1977-79, resident plastic surgery, 1979-82; fellow plastic surgery Children's Meml. Hosp., Chgo., 1982-83; instr. surgery Stritch Sch. Medicine Loyola U., Maywood, 1983, asst. prof. surgery, 1983-89, assoc. prof. surgery, pediatrics, 1989—. Mem. plastic surgery rsch. coun. Loyola U. Cleft Palate/Craniofacial Team, 1983—; attending physician Loyola U. Med. Ctr. div. Plastic Surgery, 1983—. children's Meml. Hosp. div. plastic surgery, 1983—. Contbr. articles to profl. jours. Mem. Am. Soc. Plastic and Reconstructive Surgeons, Am. Acad. Pediatrics, ACS, Am. Cleft Palate Assn., Ill. Assn. Craniofacial Teams, Chgo. Soc. Plastic Surgery, Can. Soc. Plastic Surgeons, Desmond A. Kernahan Soc. (founding). Avocations: martial arts, scuba diving, sailing, skiing. Office: Loyola U Med Ctr 2160 S 1st Ave Maywood IL 60153-3304

DAFFRON, MARYELLEN, librarian; b. Richmond, Va., Nov. 12, 1946; d. William Charles and Ellen (Ahern) D. BA, Coll. Mt. St. Joseph on Ohio, Cin., 1968; MLS, Drexel U., 1970. Libr. Richmond Pub. Libr., 1969-73, FMC, Washington, 1973—93; with U.S. Immigration and Naturalization Svc. Office of Gen. Counsel, Washington, 1993—2003; law libr. Office of Prin. Legal Advisor, U.S. Immigration and Customs Enforcement, Washington, 2003—. Vol. No. Va. Hotline, Arlington, 1974-79. City of Richmond fellow, 1968. Mem. Law Libr. Soc. Washington, Beta Phi Mu. Roman Catholic. Office: Dept Homeland Security US Immigration & Customs Enforcement Office of Prin Legal Advisor 425 I St NW Rm 6100 Washington DC 20536-0001

DAGAVARIAN-BONAR, DEBRA AGHAVNI, college administrator, consultant; b. N.Y.C., Oct. 26, 1952; d. Harry O. Dagavarian and Norma Siran (Cazanjian) Hansen; m. James B. Bonar, Dec. 26, 1988. BA, SUNY, New Paltz, 1973; MA, SUNY, Albany, 1975; EdD, Rutgers U., 1986. Transfer admissions counselor Mercy Coll., Dobbs Ferry, NY, 1976—79, asst. dir. spl. sessions, 1979—81, dir. evening programs, 1981—86, dir. acad. advising, 1986—87; asst. dean for assessment Empire State Coll., Hartsdale, NY, 1987—88; dir. testing assessment Thomas Edison State Coll., Trenton, NJ, 1988—96, dep. vice provost, 1996—2002; asst. v.p. acad. affairs Richard Stockton Coll. NJ, Pomona, 2002—. Adj. prof. Empire State Coll., Mercy Coll., 1979-95; cons. various instns. and corps., 1987—. Author: Saying It Ain't So: American Values as Revealed in Children's Baseball Stories, 1987; author, editor: A Century of Children's Baseball Stories, 1990, (jour.) Jour. of the Nat. Inst. on Assessment of Experiential Learning, 1989-2002; contbr. articles to profl. jours., periodicals, books. Mem. NAFE, Am. Sociol. Assn., Soc. for Am. Baseball Rsch., Coun. for Adult and Experiential Learning, Assn. for Continuing Higher Edn. Democrat. Avocations: baseball research, singing, jewelry making. Office: Richard Stockton Coll of NJ PO Box 195 Jim Leeds Rd Pomona NJ 08240

DAGGETT, BEVERLY CLARK, state legislator; b. Florence, S.C., Sept. 9, 1945; d. John and Beth Clark; m. Thomas A. Daggett, May 8, 1971; children: John, Page, Paul. BS in Biology, Hillsdale Coll., 1967. Mem. Maine Ho. of Reps., Augusta, 1987-96; chair commn. to study biotech. and genetic engring., 1995—; house chair joint standing com. on state and local govt., 1995-96; mem. Dist. 15 Maine Senate, Augusta, 1996—, Dem. leader, 2001—, majority leader, 2002—, pres., 2002—. Chair joint standing com. on legal and vets. affairs Maine State Senate, mem. taxation com.; mem. Substance Abuse Svcs. Commn. Bd. dirs. Dem. Legis. Campaign Com., 2000—. Coun. State Govts. Toll fellow, 1990; Flemming fellow, 1997. Democrat. Home: 16 Pine St Augusta ME 04330-5340 Personal E-mail: senatorbdaggett@aol.com. E-mail: senbeverly.daggett@legis.maine.gov.

DAGGETT, ROXANN, state legislator; b. Mar. 10, 1947; m. Dave Daggett, Aug. 20, 1967; 2 children. Student, Concordia Coll., 1965-67; BS, U. N.D., 1968. Motivational spkr.; rep. Dist. 11A Minn. Ho. of Reps., 1994—.

DAGNA, JEANNE MARIE, special education educator; b. Flushing, N.Y., July 28, 1959; d. Renato Lawrence and Norma Jeanne (Leuchtman) D. BS in Elem. and Spl. Edn., L.I. U., 1982, MS in Spl. Edn., 1984. Cert. spl. edn. tchr., N.Y., Pa. Adminstrv. asst. N.Y. State Dept. Edn., Greenvale, 1983-85; spl. edn. tchr. Baldwin (N.Y.) Sch. Dist., 1985-87, Advances of Wiley House, Reading, Pa., 1989-90; master tchr. Centennial Sch./Lehigh U., Bethlehem, Pa., 1990-92; student assistance liaison Alcohol & Adddictions Dept. of Delaware County, Media, Pa., 1992-93; spl. edn. tchr. children and adolescent units Horsham Psychiat. Clinic, Ambler, Pa., 1993-95; spl. edn. tchr. learning and emotional support Lower Merion H.S., Ardmore, Pa., 1994-2000, spl. edn. liaison in pupil svcs., 2000—. Sec. Main Line Youth Alliance, Wayne, Pa., 1996-99. Contbr. articles to profl. jours. Mem. Crohn's and Colitis Assn., United Ostomy Assn., Coun. for Exceptional Children, Pa. Coun. for Exceptional Children (conf. presenter 1998, 99, Gay, Lesbian, Straight Educators Network. Avocations: reading, flute/oboe, drawing, bicycling. Office: Lower Merion HS 245 E Montgomery Ave Ardmore PA 19003-3339 E-mail: dognaj@lmsd.org.

D'AGOSTINO, GLORIA M. secondary school educator; b. Ossining, N.Y., Mar. 13, 1950; d. Anthony and Sarah (Leary) D'Agostino. BA, SUNY, New Paltz, 1973, MA, 1977. Sci. tchr. Binghamton (N.Y.) Sch. Dist., 1974—76; tchg. fellow, biology St. Bonaventure U., Olean, NY, 1977—81; instr. biology Westchester County Coll., White Plains, NY, 1981—82; tchr. chemistry Middletown (N.Y.) Sch. Dist., 1982—. Contbr. articles to bulls. Office: Middletown High Sch Gardner Ave Ext Middletown NY 10940

DAHL, ARLENE, actress, writer, apparel designer, cosmetics executive; b. Mpls., Aug. 11, 1928; d. Rudolph and Idelle (Swan) D.; m. Marc A. Rosen; children: Lorenzo Lamas, Carole Christine Holmes, Stephen Andreas Schaum. Student, U. Minn., 1943-44, Mpls. Inst. Art, 1945, Minn. Coll. Music, 1944, Minn. Bus. Coll., 1944. Pres. Arlene Dahl Enterprises, 1952-67; v.p. Kenyon & Eckhart, 1967-72; pres. Woman's World divsn. Kenyon & Eckhart Advt. Agy., 1967-72; nat. beauty and health advisor Sears Roebuck Co., 1970-75; internat. dir. Sales and Mktg. Execs. Internat., 1972-75; fashion dir. O.M.A., 1975-78; pres. Dahlia Parfums, Inc., 1975-80, Dahlia Prodns., Inc., 1978-81, Dahlmark Prodns., 1981—, Scandia Cosmetics, Ltd., 1978-80; pres., chmn. Lasting Beauty Ltd., 1986—. Author: Always Ask a Man, 1965, 12 Beautyscope books, 1968, rev. edit., 1978, Arlene Dahl's Secrets of Hair Care, 1969, Arlene Dahl's Secrets of Skin Care, 1972, Beyond Beauty, 1980, Arlene Dahl's Lovescopes, 1983, Arlene Dahl's Weekly Astro Forecast, 1991, 92, 93, 94, 95, 96, 97, 98, 99, 2000, 01, 02, Arlene Dahl's Hollywood Horoscope internat. syndicated weekly column, 1990—; actress: (Broadway plays) including Mr. Strauss Goes to Boston, Questionable Ladies, Cyrano de Bergerac, Applause (Tony award musical), (films) including (debut) My Wild Irish Rose, The Bride Goes Wild, Reign of Terror, A Southern Yankee, Ambush, The Outriders, Three Little Words, Watch the Birdie, Scene of the Crime, Inside Straight, No Questions Asked, Desert Legion, Slightly Scarlet, Sangaree, Caribbean Gold, Jamaica Run, Diamond Queen, Here Come the Girls, Bengal Brigade, Kisses for My President, Woman's World, Journey to the Center of the Earth, Wicked as They Come, She Played with Fire, Les Poneyettes, Du Blé Enliases, The Land Raiders, The Way to Kathmandu, Fortune Is a Woman, The Big Bank Roll, Who Killed Maxwell Thorn?, Midnight Warrior, 1991, (TV shows) Lux Video Theatre, 1952-53, guest starring appearances on The Love Boat, Fantasy Island, Love American Style, One Life to Live, 1981-84, Night of 100 Stars, 1983, Happy Birthday Hollywood, 1987, All My Children, 1995, Renegade, 1995, 96, 97, Air America, 1999; hostess (TV series): Pepsi Cola Theatre, 1954, [illegible], Arlene Dahl's Beauty Spot, 1966, Arlene Dahl's Starscope, 1979-80, Arlene Dahl's Lovescope, 1980-82; played throughout U.S. in One Touch of Venus, The Camel Bell, Blithe Spirit, Liliom, The King and I, Roman Candle, I Married an Angel, Bell, Book and Candle, Applause, Marriage Go Round, Pal Joey, A Little Night Music, Forty Carats, Life with Father, Murder Among Friends, Dear Liar; nightclub acts Flamingo Hotel, Las Vegas, Latin Quarter, N.Y.C., musical stage appearances: Carnegie Hall, 1997, London Paladium, 1992, 1998, Salute to MGM Musicals; internat. syndicated beauty columnist Chgo. Tribune/ N.Y. News Syndicate, 1950-70, Arlene Dahl's Lucky Stars Column, Globe Communications, 1988-90, Arlene Dahl's Starscope Weekly Column, 1991, 92, 93, 94, 95, 96, 97, 98, 99, 2000, 01, 02, Horoscope Yearly Forecast 1991-2002; designer sleepwear for A.N. Saab & Co., 1952-57, In Vogue with Arlene Dahl (Vogue Patterns), 1980-85, Arlene Dahl Pvt. Collection Jewelry, 1989-94, Arlene Dahl's Jewels of Fortune Home Shopping Network, 1996. Hon. life mem. Father Flannagan's Boys Town; internat. amb. Pearl Buck Found.; founder, pres. Broadway Walk of Stars Found., Inc.; bd. dirs. Hollywood Mus. Recipient 10 Box Office Laurel awards, Hollywood Walk of Fame Star, 1961, Coup de Chapeau Deaville Film Festival award, 1982, 92; named Best Coiffed, Heads of Fame awards, 1967-72, 80, award Scandinavian Hall of Fame, 1997; named Woman of the Yr., Advt. Club of N.Y.C., 1969, Mother of the Yr., 1982, Lifetime Achievement award WorldFest, 1994, Leadership in the Arts, 1997; named to Scandinavian Hall of Fame, 1997. Fellow: Vesterheim Norwegian/Am. Found. (life); mem.: UNIFEM, NATAS (trustee), Film Soc., Edward Grieg Soc., Authors Guild, Acad. Motion Picture Arts and Scis. (vice chair N.Y. spl. events), Acad. TV Arts and Scis. (bd. govs., v.p.), Smithsonian Assocs., Nat. Trust for Hist. Preservation, Commanderie de Bordeaux (N.Y.), Commanderie de Bontemps du Medoc et Graves, France. Office: Dahlmark Prodns Rockland Rd PO Box 116 Sparkill NY 10976-0116

DAHL, BARBARA JEAN, psychologist; d. William Elmer Dahl and Aileen Harriet Brudevold. BA in Bus. Adminstrn., Wash. State U., Pullman, 1981; BA in Psychology, U. Wash., 1991, MS in Psychology, 1993, PhD in Clin. Psychology, 1999. Lic. psychologist Wash. Tchg. asst. U. Wash., Seattle, 1991—98; psychology intern Clin. Psychology Internship-Behavioral Medicine, Farmington/Newington, Conn., 1998—99; postdoctoral fellow Addictive Behaviors Rsch. Ctr., Seattle, 1999—2001; counselor Bedaichelh-Tulalip (Wash.) Indian Reservation, 1999—2002; psychologist Northup Group, Bellevue, Wash., 2001—02, U. Wash. Counseling Ctr., Seattle, 2001—03, Advance Behavioral Medicine and Neuropsychology Assocs., Tacoma, 2002—. Tchr., cons., presenter Addictive Behaviors Rsch. Ctr., Seattle, 1999—2001; addictive behaviors cons. U. Wash. Counseling Ctr., Seattle, 2001—03; presenter in field. Mem.: APA, Wash. State Psychol. Assn. Avocations: hiking, mountaineering, bicycling. Office: Advanced Behavioral Medicine and Neuropsychology Assocs 2013 S 19th St Tacoma WA 98405

DAHL, BREN BENNINGTON, photography studio co-owner; b. Gary, Ind., Nov. 15, 1954; d. Paul Wayland and Shirley Ann (Havard) Bennington; m. Curtis Ray Dahl; children: Austin Brooks, Darren Curtis. Student, Principia Coll., Elsah,Ill., 1972-74, Sch. of Art Inst. Chgo., 1983; BA in English with honors, U. Hawaii, 1977. Tchr. English, Peace Corps, Mbuji-Mayi, Zaire, 1977-79, Asahi Cultural Ctr., Osaka, Japan, 1981-82, Osaka Inst. Fgn. Trade, Osaka, 1981-82; tchr. English Kansai U. Fgn. Studies, Osaka, 1980-82, Matsuhita Electric, Osaka, 1982; pres., owner Video Enterprises, North Palm Beach, Fla., 1983-87; prodr.'s asst. Casady Entertainment, Hollywood, Calif., 1989-91; photo retoucher Kaish-Dahl Photography; mgr. Curtis Dahl Photography, 2000—. Screenwriter: Ties That Bind, 1991, The Spider Clock, 1993, Ticking Off Ryan, 1995. Mem. Temple Beth Haverim Choir, 1996, 97, 98; mem. Palm Beach Opera Chorus, 1984-85; mem. Ohr Hatorah Choir, 1999; bd. dirs. First Neighborhood Homeowners Assn., 1996-98. Fred Waring scholar, 1972. Mem. Exec. Women of Palm Beaches, Fla. Motion Picture and TV Assn., Am. Film Inst., No. Palm Beach County C. of C. (co-chmn. spl. events 1985-86), BBB Scriptwriters Network, Tourette Syndrome Assn. Republican. Jewish. Avocations: calligraphy, singing, gourmet cooking.

DAHL, MARILYN GAIL, psychotherapist; b. Louisville, Dec. 6, 1946; d. James Blair and Dorothy Emma (McDermott) Swartzwelder; m. Charles Dalton Weaver, Dec. 30, 1967 (div. Apr. 1969); m. Donald Allan Dahl, Sept. 18, 1985. BSN, U. Ky., 1968; MEd in Clin. Counseling, The Citadel, 1987. Lic. profl. counselor, Ill. Instr. med.-surg. nursing Sch. Nursing Ky. Bapt. Hosp., Louisville, 1973-79; child psychiat. nurse Norton's Children's Hosp., Louisville, 1980-81; asst. prof., psychiat. nurse Sch. Nursing, U. Louisville, 1981-82; primary therapist/child psychiat. nurse Children's Treatment Svc., Louisville, 1982-83; instr. psychiat. nursing Sch. Nursing Bellarmine Coll., Louisville, 1983-84; adult and geriat. therapist Seven Counties Svcs., Louisville, 1984; psychiat. nurse So. Pines Hosp., Charleston, S.C., 1985-86; rev. specialist S.C. Peer Rev. Orgn., Charleston, 1986-87; psychotherapist Ctr. for Change, Charleston, 1987-88; pvt. practice North Charleston, 1988-94; hospice nurse Condell Home Health Agy., Libertyville, Ill., 1994-95; home health nurse Manpower Temporary Agy., Waukegan, Ill., 1996-97; staff nurse Hospice of Highland Park (Ill.) Hosp., 1996-99; pvt. practice psychotherapy Goshen, Ky., 1999—; home health nurse Manpower Temp. Agy., Waukegan, 1996-97. Hospice nurse Hospice of Charleston, Inc., 1991-92; pub. health nurse Trident Home Halth Svcs., 1992; mental health profl. Charleston/Dorchester Mental Health Ctr., 1993. Vol. Hospice of Louisville, Inc., 1978-85, ARC State and Nat. Response Team, 1996—, Hospice and Palliative Care Louisville, Inc., 1999—; mem. steering com. Highlands Adult Day Ctr., Louisville, 1984-85; bd. dirs. Ashley River Fire Dept., Charleston, 1986-90, chair, 1989-90, mem. ladies aux., 1985-94; mem. test rose panel Jackson & Perkins, 1989-91. Named to Honorable Order Ky. Cols., Commonwealth of Ky., 1977. Mem. ACA, Am. Assn. for Mental Health Counselors. Avocations: cross stitching, raising roses, wildflower gardening, singing, making stained glass projects. Home and Office: 1120 Cliffwood Dr Goshen KY 40026-9558

DAHLGREN, DOROTHY, museum director; b. Coeur d'Alene, Idaho; m. Robert Eagan, 1985; 1 child, Ivan. BS in Museology and History, U. Idaho, 1982; M in Orgnl. Leadership, Gonzaga U., 1998. Dir. Mus. North Idaho, Coeur d'Alene, 1982—. Mem. Kootenai County Hist. Preservation Commn. Author: (with Simone Carbonneau Kincaid) In All the West No Place Like This: A Pictorial History of the Coeur d'Alene Region, 1996. Mem. no. region com. Idaho Heritage Trust. Office: Mus N Idaho PO Box 812 Coeur D Alene ID 83816 Office Phone: 208-664-3448. E-mail: dd@museumni.org.

DAHL REEVES, GRETCHEN, occupational therapy educator; b. Highland Park, Mich., July 20, 1949; d. Henry Raymond and Dorothy Ann (Canavan) Dahl; m. Jerry Charles Reeves, Dec. 30, 1970; children: Branden Levi, Garrett Whitney. BS magna cum laude, Mich. State U., 1970, MA, 1973; M of Occupl. Therapy, Western Mich. U., 1974; PhD, U. Mich., 1994. Cert. occupl. therapist. Staff therapist State of Mich., Howell, 1974-75, Clinton County Intermediate, St. Johns, Mich., 1975-78, City of Pontiac (Mich.) Schs., 1978-80; owner, oeprator Devel. Therapy Svc., Oxford, Mich., 1980—; asst. prof Med. Coll. Ohio, Toledo, 1996—. Vis. asst. prof. Oakland U., Rochester, Mich., 1993-96. Contbr. chpt. to books, articles to profl. jours.; presenter/spkr. in field. Bd. dirs. North Star Acad., Southfield, Mich., 1995-96. Recipient Dean's award for tchg. excellence Med. Coll. Ohio, 1997, Jane Walter award for acad. excellence Oakland U., 1998. Fellow Am. Occupl. Therapy Assn.; mem. Nat. Rehab. Assn., Soc. for Rsch. in Child Devel. Office: Med Coll Ohio Dept Occupl Therapy 3015 Arlington Ave Toledo OH 43614-2570 E-mail: greeves@mco.edu.

DAHLSTROM, NANCY, state representative; b. Balt., Md., Aug. 13, 1957; m. Kit Dahlstrom; children: Colby, Shayna, Misty, Matthew. AS in Human Svcs., Wayland Bapt. U., BS Human Svcs. and Bus., 1994; M in Orgnl. Mgmt. and Human Resources, U. LaVerne, 1997. Vocat. counselor work-force program U. Alaska, Anchorage; mgr. key accts. Chugach Electric Assn.; sr. sales mgr. GCI; mktg. mgr. and partnership devel. AT&T Alascom; acct. exec. Alascom, sales rep., support specialist; mem. Alaska Ho. of Reps., 2002—. Coord. Children's Miracle Network; vol. Winter Spl. Olympics, 2000; former pres. Relief-Soc.; advisor Young Women's Orgn.; coord. South Ctrl. Women's Conf. Mem.: NRA, Eagle River C. of C., Am. Mktg. Assn., Alaska Outdoor Coun., Young Rep. Republican. Avocations: reading, travel. Office: Rm 108 State Capitol Juneau AK 99801-1182

DAHLSTROM, PATRICIA MARGARET, real estate appraiser; b. L.A., Calif., Apr. 29, 1951; d. Colin Rose, Jr. and Patricia Rose; m. David Keith Dahlstrom, July 15, 1989; m. Peter Klaus Reese, Dec. 3, 1972 (div. Dec. 31, 1983); 1 child, Steven Eric Reese. BA in Urban Econ. Geography, Calif. State U., Northridge, 1976, MA in Urban Econ. Geography, 1984; BSN, UCLA, Westwood, Calif., 1995, MSN, 1997. Cert. profl. logistician, Soc. of Logistics Engrs., 1987; RN Calif., 1995, lic. Nurse Practitioner, Bd. of Registered Nursing, Calif., 1997, cert. Pediatric Nurse Practitioner, Nat. Certification Bd. of Pediatric Nurse Practitioners, 1997. Instr. Moorpark (Calif.) Coll., 1977—78; rsch. analyst Natelson Co., Westwood, Calif., 1976—78; logistics engr. Litton, Data Systems Divsn., Van Nuys, Calif., 1980—84; program mgr. Micom, Simi Valley, Calif., 1984—86; logistics engr. Allied Signal, Ocean Systems, Sylmar, Calif., 1986—87; logistics engr./project lead Litton, Data Systems Divsn., Van Nuys/Agoura Hills, Calif., 1987—91; PNP Children's Hosp., Los Angeles, Calif., 1997—98, Lavin and VanDopp, MDs, Tarzana/Van Nuys, Calif., 1998—99, Kaiser Permanente, Panorama City, Calif., 2000—01; part-time faculty instr. Calif. State U., Dept. Health Scis., Northridge, 1998—2002; appraiser Graphic Appraisal Svcs., Sherman Oaks, Calif., 2003—; tchg. asst. UCLA Sch. Nursing, Westwood, Calif., 1995—97. Workshop leader Profls. Plus Networking Group, Lancaster, Calif., 1991—92; cons. AMEX, Compton, Calif., 1986—86. On-screen nurse practitioner & co-author : (instructional video) Physical Assessment: Head to Toe Examination in 45 Minutes. Fundraiser Am. Stroke Assn., L.A., Calif., 2003; pres. Calif. Coalition of Nurse Practitioners, Region 16, San Fernando Valley, 1999—2000; sec. Calif. Coalition of Nurse Practitioners, Region 13, L.A., 1998—99; ch. coun. Ch. of the Foothills, Sylmar, Calif., 2002—. Fellow: Nat. Assn. of Pediatric Nurse Practitioners; mem.: Soc. for Adolescent Medicine, Am. Acad. of Pediat., Calif. Coalition of Nurse Practitioners, Golden Key, Sigma Theta Tau. Democrat. Lutheran. Avocations: travel, walking marathons, reading, gardening, music, theater, movies.

DAHME, MAUD, educational association administrator; b. The Netherlands; arrived in U.S., 1954; married; 4 children. Mem. N.J. State Bd. Edn., Trenton, 1983—, pres., 1998—. Mem. North Hunterdon Regional H.S. Bd. Edn., 1976—83; chair Interstate Migrant Edn. Coun., 1998; former v.p., pres. Hunterdon County Sch. Bds. Assn. Mem.: N.J. State Sch. Bds. Edn. (pres. 1995). Office: NJ Dept Edn State Bd Office PO Box 500 Trenton NJ 08625-0500

DAHMEN-RAY, PATRICIA, professional society administrator; Co-owner Ray's Demolition; corp. pres. Exec. Women Internat., Spokane, Wash., 2001—. Office: Executive Women International 515 South 700 East Ste 2A Salt Lake City UT 84102 also: Executive Women International 521 W Maxwell Spokane WA 99205-0393

DAHNK, JEAN PATRICIA, lawyer; b. 1958; BS in Bus. Adminstrn., George Washington U.; JD, Coll. William and Mary. Bar: Va. 1986. Ptnr. Glover & Dahnk, Fredericksburg, Va. Mem.: Va. State Bar (pres.-elect 2002). Office: Glover and Dahnk PO Box 207 Fredericksburg VA 22404-0207

DAILEY, COLEEN HALL, magistrate, lawyer; b. East Liverpool, Ohio, Aug. 10, 1955; d. David Lawrence and Deloris Mae (Rosensteel) Hall; m. Donald W. Dailey Jr., Aug. 16, 1980 (div. May 2001); children: Erin Elizabeth, Daniel Lester. Student, Wittenberg U., 1973-75; BA, Youngstown State U., 1977; JD, U. Cin., 1980. Bar: Ohio 1981, U.S. Dist. Ct. (no. dist.) Ohio 1981. Sr. libr. assoc. Marx Law Libr., Cin., 1979-80; law clk. Kapp Law Office, East Liverpool, 1979, 1980-81, assoc., 1981-85; pvt. practice East Liverpool, 1985-95; magistrate Columbiana County, Ohio, 1995—. Spl. counsel Atty. Gen. Ohio, 1985-92. Pres. Columbiana County Young Dems., 1985-87; bd. dirs. Big Bros./Big Sisters Columbiana County, Inc., Lisbon, Ohio, 1984-87, Planned Parenthood Mahoning Valley, Inc., 1993-97; trustee Ohio Women Inc., 1991-95; mem. Columbiana County Progress Coun., Inc. Mem. ABA, Ohio Bar Assn. (Ohio Supreme Ct. Joint Task Force on Gender Fairness, family law specialization bd.), Ohio Assn. Magistrates (chmn. domestic rels. sect. 1998-2000, 02-04), Columbiana County Bar Assn., East Liverpool Bus. and Profl. Women's Assn., Ohio Women's Bar Assn. (trustee 1997-99). Democrat. Lutheran. Office: Columbia County Common Pleas Court 105 S Market St Lisbon OH 44432-1255 E-mail: cdailey@ccclerk.org.

DAILEY, DIANNE K. lawyer; b. Great Falls, Mont., Oct. 10, 1950; d. Gilmore and Patricia Marie (Linnane) Halverson. BS, Portland State U., 1977; JD, Lewis & Clark Coll., 1982. Assoc. Bullivant, Houser, Bailey, et. al., Portland, Oreg., 1982-88, ptnr., 1988—, pres., 2002—. Contbr. articles to profl. jours. Mem.: ABA (chair task force on involvement of women 1990—93, governing coun. 1992—99, liaison to commn. on women 1993—97, vice chair tort and ins. practice sect. 1995—96, chair-elect tort and ins. practice sect. 1996—97, standing com. environ. law 1996—99, chair tort and ins. practice sect. 1997—98, chair sect. officers conf. 1998—2001, governing coun. 2003, del. 2003, property ins. law com., ins. coverage litigation com., chair task force CERCLA reauthorization, law practice mgmt. sect., comm. com.), Fedn. Ins. and Corp. Counsel, Def. Rsch. Inst., Internat. Assn. Def. Counsel, Multnomah Bar Assn. (bd. dirs. 1994—95), Oreg. State Bar, Wash. Bar Assn. Office: Bullivant Houser Bailey 300 Pioneer Tower 888 SW 5th Ave Ste 300 Portland OR 97204-2089

DAILEY, IRENE, actress, educator; b. New York, Sept. 12, 1920; d. Daniel James and Helen Therese (Ryan) D. Student, Uta Hagen, N.Y.C., 1951-61, Herbert Berghof, 1951-61. Cons. Am. Nat. Theatre and Acad., 1965-68; cons., coach for various theatre groups and individual artists., 1956—. Guest artist and tchr. various univ. in U.S., 1965— ; founder Sch. of the Actors Co., N.Y.C., 1961, artistic dir., 1961-72, mem. faculty, 1961-72. Appeared in: (films) Daring Game, 1967, No Way to Treat A Lady, 1968, Five Easy Pieces, 1970, The Grissom Gang, 1970, The Last Two Weeks, 1977, The Amityville Horror, 1978, Stacking, 1986; Broadway plays Andorra, 1962, The Subject Was Roses, 1964-65 (Drama Critics Cir. award), Rooms, 1966-67, (Drama Desk Award), You Know I Can't Hear You When the Water's Running, 1968, (off-Broadway) The Loves of Cass Maguire, 1982; appeared as Jasmin Adair in Tomorrow With Pictures (London Mag. Critics Award), Duke of York's, London, 1960; appeared in The Effect of Gamma Rays on Man-In-the-Moon Marigolds, Chgo., 1970 (Sarah Siddons Award), The House of Blue Leaves, Chgo., 1972 (Joseph Jefferson nomination), Lost in Yonkers, 1993, If We Are Women, Syracuse, 1993, (off-Broadway) Edith Stein, 1993-94, The Last Adam, Syracuse, 1994-95, (Broadway) The Father, 1995-96; appeared in Another World, NBC-TV, 1973-92 (Emmy Award 1980); appeared in (plays) Desire Under the Elms, Princeton, N.J., 1961; The Sea Gull, 1973; author: (play) Waiting for Mickey and Ava, 1978. Mem. Actors Equity Assn., Screen Actors Guild, Nat. Acad. TV Arts and Sci., Am. Ednl. Theatre Assn., AFTRA. Unitarian Universalist.

DAILEY, JANET, writer; b. Storm Lake, Iowa, May 21, 1944; d. Boyd and Louise Haradon; m. William Dailey; 2 stepchildren. Student pub. schs., Independence, Iowa. Sec., Nebr., Iowa, 1963-74. Author: No Quarter Asked, 1976, After the Storm, 1976, Boss Man From Ogallala, 1976, Savage Land, 1976, Land of Enchantment, 1976, Fire and Ice, 1976, The Homeplace, 1976, Dangerous Masquerade, 1977, Night of the Cotillion, 1977, Valley of the Vapors, 1977, Fiesta San Antonio, 1977, Show Me, 1977, Bluegrass King, 1977, A Lyon's Share, 1977, The Widow and the Wastrel, 1977, Giant of Mesabi, 1978, The Ivory Cane, 1978, The Indy Man, 1978, Darling Jenny, 1978, Reilly's Woman, 1978, To Tell the Truth, 1978, Sonora Sundown, 1978, Big Sky Country, 1978, Something Extra, 1978, Master Fiddler, 1978, Beware of the Stranger, 1978, The Matchmakers, 1978, For Bitter or Worse, 1979, Green Mountain Man, 1979, Six White Horses, 1979, Summer Mahogany, 1979, Touch the Wind, 1979, Strange Bedfellow, 1979, Low Country Liars, 1979, Sweet Promise, 1979, For Mike's Sake, 1979, Sentimental Journey, 1979, A Land Called Deseret, 1979, The Bride of the Delta Queen, 1979, Tidewater Lover, 1979, Lord of the High Lonesome, 1980, Kona Winds, 1980, The Boston Man, 1980, The Rogue, 1980, Bed of Grass, 1980, The Thawing of Mara, 1980, The Mating Season, 1980, Southern Nights, 1980, Ride the Thunder, 1980, Enemy in Camp, 1980, Difficult Decision, 1980, Heart of Stone, 1980, One of the Boys, 1980, Wild and Wonderful, 1981, A Tradition of Pride, 1981, The Traveling Kind, 1981, The Hostage Bride, 1981, Dakota Dreamin', 1981, For the Love of God, 1981, Night Way, 1981, This Calder Sky, 1981, Lancaster Men, 1981, Terms of Surrender, 1982, With a Little Luck, 1982, Wildcatter's Woman, 1982, Northern Magic, 1982, That Carolina Summer, 1982, This Calder Range, 1982, Foxfire Light, 1982, The Second Time, 1982, Mistletoe and Holly, 1982, Stands a Calder Man, 1983, Separate Cabins, 1983, Western Man, 1983, Calder Born, Calder Bred, 1983, Best Way to Lose, 1983, Leftover Love, 1984, Silver Wings, Santiago Blue, 1984, The Pride of Hannah Wade, 1985, The Glory Game, 1985, The Great Alone, 1986, Heiress, 1987, Rivals, 1989, Masquerade, 1990, Aspen Gold, 1991, Tangled Vines, 1992, Riding High, 1994, The Proud and The Free, 1994, Touch the Wind, 1994, Summer Mahogany, 1995, Legacies, 1996, Homecoming, 1997, Illusions: A Novel, 1997, The Prodigal Daughter, 1998, This Calder Sky, 1999, Calder Pride, 1999, A Capital Holiday, 2001, Green Calder Grass, 2002. Recipient Golden Heart award Romance Writers Am., 1981, Romantic Times Contemporary award, 1983.*

DAILEY, JUDY (JUDY ST. MARIE), mathematician, director, mathematician, consultant; b. Taunton, Mass., Oct. 5, 1943; d. George and Ruth (Padelford) Despin; m. Danny O'Neil Dailey, Nov. 24, 2001; children from previous marriage: Sean Patrick Barrett, Kerri Ann Barrett McAvay, Casey Walker Barrett. BS So. Conn. State Coll., 1965, MA U. Conn., 1985. Phys. edn. tchr. Amity Regional Sch. Dist. #5, Bethany, Conn., 1965—68; YMCA fitness instr. Norwich YMCA, 1970—77; owner craft bus. Chatterbox Wholesaler Craft Bus., 1976—80; tchr. Grade 1 Montville Bd. Edn., Conn., 1982; tchr. health Montville Bd. Edn., 1982—84, tchr. math, 1984—87, coord. math, 1987—. Fellow Project to Increase Mastery of Math and Sci. Wesleyan U., Middletown, 1989—; bd. dirs. Ct. Acad. Math., Sci. and Tech., Middletown, 1999—, fellow; tchr. in residence Ct. State Dept. Edn. ; co-developer Numeracy Acad. Primary Educators. Co-author: (book) NCTM Navigations in Geometry, 2001, NCTM Navigations in Measurement, Connecticut Pre K-12 Mathematics Program Evaluation and Implement Guide, 2001. Moderator First Congl. Ch., Norwich, 1997—2000. Recipient Robert Rosenbaum award, Associated Tchrs. Math. in Conn., 2000. Mem.: Conn. Assn. Mathematically Precocious Youth (chmn. 1998—2001, founder). Avocations: sewing, painting, creating porcelain dolls. Office: Montville HS Old Colchester Rd Oakdale CT 06370 E-mail: mathmover@cyberzone.net.

DAILEY, MARILYN, elementary school educator; b. Lucedale, Miss., Apr. 30, 1957; d. Jesse Lee and Vera Mae Chambers; m. William Harry Dailey, July 27, 1985. BS, William Carey Coll., Hattiesburg, Miss., 1982; MS, Ala. State U., 1995, EdS, 2001. Tchr. spl. edn. New Augusta (Miss.) H.S., 1982-83, Richton (Miss.) H.S., 1983-85; tchr. 1st grade Frisco City (Ala.) Elem. Schs., 1985-86; tchr. 4th grade Southside Elem. Sch., Evergreen, Ala., 1987-89, Thurgood Marshall Elem. Sch., Evergreen, 1989—. Named Tchr. of Yr., Conecuh County Bd. Edn., 1997-98. Mem. Internat. Reading Assn., Ala. Edn. Assn., Assn. Supervision and Curriculum, Nat. Assn. Elem. Sch. Prins., Nat. Coun. Tchrs. English, Sigma Gamma Rho, Kappa Delta Pi, Phi Delta Kappa. Avocations: singing, art. Home: PO Box 917 Evergreen AL 36401-0917

DAILY, EILEEN M. state legislator; b. Boston, Mar. 3, 1943; d. Mary and Jim Meade; m. Jim Daily; children: Jeff, Amy. Student, Northestern U., Cambridge Coll. Mem. staff dept. revenue svc Commr.'s Office, State of Conn., 1990-91; mem. Dist. 33 Conn. Senate, Hartford, 1993—, asst. minority leader; asst. pres. pro-tem Conn. State Senate. Asst. pres. Senate, 1997-98; chair Legis. Environ. Com.; vice-chair Fin., Revenue and Bonding Com.; ranking mem. Program rev. and Investigations Com.; mem. Edn. and Legis. Mgmt. Coms.; mem. L.I. Sound Bi-State commn., New England Recycling Coun.; Conn. vice-chair, New England dir. Order of Women Legislators. Mem. Westbrook (Conn.) Dem. Town Com.; chair pers. com. Westbrook Bd. Edn., 1977-83; first selectman Town of Westbrook, 1983-89, mem. bd. selectman, 1989-91; chmn. Lower Valley Selectmen's Assn., 1985-89; mem. exec. com. Coun. Small Towns, 1985-89; bd. dirs. Conn. Conf. Municipalities, 1987-89; mem. Friends of Libr.; hon. chair March of Dimes Walk-a-thon, 1997. Recipient Govs. Vol. Svc. award Conn. Alcohol and Drug Abuse Commn., award for outstanding svc. Coun. of Small Towns, award for svc. to boating industry Conn. Marine Trade Assn. Mem. C. of C., Soroptimists, Westbrook Grange. Office: Conn State Senate State Capitol Hartford CT 06106 also: 103 Cold Spring Rd Westbrook CT 06498-3511

DAILY, ELLEN WILMOTH MATTHEWS, technical publications specialist; b. Marfa, Tex., Aug. 13, 1949; d. Lynn Henry Sr. and Wilmoth Hamilton (Cox) Matthews; m. John Scott Daily Sr., Mar. 21, 1970; children: John Scott Jr., Kristen Michelle. BS in Physics, U. Tex., El Paso, 1971; postgrad., George Mason U., Fairfax, Va., 1980; continuing edn., North Lake Coll., Irving, Tex., 1996; MS in Computer Ednl. Cognitive Scis., U. North Tex., 1998, postgrad., 1998—. House dir., activity counselor Southwestern Children's Home, El Paso, Tex., 1965-68; analyst Schellenger Rsch. Found. Labs, El Paso, 1968-70; computer operator, supr. keypunch El Paso Nat. Bank, 1970-73; supr., progam analyst El Paso Sand Products, 1973-74; tech. rep. Xerox Corp., Jackson, Miss., 1975-77, product tech. specialist, 1977-79, tech. trainer Leesburg, Va., 1979-82, sr. tech. writer, tng. analyst Lewisville, Tex., 1982-95; tech. publs. specialist RFMonolithics, Inc., Dallas, 1995-96. Group rep. Xerox Corp., various cities, 1975-90; owner Daily Delight Cattery, Chantilly, Va. and Carrollton, Tex., 1979-89; co-owner J & M Answering Svc., Dallas, 1983-84, Triple "D" Enterprises, 1994—; tchg. fellow U. North Tex., Denton, 1997-98, 2000—, tchg. asst., 1998-99. Co-author: (electronic Bible verse) Verse of the Day, 1987-92. Team and divsn. mgr. Chantilly Youth Assn., 1980-82; bd. dirs., swim team dir. Brookfield Swim Club, Chantilly, 1980-82; vol. Metrocrest Svc. Ctr., Carrollton, 1986-89; elder Nor'Kirk Presbyn. Ch., Carrollton, 1989-91; founding mem. United We Stand Am., 1993-97; vol. Catherine the Great, 1992, Tex. Storytelling Festival, 1999-2000. Recipient Toulouse doctoral fellowship, 1998—. Mem. Internat. Platform Assn. (red carpet com. 1994—, newsletter editor 1999—), U. Tex. El Paso Cannoneers Club (sec.-treas. 1967-71), Nat. League Am. Pen Women (Dallas br. publ. chair 2001-02, Dallas br. pres. 2002-03), Xerox Bowling League (pres. 1988-89), Sigma Pi Sigma, Kappa Delta (social svc. dir. 1969-70), Kappa Delta Phi, Phi Kappa Phi. Avocations: web site development, computers, internet. Home: 3701 Grassmere Dr Carrollton TX 75007-2616 E-mail: edaily@comcast.net.

DAILY, JEAN A. marketing executive; b. Bloomington, Ill., Nov. 20, 1949; d. William H. and Niola N. (Thompson) D.; m. Ronald R. Willis, June 14, 1968 (div. 1972); m. Rodger D. Melick, Aug. 15, 1981. BS, Ill. State U., 1975. Sr. acctg. clk. Country Cos., Bloomington, 1976-78; owner, mgr. Danvers (Ill.) Motor Co., 1979-85; office mgr., ops. mgr. Goods Carpet, Bloomington, 1986-87; dir. mktg. Westminster Village Inc., Bloomington, 1987—. Chair Com. to Elect Judge Prall, Bloomington, 1996; publ. chair Danvers Days, 1982—85; bd. dirs., publ. rels. & devel. advisor Twin Cities Ballet, Bloomington, 1994—96; bd. dirs. ARC, 1991—94; pres. Chestnut Health Sys. Aux., 1995—98, 1999, treas., 1997—2001; vol. Arthritis Telethon, St. Jude Golf Tournament, 1997—2003; publicity chair Gardenwalk 97; mem. adv. bd. Arthritis Found., 1997—2001; apptd. cabinet bd. Ill. Life Svcs. Network Assisted Living, 1997—2003, sec., 1997—99, sec. housing cabinet, 2003. Mem. Women in Comms., Nat. Soc. Fund Raising Execs. (co-editor chpt. newsletter 1989-91). Avocations: reading, crafts, golf, photography, country dance. Office: Westminster Village 2025 E Lincoln St Bloomington IL 61701-5995 E-mail: jeanvillageblm@aol.com.

DAJANI, VIRGINIA, arts association administrator; Exec. dir. Am. Acad. Arts and Letters, N.Y.C., 1990—. Office: Am Acad Arts and Letters 633 W 155th St New York NY 10032-7501

DAKE, MARCIA ALLENE, retired nursing educator, university dean; b. Bemus Point, N.Y., May 22, 1923; d. Earl B. and Bernice DeLeo (Haskin) D. Diploma, Crouse Irving Hosp., 1944; BS, Syracuse U., 1951; MA, Columbia U., 1955, EdD, 1958. RN. Sch. nurse tchr. various locations, 1946-48; chmn. health dept. SUNY, Oneonta, 1952-56; dean coll. nursing U. Ky., Lexington, 1958-72; dir. dept. nursing edn. ANA, Kansas City, 1972-74; project dir. program devel. nursing ARC, Washington, 1975-79; dir. nursing edn. James Madison U. Coll. Nursing, 1981-88; prof. dean Coll. Nursing, 1981-88; ret., 1988. Editor, resident photographer: Greenspring Village Photo Directories, 2000—. Mem. Ky. Bd. Nursing Edn. Nurse Registration, 1969-72, pres., 1970-72; pres. Va. Coun. Deans of Baccalaureate Nursing Programs, 1981-84; nurse officer Civil Def. Otsego County, N.Y., 1953-56; mem. Def. Adv. Com. on Women in Svcs., 1963-65; mem. Ky. Comprehensive Health Planning Coun., 1968-71; pres. Ky. League for Nursing, 1961-65; bd. dirs. Cmty. Ch. Coll., Sun City Ctr., Fla., 1989-92, Sun City Ctr. Guardianship Found., 1990-98; trustee United Cmty. Ch., Sun City Ctr., 1993-96, chmn. pers. com., 1994-96, fin. com., 1994-95, vice chmn. bd. trustees, 1995-96, stewardship com., 1996, mem. pastoral rels. com., 1996—, mem. long range planning com., 1996-97, chmn. pastoral rels. com., 1998—; sec. Caloosa Women's Golf Assn., Sun City Ctr., 1991-92; treas. Greater Sun City Ctr. Disaster Coun., 1992-94; mem., vice chmn. resident adv. com. Greenspring Village, Springfield, Va., 1999-2000, corr. sec. resident adv. com., 2001. 1st lt. U.S. Army Nurse Corps, 1945-46. Fellow Nat. League Nursing; mem. ANA, Va. Nurses Assn. (pres. dist. 9 1983-85), Va. Soc. Profl. Nurses (treas. 1983-88), Va. Assn. Colls. of Nursing (sec. 1980-82, pres. 1982-85), Alliance of Nursing Orgns. (chmn. Va. 1985-88), LWV, Delta Kappa Gamma, Kappa Delta Pi, Pu Lambda Theta. Address: PV 222 7442 Spring Village Dr Springfield VA 22150-4444 E-mail: mdake@aeity.net.

DAKIN, CHRISTINE WHITNEY, dancer, educator; b. New Haven, Aug. 25, 1949; d. James Irving, Jr. and Jean Evelyn (Coulter) Crump; m. Robert Ford Dakin, June 21, 1969 (div. Sept. 1982); m. Stephen J. Mauer, Aug. 1, 1985. Student, U. Mich., 1967-71; D of Arts (hon.), Shenandoah U., 1996. Performer, teacher Ann Arbor Dance Theater, Mich., 1965-71; tchr. Ann Arbor Pub. Schs., 1967-70, Lincoln Ctr. Inst., N.Y.C., 1978, Guanajuato U., Mex., 1982; vis. artist USIA Vladivastock, Vladivastock, Russia, 1992; ArtsLink grantee, vis. artist Vladivastock, 1996; tchr., faculty advisor Ballet Nacional de Mex., 1993—; vis. artist USIA Ballet Contemporaneo, Buenos Aires, 1993; prin. dancer Martha Graham Dance Co., N.Y.C., 1976—. Dancer, rehearsal dir. Pearl Lang. Dance Co., 1972-76, Kazuko Hirabayashi Dance Co., 1974-76; faculty Martha Graham Sch., 1972—, Juilliard Sch., 1992—, Alvin Alley Am. Dance Ctr., 1989-93. Appeared in: It's Hard to Be a Jew, 1972, The Dybuk, 1975; appeared (with Martha Graham Dance Co.) Covent Garden, London, 1976, Met. Opera, 1980, Bklyn. Acad. Music, 1994, Sta. WNET Dance in Am. Series, 1979; Young Artist in Performance at The White House, Sta. WNET, 1982, (with Rudolph Nureyev) Paris Opera, Berlin Opera, 1984, N.Y. State Theater, 1985; NHK Film, Japan, 1990, Paris Opera Film, 1991, (documentary film) Les Printemps du Sacre, 1993; assoc. founder Buglisi/Foreman Dance, 1994, (with Buglisi/Foreman Dance) Runes of the Heart, Kennedy Ctr., 1997; assoc. artistic dir. Martha Graham Dance Co., 1997. Am. Dance Festival scholar, 1969, Garcia-Robles Sr. scholar Fulbright Found., 1999; recipient award Dance Mag., 1994; grantee Rockefeller U.S.-Mex. Fund for Culture, 1997-98. Mem. Am. Guild Mus. Artists (life, bd. govs.) Office: Martha Graham Dance Co Rm 5101 153 E 53rd St New York NY 10022-4631

DAKIN, MAUREEN P. state representative; b. Proctor, Vt., Mar. 17, 1950; m. Robert E. Dakin (dec.); 2 children. BA, U. Vt., 1972, Trinity Coll., 1989; A, Vt. Leadership Inst., 1996. State rep. State of Vt., 1997—, mem. agrl. com., 1999—2000, clk. commerce com., 2001—. Mem. Friends of Burnham Libr., Colchester Cmty. Develop. Corp.; past mem. Vt. Human Svcs. Bd., Vt. Bd. Dental Examiners; past vice chair Colchester Sch. Bd.; Justice of Peace; mem. Legis. Com. on Adminstrv. Rules, 2001—, Legis. Coun., 2001—; chair Colchester Dem. Com., Farmers Night Com., 2000—. Toll fellow, 2000. Democrat. Roman Catholic. Office: 47 Ponderosa Dr Colchester VT 05446 E-mail: dakin@innevi.com.

DAKOFSKY, LADONNA JUNG, radiation oncologist, educator; b. N.Y.C., Oct. 30, 1960; d. George S. and Kay (Han) Chung. BA magna cum laude, Columbia U., N.Y.C., 1982; MD, NYU, 1987. Bd. cert. radiation oncologist. Rsch. asst. dept. neurology UCLA, 1980-81, Harvard U., Boston, 1982; tchr. chemistry St. Ann's Sch., Brooklyn Heights, N.Y., 1982-83; resident in internal medicine Lenox Hill Hosp., N.Y.C., 1987-88; resident in radiation oncology Hosp. of U. Pa., Phila., 1988-91; instr. in radiation oncology New Eng. Med. Ctr., Boston, 1991-92; attending physician Norwalk (Conn.) Hosp., 1992—. Clin. asst. prof. radiation oncology Yale U., 1994—; prin. investigator RTOG cancer rsch. Norwalk Hosp., exec. com. hosp. staff, IPA chair of quality improvement subcom.; physician adminstr. Norwalk Radiology Cons. Mem. jr. com. Boys Club N.Y.; sponsor Mus. City of N.Y.; mem. com. Vocat. Found., N.Y.C.; mem. Jr. League of Stamford-Norwalk. Marine Biol. Lab. scholar, 1981. Mem. AMA, Assn. Therapeutic Radiology and Oncology, Fairfield County Med. Assn. (Melville Magida award 1998, Best Younger Physician in Fairfield County 1998), New Eng. Cancer Soc., Met. Breast Cancer Group. Presbyterian. Avocations: writing, sailing, voice. Home: 7 Sweetbriar Lane Sandy Hook CT 06482

DALE, BRENDA STEPHENS, gifted and talented educator; b. Hickory, N.C., Sept. 24, 1942; d. John Doyle and Bertha (Barger) Stephens; m. James Darrell Dale, June 13, 1964; children: Ginger Leigh Rizoti, Jami Lynne Price. BS in English, Appalachian State U., 1964, MA in Reading Edn., 1977; cert. edn. academically gifted, Lenoir Rhyne, Hickory, N.C., 1982. H.S. tchr. Moore County Schs., Carthage, N.C., 1964, Asheboro (N.C.) City Schs., 1964-65; 8th grade tchr. Davidson County Schs., Thomasville, N.C., 1967-68; reading specialist Randolph County Schs., Trinity, N.C., 1970-72, Wilkes N.C. Schs., Wilkesboro, 1972-82, tchr. acad. gifted, 1982—. Tchr. Davidson County C.C., Lexington, N.C., 1965-68, Wilkes C.C., Wilkesboro, 1982-87, 97—; adult literary tutor, 1997-98. Edn. chair, bd. dirs. Am. Cancer Soc., North Wilkesboro, N.C., 1985-90; mem. Wilkes Regional Med. Ctr. Aux., 1992—; adminstrv. coun. Wilkesboro Meth. Ch., 1997-1999; vol. Samaritan's Purse, 1997-99. Tchr. scholar fellow N.C. Ctr. for Advancement of Tchg., Western Carolina U., 1990; recipient C.B. Eller Tchg. award C.B. Eller Found., 1991. Mem. AAUW (charter, fundraiser 1977-78, bd. dirs., chmn. edn. found. 1992-96), NEA, N.C. Assn. Educators (state del. 2002, intellectual profl. devel. com. 2003—), Internat. Reading Assn. (sec. 1985-86), Mary Hemphill Svc. Group, So. Appalachian Leadership on Cancer, Lynnwoode Recreation Club, United Meth. Women (dist. membership chair Western N.C. conf. 1996-97, nominating com. 1997-98), Alpha Delta Kappa. Methodist. Avocations: writing, reading, piano. Home: 187 Laurel Mountain Rd North Wilkesboro NC 28659-8122 Office: Wilkes County Schs Main St Wilkesboro NC 28697

DALE, JUDY RIES, religious organization administrator, consultant; b. Memphis, Dec. 13, 1944; d. James Lorigan and Julia Marie (Schwinn) Ries; m. Eddie Melvin Ashmore, July 12, 1969 (div. Dec. 1983). BA, Rhodes Coll., 1966; M in Religious Edn., Grad. Specialist in Religious Edn., So. Bapt. Theol. Sem., 1969. Cert. tchr. educable mentally handicapped, secondary English, adminstrn. and supervision in spl. edn. EMH tchr., curriculum writer, tchr. trainer Jefferson County Bd. Edn., Louisville, 1969-88, ednl. cons., 1988-90; dist. coord. Gt. Lakes dist. Universal Fellowship Met. Cmty. Chs., Louisville, 1990—2002. Lectr. Jefferson C.C., Louisville, 1987-93, U. Louisville, 1976-77, 87-90; mem. faculty Samaritan Inst. for Religious Studies, 1992-98; mem. program adv. com. Internat. Conf. Spl. Edn., Beijing, 1987-88. Editor, writer: (handbook) Handbook for Beginning Teachers, 1989, A Manual of Instructional Strategies, 1985; author: (kit) Math Activities Cards, 1978. Bd. sec. Com. of Ten, Inc., Louisville, 1987-91; v.p. GLUE, 1988-92, pres., 1992-94; mem. Universal Fellowship of Met. Cmty. Chs., programs and budget divsn., 1990-97, mem. gen. coun., 1990-2002, mem. core team, 1993-2000, chair, 1997-2000, active Women's Secretariat steering com., 1991-95, fin. team, 2000—, bd. adminstrn., 2003—, chmn. risk mgmt. team, 2003—; dist. coord. Gt. Lakes Dist. (parliamentarian 1987-89); mem. membership com. Cmty. Health Trust, 1991-94; trustee Samaritan Inst. Religious Studies, 1992-98, chair acad. affairs com., 1996-97. Recipient Honorable Order of Ky. Cols., 1976, MCC Disting. Lay Leadership award, 1999; named Outstanding Elem. Tchr. Am., 1975. Mem. AAUW, NOW, ACLU, Nat. Gay & Lesbian Task Force, Parents, Family & Friends of Lesbians & Gays, Nat. Ctr. for Lesbian Rights, Lambda Legal Def. & Edn. Fund, Gay & Lesbian Assn. Anti-Defamation, Coun. Exceptional Children (keynote speaker 1984-88, inter nat. pres. 1986-87, exec. com. 1984-88, bd. govs. 1981-88), Ky. Coun. Exceptional Children (bd. dirs. 1976-90, Mem. of Yr. 1987), Internat. Platform Assn., Women's Alliance, Phi Delta Kappa. Democrat. Avocations: people, church work, reading, handwork. Home and Office: 1300 Ambridge Dr Louisville KY 40207-2410

DALE, KATHLEEN A. literature educator; b. Stafford, Kans., Mar. 15, 1945; m. Steven Kapelke, Jan. 14, 1984; children: Jessi Kapelke-Dale, Rachel Kapelke-Dale, Liana Kapelke-Dale. BA, Ohio Wesleyan U., 1967; MA, U. of Mich., 1968, PhD, with hons. U. Wis., 1976; MSW, U. of Wis., 1988. Sr. lectr. Academic Opportunity Ctr. U. Wis., Milw., 1981—. Contbr. poetry to profl. jours. Tutor Literacy Svcs., Milw., 2000—03. Mem.: Wis. Fellowship of Poets (assoc.), Phi Beta Kappa. Avocations: piano, sailing. Home: 2960 N Hackett Ave Milwaukee WI 53211 Office: UW Milwaukee Mitchell Hall Milwaukee WI 53201 Personal E-mail: kaplc@execpc.com. E-mail: kdale@uwm.edu.

DALE, MARCIA LYN, nursing educator; b. Ft. Dodge, Iowa, Mar. 4, 1938; d. William R. and Erma (Umland) Bradley; m. William G. Dale, Jr., June 30, 1967; children: Dori Lyn, Devin Glenn. BS, U. Wyo., 1960; M. Nursing, U. Wash., 1961; EdD, U. No. Colo., 1981. Prof. U. Wyo., Laramie, 1971—, dean sch. nursing, assoc. dean coll. health scis., 1991—. Recipient Disting. Alumni award Sch. Nursing U. Wyo., 1985. Fellow Am. Acad. Nursing; mem. Wyo. Nurses Assn. (Wyo.'s Search for Excellence Leadership award 1989), Wyo. League for Nursing, Sigma Theta Tau. Home: 827 Evergreen St Cheyenne WY 82009-3218

DALE, SHARON KAY, real estate broker; b. San Franciso, July 14, 1940; d. Terrill Odin and Alice Ernestine (Anthony) Glenn; divorced; 1 child, Kimberly Kay. AS, Fresno City Coll., Calif., 1982; student, Calif. State U., Fresno, 1983—. Lic. real estate broker, Calif. Sales assoc. Red Carpet Realtors, Fresno, 1974-77; broker, owner U.S. Cities Realtors, dba, Pierson & Planamento, Inc., Fresno, 1977-80; broker assoc. Easterbrook Constrn., Fresno, 1980-81, 1983-84; exec. sec. Valley Med. Ctr., Fresno, 1981—96; broker Assoc. Adanalian & Jackson Real Estate, Fresno, 1981—83, 1984—85. Dir. div. II U.S. Cities Realtors, Inc. No. Calif, Nev., 1978-80. Vol. St. Agnes Service Guild, Fresno, 1974—, Mental Health Assn., Fresno, 1982-83, Ednl. T.V. Channel 18, Fresno,1983, Valley Med. Ctr. Aux., Fresno, 1985-96, Holiday Guild Children's Hosp. Ctrl. Calif., 2000—. Mem. Fresno County, City C. of C. (Ambassadors Club), Calif. Assn. Realtors, Fresno Bd. Realtors, Multiple Listing Svc., Nat. Bd. Realtors, Fresno State Alumni Assn., Sierra Sport & Racquet Club (Fresno, Calif.) (charter mem.). Republican. Avocations: golf, tennis, photography, traveling. Home: 5099 W Shields Ave Fresno CA 93722-9751 Office: Adanalian & Jackson Real Estate 1515 W Shaw Ave Fresno CA 93711-3503

D'ALESSIO, JACQUELINE ANN, English educator; b. Morristown, N.J., Jan. 26, 1943; d. Clifford Corbet and Helen Ann (Chrenko) Compton; m. Harold F. D'Alessio, Oct. 28, 1967. BA in English, Coll. New Rochelle, 1964; MA in English, Seton Hall U., 1969. Tchr. Bridgewater (N.J.)-Raritan Regional Sch. Dist., 1964—. Advisor dramatics Bridgewater-Raritan Mid. Sch., Bridgewater, N.J., 1983—. Chmn. pub. rels. Mt. St. Mary Devel. Office, 1985-2000; bd. dirs. N.J. Legis Agenda for Women, Inc., 1993-94. Recipient Gov. Tchr. Recognition, N.J. Dept. Edn., Trenton, 1989, Disting. Svc. award Bridgewater-Raritan Regional Sch. Dist., 2001; named Outstanding Elem. Tchr. in U.S., 1971. Mem. AAUW (N.J. pres. 1990-94, program v.p. 1988-90, rep. Women's Agenda 1989-94, dir. pub. policy 1997-99, treas. 1999—, mid-Atlantic region dir. 2001—). Roman Catholic. Avocations: travel, golf, biking, gardening. Home: 30 Putnam St Somerville NJ 08876-2737

D'ALESSIO, VALAIDA CORRINE, artist, consultant; b. Dwight, Ill., Jan. 7, 1938; d. Roy Selmer and Agnes Irene (Seversen) Christiansen; m. Terald Ramon Stevens, July 5, 1958 (div. Dec. 1974); children: Christian Stevens, Curt Stevens, Kirsten Stevens, Karlin Stevens; m. Paul D'Alessio, July 16, 1976. Student, Joliet (Ill.) Jr. Coll., 1957, Aurora (Ill.) Coll., 1964, Am. Acad. Art, Chgo., 1969. Expereicned-based master endl. resources Joliet Twp. High Schs. Adult art educator Joliet Jr. Coll., 1980-88; art workshop leader various art leagues, Chgo. area, 1980-96, State of Ill. Gallery, Lockport, 1994. Art cons. Lockport St. Gallery, Plainfield, Ill., 1994—96, Prairie View Gallery, Lockport, 1999—. Contbr. paintings and mixed media collages Watercolor and Collage Workshop, 1988, book Layering: An Art of Time and Space, 1992, book Creative Collage Techniques, 1994, book Best of Watercolor 2, 1997, book Best of Watercolor 2 Painting Texture, 1997, book Bridging Time and Space, Essays on Layered Art, 1998, book Art and Helaing (Barbara Ganin), 1999. Vol. Crisis Line Will County, 1990—96. Mem.: North Coast Collage Soc., Soc. Exptl. Artists, Soc. Layerists Multi-Media.

DALEY, ANN SCARLETT, curator; b. Havre, Mont., Jan. 26, 1935; d. Frederick William and Clara Scarlett; m. James Burger Daley, Feb. 22, 1958 (div. 1981); children: James Bruce, Kathryn Scarlett, John Edward, Matthew Frederick; m. John Charles Emerson, June 6, 1987. AA, Colo. Womans Coll., 1955; BA, U. Wyo., 1958; MA, Denver U., 1981. Curator Am. art Denver Art Mus., 1977-81; curator Foxley & Co., Denver, 1980-81, Captiva Corp., Denver, 1985—. Advisor Holme, Roberts & Owen, Denver, 1989—; assoc. curator Denver Art Mus., 1993—; curator Nat. Western

Stock Show Art Exhibit, 1994—97; cons. in field. Contbr. articles to profl. jours. Mem. Mayor's Art Culture & Film Com., Denver, 1995-2003; bd. dirs. Met. State Coll. Ctr. Visual Arts, Denver, 1991-96. Mem.: Assn. Profl. Art Advisors, Phi Beta Kappa. Avocations: bicycle touring, skiing. Office: 1700 Lincoln St Ste 4750 Denver CO 80203-4511 E-mail: ann@captiva-[illegible]

DALEY, LINDA, lawyer; b. Newark, N.J., Jan. 19, 1954; d. Charles and Margaret Mongiovi; m. Rodger Cleveland Daley, Oct. 7, 1978. Student, Upsala Coll., 1971—74; BS, Regis Coll., 1975; JD, U. of Denver, 1982. Bar: Colo. 1982. Loan svc. clk. World Savs. & Loan Assn., Denver, 1975—76; rschr. Eleanor Roosevelt Inst. for Cancer Rsch., Denver, 1976—79; legal asst. Robert T. Hinds, Jr. & Associates, P.C., Littleton, Colo., 1979—82, assoc., 1982—86; law clerk to Hon. Donald P. Smith Colo. Ct. Appeals, 1987—89; assoc. staff atty. Colo. Ct. of Appeals, Denver, 1989—95, dep. chief staff atty., 1995—. Contbr. articles to profl. jours. Mem.: Colo. Bar Assn. (Amicus com.), YMCA, Denver Law Jour., Phi Beta Kappa. Avocations: walking, pets, knitting, crocheting.

DALEY, PAMELA, lawyer; b. Springfield, Mass., Oct. 1, 1952; d. Edward Murray and Elizabeth Bloom Daley; m. Randall Lee Phelps, Aug. 26, 1995. AB summa cum laude in Romance Langs. and Lit., Princeton U., 1974; JD magna cum laude, U. Pa., 1979. Bar: Pa. 1979, N.Y. 1991. Lectr. partnership taxation law U. Pa., Phila., 1982-89; assoc. tax sect. Morgan, Lewis & Bockius, Phila., 1979-86, ptnr., 1986-89; tax counsel GE, Fairfield, Conn., 1989-91, v.p., sr. counsel for transactions, 1991—. Bd. outside advisor Va. Tax Review assn., 1982-92. Editor-in-chief U. Pa. Law Review; contbr. articles to profl. jours. Trustee MacDuffie Sch., Springfield, 1986-92; bd. govs. Pa. Economy League, 1986-89; mem. bd. overseers Law Sch. U. Pa., 1999—; bd. dirs. G.E. Fund, 1999—; mem. nat. coun. World Wildlife Fund, 1999-. Teaching fellow Salzburg Seminar on Am. Law and Legal Instns., 1986; named to Acad. Women Achievers YWCA, 1992. Mem. Am. Corp. Counsel Assn., Order Coif, Phi Beta Kappa. Office: GE 3135 Easton Tpke #W3A Fairfield CT 06431-0002

DALEY, RUTH MARGARET, advertising agency administrator; b. Buffalo, Apr. 12, 1950; d. Russell Short and Emma Pleasant (Wear) Garrick; m. Jeffrey George Vanghel (dec. 1988); m. Patrick L. Daley. Student, Villa Maria Coll., Buffalo. Sec. McKesson & Robbins Drug Co., Cheektowaga, N.Y., 1972-78; sales rep. Nasco Inc., Springfield, Tenn., 1978-80; telemktg. sales rep. L.M. Berry & Co., Amherst, N.Y., 1980-81, mgr. telemktg. sales unit, 1981-83, mgr. telemktg. sales dept., 1984-90; mgmt. cons. Ameritech, Troy, Mich., 1990-92; mgr. tng. White Directory Pub. (The Talking Phone Book), Buffalo, 1992—2002, telephone sales mgr., 2002—. Grad. asst. Dale Carnegie Inst., Buffalo, 1985. Avocations: dance, reading, travel. Home: 66 Parktrail Ln Buffalo NY 14227-2545 Office: The Talking Phone Book 1945 Sheridan Dr Buffalo NY 14223-1203 Office Phone: 716-875-9100 x142. Business E-Mail: rdaley@talkingphonebook.com.

DALEY, SUSAN JEAN, lawyer; b. New Britain, Conn., May 27, 1959; d. George Joseph and Norma (Woods) Daley. BA, U. Conn., 1978; JD, Harvard U., 1981. Bar: Ill. 1981. Assoc. Altheimer & Gray, Chgo., 1981-86, ptnr., 1986—2003, Perkins Coie LLP, Chgo., 2003—. Mem.: ABA (real property, probate and trust law sect. 1983—, employee benefits com. taxation sect. 1984—, chmn. welfare plans com. real property, probate and trust law sect. 1989—95, chmn. employee benefits, securities law com. taxation sect. 2001—), Chgo. Coun. Fgn. Rels., Chgo. Bar Assn. (chmn. employee benefits divsn. fed. taxation sect. 1985—86, chmn. employee benefits com. 1990—91, chmn. fed. taxation com. 1992—93), Ill. Bar Assn. (chmn. employee benefits divsn. fed. taxation sect. 1984—86, chmn. employee benefits sect. 1995—96), Nat. Assn. Stock Plan Profls. (pres. Chgo. chpt. 1995—). Avocation: marathons. Home: 1636 N Wells St Apt 415 Chicago IL 60614-6009 Office: Perkins Coie LLP 131 S Dearborn St Ste 1700 Chicago IL 60604 Business E-Mail: SDaley@perkinscoie.com.

DALGLISH, LUCY ANN, lawyer, organization executive; b. Mpls., Mar. 24, 1959; d. James Mark and Joanne Elizabeth (Speikers) D. BA, U. N.D., 1980; MSL, Yale U., 1988; JD, Vanderbilt U., 1995. Bar: Minn. 1995, D.C. 2001. Reporter Grand Forks (N.D.) Herald, 1978-80, St. Paul Dispatch, 1979, 80-81, St. Paul Pioneer Press., 1981-89; night city editor St. Paul Pioneer Press, 1989-90, nat./fgn. editor, 1991-93; rsch. asst. Freedom Forum, Nashville, 1993-95; assoc. Dorsey & Whitney, Mpls., 1995-2000; exec. dir. Reporters Com for Freedom of Press, Arlington, Va., 2000—. Instr. Hamline U., St. Paul, 1989, 90. Nat. chair Project Watchdog, Greencastle, Ind., 1990-92. Inducted into Nat. Freedom of Info. Act Hall of Fame, Washington, 1996; Yale Law Sch. fellow, 1987-88. Mem. Soc. Profl. Journalists (bd. dirs. 1987-91, nat. chairwoman, freedom of info. com. 1991-95; recipient Wells Meml. Key 1995), First Amendment Congress (nat. bd. mem. 1991-97), Minn. AP Assn. (v.p. 1991-93), Sigma Delta Chi Found. (bd. dirs. 1990-91), Minn. Bar Assn. (bar/media com. 1992-93, 95-97, bar-media chairwoman 1997-2000). Roman Catholic. Avocations: downhill and water skiing, golf, reading, antiques, gardening. Office: Reporters Com for Freedom of Press 1815 N Ft Myer Dr Arlington VA 22209

DALIANIS, LINDA STEWART, judge; BA cum laude, Northeastern U., 1970; JD, Suffolk U., 1974, JD (hon.), 2001. Bar: N.H. 1974, U.S. Dist. Ct. N.H. 1974, U.S. Supreme Ct. 1974. Pvt. law practice, Nashua, N.H., 1974-79; marital master N.H. Superior Ct., 1979-80, assoc. justice, 1980—2000, chief justice, 2000; assoc. justice N.H. Supreme Ct., Concord, 2000—. Chair Interbranch Criminal and Juvenile Justice Com.; mem. edn. coms. N.H. Supreme and Superior Cts., Northern New Eng. Jud. Edn. Com.; mem. jud. adv. com. N.H. Dept. Corrections; mem. marital masters com., alternative dispute resolution com. N.H. Supreme Ct. Office: Supreme Ct Bldg One Noble Dr Concord NH 03301-6160

DALIS, IRENE, mezzo-soprano, opera company administrator, music educator; b. San Jose, Calif., Oct. 8, 1925; d. Peter Nicholas and Mamie Rose (Boitano) D.; m. George Loinaz, July 16, 1957; 1 child, Alida Mercedes. AB, San Jose State Coll., 1946; MA in Teaching, Columbia U., 1947; MMus (hon.), San Jose State U., 1957; studied voice with, Edyth Walker, N.Y.C., 1947-50, Paul Althouse, 1950-51, Dr. Otto Mueller, Milan, Italy, 1952-72; MusD (hon.), Santa Clara U., 1987; DFA (hon.), Calif. State U., 1999. Prin. artist Berlin Opera, 1955-65, Met. Opera, N.Y.C., 1957-77, San Francisco Opera, 1958-73, Hamburg (Fed. Republic Germany) Staatsoper, 1966-71; prof. music San Jose State U., Calif., 1977—; founder, gen. dir. Opera San Jose, 1984—. Dir. Met. Opera Nat. Auditions, San Jose dist., 1980-88. Operatic debut as dramatic mezzo-soprano Oldenburgisches Staatstheater, 1953, Berlin Staedtische Opera, 1955; debut Met. Opera, N.Y.C., 1957, 1st Am.-born singer, Kundry Bayreuth Festival, 1961, opened, Bayreuth Festival, Parsifal, 1963; commemorative Wagner 150th Birth Anniversary; opened 1963 Met. Opera Season in Aida; premiered: Dello Joio's Blood Moon, 1961, Henderson's Medea, 1972; rec. artist Parsifal, 1964 (Grand Prix du Disque award); contbg. editor Opera Quar., 1983. Recipient Fulbright award for study in Italy, 1951, Woman of Achievement award Commn. on Status of Women, 1983, Pres.'s award Nat. Italian Am. Found., 1985, award of merit People of San Francisco, 1985, San Jose Renaissance award for sustained and outstanding artistic contbn., 1987, Medal of Achievement Acad. Vocal Arts, 1988; named Honored Citizen City of San Jose, 1986; inducted into Calif. Pub. Edn. Hall of Fame, 1985, others. Mem. Beethoven Soc. (mem. adv. bd. 1985—), San Jose Arts Round Table, San Jose Opera Guild, Am. Soc. Univ. Women, Arts Edn. Week Consortium, Phi Kappa Phi, Mu Phi Epsilon. Office: Opera San Jose 2149 Paragon Dr San Jose CA 95131 Office Phone: 408-437-4450. E-mail: dalis@operasj.org.

DALLAS, SANDRA, writer; b. Washington, June 11, 1939; d. Forrest Everett and Harriett (Mavity) Dallas; m. Robert Thomas Atchison, Apr. 20, 1963; children: Dana Dallas, Povy Kendal Dallas. BA, U. Denver, 1960. Asst. editor U. Denver Mag., 1965-66; editl. asst. Bus. Week, Denver, 1961-63, 67-69, [illegible] 1983-90; freelance editor, 1990—2001. Book reviewer Denver Post, 1961—, regional book columnist, 1980—. Author: Gaslights and Gingerbread, 1965, rev. edit., 1984, Gold and Gothic, 1967, No More Than 5 in a Bed, 1967, Vail, 1969, Cherry Creek Gothic, 1971, Yesterday's Denver, 1974, Sacred Paint, 1980, Colorado Ghost Towns and Mining Camps, 1985, Colorado Homes, 1986, Buster Midnight's Cafe, 1990, reissued 1998, The Persian Pickle Club, 1995, The Diary of Mattie Spenser, 1997, Alice's Tulips, 2000, The Chili Queen, 2002; editor: The Colorado Book, 1993; contbr. articles to various mags. Bd. dirs. Vis. Nurse Assn., Denver, 1983-85, Hist. Denver, Inc., 1979-82, 84-87, Rocky Mountain Quilt Mus., 2001—, Historic Georgetown, Inc., 2002—. Recipient Wrangler award Nat. Cowboy Hall of Fame, 1980, Lifetime Achievement award Denver Posse of Westerners, 1996, disting. svc. award U. Colo., 1997; named Colo. Exceptional Chronicler of Western History by Women's Library Assn. and Denver Pub. Library Friends Found., 1986; finalist Spur award We. Writers of Am., 1998, recipient, 2003, finalist Willa award Women Writing the West, 2000, 2003, Colo. Book awards, 2000, Mt. Plains Booksellers Award, 2003. Mem. Women's Forum Colo., Denver Woman's Press Club, Western Writers Am. (Spur award 2003), Women Writing the West. Democrat. Presbyterian. Home and Office: 750 Marion St Denver CO 80218-3434

DALLEMAGNE-COOKSON, ELISE CAMILLE, writer; b. Tarrytown, N.Y., Mar. 31, 1933; d. Edmund Leo and Irene (Poisson) Cookson; m. Jeremy Gaige, June 6, 1951 (div. June 1955); m. Pierre Georges Dallemagne (dec. May. 1979); children: Pierre E. (dec. May 1994), Paul C. AB, Katherine Gibbs Bus. Sch., 1951; student, NYU, 1951-52, Syracuse U., 1952-54, Fla. Inst. Tech., 1973-75. Publicist, prodn. asst. United Artists, 20th Century Fox, Columbia Pictures, Robert Rossen Prodns., N.Y., Hollywood, Calif., 1955—59; ptnr. Katzka, Farrell, Gaige Films; pub. affairs officer U.S. Fgn. Svc., 1959—60; farmer Congo and Argentina, 1959-68; internat. hi-tech sales rep. Harris Computers Fla., 1975-78; registered rep. Wall Street various internat. banks, N.Y.C., 1980-89; fgn. lang. tchr. Cherry Valley (N.Y.) Schs., 1989-93. Author: Simplified Swahili, 1970, The Bearded Lion Who Roars, 1995, The Ombu Tree, 1998, The Filmmaker, 2000, The Red-Eye Fever, 2002, Marie Grandin-Sent by the King, 2003; contbr. articles to mags. and features to newspapers. Avocations: farming, teaching. Home and Office: 311 County Highway 34A Cherry Valley NY 13320-2404 Office Phone: 518-284-2270. E-mail: Elise@Dallemagne-Cookson.com.

DALLI, INALBYS R. accountant; b. Palma Soriano, Cuba, Jan. 27, 1946; d. Jose Ruben and Aurelia (Navarro) Toro; m. Joseph Dalli, June 15, 1969; children: Jason, Erik. BS in Acctg., Hunter Coll., 1970. CPA, N.Y. Cost acct. H. Kohnstamm & Co., N.Y.C., 1970—; audit supr. Lucas, Tucker & Co., N.Y.C.; controller Consolidated Biscuit Co., Malta; internal auditor Ericcson, Inc., Greenwich, Conn., 1984-85; controller Fedn. Handicapped, N.Y.C., 1989—91, City Vol. Corps., N.Y.C., 1989—91; acct. pvt. practice, White Plains, NY, 1987—94; controller Salesian Missions, New Rochelle, NY, 1995—; mgr. Lobo Acres. Avocation: painting. Home: PO Box 190 Thompsonville NY 12784-0190

DALLMAN, MARY F. physiologist, science educator; BA in Chemistry, Smith Coll., 1956; PhD in Physiology, Stanford U., 1967; postgrad., Swedish Royal Vet. Sch., 1968, U. Calif., San Francisco, 1969—70. Lectr. U. Calif. Dept. Physiology, San Francisco, 1970—72, aast., 1972—76, assoc. prof., 1976—81, prof., 1981—, vice-chair, 1987—. Assoc. editor Am. Jour. Physiol.: Endocrnology and Metabolism, 1979—85, Steroids, 1919—87, Am. Jour. Physiol.: Regulatory, Integrative and Comparative Physiology, 1990—92; contbr. articles to profl. jours. Recipient Am. Diabetes Rsch. award, 1996. Mem.: NIH (mem. endocrine study sect. 1977—81, mem. diabetes, digestive, kidney grants rev. subcom. 1988—92, chair 1992—93), Internat. Soc. Neuroendocrinology (pres. 1996), Women in Endocrinology (pres. 1993—95). Office: U Calif Dept Physiology Box 0444 HSW 747 513 Parnassus Ave San Francisco CA 94143

DALLMANN, CAROLYN E. auditor; d. Pearl Eileen and Harold Wilhelm Schroeder; m. David A. Dallmann, Sept. 24, 1966; children: Kyla Rae, Kassi Jean. AAS, U. of Wis./Baraboo-Sauk Country, 1997; AS in Math., BA in Math., Thomas Edison State Coll., Trenton, N.J., 1998. Cert. Quality Auditor Am. Soc. for Quality, 1999, Quality Mgr. Am. Soc. for Quality, 2003. Organist St. Paul's Luth. Ch., North Freedom, Wis., 1961—65; lab. technician Olin/Badger Army Ammunition Plant, Baraboo, Wis., 1966—74; profl. seamstress Baraboo, Wis., 1975—88; quality auditor Olin/Badger Army Ammunition Plant, Baraboo, Wis., 1988—. Recipient C.A.R.O.L. award, Jaycettes, 1979. Mem.: Am. Soc. for Quality, Am. Chem. Soc., Am. Ofcl. Assn. of Chemists, Wis. Lab. Assn. (pres. 1999—2000, Laboratorian of the Yr. 2002).

DALLY, LYNN, choreographer, performing company executive, educator; d. Jimmy Rawlins. Student, Honi Coles, Eddie Brown, Jimmy Rawlins. Co-founder, artistic dir. Jazz Tap Ensemble. Choreographer (film) Tribute, (ballet) Black Iris, (play) Speak Low; appearances include (film) Tapdancin'. Nat. Endowment Arts fellow, Artist fellow Calif. Arts Coun., 1991. Office: Pacific Northwest Ballet 301 Mercer St Seattle WA 98109-4600

DALPHOND-GUIRAL, MADELEINE, member of Canadian parliament; b. Monteal, Quebec, Can., June 6, 1938; BS in Nursing. Mem. parliament from Laval Centre Parliament of Canada, Ottawa, 1993. Office: House of Commons Justice Bloc-Rm 209 Ottawa ON Canada KIA 0A6

DALPINO, IDA JANE, retired secondary school educator; b. Newhall, Calif., Oct. 20, 1936; d. Bernhardt Arthur and Wahneta May (Blyler) Melby; m. Gilbert Augustus, June 14, 1963 (div. 1976); 1 child, Nicolette Jane. BA, Calif. State U., Chico, 1960; postgrad., Sacramento State, 1961-65, Sonoma State, 1970-71; MA, U. San Francisco, 1978. Cert. cmty. counselor, learning handicapped, c.c. instr., exceptional children, pupil pers. specialist, secondary tchr., resource specialist. Tchr. Chico High Sch., 1959-60; counselor Mira Loma High Sch., Sacramento, 1960-66; tchr. ESL Phoenix Ind. High Sch., 1968-69; resource specialist Yuba City (Calif.) High Sch., 1971-2000; ret., 2000. English tchr. Rough Rock Demonstration Sch., summers, 1975, 76. Office sec. Job's Daus., North Bend, Oreg., 1953—; active Environ. Def. Fund, Centerville Hist. Assn., Chico, 1991—. Mem. NEA, Calif. Tchrs. Assn., Chico State Alumni Assn., Sierra Club, Nature Conservancy, Audubon, Greenpeace, Sigma Kappa Alumni. Democrat. Mem. Science of the Mind Church. Avocations: reading, ecology, genealogy. Home: 6 Navajo Ln Corte Madera CA 94925 E-mail: idajane@comcast.net.

DALRYMPLE, CHERYL, retired computer company executive; CFO Lexis-Nexis, Dayton, Ohio, 1997—98, CFO, sr. v.p., 1998—99; CFO Oblix, Inc., Cupertino, Calif., 1999—. Office: Oblix Inc 18922 Forge Dr Cupertino CA 95014

DAL SANTO, DIANE, writer, retired judge; b. East Chicago, Ind., Sept. 20, 1949; d. John Quentin Dal Santo and Helen (Koval) D.; m. Fred O'Cheskey, June 29, 1985. BA, U. N.Mex., 1971; cert., Inst. Internat. and Comparative Law, Guadalajara, Mex., 1978; JD, U. San Diego, 1980. Bar: N.Mex. 1980, U.S. Dist. Ct. N.Mex. 1980. Ct. planner Met. Criminal Justice Coordinating Coun., Albuquerque, 1973-75; planning coord. Dist. Atty.'s Office, Albuquerque, 1975-76, exec. asst. to dist. atty., 1976-77, asst. dist. atty. for violent crimes, 1980-82; chief dep. city atty. City of Albuquerque, 1983; assoc. firm T.B. Keleher & Assocs., 1983-84; judge Met. Ct., 1985-89, chief judge, 1988-89; judge Dist. Ct., 1989-2000. Mem. faculty Nat. Jud. Coll., 1990-95, 97-, trustee, 1995-96; adj. faculty Internat. Law Enforcement Acad., Roswell, N.M., [illegible]; columnist Albuquerque Jour., 1996-98. Bd. dirs. Nat. Coun. Alcoholism, 1984, S.W. Ballet Co., Albuquerque, 1982-83; mem. Mayor's Task Force on Alcoholism and Crime, 1987-88, N.Mex. Coun. Crime and Delinquency, 1987-97, bd. dirs., 1992-94, Task Force Domestic Violence, 1987-94; pres. bench, bar, media com., 1987, pres. 1992, rules of evidence com. Supreme Ct., 1993-96, chair com. access to pub. records Supreme Ct., 1988; steering com. N.Mex. Buddy Awards, 1995—; mem. Metro. Criminal Justice Coordinating Coun., 1998—. U. San Diego scholar, 1978-79; recipient Women on the Move award YWCA, 1989, Disting. Woman award U. N.Mex. Alumni Assn., 1994, Outstanding Alumnus Dept. Sociology U. N.Mex., 1995; named Woman of Yr. award Duke City Bus. and Profl. Women, 1985. Mem. ABA (Nat. Conf. State Trial Judges Jud. Excellence award 1996), LWV, AAUW, Am. Judicature Soc., N.Mex. Women's Found., N.Mex. State Bar Assn. (silver gavel award 1997), N.Mex. Women's Bar Assn. (bd. dirs. 1991-92, Power and Caring award 2000), Albuquerque Bar Assn., Nat. Assn. Women Judges (bd. dist. dirs. 1999-00), Greater Albuquerque C. of C. (steering com. 1989), N.Mex. Magistrate Judges Assn. (v.p. 1985-89), Dist. Judges Assn. (pres. 1994-95), Pennies for Homeless. Office: Dist Ct 415 Tijeras Ave NW Albuquerque NM 87102-3252 E-mail: dianedalsanto@aol.com.

DALTCHEV, ANA RANGUEL, sculptor; b. Sofia, Bulgaria, Jan. 25, 1926; came to U.S., 1979; d. Ranguel and Struma Popov; m. Lubomir Daltchev, Jan. 23, 1949; 1 child, Lubomir. MA, Higher Inst. Visual Arts, Sofia, Bulgaria, 1952. Registered sculptor, Europe, 1953-79; free-lance sculptor, 1979—. Exhibited in group shows in U.S., Germany, Bulgaria, France, Yugoslavia, India, Greece, Rumania; prin. works include Motherhood, Fount, Weaver, Joy, Sophia, Youth, California Women, Dance; participation with sculptures in XIV World Biennial of Sculpture, Middleheim, Antwerpen, Pagani Biennial of European Sculpture Milan, European Biennial of Small Sculpture, Budapest, Hungary. Selected Biennale Internazionale dell' Arte Conteporanea, Italy. Mem. San Francisco Mus. Modern Arts, Women in Arts. Achievements include: half a century dedicated to research and creation of new feminine forms in sculpture. Office: PO Box 70054 Sunnyvale CA 94086-0054

DALTON, CLAUDETTE ELLIS HARLOE, anesthesiologist, educator, university official; b. Roanoke, Va., Jan. 18, 1947; d. John Pinckney and Dorothy Anne (Ellis) Harloe; m. Henry Tucker Dalton, May 17, 1973 (div. 1979); 1 child, Gordon Tucker; m. H. Christopher Alexander, III, April 29, 2000. BA, Sweet Briar Coll., 1969; MD, U. Va., 1974. Resident in anesthesiology U. N.C., Chapel Hill, 1974—77; med. edn. Lenoir County Meml Hosp./East Carolina U., Kinston, 1978—80; med. edn. in intensive care Presbyn Hosp., Charlotte, NC, 1981—82; practice anesthesiology Charlotte Eye, Ear, Nose and Throat Hosp., 1982—85, Medivision of Charlotte and Orthopedic Hosp. of Charlotte, 1985—89; asst. prof. U. Va. Health Scis. Ctr., Charlottesville, Va., 1992—; dir. Office of Cmty. Based Med. Edn., Charlottesville, 1994—; asst. dean for cmty. based med. edn. U. Va., Charlottesville, 1996—, med. dir. Pre-Anesthesia Clinic, 1996—, asst. prof. anesthesiology and med. edn., 1996—. Author developer patient edn. materials for illiterate patients, 1979—, emergency med. svc. tng. program, 1981. Bd. dirs. Charlottesville Family Svcs., Family Svcs. Albemarle County, 1992-93, U. Va. Women's Ctr., 1996—, Coun. on Aging, Lenoir County C.C., Am. Cancer Soc.; exec. dir. Cmty. Involvement Coun. Lenoir County, Kinston, 1979; county coord. Internat. Yr. of Child, Kinston, 1979; mem. sch. medicine com. on women U. Va. Med. Sch.; also others. Named Commencement spkr., U. Va. Sch. Medicine Graduation, 1993; recipient Gov.'s award, State of N.C., 1980, cert. of merit for svc. to children, N.C. Dept. Human Resources, Outstanding Tchg. award, U. Va. Sch. Medicine, 1993, Sharon L. Hostler U. Va. Outstanding Woman in Medicine award, 2002. Mem.: AMA (coun. med. edn. liaison to Nat. Bd. Med. Examiners adv. com. for med. 2003—), Va. Soc. Anesthesiology, Albemarle County Med. Soc., Med. Soc. Va. (bd. dirs. Va. Health Quality Coun. 1995—97, chair ad hoc com. on telemedicine 1996—99, 2d v.p. 1998—99, chair scope of practice com. 1999—2002, dist. dir. 1999—, coun. on med. edn. AMA 2003, editor med. news Va. Med. Quar., mem. legis. com., mem. health access com., del. to ann. meeting, reference com., mem. strategic planning and implementation com., mem. women's com., mem. med. affairs com., mem. bd. medicine adv. com., Cmty. Svc award 2003), Alpha Omega Alpha, U. Va. Med. Alumni Assn. (assoc. bd. dirs. 1989—92, chair women in medicine leadership conf. 1998—99). Avocations: natural history, environment, dance, writing, gardening. Office: U Va Med Sch PO Box 800325 Charlottesville VA 22908-0325

DALTON, DEBORAH WHITMORE, dean; b. Cleve., Dec. 30, 1951; BA in Landscape Architecture, U. Pa., 1974, MLA, 1976. Registered landscape architect, Calif., N.C. Staff lanscape designer Skidmore, Owings and Merrill, Chgo., 1976-78; assoc. The Planning Collaborative, Inc., San Francisco, 1978-80; staff landscape architect Brown/Heldt ASsocs., Inc., San Francisco, 1980-81; assoc. prof. landscape architecture N.C. State U., 1981-92, Temple U., 1992-94; dean Coll. of Architecture U. Okla., Norman, 1994-97, prof. landscape architecture, 1994—. Contbr. articles to profl. jours. Mem. pub. art subcom. City of Raleigh Arts Commn., 1991-92. Recipient Recognition award N.C. ASLA, 1992, Gold award Soc. Environ. Graphic Designers, 1991; grantee U.S. Dept. Edn., 1993. Mem. Am. Soc. of Landscape Architects. Office: U Okla Coll Architecture Carn Rm 306 Norman OK 73019-0001 E-mail: dalton@ou.edu.

DALTON, MARGARET STIEG, library and information sciences educator; b. Utica, N.Y., May 20, 1942; d. Lewis Francis and Mildred Graf Stieg; m. Jack Dalton (dec. July 7, 2000). AB cum laude, Harvard U., 1963; MSLS with honors, Columbia U., N.Y.C., 1964; MA, U. Calif., Berkeley, 1966, PhD, 1970. Reference libr. Harvard Coll. Libr., Harvard U., Cambridge, Mass., 1968—71; asst. prof. Sch. Libr. Svc., U. Ala., Tuscaloosa, Ala., 1972—75, Sch. Libr. Svc., Columbia U., N.Y.C., 1975—83; assoc. prof. Sch of Libr. and Info. Studies, U. Ala., Tuscaloosa, 1983—87; prof. Sch. Libr. and Info. Studies, U. Ala., Tuscaloosa, 1987—96, Bristol/Ebsco prof., 1996—. Author: (book) Laud's Laboratory: The Diocese of Bath and Wells in the Early Seventeenth Century, 1982, The Origin and Development of Scholarly Historical Periodicals, 1986, Public Libraries in Nazi Germany, 1992 (Fraenkel prize Wiener Libr., London, 1989), Change and Challenge in Library and Information Science Education, 1992; contbr. numerous articles to profl. jours. Grantee Fulbright German Studies Seminar, Fulbright Assn., 1997, research grantee, various orgns. Mem.: ALA (Justin Winsor prize Library History Round Table 1991), Assn. for Libr. and Info. Sci. Edn. (Profl. Contbn. to Libr. and Info. Sci. award. 1995). Episcopalian. Avocations: dogs, travel, quilting. Office: U Ala Sch of Libr and Info Studies Box 870252 Tuscaloosa AL 35487 Business E-Mail: mdalton@slis.ua.edu.

DALTON, PHYLLIS IRENE, library consultant; b. Marietta, KS, Sept. 25, 1909; d. Benjamin Reuben and Pearl (Travelute) Bull; m. Jack Mason Dalton, Feb. 13, 1950. BS, U. Nebr., 1931, MA, 1941, U. Denver, 1942. Tchr. City Schs., Marysville, Kans., 1931-40; reference libr. Lincoln (Nebr.) Pub. Libr., 1941-48; libr., asst. state libr. Calif. State Libr., Sacramento, 1948-72; pvt. libr. cons. Scottsdale, Ariz., 1972—. Libr. U. Nebr., Lincoln, 1941-48. Author: Library Services to the Deaf and Hearing Impaired Individuals, 1985, 91 (Pres.' Com. Employment of Handicapped award 1985), also poems; contbr. chpt., articles, reports in books and publs. in field. Mem. exec. bd. So. Nev. Hist. Soc., Las Vegas, 1983-84; mem. So. Nev. Com. on Employment of Handicapped, 1980-89, chairperson, 1988-89; mem. adv. com. Nat. Orgn. on Disability, 1982-94; mem., sec. resident coun. Forum Pueblo Norte Retirement Village, 1990-91, pres. resident coun., 1991-94; bd. dirs. Friends of So. Nev. Libraries; trustee Univ. Libr.

Soc., U. Nev.-Las Vegas; mem. Allied Arts Coun., Pres.' Com. on Employment of People with Disabilities, emeritus, 1989—, Ariz. Gov.'s Com. on Employment of People with Disabilities, 1990—, Scottsdale Mayor's Com. on Employment of People with Disabilities, 1990—, chmn., 1996—; mem. Scottsdale Publ Libr. Ams. With Disabilities Com., 1994—; coord. writers' group Pueblo Norte, 2002—. Recipient Libraria Sodalitas, U. So. Calif., 1972, Alumni Achievement award U. Denver, 1977, U. Nebr., Lincoln, 1983, Outstanding Sr. Citizen Vol. award City of Scottsdale, 1997, citation for svc. to people with disabilities Mayor of Scottsdale, 1999; named Mover and Shaker Scottsdale Mag., 1994. Mem. LWV, ALA (councilor 1963-64, Exceptional Svc. award 1981, award com. O.C.L.C. Humphreys Forest Press award 1994), AAUW, Assn. State Librs. (pres. 1964-65), Calif. Libr. Assn. (pres. 1969), Nev. Libr. Assn. (hon.), Internat. Fedn. Libr. Assns. and Instns. (chair working group on libr. svc. to prisons, standing com. Sect. Librs. Serving Disadvantaged Persons 1981-95), Nat. League Am. Pen Women (Las Vegas chpt. 1988-94, com. on qualifications for Letters membership 1994—, parlimentarian Scottsdale chpt. 1989-94, v.p. 1992-94, 96-98, v.p. state chpt. 1996-98, sec. 1998-2001), Am. Correctional Assn. (libr. svcs. instns. com. 1994—), Internat. Soc. Poets (disting.), Pilot Internat. (at-large). Home: 7108 E Mescal St #224 Scottsdale AZ 85254-6126

D'ALVIA, MARLENE, medical social worker, clinical social worker; b. Peekskill, N.Y., Aug. 10, 1941; d. Edward and Ethel (Robinson) Beisser; m. Raymond D'Alvia (div. Feb. 1975); children: Carl, Jennafer, Thea. BS in Edn., Oneonta (N.Y.) State U., 1963; MSW, Fordham U., Tarrytown, N.Y., 1986. Cert. social worker. Sr. caseworker Dept. Social Svcs., White Plains, N.Y., 1983-92; supr. child profl. svcs. Dept. Social Svcs. Westchester County, Yonkers, N.Y., 1992-95; coord. ptnrs. in parenting No. Westchester Guidance Clinic/ Mental Health Assn. Westchester County, Mt. Kisco, N.Y., 1995-99; med. social worker Hospice of Rockland, Pomona, N.Y., 1999—. Foster parent traine Dept. Social Svcs., White Plains, 1989-92. Mem. NASW. Avocations: sculpture, walking, dance. Home: PO Box 255 Cornwall On Hudson NY 12520

DALY, CHERYL, broadcast executive; b. Providence, Apr. 20, 1947; d. Francis Patrick and Mary Ann (Wallis) D.; m. Arthur James Generas, July 18, 1970; 1 child, Caroline. BA, Rutgers U., 1969; postgrad., New Sch. for Social Rsch., 1975-78. Account exec. Phil Dean Assocs., N.Y.C., 1969—72; dir. pub. rels. Kirkland Coll., Clinton, 1972—75; mgr. press svcs. CBS Radio, N.Y.C., 1976—80; assoc. dir. internal comm. CBS, Inc., 1980—81, dir. corp. info., 1981—83; v.p. pub. rels. Group W Satellite Comm., 1984—95, sr. v.p. pub. rels., 1995—97, CBS Cable, 1997—2000; sr. v.p. comm. TNN, MTV Networks, 2000—01; v.p. media relations MSNBC, 2002; pub. rels. cons. N.Y.C., 2002—. Examiner Westinghouse Quality Awards, Pitts., 1990. Recipient Best Co. Comm. award Cable TV Bus., 1986, Mktg. award Westinghouse Broadcasting Co., 1991. Mem. Cable TV Pub. Affairs Assn. (bd. dirs. 1985-87), Media Mommies (co-founder 1987). Democrat. Roman Catholic. Home: 1 W 67th St New York NY 10023-6200 Office: One West 67 st New York NY 10023-6200

DALY, JOE ANN GODOWN, publishing company executive; b. Galveston, Tex., Aug. 7, 1924; d. Elmer and Jessie Fee (Beck) Godown; m. William Jerome Daly, Jr., Jan. 25, 1958 (dec.). BA in Journalism, U. Okla., 1945, BA in Piano, 1952. Asst. editor house organ Southwestern Bell Telephone, St. Louis, 1945-47; sec. to city mgr. Okla. Daily News, Oklahoma City, 1947-49; pvt. piano tchr. Alva, Okla., 1952-54; sec. to editor Prentice-Hall, Inc., N.Y.C., 1954-55, asst. to children's book editor, 1955-58; asst. editor children's books Dodd, Mead & Co., N.Y.C., 1963, dir. children's books, 1965-88, asst. v.p., assoc. pub. children's books, 1986-88; editl. dir. Cobblehill Books affiliate Dutton Children's Books, N.Y.C., 1988-97, ret., 1997. Mem. Children's Book Council, N.Y.C., 1963, treas., 1969; mem. CBC/LA Com., N.Y.C., 1980, CBC/Prelude Com., N.Y.C., 1983 Active Bklyn. Heights Assn., 1976— ; friend Carnegie Hall, N.Y. Philharm.; mem. Met. Opera Guild, Mus. Modern Art, Mus. Natural History. Mem. Phi Beta Kappa, Sigma Delta Chi, Theta Sigma Phi, Mu Phi Epsilon Democrat. Methodist. Home: 80 Cranberry St Brooklyn NY 11201-1726

DALY, KAY R. public relations professional; b. Santa Monica, Calif., Oct. 31, 1966; d. Walter Francis and Joy Ray Ryon; m. Jack Williams Daly, Dec. 14, 1996; children: Patrick Bryan, Jack Reagan. BA in Comms., U. Calif., San Diego, 1989; postgrad., George Washington U. Prodn. intern TV show Dukes of Hazzard, fall 1982, Hill Street Blues, spring 1984; lab. asst. George C. Page Mus., summer 1983; salesperson Saks Fifth Ave., Beverly Hills, summer 1985; intern Phillips-Ramsey Advt. & Pub. Rels., fall 1987; press intern U.S. Sen. Pete Wilson Washington, summer 1988; press intern Senate campaign Californians for Pete Wilson, fall 1988; press asst. to campaign mgr. Sen. Pete Wilson's Campaign for Gov., 1989; state projects asst. U.S. Sen. Phil Gramm, 1989-91; dir. polit. analysis Booz-Allen & Hamilton, Inc., 1991-92; chief of staff Office of Tex Lezar, 1992-94; press sec., dep. campaign mgr. Tex Lezar for Lt. Gov., 1994; press sec., projects dir. U.S. Rep. Fred Heineman, 1995-96; rsch. cons. U.S. Rep. Robin Hayes' Campaign for Gov., 1996; comms. cons. N.C. Rep. Party, 1996, dir. comm., 1996-97; v.p., Wash. ops & publ. rels. dir. Signature Agy., 1997—2003. Various positions Mitsui Mfrs. Bank, summer 1984, 86, 87; rsch. dir. radio/TV talk show The Tom Joyner Show, N.C., mng. editor newsletter The Amen Corner, 1996; dir. Am. for Ashcroft Comm., 2001; spokesperson Coalitian for a Fair Judiciary. Asst. editor: (book) Making Government Work, 1992; newsletter editor: N.C. Fed. Rep. Women; frequent columnist, radio/TV guest. Mem. exec. com. Wake County GOP, 4th Congl. Dist. GOP.; bd. dirs. state coord. Ronald Reagan Legacy Project. Recipient speech and debate awards Nat. Forensics League, commendation letter U. So. Calif. Reading Ctr. for Tapes for the Blind, Top Honors in Crisis Comm., Infogroup, 2000, Ronald Reagan award Am. Conservative Union, 2003. Fellow (sr.) Ctr. for Individual Freedom; mem. Internat. Rep. Inst. (trainer issue advocacy/campaign comms. seminar in Ukraine), Internat. Assn. Bus. Communicators, Rep. Comms. Assn., Ind. Women's Forum, Mil. Order of World Wars (hereditary mem.), Delta Delta Delta. Republican. Avocations: gourmet cooking, politics, traveling. Home: 6035 Woodlake Ln Alexandria VA 22315 Office: PO Box 33973 Washington DC 20013 E-mail: krdaly@aol.com.

DALY, LINDA, artist, educator; d. Samuel O'Desky. BFA, Instituto Allende, 1964, MFA, 1965. Propr. Fibre-Concepts, NYC, 1973—; prof. Pratt Inst., Bklyn, 1973—; cons. UN, NYC, 1986—87. Artist/ designer Henri Bendel, NYC, 2001—; artist/designer Bloomingdales, Macys, Gucci, Armani, Fendi, Barneys, Ferragamo others., NYC, 1973—2001. Sept. 11th Meml. Banner. Recipient, Ednl. Honor Soc., 1963; MFA scholarship, Instituto Allende, 1965. Mem.: Nat. Assn. of Photoshop Professionals, Nat. Assn. for Female Executives. E-mail: ldalynyc@aol.com.

DALY, SARALYN R. retired humanities educator, writer; b. Huntington, W.Va., May 11, 1924; d. John Ross and Ruth (Kaufman) Daly. BA with honors, Ohio State U., 1944, MA, 1945; postgrad., Yale U., 1945—46; PhD, Ohio State U., 1950. Instr. Ohio State U., Columbus, 1947—49; prof., dept. chair Coll. Emporia, Kans., 1949—50; prof. Midwestern U., Wichita Falls, Tex., 1950—61; assoc. prof. Tex. Christian U., Ft. Worth, 1961—62; prof. Calif. State U., L.A., 1962—88; ret., 1988. Exch. prof. Université de Aix-en Provence, France, 1986, Universität Tübingen, Germany, 1986—87, U. Ottawa, Canada, 1987—88. Author: Katherine Mansfield, 1964, rev., 1994, In the Web, 1978, Love's Joy, Love's Pain, 1983; translator: (poetry) Book of True Love, 1978 (Harold Morton Landon prize Acad. Am. Poets, 1978). Grantee Fulbright, Am. U. Beirut, 1964—65, Tokyo Gakugei & Tsuda Coll., 1967—68, U. Bujumbura, 1970—71. Mem.: MLA (life), Acad. Am. Poets, Medieval Acad. Am. (life). Home: 6211 Gyral Dr Tujunga CA 91042

DALY, TYNE, actress; b. Madison, Wis., Feb. 21, 1946; d. James Daly and Hope Newell; m. Georg Stanford Brown (div.); children: Alyxandra, Kathryne, Alisabeth. Student, Brandeis U., Am. Music and Dramatic Acad. Performed at Am. Shakespeare Festival, Stratford, Conn.; appeared on Broadway in Gypsy, 1990, 91 revivals, The Seagull, 1992; films include Angel Unchained, 1970, The Enforcer, 1976, The Entertainer, 1976, Speed Trap, 1977, Telefon, 1977, Zoot Suit, 1982, The Aviator, 1985, Movers and Shakers, 1985; made TV debut in series The Virginian; guest appearances in various TV series including Veronica's Closet, 1996, appearances in TV series include Cagney & Lacey, 1982-88 (Emmy awards 1983, 84, 85, 88), Christy, 1994, (Emmy award 1996), Judging Amy, 1999-, (Emmy award best sup. actress, 2003); TV films include In Search of America, 1971, A Howling in the Woods, 1971, Heat of Anger, 1972, The Man Who Could Talk to Kids, 1973, Larry, 1974, Intimate Strangers, 1977, Better Late Than Never, 1979, The Women's Room, 1980, A Matter of Life and Death, 1981, The Great Gilly Hopkins, 1981, Your Place or Mine, 1983, Kids Like These, 1987, Stuck With Each Other, 1989, The Last to Go, 1990, Face of a Stranger, 1991, On the Town, 1993, Scattered Dreams, 1994, Colombo: Bird in the Hand, 1994, Bye Bye Birdie, 1994, Columbo: Undercover, 1994, The Forget-Me-Not Murders, 1994, Cagney and Lacey: The Return, 1994, Cagney and Lacey: Together Again, 1995, A Perfect Mother, 1996, Autumn Heart, The Simian Line, Shades of Gray, Three Secrets, Tricks, 1997, The Perfect Mother, 1997, Vig, 1998, Execution of Justice, 1999, The Wedding Dress, 2001; appearance one-woman show Mystery School. Recipient Tony award for Mama Rose role in Gypsy, 1990. Address: 272 S Lasky Dr Unit 402 Beverly Hills CA 90212-3671*

D'AMBRA, EVE, art historian; b. N.Y., Oct. 6, 1956; d. John and Rosalie D'Ambra; m. Franc Dominic Palaia, June 3, 1986. BA, U. Ariz., 1978; MA, UCLA, 1981; PhD, Yale U., 1987. Lectr. Kean Coll. N.J., 1988; asst. prof. U. R.I., 1989-90, Vassar Coll., Poughkeepsie, N.Y., 1990—. Vis. lectr. U. Pa., 1987, Rutgers U., Newark, 1987-88; vis. asst. prof. Boston U., 1989; lectr. Am. Acad. in Rome, 1986, Archaeol. Inst. Am., San Antonio, 1986, N.Y.C., 1987, Balt., 1989, Boston, 1989, New Orleans, 1992, Coll. Art Assn., N.Y.C., 1990, Barnard Coll., 1990, Brown U., 1991, NYU, 1991, Middlebury Coll., 1993, Gardner Mus. Symposium, 1994. Author: Private Lives, Imperial Virtues: The Frieze of the Forum Transitorium in Rome, 1993; editor: Roman Art in Context, 1993; contbr. articles to profl. jours. Recipient Rome prize, 1984-86; fellow Yale U., 1982-86, Fulbright, 1984-85; NEH travel grantee, 1991, rsch. grantee Vassar Coll., 1991, 93. Office: 371 4th St Jersey City NJ 07302-2224

DAMER, CARA JOY, marketing professional; d. Susan Ann Goldmeer. BA in Exercise Sci., BA in Dance, Ariz. State U., 1999. Mng. ptnr. Hart Agy., Inc., N.Y.C., 1994—; prin., pres. Cara Joy Ltd., Huntington, NY, 2001—; ptnr. Printon 56, N.Y.C., 2003—. Cons. Hart Agy., N.Y.C., 2002—. Sponsor Shop Well with You, N.Y.C., 2003, event organizer Lukemia/Lymphoma Soc., Huntington, 2003. Mem.: NAFE (Small Bus. award), Spanish Honor Soc., Italian Hon. Soc. Avocations: salsa and merengue dancing, reading, sewing, decorating, cooking. Office: Hart Agy Inc Ste 5C 45 W 21st St New York NY 10010 Office Phone: 212-989-4288. E-mail: cara@hartmodel.com.

D'AMICO, CAROL, educational administrator; MS in Adult Edn., EdD in Leadership and Policy Studies, Ind. U. Sr. program analyst Ind. Gen. Assembly; policy and planning specialist Ind. Dept. Edn.; dean workforce devel. Ivy Tech. C.C. Ind.; asst. sec. vocat. and adult edn. Dept. Edn., Washington, 2001—03; chancellor-elect Ivy Tech. State College's Ctrl. Ind. region, 2004—. Expert workforce devel. and edn. issues; testified before Congress and several state legislatures; sr. fellow Hudson Inst.; spkr. in field. Co-author: (book) Workforce 2020: Work and Workers in the 21st Century; contbr. articles to newspapers and profl. jours. Office: One W 26th St Indianapolis IN 46206-1763

DAMICO, DEBRA LYNN, college official, English and French educator; b. Passaic, N.J., Apr. 15, 1956; d. Nicholas Biagio and Eleanore Lorraine (Hugle) D. BA, Montclair State U., 1978, MA, 1989. Cert. tchr., N.J, reading specialist. Tchr. St. Francis Sch., Hackensack, NJ, 1978—79, Saddle Brook (N.J.) H.S., 1979-80, St. Dominic Acad., Jersey City, 1980-84; tchr. adult basic edn., gen. edn devel. and ESL, Montclair State U., 1974—2001, coord. EXCEL program, 1993—2001; internat. student advisor Manhattan Coll., Bronx, N.Y., 1984—, ESL instr., 1986—, instr. French, 1998—. Instr. Writing Inst. Adult Edn. Resource Ctr., Jersey City State Coll., 1987—; Outstanding Internat. Student advisor, 1989—. Mem. Dist. Wide Curriculum Council, Lodi, N.J., 1977-78; ch. cantor and musician. Named Outstanding Young Woman Am., 1986; grantee, Assn. Internat. Educators, 1985—86. Mem. Nat. Assn. Tchrs. of English as a Fgn. Lang., N.Y. Tchrs. of ESL, Assn. of Internat. Educators, Metro-Internat., Am. Assn. Tchrs. French, Kappa Delta Pi, Pi Delta Phi. Democrat. Roman Catholic. Avocations: singing, playing and teaching guitar, cantor and musician at church. Office: Manhattan Coll 4513 Manhattan College Pkwy Bronx NY 10471-4998 Fax: 718-862-8016. E-mail: debra.damico@manhattan.edu.

D'AMICO, PETRINA, sculptor; b. Borgetto, Italy, Jan. 27, 1938; came to U.S., 1947; d. Vito and Frances (Arcabascio) D'A.; children: Louis, Salvatoro. Student, Excelsia, 1965, Cerritos Jr. Coll., 1966-67, Shasta Jr. Coll., 1970-76; studied with Rafael Martine, 1983. Executive various bronze sculptures; exhibited at numerous group shows, 1988-90, at Calif. State Fair (4 First Place awards and 1 Second Place award); 1 yr. display at Disneyland, Anaheim, Calif., 1987; permanent exhbn. at Women's Refuge, Redding, Calif. Bd. dirs. Women's Refuge, 1985—. Mem. Bus. and Profl. Women. Office: 1975 Placer St Redding CA 96001-1747

DAMON, SHIRLEY STOCKTON, art gallery owner; b. San Francisco, Apr. 29, 1931; d. Andrew Benton and Melva Laverta (Harbin) Stockton; m. Terry Allen Damon, Oct. 20, 1956 (div. 1980); children: Benton Allen (dec.), Diana Clare, Denise Yvonne, Andrew Allen. BA, U. Calif., Santa Barbara, 1953; MA, Stanford U., 1956, postgrad., 1958. Tchr. Santa Barbara City Sch., 1953-54; demonstration tchr. U. Calif., Santa Barbara, 1954; dir. CIT program, asst. camp dir. Montecito Camp for Girls, Calif., 1955-57; tchr. Santa Clara County Sch., 1957; instr. Stanford U., 1958; tchr. Escambia County Sch., Pensacola, Fla., 1959; pres. Damon Galleries, Ltd., Vienna, Va., 1973—. Chair archtl. rev. bd. Town of Vienna, 1994—, mem., 1991—; mem. Police Chiefs Adv. Bd., Vienna, 1993-96; pres. Vienna Commons Assn., 1990-96; adult leader Girl Scouts USA Mem.: Am. Soc. Philat. Exhibitors, Internat. Soc. Japanest Philately, Ryukyu Philat. Soc. (charter), Profl. Picture Framers Assn. (chmn. cert. com. 1993—98, pres. 1990—93, assoc. regional dir. 1984—90, judge framing competitions 1990—, nat. instr. in tng. courses, award for svc. 1994), Am. Philat. Soc. (life). Republican. Episcopalian. Office: Damon Galleries Ltd 145 Church St NW Vienna VA 22180

DAMOUDE, DENISE ANN, postal worker; b. West Point, Nebr., Oct. 27, 1953; d. Dean Welch and Ella Marie (Knobel) DaM. BS in Edn., Chadron State Coll., 1976; MA in Cmty. Mental Health, Regent U., 1996. Cert. tchr., Nebr. Tchr. phys. edn. and health, coach Pine Ridge (S.D.) Mid. Sch., 1977—79; dorm supr. and counselor U.S. Forest Svc., Chadron, Nebr., 1980-81; city carrier U.S. Postal Svc., Chadron, 1981-83, clk., 1983-92, city carrier Portsmouth, Va., 1993—. Mem. women's program com. U.S. Postal Svc., North Platte, Nebr., 1986-90; mental health counselor; facilitator for boundaries, divorce care and sexual brokeness groups. Bd. dirs. Guilding Star coun. Girl Scouts U.S.A., Ogallala, Nebr., 1981-83, 90-92, day camp dir. Chadron coun., 1978, sr. troop leader Chadron coun., 1977-79; mem. Cmty. Chorus, Chadron; co-chmn. Christian edn. com. Chadron Cmty. Ch., 1987-88, supt. Christian edn., 1988-91, active with coll. students and single parent households, 1983-92; com. mem. Fellowship of Christian Adult Singles, West Nebr., 1986-92; deacon Evang. Presbyn. Ch., 2000—; chmn. food pantry Kempsville Presbyn. Ch., 2001-03, clothing closet, 2004—. Mem. NAFE, Nat. Food Coop. (bd. dirs., sec. 1984-86), Christian Assn. Psychol. Studies, Am. Assn. Christian Counselors, Cardinal Key, Sigma Delta Nu. Republican. Avocations: gardening, travel, tole painting, reading. Home: 941 Josephine Cres Virginia Beach VA 23464-3916 Office: US Postal Svc 933 Broad St Portsmouth VA 23707-9998 E-mail: ddamoude@juno.com.

DAMP, KATIE, actor, educator, community relations administrator; d. Robert A. and Barbara C. Damp; m. David Klossner, Dec. 31, 1996; stepchildren: Micah Klossner, Logan Klossner, Dakota Klossner. MFA theatre, W.Va. U., Morgantown, W.Va., 1989—91. Cmty. rels. mgr. Douglas County Libraries, Castle Rock, Colo., 2000—; founding artistic dir. Castle Rock Players, 1997—2001; theatre program dir. U. Colo., 1995—2000; theatre instr. SUNY Plattsburgh & North Country C.C., Adirondacks, NY, 1992—95; actor, dir. Pendragon Theatre, Merry-Go-Round Playhouse, Rutland Theatre, Lakeview Theatre, etc., 1986—95. Freelance actor, dir., tchr., coach, Colo., 1986—. Dir.: (stage) A Raisin in the Sun, 1999 (Best Dir. of the Yr., 1999). Legis. com. Arts for Colo., Denver, 2002; bd. mem. Alliance for Colo. Theatre, Colo., 2002; commr. Parker Cultural Commn., Parker, Colo., 2001—03. Office Phone: 303-688-7640. Personal E-mail: katiedamp@earthlink.net.

DAMPIER, CARYN, self-defense instructor; b. San Angelo, Tex., June 9, 1956; d. Clyde Hampton and Betty Jean Harville; m. David Anthony Dampier, Feb. 4, 1983; children: David, Michael, Nicholas. BA, U. Tex., El Paso, 1978. Teen psychiat. counselor St. Joseph Hosp., El Paso, 1978-82; vol., counselor Ft. Stewart (Ga.) Drug Abuse Program, 1984-87; vol. Ft. Stewart Children's Camp, 1984-87; adminstrv. asst. Naval Rsch. Lab., Monterey, Calif., 1988-2000; claims asst. William Beaumont Army Med. Ctr., El Paso, Tex., 1988-2000; transp. specialist The Mil. Traffic Command, Washington, 1988-2000; rape/aggression/def. instr. Fairfax (Va.) County Police, 1999-2000, Miss. State U., 2000—, com. specialist Social Sci. Rsch. Ctr., 2000—02; program dir. First United Meth. Ch., 2002—. Chief instr., regional dir. Naval Postgrad. Sch. Tae Kwondo Assn., 1997—, master instr., 1999—. Vol. First United Meth. Ch. TV Ministry Missions Team. Recipient Presdl. Sports award Pres. Coun. on Phys. Fitness, 1998, 2000, 01, 02. Mem. Am. Legion Aux., Civitan Republican. Methodist. Home: 801 Cathys Pond Starkville MS 39759-7008 E-mail: caryn@fumc.org.

DANA-DAVIDSON, LAOMA COOK, English language educator; b. Herndon, W.Va., Nov. 23, 1925; d. Virgil A. and Latha (Shrewsbury) Cook; m. William J. Davidson, Apr. 1946 (div. 1971); 1 child, Deborah Davidson Bollom. BE, Marshall U., 1946; MA in Adminstrn., Azusa U., 1981. Cert. tchr., Calif. Tchr. Cajon Valley Union Sch. Dist., El Cajon, Calif., 1958—, San Diego Diocese. Master tchr. to 50 student tchrs. Author: Reading series used in dist., 1968. Former pres. El Cajon Rep. Women Federated; chaplin San Diego County Rep. Women; mem. El Cajon Hist. Assn.; v.p. Cajon Valley Union Sch. Bd.; active literacy program Rolling Readers; mem. Spa-Wars Edn. Com. for Navy Relocation, mem. Alcohol and Drug Prevention Task Force; recent candidate Calif. State Assembly; apptd. hon. chmn. reflectice com. promoting art, music, dance and phys. edn. PTA Coun., 2000. Recipient sabbatical to study British Schs. Cajon Valley Union Sch. Dist., 1977-78. Mem. AAUW (pres. 1964-66, edn. com. 1993-94, policy com., women's issuees com., Chris Lynn Downey rsch. and projects award 1996), League of Women Voters, Grossmont Concert Assn., La Mesa C. of C. (edn. rep. Cajon Valley Sch. Dist.), Delta Kappa Gamma, Phi Delta Kappa. Avocations: travel, writing, reading, tennis, theatre. Office: 809 Ecken Rd El Cajon CA 92020-7312 Fax: (619) 447-4512.

DANAHER, MALLORY MILLETT (MALLORY JONES), actress, photographer, film producer, theater producer; b. St. Paul, 1939; d. James Albert and Helen Rose (Feely) Millett m. Thomas C. Danaher, Mar. 1985; 1 child by previous marriage, Kristen Vigard. BA, U. Minn. CFO Sheets & Co., N.Y.C., Happy Camper, N.Y.C., Everwarm, Inc., Mallory Inc. Active : N.Y. Theatre, 1971—; mem. : original cos. of Annie; mem. The Best Little Whorehouse in Texas; stage roles : Dodsworth, Berkshire Theatre Festival; House of Blue Leaves; Hedda Gabler; Kennedy's Children (dir. Olympia Dukakis); Edward Albee's Everything in the Garden (dir. Shelley Winters); Lincoln Ctr. Libr. Theatre; Stella; Cocteau's one-character play The Human Voice at Deutsches-Haus, NYU; Full Moon and High Tide (dir. Shelley Winters); (off-Broadway prodn.) Loose Connections, Judith Anderson Theatre; actor: (TV series) Love of Life, Another World, Hunter, Thirty-something, Superior Court, Divorce Court, The Judge, Eischied: Only the Pretty Girls Die (NBC Movie of the Week); (films) Tootsie, Hell Hath No Fury with Barbara Eden, Alone in the Dark; exhibitions include (photos) Third Eye Gallery, NYC, exhibitions include Modernage Discovery Gallery, Gallery of St. Clement's; author: Fatherless Child, numerous poems; co-prodr., subject : (films) Three Lives; (broadway prodn.) Epic Proportions; exec. prodr., lead actress : Best Served Cold. Mem. Creative Coalition. Mem.: Ctr. for Study of Popular Culture (bd. dirs.), Claremont Inst., Am. Women's Econ. Devel., Nat. Assn. for Self-Employed, Women in Theatre, Legatus, The Actors Studio (chmn. auditions), The Friars Club.

DANBURG, DEBRA, state legislator; b. Houston, Sept. 25, 1951; d. Stanley and Barbara Jean (Walker) D. BA, U. Houston, 1974, JD, 1979. Asst. dir., lobbyist Texans for ERA, 1974-75; atty. pvt. practice, Houston, 1979—; mem. Tex. Ho. of Reps., 1981—, house com. on state affairs, 1991—, chmn. house coms. on elections, 1991—; mem. Appropriations Com.; chair Budget & Oversight for Cultural and Hist. Resources Com., Appropriations Subcom. on AIDS; mem. Appropriations Subcom. on the State Employee Classification System; Speaker's appointments Tex. Adv. Commn. on Intergov. Rels. and Tex. Health & Human Svcs. Coord. Coun., 1992; del. Dem. Nat. Convention, 1984; mayoral appointee City of Houston's Mcpl. Arts Commn., 1991—; hon. bd. dirs. S.W. region Am. Jewish Congress; mem. Leadership Am., Tex. coun. Family Violence; ex-officio dir. San Jacinto River Assn, 1992; speaker's appointments Elections Adv. Com., State Artist Com., Select Com. on Rules; mem. faculty in residence, new leadership program Ctr. Am. Women in Politics, Eagleton Inst., Rutgers, 1994; mem. 3rd Conf. Jewish Parliamentarians in Israel, 1993; speaker Jewish Women's Leadership Conf. in Israel, 1994. Named Outstanding feminist Now, 1975, best legislator Houston mag., 1981, Vol. of Yr. KS/AIDS Found., 1984, Outstanding Houston Profl. Woman by Fedn. of Houston Profl. Women, 1988, Tex. Recreation and Park Soc. Legislator of Yr., 1987, Friend of Psychology, Tex. Psychology Assn., 1992, Alumnae of Yr., U. Houston Coll. Social Scis., 1993; recipient Spl. Presdl. award Houston Apt. Assn., 1985, Environ. Def. award Sierra Club, 1987, Outstanding Legislator award Tex. Assn. of Symphony Orchs., 1990, Good Brick award Greater Houston Preservation Alliance, 1990, Mary Polk award Tex. Coun. Family Violence, Unsung Heroine award The Women's Advocacy Project, 1991, Women's Suffrage award Houston Area Women's Ctr., 1991, Hollyfield Polit. Svc. award Tex. Human Rights Campaign Fund, 1995, cert. of appreciation Common Cause, 1995, cert. recognition Tex. Mcpl. League, 1995, Good Gal award Tex. Women's Polit. Caucus, 1995. Mem. Harris County Criminal Lawyers Assn. (bd. dirs. 1982-83), Nat. Trust Hist. Preservation (hon.), Sierra Club. Office: Tex Ho Reps PO Box 2910 Austin TX 78768-2910

DANCIK, JO MARIE, accountant, accounting company executive; m. George Dancik. CPA, Colo. With Ernst & Young, Cleve., until 1985, ptnr. Denver, 1985-91, mng. ptnr., 1991—. Mem. bd. Fed. Res. Bank Kansas City, 1996—, dep. chmn., 1998, chmn., 1998—. Trustee Boy Scouts Am., Denver; chmn. fund raising campaign Metro-Denver United Way, 1995; bd. dirs. Mile High United Way; mem. bus. adv. coun. U. Colo.; mem. Colo. Women's Forum, Wise Women's Coun., Colo. Concern, Colo. Forum; mem. Colo. Gov.'s Tech. Learning Com. Named Banking and Fin. Exec. of Yr., Denver Bus. Jour., 1996; chosen to carry Olympic torch through

Denver, 1996. Mem. Colo. Soc. CPAs (state steering com.), Econ. Club Colo. (bd. dirs.). Avocation: mountain climbing. Office: Ernst & Young LLP 370 17th St Ste 4300 Denver CO 80202-5663

DANDEKAR, SWATI, state representative; b. May 1951 in [illegible] [illegible] Dandekar; children: Ajai, Govind. BS in Chemistry/Biology, Nagpur (India) U., 1971; postgrad. diploma in dietetics, Bombay U., 1972. Mem. Iowa Ho. Reps., DesMoines, 2003—, mem. appropriations com., mem. econ. growth com., mem. edn. com. Active Linn-Mar Cmty. Sch. Dist. Bd. Edn., 1996—, Vision Iowa Bd., 2000—; bd. dir. Iowa Assn. Sch. Bds., 2000—; bd. dirs. Liars Holographic Radio Theatre, 2001—. Mem.: Jr. League Cedar Rapids (pres. sustainers, chair diversity com.). Home: 2731 28th Ave Marion IA 52302 Office: State Capitol East 12th and Grand Des Moines IA 50319

DANDOR, DENISE, newscaster; BA in comm., Mills Coll. Bureau chief, anchor, reporter Fox's KMPH-TV, Fresno, Calif., 1990—93; anchor, reporter ABC affiliate WXYZ-TV, Detroit, 1993—98; anchor, health specialist KABC, Los Angeles, 1998—. Recipient Profiles in Progress Award, Am. Cancer Soc., 1996, Best News Feature Award, Mich. Assn. of Broadcasters, 1997, Emmy Award for outstanding news feature reporting, Nat. Assn. of Broadcasters, 1998. Office: ABC7 Broadcast Ctr 500 Circle Seven Dr Glendale CA 91201*

DANDROW, ANN P. state legislator; b. Cambridge, Mass. BS, N.H. Coll. Mem. from dist. 30, asst. minority leader Conn. State Ho. of Reps., 1987—, mem. jud. com., select com. children, fin. revenue & bonding, mem. pub. health com., mem. substance abuse prevention com. Mem. Southington Bd. Edn., 1974-76; mem. Southington Town Coun., 1978-83, chmn., 1981-83. Mem. Order of Women Legislators (pres. Conn. chpt.). Home: 39 Tanglewood Dr Southington CT 06489-1844 Office: State Rep LOB Rm 4200 Hartford CT 06106-1591

DANDY, BERYL C. middle school educator; b. Savannah, Ga., Nov. 12, 1944; d. Thomas William Cook, Sr. and Roberta Fielding Cook; m. James Dandy, Jr., Mar. 3, 1965 (dec. Mar. 2003); children: Kenneth M., Janice E. Dandy-Harris. BS in Music Edn., Savannah State Coll., 1973; EdM in Integrated Studies, Cambridge Coll., 1998. Cert. tchr. Ga. Educator Chatham-Savannah Bd. Edn., 1974—80, 2001—; social worker Richmond County Dept. Family and Childrens Svcs., Augusta, Ga., 1980—82; educator Columbia County (Ga.) Bd. Edn., 1982—83, Dept. Corrections-State of Ga., Savannah, 1983—86; social worker Crudler Hosp., Savannah, 1986—94, Youth Futures Authority, Savannah, 1995—2000. Dir. Midtown Elderly Treatment Svcs. Tidelands Mental Health/Mental Retardation/Substance Abuse Ctr., Savannah, 1994—97. Recipient Cert. of Participation, Nat. Guild Piano Tchrs., 1973. Mem.: Music Educators Nat. Conf., Delta Sigma Theta. Democrat. Home: 2136 Hart Ave Savannah GA 31405 Office: George W DeRenne Middle Sch 1009 Clinch St Savannah GA 31405

DANES, CLAIRE, actress; b. N.Y.C., Apr. 12, 1979; d. Chris and Carla Danes. TV role as Angela Chase in series My So-Called Life, ABC, 1994-95 (nominee Emmy award for Best Lead in Drama Series 1995, Golden Globe award for Best Actress ina Drama 1995); appeared in HBO spl. More Than Friends: The Coming Out of Heidi Leiter, 1994, also guest appearances on TV series Law and Order, 1990; film appearances include: Dreams of Love, 1992, 30, 1993, Little Women, 1994, Dead Man's Jack, 1994, How to Make an American Quilt, 1995, Home for the Holidays, 1995, THe Pesky Suitor, 1995, I Love You, I Love You Not 1996, To Gillian on Her 37th Birthday, 1996, as Juliet in William Shakespeare's Romeo and Juliet, 1996, Mononoke-hime (voive only), 1997, U-Turn, 1997, The Rainmaker, 1997, Les Misérables, 1998, Polish Wedding, 1998, The Mod Squad, 1998, Brokedown Palace, 1999, Hercules (voice only), 1998, Igby Goes Down, 2002, The Hours, 2002, It's All About Love, 2003, Terminator 3: Rise of the Machines, 2003, The Rage in Placid Lake, 2003.

D'ANGELO, LIHONG LILLY, chemist; d. Mou Ji Li and Cui Ying Xiao. BS, Peking U., 1983; PhD, Emory U., 1989; MBA, Mercer U., 2002. Assoc. scientist Coca-Cola Co., Atlanta, 1989—95, scientist, 1995—2000, sr. scientist, 2000—. Contbr. articles to profl. publs. Bd. mem. Emory U. Grad. Sch. Arts and Scis., Atlanta, 2002—, Fulbright Assn., Ga. chpt., Atlanta, 2002—. Mem.: Am. Chem. Soc. (councilor Ga. chpt. 1994—, com. chemistry and pub. affairs 2001—). Achievements include patents for high potency sweeteners.

D'ANGELO, RENÉE YOUNG, special education educator; d. William and Iva Mae Young; m. Thomas C. D'Angelo, Aug. 15, 1981. BS, Ea. Nazarene Coll., 1981; MS, Nova U., 1991. Cert. profl. educator's cert. Fla., elem. edn. Fla., emotionally handicapped Fla., specific learning disabilities Fla., English to spkrs. of other langs. Fla. Tchr. specific learning disabilities Palm Beach County Schs., Belle Glade, Fla., 1986—88, tchr. emotionally handicapped, 1988—92, Loxahatchee, Fla., 1992—95, pre-kindergarten tchr. of autistic, 1995—. Recipient Seldon Waldo Meml. award, Fla. Jr. C. of C., 1998. Mem.: Royal Palm Beach Jaycees (sec. 1995—97, pres. 1997—98, mgmt. v.p. 1998—99), Palm Beach County Chpt. 200, Coun. for Exceptional Children (pres. Palm Beach County chpt. 2003—, sec. Palm Beach County chpt. 2001—02). Avocations: reading, travel, cooking, walking.

DANIEL, BETH, professional golfer; b. Charleston, S.C., Oct. 14, 1956; d. Robert and Lucia D. Grad., Furman U., 1978. Profl. golfer Ladies Profl. Golf Assn. tour, 1979—. Mem. U.S.A. World Cup Team, 1978, U.S.A. Solheim Cup Team, 1990, 92, 94, 96, 2000, 02, 03, LPGA Executive Com., 2002—03. Winner U.S. Amateur Title, 1975, 77; winner 33 LPGA events including World Series Women's Golf, 1980, 81, Columbia Savs. Classic, 1980, 82, LPGA Championship, 1990, Big Apple Classic, 1994; Named Rolex Rookie of Yr., 1979, Rolex Player of Yr., 1980, 90, 94, A.P. Female Athlete of Yr., 1990; recipient Vare Trophy, 1989, 90, 94, The Heather Farr Player Award, 2003. Achievements include being the leading money winner in LPGA, 1980, 81, 90; inducted into LPGA Tour Hall of Fame, 1999, inducted World Golf Hall of Fame, 2000; named in the top 50 LPGA Players All-time, 2000.

DANIEL, CATHY BROOKS, tutor, educational consultant; b. Nashville, Sept. 1, 1946; d. Conway William and Alliene Marie (Gilliam) B.; m. James Newton Daniel Jr., Dec. 29, 1967 (div. July 1988; children: Laura Marie, James Newton III. Student, Memphis State U., 1964-66; BS, George Peabody Coll., 1968, MA, 1971. Cert. elem. tchr., special edn. tchr., learning disabilities and behavior disorders. Tchr. Fairview (Tenn.) Elem. Sch., 1968-69; special edn. tchr. Ross Elem. Sch., Nashville, 1969-70, Rosebank Elem. Sch., Nashville, 1970-71, Graymar Elem. Sch., Nashville, 1971-73, Norman Binkley Elem. Sch., Nashville, 1973-74; cons. ednl. and family counseling, ednl. testing Franklin, Tenn., 1975—. Methodist. Avocation: tennis. Home and Office: 2203 Springdale Dr Franklin TN 37064-4962

DANIEL, ELNORA D. academic administrator; d. Stephen and Cecelia Bell; m. Herman Daniel, Mar. 25, 1961; 1 child, Michael. BS, N.C. Agrl. and Tech. U., Greensboro, 1964; MEd, Columbia U., N.Y.C., 1968; EdD, Columbia U., 1975. RN N.C., 1964. V.p. for acad. affairs Hampton U., Va., 1991—93, v.p. for health, 1994—95, exec. v.p. and provost, 1995—98; pres. Chgo. State U., 1998—. Bd. dirs. LaRabida Children's Hosp., Chgo., 2001—. Contbr. articles to profl. jours., chpts. to books. Mem. The LWV of Chgo., 1999, YMCA of Greater Roseland, Chgo., 2002, The Little Co. of Mary Hosp. Found., Evergreen Park, Ill., 1999. Col. Nurses Corp. U.S. Army, 1991. Named to Hall of Fame, Today's Chgo. Woman, 2002. Fellow: ANA (nat. adv. bd. 1999—); mem.: Am. Assn. of State Colls. and Univs., Nat. Assn. for Equal Opportunity in Higher Edn. (bd. dirs. 2002—), The Chgo. Network, Econ. Club of Chgo., Jr. Achievement of Chgo. Independent. Office: Chicago State Univ 9501 S King Dr ADM/313 Chicago IL 60628 E-mail: ed-daniel2@csu.edu.

DANIEL, KAREN, engineering and design company executive; BS in Acctg., N.W. Mo. State, 1980; MS in Acctg., U. Mo., Kansas City, 1981. CPA. With KPMG Peat Marwick, 1981—92, Black & Veatch, Overland Park, Kans., 1992—, now CFO. Mem. bd. commrs. Kansas City Pks. and Recreation, 1999—2003; bd. dirs. Cmty. Found., Women's Employment Network, Black Econ. Union; mem. bd. regents N.W. Mo. State U., 2003—. Recipient Nat. Profl. Achievement award, Nat. Women of Color, 2002. Office: Black & Veatch 11401 Lamar Overland Park KS 66211

DANIEL, MARILYN S. lawyer; b. Tulsa, Okla., July 30, 1940; d. Basil M. and Kathryne (Shannon) Stewart; m. John A. Daniel, June 15, 1962; 1 child, John S. BA, Rhodes Coll., 1962; JD, U. Ky. Coll. of Law, 1976. Bar: Ky. Sec. math. tchr., Ky., N.J., 1962-71; legal clerk U.S. Dist. Judge, Lexington, Ky., 1977; asst. U.S. atty. U.S. Dept. Justice, Lexington, 1978-81; gen. counsel Mason & Hanger Corp., Lexington, 1982—, v.p. adminstrn., 1992-96, sr. v.p., 1996—. Dir. Mason Techs. Inc., 1988—, The Mason Co., Lexington, 1990—, Ky. Bar Assn. for Women, 1991-93. Mem. Fayette County Bd. Edn., 1985-88; trustee Transylvania Presbytery, 1985—; elder Maxwell St. Presbyn. Ch., 1993—. Recipient Women of Achievement award YWCA, 1993. Mem. ABA, KBA (CLE chair ann. conv. 1992), Fayette County Bar Assn. (Henry T. Duncan award 1994. Avocations: gardening, cooking, hiking, quilting, handwork. Office: Mason & Hanger Corp 2355 Harrodsburg Rd Lexington KY 40504-3307

DANIEL, WINIFRED YVONNE, elementary school educator; d. William Clair Goatley and Imogene Gregory Shelby; 1 child, Jacquelyn Marie. BS in Elem. Edn., Ctrl. State U., 1960. Profl. cert. elem. edn. Ohio. Tchr. grade 1 Cleve. Pub. Schs., 1960—72; tchr. grades 1 and 4 Maple Heights Pub. Schs., Ohio, 1972—77; tchr. grades 4-8 Warren City Schs., Ohio, 1977—2000. Substitute tchr. Warren City Schs., 2000—. Jennings scholar, Martha Holden Jennings Found., 1966—67. Mem.: Delta Sigma Theta. Baptist. Avocations: reading, baking, quilting.

DANIEL-DREYFUS, SUSAN B. RUSSE, civic worker; b. St. Louis, May 30, 1940; d. Frederick William and Suzanne (Mackay) Russe; m. Don B. Faerber, Nov. 27, 1962 (div. Nov. 1968); 1 child, Suzanne Mackay; m. Marc Andre Daniel-Dreyfus, Aug. 9, 1969; 1 child, Cable Dunster. Student, Smith Coll., 1958-60, Corcoran Sch. Fine Arts, 1960-61, Washington U., St. Louis, 1961-62; MEd, Cambridge Coll., 1991. Mng. ptnr. Comm., Inc., 1980-82; asst. dir. Harvard Bus. Sch. Fund, Cambridge, 1982-86; pres. SCR Assocs. Corp., Cambridge, 1986—. Mem. bd. advisors Odysseum, Inc.; bd. dirs. Future Mgmt. Systems. Mem. St. Louis-St. Louis County White House Conf. on Edn., 1966-68; mem. Mo. 1st Gov.'s Conf. on Edn., 1966, 2d Conf., 1968; bd. dirs. Tunbridge Sch., 1973-78, St. Louis Smith Coll.; hon. bd. dirs. New Music Circle; mem. woman's bd. dirs. Washington U., New Music Circle, 1963-67; mem. woman's bd. Mo. Hist. Soc.; bd. dirs. Non-Partisan Ct. Plan for Mo., Young Audiences Inc., 1967-69; bd. dirs. Childrens Art Bazaar, 1968-70; founder St. Louis Opera Theater; chmn. Art. Mus. Bond Issue election St. Louis, 1966; jr. bd. dirs. St. Louis Symphony, 1966-68, Opportunities Indsl. Center, Boston; legis. chmn. bd. dirs. Boston LWV, 1969-72; mem. coun., bd. dirs. Jr. League Boston, 1970-72, 74-76, v.p. Bd. of Family Counseling Services-Region West, Boston, 1979—; pres. Family Counseling Bd., Brookline, Mass.; trustee Chestnut Hill Sch., Boston, Brookline Friendly Soc.; mem. steering com. ann. fund Boston Children's Hosp. Med. Center, 1980-84; v.p. Nat. Friends Bd., Joslin Diabetes Found., 1980-83; mem. corp. bd. Joslin Diabetes Ctr.; v.p. bd. dirs. Boston Ctr. Internat. Visitors, 1979-82; Boston bd. dirs. Mass. Soc. Prevention of Cruelty to Children, 1980-84; exec. v.p. Ctr. for Middle East Bus., 1978-82; pres. bd. Brookline Community Fund, 1984—; overseer Old Sturbridge Village, 1987—. Mem. Colonial Dames, Soc. Art Historians. Clubs: Women's City (dir., Boston); Vincent (dir.). Home: PO Box 638 Altona 3018 Australia

DANIELIDES, JOANNIE C. public relations executive; m. Nicholas Danielides; children: Philippe, Alexander. BA in art history, Finch Coll.; M in art history, Queens Coll. With Met. Mus. Art, NYC, lectr.; with Ruder Finn, Burson-Marsteller, Ogilvy & Mather, Spencer & Rubinow; press sec. for Donna Hanvoer (former Mrs. Rudy Giuliani), others; founder, pres. Danielides Comm., 1986—. Recipient Media award, Am. Acad. Nursing, 1998. Mem.: NY Women in Comm. (pres. 2003—04). Office: Danielides Comm 9 E 53rd St New York NY 10022-4220*

DANIELS, ALBERTINA DIANA, secondary school educator; b. Jacksonville, Fla., Aug. 30, 1948; d. David and Petronita Josephine Daniels. BS, Edward Waters Coll., Jacksonville, 1971; MA in Tchg., Marygrove Coll., Detroit, 2003. Cert. notary pub. N.J., N.J. Dept. Banking and Ins. Prodr. Bus. edn. tchr. Camden (N.J.) City Sch. Dist., 1976—, resource tchr., 1991—96, GED examiner, 1998—2001, GED chief examiner, 2001—, career counselor, 1999—. Coord. food basket drive Cmty. Sharing and Caring, Camden, 1994—, sch. book asst., 1995—, summer food program asst., 1998—. Mem.: Women's Internat. Bowling Congress, Club Docetts, Order of Ea. Star (grand organizer 1988—, assoc. matron). Baptist. Avocations: bowling, sewing, reading, travel, computer programs. Office: Cmty Sharing and Caring Corp 2656 Baird Blvd Camden NJ 08105 Personal E-mail: tindaniels@aol.com.

DANIELS, ARLENE KAPLAN, sociology educator; b. N.Y.C., Dec. 10, 1930; d. Jacob and Elizabeth (Rathstein) Kaplan; m. Richard Rene Daniels, June 9, 1956. BA with honors in English, U. Calif., Berkeley, 1952; MA in Sociology, 1954, PhD in Sociology, 1960. Instr. dept. speech U. Calif., Berkeley, 1959-61; rsch. assoc. Mental Rsch. Inst., Palo Alto, Calif., 1961-66; assoc. prof. sociology San Francisco State Coll., 1966-70; chief Center for Study Women in Soc., Inst. Sci. Analysis, San Francisco, 1970-80; mem. faculty Northwestern U., Evanston, Ill., 1975-95, prof. dept. sociology, 1975-95, dir. Women's Studies, 1992-94, prof. emerita. Vis. prof. dept. sociology U. Calif., Berkeley, 1997—; cons. NIMH, 1971-73, NEH, 1975-80, Nat. Inst. Edn., 1978-82 Editor: (with Rachel Kahn-Hut) Academics on the Line, 1970; co-editor: (with Gaye Tuchman and James Benét) Hearth and Home: Images of Women in the Mass Media, 1978, (with James Benét) Education: Straightjacket or Opportunity?, 1979, (with Rachel Kahn-Hut and Richard Colvard) Women and Work, 1982, (with Alice Cook and Val Lorwin) Women and Trade Unions in Eleven Industrialized Countries, (with Teresa Odendahl and Elizabeth Boris) Working in Foundations, 1985, Invisible Careers, 1988, (with Alice Cook and Val Lorwin) The Most Difficult Revolution: Women in the Trade Union Movement, 1992; editor: Jour. Social Problems, 1974-78; assoc. editor: Contemporary Sociology, 1980-82, Symbolic Interaction, 1979-84, Am. Sociol. Rev., 1987-90. Trustee Bus. and Profl. Women's Rsch. Found. Bd., 1980-85, Women's Equity Action League Legal and Ednl. Def. Fund, 1979-81; mem. Chgo. Rsch. Assoc. Bd., 1981-87. Recipient Social Sci. Rsch. Council Faculty Rsch. award, 1970-71; Ford Found. Faculty fellow, 1975-76; grantee Nat. Inst. Edn., 1978-79, 1979-80, NSF, 1974-75, NIMH, 1973-74 Mem. Inst. Medicine NAS, Sociologists Women in Soc. (pres. 1975-76), Am. Sociology Assn. (coun. 1979-81, chmn. occupations and orgns. 1987, chmn. pubs. com. 1985-87, sec. 1992-95, Jessie Bernard award 1995), Soc. Study Social Problems (v.p. 1981-82, pres. 1987 Lee Founders award 1988), Soc. Study Symbolic Inter-Action. E-mail: akdaniels@aol.com.

DANIELS, ASTAR, artist; b. Fostoria, Ohio, Nov. 27, 1920; d. Alfred Henry and Edna Mae (Roush) Shultz; m. Bert Franklin Daniels, May 17, 1942 (div. Sept. 1976); children: Larry Bert, Cheri Hogue-Daniels, N. Dana Rahbar-Daniels. Honor grad., Art Instrn., Inc., Mpls., 1952; student, Toledo Mus. Sch. Design, 1950-52; studied with, Emerson C. Burkhart, 1952-54; student, Thomas Moore Coll., 1971-73; grad. summa cum laude, U. Cin., 1977, student, Ohio U., [illegible] adult and youth art classes, Forest and Cin., Ohio, 1950-57; portrait demonstrator numerous galleries, colls., mus., TV nationwide, 1951-79; dir. art, tchr. Defiance (Ohio) Coll., 1956-57; tchr. art and drama Meth. Ch. Camp, Sabina, Ohio, 1960-64; lectr. on liturgical art Hyde Park Comty. Ch., Cin., 1960-79; tchr. art and drama Fairview Arts Ctr., Cin., 1977-78; tchr. art Losantiville Summer Sch. Disadvantages Youth, 1996. Judge, mem. jury art shows, 1956—70; gallery guide Contemporary Art Ctr., Cin., 1972—73; costume designer Girl Scouts Symphony Music Hall, Cin., 1960, Cin., 62, Cin., 66; dir. art Ohio State Fair, Columbus, 1955—57; nat. art dir. Sr. Girl Scout Round-up, Button Bay, Vt., 1962; founder, chairperson Fine Arts Com. Ecclesia, Cin., 1960—79. One-woman shows include mus., colls., galleries, 1954—72, exhibitions include glass sculpture Schaff Gallery, Cin., 1996, commns., include Richard Nixon, Dr. A. B. Graham, James Arnes; author, illustrator: book Aiming in His Direction, 1971; illustrator (book) Woman Spirit Bonding, 1983. Art therapist Christ Hosp. Psychiat. Ward, Cin., 1959—61; citizen diplomat Soc. Positive Future, 1986; youth liturgical dance dir. Hyde Park Cmty. Ch., Cin., 1959—66. Recipient Scouters award for tng. leadership, Boy Scouts Am., Forest, 1957, Cert. of Achievement, Charlotte R. Schmidlapp Found., Cin.. 1977, Exptl. Inst. Human Devel. award, Hyde Park Cmty. Ch., 1976. Mem.: Nat. Mus. Women in Arts, Soc. Universal Human (founding mem. 1996). Avocations: world travel, exploring Incan and Mayan sites, mentoring young women, reading, metaphysical phenomena. Home and Office: 101 Solway Ct Cary NC 27511

DANIELS, BARBARA ANN, non-profit organization executive; b. Middletown, Ohio, Apr. 8, 1968; d. Benjamin Franklin and Hazel May (Dorsey) Lewis; m. Kevin Wilson Daniels, Oct. 8, 1988; children: Kara Marie, Kaitlyn Brooke. Student, U. Phoenix, 1999—. Acctg. intern AC&D Bus. Svcs., Inc., Mesa, 1989, Switzer's Corp., Phoenix, 1991; accts. payable clk. Rockford Fosgate Corp., Tempe, 1989-91; office asst., sr. cons. Ariz. State U., Tempe, 1992, bus. cons. deans office Coll. of Bus., 1992-93; pres. Daniels Bus. Svcs., Mesa, 1992—; dir. mem. svcs. Greater Phoenix Leadership, 1993—. Chair GPL Adminstrv. Assts. Network, Phoenix, 1995—. Mem. NAFE, Profl. Secs. Internat. (chair publicity team Tempe chpt. 1995, chair cmty. svc. com. 1993-94), Nat. Trust for Hist. Preservation, Valley Citizens League, Exec. Women Internat. (Phoenix Chpt., bd. dirs., program dir.). Republican. Avocations: family, education, physical fitness, community involvement. Office: Greater Phoenix Leadership Inc 201 N Central Ave Fl 3 Phoenix AZ 85073-0073 Home: 10959 E Dover St Apache Junction AZ 85220-2250

DANIELS, CAROLINE, publishing company executive; b. San Francisco, Dec. 11, 1948; d. William L. and Gladys Daniels; m. Jack Wernick, Nov. 30, 1985 (div.); children: Martin, Katherine. Student, U. Dijon, France, 1965; BA in Psychology, U. Colo., 1970; postgrad. mgmt. program, Harvard U., 1983-85. Export agt. Air Oceanic Shippers, San Francisco, 1972-73; library supr. Aircraft Tech. Pubs., San Francisco, 1973-75, ops. mgr., 1975-80, v.p., 1980-82, exec. v.p. Brisbane, Calif., 1982-84, pres., CEO, chmn. bd. dirs., 1984—. Pres. adv. bd. Embry Riddle Aero. U.; bd. dirs. Acad. Art Coll., San Francisco. Past mem. bd. dirs. Jr. Achievement of The Bay Area. Mem. Gen. Aviation Mfg. Assn. (bd. dirs., mem. exec. com., former chmn. pub. affairs com., chmn. safety affairs com.). Office: Aircraft Tech Pubs 101 S Hill Dr Brisbane CA 94005-1251

DANIELS, CHERYL LYNN, pediatrics nurse, case manager; b. Paterson, N.J., June 15, 1951; d. Nathan and Frances Avonna (Bradshaw) D. RN, Martland Hosp. Sch. Nursing, Newark, 1971; AAS in Health and Community Svc., NYU, 1984, BA in Journalism, 1987. Cert. pediat. nurse, ANCC. Evening charge nurse Martland Hosp. Unit, Newark, 1971-73; staff nurse Heal Econs. Advancement League, Paterson, N.J., 1972-74; neonatal intensive care nurse St. Joseph's Hosp. & Med. Ctr., Paterson, N.J., 1973-77, 1977-79, pediat. neonatal ICU, 1979-89, intensive care nurse, pediatric HIV outpatient nurse, 1989-90; rsch. outpatient HIV/SJH case mgmt. nurse Aids Clin. Trial Group, 1990-2001; case mgr. outpatient pediat. HIV Clinic, 1989—; pediat. sedation nurse for CT scan procedures, 2001—02. Mentor Career Beginning Program, Paterson, 1988-90. Recipient Gobetz award, NYU, 1984. Mem. ARC, ANA, AACN (cert. pediat. nursing), Alpha Sigma Lambda. Baptist. Avocations: clarinet, swimming, reading, writing, oil painting. Office: Saint Joseph Hosp 703 Main St Paterson NJ 07503-2691 Home: 680 11Th Ave #680 Paterson NJ 07514-1202

DANIELS, CINDY LOU, space agency executive; b. Moline, Ill., Sept. 24, 1959; d. Ronald McCrae and Mary Lou (McLaughlin) Guthrie; m. Charles Burton Daniels, June 19, 1982. Student, Augustana Coll., Rock Island, Ill., 1977-78; BS cum laude, No. Mich. U., 1981; MS in Info. Sys., George Washington U., 1999, M Engring Mgmt., 2000. Field engr. Ford Aerospace, Houston, 1982-83; engr. flight ops. McDonnell Douglas Corp., Houston, 1983-85; electronics engr. Johnson Space Ctr. NASA, Houston, 1985-89, project mgr. multiple program control ctr., 1989-90, project mgr., 1989-91, mission control ctr. upgrade project mgr., 1990-91, mgr. program control office, 1991-93; mgr. ground facilities Space Sta. Program Office NASA, Houston, 1993-94; engring. and ops. mgmt., space sta. program NASA Hdqrs., Washington, 1994-96; spl. assessments and acquisition mgr. NASA Langley Rsch. Ctr., Hampton, Va., 1996—. Dynamics contr. NASA Johnson Space Ctr., 1982-83; payload data engr. NASA, 1983-84, earth radiation budget satellite joint ops. integration plan mgr., 1984; mem. payload assist module team NASA-McDonnell Douglas Corp., 1984-85. Home: 200 Barrington Ln Yorktown VA 23693 Office: NASA Langley Rsch Ctr 12 W Taylor Ave Hampton VA 23663-2206

DANIELS, CINDY LOU, writer, educator; d. Rodger Franklin and Barbara Janet Blackmer; m. Alfred Jay Daniels, June 22, 1979; children: Jay Allen, Julie Ann. AAS in Computer Info. Systems, SUNY, Canton, 1992; BA in English Writing, summa cum laude, St. Lawrence U., Canton, 1995, MEd, 1996; MFA, Norwich U., Montpelier, Vt., 1997. Coll. instr. SUNY, Potsdam, NY, 1998—2000, asst. prof. English/humanities Canton, NY, 1996—. Contbr. short stories to various lit. jours. (hon. mention, Am. Pen Women, 1993, Finalst, Southeast Rev., 1996). Mem.: Phi Theta Kappa, Phi Beta Kappa. Office: SUNY Canton Cornell Dr Canton NY 13617 E-mail: danielsc@canton.edu.

DANIELS, DAVETTA MILLS, principal; b. Austin, Tex., July 31, 1952; d. Carole Athene and David Crockett Hill; m. Ray McCoy Daniels, Feb. 17, 2001; 1 child, Joelle Devee Mills. EdD, Nova Southeastern U., 2003. Cert. tchr. Tex. Edn. Agy., 1978. Social work Houston Area Urban League, Houston, Tex., 1975—76; tchr. Houston Ind. Sch. Dist., Houston, Tex. Prin. Houston Ind. Sch. Dist., Houston, 1995—2003, Hartsfield Elem., Houston, Texas, Tex.; founder/dir. Nat. Counseling and Referral Svcs., Houston; presenter Oxford (Eng.) U., 1999. Greeter/welcome Wheeler Ave. Bapt. Ch., Houston, 2002—03; bd. mem. Women's Ctr., Houston, 2000—02; dir. Pass It On Mentorship/Guidance Program for Male Students, Houston. Fellow: Tenn. State U. (life; sec. 1999—2002); mem.: NAACP, Tex. Assn. Secondary Sch. Prins. (Outstanding Prin. of Yr. 1999—2000), Phi Delta Kappa, Delta Sigma Theta, Alpha Kappa Alpha. Home: 12714 Water Oak Drive Missouri City TX 77489 Office: Hartsfield Elem Sch 5001 Perry St Houston TX 77021 Personal E-mail: ddaniel1@houstonisd.org.

DANIELS, DEBORAH JEAN, federal agency administrator; BA, De Pauw U., 1973; JD, Ind. U. Bar: Ind., U.S. Dist. Ct. (so. dist.) Ind., U.S. Ct. Appeals (7th cir.), U.S. Supreme Ct. 1987. U.S. attorney U.S. Dist. Ct. So. Dist. Ind., 1988—; asst. atty. gen. justice programs U.S. Dept. Justice, DC, 2001—. Office: US Dept Justice Off Justice Programs 810 7th St NW Washington DC 20531

DANIELS, DIANA M. lawyer; b. Dillon, Mont. BA, Cornell U., 1971; JD, Harvard U., 1974; M of City Planning, MIT, 1974; diploma, U. Edinburgh, Scotland, 1976. Bar: N.Y. 1975, U.S. Dist. Ct. (ea. and so. dists.) N.Y. 1975, U.S. Ct. Appeals (2d cir.) 1975, D.C. 1978, U.S. Supreme Ct. 1988. Assoc. Cravath, Swaine & Moore, N.Y.C., 1975-78; asst. counsel Washington Post newspaper, 1978-79; gen. counsel Washington Post Co., 1988-89, v.p., gen. counsel, 1989-91, v.p., gen. counsel, sec., 1991—; v.p., counsel Newsweek, N.Y.C., 1979-85, v.p., gen. counsel, 1985-88. Trustee Cornell U., 1995-; trustee ABA Mus. of Law, 1997—, Appleseed Found., 1998—, Ctr. for Study of Presidency, 1997-2001, Com. Corp. Gen. Counsel, 2000—, Am. Law Inst., 2003-. Office: Washington Post Co 1150 15th St NW Washington DC 20071-0002

DANIELS, ELIZABETH ADAMS, English language educator; b. Westport, Conn., May 8, 1920; d. Thomas Davies and Minnie Mae (Sherwood) Adams; m. John L. Daniels, Mar. 21, 1942; children: John L., Eleanor B. (dec.), Sherwood A., Ann S. AB, Vassar Coll., 1941; A.M., U. Mich., 1942; PhD, N.Y. U., 1954. From instr. to prof. English Vassar Coll., Poughkeepsie, N.Y., 1948-85, dean freshmen, 1955-58, dean studies, 1965-73, chmn. dept. English, 1974-76, 81-84, acting dean faculty, 1976-78, chmn. self-study, 1978-80, Vassar historian, 1985—. Author: Jessie White Mario, Risorgimento Revolutionary, 1972, Main to Mudd, Bridges to the World, 1994, Main to Mudd, and More, 1996; co-author (with Clyde Griffen); Full Steam Ahead in Poughkeepsie, The Story of Coeducation at Vassar 1966-74, 2000, (with Maryann Bruno) Vassar College 1861-2000, 2000, also articles. Bd. dirs. Alzheimer's Assn. Mid-Hudson Valley. Recipient Grad. award Alumnae Assn. N.Y. U., 1954; Vassar fellow, 1941; Nat. Endowment Humanities summer stipend, 1981 Mem. MLA, AAUP, Poughkeepsie Tennis Club, Phi Beta Kappa. Democrat. Home: 56 Muirfield Ct Poughkeepsie NY 12603 Office: Vassar Coll PO Box 74 Poughkeepsie NY 12602-0074

DANIELS, GLENNIE OVERMAN, family and consumer educator; b. Yadkinville, NC, Mar. 27, 1945; d. Rex Thomas and Mary Blanche (Simmons) Overman; m. Michael Dean Daniels, Jan. 28, 1967. BSHE, U. NC, Greensboro, 1967, MEd, 1972, PhD, 1996; cert. in Gerontology, U. NC, 2001. Cert. tchr., NC. Asst. dir. residence halls UNCG, Greensboro, 1967; tchr. Berlin-Am. Sch., Berlin, 1969, Guilford County Schs., Greensboro, NC, 1970-83; sole proprietor Fibers and Frames, Statesville, NC, 1983-93; extension agent NC Cooperative Extension, Newton, 1995—. Bd. dir. Project HEART, Smart Start, Catawpa County, NC. Author, presenter: (symposium) Am. Ednl. Studies Assn., 1994, NC Assn. Rsch. in Edn., 1995. Recipient Terry Sanford Creative Tchg. Local award NC Public Schs., Greensboro, 1977, Tchr. Yr. award Assn. Classroom Tchrs., 1979, Hammermill Paper Creative Design award Hammermill Paper, 1989, Science Tchg. Excellence award Guilford County, NC, Greensboro, 1983, Early Career award 1999. Mem. Alpha Delta Kappa (past chpt. pres.), Kappa Omicron Nu, Epsilon Sigma Phi. Avocation: heritage crafts. Office: NC Cooperative Extension 1175 S Brady Ave Newton NC 28658-3331

DANIELS, J. YOLANDE, architectural firm executive, educator; BS in Architecture, CUNY, 1987; M in Architecture, Columbia U., 1990. With Office of Thierry Despont, NY, 1990—91, Gaetano Pesce Ltd., NY, 1991, Smith-Miller and Hawkinson Archs., NY, 1991—93, Selldorf Archs., NY, 1993—95, Ralph Appelbaum Assocs., NY, 1996—98; ptnr. SUMO, 1995—. Adj. prof. CUNY, 1992—95; adj. asst. prof. Columbia U., 1997, Pratt Inst., 1997—98; asst. prof. U. of Mich., 1998—2000; women's studies seminar lectr. Josai Internat. U., Chiba, 2000, Chiba, 01, Chiba, 03; asst. prof. Columbia U., 2000—. Contbr. numerous lectures, acad. juries, exhibitions and reviews. Finalist Young Archs. Program, Mus. of Modern Art, 2001; recipient Young Archs. award, Archtl. League of N.Y., 1999, Nat. Design award, Am. Collegiate Schs. of Architecture, 1999, Rome prize, Am. Acad. in Rome, 2003—; grantee, N.Y. Found. for Arts, 2002. Office: Studio Sumo 101 W End Ave #75 New York NY 10023 also: Sch of Architecture Planning & Preservation Columbia U 400 Avery 2960 Broadway New York NY 10027-6902 E-mail: studiosumo@rcn.com.

DANIELS, LORI S. state legislator, insurance agent; b. Burlingame, Calif., Nov. 5, 1955; d. Robert William and Sue Ann (McCowen) McCroskey; m. Stephen L. Daniels, June 19, 1976 (div. June 1980). Student, Ariz. State U., 1973-76; BA in Mgmt., U. Phoenix, 1994. CLU. Trainer Campus Crusade for Christ, San Bernadino, Calif., 1977-79; with instalment loans dept. Ariz. Bank, Mesu, 1979-80; ins. agt. State Farm Ins., Chandler, Ariz., 1980—; mem. Ariz. Ho. Reps., 1992-00; majority leader Ariz. Ho. Reps., Dist. 6, 1997-00; mem. Ariz. Senate, Dist. 6, Phoenix, 2001—. Bus. cons Jr. Achievement, Mesu, 1987-92; mem. various com. including ways and means, rules, 1997—. V.p. Valley of Sun United Way, Phoenix, 1991-93, chmn. Chandler Area Reg. Coun., 1991-92. Recipient Small Bus. Person of Yr. award Gilbert C. of C., 1989. Mem. Chandler C. of C. (v.p. cmty. devel. 1991-92, v.p. membership svc., 1992-93, Pres.'s award 1990, Chamber cup 1992). Republican. Home: 700 N Dobson Rd Unit 7 Chandler AZ 85224-6939 Office: 1700 W Washington St Ste 110 Phoenix AZ 85007-2812

DANIELS, MARYBETH ELIZABETH, nurse; b. Bryn Mawr, Pa., Jan. 24, 1960; d. Joseph Ignatius and Rita Marie (Lavan) Harkins; m. Thomas Scott Daniels, May 28, 1983; children: Ryan Thomas, Matthew Joseph. ASN, Gwynedd Mercy Coll., Gwynedd Valley, Pa., 1979. RN, Md.; cert. gen. nursing practice and med.-surg. nursing, ANCC. Insvc. edn. and infection control nurse Mallard Bay Nursing and Rehab. Ctr., Cambridge, Md., 1987-88; staff nurse insvc. edn. spl. care unit Dorchester Gen. Hosp., Cambridge, 1988-90; staff nurse ICU Meml. Hosp., Easton, Md., 1983-87, staff nurse med.-surg. unit, 1990-91, assoc. nurse mgr. critical care svcs., 1991-96, cardiac and pulmonary rehab. program mgr., 1996—. Nursing advisor Midshore Heart Club, Easton, 1990—96; CPR instr. Am. Heart Assn., Easton, 1990—; mem. Lipid Nurse Task Force. Bd. dirs. Dorchester Youth Lacoss, Cambridge, 1996—, Dorchester Shore Fins Swim Team, 1996—97, coach, 1997, 1998; bd. dirs. Talbot County chpt. Am. Heart Assn., 1993—2000. Mem.: Md. Assn. Cardiovasc. and Pulmonary Rehab., Am. Assn. Cardiovasc. and Pulmonary Rehab. Roman Catholic. Avocations: reading, sports, stenciling, fishing, her family. Office: Meml Hosp 219 S Washington St Easton MD 21601-2996 Home: 600 Edlon Park Cambridge MD 21613-1314

DANIELS, SUSAN M. commissioner; BA magna cum laude, Marquette U.; MS, Miss. State U.; PhD in Ednl. Psychology, U. N.C. Prof., head dept. Sch. Allied Health Professions, La. State U. Med. Ctr., New Orleans, 1978-88; assoc. commr. Rehab. Svcs. Adminstrn., Dept. Edn., Washington, 1988-91; assoc. commr. Adminstrn. on Devel. Disabilities, Dept. HHS, Washington, 1991-94; assoc. commr. Disability, Social Security Adminstrn., Washington, 1994, dep. commr. Disability and Income Security Programs. Spkr. in field. Avocations: reading, movies, playing cards, theater, travel. Office: Social Security Adminstrn Office Dep Commr 6401 Security Blvd Baltimore MD 21235-0001

DANIELS, SUSANNE, broadcast executive; m. Greg Daniels. Grad., Harvard U. Asst. mgr. devel. Broadway Video Entertainment, mgr. devel.; dir. variety, reality and specials ABC TV Network; dir. comedy devel. The Fox Broadcasting Co.; pres. entertainment The WB Network, Burbank, Calif. Spkr. in field; developer (for Lorne Michaels) Saturday Night Live, Kids in the Hall, Am. Detective, America's Funniest People, Living Single, Martin, Buffy the Vampire Slayer, Dawson's Creek, Felicity, Roswell, Angel, Gilmore Girls, 7th Heaven; responsible for overseeing (ABCs spls.) Academy Awards, Muhammad Ali's 50th Birthday Spl., Am. Comedy Awards. Bd. dirs. The Nat. Campaign to Prevent Teenage Pregnancy. Named in the Power Issue Entertainment Weekly, 1997, one of most powerful women in entertainment, The Hollywood Reporter, 1998, 1999, 2000. Mem.: Acad. TV Arts and Sci. Office: WB Network 4000 Warner Blvd Bldg 34-r Burbank CA 91522-0001

DANIELS-CARTER, VALERIE, food franchise executive; d. John and Katherine Daniels. Degree, Lincoln U., 1978; MS, Cardinal Stritch Coll., 1982. With Firstar Bank, 1978-81; auditor MGIC Investment Corp., 1981-84; co-founder V & J Foods, Milw., 1984—. Owner 37 Burger King restaurants, 61 Pizza Hut restaurants. Pres. bd. dirs. Milw. World Festival Inc. Named Entrepreneur of Yr., Ernst & Young and Merrill Lynch, 1994; recipient award Black Women's Network of Milw., 1997, Sacajawea award for creativity Midwest Express Airlines, 1997. Office: V & J Holding Cos 6933 W Brown Deer Rd Milwaukee WI 53223-2103

DANIELSON, JUDITH A. state legislator; b. Boise, Dec. 30, 1951; m. John Danielson; children: Jason, Jaymee. Student, Boise State U., U. Idaho, Long Beach City Coll. Nurse/LPN, 1971-81; dep. sheriff for juvenile offenders; mem. Idaho Ho. of Reps., Boise, 1989-94, Idaho Senate, Dist. 8, 1994—. Past Boise County Commr.; past City Coun. pres.; vice chair resources and environment com.; mem. fin., health and welfare, and transp. coms. Active bicycle safety program for Boy Scouts. Mem. Ida-Ore Planning Devel. Assn. (v.p.), PTA, Idaho Assn. Pvt. Industry Couns. (past chair), Adams County Devel. Corp. Republican. Office: State Capitol PO Box 83720 Boise ID 83720-3720

DANILOW, DEBORAH MARIE, realtor, vocalist, composer, musician, rancher; b. Mineral Wells, Tex., Dec. 9, 1947; d. Stanton Byron and Irval Leona (Vanhoosier) D.; m. William Paul Cook Jr., June 1965 (div. Oct. 1967); m. Chance Gentry, Oct. 1971 (div. May 1974); m. Ellis Elmer Aldridge, Dec. 3, 1977 (div. Nov. 1984); children: Chandra Desiree, Anthony Ellis; m. Carl Graham Quisenberry, Feb. 7, 1992 (div. May 1997). Student, Brantley Draughon Bus. Coll., Ft. Worth, 1965-66, Tex. Christian U., 1965-67, U. Ariz., 1967-69. Asst. to pres. Hollywood Video Ctr., L.A., 1969-72; producer Western Inst. TV, L.A., 1972-77; owner Chanelde Ranch, Weatherford, Tex., 1977-84; band musician Bonnie Raitt, Jerry Williams, Malibu, Calif., 1984, Mick Fleetwood, Malibu, 1984; lead musician Jazz Talk, Ft. Worth, 1985-96; owner Brazos Valley Ranch Inc., 1987—97, AAA Bail Bonds, Seymour, 1990-96; mgr., team leader Keller Williams Realty, Arlington, Tex., 2002—03, Mansfield, Tex., 2002—03, realtor assoc. Ft. Worth, 2003—. Composer numerous pub. songs, 1969—; lead musician Debbie Danilow and Soul Full o' Jazz, 1996—; debut solo CD Primordial Heart, 1999. Active Sheriffs Assn. Tex., Seymour, 1991-97, North Tex. Taxpayers League, Wichita Falls, Tex., 1991-96, Tex. State Notary Bd., Austin, 1990-99. Mem. NRA, Nat. Assn. Realtors, Tex. Realtors Assn., Greater Ft. Worth Bd. Realtors, Greater Lewisville Bd. Realtors, Arlington Bd. Realtors, Tex. Limousin Assn., Tex. Southwestern Cattle Raisers Assn., Tex. Cattlewomen's Assn., Am. Quarter Horse Assn. (life), Nat. Found. Quarter Horse Assn., Dallas-Ft. Worth Profl. Musicians Assn., Ft. Worth Jazz Soc. (sec. 1987-89), N.Am. Limousin Found. (life), Australian Shepherd Club Am., Marchigiana Cattle Assn. (life). Avocations: music, investments, writing, performing, real estate. Home and Office: Debbie Danilow Inc 524 Pineview Ln Fort Worth TX 76140 Personal E-mail: debbie@debbiedanilow.com.

DANIS, JULIE MARIE, writer, advertising executive; b. Dayton, Ohio, Aug. 19, 1955; d. Charles Wheaton and Elizabeth Jane (Sliter) D. BS, Northwestern U., 1977; AM, U. Chgo., 1979, MBA, 1984. Juvenile justice planner Ill. Law Enforcement Commn., Chgo., 1979-80; prin. budget analyst City of Chgo., 1980-82; account mgmt. intern Foote, Cone & Belding, Chgo., 1983; product mgr. Frito-Lay, Inc., Dallas, 1984-87; advt. account exec. Leo Burnett Co., Chgo., 1987-88; ptnr., mgmt. cons. The Everest Group, Chgo., 1988-94; writer, columnist, humorist, pub. spkr. Chicago Tribune, 1994—; sr. v.p., dir. Mind & Mood Foote, Cone & Belding Advt., Chgo., 1994—. Commentator PRI Marketplace radio. Cons. United Way of Chgo.; ex-officio Discovery Bd. Goodman Theatre; trustee Chgo. Trustee Group Goodman Theatre, active in Leadership Am., Metro Help Svcs., Am. Cancer Soc., Social Venture Ptnrs., Mercy Home for Boys and Girls, 1990-94. Mem. U. Chgo. Women's Bus. Group, Pi Beta Phi. Roman Catholic. Avocations: theatre, dance, long distance running, tennis, travel. Home: 2130 N Lincoln Park W Apt 15S Chicago IL 60614-4639 Office: Foote Cone & Belding 101 E Erie St Fl 14 Chicago IL 60611-2850

DANITZ, MARILYNN PATRICIA, choreographer, videographer; b. Buffalo; BS in Chemistry, Le Moyne Coll.; MS in Chem. Engring., Columbia U. Artistic dir. High Frequency Wavelengths/Danitz Dances, 1976—. Assoc. prof. Tainan Cheng Chuan Coll., Taiwan, 1984; profl. dancer Ballet Mcpl. Strasbourg, France, Ballet Mcpl. Geneva, Switzerland; choreography commns. performances include The 11th Internat. Ballet Comp. Varna, Bulgaria, 1983, Tbilisi Ballet co., USSR, Nat. Ballet of Colombia, Nat. Inst. Arts, Taiwan, Nanatsudera Theatre, Nagoya, Japan, Shanghai Ballet and Shanghai Jiao Tung U., People's Republic of China, Nat. Cheng Kung Dance Group, Taiwan, Jacob's Pillow Dance Festival, Mass., 6th Internat. Dance Theatre Festival, Poland, 5th Anniversary Celebration Kannon Ctr., St. Petersburg, Russia, 15th Internat. Festival of Modern Choreography, Belarus, others; master choreography workshops include Ctrl. Ballet, Beijing, Chinese Cultural U., Taipei, Taiwan, Okuda Studio, Nagoya, Ballet Philippines, Manila, NSW Coll. Dance, Sydney, The Ballet Sch., Bogota, Colombia, Lublin, Lodz, Poznan and Bytom, Poland, Vitebsk, Belarus, others; video prodn. Real Art Ways Nat. Residency, funded by NEA, 1990; video art collaboration with Allen Ginsberg. Presentations include Internat. Conf. on Dance and Tech., 1993, Naropa Inst. 20th Anniversary Celebration, 1994; video work presented at Lincoln Ctr., N.Y.C., 1995, Hanyang U., Seoul, Korea, 1997, others; video work in permanent collection Lincoln Ctr. Dance Collection; TV prodns. of works include Nat. Broadcasting, Venezuela, Colombia, Bulgaria, Poland, Russia, Belarus, Pub. Broadcasting, Albany, N.Y.C., Mpls.; works performed by Nat. Ballet with the Nat. Philharm. Orch. of Colombia Gala Performance, 1984; co. tours include China, Japan, Taiwan, Europe, Hawaii; co-editor Branching Out, Oral Histories of the Founders of Six National Dance Orgns.; juror competitions. Recipient Outstanding Dance-Theater Work of 1986 award Dance Brew-ATV Cable Manhattan, award for disting. choreography Nat. Assn. Regional Ballet, 1982; Bessie Schoenberg Lab. for Experienced Choreographers Dance Theater Workshop; NIH fellow; Gold Medal scholar Conservatoire Geneve, N.Y. State Regents scholar, Le Moyne Coll. Chemistry scholar, others. Mem. Dance Theater Workshop, Am. Dance Guild (pres., editor Am. Dance, bd. dirs., nat. conf. planning com.), Soc. Dance History Scholars, Dance Films Assn. Address: 560 Riverside Dr Apt 16E New York NY 10027-3208 also: PO Box 216 Sand Lake NY 12153-0216 also: 3200 Holly Rd Apt 2 Virginia Beach VA 23451-2926 E-mail: HFW2000@aol.com.

DANKE, VIRGINIA, educational administrator, travel consultant; b. Spokane, Wash., Mar. 9, 1925; d. William Ernest and Daisy May (Norton) Danke. BS, Wash. State U., 1947; MEd, Whitworth Coll., 1950; postgrad., LaSalle U., 1973. Cert. tchr. Counselor Clarkston (Wash.) Sch. Dist., 1948—48; head phys. edn. dept. Lewis & Clark H.S., Spokane Sch. Dist., 1948—77; travel cons. Viking Travel, Spokane, 1982—, Empire Tours, Spokane, 1982—. Co-author (editor): Marching Together, 1955. Treas. Fedn. Western Outdoor Clubs, 1980—; com. mem. Future Spokane, 1981—, bd. dirs., Pacific Crest Trail Conf., Santa Ana, Calif., 1984; mem. Friends Centennial Trial, 1992—, bd. dirs., 1994—96; mem. Am. Red Cross Disaster Unit. Named to Wash. State Officials Hall of Fame, 2003; recipient Scroll of Honor-Hall of Fame, Spokane C. of C., 1983, Greater Spokane Sports Assn., 1973, Wash. Interscholastic Activites Assn., 1990, State Officiating, 1992. Mem.: Spokane Ret. Tchrs. Assn. (pres. 1981—82), Wash. State Ofcls. Assn. (Meritorious Svc. award 2002, named to Hall of Fame 2003), Wash. State Ret. Tchrs. Assn. (bd. dirs. 1987—), Nat. Ret. Tchrs. Assn., Wash. Edn. Assn., Spokane Edn. Assn. (com. chmn. 1960—70), Soroptimist (pres. 1970), Hangman Golf Club (Spokane pres. 1997), Hobnailers Club (pres. 1966—67, 1986—87). Home: 1103 E 14th Ave Spokane WA 99202-2541

DANKO-MCGHEE, KATHERINA ELAINE, art educator, consultant; b. Derry, Pa., May 1, 1952; d. George Danko and Margaret Scholastica Mlinarchek; m. Jimmy Scott McGhee, July 31, 1977; children: Windsor Castille McGhee, Caribbea Laise McGhee. BS, W.Va. Wesleyan, Buckhannon, 1974; MS, Ind. State U., Terre Haute, 1979; PhD, Ohio State U., 1988. Art tchr. Upshur County Sch. Dist., Buckhannon, W.Va., 1974—82; art edn. coord. U. Ctrl. Fla., Orlando, 1989—95; art edn. dir. Tenn. Technol. U., Cookeville, 1995—2000; early childhood art edn. coord. U. of Toledo, 2000—. Early childhood cons. Toledo Mus. Art, 2000—; art cons. to Reggio Emilia study group NW Ohio Spl. Edn. Regional Resource Ctr., Bowling Green, Ohio, 2003—; early childhood art edn. cons. Harcourt Ednl. Pub. Co., Orlando, Fla., 2003—. Author: The Aesthetic Preferences of Young Children, 2000; contbr. articles to profl. jours. Grantee, NEA, 1999—2000; Artist in Residence project grantee, Tenn. Arts Commn., 1997—2000. Mem.: Toledo Assn. Edn. of Young Children (historian 2003—), Assn. Edn. of Children Internat. (assoc.), Nat. Assn. Edn. of Young Children (assoc.), Ohio Art Edn. Assn. (assoc.), Nat. Art Edn. Assn. (assoc.; southeast dir. higher edn. 1997—2001). Avocations: travel, jewelry making, painting, gardening. Office: U Toledo Art Dept 620 Grove Place Toledo OH 43620 E-mail: kdankom@pop3.utoledo.edu.

DANKWORTH, CLEMENTINA DINAH See LAINE, CLEO

DANNECKER, TANJA MICHAELA, electrical engineer; d. Manfred and Sieglinde Irmtraud Marianne Dannecker. MEE, Tech. U. Stuttgart, 1997. Diplom-Ingenieur/ Electrical Engineer, Stuttgart, Germany, 1997. Electronic products dir./ dir. engring. Huf N.Am., Greeneville, Tenn., 2000—03, diplom-ingenieur/ elec. engr., 1998—2000, Emirates Transformer & Switchgear Ltd., Jebel Ali Free Zone, Dubai, United Arab Emirates, 1997—98. Mem.: Aircraft Owners and Pilots Assn., Nat. Associates of Female Executives. Avocations: aerobics, swimming, travel, languages, flying of single-piston engine land airplanes. Home: 1150 Tusculum Boulevard Apt 2 Greeneville TN 37745

DANNENHOLD, KATHLEEN E. writer, director; b. Elizabeth, NJ, Mar. 21, 1947; d. Frederick Jerome and Anne Mary Jones; m. Robert E. Dannenhold, Sept. 5, 1969; children: Kara Kathleen, Robyn Rebecca. BA, U. of Calif., 1965—69. Asst. copywriter Lee & Associates, Beverly Hills, Calif., 1969—71; ednl. film reviewer Landers Film Rev. Digest, Los Angeles, Calif., 1971—73; dir. of pub. rels. & devel. Hillside Learning Ctr., La Canada, Calif., 1972—88; freelance writer & mktg. cons. Word Express, Eastsound & Seattle, Wash., 1988—98; dir. of comm. UW Sch. of Nursing, Seattle, Wash., 1998—2003; dir. of pub. info. UW Ctr. on Infant Mental Health, Seattle, Wash., 2003—. Chair, website devel. com. UW Sch. of Nursing, Seattle, 2000—02; com. mem. UW Campaign Comm., Seattle, 2002—03; website writer & cons. Collegeology, Seattle. Author: (short story) Synapse Literary Magazine, (poem) The Eclectic Muse. Sch. bond campaign co-chair Bd. of Edn., Eastsound, Wash., 1990—91; parent bd. mem. & ann. auction chair for solicitations Holy Names Acad., Seattle, Wash., 1995—98. Recipient Above & Beyond award, UW Sch. of Nursing, 1998, 2000. Mem.: Soc. of Profl. Journalists, Coun. for the Support and Advancement of Edn. Democrat-Npl. Catholic. Achievements include development of the Cybercapsule, a web-based time capsule of the UW School of Nursing; researched, wrote and published (including web version) a 100-year timeline of nursing and UW School of Nursing. Avocations: travel, fiction writing, book discussion, politics, hiking. Office: UW Center on Infant Mental Health Box 357920 Seattle WA 98195-7920 E-mail: kathyd@u.washington.edu.

DANNER, KATHLEEN FRANCES STEELE, federal official; b. Kansas City, Mo., Oct. 28, 1960; m. Steve Danner, Jan. 18, 1996. Admissions counselor N.E. Mo. State U., Kirksville, 1980-83, assoc. dir. admissions, 1983-86, programming coord. dept. pub. svcs., 1986-87; Iowa, N.H. dir. Gephardt for Pres., St. Louis, 1987-88; mem. Mo. Ho. of Reps., Jefferson City, 1988-94; state dir. Clinton for Pres., 1991-92; regional dir. U.S. Dept. HHS, Kansas City, Mo., 1994—, acting dir. intergovtl. affairs Washington, 1998—. Pres. Greater Kansas City Fed. Exec. Bd. Pres. Greater Mo. Found.; exec. com. Heart of Am. United Way; mem. White House Outreach Task Force on CHIP. Recipient Hammer award V.P. Gore, 1999, award for disting. svc. Sec. Shalala, 1998. Mem. Ctrl. Exch., Nat. Women's Polit. Caucus. Roman Catholic. Avocations: sports enthusiast, dance, reading, politics. Home: 6 Nantucket Ct Smithville MO 64089 9605 Office: US Dept Health and Human Svcs 601 E 12th St Ste 210 Kansas City MO 64106-2826

DANNER, PATSY ANN (MRS. C. M. MEYER), former congresswoman; b. Louisville, Ky., Jan. 13, 1934; d. Henry J. and Catherine M. (Shaheen) Berrer; children: Stephen, Stephanie, Shane, Shavonne.; m. C.M. Meyer, Dec. 30, 1982. Student, Hannibal-LaGrange Coll., 1952; BA in Polit. Sci. cum laude, N.E. Mo. State U., 1972. Dist. asst. to Congressman Jerry Litton, Kansas City, Mo., 1973-76; fed. co-chmn. Ozarks Regional Commn., Washington, 1977-81; mem. Mo. State Senate, 1983-1992, 103rd-106th Congress from 6th Mo. dist., 1993-2001. Mem. internat. rels. com., transp. and infrastructure com. Mem.: LWV (bd. mem., health chairwoman Columbia-Boone County, Mo.). Democrat. Roman Catholic.*

D'ANNIBALLE-HOLDREN, PRISCILLA LUCILLE, contracting company executive; b. Martins Ferry, Ohio, Oct. 28, 1950; d. James Louis and Smyrna Isabell (Prieto) D'A; m. Terrence E. Holdren. BE, U. Toledo, 1973. Credit mgr. Kabat Distbg. Co., Toledo, 1973-80; comml. ops. officer Ohio Citizens Bank, Toledo, 1980-81, credit officer, 1981-82, mktg. officer, 1982-83, mortgage banking officer, 1983-85; owner, pres. D'Ann Enterprises, Inc. dba Paul Davis Restoration, Holland, Ohio, 1985—; pres. district V Paul Davis Systems, Toledo, 1992-95, mem. nat. exec. com., 1992-95, treas. nat. exec. com., 1994-95. Chmn. arbitration com. Paul Davis Systems, 1991; dist. 3 acting pres. Paul Davis Restoration, 2002, dist. 3 v.p., 2001—. Mem. fund drive United Way, Toledo, 1982, Jr. Achievement, Toledo, 1983; bd. dirs. Voluntary Action Ctr., Toledo, 1981-82, Better Bus. Bur., 2002-03. Mem. Nat. Assn. Credit Mgmt. (bd. dirs. 1981-87, bd. dirs. Ednl. Forum 1976-82, pres. 1980, Credit Person of Yr. award 1982, Credit Exec. of Yr. award 1987), Holland-Springfield C. of C. (exec. bd. dirs. 1990-95, v.p. 1991-92, pres. 1993), Paul Davis Systems Franchisee Assn. (pres. 1991). Roman Catholic. Avocations: golf, swimming, gardening, antiques, traveling. Home: 704 Oak Park Dr Toledo OH 43617-2024 Office: D'Ann Enterprises Inc 1049 S Mccord Rd Holland OH 43528-9596

DANOFF-KRAUS, PAMELA SUE, real estate developer; b. Gallup, N.Mex., Aug. 29, 1946; d. Isadore Harry and Armida Catherine (Ceccardi) Danoff; m. Robert Warren Kraus, Nov. 30, 1985; 1 child, Jillian Amaris. BA, U. N.Mex., 1968. Lic. in real estate, Calif. Real estate rep. Kaiser Aetna, Newport Beach, Calif., 1975-76; leasing agt. Alexander Haagen Co., Rolling Hills, Calif., 1976-77; dir. leasing Warren Kellogg & Assocs., Newport Beach, 1977-81, Ctr. Devel. Co., Newport Beach, 1981-84; exec. v.p., ptnr. The Von Der Ahe Co., Newport Beach, 1984-86; ptnr., shopping center development executive Marketplace Properties, Tustin, Calif., 1986-

92; owner Danoff Kraus Enterprises, Santa Ana, 1992—. Lectr. in field; panelist various convs., univs.; condr. seminars in field. Contbr. articles to profl. jours. Sponsor Californians Working Together to End Hunger and Homelessness, L.A., 1988; mem. Orange County Performing Arts Ctr., 1983-85. Mem. Internat. Coun. Shopping Ctrs. [illegible] com., state [illegible] pub. rels. and cmty. affairs for Calif., 1989-92, chair pub. rels. and cmty. svc. Western divsn. 1992-95), Calif. Bus. Properties Assn., Calif. Redevel. Assn., Assistance League of Santa Ana, Women in Retail Real Estate, Chi Omega. Republican. Roman Catholic. Avocations: skiing, sailing, wine tasting, needlepoint, gardening. Home and Office: Danoff Kraus Enterprises 10182 Brier Ln Santa Ana CA 92705-1531 E-mail: danoffkraus@cox.net.

D'ANTONIO, CYNTHIA MARIA, sales and marketing executive; b. Chgo., Sept. 12, 1956; d. Michael Patrick and Joan Marie (Funk) D'A. BS in Natural Resource Devel., Mich. State U., 1979. Chemist Aqualab, Streamwood, Ill., 1980-83; R&D specialist Seaquist Closures, Crystal Lake, Ill., 1983-87; internat. sales & mktg. exec. Seaquist-Valois Australia, Sydney, 1987-93; internat. v.p. sales and mktg. cosmetics Pfeiffer Inc., Princeton, N.J., 1993—. Spkr. in field. Contbr. articles and photos to profl. jours. Mem. NAFE, Plastic Inst. Australia. Republican. Roman Catholic. Avocations: foreign current events, photography, golf, bike tours. Home: 5 Bradway Ave Ewing NJ 08618-2607

DANTZIC, CYNTHIA MARIS, artist, educator; b. NYC, Jan. 4, 1933; d. Howard Arthur and Sylvia Hazel (Wiener) Gross; m. Jerry Dantzic, June 15, 1958; 1 son, Grayson Ross. Student, Brooklyn Mus. Art Sch., Bklyn., 1947—50, Bard Coll., 1950—52; BFA, Yale U., 1955; MFA, Pratt Inst., 1963. Tchr. art Baldwin Sch., Bryn Mawr, Pa., 1955-58; head art dept. Bentley Sch., N.Y.C., 1958-62; coord. art prog., instr. North Shore Cmty. Arts Ctr., Roslyn, NY, 1962-64; instr. art CUNY-Bronx, N.Y.C., 1963-64; faculty L.I. U., Bklyn., 1964—, prof., 1975—, chair art dept., 1980-86. Adj. assoc. prof. art Cooper Union, 1992—99, adj. prof. art, 1999—2002; lectr., presenter in field. One-woman shows include Resnick Gallery, L.I. U., Bklyn., 1983, 89, 95, 2000, East Hampton Gallery, N.Y.C., 1965-66, St. John's U. Gallery, 1995; exhibited in group shows at Blue Mountain Gallery, N.Y.C., 1984-85, 94-98, 2001, 2002, Hillwood Gallery, Greenvale, N.Y., 1985; commd. artist edit. of photo collages Bklyn. Arts and Culture Assn., 1983; represented in permanent collections Bklyn. Mus., N.Y., Rose Art Mus., Mass., Bard Coll., N.Y.; author, illustrator: Stop Dropping BreAdcrumBs on my YaCht, 1974, Sounds of Silents, 1976, Design Dimensions: An Introduction to the Visual Surface, 1990, Drawing Dimensions: A Comprehensive Introduction, 1999, Antique Pocket Mirrors: Pictorial & Advertising Minatures, 2002; contbr. articles to profl. jours. Trustee Park Slope Civic Coun., 1991—. Mellon grantee, 1984, L.I. Univ. faculty rsch. grantee, 1985—; recipient Newton Teaching Excellence award, 1988, Trustees award single work, 1990, Trustees lifetime award for Scholarly Achievement in art and art edn. L.I. Univ., 1999. Mem. AAUP, Internat. Soc. Copier Artists, L.I. U. Faculty Fedn. (exec. com. 1975—), Coll. Art Assn., Soc. Scribes (bd. govs. 2003—). Avocations: piano, travel, collecting americana and tribal and folk art. Home: 910 President St Brooklyn NY 11215-1604 Office: LI U Art Dept University Pla Brooklyn NY 11201 E-mail: cdantzic@liu.edu.

DANTZSCHER, JAMIE, gymnast; b. Canoga Park, Calif., May 2, 1982; d. John and Joyce Dantzcher. Student, UCLA, 2001—. Mem. U.S. Nat. Team, 1994—2001, U.S. Gymnastic Team, Sydney Olympics, 2000. Mem. Charter Oaks Gliders. Named NCAA Champion, All-around, Vault and Floor Competitions, 2002, NCAA Co-Champion, Uneven Bars, 2003; recipient 1st pl. vault, Coca-Cola Nat. Championships, 1995, 1st pl. all-around, City of Popes (France) Competition, 1996, 1st pl. (tied) vault, Am. Classic, 1998, 1st pl. uneven bars, John Hancock U.S. Gymnastics Championships, 1999. Address: c/o UCLA Athletic Dept JD Morgan Ctr PO Box 24044 Los Angeles CA 90024

DANZIGER, GERTRUDE SEELIG, metal fabricating executive; b. Chgo., Oct. 24, 1919; d. Isidor and Clara (Fuchs) Seelig; widowed; children: Robert, James. With Homak Mfg. Co., Inc., Chgo., 1966-79, pres., 1979—. Patentee in field. Office Phone: 708-594-0123.

DANZIGER, LUCY, editor; married; 2 children. Grad., Harvard U. Reporter Star-Ledger, Newark, 1982—86; mag. assoc. editor, 1986—88; founding mng. editor 7 Days, 1988—90; exec. editor Manhattan, Inc., N.Y.C., 1990—92; freelance writer, 1992—95; freelance editor Allure; editor style and news dept. NY Times, N.Y.C., 1994—95; founding editor Women's Sports & Fitness, 1997—2001; editor-in-chief SELF mag., N.Y.C., 2001—. Office: Salf Mag 4 Times Sq New York NY 10036*

DANZON, PATRICIA M. medical educator; BA, U. Oxford, 1968; MA, U. Chgo., 1969, PhD of Econs., 1973. Lectr. U. Chgo., 1972; rsch. economist, instr. Rand Corp., 1974-80; sr. rsch. fellow Hoover Inst. Stanford U., 1980-84; assoc. prof., adj. prof., lectr. Duke U., Durham, N.C., 1984-85; Celia Moh prof. Health Care Mgmt. Dept. Ins. & Risk Mgmt. U. Pa., Phila., 1985—. Vis. asst. prof. econ. dept. U. Calif., 1978; vis. prof. Ctr. Study Economy and State U. Chgo., 1988-89. Office: U Pa Wharton Sch Health Care Sys Dept 3641 Locust Walk Philadelphia PA 19104-6218

DAO, KHANH PHUONG THI, automotive executive, sales professional; b. Saigon, Vietnam, Apr. 3, 1970; came to the U.S., 1975; m. Scott K. Ginsburg, 1998. Student, Tex. Christian U., 1987-88, Tarrant County Jr. Coll., Ft. Worth, 1988, 89, Austin (Tex.) C.C., 1988-90, U. Tex., Arlington, 1991. Pres. Klaus Motors/Concours Detailing, Ft. Worth, 1990-92; fleet sales mgr. Toyota of Dallas, 1992-93; broker trainee, account exec. B.T.S.-Southwest Securities, Richardson, Tex., 1993-94; sales cons. Crest Infiniti/Autogroup, Plano, Tex., 1994-95; v.p. Edwards Petroleum/Devel. Inc., Dallas, 1995-96; pres., CEO, cons. Bang Entertainment/Devel. Inc., Dallas and Wilmington, Del., 1996—; prin. The Gotham City Club Ltd., Dallas, 1996—; sales cons. Park Place Porsche, Dallas, 1996—; prin. Steel Restaurant and Lounge Ltd.; co-founder, ptnr. Voltaire Restaurant & Bar, Boardwalk Motor Car. Ptnr. The Porsche Store, Dallas; pres., CEO edirectories.com Corp., hostingonline.com Corp.; founder, CEO eDirectories USA.com. Corp, eB2Bdirectories.com., Get Auto Bio.com, PlanesToYachts.com. Mem. Rep. Presdl. Task Force, Washington, 1989—. Mem. Porsche Cars N.A. (cert. Porsche specialist), Porsche Club N.A. Avocations: tennis, golf, traveling, collecting vintage timepieces, racing cars. Home: Ste 101-18 3818 Cedar Springs Rd Dallas TX 75219-4168 Office: The Centrum Bldg 3102 Oak Lawn Ave Ste 100 Dallas TX 75219-4257

DAPPER, KAREN LYNN, psychologist, educator; b. Salzburg, Austria, Jan. 14, 1954; d. Albert Logan and Ruth Rhyner Froede; m. David Paul Dapper, Mar. 23, 1974; children: Ryan Mathew, Diane Lynn, Lauren Michelle. A of Nursing, Columbus C.C., 1974; BS in Social Psychology summa cum laude, Park U., 1991; D in Clin. Psychology, Wright State U., 1996. RN Ohio, 1974; lic. clin. psychologist Ohio, 1997. Intern Northeastern Ohio U. Coll. Medicine, 1995—96; psychology asst. Lifewell Psychol. Cons., Columbus, Ohio, 1996—97, Ohio Reformatory Women, Marysville, 1996—97; psychologist Lifewell Psychol. Cons., Columbus, 1997—2000; coord. residential treatment unit Ohio Dept. Rehab. & Corrections, Marysville, 1997—98, psychiat. nurse, supr., 1998—99, clin. dir. mental health, 1999—; forensic psychologist Psychol. Forensic & Cons. Svcs., Dayton, 2001—. Prof. behavioral scis. Park U., Parkside, Mo., 2001—; clin. prof. Wright State U., Dayton, 1999—. Mem.: Ctrl. Ohio Psychol. Assn., Ohio Psychol. Assn., APA. Presbyterian. Avocations: scuba diving, horseback riding, flying.

DARBY, BARBARA ANN-LOFTHOUSE, chemical technician; b. Phila., Sept. 15, 1961; d. Robert William and Lina Evelyn (James) Lofthouse; m. Joseph Francis Darby, Dec. 23, 1988; children: Robert Lofthouse, Joseph. GED, Phila., 1982. Cert. biocides operator, [illegible] Rohm & Haas, Phila., 1992-95, chem. technician La Porte, Tex., 1995—. Tng. coord. Bayport Biocides. Active World Wildlife Fund, Washington, 1994—, Clear Lake Ind. Sch. Dist. PTA, 1995—, Nature Conservancy, Tex., 1995; vol. United Way Campaign, Rohm & Haas Plants, 1992—; mem. Habitat for Humanity, 1996—, Natural Resources Def. Coun., 1996—; bd. dirs. Bay Area Sharks/Sharkettes, Tex. Intercity Football, Inc. Football League. Lutheran. Avocations: wildlife defense, environmental activities, cars. Home: 2800 NASA Road One Apt 1114 Seabrook TX 77586 Office: Rohm & Haas Bay Port Biocides 13300 Bay Area Blvd La Porte TX 77572 also: 2800 Nasa Rd One Apt 1114 Seabrook TX 77586 E-mail: bdarby915@aol.com., darby@rohmhaas.com.

DARBY, JOANNE TYNDALE (JAYE DARBY), arts and humanities educator; b. Tucson, Sept. 22, 1948; d. Robert Porter Smith and Joanne Inloes Snow-Smith; stepchildren: Margaret Loutrel, David Michael. BA, U. Ariz., 1972; MEd, U. Calif., L.A., 1986, PhD, 1996. Cert. secondary tchr., gifted and talented tchr., Calif. Tchr. English, chmn. dept. Las Virgenes Unified Sch. Dist., Calabasas, Calif., 1979-82; tchr. English and gifted and talented edn. Las Virgenes Unified Sch.Dist., Calabasas, Calif., 1983-84; sch. improvement coord./lang. arts/social studies/drama tchr Las Virgenes Unified Sch. Dist., Calabasas, Calif., 1991-92; tchr. English and gifted and talented edn. Beverly Hills (Calif.) Unified Sch. Dist., 1982-83, 84-89, English and drama tchr., 1994; tchr., cons. Calif. Lit. Project, San Diego, 1985-87; cons., free lance editor L.A., 1977—; dir. Shakespeare edn. and festivals project Folger Libr., Washington, 1990-91; field work supr. tchr. edn. program Ctr. X, Grad. Sch. Edn. and Info. Studies, UCLA, 1992-96, Ctr. X postdoctoral scholar, tchr. edn. program, 1996-97; asst. rschr., founding co-dir. Project HOOP, Am. Indian Studies Ctr., UCLA, 1997—2000; asst. prof. Coll. Edn. San Diego State U., 2000—. Cons. arts and edn., L.A., 1991—. Co-editor (with Hanay Geiogamah) Stories of Our Way: An Anthology of American Indian Plays, 1999, American Indian Theater in Performance: A Reader, 2000, (with Stephanie Fitzgerald) Keepers of the Morning Star: An Anthology of Native Women's Theater, 2003; contbr. articles to profl. publs. Mem.: MLA, Assn. for Theatre in Higher Edn., Nat. Coun. Tchrs. English, Am. Ednl. Rsch. Assn., Phi Beta Kappa, Alpha Lambda Delta, Phi Beta Phi. Home: 7350 Golfcrest Pl Apt 2001 San Diego CA 92119-2486

DARBY, MARIANNE TALLEY, elementary school educator; b. Adel, Ga., Nov. 8, 1937; d. William Giles and Mary (McGlamry) Talley; m. Roy Copeland Darby, Apr. 2, 1958; children: Susan, Leslie Darby Galifianakis, Allison Darby Davis. Student, Emory U., 1955-57; BS in Early Childhood Edn., Valdosta (Ga.) State Coll., 1973. Cert. early childhood and elem. edn. tchr., Ga. Tchr. 2d grade Adel Elem. Sch., spring 1973, tchr. 1st grade, 1973-98, ret., 1998. Pres. Cook County Jaycettes, Adel, 1962. Teacher of Year, Cook Elem. Sch., 1998—. Mem. Internat. Reading Assn. (South Cen. Ga. coun.), Profl. Assn. Ga. Educators, Adel Garden Club, Alpha Epsilon Upsilon, Alpha Delta Kappa (sec. 1980-82), Sigma Alpha Chi, Alpha Chi, Kappa Alpha Theta. Republican. Methodist. Avocations: sewing, piano, reading, african violets. Home: 710 S Forrest Ave Adel GA 31620-3523

D'ARCANGELO, MARCIA DIANE, educational media producer; b. Meadville, Pa., May 16, 1945; d. Terrence Benjamin and Eileene Marie (Judy) Darcangelo; m. Thomas Brown Andrews V, Sept. 16, 1989. BS in Chemistry, Grove City Coll., 1967. Info. specialist Eastman Kodak Co., Rochester, N.Y., 1967-68; singer/dancer Kids Next Door-Young Ams. Orgn. (Katand Prodns.), L.A., 1968-69, Stand Up and Cheer TV Show, The Johnny Mann Singers, L.A., 1970-74; singer, dancer, actor John Brown's Body AEA Nat. Tour, Fitzgerald Prodns., L.A., 1975-76; singer, dancer The Perry Como Show-Roncom Prodns., 1977-82; med. news journalist Physicians Radio Network, N.Y.C., 1983-84; prodn. asst., prodn. coord. ASCD, Alexandria, Va., 1985-86, producer, sr. producer, 1987-88, mgr. media prodns., 1989—. Cons. Holbrook & Kellogg, Falls Church, Va., 1990, Developmental Studies Ctr., San Ramon, Calif., 1991, Soc. for Preservation of Social Security and Medicare, Washington, 1991. Composer 4 mus. pieces (words and music); co-author 20 tng. manuals; author/co-author 46 video-based tchr. tng. programs, articles. Recipient award of merit VFW, 1971, Jack Kennedy Alumni Achievement award Grove City Coll. Alumni Assn., 1984, Clarion award Women in Comm., 1991, 6 Cine Golden Eagle awards Coun. on Internat. Nontheatrical Events, 1991, 92, 93, 94, Silver Apple award Nat. Ednl. Film and Video Festival, 1991, 93, 95, Bronze Apple award, 1993, 94, 99, Silver Screen award and Cert. for Creative Excellence U.S. Internat. Film and Video Festival, 1993, 94, 95, 96, Disting. Achievement award and Best of Category Ednl. Press Assn. Am., 1994, 95, 96, Telly Awards-Silver and Bronze, 1996, 98; award of excellence Nat. Sch. Pub. Rels. Assn., 1995, 96, Bronze award Columbus Internat. Film & Video, 1995. Mem. SAG, AFTRA, NAFE, ASCD, Am. Guild Variety Artists, Actors Equity Assn., Nat. Staff Devel. Coun., Internat. TV Assn., Internat. Interactive Comm. Soc., Women in Film and Video Internat. Avocation: singing. E-mail: mdarcang@ascd.org.

DARCE, SHIRL JOHNSON, computer sales director; b. New Orleans, Feb. 11, 1964; d. Mervin L. and Virginia A. (Scandirato) Johnson. A in Computer Programming, Phillips Jr. Coll., Metairie, La., 1983. Tech. support person Amann Bus. Machines, New Orleans, 1983-84; computer saleswoman Computer Terminal, New Orleans, 1984-85, Compumark, Metairie, 1985-86; v.p. Value Bus. Ctr., Metairie, 1986-94; gen. mgr. PC Warehouse, Metairie, 1994—; govt. sales mgr. Pelican Computer, Jefferson, La., 2004—. Cons. City of New Orleans, 1992-95, State of La., 1988-2004. Office: Pelican Computer 1417 Edwards Ave Jefferson LA 70123

DARDEN, BARBARA S. library director; b. Cleve., Apr. 6, 1947; d. Curley and Cora (Chambliss) Brown; m. Joseph S. Darden; children: Michelle, Crystal. BS, Ohio State U., 1967; MS in Ednl. Media, MLS, Kent State U., 1971; PhD, Rutgers U., 2002. Adminstrv. supr. Cleve. Pub. Schs., 1968-70; libr. Cuyahoga C.C., 1972-75, coord., 1975-77, interim dir., 1977-78, asst. dean, 1978-80, dir., 1980-84; dir. libr. Kean Coll., Union, N.J., 1984—. Cons. Dembsy Assocs., Boston, 1967-81; editl. cons. Max Pub. Co., N.Y.C., 1967-81; cons. reader U.S. Office Edn., Washington, 1979-80; editl. cons. Jossey-Bass Pub. Co., 1979. Cons. editor Probe, 1976, Sch. Media Ctr., 1968, Booklist, 1969; contbr. articles to profl. jours. Bd. dirs. N.J. Adv. Bd. on Status of Women, 1988, Africana Studies, 1988; mem. N.J. State Libr. Adv. Bd.; bd. dirs. N.J. Ednl. Activities Task Force Libr. Com. Recipient Phillips award Kent State U., 1970. Mem. ALA (chmn. pay equity com. 1996, chair LAMA-COLA 1999), Higher Edn. Reps., N.J. Acad. Libr. Network (chmn. 1987, bd. dirs. 1995—), Coun. N.J. Librs. (prs. 1987—), N.J. Libr. Assn., Oral History Soc., N.J. Hist. Soc., Libr. Adminstrn. Mgmt. Assn. (chair 1997-99, bd. dirs. 1999), Coun. N.J. Coll. and Univ. Libr. Dirs. (pres. 1999—), Jr. League (Cleve. vice chmn. 1981, 83), Concerned Parents Club (pres. 1984), Women's City Club (adv. bd. 1997—). Avocations: music, reading. Office: Kean Univ Libr Morris Ave Union NJ 07083

DARENSBOURG, MARCETTA YORK, chemistry educator; b. Artemus, Ky., May 4, 1942; m. 1967. BA, Union Coll., 1963; PhD in Inorganic Chemistry, U. Ill., Urbana, 1967. Asst. prof. inorganic chemistry Vassar Coll., 1967-69; asst. prof. SUNY, Buffalo, 1969-71; from asst. to assoc. prof. Tulane U., La., 1971-79, prof. inorganic chemistry, 1979—; prof. chemistry Tex. A&M U., 1982—. Recipient Agnes Faye Rsch. award, 1981; Am. Chem Soc. award for Disting. Svc. in the Advancement of Inorganic Chemistry, 1995. Mem. Am. Chem. Soc. (chair-elect, chair inorganic divsn., Disting. Svc. award 1995), Sigma Xi. Office: Texas A & M U Dept Chemistry College Station TX 77843-0001

DARKOVICH, SHARON MARIE, nurse administrator; b. Ft. Wayne, Ind., Dec. 10, 1949; d. Gerald Antone LaCanne and Ida Eileen (Bowman) LaCanne Cutler; m. Robert Eliot Noon, July 17, 1971 [illegible] Jan. 23, 1981 (div. May 1994); 1 child, Amy Elizabeth. BSN, Case Western Res. U., 1973, BA in Psychology, 1978; cert. in advanced bioethics, Cleve. State U., 1990, MA in Philosophy and Bioethics, 1994. RN, Ohio. Staff nurse Univ. Hosps., Cleve., 1973, asst. head nurse, 1973-76; quality improvement coord. St. Luke's Med. Ctr., Cleve., 1976-83, 84-97, dir. nursing, 1983-84, quality improvement dir., 1997-98; dir. quality svcs. Lake Hosp. Sys., Inc., Painesville, Ohio, 1998-2000, corp. quality and compliance officer, 2000—. Cons. to long-term care facilities, 1986-92, pressure ulcer dressing devel. B.F. Goodrich Co., 1988-92; cons. to ambulatory facility for Joint Commn. for Accreditation of Health Care Orgns., Oakbrook, Ill., 1994, cons. to cmty. hosp. med. staff, bylaws, 1996; lectr. U. Akron, 1992-93, Northeast Ohio U. Coll. Medicine, 1993-95; bd.dir. Bioethics Network Ohio. Mem. ANA, Am. Soc. for Healthcare Bioethics, Am. Soc. for Quality, Greater Cleve. Nurses Assn. (mem. dist. coun. on practice, 1982-84), Sigma Theta Tau. Avocations: reading, needlework, sewing, camping. E-mail: sharon.darkovich@lhs.net.

DARLING, ALBERTA STATKUS, state legislator, marketing executive, former art museum executive; b. Hammond, Ind., Apr. 28, 1944; d. Albert William and Helen Anne (Vaicunas) Statkus; m. William Anthony Darling, Aug. 12, 1967; children— Elizabeth Suzanne, William Anthony. BS, U. Wis., 1967. English tchr. Nathan Hale High Sch., West Allis, Wis., 1967-69, Castle Rock High Sch., Castke Rock, Colo., 1969-71, community vol. worker West Allis, Milw., 1971—; mem. Wis. State Assembly, 1990-92, Wis. Senate from 8th dist., Madison, 1992—. Cons. orgn. devel., Milw., 1982— ; dir. mktg. and communications Milw. Art Mus., 1981-88; exec. dir. mktg. architectural firm, 1988-90; State Rep. Wis., 1990—, mem. urban edn. com., children and human svcs. com., tourism com., homelessness com., teenage pregnancy com., vice chmn. gov.'s housing policy commn., assembly coms. Pres. Community Action Seminar for Women, 1979-80; a founder Goals for Greater Milw. 2000, 1980-84; co-chair Action 2000, 1984-86; co-chmn. Icebreaker Am. Winterfestival; chmn. Community Action Seminar for Women, 1988; bd. dirs., exec. com. United Way, Milw., 1982-1992, chair project 1985, 1984-85, chmn. policy com. 1988; founder Today's Girls/Tomorrow's Women, Milw., pres. Jr. League Milw., 1980-82, Planned Parenthood Milw., 1982-84, Future Milw., 1983-85; vice chmn. State of Wis. Strategic Planning Council, 1988—, chmn. small bus./entrpreneur com.; mem. Greater Milw. Com.'s Mktg. Task Force, 1987-88; chmn. United Way Policy Com., 1987-88; participant Bus. Ptnrs. White House Conf., 1987; mem. summerfest adv. com. on Winter Festivals, 1989; founder Women's Fund of Milw. Found; actuve Juvenile Justice Leadership Com. Recipient Vol. Action award Milw. Civic Alliance, 1984, Community Service award United Way, 1984, Leader of Future award Milw. Mag., 1988, Nat. Assn. Community Leadership Orgn. award, 1986, Today's Girls/Tomorrow's Women Leadership award, 1987, Future Milw. Community Leadership award, 1988, Friend of Edn. Leadership award Head Start, 1994, William Steiger Humanitarian award, 1994. Mem. Greater Milw. Com., TEMPO Profl. Women, Am. Mktg. Assn. (Marketer of Yr. 1984), Pub. Relations Soc. Am., Ctr. for Pub. Representation (state bd. 1988), ARC (bd. dirs., exec. fin. coms. 1987—), Women's Fund (steering com. 1988), Internat. Assn. Bus. Communicators, Greater Milw. Com. Republican. Avocations: travel, art history, contemporary american literature, golf, tennis. Home: 1325 W Dean Rd Milwaukee WI 53217-2537 Office: State Capitol PO Box 7882 Madison WI 53707-7882

DARLING, JUANITA MARIE, correspondent; b. Columbus, Ohio, Apr. 7, 1954; d. Robert Lewis and Joanne Mae (Oiler) D. BA in L.Am. Studies, BA in Comms., Calif. State U., Fullerton, 1976; MA in Internat. Journalism, U. So. Calif., L.A., 1989; bur. chief, L.A. Times, Crtl. America. Reporter Daily News Tribune, Fullerton; bus. editor The News, Mexico City; reporter Orange County Register, Santa Ana, Calif.; corr. L.A. Times, Mexico City, El Salvador, Cen. Am. bur. chief. Office: LA Times Times Mirror Sq Los Angeles CA 90053

DARLING-HAMMOND, LINDA, education educator; BA, Yale U., 1973; EdD in Urban Edn., Temple U., 1978. Dir., sr. social scientist Edn. and Human Resources Program RAND, 1985—89; prof. Columbia U., 1989—98, co-dir. Nat. Ctr. for Restructuring Edn., Schs. and Tchg., Tchrs. Coll., 1989—98, William F. Russell prof. in Founds. of Edn., 1993—98; prof. edn. Stanford U., 1998—. Chair stds. drafting panel Coun. Chief State Sch. Officers, Interstate New Tchr. Assessment and Support Consortium, 1991—; mem. Nat. Adv. Commn., The Coll. Bd., Equity 2000, 1993—, Carnegie Corp. Task Force on Learing in the Primary Grades, 1994—; exec. dir. Nat. Commn. on Tchg. and Ams. Future, 1994—; mem. adv. bd. Ctr. for Policy Rsch. in Edn., 1996—; mem. tech. rev. panel for the schs. an staffing survey U.S. Dept. Edn., 1997—; mem. Internat. Adv. Coun., San Francisco Exploratorium, 1998—; co-chair Calif. Profl. Devel. Task Force, 2000; bd. dirs. Recruiting New Tchrs. Author (with J. Ancess and B. Falk): Authentic Assessment in Action: Studies of Schools and Students at Work, 1995; author: The Right to Learn: A Blueprint for Creating Schools that Work, 1997; editor: Professional Development Schools: Schools for Developing a Profession, 1994; editor: (with Gary Sykes) Teaching as the Learning Profession: A Handbook of Policy and Practice, 1999; contbr. articles to profl. jours. Mem.: Nat. Acad. Edn. (chair com. on tchr. edn. 2000—). Office: Stanford Univ Sch Edn 485 Lasuen Mall Stanford CA 94305-3096

DARLINGTON, HILDA WALKER, real estate company officer; b. Anderson, SC, May 3, 1923; d. Dewey Columbus White and Julia Elizabeth Davis; m. Thomas M. Darlington; m. Roy Jones Walker, June 28, 1945 (div. July 1962); children: Stephen D. Walker, Karon Elaine Meehan. Diploma in History. Adminstrv. acct. So. Railway, Atlanta and Washington, 1960—76, Human Resources/State of Va., Arlington, 1978—85; real estate cons. Arlington, Va., 1986—98. Adv. for adminstrv. manual Human Resources, Richmond, Va., 1988—93. Vol. adminstrv. asst. Kennedy Ctr., Washington, 1986—96; civic assn. sec. Lyon Village, Arlington, Va., 1985—97; proprietor homeless shelter Courtlands, Arlington, Va., 1995—99. Mem.: Women's Investment Club, Profl. Business Women's Club. Republican. Avocation: aerobics, gardening, reading.

DARLOW, JULIA DONOVAN, lawyer; b. Detroit, Sept. 18, 1941; d. Frank William Donovan and Helen Adele Turner; m. George Anthony Gratton Darlow (div.); 1 child, Gillian; m. John Corbett O'Meara. AB, Vassar Coll., 1963; postgrad., Columbia U. Law Sch., 1964-65; JD cum laude, Wayne State U., 1971. Bar: Mich. 1971, U.S. Dist. Ct. (ea. dist.) Mich. 1971. Assoc. Dickinson, Wright, McKean, Cudlip & Moon, Detroit, 1971-78; ptnr. Dickinson, Wright, Moon, Van Dusen & Freeman and predecessor, Detroit, 1978—2001; sr. v.p. Detroit Med. Ctr., 2001—01; cons. mem. Dickinson, Wright PLLC, Detroit, 2002—. Bd. dirs. Internat Corp.; adj. prof. Wayne State U. Law Sch., 1974-75, 96; commr. State Bar Mich., 1977-87, mem. exec. com., 1979-83, 84-87, sec. 1980-81, v.p., 1984-85, pres.-elect 1985-86, pres. 1986-87, coun. corp. fin. and bus. law sect. 1980-86, coun. computer law sect. 1985-88; mem. State Officers Compensation Commn., 1994-96; chair Mich. Supreme Ct. Task Force on Gender Issues in the Cts., 1987-89. Bd. dirs. Hutzel Hosp., 1984—2003, chair, 2002—03; bd. dirs. Mich. Opera Theatre, 1985—, mem. exec. com., 1992—; bd. dirs. Mich. Women's Found., 1986—91, Detroit Med. Ctr., 1990—2003, Marygrove Coll., 1996—, sec., 2003—; trustee Internat. Inst. Met. Detroit, 1986—92; trustee Mich. Met. coun. Girl Scouts USA, 1988—91; trustee Detroit coun. Boy Scouts Am., 1988—; mem. exec. com. Mich. Coun. Humanities, 1988—92; mem. Blue Cross-Blue Shield Prospective Reimbursement Com., Detroit, 1979—81; v.p., mem. exec. com. United Found., 1988—95; mem. Mich. Gov.'s Bilateral Trade Team for Germany, 1992—98. Fellow Am. Bar Found. (Mich. State chair 1990-96); mem. Detroit Bar Assn. Found. (treas. 1984-85, trustee 1982-85),

Mich. Bar Found. (trustee 1987-94), Am. Judicature Soc. (bd. dirs. 1985-88), Internat. Women's Forum (global affairs com. 1994—), Women Lawyers Assn. (pres. 1977-78), Mich. Women's Campaign Fund (charter), Detroit Athletic Club. Democrat. Office: Dickinson Wright PLLC 500 Woodward Ave Ste 4000 Detroit MI 48226-3416

DARNALL, ROBERTA MORROW, association executive; b. Kemmerer, Wyo., May 18, 1949; d. C. Dale and Eugenia Stayner (Christmas) Morrow; m. Leslie A. Darnall, Sept. 3, 1977; children: Kimberly Gene, Leslie Nicole. BS, U. Wyo., Laramie, 1972. Tariff sec., ins. adminstr. Wyo Trucking Assn., Casper, 1973-75; asst. clerical supr. Wyo. Legislature, Cheyenne, 1972-77, congrl. campaign press aide, 1974; pub. rels. dir. Casper, Wyo., Wyo. Rep. Ctr. Com., 1976-77; asst. dir. alumni rels. U. Wyo., 1977-81; exec. dir. Alumni Assn., 1981—. Bd. dirs. recognition and golf coms. Ivison Meml. Hosp. Found.; mem. Altar Guild, lector, usher, former acolyte, coord. St. Matthew's Ch. Mem. Higher Edn. Assn. Rockies, Am. Soc. Assn. Execs., Laramie C. of C. (past edn.com.), U. Wyo. Alumni Assn., Cowboy Joe Club, PEO (former courtesy com., officer). Republican. Episcopalian. Home: 15 Snowy View Ct Laramie WY 82070-5358 Office: 214 S 14th St Laramie WY 82070 Office Phone: 307-766-4166. E-mail: robbie@uwyo.edu.

DARNELL, DORIS HASTINGS, performance artist; b. Chgo., Sept. 14, 1916; d. Willard Seth and Faith Emily (Olmstead) Hastings; m. Howard Clayton Darnell, Aug. 27, 1938; children: Elizabeth Loyd, John Hastings, Eric Allen. BA in Latin, Bryn Mawr Coll., 1939. Head resident, asst. to dir. Pendle Hill Grad. Sch. Religious and Social Concerns, Wallingford, Pa., 1939-40; libr. Res. Rm. and sci. Bryn Mawr (Pa.) Coll., 1950-52; acting head libr. Westtown (Pa.) Friends Sch., 1952-53; head libr. Westtown Sch., 1954-55; libr. Res. Rm. Haverford (Pa.) Coll., 1953-54; exec. dir., editor Westtown Alumni Assn., 1955-64, from coord. recruitment to assoc. exec. sec. pers. Am. Friends Svc. Com., Phila., 1964-78; creator, owner A Century of Elegance in Costume and Story, State College, Pa., 1980—. Gov. com. Pendle Hill, Westtown Sch., Friends Select Sch., Pa., 1948—78; mem. Rufus Jones Assocs., Haverford Coll.; founding trustee Allen Hilles Fund, 1982—91, trustee emerita, 1991—; lectr., exhibitor 19th and 20th century fashions, 1980— Mem.: Women's Nat. History Mus., Women in the Arts, Internat., Palmer Art Mus., Costume Soc. Am. Mem. Soc. Of Friends Quaker. Home and Office: #C 36 500 Marylyn Ave State College PA 16801 E-mail: eleganztoo@aol.com.

DARNELL, SUSAN LAURA BROWNE, retired air force officer; b. Milw., Mar. 11, 1955; d. William George Jr. and Jean Marie (Gable) Browne; m. Kevin Scott Charles Darnell, Oct. 4, 1984; children: Emily Elizabeth Browne, Katherine Maureen Browne. BSN, U. Md., 1982; MS in Sys. Mgmt., U. So. Calif., Okinawa, Japan, 1988; postgrad., Roger Williams U., 2001—. Cert. RN, Aeronautical Rating of Sr. Navigator. Commd. 2d lt. USAF, 1982, advanced through grades to maj., 1995; Army spl. 7th Army Soldiers Chorus, Heidelberg, 1975-78; AWACS navigator 964 AWAC Sqaudron, Tinker AFB, Okal., 1983-85; instr. navigator 961 AWAC Squadron, Kadena, Japan, 1985-90; flight comdr. 451 Flying Training Squadron, Mather AFB, Calif., 1990-92; chief current ops. 12 Ops. Support Squadron, Randolph AFB, Tex., 1992-94; asst. ops. officer 12 Ops. Support Squadron, Randolph AFB, Tex., 1994-95; asst. chief Comdr.'s Action Group 12 FTW, Randolph AFB, Tex., 1995; chief of counter-drug plans 24 ASG, Howard AB, Panama, 1996-97; dep. dir. for plans and policy Joint Inter-Agy. Task Force South, Howard AB, Panama, 1997—99. Leader Girl Scouts U.S., 1997—; v.p., pres. Newport Officer Spouses, 1999—2001. Recipient Appreciation award Girl Scouts of U.S., San Antonio, 1996. Mem. Air Forces Assn. (life), Women Mil. Aviators, Inc., Women Mil. Svc. for Am.Meml. Avocations: speaking on non trad. career for women.

DARNER, LESLIE KAREN, state legislator; b. Oklahoma City, Aug. 24, 1945; BS, U. Ill., 1967, MS, 1968. Mem. Va. State Senate, 1991—, mem. edn. com., mem. transp. com., mem. health welfare & insts. com., mem. claims com., mem. Chesapeake and its tricutaries com. Democrat. Methodist. Home: 969 S Buchanan St Arlington VA 22204-3086 Office: Gen Assembly Bldg Rm 711 PO Box 406 Richmond VA 23218-0406

D'ARPA, JOSEPHINE, music educator; b. Tampa, Fla., Oct. 26, 1936; d. Jerome F. and Susie G. D'Arpa. Student, U. Tampa, 1956-58; MusB, William Carey Coll., 1960; M of Ch. Music, Southwestern Theol. Sem., 1964. Min. of music 1st Bapt. Ch., Forrest City, N.C., 1964-65; assoc. prof. music William Carey Coll., Hattiesburg, Miss., 1965—, Winters endowed chair music, 1991-93. Mem., soloist Bapt. Hour Choir, So. Bapt. Conv. Radio and TV Commn., Ft. Worth; jr. choral dir. Grace Luth. Ch., Ft. Worth; min. music Bay Springs (Miss.) Bapt. Ch., 1971-75; dir. choral activities 1st Presbyn. Ch., Hattiesburg, 1975-79; interim min. music Bellevue Bapt. Ch., Hattiesburg, 1980; interim children's choral dir., soloist Broadstreet Meth. Ch., Hattiesburg, 1983; min. of music Court St. United Meth. Ch., 1997—; condr. vocal workshops; adjudicator choral festivals Ga. Bapt. Conv., 1965, 85, Miss. Bapt. Conv., 1965—, Jones Jr. Coll., Ellisville, Miss., others. Opera performances include Noye's Fludde (The Chester Miracle Play), Amahl and the Night Visitors, La Boheme; recital soloist Southwestern Bapt. Theol. Sem. and 1st Bapt. Ch. of Tampa, 1963, Harrisburg Bapt. Ch., Tupelo, Miss., Ridgecrest (N.C.) Bapt. Assembly, others. Mem. Music Tchrs. Nat. Assn. (guest collegiate artist so. divsn. 1960), Nat. Assn. Tchrs. of Singing, Miss. Music Tchrs. Assn., Ch. Music Conf. of So. Bapt. Conv., Ch. Music Conf. of Miss. Bapt. Conv., Condrs. Conf. of U. of So. Miss., Omicron Sigma chpt. Delta Omicron (chpt. advisor 1974—). Avocations: swimming, reading, singing. Home: 620 S 28th Ave Hattiesburg MS 39402-2518

DARPINO, VICTORIA GNOJEK, music educator; d. Walter Gnojek and Alice Valades; m. Fred Joseph Darpino, July 14, 1984; children: Julian Mario, Nicholas Joseph, Joseph Anthony. BA, U. No. Colo., 1975, M in Music Edn., 1979. Cert. Kodally method of tchg. music edn., Colo., 1999. Elem. music tchr. Keenesburg & Prospect Valley (Colo.) Elem. Schs., 1975—78; tchg. asst. U. No. Colo., Greeley, 1978—79; vocal music tchr. Horace Mann Jr. H.S., Colorado Springs, Colo., 1979—84, Anna M. Rudy Elem. Sch., Colorado Springs, 1984—93, Holmes Mid. Sch., Colorado Springs, 1995—96, Will Rogers Elem. Sch., Colorado Springs, 1996—97, Longfellow Elem. Sch., Colorado Springs, 1997—2003, Monroe Elem. Sch., Colorado Springs, 2003—. Elem. and secondary vocal music tchr. Sch. Dist. 11, Colorado Springs, 1978—, principal's adv. com. elem. and secondary schs., 1979—95, PTO & PTA liaison elem. and secondary schs., 1984—2002, music curriculum com. mem. Bd. dirs. Performing Arts for Youth Orgn., Colorado Springs, 1987—88. Recipient Lion's award, Tchr.'s Assn., 1984—85, Pacesetters Award for Profl. Excellence, 3D Bn. 29th Field Artilllery, 2000. Mem.: Colo. Springs Tchr's. Assn. (assoc.; tchr's. rights advocate com. chairperson 1984—89, rep. 1975—84). Office: School Distr #11 1115 N El Paso Colorado Springs CO 80903 Office Phone: 719-328-7400.

DARR, ANN RUSSELL, poet, educator; b. Bagley, Iowa, Mar. 13, 1920; d. Henry Horton and Lessie Rebecca (Hooper) Russell; m. George Campbell Darr, Nov. 7, 1941 (div. Mar. 1981); children: Elizabeth Russell, Deborah Horton, Shannon Campbell. BA magna cum laude, State U. Iowa, 1941; postgrad., Harvard Coll., 1980, Am. U., 1981. Writer/actor NBC Radio, N.Y.C., 1941-43, 45-46; tape recs. for blind Libr. of Congress, Washington, 1950-60; instr. creative writing Poets in the Schs., Md., Va. and D.C., 1970-80, 92-93; co-dir. workshop Nethers (Va.) Arts Colony, 1979; poet/dir. Georgetown U., Washington, summer 1977-78; poet The Writers Ctr., Bethesda, Md., 1981—; adj. prof. dept. lit. Am. U., Washington, 1982—. Fine arts seminar poet Montgomery (Ala.) Seminars, summer 1975; poet-in-residence Columbia (S.C.) Coll., spring 1975, 76, Am. Wind Symphony aboard Point Counterpoint II, U.S., 1976, 86, Jamaica, 1981, Europe, 1989, Eckard Coll., St. Petersburg, Fla., spring 1977; workshop poet St. Mary's (Md.) Coll., spring 1981, 82, 94, 95, 98, 99; judge for poetry Eckerd Coll., St. Petersburg, Fla., 1977, Nat. Endowment for Arts, Washington, 1979, Radcliff Coll., Cambridge, Mass., 1980, New Eng. Poetry Soc., Boston, 1981; mem. lit. panel Nat. Endowment for Arts, 1979-80; mem. adv. com. Folger Libr. Poetry Series, Washington, 1974-96. Author: St. Ann's Gut, 1971, The Myth of a Woman's Fist, 1973, Cleared for Landing, 1978, Riding with the Fireworks, 1981, Do You Take This Woman..., 1986 (Pub. award 1986), The Twelve Pound Cigarette, 1991, Confessions of a Skewed Romantic, 1993, Flying the Zuni Mountains, 1994, Gussie, Mad Hannah & Me, 1999, Love In the Past Tense, 2000; editor: Hungry As We Are, 1995; author numerous poems, 1961-99; translator (with others) Reading the Ashes, 1978, (with others) After the First Rain, 1997; featured poet Nat. Mus. Radio and TV, 1997. Mem. election com. Somerset (Md.) Town Bd., 1975-79; vol. Arena Stage, Washington, 1949-52. With U.S. Army Airforce (Women's Airforce Svc. pilot), 1943-44, WWII. Recipient Bunting fellowship Radcliffe Coll., 1979-80, Discovery 70 award Poetry Ctr., N.Y.C., 1970, Yaddo fellowship Yaddo, 1979, 86, MacDowell fellowship MacDowell Found., 1979. Mem. White House Conf. for Poets, Poetry Soc. Am., Acad. Am. Poets, Phi Beta Kappa, Zeta Phi Eta. Avocations: flying, traveling, acting, reading, collecting birds. Office: Am Univ 4400 Massachusetts Ave NW Washington DC 20016-8001 Home: 900 N Lake Shore Dr Apt 803 Chicago IL 60611-1530

DARRAGH, MARTINA, school librarian; b. Pitts., Nov. 21, 1950; d. Kim and Margaret Savage Darragh; m. Peter Inman; 1 child, Darragh Luke Inman. BA, Trinity Coll., Washington, 1972; MLS, U. Md., 1985. Cert. Montessori 1977. Group assoc. Matthew Bender & Co., Washington, SC, 1974—76; tchr. Montessori Sch. Champaign-Urbana, Champaign, Ill., 1977—78; deck attendant Libr. Congress, Washington, 1979—80; tchr. Lanham (Md.) Internat. Sch., 1981—82; rsch. asst./assoc. KBL Group, Inc., Silver Spring, Md., 1983—85, mgmt. analyst INSLAW, Inc., Washington, 1985—86; database adminstr. Nat. Med. Enterprises, Washington, 1986—88; technol. svcs. librarian Epilepsy Found. of Am., New Carrolton, Md., 1988—93; assoc. librarian Nat. Ctr. Edn. in Maternal and Child Health, Georgetown U., Arlington, Va., 1993—95; reference librarian Nat. Reference Ctr. Bioethics Lit., Kennedy Inst. for Ethics, Georgetown U., Washington, 1995—. Author: My Hands to Myself, 1975 (Creative Writing Fellowship, NEA, 1979), On the Corner to Off the Corner, 1981, Striking Resemblance, 1989, Against the Odds, 1989, Dream Rim Instructions, 1999. Fellow Watson Found., 1972—73. Home: 56-J Crescent Rd Greenbelt MD 20770 Office: Kennedy Inst Georgetown U Box 571212 Washington DC 20057-1212 Business E-Mail: darraghm@georgetown.edu.

DARROW, EMILY M. public relations executive, writer; b. Kingston, NY, Sept. 21, 1964; d. H. Van Wyck and Marianne Darrow; m. Brendon Paul McCrane, Oct. 5, 2002. Student, Vassar Coll., 1983—84; BA, Hunter Coll., 1989; postgrad. in Fine Arts, NYU, 1992. Mus. mgr., edn. mgr. Hist. Hudson Valley-Montgomery Pl., Annandale-on Hudson, NY, 1995; dir. pub. rels. and promotions Mohonk Mountain Ho., New Paltz, NY, 1997—98; pub. rels. assoc. Bard Coll., Annandale-on-Hudson, 1998—; asst. dir. Inst. Advanced Theology Bard Coll., Annandale-on-Hudson, 2001—. Rschr. Salander O'Reilly Gallery-Stuart Davis Catalogue Raisonne Project, N.Y.C., 1989—90; writer, rschr. Art Commn. City of N.Y., 1989—90; internship in pub. rels. Opera Garnier de Paris-Paris Opera Ballet, Paris, 1990—91, N.Y.C. Ballet, 1982—84; cons., writer Vikarmasila Found., N.Y.C., 1999—. Recipient Zabar grad. scholarship, Hunter Coll., 1989; fellow Leon Levy and Shelby White, Inst. of Fine Arts/NYU, 1990. Mem.: Jr. League of Kingston (rec. sec. 1991—96, pub. rels. dir. 1991—96). Home: 250 Morton Rd Rhinebeck NY 12572 Office: Bard Coll Annandale Hotel Annandale On Hudson NY 12504 Personal E-mail: EMDarrow87@alum.vassar.edu. Business E-Mail: darrow@bard.edu.

DARROW, GRETCHEN, costume designer; b. Ithaca, N.Y., Apr. 5, 1970; d. Frank William and Catherine (Twomey) D. MusB, U. Hartford, 1992; MFA, U. Conn., 1995. Asst. mgr. box office Hangar Theatre, Ithaca, 1992, mgr. box office, 1993-94, asst. shop mgr., 1995, mgr. costume shop, costume designer, 1996-99; sales assoc. JoAnn Fabrics, Ithaca, 1995; foreman costume shop Syracuse (N.Y.) Stage Co., 1996-99, mgr. costume shop, 1999—. Office: Syracuse Stage Co 820 E Genesee St Syracuse NY 13210-1508 Address: 456 Westcott St Syracuse NY 13210-2110

DARROW, JANE, artist; b. Hollywood, Calif., Apr. 9, 1936; d. Reginald Ivan and Dorothy Gertrude Bauder; m. Henry Frank Smith, Oct. 1954 (div. June 1967); children: Michael Henry, Linda Lee, Nancy Ann; m. Lee Hunter Darrow, Nov. 21, 1981. Student, U. So. Calif., 1953-55, U. Oreg., 1960-61. Art tchr. and exhibiter Los Abrigados, Sedona, Ariz., 2002—. Art instr. Sedona (Ariz.) Art Ctr., 1995. One-woman shows include Miramar, San Juan, P.R., El Dorado Gallery, San Juan, Excelsior Hotel, San Juan, Conservation Soc., P.R., Galeria Isabella, Vieques, P.R., 1992-94, Inst. Culture, San Juan, 1995, Ch. of the Red Rocks, Sedona, 1996, Creekside Gallery, Sedona, 1997; exhibited in group shows at P.R. and Fla. Watercolo Assn. Shows, 1989, 90, Phila. Watercolor, 1992, Catherine Lorillard Wolfe Art Club, 1992-95, Rocky Mountain Nat., 1992, 97, San Diego Watercolor, 1993, Ariz. Aqueous, 1993, 94, 97, La. Watercolor, 1994, Salmagundi Non-members, 1994, Ariz. Watercolor Assn., 1994-97, N.W. Watercolor, 1994-98, No. Ariz. Watercolor Assn., 1995, 97, Allied Artists, N.Y., 1995, 96, Phippen Mus., Prescott, Ariz., 1999; commd. artist Mariott Hotel, San Juan, 1994, Piñon Pointe Hyatt Hotel, Sedona; represented in permanent collections Condado Plaza Hotel, San Juan, Law Offices Guzman Esquilin and Assocs., San Juan, Crow's Nest Hotel, Vieques, Danmar Corp., San Juan; represented by Ratliff Gallery, Sedona, 1996-97, Raku Gallery, Jerome, Ariz., 1997—, Marcus Gallery, Santa Fe, 1997—, Golden Gecko Gallery, Sedona, 1999-2003. Mem. N.W. Watercolor Soc. (Miva/Walter Welt award 1997, No. Ariz. Watercolor Soc. (v.p. 1995-97, pres. 1997—, award of excellence 1996, best in show award 1997-99), Ariz. Watercolor Assn. (award of excellence 1995), Catherine Lorillard Wolfe Art Club. Home: 45 Ridge Rd Sedona AZ 86336-4035 E-mail: Janedarrow@aol.com.

DARROW, JILL E(LLEN), lawyer; b. N.Y.C., Jan. 6, 1954; d. Milton and Elaine (Sklarin) D.; m. Michael V.P. Marks, May 14, 1987. AB in English, Barnard Coll., 1975; JD, U. Pa., 1978; LLM in Tax Law, NYU, 1983. Bar: Pa. 1978, N.Y. 1979, U.S. Tax Ct. 1982. Assoc. Shearman & Sterling, N.Y.C., 1978-79, Rosenman & Colin, N.Y.C., 1979-86, ptnr., 1987—2002, Katten Muchin Zavis Rosenman, N.Y.C., 2002—. Mem. ABA, N.Y. State Bar Assn., Pa. Bar Assn., Phi Beta Kappa. Home: 860 5th Ave New York NY 10021-5856 Office: Katten Muchin Zavis Rosenman 575 Madison Ave Fl 12 New York NY 10022-2511 E-mail: jill.darrow@kmzr.com.

DARROW, MARIANNE ROSINA, speech pathology/audiology services professional, editor, writer; b. Kingston, N.Y., Dec. 11, 1925; d. Burton Jacob and Mary Anne Davis; m. H. Van Wyck Darrow, Jr., Nov. 24, 1963 (dec. July 1998); 1 child, Emily Marika. BA in English/Social Studies/Drama cum laude, SUNY, Albany, 1946; MA in Speech/Drama, Columbia U., 1952. Lic. speech-lang. pathologist N.Y., tchr. speech/hearing handicapped N.Y. Copywriter trainee J. Walter Thompson, N.Y.C., 1946—47; dancer Pitts. Ligth Opera Co., 1947, Touring Co., 1947—48; soc. editor Kingston (N.Y.) Daily Freeman, 1953—55; entertainment editor Ulster County Townsman, Woodstock, NY; pre-doctoral assoc. U. Wash. Speech and Hearing Clinic, Seattle, 1957—60; speech and hearing tchr. Kingston City Schs. Consol., 1960—64; speech-lang. pathologist Cerebral Palsy Ctr., Kingston, 1962, therapist, 1967—69; cons. Benedictine and Kingston Hosps., Kingston, 1967—72; speech cons. Ten Broeck Commons, Ulster, 2001—02; with Hutton Nursing Home, Kingston, 2002—03; speech cons. Ulster-Greene ARC, Kingston, NY. Actor: Coach House Players, 1951, Woodstock Playhouse, 1951; contbr. articles to profl. jours., to mags. including The Citizen, Antique Living. Chair pers. com. Kingston City Sch. Bd., 1970—75; founder pres. coun. PTA; chair environ. project Group Against Spraying Pesticides, Hurley, 1993—; founder, mem. prevention group Benedictine Hosp., 1995; dir. entertainment Sapporo, Japan, Nurnberg, Germany, 1948—50. Named Citizen Adv. of Yr., Mid-Hudson Options Project, Inc., 2001. Mem.: AAUW, N.Y. State Speech Hearing Lang. Assn., Am. Speech/Lang./Hearing Assn., Hillside Acres Garden Club. Avocations: gardening, swimming, travel, lecturing. Home: 436 Old Rt 209 Hurley NY 12443

DARST, MARY LOU, secondary school educator; b. Houston, Aug. 12, 1943; d. Carl Kennedy and Sara Catharine (Emmott) Hughes; m. William Maury Darst, Apr. 20, 1963 (dec. May 1990); children: Robert Maury, Catharine Fontaine Darst Knight. Student, Stephen F. Austin State Coll., 1961—63, Galveston Coll., 1970-72, 76-77, U. Tex. Med. Br., 1983—84; BA, U. Houston, Clear Lake, 1989, MS, 1993, BA, 2001; postgrad., U. St. Thomas, 1999—2002, Rice U., 2003. Cert. tchr. elem. edn., secondary English, ESL, gifted and talented, Advanced Placement. Sec. William Temple Fedn., Galveston, 1979-80; with new accounts Tex. First Bank, Galveston, 1981-84; med. sec. U. Tex. Med. Br., Galveston, 1984-87; tchr. Galveston (Tex.) Ind. Sch. Dist., 1990—2002, Galveston Coll., 1995-96; ESL tchr. Clear Lake H.S., 2002—. Mem. Jr. League of Galveston, 1966-69; bd. dirs. YWCA, 1972-73. Recipient Title VII grantee, U. Houston at Clear Lake, Houston, 1991—93. Mem.: Galveston Art League, Rock Art, Tex. Neurofibromatosis Found. (sec. 1987—89, pres. 1989—91), Assn. Tex. Profl. Educators, Mus. Fine Arts Houston, U. Houston Alumni Assn., Scenic Galveston, Sierra Club, Alpha Chi Omega, Delta Kappa Gamma (v.p. Omicron chpt. Theta Zeta 1995—96). Democrat. Episcopalian. Avocations: travel, music, swimming, walking, writing. Home: 1431 San Sebastian Ln Houston TX 77058-3451 E-mail: mldarst@juno.com.

DART, DEBORAH GORDON, artist; b. Princeton, N.J., Oct. 1, 1951; d. Henry Ward and Joyce V. (Switzgable) Gordon; m. John McRae Dart, Dec. 1, 1973; children: Sara M., Alexandra G. Student, Phila. Coll. Art, 1968-69, U. Miami, 1970-71, Ringling Sch. Art, 1971-73. Freelance artist, Sarasota, Fla., 1972-86, 95—; contractor Renovation/Rehab. of Hist. and Non-Hist. Homes, Sarasota, 1983-91; v.p. John Ringling Ctr. Found., Sarasota, 1991-95. Illustrations published in New Yorker Mag., Bon Appetit Mag., Yankee Mag. Bd. dirs. City of Sarasota Hist. Preservation Bd., 1989-95, chair, 1992; bd. dirs. Sarasota County Hist. Commn., 1991-93, mem. Sarasota Alliance for Hist. Preservation, v.p., 1987—; mem. Hist. Soc. Sarasota County, v.p., 1986—; mem. Rosemary Cemetery Project, chair, vice chair, 1986-90; mem. Fla. Trust for Hist. Preservation, 1990-96, Preservation Action, 1994-96, Nat. Trust Hist. Preservation, 1990-96. Avocation: historic preservation activist.

DASCH, PAT (ANNE), professional society administrator; b. Hampton Court, Surrey, Eng., Oct. 19, 1948; came to U.S., 1986; d. Arthur James and Eileen Dorothy (Adams) Kirk; m. Peter Malcolm Jones, Dec. 22, 1973 (div. 1981); m. Ernest Julius, Apr. 3, 1987. BA with honors, U. East Anglia, Norwich, Eng., 1975. Adminstrv. asst. Imperial Coll., London, 1968-72; adminstr. Wolfson Coll., Oxford, Eng., 1976-82; broadcaster, commentator Nat. Space Soc., Houston, 1984-88; planetary sci. rschr. Lunar Planetary Inst., Houston, 1986-88; planetary sci. analyst SAIC for NASA, Washington, 1988-94; editor in chief Ad Astra Mag., Nat. Space Soc., Washington, 1994-98; exec. dir. Nat. Space Soc., Washington, 1997—. Co-author: Images of Earth, 1984 (Best Remote Sensing Book of Yr.); editor-in-chief: Space Sciences for Students, 2000—. Avocations: geology, hiking, travel, theater. Office: Nat Space Soc 600 Pennsylvania Ave SE Ste 201 Washington DC 20003-4344 E-mail: pdasch@nss.org.

DASCHLE, LINDA HALL, transportation industry lobbyist; b. Okla., May 1955; m. Tom Daschle, 1984. Attended, Kans State U. Regional dir. Civil Aeronautics Bd. (CAB), 1980—84; sr. v.p. Am. Assn. Airport Exec.; chief lobbyist Air Transport Assn., 1984—; dep. adminstr., then acting adminstr. FAA, 1993—97; lobbyist, chair pub. policy group Baker Donelson Bearman & Caldwell, 1997—. Achievements include Miss Kans., 1976. Office: Baker Donelson Bearman & Caldwell 555 11th St NW Fl 6 Washington DC 20004 Office Phone: 202-508-3400.*

DA SILVA, ANN MARIE KATHERINE, psychotherapist, consultant; b. N.Y.C., N.Y., Sept. 2, 1954; d. Michael John Mazzarella and Eleanor May Shannon; m. Richard Joseph Da Silva, Jan. 16, 1987; children: Andrew Richard, Dylan Joseph. BA, Boston Coll., 1976; MS, Columbia U., 1982. CSW Acad. Cert. Social Workers, 1984, LCSW N.Y. State, 1985. Psychiatric social worker Carrier Found., Bellemeade, NJ, 1982—84; clinician Jewish Childcare Assn., Pleasantville, NY, 1984—85, Jewish Bd. Family & Children Svc., N.Y.C., NY, 1986—89; sch. clinician Pius XII Corp. Svc., Goshen, NY, 1994—98; pvt. practice Highland Mills, NY, 1987—. Adv. bd. Adv. Coun. on Drug Abuse, Prevention & Edn., Pinebush, NY, 1994—99; clinical supervision coord. Orange County Student Assn. Coords., Goshen, 1997—99. Mem. parent edn. & peace custody effectiveness Orange County Ct. Sys., Goshen, 1998. Recipient Appreciation award, Mayor Koch & Mayor's Voluntary Action Ctr., 1980. Mem.: NASW, Boston Coll. Alumni Assn. Home and Office: 30 Cindy Lane Highland Mills NY 10930

DASTRUP-HAMILL, FAYE MYERS, city official; b. Sanford, Colo., Dec. 15; d. Earl Dixon and Kady Florence (Cornum) Faucett; m. Sherly K. Myers (dec.); children: Carla Pearce, Susan Kitley (dec.), Mary Jane James, Elizabeth Ireland; m. Merrill E. Dastrup, Sept. 22, 1972 (dec. July 1987); m. Wayne A. Hamill, Mar. 23, 1991. Student, L.D.S. Bus. Coll., 1934-35; grad., Dale Carnegie Inst., 1953; degree in mcpl. works adminstrn., Mt. San Antonio Coll., 1960; student, Syracuse U. Inst., 1968; degree in tech. reporting, Chaffey Coll., 1970. Legal sec. W. W. Platt, City Atty., Alamosa, Colo., 1935-40; sec. pub. works dept. City of Ontario, Calif., 1957-60, dep. city clk., dep. city treas., 1960-64, city clk., 1964-73, city coun. mem., mayor and mayor pro tem, 1974-92; mem. part 150 implementation com. Ontario Airport, Calif., 1993—, chmn. noise adv. com., dept. trans. State of Calif., 1994—. Sec. pers. dept. L.A. Housing Authority, 1948; mem. legis. subcom. So. Calif. Assn. Govts., chmn. hist. preservation and cultural arts com.; mem. revenue and taxation com. League of Calif. Cities, vice-chmn., chmn. Clks. Inst., gen. resolutions com., com. on environ. quality Inland Empire divsn.; chmn. San Bernardino County Planning Com., Criminal Justice; prese. So. Calif. City Clks. Assn., chmn. legis. com.; mem. exec. com. Valley Assn. of Cities; city coun. rep. Ontario Libr. Bd. Trustees. Escort sch. classes through City Hall; judge sci. fairs and sch. and comty. events; life mem. Friends of Ontario Libr.; mem., donor Friends of Mus. of History and Art, Ontario; pres., treas., trustee Ontario (Calif.) City Libr., 1993—; choir dir., life mem. Ch. of Jesus. Recipient plaque with gold gavel So. Calif. City Clks. Assn., 1972, Women Helping Women award Soroptomist Internat. of Ontario, 1981, 1990 Woman of Yr. award State Legislature, State of Calif., 1990, Woman of Achievement award 90s Women's Conf., 1990, 1994 YWCA Woman of Achievement award West End YWCA, 1994, Elizabeth S. Genee Lifetime Achievement award, West End YWCA, 1994, Bryce Denton award Mus. of History and Art, 1996, Outstanding Effort with Calif. Water plaque San Bernardino County Waterworks Dist. #8, 1986, Outstanding Svc. plaque Ontario Air N.G., 1990, Leadership plaque San Bernardino County Sheriff's Dept., 1993, Founding, Support and Encouragement of Crime Stoppers Spl. Recognition plaque Ontario Police Dept., 1993, Outstanding Comty. Svc. plaque U.S. Congressman Jay Kim, 1994, Plaque and Spl. Cert. congratulating receipt of Elizabeth Genee Lifetime Achievement award, 1994, Pub. Svc. Award trophy Adrian Meewis, 1972, plaque for dedicated and meritorious svc. to Ontario, as mayor City Coun. and City Clk., 1986, Lifetime Achievement plaque San Bernardino County Supr. Larry Walker, 1994, Svc. plaque South Coast Air Quality Mgmt. Dist., 1987, decorated plaque Salvation Army, 1992, others. Mem. Calif. Assn. Libr. Trustees and Commrs., Comty.

Concert Assn. Pomona Valley (donor), Ontario C. of C. (life, Svc. Award plaque 1992), Musicians Club of Pomona Valley. Mem. Ch. of Jesus Christ of LDS. Avocation: vocal soloist. Home: 761 W Hawthorne St Ontario CA 91762-1510

[illegible] [illegible] artist, b. Bucharest, Romania, Apr. 22, 1944; d. Marin and Niculina Datcu; m. Vasile Porcisanu, Aug. 5, 1967 (div. 1983); 1 child, Isabelle Ioana. BA, Pedagogical Inst., Bucharest, 1967; BFA summa cum laude, U. Minn., 1987, MFA, 1991. Tchr. biology high sch., Argova, Preasna, Romania, 1967-74; photography asst. U. Minn., St. Paul, 1985-86; photographer civil rights dept. City Hall, St. Paul, 1986-87; darkroom supervisor Film in the Cities, St. Paul, 1987-88; gallery asst., curator Paul Whitney Gallery, St. Paul, 1987-91; art instr. Minn. Mus. Am. Art, St. Paul, 1993-94; instr. drawing & painting U. Minn., Mpls., 1996-97. One-woman shows include Flanders Contemporary Art, Mpls., 1994, Winona (Minn.) State U, 1995, Mont. State U., Billings, 1996, Ea. Wash. U., Cheney, 1996, Indpls. Art Ctr., 1996, Kansas City (Mo.) Artists Coalition, 1997, Grants Pass (Oreg.) Mus. Art, 1997, Trinity Presbyn. Ch., Denton, Tex., 1998, South Bend (Ind.) Mus. Art, 1998, U. Dayton, Ohio, 2000, Concordia U., Seward, Nebr., 2004, juried exhibitions include, North Park Coll., Chgo., 1991, Hist. Trinity, Detroit, 1993, 1995, 1996, Coll. St. Catherine, St. Paul, 1995, Barrett House Galleries, Poughkeepsie, N.Y., 1994, 1996, Coll. St. Catherine, St. Paul, 1995, Minot State U., N.D., 1995, St. John's U., N.Y., 1995, Katherine E. Nash Gallery, Mpls., 1992, 1995, 1996, Focal Point Gallery, N.Y.C., 1996, SoHo Photo Gallery, 1997, Greater Lafayette Mus. Art, 1997, Greater Lafayette Mus. Art., 1997, Truman State U., Mo., 1998, McNeese State U., La., 1998, Attelboro (Mass.) Mus. Art, 1998, 1999, New World Art Ctr., N.Y.C., 1999, Ctrl. Mo. State U., 1999, Am. Bible Soc. Gallery, N.Y.C., 2000, Internat. Print Triennial, Cracow, Poland, 2000, Internat. Print Triennial Krakow Nürnberg, Messezentrum Mus., Germany, 2000, Jewish Cmty. Ctr. Greater New Haven, Woodbridge, Conn., 2001, Korean Cultural Ctr., L.A., 2001, New Am. Paintings Exhibit in Print, Open Studio Press, 1995, Images of the Spirit Traveling Exhibit, 1995—97, CIVA CODEX III traveling exhibit, 1997—2001, represented in, CD-Rom collections of Art Comms. Internat., 1995, Artmax Internat., 1995, Ency. Internat. Women Artists, Alliance Women Artists, 1997, New Art Internat., Book Art Press, 1997, Christianity and the Arts Jour., 1999, Bridge to the Future, 2000, The Missing Mary, 2004, juried exhibititons include, Grand Forks Art Gallery, Can., 2004. Grantee Pollock-Krasner Found., 1992, Minn. State Arts Bd., 1994; Jerome Found. Residency fellow, 1994; McKnight Photography fellow, 1992, fellow Arts Midwest NEA, 1994-95, Clowes Fund regional residency fellow, Indpls., 1997; Vt. Studio Ctr. Residency award, Johnson, Vt., 1997. Mem. Christians in the Visual Arts, Nat. Assn. Women Artists, Inc. Mem. Eastern Orthodox Ch. Avocations: classical music, movies, yoga, books, animals. Home: 1028 E Justin St Sunsites AZ 85625 E-mail: idatcu@vtc.net.

DAUB, PEGGY ELLEN, library administrator; b. Bluffton, Ohio, Oct. 15, 1949; d. Perry J. and Olive L. (Hoover) D.; m. Jeffrey H. Cooper, Dec. 13, 1975; 1 child, William P. Cooper-Daub. MusB summa cum laude, Miami U., 1972; MA, Cornell U., 1975; MSLS, U. Ill., 1980; PhD, Cornell U., 1985. Acting asst. music libr. Yale U., 1980-81, head of music tech. svcs., rare books libr. Music Libr., 1981-82; head Music Libr. U. Mich., Ann Arbor, 1982-89, head Spl. Collections & Arts Librs., 1989-99, head Spl. Collections Libr., 2000—. Presenter Rare Books and Manuscript Sect. Pre-Conf., New Orleans, 1993, Bloomington, 1995 and others. Contbr. articles to profl. jours. Co-clk. Ann Arbor Friends Meeting, 1997-2001. Travel grantee Ctr. for Internat. Studies, Cornell U., 1977. Mem. ALA (Assn. Coll. and Rsch. Librs. rare books and manuscripts sect., mem. task force on interlibr. loan 1991-93, mem. preconf. program planning com. 1992-94), Music Libr. Assn. (bd. dirs. 1985-87, mem. resource sharing and collection devel. com. 1982-91), Rsch. Librs. Group (chairperson music program com. 1985-87, mem. steering com. 1982-87), Am. Musicol. Soc. (mem. coun. 1988-91, mem. coun. com. on minorities/diversity 1988-91), Phi Beta Kappa. Mem. Soc. Of Friends. Office: U of Mich Spl Collections Libr 711 Graduate Libr Ann Arbor MI 48109-1205 E-mail: pdaub@umich.edu.

DAUBE, LORRIE O. sales executive; b. Toledo, Ohio, Feb. 3, 1951; d. Stanley and Marian Oberlin; m. Jeffrey Daube, Aug. 31, 1975; children: Ryan Oberlin, Danielle Elyse. BS in Comm., U. Ill., 1973. Media sales WDAI-ABC-FM, Chgo., 1973—74; media sales rep. Jack Masla, Chgo., 1974—75; media sales WMET Metromedia, Chgo., 1976—79, WIND-Westinghouse, Chgo., 1980—82; copywriter Burgess, Heynssen and Oberlin, Deerfield, Ill., 1983—85; sales cons. Coldwell Banker, Deerfield, 1990—. Girls tennis coach asst. Deerfield (Ill.) H.S., 2000—. Charity fundraiser Med. Rsch. Inst., 1985—90, Jewish United Fund, Chgo., 1995—; active guest svcs. 2002 Winter Olympics, Deer Valley, Utah, 2002; asst. coach girls jr. varsity and varsity tennis Deerfield High Sch., Ill., 2002—. Mem.: Northshore Women's Tennis League Assn. (pres. 1986—88). Republican. Avocations: skiing, tennis, golf, platform tennis, swimming. Home: 8 Dunsinane Ln Bannockburn IL 60015

DAUBENAS, JEAN DOROTHY TENBRINCK, librarian, educator; b. N.Y.C., Apr. 04; d. Eduard J.A. and Margaret Dorothy (Schaffner) Tenbrinck; m. Joseph Anthony Daubenas, May 29, 1965. Grad., Am. Acad. Dramatic Arts, 1963; AB, Barnard Coll., Columbia U., 1962; MA, NYU, 1965; MLS, U. Ariz., 1972; PhD, U. Utah, 1986. Tchr. Beth Jacob Tchrs. Sem. Am., Bronx, N.Y., 1965-66; caseworker Dept. Social Svcs., N.Y.C., 1966-67; actress Boothbay (Maine) Playhouse, also others, 1967-70; reference libr. Ariz. State U., Tempe, 1972-75; grad. asst. U. Utah, Salt Lake City, 1976-77; asst. libr., asst. prof. libr. sci. Avila Coll., Kansas City, Mo., 1979-83; assoc. prof., libr. St. John's U., Jamaica, NY, 1983—99; ret., 2000. N.Y. State Regents scholar, 1958-61, U. Ariz. scholar, 1971-72. Mem. ALA, AAUP, Actors Equity Assn., Theatre Libr. Assn., Assn. Theatre in Higher Edn., Beta Phi Mu, Phi Kappa Phi. Roman Catholic.

DAUCHER, LYNN M. state official; b. Washington, D.C., Feb. 20, 1946; m. Don Daucher; children: Kelly, Carl, Jill, Brian. BS in Edn., U. Rochester, 1968. Tchr., Williamsville, NY, 1968—69; mem. Brea Olinda Sch. Bd., 1981—94, Brea City Coun., 1994—2000; state assembly mem. Dist. 72 Calif. State Assembly, 2000—. Mem. budget com.; mem. local govt. com. Mem.: State League Fiscal Funding (reform task force), State League of Cities (revenue and taxation com.), Rep. Women of Brea, League of Calif. Cities, Placentia C. of C., La Habra C. of C., Fullerton C. of C., Brea C. of C., Kiwanis Club of Brea. Republican. Lutheran. Mailing: Rm 2158 PO Box 942849 Sacramento CA 94249 Office: Ste 202 210 W Birch St Brea CA 92821

DAUER, SALLY E. small business owner, volunteer; b. Pitts., May 6, 1967; d. Stanley Lawrence Kalinowski and Barbara Jean Johnson; m. Michael John Dauer, Dec. 27, 1960; 1 child, Maddelin Jade. AS in Computer Sci., Pa. State U., New Kensington, 1987; BS in Computer Info. Sys., La Roche Coll., 1992, MS in Human Resource Mgmt., 2002. Computer programmer, analyst Mellon Bank, Pitts., 1992—93; client devel. analyst II Fiserv, Inc., Pitts., 1994—97; implementation specialist II ADP, Pitts., 1997—99; bus. analyst Sanchez Data Systems, Inc., Seven Fields, Pa., 2000—02. Head vol. resource devel. North Hills Cmty. Outreach, Allison Park, Pa., 2002—03. Roman Catholic. Avocations: fishing, reading, bowling, walking, golf. Home: 1603 Eaglewood Ct Pittsburgh PA 15237 Office: North Hills Community Outreach 1975 Ferguson Rd Allison Park PA 15101-3235

DAUGHERTY, LINDA HAGAMAN, real estate company executive; b. Denver, Jan. 25, 1940; d. Charles B. and Agnes May (Wall) Hagaman; m. Thomas Daniel Daugherty, Nov. 20, 1965; children: Patrick, Christina Marie. BS in Bus., U. Colo., 1961; postgrad., Tulane U., 1963-64, U. St. Thomas, 1990-91. Sr. systems analyst Lockheed Electronics NASA, Houston, 1966-73; sr. systems cons. TRW Systems Internat., Caracas, Venezuela, 1973-74; sy. systems cons. TRW Systems, L.A., 1974-75; sr. systems analyst Intercomp, Houston, 1979-80; cons. Daugherty Fin. Svcs. [illegible] Katy, T[illegible] 19[illegible]; pres., [illegible]-91, mng. ptnr. Motivated Child Learning Ctrs., Katy, 1976—; pres. Williamsburg Country Day Sch., Katy, 1983—2003, Nottingham Country Day Sch., Katy, 1977—2003. Pres. Mason Creek Women Reps. Club, Katy, 1980; treas. Nottingham Country Civic Club, Katy, 1979; mem. adv. bd. Nottingham Country Club, 1982-85; co-founder Friends of Archaeology U. St. Thomas, pres., 1991-93; mem. Epiphany Ch. Social Works Commn.; asst. curator Archaeology Gallery, U. St. Thomas; mem., pres. Friends of Boerne Pub. Libr., 1997—; San Antonio World Affair Coun. Mem. Houston Archeology Soc., Tex. Archeology Soc., Archaeology Inst. of Am., Boerne Women's Club. Roman Catholic. Avocations: archaeology, bridge. Office: Motivated Child Learning Ctr PO Box 489 Boerne TX 78006-0489

DAUGHERTY, PATRICIA ANN, elementary school educator; b. Rockford, Ill., May 19, 1949; d. Bjarne John and Mary Rita (Ryan) Jacobsen; m. Greg A. Kramer, June 23, 1973 (div. Apr. 1988); 1 child, Josie Kramer. BS, No. Ill. U., 1971, MS, 1978. cert. elem. tchr., Ill., spl. edn. tchr., Ill. Tchr. Aurora (Ill.) East Sch. Dist., 1971—. Mem. PTA; mem. choir Our Lady of Mercy Cath. Ch. Mem. AAUW (gift honoree 1996), Am. Fed. Tchrs. (bldg. rep. local 604 1995—). Avocations: reading, gardening, skiing, golfing. Home: 340 Inverness Dr Aurora IL 60504-6925 Office: Dieterich Sch Aurora IL 60504

DAUGHERTY, RUTH ALICE, religious association consultant; b. Shenandoah, Va., Feb. 21, 1931; d. Lee Earl and Lena Alice (Heishman) Sheaffer; m. Robert Mowery Daugherty, July 11, 1953; children: Carole Ruth Daugherty Haigh, Steven Robert, Beth Anne Daugherty Carr. AA, Shenandoah Jr. Coll., 1950; BA, Lebanon Valley Coll., 1952; HHD (hon.), Albright Coll., 1982, Shenandoah U., 1986. English and history tchr. Bruce H.S., Westernport, Md., 1952-53, Trotwood (Ohio) H.S., 1953-55; officer United Meth. Women, Pa., 1956-72, nat. pres., 1980-84; nat. chair ministry study United Meth. Ch., 1984-92; nat. v.p. United Meth. Comm. Commn., 1984-88; v.p. United Bd. for Christian Higher Edn. in Asia, N.Y.C., 1984-87. M. faculty Drew Theol. Sem., 2001; cons. for gen. commn. Christian unity and interreligious concerns United Meth. Ch., 2001—. Author: (booklet) United Methodist Women in Mission, 1994, (study guide) John Wesley Study, 1996, The Missionary Spirit: History of the Methodist Protestant Church, 2004. Trustee Lebanon Valley Coll., Annville, Pa., 1971—89; chair pers. com., chair mus. com. Scarritt-Bennett Ctr., Nashville, 1991—96, sec., 1996—99; pres. Lumina Bd., Lancaster, Pa., 1998—; co-chair addressing world and cmty. issues EPA Conf., 2000—, del. to quad gen. confs., 1972—; sec. NE jurisdiction United Meth. Ch., 2003—; bd. dirs. United Meth. Pub. House, 2003—; chair policy program com., chair directions for the '90s United Bd. for Christian Edn. in Asia, 1990—98; sec. trustees Ea. Pa. Conf. United Meth Ch., Valley Forge, 1992—98; gen. commn. Christian unity and interreligious concerns United Meth. Ch., 1992—2000, sec., 1996—2000, Otterbein dist. lay leader, 1998—2001. Recipient Disting. Alumni award Shenandoah U., 1996, Alumni award Lebanon Valley Coll., 1979, Woodrow B. Seals Laity award Perkins Sch. Theology, 1997, Anna Howard Shaw award Anna Howard Shaw Ctr., Boston U. Avocations: making yeast breads, making quilts, reading, gardening. Home: 1936 N Eden Rd Lancaster PA 17601-4952 E-mail: rdaugherty@mycyberlink.net.

DAUGHTREY, MARTHA CRAIG, federal judge; b. Covington, Ky., July 21, 1942; d. Spence E. Kerkow and Martha E. (Craig) Piatt; m. Larry G. Daughtrey, Dec. 28, 1962; 1 child, Carran. BA, Vanderbilt U., 1964, JD, 1968. Bar: Tenn. 1968. Pvt. practice, Nashville, 1968; asst. U.S. atty., 1968—69; asst. dist. atty., 1969—72; asst. prof. law Vanderbilt U., Nashville, 1972—75; judge Tenn. Ct. Appeals, Nashville, 1975—90; assoc. justice Tenn. Supreme Ct., Nashville, 1990—93; circuit judge U.S. Ct. Appeals (6th cir.), Nashville, 1993—. Lectr. law Vanderbilt Law Sch., Nashville, 1975—82, adj. prof., 1988—90; mem. faculty NYU Appellate Judges Seminar, N.Y.C., 1977—90, N.Y.C., 1994—. Contbr. articles to profl. jours. Pres. Women Judges Fund for Justice, 1984—85, 1986—87; active various civic orgns. Recipient Athena award, Nat. Athena Program, 1991. Mem.: ABA (chmn. appellate judges conf. 1985—86, ho. of dels. 1988—91, chmn. jud. divsn. 1989—90, standing com. on continuing edn. of bar 1992—94, commn. on women in the profession 1994—97, bd. editors ABA Jour. 1995—2001, Margaret Brent award 2003), Lawyers Assn. for Women (pres. Nashville 1986—87), Nat. Assn. Women Judges (pres. 1985—86), Am. Judicature Soc. (bd. dirs. 1988—92), Nashville Bar Assn. (bd. dirs. 1988—90), Tenn. Bar Assn. Office: US Ct Appeals 300 Customs House 701 Broadway Nashville TN 37203-3944*

DAUSER, KIMBERLY ANN, physician assistant; b. Detroit, Nov. 20, 1947; d. George Leonard and Jeanne (Austin) Wilkie; 1 child, Aaron Thomas. AA, Pensacola Jr. Coll., 1971; BS in Medicine, physician's asst. cert. in medicine, U. Ala., Birmingham, 1976; cert. in mgmt., Am. Mgmt. Assn., 1989; postgrad., U. West Fla., 1995—. Cert. physician's asst. Asst. mgr. Christo's, Gulf Breeze, Fla., 1966-67; teller, bookkeeper loan dept. Bank Gulf Breeze, 1967-72; med. tech. aide USN Hosp., Pensacola, 1972, physician's asst., 1972-73, John Kingsley, MD, Pensacola, 1976, Mountain Comprehensive Health Corp., Whitesburg, Ky., 1976-78, N.W. Fla. Nephrology, Pensacola, 1978-87, med. adminstr., 1987-95, Nephrology Ctr. of Pensacola, Fla., 1987-95; COO Nephrology Ctr. Inc., Crestview, Pensacola, 1995—, Nephrology Ctr., Inc., Crestview, Pensacola, 1995-96, Nephrology Ctr. Assocs., Pensacola, 1995-96; regional COO, Renal Care Group Inc., Pensacola, Fla., 1996-98; COO Nephrology Ctr. Assoc. PA, 1998-99; area adminstr. Renal Care Group Inc., Houston, 1999—2002, clin. ops. cons., 2002, dir. clin. ops., 2002, 2002—. Fellow Am. Acad. Physician's Assts. (del. nat. meeting 1978—), Nat. Commn. on Cert. Physician's Assts., Fla. Acad. Physician's Assts. (mem. jud. com. 1979-80), Natural Wildlife Assn. Republican. Roman Catholic. Avocations: photography, antiques, reading, wildlife preservation. Office: Renal Care Group Ste 600 2525 W End Ave Nashville TN 37203 Home: 600 Enterprise Ave # 1028 League City TX 77573

DAUTH, FRANCES KUTCHER, journalist, newspaper editor; b. St. Louis, Aug. 20, 1941; d. David Jacob Kutcher and Dorothy Marie (Baugh) Hedges; m. Jerry Donald Dauth, July 5, 1964 (div. Dec. 1980). BA, U. Colo., 1963; cert. mgmt. program, Smith Coll., 1989. Staff writer Alameda (Calif.) Times Star, 1966-67, Contra Costa Times, Walnut Creek, Calif., 1968-69, Oakland (Calif.) Tribune, 1969-77; project editor San Francisco Examiner, 1977-82; asst. city editor Phila. Inquirer, 1982, dep. N.J. editor, 1983, suburban editor, 1984-85, city editor, 1985-89, nat. editor, 1989-91, fgn. editor, 1991-94, assoc. mng. editor, 1994-96; mng. editor Star Ledger, Newark, 1996—. Home: 842 S 2nd St # 392 Philadelphia PA 19147-3430 Office: Star Ledger Newark NJ 07104

DAVENPORT, ANN ADELE MAYFIELD, retired home care agency administrator; b. New Orleans, Nov. 12, 1941; d. Henry Louis and Myrtie Iola (Cason) Mayfield; m. John Wayne Davenport, June 18, 1966; children: Steven Lyle, Daniel Ryan, Elaine Adele. BA, Southeastern La. Coll., 1963; MA in Edn., George Peabody C., 1965; MA in Sociology, Tex. Tech. U., 1971. Tchr. various schs., 1963-70; instr. of sociology Tex. Tech. U., Lubbock, 1970-74, James Madison U., Harrisonburg, Va., 1981-82, Ga. So. Coll., Statesboro, 1982-84; 5th grade tchr. Bulloch county Schs., Statesboro, Ga., 1985-87; gerontology project coord. Dept. of Nursing Ga. So. Coll., 1987-88; project dir. Sr. Companion Program Ctr. for Rural Health and Rsch., Ga. So. U., Statesboro, 1988-93; instr. dept. health sci. edn. Ga. So. Coll., Statesboro, 1993-95; exec. dir. Ogeechee Home Health Agy., Statesboro, 1995-96, Homebound Svcs., Statesboro, 1996—2002; ret., 2002. Editor various newsletters, 1987-2002. Bd. dirs. Citizens Against Violence, Statesboro, 1987-88, Habitat for Humanity, 1990-2002; pres. Coun. on Children and Parents, Statesboro, 1988-89, 93-94; mem. steering [illegible] Commn. on Human Svcs., 1989-2002; mem. adminstrv. bd. dirs., coun. on ministries, nominating com. Pittman Park United Meth. Ch.; pres. Ogeechee Wellness Coun., 1992-2002; bd. dirs. Ogeechee Home Health Agy., 1989-93. Mem. Ga. Rural Health Assn. (sec. 1988-89, editor state newsletter 1989-96), So. Sociol. Soc., Ga. Gerontol. Assn., Ga. Sociol. Assn., AAUW (newsletter editor Statesboro 1987-89), Am. Soc. on Aging, Nat. Coun. on the Aging, Am. Rural Health Assn. Avocations: tennis, reading. Home: 1920 Hampton Way Ada OK 74820

DAVENPORT, DEBORAH MORGAN, obstetrician, gynecologist; b. Phila., May 21, 1948; d. Michel Kerop and Gloria Anita (Kremens) Morgan; m. James Whitman Davenport, Jan. 27, 1968; children: Jesse, Christopher, Michael, Andrew. BA, Douglass Coll., 1971; MD, U. Pa., 1975. Diplomate Am. Bd. Obs.-Gyn. Resident SUNY Sch. Medicine, Stony Brook, N.Y., 1980-83, asst. prof. obs-gyn., 1983-86; physician Three Village Women's Hlth., Setauket, N.Y., 1986—. Clin. asst. prof. SUNY Sch. Medicine, 1986—, credentials com. dept. ob-gyn., 1990—; mem. med. bd. Univ. Hosp., 1997-99. Bd. dirs. Suffolk Network Adolescent Pregnancy, 1982-85, Planned Parenthood Suffolk County, 1989—, chairperson medicinal affiliate com. Recipient NY Magazine Best Doctor award, NY Metro Area, 2003, Castle Connoly Best Drs. award, N.Y. Metro Area, 1995—2003. Fellow: ACOG; mem.: NOW, N.Am. Menopause Soc. (charter mem., nat. cert. menopause practionioner 2002—), Am. Women's Med. Assn. (br. pres. 1995—, adviser student chpt. SUNY-Stony Brook), Am. Orchid Soc., Alpha Omega Alpha, Phi Beta Kappa. Democrat. Unitarian Universalist. Avocations: gardening orchids, cooking, boating, reading. Office: Three Village Womens Hlth 100 S Jersey Ave Setauket NY 11733-2034 Office Phone: 631-689-6400.

DAVENPORT, DOROTHY DEAN, retired medical/surgical nurse; b. Grandview, Idaho, Sept. 29, 1924; d. William Christian and Frances Beatrice (Campbell) Forcher; m. Richard Ellis Davenport, May 26, 1946 (dec. May 1982); children: Robert Ray, William Lee, Gary Edward, James Ellis. Student, Walla Walla Coll., 1942-44; ADN, Loma Linda U., 1946, 49-50. RN, W.Va. Office nurse, Corona, Calif., 1946-49; nursing educator Jengre (Nigeria) Hosp., 1956-58; home health nurse Appalachian OH-9, Bluefield, W.Va., 1984-86, clinic charge nurse, 1986-89, health edn. tchr., 1989-91, nutrition counselor WIC program, 1995-98, ret. Tchr. courses in field, 1998-99; tchr. sci. at k-12 sch., 1998—. Author: Who Found Klippy and Other Stories, 1960, His Guiding Hand, 1993. Trustee, mem. conf. com., mem. fin. com. Mountain View Conf. of Seventh-day Adventists, Parkersburg, W.Va., 1993—; bd. dirs. Valley View Seventh-day Adventist Ch., Bluefield, 1977—. Avocations: walking, nature crafts, bird watching, gardening, music, landscaping. Home: RR 2 Box 383-bb Bluefield WV 24701 Office Phone: 304-325-8679.

DAVENPORT, LINDSAY, professional tennis player; b. Palos Verdes, Calif., June 8, 1976; d. Wink and Ann Lindsay; m. Jon Leach, 2003. Profl. tennis player, 1993—. Named gold medalist singles, 1996, winner, WTA Doubles Championship, 1996—98, U.S. Open, 1998, Wimbledon, 1999, WTA Singles Championship, 1999, Australian Open, 2000, winner Singles Grand Slam titles, U.S. Open, 1998, Wimbldeon, 1999, Australian Open, 2000; named to, Olympic Team, 1996; ranked #1, 1998, 2001. Office: US Tennis Assn 70 W Red Oak Ln White Plains NY 10604-3602

DAVID, MARTHA LENA HUFFAKER, retired music educator, retired sales executive; b. Susie, Ky., Feb. 7, 1925; d. Andrew Michael and Nora Marie (Cook) Huffaker; m. William Edward David, June 24, 1952 (div. Jan. 1986); children: Edward Garry, William Andrew, Carolyn Ann, Robert Cook. AB in Music magna cum laude, Georgetown (Ky.) Coll., 1947; postgrad., Vanderbilt U., 1957-58; Spanish cert., Lang. Sch., Costa Rica, 1959; MEd, U. Ga., 1972. Elem. tchr. Wayne County Bd. Edn., Spann, Ky., 1944-45; music tchr. Mason County, Mayslick, Ky., 1947-49, Hikes Grade Sch., Buechel, Ky., 1949-53; English and Spanish tchr. Jefferson (Ga.) High Sch., 1961-63; music and English tchr. Athens (Ga.) Acad., 1967-71; music tchr. Barrow County Bd. Edn., Winder, Ga., 1971-88; real estate agt. South Best Realty, Athens, 1986-90; ret., 1988. Data collector Regional Ednl. Svcs. Agy., Athens and Winder, 19176-78; tchr. music Union Theol. Sem., Buenos Aires, 1957-60. Author: (poems) Parcels of Love, Book I, 1984, Book II, 1999, Poems and Reflections; composer (music plays) The B.B.'s, The Missing Tune, A Dream Come True, The Stars Who Creep Out of Orbit, 1976-86. Active cultural affairs orgns., Athens, 1962—, Athens Area Porcelain Artists, YWCO; entertainer nursing homes and civic orgns., Athens, 1962; chmn. cancer drives, heart fund drive United Way, March of Dimes, Athens, 1962—; historian, elder, pianist Christian Ch. Winner regional piano competition Ky. Philharm. Orch., 1946; nominated Tchrs. Hall of Fame, Barrow County, 1981. Mem. Ret. Tchrs. Assn., Writer's Group, Ga. Music Tchrs., Nat. Music Tchrs. Assn., Athens Music Tchrs. Assn. (pres. recital chmn.), Ga. World Orgn. China Painters, Athens Area Porcelain Artists, Women's Mus. Arts (assoc.), Women's Mus. Art (Washington), Touchdown Club, Band Boosters, Alpha Delta Kappa (Fidelis Nu chpt., historian), Delta Omicron (life, scholar 1944). Democrat. Mem. Christian Ch. Avocations: porcelain art, oil and acrylic painting, swimming, square dancing, round dancing. Home: 105 Nassau Ln Athens GA 30607-1456

DAVID, MICHELE MARIE ALINE, physician, researcher; d. Odnell and Aline (Cantave) D. BS, Roosevelt U., 1978; MBA, U. Ill., Chgo., 1985; MD, U. Chgo., 1988; MPH, Harvard U., 1994. Diplomate in internal medicine, pulmonary disease and critical care medicine Am. Bd. Internal Medicine. Resident Columbia Presbyn. Hosp., N.Y.C., 1988-91; pulmonary & critical care fellow Brigham & Women's Hosp., Boston, 1991-95; asst. prof. medicine Sch. Medicine Boston U., 1995—; staff physician Boston Med. Ctr., 1995—. Chair bd. dirs. Haitian Am. Pub. Health Initiative, Boston; co-dir. Haitian Health Inst. at Boston Med. Ctr., 1996—. Bd. dirs. First Parish Brookline, Mass., 1995—. Finalist Rising Start Annual Show, 2003, Thayer Meml. Libr. Annual Quilt Show, 2003; named an Outstanding Physician of Yr., Howard Pilgrim Healthcare, 2000. Fellow: Mass. Med. Soc.; mem.: Soc. Gen. Internal Medicine, Alpha Omega Assn. Unitarian Universalist. Avocations: reading, music, theater, cooking, hiking. Office: Boston Med Ctr 91 E Concord St Fl 2 Boston MA 02118-2335 Office Phone: 617-638-7428.

DAVIDS, JODY, pharmaceutical and medical supply executive; BBA, MBA, San Jose State U. Computer programmer Apple Computer, Inc., Cupertino, Calif., 1982, various positions, including Asia Pacific divsn., dir. supply chain reengring.; dir. tech. svcs. Nike, Inc., Beaverton, Oreg., 1997—2000; sr v.p. IT pharm. distbn. bus. unit Cardinal Health, Inc., Dublin, Ohio, 2000—03, exec. v.p., chief info. officer, 2003—. Office: Cardinal Health Inc 7000 Cardinal Pl Dublin OH 43017*

DAVIDSHOFER, CLAIRE H. college instructor; b. Bouake, Cote d'Ivoire, Oct. 1, 1946; BA in English, U. d'Aix-en-Provence, France, 1968; MA in Am. Lit., U. d'Aix-en-Provence, France, 1969. H.s. tchr. MSAD #1/Presque Isle High, Presque Isle, Maine, 1969—73, 1974—78, 1979—80; coll. instr. U. Maine at Presque Isle, 1980—. Office: Univ of Maine at Preque Isle 181 Main St Presque Isle ME 04769

DAVIDSON, ANNE STOWELL, lawyer; b. Rye, N.Y., Feb. 24, 1949; d. Robert Harold and Anne (Breeding) D. BA magna cum laude, Smith Coll., 1971; JD cum laude, George Washington U., 1974. Bar: D.C. 1975, U.S. Dist. Ct. D.C. 1975, U.S. Ct. Appeals (D.C. cir.) 1975, U.S. Supreme Ct. 1980. Asst. chief counsel drugs and enforcement FDA, Rockville, Md.,

1974-78; counsel Abbott Labs., North Chicago, Ill., 1978-79, U.S. Pharm. Ops. Schering-Plough Corp., Kenilworth, N.J., 1979-83; sr. counsel Sandoz Pharms. Corp., Inc., East Hanover, N.J., 1983-86, v.p., assoc. gen. counsel, 1987-96; assoc. gen. counsel Novartis Pharms. Corp., East Hanover, 1997—. Contbr. articles to profl. jours. Trustee N.J. Pops Orch. Recipient Dawes prize Smith Coll., 1971. Mem. ABA, Pharm. Mfrs. Assn., Food and Drug Law Inst., Non-prescription Drug Mfrs. Assn. (govt. affairs com.), Smith Coll. Club (pres. 1981-82). Republican. Presbyterian. Office: Novartis Pharms Corp 59 State Route 10 East Hanover NJ 07936-1005

DAVIDSON, BONNIE JEAN, gymnastics educator, sports management consultant; b. Rockford, Ill., Nov. 19, 1941; d. Edward V. and Pauline Mae (Dubbs) Welliver; m. Glenn Duane Davidson, June 4, 1960 (dec. Oct. 1993); children: Lori Davidson Aamodt, Wendy Davidson Seerup; m. James A. Johnson, Sept. 15, 2001. Student, Rockford Coll., 1965, Rock Valley Coll., Rockford, 1969-77. Founder, owner, dir. Gymnastic Acad. Rockford, 1977-95; pres., dir., owner Springbrook, Ltd., swim and tennis club, Rockford, 1986-95. Rep. trampoline and tumbling com. AAU, 1989-99—; coach nat. and world champion athetes; mgr., judge, head del. U.S.A. gynmastics teams, 1980—; speaker, lectr., clinician in field.; mem. organizing coms. world championships, also others, 1982-99 Contbr. World Book Ency. Bd. dirs. U.S. Olympic Com., 1995—, U.S.A. Gymnastics, 1991—; instr. ARC. Named one of Most Interesting People, Rockford mag., 1987; named to USA Gymnastics Hall of Fame, 2003; recipient YWCA Janet Lynn Sports award, 1996. Mem. Internat. Fedn. Trampoline and Tumbling (internat. judge, mem. tech. com. 1986-99—, del. to congress 1976-86, hon. lifetime mem. 1998), Internat. Fedn. Sport Acrobats (internat. judge), U.S.A. Trampoline and Tumbling Assn. (hon. life; nat. tumbling chairperson 1980-88, advisor 1988-99—, Coach of Yr. award 1980, Outsanding Contbn. to the Sport award 1987, 96, Master of Sport award 1989), U.S. Sports Acrobatics Fedn. (hon. life; v.p. 1984-95), Nat. Judges Assn. (exec. dir.). Republican. Avocations: skiing, boating, bicycling, birdwatching, flying. E-mail: davidsonbj@aol.com., davidsonbj@insightbb.com.

DAVIDSON, DONETTA, state official; County clk. and recorder Bent County, Colo., 1978-86; dir. of elections State of Colo., 1986-94; county clerk and recorder Arapahoe County, Colo., 1994-99; sec. of state State of Colo., 1999—. Republican. Office: Office of Sec of State Denver Post Bldg 1560 Broadway Ste 200 Denver CO 80202-5169 E-mail: sos.admin1@sos.state.co.us.

DAVIDSON, JANET G. telecommunications industry executive; b. Short Hills, N.J. B in Physics, Lehigh U.; M in Elec. Engring., Ga. Tech., 1979; M in Computer Sci. Joined Bell Labs., 1978; various positions Bell Labs. & Lucent Techs.; v.p. access product mgmt. Lucent Techs., Murray Hill, NJ, 1996—98, v.p. access, switching and access solutions, 1998, v.p. N.Am. emerging markets, 1999, pres. Access Networks divsn. InterNetworking Sys., 2000, group pres. InterNetworking Sys., 2000, group pres. Network Ops. Software, 2000, group pres. InterNetworking Sys. and Switching Solutions, 2001, pres. Integrated Network Solutions, 2001—. Named one of Top 50 Most Powerful Women in Bus., Fortune 500, 2001; named to Acad. Women Achievers, YWCA, N.Y.C., 1999; recipient Women Enabling Sci. and Tech. award, Working Women Found., 2001. Office: Lucent Techs 600 Mountain Ave Murray Hill NJ 07974

DAVIDSON, JEANNIE, costume designer; b. San Francisco, Mar. 21, 1938; d. Willis H. and Dorothy J. (Starks) Rich; children from previous marriage: David L. Schultz (dec. Jan. 1996), Mark P. Schultz, Seana Davidson, Michael Davidson; m. Bryan N. St. Germain, June 14, 1980. BA, Stanford (Calif.) U., 1961, postgrad., 1965-68. Resident costume designer Oreg. Shakespearean Festival, Ashland, 1969-91; owner, designer Ravenna Fabric Studio, Inc., Medford, Oreg., 1994—. Mfr. custom ch. vestments and hand-dyed wearable art. Designer over 150 prodns. including all 37 of Shakespeare's plays. Recipient numerous awards for excellence in costume design. Mem. U.S. Inst. for Theatre Tech., Phi Beta Kappa. Avocations: fabric design, painting, writing. E-mail: jsg@mind.net.

DAVIDSON, JO ANN, former state legislator; children: Julie, Jenifer. Mem. Ohio Ho. of Reps., Columbus, 1981—2001, minority whip, speaker, 1995—2001; Interim Dir. Ohio Dept. of Jobs and Family Services, 2001; owner JAD & Assoc. Government Cons. Firm, 2001. Mem. fin., ethics and stds. and rules coms., house speaker, minority leader, mem. joint com. on mental retardation and devel. disabilities. Mem. Reynoldsburg (Ohio) City Coun., 1968-77; former vice chmn. Ohio Turnpike Commn.; trustee Franklin U., U. Findlay, Ohio; mem. Columbus Area Women's Polit. Caucus. Named Legislator of Yr., Nat. Rep. Legislators Assn., 1991; named to Ohio Women's Hall of Fame, 1991. Mem. Oho C. of C. (v.p. spl. programs), Rotary. Republican. Home: 6639 Forrester Way Reynoldsburg OH 43068-4315 Office: 37 W Broad St Ste 970 Columbus OH 43215-0001

DAVIDSON, JOY ELAINE, mezzo-soprano; b. Ft. Collins, Colo., Aug. 18, 1940; d. Clarence Wayne and Jessie Ellen (Bogue) Ferguson; m. Robert Scott Davidson, Aug. 9, 1959; children: Lisa Beth, Robert Scott II, Jeremy Fergus, Bonnie Kathleen, Jordan Christian. BA, Occidental Coll., Los Angeles, 1959; postgrad., Fla. State U., 1961-64. Dir. vocal/opera dept. New World Sch. Arts Coll./Conservatory Divsn., Miami, Fla., 1992—2002; ret., 2001. Robert A. Carrie Mastronardi endowed prof., 1995—. Debut 1965 with Miami Opera; has performed with Met. Opera, opera cos. throughout U.S. and Can., La Scala, Vienna State Opera, Bayerische State Opera, Lyons (France) Opera, Welsh Opera, Florence (Italy) Opera, Torino (Italy) Opera. (recipient Gold medal Internat. Competition Young Opera Singers, Sofia, Bulgaria 1969), Rio de Janeiro; performed with numerous orchs. including N.Y. Philharm., Los Angeles Philharm., Boston Orch., Pitts. Orch., Columbus (Ohio) Orch.; rec. artist. Named Outstanding Miami Artist at Orange Bowl; recipient Mastronardi endowed chair, 1995, NISOD award for tchg. excellence, 1996, Roberta Rymer Balfe award Fla. Grand Opera. Mem. PEO, United Meth. Women, Sigma Alpha Iota, Zeta Tau Zeta. Methodist. Avocations: swimming, camping, cycling, church activities. Home: 413 Walnut St #5032 Green Cove Springs FL 32043 E-mail: davidsons123@hotmail.com.

DAVIDSON, JUDI, public relations executive; b. Bklyn., June 06; d. Samuel Lewis and Esther (Friedman) Swiller; m. Gordon Davidson, Sept. 21, 1958; children: Adam, Rachel Davidson-Janger. BA, Vassar Coll., 1957. Writer Charm Mag., N.Y.C., 1957-59; press agt. various theatrical prodns., N.Y.C., 1959-64; prin. Judi Davidson Publicity, L.A., 1972-84; ptnr. Davidson & Choy Publicity, L.A., 1984—. Bd. dirs. Bet Tzedek Ho. Justice, L.A., 1989—99, Blue Ribbon, L.A., 1990—93, L.A. Music Ctr., 1995—99. Mem.: Pub. Rels. Soc. Am. (bd. dirs. 1997—98), Entertainment Publicists Profl. Soc. (bd. dirs. 1996—99), Assn. Theatrical Press Agts. and Mgrs. (bd. dirs. 1996—97). Democrat. Jewish. Avocations: cooking, gardening, reading. Office: Davidson and Choy Publicity 4311 Wilshire Blvd Los Angeles CA 90010-3708

DAVIDSON, KAREN LEA, music educator; b. Hutchinson, Kans., Oct. 2, 1952; d. Scott and Frances (Hill) Hester; m. Byron Davidson, Nov. 24, 1987; children: Jillian, Ariel Marie. BA, Ft. Hays State U., 1974; MA in Sch. Counseling, Wichita State U., 1989, cert., 1999. Cert. K-12 vocal/instrumental music tchr. Kans., sch. counselor K-9 Kans., sch. counselor 10-12 Kans. Vocal music tchr. 1-8 Unified Sch. Dist. #504, Oswego, Kans., 1974—75, Unified Sch. Dist. #396, Douglass, Kans., 1975—78; elem. sch. music tchr. pre K-6 Unified Sch. Dist. #394, Rose Hill, Kans., 1975—. Rep. committeewoman, Wichita, 1998—2003. Mem.: NEA (assoc.), Rose Hill Edn. Assn. (negotiator, spokesperson 1984—2001, v.p. 1995—97, pres. 1997—2000, tchr. adv. 1999—), Music Educators Nat. Conf. Republican. Methodist. Avocations: horseback riding, YMCA. Office: Unified Sch Dist #394 104 N Rose Hill Rd Rose Hill KS 67133

DAVIDSON, KAREN SUE, computer software designer; b. Chgo., July 24, 1950; d. Woodrow Wilson and Velma Louise (Dickinson) D. BS in Comm., U. Ill., 1972; MBA, De Paul U., 1977. Microsoft cert. profl. News prodr. Sta. WIND, Westinghouse Broadcasting Co., Chgo., 1973-75; mktg. rep. divsn. data processing IBM, Chgo., 1977-80, process industry specialist, 1980, industry applications specialist White Plains, N.Y., 1981-83; sr. sales rep. Wang Labs., Chgo., 1983-84; ptnr. KDA-K Davidson & Assocs., Centralia, Ill., 1984-88; pres. KDA Software Inc., Centralia, 1988—. Instr. Belleville (Ill.) Area Coll., 1992, mem. office and tech. adv. bd., 1998—, chair, 1999—; vis. lectr. So. Ill. U., Carbondale, 1994; mem. rev. bd. State of Ill. Pvt. Enterprise. Author/designer software programs; contbr. articles to profl. pubs. State of Ill. Small Bus. Adv. Bd., Internat. Trade/Export Rep., 1990-93; WordPerfect cert. resource instr. WordPerfect Corp., 1991—; apptd. to State of Ill. Small Bus. 100, 1996. Named Outstanding Working Woman of Ill. Fedn. Bus. & Profl. Women's Clubs, 1990. Mem. Soc. Profl. Journalists, Ind. Computer Cons. Assn. (pres. St. Louis chpt. 1998-99), Ill. Software Assn., Chgo. High Tech. Assn. Assn. St. Louis Info. Sys. Trainers (v.p. 1988), Centralia Cultural Soc., Inventors' Assn. St. Louis, Greater Centralia C. of C. (bd. dirs. 1990-93, good will amb. 1990), Rotary, Zeta Tau Alpha. Presbyterian. Office: KDA Software Inc PO Box 1163 315 E 3rd St Centralia IL 62801-3919

DAVIDSON, MARY ANN, information technology executive; BSME, U. Va.; MBA, U. Pa., Wharton Sch. Commd. officer U.S. Navy Civil Engineer Corps; various positions in product devel. and security Oracle Corp., 1988—2001, chief security officer, 2001—. Ed. review bd. Secure Business Quarterly; testified before Congress on info. security four times. Recipient Navy Achievement Medal, U.S. Navy Civil Engr. Corps. Mem.: Info. Tech. Info. Security Analysis Ctr. (bd. dirs.). Avocations: outdoors, surfing, skiing. Office: Oracle Corp 500 Oracle Pkwy Redwood City CA 94065*

DAVIDSON, NANCY BRACHMAN, artist, educator; b. Chgo., Nov. 3, 1943; d. Philip and Jane (Blanch) Brachman; m. Donald Davidson, July 15, 1961 (div. 1977); 1 child, Lance A.; m. Greg Drasler, June 15, 1985. BEd, Northeastern Ill. U., 1965; BA, U. Ill., Chgo., 1972, MFA, Sch. Art Inst., Chgo., 1975. Vis. asst. prof. U. Ill., Champaign, 1977-79, Williams Coll., Williamstown, Mass., 1980-84; vis. artist, assoc. prof. SUNY, Purchase, 1984—. One-woman shows include Berkshire Mus., Pittsfield, Mass., 1982, Marianne Deson Gallery, Chgo., 1978, 1981, 1983, 1988, Richard Anderson Gallery, N.Y.C., 1991, 1993, 1995, Shoshana Wayne Gallery, Santa Monica, Calif., 1997, Nova Sin Gallery, Prague, Czech Republic, 1998, Neuberger Mus., Purchase, N.Y., 1998, Dorsky Gallery, N.Y.C., Inst. Contemporary Art, U. Pa., Phila., 1999, Vedanta Gallery, Chgo., 2000, The Contemporary Arts Ctr., Cin., 2001, Robert Miller Gallery, N.Y.C., 2001, Regina Gouger Miller Gallery, Carnegie Mellon U., Pitts., 2002, exhibited in group shows at Albright-Knox Gallery, Buffalo, 1980, Mus. Contemporary Art Chgo., 1984, Art Inst. Chgo., 1974, 1978, 1979, Bad Girls West-UCLA, 1994, Corcoran Biennial, 2002. Fellow NEA, 1978, Mass. Coun. Arts, 1981, Ford Found., 1978; Mass. Coun. Arts grantee, 1984, Anonymous Was a Woman grantee, 1997, Pollock-Krasner grantee, 2001. Home: 137 Duane St Apt 4W New York NY 10013-3892

DAVIDSON, SARAH J. health services administrator; b. North Little Rock, Ark., Nov. 26, 1947; d. Earnest Jefferson and Alice Sanders D.; 1 child, DeAngelo Kinard. BA in Sociology, Howard U., 1970; MA in Edn., Catholic U., 1971. Elem. sch. tchr. DC Pub. Schs., 1971-72; rsch. assoc. Pres. Nat. Adv. Coun. on Edn., Washington, 1972-74; sr. info. specialist Howard U. Children's Ctr., Washington, 1974-75; head start edn. dir. Wash., DC Parent Child Ctr., Washington, 1975-77; dir. office of field svcs. Child Devel. Assn. Consortium, Washington, 1977-78; child devel. assoc. Enterprise for New Directions, Washington, 1978-79; state coord. children's health DC Dept. of Health Medicaid, Washington, 1979—. Child devel. assn. rep. Coun. for Early Childhood Recognition, Wash., 1976—; proposal reader Dept. Edn., 1979; review panelist Dept. Edn., 1986. Assoc. editor: (nat. newsletter) Parent Preschool Press, 1981. Bd. sec. Nat. Fed. Black Women Bus. Owners, 1992—; pub. rels. coord. Coun. of 100 Black Repubs., 1986-91. Named Outstanding Arkansan Living in DC Arkansas Dem. Gazette, Little Rock, 1993; participant Nat. Security Seminar, U.S. Army War Coll., Carlisle, Pa., 1994. Mem. Nat. Black Child Devel. Inst., Delta Sigma Theta. Republican. Baptist. Avocations: writing, reading, tennis, travel. Office: Dist Government 825 N Capitol St NE Washington DC 20002-4210 E-mail: sdavidson.doh@dcgov.org.

DAVIDSON, SUSAN BETTINA, editor, writer; b. Wolverhampton, Eng., June 6, 1942; came to U.S., 1957; d. Basil Thomas and Hedi (Liebermann) Goldfarb; m. Daniel Ira Davidson, Mar. 13, 1966; 1 child, Jill. Student, Nat. U. Mex., Mexico City, 1962; BA in Langs., Ohio State U., 1963; postgrad., New Sch. for Social Rsch., 1963, Columbia U., 1963—65, Alliance Française, Paris, 1968, George Washington U., 1995—97. Editl. asst. Harcourt, Brace & Co., N.Y.C., 1963-64; asst. to prodr. ABC-News, N.Y.C., 1964-65; prodn. asst. UPI, N.Y.C., 1965-66; news prodr. Ind. TV News, Washington, 1966-69; freelance prodr. London Weekend TV, Washington, 1969-75; arts editor Washingtonian mag., Washington, 1977—. Contbg. editor Women's Work, 1972—75; Washington editor Changing Homes, 1985—87; nominator Helen Hayes Awards, Washington, 1983—99, Ortho 21st Century Women Awards; judge Washington Craft Show, 1996; reader Fund for New Am. Plays, Washington, 1997, Washington, 98, Washington, 99, Washington, 2000, Washington, 01; reviewer, rschr., editor books and plays. Contbr. articles to newspapers and various publs., including N.Y. Times, Washington Post, L.A. Times, Stagebill, Nat. Geographic Traveler, Savvy Traveler, Art & Antiques. Panelist Prince George's County Arts Awards, Washington, 1992, Mayor's Arts Awards, Washington, 1993, Mayor's Arts Edn. Awards, Washington, 1996, USIA Selection Bd., Washington, 1997; vol. Women's Health Initiative. Democrat. Jewish. Avocations: theater, reading, music, dance, travel. Home: 2900 Brandywine St NW Washington DC 20008-2138 Office: Washingtonian Mag 1828 L St NW Ste 200 Washington DC 20036-5169 Office Phone: 202-296-3600. E-mail: sdavidson@washingtonian.com., s.davidson@starpower.net.

DAVIDSON, SUZANNE MOURON, lawyer; b. Oxford, Miss., Aug. 5, 1963; d. Bertrand D. Jr. and Barbara Jean (Baca) Mouron; m. Garrison H. Davidson III, Dec. 12, 1987; children: Jane Harrington, Catherine Stender. AB in English Lit., U. Calif., 1985, JD, 1988. Assoc. Peterson, Ross, L.A., 1988-89; asst. litigation counsel Ticor Title Ins., Rosemead, Calif., 1989-91; corp. counsel Forest Lawn, Glendale, Calif., 1991—. Deacon San Marino Cmty. Ch., 1995-98, elder, 2000-2003; bd. dirs. San Marino Cmty. Ch. Nursery Sch., 1995-2000; mem. Jr. League, Pasadena, Calif., 1989—, Nat. Charity League Jrs. (San Marino), 2002—, bd. dirs, 2003—. Mem. Calif. State Bar Assn., L.A. County Bar Assn., Pasadena Athletic Club, Salt Air Club, Chi Omega (chmn. nat. area exch info. 1988-95). Presbyterian. Office: Forest Lawn Co Legal Dept 1712 S Glendale Ave Glendale CA 91205-3320

DAVIDSON, THYRA, artist, sculptor; b. Bklyn., Oct. 15, 1926; m. George Wexler, Jan. 4, 1947; children: Andrew, James, Daniel. Student, Bklyn. Coll., 1943-45, Nat. Acad. Art, 1943-45, Bklyn. Mus. Art Sch., 1946, New Sch. for Social Rsch., 1946. Adj. lectr. Bklyn. Coll., 1973-76, Dutchess C.C., Poughkeepsie, N.Y., 1974, SUNY, New Paltz, 1975-76; graphic artist Hudson Valley Newspapers, Highland, N.Y. One person shows include Schoelkopf Gallery, N.Y.C., 1967, Simon's Rock Coll., Great Barrington, Mass., 1972, Dutchess C.C., 1973, First St. Gallery, N.Y.C., 1972, 75, 79, 82, Mus. of Hudson Highlands, Cornwall, N.Y., 1982, Company Hill Gallery, Kingston, N.Y., 1986; exhibited in group shows at Davis-Long Gallery, N.Y.C., 1977, Schoelkopf Gallery, 1977, 86, Albany (N.Y.) Art Inst., 1973, 84, FAR Gallery, N.Y.C., 1974, SOHO Ctr., N.Y.C., 1976, First St. Gallery, 1984, Chesterwood, Stockbridge, Mass., 1989, Mountain Gallery, New Paltz, 1990, Knowles Gallery, La Jolla, Calif., 1991, 92, Connoisseur Gallery, Rhinebeck, N.Y., 1993, Park West Gallery, Kingston, N.Y., 1995, Watermark-Cargo Gallery, Kingston, N.Y., 1995; exhbns. include Lyric Gallery, Highland, N.Y., 1998, Dorsky Mus., New Paltz, 2002; represented in permanent collections at Albany Inst. History and Art, SUNY, Albany Art Gallery. Avocation: gardening. Home: 180 Portuese Ln New Paltz NY 12561-3053

DAVIDSON-MEYER, NOREEN HANNA, financial services company executive; b. Hartford, Conn., Sept. 13, 1950; d. Morris A. and Allene Sullivan (Gotis) Bezzini; m. Herbert L. Davidson, May 27, 1983 (div. 1991); m. Bradley P. Meyer, Nov. 20, 1998; 1 child, Stephanie Wells. BA, Stephens Coll., 1972. Senate intern U.S. Senator Thomas Dodd, Washington, 1970; legis. aide Mo. State Senate, Jefferson City, 1972; liaison econ. stabilization and White House Exec. Office of Pres., Washington, 1972-74; senate staff U.S. Senator Jacob Javitts, Washington, 1974; dir. legislation Nat. Assn. Plumbing, Heating and Cooling Contractors, Washington, 1975-77, Am. Aviation Found., Washington, 1977-81; mgr. nat. sales Nat. Standards, Bethesda, Md., 1981-84; v.p. Great Lakes Investment, Reston, Va., 1984-91; dir., v.p., br. mgr. Meyers, Pollack, Robbins, Inc., McLean, 1991-97; v.p. First Union Securities, Leesburg, Va., 1998-2000, Morgan Stanley Dean Witter, 2000—. Mem. adv. bd. Heritage Fin. Corp., McLean, 1988-90. Author, editor Fixed Income newsletter Fin. Mgmt. Group, 1990, 91, Legislative News newsletter Nat. Assn. Plumbing, Heating and Cooling Contractors, 1976. Mem. exec. staff Presdl. Inaugral for Reagan, Washington, 1984, mem. staff, 1980, Presdl. Inaugral for Nixon, Washington, 1972; mem. PTA. Recipient cert. of appreciation Presdl. Inaugral Com., 1984. Mem. Nat. Assn. Security Dealers (cert. series 7, 63, 24), Hunt Club Assn. (fin. advisor), Stephens Coll. Alumni, Hunt Club Girls Club (pres. 1988-89), Rotary Internat. Republican. Roman Catholic. Avocations: contract bridge, golf, sailing, travel, skiing. Office: Morgan Stanley Dean Witter 45985 Regal Plz Ste 160 Sterling VA 20165-6144

DAVIES, ALMA (ALMA ROSITA), producer, playwright, lyricist, composer, designer, sculptor; b. Bloemfontein, South Africa; d. Walter David Davies and Elizabeth (Van der Kar); m. Lee Kaye, Dec. 9, 1956 (dec. Jan. 1967); children: Walter Ian Kaye, Elena-Beth Kaye; m. Edwin William Williams, June 22, 1985 (dec. Mar. 1997). Tchr., choreographer Spanish dance, ballet Sch. Dance Arts, Carnegie Hall, N.Y.C. Toured as solo dancer, actress with Manhattan Opera Co. in Desert Song, with Ana Maria Spanish Dance co.; soloist Dances of Spain, Am. Mus. Natural History, N.Y.C., featured soloist Jose Greco Dance Co., Washington; soloist, choreographer Jacobs Pillow Dance Festival, Mass., Radio City Music Hall; soloist Am. Youth Ballet, N.Y.C.; guest artist, soloist, choreographer Syracuse (N.Y.) Philharm. Orch.; soloist, dancer, actress Voice of Firestone NBC-TV, N.Y.C.; guest artist Simmons Cruise Concert-S.S. Olympia, Caribbean Seas; exhbns. for sculpted 3-D pictures include Schumacher Fabrics, N.Y.C., Warner Bros., Hollywood others; puppeteer Rose Rivero Charity Showcase, N.Y.C.; jewelry designer, manufacturer; author, composer, dir., prodr. musicals: Princessa, Moon Holiday, Little Lord, Dorinmore, Lord Fauntleroy, (TV film) Clash of Wills; author: I Blow Myself Away, Memoirs of a Remarkable Diva; composer, United In Spirit, We'll Never Forget. Recipient First prize for costume design Beaux Arts Ball, N.Y., Internat. Beaux Arts Ball, N.Y.. Mem. ASCAP, Dramatists Guild, The Drama League, Comml. Theatre Inst., Internat. Platform Assn. Avocations: sculpture, scenic design, costume design. Home: 2857 S Paradise Rd #1001 Las Vegas NV 89109

DAVIES, GRACE LUCILLE, real estate educator; b. Providence, Apr. 6, 1926; d. Leonard Cerulle and Eleanor De Prete; m. David John Davies, Feb. 8, 1948; children: Mary Ellen, David L., Pamela, Amy. AA, Long Beach City Coll., 1946; BA, U. Calif., Berkeley, 1948; MA, Calif. State U., Long Beach, 1965. Gen. elem. credential Calif., life elem. credential Calif., elem. sch. adminstr. credential Calif., life elem. sch. adminstr. Calif. Elem. educator ABC Unified Sch. Dist., Artesia, Calif., 1956—85, MGM coord., 1960—70, bilingual coord., 1960—70, asst. prin., 1970—80; real estate, bus., investment D. Davies & Assoc., Long Beach, Calif., 1985—. Clk. Long Beach (Calif.) Election Bd., 1990—; mem., vol. Long Beach City Campaign, 1998. Mem.: Calif. Ret. Tchrs. Assn. (legis. chair 1985—, pres. 2000—), Apt. Mgmt. Assn., Delta Kappa Gamma (v.p., pres., Golden Rose award 1996), Pi Lambda Theta (treas., v.p., pres., Outstanding Contbn. Edn. award 1996). Avocations: travel, reading, theater, camping, music. Home: 6215 Parima St Long Beach CA 90803

DAVIES, HELEN C. microbiology educator; Mem. faculty U. Pa. Sch. Medicine, Phila., prof. microbiology, former assoc. dean for students and housestaff affairs, now acad. coord. dept. microbiology, organizer, adminstrn. health edn. program, 1968—. Recipient mentor award for lifetime achievement AAAS, 1998. Mem. Assn. for Women in Sci. (nat. pres.). Achievements include research on biochemistry of prokaryotic organisms, with special focus on bacterial energetics, electron transfer and cytochrome system. Office: U Pa Med Ctr Dept Microbiol 201 A Johnson Pavilion Philadelphia PA 19104-6076 Fax: 215-573-9068. E-mail: daviesh@mail.med.upenn.edu.

DAVIES, LAURA, professional golfer; b. Coventry, Eng., Oct. 5, 1963; Profl. golfer LPGA, 1987—. Mem. European Solheim Cup Team, 1990, 92, 94, 96, 98. 15 career victories, including Circle K LPGA Tucson Open, 1988, Jamie Farr Toledo Classic, 1988, Lady Keystone Open, 1989, Inamori Classic, 1991, McDonald's Championship, 1993, Standard Register Ping, 1994, 95, 96, 97, Sara Lee Classic, 1994, Chick-fil-a Charity Championship, 1995, Star Bank LPGA Classic, 1996, LPGA Tour Championship, 1996, L.A. Womeen's Championship, 2000, The Philips Invitational, 2000; recipient Rolex Player of Yr. award, 1996; named Mem. Brit. Empire, Queen Elizabeth II, 1988. Office: care LPGA 100 International Golf Dr Daytona Beach FL 32124-1082

DAVIES, LOIS A. educational association administrator, adult education educator; b. Lakeview, Oreg., Dec. 15, 1955; d. Delbert M. and Alice L. Milholland; m. Paul E. Davies; 1 child, Jon ; children: Jessica, Luke, Eric. MEd, Lesley Coll., Cambridge, Mass., 1998. Cert. tchr. Wash., 1979. Coord. gifted edn. N. Ctrl. Ednl. Svc. Dist., Wenatchee, Wash., 1999—2002; dir. Adult Consumer Edn. Telecomms. N. Ctrl. Ednl. Svc. Dist., Wenatchee, Wash., 2001—02; sch. improvement facilitator Sadrington Office Supt. Pub. Instructing, 2003—06; schl. improvement specialist N. Ctrl. Ednl. Svc. Dist., 2002—. Coord. acad. events N.Ctrl. ESD, Wenatchee, Wash., 1998—2002. Editor: (monthly publ.) Gift Rap, 2001—. Founding bd. mem. Orondo (Wash.) Dollars for Scholars, 1993—99; exchange tchr. in China Orondo Sch. Dist., Zibo, China, 1995; mem. team Wenatchee (Wash.) Relay for Life, 2000—02. Mem.: ASCD, Nat. Assn. Gifted Children, Ctr. for Exceptional Children, WERA, WASCD (Conference Chair/Board member 1999—2000), NCCE. Office: North Central ESD PO Box 1847640 Mission Street Wenatchee WA 98807-1847 Office Fax: 509-662-9027. Business E-Mail: loisd@ncesd.org.

DAVIES, TERRI LYNN, pharmaceutical sales representative; b. Detroit, Dec. 30, 1966; d. Gary James and Nadine (West) McMullen; m. Rodney Charles Davies, Aug. 25, 1991. BS in Econs., Mich. State U., 1989; MA in Edn., Chestnut Hill Coll., 1992. Pharm. sales Parke-Davis, Phila., 1990-91, Abbott Labs., Camden, N.J., 1991-92, Wyeth-Ayerst, San Diego, 1992-97; pharm. sales rep. Profl. Detailing, Inc., Phila., 1998—.

DAVIES-MCNAIR, JANE, retired educational consultant; b. Topeka, May 21, 1922; m. K. Robert Davies, Aug. 27, 1949; m. John D. McNair June 4, 1989. BE, Nat. Louis U. (formerly Nat. Coll. Edn.), Evanston, Ill., 1944, ME, 1958; postgrad., Columbia U., Ill. State U., Nat. Coll. Edn. Tchr. various schs., Oak Park, Ill., Hillside, N.J., Elmont, N.Y., 1944-58, Sch. Dist. Dwight, Ill., [illegible]; asst. county supt. Livingston County, Pontiac, Ill., 1969-72; project cons., supr., trainer early prevention of sch. failure K W Curriculum Svc. Office, Peotone, Ill., 1972-77; freelance cons., speaker early childhood edn. Ill., 1977-80; ret., 1980. Author: Resource Guide for Developing Pre-Academic, Learning Skills and Other guides for the Early Prevention of School Failure, The Gifted and the Biligual and Migrant Programs. Mem.: DAR, ASCD, AAUW, Childhood Edn. Internat., Internat. Platform Assn., Ill. Edn. Assn. (life and ret. life com.), Ill. Ret. Tchrs. Assn. (dir. region II), Assn. Childhood Edn. (early childhood), Nat. Assn. Edn. Young Children, State Evaluation Team, U.S. Holocause Meml. Mus. Circle of Life (charter supporting mem.), Nat. Mus. Am. Indian (charter), Smithsonian Mus. Am. India, Nat. Soc. Sons and Daus. of Pilgrims, Am. Assn. Ret. Persons, Gen. Fedn. Women's Club, Delta Kappa Gamma, Order Eastern Star.

DAVILA, ELISA, language educator, literature educator; b. Libano, Tolima, Colombia, May 29, 1944; arrived in U.S., 1974; d. Rafael Antonio Davilla and Amalia Parra; m. Bruce Roger Smith, Oct. 17, 1973 (div. 1981). BA, U. Pedagogica Nat., Bogota, Colombia, 1966; MA, U. Pacific, 1972; PhD, U. Calif., Santa Barbara, 1983. Asst. prof. U. Valle, Cali, Colombia, 1968-73; rschr. Inst. Colombiano de Pedagogia, Bogota, Colombia, 1973-73; assoc. U. Calif., Santa Barbara, 1974-78, 78-80; instr. W. Tex. State U., Canyon, Tex., 1978-80, Def. Lang. Inst., Calif., 1981-82; prof. SUNY, New Paltz, 1999—, chair fgn. langs., 1990-94, 96—, dir. Latin Am. studies, 1991—. Vis. lectr. U. Calif., Santa Cruz, 1982—; reader, evaluator N.J. Dept. Higher Edn., Princeton, 1987—89; reader Ednl. Testing Svc., Princeton, 1987—89; acad. dir. Spanish Immersion Inst. Bd. Edn. and Office Mental Health, N.Y.C., Albany, 1987—90; project dir. title VI grant undergraduate internat. and fgn. lang. program U.S. Dept. Edn., 2000—. Recipient Disting. Tchr. award, Alumni Assn., 1996; scholar Heloise Brainer, 1964, Latin-Am. Scholarship Program, Am. Univs. Mem.: MLA, Latin-Am. Studies Assn., Am. Assn. Tchrs. Spanish and Portuguese. Avocations: creative writing, poetry. Home: PO Box 423 Hurley NY 12443-0423 Fax: (845) 257-3512. Office Phone: 845-257-3489. E-mail: davilae@newpaltz.edu.

DAVILA, REBECCA TOBER, physical education educator; b. Dallas, Apr. 10, 1942; d. Antonio M. and Aurora Tober (Benavides) D. BS, Tex. Woman's U., 1964, MA, 1969; Cert. in Mgmt. and Adminstrn., North Tex. State U., 1983. Cert. health edn. specialist. Camp counselor Heart O the Hills, Kerrville, Tex., 1962-67; tchr. San Antonio Ind. Sch. Dist., 1964-67; grad. asst. Tex. Woman's U., Denton, 1967-68; tchr., dept. chair Lewisville (Tex.) Ind. Sch. Dist., 1968—. Vol. Am. Heart Assn., Lewisville, 1980s, 90s, Kidney Found., Lewisville, 1980s, Christian Comty. Action, Lewisville, 1980s, 90s. Mem. Tex. Assn. for Health, Phys. Edn., Recreation and Dance (v.p. health divsn. 1994, workshop dir. region XI 1990, 91, 92, membership chair 1992-93, pres. 1999, Health Tchr. of Yr. 1991), Tex. State Tchrs. Assn. (pres. local chpt. 1984-85), Delta Kappa Gamma (pres. local chpt. 1988-90, Achievement award 1989). Democrat. Roman Catholic. Avocations: gardening, reading, fishing, golf, refinishing antique furnisher.

DAVION, ETHEL JOHNSON, school system administrator, curriculum specialist; b. Raleigh, N.C., July 21, 1948; d. John Arthur and Ethel Mae (Morgan) Johnson; 1 child, Laura Christal. BA, Livingstone Coll., 1971; MA, Glassboro (N.J.) State U., 1983. Cert. tchr., prin., supr., N.J. Sr. English tchr. Camden (N.J.) Bd. Edn., 1977-81; tchr. of English Westfield (N.J.) Bd. Edn., 1982-85, Union County Regional Dist. 1, Berkeley Heights, N.J., 1981-82, Hillside (N.J.) Bd. Edn., 1985-87; supr. English, lang. arts Irvington (N.J.) Bd. Edn., 1987-92; vice prin. Frank H. Morrell H.S., Irvington, N.J., 1992-95, prin., 1996—; asst. supt. Acad. Affairs, 2001—. Writer, researcher Collegiate Rsch. Systems, Camden, 1976-77; participant profl. devel. programs Harvard U., 1989, Notre Dame U., 1990; participate Oxford Univ. Roundtable, Oxford, Eng., 2002. Author: A Tutorial Approach to Teaching English, 1983, Teachers' Resource Manual, 1987; contbr. articles to jours. Bd. dirs., sec. Emmanuel Tabernacle, Linden, N.J., 1988. Recipient Resolution Town Coun. Irvington, 1992. Fellow N.J. Edn. Assn., Nat. Coun. Tchrs. English; mem. Linden Scholarship Guild (sec. 1985—), Assn. for Supervision and Curriculum Devel., Prin. and Suprs. Assn., Irvington Adminstrs. Assn. (treas.), Internat. Platform Assn., Good Samaritans Club, Obsidian Civic Club (Westfield, historian 1985—), Diversity 2000 Coun. (sec. 1997—). Democrat. Baptist.

DAVIS, ADA ROMAINE, nursing educator; b. Cumberland, Md., June 7, 1929; d. Louis Berge and Ethel Lucy (Johnson) Romaine; m. John Francis Davis, Aug. 1, 1953; children: Kevin Murray, Karen Evans-Romaine, William Romaine. Diploma in nursing, Kings County Hosp., Bklyn., 1949; BSN, U. Md., Balt., 1973, MS, 1974; PhD, U. Md., College Park, 1979, postdoctoral student, 1985-89. Cert. editor in life scis. Asst. prof. grad. program U. Md., Balt., 1974-79; chmn. dept. nursing Coll. of Notre Dame, Balt., 1979-82; assoc. dean grad. program Georgetown U. Sch. Nursing, Washington, 1982-87; nurse cons. Health Resources and Svcs. Adminstrn., Rockville, Md., 1987-93, HHS, USPHS, Bur. Health Profls., Rockville, 1987-93; assoc. prof. and dir. undergrad. program Johns Hopkins U. Sch. of Nursing, Balt., 1993-98, prof. emeritus, 1998—. Reviewer Choice, ALA; evaluator methodology and findings for rsch. studies; hist./med. biographer; prof., editor Johns Hopkins U. Sch. Nursing, 2003—. Author: John Gibbon and His Heart-Lung Machine, 1992, Advanced Practice Nurses: Education, Roles and Trends, 1997; editor: Ency. of Home Care for the Elderly, 1995; contbr. articles to nursing jours.; assoc. editor Hopkins InteliHealth, Johns Hopkins Family Health Guide, 1999, Johns Hopkins Insider, 1998. Recipient excellent performance award HRSA; rsch. grantee U. Md. Grad. Sch. Mem. AAAS, ANA (cert. adult nurse practitioner), Soc. for Neoplatonic Studies, Nat. Orgn. Nurse Practitioner Faculties, Am. Acad. Nurse Practitioners, Am. Pub. Health Assn., Gerontol. Soc. Am., Nat. Trust for Hist. Preservation, Am. Geriat. Soc., Md. History of Medicine Soc., Soc. for the Social History of Medicine (Oxford U.), N.Y. Acad. Scis., Coun. Sci. Editors, Sigma Theta Tau. E-mail: adarom@earthlink.net.

DAVIS, ALISON B. company executive; BA, Douglas Coll. Pres. Davis-Hays & Co. Inc., 1984—. Office: Davis & Company 11 Harristown Rd Glen Rock NJ 07452-3319

DAVIS, ANDREA BARBARA, language educator; b. Vienna, Sept. 13, 1960; arrived in U.S., 1981; d. Gerhard Richard Rudolf Wiedermann and Elisabeth Johanna Maria Pichler; m. Adam Brooke Davis, Aug. 26, 1983; children: Naomi, Clement, Paul, August. BA in German and French, U. Mich., 1983; MA in French, U. Mo., 1987. Tchr. German Pioneer H.S., Ann Arbor, Mich., 1983; instr. German and French Truman State U., Kirksville, Mo., 1991—. Tutor English, Freiburg, Germany, 1990—91. Active Mary Immaculate Ch., Kirksville, 1991—. Mem.: Phi Beta Kappa (treas. 2002—03, resident mem.). Roman Catholic. Avocations: hiking, reading, movies. Home: 804 E Illinois St Kirksville MO 63501 Office: Truman State U MC 311 Normal/Franklin St Kirksville MO 63501

DAVIS, ANN CALDWELL, history educator; b. Alliance, Ohio, June 3, 1925; d. Arthur Trescott and Jane Caldwell D. BA, Western Reserve U., 1947; MA, Columbia U., 1955; PhD, Columbia Pacific U., 1987. Cert. tchr., Ill., Ohio. Pres. The Clio Found. Inc., Gulfport, Fla., 1955—; tchr. Supr. Child Enterprise, Evanston, Ill., 1956-60; human rels. coun. U. Chgo., 1957-58, asst., 1961; tchr., dept. chair Evanston Pub. Schs., 1961-85; project English Northwestern U., Evanston, 1963-64. Cons. Dist. #65 Sch., Evanston, 1985-90. Presenter, author: (speech) Do-it-Yourself Help For The Top 10%, 1964, The Non-Graded School, 1976, Social Studies Reading & Reference Skills, 1979; author: (video) U.S. & Ill. Constn., 1986. Vol. Meals ON Wheels, Treasure Island, Fla., 1990-94, Pinellas County Schs., Fla., 1991, steering com. St. Petersburg, Fla., 1995, health care chair Older Women's [illegible] Assn. of U. Women, Orgn. of Am. Historians, Ill. & Nat. Edn. Assn. Office: The Clio Found Inc PO Box 5110 Gulfport FL 33737-5110 E-mail: cliofdn@aol.com.

DAVIS, ANN RICHARDSON, artist, sculptor, book dealer, writer; b. Savannah, Ga., Nov. 27, 1942; d. Charles Clifford and Nancy Lee (Powell) Richardson; m. Charles Hamilton Davis, July 13, 1962; children: Rhett, Christy Lee Davis Heatherly. Grad. high sch., Savannah. Represented by Sea Griffin Gallery & Books, Darien, Ga., 1997—. Author: (juvenile) The Tale of the Altamaha "Monster," 1997, Richardson and Allied Lines of the Southeast, 2000, McIntosh County Georgia Marriage and Deeds Reference Books, fiction) Heaven In A Hole In The Ground and Other Earthy Stories, 2003; one-woman shows include Parthenon Galleries, Nashville, 1984, Tenn. Art League Galleries, Nashville, 1983; represented in permanent collections First Am. Bank, Nashville, Blue Grass Reg. Libr., Columbia, Tenn. Mem. arts com. Ashantilly Ctr., Darien, 1997. Recipient 2d place for sculpture Exhbn. South, Tuscumbia, Ala., 1981, Tallix Foundry award Pen and Brush Club, N.Y.C., 1982, hon. mention for painting and sculpture Tenn. All-State Exhbn., Nashville, 1982, 83, award Chautauqua, N.Y., 1986. Mem. Acad. Artists Assn. (coun. Am. Artists award 1984). Avocation: genealogical and historical research. Office: Sea Griffin Gallery & Books 206 Ft King George Dr Darien GA 31305

DAVIS, ANNA JANE RIPLEY, elementary school educator; b. Uhrichsville, Ohio, Sept. 7, 1931; d. Emmet Frank and Lillie Hazel (Kinsey) Ripley; m. H. Joe Davis, Mar. 16, 1951; children: Alan Joe, Kendal Jay. Assoc., Asbury Coll., 1953; BS with honors, Kent State U., 1962, MEd with honors, 1978, postgrad., 1980—94; student, Richmond Coll., London U., St. Andrews U., Dundee U., Cambridge U., U. Paris, U. Rome, Ohio U. Cert. elem. tchr., Ohio. Tchr. Kenston Schs., Chagrin Falls, Ohio, 1953-55, 58-62, Firestone Rubber Plantation, Harbel, Liberia, West Africa, 1962-64, Newbury (Ohio) Schs., 1964-65, Orange Schs., Pepper Pike, Ohio, 1965-99. Chaperone, counselor Am. Inst. for Fgn. Study, British Isles and Europe, summers 1968-81. Author children's books. Active Kenston PTA, Chagrin Falls and Pepper Pike PTA, Am. Field Svc., Chagrin Falls, Geauga County Personal Growth Com. for workshops; bd. dirs. Friends Geauga County Pub. Libr.; bookmobile project vol. traveling libr. Geauga County Pub. Libr. for Amish Schs., traveling libr., 1994—; elem. sch. tutor, 1998—; vol. ARC, 1955—, Food Pantry and Clothing for Needy, Kiwanis, bookmobile projects Geauga County Pub. Lib. Friends; mem. edn. com., libr., home care, Care Bears com., Prayer Chain, Sunday sch. com., Sunday Sch., membership com., Pepper Pike Garfield Meml. United Meth. Ch. Mem. NEA (life), ASCD, Ohio Edn. Assn., N.E. Ohio Tchrs. Assn., Orange Tchrs. Assn. Avocations: family, travel, cycling, hiking, reading, writing.

DAVIS, ANNE LOUISE, music educator; b. Alton, Ill., Feb. 6, 1952; d. Robert William and Bette Ann Schrimpf; m. S. Wiley Davis, Sept. 9, 1972; children: Katherine Anne, Andrew Wiley, John Wiley. B in Music Edn., So. Ill. U., 1974. Cert. spl. music K-12 State of Ill. Elem. music tchr. Ferguson/Florissant (Mo.) Sch. Dist., 1974—76; pvt. piano tchr. Alton, 1976—82; elem. music tchr. Evang. Elem. Sch., Godfrey, Ill., 1984—92; choral dir. Alton H.S., 1995—. Vol. Alton Cmty. Unity Sch. No. 11, Alton, 1992—95; sponsor Encounter Youth Group, Alton, 1993—2000, 2003; leader Stephen Ministry Program, Alton, 2000—03. Named Women of Yr., Main St. Meth., Alton; named one of Women of Dist., YWCA, Alton. Mem.: Am. Choral Dirs. Assn., Music Educators Nat. Conv., Ill. Music Educators Assn. Methodist. Home: 4407 Bluffdale Ct Godfrey IL 62035 Office: Alton High Sch 220 College Ave Alton IL 62002 E-mail: ADavis252@aol.com.

DAVIS, BARBARA JEAN SIEMENS, service company executive; b. Louisville, Ky., Nov. 12, 1931; d. Gustav Adolph Siemens and Alberta Jeanette (McAdams) Simon; m. Donald Elmore Davis, Aug. 4, 1950 (dec. 1995); children: Dale Montgomery, Gale Sue Davis Beaty. Mktg. and personnel mgr. Kelly Svcs., Louisville, 1962-65; tchr. asst. TV English Jefferson County Schs., Louisville, 1965-70; wedding and floral designer Wedding Ring, Louisville, 1971-73; owner, designer Nook Flowers and Gifts, Memphis, 1973-75; cons. pub. rels. Dixie Rents, Memphis, 1975-79; div. mgr. pres. Party Concepts, Inc., Memphis, 1980-88; pres., CEO, 1993-94; pres. Siemens-Davis Assoc., Cordova, Tenn., 1989-91; cons. Leon Loard, 1992; facilitator/trainer Motivational Concepts Internat., 1993; cons. Interim Personnel, Montgomery, Ala., 1994-95; chmn., bd. dirs. sdb Greenscape, Fla., 1996-99; dir., sec., treas. Cobblestone Walk, Coral Springs, Fla., 1996—2003. Author: Wedding Workshop Brides Work Book, 1984, Wedding Party Consultants Certification Program, 1984, Wedding Directors and Party Consultant Program, 1995. Mem. Am. Rental Assn. (mem. party coun. 1985-88), Nat. Assn. Wedding Cons. (pres. 1983-87), NAFE (dir. Memphis network), Internat. Platform Assn., Sales and Mktg. Execs. Republican. Presbyterian.

DAVIS, BARBARA M(AE), librarian; b. Cranston, R.I., Dec. 23, 1926; d. Harrie S. and Marguerite M. (Cameron) D. BS in Chemistry, Brown U., 1948; MS in Libr. Sci., Simmons Coll., 1956. Asst. rsch. libr. R&D Dept. Cabot Corp., Cambridge, Mass., 1948-57, rsch. libr., 1957-61, Billerica (Mass.) Rsch. Ctr., Cambridge, Mass., 1961-68, head tech. info. svcs., 1968-81, mgr. tech. info. ctr., 1981-87. Dir. Cabot Boston Credit Union, 1956-59, 61-64, 72-78, clk., 1961-64, 72-77, v.p., 1977-78. Vol. Lexington Coun. Aging, 1990-2000, Lexington Hist. Soc., 1991-2003; chmn. rsch. com. Greater Boston Young Rep. Club, 1959-61; treas. Women's Rep. Club Lexington, 1988-2001; mem. Lexington Rep. Town Com., 1993-98; del. Mass. Rep. Conv., 1994, 98. Mem. Am. Chem. Soc. (sec. div. chem. lit. 1961-65), Simmons Coll. Libr. Sch. Alumni (v.p. 1965-66). Home: 37 Drummer Boy Way Lexington MA 02420-1222

DAVIS, BARBARA SNELL, education educator; b. Painesville, Ohio, Feb. 21, 1929; d. Roy Addison and Mabelle Irene (Denning) Snell; children: Beth Ann Davis Schnorf, James L., Polly Denning Davis Spaeth. BS, Kent State U., 1951; MA, Lake Erie Coll., 1981; postgrad., Cleve. State U., 1982-83. Cert. reading specialist, elem. prin., Ohio. Dir. publicity Lake Erie Coll., Painesville, 1954-59; tchr. Mentor (Ohio) Exempted Village Sch. Dist., 1972-86, prin., 1986-97; prof., field dir. Lake Erie Coll., 1997—. Contbr. articles to profl. jours. Former trustee Mentor United Meth. Ch. Mem. Delta Kappa Gamma (pres. 1982-84), Phi Delta Kappa (pres. 1992-93), Theta Sigma Phi (charter). Home: 7293 Beechwood Dr Mentor OH 44060-6305 Office: 326 College Hall Lake Erie Coll Painesville OH 44077 E-mail: beachbumbarb@aol.com.

DAVIS, BERTHA LANE, psychiatric nursing educator; b. Mobile, Ala., Sept. 3, 1950; d. James W. and Marie (Woods) Lane; m. George Willard Davis, June 26, 1976; 1 child, Geoffrey Jerard. BSN, Tuskegee U., 1972; MEd in Counseling, Coppin State Coll., 1975; MS in Psychiat. Nursing, U. Md., 1977; PhD in Higher Edn., Wash. State U., 1983. Charge nurse med.-surg. dept. Provident Hosp., Balt., 1972-73; instr. Helene Fuld Sch. Nursing, Provident Hosp., Balt., 1973-77; asst. prof. Coppin State Coll., Balt., 1977-78, assoc. prof., 1983-84; predoctoral lectr. Intercollegiate Ctr. Nursing Edn., Spokane, 1981-83; prof. Sch. Nursing Hampton (Va.) U., 1984-85, chair dept. grad. nursing, 1985-91, prof., dean Sch. Nursing, 1991-97, prof. Sch. Nursing, 1997—, asst. dean for rsch., 2001—. Office: Hampton U Sch Nursing Hampton VA 23668 E-mail: bertha.davis@hamptonu.edu.

DAVIS, BETH, elementary school educator; b. Collins, Miss., Sept. 24, 1940; d. Richard Alexandria McDonald and Vaudril Lindell Taylor; m. James Stancel Davis, Oct. 28, 1960; children: James Stancel II, Tracy Lynd Davis-Blomgrist. AS, Brevard C.C., Cocoa, Fla., 1973; BS in [illegible] Rollins Coll., 1975; M in Adminstrn., Nova U., 1978. Tchr. Golfview Elem., Rockledge, Fla., 1975-93, 97—, Saturn Elem., Cocoa, Fla., 1993-96, Riverview Elem., Titusville, Fla., 1996-97. Tchr. TK-1 workshops Brevard County Sch., Rockledge; spkr. Fla. Reading Assn., Orlando, 1985, U. Ctrl. Fla., 1994. City coun. candidate City of Rockledge. Mem. Elks (Cocoa, Lady Elk of Yr. lodge 1532, 1st Woman Exalted Ruler 1999), Delta Kappa Gamma, Phi Delta Kappa. Republican. Presbyterian. Avocations: decorating, flower garden, college football, fishing, golf. Home: 1675 Fiske Blvd Apt 242J Rockledge FL 32955-2500

DAVIS, BETTY BOURBONIA, real estate investment executive; b. Ft. Bayard, N.Mex., Mar. 12, 1931; d. John Alexander and Ora M. (Caudill) Bourbonia; children: Janice Cox Anderson, Elizabeth Ora Cox. BS in Elem. Edn., U. N.Mex., 1954. Gen. ptnr. BJD Realty Co., Albuquerque, 1977—. Bd. dirs. Albuquerque Opera Build, 1977-79, 81-83, 85-87, membership co-chair, 1977-78; mem. Friends of Art, 1978-85, Friends of Little Theatre, 1973-85, Mus. N.Mex. Found.; mem. grand exec. com. N.Mex. Internat. Order of Rainbow for Girls; mem. Hodgin Hall Preservation com. U. N.Mex.; sustainer Albuquerque Jr. League. Recipient Matrix award for journalism Jr. League. Mem. Albuquerque Mus. Assn., N.Mex. His. Soc., N.Mex. Symphony Guild, Jr. League Albuquerque (sustaining mem.), Alumni Assn. N.Mex., Albuquerque Petroleum Club, Albuquerque Knife and Fork Club, Internat. Platform Assn., Order Eastern Star, Order Rainbow for Girls (past grand worth adv. N.Mex., past mother adv. Friendship Assembly 50, state exec. com. N.Mex. Order 1986-2002, chair pub. rels. com., co-chair gen. arrangements com. 1990-97), Tanoan Country Club, Las Amapolis Club, Mt. Vernon Ladies Assn., Albuquerque Guild Santa Fe Opera, Alpha Chi Omega (chpt. advisor, bldg. corp. 1962-77). Republican. Methodist. Home: 9505 Augusta Ave NE Albuquerque NM 87111-5820

DAVIS, BETTYE JEAN, academic administrator, state official; b. Homer, La., May 17, 1938; d. Dan and Rosylind (Daniel) Ivory; m. Troy J. Davis, Jan. 21, 1959; children: Anthony Benard, Sonja Davis Wade. Cert. nursing, St. Anthony's, 1961; BSW, Grambling State U., 1971; postgrad., U. Alaska, 1972. Psychiat. nurse Alaska Psychiat. Inst., 1967-70; asst. dir. San Bernardino (Calif.) YWCA, 1971-72; child care specialist DFYS Anchorage, 1975-80, soc. worker, 1980-82, foster care coordinator, 1982-87; dir. Alaska Black Leadership Edn. Program, 1979-82; exec. dir. Anchorage Sch. Bd., 1982-89; mem. Alaska Legislature, 1990—. Chair Children's Caucus Alaska Legis., 1992—. Pres. Anchorage Sch. Bd., 1986-87; bd. dirs. Blacks in Govt., 1980-82, March of Dimes, 1983-85, Anchorage chpt. YWCA, 1989-90, Winning with Stronger Edn. Com., 1991, Alaska 2000, Anchorage Ctr. for Families, 1992—, active Anchorage chpt. of NAACP, bd. dirs. 1978-82. Toll fellow Henry Toll Fellowship Program, 1992; named Woman of Yr., Alaska Colored Women's Club, 1981, Child Care Worker of Yr., Alaska Foster Parent Assn., 1983, Social Worker of Yr., Nat. Foster Parents Assn., 1983, Outstanding Bd. Mem, Assn. Alaska Sch. Bds., 1990,; recipient Outstanding Achievement in Edn. award Alaska Colored Women's Club, 1985, Outstanding Women in Edn. award Zeta Phi Beta, 1985, Boardsmanship award Assn. Alaska Sch. Bds., 1989, Woman of Achievement award YWCA, 1991, Outstanding Leadership award Calif. Assembly, 1992. Mem. LWV, Nat. Sch. Bd. Assn., Nat. Caucus of Black Sch. Bd. Mems. (bd. dirs. 1986-87), Alaska Black Caucus (chair 1984—), Alaska Women's Polit. Caucus, Alaska Black Leadership Conf. (pres. 1976-80), Alaska Women Lobby (treas.), Nat. Caucus of Black State Legis. (chair region 12, 1994—), Women Legislators Lobby, Women's Action for New Directions, North to Future Bus. and Prof. Women (pres. 1978-79, 83), Delta Sigma Theta (Alaska chpt. pres. 1978-80). Clubs: North to Future Bus. and Profl. Women (past pres.). Democrat. Baptist. Avocations: cooking, Scrabble, collecting stamps, coins and matches, reading. Home: 2240 Foxhall Dr Anchorage AK 99504-3350

DAVIS, BEVERLY WATTS, government agency administrator; BA in Econs., Polit. Sci. and Social Sci., Trinity U., San Antonio; postgrad., Webster U., Jeffersonville, Ind. Statewide coord. Texans' War on Drugs, 1988; cons., then dir. cmty. health Travis County Tex. Health Dept.; exec. dir. San Antonio Fighting Back Anti-Drug Cmty. Coalition; sr. v.p. United Way of San Antonio and Bexar County; dir. Ctr. for Substance Abuse Prevention, Substance Abuse and Mental Health Svcs. Adminstrn., Rockville, Md., 2003—. Mem. Minority-and Women-Owned Bus. Commn. Named Vol. of the Yr., Pres. Bill Clinton, 1997, Advocate of the Yr., Palmer Drug Abuse Program, Yellow Rose of Tex., Gov. of Tex., Outstanding Minority Bus. Owner, Greater Austin C. of C., 1985; named to San Antonio Women's Hall of Fame, 1998; recipient Dir.'s Award for Cmty. Leadership, FBI, Commendation award, U.S. Dept. Justice, Comdr.'s Award for Outstanding Leadership, Dept. Def., Vol. award, Gov. Tex., Award for Neighborhood Action, Tex. Atty. Gen.'s Office, Outstanding Citizen Advocate award, Nat. Crime Prevention Coun. Office: Substance Abuse and Mental Health Svc Adminstrn Rm 12-105 Parklawn Bldg 5600 Fishers Ln Rockville MD 20857*

DAVIS, BONNIE CHRISTELL, judge; b. Petersburg, Va., July 13, 1949; d. Robert Madison and Margaret Elizabeth (Collier) D. BA, Longwood Coll., 1971; JD, U. Richmond, 1980. Bar: Va. 1980, U.S. Dist. Ct. (ea. dist.) Va. 1980, U.S. Ct. Appeals (4th cir.) 1982. Tchr. Chesterfield County Schs., Chesterfield, Va., 1971-77; pvt. practice, Chesterfield, 1980-83; asst. commonwealth atty. Chesterfield County, 1983-93; judge Juvenile and Domestic Rels. Ct. for 12th Jud. Dist. Va., 1993—. Adviser Youth Svcs. Commn., Chesterfield, 1983-93; cons. Task Force on Child Abuse, 1983-93, Met. Richmond Multi-Discipline Team on Spouse Abuse, 1983-93, Va. Dept. of Children for handbook "Step by Step Through the Juvenile Justice System in Virginia, 1988; mem. nat. adv. com. for prodn. on missing and runaway children Theatre IV; mem. adv. group to set stds. and tng. for Guardians Ad Litem, Supreme Ct. Va., 1994; chmn. jud. adminstrn. com. Jud. Conf. Va. for Dist. Cts., 1995-97, 2001-2003; mem. state adv. com. for CASA and children's Justice Act, 1998-2002. Co-author: Juvenile Law and Practice in Virginia, 1994. Mem. Chesterfield County Pub. Schs. Task Force on Core Values, 1999. Mem.: Chesterfield-Colonial Heights Bar Assn., Met. Richmond Women's Bar Assn., Va. Trial Lawyers Assn., Va. Bar Assn., Va. State Bar (bd. govs. family law sect. 1997—2001), State-Fed. Jud. Coun. Va. Home: 415 Lyons Ave Colonial Heights VA 23834-3154 Office: Chesterfield Juvenile and Domestic Rels Dist Ct 7000 Lucy Corr Blvd Chesterfield VA 23832-6717 Office Phone: 804-751-4115.

DAVIS, CAROL, educational association administrator, educator; English tchr.; English curriculum specialist Terrebonne Parish Pub. Sch.; pres. La. Assn. Educators, Baton Rouge, 2000—. Trainer instrn. and profl. devel. La. Assn. Educators; field site coord. Nicholls State U. Mem.: Terrebonne Assn. Educators (pres.), La. Assn. Educators (v.p., bd. dirs., chair program and budget com., co-chair strategic planning com.). Office: La Assn Educators PO Box 479 1755 Nicholson Dr Baton Rouge LA 70802

DAVIS, CAROL LYN, administrative assistant; b. West Palm Beach, Fla., Oct. 22, 1953; d. Robert Lee and Barbara Jean (Collett) D. BFA in Studio Arts, Tex. Christian U., Ft. Worth, 1975; MA in Am. Studies, Tex. Christian U., 1977. R&D product line designer Am. Handicrafts/Merribee Needlearts, Ft. Worth, 1977-81; ceramics/china sales cons. Dillard's, Ft. Worth, 1981-82; dept. mgr. Stripling-Cox, Ft. Worth, 1982-83; freelance ceramic and string art designer, 1982-83; rschr. with phase III, IV, V hist. sites inventory Tarrant County (Tex.) for Hist Preservation Coun., 1983-86, Page, Anderson & Turnbull, Inc., San Francisco, 1983-86; rschr. Tarrant County Greater Ft. Worth Housing Starts Tex. Update, Inc., 1987-94; rschr. M/PF Rsch., Inc., Dallas, 1989-94; sales adminstrv. asst. Trail Ridge,

Bellaire Park, Summer Creek, Hulen Bend subdiv., Ft. Worth, 1994-2001, Summer Creek Ranch subdiv. Perry Homes, A Joint Venture, Ft. Worth, 2001—. Author pamphlets in field. Mem. mgmt. adv. panel Chem. Week, 1981; alternative precinct election judge Dem. Party, 1994—; mem. Tarrant County Dem. Party; mem. Arts Coun. Ft. Worth and Tarrant County. Mem. Royal Over-Seas League (London). Democrat. Episcopalian. Home: 7800 Garza Ave Fort Worth TX 76116-7717

DAVIS, CARYLON LEE, mortgage company executive, real estate broker; d. Palmus Dupree and Alice Enolia Strickland Dupree; m. Willie Davis, June 2, 1973. AA, L.A. City Coll., 1966; student, L.A. State Coll., 1967—69. Clk.-typist Gold's Furniture and Appliances, L.A., 1960—63, Dept. Def., L.A., 1963—69, sec., 1969—72, adminstrv. asst., 1972—78, exec. sec., 1983—85; office mgr. Dept. Air Force, L.A., 1978—83; bus. owner, pres. Kari's Profl. Svcs., Carson, Calif., 1989—98; real estate agt. Frank Jones Realty, Carson, 1989—98; real estate broker Kari's Enterprises, Carson, 1998—; mortgage broker A Plus Fin., Carson, 1998—. Avocation: piano. Office: A Plus Fin 20715 S Avalon Blvd #300 Carson CA 90746 Office Phone: 310-538-5254. E-mail: carylon@sbcglobal.net.

DAVIS, CATHY, publishing executive; Sr. v.p. mktg. and devel., Ariz. Republic, Phoenix; pres. and CEO Tucson Newspapers, Tucson, 2000—. Office: Tucson Citizen Newspaper 1640 E River Rd Ste 201 Tucson AZ 85718-7645

DAVIS, CHARLOTTE MACLEAN, secondary school educator; b. Detroit, May 30, 1964; d. Peter Vincent MacLean and Dorothy May Denny; m. George Davis, Aug. 22, 1993; 1 child, Katherine. B in Bus. Adminstrn., Ea. Mich. U., 1987, bus. and tech. tchg. cert. Acct. Mexican Industries, Detroit, 1987—91; technician Decision Consultants, Troy, Mich., 1991—93; tchr. Ann Arbor (Mich.) Pub. Schs., 2001—03. Judge, mentor Bus. Profls. Am., Mich., 2001—03. Mem.: Mich. Edn. Assn., Kappa Delta Pi.

DAVIS, CLARICE MCDONALD, lawyer; b. New Orleans, Jan. 20, 1941; d. James A. and Helen J. (Ross) McDonald. BA, U. Tex., 1962, MA, 1964; JD, So. Meth. U., 1968. Bar: Tex. 1969, U.S. Dist. Ct. (no. dist.) Tex. 1970, U.S. Ct. Appeals (5th cir.) 1971, U.S. Supreme Ct. 1973. Law clk. to presiding justice U.S. Ct. Appeals (5th cir.), Dallas, 1969-71; ptnr. Akin, Gump, Strauss, Hauer & Feld, Dallas, 1971—. Comments editor Southwestern Law Jour., 1967-68; instr. Southern Methodist Univ. Sch. of Law, 1968-69. Bd. visitors So. Meth. U., Dallas, 1979-82, v.p. Law Sch. Alumni Adv. Coun., 1992, pres. 1993-94, mem. bd. govs., 1995-98. Avocations: photography, swimming, running, golf. Home: 6317 Churchill Way Dallas TX 75230-1807 Office: Akin Gump Strauss Hauer & Feld 1700 Pacific Ave Ste 4100 Dallas TX 75201-4675

DAVIS, CONNIE WATERS, public relations executive, marketing professional; b. Gainesville, Ga., July 3, 1948; d. Starling Randolph and Evelyn Jeanette (Bonds) Waters; m. John W. Davis Jr., Sept. 24, 1971; 1 child, John Christopher. AA, Gainesville Jr. Coll., 1968; BA in Human Resources Mgmt., Brenau U., 1988; postgrad., Student Evaluation Inst. of Washington, 1988, U. Ga., 1972-73, 85—. Project evaluator Model Cities Program, Gainesville, 1970-74; pers. dir. Lanier Pk. Hosp., Gainesville, 1977-79; asst. dir. Ga. Mountains Ctr., Gainesville, 1979-83; owner, CEO Models by Davis and Davis, Gainesville, 1979—; dir. pub. rels. and sales Ramada Hotel, Gainesville, 1985—; dir. corp. devel. Chestatee Regional Hosp. Dir. Fashion Works, Gainesville; pres. Davis Consulting; owner & pres. Tastefully & Properly Growing Up, 1998—; cons. pub. rels. and mktg; dir. of pub. rels. UP Corp. Deve. Wakkins Chiropractic. Prodr., writer, implementor Gracefully and Properly Growing Up; contbr. articles to mags. and newsletters; writer nat. poulty industry publ., 1990, 95. Publicity chmn. Cancer Soc., 1982, 83, 85; mem. Theatre Wings and Arts Coun.; bd. dirs., mem. mktg. com. Gainesville Jr. Coll., 1985—, trustee, 1995—; bd. dirs. ARC, 1978-79; co-chmn. Flag Com. for Olympics; bd. dirs. Greater-Hall C. of C., 2003—. Recipient Peach award Lions Club, 1979, Vol. award ARC, 1978, various modeling awards So. Models Assn., 1983, 2 Silver Shovel award 1993, 94, state vol. award, 1995; named Best Dressed Woman, Fashion Tour Group, 1984. Mem. Am. Heart Assn. (pres. 1995-96), Am. Lung Assn. (state bd. dirs., Vol. of Yr.), Greater Hall C. of C. (bd. dirs.), Gainesville C. of C., Gainesville Coll. Exec. Coun., Tourism and Conv. Bur. (chmn. 1983-84), N.E. Ga. Advt. Club, Pers. Adminstrs. Group, Ga. Hospitality and Travel Assn., Phoenix Soc., Greater Hall C. of C. (bd. dirs. 2003-), Rotary (cotillion dir. 1998—), Fashion Club (bd. dirs.). Avocations: exercising, skiing, boating, jogging, writing, music, arts. Home: 1214 Chestatee Rd Gainesville GA 30501-2816

DAVIS, DAISY SIDNEY, history educator; b. Matagorda County, Tex., Nov. 7, 1944; d. Alex C. and Alice M. (Edison) Sidney; m. John Dee Davis, Apr. 17, 1968; children: Anaca Michelle, Lowell Kent. BS, Bishop Coll., 1966; MS, East Tex. State U., 1971; MEd, Prairie View A&M, 1980; postgrad., U. Tex., Tex. A&M U. Cert. profl. lifetime secondary tchr., Tex.; mid-mgmt. adminstr. Tchr. Dallas pub. schs., 1966—, history dept chairperson, 1998—. Instr. Am. History El Centro Coll., 1991-98; adv. Am. history telecourse Dallas County C.C. dist. Coord. Get Out the Vote campaign, Dallas, 1972, 80, 84, 88, 92, 94, 96, 98, 2000, 02; sec., bd. trustees St. John Bapt. Ch., 1995-98; pres. The Amazons. Recipient Outstanding Tchr. award Dallas pub. schs., 1980, Jack Lowe award for ednl. excellence, 1982; Free Enterprise scholar So. Meth. U., 1987; Constl. fellow U. Dallas, 1988; named to Hall of Fame, Holmes Acad., 1979. Mem. NEA, Tex. State Tchrs. Assn., Classroom Tchrs. Dallas (faculty rep. 1971-77, 95—), Dallas County History Tchrs., Afro-Am. Daus. Republic of Tex. (founder), Top Ladies of Distinction, Zeta Phi Beta. Clubs: Jack & Jill Assocs., (Dallas) (rec. sec., v.p., chair Beautillion Ball, pres., Disting. Mother award, Nat. Committment award 1997). Democrat. Baptist. Home: 1302 Mill Stream Dr Dallas TX 75232-4604 Office Phone: 972-224-5675.

DAVIS, DEBRA GREER, music educator, pianist; b. Crocker, Mo., Mar. 4, 1956; d. Clifford Eugene and Emogene Telitha (Bullock) Greer; m. Rodney Neal Davis, July 1, 1978; children: Neal Stephen, Kimberly Reneé, Paul Andrew. B of Music Edn., S.E. Mo. State U., 1978. Cert. vocal music educator, K-12; cert. tchr., Mo., Iowa. Pvt. piano instr., Cape Girardeau, Mo., 1980-96; ch. pianist First Bapt. Ch., Cape Girardeau, Mo., 1987-90; music educator Cape Girardeau (Mo.) Pub. Sch., 1987-91, St. Augustine Sch., Kelso, Mo., 1991-93, Altenburg (Mo.) Pub. Sch., 1991-96; nursing libr. St. Francis Med. Ctr., Cape Girardeau, 1992-96; music educator Spickard (Mo.) R-2 Sch., 1996-97, Harrison R-IV Sch., Gilman City, Mo., 1997. Instr. Music Preparatory Program, S.E. Mo. State U., Cape Girardeau, 1990-92; dist. music try-out judge S.E. Mo. Dist. Music Educators, Cape Girardeau, 1992; sr. grant coord. disease prevention com. St. Francis Med. Ctr., Cape Girardeau, 1995-96, mem. healing environment, 1994-96. Accompanist: (cassette tape) Open Your Hear's Door-Charlene Peyton, 1994; editor: (booklet) Ann. Nursing Report-St. Francis Med. Ctr., 1995. Accompanist L.J. Schultz Mid. Sch. Choir, Cape Girardeau, 1992-93, Cape Girardeau H.S. Chamber Choir, 1993, Charles Clippard Elem. Sch. Choir, Cape Girardeau, 1996, Mo. Bapt. Conv., Cape Girardeau, 1994. Mem. Mo. Educators Assn., Music Educators Nat. Conf. Avocations: counted cross stitch, music.

DAVIS, DEIDRE, advocate; Dir. tech. asst. svc. U.S. Equal Opportunity, Washington, 1991-94; asst. sec. EEO & Civil Rights, Washington, 1999—. Office: EEO & Civil Rights 2201 C St NW Rm 4216 Washington DC 20520-0001

DAVIS, DIANN HOLMES, elementary school educator; b. N.Y.C., July 5, 1949; d. Henry F. and Pearl B. Holmes; m. Milton Davis, July 24, 1973; children: Milton, Keith, Madelyn. AA, N.Y. Tech. Coll., 1971; BS cum laude, Medgar Evers Coll., 1981; MA, Columbia U., 1994. Lic. reading and early childhood. Sci. tchr. JHS 166, IS 302 Future Day Care, Bklyn.; tchr. N.Y. Bd. Edn., Bklyn. Dance tchr. Faith Hope and Charity Day Care Ctrs.; parent rep. Start Smart; mem. Bklyn. (N.Y.) Reading Coun. Common Brs. Mem. Hall of Sci., Bklyn. Children's Museum, Assn. for Study of Curriculum Devel. Avocations: bicycle riding, ice skating, roller skating, dance, sewing.

DAVIS, DIANNE, music educator; b. Cleve. d. Lee Frederick and Mary Kate McQueen; 1 child from previous marriage, Travis. BS in Music Edn., Ky. State U., 1966. Cert. Ohio Bd. Edn. Vocal music tchr., Gary, Ind., 1966—68; vocal instr. Cleve. Music Sch. Settlement, 1977—82; dir. Sanaa Music Sch., Cleve., 1982—, Music Inc., Cleve., 1991—; vocal music tchr. East Cleveland City Schs., 1997—. Bd. dirs. The Cleve. Fine Arts Soc., 1995. Mem.: Ohio Edn. Assn., Music Educators Nat. Conf. Baptist. Avocations: cooking, designing, home remodeling, gardening, entertaining. Home: 24412 Emery Rd Cleveland OH 44128 Office: East Cleveland City Schs 15320 Euclid Ave East Cleveland OH 44112 E-mail: diannedavis@msn.com.

DAVIS, DIANNE LOUISE, marketing professional; b. Fresno, Calif., Mar. 1, 1940; d. Edwin L. and Adeline (Irvin) Gribble; m. John R. Jansen, June 11, 1960 (dec. 1966); children: Anthony, Julia; m. Edward Kent Davis, May 13, 1967 (div. 1977); 1 child, Edward Kent Jr. AA cum laude, Colo. Woman's Coll., 1957; student, Minot State Coll., 1968, Ottawa State U., 1987—. Cert. real estate broker, Mo., Kans; cert. resdl. specialist. Co-ptnr. Key Realty, Warrensburg, Mo., 1973-77; residential broker, assoc. DeLozier Realty, Warrensburg, 1977-78; owner, broker Old Drum Realty, Warrensburg, 1978-81; comml. broker, assoc. Varnum-Armstrong-Deeter, Overland Pk., Kans., 1981-82; residential broker, assoc. Kroh Bros. Realty, Overland Pk., 1982-83, Re/Max-Overland Pk., 1983-87, J. D. Reece Real Estate, Overland Pk., 1987-89; dir. mktg. Riss Lake Realty, Parkville, Mo., 1989-92; broker-salesperson JC Nichols Real Estate, 1992-93, Prudential Henry & Burrows Realtors, Overland Park, Kans., 1993—. Mem. Friends of Art Nelson Art Gallery, Kansas City, 1989-90, Friends of the Zoo, Kansas City, 1989-90. Mem. nat. Assn. Home Bldrs. (mem. Inst. Res. Mktg. designation), Met. Kansas City Home Bldrs. Assn. (sales and mktg. coun. 1989-92), Met. Kansas City Bd. Realtors (profl. standards com. 1990-92, chmn., 1992), Johnson County Bd. Realtors, Nat. Assn. Realtors (state del. 1991-92). Republican. Episcopalian. Avocations: painting, piano, travel, bridge, reading. Office: Prudential Henry & Burrows Realtors 8101 College Blvd Ste 100 Overland Park KS 66210-2671 Fax: 913-661-1468. E-mail: dianne@diannedavis.com.

DAVIS, DOLLY, religious organization administrator; Dir. Ladies Auxiliary of the Pentecostal Free Will Baptist Ch., Dunn, N.C. Office: Pentecostal Baptist Ch PO Box 1568 Dunn NC 28335-1568

DAVIS, DONNA LEE, small business owner, writer; b. Phila., May 19, 1945; d. Cecelia E. Davis. Studied, Mary Wash. Coll., Fredericksburg, Va., 1979—80. Ct. reporter USMC, Quantico, Va., 1973—99; owner Paradise Tree, Hartwood, Va., 2002—. Author: (poetry collection) Sheer Poetry, 1981. Recipient Meritorious Civilian Svc. Award, Dept. of Navy, 1999. Achievements include design of Paradise Tree Collectible Christian Ornaments. Office Phone: 540-752-5502.

DAVIS, DORIS JOHNSON, retired music educator; b. Yazoo City, Miss., Nov. 26, 1947; d. Floyd Lee and Bessie Louvenia Johnson B of Music Edn., Jackson State U., 1970; B of Music Therapy, Loyola U., 1973; M of Music Edn., William Carey Coll., 1975; postgrad. in Computer Tech. and Adult Edn., U. So. Miss. Cert. tchr. spl. subjects, Miss.; registered music therapist. Music tchr. Ft. Wayne (Ind.) Cmty. Schs., 1970-71; clin. intern, music therapy Cen. La. State Hosp., 1973; music therapist Ellisville (Miss.) State Sch., 1974-75; music tchr. Forrest County Sch. Sys., Hattiesburg, Miss., 1976-81; music instr. Prentiss (Miss.) Jr. Coll., 1975-76, 81-82; clk. typist Hattiesburg Pub. Libr., 1983-87; ch. musician Zion Chapel AME Ch., Hattiesburg, 1982-95, True Light Bapt. Ch., Hattiesburg, 1995-2000; music tchr. Hattiesburg Pub. Sch. Dist., 1987—2002; ret., 2002. Tchr. from home, Hattiesburg, 1998—. Vol. youth dept. Star Light Band, True Light Bapt. Ch., Hattiesburg, 1999—; mem. NAACP, Hattiesburg. Named to Outstanding Young Women of Am., 1979, 82; recipient scholarship So. Ill. U., 1965. Mem. Am. Fedn. Tchrs., Music Educators Nat. Conf. Democrat. Avocations: genealogy, computers, reading, walking. Home: 703 Myrtle St Hattiesburg MS 39401-4850 E-mail: djdavis@megagate.com.

DAVIS, DORIS ROSENBAUM (DEE DAVIS), artist, writer; b. N.Y.C., Nov. 7, 1919; d. Lewis Newman and Bella (Wretnikow) Rosenbaum; m. Lewis F. Davis, Aug. 13, 1940 (div. Dec. 1989); children: Laurie, Peter. BA, Sarah Lawrence Coll., 1941. Crafts instr. Cooper Hewitt Mus., N.Y.C., 1977-87, Pratt Inst., N.Y.C., 1988-92, Am. Craft Mus., N.Y.C., 1996—2004, Adventures in Crafts, N.Y.C., 1971—. Represented in permanent collections Cooper-Hewitt Mus., Am. Craft Mus., Mus. City of N.Y., Gracie Mansion, Sarah Lawrence Coll.; author: Découpage, 1995, Decoupage, A Practical Guide, 2000; co-author: Step by Step Découpage, 1976, The Découpage Gallery, 2001, The Victorian Scrap Gallery, 2003; contbr. articles on découpage, faux finishes, gilding to craft mags.; appeared in (TV series) Our Home, 1997—98, HGTV, 2001. Democrat. Jewish. Avocations: traveling abroad, visiting museums, galleries, reading, classical music. Office: Adventures in Crafts PO Box 6058 New York NY 10128-0001 Office Phone: 212-410-9793. E-mail: deecoupage@webtv.net.

DAVIS, DOROTHY SALISBURY, writer; b. Chgo., Apr. 26, 1916; d. Alfred Joseph and Margaret Jane (Greer) Salisbury; m. Harry Davis, Apr. 25, 1946 (dec.). AB, Barat Coll., Lake Forest, Ill., 1938. Mystery and hist. novelist, short story writer. Author: A Gentle Murderer, 1951, A Town of Masks, 1952, Men of No Property, 1956, Death of an Old Sinner, 1957, A Gentleman Called, 1958, The Evening of the Good Samaritan, 1961, Black Sheep, White Lamb, 1963, The Pale Betrayer, 1965, Enemy and Brother, 1967, God Speed The Night, 1968, Where the Dark Streets Go, 1969, Shock Wave, 1972, The Little Brothers, 1973, A Death in the Life, 1976, Scarlet Night, 1980, A Lullaby of Murder, 1984, Tales for a Stormy Night, 1985, The Habit of Fear, 1987, In the Still of the Night, 2000. Recipient Life Achievement award Bouchereon, 1989. Mem. Authors Guild, Mystery Writers of Am. (former pres., recipient Grand Master award 1985), Adams Roundtable. Home: PO Box 595 Palisades NY 10964-0595

DAVIS, ELBA LUCILA, veterans affairs nurse; b. San Juan, P.R., Feb. 25, 1945; d. Eladio Millan and Fidencia Walker; m. Joseph Edward Davis; children: Pauly Lucille, Joelyne Lucille. BS Mgmt., Columbian Union Coll., 1995; Cosmetology degree, Hollywood Acad., College Park, Md., 1988; Principles of Real Estates degree, Prince Georges C.C., Largo, Md., 2001. RN P.R., 1971. Student aide Columbus Hosp., N.Y.C., 1963—64; med. asst. Dr. Durruthy's Office, Bronx, NY, 1964; officinist P.R. Lottery, Rio Piedras, 1965—67; nurse Saint Martin's Hosp., Rio Piedras, PR, 1971, Carolina (P.R.) Mcpl. Hosp., 1971—76, Walter Reed Army Med. Ctr., Silver Spring, Md., 1976—80; cosmetologist Hair Cuttery, Wheaton, Md., 1993—93; nurse VA Med. Ctr., Washington, 1980—. Unit preceptor VA Med. Ctr., Washington, 1985—, chairperson edn. IV Team, 2001—, rep. safety com., 1995—96, rep. product com., 1995—96, rep. standard of care com., 1992—94, rep. quality assurance com., 1981—83, rep. scheduling com. IV Team, 2001—. Actor: (video prodn.) Annual Infection Control Review Video, 1997, (Video) VA Med. Ctr. BCMA Sys./Japanese Prodn., 2001; (films) The Replacements, 1999. Active Wild Life Defendant, Washington, 2001; RN Anthrax Hotline Channel 9 News on Anthrax, Washington, 2001. Mem.: Fed. Women's Program, Washington DC Nurses Assn. Mem. Seventh Day Adventist. Avocations: reading, bicycling, exercise, crafts, singing.

DAVIS, ELEANOR KAY, museum administrator; b. Rome, Nov. 10, 1935; d. Fred H. and Hazel (Turner) D.; m. Walter H. Dunn; children: Victoria Elaine Davis Reich, Gregory Brian. BA, Berry Coll., 1957; MA, Western Md. Coll., 1962; PhD, Ga. State U., 1975. Tchr. biology and physics Jonesboro High Sch., Clayton, Ga., 1957-58; tchr. physics and biology S.W. DeKalb High Sch., Decatur, Ga., 1958-59; tchr. biology, physics and phys. sci. Taneytown High Sch., Carroll County, Md., 1959-61; chmn. physics and biology Coosa High Sch., Rome, Ga., 1961-62, tchr. biology and physics, 1962-65; tchr. physics Briarcliff High Sch., Decatur, 1966-72; adminstrv. coord. Fernbank Sci. Ctr., Atlanta, 1972-84; exec. dir. Fernbank Mus. Natural History, Atlanta, 1984—, 1992—. Named Outstanding Mus. Profl., Ga. Assn. Mus. and Galleries, 1983, Woman of Achievement, Atlanta Bus. Women's Assn., 1984; mem. Acad. of Women Achievers, Atlanta YWCA, 1987. Mem. AAAS, AAUW, Ga. Assn. Mus. and Galleries, Am. Assn. Mus., Southeastern Mus. Conf. Office: Fernbank Mus Natural History 767 Clifton Rd NE Atlanta GA 30307-1221

DAVIS, ELENA DENISE, accountant; b. Rome, NY, June 24, 1953; d. Robert Frederick and Arlene Ruth (Fravor) Vrooman; m. Joseph E. Davis, Dec. 24, 1975 (div. Nov. 1988); children: JoAnna Lynn, Robert George, Crystal Leigh. AS, Jefferson C.C., Watertown, N.Y., 1975; BSBA, BS in Acctg., Orlando Coll., 1995; MBA in Acctg., Fla. Met. U., 2001. Staff acct., asst. mgr. Vrooman's Tire & Rd. Svc. Inc., Adams, N.Y., 1975-89; claim assoc. Hartford Ins., Maitland, Fla., 1989-97; acct. Raybob Plumbing Co. Inc., Orlando, 1997-98, Ctrl. Sweeping Svc., Inc., Winter Garden, Fla., 1998-99; staff acct., office mgr. Engelmeier Roofing & Sheet Metal Co., Inc., Lockhart, Fla., 1999—2003. Active Boy Scouts Am., Girl Scouts Am., PTA; Sunday sch. tchr. Methodist Ch., 1984-89; coord. Meth. Ch. Nursery. Home: PO Box 721 Ocoee FL 34761-0721

DAVIS, ELIZABETH HAWK, English language educator; b. Ft. Smith, Ark., Sept. 6, 1945; d. Arthur Carlton and Lolitta (Poe) Hawk; m. Leo Carson Davis, Aug. 31, 1960. BA, BM, U. Ark., 1967, MA, 1969; EdD, East Tex. State U., 1989. Classroom tchr. Springdale (Ark.) Pub. Schs., 1967-68; lectr. U. Md., Heidelberg, Fed. Republic Germany, 1978-79; from instr. to asst. prof. performing arts So. Ark. U., Magnolia, 1981-92, assoc. prof., 1992-96, chair English and fgn. langs. dept., 1993—, prof., 1996—. Contbr. articles to profl. jours. Organist First Presbyn. Ch., Magnolia, 1984—. Mem.: MLA, Ark. Philol. Assn., Nat. Coun. Tchrs. English, Phi Beta Kappa. Office: So Ark U PO Box 9356 Magnolia AR 71754-9356 E-mail: ehdavis@saumag.edu.

DAVIS, EMILY S. lawyer; m. Matthew I. Levine; 2 children. BA cum laude, U. Mass., 1978; JD cum laude, Boston Coll., 1982. Bar: Vt. 1982, N.H. 1990, U.S. Dist. Ct. Vt., U.S. Dist. Ct. N.H. Assoc. Downs, Rachlin & Martin, 1982-84; dep. state's atty. Windsor County State's Atty.'s Office, 1984-86; ptnr. Black Black & Davis, White River Junction, Vt., 1990-99, Davis & Steadman, White River Junction, Vt., 1999—. Adj. faculty Vt. Law Sch., 1991-94. Co-chair Citizens Justice Conf., 1998-99; mem. Commn. on the Future Vt.'s Justice Sys., 1998-99; bd. dirs. ProChoice Ct., 1982-92, co-chair, 1989-91. Mem. ABA (family law sect.), Vt. Bar Assn. (pres.-elect 1997-98, pres. 1998-99, bd. mgrs. 1993-2000, family law com. 1993—, long range/scope and program com. chair 1997-98, family ct. rev. com., chair rules and statutes subcom. 1997), Vt. Bar Found. (bd. dirs. 1995-98), New Eng. Bar Assn. (bd. dirs. 1995-98, 2000—), Vt. Trial Lawyers Assn. (bd. dirs. 1999—), Vt. Vol. Lawyers Project (Pro Bono Svc. award 1996), Windsor County Bar assn. (pres. 1991-92, v.p. 1989-91, sec.-treas. 1988-89), N.H. Bar Assn. Office: Davis & Steadman PO Box 796 White River Junction VT 05001-0796 E-mail: Davis@WhiteRiverLawyers.com.

DAVIS, ERLYNNE P. social work educator; b. Cleve., Oct. 16, 1925; d. Earle Vernon and Margaret Ruth (Sanders) Poindexter; m. Charles E. Davis Sr. (dec.); 1 child, Charles E. Jr. AB, Oberlin Coll., 1947; MS in Social Adminstrn., Western Res. U., 1950. Case worker Cuyahoga County Welfare Dept., Cleve., 1947-48, Family Svc. Assn., Cleve., 1950-54; supr. Cuyahoga County Welfare Dept., Cleve., 1956-63; instr. Sch. Applied Social Scis. Case Western Res. U., Cleve., 1963-66, asst. prof., 1966-69, assoc. prof. Sch. Applied Social Scis., 1969-87, assoc. prof. emerita Mandel Sch. Applied Social Scis., 1987—. Cons., staff devel. trainer, continuing edn. instr., spkr. in field, 1957-99. Bd. trustees Project Friendship, Cleve., 1986—91, pres., 1987, Youth Visions, 1991—95; bd. dirs. Met. YWCA, Cleve., 1987—92; vol. Ret. Srs. Vol. Program, 1989—2002; mem. adv. coun. Ret. Srs. Col. Program, Cleve., 1991—94, 1995—2001; active Cmty. Coun., 1993—95, Fairhhill Exec. Coun. Fairhill Ctr. for Aging, 1996—97; vol. Intergenerational Resource Ctr., 1994—99; mem. adv. coun. on sr. and adult svcs. Cuyahoga County, 1996—2000; coun. on older persons Fedn. Cmty. Planning, 1995—2001; mem. IRC Adv. Team, 1997—99; mem. African Am. adv. coun. Cleve. Alzheimer Assn., 1999—2002; mem. St. James African Meth. Episcopal Ch. Recipient Women of Distinction award, Women's Missionary Soc. African Meth. Episcopal Ch., 1983, Disting. Alumni award, Sch. Applied Social Scis. Case Western Res. U., 1987, 20th Ann. Founders Recognition, Ctr. for Human Svcs., Cleve., 1990, Ebony Rose Edn. award, Murtis Taylor Multi-Svc. Ctr., Cleve., 1990, Ebony Rose Honored award, 1995, Anna V. Brown Cmty. Svc. award, Dept. Social Work Cleve. State U., 1999. Mem.: NAACP (life), Alpha Kappa Alpha (Achievement award Alpha Omega chpt. 1963, 1974, 1999, Gold mem.).

DAVIS, EVELYN MARGUERITE BAILEY, artist, musician; d. Philip Edward and Della Jane (Morris) Bailey; m. James Harvey Davis, Sept. 22, 1946. Student pub. schs., Springfield; student art, Drury Coll.; piano, organ student of Charles Cordeal. Sec. Shea and Morris Monument Co., before 1946; past mem. sextet, soloist Sta. KGBX. Tchr. Bible, organist, pianist, vocal soloist, dir. youth choir Bible Bapt. Ch., Maplewood, Mo., 1956-69; pvt. instr. piano and organ, voice Croma Harp, Affton, Mo., 1960-71, St. Charles, Mo., 1971-83; Bible instr. 3d Bapt. Ch., St. Louis, 1948-54; pianist, soloist, tchr. Bible Temple Bapt. Ch., Kirkwood, Mo., 1969-71; asst. organist-pianist, vocal soloist, tchr. Bible, Bible Ch., Arnold, Mo., 1969; faculty St. Charles Bible Bapt. Christian Sch., 1976-77; organist for Dr. Jack Van Impe Crusades and Dr. Oliver B. Green Crusades; organist, pianist, soloist, Bible tchr., dir. youth orch., music arranger, floral arranger Bible Bapt. Ch., St. Charles, 1971-78; organist, vocal soloist, floral arranger, Bible tchr. Faith Missionary Bapt. Ch., St. Charles, 1978-82; organist, floral arranger, vocal soloist Belleview Bapt. Ch., Springfield, Mo., 1984-90; tchr. piano, organ, voice, organist, Springfield, 1983—; pianist Golden Agers Pk. Crest Bapt. Ch., Springfield, 1991; interior decorator, floral arranger, organist, vocal soloist for weddings and funerals. Composer: I Will Sing Hallelujah, (cantata) I Am Alpha and Omega, Prelude to Prayer, My Shepherd, O Sing unto the Lord a New Song, O Come Let Us Sing unto the Lord, The King of Glory, The Lord Is My Light and My Salvation, O Worship the Lord in the Beauty of Holiness, The Greatest of These Is Love, Prayer to the Lord Our God, We Will Sing Praises, His Name Is Jesus, From Bethlehem's Manger to the Cross, The King of Kings Is Coming! Alleluia! To the Throne You Go, The Eyes of God, The Most Holy, Dearly Beloved, Precious, Loving Lamb of God, Devine, also numerous hymn arrangements for organ and piano. Past pianist, Sunday sch. tchr., mem. choir East Ave. Bapt. Ch. Fellow Internat. Biog. Assn. (life), Am. Biog. Inst. Rsch. Assn. (life); mem. Nat. Guild Organists, Nat. Guild Piano Tchr. Auditions, Internat. Platform Assn. Home: 5135 E Farm Road 174 Rogersville MO 65742-8220

DAVIS, EVELYN Y. editor, writer; b. Aug. 16; d. Herman H. and Marian (Witteboom) DeJong; m. William Henry Davis, 1957 (div. 1958); m. Marvin Knudsen, 1969 (div. 1970); m. Walter O. Froh Jr., 1991 (div. 1994). Student, Western Md. Coll., George Washington U., N.Y. Inst. Fin. Editor, pub., Highlights and Lowlights, 1964— . Pres. Evelyn Y. Davis Found., 1980 [illegible] Washington U. Med. Ctr., hon. bd. govs. Art Inst. of Chgo. Fellow JFK Ctr. for Performing Arts. Mem.: Smithsonian Benefactors Cir., Andrew Carnegie Soc. (life), George Washington U. Club (life), Capitol Hill Club (life). Home: Watergate East 2510 Virginia Ave NW Washington DC 20037-1904 Office: Highlights and Lowlights Watergate Office Bldg 2600 Virginia Ave NW Ste 215 Washington DC 20037-1905

DAVIS, FLOREA JEAN, social worker; b. Crossett, Ark., Jan. 10, 1953; d. Richard Davis and Geneva (Bedford) Williams. BA in Psychology and Social Work cum laude, Park Coll., Parksville, Mo., 1975; MSW, Kans. U., 1982. Cert. secondary tchr. social studies; lic. social worker, Kans.; lic. specialist clin. social work. Asst. dir. Northeast Coordination and Devel. Ctr., Kansas City, Kans., 1975; asst. dir., clin. supr. DRAG Alcohol Ctr., Kansas City, 1975-83; substance abuse counselor Johnson County Substance Abuse Ctr., Shawnee, Kans., 1983-85; clin. social worker Family & Children Services, Inc., Kansas City, 1975-88; area svc. mgr. Agy. Heart of Am. Family Svcs., Kansas City, 1988-90; sr. practitioner Crittenton, Kansas City, Mo., 1990—; dir. Wyandotte Christian Counseling Ctr., Kansas City, Kans., 1995—. Instr. U. Kans., Lawrence, 1976: substance abuse specialist, cons. Kansas City area, 1985—; part-time instr. Avila Coll., Kansas City, Mo., 1987—; sr. practitioner Kansas City Outpatient Clinic, Crittenton, Kans., 1990—; behavioral health cons. KCMC Child Devel. Ctr., 1999-2000; counselor Saint Luke EAP Office, Kansas City, 2002—; ednl. cons., presenter Donnelly Coll., 2002--. Co-author: Human Services and Social Change: An African-American Church Perspective, 1992. Vol. United Way Spkrs. Bur., 1986—. Named to Wall of Tolerance, Nat. Campaign for Tolerance, 2004. Mem. NASW (clin. diplomat), Acad. Cert. Social Workers, Next Step Counseling & Consulting Assn. (pres., founder). Avocations: reading, singing, tennis, travel. Home: 1216 N 77th St Kansas City KS 66112-2408 Office: Crittenton S Kans City 10920 Elm Ave Kansas City MO 64134-4108

DAVIS, GAIL SHELL, gifted and talented educator; b. Century, Fla., Aug. 3, 1950; d. Loyd Truss and Fanny Hall Shell; m. Clay Savelle Davis, Aug. 21, 1981; 1 child, Donna Lee. AA, Jefferson Davis State Jr. Coll., Brewton, Ala., 1970; BS, Auburn U., 1973; MS in Tchg., U. West Fla., 1991, EdD, 2003. Cert. tchr. Fla., edn. specialist Fla. Tchr. Gulf Breeze (Fla.) Mid. Sch., Gulf Breeze, 1973—84, head sci. dept., 1977—84; tchr. Woodham HS, Pensacola, Fla., 1984—87, Tate HS, Pensacola, 1987—94; tchr. gifted Pea Ridge Elem./ S.S. Dixon Intermediate, Pace, Fla., 1994—. Author: Environmental Education in Santa Rosa County, 1980, Searching for TWM in a Northwest Florida School, 1996, Development of a Formative Assessment Instrument for Elementary Science in Florida Schools, 2003. Nominating com. Wallace Bapt. Ch., Pace, 1997, nursery coord., 1998—, youth pastor search com. chair, 2002. Named Woman of Yr., Am. Bus. Womens Assn. West Fla., 1982. Mem.: ASCD, NSTA, Fla. ASCD. Democrat. Southern Baptist. Avocations: travel, cooking. Home: 5225 Rowe Tr Pace FL 32571 Office: Pea Ridge Elem Sch 4575 Sch Ln Pace FL 32571 Personal E-mail: wegl@aol.com.

DAVIS, GEENA (VIRGINIA DAVIS), actress; b. Wareham, Mass., Jan. 21, 1957; m. Richard Emmolo, 1981 (div. 1983); m. Jeff Goldblum, 1987 (div. 1990); m. Renny Harlin, 1993. BFA, Boston U., 1979; attended, New England Coll., Henniker, N.H. Founder Genial Pictures; mem. My. Washington (N.H.) Repertory Theatre Co. Motion picture appearances include Tootsie, 1982, Fletch, 1985, Transylvania 6-5000, 1985, The Fly, 1986, Beetlejuice, 1988, The Accidental Tourist, 1988 (Academy award Best Supporting Actress, 1989), Earth Girls Are Easy, 1989, Quick Change, 1990, Thelma and Louise, 1991 (Acad. award nominee Best Actress 1991, British Acad Film and TV Arts award Best Actress in leading role 1991, Golden Globe award nominee Best Actress 1991), A League of Their Own, 1992, Hero, 1992, Angie, 1994, Speechless, 1994, Cutthroat Island, 1995, The Long Kiss Goodnight, 1996, Stuart Little, 1999; TV series: Buffalo Bill, 1983-84, Sara, 1985; appeared in TV film Secret Weapons, 1985, episodes series Family Ties, 1984.

DAVIS, GLENNA SUE, human resources director; b. Elk City, Okla. d. Toney and Wilma (Jansson) Wilcox; m. Wayne Milton Davis, Apr. 15, 1962 (div. Jan. 1984); children: Jeffrey, Bradley, Scott. BABA, Adams State Coll., 1982. Registered ombudsman, Ill. Dept. on Aging, 1993-95. Acct. Louis Moffett, CPA, Amarillo, Tex., 1961-65, J.H. Cochran, CPA, Monte Vista, Colo., 1968-69, T&W Ranch, Inc., Monte Vista, Colo., 1969-79; quality control mgr. A.E. Staley mfg. Co., Monte Vista, 1979-93, prodn. planner, 1993-95; dir. human resources Adams State Coll., Alamosa, 1995—99; mgr. human resources U. No. Colo., Greeley, 1999—2002; exec. dir. San Luis Valley Cmty. Connections, Alamosa, 2002—. Pres. Liberty Cons., Alamosa, 1993—; presenter Nat. Con. on Adult Learning, 1995, other confs. in field. Co-dir. San Luis Valley Kids Against Drugs, Alamosa, 1990-92; mem./treas. Monte Vista Community hosp. Bd., 1989-93; dir. San Luis Valley Network, Monte Vista, 1984-93; vol. Am. Cancer Soc., 1992-96; mem. Colo. 12th Dist. Jud. Performance Rev. Bd., 1992-93. Mem. AAUW (dist. dir. 1996—98, state sec. 1990-92), Boys and Girls Club (exec. bd. 1995—). Republican. Baptist. Avocations: golf, travel, reading, exploring southwest indian ruins. Home: 2029 E County Road 8 N Monte Vista CO 81144-9735 Office: San Luis Valley Cmty Connections 128 Market St Alamosa CO 81101

DAVIS, GLORIA ZEAL, counseling administrator, educator; b. Flushing, N.Y., Aug. 22, 1926; d. Robert Edward Miller and Lillian Louise Aufenger; m. Edward Gale Zeal, May 31, 1952 (dec. Nov. 1957); children: Robin Zeal, Katie Zeal, Douglas Zeal; m. Elvin Albert Davis, June 24, 1973 (dec. Aug. 1998); 1 child, Jeffrey. BA in English Composition, Wellesley Coll., 1947; MS in Edn. and Counseling, Portland State U., 1969. Cert. tchr. Oreg., standard personnel svc., standard counselor. Asst. editor dept. boys and girls books Harper & Bros. (now Harper-Collins), N.Y.C., 1947—51; program dir. young adults YWCA, Portland, Oreg., 1958—60; tchr. English Catlin Gabel Upper Sch., Portland, 1963—67; counselor David Douglas H.S., Portland, 1968—76; dyslexia therapist Lang. Skills Therapy, Portland, 1977—87; editor-in-chief Wistaria Press, Portland, 1981—; learning disabilities assessment Lewis and Clark Coll., Portland, 1988—. Del. Single Parents and the Schs., Washington, 1983; elder Westminster Presbyn. Ch., 2000—01, bd. dirs.; program chair Chief Supreme Ct. Justice Peterson's All Day Symposium, Portland, 1991. Mem.: Internat. Dyslexia Assn. (nat. bd. dirs. 1987—93, coun. advisors Oreg. br. 1993—, pres. Oreg. br. 1984—85, bd. dirs. 1981—87, Appreciation award 1995), Cascade Ski Club (former bd. dirs.), Irvington Tennis Club. Avocations: tennis, swimming, ice skating, skiing. Office: Wistaria Press 4373 NE Wistaria Dr Portland OR 97213

DAVIS, GRACE W. state legislator; d. Frank and Grace (Worthy) Wilkinson; 1 child, Curtis Davis Jr. Student, Tuskegee Inst., Hunter Coll. Rep. 48th dist. Ga. Ho. of Reps., 1986-99; dep. dir. aging City of Atlanta, 2000—. Vice chmn. house human rels. and aging com., mem. house appropriations com., house pub. safety com., house spl. rules com. Mem. Atlanta Women Against Crime; former bd. dirs. United Youth Adult Conf., Inc.; former adolescent dir. West End Med. Ctr. Democrat. Baptist. Home: 2 Peachtree St Atlanta GA 30303-3142 Office: State Capitol Rm 401 Atlanta GA 30334

DAVIS, GWENDOLYN LOUISE, air force officer, English educator; b. Toledo, Dec. 8, 1951; d. Robert Louis and Marietta Beatrice (Sautter) Davis; m. Barry Dennis Fayne, Jan. 6, 1979 (div. Feb. 2001); children: Ashleigh Elizabeth, Zachary Alexandur-John. BFA, So. Meth. U., 1972; MEd, U. North Tex., 1978; MA, U. Denver, 1987. Cert. tchr., Tex., Ala.; cert. secondary tchg. Am. Montessori Soc. Substitute tchr., Toledo and Dallas, 1972-73; film dir. Channel 39 Christian Broadcasting Network, Dallas, 1973-75; engr., air operator Channel 40 Trinity Broadcasting Network, [illegible] Dallas, 1976; commd. 2d lt. USAF, 1978, advanced through grades to maj., 1989, ret., 1995; mgr. western area Hdqrs. USAFR Officers Tng. Corp., Norton AFB, Calif., 1979-81; chief tng. systems support Hdqrs. Air Force Manpower Pers. Pentagon, Washington, 1981-84; pers. policies officer J1, Orgn. of Joint Chiefs of Staff Pentagon, Washington, 1984-85; asst. prof. English, dir. forensics USAF Acad., Colorado Springs, Colo., 1987-92; adj. faculty mem. dept. English Auburn U., Montgomery, Ala., 1994-95; adj. faculty mem. dept. arts and scis. Troy State U., Montgomery, 1994-96; dir. Bullock County HS Learning Ctr., Union Springs, Ala., 1995-96; tech. and acad. tchr. Ctr. for Advanced Tech. Booker T. Washington Magnet H.S., Montgomery, 1996; tchr. speech and English Mountain Brook H.S., Birmingham, Ala., 1997-98; tchr. humanities Joseph Bruno Montessori Acad., Birmingham, 1998-2000; upperschool director Sacred Heart Church Sch., 2000-2001, ednl. cons., 2001—02; founder, dir. Shiloh Village Montessori H.S., 2002—. Assoc. editor Airpower Jour., Maxwell AFB, Ala., 1992-94, mil. doctrine analyst, 1994-95; chmn. mil. affairs Jr. Officer's Coun., Norton AFB, 1981; invited spkr. in field; chmn. program devel. com. for nat. orgn. Cross Exam. Debate Assn., 1990-91. Contbr. articles to profl. jours. Teacher, mem. choir, soloist various chs., 1973; chair publicity com. Birthright, Inc., Woodbridge, Va., 1983. Named Command Jr. Officer of Yr., Hdqrs. USAFR Officers Tng. Corps, 1979. Mem. Nat. Parliamentary Debate Assn. (co-founder, editor Parliamentary Debate jour. 1992-95), Am. Montessori Soc., Phi Upsilon Omicron. Avocations: reading, antiques, sight-seeing, family. Home: 1532 Cahaba River Parc Birmingham AL 35243 E-mail: gwendavis1@aol.com.

DAVIS, HELEN GORDON, former state senator; b. N.Y.C., 1926; m. Gene Davis; children: Stephanie, Karen, Gordon. BA, Bklyn. Coll.; postgrad., U. South Fla., 1967—70. Tchr. High Sch. Commerce, N.Y.C., Hillsborough High Sch., Tampa, Fla.; grad. asst. U. South Fla., 1968; mem. Fla. Ho. of Reps. (1st woman to be elected in 1974 from Hills Co., 1st woman to chair the legis. del.), 1974-88; state senator Fla., 1988-92; mem. Fla. Supreme Ct. Commn. on Gender Bias in the Cts., 1988-90, Fla. Supreme Ct. Commn. on Mediation and Arbitration, 1987—. Chmn. senate appropriations subcom. human svcs., mem. rules com., internat. trade and econ. devel. com., health and rehab. svcs. com. Jud. chmn. Local Govt. Study Commn. Hillsborough County (Fla.), 1964; mem. Tampa Commn. on Juvenile Delinquency, 1966-69, Mayor's Citizens Adv. Com., 1966-69, Quality Edn. Commn., 1966-68, Gov.'s Citizen Com. for Ct. Reform, 1972, Hillsborough County Planning commn., 1973-74; mem. Gov.'s Commn. on Jud. Reform, 1976; mem. employment com. Commn. Cmty. Rels., 1966-69; by-laws chmn. Arts Coun. Tampa, 1971-74; 1st v.p. Tampa Symphony Guild, 1974; bd. dirs. U. South Fla. Found., 1968-74, Stop Rape, 1973-74; past pres. PTA; active adv. commn. Nat. Child Care Action Campaign, Nat. Ctr. for Crime and Delinquency; chair Hillsborough Dem. Exec. Com., also pres. Recipient U. South Fla. Young Dems. Humanitarian award, 1974, Diana award NOW, 1975, Woman of Achievement in Arts award Tampa, 1975, Tampa Human Rels. award, 1976, Hannah G. Solomon Citizen of Yr., 1980, St. Petersburg Times/Fla. Civil Liberties award, 1980, Friend of Edn. award, 1981, Fla. Alliance for Responsible Parenting award, 1981, Humanitarian award Judeo-Christian Clinic, 1984, Fla. Network of Runaway Youth award, 1985, Ctr. for Women Leader-adv. Friend award, 1985, Nat. Assn. Juvenile Ct. Judges Appreciation award, 1987, AAUW Leadership award, 1987, Hillsborough County Halfway House appreciation award, 1988, Martin Luther King award City of Tampa, 1988, Nat. Fedn. Dem. appreciation, 1989, Dept. Legal Affairs appreciation, 1990, Superwoman award Mus. Sci. and Industry, 1990, Nat. Childcare Merit award NASP, 1992, Am. Judicature award Am. Judicature Assn., 1993, Woman of Courage award City of Tampa, 2000; named Fla. Motion Picture and TV Outstanding Legislator, 1990. Mem. LWV (pres. Hillsborough County 1966-69, lobbyist, Fla. adminstrn. of justice chmn. 1969-74), Am. Arbitration Assn., Hills County Expy. Authority, Fla. Supreme Ct. Commn. Arbitration. Democrat. Home: 45 Adalia Ave Tampa FL 33606-3301 Fax: 813-253-0393. E-mail: hegordav@aol.com.

DAVIS, JANET MARIE GORDEN, secondary school educator; b. Springfield, Mo., Jan. 6, 1938; d. Ura Arlond and Evelyn Ruby (Nickols) Gorden; m. Benjamin George Davis, June 21, 1980; children: Leslie Anne, John Nathan. BS, S.W. Mo. U., 1960, MA, 1969; PhD, U. Md., 1992. Tchr. Springfield Schs., 1960-64; instr. USAFE-U. Md., Germany, 1965-67, S.W. Mo. U., Springfield, 1969-70; tchr., dept. chair Baltimore County, 1977—. Cons. in internat. edn. World Relief Corp., Wheaton, Ill., 1984; asst. prof. Balt. Internat. Coll., 1993-95. Author: For the Love of Literature: A Survey of Fiction, 1989, For the Love of Literature: Reading and Writing Nonfiction, 1989. Fulbright fellow, Eng., 1980-81. Mem. Dickens Fellowship, Fulbright Assn., Phi Kappa Phi. Baptist. Avocations: piano, animal rights, victorian poetry, hymnology. Home: 6580 Madrigal Ter Columbia MD 21045-4628

DAVIS, JANET R. BEACH, science educator; b. Davenport, Iowa, Jan. 25, 1960; d. James R. and Fern Louise Munday Beach; m. Dennis Kay Davis, Jan. 31, 1978; 1 child, Matthew Glenn. AA, Heartland C.C., Bloomington, Ill., 1995. Sr. sci. lab. tech. Heartland C.C., Bloomington, 1994-99, supr. sci. lab., 1999—. Founder, pres. environ club Heartland C.C., Bloomington, 1993—99; advisor First STEP Environ. Club, 2000—; facilitator Ill. Dept. Natural Resources, 1998—, citizen scientist forest watch, 1999. Author: Earth Science Lab, 1999. Vol. worker Audubon Soc., Bloomington, 1996—; adv. bd. Ecology Action Ctr., Normal, Ill., 1997—, bd. dirs., 2002— Recipient Paul Simon award Ill. C.C. Trustee Assn., 1996; mem. USA Today Ill. Acad. Team, 1995, 96. Mem.: Am. Assn. Women in C.C. (pres.-elect 2001, pres. 2002), Bloomington Normal Women Writers Group (founder), Ill. Power Customers United to Save Our Trees (founding mem.), First Step Environ. Club (founder, pres. 1993—), Phi Theta Kappa (founder). Avocations: needlework, reading, mahjong. Office: Heartland CC ICB 1006 1500 W Raab Rd Normal IL 61761 E-mail: janet.beachdavis@heartland.edu.

DAVIS, JEAN E. bank executive; b. Durham, N.C., Dec. 9, 1955; BA in Polit. Sci. and Indsl. Rels., U. N.C.; MBA, Duke U. Joined Wachovia Corp., Charlotte, NC, 1985, regional v.p. Piedmont Triad Region, 1996—98, merger coord. Va. ops., 1998, exec. v.p., dir. human resources, 1998—99, sr. exec. v.p., dir. human resources, 1999—2000, sr. exec. v.p., chief tech. and ops. officer, 2000—01, sr. exec. v.p., divsn. head info. tech., e-commerce and ops., 2001—. Mem. Fin. Svcs. Roundtable; bd. trustees U. N.C., Greensboro, bd. visitors, Chapel Hill. YMCA of Greater Charlotte. Named one of 25 Women to Watch, US Banker Mag., 2003. Office: Wachovia Corp 301 South College St Charlotte NC 28288-0570*

DAVIS, JESSICA G. clinical geneticist, pediatrician; b. Bklyn., Apr. 3, 1934; d. Nathan S. and Sylvia (Teplitz) Grosof; m. Andrew R. Davis, June 17, 1956; children: Jennifer Davis Hall, David. BA, Wellesley Coll., 1955; MD, Columbia U., 1959. Diplomate Am. Bd. Med. Genetics. Intern pediatrics St. Luke's Hosp.-Columbia U.; fellow Albert Einstein Coll. Medicine Yeshiva U., N.Y.C., 1961-68, instr. Albert Einstein Coll. Medicine, 1962, asst. prof. Albert Einstein Coll. Medicine, 1968-74; assoc. prof. clin. pediatric Weill Coll. Medicine Cornell U., N.Y.C., 1974—. Cons. March of Dimes, N.Y.C., 1974—, Hastings Inst., Garrison, N.Y., 1979—; mem. sickle cell adv. com. NIH. Contbr. articles to profl. jours. Recipient numerous grants. Fellow: Am. Coll. Med. Genetics (founding fellow, CME officer); mem.: N.Y. Acad. Medicine, Coun. Regional Genetics Network (pres. 1991—94), Am. Soc. Human Genetics. Office: Weill Med Coll Cornell U Presbyn Hosp 525 E 68th St Rm Box #128 New York NY 10021-4870 Office Phone: 212-746-1496. E-mail: [illegible]

DAVIS, JO ANN S. congresswoman; b. Rowan County, N.C., June 29, 1950; m. Charles E. Davis II; children: Charloe, Chris. Attended, Hamtpon Roads Business Coll. Mem. Va. State Legis., 1998-2001, mem. gen. laws com., mem. health welfare & insts., mem. sci. & tech. com., mem. claims com, mem. Chesapeake and its tributaries com.; mem. U.S. Congress from 1st Va. dist., 2001—; mem. armed svcs. com., govt. reform com., internat. rels. com. Republican. Mem. Assembly Of God Ch. Office: 1123 Longworth Ho Office Bldg Washington DC 20515-4601*

DAVIS, JOAN CARROLL, retired museum director; b. Sept. 20, 1931; d. Homer Leslie and Ruby Isabelle (Stone) G.; m. Frederic E. Davis, Aug. 22, 1953; children: Timothy, Terri, Tami, Traci, Todd, Tricia. Student, Bob Jones U., 1949-52. Supr. Day Care Ctr. Bob Jones U., Greenville, S.C., 1953-63; docent Univ. Art Gallery, Greenville, 1964-73, dir., 1974—; ret. Republican. Baptist. Office: Bob Jones Univ 1700 Wade Hampton Blvd Greenville SC 29614-1000

DAVIS, JOAN ELAN, artist; b. Queens, N.Y., June 6, 1963; d. Gerald and Selma Pearl Kushel; m. James Clarke Davis, Nov. 26, 1989; children: Matthew, Alexander. BS in Journalism, Ohio U., Athens, 1985. Painter, fine artist Linda Zweig Fine Art (Art Smart), San Francisco, 1998—2001, Sightings Gallery, San Francisco, 1997—2001, Lionheart Gallery, Louisville, 1999—, Ebert Gallery, The Project Rm., San Francisco, 1999—, North Beach Galllery, San Francisco, 2002—. Co-chair, art from the heart com. Schs. of the Sacred Heart, San Francisco, 2000—01; docent San Francisco Mus. Modern Art, 1999—; pub. spkr., lectr. on art appreciation, nationwide; fall lectr. series chair San Francisco Art Inst. One-woman shows include San Francisco Sch. Art Gallery, 1999—, San Bernardino County Mus., Redlands, Calif., 2000—01, Period Gallery, Omaha, 2000, Walter Anderson Mus. Art, Ocean Springs, Miss., 2000, Bolinas (Calif.) Mus., 2000, Southeastern C.C., Whiteville, N.C., 2000, Coos Art Mus., Coos Bay, Oreg., 2000, Chatahoochee Valley Art Mus., LaGrange, Ga., 2000, Nathan B. Rosen Mus. and Gallery, Boca Raton, Fla., 2000, eklektikos gallery of art, Washington, 2000, Springfield (Mo.) Mus. Art, 2001, Lionheart Gallery, Louisville, 2001, North Beach Gallery, San Francisco, 2002, San Francisco Mus. Modern Art Auction, 2002, San Francisco Art Inst. Auction, 2002, many others, —. Represented in permanent collections Chevron Energy Solutions, San Francisco, Joseph Piedot Advt., San Francisco, Represented in permanent collections numerous pvt. owners, Artfully Yours, Inc., San Francisco, Am. Embassy, Budapest, Hungary. With U.S. in Embassies art program, Budapest, 2002—; docent Columbus (Ohio) Mus. Art, 1994—96, Houstong Mus. Fine Art, 1996—97, San Francisco Mus. Fine Art, 1998—; Edgewood vol. children's orgn., San Francisco, 2000—01; pres. Joan Davis Art.com. Republican. Jewish. Avocations: exercise, reading, writing, skiing. Home: The Presidio 337 Infantry Terr San Francisco CA 94129

DAVIS, JOANNE FATSE, lawyer; m. Thomas J. Davis, Jr. BS, Boston U., 1977; JD, U. Bridgeport, 1982. Bar: Conn. 1982, N.Y. 1983. Motions law clk. U.S. Ct. Appeals (2d cir.), N.Y.C., 1982-83; assoc. Debevoise & Plimpton, N.Y.C., 1983-89; sr. corp. counsel Uniroyal Chem. Co., Middlebury, Conn., 1989-99; asst. gen. counsel, fin. and adminstrn. Crompton Corp., 1999—. Mem. Am. Corp. Counsel Assn., Conn. Bar Assn., The Corporate Bar, Assn. Bar City of N.Y., Soc. Farsarotul. Eastern Orthodox.

DAVIS, JONNI K. secondary school educator, writer; b. Crane, Tex., May 22, 1956; d. Norman E. and Emily Bradford; m. George Jefferson Davis; 1 child, Patrick. BA, Baylor U., 1978. Cert. tchr.secondary edn.-English/History. Tchr. English and drama Teague (Tex.) H.S., 1979—81; tchr. English James Martin H.S., Arlington, Tex., 1985—87; tchr. Brit. lit./English and leadership Arlington H.S., 1987—. Co-facilitator, site-based decision making com. Arlington H.S., 1994—97, varsity cheerleader sponsor, 1994—95, dir. sr. class variety show, 1994—, student leadership advisor, 1999—, class of 2005 lead sponsor, 2001—. Author: ParenTime Educational Video Series, Harris Hospital-Methodist, 1983; dir.: (educational videos) ParenTime I, 1983, ParenTime II - Feeding Your Baby, 1983 (Bronze Quill award for excellence in comm. IABC Ft. Worth, 1983). Mem.: Okla. Writers' Fedn., Inc. (contest category chair 2001), United Educators' Assn., Baylor Alumni Assn. (life). Methodist. Avocation: writing.

DAVIS, JOY LEE, English language educator; b. N.Y.C., Apr. 3, 1931; d. William Henry and Genevieve (Rhein) Belknap; m. Peter John King, Aug. 26, 1955 (div. Feb. 1985); children: William Belknap King, Russell Stuart King; m. John Bradford Davis, Jr., July 5, 1986. AB, Wellesley Coll., 1952, AM, 1953; PhD, Rutgers U., 1968; postgrad., Oxford (Eng.) U., 1978. Tchr. English Dana Hall Sch. for Girls, Wellesley, Mass., 1953-54; instr. English U. Mo., Columbia, 1954-55, Boston U., 1955-56; tchr. English Brookline (Mass.) High Sch., Spartanburg (S.C.) High Sch., 1956-60; prof. English Ohio Wesleyan U., Delaware, 1966-71, Hamline U., St. Paul, 1972-74, U. Minn., Mpls., 1974-77, Coll. St. Thomas, St. Paul, 1977-88; lectr., dir. Joy Davis Seminars, St. Paul, 1988—. Author: Everything But: An Education Memoir, 1999, The Hero in Literature: Prometheus to Prufrock, 2003; pub. poetry in New World Writing and Crisp Pine Anthology; lit. criticism in Midwest Quar., 1993, Jour. Grad. Liberal Studies, 1996. Wellesley Coll. scholar, 1952. Mem. AAUW (bd. dirs., v.p. ways & means, 2003—, Svc. awrd St. Paul br. 1983), Midwest MLA, Mpls. Inst. Fine Arts, Minn. Club (bd. dirs. 1982-88), New Century Club (bd. dirs., spl. subjects chmn.) Schubert Club (bd. dirs., chmn. mus. com.), Wellesley Coll. Club (regional campaign com.), Delta Kappa Gamma. Republican. Presbyterian. Avocations: reading, travel, creative cuisine. Home and Office: 4312 Pond View Dr Saint Paul MN 55110-4155

DAVIS, JOY MORGAN, actress, writer; b. Fort Worth, Tex., Sept. 19, 1930; d. William Claude and Kate Durham (Polk) Morgan; m. Jewell Andrew Davis, Jr., Nov. 21, 1953; 1 child, William Jewell ; 1 child, Drew Ann Borsos. BA, Miss. Coll., Clinton, 1952. Tchr. Christian Drama Glorietta Bapt. Assembly, N.Mex. Actor: (performs one-woman readings of books and plays), 1966—; author: (women's book) A Woman's Song, 1984—, (book of prayers, poetry) You Bring the Umbrellas, Lord, 1992—, (book of poetry) Could Hurry Up the Dawn, Lord?, 1994—, A Mother's Precious Moments, 1996, I'm Ready for my Rainbow, Lord, 1998. Mailing: 2108 Kessler Ct Dallas TX 75208-2951

DAVIS, JUDY, actress; b. Perth, Australia, Apr. 23, 1955; m. Colin Friels, 1984; children: Jack, Charlotte. Student, Nat. Inst. Dramatic Art, Sydney, Australia. Appearances include: (films) High Rolling, 1976, My Brilliant Career, 1979 (Best Actress Sammy award Australian Film and TV Awards 1979, Best Actress award Brit. Acad. Film and TV Arts 1981, Best Newcomer Brit. Acad. Film and TV Arts 1981), Hoodwink, 1981 (Best Supporting Actress Sammy award Australian Film and TV Awards 1981), Winter of Our Dreams, 1981 (Best Actress Sammy award Australia Film and TV Awards 1981), Heatwave, 1982, The Final Option, 1983, A Passage to India, 1984 (Acad. award nominee for best actress 1984), Kangaroo, 1986, High Tide, 1987, Georgia, 1988, Alice, 1990, Impromptu, 1991, Barton Fink, 1991, Naked Lunch, 1991 (Best Supporting Actress award N.Y. Critics Cir. 1991), Where Angels Fear to Tread, 1991, Husbands and Wives, 1992 (Acad. award nominee for best supporting actress 1992), The Ref, 1994, The New Age, 1994, Children of the Revolution, 1996, Absolute Power, 1996, Blood and Wine, 1996, Deconstructing Harry, 1996, Celebrity, 1997, The Echo of Thunder, 1998, Gaudi Afternoon, 2000, The Man

Who Sued God, 2001, Swimming Upstream, 2003; (TV movies) A Woman Called Golda, 1982 (Emmy award nominee 1982), The Merry Wives of Windsor, 1982, Rocket to the Moon, 1986, One Against the Wind, 1991, Serving in Silence: The Margarethe Cammermeyer Story, 1995 (Emmy award), Swimming Upstream, 2001; (TV movie) Coast to Coast, 2002; (TV miniseries) Water Under the Bridge, 1982; (stage) Lulu (Frank Wedekind), Piaf (Pam Gem), Insignificance (Terry Johnson), 1982, Echo of Thunder (Emmy nomination), 1997, (TV prodn.) Dash & Lily, 1997 (Emmy nomination), A Cooler Climate, 1998, Me and My Shadows, 2000 (Golden Globe award, Am. Screen Actors award, Golden Satellite award, Broadcast Critics Choice award, Am. Film Inst. award, Emmy award). Office: care Shanahan Mgmt PO Box1509 Darlinghurst NSW 1300 Australia*

DAVIS, JULIA MCBROOM, college dean, speech pathology and audiology educator; b. Alexandria, La., Sept. 29, 1930; d. Guy Clarence and Addie (McElroy) McBroom; m. Cecil Ponder Davis, Aug. 25, 1951 (div. 1981); children: Mark Holden, Paul Houston, Anne Hamilton; m. David G. Reynolds, Aug. 26, 1987. BA, Northwestern State U., Natchitoches, La., 1951, MS, U. So. Miss., 1965, PhD, 1966. Asst. prof. U. So. Miss., Hattiesburg, 1966-69, assoc., 1969-71; assoc. prof. Southwestern State U., Hammond, 1971; faculty U. Iowa, Iowa City, 1971-87, prof., chmn. dept. speech pathology and audiology, 1980-85, assoc. dean Coll. Liberal Arts, 1985-87, dir. Speech and Hearing Ctr., 1979-80; dean Coll. Social and Behavioral Scis. U. South Fla., Tampa, 1987-90, assoc. provost, 1990-91; dean Coll. Liberal Arts, U. Minn., Mpls., 1991-96, prof., 1991-97. Author (with Edward J. Hardick)): Rehabilitative Audiology for Children and Adults, 1981; editor: Our Forgotten Children, 3d edit., 2001; assoc. editor: Jour. Speech Hearing Research, 1975—77, Jour. Speech Hearing Disorders, 1982—83. Pres., bd. of trustees Minn. Foun. for Better Hearing & Speech; bd. trustees Mpls. Found., Ballet Arts of Minn., Johnson County Crisis Ctr., Am. Speech-Lang.-Hearing Assn. Found.; bd. dirs. Crisis Intervention Ctr. Fellow Am. Speech-Lang.-Hearing Assn. (cert. in clin. competence in audiology, chmn. program com. 1980-81, found. trustee 2001-), Iowa Speech and Hearing Assn. (v.p.-liaison 1972-73, honors 1985); mem. Acad. Rehabilitative Audiology (pres. 1979-80), Iowa Conf. for Hearing Impaired (pres. 1975-76), Sigma Xi. Democrat. Methodist. Home: 55 Rita Lyn Ct Iowa City IA 52245-3504

DAVIS, JUNE FIKSDAL, medical facility owner, floral designer; b. Alexnadria, Minn., June 18, 1944; d. Mads and Gladys Lillian Katherine (Engstrom) Fiksdal; m. Merrill Nathaniel Davis III, June 20, 1971; adopted sons: Kim Geoffrey, Marc Lee. Cert. with highest honor, Am. Sch. Floral Arts, Chgo., 1965. Floral designer Fiksdal Flowers, Rochester, Minn., 1960-70; prin. floral designer, nat. design tchr. Retail Florists, Kansas City, Mo., Houston, 1970-81; pres. owner, founder The Gables Found., Inc., Rochester, 1982—; floral designer, 1981—. Author: Floral Design, 1973 (Am. Inst. Floral Design award 1974). Cellist Rochester Symphony Orch., 1960-69; bd. dirs., fin. planner United Way, 1974; real estate placement Riverplace Devel., 1980; bd. dirs. Rochester Ballet, 1975; chair Symphony Ball, Rochester Symphony, 1975; coord. music program, new pipe organ, harpischord Unitarian Ch., 1975-81 (Outstanding Svc. award 1977), project pres. Walden Hill Bach Soc., 1975-82; vol. Mayo Clinic Visitors Bur. Mem. Am. Inst. Floral Design, Bus. and Profl. Women. Avocations: gourmet cooking, water sports, winter sports, skiing, European travel.

DAVIS, KAREN, fund executive; b. Blackwell, Okla., Nov. 14, 1942; d. Walter Dwight and Thelma Louise (Kohler) Padgett; 1 child, Kelly Denise Collins. BA, Rice U., 1965, PhD, 1969. Asst. prof. econs. Rice U., 1969-70; econ. policy fellow Social Security Adminstrn. Brookings Instn., Washington, 1970-71, rsch. assoc., 1971-74, sr. fellow, 1974-77; dep. asst. sec. for planning and evaluation, health HEW, Washington, 1977-80; adminstr. health resources adminstrn. USPHS, Washington, 1980-81; prof. Johns Hopkins U., Balt., 1981-92; chmn., 1983-92; exec. v.p. Commonwealth Fund, N.Y.C., 1992-94, pres., 1995—. Mem. Physican Payment Rev. Commn., 1986-94; dir. Commonwealth Fund Commn. on Elderly People Living Alone, 1985-91; vis. lectr. Harvard U., 1974-75; mem. nat. adv. com. Agy. for Health Care Rsch. and Quality, 1999-2003. Author: National Health Insurance: Benefits, Costs and Consequences, 1975, Health and the War on Poverty, 1978, Medicare Policy: New Directions for Health and Long-Term Care, 1986, Health Care Cost Containment, 1990. Mem. Inst. Medicine, Phi Beta Kappa. Democrat. Methodist. Home: 200 E 62 St New York NY 10021 Office: The Commonwealth Fund The Harkness House 1 E 75th St New York NY 10021-2692 Office Phone: 212-606-3825. E-mail: kd@cmwf.org.

DAVIS, KAREN ANN (KAREN ANN FALCONER), special education educator; b. Rockford, Ill., Sept. 24, 1948; d. Duane Fay and Vivian Marie (Milani) Falconer. BS in Edn., Ill. State U., 1971; MBA in Mgmt., Kennedy-Western U., 1994; MA in Tchg., Rockford Coll., 1996. Cert. Ill. assessing ofcl. Spl. edn. tchr. Winnebago Co-op, Rockton, Ill., 1971-76; assessor Winnebago Twp., Ill., 1977-85; program coord. Ill. Growth Enterprises, Rockford, Ill., 1977-87; substitute tchr. Rockford Pub. Schs., 1987-89, 92—; estate planner Bradford and Assocs., Rockford, 1988-89, A. Bergners, Rockford, 1989-91; spl. edn. tchr. Eisenhower Middle Sch., Rockford, 1992—. Pub. ofcl. Assessor-Winnebago Twp., 1977-85. Mem. Twp. Assessor's Assn. (treas. 1985), Nat. Audubon Soc. Roman Catholic. Avocations: photgraphy, bird watching, gardening, traveling, antiquing.

DAVIS, KATHERINE LYON, lieutenant governor; b. Boston, June 24, 1956; d. Richard Harold and Joy (Hallum) Winer; m. John Marshall Davis, Feb. 22, 1992; 1 child, Madeline Felton. BS, MIT, 1978; MBA, Harvard U., 1982. Engr. Cambridge (Mass.) Collaborative, 1978-80; mfg. mgr. Cummins Engine Co., Columbus, Ind., 1982-87, bus. dir., 1987-89; dep. commr. Ind. Dept. Transp., Indpls., 1989-95; budget dir. State of Ind., Indpls., 1995-97; exec. sec. Ind. Family and Social Svcs. Commn., Indpls., 1997-99; city contr. City of Indpls., 1999—2003; lt. gov. State of Ind., Indpls., 2003—. Mem. Transp. Rsch. Bd., 1990-93. Recipient commendation Dept. Transp., Fed. Hwy. Adminstrn., 1991. Democrat. Avocations: running, swimming, bicycling, hiking, photography. Office: 333 State Capitol Indianapolis IN 46204-2790 E-mail: kldavis@lg.state.in.us.*

DAVIS, KATHERINE SARAH, physical therapy educator; b. Landstuhl, Germany, Oct. 14, 1960; (parents Am. citizens); d. Quentin Duane and Jean Elizabeth (Marshall) D. BS in Health and Phys. Edn., West Chester U., 1982; MA in Phys. Edn., U. No. Colo., 1983; BS in Phys. Therapy, U. Md., Balt., 1991. Lic. phys. therapist, Colo., Md. Tchr. phys. edn. Baltimore County Pub. Schs., Essex, Md., 1983-85, St. Joseph Sch., Perry Hall, Md., 1985-89; phys. therapist Meml. Hosp., Colorado Springs, Colo., 1991-93; asst. prof. phys. therapy, acad. coord. clin. edn. U. Md., Balt., 1993—. Mem. Am. Phys. Therapy Assn., Am. Assn. Therapeutic Humor, Kappa Delta Pi. Avocations: golf, hiking, cycling. Office: U Md Dept Phys Therapy 100 Penn St Baltimore MD 21201-1082

DAVIS, KATHRYN WASSERMAN, foundation executive, writer, lecturer; b. Phila., Feb. 25, 1907; d. Joseph and Edith (Stix) Wasserman; m. Shelby Cullom Davis, Jan. 4, 1932; children: Shelby M. Cullom, Diana Davis Spencer, Priscella Alden (dec.). BA, Wellesley Coll., 1928; MA, Columbia U., 1931; D of Polit. Sci., U. Geneva, 1934; law degree (hon.), Columbia U., 1997. Researcher Coun. on Fgn. Rels., N.Y.C., 1934-36, State of Pa., Phila., 1936-37; writer and lectr. on fgn. affairs N.Y., 1937—; ptnr. Shelby Cullom Davis & Co., N.Y.C., 1985—; pres. The Shelby Cullom Davis Found., N.Y.C., 1985—. Lectr. on fgn. affairs. Author: Soviets at Geneva, 1934. Trustee Wellesley Coll., 1983— ; v.p. Women's Nat. Rep. Club, 1976—, chmn. internat. affairs com.; bd. govs. Harvard U., mem. vis. com. Russian studies, 1986—; past pres. LWV. Recipient life achievement award Women's Nat. Rep. Club, 1990, gold medal for disting. svc. to humanity Nat. Inst. Social Scis., 1990, Claire Booth Luce medal Heritage Found., 1991, Plymouth Com. award Mayflower Soc., 1992, Life Accomplishment award Internat. House, 1995. Mem. Cosmopolitan Club (N.Y.C., com. fgn. visitors), Sleepy Hollow Club (Scarborough N.Y.), N.Y. Harbor Club, Seal Harbor Club (Maine), Jupiter Island Club (Hobe Sound, Fla.), The Everglades Club, Inc. (Palm Beach, Fla.), Knickerbocker Club, Univ. Club. Avocations: skiing, tennis, swimming, travel. Home: PO Box 689 Hobe Sound FL 33475-0689 Office: Shelby Cullom Davis & Co LP 609 5th Ave New York NY 10017-1021

DAVIS, KATHY E. information analyst; b. Kansas City, Kans., Sept. 14; d. James Thomas and Mary Katherine Davis. AA in Computer Sci./Data Processing, Kansas City Kans. C.C., 1980; BS in Computer Sci./Data Processing, Avila Coll., 1982. Supr. ops. Western Auto, Kansas City, Mo., 1979-85; info. analyst Electronic Data Sys., Kansas City, Kans., 1985—. Democrat. Mem. Assembly of God Ch. Avocations: singing, bible teaching, embroidery, cooking, aerobics. Office: Electronic Data Sys 3201 Fairfax Trfy Kansas City KS 66115-1307

DAVIS, KEIGH LEIGH, aerospace engineer; b. Mitchell, S.D., Oct. 6, 1954; d. Clarence Ralph and Katherine Lee Schilling; m. Glenn Nickerson Davis, Nov. 24, 1992; children: Tasha Clare Marie, Anastasia Lynn Marie. BS in Aerospace Engrng. & Mechanics, U. Minn., 1976; MS in Aerospace Engrng., U. Dayton, 1983. Stability and control project engr. Flight Stability and Control Br., USAF, Wright Patterson AFB, Ohio, 1976-85, E-3/Joint Stars Program Office, Wright Patterson AFB, 1985-86; lead stability, control & flying qualities project engr. Advanced Tactical Fighter Program, Wright Patterson AFB, 1986-88, Advanced Tactical Fighter Sys. Program Office, Wright Patterson AFB, 1988-90; stability and control project engr. Joint Tactical Autonomous Weapon Sys. Program Office, Wright Patterson AFB, 1990-91; lead br. engr. Flight Stability and Control Br., Wright Patterson AFB, 1991-94; stability and control tech. specialist Flight Mechanics Br., Wright Patterson AFB, 1993—. Chmn. MIL-STD-1797 pilot-in-the-loop oscillation update team ASC/ENFT, Wright Patterson AFB, 1992-95, responsible engr. for flying qualities of piloted aircraft mil. std., 1992-97, mil. handbook, 1997-2003; co-chmn. USAF flying qualities devel. process team, 1995-97. Mem. AIAA (sr.), Nat. Mgmt. Assn., Soc. Women Engrs. (life), Order of Ea. Star (pres.).

DAVIS, KRISTIN, actress; b. Boulder, Feb. 23, 1965; d. Keith and Dorothy Davis. BFA, Rutgers U Mason Gross Sch of the Arts, 1987. Actor: (TV series) General Hospital, 1991, "Melrose Place", 1995—96, Sex and the City, 1998—2004 (Women in Film Lucy Award, 1998, Award for Outstanding Ensemble in a Comedy Series, 2001); (TV films) N.Y.P.D. Mounted, 1991, Alien Nation: Body and Soul, 1995, The Ultimate Lie, 1996, Deadly Vision, A., 1997, Atomic Train, 1999, Take Me Home: The John Denver Story, 2000, Sex and the Matrix, 2000, Someone to Love, 2001, Three Days, 2001; (films) "Doom Asylum", 1987, Nine Months, 1995, Sour Grapes, 1998, Traveling Companion, 1998, Blacktop, 2000. Office: Endeavor Talent Agency 9701 Wilshire Blvd Ste 2700 Los Angeles CA 90010 also: HBO 1100 6th Ave New York NY 10036*

DAVIS, LAURA ARLENE, retired foundation administrator; b. Battle Creek, Mich., Apr. 14, 1935; d. Paul Bennett and Daisy E. (Coston) Borgord; m. John R. Davis, Aug. 7, 1955; children: Scott Judson, Cynthia Ann Davis Welker. BS, Ctrl. Mich. U., 1986. Sec. Mich. Loan Co., Battle Creek, 1952-56; legal sec. Ryan, Sullivan & Hamilton, Battle Creek, 1957-64; exec. sec. W.K. Kellogg Found., Battle Creek, 1965-76, adminstrn./program asst., 1976, fellowship dir., 1977, asst. v.p. adminstrn., asst. corp. sec., 1978-84, v.p. corp. affairs, corp. sec., 1984-95, spl. asst. to pres., CEO, 1996-97. Cons. Mich. State U., 1998—. Pres. bd. dirs. Charitable Union, Battle Creek, 1983-85; mem. allocations panel United Way of Battle Creek, 1983, v.p. cmty. rels., 1990-91, 1st v.p., 1994, pres. of bd., 1995-97; bd. dirs. Battle Creek Gas Co., 1988—, Riding for the Handicapped Cheff Ctr., 1991-96, sec., 1992; trustee Binder Park Zoo; mem. adv. coun. Argubright Bus. Coll., 1989-90; mem. Visionquest 5000, 1989; mem. selection com. Cmty. Leadership Acad.; bd. dirs. Coun. Mich. Founds., 1994-97; mem. membership com. Recipient Athena award C. of C., Cmty. Svc. award J.C. Penney. Mem. Adminstrv. Mgmt. Soc. (pres. chpt. 1982-83), Am. Mgmt. Assn., Nat. Touring Network (bd. mem. 1997-99, sec. 1998-99), Battle Creek C. of C. Home: 101 Brighton Park Battle Creek MI 49015-9615

DAVIS, LINDA L. social welfare executive director; b. Balt., Mar. 6, 1954; m. Joseph K. Davis Jr., Jan. 13, 1973. AA, Dundalk C.C., Balt., 1996. Exec. dir. Survivors of Incest Anonymous World Svc. Office Inc., Balt., 1982—. Recipient Gov. Victim Assistance award State of Md., 1993. Office: Survivors of Incest Anonymous World Svc Office Inc PO Box 21817 Baltimore MD 21222-6817

DAVIS, LISA ANNE, secondary school educator; b. El Paso, Dec. 3, 1955; d. William Arthur and Betty Lu (Hood) D. BS in Edn., Lock Haven (Pa.) State Coll., 1977; MA in French, Millersville U., 1991. Tchr. French, Girard (Pa.) H.S., 1978; tchr. French and English, Northeastern H.S.., Manchester, Pa., 1978-80, So. Huntingdon County High Sch., Three Springs, Pa., 1980—. Mem. Dem. County Com., Huntingdon, 1994-99; mem. fin. com. Huntingdon County Arts Festival, Saltillo, Pa., 1990. Mem. So. Huntingdon County Educators Assn. (pres. 1996-97). Avocation: reproduction Victorian needlework. Office Phone: 814-447-5529. E-mail: tantelise@pa.net.

DAVIS, LISA CORINNE, artist; b. Balt., Jan. 22, 1958; d. Robert Clarke and Elaine C. (Carsley) D.; m. Colin Murray Cathcart, Oct. 25, 1986; children: G. Davis Cathcart, Corinne Davis Cathcart. BFA, Pratt Inst., 1980; MFA, CUNY, 1983. Asst. prof. School of Art, Yale U., New Haven, 1997—2002; critic Yale U., New Haven, 2002—; asst. prof. CUNY, 2002—. One-man shows include Marlborough Gallery, NYC, June Kelly Gallery, N.Y.C., Print Club, Phila., 1993, 2d St. Gallery, Charlottesville, Va., 1994, Mcpl. Gallery, Atlanta, 1994, Halsey Gallery, Charleston, S.C., 1994, Dell Pryor Galleries, Detroit, 1994, Project Room Bronx Coun. on the Arts, N.Y., 1996; group shows include Inroads Gallery, N.Y.C., 1984, U.S. Capitol Bldg., Washington, 1986, The Schenectady Mus., N.Y., 1986, Ridge St. Gallery, N.Y.C., 1987, 88, Christie's, N.Y.C., 1989, 90, Artist's Space, N.Y.C., 1990, 91, Okeanos Gallery, Berkeley, Calif., 1992, Pyramid Atlantic Workshop, Washington, 1992, Print Club, Phila., 1992, Granary Books, N.Y.C., 1993, Kenkeleba Gallery, N.Y.C., 1993, Orgn. Ind. Artists, N.Y.C., 1993, Art in General, N.Y.C., 1993, 94, The Bronx Mus. Arts, 1993, 96, Butters Gallery, Portland, Oreg., 1993, Barrett House Galleries, Poughkeepsie, N.Y., 1994, Gallery Annext, N.Y.C., 1994, City Without Walls, Newark, 1994, Papermill, N.Y.C., 1995, Ctr. Contemporary Art, Newark, 1996. Regional fellow Mid-Atlantic Arts Found., 1992, fellow NEA, 1995-96, artists' fellow N.Y. Found. for Arts, 1997, 2000, Louis Comfort Tiffany Found. fellow, 2001. Studio: 323 West 39th St New York NY 10018

DAVIS, LISA RENE, special education educator, consultant; b. Tracy, Calif., Aug. 23, 1970; d. Buddy Ray and Shirley Mae Davis. BA in Psychology, U. Calif., San Diego, 1994; MS in Edn. and Psychology, Calif. State U., Hayward, 1997. Cons., contractor, Calif., 1994—; spl. edn. tutor, 1994—. Cmty. health analyst First Steps Collaborative, Tracy, 1994-95; student health educator U. Calif., San Diego. Author reports; contbr. essays, poetry, screenplays and book revs. to various publs. Chair Libr. Adv. Bd., Tracy, 1999—2001; mem. Deuel Vocat. Inst. Literacy Program, Tracy, 1995—96; advisor San Joaquin Family Preservation and Family Support Program Survey, Stockton, Calif., 1994; mem. Hosp. Found. Com., Tracy, 1994. Recipient Recognition awards Sierra Health Found., 1995, City of Manteca, 1995, U. Calif., San Diego, 1992, Excellence award Give Every Child a Chance, 1998. Mem.: APA, Toastmasters Internat. (v.p. edn. 1999—2001). Avocations: arts and crafts, sailing, tennis, golf. Office: 3550 Pacific Ave Apt 910 Livermore CA 94550-4889

DAVIS, LORI, foundation executive; m. Scott; children: Jacob, Josh, Caitlin, Michael, Eric, Travis. Grad. in acctg., Fresno State C.C., Fresno, Calif. Acctg. position with a cons. co.; acctg. position with a bank; engring. asst. for an ind. oil prodr.; asst. dir. Trend Lightly!, Ogden, Utah, interim exec. dir., exec. dir. Office: Trend Lightly 298 24th St Ste 325 Ogden UT 84401-1482

DAVIS, LORRAINE JENSEN, writer, editor; b. Omaha, Apr. 2, 1924; d. Theron R. and L. Mildred (Henkel) Jensen; m. Richard Morris Davis, Apr. 4, 1959 (dec.); 1 child, Laura Jensen. BA, U. Denver, 1946. Copywriter Glamour mag., N.Y.C., 1946-54, prodn. editor, 1954-61, Vogue Children mag., N.Y.C., 1963-66. Writer, assoc. features editor, Vogue mag., N.Y.C., 1966-77; mng. editor, writer women's news column, 1977-88; editorial dir. Condé Nast Books, 1988-91; editor: Vogue Living and Food Guide, 1975; editorial cons.: Vogue Beauty and Health Guide, 1979-82; editor: Cooking with Colette (by Colette Rossant), 1975, Fairchild Dictionary of Fashion (by Charlotte Calasibetta), 1975, English translation Paul Bocuse's French Cooking, 1977. Recipient Disting. Citizen award Alpha Gamma Delta, 1981 Mem. NOW, Phi Beta Kappa. Democrat. Episcopalian. Home: 200 Leeder Hill Dr Apt 538 Hamden CT 06517-2729

DAVIS, LUANN RAELENE, fund raising executive; b. Jamestown, N.D., Apr. 15, 1960; d. Wilbert and Lualla (Kungel) W.; m. Lynn Alan Davis, Dec. 12, 1993; 1 chld, Citlynn Paige. BS, Union Coll., 1982; MBA, U. Nebr., 1996. Cert. fund raising exec. Devel. assoc. Union Coll., Lincoln, 1982-86, v.p. for advancement, 1992—; assoc. dir. Philanthropic Svc. for Instns., Silver Spring, Md., 1986-92, also bd. dirs. Bd. dirs. Milton Murray Found. for Philanthropy, Fla. Editor (manual) Schools That Are Ready to Undertake Philanthropy, 1991. Named Trailblazer in Philanthropy, 1999. Mem. Assn. Fund Raising Profls., Kiwanis Club of Lincoln S.E. (bd. dirs. 1993-2003). Mem. Seventh-day Adventist. Office: Union Coll 3800 S 48th St Lincoln NE 68506-4316

DAVIS, LYNN ETHERIDGE, political scientist, educator; b. Miami, Fla., Sept. 6, 1943; d. Earl DeWitt and Louise (Featherston) Etheridge. BA, Duke U., 1965; MA, Columbia U., 1967, PhD, 1971; DHL (hon.), Va. Theol. Sem., 2000. Lectr. Miles Coll., Birmingham, Ala., 1966-67; asst. prof. polit. sci. Barnard Coll., Columbia U., N.Y.C., 1970-74; rsch. assoc. Internat. Inst. for Strategic Studies, London, 1973; program analysis staff Nat. Security Council, 1974; asst. prof., lectr. dept. polit. sci. Columbia U., 1974-76; prof., staff mem. Senate Select Com. on Intelligence, 1975-76; dep. asst. sec. of def. for policy plans and nat. security affairs Office of the Under Sec. for Policy, Dept. Def., Washington, 1977-79, asst. dep. under sec. for policy planning, 1979-81; rsch. Internat. Inst. Strategic Studies, London, 1981-82; prof. national security affairs National War Coll., Washington, 1982-85; dir. studies Internat. Inst. Strategic Studies, London, 1985-87, hon. sr. rsch. fellow, dept. war studies Kings Coll., London, 1988-90; rsch. fellow John Hopkins Fgn. Policy Inst, Paul H. Nitze Sch. Advanced Internat. Studies, 1988-91; v.p. army rsch. divsn., dir. Arroyo Ctr. RAND, Santa Monica, Calif, 1991-93, sr. fellow Washington, 1997—2001, sr. polit. scientist, 2001—; under sec. for arms control and internat. security affairs Dept. State, Washington, 1993-97. Author: The Cold War Begins, Soviet American Conflict Over Eastern Europe, 1974. Woodrow Wilson fellow, 1965-66, 69-70, 81-82; Columbia U. fellow, 1965-66, 68-69; recipient David D. Lloyd prize Harry S. Truman Library, 1976 Mem. Coun. on Fgn. Rels., Phi Beta Kappa. Home: 827 S Lee St Alexandria VA 22314-4333 Office: RAND 1200 S Hayes St Arlington VA 22202-5050 E-mail: Lynn_Davis@rand.org.

DAVIS, MAGGIE (MARIE HILL), writer; b. Norfolk, Va. d. George Blair and Dorothy Austin (Mason) Hill; children: Stuart, Richard, David, Cambren. Advt. copywriter Young and Rubicam, N.Y.C.; asst. in rsch. to chmn. dept. psychology Yale U., New Haven. Instr. creative writing courses Yale U.; guest writer/artist Internat. Cultural Ctr., Hammamet, Tunisia. Author: The Far Side of Home, 1992, Daggers of Gold, 1993, Moonlight and Mistletoe, 1993, The Amethyst Crown, 1994, Blood Red Roses, 1991 (named Best Medieval Novel by Romantic Times mag.), A Christmas Romance, 1991 (dramatized as CBS Sunday Night Movie 1994), Eagles, 1980, The Sheik, 1977, Rommel's Gold, 1971, Enraptured, 1999, Masquerade, 1999, Strangers in the Night, 2000, Out of the Blue, 2002, Stage Door Canteen, 2003; feature writer Atlanta Jour. Constn.; contbr. articles and short stories to Ga. Rev., Cosmopolitan, Ladies Home Jour., Good Housekeeping, Holiday, Venture mags. Named Ga. Author of Yr., 1963; recipient Silver Pen award Affaire de Coeur Mag., 1987, Lifetime Achievement award Romantic Times Mag., 1987. Mem. Medieval Acad. Am., Authors Guild, Romance Writers of Am., Pub. Rels. Soc. Am., Acad. Am. Poets, Women's Polit. Caucus, Caledonian Club. Democrat. Mem. Soc. Of Friends. Avocations: hiking, swimming. E-mail: madav1@aol.com.

DAVIS, MAGGIE L. elementary teacher; b. Bastrop, La., July 13, 1939; m. Killion C. Davis II, May 1, 1961. BA, U. Calif, 1982, postgrad.; PhD, Grambling State U., 1961. Cert. elem. tchr. Tchr. Berkeley (Calif.) Unified Sch. Dist., 1987—. Head supr. Willie Youth Field O.E.S., 1983—. Mem. Alpha Kappa Alpha (sec. 1959), NCNW. Lodges: Pride Alameda, O.E.S. (worth matron 1983—), Queen Sheba L.K.T. (fin. sec. 1982—), Queen Adah Grand Chpt. (grand recorder 1984—, fin. sec. 1983—). Democrat. Baptist. Avocations: sewing, reading, solving puzzles, swimming, tennis. Office: 1501 Harmon St Berkeley CA 94703-2619

DAVIS, MARGARET BRYAN, paleoecology researcher, educator; b. Boston, Oct. 23, 1931; AB, Radcliffe Coll., 1953; PhD in Biology, Harvard U., 1957; DSc (hon.), U. Minn., 2002. NSF fellow dept. biology Harvard U., Cambridge, Mass., 1957-58; dept. geosci. Calif. Inst. Tech., Pasadena, 1959-60; rsch. fellow dept. zoology Yale U., New Haven, 1960-61, prof. biology, 1973-76; rsch. asoc. dept. botany U. Mich., Ann Arbor, 1961-64, assoc. rsch. biologist Gt. Lakes Rsch. divsn., 1964-70, rsch. biologist, assoc. prof. dept. zoology, 1966-70, rsch. biologist, prof. zoology, 1970-73; head dept. ecology and behavioral biology U. Minn., Mpls., 1976-81, prof. dept. ecology, evolution and behavior, 1976-82, Regents prof. ecology, 1983—2000. Vis. prof. Quaternary Rsch. Ctr., U. Wash., 1973; vis. investigator environ. studies program U. Calif., Santa Barbara, 1981-82; adv. panel ecology NSF, 1976-79; sci. adv. com. biology, behavior and social scis., 1989-91; adv. panel geol. record of global change, NRC, 1991-92, planetary biology com., 1981-82, global change com; 1987-90, mem. screening com. in plant scis., internat. exch. of persons com., 1972-75, sci. and tech. edn. com., 1984-86, vis. rsch. scientist scholarly exch. com. NAS/NRC, People's Republic China, mem. grand challenges in environ. sci. com., 1999-2000; U.S. nat. com. internat. Union Quaternary Rsch., 1966-74; bd. trustees Inst. for Ecosys. Studies, 2000—. Mem. editl. bd. Quaternary Rsch., 1969-82, Trends in Ecology and Evolution, 1986-92, Ecosystems, 2000—. Recipient Sci. Achievement award Sci. Mus. Minn., 1988, alumnae Recognition award Radcliffe Coll., 1988, Nevada medal, 1993, Merit award Bot. Soc. Am., 1998, award for Contbn. Grad. Edn., U. Minn., 1999. Fellow: AAAS, Geol. Soc. Am., Am. Acad Arts and Scis.; mem.: NAS, Am. Quaternary Assn. (councillor 1969—70, 1972—76, pres. 1978—80, Dist. Career award 2001), Brit. Ecol. Soc. (hon.), Am. Soc. Naturalists (hon.), Ecol. Soc. Am. (pres. 1987—88, Eminent Ecologist award 1993), Nature Conservancy (bd. dirs. Minn. chpt. 1979—85), Internat. Assn. Gt. Lakes Rsch. (bd. dirs. 1970—73), Sigma Xi, Phi Beta Kappa. Office: U Minn Dept Ecology Evolution & Behavior 100 Ecology Bldg 1987 Upper Buford Cir Saint Paul MN 55108-1051

DAVIS, MARGARET SCHLITT, social services administrator; b. Pilot Point, Tex., Aug. 10, 1951; d. Andrew J. and Billie M. (Hanes) Schlitt; m. Joe Russell Davis, July 26, 1974; children: Jeffrey, Scott. Student, Midwestern U., 1975; degree in Med. Receptionist/Terminology, Lafayette Acad., 1975. Phys. therapy aide, phys. therapy/radiologgy receptionist Grady Meml. Hosp., Chickasha, Okla., 1980-[illegible] dir. activity, phys. therapy aide Christian Care Retirement Village, Chickasha, 1989—. Mem. regional adv. bd. Abuse Svcs. Trustee Chickasha Pub. Sch. Found.; mem. Santa's Work Shop, Festival of Light, Inc.; mem. Chickasha City Coun.; active Am. Cancer Soc.; mem. adv. bd. Chickasha Area. Named Chamber Amb. of Yr., 1991, 93, 94, Female Grady Countian of Yr.; recipient Readers Choice awards, 1998. Mem. Am. Bus. Women Assn. (Bus. Woman of Yr. 1995), Chickasha C. of C. (bd. dirs.), Optimist Internat. (Chickasha chpt. bd. dirs., pres.), State of Okla. Social Svcs./Activity Sect. Dirs. (bd. dirs. 1991—), Southwest Okla. Blood Inst., Beta Sigma Phi Internat. (Woman of Yr. 1995). Office: Christian Care Retirement Village 3003 W Iowa Ave Chickasha OK 73018-6026

DAVIS, MARGARET THACKER, retired critical care, medical and surgical nurse; b. Greensboro, N.C., June 7, 1925; d. Tiller Foltz and Lucy Wright (Spencer) Thacker; m. Joe Southard Davis, Feb. 4, 1961; 1 child, Dana Lee. Diploma in nursing, Baylor U., Dallas, 1947; student, Ea. N.Mex. U., Roswell, 1978. RN, N.Mex., Tex., Fla. Office nurse Drs. Britt & Cafaro, St. Augustine, Fla., 1947-50, Dr. Robert J. Rowe, Dallas, 1950-61, Dr. F.A. English, Roswell, 1964-74; charge nurse post anesthesia care unit Ea. N.Mex. Med. Ctr., Roswell, 1990-91, ret., 1991. Named Employee of Month, Ea. N.Mex. Med. Ctr., 1985. Mem. ANA, Am. Soc. Post Anesthesia Nurses (charter), Post Anesthesia Nurses Assn. N.Mex. (bd. dirs. 1980-86, sec. 1986-87, legis. com. 1989-90), N.Mex. Nurses Assn. (dist. 5 sec. 1983-85, 91-93, pres. 1986-88, bd. dirs. 1988-90, 92-94, 96-98, membership chmn. 1988-90, chmn. nominating com. 1990, Nurse of Yr. award 1989, search for excellence award 1990, dist. 5 honored nurse 1995), Baylor U. Sch. Nursing Alumni Assn. E-mail: maggied53@aol.com.

DAVIS, MARICA NANCI ELLA RIGGIN, retired artist; b. Phila., Apr. 13, 1934; d. Dale Thomas and Anna (Kudla) Purtle; m. Donald Allen Riggin, Sept. 11, 1954 (dec. Nov. 10, 1970); children: Ralph Allen Riggin, Ronald Dale Riggin, David Wayne Riggin; m. Leonard Nettleton Davis, July 3, 1976; 3 stepchildren. Student, Montgomery Coll., Rockville, Md., 1975—78, student, 1983, student, 1988, student, 1993. Electro-mech. drafter Philco, Phila., 1952—55, Vitro Labs. Automated Industries, Aspen Hill, Md., 1971—73; designer, printer Sears Roebuck, Bethesda, Md., 1970; drafer, illustrator Watkins-Johnson Co. divsn. CEI, Gaithersburg, Md., 1973—86, IDEAS/SAIC, Columbia, Md., 1987—98. Instr. adult edn. craft class Montgomery County, Md.; jury Damascus County Fair Art Show. One-woman shows include Sugar & Frichtle, Kensington, Md., Town Ctr., Ten Oaks, Md., Gurmukh Galleries, Md., Gaithersburg Coun. Arts, Woodlawn Mansion, Md., Kentland Mansion, McCrillus Gardens, Audubon Soc., Unitarian Universalitic Ch., Pyramid Atlantic, Sandy Spring Mus., Visual Sys. Art Ctr., Strathmore Hall, Rockville Arts Pl., Delapaine Visual Arts Ctr., Md., Café Monet, Kensington, Kent Island Federation Art, Sumner Mus., Washington, Saxon Swan Gallery, Del., Dietricks Gallery, Sta. Gallery, Dover (Del.) Art League, Open Studio Gallery, 1999, 2000, 2001, 2002, 2004, Kent Island Fedn. Art, 2003. Pres. Episcopal Ch. Women, Beathany Beach, Del., 2003. Mem.: Ga. Miniature Art Soc., Miniature Art Soc. Fla. Inc., Cider Painters Am., Printmakers Plus, Olney Art Assn. (pres. 1995, 1996), S. Ea. Del. Artists Studio Tour, Miniature Painters Sculptors and Gravers Soc. (receiver 1989—98), Nat. League Am. Pen Women (membership chair Holly chpt.), Md. Printmakers (assoc.; folio chair 1996), Phi Theta Kappa. Home: 306 Steamboat Ln Dagsboro DE 19939-9226 Personal E-mail: ezdavis306@aol.com.

DAVIS, MARIE ELAINE, elementary school educator; b. Washington, Oct. 28, 1960; d. Eugene Carter and Esther Marie Davis; children: Teresa, Travis Cameron Newsome. AA, Montgomery Coll., 1982; BS, Towson State U., 1987; Masters equivalency, Trinity Coll., Washington, 1998. Substitute tchr. Bucklodge Mid. Sch., Prince Georges County, Md., 1988—89; long term substitute tchr. Sligo Mid. Sch., Montgomery County Pub. Schs., Wheaton, Md., 1990—91, sci. tchr., 1991—. Environ. club sponsor Sligo Mid. Sch., Wheaten, 1997—2003, heritage proud club, 1998—2003, drama club dir., 2001—02. Fellow: Md. Tech. Acad.; mem.: Nat. Sci. Tchr. Assn. Avocations: writing, billiards, snorkeling, designing web pages. Office: Sligo Mid Sch 1401 Dennis Ave Wheaton MD 20902

DAVIS, MARILYN RUTH, artist; b. Ill., Feb. 22, 1940; d. Hibbs Foster and Vivien Goedelmann; m. Arthur W. Davis, Jr., 1962; children: Arthur III, Caralyn, Benjamin. BS in Occupl. Therapy, Washington U., 1962. Occupl. therapist Easter Seals, Albany, Ga., 1962; adult protective svc. Family and Children Svc., Toccoa, Ga., 1985—87; svc. asst. Toccoa Dialysis Facility, 1987—2000. Exhibitions include Ga. Heritage Gallery, Tallulah Falls, 2004, Currahee Artists Guild Shows. Recipient Coats Merit award in art, Coats N.Am., 2003. Mem.: Currahee Artists Guild (past v.p., various awards 1991—), United Meth. Women (Clarkesville Circle leader 2003—). Avocations: gardening, dried flower arranging, needlecrafts. Home: 172 Settlers Point Dr Clarkesville GA 30523

DAVIS, MARINA WINN, psychotherapist; b. Laredo, Tex., Aug. 30, 1945; d. Seaborn Lafayette and Lucy Curtis (Winn) Faulk; m. Donnie Fayy Smith, Aug. 21, 1967 (div. Jan. 1988); 1 child, Susan Ellene Smith. BS, U. Montevallo, Ala., 1970; MS, Tex. A&M U., 1991. Lic. prof. counselor, lic. chem. dependency counselor, cert. social work assoc., Tex. Tchr. ACISD, Rockport, Tex., 1989-93; psychotherapist in pvt. practice, Corpus Christi, 1994—. Vol., Family Outreach, Corpus Christi; primary therapist, geropsychiat. unit Columbia Northbay Hosp.; bd. dirs. YMCA New Orlans East, La., 1976, YMCA, Rockport, Tex., 1992. Mem. Phi Delta Kappa, Psi Chi. Methodist. Avocations: collecting aphorisms and illusions, rock climbing. Office: PO Box 881 Corpus Christi TX 78403 E-mail: MarinaDavisTexas@netscape.net.

DAVIS, MARY BRONAUGH, music educator; b. Kansas City, Kans, June 28, 1937; d. John Esme and Martha Lucinda (Wilson) Bronaugh; m. William D. Davis, Jr., Jan. 1, 1983. AB, William Jewell Coll., Liberty, Mo., 1959; MA, Conservatory Music, U. Mo., Kansas City, 1974. Cert. tchr. piano. Piano tchr. Leshosky Music Store, Gladstone, Mo., 1959-61; organist Pres. Hotel, Kansas City, 1965-67; piano tchr. Maple Woods C.C., Kansas City, 1972-81; ind. piano/organ tchr. Gladstone, Mo., 1962—; min. music, organist Barry Christian Ch., Kansas City, 1960—. Mem. Music Tchrs. Nat. Assn. (bd. dels. 1995-96), Am. Guild Organists (youth chair Greater Kansas City chpt. 2003—, Mo. Fedn. Music Clubs (handbell chair 1999-2003, Ch. Musician of Yr. 1998, 99), Mo. Music Tchrs. Assn. (pres. 1995-96), Kansas City Music Tchrs. Assn. (pres. 1988-90), Federated Music Tchrs. Greater Kansas City (pres. 1969-70, 84-85). Home: 1400 NE 76th Ter Kansas City MO 64118-1907

DAVIS, MARY BYRD, conservationist, researcher; b. Cardiff, Wales; came to U.S., 1947; d. John Dymond and Joanna Inger (Falconer) Byrd; m. Robert Minard Davis; children: Carol, John. BA, Agnes Scott Coll., 1958; MA, U. Wis., 1968, PhD, 1972; MLS, Simmons Coll., 1974. Acquisitions libr. No. Mich. U., Marquette, 1974-75; asst. libr. Georgetown (Ky.) Coll., 1975-78; libr. U. Ky., Lexington, 1978-83; freelance writer and editor Georgetown, 1983-90, 93—; staff writer, office mgr. Earth First Jour., Canton, N.Y., 1990; co-founder and pub. Wild Earth, Canton, N.Y., 1991-92, assoc. editor Richmond, Vt., 1993—; dir. Yggdrasil Inst., Georgetown, Ky., 1994—. Author: The Military Civilian Nuclear Link, 1988, Guide de L'Industrie Nucleaire Francaise, 1988, The Green Guide to France, 1990, Going Off the Beaten Path: An Untraditional Travel Guide to the U.S., 1991, Old Growth in the East: A Survey, 1993, La France nucléaire: matières et sites, 1997, 2002, The U.S. Enrichment Establishment 1999, 1999; co-author: Les Déchets nucléaires militaires Français, 1994; editor: Eastern Old-Growth Forests: Prospects for Rediscovery and Recovery, 1996, Eastern Old-Growth Notes, 1997-2000. Bd. dirs. Centre de Documentation et de Recherche sur la [illegible], Lyon, France, 1989—, Wildlands Ctr. for Preventing Roads, Missoula, Mont., 1996-99. Mem. Nat. Writers Union, Sierra Club (editor energy report 1986-87, exec. com. Cumberland chpt. 1982-84), Phi Beta Kappa. Home: 2900 Runnymede Way Lexington KY 40503-2813 E-mail: mdavis@old-growth.org.

DAVIS, MARY ELLEN K. library director; MLS, U. Ill.; MA, Ctrl. Mich. U. Sr. assoc. exec. dir. Assn. Coll. and Rsch. Librs., 1993—2001, exec. dir., 2001—, dir. comm. and systems, publs. program officer; ref. libr., bibliographer Ctrl. Mich. U. Recipient Girl Scouts Outstanding Vol. award. Mem.: ALA, Am. Soc. Assn. Execs., Soc. Scholarly Publishing, Profl. Conv. and Meeting Planners Assn., Phi Kappa Phi, Beta Phi Mu. Office: 50 East Huron St Chicago IL 60611 Office Phone: 800-545-2433. E-mail: acrl@ala.org.

DAVIS, MARY HELEN, psychiatrist, psychoanalyst, educator; b. Kingsville, Tex., Dec. 2, 1949; d. Garnett Stant and Emogene (Campbell) D. BA, U. Tex., 1970; MD, U. Tex., Galveston, 1975; grad. in adult and child psychoanalysis, Inst. for Psychoanalysis, Chgo., 1982-92. Cert. Nat. Bd. Med. Examiners, Am. Bd. Psychiatry and Neurology, Child and Adolescent Psychiatry. Intern, then resident in psychiatry SUNY, Buffalo, 1975-78; fellow in child psychiatry U. Cin., 1978-80; asst. prof. Med. Coll. Wis., Milw., 1980-89, clin. assoc. prof., 1989-93; med. dir. adolescent treatment unit Milw. Psychiat. Hosp., 1981-86, Schroeder Child Ctr., 1986-89; pvt. practice, 1989-93; med. dir. Devereux-Victoria (Tex.) Psych. Residential Treatment Ctr., 1993-94; pvt. practice Lancaster, Pa., 1995—. Cons. Milw. Mental Health Cons., 1980-93, Children's Svc. Soc., Milw., 1982-93, Cath. charities, Harrisburg, Pa., 1996—, Sch. Dist. Lancaster, 1998—. Bd. dirs. Next Generation Theatre, Milw., 1988-90, Next Act Theatre, Milw., 1990-92, Lancaster Guidance Ctr., 2002--. Mem. Am. Psychiat. Assn., Am. Soc. Adolescent Psychiatry, Am. Med. Women's Assn., Assn. for Child Psychoanalysis, Am. Psychoanalytic Assn. Baptist. Avocations: science fiction, music, computers, crochet.

DAVIS, MARY KATHRYN, marketing professional; b. Clearwater, Fla., Jan. 10, 1966; d. John Minor, Lee Marie Zuberer; m. James R. Davis (div.); children: Rachel Frances, Joshua Edward Leo; m. Michael C. Sultzbach, Sept. 8, 2001. BA in Mass Comm., U. Denver, 1987. Reporter Del. Bus. Rev., Wilmington, 1988—90; mktg. coord. Del. Dept. Transp., Dover, 1990—93; mktg. mgr. MBNA Am. Bank, Wilmington, 1993—99; mktg. and pub. rels. dir. The Grand Opera House, Wilmington, 1999—. Contbr. articles to profl. jours. Bd. dirs. Wilmington Drama League, Chapel St. Players. Avocations: writing, community theatre. Office: The Grand Opera House 818 N Market St Wilmington DE 19801

DAVIS, MARY LOU, secondary school educator; b. Lansford, Pa., Aug. 25, 1943; d. Lester Earl and Susan (Depuy) Snyder; m. David Hugh Davis, June 29, 1968; children: Scott David, Sean Geoffrey. BA in Math., Susquehanna U., 1965; MEd in Math., West Chester Coll., 1969. Cert. tchr. N.Y., Pa. Math. tchr. Marple Newton Sch. Dist., Broomall, Pa., 1965-68, Arlington Ctrl. Sch. Dist., Poughkeepsie, NY, 1968—73, 1977—79, 2003, Spackenkill Union Free Sch. Dist., Poughkeepsie, 1979—2000, dept. chmn., 1988-91, ctrl. treas., 1994—2000. Adj. math. tchr. Dutchess C.C., Poughkeepsie, 1973-77, Marist Coll., Poughkeepsie, 1983, 1992-93. With Jr. League of Poughkeepsie, 1979—; mem. Arlington Sch. Bd., Poughkeepsie, 1988-94, v.p., 1993-94; budget com., past program chmn. Dutchess County Sch. Bd., Poughkeepsie, 1988-94; active Mid-Hudson Alumnae Panhellenic, 1988—; mem. pub. rels. com. Habitat for Humanity, 1995—; auditing chmn., past treas., past trustee Poughkeepsie United Meth. Ch. Recipient Vision award IBM-Semiconductor Rsch. Corp. Competitiveness Found. Edn. Alliance, 1991. Mem. AAUW (v.p. for membership 1999-2001, pres. 2002—), Am. Fedn. Tchrs., Nat. Coun. Tchrs. of Math., N.Y. State Tchrs. Union Spackenkill (retirement del., chmn. pub. rels. and polit. action com. 1995-99, pres. 2001—), Assn. Math. Tchrs. of N.Y. State, Dutchess County Math. Tchrs. Assn., Dutchess County United Tchrs. Coun. (v.p. pub. rels. 1999—), Dutchess-Ulster-Sullivan-Orange Math. League (pres. 1984-98), Dutchess County Ret. Tchrs. Assn. (treas. 2003—). Republican. Avocations: reading, skiing, travel, bridge. Home: 125 Andrews Rd Lagrangeville NY 12540-6064

DAVIS, MICHELE, federal agency administrator; b. Louisville, Ky. BS in Fgn. Svc., Georgetown U., Washington, 1988; M in Econs., Am. U. Economist Citizens for Sound Economy; economist minority leader staff Joint Econ. Com. Washington; chief spokesperson majority leader's office; advisor house Rep. leadership; comms. dir. house majority leader Dick Armey, 1997—2001; asst. sec. pub. affairs U.S. Dept. Treasury, Washington, 2001—. Republican. Office: US Dept Treasury Pub Affairs 1500 Pennsylvania AveNW Washington DC 20220

DAVIS, MINNIE LOUISE, writer; b. Chattanooga, Tenn., Sept. 5, 1935; d. Moses McKelton and Lillie Mae (Glover) Smith; m. Robert Lee Martin, 1952 (div. 1964); children: Bobby Lee, Loretta, Enrico, Alexander, Jacqueline; m. Will Davis Jr., Feb. 18, 1979. BS, Va. State U., 1979. Lic. cosmetologist, Ohio, Va. Background artist various films. Author: (books) Brittini in ABC Land, 1994, (poem) Green & Gold, 1997, A Mother's Prayer, 1998, (screenplay) A Mother's Prayer, 2002. Mem., tchr. Meml. Chapel, Ft. Lee, 1980—; vol. Am. Red Cross. Mem. Ladies Auxilliary VFW, Disabled Am. Vets., NCO Wives Club (v.p. 1997-98), Sigma Gamma Rho. Home: 20124 Gandy Ave Ettrick VA 23803-1666

DAVIS, MONIQUE D. (DEON DAVIS), state legislator; b. Chgo., Aug. 19, 1936; d. James and Constance (Dutton) McKay; divorced; children: Robert Jr., Monique C. Conway. BS in Edn., Chgo. State U., 1967, MS in Guidance and Counseling, 1976. Tchr. Chgo. Bd. Edn., 1967-86, coordinator, 1986—; mem. Ill. Ho. of Reps. from 27th dist., 1987—, vice chmn. elem. and secondary edn. com. Mem. legis. com. Chgo. Area Alliance Black Sch. Edn., 1982-84, Independent Voters of Ill.-Independent Precinct Orgns., Chgo., 1982-83; coordinator 21st ward, Citizens for Mayor Washington, 1985, 87. Recipient GRIT award Roseland Womens Orgn., 1987; named a Tchr. Who Makes a Difference PTA, 1978, 85, 2002 March Monique Davis Named best Legislature of the year by Chicago Area Proseet Mem. Chgo. Area Tchrs. Alliance (chmn.), Christian Bd. Edn. (bd. dirs. 1978-82), Phi Delta Kappa. Mem. United Ch. of Christ. Office: Ill Ho of Reps 2040-j Stratton Bldg Springfield IL 62706-0001

DAVIS, N. JAN, astronaut, mechanical engineer; b. Cocoa Beach, Fla., Nov. 1, 1953; d. B. Bryce and Dolly Jo Davis; m. Mark Lee. BS in Applied biology, Georgia Inst. Tech., 1975; BS in Mech. eng., Auburn U.; MS in Mech. eng., U. Ala., 1983, D of Mech. eng., 1985. Petroleum engr. Texaco, Bellaire, Tex, 1977-79; aerospace engr. Marshall Space Flight Ctr., NASA, 1979-1986; team leader Structural Analysis Div., NASA, 1986—, lead engr. redesign Solid Rocket Booster external tank attach ring, 1987—; astronaut Astronaut Office Mission Devel. Branch, NASA, 1987—; mission specialist on STS-47, Spacelab-J, 1992. Contr. articles to profl. jours. Recipient Marshall Space Flight Ctr. Dirs. Commendation, 1987. Fellow ASME, mem. Tau Beta Pi, Omicron Delta Kappa, Pi Tau Sigma. Avocations: flying, ice skating, aerobics, bicycling, snow skiing. Office: NASA Johnson Space Ctr Astronaut Office Houston TX 77058

DAVIS, NANCY COSTELLO, retired educator; b. Manchester, Conn., May 16, 1939; d. Lawrence Fredrick Costello and Agnes Imalda (Dailey) Schmidt; m. Paul Hawley Davis, Aug. 23, 1958; children: Mark A., Susan A., Linda J., Dianne M., Maryellen L. BS, Cen. Conn. State U., 1978, MS, 1986, 6th yr. diploma adminstrn.-supervision, 1990. Computist UTC div. Pratt & Whitney, East Hartford, Conn., 1958-59; program dir. YWCA, East Hartford, 1966-68; dean mid. age religious edn. St. Mary's Ch., East Hartford, 1972-77, John Bennet Jr. High Sch., [illegible] 1978—91, chmn. data processing, 1983—91, also dir. computer edn.; vice prin. Bennet Middle Sch., 1991—2000; ret., 2002. Insvc. instr. Manchester Bd. Edn., 1981, 83—; adj. instr. Cen. Conn. State U., 1987, program coord., Vernon Adult Edn., 2000-. Treas. Lullaby Club of Hartford, Conn., 1966, 2d v.p., 1967, pres., 1968. Mem. NEA, ASCD, Conn. Edn. Assn., Manchester Edn. Assn. Democrat. Roman Catholic. Avocations: sewing, gardening, golf, dance. Office: Vernon Adult Edn 70 Loveland Hill Rd Vernon Rockville CT 06066

DAVIS, NICOLE D. executive secretary, entrepreneur; d. Mace Green and Anna L. Davis; children: Anthony R, David T, Thomas J. AAS in Secretarial Arts, Gibbs Coll., 1992; BTh, MDiv, Christian Life Sch. Theology, 1999. Min. Shabach Christian Ctr., 2000. Sec. Shabach Ministries, Norwalk, Conn., 1992—; exec. sec. Fairfield County Coun., Boy Scouts Am., Norwalk, 1992—94; adminstrv. sec. Norwalk Pub. Schs., 1994—2000, exec. sec., 2000—. Owner secretarial svcs. AnRay Tobiah, Norwalk, 1998—. Vol. Shabach Christian Ctr., Norwalk, 1992—2000. Scholar, Katharine Gibbs Sch.-Gibbs Coll., 1990. Avocations: dance, reading, writing. Personal E-mail: ndavis29@optonline.net.

DAVIS, NORMA STITES, conductor, music educator; b. Dover, N.J., July 4, 1968; d. Theodore Joseph and Barbara Tobias Stites; m. Steven Albert Davis, June 24, 1995. MusB, Rutgers U., 1993. Cert. tchr. NJ., 1993. Orch. performer, sectionals coach Delbarton Abbey Orch., Morristown, NJ, 1986—. Condr. Delbarton Summer Orch., Morristown, Abbey Orch., Morristown, 1999—, Young Musicians Orch., Morristown, 1999—; pvt. tchr., Randolph, NJ; string specialist Piscataway (N.J.) Twp. Schs., 1993—98, Dover (N.J.) Schs., 1998—99; performer Delbartton Abbey Orch., 1986—, coach sectionals, 1986—. Sunday sch. tchr. Founders Bapt. Ch., Dover, christmas program dir., vacation bible sch. tchr. Recipient Tchr. Recognition award, Morris Edn. Found., 1999—2003; scholar Paul Douglas Tchr. scholarship, State of NJ., Meta Thorne Waters Music scholarship, County Coll. of Morris, Marcus & Lillian Ossre Cohen Music scholarship. Mem.: Nat. Sch. Orch. Assn., Music Educators Nat. Conf., Am. String Tchr. Assn. (sec. N.J. chpt. 1994—98).

DAVIS, PAIGE, television host/personality; b. Phila. married. Grad., Meadows Sch. Arts, So. Meth. U., Dallas. Host TLC's Trading Spaces series, 2001—; dancer Broadway prodn. Chicago; with nat. touring co. Broadway prodn. Beauty and the Beast; appeared in commls. and videos and toured with The Beach Boys. Office: Trading Spaces Banyan Prodns 530 Walnut St Ste 276 Philadelphia PA 19106*

DAVIS, PAMELA BOWES, pediatric pulmonologist; b. Jamaica, N.Y., July 20, 1949; d. Elmer George and Florence (Welsch) Bowes; m. Glenn C. Davis, June 28, 1970 (div. Mar. 1987); children: Jason, Galen. AB, Smith Coll., 1968; PhD, Duke U., 1973, MD, 1974. Internal medicine intern Duke Hosp., 1973-74, resident in internal medicine, 1974-75; sr. investigator NIAMD/NIH, Bethesda, Md., 1977-79; asst. prof. U. Tenn. Coll. Medicine, Memphis, 1979-81, Case Western Res. U. Sch. Medicine, Cleve., 1981-85, assoc. prof., 1985-89, prof., 1989—, Arline H. and Curtis F. Garvin Rsch. prof., 2002—, sr. assoc. dean for rsch., chief pediatric pulmonary divsn., 1985—, vice chmn. rsch. dept., 1994-96. Pres. Am. Fedn. for Clin. Rsch., Thorofare, NJ, 1989—90; trustee Rsch. Am, Arlington, Va., 1989—90; mem. adv. coun. Nat. Inst. Diabetes, Digestive and Kidney Diseases, 1992—96; mem. bd. sci. counselors NHLBI, 2001—. Contbr. articles to profl. jours. Chmn., med. adv. coun. Cystic Fibrosis Found., Bethesda, 1988-90. Named to, Clevel. Med. Hall of Fame, 2001; recipient Samuel Rosenthal award in acad. pediat., 1996, Maurice Saltzman award, Mt. Sinai Health Care Found., 1998, Smith Coll. medal, 2001, Rainmaker of Yr., Edn. Rsch. Northeast Ohio Live Mag., 2002. Fellow ACP; mem. Am. Pediatric Soc., Am. Acad. Pediatrics, Am. Physiol. Soc., Am. Thoracic Soc., Am. Soc. Gene Therapy, Biophys. Soc., Soc. for Pediatric Rsch., Phi Beta Kappa, Sigma Xi, Alpha Omega Alpha. Office: Rainbow Babies/Child Hosp 2101 Adelbert Rd Cleveland OH 44106-2624 Business E-Mail: pamela.davis@case.edu.

DAVIS, PAMELA JO, special education educator; b. Canadian, Tex., Feb. 9, 1957; m. Charles Davis, 1979; 5 children. BA in Math., Baker U., 1979; MS in Spl. Edn., Emporia State U., 2003. Cert. H.S. Math. Tchr. Kans., 1979. H.S. math. tchr., 1979—85; math tchr. Johnson County C.C., Overland Park, Kans., 1989—; spl. edn. tchr. Anderson County H.S., Garnett, Kans., 2000—. Home: 8600 Hilltop Rd De Soto KS 66018

DAVIS, PAMELA MARIE, administrative analyst; b. New Orleans, Jan. 22, 1961; d. David James Davis Sr. and Anita Hurst Davis. B in Pub. Adminstrn., Loyola U., 1983. Adminstrv. analyst divsn. housing and neighborhood devel. City of New Orleans, 1988—2002, prin. analyst divsn. housing and neighborhood devel., 2003—; civil svc. trainer Civil Svc. Dept., New Orleans, 1991—. Mem. City Civil Svc. Commn., New Orleans, 1999—. Contbr. (employee newsletters) The Link/Our Beat, 1999—. Lector St. Peter Claver Ch., New Orleans, 1971—, lector tng. coord., 1991—, chairperson worship commn., 1988—92; assoc. mem., pres. St. Vincent de Paul Conf., New Orleans, 1994—99; del. Nat. Black Cath. Congress, 1992; mem. parish coun. St. Peter Claver Ch., New Orleans, 1985—97; bd. dirs. Outstanding Young Ams., 1996—98. Named one of Outstanding Young Women of Am., 1983, 1988; recipient Order of St. Louis medallion, Archdiocese of New Orleans, 1988, Hibernia Merit award, Bur. Govtl. Rsch., 1997. Mem.: Legion of Mary (assoc.). Democrat. Roman Catholic. Avocations: reading, playing table tennis, traveling. Office: Divsn Housing and Neighborhood Devel 1340 Poydras St 10th Fl New Orleans LA 70112

DAVIS, PATRICIA ANNE, secondary school educator, art educator; b. Norfolk, Va., Dec. 7, 1942; d. Robert Aloysius Davis III and Audrey Rowe. BA in Art, Caldwell Coll., 1968; MA in Art, Ball State U., 1976. Cert. tchr. Md. 2nd grade tchr. Sacred Heart Elem. Sch., Lyndhurst, NJ, 1963—66; 1st grade tchr. Holy Spirit Elem. Sch., Union, NJ, 1966—68; art tchr. grades 1-8, lang. arts tchr. grades 1-3 Mt. St. Dominic Acad. Grad. Sch., Caldwell, NJ, 1968—70; arts chair, educator St. Mary's H.S., Rutherford, NJ, 1970—77, Caldwell (N.J.) Coll., 1977—78, George Mason Jr./Sr. H.S., Falls Church, Va., 1978—79, Our Lady of Good Counsel H.S., Wheaton, Md., 1979—. Supr., student art tchr. Caldwell Coll., 1975—78; trustee Lacordaire Acad., Montclair, NJ, 1976—78; evaluator, middle states teams Chesapeake Riverdale H.S. Mem.: Md. Art Edn. Assn., Nat. Art Educators Assn. Roman Catholic. Avocations: calligraphy, painting, reading, gardening, visiting museums and galleries. Home: 20305 Cabana Dr Germantown MD 20876 Office: Our Lady of Good Counsel HS 11601 Georgia Ave Wheaton MD 20902

DAVIS, PATTI, writer; b. L.A., Oct. 22, 1952; d. Ronald Reagan (former U.S. pres.) and Nancy Davis Reagan; m. Paul Grilley, 1984 (div. 1990). Attended, Northwestern U., U. So. Calif. Hostess, singer Gt. Am. Food and Beverage Co., Santa Monica, Calif. Conducted seminars on dysfunctional families. Appeared in Vega$, Nero Wolfe, Trapper John, M.D.; author: Home Front, 1986, Deadfall, 1989, A House of Secrets, 1992, The Way I See It, 1993, Bondage, 1994; featured in Playboy Mag., June 1994. Office: Simon & Schuster Ste 383 1230 Avenue Of The Americas Fl Concl New York NY 10020-1586

DAVIS, PAULA MAY, music educator; b. Huntington, W.Va., Feb. 17, 1957; d. Paul Adair and Frances Edwards Warren; m. Donald Allen Davis, June 17, 1996; 1 child, Christina Marie Lewis. B.A. in music edn., Marshall

U., 1984—88, M.S. in adult and tech. edn., 1998—99. Choral dir. Vinson H.S., Huntington, W.Va., 1988—89; elem. music tchr. Prichard Elem. Sch., Prichard, W.Va., 1988—89; choral dir. Buffalo H.S., Kenova, W.Va., 1989—91; gen. music Buffalo Mid. Sch., Kenova, W.Va., 1991—2000; choral dir. Spring Valley H.S., Huntington, W.Va., 2000—. Choral dir. Lavalette United Meth. Ch., W.Va., 1997—2000, Steele Meml. United Meth. Ch., Barboursville, W.Va., 1991—97, music ministry dir., 2003—. Scholarship com. mem. Huntington Area Postal Credit Union, W.Va., 1999—2003; sec. Western Bd. of Ordained Ministries, Huntington, W.Va., 1999—2003; corr. sec. WV Alpha Delta Kappa, 2000—02; altruistic chmn. Alpha Delta Kappa, Huntington, W.Va., 1998—2000. Mem.: Music Educators Nat. Assn., KYOVA Quilt Soc., WV Alpha Delta Kappa (historian 2002—04). Democrat-Npl. Meth. Avocations: reading, quilting, singing. Office: Wayne County School System PO Box 79 Wayne WV 25570 Personal E-mail: singingquilter96@yahoo.com.

DAVIS, ROBIN JEAN, state supreme court justice; b. Boone County, W.Va., Apr. 6, 1956; m. Scott Segal; 1 child, Oliver. BS, W.Va. Wesleyan Coll., 1978; MA in Indsl. Rels., JD, W.Va. U., 1982. With Segal & Davis L.C., 1982-96; justice W.Va. Supreme Ct. of Appeals, 1996—, chief justice, 1998—2002. Mem. W.Va. U. Law Inst., W.Va. Bd. of Law Examiners, 1991—. Contbr. articles to W.Va. Law Rev. Mem. ABA, Assn. of Trial Lawyers of Am., Kanawha County Bar Assn., Am. Acad. Matrimonial Lawyers. Office: Supreme Ct of Appeals Bldg 1 Rm E 301 State Capitol Charleston WV 25305

DAVIS, RUBY DEE See DEE, RUBY

DAVIS, RUTH A. federal agency administrator; b. Phoenix, May 28, 1943; BA, Spelman Coll., 1966; MSW, U. Calif., Berkeley, 1968. Consular officer, Kinshasa, Zaire, 1969-71, Nairobi, Kenya, 1971-73, Tokyo, 1973-76, Naples, Italy, 1976-80; spl. asst. internat. affairs Mayor of Washington, 1980-82; sr. watch officer ops. ctr. Dept. State, 1982-84, chief tng. and liaison, bur. pers., 1984-86; consul gen. Barcelona, 1987-91; amb. to Benin, 1992-96; prin. dept. asst. Sec. State. for Consular Affairs U.S. Dept State, Washington, 1995-97, dir. nat. fgn. affairs tng. ctr., 1997—2001; dir. gen. of foreign serv. U.S. Dept. State, Washington, 2001—. Mem. sr. seminar Fgn. Svc. Inst., 1992. Office: US Dept State Bureau of Human Resources 2201 C St NW Washington DC 20520

DAVIS, RUTH CAROL, pharmacy educator; b. Wilkes-Barre, Pa., Oct. 27, 1943; d. Morris David Davis and Helen Jane Gillis. BS, Phila. Coll. Pharmacy and Sci., 1967; PharmD, Ohio State U., 1970; AA in Elec. Engring., ITT Tech. Inst., 1999. Cert. pharmacist, Pa., Md. Mgr. pharmacist Fairview Pharmacy, Etters, Pa.; mgr., pharmacist Neighborcare Pharmacy, Balt.; dir. ambulatory svcs. Rombro Health Svcs., Balt.; tchr., pharmacist Boothwyn Pharmacy, Phila.; pharm. cons. Nat. Rx Svcs. of Pa.; Eagle Managed Care, 1996; pharmacist Pharmastat Inc., 1996—; pharmacy supr. Johns Hopkins Hospice Pharmacy, 2000—; asst. prof. pharmacy Anne Arundel C.C., 2001—. Adj. prof. Essex C.C., 1999, Balt. City C.C., 2000. Republican. Baptist. Avocations: music, reading. Home and Office: 75 Lion Dr Hanover PA 17331-3849

DAVIS, RUTH MARGARET (MRS. BENJAMIN FRANKLIN LOHR), information technology executive; b. Sharpsville, Pa., Oct. 19, 1928; d. W. George and Mary Anna (Ackermann) D.; m. Benjamin F. Lohr, Apr. 29, 1961. BA, Am. U., 1950; MA, U. Md., 1952, PhD, 1955, CMU, 1978, U. Md., 2000. Statistician FAO, UN, Washington, 1946-49; mathematician Nat. Bur. Standards, 1950-51; head ops. rsch. div. David Taylor Model Basin, 1955-61; staff asst. Office Dir. Def. Rsch. and Engring. Dept. Def., 1961-67; asso. dir. rsch. and devel. Nat. Libr. Medicine, 1967-68; dir. Lister Hill Nat. Center for Biomed. Communications, 1968-70; dir. Inst. for Computer Scis. and Tech. Nat. Bur. Standards, 1970-77; dep. undersec. def. for rsch. and engring., 1977-79; asst. sec. resource applications U.S. Dept. Energy, 1979-81; chmn., pres., CEO Pymatuning Group Inc. FMR, 1981-2000. Chmn. Aerospace Corp., 1994—2001; lectr. U. Md., 1955—57, Am. U., 1957—58; vis. prof. computer sci. U. Pa., 1969—72; adj. prof. U. Pitts.; mem. Md. Gov.'s Sci. Adv. Coun., 1971—77; chmn. nat. adv. coun. Elec. Power Rsch. Inst., 1975—76. Contbr. articles to profl. jours. Recipient Rockefeller Tech. Mgmt. award, 1973, Fed. Woman of the Yr. award, 1973, Systems Profl. of Yr. award, 1979, Disting. Svc. medal, U.S. Dept. Def., 1979, U.S. Dept. Energy, 1981, Gold medal, 1981, Ada A. Lovelace award, 1984, Disting. Alumnus award, U. Md., 1993; inducted into Computer News Hall of Fame, 1988. Fellow AIAA, Soc. for Info. Display; mem. AAAS, Am. Math. Soc., Math. Assn. Am., Nat. Acad. Engring. (counselor), Nat. Acad. Pub. Adminstrn., Nat. Acad. Arts and Scis., Washington Philos. Soc., Sigma Pi Sigma, Tau Beta Pi. Office: Pymatuning Group Inc 1500 N Beauregard St Ste 101 Alexandria VA 22311-1878 Office Phone: 703-671-3500. E-mail: rmdavis5@aol.com.

DAVIS, SARA LEA, pharmacist; b. Knoxville, Tenn., Aug. 1, 1951; d. Horace William and Margaret Jewel (Hill) D. BS in Liberal Arts, U. Tenn., 1973; BS in Pharmacy, U. Tenn., Memphis, 1976, PharmD, 1977. Asst. mgr. Pharmaco Nuclear, Inc., Chgo., 1977-79; nuclear pharmacist Kansas City, Mo., 1979, Bapt. Meml. Hosp., Memphis, 1979-83; asst. mgr. Syncor, Inc., Washington, 1983-84; staff pharmacist Rite Aid Corp., Knoxville, 1984—2002, pharmacist-in-charge, 1987—. Rep. 3d High Country Nuclear Medicine Conf., Vail, Colo., 1983; mem. adv. bd. V.I.P. Home Nursing & Rehab., Knoxville, 1985-86. Active Leconte Exec. Women's Coun. Mem. Am. Pharm. Assn., Acad. Pharm. Sci. (sect. nuclear pharmacy), Soc. Nuclear Medicine, Memphis Bus. and Profl. Women's Assn. (bd. dirs. 1982-83), Club Leconte, U. Tenn. Century Club, Mortar Bd., Phi Beta Kappa, Phi Kappa Phi, Rho Chi, Alpha Lambda Delta. Baptist. Office: Rite Aid Pharmacy 508 E Tri County Blvd Oliver Springs TN 37840-2018

DAVIS, SARAH IRWIN, retired English language educator; b. Louisburg, N.C., Nov. 17, 1923; d. M. Stuart and May Amanda (Holmes) D.; m. Charles B. Goodrich, Nov. 18, 1949 (div. 1953). AB, U. N.C., 1944, AM, 1945; PhD, NYU, 1953. Tchg. asst. English dept. NYU, 1948-51; tchr. English Elizabeth Irwin H.S., N.Y.C., 1951-53; editor coll. texts Henry Holt, N.Y.C., 1953-55; editor coll. texts, encylopedias McGraw-Hill, N.Y.C., Rome, 1955—60; asst. prof. English Louisburg (N.C.) Coll., 1960-63, Randolph-Macon Woman's Coll., Lynchburg, Va., 1963-70, assoc. prof. English, 1970-75, chairperson Am. studies, 1971-87, prof. English and Am. studies, 1975-87, ret., 1987. Contbr. articles to profl. jours. Mem. MLA, Am. Studies Assn., N.C.-Va. Coll. English Assn. (various coms.), Franklin County Hist. Soc. (pres. 1989-94). Address: Carol Woods 139 750 Weaver Dairy Rd Chapel Hill NC 27514

DAVIS, SHARON CADE, secondary school educator; b. Tyler, Tex., Sept. 27, 1948; d. Bert Goodwin and Maurine Cade; m. James Larry Davis, Feb. 6, 1977; 1 child, Sheryl Rene. BS in Vocat. Home Econs., Stephen F. Austin State U., 1971, EdM in Early Childhood Edn., 1977. Cert. tchr. home econs., kindergarten, early childhood, mental retardation Tex. Early childhood specialist Galveston (Tex.) Ind. Sch. Dist., 1971—73; dir. Project Imagine Infant Devel. Ctr., Nacogdoches, Tex., 1973—76; therapist technician Rusk (Tex.) State Hosp., 1977—79; spl. edn. resource tchr. Westwood Primary Sch., Palestine, Tex., 1979—81, Maydelle (Tex.) Ind. Sch. Dist., 1981—83; kindergarten tchr. Rusk Primary Sch.-Palestine Ind. Sch. Dist., 1983—87; co-dir., tchr. New Horizons Pvt. Sch., Palestine, 1987—90; prekindergarten tchr. for children with disabilities Elkhart (Tex.) Elem. Sch.-Elkhart Ind. Sch. Dist., 1990—98; edn. coord. Region VII Edn. Svc. Ctr. Head Start, Jacksonville, Tex., 1998—. Adj. instr. child devel. Trinity Valley C.C., Palestine, 1988—. Del. Tex. Dem. Party, Palestine, 2000—00; sec. Anderson County Dem. Women's Orgn., Palestine, 2001—03; bd. mem. Anderson County Champions for Children, Palestine, 2000—03. Recipient Promising Practice award, Tex. Edn. Agy., 1994, 1997. Mem.: Tex. Elem. Prins. and Suprs. Assn. (assoc.), Nat. Assn. for the Edn. Young Children (assoc.), Beta Sigma Phi (assoc.; Alpha Phi Kappa chpt.). Presbyterian. Avocations: photography, travel, music, amateur radio, gardening.

DAVIS, SHEILA KAY, administrative assistant; b. Elkins, W.Va., Dec. 18, 1966; d. Darl Timmie Sr. and Gloria Becky (Armstrong) Kelley; m. Howard William Davis Sr., Nov. 23, 1985; 1 child, Howard William Jr. Diploma, Randolph County Vo-Tech., 1985, Computer Tng. Ctr., 1992. Office mgr., legal sec. Carlton K. Rosencrance Law Office, Elkins, 1986—97; adminstrv. asst. U.S. Fish and Wildlife Svc., Elkins, W.Va., 1997—. Sec. Elkins Jaycees, 1989, v.p., 1990. Avocations: computers, sports, dance.

DAVIS, SHIRLEY ROSS See SULLIVAN, SHIRLEY ROSS

DAVIS, SUE ELLEN H. elementary and secondary music educator; b. Girard, Ohio, May 26, 1952; d. Edgar J. and Jane A. (O'Brien) Harris; 1 child, Heidi Elizabeth. BM, Youngstown (Ohio) State U., 1975, MS in Edn./Sch. Counseling, 1985. Cert. counselor, music tchr. K-12, sch. counselor. Tchr. vocal music, kindergarten-12th grade Girard City Schs. Grant coord. Tng. Ohio Parents for Success, Girard City Schs. Active in ch. and community orgns.; co-founder Cmty. Band, 2002. Mem. NEA, Ohio Edn. Assn., Girard Edn. Assn., Nat. Assn. Tchrs. Singing (high sch. div. competition judge), Music Educators Nat. Conf., ASCD, Ohio Sch. Counselor Assn., Ohio Career Devel. Assn., Ohio Assn. Counseling and Devel., Eastern Ohio Counselor's Assn., Ohio Assn. Counselor Educators and Suprs., Ohio Coll. Pers. Assn., Ohio Mental Health Counselors Assn., Ohio Assn. for Specialists in Group Work, Phi Delta Kappa, Delta Kappa Gamma, Sigma Alpha Iota.

DAVIS, SUSAN A. congresswoman; b. Cambridge, Mass., Apr. 13, 1944; m. Steve, 1970; children: Jeffrey, Benjamin. Degree in Sociology, U. Calif., Berkeley; MA in Social Work, U. N.C. Social worker; exec. dir. Aaron Price Fellowship Program, 1990-93; served Calif. State Assembly, 1994-2000; congresswoman Calif. 53rd Dist., 2000—; mem. Ho. Com. on Veteran Affairs. Mem. Congressional com. House Armed Svcs., Edn. and Workforce; chaired Women's Caucus for Senate and Assembly, Consumer Protection, Govt. Efficiency, Econ. Devel. com.; created and co-chaired Select com. on Adolescence. Mem. San Diego City Sch. Bd., 1983-1992, pres. and v.p.; pres. League of Women Voters San Diego., Democrat. Office: 1224 Longworth House Office bldg Washington DC 20515*

DAVIS, SUSAN F. human resources specialist; BS, MS, Beloit Coll.; MBA, U. Mich. From strategic planner to corp. mgr. tng. and devel. Hoover Universal Corp., 1983-85; various positions Johnson Controls, Inc., Milw., 1985-94, corp. officer, v.p. human resources, 1994—. Bd. dirs. Quanex Corp. Office: Johnson Controls Inc 5757 N Green Bay Ave Milwaukee WI 53209-4408

DAVIS, SUZANNE SPIEGEL, retired information specialist; b. St. Louis, Sept. 27, 1935; d. Albert Louis Jr. and Dorothy Lydia (Grafeman) Spiegel; m. Glenn Guy Davis Jr., Sept. 23, 1961 (div. Mar. 1986); 1 child, Wendy Sue. BA, U. Okla., 1957; MLS, U. Ill., 1958. Reference asst. Atlanta Pub. Libr., 1958-59, head adult dept. Ida Williams br., 1959-61, head Fulton County depts, 1961-62; pub. svcs. and documents libr. Queens Coll. Libr., Charlotte, 1969-83; info. specialist Pub. Libr. Charlotte and Mecklenburg, NC, 1983—96. Pres. Charlotte Panhellenic Congress, 1965-66, Charlotte Nature Mus. Guild, 1969-70; rec. chmn. ARC, Mecklenburg County Unit, Charlotte, 1968-69, tng. chmn., 1969-70. Mem. Southeastern Libr. Assn., N.C. Libr. Assn., Charity League, Guild of Nature Mus. and Discovery Place, Beta Phi Mu, Phi Alpha Theta, Alpha Phi. (Michaelanean award 1984). Republican. Presbyterian.

DAVIS, TERRI LEE, graphics designer, writer, artist; d. Arthur George and Frances Ardele Smith; m. Michael Paul Davis, Oct. 22, 1977; children: Jodie Lynn Hammond, David James McMullen. Freelance graphic artist, Milwaukie, Oreg., 1996—; graphic artist Oreg. Health Scis. U., Portland, 1997—. Author: The Path of Grief, A Journey From Mourning to Life. Avocations: reading, photography. Home: 11988 SE Wood Ave Milwaukie OR 97222 Office Phone: 503-513-6197. Personal E-mail: tdavis@spiritone.com.

DAVIS, TUFTS, artist; b. Oct. 9, 1938; d. Helen Tufts; m. Richard McLaren Colwell, Jan. 30, 1994; m. Robert Whelihan, Nov. 7, 1950 (div. Nov. 1990); children: Harriet Tufts Whelihan, Elizabeth Whelihan. AA, San Diego City Coll.; student, Atelier Fougerat, Paris, France, Rhonde Island Sch. of Design, Guam Territorial Coll., Agana, Guam, Coronado Sch. of Fine Arts, Silvermine Sch. for the Arts, New Canaan, Conn., Studio II, Westport, Conn., Ringling Sch. of Art, Sarasota, Fla., 2001—03. Tchr. watercolor Ridgefield (Conn.) Guild of Arts, 1992—94, Grenwich. Conn. Adult Edn., 1993—94, Adult Edn., Wilton, Conn., 1993—94, Hilton Beach Watercolor Studio Satelite Classes, Sarasota, Fla., 1995—96. One-woman shows include Wilton Gallery, Wilton, Conn. (First Place, 1979, Second Place, 1981), Ye Old Drugstore Gallery, Vinalhaven, Maine, Adair Gallery, Faience, Norwalk, Conn., Maine Maritime Acad., Castine, Maine, exhibited in group shows at Thirty-Fifth New England Exhibition 1984, Thirty-Third New England Exhibition 1982 (Watercolor Medium, 1984), Thirty-First New England Exhibition 1980, Salmagundi Club, N.Y.C., 1980, 59th Conn. Women Artist, 1988, Conn. Watercolor Soc., New Britian Mus., 1990, Univ. of Hartford, 1982—87, John Slade Ely House, New Haven, Conn., 1991, Katherine Butler Gallery, Sarasota, Fla., 2001—03, Brooksville, Maine, 2001—03, Art in the Park, Sarasota, Fla., 2001—03 (Honorable Mention, 2001, Second Place, 2002, 2003), Old Post Office Gallery, South Thomaston, Maine, 2001—03, Represented in permanent collections Marketing Corp. of Am., Hearst Corp. Established Safe Rides For Teenagers Wilton (Conn.) HS, 1982; vol. Safe Place & Rape Crisis Ctr., 1998—2003. Recipient First Place, Sunnyvale, Calif. Arts Festival, Palo Alto, Calif. Art Club, Rowayton, Conn. Arts Ctr., 1989, Second Place, SCAN - Mary Sanford Memorial award, 1981. Republican. Congregational. Avocations: gardening, golf, swimming, tennis. Home: 7209 Churston Lane University Park FL 34201

DAVIS, VIRGINIA, trade show producer; b. Waycross, Ga., Nov. 14, 1933; d. Arthur Lewis and Mina (Hyers) Davis; m. Edward Anthony Carfano, July 3, 1954 (div. June 1976). Adminstrv. asst. Mills Music Ltd., N.Y.C., 1960-67; v.p. Edward Carr Prodns., Ltd., N.Y.C., 1990-96; owner Virginia Davis Trade Shows, Convs., Meetings, N.Y.C. and Phoenix, 1973—; asst. at trade shows and press confs. William Campeau Pub. Rels., 1983—. Democrat. Avocations: reading, dance, yoga, animals. Home: 5301 W Camelback Rd Sun City AZ 85351

DAVIS, VIVIAN, English language educator; Tchr. Spanish Prairie View Coll., Tex.; secondary sch. tchr. English; prof. English Eastfield Coll., Mesquite, Tex. Mem. Nat. Coun. Tchrs. English (exec. com., dir. Comm. on Lang., mem. Achievements Awards in Writing adv. com., adv. com. People of Color, com. Status and Role of Women in the Profession, leadership roles Conf. Coll. Compsition and Comm. Office: Eastfield Coll Dept English 3737 Motley Dr Mesquite TX 75150-2033

DAVIS, WANDA ROSE, lawyer; b. Lampasas, Tex., Oct. 4, 1937; d. Ellis DeWitt and Julia Doris (Rose) Cockrell; m. Richard Andrew Fulcher, May 9, 1959 (div. 1969); 1 child, Greg Ellis ; m. Edwin Leon Davis, Jan. 14, 1973 (div. 1985). BBA, U. Tex., 1959, JD, 1971. Bar: Tex. 1971, Colo. 1981, U.S. Dist. Ct. (no. dist.) Tex. 1972, U.S. Dist. Ct. Colo. 1981, U.S. Ct. Appeals (10th cir. 1981), U.S. Supreme Ct. 1976. Atty. Atlantic Richfield Co., Dallas, 1971; assoc. firm Crocker & Murphy, Dallas, 1971-72; prin. Wanda Davis, Atty. at Law, Dallas, 1972-73; ptnr. firm Davis & Davis Inc., Dallas, 1973-75; atty. adviser HUD, Dallas, 1974-75, Air Force Acctg. and Fin. Ctr., Danver, 1976-92; co-chmn. regional Profl. Devel. Inst. Am. Soc. Mil. Comptrollers, Colorado Springs, Colo., 1982; chmn. Lowry AFB Noontime Edn. Program, Exercise Program, Denver, 1977-83; mem. speakers bur. Colo. Women's Bar, 1995—, Lowry AFB, 1981-83. Mem. fed. ct. liaison com. U.S. Dist. Ct. Colo., 1983; mem. Leaders of the Fed. Bar Assn. People to People Del. to China, USSR and Finland, 1986. Contbr. numerous articles to profl. jours. Bd. dirs. Pres.'s Coun. Met. Denver, 1981-83; mem. Lowry AFB Alcohol Abuse Exec. Com., 1981-84. Recipient Spl. Achievement award USAF, 1978; Upward Mobility award Fed. Profl. and Adminstrv. Women Denver, 1979, Internat. Humanitarian award CARE, 1994. Mem. Fed. Bar Assn. (pres. Colo. 1982-83, mem. nat. coun. 1984—, Earl W. Kintner Disting. Svc. award 1983, 1st v.p. 10th cir. 1986-97, Internat. Hummanitarian award CARE, 1994), Zach Found. for Burned Children (award 1995), Colo. Trial Lawyers Assn., Bus. and Profl. Women's Club (dist. IV East dir. 1983-84, Colo. pres. 1988-89), Am. Soc. Mil. Comptrollers (pres. 1984-85), Denver south Met. Bus. and Profl. Women's Club (pres. 1982-83), Denver Silver Spruce Am. Bus. Women's Assn. (pres. 1981-82; Woman of Yr. award 1982), Colo. Jud. Inst., Colo. Concerned Lawyers, Profl. Mgrs. Assn., Fed. Women's Program (v.p. Denver 1980), Colo. Woman News Community adv. bd. 1988—), Dallas Bar Assn., Tex. Bar Assn., Denver Bar Assn., Altrusa, Zonta, Denver Nancy Langhorn Federally Employed Women (pres. 1979-80). Christian.

DAVIS, YVONNE D. county official; b. Orange, N.J., Sept. 21, 1947; d. William J. and Alice-Ruth Patterson; m. Royce Davis; children: Shannon K., Sarah K. BA in Spanish, Montclair State Coll., Upper Montclair, N.J., 1975; cert. pub. mgmt., Kean Coll., Union, N.J., 1982; cert. equal employment, Rutgers U., 1984. Bilingual family svc. worker dept. citizen svcs. Essex County Divsn. Welfare, Newark, 1971-78, family svc. supr., 1978-81, adminstrv. analyst, 1981-83, prin. personnel technician, 1983-86, pers. mgr., supr. prin. pers. technician, 1984—, adminstrv. dep. dir. welfare, 1992-93, dir. dept., 1994-95, pers. mgr., 1995-99, chief pers. and labor rels., 1999, dep. dir. welfare, 2000—. Mem. exec. bd. Essex County Minority Employees Assn., Newark, 1984-85; mem. employment coun. Tng., Inc., Newark; mem. Essex County Adv. Bd. on Status of Women; mem. Coordinating Coun. for Social Svcs., Essex County, N.J.; mem. Essex County Ins. Commn.; mem. Essex County Juvenile Justice Detention Ctr. Policy Reform Task Force, 1997—; active Epilepsy Found. Am., Trenton; vol. Isaiah Ho. Homeless Shelter, 2000. Recipient Excellence in Personnel Mgmt. award Essex County Minority Employees Assn., 1986, Excellence in Spanish award Nat. Assn. Tchrs. Spanish, 1964, 65, Excellence in French award Nat. Assn. Tchrs. French, 1965, Recognition award United Way, 1984-2000; cert. of appreciation U.S. Dept. Treas., 1984, tng. cert. N.J. Div. Civil Rights, 1988. Mem. NAFE, NAACP, Am. Mgmt. Assn., Am. Assn. Affirmative Action, Nat. Assn. Pub. Sector Equal Opportunity Officers, Nat. Assn. Negro Bus. and Profl. Women Inc., Mcpl. Career Women Newark Inc. Democrat. Baptist. Avocations: photography, theater workshop. Office: Essex County Dept Citizen Svcs Divsn Welfare Admin Offices 18 Rector St 9th Fl Newark NJ 07102-4512

DAVIS-GOGA, MURIEL E. elementary school educator; b. Louisburg, Ky., July 4, 1966; d. Revie V. Davis and Edward M. Madison; m. Joseph E. Goga, July 22, 2000. AAS in Child Devel., Harold Washington Coll., Chgo., 2001. Advanced Certificate Child Development Pre School Harold Wash. Coll., 2001. Tchr. asst./ head tchr. Chgo. Commons, 2000—02; tchr. asst. Chgo. Pub. Schools, 2002—. Head tchr. The Children's Ho., Chgo., 2000. Adv. for young children Chgo. Commons, 2001—02. Mem.: Phi Theta Kappa (life).

DAVIS-JEROME, EILEEN GEORGE, principal; b. N.Y.C., Nov. 10, 1946; d. Rennie and Flora May (Compton) George; m. Bruce Davis, Aug. 8, 1970 (div. 1978); m. Frantz Jerome, Sept. 7, 1982; 1 child, Thais Davis. BFA, Pratt Inst., 1968; MA, CUNY, 1971, PD, 1990; EdD, Nova Southeastern U., 1998. Lic. ednl. adminstr., prin., instrn. specialist, N.Y. Tchr. fine arts Herbert Lehman High Sch., Bronx, N.Y., 1971-75; tchr. English/fine arts Jr. High Sch. 131, Bronx, 1975-76; tchr. English Jr. High Sch. 22, Bronx, 1976-79; tchr. fine arts Andrew Jackson High Sch., Cambria Heights, N.Y., 1979-83, coord. art dept., 1986-92; admissions counselor Fashion Inst. Tech., SUNY, N.Y.C., 1983-85; coord. Queensborough Coll. Project Prize, Bayside, N.Y., 1991-92; project dir. Andrew Jackson Magnet High Sch., Cambria Heights, N.Y., 1993—, project dir. Humanities and the Arts, 1994—; ednl. adminstr. Queens High Sch. Office, N.Y.C. Pub. High Schs., Corona, N.Y., 1993-94; prin. Humanities and the Arts Magnet H.S., Cambria Heights, NY, 1994—2003. Coord. internat. studies Friends of Jackson High Sch., Cambria Heights, 1986-93, equal opportunity coord., 1989-92; exam asst. N.Y. C. Bd. Edn., Bd. Examiners, Bklyn., 1983-87; curriculum/career cons. Fashion Inst., SUNY, Detroit, Washington, Phila., 1983-86. Curriculum writer N.Y. State Project ot Implement Career Edn., 1975, N.Y. State Futuring, 1984; proposal writer Magnet Sch. Funding, 1993; author: Resource Book, 1989. Mem., speaker Cambria Heights Civic Assn., 1983; mem. N.Y. Urban League, N.Y.C.; vol. Mayor's Vol. Action/Alpha Sr. Cr., Cambria Heights, 1984; vol. Black Spectrum Theatre Co., 1983-86; mem. coord. coun. h.s. divsn. N.Y.C. Bd. Edn., 1997—; v.p. for edn. Madam C.J. Walker Found., 2001—. Named Educator of Yr., NAACP/ACT-S0, N.Y.C., 1992; recipient Recognition award, Black Spectrum Theatre Co., 1983, Speakers award, N.Y.C. Bd. Edn. Open Doors, 1983—84, Black Exec. Exch. Program Nat. Urban League, N.Y.C., 1984, Developer Grant award, Impact II Grant, N.Y.C., 1989, Laurelton Club Prol. award, 1996, Disting. Educator award, L.I. br. Nat. Assn. Univ. Women, 2001, Life Membership award, NAACP, N.Y.C., 2001, Excellence in Edn. award, Omega Psi Phi, 2002, Disting. Educator award, Newsday, 2003, Outstanding Citizen citation, N.Y.C. Coun., 2003. Mem. ASCD, N.Y. State Art Tchrs. Assn., N.Y.C. Art Tchrs. Assn. (v.p., sec. 1983-85, cert. 1983-86), Cultural Heritage Alliance (assoc., Recognition award 1986), Greater Queens Chpt. The Links, Inc., Delta Sigma Theta (chair arts and letters 1991-97, Golden Life award 1991), Phi Delta Kappa (Disting. Cert. 1994). Democrat. Episcopalian. Avocations: painting, travel, dance, writing, theater. Office: Magnet HS Humanities and the Arts 20701 116th Ave Jamaica NY 11411-1038

DAVIS-KALUGIN, DORINNE SUE, audiologist; b. East Orange, N.J., Mar. 29, 1949; d. William Henry and Evelyn Doris (Thorp) Taylor; children: Larissa Louise, Peter Alexander; m. Eric S. Kalugin. BA, Montclair State Coll., 1971, MA, 1973. Cert. tchr. of hearing impaired, speech correctionist, tchr. speech and drama, supr. nursery sch. endorsement, N.J. Ednl. audiologist Kinnelon (N.J.) Bd. Edn., 1972-94, kindergarten tchr., 1994-97; ednl. audiologist Inst. for Career Advancement, Inc., 1980-82, Dover Gen. Hosp., 1984-86; pres. Hear You Are, Inc., 1987-98, Davis Ctr. Hearing Speech and Learning, Inc., Budd Lake, NJ, 1998—2002; with Davis Ctrs., Inc., 2002—. Adj. prof. Kean Coll., Union, NJ, 1993—95. Mem. NEA, Internat. Orgn. Educators Hearing Impaired, Am. Speech and Hearing Assn. (cert. clin. competence in audiology), Am. Acad. Audiology, N.J. Speech and Hearing Assn., N.J. Edn. Assn., Ednl. Audiology Assn. (past pres.). Methodist. Home: 51 King Rd Landing NJ 07850-1308 Office: Davis Ctrs Inc 98 Rt 46W Budd Lake NJ 07828

DAVIS-LEWIS, BETTYE, nursing educator; b. Egypt, Tex., Sept. 19, 1939; d. Henry Sr. and Eliza (Baylock) Davis; divorced; children: Kim Michelle, Roderick Trevor. BS, Prarie View A&M U., 1959; BA in Psychology, U. Houston, 1972; MEd, Tex. Southern U., 1974, EdD, 1982. Dir. edn. Houston Internat. Hosp., 1987—; dir. nurses Mental Health & Mental Retardation Auth. Harris County, Houston, 1982-87, Riverside Gen. Hosp., Houston; CEO, owner Diversified Health Care Systems, Inc., Houston, 1985—; asst. clin. prof. psychiat. nursing U. Tex., 1987-88; asst.

prof. allied health sci. Tex. So. U., Houton, 1989—. Adj. prof. Coll. Nursing, Prairie View (Tex.) A&M U., 1986—; lectr. in field; leadership extern. Mem. Harris County Coun. Orgns., 1987—; mem. polit. action com. Coalition 100 Black Women, 1988—; founder, mem. Hattie White Aux. br. NAACP, 1988; mem. grievance com. State Bar Tex., 1988—; chmn. S.W. Regional Nat. Black Ng'l Lobbyist on council, 1988—, grad. Leadership Tex.; bd. dirs. Theatre Under the Stars. Recipient Disting. Rsch. award Internat. Soc. Hypertension, Disting. Crystal award, Impact award Wheeler Ave. Bapt. Ch.; fellow Internat. Leadership Forum, Am. Leadership Forum. Fellow Internat. Soc. Hypertension in Blacks; mem. ANA, Nat. Black Nurses Assn. (bd. dirs.), Sigma Theta Tau, Chi Eta Phi. Home: 9114 Mcafee Dr Houston TX 77031-1104*

DAVISON, AUDREY M. lawyer, consultant; b. Flasher, N.D., Dec. 30, 1919; d. Frank and Laura Wyman Colegrove; m. John Roats, June 5, 1938 (div. June 1949); 1 child, Gary Charles Roats; m. Kenneth Bradley Davison (dec.); 1 child, Nelson Bradley. BA in Music, U. Wash., 1950; MA, Stanford U., 1963; JD, San Francisco Law Sch., 1992. Rsch. assoc. Vets. Hosp. and Stanford U., Palo Alto, Calif., 1965—67; sr. clin. lab. scientist Cmty. Hosp. of Los Gatos/Saratoga, Calif., 1973—85, San Jose Med. Group, 1986—94; cons. in environ. law Seattle, 1994—. Rsch. scientist VA, Palo Alto, 1967—73; instr. DeAnza C.C., Cupertino, Calif., 1974—79. Organizer citizen participation for preservation of foothills, Santa Clara County, Calif., 1970—75. Mem.: Assn. Women in Sci. Seattle chpt. 1997—99, co-chair outreach com.), Toastmasters Internat. (Dist. 2 officer 1997—, Area 3 Gov. 1997—, com. chair Success/Leadership Program 1998—99, Outstanding Mem. cert. and pin 1998). Achievements include development of 2.5% agarose column separation of anti-hemophilic globulin separation from frozen human plasma. Home: 320 Valley St #5 Seattle WA 98109

DAVISON, DAWN SHERRY, correctional administrator, educator; b. Chgo., Nov. 3, 1956; d. Henry and Teresa (Lombardo) Foreman; m. Wayne Thomas Davison, Apr. 21, 1979; children: Laurenne Teresa, Celise Arielle. BS, Loyola Marymount U., 1978; MS, Calif. State U., Fullerton, 1982. Personnel officer Calif. Inst. Women, Frontera, 1986-93; correctional bus. mgr. Calipatria (Calif.) State Prison, 1994-97; assoc. warden, correctional administrator Calif. State Prison L.A. County, Lancaster, 1997—, equal employment opportunity program coord. Mem. NAFE, Chicano Correctional Workers Am., Assn. Black Correctional Workers. Democrat. Avocations: theatre, jazz music, reading, sketching. Office: Calif State Prison L A County 44750 60th St W Lancaster CA 93536-7619

DAVIS-TOWNSEND, HELEN IRENE, retired art educator; b. North Adams, Mich., July 25, 1910; d. Bert and Jennie Louisa (Martin) Smith; m. Donald Hicks Davis, Mar. 21, 1931 (dec. Nov. 1944); children: Donald H. Jr., Bernard S., Bruce M., William J.; m. Loal Wendell Townsend, Dec. 27, 1971. BA, Mich. State U., 1952, MA, 1959. Permanent tchg. cert., Mich. Typist, sec. Buermann-Marshall Co., Lansing, Mich., 1928-30; pvt. sec. Frank L. Young, Jr., LLD, Lansing, 1930-31; typist Buermann-Marshall Co., Lansing, 1932-36, Olds Motor Co., Lansing, 1936-37; art tchr. Okemos (Mich.) Pub. Schs., 1952-72. Art club dir. Okemos H.S., 1952-72, tchr. adult edn. classes, 1962-70; supervising tchr. tchr. edn. program Mich. State U., East Lansing, 1960-72; region 8 rep., liaison officer Mich. Art Edn. Assn. State Bd., East Lansing, 1962-70; vis. artist John Wesley Coll., Owosso, Mich., 1979. Author, composer: (children's mus.) That Star Is Shaking Up Our Town, 1974, (song and music) Life Is a Road, 1974; artist numerous paintings. Sec.-typist Mich. Rep. Party, Lansing, 1932; children and youth choir dir. Wesleyan Meth. Ch., Lansing, 1939-72, choir mem., 1929-72; choir mem. Stockbridge (Mich.) United Meth. Ch., 1972-80. Recipient Bonderenco award, 1987; Hinman scholar Mich. State U., 1950, Alumni scholar, 1951-52. Mem. NEA (life), Mich. Edn. Assn. (life), Nat. Mus. of Women in Arts (charter), Art League of Manatee County, Lansing Art Gallery (charter). Methodist. Avocations: painting, playing piano and organ, bowling, theater, traveling.

DAVIS-YANCEY, GWENDOLYN, lawyer; b. Jackson, Mich., Apr. 6, 1955; d. Wendell Norman Sr. and Jean Davis; children: Natosha, Michael, Nicole, Jennifer, Cyril; m. Kenneth Donald Yancey, Dec. 9, 1995. BS, Wayne State U., 1990; JD, U. Detroit-Mercy, 1994. Bar: Mich., U.S. Dist. Ct. (ea. dist.) Mich.; cert. tchr. Mich. Legal sec. Dykema, Gossett, Detroit; chemistry tchr. Detroit Bd. Edn., 1990-92; atty. Misdemeanor Def.'s Office, Detroit, 1994-95, Legal Aid and Def.'s Office, Detroit, 1995-96. Davis-Yancey Law Office P.L.L.C., Southfield, Mich., 1996—; ptnr., owner Men's Legal Svc., 1999—. Mem. ABA, State Bar of Mich. (family law sect., real estate sect., bus. law sect., litig. sect.), Wayne County Family Law Bar. Office: Davis-Yancey Law Office PLLC # 703A W 15565 Northland Dr Southfield MI 48075

DAWES, DOMINIQUE, Olympic athlete; b. Silver Spring, Md., Nov. 20, 1976; BS, U. Md., 1999. Mem. U.S. Olympic Team, Barcelona, 1992, Atlanta, 1996. Named U.S.A. Gymnastics Athlete of Yr., 1993, Sportsperson of Yr., USA Gymnastics, 1994, 3d pl. team, Olympic Games, Barcelona, Spain, 1992, 2d pl. all around and floor exercise, 1st in vault and balance beam, 3d uneven bars, Coca Cola Nat. Championships, Salt Lake City, 1993, 2d in uneven bars and balance beam, World Gymnastics Championships, Birmingham, Eng., 1993, 1st pl. in all around, vault, balanve beam and floor exercise, McDonald's Am. Cup, Orlando, Fla., 1994, 1st pl. in all around, vault, uneven bars, balance beam and floor exercise, Cola Cola Nat. Championships, Nashville, 1994, 1st pl. in all around, NationsBank World Team Trials, Richmond, Va., 1994, 2d pl. team, World Championships, Dortmund, Germany, 1994, 1st pl. in uneven bars and floor exercise, 3d pl. in balance beam, Coca Cola Nat. Championships, New Orleans, 1995; recipient Arch McDonald award, Touchdown Club Washington, 1995, McDonald's Balancing It All award, 1995, Harry P. Iba Citizen Athlete award, 1995, Gold medal Team Competition, Olympic Games, Atlanta, 1996. Avocations: reading, dance, acting. Office: care USA Gymnastics Pan Am Plz 201 S Capitol Ave Ste 300 Indianapolis IN 46225-1058

DAWICKI, DOLORETTA DIANE, analytical chemist, research biochemist, educator; b. Fall River, Mass., Sept. 13, 1956; d. Walter and Stella Ann (Olszenski) D. BS, S.E. Mass. U., 1978; PhD, Brown U., 1986. Rsch. assoc. Meml. Hosp. R.I., Pawtucket, 1986-92; asst. prof. Brown U., Providence, 1986-96; rsch. assoc. VA Med. Ctr., Providence, 1992-96; quality control tech. svcs. prin. scientist Genzyme Corp., Framingham, Mass., 1996—. Contbr. articles to profl. jours. Mem. AAAS, Am. Soc. for Biochemistry and Molecular Biology, Parenteral Drug Assn. Achievements include research on in vivo antiplatelet mechanism of action of the clinical agent dipyridamole, endothelial cell injury, effects of nucleotides on leukocyte-endothelial cell interaction; assay development, optimization, and validation to monitor drug identity, safety, and efficacy; product testing and quality control release of commercial therapeutic finished drug products. Home: 3 Odyssey Ln Franklin MA 02038-2460 Office: Genzyme Corp PO Box 9322 Framingham MA 01701-9322 E-mail: dale.dawicki@genzyme.com.

DAWKINS, AMY, artist; b. Moberly, Mo., May 11, 1969; d. Frederick Eugene and Carol June D.; 1 child, James Eugene Dorman. BFA, Md. Inst. Coll. Art, 1991. Delivery truck driver UPS, Columbia, Mo., 1995-99; artist Dogkins Studio, Sturgeon, Mo., 1999—. Author: poems. Juror State of Mo., Columbia, 1999; student youth amb. People to People (Eisenhower) Program, Moberly, 1987. Scholar, grantee Md. Inst. Coll. Art, 1987-91; scholar Little Dixie Art Assn., 1987; named Honor Top of Class Moberly Rotary Club, 1991. Mem. Columbia Art League, Women in Arts Mus.,

Humane Soc. Columbia, Nat. ARbor Day Found. Avocations: painting, drawing, writing, photography, running. Home and Office: Dogkins Studio 19101 N Route V Sturgeon MO 65284-9470

DAWKINS, DEBORAH JEANNE, state legislator; b. Mobile; m. Senate from 48th dist., Jackson, 2000—. Vice chair com. environ. protection, conservation and water resources, exec. contingent fund, appropriations com.; active numerous coms. Democrat. Office: 22383 Meadowlark Dr Pass Christian MS 39571

DAWKINS, MARVA PHYLLIS, psychologist, educator; b. Jacksonville, Fla., Apr. 12, 1948; d. Ralph and Altamese (Padgett) Dawkins. Student U. Freiburg, Germany, 1969—70; BS Stetson U., 1971, MS Fla. State U., 1972, PhD Fla. State U., 1975. Registered psychologist Ill. Rsch. asst. Fla. State U., Tallahassee, 1970—72; clin. intern dpt. psychology Presbyn.-St. Luke's Med. Ctr., 1973—74; clin. intern dept. mental health Mile Square Health Ctr., Chgo., 1973—74, staff psychologist, dir. aftercare treatment program dept. mental health, 1974—75, staff psychologist, coord. devel. disabilities program, 1976—79; asst. prof. psychology U. N. Fla., Jacksonville, 1975—76, Rush U.-Presbyn. St. Luke's Med. Ctr., Chgo., 1976—; pvt. practice clin. psychology, 1977—. Exec. dir. Inst. Cmty. Mental Health, 1979—89; cons. safety evaluation program Isaac Ray Ctr., 1986—91; dir. Ctr. Applied Psychology and Forensic Studies, 1991—; psychology cons. Disability Policy Br. Social Security Adminstrn., Chgo., 1980—; med. expert Social Security Administrn., Chgo., 1995—; cons. in field. Mem.: APA, Assn. Black Psychologists.

DAWSON, CAROL GENE, former commissioner, writer, consultant; b. Indpls., Sept. 8, 1937; d. Ernest Eugene (dec.) and Hilda Lou (Carroll) D.; m. Robert Edmund Bauman, Nov. 19, 1960 (div. 1982); children: Edward Carroll, Eugenie Marie, Victoria Ann, James Shields; m. Franklin Dean Smith, Aug. 2, 1986. BA, Dunbarton Coll., Washington, 1959, Cath. U., 1960; MA in Internat. Transactions, George Mason U., 1994. Staff asst. Senator Kenneth B. Keating, Washington, 1959; exec. asst. Americans for Constl. Action, Washington, 1959; exec. sec. Youth for Nixon Lodge, Washington, 1959-60; legis. asst. Rep. Donald C. Bruce, Washington, 1961-63; dep. dir., pub. info. Goldwater for Pres. Campaign and Rep. Nat. Com., Washington, 1963-64; editor, assoc. editor The New Guard Mag., Washington, 1965-66; dir. info. Am. Conservative Union, Washington, 1966-67; publs. and news analyst White House, Washington, from 1969; staff reporter Easton (Md.) Star-Democrat, 1971-72; freelance writer Easton, 1972-77; real estate salesperson Latham Realtors, Easton, 1977-80; sr. staff asst. presdl. transition U.S. Office of Personnel Mgmt., Washington, 1980-81; dep. press sec. U.S. Dept. Energy, Washington, 1981-82, dep. spl. asst. to sec., 1982-84; commr. U.S. Consumer Product Safety Commn., Washington, 1984-93. Editor Cath. Currents newsletter, Washington, 1969-70. Bd. visitors Inst. Polit. Journalism Georgetown U., 1985—89; mem. Nat. Policy Forum, Coun. of Free Individuals in a Free Soc., Coun. on Internat. Trade, 1994—97; bd. dirs. Consumer Alert, 1995—; mem. Commonwealth of Va. Bd. Phys. Therapy, 2000—; bd. dirs. Nat. Conservative Campaign Fund, Washington, 1999—; chmn. Lancaster County (Va.) Rep. Com., 1996—2002, 99th Legis. Dist. Rep. Com., 2000—; mem. Va. Rep. State Ctrl. Com., 2001—. Recipient Award of Merit Young Americans for Freedom, 1970. Mem. The Charter 100, Reagan Appointees Alumni, The Fairfax Hunt Club (bd. govs. 1989-91). Roman Catholic. Home and Office: PO Box 2 Morattico VA 22523-0002 E-mail: cdawson@rivnet.net.

DAWSON, CINDY MARIE, lawyer; b. Oklahoma City, May 3, 1960; d. Alva Glenn and Ethel Estelle Horner; m. Ronnie L. Dawson, July 14, 1977; children: Kristina Lee Ann, Kathryn DeeAnn, Shaunna Renee. AA, Rose State Coll., Midwest City, Okla., 1993; BBA, U. Ctrl. Okla., 1994, postgrad., 1997—; JD, Oklahoma City U., 1997. Bar: Okla. 1997. Leasing agt. Brentwood Apts., Shawnee, Okla., 1988; bus. advisor Triple H Constrn., Eufaula, Okla., 1989-96; pvt. practice atty. Edmond, Okla., 1997-2000; asst. dist. atty. Shawnee, Okla., 2000—01; pvt. practice atty. Eufaula, 2001—. Mem.: ATLA, Legal Aid Western Okla., Okla. Criminal Def. Lawyers Assn., Okla. Trial Lawyers Assn., Okla. Bar Assn., Eufaula Alumni Assn., Phi Delta Phi. Avocations: reading, cooking, sports, travel. Office: 112 Selmon Rd Eufaula OK 74432 E-mail: dawsonpc@hotmail.com.

DAWSON, DIANNE, education educator, writer; d. Janita Mae Haffner and Leo Arthur Dawson; 1 child, Amanda Jean Hammack. BS, U. of SC., Charleston, SC, 1969—73; MA, Citadel, Charleston, S.C., 1980. Cert. Math/English tchr. S.C., 1990, Radiological Control Technician U.S. Navy, 1990. Instr. Program for Afloat Coll. Edn., Charleston, SC, 1981—83, Trident Tech. Coll., Charleston, SC, 1974—83, Berkeley County Sch., Charleston, SC, 1984—88; phys. sci. technician U.S. Navy, Charleston, SC, 1988—90; edn. specialist Bethesda Naval Med. Ctr., Md., 1990—92; pub. affairs specialist/writer Indian Health Svc., Rockville, Md., 1992—. Editor Md. Reservist Newsletter, Gaithersburg, Md., 1996—97. Editor guidelines for indian health service, author guidelines for indian health svc., poems. Com. mem. Nat. Indian Heritage Month Planning Com., Rockville, Md., 2000—03; pres. and cofounder Coastal Carolina MENSA, Charleston, SC, 1981—82. Recipient Meritorious Unit Commendation Award, U.S. Navy, 1989, Spl. Achievement Award, 1990, Spl. Svc. Awards, Indian Health Svc., Dept of Health and Human Svcs., 1998, 1999, 2000, President's Award (Group Award), Bill Clinton, 2000; Grad. Fellowship in Biometry, Med. U. S.C., 1984. Mem.: MENSA (life; pres., coastal carolina chpt. (1981-1982) 1980—2003). Office: Indian Health Svc 801 Thompson Ave Rockville MD 20852-1627 Office Phone: 301-443-1635. E-mail: dianne.dawson@ihs.hhs.gov.

DAWSON, DONNA L. secondary school educator; d. Donald William and Louise Elizabeth Dawson. Assoc. in Office Adminstrn., No. Ky. U., 1977, BA in English summa cum laude, 1979, MA in Secondary Edn., 1985. Cert. rank I in secondary edn., gifted and talented edn. Tchr. English Ockerman Mid. Sch. Boone County Schs., Florence, Ky., 1980—92, tchr. English Ryle H.S. Union, Ky., 1992—. Mem.: Nat. Coun. Tchrs. English, Kappa Delta Pi. Republican. Southern Baptist. Avocations: reading, historical and folk dance, travel.

DAWSON, KIM, reporter; Degree, Howard U. Reporter WISN, Milw., 2001—. Recipient Michele Clark fellowship, Radio and TV News Dirs. Assn. Office: WISN PO Box 402 Milwaukee WI 53201-0402

DAWSON, M. SUSAN, nursing educator, psychiatric clinical specialist; b. St. Louis, June 9, 1950; d. Lester A. and Natalie J. (Federer) Liebmann; m. W.M. Mark Dawson, Jan. 1, 1993; children: Jessica M. Patton, Jillian L. Countryman. ADN, St. Louis C.C., 1974; BSN, Webster U., 1988, MA in Edn., 1990; MSN, So. Ill. U., 1993; EdD, U. Mo., 1997. RN;bd. cert. psychiat. advanced practice nurse. Nurse, various locations, 1974—; nursing instr. Luth. Sch. Nursing, St. Louis, 1990-93, Lewis and Clark C.C., Godfrey, Ill., 1993-95; prof. nursing St. Louis C.C., 1992—; prof. Goal Program Greenville Coll., Ill., 1997—; assoc. faculty Jewish Coll. Nursing/Washington U., St. Louis, 1998—. Mem. Nat. League of Nurses, Sigma Theta Tau. Office: St Louis CC at Meramec 11333 Big Bend Rd Saint Louis MO 63122-5720

DAWSON, MARTHA BROMLEY, administrative assistant, software developer; b. Whitewater, Wis., Feb. 25, 1940; d. Fred G. and Ruth O. (Hackett) Bromley; m. James R. Dawson, June 10, 1959; children: Heather Joy Dawson Cudworth, Jamie Ruth Dawson Strebing. Student, U. Wis.-Stout, Menomonie, 1957-59, Ind. U., 1977-78. Cert. computer profl. Inst. for Cert. Computing Profls. Sys. analyst, programmer Johnson Controls, Milw.; 1963-69; software developer various orgns., Bloomington, Ind.,

1969—2000; sys. analyst, programmer Westinghouse Electric, Bloomington, 1973-75; adminstrv. asst. Bloomington (Ind.) Twp., 1979-2000; mem. com. new ch. devel. South Ind. conf. United Meth. Ch., 1998—, bd. ch. location and bldg. Bloomington dist., 2001—. Bd. dirs. Youth For Christ Ill. collegium 1983-85. Methodist. Avocation: genealogy. E-mail: mdawson@bluemarble.net.

DAWSON, MARY E. lawyer; b. Halifax, N.S., Can., June 23, 1942; d. Thomas Paul and Florence Margaret (Thurston) McMillan; m. Peter Dawson, Aug. 30, 1969; children: David, Emily. BA in Philosophy with honors, McGill U., 1963, BCL, 1966; DESD, U. Ottawa, 1968; LLB, Dalhousie U., 1970. Tax rschr. Revenue Can., Ottawa, 1967-68, legal counsel, 1968-69; tchg. fellow Dalhousie U., 1969-70; legis. drafter Dept. of Justice, Ottawa, 1970-79, assoc. chief legis. counsel, 1980-86, asst. dep. minister pub. law, 1986-88, assoc. dep. minister, 1988—. Mem. adv. bd. Ctr. Rsch. and Edn. Women and Work, Sch. Bus.; Carleton U. Recipient Lyon William Jacobs Q. C. award, 1965, 1978; scholar, McGill U., 1960. Mem.: Ont. Bar, Que. Bar, N.S. Bar, Internat. Bar Assn. (chmn. govt. law com. 1998—2002, mem. coun. 2002—). Avocations: nordic skiing, swimming, theater, reading. Home: 97 Reid Ave Ottawa ON Canada K1H 1T1 Office: Dept Justice Rm EMB-4175 Ottawa ON Canada K1A 0H8 E-mail: mary.dawson@justice.gc.ca.

DAWSON, MARY RUTH, curator, educator; b. Highland Park, Mich., Feb. 27, 1931; d. John Elson and Olga Josephine (Down) D. BS, Mich. State Coll., 1952; postgrad., U. Edinburgh, 1952-53; PhD, U. Kans., 1957; D of Humanities (hon.), Chatham Coll., 1983. Instr. zoology Smith Coll. 1958-61; asst. program dir. NSF, Washington, 1961-62; mem. staff Carnegie Mus., Pitts., 1962—, curator, 1971—, chmn. earth sci. div., 1973-97, acting dir., 1982-83, curator emeritus, 2003. Adj. prof. earth scis. U. Pitts., 1971—. Named Disting. Dau. Pa., 1987; recipient Arnold Guyot award, Nat. Geog. Soc., 1981, Woman in Sci. award, Chatham Coll., 1983, Disting. Alumni award, Mich. State U., 2003, Romer-Simpson medal, Soc. Vertebrate Paleontology; fellow, AAUW, 1958—59: Fulbright scholar, 1952—53, rsch. grantee, NSF, 1961—62, 1965—. Fellow Geol. Soc. Am., Arctic Inst. N.Am.; mem. Soc. Vertebrate Paleontology (hon.; v.p. 1972-73, pres. 1973-74), Paleontol. Soc., Paläontologische Gesellschaft, Bernese Mountain Dog Club Am., Am. Soc. Mammalogists, Phi Beta Kappa. Achievements include research and publication on Tertiary Lagomorpha, 1957—, early Tertiary Holarctic rodents, 1960—, Arctic paleontology, 1975—. Office: Carnegie Mus 4400 Forbes Ave Pittsburgh PA 15213-4080 E-mail: dawsonm@carnegiemuseums.org.

DAWSON, MIMI WEYFORTH, public policy consultant; b. St. Louis, Aug. 31, 1944; d. Francis Griffin and Jeanne (Gething) Weyforth; m. Rhett Brewer Dawson, Jan. 15, 1976; 2 children: Elizabeth Stuart, Andrew Brewer. AB, Washington U., St. Louis, 1966. Press sec., legis. asst. to Rep. James Symington, Mo. Dist., 1973; pres. sec., chief staff Sen. Bob Packwood, Oreg., 1973-81; commr. FCC, Washington, 1981-87; dep. Sec. U.S. Dept. Transp., Washington, 1987-89; sr. pub. policy cons. Wiley Rein and Fielding LLP, Washington, 1989—. Apptd. U.S. Holocaust Meml. Coun., 1992-98; adj. fellow Ctr. for Strategic and Internat. Studies. Mem. Atlantic Coun. U.S. (bd. dirs. 1995—). Republican. Roman Catholic. Office: Wiley Rein and Fielding LLP 1776 K St NW Washington DC 20006-2304 E-mail: mdawson@wrf.com.

DAWSON, MURIEL AMANDA (MANDY DAWSON), state legislator; b. Ft. Lauderdale, Fla., July 18, 1956; d. Clifford and Altemease (Laws) Hardy; divorced; children: Shateras (Tibby), Colongie, Ashley. Student, Fla. A&M U., 1975—80; degree in liberal arts, Barry U. Legis. asst. Fla. Ho. of Reps., Ft. Lauderdale, 1988-92, state legislator Dist. 93, 1992-98; mem. Fla. State Senate Dist. 30, 1998—. Mem. budget subcom. on transp. and econ. devel., commerce and econ. opportunities, health, aging and long-term care, regulated industries, apportionment and redistricting coms. Chairperson Fla. Commn. Minority Health, 1993-95; mem. children, families and health com. Nat. Conf. State Legis., 1995-96; co-vice chair Fla. Women's Legis. Caucus, 1995-96, mem. select com. on telecom., 1994-95; assoc. trustee Bethune-Cookman Coll., 1994; mem. north area adv. bd. Sch. Bd. Broward County, 1992—; mem. health care task force Nat. Black Caucus of State Legislators, 1993—; mem. Fla. Conf. Black State Legislators, 1992—; bd. dirs. Broward County Urban League, Ft. Lauderdale, 1994—, Friends of Children, Youth and Families, Ft. Lauderdale, 1996, Voice of Choice Adv. Bd., 1995, Ft. Lauderdale Children's Theatre, 1994-96, Healthy Mothers/Healthy Babies Coalition of Broward County, 1993—, Minority Bus. Enterprise, 1991-92, Child Care Connection; mem. exec. adv. bd. Nat. Black Police Assn., 1994; adv. bd. Child Care Connection, 1992—; founding mem. Multicultural Women's Issues Group, 1993; mem. Broward Healthy Start Coalition, 1993—, Women's Polit. Caucus, Gwen Cherry chpt., 1990—, Ctrl. Broward Dem. Club, 1990—, Boisey Waiters Black Caucus Dem. Club of Broward County, 1990—, Young Dems. of Broward County, 1990—, Greater Ft. Lauderdale Dem. Club; founder Positive Images, 1996—; vice chair Broward County Legis. Del.; chmn. Nat. Task Force on Health Care Reform, Nat. Conf. Black State Legislators, 1999. Recipient Merit award M.A.D.D., 1991, Woman of the Yr. award Fla. Fedn. Bus. and Profl. Women, 1992, Competitive Edge Program award Broward C.C., 1991-92, 92-93, Trailblazer of Yr. award Broward County Young Dems., 1993, Margaret Roach Leadership award Broward County Urban League, 1993, Hon. McKnight Achiever award, 1993, Outstanding Svc. award Sickle Cell Disease Found. of Broward County, 1993, 94, With the Multitude of Her Being tribute African Am. Women of South Fla., 1993, Ashanti Cultural Arts Cmty. Svc. award, 1994, Woman of Distinction award Women's Polit. Caucus Gwen Cherry chpt., 1994, Impact award New Rep. Club of Broward County, 1994, Legis. Advocate award Fla. Assn. Cmty. Health Ctrs., Inc., 1994, Humanitarian of the Yr. award Sunshine Health Ctr., 1994, Legis. Roll Call award Fla. C. of C., 1993, 94, Legis. award Fla. Assn. C.C.'s, 1994, Legislator of the Yr. award Fla. Coll. Emergency Physicians, 1995, Commendation for Svc. award Ft. Lauderdale Mayor Jim Naugle and City Commrs., 1995, Advocate Appreciation award Broward County Walk a Mile for Edn., 1996, Advocate award Broward Pediat. Soc., 1996, Elderly Advocate award N.W. Federated Women's Club, 1996, Criminal Justice Image award Cmty. Reconstrn. Inst., 1998, Govt. award Family Ctrl., Inc., 1998, Alpha award Alpha Phi Alpha, 1999, African-Am. Achievers award JM Family Enterprises, Inc., 1999, Women and Children Advocacy award Greater Fla. region B'nai B'rith Internat., 1999, Trailblazer award Palm Beach County Urban League, 1999, Lifesaver award First Call for Help of Broward County, 1999, award of excellence Nostalgia in Gold, 1999, Elaine Gordon Lifetime Achievement award Bus. & Profl. Women of Fla., 1999, Disting. Legislator award Fla. Legal Svcs. Inc., 1999, Senator of Yr. award Fla. Assn. Rehabilitative Facilities, 1999, Great Svc. award Women's Pastoral Alliance, 2000, Outstanding Cmty. Svc. award North Broward NAACP, 2000. Mem. NOW, NAACP (subscribing life mem.), Bus. and Profl. Women (Woman of the Yr. 1995), Broward Assn. Black Social Workers (founding mem.), Optimists, Kiwanis, Order of Ea. Star., Democrat. Baptist. Avocations: reading, writing short stories for children, traveling. Home: 33 NE 2d St Ste 209 Fort Lauderdale FL 33301

DAWSON, PATRICIA LUCILLE, surgeon; b. Kingston, Jamaica, W.I., Sept. 30, 1949; arrived in U.S., 1950; d. Percival Gordon and Edna Claire (Overton) D.; children: Alexandria Zoe, Wesley Gordon. BA in Sociology, Allegheny Coll., 1971; MD, N.J. Med. Sch., Newark, 1977; MA in Human and Orgn. Devel., The Fielding Inst., 1996, PhD in Human and Orgnl. Sys., 1998. Membership dir. N.J. ACLU, Newark, 1972; resident in surgery U. Medicine and Dentistry N.J. N.J. Med Sch., 1977-79; resident in surgery Virginia Mason Med. Ctr., Seattle, 1979-82; pvt. practice specializing in surgery Arlington, Wash., 1982-83; dir. med. staff diversity Group Health Coop., Seattle, 1993-98, staff surgeon, 1983-98; pvt. practice Seattle,

1998—2003; breast surgeon Swedish Cancer Inst., 2004—. Author: Forged by the Knife—The Experience of Surgical Residency from the Perspective of a Woman of Color. Fellow ACS, Seattle Surg. Soc.; mem. Physicians for Social Responsibility, Assn. Women Surgeons, Wash. Black Profls. in Health Care, NOW. Avocations: fiction, walking, cooking. Office: Providence Comp Breast Ctr Jefferson Twr 1600 E Jefferson St Ste 300 Seattle WA 98122-5645 Office Phone: 206-320-4880.

DAWSON, STEPHANIE ELAINE, city manager; b. Norwalk, Conn., Nov. 12, 1956; BA, Cornell U., 1979; MPA, Marist Coll., 1994. Cert. Project Mgmt. Inst., Inst. for Cert. Computing. Ops. analyst Irving Trust Co., N.Y.C., 1981-82, ops. mgr., 1982-85; sys. analyst Dept. Gen. Svcs., N.Y.C., 1986-88, sr. project mgr., 1988-91, dir., 1991-95; project mgr., cons. Port Authority N.Y. and N.J., N.Y.C., 1995-98, mgr. capital programs, 1998—. Dir. projects, chpt. liaison Project Mgmt. Inst.-Info. Sys. Spl. Interest Group, Panel leader emerging tech. Am. Soc. Pub. Adminstrn., 1993; mem. Emerging Tech. Adv. Group Assn. for Info. and Image Mgmt., 1995-99; del. to South Africa, People to People Mission, 1997. Maj. Army Nat. Guard, 1979—. Recipient Women in Law and Govt. recognition Nat. Assn. Negro Bus. and Profl. Women's Clubs, N.Y., 1999. Mem. Alpha Kappa Alpha. Office: 1 World Trade Ctr New York NY 10048-0202 Fax: 212-435-4537. E-mail: srpdawson@aol.com., sd@panynj.gov.

DAWSON, SUZANNE STOCKUS, lawyer; b. Chgo., Dec. 29, 1941; d. John Charles and Josephine (Zolpe) Stockus; m. Daniel P. Dawson Sr., Sept. 1, 1962; children: Daniel P. Jr., John Charles, Michael Sean. BA, Marquette U., 1963; JD cum laude, Loyola U., Chgo., 1965. Bar: Ill. 1965, U.S. dist. Ct. (no. dist.) Ill. 1965. Assoc. Kirkland & Ellis, Chgo., 1965-71, ptnr., 1971-82, Arnstein & Lehr, Chgo., 1982-89, Foley & Lardner, Chgo., 1989-94; spl. counsel publicly held corps. Glenview, Ill., 1995-97; corp. counsel Baxter Healthcare Corp., Deerfield, Ill., 1997-98, sr. counsel, 1998—. Mem. various coms. United Way Chgo.; corp. adv. bd. Sec. State of Ill., 1973; past mem. bd. advisors Loyola of Chgo. Law Sch.; trustee Lawrence Hall Youth Svcs., Chgo., 1983-98, pres., 1991-93, chair 1993-96; mem. adv. bd. Cath. Charities Chgo., 1985—, bd. dirs., 2002—, chair north suburban regional adv. bd., 2002—; mem. exec. com., bd. governance Notre Dame High Sch., Niles, Ill., 1990-97. Recipient Founder's Day award Loyola U., 1980, St. Thomas More award Loyola of Chgo. Law Sch., 1983. Mem. ABA, Am. Arbitration Assn. (appointed mem. nat. panel of comml. arbitrators 1996—), Ill. Bar Assn. Roman Catholic. Avocations: piano, choir singing, gardening, skiing, gourmet cooking. Home: 2113 Valley Lo Ln Glenview IL 60025-1724 Office: Baxter Healthcare Corp One Baxter Pkwy Deerfield IL 60015-4633 E-mail: suzanne_dawson@baxter.com.

DAWSON, VALINA L. science educator; BS in Environ. Toxicology, U. Calif., Davis, 1983; PhD in Pharmacology, U. Utah, 1989. Fellow dept. neurology Hosp. of U. Pa., Phila., 1989—90; fellow Addiction Rsch. Ctr. Nat. Inst. Drug Abuse, Balt., 1990—93; dir. neurobiology of disease program dept. neurology Johns Hopkins U. Sch. Medicine, Balt.; assoc. prof. neurology, neurosci., and physiology Johns Hopkins Hosp., 1994—2001, prof., vice chmn. neurology, prof. neurosci. and physiology, 2001—. Contbr. articles to profl. jours. Named Internat. Soc. for Neurochemistry Young Investigator, 1999, Staglin Music Festival Investigator, 1998; recipient Mary Lou McIlhany scholarship, 1999, Am. Heart Assn. Grant-in-Aid award, 1990, award, Muscular Dystrophy Assn., 1995, Alzheimer's Assn. Scholar award, 1994, Am. Heart Assn. Grant-in-Aid award, 1994, AmFar Scholar award, 1994, ADAMHA Intramural Rsch. Tng. award, 1992, Nat. Inst. Drug Abuse Staff Fellow award, 1992, Winter Conf. on Brain Rsch. fellowship, 1991, NIH PRAT fellowship, 1990. Achievements include research in molecular mechanisms of neurodegeneration and regeneration; experimental models of stroke; gene discovery of novel cell survival pathways; cell based therapies for the treatment of neurologic disorders. Office: Inst for Cell Engring Dept Neurology 733 N Broadway St Ste 711 Baltimore MD 21205

DAWSON, VIRGINIA SUE, retired editor; b. Concordia, Kans., June 6, 1940; d. John Edward and Wilma Aileen (Thompson) Morgan; m. Neil S. Dawson, Nov. 28, 1964; children: Shelley Diane Dawson Sedwick, Lori Ann Dawson Hughes, Christy Lynn. BS in Home Econs. and Journalism, Kans. State U., 1962. Asst. publs. editor Ohio State U. Coop. Ext. Svc., Columbus, 1962-64; home editor Ohio Farmer mag., Columbus, 1964-78; food editor Columbus Dispatch, 1978—2000, ret. Recipient Commn. award Ohio Poultry Assn., 1980. Mem. Assn. Food Journalists. Avocations: biking, running, reading, cooking. E-mail: ndaws2@aol.com.

DAWSON-HUGHES, BESS, scientist; Recipient Bolton L. Carson medal Franklin Inst., 1995. Office: Nutrition Rsch Aging Ctr USDA 711 Washington St Boston MA 02111-1524

DAY, ADRIENNE CAROL, artist; b. Jackson, Miss., Dec. 13, 1955; d. Robert Maxwell and Phyllis Mary (Roberts) D. BFA, U. Okla., 1986; MFA, Ariz. State U., 1990. Adj. instr. Mesa (Ariz.) C.C., 1990; artist-in-residence Arts Coun. Okla., Okla. City, 1991—; vis. lectr. dept. art U. Ctrl. Okla., Edmond, 1993-98; adj. prof. art Okla. City U., 1996—; adj. asst. prof. U. Okla. Coll. Liberal Studies, Norman, 1997—2001; art specialist Western Village Acad., Oklahoma City, 2001—. Coord., organizer Suite Okla. exchange portfolio, 1997. One-woman shows include Ariz. State U., Tempe, 1990, Individual Artists of Okla. exhbn., Okla. City, 1993, ARC Gallery, Chgo., 1995, Leslie Powell Gallery, Lawton, Okla., 1996, U. Southeastern Okla., Durant, 1998; exhibited in group shows at Ariz. State U., Tempe, 1989 (purchase award), Guadalupe Cultural Arts, Ctr., San Antonio, 1989 (cash award), Greenville (N.C.) Mus. Art, 1989, Ind. U., 1989, Shemer Art Ctr. and Mus., Phoenix, 1990, Kirkpatric Ctr. Gallery, Okla. City, 1991, Okla. City Art Mus., 1992, Fla. State U. Mus., Tallahassee, 1993, Corcoran Sch. Art, Washington, 1994-97, U. Ctrl. Okla. Faculty Exhibit, Edmond, 1994-97, Austin Peay U., Clarksville, Tenn., 1994, I.A.O/M.A.R.S. Exchange Exhibit, Phoenix, 1995, Alexander Hogue Gallery, U. Tulsa, Okla., 1997, Truman State U., 1998, Columbia (Mo.) Coll., 1998, Morgan Gallery, Kansas City, 2000, Wichita, Kans., 2001; represented in permanent collections Haarmann and Reimer Corp., Germany, Corcoran Mus., Washington, U. Ctrl. Okla., Fred Jones Mus., Carol Reese Mus., East Tenn. State, U. Tenn., Knoxville, Miss. State U., U. Texas, Tyler, Fellers & Co., Okla. City, U. Fla., Gainsville, Bradley U., Peoria, Ariz. State U., Ohio U., Athens, Brigham Young U., U. Utah, U. Alberta. Recipient Letzeiser Gold medal U. Okla. Sch. Art, Norman, 1987, Abraham and Bessie Lehrer Meml. award Ariz. State U., 1989, faculty purchase award Presdl. Ptrns. U. Ctrl. Olka., Edmond, 1995; first alt. Fourth Annual Nathan Cummings Travel fellow Ariz. State U., 1989; Artist Project grantee Ariz. Commn. on the Arts, 1991, Sudden Opportunity grantee Okla. Visual Arts Coalition, Okla. City, 1992. Democrat. Home and Office: PO Box 6354 Norman OK 73070-6354

DAY, ANN, state legislator; b. EL Paso, Tex. BAEducation, Ariz. St. U.; M.Ed, U. Ariz. Former tchr., counselor; mem. Ariz. Senate, Phoenix, 1990-. Republican. Home: PO Box 65417 Tucson AZ 85728-5417 Office: Arizona State Senate 1700 W Washington St Ste S Phoenix AZ 85007-2890

DAY, ANN ELIZABETH, artist, educator; b. Valetta, Malta, June 1, 1927; came to U.S., 1940; d. John Dwight and Joyce Elizabeth (Marett) Harvey; m. George Frederick Day, Oct. 23, 1948 (div. Oct. 1979); children: Georgianna Day Ludcke, John F., David S.; m. Donald Monturean Mintz, Dec. 30, 1980. BA, Mt. Holyoke Coll., 1948. Asst. to dir. advanced studies Nat. Ctr. Atmospheric Rsch., Boulder, Colo., 1962-67; edn. dir. Waterloo (Iowa) Recreation and Arts Ctr., 1967-76; curator edn. svcs. Utah Mus. Fine Arts, Salt Lake City, 1976-80; lectr. art history YMHA of No. N.J., Wayne, 1982—, RSVP, Paramus, N.J., 1994—, Art History Tours of France, Tour de France, Ltd., 1994—, Classic Residence, Teaneck, N.J., 1995—, Belleville (N.J.) Libr., 1995—, Montclair (N.J.) Adult Sch., 2001—, Teaneck (N.J.) Sr. Ctr., 2003—; freelance artist Ringwood, N.J., 1982—; represented by Nathans Gallery, West Paterson, NJ. Vice chair, panelist Fed. State Ptnrship., NEA, Washington, 1972-77; mem. exec. com. Nat. Assn. Community Arts Agys., Washington, 1975-77. Author of poems; represented in permanent collections Utah Mus. of Fine Arts, also U.S. and abroad. Recipient Silver medal Utah Watercolor Soc., Salt Lake City, 1976, Lake Mohawk Club award Sussex County Art Assn., Sparta, N.J., 1992, 93, Best in Show award Sussex County Art Assn., 1997, Artists Mag. award (NWS juried exhibition), 1996. Mem. Nat. Watercolor Soc., N.J. Watercolor Soc. (Heimrod award for NJWSC exhibit 1991), Phi Beta Kappa. Democrat. Avocations: walking, swimming, collecting tribal art. Home and Office: 117 Cedar Rd Ringwood NJ 07456-1800

DAY, ANNE WHITE, retired nurse; b. Cin., July 9, 1926; d. Pinkney McGill and Anna Pearl (Glendenning) White; m. Raymond Eric Parker, Mar. 6, 1948 (div. 1969); children: Douglas McGill, Stephanie Morse. Diploma, Christ Hosp. Sch. Nursing, Cin., 1947. RN, Ohio; cert. chem. dependency nurse Consol. Assn. Nurses in Substance Abuse. Staff nurse to asst. head nurse Holmes divsn. U. Cin., 1948-84; nursing supr. Villa Hope Extended Care Facility, Cin., 1970-72; staff nurse Hillenbrand Nursing Home, Cin., 1980-82, Emerson A. North Hosp., Cin., 1982-94. Vol. Group Against Smoke Pollution, Cin., 1989—; donor Zoo, Cin., 1989—, Voters for Choice, Ohio, 1989—, Ams. for Non-Smokers Rights, Calif., 1989—, Action on Smoking or Health, 1989—, Stop Teenage Addiction to Tobacco. Mem. DAR (life). Episcopalian. Avocations: swimming, reading, knitting, crocheting, pattern dancing.

DAY, CHRISTINE SUSAN, music educator; d. Arvel Muriel and Frances Ruth Lake; m. Thomas Robert Day, Aug. 3, 1974; children: Meghann Christine, Joshua Thomas. MusB, IA State U., 1974. Cert. Edn. Orff, 1984. Tchr. music k-12 grade Urbana Sch. Dist., Urbana, Iowa, 1975—76; tchr. elem. and H.S. music Red Oak Sch. Dist., 1976—80; tchr. elem. music United Sch. Dist. 320, Wamego, Kans., 1980—2000, Geary County Sch. Dist. #475, Junction City, 2000—. Mem. orch. Tarkio Symphony, Mo., 1976—80; ch. choir accompanist United Presbyn. Ch., Red Oak, Iowa, 1976—80; dir. chancel choir United Meth. Ch., Wamego, Kans., 1982—, dir. choral music Flint Hills Messiah Chorus, 1992—; dir. music piano accompianist Columiban Theatre, 1994—; prairie rose quartet Sweet Adelines Internat., 1995—; dir. Columbian youth choir Columiban Theatre, 2002—; chairor elem. music tchrs. Geary County Sch. Dist. #475, Junction City, Kans., 2003—. Mem. worship com. United Meth. Ch., Wamego, Kans., 1982. Recipient North Ctrl. Elem. Music Tchr. Yr., Kans. Music Educator's Assn., 1998, Tchr. Edn. award, Santa Fe Trail Assn., 1999; grantee Opera Workshop, Met. Opera Co., 1997, Santa Fe Trail Tchr. Workshops, Nat. Pk. Svc., 2003—04. Mem.: Elem. Music Tchrs. Assn. (chair 2003—), North Ctrl. Region Kans. Music Educators Assn. (chair 1998—2000), NEA, Kans. Corral Westerners, Music Educators Nat. Conf., Orgn. of Am. Kodaly Edcuators, Am. Orff-Schulwerk Assn., Santa Fe Trail Assn. (co-chair 1999—), Delta Kappa Gamma. Methodist. Avocations: acting, gardening, researching american history, teaching private music lessons. Home: Po Box 118 Wamego KS 66547 Office: Geary County Sch Dist #475 Eisenhower Rdd Junction City KS 66441 Personal E-mail: dosdays@kansas.net. E-mail: dayc@usd475.k12.ks.us.

DAY, COLIEN, retired secondary school educator; b. Roxboro, N.C., Nov. 3, 1927; d. Luther Davis and Cornelia Lou (Allen) Long; m. Russell Van Buren Day (dec. 1981). AB in English, Trevecca U., Nashville, 1951; MEd, U. N.C., 1955; Sectl. Cert., Elon Coll., 1944-45. With Burlington Ind., Burlington, N.C., 1945-48; tchr. Bartlett-Yancey High Sch., Yanceyville, NC, 1951-53, Sumner High Sch., Greensboro, N.C., 1953-59; tchr. English Asheboro (N.C.) City Schs., 1959-61; librarian Randolph County Schs., Asheboro, 1961-64; tchr. English Marysville (Calif.) Joint Unified Sch. Dist., 1964—91. Tutor in English to Asian immigrants, 1988—. Mem. AAUW, Nat. Geographic Soc., Nat. Edn. Assn., Smithsonian Instn. Democrat. Home and Office: 1739 Glen St Marysville CA 95901-4018

DAY, DORIS (DORIS VON KAPPELHOFF), singer, actress; b. Cin., Apr. 3, 1924; d. Frederick Wilhelm and Alma Sophia von Kappelhoff; m. Al Jorden, Mar. 1941 (div. 1943); 1 son, Terry; m. George Weilder, 1946 (div. 1949); m. Marty Melcher, Apr. 3, 1951 (dec. 1968). Student pub. schs., Cin. Made profl. dancing appearance with Doherty & Kappelhoff, Glendale, Calif.; singer Karlin's Karnival, Sta. WCPO-Radio, with bands Barney Rapp, Bob Crosby, Fred Waring, Les Brown; singer, leading lady, Bob Hope NBC radio show, 1948-50, Doris Day CBS show, 1952-53; singer Columbia Records, 1950—, Hooray for Hollywood col.1, 1988, A Day At The Movies, 1989, The Essence of Doris Day, 1993, Duet with The Andre Previn Trio, 1996; star Warner Bros. Studio; motion pictures include Romance on the High Seas, 1948, My Dream is Yours, 1949, Young Man With a Horn, 1950, Tea For Two, 1950, West Point Story, 1950, Lullaby of Broadway, 1951, On Moonlight Bay, 1951, I'll See You in My Dreams, 1951, April in Paris, 1952, By the Light of the Silvery Moon, 1953, Lucky Me, Yankee Doodle Girl, 1954, Love Me or Leave Me, 1955 (selected as 1 of 10 best films by N.Y. Herald Tribune), Pajama Game, 1957, Teacher's Pet, 1958, Tunnel of Love, 1958, It Happened to Jane, 1959, Pillow Talk, 1959, Midnight Lace, 1960, Jumbo, 1962, That Touch of Mink, 1962, The Thrill of It All, 1963, Please Don't Eat the Daisies, 1960, Lover Come Back, 1962, Send Me No Flowers, 1964, Do Not Disturb, 1965, The Glass Bottom Boat, 1966, Caprice, 1967, The Ballad of Josie, 1968, Where Were You When The Lights Went Out, 1968, With Six You Get Eggrolls, 1968, Sleeping Dogs, Hearts and Souls, 1993, That's Entertainment III, 1994; TV series The Doris Day Show, 1970-73, Doris Day & Friends, 1985-86, Doris Day's Best, 1985-86; appeared on TV spl. The Pet Set, 1972. Founder Doris Day Animal League, Washington, 1987. Winner 1st prize (with Jerry Doherty) as best dance team in Cin.; recipient Laurel award as leading new female personality in motion picture industry, 1950; named top audience attractor, 1962; recipient Am. Comedy Lifetime Achievement award, 1991. Christian Scientist. Office: care Doris Day Animal League Ste 100 227 Massachusetts Ave NE Washington DC 20002-4963 also: Columbia Records 550 Madison Ave New York NY 10022-3211

DAY, ELIZABETH AGALL, press secretary; b. Pensacola, Fla., May 25, 1967; m. Dennis Scott Day; 1 child. BS in Comm. cum laude, Fla. State U., 1989. Asst. to dirs. congl. rels. The Heritage Found., 1990-92; personal asst. to chief of staff Office of Senator Thad Cochran, Washington, 1992-94, press asst., 1994-96, pres sec., 1997—. Office: 326 Senate Russell Ofc Washington DC 20510-0001

DAY, FRANCES ANN, writer, educator; b. Grant, Nebr., June 30, 1942; d. Jay and Rachel Ellen Day. BA magna cum laude, Kearney (Nebr.) State Coll., 1964; MA, U. Colo., 1969, EdS, 1979. Cert. lang. and culture tchr., Colo. Tchr. Kearney Pub. Schs., 1961-64, Cherry Creek Schs., Englewood, Colo., 1965-93; lectr. Sonoma State U., Rohnert Park, Calif., 1999—. Grant dir. Village East Schs., Englewood, 1984-90; chair Village East Multicultural Edn. Com., Aurora, Colo., 1989-91. Author: Multicultural Voices, 1994, 2d edit., 1999, Latina and Latino Voices, 1998, Lesbian and Gay Voices, 2000; author column and revs. Sec., East Arapahoe County Coun. on Human Rels., 1971-73; mem. adv. bd. U. San Francisco Ctr. for Multicultural Lit., U.S. Bd. on Books for Young People. Recipient Colo. Tchr. of Yr. Honorable Mention award Colo. Dept. Edn., 1974, Women's History award of excellence Colo. Com. for Women's History, 1988, Denali Press award Am. Libr. Assn., 1998. Mem. Nat. Assn. for Multicultural Edn., Calif. Assn. for Bilingual Edn. Avocations: reading, walking. Office: Heinemann Pubs 361 Hanover St Portsmouth NH 03801-3959

DAY, JACQUELINE FRANCES, museum director; BA in English, Antioch Coll.; MA in Folklore, Ind. U.; student, Tulane U., Wash. State U. Instr. N.D. State U., Fargo, 1973-75; Curator Idaho State Historical Soc., Boise, 1975-77; program officer Assn. Humanities Idaho, Boise, 1977-84; field rschr. Mont. Historical Soc., Helena, 1984; dir. Beall Park Art Ctr., Bozeman, Mont., 1984-86; exec. dir. Regional Council of Historical Agencies, Syracuse, N.Y., 1986-90, Gallery Assn. of N.Y. State, Hamilton, 1990-92; dir. Adirondack Mus., Blue Mountain Lake, N.Y., 1992—. Mem. State Historical Records Advisory Bd., N.Y., 1996—. Bd. dirs. Adirondack Architectural Heritage Consortium, 1993-95, Friends and Visitors Interpretive Ctr., 1993—. Mem. Am. Assn. State Local History, Museum Assn. N.Y. (bd. dirs.). Office: Adirondack Museum Rt 28 N & 30 Box 99 Blue Mountain Lake NY 12812

DAY, LUCILLE LANG, museum administrator, educator, writer; b. Oakland, Calif., Dec. 5, 1947; d. Richard Allen and Evelyn Marietta (Hazard) Lang; m. Frank Lawrence Day, Nov. 6, 1965 (div. 1970); 1 child, Liana Sherrine ; m. Theodore Herman Fleischman, June 23, 1974 (div. 1985); 1 child, Tamarind Channah Fleischman ; m. Richard Michael Levine, Aug. 25, 2002. AB, U. Calif., Berkeley, 1971, MA, 1973, PhD, 1979; MA, San Francisco State U., 1999. Tchg. asst. U. Calif., Berkeley, 1971-72, 75-76, rsch. asst., 1975, 77-78; tchr. sci. Magic Mountain Sch., Berkeley, 1977; specialist math. and sci. Novato (Calif.) Unified Sch. Dist., 1979-81; instr. sci. Project Bridge Laney Coll., Oakland, 1984-86; sci. writer and mgr. precoll. edn. programs Lawrence Berkeley Nat. Lab., 1986-90, life scis. staff coord., 1990-92, mgr. Hall of Health, Children's Hosp. and Rsch. Ctr. at Oakland, 1992—. Lectr. St. Mary's Coll. Calif., Moraga, 1997—2000. Author: numerous poems, articles and book reviews; author: (with Joan Skolnick and Carol Langbort) How to Encourage Girls in Math and Science: Strategies for Parents and Educators, 1982; author: (poetry) Self-Portrait with Hand Microscope, 1982, Fire in the Garden, 1997, Wild One, 2000, Lucille Lang Day, Greatest Hits, 1975-2000, 2001, Infinities, 2002. Recipient Joseph Henry Jackson award in lit., San Francisco Found., 1982; Grad. fellow, NSF, 1972—75. Mem.: Soc. Pub. Health Edn. (No. Calif. chpt.), Math./Sci. Network, Nat. Assn. Sci. Writers, No. Calif. Sci. Writers Assn., Phi Beta Kappa, Iota Sigma Pi. Home: 1057 Walker Ave Oakland CA 94610-1511 Office: Hall of Health 2230 Shattuck Ave Berkeley CA 94704-1416 Office Phone: 510-549-1564. Personal E-mail: lucyday@earthlink.net. Business E-Mail: lucyday@hallofhealth.org.

DAY, MARGARET ANN, research librarian, information specialist; b. Butler, Pa., Nov. 15, 1941; d. Edwin James and Helen Louella (Christy) Longwell; m. Donald Emery Day, Dec. 15, 1961; children: Catherine Anne (dec.), Donna Lau, Donald Edwin. BS in Edn. magna cum laude, Clarion U. Pa., 1972, MS in Libr. Sci., 1986. Cert. tchr., profl. libr., Pa.; lic. real estate salesperson, Pa. Substitute tchr. Karns City (Pa.) Area Schs., 1976, 79-85; grad. asst. Clarion U. Pa., 1985-86; libr., info. specialist Interactive Media Corp., Butler, 1987—94. Real estate sales assoc. Ed Shields, Realtor, Butler, 1994. Pres. Bruin (Pa.) Borough Coun., 1984. DAR, Breth and Wahr scholar, 1959. Mem. Beta Phi Mu. Avocations: reading, gardening, sewing, cooking and nutrition, continuing education. Home: PO Box 85 Bruin PA 16022-0085 Office: Interactive Media Corp 292 Three Degree Rd Butler PA 16002-3860

DAY, MARY, artistic director, ballet company executive; b. Wash. Trained by Lisa Gardiner, ArtsD (hon.), Shenandoah Conservatory; DHL (hon.) Mount Vernon Coll. Co-founder Washington Sch. of Ballet, 1944—; founder Washington Ballet, 1976—. Named Washingtonian of Yr., Washingtonian mag.; recipient Mayor's award, Woman of Achievement award, WETA-TV, Met. Dance award, Founders award, Cultural Alliance, Excellence in Teaching Chautauqua Dance award, sr. Svcs. Disting. award IONA. Office: Washington Ballet 3515 Wisconsin Ave NW Washington DC 20016-3085*

DAY, MARY ANN, medical/surgical nurse; b. Covington, Tenn., Apr. 9, 1944; m. George Day, Jan. 17, 1980; children: Maurice, Michele, Shawn, Corey. AAS, Joliet (Ill.) Jr. Coll., 1989; BSN, Lewis U., 1995; student, U. St. Francis, 1998—. RN, Ill.; cert. emergency nurse pediat. course. Staff nurse Michael Reese Hosp., Chgo., 1989-91, MacNeal Hosp., Berwyn, Ill., 1991-99, Westlake Hosp., Melrose Park, Ill., 1999—; adj. faculty/LPN program Triton Coll., River Grove, Ill., 1996—, instr. RN continuing edn. course, 1998—; asst. patient care mgr. St. Joseph Hosp., Joliet, Ill., 1999—; IV therapist Ctrl. Dupage Hosp., Winfield, Ill., 1999—; nursing supr. St. Anthony's Hosp., Chgo., 2001—. Mem. diversity task force com., Westlake Hosp., 1999; instr. in nursing assistance Waubonsee Coll., 2002. Nominee Black Profl. Female scholarship, Minority Student of Yr., 1989. Avocations: classical music, classical pianist. Home: 6 Puffin Cir Bolingbrook IL 60440-1236 E-mail: mhoneyday@aol.com.

DAY, MARY JANE THOMAS, cartographer; b. Connors, New Brunswick, Can., Oct. 12, 1927; d. Angus and Delina (Michaud) Thomas; m. Howard M. Day, July 1, 1949 (dec. April 27, 2003); children: Laurie Anne Day Greene, Angus Howard. BS in Geography, U. Md., 1974, BS in Bus. & Mgmt., 1977. Meteorol. aide Hangar 8 Eastern Airlines, N.Y.C., 1946-47, U.S. Weather Bur., Washington, 1948-50; cartographic aide U.S. Navy Hydrographic Office, Suitland, Md., 1950-57, cartographer, 1957-62, U.S. Navy Oceanographic Office, Suitland, 1962-72, Def. Mapping Agy., Suitland/Brookmont, 1972-93; ret., 1994. Cartographer USNS Harkness, 1978, Indonesian Naval Personnel, Jakarta, Indonesia, 1981-82. Compiled, wrote and published; The Descendants of John Thomas of Connors, N.B., 1988; author numerous poems. Mem. Andrews Officers Club (Md.). Avocations: travel, genealogy, foreign languages. Home: 3532 28th Pky Temple Hills MD 20748-2922

DAY, MARYLOUISE MULDOON (MRS. RICHARD DAYTON DAY), appraiser; b. St. Louis; d. Joseph A. and Dorothy (Lang) Muldoon; A.B., Washington U., St. Louis, 1940; postgrad. Air U., 1958, George Washington U., 1963-64; grad. Real Estate Inst. Md., 1972; m. Richard Dayton Day, Aug. 15, 1959. Intelligence specialist U.S. Air Force, Washington, 1947-60; program officer, spl. asst. to dir. project devel. VISTA, OEO, 1965-67; with Joint Intelligence Bur., London, Eng., 1953; appraiser, cons. on antiques, fine arts, 1969—; Marylouise M. Day, Inc., 1978—. Recipient citation U.S. Air Force, 1960. Fellow Am. Soc. Appraisers (chpt. 1st v.p. 1977-78, pres. 978-79, chmn. fine arts forum 1976-78, gov. Region 3 1980-82, internat. sec. 1982-84, treas. ednl. found. 1986-91); mem. Appraisers Assn. Am., Irish Georgian Soc., Winterthur Guild, Assn. Former Intelligence Officers, Decorative Arts Trust, Delta Gamma. Club: Kenwood Golf and Country (Bethesda, Md.). Home: 4928 Sentinel Dr Bethesda MD 20816-3591

DAY, VICTORIA LYNN, principal; d. William Vasil and Florence Hassis Vissar; m. Scott Roger Day, Feb. 18, 1990. MusB, SUNY, Potsdam, 1987, MusM, 1992; EdM, St. Lawrence U., 1999. Cert. sch. dist. adminstr. N.Y., sch. music tchr. N.Y. Music tchr. Gouverneur (N.Y.) Ctrl. Schs., 1987—98; asst. prin. Gouverneur Mid./H.S., 1998—2000; elem. prin. Fowler Elem. Sch., Gouverneur, 2000—.

DAYA, JACKIE, publishing company executive; Sr. v.p., CFO Cahners Pub. Co., Newton, Mass., 1999; exec. v.p. Robert Barghaus, 1999—2000; sr. v.p., fin. adminstrn. Hasbro Interactive, 2000—. Office: Hasbro Interactive 50 Dunham Rd Beverly MA 01915-1894

DAYA MATA, SRI (FAYE WRIGHT), clergywoman; b. Salt Lake City, Jan. 31, 1914; d. Clarence Aaron and Rachel (Terry) Wright. Grad. high sch., 1931. Ordained to ministry Self-Realization Fellowship, 1935. Min.

Self-Realization Fellowship, L.A., 1935—, bd. dirs., 1941—, sec., 1944-45, treas., 1945-71, lectr., 1952—; pres. brs. U.S., Can., Mex., S.Am., Europe, Africa, Asia, Australia and New Zealand Self-Realization Fellowship/Yogoda Satsanga Soc. of India, 1955—. Gemeinschaft der Selbst-Verwirklichung, 1974—, Self Realization Inst. of Va., Inc., 1981—. Author: Only Love, 1976, Finding the Joy Within [illegible] Enter The Quiet Heart, 1998, Intuition: Soul-Guidance for Life's Decisions, 2003; (videocassettes) Security in a World of Change, 1989, Him I Shall Follow, 1997, Living in the Love of God, 2002; contbr. articles to mags. Pres. Yogoda Satsanga Homeopathic Mahavidyalaya, Yogoda Satsanga Mahavidyalaya, Yogoda Satsanga Vidyalaya, Yogoda Satsanga Kanya Vidyalaya, Yogoda Satsanga Sangeet Kala Bharati, Yogoda Satsanga Shilpa Kala Bharati, Yogoda Satsanga Balkrishnalaya, Yogoda Satsanga Sevashram Hosp., Worldwide Prayer Circle, others. Home and Office: Self-Realization Fellowship 3880 San Rafael Ave Los Angeles CA 90065-3298

DAYHOFF, NANCY BELMONT, artist; b. West Depford Township, N.J., Apr. 30, 1922; d. Donald Johnston and Ann Catherine (Gorry) Mackinnon; m. Thomas Simon Belmont, Nov. 15, 1944 (dec. Aug. 1982); children: Paul Thomas, Ann Frances, Thomas Matthew, Matthew Peter; m. Edward Samuel Dayhoff, Dec. 8, 1987. Student, Douglas Coll., 1940-43, Art Students League, N.Y.C., 1943; BA summa cum laude, SUNY, Utica, 1981. Tchr. art Catskill Art Soc., Hurleyville, N.Y., 1972-78, dir. publicity, 1974-80, exec. dir., 1978-80; asst. designer dept. pub. rels. SUNY, Utica, 1980-81. One woman shows include Herkimer (N.Y.) County Libr., 1984, Cedar Lane Unitarian Ch., Bethesda, Md., 1993, European Art Cafe, Bethesda, 1995, Robert's Gallery on 10th Ave., N.Y.C., 1995, Rockville (N.Y.) Sr. Ctr., 1997, Collington, Michelville, Md., 1997; exhibited in group shows at Catskill Art Soc., Hurleyville, 1972-80, N.Y. State Legislature bldg., Albany, 1978, Middletown (N.Y.) Art Group, 1978, Woodstock (N.Y.) Art Soc., 1983, St. Nicholas Parish House, Washington, 1995; author: (children's play) Small World, Glad World, 1971. Mem. Rockville Arts Place, Strathmore Hall Art Ctr., Strathmore Hall Artists. Democrat. Unitarian Universalist. Avocations: walking, travelling, visiting art galleries, strength training. Home and Office: 7716 Bells Mill Rd Bethesda MD 20817-1406

DAYMON, JOY JONES, school psychology specialist; b. Prescott, Ark. d. Coy A. and Alma E. (Honea) Jones; m. Jack C. Daymon, May 3, 1947; children: Jim, Michael, David, Deborah. BA, Long Beach State Coll.; MS in Ednl. Psychology, U. So. Calif., 1974; student, UCLA. Cert. elem. tchr., sch. psychologist specialist, Ark.; lic. profl. counselor, Ark. Tchr. Redondo Beach (Calif.) Sch. Dist.; ednl. examiner El Dorado (Ark.) Schs. Adj. instr. So. Ark. U., Magnolia; presenter workshop on assessment of severe and multi-handicapped various state and nat. convs. Author: Rabbit Pancakes, 1995, Princess Diana the Lamb to the Slaughter, 2002. Mem. NASP (state del., 1984-86), APA, Ark. Psychol. Assn. (treas. 1978-80), Ark. Sch. Psychologists Assn. (state del.), Ark. Counseling Assn., Nat. Bd. Cert. Counselors, Ark. Assessment in Counseling (pres., 1980-81), Delta Kappa Gamma (pres, 1986-87), Phi Delta Kappa. Home: 2202 N Wyatt Dr El Dorado AR 71730-9262 Office: 108 Randolph El Dorado AR 71730

DAYS, RITA DENISE, state legislator; b. Minden, La., Oct. 16, 1950; d. Marion and Juliette (Mitchell) Heard; m. Frank S. Days, June 17, 1972; children: Elliott Charles, Natalie Rechelle, Evelyn Jeanine. BMus, Lincoln U., 1972. Tchr. Webster Parish Sch. Bd., Minden, La., 1972; clk. typist Urban League of St. Louis, 1973-74, asst. dir. pub. info., 1974, placement interviewer, 1974-76; office supr. Burroughs Corp., St. Louis, 1976-80; sec., admissions counselor Jewish Coll. of Nursing, St. Louis, 1989-93; mem. Mo. Ho. of Reps., St. Louis, 1993—. Chair elections com. Mo. Ho. of Reps., St. Louis, treas. Mo. Legis. Black Caucus, mem. Supreme Ct. Task Force on Children and Families; mem. Interagy. Coordinating Coun. part H. Active Ptnrs. for Kids, 1993—, New Sunny Mount Bapt. Ch.; sec. Women Legislators Mo.; bd. mem. Project Respond.; past bd. dirs. Normandy Sch. Dist. Mem. Alpha Kappa Alpha. Democrat. Office: Mo Ho of Reps State Capitol Building Jefferson City MO 65101-1556

DAY-SALVATORE, DEBRA LYNN, medical geneticist; b. Hoboken, N.J., Oct. 23, 1953; m. Francis P. Salvatore, Sr., Dec. 24, 1988. BA in Biology, Harvard U., 1975; MS in Pharmacology, NYU, 1979, PhD in Pharmacology, 1982; MD, Case Western Res. U., 1986. Diplomate Am. Bd. Med. Genetics, Am. Bd. Pediats. Grad. fellow dept. pharmacology NYU Med. Ctr., 1978-79; sr. rsch. asst. dept. medicine Case Western Res. U., Cleve., 1979-82, rsch. assoc. dept. molecular biology and microbiology, 1982-84; pediatric and adolescent medicine resident Cleve. Clinic Found., 1986-89; med. genetics fellow Robert Wood Johnson Med. Sch., New Brunswick, N.J., 1990-91, asst. prof. pediatrics, 1990—, coord. perinatal genetics dept. ob-gyn., 1991-92, dir. divsn. reproductive and perinatal genetics dept. ob-gyn., 1992—, asst. prof. ob-gyn. and reproductive scis. and pediatrics, 1992—, acting chief divsn. clin. genetics, dept. ob-gyn. and reproductive scis., 1993—; physician Robert Wood Johnson Univ. Hosp., New Brunswick, 1990—, St. Peter's Med. Ctr., 1992—, chief divsn. clin. genetics, 1996—. Mem. genetic adv. bd. N.J. State Dept. Health's Parental and Child Adv. Com.; mem. med. adv. bd. Cryo-Cell Internat. Genetics editor Jour. of Perinatology, 1993—; contbr. articles, abstracts to profl. jours. Cons. N.J. Interagency Adoption Coun. Mem. AAAS, AMA, Am. Acad. Pediatrics (mem. N.J. chpt.), Am. Soc. Cell Biology, Am. Soc. Human Genetics, Human Genetics Assn. N.J. (mem. legis. com.), N.Y. Acad. Sci. Office: Saint Peter's Univ Hosp 254 Easton Ave # 4410 New Brunswick NJ 08901-1766 E-mail: Day-Salva@comcast.net.

DAYSON, DIANE HARRIS, superintendent, park ranger; b. N.Y.C., Feb. 14, 1953; d. Robert Gene and Dessie Lee (Osborne) Harris; m. Kevin Maurice Dayson, Sept. 15, 1978; children: Dayna Renee, Kyle Ryan. BA in Early Secondary Edn. and Am. History, SUNY, Cortland, 1975; MS, NYU, 2000; Sr. Exec. Svc. grad., U.S. Dept. Interior, 2000. With Nat. Pk. Svc. U.S. Dept. Interior, 1975—, law enforcement ranger, 1977-79, concessions specialist, 1979-81, site mgr. Nat. Pk. Svc., 1984-87, supt. Nat. Pk. Svc. Oyster Bay, N.Y., 1987-90, Morristown, N.J., 1990-93, Hyde Park, N.Y., 1993-95; supt. Statue of Liberty Ellis Island, N.Y.C., 1996—. Adj. prof. NYU Wagner Sch. of Pub. Adminstrn.; ambassador to Amsterdam, 1998; ambassador on geneology to Paris, France, 2000, Bremehaven, Germany, 2000, San Marino, Italy, 1997. Active United Way, Dutchess County; exch. steward, Manchester, Eng., 1994; bd. dirs. Christian Ministry in Nat. Parks, 1997—. Mem. NAFE, Oyster Bay C. of C. Republican. Roman Catholic. Avocations: travel, knitting, reading. Office: Statue of Liberty Ellis Island Liberty Is New York NY 10004-1467

DAYTON, JEAN, elementary school principal; b. Belleville, Ill., Jan. 6, 1957; d. Charles John and Marjorie Jane Hempen Mueth; m. Michael Louis Dayton, Oct. 26, 1996. BS in Spl. Edn. & Elem. Edn., So. Ill. U., 1980, MS in Spl. Edn., 1993; PhD in Edn., St. Louis U., 1998. Tchr. spl. edn. Cmty. Consol. Sch. Dist. 110, Fairview Heights, Ill., 1980-92, behavior devel. coord., 1992-93; spl. edn. advisor So. Ill. U., Edwardsville, 1993-98; supr. spl. edn. program Cmty. Unit Sch. Dist. #10, Collinsville, Ill., 1998-2000; prin. Caseyville (Ill.) Elem. Sch., 2000—. Leader Tchr. Support Team, St. Clair County, Ill., 1989-91; mem. Transition Planning Com., St. Clair County, 1992-93. Tchr. in space applicant NASA, Cape Canaveral, Fla., 1985. Mem. Coun. Exceptional Children. Office: Caseyville Elem Sch 433 S 2d St Caseyville IL 62232

DAYTON, LEAH JANE, secondary school educator; b. Fort Worth, Tex., Apr. 27, 1953; d. Robert Hartwell and Vernon Elizabeth Mitchell; m. John Leon Dayton, Aug. 21, 1971; children: Amy E. Gausin, Jonathan L. Cert. tchr. psychology and English. Med. transcriptionist Robert H. Mitchell, MD, Plainview, Tex., 1970—84, Carl P. Weidenbach, MD, Plainview, Tex., 1984—91; English tchr. Plainview (Tex.) Ind. Sch. Dist., 1995—. Mem. dist. writing com. Plainview (Tex.) Ind. Sch. Dist., 1995—, mem. ednl. improvement coun., 1997—2000, mem. textbook adoption com., 2000—01; adv. bd. dirs. Houston Sch., Plainview, Tex.; mem. TAKS II com. Tex. Edn. Agy., Austin, 2000—01. Life mem. PTA, Plainview, Tex., 1978—. Recipient Outstanding E[illegible] award Plainview Daily Herald, 1998, Tchr. of Yr. award, Walmart Distbn., Plainview, Tex., 1998—99. Mem.: AAUW (sec. 1995—2001), Tex. Classroom Tchrs. Assn. (campus rep.), Tex. Assn. Alternative Schs., Psi Chi (life). Republican. Episcopalian. Avocations: reading, camping, water activities. Home: 513 W 8th Plainview TX 79072 Office: Houston Sch 2417 Yonkers Plainview TX 79072 Business E-Mail: ldayton@plainview.k12.tx.us. E-mail: ldayton@cox.net.

DE, DEVASMITA, research aquarist; b. Calcutta, India, Nov. 6, 1966; d. Kamal Chandra and Sheila D.; m. Arijit Das, June 2, 1990. BS, U. Calcutta, 1990; MS in Human Ecology, Vrije U., Brussels, 1994. Aquarist J.G. Shedd Aquarium, Chgo., 2000—; lead rsch. aquarist project seahorse McGill U., Montreal, Can., 2001—. Recipient Internat. Cert. Human Ecology, 1994. Mem. AAAS. Avocations: astronomy, reading, cookery, swimming, classical music. Office: JG Shedd Aquarium 1200 S Lake Shore Dr Chicago IL 60605

DEAL, AMY SUZANNE, choral director; b. Statesboro, Ga., Oct. 4, 1972; d. Robert Daniel and Lyn Jo Deal; m. Chad Andrew Deal, June 28, 2003. MusB in Music Edn. and Music Theory, U. Ga., 1996; MA in Musicology and Music Theory, Pa. State U., 1998. Instr. Pa. State U., State College, 1996—98; choral dir. Langston Chapel Mid. Sch., Statesboro, Ga., 1998—2001; choir dir. Brooklet United Meth. Ch., Brooklet, Ga., 1999—2002; choral dir. Statesboro H.S., 2001—02, KO Knudson Acad. Performing Arts, Las Vegas, Nev., 2002—. Nat. Merit scholar, State Farm Ins., 1991—95, Ga. scholar, 1991—96. Mem.: Ga. Music Educators Assn., Music Educators Nat. Conf., Phi Kappa Phi. Methodist. Avocations: reading, travel, piano. Office: KO Knudson Acad Performing Arts 2400 Atlantic St Las Vegas NV 89104

DEAL, KAREN LYNNE, conductor; b. Richmond, Va. d. John F. Deal, Jr.. BA, Oral Roberts U.; MA in Conducting, Va. Commonwealth U., 1982; student, Hochschule Musick and Darnstellende Kunst, Frankfurt, Germany, Peabody Conservatory Music. Assoc. condr. Annapolis Symphony Orch., 1986—92; founding music dir. Sinfonia Concertante; music dir., condr. Nashville (Tenn.) Ballet, 1992—2000; assoc. condr. Nashville (Tenn.) Symphony, 1992—2000; musical dir. Ill. Symphony Orch., Springfield, Ill., 2000—, dir., 2000—. Asst. condr. Frankfurt (Germany) State Opera, Nat. Repertory Orch., 1990—91; guest condr. in field. Condr.: TV series PBS Nova. Founder Sneakers and Jeans Initiative. Named one of Coolest People, Nashville (Tenn.) Life Mag., 1997; recipient Biennial Conducting Competition award, Nat. Repertory Orch., 1989, Woman of Achievement award, Mid. Tenn. State U., 1995, Citation of Appreciation, Mayor of Nashville, 2000, Nashville (Tenn.) Pub. Schs. Bd. Edn., 2000, Coun. Met. Govt. Nashville, 2000, Mayor's award, Springfield (Ill.) Arts Coun., 2002, Ill. Coun. Orchs. award, 2002; scholar, Aspen Music Festival, Tanglewood Music Festival. Office: Illinois Symphony Orchestra PO Box 5191 Springfield IL 62705-5191*

DEAL, PATRICIA MARIE, political activist; b. Boston, Mar. 6, 1943; d. Paul Albert and Esther Helen (Hines) D. BS, Boston U., 1964; MEd, Salem State Coll., 1972; MBA, Bentley Coll., 1984. Cert. tchr., Mass. Tchr. Boston Pub. Schs., 1966-67, Sts. Peter & Paul H.S., St. Thomas, V.I., 1967-68, Wakefield (Mass.) Pub. Schs., 1968-71, Gloucester (Mass.) Pub. Schs., 1972-74; tchr., adminstr. St. Anne's Sch., Arlington, Mass., 1975-79; customer support supr. Educators Cons. Svcs., Burlington, Mass., 1979-82; project mgr. SEI Corp., Cambridge, Mass., 1982-86; ops. mgr. Bank of Boston, 1987—98; asst. treas. Office of Mass. State Treas., Boston, 1999—. Town meeting mem. Town of Arlington, 1988—; Dem. state committeewoman Mass. Dem. Party, 1988—, mem. exec. com., 1992—; libr. trustee Robbin Libr., Arlington, 1994—; active Mass. Women's Polit. Caucus, 1984—, Nat. Women's Polit. Caucus, 1985—, v.p., 1995-99; co-chair Dem. Task Force, 2003—. Home: 9 Ronald Rd Arlington MA 02474-1421

DEAL, SARAH R. psychotherapist, educator; b. Houston, Tex., Mar. 14, 1974; d. Harry Stephen and Amanda Moore Deal. BS in Psychology cum laude, Tex. Christian U., 1996; MA in Clin. Psychology, St. Mary's U., 1999, postgrad., 2003—; PhD in Counseling, 2003. Intern Tarrant County Women's Ctr., Ft. Worth, 1994—96; clin. rschr. U. Tex. Health Sci. Ctr., San Antonio, 1997—99; intern U. Tex. Mental Svcs. Inst., Houston, 1998—99; instr. psychology Lee Coll., Baytown, 2000—01; counselor Cmty. Based Counseling, San Antonio, 2001—02; adj. faculty psychology St. Mary's U., 2001—. Rsch. asst. St. Mary's U., 2003—. Named Disting. Grad., St. Mary's U., 1999. Mem.: APA, Tex. Counseling Assn., Sigma Chi Iota. Avocations: gardening, travel, animal rescues. Office: St Marys U Psychology Dept 1 Camino Santa Maria San Antonio TX 78228 E-mail: doccounseling@aol.com.

DEALBUQUERQUE, JOAN MARIE, band director; b. Grosse Pointe, Mich., Feb. 1, 1967; d. Angela May and Anthony Joseph deAlbuquerque. MusB in Edn., Mich. State U., East Lansing, 1993, MusM in Wind Conducting, 1999; postgrad., U. North Tex., Denton, 2000—03. Tchg. fellow U. North Tex., Denton, 2000—03; assoc. dir. of bands Calif. State U., Long Beach, 2003—. Music dir, choir dir., vocal soloist Unity Ch. of Rochester, Mich., 1994; asst. condr. Mich. State U. Concert Band, East Lansing, 1997—99; H.S. band adjudicator No. N.Mex. Dist., 2000; condr. U. North Tex. Concert Band, Denton, 2000—03, H.S. Honor Band, Alamosa, Colo., 2000—00; cantor/vocal soloist Immaculate Conception Cath. Ch., Denton, Tex., 2001—03; rec. prodr. John Wacker, solo trumpet, Denton, Tex., 2002—02; mgr. Conductors Collegium, Denton, Tex., 2002—03; condr. Octet by Stravinsky/Grad. Chamber Group, Denton, Tex., 2003—03. Author: (book) 3 articles in Teaching Music Through Performance in Band. Scholar, Macomb C.C., 1990-1991, Toulouse Grad. Dept., 2000; Tchg. fellowship, U. North Tex., 2000-2003. Mem.: Music Educators Nat. Conf., So. Calif. Sch. Band and Orchestra Assn.., Calif. Band Dirs. Assn., Coll. Band Dirs. Nat. Assn., Golden Key Nat. Honor Soc., Pi Kappa Lambda, Phi Kappa Phi. Roman Catholic. Home: 35444 Stillmeadow Ln Clinton Township MI 48035 Office: Calif State Univ 1250 Bellflower Blvd Long Beach CA 90840-7101 Office Phone: 562-985-4533. Personal E-mail: jdealbuq@csulb.edu.

DEALEY, AMANDA MAYHEW, former foundation administrator; b. Dallas, July 17, 1950; d. Charles Milton and Audrey (Overton) Mayhew; m. Joe M. Dealey Jr., Nov. 4, 1972 (div. 1978); 1 child, Christopher Charles; m. Lawrence W. Speck, Oct. 3, 1992. BA in Art History, U. Tex., 1972. Bd. dirs. Mid Am. Arts Alliance, Kansas City, Mo., 1987-90, James Dick Found., 1978—; mem. adv. coun. Sch. Nursing U. Tex., Austin, 1987—; sec.-treas. Tex. Assn. for Symphony Orchs., Austin, 1988-89, vice-chmn. Tex. Arts Alliance, 1986-89. Mem. Mental Health Assn. Tex. (v.p. 1995—), Tex. Lyceum Assn. (pres. 1995, chair 1996). Home: 1210 W 13th St #A Austin TX 78703-4106

DE AMORIM, VALDIVIA VÂNIA SIQUEIRA, translator; b. Recife, Brazil, June 17, 1944; d. Francisco Targino and Angelica (Lucas) De Siqueira; m. Jimmie Willis Beauchamp (div. 1970); 1 child, Angélica R. Beauchamp-Ringeisen; m. Joāo Mendonca de Amorim Filho, 2002. BS in Journalism, CEUB, 1978; MA in Portuguese and Spanish Lit., NYU, 1992. Registered profl. journalist. Social comm. sec. Office of Brazilian Presidency, Brasilia, Brazil, 1984-90; Portuguese translator Family Court, N.Y.C., 1993; translator, broker asst. Josephthal Lion & Ross, N.Y.C., 1995, U.S. Securities and Futures, N.Y.C., 1996—99; in flight translator, internat. flight attendent Am. Airlines. Reporter, corr. Revista Aerea, N.Y.C., 1984—; founder, tchr. Lang. Sch. Multi Lingua, Brazil; tchr. Portuguese and Spanish, Sigma Delta Pi, Purdue U., Ind., 1982-84, NYU, 1990-92. Author: Stigma, Saga for a New World, 1000-2003, 2003. Founder literary hour NYU; liberal artist Lafayette Art Mus., 1982-84 [illegible] C. of the Rockways (exec. dir. 1998). Presbyterian. Avocations: oil painting, piano, horseback riding, boating/fishing.

DEAN, ANN MARIE BUTZ, secondary school educator; b. Indpls., Dec. 8, 1948; d. Charles Theodore and Rebecca Jean Butz; m. Carl Wilde Dean, June 1, 1974; children: Heather Ann, Abigail Rebecca Dean Ferretti, Laura Louise. BA, Hanover Coll., 1971; exec. sec., Ind. Bus. Coll., 1973. Lic. tchr. history and English 7-12. Legal sec. Rocap, Rocap, Reese & Young, Indpls., 1973; exec. asst., asst. evaluator Lilly Endowment, Inc., Indpls., 1973—76; vol. IPS, Westfield Schs., Agape PTO, Therapeutic Riding Neighborhood Assn., Indpls. and Westfield, Ind., 1976—2000; substitute tchr. Westfield/Washington Schs., 2000—03; instr. asst. spl. edn. Warren Twp. Schs., 2003—. Mem. prin. selection bd. Westfield Mid. Sch., 1994. Founder PTO, Westfield H.S., 1997—99; bd. dirs. Village Farms Neighborhood Assn., Carmel, Ind., 1996—2002; team mom 3 soccer orgns. Westfield and Indpls., 1990—98. Mem.: Women's Recreation Soc., Hanover Coll. (pres. 1970—71), Contemporary Club, Players Club, Dramatic Club. Republican. Methodist. Avocations: tennis, horseback riding, camping, swimming, sewing. Home: 77 Greyhound Pass Carmel IN 46032 Personal E-mail: cadeanfamily@hotmail.com

DEAN, BONNIE BLANDER, epidemiologist; b. Panorama City, Calif., Aug. 18, 1969; d. Robert E. and Phyllis Blander; m. Steven Jay Dean. BA, Calif. State U., 1992; MPH, U. Calif., L.A., 1996, PhD, 2000. Rsch. asst. Calif. State U., Northridge, 1991—93; rsch. assoc. So. Calif. Injury Prevention Rsch. Ctr., L.A., 1994—2000; assoc. dir. rsch. Zynx Health Inc., Beverly Hills, Calif., 2000—. Tutor Calif. State U., L.A., 1998—99. Contbr. articles to profl. jours. Mem. East L.A. injury prevention consortium and older adult project Royal Inst. Applied Gerontology, 1997—2000; Member National Foundation of Ileitis and Colitis, Los Angeles, CA, 1985—2002; Counselor Human Efforts Aimed at Preventing Violence Among Youth (Project HEAVY), Los Angeles, CA, 1991—91. Fellow, U. Calif., L.A., 1996—99. Mem.: Am. Pub. Health Assn. (edn. com. 1998—2000, abstract reviewer 1999), Psi Chi, Golden Key (life). Office: Zynx Health Inc 9100 Wilshire Blvd Beverly Hills CA 90212 Office Fax: 310-247-7710. Business E-Mail: bdean@cerner.com.

DEAN, CAROL, secondary school educator; b. Omaha, Jan. 16, 1953; 1 child, William Dean Nassau. BA in Translation, U. Nebr., 1976; MA in Comparative Lit., Binghamton (N.Y.) U., 1983, MAT in Fgn. Lgn., 1987; EdD in Ednl. Theory and Practice, SUNY, Binghamton, 2003. Cert. tchr., N.Y. Translator Mutual of Omaha Ins. Co., Omaha, 1976-78; tchr. Unatego Ctrl. Schs., Wells Bridge, N.Y., 1987-88, Oneonta (N.Y.) City Schs., 1988—2000; coord. data analysis svcs. Broome-Tioga BOCES, Binghamton, NY, 2000—. Nat. trainer Generating Expectations Student Achievment. Contbr. articles to profl. jours.; actress (TV series) Susquehanna Stories, 1990. Couper fellowship Binghamton U., 1994; recipient essay contest award N.Y. State Founds. in Edn. Assn., 1998. Mem. NEA, AAUW, ASCD, Am. Ednl. Rsch. Assn., N.Y. Schs. Data Analysis Tech. Assistance Group (founding mem.). Democrat. Avocations: acting, skiing, travel. Home: 16 Hazel St Oneonta NY 13820-1307

DEAN, CAROLE LEE, film company executive; b. Dallas, Mar. 23, 1939; d. Roy Webster and Dorothy Lee Dean; children: Richard Dean, Carole Joyce. Student, UCLA. Pres. Studio Film and Tape, L.A., 1969-2000, N.Y.C., 1970-2000, Chgo., 1994—2000, From the Heart Prodn., L.A., 1992—. Prodr., host Health Styles, 1994-97; author: Heal Thyself, 1999, Art of Funding Your Film, 2003. Mem. Nat. Arts Club. Republican. Avocations: skiing, equesterian. E-mail: caroleedean@att.net.

DEAN, DELORES A. director; 2 children. Bachelors Degree, Fla. State U., 1980; Masters Degree, Fla. A&M U., 1996, PhD, 2004. Pers. technician Fla. State U., Tallahassee, 1983—86; med. disability specialist Health and Rehab. Svcs., Tallahassee, 1986—90; asst. dir. Fla. A&M U. Career Ctr., Tallahassee, 1990—98, dir., 1998—. Bd. dirs. Alpha Data Svcs., Tallahassee, Campus Ministry, Tallahassee. Contbr. articles to profl. jours. Participant March of Dimes, Tallahassee, 2002, 2003. Mem.: Fla. Career Ctr. Consortium, Fla. Career Profls. Assn., Nat. Assn. Colls. and Employers. Avocations: reading, travel, shopping, exercise, walking. Office: Fla A&M U The Career Ctr M L King Blvd Ste 100 Tallahassee FL 32307

DEAN, DIANE (H.) SWEET, artist, retired credit manager; b. Glendale, Calif., May 7, 1953; m. Bill J. Dean, Aug. 27, 1994; children: Aaron J., Brian W. Wallace. AA in Graphics, Pierce Coll., 1971; studied with The Samsel's, Calif., 1963—69; studied with Vel Miller, Reseda, Calif., 1969—73; studied with Hal Reed, Van Nuys, Calif., 1971—74; studied with Lisette De Winne, L.A., 1973—. Credit mgr. Syncor Internat., Woodland Hills, Calif., 1984—2000. Exhibited in group shows at Santa Clarita Art Guild (1st Place award, 1978, Best of Show award, 1979, 1st Place award, 2000, 2001), 1979, Art Classic XII, Santa Clarita, 2001 (1st in Theme award, 1st in Colored Graphics award, 2d in Peoples' Choice award), Santa Paula Art Exhibit, 2002 (1st People's Choice award, 1st jury of peers award, 2002), Southwest Art Mag., 2002. Recipient Artist of Yr., San Gabriel Fine Art Assn., 2001, Don Roche Meml. award, 2002. Mem.: River Valley Art Assn. (1st pl. award 2003), Pastel Soc. Am. (signature), Havasu Art Assn. (1st Pl. award 2003, People's Choice award 2003). E-mail: ddsweet7@frontiernet.net.

DEAN, JEAN BEVERLY, artist; b. South Paris, Maine, Aug. 23, 1928; d. Henry Dyer and Doris Filena (Judd) Small; m. Samuel Lester Dean. AS, Becker Coll., Worcester, Mass., 1948; AA, Edison Coll., Ft. Myers, Fla., 1980. Artist, Ft. Myers, 1963—. (one-woman shows) Edison C.C. Gallery, Ft. Myers, Joan Ling Gallery, Gainesville, Fla., Berry Coll., Mt. Berry Ga., Gallery 10, Asheville, N.C., Sanibel Gallery, Fla., 1993, Barrier Island Group for the Arts, Sanibel, 1994, 1996, Sanibel Gallery, 1995, Gallery Mido, Belleview Mido Resort, Belleair, Fla., 1996, No. Trust Bank, Ft. Myers, 1996, Lee County Alliance of the Arts, 1996, Art League of Manatee County, Fla., 1996, Naples Libr., 1997, Sy Zy Gy Gallery, Ft. Myers, 1998, 2000, Barnes and Noble, 2000, Captiva Civic Assn., Fla., 2000, So. Co. Ctr. for the Arts, Ft. Myers, Fla., 2000, Viva Gallery, Captiva, Fla., 2000, Broadway Palm Dinner Theatre, Ft. Myers, Fla., 2001, Art House, 2002, Tower Gallery, Sanibel, Fla., 2002; one-woman shows include Alliance for the Arts, Ft. Myers, Fla., 2004; exhibited (group shows) S.E. Painting and Sculpture Exhbn., Jacksonville, Fla., Southeastern Ctr. for Contemporary Art, Ybor City, S.W. Fla. Internat. Airport, 1991, 1995, Ctr. Art Show, St. Petersburg, Fla., 1991, Ridge Juried Art Show, Winter Haven, Fla., 1992, Artists Group, Sarasota, 1992, Women's Caucus for Art, 1993, Polk Mus., Lakeland, Fla., 1993, Daytona Mus., Fla., 1994, Women's Caucus Art Nat. Show, San Antonio, 1995, Capitol Gallery, Tallahassee, 1995, Women's Caucus Art State Show, Sarasota, 1995, Women's Caucus for Art, Miami, 1996, 1998, Fla. Artist Group, Winter Haven, 1996, Jacksonville Art Mus., 1998, Edison Coll., Ft. Myers, 1999, Fla. So. Coll., Lakeland, 1999, Art Ctr., St. Petersburg, Fla., 1999, Viva Gallery, Captiva, Fla., 2000, Charlotte County Nat., Fla., 2000, Nat. Exhibit, Winter Haven, Fla., 2000, The Capitol, Tallahassee, Fla., 2001, Venice Art Ctr., 2001, Captiva Art Ctr., 2001; Exhibited in group shows at Charlotte County National, Fla., 2002, Alliance of the Arts, Ft. Myers, Fla., 2002—03, Barrier Island Group for the Arts, Sanibel, Fla., 2002, Gallery on Broadway, Ft. Myers, Fla., 2002, Florida Gulf Coast U., Ft. Myers, 2003, Bonita Arts Ctr., Bonita Springs, Fla., 2003, Crossed Palms Gallery, Bookelia, Fla., 2002—03, Represented in permanent collections Am. Embassy, Madrid, Edison Coll., Ft. Myers, Fla., First Fed. Savs. and Loan, Ft. Myers, Naples, Fla., NCNB Bank, Tampa, Health Park, Ft. Myers, Clara Barton House, Washington, Hirshhorn Collection, ArtServe Gallery, Ft. Lauderdale, Fla. Active Lee County Alliance for Arts, 1994-2003; chair invitational com. Barrier Island Group for Arts, Sanibel, 1994-99; founder Open Doors Lee County Alliance of the Arts, Fla., 1990—. Recipient more than 100 awards. Mem. Nat. Mus. Women in the Arts (charter mem.), Fla. Artists Group. Democrat. Unitarian Universalist. Home: 17643 Captiva Island Ln Fort Myers FL 33908-6115

DEAN, LISA, foundation executive; b. New Castle, Pa., Aug. 8, 1968; d. Wayne Ernest and Theresa May Dean. BA, St. John's U., 1992; postgrad., Columbia U., 1992-94. V.p. for tech. policy Free Congress Found., Washington, 1994—. Editor The Privacy Papers, 1997—; host nat. syndicated TV show Endangered Liberties, 1997-99; bd. dirs. Am.'s Voice TV Network, Free Congress PAC, Com. for an Effective State Govt. Republican. Eastern Orthodox. Avocations: travel, orgnizational and charitable work. Office: Free Congress Found 717 2d St NE Washington DC 20002

DEAN, PATRICEA LOUISE, lawyer, law educator, small business owner; b. Kansas City, Mo., Sept. 25, 1928; d. Merville Francis Davies and Marie Margaret (Dorsch Davies) Damron; m. Richard Wallace Dean, Mar. 14, 1948 (dec. July 20, 1987); children: Phyllis Carol(dec.), Katherine Ann, Carol Anne. AA, Met. Jr. Coll., Kansas City, 1947; BA, Pepperdine U., 1968, JD, 1971. Bar: Calif. 73, U.S. Supreme Ct. 87, U.S. Tax Ct. 92. Pvt. practice, Anaheim and Sacramento, Calif., 1973—2001; instr. various colls. and law schs., Calif., 1975—2001; continuing edn. instr. N.W. Coll., Powell, Wyo., 2001—. Legis. coord. Western Manufactured Housing Inst., 1977—83; atty., lobbyist, presenter seminars Calif. Manufactured Home Owners League, 1984—89; dir., pres. telecomms., software and internet businesses, 1990—. Author: Guide to Manufactured Housing, 1980; contbr. articles to profl. publs. Pres. Friends of Cody Libr., 2002—; precinct worker Dem. Party, Mo. and Calif., 1949—53; campaign mgr. Dist. Atty. race, Iron County, Utah, 1962—63; precinct committeewoman Rep. Party, Park County, Wyo., 2002—03. Achievements include helped draft federal and state laws on building, siting, zoning and taxation of manufactured homes. Office: Office@Home Inc PO Box 836 Powell WY 82435

DEAN, SHERRY LYNN, language educator, speech professional; b. New Albany, Ind., July 1, 1960; d. Oscar L. Brown and Betty L. Roberts; m. A. L. Dean Jr.. BA inFrench, Speech Comm., Secondary Edn., Asbury Coll., 1983; MA in French, U. Tex., Arlington, 1990; Cert. pratique de francais commercial, Chambre de Commerce de d'Industries, Paris, 1990; MA in Interdisciplinary Studies, U. Tex., Arlington, 1999—; PhD in Higher Edn. Adminstrn., U. Tex., Austin, 2003. Mem. adj. French faculty Mountain View Coll., Dallas, 1986—91, mem. French faculty, 1991—, prof. French and speech comm., 1993—. Sponsor French Club, Mountain View Coll., 1989—, chair honors program, 1996—98, sponsor Senegal Studies Club, 1997—98, 1999—2000, coord. Study Abroad Programs, 1998—, mem. study abroad coords., 1998—, chair cultures course com., 1999—, mem. core curriculum cultures course com., 1999—, coord. intercultural spkr. series, 1995, coord. Europe 1992 Conf., 1991—92, mem. numerous other coms.; mem. North Tex. C.C. Consortium for Internat. Edn., 1997—; presenter in field. Compiler AATF Travel Guide, 1996, reviewer Little-known Museums In and Around Paris; author: (book) Discover French-speaking Louisiana: A Brief Guide to Creating An Acadiana Adventure Tour. Named Outstanding Young Woman of Yr., 1986, Chevalier, Knight of the Acad. Palms French Govt., 2003; recipient internship, French Cultural Svcs., Washington, 1981; grantee, Dallas County C.C. Dist., 1993—2000. Mem.: Am. Assn. Tchrs. of French (v.p. North Tex. chpt. 1994—96, com. chair Task Force for Promotion of French in U.S. 1995—97, pres. North Tex. chpt. 1996—98, mem. Commn. for Promotion of French 1999—2000, mem. Nat. French Week Commn. 1998—, co-chair Nat. C.C. Commn. 2000, Coll. Tchr. of Yr. award 1999, Dorothy S. Ludwig Excellence inTchg. award 2000), Tex. Fgn. Lang. Assn. (Coll. Tchr. of Yr. award 1998), l'Alliance Francaise (hon.). Home: 1329 Primrose Ln De Soto TX 75115 Office: Mountain View Coll 4849 W Illinois Ave Dallas TX 75211

DEANE, DEBBE, psychologist, journalist, editor, consultant; b. Coatesville, Pa., July 30, 1950; d. George Edward and Dorothea Alice (Martin) Mays; widowed; children: Theo, Vonisha, Lorise, Voniece. AA in Psychology, Mesa Coll., 1989; BA Psychology, San Diego State U., 1993; MA in Psychology, Nat. U., 1995; postgrad., U.S. Internat. U., 1995—. Announcer Sta. KBPI, Denver, 1969-70, Sta. WKXI, Jackson, Miss., 1970-72; news anchor Sta. WNGE-TV, Nashville, 1973-76; news dir. Sta. KLDR, Denver, 1976-78; host, reporter Sta. KMGH-TV, Denver, 1978-81; news anchor, editor Sta. KHOW, Denver, 1978-79; news & pub. affairs dir. Sta. KLZ, Denver, 1979-80, Sta. KCBQ, San Diego, 1980-82; news anchor Sta. KOGO, San Diego, 1983-84; news anchor, reporter Sta. KCST-TV, San Diego, 1984-87; dir. comm. Omni Corp., San Diego, 1987—; news anchor Sta. KFI, L.A., 1990-91; sr. psychiat. therapist Behavioral Health Group, San Diego, 1993—. Media liaison United Negro Coll. Fund, San Diego, 1990-92; dir. comm. United Chs. of Christ, San Diego, 1989-92; cons. San Diego Assn. Black Journalists, 1985-92, San Diego Coalition Black Journalists, 1985-92; cons. in field. Campaign fin. analyst San Diego County Registrar of Voters, San Diego, 1990; cons. San Diego County Office Disaster Preparedness, 1990-91, Nu Way Youth Ctr. & Neighborhood House, Inc., San Diego, 1991-92; counselor Project STARRT, San Diego, 1991-92; cons. United Way Home Start, Inc. Family Self-Sufficiency Program, 1996—; cons. and program coord. San Diego Healthy Start, Inc., 1997—, Samuel L. Gompers Secondary Inst. Math., Sci. & computer Tech., 1997—. Recipient San Diego Black Achievement award Urban League, 1989, Best News Show & Spot News award San Diego Press Club, 1985, Golden Mike award So. Calif. Broadcast Assn., L.A., 1986; named one of Top 25 Businesswomen Essence Mag., 1978, Outstanding Humanitarian Worldvision, 1993, Outstanding Humanities Alumna Mesa Coll., 1993, Woman of the Year. Mem. AFTRA, APA, Am. Psychol. Assn., Am. Women in Radio & TV, Women in Comm., Black Students Sci. Orgn. (sec. 1989-91), Africana Psychol. Soc. (media coord. 1990-92), Psi Chi. Democrat. Achievements: first African-Am. in U.S. lic. to teach radio & TV broadcast prodn. Home: 3545 Valley Rd No 1 Bonita CA 91902-4164 E-mail: debbedeane@worldnet.att.net

DEANE, ELAINE, lawyer; b. Washington, Sept. 10, 1958; d. William Francis Goode and Elizabeth Anne (Downes) Deane. AB, U. Calif., Berkeley, 1980; JD, U. San Francisco, 1986. Bar: Calif. 1986. Assoc. Parkinson, Wolf, Lazar & Leo, L.A., 1985-89, Peltit & Martin, San Francisco, 1989-91, Frandzel & Share, San Francisco, Calif., 1992-93, Arter & Haddon, San Francisco, 1994—. Mem. Calif. Bar Assn., L.A. County Bar Assn., Century City Bar Assn., Beverly Hills Bar Assn., San Francisco Bar Assn., Lawyers' Com. for Urban Affairs, Sierra Club, Amnesty Internat., Wilderness Soc., Greenpeace. Avocations: ballet, theatre, environment. Office: Arter & Hadden LLP Ste 3130 555 California St San Francisco CA 94104-1607

DEANE, SALLY JAN, health services management, consultant; b. Downey, Calif., Sept. 24, 1948; d. Virgil Eldred and Pearl Jan (Kettell) D. BA, Whittier Coll., 1970; MEd, Boston U., 1971, MPH, 1988. Mgr. community health Peter Bent Brigham Hosp., Boston, 1974-76; coord. WIC program Martha Eliot Health Ctr., 1976-78; dir. S.W. Boston WIC program Shattuck Hosp. Corp., 1978-80; exec. dir. Fenway Community Health Ctr., 1980-84; exec. asst. commr. Boston Dept. Health & Hosps., 1984-86; assoc. dir. spl. projects Health Policy Inst. Boston U., 1986-87; dir. ambulatory reimbursement Mass. Medicaid, 1987-88; assoc. Cambridge (Mass.) Mgmt. Group, 1989; ptnr. Integrated Health Strategies Inc., Cambridge, Mass., 1990-96; adj. asst. clin. prof. Pub. Health Boston U., 1994—; v.p. Chadwick Martin Bailey, Boston, 1996-98; mng. ptnr. Strategic Healthcare Innovations LLC, Boston, 1999—; instr. Boston U., 1999—. Cons. Mass. Dept. Pub. Health, Boston, 1978-80, Citicorp Hdqrs., N.Y.C., 1986; lectr. Grad. Sch. Mgmt., Boston U., 1999—; bd. visitors Boston U. Sch. Pub. Health, 1999—; innkeeper Charles St. Inn. Mem. Mayor's Task Force on AIDS, Boston, 1983—86; v.p. Trustees Charitable Donations, Boston, 1984—88; chair bd. dirs. Boston Women's Health Book Collective, 2000—; chmn. bd. dirs. N.E. Eye Inst., 2001—. Mem.: Boston Club. Presbyterian. E-mail: sallydeane@yahoo.com.

DEANER, NANCY MARCY, religious studies educator, religious organization administrator; d. Harry K. and Lillian C. Marcy; m. Francis Reed Deaner, June 8, 1974; children: Jeremy, Jason. BA, Albright Coll., 1974; M in Christian Edn., Garrett-Evang. Theol. Sem., 1977. Dir. christian edn. United Meth. Ch., Elm Grove, Wis., 1979—81; camping and retreat ministries coord. Wis. Conf., United Meth. Ch., Sun Prairie, 1998—. Sch. bd. mem. Lake Geneva Schools, Joint #1, 1993—96, sch. bd. pres., 1995—96. Recipient Wis. Women Leaders in Edn. award, AAUW, Geneva Lake chpt., 1995—96. Mem.: Am. Camping Assn. Methodist. Avocation: travel. Office: Wis Conf United Meth Ch PO Box 620 Sun Prairie WI 53590

DEANGELIS, CATHERINE D. pediatrics educator; b. Scranton, Pa., Jan. 2, 1940; m. James C. Harris. BA, Wilkes Coll., 1965; MD, U. Pitts., 1969; MPH, Harvard U., 1973. Diplomate Nat. Bd. Med. Examiners, Am. Bd. Pediat.; RN Pa., N.Y. Intern in pediat. Children's Hosp., Pitts., 1969—70; resident in pediat. Johns Hopkins Hosp., Balt., 1970—72, teaching fellow pediat. dept. internat. health Sch. Pub. Health, 1972; pediatrician Roxbury Comprehensive Health Clinic, Boston, 1972—73; asst. prof. pediat. Coll. Physicians and Surgeons, asst. prof. health svc. adminstrn. Sch. Pub. Health Columbia U., 1973—75; mem. staff divsn. pediatric ambulatory care, dir. med. edn. Child Care Project Columbia Presbyn. Med. Ctr., 1973—75; asst. prof. pediat. Sch. Medicine U. Wis., 1975—77, assoc. prof. pediat. Sch. Medicine, 1977—78; dir. ambulatory pediatric svcs. U. Wis. Hosps., 1975—78; assoc. prof. pediat. Johns Hopkins Sch. Medicine, 1978—85; dir. pediatric primary care and adolescent medicine Johns Hopkins Hosp., 1978—84, co-dir. adolescent pregnancy program, 1979—82; with dept. health svcs. administrn. and dept. internat. health Johns Hopkins Sch. Hygiene and Pub. Health, 1980—90; dir. residency tng. dept. pediat. Johns Hopkins Hosp., 1983—90, dir. divsn. gen. pediat. and adolescent medicine, 1984—90; deputy chmn. dept. pediat. Johns Hopkins Sch. Medicine, 1983—90, prof. pediat., 1986—, assoc. dean acad. affairs, 1990—93, sr. assoc. dean acad. affairs and faculty, 1993—94, vice dean acad. affairs and faculty, 1994—; editor Jour. AMA, 2000—. Mem. Gov.'s Task Force to Evaluate Health Care in Wis. State Prisons, 1975—78; chmn. ambulatory care com. U. Wis. Hosp., 1976—78; mem. med. sch. admissions com. U. Wis. Sch. Medicine, 1976—78, chmn., 1977—78; mem. exec. coun. dept. pediat. and Children's Ctr. Johns Hopkins U. Sch. Medicine, 1982—90, chmn. fin. com. dept. pediat., 1984—85, chmn. assoc. prof.'s promotion com., 1985—88, chmn. com. developing Women's Health Ctr. at Johns Hopkins Med. Instns., 1993—; mem. Md. Gov.'s Task Force on Women's Health, 1993—, chair, 1994—; mem. search com. U. Wis., 1976, Johns Hopkins Sch. Medicine, 1984, 88, 92, 93; mem. nat. rev. com. for accreditation of nurse practitioners Am. Nurses' Assn., 1975—79, co-chmn., 1977; mem. peer rev. com. nurse practitioner programs divsn. nursing Health Resources Agy., Dept. HEW, 1979—81. Author: Basic Pediatrics for the Primary Care, 1984; editor: An Introduction to Clinical Research, 1990; editor: (with others) Principles and Practice of Pediatrics, 1990, 1994; assoc. editor Pediatric Annals, 1990—, editor Archives of Pediatrics and Adolescent Medicine, 1993—. Cons. Robert Wood Johnson Found., 1972—; mem. adv. group on improving outcomes for children Pew Charitable Trusts, 1991—92; mem. adv. panel medicine Pew Health Profn.'s Commn.; mem. nat. adv. com. Robert Wood Johnson Clin. Scholars Program, 1992—; mem. steering com. Rural Health Planning, Wis. Recipient George Armstrong award, Ambulatory Pediatric Assn., scholarship, Acad. Adminstrn. and Health Policy, Assn. Health Ctrs., 1993; fellow NIH, 1973. Fellow: APHA, Am. Acad. Pediat. (govt. affairs com. 1984—88, chpt. III youth com. N.Y. chpt. 1974—75, chmn. adolescent com. Md. chpt. 1981—84); mem.: Inst. Medicine Coun., Soc. Adolescent Medicine, Am. Bd. Pediat. (examiner 1986—, long-range planning com. 1990—91, chmn. long-range planning com. 1992—, bd. dirs. 1990—, fin. com. 1991—, sec., treas. 1993—95, chair-elect 1995—96, chair 1996, search com. 1990), Am. Pediatric Soc. (sec., treas. 1989—), Alpha Omega Alpha. Address: JAMA 515 N State St Chicago IL 60610-4325 Office: Johns Hopkins Sch Medicine 720 Rutland Ave Ste 106 Baltimore MD 21205-2109*

DE ANGELIS, DEBORAH ANN AYARS, university athletics official; b. San Diego, July 2, 1948; d. Charles Orvil and Janet Isabel (Glithero) Ayars; m. David C. De Angelis, Sept. 29, 1984. BA, U. Calif.-Santa Barbara, 1970, Eligibility worker Certificate in Social Services, 1972; MS, U. Mass., 1979. Eligibility worker County Welfare Dept., Santa Barbara, Calif., 1970-73; women's crew coach U. Mass., 1978-79, Northeastern U., Boston, 1979-83, bus. mgr. women's athletics, 1983-87, asst. dir. bus., 1987-89; mgr. athletics bus. Calif. State U., Northridge, 1989-93, assoc. dir., 1993-96; assoc. athletic dir. for internal affairs Towson State U., 1996—2001; diversity affirmative action com. Towson State U., 1996—; athletic dir. Calif. State U., Hayward, 2001—. Com. mem. Women's Olympic Rowing Com., 1976-84; life trustee Nat. Rowing Found., 1984; life mem. selection com. Rowing Found. Hall of Fame, 1984—, bd. dirs., 1994-99; rowing mgr. Women's Olympic Team, 1976, 80; head mgr. U.S. Olympic Festival, Syracuse, N.Y., 1981, coach, Indpls., 1982, Colorado Springs, Colo., 1983; mem. alcohol and drug awareness com. Northeastern U., 1983; mem. intercoll. athletics oversignt adv. bd. Calif. State U. Northridge; chmn. cmty. policing adv. bd. Calif. State U. Hayward, 2003-04. Mem. Nat. Women's Rowing Assn. (pres. 1976-80, Woman of Yr. award 1983), Fedn. Sociétés d'Aviron (women's commn. 1978—, U.S. del. to ann. congress 1978, 80-88, 95-98, del. 2000-01), U.S. Rowing Assn. (del. 1988, bd. dirs. 1975-80, 85-98, co-chmn. internat. div., co-chmn. events div. 1985-98, chmn. internat. div. 1986-88, women's v.p. 1985-88, mem. exec. com. 1985-89, exec. v.p. 1988-89, sec. 1995-96), ZLAC Rowing Club. Home: 30113 Treeview St Hayward CA 94544-7212 Office: Dept Kinesiology & PE 25800 Carlos Bee Blvd Hayward CA 94544

DE ANGELIS, JUDY, anchorwoman; b. Passaic, N.J., Oct. 1, 1949; d. Fredrick and Patricia (Zollo) De An.; m. Barry Sheffield, Aug. 28, 1977; children: Alexader, Katelin, Corrine. Student, Hartt Sch. Music, Hartford, Conn., 1968-69; BA in Speech and Drama, U Hartford, 1971; MA in Edn., Montclair State U., 1973. Lic. 3d class operator FCC. Anchor Sta. WALK-AM-FM, Patchogue, N.Y., 1978-79, Sta. WGBB-FM, Freeport, N.Y., 1979-80, Sta. WKJY-FM, Hempstead, N.Y., 1980, Sta. WHLI, Hempstead, 1980, Sta. WCBS-FM, N.Y.C., 1980-81; reporter, anchor Sta. WNBC, N.Y.C., 1981-88; morning anchor Sta. WINS, N.Y.C., 1988—2004; morning drive anchor WNEW-FM, N.Y.C., 2004—; co-owner Sheffield Studios, Mahwah, N.J. Freelance anchor The Source, 1982-88; freelance anchor NBC Radio Network, 1982-888, host talk-net, 1989-90; news anchor HBO Entertainment, 1988; indsl. voice-over Odyssey Prodns., N.Y.C., 1981-88; comml. voice-over DWJ, Ridgewood, N.J., 1994—, Gourvitz Comm., N.Y.C., 1995—; cons. Media Placement Svcs., Glen Rock, N.J., 1994—. Author: (documentary) Child Abuse: The Darker Side of Growing Up, 1982 (Olive awrd N.Y.C. Coun. of Chs., 1983; appeared on Broadway in Rockabye Hamlet, 1976. Lectr. on broadcasting all ednl. levels, 1985—; dir. religious edn. Christ Episcopal Ch., Ridgewood, 1995—; troop leader Girl Scouts U.S.A., 1994—. Recipient award for pub. svc. N.Y. Deadline Club,, 1982, spl. citation Office N.Y.C. Comptr., 1983; name Best Radio Newscaster, N.Y. AIR, 2000, 01. Mem. AFTRA, Actors Equity, Ramapo-Bergen Animal Refuge. Democrat. Avocations: carpentry, swmming, gardening, crossword puzzles, sailing. Office: 1010 WINS Radio 888 7th Ave New York NY 10106-0001

DEANGELIS, SUSAN PENNY, human resources professional; b. N.Y.C., Nov. 20, 1950; d. Milton Abraham and Anne Pearl (Fleischer) Zwilling; m. Ivo DeAngelis, July 25, 1971 (div. Feb. 1982); m. Benjamin H. Pfeffer, May 17, 1985. BA cum laude, Bklyn. Coll., 1971. Spl. projects coord., customer svc. rep. N.Y. Property Ins. Underwriting Assocs., N.Y.C., 1971-72; office mgr. Pyramid Personnel Agy., N.Y.C., 1972-73; v.p. human resources Feature Enterprises Inc., N.Y.C., 1973-92; cons. JWJ Enterprises Inc., N.Y.C., 1984-85; dir. human resources Hebrew Immigrant Aid Soc. Inc., N.Y.C., 1992-2000, Girls Inc., N.Y.C., 2000—. Mem. bus. adv. com. RUSK Inst. of Rehab., 1993—. N.Y. State Bd. Regents scholar, 1967. Mem.: Soc. for Human Resource Mgmt., Pers. Assn. Non-Profit Orgns. (exec.com. 1993—96, v.p. 1999—), N.Y. Assn. New Ams. (chmn. pvt. sector adv. com. 1985—93), U.S. Power Squadrons (past lt. comdr.). Avocations: photography, fitness, painting, boating. Home: 2258 E 27th St Brooklyn NY 11229-5030 Office: Girls Inc 120 Wall St New York NY 10005

DEANGELO, JUDITH, artist; b. Conn., July 17, 1944; d. Carl Carlson and Mildred Baker; m. Lawrence DeAngelo, Sept. 29, 1990; children: Robin Dawson, Kirsta Migliaro. Oil/alkyd paintings on exhbn. at Hargis Unique Art Gallery, Corona, Calif.; other exhbns. include Spectrum Fine Art, Westhampton Beach, N.Y., 1996, Mus. of Modern Art, Miami, Redding Mus. of Art, Calif., Art for AIDS, Milw., 1995; work displayed in pvt. collections of Sally Marr, Kitty Bruce, John Cestare, Ed Zwirn, Hugo DeVillar. Recipient award of Excellence, Manhattan Arts Internat. Competition, 1998.

DEAN-TOLER, BETHANY FRANCINE, psychologist; b. Charleston, W.Va., Feb. 17, 1974; d. Sandra Sue Dean; m. Tracy Anderson Toler, Oct. 12, 2002; 1 child, Magnolia Sunshine Toler. BA in Psychology, U. Ky., 1996; MA in Somatic psychology with specialization in dance movement therapy, Naropa U., Boulder, Colo., 2002. Cert. supervised psychologist W. Va., 1996, temp. lic. pyschol. assoc. Ky., 2003. Residential living specialist Carmel Cmty. Living Corp., Boulder, Colo., 1998—99; mental heath worker Centennial Pk. Hosp., Louisville, Colo., 1999; mental heath worker and clin. intern Devereux Cleo Wallace Ctr., Westminster, Colo., 2000—01; supervised psychologist Braley and Thompson, Inc., St. Albans, W.Va., 2002, Radical Rehab. Solutions, LLC, Huntington, W.Va., 2003—. Yoga instr. Mem.: Coun. for Exceptional Children. Avocations: dance, hiking, yoga. Office: Radical Rehab Solutions LLC Huntington WV Office Phone: 304-525-3310. E-mail: d_bethany@excite.com.

DEANY, DONNA JEAN, radiology technologist; b. Fairbury, Ill., Aug. 14, 1959; d. Paul Leroy and Jean Avis (Donley) D. Cert., Bloomington-Normal Sch. Radiog, 1979. Registered radiologic technologist. Staff technologist Mennonite Hosp., Bloomington, Ill., 1979-80, asst. chief technologist, 1981-85; radiology mgr. BroMenn Healthcare, Normal, Ill., 1985—. Clin. instr. Bloomington-Normal Sch. Radiography, 1980-85. Mem. Am. Registry Radiologic Technoloigsts, Ill. State Soc. Radiologic Technologists (sec. 1985-87, v.p. 1989-91, pres. 1992-94, treas. 1994-95). Avocations: skiing, reading, gardening. Home: 3 Reading Rd Bloomington IL 61701-1426 Office: BroMenn Healthcare Virginia at Franklin Normal IL 61761

DEARBORN, MAUREEN MARKT, speech and language clinician; b. Brockton, Mass., Jan. 19, 1948; d. Francis Joseph and Marjorie Agnes (White) M.; m. James Clement Bovin, Nov. 6, 1970 (div. June 1973); m. David C. Dearborn, Jan. 14, 1989. BA in Speech Pathology and Audiology, U. Mass., 1970; MA in Ednl. Psychology, Am. Internat. Coll., Springfield, Mass. Speech and lang. clinician Holyoke (Mass.) Pub. Schs., 1970—. Chmn. Holyoke Cancer Crusade, 1985; voter registration chmn. Holyoke Dem. Com., 1987; chmn. deaconesses 2d Congl. Ch. Holyoke. Mem.: DAR (historian Eunice Day 1984—), Mass. Tchrs. Assn., Mass. Speech, Hearing and Lang. Assn., Am. Speech, Hearing and Lang. Assn. (continuing edn. adv. bd. 1988—91, congl. action contact 1988—90), Holyoke Tchrs. Assn., Hampden County Tchrs. Assn. (pres. 1981, 1987, sec. 1982, v.p. 1984—86, treas. 1988—), Dorchester Hist. Soc., Wrenthan Hist. Soc., Assn. for Gravestone Studies, Friends of the Libr. Coun. (treas. 1992—2000), Mass. Geneal. Soc., New Eng. Hist. and Geneal. Soc. Avocations: bicycling, antiques, genealogy, aerobics. Home: 257 W Franklin St Holyoke MA 01040-2210 Office: Holyoke Pub Schs 57 Suffolk St Holyoke MA 01040-5015

DEARHAMMER, NANCY ELLEN, educational consultant; b. Chgo., July 12, 1968; d. John Howard and Mary Ellen Dearhammer. BA in Elem. Edn., Concordia U., River Forest, Ill., 1990; MA in Edn., U. Mich., 1996; D of Edn., Loyola U., Chgo., IL, 2001. Cert. tchr. Ill., adminstr. Ill., supr. Ill. Tchr. Archdiocese of Chgo., 1990—92; tchr. trainer, cmty. developer U.S. Peace Corps, St. John's, Antigua and Barbuda, 1992—94; tchr. Detroit Pub. Schs., 1994—96; prin. Archdiocese of Chgo., 1996—98; v.p. curriculum, prin. Chgo. Internat. Charter Schs., 1998—2000; exec. dir., founder LEARN Charter Sch., Chgo., 2000—02; guide KIPP Found., San Francisco, 2002—; pres. Sch. Solutions, Inc., Brookfield, Ill., 2002—. Author: The State of Special Education in Our Nation's Charter Schools. Lobbyist for charter legis. LEARN Charter Sch./Leadership for Quality Edn., Chgo., 2000—02; founding bd. mem. KIPP Sankofa Charter Sch., Buffalo, 2002—03. Peace Corps fellow, DeWitt Wallace/Reader's Digest, 1994—96, Cardinal's Educator scholar, Archdiocese of Chgo., 1998—2001. Mem.: ASCD, Hispanic Coun. for Reform and Ednl. Options, Black Alliance for Ednl. Options, Returned Peace Corps Assn., Phi Delta Kappa. Buddhist. Avocations: scuba diving, reading, travel. Home: 79 Honeysuckle Round Lake Beach IL 60513 Office: Sch Solutions Inc 9026 W 31st St Brookfield IL 60513 E-mail: nancydearhammer@hotmail.com.

DEARMOND, PATTI JO, hotel administrator; b. Joplin, Mo., Oct. 28, 1959; d. Lloyd Glen and Margie Dale DeArmond. BS in Edn., Mo. So. State Coll., 1983; EdM, S.W. Mo. State U., 1994, postgrad., 1996—98. Cert. libr. specialist Mo., lifetime tchg. cert. Mo. Tchr. instrumental and vocal music Liberal (Mo.) R-3 Schs., 1983—85, Diamond (Mo.) R-4 Schs., 1985—88; elem. vocal tchr. Crane (Mo.) R-3 Schs., 1988—89; asst. band dir. Carl Junction (Mo.) R-1 Schs., 1989—91, jr. h.s. libr. media specialist, 1996—98; vocal music tchr. N.E. Unified Sch. Dist. 246, Arma, Kans., 1991—96; jr. h.s./h.s. libr. media specialist Neosho (Mo.) R-5 Schs., 1998—2000; vocal music tchr. grades 5-6 Ozark (Mo.) Schs., 2000—01; gen. mgr. Drury Hotels, Houston, 2001—. Coord. edn. travel Carl Junction Jr. H.S., 1996—98; coor. sch. History Day program Carl Junction Schs., 1996—97; del. Mo. State Tchrs. Assn., 1997—98, 1999—2000; clinician Jr. High Mass Choir Festival. Recipient Dir.'s Choice award, Stained Glass Theatre, Joplin, Mo., 1999. Mem.: Pasadena C. of C., Hobby/Pearland C. of C., Greater Houston Conv. and Visitors' Bur. Republican. Avocations: travel, acting in Christian theater. Home: 2323 Fairwind Rd apt 645 Houston TX 77062-6249

DEASON, LUCINDA MARIE, accountant, educator; b. Eloise, MI, Feb. 20, 1963; d. William Berry, Almeda White; children: Brandon Ramsey, Kareemah Garba. PhD, Mich. State U., East Lansing, 2000; MPA, U. Mich.-Dearborn, 1994; BSBA-Finance, Wayne State U., Detroit, 1990. Acct. Wayne State U., Detroit, 1990—92; instr. Mich. State U., East Lansing, Mich., 1996—98; lectr. U. Mich.-Flint, 1996—2000; asst. prof. U. Akron, Akron, Ohio, 2000—02. Lectr. U. Mich.-Flint, 1996—2000; evaluator/Cons. City of Akron, 2001; survey devel. and analysis subcontractor State of Mich., Lansing, 1996—2000. Mem. editl. rev. bd.: The Jour. Multicultural Nursing and Health, 2003—; contbr. articles to profl. jours. and publs. Adv. APHA, Washington, 1996—2002. Specialist U.S. Army, 1981—84. Recipient Honorable Mention, NSF, 1994, Good Conduct Medal, U.S. Army, 1983, Betty Jane Cleckley Minority Rsch. Issues award, 2002; fellow King, Chevas, Parks Grad. fellow, State of Mich., 1992—98, Minority Doctoral Student Leadership Devel. Program Fellow in Aging, AARP Andrus Found. and Nat. Inst. on Aging, 1998, Polit. Instns. and Pub. Choice Program Fellow, Mich. State U., 1995, Summer Rsch. Acceleration Fellow, 1994; grantee Rsch. Grant, U. Akron, 2001, Blue Cross Blue Shield Found., 1994; scholar Scholarship, AICPA, 1985—87. Fellow: Inst. of Life

Span Devel. and Gerontology (Co-chair Rsch. Com. 2001—02); mem.: PTA, APHA (Gerontol. Health Sect. Listserv Chair 1993—2002), AARP, Midwest Polit. Sci. Assn., Am. Polit. Sci. Assn., Nat. Citizen's Coalition for Nursing Home Reform, Gerontol. Soc. Am. Avocation: Hiking, biking, gardening, travel, fishing. Home: 220 Best St Bedford OH 44146 Office: The Univ Akron 225 S High St Rm 266 Polsky Bldg Akron OH 44325-7904 Office Phone: 330-972-5596. Home Fax: 440-439-3279; Office Fax: 330-972-6376. Personal E-mail: deason@uakron.edu. Business E-Mail: deason@uakron.edu.

DEATON, VALERIE L. financial researcher, consultant; b. Des Moines, Sept. 19, 1960; d. C. Ray and Patricia Ruth Deaton; m. Stephen R. West, Dec. 22, 1996. BFA magna cum laude, Drake U., 1984. Asst. fin. officer Iowa State Senate, Des Moines, 1984; field dir. Edgar U.S. Senate Campaign, Media, Pa., 1985; mgr. Vanguard Group, Valley Forge, Pa., 1985-86; sr. rsch. assoc. Opinion Rsch. Corp., Princeton, N.J., 1986-89; sr. rsch. mgr. Prin. Fin. Group, Des Moines, 1989-96; prin. Deaton Rsch., Lambertville, N.J., 1996-99; bus. devel. and fin. rsch. cons. Matthew Greenwald and Assocs., Washington/Lambertville, 1999—. Lectr., cons. in field; mktg. advisor U.S. AID, CNFA, Nakhodka, Russia, 1994-96. Bd. dirs. Project Mgmt. inst., Des Moines, 1992-94; rsch. advisor Des Moines C. of C., 1990-93, VA, Des Moines, 1994; mem. comms. com. Planned Parenthood, Des Moines, 1992-95. Mem. Am. Mkgt. Assn., Assn. Profl. Ins. Women, Soc. Ins. Rsch. (v.p. ann. conf. 1998-99), Rock Creek Woods Homeowner Assn. (sec. bd. dirs. 1999—, trustee), Omicron Delta Kappa, Alpha Lmabda Delta, Phi Eta Sigma. Democrat. Avocation: horticulture. Office: Mathew Greenwald & Assocs 4201 Connecticut Ave NW Washington DC 20008-1158 Home: PO Box 3010 Arnold CA 95223-3010 E-mail: valeriedeaton@yahoo.com.

DEBAKEY, LOIS, science communications educator, editor, writer; b. Lake Charles, La. d. S. M. and Raheeja (Zorba) DeBakey. BA in Math., Tulane U., MA in Lit. and Linguistics, 1959, PhD in Lit. and Linguistics, 1963. Asst. prof. English Tulane U., 1963—64; asst. prof. sci. communication Tulane U. Med. Sch., 1963-65, assoc. prof. sci. communication, 1965-67, prof. sci. comm., 1967-68, lectr., 1968-80, adj. prof., 1981-92; prof. sci. comm. Baylor Coll. Medicine, Houston, 1968—. Mem. biomed. libr. rev. com. Nat. Libr. Medicine, Bethesda, Md., 1973-77, bd. regents, 1981-86, cons., 1986—, co-chmn. permanent paper task force, 1987—, lit. selection tech. rev. com., 1988-93, chmn., 1992-93, outreach planning panel, 1988-89; dir. courses in med. comm. ACS and other orgns.; trustee DeBakey Med. Found., 1995--; exec. coun. Commn. on Colls. So. Assn. Colls. and Schs., 1975-80; mem. nat. adv. coun. U. So. Calif. Ctr. Continuing Med. Edn., 1981, steering com. Plain English Forum, 1984, founding bd. dirs. Friends Nat. Libr. Medicine, 1985—, chmn. med. media award of excellence com. FNLM, 1992—, adv. com. Soc. for Preservation English Lang. Lit., 1986, Nat. Adv. Bd. John Muir Med. Film Festival, 1990-92, The Internat. Health and Med. Film Festival, Acad. of Judges, 1992-93; mem. adv. coun. U. Tex. at Austin Sch. Nursing Found., 1993—; cons. legal writing com. ABA, 1983—, Ency. Brit. Biomed. and Health Database, 1999--; former cons. Nat. Assn. Std. Med. Vocabulary; pioneered instruction in sci. comm. in med. sch. Sr. author: The Scientific Journal: Editorial Policies and Practices, 1976; co-author: Medicine: Preserving the Passion, 1987; Medicine: Preserving the Passion in the 21st Century, 2004; mem editl. bd.: Tulane Studies in English, 1966-68, Cardiovascular Research Center Bull., 1971-83, Health Communications and Informatics, 1975-80, Forum on Medicine, 1977-80, Grants Mag, 1978-81, Internat. Jour. Cardiology, 1981-86, Excerpta Medica's Core Jours. in Cardiology, 1981—, Health Comm. and Biopsychosocial Health, 1981-82, Internat. Angiology, 1985—, Jour. AMA, 1988-2002; mem. usage panel Am. Heritage Dictionary, 1980—; cons. Webster's Med. Desk Dictionary, 1986; editl. advisor Ency. Brit.; contbr. articles on biomed. comm. and sci. writing, literacy, also other subjects to profl. jours., books, encys., and pub. press. Active Found. for Advanced Edn. in Sci., 1977—. Recipient Disting. Svc. award, Am. Med. Writers Assn., 1970, Bausch & Lomb Sci. award, 1st John P. McGovern award, Med. Libr. Assn., 1983, Outstanding Alumna award, Newcomb Coll., 1994. Fellow Am. Coll. Med. Informatics, Royal Soc. for Encouragement of Arts, Mfrs., and Commerce; mem. Internat. Soc. Gen. Semantics, Med. Libr. Assn. (hon.), Coun. Biology Editors (dir. 1973-77, chmn. com. on editl. policy 1971-75), Coun. Basic Edn. (spl. com. writing 1977-79), Assn. Tchrs. Tech. Writing, Dictionary Soc. N.Am., Nat. Assn. Sci. Writers, Soc. for Health and Human Values, Com. of Thousand for Better Health Regulations, Golden Key, Phi Beta Kappa. Office: Baylor Coll Medicine 1 Baylor Plz Houston TX 77030-3411

DEBAKEY, SELMA, science communications educator, writer, editor, lecturer; b. Lake Charles, La. BA, postgrad., Newcomb Coll., Tulane U., New Orleans. Dir. dept. med. communication Ochsner Clinic and Alton Ochsner Med. Found., New Orleans, 1942-68; prof. sci. communication Baylor Coll. Medicine, Houston, 1968—; editor Cardiovascular Research Ctr. Bull., 1970-84. Mem. panel judges Internat. Health and Med. Film Festival, 1992. Author: (with A. Segaloff and K. Meyer) Current Concepts in Breast Cancer, 1967; past editor Ochsner Clinic Reports, Selected Writings from the Ochsner Clinic; contbr. numerous articles to sci. jours., chpts. to books. Named to Tex. Hall of Fame. Mem. AAAS, Soc. Tech. Communication, Assn. Tchrs. Tech. Writing, Am. Med. Writers Assn. (past bd. dirs.; publ., nominating, fellowship, constn., bylaws, awards, and edn. coms.), Council Biol. Editors (past mem. trn. in sci. writing com.), Soc. Health and Human Values, Modern Med. Monograph Awards Com., Nat. Assn. Standard Med. Vocabulary (former cons.). Office: Baylor Coll Medicine 1 Baylor Plz Houston TX 77030-3411

DE BARBIERI, MARY ANN, nonprofit management consultant; b. Winston-Salem, N.C., May 1, 1945; d. Robert Carroll and Annie Louise (Neal) Hutcherson; m. Alfredo Emanuelle De B.; children: Maria Luisa, Riccardo Roberto. BA in Theatre Arts, Mary Washington Coll., 1967; student, Herbert Berghof Studio, 1967—69. With J. Walter Thompson, N.Y.C., 1967-68; asst. to prodr. Norman Twain Prodns., N.Y.C., 1968-69, Contemporary Theatre Co., N.Y.C., 1971-74; co. mgr. Folger Theatre Group, Washington, 1974-77, bus. mgr., 1977-80; mng. dir. Shakespeare Theatre at the Folger, Washington, 1980-90; performing arts cons. Alexandria, Va., 1990-92; dir. The Found. Ctr., Washington, 1992-94; pres. De Barbieri and Assocs., 1994—. Adj. prof. arts mgmt. grad. program Am. U., 1994—; treas. League of Washington Theatres, 1983-86; chair selection com. The Washington Post/Washington Coun. Agys. Award for Excellence in Nonprofit Mgmt., 1997, 98, 99, mem. selection com. 1996-99, The Washington Post Grants in the Arts, 1997—; curriculum design cons., core faculty Choral Mgmt. Inst. of Chorus Am., 2002-04; presenter in field. Bd. dirs. Washington Area Lawyers for Arts, 1984-94; bd. dirs. Cultural Alliance Greater Washington, 1986-96, v.p., 1990-96; bd. dirs. Nat. Soc. Fundraising Execs., 1993-96, v.p. edn., 1995, treas., 1996; bd. dirs. Washington Coun. Agys., 2000—, pres., 2004-; chair Performing Arts Coun., Alexandria, Va., 1981-84; founder, first chair Alexandria Commn. for Arts, 1984-88, theatre commr., 1984-94; contbr. to study of downtown stages for new theatre in Washington, 1985; mem. panel Va. Commn. for the Arts, 1990-96. Recipient Outstanding Svc. to Theatre Cmty. award League of Washington Theatres, 1990. Office: 3812 Fort Worth Ave Alexandria VA 22304-1709 Office Phone: 703-370-3251. E-mail: debarasso@aol.com.

DEBARLING, ANA MARIA, language educator; b. Del Rio, Tex., Apr. 30, 1938; d. Octaviano and Guadalupe Dominguez; m. Peter Wesley Barling, June 4, 1968 (div. Oct. 1988); children: Laura Blanche, Wesley Peter. BA, San Jose State U., 1968, M in Hispanic Lit., 1970; DEd, U. Pacific, 2001. Cert. sch. administrn. Calif. Secondary tchr. Fremount Union H.S. Dist., Sunnyvale, Calif., 1968—94, dir. gifted edn., 1980—83; lang. prof. West Valley Coll., Saratoga, Calif., 1994—. Cons. Edn. Testing Svcs., San Antonio, 1992—; bilingual proficiency testing City of Morgan Hill and Campbell, Calif., 1995—. Editor: (booklet) Gifted & Talented Education, 1991. Mem. Latina Leadership, San Jose, 1988—, Immigration Edn. Task Force, Santa Clara, Calif., 1999—. Mem.: Am. Tchrs. Fgn. Lang., Faculty Assn. C.C. Democrat. Roman Catholic. Home: 373 Redwood Ave Santa Clara CA 95051 Office: West Valley Coll 14000 Fruitvale Ave Saratoga CA 95070 E-mail: and_maria_de_baring@wuv.edu.

DEBARTOLO-YORK, DENISE, sports team executive; m. John C. York II; 4 children. Grad., Notre Dame U. Team pres. Pitts. Penguins; exec. v.p. personnel and corp. mktg./comm. The Edward J. Bartolo Corp., vice chmn., 1994; chmn. The Edward J. DeBartolo Corp., 1994—. Supporter DeBartolo Family Found. Mem. fin. adv. bd. Ursuline Sisters; mem. MADD; recognized for contbn. to St. Charles Elem. Sch., Boardman, Ohio. Named to Italian American Sports Hall of Fame, 2003. Office: care San Francisco 49ers 4949 Centennial Blvd Santa Clara CA 95054-1229*

DEBAUGE, JANICE B. musician; MusB magna cum laude, Southern Mo. U. Classical musician, soprano. Bd. regents Washburn U., 2001—. Home: 1966 Morningside Dr Emporia KS 66801

DEBAUN, LINDA LOUISE, performing arts educator; b. L.A., Nov. 11, 1946; d. James Irving and Katherine Adeliade deBaun; life ptnr. Heidi Annette Wilson, June 15, 1996. AA, Mt. San Antonio Jr. Coll., 1966; BA in Writing, Pitzer Coll., 1968; MLitt of English, Clairemont U., 1972; M of Theatre, Calif. State U., 1998. Tchr. Azusa (Calif.) H.S., 1972—73, Vol. State Coll., Gallatin, Tenn., 1973—75; tchr., dir. drama Yucaipa (Calif.) H.S., 1980—. Recipient Tchr. of Yr., San Bernadino County, Calif., 2000. Mem.: Internat. Thespian Soc. (state bd. dirs.). Avocations: writing, music. Home: 11666 Pendelton Rd Yucaipa CA 92399 Office: Yucaipa High Sch 33000 Ycuaipa Blvd Yucaipa CA 92399

DEBERRY, LOIS MARIE, state legislator; b. May 5, 1945; d. Samuel and Mary (Page) DeBerry. BA in Elem. Edn., Lemoyne-Owen Coll., 1971. Mem. Tenn. Ho. of Reps.; spkr. pro. tempore; chmn. ad hoc com. to study sch. safety issues; mem. select com. on children & youth. Mem. Tenn. Ho. of Reps. Health and Human Resources Com., Govt. Ops. Com., Calendar and Rules Com., Corrections Oversight Com., Tenncare Oversight Com., Ethics Com., Rules Com., State Commn. on Aging; spkr. in field. Bd. dirs. State Legis. Leaders Found.; mem. Nat. Conf. of State Legis.; pres. emeritus Nat. Black Caucus of State Legis.; founder, chairperson annual legis. retreat Tenn. Black Caucus of State Legislators. Mem. Links, Delta Sigma Theta. Office: Tenn Ho of Reps Legis Plz Ste 15 Nashville TN 37243-0191

DEBIAGI, ANNA LILLIAN, retired educator; b. N.Y.C., July 21, 1930; d. Giovanni-Battista and Michelina (Caramanna) Pollara; m. Giovanni De-Biagi, Nov. 19, 1955; children: Gianni Deo, Maria-Michelina Cologera. BA, CUNY, 1952; MA, Columbia U., 1957; postgrad., L.I. U., 1977. Tchr. Massapequa (N.Y.) Pub. Schs., 1953-87. Exhibited in Massapequa Pub. Libr.; group shows in Huntington, Babylon. Tchr. Ch. St. John the Bapt., Bronx, 1952-54, supt. 1954-56; instr. CPR, Am. Heart Assn., 1976-78; tchr. rep. PTA; arts & culture bd. City of Pembroke Pines, Fla., 1999-2001; active Friends Libr., 1999—; artist sel. panel Southwest Libr. Acad. Village, Pembroke Pines, 1999; co-founder Culture Vultures, 2001—. Mem. AAUW (chmn. 1964-65, pres. 1977-79, chmn. 1981-96, Commendation award 1982, Eleanor Roosevelt Found. name grant 1990; v.p. membership 1998-2000), Am. Italian Hist. Soc., Hist. Soc. Massapequas, Massapequa Fedn. Ret. Tchrs., Art League of L.I., Pequa Art Assn., Wantagh Arts Coun. Avocations: writing poetry, painting, music, needlework. Home: 662 SW 159th Dr Pembroke Pines FL 33027-1145

DE BLASIO, MARIA P. physician; b. Naples, Italy, May 4, 1940; came to U.S., 1967; d. Agnello and Sophia (Recchia) de B. BA, St. Jeanne D'Arc Coll., Naples, 1958; MD, U. Naples, 1966; M in Piano and Composition, San Pietro A Maiella, Conservatory of Music, 1963. Resident Mt. Vernon (N.Y.) Hosp., 1967-72, Union Hosp., Bronx, N.Y., 1972, Misericordia Hosp., Bronx, 1968; fellow U. Pa., Phila., 1972; attending physician Our Lady of Mercy, Bronx, N.Y., 1982—, St. Barnabas Hosp., Bronx, N.Y., 1981—. Med. dir. Jean Jugan Residence, Bronx. Named Best Physician of Yr., New Yorker mag., 1996, N.Y. mag., 2002. Mem. AMA, Bronx County Med. Soc., N.Y. State Med. Soc. Avocations: concerts, opera, reading. Home: 2226 Valentine Ave Bronx NY 10457-1106 Office: 3065 Grand Concourse Bronx NY 10468

DEBOEF, BETTY, state representative; b. Feb. 1951; Mem. Iowa Ho. Reps., DesMoines, 2001—, vice chair agr. com., mem. environ. protection com., mem. health and human rights com., mem. appropriations com., mem. human resources com. Republican. Office: State Capitol East 12th and Grand Des Moines IA 50319 also: 203 Sleeper St New Sharon IA 50207

DE BONO, LUELLA ELIZABETH, music educator; b. Argyle, Iowa, May 15, 1920; d. Albert Fred and Bessie Mae (Langwith) Haffner; m. Charles De Bono, July 26, 1947; 1 child, Douglas. MMus, Sherwood Conservatory Music, Chgo., 1945; M in Counseling and Guidance, U. St. Thomas, St. Paul, 1966; postgrad., U. Minn. Lic. music instr. of keyboard, voice and instrumental. Dir. music Am. Girl's Coll., Assiut, Egypt, 1945-48; music tchr. Argyle Pub. Sch., 1949-54; instr. music MacPhail Coll. Music, 1956-66; counselor various pub. schs., Minn., 1966-82; pvt. music instr. Eden Prairie, Minn., 1982—. Profl. accompanist and pianist; adjudicator state music contests, Mpls., 1958—. Nat. honor soc. advisor St. Paul Pk. H.S., 1966-68; Am. field svc. adviser St. Paul Pk. H.S.; counselor Am. Youth Hostel Camp, Europe, 1946. Presbyterian. Avocations: animals, showing horses, volunteering. Home and Office: 17325 Pioneer Trail Eden Prairie MN 55347-3403

DE BOTH, TANYA, statistician; b. Green Bay, Wis., Nov. 27, 1972; d. Richard L. and Louise A. De Both. BA in Psychology, U. Wis., 1996; student, Frostburg (Md.) State U., 1996—97; MSc in Exptl. Psychology, U. Wis., 2000. Outcomes specialist Family Svcs., Green Bay, Wis., 2000—01; data rsch. analyst Agnesian Health Care, Fond du Lac, Wis., 2001—. Mem. Wis. Forum Healthcare Strategy, 2001—. Contbr. articles to profl. jours. Mem.: AAUW, NOW, APA, ACLU, LWV, NAFE, Phi Kappa Phi. Avocations: walking, volleyball, golf, camping, bicycling.

DE BRIGARD, EMILIE, anthropologist, consultant; b. N.Y.C., Dec. 11, 1943; d. A. Lincoln and Ruth Emilie (Jaeger) Rahman; m. Raul de Brigard, June 11, 1966; 1 child, George. BA, Harvard Coll., 1963; MA, U. Calif., 1972. Guest curator dept. of film Mus. of Modern Art, N.Y.C., 1972-73; asst. to dir. human studies film archives Smithsonian Instn., Washington, 1975-77; prin. programmer Margaret Mead Film Festival Am. Mus. Natural History, N.Y.C., 1977-78; faculty Harvard Summer Sch., Cambridge, Mass., 1980-86; pres. Internat. Film Seminars, Inc., N.Y.C., 1981-83; vis. lectr. dept. anthropology Yale U., New Haven, Conn., 1989-91; pres. Soc. for Visual Anthropology, Washington, 1995-97, FilmResearch, Higganum, Conn., 1970—. Cons. Choreometrics Project, N.Y.C., 1970-73; mem. Comité Internat. des Films de l'Homme, Paris, 1977—. Author: (books) The History of Ethnographic Film, 1971, Anthropological Cinema, 1973, Cine Antropológico, 1978; producer (film) Margaret Mead: A Portrait by a Friend, 1978. Trustee Wadsworth Atheneum, Hartford, Conn., 2000—; corporator Conn. Inst. for the Blind-Oak Hill, Hartford, Conn., 1996—; bd. dir. Friends of the Ixchel Mus., Guatemala, 2003—. Recipient scholarship Harvard U., Cambridge, Mass., 1963-64, fellowship, Yale U., New Haven, Conn., 1987-88; grantee: Wenner-Gren Found., N.Y.C., 1970-72, Tinker Found., N.Y.C., 1976. Fellow Am. Anthrop. Assn., Royal Anthrop. Inst.; mem. Soc. Woman Geographers, Harvard Alumni Assn. (dir. 2002-2005, Hiram S. Hunn award 2002), Town and County Club, Harvard Club of So. Conn. (v.p. 1995—), Saturday Morning Club (pres. 2003—). Avocation: costume and textiles. Home: 285 Riverside Dr Apt 7E New York NY 10025-5227 Office: FilmResearch 0 Christian Hill Rd Higganum CT 06441-4030 E-mail: debrigard@att.net.

DEBROSKY, CHRISTINE ANNE, painter, educator; b. Kingston, NY, Dec. 10, 1951; d. John Michael and Eileen Mary Schupp; m. Wayne William Debrosky, Feb. 13, 1971; 1 child, Eric Conan. AA, Ulster Co C.C., N.Y., 1971. Staff instr. Woodstock Sch. of Art, Woodstock, NY, 1998—. Exhibitions include Southern Vermont Arts Ctr., The Hudson Valley, A New light, Pastels at Butler Ins. of Am. Art, Europastel, Italy, and St. Petersburg, Russia, Art du Pastel en France, Am. Women Artists, Santa Fe, NM, and Sorrento, Italy, Pastel Soc. of the West Coast, North and South, Fountainside Fine Art, N.C., Pastel soc. of Am. juried international exhibitions. Bd. mem. Environ. Rev. Bd., Esopus, NY, 1988—90. Recipient Toh-Atin Poster, Am. Women Artists, 1998, Prix du Pastel, Art du Pastel en France, 2002, 2003. Master: Pastel soc. of the West Coast (licentiate; signature mem., Disting. Pastellist 2002, Exhbn. Awards of Distinction 1998, 2000, 2001, 2002, 2003); mem.: Pastel Soc. of Am. (licentiate; signature mem., Barbara & Gary Scott 1992). Achievements include Collection, Pfizer Chemical, world corporate headquarters; Corporate collection, Standard & Poor's; Corporate collection, McGraw- Hill, Inc; Corporate collection, Key Bank, Inc. Avocations: writing, travel, photography, crafts, hiking. Home: Mt View Rd Tillson NY 12486 Office: S Scape Studio Mt View Rd Tillson NY 12486

DE BRUN, SHAUNA DOYLE, industrialist, investment banker; b. Boston, June 3, 1956; d. John Justin and Marie Therese (Carey) Doyle; m. Seamus Christopher de Brun, July 24, 1982; children: Brendan Joseph, Kieran Christopher. Student, U. Salzburg, 1974-75; BA, Mt. Holyoke Coll., 1978; postgrad., Harvard U., 1981-82; M in Internat. Fin., Columbia U., 1984. Cert. fin. analyst, 1987. Assoc. Salomon Bros., N.Y.C., 1978; rsch. assoc. Kennedy Sch. Govt., Cambridge, Mass., 1979-80; faculty assoc. Harvard Bus. Sch., 1980-81; fgn. expert Beijing Normal U., Peoples Republic China, 1981-82; assoc. dir. N.Y. Capital Resources, N.Y.C., 1984-85; ptnr. Eppler & Co., Denver, 1985-87, pres. Teaneck, N.J., 1987-88; v.p. fin. Patten Corp., Stamford, Vt., 1988-91; pres. Serfimex USA, Inc., 1991-92; pres., CEO Pliana Holdings, Mexico City, 1992—. Columbia U. Internat. fellow, 1982; Sarah Williston scholar Mt. Holyoke Coll., 1975. Mem. AACCLA (v.p., treas.), Am. C. of C./Mex. (past pres., dir.), Navy League U.S., Phi Beta Kappa, Harvard Club. Avocations: piano, horseback riding. Office: Pliana Holdings SA de CV 275 Palmas 5th Fl 11000 Mexico City Mexico

DEBS, BARBARA KNOWLES, former college president, consultant; b. Eastham, Mass., Dec. 24, 1931; d. Stanley F. and Arline (Eugley) Knowles; m. Richard A. Debs, July 19, 1958; children: Elizabeth, Nicholas. BA, Vassar Coll., 1953; PhD, Harvard U., 1967; LLD, N.Y. Law Sch., 1979; LHD, Manhattanville Coll., 1985. Freelance translator editor Ency. of World Art divsn. McGraw-Hill Pub., N.Y.C., 1959-62; from asst. prof. to prof. Manhattanville Coll., Purchase, N.Y., 1968-86, pres., 1975-85; trustee, chmn. collections com. N.Y. Hist. Soc., 1985-87, pres., CEO, 1988-92; cons. non-profit orgns. pvt. practice, 1992—. Contbr. articles on Renaissance and contemporary art to profl. publs. Mem. N.Y. Coun. Humanities, 1978-85; mem. Westchester County Bd. Ethics, 1979-84; trustee N.Y. Law Sch., 1979-89; trustee Geraldine R. Dodge Found., 1985—; bd. dirs. Internat. Found. for Art Rsch., 1985-92; trustee Com. Econ. Devel., 1985-94, Bklyn. Mus. Art, 1996—; mem. Coun. Fgn. Rels., 1983—; mem. exec. bd. Bard Ctr. for Decorative Arts, 1995—; bd. govs. Fgn. Policy Assn., 1996-2002; hon. trustee Manhattanville Coll., 1996—, Midori Found., 1998—. AAUW Nat. fellow and Ann Radcliffe fellow, 1958-59; Am. Council Learned Socs. grantee, 1973; Fulbright fellow, Pisa, Italy, 1953, U. Rome, 1954. Mem. Am. Coun. on Edn. (chmn. commn. acad. affairs 1977-79), Young Audiences (nat. dir. 1977-80), Renaissance Soc. Am., Coll. Art Assn., Phi Beta Kappa. Clubs: Cosmpolitan, Century Assn.

DEBUONO, BARBARA ANN, physician, state official; b. N.Y.C., Apr. 13, 1955; d. Richard Francis and Catherine (Brutto) DeB.; m. David Lavington Farren, June 1, 1980; children: Adam, Douglas. BS, U. Rochester, 1976, MD, 1980; MPH, Harvard U., 1984. Diplomate Am. Bd. Internal Medicine, Nat. Bd. Med. Examiners. Intern in internal medicine New Eng. Deaconess Hosp., Boston, 1980-81, jr. med. resident, 1981-82, sr. med. resident, 1982-83; clin. fellow Brown U., Providence, 1984-86, clin. instr. dept. medicine, 1987-90, clin. asst. prof. medicine, 1990; med. epidemiologist R.I. Dept. Health, Providence, 1986, state epidemiologist, med. dir. Office Disease Control, 1986-91; dir. dept. health State of R.I., 1991—95; commr. NY State Dept. Health, Albany, 1995—98; CEO N.Y. Presbyn. Healthcare Network, 1998—2000; exec. v.p. N.Y. Presbyn. Healthcare System, 1998—2000; sr. med. dir. pub. health Pfizer Inc., 2001—; clin. prof. medicine Columbia U. Coll. Physicians and Surgeons. Lectr. in field; adv. com. to dir. Ctrs. for Disease Control; bd. mem. Ctr. Health Policy Devel.; nat. adv. com. Healthy Steps. Contbr. articles to profl. jours. Robert Wood Johnson Found. Ednl. scholar U. Rochester Sch. Med., 1976-80; recipient James L. Tulis Disting. Study Lectureship award New Eng. Deaconess Hosp., 1992; named Women of Yr. by Bus. and Profl. Women's Club Providence, 1989, Person of Yr. by The Women's Youth League R.I., 1990, Woman of Yr. by R.I. Fedn. Bus. and Profl. Women's Clubs, 1991. Fellow Am. Coll. Internat. Physicians, Am. Coll. Physicians; mem. AMA, APHA, Am. Soc. Microbiology, Infectious Disease Soc. Am., Providence Med. Assn., R.I. Med. Soc., R.I. Med. Women's Assn. (R.I. Women Physician of Yr. 1988), R.I. Environ. Health Assn., Hosp. Assn. R.I., Women Execs. in Govt. Avocations: swimming, tennis, gardening. Office: NY State Dept of Health Corning Tower Empire State Plz Albany NY 12237-0001*

DEBUS, ELEANOR VIOLA, retired business management company executive; b. Buffalo, May 19, 1920; d. Arthur Adam and Viola Charlotte (Pohl) D. Student, Chown Bus. Sch., 1939. Sec. Buffalo Wire Works, 1939-45; home talent prodr. Empire Producing Co., Kansas City, Mo.; sec. Owens Corning Fiberglass Buffalo; pub. rels. and publicity Niagara Falls Theatre, Ont., Can.; pub. rels. dir. Woman's Internat. Bowling Congress, Columbus, Ohio, 1957-59; publicist, sec. Ice Capades, Hollywood, Calif., 1961-63; sec. to contr. Rexall Drug Co., L.A., 1963-67; bus. mgmt. acct. Samuel Berke & Co., Beverly Hills, Calif., 1967-75, Gadbois Mgmt. Co., Beverly Hills, 1975-76; sec., treas. Sasha Corp., L.A., 1976-92; former bus. mgr. Dean Martin, Eleanor Powell, Debbie Reynolds, Shirley MacLaine. Contbr. articles to various mags. Mem.: Am. Film Inst. Republican.

DEBUSK, F. AMANDA, export administration executive; BA, U. Richmond; JD, Harvard U. Ptnr. internat. trade dept. O'Melveny & Myers, LLP; asst. sec. export enforcement Dept. of Commerce, Washington. Office: Dept of Commerce Bur Export Adminstrn 14th And Constitution NW Washington DC 20230-0001

DE CACHO, GRACIELA ELETA, marketing executive; b. Panama; BA in econ. magna cum laude, Wellesley Coll.; MBA, Boston Coll. Dir. mktg. Proctor & Gamble, PR, 1987—2001, v.p. multicultural devel. orgn., 2001—. Mem.: SER Jobs for Progress, San Juan Rotary Club, Fondos Unidos. Achievements include launched several successful brands in PR including Pantene, Vidal Sassoon, Swifter; developed innovative and holistic mktg. strategies for Hispanic and Ethnic markets in N. Am; highest ranking Latina exec. in Proctor & Gamble. Office: P&G Comml Co City View Plz Piso 6 Carretera 165 Km 1.2 Guaynabo PR 00968 Office Phone: 787-620-7070. Office Fax: 787-620-7399.*

DECARO, MONICA WARD, finance administrator; b. Norristown, Pa., May 9, 1958; d. Thomas F. and Elizabeth Mary (Marino) Ward; m. Howard J. Lothrop, June 22, 1980 (div. Nov. 1991); m. James J. DeCaro, May 18, 2002. BS, St. Joseph's U., 1980; MBA, Memphis State U., 1990. Cert. mgmt. acct. Trainee York (Pa.) Bank and Trust Co., 1980-81; acct. Volvo White Truck Corp., Greensboro, N.C., 1981-84; fin. analyst Dairymen Inc., Greensboro, N.C., 1984-86; acctg. mgr. Kraft Dairy Group, Memphis, 1986-88; contr. Green Duck Corp., Hernando, Miss., 1988-89; divisional contr. Am. Signature, Olive Branch, Miss., 1992-93; plant contr. Smurfit Recycling, Memphis, 1992-94; fin. dir. Borough of Norristown, Pa., 1995—. Instr. Data Processing Trainers, Phila., 1995—; dir. Dairymen Credit Union, Greensboro, 1986; mem. adv. bd. Montgomery County Office Children and Youth, 1996-97; chmn. spl. events com., bd. dirs. Superkids of Montgomery County. Chpt. treas. Amigos de las Americas, Memphis, 1994-95; vol. Bridge of Hope, 2002—; host family AYUSA, 1998-2000; vol. Hays Ave. United Meth. Ch. Soup Kitchen, 2001—. Mem. Inst. Cert. Mgmt. Accts. (cert., North Pa. chpt.), Govt. Fin. Officers Assn., Assn. Cert. Fraud Examiners, Pa. State Tax Collectors Assn. Home: 915 Cooke Ln Norristown PA 19401-4136

DECATUR, RAYLENE, former museum director; BA, U. Va.; MA, George Washington U. Various positions Md. Sci. Ctr., Balt., Acad. Natural Scis., Phila., Renwick Gallery; pres., CEO Denver Mus. Nature and Sci. (formerly Denver Mus. Natural History), 1995—2004. Office: Denver Mus of Nature & Sci 2001 Colorado Blvd Denver CO 80205-5732*

DECHANE, MARLENE M. state legislator; b. Methuen, Mass. BS, Plymouth State Coll., 1978. Mem. dist. 6 N.H. Ho. of Reps., mem. public works and hwys. com.; nursing asst. Home: 136 Berry River Rd PO Box 123 Barrington NH 03825-0123

DECHAUD, CHRISTINA RITA, marketing specialist, consultant; b. Aurora, Ill., Apr. 24, 1966; d. Hermann and Rita Marie Anne (Bauernfeind) Golter; m. Stephen Joseph deChaud, Sept. 18, 1999. BA in Internat. Studies, Am. U., 1988; MBA, Northwestern U., 1992. Intern in cultural svcs. Embassy of France, Washington, 1985; intern Office of Fgn. Policy U.S. Senator Edward Kennedy, Washington, spring 1986; intern security and fgn. policy German Fed. Govt., Bonn, fall 1986; intern Blue Danube Radio Austrian Fed. Broadcast Sys., Vienna, 1987; account exec. Lufthansa German Airlines, Chgo., 1988-93; dir. world capitals programs Am. U., Washington, 1993-94; market devel. mgr. Ragold Inc., Chgo., 1994-96; sr. mktg. analyst/account mgr. Lee Hill Inc., Chgo., 1996-97; sr. v.p., mgr. worldwide mktg. and resource svcs. Draft, Chgo., 1997—. Host com. vol. World Cup Soccer '96, Chgo., 1993, Nat. Dem. Conv., Chgo., 1996. Recipient Cert. of Appreciation, Golden Kiwanis, 1996. Mem. NAFE, Am. Mktg. Assn., Am. Mgmt. Assn., Chgo. Assn. Direct Mktg., Kellogg Exec. Mgrs. Program Alumni Club, Phi Kappa Phi. Avocations: cooking, playing piano, language tutoring in german, french, and spanish. Home: 47 Briargate Cir Aurora IL 60506-9178 Office: Draft 633 N St Clair St Chicago IL 60611-3234 E-mail: cdechaud@draftnet.com.

DE CHESNAY, MARY, nursing educator; BSN, Coll. St. Teresa, 1969; MS in Psychiat. Nursing, Rutgers U., 1973; postgrad., Ga. State U., 1979; DSN in Cmty. Mental Health Nursing, U. Ala., 1982. Instr. psychiat./mental health nursing, U. Ariz., Tucson, 1973-75; pvt. practice, 1973—; clin. specialist Northeast Kingdom Mental Health Co., Newport, Vt., 1975-76; head dept. nursing Clayton Jr. Coll., 1976-79; asst. prof. Emory U., Atlanta, 1981-90; assoc. prof. U. Ala., Birmingham, 1983-89, prof., 1989; prof., head dept. rsch. Clemson (S.C.) U. Coll. Nursing, 1989-94, with dept. continuing edn., 1991, acting head, 1992; sr. scientist Birmingham Sch. Medicine Ctr. Injury Prevention and Control, 1990; prof., dean Duquesne U. Sch. Nursing, Pitts., 1994—2002; endowed chair for vulnerable populations Seattle U., 2002—. Lectr., cons. in field. Mem. editl. bd. various jours.; contbr. articles to profl. jours., chpts. to books. Ill. State scholar, 1965; Nurse fellow NIMH, 1972-83; named one of Outstanding Young Women of Am., 1978, 79; grantee Clayton Jr. Coll., 1977, 78, Ga. Endowment Humanities, 1981, U. Ala., 1982, 83-84, 85-86, NIH, 1988, Clemson U., 1995. Fellow Am. Acad. Nursing, Soc. Applied Anthropology; mem. ANA (cert. specialist adult psychiat./mental health nursing), Am. Acad. Nursing, Caribbean Studies Assn., Southeast Coun. Latin Am. Studies, So. Nursing Rsch. Soc. (founder, v.p. 1988-90), Sigma Theta Tau. Office: Seattle U Sch Nursing 900 Broadway Seattle WA 98122-4340 E-mail: dechesna@seattleu.edu.

DECKER, CAROL ARNE, magazine publishing consultant; b. Rochelle, Ill., Apr. 3, 1946; d. Irvin Norman Arne and Edna (Olsen) Stein; m. Charles Levitt Decker, Feb. 17, 1979; children: Katharine Elizabeth. BS, So. Ill. U., 1969. Advt. sales rep. Travel Agent mag., N.Y.C., 1971-74, Business Week mag., N.Y.C., 1974-80, Reader's Digest Publs., N.Y.C., 1980-82; assoc. pub. The Atlantic Monthly, N.Y.C., 1982-84; pub. Personal Investor, N.Y.C., 1984-86, Lear's Mag., 1992-93; pub. cons. C.A. Decker & Assocs., N.Y.C., 1986-94; founder, CEO Western Interiors and Design Mag., LLC, Jackson, Wyo., 1999—. Office: POBox 14610 Jackson WY 83002

DECKER, JOSEPHINE I. health clinic official; b. Barling, Ark., May 24, 1933; d. Ralph and Ada A. (Claborn) Snider; m. William Arlen Decker, Feb. 4, 1952; 1 child, Peter A. BS in Health Mgmt., Kennedy Western U., 1986, MS in Bus. Adminstrn., 1987. With Southwestern Bell Tel. Co., Ft. Smith, Ark., 1951-52, Sparks Med. Found. (formerly Holt Krock Clinic), Ft. Smith, 1952—, bus. adminstr., 1970—; reg. dir. Sparks Med. Found., Ft. Smith, 1999—. Bd. dirs. Sparks Credit Union, Bost Found., Crisis Ctr. for Women, Sparks Women's Ctr., Leadership Ft. Smith; mem. adv. coun. Northside H.S., Ft. Smith, Ft. Smith Girls Shelter, Ft. Smith Credit Bur. Mem. Credit Women Internat., Soc. Cert. Consumer Credit Execs. Office: Sparks Medical Plaza PO Box 17030 Fort Smith AR 72917-7030 Office Phone: 479-709-1900. E-mail: jdecker@sparks.org., decker02@quixnet.net.

DECKER, SUSAN, Internet company executive; BS, Tufts U.; MBA, Harvard U. Cert. Charterd Fin. Analyst. With Donaldson, Lufking & Jenrette (DLJ), 1986—2000, publ. and advtsg. rsch. anlayst, global head rsch.; CFO, sr. v.p. fin. and adminstrn. Yahoo!, Sunnyvale, Calif., 2000—. Apptd. to acctg. stds. adv. coun. Fin. Acctg. Fedn. Office: Yahoo! 701 1st Av Sunnyvale CA 04089

DECKERT, MYRNA JEAN, small business owner, consultant; b. McPherson, Kans., Nov. 4, 1936; d. Francis J. and Grace (Killion) George; m. Ray A. Deckert, Sept. 29, 1957; children: Rachelle, Kimberly, Charles, Michael. AA, Coll. of Sequoias, 1956; BA, U. Beverly Hills, 1983, MBA, 1984. Youth dir. Asbury Meth. Ch., El Paso, Tex., 1960-63; teen program dir. YWCA, El Paso, 1963-69, assoc. exec. dir., 1969-70, CEO, 1970—2002; chair strategic planning com. Tex. Dept. Pub. and Regulatory Svcs., 1994-97; owner, prin. MJD and Assocs., 2002—. Cons. to nonprofits; exec. cons. Bus. Leadership Coun., 2002—. Pres. Exec. Forum, 1991—92; commr. Housing Authority City of El Paso, 1989—92; former chair bd. trustees Columbia Med. Ctr. East, 1992—97; deans adv. com. Tex. Tech. Med. Ctr.; past trustee Dues/High Tower Found.; chair Leadership EP, 1994—95; past mem. Tex. Challenge Adv. Com., 1998; chair Change Initiative Com., 1998—2000; adv. dir. M.D. Anderson Hosp., Houston; co-chair El Paso Ind. Sch. Dist. Bd. Com., 2000; mem. City of El Paso Bond Com., 1999—2000; mem. nat. coordinating bd. YWCA of the USA, 2002—, chair global campaign; bd. dirs. Chase Bank of Tex., El Paso, Blue Cross/Blue Shield Tex., 1999—. Recipient Hannah Soloman Cmty. Svc. award Nat. Coun. Jewish Women, Sertoma Club award Svc. to Mankind, 1974, Cmty. Svc. award League United L.Am. Citizens, 1980, Humanitarian award, 1994, Vol. Svc. award Vol. Bur., 1984, Merit award Adalante Mujer, 1986, Social Svc. award KVIA/Sunturians, 1986, Excellence award Nat. Assn. YWCA Execs., 1990, Racial Justice award YWCA of the U.S.A., 1991, Disting. Svc. award Rotary of El Paso, 1997, Citizen of Yr. award Greater El Paso Assn. Realtors, 1998; named Woman of Yr., AAUW, 1975, Dir. of Yr., United Way El Paso County, 1985, Philanthropy Exec. of Yr., 2003, First Lady of El Paso, Beta Sigma Phi, 1991, One of 10 Most Influential Women, El Paso Times, 1995, Citizen of Yr., Mil. Order of World Wars, 1996; inducted into El Paso Women's Hall of Fame, 1990, El Paso Hist. Soc. Hall of Honor, 1995, Hall of Fame/Coll. of Sequoias, 1995, Hall of Honor, 1996, Jr. Achievement Bus. Hall of Honor, 1998, Bravo award LWV, 1999, Myrna J. Deckert Living Legacy award, 2003; named Citizen of Yr., El Paso Bd. Realtors, 1999; Conquistador award, City of El Paso, 2002; named El Pasoan of Yr., 2003, Philanthropy Exec. of Yr., 2003. Methodist. Home: 4276 Canterbury Dr El Paso TX 79902-1352 Office Phone: 915-203-5762. Personal E-mail: mjdeckert@aol.com. Business E-Mail: mdeckert@ywcaelpaso.org.

DECLERCQ, MARISSA HELENA, actress; b. San Francisco, Sept. 21, 1979; d. John and Kathleen DeClercq. BA in Theatre Arts cum laude, San Jose State U., 2003. Profl. actress Willows Theatre Co., Concord, Calif., 1995—98, Woodminster Theatre, Oakland, Calif., 1996—96, Sacramento Theatre Co., Sacramento, 1998—98, Utah Musical Theatre, Ogden, 2000—01. Profl. singer, Bay Area, Calif., 1996—. Recipient Youth Leader award, City of Concord, 1996. Mem.: Alpha Gamma Sigma, Phi Kappa Phi.

DECONCINI, BARBARA, association executive, religious studies educator; b. Phila., Feb. 15, 1944; d. Edwin Francis and Anne Marie (Farrell) DeC.; m. Walter James Lowe, June 30, 1979. AB in English, Rosemont Coll., 1968; MA in English, Bryn Mawr Coll., 1973; PhD in Humanities, Emory U., 1980. Assoc. dean Rosemont (Pa.) Coll., 1971-74; from lectr. to prof. Atlanta Coll. of Art, 1975-91, interim pres., 1985, acad. dean, 1986-91; prof. religion and culture Emory U., Atlanta, 1991—; exec. dir., treas. Am. Acad. Religion, Atlanta, 1991—. Coord. long-range instnl. and ednl. planning Soc. of the Holy Child, 1973-75; treas. Southeastern Commn. for Study of Religion, 1989-91; chair various acad. sessions in field. Author: Narrative Remembering, 1990; contbr. numerous articles to profl. publs. Bd. dirs. Art Papers, Atlanta, 1988-91, Rosemont Coll., 1992—, chmn. acad. com.; trustee Scholars Press, Atlanta, 1991—, chmn. bd. trustees, 1994-97; bd. dirs. Ga. Artists Internat. Exhibit Fund, 1988-92. Alliance of Ind. Colls. of Art grantee. Mem. Am. Coun. Learned Socs. (chmn. exec. com. coun. adminstrv. officers 1995-97, bd. dirs. 1996-98), Am. Acad. Religion (bd. dirs. 1989—, cons. for reorgn. arts, lit. and religion sect. 1990, mem. program com. 1986-89, pres. S.E. sect. 1984-85, program chair 1983-84, 84-85, exec. com. 1980-83), So. Assn. Colls. and Schs. (accreditation evaluator), Mid. States Assn. Colls. and Schs. (accreditation evaluator), Phi Beta Kappa, Omicron Delta Kappa. Office: Am Acad Religion 825 Houston Mill Rd NE Ste 300 Atlanta GA 30329-4246

DECOPPET, LAURA, writer, editor; b. N.Y.C., June 21, 1946; d. André and Eileen (Johnston) de C; m. Kenneth Archer LaBarre; 1 child, Susanna Jane. BA, Barnard Coll., N.Y.C., 1968. Asst. Avant Guard Art Gallery, N.Y.C., 1972-76; writer, editor Interview Mag., 2003—. Author, editor: The Art Dealers, 1984. Mem. Ch. Of Eng. Avocations: backgammon, biking, art collecting, mahjonga, bridge. Home: 50 E 10th St New York NY 10003-6221 Office: Interview Mag 500 Broadway New York NY 10012-4416

DECOSTA WILLIS, MIRIAM, education educator, writer; b. Florence, Ala., Nov. 1, 1934; d. Frank Augustus and Beautine Hubert DeCosta; m. Russell Bertram Sugarmon, June 25, 1955 (div. Apr. 4, 1968); m. Archie Walter Willis, Oct. 20, 1972 (dec. July 14, 1988); children: Tarik Brant Sugarmon, Elena Sugarmon Williams, Erika Marie Sugarmon, Monique Ariel Sugarmon. BA, Wellesley Coll., 1952—56; MA, Johns Hopkins U., 1959—60, PhD, 1965—67. Instr. of french LeMoyne Coll., Memphis, 1957—58; prof. of spanish Howard U., Washington, 1970—76; prof. of romance languages LeMoyne-Owen Coll., Memphis, 1979—89; prof. of africana studies U. of Md., Balt. County, 1991—99; commonwealth prof. of spanish George Mason U., Fairfax; assoc. prof. of spanish Memphis State U.; instr. of english and french Owen Jr. Coll., Memphis. Chair, dept. of romance languages Howard U., Washington, 1974—76; dir. of the dubois scholars program LeMoyne-Owen Coll., Memphis; chair Tenn. Humanities Coun., Nashville, 1986—87; dir. of grad. studies, dept. of african am. studies U. of Md., Balt. County, 1991—95. Editor: (anthology) Homespun Images: An Anthology of Black Memphis Artists and Writers, Daughters of the Diaspora: Afra-Hispanic Writers, Erotique Noire / Black Erotica, (diary) The Memphis Diary of Ida B. Wells, (collection of essays) Blacks in Hispanic Literature, Singular Like a Bird: The Art of Nancy Morejón. Mem. bd. Fedn. of State Humanities Councils, Washington, 1985—86; mem bd. Memphis Br. of NAACP, 1956—70; mem. bd. Shelby County Hist. Commn., Memphis, 1979—85, Shelby County Dem. Club, Memphis, 1956—66, MSU Ctr. for Rsch. on Women, Memphis, 1983—89. Recipient Torchbearer of Afro-Hispanic Studies, Coll. Lang. Assn., 1998, Leadership Award in Afro-Hispanic Studies, Howard U., 1998, Prominent Black Women, Memphis State U., 1984. Mem.: Afro-Latin/Am. Rsch. Assn., Coll. Lang. Assn. (fgn. lang. rep. 1974—76), Phi Beta Kappa. D-Liberal. Achievements include research in Blacks in Afro-Hispanic Literature. Home: 700 7th St S W #205 Washington DC 20024

DECOTIS, RUTH JANICE, career planning administrator, educator; b. Lebanon, N.H., July 3, 1949; d. David Gilman Fowler and Olive Leonie Greenwood; m. Terry L. DeCotis, Sept. 2, 1967; children: Gregory, Curtis, Erin. AS magna cum laude in Sec. Sci., Plymouth State Coll., 1989, BS magna cum laude in Adminstrn. Mgmt. & Comm., 1995, MEd magna cum laude in Counselor Edn. & Human Rels., 1998. Sec. Equity Pub., Orford, NH, 1969—79; sec. social sci. dept. Plymouth State Coll., Plymouth, NH, 1980—86, from program asst. to academic & career adv. ctr., 1986—. Travel agt. Plymouth Travel, Plymouth, 1991—. Co-author: Great Jobs for Math Majors, 1998. Mem.: Assn. for Psychol. Type, Nat. Academic Adv. Assn., Nat. Soc. Experiential Edn., Am. Counseling Assn. Avocations: travel, antiques, restoration of old homes. Office: Plymouth State Coll Academic & Career Adv Ctr 17 High St MSC 44 Plymouth NH 03264 E-mail: rdecotis@mail.plymouth.edu.

DE COURTEN-MYERS, GABRIELLE MARGUERITE, neuropathologist; b. Fribourg, Switzerland, Aug. 8, 1947; came to U.S., 1979; d. Maurice Edmond and Margrit (Wettstein) De Courten; m. Ronald Elwood Myers, Apr. 18, 1981; 1 child, Maximilian. BSBA, Akademikergemeinschaft, Zurich, Switzerland, 1967; MD, U. Zurich, 1974. Resident in psychiatry Hopital Psycho-Geriatrique, Gimel, Switzerland, 1974-75; resident in pediatrics U. Hosp. Zurich, 1977; resident in neuropathology U. Hosp. of Lausanne, Switzerland, 1976-78; rsch. assoc. NIH, Bethesda, Md., 1979-80; fellow in neuropathology Coll. of Medicine U. Cin., 1980-83, asst. prof. neuropathology Coll. of Medicine, 1983-88, assoc. prof. neuropathology Coll. of Medicine, 1988-89, tenured assoc. prof. Coll. of Medicine, 1989—. Cons. Vets. Affairs Med. Ctr., Cin., 1983—, Children's Hosp. Med. Ctr., Cin., 1984—, Good Samaritan Hosp., Cin., 1990—. Grantee VA, 1985—, NIH, 1986-90, 93—, Am. Heart Assn., 1991-94, Am. Diabetes Assn., 1995. Mem. AAAS, Am. Assn. Neuropathologists, Am. Acad. Neurology, AAUP, Soc. Acad. Emergency Medicine, Soc. Exptl. Neuropathology. Office: U Cin Coll of Medicine Dept Pathology PO Box 670529 231 Bethesda Ave Cincinnati OH 45267-0529 E-mail: gabrielle.decourten@uc.edu.

DECROSTA, SUSAN ELYSE, graphic designer; b. Cambridge, Mass., Aug. 28, 1956; d. Joseph Mario and Gertrude Ermelinda (Galligani) DeC. BFA, Mass. Coll. Art, 1980. certified art tchr., supr. Graphic artist Nixdorf Computer Corp., Burlington, Mass., 1981-86; artist, illustrator Rivers, Trainor, Doyle, Providence, 1987; lead artist, illustrator Raytheon Co., Andover, Mass., 1986-94; graphic designer Raytheon Svc. Co., Burlington, Mass., 1994—2004; sr. graphic designer Rhytheon Tech. Svc., 2004—. Freelance graphic artist, 1980—; guest spkr. to design and illustration students Northeastern U., 1992. Publ. Graphic Design U.S.A. Mag., 2000 (Am. Graphic Design award, 2000, 2003). Vol. AIDS Action Com., Boston; bd. dirs. Jeannette Neill Dance Scholarship Program, Boston, 1999—. Recipient Excellence award Soc. Tech. Comm. & Art Direction, 1986. Mem.: Women's Initiative Network, Art Alumni Assn. Avocations: dance, painting. Office: Raytheon Svc Co 3 Van DeGraaff Dr Burlington MA 01803-4607 Office Phone: 781-238-3070. E-mail: susan_e_decrosta@raytheon.com., susandecrosta@rcn.com.

DECROW, KAREN, lawyer, writer, educator; b. Chgo., Dec. 18, 1937; d. Samuel Meyer and Juliette (Abt) Lipschultz; m. Alexander Allen Kolben, 1960 (div. 1965); m. Roger DeCrow, 1965 (div. 1972, dec. 1989). BS, Northwestern U., 1959; JD, Syracuse U., 1972; DHL (hon.), SUNY, Oswego, 1994. Bar: N.Y., U.S. Dist. Ct. (no. dist.) N.Y. Resorts editor Golf Digest mag., Evanston, Ill., 1959-60; editor Am. Soc. Planning Ofcls., Chgo., 1960-61; writer Ctr. for Study Liberal Edn. for Adults., Chgo., 1961-64; editor Holt, Rinehart, Winston, Inc., N.Y.C., 1965; textbook editor L.W. Singer, Syracuse, N.Y., 1965-66; writer Ea. Regional Inst. for Edn., Syracuse, 1967-69, Pub. Broadcasting System, 1977; tchr. women and law, 1972-74; nat. bd. mem. NOW, 1968-77, nat. pres., 1974-77, also nat. politics task force chair; cons. affirmative action; pvt. practice, 1974—. Lectr. topics including law, gender, internat. feminism to corps., polit. groups, colls. and univs., U.S., Can., Mex., Finland, China, Greece, former USSR; nat. coord. Women's Strike for Equality, 1970; moot ct. judge, 1974-; N.Y. State del. Internat. Women's Yr., 1977; originator Schs. for Candidates; participant DeCrow-Schlafly ERA Debates, from 1975; founder (with Robert Seidenberg, MD) World Woman Watch, 1988; gender issues advisor Nat. Congress for Men; mem. Task Force on Gender Bias. Author: (with Roger DeCrow) University Adult Education: A Selected Bibliography, 1967, American Council on Education, 1967, The Young Woman's Guide to Liberation, 1971, Sexist Justice, 1974, First Women's State of the Union Message, 1977, (with Robert Seidenberg) Women Who Marry Houses: Panic and Protest in Agoraphobia, 1983, Turkish edit., 1988, 2d Turkish edit., 1989, United States of America vs. Sex: How the Meese Commission Lied About Pornography, 1988, (with Jack Kammer) Good Will Toward Men: Women Talk Candidly About the Balance of Power Between the Sexes, 1994; editor: The Pregnant Teenager (Howard Osofsky), 1968, Corporate Wives, Corporate Casualties (Robert Seidenberg, MD), 1973; contbr. articles to USA Today, N.Y. Times, N.Y. Times Bus. Sect., L.A. Times, Chgo. Tribune, Nat. Law Jour., Women Boston Globe, Vogue, Mademoiselle, Ingenue, Newsday, Chgo. Sun Times, Penthouse, Washington Post, L.A. Times Mag., Policy Review, Miami Herald, Internat. Herald Tribune, Social Problems, Houston Chronicle, Pitts. Press, Nat. NOW Times, Syracuse U. Mag., San Francisco Chronicle, Civil Rights Quar., Women Lawyers Jour., other newspapers, mags.; regular columnist: Syracuse New Times; columnist N.Y. Times Spl. Features; recording: Opening Up Marriage, 1980. Hon. trustee Elizabeth Cady Stanton Found.; active Hon. Com. to Save Alice Paul's Birthplace; Liberal party candidate for Mayor of Syracuse, 1969. Recipient Profl. Recognition award for best newspaper column Syracuse Press Club, 1990, 94, 95, 96, 2000, Best Column award, 1994-95, 99, 2001, 02, Best Column award N.Y. Press Assn., 1991-92, 95, award Barnard Coll., Vet. Feminists of Am. and the Barnard Ctr. for Rsch. on Women, Woman of Achievement/Distinction award Gov. George E. Pataki, 1998; Svc. to Soc. award Northwestern U. Alumni Assn., 2002, Achievement award The Post-Standard, Syracuse, 2003. Mem. NOW (pres.), Onondaga County Bar Assn. (profl. ethics com.), N.Y. Women's Bar Assn. (ctrl. N.Y. chpt. pres. 1989-90, jud. screening com., Joan L. Ellenbogen Founder's award 2003), N.Y. Bar Assn., ACLU (Ralph E. Kharas Disting. Svc. in Civil Liberties award 1985), Elizabeth Cady Stanton Found. (trustee), Working Women's Inst. (bd. advisors), Syracuse Friends Chamber Music, Atlantic States Legal Found., Yale Polit. Union (hon. life), Nat. Congress Men (gender issues advisor), Mariposa Edn. and Rsch. Found., Nat. Coun. Children's Rights (adv. panel), Wilderness Soc., Northwestern U. Alumni Assn., Women's Inst. Freedom Press, Art Inst. Chgo., Nat. Women's Polit. Caucus, Theta Sigma Phi. Address: 7599 Brown Gulf Rd Jamesville NY 13078-9636

DECTER, MIDGE, writer; b. St. Paul, July 25, 1927; d. Harry and Rose (Calmenson) Rosenthal; m. Norman Podhoretz, Oct. 21, 1956; children[00bf] Rachel, Naomi, Ruth, John. Student, U. Minn., 1945-46, Jewish Theol. Sem. Am., 1946-48. Asst. editor Midstream mag., 1956-58; mng. editor Commentary, 1961-62; editor Hudson Inst., 1965-66, CBS Legacy Books, 1966-68; exec. editor Harper's mag., 1969-71; book review editor Saturday Rev./World mag., 1972-74; sr. editor Basic Books, Inc., 1974-80; exec. dir. Com. for Free World, 1980-90; sr. fellow Inst. on Religion and Pub. Life, 1991—. Author: The Liberated Woman and Other Americans, 1971, Liberal Parents, Radical Children, 1975, The New Chastity and Other Arguments Against Women's Liberation, 1997, An Old Wife's Tale: My Seven Decades in Love and War, 2001, Losing the First Battle, Winning the War, 2002, Rumsfeld: A Personal Portrait, 2003; mem. editl. bd.: First Things. Bd. dirs. Heritage Found., Ctr. for Security Policy, Inst. on Religion and Pub. Life; founding mem. Coalition for Dem. Majority; mem. bd. overseers Hoover Instn.; former dir. Nicaraguan Freedom Fund. Recipient Nat. Humanities medal, 2003. Home: 120 E 81st St New York NY 10028-1428 Office: Inst on Religion and Pub Life Ste 400 156 Fifth Ave New York NY 10010*

DEDE, BONNIE AILEEN, librarian, educator; b. Racine, Wis., Mar. 21, 1942; d. Edward Charles and Gracebelle Roeber; children: Suzan A., Ercan M. BA, U. Mich., 1963, MA, 1966, AM in Libr. Sci., 1968; cert., U. Ill., 1970. Various positions U. Mich. Libr., Ann Arbor, 1967—88, head spl. formats cataloging, 1988—99, adj. lectr. sch. info., 1989—, head monograph cataloging prodn., 1999—, adj. lectr. Law Libr., 2003—. Mem. part-time faculty libr. and info. sci. program Wayne State U., Detroit, 1993—; vis. lectr. Grad. Sch. Libr. and Info. Sci. U. Ill., Urbana-Champaign, 2003—; cons. Gale Rsch., Detroit, 1993; reviewer Am. Reference Books Ann., 1992—; cons. grant projects OCLC, 1991—92, 1994—96. Mem. editl. bd. MC, Jour. Acad. Media Librarianship, 1992-2002. Grantee Title II-B, U.S. Office Edn., 1970, faculty-libr. coop. rsch. grantee Coun. on Libr. Resources, 1986-88, access grantee NEH, 1990-93. Mem. ALA, Alpha Lambda Delta, Beta Phi Mu (pres. Mu chpt. 1991-96). Office: U Mich 100 Hatcher Libr North Ann Arbor MI 48109-1205

DEDMON, ANGELA MARIE MAXINE, psychologist; b. Oklahoma City, May 25, 1971; d. Hubert Carlton and Patricia Ann Bryan; m. Brian Todd Dedmon, June 15, 1991; children: Caeli Ann Louise, Joshua Todd. BA in Psychology and Sociology magna cum laude, Okla. State U., 1993; MA in Clin. Psychology, Tex. Tech. U., 1997, PhD in Clin. Psychology, 1999. Lic. psychologist Okla. Rsch. asst. Tex. Tech. U., Lubbock, 1995—96; clinic co-dir. Tex. Tech. Psychology Clinic, Lubbock, 1995—97; psychologist in tng. Lubbock County Youth Ctr., 1996—97, Lubbock Ind. Sch. Dist., 1997—98; intern psychology Children's Mercy Hosp., Kansas City, Mo., 1998—99, fellow psychology, 1999—2000; pvt. practice clin. child psychologist Edmond, Okla., 2001—. Clin. child psychologist psychol. evaluations Pauline Meyer Shelter, Oklahoma City, 2001—; spkr. Okla. Foster Care Assn., Oklahoma City, 2002. Contbr. articles to profl. jours. Vol. disaster recovery ARC, Oklahoma City; vol. disaster hotline local TV sta., Oklahoma City, 2001. Mem.: APA, Okla. Psychol. Assn. Avocations: swimming, reading, church activities. Office: 2500 S Broadway #200 Edmond OK 73013

DEE, DIANE MARIE, rancher, farmer; b. Evansville, Ind., Dec. 24, 1952; d. George William Fox and Thelma Ann Richter; m. Jonathan Dee, Nov. 2, 1979 (div. Mar. 1998); children: Brian Daniel, Sarah Ruth. Student, Ind. U. Cert. homeopathic educator. Life guard Recreation Dept., Evansville, Ind.,

1968—70; waitress Ladyman's Cafe, Bloomington, 1971—76; fitness trainer Europeaw Health Spa, Short Hills, NJ, 1976—78; libr. Far Brook Sch., 1987—99, substitute tchr., 1993—99; homeopath pvt. practice, Morristown, 1992—; rancher, farmer The Rising Sun Ranch, Van Buren, Mo., 1999—. Educator Cherokee and other Native Tribes local schs., 1985—. Independent. Avocations: gardening, sewing, beeding. Home: Rt 2 Box 2174 Van Buren MO 63965

DEE, PAULINE MARIE, artist; b. Concord, N.H., Jan. 9, 1933; d. Arthur Joseph and Anna Marie (Marquis) Champagne; m. Edmond Francis Dee, July 2, 1955; children: James Francis, Diane Mary. Bus. Cert., Burdett Coll., Lynn, Mass. Membership chmn. Danvers (Mass.) Art Assn., 1986-92, v.p., 1990-92; founder Pauline Dee Studio for Oil Painting, 1989; v.p. Lynnfield (Mass.) Art Guild, 1991-93, pres., 1994-96; v.p. Saltbox Gallery, Topsfield, Mass., 1995-2000, pres., 2000—. Demonstrator in field; cons. Kohinor Accent Program, Bloomsbury, N.J., 1995—; founder Pauline Dee Studio, 1989; instituted Lynnfield Art Guild Scholarship Fund, 1993. Exhibited in solo shows at Woman's Club of Boston, 1980, Naval Officers Club, Pearl Harbor, Hawaii, 1994; represented in numerous pvt. collections. Cons. Peabody (Mass.) Internat. Festival, 1995; bd. dirs. North Shore Art Assn., Gloucester, Mass., 1996. Recipient achievement awards, 1985-95; Lynnfield Arts Lottery grantee, 1996. Mem. Our Lady Guadalupe Sodality (prefect 1966-68). Roman Catholic. Avocations: art, golf, swimming, photography, walking. Home: 16 Samoset Rd Peabody MA 01960-3504

DEE, RUBY (RUBY DEE DAVIS), actress, writer, director; b. Cleve. d. Marshall Edward and Emma (Benson) Wallace; m. Ossie Davis, Dec. 9, 1948; children: Nora, Guy, Hasna. BA, Hunter Coll., 1945; ArtsD (hon.), Fairfield U.; BA (hon. doctorate), Iona Coll., Va. State U.; apprentice, Am. Negro Theatre, 1941-44; LHD (hon.), SUNY, Old Westbury, 1990; DFA, Spelman Coll., 1991. Ind. actress, writer, dir., v.p. Emmslyn II Prodns., 1945—. Author: (poetry) Glowchild, 1972, (musical) Take It from the Top, (collected poetry, humor, short stories) My One Good Nerve; adaptor: (African folk tales) Two Ways to Count to Ten, The Tower to Heaven, (play) Books With Legs, 1993; contbr. column N.Y. Amsterdam News; co-writer (film) Uptight; dir., adaptor (stage prodn.) Zora is my Name!, 1983; stage appearances include Jeb, 1946, Raisin in the Sun, 1959, Purlie Victorious, 1961, The Imaginary Invalid, 1971, Wedding Band, 1972 (Drama Desk award 1972), Boesman and Lena, 1970 (Obie award 1971), Anna Lucasta, Taming of the Shrew, Checkmates, 1988, The Glass Menagerie, 1989, Flyin West, 1994, Two Hah-Hahs and a Homeboy, 1995; actress: (films) Gone are the Days, The Jackie Robinson Story, Take a Giant Step, St. Louis Blues, A Raisin in the Sun, Purlie Victorious, To Be Young, Gifted and Black, Buck and the Preacher, Countdown at Kusini, Cat People, 1982, Do the Right Thing, 1989 (NAACP Image award as best actress 1989), Jungle Fever, 1991, Cop & 1/2, 1993, Whitewash, 1994, Just Cause, 1995, Simple Wish, A, 1997, Baby Geniuses, 1999; narrator: Time to Dance: The Life and Work of Norma Canner, A, 1998, Unfinished Journey, 1999; numerous TV appearances including It's Good to be Alive, 1974, Today Is Ours, 1974, The Defenders, Police Woman, Peyton Place, (TV films) To Be Young, Gifted and Black, All God's Children, The Nurses, Roots: The Next Generation, I Know Why the Caged Bird Sings, Wedding Band, It's Good to Be Alive, Decoration Day (Emmy award for Supporting Actress in a Miniseries or Special 1991), The Atlanta Child Murders, (TV spl. with Ossie Davis) Martin Luther King: The Dream and the Drum, The Winds of Change, Windmill of the Gods, TV miniseries Stephen King's The Stand, 1994, Tuesday Morning Ride, 1995, Mr. & Mrs. Loving, 1996, Captive Heart: The James Mink Story, 1996, Porgy and Bess: An American Voice, 1998, Passing Glory, 1999, Having Our Say: The Delany Sisters' First 100 Years, 1999, Finding Buck McHenry, 2000, A Storm in Summer, 2000; co-producer: (TV spl.) Today is Ours, The Ernest Green Story, 1993, (radio show) Ossie Davis and Ruby Dee Story Hour, 1974-78, (TV series) With Ossie and Ruby, 1981, (home videotape) Hands Upon The Heart, 1991, Middle Ages, 1992, Hands Upon The Heart II, 1993; rec. artist poems and stories; host (with Ossie Davis) African Heritage Movie Network. Recipient Martin Luther King Jr. award Operation PUSH, 1972, Drama Desk award, 1974, (with Ossie Davis) Frederick Douglass award N.Y. Urban League, 1970, (with Ossie Davis) NAACP Image award Hall of Fame, Master Innovator For Film award Sony, 1991, Nat. Medal of Arts, 1990. Mem. NAACP, CORE, Student Non-Violent Coordinating Com., SCLC. Address: The Artists Agy 10000 Santa Monica Blvd Los Angeles CA 90067-7007

DEEB, MARY-JANE, editor, educator; b. Alexandria, Egypt, Aug. 27, 1946; came to U.S., 1973; d. Alix and Stephanie (Klanscek) Anhoury; m. Marius K. Deeb, Sept. 27, 1969; 1 child, Hadi K. BA in Sociology, Am. U., Cairo, 1967, MA in Sociology, 1972; PhD in Internat. Rels., Johns Hopkins U., 1987. Rsch. assoc. Ford Found., Beirut, 1972-73; cons. UN Econ. Commn. for Western Asia, Beirut, 1980, UNICEF, Beirut, 1980-81; project dir. U.S. AID, Beirut, 1982-83; asst. professorial lectr. George Washington U., Washington, 1988-89, 93, 97, Georgetown U., Washington, 1991, 94; asst. prof. Am. U., Washington, 1989-94, adj. assoc. prof., 1994—; editor Mid. East Jour., Washington, 1995-98; Arab world area specialist Libr. of Congress, Washington, 1998—. External reviewer for grant proposals U.S. Inst. Peace, Washington, 1991, 92, 97; testified on subcom. on Africa fgn. rels. com. U.S. Ho. of Reps., 1991, 92, 98; testified before the select com. on intelligence, U.S. Senate, 1996; testified on fgn. rels. com. U.S. Senate, 1997, UN Monitor of Algerian legislative elections, 1997; dir. Algeria program Corp. Coun. on Africa; leader Libr. of Congress Mission to Iraq, 2003. Author: Libya Since the Revolution, 1982, Libya's Foreign Policy, 1991; co-editor: Hasib Sabbagh from Palestinian Refugee to Citizen of the World, 1996, Cocktails and Murder on the Potomac, 2001, (novel) Murder on the Riviera, 2004; rev. editor Internat. Jour. Mid.-East Studies, 1989-94; contbr. articles, revs. to profl. jours. and encys., and chpts. to books; interviewed on numerous TV programs, including CBS Evening News, ABC News, NBC Nightly News, CNN Headline News, Fox Morning News, PBS, and in news publs., including N.Y. Times, Washington Post, Time mag., L.A. Times, The Christian Sci. Monitor, U.S.A. Today, Boston Globe, Tokyo Shimbum, Yomouri, others. Mem. UN Assn., Am. Polit. Sci. Assn., Internat. Studies Assn., Mid. East Studies Assn. N.Am., Women's Caucus for Polit. Sci., Am.-Tunisian Assn. (exec. bd. 1989—), Hannibal Club (founding mem. 1999), World Affairs Coun., Women in Fgn. Policy. Roman Catholic. Office: Libr Congress African and Middle Ea Divsn Jefferson Bldg 101 Independence Ave SE Washington DC 20540-0002 E-mail: mdee@loc.gov.

DEEDS, VIRGINIA WILLIAMS, volunteer; b. Newark, Ohio, June 28, 1934; d. Theodore Nelson and Nell Elizabeth (Hoover) Williams; m. Charles Lemoin Deeds, Aug. 7, 1955; children: Melinda, Jennifer Giesen, C. Jason, Stephanie Sanda. RN, White Cross Sch. Nursing, 1955. RN, Ohio. RN obstet. dept. Berea (Ohio) Cmty. Hosp., 1955-56; RN emergency dept. White Cross Hosp., Columbus, Ohio, 1956; RN med. & obstetrics Union Hosp., Dover, Ohio, 1961-62; vol. RN United Health Found. Sr. Ctr., Dover, Ohio, 1961—, Office Roy Geduldig, Dover, Ohio, 1967-68. Co-founder, co-dir. Tuscarawas County Teen Pregnancy Prevention Taskforce, 1985-92. Co-editor The Chart newsletter, 1991-98. Bd. dirs. United Health Found., New Philadelphia, YMCA, Dover, Union Hosp. Aux., Chestnut Soc. Kent State U., 1996—, Juvenile Ct. Citizens Review Bd., 1989—; mem. bd. Chestnut Soc. Kent State U., Tuscarawas Campus, 1996-98; mem. Alcohol-Drug Addiction Mental Health Svcs. Bd., 1996—. Recipient Zeisberger award Tusc. County Hist. Soc., 1994. Avocations: golf, reading, needlework.

DEEL, FRANCES QUINN, retired librarian; b. Pottsville, Pa., Mar. 9, 1939; d. Charles Joseph and Carrie Miriam (Ketner) Q.; m. Ronald Eugene Deel, Feb. 5, 1983. BS, Millersville State Coll., 1960; M.L.S., Rutgers U., 1964; M.P.A., U. West Fla., 1981. Post librarian U.S. Army Armor (Desert Tng. Ctr.), Ft. Irwin, Calif., 1964-66; staff librarian Mil. Dist. of Washington, 1966-67; supervisory librarian 1st Logistical Command, APO San Francisco, 1967-68; tech. process specialist Naval Edn. and Tng. Supervisory Command, Washington, 1968-77, Pensacola, Fla., 1968-77; chief tech. library USAF Armament Lab., Eglin AFB, Fla., 1977-81; dir. command libraries Air Force Systems Command (Andrews AFB), Washington, 1981-92; mem. exec. adv. council Fed. Library and Info. Network, Washington, 1983-86; libr. Air Force Dist. of Washington (Bolling AFB), Washington, 1992-94; dir. Navy Dept. Libr., Washington, 1994; ret., 1994. Mem. ALA (dir.-at-large armed forces libraries sect. Chgo. 1983-86), Spl. Libraries Assn., D.C. Library Assn. Roman Catholic. Home: 99 Country Club Dr W Destin FL 32541-4433

DEEMER, (NORMA) JEAN, artist; b. Cleve., Sept. 5, 1929; d. Harold Charles and Erma Marie (Kaiser) Daniels; m. Fred Orlo Deemer Jr., Apr. 20, 1957 (div. Aug. 1991); 1 child, Fred Webster. Master classes with, Glen Bradshaw. Co-owner art gallery and frame shop, 1987. Tchr. OASIS; presenter, demonstrator, lectr. at workshops, juror of selection and awards in field. One-woman shows at Women's City Club of Akron, Ohio, Akron Jewish Ctr., Little Art Gallery, North Canton (Ohio) Libr., Akron Gen. Med. Ctr., Taylor Libr., Cuyahoga Falls, Ohio, Twinsburg (Ohio) Libr., North Hill Libr., Akron, Martel's, Akron, Rocky Knoll, Hudson (Ohio) Galleries, 1997, Lawrence Churski Gallery, Akron, Ohio, 2000, others; exhibited in group shows (25 awards) at Case Western Res. U., Cleve., 1996, 20th Century Gallery affiliate Va. Mus. Art, Williamsburg, 1998, Nicolet Coll., Rhinelander, Wis., 1992, Soc. Layerists in Multi Media, Bradford, Mass., 1994, Ohio Dept. Mental Health, Columbus, 1994, Johnson-Humrick House, Coshocton, Ohio, 1994, Sandusky (Ohio) Cultural Ctr., 1994, U. Ark. Art Galleries, Fayetteville, 1994, Stocker Ctr., Lorain C.C., Elyria, Ohio, 1995, Tubac (Ariz.) Ctr. for Arts, 1994-95, 98, Kirkpatrick Ctr. Mus. Complex, Oklahoma City, 1991-92, 95, Western U. N.Mex., Silver City, 1996, Lakeland C.C., Kirtland, Ohio, 1996, Brea (Calif.) Civic Cultural Ctr., 1997, Van Vechten-Lineberry Taos (N.Mex.) Art Mus., 1997, Nat. Soc. Painters in Casein and Acrylic (2 awards), Salamagundi Club, NYC, 2000-02, Canton Mus. Art, 2001; represented in permanent collections at FirstMerit Corp., Ohio, Akron-Summit County Pub. Libr., Portage Lakes, Ohio, Soc. Nat. Bank, Cleve., Colony Savs. Bank, Pitts., Columbia-Greene C.C., Hudson, N.Y., Anthony Cerny Archtl. Design Studios, Medina, Ohio, Ohio Arts and Crafts Found., Ohio Watercolor Soc., SAS Inst. One, Cary, NC; contbr. art to jours. cover and books in field. Mem. faculty, edn. chmn. Cuyahoga Valley Art Ctr., Cuyahoga Falls, 1986-88, also workshop chmn., v.p. Recipient Silver medal Watercolor Ohio, 1993, Merit award Watercolor Ohio, 1995, Juror's award Nat. Watercolor Okla., 1995, GE award Ky. Aqueous Nat., 1990, hon. mention; travel award, 1997. Mem. Nat. Watercolor Soc., Nat. Soc. Painters in Casein and Acrylic, Ky. Watercolor Soc., Soc. Layerists in Multi-Media, Ohio Watercolor Soc. (corr. sec. 1983-84, coord. ann. state juried exhbn. 1991, workshop coord. 1992, trustee 1991-94, 1st v.p. 1994-96, exhbn. liaison officer 1994-96, pres. 1996-2000, bd. dirs. 2001—, Hunt Mfg. award 1980, Bronze medal 1988, Award of Excellence 1991, 99, 2001, Silver medal 1993, Merit award 1995, award of distinction 2000). Avocations: travel, music, reading, interest in healing connection of art and medicine. Home: 1537 Briarwood Cir Cuyahoga Falls OH 44221-3623

DEEN, PAULA H. television personality, chef, restaurant owner; b. Albany, Ga. children from previous marriage: Bobby, Jamie. Owner catering bus. The Bag Lady; owner The Lady and Sons restaurant, Savannah, Ga., 1990—. Host (TV series) Paula's Home Cooking, Food Network, 2002—; author: (cookbooks) The Lady and Sons Savannah Country Cookbook, The Lady and Sons Too, The Lady and Sons Just Desserts, 2002. Provided sponsorships and donations of money, cookbooks and other services to cmty. groups and causes. Named Most Memorable Meal Yr. at The Lady and Sons restaurant, USA Today, 1999, Small Bus. Person Yr. in Ga., US Small Bus. Adminstrn., 2003; recipient Ga. Women Entrepreneurs (GWEN) award, Ga. Small Bus. Devel. Ctr., 2003. Mailing: Food Network Studios 604 W 52nd St New York NY 10019*

DEER, ADA E. former federal agency official, social worker, educator; b. Menominee Indian Reservation, Wis., Aug. 7, 1935; d. Joe and Constance (Wood) D. BA in Social Work, U. Wis., 1957, LDH (hon.), 1974; MSW, Columbia U., 1961; postgrad., U. N.Mex., 1971, U. Wis., 1971-72; D in Pub. Svc. (hon.), Northland Coll., 1974. Group worker Protestant Coun. N.Y., N.Y.C. Youth Bd., 1958-60; program dir. Edward F. Waite Neighborhood House, Mpls., 1961-64; community svc. coord. bur. Indian affairs Dept. of Interior, Mpls., 1964-67; coord. Indian affairs Tng. Ctr. Cmty. Programs U. Minn., Mpls., 1967-68; trainer Project Peace Pipe Peace Corps., Arecibo, P.R., 1968; sch. social worker Mpls. Pub. Schs., 1968-69; dir. Upward Bound U. Wis., Stevens Point, 1969-70, dir. Program Recognizing Individual Determination through Edn., 1970-71; v.p., lobbyist Nat. Com. Save Menominee People and Forest, Inc., Washington and State of Wis., 1972-73; chair Menominee Restoration Com., Wis., 1974-76; lectr. Sch. Social Work, Am. Indians Studies Program U. Wis., Madison, 1977—93, 1997—, dir. Am. Indian Studies program, 2000—; asst. sec. Indian Affairs U.S. Dept. Interior, Washington, 1993—97. Legis. liaison Native Am. Rights Fund, Washington, 1979-81; cons., trainer Nat. Women's Edn. Fund, Washington, 1979-85; founding mem. Am. Indian Scholarships, Inc., Albuquerque, 1973-85; apptd. Joint Commn. on Mental Health of Children, Inc., Washington, 1967-68, Youth for Understanding, Wis., 1985-90; mem. adv. panel Office Technology Assessment, Washington, 1984-86; mem. Nat. Indian Adv. Com., Washington, 1989-91, Milw., 1990—, numerous other coms.; spkr. in field. Vice chair Nat. Mondale/Ferraro Presdl. Campaign, Washington, 1984; del.-at-large Dem. Nat. Conv., San Francisco, 1984; mem. spl. com. minority presence Girls Scouts U.S.A., N.Y.C., 1975-77, mem., 1969-75; bd. dirs. Planned Parenthood, Mpls., 1965-66, Indian Cmty. Sch., Milw., 1989—, Native Am. Rights Fund, Boulder, 1984-90, chmn., 1989-90, chair nat. support com., 1990—; mem. bd. improving health Native Ams. Robert Wood Johnson Found., Princeton, N.J., 1988—; bd. dirs. Quincentenary Com. Smithsonian Instn., Washington, 1989—, Hunt Commn. Dem. Nat. Com., Washington, 1981-82, Ind. Sector, Washington, 1980-84, Rural Am., Washington, 1978-85, Ams. for Indian Oppty., 1970-83; apptd. Pres. Commn. White House Fellowships, 1977-83; active Common Cause, Washington, 1974-78, Wis. Women's Coun., Madison, 1983-84, Camp Miniwanca, Stony Lake, Mich., 1953-57, Coun. Founds., Washington, 1977-83, Madison Urban League; Dem. candidate Wis. Sec. State, 1982; chair Menominee Nation, Wis., 1974-76. Recipient White Buffalo Coun. Achievement award, 1974, Politzer award Ethical Culture Soc., 1975, Wonder Woman Found. award, 1982, Indian Coun. Fire Achievement award, 1984, Nat. Disting. Achievement award Am. Indian Resources Inst., 1991; named Woman of Yr. by Girl Scouts Am., 1982; honoree Nat. Women's History Month Poster, 1987, Heroine Calendar Nat. Women's Studies Assn., 1987; Harvard U. fellow, 1977-78, Delta Gamma Found. Meml. fellow, 1960, John Hay Whitney Found. Meml. fellow, 1960; Menominee Tribal scholar, 1953-55. Mem. ACLU, NOW, Nat. Women's Polit. Caucus, Nat. Congress Am. Indians, Nat. Assn. Social Workers (pres. Wis. chpt. 1988-90, nat. com. women's issues 1988-90, decision making task force 1988-90, minorities com. 1977-81), Assn. Am. Indians and Alaska Native Social Workers (pres. Wis. 1978-80), Common Cause, Nature Conservancy. Avocations: reading, traveling. Office: Ethnic Studies Coll Letters and Sci 318 Ingraham Hall M 1155 Observatory Dr Madison WI 53706

DEERE, KELLI BETH, music educator; b. Lexington, Tenn., Dec. 30, 1977; d. James L. and Beth A. White; m. David Neal Deere, Mar. 2, 2002. Bachelor of Music in Music Edn., Union U., 2000, MEd, 2002. Music educator W. Carroll Primary/Elem. Sch., McLemoresville, Tenn., 2000—02, Paul G. Caywood Sch., Lexington, 2002—. Dir. children's choir Mt. Gilead Bapt. Ch., Cedar Grove, Tenn., 1999—. Mem.: W. Tenn. Vocal Music Assn., Music Edn. Nat. Conf., Tenn. Edn. Assn. Democrat. Baptist. Avocations: singing, piano, motorcycling.

DEERING, ANNE-LISE, artist, retired real estate salesperson; b. Oslo, June 20, 1935; d. Reidar Ingolf Dahlsrud and Dagny Elfrida (Grönneberg) Nilsen; m. Reginald Atwell Deering, Oct. 20, 1956 (div. July 1992); children: Eric, Mark, Linda, Norman. BA in Art, Pa. State U., 1977, postgrad., 1990—91. Rsch. asst. Yale U., New Haven, 1955-57; ceramic artist/potter State College, Pa., 1977-98. Real estate agt. Coldwell Banker Univ. Realty, State College, 1992-93, Century 21 Corman Assocs., State College, 1993-99; artist mem. Art Alliance Ctrl. Pa., 1977-2000. Editor Ctrl. Pa. Guild of Craftsmen newsletter, 1994; exhibited in group shows at Newark Mus., 1990, Montain Top Gallery, Cresson, Pa., 1998, Pen and Brush Gallery, N.Y.C., 1998, 99, 2000, 01, Queensborough C.C., 2000, FIDEM, Weimar, Germany, 2000, FIDEM, Paris, 2002, FIDEM Seixal, Portugal, ANA, Colorado Springs, 2001, Penn State U., 2002, Wroclav, Poland, 2002, AMSA mems. exhibit, Nat. Ornamental Metal Mus., Memphis, 2003, Ford Gallery, Eastern Mich. U., 2003, Gallery North, Edmonds, Va. Mem. visual arts adv. com. Ctrl. Pa. Festival of Arts, 1989-93, co-chair, 1991-93, jury and rules co-chmn. for sidewalk sales com., 1993-97, chair AMSA mems. juried exhibit, Nordic Heritage Mus., Seattle, 2004. Mem.: Internat. Fedn. Medal Art, Wash. Potters Assn. (bd. dirs. 2000—), Art Alliance Ctrl. Pa. (chair mems. juried exhibit 1978, bd. dirs. 1978—79, participant Gallery Shop 1989—99, steering com. 1994—97), Am. Medallic Sculpture Assn. (newsletter editor 2000—03, co-chmn. Hands Across the Sea Am./Polish Medals Exhibit 2001—02, sec. 2002—), Am. Mus. Women in Arts (charter), Ctrl. Pa. Guild Craftsmen (pres. 1986—87, 1993—94), Pa. Guild Craftsmen (bd. dirs. 1980—83, v.p. 1985, bd. dirs. 1985—98, v.p. 1991, 1992, coord., chair ann. Christmas sale). Avocations: photography, music, sailing, gardening, wine making. Home: 24229 92nd Ave W Edmonds WA 98020-6503 E-mail: superpotr@aol.com.

DEERMAN, RUTH GILLETT, sales executive; b. El Paso, Tex., June 17, 1915; d. Otis Theodore and Katie Yvette (Textor) Gillett; m. Charlie Luther Deerman, Nov. 25, 1933 (dec. June 1992). Student, U. Tex., El Paso, 1966. Flight instr. Border Aviation, El Paso, 1944; flight and ground instr. S.W. Air Rangers, El Paso, 1968; beauty cons. Mary Kay Cosmetics, El Paso, 1969-70, ind. sales dir., 1970-75, ind. sr. sales dir., 1975—. Tchr. flying and ground sch., 1945—; accident prevention councilor FAA, 1972-80. Bd. dirs. Am. Cancer Soc., 1957-67; pres. Providence Meml. Hosp. Aux., 1960-61; past treas. Womans Club El Paso; past bd. dirs. YWCA, El Paso; past pres. Women's Missionary Union, 1st Bapt. Ch. Named Tex. Flying Farmers State Queen, 1955; winner All Woman Transcontinental Air Race, 1954; inducted into El Paso Aviation Hall of Fame, 1983; honored with granite plaque Internat. Forest of Friendship, 1977; recipient Jimmie Kolp award for contbg. to aviation and 99s, 1975. Mem. NAFE, Nat. Assn. Flight Instr., 99s (lic. women pilots, past internat. pres.), Whirly Girls (Whirly Girl # 78), Silver Wings, El Paso Aviation Assn. (v.p. 1947), 66s (founder), Clowns of Am. Internat., El Paso C. of C. (coms. woman's dept.), PEO, Ladies Oriental Shrine Am. (FAA accident prevention councilor 1972-80), Daus. of Nile (queen 1951-52), Order Ea. Star (worthy matron 1945). Republican. Avocations: bowling, golf. Home and Office: 405 Camino Real Ave El Paso TX 79922-2003

DEERNOSE, KITTY, curator; b. Crow Agency, Mont., Apr. 14, 1956; AA in Mus. Studies, Inst. Am. Indian Arts, Santa Fe, 1985. Mus. intern Heard Mus. Anthropology and Primitive Art, Phoenix, 1984; interpreter Little Bighorn Battlefield Nat. Monument, Crow Agency, Mont., 1985-90, mus. curator, 1990—. Mus. intern in Crow studies Smithsonian Instn., Washington, 1988. Recipient White Glove award Nat. Park Svc., 1995. Mem. Am. Assn. Muss., Am. Assn. State and Local History, Mountain Plains Mus. Assn., Smithsonian Nat. Mus. Am. Indian, Internal Coun. Museums. Office: Little Bighorn Battlefield Nat Monument PO Box 39 Crow Agency MT 59022-0039 E-mail: Kitty-Deernose@nps.gov.

DEES, SANDRA KAY MARTIN, psychologist, research scientist; b. Omaha, Apr. 18, 1944; d. Leslie B. and Ruth Lillian (May) Martin; m. Doyce B. Dees. BA magna cum laude, Tex. Christian U., 1965, MA, 1972, PhD, 1989. Cert. Montessori Soc., 1977. Adminstrv. asst., rsch. coord. Hosp. Improvement Project, Wichita Falls (Tex.) State Hosp., 1968-69; caseworker adoptions Edna Gladney Home, Ft. Worth, 1970-71; psychologist Mexia (Tex.) State Sch., 1971-72; sch. psychologist Ft. Worth Ind. Sch. Dist., 1971-78, program evaluator, 1978-86; pvt. counselor, 1986-88; rsch. scientist Tex. Christian U., Ft. Worth, 1989—, mem. adj. faculty, 1991-92, mem. grad. faculty, 1994—. Bd. dirs Because We Care, Ft. Worth, 1988-97, Hill Sch., 1994—. Contbr. articles to profl. jours. Dallas TCU Women's Club creative writing scholar, 1962-64, Virginia Alpha scholar, 1963; NASA rsch. asst., 1965-67; USPHS trainee, 1967-68. Mem. APA, Am. Ednl. Rsch. Assn., Mental Health Assn., Mortar Board, Mensa, Sigma Xi, Alpha Chi, Phi Alpha Theta, Psi Chi, Phi Delta Kappa. Home: 29 Bounty Rd W Fort Worth TX 76132-1003 Office: Tex Christian U Dept Psychology Fort Worth TX 76129-0001 E-mail: s.dees@tcu.edu.

DEFATTA-BARATTINI, KATHRYN, communications educator; d. Vincent DeFatta and Lucille Marabella; m. Gene Barattini, Sept. 3, 1994; 1 child, Rachel Barattini. BA, La. State U., Shreveport, 1990; MA, U. N.C., Chapel Hill, 1992. Instr. pub. speaking Bossier Parish C.C., Bossier City, La., 1992—97, asst. prof. pub. speaking, 1997—2000, assoc. prof. pub. speaking, 2000—. Author: The Relationship of Ethnic Self-Identification of Latter Generations of Louisiana's Sicilian-Americans to Their Use of Ethnic Colloquial Phrases, 2000; reviewer (acad. books). Founding mem. nat. campaign for tolerance So. Poverty Law Ctr., Montgomery, Ala., 2001—02; mem. bishop's diocesan coun. Cath. Diocese of Shreveport, 1994—97. Independent. Avocations: writing, art and graphic design, Italian-American research. Office: Bossier Parish Community College 2719 Airline Dr North Bossier City LA 71111 E-mail: kdefatta@bpcc.edu.

DEFAZIO, LYNETTE STEVENS, dancer, educator, choreographer, violinist, actress; b. Berkeley, Calif., Sept. 29, 1930; d. Honore and Mabel J. (Estavan) Stevens; children: J.H. Panganiban, Joanna Pang. Student, U. Calif., Berkeley, 1950-55, San Francisco State Coll., 1950-51; studied classical dance teaching techniques and vocabulary with Gisella Caccialanza and Harold and Lew Christensen, San Francisco Ballet, 1952-56; D in Chiropractic, Life-West Chiropractic Coll., San Lorenzo, Calif., 1983; cert. techniques of tchg., U. Calif., 1985; BA in Humanities, New Coll. Calif., 1986. Lic. chiropractor, Mich.; diplomate Nat. sci. Bd.; eminence in dance edn., Calif. C.C. dance specialist, std. svcs., childrens ctrs. credentials Calif. Dept. Edn., 1986. Contract child dancer Monogram Movie Studio, Hollywood, Calif., 1938-40; dance instr. San Francisco Ballet, 1953-65; performer San Francisco Opera Ring, 1960-67; performer, choreographer Oakland (Calif.) Civic Light Opera, 1963-70; dir. Ballet Arts Studio, Oakland, 1960; tchg. specialist Oakland Unified Sch. Dist., 1965-80; fgn. exch. dance dir. Academie de Danses-Salle Pleyel, Paris, 1966; instr. Peralta C.C. Dist., Oakland, 1971—, chmn. dance dept., 1985—. Cons., instr. ext. courses UCLA, Dirs. and Suprs. Assn., Pitts. Unified Sch. Dist., 1971-73, Tulare (Calif.) Sch. Dist., 1971-73; rschr. Ednl. Testing Svcs., HEW, Berkeley, 1974; resident choreographer San Francisco Childrens Opera, 1970—, Oakland Civic Theater; ballet mistress Dimensions Dance Theater, Oakland, 1977-80; cons. Gianchetta Sch. Dance, San Francisco, Robicheau Boston Ballet, TV series Patchwork Family, CBS, N.Y.C.; choreographer Ravel's Valses Nobles et Sentimentales, 1976. Author: Basic Music Outlines for Dance Classes, 1960, Basic Music Outlines for Dance Classes, rev., 1968, Teaching Techniques and Choreography for Advanced Dancers, 1965, Basic Music Outlines for Dance Classes, 1965, Goals and Objectives in Improving Physical Capabilities, 1970, A Teacher's Guide for Ballet Techniques, 1970, Principle Procedures in Basic Curriculum, 1974, Objectives and Standards of Performance for Physical Development, 1975, Techniques of the Ballet School, 1970, Techniques of the Ballet School, rev., 1974, The Opera Ballets: A Choreographic Manual Vols. I-V, 1986; assoc. music arranger: Le Ballet du Cirque, 1964, assoc. composer, lyricist: The Ballet of Mother Goose, 1968; choreographer Valses Nobles Et Sentimentales (Ravel), Transitions (Kashevaroff), 1991, The New Wizard of Oz, 1991, San Francisco Children's Opera (Gingold), Canon in D for Strings and Continuo (Pachelbel), 1979, Oakland Cmty. Orch. excerpts from Swan Lake, Faust, Sleeping Beauty, 1998, Rodeo, Alameda Coll. Cultural Affairs Program, 2000, dancer solo dancer Three Stravinsky Etudes, Alameda Coll. Cultural Affairs Program, 1999, appeared in Flower Drum Song, 1993, Gigi, 1994, Fiddler on the Roof, 1996, The Music Man, 1996, Sayonara, 1997, Bye Bye Birdie, 2000, Barnum, the Circus Musical, 2001; musician (violinist): Oakland Cmty. Concert Orch., 1995—; condr. Gil Gleason:. Bd. dirs. Prodrs. Assocs., Inc., Oakland, 1999—. Recipient Foremost Women of 20th Century, 1985, Merit award San Francisco Children's Opera, 1985, 90. Mem. Calif. State Tchrs. Assn., Bay Area Chiropractic Rsch. Soc., Profl. Dance Tchrs. Assn. Home and Office: 4923 Harbord Dr Oakland CA 94618-2506 Personal E-mail: balletarts@bigplanet.com.

DEFEIS, ELIZABETH FRANCES, law educator, lawyer; b. N.Y.C. d. Francis Paul and Lena (Amendola) D. BA, St. John's U., 1956, JD, 1958, JSD (hon.), 1984; LLM, NYU, 1971; postgrad., U. Milan, Italy, 1963-64, Inst. Internat. Human Rights, 1991. Bar: N.Y. 1959, U.S. Dist. Ct. (fed. dist.) 1960, U.S. Dist. Ct. (so. dist.) N.Y. 1961, U.S. Supreme Ct. 1965, U.S. Dist. Ct. (ea. dist.) N.Y. 1978, N.J. 1983. Asst. U. S. atty. So. Dist. N.Y., Dept. Justice, 1961-62; atty. RCA Corp., 1962-63; assoc. Carter, Ledyard & Milburn, N.Y.C., 1963-69; atty. Bedford Stuyvesant Legal Svcs. Corp., 1969-70; prof. law Seton Hall U., Newark, 1971—, dean Sch. Law, 1983-88. Vis. prof. St. Louis U. Sch. Law, 1988, St. John's U. Sch. Law, 1990, 2001, U. Milan, Italy, 1996; Fulbright-Hays lectr., Iran, India, 1977-79; lectr. Orgn. Security and Cooperation in Europe, Russia, Turkmenistan, Tajikistan, Azerbaijan; vis. scholar Ctr. Study of Human Rights, Columbia U., 1989; project dir. TV series Women and Law, 1974-80; narrator TV series Alternatives to Violence, 1981; mem. com. women and cts. N.J. Supreme Ct., 1982-95; trustee Legal Svcs. N.J., 1983-88; mem. 3rd Cir. Task Force on Equality in the Cts., 1995-90, tech. cons. on Constitution of Armenia, 1992-95; project dir. T.V. series Pub. Internat. Law.; legal expert Armenia election OSCE, 1998. Chair Albert Einstein Inst., Boston, 1995—2001. Fulbright-Hays scholar Milan, Italy, 1963-64, Fulbright-Hays, Orgn. for Security and Cooperation in Europe scholar, Armenia, Russia, Italy, 1996; Ford Found. fellow, 1970-71. Mem. ABA, Nat. Italian Am. Bar Assn., Columbian Lawyers Assn., Assn. of Bar of City of N.Y. (internat. law com., coun. internat. affairs), N.J. Bar Assn., Nat. Italian Am. Found. Office: Seton Hall U Law Sch One Newark Ctr Newark NJ 07102 E-mail: defeisel@shu.edu.

DE FERRARI, GABRIELLA, curator, writer; b. Tacna, Peru, June 3, 1941; came to U.S., 1959, naturalized, 1964; d. Armando and Delia De Ferrari; children: Nathaniel, Gabriella, Jeppson. BA, St. Louis U., 1962; MS, Tufts U., 1965; MA, Harvard U., 1981. Dir. Inst. Contemporary Art, Boston, 1975-77; acting curator Busch Reisinger Mus., Harvard U., Cambridge, Mass., 1978-79; asst. dir. for curatorial affairs and program Fogg Art Mus., 1979-82. Cons. editor Travel and Leisure; mem. bd. visitors Harvard U. Art Museums, Cambridge, Mass.; trustee New Sch. U., N.Y.C., Wadsworth Atheneum, Hartford, Conn. Author: A Cloud on Sand, 1990, Gringa Latina A Woman of Two Worlds, 1995. Office: 10 Jay St New York NY 10013-2861

DEFLEUR, LOIS B. university president, sociology educator; b. Aurora, Ill., June 25, 1936; d. Ralph Edward and Isabel Anna (Cornils) Begitske; m. Melvin L. DeFleur (div.) AB, Blackburn Coll., 1958; MA, Ind. U., 1961; PhD in Sociology, U. Ill., 1965; HHD (hon.), U. Alaska, 1999. Asst. prof. sociology Transylvania Coll., Lexington, Ky., 1963-67; assoc. prof. Wash. State U., Pullman, 1967-74, prof., 1975-86, dean Coll. Liberal Arts, 1981-86; provost U. Mo., Columbia, 1986-90; pres. Binghamton U., SUNY, 1990—. Disting. vis. prof. USAF Acad., 1976-77; vis. prof. U. Chgo., 1980-81; bd. dirs. Energy East Corp., HealthNow, N.Y. Author: Delinquency in Argentina, 1965; (with others) Sociology: Human Society, 3d edit. 1981, 4th edit., 1984, The Integration of Women into All Male Air Force Units, 1982, The Edward R. Murrow Heritage: A Challenge for the Future, 1986; contbr. articles to profl. jours. Mem. Wash. State Bd. on Correctional Svcs. and Edn., 1974-77, State of N.Y. Edn. Dept. Curriculum and Assessment Coun., 1991-94, Trilateral Task for N.Am. Ednl. Collaboration, USIA, 1993-95. Recipient Disting. Alumni award Blackburn Coll., 1991, Chief Exec. Leadership awrd Coun. for Advancement and Support of Edn., 1999, Civic Leadership award Greater Binghamton C. of C., 2003, Woman of Distinction award Girl Scout Coun., 2002; grantee NIMH, 1969-79, NSF, 1972-75, Air Force Office, 1978-81. Mem. NCAA (pres. commn. 1996, exec. com. 1997-98), Am. Sociol. Assn. (publs. com. 1979-82, nominations com. 1984-86, coun. mem. 1987-90), Pacific Sociol. Assn. (pres. 1980-82), Coun. Colls. of Arts and Scis. (bd. dirs. 1982-84, pres. 1985-87), Aircraft Owners and Pilots Assn., Internat. Comanche Soc., Nat. Assn. State U. and Land-grant Colls. (exec. com. 1990-93, chair coun. of pres. 1994-95, chmn. bd. dirs. 1996-97), Am. Coun. Edn. (bd. dirs. 1994-2000, v.p. chair-elect 1997-98, chair bd. dirs. 1998-99), Consortium Social Sci. Assns. (bd. dirs. 1993-96). Office: Binghamton U Office of Pres PO Box 6000 Binghamton NY 13902-6000

DE FOX, MARTA SAHAGUN, First Lady of Mexico; b. Zamora, Mexico, Apr. 10, 1953; d. Alberto Sahagun; m. Manuel Bribiescal, 1971 (div. 2000); 3 children ; m. Vicente Fox (president of Mexico), July 2, 2001; 4 stepchildren. Tchr. English La Salle U., Celaya, Konrad Adenauer Found.; mem. Nat. Action Party, Mexico, 1988—, nat. and state party coun. mem., sec. women's polit. promotion, coord. citizen's environ. protection com., candidate for mcpl. pres. city of Celaya; spokesperson Gov. of Guanajuato Vicente Fox, Mexico, 1995—99; pres. sec. Pres. Vicente Fox, Mexico, 2000—01; head social work found. Vamos Mex., 2001—; first lady of Mex., 2001—. Office: Presidencia de la Republica Residencia Oficial de los Pinos Puerta 1 Col San Miguel Chapultepec 11850 Delegacion Miguel Hidalgo CP Mexico*

DEFRANCIS, SUELLEN MARIA, interior architect; b. Bklyn., Sept. 21, 1946; d. Joseph Agustino and Mary DeF.; m. James D. Block, Apr. 23, 1965 (div. 1983); children: Melissa, Louis, Maximillian. BS, CCNY, 1982; BArch, CUNY, 1982, MS in Urban Design, 1983. Designer John Burgee Architects, N.Y.C., 1985-86; prin., owner Suellen DeFrancis Archtl. Interiors, Scarsdale, 1986—. Real estate investment advisor; lectr. Iona Coll., New Rochelle, N.Y., in field of architecture. Major projects include N.Y. Yacht Club, N.Y.C., Nippon Steel, N.Y.C., Mitsubishi Estate Housing, Ashiya, Japan, Asahi Breweries, Kobe, Japan, Sakikawa residences, Tokyo, Atlanta, and N.Y.C., Okada residences, Iwaki, Japan, N.Y.C., Met. Tower, N.Y.C., Genex Hdqs., N.Y.C., Hilcrest by Hilton, Tarrytown, N.Y., The Castle Restaurant and Inn, Tarrytown, Berkshire Place Hotel, N.Y., IBM Milford (Conn.) Campus, archtl. restoration 1923 Young Apts. Bldg., Scarsdale, N.Y.; works pub. in (book) 100 Designers' Favorite Rooms, 1993, 1st and 3d edits., (mag.) Kukan, Japan, N.Y. Times, Wall St. Jour. Trustee St. Christopher's-Jennie Clarkson Childcare Svcs., Inc. Recipient del Gaudio award N.Y. Soc. Architects, 1982; AIA scholar, 1982. Mem. AIA (assoc., N.Y.C. AIA interiors com.), Internat. Interior Design Assn., Internat. House of Japan, Far East Soc. Architects and Engrs., Nippon Club, Cosmopolitan Club (N.Y.C.). Avocations: travel, tennis.

DEFRANTZ, ANITA, sports association executive, lawyer; b. Phila., Oct. 4, 1952; d. Robert and Anita DeFrantz. BA in Political Philosophy, Conn. Coll., 1974; JD, U. Penn., 1977; PhD (hon.), U. RI, Pepperdine U., Mills Coll., Mount Holyoke Coll. Atty. Juvenile Law Center of Phila., 1977—79; admin. Princeton U., 1979—81; counsel Corp. for Enterprise Develop., 1980—81; v.p. L.A. Olympic Organizing Comm., 1981—85; pres. Amateur Athletic Found., 1987—. Mem. U.S. Women's Rowing Team, 1975—80; captain U.S. Olympic Women's Rowing Team, Montreal, 1976, mem., Moscow, 80. Recipient Olympic Bronze medal in rowing, 1976, Olympic Bronze medal of the Olympic Order, 1980, Olympic Torch award, U.S. Olympic Comm., 1988, Black Women of Achievement award, NAACP Legal Defense and Ednl. Fund, Martin Luther King Jr. Brotherhood award, L.A. YMCA, 1990, Award of Excellence, Sports Lawyers Assoc., 1992, Turner Broadcasting Trumpet award, 1993, Billie Jean King Contribution award, 1996. Mem.: Internat. Rowing Fed. (v.p. 1993), U.S. Rowing Assoc. (Jack Kelly award 1991), Vesper Rowing Club, S. Calif. Olympian Soc. (former pres.), Kids in Sports (pres.), Internat. Olympic Comm., 1986- (exec. bd. 1992—2001, v.p. 1997—2001). Office: Amateur Athletic Found 2141 W Adams Blvd Los Angeles CA 90018*

DEGANN, SONA IRENE, obstetrician, gynecologist, educator; b. Homs, Syria, 1952; d. Papken Stephan and Helen Irene (Wadsworth) Mugrditchian; m. A. David Degann, May 11, 1983; children: Alexander, Seta. BSc, Am. U. Beirut, Lebanon, 1975; MS, U. Mich., 1976; MD, Johns Hopkins U., 1983. Diplomate Am. Bd. Ob-Gyn. Resident in ob-gyn. N.Y. Hosp., N.Y.C., 1983-87, staff. Clin. instr. Cornell U. Sch. Medicine, N.Y.C., attending Ob-Gyn New York Presbyn. Hosp., N.Y.C. Fellow Am. Coll. Ob-Gyn.; mem. AMA, Med. Soc. State N.Y., N.Y. County Med. Soc.

DE GARCIA, LUCIA, marketing professional; b. Medellin, Colombia, June 26, 1942; came to the U.S., 1962; d. Enrique Giraldo Botero and Carolina (Vega) Estrada; m. Alvaro Garcia Osorio, July 30, 1962; children: Carolina Alexandra, Claudia Maria. BS, Nat. U., 1962. Engring. arch. designer VTN, Newport Beach, Calif., 1974-78; pres., CEO Elan Internat., Newport Beach, 1984—. Speaker, lectr. on success, protocol in bus. with Latin Am., free trade agreement between U.S. and Mexico. Editor: Elan mag., 1988-90. Trustee Nat. U., Calif., 1989-93; area campaign mgr. Bush for Pres., Orange County, Calif., 1988, Christopher Cox for Congress, 1988, Pete Wilson for Gov., 1990, People to Watch, 1994; bd. dirs. ARC, 1985-90, Am. Cancer Rsch. Ctr., 1986—; active South Coast Repertory Theater, 1982—. Named Dama de Distincion U.S./Mexico Found., 1991, Hispanic Woman of Yr. LULAC, 1986, One on the 10 Most Influential Women in Orange County, Orange County Metropolitan, 1994, One of the Hispanic 100 Most Influential in the U.S., Hispanics Bus. Mag., 1994; recipient Internat. award U.S. Hispanic C. of C., 1992, Mgr. of Yr. 2000 award Soc. Advancement of Mgmt. Mem. U.S./Mexico Found. (trustee 1990—), Latin Bus. Assn. (bd. dirs. 1992-93), World Trade Ctr. Assn. Republican. Roman Catholic. Avocations: travel, arts, hiking, walking on the beach. Home: 17532 Wayne Ave Irvine CA 92614-6658 Office: Elan Internat 620 Newport Center Dr Fl 11 Newport Beach CA 92660-6420

DEGENER, CAROL M. lawyer; d. John Michael and Marie-Laure Degener. BA, MA, Columbia U.; JD, Harvard U. Bar: Mass. 1988, N.Y. 1990. Assoc. corp. fin. Goldman Sachs & Co., N.Y.C.; assoc. corp. dept. Donovan Leisure Newton & Irvine, N.Y.C., counsel corp. fin. dept. Seward & Kissel LLP, N.Y.C. Office: Seward & Kissel LLP 1 Battery Park Plz Fl 20 New York NY 10004-1405

DEGENERES, ELLEN, actress, comedienne; b. Metairie, LA, Jan. 26, 1958; d. Elliott and Betty DeGeneres. Began career as emcee local comedy club, New Orleans; performer various comedy clubs. Comedian (TV spls.) Young Comedians Reunion, HBO, Women of the Night, 1986, Command Performances: One Night Stand, 1989; author: My Point...And I Do Have One, 1995, The Funny Thing Is..., 2003; actor: (films) Coneheads, 1993, Mr. Wrong, 1996, Goodbye Lover, 1998, (voice) Dr. Doolittle, 1998, EDtv, 1999, The Love Letter, 1999, Reaching Normal, 1999, (voice of Dory) Finding Nemo, 2003 (Annie award for Outstanding Voice Acting in Animated Feature Prodn., 2004), : (TV films) On the Edge, 2001; (TV series) Open House, 1989, Laurie Hill, 1992; actor, exec. prodr. (TV films) If These Walls Could Talk 2, 2000, (TV series) The Ellen Show, 2001—02, actor, prodr., writer Ellen (originally named These Friends of Mine from 1993-94), 1993—98 (Emmy award for Outstanding Writing for Comedy Series, 1997, Peabody award, 1997), host, exec. prodr. The Ellen DeGeneres Show, 2003—, star, exec. prodr. (TV spls.) Ellen DeGeneres: The Beginning, 2000 (Am. Comedy award for Funniest Female Peformer in TV spl., 2001), Ellen DeGeneres: Here and Now, 2003, co-host 46th Annual Primetime Emmy Awards, 1994 (Am. Comedy award for Funniest Female Peformer in TV spl., 1995), host 53rd Annual Primetime Emmy Awards, 2001, 54th Annual Primetime Emmy Awards, 2002, 38th Annual Grammy Awards, 1996, 39th Annual Grammy Awards, 1997, VH1 Fashion Awards, 1998, VH1 Divas Las Vegas, 2002, appeared as herself (documentaries) Wisecracks, 1991. Recipient Funniest Person Am. for videotaped club performances in New Orleans, Showtime, 1982, Am. Comedy award for Funniest Female Stand-Up Comic, 1991, Golden Apple award as Female Discovery Yr., Hollywood Women's Press Club, 1994, Lucy award, 2000, Enduring Spirit award, Amnesty Internat., 2000.*

DE GETTE, DIANA LOUISE, congresswoman, lawyer; b. Tachikawa, Japan, July 29, 1957; came to U.S., 1957; d. Richard Louis and Patricia Anne (Rose) De G.; m. Lino Sigismondo Lipinsky de Orlov, Sept. 15, 1984; children: Raphaela Anne, Francesca Louise. BA magna cum laude, The Colo. Coll., 1979; JD, NYU, 1982. Bar: Colo. 1982, U.S. Dist. Ct. Colo. 1982, U.S. Ct. Appeals (10th cir.) 1984, U.S. Supreme Ct. 1989. Dep. state pub. defender Colo. State Pub. Defender, Denver, 1982-84; assoc. Coghill & Goodspeed, P.C., Denver, 1984-86; sole practice Denver, 1986-93; of counsel McDermott & Hansen, Denver, 1993-96; mem. Colo. Ho. of Reps., 1992-96, asst. minority leader, 1995-96; mem. U.S. Congress from 1st Colo. dist., 1997—; mem. commerce com. Editor: (mag.) Trial Talk, 1989-92. Mem. Mayor's Mgmt. Rev. Com., Denver, 1983-84; resolutions chair Denver Dem. Party, 1986; bd. dirs. Root-Tilden Program, NYU Sch. Law, N.Y.C., 1986-92; bd. trustees, alumni trustee Colo. Coll., Colorado Springs, 1988-94. Recipient Root-Tilden scholar NYU Sch. Law, N.Y.C., 1979, Vanderbilt medal, 1982. Mem. Colo. Bar Assn. (bd. govs. 1989-91), Colo. Trial Lawyers Assn. (bd. dirs., exec. com. 1986-92), Colo. Women's Bar Assn., Denver Bar Assn., Phi Beta Kappa, Pi Gamma Mu. Democrat. Avocations: reading, backpacking, gardening.*

DEGIOVANNI-DONNELLY, ROSALIE FRANCES, biology researcher, educator; b. Bklyn., Nov. 22, 1926; d. Frank and Rose (Quartuccio) DeGiovanni; m. Edward Francis Donnelly, Sept. 23, 1961; children: Edward F. Jr., Francis M. BA, Bklyn. Coll., 1947, MA, 1953; PhD, Columbia U., 1961. Adj. prof. microbiology and genetics George Washington U., Washington, 1968—; rsch. biologist FDA, Washington, 1968-88. Contbr. articles to profl. jours. Recipient Merit award FDA, 1970. Mem. AAAS, AAUW, Italian Cultural Soc., Environ. Mutagen Soc., N.Y. Acad. Scis., Am. Soc. Microbiology, McLean Indoor Club, Sigma Xi, Sigma Delta Epsilon. Democrat. Roman Catholic. Avocations: theater, swimming, tennis, travel, photography. Home: 1712 Strine Dr Mc Lean VA 22101-4744 Office: George Washington U Microbiology Dept Washington DC 20052-0001 E-mail: edndol@earthlink.net.

DE GRAMONT, CAROL CARMEL, writer; b. Cin., Dec. 15, 1934; d. A. Gerson and Cyrilla Elaine Carmel; m. Georges Louis de Gramont, Nov. 3, 1961; children: Alexandre, Nina. BA, Sarah Lawrence Coll., 1956; postgrad., U. Cin., 1958. Copywriter Reader's Digest, N.Y.C., 1958—61. Contbr. stories to literary mags. Mem.: Englewood Writers Club. Avocations: theater, films, reading literature, physical fitness. Home: 182 E Linden Ave Englewood NJ 07631

DEGRENIA, LISA ANN MOSS, minister; d. Kent Evan and Lee Oma Russell Moss; m. Edward Arthur Degrenia, Mar. 18, 1989; children: Elyse Christine, Laura Kathleen. BS Music Edn. summa cum laude, U. So. Fla., Tampa, FL, 1984—88; MDiv summa cum laude, Duke Div. Sch., Duke U., Durham, NC, 1996—2000. Ordination as Elder United Meth. Ch., Fla. Conf., 2003. Assoc. pastor St. Paul United Meth. Ch., Largo, Fla., 2000—01; sr. pastor Allendale United Meth. Ch., St. Petersburg, Fla., 2001—. Hymn resources Sermonwriter, 1999—. Recipient Hoyt Hickman Award for Excellence in Liturgics, Order of St. Luke, 2000.

DEHART, DEBORAH LEE, private school educator, composer; b. Woodbury, N.J., Nov. 26, 1953; d. John Walter and Doris Ray DeH.. Cert. music tchr. K-12 Del., 1977. Theory tchr. dept. chair Wilmington (Del.) Music Sch., 1976—84; mgr. Minikin Opera Co., Wilmington, Del., 1976—80; music tchr. St. Edmond's Acad., Wilmington, 1977—, dept. chair, 2001—; founder, pres., gen. mgr. Shoestring Prodns., Ltd., Wilmington, 1977—; pvt. tchr., 1977—. Author, composer: music theater for youth, 30 titles, 1981—; composer: (commd. works for) Longwood Gardens, Hellenic Soc., Del. Assn. Early Childhood. Mem.: Del. Music Educators Assn., Music Educators Nat. Conf. Avocations: costuming, gardening, travel, history, reading. Office: 705 Brandywine Blvd Wilmington DE 19809

DEHART, EILEEN, state legislator; b. Sept. 15, 1948; Grad., Mich. State U. Staff Rep. Justine Barns; rep. Mich. State Dist. 18, 1995—. Conservation, environ. and Great Lakes com. Mich. Ho. Reps., sr. citizens com., vet. affairs com. Address: Mich Ho of Reps PO Box 30014 Lansing MI 48909-7514

DEHART, KAREN TRAUTMANN, artist, educator; b. Pitts., Nov. 11, 1953; d. Elmer Martin and Jane Anne (Hesse) T.; m. Shannon Dean DeHart, May 23, 1976; children: Allison Anne, Rebekah Ellen, Rachel Elisabeth. AA, Miami U., 1975, BFA summa cum laude, Wright State U., 1991. Art instr. Troy-Hayner Cultural Ctr., Troy, Ohio, 1991-94; artist Troy, Ohio, 1990—; art tchr., 1991—; drawing tchr. Troy Christian Schs., Troy, Ohio, 1991-92; teaching asst. Wright State Univ., Dayton, Ohio, 1993. Exhibition comm. Troy-Hayner Cultural Ctr., 1991—; chmn. Through Our Eyes Exhibit, 1993-95; adj. instr. Wright State U., 1996. Solo exhbns. include Preble County Fine Arts Ctr., Eaton, Ohio, 1994, The Crandall Gallery Mount Union Coll., Alliance, Ohio, 1995, MacMurray Coll. Art Gallery, Jacksonville, Ill., 2002; exhibited in group shows at Bowery Gallery, N.Y., 1992, Butler Inst., 1994, 95, 96, 97, 98, Margaret Kaulback exhibitor, Trumbull Art Gallery, 1994, Dayton Visual Arts Ctr., 1992, Mus. of Contemporary Art, Wright State U., 1991, 97, Dayton Visual Arts Ctr., 1992, 97, Butler Inst. Am. Art, 1993, 94, 95, 97, 98, Pearl Conard Gallery, 1993, 94, Rosewood Art Ctr. Gallery, Kettering, Ohio, 1993, Olin Fine Arts Ctr. Gallery, Washington and Jeffrson Coll., Washington, Pa., 1994, 97, Books & Co., Kettering, Ohio, 1994, Fine Arts Inst. San Bernardino County Mus., Redlands, Calif., 1994, Evansville (Ind.) Mus. Arts and Sci., 1994, Wichita (Kans.) Ctr. Arts, 1994, Stables Art Gallery, Taos, N. Mex., 1995, Gallery Alexy, Phila., 1996, Hoyt Inst. Fine Arts, New Castle, Pa., 1997, Troy (Ohio)-Hayner Cultural Ctr., 1997, Valdosta State U. Gallery, Valdosta, Ga., 2002; featured in Nexus Mag., 1990, Art Duck, 1989-91, Dayton Daily News, 1992, 98, Alliance Review, 1995. Com. mem. Troy C. of C., 1993; ad hoc mem. Troy-Hayner Cultural Ctr., 1992, chamn. photography exhibit, 1993-95, chmn. sister-city art exchange Troy-Takahashi City, Japan, 1995-96, mem. exhib. com., 1991-96; curriculum com. Troy Christian Schs., 1992-94. Recipient Grumbacher Gold medallion 16th ann. Hoyt Nat., 1997, 26th Nat. Painting Show, 1994, Winsor Newton award Fine Arts Inst., 1994, Evansville Mus. Contemporaries Purchase award, 1994, Jurors Choice award Butler Inst. Am. Art, 1994, Margaret Kaulback award, 1997, Best of Show award Rosewood Art Ctr., 1992, Award of Excellence Edison State C.C., 1989; Spl. Talent scholar Wright State U., 1989-91. Mem. Dayton Visual Arts Ctr., Phi Kappa Phi, Chi Omega. Home and Office: 1498 Cheshire Rd Troy OH 45373-2602

DE HARVEN, GERRY S. healthcare educator, consultant; b. Chgo. BS in Psychology, U. Ill., 1949. Adminstrv. asst. Sloan-Kettering Inst. Cancer Rsch., 1962—66, Am. Cancer Soc., 1966—93, v.p. internat. activities, 1982—93; staff asst. fgn. svc. Dept. State, Wash., Italy, Egypt, Thailand, 1954—61. Cons. Commn. on Cancer Control, Com. on Voluntary Orgns. Internat. Union Against Cancer, Geneva, 1970—93. Vol. coord. Atlanta Humane Soc. Recipient Disting. Svc. award, Internat. Union Against Cancer. Mem.: Cancer Soc. New Zealand (life; hon.), Israel Cancer Assn. (life; hon.), Queensland (Australia) Cancer Fund (life; hon.). Home: 1804 Rockridge Pl NE Atlanta GA 30324

DEHAVEN-BINGER, JEANINE KAY, special education educator; b. Monroe, Wis., Dec. 1, 1977; d. William Don and Debra Kay DeHaven; m. Daniel Ray Binger, June 15, 2002. AA, Highland C.C., 1998; BS in Edn., No. Ill. U., 2000. Paraprofl. Walter Lawson Children's Home, Loves Park, Ill., 1998—2000, day tng. instr., 2000; spl. edn. tchr. Hononegah H.S. Dist. 207, Rockton, Ill., 0200—. Salesperson Mary Kay Cosmetics, Roscoe, Ill., 0002—; volleyball coach Hononegah Indians, Rockton, 2000—03. Home: 9573 Cinnabar Dr Roscoe IL 61073

DE HAVILLAND, OLIVIA MARY, actress; b. Tokyo, July 1, 1916; naturalized, 1941; d. Walter Augustus and Lilian Augusta (Ruse) de H. (parents British subjects); m. Marcus Goodrich, Aug. 26, 1946 (div.); 1 child, Benjamin Briggs Goodrich (dec.); m. Pierre Galante, Apr. 2, 1955 (div.); 1 child, Gisele. Student schs. and convent in, Calif.; Ph.D (hon.), Am. U., Paris, 1994. Made stage debut as Hermia in: Midsummer Night's Dream (Max Reinhardt prodn.), Hollywood Bowl, 1934; 1st motion picture in same role, 1935; actress: (films) including Captain Blood, Anthony Adverse, Robin Hood, Gone With the Wind (nominated for Acad. award 1939), Strawberry Blonde, Hold Back The Dawn (nominated for Acad. award 1941), Princess O'Rourke, To Each His Own (Acad. award for best actress 1946), Dark Mirror, The Snakepit (nominated for Acad. award 1948, N.Y. Critics Award 1948, Laurel Award for best performance 1948-53), The Heiress (Acad. award for best actress 1949, N.Y. critics award), My Cousin Rachel 1952, Not As A Stranger, 1954, Ambassador's Daughter, 1955 (Belgian Critics Prix Femina), Proud Rebel, 1957, Light in the Piazza, 1961, Lady in a Cage, 1963 (British films and filming award), Hush, Hush Sweet Charlotte, 1964, Airport '77, 1976, The Swarm, 1978, The Fifth Musketeer, 1979; TV appearances include Noon Wine, 1966, The Screaming Woman, 1972, Roots: The Next Generations, 1979, Murder is Easy, 1981, Charles and Diana: A Royal Romance, 1982, North and South, II, 1986, Anastasia: The Mystery of Anna, 1986 (Golden Globe award, Emmy nomination), The Woman He Loved, 1988; theatre includes (on Broadway) Romeo and Juliet, 1951, Candida, 1952, A Gift of Time, 1962, (summer stock) What Every Woman Knows, Westport, Conn., Easthampton, Long Island, 1946, Candida, same plus 9 other summer theatres, 1951; (legitimate) Transcontinental Tour Candida 1951-52, (245 Performances); lecture tours, U.S., 1971-80; toured Army and Navy hosps. in U.S., Alaska, Aleutians, South Pacific, 1943-44, Europe, 1957-61; pres. jury Cannes Film Festival, 1965; participant: narration of France's Bicentennial gift to U.S. Son et Lumiere, 1976, Bicentennial Service, Am. Cathedral in Paris, 1976; author: Every Frenchman Has One, 1962. Trustee Am. Coll. in Paris, 1970-71, Am. Libr. in Paris, 1974-81. Recipient Women's Nat. Press Club award for outstanding accomplishment in theater presented by Pres. Truman, 1950; Am. Legion Humanitarian award, 1967; Hon. degree of Doctor of Humane Letters from The Am. U. of Paris, 1994. Mem. Screen Actors Guild, Acad. of Motion Picture Arts and Scis. Democrat. Address: BP 156 75764 Paris Cedex 16 France

DEHN, VIRGINIA, visual artist; b. Nevada, Mo. d. Finis Ewing and Ruby Grayson (Lane) Engleman; m. Adolf Arthur Dehn, Nov. 12, 1947 (dec. May

1968). AA, Stephens Coll., 1941; student, Traphagen Sch Design, 1941-42, Art Students League, N.Y.C., 1953, 54. One-woman shows include Caravan Galleries, N.Y.C., 1974, Discovery Gallery, Montclair, N.J., 1977, Capicorn Gallery, Bethesda, Md., 1979, Washington Coll., Chestertown, Md., 1983, Carlin Gallery, Ft. Worth, Susan Teller Gallery, N.Y.C., 1989, Mus. Fine Arts, [illegible], 1993, Horwitch-Lew Allen Gallery, 1996, Richmond Art Ctr., Windsor, Conn., 1996, Cline-Lew Allen Contemporary Gallery, 1997, Lew Allen Contemporary Gallery, 2001, Am. Inst. Arts and Letters; group shows include Fine Arts Am., Gallery, Richmond, Va., 1983, Hick St. Gallery, Bklyn., others; represented in permanent collections Herbert F. Johnson Mus., Ithaca, N.Y., Columbus Mus. Art, Ohio, Butler Inst. Am. Art, Youngstown, Ohio, U. Calif. Berkeley, Castellon Meml. Collection, Columbia U., N.Y.C., N.Y. Pub. Libr., N.Y.C., State of Minn. Hist. Soc., Vivian and Gordon Gilkey Graphic Art Collection, Portland Art Mus., Oreg., AmerWest Fin. Ctr., Albuquerque, Springfield (Mass.) Mus. Fine Art, Albuquerque Internat. Airport, others. MacDowell Colony fellow, Yaddo fellow, Ossabaw Island Project fellow. Mem. Soc. Layerists in Multi-Media (a founder). Home: 524 Camino Militar Santa Fe NM 87501-5972

DEHN-WITTKE, BARBARA ANN, music educator; b. Buffalo, Aug. 27, 1947; d. George John Schiller and Thelma Dorothy Schiller-Barnes; m. Oskar Wittke, July 21, 2001; children: Richard William Dehn, John Charles Dehn, Bardley Aaron Dehn. BME magna cum laude, U. Tulsa, 1992. Dir. cir. state with song OMEA, Tulsa, 1996—98; vol. ARC, 1980—95. Clarinetist Tulsa Starlight Band, 1999—2002. Soloist performer Immanuel Luth. Ch., Broken Arrow, Okla., 1992—2003. Scholar, Sigma Alpha Iota, 1991, Okla. Fall Arts Inst., Okla. Arts Coun., 1992, 1994, 1995, 1996. Mem.: Am. Fedn. Musicians, Music Educators Nat. Conf., Sigma Alpha Iota (life; v.p. programs 1999—2001). Conservative. Lutheran. Avocations: travel, needlecrafts, painting, reading. Home: 6505 E 27th St Tulsa OK 74129-6109 Office: Mannford Pub Schs 220 Evans Mannford OK 74044 E-mail: dwitkeb@mannford.k12.ok.us.

DEHORITY, MIRIAM A. (MIRIAM NEWMAN), artist; b. Hampton, Ga., Jan. 6, 1928; d. David Johnson and Ethel (Sloan) Arnold; m. William Truslow Newman, Feb. 12, 1954 (dec.); children: David Arnold Newman, William Truslow III Newman; m. Edward Havens DeHority, Jr., Jan. 1, 1984. BA, Agnes Scott Coll., 1949; student, Atlanta Sch. Art, 1953-55, Ga. State U., 1959-60, Chatov Studios, 1961-63. One-woman shows include Water Color Soc. Ala., Mont., 1963 (1st award), Am. Water Color Soc.-Nat. Acad. Galleries, NYC, 1966, Patricia Cloutier Gallery, 2000, 2002, 2 person show, Heath Gallery, Atlanta, 1968, Soc. Fine Arts, Palm Beach, Fla., 1999, Soc. of 4 Arts, Palm Beach., 1999, Patricia Cloutier Gallery, 2002, William Truslow Newman II, exhibited in group shows at Atlanta Art Assocs., 1958—62, High Mus. Art, Atlanta, 1965, 1971, Soc. Contemporary Art, Mobile, Ala., 1969, Mus. Arts and Sci., Macon, Ga., 1972, Heath Gallery, 1972, Swan Coach House Gallery, Atlanta, 1983, 1988, Patricia Cloutier Gallery, Jupiter, Fla., 1992, 1999—2000, Lighthouse Gallery, Jupiter, 1997, John Collette Gallery, Highland, N.C., 2003, Patricia Cloutier Gallery, 2003, represented in permanent collections. Founding pres. Members Guild High Mus., Atlanta, 1966; bd. dirs. High mus. Art, Atlanta, 1966-67, Atlanta Arts Alliance, 1966-67, Jr. League of Atlanta, 1958-68. Recipient First award Ala. Water Color Soc., 1963. Avocations: gardening, cooking, design, tennis, golf.

DE HOYOS, DEBORA M. lawyer; b. Monticello, N.Y., Aug. 10, 1953; d. Luis and Marion (Kinney) de Hoyos; m. Walter C. Carlson, June 20, 1981; children: Amanda, Greta, Linnea. BA, Wellesley Coll., 1975; JD, Harvard U., 1978. Bar: Ill. 1978, U.S. Dist. Ct. (no. dist.) Ill. 1980. Assoc. Mayer, Brown & Platt, Chgo., 1978—84, ptnr., 1985—, mng. ptnr., 1991—. Bd. dirs. Evanston Northwestern Healthcare; bd. trustees Providence St. Mel. Sch. Contbr. chpt. to Securitization of Financial Assets, 1991. Trustee Chgo. Symphony Orch. Office: Mayer Brown & Platt 190 S La Salle St Ste 3100 Chicago IL 60603-3441

DEILY, LINNET FRAZIER, ambassador; b. Dallas, June 20, 1945; d. William Harold and Ruth (White) Frazier; m. Myron Bonham Deily, Apr. 18, 1981. BA, U. Tex. Austin, 1967; MA, U. Tex. Dallas, 1976. Banking officer, asst. v.p., v.p. Republic Bank, Dallas, 1975—80, sr. v.p., 1980—81; v.p. First Interstate Bancorp, L.A., 1981—83; sr. v.p., divsn. mgr. First Interstate Bank of Calif., L.A., 1983—84, exec. v.p., 1988; chmn., pres., CEO First Interstate Bank of Tex., 1988—96; pres. Schwab Institutional, 1996—98, Schwab Retail Group, 1998—2001; vice chmn. Charles Schwab Corp., 2000—01; dep. U.S. trade rep. Geneva, 2001—. Bd. dirs. First Interstate Inst., L.A. Mem.: Univ. Club L.A. (fin. com.). Office: World Trade Orgn Centre William Rappard Rue de Lausanne 154 CH-1211 21 Geneva Switzerland*

DEIOTTE, MARGARET WILLIAMS TUCKEY, nonprofit consultant, grants writer; b. Lafayette, Ind., Mar. 6, 1952; d. Ronald B. and Elizabeth A. (Williams) Tukey; m. Charles E. Deiotte, Sept. 11, 1971 (dec.); children: Raymond, Karl, Ronald. Student, U. Wash., 1969-72, 77-79. V.p., treas. Logical Systems, Inc., Colorado Springs, 1982-86; v.p. CEDSYS, Inc., Colorado Springs, 1987-92; pres. Penrose Enrichment Program Found., Colorado Springs, Colo., 1988-89; free lance tech. and grant proposal writer, 1990—; dir. Rexall Showcase Internat., Boca Raton, Fla., 1994—. Conf. coord. Colo. Assn. Ptnrs. in Edn., 1994; editor Am. Boarding Kennels Assn., 1995-98; owner Outside The Box, 1996—, presenter seminar Pikes Peak Pace Conf., 1991, 92; presenter 20th annual nat. conf. Am. Boarding Kennels Assn. Mem. adv. bd. gifted and talented Sch. Dist. 11, 1989—, mem. dist. II found. bd., 1997—2004, OS/CR adv. coun. dist. II, 1999—2001; pres. Penrose Elem. PTA, 1989—91; 1st v.p. El Paso Coun. PTA, 1990—91, treas., 1991—92; mem. grants commn. Colo. State PTA, 1990—91; coach Odyssey of the Mind, 1990, 1991—92, 1995—96; mem. dist. accountability com. Sch. Dist. 38, 1993—94; accountability chmn. Lewis-Palmer Mid. Sch.; mem. gifted and talented com. Sch. Dist. # 38; mem. parent bd., internat. baccalaureate Palmer High Sch., Colorado Springs, Colo., 1994—97, treas., 1995—96, pres., 1996—97; bd. dir. YMCA Youth Leadership Inst., 1990—92, 1992—93, Independence Cmty. Fund, 2001—. Mem.: Assn. Fundraising Profls., Assn. Fundraising Profls. Home and Office: 1221 Mount View Ln Colorado Springs CO 80907-4722

DEISSLER, MARY ALICE, foundation executive; b. Oneanta, N.Y., Dec. 30, 1955; d. George W. and Carol (Zorda) Baker; m. James N. Deissler, Nov. 24, 1987; children: Benjamin, Eliza. BA, U. Mass., 1978; MBA, Babson Coll., 1982. Fin. analyst Digital Equipment Corporation, Maynard, Mass., 1978-82; devel. dir. Handel & Haydn Soc., Boston, 1984-89, gen. mgr., 1984-89, exec. dir., 1990—. Pres., bd. dirs. Studebaker Movement Theatre Co., Boston, 1986-88. Bd. dirs. Early Music Am., N.Y.C., 1989—, v.p., 1991—, pres., 1994; bd. dirs. Babson Coll., 1990-94, Chorus Am., 1991—, v.p., 1992, pres.-elect, 1996, pres., 1997, pres. bd. dirs., 1997; mem. bd. Arts/Boston, 1994—, pres. bd. dirs., 2003; bd. dirs. Am. Composers Fourm, 2000, Berkshire Choral Soc., 2000—; treas. Handel House of Am. Found. Mem. Am. Symphony Orch. League. Office: Handel & Haydn Soc 300 Massachusetts Ave Boston MA 02115-4544

DEITERS, SISTER JOAN ADELE, psychoanalyst, nun, chemistry educator; b. Cincinnati, Apr. 28, 1934; d. Alfred Harry and Rose Catherine (Rusche) D. BA, Coll. Mt. St. Joseph, Cin., 1963; PhD, U. Cin., 1967; M in Christian spirituality, Creighton U., Omaha, 1985. Joined Sisters of Charity, Roman Cath. Ch., 1952; cert. psychoanalyst, Westchester Inst. for Tng. in Psychoanalysis and Psychotherapy, 2000. Prof. chemistry Coll. Mt. St. Joseph, Cin., 1969-78; Matthew Vassar Jr. chair Vassar Coll., Poughkeepsie, NY, 1978-96. Contbg. articles to profl. jour. Mem. Am. Chem. Soc., Sisters of Charity, Sigma Xi; Nat. Assn. for Advancement of Psychoanalysis. Home: 73A Raymond Ave Poughkeepsie NY 12603-3117 Office: 39 Collegeview Ave Poughkeepsie NY 12603-2415

DEITZ, PAULA, magazine editor; b. Trenton, N.J., Apr. 26, 1938; d. David and Rosalie (Nathanson) D.; m. (George) Frederick Morgan, Nov. 30, 1969. BA, Smith Coll., 1959; MA, Columbia U., 1969. Asst. editor Bollingen series Bollingen Found., N.Y.C., 1962-67; assoc. editor The Hudson Rev., N.Y.C., 1967-75, co-editor, 1975-98, editor, pres., 1998—. Rsch. asst. Pakistan Mission to UN, N.Y.C., 1961; lectr. Columbia U., N.Y.C., 1962. Contbr. articles on art, architecture, landscape design to newspapers and mags. Bd. counselors Smith Coll., 1992-96. Mem. Cosmopolitan Club, Colony Club. Avocation: swimming. Office: The Hudson Rev 684 Park Ave New York NY 10021-5043

DEITZ, SUSAN ROSE, columnist; b. Far Rockaway, N.Y., Mar. 21, 1934; d. Emanuel and Florence Jean (Goodstein) Davis; m. Morris J. Mandelker, Nov. 29, 1975; 1 child, Scott Richard; m. Richard Alan Deitz, Dec. 22, 1958 (dec. 1967). Student, Smith Coll., Barnard Coll., N.Y.C., Art Students League, Stella Adler Theater Studio. Advice columnist L.A. Times Syndicate, 1975-2000; syndicated columnist Creators Syndicate, 2000—. Faculty New Sch., N.Y.C., 1977-79; radio personality, 1979; singles expert Prodigy Svcs., White Plains, N.Y., 1987-93; spkr. satellite conf. NAFE, 1990; lectr. L.A. Times Syndicate Spkrs. Bur.; guest expert iVillage.com. Author: Valency Girl, 1976, Single File, 1989, paperback edit., 1990. Honored Single Parent Resource Ctr., N.Y.C., 2001. Mem. Women in Comm. (Outstanding Member award 1984), Authors Guild, Newspaper Features Assn., Overseas Press Club (elect.), Smith Coll. Club. Achievements include being online resident expert fidget.com., southJersey.com, Lipetnights.com, divorceinteractive.com, ivillage.com. E-mail: sumor123@aol.com.

DEJA, HEIDI, newscaster; Reporter, Wilkes-Barre, Pa., Erie, Pa., St. Louis; anchor, reporter Mpls.; anchor NBC 17, Raleigh, NC, 1999—. Announcer Spl. Olympics; vol. Exploris, Raleigh. Office: NBC 17 Studios 1205 Front St Raleigh NC 27609

DEJACK, JACQUELINE ELVADEANA, artist, educator; b. St. Louis, Oct. 9, 1938; d. John Allen and Margie Louise (Cooksey) Williams; m. James Patrick DeJack (dec. June 1994); children: Jennifer Lynn, John Patrick. Student, St. Louis U, 1966-67, Webster Coll., 1978-79; AA, East Ctrl. U., 1979; student, U. Mo., 1998. Lic. real estate agt., Mich.; cert. broker sales and tchr. broker, Mo. Sales staff Hudsons Dept. Store, Detroit, 1957; with First Fed. Savs., Detroit, 1961-62; cons. to libr. dir. St. Louis U., 1965-66; bank cons., ins. mgr. Willston (Mo.) State Bank, 1967-68; co-founder, broker, cons. Tri County Real Estate, Pacific, Mo., 1971-89; pvt. practice artist and writer Jacqueline's Affordable Graphics, Pacific, Mo., 1993-2001; broker, sales Hickenbotham Real Estate, 2000-2001. Fine art tchr., cons. Six Flags Over Mid-Am., Eureka, Mo., summer 1982. Supr. youth corp. St. Louis U., 1964; bd. mem. U. Mo., St. Louis, 1980; mem. Sears (Mich.) Writer's Guild, 1987. Mem. Cadillac Artis Guild, Phi Theta Kappa. Avocations: writing, art, history research, music, swimming.

DEJARNETTE, SHIRLEY SHEA, treasurer; b. Bradford, Pa., Feb. 21, 1943; d. James H. and Jean L. (Dennis) Shea; m. Jaquelin Harrison DeJarnette, Mar. 21, 1978; 1 child, Shea Ann. AA, Stephens Coll., Columbia, 1963; BS in Bus. Adminstrn., U. Mo., 1966; Program for Mgmt. Devel. Cert., Harvard U., 1982. CFA. Asst. trust officer Boatmen's Nat. Bank St. Louis, 1966-74; mgr. investor rels. Kraft, Inc., Glenview, Ill., 1974-77; dir. investment rsch. Cummins Engine Co., Columbus, Ind., 1977-78; asst. treas. Mead Corp., Dayton, Ohio, 1978-86; v.p., exec. Chase Manhattan Bank, N.Y.C., 1986-89; mng. dir. DeJarnette Inv Adv, Wintergreen, Va., 1989-90; asst. v.p. investment and banking U. Mo., Columbia, 1990—. Mem. adv. bd. TA Assocs. Realty, Boston, 1995-99, treas. 1999—. Mem. Leadership Dayton, 1983—; bd. trustees Stephens Coll., Columbia, Mo., 1992-96; bd. dirs. Mead Corp Found., Dayton, Ohio, 1986. Mem. Assn. Investment Mgmt. and Rsch. (mem. disciplinary review com.), St. Louis Soc. Fin. Analysts, Fin. Mgmt. Assn. Home: 2616 Johnson Dr Columbia MO 65203-1520 Office: U Mo Sys 215 University Hall Columbia MO 65211-3020

DEJESUS-BURGOS, SYLVIA TERESA, security and risk management officer; b. Rio Piedras, P.R., Puerto Rico, Jan. 13, 1941; came to U.S., 1961; d. Luis deJesus Correa and Maria Teresa (Burgos) deJesus. BA, Cen. U., Madrid, 1961. Sr. systems analyst H.D. Hudson Mfg. Co., Chgo., 1974-76; mgr. software engring. Morton Internat. Corp., Chgo., 1976-87; prodn. and dist. systems mgr. Kraft Foods divsn. Phillip Morris, Glenview, Ill., 1987-94; mgr. info. tech. svcs. Equate Petrochem. Corp. (Kuwait) joint venture Dow Chemical Co./ Union Carbide, 1994—2001; chief info. security and privacy officer Visteon Corp., 2001—. Editor U. Minn. Mgmt. Info. Systems Jour., 1984—. Pres. Chgo. chpt. Nat. Conf. Puerto Rican Women, 1980-83, nat. v.p. 1981-82; bd. dirs. Midwest Women's Ctr., 1980-82, YWCA, Chgo., 1982-84, Gateway Found. Substance Abuse Prevention and Rehab., 1986-87; v.p. communications Hispanic Alliance for Career Enhancements, 1986-87, bd. dirs. 1982-84, 91-92, chmn. bd., 1991-93; 1st v.p. Campfire Met. Chgo., 1982, bd. dirs. 1980-82; appointed to Selective Svc. Bd. by Ill. Gov. James Thompson, 1982; alt. del. Dem. Nat. Conv., N.Y.C., 1980; rep. Women in Mil. Svc. for Am. Meml., 1990-92. Served with USN, 1961-64. Recipient Youth Motivation award Chgo. Assn. Commerce and Industry, 1978-82, 86, YWCA Leadership award, 1980, 84, H.L. Kroft Achievement award, 1994. Mem. Women in Computing, Info. Systems Planners Assn., Navy League, Am. Legion. Republican. Roman Catholic. Office: PO Box 1449 Ann Arbor MI 48104-1449 also: Visteon Corp 5900 Mercury Dr Dearborn MI 48126

DE KANTER, ADRIANA ALISON, federal agency administrator; BA in hist., Mount Holyoke Coll., 1977; MPA, U. Tex., Austin, 1980. Dir. policy tech. analysis, support, planning evaluation svc. US Dept Edn., Under Sec. Edn., Wash., 2002—; partnership liaison US Dept. Edn., Elem. Secondary Edn., Academic Improvement Demo. Programs, Wash., 2001—03; spec. adv. afterschool issues US Depte. Edn., Off. of Sec., 1999—2001; dep. dir. US Dept. Edn., Planning Evaluation Svc., 1993—99; dir. State Tex. Off. Gov., Austin, 1993—94, US Dept. Edn., Nat. Assessment Planning Evaluation Svc., Wash., 1991—93; lead program analyst to planning studies br. chief US Army, V Corps, Asst. Chief of Staff for Resources Mgmt., Frankfurt, Germany, 1987—91; regional rep. US Dept. Edn., Kans. City, Mo., 1986—87; program analyst US Dept. Edn. Planning Evaluation Svc., Wash., 1983—86; profl. staff mem. Subcom. Edn., Arts, and Humanities, US Senate, Wash., 1982—83; pres. mgmt. intern US Dept. Edn., Off. Planning and Budget, Wash., 1980—82; sec. Dept. Spanish and other Languages, U. Houston, Houston, 1977—78. Contbr. articles various profl. jours. Recipient Presidential Mgmt Internship award, 1980—82, US Meritorious Civilian Svc. award, 1990, Contribution award, Nat. Cmty. Edn. Assn., 2000, Publ. Svc. Excellence award, Pub. Pvt. Partnerships, 2002. Office: US Dept Edn Under Sec Edn 400 Maryland Ave SW FOB-6 Rm 6W115 Washington DC 20202

DE KANTER, ELLEN ANN, English and foreign language educator; b. Spokane, Wash., Mar. 10, 1926; d. George L. and Alison P. (Christy) Tharp; m. Scipio de Kanter, Feb. 2, 1949 (dec.); children: Scipio, Georgette, Robert, Adriana. BA, Mexico City Coll.-U. of Ams., 1947; MEd, U. Houston, 1972, MA in Spanish, 1974, EdD, 1979. Dir. bilingual edn., prof. U. St. Thomas, Houston, dir. bilingual edn., 1979—. Contbr. articles to profl. jours. 11 Tchr. Tng. grants undergrad. and grad. students, U. St. Thomas, 1986—. Mem. Nat. Assn. Bilingual Edn. (chmn. 1989 conf., program chair 1993 conf.), Houston Area Assn. Bilingual Edn. (pres. 1987-88), Inst. Hispanic Culture (bd. dirs. 1989-90). Home: 3015 Meadowview Dr Missouri City TX 77459-3308 Office: U St Thomas 3800 Montrose Blvd Houston TX 77006-4626 E-mail: dekanter@stthom.edu

DEKIEFFER, KITTY, volunteer; b. San Diego, Nov. 12, 1956; d. Robert Paul and Beverly Ann Cannon; m. Robert Coffin deKieffer, May 18, 1985; 1 child, Hunter Coffin. BA in Acctg., Calif. State U., Fullerton, 1979. Fin. mgr. NREL, Golden, Colo., 1981-84; asst. contr. Boulder (Colo.) Daily Camera, 1984-89; acctg. mgr. Career Track, Boulder, 1989-91. Hon. trustee Boulder Philharm. Orch., pres., 1991—96; dir. Humane Soc. Blair Valley, pres., 1995—96; treas. Fran Ravanbush for Senate, Boulder, 1996; dir. YWCA Boulder County, pres., 1996—; trustee Womens FO of Colo., 1996—; dir. FO for Boulder Valley Schs., sec. and devel. chair and endowment chair, 1998—2002; vol. Douglas Elem. Sch., 1994—2000, Platt vol., 2000—03; dir. Women in the Wilderness Inst., 2000—, pres.; project team Boulder County Attention Homes; fundraising chair Boulder Cmty. Hosp. Aux.; capital campaign chair YWCA Boulder County, 2000—04, Peak to Peak chpt., 2003—; trustee Boulder County Mental Health Found., 2003—04; com. mem. Cmty. for Devel.; treas. Trinity Luth. Ch., 1997—99. Recipient Women Who Light Up Cmty. award Boulder C. of C., 1997, Vol. award 2000 Pacesetter of Boulder County, award Channel 9 (NBC) 9 Who Care, 2000. Mem.: Alpha Chi Omega (past officer and current trustee of AXR Found.). Republican. Lutheran. Home: 3002 Melissa Ln Boulder CO 80301-4841

DEKUYPER, MARY HUNDLEY, non-profit consultant; b. Syracuse, N.Y., Feb. 23, 1939; d. Edwin Graves and Edna Thompson (Smith) Hundley; m. Frederick Timothy DeKuyper, June 17, 1961; children: Gordon, Sarah. AB, Wellesley Coll., 1960. Adminstr. Calvert Sch., Balt., 1960-65; cons., 1981—. Cons. Assn. Governing Bds., Washington, 1992—, BoardSource, Washington, 1992—; nat. chair vols. ARC, 2000—. Author: Trustee Handbook, 1998, 2003. Pres. Bryn Mawr Sch. Bd., 1984—88; mem. exec. com. Planned Parenthood Md., 1989—98, chair nominating com., 1989—90, chair devel. com., 1990—92, chair strategic planning com., 1992—94, vice chair bd., 1990—96, chair com. bd. devel., 1994—96, vice chair, 1997—98; chair bd. dirs. ARC Greater Chesapeake and Potomac Blood Region, 1992—94, chair bd. devel. com., 1994—96, ex-officio, 1997—99, bd. dirs., 1999—2000; exec. com. ARC Ctrl. Md. chpt., 1989—92, chair blood svcs. com., 1988—92, vice chair bd., 1990—92, chair transition com., 1991, vice chair bd., 1996, chair bd., 1996—98, hon. bd. dirs., 1999—; pub. support com. ARC Nat. Bd. Govs., 1993—99, ex-officio, 2000—, vice chair biomed. svcs. bd., 1994—96, vice chair audit com., 1996—99, history and edn. ctr. adv. bd., 1996—, exec. com., 1996—99, ex-officio, 2000—; pres. nat. bd. Girls, Inc., 1986—90, chair nat. adv. com. trustee edn. project, 1992—95, trustee educator, 1995—; bd. dirs. United Way of Ctrl. Md., 1996—, mem. exec. com.; bd. dirs. Union Meml. Hosp. Found., 1999—2001, Planned Parenthood Md. Found., 1997—2000; vol. Ctrl., 2000, Far Hills Country Day Sch., 2000—, Clara Barton Fed. Credit Union, 2001—; Trustee Enoch Pratt Free Libr., Balt., 2002—; mem. fin. commn. Episcopal Diocese Md., 1993—97, chair program and budget com., 1995—98. Named to, Md.'s Top 100 Women, 1996, 2002; recipient William J. Casey award, 1989, Mary H. DeKuyper Trustee Svc. award, Bryn Mawr Sch., 1989, Exemplary Cmty. Svc. award, Health and Welfare Coun., 1990, Mary H. DeKuyper award, ARC Greater Chesapeake and Potomac Blood Region, 1994, Clementine Peterson award, United Way Ctrl. Md., ARC Nat. Harriman award, 2000. Mem. Jr. League Balt. (pres. 1975-77, Sustainer award 1988), Hamilton St. Club (treas. 1991-95), Wellesley Coll. Club. Democrat. Episcopalian. Home: 4422 Underwood Rd Baltimore MD 21218-1150 Office: ARC 2025 E St NW Washington DC 20006 E-mail: dekuyperm@usa.redcross.org., deluyper@ix.netcom.com.

DELACATO, JANICE ELAINE, learning consultant, educator; b. Bklyn., June 6, 1926; d. Frode Siegfried and Vilma (Rili) Fernstrom; m. Carl Henry Delacato, June 20, 1951; children: Elizabeth Delacato Putnam, Carl Henry, David Fernstrom. AB, Bryn Mawr Coll., 1948. Tchr. Rydal Hall, Ogontz Sch., Pa., 1948-49, The Spence Sch., N.Y.C., 1949-50, Chestnut Hill Acad., Phila., 1950-52; co-dir. The Chestnut Hill Reading Clinic, Phila., 1951-65, Delacato & Delacato Cons. in Learning, Phila., 1972-88; mgr. Morton (Pa.) Book Store, 1972-88; co-dir. The Delacato & Delacato Conf. Autism & Learning Disabilities, 1979-82. Editor newsletter Temple U. Med. Ctr. Women's Aux., Phila., 1953-65; class editor Bryn Mawr Coll. Alumnae Bull., 1966-79. Chmn. fund-raising com. Springside Sch., 1969-71; treas. Main St. Fair Antiques Booth, Chestnut Hill Hosp., 1965-77. Recipient Main St. Fair award Chestnut Hill Hosp., 1972. Mem. AAUW, Phila. Cricket Club. Republican. Unitarian Universalist. Home: Apt 1014 Lincoln Woods 9801 Germantown Pike Lafayette Hill PA 19444

DE LACERDA, MARIA ASSUNÇAÕ ESCOBAR, social worker, consultant; b. Cedros, Faial, Portugal, Aug. 15, 1944; came to U.S., 1948; d. Antonio Garcia de Lacerda and Filomena Escobar de Lacerda. BA in Polit. Sci., U. R.I., 1966; MSW, U. Conn., 1972. Cert. ind. social worker, R.I. Social worker R.I. Dept. Social and Rehab. Svcs., 1969-78, supr., 1978-81, R.I. Dept. for Children and Their Families, 1982; supr. div. retardation and devel. disabilities R.I. Dept. Mental Health, Retardation and Hosps., 1982-90; social worker cons. Alternatives Inc., North Kingstown, R.I., 1990-92, Avatar, Inc., Warwick, R.I., 1992-97. Vol. Peace Corps, Paraguay, 1966-69; pres. bd. dirs. East Bay Community Mental Health Ctr., Barrington, R.I., 1982-85; mem. R.I. Coun. for Mental Health Ctr., 1982-85; chair phonathon U. R.I. Ann. Fund, 1988. Recipient Profl. Recognition award Ocean State Assn. Residential Resources, 1990. Mem. U. R.I. Alumni Assn. (sec. 1990-91). Democrat. Roman Catholic. Avocations: reading, gardening, cycling, travel. E-mail: mdelacerda@aol.com.

DELACERDA, MELISSA GRINER, lawyer; b. St. Petersburg, Fla., Mar. 17, 1952; d. Joseph Henry and Dorothy Jean (Stephens) G.; m. Fred G. DeLacerda, June 17, 1972. BS, Memphis State U., 1973; JD, U. Tulsa, 1979. Bar: Okla. 1979. Tchr., elem. sch., Crowley, La., 1974-75; sports reporter Daily Advertiser, Lafayette, La., 1974-75; assoc. firm Bird & Hochderffer, Stillwater, Okla., 1979-80; sole practice law, Stillwater, 1980— . Bd. dirs. Alcoholism Council Area Okla., 1981-82, Stillwater Domestic Violence Svcs., 1979—. Mem. Okla. Bar Assn. (pres. elect, 2002-03, pres. 2003-), Payne County Bar Assn. (sec. 1984), Am. Trial Lawyers Assn., Bus. and Profl. Women Stillwater (pres. 1985), Stillwater C. of C. (ambassador 1982-84). Office: Law Office of Melissa DeLacerda 301 S Duck St PO Box 1252 Stillwater OK 74076

DELACOUR, JONELL, music educator; b. St. Joseph, Mo., Jan. 14, 1952; d. John David and Nellie Mae Roberts; m. Michael Gene Delacour, Nov. 8, 1975; 1 child, Jerad William. B in Music Therapy, U. Kans., 1974; MAT, St. Mary Coll., Leavenworth, Kans., 2002. Music therapist Larned (Kans.) State Security Hosp., 1975—83; paraprofl. Larned Sch. Dist., Garfield, 1983—90; vocal music tchr. United Sch. Dist. 447, Cherryvalle (Kans.) Middle/High Sch., 1991—2000; vocal/gen. music tchr. United Sch. Dist. 446, Independence (Kans.) Middle Sch., 2000—. Accompanist children's choir Ind. Area, 2002—. Bd. dirs. Independence Area Childrens' Choir, 2001—03. Mem.: Music Educators Nat. Conf., Kans. Choral Dirs. Assn., Kans. Music Educators Assn. (state tri-m chair 1999—2002, S.E. dist. ms choral chair 2001—03, S.E. dist. pres.-elect 2003—, SE Dist. Middle Sch. Outstanding Tchr. 2000). Office: Independence Middle Sch 300 W Locust Independence KS 67301 E-mail: jdelacour@indyschools.com.

DELAGARDELLE, LINDA, food executive; b. Waterloo, Mar. 15, 1953; d. Donald Leo D. and Leona Ann Reuter. AA in Biotechnology, Ellsworth C.C., Iowa Falls, Iowa, 1992; BS in Agronomy, Iowa State U., 1994. Owner, operator dairy farm, Jesup, Iowa, 1979-86; barber, stylist Kathy's Barber Shop, Alden, Iowa, 1986-94; rsch. lab asst. USDA, Ames, Iowa, 1992-94; intern Pioneer Hi-Bred Int., Kekaha, Hawaii, 1995; asst. agronomist Hudson (Iowa) Co-op, 1995-96; area supr. Seneca Foods Corp., Glencoe, Minn., 1996—. Carver scholar, 1992, Transfer scholar, 1992; Pell grantee, 1992. Mem. Nat. Rep. Com., 1996—; co-chair Children's Christmas Party, Glencoe, 1996-98; vice-chair Employee Fund Com., Glencoe, 1996-98; mem. United Fund Com., Glencoe, 1996-98. Mem. Glencoe C. of C. (annual banquet com.), Glencoe Country Club. Roman Catholic. Avocations: golf, biking, skiing, organ. Home: 210 Pleasant Ave Glencoe MN 55336

DE LAGUNA, FREDERICA, anthropology educator emeritus, writer, publisher; b. Ann Arbor, Mich., Oct. 3, 1906; d. Theodore and Grace Mead (Andrus) de L. AB, Bryn Mawr Coll., 1927; PhD, Columbia U., 1933; LHD (hon.), U. Alaska, Anchorage, 1982. Asst., field dir. U. Pa. Mus., Phila., 1931-35; assoc. soil conservationist U.S. Soil Conservation Svc., 1936; lectr. anthropology Bryn Mawr (Pa.) Coll., 1938-41, asst. prof., 1941-42, 46-49, assoc. prof., 1949-55, prof. anthropology, 1955-75, William R. Kenan, Jr. prof. emeritus, 1975—. Pub., Frederica de Laguna Northern Books Pub.; vis. lectr., vis. prof. U. Pa., U. Calif., Berkeley, Bryn Mawr Coll.; hon. curator Am. sect. U. Pa. Mus., 1983—. Author: The Thousand March: Adventures of an American Boy with Garibaldi, 1930, The Archaeology of Cook Inlet, Alaska, 1934, 1975, The Arrow Points to Murder, 1937, 1999, Fog on the Mountain, 1938; author Frederica de Laguna, 1995; co-author (with Kaj Birket-Smith): The Eyak Indians of the Copper River Delta, Alaska, 1938, Prehistory of North America as Seen From the Yukon, 1947, Chugach Prehistory: The Archaeology of Prince William Sound, 1956, 1967, The Story of a Tlingit Community, 1960; co-author: (with others) The Archaeology of the Yakutat Bay Area, Alaska, 1964, Under Mount Saint Elias: The History and Culture of the Yakutat Tlingit, 1972, Voyage to Greenland: A Personal Initiation Into Anthropology, 1977, 1995, Tales from the Dena, 1995, Travels Among the Dena: Exploring Alaska's Yukon Valley, 2000; editor: Selected Papers from the American Anthropologist 1888-1920, 1960, 1976, The Tlingit Indians (George Thornton Emmons), 1991, reprint, 2002; advisor, participant documentary film More Than Words, 1994, subject of documentary film Reunion Under Mt. St. Elias, 1996, subject spl. exhibit Pratt Mus., Homer, Alaska, 2000. Lt. comdr. USNR, 1942-45. Recipient Lindback award for disting. tchg., Bryn Mawr Coll., 1975, Rochester Mus. award and fellow, 1941, Inaugural award Contbn. to Alaska History award, Alaska Hist. Soc., 2001, Lucy Wharton Drexel medal for archaeology, U. Pa. Mus., 1999, fellow, Columbia U., 1930—31, NRC, 1936—37, Rockefeller Found., 1945—46, Wenner-Gren Found., 1949—50, Social Sci. Rsch. Coun., 1962—63; grantee, Am. Philos. ., Arctic Inst. of N.Am., 1973, Bryn Mawr Coll., NEH, NSF, U. Pa. Mus., Wenner-Gren Found. for Anthrop. Rsch. Fellow AAAS; mem. Am. Anthrop. Assn. (pres. 1966-67, Disting. Svc. award 1986), Arctic Inst. N.Am. (hon. life), NAS, Soc. for Am. Archaeology (1st v.p. 1949-50, 50th Ann. award 1986), No. Studies Assn. (internat. secretariat, hon. pres. 1991—), Phila. Anthropology Soc. (pres. 1939-40), Alaska Anthrop. Assn. (hon. life, award for lifetime contbn. to Alaskan anthropology 1993), Homer (Alaska) Natural History Soc. (hon. life, Silver Trowel award), Before Columbus Found. (Am. Lifetime Book award 1995). Democrat. Home and Office: 3300 Darby Rd # 1310 Haverford PA 19041-1067

DELAHANTY, LINDA MICHELE, dietician; b. Boston, Feb. 8, 1957; d. John Joseph and Helen Mary (Salami) D.; m. Paul Joseph Gorski, June 14, 1987. BS summa cum laude, U. Mass., 1978; MS summa cum laude, Boston U., 1980. Adminstrv. dietitian Joslin Diabetic Camp, Charlton, Mass., 1978; nutritional research asst. Lemuel Shattuck Hosp., Jamaica Plain, Mass., 1979; nutrition educator Home Med. Service-Univ. Hosps., Boston, 1980, Boston City Hosp., 1980-81; clin. dietitian Mass. Gen. Hosp., Boston, 1981-88, nutrition counselor, 1988—, rschr. Mass. Gen. Hosp. Diabetes Ctr., Boston, 1983—, chief dietitian, dir. nutrition and behavioral rsch., 2003—. Nutrition coord. Diabetes Control and Complications Trial, NIH, 1987—93, co-investigator Diabetes Prevention Program, 1996—2002; co-investigator LOOK AHEAD (Action for Health in Diabetes), 1999—; cons. New Eng. Diabetes and Endocrinology Ctr., Brookline, Mass., 1985—86; panelist NIH Consensuc Devel. Conf., Bethesda, Md., 1986, Am. Diabetes Assn. Consensus Statement on Self Monitoring of Blood Glucose, 1993; expert panelist TV series Doctors on Call, 1997; assoc. lectr. Harvard U. Geriatric Edn. Ctr., 1984—89; instr. Med. Sch. Harvard U., Cambridge, 2002—. Mem. editl. bd. Diabetes Spectrum, 1994-96, Diabetes Forecast, 2001—, Jour. Am. Dietetic Assn., 2002--; contbr. articles to profl. jours. Recipient Charles H. Best medal for Disting. Svc., Am. Diabetes Assn., 1994, Rschrs. award Am. Dietetic Assn., 1998, Mary P. Huddleston award, 2002; named Young Dietitian of Yr. Am. Dietetic Assn., 1984. Mem. Mass. Area Rehab. Dietitians (co-chair 1983-84), Diabetes Care and Edn. Practice Group (sec. 1985-87), Mass. Gerontol. Nutrition Practice Group (chair 1984-85), Mass. Dietetic Assn. (chair community dietetics div. 1983-84, coun. on practices), Am. Dietetic Assn. (area coord. gerontol. nutrition and dietetic practice group 1988-90). Roman Catholic. Avocations: skiing, photography, travel. Home: 18 Saybrook Rd Framingham MA 01701-7835 Office: Mass Gen Hosp Diabetes Ctr 50 Staniford St Ste 340 Boston MA 02114-2620 E-mail: ldelahanty@partners.org.

DELAHUNT, SUZANNE MARY, music educator, musician; b. Rockville Center, New York, June 19, 1958; d. Robert Joseph and Margaret Ann (Crown) Delahunt. BFA in Theatre, Adelphi Univ., Garden City, N.Y., 1980; MA, Bklyn. Coll., N.Y., 2004. Music tchr. N.Y.C. Bd. of Edn., N.Y.C., 1984—; dir. of music, organist St. Savior's, R.C., Bklyn., 1988—90, St. John Vianney, R.C., Queens, NY, 1992—96, St. Rose of Lima, R.C., Bklyn., 1996—2000, St. Vincent de Paul, R.C., Bklyn., 2000—03; magnet music dir., tchr. N.Y.C. Dept of Edn., Bklyn., 2000—. Musician, choral dir. Eyewitness News 7, N.Y.C., 1994, Fox 5 T.V. Sunday Mass, N.Y.C., 1996, Lunchtime Concerts Bklyn. boro pres. Markowitz, 2003; tchr. Music Memory, 2003 Riverside Symphony; choral dir. Met. Opera Guild, N.Y.C., 2002; coord. PAAP grant CAE, N.Y.C., 2002—. Composer (miscellaneous) songs; composer: Peace Please, 1992 (hon. mention, John Lennon Songwriting Contest, 1992); grant writer (parent string instrument) String Fling, PAAP, 2004. Musician, performer Guiliani's re-election cmty., St. Charles Boro, NY, 1998, Bridges to Learning Fund Raiser Roman Cath. Schools, Waldorf Astoria Hotel, NY, 2000; musician, choral dir. Bklyn. Boro Pres. Office, 2003. Mem.: Music Educators Nat. Cmty., N.Y.C. Music Teachers Assn., United Fedn. of Teachers. Democrat. Roman Catholic. Achievements include actor and singer in Pericles on permanent collection at Lincoln Ctr. Fine Arts Libr., N.Y.C., Artist Affiliate BMI, N.Y.C; composer of the P.S. 206 Sch. song, Bklyn., Guiness Book of Records Carol Sing, also an actor T.V., films, and movies i.e. HBO, NBC, Cinemax. Avocations: fitness, swimming, sailing, guitar, piano. Home: 6 New Lane Apt 1A Staten Island NY 10305-3128 Office: PS 206 2200 Gravesend Neck Rd Brooklyn NY 11229-4821 E-mail: delagirl2@aol.com.

DELANEY, ANNA T. director; b. Phila., May 5, 1963; d. John Ennis S. and Mary Agnes Schmidt; m. Daniel Robert Delaney, June 21, 1985; children: Daniel Robert Jr., Erin Rose. BS, St. John's U., Phila., 1985; postgrad., West Chester (Pa.) U. Dept. asst. Macy's Inc., Mays Landing, NJ, 1987—89; mgr. Nutri/Sys., Inc., Northfield, NJ, 1990—92, Paoli, Pa., 1992—93; office mgr. Leo J. McCormick, D.C., Wayne, Pa., 1993; sr. sec. to vice dean edn. Office Acad. Programs U. Pa. Sch. Medicine, Phila., 1994—95, adminstrv. coord. I, 1995—96, adminstrv. coord. III, 1994—98, assoc. dir. curriculum office, 1998—2000, dir., chief adminstrv. officer, 2000—. Office: U Pa Sch Medicine 3450 Hamilton Walk Philadelphia PA 19104 Office Phone: 215-898-8091.

DELANEY, KIM, actress; b. Phila., Nov. 29, 1961; 1 child, Jack. Appeared in (TV series) All My Children, 1981-84, 94, Tour of Duty, 1987, The Fifth Corner, 1992, NYPD Blue, 1995-2001 (Emmy award 1997), Philly, 2001, CSI: Miami, 2002 (TV movies) First Affair, 1983, Perry Mason: The Case of the Sinister Spirit, 1987, Cracked Up, 1987, Christmas Comes to Willow Creek, 1987, All My Darling Daughters, Please Take My Daughters, 1988, Something Is Out There, 1988, The Broken Cord, 1992, Lady Boss, 1992, Closer and Closer, The Disappearance of Christina, 1993, Tall, Dark, and Deadly, 1995, Tall Dark and Deadly, 1995, All Lies End in Murder, 1997, The Devil's Child, 1997, Love and Treason, 2001, (films) That Was Then...This Is Now, 1985, The Delta Force, 1986, Hunter's Blood, 1987, Campus Man, 1987, The Drifter, 1988, Hangfire, 1991, Body Parts, 1991, The Force, 1994, Inferno, Darkman II: The Return of Durant, 1994, Dark Goddess, 1994, Serial Killer, 1995, Project: Metalbeast, 1995, Closer and Closer, 1995., Mission to Mars, 2000. Avocations: biking, swimming, working out, watching films. Office: care The Gersh Agy attn Bob Gersh 232 N Canon Dr Beverly Hills CA 90210-5302 also: care Melissa Prophet Mgmt 1041 N Formosa Ave Los Angeles CA 90046 also: CSI Miami Prodn Office El Segundo Studios 2265 E El Segundo Blvd El Segundo CA 90245

DELANEY, MARION PATRICIA, retail executive; b. Hartford, Conn., May 20, 1952; d. William Pride Delaney Jr. and Marian Patricia (Utley) Murphy. BA, Union Coll., Schenectady, N.Y., 1973. Adminstrv. asst. N.Y. State Assembly, Albany, 1973-74; account exec. Foote, Cone & Belding, N.Y.C., 1974-78; sr. account exec. Dailey & Assocs., L.A., 1978-81; pub. rels. cons. NOW, Washington, 1981-83; account supr. BBDO/West, L.A., 1983-85; v.p. Grey Advt., L.A., 1985-87, San Francisco, 1987-89; sr. v.p. McCann-Erickson, San Francisco, 1989-95; sr. v.p., dir. advt./mktg. comms. Bank of Am., San Francisco, 1995-99; mng. dir. doodlebug LLC, San Anselmo, Calif., 2001—; cons. Brand Strategy, 1999—2000. Del. Dem. Nat. Conv., San Francisco, 1984; bd. dirs. JED Found., Hartford, Conn., 1989—, Easter Seals Soc., Bay Area, 1995-97. Mem. NOW (v.p. L.A. chpt. 1980-83, pres. 1984, advisor 1985-87), Marin Assn. Female Execs., Contemporary Ceramics Studio Assn., Am. Splty. Toy Retailers Assn., Hobby Industries Assn., Toy Industry Assn., San Anselmo C. of C.

DELANEY, MARY ANNE, retired theology studies educator; b. Waltham, Mass., Feb. 15, 1926; d. Thomas Joseph and Mary Teresa (Berry) D. BA, Regis Coll., 1953; MEd, U. Mass., Boston, 1973; MDiv, Andover Newton Theol. Sch., Newton Ctr., Mass., 1978. Tchr. various schs., Mass., 1953-73; pastoral counselor Boston City Hosp., 1974-76; dir. pastoral care Cape Breton Hosp., Sydney River, Canada, 1978-81, Nova Scotia Hosp., Dartmouth, 1981-86, Misericordia Hosp., Edmonton, Canada, 1986-91; pastoral counselor Assn. Pastoral Edn., Waltham, Mass., 1992-96, Emmanuel Coll., Boston, 1996—2001; supr. pastoral edn. Leland Retirement Home, Waltham, 1992—2001; ret., 2001. Vice chair bioethics consultative svc. Misericordia Hosp., Edmonton, 1987-91; vis. scholar Andover Newton Theol. Sch., 1991-92. Trustee Pastoral Inst., Halifax, N.S., Can., 1981-86; mem. commn. on ecumenism Archdiocese of Halifax, 1982-86; mem. of the Congregation of Sisters of St. Joseph, Boston, 1945—. Mem. Can. Assn. Pastoral Edn. (cert. com. 1987-91), Assn. for Clin. Pastoral Edn. (cert. supr., accreditation com. 1993-98, cert. com. 1998-2001). Roman Catholic. Avocations: international travel, classical music, art. Home and Office: 16 Cutter St Waltham MA 02453-5911 E-mail: sr.marydelaney@mediaone.net.

DELANEY, PAMELA DELEO, foundation administrator; b. Providence, May 14, 1947; d. Raymond S. and Anna A. Santulli DeLeo; m. Carroll J. Delaney Jr., Sept. 12, 1970; 1 child, Carroll J. III. BA, Newton (Mass.) Coll., 1969; MA, Rutgers U., 1970; M in Philosophy, Columbia U., 1978. Dept. sec., asst. to police commr. N.Y.C. Police Dept., 1971-80, dir. civilian programs, 1980-83; pres. N.Y.C. Police Found., 1983—. Chmn. N.Y.C. Civilian Complaint Review Bd, 1974-83; mem. N.Y.C. cmty. Bd., 1998-02. Office: NYC Police Found 345 Park Ave New York NY 10154-0004 E-mail: pdelaney@nycpolicefoundationl.org.

DELANEY, SHARON, newscaster; Grad. in Comm., Fla. State U. Reporter, Tallahassee; anchor Monroe, La., Shreveport, La., Orlando, Fla., NBC 17, Raleigh, NC. Office: NBC 17 Studios 1205 Front St Raleigh NC 27609

DELAP, MIRIAM ANNE, music educator; b. Wichita, Kans., Jan. 9, 1944; d. Ewald William and Norine Bertha (Scar) Nath; m. David Frank, Jr. DeLap, Dec. 21, 1968; children: David William, Lora Colleen. BA, MA, Wichita (Kans.) State U., 1966. Cert. elem. tchr. Kans., 1968. Tchr. Wichita (Kans.) Sch. Dist. McLean Elem., 1966—68; 6th grade tchr. Anchorage (Alaska) Sch. Dist. Nunaka Valley, 1969—71; 5th and 6th grade tchr. Lake Otis Elem., Anchorage, 1971—73, music tchr., 1983—. Prin. bassist Anchorage Symphony Orch., 1969—; adj. faculty bass tchr. U. of Alaska, Anchorage, 1996—; instr. record for Anchorage (Alaska) Sch. Dist., 1997—; adj. faculty music edn. Alaska Pacific U., 2004—. Recipient Oustanding Alaska Music Educators, Alaska Music Educators Assn., 2000, Tchr. of Excellence award, Brit. Petroleum Exploration Inc., 2000. Mem.: Alaska Orff Schulwerk (v.p. 1997—99), Am. Orff Schulwerk Assn., Music Educators Nat. Conf. Achievements include Created Miss Mimi's Music Room, thirty minute music program for preschool children, for sch. dist. TV channel in Anchorage. Office: Lake Otis Elem Sch 3331 Lake Otis Pkwy Anchorage AK 99508 E-mail: delap_miriam@asdk12.org.

DELAPA, JUDITH ANNE, business owner; b. Bad Axe, Mich., Feb. 1, 1938; d. John Vincent and Ellen Agatha (Peters) McCormick; m. James Patrick DeLapa, Jan. 10, 1959; children: Joseph Anthony, James P. II, John M., Gina M. BS, Mich. State U., 1959, MA, 1985. Tchr. various schs., Mich., 1959-64; co-founder Saluto Foods Corp., Benton Harbor, Mich., 1963-76; founder Earthtone Interiors, St. Joseph, Mich., 1977-82, High Impact Mktg. Svcs., Grand Rapids, Mich., 1987—2002. Mktg. rsch. and mgt. cons., writer various clients, nationwide. Author: High-Impact Business Strategies, 1993, The McCormick-DeLapa Family Cookbook, 1997, A Place Called Ireland, 2000, Was That Really Us God?, 2001. Past vice chair exec. bd. Grand Rapids Symphony Orch.; bd. dirs., pres. The Samaritan Found.; bd. dirs. Grand Rapids Art Mus. Judith A. DeLapa Perennial Garden named in her honor Mich. State U. Avocations: reading, travel, theater. Office: High Impact Mktg Svcs 2505 E Paris Ave SE Grand Rapids MI 49546-6100

DELAPP, TINA DAVIS, retired nursing educator; b. L.A., Dec. 18, 1946; d. John George and Margaret Mary (Clark) Davis; m. John Robert DeLapp, May 31, 1969; children: Julia Ann, Scott Michael. Diploma, Good Samaritan Hosp., Phoenix, 1967; BSN, Ariz. State U., 1969; MS, U. Colo., Denver, 1972; EdD, U. So. Calif., 1986. Health aide instr. Yukon-Kuskokwim Health Corp., Bethel, Alaska, 1970-71; asst. prof. nursing Bacone Coll., Muskogee, Okla., 1972-74; instr. nursing Alaska Meth. U., Anchorage, 1975-76; prof., assoc. dean for nursing U. Alaska, Anchorage, 1976-96, dir. sch. nursing, 1996—2004; ret. Mem. Alaska Bd. Nursing, 1989-92. Contbr. articles to profl. jours. Recipient Jo Elinor Elliott Leadership award, Western Inst. of Nursing, 2002. Fellow: We. Acad. Nursing; mem.: Am. Assn. Coll. Nursing (mem. nominating com. 2003), Nat. League for Nursing Accreditation Comn. (program evaluator 1986—, review panel mem. 2000—), We. Inst. Nursing (chair program com. 1994—95, sec.-treas. 1995—), Sigma Theta Tau (pres. chpt. 1986—88, v.p. 1988—93, counselor 1995—2000).

DE LAPPE, PELE PHYLLIS, retired journalist, artist; b. San Francisco, May 4, 1916; d. Wesley Raymond and Dorothy (Sheldon) de L.; m. Bertram Edises, 1935 (div. 1949); Steve Murdock, 1953 (div. 1969); children: Nina Sheldon Edises, Peter Edises. Student, Calif. Sch. Fine Arts., San Francisco, 1929-31, Art Students League, N.Y.C., 1931-33. Cartoonist New Masses, Daily Worker, N.Y.C., 1934-40; cartoonist, illustrator San Francisco Chronicle, Peoples World, 1934-75, Marine Workers Voice, San Francisco Mag., San Francisco, 1934-50; feature editor People's World, San Francisco, 1940-53, 73-91; layout artist Moore Bus. Forms, Emeryville, Calif., 1953-72. Caricaturist of authors San Francisco Chronicle Book section, 1940's. Artist, lithographer: one-person shows include: Art Center Gallery, Montgomery St., San Francisco, 1935, Book Shop Coop. Gallery, Washington, 1939; prints exhibited Annex Galleries, Santa Rosa, Calif., Ron Quercia, Duncan's Mills, Calif., Claudia Chapline Gallery, Stinson Beach, Calif., Dore Gallery, San Francisco, Bolinas Mus., Susan Teller Gallery, N.Y.C., Meridien Gallery, San Francisco; included in collections of Achenbach Found. for Graphic Art, Calif. Palace of Legion of Honor, San Francisco, Woodstock Artists Assn. permanent collection, Cameron Woo, Berkeley, Hazel and Aubrey Grossman, San Francisco, Marc Clavland, Marshall, Calif., Charles and Raquel Rasor, Santa Rosa, Calif, Lynn Cooper, Berkeley, Trudy O'Brien, San Francico, Ben and Bea Goldstein, N.Y.C., Brom and Sandy Dijkstra, Del Mar, Calif; author: Pele: A Passionate Journey Through Art & The Red Press, 2000. Home: 41 Acorn Cir Petaluma CA 94952-6310

DE LARIOS, DORA, artist; b. L.A., Oct. 13, 1933; d. Elpidio and Concha (Martinez) De L.; 1 child, Sabrina. BFA, U. So. Calif., 1957. Tchr. ceramics UCLA, 1979, U. So. Calif., L.A., 1959; curator 1st internat. ceramic exhbn., L.A., 1988. Ceramic artist, commd. work for site specific areas, including Montage Resort and Spa, Laguna Beach, Calif., 2003; over 40 major works located in Tahiti, Hawaii, Japan, N.J., Fla., pvt. residential projects. Democrat. Avocations: reading, collecting cook books, cooking, drawing edwin the rabbit. Studio: 8560 Venice Blvd Los Angeles CA 90034-2549 Office Phone: 310-839-8305.

DE LA RIVA, MYRIAM ANN, artist; b. Mexico City, Mex., Oct. 8, 1940; arrived in U.S., 1989; d. Adolfo De La Riva and Marianne Kayser; m. Conrado Gallegos, Feb. 26, 1961; children: Conrado Bernardo, Aileen, Eugenio Eduardo. Grad. in Fine Arts, IberoAm. U. V.p. World Coun. Visual Artists, Mexico City, 1994—96; bd. dirs. Latin Am. Art Mus. One-woman shows include, 1988—2003, exhibited in group shows, 1988—2003, prin. works include mural Today XXist Century. Vol. Tamayo Comtemporary Art Mus., Mexico City, 2000—03, Munal Mus., San Carlos, 2000—02; mem. Miami Art Mus., 1991—2003, Nat. Mus. Women in Arts, 1991—2003, Global Culture Ctr., 1991—98. Named Hon. Mention Women in the Arts, Latinam. Art Mus., Fla., 1994; recipient 1st prize, Sor Juana Found. Mex.-Lebanon Inst. Cultural, 1998, 3d prize, Francisco Goitia prize, 1994, Francisco Goitia prize, Ateneo del Anahuac, 1991, 1992. Mem.: Assn. Artes Aiap-Unesco, Soc. Mex. de Artistas Plasticos. Home: 10150 SW 139 Ct Miami FL 33186 Office: Delariva Bosque de Guayacanes #57 11700 Mexico City Mexico E-mail: delarivamyriam@hotmail.com.

DELATEUR, BARBARA JANE, medical educator; b. Hoquiam, Wash., Nov. 17, 1936; Student, Marylhurst (Oreg.) Coll., 1954-56; BS in Philosophy, St. Louis U., 1959; MD, U. Wash., 1963, MSc, 1968. Cert. Am. Bd. Phys. Medicine and Rehab.; lic. physiatrist, Wash., Md. Rotating intern U. Hosp., U. Wash., 1963-64; resident dept. phys. medicine and rehab. U. Hosp., 1964-67; instr. dept. phys. medicine and rehab. U. Wash. Sch. Medicine, 1967-68, asst. prof., 1968-71, assoc. prof., 1971-76, prof. dept. rehab. medicine, 1976-93; prof., dir. dept. phys. medicine and rehab. Johns Hopkins U. Sch. Medicine, Balt., 1993—, Lawrence Cardinal Shehan chair phys. medicine and rehab., 1993—, joint prof. health policy & mgmt. Sch. Hygiene & Pub. Health, 1994—; acting physiatrist-in-chief Rehab. Medicine Svc. Harborview Med. Ctr., Seattle, 1970-72, physiatrist-in-chief, 1972-93; dir. Muscular Dystrophy Clinic Meml. Hosp., Yakima, Wash., 1979-88; dir. dept. phys. medicine and rehab. Johns Hopkins Hosp., Balt., 1993—; med. dir. dept. rehab. medicine Good Samaritan Hosp., Balt., 1993—. Vis. prof. dept. rehab. medicine and dept. internal medicine SUNY, Syracuse, 1988; cons. physiatrist Johns Hopkins Geriatrics Ctr., Johns Hopkins Bayview Med. Ctr., Balt., 1994—; vis. lectr. dept. phys. medicine Coll. Medicine, Ohio State U., 1985; Arthur Grant lectr. U. Tex., San Antonio, 1992; Marquette lectr. Jefferson Med. Coll., Phila., 1993; spkr. various univs. and orgns.; pres. Phys.Medicine and Rehab./Edn. and Rsch. Found., 1990-94; mem. governing coun. sect. rehab. hosps. and programs Am. Hosp. Assn., 1993—; mem. adv. bd. Wash. State Divsn. Vocat. Rehab., 1979-84. Contbr. articles to profl. jours.; mem. editl. bd. Archives Phys. Medicine and Rehab., 1978-84, Health After 50, Johns Hopkins Hosp., 1994—; reviewer Jour. Am. Geriatrics Soc., 1994—. Recipient Elizabeth and Sidney Licht award for sci. writing, 1990, Excellence in Tchg. award N.J. Med. Sch., 1992, Excellence in Rsch. Writing award Assn. Acad. Physiatrists and Am. Jour. Phys. Medicine and Rehab., 1992, Golden Goniometer award Phys. Medicine and Rehab. Residents, 1995, Labe Scheinberg award, Meeting of Consortium of MS Ctrs., Portland, Oreg., 1995. Fellow Am. Acad. Phys. Medicine; mem. AMA, Am. Acad. Phys. Medicine and Rehab. (bd. govs. 1983-90, v.p. 1986-887, pres-elect 1987-88, pres. 1988-89, past-pres. 1989-90, Disting. Clinician award 1998), NAS, Am. Burn Assn., Am. Congress Rehab. Medicine, Assn. Acad. Physiatrists (Disting. Academician award 1998), Internnt. Assn. for Study of Pain, King County Med. Assn., Northwest Assn. Phys. Medicine and Rehab. (pres. 1974-76), Gerontol. Soc. Am. (clin. medicine sect.), Wash. State Med. Assn. Office: JHPM & R Good Samaritan Profl Bldg 5601 Loch Raven Blvd Ste 406 Baltimore MD 21239-2905

DE LA TIERRA, TATIANA, librarian, writer; b. Villavicencio, Colombia, May 14, 1961; d. Fabiola Restrepo and Gustavo Barona. MFA, U. Tex., El Paso, 1999; MLS, U. Buffalo, 2000. Info. literacy libr. U. Buffalo, 2000—. Author: For the Hard Ones: A Lesbian Phenomenology / Para las duras: Una fenomenologia lesbiana, 2002, Gustavo Alvarez Gardeazabal: Prisoner of Hope, (non-fiction) La Violencia (Associated Writing Programs Intro Jours.Project Nonfiction Winner, 1998), Love Me Dis-Embodied (Vincent J. Lovett Meml. Essay Contest Winner, 1998); contbr. to mags. Recipient Money for Women award, Barbara Deming Meml. Fund, 1997, 1st pl., Chip Jordan Lit. Fiction Contest, 1998, Just Buffalo Lit. award for creative non-fiction, 2001, New Calif. Media award for internat. affairs, 2002; Writing Residency fellow, Cottages at Hedgebrook, 1990, 1997, Audre Lorde fellow for women of color writers and activists, 1998, Zora Neale Hurston Writing scholar, Naropa Writing Inst., 1996. Mem.: The Beauty Salon / El Salon de Belleza (life), Latino Grad. Student Assn. (assoc.; sec. 1999—2001). Home: 266 Elmwood Ave #104 Buffalo NY 14222 Personal E-mail: td6@buffalo.edu.

DELAURENTIS, LOUISE BUDDE, writer; b. Stafford, Kans., Oct. 5, 1920; d. Louis and Mary (Lichte) Budde; m. Mariano Anthony DeLaurentis, Mar. 26, 1948 (dec. Oct. 1991); 1 child, Delbert Louis. BA, Ottawa (Kans.) U., 1942. Airport traffic contr. FAA, various cities, 1943-55. Author: Etta Chipmunk, 1962, A Peculiarity of Direction, 1975, Traveling to the Goddess, 1994; editor: Gentle Sorcery by Bessie Jeffery, 1972; author numerous poems various periodicals; contbr. articles to profl. jours. Chairperson Tompkins County Liberal Party, Ithaca, N.Y., 1969-72; mem. local women's spirituality groups. Mem. LWV, AAUW, Writers Assn. of Ithaca Area (pres. 1964-65, co-editor anthology 1967, 95). Avocations: swimming, camping, backpacking, making lunar calendars. Home: 983 Cayuga Heights Rd Ithaca NY 14850-1044

DELAURO, ROSA L. congresswoman; b. New Haven, Conn., Mar. 2, 1943; m. Stanley Greenberg. Student, London Sch. Econs. & Polit. Sci., 1962-63; BA in History and Polit Sci. cum laude, Marymount Coll., 1964; MA in Internat. Politics, Columbia U., 1966. Tng. assoc. Community Progress Inc., New Haven, Conn., 1967-69; instr. in internat. rels. Albertus Magnus Coll., 1967-68; adminstrv. asst. Nat. Urban Fellows, 1969-72, asst. dir., dir., 1972-75; city coord. Carter-Mondale Presdl. Campaign, New Haven, 1976; exec. asst. Mayor Frank Logue, New Haven, 1976-77, campaign mgr., 1977; exec. asst., devel. adminstr. City of New Haven, 1977-79; campaign mgr. Chris Dodd for U.S. Senate, 1979-80, 86; adminstrv. asst. U.S. Senator Christopher J. Dodd, Washington, 1981-87;

state dir. Mondale-Ferraro Presdl. Campaign, N.J., 1986; ptnr. DeLauro-Geller, 1987-88; regional dir. Dukakis for Pres. Campaign, N.Y., N.J., Con.., 1988; exec. dir. EMILY's List, 1989; mem. U.S. Congress 3rd Conn. dist., 1991—; mem. house appropriations com.; chief dep. minority whip. Del. to Dem. Nat. Conv., 1984; bd. dirs. Pax Ams. Past pres. New Haven [illegible] Timothy Dwight Coll., Yale U., recipient Leadership award Am. Com. on Italian Migration. Mem. Nat. Italian-Am. Found., Dem. Women for Progress. Democrat. Office: US House of Reps 2262 Rayburn Ho Office Bldg Washington DC 20515-0703 also: District Office 59 Elm Street New Haven CT 06510*

DE LA VERGNE, MARIE LOUISE BEATRICE, antiques and fine art consultant; b. New Orleans, Jan. 15, 1972; d. Hugues Jules and Beatrice Badger de la Vergne. BBA, So. Meth. U., 1994; Cert. for Am. Art, Sotheby's Inst., N.Y.C., 1999; postgrad., NYU, 2000. Sales exec. Pitney Bowes, New Orleans, 1994—95; property mgr. 1st Lake Properties, New Orleans, 1995—98; mktg. coord. Sothebys.com, N.Y.C., 1999—2000; antique furniture expert Neal Auction Co., New Orleans, 2000—02; antiques and fine art cons., auctioneer Matthew Clayton Brown, New Orleans, 2003—. Vol. Preservation Resource Ctr., New Orleans, 2001—03, Smart Growth, New Orleans. Republican. Roman Catholic. Avocations: running, travel, scuba diving. Home: 4617 Hessmer Ave Metairie LA 70002 Office: 1724 St Andrew St New Orleans LA 70113

DELBANCO, SUZANNE F. human services administrator; MPH, U. Calif., Berkeley; PhD in Pub. Policy, Goldman Sch. Pub. Policy. With Henry J. Kaiser Family Found.; sr. mgr. Pacific Bus. Group on Health; exec. dir. The Leapfrog Group, Washington, 2000—. Office: Leapfrog Group 1801 K St NW Ste 701L Washington DC 20006

DELBOURGO, JOËLLE LILY, publishing executive; b. Alexandria, Egypt, Sept. 10, 1953; came to U.S., 1960; d. Edward Daniel and J. Andrée (Domergue) D.; m. Lewis Foster Patton, May 16, 1976 (div. May 1996); children: Caroline Emily, Andrew David. Student, Vassar Coll., 1970-72; BA, Williams Coll., 1974; MA, Columbia U., 1975. Editorial asst. Bantam Books, N.Y.C., 1975-76, asst. editor, 1976-78, assoc. editor, 1978-80; sr. editor Ballantine Del Rey Fawcett Ivy Books div. Random House Inc., N.Y.C., 1980-81, exec. editor, 1981-83, editor-in-chief, 1983-86, v.p., editor-in-chief trade books, 1986-89, editor-in-chief hard cover books and trade paperback, 1990-95; v.p., editl. dir. HarperCollins, N.Y.C., 1996, sr. v.p., assoc. publ., editor-in-chief, 1997-99; CEO, pres. Joëlle Delbourgo Assocs. Inc. Lit. Mgmt., Pub. Cons., 1999—. Columbia faculty fellow, 1974-75. Mem. Women's Media Group (bd. dirs.), Phi Beta Kappa. Office: 450 7th Ave Ste 3004 New York NY 10123-3004 E-mail: joelle@delbourgo.com.

DEL COLLO, MARY ANNE DEMETRIS, school administrator; b. Norristown, Pa., May 10, 1949; d. John and Julia (Chale) Demetris; m. William Paul Del Collo, July 1, 1973; children: Margaux, Julia, Nicole. BS, West Chester State U., 1971; MEd, Rosemont Coll. Tech., 1995; EdD, Widener U., 2001. Cert. elem. tchr. and sch. adminstr., Pa. Tchr. Phoenixville (Pa.) Area Sch. Dist., 1971-97, adminstr., 1997—, Methacton Sch. Dist., Norristown, Pa., 1998—. Mem. AAUW, Pa. Assn. Elem. and Secondary Sch. Prins., Hellenic Univ. Club, Nat. Middle Sch. Assn., Kappa Delta Pi (v.p. Chi Gamma chpt. 1998-2000, pres. 2000-02, past pres. 2002-). Avocations: technology, walking, reading, antiquing, traveling. Office: Methacton Sch Dist Eagleville Rd Norristown PA 19403

DEL CONTE, L. CATHERINE, special education educator; b. Montour Falls, N.Y., June 8, 1955; d. Leon Clarence and Dorothy Louise May; m. Douglas Kelsey, Aug. 2, 1973; children: Henry Lee Kelsey, Bryon Douglas Kelsey; m. Richard Ralph Del Conte, Apr. 8, 1995. AA in Human Svcs., Genesee C.C., Batavia, N.Y., 1981; BSW, SUNY-Brockport, 1983, MPA in Geriatrics, 1986; M.Spl. Edn., George Mason U., Fairfax, Va., 2000. Case mgr. We Care, Inc., Washington, 1991—92, Brice Warren Corp., Washington, 1992—94, State of Md./Great Oaks MR Ctr., 1994—95, Jewish Social Svcs., Rockville, Md., 1995—97; learning disabilities/ED tchr. Fairfax County Pub. Schs., Annandale, Va., 1998—. Historian Phi Delta Kappa/George Mason U., 1998—2000, rsch. coord., 2000—; ct. apptd. specialist Fairfax County, Fairfax, Va., 1991—93; lead tchr. remediation program Annandale H.S., 1999—2002, mem. attendance adv. com., 2003—. Avocations: hiking, reading, working out, writing poetry. Home: 6006 Scarborough Commons Ln Burke VA 22015 Office: Fairfax County Public Schs 4700 Medford Dr Annandale VA 22003

DEL DUCA, RITA, language educator; b. NYC, Apr. 1, 1933; d. Joseph and Ermelinda (Buonaguro) Ferraro; m. Joseph Anthony Del Duca, Oct. 29, 1955; children: Lynn, Susan, Paul, Andrea. BA, CUNY, 1955. Elem. tchr. Yonkers (N.Y.) Pub. Schs., 1955-57; tchr. kindergarten Sacred Heart Sch., Yonkers, 1962-64; tchr. piano, Scarsdale, N.Y., 1973-79; asst. office mgr. Foot Clinic, Hartsdale, N.Y., 1977-85; tchr. ESL, Linguarama Exec. Sch., White Plains, N.Y., 1985-89; ESL tutor, Scarsdale, 1989—. Dist. leader Greenburgh (N.Y.) Rep. Com., 1991-92. Mem.: ASCAP. Avocations: oil painting, piano teaching, tennis, theatre arts. Home and Office: Unit 79 10 Old Jackson Ave Hastings On Hudson NY 10706

DELEHANTY, MARTHA, human services administrator; B in Psychology, Mount Holyoke Coll.; M in Bus., U. Tex. With GTE, 1991—2000; field dir. Midwest Area GTE Wireless; joined Verizon Wireless, 2000; exec. dir. employee rels. Verizon Wireless LLC, Bedminster, NJ, 2000—04, v.p. human resources, 2004—. Office: Verizon Wireless LLC 180 Washington Valley Rd Bedminster NJ 07921*

DE LEON, LIDIA MARIA, magazine editor; b. Havana, Cuba, Sept. 10, 1957; d. Leon J. and Lydia (Diaz Cruz) de L. BA in Communications cum laude, U. Miami, Coral Gables, Fla., 1979. Staff writer Miami Herald, Fla., 1978-79; editorial asst. Halsey Pub. Co., Miami, 1980-81, assoc. editor, 1981, editor, 1981—, editor Delta Sky mag., 1983-95. Mem. Am. Soc. Mag. Editors, Am. Assn. Travel Editors, Golden Key, Sigma Delta Chi. Roman Catholic. Avocation: tennis. Office: 12550 Biscayne Blvd # 212 Miami FL 33181

DE LEON, MARITA BERNARDO, psychologist, researcher; b. Manila, Philippines, July 3, 1961; d. Mariano Lacson and Socorro Depante Bernardo; m. Aderito T. de Leon, Jr., Feb. 7, 1961; children: Maya Bernardo, Marco Bernardo. PhD in Devel. Psychology, Mich. State U., 1994, MA in Psychology, 1987; BS in Psychology cum laude, U. Philippines, 1982. Assoc. prof. De La Salle U., Manila, Philippines, 1989—95; dir. rsch. Psychol. & Neuropsychological Services, Lansing, Mich., 1995—. Mem. Capital Area Brain Injury Spl. Interest Group, Greater Lansing area, Mich., 2002—. Contbr. book A Guide to Thesis Writing. Lang. tchr. Philippine Am. Club of Greater Lansing, Lansing, Mich., 2003—03; Sunday sch. tchr. U. Ref. Ch., East Lansing, Mich., 1997—2003. Mem.: Philippine Am. Club Greater Lansing, Phi Kappa Phi, Pi Gamma Mu. Achievements include development of a model of cognitive rehabilitation; research in neurofatigue after brain injury. Office: Psychological & Neuropsychological Svcs 1200 E Michigan Ave Suite 630 Lansing MI 48912 Personal E-mail: bernar19@msu.edu. E-mail: bernar19@msu.edu.

DE LEON, SYLVIA A. lawyer; b. Corpus Christi, Tex., Mar. 2, 1950; BA, Briarcliff Coll., 1972; JD, U. Tex., 1976. Bar: Tex. 1976, D.C. 1977. Ptnr. Akin, Gump, Strauss, Hauer & Feld LLP, Washington. Adj. prof. law Georgetown U. law ctr., 1988-90; bd. dirs. (pres. apptd. senate confirmed) Amtrak, Nat. Railroad Passenger Corp., 1994—, vice chmn. 2003-, chair corp. strategy com. Bd. trustees U. Tex. Law Sch. Found. 2002-, U. Tex. Law Assn., 1985-89, 92-96, 2000-03, U. Tex. Devel. Bd., 1996—, bd. dirs. Washington Ballet, 2001-; coord. issues transp. Clinton-Gore Presdl. Transition Team, 1992; presdl. appointee Nat. Commn. Ensure Strong Competitive Airline Industry, 1993, White House Conf. on Travel and Tourism. Mem. Bar Assn. D.C., State Bar Tex. (chmn. fed. law and regulations com. 1984-87), Nat. Civil Aviation Bar [illegible] Gump Strauss Hauer & Feld Ste 400 1333 New Hampshire Ave NW Washington DC 20036-1564

DELEUZE, MARGARITA, artist; b. Caracas, Miranda, Venezuela, May 11, 1943; arrived in US, 1982, naturalized, 1992; d. Ivor Hauck and Margarita Schnell; m. Felipe Silén, July 3, 1964 (div. Nov. 1982); children: Anabella, Margarita; m. Eric Charles Deleuze, Nov. 12, 1988. AAS, Bennett Coll., 1962. Recipient Arts awards Venezuelan VAAUW, Caracas, 1971, 72, San Francisco Mus. Contemporary Hispanic Art award, 1998, Premio Nosotros award, ALAS, Miami, 2000, Artistic Achievement award Five Part Nat. Juried Competition, Artscape Naples, Fla.; named Dressage Nat. Champion, Venezuelan Riding Fedn., Caracas, 1972, 73, 74, 75. Mem. World Wildlife Fund, Nat. Audubon Soc., Humane Soc. Broward County, Defenders Wildlife, Cousteau Soc., Nat. Mus. Women in Arts. Avocations: photography, gardening, traveling, music, gourmet cooking. Home: 2698 Cypress Ln Weston FL 33332-3423 Studio: MD Fine Arts Studio 2698 Cypress Ln Weston FL 33332-3423 E-mail: margarita@deleuze.com.

DELGADO, GRACIELA, court interpreter; b. Chihuahua, Mexico, Oct. 9, 1939; d. Francisco Rios and Adela Navarro; m. Tito Joel Delgado, Jan. 17, 1970; 1 child, Aixa. BA, U. Tex., El Paso, 1961, MEd, 1986. Tchr. h.s. El Paso Ind. Sch. dist., 1961-96; interpreter County of El Paso, 1998-99. Conf. interpreter, El Paso, 1993-99. Mem. AAUW (program pres. 1994-95, pres. 1998—), El Paso Interpreters and Translation Assn. (pres.-elect 1993-99), Am. Translators Assn. (cert.). Avocation: travel. Home: 1003 Alethea Park Dr El Paso TX 79902-2136

DELGADO, JANE, health facility administrator, writer; b. Havana, Cuba, June 17, 1953; d. Juan Lorenzo Delgado Borges and Lucila Aurora Navarro Delgado; m. Mark A. Steo, May 15, 1999; 1 child, Elizabeth A. Steo. BA, SUNY, New Paltz, 1973; MA, NYU, 1975; MS, W. Averell Harrimann Sch., 1981; PhD in Clin. Psychology, SUNY, Stony Brook, 1981. Children's talent coord. Children's TV Workshop, 1973-75; rsch. asst. SUNY, Stony Brook, 1975-79; social sci. analyst U.S. Dept. Health and Human Svcs., 1979-83, health policy advisor, 1983-85; pres., CEO Nat. Alliance for Hispanic Health, 1985—; pvt. practice in psychology, 1979—. Bd. dirs. Nat. Health Coun., 1986—97, Carter Ctr. Mental Health Taskforce, 1991—2000, Patient Safety Inst., 2001—; trustee The Kresge Found, 1997—, Found. Child Devel., 1989—97. Author: Salud! A Latina's Guide to Total Health, 1997, 2d edit., 2002. W.K. Kellogg Found. Nat. fellow, 1988, NIMH fellow, 1975-79; recipient Surgeon Gen.'s award, 1992, Florence Kelley award, 2002, Health and Sci. Latina Excellence award, 1995; named SUNY Alumna of Yr., 1993 Office: Nat Alliance for Hispanic Health 1501 16th St NW Washington DC 20036-1401

DELGADO, MARICA LADONNE, librarian, educator; b. Murray, Ky., Nov. 28, 1959; d. Billie Ray Roberts and Ada Sue Ross Roberts; m. Jon E. Delgado; children: Maurya, Jessamyn, Ian. BS, Murray State U., 1981; ML, Vanderbilt U., 1982. Libr. spl. projects Tenn. Tech. U., Cookeville, Tenn., 1982; libr. collection develop./spl. projects Tenn. Tech. U. Libr., Cookeville, Tenn., 1983—88, exch. libr. head periodicals and gifts, 1986—88; libr. gifts and exch., instr. Miss. State U. Libr., Starkville, Miss., 1988—92, libr. govt. documents, asst. prof., 1992—97, coord. govt. documents and microforms, assoc. prof., 1997—. Contbr. articles to profl. jours. Mem.: ALA (poster sessions rev. panel 1992—2002), MSU Robert Holland Faculty Senate (sec. 1999—), Miss. Libr. Assn. (GODORT sec. 1996—97, chair 2004), Southeastern Libr. Assn. (SELA poster sessions coord. 1998—2000). Avocations: boating, travel, camping, hiking. Home: 507 Sycamore St Starkville MS 39759 Office: Miss State U Libr Hardy Rd Mississippi State MS 39762 Office Phone: 662-325-7660. Office Fax: 662-325-3560. Personal E-mail: Ldelgado@library.msstate.edu. Business E-Mail: Ldelgado@library.msstate.edu.

DELGADO, MARY LOUISE, elementary school educator, secondary school educator, consultant, Internet company executive; b. Manitowoc, Wis., June 6, 1943; d. Walter Anthony and Jane Mary Jagodensky; 1 child, Daniel David. BA in English, Edn., Silver Lake Coll., 1971; MA, Govs. State U., Park Forest, Ill., 1983. Cert. tchr. Wis., Ill. Tchr. Colegio San Antonio Abad, Humacao, PR, 1973—75, Chgo. Pub. Schs., 1984—88, Milw. Pub. Schs., 1988—; pres., cons. Quality Online Connections, Milw., 2000—. Presenter in field. Pres. Lenox Heights Neighborhood Assn., Milw., 1999—2002. Fellow, Am. Coun. Learned Socs., 1994, 1995; grantee, Coun. Basic Edn. Ind. Study, 1994, NEH, 2000; Eleanor Roosevelt Tchr. scholar, 1999. Mem.: ASCD, AAUW, Wis. Tchrs. English to Students Second Langs. Democrat. Avocations: bicycling, reading, weaving. Office: Quality Online Connections 6333 W Chambers St Milwaukee WI 53210 Personal E-mail: mdelgado1@wi.rr.com.

DELGADO-COLON, AIDA M. federal judge; b. 1955; BA, U. P.R., 1977; JD, Cath. U. P.R., 1980. Bar: P.R. 1980. Dir. investigations P.R. Gov.'s Adv. Bd. on Labor Policy, 1980-82; asst. fed. pub. defender, 1982—93; 1st asst. fed. pub. defender, 1992—93; magistrate judge U.S. Dist. Ct. for P.R., San Juan, 1994—. Mem. Fed. Bar Exam. Com., 1986—; mem. local rules com. U.S. Dist. Ct. for P.R., 1991—; chmn. interpreters and ct. reports com., 1994-96, mem. criminal justice act com., 1994-96, EEO coord., 1995-99, EDR coord., 1999—. Mem. Fed. Magistrate Judges Assn., Women Judges Assn., P.R. Bar Assn., Cath. U. P.R. Law Sch. Alumni Assn., Nat. Hispanic Bar Assn. Office: Ruiz-Nazario Fed Bldg 150 Ave Carlos Chardon # 495 San Juan PR 00918-1703

DELI, ANNE TYNION, marketing executive; b. Milw., Apr. 18, 1956; m. Steven F. Deli; 2 children. BA in History and French, Georgetown U., 1978. Acct. exec. Dancer Fitzgerald Sample, N.Y.C., 1978-80; acct. supr. Grey Advt., N.Y.C., 1980-82; v.p. Wells Rich Greene, N.Y.C., 1982-84; sr. v.p. Lawrence Charles Free, N.Y.C., 1984-86; prin. Anspach Grossman Portugal, N.Y.C., 1986-88; sr. v.p. Siegel & Gale, N.Y.C., 1988-93; v.p., global mktg. Harley-Davidson, Inc., Milw., 1993-95; pres., founder North River Strategies, Milw./Chgo., 1995—2000; owner Orlando Harley-Davidson, 2000—. Dir. Milw. Zool. Soc.; bd. dirs. Chgo. Shakespeare Theatre, 2001—02, Orlando Mus. Art, 2002—. Honoree, Orlando Women Who Mean Bus., 2004. Mem.: Orlando Regional C. of C. (exec. com. 2003—). Republican. Avocations: world travel, decorative arts, tennis. Office: 30 S Wacker Dr Ste 2318 Chicago IL 60606-7405

DE LIMANTOUR, CLARICE BARR, food scientist; b. Allentown, Pa., Dec. 24, 1918; d. Joseph Robert and Laura (Wirthlin) Barr; m. Julio Edwardo Iturbide Limantour, Sept. 13, 1940 (dec. 1972); children: Jose' Ignacio, Julio Edwardo. BS, Rutgers U., 1938, MS, 1940; postgrad., U. Mexico, 1946-49, Rutgers U., 1949-50. Advisor Nat. Sch. Feeding Program, Mexico City, 1947-49; pres. Factory Feeding Corp., Mexico City, 1950-58; advisor Nat. Factory Feeding Program, Mexico City, 1958-60; developer New Food Product-Gen. Foods, White Plains, N.Y., 1960-61, New Food Product-Gen. Mills, Reynolds, 1961-63, New Food Product-Miles Labs., 1963-64; cons. New Food Products-various cos., 1964-78; pres., researcher Limantour Devel. Corp., Pa., 1966-91, chmn. of bd., 1988—; developer Cliffdale Farms, Quakertown, Pa., 1988—; pvt. practice cons. Durham, Pa. Inventor in field of freezing of all classes of emulsions. Mem. Bucks County Conservancy Assn., Doylestown, Pa., 1989-91, Fine Arts Club, N.Y.C., 1984-88, Acad. Sci., N.Y.C., Republican Club, Pa., 1982-89, Citizens Against Govt. Waste, Washington, 1988-91. Republican. Episcopalian. Avocations: reading, music, traveling, sailing, bird watching. Home: 905 Durham Rd Durham PA 18039 Office: Cliffdale Farms 35 Tillage Rd Breinigsville PA 18031-1829

DE LISI, JOANNE, media consultant, educator; b. Bklyn. d. Louis Anthony and Maria Anna De Lisi. BA, Hunter Coll., 1972, MA, 1977; postgrad., NYU. Cert. tchr. N.Y. Asst. instr. Hunter Coll., N.Y.C., 1974-75; instr. NYU, N.Y.C., 1974-78; cons. communication N.Y.C., 1976—; instr. Bklyn. Coll., 1978-82, dir. forensics, 1981-82, asst. dir. acad. prep. program, 1980-82; adj. lectr. City U. Sys., N.Y.C., 1983-91. Profl. entertainer, 1953—75; faculty advisor Alpha Tau Omega, Bklyn. Coll., 1980—82. Contbr. articles to profl. jours., poems to anthologies, radio programs, newspapers. Dep. rep. St. Albans Campus NYVA Harbor Health Care Sys.; mem. adv. bd. N.Y. State Senator Serphin Maltese. Recipient Nat. award of excellence, POW/MIA, Am. Legion Aux., 1995, Nat. award, USO and Savs. Bonds Jr. Activities Am. Legion Aux., 1996—98, Vets. Affairs, 1998—2000. Mem.: Metro N.Y. Database Internet Users Group, Fencers Am., Hunter Alumni Orgn., Am. Legion (pub. rels. officer Queens County 1991—93, treas. 1991—2001, v.p., girls state chmn. 1993—94, pub. rels. officer, newsletter editor, sec. Leonard unit 1993—94, pres. 1994—95, del. N.Y. state Dept. Conv. 1995, judge Forensics Tournament 1995—2003, pres. unit 104 1996, nat. security chmn., jr. activity chmn., pub. rels. dir. 1996—98, 10th dist. sgt-at-arms, sec., v.p. 2001—), Kappa Delta Pi. Roman Catholic. Avocations: antique collector, travel, jewelry making, fencing dir. Office: Wyckoff Heights Sta PO Box 370029 Brooklyn NY 11237-0029

DE LISI, NANCY, corporate financial executive; BA in Psychology, MS in Profl. Acctg., U. Tex., Austin. Various executive positions in multinational companies and Citibank in internat. fin. and bus. development, 1976—85; from asst. treas. to v.p. fin. and treas. Altria Group, Inc., N.Y.C., 1985—2002, sr. v.p. mergers and acquisitions N.Y. C., 2002—. Bd. dirs. SABMiller, PLC. Office: Altria Group Inc 120 Park Ave New York NY 10017-5592

DELL, DIANA JEAN, writer; b. East Vandergrift, Pa., Feb. 11, 1946; d. James Albert Dell and Clara Dorothy Masgay; 1 child, Mark Clark. BS, W.Va. U., 1967. Dir. USO, Washington, 1970—75; instr. Tampa (Fla.) Coll., 1995—96; pres. VietnamWar.net, Boston, 1996—. Freelance writer, Boston, 1976—. Author: (book) A Saigon Party: And Other Vietnam War Short Stories, 1999, Memories Are Like Clouds, 2000; editor: Memorable Quotations: American Women Writers of the Past, 2000, Memorable Quotations: Famous Teachers of the Past, 2001, Memorable Quotations: Humorists, Wits, and Satirists of the Past, 2000, (web site) IntelligentsiaNetwork.com, 1997, MemorableQuotations.com, 2000, VietnamWar.net, 1996. Recipient Outstanding Civilian Svc. medal, U.S. Dept. of Army, 1972. Home and Office: 21 Elm St #2 Malden MA 02148 Personal E-mail: dianajdell@aol.com.

DELL, WILLIE JONES, social services executive, educator; b. Rocky Mt., N.C., May 8, 1930; d. Willie Aikens and Emma Mae (Anderson) Grant; m. James A. Jones; 1 child, Wayne; m. Nathan Dell, June 19, 1967. BA, St. Augustine Coll., 1952; MSW, Coll. William and Mary, 1961. Lic. social worker, Va. Tchr. Enfield (N.C.) Sch. System, 1955-56; case worker Va. Dept. Welfare, Richmond, 1956-59; student advisor Va. Union U., Richmond, 1964-65; chief med. social worker Med. Coll. Va., Richmond, 1961-67, Pub. Health Dept., Richmond, 1967-69; asst. prof. Va. Commonwealth U., Richmond, 1969-74; assoc. prof. U. Richmond, 1974-95; exec. dir. Richmond Cmty. Sr. Ctr., 1976-94. Contbr. articles to profl. jours. Mem. Richmond City Coun., 1973-82; v.p. Richmond Crusade Voters, 1983; pres. Richmond chpt. Nat. Caucus Black Aged, 1987, Human Resources, Inc., Richmond, 1987—; bd. dirs. St. Joseph's Home for Boys, Port Au Prive, Haiti, Heifer Project Internat., Family and Children Svcs., Fan Fee Clinics, United Givers Funds, Richmond's One to One. Recipient Good Govt. award Delta Sigma Theta, 1982; named Outstanding Woman in Govt., YWCA, 1982, Outstanding Vol., Powhattan Correctional Ctr., 1988. Mem. NAACP (life), Nat. Black Presbyn. Caucus (pres. 1986-91). Democrat. Avocations: foreign travel, sewing, reading, walking. Home: 2956 Hathaway Rd Apt 805 Richmond VA 23225-1731 Office: U Richmond Richmond VA 23173

DELLAS, MARIE C. retired psychology educator and consultant; b. Buffalo; d. Theodore Andrew and Katherine (Callos) D. BS cum laude, State U. Coll., Buffalo, 1945; MEd, U. Buffalo, 1967; PhD, SUNY, Buffalo, 1970. Asst. editor Urban Edn. Jour., Buffalo, 1966-67; rsch. asst. SUNY, Buffalo, 1967-69; asst. prof. psychology Ea. Mich. U., Ypsilanti, 1969-73, assoc. prof., 1973-79, prof., 1979-93. Mem. adv. bd. Inst. Study Children and Families, 1983-93. Author: Dellas Identity Status Inventory, 1979, 81, Creative Thinking Applied to Problem Solving Manual, 1993; contbr. articles to profl. jours.; mem. bd. editors Midwestern Ednl. Researcher, 1980-87, Urban Edn. Jour., 1977-94. Recipient Josephine N. Keal award Women's Commn., 1980, 85, 86; Grad. Rsch. grantee Ea. Mich. U., 1980-84. Mem. APA, Am. Ednl. Rsch. Assn., Nat. Assn. Gifted Children, Midwestern Ednl. Rsch. Assn., Midwestern Psychol. Assn., Mich. Acad. Gifted, Am. Assn. Univ. Women, Women's Coun. Cleveland Mus. of Art, Pi Lambda Theta. Home and Office: 2201 Acacia Park Dr Apt 312 Lyndhurst OH 44124-3840

DELLA SANTA, LAURA, principal; Prin. Mater Christi Sch., Burlington, Vt. Recipient Elem. Sch. Recognition award U.S. Dept. Edn., 1989-90. Office: Mater Christi Sch 50 Mansfield Ave Burlington VT 05401-3389

DELMONTE, FRANCINE, state legislator; m. Douglas M. Clarke. BA, Buffalo State Coll.; MA, SUNY. Chief of staff Joseph T. Pilittere; staff aide Paul A. Tokasz. Democrat. Office: 1700 Pine Ave Niagara Falls NY 14301

DELMORE, LOIS M. state legislator; m. Michael Delmore; 2 child. Student, U. N.D. Tchr. English Red River H.S.; mem. Dist. 43 N.D. Ho. of Reps.; mem. judiciary and polit subdivsn. coms. N.D. State Senate. Mem. N.D. State Tchrs. Assn. Home: 714 S 22nd St Grand Forks ND 58201-4138

DELO, ELLEN SANDERSON, lawyer; b. Nassawadox, Va., Nov. 29, 1944; d. Robert G. and Daisy B. (Hitchens) Sanderson; m. Arthur C. Delo Jr., Mar. 20, 1971; 1 child, Marjorie Cotton Delo. BA, U. Richmond, 1966; JD, Rutgers U., 1977; LLM, NYU, 1985. Bar: N.J., 1977, U.S. Dist. Ct. N.J., 1977, U.S. Tax Ct., 1987, U.S. Ct. Appeals (2nd cir.) 1997, D.C. 1999, N.Y. 1999. Law clk. to Hon. John J. Geronimo N.J. Superior Ct., 1977-78; assoc. Lamb Hutchinson Chappell Ryan & Hartung, Jersey City, 1978-80, Chasan Leyner Holland & Tarrant, Jersey City, 1980-84, Stryker Tams & Dill, Newark, 1985-92, ptnr., 1993-98; exec. compensation assoc. Bachelder Law Offices, N.Y.C., 1998—2002, of counsel, 2002—. Lectr. on tax issues. Contbr. articles to profl. jours. Lay reader Ch. St. Andrew and Holy Communion, South Orange, N.J. Democrat. Episcopalian. Avocation: animal welfare organizations and activities. Home and Office: 340 Montrose Ave South Orange NJ 07079-2439 E-mail: esdelo@msn.com.

DELONG, DEBORAH, lawyer; b. Louisville, Sept. 5, 1950; d. Henry F. and Lois Jean (Stepp) D.; children: Amelie DeLong, Samuel Prentice. BA, Vanderbilt U., 1972; JD, U. Cin., 1975. Bar: Ohio 1975, Ky. 1999, U.S. Dist. Ct. (so. dist.) Ohio 1975, U.S. Ct. Appeals (Fed. cir.) 1990, (11th cir.), 1995, U.S. Ct. Appeals (6th cir.) 1991, U.S. Supreme Ct. 1982. Assoc. Paxton & Seasongood, Cin., 1975-82, ptnr., 1982-88, Thompson, Hine & Flory, 1989—2001. Contbr. articles to profl. jours. Bd. dirs. Cin. Opera, Cin. Shakespeare Festival, Clovernook Ctr. for the Blind. Mem. ABA, Ohio State Bar Assn., Cin. Bar Assn., Arbitration Tribunal U.S. Dist. Ct., Ohio, 1984. Republican. Episcopalian. Office: Dinsmore & Shohl LLP 1900 Chemed Ctr 255 E Fifth St Cincinnati OH 45202-4089

DELONG, MARGARET DOHERTY, psychologist, consultant; b. Plainfield, NJ, Feb. 21, 1968; d. William Thomas and Carol Lou Doherty; m. John Richard DeLong, Aug. 1, 1998; children: Caroline Mary, Morgan Elizabeth. BA in Psychology magna cum laude, U. Vt., 1990; MA in Clin. Psychology, Fairleigh Dickinson U., 1992; MSEd in Sch. Psychology, Pace U., 1998, PsychD in Clin. Child/Sch. Psychology, 2000. Lic. psychologist NJ. Therapeutic tchr. Therapeutic Learning Ctr., Newark Beth Israel Med. Ctr., 1993—98; psychology intern Family Enrichment Program, Morristown, NJ, 1999—2000; sch. psychologist Livingston (NJ) Pub. Schs., 2000; psychologist, program dir. Family Connections, Orange, NJ, 2001—; pvt. practice psychology Liberty Corner, NJ, 2002—. Dir. comprehensive mental health program Presch. Psychol. Assessment Resources and Edn., 2001. Scholar, Bernardsville Bus. and Profl. Women's Assn., 1995. Mem.: APA, Am. Profl. Soc. of Abuse of Children, Morris County Psychol. Assn., Phi Beta Kappa. Avocations: telemark skiing, mountain biking, hiking, crafts. Office: 3640 Valley Rd PO Box 32 Liberty Corner NJ 07938 Office Phone: 908-832-7380. Office Fax: 908-832-7585.

DELONG-SMITH, STEPHANIE K. secondary school educator; b. Chadds Ford, Pa., Dec. 20, 1969; d. Warren Earl and Carla Jean (Douthat) DeLong; m. Carl E. Smith, July 27, 1996; 1 child, Laura Eden. BA in History and Social Studies Edn., York Coll. of Pa., 1992; MA in History, U. Ky., 1996. Tchr. 7th grade McCurdy Mission Sch., Espanola, N.Mex., 1992-94; dance instr. Lexington, 1993-94; tchr. 7th grade Woodland Hills Christian Sch., Harlan, Ky., 1996-97; tchr. high sch. social studies-AP U.S. history Cawood H.S., Harlan County Bd. Edn., 1997-99. Intern in mus. edn. Hagley Mus., Wilmington, Del., 1991. Lifeguard and Red Cross swim instr. Kendal and Crosslands, Kennett Square, Pa., 1986-96; advisor Y-Club, Cawood High Sch., 1997—. James Madison Meml. fellow Madison Found., 1993; recipient Ashland Golden Apple Teaching award Ashland Oil, 1999. Mem. Nat. Coun. History Edn., Orgn. Am. Historians, Ky. Assn. Tchrs. of History, Pa. Hist. Assn., Ladies Golf Assn. (v.p. 1999—), Beta Sigma Phi (Zeta Beta chpt.), Phi Sigma Pi. Avocations: ballet dancing, reading, golfing, cooking international cuisine, singing in church choir. Home: 1345 Ivy Hl Harlan KY 40831-1550 E-mail: Sdelong@Eastky.net.

DELORGE, AMY BETH, music educator; d. Arthur Frank and Mary Golden; m. Douglas Michael Delorge, June 25, 2000; 1 child, Michael Paul. B.Mus.Edn., U. of Mass., 1992. Cert. music tchr. Maine, N.H., Mass., 1992. Music tchr. Claremont (NH) Sch. Sys., 1992—95, Biddeford (Maine) Mid. Sch., 1995—. Arts grantee, Music Educators Nat. Conf., 1999—. Fellow: Ptnrs. in Arts and Learning (sch. rep. 1998—2001); mem.: Music Educators Nat. Conf. Office: Biddeford Middle Sch 335 Hill St Biddeford ME 04005 E-mail: adelorge@biddschools.org.

DELORME, DENISE ELIZABETH, communications educator; b. Alexandria, Va., May 19, 1968; d. Charles DuBose and Betty (Rush) DeLorme; m. Scott Charles Hagen, Dec. 18, 1999. ABJ cum laude, U. Ga., 1989, MA, 1991, PhD, 1995. Instr. advt. U. Ga., Athens, 1993—96; asst. prof. U. Ctrl. Fla., Orlando, 1996—2002, assoc. prof., 2002—. Mem. editl. bd. Jour. Advt. Edn., 2001—; contbr. articles to profl. jours. Grantee, Adv. Coun. Environ. Edn., 1999, Fla. Fish & Wildlife Conservation Commn., 2000. Mem.: Assn. Edn. Journalism and Mass Comm., Am. Mktg. Assn., Am. Acad. Advt. (mem. rsch. com., mem. awards com. 2001, Rsch. Fellowship award 2002). Avocations: travel, reading, aerobics. Home: 1624 Magnolia Ave Winter Park FL 32789 Office: U Ctrl Fla Nicholson Sch Comm 4000 Central Florida Blvd Orlando FL 32816-1344

DELOZIER, DORIS M. retired secondary school educator; b. Hartford, Vt., June 11, 1933; d. Arthur James and Lena Anne Moffitt; m. A. John Lacaillade, Aug. 19, 1958 (div. Sept. 6, 1964); m. Dean K. Delozier, July 9, 1969; 1 child, Tracy. BA, Plymouth State Coll., 1957; MEd, Boston U., 1968; advanced grad. studies, Harvard U., 1987. Lic. tchr. N.H., Mass. Tchr. English Laconia (N.H.) Sch. Dist., 1958—68, reading specialist, 1969—96; English as Second Lang. specialist Harvard U., Cambridge, Mass., 1984—87; reading cons. Coll. Park Elem. Sch., Ocala, Fla., 1999—2001; ret. Head Right to Read program Supervisory Assn. Union # 30, Laconia, 1970—80; mem. adv. bd. N.H. Edn. Assn., Concord, NH, 1975—85; literacy chmn. Delta Kappa Gamma, Laconia, 1970—80; reading curriculum devel. Laconia Sch. Sys., 1979; literacy sec. AAUW, Laconia, 1967—77; literacy chmn. Zonta Internat., Laconia, 1990—. Co-author: (booklet) Sign Posts in Reading, 1975; author: (study skills book) Fishing for Success, 1992, (guide booklet) Keep It Simple, 2001 (Am. Assn. Ret. Persons award, 2001). Recipient tchg. fellowship, Harvard U., 1984. Republican. Episcopalian. Avocations: golf, bridge, reading, antiques. Home: 11558 SW 72 Cir Ocala FL 34476-9487

DEL PAPA, FRANKIE SUE, former state attorney general; b. 1949; BA, U. Nev.; JD, George Washington U., 1974. Bar: Nev. 1974. Staff asst. U.S. Senator Alan Bible, Washington, 1971—74; assoc. Law Office of Leslie B. Grey, Reno, 1975—78; legis. asst. to U.S. Senator Howard Cannon, Washington, 1978—79; ptnr. Thornton & Del Papa, 1979—84; pvt. practice Reno, 1984—87; sec. of state State of Nev., Carson City, 1987—91, atty. gen., 1991—2002. Active Nev. Women's Fund; bd. dirs. Sierra Arts Found.; adv. com. Trust for Pub. Land. Democrat. E-mail: renofsdp@aol.com.*

DEL ROSSO, JEANA MARIE, literature educator; b. Binghamton, N.Y., Dec. 21, 1970; d. Paul Joseph and Roseann A. Del Rosso; m. David M. Freeman, June 18, 1994. BA in English, Binghamton U., 1992; MA in English, U. Md., 1993, women's studies cert., 1998, PhD in English, 2000. Tchg. asst. U. Md., College Park, 1994—2000; asst. prof. Coll. Notre Dame of Md., Balt., 2001—. Adj. faculty UMBC, Balt., 2000—01, Trinity Coll., Washington, 2000—01. Contbr. articles to jours. Mem.: MLA, Nat. Women's Studies Assn., Nat. Assn. Univ. Women, Golden Key, Phi Kappa Phi, Sigma Tau Delta (sponsor), Phi Beta Kappa. Office: Coll Notre Dame Md Dept English 4701 N Charles St Baltimore MD 21210

DEL SESTO, JANICE MANCINI, opera company executive; Grad., New England Conservatory. Dir. development and comm. New England Foundation for the Arts, 1983—89; dir. development and public relations Computer Museum, 1989—92; gen. dir. Boston Lyric Opera Co., Boston, 1992—. Office: Boston Lyric Opera Co 45 Franklin St Boston MA 02110-1301*

DEL TIEMPO, SANDRA KAY, sales executive; b. Willoughby, Ohio, Nov. 21, 1962; d. Charles Soloman and Lacey Marie (Webb) Eggers; m. Robert Joseph Craig, June 28, 1986 (div. Jan. 1993); 1 child, Misty Marie Mangus; m. Robert David Del Tiempo, Feb. 14, 1995; stepchildren: Jaime Brandon, Joseph David Del Tiempo. AAB cum laude, Shawnee State U., 1985; BBA summa cum laude, Ohio U., 1987; postgrad., Pepperdine U., 1998-2000. From ter. mgr. to sales mgr. ARA Cory, San Diego, 1988-90; sales rep. Rsch. Inst. Am., Riverside, Calif., 1990-92, 96-00, regional sales mgr. So. Calif., L.A., 1992-95, leader's coun. Culver City, 1996-2000, pres. bd. dirs., 1996-97, asst. mgr., 1997, 1999-2000, corp. acct. mgr., 1997-2000; mem. sales adv. bd. RIA/CLR Group (formerly Rsch. Inst. Am.), Culver City, 1998-2000; sr. v.p. Media Strategy Lawnmower Media, Culver City, 2000; sr. account exec. SAP Am., Irvine, Calif., 2000—. Cons. Video Ave., Paradise Pizza, Chillicothe, Ohio, 1987-88; sales rep. to corp. acct. mgr. Rsch. Inst. Am. Orange County, L.A., 1990-2000. Active Girl Scouts U.S., Menifee, 1988-92, Jr. All Am. Football. Mem. NAFE, NOW, Phi Kappa Phi, Phi Theta Kappa, Delta Mu Delta. Democrat. Avocations: travel, reading, jazz. Home: 6732 E Ashler Hills Cave Creek AZ 85331-3130 Office: CCH Inc 2700 Lake Cook Rd Riverwoods IL 60015 E-mail: sdeltiempo@yahoo.com.

DEL TORO-POLITOWICZ, LILLIAN, medical association administrator, geriatric counselor; b. Bronx, N.Y., Feb. 23, 1954; d. Billie Antonio Del Toro and Eva Luz (Guasp) Toro; 1 child, Yvelise Delilah Chandler; m. Walter Politowicz, Nov. 23, 1997; 1 stepchild, Sebastian. BS in Psychology summa cum laude, Mercy Coll., 1981; postgrad., L.I. U., 1982-83, Harvard U., 1973-74, Lehman Coll., 1972, 75, Nova South-Eastern U., 1998—. Lic. adminstr. adult care facilities, Fla. Mental hygiene therapist Rockland Psychiat. Hosp., Orangeburg, N.Y., 1975-81; office mgr. Frankart Furniture, Inc., Pelham Pkwy., N.Y., 1979-84; regional office mgr. W.J. Sloane, Inc., Ridgewood, N.J., 1984-86; bookkeeper, asst. dir. mgmt. info. sys. Midland Lumber Supply Co., Midland Pk., N.J., 1986-89; adminstr. Fla. Golden Years, Spring Hill, 1991-92, Gallo House II, River Lodge, New Port Richey, Fla., 1994-95, Ranch House, Tarpon Springs, Fla., 1993-94; co-owner Elder Care Foster Home, Spring Hill, Fla., 1992—. Grad. admissions counselor L.I. U., Bklyn., 1981-82; elder-care cons. Fla. Golden Years, Spring Hill, 1991-92. Harvard U. scholar, 1973-74; recipient outstanding achievement, health & human svcs.- cmty. svc. award YWCA and St. Petersburg Times, Tampa, 1997; undergraduate pre-medicine scholar Lehman Coll., Bronx, N.Y., 1972, 75, Harvard U., 1973-74. Mem. AAUW, NAFE, Altrusa Internat. (mem. cmty. projects com. 1997), Fla. Assisted Living Adminstrs. Assn., Alpha, Psi Chi. Avocations: world music and dance, opera, ballet, reading, nature. Home and Office: Elder Care Foster Home 6427 Mayhill Ct Spring Hill FL 34606-6028 E-mail: politowicz@yahoo.com.

DELUCA, ANNETTE, professional golfer; b. North Bergen, N.J., May 13, 1968; Golfer LPGA, 1989—; mem. Asian Tour, 1993; mem. Gold Coast Tour, 1994, 95; 3 Gold Coast victories, 1995; qualifier U.S. Women's Open, 1994, 95. Avocations: fishing, water sports, harley davidson motorcycles, movies, working out. Office: c/o LPGA 100 International Golf Dr Daytona Beach FL 32124-1082

DE LUCA, EVA, vocalist, writer, composer; d. John Adolph De Luca and Rosa Maria Litrenta; m. Alfred A. Sirna, May 11, 1975 (dec. Dec. 1984); m. Russell Frederick Du Laux, Dec. 24, 1985. Student, Peabody Inst., 1936-37, Juilliard Sch., 1943-44, Marymount Coll., 1985; Doctorate (hon.), Dewey Internat. Consortium, 1999. Pres. Eva De Luca Co., N.Y.C., 1950, Greeting Scrolls, Ltd., N.Y.C., 1960; cons. Creative Consultations, N.Y.C., 1994; mem. adv. bd. Humanity Against Hatred, N.Y.C., 1992-96; CEO/creative dir. Ideas Unlimited U.S.A., 2001. Profl. operatic debut Phila. La Scala Opera Co.; European opera debut La Boheme and Madama Butterfly; starred in 1st rec. of La Rondine (Puccini) for Columbia Records, 1955; author poetry. Com. mem. Women's Nat. Rep. Club, N.Y.C., 1978-85; active Italian Welfare League, N.Y.C., 1978, Met. Opera Guild, N.Y.C., 1979. Recipient Editor's Choice award for outstanding achievement in poetry Nat. Libr. Poetry, 1997, awarded 2 design patents Mirror-View Measuring Stick, 1972. Mem. The Famous Poets Soc., The Russian Nobility Assn. in Am., Inc. (benefit com. mem.), Nat. Orgn. of Italian-Am. Women, Sovereign Order of Orthodox Knights Hospitaller of St. John of Jerusalem (dame comdr.). Roman Catholic. Achievements include patents for mirror-view measuring stick, personal dental aid; inventor in field; patents for personal dental aid. Avocations: reading, political campaign activity, theater, opera. Home: FDR Sta Box 477 New York NY 10150-0477

DELUCCIA, PAULA, artist; b. Paterson, N.J., Sept. 9, 1953; d. Ralph Lincoln and Isabel Miriam (Santucci) DeLuccia; m. Larry Poulin, Dec. 19, 1981. Student, Ridgewood (N.J.) Sch. Art, 1971-73, Kansas City (Mo.) Art Inst., 1973-74. Exhibited in group shows at Nelson Atkins Mus., Kansas City, 1974, Ridgewood Sch. Art, 1978, Soghor Leonard & Assocs., N.Y.C., 1985, Art & Design, Phila., 1985, Jerusalem Gallery, N.Y.C., 1986, Helander Gallery, Palm Beach, Fla., 1990, 91, 92, 93, Wetherholt Gallery, Washington, 1991, Perspectives, Ghent, N.Y., 1991, Schulte Galleries, South Orange, N.J., 1992, Greene County Coun. on the Arts, Catskill, N.Y., 1992-93, Lorraine Kessler Gallery, Poughkeepsie, N.Y., 1992-93, Philharmonic Ctr. for the Arts, Naples, Fla., 1993, Farah Damji Fine Art, N.Y.C., 1993, Mountaintop Gallery, Windham, N.Y., 1994, 95, Roger Smith Gallery, N.Y.C., 1994, Art/Omi Studios, Omi, N.Y., 1994, Planet Thailand, Bklyn., 1995, Mountain Top Gallery, Windham, N.Y., 1995, 98, Tribes Gallery, N.Y.C., 1996, Planet Thailand, Bklyn., 1997, 98, Sideshow, Bklyn., 1998, Claudia Carr Gallery, N.Y.C., 1998, Steinboum Kraus Gallery, N.Y.C., 1999, Greene City Coun. on Art Small Works, Catskill, N.Y., 2000, 01, Side Show Gallery, 2001, Greene County Coun on Arts, 2002, Phoenix Gallery, 2002, Perrella Gallery, Johnstown, NY, 2003, others; two-person exhbns. include Farah Damji Fine Art, 1993, LaCappelli, Cambridge, Mass., 1995; one-woman shows include The Bentley Inn, Bay Head, N.J., 1993, Hair Gallery, N.Y.C., 1995, Side Show Gallery, Bklyn., 2001, 2002, C.W. White Gallery, Portland, 2003, Side Show Gallery, 2003, Phoenix Gallery, 2003, Richard Sena Gallery, Hudson, N.Y., 2003, Deborah Davis Fine Art, Hudson, 2004, AAWAA Gallery, Bklyn., 2004, Studio 18, N.Y., 2004; represented in permanent collections of City of Barcelona, Art Omi, Leshanski, O'Sullivan & Maybaum, N.Y.C., and numerous private collections; drawing reproduced in Cover Mag., 1982; paintings reproduced in Long Shot, 1993. Recipient Art Triangle Barcelona, Spain, 1987, Inaugural Yr. award Art/Omi, 1992. Home: 831 Broadway New York NY 10003-4706

DE LUNA-GONZALEZ, ELMA, accountant; b. Edinburg, Tex., June 22, 1950; d. Emilio De Luna and Julia Andaverde; m. Antonio Gonzalez, Oct. 10, 1975; 1 child, Julissa Priscilla Gonzalez. AA, Houston C.C., 1986; BA, Houston Internat. U., 1990, U. Houston, 1997; MA, Prairie View A&M U., 1999. Bookkeeper Aluminum Industries, McAllen, Tex., 1973—75; estimator Clow Corp., Tarrant City, Ala., 1975—79; acct. Freeman Design and Display Co., Houston, 1980—86, Forrest Mfg. Co., Houston, 1988, Hispanic Bus. and Acctg. Svcs., Houston, 1988—2001; asst. to dean Prairie View (Tex.) A&M U., 2001—. Musician, vocalist De Luna Band, Dekalb, Ill., 1968—88. Composer: Impossible Love, 1987. Chair, treas. Gonzalez for Tex. Ho. Reps. Campaign, Houston, 1994. Named Women of the Yr., Ala. Women Soc., 1988; recipient Mayors award, City Kendelton, Tex., 2002. Mem.: ACA, AAUW, Tex. Counseling Assn., Nat. Soc. Pub. Accts., League United L.Am. Citizens, No. Ill. U. Women Club, Phi Delta Kappa, Chi Sigma Iota. Avocations: writing, music, reading. Home: 16614 Dounreay Dr Houston TX 77084 Office: Prairie View A&M U PO Box 4207 Prairie View TX 77446 Office Phone: 936-357-2014.

DE LUNG, JANE SOLBERGER, independent sector executive; b. Anniston, Ala., July 9, 1944; d. Samuel and Margaret Polk (Oldham) S.; m. Harry Leonard De Lung, Apr. 23, 1965 (div. 1972); m. Charles F. Westoff, May 2, 1997. BA in History, Emory U., 1966; MA in Urban Planning, Roosevelt U., Chgo., 1972. Exec. asst. Cook County Legal Assistance, Chgo., 1967-69; asst. dir. family planning Am. Coll. Ob-gyn., Chgo., 1969-71; v.p. Ill. Family Planning Coun., Chgo., 1971-80; asst. commr. Chgo. Dept. Pub. Health, 1981-82; pres. Pub. Solutions, Princeton, NJ, 1982-88, Population Resource Ctr., N.Y.C., 1988—. Bd. dirs. Planned Parenthood Mercer County, Trenton, N.J., 1986-96, Population Resource Ctr., 1989—, Trenton Head Start, 1993—; mem. adv. bd. dept. sociology Princeton U., 1991—. Mem. APHA, AAUW, LWV, Internat. Union Sci. Study of Population, Population Assn. Am., UN Assn. of U.S.A. (nat. adv. com. 1998-). Democrat. Episcopalian. Office: Population Resource Ctr 15 Roszel Rd Princeton NJ 08540-6248 Office Phone: 609-452-2822. E-mail: jdelung@prcnj.org.

DELYRA, ELIZABETH M. product designer; b. Greenfield, Mass., Apr. 29, 1930; d. Michel A. and Harriet M. (Couture) Morvant; m. J. George DeLyra, Apr. 16, 1951 (div. May 1970); children: Michel DeLyra, Geoffrey DeLyra, Martha DeLyra. Legal sec. Jacobus & Seibert, Greenfield, Mass., 1948—51; owner, operator Studio, S. Harpswell, Maine, 1960—68; exec. sec. Econ. Opportunity Office, Bath, Maine, 1968—72; designer, craftsmen textile/lampshade products Brunswick, Maine, 1972—. Mem.: Craft Guild Maine (treas. 1990—2000), United Maine Craftsmen (Pres. 1982—84, treas. 1988—94). Home: 31 Garrison St Brunswick ME 04011 Office Phone: 207-725-6727.

DEMARAIS, KARIN, financial analyst; d. Patricia and James Demarais. BA, U. New Hampshire, 1994—98. Bus. process analyst Doctor's Associates Inc., Milford, Conn., 2001—, internat. R&D adminstr., 1999—2001. Recipient Dean's Scholarship, U. New Hampshire, 1994 - 1998. Office: Doctor's Associates Inc 325 Bic Drive Milford CT 06460 E-mail: demarais_k@subway.com.

DEMARCO, CAROLYN BETH, human resources specialist; b. Cheyenne, Wyo., Feb. 21, 1978; d. T. J. DeMarco and Irene F. French. BS in Bus. Adminstrn., Rowan U., Glassboro, NJ, 2000, post grad. in Bus. Adminstrn., 2003—. Mng. dir. Huntington Learning Ctr., Lawrenceville, NJ, 2000—01; human resources assoc. excelleRx, Inc., Phila., 2001—. Mem.: Soc. For Human Resource Mgrs. Office: excelleRx Inc 530 Walnut Street Suite 550 Philadelphia PA 19106 Personal E-mail: cdemarco221@netscape.net. E-mail: cdemarco@excellerx.com.

DEMARCO, PATRICIA M. state agency administrator; m. Joseph Barkoski. BSc, PhD in Biology. Prin., owner Alaska Joe Fishing Charters; pres. Anchorage Econ. Devel. Corp., 1995—99; commr. Regulatory Commn. Alaska, Anchorage, 1999—. Bd. dir. Anchorage Symphony Orch., Downtown Rotary. Office: RCA 701 West 8th Ave Ste 300 Anchorage AK 99501

DEMAREST, CYNTHIA, music educator; m. Gerald Demarest. BA in Music Edn., East Ctrl. U., Ada, Okla., 1979; MusM, Southwestern Okla. State U., 1994. Cert. tchr. Okla., Tex., Ga. Choral dir. / English tchr. Holdenville (Okla.) Pub. Schs., 1979—90; dir. choral activities / choral coord. Denison (Tex.) HS, 1990—92; elem. music specialist Thomas (Okla.) Elem. Sch., 1992—94; dir. music Darren Patterson Christian Acad., Buena Vista, Colo., 1995—98; faculty Colo. Mountain Coll., Buena Vista, Colo., 1995; dir. choral activities Effingham County HS, Springfield, Ga., 2000—. Piano instr., 1970—. Mem.: Ga. Music Educators Assn. (dist. solo and ensemble festival chmn. 2003), Nat. Fedn. of Music Clubs (festival chmn. Colo. chpt. 1998—2000), Ga. Fedn. of Music Clubs (festival chmn. 2003), Am. Choral Directors Assn. (Ga. chpt. newsletter editor, mem. state bd. 2001), Delta Kappa Gamma (1st v.p. Sigma chpt. 1988—90, pres. Upsilon chpt. 1996—2000). Office: Effingham County High Sch 1589 Hwy 119 S Springfield GA 31329 Office Phone: 912-754-6404.

DEMAREST, SYLVIA M. lawyer; b. Lake Charles, La., Aug. 16, 1944; d. Edmand and Emily Demarest; m. James A. Johnston, Jr., Oct. 31, 1975 (div. Dec. 1979). Student, U. S.W. La., 1963-66; JD, U. Tex., 1969. Bar: Tex. 1969, U.S. Supreme Ct. 1973, U.S. Ct. Appeals (5th cir.) 1970, U.S. Ct. Appeals (7th cir.) 1979, U.S. Ct. Appeals (11th cir.) 1980, U.S. Dist. Ct. (no. dist.) Tex. 1970, U.S. Dist. Ct. (ea. dist.) Tex. 1970, U.S. Dist. Ct. (so. dist.) Tex. 1972. Reginald H. Smith Cmty. Lawyer fellow, Corpus Christi and Dallas, 1969-71; house counsel Tex. Inst. Ednl. Devel., San Antonio, 1972-73; staff atty. Dallas Legal Svsc. Found., Inc., 1973, exec. dir., 1973-76; sole practice Dallas, 1977-78; mgr. product litig., dir. Windle Turley, P.C., Dallas, 1978-83; sole practice Dallas, 1983-85; ptnr. Demarest & Smith, Dallas, 1985—. Mem. faculty trial advocacy program So. Meth. U. Law Sch., 1984; lectr. Contbr. articles to profl. jours. Mem. ABA, State Bar Tex., ATLA, Dallas Bar Assn., Dallas Trial Lawyers Assn. (past pres.), Dallas Inn of Ct. (master of the bar 1989—). Democrat. Home: 1812 Atlantic St Dallas TX 75208-3002 Office: 4040 N Central Expwy Ste 800 Dallas TX 75204

DEMARINIS, NANCY ANN, state legislator; b. Glen Ridge, N.J. BS, U. Conn., 1975; MS, So. Conn. U., 1981. Ret. tchr., gudiance counselor; mem. Conn. Ho. of Reps., 1993—. Mem. Groton City Coun., 1987-89, Town Coun., 1981-89. Home: 898 Shennecossett Rd Groton CT 06340-6047

DEMARIS, HEATHER, occupational therapist; b. St. Paul, Aug. 20, 1974; d. Florann Irene Singer. BA in Psychology, Coll. of St. Benedict, St. Joseph, Minn., 1996; MA in Occupl. Therapy, Coll. of St. Catherine, St. Paul, 1999. Lic. occupl. therapist Minn., registered Nat. Bd. Cert. Occupl. Therapists, 1999. Therapeutic recreation program St. Benedict's Ctr., St. Cloud, Minn., 1998; program aide, day treatment Courage Ctr., Mpls., 1998; occupl therapy intern VA Med. Ctr., Albuquerque, 1999, Marquette (Mich.) Gen. Hosp., 1999; mental health counselor Hoikka Ho., Inc., St. Paul, 1999; occupl. therapist PRO Rehab., St. Paul, 1999—2000; occupl. therapy dir. Hoikka Ho., Inc., 2000—02; resident svcs. coord. Wilder Found., 2002—. Mem. safety com. Hoikka Ho., Inc., 2000—; presenter in field. Emergency rm. vol. Regions Hosp., St. Paul, 2001—; VISTA vol. Coll. St. Benedict, 1993. Christian. Avocations: hiking, camping, travel, reading, music. Office: Wilder Found 516 Humboldt Ave Saint Paul MN 55107

DE MARR, MARY JEAN, English language educator; b. Champaign, Ill., Sept. 20, 1932; d. William Fleming and Laura Alice (Shauman) Bailey. BA, Lawrence Coll., 1954; MA, U. Ill., 1957, PhD, 1963; postgrad., U. Tuebingen, 1954-55, Moscow State U., 1961-62. Asst. prof. English Willamette U., 1964-65; asst. prof. English Ind. State U., 1965-70, assoc. prof., 1970-75, prof., 1975-95, prof. emerita English and women's studies, 1996—. Author: Colleen McCullough: A Critical Companion, 1996, Barbara Kingsolver: A Critical Companion, 1999, Kaye Gibbons: A Critical Companion, 2003; co-author: Adolescent Female Portraits in the American Novel, 1961-81: An Annotated Bibliography, 1983, The Adolescent in The American Novel Since 1960, 1986; Am. editor: Annual Bibliography of English Language and Literature, 1979-90; editor, contbr. In the Beginning: First Novels in Mystery Series, 1995. Recipient Fulbright assistantship, 1954—55, Dove award, Popular Culture Assn., 1996, Midam. award, Soc. for the Study of Midwestern Lit., 2000. Mem.: ACLU, AAUP, MLA, Modern Humanities Rsch. Assn., Phi Kappa Phi, Phi Beta Kappa. Home: 594 Woodbine Terre Haute IN 47803-1760 E-mail: mjd594@msn.com.

DEMARS, BONNIE MACON, librarian; b. Pensacola, Fla., Jan. 13, 1943; AA Pensacola Jr. Coll., 1963; BS, U. West Fla., 1968; M in Libr. Sci., Fla. State U., 1983. Head cataloging dept. W. Fla. Regional Library, 1969—79, asst. head tech. svcs., 1979—92, head reference dept., 1992—. Office: W Fla Regional Library 200 W Gregory St Pensacola FL 32502

DEMARS, JUDITH M. elementary school educator; b. Cleve., Mar. 17, 1947; d. Edward C. and Ann J. (Sedivy) Nau; m. Gordon DeMars, Mar. 10, 1973; 1 child, Darren Jay. BS in Edn., Cleve. State U., 1969; MA in Edn., Baldwin Wallace Coll., Berea, Ohio, 1984; PhD, U. Akron, 1990. Cert. tchr. Nat. Bd. Edn., early childhood generalist Nat. Bd. Edn. Tchr. Garfield Heights City Sch., Ohio; tchr. 2nd and 3rd grades Warrensville Heights City Sch., Ohio; tutor developmental reading, 6th-8th grades Medina, Ohio; tutor Chpt. I reading, 1st and 2nd grade, multiage tchr. Highland Local Schs., Medina. Ohio Reads coord. Sharon Elem.; presenter in field. Rsch. on beginning reading methods. Mem. adv. com. Medina County Tchrs. Acad. Martha Holden Jennings grantee. Mem. Internat. Reading Assn. (Ohio coun.), Assn. for Supervision and Curriculum Devel., Assn. for Childhood Edn. Internat. Home: 6704 Kennard Rd Medina OH 44256-8559

DE MARS, SUSAN S. lawyer, health products executive; BA, Claremont (Calif.) McKenna Coll.; JD, Harvard U., Cambridge, Mass. Ptnr. Sacks, Tierney, Phoenix, 1993—95; asst. gen. counsel PCS Health Systems, Irving, Tex., 1995—97, v.p. corp. accounts, 1997—99; v.p., gen. counsel Advance PCS Health Systems, Irving, Tex., 1999—2000; sr. v.p., gen. counsel Advance PCS, Irving, Tex., 2000—. Office: Advance PCS Inc Ste 1200 750 W John Carpenter Fwy Irving TX 75039

DE MARTIN, COLLEEN DIANNE, college official, interior designer, consultant; b. Detroit, Mar. 18, 1950; d. F. Robert and Jeanne Claire Maxwell; m. Gerald John De Martin (div. 1984); children: Jessica Marie, Timothy Robert. BS in Interior Design and Home Econs., Ea. Mich. U., 1972; MA in Housing and Interior Design, Wayne State U., 1975; postgrad. [illegible] Mich. Hypnosis Assn. Program coord. interior design U. Minn. Tech. Coll., Crookston, 1977-84; instr. interior design Calif. Poly. State U., San Luis Obispo, 1984-89, Wayne State U., Detroit, 1990-93; counselor, student advisor Ross Tech. Inst., Ann Arbor and Taylor, Mich., 1993-96; program dir. interior design, student advisor Baker Coll., Auburn Hills, Mich., 1994—. V.p., historian Ctrl. Coast Interior Designers, 1983-85; CAD coord., kitchen designer Grahl's Kitchen & Bath, Woodhaven, Mich., 1990-91; hist. cons. Avila Lighthouse Restoration/Harbor Commn., Avila Beach, Calif., 1987-88, Hart House Restoration, Santa Maria, Calif., 1988-89; com. me., organizer State Conf. East Faces West, San Luiis Obispo, 1986; asst. counselor Job Tng. Placement Assn., Southgate, Mich., 1995; owner Maxwell Design Cons., Grosse Ile, Mich., 1996—; spkr. Stroheim & Rohamm, Troy, Mich., 1998. Editor slide/tape series The French Monarchy: The Study of French Furnishings, 1981. Handbell player El Morro Nazarene Ch., Los Osos, Calif., 1987-89, dir. children;s handbell, 1988; panel participant on teenage drugs Grosse Ile TV, 1996; tour hostess Garden Club, Grosse Ile, 1998; instr., advisor Habitat for Humanity, Auburn Hills, 1999. Recipient outstanding svc. award Distinction Edn. Clubs Am., 1981, Interior Design Club, U. Minn., 1984, Am. Soc. Interior Designers, 1985; scholar Presbyn. Ch. U.S.A., 1968-69. Mem. Interior Design Soc. (profl. mem., edn. rep. 1975—). Mem. Nazarene Ch. Avocations: basket weaving, paper making, sewing, piano. Home: 28731 Elbamar Dr Grosse Ile MI 48138-2070 Office: Baker Coll 1500 University Dr Auburn Hills MI 48326-2642

DEMARY, JO LYNNE, state official, elementary school educator; BEd, DEd, Coll. of William and Mary; MS in Spl. Edn., U. Va. Commonwealth. Tchr. Fairfax County Schs., Va., Henrico County Schs., Va., from tchr. to asst. supt.; asst. supt. instruction Commonwealth of Va., 1994—99, acting supt. instruction, 1999—2000; supt. of instruction, 2000—. Office: Va Dept Edn PO Box 2120 Richmond VA 23218

DE MASSA, JESSIE G. media specialist; BJ, Temple U.; MLS, San Jose State U., 1967; postgrad., U. Okla., U. So. Calif. Tchr. Palo Alto (Calif.) Unified Sch. Dist., 1966; librarian Antelope Valley Joint Union High Sch. Dist., Lancaster, Calif., 1966-68, ABC Unified Sch. Dist., Artesia, Calif., 1968-72; dist. librarian Tehachapi (Calif.) Unified Sch. Dist., 1972-81; media specialist, free lance writer, 1981—; assoc. Chris DeMassa & Assocs., 1988—. Author: (novel) The Haunting and Murder in Aruba, 2002; contbr. articles to profl. jours. Mem. Statue of Liberty Ellis Island Found., Inc.; charter supporter U.S. Holocaust Meml. Mus., Washington; supporting mem. U.S. Holocaust Meml. Coun., Washington; mem. Nat. Trust for Hist. Preservation. Named to Nat. Women's Hall of Fame, 1995. Fellow Internat. Biog. Assn.; mem. Calif. Media and Libr. Educators Assn., Calif. Assn. Sch. Librs. (exec. coun.), AAUW (bull. editor chpt., assoc. editor state bull., chmn. publicity, 1955-68), Nat. Mus. Women in Arts (charter), Hon Fellows John F. Kennedy Libr. (founding mem.), Women's Roundtable of Orange County, Nat. Writer's Assn. (so. Calif. chpt.), Calif. Retired Tchrs. Assn. (Harbor Beach divsn. 77), The Heritage Found., Claremont Inst., Nat. Women's History Mus. (charter mem.), Libr. of Congress (nat. charter mem.). Home: 9951 Garrett Cir Huntington Beach CA 92646-3604 Personal E-mail: jdwriter10@aol.com.

DE MATTEO, DREA, actress; b. Queens, NY, 1973; BFA in film prodn., NYU, Tish Sch. Arts. Owner Filth Mart Clothing, NY. Actor: (TV series) The Sopranos, 1999—; (films) Meet Prince Charming, 1999, Sleepwalk, 2000, Swordfish, 2001, The Perfect You, 2002, Deuces Wild, 2002, Love Rome, 2002, Prey for Rock & Roll, 2003, Dirty Love, 2003, Beacon Hill, 2003. Office: 1100 Ave of the Americas New York NY 10036*

DEMATTEO, GLORIA JEAN, financial counselor; b. Perth Amboy, N.J., May 23, 1943; d. John J. and Helena (Elias) Kancz; m. Ronald D. DeMatteo, Feb. 20, 1965 (div. Nov. 1987); children: Douglas J., Keith G. Student, Berkeley Sch., 1961. CLU. Exec. sec. Rhodia Inc., New Brunswick, N.J., 1961-65; real estate saleswomen Mid-Jersey Realty, East Brunswick, N.J., 1974-79; pntr. Realty World Garden of Homes, East Brunswick, 1979-81; spl. agt. Prudential Ins. Co. Am., Iselin, N.J., 1981-2000; agt. Rahway (N.J.) Savs. and Ins. Agy., Inc., 2000—01; account exec. retirement svcs. divsn. Citistreet Travelers Educators Retirement, Woodbridge, NJ, 2002—. V.p. Belcourt Condo Assn., North Brunswick, N.J., 1987-88. Mem. Nat. Assn. Life Underwriters (nat. sales achievement award, nat. quality award), Soc. Fin. Svc. Profls., Prudential Leaders Club. Avocations: bridge, hiking, dance, theater. Home: 463 Andover Pl East Brunswick NJ 08816-5121 Office: 581 Main St Woodbridge NJ 07095 E-mail: gdematteo@citistreetonline.com.

DEMBROW, DANA LEE, lawyer; b. Washington, Sept. 29, 1953; parents: Daniel William and Catherine Louise (Carder) D. BA, Duke U., 1975; JD, George Washington U., 1980. Bar: D.C., Md., W.Va. Law clk. D.C. Superior Ct., Washington, 1979-80; assoc. Smink & Scheuermann, Washington, 1980-81, Reback & Parsons, Washington, 1981-82, Howard M. Rensin, Hyattsville, Md., 1984-86; mem. com. on constitutional and adminstrv. law Md. Ho. of Dels., 1986-92; mem. jud. com. Md. State Legis., 1993—. Chair county affairs com., Montgomery Del., 1994—; can. for congress, Md.'s 4th Congl. Dist., 1992; chair subcom. on civil law and procedure House Judiciary Com., 1994—, chair Intergovernmental Affairs Com., Southern Legis. Conference, 1999-2000. Chair Colesville Strawberry Festival, 1998, 99. Office: 220A Lowe House Office Bldg Annapolis MD 21401 E-mail: dana_dembrow@house.state.md.us., del.dem.@erols.com.

DEMBROWSKI, NANCY J. state senator; m. Ed Dembrowski (dec.); children: Michael, Rebecca, Patrick. With WKVI Radio, Knox, Ind.; mayor Knox, Ind.; state sen. 5th dist. Ind. State Senate, Indpls., 2002—, mem. elections and civic affairs com., civic affairs subcom., mem. judiciary com., cts. and juvenile justice subcom., mem. govtl. affairs and interstate cooperation com, govtl. affairs subcom. Mem.: numerous C. of C., Starke County Jr. Achievement (pres.), Starke United (chair), Starke County Youth Club (sec.), Kiwanis Club. Democrat. Roman Catholic. Avocations: reading, gardening. Office: Indiana State Senate 200 W Washington St Indianapolis IN 46204-2787

DEMEGRET, A. JEAN HUGHES, secondary education educator, artist; b. Hancock County, Ind., Oct. 22, 1927; d. Harlin E. and Melva L. Hughes. BAE, Butler U., 1949; student, John Herron Art Inst., Indpls.; MA, Columbia U., 1965; postgrad., No. Ill. U., Europe, 1966. Tchr. art Indpls. Pub. Schs., 1949-51; tchr. art and English Fortville (Ind.) Sch. Sys., 1951-62; supr. art dept. Greenfield (Ind.) Ctrl. H.S., 1962-84; tchr. adult art high schs., Indpls. and Greenfield. Exhibited paintings in Hoosier Art Show, 1960s and 70s, Ind. State Fair, 1960s and 70s, Columbia U. Art Gallery, 1963-66, others. Mem. Indpls. Mus. Art. Mem. Hancock County Ret. Tchrs., Bus. and Profl. Women (past pres.), Order Eastern Star, Ind. Sch. Women's Club, Nat. Art Educators Assn., Nat. Women in Art, Internat. Soc. Educators in Art, Delta Kappa Gamma (past pres.). Methodist. Avocations: painting portraits and horses, music, travel. Home: 411 S Main St Fortville IN 46040-1610

DEMENT, IRIS, vocalist, songwriter; b. Paragould, Ark., Jan. 5, 1961; d. Patric Shaw and Flora Mae DeM. Represented by Rounder/Philo, 1991-92, Warner Bros., 1993—. Songwriter, 1986—; performer open mic. nights, Kansas City. Albums include Infamous Angel, 1992, rereleased 1993, My Life, 1994, The Way I Should, 1996. Home: PO Box 28856 Kansas City MO 64188-8856 Office: Warner Bros 3300 Warner Blvd Burbank CA 91505-4694

DE MERE-DWYER, LEONA, medical illustrator; b. Memphis, May 1, 1928; d. Clifton and Leona (McCarthy) De M.; m. John Thomas Dwyer, May 10, 1952; children: John, DeMere, Patrice, Brian, Anne-Clifton DeMere Dwyer, McCarthy-DeMere Dwyer. BA, Rhodes Coll., Memphis, 1949; MSc, U. Memphis, 1984; PhD, Kennedy-Western U., 1990. Lic. embalmer, funderal dir. Med. artist McCarthy DeMere, Memphjis, 1950-80; pres. Aesthetic Med. & Forensic Art, 1984—; speech therapist Memphis, 1950-82. Lectr. on med. art univs., confs., assns.; cons. in prostheses Vocat. Rehab. Svcs., in plastic surgery, 2001; elected expert witness in funeralization Nat. Forensic Ctr. Author: AIDS; Care of Health Care Workers in the Workplace; contbr. articles to profl. jours. Bereavement counselor, organizer Ladies of St. Jude, Memphis, 1960; active Brooks Art Gallery League of Memphis; emm. God's Unfinished Bus. com. Temple Israel; vice dir. Tellico Hist. Found., 1980; mem. exec. bd. Chickasaw coun. Boy Scouts Am.; active Rep. campaign coms. Recipient Disting. Svc. award Gupton-Jones Coll. Mortuary Sci., 1981, Silver medal Sons of the Am. Revolution medal, 1985, Martha Washington medal. Mem. Nat. Forensic Ctr. (expert witness funeralization 1991—), Fedn. Internat. d'Automobile (internat. car racing 1972, lic.), Assn. Med. Illustrators, Am. Assn. Med. Assts., Emergency Dept. Nurses Assn., Am. Physicians Nurses Assn., Am. Soc. Plastic and Reconstructive Surgeons Found. (guest mem. cons.), Women in Law (chmn. assocs.), Exec. Women Am., Brandeis U. Women, DAR (1st v.p. regent 1980), UDC (pres. Nathan Bedford Forrest chpt.), Cotton Carnival Assn. (chairperson children's sect. 1968-70), Tenn. Club, Royal Matron Amaranth (Faith Ct.), Sertoma (1st female mem. Memphis, elected pres. 1989-90), Pi Sigma Eta, Kappa Delta (adv.), Kappa Delta Pi. Home: 106 Pinehurst st Memphis TN 38117-2336

DEMERS, CATHERINE MARY, parochial school educator; b. Boston, Apr. 13, 1962; d. Martin Joseph and Catherine Veronica (Doherty) Costello; m. John Robert Demers, June 25, 1988; children: Timothy, Thomas, Peter, Lilyana. BA in English, Regis Coll., Weston, Mass., 1984; MA in Pastoral Ministry, Boston Coll., 1986. Tchr. Cardinal Spellman High Sch., Brockton, Mass., 1985—93, 2000—; dir. religious edn. Sacred Heart Ch., Weymouth, Mass., 1993—98; tchr. St. Frances Cabrini Ch., Scituate, Mass., 1999—2000. Mem.: Nat. Cath. Ednl. Assn. Office: Cardinal Spellman High Sch 738 Court St Brockton MA 02302

DEMERS, JUDY LEE, former state legislator, university dean; b. Grand Forks, North Dakota, June 27, 1944; d. Robert L. and V. Margaret (Harming) Prosser; m. Donald E. DeMers, Oct. 3, 1964; div. Oct. 1971; 1 child, Robert M.; m. Joseph M. Murphy, Mar. 5, 1977; div. Oct. 1983. BS in nursing, U. N.D., 1966; M in Edn., U. Wash., 1973, post grad., 1973-76. Pub. health nurse Govt., Wash., DC, 1966-68; Combined Nursing Svc., Mpls., 1968-69; instr. pub. health nursing U. N.D., Grand Forks, ND, 1969-71; assoc. dir. Medex program, 1970-72; rsch. assoc. U. Wash., Seattle, 1973-76; dir. family nurse practitioner program, 1977-82; dir. under grad. med. edn., 1982-83; assoc. dir. rural health, 1982-85; mem. N.D. Ho. of Reps., 1982-92; assoc. dean, 1983—; mem. N.D. Senate, 1992-2000. Cons. health manpower devel. staff, Honolulu, 1975-81, Assn. Physician asst. programs, Washington, 1979-82; site visitor cons., AMA Com. Allied Health Edn. Accreditation, Chgo.,1979-81. Author: Educating New Health Practitioners, 1976; mem. editl. bd.: P.A. Jour., 1976-78; contbr. articles to profl. jours. Sec., bd. dirs. Valley Health, Grand Forks, N.D., 1982—; mem. exec. com., bd. dirs. Agassiz Health Systems Agy., Grand Forks, 1982-86; mem. N.D. State Daycare Adv. Com., 1983-93, Mayor's Adv. com. on Police Policy, Grand Forks, 1983-85, N.D. State Foster Care Adv. Com., 1985-87, N.D. State Hypertension Adv. Com., 1983-85, Gov.'s Com. on DUI and Traffic Safety, 1985-91, State wide Adv. Com. on AIDS, 1985-90; bd. dirs. Casey Found., Families First Initiative, 1988-97, Comprehensive Health Assn. N.D., 1993-95, United Health Found., 1990-97, Northern Valley Mental Health Assn., 1994-00, bd. dir., Grand Forks Girl's and Women's Hockey Assn., 1999-2002; bd. dirs., sec.-treas., exec. com., program com., fundraising com., sec.-treas. Devel. Homes, 1999—; adv. bd. Mountainbrooke (formerly Friendship Place), 1992-96; adv. com. Ruth Meiers Adolescent Ctr., Grand Forks, 1988-2002, Altru Health Sys. Corp. Bd., 1997—; mem. Commn. on Future Structure of VA Health Care, 1990-91; bd. dirs. Red River Valley Cmty. action Program, 1991—; mem. Resource and Referral Bd. Dirs., 1990—; caring coun. N.D. Blue Cross and Blue Shield Caring Program for Children, 1995-99; coun. mem. N.D. Health Task Force, 1992-94; healthcare subcom. Northern Gt. Plains Econ. Devel. Commn., 1995-96; adv. com. on telecomms. and healthcare FCC, 1996; mem., chmn. Grand Forks City and County Bd. Health, 2000—. Recipient: Pub. Citizen of Yr. Award, N.D. chpt., Nat. Assn. Social Workers, 1986, Golden Grain Award, N.D. Dietetic Assn., 1988, Person of Yr. Award, U. N.D., Law Women Caucus, 1990, Legislator of Yr. award North Valley Labor Coun., 1990, N.D., Martin Luther King Jr. Award, 1990, Legislator of Yr. Award, Mental Health Assn., N.D., 1993, N.D. Libr. Assn. Legislator of Yr., 1999, Friend of Medicine Award N.D. Med. Assn., 1999, Legislator of Year Award, N.D. Pub. Employees Assn., 1999, Friend of Counseling Award, N.D. State Counseling Assn., 2000, Legislative Svc. Award, ARC of N.D., Friend of Higher Edn. Award, AAUP, 1995. Mem. N.D. Nurses Assn., Alpha Lambda Delta, Sigma Theta Tau, Pi Lampda Theta. Home: Unit 92 N 2200 S 29th St Apt 92N Grand Forks ND 58201-5869 Office: UND Sch Medicine PO Box 9037 501 N Columbia Rd Grand Forks ND 58202-9037 E-mail: jdemers@medicine.nodak.edu.

DEMERY, DOROTHY JEAN, secondary school educator; b. Houston, Sept. 5, 1941; d. Floyd Hicks and Irene Elaine Burns Clay; m. Leroy W. Demery, Jan. 16, 1979; children: Steven Bradley, Rodney Bradley, Craig Bradley, Kimberly Bradley. AA, West L.A. Coll., Culver City, Calif., 1976; AS, Harbor Coll., Wilmington, Calif., 1983; BS in Pub. Adminstrn., Calif. State U., Carson, 1985; MS in Instructional Leadership, Nat. U., San Diego, 1991. Cert. real estate broker, tchr. math. and bus. edn., bilingual tchr., crosscultural lang. and acad. devel.; lang. devel. specialist. Eligibility social worker Dept. Pub. Social Svcs., L.A., 1967-74; real estate broker Dee Bradley & Assocs., Riverside, Calif., 1976—; tchr. math L.A. Unified Sch. Dist., 1985-91; math/computer sci. tchr. Pomona (Calif.) Unified Sch. Dist., 1991—. Adj. lectr. Riverside C.C., 1992—93; mem. Dist. Curriculum Coun./Report Card Task Force, Pomona, 1994—; del. rep. assembly NEA, 1991—2003. Chairperson Human Rights Com., Pomona, 1992—, sec. steering com., 1993—, adv. bd., 1993—; mem. polit. action com. Assoc. Pomona Tchrs., 1993-94. Recipient Outstanding Svc. award Baldwin Hills Little League Assn., L.A., 1972. Mem.: Calif. Tchrs. Assn. (state coun. 2000, chair site base, chair dept. math.), Associated Pomona Tchrs. (site base chairperson, math. chairperson 1994—, nominee to Nat. Coun. Tchrs. of Math. 2001, bd. dirs. 1998—), Aux. Nat. Med. Assn., Nat. Coun. Tchrs. Math., Nat. Bus. Assn. Avocations: hiking, tennis, walking. Office: Simons Middle School 900 E Franklin Ave Pomona CA 91766-5362

DEMESME, RUBY BUTLER, civilian military executive; b. Clinton, N.C. married; 2 children. BA magna cum laude, St. Augustine's Coll., Raleigh, N.C., 1969; MSW, U. N.C., 1979. Exec. adminstr. Cumberland County Dept. Social Svcs., Fayetteville, N.C., 1969-80; clin. social worker Womack Army Hosp., Ft. Bragg, N.C., 1973; adjutant and divsn. chief for force structure and manpower U.S. Army, Mainz, Germany, 1980-84; mgmt. and manpower analyst Army Materiel Command, Alexandria, Va., 1984, program mgr., 1984-85; family programs adviser, dep. chief staff for pers. Hdqs. Dept. Army, Washington, 1985-88; congl. fellow, mem. profl. staff Sen. John Glenn, U.S. Senate, Washington, 1989-90; asst. dep. for morale, welfare, recreation-family programs Office Asst. Sec. Army for Manpower and Rsch. Affairs, Washington, 1990-91; asst. dept. sec. morale, welfare, recreation-health affairs USAF, Washington, 1991-93, acting dep. asst. sec. for force mgmt. and pers., 1993-94, dep. asst. sec. for force mgmt. and pers., 1994-98, asst. sec. manpower, Res. affairs, installations-environ., 1998—. Instr. adult continuing edn. [illegible]; mem. subgroup on children and families Sr. Exec. Svc. Women Appointees; mem. Senate Black Legis. Staff Caucus. Recipient cert. of achievement Sec. of Army, 1997, Disting. Leader award Thomas W. Anthony chpt. Air Force Assn., 1998, Disting. Alumni award U. N.C., 1998, 25th Anniversary of All Vol. Force award, 1998, Disting. Svc. award Tuskegee Airman, 1999, Meritorious Civilian Svc. awards 1994-98. Mem. Women in Def., Nat. Mil. Family Assn., Phi Beta Lambda, Delta Sigma Theta. Office: Asst Sec of the Air Force 1660 Air Force Pentagon Washington DC 20330-1660

DEMETRAKEAS, REGINA CASSAR, social worker; b. Detroit, Jan. 23, 1969; d. Rene Antoine and Carol Ann Cassar; m. David Demetrakeas, June 4, 1993. BSW, Wayne State U., 1992, MSW, 1993. Cert. social worker ACSW. Therapist intern Cath. Svcs. Macomb, Sterling Heights, Mich., 1992-93; therapist Judson Ctr., Royal Oak, Mich., 1993-96, supr., 1996—, supr. interns, 1996-97. Contractual therapist Eastwood Clinics, Clinton Twp., Mich., 1999. Mem. NASW, Nat. Honor Soc. Avocations: archery, hunting, nature walks, reading.

DEMILLO, ERNABEL, reporter; M in Broadcast Journalism, Northwestern U. Gen. assignment reporter Orange County News Channel, Sta. KOVR-TV, Sacramento, 1995—96; news reporter Sta. WNYW-TV, N.Y.C., 1996—. Vol., bd. dirs. APEX; bd. dirs. Coalition Asian-Am. Children and Families. Recipient Gov.'s award Excellence, 1999. Mem.: Asian Am. Journalists Assn. (bd. dirs.), N.Y. Roadrunner's Club. Office: WNYW 205 E 67th St New York NY 10021

DEMING, JODY WHEELER, oceanography educator; b. Houston, July 2, 1952; d. Samuel Henry Wheeler and Laverne (Lewis) Kraft. BA in Biol. Scis., Smith Coll., 1974; PhD in Microbiology, U. Md., 1981. Rsch. asst. biology Sloan Found. Rsch. Smith Coll., Northampton, Mass., 1973; field biologist Water Quality Div. Md. State Dept. Natural Resources, Annapolis, 1974; rsch. technician Div. Infectious Diseases Tufts/New Eng. Med. Ctr. Hosp., Boston, 1974-75; rsch. assoc. Bioluminescence Lab. NASA/Goddard Space Flight Ctr., Greenbelt, Md., 1975-77; grad. teaching and rsch. asst. microbiology U. Md., College Park, 1977-81; NSF postdoctoral fellow Marine Biology Rsch. Div. Scripps Inst. Oceanography, La Jolla, Calif., 1981-82; NOAA postdoctoral fellow Office of Marine Pollution and Assessment, Rockville, Md., 1982-83; assoc. rsch. scientist Chesapeake Bay Inst. Johns Hopkins U., Shady Side, Md., 1981-86, rsch. scientist Chesapeake Bay Inst., 1986-88, asst. prof. biology, 1983-86; scientist Ctr. Marine Biotech., U. Md., Balt., 1986-88; dir., Marine Bioremediation Program U. Wash., Seattle, 1993—99; assoc. prof. U. Wash. Sch. Oceanography, Seattle, 1988—95, prof., 1995—. Mem. internat. com. U.S. Task Group, U.S./France Bilateral Agreement for Coop. in Oceanography, 1987-89; mem. nat. com. ALVIN Rev. Com., 1984-87; mem. sci. rev. panel for NOAA Nat. Undersea Rsch. Program, U. Hawaii, 1986, NSF Polar Programs Rev., 1986, NSF Biol. Oceanography Rev. Panel, 1991; reviewer jours. Sci., Nature, Applied Environ. Microbiology, others. Contbr. numerous chpts. to books and articles to profl. jours. Recipient award for Sci. Achievement in the Biol. Scis., Wash. Acad. Scis., 1987, Presdl. Young Investigator NSF award, 1989-94. Mem. AAAS, Am. Soc. for Microbiology, Am. Acad. of Microbiology, Am. Soc. of Limnology and Oceanography, Am. Geophys. Union, The Oceanography Soc., Sigma Xi. Achievements include patents for rapid quantitive determination of bacteria and their antibiotic susceptibilities in a variety of fluid samples. Office: U Wash Sch Oceanography Wb 10 Seattle WA 98195-0001*

DEMIR, SEMAHAT SIDDIKA, engineering educator; BSEE, Istanbul Tech. U., 1988; MS in Elec. and Computer Engring., Rice U., 1992, PhD in Elec. and Computer Engring., 1995; MS in Biomedical Engring., Bogazici U., 1996; cert. in Biomedical Engring., Johns Hopkins U., 1996. Postdoctoral fellow Dept. Biomedical Engring. Johns Hopkins U., Balt., 1995—96; asst. prof. biomedical engring. U. Memphis and U. Tenn., Memphis, 1996—2000, assoc. prof. biomedical engring., 2000—. Vis. assoc. prof. Faculty Elec. and Electronics Engring. Istanbul (Turkey) Tech. U., 2000—01; vis. rsch. assoc. prof. Inst. Biomedical Engring. Bogazici U., Istanbul, 2001; assoc. prof. Elec. Engring. Interuniversity High Coun. Turkish Univs., Ankara, Turkey, 1998—. Mem.: Soc. Women Engrs. (Disting. New Engr. award 2003). Office: Dept Biomed Engring Joint Biomed Engring Program Univ Memphis & Univ Tenn 330 Engring Technology Bldg Memphis TN 38152-3210*

DEMITA, GERALDINE, librarian; b. N.Y.C., July 30; d. Michael DeMita and Philomina Pastore. BA, Nazareth Coll., 1973; MLS, Pratt Inst., 1975. Cert. libr., N.Y. Librarian Franklin Nat. Bank, N.Y.C., 1974, Seagrams & Co., N.Y.C., 1975-77, GM, N.Y.C., 1978-80, Queens Borough Pub. Libr., N.Y.C., 1982—. Tutor Children's Devel. Fund, N.Y.C., 1990-91. Rsch. book: Swelling Tide, 1998. Mem. Meadows Spa, North Shore Tennis and Racquet Club, Wildwood Pool and Tennis Club. Roman Catholic. Avocations: tennis, reading, music, jogging, gardening.

DEMITCHELL, TERRI ANN, law educator; b. San Diego, Apr. 10, 1953; d. William Edward and Rose Annette (Carreras) Wheeler; m. Todd Allan DeMitchell, Aug. 14, 1982. AB in English with honors, San Diego State U., 1975; JD, U. San Diego, 1984; MA in Edn., U. Calif., Davis, 1990; EdM, Harvard U., 1997. Bar: Calif. 1985, U.S. Dist. Ct. (so. dist.) Calif. 1985; cert. elem. tchr., Calif. Tchr. Fallbrook (Calif.) Union Elem. Sch. Dist., 1976-86; adminstrv. asst. gen. counsel San Diego Unified Sch. Dist., 1984; assoc. Biddle and Hamilton, Sacramento, 1986-88; instr. U. N.H., 1990-93. Teaching asst. U. Calif., Davis, 1987. Author: The California Teacher and the Law, 1985, The Law in Relation to Teacher, Out of School Behavior, 1990, Censorship and the Public School Library: A Bicoastal View, 1991. Mem. Calif. Bar Assn., Am. Bar Assn.

DEMONTE, CLAUDIA ANN, artist, educator; b. Astoria, N.Y., Aug. 25, 1947; d. Joseph James and Ammeda Ellen (Heiss) DeM.; m. William Edward McGowin, May 28, 1977. BA, Coll. Notre Dame, 1969; MFA, Cath. U., 1971. Instr. Bowie State Coll., Md., 1971-72, Prince Georges C.C., Largo, Md., 1972; prof. dept. art U. Md., College Park, 1972—. Dir. Art Workshops, New Sch. Social Rsch., N.Y.C., 1980-94; USIA artist in residene (Sofia) Bulgaria, 1982; mem. art bd. Queens Coll., N.Y. Selected exhbns.: Corcoran Gallery Art, 1976, Contemporary Arts Ctr., New Orleans, Cranbrook Acad., 1978, Marianne-Deson Gallery, 1979, Miss. Mus., Fort Worth Mus., Washington Project for Arts, 1980, Marion Locks Gallery, Miami Dade Gallery, Xochipilli, 1981, 86, 95, New Sch. Social Rsch., 1982, Queens Mus., N.Y., Stamford Mus., Conn., Gallery 121, Antwerp, Belgium, 1985, Gracie Mansion Gallery, N.Y., 1987, Brentwood Art Gallery, St. Louis, 1987, Nina Freunenheim Gallery, Buffalo, N.Y., 1987, 92, 94, Internat. Rev. of Arts Arsenal, Amalfi, Italy, 1987, Esbo Mus., Helsinki, Finland, 1988, Evanston (Ill.) Art Ctr., 1989, Barbara Gillman Gallery, Miami, 1991, 92, 94, Gallery 86, Lodz, Poland, Slow Art, Painting in N.Y. Now, P.S. 1 Mus., N.Y., 1991, Haggerty Mus., Wis., 1993, Nina Freudenheim Gallery, Buffalo, 1994, Leedy Voulkos Gallery, Kansas City, Mo., 1996, Panaroma Gallery, Barcelona, Spain, Silpakorn U., Bangkok, 1997, Retrospective, Choklalfabuken, Malmo, Sweden, 1998, Liesbeth Lip Gallery, Rotterdam, The Netherlands, 1999, Retrospective Rosemont Coll., Pa., 2000, U. New Eng., Tucson Mus., Ariz., 2001, Mus. of S.W., Midland, Tex., 2002, Internat. Mus. of Women, San Francisco, 2003, Talinn Kunsit House, Estonia, 2004; pub. collections include Indpls. Mus., Stamford Mus., Miss. Mus., Prudential Life Ins., Hyatt-Regency, Chem. Bank, Best Products, U. Md., Mus. Modern Art, New Orleans Mus., Minn. Mus., Grand Rapids Mus., Mich., UCLA, Corcoran Gallery of Art, Bklyn. Mus., Mus., Bass Mus., Tucson Mus., Boca Raton Mus.; author: (with Judy Bachrach)

The Height Report, 1983, (pomegranate) Women of the World: A Global Collection of Art, 2000; commd. works include: U. No.Iowa, 2003. Mem. art bd. Queens (N.Y.) Coll. Recipient award Am.-Italian Assn., 1971, Head Balt. Bus., 1972, Creative award Me., 1974, 77, 83, 87; N.Y. Found. for the Arts fellow, 1989—, N.Y.C. Dept. Cultural Affairs Art in Pub. Places Sculpture Commn., 1991, N.Y.C. Dept. Cultural Affairs Mural Commn. fellow 1993, sculpture commn. N.Y.C. Dept. Cultural Affairs, 1997, N.Mex. State Art Commn., Sculpture Commn., Socorro, 1998, U. No. Iowa Commn., 2003, Gund Found. grant, 1998, Ancohrage Found. of Tex. grant, 1999. Democrat. Home: 96 Grand St New York NY 10013-2633 Office Phone: 301-405-1464. E-mail: mcmonte2@aol.com., demonte@umd.edu.

DEMONTE, CYNTHIA MARIA, investor relations and management consultant; b. N.Y.C., May 23, 1956; d. Joseph James and Ammeda Ellan (Heiss) DeM.; m. Abraham Figueroa, Mar. 8, 1991. BA, NYU, 1978. Asst. dir. mktg. Tandem Computers, N.Y.C., Cupertino, Calif., 1978-82; v.p. corp. fin. Gruntal & Co., N.Y.C.; pres. DeMonte Assocs. Cons., N.Y.C., 1995—; v.p. Investor Access Corp., 1992-94; v.p. investor rels., corp. commn. Ruder Finn, 1994—; sr. v.p. investor rels. Fin. Rels. Bd., 1995; pres., founder Cynthia DeMonte Assocs Ltd./DeMonte Assocs., 1996—. Mem. Dinkin's Com., 1990—; Dem. nat. com. Women's Leadership Forum. Mem. NAFE, Nat. Investor Rels. Inst., Nat. Assn. Profl. Organizers, Am. Women's Econ. Devel. Corp., Am. Mgmt. Assocs., Ctr. for Entrepreneurial Mgmt., Am. Mgmt. Assn. Avocations: european travel, foreign language. Home: 138 Tatum Dr Middletown NJ 07748-3126 Office: Cynthia M DeMonte & Assoc 161 W 54th St New York NY 10019-5322

DE MONTEIRO, NADSA, chef; b. Cambodia; d. Longteine de Monteiro; m. Bob Perry, Dec. 1986. Travel agt., Boston, 1986—92; owner, sous chef The Elephant Walk, Somerville, Mass., 1992—94, owner, exec. chef Boston, 1994—; owner, chef Carambola, Waltham, Mass., 1997—. Office: The Elephant Walk 2067 Massachusetts Ave Cambridge MA 02140

DEMORO, ROSE ANN, nursing administrator; Former dir. collective bargaining Calif. Nurses Assn., Oakland, Calif., exec. dir., 1993—. Office: Calif Nurses Assn 2000 Franklin St Oakland CA 94612

DEMORUELLE, CHARMAINE, music educator; b. New Orleans, Sept. 30, 1952; d. James Ivon and Nell Marie (Porbes) deMoruelle; m. Oren Francis Benedic, Nov. 10, 1973 (div. July 1976); m. John Joseph Brion, Oct. 29, 1989; children: Yvette Jeanne Brion, Jean-Paul deMoruelle Brion. AS, Delgado Jr. Coll., New Orleans, 1973; BA, U. New Orleans, 1979. Tchr. instrumental music Jefferson Parish Sch. Bd., Metairie, La., 1979—. Clarinetist Jefferson Parish Cmty. Band, Am. Legion Post 175 Band; chief of Kickapoo YMCA Indian Guides, Metairie; bd. mem. at large 1st Unitarian Universalist Ch. of New Orleans, 1987. Scholar Seymore Weiss scholar, Delgado Jr. Coll., 1972—73. Mem.: La. Band Masters Assn., La. Music Educators Assn. Unitarian Universalist. Avocations: camping, soccer, karate. Home: 1437 Gardenia Dr Metairie LA 70005 Office: J D Meisler Middle Sch 3700 Cleary Ave Metairie LA 70002

DEMOSS, DOROTHY DELL, historian, educator; b. Houston, Feb. 17, 1942; d. Harold Raymond and Jessy May (Cox) DeMoss. BA, Rice U., 1963; MA, U. Tex., 1966; PhD, Tex. Christian U., 1981. Prof. history Tex. Woman's U., Denton, 1966-2004. Author: The History of Apparel Manufacturing in Texas, 1897-1981, 1989; contbr. chpt. to book Profiles in Power: Twentieth Century Texans in Washington, 1993. Mem.: AAUW, Tex. State Hist. Assn., So. Hist. Assn. Republican. Presbyterian. Home: 2228 Picadilly Ln Denton TX 76209 Office: Texas Woman's U PO Box 425889 Denton TX 76204

DEMOTT, DEBORAH ANN, lawyer, educator; b. Collingswood, N.J., July 21, 1948; d. Lyle J. and Frances F. (Cummings) DeM. BA, Swarthmore Coll., 1970; JD, NYU, 1973. Bar: N.Y. 1974. Law clk. U.S. Dist. Ct. (so. dist.) N.Y., 1973; assoc. Simpson, Thacher & Bartlett, N.Y.C., 1974-75; from asst. prof. to assoc. prof. Duke U., Durham, N.C., 1975-80, prof. law, 1980—, David F. Cavers prof. law, 2000—. Vis. asst. prof. U. Tex., Austin, 1977-78; Bost rsch. prof. law, 1981; vis. prof. U. Calif. Hastings Coll. Law, 1986, U. Colo., 1989, U. San Diego, 1991; James L. Lewtas vis. prof. law Osgoode Hall Law Sch., Toronto, Ont., Can., 1991; vis. fellow U. Melbourne, 1993, 95, 98; Huber C. Hurst Eminent vis. scholar U. Fla. Coll. Law, 1996; Frances Lewis Scholar-in-Residence Washington & Lee Law Sch., 1998; centennial vis. prof. law dept. London Sch. Econs., 2000-2002. Author: Shareholder Derivative Actions, 1987, Fiduciary Obligation Agency and Partnership, 1991; editor: Corporations at the Crossroads: Governance and Reform; contbr. articles to profl. jours.; bd. advisors Jour. Legal Edn., 1983-86. Trustee Law Sch. Admission Coun., 1984-88; mem. N.C. Gen. Statutes Commn., 1990-98; mem. selection com. Coif Book Award, 1988-90. Recipient Pomeroy prize NYU Sch. Law, 1971-73; AAUW fellow, 1972-73; Fulbright Sr. scholar Sydney U. and Monash (Australia) U., 1986. Mem. ABA, Am. Law Inst. (reporter restatement of agy. 1995—). Office: Duke U Law Sch PO Box 90360 Durham NC 27708-0360

DEMPSEY, B. artist; b. Ada, Okla., Nov. 24, 1926; d. John Benjamin Foster and Alma Lula Hubbard; m. Loyd Dempsey, Apr. 21, 1949; children: Ronny DeWayne, Johnny DeWight, Loyd Raymond, Novelia Dianne, Kevin Wendell. Diploma, Byng H.S., Ada, 1945. Sec. First Nat. Bank, Ada, 1945, Ada Welfare Dept., 1946; sorter/packer Hazel-Atlas Glass Co., Ada, 1946-48; tailor, seamstress S & Q Clothiers, Ada, 1971-86. Exhibited in group shows at Okla. State Capitol, 1981-93, Festival of Lights, Oklahoma City, 1983-86, Folklife Festival Art Show, Oklahoma City, 1983-86, Oklahoma City Meml. Bldg.; ehxibits in 12 area shows annually. Mem. Ada Artists Assn. (publicity chair), Magic Brush Art Guild (publicity chair), Holdenville Soc. Painters. Democrat. Baptist. Avocations: church choir, sewing and painting crafts, creative doll making. Home: 921 Williams St Ada OK 74820-1822

DEMPSEY, JOAN, federal agency administrator; BA Polit. Sci., So. Ark. U.; MA Pub. Adminstrn., U. Ark. Deputy dir. Gen. Defense Intelligence Program Staff; dir. Mil. Intelligence Staff, Nat. Mil. Intelligence Prodn. Ctr.; acting asst. sec. defense Command, Control, Comm. and Intelligence; deputy asst. sec. Defense for Intelligence and Security; deputy dir. cmty. mgmt. CIA, Washington, 1997—. With USN. Office: DDCI/CM Intelligence Cmty Washington DC 20505

DEMPSEY, MARY A. library commissioner, lawyer; m. Philip Corboy, Sept. 4, 1992. BA(hon.), St. Mary's Coll., Winona, Minn., 1975; MLS, U. Ill., 1976; JD, De Paul U., 1982. Bar: Ill. 1982. Libr. Hillside Pub. Libr., Ill., 1976-78; assoc. Reuben and Proctor, Chgo., 1982-85; assoc. gen. counsel Michael Reese Hosp. and Med. Ctr., Chgo., 1985-86; pvt. practice Chgo., 1987-89; counsel Sidley and Austin, Chgo., 1990-93; commr. Chgo. Pub. Libr., 1994—. Adj. prof. law DePaul U. Coll. Law and Health Inst., Chgo., 1986-90; spl. counsel Chgo. Bd. Edn., 1987-89; mem. adv. bd. Dominican U. Grad. Sch. Libr. and Info. Sci., River Forest, Ill. Mem. State Street Commn., Chgo.; bd. dir. Big Shoulders Fund (for inner city Cath. sch.), Urban Libr. Coun.; trustee DePaul U., Chgo.; mem. Ill. State Libr. Adv. Coun. State libr. scholar in Ill. Mem. Chgo. Bar Assn., Chgo. Network. Office: Chgo Pub Libr 400 S State St Chicago IL 60605-1203

DEMUNBRUN-HARMON, DONNE O'DONNELL, retired family physician; b. St. Paul, Aug. 26, 1926; d. Francis Joseph and Julia (Hoffmann) O'Donnell; m. Truman Weldon DeMunbrun, Mar. 17, 1948 (dec. Aug. 1996); children: Michael J., Steven M., Julie F., Suzanne B.; m. Donald Laurance Harmon, Aug. 26, 1997. BS, U. Ky., 1948, MS, 1949; MD, U. Louisville, 1954. Diplomate Am. Bd. Family Practice. Rotating intern St. Anthony Hosp., Louisville, 1955—56; pvt. practice Louisville, 1956—85; med. dir. St. Mary and Elizabeth Hosp., Louisville, 1971—76, Parkway Med. Ctr., Louisville, 1976—99, Family Health Ctrs., Louisville, 1985—90; ret., 1999. Case reviewer Health Care Rev., Louisville, 1995-96; criteria writer Nat. Health Svc., Louisville, 1995-96; asst. clin. prof. family practice, U. Louisville Med. Sch., 1987-90. Pres. Jacques Timothe Boucher Sieur de Montburn Heritage Soc., Nashville, 1996-97. Recipient mayor's citation Cify of Louisville, 1990, proclamation of tribute Jefferson County, Ky., 1990. Mem.: Jefferson County Med. Soc. (life; v.p. 1976—77), Ky. Acad. Family Practice (life), Ky. Med. Assn. (life; del.), Am. Acad. Family Practice (life), Filson Club, Execs. Club, Univ. Club, Sigma Pi Sigma, Pi Mu Epsilon, Alpha Lambda Delta. Avocations: gardening, reading, travel, family, dogs. Home: 3004 Beals Branch Dr Louisville KY 40206-2902 E-mail: d2d.harmon@att.net.

DENDY, TERRI ANITA, secondary school educator; b. Wilmington, Del., May 8, 1965; d. Jesse Lee and Rosalie Dendy. BS, George Mason U., Fairfax, Va., 1988; MA, U. Del., Newark, 1991; BS, U. Del., 1997. Sales assoc. J.C. Penney Co., Wilmington, 1995—99; tchr. N.Y.C. Bd. Edn., 1999—. Track coach U. Del., Newark, 1995—97. Named Coach of the Yr., 1999, World Champion in 4 x 400, 1993; recipient Trail Blazer award, 1999, Pan Am. Silver medalist in 4x400, 1995. Mem.: Golden Key. Achievements include 1988 USA Olympian in relay; Indoor 400m Champion, 1988. Home: 177-43 106th Ave Jamaica NY 11433 Office: Life Sciences Secondary Sch 320 E 96th St New York NY 10128

DENENBERG, KATHARINE W. HORNBERGER (TINKA DENENBERG), artist, educator; b. Ann Arbor, Mich., Nov. 2, 1932; d. Theodore Roosevelt and Marian Louise (Welles) Hornberger; m. Allan Neal Denenberg; children: Peter David, Thomas Andrew. Student, Brown U., 1950-51; BA, U. Minn., 1953; MAT, Harvard U., 1954. Intern tchr. art Concord (Mass.) H.S., 1954-55; tchr. art Bedford and Pound Ridge (N.Y.) Schs., 1955-56, New Lincoln Sch., N.Y.C., 1956-62, Mus. Modern Art, N.Y.C., 1964-71, Children's Art Workshop, Mamaroneck, N.Y., 1971-81, Pelham (N.Y.) Art Ctr., 1981. One-woman shows include Manhattanville Coll., Purchase, N.Y., 1975, Rye (N.Y.) Libr., 1975, 85, West Cornwall (Conn.) Gallery, 1978, 79, West Cornwall Libr., 1979, 84, Condeso Lawler Gallery, N.Y., 1982, 84, Moviehouse Gallery, Millerton, N.Y., 1987, Larchmont Libr., 1988, St. Peter's Ch., N.Y., 1990; exhibited in group shows at Duffy-Gibbs Gallery, N.Y., Nat. Mus. of Taiwan, Bridge Gallery, White Plains, N.Y., Westport-Weston Arts Coun., Manhattanville Coll., New Britain (Conn.) Mus., Sarah Rentzler Gallery, Condeso-Lawler Gallery, Silvermine Gallery, The Castle Gallery, Coll. New Rochelle, N.Y.; represented in permanent collections at Credit Lyonais, Bank of Boston, Chermayeff and Geismar, Great Lakes Corp., Tex. Comml. Bank, Sohio Petroleum, Cleary Gottlieb. N.Y.State Coun. for the Arts grantee, 1975. Mem. Phi Beta Kappa.

DENES, AGNES C. environmental artist; b. Budapest, Hungary, 1931; Student, CCNY, New Sch. Social Research, Columbia U., 1964-66; DFA, Ripon Coll., 1994. Lectr. NYU, 1971, CUNY, 1972, 76Oberlin (Ohio) Coll., 1973, N.Y. Inst. Tech., N.Y.C., 1973, Corcoran Sch. Art, Washington, 1973, 74, U. Mass. Amherst, 1974, Ohio Wesleyan U., Delaware, 1974, Pratt Inst., N.Y.C., 1974, 76, 81, Ohio State U., Columbus, 1974, Moore Coll. Art, Phila., 1974, San Francisco Art Inst., 1975, 76, Kensington Arts Assn., Toronto, 1975, U. Calif. Berkeley, 1976, 80, U. Akron, Ohio, 1976, San Jose (Calif.) State U., 1976, Pratt Inst., N.Y.C., 1976, Newport Harbor Art Mus., Newport Bch., Calif., 1976, 81, Rutgers U., New Brunswick, N.J., 1976, Temple U., Phila., 1977, Art Gallery, Toronto, 1977, UCLA, 1978, Birmingham Poly. Inst., Eng., 1978, Rochester (N.Y.) Inst. Tech., 1979, St. Laurence U., Canton, N.Y., 1980, 82, Hunter Coll., N.Y.C., 1980, 81, MIT, Cambridge, Mass., 1980, Skidmore Coll., Saratoga Springs, N.Y., 1980, Wabash Coll., Crawfordsville, Ind., 1983, Miami (Fla.)-Dade C.C., 1984, Harvard U., Cambridge, Mass., 1984, Cooper Union Advancement Sci. and Art, N.Y.C., 1985, U. Hawaii, Honolulu, 1985, 1993, U. Genoa, Italy, 1986, Nat. Inst. Fine Arts, Guadalajara, Mex., 1986, U.N.D., Grand Forks, 1989, Architects House, Moscow, 1990, Fla. State U., Tallahassee, 1991, Royal Acad., Stockholm, 1992, Fine Arts Acad., Helsinki, Finland, 1992, Cornell U., Ithaca, N.Y., 1993, SUNY Albany, 1993, Great Hall, Cooper Union, 1993, 99, 2000, Boston U., 1994, Tufts U, Medford, Mass., 1995, Kansas City Art Inst. Mo., 1995, SUNY Potsdam, N.Y., 1996, U. Sao Paulo, Brazil (Visual Arts Congress), 1996, San Franciso Art Inst., 1997, N. Tex. U., Denton, 1997, Modern Art Mus., Ft. Worth, Tex., 1997, Centro Studi Americani, Rome, Italy, 1998, Pusan Met. Mus., Korea, 1998, Chinese Cultural Ctr., N.Y., 1999, Fort Asperen Found., Holland, 2000, Bayly Art Mus., U. Va., Charlottesville, 1999, Carnegie Mellon U., Pittsburgh, 1999, Russian State U. Humanities, Moscow, 2001, Modern Art Mus., Ft. Worth, Tex., 2002, Herron Sch. Art, U. Ind., Indianapolis, 2003, CAA Coll. Art Assn.Conf., N.Y., 2003, Haggerty Mus. Art, Marquette U., Milwaukee, 2003, Naples Mus. Art, Fla., 2004; vis. critic sch. archtecture U. Pa., 1991; tchr. art Sch. Visual Arts, N.Y.C., 1974-79, San Francisco Art Inst., 1976, Skowhegan (Maine) Sch. Painting and Sculpture, 1979, Universita degli Studi di Genoa, Italy, 1986, Hartford (Conn.) Art Sch., 1988; speaker at numerous global confs. One-person shows include Columbia U., N.Y.C., 1965, Ruth White Gallery, N.Y.C., 1968, A.I.R. Gallery, N.Y.C., 1972, Ohio State U., Columbus, 1974, Corcoran Gallery Art, Washington, 1974, Stefanotty Gallery, N.Y.C., 1975, U. Akron, Ohio, 1976, Newport Harbor Art Mus., Newport Beach, Calif., 1976, Rutgers U., 1976, 112 Green St. Gallery, N.Y.C., 1977, Temple U., 1977, Centre Culturel Americain, Paris, 1978, Franklin Furnace, N.Y.C., 1978, Ikon Gallery, Birmingham, Eng., 1978, Amerika Haus, Berlin, 1978, Studio d'Arte Cannaviello, Milan, 1979, Inst. Contemporary Art, London, 1979, Gallerie Aronowitsch, Stockholm, 1980, Galleriet, Lund, Sweden, 1980, Elise Meyer Gallery, N.Y.C., 1980, 81, MIT, 1980, Kunsthalle, Nurnberg, Germany, 1982, No. Ill. U. Art Gallery, Chgo., 1985, U. Hawaii Art Gallery, 1985, Ricardo Barreto Arte Contemporaneo, Guadalajara, Mex., 1986, Arts Club Chgo., 1990, Anselmo Alvarez Galeria de Arte, Madrid, Spain, 1990, Cornell U., Ithaca, N.Y., 1992, Wynn Kramarsky, N.Y.C., 1994, Joyce Goldstein Gallery, N.Y., 1995 & 1997, Gibson Gallery, SUNY Potsdam, N.Y., 1996, View Gallery, N.Y., 1997, Gallerie Il Bulino, Rome, 1998, 2003, Herron Sch. Art, Indiana U., 2003, Haggerty Mus. Art, Marquette U., Milwaukee, 2003, Naples Art Mus., Fla., 2004; group exhbns. include Hundred Acres Gallery, N.Y.C., 1970, Nat. Acad. Galleries, N.Y.C., 1970, 80, Dwan Gallery, N.Y.C., 1970, Jewish Mus., N.Y.C., 1970, Finch Coll. (N.Y.) Mus., 1971, Whitney Mus. Art, N.Y.C., 1971, 73, 76, Mus. Modern Art, Buenos Aires, 1971, Mus. Fine Arts, Santiago, Chile, 1971, Inst. Contemporary Art, Lima, Peru, 1971, NYU, 1972, Albion Coll., Mich., 1972, N.Y. Cultural Ctr., N.Y.C., 1972, 73, Kent State U., 1972, Oberlin Coll., 1972, N.Y. Inst. Tech., N.Y.C., 1972, Bklyn. Mus., 1972, 76, 80, Kunsthaus, Hamburg, Germany, 1972, Pace Coll., 1973, 78, Mus. Modern Art, 1973, 77, Kunstverein, Berlin, 1973, Calif. Inst. Arts, Valencia, Calif., 1973, Wadsworth Atheneum, Hartford, Conn., 1973, Kunsthalle, Cologne, 1974, Indpls. Mus., Ofart, Ind., 1974, San Francisco Mus. Art, 1974, Stadtisches Mus., Leverkusen, Germany, 1975, Grey Art Gallery N.Y.U., 1975, Inst. Contemporary Art, U. Pa., Phila., 1975, Michael C. Rockefeller Arts Ctr., Fredonia, N.Y., 1976, Arts Gallery, New South Wales, Sydney, Australia, 1976, Mus. Natural Hist., N.Y.C., 1977, Documenta VI, Kassel, Germany, 1977, Cleve. State U., 1977, Venice Biennale, Italy, 1978, 80, Yale U. Art Gallery, New Haven, 1978, Leo Castelli Gallery, N.Y.C., 1978, Rose Esman Gallery, N.Y.C., 1978, 79, Nat. Gallery, Wellington, Australia, 1978, Mus. Contemporary Arts, Brisbane, Australia, 1978, Seibu Art Mus., Tokyo, 1979, Gallerie AIX, Stockholm, 1979, Ackland Art Mus., Chapel Hill, N.C., 1979, Kunstmuseum, Berne, Switzerland, 1979, Mus. Ludwig, Cologne, 1979, Gulbenkiam Found., Lisbon, Portugal, 1979, Museo Espanol de Arte Contemporaneo, Madrid, 1979, Tel Aviv Mus., 1979, Vienna Mus. des 20 Jahrhunderts, Austria, 1979, New Mus., N.Y.C., 1980, Albright Coll., Reading, Pa., 1980, 81, Wright State U., Dayton, Ohio, 1980, U. Pa., 1980, Kunstforeninger Mus., Copenhagen, 1980, Biblioteca Nacional, Madrid, 1980, Musee Nat. d'art Moderne, Paris, 1980, Museo de Arte Contemporanea, Brazil, 1980, Rutgers U., 1981, 86, Hofstra U., N.Y.C., 1981, 92, Aldrich Mus. Contemporary Art, Ridgefield, Conn., 1981, Palais des Beaux Arts, Brussels, 1981, U. Colo. Art Galleries, Boulder, 1981, Toledo (Ohio) Mus. Art, 1981, Galerie Nacional de Arte Moderna, Lisbon, 1981, New Gallery Contemporary Art, Cleve., 1981, Galleriet, Lund, Sweden, 1982, Nat. Acad. Design, N.Y.C., 1982, Va. Commonwealth U., Richmond, 1982, John Michael Kohler Art Ctr., Sheboygan, Wis., 1982, San Francisco Mus. Modern Art, 1983, Osaka U. Arts, Japan, 1983, Tacoma (Wash.) Art Mus., 1983, Nat. Mus. Art, Smithsonian Inst., Washington, 1984, 85, San Antonio Mus. Assn., 1984, Dayton (Ohio) Art Inst., 1984, Rhona Hoffman Gallery, Chgo., 1984, Germans van Eck Gallery, N.Y.C., 1984, Bard Coll., N.Y., 1984, 90, Ronald Feldman Fine Arts, N.Y.C., 1984, Am. Inst. Arts & Letters, 1985, 86, Moderna Museet, Stockholm, 1985, Rosemont (Pa.) Coll., 1985, Bass Mus. Art, Miami Bch., Fla., 1985, Winnipeg (Can.) Art Gallery, 1985, Anchorage (Alaska) Hist. & Fine Arts Mus., 1985, U. Minn., Duluth, 1985, Stamford (Conn.) Mus., 1985, Nurnburg, Kunsthalle, Germany, 1986, Print Club, Phila., 1986, Museo de Artes Moderno La Tertulia, Cali, Colombia, 1986, Santa Maria di Castello, Genoa, Italy, 1986, Ethnographic Mus., Belgrade, Yugoslavia, 1986, Nat. Acad. Design, N.Y.C., 1987, Circulo de Bellas Artes, Madrid, 1987, Kolnischer Kunstverein, Cologne, 1987, Goteborgs Kontsmuseum, Sweden, 1987, Sonya Henie-Neils Onstad Found., Hovikodden, Norway, 1987, Minn. Mus. Art, St. Paul, 1987, Kjarvalsstadir, Reykjavik, Iceland, 1987, Circulo de Bellas Artes, Madrid, 1987, Museu de Arte, Sao Paulo, Brazil, 1987, Cin. Art Mus., 1989, Denver Art Mus., 1989, 91, Pa. Acad. Fine Arts, Phila., 1989, L.I. U., Brookville, N.Y., 1989, Brandeis U., Waltham, Mass., 1991, Mus. Contemporary Art, Helsinki, Finland, 1992, The Mus. Tampere, Finland, 1992, Art Gallery, Hamilton, Can., 1992, Expo '92, Moguer, Spain, 1992, Laumeier Sculpture Park & Gallery, St. Louis, 1993, Dallas Mus. Nat. Hist., 1993, Epad, La Defénse, Paris, 1993, Tufts U., Medford, Mass., 1995, Rutgers U., 1996, Staatsgalerie, Stuttgart, Germany, 1997, Am. Acad., Rome, Biennale dei Parchi, Palazzo delle Esposizione, Rome, Wexner Ctr. for Arts, Ohio State U., Pusan Met. Arts Mus., Korea, 1998, Mus. Contemporary Art, L.A., 1999, Simmons Visual Art Ctr., Grenau U., Gainesville, Ga., 1998, Nat. Mus. Women in Arts, Washington D.C., 1999, Mus. Contemporary Art (MOLA), Los Angeles, 1999, Contemporary Art Mus., Houston, 2000, Huntington Gallery, Mass.Coll. Art, Boston, 2000, Boulder Mus. Contemporary Art, Colo., 2000, Mus. Modern Art, N.Y.C., 2000 & 2001, Museo D'Art Contemporani (MACBA), Barcelona, 2000, Hayward Gallery, London, 2000, Achim Möller Gallery, N.Y., 2000, Denver Art Mus., Colo., 2000, Cooper Union Sch. Engring., N.Y., 2000, Ft. Asperen Found., The Netherlands, 2000, Venice Biennale, Italy, 2001, Herter Callery, U. Mass., Amherst, 2001, Göteborgs Internationelle Konstbiennal, Sweden, 2001, Gallery L, Moscow, 2001, Internat. Art Biennal, Buenos Aires Museo Nacional de Bellas Artes, Argentina, 2002, Ringling Sch. Art & Design, Sarasota, Fla., 2002, Contemporary Art Ctr., Cincinnati, Ohio, 2002, House of Docs Gallery, Sundance Film Festival, Utah, 2002; commns. and installations include Artpark, Lewiston, N.Y., 1977, 79, Container Corp. Am., Chgo., 1979, Manhattan Pub. Art Fund, N.Y.C., 1982, Dept. Cultural Affairs, Genoa, Italy, 1986, First Nat. Bank Chgo, N.Y.C., 1986-87, Am.-Scandinavian Found, Sweden, 1988-89, NSW Masterplan City of Berkeley, Calif., 1988-91, City of Chgo. Pub. Art Program, 1990-91, Internat. Ctr. Preservation Wild Animals, Columbus, Ohio, 1990-93, Ministry Environment & United Nations, Tree Mountain, Pinsiö gravel pit, Ylöjarvi, Finland, 1992-96, Mahtesh Ramon Crater, Israel, 1995, Mus. Contempory Art, Helsinki, Finland, 1992, Sheep, Am. Acad. Rome, Italy, 1998, A Forest for Australia, Melbourne, 1998, Poetry Walk, U. Va. Art Mus., Charlottesville, 2000, Nieuwe Hollandse Waterline, Ft. Asperen Found., Holland, 2000, Göteborgs Internat. Konstbiennal, Sweden, 2001, Venice Biennale, Italy, 2001; author: Paradox and Essence, 1976, Sculptures of the Mind, 1976, Isometric Systems in Isotropic Space: Map Projections, 1979, Book of Dust -- The Beginning and the End of Time and Thereafter, 1989, Notes on a Visual Philosophy in Symmetry-Unifying Human Understanding, 1986. Creative Artists Pub. Svc. grantee N.Y. State Coun. Arts, 1972, 74, 80, Visual Arts Program grantee, N.Y. State Coun. Arts, 1979, 84, The Thord-Gray Meml. Fund, Rsch. and Devel. grantee Am.-Scandinavian Found., 1987, Herbert F. Johnson Mus. Art Purchase prize Richard A. Florscheim Art Fund, 1992; Individual Artists fellow NEA, 1974, 75, 81, 89, Collaboration in Art, Sci. and Tech. fellow Syracuse U., 1977, Deutscher Akademischer Austausdienst fellow Berlin, 1978, Rsch. fellow Ctr. Advanced Visual Studies, MIT, 1980, Studio for Creative Inquiry, Carnegie-Mellon U., 1993—, fellow Carnegie Mellon U., 1993, Courant Inst., 1996, Am. Acad., Rome, Prize Fellow, 1998, 4 fellowships Nat. Endowment; recipient Nat. Drawing Competition Purchase prize Rutgers U., 1974, Internat. Women's Yr. award Internat. Women's Art Festival, 1975-76, Berthe Von Moschzisker prize Print Club, 1980, The Ann and Donald McPhail award Print Club, 1982, Hassam and Speicher Fund Purchase award Am. Acad. Arts & Letters, 1985, The Eugene McDermott Achievement award MIT Coun. for Arts, 1990, Young Lawyers Pub. Art award Chgo. Bar Assn., 1992, Watson award, 1999. Address: 595 Broadway New York NY 10012-3222

DENHAM, JILL H. bank executive; BBA, U. Western Ont.; MBA, Harvard U., 1990. From asst. v.p. to exec. v.p. CIBC Wood Gundy, Toronto, 1983—2001, sr. exec. v.p. retail markets and small bus. banking, 2001—03, vice chair retail markets, 2003—. Office: CIBC Commerce Ct Toronto ON Canada M5L 1A2

DENHART, GUN, direct mail order company executive; b. Lund, Sweden, July 14, 1945; came to U.S., 1975; d. Gunnar Arnold and Elsa (Bjôrklund) Brime; m. Thomas E. Denhart, Aug. 29, 1975; children: Philip, Christian. MBA, Lund U., Sweden, 1967. Tchr. Swedish Pub. Sch., Landskrona, Sweden, 1972-73; asst. to sec. gen., bus. and industry adv. com. OECD, Paris, 1973-75; fin. mgr. EF Colls. Ltd., Greenwich, Conn., 1978-84; chief exec. officer Hanna Andersson Corp., Portland, Oreg., 1984—. Trustee Ednl. Fund for Fgn. Colls., Greenwich, Conn. Mem. Young Pres. Orgn. Office: Hanna Andersson Corp 1010 NW Flanders St Portland OR 97209-3119

DENHOLTZ, ELAINE GRUDIN, literature educator, writer; b. NJ; d. Maurice and Lillian (Sachs) Grudin; m. Melvin Denholtz; children: Jeffrey, Steven, Lisa. BA, Bucknell U.; MA, Seton Hall U. Adj. prof. English Fairleigh Dickinson U., Madison, NJ, 1966—. Author: (plays) The Highchairs, 1977, (book) How to Save Your Teeth & Money, 1977, The Dental Facelift, 1981, Having It Both Ways, 1981, Playing for High Stakes, 1986, Balancing Work & Love, 2000, The Zaddik, 2001; contbr. articles to profl. publs. Named to, N.J. Lit. Hall of Fame; recipient numerous lit. and dramatic awards, grants. Mem.: Phi Beta Kappa. Avocation: swimming. Office: Fairleigh Dickinson U Madison Ave MDBO-01 Madison NJ 07940

DENICE, MARCELLA L. counseling administrator; b. 1933; BA in English, Our Lady of the Lake U., 1973, MA in Counseling, 1990. Head basketball coach Alamo Heights H.S., 1980—81; English tchr., cross-country track coach Burbank H.S., San Antonio, 1983—90; guidance counselor Highland Park Elem. Sch., San Antonio, 1990—. Bd. dirs. Nat. Bd. for Profl. Tchg. Stds.; mem. adv. com. for counselors SAISD, mem. dist. leadership team, 2002—. Mem. spkrs. bur. Am. Cancer Soc. Named Outstanding Counselor of Yr., Tex. Counseling Assn., 1991; recipient Remarkable Woman award, Our Lady of the Lake, 1995. Office: Highland Park Elem 635 Rigsby San Antonio TX 78210

DENIGRIS, CAROLE DELL CATO, artist; b. N.Y.C., May 26, 1936; d. Frederick and Elsie Helen (Dell) Cato; m. Daniel Anthony DeNigris, June 30, 1957; children: Daniel Cary, Carole Lynn. Student, Hunter Coll., 1954-57; studied with Richard Lippold, William Baziotes,, 1954-57, studied

Oriental art with Diana Kan, 1969-75; grad., Silva Mind Control. Buyer, salesperson Ethel Allan, Stamford, Conn., 1976-79; asst. mgr., buyer Jean Hutchinson, Greenwich, Conn., 1977-85; dir. Decker Studio and Art Gallery Ltd., Glenville, Conn., 1985-88; mgr. Odetta-Women's Fine Apparel, Greenwich, 1988-90; freelance fragrance model Guerlain of Paris, Stamford, [illegible] One-woman shows include Greenwich Hosp., 1995, Greenwich (Conn.) Beauty Salon and Spa, 2003, 2 person show, Town and Country Club, Hartford, Conn., 2001, exhibited in group shows at Hammond Mus., North Salem, N.Y., Ferguson Libr., Stamford, Hurlbert Gallery, Greenwich, Wilton (Conn.) Libr., Greenwich Art Soc., Conn. Cmty. Bank, Greenwich, Old Bergen Art Guild, 1977—78, Hobe Sound (Fla.) Art Gallery, Pen and Brush Club, N.Y.C., Port Chester (N.Y.) Libr., Greenwich YWCA. Pres. Newcomers of Port Chester, 1969-70. Mem. Oriental Brush Artists Guild (v.p. 1995-96, pres. 1996-98, publicity chairperson, advisor to pres., asst. treas. art exhibit com., asst. hostess art exhibit com.). Republican. Avocations: mycology, methaphysics. Home: 12 Nutmeg Dr Greenwich CT 06831-3211

DENIOUS, SHARON MARIE, retired publishing executive; b. Rulo, Nebr., Jan. 27, 1941; d. Thomas Wayne and Alma (Murphy) Fee; m. Jon Parks Denious, June 17, 1963; children: Timothy Scot, Elizabeth Denious Cessna. Grad. high sch. Operator N.W. Pipeline co., Ignacio, Colo., 1975-90; pub. The Silverton Standard & The Miner, Colo., 1990-99. Avocations: reading, hiking. E-mail: denious@frontier.net.

DENIRO, MARY LYN S. lawyer; b. Salt Lake City, Feb. 15, 1959; d. Ted Gordon and Marilyn Valoe (Butcher) Symes; m. Dan DeNiro. BS magna cum laude, U. Utah, 1980; JD magna cum laude, Fordham U., 1992. Bar: N.Y. 1993. Exec. asst. to chmn. ASARCO Inc., NYC, 1983-91, legal asst., 1991-92; jud. clk. US Dist. Ct. (ea. dist.), Bklyn., 1992-93; assoc. Davis Polk & Wardwell, NYC, 1993-99; v.p., legal counsel Zurich Centre Group, NYC, 1999—2003; v.p. Counsel Ace Capital Re Inc., 2003. Mem. Order of Coif, Phi Kappa Phi, Phi Eta Sigma. Office: Ace Fin Svc 1325 Ave of the Americas New York NY 10019

DENISH, DIANE D. lieutenant governor; d. Libby Donley and Jack Daniels; m. Herb Denish; 3 children. Assoc. pub., bus. devel. and advt. sales Starlight Pub. Ltd., Albuquerque Living and NMex. Monthly, Albuquerque; state chmn. N.Mex Dem. Party, 1999—2001; former owner Target Group; lt. gov. State of Nev., 2003—. Chair Children's Cabinet, Mortgage Fin. Authority, Mil. Base Planning Commn., Ind. Devel. Account Adv. Coun.; active Equal Pay Task Force, Spaceport Commn., Border Authority, Fin. Independence Task Force, Workforce Devel. Bd., Commn. on Volunteerism; trustee N.Mex. Mil. Inst. Found. Bd.; former chair N.Mex. First, N.Mex. Cmty. Found., N.Mex. Tech. Bd. Regents; former mem. N.Mex. Commn. on the Status of Women; former mem. nat. adv. bd. Small Bus. Adminstrn.; pres. N.Mex. State Senate; bd. mem. Daniels Fund. Named 2003 YWCA New Mexican of Vision; named one of Top 100 New Mexicans in honor of her cmty. leadership. Address: 1301 San Pedro Albuquerque NM 87110 Office: State Capitol, Ste 417 Santa Fe NM 87501*

DENISON, CYNTHIA LEE, accountant, tax specialist; b. Hyannis, Mass., Feb. 1, 1956; d. Gordon Avery Denison, Elizabeth Theresa Bourque-Denison; children: Randall Wayne Brown, Shaun Avery Brown, Kelly Joseph Brown. BS in Bus. Adminstrn., Hawaii Pacific U., 1990. Office mgr., tax preparer H&R Block, Fayetteville, NC, 1979—83; asst. acct., acctg. supr. Dept. of Def. Acctg. and Fin., Germany, 1984—86; revenue agt. IRS, Bailey's Crossroads, Va., 1990—91, taxpayer rep., 1991—97, lead tax specialist, 1997—2000, sr. tax specialist, taxpayer rep., 2000—. Electronic filing No. Va. coord. IRS, Bailey's Crossroads, 1998—. Unofficial scoutmaster and cubmaster, den mother, com. mem., counselor Boy Scouts Am., Honolulu, 1986—90; football, baseball, soccer coach Moral, Recreation & Welfare, Honolulu, 1986—90; baseball coach Youth Sports, Spring Lake, NC, 1981—83. Mem.: AAUW, Statue of Liberty/Ellis Island Soc., Smithsonian Instn., Nat. Preservation Soc., Nat. Geog. Soc., Denison Soc., Nat. Geneal. Soc., New Eng. Hist. and Geneal. Soc. Avocations: genealogy, historic preservation, animal preservation, reading, crafts. Home: 2909 Marsala Ct Woodbridge VA 22192 Personal E-mail: cyndidenison1@msn.com.

DENISON, MARY BONEY, lawyer; b. Wilmington, N.C., June 8, 1956; d. Leslie Norwood Jr. and Lillian (Bellamy) Boney; children: Mary Catesby Bellamy, James Wholley IV. AB, Duke U., 1978; JD, U. N.C., 1981. Bar: N.Y. 1982, U.S. Dist. Ct. (so. and ea. dists.) N.Y. 1983, U.S. Ct. Appeals (2d cir.) 1984, DC 1988, U.S. Dist. Ct. DC 1988, U.S. Ct. Appeals (DC cir.) 1988. Assoc. Law Office William G. Kaelin, N.Y.C., 1981-82, Smith, Steibel, Alexander & Saskor, N.Y.C., 1982-86, Graham & James, Washington, 1986-91, ptnr., 1992-96, Farkas & Manelli PLLC, Washington, 1996-2000, Manelli, Denison & Selter, PLLC, Washington, 2001—. Vol. Legal Aid Soc., N.Y.C., 1983—86. Mem.: ABA, Internat. Trademark Assn. (vice chair treaty analysis com. 2000—01, chair treaty analysis com. 2001—03, bd. dirs. 2003—), French Am. C. of C. Washington (treas. 1991—97). Democrat. Episcopalian. Office: Manelli Denison & Selter PLLC 2000 M St NW Ste 700 Washington DC 20036-3364 E-mail: mdenison@mdslaw.com.

DENLINGER, ANN T. school system administrator; b. Waynesville, N.C., July 15, 1944; m. Robert Denlinger; 1 child. B in Elem. Edn., Campbell Coll., 1966; M in Ednl. Adminstrn., Campbell U., 1982, D in Ednl. Adminstrn., 1992. Tchr. Harnett County Schs., 1966—68, Wake County Schs. and Raleigh (N.C.) City Schs., 1968—80; prin. A.V. Baucom Elem. Sch., 1980—82, Lynn Rd. Elem. Sch., 1982—85, Fuquay-Varina Mid. Sch., 1985—87; asst. supt. for elem. curriculum and instrn. Wake County Schs., 1990—92; supt. Wilson County Schs., 1992—97, Durham (N.C.) Pub. Schs., 1997—. Named Supt. of Yr., N.C. Assn. Sch. Adminstrs., 2000; recipient Disting. Alumna award, Campbell U., Reading Recovery Tchr. Leader award, Boston Tchr. Leader Inst., 2002. Avocations: following U. N.C. basketball and football, reading, landscaping, gardening. Office: Durham Pub Schs 511 Cleveland St PO Box 30002 Durham NC 27701

DENLINGER, VICKI LEE, secondary school educator, physical education educator; b. Dayton, Ohio, June 13, 1961; d. David Lee and Barbara Ann (Zimmerman) D.; 1 child, David Micheal. Student, Ohio State U., 1979-82; BS in Edn., Wright State U., 1982-85; postgrad. studies, Miami U., Oxford, Ohio, 1986-87, U.S. Sports Acad., Daphne, Ala., 1996-97, U. Dayton, 2001—. Cert. phys. edn. and health tchr., Ohio; lic. athletic trainer, Ohio. Student athletic trainer Wright State U., Dayton, Ohio, 1983-85; asst. athletic trainer Oakwood (Ohio) City Sch., 1984-86; grad. asst. athletic trainer Miami U., Oxford, Ohio, 1986-87; subst. tchr. Oakwood City Sch., Kettering Moraine City Schs., Ohio, 1987-89; athletic trainer Kettering Moraine City Schs., Kettering, Ohio, 1987-96, tchr., 1989—; owner InnerPrize, Kettering, 1996—. Pub. spkr. Greater Dayton Athletic Trainers, 1987—, InnerPrize, 1996—; advisor Kettering Fairmont Student Athletic Trainers Assn., Kettering Moraine City Schs., 1989—96; facilitator Student Assistance Support Group, Kettering-Moraine City Schs., 1994—2000; instr. Kettering Awareness Tobacco Edn. Program, 1997—2001; advisor Students Against Destructive Decisions, 1997—. Mem. PTA Assns. of various Kettering-Moraine Pub. Schs., 1989-00; co-dir. Kettering 24-Hour Relay Challenge, 1999. Named Jaycee of the Month Region E, 1996, Ohio Jaycees, Most Outstanding Write-Up of the First Quarter, 1996, Ohio Jaycees. Mem. NEA, ASCD, Nat. Athletic Trainer's Assn. (cert. athletic trainer), Ohio Athletic Trainers Assn., Greater Dayton Athletic Trainers Assn., Nat. Strength and Conditioning Assn., Internat. Weight Lifting Assn. (cert. weight trainer), Ohio Edn. Assn., Kettering Edn. Assn., Ohio Assn. for Health, Phys. Edn., Recreation and Dance, Am. Coll. Sports Medicine, Nat. Fedn. Interscholastic Coaches Edn. Program/Am. Coaching Effectiveness Program, Sports First Aid Instr. Avocations: Christian studies, fitness, personal devel. and sports, athletics. Home: 3489 Valleywood Dr Kettering OH 45429-4234 Office: Kettering Fairmont HS 3301 Shroyer Rd Kettering OH 45429-2635 E-mail: denlingerv@aol.com.

DENMARK, FLORENCE HARRIET LEVIN, psychology educator; b. Phila., Jan. 28, 1931; d. Morris and Minnerva (Sharkis) L.; m. Stanley J. Denmark, June 7, 1953 (div. Apr. 1973); children: Valerie, Pamela (dec.) and Richard (twins); m. Robert W. Wesner, Sept. 5, 1973; stepchildren: Kathleen, Michael, Wendy. AB, U. Pa., 1952, AM, 1954, PhD, 1958; DHL, Mass. Sch. Profl. Psychology, 1985, Cedar Crest Coll., 1988; D of psychology, Ill. Sch. Profl. Psychology, 1995; DHL, Alleghany Coll., 1998. Lectr. psychology CUNY, Queens, 1959-66, instr. to prof. N.Y.C., 1964-90, doctoral faculty psychology, 1967-87, prof. psychology, 1984-90; Robert Scott Pace Disting. prof. psychology, chair Pace U., N.Y.C., 1988—; adj. prof. CUNY, N.Y.C., 1990—. Editor: Who Discriminates Against Women?, 1974, Psychology: The Leading Edge Into the Unknown, 1980, (with L.L. Adler) Violence and the Prevention of Violence, 1995, (with M.B. Nadien) Females and Autonomy: A Life-span Perspective, 1999, (with V. Rabinowitz and J. Sechzer) Engendering Psychology, 2000, others; co-editor: Women: Dependent or Independent Variable?, 1975; contbr. various chpts. to books and numerous articles to profl. jours. Mellon scholar St. Olaf Coll., 1977; grantee Ctr. Human Rels. U. Pa., U.S. Office Edn., Rsch. Found. State of N.Y., N.Y. Cmty. Trust, Nat. Sci. Found., Ford Found., Nat. Endowment for Humanities, Nat. Inst. Mental Health, Muskowini Fund, Pace U. Fellow APA (com. on accreditation 1998—, pres. divsn. 52 internat. psychology 1999, pres. 1980, mem. various coms.; Centennial award 1992, disting. contbns. to psychology in pub. interest 1993, disting. contbns. to internat. psychology award 1996, 99), Am. Psychol. Soc. (charter); mem. Internat. Coun. Psychologists (pres. 1989-90), Interamerican Soc. Psychology (Interamerican award in Psychology 1997), Internat. Orgn. for Study of Group Tensions (v.p.), N.Y. State Psychol. Assn. (pres. divsn. social psychology 1989-90, acad. divsn. 1990-91; Kurt Lewin award 1978, Wilhelm Wundt award 1988, Carolyn Wood Sherif award 1992, Allen V. Williams Jr. Meml. award 1994, Margaret Floy Washburn award 1996), N.Y. Acad. Scis. (fellow 1966, v.p. 1984-87, Psychology Adv. Com. 1971—), Eastern Psychol. Assn. (pres. 1986, bd. dirs. 1988-91), Coun. Sci. Pres. (sec., exec. bd. mem. 1983-84), Internat. Coun. Psychologists, Assn. Women in Psychology (Outstanding Women in Sci. award 1980, disting. career award 1996), Soc. for Advancement of Social Psychology, Nat. Coun. of Chairs of Grad. Depts. Psychology, Soc. for Psychol. Study of Social Issues (mem. Otto Klineberg Intercultural and Internat. Rels. Award. Com.), Century Club, Chemists Club, Psi Chi (nat. pres. 1978-80). Avocations: opera, ballet, theatre, travel, sports. Office: Pace U 41 Park Row Fl 13 New York NY 10038-1508 E-mail: Fdenmark@pace.edu.

DENNANY, KELLY, mechanical engineer, test engineer; b. Kalamazoo, Sept. 26, 1972; d. Robert Dale Jr. and Debra Lee Dennany. BS in Mech. Engring., GMI Engring. and Mgmt. Inst., Flint, MIch., 1995. ABS lab. sr. test engr. Continental Teves, Auburn Hills, Mich., 1995—. Mem. Soc. Automotive Engrs. Republican. Baptist. Avocations: rubber stamping, cooking, crafts.

DENNERY, LINDA, newspaper publishing executive; b. Phila., July 7, 1947; V.p., gen. mgr. Times-Picayune, New Orleans, 1987—97, pres., mem. of advisory bd., 1997—99; pub. Star-Ledger, Newark, 1999—. Bd. dirs. Kingsley House, Touro Infirmary, Bur. Govtl. Rsch., So. Newspaper Pub. Assn., Internat. Women's Forum. Mem.: bd. of dir. of Kingsley House, Touro Infirmary, Bureau of Governmental Research, Southern Newspaper Pub. Assoc., International Women's Forum. Office: Star Ledger 1 Star Ledger Plz Newark NJ 07102-1200*

DENNEY, SHAWNA LEANN, music educator; b. Colorado Springs, Colo., July 14, 1971; d. George Howard and Rosemarie Gertrude Vanaman; m. William Malcolm Denney, July 1, 1999; children: Payton Chrystine, Carson Rebekah. MusB Edn., N.Mex State U., 1998. Cert. level 3 educator State Bd. Edn. N.Mex., 2003. Asst. band dir. Alamogordo (N.Mex.) H.S./Chaparral Mid. Sch., 2000—01; dir. bands Chaparral Mid. Sch., Alamogordo, 2001—. Pvt. lesson instr. Milanos Music, Tempe, Ariz., 1999—2000. Mem.: N.Mex Music Educators Assn. Republican. Avocation: music. Home: 300 Chipmunk Cloudcroft NM 88317 Office: Chaparral Middle School 1401 College Ave Alamogordo NM 88317 Personal E-mail: saxdiva7@yahoo.com. E-mail: sdenney@aps4kids.org.

DENNICK, LORI ANN (L. ANNE CARRINGTON), editor; b. Cannonsburg, Pa., Feb. 8, 1962; d. Albert William and Mary Alice (Baldwin) D. AS, Pa. Comml. Bus. Coll., Washington, 1987; BA, U. Md., 1992; MFA, Hunter Coll., N.Y.C., 1999. Editor, art dir. Common Ground, Pitts., 1995-96; editor wrestling MopSquad Sports, 2004—. Holdenlog guest product reviewer, 2003. Editor: (Paul London's ofcl. website) London: Not the City; freelance contbr. Observer Reporter, Washington, Pa., 1980—97. Mem. daffodil days com. Am. Cancer Soc., Pitts., 1999. Named Miss 16 Plus-Model of Yr., Miami, Fla., 1995, Ms. Plus Internet World, 2002, Ms. Elegant Pa., 2002, Ms. Plus Pa., 2002, Miss Pa. Galaxy, 2002, Miss Pa Galaxy, 2003, Miss Am. Rose McKeesport City Queen, 2003, Ms. Picture Perfect Pa., 2003; recipient Ms. McKeesport Am. States, 2003. Mem.: Models United. Democrat. Presbyterian. Avocations: theater arts, travel, painting, jewelry design. E-mail: thewrestlingbabe@mopguad.com.

DENNIES, SANDRA LEE, city official; b. Buffalo, Dec. 26, 1951; d. Norman John and Shirley Edith (Dils) D.; m. Robert Francis Gilbane, Sept. 21, 1974 (div. Apr. 1987); children: Brandon Michael, Gianpatrick. AS in Dental Hygiene, U. Bridgeport, Conn., 1972, BS in Dental Hygiene Edn., 1973; MS in Health Scis., So. Conn. State U., 1979. Dental hygienist various orgns., New Haven, 1972-73, Leonard B. Zaslow, DDS, Westport, Conn., 1973-81; lectr. U. Bridgeport, 1973-76; planner City of Bridgeport, 1977-79, planning asst., 1979-81; grants dir. City of Stamford, Conn., 1981—. Sec. Com. on Emergency Med. Disaster Planning, Bridgeport, 1978-79; dir., dep. dir. Stamford Coliseum Authority, 1982-91; dep. dir. Stamford Film Commn., 1986-88. Editor, chief Hy-Light Jour., 1973-76. Mem. Stamford Youth Planning and Adv. Bd., 1981-91, Stamford Youth Svc. Bur., 1991-95, United Way Corp., Stamford, 1986-93; pres., sec. Alcohol and Drug Abuse Coun., 1987-92; mem. bd. Christian Outreach North Stamford Congl. Ch., 1988-92, 95-2000, mem. pastoral rels. com., 1995—; mem. Coun. Chs. and Synagogues Assembly, Stamford, 1989; pres. Stamford Mcpl. Supervisory Employees Union, 1991-99, mem. 1981—; v.p., sec. Stamford Sch. Readiness Found., 1998—. Democrat. Avocations: piano, clarinet, guitar, skiing. Home: 171 Shadow Ridge Rd Stamford CT 06905-1813 Office: City of Stamford 888 Washington Blvd PO Box 10152 Stamford CT 06904-2152 E-mail: sandra171@aol.com.

DENNIS, DONNA FRANCES, sculptor, art educator; b. Springfield, Ohio, Oct. 16, 1942; d. Donald Phillips and Helen Frances (Hogue) D. BA in Art, Carleton Coll., 1964; student, Coll. Art Studies Abroad, Paris, 1964-65, Art Students League, N.Y.C., 1965-66. Instr. Skowhegan Sch. Painting and Sculpture, Maine, 1982, Sch. Visual Arts, N.Y.C., 1983-90, SUNY, Purchase, 1984-85, 87, Princeton U., N.J., 1984; assoc. prof. SUNY Purchase Coll., 1990-96; prof. SUNY, 1996—, Doris and Karl Kempner disting. prof., 2001—03. One-woman shows include Holly Solomon Gallery, N.Y.C., 1976, 80, 83, 98, Contemporary Arts Ctr., Cin., 1979, Neuberger Mus. of SUNY-Purchase, 1985, Univ. Gallery, U. Mass., Amherst, 1985, Bklyn. Mus., 1987, Del. Art Mus., Wilmington, 1988, Indpls. Mus. Art, 1991-98, Sculpture Ctr., N.Y.C., 1993, Dayton Art Inst., 2003; exhibited in group shows Venice Biennale, Italy, 1982, 84, Whitney Mus., N.Y.C., 1979, 81, Tate Gallery, London, 1983, Hirshhorn Mus., Washington, 1979, 84, Biennial of Pub. Art, Neuberger Mus., 1997, Asheville (N.C.) Mus. Art, 1998; permanent commns. include decorative fence P.S. 234, N.Y.C., I.S. 5, Queens, N.Y., Wonderland Sta., MBTA, Boston, North Plaza, Klapper Hall, Queens Coll., Queens, N.Y., Am. Airlines Terminal, Terminal One, Kennedy Airport, N.Y.C. Recipient Art award for excellence in design N.Y.C. Art Commn., 1987, Art award Am. Acad. and Inst. of Arts and Letters, 1991, [illegible] Design award, 1992; grantee N.Y. State Creative Artists, 1975, 81, N.Y. Found. for Arts, 1985, 92; fiscal sponsorship, N.Y. Found. for Arts, 2002-; fellow Guggenheim Found., 1979, NEA, 1977, 80, 86, 94, Pollock-Krasner award, 2001; Doris and Karl Kempner Dist. Prof. award Purchase Coll. SUNY, 2001-03. Democrat. Home: 131 Duane St New York NY 10013-3850 E-mail: tunnelsandtowers@att.net.

DENNIS, GINETTE E. (GIGI), state legislator; b. Kansas City, Mo., Nov. 28, 1961; m. Dean Dennis. Student, Adams State Coll., U. So. Colo., Harvard U. With Band of Monte Vista, 1982-87; customer svc. rep. Pub. Svc. Co. Colo., Alamosa, 1987-91, Pueblo, 1991-94; mem. Colo. Senate, Dist. 5, Denver, 1994—. Bd. mem. El Pueblo Boys and Girls Ranch; active Sangre de Cristo Arts Ctr., Rosemount Mus.; sec., past sec. Rio Grande County Reps.; past chair Ho. Dist. 60; mem. Local, State and Nat. Campaign Com., 1984—. Mem. Pueblo Zool. Soc., Bel Nor Rep. Women, Monte Vista C. of C., Pueblo West Rotary, Colo. Cattle Assn. Republican. Roman Catholic. Office: State Capitol 200 E Colfax Ave Ste 263 Denver CO 80203-1716 also: 7166 S Eagles Nest Cir Littleton CO 80127-3212 Fax: 719-547-9330.

DENNIS, KAREN MARIE, plastic surgeon; b. Cleve., Dec. 23, 1948; d. Chester and Adele (Wesley) D.; m. Miles Auslander, June 21, 1974; 1 child, Kristin. BS, Ohio State U., 1971, MD, 1974. Diplomate Am. Bd. Plastic Surgery, Am. Bd. Otolaryngology. Intern Kaiser Permanente, L.A., 1974-75; resident in otolaryngology Roosevelt Hosp., N.Y.C., 1976-79; resident in plastic surgery Ohio State Univ. Hosps., Columbus, 1979-81; pvt. practice Beverly Hills, Calif., 1981—. Mem. Am. Soc. Reconstructive and Plastic Surgeons, Calif. County Med. Assn., L.A. County med. Assn., L.A. Soc. Plastic Srugeons (sec. 1993-94), Phi Beta Kappa. Avocations: tennis, golfing, traveling, reading. Office: 433 N Camden Dr Beverly Hills CA 90210-4426

DENNIS, LINDA SUSAN, nonprofit organization executive; b. Chgo., Mar. 26, 1948; d. William Evert and Edwina Louise (Franke) Dennis; m. William Raymond Parker, Feb. 15, 1969 (div. 1999); children: Anthony Wade, Kathleen Louise, Elizabeth Irene, Sarah Miriam. AA magna cum laude, Kenai Peninsula Coll., 1996; BA, Evergreen State Coll., 1999; postgrad., U. Wash., 1999. Founder, dir. Kenai Peninsula Food Bank, Soldotna, Alaska, 1987-98; co-chmn. Kenai Healthy Start, Soldotna, 1991-98; pres., bd. dirs. Green Stor, 1997-98. Bd. dirs. Bishop's Attic, Soldotna, 1993-98, Fed. Emergency Mgmt. Agy., Soldotna, 1992-98; vol. Boy Scouts Am., Soldotna, 1980-93, Girl Scouts Am., Soldotna, 1980-87, Kenai Peninsula Sch. Dist., Soldotna, 1980-90; co-chair Alaska Food Coalition, 1996-98; established 1st St. Soup Kitchen, 1997. Recipient Vol. of the Yr. award State of Alaska, 1986, Points of Light award Points of Light Found., 1992, Gold award United Way, Kenai, 1990-95, Woman of Distinction award Soroptimist, Person of Yr. award Soldotna C. of C., 1996. Mem. Soldotna C. of C. (bd. dirs. 1996-98, sec.-treas. 1998), Phi Theta Kappa (treas.). Methodist. Avocations: reading, travel, education. Home: 155 SE Washington Ave Chehalis WA 98532-3049

DENNIS, PATRICIA DIAZ, lawyer; b. Santa Rita, N.Mex., 1947; d. Porfirio Madrid and Mary (Romero) Diaz; m. Michael John Dennis, Aug. 3, 1968; children: Ashley Elizabeth, Geoffrey Diaz, Alicia Sarah Diaz. BA in English, UCLA, 1970; JD, Loyola U. LA Sch. Law, 1973. Bar: Calif. 1973, DC 1984, Tex. Law clk. Calif. Rural Legal Asst., McFarland, 1971; assoc. Paul, Hastings, Janofsky & Walker, LA, 1973-76; atty. Pacific Lighting Corp., LA, 1976-78; atty., asst. gen. atty. ABC, Hollywood, 1978-83; commr. FCC, Washington, 1986-89; ptnr., head comm. Jones, Day, Reavis & Pogue, Washington, 1989-91; v.p. govt. affairs US Sprint/United Telecom, Washington, 1991-92; asst. sec. State for Human Rights and Humanitarian Affairs Dept. State, Washington, 1992; special coun. comm. Sullivan & Cromwell, Washington, 1991—98; sr. v.p. regulatory and pub. affairs SBC Comm., San Antonio, 1998—2002; mem. bd. dirs. Entravision Comm. Corp., 2001—, 2001—. Chmn. US del. Internat. Telecomm. Union Region 2 Broadcasting Conf., Rio de Janeiro, 1988; bd. dirs. Telemundo Group Inc., 1989-92, Conn. Mut. Life Ins. Co., Nat. Pub. Radio, 1992, PR Legal Def. and Edn. Fund, 1991-92, Nat. Labor Rels. Bd., Regan adminstrn.; mem. adv. bd. Ctr. for Telecomm. and Info. Studies, Columbia U., 1991-92, Latin Am. Inst., Loyola U. (LA Sch. Law), 1991-92, Bur. Nat. Affairs, Media Law Reporter, 1990-92; mem. Nat. Adv. Com. (Women Judges' Fund for Justice), 1990-92. Exec. editor: Loyola Law Rev., 1972-73. Com. mem. Hispanic leadership program Coro Found., LA, 1981-82; US del. UN Commn. on Status of Women, 30th session Econ. and Social Coun., Vienna, Austria, 1984, World Conf. UN Decade for Women, Nairobi, Kenya, 1985; bd. dirs. Resources for Infant Educators, 1981-83, Nat. Network Hispanic Women, LA, 1983-92, Reading is Fundamental, 1991—; mem. exec. com., nat. adv. bd. Leadership Am., Found. for Women's Resources, 1987—, bd. mem., trustee; bd. visitors Pepperdine U. Sch. Law, 1988-92; mem. adv. coun. Ctr. for Pub. Utilities, N.Mex. State U., 1988-92; bd. mem. and trustee Thomas Rivera Policy Inst., 1991—, Radio and Television News Dirs. Found., 1992—, Women's Mus., Bexar County Women's Bar Assn., Tex. State U. Sys. Bd. Regents, Hispanic Scholarship Fund, Mex. Am. Legal Defense and Ednl. Fund, Mass. Mutual Life Ins. Recipient cert. achievement YWCA, LA, 1979, Woman Yr. award merit Mex. Am. Opportunity Found., 1984, Recognition Outstanding Achievements award Nat. Coun. Hispanic Women, 1986, Woman Achievement award City Club Cleve., 1986, Friend Family award The Family Place, 1987, Woman Yr. award Hispanic Women's Coun., Inc., 1989, Belva Lockwood Outstanding Lawyer award, Bexar County Women's Bar Assn., 2000, Pub. Endeavor award, Assn. Women in Comm., 2001; named one of 100 Influentials, Hispanic Bus. mag., 1987, 88, 90, 96; named Hispanic Woman Yr., Houston YMCA, 1992, Alumna Yr., UCLA Latino Alumni Assn., 1999, Corp. Exec. Yr., San Antonio Women's C. of C., 1999. Mem. Mex.-Am. Bar Assn. (sec. 1980-81, trustee 1979-80, 81-82), LA County Bar Assn. (child abuse subcom. chmn. barristers sect. 1980-81, exec. com. barristers sect. 1980-82), Hispanic Bar Assn. DC, ABA (com. labor arbitration and law of collective bargaining agreements, labor law sect. 1979-82), Women's Forum Wash., Am. Bar Assn. Commn. (on opportunities for minorities in the profession 1991-92, mem. nominations com., 1991-92, co-chmn. common carrier com., 1990-91), Fed. Comm. Bar Assn. Democrat. Roman Cath. Office: 2410 Camino Ramon Ste 257 San Ramon CA 94583 Office Phone: 925-806-4090. Office Fax: 925-866-2030.*

DENNIS, PATRICIA LYON, adult education educator; b. Rockford, Tenn., June 13, 1933; d. Howard Stanton and Dora Hester (Maynard) Lyon; m. Norman Bryan Dennis Jr., Jan. 12, 1957 (dec. Jan. 1985); children: Sarah Dennis Banks, Rebecca Dennis Hampton. BS, George Peabody Coll., 1955; MA, U. Mo., 1977; postgrad., Auburn U., 1977-73, U. Kans., 1982-92, U. Mo., Kansas City, 1994, 96. Cert. tchr.; cert. libr. media specialist, Kan; elem. classroom tchr., N.C., Mich., Mo., Ala. 3d grade tchr. Ray Street Elem. Sch., High Point, N.C., 1955-56; kindergarten and 3d grade tchr. Wurtsmith Dependent Sch., Clark AFB, Philippines, 1957-59; spl. reading tchr., 1st grade tchr. McDonald Elem. Sch., K.I. Sawyer AFB, Mich., 1961-63; kindergarten tchr. Gladden Elem. Sch., Richards-Gebaur AFB, Mo., 1964-65; 2d grade tchr., libr. Goose AFB Dependent Sch., Labrador, 1965-67; 2d grade tchr. Edgewood Acad., Wetumpka, Ala., 1969-70; 1st and 4th grade tchr. Trinity Christian Day Sch., Montgomery, Ala., 1970-72; 2d and 3d grade tchr. Fairview Elem. Sch., Olathe, Kans., 1974-77; libr. media specialist Wash. Elem. Sch., Olathe, Kans., 1977-99; instr. continuing edn. Johnson County C. C., Overland Pk., Kans., 1999—. Pres. Pre-Sch. Bd., Gunter AFB, 1968-69; children's choir dir. Leawood (Kans.) Bapt. Ch., 1979-84, Sunday sch. dept. dir., 1987-88, ch. libr., 1990-93; bd. dirs.

Scholarship Pageant, Kansas City, 1988-96; chaperone, traveling companion Miss Am.-Kans. Scholarship Pageant, Pratt, Kans., 1989-98; commr., book rev. com. Kans. State Reading Cir. Commn., Topeka, 1985-91, 94-96, 97-99; primary subcom. chairperson Kans. State Reading Circle, 1998-99. Mem.: MLA, NEA, Kans. Reading Assn., Kans. Assn. Sch. Librs. (presenter 1990—97), Olathe Culture Group (v.p. 2002—), Sigma Alpha Iota (treas. 1954), Alpha Delta Kappa (sec. 1999—2002, pres. 2002—, mem. cmty. scholarship bd. 2002—03). Republican. Baptist. Avocations: harp, piano, voice, dance, physical fitness. Home and Office: 10525 Chesney Ln Olathe KS 66061-2775

DENNIS-MCDONNELL, LYNN MARIE, environmetal health practitioner, biologist; b. Clinton, Iowa, May 31, 1968; d. Robert Harry and Judith Ann Dennis; m. Donald Richard McDonnell, Dec. 1, 1990; children: Payton Scarlett McDonnell, Shay Judith McDonnell. AA, South C.C., Betlendorf, Iowa, 1994; BS in Biology, St. Ambrose, Davenport, Iowa, 1996. Rschr. Clinton County Health Assesment Vis. Nurses Assn., Clinton, Iowa, 1997—98; water lab tech. Quad City Metalurgical Lab, Eldndge, Iowa, 1998—99; programmer, staff biologist CTR, Davenport, Iowa, 1999—2000; lic. environ. health practitioner Whiteside County Health Dept., Morrison, Ill., 2000—. Avocations: reading, gardening. Home: 1004 17th St Port Byron IL 61275

DENNISON, NORMA MAE, art educator; b. Loraine, Tex., Nov. 5, 1926; d. John Luther Croslin and Twila Rebecca Walker; m. Robert Manley Dennison, Jan. 27, 1946; children: Laura Denise, Robert Glenn, Manley Brent. Grad. h.s., Coachella, Calif. Advt./comml. artist Kelly Foods, Proctor & Gamble, Rosenbloom's Fashion Store, The Jackson Sun, Jackson, Tenn., 1943—66; art tchr. Jackson, 1966—72, Jackson State Coll., 1972—2003; judge local, state, and nat. art shows. Featured on 6 nat. mag. covers, drawings, Perspectives 1 and 2, 1996, videos, Watercolor 1 and 2, 1996, Watercolor Video on Portraits, 1998, Oil Video on Portraits, 1998. Recipient 1st pl. award, Midwest Arts in the Park, Wash., others. Mem.: Women in Arts (charter mem., founder), Memphis and German Town Art League, Jackson Art Assn. (co-founder), Nat. Pen Women (nat. bd. dirs. 1982—96, nat. art chmn. 1994—96), Nat League Am. Pen Women (pres.), Zeta Tau Alpha (nat. life mem., featured cover nat. mag.). Baptist. Home: 108 Odell Rd Jackson TN 38301 Office: Art with Norma Dennison Jackson TN 38301

DENNISTON, MARTHA KENT, small business owner, writer; b. Phila., Feb. 8, 1920; d. Samuel Leonard and Elizabeth (Cryer) Kent; m. Edward Shippen Willing, May 14, 1942 (div. 1972); children: Peter, Matthew, Thomas, Stephen; m. George C. Denniston, July 5, 1974. BA, Bryn Mawr (Pa.) Coll., 1941; MA, U. Wash., Seattle, 1965. Clinic dir. Population Dynamics, Seattle, 1973-84; pvt. practice investor, 1950—; resort owner Ecologic Pl., Port Townsend, Wash., 1972—. Sec. bd. dirs. Ctr. for Population Communications, N.Y.C., 1983-86. Author: Beyond Conception, Our Children's Children, 1971, (poems) The Bladed Quiet, 1994. Bd. dirs. Population Action Coun., Washington, 1977-80. Mem. Nat. Soc. Colonial Dames Am. Avocation: genealogy. Home: 45 Robbins Rd Nordland WA 98358-9607

DENNY, JUDITH ANN, retired lawyer; b. Lamar, Mo., Sept. 18, 1946; d. Lee Livingston and Genevieve Adelpha (Falke) D.; m. Thomas M. Lenard, May 29, 1976; children: Julia Lee, Michael William. BA, La. Tech. U., 1968, JD, George Washington U., 1972. Bar: D.C. 1973. Asst. spl. prosecutor Watergate Spl. Prosecution Force, Washington, 1973-75; pros. atty. U.S. Dept. Justice, Washington, 1975-78; dir. div. compliance U.S. Office Edn. HEW, Washington, 1978-80; acting asst. insp. gen. for investigations U.S. Dept. Edn., Washington, 1980; dep. dir. policy and compliance, office of revenue sharing U.S. Dept. Treasury, Washington, 1980-83, counselor to gen. counsel, 1983-89; insp. gen. ACTION, Washington, 1989-94; cons. Fed. Quality Inst., 1994-95. Mem. D.C. Bar Assn. Home: 2816 Arizona Ter NW Washington DC 20016-2642

DENNY, MARY CRAVER, state legislator, business owner; b. Houston, July 9, 1948; d. Kenneth and Lois (Skiles) Craver; m. Henry William Denny, Jan. 26, 1969 (div. Aug. 1990); 1 child, Bryan William. Student, U. Tex., 1966—70; BS in Elem. Edn. magna cum laude, U. North Tex., 1973. Cert. tchr. Tex. Mem. Tex. Ho. of Reps., Austin, 1993—. Mem. numerous other civic orgns.; del. state and nat. Rep. convs., 1972—; chmn. Denton (Tex.) County Rep. Com., 1983—91; bd. dirs. Tex. Fedn. Rep. Women, 1988—2003, Tex. Com. Humanities, 1990, YMCA, Denton, 1985—; life mem. pres.'s coun. U. N. Tex., Denton, 1974—, chmn., 1983; mem. Denton Benefit League, 1976—, Denton Arts Coun., 1986—. Named Outstanding Rep. Vol., Denton County Rep. Com., 1985, Outstanding Alumna in Edn., U. N. Tex. Coll. Edn., 1993; named one of 10 Outstanding Rep. Women, Tex. Fedn. Rep. Women, 1991. Mem.: Nat. Conf. State Legislature, Am. Legis. Exch. Coun., Ariel Club, Delta Zeta. Episcopalian. Avocations: swimming, bridge. Address: 8684 FM 2153 Aubrey TX 76227-3029 Office: PO Box 2910 Austin TX 78768-2910 also: 1001 Cross Timbers Rd Flower Mound TX 75028 E-mail: mary.denny@house.state.tx.us.

DENOBRIGA, KATHIE ELIZABETH, consultant; b. Atlanta, Dec. 4, 1950; d. Frank Herbert and Eleanor Patricia (Upchurch) deNobriga; m. William Russell Brantley, Aug. 21, 1971 (div. 1974); life ptnr. Alice Lynn Teeter, July 4, 1999. BA, Wake Forest U., 1972, MA, 1974. Performer, stage mgr. Winston-Salem Arts Coun., NC, 1972—75; artist-in-residence Johnston County Tech. Coll., Smithfield, 1974—76; ensemble, treas. The Rd. Co., Johnson City, Tenn., 1976—79; theatre specialist Lee County Parks & Recreation, Sanford, NC, 1979—84; artistic mng. dir. Temple Theatre, 1984—88; exec. dir. Alternate ROOTS, Atlanta, 1988—97; cons. pvt. practice, 1997—. Bd. dirs. Art in Pub. Interest, Saxapahaw, NC, 1999—, Alternate ROOTS, exec. com., 1980—82; site reviewer NEA, Washington, 1989—. Co-editor: Alternate ROOTS: Plays from the Southern Theatre, 1994. Mem. city coun., Pine Lake, Ga., 2002—; bd. dirs. Little Five Point Cmty. Ctr., Atlanta, 1997—99, chair bd. dirs., 1999—. Next Generation Leadership fellow, Rockefeller Found., N.Y.C., 1999.

DENSEN-GERBER, JUDIANNE, psychiatrist, lawyer, educator; b. N.Y.C., Nov. 13, 1934; d. Gustave A. and Beatrice D.; m. Michael M. Baden, June 14, 1958; children: Trissa Austin Baden, Judson Michael, Lindsey Robert Baden, Sarah Densen Baden AB cum laude, Bryn Mawr Coll., 1956; LLB, Columbia U., 1959, JD, 1969; MD, NYU, 1963. Bar: N.Y. 1961. Rotating intern French Hosp., N.Y.C., 1963-64; resident psychiatry Bellevue Hosp., N.Y.C., 1964-65, Met. Hosp., N.Y.C., 1965-67; ethics com. Park City Hosp., Bridgeport, Conn., 1988-93; mem. core staff Addiction Services Agy., N.Y.C., 1966-67; founder Odyssey House (psychiat. residence for rehab. narcotics addicts), N.Y.C., Mich., Maine, N.H., Utah, La., Australia, N.Z., 1967, from clin. dir. to pres. bd., 1967-82, exec. dir., 1967-74; pres., founder, CEO Odyssey Inst. Am., 1974-82; pres. Odyssey Inst. Australia, 1977-86, Odyssey Inst. Internat., Inc., 1978—2003; chair Odyssey Inst. Corp. Conn., 1974—2003; attending physician Gracie Sq. Hosp., N.Y.C., 1982-93, Park City Hosp., Bridgeport, Conn., 1985-93; mem. ethics com. Bridgeport Hosp., 1985—2000, attending physician, 1985—2000, Northwest Gen. Hosp., Detroit, 1985-86; active staff St. Vincent's Hosp., Bridgeport, 1987-2000; courtesy staff Norwalk Hosp., 1993—2000. Assoc. vis. prof. law U. Utah Law Sch., 1973-75; adj. prof. law N.Y. Law Sch., 1973-76; chairperson plenary session drug abuse Am. Acad. Forensic Scis., 1972, sec. psychiatry sect., 1973, chmn. sect., 1974-2003; founder, 1973, since pres. Inst. Women's Wrongs; founder, since pres. Odyssey Inst. (health care for socially disadvantaged), 1974-80; bd. dirs. Simpson St. Devel. Assn., An Extraordinary Event (One to One for Mental Retardation), Bridge House; mem. Nat. Adv. Commn. Criminal Justice Standards and Goals, 1971-74, Pres.'s Commn. on White House Fellows, 1972-76; mem. drug experience adv. com. HEW, 1973-76; v.p. psychiat. sect. Internat. Forensic Medicine Conf., Budapest, 1967; pres. N.Y. Council Alcoholism, 1978-2003; co-chair com. on reproductive rights vs. best interest of the child Mich. State Senate, 1984-86; trustee Nat. Forensic Ctr., Princeton, N.J., 1985-2003, keynote speaker nat. conf., 1988, lectr., 1988; speaker Conf. for Multiple Personality Disorder, Chgo., 1985-2003; cons. to Mich. State Legislature to draft legislation on The Best Interests of the Child vs. the New Reproductive Techs., 1986; amicus curiae brief in Mary Beth Whitehead appeal Surrogate Mothering, 1987; sr. non-govt. psychiatrist L'Ambiance Plaza disaster, Bridgeport, 1987; guest lectr. narcotics addiction NYU Sch. Medicine, also Sch. Law.; in field dir. Daitch Shopwell, Inc.; cons. substance abuse Insight Inc., Flint, Mich., 1987-88; guest speaker Cornell U., 1989, Internat. Hypnosis Soc. of Yale, 1989, Cumberland Law Sch., 1989, Sacred Heart U., 1994; founder, CEO, pres. The Family Maintenance Health Orgn., LLC; guest speaker Nat. Ctr. Forensic Scis. Author: (with Trissa Austin Baden) Drugs, Sex, Parents and You, 1972, We Mainline Dreams, The Odyssey House Story, 1973, Walk in My Shoes, 1976; (with David Sandberg) The Role of Child Abuse in Delinquency and Juvenile Court Decision-Making, 1984, Chronic Acting-Out Students and Child Abuse: A Handbook for Intervention, 1986, Shortened Forms: A Manual for Teachers On; (with John Dugan) Issues in Law and Psychiatry, 1988; contbr. articles to profl. jours.; editor: Jour. Corrective and Social Psychiatry, 1975; co-developer, co-inventor virocidal surface cleaner against AIDS, 1988 Mem. N.Y.C. Crime Control Commn., 1975-79, Gov.'s Task Force on Crime Control, Albany, N.Y., 1977-79, N.Y. State Crime Control Planning Bd., 1975-79; del. White House Conf. on Youth, 1971; bd. dirs. Nat. Coalition for Children's Justice, 1975-2003, Am. Soc. for Prevention of Cruelty to Children, 1979-2003, Mary E. Walker Found., 1978; psychiat. cons. Good Shepherd Home for Girls, 1989-90. Recipient Woman of Achievement award AAUW, 1970; Myrtle Wreath award Hadassah, 1970; B'nai B'rith Woman of Greatness award, 1971; Otty award for service to N.Y.C. Our Town Newspaper, 1977; named Dame of White Cross Australia, #1 Dame of Malta, Ky. Col., N.Y. State Hon. Fire Chief. Fellow Am. Coll. Legal Medicine (Congl. cert. merit 1990, #2 Rep. gold medal, 2002); mem. AMA, Conn. State Soc., Fairfield County Med. Soc., Soc. Med. Jurisprudence, Therapeutic Communities Am. (founding mem., 1st v.p. 1975-2003), Am. Acad. Psychiatry and Law (mem. AIDS ad hoc com 1988-2003), Am. Psychiat. Assn., Women's Forum N.Y. (founding mem.), Nat. Women's Forum, Internat. Women's Forum, Internat. Soc. Multiple Personality and Dissociative States, Conn. Med. Assn., Am. Orthopsychiat. Assn., ABA, N.Y. State Bar Assn., N.Y. County Women's Bar Assn., N.Y. Assn. Vol. Agys. Narcotics Addiction and Substance Abuse (dir. 1968-2003), Am. Psychiat. Assn., N.Y. Med. Assn., Post Traumatic Stress Syndrome Soc., Fairfield County Med. Soc. (physicians health subcom. 1986-92), Congl. Physicians Advisory Coun. (hon. chmn) 2001-2003, Congl. Bus. Commn. (hon. chmn) 2001-2003, Womens City Club N.Y.C. Republican. Unitarian Universalist. Died May 11, 2003.

DENSLEY, COLLEEN T. principal; b. Provo, Utah, Apr. 12, 1950; d. Floyd and Mary Lou (Dixon) Taylor; m. Steven T. Densley, July 23, 1968; children: Steven, Tiffany, Landon, Marianne, Wendy, Logan. BS in Elem. Edn., Brigham Young U., 1986, MEd in Tchg. and Learning, 1998. Cert. in elem. edn., K-12 adminstrn. Utah. Substitute tchr. Provo Sch. Dist., 1972-85, curriculum specialist, 1999-2001; tchr. 6th grade, mainstreaming program Canyon Crest Elem. Sch., Provo, 1985—94; instructional facilitator Campus Crest Elem., 1994—99; prin. Wasatch Elem. Sch., Provo, 2001—. Tchr. asst., math. tutor Brigham Young U., 1968—69; attendee World Gifted and Talented Conf., Salt Lake City, 1987, Tchr. Expectations and Student Achievement, 1988—89, Space Acad. for Educators, Huntsville, Ala., 1992; supr. coop. tchr. for practicum tchrs., 1987—90; co-chmn. accelerated learning and devel. com.; trainee working with handicapped students in mainstream classroom, 1989; mem. elem. sch. lang. arts curriculum devel. com., 90; mem. task force Thinking Strategies Curriculum, 1990—91; extensions specialist gifted and talented, 1990—91; math, 1991—; master tchr. Nat. Tchr. Tng. Inst., 1993. Co-author: (curricula) Provo Sch. Dist.'s Microorganism Sci. Kit, 1988, Arthropod Sci. Kit, 1988, Tchg. for Thinking, 1990—, PAWS Presents the Internet and the World Wide Web, 1997. Named Utah State Tchr. of the Yr., 1992; recipient Honor Young Mother of Yr. award, State of Utah, 1981. Mem.: NEA, Provo Edn. Assn. (Tchr. of the Yr. 1991—92), Internat. Space Edn. Initiative (adv. bd.), Utah Coun. Tchrs. Math., Utah Edn. Assn., Nat. Coun. Tchrs. Math. Republican. Mem. Lds Ch. Office: Wasatch Elem Sch 1080 N 900 E Provo UT 84604 E-mail: colleend@provo.EDU.

DENSLOW, DEBORAH PIERSON, primary education educator; b. Phila., May 2, 1947; d. Merrill Tracy Jr. and Margaret (Aiman) D.; m. James Tracy Grey III, Nov. 24, 1972 (div. Dec. 1980); 1 child, Sarah Elizabeth. BS, Gwynedd Mercy Coll., 1971; MA, Marygrove Coll., Detroit, 2000. Tchr. Willingboro (N.J.) Bd. Edn., 1971—. Union rep. Burlington County Edn. Assn., Willingboro, 1981-82, ednl. adv. Nat. Constitution Ctr., Phila., 2002-; mem. task force for reoganization Morrisville Sch. Dist., 1991-92. Mem. Borough Coun., Morrisville, 1988—94, pres., 1992—94, rep. candidate, 1986; borough chmn. Am. Cancer Soc., 1986—87; sec. bd. dirs. Morrisville Free Libr., 1988—90, bd. dirs., 1988—2001; mem. Morrisville Mcpl. Authority, chmn., 1994—95, 1996—2000, asst. sec., treas., 1995—96, 2001; judge City Gardens Contest The Pa. Horticultural Soc., Phila., 2002; committeewoman 1st ward Morrisville (Pa.) Rep. Com., 1986—98. Mem. NEA, N.J. Edn. Assn., Willingboro Edn. Assn. (union rep. 1981-82, alt. union rep. 1988-89), Parents without Ptnrs. (bd. dirs. Mercer County chpt. 1981-82, sec. 1982-84), Bucks County Boroughs Assn. (bd. dirs. 1989—, v.p. 1990-92, pres. 1992-93), Pa. Mcpl. Authorities Assn. (profl. devel. com. 2000-2001). Presbyterian. Avocations: swimming, sailing. Home: 1 Garrett Lane Willingboro NJ 08046

DENSMORE, JACQUELINE JEAN, financial accountant; b. Media, Pa., July 20, 1968; d. Robert Edward and Jean Alberta (Hoch) Wehner; married, July 12, 1997; 1 child, Luke Evan. AS in Acctg., Delaware County C.C., 1991; BS in Acctg., Widener U., 1994. Payroll clk. SCT, Malvern, Pa., 1988-89; payroll tax acct. SmithKline Beecham, Phila., 1989-92, fixed asset acct., 1993-94, fin. acct. Exton, Pa., 1994-95, Pfizer Inc., Exton, Pa., 1995-97, Memphis, 1997—2000. Avocations: piano, guitar, country line dancing, scuba diving, travel. Home: 310 Hawksbill Dr Easley SC 29642-8012

DENT, ELLEN MARGARET, writer; b. Columbus, Ohio, Aug. 3, 1932; d. Raymond William and Mary Elizabeth Quinlivan; m. Robert William Dent, Aug. 10, 1957; children: Vivian Catherine, Paul Harden, Mary Jean, John Robert, Sheila Joy. BA summa cum laude, Ohio Dominican Coll., 1954; MA, UCLA, 1956. Tech. editor Hughes Aircraft Co., Culver City, 1956—58, sr. editor/writer, head proposal ops., mgr. tech. comm. space and comm. group El Segundo, 1970—83; freelance sci. writer, instr., 1958—70; fit., v.p., pres. H. Silver and Assocs., L.A., 1983—97. Co-author: Readings in Science and Engineering, 1958, (textbook) Proposal Management for the 90s, 1990, (software) TOP-MAN-X, A Management Simulation, 1961. Bd. dirs., pres. Open Paths Counseling Ctr., L.A., 1990—2001. Home: 15450 Deerhorn Rd Sherman Oaks CA 91403

DENT, JULIE, director; d. Ernest and Elaine (King) Dent; m. Barry Morrow; 1 child, Christopher Dent Morrow. AAS, Borough Manhattan C.C., N.Y.C., 1988; BS in Edn., Empire State Coll.; MS in Edn., CUNY. Tchr. Horace E. Greene Day Care Ctr., Bklyn., 1983—88, adminstrv. dir., 1988—97; exec. dir. Audrey Johnson Day Care, Bklyn., 1997—. Domestic violence prevention counselor Women Working for a Better Cmty., 1996—; exec. bd. 1st vice chair Woodhull Hosp., Bklyn., 1999—; exec. vice chair Cmty. Sch. Bd. Dist. # 32, Bklyn., 2002—. Recipient award for excellence in early childhood edn., Profl. Assn. Day Care Dirs. Inc., 1989, award for outstanding cmty. svc., City Coun. N.Y., 1996, Key Stone award, Fedn. Protestant Welfare Agy. Inc., 2000, Citation of Honor, Charles J. Hynes, Dist. Atty., 2002, award for dedicated svc. to children, State Senator Martin M. Dilan, 2003, Citizenship award, Assemblyman Vito Loper. Mem.: Phi Delta Kappa (mem. Beta Omicron chpt.). Avocations: reading, dance. E-mail: audreyjo272@aol.com.

DENT, LEANNA GAIL, secondary art educator; b. Manhattan, Kans., Oct. 21, 1949; d. William Charles and Maxine Madeline Payne; children: Laura Michelle, Jeffery Aaron. BS in Edn., U. Houston, 1973; postgrad., U. Tex., 1975-76; MS in Edn., Okla. State U., 1988. Cert. elementary and secondary art tchr., Okla., Tex. Tchr. art Popham Elem. Sch., Del Valle, Tex., 1973-77; graphic artist Conoco, Inc., Ponca City, Okla., 1987-88; tchr. art Garfield Elem. Sch., Ponca City, Okla., 1988-91, Reed Elem. Sch., Houston, 1991-92, Copeland Elem. Sch., Houston, 1992-94, Campbell Jr. High Sch., Houston, 1994—. Cons. and specialist in field. Author: Using Synectics to Enhance the Evaluation of Works of Art, 1988; group exhibitions in Ala., Kans., Nebr., Okla., Tex. and Pa. Vol. 1st Luth. Day Sch., Ponca City, 1977-91, Ponca City Inds. Sch. Dist., 1987-91; work com. Cy-Fair Ind. Sch. Dist., Houston, 1991-94. Acad. and Mem. scholar Okla. State U., 1986-88; named Spotlight Tchr. Yr., 1992-93. Mem. Nat. Art Edn. Assn., Tex. Art Edn. Assn. (judges commendation 1993), Assn. Tex. Profl. Educators, Houston Art Edn. Assn. (v.p. 1992-93, pres.-elect 1993-95, pres. 1995-97, past pres. 1997-99), Phi Delta Kappa, Phi Kappa Phi. Republican. Lutheran. Avocations: riding horses, camping, art, museums, black and white movies. Office: Campbell Jr High Sch 11415 Bobcat Rd Houston TX 77064-3097

DENTON, JOY GRIGG, music educator; b. Marianna, Fla., Dec. 21, 1943; d. Jesse Edward and Inez Martin Grigg; m. William Warren Denton, June 4, 1965; children: Kathryn Jessica Acree, William Drake. Student, Judson Coll., Marion, Ala., 1962—64; BS in Music Edn., U. Ala., 1966; M.Music Edn., U. Montevallo, Ala., 1994; Cert. Edn. Adminstrn., Samford U., Birmingham, Ala., 1996—97. Elem. music tchr. DeKalb County Schs., Decatur, Ga., 1966—67, Dekalb County Schs., Decatur, 1975—76; pvt. piano tchr. Decatur, 1967—75; presch. tchr. Mountain Park Bapt. Ch., Stone Mountain, Ga., 1976—80; pvt. piano tchr. Stone Mountain, 1980—85; elem. music tchr. Gwinnett County Schs., Lawrenceville, Ga., 1985—88, Jefferson County Bd. Edn., Birmingham, 1989—. Guest presenter music methods class U. Montevallo, 1998; guest presenter Jefferson County Bd. Edn., Birmingham; resource/curriculum presenter Birmingham Internat. Festival for Jefferson County Bd. Edn., 2000—. V.p. Leeds Music Study Club, Ala., 1990—; choir and com. mem. Meadow Brook Bapt. Ch., Birmingham, 1989—. Named Second Mile Tchr., Jefferson County Bd. Edn., 1994, Outstanding Grad. Student in Music, U. Montevallo, 1994; grantee Multicultural Fine Arts grantee, Ala. State. Coun. on the Arts, 1994, Jefferson County Bd. of Edn. Found., for Hansel and Gretel musical prodn., Birmingham Internat. Festival, 1996, for sch.-wide Native Am. Festival, 2000. Mem.: Ala. Music Educators Assn., Ala. Orff Assn., Music Educators Nat. Conf., Am. Fedn. Tchrs., Delta Kappa Gamma, Delta Omicron (life). Baptist. Avocations: southern history, antiques. Office: Leeds Elementary Sch 201 Ashville Rd Leeds AL 35094

DENTON, JUDY ANN, art educator; d. John Lewis and Nellie Ann Yates; m. Charles Theodore Denton, May 31, 1975, children: Janel, Jessica. BS magna cum laude in Art Edn., N.E. Mo. State U., 1977, MA in Art Edn., 1984. Art educator Marceline (Mo.) Sch. Dist., 1977—86, libr., 1986—89; art educator Marshall (Mo.) Sch. Dist., 1989—. Asst. coach cross country Marshall (Mo.) Sch. Dist., 1998—; mem. fine arts project Dep. Elem. and Secondary Edn., Jefferson City, Mo., 1999—2000; educator Marshall (Mo.) Philharmonic Orch., 1993—. Mem.: Marshall (Mo.) Cmty. Tchrs. Assn., Mo. Art Edn. Assn., Nat. Art Edn. Assn. Avocations: reading, gardening, travel, exercise, artwork.

DENTON, MICHELE ANNE, music educator; b. Huntington, N.Y., Jan. 28, 1967; d. Robert John Luther and Frances Theresa Perry; m. Adam Stephen Denton; children: Erica, Andrew. BA in Music Edn., Fla. State U., 1989, BS in Music Performance, 1990; MA in Music Edn., Ithaca Coll., 1993; M in Arts and Liberal Studies, SUNY, Stony Brook, 1994. Music tchr., orch. dir. Sayville (N.Y.) Pub. Schs., 1990—2001, Syosset (N.Y.) Pub. Schs., 2001—. Scholar, Fla. State U. Mem.: Suffolk County Music Educators Assn. (all-county chairperson divsn. III 1993, 1994), Nassau Music Educators Assn. (all-county chairperson divsn. III 2001), Music Educators Nat. Conf. Avocations: music, conducting, reading, sewing, knitting. Home: 49 Unqua Rd Massapequa NY 11758 Office: Syosset Pub Schs 70 Southwoods Rd Syosset NY 11791

DENTON, PEGGY, occupational therapy educator, researcher; b. Moose Lake, Minn., Apr. 19, 1950; d. Donald Duane and Ruth Elaine (Stewart) D.; m. Frank William Johonnott, Feb. 22, 1986; 1 child, James Ryan. BS in Occupl. Therapy, U. Minn., 1972; MS in Occupl. Therapy, Boston U., 1979; PhD in Urban Edn., U. Wis., Milw., 1997. Registered occupl. therapist, Wis. Staff occupl. therapist Rogers VA Hosp., Bedford, Mass., 1973-78; asst. prof. U. Wis., Madison, 1979-83; staff occupl. therapist Meth.-Meriter Hosp., Madison, 1983-86, supr. occupl. therapy, 1986-87; occupl. therapy adminstrv. cons. Rock County Health Care Ctr., Janesville, Wis., 1988-99; assoc. prof. occupl. therapy Concordia U., Mequon, Wis., 1995-99, prof., 1999—, dir. divsn. occupl. therapy, 1999—. Bus. dir. Images of Madison, 1981-85; mem. accreditation rev. bd. Accreditation Coun. for Occupl. Therapy Edn., Bethesda, Md., 1995—; mem. profl. jour. rev. bd. Am. Jour. Occupl. Therapy, Bethesda, 1998—. Author: Psychiatric Occupational Therapy: A Workbook of Practical Skills, 1987; co-author: Occupational Therapy for Mood Disorders, 1999; contbr. articles to profl. jours., including Devel. Rev., Hosp. and Cmty. Psychiatry. Mem. employment task force Joint One Sch. Bd., Lake Geneva, Wis., 1998-991 mem. United Ch. Christ Bell Choir. Grantee Aid Assn. for Luths., 1999. Fellow Am. Occupl. Therapy Assn.; mem. Soc. for Rsch. in Child Devel., Wis. Occupl. Therapy Assn. (bd. dirs. 1986-92), award of distinction 1987), Lakeland Players Assn. Avocations: quilting, needle arts, gardening, community theater, music. Office: Concordia U 12800 N Lake Shore Dr Mequon WI 53097-2418

D'ENTREMONT, AMY, professional figure skater; b. Stoneham, Mass., May 2, 1977; Placed 17th Nat. Sr. Competition, 1997, 4th Ea. Sr., 1997, 5th New Eng. Sr., 1997, 3rd U.S. Olympic Festival, 1995, 4th nat. Jr., 1995, 1st, New England Jr., 1995, 6th U.S. Olympic Festival, 1994, 6th Nat. Jr., 1994, 2nd Ea. Jr., 1994, 1st New England Jr., 1994, others. Mem. U.S. Figure Skating Assn. Avocations: white water rafting, rollerblading, dance, friends. Office: 20 1st St Colorado Springs CO 80906-3624

DENTZER, SUSAN, journalist; b. Phila., 1955; BA in English Lit., Dartmouth Coll., 1977; Nieman fellow, Harvard U., 1986-87. Reporter Southampton (N.Y.) Press/Hampton Chronicle-News, 1977-78; sr. writer Newsweek, N.Y.C., 1979-87; sr. writer/chief econ. corr. U.S. News and World Report, Washington, 1987-97; health policy corr. The News Hour with Jim Lehrer, Arlington, Va., 1998—. Office: The News Hour with Jim Lehrer Ste 240 2700 S Quincy St Arlington VA 22206-2226 E-mail: sdentzer@newshour.org.

DENVER, EILEEN ANN, retired magazine editor; b. N.Y.C., Nov. 16, 1942; d. Daniel Joseph and Katherine Agnes (Boland) D.; m. Duncan C. Stephens, July 2, 1988. BA, Coll. New Rochelle, 1964; certificate, Radcliffe Sch. Pub., 1964; MA, Ind. U., 1967. Editorial asst. Mass. Inst. Tech. Tech. Review, Boston, 1965-66; instr. English St. Peter's Coll., Jersey City, 1967-70; assoc. editor, writer Am. Home mag., N.Y.C., 1971-75; asst. editor Consumer Reports, Mt. Vernon, NY, 1975-77, asst. mng. editor, 1977-79, mng. editor, 1979-91, exec. editor, 1991-96, dir. editl. ops., 1997-2000, assoc. editl. dir./exec. editor, 2000—, ret. Office: Consumer Reports 101 Truman Ave Yonkers NY 10703-1044

DENZEL, NORA, information technology executive; Graduate, SUNY, [illegible] in bus. admin., Santa Clara U., Calif. Various tech. and bus. roles to dir. storage-mgmt. products IBM; sr. v.p. product operations Legato Systems, 1997—2000; v.p. storage Hewlett Packard Co., 2000—03, sr. v.p. adaptive enterprise and software group, 2003—. Named one of the 50 Most Powerful People in Networking, Network World mag., 2003. Office: Hewlett-Packard Co 3000 Hanover St Palo Alto CA 94304*

DENZLER, MARY JOANNE, special education educator; b. Tacoma, Apr. 19, 1940; d. Sherman Russ and Mary Lucille (Senour) D. (dec.); divorced; children: Jeanette Deborah Hughes, John Edward Hughes III. B of Univ. Studies with honors, U. N.Mex., 1992, MA in Spl. Edn., 1995. Cert. spl. edn. tchr., N.Mex. Sec. Albuquerque Boy's Acad., 1959; co-owner Alamo Sales, Albuquerque, 1985-86; temp. jobs U. N.Mex., Albuquerque, 1986-95; with Presbyn. Ear Inst. Preschool, Albuquerque, 1995; spl. edn. tchr. Los Lunas (N.Mex.) Sch. Dist., 1995—, extended sch. year spl. edn. tchr., 1995—. Mem. St. Michael and All Angels Episcopal Ch., 1987-94, group facilitator spiritual recovery and healing for female survivors of sexual abuse; lay Eucharist min. St. Michael; lay Eucharist min., lector Cathedral Ch. St. Johns, 1994—, Soc. Mary, Altar Guild, Healing Team; Cursillo candidate Episcopal Diocese of Rio Grande, 1992, Cursillo team, 1994; lay eucharist, min. The Cathedral Ch. of St. John, 1994—; mem. Summer Harvest Healing Team, Episcopal Diocese of Rio Grande; assoc. mem. Internat. Order of St. Luke, 1997—, Friends of Religious Studies, U. N.Mex., AAUW, 1997—. Multicultural tchr. tng. prog. grad. sch. fellow U. N.Mex., 1993-95. Mem. Blue Key Nat. Honor Fraternity (life), Golden Key Nat. Honor Soc. (life). Avocations: painting, drawing, ceramics, listening to chamber music, opera. Home: 1135 1/2 Cinder Ln Los Lunas NM 87031-6510

DEOUL, KATHLEEN BOARDSEN, publishing executive; b. New London, Conn., May 5, 1944; d. Harry Kostrope Boardsen and Elizabeth (Conti) Dunham; m. Neal Deoul, June 20, 1982; 1 child, Shannon Rae. Grad. high sch., New London. Br. mgr. Qwip Sys. divsn. Exxon, Balt.; br. ops. mgr. Exxon Office Sys., Pitts., 1977-82; owner, pres. Bus. Quars., Crystal City, Va., 1983-95, Wellness Alternatives, Balt., 1993—, Cassandra Books, LLC, 2001. Author: (book) Cancer Cover-up, 2001. Mem. Team Diamond; co-chair Found. Alternative and Complementary Treatments. Mem.: Pres.'s Club Nikken, Inc. (Distbr. of Yr. 1999), Pres.'s Club Exxon. Avocations: venture capitalist, travel, writing, interior decorating, public speaking. E-mail: kathleendeoul@comcast.net.

DEPAN, MARY ELIZABETH, civic volunteer, nurse; b. Boston, Oct. 5, 1927; d. Frank and Josephine Madeline (Lennon) Natter; m. Harry McCarthy Depan, Apr. 26, 1952 (div. Aug. 1981); children: Harry, Madeline, Mark, Andrew. Student, Notre Dame Acad., 1945; diploma in nursing, St. Elizabeth Hosp., Boston, 1948; student, Skidmore Coll., 1960—. RN, Mass. Oper. rm. supr. Gt. Lake Naval Sta., Chgo., 1949; staff nurse Beth Israel Hosp., Boston, 1949. Monitor, leader Gt. Books Found., Glens Falls, N.Y., 1960—, Adirondack C.C., Glens Falls, 1960—; vol., bd. dirs. Literacy Vols., Glens Falls, 1983—; vol. nurse ARC, Glens Falls, 1985—; active area sr. citizen's orgn., 1992—. Lt. (j.g.) USN, 1949-52. Recipient cert. for porcelain painting, 1991. Mem. Women in Arts (chartered), Porcelain Artists, Nat. Mus. Women in the Arts (charter), Women's Meml. (charter). Roman Catholic. Avocations: painting, travel, museums, volunteering. Home: #142 Glen Hiland Mdws Queensbury NY 12804

DEPAOLI, GERI M. (JOAN DEPAOLI), artist, art historian; b. June 8, 1941; m. Alexander DePaoli, July 4, 1961; children: Alexander Mark, Michael Alexander. BA, U. Md., 1974, MA, 1978; student, U. Calif., Davis, 1965-68. Art history educator, artist, curator slides and photos Nat. Mus., Bangkok, Thailand, 1968-71; art prof. Montgomery Coll., Rockville, Md., 1978-82; cons. oriental slide and photo collection Princeton U., 1983-84; lectr. Princeton Sch. Visual Arts, 1986-90; curator The Mus. Art, Ft. Lauderdale, Fla., 1986; dir. Coun. for Creative Projects, N.Y.C., 1989-91; faculty artworks Princeton Sch. Visual Arts, 1984-91; exec. dir. EducArt Projects Inc., Davis, Calif., 1991—. Cons. in field. Author: Emmy Lou Packard: A Woman and a Century, 1998, Barbara Spring, Populations from the Collective Unconscious, 1998, Donna Billick: Making Art out of Stone, 1999, Clayton Bailey: Happenings in the Circus of Life, 2000; editor (exhbn. catalog): Elvis & Marilyn: 2 X Immortal, Rizzoli, 1994; author (ednl. resource guide) Elvis & Marilyn: 2 X Immortal, 1994, (ednl. program) Images of Power, 1994, video prodr. Images of Power: Balinese Paintings made for Gregory Bateson and Margaret Mead, 1994, editor/co-curator (exhbn. catalog) Transcending Abstraction, 1986, reviewer ArtMatters Newspaper, Phila., 1987—90, author-curator The Trans Parent Thread: Asian Philosophy in Recent Am. Art, 1990, contbg. author Art of Calif. Mag.; one-woman shows include E.W. Gallery, Bethesda, Md., 1978, Upstairs Gallery, Kingston, N.J., 1982, Gallery at the Purple Barge, N.Y.C., 1984, The Art Gallery, Kingston, 1985, Back Door Gallery, Princeton, 1986, Campion Gallery of Art, 1987, AT&T Corp. Gallery, Princeton, 1989, Rider Coll. Gallery, Lawrenceville, N.J., 1990; also numerous group shows. Councilor Nat. Abortion Rights Action League, 1989—. Recipient award for excellence in pub., Office of Pres. of U.S., 1969. Fellow Soc. for Arts Religion and Contemporary Culture; mem. Assn. Ind. Historians of Art (v.p. 1988—), Coll. Art Assn., Princeton Rsch. Forum, Nat. Coalition of Ind. Scholars, Sierra Club, Greenpeace. Buddhist. Avocations: skiing, philosophy discussion groups, intellectual history. Office: EducArt Projects Inc PO Box 267 Davis CA 95617-0267

DEPAOLO, ROSEMARY, dean, academic administrator; b. Bklyn., July 17, 1947; d. Nunzio and Edith (Spano) DeP.; m. Dennis B. Smith, 1977 (div. 1983); m. T. Frederick Wharton, 1984. BA, CUNY, Flushing, 1970; MA, Rutgers U., 1974, PhD, 1979. Asst. prof. to prof., dir. Ctr. for Humanities Augusta (Ga.) Coll., 1975-90; asst. dean Coll. Arts and Sci. Ga. So. U., Statesboro, 1990-93; dean Coll. Arts and Scis. Western Carolina U., Cullowhee, N.C., 1993-97; pres. Ga. Coll. and State U., Milledgeville, 1997—2003; chancellor U. North Carolina, Wilmington, NC, 2003—. Office: 601 S College Rd Wilmington NC 28403-3297

DEPARLE, NANCY-ANN MIN, former federal agency administrator, lawyer; b. Rockwood, Tenn., Dec. 17, 1956; m. Jason DeParle. BA, U. Tenn., 1978; JD, Harvard U., 1983; BA, MA, Balliol Coll., Oxford U., Eng., 1981. Past pvt. practice in law; commr. human svcs. Gov. Ned McWherter State of Tenn., 1987-89; past assoc. dir. health and pers. White House OMB, Washington; administr. Health Care Financing Adminstrn. HHS, Washington, 1997—2000; mem. board of dir. Cerner Corp., Kansas City, Mo., 2001—. Rhodes scholar, 1979-81. Office: Cerner Corp 2800 Rockcreek Pkwy Kansas City MO 64117

DEPEW, CAROL ANN, pharmaceutical sales representative; b. Kalamazoo, Mar. 2, 1962; d. Norman Sylvester and Margaret Ann (Mitscher) D. BA, U. Tenn., Knoxville, Tenn., 1986; MEd, U. Va., 1988. Nat. cert. counselor. Transition resource specialist Project PERT, Woodrow Wilson Rehab. Ctr., Fishersville, Va., 1989-1991; social worker Victor C. Newman Sch., Chgo., 1992-93; marriage and family couns. Community Svcs. Bd., Appomattox, VA, 1993-94; sales rep. Eli Lilly Co., 1994-98, Hoffman LaRoche, 1999—. Home: 25 Easton Ave Lynchburg VA 24503-1605 E-mail: cdepewmed@aol.com.

DEPEW, MARIE KATHRYN, retired secondary school educator; b. Sterling, Colo., Dec. 1, 1928; d. Amos Carl and Dorothy Emelyn (Whiteley) Mehl; m. Emil Carlton DePew, Aug. 30, 1952 (dec. 1973). BA, U. Colo., 1950, MA, 1953. Post grad. Harvard U., Cambridge, Mass., 1962; tchr. Jefferson County Pub. Schs., [illegible] Accountability Program, Denver, 1973-83; sr. cons. Colo. Dept. Edn., Denver, 1973-85, ret., 1985. Author: (pamphlet) History of Hammil, Georgetown, Colorado, 1967; contbr. articles to profl. jours. Chmn. Colo. State Accountability Com., Denver, 1971-75. Fellow IDEA Programs, 1976-77, 79-81. Mem. Colo. Hist. Assn., Jefferson County Edn. Assn. (pres. 1963-64), Colo. Edn. Assn. (bd. dirs. 1965-70), Ky. Colonels (hon. mem.), Phi Beta Kappa. Republican. Methodist. Avocations: historical research, writing, travel, collecting antiques. Home: 920 Pennsylvania St Denver CO 80203-3157

DE PLANQUE, E. GAIL, physicist; b. Orange, N.J., Jan. 15, 1945; d. Martin William and Edna de Planque. AB, Immaculata Coll., 1967; MS in Physics, N.J. Inst. Tech., 1973; PhD in Environ. Health Scis., NYU, 1983. Physicist U.S. AEC, U.S. Dept. Energy, N.Y.C., 1967-82; dep. dir. environ. measurement lab. U.S. Dept. Energy, N.Y.C., 1982-87, dir. environ. measurement lab., 1987-91; mem. Energy Strategists Consultancy, Ltd., 2000—. Adj. prof. NYU, N.Y.C., 1986—; pres. Pacific Nuclear Coun., 1989-91; mem. engring. sci. dept. adv. com., bd. trustees N.J. Inst. Tech., Newark, 1985-91; bd. dirs. British Nuclear Fuels, Inc.; mem. visiting com. dept. nuclear engring. MIT, Diablo Canyon Ind. Safety Commn.; mem. TU Electric Ops. Rev. Com.; cons. in field. Contbr. articles to profl. jours. Commr. U.S. Nuclear Regulatory Commn., 1991-95; bd. trustees Northeast Utilities, 1995—; bd. dirs. British Nuclear Fuels, Inc., 1996—; Tex. Utilities Elec. Ops. Review Com., 1996—; cons. United Nation's Internat. Atomic Energy Agy., 1996—; mem. external adv. com., Amarillo Nat. Resource Ctr. for Plutonium, 1996—. Fellow Am. Nuclear Soc. (bd. dirs. 1977-80, 84-91, v.p. 1987-88, pres. 1988-89), Health Physics Soc., AAAS, Am. Phys. Soc., Assn. for Women in Sci. (v.p. N.Y. met. sect. 1980-82), Internat. Nuclear Energy Acad., (sec. 1996—). Achievements include research in environmental radiation, radiation protection, solid state dosimetry, thermoluminescence.

DE PLANQUE, J. KATHRYN, psychologist; b. Union, NJ, Nov. 5, 1947; d. Lawrence Frazier and Matilda Katherine (Kern) de P.; m. Ronald Jay Losch, July 24, 1974; 1 child, Ashley Katherine Losch ; m. Ralph Joseph Rudzinski. BA in Spl. Edn., William Patterson Coll., Wayne, NJ, 1970; MS in Counseling and Sch. Psychology, Calif. State U., LA, 1976; PhD in Holistic Health Scis., Clayton Coll. Natural Health, Birmingham, Ala., 1998. Cert. tchr. N.J., Calif., sch. psychologist Calif., hypnotherapist Am. Bd. Hypnotherapy, Reiki 2nd degree The Radiance Technique internat. Resource specialist spl. edn. Springfield (N.J.) Pub. Schs, 1970—72; tchr. emotionally disturbed L.A. Child Achievement Ctr., Sherman Oaks, Calif., 1972—73; sch. psychologist La Cañada (Calif.) USD and Santa Monica, 1975—78; pvt. practice edn. therapy Lakeside Learning Lab., Westlake Village, Calif., 1978—83; inpatient psychol. evalns. Neurpsychiatric Inst. UCLA, Westwood, Calif., 1983—86; coord. psychol. svcs., spl. edn. La Cañada USD, 1986—99; ednl. psychologist, hypnotherapist Pediat. Pain Team UCLA, Westwood, 1999—; group facilitator for cancer patients Ted Mann Resource Ctr. UCLA, Westwood, 1999—, John Wayne Cancer Inst. St. John's Hosp., Santa Monica, Calif., 2000—. Charter sch. cons. Opportunities for Learning, Odyssey Charter Sch., Pasadena, Calif., 2000—; kindness cons. Sydney & Me puppet class presentation, 1999—. Avocations: singing, travel.

DEPRIEST, TIFFANY BOALS, music educator, music director; b. Jackson, Tenn., Mar. 13, 1971; d. Harry Lee and Virginia Dare Boals; m. Douglas B. DePriest, Dec. 27, 1997 (div. Jan. 8, 2001); 1 child, Mackenzie Nicole. BMus, U. Tenn., Martin, 1993, M, 1996. Music educator Dyer County Schs., Dyersburg, Tenn., 1994—96, Ft. Zumwolt Schs., O'Fallon, Mo., 1996—99, Sumner County Schs., Hendersonville, Tenn., 1999—. Colorguard instr. Mem.: Music Educators Nat. Conv., Middle Tenn. Elem. Music Tchrs. Assn. (treas./sec. 2000—), Middle Tenn. Vocal Assn. (elem. mass choir rep. 2001—03), Am. Orff Schubert Assn. Avocations: scrapbooks, reading, web design, computers. Office: Sumner County Schs 1040 Madison Creek Rd Goodlettsville TN 37072

DERAISMES, ANN M. insurance company executive, human resources specialist; BA, Keuka Coll., Keuka Park, N.Y.; MA in Human Resources, Western Conn. State U. Mgr. staffing Hartford (Conn.) Life, 1984—87, asst. dir. personnel, 1987—91, dir human resources, 1991—92, asst. v.p. human resources, 1992—94, v.p. human resources, 1994—97; sr. v. p. human resources Hartford (Conn.) Life, 1997—2003; group sr. v.p. human resources Hartford Fin. Svcs. Group, 2003—. Office: Hartford Fin Svcs Group Hartford Plz 890 Asylum Ave Hartford CT 06115

D'ERASMO, MARTHA JEAN, health company executive; b. Newark, Dec. 6, 1939; d. Harry Eugene and Phyllis Guy (Wing) Aldrich; m. Joseph John D'Erasmo, 1995 (div.); children: Stacey, Nancy; m. Robert Gordon Rosenberg, Sept. 27, 1987; stepchildren: David, Daniel. BA, Antioch U., Columbia, Mo.; RN, St. Lukes Hosp. Sch. Nursing, N.Y.C., 1961; MPH, Johns Hopkins U., Balt. Dir. nursing svcs. Washington Ctr. Aging Svcs., 1982-83; dir. clin. svcs. Group Health Assocs., Washington, 1983-87; mgr. Coopers & Lybrand, Washington, 1987-89; prin. Birch & Davis, Silver Spring, Md., 1989-94; v.p., ptnr. Hewalth Care Resources Internat., Moorestown, N.J., 1994-96; pres., CEO Johns Hopkins Med. Svcs. Corp., Balt., 1996—. Chmn. bd. Pharmequip, Balt., 1997—; cons. Bur. Primary Health Care, Washington, 1993-96. Co-author: Living in a Nursing Home; contbg. author: A Guide to Management and Supervision in Nursing Homes, 1986. Grantee Nat. Inst. Aging, 1993. Democrat. Avocation: exercise. Office: Johns Hopkins Med Svcs 3100 Wyman Park Dr Baltimore MD 21211-2803

DERBY, DEBORAH, retail executive; BA in Econs., Harvard U.; MBA, JD, U. Notre Dame. Fin. analyst Goldman Sachs; atty. Miller, Canfield, Paddock and Stone; with human resources Whirlpool Corp., 1992—2000; from v.p. human resources Babies "R" Us Divsn. to exec. v.p. human resources Toys "R" Us, Inc., Wayne, NJ, 2000—03, exec. v.p. human resources, 2003—. Mem.: ABA, Soc. Human Resource Profls., Mich. Bar Assn. Office: Toys R Us Inc 1 Geoffrey Way Wayne NJ 07470-2030

DERCHIN, DARY BRET INGHAM, writer; b. Camden, N.J., Sept. 15, 1941; d. Charles and Dorothy Roberta (Ingham) Lambiase; m. Michael Wayne Derchin, Dec. 29, 1970; children: Taylor-Leigh, Danielle Ashlin Lacey. BA, Montclair State Coll., 1962; postgrad., NYU, 1965, New Sch., 1966. Tchr., Randolph, N.J., 1962-64; rsch. asst. NYU, N.Y.C., 1965-67, Bolivian Peace Corps Project, N.Y.C., 1966; co-head rsch. Derchin Enterprises, N.Y.C., 1970-75. Author: Real Talk, 1992; playwright Blue No More; contbr. articles to the N.Y. Times, Harper's and book the Big Picture, others; talk show host: The Better Sex with Danna Day, Sta. WALE, 1999—, KFNY, WEVD; spkr., guest talk shows. Mem. Drama League, Lincoln Ctr. Film Soc., Am. Film Inst., Friends of Poets and Writers, Univ. Club, Nat. Art Club (lit. com., film com., Joseph Kesselring Playwright award com.). Home: Laurel Cove PO Box 200 Fair Haven NJ 07704-0200

DERITTER, MARGARET CATHERINE, journalist; b. Paterson, N.J., May 14, 1957; d. Elmer and Lena (Soodsma) DeR. BA in Philosophy, Calvin Coll., 1979. Assoc. editor Ch. Herald, Grand Rapids, Mich., 1980-83; reporter, copy editor Advance Newspapers, Jenison, Mich., 1983-84, asst. editor, 1985-86, sr. news editor, 1986-88; state wire editor Kalamazoo (Mich.) Gazette, 1988-89, metro copy editor, 1989-91, entertainment and health and sci. copy editor, 1991—99, entertainment editor, 1999. Mem. spkrs. bur. Dreaming Me, Kalamazoo, 1994—. Recipient Sch. Bell award Mich. Edn. Assn., 1986, 87, 3d Pl. award Mich. Press Club, 1987, Hon. Mention award Mich. Press Assn., 1995, 2d Pl. award Mich. Press Assn., 1993, 97,2d Pl. award Penney-Mo. awards, 1992, 1st Pl. award Mich. Press Assn., 1993, Hon. Mention award Women In Comms., Inc., 1993. Mem. NAFE, Nat. Lesbian and Gay Journalists Assn.[illegible] Office: Kalamazoo Gazette 401 S Burdick St Kalamazoo MI 49007-5279

DE RIVAS, CARMELA FODERARO, psychiatrist, health facility administrator; b. Cortale, Italy, Nov. 25, 1920; came to U.S., 1935, naturalized, 1942; d. Salvatore and Mary (Vaiti) Foderaro; m. Aureliano Rivas, Oct. 30, 1948; children: Carmen, Norma, Sandra, David. Student, U. Pa., 1940-42; MD, Women's Med. Coll. Pa., 1946. Diplomate: Am. Bd. Psychiatry and Neurology. Intern women's Med. Coll. Pa. Hosp., 1946-47; gen. med. resident Chestnut Hill Hosp., Phila., 1947-48; gen. practice Tex., 1948-49; mem. staff Norristown (Pa.) State Hosp., 1949-63, supt., 1963-70, dir. family planning, 1979-87, clin. dir. spl. assignments, 1979-82; assoc. psychiatry U. Pa., 1963-75. Psychiatrist Penn Found. Mental Health, Sellersville, Pa., 1970—72; dir. intake coping svcs. Ctrl. Montgomery Mental Health/ Mental Retardation Ctr., Norristown, Pa., 1972—77, med. dir., 1977—82, psychiatrist, 1980—82; cons. surveyor Health Care Fin. Adminstrn., 1987—2001; dir. program evaluation Norristown State Hosp., 1979—82, med. dir., 1982—87. Named to Hall of Fame S. Phila. H.S., 1968; recipient citation Women's Med. Coll. Pa., 1968, Amita achievement award, 1976, achievement award Grad. Club Phila., 1976; named Woman of Yr. Pa. Fedn. Bus. and Profl. Women, 1979. Disting. life fellow Am. Psychiat. Assn., Pa. Psychiat. Soc. (rep. assembly of dist. brs. 1979-88); mem. AMA, Phila. Psychiat. Soc. (councilor), Montgomery County Med. Soc. (bd. dir., past pres.), Pa. Med. Soc. (chmn. adv. com. to aux. 1981-88, mem. ho. of dels., mem. commn. on med. edn. 1991-94, mem. com. on continuing med. edn. 1994-98). Home: Dunwoody Village-CH 112 3500 W Chester Pike Newtown Square PA 19073-4101

DERKSEN, CHARLOTTE RUTH MEYNINK, librarian; b. Newberg, Oreg., Mar. 15, 1944; BS in Geology, Wheaton (Ill.) Coll., 1966; MA in Geology, U. Oreg., 1968, MLS, 1973. Faculty and libr. Moeding Coll., Ootse, Botswana, 1968-70, head history dept., 1970-71; tchr. Jackson (Minn.) Pub. High Sch., 1975-77; sci. libr. U. Wis., Oshkosh, 1977-80; libr. and bibliographer Stanford (Calif.) U., 1980—2004. Acting chief scis., 1985-86, head Sci. and Engring. Librs., 1992-97. Contbg. author: Union List of Geologic Field Trip Guidebooks of North America; contbr. articles to profl. jours. Mem. ALA, Western Assn. Map Librs., Geosci. Info. Soc. (v.p. 1997-98, pres. 1998-99), Am. Geol. Inst. (soc. coun. 2000-02), Geol. Soc. Am. (publ. com. 2002—), Cartographic Users Adv. Coun. (chair 1988-90), GeoRef Adv. Bd. (chair 1998-2004). Republican. Lutheran. Office: Stanford U Branner Earth Scis Library Stanford CA 94305 Home: 12522C 26th Ave NE Seattle WA 98125-8803 E-mail: cderksen@stanford.edu.

DERN, LAURA, actress; b. Santa Monica, Calif., Feb. 10, 1967; d. Bruce Dern and Diane Ladd. Student, Lee Strasberg Inst., Royal Acad. Dramatic Art, London. Appeared in films Alice Doesn't Live Here Anymore, 1975, Foxes, 1980, Ladies and Gentlemen, The Fabulous Stains, 1982, Teachers, 1984, Mask, 1985, Smooth Talk, 1985, Blue Velvet, 1986, Haunted Summer, 1988, Fat Man & Little Boy, 1989, Wild At Heart, 1990, Rambling Rose, 1991 (Acad. award nomination for best actress, Golden Globe nomination for best actress in a drama), Jurassic Park, 1993, A Perfect World, 1993, Citizen Ruth, 1996, Bastard Out of Carolina, 1996, October Sky, 1999, Daddy and Them, 2001, Jurassic Park III, 2001, Novocaine, 2001, I Am Sam, 2001, We Don't Live Here Anymore, 2004; TV appearances include: Afterburn, 1992 (Golden Globe award for best actress in TV movie or mini series), Fallen Angels (Murder, Obliquely), 1993 (Emmy nomination, Best Actress - Drama, 1994), Ruby Ridge, 1996, The Baby Dance, 1998, Damaged Care, 2002; TV guest appearances include Shannon, 1981, Fallen Angels, 1993, Frasier, 1995, Ellen, 1997, The West Wing, 2002; stage appearances include The Palace of Amateurs (N.Y.), 1988, Brooklyn Laundry (L.A.); dir. The Gift.*

DERNER, CAROL A. retired librarian; b. Evansville, Ind., May 12, 1934; d. Jacob Christopher and Catherine Loretta (Grant) Niedhammer; m. George Bendix Derner, May 4, 1957. BA in Am. Lit., Ind. U., 1956, MA in Libr. Sci., 1958. Children's libr. Monroe County Pub. Libr., Bloomington, Ind., 1958-59, Pub. Librs. of Lake County, Merrillville, Ind., 1959-60; sch. libr. Valparaiso (Ind.) Cmty. Schs., 1960-63; head popular libr. Gary (Ind.) Pub. Libr., 1963-64, head extension dept., 1964-67; head libr. Elmwood Park (Ill.) Pub. Libr., 1968-76; asst. dir. Lake County Pub. Libr., Merrillville, 1976-85, dir., 1985-91. Adj. faculty Ind. U. Sch. Libr. and Info. Sci., Bloomington, 1982-94. Contbr. articles to profl. jours. Mem. edn. com. N.W. Ind. Forum, Portage, 1992-99; mem., sec. Ednl. Referral Ctr., Highland, Ind., 1996-99. Named Woman of Yr., Merrillville Bus. and Profl. women, 1990. Mem. ALA (coun. 1983-87), Ind. Libr. Fedn. (Libr. of Yr. 1997), Exec. Coun., Altrusa Club of Ind. Dunes (pres. 1998-99). Avocations: reading, travel, antiques. Home: 2558 Shellsburg Ave Henderson NV 89052-6442 E-mail: caderner@aol.com.

DEROCCO, EMILY STOVER, federal agency administrator; BA Journalism, Pa. State U.; JD, Georgetown U., 1982. Bar: D.C. 1983. Exec. dir. Nat. Assn. State Workforce Agys.; asst. sec. employment and tng. adminstrn. U.S. Dept. Labor, Washington, 2001—. Office: US Dept Labor 200 Constitution Ave NW Washington DC 20210

DERRICKSON, DENISE ANN, secondary school educator, educator; b. Seaford, Del., Sept. 20, 1956; d. William Hudson and Patricia Ann (Adkins) D. BS, James Madison U., 1978; MEd in Counseling and Human Devel., George Mason U., 1990, MEd in Curriculum & Instrn., 1994. Social studies instr. Brentsville Dist. High Sch., Nokesville, Va., 1978-91, Woodbridge (Va.) Sr. High Sch., 1991-99. Faculty liaison Parent-Tchr. Action Coun., 1990-91; prin.'s adv. coun., 1994-96. Vol. Childrens Hosp., Washington, 1983-86, Action in the Community through Svc., Inc.-Helpline, Manassas, Va., 1988-92. Recipient Cert. Appreciation Prince William County Sch. Bd., 1989, Outstanding Educator award Va. Govs. Sch., 1990, ACTS-Helpline Outstanding Vol. Svc. award, 1990; presented with U.S. Flag Armed Svcs. Hall of Honor at the dedication of the U.S. Women's Meml., 1998. Mem. NEA, AAUW, ASCD, VFW, Am. Assn. Curriculum Devel., Nat. Soc. for Study of Edn., Va. Edn. Assn., Va. Assn. Supervision and Curriculum Devel., Prince William Edn. Assn., Internat. Platform Assn., Kappa Delta Phi, Phi Delta Kappa. Avocations: sewing, crafts, travel.

D'ERRICO, DIDI, public relations executive; BA in Mass Comm., MA in Pub. Rels., Ball State U. Mgr. employee comm. Ball Corp.; v.p. Blanc & Otus, San Francisco. Office: 4 Embarcadero Ctr Lbby 8 San Francisco CA 94111-4112

DERRICO, GEORGIA SANTANGELO, banker; b. N.Y.C., Oct. 6, 1944; d. George M. Derrico and Rose Mary (Rao) Santangelo; m. R. Roderick Porter, Feb. 6, 1982. BA, St. Mary's Coll., Notre Dame, Ind., 1966; deg. Internat. Affairs, Johns Hopkins U., Bologna, Italy, 1969; M Internat. Affairs, Columbia U., 1970; postgrad. exec. seminar, Harvard U., 1977. Various positions including lending officer, dist. head corp. divsn., chief adminstrv. and credit officer multinat. divsn. Chem. Bank, N.Y.C., 1971—, sr. v.p., 1982—84, dir. corp. affairs, 1982—84; chmn. So. Fin. Fed. Savs. Bank, N.Y.C., 1985—. Bd. dirs. Oneida, Ltd. Contbr. articles to profl. jours. Bd. dirs. Nat. Dance Inst. Mem.: Assn. MBA Execs.

DERSCH, CHARETTE ALYSE, marriage and family therapist; b. Houston, Feb. 21, 1971; d. Albert and Sharon Beth (Bradley) Rofé; m. John Stephen Dersch, May 27, 1995; 1 child, Sloane Elizabeth. BA in Psychology and French, Tex. Tech U., 1994, MS in Human Devel. and Family studies, 1996, postgrad., 1996—. Rsch. asst. Tex. Tech U., Lubbock, 1993-97, instr., clin. intern, 1996-98, therapist, asst. dir. rsch. and grants, 1999—. Computer cons., Lubbock, 1994-97; conf. presenter San Diego Cconf. on Responding to Child Maltreatment, 1996, Am. Assn. Family and Consumer Scis., 1996; program coord. Parent Empowerment Program, 1998-99; transition counselor Transition to 7th Grade Program, 1998-99. Contbr. chpt. to book and articles to profl. jours. Vol. ccaseworker Family Outreach Ctr., Lubbock, 1995-96. Scholar Alpha Chi Omega, 1990-92, Family Outreach Ctr., 1995-96, Gladys M. Haley scholar, 1995-96, C.M. and Virginia Hucheson scholar, 1996-97, Lola Drew scholar, 1998-99. Mem. Am. Assn. for Marriage and Family Therapy (conf. presenter nat. conf. 1997, 98), Tex. Assn. for Marriage and Family Therapy, Lubbock Assn. for Marriage and Family Therapy (conf. presenter 1998, Golden Key, Phi Upsilon Omicron, Psi Chi, Pi Delta Phi. Office: Tex Tech U Health Sci Ctr Dept Neuropsych/Behav Scis 3601 4th St Lubbock TX 79430-0001 Home: 5213 Promise Land Dr Frisco TX 75035-7604

DERUBERTIS, PATRICIA UHL, software company executive; b. Bayonne, N.J., July 10, 1950; d. George Joseph and Veronica (Lukaszewich) Uhl; m. John Stryker, 1975; m. Michael DeRubertis, 1986. BS in Bus. Adminstrn., U. Md., 1972. Account rep. GE, San Francisco, 1975-77; tech. rep. Computer Scis. Corp., San Francisco, 1977-78; cons., pres. Uhl Assocs., Tiburon, Calif., 1978-81; cons. mgr. Ross Sys., Palo Alto, Calif., 1981-83; COO, exec. v.p. Distributed Planning Sys., Calabasas, Calif., 1983-92; pres. DeRubertis & Assocs., Thousand Oaks, Calif., 1992-94, DeRubertis Software Sys., Inc., Windermere, Fla., 1995—. Author: Rose Gardening By Color, 1994. Troop leader San Francisco coun. Girl Scouts Am., 1974; participant Woman On Water, Marina Del Rey, Calif., 1983; vol. Martin County Coun. for the Arts, 1995, Habitat for Humanity, 2002, Gayle Harrell campaign for state legis., 2000. Mem. AAUW, NAFE, Windermere Garden Club, Delta Delta Delta. Democrat. Office: 109 Main St Windermere FL 34786 Office Phone: 800-411-7213. E-mail: dssincpd@aol.com.

DERUYTER, MARILYN, real estate broker; b. Canandaigua, N.Y., May 8, 1942; d. Ernest Robert and Alice Zereda Mason Prober; m. Paul C. DeRuyter, Dec. 29, 1961 (div. July 1990); children: Kristin M. Walters, Paul R. Grad., high sch., Shortsville, N.Y., 1960, Real Estate Inst., 1982. Cert. residential specialist; grad. Real Estate Inst. Exec. sec. Red Jacket Tel., Shortsville, 1966-72; paralegal David G. Retchless Esq., Clifton Springs, N.Y., 1972-80; real estate broker M. DeRuyter Real Estate, Shortsville, 1978—. Recipient Sales Master Gold and Zenith awards for Sales Excellence. Mem.: Clifton Springs Rotary, Lions. Avocations: reading, shopping, family. Home: 74 E Main St Clifton Springs NY 14432 Office Phone: 315-462-6191. E-mail: mderuyte@rochester.rr.com.

DERVIN, BRENDA LOUISE, communications educator; b. Beverly, Mass., Nov. 20, 1938; d. Ermina Diluiso; adopted d. John Jordan and Marjorie (Sullivan) D. BS, Cornell U., 1960; MA, Mich. State U., 1968, PhD, 1972; PhD (hon.), U. Helsinki, 2000. Pub. info. asst. Am. Home Econ. Assn., Washington, 1960-62, pub. info. specialist Ctr. Consumer Affairs, U. Wis., Milw., 1962-65; instr., rsch. and teaching asst. dept. communications Mich. State U., E. Lansing, 1965-70; asst. prof., Sch. Info. Transfer Syracuse (N.Y.) U., 1970-72; asst. to assoc. prof. U. Wash., Seattle, 1972-85; prof. comm. Ohio State U., Columbus, 1985—. Co-author: The Mass Media Behavior of the Urban Poor, 1980; editor: Rethinking Communication, 1989, Communication A Different Kind of Horserace, 2003, Sense-making Methodology Reader, 2003; editor Progress in Communication Sci., 1981-92; contbr. articles to profl. jours. Grantee U.S. Office Edn., 1974-76, Calif. State Libr., 1974-84, Nat. Cancer Inst., 1984, Ameritech, 1992, Inst. Mus. and Libr. Svc., 2003—. Fellow Internat. Communication Assn. (pres. 1986-87); mem. Internat. Assn. Mass Communications Rsch. (governing coun. 1988-97). Home: 4269 Kenridge Dr Columbus OH 43220-4157 Office: Ohio State U 3016 Derby 154 N Oval Mall Columbus OH 43210-1330 Office Phone: 614-292-3192. E-mail: dervin.1@osu.edu.

DE SA E SILVA, ELIZABETH ANNE, secondary school educator; b. Edmonds, Wash., Mar. 17, 1931; d. Sven Yngve and Anna Laura Elizabeth (Dahlin) Erlandson; m. Claudio de Sá e Silva, Sept. 12, 1955 (div. July 1977); children: Lydia, Marco, Nelson. BA, U. Oreg., 1953; postgrad., Columbia U., 1954-56, Calif. State U., Fresno, 1990, U. No. Iowa, 1993; MEd, Mont. State U., 1978. Med. sec., 1947-49; sec. Merced (Calif.) Sch. Dist., 1950-51; sec., asst. Simon and Schuster, Inc., N.Y.C., 1954-56; tchr. Casa Roosevelt-União Cultural, São Paulo, Brazil, 1957-59, Coquille (Oreg.) Sch. Dist., 1978-96; music tchr. Cartwheels Presch., North Bend, Oreg., 1997—99, 2001. Tchr. piano, 1967—78; instr. Spanish Southwestern Oreg. C.C., Coos Bay, 1991—94; pianist/organist Faith Luth. Ch., North Bend, Oreg., 1995—2002, New Life Luth. Ch., Florence, Oreg., 2002—04; vocal soloist, 1996—; voice tchr., 1997—99. Chmn. publicity Music in Our Schs. Month, Oreg. Dist. VII, 1980-85; sec. Newcomer's Club, Bozeman, Mont., 1971. Quincentennial fellow U. Minn. and Found. José Ortega y Gasset, Madrid, 1991. Mem. AAUW (sec., scholarship chmn., co-pres., pres., treas., editor newsletter), Nat. Trust Hist. Preservation, Am. Coun. on Tchg. Fgn. Langs., Am. Assn. Tchrs. Spanish and Portuguese, Nat. Coun. Tchrs. English, Music Educators Nat. Conf., Oreg. Music Educators Assn., Oreg. Coun. Tchrs. English, Confedn. Oreg. Fgn. Lang. Tchrs., VoiceCare Network, Am. Guild Organists. Democrat. Avocations: swimming, walking, travel, drama. Home: 14425 SW Arabian Dr Beaverton OR 97008

DESAI, ANITA, writer; b. Mussoorie, India, June 24, 1937; came to U.S., 1987; d. D.N. and Toni (Nime) Mazumdar; m. Ashvin Desai, Dec. 13, 1958; children: Rahul, Tani, Arjun, Kiran. BA, Delhi U., 1957. Tchr. Smith Coll., Mount Holyoke Coll.; prof. of writing MIT, Cambridge, 1993—2002. Author: Cry, the Peacock, 1963, Voices in the City, 1965, Bye-Bye Blackbird, 1968, The Peacock Garden, 1974, Where Shall We Go This Summer?, 1975, Cat on a Houseboat, 1976, Fire on the Mountain, 1977, Games at Twilight and Other Stories, 1978, Clear Light of Day, 1980, The Village by the Sea, 1982, In Custody, 1985, Baumgartner's Bombay, 1989, Journey to Ithaca, 1995, Fasting, Feasting, 1999, Diamond Dust and Other Stories, 2000. Recipient Winifred Holtby prize Royal Soc. Lit., 1978, Sahitya Acad. award, 1979, Guardian award for children's book, 1982, Lit. Lion award N.Y. Pub. Libr., 1993, Neil Gunn fellowship Scottish Arts Coun., 1994, Moravia prize, Italy, 1999; Girton Coll. and Clare Hall fellow Cambridge U., Eng. Fellow Am. Acad. Arts and Letters (hon.), Royal Soc. Lit. Eng. Home: Rogers Coleridge and White Ltd 20 Powis Mews London W11 1JN England

DESAI, PANKAJA MOHAN, epidemiologist; b. Honavar, Karnataka, India, July 8, 1976; d. Mohan and Radha Desai; m. Deepak H. Bapu. BS, U. Ill., 1998; MSW, U. Mich., 1999; MPH, U. Ill., Chgo., 2003. Cert. specialist in aging 1999. MSW intern U. Mich. Hosps., Ann Arbor, 1999—2000; work-life cons. ComPsych - Employee Assistance Program, Chgo., 2000—01; rsch. asst., Health Rsch. and Policy Ctrs. U. Ill., Chgo., 2001—03; epidemiologist Cook County Dept. Pub. Health, 2003—. Shelter vol. Vol. Illini Projects, 1995—96. Mem.: NASW, Gerontol. Soc. Am., Student Pub. Health Assn., Undergrad. Psychiatry Assn., Sigma Phi Omega. Hindu. Avocations: dance, mystery novels, travel, tennis. Home: 632 Highland Ave # 2N Oak Park IL 60304 Personal E-mail: pankajadesai@hotmail.com.

DESAI, VEENA BALVANTRAI, obstetrician, gynecologist, educator; b. Karvan, Gujarat, India, Oct. 5, 1931; came to U.S., 1973; d. Balvantrai P. and Maniben (Vashi) Desai; m. Vinay D. Gandevia, Sept. 19, 1964. MBBS, Seth G.S. Med. Coll., Bombay, 1957, MD, 1961. Jr. resident Bombay U., 1957-59; house officer gyn. Chalmer's Hosp., Edinburgh, Scotland, 1962-63; registrar ob-gyn. Neath (U.K.) Gen. Hosp., 1963-64, Scunthorpe (U.K.) Gen. Hosp., 1964-66; chief resident ob-gyn. St. John (Can.) Gen. Hosp., 1973-74; attending ob-gyn. Portsmouth (N.H.) Hosp., 1975-84; assoc. prof. Boston U., 1985-86; sr. staff ob-gyn. Santa Clara (Calif.) Valley Med. Ctr., 1986-87; mem. staff ob-gyn. West Anaheim (Calif.) Med. Ctr., 1988-98, chief dept. ob-gyn., 1992-93, vice chief of gen. med. staff, 1994—95; ob/gyn Bay State Med. Ctr., Springfield, Mass., 1998—; chief ob-gyn. Mercy Med. Ctr., Springfield, 2002—03. Assoc. clin. prof. ob-gyn. U. Calif., Irvine, 1990-98; pres. Desai Med. Corp., Anaheim, 1989—. Chmn.'s advisor Nat. Security Coun.; charter mem. Presdl. Task Force; mem. Rep. Party Inner Cir., 1984-2003. Recipient Presdl. Medal of Merit, 1982, award Spl. Congl. Adv. Bd., 1984, Order of Liberty, U.S. Congress, 1995, Medal of Freedom, U.S. Senate, 1994, medal Ronald Wilson Reagan Eternal Flame of Freedom, 1996, Millennium Medal of Freedom, Rep. Senate, 1999, Internat. Peace prize United Cultural Conv., 2003. Fellow ACS, Internat. Coll. Surgeons, Am. Coll. Ob-Gyn., Western Mass. Ob-Gyn. Soc. (pres. 2002—), Royal Coll. Ob-Gyn. (chmn. Am. rep. com. 1997-2002); mem. Buena Park Rotary (pres. 1994, chair internat. svc. 1992-93). Avocations: latchhook work, international politics, travel. Home: 35 Sean Louis Cir West Springfield MA 01089-4547 E-mail: veenadesai@comcast.net.

DESAI, VISHAKHA N. museum director, professional society administrator; b. Ahmedabad, Gujarat, India, May 1, 1949; came to U.S., 1966; m. Robert B. Oxnam, 1993. BA, Bombay U., Elphinstone Coll., 1970; MA in History of Art, U. Mich., 1975, PhD in History of Art, 1984. With edn. div. Bklyn. Mus., N.Y.C., 1972-74; head exhibit resource Mus. sect. edn. dept. Fine Arts, Boston, 1977-80; acting dir. edn. dept. Mus. Fine Arts, Boston, 1980-81, coord. acad. program, 1981-88, asst. curator, 1981-90; dir. Asia Soc. Galleries, N.Y.C., 1990—; v.p. Asia Soc., 1993—. Adj. asst. prof. Boston U., 1982-87; assoc. prof. U. Mass., Boston, 1986-90; adj. prof. Columbia U., 1995-96, 97; bd. dirs. Am. Com. South/S.E. Asia Art; reviewer Bunting Inst., Radcliffe Coll., Boston, 1990—; bd. dirs. Art Table, N.Y.C., 1991-94. Contbr. articles to profl. jours. Pres. Mass. Found. for Humanities, 1989-91. Outstanding Teaching fellow U. Mich., 1977, Am. Inst. of Indian Studies fellow, 1978; grantee, Nat. Endowment for the Arts, NEM, 1979—, Mus. Sabbaticatal grantee Nat. Endowment for the Arts, 1982. Mem. Coll. Art Assn. (bd. dirs. 1995—), Am. Assn. Art Mus. Dirs. (bd. dirs. 1995—. pres. 1998—). Office: Asia Soc and Mus 725 Park Ave New York NY 10021-5025

DESANTIS, SHEROLYN SMITH, foundation executive; b. Ontario, Oreg., Feb. 7, 1949; d. Ronald Duane Smith and Dorothy Lorene Hergert Smith; divorced; children: Louie Duane, Rhonda Marie, Paul Nunzio. BA, Idaho State U., 1971. Chmn., founder, exec. dir. Diagnostek Charitable Found., Albuquerque, 1990-95, Joshua Chariable Found., Albuquerque, 1995—; chmn., founder, ex-dir. Albuquerque Women's Resource Ctr., 1998—. Bd. dirs. Caballero Norte Neighborhood Assn., Albuquerque, 1985-87; mem. fundraising Albuquerque Pregnancy Ctr., 1984-99, bd. dirs., 1996-98, sec. bd. dirs., 1997-98; mem., del. Rep. State Ctrl. Com., Albuquerque, 1998—; mem. Rep. Assembly, Albuquerque, 1998—, Rep. Ward vice-hmn.; mentor Wise Men & Women, Albuquerque, 1998-99. Mem. N.Mex. Soc. Fundraising Execs. Baptist. Avocations: reading, cooking, entertaining, politics, fundraising. Office: Joshua Charitable Found PO Box 94298 Albuquerque NM 87199-4298

DE SANTIS, SYLVIA, library director; b. Palmer, Mass., Mar. 27, 1920; d. Ezio DeS. and Josephine Alonzo. BA in Chemistry, Mt. Holyoke Coll., 1942. Chem. rsch. libr. Jackson Lab., E.I. DuPont, Wilmington, Del., 1942-43, Naugatuck (Conn.) Chem., 1944-45, libr. dir., 1944—49, Monson (Mass.) Free Libr. & Reading Room Assoc., 1949-97; retired, 1997. Cons. in field. Mem. Monson Arts Coun.; Trustees of Reservations Mass. Mem.: Monson Hist. Soc., Western Mass. Libr. Club. Avocations: collecting art, books, photography, gardening. Home: PO Box 358 Monson MA 01057-0358

DE SAVORGNANI, ADRIANE ALDRICH, health care administrator, nurse; b. Boston, Dec. 17, 1940; d. Merritt James Aldrich and Edith Carolyn (Borrebach); m. Luciano de Savorgnani, Aug. 1, 1979 (dec. Aug. 2002); children: Andrew, Alexia, Miranda. AB, Radcliffe Coll., 1962; diploma in nursing coord. program, Radcliffe Coll./Mass. Gen Hosp, 1965; MPH, U. Hawaii, 1974; DBA, Nova U., 1992. RN, Hawaii; cert. nursing adminstrn. advanced. Clin. nurse Dept. Public Health, Washington, 1966-67; staff nurse pediat., obstetrics, nursery, med.-surg. U.S. Naval Hosp., Naples, Italy, 1967-69; pub. health nurse Dept. Human Resources, Washington, 1969-72; staff nurse, ob-gyn., nursery, recovery rm. Kapiolani Hosp., Honolulu, 1972-75; rsch. nurse U. Hawaii Newborn Psychology Rsch. Lab, Honolulu, 1974-75; staff nurse, med. and gynecol. oncology Naval Regional Med. Ctr., San Diego, 1975-78; staff nurse emergency rm. Naval Aerospace Reg. Med. Ctr., Pensacola, Fla., 1978-79; charge nurse, emergency rm. outpatient-inpatient care coord. U.S. Naval Hosp., Naples, Italy, 1979-83; charge nurse military med. dept., utilization rev., discharge planning Naval Hosp., Newport, R.I., 1983-86; head, Reg./Fleet Support, Naval Med. Command N.E. Region, Great Lakes, Ill., 1986-89; head health care plans spl. projects, head preventive med. health promotion br. Bur. Medicine and Surgery, Washington, 1989—92; exec. officer Naval Med. Clinic, Key West, Fla., 1993—. Asst. dir. nursing svcs. Naval Hosp., Jacksonville, Fla., 1992—95, exec. officer, Lemoore, Calif., 1995—98; comdg. officer U.S. Naval Med. Clinics, U.K., 1998—2001; head clin. plans and mgmt., acting asst. dep. chief med. ops. support Bur. Medicine and Surgery, Washington, 2001—03; adminstrv. asst. to Def. Attaché Office Am. Embassy, London, 2003—. Contbr. articles to profl. jours. Lector, lay eucharistic minister, choir accompanist; vol. local sch.; vol. tchr. ESL; vol. women's homeless shelter. Capt., Nurse Corps, U.S. Navy, 1975-2003. Decorated Legion of Merit, Meritorious Svc. medal (5), Navy and Marine Corps Commendation medal (2), Nat. Def. medal (2), Vol. Svc. medal, Navy and Marine Corps Overseas Svc. Ribbon (7 stars);; recipient Clara Barton award, ARC, Naples, 1983, cert. of appreciation, Operation Desert Storm, Washington, 1991, Jane A. Delano award, ARC London, 2001, dir.'s award, Human Resources Svc. Ctr., Europe, 2001. Fellow Am. Coll. Healthcare Execs.; mem. ANA, APHA, Assn. Mil. Surgeons U.S. (life), Acad. Mgmt., Internat. Tng. in Comm., ARC (instr.), Navy Nurse Corps. Assn., Coll. Alumnae Assns., Sigma Theta Tau. Republican. Roman Catholic. Avocations: piano, theatre, art, travel, physical fitness. Home: 14 Bardsley Ln Greenwich London SE10 9RF England

DESCHNER, JANE WAGGONER, photo artist, public relations consultant; b. Bellefont, Pa., Feb. 9, 1948; d. George Ruble and Helen Louise (Talbert) Waggoner; m. William Henry Deschner, July 26, 1969 (div. Dec. 1987); children: John William, Elisabeth Anne. BA in Geography, U. Kans., 1969; BA in Art, Mont. State U., Billings, 1987; MFA in Visual Art, Vt. Coll., 2002. Economist Mid-Am. Regional Coun., Kansas City, Mo., 1970-73; ptnr., owner Castle Art Gallery, Billings, Mont., 1982-88; asst. dir. client svcs. Mont. Inst. of Arts Found., Billings, 1988-89; account exec., artist, writer Exclamation Point Advt., Billings, 1989-94; artist, project coord. Billings, 1981—; project coord., cons. pub. rels./graphic design, 1994—; curator Women's Ctr. Gallery and D.A. Davidson & Co. Gallery, Billings, 2003—. Coord. Art in the Libr. program, adj. art faculty Rocky Mountain Coll., Billings, creative coord. Arts in Medicine St. Vincent Healthcare. Exhibited at Nicolaysen Art Mus., Casper, Wyo., Toucan Gallery, Billings, U. Mont., Missoula, Mont., Art Mus. Missoula, Mont. State U., Billings, Holter Mus. Art, Helena, Mont., Broken Diamond Gallery, Billings, Mont. State U., Bozeman, Deering Galleries, Taos, N.Mex., Contemporary Art Mus., Sacramento, St. Vincent Healthcare, Billings, Mont. Art of Survival, Healing in Life, 2000-. Bd. dirs. Billings Mental Health Assn., 1988-92, v.p., 1989, 90; gallery dir., bd. dirs. The Women's Ctr., St. Vincent Healthcare, Billings, 1991—; mem. Youth Ct. Conf. Com. 13th Jud. Dist. Mont., Billings, 1992—; Poets on the Prairie artist YMCA Writer's Voice; bd. dirs. InterMountain Planned Parenthood, 1998-2001. Recipient 1st pl. award in non-comml. art Billings Advt. and Mktg. Assn., 1992, 93; Sam and Alfreda Maloof scholar Anderson Ranch Arts Ctr., 1998-99; State of Mont. profl. devel. grantee, 1999. Mem. Yellowstone Print Club (bd. dirs., pres. acquisitions chair), Yellowstone Art Ctr. (Auction Artist 1989-2002), Soc. for the Arts in Healthcare (bd. dirs.). Unitarian Universalist. Avocations: travel, cooking, reading. Studio: 1313 Granite Ave Billings MT 59102-0869 E-mail: janed@wtp.net.

DESCOTEAUX, CAROL J. health facility administrator; b. Nashua, N.H., Apr. 5, 1948; d. Henry Louis and Therese (Arel) D. BA, Notre Dame Coll., 1970; MEd, Boston Coll., 1975; MA, U. Notre Dame, 1984, PhD, 1985. Jr. high sch. instr., dir. religious studies St. Joseph's Sch., North Grosvenordale, Conn., 1970-73; jr. high sch. tchr., dir. religious edn. Notre Dame Sch., North Adams, Mass., 1973-77, 1978—81; chairperson religious studies discipline Notre Dame Coll. Grad. Theol. Union, U. Notre Dame, Ind., 1982-83, 84-85; jr. high sch. instr. Sacred Heart Sch., Groton, Conn., 1977-78; pres. Notre Dame Coll., Manchester, NH, 1985—99; v.p. mission integration St. Joseph Hosp., Nashua, NH, 2000—. Trustee King's Coll., Wilkes-Barre, Pa., 1987-95; pres. Fedn. of Holy Cross Colls., 1985-96; mem. adv. bd. Manchester Christian Life Ctr., 1978-80; treas. N.H. Coll. and Univ. Council, Manchester, 1985-86; trustee N.H. Higher Edn. Assistance Found., 1986—. Mem. Manchester United Way campaign, 1985—; bd. incorporators, mem. ethics com., instl. research com. Cath. Med. Ctr., Manchester, 1986—99; mem. bd. trustees Dartmouth-Hitchcock Med. Ctr., Marguerite's Place, St. Joseph Cmty. Svcs., N.H. Partnership for End-of-Life Care, Stonehill Coll., Rivier Coll. Named Disting. Woman Leader of Yr., So. N.H. region YWCA, 1985, N.H. Disting. Woman Educator, 1994, Manchester Citizen of Yr., 1995, N.H. Boston Coll. Alumna of Yr., 1990, N.H. U. Notre Dame Alumna of Yr., 1992. Mem. Am. Acad. Religion, Coll. Theology Soc. Am., N.H. Women's Forum, Soc. Christian Ethics, Nat. Hospice and Palliative Care Assn., Cath. Hosp. Assn. Am. Democrat. Roman Catholic. Avocations: art, music, theater, fishing, bowling. Office: St Joseph Hosp 172 Kinsley St Nashua NH 03060-3688

DESFORGES, JANE FAY, internist, hematologist, educator; b. Melrose, Mass., Dec. 18, 1921; d. Joseph Henry and Alics Maher (Fay) Desforges; m. Gerard Desforges, Sept. 11, 1948; children: Gerard Joseph, Jane Alice. BA cum laude (Durant scholar), Wellesley Coll., 1942; MD cum laude, Tufts U., 1945; ScD (hon.), Holy Cross Coll., 1990. Diplomate Am. Bd. Internal Medicine, Am. Bd. Hematology. Intern in pathology Mt. Auburn Hosp., Cambridge, Mass., 1945—46; intern in medicine Boston City Hosp., 1946—47, resident in medicine, then chief resident, 1948—50; USPHS research fellow in hematology Salt Lake Gen. Hosp., Salt Lake City, 1946—47; research fellow in hematology hosp. Thorndike Lab., 1950—52; physician-in-charge RH lab., 1952—53; mem. faculty Tufts U. Med. Sch., 1952—, prof. medicine, 1972—, disting. prof., 1992—, prof. emerita, 1994; asst. dir. Tufts Med. Svc., Boston City Hosp., 1952—67; assoc. dir. Tufts Med. Svc., 1967—68; acting dir., physician in charge, 1968—73; dir. Tufts Med. Svc., 1968—69; assoc. dir. Tufts hematology lab., 1954—67, asst. dir. hosp. labs., 1958—67, acting dir. labs., 1967—68. Sr. physician in hematology New Eng. Med. Ctr. Hosp., Boston, 1973—, rsch. assoc. blood resch. lab, 1973—92; attending physician VA Hosp., Jamaica Plain, cons. in hematology to various area hosps., 1955—72. Contbr. numerous articles to med. jours. Bd. dirs. Med. Found., Inc., 1976—82; bd. trustees Boston Med. Libr., 1977—81; chmn. automation in med. lab. scis. rev. com. Nat. Inst. Gen. Med. Scis., 1974—76; chmn. consensus com. of infectious disease testing for blood transfusions NIH, 1995—96; mem. subcom. on hematology Am. Bd. Internal Medicine, 1976—82, bd. dirs., 1980—88, exec. com., 1984—88; chmn. blood diseases and resources adv. com. Nat. Heart, Lung and Blood Inst., 1978—81. Named to Internat. Women in Medicine Hall of Fame, Am. Med. Women's Assn., 2003; recipient Disting. Alumna award, Wellesley Coll., 1981; grantee NIH, 1955—88. Fellow: AAAS; mem.: Inst. Medicine, Am. Assn. Physicians, N.Y. Acad. Scis., Mass. Med. Soc. (mem. publs. com. 1995—99), Lifetime Achievement award 2001), Internat. Soc. Hematology, Am. Soc. Hematology (exec. com. 1975—78, adv. bd. 1980—82, v.p. 1982—83, pres. 1984—85), Am. Soc. Clin. Pathology, Am. Fedn. Clin. Rsch., ACP (chmn. med. knowledge self assessment program IX 1989—92, Master 1983, Disting. Tchr. award 1987), Alpha Omega Alpha (Outstanding Tchr. award 1994), Phi Beta Kappa. Home: 49 Lake Ave Melrose MA 02176-2701

DESHA, DORIS HOLLINGSWORTH, retired elementary school educator; b. Sept. 7, 1927; d. Carl and Sallie Jane (Burmeister) Hollingsworth; m. George K. Desha, Jr., May 12, 1951 (dec. Nov. 1993); children: Paul Alan, George K. III. Student, U. Tex., 1944-46, 47-48, Sam Houston U., 1949, Tarleton U., 1961-62; BS, U. N. Mex., 1969, postgrad., 1971-72; MEd, Tex. Christian U., 1980. Tchr., Jourdanton, Tex., 1946-47, Leming, Tex., 1949-50, Cost, Tex., 1951; substitute tchr. Big Spring, Tex., Albuquerque, Crowley, Tex., 1964-66, 76-77, 1991-99; tchr. McCollum Elem. Sch., Albuquerque, 1969-75, S.W. Christian Sch., Ft. Worth, Tex., 1975-76; elem. tchr. St. Andrews Interparochial Sch., Ft. Worth, 1977-91, also reading coord. kindergarten through 4th grade, 1977-91, substitute tchr., 1991-92, 1992-96, ret., 1996—. Author children's books. Vol. libr. storyteller, 1995-98, vol. Alzheimers Assn., 1997-99. Mem. soil conservation Svc. Alumni, Am. Assn. Ret. Persons, Alphaah Delta Kappa et. Fidelis Alpha), Ch. of Christ. Democrat. Home: 1501 Linwood Ln Fort Worth TX 76134-2851

DESHAZER, RUTH SHOMLER, health facility administrator, consultant; b. Glendale, Calif., July 17, 1954; d. Russell Paul and Pauline April (Lathrop) Shomler; 1 child, Michael Jr. BA magna cum laude, San Diego State U., 1982; AS, San Diego Mesa Coll., 1993. Registered health info. adminstr.; cert. profl. of healthcare quality; cert. med. staff coord. Med. records technician, coder Scripps Healthcare, La Jolla, Calif., 1993-94; cont. quality improvement coord. Adventist Health Systems, National City, Calif., 1994-96; applications specialist MED Data Systems Inc., San Diego, 1996-97; health info. mgmt. cons. Pyramid Healthcare Cons., L.A., 1997; health info. mgmt. sr. cons. Elacor Resources Group, L.A., 1997-98; health info. mgmt. dir. Brea (Calif.) Cmty. Hosp., Pacifica Hosp. of the Valley, Burbank, Calif., 1998-99; ind. cons. in healthcare quality, info. mgmt. and survey preparation, L.A. and Orange County, Calif., 1999—; med. staff coord. MemorialCare Health Systems, Orange County, Calif., 1999—. Med. staff coord. MemorialCare Health Sys., Orange County, Calif., 1999—. Contbr. articles to profl. jours. Mem. Calif. Assn. Quality Profls., San Diego Health Info. Assn. (various offices 1994-97), Greater Orange Counth Health Info. Assn. (pres.-elect 1998-99, pres. 1999-2000, past pres. 2000-01), Calif. Health Info. Assn. (nominating com. 1995-96, legis. com. 1996-97, convention com. 1997-98, chair convention com. 1998-99, membership com. 1998-99), Am. Health Info. Assn., Phi Beta Kappa, Phi Kappa Phi. Avocations: landscaping, floral design, swimming, travel. Home: 1109 Augusta Ln Ottawa KS 66067-1694 E-mail: cooknruth@aol.com.

DESHAZO, MARJORIE WHITE, occupational therapist; b. Syracuse, N.Y., Apr. 25, 1941; d. Rexford Everett and Joyce Winifred Ella (Brown) Young White; m. Del DeShazo, Dec. 22, 1966; stepchildren: Chad A., Karen A. Lynch. BS in Occupl. Therapy, U. Puget Sound, 1964. Lic. occupl. therapist, 1996. Occupl. therapist VA Med. Ctr., Roseburg, Oreg., 1965-70, Salisbury, N.C., 1970-78; occupl. therapist, co-chief VA Domiciliary, White City, Oreg., 1978-80; chief occupl. therapist VA Med. Ctr., Lexington, Ky., 1980-87; pvt. cons. occupl. therapy Camdenton, Mo., 1987—. Coord. TV21 Art Collections, Springfield, Mo. Inventor (in field); exhibitions include Lexington Art League, 1986—87, Laurie Fine Arts Show, 1993, Ozark Art and Palette, 1996, Lisa Frick Gallery, 1996—98, Osage Beach City Hall Mural, Represented in permanent collections First Nat. Bank, Lake Ozark, Mo., Ozark Ford Bldg., private collections. Active Greater Lake Area Arts Coun., Osage Beach, Mo., 1987—. Kappa Kappa Gamma scholar U. Puget Sound. Mem. Ozark Art and Palette Club (treas. 1998-2000), Creative

Artists Guild (coord. art hanging 1998—), Mo. Watercolor Soc., Nat. Oil and Acrylic Soc. Democrat. Methodist. Avocations: sewing, art, gardening, gourmet cooking. Home: 12 Brookfield Ln Lake Ozark MO 65049-8673

DESHIELDS, ELIZABETH PEGGY BOWEN, artist, educator, poet; b. Ada, Okla., Nov. 11, 1928; d. Samuel Archie and Etta Berthel (Flowers) Bowen; m. Amos Jack DeShields, Sept. 19, 1947; children: Dennis Jack, Sheila Beth. BA in English, East Ctrl. Okla. U., 1947, BS Edn., 1947, EdM in counseling, 1977. Bus. tchr. Bearden HS, Okla., 1947-48; confidential sec., prodn. supt. Phillips Chem. Co., Borger, Tex., 1949-53; English tchr. Borger HS, 1954-55; co-owner, bookkeeper Jack DeShields' Bldg. Stone, Cromwell, Okla., 1955—; asst. prin., tchr. Ctrl. Oak Elem. Sch., Oklahoma City, 1955-68; tchr. Will Roger's Sch., Shawnee, 1968-70, Butner Pub. Schs., Cromwell, 1970-74; co-owner, bookkeeper DeShields' Energy, 1970—, Rainbow Hills Ranch, 1970—; tchr. Castle Pub. Schs., 1976-79; counselor Okemah Pub. Schs., Okemah, 1979-85. Reporter Ada Times Democrat, 1947; news corr. Daily Oklahoman, Oklahoma City Times, 1947; abstracting asst. Pontotoc Co. Abstract Co., Ada, 1946; legal sec. C.F. Green Law Offices, Ada, 1944-46. Contbr. poems to profl. publs.; artist, illustrator for books. Mem. choir, Sunday sch. tchr. First Bapt. Ch., Cromwell, chmn. trustees, 1991; tchr. Cromwell Art Club. Named Ret. Tchr. of Yr., Okemah Alumni Assn., 2002; recipient scholarship, Nat. Sch. Bus., 1944, East Ctrl. U., 1944, Spl. Recognition Appreciation of Svc. award, Crooked Oak PTA, 1967, Yearbook Dedication, 1966, Svc. award, 1967, Leadership Svc. award, Girl Scouts U.S., 1968, Leadership Am. Secondary Edn., 1972, Yearbook award, 1971—73, Golden Eagle award for outstanding contbn. to journalism, 1973, Silver award, Columbia Scholastic Press Assn., numerous art awards, Okmulgee, Seminole and Hughes Counties, Okla., 1979—2003, Butner Yearbook Dedication, Appreciation Plaque, Cromwell Headstart, 1985, FFA, 1985, Plaque, First Bapt. Ch., 1991, Editor's Choice award, Nat. Libr. Poetry, 1996, Recognition award, Famous Poets Soc., 1999—2003. Mem. Okla. Ret. Tchrs., Okfuskee County Ret. Tchrs., Nat. Mus. Women in Arts (charter). Democrat. Avocations: painting, writing, gardening. Home: RR 2 Box 71 Okemah OK 74859-9623

DESHIELDS, SHEILA BETH, writer; b. Borger, Tex., Dec. 31, 1952; d. Amos Jack and Elizabeth Peggy DeShields; m. David Ian Hildreth, Sept. 10, 1978; children: Ian Andrew DeShields Hildreth, Taylor Bryn DeShields Hildreth. BA with honors, Okla. Bapt. U., 1974; MA, U. Wales, 1976. Cert. data sys. engr., data sys. design developer. Editor Nimrod Mag., Tulsa, 1976—78; secondary tchr. Anderson Jr. H.S., Tulsa, 1976—78; reporter The Chronicle Herald, Halifax, Canada, 1978; editor Writers Fedn. of N.S., Halifax, 1978—79; tech. editor Ramtek, Santa Clara, Calif., 1979—80; software sys. engr. Lockheed Missiles and Space Co., Sunnyvale, Calif., 1980—87; freelance writer San Jose, Calif., 1987—. Tech. cons. freelance, Silicon Valley, Calif., 1979—80. Author: At Grandmother's Table, 2000, 2001. Co-coord. Young Authors' Faire, 1994—2003. Named Vol. of Yr., Moreland Sch. Dist., 2001; recipient Hedgebrook Writers Residency, Whitbey Island Selection Com., 1994; Rotary Internat. fellowship, England, 1974—76. Avocations: bicycling, gardening, snorkeling.

DE SHIELDS-MINNIS, TARRA RAMIT, lawyer; b. Balt. d. Lawrence Franklin DeShields and Ramona Fleurette Brown. BA, U. Md., 1984; JD, U. Balt., 1987. Bar: Md. 1988, U.S. Dist. Ct. Md. 1990, U.S. Ct. Appeals (4th cir.), U.S. Supreme Ct. 1993. Jud. clk. Md. Ct. of Spl. Appeals, 1987-88; asst. state's atty. Office of the State's Atty., Montgomery County, 1988-90; asst. atty. gen. Office of the Atty. Gen., Balt., 1990-96; asst. U.S. atty. U.S. Atty.'s Office, Balt., 1996—. Recipient Am. Jurisprudence award Lawyer's Cooperative Pub. Co., 1988; Supreme Ct. fellow Nat. Assn. of Attys. Gens., 1993. Mem. Md. State Bar Assn., Nat. Bar Assn. Roman Catholic. Avocations: reading, antique shopping, racquetball. Office: US Attys Office 101 W Lombard St Baltimore MD 21201-2605

DESIATO, DONNA JEAN, school system administrator; b. Bridgeport, Conn., Nov. 28, 1949; d. William Joseph and Elvira Rosemarie (Cerreta) Gilberti; 1 child, Danielle DeSiato Creveling. BEd, U. Miami, 1971; MS in Edn., SUNY Cortland, 1977; cert. advanced study, SUNY Oswego, 1983; postgrad., Syracuse U. Cert. permanent tchr. cert. N.Y., 1976, sch. dist. adminstr. N.Y., 1983. Tchr. Syracuse (N.Y.) City Sch. Dist., 1974—79, instrl. specialist, 1979—83, vice prin., 1983—84, prin., 1984—94, dir. elem. edn., 1993—2000, asst. supt., 2000—. Mem. reading and lit. partnership N.Y. State Edn. Dept., Albany, 1999—; mem. lit. collaborative Success By Six, Syracuse, NY, 1999—; mem. edn. adv. bd. Syracuse Newspapers, 1990—95. Mem. Corinthian Club, Syracuse, 2000—. Recipient Outstanding Educator award, Supervisors and Adminstrs. Assn. N.Y. State, 1999, Adminstrs. Excellence award, Supervisors and Adminstrs. Assn. Syracuse, 1996, 1997, 1998, Leadership Recognition award, Commn. on Women in Leadership, 1995, Disting. Alumni award, Onadaga C.C., 2003. Mem.: N.Y. State Assn. Women in Adminstrn. (chair chpt.), Delta Kappa Gamma (Alpha Omega chpt.), Phi Delta Kappa. Office: Syracuse City Sch Dist 725 Harrison St Syracuse NY 13210

DESIREE, LAURA, dancer; Studies with, Natalia Clare; student, Joffrey Ballet Sch. Former mem. Joffrey Ballet Concert Group; mem. Pitts. Ballet Theatre, 1982—, 1st soloist, 1986, prin. dancer, 1990. Originated role of Jordan Baker in Prokovksy's The Great Gatsby. Office: Pitts Ballet Theatre 2900 Liberty Ave Pittsburgh PA 15201-1511

DESJARDINS, JUDITH ANNE, psychotherapist; b. Colorado Springs, Colo., Dec. 21, 1943; d. Herbert T. and Sally H. King; m. Sherwyn L. Drucker, Sept. 3, 1993; children from previous marriage: André, Danielle Anne. BA with honors, U. Wyo., 1965; MSW, Ariz. State U., 1972. Diplomate Acad. Managed Care Providers; LCSW Calif. Bd. Behavioral Sci. Examiners, bd. cert. diplomate in clin. social work Am. Bd. Examiners Clin. Social Work, master social work addiction counselor Nat. Bd. Addiction Examiners. Counselor, instr. Phoenix Opportunities Industrialization Ctr., 1972—73; med. social worker Maricopa County Hosp., Phoenix, 1973—75; psychiat. social worker St. Joseph's Hosp., Phoenix, 1975—76; oncology social worker St. John's Hosp., Santa Monica, Calif., 1976—78; pvt. practice psychotherapist Santa Monica, 1978—; clin. supr. Turning Point Shelter, Santa Monica, 1987—91; clin. supr. outpatient substance abuse svcs. Didi Hirsch, Venice, Calif., 1990—98; dir. Addiction Recovery Ctr., Santa Monica, 1998—2000. Lectr. Mt. St. Mary's Coll., L.A., 1979, Loyola Marymount U., L.A., 1993—96; instr. St. Martin Tours Sch., L.A., 1982—88; presenter in field. Contbr. articles to profl. jours. Vol. therapist Pacific Counseling Ctr. AIDS/HIV, L.A., 1991—98; mem. disaster mental health team Am. Red Cross, Santa Monica, 1999—. Fellow: NASW; mem.: AFTRA, Screen Actors Guild. Avocations: rollerblading, Native Am. art, jewelry, deerskin, pillow creations.

DES JARDINS, TRACI, chef, restaurant owner; b. Calif. Student, U. Calif., Santa Cruz. Formerly mem. staff 7th St. Bistro, L.A.; former apprentice Michel and Pierre Troisgros, Lucas Carton, Alain Ducasse, Alain Passard, France; former mem. staff Montrachet, N.Y.C.; former chef de cuisine Patina, Calif.; former chef Aqua, San Francisco, Elka, San Francisco; exec. chef Rubicon, San Francisco, 1993—97; ptnr., chef Jardiniere, San Francisco, 1997—. Environ. activist. Named a Rising Star Chef of Yr., James Beard Found.; named Chef of Yr., San Francisco Mag.; named one of Best New Chefs, Food & Wine Mag., Top 3 Chefs in Bay Area, San Francisco Chronicle. Office: Jardiniere 300 Grove St San Francisco CA 94102

DESJARLAIS, GEORGIA KATHRINE, retired military officer; b. Chattanooga, Tenn., Oct. 31, 1958; d. Lowell and Lucy Caroline (Brown) Lawson; m. Daniel Eugene Desjarlais, Apr. 22, 1978 (div. May 1985). AA, Hawaii Pacific Coll., 1980, BS, 1982; MPA, Auburn U., Montgomery, 1999; student, Air U., 1999, Air Command and Staff Coll., 1998—99. Enlisted as E-1 USN, 1976, commd. as ensign, 1983, advanced through ranks to lt. comdr., 1994, ret., 2000; supply officer, food svc. officer NSGA Adak, Alaska, 1984—86; disbursing and stores officer USS Dixon (AS 37), San Diego, 1986—88; material officer COMNAVSUPPFORANTARCTICA, Oxnard, Calif., 1988—91; stock control and AOIC USNS Sirius (TAFS 8), Norfolk, Va., 1991—94; load mgr. COMNAVSURFLANT, Norfolk, 1994—96; asst. supply officer USS Emory S. Land (AS 39), Norfolk, 1996—98; logistics supr. Corning Inc., Oneonta, NY, 1999—2002. Mentor Ret. Officer's Assn., Washington, 1999—. Mem.: AAUW (sec. Oneonta br. 2001—02, membership chmn. Memphis br. 2002—). Methodist. Avocations: reading, history, wildlife. Home: 784 Canterbury Ln Oneonta NY 13820

DESLAURIERS, SUZANNE DAWSEY, secondary school educator, artist; b. Wilmington, N.C., Sept. 13, 1950; d. Cyrus Bassett and Marshlea (Cottingham) Dawsey; m. Cecil Hörger Knight, Dec. 28, 1972 (dec. Nov. 25, 1995); 1 child, Jesse Hörger Knight ; m. E. Joseph Deslauriers, Dec. 16, 1996. BA in Fine Arts, Fla. So. Coll., Lakeland, Fla., 1972; MA in Art Edn., U. S.C., Columbia, S.C., 1985. Cert. Nat. Bd. Cert. Tchr., 99. Child care program dir. Appalachia State Wesley Found., Boone, NC, 1977—78; supr. aftercare sch. program Hardin Park Elem., Boone, 1977—78; art tchr., asst. soccer coach Holly Hill-Roberts High Sch., Holly Hill, SC, 1979—88; art tchr., social studies tchr. Hiwassee Dam Sch., Murphy, NC, 1988—, A+ Schs. coord., 1994—. Presenter, cons. on integrated instrn. Cherokee County Schs., Murphy, 1994—; mentor for nat. bd. tchr. cert. NEA, Western, NC, 2000—; adj. prof. West Carolina U., Cullowhee, NC, 2002; painting and drawing tchr. John C. Campbell Folk Sch., Brasstown, NC, 1995—. Recipient Creative Tchr. of the Yr., Western North Carolina, 1996. Mem.: North Carolina Art Educator Assn. (Secondary Art Educator of the Yr. 1999—2000). Home: 24 Lady Slipper Ln Brasstown NC 28902-8073

DE SMET, LORRAINE MAY, artist; b. Passaic, N.J., May 5, 1928; d. Peter John and Mary (Lovas) Prevelige; m. Louis John de Smet, May 17, 1952; children: Mary Lizabeth, Jean Marie, Carolyn, Allise Marie. Student, Berkeley Sch., 1945, Art Students League, 1979-82. One woman show Pen and Brush Club, 1984 (Solo Show award). Bd. dirs. Art Ctr. of N.J., 1993—. Recipient 1st prize, Livingston (N.J.) Art Assn., 1987, 1988, Am. Artist award, Ridgewood Art Inst., 1998, Caldwell Progress award, 1998, 2003, LAA merit award, 1998, 1999, 2001, 2002, 2003, WEAA award, Caldwell Coll., 1999, merit award, 2000, Best of the Best exhbn., Trenton Mus., 2001, numerous other awards. Mem. U.S. Coast Guard Artists, Am. Artists Profl. League (Ann Waldron N.J. award 1998, N.J. Disting. Merit award 2002), Ringwood Manor Art Assn. (award 2000), Pen and Brush Club of N.Y. (bd. dirs. 1985-92, v.p. 1989-92, dir. brush divsn. 1987-89, mem. dir. 1990-92, co-chair brush sect. 1994-95, 97), Art Ctr. of N.J. (bd. dirs., sec., membership chair), West Essex Art Assn. (bd. dirs. 1992-98), Art Students League of N.Y. (life), Millburn-Short Hills Art Assn.(award of excellence 2001, 2002, Louise Melrose Gallery award 2002). Home: 33 Campbell Rd Fairfield NJ 07004-1735

DESMOND, KATHLEEN KADON, critic, educator, artist; b. Marshfield, Wis., Sept. 2, 1950; d. John Charles and Ann Preller Kadon; m. William Dean Desmond, Aug. 8, 1970 (dec. Mar. 1981). BS in Art Edn., U. Wis., 1973; MA in Art Edn., Ariz. State U., 1976, EdD in Art Edn., 1981. From asst. prof. to assoc. prof. art edn. Ohio State U., Newark, 1981—89; assoc. prof. Ctrl. Wash. U., Ellensburg, 1989—90, chair dept. art, 1989, assoc. dean grad. sch., 1990; prof. art Ctrl. Mo. State U., Warrensburg, 1991—, dean grad. sch., 1991—93, asst. provost, 1993—94. Dir. Maastricht Ctr. Transatlantic Studies, Netherlands, 1999; instr. Missouri London Program, 1997. Contbr. critical revs. and articles to profl. jours., chapters to books, exhbn. catalogues;, editor articles. Recipient many rsch. and tchg. awards. Mem.: Soc. for Contemp. Photography (bd. dirs. 1999—2003), Nat. Art Edn. Assn. (pres. women's caucus 2000—02), Coll. Art Assn. (chair edn. com. 1999—2003). Avocations: travel, walking dogs, reading, art museums and galleries. Home: 6820 Holmes Kansas City MO 64131 Office: Central Missouri State U Art Ctr 121 Warrensburg MO 64093 Office Phone: 660-543-4620.

DESMOND-HELLMANN, SUSAN, medical products manufacturing executive; b. 1958; Bachelors Degree, MD, U. Nev.; M in Epidemiology and Biostats., U. Calif., Berkeley. Bd. cert. internal medicine and med. oncology. Trainee U. Calif., San Francisco; assoc. dir. clin. cancer rsch., project team leader Taxol Bristol-Myers Squibb Pharm. Rsch. Inst.; clin. scientist Genentech, Inc., South San Francisco, 1995-96, sr. dir. clin. sci., 1996, v.p. med. affairs, 1996, chief med. officer, 1996—, v.p. devel., 1997, sr. v.p. devel., 1997, exec. v.p. devel. and product ops., 1999—. Vis. faculty Uganda Cancer Inst.; asst. prof. hematology-oncology U. Calif. San Francisco, adj. assoc. prof. epidemiology and biostats; adv. com. regulatory reform, HHS; bd. dirs. Biotechnology Industry Orgn. Office: Genentech Inc One DNA Way South San Francisco CA 94080-4990 Office Fax: 650-225-6000.

DESNOYERS, MEGAN FLOYD, archivist, educator; b. N.Y.C., Oct. 31, 1945; d. Lawrence Clifford and Frances Irene Floyd; m. David George Desnoyers, Sept. 2, 1967; 1 child, Adam O'Neil. AB, Vassar Coll., 1967; MLS, Rutgers U., 1968. Cert. archivist. Libr. John Jay H.S., Wappingers Falls, N.Y., 1968-69; archivist Franklin D. Roosevelt Libr., Hyde Park, N.Y., 1969, John F. Kennedy Libr., Boston, 1970—, curator Ernest Hemingway Collection, 1987—96, 2000—01; instr. in archives adminstrn. Nat. Archives Modern Archives Inst., Washington, 1982-2000. Lectr. archives adminstrn. U. Mass., Boston, 1978-80; lectr. on Hemingway, 1992—2000; mem. Archives Adv. Commn., Boston, 1977-2000; archival advisor Girl Scouts U.S., N.Y.C., 1991—. Contbr. chpt. to book, articles to profl. jours. Mem. adv. bd., chmn. com. Voluntary Action Ctr., Mass. Bay United Way, Boston, 1974-80; mem., chair bd. trustees Randall Libr., Stow, Mass., 1976-80; mem. Mass. Hist. Records Adv. Bd., 1979-2000. Nat. Def. fellow, 1967-68. Fellow Soc. Am. Archivists; mem. New Eng. Archivists (sec. 1976-78), Soc. Am. Archivists (workshop instr. 1978-2000), Acad. Cert. Archivists (task force on recert. 1991-92), Beta Phi Mu. Democrat. Roman Catholic. Office: John F Kennedy Libr Columbia Point Boston MA 02125

DESOER, BARBARA J. bank executive; BA in Math., Mount Holyoke Coll.; MBA, U. Calif., Berkeley. Various positions to mng. strategy devel. and implementation, consumer banking unit Bank Am. Corp., 1977—96, exec. v.p., Calif. retail banking group, 1996—98, pres., No. Calif. banking, 1998, mktg. exec., 1999—2001, pres. consumer products, 2001—. Chmn. internat. diversity adv. coun. Bank Am. Corp.; mem. adv. coun. Haas Sch. Bus. U. Calif., Berkeley; mem. bus. adv. coun. Belk Coll. Bus. Adminstrn. U. NC, Charlotte. Bd. dir. NC Dance Theatre, Presbyn. Hosp. Found., United Way Ctrl. Carolinas. Office: Bank Am Corp 100 N Tryon St Charlotte NC 28255*

DESOMBRE, NANCY COX, academic administrator, consultant; b. Lake City, Minn., Sept. 7, 1939; d. Ray Ronald and Marjorie Mae (Lipa) C.; m. Eugene DeSombre, Sept. 10, 1960; children: Elizabeth DeSombre, Michael DeSombre. BA, U. Chgo., 1961, MA, 1962. Prof. English dept. Wilbur Wright Coll., Chgo., 1962—, chair English dept., 1976—, dean vocat. program, 1981-82, dean of instrn., 1982-86, v.p. faculty, instr., 1987-94; pres. Harold Washington Coll., Chgo., 1994—. Cons. evaluator North Cen. Assn. of Coll./Schs., Chgo., 1987—; dir. LaSalle Bank, N.A., Chgo., 1994—; mem. bd. dirs. Greater State St. Coun., Chgo., 1995—, State Univ. Retirement System, Champaign, Ill., 1995—. Mem. bd. dirs. Frank Lloyd Wright Found., Oak Park, 1987—. Recipient Inst. Ednl. Mgmt. award Harvard U., 1990, Project Enhance award Wright Coll., 1991, Woman of the Yr. award Exec. Leadership Inst.-League for Innovation, 1993, 94. Avocation: gardening. Office: Harold Washington Coll 30 E Lake St Chicago IL 60601-2403

DESPANZA-SPRENGER, LYNETTE CHARLIE, small business owner; b. New Orleans, June 7, 1948; d. Sylvester Issac and Yverdelle Ida Despanza; m. Charles Ricard II, May 1970 (div. May 18, 1978); m. Paul Henri Sprenger, Oct. 28 (div. June 2002); 1 child, Charles Ricard III. BSN, U. Hawaii, 1995; ASN, St. Pete Jr. Coll., 1988; student, Delgado Jr. Coll., 1972. Cert. respiratory therapist La.; RN La. Sedation rn. dir. King Khalid Eye Specialist Hosp., Riyadh, Saudi Arabia, edn. clin. instr. and stress mgmt. instr., 1989—98; ballroom dance and exercise instr. Inst. Royal Family and We. and European Families in Saudi Arabia, Saudi Arabia, 1990—98; clinic adminstr., dir. Columbia Gia Diah Internat., Vietnam; respiratory therapist Bay Front Hosp., St. Petersburg, Fla.; emergency nurse, ICU nurse Maxim Healthcare Agy. and Agy. Personnel, St. Petersburg, Fla., 1999—2000; owner, chef, operator Lagniappe Bistrot, St. Petersburg; co-operator Swiss Creole Connection, 2002—. Art restorer Leppa Rathner Mus., St. Petersburg. Vol. St. Petersburg Jr. Coll. N.O.L.A., Fla. Recipient pastels and oil painting award, Art Soc. of St. Petersburg, U. New Orleans. Roman Catholic. Avocations: jazz, tap, ballroom dancing, painting, fencing. Home: 732 17th Ave N Saint Petersburg FL 33704 E-mail: despanzalynette@hotmail.com.

DESROSIERS, ANNE BOOKE, performing arts administrator, consultant; b. Bradford, Pa., Sept. 30, 1938; d. Benjamin and Twila Mae (Schwab) Booke; m. Roger Isadore DesRosiers, Dec. 27, 1960 (div. 1994); children Marc (dec.), Diana, Berinthia. BA in English, U. Fla., 1960. Tchr. Rantoul (Ill.) Elem. Sch., 1961-63, Oogontz Jr. H.S., Phila., 1969-73; dir. adult edn. Guadaloupe Ctr., Salt Lake City, 1974-77; dir. devel. Repertory Theater of St. Louis, 1977-85, St. Louis Zoo, 1985-88; pres. DesRosiers & Assocs., Cleve., 1988—; mng. dir. Great Lakes Theater Festival, Cleve., 1993-98; acting exec. dir. Cleve. Cultural Coalition, 1999-2000. Mem. Nat. Soc. Fund Raising Execs. (cert., Exec. Leadership Inst. 1990, Outstanding Fund Raising St. Louis chpt. 1988), Cleve. Cultural Coalition (vice chair 1995-98). Republican. Jewish. Avocations: golf, travel, sailing. Home and Office: 1 Bratenahl Pl Apt 1102 Bratenahl OH 44108-1155 Fax: 216-541-0344. E-mail: abdesr@megsinet.net.

DESROSIERS, MURIEL C. music educator, retired nursing consultant; b. Woonsocket, R.I., Jan. 15, 1934; d. Rodolphe J. Desrosiers and Rhea M. Archambault; m. Albert A. Desrosiers; 6 stepchildren. BSN, Boston Coll., 1965; MSN, Boston U., 1967, cert. advanced grad. studies, 1975, EdD, 1977. Instr. St. Anselm's Coll. Sch. Nursing, Manchester, NH, 1968—74; cons. drug abuse prevention N.H. State Dept. Edn., Concord, 1974—75, sch. health cons., 1976—89; instr. piano performance, theory and technique. In-svc. educator N.H. Hosps., 1968—75; instr. leadership workshops, 1968—75; grant writer Sch. Nurse Achievement Program. Vol. Home for Little Wanderers; chair Am. Sch. Health Assn., 1984—87; pres. Nat. Assn. Sch. Health Consultants, 1984—87. Recipient Disting. Svc. award, Am. Sch. Health Assn., 1987, Sch. Nurse Achievement award, 1988. Mem.: N.H. Nurses Assn., Maine Nurses Assn., Maine Music Tchrs. Assn. (chair program 1990—95), Nat. Assn. Music Tchrs. (emeritus). Avocation: writing. Home: RR 4 Box 2350 Waterville ME 04901

DESSASO, DEBORAH ANN, freelance/self-employed writer, corporate communications specialist; b. Washington, Feb. 6, 1952; d. Coleman and Virginia Beatrice (Taylor) Dessaso. AS in Bus. Adminstrn., Southeastern U., 1986, BSBA, 1988; MA in English Composition and Rhetoric, U. DC, 1997. Clk.-stenographer FTC, Washington, 1969—70; sec. NEA, Washington, 1970—72, AARP, Washington, 1972—79, assoc. adminstrv. specialist, 1979—80, adminstrv. specialist, 1979—89, legis. comm. specialist, 1989—2000, mgr. issue response, 2000—01; cons., 2000—. Founding mem., sec. Andrus Fed. Credit Union, 1980; adj. prof. English U. DC, 2002—03, dir. Writing Ctr., 2003—. Mem.: Associated Writing Program. Mem. Faith Outreach Cmty. Ch. Home: 3042 Stanton Rd SE Washington DC 20020-7883 E-mail: dessaso749@verizon.net.

DESSEREAU, APRIL, art educator; b. Port Chester, N.Y., Mar. 4, 1952; d. Francis Gregory and Ruth Helen (Sundberg) Dessereau. BA, SUNY, Oswego, 1975; MS in Art Edn., U. Bridgeport, 1978; MA in Humanities, Manhattanville Coll., 1992. Cert. art tchr. N.Y. Adult edn. instr. art Port Chester (N.Y.) Bd. Edn., 1979-83, art/photography tchr., 1982—. Freelance calligrapher, 1978—92. Mem.: NEA, Westchester Coun. of the Arts, Am. Fedn. Tchrs., N.Y. State Art Tchrs. Assn., Nat. Art Edn. Assn. Avocations: photography, quilting, gardening, drawing, painting. Office: Port Chester HS Tamarack Rd Port Chester NY 10573

DESSYLAS, ANN ATSAVES, human resources and office management executive; b. Bklyn., Jan. 28, 1927; d. Charles and Agnes (Cocoros) Atsaves; m. George Dessylas, Dec. 28, 1969. BA, Bklyn. Coll., 1957; MA, NYU, 1961, MBA, 1977. Exec. asst. W.R. Grace & Co., N.Y.C., 1950-70; asst. sec. St. Joe Minerals Corp., N.Y.C., 1970-81, asst. v.p., 1981-85; cons. Cyprus Minerals, Denver, 1985-91; pres. AAD Enterprises, Forest Hills, N.Y., 1992—. Dir. Continental Owners Corp.; sec. Plato Malozemoff Found. Avocations: music, theater, golf, art, tennis. Home and Office: 70-20 108th St Ste 8-p Forest Hills NY 11375-4449

DESTAFFANY, SANDRA RUSSELL, childbirth educator, author; b. Billings, Mont., Mar. 15, 1957; d. Alexander Emmett and Cleora Jean (Saunders) Russell; children: Naomi Jo, Andrea Renee, James Russell. BS, Mont. State U., 1979, postgrad. cert. childbirth educator. Childbirth educator Conrad (Mont.) Childbirth Edn. Assn., 1983—94. U.S. western dir. Inter Childbirth Edn. Assn., Mpls., 1990-92, pres. elect 1992-94, pres. 1994-95. Contbr. numerous articles to profl. jours. Avocations: skiing, reading, writing, needlework, quilting.

DESTITO, ROANN M. state legislator; b. Jan. 15, 1956; m. Chris Destito; 1 child. BS in Industrial Relations, LeMoyne Coll. Assemblywoman dist. 116 N.Y. State Assembly, 1992—. Chmn. Governmental Operations Comm., Displaced Homemakers Sub-Comm.; mem. Aging Comm., Agriculture, Labor Comm., Mental Health Comm., Small Business Comm., Economic Development Comm., Job Creation Comm., Commerce and Industry Comm., Ways and Means Comm. Mem. NOW, Bus. & Profl. Women. Office: NY State Assembly Rm 704 Legis Office Bldg State Capitol Albany NY 12248*

DESVIGNES-KENDRICK, MARY, municipal official; m. Ernest A. Kendrick; children: Aziza, Jelani, Shomari. BA, NYU, 1974; MD, Meharry Med. Coll., 1978; MPH, U. Tex., 1988. Diplomate Nat. Bd. Med. Examiners, Am. Bd. Pediatrics. Intern Baylor Coll. Medicine Affiliated Hosps., Houston, 1978, resident in pediatrics, 1979-81, staff pediatrician Martin Luther King Cmty. Clinic, 1982-86, instr. Dept. Cmty. Medicine, 1982-84, asst. prof. Dept. Cmty. Medicine, 1984-86; med. dir. Northside Health Ctr. City of Houston Dept. Health and Human Svcs., 1986-88, asst. dir. Personal Health Svcs., 1990-92, interim dir., 1992, dir., 1992—. Adj. faculty U. Tex. Sch. Pub. Health, Houston, 1993—; chair City of Houston Dept. Health and Human Svcs. Com. for the Protection of Human Subjects, 1990-91, Exec. Quality Assurance Com., 1990-91; mem. Baylor Coll. of Medicine Affiliated Hosps. Affirmative Action Com., 1985-86, Com. on Adolescent Health Issues, 1985-86. Mem. Class XI Am. Leadership Forum, 1993, Leadership Tex. Class of 1991, adv. bd. Tex. Nurses Assn. Dist. 9, 1993, adv. bd. U. Houston Health Law and Policy Inst., 1992—, bd. dirs. Leadership Tex. Alumnae Assn., 1992-94, adv. bd. Greater HoAIDS Alliance, 1992, chair Houston Area Immunization Task Force, 1992, mem. adv. bd. Houston

Assn. for Communication Disorders, 1991, mem. project adv. group U. Tex. Health Sci. Ctr. at Houston Sch. Pub. Health, 1991, bd. dirs. Children at Risk, 1991, Am. Lung Assn. Tuberculosis Ctrl., 1990-91, adv. bd. United Way of Tex. Houston/Gulf Coast chpt., 1993—, adv. bd. CORE, U. Houston Grad. Sch. Social Work, 1993—. Fellow Am. Acad. Pediatrics; mem. APHA (Milton and Ruth Roemer prize 1997), Nat. Med. Assn., Am. Coll. Physician Execs., Tex. Pediatric Soc., Nat. Forum Black Pub. Adminstrs. (cert. for Commitment to Excellence and Svc. to the Pub. 1993), Nat. Assn. County and City Health Officials (pres. 1997), Forum Club of Houston, Rotary. Office: Dept Health and Human Svcs City of Houston 8000 N Stadium Dr Houston TX 77054-1823

DE TABOAS, HILDA RIVERA, occupational health nurse; b. Coamo, P.R., Dec. 19, 1919; d. Dàmaso and Ramona (Zayas) Rivera; m. Julio Oscar Taboas; children: Julio Oscar, Alberto Jose, Carlos E. Cert., Bishop Willinger Sch. Nursing, 1941, Presbyn. Hosp., 1962, Met. Hosp., 1969, Coutinuos Edn., 1980. RN, P.R. RN U.S. Vet. Hosp., San Juan, P.R.; coronary care nurse Presbyn. Hosp., San Juan, P.R.; pvt. nurse Directory Nurses, San Juan, P.R.; first aid nurse Airport Internat. Islavarda, San Juan, P.R. Contbr. articles to profl. jours. Mem. Colegio Profesionales de Enfarmaria de P.R. Home: Purus 1687 Rp Hts San Juan PR 00926

DETERMAN, SARA-ANN, lawyer; b. Palmerton, Pa., Aug. 17, 1938; d. Albert H. and Evelyn (Tucker) Heimbach; m. Dean W. Determan, July 28, 1957 (div. Nov. 1981); children: Dann, David, Steven (dec.); m. Gary Sellers, May 21, 1988. Student, Conn. Coll., 1956-57, Stanford U., 1958; AB, U. Del., 1960; LLB, George Washington U., 1967. Bar: U.S. Dist. Ct. D.C. 1968. Law clk. to sr. judge U.S. Ct. Appeals (D.C. cir.), Edgerton, 1967-68; assoc. Hogan & Hartson, Washington, 1968-75, ptnr., 1975—. Trustee Lawyers Com. for Civil Rights Under Law, Washington, 1982-94, co-chmn., 1994—. Bd. dirs. Mex.-Am. Legal Def. and Ednl. Fund, 1983-88, Women's Legal Def. Fund, 1980-2002. Fellow Am. Bar Found.; mem. ABA (chmn. individual rights sect. 1985-86, commr. legal programs for elderly 1983-89, com. on delivery of legal svcs. 1989-93, mem. consortium on legal svcs.), ACLU (bd. dirs. 1975-92), D.C. Bar (pres. 1990-91). Democrat. Unitarian Universalist. Office: Hogan & Hartson Columbia Square 555 13th St NW Ste 800E Washington DC 20004-1161

DETERT, MIRIAM ANNE, chemical analyst; b. San Diego, Calif., Sept. 16, 1925; d. George Bernard and Margaret Theresa Zita (Lohre) D. BS, Dominican Coll., San Rafael, Calif., 1947. Chem. analyst Shell Devel. Co., Emeryville, Calif., 1947-72, Houston, 1972-86. Photo participant Wax Rsch.: Quest, 1981; exhibited etchings Sight and Insight Art Studio, Mill Valley, Calif., 2002; contbr. poetry to books including The International Library of Poetry - Best Poems of the 90's, Spirit of the Age, The Nightfall of Diamonds, The Long and Winding Road, Through Oceans of Time. Vol. Falkirk Cultural Ctr., San Rafael, 1987-91, M.D. Anderson Tumor Inst., Houston, 1978-86, Rep. Party, San Rafael, 1990, 94; mem. Jewish Comm. Ctr. Recipient Disting. Alumni award Dominican Coll., 1994. Mem. Marin Geneal. Soc. Republican. Roman Catholic. Avocations: etching, oil painting, genealogy, swimming.

DETERT-MORIARTY, JUDITH ANNE, graphic designer, educator, volunteer; b. Portage, Wis., July 10, 1952; d. Duane Harlan and Anne Jane (Deville) Detert; m. Patrick Edward Moriarty, July 22, 1978; children: Colin Edward Moriarty, Eleanor Grace Moriarty, Dylan Joseph Moriarty. BA, U. Wis., Madison, 1973, U. Wis., Green Bay, 1991. Cert. in no-fault grievance mediation Minn. Legis. sec., messenger State of Wis. Assembly, Madison, 1972, 74-76; casualty-property divsn. clk. Capitol Indemnity Corp., Madison, 1977-78; word processor consumer protection divsn. Wis. Dept. Agr., Madison, 1978; graphic arts composing specialist Moraine Park Tech. Inst., Fond du Lac, Wis., 1978-79; freelance artist Picas, Pictures and Promotion (formerly Detert Graphics), 1978-90; prodn. asst. West Bend News, 1980-83; devel. asoc. Riveredge Nature Ctr., Inc., Newburg, Wis., 1983-84; exec. dir. Voluntary Action Ctr. Washington County, West Bend, 1984-86; instr. cmty. svcs. Austin (Minn.) CC, 1988; art and promotional publs. dir. Michael G. and Co., Albert Lea, Minn., 1988-89; corp. art dir. Newco, Inc., Janesville, Wis., 1989-91; owner, artist Art Graphica, 1991-00. Cartooning instr., contbg. artist Janesville Sch. Dist., 1989—93, substitute tchr., 1999—. Contbr. articles to profl. jours. Newsletter editor, artist Friends of Battered Women, West Bend, 1983—86; rep. Planned Parenthood of Wis. Bd., 1984—85; artist LWV Washington County, 1984—86; apptd. Austin (Minn.) Human Rights Commn., 1987—88; fundraiser Victims Crisis Ctr., 1987; cmty. contact, v.p. Caths. Free Choice Wis., 1990—92; apptd. Janesville Hist. Commn., 1993—95, sec., 1992—95; vol. bd. dirs., chmn. advt. com. Janesville Concert Assn., 1994—97; newsletter editor Roosevelt Elem. Sch. PTA, 1996—2002, sec., 1999—2001; vol. newsletter editor Badger Coun. Girls Scouts, Inc., 1996—98; founder United Arts Alliance, 1996, pres., 1997—98, sec., 1998—2001, editor Artsrock, 2000—04; founder, bd. mem., sec. Bower City Preservation Assn., 1999—; chpt. coord. Project Linus-Janesville, 2000—; founder, instr. after-school knitting clubs Roosevelt and Jefferson Elem. Schs. and Boys and Girls Club, Janesville, 2001—04; organizer Lysistrata Project, Janesville, 2003; vol. Austin Pub. Sch. Omnibus Program, 1987—88; bd. dirs. Montessori Childrens House-West Bend, Wis., 1983—85, newsletter editor, 1983—85; founder, pres. Parents' Assn. Montessori Childrens House-Janesville, Wis., 1994—97, newsletter editor, 1994—97; bd. pres. Washington County, 1984—85; student vol. McCarthy for Pres., U. Wis., Madison, 1968; coord. student residences McGovern for Pres., 1972; vol. Udall for Pres., 1976; Washington County Campaign coord. Nat. Unity Campaign for John Anderson for Pres., 1980; publicity coord. Wis. Intellectual Freedom Coalition, 1981; pres., founder People of Washington County United for Choice, 1981—83; bd. dirs., v.p. Wis. Pro-Choice Conf., 1981—82; Washington County ward coord. Earl for Gov., 1982, Mondale/Ferraro, 1984; Washington County campaign chmn. Peg Lautenschlager for Wis. State Senate, 1984; sec., newsletter editor Manitowoc County Dems., Wis., 1986; precinct ofcl., affirmative action ofcl. Mower County Dems., Minn., 1986—88; local chair Women's Polit. Caucus, 1997—98; v.p. commn. officer, newsletter editor Rock County Dems., Wis., 1988—; vol. coord. Rock County Dukakis for Pres., 1988; campaign chair Lew Mittness for Wis. State Assembly, 1990; newsletter editor Rock County Voice for Choice, 1990—94; founding exec. bd. dirs., newsletter editor Moral Alternatives, 1990—92; vol. Rock County Clinton for Pres., 1992, 1996; 1st C.D. 4th vice chair Wis. Dems., 1999—2001; mem. campaign coordinating com. Vote Graf, 2000; Rock County coord. Ralph Nader for Pres., 2000; mem. steering com., bd. mem. Rock County Citizens for Peace, 2001—; Rock County campaign coord. John Kerry for Pres., 2004; newsletter editor, mem. coms. Planned Parenthood of Washington County, 1980—85, bd. dirs., 1984—85. Nominee Woman of Distinction, YWCA, 1996—98; recipient award of Excellence, Bd. Report Graphic Artists, 1994, Gov.'s award in support of arts, 1995, Comm. Arts Devel. award, 1997. Mem.: NOW (newsletter editor Dane County 1977—78, coord. reproductive rights task froce North Suburban chpt. 1981—84, coord. Wis. state reproductive rights task force 1982—84, Minn. pub. rels. coord. 1987—88, Wis. state 1994—99), Green-Rock Audubon Soc. (bd. dirs., newsletter editor), Forward Janesville (mem. steering com. Celebrate Janesville 1992—94). Mem. Soc. Of Friends. Avocations: reading, bicycling, gardening, knitting, world wide correspondence. Office: 23 S Atwood Ave Janesville WI 53545-4003 E-mail: proartist@aol.com.

DETIEGE-CAMPOS, ALICEA LYNNETTE, special education educator; b. Liberty, Tex., Jan. 6, 1970; d. Clifton Tom and Ella Mae deTiege; m. Martin Jesus Campos, June 27, 1998. BA in History, U. Tex., San Antonio, 1995; MEd, Our Lady of the Lake U., 2003. Cert. classroom tchr. spl. edn. K-12 State Bd. for Educator Certification, 2003. Content mastery ctr. tchr. Natalia (Tex.) Ind. Sch. Dist., 2000—01; spl. edn. history tchr. Northside Ind. Sch. Dist., San Antonio, 2001—. Active Childreach, Brazil, The Nature Conservancy, Tex., World Wildlife Fund; vol. Animal Def. League, San Antonio, 1991; delivery person St. Matthew's Cath. Ch. Meals on Wheels, San Antonio, 1992—93. Grantee Women and Minority Undergraduate Rsch. Program, U. Tex. San Antonio, 1994. Mem.: Coun. for Exceptional Children, Alphi Pi chpt. Alpha Chi, Golden Key. Democrat. Roman Catholic. Avocations: reading, historical research, cooking, gardening, movies. Office: HB Zachry Middle School 9410 Timber Path San Antonio TX 78250 Personal E-mail: ladybug88888888@hotmail.com.

DETMAR-PINES, GINA LOUISE, business strategy and policy educator; b. S.I., N.Y., May 3, 1949; d. Joseph and Grace Vivian (Brown) Sargente; m. Michael B. Pines, Sept. 11, 1988; 1 child, Drue Joseph Pines. BS in Edn., Wagner Coll., 1971, MS, 1972; MA in Urban Affairs and Policy Analysis, New Sch. for Social Rsch., 1987; MPhil, CUNY, 1995; PhD in Bus./Orgn. and Policy Studies, CUNY-Baruch Coll., 1997. Cert. adminstr. and supr., sch. dist. adminstr. Tchr. pub. schs., N.Y.C., 1971-82; coord. spl. projects, pub. affairs N.Y.C. Bd. Edn., 1982, spl. asst. to exec. dir. pupil svcs., 1983, asst. to chancellor, 1983-84, exec. dir. tchr. Summer Bus. Industry Program, 1984-93; prof. pub. adminstrn. and mgmt. John Jay Coll. Criminal Justice CUNY, 1992-93; prof. bus. Cen. Conn. State U., 2000—. Vis. prof. Rensselaer at Hartford, 1993—98, Fairfield U., 1998—2000; liaison for the Tech. Industry Program N.Y.C. Partnership, 1985—93. Mem. com. to re-elect Borough pres. Lamberti, S.I., 1985-86; chairperson Crystal Ball event Greater Hartford Easter Seals Rehab. Ctr., 1994, trustee, 1994—; bd. dirs. Hartford Symphony, com. mem. 50th Anniversary Gala, 1993. Mayor's scholar City of N.Y., 1984-96. Mem. ASPA, Fgn. Lang. Instrs. Assn., Strategic Mgmt. Soc., Acad. Mgmt., U.S. Seaplane Pilot's Assn., Internat. Orgn. for Lic. Women Pilots, Jr. League of Hartford, Hartford Task Force on Healthy Families, Chinese-Am. Soc., Am. Mgmt. Soc., Ea. Acad. Mgmt., Acad. of Internat. Bus., Cambridge Flying Group Club. Episcopalian. Avocations: flying, scuba diving, skiing. Office: Ctrl Conn State U 1615 Stanley St New Britain CT 06053-2439

DE TOLEDO, CATHERINE HOLT, medical writer; b. Columbus, Ohio, May 16, 1954; d. Golden Jr. and Petrea (Giles) Holt; m. Luiz Carlos de Toledo, Mar. 10, 1979; 1 child, Laura Holt. BS, Stanford U., 1976. Med. writer Alfred I. duPont Inst., Wilmington, Del., 1976-79; tchr. English Mich. Lang. Inst., Campinas, Brazil, 1980-81; propr. Belladerme Skin Care, Campinas, 1981-84; med. writer Louisville Hand Surgery, 1984-85; freelance med. writer Ft. Worth, 1985-98. Owner MedShare Office Concepts, 1998—. Asst. editor: Reconstruction of the Child's Hand, 1989; contbr. articles to various publs. Polit. Campaign Mgmt. Bd. dirs. North Tex. Planned Parenthood, 1992—, chmn. bd. 1998-2000. Mem. NAFE, Am. Med. Writers Assn., Soc. Profl. Journalists, Texpac Alliance (dist. chmn. 1989—, exec. com. 1990 2000), Tarrant County Med. Soc. Alliance (chmn. health fair 1988, v.p. publicity 1989, rep.-at-large 1990, pres.-elect 1992, pres. 1993), Tex. Med. Assn. Alliance (publ. editor 1990-92, legis. chmn. 1992, pres. 1993, v.p. legis. 1997), Women's Club Ft. Worth, Etta Newby Club. Avocations: running, sewing, biking, reading. Home and Office: 6651 Mike Lane Ct Fort Worth TX 76116-8112

DE TORNYAY, RHEBA, nursing educator, retired dean; b. Petaluma, Calif., Apr. 17, 1926; d. Bernard and Ella Fradkin; m. Rudy de Tornyay, June 4, 1954. Student, U. Calif., Berkeley, 1944-46; diploma, Mt. Zion Hosp. Sch. Nursing, 1949; AB, San Francisco State U., 1951, MA, 1954; Ed.D., Stanford U., 1967; Sc.D. (hon.), Ill. Wesleyan U., 1974; LHD (hon.), U. Portland, 1974, Georgetown U., 1994. Mem. faculty San Francisco State U., 1957-67, prof. nursing, 1966-67, chmn. dept., 1959-67; assoc. prof. U. Calif. Sch. Nursing, San Francisco, 1968-71, prof., 1971; dean, prof. Sch. Nursing UCLA, 1971-75; dean emeritus, prof. U. Wash., Seattle, 1986—. Author: Strategies for Teaching nursing, 1971, 3rd edit., 1987, Japanese transl., 1974, Spanish edit., 1986; co-author: (with Heather Young) Choices: Making a Good Move to a Retirement Community, 2001. Trustee emeritus Robert Wood Johnson Found. Mem. ANA, Am. Acad. Nursing (charter fellow, pres. 1973-75), Inst. Medicine (governing coun. 1979-81). Home: 4540 8th Ave NE Apt 1001 Seattle WA 98105-4795 E-mail: rheba@u.washington.edu.

DETTMER, HELENA R. classics educator; d. Terry Stone; children: Dan, Heather, Mike, Anne, Alex. BA in Classics, Ind. U., 1972; MA/PhD, U. Mich., 1976. Asst. prof. U. Iowa, Iowa City, 1976-83, assoc. prof., 1983-97, chair, 1993—, prof., 1997—, dir. interdisciplinary program, 2001—; co-editor Syllecta Classica, 1989—98. Author: Horace: A Study in Structure, 1983, Love By the Numbers: Form and Meaning in the Poetry of Catullus, 1997; contbr. articles to profl. jours. Mellon fellowship Duke U., 1977-78; faculty scholarship, 1986-89. Mem. Classical Assn. of Middle West and South (pres.-elect 1995-96, pres. 1996-97). Am. Philolog. Assn. Office: Univ Iowa 212 Schaeffer Hall Iowa City IA 52242-1409

DETWEILER-BEDELL, JERUSHA BETH, social sciences educator; b. Princeton, N.J., Sept. 10, 1973; d. Richard Allen and Carol Sue Detweiler; m. Brian Thomas Bedell, June 26, 1999. BA, MA, Stanford U., 1995; PhD, Yale U., New Haven, Conn., 1995—2001. Asst. dir. Yale Psychol. Svcs. Clinic, New Haven, 1998—99; clin. fellow and psychology intern McLean Hosp. Harvard Med. Sch., Belmont, Mass., 2000—01; asst. prof. of psychology Lewis and Clark Coll., Portland, Oreg., 2001—. Psychologist resident Lewis and Clark Coll. Counseling Ctr., Portland, Oreg., 2002—04. Author: Treatment Planning in Psychotherapy: Taking the Guesswork Out of Clin. Care, 2003; contbr. articles to profl. jours. Grad. Fellowship, Yale U., 1995-1999, Dissertation Fellowship, 1999-2000. Fellow: Bush Fellows of Yale U.; mem.: APA, Assn. for Advancement of Behavior Therapy, Am. Psychol. Soc. Achievements include research in message framing and sunscreen use. Avocation: travel. Office: Lewis and Clark College 0615 SW Palatine Hill Road Box 16 Portland OR 97219

DETWILER, CHRISTINA LEFEVRE, elementary school educator; b. Richmond, Va., July 27, 1968; d. Michael Roy and Linda Harris LeFevre; m. Scott Douglas Detwiler, Aug. 1, 1998; children: Sarah Catherine, Grayson Scott. Student, Longwood Coll., 1986—88, J. Sargeant Reynolds, Richmond, 1988—90, Va. Commonwealth U., 1990—91, BS in Psychology, MT in Elem. Edn., 1994. Postgrad. profl. lic. in early edn. NK-4. Kindergarten tchr. Elmont Elem., Ashland, Va., 1995—97, 1st grade loop tchr., 1997—98, 1st grade tchr., 1998—99, Acquinton Elem., King William, Va., 1999—2001. Active March of Dimes, Aylett, Va., 1998—, VFW, 1998—, Save the Mattaponi Orgn., King William, 1999—2003, Sept. 11 Fund, 2001, Va. Food Bank, 2003—. Mem.: NEA, Psi Chi, Sigma Kappa.

DEUSCHLE, CONSTANCE JOAN, counselor, educational consultant; b. Indpls., July 16, 1945; d. Delmar Sanford and Mildred Cynthia (Kreis) Gray; m. John Hanlan Deuschle, Nov. 12, 1966; children: Peter John, Thomas Scott, Matthew James. ASN, Southwestern Mich. U., 1976; BS, Ind. U., 1989, MS, 1991, EdD, 1999. Counselor Concord Cmty. Schs., Elkhart, Ind., 1986-92; cons. Ind. Dept. Edn., Indpls., 1992—; counselor Elkhart, 1992—. Cons. C.J. Cons., Goshen, Ind., 1992—; asst. prof. Ind. U., South Bend, 2000—. Co-author: Handbook for School Counselors: Stop the Bus, 2000; contbr. articles to profl. book. Educator drug & Alcohol awareness Concord Schs., 1983-92. Mem. Nat. Student Assistance Assn. (sec. 1995—), Ind. Assn. Student Assistance Programs (bd. dirs. 1994—). Roman Catholic. Avocations: writing, poetry, walking, travel. Home and Office: 58112 Orchard Ln Goshen IN 46528-9078 E-mail: cdeuschl@iusb.edu.

DEUSER, JANE, marketing professional; BA in French, U. Colorado. Mktg. mgr. N. Am. Meridien Hotels; consultant MindForce, N.Y.C. Sloan fellow London Business School; bd. mem. Am. Womens Econ. Devel. Corp. Office: Am Womens Econ Devel Corp 71 Vanderbilt Ave Ste 320 New York NY 10169-0005 also: MindForce Consulting 244 5th Ave Ste 2675 New York NY 10001

DEUTERMANN, JULIE CATERSON, social worker; b. Binghamton, N.Y., Sept. 5, 1962; d. Robert Kenneth and Mary Lee (Sterling) Caterson; m. Craig Charles Deutermann, May 19, 1989; children: Kevin Sterling, Tess Elizabeth. BA in Psychology cum laude, Gettysburg Coll., 1984; MSS, Bryn Mawr Coll., 1989. LCSW Pa., home and sch. visitor Pa. Ednl. cons., puppeteer The Kids on the Block, Inc., Alexandria, Va., 1984—86; social worker Bucks County Children & Youth, Doylestown, Pa., 1989—91; adoption coord. Pearl S. Buck Internat., Perkasie, Pa., 1993—2003; sch. social worker Lakeside Ednl. Network, Ft. Washington, Pa., 2002—03; home and sch. vis. Spring-Ford Sch. Dist., Royersford, Pa., 2003—. Meeting planner Caterson Consulting, Perkiomenville, Pa., 1999—2001. Recipient charter grant, Gettysburg Coll., 1984. Mem.: NASW. Presbyterian. Avocation: piano. Home: 1841 Perkiomenville Rd Perkiomenville PA 18074-9683 E-mail: jdeut@spring-ford.net.

DEUTSCH, NINA, pianist, vocalist; b. San Antonio, Mar. 15; d. Irvin and Freda (Smukler) Deutsch. BS, Juilliard Sch. Music, 1964; MMA, Yale U., 1973. Concert pianist internat. and U.S. tours, 1965-82; entertainer, solo pianist Holland Am. Cruise Lines, 1987, 89-90; freelance pianist, lectr. music, 1990—. Exec. v.p. Internat. Symphony, N.Y.C., 1978—82. Musician (pianist): (albums) Charles Ives, 1976; author: (plays) Portrait of Clara Schumann, 1987, Portrait of Liberace, 1995; contbr. articles to mags. and newspapers. Bd. dirs. Metzner Found. Overseas Relief; Ft. Lee coord. Channel 13, 1974. Recipient award for Am. music, Nat. Fedn. Music Clubs, 1975; grantee, Philips Petroleum Found., 1982; scholar, Oberlin Coll.; Tanglewood fellow, Wulsin Fellowship, 1966. Mem.: Yale Alumni Assn. Bergen County. Achievements include first American pianist to play all American music in communist China, 1982; first woman pianist to entertain for Holland America; first woman to record complete solo piano music of Charles Ives. Avocations: swimming, hiking, baking. Home: PO Box 405 Leonia NJ 07605-0405 Office Phone: 201-947-0087. E-mail: ianist100@aol.com.

DEUTSCHMAN, LOUISE TOLLIVER, curator; b. Taylorville, Ill., Sept. 6, 1921; arrived in France, 1950,arrived in U.S., 1966; BA MacMurray Coll., 1937; postgrad., Northwestern U., Sorbonne, Paris. Assoc. dir. Waddell Gallery, N.Y.C., 1966—74, Sidney Janis Gallery, N.Y.C., 1975—78; dir. Alex Rosenberg Gallery, N.Y.C., 1978—80; assoc. dir. Sidney Janis Gallery, N.Y.C., 1980—2000, curator Pace Wildenstein, N.Y.C., 2000—.

DEUTZ, NATALIE RUBINSTEIN, actress, consultant; b. Plymouth, Mass., Sept. 26; d. Louis and Lillian Rubinstein; m. Nov. 29, 1947 (dec.). Student, Simmons Coll., Modern Sch. Applied Art. Fashion buyer Wm. Filene's Sons Co., Boston, 1940-47; asst. to corp. pres. Columbia Textiles, Inc., N.Y.C., 1956-58; dir. John Robert Powers Sch., N.Y.C., 1968 72; v.p., nat. dir. fashion merchandising, dir. advt. workshop Barbizon Internat., Inc., N.Y.C., 1972-83. Cons. 1983— Films include Arthur on the Rocks, Crocodile Dundee, Moonstruck, Six Degrees of Separation; appeared on (TV) Sopranos; appeared in Super Elderly People for Japanese TV; commls. include Rogaine, Levis, Blockbuster. Mem.: AFTRA, SAG.

DEVAN, DEBORAH HUNT, lawyer; b. Allentown, Pa., Jan. 22, 1950; d. Valerio R. and Audrey (Miller) H.; m. Mark S. Devan, May 30, 1981; children: Emily, David, Eric. BA in Econs. magna cum laude, U. Md., 1972, JD cum laude, 1975. Bar: Md. 1975, D.C. 1976, U.S. Dist. Ct. Md. 1976, U.S. Dist. Ct. D.C. 1987, U.S. Ct. Appeals (4th cir.) 1988, U.S. Ct. Appeals (2d cir.) 1991, U.S. Supreme Ct. 1980, Md. Ct. Appeals 1975, D.C. Ct. Appeals 1976. Ptnr. Weinberg and Green, Balt., 1974-94; prin. Neuberger, Quinn, Gielen, Rubin & Gibber, P.A., Balt., 1994—. Bd. dirs. Lutheran Hosp. Md., Inc., 1981-86, Cystic Fibrosis Found., 1983 (Community Svc. Gold award), Lutheran Health Care Corp., 1988-91, U. Md. Law Sch. Fund, 1991, Balt. Devel. Corp., 1999—, U. Md. Sch. Law Alumni Assn., 2000—; trustee Merry-Go-Round Enterprises, Inc. Fellow Am. Coll. Bankruptcy; mem. ABA (bus. bankruptcy com., subcommittee bankruptcy litigation, subcommittee claims and priorities), Am. Bankruptcy Inst., Turnaround Mgmt. Assn., Women's Bar Assn., Assn. Comml. Fin. Attys., Md. State Bar Assn., Inc. (subcommittee creditor's rights, bankruptcy and insolvency), Bankruptcy Bar Assn. Md. (corp. sec., bd. dirs., pres. 1996-97), Exec. and Profl. Women's Coun. Md. (1st v.p. 1984), Network 2000, Comml. Real Estate Women, Bar Assn. Balt. City (profl. ethics com. 1980, publicity com. 1981). Office: Neuberger Quinn Gielen Rubin & Gibber 1 South St Fl 27 Baltimore MD 21202-3282

DEVANE, MINDY KLEIN, financial planner; b. Detroit, May 4, 1954; d. Myer and Maxine (Gold) Klein; m. Kenneth Manuel DeVane, Nov. 20, 1993. BS in Journalism, U. Fla., 1976, MBA in Fin., 1981. CFP. Mktg. rep. IBM, Tampa, 1981-85; account exec. Thomson McKinnon, Tampa, 1985-88, Smith Barney, Miami, 1988-89; underwriter Cigna, North Miami, Fla., 1989-92; sr. account exec. Cohig & Assocs., Tampa, 1992-93; v.p. Josephthal Lyon & Ross, Tampa, 1993-96; v.p. investments Raymond James, Tampa, 1996-99; fin. planner Griffith Bowles Fin. Mgmt. First Union Securities, Tampa, 1999—2001; proprietor DeVane Fin. Advisors, Tampa, 2001—. Allocations com. mem. United Way, Pinellas County, Fla., 1998, Hillsborough County, Fla., 1999; founder Hyde Park Exec. Women Leader Club, 1999-2002; bd. dirs. Vivo Fla. Orch. Guild, Sword of Hope; mem. ACS Guild. Recipient Outstanding Fin. Advisor award Asset Mgmt. Svcs. RJF, 1996-97. Mem. Fin. Planners Assn. (pres.-elect), Bus. and Profl. Women (editor 1986-88). Avocations: bicycling, swimming, collectibles. Home: 6308 Jacqueline Arbor Dr Temple Terrace FL 33617-3164 Office: PO Box 16626 Tampa FL 33687 E-mail: mdevane@tampabay.rr.com.

DEVANEY, CYNTHIA ANN, elementary school educator, secondary school educator, real estate broker; b. Gary, Ind., Feb. 6, 1947; d. Charles Barnard and Irene Mae (Nelson) Burner; m. Harold Verne DeVaney, Nov. 23, 1974 (dec. 1981). BS, Ball State U., 1970, MS, 1972; postgrad., Ind. U. and Purdue U., 1974-76. Cert. real estate broker, Ind. Real estate broker Century 21 McColly Realtors, Highland, Ind., 1979-86, GMAC McColly Realtors, Merrillville, 1986—, with Pres.' Coun.; tchr. Merkley Elem. Sch., Highland, Ind., 1969—2002; student tchr. supr. Ind. U., Bloomington, 2002—. Supr. student tchrs., Ind. U. Active Schubert Theater Guild, Chgo. Mem. N.W. Ind. Bd. Realtors (Million Dollar Club), Nat. Bd. Realtors, Jr. Ind Hist. Soc., Innsbrook Country Club, Match Point Tennis Club. Democrat. Methodist. Avocations: golf, tennis, traveling, gardening, theater. Home: 607 E 78th Pl Merrillville IN 46410-5624 Office: McColly GMAC 2000 W 45th Ave Highland IN 46322-2504 E-mail: cindevaney@aol.com.

DEVARD, JERRI, marketing professional; BA in Econs., Spelman Coll., 1979; MBA in Mktg., Atlanta U., 1983. Mktg. asst. The Pillsbury Co., Mpls., 1983—92, group mktg. mgr. cake mixes divsn., 1992—93; dir. suites mktg. Minn. Vikings, 1993—94; v.p. mktg. Harrah's Entertainment, New Orleans, 1994—96; v.p. mktg. Color Cosmetics Revlon, 1996; with Citigroup, chief mktg. officer e-Consumer line of bus.; sr. v.p. brand mgmt. and mktg. comm. Verizon Comms., N.Y.C., 2003—. Bd. dirs. Exec. Leadership Coun. Found. Mem.: Nat. Black MBA Assn., Spelman Coll. Alumnae Assn. Office: Verizon Communications Inc 1095 Ave of the Americas New York NY 10036-6797*

DEVARIS, JEANNETTE MARY, psychologist; b. Burbank, Calif., Jan. 7, 1947; d. Nicholas Propper Klein and Elizabeth (Von Lichtenberg) Schaeffer; m. Robert Lee Blake, May 20, 1967 (div. 1979); 1 child: Brendon; m. Panayotis Eric DeVaris, Dec. 5, 1988. BA, Adelphi U., 1968; MA, Fairleigh Dickinson U., 1977; PhD, Seton Hall U., 1987. Lic. psychologist, N.J. Caseworker [illegible], 1966-72, alcohol and drug rehab. counselor U.S. Army, Ft. Monmouth, NJ, 1972-76; psychol. intern N.J. State Intern Program, Trenton, 1977-78; psychologist Greystone Psychiat. Hosp., Greystone Park, NJ, 1979; sr. psychologist R. Hall Cmty. Mental Health Ctr., Bridgewater, NJ, 1979-90; pvt. practice South Orange and Somerset, NJ, 1988—. Tng. supr. Grad. Sch. Applied and Profl. Psychology; adj. prof. Seton Hall U.; sponsor and participant in Cable TV program; mem. South Orange Critical Support Team Vol. Group of Psychologists. Contbr. articles to profl. jours. Mem. APA, Nat. Register Health Svc. Providers, N.J. Psychol. Assn. (bd. dirs., interprofl. rels. com.), Soc. Psychologists in Pvt. Practice (bd. dirs., spkrs. bur. com.). Avocations: travel, reading. Office Phone: 973-762-3149. E-mail: drdevaris@aol.com.

DE VARONA, DONNA, sports reporter, former Olympic swimmer; b. San Diego, Apr. 26, 1947; m. John Pinto; 2 children. BA in polit. sci., UCLA; four doctoral degrees (hon.). On-air analyst, commentator, host, writer ABC Sports, 1965—76, 1983—98, Olympic Coverage NBC, 1976—83; radio host Donna de Varona on Sports. Chair Women's World Cup Soccer Tournament Organizing Com., 1999; served on US Sec. Edn. Commn. on Opportunity in Athletics, 2002—03; founding mem., first pres. Women's Sport Found., 1979—84; served four terms Pres. Coun. Physical Fitness and Sports. Named Most Outstanding Female Athlete World, AP, 1964, United Press Internat. (UPI), 1964; named to US Olympic Hall Fame, Bay Area Hall Fame, San Jose Hall Fame, Woman's Hall Fame, 2003; recipient Internat. Swimming Hall Fame Gold Medallion, Olympia Award for contbn. to Olympic Movement, Olympic Order, Internat. Olympic Com., Susan B. Anthony Trailblazer award, Overcoming Obstacle award, Cmty. Edn. Found., 2002, Theodore Roosevelt (Teddy) award, Nat. Collegiate Athletic Assn. (NCAA), Emmy award for Special Olympics coverage, 1991. Achievements include youngest competitor at 1960 Olympics games; broke 18 world swimming records; won 2 Olympic Gold medals, 400-meter individual medley and 4 by 100 meter relay, 1964 Olympics; won 37 national championships; first female sports broadcaster on network TV, 1965; first woman to do TV commentary on Olympics, 1968; active in passing 1978 Amateur Sports Act by US Congress and 1972 landmark "Title IX" legis.*

DEVAUD, JUDITH ANNE See HALVORSON, JUDITH

DEVAUGHAN, JEWELL L. music educator; b. Lookeba, Okla., Dec. 27, 1920; d. Wilburn Elijah and Charity May (Dorrough) D. Piano tchr. Okla. Fedn. Music Clubs, Sulphur, 1964—, Okla. Music Tchrs. Assn., Sulphur, 1966—. Tchr. pvt. piano lessons for 38 yrs. Recreation hostess Salvation Army, 1945; pianist spl. svc. civilian 97th U.S. Army Dance Band, Ft. Sill, 1946-50; pianist Sr. Citizens Hospitality, 1963-66, sr. citizens clubs, 1971-73. Avocations: choir, group singing, vocal accompanist.

DEVAUL, DIANE D. policy director; b. Ames, Iowa, July 12, 1943; d. Wayne Allen DeVaul and Ruth Louise Dana; m. Thomas Andrew Twomey, June 6, 1965 (div. Oct. 1978); children: Heather B. Twomey, Antonio DeVaul; m. Hagos Alemayehu, Apr. 30, 1982; 1 chlid, Victor Hagos DeVaul. BA, U. Iowa, 1965; MA, U. Md., 1972, PhD, 1998. Instr. Am. U., George Mason U., U. Md., 1976-77; policy analyst N.E.-Midwest Inst., Washington, 1978-86, dir. policy, 1986—; cons. to asst. sec. U.S. Dept. HUD, Washington, 1979. Dir. N.E. Regional Resource Ctr. for Innovation, U.S. Dept. Energy, Washington, 1997-2002, mem. grant rev. panel, 1998-2001; presenter in field. Author poetry book, 1979; contbr. articles to profl. jours. Recipient Commendation, Gov. of N.H., 1998. Mem. Am. Studies Assn. Office: NE-Midwest Inst 218 D St SE Washington DC 20003 E-mail: ddevaul@nemw.org.

DEVAULT, KATHY, psychiatric consultant, liaison nurse; b. Bklyn., July 30, 1943; children: David S. IV, Megan. BS in Health Arts, Coll. St. Francis, Joliet, Ill., 1991; MS in Psychiat. Mental Health Nursing, Rush U., Chgo., 1996, DNursing, 1997. RN, N.Y.; cert. clin. specialist. Head nurse Caledonian Hosp., Bklyn., 1966-67, recovery rm. supr., clin. instr., 1967-69; intensive care supr. Arnold Gregory Meml. Hosp., Albion, N.Y., 1969-72; nurse practitioner in pvt. practice, Albion, 1972-74, Batavia (N.Y.) VA Hosp., 1974-77, Buffalo VA Hosp., 1978-79, Cook County Hosp., Chgo., 1981-98, psychiat. cons.-liaison nurse, 1998—. Mem. Town Coun., Beverly Shores, Ind., 1996—, mem. Plan Commn., 1998—; bd. officer Assn. Beverly Shores Residents, 1988-98. Mem. ANA, AAUW, Am. Psychiat. Nurses Assn., Internat. Soc. Psychiat. Nurses. Avocations: photography, reading. Office: Adminstrn Bldg 1900 W Polk St Rm 839 Chicago IL 60612-3736

DEVENY, CHARLOTTE PERRY, musician, educator; b. Maywood, Ill., Apr. 29, 1930; d. Lester Earl Perry and Armede Cooper Draper; m. Glenn Lindquist Harris, Aug. 5, 1950 (div. Apr. 1963); children: Charlotte Armede, Catherine Elizabeth; m. Edwin Rountree Deveny, Feb. 16, 1991. Student Piano Lower Conservatory, Chgo. Mus. Coll., 1936-42; MusB, Northwestern U., 1951. Performer, accompanist, Chgo., 1942—; cellist San Antonio Symphony, 1949; tchr. class piano and strings Park Ridge (Ill.) Sch. Dist., 1951-52; freelance musician various movie, TV, and rec. studios, L.A., 1952-61; cellist Lawrence Welk Orch., L.A., 1961-78; pvt. tchr. piano and cello Palos Verdes, Calif., 1978—; co-dir. Deveny Music Sc., Palos Verdes, 1991—. Recipient over 30 first-pl. medals in piano and cello, Ill., 1936-42. Mem. DAR, Music Tchrs. Nat. Assn., Music Tchrs. Assn. Calif. (pres. South Bay 1983-87, 91-92, 1999-2000). Avocations: reading, writing short stories. Home and Office: PO Box 4328 Palos Verdes Peninsula CA 90274

DEVER, MAUREEN BRIGID, pediatric nurse practitioner; b. Phila., Mar. 4, 1965; d. Raymond and Margaret Mary (Ryan) Wright; m. Daniel Mersiowsky (div.); 1 child, Ashley Margaret Mersiowsky ; m. Michael J. Dever, Feb. 3, 2001; 1 child, Sean Michael. BSN, Temple U., 1987; MSN, Hahnemann U., 2000. RN 1987, cert. Nephrology Nurse, 1997, Cert. Registered Nurse Practitioner, 2000. Pediatric nurse St. Christopher's Hosp. for Children, Phila., 1987—90, pediatric dialysis nurse, 1990—2000, pediatric endocrinology nurse practitioner, 2000—. Mem.: Am. Diabetic Assn., Pediatric Endocrine Nurse Soc. (participant mentor/preceptorship program), Am. Nephrology Nurse Assn., NAPNAP, Sigma Theta Tau. Office: St Christophers Hosp for Children Front St & Erie Ave Philadelphia PA 19134 Office Phone: 215-427-8100. E-mail: Maureen.Dever@tenethealth.com.

DEVERA, GERTRUDE QUENANO, education educator; b. Malasiqui, Pangasinan, Philippines, Dec. 15, 1924; came to U.S., 1950; d. Paulino Castro and Filomena (del Rosario) Magsanoc; m. Perfecto Tamondong DeVera, June 23, 1946 (dec. Sept. 1976). BA, San Francisco State U., 1952; postgrad., U. Calif., Berkeley, 11952-54; MA in English Lit., San Francisco State U., 1956. Calif. tchrs. cert. and life diploma. Tchr. San Francisco Unified Sch. Dist., 1956-88, demonstration tchr., 1958-59; mem. aux. bd. trustees Don Adriano Geslani Montessori Sch., Malasiqui, Luzon, The Philippines, 1997—. Tchr. participant Project Read Behavioral Rsch. Labs., Palo Alto, Calif., 1967-68; cert. demonstrator Astra's Magic Math-Alphaphonics, 1987-88; rschr. in preventive medicine, San Francisco, 1975—. Editing chmn.: Guidelines for Use of the Eudcational Facilities Planning model, 1968 (NDEA award 1968). Summer Inst. grantee NDEA, U. Wash., Seattle, 1968; recipient Hon. Svc. awards Calif. Congress Parents and Tchrs. Inc., Sacramento, 1975, San Francisco 2nd Dist., 1980. Mem. AAUW (legis. interview com. 1970's), Internat. Platform Assn., World Affairs Coun. No. Calif., Libr. of Congress. Democrat. Roman Catholic. Avocations: reading, creative writing, public speaking, attending lectures, various cultural pursuits.

DEVERAUX, JUDE (JUDE GILLIAM WHITE), writer; b. Louisville, Sept. 20, 1947; d. Harold J. and Virgina (Berry) Gilliam; m. Richard G. Sides, 1967 (div. 1969); m. Claude B. White, 1970 (div. 1993). BS Fine Arts, Murray State U., 1970; Cert. in Teaching, Coll. Santa Fe, 1973. Cert. remedial reading tchr. Tchr. elem. sch., Santa Fe, 1970-76; writer, 1976—. Author novels including: The Enchanted Land, 1978, The Black Lyon, 1980, The Velvet Promise, 1981, Casa Grande, 1982, Highland Velvet, 1982, Velvet Song, 1983, Velvet Angel, 1983, Sweetbriar, 1983, Countefeit Lady, 1984, Lost Lady, 1985, River Lady, 1985, Twin of Ice, 1985, Twin of Fire, 1985, The Temptress, 1986, The Raider, 1987, The Princess, 1987, The Maiden, 1988, The Awakening, 1988, The Taming, 1989, A Knight in Shining Armor, 1990, Wishes, 1990, Mountain Laurel, 1990, The Conquest, 1991, The Duchess, 1991, Sweet Liar, 1992, Eternity, 1992, The Invitation, 1993, Remembrance, 1994, Legend, 1996, An Angel for Emily, 1998, The Blessing, 1999, High Tide, 2000, Temptation, 2000, Twin of Fire/Twin of Ice, 2001, The Summerhouse, 2001, A Knight in Shining Armor, 2002, The Mulberry Tree, 2002, Forever, 2002, Wild Orchids, 2003, Forever and Always, 2003, Holly, 2003, Eternity, 2004, The Princess, 2004, Wishes, 2004, River Lady, 2004. Mem. Costume Soc. Am. Avocations: cooking, computers, travel, collecting books on costume history, reading english history. Office: Pocket Books Simon & Schuster Inc 1230 Avenue Of The Americas New York NY 10020-1586*

DE VERITCH, NINA, cellist, music educator; b. Montclair, N.J., Aug. 18, 1941; Student, U. So. Calif., 1959-61, Juilliard Sch. Music, 1961-63. Mem. Detroit Symphony Orch., 1968-70; recording artist movies, records, TV, 1971-74; prin. cellist Utah Symphony, 1964-68; mem. faculty U. Utah, 1964-67, Brigham Young U., 1964-68; studio tchr., adjudicator I, master classes, 1980—; freelance cellist, artist tchr., 2002—. Vis. assoc. prof. U. Mich., 1990-91; prin. cellist Ann Arbor Chamber Orchestra, 1988-90. Mem.: Michiana Cello Soc. (past sec., bd. dirs.), Mich. Music Tchrs. Assn., Am. Fedn. Musicians, Am. String Tchrs. Assn. Home: 9800 Adolphus Dr Frisco TX 75035-7073

DEVERS, GAIL, track and field athlete; b. Seattle, Nov. 19, 1966; BA in Sociology, UCLA, 1988. Gold medalist, 100m Track and Field Barcelona Olympic Games, 1992; Gold medalist 100m, 100m Hurdles World Track and Field Championships, Stuttgart, Germany, 1993; Gold medalist, 100m Track and Field Atlanta Olympic Games, 1996, Gold medalist 4x100m relay, 1996, World Championships, 1997; founder, CEO Gail Force, Inc. Founder Gail Devers Found. Named Nat. champion 100m hurdles, 1991, 1992, 1993, 1993, 1995, 1996, Nat. indoor champion 60m, 1993, World indoor champion 60m, 1993, World champion 100m, 1993, 1995, World champion 100m hurdles, 1993, Athlete of Yr., Women's Sports Found., 1997. Achievements include overcoming Graves disease to win multiple Olympic medals. Office: Elite Intl Sports Mkt PO Box 69047 Saint Louis MO 63169-0047

DEVI, AMRITANANDAMAYI (SRI MATA AMRITANANDAMAYI DEVI), spiritual advisor; b. Kerala, India, 1953; Founder Amrita Inst. Med. Scis., Mata Amritanandamayi Mission Trust, Gujarat Earthquake Relief Effort; pres. Centenary Parliament of World Religions, Chgo.; spkr. UN. Recipient Gandhi-King award for Non-Violence, 2002. Office: Sri Mata Amma Amritapuri PO Box Kallam Kerala India also: MA Ctr PO Box 613 San Ramon CA 94583

DEVIGNE, KAREN COOKE, retired amateur athletics executive; b. Phila., July 31, 1943; d. Paul and Matilda (Rich) Cooke; m. Jules Lloyd Devigne, June 26, 1965; children: Jules Paul, Denise Paige, Paul Michael. AA, Centenary Coll., Hackettstown, 1963; student, Northwestern U., 1963-65; BA, Ramapo Coll., Mahwah, 1976; MA, Emory U., Atlanta, 1989. Founder GYMSET, Marietta, Ga., 1981—. Cons. Girls Club Am. Marietta, 1989; vol. Cobb County Gymnastic Ctr., Marietta, 1976-95, Ga. Youth Soccer Assn., Atlanta, 1976-95; fundraiser Scottish Rite Children's Hosp., Atlanta, 1989. Recipient recognition awards from various youth groups, Atlanta, 1976—; named Nominee Woman of Yr. ABC News, Atlanta, 1984. Avocations: skiing, tennis, bridge. Home: 4662 Wynmeade Pk NE Marietta GA 30067 also: 7 Sunrise Point Dr Breckenridge CO 80424

DEVIN, IRENE K. state legislator, nurse; b. Sumter, S.C., Jan. 24, 1943; m. Jerry Devin. BSN, U. Iowa, 1965. RN. Mem. Wyo. Ho. Rep., Cheyenne, 1992-96, Wyo. Senate, Dist. 10, Cheyenne, 1996—; mem. edn. com. Wyo. Senate, Cheyenne, mem. labor, health, and social svcs. com. Trustee Dist. Hosp., 1986-92, past pres.; mem. Laramie Econ. Devel. Corp., Friends of 4-H; pres. Ivinson Meml. Hosp. Found.; mem. state adv. bd. Medicaid, Rural Health TB Program; mem. adv. bd. Cmty. Pub. Health. Mem. Laramie C. of C., Soroptomists Internat. Republican. Home: 3601 Grays Gable Rd Laramie WY 82072-5032 Office: Wyo Senate State Capitol Cheyenne WY 82002-0001

DEVINE, BARBARA ARMSTRONG, risk manager; b. Lawrence, Kans., Mar. 2, 1965; BS in Microbiology, U. Ill., 1987; MBA, Lake Forest (Ill.) Grad. Sch., 1997; postgrad., George Washington U. Cert. purchasing mgr. R & D technician Abbott Labs., Abbott Park, Ill., 1987-90, asst. scientist, 1990-91, assoc. biochemist, 1991-93, purchasing agt., 1993-95, sr. purchasing agt., 1995-96, sect. head med. writing, 1996-97, sr. label editor, 1997-99, labeling group leader, 1999; chem. sales rep. AIC, Inc., Natick, Mass., 1999-2001; sr. purchasing agt. TAP Pharm. Products, Lake Forest, Ill., 2000—02, risk manager, 2002—. Patentee in field. Vol. Choices program Abbott Labs., 1994-99; bd. dirs. HIV Coalition, Wheeling, Ill., 1997. Named Outstanding Buyer, Chgo. Minority Bus. Devel. Coun., 1996. Mem. NAFE, AAUW, Risk and Ins. Mgmt. Soc., Inst. for Supply Mgmt., Project Mgmt. Inst. Achievements include patents in field. Home: 1903 S Warbler Ct Libertyville IL 60048-4612 E-mail: barbara.devine@tap.com.

DEVINE, CHRISTINE, newscaster; BA in journalism, Walter Cronkite Sch. Journalism and Telecom. Ariz. State U. Anchor, co-prodr. weeknight news 6pm and 10pm KLST-TV, San Angelo, Tex., 1988; anchor KVOA-TV, Tucson, 1988—90; weekend anchor, gen. assignment reporter KTTV, LA, 1990—92, co-anchor Fox 11 10 O'Clock News, 1992—. Named Best Anchor Team, AP, 1996. Office: KTTV FOX 11 1999 S Bundy Dr Los Angeles CA 90025-5235*

DEVINE, KATHERINE, environmental consultant, educator; b. Denver, Oct. 15, 1951; BS, Rutgers U., 1973, MS, 1980; postgrad., U. Md., 1981-82. Lab. technician Princeton (N.J.) U., 1974-76; econ. and regulatory affairs analyst, program mgr. U.S. EPA, Washington, 1979-89, cons., 1989-99; exec. dir. Applied BioTreatment Assn., Washington, 1990-91; pres. DEVO Enterprises, Inc., Washington, 1990-99; sr. editor Scientist, Phila., 2000—01; tchr. Phila. Sch. Dist., 2001—. Chair adv. bd. Applied Bioremediation Conf., 1993; co-chair Environ. Biotech. Conf., 1996, 97, others. Author: N.J. Agricultural Experiment Station of Rutgers Uniersity, 1980, Bioremediation Case Studies: An Analysis of Vendor Supplied Data, 1992, Bioremediation Case Studies: Abstracts, 1992; co-author: Biomediation: Field Experiences, 1994, Bioremediation, 1994; founder, pub., editor (mag.) Biotreatment News, 1990-97; pub. The Gold Book; editor Indsl. Biotech. News, 1998; contbr. articles to profl. jours., chpts. to books; co-sponsor over 20 confs. Mem. Women's Coun. on Energy and the Environment, 1991-93. Recipient numerous fed. govt. and non- govt. awards. Mem. Am. Chem. Soc., Futures for Children, Alpha Zeta. E-mail: devoinc@aol.com.

DEVINE, LIBBY, art educator, consultant; b. Indpls., Jan. 31, 1952; d. Taylor William and Elizabeth Josephine Jackson; m. Douglas M. Devine, June 12, 1976. BFA, U. Ga., 1974; M of Visual Arts, Ga. State U., 1980. [illegible] Adolescence through Young Adult. Tchr. art, dept. chair Roswell (Ga.) H.S./Fulton County Schs., 1980—; cons. Ga. Dept. of Edn. Test Devel., Tchr. Cert. Test in Art, 1988—90; sch. arts program coord. Fulton County Dept. of Edn., Fulton County Arts Coun., 1988—, cons. coll. bd., 2002—03; presenter in field. Contbr. articles;, editor curriculum guide. Grantee, Fulton County Arts Coun., 2003—04. Mem.: Profl. Assn. Ga. Educators, Ga. Art Edn. Assn., Nat. Art Edn. Assn. (grant 1991). Office: Roswell HS 11595 King Rd Roswell GA 30075

DEVINE, NANCY, postmaster; b. Hyannis, Mass., Feb. 8, 1949; d. Joseph Peter and Rose (Almeida) Cabral; m. Michael G. Devine, Mar. 20, 1971 (div. 1975); 1 child, Paul. Student, U. Mass., 1967-70. Postal clk. U.S. Postal Svc., Centerville, Mass., 1977-80, postmaster West Hyannisport, Mass., 1980—. Affirmative Action planner U.S. Postal Svc., Brockton, Mass., 1979-80, prin. rep /exec. bd., Providence, 1993. Painter in acrylics. Art and Humanities grantee Barnstable Arts Coun., Mass. Art Coun., Nat. Endowment for the Arts. Mem. Nat. Assn. Women Artists, Cape Cod Art Assn., Smithsonian Instn. Home: PO Box 361 West Hyannisport MA 02672-0361 E-mail: ncdevine@mailcity.com.

DEVINE, SHARON JEAN, lawyer; b. Milw., Feb. 27, 1948; d. George John Devine and Ethel May (Langworthy) Devine Chase; children: Devin Curtiss, Katharine Langworthy. BS in Linguistics magna cum laude, Georgetown U., 1970; JD, Boston U., 1975. Bar: Ohio, Colo. Staff atty. FTC, Cleve., 1975-79, asst. regional dir. Denver, 1982-84; atty. Mountain Bell, Denver, 1982-84, U.S. West Direct, 1984-85, assoc. gen. counsel, 1985-87, Landmark Pub. Co., Denver, 1987-88; antitrust counsel U.S. West, Denver, 1988-91, corp. counsel, 1991-99, assoc. gen. counsel, 1999-2000, 2 West Commns. Internat. Inc., 2000—. Dir. Denver Consortium, 1982-83, Ctr. for Applied Prevention, Boulder, Colo., 1982-90; dir. Legal Aid Found. of Colo., 1990-96, Suzuki Assn. of Colo., 1990-94. Active mem. Jr. League, Denver, 1980-87. Mem. Am. Corp. Counsel Assn. (dir. Colo. chpt. 1994-2000, pres. 1999-2000), Colo. Bar Assn., Denver Assn., Colo. Women's Bar Assn.- Home: 118 Pika Rd Boulder CO 80302-9517 Office: 2West 1801 California St Ste 4900 Denver CO 80202-2610 E-mail: sjdevine@qwest.com.

DEVITO, TERESA MARIE, artist; b. Bangoli del Tigino, Italy, June 11, 1920; came to U.S., 1924, naturalized, 1926; d. Bartolomeo and Santo Donatello Cimaglia; m. Americao DeVito; children: Richard (dec.), Sandra Ann DeVito King. BA inEdn., Fairmont State Coll., 1960, MA, W.Va. U., 1964; postgrad., Wagner Coll., 1968; D (hon.), Minsitry Fgn. Affairs of Malta. Tchr. East Fairmont (W.Va.) High Sch., 1960-68, Miller Jr. High Sch., Rivesville, W.Va., 1969-70; instr. art Fairview H.S., 1970-86, Barrockville H.S., Farmington H.S. One-woman shows include Lynn Katler Gallery, N.y.C., 1975; exhibited at group shows at Morgantown Art Assn. Exhbn., 1960; commd. work includes paintings on cloth at Immaculate Conception Ch., Fairmont, Fairmont Bowling Ctr., 1988, Disney World. Recipient Internat. Statue of Victory, Einstein Peace Medal, Rhodeodendron Festival award, Honoris Causea, Internat. Found., 1987. Mem. AAUW, NEA, Nat. Art Edn. Assn., Tole Painters Am., W.Va. Art Assn., W.Va. Artist and Craftsman Guild, Artists Equity, League Ind. Artists (past v.p.), Village Garden Club, Cath. Daus. Am. (State Ct. of W.Va. award, Nat. Merit award for "Face in a Cloud" entry in poster contest, 2000), Quota Internat. Orgn. Roman Catholic. Home: 417 Newton St Fairmont WV 26554-5218

DEVLIN, BARBARA JO, school district administrator; b. Milw., Oct. 6, 1947; d. Raymond Peter Seeley and Lois Elsa Young; m. John Edward Devlin, June 23, 1973; 2 children. BA, Gustavus Adolphus Coll., 1969; MA, U. Mass., 1971; PhD, U. Minn., 1978. Cert. tchr., sch. prin., supt., Minn.; cert. supt., Ill., Minn. Tchr. Worthington (Minn.) High Sch., 1971-75; rsch. assoc. Ednl. R & D, Mpls.-St. Paul, 1975-76, 76-77; coord. edn. svcs. Ednl. Coop. Svc., Mpls.-St. Paul, 1977-79; dir. personnel Minnetonka Pub. Schs., Excelsior, Minn., 1979-85, asst. supt., 1985-87; supt. Sch. Dist. 45, Villa Park, Ill., 1987-95, Ind. Sch. Dist. 280, Richfield, Minn., 1995—. Editor working papers Gov.'s Coun. on Fluctuating Enrollments, St. Paul, 1976. Contbr. articles to ednl. jours. Bd. dirs. Richfield Found., 1995—. Ednl. Policy fellow George Washington U., 1977-78; mem. fellow program Bush Found. Pub. Schs., 1984-85; named Ill. Supt. of the Yr., 1994; recipient Disting. Alumni award Gustavus Adolphus Coll., 1994. Mem. Richfield C. of C. (bd. dirs. 1996-99), Rotary Internat. (membership chair Villa Park unit 1989-91, vocat. dir. 1991-92, sec. 1992-93, pres. 1994-95), Rotary Dist. 5950 (leader), Optimists Internat. (pres. elect Richfield unit 1998-99, pres. 1999-2000). Methodist. Office: Richfield Pub Schs 7001 Harriet Ave Richfield MN 55423-3061 E-mail: Barbara.Devlin@richfiedl.k12.mn.us.

DEVLIN, JEAN THERESA, education educator, storyteller; b. Jamaica, N.Y., Apr. 14, 1947; d. Edward Philip and Frances Margaret (Tillman) Creagh; children: Michael, Bernadette, Patrick. BA magna cum laude, Queens Coll., 1972, postgrad., 1994—95; MA, St. John's U., Jamaica, 1987; PhD, So. Ill. U., 1991. Substitute tchr. Diocese of Bklyn., 1969-75; tchr. St. Gregory's Sch., Bellerose, N.Y., 1975-82; dist. mgr. Creative Expressions, Robesonia, Pa., 1980-83; asst. to dean, adj. instr. workshop supr. Spl. Univ. Program St. John's U., Jamaica, 1983-87, asst. prof. dept. English, 1992; asst. dean St. John's Coll. Liberal Arts, St. Johns U., 1993-94; owner Tara's Tees and Golden Hands Embroidery, 1984-87; from grad. asst. to doctoral fellow English dept. So. Ill. U., Carbondale, 1987-89, storytelling tchr. Continuing Edn., 1992; adj. asst. prof. St. John's U., Jamaica, 1992-94, Poly. U., N.Y., 1995-96, Bayside Acad., N.Y., 1995-97, St. Anthony's H.S., Huntington, N.Y., 1996-99; tchr. SCOPE (gifted and talented program) South Huntington Dist., N.Y., 1999-2000; tchr., asst. prin., tchr. Rambam Mesivta Maimonides H.S., Lawrence, NY, 1999—2001; tchr. Hicksville H.S., 2002, North Shore Hebrew Acad. H.S., 2002—; asst. prof. L.I. Conservatory, 2002—03. Cons. Family Lit. Project; supr. workshops Popular Culture, 1991-94, Children's Lit. Assn., 1990-92, Midwest Popular Culture, 1991, Wyo. Centennial, 1990; presenter poetry readings, dramatic interpretation, storytelling, including Internat. Rsch. Soc. in Children's Lit., Paris, 1991, Nat. Coun. Tchrs. English Conf., 1992, Ill. Assn. Tchrs. of English, 1990, 91, 92, South Atlantic MLA, 1992, Mid Atlantic Popular/Am. Culture, 1993; speaker Speak Easy Workshop, 1981; showcased Nat. Congress Storytelling, Children's Reading Roundtable, 1990; world-wide storyteller, 1991—; featured spkr. Puppet Guild of L.I., 1997; adj. asst. prof. So. Ill., St. John's U., Polytechnic U., Molloy Coll., 1998—, SUNY, Farmingdale, 2002—. Author: Gabby Diego, 1992, repub. 1994, Rainbows Stories and Customs from Around the World, 1996; contbr. articles to profl. jours. and children's mags.; contbg. photographer Eye of the Beholder, 2000; actress (videotape and audiocassette) Peter Kagan and the Wind, 1990, 91, played at White House, 1992, Sta. WKTS, 1992-94, Excerpts from Shakespeare, 1999, (videotape) Puppets from A to Z, 2000; performed as storyteller on 5 continents, 1991—;singer with North Shore Hebrew Acad. Choir, CD, Shiryla, 2003; mem. editl. bd. Habari Gari: A Newsletter for Catholics of African Ancestry, 1999-2000. Den leader Boy Scouts Am., Bayside, N.Y., 1975-80; troop leader Girl Scouts U.S.A., Flushing, N.Y., 1976-78; vol. Elderwise Day Care, Carbondale, Ill., 1992, Alice Wright Day Care Ctr., Carbondale, 1989-92, ABC Quilts (A Pediatric AIDS group), 1991-2000; mem. The Stage Co., Cill Cais Players. Honored for outstanding svc. Boy Scouts Am., 1978; recipient Outstanding Cmty. Svc. award, named Most Admired Woman of the Decade Sta. WPSD-TV, 1991, Internat. Women of Yr., 1993; grantee So. Ill. Art Coun., 1992; named Educator of Excellence, N.Y. State English Coun., 2000, L.I. Lang. Arts Coun., 2001. Mem.: AAUW, MLA, United Fedn. Tchrs., Am. Fedn. Tchrs., N.Y. State United Tchrs., United Univ. Profs., L.I. Lang. Arts Coun., NY

State English Coun., Puppet Guild L.I., Nat. Theatre for Puppet Arts, Children's Lit. Assn., Nat. Assn. Preservation and Perpetuation of Storytelling, Nat. Coun. Tchrs. English, Phi Delta Kappa, Sigma Tau Delta, Alpha Sigma Lambda, Skull and Circle Honor Soc. (St. John's U.). Avocations: needlework, acting, puppetry. Home: 193 W 19th St Huntington Station NY 11746-2118

DE VOE, MILDA M. writer; m. Lawrence Harkness De Voe, Jr., Oct. 17, 1992; 1 child, Erazmas Lan. BA magna cum laude, Coll. Notre Dame, Balt., 1990; MFA, Columbia U., 2001. Pub. rels. rep. Third Eye Repertory, Inc., N.Y.C., 1993—97; mgmt. com. chair Genesis Repertory Ensemble, Inc., N.Y.C., 1997—2000; freelance book dr. N.Y.C., 2000—. Prodr.: (plays) Waiting, 1997—2000;, author short stories and essays; actor: (plays) The Heidi Chronicles, A Lie of the Mind, Baby with the Bathwater, Macbeth. Recipient $500 - Raymond Carver Short Story Contest, Humbolt State U., 1998; fellow Writing Divsn. fellow, Columbia U., 1997—98; Presdl. scholar, Coll. Notre Dame Md., 1986—90. Mem.: Sigma Tau Delta. Home: 176 Broadway #14F New York NY 10038

DE VOE, PAMELA ANN, anthropologist, educator; b. Chgo., Ill., Sept. 22, 1946; d. Edward George De Voe and Evelyn Francis De Grave; m. Ronald E. Mertz, Aug. 1971; 1 child, Renée De Voe. BA, U. Wis., 1967; MA, U. Mo., 1971; PhD, U. Ariz., 1979; student, U. Mo., 1980—82. Cons., St. Louis, 1995—99; parent coord. St. Louis Pub. Sch., St. Louis, 1998—99; info. specialist St. Louis C.C., St. Louis, 1999—2001; asst. prof. St. Louis U., St. Louis, 2001—. Adj. faculty Webster U., St. Louis, 2000—, St. Louis C.C., St. Louis, 2000—. Co-prodr.: Refugee Studies Newsletter, 1984—86; editor: Selected Papers in Refugee Issues 1992, 1992; contbr. articles to profl. jours. Fellow Tchg. fellow, U. Ariz., 1976—77, U. Mo., Columbia, 1980—82; grantee HEW Fulbright-Hays grantee, 1977—78, Mo. Humanities Coun., 1989—90. Mem.: Soc. Applied Anthropology, Am. Anthropological. Assn. (com. refugee issues 1986, editor CORI 1988—94, bd. dir. gen. anthropology divsn. 1992—96, com. on refugees & immigrants 1994—96, 2000—), Asian Art Soc. (v.p. 1996—98, pres. 1998—99, bd.dir. 1993—2001). Democrat. Avocations: writing poetry, spinning wool. Home: 165 Bonchateau Dr Saint Louis MO 63141 Office: Internat Inst St Louis 3651 S Grand Blvd Saint Louis MO 63118 Business E-Mail: devoemertz@sbcglobal.net.

DE VOE, TAMARA LYNNE, art director, painter; b. Plainfield, NJ, Feb. 14, 1967; d. Robert James De Voe and Maureen Elizabeth Harrington; m. Mark Andrew Caccavo, May 12, 2000; 1 child, Simone Elizabeth. BFA, U. of the Arts, 1989. Freelance designer, Phila., 1989—92; designer Engraph, Moorestown, NJ, 1992—94; package designer Calvin Klein Cosmetics, Mt. Olive, NJ, 1995—96; freelance design N.Y.C., 1996—97; package designer Landor N.Y., divsn. of Young & Rubicam, N.Y.C., 1997—98; sr. art dir. L'Oreal Profl. divsn. Cosmair NY, N.Y.C., 1998—99, Nine West Group Inc., White Plains, 1999—2002. Mem.: Nat. Mus. Women in the Arts (charter mem.). Avocations: painting, skiing, hiking, music, museums.

DEVOL, LUANA, vocalist, consultant; b. San Mateo, Calif., Nov. 30, 1942; AA, Coll. San Mateo, 1960; postgrad., San Francisco State U., 1962, U.S. Internat. U., San Diego, 1970. Asst. to bd. dirs. Spring Opera Theatre, San Francisco, 1972-75; asst. gen. mgr. Paramount Theatre, Oakland, Calif., 1973-84, soprano Mannheim Nat. Theater, Germany, 1987-91. Opera singer Bayreuth, Berlin, Hamburg, Munich, Dresden, Leipzig, San Francisco, Florence, La Scala, Vienna, Paris, Helsinki, others; pvt. voice cons.; guest lectr. U. Md., Mannheim, 1991, 94 Seminar, European Singing Career, 1987, master class U. Nev., Las Vegas, 1996, 98, N.Y., 1999; mem. editl. bd. The Oakland Paramount, 1988. Made European debut as Leonore in Fidelio, Württembergische Staatsoper, 1983; roles include Isolde, Senta, Elsa, Elisabeth, Brunnhilde, Elektra, Faerberin, Kaiserin, Ariadne, Norma, Aida, Amelia, Tosca, Donna Anna and Donna Elvira. Trustee Young Artists Festival, Bayreuth, Germany. U.S. Internat. U. scholar, 1971; named Singer of Yr. Opern Welt, 1997, 2000, nom. 2003. Mem. Richard Wagner Soc. (hon.), Am. Guild Musical Artists, Am.-German C. of C. Home: 1908 Grey Eagle St Henderson NV 89074-0670

DEVOLITES, JEANNE MARIE ARAGONA, state legislator; b. Swindon, England, Feb. 28, 1956; m. John Arthur Devolites; children: Nichole, Ashley, Cassandra, Alexandra. BA in Math., U. Va., 1978. Mem. Va. State Legis., 1998—, mem. privileges & elections com., mem. health welfare & insts. com., mem. militia & police com., mem. claims. com. Republican. Roman Catholic. Office: Gen Assembly Bldg PO Box 406 Richmond VA 23218-0406

DEVONE, DENISE, artist, educator; BFA cum laude, Temple U., 1975; MFA, U. Hawaii, 1978. Instr. Newark Mus., 1990-97; art tchr. Holy Cross Sch., Harrison, 1995—. Adj. prof. County Coll. of Morris, Randolph, NJ, 1994—; cons. Donald B. Palmer Mus., Springfield, NJ, 1992-95. Executed murals Kaiser Hosp., Honolulu, 1985, Kaiser Pensacola Clinic, Honolulu, 1986, Distinctive Bodies Fitness, Warren, NJ, 1993, Ambulatory Pediatric Clinic, Overlook Hosp., Summit, NJ, 1994; Sole proprietor of Amalgamated Cocoanuts; one-woman shows include Contemporary Mus., Honolulu, 1992, ETS, Princeton, 1995, Montclair Kimberly Acad., NJ, 1995, 98, ADP Gallery, Roseland, NJ, 1997, Palmyra Gallery, Bound Brook, NJ, 1999; illustrator: Japanese Pilgramage, 1983, The Art of Featherwork in Old Hawaii, 1985. Recipient Purchase awards Hawaii State Found. on Culture and the Arts, 1976, 78, 80, 86, award of merit City and County of Honolulu, 1988; NJ State Coun. on Arts, Dept. State fellow, 1994-95. Mem. Nat. Assn. Women Artists, Inc., Studio Montclair, Inc., City Without Walls, Artists Space. Avocation: piano. Home: 33 Kew Dr Springfield NJ 07081-2530 E-mail: Ddevone@aol.com.

DEVORAH, RUTH, vocalist, actress, composer, artist, costume designer; b. N.Y.C., Dec. 28, 1930; d. Albert and Gladys (Chayet) Cohen; m. Marvin Abraham Trelin, Dec. 1, 1951 (div. Aug. 1967); children: Jayne Susan, Steven Ira; m. Harold Israel Glick, June 6, 1976. Cantorial cert., Herzliah Hebrew Seminary, N.Y.C., 1978. Cantor: conservative, reform synogogues; moderator, panelist: Women in Jewish Music; singer at festivals and spl. events including Nat. Coun. Women of U.S. Inauguration Ceremony Susan B. Anthony Coin Day, 1979, Unionia Israelita ann. concert to benefit Jerusalem Med. Ctr., Caracas, Venezuela, 1985; spl. performances Hosp. Audiences, Inc., N.Y.C. Sr. Outreach, N.Y. State Dept. Pks. and Recreation, U.S. Army base shows, Bankers Trust Pub. Svc. programs, 1975—; appearances on variety shows, theater, radio and TV prodns., voice-overs; composer: (songs) La La Songs, I Love America, Inspirational, Seven Heavenly Prayers; Author: (poems) A Few Expressions of My Impressions; Artist: (Exbtn.) Chelsea Art Show, N.Y.C. Mem. Am. Soc. for Jewish Music, Actors Equity Assn., Screen Actors Guild, Soc. Singers. Avocation: photography. Home: 240 Central Park S # 5Q New York NY 10019-1413 E-mail: rdevorah@yahoo.com.

DEVORE, BARBARA JANE EGAN, corporate finance executive; b. Harrisburg, Pa., Aug. 15, 1958; d. John Joseph and Pearl Catherine (Schaeffer) Egan; m. Timothy Dale DeVore, Oct. 22, 1983; children: Dale Vincent, Jessica Lynne. BS in Bus./Acctg., Wright State U., Dayton, Ohio, 1980. CPA, Ohio, CMA. Acctg. intern Delco Air divsn. GM, Dayton, 1979-80; from auditor to fin. and adminstrv. tng. analyst NCR Corp., Dayton, 1980—95, fin. and adminstrv. tng. analyst office corp. controller, 1995; fin. mgr. sales and mktg. O-Cedar/Vining, Springfield, Ohio, 1996—97; decision support analyst The Cmty. Hosp., Springfield, 1997—99; mgr. fin. projects The Ohio Masonic Home, Springfield, 1999—2000, controller, 2000—02, dir. fin. planning and analysis, 2002—. Fin. sec. Knob Prairie Ch., Enon, Ohio, 1990-91, choir dir., 1991-98; song leader Enon Cmty. Hist. Soc., 1991-98; dir. Enon Sesquicentennial Chair, 2000, piano choral composer, 1996—. Mem. Wright State Alumni Assn. Republican. Avocations: piano and vocal music, candle-making, needlework, leathercrafting, hiking. Home: 560 Brunswick Dr Enon OH 45323-1802

DEVORE, KIMBERLY K. business executive; b. Louisville, June 19, 1947; d. Wendell O. and Shirley F. DeV. Student, Xavier U., 1972-76; AA, Coll. Mt. St. Joseph, 1979; BA, Internat. U. Metaphysics, 1999. Patient registration supr. St. Francis Hosp., Cin., 1974-76; cons., bus. mgr. Family Health Care Found., Cin., 1976-77; exec. dir. Hospice of Cin., Inc., 1977-80; pres. Micro Med, 1979-86; v.p. Sycamore Profl. Assn., 1979-86; ptnr. Enchanted House, 1979-86, sec., 1979-80, treas., 1980-83; dist. sales rep. Control-O-Fax, 1986; br. sales mgr., 1987; nat. dealer devel. rep., 1987; nat. computer field sales trainer, 1987-90; pres. U.S. Exec. Leasing and U.S. Med. Leasing, Inc., 1991—2001, Accu Svcs., Inc., 1993—, U.S. Med. Mgmt., Inc., 1994-98. Pres. U.S. Med. Mgmt. of Ga., Inc., 1996—. Pres. Saddle Creek Homeowners Assn., Inc., 1992-95, parliamentarian, 1995-96;; chairperson Citizen's Police Adv. Com. City of Roswell, 1997-99; chairperson found. grants Orch. Atlanta, 1998-99, pres., 1999-03, vice-chmn., pres. & CEO, chaplin Unity N. Atlanta, 2000-02, emeritus, 2003; bd. dirs., membership chairperson Smith Plantation City of Roswell, 1996-97; pres. Roswell Citizen's Police Acad., Inc., 1994-95; mem. City of Roswell Med. Devel. Dist. Coun., 1995—; mem. North Fulton Civic League, Inc., 1995-96, 2001-; bd. dirs. Nat. Hospice Orgn., 1979-82, chmn. long-term planning com., fin. com., ann. meeting com., 1979-82, sec., 1980-81, treas., 1981-82; bd. dirs. Hospice of Miami Valley, Inc., 1982-86, also chmn. pers. com., by-laws com.; bd. dirs. Orch. Atlanta, 1998—. Mem. Greater Clin. Soc. Fund Raisers, Better Housing League; mem. service and rehab. com. Hamilton County Unit, Am. Cancer Soc., 1977-78; chair road com. Saddle Creek Homeowners Assn., 1991-92. Mem. Ohio Hospice Assn. (co-founder, state chmn., pres., 1978-83), Nat. League for Nursing, Ohio Hosp. Assn., Nat. Fedn. Bus. and Profl. Women's Clubs, Ohio Fedn. Bus. and Profl. Women's Clubs, Cin. Bus. and Profl. Women's Clubs (pres. 1973-75).

DEVOS, ELISABETH (BETSY), political association executive; b. Holland, Mich., Jan. 8, 1958; d. Edgar Dale and Elsa D. (Zwiep) Prince; m. Richard M. DeVos Jr., 1979; four children. BSc in Bus. Adminstrn., Calvin Coll., 1979. Co-chmn. Kent County (Mich.) Rep. Finance Com., 1983-84, chmn., 1985-88, 96—; Rep. Nat. Committeewoman State of Mich., 1992-97; chmn. Mich. State Rep. Party, 1996—2000; mem. Nat. Rep. Com., 1996—; chmn. Mich. State Rep. Party, 2003—. Market rsch. analyst Amway Corp., 1979-81; pres. Windquest Group. Bd. dirs. Blodgett Meml. Med. Ctr., 1986—, Ada (Mich.) Christian Sch., 1992—; mem. Rep. Congl. Leadership Coun. Mem. Econ. Club of Grand Rapids. Avocations: travel, boating, skiing.

DE VRIES, MADELINE, public relations executive; Founder, pres. DeVries Pub. Rels., N.Y.C., 1978—; chmn., CEO DeVries Pub. Rels. (acquired by Interpublic Group), N.Y.C.; public relations dir. Bergdorf Goodman, N.Y.C. Bd. dirs. and trustee Brooklyn Botanic Garden. Named an honoree Matrix Award, New York Women in Communications, 2002. Mem.: Cosmetic Exec. Women (mem. exec. com., chair, mktg. com.). Office: DeVries Public Relations 30 E 60th St New York NY 10022-1008

DE VRIES, MARGARET GARRITSEN, economist; b. Detroit, Feb. 11, 1922; d. John Edward and Margaret Florence (Ruggles) Garritsen; m. Barend A. de Vries, Apr. 5, 1952; children: Christine, Barton. BA in Econs. with honors, U. Mich., 1943; PhD in Econs., MIT, 1946. With IMF, Washington, 1946-87, sr. economist, 1949-52, asst. chief multiple currency pratices div., 1953-57, chief Far Eastern Div., 1957-59, econ. cons., 1963-73, historian, 1973-87. Professorial lectr. econs. George Washington U., 1946-49, 58-63 Author: The International Monetary Fund, 1966-71, The System Under Stress, 2 vols., 1977, The International Monetary Fund, 1972-78, Cooperation on Trial, 3 vols., 1985, The IMF in a Changing World, 1945-85, transl. into Chinese, 1986, Balance of Payments, Adjustment: The IMF Experience, 1945-86, transl. into Chinese, 1989, (with I.S. Friedman) Foreign Economic Policy of the United States in the Postwar, 1947, (with J.K. Horsefield) The International Monetary Fund, 1945-65, Twenty Years of International Monetary Cooperation, 3 vols., 1969; contbr. articles to profl. jours. Recipient Disting. Alumni award U. Mich., 1980, Cert. of Appreciation George Washington U., 1987, Outstanding Washington Woman Economist award, 1987; AAUW scholar, 1939-42; U. Mich. Univ. scholar, 1942; Phi Kappa Phi fellow, 1943; MIT fellow, 1943-46; Ford Found. grantee, 1959-62. Mem. Am. Econ. Assn. (CSWEP - Carolyn Shaw Bell award 2002), U. Mich. Alumni Assn., MIT Alumnae Assn., Phi Beta Kappa, Phi Kappa Phi. Mem. United Church of Christ. Home: 10018 Woodhill Rd Bethesda MD 20817-1218

DE VRIES, ROBBIE RAY PARSONS, writer, illustrator, international consultant; b. Idabel, Okla., Sept. 11, 1929; d. General Forrest Sr. and Jessie Demma (Burch-Oldham) Parsons; m. Douwe de Vries, Apr. 2, 1953; children: Jessica Joan de Vries Kij, Peter Douwe. BS in Bus. Adminstrn. and Journalism, Okla. State U., 1952; postgrad., U. Houston, 1987, 88, Rice U., 1988, 89, U. St. Thomas, 1996, 97. Sec. to mgr. drafting and survey Shell Oil Co., Houston, 1952-53; sub. tchr. Spring Br. Ind. Sch. Dist., Houston, 1989-92; pres., owner Robbie P. de Vries Interests, Houston, 1983—, author, illustrator, pub., internat. cons., 1989—. V.p. Systems, Inc., Houston, 1981—, internat. studies dept. U. St. Thomas; bd. dirs. Friends of Okla. State U. Libr., Stillwater; mem. Friends of U. Houston Libr., 1981—; bd. dirs., cons. Ctr. for Internat. Trade, Okla. State U., Stillwater, 1990—; invited guest Peoples Republic of China/U.S. State Dept., China, 1992; bd. assocs. New Internat. Sch. Okla. State U., 1999; lectr. on intercultural comms. Okla. State U., 1999, 2000; cons. Habitat for Humanity Internat.; invited guest to Egypt, Israel and Jordan by U.S. State Dept., 1999. Columnist Conroe, Tex. Daily Courier, 1988-89; editor Idabel Warrior newspaper (Gold medal), 1947, Houston Symphony League newspaper, 1974-75; author, illustrator, pub.: A Cultural Exchange: American and Chinese Weddings, English edit., 1993, Chinese edit., 1995; author, pub.: Regional Study of Russian and the Eurasian States, 1997. Internat. coord. Habitat for Humanity, Philippines, internat. coord. for better housing; vol. cultural and internat. areas New Orleans, 1960—69, Houston, 1969—; home host internat. youth exch., Netherlands, 1978; grand jury mem. Harris County, Tex., 1986—87; patron Jr. League, Houston, 1970—; docent Mus. Fine Arts, Houston, 1974—; co-chmn. Houston-Baku, Azerbaijan, USSR Sister City, 1979—89; mem. magic cir. Greater Houston Women's Found.; mem. donor Baylor Med. Sch. Devel., 1990—; mem. magic cir. Rep. Women Houston, 1989—; bd. dirs. New Orleans C. of C., 1964—69, Houston Symphony Soc. League, 1972, Inst. Internat. Edn., Houston, 1969—, Boy Scouts Am., Houston, 1980—; bd. dirs., chair internat. conf. YWCA, Houston, 1986—87. Recipient Ann. Fund Silver Tray award Houston Symphony League, 1972, Miss Ima Hogg Orchid award Houston Symphony Soc., 1975, Gen. Maurice Hirsch Leaf and Letter award Symphony Soc., 1980, 81, 82, Tex. Mother of Yr., Alpha Delta Pi, 1982, Mayor's award Baku, Azerbaijan USSR, 1979, 83, 87, 89, U.S. State Dept. pin, 1986, 10-Yr. Leadership award Mayor of Baku, 1988, U. Houston Ball Merit/Honor, 1991, Merit award Boy Scouts of Am., 1993, 10-Yr. Svc. award, 1995; named Acting First Lady of Houston for goodwill trip to Baku, Azerbaijan, USSR, by Mayor of Houston Jim McConn, 1979; named Hon. Dep. Sheriff, Harris County Sheriff Johnny Klevenhagen, 1986, Harris County Sheriff Tommy B. Thomas, 1996; feature Honor Villages mag., 1994; certificate of appreciation, Okla. State U. Habitat for Humanity; named hon. lt. gov. of Okla., 2001. Mem.: AAUW (past pres.), Nat. Mus. Women in the Arts (charter), Tex.-Netherlands Bus. Assn., Houston Coun. Writers, Inspirational Writers, Tex. Fine Arts Assn., Nat. Women's Hall of Fame, Forum Club Houston, Tuesday Music Club (yearbook cover designer 1975—78), Étoffe Littéraire (founder, Founder's award 1985), Mu Kappa Tau. Republican. Presbyterian. Avocations: classical music, international entertaining, travel, interior decorating, art. Home and Office: Robbie P de Vries Interests 802 Piney Point Rd Houston TX 77024-2725 Fax: 713-467-7631.

DEW, JOAN KING, freelance/self-employed writer; b. Columbus, Ga., June 24, 1932; d. Henry Grady and Vivian Pauline (Cook) King; m. Clifford Dew (div.); children: Clifford L. Jr., Michael David; m. Albert Schmitt (div.); 1 child, Christopher Thomas. Student, Fla. State U., 1949—51. Reporter, feature writer Ft. Lauderdale (Fla.) Daily News, 1950—56; editor Nassau (Bahamas) Guardian, 1956—58; stringer UPI, 1956—58; copy chief Art and Publicity, Ltd., Kingston, Jamaica, 1958—60; feature writer, author column Male Call, Valley Times Today, North Hollywood, Calif., 1960—66; freelance writer Hollywood, Calif., 1966—77, Nashville, 1977—88; editor food and wine LA Herald Examiner, 1988—89; exec. editor Ctrl. Coast Adventures, Monterey Peninsula, Calif., 1992—2002; ret., 2002; with Peace Corps, 2003—. Author: Singers and Sweethearts: The Women in Country Music, 1977, Stand By Your Man: The Autobiography of Tammy Wynette, 1978, Minnie Pearl, The Autobiography of Minnie Pearl, 1980, 3 books on wine and food, 1984—88, Christmas, 1987; author: (with David Fox) Follow Your Heart, 1988; columnist Nashville Tennessean, 1988; contbr. numerous articles to nat. mags. Address: 1920 Whitley Ave Los Angeles CA 90068-3233

DE WALD, VICKY COLEEN, theater director, performing company executive, theater educator; b. Superior, Neb., Dec. 26, 1962; d. William A. and Dorothy P. (Bjornstad) Kegle; m. Jason P. De Wald; children: Nathaniel, Ryan. AA theatre, Ctrl. Cmty. Coll., Hastings, Neb.; BA theatre, tech. theatre minor, U. of Neb. at Kearney, Kearney, Neb. Box office assoc. Univ. of Nebr. at Kearney, Kearney, Nebr., theatre scene shop technician, theatre dept., theatre costume shop asst., theatre dept.; exec. dir. The Tassel Performing Arts Ctr., Holdrege, Nebr.; tchr. aide, instr. No. Slope Borough Pub. Schools, Kaktovik, Alaska, artist dir. Kearney Cmty. Theatre, Kearney, Nebr. Children's theatre dir. No. Slope Borough Pub. Schools, Kaktovik, Alaska; actress Cheyenne Cmty. Theater, Cheyenne, Wyo.; stage mgr. Univ. of Nebr. at Kearney, Kearney, Nebr.; guest tchr. Elm Creek HS, Elm Creek, Nebr.; adult sponsor Holdrege Thespians, Troupe 737, Holdrege, Nebr. Pub. poetry, The Only Thing That's Valuable; contbr. columns in newspapers Barrow Sun; artwork, cartoon copywrited, Faith is....Glory B. Bunny. Fundraising chair, sec., treas., hist., Prairie Players of Phelps County, Holdrege, Nebr.; speakers bur. Life Choice, Cheyenne, Wyo.; v.p. Alpha Psi Omega, Pi Upsilon Chpt., Kearney, Nebr., 2001—02; speech, drama coach Holdrege Speech, Drama Team, Holdrege, Nebr.; mem. Music Boosters, Holdrege, Nebr.; judge Nebr. State Dramatic Competition, Nebr.; student advisor Univ. of Nebr. at Kearney, Kearney, Nebr.; co-founder Children's Peanut Butter Theatre, Holdrege, Nebr.; counselor Stress Debriefing Team, Kaktovik, Alaska; troupe leader, summer camp dir. Girl Scouts, Crete, Nebr. Nominee Regional Costume Design, Kennedy Ctr. Am. Coll. Theatre Festival, Region V, Regional Scenic Design; recipient Alpha Psi Omega Scholarship, Alpha Psi Omega, Pi Upsilon Chpt., Univ. of Nebr. at Kearney, Dean's Academic Excellence, Dean's Office, Fine and Performing Arts Coll., Univ. of Nebr. at Kearney, Campus Pres. Academic Excellence award, Campus Pres. Office, Ctrl. Cmty. Coll./Hasting, Nebr., Best Supporting Actress Nominee, Alpha Psi Omega, Pi Upsilon Chpt., Best Stage Mgmt., Silver Medalist, Nebr. State Dramatic Competition, Stage Mgmt., 1st Pl., Kennedy Ctr. Am. Coll. Theater Assn. Mem.: Nebr. Assn. for Arts in Edn., Nebr. Assn. of Cmty. Theatres, Alpha Psi Omega, Pi Upsilon Chpt. (v.p.), Phi Theta Kappa, Phi Kappa Phi. R-Conservative. Protestant. Avocations: travel, theater. Office: The Tassel Perfoming Arts Ctr PO Box 526 1324 Tilden St Holdrege NE 68949 E-mail: info@thetassel.org., vcnjpd@hotmail.com.

DEWANE-POPE, PEGGY, elementary school educator, public relations executive, consultant; b. Evanston, Ill., Nov. 1, 1958; d. James N and Patricia A Dewane; m. Craig M. Pope, Dec. 12, 1981; children: Thomas, Shannon, Corinne. BS, Calif. Poly. State U., San Luis Obispo, 1980; degree in tchg., Calif. State U., 2001. News dir. KGEO-KGFM Radio, Bakersfield, Calif., 1981—83; exec. dir. Soc. Crippled Children, Bakersfield, Calif., 1983—85; pub. rels. specialist Contel, Bakersfield, Calif., 1985—88; pub. rels. cons. Bakersfield, Calif., 1988—97, Houghton Covey Group, Bakersfield, Calif., 1999—2000; tchr. Earl Warren Jr. High, Bakersfield, Calif., 2001—. Recipient Highest Honors, Secondary Sch. Of Edn., Calif. State U., 2001. Mem.: AAUW (pres. 1997—98, mem. state bd. 1998—2000).

DEWAR, HELEN, reporter; b. Stockton, Calif., 1936; BA in Polit. Sci., Stanford U. Reporter The Northern Virginia Sun; metro reporter The Washington Post, Washington, 1961-77, nat. staff reporter, 1977—. Office: The Washington Post 1150 15th St NW Washington DC 20071-0001

DEWAR, MILDRED JO ELLER (MRS. DONALD NORMAN DEWAR), librarian; b. Wilkesboro, N.C., Nov. 9, 1925; d. Charles Franklin and Golda (Velt) Eller; m. Donald Norman Dewar, Mar. 6, 1954; 1 dau., Heather. Student, Brevard Coll., 1942-44; diploma, Jr. Coll., 1944; AB, Berea Coll., 1946; BSLS, U. NC., 1948; postgrad., Barry Coll., U. Fla., U. Miami. Tchr., librarian Mountain View High Sch., Hays, N.C., 1946-47; chief librarian Tenn. Wesleyan Coll., Athens, 1948-50; dept. head U. Tex. Library, Austin, 1951; librarian U.S. Army Spl. Services, Ft. Jackson, S.C., 1951-52, chief post library system Ft. Stewart, Ga., 1952-54; librarian Olsen Jr. High Sch., Dania, Fla., 1955-56, Lauderdale Manors Sch., Ft. Lauderdale, Fla., 1956-63; head reader's services Miami-Dade Community Coll. Library, Miami, Fla., 1963-70, library dir. South Campus, 1970-90. Vis. instr. U. Ga., summer 1967; co-exec. dir. Nat. Library Week in Fla., 1965-66; mem. Fla. learning resources standing com. Council on Instructional Affairs. Contbr. articles to profl. jours.; mem. editorial bd. Community and Jr. Coll. Libraries. Mem. AAUW (past br. v.p.), ALA, Fla. Library Assn., Am., Fla. (past pres.) assns. sch. librarians, SE Fla. Ednl. Consortium (library task force), Delta Kappa Gamma. Home: 1340 Magnolia Ave Annapolis MD 21403-4914

DEWEY, ARIANE, artist, illustrator; b. Chgo., Aug. 17, 1937; d. Charles S. Dewey, Jr. and Marjorie G. Graff; m. Claus Dannash, Feb. 7, 1976; m. Jose Arugeo, Jan. 27, 1960; 1 child, Juan Dewey Aruego. BA, Sarah Lawrence Coll., 1959. Rsch. and publicity asst. George Nelson, N.Y.C., 1960—62; art editor Harcourt, Brace, Jovanovich, Inc., N.Y.C., 1963—65; freelance artist, illustrator, 1968—. Author, illustrator: Naming Colors, 1995, The Sky, 1993, The Narrow Escapes of Davy Crockett, 1990, The Tea Squall, 1988, Gib Morgan, Oilman, 1987, Febold Feboldson, 1984, Pecos Bill, 1983, Dorin and the Dragon, 1982, The Thunder God's Son, 1981, The Fish Peri, 1979, illustrator: Sally Ann Thunder Ann Whirlwind Crockett, 1985, co-author, co-illustrator: Weird Friends, 2002, Rockabye Crocodile, 1988, We Hide, You Seek, 1979, A Crocodile's Tale, 1972, Pilyo the Piranha, 1971, Symbiosis, A Book of Unusual Friendships, 1970, Juan & the Asuangs, 1970, The King and His Friends, 1969, co-illustrator with Jose Aruego: They Thought They Saw Him, by Craig Kee Strete, 1996, The Littlest Wolf, by Larry Dane Brimner, 2002, Gregory the Terrible Eater, by Mitchell Sharmat, 1980, co-author, co-illustrator: Splash, 2000, co-illustrator with Jose Aruego: Rum Pum Pum, by Maggie Duff, 1978, co-illustrator: Lizard's Home, by George Shannon, 1999, Where Does the Sun Go At Night?, by Mirra Ginsburg, 1992, Alligators and Others All Year Long, by Cresent Dragonwagon, 1993, Musical Max, by Robert Kraus, 1990, Another Mouse to Feed, by Robert Kraus, 1980, co-illustrator with Jose Aruego: One Duck, Another Duck, by Charlotte Pomerantz, 1984, Runaway Marie Louise, by Natalie Savage Carlson, 1977; co-illustrator Rosa Reposa by Isabel Campoy, 2002, Antarctic Antics, A Book of Penguin Poems by Judy Sierra, 1998, Safe, Warm and Sung by Stephen R. Swinburne, 1999, How Chipmunk Got His Stripes by Joseph Bruchae and James Bruchac, 2001, Turtle's Race with Beaver by Joseph Burchac &

James Bruchac, 2003, Lizard's Guest, 2003. Recipient Goldmedaille, Internat. Buchkunst-Ausstellung, Leipzig, Germany, 1977. Mem.: Soc. Illustrators, PEN, Authors Guild. Avocation: kayaking. E-mail: adewey@mindspring.com.

DEWEY, [illegible] SCAMELL, retired humanities educator; d. Ralph Eugene Scamell and Eva Charlotte Bernhard; m. Ernest Wayne Dewey, Apr. 11, 1949 (dec. Mar. 1982); children: Ernest Ralph, William Frederick, James Franklin. BA with honors in Philosophy, U. Kans., 1948, MA in Philosophy, 1949; postgrad., U. Tex., 1951, U. Toledo, 1972—82. With U. Kans., Lawrence, 1948—50; part-time instr. Okla. State U., Stillwater, 1956—60. Vol. Dem. Party, Stillwater, 1954—. With U.S. Navy WAVES, 1944—46. Mem.: WAVES (nat.), LWV, Women in Mil. Svc. to America, Friendship Force, Phi Alpha Theta, Phi Beta Kappa. Democrat. Avocations: reading, camping, travel, swimming, cooking.

DEWITT, BARBARA JANE, journalist; b. Glendale, Calif., Aug. 5, 1947; d. Clarence James and Irene Brezina; m. Don DeWitt, Apr. 21, 1974; children: Lisa, Scarlett. BA in Journalism, Calif. State U., Northridge, 1971. Features editor The Daily Ind. Newspaper, Ridgecrest, Calif., 1971-84; fashion editor The Daily Breeze, Torrance, Calif., 1984-89; freelance fashion reporter The Seattle Times, 1990; fashion editor, columnist The Los Angeles Daily News, L.A., 1990—. Instr. fashion writing UCLA, 1988, Am. InterContinental U., L.A., 1996—. Dir. Miss Indian Wells Valley Scholarship Pageant, 1980-84. Recipient 1st Pl. Best Youth Page, Calif. Newspaper Pubs. Assn., 1980, 1st Pl. Best Fashion, Wash. Press Assn., 1989, The Internat. Aldo award for fashion journalism, 1995, 96. Republican. Lutheran. Avocations: antiques, reading, swimming. Office: The Daily News 21221 Oxnard St Woodland Hills CA 91367-5081

DEWITT, MARY THERESE, forensic anthropologist, archaeologist; b. Chgo., Aug. 25, 1948; d. Robert Baldwin and Helen (Rossman) DeW. BA in Anthropology, U. Tex., Arlington, 1995, MA in Interdisciplinary Studies, 1997. Dir. mktg. Homart Devel. Co., Florence, Ky., 1975—76, Melvin Simon & Assocs., Inc., Hurst, Tex., 1976-79; pres. Mary DeWitt Co., Ft. Worth, 1979-85; v.p. mktg. Southmark Comml. Mgmt., Dallas, 1986-87; prin. DeWitt Group and subs. Cat's-Eye Intelligence Svc., Dallas and Ft. Worth, 1988-98; coord. program advisement U. N.Mex., Albuquerque, 1998—. Cons. logistics and documentation one team Internat. Group for Hist. Aircraft Recovery, The Phoenix Group South Pacific, 1989; mem. hist. survey and exhumation team Smithsonian and U. Tex., Giddings, Tex., 1998. Mem. Am. Coll. of Forensic Examiners, Archaeol. Inst. of Am., Internat. Assn. for Identification, Am. Assn. of Phys. Anthropologists, N.Mex. Academic Advising Assn., Lambda Alpha (v.p. 1994-97), Alpha Phi Omega (staff advisor). Home: 612 6th St SW Albuquerque NM 87102-3808 Office Phone: 505-277-1514. E-mail: mdewitt@unm.edu.

DEWITT, SALLIE LEE, realtor; b. Ft. Smith, Ark., Oct. 11, 1923; d. Lee and Claudia Cordelia Victoria (Vest) DeWitt. BS, U. Tex., 1944; student, U. Houston, 1971; postgrad. in Computers, Del Mar Coll., 1989. Real estate broker, Tex.; cert. profl. sec. Layout artist, copywriter Corpus Christi (Tex.) Caller-Times, 1945-56; exec. sec. to chief geologist Exxon Co., Houston, 1956-73; adminstrv. asst. to gen. mgr. Valley Telephone Coop., Inc., Raymondville, Tex., 1976-89; owner, mgr. Sallie Lee DeWitt Real Estate, Raymondville, Tex., 1980-89; broker assoc. Alfred Edge Realtors, Corpus Christi, 1990-95; broker, owner Sallie Lee DeWitt Real Estate, 1996—. Property tax cons., Corpus Christi, 1992-94. Mem. Nueces County Hist. Soc., Corpus Christi, 1990—. Mem. AAUW, Women's Coun. Realtors, Corpus Christi Bd. Realtors, C.C. Town Hall, C.C. Bus. and Profl. Women, Civitan Internat., Tropical Trails Investment Club/Harlingen, Tex., Internat. Soc. Poets, Interna. soc. Photographers. Republican. Baptist. Avocations: poetry, piano, art, photography, genealogy.

DEWITT-MORETTE, CÉCILE, physicist; b. Paris, Dec. 21, 1922; came to U.S., 1948; d. André and Marie Louise (Ravaudet) Morette; m. Bryce S. DeWitt, Apr. 26, 1951; children: Nicolette, Jan, Chris, Abigail. BS, U. Caen, 1943; PhD, U. Paris, 1947. With Centre Nat. de la Recherche Sci., 1944-65, Maitre de Confs. prof., 1965-88. Mem. Inst. Advanced Studies, Dublin, 1946—47, Copenhagen, 1947—48, Princeton, 1948—50; lectr. U. Calif., Berkeley, 1952—55, U. N.C., Chapel Hill, 1956—71; prof. U. Tex., 1972—93, Jane and Roland Blumberg Centennial prof. physics, 1993—2000, prof. emeritus, 2000—; founder, dir. Ecole d'ete de Physique Theorique, Les Houches, France, 1951—72. Author: Particules Elementaires, 1951, (with Y. Choquet-Bruhat and M. Dillard-Bleick) Analysis, Manifolds and Physics, 1977, rev. edit., 1982, (with A. Maheshwari, B. Nelson) Path Integration in Non Relativistic Quantum Mechanics, 1979, (with Y. Choquet Bruhat) Analysis, Manifolds and Physics, Part II, 92 Applications, 1989, rev. edit., 2000, also articles. Decorated chevalier Ordre Nat. du Mérite, chevalier Ordre des Palmes Académiques; chevalier Ordre Nat. Legion d'Honneur; Rask-Oersted fellow, 1947-48, Prix des Sciences Physiques et Mathematiques (Comite du Rayonnement Français, 1992); recipient (with Bryce DeWitt) Marcel Grossman award, 2000. Fellow Am. Phys. Soc.; mem. Internat. Astron. Union, European Phys. Soc., Inst. Hautes Etudes Scientific (trustee), French Soc. Physics (Membre d'honneur). Home: 2411 Vista Ln Austin TX 78703-2343 Office: U Tex Dept Physics Austin TX 78712 E-mail: cdewitt@physics.utexas.edu.

DEWITZ, LYNN MARLENE, art educator, consultant; b. Woodworth, N.D., Jan. 29, 1947; d. Harold Herman Neustel and Helen Jeanette Madson Neustel; m. Richard Allen Dewitz, June 13, 1970; children: Jon Allen, Chad Aron, Neal Richard, Scot James. BS in Edn., Valley City State U., 1969; postgrad., U. N.D., 1992—99, N.D. State U., 1992—2002, Savannah Coll. Art & Design, 2001. Elem./secondary art tchr. Ada (Minn.) Pub. Schs., 1969—70; kindergarten tchr. Tappen (N.D.) Pub. Schs., 1979, art instr., 1989—90, Ctrl. Dakota TeleComm., Tappen, ND, 1994—95; elem./secondary art instr. Langdon (N.D.) Pub. Schs., 1995—96; art instr. Ctrl. Dakota Telecomm./Great We. Network, ND, 1996—2000, Great We. Network, Steele, ND, 2000—. Chmn. Tappen Art Found., Tappen, 2001—; cons., instr. Edu Tech, Valley City, ND, 2002—; adv. bd. Acres for Aaron Scholarships, Tappen, 2002—. Mem. Nat. Family & Cmty. Edn., Tappen, 1970—; artwork coord. Tappen's 125th Celebration, 2001—. Recipient Merit award for painting, Mandan Art Assn., N.D., 2003. Mem.: Bismarck Art & Galleries Assn., N.D. Edn. Assn., Nat. Art Edn. Assn., Am. & UFW Auxiliary. Lutheran. Avocations: painting, drawing, camping, gardening, reading. Home: 3663 39th Ave SE Tappen ND 58487 Office: Great Western Network 101 4th St SE Steele ND 58487

DEWOLFE, MARTHA, singer, songwriter, publisher, producer; b. Arlington, Tex., Nov. 30, 1959; d. Homer C. and Grace R. DeWolfe. Student, N. Tex. State U., 1978-79, Larimer County Vocat.-Tech., Ft. Collins, Colo., 1983; cert. peace officer, Tarrant County Jr. Coll., Euless, Tex., 1984; student, North Ctrl. Tex. Coun. Govts., 1984-94, Southwestern Law Enforcement Sch. of Police Supervision. Police officer Grand Prairie (Tex.) Police Dept., 1984-94, sgt., 1989-94, supr. crime prevention unit, 1991-92. Mem. Police Employee Rels. Bd., 1990-91; BMI assoc.; estabished Maui Records, 1992, Midnight Tiger Music, BMI, 1994. Albums include That Flame Keeps Burning, 1992, Take Good Care of My Heart, 1995, Mama Look, 1997; songs include Adrianna, Worse Than Being Lonely, All the Blue, Patsy Come Home, River of Tears, Take Good Care of My Heart, Once a Year, The Drought; acting credits include Paramount's "Denton County Massacre", 1993, and commercials; lead singer Wildcat Canyon Band, 1997—. Sec. Grand Prairie Police Assn., 1985-86. Recipient 1st place Tex. Comml. Art Skill Speed Competition, 1977-78. Mem. Fraternal Order Police, Grand Prairie Police Assn., Tex. Assn. Vet. Police Officers, Country Music Assn., Broadcast Music Internat., Nashville Songwriter's Assn. Internat., No. Calif. Songwriters Assn., Mensa. Avocations: pvt. pilot, cats, photography. Home: PO Box 266 Martinez CA 94553-0026

DEWULF NICKELL, KAROL, editor; m. Don Nickell; children: Lauren, Alexander. BA in Journalism, Iowa St. U. Furnishings editor Better Homes and Gardens mag., 1979—87; editor-in-chief Traditional Home mag., 1987—2001; columnist Country Home mag., 1987—2001; editor in chief Better Homes and [illegible] 2001 [illegible]; Editor Renovation Style mag., Decorator Showhouse mag. Avocations: gardening, reading, cooking. Office: 1716 Locust St Des Moines IA 50309-3023

DEXTER, DEIRDRE O'NEIL ELIZABETH, lawyer; b. Stillwater, Okla., Apr. 15, 1956; d. Robert N. and Paula E. (Robinson) Maddox; m. Terry E. Dexter, May 14, 1977; children: Daniel M. II, David Maddox. Student, Okla. State U., 1974-77; BS cum laude, Phillips U., 1981; JD with highest honors, U. Okla., 1984. Bar: Okla. 1984, U.S. Dist. Ct. (no. and ea. dists.) Okla. 1985, U.S. Dist. Ct. (we. dist.) Okla. 1987, U.S. Ct. Appeals (10th cir.) 1987; grad. Nat. Inst. Trial Advocacy Advanced Trial seminar. Jud. intern Supreme Ct. Okla., Oklahoma City, summer 1983; assoc. Conner & Winters, Tulsa, 1984-90, ptnr., 1991, shareholder, 1991-2000; assoc. dist. judge Tulsa County Dist. Ct., 2000—03; assoc. Frederic Dorwart, Lawyers, Tulsa, 2003—. Article editor Okla. U. Law Rev., 1982-84. U. Okla. scholar, 1983. Mem. Okla. Bar Assn. (advising atty. state champion H.S. mock trial team competition 1992), Tulsa County Bar Assn., mem. bd. dirs., Order of Barristers, Order of Coif, Am. Inns of Ct. (master), Delta Theta Phi. Republican. Baptist. Office: Old City Hall 124 E 4th St Tulsa OK 74103 E-mail: Ddexter@fdlaw.com.

DEXTER, HELEN LOUISE, dermatologist, consultant; b. Cin., July 28, 1908; d. William Jordan and Katherine (Weston) Taylor; m. Morrie W. Dexter, Jan. 27, 1937; children: Katharine, Helen Dexter Dalzell, Elizabeth Taylor, William Taylor. AB, Bryn Mawr Coll., 1930; MD, Columbia U., 1937; postgrad., U. Cin., 1948-50. Intern Jersey City (N.J.) Med. Ctr., 1938-39; internist Cin. Babies Milk Fund Maternal Health Clinic, 1938-45; clinician U. Cin. Med. Sch., 1938-48; lectr. dept. dermatology, 1948-53; practice in medicine specializing in dermatology, 1954—. Dermatology cons. VA, 1955—; investigation of carcinogenic effects of shale oil U.S. Bur. Mines, Rifle, Colo., 1950. Contbr. articles to profl. jours. Mem. Clearwater Power Squadron Aux.; commr. Town of Belleair, 1980. Recipient Ina Clay trophy Intercollegiate Ski Champion, 1928-30. Mem. AMA, Soc. Investigation Deramtology, Am. Acad. Dermatology, S.E. Dermatol. Assn. (v.p. 1963-65), Fla. Dermatol. Soc., Pan-Am. Dermatol. Soc., Am. Archaeol. Soc., Soc. Tropical Dermatology, Clearwater Yacht Cariouel Yacht. Presbyterian. Address: 409 Bayview Dr Belleair FL 33756-1409

DEXTER, JANE MEISER, physical education educator; b. Jamacia Plain, Mass., Nov. 3, 1944; d. Carl Joseph and Ellen Margaret Meiser; m. George Thomas Dexter, May 19, 1967; children: Karen, Adam. BS, U. Mass., 1967. Elem. edn. tchr., Coconut Creek, Fla., 1981—82; physical edn. tchr. Coral Springs, Fla., 1982—, Coconut Creek, 2003—. Adv. chairperson Coconut Creek (Fla.) HS, 1983—98. Pres. Margate Softball, 1975—2003, Margate Soccer, 1979—2003. Recipient Citizen of Yr., local newspaper, 1992. Mem.: Broward Tchrs. Union. Democrat. Roman Catholic. Avocations: walking, bicycling. Home: 480 SW 49 Ter Margate FL 33068

DEY, CHARLOTTE JANE, retired community health nurse; b. Benson, Minn., Dec. 14, 1927; d. Elmer Ellsworth and Charlotte Iona (Eastman) Bowers; m. Thomas A. Dey, June 25, 1948 (dec. Mar. 1973); children: Thomas A. Jr., Scott E. (dec.). Grad., St. Luke's Hosp. Sch. Nursing, 1948; student, Kansas City (Kans.) Jr. Coll., 1968; BS in Nursing with distinction, U. Kans., 1970; MPA, U. Mo., Kansas City, 1975. RN, Mo.; ordained deacon, Episcopal Ch., 1993. Head nurse communicable disease ward St. Luke's Children's Hosp., Kansas City, Mo., 1948-49; head nurse newborn nursery Providence Hosp., Kansas City, Kans., 1949-51; pub. health nurse Johnson County Health Dept., Olathe, Kans., 1951-52, 66-68, pub. health nurse, supr., 1970-72; evening supr. Olathe Community Hosp., 1953-55; office nurse B. Albert Lieberman, Jr., MD, Kansas City, Mo., 1960-66; coord. clin. confs. ANA, Kansas City, 1973-76; chief Bur. Community Health Nursing Mo. Dept. Health, Jefferson City, 1976-93; ret., 1993. Sem. expert panel to review and update criteria to estimate future requirements for nursing pers. div. nursing Dept. Health and Human Svcs., 1984, mem. nat. adv. coun. nursing edn. and practice div. nursing, 1998-2002; chair Mid-Am. Community Health Nursing Leadership Group. Recipient award of merit Assn. State and Territorial Dirs. Nursing, 1992. Mem. ANA (cert. nursing adminstrn. advanced, chairperson exec. com. coun. community health nursing 1989-92), APHA, Nat. League Nursing, Nat. Perinatal Assn., Am. Acad. Health Adminstrn. (pres. Mo. chpt. 1980-82), Mo. State Nurses Assn. (coun. nursing svc. facilitors exec. com. 1983-92), Mo. Pub. Health Assn., Mo. League Nursing, Mo. Perinatal Assn., Kans. State Nurses' Assn. (vice chairperson community health conf. group), Kans. Pub. Health Assn. (legislative com.), Sigma Theta Tau. Mem. Episcopal Ch. Home: 8090 Granite Falls Ct Redmond OR 97756-7389

D'HAITI, FELICIA KATHLEEN (FELICIA KATHLEEN MESSINA), fine arts educator; BA, Georgetown U., Washington, DC, 1987—91; MA, Rutgers U., New Brunswick, NJ, 1992—95. Cert. Advanced Profl. Md. State Bd. of Edn., 2003. Edn. program specialist Smithsonian Office of Edn., Washington, 1995—97; contractor Smithsonian Mag., Washington, 1997—98; fine arts tchr. Prince George's County Pub. Schools, Forestville, Md., 1999—. Recipient Armed Forces Comm. and Electronics Ednl. award, Dept. of Def. Summer Engrng. and Sci. Program, 1987, Ford Found. Predoctoral Fellowship (Hon. Mention), Ford Found., 1992, Smithsonian Instn. award, Smithsonian Office of Edn., 1996, Letter of Commendation, Andrew Jackson Mid. Sch., 2000, 2001; fellow Ralph J. Bunche Fellowship, Rutgers U., 1992-1994, Trustees Fellowship, 1994-1995; grantee Georgetown U. Grant, Georgetown U., 1987-1991, U. of Md. Student Support Grant-Assistantship, U. of Md. Coll. Pk., 1997-1999; scholar Cath. Negro Scholarship, Cath. Negro Scholarship, 1987-1991, Md. State Scholarship, Md. State Govt., 1989, Fulbright Meml. Fund Tchr. Program, Fulbright Meml. Fund, 2002. Mem.: Am. Assn. of Museums, Assn for Supervision and Curriculum develop. (ASCD), Am. Ednl. Rsch. Assn., Prince George's County Educators Assn., Md. State Teachers Assn., Nat. Edn. Assn. (NEA), Nat. Art Edn. Assn., Alpha Delta Kappa, Phi Delta Kappa. Independent. Roman Catholic. Avocations: travel, piano, museums, theater. Personal E-mail: fkmdhaiti@aol.com. E-mail: felicia.dhaiti@pgcps.org.

D'HARNONCOURT, ANNE, museum director, museum administrator; m. Joseph J. Rishel, June 19, 1971. BA, Radcliffe Coll., 1965; MA with distinction, Courtauld Inst. Art, U. London, 1967. Curatorial asst. Phila. Mus. Art, 1967-69; asst. curator 20th Century art Art Inst. Chgo., 1969-71; curator 20th Century art Phila. Mus. Art, 1971-82, George D. Widener dir., 1982—. Mem. mus. panel NEA, 1976-78, mem. indemnity panel, 1985-88, mem. mus. program overview panel, 1986-87; mem. Indo-U.S. Subcommn. Edn. and Culture, 1983-87; bd. advs. Ctr. Advanced Study in the Visual Arts Nat. Gallery Art, 1987-89. Organizer: (with McShine) exhbn. Marcel Duchamp, 1973-74, (with others) Philadelphia: Three Centuries of American Art, 1976, Eight Artists, 1978, (with Percy) Violet Oakley, 1979, Futurism and the International Avant-Garde, 1980, (with Sims) John Cage: Scores and Prints, 1982; author: (with Walter Hopps) Etant Donnes. Reflections on a New Work by Marcel Duchamp, 1969, The Cubist Cockatoo: Preliminary Exploration of Joseph Cornell's Hommages to Juan Gris, 1978, John Cage: Paying Attention, 1993, also prefaces for various books. Bd. dirs. Henry Luce Found., Inc., N.Y.C.; trustee Fairmount Park Art Assn. Phila., Georgia O'Keeffe Found.; bd. trustees Japan Soc. N.Y.C.; bd. regents Smithsonian Instn. Fellow AAAS; mem. Am. Philos. Soc., Pa. Coun. Arts, 1992-99, Assn. Art Mus. Dirs. Office: Phila Mus Art Benjamin Franklin Pkwy PO Box 7646 Philadelphia PA 19101-7646*

DHILLON, SUKHBANS K. retired computer services executive; b. Lahore, Punjab, India, Sept. 17, 1926; came to U.S., 1964; divorced; 1 child, Surinder S. (dec.). BA in History and Polit. Sci., Punjab U., Amritsar, 1942, MA in History, 1945, [illegible] specialist, asst. prof., prof. Bangala Sahib Degree Coll., Amritsar, 1948-52, prin., 1953; edn. specialist Dept. Edn., Delhi, India, 1964-72; sr. v.p., CEO, chmn. REHAB Computer Svcs. Co., Arlington, Va., 1972-86. Grantor Surinder S. Dhillon Cardiovasc. Lab., Washington Hosp. Ctr., Washington, 1986, Sukhbans K. Dhillon Cardiology Fellowship, Washington Hosp. Ctr., Washington, 1990, Surinder S. Dhillon & Sukhbans K. Dhillon Phys. Edn. Ctr., Edinboro (Pa.) U., 1994; mem. Rep. Senatorial Inner Cir., Washington, 1990—, Rep. Nat. Com., Washington, 1994—, Rep. Party Va., Richmond, Friends of the Ronald Wilson Reagan Presdl. Libr. and Mus., Calif., 1996—; assoc. George W. Bush Presdl. Libr. and Mus., Tex., 1998—. Recipient Rep. Senatorial Medal of Freedom, Rep. Party, 1994, Ronald Wilson Reagan Eternal Flame of Freedom Commemmorative medallion Rep. Party, 1995, Eisenhower Commn, Rep. Nat. Com., 1995, Senatorial Commn., U.S. Senate Reps., 1996, Citation of Leadership award Rep. Nat. Conv., 1996, Rep. Majority medal Nat. Rep. Senatorial Com., 1997, Rep. Senatorial Inner Cir., 1998, Rep. Senatorial Medal of Freedom, Rep. Senatorial Inner Cir., 1999; inductee Nat. Hall of Honor, Rep. Party, 1992. Mem. ASPCA, World Affairs Coun., Am. Humane Soc., John F. Kennedy Ctr., Wolf Trap Ctr. for Performing Arts. Avocation: supporting fine arts.

DIA, MABEL PERILLO, dietician; b. Asingan, Philippines, July 5, 1935; came to U.S., 1974; d. Julian and Feliza (Escorpizo) Perillo; m. Januario D. Dia, Oct. 29, 1958. BS in Home Econs., U. Philippines, 1954; MS in Foods and Nutrition, Centro Escolar U., 1968; St. Masters cert., NYU, 1981. Registered dietician. Dietician Quezon Inst., Quezon City, Philippines, 1954-62; dietary cons. Cebu Cmty. Hosp., Cebucity, Philippines, 1966-74; asst. prof., head dept. of nutrition and home econs. U. So. Philippines, Cebu City, 1962-74; therapeutic dietitian Med. Arts Hosp., N.Y.C., 1974-75; chief therapeutic dietitian Astoria Gen. Hosp., L.I., N.Y., 1975-86; registered dietician Brookhaven Beach HRF, Far Rockaway, N.Y., 1986-88; asst. dir. of food and nutrition svcs. Neponsit (N.Y.) Health Care Ctr., 1988-90; nutrition cons. Ind. Living Assoc., Bklyn., 1992-95; nutrition cons., lectr. Johnson Home Care Svcs., Bklyn., 1994—. Nutrition cons. Episcopal Social Svcs., N.Y.C., 1978—, Young Adult Inst., N.Y.C., 1995—; dir., owner MPD Nutrition Svc., Bklyn., 1992—; chief clin. dietitican Seacrest Health Care Ctr., Bklyn., 1990—. Contbr. articles to profl. jours. Fellow Am. Dietetic Assn.; mem. Am. Dietetic Assn., Am. Diabetes Assn., Filipino-Am. Dietetic Assn. Avocations: reading, cooking. Office: MPD Nutrition Svc 115A George St Brooklyn NY 11237-1905

DIACHENKO, MARGE, political organization administrator; 2 children. 1st v.p., 2nd v.p., 3rd v.p., treas. Nat. Fedn. Rep. Women, mem.-at-large exec. com., 1995-96, regent, sec., dir. region 1. Past pres. Conn. Fedn. Rep. Women; mem. Conn. Rep. Ctrl. Com., 1995—, treas. state senate campaign com.; legis. asst. House Rep. Office Conn. Gen. Assembly; with Govt. Adminstrn. and Elections com. Town Clk.'s Office, Simsbury, Conn. Vol. coach Spl. Olympics; active Commn. on Aging and Disabilities Town of Simsbury, State Elections Study LWV; vol. chair Conn. State Employees Campaign for Charitable Giving; gov.-elect Civitan New England Dist. Mem. Order of Eastern Star (past matron). Office: Nat Fedn Rep Women 124 N Alfred St Alexandria VA 22314-3011 Fax: 703-548-9836.

DIAL, CARMEN MIRANDA, financial counselor, evangelist; b. Bessemer, Ala., May 12, 1950; d. Clifton and Idella Dial; 1 child, Clifton Millard Wright. BS, Ala. A&M U., 1972. Addressograph operator Fulton-Dekalb Hosp. Authority, Atlanta, 1972—77; fin. counselor Grady Health Sys., Atlanta, 1977—. Pres. Word of Knowledge, Atlanta, 1995. Author: Walking with Jesus, Crystal Fountain of Love, Jesus is The Light, Our Father, Rain Drops, To the Living God, I Give You Praise, To the Man of My Life. Mem. Chosen Vessel, Atlanta, 1992—; Bible tchr., chmn. Green Forest Cmty. Bapt., Decatur, Ga., 2001. Avocations: tennis, volleyball. Home: # D54 3000 Continental Colony Pky Atlanta GA 30331

DIAL, ELEANORE MAXWELL, foreign language educator; b. Norwich, Conn., Feb. 21, 1929; d. Joseph Walter and Irene (Beetham) Maxwell; m. John E. Dial, Aug. 27, 1959. BA, U. Bridgeport, Conn., 1951; MA in Spanish, Mexico City Coll., 1955; PhD, U. Mo., 1968. Mem. faculty U. Wis.-Milw., 1968-75, Ind. State U., Terre Haute, 1975-78, Bowling Green (Ohio) State U., 1978-79; asst. prof. dept. fgn. langs. and lit. Iowa State U., Ames, 1979-85, assoc. prof., 1985-96, emerita assoc. prof., 1996—. Cons. pub. cos.; participant workshops; del. 1st World Congress Women Journalists and Writers, Mex., 1975, also mem. edn. commn. Contbr. articles, anthologies and revs. to scholarly jours. Active Gov.'s Commn. on Fgn. Langs. and Internat. Studies, 1988-95. NDEA grantee, 1967, Ctr. Latin Am. grantee, 1972, NEH summer seminar UCLA, 1981, U. Calif.-Santa Barbara, 1984. Mem. MLA, Am. Assn. Tchrs. Spanish and Portuguese, Midwest MLA, N. Ctrl. Coun. Latin Americanists, Midwest Assn. Latin Am. Studies, Clermont County Geneal. Soc., Ohio Geneal. Soc., Story County (Iowa) Geneal. Soc., Caribbean Studies Assn., Phi Beta Delta, Phi Sigma Iota, Sigma Delta Pi. Office: Iowa State U Ames IA 50011-0001 Home: 190 Norht st Batavia OH 45103-2911

DIALLESANDRO, CONNIE LYN, family practice nurse practitioner; b. Phoenix, Aug. 9, 1959; d. Elroy McClung Cooksey and Marilyn Louise Ewing-Cooksey; m. Louis James DiAllesandro Jr., Apr. 24, 1982; children: Angelo Rafael, Andrew James Lee. LPN, Phoenix Area Vocat. Ctr., 1978. LPN staff relief nurse Med Pro Svcs., Phoenix, 1978—90; LPN staff nurse Paradise Valley Nursing Home, Phoenix, 1990—95, Dakota Clinic Moorhead, Minn., 1995—. Contbr. poetry to anthologies (3 Pres.'s Choice awards). Dilworth city planner, Moorhead, 1997—2001; mem. Clay County Permit Bd., Dilworth, Minn., 1999—2001. Baptist. Avocations: gardening, travel, reading, poetry. Home: 424 1st Ave SE Dilworth MN 56529

DIAMANT, ANITA, writer; b. N.Y.C., June 27, 1951; d. Maurice and Helene Diamant; m. James R. Ball, June 11, 1982; 1 child, Emilia. AB, Washington U., St. Louis, 1973; MA, SUNY, Binghamton, 1975. Sr. staff writer Boston Mag., 1986-88; columnist Boston Globe mag., 1988-95; freelance writer, 1988—; columnist Jewishfamily.com., Boston, 1998-99; commentator WBUR-FM, Boston, 1994-96; contbg. editor Parenting Mag., 1994-95. Author: The New Jewish Wedding, 1985, Living a Jewish Life, 1991, The New Jewish Baby Book, 1994, Bible Baby Names, 1996, Choosing a Jewish Life: A Handbook for People Converting to Judaism and Their Family and Friends, 1997, The Red Tent, 1997, Saying Kaddish: How to Mourn as a Jew, 1998, How to be a Jewish Parent, 2000, Good Harbor, 2001; editor: Equal Times, 1977—78; contbr. to profl. publs. and mags. Recipient Book of Yr. award Boston Author's Club, 1998, Significant Jewish Book of Yr. award UAHC Reform Judaism Mag., 1999, Booksense Book of Yr. award, 2001. Jewish. E-mail: anitaweb@aol.com.*

DIAMANT, AVIVA F. lawyer; b. N.Y.C., Mar. 13, 1949; d. Herman and Anni (Silbermann) D.; m. Steven Kaufman, May 31, 1976; 2 children. BS cum laude, CCNY, 1969; JD, Columbia U., 1972. Bar: N.Y. 1973, U.S. Ct. Appeals (2d cir.) 1975, U.S. Dist. Ct. (so. dist.) 1976. Assoc. Fried, Frank, Harris, Shriver & Jacobson, N.Y.C., 1972-79, ptnr., 1979—. James Kent scholar, 1972. Mem. Assn. of Bar of City of N.Y. (com. on corps. 1982-85), Phi Beta Kappa. Jewish. Office: Fried Frank Harris Shriver & Jacobson 1 New York Plz Fl 22 New York NY 10004-1980

DIAMOND, DIANA LOUISE, editor, graphic artist; b. Floral Park, NY, Feb. 4, 1937; d. Louis Bartholomew and Helen Stephanie (Strzelecki) Chmielewski; m. Horace Williams Diamond, Jr., June 29, 1958 (div. 1975); children: Bruce Williams, Scott Kenneth, Kent Christopher, Mark Patrick.

BA in English, U. Mich., 1958. Reporter Lerner Newspapers, Highland Park, 1970-72, mng. editor, 1972-78, suburban coord., 1974-78; corr. (part-time) The N.Y. Times, 1975-78; prof. journalism fellow Stanford U., 1978-79, sr. writer, editor, spl. asst. to pres., 1983-88, exec. asst. to v.p. and dean Sch. of Medicine, 1988-89; writer, editl. bd. San Jose (Calif.) Mercury News, 1979—81; editor, sect., spl. projects editor Sunday Opinion, 1981; editor-in-chief Calif. Lawyer, 1981—83; spl. asst. to pres. Stanford U. Hosp., 1990-93, mgr. publs., 1993-94; pres. Diamond Comm. and Design, Palo Alto, Calif., 1994—. Columnist Palo Alto Daily News, 2001—. Bd. dirs. Midpeninsula Citizens for Fair Housing, pres., 1983-86; bd. dirs. New Forum, 1985-90, pres., 1987-89; bd. dirs. Pacific Art League, 1989-94, Palo Alto Centennial '94, 1990-94, Palo Alto chpt. ARC, 2000—, YMCA of Midpeninsula, 2002—; founder, chmn. bd. dirs. RotaCare Internat., 1992—. Recipient Nat. Blue Ribbon Newspaper award, 1976-78; 3rd pl. Ill. Editor of Yr. contest, 1974; 1st pl. for best feature story, Ill. Press Assn., 1976, Suburban Newspapers Am., 1977; 2d pl. for best column Nat. Newspaper Assn., 1977, Maggie award We. Pubs. Assn., Silver Six award Internat. Bus. Comm., 1996, Crystal award Communicators Group, 1998, 1st pl. best column Pa. Press Assn., 2002. Mem. YMCA, Palo Alto Red Cross (bd. dirs.), Rotary (pres. Palo Alto chpt. 1999-2000). Home: 2512 Cowper St Palo Alto CA 94301-4218 Office: Diamond Comm & Design 550 Hamilton Ave Ste 338 Palo Alto CA 94301-2031 Office Phone: 650-322-9090. E-mail: diana@dianadiamond.com.

DIAMOND, ESTELLE, education educator, state legislator; b. N.Y., Mar. 20, 1924; d. Jacob and Edna Fischer Diamond; m. Milton Goldberger, Mar. 24, 1945 (div. Apr. 1, 1970); children: Janet, Jesse, Margaret. BA, Harpur Coll., Bushtown, N.Y., 1966; MAT, Burghampton Univ., Burghampton, N.Y., 1972. Cert. H.S. tchr. English tchr. Vestal H.S., NY, 1966—86, Binghamton Univ., NY, 1986—87, 1990—93; Broome County Legis. Binghampton, NY, 1987—89; N.H. State Legis. Grafton County, N.H. House, Concord, NH, 2003—. Recipient exemplary tchg. award, Bd. Coop. & Educators Broome County Svcs., 1985, Women of Achievement, Broome County Status of Womens Coun., 1986. Avocation: american quilts collector.

DIAMOND, JESSICA, artist; b. Bronx, N.Y. BFA, Sch. Visual Arts, N.Y.C., 1979; MFA, Columbia U., N.Y.C., 1981. One-woman shows include Standard Graphic, Cologne, Germany, 1990, Jablonka Gallery, Cologne, 1991, Gallery Fahnemann, Berlin, 1991, Gallery Massimo De-Carlo, Milan, 1993, Ynglingagatan 1, Stockholm, 1994, Rix, Linköping, Sweden, 1996, Galerie Analix, Geneva, 1996, Deitch Projects, N.Y., 1996, le Consortium, Dijon, France, 1997, Vera Van Laer Gallery, Antwerp, Belgium, 1998, Ota Fine Arts, Tokyo, 1999, Mus. Het Domein, Sittard, The Netherlands, 1999, Birmingham (Ala.) Mus. of Art, 2000, Art Gallery-York U., Toronto, Ont., Can., 2001, Montreal (Can.) Mus. of Fine Arts, 2002; exhibited in group shows at Mus. van Hedendaagse Kunst Ghent, Belgium, 1993, Venice (Italy) Biennale, 1993, Vorarlberger Kunstverein, Bregenz, Austria, 1993, Corner House, Manchester, Eng., 1994, Deichtorhallen Hamburg, Germany, 1994, Mus. Contemporary Art, Sydney, Australia, 1994, Serpentine Gallery, London, 1994, Watari-um Mus., Tokyo, 1995, Kunsthalle Bern, Switzerland, 1995, Galerie Fahnemann, Berlin, 1996, Whitney Mus. Am. Art, N.Y.C., 1997, Stedelijk Mus. voor Actuele Kunst, Ghent, Belgium, 1999, Paula Cooper Gallery, N.Y.C., 1999, Tate Gallery Liverpool, Eng., 1999, Kunstmuseum Bonn, Germany, 1999 Kunstlerhaus Wien, Vienna, 2000, Sonsbeck 9, Arnhem, The Netherlands, 2001, The Tang Tchg. Mus. and Art Gallery, Skidmore Coll., Saratago Springs, N.Y., 2001, Casino Luxembourg, 2002, Neues Mus., Germany, 2002, MIT List Visual Arts Ctr., Cambridge, Mass., 2003, Inst. of Contemporary Art, Phila., 2004. Recipient award Nat. Endowment for Arts, 1989; John Simon Guggenheim Meml. Found. fellow, 2000. Home: 549 83d St Brooklyn NY 11209-4503

DIAMOND, MARIAN CLEEVES, anatomy educator; b. Glendale, Calif., Nov. 11, 1926; d. Montague and Rosa Marian (Wamphler) Cleeves; m. Richard M. Diamond, Dec. 20, 1950 (div.); m. Arnold B. Scheibel, Sept. 14, 1982; children: Catherine, Richard, Jeffrey, Ann. AB, U. Calif., Berkeley, 1948, MA, 1949, PhD, 1953. With Harvard U., Cambridge, 1952-54, Cornell U., Ithaca, N.Y., 1954-58, U. Calif., San Francisco, 1959—62, prof. anatomy Berkeley, 1962—. Asst. dean U. Calif., Berkeley, 1967-70, assoc. dean, 1970-73, dir. The Lawrence Hall of Sci., 1990-95, dir. emeritus, 1995—; vis. scholar Australian Nat. U., 1978, Fudan U., Shanghai, China, 1985, U. Nairobi, Kenya, 1988. Author: (with J. Hopson) Magic Trees of the Mind, 1998; author: Enriching Heredity, 1989; co-author: The Human Brain Coloring, 1985; editor: Contraceptive Hormones Estrogen and Human Welfare, 1978; contbr. over 155 articles to profl. jours. V.p. County Women Dems., Ithaca, 1957; bd. dirs. Unitarian Ch., Berkeley, 1969. Recipient Calif. Gifted award, 1989, C.A.S.E. Calif. Prof. of Yr. award, Nat. Gold medalist, 1990, Woman of Yr. award Zonta Internat., 1991, U. medal La. Universidad Del Zulia, Maricaibo, Venezuela, 1992, Alumna of the Yr. award U. Calif., Berkeley, 1995; Calif. Acad. Scis. fellow, 1991, Calif. Soc. Biomedical Rsch. Dist. Svc. award, 1998, Alumnae Resources-Women of Achievement Vision and Excellence award, 1999, Benjamin Ide Wheeler award 1999, Achievement award Calif. Child Devel. Adminstrs. Assn., 2001; named to Internat. Educators Hall of Fame, 1999. Fellow AAAS, AAUW (sr.; fellowship chair 1970-85, 1st Sr. Scholar award 1997); mem. Am. Assn. Anatomists, Soc. Neurosci., Philos. Soc. Washington, The Faculty Club (Berkeley, v.p. 1979-85, 90-95). Avocations: hiking, sports, painting. Home: 2583 Virginia St Berkeley CA 94709-1108 Office: U Calif Dept Integrative Biology 3060 Valley Life Sciences Bldg Berkeley CA 94720-3116 Business E-Mail: diamond@socrates.berkeley.edu.

DIAMOND, MARY E(LIZABETH) B(ALDWIN), artist; b. Detroit, Sept. 2, 1951; d. Harold Barber and Evelyn (Glenn) Weaver; m. David Baldwin III, June 24, 1972 (div. Nov. 1982); 1 child, David Damar; m. Robert Proctor Diamond, Oct. 6, 1986; 1 child, Angelique Krista. Freelance artist, cartoonist, photographer Phase II Mag., Detroit, 1981-85; artist Montague Art Galleries Inc., Locust Valley, N.Y., 1989-99; adminstrv. asst., gallery dir. East End Arts and Humanities Coun., Riverhead, N.Y., 1996, 97; gallery dir. East End Arts Coun., Riverhead, 1997. Auditor N.Y. State Coun. on Arts, Huntington, 1995-99, chair decentralization regrant program, Suffolk County, 1999; mem. The Chase Manhattan Smarts Regrant program, Huntington, N.Y., 1999-2001; curator Black History Month exhbn. East Hampton (N.Y.) Artist Alliance, 1999; instr. Parish Art Mus., Southampton, N.Y., 1990-2001; guest spkr. and panelist "African-Am. Artists and Writers", Eastville Hist. Soc., Sag Harbor, N.Y., 1996; guest spkr. L.I. U., Southampton, N.Y., 1995, Jimmy Ernst Artists Alliance, East Hampton, N.Y., 1991, Southampton (N.Y.) Intermediate Sch., 1994, Galerie "Die Treppe", Stuttgart, Germany, "New York, New York" Exhibit, 1995, judge Parrish Art Mus., Southampton, 1993; vis. artist Southampton Adventures in Learning Southampton Elem. Sch., 1996, Adventures in Learning, Southampton Elem. Sch., 1997, internat. exhbn. Galerie "Die Treppe", Reudern, Germany, 1994-97, Salon De Femme Invitational Exbn. Southampton Cultural Ctr., 1997, East End Arts Coun., 1997, Sundance Gallery, Season Opening Invitational Exhbn., 1995, Havre De Grace, Md., 1995, Nat. Jr. Duck Stamp Competition, 1995, Adventures in Learning, Southampton Elem. Sch., 1997-98; bd. dirs. Southampton Cultural and Civic Ctr., 1995; vis. artist Salon at Siena Ctr., Water Hill, N.Y., 1998, What is Kwanzaa, Southampton, 1999, others; guest spkr., presenter, studio tour leader Art Out East, 1997-2001, L.I. Art Tchrs. Assn. Spring Conf., East Hampton, 1997; guest lectr. Studio Tour for Friends of Guild Hall Mus., East Hampton, 1997; judge traveling exhbn. UNICEF, Southampton, 1998; judge Southampton artists student exhbn., N.Y., 2001. Exhbns. include Sundance Gallery, Season Opening Invitational Exhbn., Bridgehampton, N.Y., 1996, Southampton Cultural Ctr., 1995, Clayton & Liberatore Gallery 75th Anniversary Invitational Exhbn., Bridgehampton, N.Y., 1995, Landscape Today; East End Views Guild Hall Mus., East Hampton, N.Y., 1994, 39th Ann. L.I. Artists Juried Exhbn., Hecksher Mus., Huntington, N.Y., 1994, Landscape Observed, Landscape Transformed, Islip Art Mus., East Islip, N.Y., 1992, Nat. League Am. Pen Women, 12th Juried Exhibit, Vanderbilt Mus., Centerport, N.Y., 1992, Art Assn. Harrisburg (Pa.) 66th Ann. Exhibit, 1994, Southampton Cultural Ctr., 1997, Simply Art Gallery, Bklyn., 1997-2001, Shifflett Gallery, L.A., 1999-2001; 2d Place award in oil painting Mather Meml. Hosp. Juried Auction, 1997, 1st Place award in oil painting L.I. Artists Open Juried Art Competition, Brookhaven Cultural Ctr., 1995, Hon. mention North Shore Art Guild Ann. Mems. Exhbn., Brookhaven, 1995, Lynn Shifflett Gallery, L.A., 1995-99, 2000, East End Arts Coun., Riverhead, N.Y., 1997, Elaine Benson Gallery, Bridgehampton, N.Y., 1997-99, Jonkonnu Gallery, Sag Harbor, 1998, Image Gallery, Riverhead, N.Y., 1999, L.I. U., Southampton, 2000. Bd. dirs. Cultural and Civic Ctr., Southampton, N.Y., 1995-2001; trustee Colonial Soc. of Southampton Hist. Soc., 1997-99. Named Outstanding Woman of Eastern L.I., Hero award Southampton Ind. Newspaper, 1996; grantee N.Y. Found. for the Arts, 1994; mem. Southampton Hist. Mus., 1997-2000. Mem. Am. Soc. Portrait Artists, East End Arts Coun., Allied Artists of Am., Southampton Artists Assn. (organized life drawing workshop 1989-94, v.p. 1991, pres. 1992, bd. dirs. 1999-2001, mus. liaison 1999), The Onyx Group (founder, treas., pres. 1992-94), The Artists Alliance of East Hampton, North Shore Art Guild, Guild Hall Mus. Home: 83 Northside Dr Sag Harbor NY 11963-2003

DIAMOND, NANCY KAY, environmentalist, consultant; b. Detroit, July 16, 1956; d. Philip and Norma (Basof) D. BS in Forest Sci., Humboldt State U., 1980; MS in Agr., Calif. Poly State U., San Luis Obispo, 1988; PhD in Wildland Resource Sci., U. Calif., Berkeley, 1992. Agroforestry cons. Internat. Union for Conservation Nature & Natural Resources, Tanzania, 1988; social forestry advisor Office Economic & Internat. Devel. U.S. Agy. Internat. Devel., Washington, 1991-93; gender & environ. advisor Office Women Devel. AID, Washington, 1993-96, rsch. & evaluation officer Acad. for Edn. Devel., Washington, 1996-97. Grad. student instr. U. Calif., Berkeley, 1986-91, rschr., Kenya, 1989-90. Vol. Doing Something, Washington, 1995-96; mem. adv. bd. Urban Creeks Coun., 1983-87. Recipient Doctoral Dissertation Rsch. award Fulbright-Hays, 1989-90; pre-dissertation rsch. fellow Social Sci. Rsch. Coun., 1987, dissertation fellow, 1990, Fgn. Lang. & Area Studies fellow U.S. Dept. Edn., 1987-88; Nat. Merit scholar, 1974-78. Democrat. Avocations: collecting folk art, travel.

DIAMOND, SARA ROSE, lawyer, writer; b. 1958; BA in Spanish, U. Calif., Irvine, 1979; MA in Sociology, U. Calif., Berkeley, 1988, PhD in Sociology, 1993; JD, U. Calif., 2003. Bar: Calif. 2003. Elder law and estate planning lawyer. Lectr. U. Calif., Santa Cruz, 1988, 91, 94, U. Calif., Berkeley, 1994, Calif. State U. Hayward, 1995—2000. Author: Spiritual Warfare: The Politics of the Christian Right, 1989, Roads to Dominion: Right-Wing Movements and Political Power in the United States, 1995, Facing the Wrath: Confronting the Right in Dangerous Times, 1996, Not By Politics Alone: The Enduring Influence of the Christian Right, 1998. Mem.: Alameda County Bar Assn. (trusts and estates sect.). Home: PO Box 6006 Albany CA 94706-0006 Office: 827 Broadway Ste 200 Berkeley CA 94607

DIAMOND, SHARI SEIDMAN, law educator, psychology educator; b. Chgo., Mar. 17, 1947; d. Leon Harry and Rita (Wolff) S.; m. Stewart Howard Diamond, Nov. 1, 1970; 1 child, Nicole. BA in Psychology, Sociology, U. Mich., 1969, MA in Psychology, Northwestern U., 1970, PhD in Social Psychology, 1972; JD with honors, U. Chgo., 1985. Bar: Ill. 1985. Rsch. assoc. Sch. Law U. Chgo., 1972-73; asst. prof. psychology and criminal justice U. Ill., Chgo., 1973-79, assoc. prof., 1979-90, prof., 1990-2000; assoc. Sidley & Austin, Chgo., 1985-87; sr. rsch. fellow ABF, Chgo., 1987—; lectr. U. Chgo. Law Sch., 1994-96; prof. law and psychology Northwestern U., 1999—, Stanton Clinton sr. rsch. prof., 2000-01, Howard J. Trienens prof. law, 2002—. Cons. govtl. and pub. interests groups including Rsch. Adv. Panel for U.S. Sentencing Commn., 1987-91; acad. visitor dept. law London Sch. Econs., 1981; hon. fellow Ctr. for Urban Affairs Northwestern U., Evanston, Ill., 1973-73; hon. rsch. assoc. U. London, 1970; speaker, lectr. in field; mem. NAS panel on sentencing rsch., 1981-83, panel on forensic DNA evidence, 1994-96. Editor Law and Soc. Rev., 1988-91; past mem. editorial bd. Law and Soc. Rev., 1983-88, Law and Human Behavior, Crime and Justice Annual, Evaluation Rev.; reviewer NSF; contbr. articles to profl. jours. Chair Coll. Edn. Policy Com., 1979-80; dir. tng. grant NIMH Crime and Delinquency, 1979-80. Fellow Northwestern U., 1968-69, NIMH, 1969-71; grantee Spencer Found., 1972-74, disting. scholar, grantee, U. Ill., 1995-98, Law Enforcement Assistance Adminstrn., 1974-76, Ctr. for Crime and Delinquency NIMH, 1976-81, NSF, 1980-83, 90-92, 99—; B. Kenneth West U. scholar, 1995-98. Fellow APA (Award for Disting. Contbns. to Rsch. in Pub. Policy 1991), Am. Psychol. Soc.; mem. ABA, Am. Psychology-Law Soc. (pres. 1987-88), Law and Soc. Assn. (trustee 1979-82). Office: Northwestern U Law Sch 357 E Chicago Ave Chicago IL 60611

DIAMOND, SUSAN ZEE, management consultant; b. Okla., Aug. 20, 1949; d. Louis Edward and Henrietta (Wood) Diamond; m. Allan T. Devitt, July 27, 1974. AB, U. Chgo., 1970; MBA, DePaul U., 1979. Dir. study guide prodn. Am. Sch. Co., Chgo., 1972—75; supr. publs. Allied Van Lines, Broadview, Ill., 1975—78, sr. account svcs. rep., 1978—79; pres. Diamond Assocs. Ltd., Bensenville, Ill., 1978—. Author: Records Management: A Practical Guide, 3d edit., 1995, Seventeen Steps to Slimness: A Sherlockian Guide to Dieting, 2002; editor: The Serpentine Muse, 1996, Serpentine Muse-ings, 2004. Mem.: Assn. Record Mgrs. and Adminstrs., Inst. Mgmt. Accts., Baker St. Irregulars, Adventuresses of Sherlock Holmes.

DIAMONSTEIN-SPIELVOGEL, BARBARALEE, writer, television interviewer/ producer; b. New Yprk City; d. Rubin Robert and Sally H. Simmons; m. Alan A. Diamonstein, July 22, 1956; m. Carl Spielvogel, Oct. 27, 1981. BA, BC, MA, Doctorate, N.Y. U., 1963; DHL (hon.), Md. Inst. Coll. Art, 1990, Longwood U., 1995. Staff asst. The White House, Washington, 1663—1966; 1st dir. dept. cultural affairs City of New York, 1966—67; dir. of forums McCall Corp., 1967—69; editor spl. supplements, columnist Harper's Bazaar, 1969—71; spl. project dir., guest editor Art News, 1971—93. Columnist Ladies Home Jour., 1979-84; contbr. to Saturday Rev., Vogue, Ms., Partisan Rev., N.Y. Times, Condé Nast, Traveller, House and Garden, others; mem. faculty Hunter Coll., City U. N.Y., 1974-76, New Sch., 1976-84, Duke U. (Inst. Policy Sci.), 1978; arts cons. Sunday Morning CBS-TV, 1978-82; curator Buildings Reborn, Collaborations, Visions and Images, Remaking America, The Landmarks of N.Y. I, II, and III (internat. travelling museum exhibitions.), 1978—, and numerous others. Author: Open Secrets: 94 Women in Touch With Our Time, 1972; editor: Our 200 Years: Tradition and Renewal, 1975; TV interviewer, prodr. About the Arts, WNYC-TV, 1975—79; author: The World of Art, 1902-77, 75 Years of Art News, 1977; Leo Castelli Gallery, 1978; author: Buildings Reborn: New Uses, Old Places, 1978, Inside New York's Art World, 1979; editor: MOMA at 50, 1980; TV interviewer, prodr. ABC-TV Arts, 1980—88, A and E Network, 1980—89; author: Collaboration: Artists and Architects, 1981, Visions and Images: Am. Photographers on Photography, 1981, Interior Design: The New Freedom, 1982, Handmade in Am., 1983; Leo Castelli Gallery, 1984; author: Fashion: The Inside Story, 1985, Am. Architecture Now, 1985, Remaking Am., 1986; Leo Castelli Gallery, 1988; author: The Landmarks of N.Y., 1988, 18 Wonders of the N. Y. World, 1992, The Landmarks of N.Y.: Vol. II, 1993; Leo Castelli Gallery, 1994; author: Inside the Art World: Conversations with Barbaralee Diamonstein, 1994, Skills, Values, Dreams, 1995, Singular Voices: Americans Who Make a Difference, 1997, The Landmarks of N.Y.: Vol. III, 1998, Barbaralee's Rules of the Rd.: 59 Simple Ways to Cope with a Complex World, 2001. Nat. judge Vietnam Vet. Meml. Edn. Ctr. Competition, 2004; bd. advisors Film Anthology Archives, 1969—; Commr. N.Y.C. Landmarks Preservation Commn., 1972—87, N.Y.C. Cultural Commn., 1975—86; bd. dir. PEN Am. Ctr., 1980—96; vice-chmn. N.Y. Landmarks Conservancy, 1983—87; mem. Pres. coun. Rockefeller U., 1987—; bd. visitors Pub. Policy Inst. Duke U., Durham, NC, 1987—93; mem. U.S. Holocaust Meml. Mus., 1987—93; chmn. N.Y. Landmarks Preservation Found., 1987—95; chair art pub. spaces com. Holocaust Mus., 1987—96; mem. drawing com. Met. Mus. Art, 1990—; Commr. N.Y.C. Arts Commn., 1991—94; trustee Ctrl. Pk. Conservancy, 1993—95, N.Y. Hist. Soc., 1993—95; chair Hist. Landmarks Preservation Ctr., 1995—; mem. drawing com. Whitney Mus. Am. Art, 1995—98, bd. dir., 1995—98, White House Endowment Fund, 1995—98; mem. U.S. Commn. Fine Arts, 1996—; bd. trustees Mus. of Women, the Leadership Ctr., N.Y.C., 1999—; co-chair Assn. Culture Edn. and Comm., 2001—; vice chmn. U.S. Commn. Fine Arts, 2001—02; bd. dir. Mcpl. Art Soc., 1973—83, Am. Coun. Arts, 1982—89, N.Y.C. Bicentennial Commn., 1973—77, Bklyn. Acad. Music, 1969—74, N.Y. Landmarks Conservancy, 1973—97, Fresh Air Fund, 1983—, Big Apple Circus, 1989—92, Corcoran Gallery Art, Washington, 1992—99, N.Y. State Hist. Archive's Trust, 1994—, Friends of the High Line, 2003—; chair Nat. Competition for Low Cost Housing, N.Y.C., 2004—. Recipient Founder's Day Award Pratt Inst., 1994, Outstanding Citizen Award Citizen Ctr., 1996, Heritage Trails Award, 1998, Spirit of the City Award Women's City Club, 1998, Manhattan Award, 1999, New Millenium Humanitarian Award HELP, 1999, Gen. Milan R. Stefanik Award Slovak Am. Cultural Ctr., 2002, Aging in Am. Humanitarian Award, 2003. Home: 720 Park Ave New York NY 10021-4954

DIAS, FIONA P. retail executive; m. Floyd Dias. Grad., Harvard U., 1987; MBA, Stanford U. Sr. fin. analyst Merrill Lynch Capital Markets, Inc.; sr. asst. brand mgr. Fixodent and Fasteeth denture adhesives Proctor and Gamble Co.; dir. brand mktg. Pennzoil Quaker State Co., 1996; with Pepsico, Inc.; chief mktg. officer Stick Networks, Inc.; sr. v.p. Circuit City, 2000—; pres. Circuit City Direct, 2003—. Office: Circuit City 9950 Mayland Dr Richmond VA 23233-1464*

DIAS, MARI NARDOLILLO, education educator, consultant; b. Providence, July 21, 1952; d. Robert Anthony and Dorothy Ann Nardolillo; m. Raul Dias; children: Lindsay, Adam. BA in Secondary Edn., R.I. Coll., 1974, MA in Vocat. Counseling, 1983; EdD, Johnson & Wales U., 2003—. Cons. Dias & Assocs., N. Kingstown, RI, 1985—; instr. emotional intelligence MotoRing Tech. Tng. Inst., E. Providence, RI, 1995—2000; prof. Johnson & Wales U., Providence, 2000—01; prof. grad. sch. Endicott Coll., Beverly, Maine, 2000—; prof., facilitator Duke U., Durham, NC, 2001. Mentor Feinstein Making a Difference Program, N. Kingstown, 2000—. Actor: (stage play) Talking With, 1996 (Irene Ryan nominee), (musical) The Best Little Whorehouse in Texas, 1996; prodr.: (plays) The Lottery, 1995; dir.: Nicholas Nickelby, 1995, The Monkey's Paw, 1995, James and the Giant Peach, 1997, Patient rep. vol. R.I. Hosp., Providence, 1999—; vol. instr. Odyssey of the Mind; vol. N. Kingstown Sch. Dept. Lights, Camera, Action; vol. performing arts instr. N. Kingstown Recreation Dept.; guest spkr. AIDS Respite Program; vol. cons. R.I. Cambodian Soc.; bd. dirs. St. Mary's Sch., Cranston, RI. Named Outstanding Woman of Yr. in Arts and Edn., Greater Providence YWCA, 2001; recipient Town Hero award, North Kingstown, 1998, Citizen citation, City of Providence, 2001, scholar, Johnson & Wales U., 2000. Mem.: NEA, AAUW (mem. Diversity Task Force, co-author, dir. Reviving the D 1999—, rsch. and projects endowment 2001), Am. Soc. Tng. and Devel., Friends of Oceanography (chair publicity com. 1985—88), Academy Players (bd. dirs. 1992), CCRI Players Club (pres. 1995—96). Avocations: scuba diving, aerobics (cert. instr.), world travel. Personal E-mail: teachdias@home.com. Business E-Mail: MDias@jwu.edu.

DIAS, MICHELE C. primary educator; b. Ft. Bragg, Calif., Jan. 14, 1949; d. Dana and Jessie Kathryn (Pacini) Coverston; 1 child, Adam Russell. AA, Santa Rosa Jr. Coll., 1970; BA in Spanish, Calif. State U., Sonoma, 1973; clad credential, U. San Diego, 1999. Cert. elem. tchr., Calif. 4th grade tchr. Ft. Bragg Unified Sch. Dist., 1973-74, kindergarten bilingual tchr., 1980—; bilingual tchr. Migrant Edn. Summer Sch., Ft. Bragg, 1988-98. Dist. rep. Nat. Bilingual Edn. Conf., L.A., 1994. Mem. NEA, Calif. Tchrs. Assn., Parents Club (grade level rep. 1999, chair com. 1999). Avocations: music, reading, walking, tutoring, computers. Office: Redwood Elem Sch 324 S Lincoln St Fort Bragg CA 95437-4498

DIASIO, ILSE WOLFARTSBERGER, volunteer; b. Linz, Austria, Nov. 12, 1946; came to U.S., 1967; d. D.I. Gottfried and Elfriede (Stuchlik) Wolfartsberger; m. Robert B. Diasio, July 4, 1970; children: Christoph, Thomas, Michael. Grad. in Phys. Therapy, U. Vienna, 1967. Phys. therapist Yale-New Haven Hosp., 1968-71, Vis. Nurse Assn., Rochester, NY, 1971-72; symposium coord. dept. pharmacology U. Ala., 1988. Vol. tchr. German, Pemberton Elem. Sch., Richmond, Va., 1980-84, Vestavia Hills Elem. and H.S., 1985-93; organizer student exch. program between Vestavia Hills H.S. and Seebacher Gymnasium, Graz, Austria, 1990, 91, 94; bd. dirs. World of Opportunity. Bd. dirs. Pemberton (Va.) Elem. Sch. PTA, 1979-84, pres., 1982-84; bd. dirs. Va. Commonwealth U. Faculty Woman's Club, 1978-84, Greater Birmingham Ministries, 1998—, chmn. direct svcs. work group, 1999—02, Ala. chpt. Fulbright Assn., 1999—, LWV Greater Birmingham, 1999-2000, World of Opportunity, 2002—; pres. Childrens Svc. League, 1991-92, treas. 1991-92, asst. treas. 1990-91, 2nd v.p., rec. sec., 1998-99; vol. Our Lady Queen of the Universe and Sacred Heart of Jesus Cath. Chs., 1988-90; St. Peter's rep. Ala. Arise, diocesan rep., rec. sec., 1988-94; mem. Peace and Justice Commn. of the Cath. Diocese of Birmingham, 1989-95, chair of commn., 1994-95; bd. dirs. Be an Apostle of Christ, 1988—, vice chair, 2003-; chair human concerns com. St. Peter's, 1988—; mem. Direct Svc. Network, 1989—; mem. Greater Birmingham Ministries program, 1989—; treas., membership chair Greater Birmingham UNA-USA chpt., 1992—, mem. coun. chpts. and divsns. steering com., 2001—; mem. COMPEER Bd., Birmingham, Ala., 1990-99; mem. WOC, Call to Action, Bread for the World, CALC, Pax Christi, Amnesty Internat., Nat. Conf. of Cmty. and Justice, Smithsonian Inst., UNICEF, Coalition Against Hate Crimes, 1997—, Birmingham Com. on Fgn. Rels., 1998—; organizer Christmas gift drive for needy families Angel Tree project St. Peter's Cath. Ch., 1988—; mem. steering com. UNA-USA CCD, 2001—; bd. dirs. The World of Opportunity, sec., 2002—; vol. tchr. for GED preparation. Recipient resolution City of Birmingham, 1999. Mem. AAUW, Nat. Mus. of Women in the Arts, U.S. Holocost Mus., Vereinigung Ehemaliger Körnerschülerinnen, LWV (bd. dirs. Greater Birmingham 1999-2000). Roman Catholic. Avocations: reading, music, skiing, cooking, travelling. Home: 1225 Branchwater Ln Birmingham AL 35216-2001 E-mail: idiasio@aol.com.

DIAZ, ANNE MARIE THERESA, music educator, musician; d. Francis Joseph and Anne Patricia DeMase; m. Carl Anthony Diaz, May 3, 1975 (div. Oct. 2000); children: Christina Bianca Diaz Bailey, Lisa Marie Diaz Gibson. Attended, Carnegie-Mellon U., 1971—73. Sales/mgmt. Bloomingdale's, N.Y.C., 1973—75; owner and designer Sunny Days Creations, Vestal, NY, 1982—85; pvt. tchr. music Seaville, NJ, 1986—90; tchr. spl. edn., art, and music Uppertownship Sch. Sys., Seaville, 1986—90; tchr. music Jennings Music, Marietta, Ga., 1992—96; owner, tchr. music Tchg. Little Fingers to Play, Marietta, 1996—2004. Musician: Syracuse Civic Light Opera Co., 1970—71, Syracuse Symphony, 1971, Atlanta Wind Symphony, 1998—2000. Pres. Bells Ferry Elem. Sch. PTA, Marietta, 1986—87. Mem.: Lexington Home Owners Assn. (pres. 2002—04), Kappa Alpha Theta, Sigma Alpha Iota. Home: 4318 Nesbin Kennesaw GA 30144

DIAZ, CAMERON, actress; b. Long Beach, Calif., Aug. 30, 1972; Grad. high sch., Long Beach, Calif. Appeared in (films) The Mask, 1994, Feeling Minnesota, 1996, She's the One, 1996, The Last Supper, 1996, Keys to Tulsa, 1996, Head Above Water, 1996, My Best Friend's Wedding, 1997 (Blockbuster Entertainment award), a Life Less Ordinary, 1997, (television)

Space Ghost Coast to Coast, 1994, Very Bad Things, 1998, Fear and Loathing in Las Vegas, 1998, There's Something About Mary (Golden Globe nomination Best Performance by an Actress in a Comedy or Musical Motion Picture), 1998 (N.Y. Film Critics Cir. award, MTV Movie award, Am. Comedy award), Invisible Circus, 1999, Being John Malkovich (Golden Globe nomination Best Supporting Actress in a Motion Picture), 1999, Any Given Sunday, 1999, Charlie's Angels: The Movie, 2000, Things You Can Tell Just by Looking at Her, 2000, Shrek (voice), 2001, Vanilla Sky, 2001, The Sweetest Thing, 2002, Gangs of New York, 2002, Charlie's Angels: Full Throttle, 2003. Named Female Star of Tomorrow, Nat. Theatre Owners Assn., 1996, Boston Soc. of Film Critics best supporting actress award, 2001, Chicago Film Critics Award for best supporting actress, 2002. Office: Internat Creative Mgmt 8942 Wilshire Blvd Beverly Hills CA 90211*

DIAZ, CONSUELO, health facility administrator; BA, U. So. Calif., 1966, MPA, 1989. Chief of staff LAC/USC Medical Center; with Department of Health Services, Los Angeles; administrative officer Women's Hospital, Los Angeles; CEO Rancho Los Amigos Nat. Rehab. Ctr., 1993—. Mem. Rehabilitation Advisory Council, Calif., 2000—; dir. Calif. Assoc. of Public Hospitals and Health Systems. Mem.: Nat. Assoc. of Public Hospitals, Healthcare Assoc. of S. Calif., Governing Council for Long Term Care and Rehab., Governing Council for Metropolitan Hospitals, Am. Hospital Assoc. Office: 7601 E Imperial Hwy Downey CA 90242-3456

DIAZ, ELENA R. community health nurse; b. Albuquerque; d. Mariá E. Lopes. BSN, U. Ariz., 1975. RN Ariz., cert. cmty. health nurse, Ariz. Community health nurse Pima County Health Dept., Tucson, 1975—. Mem. ad hoc com. minority recruitment and retention Coll. Nursing U. Ariz., Tucson. Recipient St. Cyril's Clari Dunn/Judith Lovchick award, Peace and Justice Com., 1987, La Esperanza award, 1987. Mem.: Phi Beta Kappa. Office: Pima County Health Dept South Office 175 W Irvington Tucson AZ 85714

DIAZ, LAURA, newscaster; b. Santa Paula, Calif. BA in English, Cal Poly State, San Luis Obispo. Reporter KABC-TV, Los Angeles, 1983—85, anchor, 1985—, lead anchor, Eyewitness News at 5 and 11pm, 1997—2002; co-anchor, CBS 2 News at 5 and 11pm KCBS, Los Angeles, 2002—. Recipient Best News Reporting Award, L.A. Press Club, 1992, Joseph M. Quinn Award, 2003. Office: CBS 2 News 6121 Sunset Blvd Los Angeles CA 90028*

DIAZ, SHARON, education administrator; b. Bakersfield, Calif., July 29, 1946; d. Karl C. and Mildred (Lunn) Clark; m. Luis F. Diaz, Oct. 19, 1968; children: Daniel, David. BS, San Jose State U., 1969; MS, U. Calif., San Francisco, 1973; PhD (hon.), St. Mary's Coll. Calif., 1999. Nurse Kaiser Found. Hosp., Redwood City, Calif., 1969-73; lectr. San Jose (Calif.) State Coll., 1969-70; instr. St. Francis Meml. Hosp. Sch. Nursing, San Francisco, 1970—71; pub. health nurse San Mateo County, 1971—72; instr. Samuel Merritt Hosp. Sch. Nursing, Oakland, Calif., 1973—76; asst. dir. Samuel Merritt Hosp. Sch. of Nursing, Oakland, 1976—78, dir., 1978—84; founding pres. Samuel Merritt Coll., Oakland, 1984—; interim pres. Calif. Coll. Podiatric Medicine, 2001. V.p. East Bay Area Health Edn. Ctr., Oakland, 1980-87; mem. adv. com. Calif. Acad. Partnership Program, 1990-92; mem. nat. adv. com. Nursing Outcomes Project; bd. dirs. Calif. Workforce Initiative, U. Calif. San Francisco Ctr. for the Health Professions, 2000–. Bd. dirs. Head Royce Sch., 1990-98, vice chair, 1993-95, chair, 1995-97; bd. dirs. Ladies Home Soc., 1992—, sec. 1994-95, treas., CFO 1995-97, 2nd v.p. 1997-99; bd. dirs. George Mark Children's House, 2001–; mem. adv. bd. Ethnic Health Inst., 1997—; mem. com. minorities higher edn. Am. Coun. Edn., 1998—. Named Woman of Yr., Oakland YWCA, 1996. Mem. Am. Assn. of Pres. Ind. Colls. and Univs., Sigma Theta Tau (Leadership award Nu Xi chpt. 2001). Office: Samuel Merritt Coll 450 30th St Oakland CA 94609-3302 E-mail: sdiaz@samuelmerritt.edu.

DIAZ MEYER, CHERYL, photojournalist; b. Phillipines; arrived in US, 1981; BA in German, U. Minn., 1990; BA in journalism, Western Ky. U., 1994. Staff photographer Mpls. Star Tribune, 1994—2000; sr. staff photographer Dallas Morning News, 2000—. Named Minn. Photographer Yr., 1999; recipient Pulitzer Prize for breaking news photography, 2004. Office: Dallas Morning News 508 Young St PO Box 655237 Dallas TX 75265-5237

DIBATTISTE, CAROL A. lawyer; b. Phila., Dec. 28, 1951; d. Peter Martin DiBattiste and Hilda Yolanda (Battilana) Mignogna. BA magna cum laude, LaSalle U., 1976; JD, Temple U., 1981; LLM, Columbia U., 1986. Bar: Pa. 1982, U.S. Ct. Mil. Appeals 1982, U.S. Supreme Ct. 1985, N.Y. 1989, D.C. 1989, Fla. 1990, U.S. Dist. Ct. (so. dist.) Fla. 1991, U.S. Ct. Appeals (11th cir.) 1991. Commd. 2d lt. USAF, 1976, advanced through grades to maj., 1987, cir. trial counsel Pacific Region, 1982—85; mem. faculty USAF JAG Sch., Maxwell AFB, Ala., 1986—89; chief recruiting atty. Office of Judge Advocate Gen. USAF, Washington, 1989—91; asst. U.S. atty. So. Dist. Fla., Miami, 1991—92; dir. Office of Legal Edn. Dept. Justice, 1992—93; prin. dep. gen. coun. Dept. of Navy, 1993—94; dir. Exec. Office for U.S. Attys., Washington, 1994—98; dep. U.S. atty. So. Dist. Fla., Miami, 1998—99; undersec. USAF, Arlington, Va., 1999—2001; ptnr. Holland & Knight, LLP, 2001—03; chief of staff Transp. Security Adminstrn., 2003—. Adj. faculty U. Miami Sch. Law Trial Skills, 1998—99; bd. dirs. Holland & Knight Cons. Editor: The Reporter, 1986—87; mem. editl. bd.: Air Force Law Rev., 1984; contbr. articles to profl. jours. Mem. bd. visitors Temple U. Sch. Law, 1996-99; trustee USAF JAG Sch. Found., 1993-96. Mem. ABA (chmn. standing com. on mil. law 1989-91), Fed. Bar Assn. (Young Fed. Lawyer award 1985), Nat. Inst. for Trial Advocacy (faculty 1986-92), USAF Assn. Roman Catholic. Business E-Mail: carol.dibattiste@dhs.gov.

DI BENEDETTO, ANN LOUISE, accounting administrator; b. Knoxville, Tenn., Jan. 26, 1954; d. William Brown and Louise (Emerson) Nixon; m. Raymond Peters, July 11, 1975 (dec.); m. Robert Di Benedetto, Sept. 22, 2002. BBA, Miami U., Oxford, Ohio, 1976; MBA, Xavier U., 1985. Cert. internal auditor. Acctg. officer Soc. Bank (formerly Citizens Bank), Hamilton, Ohio, 1977-85; internal auditor Procter & Gamble Co., Cin., 1985-86, audit sect. mgr., 1986-88, sr. cost analyst, beauty care, 1988-90; plant fin. mgr. Procter & Gamble Mfg. Co., Phoenix, 1990-92; sr. fin. analyst, beauty care Procter & Gamble Co., Cin., 1992-93, group mgr., gen. acctg., 1993-96, group mgr. R&D fin., 1996-99, group mgr., global fin., paper divsn., 1999—2002, group mgr. global fin. governance, 2002—03, group mgr., fin., global bus. svcs., 2003—. Mem. Inst. Internal Auditors, Inst. Mgmt. Accts. Republican. Congregationalist. Avocations: golf, swimming. Home: 7889 Ironwood Way West Chester OH 45069-1623 Office: Procter & Gamble Co PO Box 599 Cincinnati OH 45201-0599

DIBERARDINO, MARIE ANTOINETTE, developmental biologist, educator; b. Phila., May 2, 1926; d. Henry and Adelina (Belfi) DiB. BS in Biology, Chestnut Hill Coll., 1948, JD (hon.), 1990; PhD in Zoology, U. Pa., 1962. Rsch. asst. Fox Chase Cancer Ctr. (formerly Inst. Cancer Rsch.), 1948-58, rsch. assoc., 1960-64, asst. mem., 1964-67; assoc. prof. anatomy Drexel U. Coll. Medicine, Phila., 1967-71, prof. anatomy, 1971-81, prof. physiology, 1981-92, prof. biochemistry, 1992-96, prof. emerita, 1996—. Adv. bd. Internat. Rev. of Cytology, 1976-2000, Differentiation, 1981—, Series: Developmental Biology, A Comprehensive Synthesis, 1982-94; assoc. editor Jour. Exptl. Zoology, 1984-86; Contbr. articles on devel., genetics and cell biology to sci. jours.; contbr. book revs. in field. Mem. NIH Fogarty Internat. Fellowship Study Group, 1984. NSF grantee, NIH grantee; recipient Jean Brachet Meml. award. Fellow AAAS; mem. Am. Soc. Cell Biology (emerita), Soc. for Devel. Biologists (emerita, treas., trustee 1975-78), Internat. Soc. Devel. Biologists, Internat. Soc. of Differentiation (emerita, exec. com. 1978-85, 87-90, bd. dirs. 1980-94). Office: Drexel U Coll Medicine 2900 W Queen Ln Philadelphia PA 19129-1033 E-mail: mad26@drexel.edu.

DIBLASI, DIANNE CLARK, editor; b. Bklyn., May 3, 1960; d. Arthur J. and Constance C. (Clark) Mandick; m. Paul J. DiBlasi; 1 child, Bryan Gene. BA in Journalism, NYU, 1982. Asst. editor Random House/Fodor's Travel Guides, N.Y.C., 1983-85; writer, editor Constrn. Products Rev. Mag., Boston, 1986-88; prodn. editor Prentice Hall, Englewood Cliffs, N.J., 1988-91; owner, cons. D. DiBlasi Editl. Svcs., Allendale, NJ, 1991—. Copy editor: Take My Word For It, 1986; prodn. editor: Creativities! Elementary Curriculum Art Activities, 1991, Parenting Toward Solutions, 1997; editor, writer Constrn. Products Rev., 1986-88. Mem. Hillsdale Playground Assn., 1994-96, Hillsdale Centennial Com., 1996; mem., chair com. Meadowbrook Faculty and Family Assn., Hillsdale, 1996—; host Fresh Air Fund, 1997—; docent Wildlife Conservation Soc., Bronx Zoo. Mem.: Editl. Freelancer Assn., Brookside Music Assn. (chmn.). Avocations: animal wildlife outreach programs, fundraising. Home and Office: 222 E Crescent Ave Allendale NJ 07401

DIBLE, ROSE HARPE MCFEE, special education educator; b. Phoenix, Apr. 28, 1927; d. Ambrose Jefferson and Laurel Mabel (Harpe) McFee; m. James Henry Dible, June 23, 1951 (div. Jan. 1965); 1 child, Michael James. BA in Speech Edn., Ariz. State U., Tempe, 1949; MA in Speech and Drama, U. So. Calif., L.A., 1950; fellow, Calif. State U., Fullerton, 1967. Cert. secondary tchr., spl. edn. tchr. English and drama tchr. Lynwood (Calif.) Sr. High Sch., 1950-51, Montebello (Calif.) Sr. High Sch., 1952-58; tchr. English and Social Studies Pioneer High Sch., Whittier, Calif., 1964-65; spl. edn. tchr. Bell Gardens (Calif.) High Sch., 1967-85, spl. edn. cons., 1985-90. Mem. DAR, Daus. Am. Colonists, Whittier Christian Woman Assn., La Habra Womans Club, Eastern Star Lodge, Kappa Delts, Phi Delta Gamma. Republican. Presbyterian. Avocations: church choir, tap dancing, doll collecting, travel. Home: 1201 Russell St La Habra CA 90631-2530 Office: Montebello Unified Sch Dist 123 Montebello Blvd Montebello CA 90640

DIBONA, LESLIE FAYE, librarian; b. Quincy, Mass., Sept. 7, 1953; d. Ferrer I.M. DiBona and Doris Louise (Mikkelsen) Boyes; m. Douglass Blake Payne, May 24, 1980 (div. Sept. 1987); m. Steven T. McGivern, July 31, 1993. AB, Boston U., 1975; MS in LIS, Simmons Coll., 1980. Serials libr. Tufts U.-Wessell Libr., Medford, Mass., 1980-84; head of tech. svcs. Harvard Grad. Sch. of Edn.-Libr., Cambridge, Mass., 1985-91, U.S. Dept. of Edn. Rsch. Libr., Washington, 1991-94; dir. libr. devel. U. Libr.-San Diego State U., 1994—2001; rsch. mgr. major gifts San Diego (Calif.) State U., 2001—. Founding mem. Calif. State U. Libr. Devel. Dirs., 1994, Acad. Libr. Advancement and Devel. Network, 1995-2001. Mem. ALA, Calif. Assn. of Rsch. Libs., Phi Beta Kappa. Avocations: theatre, photography, travel. Office: San Diego State Univ 5500 Campanile Dr San Diego CA 92182-8045

DIBONA, MARGARET ROSE, retired state official; b. Phila., Jan. 21, 1946; d. Peter Gerardo and Margaret E. (Moffett) DiB. BA, Cabrini Coll., Radnor, Pa., 1993. Inside sales rep. Arthur H. Thomas Co., Phila., 1965-69; sales corr. TRW Electronics, Villanova, Pa., 1969-71; pharmacy technician DiBona Pharmacy, Havertown, Pa., 1959-73; UC claims interviewer Upper Darby (Pa.) Job Ctr., 1973-76; UC claims examiner I Chester (Pa.) Job Ctr., 1976-87; employment svc. program supr. U.S. Dept. Labor, Commonwealth of Pa., Bur. Chester County Job Ctr., Coatesville, Pa., 1987—. Prodr. report linking tobacco smoke and asthma emergencies for WHO, 1990. Cmty. coun. Am. Lung Assn., West Chester, Pa., 1995—; primary educator at Camp Superstuff for Asthmatic Children, 1995—; facilitator of support group to redefine asthma, asthma educator Southeastern Pa., 1989—; cons., 1989—; cert. Laubach Literacy Tutor, 1988—; continuing edn. adv. bd. Cabrini Coll, chair accelerated degree program. Avocations: fine art, drawing sculpting, biking, hiking. Office: Bur Disability Retirement UISC Philadelphia PA 19114 E-mail: lungevity@hotmail.com.

DICAMILLO, KATE, writer; b. Phila. Degree, U. Fla., Gainesville, Fla. Author: The Tiger Rising, 1999 (named Newbery Honor Book, 2000), Because of Winn-Dixie, 2000 (named Newbery Honor Book, 2001), The Tale of Despereaux: Being the Story of a Mouse, a Princess, Some Soup, and a Spool of Thread, 2003 (Newbery medal, 2004). Fellow McKnight Artist fellowship, 1998. Office: Candlewick Press Inc 2067 Massachusetts Ave Cambridge MA 02140*

DICARLO, LAURETTE MARY, nurse; b. Cleve., Aug. 19, 1950; d. Amerigo and Helen (Senuta) DiC. LPN, Willoughby-Eastlake Sch., 1976; AS in Nursing, Santa Fe C.C., Gainesville, Fla., 1982; BSN magna cum laude, U. South Fla., 1991, MS in Nursing, 1997. RN, Fla., advanced registered nurse practitioner. Nurse Riverside Meth. Hosp., Columbus, Ohio, 1976-78, Lakeland (Fla.) Gen. Hosp., 1978-79, Alalhua Gen. Hosp., Gainesville, 1979-82; nurse mgr. progressive care Humana Northside Hosp., St. Petersburg, Fla., 1991-92; critical care nurse Columbia Largo (Fla.) Med. Ctr., 1982-91; med. supr. TGC Home Health, Clearwater, Fla., 1994-95; charge nurse cardiovascular intensive care, emergency nurse Columbia Largo Med. Ctr., 1992-98, nurse practitioner internal medicine and infectious disease, 1998—. Vol. Soc. for Prevention of Cruelty to Animals, Largo, 1991—. Santa Fe scholar, 1982, Joan K. Stout scholar Miami Heart Inst./U. South Fla., 1996-97. Mem. AACN, ANA, Am. Acad. Nurse Practitioners, Fla. Nurses Assn., Phi Kappa Phi, Sigma Theta Tau. Avocation: oil painting.

DICARLO, SUSANNE HELEN, financial analyst; b. Greensburg, Pa., Nov. 24, 1956; d. Wayne Larry and Clara Emogene (Weaver) Gower; m. John Joseph DiCarlo, June 21, 1980; children: Sarah Rose, Kristen Marie. BS in Acctg., Va. Tech., 1978. Auditor U.S. Army Audit Agy., Ft. Monroe, Va., 1978-79; acct. technician Fleet Combat Tng. Ctr., Virginia Beach, Va., 1980-82, supervisory auditor, 1982-83; fin. analyst Comml. Activity Mgmt. Team, Norfolk, Va., 1983—. Fed. women's program mgr. Fleet Combat Tng. Ctr., 1980—83. Creator newsletter: Fed. Women's Program Mgr., 1980—83. Mem.: Southeastern Assn. Trailriders, Am. Soc. Mil. Comptrollers, Seaside Mountaineers Club (Virginia Beach) (treas. 1986—88). Home: 4013 Dillaway Ct Virginia Beach VA 23456-1257

DICCIANI, NANCE KATHERINE, chemical company executive, chemical engineer; b. Phila., Oct. 18, 1947; d. Augustine Joseph and Josephine Cecila (Maggiano) D.; m. Joseph William Kunz, Oct. 31, 1970 (div. 1984). B in Chem. Engring., Villanova U., 1969; MS in Chem. Engring., U. Va., 1970; PhD in Chem. Engring., U. Pa., 1977, MBA, 1986. Registered profl. engr., Pa. Engr. Phila. Water Dept., 1971-72, supt., 1972-74; with Air Products and Chems., Inc., Allentown, Pa., 1991, dir. research and devel., 1984-86, gen. mgr., 1986—91; sr. v.p. & head of European operations Rohm & Haas, Paris, 1991—2002; pres. & CEO specialty materials Honeywell, Morristown, NJ, 2002—. Mem. adv. com. U. Va., Charlottesville, 1987—. Contbr. articles to tech. publs.; patentee in field. Mem. Allentown Com. on Sci. Edn., 1984-85, adv. com. Allentown Women's Health Ctr., 1987, previous bd. mem. of European Chemical Industry Fedn. (CEFIC), PP&L Resources Inc., Villanova U. Trustees. Mem. Am. Inst. Chem. Engrs., Soc. Women Engrs. (nat. adviser 1984-86, Achievement award 1987). Avocations: archaeology, tennis, skiing, golf, sailing.

DICICCO, MARGARET C. lawyer; b. Bklyn., Mar. 22, 1961; d. Vincent Richard and Margaret Josephine (Ciullo) DiC.; m. James Louis O'Rourke, Sept. 18, 1994. BA in Polit. Sci., Bklyn. Coll., CUNY, 1983; JD, U. Bridgeport, 1987. Bar: N.Y. 1989, Conn. 1994, U.S. Dist. Ct. (so. dist.) N.Y. 1989, U.S. Dist. Ct. (ea. dist.) N.Y. 1990, U.S. Dist. Ct. Conn. 1995, U.S. Supreme Ct., 1998. Assoc. Ginsberg & Caesar, N.Y.C., 1988-89, Abrams & Martin P.C., N.Y.C., 1989-93, Chesney, Murphy & Moran, Westbury, N.Y., 1993-94, Law Offices of James L. O'Rourke, 1994—. Mem. ABA, NYSBA, Greater Bridgeport Bar Assn. Roman Catholic. Home: 221 Nells Rock Rd Shelton CT 06484-3831 Office: Law Offices James L O'Rourke 1825 Barnum Ave Ste 201 Stratford CT 06614-5333

DICKENS, ALICE MCKNIGHT, minister; b. Edgecombe County, N.C., May 6, 1935; d. John and Candis Moore McKnight; m. Ernest Dickens, 1954; children: Ernest Douglas, Ronald, John, Larry, Candice, Mark. Degree in nursing, Edgecombe C.C., 1981. Lic. nurse, N.C. Founder, pastor Ch. of God of Deliverance, Rocky Mount, NC, 1971—; pres. N.C. Dist. Union Apostolic Faith Ch. of God, 1994—. Mem. pastoral staff Apostolic Faith Ch. of God, Franklin, Va., 1982—. Supporter Crisis Ministry/homeless shelter, Rocky Mount; bd. dirs. New Sources, Rocky Mount, NC, 2001—, Meals on Wheels, Rocky Mount, 1998—2000. Recipient hon. mention, Jefferson awards, WTVD-TV, Durham, N.C., 1995, tribute plaque, OIC HIV/AIDS Program, Rocky Mount, 1999. Home: 909 Columbia Ave Rocky Mount NC 27804 Office: Ch of God of Deliverance 900 Columbia Ave Rocky Mount NC 27804

DICKENS, ALYCIA THOMPSON, nurse practitioner; b. Norfolk, Va., July 31, 1968; d. Freeman Robert and Doris Kennedy Thompson; m. Byron Patrick Dickens, Mar. 20, 1991; children: Schuyler Kennedy, Logan Alexandria. BSN, Hampton U., 1995, MS, 1997. RN, Va.; cert. family nurse practitioner. Nurse Ea. State Hosp., Williamsburg, Va., 1995-96, Med. Coll. Va. at Va. Commonwealth U., Richmond, 1996—; nurse bon secours Med. ICU, Depaul Med. Ctr., 1997-99; nurse practitioner infectious disease divsn. Ea. Va. Med. Sch., 1999—. Recipient grant Ea. State Hosp., 1994, 95, William Freeman scholarship Hampton U., 1995. Mem. ANA, Assn. Reproductive Health Profls., Va. Nurses Assn., Va. Coun. for Nurse Practitioners, Sigma Theta Tau, Alpha Kappa Alpha. Democrat. Baptist.

DICKENS, JANIS, media services administrator; b. Des Moines, June 4, 1949; d. M. Wesley and Lenita Bird (Heath) Jordan BS, Iowa State U., 1971; AMLS, U. Mich., 1972. Libr. Monterey (Calif.) Inst. Internat. Studies, 1972-73, Contra Costa Pub. Libr., Pleasant Hill, Calif., 1973-74, L.A. Pub. Libr., 1974-75; br. mgr. San Jose (Calif.) Pub. Libr., 1975-79; head libr. pub. svcs. DeAnza C.C., Cupertino, Calif., 1979-85; dir. libr., instructional svcs. Hartnell C.C., Salinas, Calif., 1985-89; dir. instructional media svcs. U. Calif., Santa Cruz, 1989—2000; dir. U. Calif. Davis, Classroom Tech. Svc., 2000. Pres. Dirs. Edn. Tech. in Calif. Higher Edn., Santa Barbara, 1992-93; bd. dirs. Consortium Coll. and Univ. Media Ctrs., Ames, Iowa, 1995-97. Co-author: (reference book) Classroom Guidelines, 1995; contbr. articles to Coll. and Univ. Media Rev., 1995—. Mem. Fremont Bd. Edn. Task Force on Librs., 1988-91; mem. Alameda County Libr. Commn., Alameda, Calif., 1986-89; mem. People for a Permanent Libr., Fremont, 1987-90. Mem. Am. Libr. Assn., Calif. Libr. Assn., No. Calif. Telecomm. Consortium, Methodist. Avocations: gardening, travel, sports, sailing. Office: U Calif Davis One Shields Ave Davis CA 95616

DICKENS, JOYCE REBECCA, addictions therapist, educator; b. Roanoke Rapids, N.C. d. Lydia Marie Dickens. M in Addiction Psychology with honors, Capella U., 2000, postgrad., 2000—. Cert. addiction profl. Adj. instr. Broward CC, Ft. Lauderdale, Fla., 1991—; primary therapist addictions Treatment Works, Ft. Lauderdale, 2002—. Mem.: AAUW, Phi Theta Kappa, Alpha Chi. Avocations: tennis, travel, public speaking. Office Phone: 954-806-9864. E-mail: joyced@bellsouth.net.

DICKENSON-HAZARD, NANCY ANN, pediatric nurse practitioner, consultant; b. Ashland, Ky., Sept. 25, 1946; m. John H. Hazard Jr., May 28, 1977; 2 children. BSN, U. Ky., 1968; cert., U. Mo., 1971, U. Va., 1976, MSN, 1977. RN, Md.; PNP. Asst. program dir., instr. nursing Ea. Ky. U., Richmond, Va., 1973-75; PNP Cen. Va. Community Health Plan, New Canton, 1976-77; PNP nurse coord. Georgetown U. Health Plan, Kensington, Md., 1977-79; PNP Kaiser Health Plan, Kensington, Md., 1979-81; exec. dir. Nat. Cert. Bd. PNP/Nurses, Rockville, Md., 1981—. Ind. nurse cons. Continuing Edn. and Quality Assurance, Rockville, 1978-81; cons. to Student Nurse Assn., Ea. Ky. U., Richmond, 1974-75; speaker numerous convs. and confs. Contbg. author: Fundamentals of Nursing, 1989, Basic Nursing: Theory and Practice, 1987, Community Health Nursing, 1991; mem. editorial bd. Ped. Nursing Jour., 1986—, Jour. Pediatric Health Care, 1987; chmn. humanitarian award com. Pediatric Nursing Jour.; contbr. articles to profl. jours. Pres., Home and Sch. Assn., Rockville, 1990; mem. com. St. Elizabeth Parish and Sch., Rockville, 1984-92. Fellow Nat. Assn. Pediatric Nurse Assocs. and Practitioners (Henry K. Silver award for nat. excellence 1983), Am. Acad. Nursing; mem. ANA, Leadership Roundtable for Advanced Nursing Practice, Sigma Theta Tau. Roman Catholic. Avocations: crafts, sewing, reading, gardening. Office: Sigma Theta Tau Intl 550 W North St Indianapolis IN 46202-3191

DICKERMAN, SERAFINA POERIO, real estate broker, consultant; b. Camden, N.J., Sept. 20, 1920; d. Giuseppe Francesco Poerio and Christina Audia; m. John M. Dickerman, Oct. 27, 1956; 1 child, Dorothea Wilhelmina. Student, Seton Hill Coll., Greensburg, Pa., 1938—39, St. Vincent Coll., Latrobe, Pa., 1939—40, Barnard Coll., 1941, Northwestern U., 1943, Strayer Coll., 1951, U. Md., 1971, Am. U., 1953, student, 1965, student, 1966, student, 1967, student, 1972, student, 1973. Lic. pvt. pilot, radio operator, meteorologist, radio tel. operator, real estate agt. Md., D.C., Va., N.Y., Fla., Fedn. Internat. Professions Immobilieres, France, cert. internat. property specialist Nat. Assn. Realtors. Mem. Civil Air Patrol, Civil Aeronautics Authority, Latrobe, 1939—41; control tower radio operator TWA, Columbus, Ohio, 1941—42; meteorologist Pan Am. Airlines and Colonial Airlines, N.Y.C., 1942—43; stewardess Ea. Airlines, N.Y.C., 1943—45; part-time high fashion model Harry Conover Agy., N.Y.C., 1943—45; negotiator, organizer Airline Stewards and Stewardesses Assn. of U.S., Chgo., 1944—46; pres. Dickerman Real Estate/Investment Co., Potomac, Md., 1972—. Participant European Bldg. and Real Estate Study Nat. Assn. Home Builders and European builder orgns., 1963. Contbr. articles to mags. in field. Driver blood mobile, life saver swimmer Nat. Red Cross, Washington, 1955; hostess USO, N.Y.C., 1941; mem. Young Rep. Club, N.Y.C., 1941, Potomac Women's Rep. Club, 1960. Recipient Civil Air Patrol Silver Wings, Fed. Aeronautics Authority, 1939—40. Mem.: Nat. Mus. Women in the Arts (charter), Italian Culture Soc. of Washington, Capital Spkrs. Club (Washington), Women's Golf Assn. of Congl. Country Club, Congl. Country Club (hon. life). Presbyterian. Avocations: music, art, golf, tennis, swimming. Office: Dickerman Real Estate/Investment Co 9030 Bronson Dr Potomac MD 20854 Office Phone: 301-983-2546.

DICKERSON, BETTY, secondary education educator, consultant, tester; b. Warrenton, Va., May 7, 1948; d. Early Columbus Jr. and Mary Elizabeth (Kendrick) Griffith; m. Douglas Jerry Dickerson, Sept. 27, 1991. BS, So. Conn. State U., 1972; MEd, Fla. Atlantic U., Boca Raton, 1978; DDiv (hon.), Word Christianship Ministries, Fresno, Calif., 1993. Cert. tchr., Va., N.C. Home/hosp. tchr. Palm Beach County Pub. Schs., West Palm Beach, Fla., 1978-93; tchr. of the emotionally disturbed Prince William County Pub. Schs., Manassas, Va., 1993-98; substitute tchr. Warren County H.S., Front Royal, Va., 1998-99; math. tchr. Davie County H.S., Mocksville, N.C., 1999—. Contbg. author The Light, 1999. Literacy Missions assoc. Ch. and Cmty. Ministries, So. Bapt. Conf., 1982-99; vol. tutor ESL, Davie

County H.S., 1999—. Mem. N.C. Coun. Tchrs. Math. Avocations: horseback riding, writing an ethnographic history of the chickahominy indians, math and logic puzzles, reading. E-mail: bettydickerson@iname.com.

DICKERSON, CLAIRE MOORE, lawyer, educator; b. Boston, Apr. 1, 1950; d. Roger Cleveland and Ines Idelette (Roullet) Moore; m. Thomas Pasquali Dickerson, May 22, 1976; children: Caroline Anne, Susannah Moore. AB, Wellesley Coll., 1971; JD, Columbia U., 1974; LLM in Taxation, NYU, 1981. Bar: N.Y. 1975, U.S. Dist. Ct. (ea. and so. dists.) N.Y. 1975, U.S. Ct. Appeals (2d cir.) 1975, U.S. Supreme Ct. 1980. Assoc. Coudert Brothers, N.Y., 1974-82, ptnr., 1983-86, Schnader, Harrison, Segal & Lewis, N.Y., 1987-88, of counsel, 1988—; assoc. prof. law St. John's U., Jamaica, N.Y., 1986-88, prof., 1989-2000; prof law Rutgers U., Newark, 2000—. Author: Partnership Law Adviser; contbr. articles to profl. jours. Scholar Arthur L. Dickson scholar. Mem.: ABA, Soc. for Advancement of Socio-Econs., Law and Soc. Assn., Assn. of Bar of City of N.Y., Shenorock Club. Democrat. E-mail: cmdckrsn@rci.rutgers.edu.

DICKERSON, CYNTHIA ROWE, marketing executive, consultant; b. Cin., Apr. 14, 1956; d. Richard Emmett and Frances Jeanette (Ellwanger) Rowe; m. Mark Alan Dickerson, Oct. 24, 1981; children: Shannon Gayle, Meredith Lynne. BSBA, U. So. Calif., 1979. Mgmt. asst. Computer Scis. Corp., Pasadena, Calif., 1974-78; rsch. asst. Dailey & Assocs., L.A., 1978-79; account exec. Young & Rubicam, L.A., 1979-81, Rowley & Linder Advt., Wichita, Kans., 1981-82, Chiat/Day Inc. Advt., San Francisco, 1983-85; product mgr. Sun-Diamond Growers of Calif., Pleasanton, 1985-88; mktg. cons. San Francisco, 1988-90; sr. bus. mgr. Del Monte Foods, San Francisco, 1990-93; dir. mktg. Yorkshire Dried Fruit & Nuts, Inc., San Francisco, 1993-94, Potlatch Corp., 1995-98; dir. category mgmt., dir S. & W. brand bus. unit Tri Valley Growers, 1999-2001; mktg. cons., 2001, v.p. mktg. and sales John Laing Homes, Greenwood Village, Colo., 2002—03, dir. mkt. rsch., 2003—. Named Outstanding Youth Women of Am., Jr. C. of C., 1985. Mem. Am. Mktg. Assn., Soc. Consumer Affairs Profls., Am. Rose Soc., Heritage Rose Group. Republican. Avocations: gardening, youth sports, playing piano, gourmet cooking. Office: John Laing Homes 7000 E Belleview Ave Ste 200 Greenwood Village CO 80111 E-mail: cdickerson@johnlainghomes.com.

DICKEY, BETTY C. judge; b. 1940; m. Jay Dickey, 1960 (div. 1987); 1 adopted child, John 1 foster child, Cindy children: Laura, Ted, Rachel. BA in English, U. Ark., JD, 1985. Former tchr., Pine Bluff and Watson Chapel, Ark.; former pvt. practice atty.; former atty. State Soil and Water Commn., Ark.; former Pine Bluff asst. atty.; former Redfield city atty.; prosecutor 11th Jud. Dist., 1995—99; Ark. Pub. Svc. commr., 1999—2003; chief legal counsel Ark. Gov's Office, 2003; interim chief justice Ark. Supreme Ct., 2003—. Recipient Atty. Gen.'s Top Prosecutor award, 1997, Top 100 Women in Ark. award, 1998, 1999. Office: Adminstrv Office of the Cts 625 Marshall St 120 Justice Bldg Little Rock AR 72201

DICKEY, JEANNETTA BURKETT, social worker; b. Murphy, N.C., Oct. 19, 1928; d. Arthur Bascomb and Jenny Thelma (Mulcay) D.; m. John Arnette (div. 1967); children: John Arnette, Jeannetta Dickey Arnette, Claiborne Burkett Arnette, Benjamin Harrison Arnette. BA, Brenau Coll., 1949; MSW, U. N.C., 1969; postgrad., Duke U., 1970. Lic. clin. social worker, Calif.; cert. clin. social worker, N.C.; cert. Am. Assn. State Social Work Bds. Tchr. secondary edn., various locations, 1950-03, chief social worker, then sr. adminstr. Vance, Warren, Granville & Franklin CMHC, John Unstead Hosp., Henderson, N.C., 1969-72; chief social worker areas A, B, & C Mental Health Adminstrn., Washington, 1972-78; clin. social worker Met. State Hosp., Norwalk, Calif., 1981-88, Camarillo (Calif.) State Hosp., 1988-90; social worker Mental Health Adminstrn., Washington, 1990-92. Mem. exec. planning commn. Mental Health Adminstrn., Washington, 1974-78, mem. evaluation and cert. com., 1975-79; NIMH rsch. project for rural mental health, U. N.C., Chapel Hill, 1969-72. Author: The Multi Problem Family in Child Guidance, 1969; contbr. articles on rural mental health to profl. jours. Docent Nat. Gallery of Art, Washington, 1963, 64, 65; vol. family liaison Western Carolina Ctr., Black Mountain, N.C., 1980; vol. English as Second Lang., Washington, 1963-64; vol. United Fund-Meals on Wheels. Mem. AAUW (Cherokee County chpt.), DAR (various chpts.), Delta Delta Delta. Episcopalian. Home: 37 East Ave Murphy NC 28906-2967

DICKEY, LINDA ANN, learning center director; b. Chgo., Sept. 11, 1950; d. Edwin John and Bertha Melvina (Kryspin) Latos; m. Michael Dene Dickey, June 16, 1973; children: Beth Marie, Melissa Lynn, Jonathan Michael. BA in Secondary Edn., Social Scis., U. Ill., 1972, MLS, 1973. Media specialist Indian Trail Jr. H.S., Plainfield, Ill., 1973-77; dir learning resource ctr. St. Pius X Sch., Lombard, Ill., 1989-95; learning ctr. dir. Hinsdale (Ill.) Middle Sch., 1995-96; dir. Learning Resource Ctr. St. Pius X Sch., Lombard, 1996—98; LMC dir. White Eagle Elem. Sch., Naperville, Ill., 1998—. Pres. Pleasant Lane PTA, Lombard, Ill., 1987-89; trustee Helen Plum Meml. Libr., Lombard, 1987—, pres. bd. trustees, 1995—. Named Lombard Woman of Yr., Lombard Svcs. League, 2003. Mem. Ill. Libr. Assn., Ill. Sch. Libr. Media Assn., Phi Beta Kappa. Roman Catholic. Avocations: reading, hiking, crocheting.

DICKINSON, CAROL RITTGERS, arts administrator, writer, executive director; b. Des Moines, Apr. 16, 1933; d. Robert Johnson and Cecil Marjorie (Snyder) Rittgers; m. Donald Ira Dickinson, June 6, 1959; 1 child, Lauren Lucy. BA in English with honors, Drake U., 1954; MA in Art History, U. Hawaii, 1964. Lydia Roberts fellow Columbia U., N.Y.C., 1954-56; instr. Iowa State U., U. Hawaii, Colo Women's Coll., U. Petroleum and Minerals, Dhahran, Saudi Arabia, Colo. Sc. Mines, Golden, 1956-76; dir. pub. programs Denver Art Mus., 1980-83; dir. publicity and edn. Mus. Western Art, Denver, 1985-86; freelance writer, 1979—. Lectr., panelist numerous mus., univs. and profl. groups, Colo., 1980—. Co-editor, contbg. author: Colorado and the American Renaissance, 1980, Walking in Beauty, 1990, The Art of Dean Mitchell, 1999; founding editor Denver Urban Design Forum Newsletter, 1984, 85; contbr. more than 400 articles to nat. and regional newspapers and mags.; art critic Denver Rocky Mountain News, 1990-92. Exec. dir. Foothills Art Ctr., Golden, 1992-2003. Named in honor The Carol and Don Dickinson Sculpture Garden, Foothills Art Ctr., Golden, Colo., 2004; recipient Denver Mayor's Award for Excellence in Arts, 2000, 1st Cultural award, Jefferson Symphony, 2000, medal, Colorado Sch. Mines, 2000. Mem. Colo. Press Women (first pl. awards, revs./features), Golden Fortnightly Club, Asian Art Assn. Democrat. Episcopalian. Avocations: Asian philosophies and history, Chinese brush painting, international hosting, films, felines.

DICKINSON, ELEANOR CREEKMORE, artist, educator; b. Knoxville, Tenn., Feb. 7, 1931; d. Robert Elmond and Evelyn Louise (Van Gilder) C.; m. Ben Wade Oakes Dickinson, June 12, 1952; children: Mark Wade, Katherine Van Gilder, Peter Somers. BA, U. Tenn., 1952; postgrad., San Francisco Art Inst., 1961—63, Academié de la Grande Chaumière, Paris, 1971; MFA, Calif. Coll. Arts, Crafts, 1982, Golden Gate U., 1984. Cert. Recognition El Consejo Mundial de Artistas Plasticos, 1993. Escrow officer Security Nat. Bank, Santa Monica, Calif., 1953-54; mem. faculty Calif. Coll. Arts, Crafts, Oakland, 1971-2001, assoc. prof. art, 1974-84, prof., 1984-2001, prof. emerita, 2001—, dir. galleries, 1975-85. Artist-in-residence U. Tenn., 1969, Ark. State U., 1993, Fine Arts Mus. of San Francisco, 2000; faculty U. Calif. Ext., 1967-70; lectr. in field. Co-author, illustrator: Revival, 1974, That Old Time Religion, 1975; also mus. catalogs; illustrator: The Complete Fruit Cookbook, 1972, Human Sexuality: A Search for Understanding, 1984, Days Journey, 1985; commissions: University of San Francisco, 1990-2001; one-woman shows include Corcoran Gallery Art, Washington, 1970, 74, San Francisco Mus. Modern Art, 1965, 68, Fine Arts Mus. San Francisco, 1969, 75, Poindexter Gallery, NY, 1972, 74, Smithsonian Inst., 1975-81, U. Tenn., 1976, Galeria de Arte y Libros, Monterrey, Mex., 1978, Oakland Mus., 1979, Interart Ctr., NY, 1980, Tenn. State Mus., 1981-82, Hatley Martin Gallery, San Francisco, 1986, 89, Michael Himovitz Gallery, Sacramento, Calif., 1988-89, 91, 93, 97-98, Gallery 10, Washington, 1989, Diverse Works, Houston, 1990, Ewing Gallery, U. Tenn., 1991, G.T.U. Gallery, U. Calif., Berkeley, 1991, Mus. Contemporary Religious Art, St. Louis, 1995, Thacher Gallery, U. San Francisco, 2000; represented in permanent collections Nat. Collection Fine Arts, Corcoran Gallery Art, Libr. of Congress, Smithsonian Instn., San Francisco Mus. Modern Art, Butler Inst. Art, Oakland Mus., Santa Barbara Mus., Nat. Mus. Women in Arts, Washington; prodr. (TV) The Art of the Matter-Professional Practices in Fine Arts, 1986—. Bd. dirs. Calif. Confedn. of the Arts, 1983-88; bd. dirs., v.p. Calif. Lawyers for the Arts, 1986—; mem. coun. bd. San Francisco Art Inst., 1966-91, trustee, 1964-67; sec., bd. dirs. YWCA, 1955-62; treas., bd. Westminster Ctr., 1955-59; bd. dirs. Children's Theater Assn., 1958-60, 93-94, Internat. Child Art Ctr., 1958-68. Recipient Disting. Alumni award San Francisco Art Inst., 1983, Master Drawing award Nat. Soc. Arts and Letters, 1983, Pres.'s award Nat. Women's Caucus for Art, 1995, Lifetime Achivement award Nat. Women's Caucus for Art, 2003; grantee Zellerbach Family Fund, 1975, NEH, 1978, 80, 82-85, Thomas F. Stanley Found., 1985, Bay Area Video Coalition, 1988-92, PAS Graphics, 1988, San Francisco Cmty. TV Corp., 1990, Skaggs Found., 1991. Mem.: Nat. Women's Caucus for Art (nat. Affirmative Action officer 1978—80, nat. bd. dirs. 2000—, Pres.'s award, Lifetime Achievement award 1995), Arts Advocates, NOW Artists Equity Assn. (nat. v.p., dir. 1978—92), San Francisco Art Assn. (sec., dir. 1964—67), Calif. Lawyers for Arts (v.p. 1986—), Calif. Confederation of Arts (bd. dirs. 1983—89), Coll. Art Assn. (chair com. on Women in the Arts), Coalition Women's Art Orgns. (dir. 1978—80, v.p. 2000—), AAUP. Democrat. Episc. Office: Calif Coll Arts and Crafts 1111 8th St San Francisco CA 94107-2247 E-mail: eleanordickinson@mac.com.

DICKINSON, GAIL KREPPS, communications educator; b. Lewistown, Pa., June 10, 1956; d. Harold and Esther (Bourdess) Krepps; m. Willis H. Dickinson, Dec. 22, 1979 (div. 1998); children: Margaret Lee, Elizabeth Ann; m. Michael G. Colson, Sr., June 9, 2003. BS, Millersville U. Pa., 1977; MSLS, U. N.C., 1987; PhD, U. Va., 2000. Libr. Cape Charles (Va.) Pub. Sch., 1977-81, Broadwater Acad., Exmore, Va., 1981-85; instrnl supervisor Union-Endicott Sch. Dist., Endicott, N.Y., 1987-96; asst. prof. U. N.C., Greensboro, 2000—. Adj. prof. James Madison U., Harrisonburg, Va., 1997-99. Mem. AAUW, ASCD, Am. Ednl. Rsch. Assn., Am. Assn. Sch. Librs. (bd. dirs. 1994-97), N.Y. Libr. Assn. (pres. sch. libr. media sect. 1994), Phi Delta Kappa. Avocations: reading, word and video games.

DICKINSON, JANE W. social services administrator; b. Sept. 27, 1919; d. Charles Herman and Rachel (Whaler) Wagner; m. E. F. Sherwood Dickinson, Oct. 23, 1943; children: Diane Jane Gray Clem, Carolyn Dickinson Vane. BA, Duke U., 1941; MEd, Goucher Coll., 1965. Exec. sec. Petroleum Industry Com., Balt., 1941-43, Sherwood Feed Mills Inc., Balt., 1943-79. Mem. exec. com. Children's Aid Md., 1960-61; mem. bd. women's aux. Balt. Symphony Orch., 1958-60; dist. chmn. Balt. Cancer Drive, 1957; co-chmn. Balt. United Appeal, 1968; bd. mgrs. Pickersgill Retirement Home. Mem. Three Arts Club (Balt., sec. 1958-60, bd. govs. 1960-64, 67-70, pres. 1970-72), Women's Club of Roland Park (bd. govs. 1960-64, 86-88, 92-94), Cliff Dwellers Garden Club, Alpha Delta Phi Home: Apt 609 1055 W Joppa Rd Baltimore MD 21204-3748

DICKINSON, MAE, state legislator; b. Feb. 8, 1933; Student, Ind. U., Martin Coll., Ivy Tech. Coll. Retired quality inspector GM; rep. Dist. 95 Ind. Ho. of Reps., 1992—, mem. elections and apportionment, cities and towns com., mem. families, children and human affairs, pub. safety coms., vice chmn. labor and employment com. Precinct committeewoman; del. Dem. Nat. Conv.; ward chmn. Named Breakthrough woman in Area of Polit. Coalition of 100 Black Women. Mem. NAACP, Urban League, United Auto Workers, A. Philip Randolph Inst. (Pres.'s award 1990), Flamingo Social and Charity Club, Coalition of Black Trade Unionists. Home: 5455 N Arlington Ave Indianapolis IN 46226-1607 Office: Ind Ho of Reps State Capitol Indianapolis IN 46204

DICKSON, EVA MAE, credit manager; b. Clarion, Iowa, Jan. 16, 1922; d. James and Ivah Blanche (Breckenridge) D. Grad. Interstate Bus. Coll., Klamath Falls, Oreg., 1943. Reporter, Mchts. Credit Service, Klamath Falls, 1941; credit dept. Montgomery Ward, Klamath Falls, 1941-42; bookkeeper Heilbronner Fuel Co., Klamath Falls, 1942; stenographer City of Klamath Falls, 1943, bookkeeper, office mgr., 1943-52; owner, operator All Star Bus. Service, Klamath Falls, 1953-58, Ace Mimeo Service, Klamath Falls, 1958-73; mgr. Mchts. Credit Service, 1973-87; customer service rep. CBI/Credit N.W., 1987-91. Bd. dirs. United Way, Klamath Falls, 1980-97; sec. Klamath Community Concert Assn., 1956-99; treas., memls. chmn. Klamath County chpt. Am. Cancer Soc.; bd. dirs., treas. Hope in Crisis; mem. Klamath County Centennial Com., 1982, Unification for Progress Joint Planning Com., 1985; mem. nursing adv. com. Oreg. Inst. Tech., 1982—; mem. Klamath Employment Tng. Adv. Com., 1983-86; bd. dirs., sec., treas. Klamath Consumer Council; sec. Unified City for Progress Task Force, 1983-84, Snowflake Winter Festival, 1984—; sec. First Presbyn. Ch., 1992—. Recipient Bronze Leadership award Assoc. Credit Burs., Inc., 1976. Mem. Daughters of Am. Colonists (past regent local chpt.), Consumer Credit Assn. Oreg. (pres. 1984-85), Credit Profl. Internat. (treas. dist. 10 1984-85, 2d v.p. dist. 10 1987-88, 1st v.p. 1988-89, pres. 1989-90, internat. bull. chmn. 1990-91, 92—), Assoc. Credit Bur. Pacific N.W. (pres. 1981-82), Assoc. Credit Bur. Oreg. (pres. 1978-80), Klamath Basin Credit Women-Internat. (pres. 1976-78), Soc. Cert. Consumer Credit Exec., Internat. Consumer Credit Assn., Klamath County C. of C. (pres. 1979, ambs. com. 1980—, Nat. Fedn. Bus. and Profl. Women's Club (chmn. nat. fin. com. 1983-84, nat. fin. com. 1982-83), Oreg. Fedn. Bus. and Profl. Women's Club (state pres. 1971-72), Klamath Falls Bus. and Profl. Women's Club (pres. 1966-67, 76-77, 1996—). Republican. Presbyterian. Club: Quota (pres. 1958-59, dist. gov. 1969-70). Avocations: painting, traveling.

DICKSON, KATHARINE HAYLAND, dance educator; b. East Hartford, Conn., Dec. 4, 1904; d. George Wentworth and Marguerite Moore (Stockman) D.; m. Harry Burton Ashenden, June 23, 1928 (dec. 1967); 1 child, David Dickson; m. Theodore Henry Brown, Oct. 26, 1968 (dec. 1973); m. Charles Thomas Alverson, Feb. 18, 1978 (dec. Mar. 1985). BEd, Boston U., 1948. Tchr. Ballroom dance Model Sch. of Modern Dance, Boston, 1923-26; tchr. ballroom, ballet, tap Hazel Boone Sch. Dancing, Boston, 1926-28; tchr. mus. comedy and tap Knickerbocker Sch., Boston, 1928-31; dir. Katharine Dickson Dance Studio, Cambridge, Mass., 1934-68; tchr. ballroom dance Boston Ctr. for Adult Edn., Boston, 1943-74; tchr. ballet and tap Newton Community Ctr., Mass., 1955-74, Hayden Recreation Ctr., Lexington, Mass., 1957-74; ballroom dance tchr. Englewood (Fla.) Recreation Ctr., 1975-88; tchr. ballroom dance Venice, Fla., 1989-94. Tchr. Ramblers Rest Resort, Venice. Author: Stockman-Gallison Ancestral Lines, 1984, Downeast Dicksons, 1987, Burton-Tyler, 1990, The Stockman Story, 1992, My Very Own 20th Century Rag, 1995, Ashenden, the English Background of Harry Burton Ashenden, 1997, A 1998 Sawyer Fickett Update to Downeast Dicksons of 1987; contbr. articles to profl. jours. Mem. Nat. Coun. Dance Tchr. Orgn. (early chmn.), Dance Tchrs. Club Boston (past pres., hon.), N.Y. Soc. Tchrs. Dancing. Unitarian. Avocations: swimming, gardening, growing wildflowers. Home (Winter): 2101 S Pine St Englewood FL 34224 Home: 2101 S Pine St Englewood FL 34224-5303

DICKSON, KATHRYN, science educator; PhD in Comparative Animal Physiology, U. Calif., San Diego, 1988. Assoc. prof. biology Calif. State U., Fullerton, 1988—. Recipient award Women in Sci. and Tech., 1999. Achievements include research in development and evolution of endothermy in marine fishes and energetics and morphology associated with locomotion in fishes. Office: U Calif Dept Biology 800 N State College Blvd Fullerton CA 92831-3547

DICKSON, LINNEA E. music educator; b. Lovell, Wyo., Oct. 19, 1952; d. Glenn Ernest and Carmel Sater Engelking; m. Brian Earl Dickson, July 19, 1974; children: Jeremy Brian, Kevin Brian, Michele. BS in Music Edn., U. No. Colo., 1975; MA in Music Edn., U. Wyo., 2000. Pvt. practice piano and vocal tchg., Lovell, 1975—90; elem. music tchr. grades K-3 Big Horn County Sch. Dist. #2, Lovell, 1989—99, mid./H.S. music tchr., 1997—. Pres. North Big Horn Arts Coun., Lovell, 1999—2001. Named Vocal Music Tchr. of the Yr., North Big Horn Basin Wyo. Music Tchrs., 2002. Mem.: Wyo. Music Tchrs. Assn., Nat. Music Tchrs. Assn. Mem. Lds Ch. Avocations: crocheting, reading, piano, astronomy, photography. Home: 730 Montana Ave Lovell WY 82431 Office: Big Horn Sch Dist #2 502 Hampshire Lovell WY 82431

DICKSON, REECY L. state legislator; b. Macon, Miss. m. Billie C. Dickson. Student, Miss. Valley State, Miss. State U. State legislator Miss. Ho. of Reps., Jackson, 1993—. Mem. conservation, edn., judiciary B, juvenile justice, penitentiary coms. Miss. Ho. of Reps. Former county supt. of edn. Mem. NAACP, Order of the Ea. Star. Democrat. Baptist. Home: PO Box 293 Macon MS 39341-0293 Office: State Capitol Bldg Rm 400-F PO Box 1018 Jackson MS 39215-1018

DICKSTEIN, BETH J. lawyer, accountant; b. 1963; BS with highest honors, U. Ill., 1985; JD cum laude, U. Pa., 1988. Bar: Ill. 1988; CPA, Ill. Ptnr. Sidley & Austin, Chgo. Office: Sidley & Austin 1 S First National Plz Chicago IL 60603-2000 Fax: 312-853-7036.

DICKSTEIN, JOAN BORTECK, arbitrator, conflict management consultant; b. Phila., June 20, 1919; d. Joseph and Mary (Leibovitz) Borteck; m. Benjamin Dickstein, Dec. 24, 1939; children: Howard, Kenneth, Mary. BA, Antioch Coll., 1974; MA in Sociology, U. Pa., 1978. Phila. coord. Gt. Books Found., Chgo., 1960-64; moderator, panelist Panel of Am. Women, Phila., 1964-73; trainer sensitivity courses Phila. Fellowship commn., 1966-69; rsch. assoc., cons. U. Pa. Human Resources Ctr., Phila., 1969-73; arbitrator comty. disputes Am. Arbitration Assn., Phila., 1969-82, Mcpl. Ct. of Phila., 1974-80, Commn. on Human Rels., Phila., 1979-82; facilitator interfaith dialogue Elkins Park (Pa.) Interfaith Dialogue, 1987—. Guest lectr. conflict mgmt. La Salle Coll., Phila., 1971-74; mem. adv. com. Episcopal Comty. Svcs., Phila., 1972-73; cons. staff devel. Covenant House Health Svc., Phila., 1979-80. V.p. Phila. chpt. Am. Jewish Com., Phila., 1970-73; study tour mem. Scandinavia, World Future Soc., Washington, 1974; study tour mem. Mid. East, United Presbyn. Ch., Roman Cath. Conf., Am. Jewish Com., N.Y.C., 1976; bd. dirs. Or Hadash Congregation, Ft. Washington, Pa., 1990-93; peer counselor Women's Ctr., Jenkintown, Pa., 1987—. Recipient Human Rights award City of Phila. Commn. on Human Rels., 1982. Democrat. Jewish. Avocations: great books discussion programs, interfaith dialogue, aerobics, crossword puzzles, volunteering at women's ctr. Home: 1250 Greenwood Ave Jenkintown PA 19046-2901

DICLAUDIO, JANET ALBERTA, health information administrator; b. Monroeville, Pa., June 17, 1940; d. Frank and Pearl Alberta (Wolfgang) DiC. Cert. in Med. Rsch. Libr. Sci., Luth Med. Ctr., 1962; BA, Thiel Coll., 1975, MS, SUNY, Buffalo, 1978. Registered record adminstr. Dir. med. records Bashline Hosp., Grove City, Pa., 1962, St. Clair Meml. Hosp., Pitts., 1963-73; asst. prof. Ill. State U., Normal, 1976-81; corp. dir. med. records Buffalo Gen. Hosp., 1981-85; dir. med. records Candler Hosp., Savannah, Ga., 1985-94, med. records analyst, 1994-98; pres. prn Assocs., Savannah, Ga., 1998—. Med. record cons. White Cliff Nursing Home, Greenville, Pa., 1973—75; mgmt. cons. Gifford W. Lorenz MD, Savannah, 1992—94; Medicare compliance officer and coder Health Claims, Inc., Savannah, 1999—2001; mgmt. cons. John D. Northup, Jr., MD, Savannah, 2001—02; auditor, cons. Healthpac Computer Sys., Inc., 2001—. Contbr. articles to periodicals. Bd. dirs. Mid-Ill. Areawide Health Planning Corp., Normal, 1979-81. Mem. Am. Health Info. Mgmt. Assn., Ga. Health Info. Mgmt. Assn., S.E. Ga. Health Info. Mgmt. Assn. Avocations: painting, story telling, dance, reading. Office: Ste 705 PMB 153 7400 Abercorn St Savannah GA 31406

DICOSIMO, PATRICIA SHIELDS, secondary school educator; b. Hartford, Conn., June 27, 1946; d. Richard Nichols and Rose Aimee (Roy) Shields; m. Joseph Anthony DiCosimo, Apr. 18, 1970. BFA in Art Edn. and Printmaking, U. Hartford, 1969; MS in Edn. and Art, Ctrl. Conn. State Coll., 1972; postgrad., Rochester Inst. Tech., 1986-87. Cert. tchr., Conn. Tchr. art Simsbury (Conn.) H.S., 1969—. Tchr. Farmington Valley Art Ctr., Avon, Conn., 1989-95; supr. Nat. Art Honors Soc., Simsbury, 1989-2004; mem. Conn. regional adv. bd. Scholastic Art Awards, 1991, 93—; mem. Conn. Scholastic Arts Awards Com., 1989—, co-chair exhibit, 1994—, prin.'s faculty adv. com., 1969-2004; guest lectr. secondary methods in art edn. Ctrl. Conn. State U., 1994; presenter in field; mem. Conn. Curriculum in Arts, 1995-96, writer, 1995. One-woman shows include Farmington Woods, 1972, Ellsworth Gallery Simsbury, 1974, Annhurst Coll., 1976, Canaan Nat. Bank, 1991, Terryvill Libr., 1994, Henry James Meml. Gallery, 2004; exhibited in group shows at Ctrl. Conn. State Coll., 1969-72 (Best in Show award 1972), Bristol Chrysanthemum Festival Art Show, 1973-84 (Non-objective award 1973, Graphic award 1975, Mixed Media award 1977, Tracy Driscoll Co. Inc. award 1981, Plymouth Spring award 1983, Dick Blick award 1984), Hartford Ins. Co. Art Educators Exhibit, 1990, Simsbury Libr. Gallery Art Educators Exhibit, 1991, 92, 93, Henry James Meml. Gallery, 1992, Riverview Gallery, 1993, Simsbury Dinner Theater, 1994-2004, Canton Gallery on the Green, 1996, 98 (Best of Conn. Mural Contest 1996), Simsbury Mall Mural, 1999, ENO, 2003; author: Design as a Catalyst for Learning, 1997. Sec. Greater Bristol (Conn.) Condo Alliance, 1990-95; mem. Family Life & Marriage Enrichment, New Britain, Conn., 1970-77; vol. painter Boundless Playground for Handicapped, Simsbury, Conn., 2002, Turkey Trot Food Dr., Simsbury, Conn., 1993-03, W. Hartford Cow Parade, 2003. Named Conn. Art Tchr. of Yr., 1993, Patricia Shields DiCosimo Day in her honor, Town of Simsbury, 1993, Conn. Beginning Educator Support Tchr., Conn. Alliance for Arts Edn. Sch. Dist., 1995—96, Simsbury C. of C. Educator of Yr., 2000; recipient Book award, Hartford Art Sch., 1969, Recycling Cmty. Svc. award, Simsbury, 1999, K-12 Sculpture Tchr. 1st pl., Internat. Sculpture Com. Ctr., 2001, Hon. mention, 2001, 1st prize, 2003; grantee, Simsbury Edn. Enhancement Found., 1996—97. Mem. NEA, Nat. Art Edn. Assn., Nat. Art Honor Soc. (advisor 1983—), New Eng. Assn. Schs. and Colls. (evaluator 1998-99, 2001, 03), Conn. Art Edn. Assn. (H.S. rep. 1983-85, sec. 1985—, Conn. Art Educator 1993, Conn. Alliance for Arts Edn. award for Simsbury Art and Music 1995), Conn. Art Alliance Assn., Conn. Edn. Assn. (mem. 3-D curriculum project 1995-96, portfolio rev. com. 1999, Goals 2000 edn. project 1999-2004), Conn. Craftsman, Farmington Art Guild (tchr. 1992-95), U. Hartford Alumni Assn. Roman Catholic. Avocations: jewelry, painting, golf, travel. Home: 19 Hampton Ct Bristol CT 06010-4738 Office: Simsbury High Sch 34 Farms Village Rd Simsbury CT 06070-2399 Personal E-mail: pat46art@aol.com.

DIDION, CATHERINE JAY, science association administrator; Also ofcl. rep. to UN Assn. for Women in Sci., Washington, exec. dir., 1990—. Spkr. numerous profl. meetings.; presenter testimony to Congress; frequent spkr. tomedia on women in sci. issues; chmn. environ. and sci. task forces Coalition for Women's Appointments; head del. to 4th World Conf. on Women, Beijing; co-chmn. 1st sci. and tech. caucus UN women's Conf.; mem. adv. bd. Sci. Linkages in the Cmty.; mem. survey com. Soc. for Neurosci.; mem. Athens project Am. Chem. Soc.; mem. mentoring award rev. com. AAAS. Bimonthly columnist Women in Sci., Jour. Coll. Sci.

Tchg.; contbr. articles to profl. jours., including The Scientist, Sci., Initiatives. Grantee NSF, Alfred P. Sloan Found., Office Naval Rsch. Office: Assn for Women in Sci 1200 New York Ave NW Ste 650 Washington DC 20005-3929 Fax: 212-326-8960. E-mail: didion@awis.org.

DIDION, JOAN, writer; b. Sacramento, Calif., Dec. 5, 1934; d. Frank Reese and Eduene (Jerrett) D.; m. John Gregory Dunne, Jan. 30, 1964; 1 child, Quintana Roo. BA, U. Calif., Berkeley, 1956. Assoc. feature editor Vogue mag., 1956-63; former columnist Saturday Evening Post, Life, Esquire; now contbr. The N.Y. Rev. of Books, The New Yorker. Novels include Run River, 1963, Play It As It Lays, 1970, A Book of Common Prayer, 1977, Democracy, 1984, The Last Thing He Wanted, 1996; books of essays: Slouching Towards Bethlehem, 1968, The White Album, 1979, After Henry, 1992; nonfiction Salvador, 1983, Miami, 1987, Political Fictions, 2001, Fixed Ideas, 2003, Where I Was From, 2003; co-author: (with John Gregory Dunne) Screenplays for films The Panic in Needle Park, 1971, Play It As It Lays, 1972, A Star Is Born, 1976, True Confessions, 1981, Hills Like White Elephants, 1991, Broken Trust, 1995, Up Close and Personal, 1996. Recipient 1st prize Vogue's Prix de Paris, 1956, Morton Dauwen Zabel prize AAAL, 1978, The Edward MacDowell medal, 1996, Columbia Journalism award, 1999. Mem. Am. Acad. Arts and Letters, Am. Acad. Arts and Scis., Coun. Fgn. Rels. Office: care Janklow & Nesbit 445 Park Ave New York NY 10022-2606

DIDOMENICO, MAUREEN ELLEN, art educator, muralist; b. Bridgeport, Conn., Aug. 25, 1957; d. Thomas Francis and Sallye Ann (Shaw) Devitt; m. Gary Anthony DiDomenico, June 30, 1979; children: Lynne Ann, Kaitlin Marie. BS in Art Edn., So. Conn. U., New Haven, 1979; M in Elem. Edn., Sacred Heart U., Fairfield, Conn., 1989. Cert. tchr., Conn. Classrm. tchr. grade 7 St. Charles Sch., Bridgeport, Conn., 1979-80, classrm. tchr. grade 3, 1982-85; substitute tchr. Stratford (Conn.) Bd. Edn., 1985-86; art educator Franklin and Nichols Elem. Schs., Stratford, 1986-94, Flood Mid. Sch., Stratford, 1994—. Mem. Dem. Town Party, Stratford, 1990-95; vol. Am. Heart Assn., New Haven, 1993-95; coord., creator of scenery Stratford Acad. Dance, 1986-92; judge of local art show Sterling House Cmty. Ctr., Stratford, 1994. Recipient Achievement award Kodak Co., 1993, others. Mem. NEA, Conn. Edn. Assn., Nat. Art Edn. Assn., Conn. Art Edn. Assn. Roman Catholic. Avocations: watercolor painting, golf, gardening, decorating. Home: 150 Cutspring Rd Stratford CT 06614-2833

DIEBOLT, JUDITH, newspaper editor; b. Atchison, Kans., Oct. 6, 1948; d. George Edward and Mary Lou (Hill) D.; m. John C. Aldrich, Oct. 25, 1985. BSJ, U. Kans., 1970. Reporter Detroit Free Press, 1970-80, columnist, 1980-82, asst. city editor, 1982-85; reporter Detroit News, 1986-88, asst city editor, 1988-89, suburban editor, 1989-91; mng. editor Burlington (Vt.) Free Press, 1991-94; city editor Detroit News, 1994-98. Recipient Pub. Svc. award AP, 1978. Mem. AP Mng. Editors, Detroit Press Club (bd. govs., 1990-91), Univ. Club Detroit. Roman Catholic. Office: The Detroit News 615 W Lafayette Blvd Detroit MI 48226-3197

DIEDE, NORMA DALE, retired private school educator; b. Kyle, S.D., Nov. 18, 1930; d. Everette Edwin Dale and Mathilde Stenger; m. Ernest Frank Diede, June 6, 1950 (dec. Aug. 1, 1990); children: Dale Jean, Scott Warren. BS in Math., Lewis and Clark Coll., 1953. Resource tchr. Murray Sch., Calif., 1965—70; ret. Editor: (video) Living with Septics, 2001. Sec., treas. Valley Water and Sewer, Rapid City, SD, 1994—2001; mem. water ops. Eastridge Water Assn., Black Hawk, SD, 1990—; chmn. Black Hills Resource Conservation and Devel., Rapid City, 1998—; active Fire Recovery Assistence Ctr., Rapid City, 2002. Named Outstanding Coun. Person, Black Hills Resource Conservation and Devel., 2003; recipient Outstanding Coun. Person award, Western Region Assn. RC&D's, 2004. Mem.: AAUW (sec. 1999—), S.Dak. Assn. Resource Conservation and Devel. (v.p. 2002, Outstanding Coun. Person 2003). Republican.

DIEDERICHS, JANET WOOD, public relations executive; b. Libertyville, Ill. d. J. Howard and Ruth (Hendrickson) Wood; m. John Kuensting Diedrichs, 1953. BA, Wellesley Coll, 1950. Sales agt. Pan Am. Airways, Chgo., 1951-52; regional mgr. pub. relations Braniff Internat., Chgo., 1953-69; pres. Janet Diederichs & Assocs., Inc.; pub. rels. cons. Chgo., 1970—. Lectr. Harvard U.; mem. exec. com. World Trade Conf., 1983, 84. Com. mem. Nat. Trust for Historic Preservation, 1975-79, Marshall Scholars (Brit. Govt.), 1975-79; trustee Sherwood Conservatory Music, 2000—, Northwestern Meml. Hosp., 1985—, mem. exec. com., 1995-2000; trustee Fourth Presbyn. Ch., mem. bd. dirs. 1990-93; bd. dirs., mem. exec. com. Chgo. Conv. and Visitors Bur. 1978-87; bd. dirs. Internat. House, U. Chgo., 1978-84; bd. dirs., founder Com. of 200, 1982—; bd. dirs. Latino Inst., 1986-89, Chgo. Network, Albert Pick Jr. Found.; founders coun. Field Mus., 1999—; com. mem. Art Inst. Chgo., 1980-83; mem. exec. com. Vatican Art Coun. Chgo., 1981-83; pres. Jr. League Chgo., 1968-69. Mem. Chgo. Assn. Commerce and Industry (bd. dirs. 1982-89, exec. com. 1985-88), Internat. Women's Forum, Pub. Rels. Soc. Am., Pub. Rels. Exch. Internat. (founder), Publicity Club Chgo., Chgo. Network, Econ. Club, Woman's Athletic Club of Chgo., Comml. Club of Chgo., The Casino Club (Chgo.), The River Club (N.Y.), The Exec. Svc. Corps. (mem. adv. com. 1993-97), Chgo. Club. Office: Diederichs & Assocs 333 N Michigan Ave Ste 1205 Chicago IL 60601-4002

DIEHL, ANN, radio personality; m. Bob Diehl; 2 children. Adminstrv. asst. Family Life Radio WUGN, Midland, Mich., 1990—96, sports reader, 1996—2001, radio personality, 1997—, cohost Morning Show, 2001—. Office: WUGN 510 E Isabella Rd Midland MI 48640

DIEHL, DEBORAH HILDA, lawyer; b. Troy, N.Y., Feb. 13, 1951; d. Warren S. and Norma K. (Apple) D.; 1 child, Alexandra Ellen. Student, U. de Rouen, France, 1971-72; BA, St. Lawrence U., 1973; JD, Syracuse U., 1976; postdoctoral, George Washington U., 1978-79. Bar: N.Y. 1977, D.C. 1981, Ohio 1982, Md. 1987. Atty. USDA, Washington, 1976-81; assoc. Thompson, Hine & Flory, Columbus, Ohio, 1981-87, Semmes, Bowen & Semmes, Balt., 1987-90, ptnr., 1990-95, Whiteford, Taylor & Preston, Balt., 1995—. Pres. Mt. Royal Improvement Assn., 1995—97; chair Midtown Cmty. Benefits Dist. Mgmt. Authority, 1998—2000, dir., 1995—2001, Midtown Devel. Corp., 2000—; participant Leadership Md., 1997; mem. U. Md. Balt. County Tech. Ctr. Adv. Bd., 2001—. Mem.: ABA, Bar Assn. City Balt., Md. State Bar Assn. (bus. law sect. coun. 1998—, chair 2002—03). Avocations: bicycling, travel, economic development.

DIEHL, DOLORES, communication arts director; b. Salina, Kans., Dec. 28, 1927; d. William Augustus and Martha (Frank) D. Student pub. schs., Kans., 1941-45. Bus. rep. Southwestern Bell Telephone Co., St. Louis and Kansas City, Mo., 1948-49, Mountain States Telephone Co., Denver, 1949-50; edn. coord. pub. rels. Pacific Telephone/AT&T, L.A. and San Diego, 1950-83; cons. Bus. Magnet High Sch., L.A. Unified Sch. Dist., 1977-79; pres. First Calif. Acad. Decathlon, 1979; owner Community Connection, L.A., 1983—; mgr., dir. DelMar Media Arts, Burbank, Calif., 1985-89; mgr. Susan Blu workshops Blupka Prodns., L.A., 1989—; ptnr., dir. animation and commls. voiceover workshops Elaine Craig Voicecasting, Hollywood, Calif., 1989—; freelance performer, voiceover L.A., 1990—; mgr. Sounds Great Film Looping Workshops, L.A., 1992-93; owner Voiceover Connection, L.A., 1994-95; pres. Voiceover Connection, Inc., L.A., 1995—. V.p. pub. rels. San Diego Inst. Creativity, 1965-67; exec. com. San Diego's 200th Anniversary Celebration, 1967; pub. rels. dir. Greater San Diego Sci. Fair, 1963-68. Mem. Better Bus. Bur. Recipient Dedication to Edn. award Industry Edn. Coun., Calif., 1964; named one of seven top voiceover trainers Animation Mag., 1999. Mem. L.A. Area C. of C. (bd. dirs. women's coun.), Calif. Magnet Sch. Consortium of Cities (chairperson), Industry Edn. Coun. Calif., L.A. and San Diego (past pres.), Bus. and Profl. Women's Club, Delta Kappa Gamma (hon.). Republican. Methodist. Home and Office: 691 Irolo St Apt 212 Los Angeles CA 90005-4110 E-mail: doloresdiehl@earthlink.net.

DIEHL, JENNIFER L., counselor; d. William Theodore and Beverly Jane (Eggers) Diehl. BA, Boise State U., 1976; MEd in Counseling, U. Idaho, 1989. Lic. marriage and family therapist Idaho Bd. Occupl. Licensing, 2002. Supervising coord. Clearwater Interagency Coun. on Youth, Orofino, Idaho, 1990—98; counselor Positive Connections, Twin Falls, Idaho, 2001—03. Recipient Cmty. Svc. award, Lewis Clark State Coll., 1994, Region II Prevention award, State of Idaho, 1998. Mem.: Am. Assn. of U. Women, Am. Assn. for Marriage and Family Therapy. Presbyterian.

DIEHL, KIMBERLY A. researcher; b. Evanston, Ill., Feb. 8, 1974; d. Richard Lee Diehl and Susan Clare Roller. BA, Ea. Ill. U., 1996; MA, U. Kans., 1998, PhD, 2002. Rsch. dir. Psychol. Corp., San Antonio. Warren Willingham Rsch. fellow, Ednl. Testing Svc., 1998—99. Mem.: APA. Office: Harcourt Assessment Inc 19500 Bulverde Rd San Antonio TX 78259 Personal E-mail: kimberlydiehl@hotmail.com. Business E-Mail: kim_diehl@harcourt.com.

DIEKEMPER, RITA GARBS, landscape company executive; d. Donald Richard and Carol Ann Garbs; m. Gregory Robert Diekemper, Feb. 14, 1987; children: Madelyn Garbs, Thomas Garbs, Grace Rickert. BS in Acctg., U. Mo., 1983. CPA Mo. Auditor Touche Ross & Co., St. Louis, 1983—89, Aslage Kiefer and Co., St. Louis, 1990—95; pres., owner Gardens of Grace LLC, St. Louis, 1995—. Chmn. For Our Future...For Our Kids, St. Louis, 1987—2000; chmn. citizen's adv. com. Mehlville Sch. Dist., St. Louis, 1988, 1989; chmn. Homes for Holidays Ho. Tour, St. Louis, 2001; treas. Renew Oakville, St. Louis, St. Mark's Episcopal Ch., St. Louis, 1986—2000, vestry mem., 1986—89, endowment pres., 2000—03; mem., bd. dirs. Mehlville Sch. Dist., St. Louis, 2001—. Recipient Disting. Svc. award, Mehlville Sch. Dist., 2000. Avocations: gardening, half-marathon runner, triathelete, travel. Home and Office: 2571 Cripple Creek Dr Saint Louis MO 63129

DIEMER, EMMA LOU, composer, educator; b. Kansas City, Mo., Nov. 24, 1927; d. George Willis and Myrtle (Casebolt) D. MusB, Yale U., 1949, MusM, 1950; PhD, Eastman Sch. Music, 1960; LHD (hon.), Ctrl. Mo. State U., 1999. Composer-in-residence Arlington (Va.) Schs., 1959-61; composer, cons. pub. schs., Arlington and Balt., 1964-65; prof. theory and composition U. Md., College Park, 1965-70, U. Calif., Santa Barbara, 1971-91. Organist Ch. of the Reformation, Washington, 1962—71, Ch. of Christ, Santa Barbara, 1973—84, 1st Presbyn. Ch., Santa Barbara, 1984—2001. Composer of over 100 choral and instrumental compositions including Music for Woodwind Quartet, 1976, Four Poems of Alice Meynell for Soprano and Chamber Ensemble, 1977, Symphony No. 2, 1980, Suite for Orchestra, 1981, Suite of Homages, 1985, Church Rock, 1986, Variations for Piano, 4 Hands, 1987, String Quartet No. 1, 1987, Serenade for String Orch., 1988, Concerto for Marimba, 1990, Concerto for Piano, 1991, Sextet, 1992, Four Biblical Settings for Organ, 1992, Fantasy for Piano, 1993, Kyrie for Mixed Chorus, Organ, and Piano - 4 Hands, 1993, Santa Barbara Overture, 1995, Gloria for Mixed Chorus, 2 Pianos and Percussion, 1996, Psalm 122 for Bass Trombone and Organ, Psalm 121 for Organ, Brass and Percussion, Psalms for Flute and Organ, Psalms for Trumpet and Organ, Psalms for Percussion and Organ, 1998, Latin Mass, 2000, Homage to Tschaikovsky, 2000, Piano Trio, 2000, Quartet for Piano and Brass, 2001, Songs for the Earth, 2002, Toccata for Six, 2004, Chumask Indian Dance Celebration, 2004; composer-in-residence Santa Barbara Symphony, 1990-92. Fulbright scholar, 1952-53; grantee Ford Found. Young Composers, 1959-61, Kindler Found. Commn., 1963, Nat. Endowment Arts, 1980-81; Kennedy Ctr. Friedheim award, 1992. Mem. ASCAP (ann. awards 1962—), Am. Guild Organists (Composer of Yr. 1995), Internat. Alliance for Women in Music, Am. Music Ctr., Mu Phi Epsilon (award of merit 1995). Democrat. Presbyterian. Avocations: reading, electronic and computer music. E-mail: eldiemer@cox.net.

DIENEL, NANCY ALDUMA ROBERTS, health insurance underwriter; b. Camden, N.J., July 25, 1954; d. Charles Harold and Susan Jane (Kelley) Roberts; m. Philip Bruce Dienel, Apr. 22, 1987; 1 child, Samuel James. BA in Polit. Sci. cum laude, Moravian Coll., Bethlehem, Pa., 1976. Asst. mgr. Dempsey's Restaurant, Bethlehem, 1977-87; svc. rep. JP Food Svc., Allentown, Pa., 1990-92; group claims approver Guardian Life, Bethlehem, 1992-95, group life and health underwriter, 1995—. Mentor/acad. recovery Lehigh Valley Bus. Edn. Ptnrs., 1996—. Bd.dirs. Girls Inc., Bethlehem, 1996—; coord. Women for Ridge for Gov., Lehigh Vallye, 1994; elected com. person Northampton County Rep. Com., 1996-98; capt. blood drive Miller Meml. Blood Ctr., Bethlehem, 1997. Mem. Health Ins. Assn. Am. (assoc.),George Bush Presdl. Libr. and Mus., Phi Alpha Theta. Republican. Presbyterian. Avocation: martial arts. Home: 4480 Bayard St Easton PA 18045-4906 Office: Guardian Life 3900 Burgess Pl Bethlehem PA 18017-9097

DIENER, BETTY JANE, finance educator; b. Washington, Sept. 15, 1940; d. Edward George and Minnie (Feild) Diener; m. Robert D. Bell, 1987 (dec. 1993). AB, Wellesley Coll., 1962; MBA, Harvard U., 1964, DBA, 1974. Account exec. Young & Rubicam, Inc., N.Y.C., 1964-70; product mgr. Am. Cyanamid Co., Wayne, NJ, 1970-72; asst. dean Sch. Bus. Case Western Res. U., Cleve., 1974-79; dean Sch. Bus. Adminstrn. Old Dominion U., Norfolk, Va., 1986-87; provost, vice-chancellor acad. affairs U. Mass., Boston, 1987-88, prof. mktg., 1987—2002, spl. asst. to chancellor econ. devel., 1993-94. Pres. Environ. Bus. Coun. New Eng., Inc., 1995—97. Contbr. articles to profl. publs. Mem. Citizens Coun. Chesapeake Bay, 1986—87; adviser Jr. League, 1963—64, Plans for Progress, 1968—70, Leadership Met. Richmond, 1980—82; mem. Mass. Gov.'s Adv. Com. Sci. and Tech., 1988—90, Mayor's Task Force Empowerment Zones, 1994; mem. cmty. working group Mass. Mil. Reservation, 1997—2000; pres. Provincetown (Mass.) Repertory Theater, 2002, bd. dirs., 2001—03; commr. Norfolk Indsl. Devel. Authority, 1979—82; bd. dirs. Norfolk Conv. and Visitors Bur., 1979—82, Norfolk C. of C., 1979—82, Greater Norfolk Corp., 1986—87, Va. Orch. Group, 1982—87, Va. Stage Co., 1986—87, Karamu Ho., 1975—79, Woodruff Hosp., 1975—79, Women's City Club Cleve., 1976—79, Coun. Sustainable Fla., 2003—; mem. adv. com. state and local govt. programs John F. Kennedy Sch. Govt., Harvard U., 1986—88. Named Outstanding Working Woman, Glamour Mag., 1979; named one of 10 Outstanding Career Women of Decade, 1984; recipient Honor award, Soil Conservation Soc., 1984; Fulbright scholar, 2001. Democrat. Home: 9304 NE 9th Pl Miami Shores FL 33138 Office: Barry Univ Andreas Sch of Business Miami Shores FL 33138 E-mail: bejade@aol.com.

DIENSTAG, ELEANOR FOA, corporate communications consultant; b. Naples, Italy; d. Bruno Garibaldi and Lisa (Haimann) Foa; m. Jerome Dienstag (div. 1978); children: Joshua Foa, Jesse Paul. BA, Smith Coll., Northampton, Mass. Asst. editor Random House/Harper & Row, N.Y.C.; editor/writer Monocle Mag., N.Y.C.; cultural columnist Genesee Valley Newspapers, Rochester, NY; sr. mgr., speechwriter Am. Express, N.Y.C., 1978-83. Freelance journalist, N.Y.C., 1983—; lit. resident Yaddo Y., Va. Ctr. for Creative Arts, 95; lectr., book pub. columnist and reviewer in field. Author: Whither Thou Goest, 1976, In Good Company: 125 Years at the Heinz Table, 1994; contbr. articles, essays and feature stories to N.Y. Times, Harper's, N.Y. Observer, McCalls; columnist New Choices Mag. Recipient Merit award for speechwriting Internat. Assn. Bus. Comm., N.Y., Merit award Am. Express Mgmt. Newsletter, Outstanding Mem. award Women in Comm. Mem. Am. Soc. Journalists and Authors (past pres.). Home and Office: Eleanor Foa Assocs 435 E 79th St New York NY 10021-1034 Office Phone: 212-879-1542. E-mail: efoa@usa.net.

DIERCKS, ELIZABETH GORMAN, elementary school educator; b. Harrisburg, Pa., Aug. 12, 1944; d. Jerome Clement and Martha (Stoll) G.; m. Gregory Louis Diercks, July 24, 1982. BS, Pa. State U., University Park, 1966; MEd, U. Md., 1975, Advanced profl. cert. Tchr. Fairfax County (Va.) Pub. Schs., 1966-68, Prince George's County (Md.) Pub. Schs., 1968—, grade level chairperson, 1970-97. Early intervention coord. Ft. Washington Elem. Sch., Prince George's County, 1997—. Assoc. Nat. Trust for Historic Preservation, Washington; resident assoc. Smithsonian Assocs., Washington; sustainer The Kennedy Ctr., Washington. Mem. NEA, Md. State Edn. Assn., Prince George's County Edn. Assn., Nat. Mus. Women in the Arts (charter mem.), Nat. Mus. of the Am. Indian (charter mem.), Kappa Delta. Avocations: travel, hiking, swimming, fitness training. Office: Ft Washington Forest Elem Sch 1300 Fillmore Rd Fort Washington MD 20744-2935

DIERICKX, CONSTANCE RICKER, psychologist, management consultant; b. Evanston, Ill, June 26, 1952; d. Benjamin Franklin Ricker and Betty June Caldwell; m. Michael James Dierickx; children: Amy Gambill, April Gambill. PhD, Ga. State U., Atlanta, GA, 1998. Psychologist self employed, Marietta, Ga., 1990—98; cons. RHR Internat.Co., Atlanta, 1998—. Spkr. in field; presenter in field. Vol. Save the Park, Marietta, 2001; member, vol., adv. Ga. Coun. for Hearing Impaired., Atlanta, 1995—98; vol. Citizens to Rescind the Resolution, Marietta; Chair, Selection Com/ Habitat for Humanity, Asheville, NC, 1989—90. Grantee, Undergraduate Research Council - University of North Carolina - Asheville, NC, 1989. Mem.: APA, Soc.for Consulting. Psychology, Bd. Dirs. Network, National Assn. Corp. Dirs. Unitarian Universalist. Avocations: cooking, reading, walking, boxing fan. Office: RHR Internat Co 1355 Peachtree St Ste 1400 Atlanta GA 30064 Personal E-mail: cdierickx@rhrinternational.com. Business E-Mail: cdierickx@rhrinternational.com.

DIERS, DONNA KAYE, nursing educator; b. Sheridan, Wyo., May 11, 1938; d. Don Carlos and Ilene Helen (Poffenberger) D. BSN, U. Denver, 1960; MSN, Yale U., 1964. Staff nurse Yale Psychiat. Inst., New Haven, 1960-62; mem. faculty Yale U. Sch. Nursing, New Haven, 1964—, Anne W. Goodrich prof., 1979—, dean, 1972-75; dir. Yale Health Services, Cmty. Health Care Plan, New Haven, 1972—. Author: Research in Nursing Practice, 1979. Mem. adv. com. Robert Wood Johnson Found., Princeton, N.J., 1980-86; mem. research rev. com. Nat. Ctr. Health Services Research, Washington, 1981-86. Recipient Henderson award Conn. Nurses Assn., 1980, Disting. Alumna award Yale U. Sch. Nursing, 1983. Fellow Am. Acad. Nursing; mem. Am. Nurses Assn. (J.M. Scott award 1986), Inst. Medicine of Nat. Acad. Scis. Home: 220 Osborn Ave New Haven CT 06511-2848 Office: Yale U Sch Nursing 100 Church St S PO Box 9740 New Haven CT 06536-0740

DIERSING, CAROLYN VIRGINIA, educational administrator; b. Rushville, Ohio, Sept. 13; d. Carl Emerson and Wilma Virginia (Neel) Deyo; m. Robert J. Diersing, Dec. 22, 1962; children: Robert, Timothy, Charles, Sheila, Christina. BA, Ohio State U., 1963; state cert., Ohio Dominican, 1985. Cert. tchr., Ohio. Libr. St. Mary's Sch., Delaware, Ohio, 1979-87; tech. svcs. asst. Beeghly Libr. Ohio Wesleyan U., Delaware, 1987-90, dir. curriculum resource dept. edn., 1990-96; libr. assoc. Westerville Pub. Libr., 1997—. Contbr. poetry to Voices. Mem. ALA, Del. Area Recovery Resources (bd. dirs. 1994-96, treas. 1995, sec. 1996), Ohio Libr. Coun. Office: Westerville Pub Libr Adult Svcs Dept 126 S State St Westerville OH 43081-2095 E-mail: cdiersin@wpl.lib.oh.us.

DIESTELKAMP, DAWN LEA, government agency administrator; b. Fresno, Calif., Apr. 23, 1954; d. Don and Joy LaVaughn (Davis) Diestelkamp. BS in Microbiology, Calif. State U., Fresno, 1976, MS in Pub. Adminstrn., 1983, cert. in tng. design and mgmt., 1992, MBA, 1995. Lic. clin. lab. technologist, Calif.; cert. clin. lab. dir. Clin. lab. technologist Valley Med. Ctr., Fresno, 1977-82, info. sys. coord., 1983-84, quality control coord., 1984-90, sys. and procedures analyst, 1990-91, Fresno County Superior Ct., 1991-98, ct. info. sys. mgr., 1998—2003, dir. tech., 2003—. Chair mid-level mgrs. edn. com. Jud. Coun. Calif., Ctr. for Jud. Edn. and Rsch.; faculty U. Phoenix, 1997; instr. Fresno City Coll. Tng. Inst., 1993—98; faculty Calif. State U., Fresno, 1999—2003; pres. North Calif. Ct. Assoc., 2003—04; cons., instr. in field. Mem.: Calif. Ct. Assn., U.S. Holocaust Meml. Mus., Fresno Met. Mus. Soc. Democrat. Office: 1100 Van Ness Ave Fresno CA 93724-0002 Office Phone: 559-488-2655. E-mail: ddiestelkamp@co.fresno.ca.us.

DIETDERICH, SHIRLEY (JANE ROHLFING), interior decorator; b. San Dimas, Calif., Oct. 15, 1926; d. Rudolf Frederick Rohlfing and Helen Rebekah (Higgins) Stephenson; m. Rex Dietderich, Aug. 3, 1952; children: Frank, Jean. BA in Decorative Arts, U. Calif., Berkeley, 1950. Cert. interior designer, Calif. From decorator to head decorator Mauerhan's Decorating Studio, Berkeley, 1950-55; freelance interior decorator Shirley Dietderich Interiors, Berkeley, 1957—2002. Leader Campfire Girls, 1964-72; statistician Masters Age Records, 1983—. Named Sports Master of Yr., Bay Area Women's 'Sports Coun., 1994. Mem. Delta Zeta. Democrat. Presbyterian. Avocations: track and field (sprint, javelin, discus).

DIETRICH, DAWN, software company executive; Systems engr. Software AG, Washington, 1986-88; profl. svcs. IS Orgn., Denver, 1988-91, implemented help desk, 1991-97; v.p. customer support Saga Software, Inc., Reston, Va., 1997—. Office: Saga Software Inc 11190 Sunrise Valley Dr Reston VA 20191-5453

DIETRICH, RENÉE LONG, fund raising executive; b. Emerald, Pa., Oct. 10, 1937; d. Emmett A. and Arlene I. (Fenstermaker) Long; m. Bruce L. Dietrich, Nov. 25, 1959; children: Dodson, Katie. BS, Kutztown (Pa.) U., 1959; MLS, Rutgers U., 1966. Cert. fund raising exec., ednl. specialist. Tchr. history Reading (Pa.) Pub. Schs., 1959-65, libr., 1965-69; coord. coop. ed. Reading Area C.C., 1978-81, program adminstr. title III grant, 1982-92, coord. cmty. and legis. rels., 1983-98, dir. instnl. advancement, 1991-98, exec. dir. Found. for Reading, 1986—98; dir. planned giving LUTHERCARE, Lititz, Pa., 1999—. Cons. U.S. Office of Edn., Washington, 1990—. Contbr. articles to profl. jours. Bd. dirs. Kutztown U. Found., 1981-90, LWV Pa., 1997-99, Great Valley Coun. Girl Scouts U.S., 1999—; chair bd. trustees Kutztown U., 1976-81; mem. Berks County Commn. for Women, 1993-96; pres. LWV Berks County, 1995-97. Recipient Disting. Alumni award, Kutztown U., 1981; named to Pa. Honor Roll of Women, 1996. Mem. Assn. Fundraising Professionals, Nat. Planned Giving Coun. Mem. United Ch. of Christ. Avocations: music, reading, politics. Home: 1546 Dauphin Ave Reading PA 19610-2118

DIETRICH, SUZANNE CLAIRE, instructional designer, communications consultant; b. Granite City, Ill. d. Charles Daniel and Evelyn Blanche (Waters) D. BS in Speech, Northwestern U.; MS in Pub. Comm., Boston U., 1967; postgrad., So. Ill. U., 1973-83. Intern prodn. staff Sta. WGBH-TV, Boston, 1958-59; asst. dir., 1962-64; asst. dir. program invitation to art, 1958; cons. producer dir. dept. instructional tv radio Ill. Office Supt. Pub. Instrn., Springfield, 1969-70; dir. program prodn. and distbn., 1970-72; instr. faculty call staff, speech dept. Sch. Fine Arts So. Ill. U., Edwardsville, 1972-73; grad. asst. for doctoral program office of dean Sch. Edn., 1975-78; rsch. asst. Ill. pub. telecomms. study for Ill. Pub. Broadcasting Coun., 1979-80; cons., rsch. in comm., 1980—. Pub. advisor Bradly Pub., Inc., 1996. Exec. prodr., dir. tv programs Con-Con Countdown, 1970, The Flag Speaks, 1971. Mem. sch. bd. St. Mary's Cath. Sch., Edwardsville, 1991-92; cable tv adv. com. City of Edwardsville, 1994—, co-chair, 1996-98; bd. dirs. Goshen Preservation Alliance, Edwardsville, 1992-94, pres., 1995-97; dir. Madison County Hist. Mus. and Archival Libr., 1999—. Recipient Athena award, Edwardsville/ Glen Carbon C. of C., 2004. Mem. Mdison

County Hist. Soc. (bd. dirs. 1997-99), Glen Carbon C. of C. (Athena award 2004). Roman Catholic. Home: 1011 Minnesota St Edwardsville IL 62025-1424 Office: 715 N Main St Edwardsville IL 62025-1111 Office Phone: 618-656-7562.

DIETZ, JANIS CAMILLE, business educator; b. Washington, May 26, 1950; d. Albert and Joan Mildred (MacMullen) Weinstein; m. John William Dietz, Apr. 10, 1981. BA, U. R.I., 1971; MBA, Calif. Poly. U., Pomona, 1984; PhD, Claremont Gard. Sch., 1997. Customer svc. trainer People's Bank, Providence, 1974-76; salesman, food broker Bradshaw Co., L.A., 1976-78; salesman Johnson & Johnson, L.A., 1978-79, GE Co., L.A., 1979-82; regional sales mgr. Leviton Co., L.A., 1982-85; nat. sales mgr. Jensen Gen. divsn. Nortek Co., L.A., 1985-86; retail sales mgr. Norris divsn. Masco, L.A., 1986-88; nat. sales mgr. Thermador Waste King divsn. Masco, L.A., 1988-91; nat. accounts mgr. Universal Flooring divsn. Masco, 1991-92; western regl. mgr. Peerless Faucet divsn. Masco, 1992-95; performance devel. cons. Delta Faucet divsn. Masco, 1995—. Assoc. prof. bus. adminstrn. U. LaVerne, 1995-2002, prof., 2002—; sales trainer, Upland, Calif., 1985—; instr. Calif. Poly. U., 1988-91; lectr. Whittier Coll., 1994. Dir. pub. rels. Jr. Achievement, Providence, 1975-76; trustee Soc. Calif. chpt. Nat. Multiple Sclerosis Soc. Recipient Sector Svc. award GE Co., Fairfield, Conn., 1980, Outstanding Achievement award, 1980. Mem. NAFE, Sales Profls. L.A. (v.p. 1984-86), Toastmasters (adminstrv. v.p. 1985). Unitarian Universalist. E-mail: dietzj@ulv.edu.

DIETZ, LAUREL PATRICIA, music educator; b. Portsmouth, Va., June 9, 1978; d. James Alan and Shelia-Gene Dietz. BA in Music, St. Mary's Coll. Md., 2000. Cert. tchr. Md. State Dept. of Edn., 2000. Choral dir. Leonardtown (Md.) H.S., 1998—2000; gen. music tchr. Hollywood (Md.) Elem. Sch., 2000—02, band dir., 2000—02; choral dir. Great Mills (Md.) H.S., 2002—. Asst. marching band dir. Leonardtown H.S. Marching Band, 1999—2000; accompanist St. Mary's Musica, California, Md., 2001—03; asst. marching band dir. Great Mills H.S. Marching Band, 2002—; honor chorus dir. St. Mary's County All County Elem. Sch. Honors Chorus. Recipient Outstanding Tchr. award, LDS Ch., 2000, 2003; grantee in arts edn., Wash. Post, 2000—01. Mem.: Md. Music Educators Assn., Music Educators Nat. Conf. Avocations: tennis, travel, music. Home: 26362 Cherry Ln Hollywood MD 20636 Personal E-mail: dietzlp@yahoo.com. E-mail: dietzlp@yahoo.com.

DIETZ, MARGARET JANE, retired public information director; b. Omaha, Apr. 15, 1924; d. Lawrence Louis and Jeanette Amalia (Meile) Neumann; m. Richard Henry Dietz, May 30, 1949 (dec. July 1971); children: Henry Louis, Frederick Richard, Susan Margaret, John Lawrence (dec.). BA, U. Nebr., 1946; MS, Columbia U., 1949. Wire editor Kearney (Nebr.) Daily Hub, 1946-47; state soc. editor Omaha World-Herald, 1947-48; libr. aide Akron (Ohio) Pub. Libr., 1963-66, publicity and display dir., 1966-74; editor Owlet, 1966-74; pub. info. officer Northeastern Ohio Univs. Coll. Medicine, Rootstown, 1974-85, dir. Office Commn., 1985-87, ret., 1987. Writer Ravenna (Ohio) Record-Courier, 1988-92; cons. Kent (Ohio) State U. Sch. Music, 1988-91. Author: Akron's Library: Commemorating Twenty Five Years on Main Street, Silver Reflections: A History of the Northeastern Ohio Universities College of Medicine, 1973-98. Mem. culture and entertainment com. Goals for Greater Akron, 1976; pres. bd. Weathervane Cmty. Playhouse, Akron, 1982-85, sec. to the bd., 1988-93, trustee, 1991-93, historian, 1993—, chair 60th anniversary season, 1994-95; trustee Family Svcs. Summit County, Ohio, 1980-84, dist. trustee, 1994—, Am. Heart Assn., Akron dist., 1986-91, Mobile Meals Found., Akron, 1988-91; v.p. Friends of Akron-Summit County Pub. Libr., 1988-94, pres., 1994-95, bd.dirs., 2003—; student tutor LEARN Literacy Coun., 1988-94, trustee, 1988-95. Recipient Trustee award Weathervane Cmty. Playhouse, 1985, Family Svcs. Bernard W. Frazier award, 1994, John S. Knight award Soc. Profl. Journalists, 1995. Mem. Women in Comm. (Mary Kerrigan O'Neill award 1995), LWV (edn. found. 1989-92, newsletter editor Akron 1957-60), Coll. Club, Press Club, Akron Women's City Club. Home: 887 Canyon Trl Akron OH 44303-2401 E-mail: mjd887@earthlink.net.

DIFRANCO, ANI, music executive, musician; b. Buffalo, N.Y., Sept. 23, 1970; Founder Righteous Babe, 1990—. Albums include: Ani DiFranco, 1989, Not So Soft, 1991, Imperfectly, 1992, Puddle Drive, 1993, Out of Range, 1994, Like I Said, 1994, Not A Pretty Girl, 1995, More Joy Less Shame, 1996, Dilate, 1996, Living in Clip, 1997, Little Plastic Castle, 1998, Up, 1999, Little Plastic Remixes, 1999, Fellow Workers, 1999, To the Teeth, 1999, Swing Set, 2000, Revelling/Reckoning, 2001, So Much Shouting, So Much Laughter, 2002, Evolve, 2003, Educated Guess, 2003. Office: c/o Righteous Babe Records PO Box 95 Buffalo NY 14205-0095

DIGESO, AMY, mail order company executive; BS in Behavioral Sci., Pa. State U., 1974; MBA in Internat. Mgmt., Fordham U., 1982. Former mgmt. positions Am. Express, Estee Lauder, Banker's Trust; various positions including CEO Mary Kay, 1991-98; pres. Popular Club Plan Fingerhut Cos. Inc., Minnetonka, Minn., 1999—. Office: Fingerhut Cos Inc 4400 Baker Rd Minnetonka MN 55343-8684

DIGGS, BEATRICE M. research assistant; b. Rochester, N.Y., Apr. 10, 1904; d. Alfred Mark and Agnes (Pettengill) Moshier; m. L. W. Diggs, Nov. 30, 1929 (dec.); children: Walter, Alice, John, Margaret. A, Wellesley Coll., 1926. Rsch. asst. U. Rochester, 1926—29, U. Tenn., Memphis, 1929—95. Mem.: AAUW (pres. 1942—43). Republican. Unitarian Universalist. Avocation: gardening. Home: 7340 Raleigh Lagrange Rd Cordova TN 38018-6222

DIGGS, ELIZABETH F(RANCIS), playwright, educator; b. Tulsa, Okla., Aug. 6, 1939; d. James Barnes and Virginia Francis Diggs; m. Will Mackenzie, June 8, 1961 (div. 1964); 1 child, Jennifer Evans Mackenzie. BA, Brown U., 1961; MA, Columbia U., 1965, PhD, 1982. Assoc. prof. dramatic writing N.Y. U.-Tisch Sch. Arts, N.Y.C., 1987—. Author: (plays) Close Ties, 1984, Goodbye Freddy, 1986, Nightingale, 1990. Grantee, Sundance Playwrights Lab, 1995—96; Guggenheim fellow, 1988, NEA grant, 1989. Democrat. Avocations: gardening, tennis, travel. Home: 2092 Rt 9 Chatham NY 12037 Office: Tisch NYU Dept Dramatic Writing 721 Boran New York NY 10003

DI GIACOMO, FRAN, artist; b. Miami, Ariz., Oct. 24, 1944; d. B.J. and LaVenia Marilyn (Beavers) Fain; m. Leonard May 9, 1970; children: Marc, Eric. Student, Scottsdale Artist's Sch., 1985—2000; studied, with David Leffel, with Joe Anna Arnette, with Greg Kreutz, with Howard Terpning. Artist, 1970—; represented by Gallerie Amsterdam, Carmel, Calif., Southwest Gallery, Dallas, Heritage Gallery, Scottsdale, Ariz., Downey Gallery, Santa Fe. Commissions include portraits of Supreme Court Chief Justice Warren E. Burger, Dist. Atty., 1994, Henry Wade, 1995, Haggar Apparel, Dallas Cowboys' Emmitt Smith, 1993; author: I'd Rather Do Chemo Than Clean Out the Garage; subject of numerous articles. Recepient 2nd place, 1993, Hon. Mention, 1994, 1st place, 1996, Plano Art Assn.,1st place, 1994, Assoc. Creative Artists, Grumbacher Gold, 1997, 2nd place, 1994, Trinity Arts Guild, 1st place, 1998, 3rd place, 1999, Richardson Civic Art, 3rd place, 1995, Tex. and Neighbors 5 state. Mem. Oil Painters Am. (assoc., signature), Am. Soc. (assoc.), Classical Realism, Portrait Soc. Am., Assoc. Creative Artists (signature). Avocation: tennis.

DIGIAMARINO, MARIAN ELEANOR, retired realty administrator; b. Camden, N.J., July 23, 1947; d. James and Concetta (Biancosino) DiG. BS in Mgmt., Rutgers U., 1978. Clk. stenographer transp. div. Dept. of Navy, Phila., 1965-70, sec., 1970-73, realty asst. Profl. Devel. Ctr. program, 1973-75, realty specialist, 1975-81, supervisory realty specialist, head acquisition and ingrant sect., 1981-85, supervisory realty specialist, mgr. ops. br., 1985-92, spl. asst. for real estate, 1992-99; ret., 1999; pastoral assoc. Ch. of St. Isaac Jogues, Marlton, N.J., 1999—. Instr. USNR, Phila., 1983, 88. Contbr. articles to profl. jours. Mem. AAUW, Soc. Am. Mil. Engrs., Nat. Assn. Female Execs., Phi Chi Theta (pres. Del. Valley chpt. 1984-86, nat. councillor 1984, nat. fundraising com., pres. and corr. sec. (Alpha Omega chpt. 1976-78). Avocations: theatre, sports, needlework, reading, beach combing.

DIGIOVANNI, ELEANOR ELMA, scaffold installation company executive; b. L.I., N.Y., May 14, 1944; d. Charles and Josephine (Laureni) DiGiovanni. Student, Queensboro Coll. Collector Atlas/Re/Sun Ins. Co., N.Y.C., 1965-69; instr. Oak Manor Equitation, Weyers Cave, Va., 1970-76; dispatcher, salesperson Safway Steel Products, L.I., N.Y., 1977-83; ops. mgr. York Scaffold, L.I., 1983—95; scaffold sales rep. Safway Steel Prod., Bklyn., 1977—83; ptnr. E-Z Scholarship Data Svs., 1992-94; scaffold sales rep. R&R Scaffolding, Moonachie, NJ, 2001—02, Highrise Hoisting and Scaffolding Inc., Long Island City, NY, 2002—. Mem.: NAFE, Women in Constrn., Mus. Natural History, Internat. Platform Assn. Democrat. Roman Catholic. Avocations: reading, horseback riding, needlepoint. Home: 14-34 30th Rd Astoria NY 11102-3640 Office: Highrise Hoisting and Scaffolding Inc 2800 Borden Ave Long Island City NY 11101 E-mail: ellie2002@aol.com.

DIGNAC, GENY (EUGENIA M. BERMUDEZ), sculptor; b. Buenos Aires, June 8, 1932; came to U.S., 1954; d. Jose Victor Marenco and Margarita Eugenia D.; m. Jose Y. Bermudez, Apr. 7, 1958; children—Alexander, Melanie. Ed., U. Buenos Aires, 1952-54. Lectr. in field. Exhibited in one-woman shows at Galeria 22, Caracas, Venezuela, 1967, Michael Berger Gallery, Pitts., 1969, Cinema 2, Caracas, 1971, Pyramid Gallery, Washington, 1971; exhibited in numerous group shows including Corcoran Gallery of Art, Washington, 1958, 59, Inst. Contemporary Arts, Washington, 1967, Bklyn. Mus., 1968, Mus. Modern Art, Buenos Aires, 1971, Mus. Fine Arts, Boston, 1971, Palais des Beaux Arts, Brussels, 1974, Inst. Contemporary Arts, London, 1974; represented in permanent collections including Fundacio Joan Miro, Barcelona, Spain, Palazzo Dei Diamanti, Ferrara, Italy, Museo La Tertulia, Cali, Colombia, Galeria del Banco Central, Guayaquil, Ecuador, The Latinoamerican Art Found., San Juan, P.R., and others in Argentina, Chile, Germany, Italy, Ireland, Spain, U.S. and Venezuela; works include 27 Fire Gestures-, 1970-2000; radio and TV interviews, U.S. and abroad; works with lights, fire and temperatures; subject of profl. articles, films. Recipient prize for light sculpture IX Festival of Art, 1969 Home: 4109 E Via Estrella Phoenix AZ 85028-4515 E-mail: gdignac@aol.com.

DIGNAN, ELEANOR A. artist; b. Balt., Dec. 14, 1918; d. William M. Lobrano and Eleanor M. Seymore; m. Joseph J. Dignan; 1 child, Joseph H. Illustrator: Gold Spike Album, 1965; group exhibitions include San Francisco Mus. Modern Art, De Youg Mus., San Francisco, El Paso Mus. Art, Salamungui Art, N.Y., Maraetta Art, Ohio, New Orleans Towers. Mem. Soc. Western Artists (bd. dirs. 1962-72), San Francisco Women Artists (bd. dirs. 1965-70), Marin Soc. Artists, Marin Watercolor Soc. Roman Catholic. Home: 1018 Lombard St San Francisco CA 94109-1515

DIKE, MARGARET HOPCRAFT, retired education administrator; b. Prescott, Ariz., July 15, 1921; d. Walter Irving and Margaret Jennie (Lindsay) Hopcraft; m. Sheldon Holland Dike, Nov. 20, 1941 (div. 1971); children: Lawrence, Walter, Robert, Martin, Martha. BA, U. N.Mex., 1941, MA, 1975. Draftsman U. Calif., Los Alamos, N.Mex., 1943-45; coord. Albuquerque Pub. Schs., 1972-85; ret., 1985. Chair pub. adv. com. U. N.Mex., Albuquerque, 1973-74, chair search com. regional v.p., 1975. Co-editor: Bicentennial '76 - Albuquerque, 1977; editor booklet New Mexico Arts Resources Survey, 1957. Trustee Albuquerque Mus., 1969-81; chmn. Albuquerque R.R. Centennial, 1979-80, Keep Albuquerque Beautiful Edn., 1984—; pres. Albuquerque Sister Cities Found., 1985-87; Albuquerque Hist. Soc., 1971-78; N.Mex. Assn. for Cmty. Edn. Devel., 1980-82; chair Albuquerque Sister Cities Bd., 1988-91, 96—; life mem. N.Mex. PTA, pres., 1977-79, 92-95; sec. Edn. Forum N.Mex., 1988-89; chair, Ednl. Success Alliance, 1996-97. Recipient Lobo award U. N.Mex., 1968, Gov.'s award for outstanding N.Mex. women, Commn. on Status of Women, 1986, 90, 1st Lifetime Achievement award, 2002, N.Mex. Disting. Svc. award, 1996, Paragon award N.Mex. Assn. Ednl. Retirees, 2000, Cmty. Svc. award, AARP, 2001; named Woman on the Move for cmty. svc. YWCA, 1995, to Sr. Hall of Fame, 1995, Zia award U. N. Mex. Alumni Assn., 1999. Mem.: AAUW (pres. Albuquerque br. 1968—70, pres. N.Mex. 1989—93, pres. Albuquerque br. 2000—01, Grace Barker Wilson award N.Mex. 2001), La Luz Am. Bus. Womens Assn., Albuquerque Assn. Ednl. Retirees (pres. 1998—99, 2002—03), Mortar Bd. (pres. alumni chpt. 1988—90, 1996—, Nat. Cmty. Svc. award 1993), Exec. Women Internat. (treas. 1983—85), Phi Kappa Phi, Phi Alpha Theta, Phi Delta Kappa. Methodist. Avocations: travel, reading, camping, sewing.

DILEONE, CARMEL MONTANO, dental hygienist; b. New Haven, Aug. 24, 1926; d. Nicholas and Martha (Ercolano) M.; m. Eugene Francis Dileone, Jan. 28, 1948; children: Gina, Richard. Dental Hygienist, Temple U., 1945; AA, Albertus Magnus Coll., 1980; BS, U. Bridgeport, 1983; MS, So. Conn. State U., 1985. Registered dental hygienist. Dental hygiene practitioner George M. Montano, DDS, New Haven, 1946-50, George V. Montano, DDS, Orange, 1959-2000, Francis R. Mullen, DDS, West Haven, 1950-55; dental hygiene practioner Herbert Saunders, DDS, Orange, Conn., 1958-63, Children's Dental Assocs., Hamden, 2000—03, Children's Dental Group, New Haven, 2000—; G. Instr. Huntington Inst., North Haven, Conn., 1983; adj. assoc. prof. U. Bridgeport, Conn., Fones Sch. Dental Hygiene, 1985-96; adj. faculty U. New Haven, 1994—. Dir., treas. Conn. Hygienists' Polit. Action Com., 1996—2002. Recipient Profl. Recognition award U. New Haven, 1999. Mem.: New Haven Dental Hygienists Assn. (pres. 1949, 1975), Conn. Dental Hygienists Assn. (treas. 1986—88, v.p. 1988—89, pres.-elect 1989—90, pres. 1991, Mabel C. McCarthy award 1983, Pres. award 1994), Am. Dental Hygienists Assn., Am. Soc. Dentistry for Children, Conn. Pub. Health Assn., Sigma Phi Alpha. Roman Catholic. Home: 348 Racebrook Rd Orange CT 06477-3109

DILGEN, REGINA MARIE, English educator; b. Bklyn., Feb. 9, 1954; d. John C. and Frances M. (Mollo) D.; m. William A. Tignor, Jan. 8, 1988; children: Mia Stephanie, Francesca Maria. BA, U. Fla., 1976; MA, Fla. Atlantic U., 1985; MA in Libr. Sci., U. South Fla., 1990. Adj. instr. English, Palm Beach C.C., Lake Worth, Fla., 1988-97, assoc. prof., 1997—. Mem. ALA, Nat. Coun. Tchrs. English, Fla. Coll. English Assn. Democrat. Office: Palm Beach CC 4200 Congress Ave Lake Worth FL 33461-4705

DILIBERTI, LARA MARIE, music educator; d. Mark Michael Medvedev and Ludmilla Sokolov; m. Charles Ernest DiLiberti, July 24, 1983 (div.). BS, William Paterson State U., 1980; MA, Columbia U., 1985. Cert. gen. edn. grades K-8. Band dir. Ben Franklin Jr. H.S., Teaneck, NJ, choir dir.; musical dir. Teaneck H.S.; gen. music tchr. Radburn Sch., Fairlawn, NJ; tchr. summer music theatre Fairlawn H.S.; summer vocal dir. Summit (N.J.) H.S., vocal musical dir.; choral dir. Matawan (N.J.) Regional H.S. Mem.: Music Educators Nat. Conf., Am. Choral Dirs. Assn., Adoptees Liberty Movement Assn., Reunited Twins Assn., Kappa Delta Pi. Avocations: writing, running, target shooting. Office Phone: 732-290-2800.

DILL, BONNIE THORNTON, sociology educator; BA in English, U. Rochester, 1965; MA in Human Relations/Edn., PhD in Sociology, NYU, 1979. Trainer and course asst. Ctr. for Human Rels. NYU, 1969-71; adj. lectr. Black and Hispanic Studies Program Bernard M. Baruch Coll., 1972-73; tchg. asst. Sociology Dept. NYU, 1974-75, adj. instr. Sociology Dept., 1976-77; counselor/lectr. Dept. Compensatory Programs Bernard M. Baruch Coll., CUNY, 1970-77; dir. and founder Ctr. for Rsch. on Women Memphis State U., 1982-88, prof. sociology Dept. Sociology and Social Work, 1978-91; prof. dept. women's studies, affiliate prof. sociology U. Md., 1991—, dir. Consortium on Race, Gender & Ethnicity. Mem. adv. bd. on rsch., scholarship and edn. Ms. Mag., 1985-91; mem. editl. bd. Signs: Jour. of Women and Culture in Soc., 1979-89, mem. selection adv. com. U. Chgo. Press; cons. numerous orgns.; presenter and lectr. in field. Co-editor: Women of Color in U.S. Society, 1994, Across the Boundaries of Race and Class: An Exploration of Work and Family Among Black Female Domestic Servants, 1994; contbr. numerous articles to jours. in field. Recipient numerous grants and fellowships including The Ford Found., 1988-89, 1989-91, 1992-94, 1999-2003, Jessie Bernard Disting. Contributions to Teaching, Am. Soc. Assn., Robin Williams Jr. Lectr. Women & Achievement. Mem. Am. Sociol. Assn. (com. on status of women in sociology, com. on noms. 1984-85, task force on minority fellow program 1986-87, Jessie Bernard award com. 1986-89, chair com. on coms. 1995, numerous others), Assn. Black Sociologists (bd. dirs. 1977-79), Nat. Coun. Rsch. on Women (bd. dirs. 1983-86), Nat. Women's Studies Assn., Soc. for the Study of Social Problems (editl. and publs. com. 1986-89, Lee-Founder's award com. 1985, 87, C. Wright Mills award com. 1980-81). Office: U of Md Womens Studies Program 2101 Woods Hall College Park MD 20742-0001 Business E-Mail: bd36@umail.umd.edu.

DILLARD, ANNIE, writer; b. Pitts., Apr. 30, 1945; d. Frank and Pam (Lambert) Doak; m. R.H.W. Dillard, 1965 (div.); m. Gary Clevidence, 1980 (div.); 1 child, Cody Rose; stepchildren: Carin, Shelly; m. Robert D. Richardson, Jr., 1988. BA, Hollins Coll., 1967, MA, 1968. Contbg. editor Harper's Mag., N.Y.C., 1974-81, 83-85; scholar-in-residence Western Wash. U., Bellingham, 1975-78; disting. vis. prof. Wesleyan U., 1979-83, adj. prof., 1983—, writer-in-residence, 1987—98, writer emeritus, 1998—, bd. dirs. Writers Conf., 1984—, chmn., 1991—. Fellow Calhoun Coll., Yale U., New Haven, Conn.; Phi Beta Kappa orator Harvard-Radcliffe U., 1983; mem. U.S. writers del. UCLA US.-Chinese Writers Conf., 1982; mem. U.S. cultural del. to China, 1982; bd. dirs. The New Press, Key West Writers Conf., Wesleyan Writers Conf., Key West Literary Seminars; mem. usage panel Am. Heritage Dictionary. Author: Tickets for a Prayer Wheel, 1974, 3d edit., 2002, Pilgrim at Tinker Creek, 1974 (Pulitzer prize for gen. non-fiction 1975, Best Fgn. Book Pub. in France 1990), Holy the Firm, 1978, Living by Fiction, 1982, Teaching a Stone to Talk, 1982, Encounters with Chinese Writers, 1984, An American Childhood, 1987 (Nat. Book Critics award finalist 1987), The Writing Life, 1989 (English-speaking union Amb. Book award 1990), The Living, 1992, The Annie Dillard Reader, 1994, Mornings Like This, 1995, For the Time Being, 1999 (Maurice Coindreau prize 2001); editor: (with Robert Atwan) Best Essays, 1988; (with Cort Conley) Modern American Memoirs, 1995. Mem. Nat. Com. on U.S.-China Rels., 1982—, St. Mary's Soup Kitchen, Key West, Fla.; bd. dirs. Milton Ctr., Authors League Fund, Key West Literary Seminars, Wesleyan Writers Conf. Recipient N.Y. Presswomen's award for excellence, 1975, Wash. Gov.'s award for contbn. to lit., 1978, Appalachian Gold medallion U. Charleston, 1989, Found. award St. Botolph's Club, 1989, History Maker award Hist. Soc. Western Pa., 1993, Conn. Gov.'s award in the arts, 1993, Milton Ctr. prize, 1994, Campion award Am. Mag., 1994, Am. Acad. Arts and Letters award in Lit., 1998; grantee NEA, 1980-81, Guggenheim Found., 1985-86. Mem. NAACP, Soc. Am. Historians, Authors Guild, Am. Acad. Arts and Letters, Key West Volleyball Assn.,Phi Beta Kappa. Democrat. Address: c/o Timothy Seldes Russell & Volkening 50 W 29th St New York NY 10001-4227

DILLARD, MARILYN DIANNE, property manager; b. Norfolk, Va., July 7, 1940; d. Thomas Ortman and Sally Ruth (Wallerich) D.; m. James Conner Coons, Nov. 6, 1965 (div. June 1988); 1 child, Adrienne Alexandra Dillard Coons (dec.). Studied with Russian prima ballerina, Alexandra Danilova, 1940's; student with honors at entrance, UCLA, 1958-59; BA in Bus. Adminstrn. with honors, U. Wash., 1962. Modeling-print work Harry Conover, N.Y.C., 1945; ballet instr. Ivan Novikoff Sch. Russian Ballet, 1955; model Elizabeth Leonard Agy., Seattle, 1955-68; mem. fashion bd., retail worker Frederick & Nelson, Seattle, 1962; retail worker I. Magnin & Co., Seattle, 1963-64; property mgr. Kirkland, Wash., 1961—; antique and interior designer John J. Cunningham Antiques, Seattle, 1968-73; owner, interior designer Marilyn Dianne Dillard Interiors, 1973—. Rsch. bd. advisors Am. Biog. Inst., Inc., 1990—. Author: (poetry) Flutterby, 1951, Spring Flowers, 1951; contbr., asst. chmn. (with Jr. League of Seattle) Seattle Classic Cookbook, 1980-83. Charter mem., pres. Children's Med. Ctr., Maude Fox Guild, Seattle, 1965—, Jr. Women's Symphony Assn., 1967-73, "200+1" Org., 1967-70, Va. Mason Med. Ctr. Soc., 1990—, Nat. Mus. of Am. Indian, Smithsonian Instn., 1992—; mem. Seattle Jr. Club, 1962-65, 97—; mem. Friends of the Pike Place Market (saved the market from demolition), 1971; bd. dirs. Patrons N.W. Civic, Cultural and Charitable Orgns., chmn. various coms., Seattle, 1976—, prodn. chmn., 1977-78, 84-85, auction party chmn., 1983-84, v.p. party/prodn., 1984-85, exec. com., 1984-85, chmn. bd. vols., 1990-91, adv. coun., 1991—; mem. U. Wash. Arboretum Found. Unit, 1966-73, pres., 1969; bd. dirs. Coun. for Prevention Child Abuse-Neglect, Seattle, 1974-75; bd. dirs., v.p., mem. coms. Seattle Children's Theatre, 1984-90, asst. in lighting main stage plays, 1987-93, adv. coun., 1993—, asst. in lighting main stage plays Bathhouse Theatre, 1987-90; adv. bd. N.W. Asian Am. Theatre, 1987-2001, Co-Motion Dance Co., 1991—; organizer teen groups Episcopal Ch. of Epiphany, 1965-67; provisional class pres. Jr. League Seattle, 1971-72, next to new shop asst. chmn., 1972-73, bd. dirs., admissions chmn., 1976-77, exec. v.p., exec. com., bd. dirs. 1978-79, sustaining mem., 1984—; charter mem. Jr. Women's Symphony Assn., 1967-73; mem. Seattle Art Mus., 1975-90, Landmark, 1990—, Corp. Coun. for Arts, 1991—; founding dir. Adrienne Coons Meml. Fund, 1985, v.p. 1985-92, 95—, pres. 1992-95; mem. steering com. Heart Ball Am. Heart Assn., 1986, 87, auction chmn., 1986; mem. steering com. Bellevue Sch. Dist. Children's Theatre, 1983-85, pub. rels. chair, 1984, asst. stage mgr., 1985; mem. Hist. Seattle Preservation and Devel. Authority, 1997—; mem. Eastlake Cmty. Coun., 1997—; mem. Steamship Virginia V. Found., 1997—; mem. Floating Homes Assn., Seattle, 1999—; mem. Queen Anne Hist. Soc., 2000—; com. chmn. Rep. Precinct, 2000; mem. Kirkland Downtown on the Lake Orgn., 1999—; apptd. City of Kirkland Downtown Strategic Planning Action Com., 2001—; mem. City of Kirkland Transit Ctr. location com., 2001-03. Named Miss Greater Seattle, 1964; honored for leadership in the arts Jr. League of Seattle, 2002. Mem. U. Wash. Alumnae Assn. (life), Pacific N.W. Ballet Assn. (charter), Progressive Animal Welfare Soc., Associated Women (student coun. U. Wash. 1962), Husky Honeys (U. Wash. rep. 1961-62), Profl. Rodeo Cowboys Assn. (assoc.), Seattle Tennis Club. Republican. Episcopalian. Avocations: needlepoint, horseback riding, theatre, travel, antique restoration. Home and Office: 2053 Minor Ave E Seattle WA 98102-3513

DILLARD, SUZANNE, interior designer; d. Jerome Wallace and Mary Mae (Price) Sorenson; m. Warren Marcus Dillard; 1 child, Jeremy Blake. Student, Tex. A&M U., 1961—65; BS, U. Tex., 1965; student, Pepperdine U., 1974, UCLA, 1977-78. Interior designer Pepperdine U., Malibu, Calif., 1982-95, exec. bd. dirs. Ctr. Arts, 1993—2002; cons., interior design Neptune and Thomas, Architects, Pasadena, Calif., 1979—; pres. Suzanne Dillard Interiors, Pacific Palisades, Calif., 1974—. Prin. on camera designer TV pilot, Dream House, Forecast Group Prodns., 1983; speaker in field. Treas. Nat. Arts Assn., L.A., 1982—83, benefit chair, 2001; pres. Fine Arts aux. Assistance League So. Calif., L.A., 1984; patron, sponsor, prodn. chmn. The Footlighters, L.A., 1985—86, pres., 1992—93, League for Children, 1991—93, benefit chair, 2002; pres. Achievement Awards Coll. Scientists, 1994—96; 1st v.p. Freedoms Found., 1997—98, pres., 1997—99; bd. dirs. Ctr. for Arts, Pepperdine U. Mem.: NATAS (Acad. Emmy Blue Ribbon panel 2001—03), AFTRA, SAG (nominating com. Acad. awards 2003), Internat. Found. for Ednl. and Performing Arts (adv.

bd.), Acad. TV Arts and Scis., Delta Delta Delta (pres. L.A. chpt. 1970—72, pres. sleighbell 1993—94). Republican. Mem. Ch. of Christ. Avocations: piano, voice, oil painting, reading, skiing. Office: 9620 Arby Dr Beverly Hills CA 90210-1202

DILLASHAW, EULA CATHERINE, artist, graphic artist; b. Memphis, Feb. 19, 1947; d. John Clemons and Catheryn Livingston (Murdock) Ballew; m. Stanley Neil Williams, July 29, 1968 (div. Sept. 1982); children: John C., Eric N., Heather L.; m. William Alfred Dillashaw, Oct. 22, 1986. Student, Art Instrn. Sch., 1959-63, Memphis State U., 1965-67, Daytona Beach C.C., 1986-89. Exec. sec. Franklin Simon, N.Y.C., 1973-78, Benefit Providers for Local Unions, Memphis, 1979-82; tchr. Eula's Art Studio & Gallery, Lake Helen, 1993—. Tchr. pvt. art classes for children and adults. One-person shows include Daytona Beach Airport, 1996, Daytona Beach Shores City Hall/C. of C., 1997, 00; represented in pvt. collections. Supt. fine arts Volusia County Fair, Deland, 1995—; pres. Lake Helen League of Artists & Crafters, 1994—; supt., bd. dirs. Volusia County Fair Assn. Bd. Recipient Best in Show profl. divsn. Volusia City Fair, 1997. Mem. Lake Helen C. of C. Democrat. Avocations: gourmet cooking, canning, raising pedigree birds, travel. Home: 291 S Euclid Ave Lake Helen FL 32744-2920 Fax: 904 228-0364.

DILLEN, NANCY BAUR, art educator, artist; b. Quincy, Fla., Jan. 27, 1947; d. Joseph Augustus and Edna Carolyn (Adams) Baur; m. Fredrick Leon Dillen, Sept. 27, 1974. BS, Fla. State U., 1969, MA, 1971. Cert. tchr. Fla. From instr. to prof. art Brevard Cmty. Coll., Melbourne, Fla., 1971—, gallery dir., 1982—88. Adj. art instr. Fla. State U., Tallahassee, 1971; juror, 2-D panelist Visual Arts Fellowships, Tallahassee, 2001, 02; tchr. Arrowmont Sch. Arts and Craft, Gatlinburg, Tenn., various yrs.; exch. instr. Malaspina Coll., Nanaimo, B.C., Canada, 1977—78. Job Ready mag., featured in Am. Artist Mag., 1990, paintings in corp., pub. and pvt. collections, various exhbns. of paintings. Recipient Best of Show award, Fla. Art Edn. Assn. Juried Mems. Exhibit, 2003. Mem.: Ten Women in Art (founding 1983), Strawbridge Art League (Best of Show 2003), Brevard Cultural Alliance, Fla. Art Edn. Assn. (dir. higher edn. divsn. 2001—03, sec. 2003—). Avocations: reading, walking, painting. Office: Brevard Cmty Coll 3865 N Wickham Rd Melbourne FL 32935

DILLER, ELIZABETH E. architect, educator, artist; b. Poland, 1954; B in Arch., Cooper Union Sch. of Arch., 1979. Ptnr. Diller & Scofidio, N.Y.C., 1979—; assoc. prof. arch. design Princeton U., NJ, 1990—. Work includes Inst. of Contemporary Art, Boston, Seagram's, N.Y., Museum of Art & Technology, N.Y. Co-creator JETLAG, 1998 (Obie Award for creative achievement), co-pub. Back to the Front: Tourisms of War, Flesh: Architectural Probes, Blur: the making of nothing. Recipient Brunner Prize in Arch., Am. Academy of Arts and Letters., 2003, MacDermott award for creative achievement, MIT, Progressive Arch. Design award; fellow MacArthur Foundation, 1999. Office: Princeton U Sch Architecture 5116 Architecture Princeton NJ 08544-0001

DILLER, PHYLLIS, actress, writer; b. Lima, Ohio, July 17, 1917; d. Perry Marcus and Frances Ada (Romshe) Driver; m. Sherwood Anderson Diller, Nov. 4, 1939 (div. Sept. 1965); children: Peter II, Sally, Suzanne Diller Mills, Stephanie Diller Waldron, Perry; m. Warde Donovan, Oct. 7, 1965 (div. July 1975). Student, Sherwood Music Conservatory, Chgo., 1935-37, Bluffton (Ohio) Coll., 1938-39; D.H.L., Nat. Christian U., 1973; PhD (hon.), Bluffton Coll., 1993. (Best TV Comedienne award TV Radio Mirror 1965); Author: Phyllis Diller Tells All About Fang, 1963, Phyllis Diller's Housekeeping Hints, 1966, Phyllis Diller's Marriage Manual, The Complete Mother, The Joys of Aging and How to Avoid Them, 1981; Accompanied Bob Hope entertainment group to South Vietnam, Christmas, 1966, symphony appearances soloing on piano.; Theatrical prodns. include Dark at the Top of the Stairs, 1961, Wonderful Town, 1962, Happy Birthday, 1963, Hello, Dolly!, 1970, Everybody Loves Opal, 1972, What Are We Going to Do With Jenny, 1977, Nunsense, 1989, The Wizard of Oz, 1990-92; numerous appearances TV and radio, concerts, supper clubs and hotels, 1955-; producer, writer: Phyllis Diller Show, 1963, 64; rec. artist, Verve Records, Columbia Records, pres., BAM Prodns., Ltd., from 1965, PhilDil Prodns., Ltd., 1966-; motion pictures include Eight on the Lam, 1967, The Private Navy of Sergeant O'Farrell, Hungry Reunion, 1981, Pink Motel, 1983, The Nutcracker Prince, 1990, The Boneyard, 1991, The Perfect Man, 1993, The Silence of the Hams, 1994, A Bug's Life (voice), 1998, The Debtors, 1999, Everything's Jake, 2000, The Last Place on Earth, 2002, Hip! Edgy! Quirky!, 2002, West From North Goes South, 2002, Motocross Kids, 2004; star: TV series The Pruitts of Southampton, 1966-67, Beautiful Phyllis Diller Show, 1968-69 (Recipient honors including Star of Year award Nat. Assn. Theatre Owners), The Bold and the Beautiful (recurring role), 1995-, Titus, 2002; video appearance: How to Have a Moneymaking Garage Sale, 1987. Recipient Minuteman award U.S. Treasury Dept., Disting. Service citation Ladies Aux. VFW, Woman of Year award Variety Club Women Balt.; Golden Apple Hollywood Women's Press Club, 1967, Woman of Year award St. Louis chpt. Nat. Bus. and Profl. Women's Club, 1971; named hon. mayor Brentwood, Calif., 1971; Hon. life mem. San Francisco Press and Union League Club; named Walk of Fame Star on Hollywood Blvd., 1975, Hon. Chair for Outstanding Svc. to Calif. State U. at Los Angeles, Friends of Music Scholarship Auction, 1982; recipient Doctor of Comedy award Kent State U., 1980, AMC Cancer Rsch. Ctr. Humanitarian award, 1981, Child-Help USA Woman of Yr. award, 1989; City of Los Angeles Proclamation of Phyllis Diller Week Mayor Tom Bradley, 1979; named to Ohio's Hall of Fame, 1981; Commonwealth scholar, 1964. Office: c/o The Sychin Co Ste 208 12747 Riverside Dr Valley Village CA 91607-3303*

DILLEY, BARBARA JEAN, college administrator, choreographer, educator; b. Chgo., Mar. 13, 1938; d. Robert Vernon and Jean Phyllis (Fairweather) D.; m. Lewis Lloyd, May 1961 (div.); 1 child, Benjamin Lloyd; m. Brent Bondurant, Mar. 1977 (div.); 1 child, Owen Bondurant. BA, Mt. Holyoke Coll., 1960. Dancer Merce Cunningham Dance Co., N.Y.C., 1963-68; ind. dancer, choreographer N.Y.C. and Boulder, Colo., 1966-82; dancer Yvonne Rainer Co., N.Y.C., 1967-70; dancer, choreographer The Grand Union, N.Y.C., 1970-76; mem. faculty dance program Naropa Inst., Boulder, 1974—, dir. dance program, 1974-84. Condr. pvt. workshops Toronto, Ont., Can., Montreal, Que., Can., Halifax, N.S., Can., The Netherlands, Eng., Switzerland, Germany, 1978—; vis. faculty European Dance Devel. Ctr., Arnheim, The Netherlands, 1993-94; artistic dir. Crystal Dance, Boulder, 1978-81; mem. vis. faculty NYU, Radcliffe Coll., Cornell U., U. Colo., George Washington U., others; dir. dance symposium, 1981; adjudicator S.W. divsn. Am. Coll. Dance Festival, Loretto Heights, Colo., 1986. Mem. grants selection panel Colo. Coun. of Arts and Humanities, 1981, mem. panel on policy devel. for individual grants, 1983. NEA Choreographic fellow, 1974, 76, 81; Boulder City Arts Coun. grantee, 1981. Democrat. Buddhist. Office: Naropa Inst 2130 Arapahoe Ave Boulder CO 80302-6697

DILLITZER, DIANNE RENÉ, sales executive; b. Downey, Ill., Oct. 6, 1956; d. Alvin Lee and Mary Alice (DuVaul) Pollard; m. Ulrich Dillitzer, Oct. 20, 2001. AAS, Coll. St. Catherine, St. Mary's Campus, Mpls., 1991; BA in Applied Behavioral Scis., Nat. Louis U., 1998, MA in Adult Edn., 2000. Word processing operator Debbie Temporaries, Naperville, Ill., 1985-86, Word Processors Personnel-ADIA, Mpls., 1986-88; computer lab. asst. Coll. St. Catherine, St. Mary's Campus, Mpls., 1989-91; adminstrv. asst. First Trust Ctr., St. Paul, 1992-93, Dolphin Temporaries, Mpls., 1993-94; receptionist, adminstrv. asst. Dain Bosworth, Mpls., 1994-96; reading devel. instrnl. asst. Hubble Mid. Sch., 1998-99; computer lab. asst. Franklin Mid. Sch., Wheaton, 1999-2000; inside sales/ednl. materials Scholastic, Inc., St. Charles, Ill., 2002—. Recipient Dirs. award Minn. Inst. Med. & Dental Careers, 1988, Women's Leadership award Abigail Quigley Women's Ctr., 1991, Minority Leadership award U.S. Achievement Acad., 1991, Judson Bemis Visionary award United Negro Coll. Fund, 1995. Mem. NAACP, Nat. Wildlife Fedn., Library of Congress Assocs., Minority Employee Assn. (sec. 1995-96), Smithsonian Assocs. Avocations: reading, working out, gardening [illegible] planning. Home: 1304 Foxcroft Dr Aurora IL 60506-1267

DILLMAN, KARIN CHRISTINE, elementary school educator; b. Dayton, Ohio, Mar. 21, 1948; d. Henry Francis and Evelyn Christine Henderickson; m. Daniel Lee Orr, Sept. 26, 1970 (div. Feb. 28, 1984); children: Julia Noelle Orr, Ryan Nathan Orr; m. James Michael Dillman, Mar. 2, 1991. BS in Elem. Edn., Ohio No. U., Ada, 1970; MEd, U. Dayton, 1989. Tchr. Kettering (Ohio) City Schs., 1970—71, New Lebanon (Ohio) Local Schs., 1971—. Pathwise trainer State of Ohio Dept. Edn., 1999—. Martha Holden Jennings scholar, 1997—98. Home: 7551 Turtleback Dr Dayton OH 45414 Office: New Lebanon Elem 1150 W Main St New Lebanon OH 45345

DILLMAN, KRISTIN WICKER, elementary and middle school educator, musician; b. Ft. Dodge, Iowa, Nov. 7, 1953; d. Winford Lee and Helen Caroline (Brown) Egli; m. Kirk Michael Wicker, Jan. 1, 1982 (dec. June 1982); m. David D. Dillman, Apr. 13, 1990; adopted children: Alek Joseph, Andrew Mikhail. AA, Iowa Cen. Coll., 1974; B in Music Edn., Morningside Coll., 1976; M in Mus., U. S.D., 1983. Cert. tchr., Iowa. Tchr. instrumental music Garrigan Affiliated Schs., Algona, Iowa, 1976-77, Sioux City (Iowa) Community Schs., 1977—. Sr. beauty cons. Mary Kay Cosmetics. Asst. prin. bassist Sioux City Symphony, 1974-93, 95—, prin. bassist, 1993-95; freelance bassist Sioux City, 1976—; pianist and accompanist, St. Mark Luth. ch., Sioux City. Named Tchr. of Yr. Sioux City Community Schs., 1988-89. Mem. NEA, Iowa Edn. Assn., Sioux city Edn. Assn., Iowa Bandmasters Assn., Sioux City Musicians Assn., Zeta Sigma, Mu Phi Epsilon. Republican. Lutheran. Avocations: golf, walking, gardening, skiing. Office: Bryant Elem Sch 821 30th St Sioux City IA 51104 E-mail: DunesDave@aol.com.

DILLMAN, LINDA, retail executive; Student, U. Indpls. With Hewlett-Packard, Wholesale Club (acquired by Wal-Mart Stores, Inc.), Indpls.; application devel. mgr. Wal-Mart Stores, Inc., 1991—97, dir. applications devel., 1997—98, v.p. applications devel., 1998—99, v.p. internat. sys., 1999—2002, sr. v.p., CIO info. sys. divsn., 2002—03, exec. v.p., CIO, 2003—. Bd. dirs. Northwest Ark. Community Coll. Mem.: Uniform Code Council (bd. mem.). Office: Wal-Mart Stores Inc 702 SW Eighth St Bentonville AR 72716*

DILLON, DORIS (DORIS DILLON KENOFER), artist, art historian, educator; b. Kansas City, Mo., Dec. 1, 1929; d. Joseph Patrick and Geraldine Elizabeth (Galligan) D.; m. Calvin Louis Kenofer, Aug. 25, 1950; children: Wendy Annette Kenofer Barnes, Bruce Patrick Kenofer. BA in Art, U. Denver, 1950, MA in Art History, 1965. Stewardess United Air Lines, 1950-51; founder, chmn. fine arts dept. Regis Coll., Denver, 1970-74; cons. Sarkisian's Oriental Imports, Denver, 1975-93; mus. curator Van Vechten-Lineberry Taos Art, Taos, N.Mex., 1995. Coord. Inter-Relationship Between the Fine Arts and Science Seminars, 1970-74, Colo. Coun. on Arts & Humanities, Denver, 1980, adv. panel, 1981; consular rep. United Cultural Conv; dep dir. gen. Internat. Biog. Ctr., Eng., 1997; rsch. bd. advisors Am. Biog. Inst., 1997; lectr. in field. One-woman shows include El Pueblo Art Gallery/Mus., Pueblo, Colo., 1970, Heard Mus., Dallas, 1984, Nelson Rockefeller Collection, N.Y.C., 1984, Amparo Gallery, Denver, 1985, Veerhoff Gallery, Washington, 1986, Colo. Gallery the Arts Mus., Littleton, 1987, Highland Gallery, Atlanta, 1988, The Earth Sci. Mus., Asheville, N.C., 2003, two-person shows, E Margo Gallery, N.Y.C., 2003, exhibited in group shows at U. Denver, 1970, Denver Art Mus., 1970, Denver Mus. Natural History, 1976, U. Colo., 1986, Denver C. of C., 1987, Cadme Gallery, Phila., 1987, Internat. Platform Assn., Washington, 1998—2001, Internat. Exhbn. Gallery, Lisbon, 2000, exhibitions include St. Johns Coll., Cambridge, Eng., 2001, Vancouver, Can., 2002, 30th Internat. Congress on Sci., Culture and Arts in the 21st Century, Dublin, Ireland. Recipient 1st place drawing award, 4 States Conf. Ctr., Colo., 1960, Salute to Women award, AAUW, 1997, Key award, Excellence Arts, Rsch., Tchg., 1997, Best of Show award, Internat. Platform Assn., Washington, 2001, 2002, Internat. Visual Artist of the Yr., 2004. Mem.: Denver Art Mus., Asian Art assn. (bd. dirs. 1982—84, treas. 1985), Fine Arts Guild (v.p. 1982), Soc. for Arts, Religion and Contemporary Culture, Nat. Mus. for Women in the Arts (assoc.), Mensa (scholarship juror 1993—94). Avocations: piano, travel, bridge, swimming, hiking. Home and Office: 135 Delphia Dr Brevard NC 28712

DILLON, JEAN KATHERINE, executive secretary, small business owner; b. Birmingham, Ala., May 18, 1925; d. Andrew Crawford and Nell (Cook) Dillon; m. Roy Lerone Morris, June 12, 1946 (div. May 1969); children: Norma Jean, Elizabeth Annell. BA in Bus. and Edn., Huntingdon Coll., 1950. Cert. tchr. secondary edn., Ala. Sec./bookkeeper H.T. Fitzpatrick CPA, Atty., Montgomery, Ala., 1948-50; sec., budget technician Dir. Budget, HQ Air Univ., Maxwell AFB, Ala., 1950-58; exec. sec., adminstrv. asst. Comptroller, HQ Air Univ., Maxwell AFB, Ala., 1958-86; adminstrv. asst. Family Violence Program, State Coalition, Montgomery, 1986; owner/operator The William Cook House, Nauvoo, Ala., 1989—. Pres. Nauvoo Hist. Soc., Inc., 1989—98, bd. dirs., 1998—2001; mem., patron Birmingham Hist. Soc., 1991—; mem. Nat. Hist. Preservation Forum, 1995—; mem.-at-large, bd. dirs. Jasper Scottish Heritage Soc., 1999—2001; sec., bd. dirs. Ofcl. State of Ala. Highland Games, Montgomery, 1992—2001; treas. Capital City Rep. Women, 1995—96, v.p., 1997—98, chmn. budget and fin. com., 1997—2003, mem. budget and fin. com., 2003—, Montgomery County Ala. Rep. Exec. Com., 2003—, active, 1998—; bd. dirs. St. Andrew's Soc., Montgomery, 1995—, Walker County Arts Coun., 1996—, Montgomery Landmarks Found., Nat. Trust for Hist. Preservation, Nat. Parks Svc. Mem. Huntingdon Coll. Alumni Assn. (life), Walker County C. of C. (sec.-treas., vice chair tourism task force 1990-98). Methodist. Avocations: travel, geneology, historical research, writing, heritage. Home and Office: 929 Parkwood Dr Montgomery AL 36109-1228

DILLON, JOAN KENT, civic worker, volunteer consultant; b. Lafayette, Ind., Apr. 30, 1925; d. Richard and Gladys (Schroeder) Kent; m. George Chaffee Dillon, Sept. 11, 1948; children: Kent Chaffee, Courtney Pedersen, Emily Lorillard Berry. BA, Smith Coll., 1947; MA, U. Mo., 1969. Chmn. sales & rental gallery Nelson Art Gallery, Kansas City, Mo., 1956-63; tchr. history Sunset Hill Sch., Kansas City, 1958-69; chmn. Performing Arts Found., 1974-84; pres. Folly Theater Restoration, Kansas City, 1974-85, Kansas City Arts Coun., 1980-82. Active Mo. Adv. Coun. for Hist. Preservation, 1978-81; trustee Nat. Trust for Hist. Preservation, 1978-87; bd. trustees Smith Coll. 1994-99, Smithsonian Nat. Bd. 1993—; bd. dirs. League Historic Am. Theaters, 1975-98, Centerre Bank of Kansas City, 1984-87; active Kansas City Mcpl. Art Commn., 1970-80, Nat. Assn. Schs. of Dance and Theater Accreditation Commn., 1979-81; bd. dirs. Pres.'s Com. Arts and Humanities, 1982-88, Archives of Am. Art, 1983-87, Kansas City Cmty. Found., 1984-87, Ptnrs. for Liveable Places, 1987-95, Acting Co., 1987-91; bd. commrs. Smithsonian Nat. Portrait Gallery. Mem. Ctr. Exch., Kansas City Country Club, Eastward Ho Club, Women's Club. Episcopalian. Avocations: tennis, sailing, reading, travel.

DILLON, PATRICIA ANNE, state legislator; b. Flushing, N.Y., July 9, 1948; d. Raymond Walter and Patricia Marie (Kuhlmann) D.; m. John Schley Hughes, July 5, 1977; 1 child, Patrick John. BA, Marymount U., 1970; MA, Ohio State U., 1974; MPH, Yale U., 1998. Researcher Yale Sch. Medicine, New Haven, 1974-77; dir., founder New Haven Project Battered Women, 1977-80; devel. adminstr. City of Norwalk (Conn.), 1980-82; state legislator State of Conn., Hartford, 1984—, chmn. pub. health com., 1990—, chmn. appropriations subcom. health and hosps., 1992—, dep. majority leader, 1992—. Contbr. articles on family violence, health, taxation, solid waste, AIDS and Irish issues to various publs.; author: (with others) Blood Feuds, 1990. Word [illegible] New Haven, 1976-86; alderwoman New Haven Bd. Alderman, 1979-85; mem. Health Policy Faculty Rutgers U., 2000—. Roman Catholic. Avocations: bibliophile, gardening. Home: 68 W Rock Ave New Haven CT 06515-2221 Office: Lt Gen Assembly Legion Office Bldg Capitol Ave Hartford CT 06106

DILLON, TERRI L. consulting firm executive; b. Winston-Salem, N.C., Sept. 12, 1962; d. Dallas Eugene and Opal Wall Shields; m. Victor Ray Dillon, Apr. 18, 1992; children: Mary Abigail, Leslie Gray, Summer Rae, Dalton Levi. Student, High Point U., 1984-88, Vanderbilt U., 1998, U. N.C., Greensboro, 1999. Proof operator, teller, customer svc. and consumer loan rep. Northwestern Bank (First Union Nat. Bank), Winston-Salem, N.C., 1979-86; adminstrv. asst., grant writer, sr. project mgr. Whitney jones, Inc., Winston-Salem, 1986-97, v.p. fin. and adminstrn., 1997-2001; v.p. adminstrn. Management Recruiters of Greensboro, 2001—. Mem. steering com., chair spkrs. bur. Leave A Legacy of the Triad, Winston-Salem, 1998-99; com. mem. Colfax (N.C.) Inc. Com., 1999; grad. Winston Class of Leadership, Winston-Salem, 2001. Mem. Nat. Ctr. for Non-Profit Bds., Nat. Soc. Fund Raising Execs. (cert., chair 1999 fund-raising day conf. 1999, charter N.C.-Triad chpt., treas. and 1st v.p. 1996-99, pres. 1999-2001), New Garden Moose Lodge, Jr. Achievement N.W. N.C., Inc. (bd. dirs. 1999-2000), Rotary Club of Winston-Salem (sec. 2001). Republican. Methodist. Office: Management Recruiters Greensboro 324 W Wendover Ave Ste 230 Greensboro NC 27408

DILLON, TONI ANN, emotional support educator; b. Point Pleasant, N.J., Jan. 7, 1962; d. Thomas Joseph and Anita Marie Dillon. BA in Edn., Mercyhurst Coll., 1983; M, 1991. Cert. elem. educator Pa., tchr. mentally and/or physically handicapped Pa. Emotional support tchr. Sch. Dist. of the City of Erie, Pa., 1983—. Contbr. articles to profl. jours.; author: (1 page in storybook) GoFish! The Official Tale, 2001. Walktahon participant Crop-Walk, Erie, 1990—92, Am. Cancer Society, Erie, 2001—03, Presque Isle State Pk., Erie, 2002—03, March of Dimes, Erie, 1997; leader Penn Lakes Girl Scout Coun., Erie, 1979—. Nominee Disney's Am. Tchr. award, 2000; named Tchr. of Yr., Burton Elem. Sch., 1989, Lincoln Elem. Sch., 1992; recipient St. Elizabeth Ann Seton award, Penn Lakes Girl Scouts, 1990, Outstanding Leader award, 1991, Class Rm. award, Erie Met. Transit Authority, 1997—98, Arts in Edn. award, Lincoln Elem. Parent Tchr. Assn., 1998—99, Bread Box award, Second Harvest Food Bank, 2000. Avocations: photography, gardening, collecting N.Y. Yankee baseball cards, arts and crafts. Personal E-mail: teacherinpink@aol.com. E-mail: tdillon@eriesd.iu5.og.

DILLON-RIDGLEY, DIANNE GRANVILLE, mediator, consultant, association executive; b. Dallas, Tex. d. Harold Bishop and Evelyn (Hardin) Dillon; children: Karima Afia, Dasal Hardin. BA in Philosophy, Howard U., 1972; student, Iowa Mediation Svc., 1986, 90, 91. Cert. farmer/creditor and family matrimonial mediator. Mediator The Iowa Mediation Svc., 1986—, edn. mktg. specialist, 1991; workshop instr. Kettering Family Found., Dayton, Ohio, 1988—, cons., 1991-94; with office of student affairs U. Iowa, 1991-94; pres., dir. Zero Population Growth, Washington, 1994-2000; ret., 2000. Chmn., Human Rights Commn., Burlington, Iowa, 1986-90; mem. Iowa Humanities bd. state divsn. of NEH, 1984-90, v.p. prog. com., exec. com., chmn. mem. com.; com. profl. ethics Iowa Supreme Court, Iowa Bar Assn.; U.S. del. to UNCED, 1991, N.Y.C., adv. and mem. U.S. del. to the UN conf. on environ. and devel., Rio de Janeiro, 1992; bd. dirs. Child & Family Policy Ctr., Iowa divsn., 1989—; chair target small bus. bd. Iowa Dept. Econ. Devel., 1987—; vice chmn. bd. dirs. Nat. Summit on Africa, Washington, 1997—; mem. coun. sustainable devel. U.S. Pres.'s Coun., Washington, 1994—; sr. policy analyst WEDO, N.Y.C., 1993—; bd. dirs. Interfac Inc., Atlanta, 1997—; adj. lectr. U. Ind. Sch. Pub. and Environ. Affairs, 1997—; interim dir. WEDG, N.Y.C. Mem. nat. bd. dirs. YWCA of the U.S.A., N.Y.C., 1988—, pub. policy com., 1988-91, co-chair racial justice com., 1991—, rep. to UN conf. on environ. and devel. for YWCA of U.S.A., bd. dirs. YWCA Burlington, 1981-87, chair adult com., fin. com. chair bldg. corp. bd.; friends devel. coun. U. Iowa Mus. of Art, Burlington Fine Arts League, scholarship com. 1986-89, bd. dirs. Mus. African Am. Hist., Boston, 1976-89; bd. dirs. Burlington Civic Mus. Assn., v.p. 1985-91; bd. dirs. U. Iowa libs., 1991—, mem. human needs commn. Episcopal Diocese of Iowa; vestry bd. Christ Episcopal Ch., Burlington; bd. dirs., selection com., Martin Luther King Scholarship of Iowa, 1987—; co-chair racial justice YWCA, N.Y.C., 1994—; mem. internat. steering com. Global Water Partnership, Stockholm, 1998—. Recipient of Outstanding Woman of the Year in Politics award, 1985. Mem. Assn. Iowa Human Rights Agys. (lobbyist 1990, pres. 1986-90). Office: Zero Population Growth 1400 16th St NW Ste 320 Washington DC 20036-2290

DIMANT, ROSE JEAROLMEN, personnel testing specialist, psychometrician; b. N.Y.C. d. Bernard L. and Lillian (Herskowitz) Jearolmen; m. Jacob Dimant, Sept. 11, 1974; children: Kevin, Elliot. BA in Psychology magna cum laude, Bklyn. Coll., 1971; MA in Psychology, New Sch. for Social Rsch., N.Y.C., 1974; PhD in Psychology, CUNY, 1985. Rsch. assoc. CUNY Grad. Ctr. for Gerontological Studies, N.Y.C., 1978-80; from adj. lectr. to asst. prof. Kingsboro C.C., Bklyn., 1983-86; tests and measurement specialist N.Y.C. Dept. Personnel, 1985-88, adminstrv. tests and measurement specialist, 1988—. Cons. The Rheumatology Ctr., Bklyn., 1980-83, Keenan Rsch. & Consulting, N.Y.C., 1984-85; bd. dirs. Crown Nursing Home Assocs., Inc., Bklyn., 1991—. Office: Dept Citywide Adminstrv Svcs Divsn Citywide Pers Svcs 1 Centre Street 14th Fl North New York NY 10007

DI MARCO, BARBARANNE YANUS, principal; b. Jersey City, Nov. 16, 1946; d. Stanley Joseph and Anne Barbara (Dalack) Yanus; m. Charles Benjamin DiMarco, Mar. 15, 1986; 1 child, Charles Garrett. BA in Music Edn., Trenton State Coll., 1968; MA in Spl. Edn., Kean Coll., 1971, elem. edn. cert., 1974, adminstrv. cert., 1976. Cert. elem., music, adminstrn., spl. edn., N.J. Vocal music educator Roselle (N.J.) Bd. Edn., 1968-69, tchr. trainable mentally retarded, 1969-76, tchr. multiple handicapped, 1976—95, tchr. neurologically impaired, 1995—2003; prin. Grace Wilday Mid. Sch., Roselle, 2003—. Color guard instr. Roselle Bd. Edn., 1973—88, elem. tutor, 1976—92, adminstrv. asst. to supt., 1980—85; program dir., sec. Expanded Dimensions in Gifted Edn., Westfield, NJ, 1978—85. Vestryperson St. Luke's Ch., Roselle, 1989-91. Recipient Govs. Tchr. Recognition award, Gov. Florio, N.J., Trenton, 1992-93. Mem. NEA, N.J. Edn. Assn., Roselle Edn. Assn., N.J. Assn. for Retarded Children, Eastern Star (25-yr award 1991), Delta Omicron. Republican. Episcopalian. Avocations: skiing, flying, oil painting, travel, swimming, music, golf. Home: 13 Gentore Ct Edison NJ 08820-1029 Office: Grace Wilday Middle Sch 400 Brooklawn Ave Roselle NJ 07203 Office Phone: 908-298-3330., 908-298-2066.

DI MARIA, VALERIE THERESA, public relations executive; b. Bronx, N.Y., Apr. 5, 1957; d. Victor Joseph and Vivian Roslyn (D'Amico) Di Maria. BA in Journalism, NYU, 1978. Asst. dir. U.S. Div. Sidonie S. Ltd., N.Y.C., 1978—79; acct. supr. The Rowland Co., N.Y.C., 1979—82, Ketchum Pub. Rels., N.Y.C., 1982—83; pub. rels. dir. Charles of the Ritz Group Ltd., N.Y.C., 1983—84; sr. v.p. Porter/Novelli Pub. Rels., N.Y.C., 1984—89; mng. dir. GCI Group, N.Y.C., 1989—, now pres., 1996; v.p. pub. rels. & advt. GE Capital, Stamford, Conn. Mem.: Advt. Women of N.Y., Women in Comms., Women Execs. in Pub. Rels. (bd. dirs.), Am. Film Inst., Pub. Rels. Soc. Am. (Silver Anvil award 1986), Women's Sports Fund, The Fashion Group, Phi Beta Kappa. Office: GE Capital 260 Long Ridge Rd Stamford CT 06927-1600

DIMARTINO, SANDRA LOUISE, theater educator; b. Newton, Mass., July 9, 1958; d. Joseph Anthony and Audrey Constance DiMartino. BA in Theatre, Music Education, Regis Coll., 1980; MA in Theatre, Northwestern U., 1982. Tchr. drama Waltham High Sch., Mass., 1982—85; devel. officer Alaska Rep., Anchorage, 1985—86, Hartman Theatre, Stamford, Conn., 1986—87; mktg. staff Lyric Stage, Boston, 1987—89; tchr. drama Lexington High Sch., 1987—. Adj. prof. Emerson Coll., Boston, 1997—; dir. Lexington High Sch., 1987—. Dir.(over 30): (plays), 1974—;, performer (over 30) plays. Mem.: Theatre Cmty. Group, Am. Assn. Theatre Educators. Achievements include invititation to perform with students at Edinburgh Fringe Festival, 2004. Avocations: jewelry designing, scuba diving, singing, acting.

DIMASI, LINDA GRACE, epidemiologist; b. Trenton, N.J., Feb. 7, 1949; d. Nick and Pearl LaVerne (White) D. BS in Biology, Alderson-Broaddus Coll., 1970; MPA, Rutgers U., 1992. Cert. pub. mgr. Field rep. N.J. State Dept. of Health, Trenton, 1971-85, epidemiologist, 1985—. Contbr. articles to profl. jours. Mem. ASPA, APHA, Phi Alpha Alpha. Avocations: flying, auto racing, traveling. Home: 35 Jennifer Ln Burlington NJ 08016-1144 Office: NJ State Dept Health Divsn AIDS Prevention and Control PO Box 363 Trenton NJ 08625-0363

DIMENGO, JOSEPHINE, medical/surgical nurse; b. Cleve., Jan. 9, 1954; d. Joseph and Mary (Rihtar) Staric; m. Mark Dimengo, May 25, 1979; children: Cristina, Nicholas, Alexa. Diploma, St. Vincent Charity Hosp., Cleve., 1975; MSN, Frances Payne Bolton Sch., Cleve., 1990. Clinical dir. heart failure Am. Heathways, 2002—. Recipient Helen Lathrope Bunge award. Mem. AACN, Heart Failure Soc. Am., Am. Heart Assn., Sigma Theta Tau. Home: 2828 Old Hickory Blvd Apt 1904 Nashville TN 37221-3727

DIMENTO, CAROL A.G. lawyer; b. Salem, Mass., Dec. 5, 1942; B in Edn., Salem State Coll., 1965, M in Edn., 1967; JD, Suffolk U., 1977. Bar: Mass. 1977. Tchr. Town of Hamilton, 1965—67, Town of Marblehead, 1967—74; ptnr. DiMento & DiMento, Swampscott, Mass., 1977—. Mem.: ABA (house of delegates 1995—), Essex County Bar Assn. (pres. 1992—94), Mass. Bar Assn. (sec. 1996—97, v.p. 1997—98, treas 1998—99, 1st v.p. 1999—2000, pres.-elect 2000—01, pres. 2001—02).

DIMINO, SYLVIA THERESA, elementary and secondary educator; b. N.Y.C., June 6, 1955; d. John Anthony and Elena (Berardesca) D. BA, St. John's U., 1977; MPA, NYU, 1980, MA in Elem. and Secondary Edn., 1982, cert. advance studies in ednl. adminstrn., 1986, cert. in advanced studies in mgmt., 1992; MA in Tchg. ESL, Adelphi U., 1984; MA in Libr. Sci., Pratt Inst., 1998; chef, Nat. Gourmet Cooking Sch., 1999. Cert. elem. and secondary tchr., sch. adminstr., in mgmt. practices, social studies, math., N.Y. Traffic coord. Creamer Inc., N.Y.C., 1977-79; tchr. St. Patrick's Sch., N.Y.C., 1979-82, IS 131, Manhattan, N.Y.C., 1984-90, adminstr., coord., 1985-90, asst. prin., 1990-99; tchr. high sch. ESL, N.Y.C. Bd. Edn., 1995-99, libr. sci. tchr., 1999—; chef Natural Gourmet Cookery Sch., 1999—; City Harvest chef for children's programs, 2000—; tchr. Hatha Yoga for Kids, 2000—; integrative nutrition holistic counselor, 2004. Prana yoga tchr., 1998; Thai yoga body massage therapist, 1998. Named to 2000 Most Notable Women. Mem. NAFE, AAUW, Nat. Orgn. Women in Adminstrn., Bus. Cir. N.Y., Nat. Coun. Adminstrv. Women in Edn., Nat. Orgn. Italian-Am. Women (mentoring dir.), Yoga Tchrs. Assn. Roman Catholic. Avocations: walking, hiking, yoga. Address: FH LaGuardia HS Music Arts Performing Arts 100 Amsterdam Ave New York NY 10023-6406 Office Phone: 212-496-0700 608.

DIMITRIOU, DOLORES ENNIS, computer consultant; b. Phila., Apr. 7, 1932; d. Charles Adair and Rubye Stanton (Greene) Ennis; m. John Alexander Dimitriou, Sept. 25, 1954 (div. Aug. 1983); 1 child, Sandra Irene Dimitriou Falor. BS in Math., U. Miami, 1954; MA in Linguistics, U. Tex., 1994. Jet engine supr. GE, Evendale, Ohio, 1954-58; rsch. aide Marine Lab. U. Miami, Coral Gables, 1959-65; supr. tests Weathering Rsch. Svc., Princeton, Fla., 1959-87; income tax preparer H&R Block, Homestead, Fla., 1981-83; small bus. cons., pres., co-founder Facts & Figures Svcs., Homestead, 1983-87; computer cons., trainer Wycliffe Bible Translators, Orlando, Fla., 1987-97. Sec., treas., co-founder Weather Rsch. Svcs., Perrine, Fla., 1959-95; treas. GILLBT, Ghana, 1994-96. Bd. dirs. Ch. Women United, 1999—2003; state coun. dist. chair ombudsman, 2004—; tax aide Am. Assn. Ret. Persons, 1998—; mem. state coun., 2000—01, 2003—; dist. chair, 2000—01, 2003—; mem. ch. rels. Wycliffe Bible Translators, 1998—2003. Named Outstanding Woman in Religion YWCA, U. Miami, 1953-54. Mem.: Cutler Ridge Woman's Club, Mortar Board, Phi Mu Epsilon. Democrat. Avocations: computers, travel, reading, crafts. Home and Office: 10381 SW 209 Ln Miami FL 33189-3612 Personal E-mail: dolores-dimitriou@att.net.

DIMM, SUSAN TYNER, art educator, artist; b. Orange, N.J., Nov 7, 1960; d. Wayne Foreman and Margaret Mitchell (Browne) D. AA, Simon's Rock Coll., 1980; student, Alfred U., 1982; BA, Bennington Coll., 1984. Student tchr. Early Learning Ctr., Stamford, Conn., 1981; asst. tchr. Cambridge Sch. Weston, Mass., 1993; tchr. Eng. Art Edn. Biennial Conf., Hyannis, Mass., 1993, Creative Arts Ctr., Chatham, Mass., 1992—, Truro (Mass.) Adult Edn., 1995—96, Truro Elem. Sch., 1995—96, Monomoy Youth Svcs., Chatham, 1996; with Barn Hill Pottery, West Chatham, Mass., 1996—. Pres. Cape Cod Potters, Chatham, 1995-96, sec., 1996-97, v.p., 1994-95; bd. dirs. Creative Arts Ctr., Chatham. Mem. Nat. Coun. Edn. Ceramic Arts, Am. Craft Coun., Falmouth Artists Guild, Truro Ctr. Arts. Home: 46 Barn Hill Rd West Chatham MA 02669 Office: Barn Hill Pottery 46 Barnhill Rd West Chatham MA 02669-0238

DIMMICK, CAROLYN REABER, federal judge; b. Seattle, Oct. 24, 1929; d. Maurice C. and Margaret T. (Taylor) Reaber; m. Cyrus Allen Dimmick, Sept. 10, 1955; children: Taylor, Dana. BA, U. Wash., 1951, JD, 1953; LLD, Gonzaga U., 1982, CUNY, 1987. Bar: Wash. 1953. Asst. atty. gen. State of Wash., Seattle, 1953-55; pros. atty. King County, Wash., 1955-59, 60-62; sole practice Seattle, 1959-60, 62-65; judge N.E. Dist. Ct. Wash., 1965-75, King County Superior Ct., 1976-80; justice Wash. Supreme Ct., 1981-85; judge U.S. Dist. Ct. (we. dist.) Wash., Seattle, 1985-94, chief judge, 1994-97, sr. judge, 1997—. Chmn. Jud. Resources Com., 1991-94, active, 1987-94. Recipient Matrix Table award, 1981, World Plan Execs. Council award, 1981, Vanguard Honor award King County of Washington Women Lawyers, 1996, Disting. Alumni award U. Wash. Law Sch., 1997, Outstanding Jurist award King County Bar Assn., 2003; named Wash. Women of Yr. Seattle U. Women's Law Caucus, 2004. Mem. ABA, Am. Judges Assn. (gov.), Nat. Assn. Women Judges, World Assn. Judges, Wash. Bar Assn., Am. Judicature Soc., Order of Coif (Wash. chpt.). Office: US Dist Ct 407 US Courthouse 1010 5th Ave Seattle WA 98104-1189 Office Phone: 206-553-2469. E-mail: carolyn_dimmick@wawd.uscourts.gov.

DIMOND, ROBERTA RALSTON, psychology and sociology educator; b. Bakersfield, Calif., Mar. 25, 1940; d. Robert Leroy Vickers and Gail Anderson (Tritch) Ralston; m. James Davis, June 18, 1963 (div. 1970); 1 child, Jamie Amundsen Davis; m. Frederick Henry Dimond, Oct. 20, 1970; children: Frederick Ralston, Robert Vickers (div. 1991). BA in History and English, Stanford U., 1962, MAT in Edn., 1963; MS, U. Pa., 1970, EdD, 1973. Cert. secondary educator, ednl. specialist, counselor, coll. personnel adminstr. Thcr. Kamehameha Sch., Honolulu, 1965-67; asst. to dean of women U. Pa., Phila., 1969-70; asst. prof. Temple U., Ambler, Pa., 1970-87, Montgomery County Coll., Blue Bell, Pa., 1975-80; prof. psychology, speech, sociology Delaware Valley Coll., Doylestown, Pa., 1987—, assoc. prof. liberal arts. Cons. ETS, Princeton, N.J., 1989—; speaker in field; lectr. on sexual responsibilities in the 90s and assertive affirmative action topics; researcher on athletics and aging females syngerism. Author: Gender & RAcial Bias by Vocational Counselors, 1973. Bd. dirs. Concerned Citizens of Upper Dublin, Maple Glen, Pa., 1980-91, Arrowhead Assn., Ambler, Pa., 1990-91. Fellow Newhouse Found., 1960-63; grantee APA, 1969-70. Mem.: MADD, AAUP, APA, Phila. Tennis Assn. (pres.), Stanford Alumni Assn., Phila. Tennis Patrons, U.S. Tennis Assn., Middle States Tennis Assn. (life). Episcopalian. Avocations: tennis (ranked #6 in U.S. in women's 50 and over tennis, # 1 in over 45, # 1 MSTA over 60., duplicate bridge. Home: 236 Amherst Dr Doylestown PA 18901-2381 Office: Delaware Valley Coll Rte 202 Doylestown PA 18901

DIMOPOULOS, LINDA J. food service executive; b. 1951; With Darden Restaurants, Inc., 1982, sr. v.p. fin. ops. Red Lobster, 1993—98, sr. v.p., corp. controller, bus info. sys., 1998—99, sr. v.p., chief info. officer, 1999—2002, chief fin. officer, 2002—. Office: Darden Restaurants Inc 4800 Lake Ellenor Dr Orlando FL 32809

DI MUCCIO, MARY-JO, retired librarian; b. Hanford, Calif., June 16, 1930; d. Vincent and Theresa (Yovino) DiMuccio. BA, Immaculate Heart Coll., 1953, MA, 1960; PhD, U.S. Internat. U., 1970. Tchr. parochial schs., Los Angeles, 1949-54, San Francisco, 1954-58; tchr. Govt. of Can., Victoria, 1958—60; asst. libr. Immaculate Heart Coll. Libr., Los Angeles, 1960-62, head libr., 1962—72; adminstrv. libr. City of Sunnyvale, Calif., 1972-88; ret., 1988. Instr. Foothill C.C., Los Altos, 1977—95. Exec. bd., past pres. Sunnyvale Community Services. Mem. ICF (past pres.), Cath. Libr. Assn. (past pres.), Sunnyvale Bus. and Profl. Women, Peninsula Dist. Bus. and Profl. Women (past pres.). Home: 736 Muir Dr Mountain View CA 94041-2509 E-mail: JO736@aol.com.

DIN, HERMINIA, art educator, museum staff member, researcher; b. Taipei, Taiwan, Feb. 14, 1968; d. Jose Ta-San and Monica Din. PhD, Ohio State U., 1998. Web prodr. The Children's Mus. of Indpls., 2000—03; asst. prof. art U. Alaska, Anchorage, 2003—. Asst. prof. of mus. studies Ind. U., Indpls., 2000—, Purdue U., Indpls., 2000—; fed. grant reviewer IMLS; children's and family web site developer. Prodr.: (exhibition) Bones: An Exhibit Inside You; web site, Biotechnology Learning Ctr., Bones: An Exhibit Inside You. Scholar, The Met. Mus. of Art. Mem.: Am. Assn. of Museums (MUSE award chair), Phi Kappa Phi (Grad. Enrichment award 1996). Office: U of Alaska Anchorage Dept of Art 3211 Providence Drive Anchorage AK 99508

DINA, GWENDOLYN JUDITH, special education educator; b. Evergreen Park, Ill., Feb. 28, 1943; d. Harold Karl and Constance Pauline Doering; m. Michael George Dina, Feb. 29, 1984; 1 child, Daniel Joseph Mathews. BS in Edn., Ea. Ill. U., 1964; MS in Edn., No. Ill. U., 1980. Lic. tchr. of blind and partially sighted State Bd. of Edn., Ill., cert. std. secondary tchr. State Bd. of Edn., Ill., std. elem. tchr. State Bd. of Edn., Ill. Phys. edn. and spl. edn. tchr. Dubuque (Iowa) Sr. H.S., 1967—80; dir. habilitative svcs. Holy Angels Resdl. Facility for Mentally Retarded, Shreveport, La., 1985—92; tchr. of visually impaired Mid-Ctrl. Assn., Peoria, Ill., 1992—96, Spl. Edn. Assn. of Peoria County, Bartonville, Ill., 1996—; early intervention devel. therapist Child and Family Connections, Springfield, Ill., 1998—2002. Author: Mathew's Story: The Early Years of a Child with Asperger's Syndrome, Vision and Hearing Problems, 2001, The Magical Letter L, 2001; editor: Frugal Me: How Teachers Save Their Students and Other Memories, 2002. Named Educator of Yr., Peoria Assn. Retarded Citizens, 1994; grantee, State of Iowa, 1978, 1979. Mem.: Coun. Exceptional Children, Delta Kappa Gamma (state corr. sec. 2001—03, tchg. scholar 1978, 1979, 1980). Avocations: storytelling, writing, swimming, sewing, knitting. Office: Spl Edn Assn Peoria 6000 S Adams Bartonville IL 61607 Personal E-mail: mgdina@famvid.com. E-mail: gdina@scapco.org.

DINCECCO, JENNIE ELIZABETH WILLIAMS SWANSON, healthcare administrator, mentor, healthcare educator, volunteer; b. Atlanta, Aug. 5, 1932; d. Chester Arthur and Cleo Annie Williams; m. Richard Edward Swanson, Apr. 24, 1954 (div. 1994); children: Laurel Dee Swanson, Jeffrey Richard Swanson, Scott Edward Swanson; m. Thomas M. Dincecco, Aug. 26, 2000. BS, Northwestern U., 1954; MS, No. Ill. U., 1972, EdD, 1976. Pub. sch. tchr., 1954-69; psycho-ednl. diagnostician, 1969-72; faculty Loyola U., Chgo., 1976-82, asst. prof. ob-gyn and pediat., 1979-82; dir. pre-start project depts. ob-gyn and pediat. Stritch Sch. Medicine, 1978-82; dir. spl. svcs. Cmty. Unit Sch. Dist. 220, 1982-92. Hospice bereavement vol., 1997—; coun. mem., mentor Cong. Unitarian Ch.; antique dealer; mem. Gov. Ill. Com. Preventive Svcs., 1979-80; chair B-3 subcom. First Chance Consortium, 1978-80; chair INTER-ACT, 1979-80; cons. in field. Author: (with others) Partners in Child Development, 1978. Grantee HEW, 1973-76, 78-82. Mem.: Ret. Tchrs. McHenry County, Nat. Assn. Edn. Young Child, Nat. Acad. Neuropsychology, Nat. Perinatal Assn., Assn. Maternal and Child Health, Coun. Exceptional Children, Golden Cir., Woodstock Opera House Commn. (chairperson, chmn.), Northwestern U. Alumni Assn., Nu Alumni Club, Delta Kappa Gamma (scholar 1974), Delta Delta Delta. Unitarian Universalist.

DINERMAN, MIRIAM, social work educator; b. N.Y.C., Apr. 13, 1925; d. Abraham J. and Frances (Shostac) Goldforb; m. Harold Dinerman, June 12, 1951 (dec. June 1976); children: David, Ellen, Ruth. BA with honors, Swarthmore Coll., 1945; MSW, Columbia U., 1949, D of Social Work, 1972. Youth dir. Jewish Assn. for Neighborhood Ctrs., N.Y.C., 1949-50, program dir., 1951-54; various social work part time positions, 1955-60; asst. prof. Rutgers U. Grad. Sch. Social Work, New Brunswick, NJ, 1961-72, assoc. prof., 1972-76, prof., 1976-99, asst. dean for acad. planning, 1973-75, assoc. dean, 1975-81, acting dean, 1978, chmn. health care sequence, mem. New Brunswick faculty coun., 1989-93, chair, 1991-92; dir. PhD program Rutgers U. Sch. Social Work, 1992-97, emerita, 1999—. Mem. grants rev. panel Office Human Devel. Svcs., HHS, 1986—90; cons. on health and social svcs. N.J. Legis. Task Force on 21st Century; mem. task force on std. of need N.J. Divsn. Econ. Assistance, 1989—91; manuscript rev. editor Longman's Press, Methuen Press; dir. Ctr. for Internat. and Comparative Social Work, 1977—99; adj. prof. Yeshiva U. Sch. Social Work, 1999—. Editor: Social Work Futures, 1983; mem. editl. bd. Affilia: Jour. Women and Social Work, 1985-94, 95—, book rev. editor, 1995-00, editor-in-chief, 2000—; contbr. articles to profl. jours., chpts. to books. Bd. dirs. Def. for Children Internat., 1980—88. Grantee NIMH, 1966-67, Rutgers U. Rsch. Coun. and Samuel Silberman Fund, 1979-80. Mem.: AAUP (N.J. task force on health care policy), NASW (chpt. pres. 1984—86, nat. com. on nominations and leadership identification 1988—97, editl. com. 1991—95, steering com. polit. action for candidate election 1996—2001, bd. dirs. N.Y.C. chpt. 1999—2001, sec. bd. dirs. 2003—, bd. dirs. N.Y.C. chpt. 2003—), Group for Advancement of Doctoral Edn. (sec. steering com. 1990—96), Coun. on Social Work Edn. (program planning com. 1984—89, ednl. policy and planning commn. 1989—94), Internat. Assn. Schs. Social Work (agt. 1988—95, bd. dirs.), Acad. Cert. Social Workers. Home: 353 W 29th St New York NY 10001-4784 Office Phone: 212-960-5289. E-mail: dinerma@ymail.yu.edu.

DING, AI-YUE, conductor, music educator; b. Beijing, Dec. 17, 1942; arrived in U.S., 1990; d. Depan Ting and Susan Cheng; m. Chenghua Sun, Jan. 17, 1968; children: Tian, Sun. B in Conducting, Conservatory of Music, Shanghai, 1966; M in Sacred Music, So. Meth. U., 1993; postgrad., U. North Tex., 1993—96. Prin. condr. Hunan Symphony Orch., Chang Sha, China, 1967—83, Jiangsu Symphony Orch., Nanjing, China, 1983—90; finding condr. 100 Voice Choir of Ambassadors for Christ, Dallas, 1993—94, Chinese Youth Orch., Dallas, 1995—99, Great Land Choral Soc., Dallas, 1995—. Guest condr. Broadcast Symphony Orch., Shanghai, 1996, Symphony Orch of Shanghai Conservatory of Music, Shanghai, 1997; condr. North Tex. Philharm. Orch., Tex., 1997; guest condr. Voice of Change Inc., Dallas, 1998; condr. United Choir, Dallas, 2000, 1st Dallas Chinese Music Festival, 2004. Named one of Ten Top-Ranked Women Condrs., People's Music Jour., Beijing, 1980; recipient Grand Prize for Condr., 1st Music and Dance Festival, Jiangsu, China, 1987. Mem.: Chinese Musicians Assn., Tex. Music Tchrs. Assn., Music Tchrs. Nat. Assn. Avocations: sports, dance. E-mail: sunding@juno.com.

DINGER, ANN MONROE, association executive, interior designer; d. Hoke Jefferson and Florence Parsons Monroe; m. Donald Brackett Dinger, Aug. 13, 1960; 1 child, Lynn Ann Dinger Edmonds. BA in Edn. and Art, Mary Washington Coll. U. Va., Fredericksburg, 1958. Cert. tchr. Va. Art tchr. Alexandria (Va.) Pub. Schs., 1958—61; pvt. interior design cons. Alexandria, Charlottesville, Great Falls, Va., 1958—. Docent Robert E. Lee Boyhood Home, Alexandria, 1967—68; chair D.C. Embassy Tour Alexandria Jr. Women's Club, 1967—68; floral chmn. Pres. James Monroe Home, Charlottesville, Va., 1982—86; hospitality chmn. Newcomers Great Falls, 1987—88; dir., pres., adv. bd. mem. Clan Munro Assn., 1992—, mem. Scottish coun., 1992—. Fellowship com. chmn. Immanuel Presbyn. Ch., McLean, Va., 1994—98. Mem.: Great Falls Citizens' Assn. Republican. Avocations: antiques, gardening, travel. Home: 9100 Potomac Woods Ln Great Falls VA 22066

DINGFELDER, JACKIE, state representative; m. Tom Gainer. BA in Geography, UCLA; M in Regional Planning, U. NC. Mem. Oreg. Ho. of Reps., 2001—. Cons. environ. planning. Mem. Oreg. Hunger Relief Task Force; past watershed program mgr. For the Sake of the Salmon; past coord. Tualatin River Watershed Coun.; mem. bond task force Portland Pub. Schs.; mem. stormwater policy adv. com. City of Portland; mem. water resources policy adv. com. Metro; past bd. dirs. Interstate Firehouse Cultural Ctr., Oreg. Leagure Conservation Voters. Democrat. Avocations: hiking, bicycling, gardening, reading. Office: 900 Court St North East H-383 Salem OR 97301

DINGLE, PATRICIA A. education educator, artist; b. Washington, Apr. 19, 1954; d. Asbery and Loretha (Bryant) D. BA, Conn. Coll., 1976; MA in Tchg., RISD, 1977; PhD in Curriculum and Instrn., U. Md., 1996. Cert. art and dance tchr., Md.; ordained to ministry Bapt. Ch., 1998. Instr. dance RISD, Providence, 1976-77; visual artist, dancer R.I. Coun. on Arts, Providence, 1977-78; tchr. art Ctrl. H.S., East Providence, R.I., 1978-79, Friendly H.S., Prince Georges County, Md., 1979-82, Prince George's County Pub. Schs., Upper Marlboro, Md., 1987—; chair dept. fine arts High Point H.S., 2000—02; asst. prof. dept. edn. Clarion U. of Pa., 2002—. Dir. summer playground Md. Nt. Capital Park and Planning Commn., Prince Georges County, 1999; adj. prof. Western Md. Coll., Westminster, 1999; propr. Ding La Gift Studio, Bowie, Md., 1994—; presenter Md. Art Edn. Assn., Towson, 1997, 98, Nat. Coun. Tchrs. Math., Springfield and Phila., Success 2002 Conf., U. Md.; mem. discussion panel Conn. Coll., New London, 1998; vis. minority scholar/artist U. Wis., Eau Claire, 2000; lectr. Cath. U. Am., summer 2000; presenter in field. Exhibited in solo shows at Office of Cmty. Affairs, New London, Conn., 1973, Parkview Bapt. Ch., Landover, Md., 1975, First Bapt. Ch. in Am., Providence, 1978, others; group shows include Marlborough (Conn.) Arts Festival, 1974, Cummings Art Ctr., New London, 1976, Woods-Gerry Gallery, Providence, 1977, Marlboro Gallery/Prince George's C.C., 1981, Montpelier Mansion, Laurel, Md., 1998, Bowie Arts Expo, Allen Pond, 1999, Electronic Exhibit, N.Y., 2001, NAEA Women's Caucus Womens Artwork, N.Y., 2001, Art Celebrating Women, PA-SSHE Conf., 2002; works represented in permanent collections Carlson Libr. Clarion U.; dir. Young Designers Am. program Ashton-Drake Gallery, 2000. Facilitator youth study circle Prince Georges County Human Rels. Commn., Landover, 1998; mem. grants in comtys. adv. panel Md. State Arts Coun., 2000-01; active In Touch Ministries, 1998—; mem. mission trip Appalachian Outreach Ctr., Jefferson City, Tenn., 2003 Sgt. U.S. Army, 1983-87; assoc. min. Amazing Grace Bapt. Ch., 1998-2002; youth min. Village Bapt. Ch., 2002-2003. Recipient Anna Lord Strauss award for cmty. svc., 1976, awards for art; grad. fellow U. Md., 1989; Md. Tech. fellow, 2000; NEH summer seminar faculty profl. devel. project grantee, 2001, 03; faculty profl. devel. grantee, 2003. Mem.: Nat. Art Edn. Assn. (book reviewer 2002—03). Avocations: research, writing, piano playing, painting. Office: Clarion Univ Pa Dept of Education Clarion PA 16214 Office Phone: 814-393-1978.

DINKINS, CAROL EGGERT, lawyer; b. Corpus Christi, Tex., Nov. 9, 1945; d. Edgar H. Jr. and Evelyn S. (Scheel) Eggert; m. Bob Brown; children: Anne, Amy. BS, U. Tex., 1968; JD, U. Houston, 1971. Bar: Tex. 1971. Prin. assoc. Tex. Law Inst. Coastal and Marine Resources, Coll. Law U. Houston, Tex., 1971-73; assoc., ptnr. Vinson & Elkins, Houston, 1973-81, 83-84, 85—, mem. mgmt. com., 1991-96; asst. atty. gen. environ. and natural resources Dept. Justice, 1981-83, U.S. dep. atty. gen., 1984-85. Chmn. Pres.'s Task Force on Legal Equity for Women, 1981-83; mem. Hawaiian Native Study Commn., 1981-83; dir. Nat. Consumer Coop. Banks Bd., 1981 Contbr. articles to profl. jours. Chmn. Gov.'s Conservation Task Force, 2000, Tex. Gov.'s Flood Control Action Group 1980-81; commr. Tex. Parks and Wildlife Dept., 1997-2001; bd. govs. The Nature Conservancy, 1996—, vice chmn. 2002-2004, Oryx Energy Co., 1990-95, (dir.) U. Houston Law Ctr. Found., 1985-89, 96-98, Environ. and Energy Study Inst., 1986-98, Houston Mus. Natural Sci., 1986-98, 2000—, Tex. Nature Conservancy, 1985—, chmn., 1996-99. Mem. ABA (ho. of dels., past chmn. state and local govt. sect., past chair sect. nat. resources, energy, and environ. law, standing com. on fed. judiciary 1997-98, chair 2002-03, bd. editors ABA Jour., chair 2003—), Fed. Bar Assn. (bd. dirs. Houston chpt. 1986), State Bar Tex., Houston Bar Assn., Tex. Water Conservation Assn., Houston Law Rev. Assn. (bd. dirs. 1978). Republican. Lutheran. Office: Vinson & Elkins 2300 First City Tower 1001 Fannin St Houston TX 77002-6706 E-mail: cdinkins@velaw.com.

DINKINS, JENNIFER LYNN, special education educator; b. Louisville, July 1, 1977; d. Gary Wayne and Mary Denise Turner; m. Thomas Jefferson Dinkins Jr., Apr. 23, 1977. BA in Spl. Edn., U. North Fla., 1999. Spl. edn. tchr. Orange Pk. (Fla.) Jr. H.S., 2000—00, D.C. Virgo Mid. Sch., Wilmington, NC, 2000—. Total youth ministry leader St. Mark's Cath. Ch., Wilmington, 2002—03. Mem.: Coun. for Exceptional Children, Golden Key Nat. Honor Soc.

DINKINS, M. JEAN, goverment official; b. Sevierville, Tenn., Jan. 31, 1956; d. Hugh Melvin and Trula Mae (Williams) Dinkins. Cert. payroll profl. Clk., typist City of Knoxville, Tenn., 1974-76; facilities customer svcs. mgr. TVA, Knoxville, 1976-97, facilitator, 1991-97, coord. facilities mgmt. ea. area space, 1997—. Bd. dirs., treas. Tenn. Valley Kennel Club, Knoxville, 1986—. Avocation: raising and showing great danes. Home: 154 Winddrift Way Walland TN 37886-2018 Office: TVA 400 E Summit Hill Dr Knoxville TN 37915-1027 E-mail: mjdinkins@tva.gov.

DINNEN, MAUREEN, educational association administrator, educator; Pres. Fla. Edn. Assn.; history, govt. prof. Broward C.C., Ft. Lauderdale, Fla. Mem.: FTP-NEA (pres.). Office: Fla Edn Assn 213 S Adams St Tallahassee FL 32301

DINSMORE, ROBERTA JOAN MAIER, library director; b. Phila., Sept. 30, 1934; d. Bert Faust and Emma Baker (Keen) Maier; m. Ray W. Dinsmore, Sr., Oct. 20, 1956; children: Ray Wilson Jr., Jeffrey Maier, Debra Joan, Matthew Bert. BA, Pa. State U., 1956; MLS, Clarion U. Pa., 1990. Proofreader Aluminum Co. Am., Pitts., 1957-60; office mgr. Dinsmore, Lithographer, Punxsutawney, Pa., 1969—; dir. Punxsutawney Meml. Libr., 1978—. Freelance writer Greenburg (Pa.) Tribune Rev., 1980—81; adult edn. tchr. Jeff Tech., Reynoldsville, Pa., 1981—82. Mem. Jefferson County Constrn. Com., Jefferson County Heritage Com.; mem. sch. dist. strategic planning com.; chair, sec. Civil Svc. Commn., Punxsutawney; exec. bd.

Theatre Arts; accreditation team Clarion Univ. of Pa.; ch. libr. Punxsutawney Presbyn. Ch., 1985—; elder Presbyn. Ch.; mem. com. on ministry Kiskiminetas Presbytery; mem. exec. bd. Punxsutawney Area Arts Coun.; head hostess Welcome Wagon Internat., Memphis, 1976—80; mem. libr. sci. accreditation team Clarion U., Pa.; v.p., treas. Punxsutawney Area Arts [illegible] class, coun. mem. R.S.V.P., chair; chairperson numerous orgns. Mem.: AAUW (Woman of the Yr. 1987), RSVP (mem. coun., chair), ALA, Goschenhoppen Historians, Bus. and Profl. Women, Punxsutawney Area Hist. and Geneol. Soc. (sec. bd. dirs., charter), Clarion Dist. Libr. Assn. (pres. 1984—86), Pa. Libr. Assn. (past chair pub. libr. divsn.), Punxsutawney Hosp. Aux., Pa. Citizens for Better Librs., Friends of Libr., Irving Club (past pres.), Garden Club (past pres. Punxsutawney chpt.), PEO. Republican. Avocations: reading, making and selling crafts in small, self-owned business, genealogy. Home: 808 E Mahoning St Punxsutawney PA 15767-2320 Office: Punxsutawney Meml Libr 301 E Mahoning St Punxsutawney PA 15767-2142

DION, CELINE, musician; b. Charlemagne, Quebec, Can., Mar. 30, 1970; m. Rene Angelil, 1994; 1 child. Singer: (albums) Unison, 1990 (album of the year, 1990), Celine Dion, 1992, Colour of My Love, 1993 (multi-platinum, 1994), Premieres Anees, 1994, Dion Chante Plamondon, 1994, Des Mots Qui Sonnent, 1995, Power of Love, 1995, French Album, 1995, Live A Paris, 1996, Falling Into You, 1997 (Grammy award album of the yr. & best pop album, 1997), C'est Pour Vivre, 1997, The Collection, 1982—88, 1997, Let's Talk About Love, 1997 (Billboard Music award best album, 1998), S'il suffisait d'aimer, 1998, These are Special Times, 1998 (Grammy & Juno awds., 1999), All The Way, 1999, The French Album, 2001, Classique: A Love Collection, 2001, A New Day Has Come, 2002, One Heart, 2003, 1 Fille & 4 Types, 2003, (Soundtracks) Real Love, 1979, Beauty & the Beast, 1991 (Grammy award, 1992, best selling single, 1992, Acad. award, 1992), Sleepless in Seattle, 1993, Through the Fire, 1994, Titanic (single My Heart Will Go On), 1999 (Grammy award record of yr., 1999, Grammy award best female pop vocal, 1999, Billboard Music award best soundtrack single, 1998), (shows) The Colosseum, Caesars Palace, Las Vegas, 2003—. Recipient Favorite Female Pop/Rock Artist award, Music awards, 1999, Favorite Adult Contemporary Artist award, Am. Music awards, 1999, Album of Yr. for Titanic, Billboard Music awards, 1999, Album Artist, Billboard Music award, 1999, Adult Contemporary Artist Billboard Music award, 1999. Office: Sony Music 550 Madison Ave New York NY 10022-3211*

DIORIO, EILEEN PATRICIA, retired medical technologist, philosophy educator; b. Pitts., Mar. 17, 1938; d. Charles Frederick and Elizabeth (Maturkanich) Kozlowski; m. David Robert Kaslewicz, June 21, 1958 (div. May 1965); m. Alfred Frank Diorio, June 11, 1983; children: Suzanne C. Kaslewicz Ickes, Fredric C. Kaslewicz, Warren G. Kaslewicz, Jennifer Kaslewicz Dalessandro. Student, Duquesne U., 1956-58. Reg. Med. Technologist, Pa. Microbiology technician Presbyn. U. Hosp., Pitts., 1967-70; supr. virology/immunology lab. Allegheny Gen. Hosp., Pitts., 1970-90. Co-dir. Himalayan Inst. Yoga Science & Philosophy of Pitts., 1977-96. Vol. med. lab. mgr. Himalayan Inst. Hosp., India, 1992-96. Avocations: violin, cooking, meditation.

DI PAOLO, MARIA GRAZIA, language educator, writer; d. Alfredo and Giosina (Di Cicco) Di P.; m. Gianroberto Sarolli; 1 child, Giandomenico Sarolli. BA, Hunter Coll., 1969; MA, Columbia U., 1972, PhD, 1977. Instr. Columbia U., N.Y.C., 1973-77; asst. prof. Vassar Coll., Poughkeepsie, N.Y., 1977-85, CUNY, N.Y.C., 1985-90, assoc. prof., 1990-94, prof., 1994—, chair dept. langs. & lit. Lehman Coll., 2001—. Mem. pers. & budget com. Lehman Coll., CUNY, 1986—; chair Italian Rev. Panel CUNY Rsch. Found., 1988-89, 90-91, 96-97; mem. editl. bd. Can. Jour. Italian Studies, 1988—; pres. Italian Culture Soc. Lehman Coll., 1996-98. Author: B. Fenoglio, 1988; translator: Fenoglio's a Private Matter, 1988; editor: D'Annunzio's Correspondence with Son Veniero, 1994; contbr. articles to various publs. Recipient Faculty fellowship Columbia U., 1970-75, Sabbatical grant Vassar Coll., 1982-83, PSC-CUNY Rsch. award, 1988-89, 90-91, 2001—. Mem. MLA, Am. Assn. Tchrs. Italian. Roman Cath. Avocations: tennis, reading club, opera. E-mail: mgdipaolo@cuny.edu.

DIPARDO, ANNE, English language and education educator; BA in English magna cum laude, Calif. State U., Northridge, 1976; MA in English, UCLA, 1977; EdD in Lang. and Literacy, U. Calif., Berkeley, 1991. Assoc. prof. English and edn. U. Iowa, Iowa City, 1991—2002, full prof., 2002—. Author: A Kind of Passport, 1993, Teaching in Common, 1998; co-editor Research in the Teaching of English, 2003—; contbr. articles to profl. jours. Recipient Outstanding Scholarship award Nat. Writing Ctrs. Assn., 1993; NAE/Spencer postdoctoral fellow, 1995—. Mem. MLA, Am. Ednl. Rsch. Assn., Nat. Conf. on Rsch. in English, Nat. Coun. Tchrs. English (Promising Rschr. award 1992, Meade award 2000). Office: U Iowa N246 Linquist Ctr Iowa City IA 52242

DIPIRRO, JONI MARIE, artist; b. Clarion, Pa., Jan. 7, 1940; d. Edmund Paul and Laura Genevieve (Nietsche) DiP.; children: Paul Edmund Herman, Joni Maria Herman. Student, Acad. of Florence, Italy, 1969-71, U. Buffalo, 1977-78; studied with, Pietro Annigone, Florence, 1969-72. Dir. Sisti Gallery, Buffalo, 1974-76; curator Castellani Art Mus., Lewiston, N.Y., 1979-96. Restored statue at Niagara U., 1975; painted mural at House of Chauncey Stillman, 1979; represented in permanent collection at Castellani Mus., 1978, The White House, Washington, D.C., Womens Hall of Fame, N.Y.; paintings in the Terwilliger Mus., Waterloo, N.Y. Mem. Amherst Soc. Artists, Kenmore Soc. Artists, Societa Delle Belle Arti, Casa di Dante Florence, Art Ctr. Sarasota. Home: 3204 24th Pkwy Sarasota FL 34235-8804

DIRKSEN, MARLENE KAY, music educator; b. Hudsonville, Mich., May 15, 1941; d. Richard Jelsema and Katherine Brinks; m. Paul Irvin Dirksen, Apr. 19, 1963; children: Paul Irvin Jr., Susan Kay Dirksen-Singel. AA, Cuyahoga C.C., Cleve., Ohio, 1987; MusB Edn., Cleve. State Univ., Cleve., Ohio, 1993. Dir., music tchr. West Side Ecumenical Ministry, Cleve., 1972—94; organist Bethany Presbyn. Ch., Cleve., 1981—96; tchr. Urban Cmty. Sch., Cleve., 1993—; organist, dir. of music Westlake Christian Ch., Ohio, 1996—. Kilometers for kids walkathon Westside Ecumenical Ministry, Cleve., 1989—96; canvaser for cancer dr. Am. Cancer Soc., Cleve., 1990. Grantee Recorder grant, McGinty Found., 1999—2000, Handbell grant, Am. Handbell Assn., 2002. Mem.: Music Educators Nat. Conf., North Coast Kodály Assn. (bd. mem.), Am. Guild of Organist (bd. mem.). Protestant-Presbyn. Avocations: sewing, reading. Home: 11907 Marne Ave Cleveland OH 44111

DI RUSSO, TERRY, communications educator, writer; b. Trenton, N.J., Nov. 1, 1947; d. Joy (Urban) Rooy; m. Dennis John, June 23, 1973 (div. July 1985); 1 child, Elaine Marie; m. Robert L. DiRusso, Aug. 17, 2002. BS in Comm., Psychology, Edn., Murray State U., 1970, MS in Comm., 1971; postgrad., Cen. Conn. State U., New Britain, 1972. Tchr., teaching asst. Murray (Ky.) State U., Murray, Ky., 1970-71; instr. adult edn. Wincester Bd. of Edn., Winsted, Conn., 1973-76; special lectr. Central Conn. State U., New Britain, Conn., 1975-85; lectr. comm. dept. Tunxis C.C., Farmington, Conn., 1986—; comm. lectr. U. Conn., Waterbury, 1986, Torrington, 1986—; English educator Wincester Bd. of Edn., Conn., 1971—. Cons., lectr. Vets. Hosp. Nursing Staff, Meridan, 1981, Bus. and Profl. Women, 1982; faculty cons. Conn. State Conf. Emergency Med. Techs., Hartford, 1988-96; cons. Pvt. Individuals Pub. Speaking Coach, 1976—; comms lectr. gender comms. and sexual harassment United Techs., E. Hartford, Conn., 1995; presenter in field. Author: (mystery novel, as Terry Finello) Absolute Vengeance, 1999; mem. editl. bd. Elements of Speech Comm., 3rd edit., 1995. Mem. AAUP, NEA, Conn. Edn. Assn., Winsted Edn. Assn., Nat. Coun. Tchrs. English, New Eng. League Mid. Schs., Litchfield County Women's Network, Conn. Assn. Pubs. and Authors. Avocations: tennis, writing. Home: 126 Winterbourne Ln Canton CT 06019 Office: Univ Conn University Dr Torrington CT 06790 E-mail: tdirusso@snet.net.

[illegible] (CAROL LA CHIUSA), artist; b. Cleve., July 26, 1930; d. Theodore Christian Jenks and Evelyn Mildred Bushnell; m. Salvatore A. Lachiusa, Sept. 14, 1950 (dec. Feb. 1991); children: Drew, Cyd Marie, Dean, Dane; m. Paris Di Santo, June 28, 1992. Student, Cleve. Inst. Art, 1948-50, U. Mexico, Puebla, 1992. Art instr. Grosse Pointe (Mich.) War Meml., 1969-99; watercolor instr. The Art Ctr., Mt. Clemens, Mich., 1988-99, instr., 1988—2002. Host watercolor workshop program Grosse Pointe Cable TV-Comcast, 1986—2002; workshop lectr. Crooked Tree Art Assn., Petoskey, Mich., 1986—87; exhbn. lectr. Kettering U., Flint, Mich., 1999; lectr. various art assns., Mich., 1981—99; artist-in-residence Grosse Pointe War Meml., 1996—98. One-woman shows include Troy Art Gallery, Royal Oak, Mich., 1979, 1984, 1991, 1994, Venice, Italy, 2001, Mich. Women's Hist. Ctr. and Hall of Fame, Lansing, 2002, Remember Mama, 2002, The Art Ctr., Mt. Clemens, Mich., 2003, Grosse Artists Ctr., Mich., 2003, prin. works include Rockport Best of Watercolor, 1997, Encyclopedia of Living Artists, 11th edit., 1998, Am. Artist Mag., 1999, Grace Mag., 1999, Encyclopedia of Living Artists, 12th edit., Grosse Pointe News, 1995—97, exhibited in group shows at Gallery Bai, N.Y., N.Y., 1998, Mich. Watercolor Travelling Show, 2001, Women's Show, Plymouth, Mich., 2003 (1st prize, 03), Great Lakes Juried Show, 2003 (3d prize, 03), Detroit (Mich.) Women Painters and Sculptors, 2003 (1st prize, 03). Co-founder Grosse Pointe Arts Coun., 1993, pres., 1995-97. Mem.: Mich. Coun. Arts and Cultural Affairs, Grosse Pointe Artists Assn. (v.p. 1988—90), Detroit Soc. Women Painters and Sculptors (pres. 1998—2000), Mich. Watercolor Soc., Mich. Assn. Cmty. Arts Agys., Grosse Pointe United Ch. Womens Assn. (bd. 1999—, pres. 2001—). Home: 418 Barclay Rd Grosse Pointe MI 48236-2814

DISCALA, JAMIE LYNN, actress; b. Jericho, NY, May 15, 1981; m. A.J. DiScala. Student, NYU. Actor: (films) A Brooklyn State of Mind, 1997, Campfire Stories, 2001, Death of a Dynasty, 2003; (TV films) Call Me: The Rise and Fall of Heidi Fleiss, 2004; (TV series) The Sopranos, 1999—; (Broadway plays) Beauty and the Beast, 2002—03; author: (autobiography) Wise Girl, 2002. Achievements include started acting at NY regional theaters; starred in over two dozen theatrical prodns. including Annie, The Wizard of Oz, The Sound of Music, The Wiz, and Gypsy. Office: 1100 Ave of the Americas New York NY 10036*

DISHMAN, ROSE MARIE RICE, academic administrator, researcher; BS in Physics with honors, U. Mo., 1966; MS in Physics, U. Calif., Riverside, 1968, PhD, 1971; MBA, San Diego State U., 1979. Physics instr., elem. particle rsch. assoc. U. Tenn., Knoxville, Oak Ridge, 1968-71; computer programmer, analyst Signal Processing Divsn. Sys. Ctrl., Inc., Palo Alto, Calif., 1971-72; instr. physics San Diego State U., 1974-75; instr. algebra, calculus, physics San Diego C.C., Navy Tng. Ctr., Marine Corps Recruit Depot, 1975-78; instr. Grossmont Coll., San Diego, 1976-77; prof., dept. head Sch. Engring. and Applied Sci. U.S. Internat. U., San Diego, 1977-92, dean Sch. Engring. and Applied Sci., 1989-92, acting provost, v.p. acad. affairs, 1991-92; dean acad. affairs DeVry Inst. Tech., Pomona, Calif., 1992-94, pres. Pomona, Long Beach, Calif., 1994—. Supr. world-wide acad. progs. including campuses in Mex., Eng., Kenya, U.S. Internat. U., primary supr. deans Schs. of Edn., Bus., Visual and Performing Arts, Human Behavior, Hotel and Restaurant Mgmt., Libr., Learning Resource Ctr., developer civil engring., engring. mgmt., electronics tech., elec. engring. progs. resulting in Engring. Accreditation Commn. of the Accreditation Bd. for Engring. and Tech. accreditation for civil engring. prog. for San Diego, London campuses, mem. curriculum coun. for all univ. progs., advisor U.S. Internat. U. Engring. Club; elected mem. Calif. Engring. Liaison Com., pres. pvt. univ. segment. Named outstanting engring. educator Am. Soc. Engring. Edn., 1989; rsch. grantee Fulbright-Hayes, 1972-73, grantee Am. Soc. Engring. Edn., NASA, 1979, Am. Soc. Engring. Edn., Dept. Energy, 1981, 82, 1984-85, Fed. Emergency Mgmt. Agy., 1983, 86. Office: DeVry Inst Tech Univ Ctr 901 Corp Ctr Dr Pomona CA 91768-2642 Fax: 909-623-5666.

DISHONG, LINDA S. estate planner; b. Bluffton, Ind., July 2, 1948; d. George William Dishong and Mary Kathryn Randol; children: Loni Marie, Marlou Reneé. Student various schs. for estate and fin. planning, Ind. Cert. estate planning specialist, sr. adv., real estate rep., NASD Series 7 & 63 broker. Pres. estate planning Genesis Projects, Indpls., 1982—89; adminstrn. and customer svc. rep. MR, Inc., Indpls., 1990—99; real estate profl. Coldwell Banker, Indpls., 1998—2000; broker Charles Schwab, Indpls., 2000—01; estate planning, regulation dir. United Fin. Sys. Corp., Indpls., 2001—. Motivational svc. profl., bus. cons. Genesis Projects, Indpls., 1982—89. Mem.: Westfield-Washinton Kiwanis Club, N.W. Kiwanis Club (sec. 1989—95, v.p. 1995—96, pres. 1996—97, Disting. Sec. 1989—95, Disting. Pres. 1996—97). Republican. Avocations: family, hiking, bicycling, travel, whitewater rafting. Office: United Fin Sys Corp 7602 Woodland Dr Indianapolis IN 46278 E-mail: ldishong@unitedfin.com.

DISMUKES, CAROL JAEHNE, county official; b. Giddings, Tex., July 17, 1938; d. Herbert Emil and Ruby (Alexander) Jaehne; m. Harold Charles Schumann, Feb. 7, 1959 (div. May 1970); children: Timothy, Michael, Keith, Gregory; m. Milton Brown Dismukes, Mar. 19, 1971. Student Tex. Lutheran Coll., 1958. Dep. Lee County Clk., Giddings, Tex., 1970-74, chief dep., 1975-77; accounts receivable clk. Invader Inc., Giddings, 1977-79; prodn. sec. Humble Exploration, Giddings, 1979-80; county clk. Lee County, Giddings, 1980— . Mem., Dime Box Ind. Sch. Dist. Trustees, Tex., 1972-80, pres., 1977-80; chmn. Dime Box Homecoming and Mini-Marathon, 1978—2000; chmn. scholar com. Lee Co. Jr. Livestock Show, 1982—; v.p. coun. St. John's Luth. Ch., 1982-84, sec., 1986, treas., 1987-89, chmn., 1991-93, 97-99. Mem. County and Dist. Clks Assn. Tex., Dime Box Lions Club (charter, pres. 1996-97, sec. 1999-2003). Democrat. Avocations: reading; sewing. Office: Lee County Clk PO Box 419 Giddings TX 78942-0419 Office Phone: 979-542-3684.

DISMUKES, VALENA GRACE BROUSSARD, photographer, former physical education educator; b. St. Louis, Feb. 22, 1938; d. Clobert Bernard and Mary Henrietta (Jones) Broussard; m. Martin Ramon Dismukes, June 26, 1965; 1 child, Michael Ramon. AA in Edn., Harris Tchrs. Coll., 1956; BS in Phys. Edn., Washington U., St. Louis, 1958; MA in Phys. Edn., Calif. State U., L.A., 1972; BA in TV and Film, Calif. State U., Northridge, 1981. Cert. phys. edn. tchr., standard svc. supr. Phys. edn. tchr., coach St. Louis Pub. Sch., 1958-60, L.A. Unified Sch. Dist., 1960-84; health and sci. tchr., mentor tchr. LA Unified Sch. Dist., 1984-93; coord. gifted and talented program 32d St./U. So. Calif. Magnet Sch., 1993-95, magnet coord., 1995; adminstrv. asst. Ednl. Consortium of Ctrl. LA, Calif., 1993-95; free-lance photographer, 1970—; owner, bus. cons. Grace Enterprises, 1994-95; owner World Class Images, 1997—. Coord. Chpt. I, 1989—93; mem. sch. based mgmt. team, 1990—93; lectr. in field. Author: (photography book) As Seen, 1995; editor: parent newsletter, 1975—80; one-woman shows include The Olympic Spirit, 1984, LA-The Ethnic Pl., 1986, Native Am.: Red Black Connection, 1999, Tibet-Photos from the Roof of the World, 2000, Chocolate Women, 2001, The Tarahamara of Copper Canyon, 2001; photographer (photo montage) Homeless on the Street, 2002, Views from West Africa, 2003, (film) Black Indians: An American Story, 2001; contbr. articles to profl. jour. Mem. adv. coun. Visual Comm., LA, 1980; mem. Cmty. Consortium, LA, 1986—87; mem. adv. com. LA Edn. Partnership, 1986—87; mem. adv. bd. Espo Sports Club, LA, 1994; co-founder Alliance of Native Am. of So. Calif. (ANASCA), 1999; v.p. Alliance of Native Am. of So. Calif., 1999—2003; mem. adv. coun. Ne'ayah, 2001—03; bd. dir. NACHES Found., Inc., LA, 1985—86. Marine Educators fellow, 1992; photography grantee LA Olympic Organizing Com., 1984, See's Candies, 2000, Long Beach Fine Arts, 2001, Teaching grantee L.A. Edn. Partnership, 1987-89; recipient Honor award LA-Calif. Assn. Health, Phys. Edn. and Recreation, 1971. Mem. ACLU, NAACP, Urban League, Sierra Club [illegible], collecting dolls and baskets, ethnic art. Home: 3800 Stocker St Apt 1 Los Angeles CA 90008-5119 E-mail: vdismukes@netzero.net.

DISNEY, ANTHEA, publishing executive; b. Dunstable, Eng., Oct. 13, 1946;, naturalized, U.S., 1973; d. Alfred Leslie and Elsie (Wale) Disney; m. Peter Robert Howe, Jan. 28, 1984. Ed., Queen's Coll., Eng. Fgn. corr. London Daily Mail, N.Y.C., 1973-75, features editor London, 1975-77, bur. chief N.Y.C., 1977-79; columnist London Daily Express, N.Y.C., 1979-84; dep. mng. editor N.Y. Daily News, N.Y.C., 1984-87; editor Sunday Daily News, 1984-87, US Mag., 1987-88; editor-in-chief Self mag., 1988-89; mag. developer Murdoch Mags., 1989-90; exec. producer Fox TV's A Current Affair, 1990-91; editor-in-chief TV Guide mag., N.Y.C., 1991-95; editorial dir. Murdoch Mags., 1993-95; editor-in-chief I-Guide, Newscorp's Internet Svc., 1995-96; pres., CEO Harper Collins Publishers, 1996-97; chmn., CEO News Am. Pub. Group, N.Y.C., 1997—99, TV Guide, Inc., 1999; exec. v.p. content News Corp., N.Y.C., 1999—. Bd. dirs. Household Internat. Inc., 2001—. Office: News Corp Ste 300 1211 Avenue Of The Americas New York NY 10036-8795*

DISTECHE, CHRISTINE M. geneticist; b. Liege, Belgium, July 22, 1949; PhD, U. Liege, Belgium, 1976. Genetics fellow Harvard U., Boston, 1977-80; now med. geneticist U. Wash. Hosp., Seattle. Prof. pathology U. Wash., Seattle. Office: U Wash Hosp Dept Pathology PO Box 357470 Seattle WA 98195-7470

DISTON, LORRAINE DIANA, clinical psychologist, educator; b. N.Y.C., Dec. 16; d. Leo and Frances Diston; m. Philip Joseph Consolo (div.); children: Karen Consolo, Joseph Consolo. AA in Psychology and Fine Arts summa cum laude, Miami-Dade C.C., 1979; BA in Psychology magna cum laude, Fla. Internat. U., 1982; MS in Psychology cum laude, Nova Southeastern U., 1987, D in Psychology cum laude, 1990. Lic. clin. psychologist Fla., cert. hypnotherapist Nat. Guild Hypnotherapists. Rsch. asst. Miami Childrens Hosp., 1986; psychologist Cotler Health Care, Hollywood, Fla., 1995—98, Northwest Dade CMHC, Hialeah, Fla., 1989—95; adj. faculty St. Thomas U., Miami, 1993—, staff psychologist, 1995—2003; lic. clin. psychologist DR's & Assocs., Miami, 1995—. Psychologist, instr. Episc. Diocese S.E. Fla., Miami, 1993—. Episcopalian. Avocations: painting, textiles, writing.

DI TRAPANI, MARCIA A. health facility administrator, community health nurse, educator; b. Madison, Wis., Mar. 7, 1938; d. Alfred H. and Margaret E. Dvorak; m. Anthony R. Di Trapani, Nov. 12, 1960; children: Anthony R. Di Trapani, Jr., Laura M. Clairmont, Nancy A. Erickson. BSN, U. of Wis., 1960; MA, George Mason U., 1994. RN Va., 1974, Wash., DC, 2000. Staff nurse U. Hosps., Madison, Wis., 1960, D.C. Dept. Pub. Health, Washington, 1961—62, Columbia Hosp. for Women, Washington, 1966—68; case mgr. Internat. Rehab. Assn., Inc., Towson, Md., 1976—77; pub. health nurse Arlington (Va.) County Health Dept., 1978—83, Fairfax (Va.) County Health Dept., 1983—90, nursing supr., 1990—95; cmty. health cons. No. Va. C.C., Annandale, Va., 1995—97; exec. v.p., sec., treas. T&MCorp, Reston, Va., 1997—. Profl. practice adv. bd. mem. Va. State Bd. of Nursing, Richmond, Va., 1992—95; nurses leadership planning group mem. Child Devel. Resources, Norge, Va., 1998—2001; instr. George Mason U., Fairfax, 1998—. Contbr. articles to profl. jours. Sec. Marjorie F. Hughes Fund for Children, Arlington, Va., 1996—2003; family assistance coord. Herndon/Reston (Va.) FISH, Inc., 2003. Mem.: DAR, ANA (del. to nat. conv. 2001—03), Coalition Va. Nurses, Va. Nurses Assn. (various positions 1994—2003, pres. dist. 8 2001—03, named one of 99 Outstanding Nurses in Va. 1999, Dist 8 Outstanding Nurse award in Nursing Edn. 2000), Va. Pub. Health Assn., Sigma Theta Tau (corr. sec., eta alpha 2002—). Avocations: travel, genealogy, knitting, geocaching. Home: 11500 Drop Forge Lane Reston VA 20191

DITTA, PHYLLIS ANN, treasurer; b. New Orleans, La., July 7, 1939; d. Carlo John and Felicia Rita (Trupiano) D.; children: Phyllis Ann Ditta, Melanie Arthemise, Richard John Adams, Alexis Quincy Adams Andrews, Loretta Annette, Truman Heathcliff Woolfolk. BS, St. Mary's Dominican Coll., 1961, BA, 1967. Secondary history tchr. Jefferson Parish Schs., Orleans Parish Schs., New Orleans, La., 1967-68; owner,operator Italia Expresso Restaurant, Westwood, Calif., 1983-92; food catering cons. Maria's Italian Kitchen, Van Huys, Calif., 1992; food writer; food restaurant cons., 1992—; corp. treas. Carlo Ditta, Inc., Harvey, La., 1955—. Bd. dirs. Ciao Italia, L.A., 1984-88. Sr. food editor Italian Am. Digest, 1994—; contbr. articles to profl. jours. Mem. Gli Amici. Democrat. Roman Catholic. Avocations: interesting conversation, sports, cooking, reading, travel. Office: Carlo Ditta Inc 1445 Macarthur Ave Harvey LA 70058-2498

DIVINCENZO, SISTER MARY ANNE, chaplain, therapist; d. Dominick DiVincenzo and Mary Katherine Hayes(Stepmother). MS Religious Edn., Duquesne U., 1972—73. Reiki II Practitioner Usui Sys. of Natural Healing, 1992; cert. Chaplain Nat. Conf. of Cath. Bishops/Washington, D.C., 1989, Shiatsu Therapist Calif. Med. Sch. of Shiatsu, 1996. Staff chaplain St. Agnes Med. Ctr., Fresno, Calif., 1987, Rush Presbyn./St. Luke Med. Ctr., Chgo., 1985; reiki practitoner/shioatsu therapist Healing Moments by Mary Anne, Fresno, Calif., 1996—2003. Dir. of religious edn. St. Joseph Ch., Coraopolis, Pa., 1974—83. Regional rep. Nat. Assn. of Cath. Chaplains, Milw., 1996—2000; pres. Fresno Womens Network, Fresno, Calif., 2003—. Mem.: Nat. Assn. of Cath. Chaplains (regional dir. 1996—2000), Internat. Massage Assn. (licentiate). D-Liberal. Roman Catholic. Home: 5134 North College Ave Fresno CA 93704 Office: Saint Agnes Medical Center 1303 East Herndon #330 Fresno CA 93720 Personal E-mail: maryanned@peoplepc.com.

DIVINSKY, MIRIAM, psychotherapist; b. Novosibirsk, Russia, Oct. 14, 1944; came to U.S., 1980; d. Michael and Friderika (Schpatz) Gershman; m. Igor Pesochinsky, Apr. 14, 1982 (div. May 1989); 1 child, Alexander Michael. MS in Linguistics with honors, Kiev (Ukraine) U., 1966; PhD in Cybernetics, Anti-Aircraft Mil. Coll., Kiev, 1978; MA in Psychology, NYU, 1983, ABD in Psychology, 1985. Cert. clin. advanced hypnotherapist. Rschr. Anti-Aircraft Mil. Coll., Kiev, 1967-74; sr. rschr. Moscow U., 1975-76, Moscow Libr. Social Scis., 1976-79; tchg. asst., fellow U. Pa., Phila., 1980-81; rsch. asst., fellow psychology dept. NYU, N.Y.C., 1981-85; sr. cons. Omni Psych, Inc., Stockholm, N.J., 1985-90; dir. Ctr. for Wellnes and Creative Living, Newfoundland, N.J., 1993—. Condr. workshops Experience of Wellness, Past Life, Future Life, Purpose of Life. Contbr. articles to newspapers and profl. jours. Fellow of distinction Kiev (Ukraine) U., 1961-66. Mem. Assn. Past Life Rsch. and Therapies, Internat. Assn. Counselors and Therapists (life), Nat. Assn. Cert. Hypnotherapists. Office: Ctr for Wellness Ste 7A PO Box 615 2713 Rt 23 S Newfoundland NJ 07435

DIVITA, ANGELA MARIE, music educator; b. Lewiston, N.Y., June 28, 1978; d. Michael Louis and Jessie Wrobel DiVita. B of Music Edn., SUNY, Potsdam, 2000; M of Music Edn., U. Ill., Urbana-Champaign, 2003; MSc in Ednl. Adminstrn. and Supervision, Niagara U., 2004. Cert. music tchr. K-12 Ga., music tchr. K-12 permanent N.Y., elem. tchr. pre-K-6 provisional N.Y. Freelance clarinet, woodwind tchr., 2000—; music tchr. Niagara Falls (NY) City Schs., 2000—01, band dir., 2001—02, Cobb County Sch. Dist., Marietta, Ga., 2002—. Wish coord. Make-A-Wish Found., Marietta, 2002—; French horn player Cobb Wind Symphony, Marietta, 2002—.

Mem.: Music Educator's Nat. Conf., Ga. Music Educator's Assn. (chair all-state auditions 2002), Kappa Delta Pi, Sigma Alpha Iota. Republican. Roman Catholic. Avocations: reading, remodeling homes. Home: 77 Queens Dr Grand Island NY 14072

DIXON, ARMENDIA PIERCE, school program administrator; b. Laurel, Miss., July 15, 1937; d. L.E. and Denothras (Pickens) Pierce; m. Harrison D. Dixon Jr., Aug. 28, 1971; 1 child, Harrison D. III BS in Edn., Jackson (Miss.) State U., 1960; postgrad., No. Ill. State U., 1965-66; MEd, Edinboro (Pa.) U., 1978; PhD, PhD, Kent State U., 1994. Cert. English and secondary edn., Miss. Tchr. English, libr. Laurel City Schs., 1962-67; tchr. English, dir. summer pre-sch. Erie (Pa.) Pub. Schs., 1967-72; tchr. English, drama, journalism, forensic coach Crawford Cen. Schs., Meadville, Pa., 1972-85, asst. prin., facilitator sch. improvement coun., 1985-89, coord. successful student partnership, 1988—; prin. Meadville Area Sr. High, 1993. Exec. dir. Meadville Latch-Key Program, 1985—; coord. Urban Tchrs. Project, Kent State U., adj. asst. prof., 1989—, dir. Prospective Tchrs. Program for Phi Delta Kappa; charter mem. Results chpt., Kent State U., 1990; dir. high sch. edn. Sch. dist. City of Erie, 1993-2001; instr. English Edinboro U. Pa.; dir. of high sch. edn., The Sch. Dist. of the City of Erie, Pa., 1993—. Fundraiser Cystic Fibrosis Found., Pitts., 1976. 79, 81, Sickle Cell Anemia, Erie, 1978-83; pres. Martin Luther King Jr. Scholarship Fund, Inc., 1979-89; bd. dirs. ARC, Erie, 1996—, Villa Marie Coll., Erie, 1995—, Internat. Inst., 1994—; mem. adv. bd. Am. Enterprise, Erie, 1993—; mem. alumni bd. dirs. Edinboro U. Alumni, 1997—. Mem. NAACP (pres. Meadville chpt. 1984—), Nat. Assn. Secondary Sch. Prins., Pa. Assn. Secondary Sch. Prins., Order Eastern Star (worthy matron), Navy Mothers, Rainbow Ill, Burres, Phi Delta Kappa, Alpha Kappa Alpha. Methodist. Avocations: collecting dolls, writing, gardening. Office: Crawford Ctrl Schs 847 N Main St Meadville PA 16335-2655 Address: 716 Jefferson Street Meadville PA 16335 E-mail: armendia@alltel.net.

DIXON, BARBARA BRUINEKOOL, academic administrator; b. Sparta, Wis., June 14, 1943; MusB magna cum laude in Applied Piano, Mich. State U., 1966, MusM, 1969; MusD, U. Colo., 1991. Instr. vocal music K-12 Capac (Mich.) Cmty. Schs., 1970-71; tchr. dept. music Ctrl. Mich. U., Mt. Pleasant, 1971-89, assoc. dean coll. arts and scis., 1989-95, interim dean coll. arts and scis., 1995-97; provost, v.p. acad. affairs SUNY, Geneseo, 1997—2003; pres. Truman St. U., Kirksville, Mo., 2003—. Rep. acad. senate exec. bd., acad. senate liaison com., univ. acad. planning coun. Ctrl. Mich. U., 1986-89; dir. tchr. edn. search com., 1990, 95; chair faculty load equity study com., 1988-89, undergrad. curriculum com., 1992-93, formal hearing com. for grievance under senate rules, 1988-89; mem. profl. edn. coun., 1990-95, honors coun., 1989-94, task force on distance learning, 1992-93, piano search com., 1989, 90, 92, 95, music awards policy com., 1980-81, numerous others. One-woman performances include Kirtland C.C., Roscommon, Mich., 1986, Lansing (Mich.) C.C. Artist Series, 1987, Wurlitzer Hdqs., Holly Springs, Miss., 1989, Benefit for Cmty. Arts Coun., Pigeon, Mich., 1991, Beethoven Festival, Lansing, 1993, and others; accompanying performances include Backstage Recital Series, Jasper, Ind., 1984, Bridgeport (Mich.) Voice Symposium, 1986, Manistee (Mich.) Opera House, 1986, Saginaw (Mich.) Choral Soc., 1987, Alma (Mich.) Coll. Faculty, 1995, Black Forest Music Festival (Broadway rev.), Harbor Springs, Mich., 1995, and others. Active Art Reach Mid-Mich. (gallery com. 1995-96, chamber music com. 1995-97, fund drive com. 1996-97, bd. dirs. 1996-97, treas. 1996-97), Lions Club (chair spl. events com., bd. dirs. 1995-97), United Way (liaison to campus campaign); vol. Mich. Spl. Olympics. Mem. Mich. Music Tchrs. Assn. (bd. of certification 1976-79, 84-90, 95-97, chair 1996-97, pres. local chpt. 1991-92; chmn. collegiate activities 1979-81; mem. spkrs. bur. 1974-97, adjudicators bur. 1975-97, exec. bd. 1979-81, 96; rep. Mich. Youth Arts Festival bd. 1976-81, Mich. Alliance for Arts in Edn. 1988-89), Dalcroze Soc. Am., Delta Omicron, AAUW, Am. Assn. Higher Edn., Phi Beta Delta, Pi Kappa Lambda, Phi Kappa Phi Mortar Bd. Office: Truman St U 100 E Normal St MC200 Kirksville MO 63501 E-mail: dixon@truman.edu.

DIXON, DOTTI S. school counselor; d. William D. and Shirley A. Dixon; m. Randy W. Schmeling, Aug. 27, 1977; 1 child, Brock W. Schmeling. BS, N.D. State U., 1977, EdM in Guidance and Counseling, 1987; PhD in Ednl. Leadership, U. N.D., 2002. Lic. profl. educator N.D. Edn. Stds. and Practices Bd., profl. sch. counselor credential N.D. Dept. Pubic Instrn., elem. prin.'s credential N.D. Dept. Pub. Instrn., secondary prin.'s credential N.D. Dept. Pub. Instrn. Counselor, instr. U. Mary, Bismarck, ND, 1986—88; sch. counselor United Tribes Tech. Coll., Bismarck, 1988—91, Bismarck Pub. Schs., 1991—. Chair student svc. com. Bismarck Pub. Schs., 1992—2002; chair North Ctrl. accreditation bldg. improvement plan Wachter Mid. Sch., Bismarck, 1998—; continuing edn. instr. Minot (N.D.) State U., 2002—; dir. mid. sch. puppetry program Prevention Through Edn. Ednl. programming cons. Ft. Abraham Lincoln, Mandan, ND, 2003; mem. Rep. Women, Mandan, 1979—2003; mem. fine arts coordinating adv. com. First Luth. Ch., Mandan, 1987—2003. Recipient Prevention Through Edn. award, Mental Health Assn. N.D., 1999. Mem.: ASCD, N.D. Sch. Counselors Assn. (curriculum devel. 2003—, pub. policy and govt. rels. chair 2001—), N.D. Coun. Ednl. Leaders, Am. Sch. Counselor Assn., U. N.D. Alumni Assn., N.D. State Alumni Assn., Alpha Omicron (scholarship chair Delta chpt. 1995—2002, Adeline Stevenson Nurse and Hazel B. Nielson grad. scholar 1998), Delta Kappa Gamma (Delta chpt. pres. 2002—, N.W. regional steering com. 2002—03, scholar 2000—01). Republican. Lutheran. Avocations: gourmet cooking, travel, interior design, boating, reading and research. Home: 1512 River Dr Mandan ND 58554 Office: Wachter Mid Sch 1107 S 7th St Bismarck ND 58504

DIXON, ERNESTINE OTHREE, secondary school educator; b. Dial, Tex., May 8, 1923; BS in Econ., Prairie View U., 1946; MA in Edn., Tchrs. Coll., Columiba U., 1950; PhD, Tex. Women's U., 1971. Homemaking tchr., child devel., vocational counselor Ft. Worth Pub. Schs. Vol. Harris Hosp., Family Svcs., Wesley Cmty. Ctr., Ecumenical Ctr., San Antonio, Ft. Worth, Tex. Mem.: Ret. Tchrs. Assn. Tex., Prairie View A&M U. Alumni Chpt. Meth. Home: 9507 Burwick Dr San Antonio TX 78230

DIXON, KATHRYN A. social worker; b. Danbury, Conn., Mar. 8, 1966; d. Thaddeus Edward and Mary Kathryn (Mc Ginley) D. BS in Social Work, U. N.H., 1988; MS in Social Work, Fordham U., 1991. Lic. clin. social worker, N.J., N.Y. Psychotherapist pvt. practice, 1991—; staff Rockland Family Shelter, Spring Valley, N.Y., 1990-91; residential social worker St. Christophers Child Care Facility, Dobbs Ferry, N.Y., 1988-90; youth svcs. counselor Bergen County Divsn. Family Guidance, Paramus, NJ, 1991-97; adolescent therapist High Focus Ctrs., Inc., SaddleBrook, N.J., 1997-99; family counseling specialist State of N.J., Hackensack, 1999—2003, drug ct. coord., 2003—. Vol. Girl Scouts USA. Recipient U. Women's award, U. N.H., 1988. Mem. Am. Coll. Forensic Examiners, NASW (past chair Bergen County). Avocations: camping, jewelry making, whitewater rafting. Office: Hughes Justice Complex Criminal Practice Divsn Trenton NJ 08625

DIXON, LUGENIA, psychology educator; b. Columbus, Ga., Jan. 20, 1949; d. Sam and Ola (Bowman) Dixon; m. Willie Cornelius Ladner, 1969 (div. Aug. 1973); children: Dexteralan Keith Ladner, Craig Jeffrey Ladner, Olivia Dara Young. Student, Harris Jr. Coll., Meridian, Miss., 1967-68, Columbus (Ga.) Coll., 1971-78; BA in Psychology, U. Ga., 1980, MEd in Early Childhood Edn., 1982, PhD in Ednl. Psychology, 1985; postgrad., Ft. Valley (Ga.) State Coll., 1989; course grad., Art Instrn. Schs., Mpls., 1997. Medicare claims approval clk. Blue Cross/Blue Shield, Columbus, 1969-71, Medicare unit leader, 1975-77; collector Sears, Columbus, 1971-75; substitute tchr. Clarke County Sch. Dist., Athens, Ga., 1981, instrnl. aide, substitute tchr., 1984-85; work/study (rschr.) U. Ga., Athens, 1981-83; substitute tchr. Ga. Retardation Ctr., Athens, 1983-84; asst. prof. psychology Gordon Coll., Barnesville, Ga., 1985-89; assoc. prof. psychology Bainbridge (Ga.) Coll., 1989—2001, promoted to full prof., 2001; E.T.S. reader AP in psychology, 2004. Coord. judging Social Sci. Fair, Bainbridge Coll., 1992—, dir., 1997—; coord. minority achievement program Bainbridge Coll., 1992-97; mem. adv. com. on psychology Regents Acad. Co-author: Living Psychology: An Introduction, 1995; co-author: (handbook) Handbook for Living Psychology: An Introduction, 1995. Sec. Decatur County Artist Guild, 1994; gender equity liaison AAUW, Bainbridge br., 1995-96. MRecipient cmty. svc. cert. Athens Recreation Dept., 1984, internat. scenario writing contest award 5th World Conf. on Children, Youth and Adults, Athens, 1984; ini-grant Bainbridge Coll., 1996;, Regents minority scholar U. Ga., 1983-84; Univ. Sys. Ga. grantee Summer Inst., Brazil. Mem. AAUW (Ga. coll.-univ. rep.). Coun. Tchrs. of Undergrad. Psychology, Ga. Assn. Educators. Democrat. Roman Catholic. Avocations: gardening, drawing and painting. Home: 261 Dollar Dr Bainbridge GA 31717-6438 Office: Bainbridge College Hwy 84 Bainbridge GA 31717 Office Phone: 229-248-2571.

DIXON, PAULINE K. retired secondary school educator; b. Pittsburg, Tex., Aug. 14, 1926; d. Lonnie H. Earl and Annie Kate Young; m. Frank Dixon, Dec. 22, 1946. Oper. and instr.'s lic., Madame C.J. Walker Beauty Coll., Dallas, 1945; BS in Math. and History, Bishop Coll., 1968; MEd in Ednl. Adminstrn., East Tex. State U., 1973. Tchr. math. grades 7-8 Pearl C. Anderson Jr. H.S., Dallas, 1968—71; tchr. math. and computer applications Hill Mid. Sch., Dallas, 1971—84; tchr. math. and pre-algebra Florence Mid. Sch., Dallas, 1987—2000; ret. Candidate-at-large Dallas County Sch. Bd., 2003; candidate 32 congl. dist. U.S. Ho. Reps., Dallas, 2002. Mem.: NAACP, NOW, NEA (dir. State of Tex. 1994—99), Tex. State Tchrs. Assn. (dist. 10 pres. 1990—99), Classroom Tchrs. of Dallas (pres. 1985—87). Democrat. Baptist. Avocation: playing cards. E-mail: paulined6201@yahoo.com.

DIXON, SHIRLEY JUANITA, retired restaurant owner; b. Canton, N.C., June 29, 1935; d. Willard Luther and Bessie Eugenia (Scroggs) Clark; m. Clinton Matthew Dixon, Jan. 3, 1953; children: Elizabeth Swanger, Hugh Monroe III, Cynthia Owen, Sharon Henson. BS, Wayne State U., 1956; postgrad., Mary Baldwin Coll., 1958, U. N.C., 1977. Acct. Standard Oil Co., Detroit, 1955-57; asst. dining room mgr. Statler Hilton, Detroit, 1958-60; bookkeeper Osborne Lumber Co., Canton, N.C., 1960-61; bus. owner, pres. Dixon's Restaurant, Canton, 1961-99, ret. Judge N.C. Assn. Distributive Edn. Assn., state and dist., 1982—; owner Halbert's Family Heritage Ctr., Canton; dir. rep. Avon. Past Pres. Haywood County Assn. Retarded Citizens Bd., 1985-94, past v.p., chmn. bd. dirs.; bd. commrs. Haywood Vocats. Opportunities, 1985-94, treas. bd. dirs.; Haywood Sr. Leadership Council; dist. dir. 11th Congl. Dist. Dem. Women, 1982-85; state Teen-Dem. advisor State Dem. party, 1985-90; del. 1988 Dem. Nat. Conv., Atlanta; alderwoman Town of Canton, N.C.; vice-chair Gov.'s. Adv. Coun. on Aging, State N.C., 1982-89; 1st v.p. crime prevention Community Watch Bd., State N.C., 1985, 86; mem. Criminal Justice Bd., N.C. Assembly on Women and the Economy; chair Western N.C. Epilepsy Assn., Haywood County N.C. Mus. History, 1987—; bd. dirs. W.N.C. Women's Coalition, 1999-2000; co-chair Haywood County Commn. on the Bi-Centennial of Constn., 1987-92; Haywood County Econ. Strategy Commn.; v.p., bd. dirs. Haywood County Retirement Coun., Region A Coun. on Aging; bd. dirs. Haywood County Sr. Housing, C.B.C. United Way (mem. chair); chair bd. Canton Sr. Citizen's Ctr.; mem. Haywood County Ease Retirement Com.; pres., chairwoman bd. Haywood County Assn. Retarded Citizens; bd. dirs. W.N.C. Womens Coalition, 1999, pres. N.C. [illegible] Alzheimer's Disease and Related Disorders Assn.; bd. dirs. Canton Recreation Dept., Western N.C. Alzheimer's Disease and Related Disorders Assn., 1987-91, v.p., C.B; bd. dirs. Haywood Literary Coun., Haywood Sr. Leadership Coun., Haywood County Block Grant Com., W.N.C. Econ. Devel. Com., United Way, 1991—, drive chmn.; mem. legis. subcom. Alzheimer's-State of N.C.; bd. dirs. N.C. Conf. for Social Svcs., 1987-91; v.p. bd. Western N.C. Alzheimer's Assn., 1987-91; pres. State Coun. on Alzheimer's; apptd. mem. Legis. Study Com. on Alzheimer's; apptd. mem. State of N.C. Adv. Bd. on Community Care and Health; mem. Habitat for Humanity Haywood County; bd. chair Pigeon Valley Optimist Club; apptd. by Senate Western N.C. Econ. Devel. Commn.; appointee Haywood County Econ. Devel. Commn., Canton Hist. Commn.; judge U.S. Olympic Torch Bearers. Recipient Outstanding Svc. award Crime Prevention from Gov., 1982, Gov.'s Spl. Vol. award, 1983, Outstanding Svc. award N.C. Cmty. Watch Assn., 1984, Cmty. Svc. award to Handicapped, 1983-84, Outstanding Svc. award ARC, 1988; named Employer of Yr. for Hiring Handicapped N.C. Assn. for Retarded Citizens, 1985, Cmty. Person of Yr. Kiwanis Club, 1991, Citizen of Yr. in Western N.C., 1995, Rec. Outstanding award Haywood Co. Sr. Games, 1992, Roy A. Taylor award for disting. svc., 1999; inducted into N.C. Softball Hall of Fame, 1997. Mem. AAUW, NAFE, Women's Polit. Caucus (So. Women's Leadership award 1998), Internat. Platform Assn., Women's Forum N.C., Nat. Bd. Alzheimers Assn. (regional del.), Canton Bus. and Profl. Assn. (pres. 1974-79, Woman of Yr. 1984), Altrusa (Woman of Yr. in N.C. 1989). Democrat. Episcopalian. Avocation: softball club. Home: 104 Skyland Ter Canton NC 28716-3718 Office: Dixons Restaurant 30 N Main St Canton NC 28716-3805 E-mail: sjdixon28716@yahoo.com.

DIXON, SHIRLEY LEE, emergency physician; b. NYC, Dec. 10, 1947; d. Henry Ester and Ethel Mae (Samuels) D. BS in Biology, CCNY, 1969; MD, Howard U., 1976; MPH, Columbia U., 1983. Intern Harlem Hosp. Ctr., NYC, 1976-77, resident in internal medicine, 1979-81, attending physician dept. ambulatory care, 1981-83; attending physician La Guardia Med. Group PC, 1983-85; emergency rm. attending Interfaith Med. Ctr., 1985-87; med. dir. Triboro Divsn. US Postal Svc., Flushing, NY, 1986-93, med. officer, 1993-96; attending emergency room VA Hosp., Bronx, 1993-96. Mem. cmty. adv. bd. Harlem Hosp., 1981—83; attending physician night screening clinic Lincoln Hosp., 1989—91. Active People to People Citizen Amb. Program, Spokane, Wash., 1991; mem. People to People Internat. Commd. officer USPHS, 1977-79. Scholar Health Professions scholar; USHPS scholar, Nat. Med. fellow. Fellow: Fgn. Policy Rsch. Assn., Am. Acad. Experts in Traumatic Stress (cert. illness trauma 2001, cert. disability trauma 2001, cert. stress mgmt. 2001, diplomate), Am. Bd. Forensic Examiners (life; diplomate); mem.: APHA, Assn. Clinicians for Underserved (charter), Am. Profl. Practice Assn. (life), Am. Bd. Disability Analysts (life; diplomate, sr. analyst), NY Acad. Sci. Home: 752 West End Ave New York NY 10025-6230 Personal E-mail: vze34pbn@msn.com.

DIXON, TAMECKA, professional basketball player; b. Dec. 14, 1975; Grad., Kans. State U., 1997. Basketball player Los Angeles Sparks Women's NBA, Inglewood, Calif., 1997—. Mem. Olympic Festival Team South, 1995. Avocations: dance, shopping. Office: Los Angeles Sparks Gt Western Forum 3900 W Manchester Blvd Inglewood CA 90305-2200

DIXSON, J. B. communications executive; b. Norwich, N.Y., Oct. 19, 1941; d. William Joseph and Ann Wanda (Teale) Barrett. BS, Syracuse U., 1963; postgrad. in bus. adminstrn., Wayne State U., 1979-81; MBA, Ctrl. Mich. U., 1984. Pub. rels. edit. asst. Am. Mus. Natural History, N.Y.C., 1963-64; writer, prodr. Norman, Navan, Moore & Baird Advt., Grand Rapids, Mich., 1964-67; prin. J.B. Dixson Comm. Cons., Detroit, 1967-74; dir. Pub. Info. Svcs. divsn. Mich. Employment Security Commn., Detroit, 1974-82; news rels. mgr. Burroughs Corp., 1982-83, dir. creative svcs., 1983-85, dir. pub. rels., 1985-86; prin. Dixson Comm., Detroit, 1986-93, Durocher Dixson Werba, LLC, Detroit, 1994—. Lectr., spkr. in field at colls, univs., cmty. orgns. Author: Guidelines for Non-Sexist Verbal and Written Communication, 1976, Sexual Harassment on The Job, 1979, The TV Interview: Good News or Bad?, 1981. Mem. Detroit Mayor's Transition Com. of 100, 1972; mem. bd. mgmt. Detroit YWCA, 1974; chmn. Detroit Women's Equality Day Com., 1975; bd. dirs., founding mem. Feminist Fed. Credit Union, Detroit, 1976; centennial chair Indian Village Assn., 1993-95; founding mem. Mich. Women's Campaign Fund, 1980; active Mich. Task Force on Sexual Harassment in Workplace, Mich. Women's Com. of 100, Mich. Women's Polit. Caucus, Mich. Women's Found. Named Outstanding Sr. Woman in Radio and TV, Syracuse U., 1963; recipient Five Watch award Am. Women in Radio and TV, Mich., 1969, 75, Outstanding Women in Comm. Women's Advt. Club, 1998, cert. of recognition Detroit City Coun., 1976, Feminist of Yr. award NOW, 1977, City of Detroit Human Rights Commn., 1988, Design in Mich. award Mich. Coun. of Arts/Gov. William G. Milliken, 1977, Achievement award U.S. Dept. Labor, 1979, Spirit of Detroit award Detroit City Coun., 1980, PR Casebook, 1983, PR News Case Study, 1986, Pinnacle award Mich. Hosp. Pub. Rels. Assn., 1987, award Nat. Sch. Pub. Rels. Assn., 1992, 21st Century award Corp. Detroit Mag., 1995, Creativity in Advt. award Detroit Newspapers Assn., 2000; subject of Mich. Senate Resolution 412, 1979. Fellow Pub. Rels. Soc. Am. (accredited, pres. chpt. 1983-84, Dist. award and citation 1984, 86, 87, 93, exec. com. corp. sect. 1996-2001, Disting. Svc. award 1999), Internat. Assn. Bus. Communicators (Silver Quill award chpt. 1987, 88, 91, 93, dist. 1987, Renaissance award 1988, 91, Mercury award 1987), Nat. Assn. Govt. Communicators (Blue Pencil award 1977, Gold Screen award 1980), Automotive Press Assn., Women's Advt. Club (Top 75 Women in Comm. 1999), Econ. Club Detroit, Maple Grove Gun Club, Detroit Athletic Club. Office: Durocher Dixson Werba LLC 16th Fl Buhl Bldg 535 Griswold St Detroit MI 48226-3604 E-mail: dixson@ddwpr.com.

DLOTT, SUSAN JUDY, judge, lawyer; b. Dayton, Ohio, Sept. 11, 1949; d. Herman and Mildred (Zemboch) D.; m. Austin E. Knowlton, July 11, 1986 (div. 1988); m. Stanley M. Chesley, Dec. 7, 1991. BA, U. Pa., 1971; JD, Boston U., 1973. Bar: Ohio 1973, U.S. Dist. Ct. (so. dist.) Ohio 1975, U.S. Ct. Appeals (6th cir.) 1976, U.S. Supreme Ct. 1980, U.S. Dist. Ct. (ea. dist.) Ky. 1984, U.S. dist. Ct. (no. dist.) Ohio 1989, Ky. 1990. Law clk. Ohio Ct. of Appeals, Cleve., 1973-74; asst. U.S. atty. U.S. Dist. Ct. (so. dist.) Ohio, Dayton, 1975-79; ptnr. Graydon, Head & Ritchey, Cin., 1979-95; dist. judge U.S. Dist. Ct. for So. Dist. Ohio, Cin., 1995— Legal reporter Multimedia Program Prodn., Inc., 1982-84. Mem. Ohio Bldg. Authority, 1988-93, vice chmn., 1990-93, Jewish Fedn. Cin., trustee and mem. com. 1979-93, Jewish Cmty. Rels. Coun. Cin., 1980-90, Hamilton County Park Dist. Vol. in Parks, 1985-86; mem. Dress for Success Bd., Fine Arts Fund Bd. Recipient U.S. Postal Serv. Commendation, 1977, Service award Dayton Bar Assn., 1975-76. Mem. ABA, FBA (asst. treas. 1981-82, treas. 1982-83, sec. 1983-84, v.p. 1984-86), Ohio Bar Assn., Ky. Bar Assn., Dayton Bar Assn., Dayton Women's Bar Assn., Cin. Bar Assn., Leadership Cin. Alumni Assn., Queen City Dog Tng. Club, 6th Cir. Jud. Conf. (life), NAACP (life), Hadassah (life). Jewish. Office: 100 E 5th St Cincinnati OH 45202-3927

DLUGOSZEWSKI, LUCIA, artistic director; b. Detroit, June 16, 1934; Student, Wayne State U.; studied with, Carl Beutel, Edward Bredshall, Ktja Andy, Grete Sultan, Felix Salzer, Edgard Varese. Composer: (structure for the Poetry) Everyday Sound, 1949, Archaic Timbre Piano Music, 1958, Space Is a Diamond, 1970, Tender Theatre Flight Nageire, Densities, Nova, Corona, Clear Core, Amos Elusive Empty August, Strange Tenderness of naked Leaping, (commd. by Mikhail Baryshnikov), Disparate Stairway Radical other Quartet, 1994, Radical Quidditas Dew Tear Duende; artist dir. Erik Hawkins Dance Co., 1998—; recording artists: various labels. Named Musician of Yr. Musical Am., Village Voice, 1975; recipient Recipient Koussevitzky Internat. Recording award, 1979, Phoebe Kechum Thorne award, others; Guggenheim fellow. Office: Erick Hawkins Sch Dance PO Box 1117 New York NY 10013-0866

DLUHY, DEBORAH HAIGH, college dean; b. Summit, NJ, Mar. 4, 1940; d. Richard Hartman Haigh and Elin Frederika Anderson Neumann; m. Robert George Dluhy, June 11, 1962; 1 child, Leonore Alexandra. BA, Wheaton Coll., 1962; postgrad., Boston U., 1962—63, U. Heidelberg, Germany, 1963—65; PhD, Harvard U., 1976. Instr. fine arts Wheaton Coll., Norton, Mass., 1975—76, Radcliffe Coll., Cambridge, Mass., 1977, Boston Coll., Newton, Mass., 1976—78; devel. officer Mus. Fine Arts, Boston, 1978—84, asst. dir. devel., 1984—86; assoc. dean adminstrn. Sch. Mus. Fine Arts, Boston, 1986—87, dean acad. programs and adminstrn., 1987—93, dean, 1993—; dep. dir. Mus. Fine Arts, Boston, 1999—. Trustee Cultural Edn. Collaborative Boston, 1987—90, Wheaton Coll., Norton, Mass., 1988—; pres. Wheaton Coll. Alumni Assn., Norton, Mass., 1994—2000; visitor Walnut Hill Sch., Natick, Mass., 1996—; pres. Pro Arts Consortium, 1999—2000; exec. com., chair faculty and staff com., governance bd. affairs Wheaton Coll., Norton, Mass.; bd. dirs. Boston Arts Acad., 1999—. Woodrow Wilson fellow, 1963. Mem.: Assn. Ind. Coll. Art and Design (program com. 1995—2001, bd. dirs., exec. com., chair), Copley Soc. Boston (hon. trustee 1997—), Nat. Assn. Schs. Art and Design (rsch. com. 1990—96, evaluator 1996—, bd. dirs. 1996—, sec. bd. dirs. 2001—, exec. com. 2001—). Home: 104 Fletcher Rd Belmont MA 02478-2018 Office: Sch Mus of Fine Arts 230 Fenway Boston MA 02115-5534 Office Phone: 617-369-3611. E-mail: ddluhy@mfa.org, ddluhy@earthlink.net.

DOAN, MARY FRANCES, advertising executive; b. Vallejo, Calif., Apr. 16, 1954; d. Larry E. and Dudley (Harbison) D.; m. Timothy Warren Hesselgren, Mar. 19, 1988; children: Edward Latimer, Clinton Robert. BA in Linguistics, U. Calif., Berkeley, 1976; M in Internat. Mgmt., Am. Grad. Sch. Internat. Mgmt., 1980. Trading asst. The Capital Group, L.A., 1980-81; fin. analyst Litton Industries, Beverly Hills, 1981-82; account exec. Grey Advt., San Francisco, L.A., 1982-84, J. Walter Thompson, San Francisco, 1984-85, Lowe Marshalk, 1985-86; account supr. Young & Rubicam, 1986-89; acct. mgr. Saatchi & Saatchi, 1989—95, CEO, pres., 1995—96, worldwide dir. client svc. applications, 1997—98; cons., 1999; v.p. mktg. Roundl, San Francisco, 1999-2000; cons., 2001—02; dir. advt. Good Guys, Alameda, Calif., 2002—03, v.p. mktg. and advt., 2003—. E-mail: mfdoan@hotmail.com.

DOANE, EILEEN MALONEY, learning disabilities teacher consultant; b. Welcome, Md., Dec. 5, 1933; d. John Laurence and Lillian Marion (Posey) Maloney; m. Allan Hammond Doane, June 12, 1954; children: Kathleen, Sharon, Elizabeth. BA in Speech Arts, George Washington U., 1955; MA in Edn., Seton Hall U., 1983; postgrad. studies Learning Disabilities, Kean Coll., 1987; PhD, Berne U., 2002. Cert. tchr. of handicapped, speech correction, prin., supr., learning cons., N.J. Mem. child study team Elizabeth (N.J.) Bd. Edn. Spl. Svcs., 1990-95; learning disability tchr. cons., instrnl. supr. Matheny Sch. and Hosp., Peapack, N.J., 1995—; owner, dir. Randolph Denville Ednl. Ctr., Denville. Mem. Outreach Com. St. Peter's Episcopal Ch., Mountain Lakes, N.J., adult edn. com. Mountain Lakes. Recipient cert. appreciation Vol. Action Ctr., Morristown, NJ, Mental Health Players, Morris County Mental Health Assn., Madison, N.J., 1987, Benefactor award Rotary Found., Evanston, Ill., 1995; named Paul Harris fellow Rotary Found., 1984. Mem. AAUW, N.J. Assn. Learning Cons., Coun. Exceptional Children, Kappa Delta Pi. Democrat. Avocations: bridge, reading, travel. Home: 38 Cobb Rd Mountain Lakes NJ 07046-1143 Office Phone: 973-328-8088.

DOBB, LINDA SUE, university official, librarian; b. Reading, Pa., Aug. 6, 1952; d. Rhea Beverly Blachman; m. Arthur Michael Small, Aug. 14, 1985; 1 child, Lorelei Small. AB, U. Calif., Berkeley, 1973; MLS, Simmons Coll., 1974; JD, Hastings Coll., 1983. Cataloging libr., instr. libr. sci. City Coll. San Francisco, 1974-83; processing libr. Libr. Congress, Washington, 1984-85; chief bibliographic control sect. Govt. Printing Office, Washington, 1985-87; asst. univ. libr. San Francisco State U., 1990-95; dean librs. Bowling Green (Ohio) State U., 1995-99, exec. v.p., 2000—. Fellow Coro Found-City Focus Program, San Francisco, 1993-94; adv. bd. Kent (Ohio) State Sch. Libr. and Info. Sci., 1997—; reviewer NSF and Inst. for Mus. and Libr. Svcs., Washington, 1998-2000. Bd. dirs. Calif. Libr. Authority for Sys. and Svcs., San Jose, Calif., 1990-95, OhioNet, Columbus, 1996-2000,

Horizon Youth Theatre, Bowling Green, 1999-2001. Mem. ALA, AFTRA, Libr. Adminstrn. and Mgmt. Assn. (v.p./pres.-elect 2001—), Kiwanis. Avocation: acting. Office: Bowling Green State U McFAll Ctr 220 Bowling Green OH 43403 Home: PO Box 743 Bowling Green OH 43402-0743 Fax: 419-372-7723. E-mail: ldobb@bgnet.bgsu.edu., bgsulib@wcnet.org.

DOBBS, YVETTE MARIE, director; d. Gary Leon and Mary Lee Dobbs; m. Thomas Anthony Lowe, June 19, 1999. BA, Dillard U., New Orleans, 1988; MS, Concordia U., Mequon, Wis., 1999. Student svcs. specialist U. Wis., Milw., 1990—95; program dir. Social Devel. Commn., Milw., 1995—97; head start dir. Urban Day Sch., Milw., 1997—99, early childhood dir., 1999—. Mem. Leaves of Learning, Milw., 1995—2003; cons. vol. Non-Profit Ctr. of Greater Milw., Milw., 1996—99; mem. early care and edn. adv. bd. Milw. Area Tech. Coll., Milw., 1998—2003; founding dir. Gary Dobbs Family Resource Ctr., Milw., 2001—03. Named one of Americorps Tomorrow Leaders Today, Pub. Allies, 1995; fellow Head Start Mgmt., U. Calif. at L.A., 2000. Mem.: Nat. Head Start Assn. (assoc.), Nat. Assn. for the Edn. of the Young Child (assoc.), Nat. Black Child Devel. (assoc.). Baptist. Avocations: travel, scrapbooks. Office: Urban Day School 3774 North 12th St Milwaukee WI 53205

DOBERSTEIN, AUDREY K. college president; b. June 12, 1932; m. Stephen C. Doberstein; children: Carole, Stephen, Anne, Curt. BS, East Stroudsburg State Coll., 1953; M.Ed., U. Del., 1957; Ed.D., U. Pa., 1982. Exec. dir. Title I ESEA, Del. Dept. Public Instrn., 1965-69; pres. Ednl. Research and Services, Inc., 1969-79; asso. prof. Cheyney State Coll., 1969-79; pres. Wilmington Coll., New Castle, Del., 1979—. Bd. dirs. Blue Cross Blue Shield Del., Mellon Bank, Conectiv, Inc. Mem. NEA, Am. Assn. Higher Edn., AAUW, Phi Delta Kappa. Office: Wilmington Coll Office of the President 320 Dupont Hwy New Castle DE 19720

DOBIS, JOAN PAULINE, education administrator; b. S.I., N.Y., Sept. 11, 1944; d. Victor Raymond and Rosanna Elizabeth (Dandignac) Mazza; m. Robert Joseph Dobis, Dec. 21, 1968. BA in History, Notre Dame Coll., S.I., 1966; MS in Advanced Secondary Edn. and Social Studies, Wagner Coll., 1968; profl. diploma in ednl. adminstrn. supervision, Fordham U., 1979, postgrad. Cert. adminstr. and supr. K-12, social studies and math. tchr. K-12, elem., intermediate and jr. high sch. asst. prin., elem., intermediate and junior high sch. prin., N.Y. Tchr. Prall Intermediate Sch., Staten Island, 1966-98, administrv. asst., 1977-82; coord. social studies Dist. 31, Staten Island, NY, 1998—2003; ret., 2003. Mem. S.I. Hist. Soc., 1968-, Friends of Down's Syndrome Found., S.I., 1978—, Sister Helen Flynn Scholarship Com., S.I., 1981—, Friends Seaview Hosp. and Home, S.I., 1984—, Friends S.I. Coll., 1979—, Friends Staten Isl. Greenbelt, 1995-, Friends Staten Isl. Botanical Garens, 1995-; adv. bd. Staten Isl. Advance NIE, 1998-. Recipient St. John's U. Pietas medal, 1991; scholar N.Y. State Bd. Regents, 1962, Can. Consulate St. Lawrence U., 1987, Internat. Brotherhood Teamsters U. Calif., 1988, Nat. Geog. Soc. Geography Edn. Program SUNY, Binghamton, 1989, Women in History Program, N.Y. State Coun. for the Humanities, Albany, 1992, Immigration Program, Bard Coll., 1999; Impact II grantee N.Y.C. Bd. Edn., 1992, 98. Mem. ASCD, Nat. Coun. Social Studies, N.Y. State Coun. Social Studies, N.Y.C. Coun. Social Studies, S.I. Coun. Social Studies, United Fedn. Tchrs., Am. Fedn. Tchrs., N.Y. State Hist. Soc., Notre Dame Coll. Alumnae Assn. (regent 1978-80, pres. 1982-84), St. John's U. Alumni Fedn. (del. 1980-88, sec. exec. bd. 1988-90, chmn. bd. 1990-94), Phi Delta Kappa (co-founder S.I. chpt., pres. 1985-87, other offices, Tchr. of Yr. award Fordham U. 1993, named Disting. Kappan 1994, Tchr. of Yr. award S.I. chpt. 1998, Kappan of Decade, 1999). Republican. Roman Catholic. Home: 174 Bertha Pl Staten Island NY 10301-3807

DOBLER, JANIS DOLORES, small business owner; b. Dearborn, Mich., June 7, 1946; d. Ralph Orville and DeLoris (Frederick) Yager; m. Gordon John Dobler, June 24, 1977; children Curtis John, Kristin Marie. BS, Wayne State U., 1966. Cert. tchr., Mich. Owner, mgr. Mark Travel, Portage, Mich., 1982—. Grad. asst. Dale Carnegie, Kalamazoo, 1982-84. Bd. dirs. Davenport Coll., Kalamazoo, 1985-87. Named tchr. yr. State of Mich, 1965. Mem. Assn. Retail Travel Agts., Airlines Reporting Corp., Internat. Assn. Travel Agts., Cruise Lines Internat. Assn., Travel Savers, Portage C. of C., Nat. Fedn. Indt. Bus., Better Bus. Bur., Jr. Achievement (bd. dirs. 1985-87). Republican. Roman Catholic. Avocations: knitting, reading, watersports, travel, genealogy. Office: The Mark of Travel 1595 West Center Suite 105 Portage MI 49024-5375

DOBRIANSKY, PAULA JON, federal agency administrator; b. Sept. 14; d. Lev Eugene and Julia Kusy Dobriansky. BS summa cum laude, Georgetown U., 1977; MA, Harvard U., 1980, PhD, 1991; LHD (hon.), Fairleigh Dickinson U., 2002; LLD (hon.), Flagler Coll., 2003. Adminstrv. aide Dept. Army, Washington, 1973-76; staff asst. Am. Embassy, Rome, 1976; rsch. asst. joint econ. com. U.S. Congress, Washington, 1977-78; NATO analyst Bur. Intelligence and Rsch. Dept. State, Washington, 1979; staff mem. NSC, White House, Washington, 1980-83, dep. dir. European and Soviet affairs, 1983-84, dir. European and Soviet affairs, 1984-87; dep. asst. sec. of state Human Rights and Humanitarian Affairs, 1987-90; dep. head U.S. Del. to Conf. on Security and Cooperation in Europe, Copenhagen, 1990; assoc. dir. for policy and programs U.S. Info. Agy., 1990-93; co-chair internat. TV coun. Corp. Pub. Broadcasting, 1993-94; sr. internat. affairs and trade advisor Hunton and Williams, Washington, 1994-97; sr. v.p., dir. Washington Office Coun. on Fgn. Rels., 1997—2001; under sec. of state for global affairs U.S. State Dept., Washington, 2001—. Commr. U.S. Adv. Commn. on Pub. Diplomacy, 1997-2001; adj. fellow Hudson Inst., 1993-2001. Host: Freedom's Challenge, Nat. Empowerment Television, 1994-96; co-host: Worldwise, 1997. Bd. dirs. Congl. Human Rights Found., 1994-95, Freedom House, 1999-2001, Western NIS Enterprise Fund, 1994-2001, Am. Com. for Aid to Poland, 1994-95, ABA Ctrl./East European Law Initiative, 1994-99; mem. bd. visitors George Mason U., 1994-98; mem. adv. bd. Horton Internat. Inc., 1998-99. Named Ethnic Woman of Yr., 1990; named one of 10 Most Outstanding Young Women in Am., 1982, 10 Outstanding Working Women of 1990; recipient Georgetown U. Alumni Achievement award, 1986, State Dept. Superior Honor award, 1990, Poland's Highest medal of Merit, 1998, Democracy Svc. medal, Nat. Endowment Democracy, 2002, Dialogue on Diversity Internat. award, 2001, Grand Cross of Comdr., Order of Lithuanian Grand Duke Gediminas, 2003; fellow, Rotary Found., 1979, Ford Found., 1980; scholar Fulbright-Hays scholar, 1978. Mem. Internat. Inst. Strategic Studies, Coun. Fgn. Rels., Am. Polit. Sci. Assn., Fulbright Assn., Nat. Endowment for Democracy (bd. dirs. 1993-2001, vice-chmn. 1995-2001), Am. Coun. on Young Polit. Leaders (trustee 1993-2001), U.S. Environ. Tng. Inst. (bd. adv. 1992-93), Harvard Club (bd. dirs. 1982-85), Univ. Club, Phi Beta Kappa, Phi Alpha Theta, Pi Sigma Alpha. Office: US State Dept Washington DC 20520

DOBRINSKY, SUSAN ELIZABETH, human resources director; b. Warren, N.J., Sept. 25, 1943; d. Samuel Henry Jr. and Janet Adeline (Ryder) Christie; m. Stanley Dobrinsky, Feb. 12, 1972; children: David Stanley, Mark Alan. BA, Lycoming Coll., 1965. Cert. for Sr. Execs., John F. Kennedy Sch. of Govt. of Harvard U., 1994, PHR Cert. by SHRM, Profl. in Human Resources, 1997—. Pers. asst. County of Somerset, Somerville, N.J., 1970-74, pers. mgr., 1974-82, pers. dir., 1982-90, dir. adminstrn., 1991-95, dir. human resources, 1995—. Gov. apptd. Pub. Employees Occupl. Safety and Health Adv. Bd., Dept. of Labor, Trenton, N.J., 1984—; bd. trustees, treas. N.J. Pub. Employer Labor Rels. Assn., Somerville, N.J., 1993—; mem. Soc. Human Resource Mgmt. Cen. Jersey, Somerset, 1978—; pres. Cmty. Indsl. Rels. Orgn., Somerset, 1990-92; apptd. senate pres., mem. Pension Commn., Trenton, 1992-2001. Mem., dep. mayor Green Brook Twp. Commn., 1987-88, mayor, 1989-92; v.p. Somerset County Governing Offcls., 1990, pres., 1991; mem. Somerset County Mcpl. Com., 1999-01, 2002—; sec. Rep. Club, Green Brook, 1977; mem. staff parish com. Meth. Ch. Recipient N.J. Alumni award 4-H Youth Devel. Program, 1992. Mem. Nat. Pub. Employer's Labor Rels. Assn., N.J. Pub. Employer Labor Rels. Assn. (bd. trustees, treas. 1993—), Soc. Human Resource Mgmt. Ctrl. N.J. Soc. Human R[illegible] Personnel Mgmt. Assn., N.J. Pension and Health Commn., Cmty. Indsl. Rels. Orgn. (treas. 1988-90, pres. 1990-92), Pub. Pers. Orgn. (pres. 1990-2000), DAR (Elizabeth Snyder chpt. regent 1998-99, 2001-2003). Republican. Methodist. Avocations: skiing, genealogy, reading, crafts. Home: 11 Glenn Ave Green Brook NJ 08812-2431 Office: County of Somerset 20 Grove St Somerville NJ 08876-2306

DOBRZYNSKI, JUDITH HELEN, journalist, commentator; b. Rochester, N.Y., Mar. 8, 1949; d. Francis Anthony and Theresa (Contino) Dobrzynski. BS cum laude, Syracuse U., 1971. Corr. McGraw-Hill, San Francisco and N.Y.C., 1971—75, Bus. Week, Washington, 1976—79, London, 1979—83, corp. strategies editor, assoc. editor N.Y.C., 1983—88, sr. writer, 1988—91, sr. editor, 1991—94; bus. reporter N.Y. Times, N.Y.C., 1995—97, culture reporter, 1997—2000, dep. bus. editor and editor Sunday Money and Bus. sect., 2000—03; mng. editor CNBC, Englewood Cliffs, NJ, 2003—. Adj. instr. Columbia U. Sch. Journalism, 2002; mem. New Founds. Corp. Governance Group Harvard U., Boston, 1992—95; adv. panel Corp. Investment Project U.S. Coun. on Competitiveness, Washington, 1990—92. Contbr. articles to profl. jours. and book revs. Trustee CEC Internat. Ptnrs., N.Y.C., 1993—96; bd. dirs. City Lights Youth Theatre, N.Y.C., 1994—96. Named Knight Found. fellow, Salzburg Seminar, 2002; recipient Nat. Headliner award, First Place, Bus. & Consumer Reporting, 2004. Mem.: Syracuse U. Newhouse Sch. Alumni Assn. (bd. dirs. 1991—94, pres. 1992—93), Century Assn. Office: CNBC 900 Sylvan Ave Englewood Cliffs NJ 07632

DOBSON, BRIDGET MCCOLL HURSLEY, television executive, writer; b. Milw., Sept. 1, 1938; d. Franklin McColl and Doris (Berger) Hursley; m. Jerome John Dobson, June 16, 1961; children: Mary McColl, Andrew Carmichael. BA, Stanford U., 1960, MA, 1964; CBA, Harvard U., 1961. Assoc. writer General Hospital ABC-TV, 1965-73, head writer General Hospital, 1973-75; producer Friendly Road Sta. KIXE-TV, Redding, Calif., 1972; head writer Guiding Light CBS-TV, 1975-80, head writer As the World Turns, 1980-83; creator, co-owner Santa Barbara NBC-TV, 1983—, head writer Santa Barbara, 1983-86, 91, exec. producer Santa Barbara, 1986-87, 91, creative prodn. exec. Santa Barbara, 1990-91; pres. Dobson Global Entertainment, L.A., 1994—. Bd. dirs. Emory U. Carlos Mus.; bd. advisors Atlanta Internat. Sch., 1997-2000. Author, co-lyricist: Slings and Eros, 1993; prodr. Confessions of a Nightingale, 1994; exhibited in gallery show acrylic paintings Swan Coach House, Atlanta, 1997, exhibited oil paintings Raymond Lawrence Gallery, Atlanta, 1999, Fay Gold Gallery, Atlanta, 1999, Tippy Stern Fine Art, Charleston, S.C., 2002; one-woman shows include Mus. S.W., Midland, Tex., 2001, Midwest Mus. Am. Art, Elkhart, Ind., 2001, Charles Allis Art Mus., Milw., 2001, Albrecht-Kemper Mus. Art, St. Joseph, Mo., 2001, Walter Wickiser Gallery, N.Y.C., 2001, Danville (Va.) Mus. Fine Art, 2002, Burroughs-Chapin Art Mus., Myrtle Beach, S.C., 2002, Tippy Stern Fine Art, 2002, Anderson (Ind.) Fine Art Ctr., 2002, Ella Sharp Mus., Jackson, Miss., 2002. Bd. dirs. Carlos Mus., 1998-2001. Walter Wickiser Gallery, N.Y.C., 2003. Recipient Emmy award, 1988. Mem. Nat. Acad. TV Arts and Scis. (com. on substance abuse 1986-88), Writers Guild Am. (award for Guiding Light 1977, for Santa Barbara 1991), Am. Film Inst. (mem. TV com. 1986-88). Office: PO Box 52813 Atlanta GA 30355-0813

DOBSON, DOROTHY LYNN WATTS, elementary school educator; b. Santa Monica, Calif., Nov. 29, 1954; d. Seymour Locke and Margaret (Cheeseman) Watts; m. J. Cody Dobson, June 5, 1982; children: Jeremiah, Hannah. BS, Utah State U., 1975; MEd, U. Utah, 1982. Cert. tchr. intellectually handicapped and behaviorally handicapped, elem., Utah. Tchr. San Juan Sch. Dit., Blanding, Utah, 1974-76; behavioral specialist Salt Lake Sch. Dist., Salt Lake City, 1976-77; tchr. Granite Sch. Dist., Salt Lake City, 1977-82; instr. Utah State U., Logan, 1987—; tchr. Edith Bowen Lab. Sch., Logan, 1982—. Team coord. First Amendment Schs., Bowen Lab. Sch., Logan, 2002—. Author: Utilizing Newspapers in Social Studies, Math. and Science and Language Arts, 1983; also articles. Mem. Nat. Coun. for Social Studies (bd. dirs. 1996-99, Nat. Elem. Tchr. of Yr. 1992, State Farm Good Neighbor award 1993), Utah Coun. for Social Studies (State Elem. Tchr. of Yr. 1991), Nat. Assn. Lab. Schs. Episcopalian. Office: Edith Bowen Sch Utah State U Logan UT 84322-0001

DOBSON, JANET LOUISE, writer; b. Columbus, Ohio, Aug. 10, 1951; d. Vernon Richard and Betty Jean (Hames) Schmitt; m. John William Dobson, Dec. 22, 1973; children: Evan Michael, Colin Richard. BA in Music with high distinction, U. Mich., 1973; postgrad., Ohio State U., 1975-77; MD, Med. Coll. of Ohio, 1980. Diplomate Am. Bd. Pathology. Pathology resident Mercy Hosp., Toledo, 1980-84; pathology fellow Ohio State U., Columbus, 1984-85, rschr., flow cytometry, 1985-86; in-house med. cons. Porter, Wright, Morris & Arthur Attys., Columbus, 1987-92; medicolegal cons., freelance Springfield, Ohio, 1992—; med. writer, 1995—. Author: (biography) Rolf Armstrong-Giant of American Glamour Art, 1997, (novels) Pin-Up Dreams-The Glamour Art of Rolf Armstong, 2001. Trustee Planned Parenthood of the Greater Miami Valley, Dayton, Ohio, 1995-00; mem. Springfield Mus. of Art, 1989—, Nature Conservancy, Columbus, 1991—. Fellow Coll. of Am. Pathologists; mem. Am. Soc. Clin. Pathologists, Western Ohio Watercolor Soc. (Best of Show award 1995, Hon. Mention 1997). Avocations: painting, gardening, antiques. Office: 2330 E High St Springfield OH 45505-1322

DOBSON, PARRISH, photographer, educator; d. Peyton Hoge and Parrish Cummings Houston; m. Eugene Hillhouse Pool, May 9, 1943; 1 child, Miranda Parrish Pool. BA, Yale U., 1971; MA, Brandeis U., Waltham, Mass., 1980. Dir. careers for girls W.I.S.E., Hanover, NH, 1973—75; dir. women's studies programs Colby-Sawyer Coll., New London, NH, 1975—78; English tchr. Philips Acad., Andover, Mass., 1980—84; photograhy tchr. Buckingham, Browne and Nichols Sch., Cambridge, 1986—. Bd. mem. Kendall Ctr. for Arts, Belmont, Mass., 1996—99; steering com. North Haven (Maine) Arts and Enrichment, 1999—; chair arts dept. Buckingham, Browne and Nichols Sch., Cambridge, 2001—. Exhibitions include The Gallery at 357 Main St., Rockland, Maine, 2003. Grantee Kenan grant, Philips Acad., 1983, Artist grant, Mass. Cultural Coun., 1998. Mem.: New Eng. Women in Photography Steering Com., St. Batolph Club (artist assoc. hon. mem.). Avocations: travel, walking, gardening. Home: 263 Payson Rd Belmont MA 02478 Office: Buckingham Browne and Nichols Sch Gerry's Landing Rd Cambridge MA 02138 Studio: 4 Bradley St Somerville MA Office Phone: 617-800-2291.

DOBSON, WENDY KATHLEEN, economics educator; BSN, U. B.C., 1963; MPA, Harvard U., 1971, SM, 1972; PhD in Econs., Princeton U., 1979. Pres. C.D. Howe Inst., Toronto, 1981-87; assoc. dep. minister Dept. Fin., Govt. of Can., Ottawa, Ont., 1987-89; prof., dir. Inst. for Internat. Bus. Rotman Sch. Mgmt., U. Toronto, 1993—. Bd. dirs. Toronto-Dominion Bank, TransCan. Pipelines, MDS Inc., Can. Pub. Accountability Bd.; steering com. Pacific Trade Devel. Network; adv. com. Inst. Internat. Econs., Washington; mem. Trilateral Commn. Author: Shaping the Future of North American Economic Space: A Framework for Action, 2002, Japan in East Asia: Trade and Investment Strategies, 1993, Multinationals and East Asian Integration, 1997 (Ohira prize 1998), Financial Services Liberalization in the WTO, 1998, (chpts.) Bretton Woods: Looking to the Future, 1994, A Part of the Peace, 1994, Trade Technology and Economics: Essays in Honour of Richard G. Lipsey, 1997, Fifty Years After Bretton Woods: The Future of the IMF and the World Bank, 1995, The Growing Importance of the Asia Pacific Region in the World Economy: Implications for Canada, 1997, Trade Technology and Economics, 1997, Whither APEC?, 1997, Prisoners of the Past: Canada's Policy Framework for the Financial Services Sector, 1999; co-editor: Shaping Comparative Advantage, 1987, East Asian Capitalism: Diversity and Dynamism, 1996, Managing U.S.-Japanese Trade Disputes, 1996, The People Link, 1997, Fiscal Framework and Financial Systems in East Asia, 1998, East Asia in Transition, 1999; contbr. articles to profl. jours. Office: Rotman Sch Mgmt U Toronto 105 St George St Toronto ON M5S 3E6 Canada Business E-Mail: dobson@rotman.utoronto.ca.

DOCKERY, PAULA, state legislator; b. Queens, N.Y., June 6, 1961; BA in Polit. Sci., U. Fla., 1983, MA in Mass Comm., 1987. V.p. Dockery Mgmt.; mem. Fla. Ho. of Reps., Tallahassee, 1996—; mem. acad. excellence, econ. impact, justice couns.; mem. select com. ednl. facilities. Vice chmn. Polk Coutny Edn. Found., Lakeland Family YMCA; bd. dirs. Found. Fla. Future, City of Lakeland Pension Bd.; dir. Polk County Family Caregivers Inc.; chmn. City of Lakeland Civil Svc. Bd. Mem. Pi Rho Sigma, Leadership Lakeland, Leadership Ctrl. Fla., Lakeland C. of C. (bd. dirs.), Jr. League. Roman Catholic. Avocations: fishing, hiking, traveling, volleyball. Office: Fla Capitol 402 S Monroe St Rm 1201 Tallahassee FL 32399-6526 also: PO Box 2395 Lakeland FL 33806-2395 E-mail: dockery.paula@leg.state.fl.us.

DOCKERY-SCHILLIG, LINDA, writer; b. Louisville, Sept. 23, 1952; d. Willie Dockery and Minnie Cotton; m. Roger Lee Schillig. Freelance consulting tchr., Louisville, 1975—2002; spkr. in field. Author: Distant Drums, 1997 (Can.n Fiction award, 1997), Three Little Words, 2002 (Adcott Publishing award Fiction, 2002), Anna Claus (The Woman Behind the Legend), 2003, Cowgirl UP, 2003, An Angel for Christmas, 2003, North Pole Kitchen, 2003, (screenplays) My Special Angel, 1977, Wilderness Love, 1976 (Lippincott award for most promising new screenplay, 1976), Children of Darkness, 1977, Inherit the Devil, 1978 (Sun Burst award Best Screenplay, 1978), Welcome to Hell, 1978, Rain Softly Till Then, 1984, (TV series) A Time for Love, 1981, (film) Inherit the Devil, 1985, (documentary film) For Our Land, 1991, singer country music. Recipient Faith and Love award Best Christian Short Story, 1980, Golden pen, 1991, Marshal award Poetry, 1992. Mem.: American Film Inst., Ind. Film Inst., Nat. Hist. Soc., Women Writing the West, Women's Writers Guild. Home and Office: 11117 E Old 56 Scottsburg IN 47170 Personal E-mail: dockery002@aol.com.

DOCKSTADER, DEBORAH RUTH, minister; b. Elmira, N.Y., Oct. 12, 1948; d. E. Stanley and Ruth Emery Dockstader. BA, Mercyhurst Coll., 1974; MDiv, Princeton Theol. Sem., 1977. Ordained to ministry Presbyn. Ch., 1977. Pastor Lake Champlain Islands Parish, North Hero, Vt., 1977—79, East Greene Presbyn. Ch., Eric, Pa., 1979—84; dir. edn. St. Stephen's Ch., Fairview, 1984—85; assoc. exec. dir. Inter-Ch. Ministries, Erie, 1985—93; interim pastor Ross Meml. Presbyn. Ch., Binghamton, NY, 1993—96; pastor Southside Presbyn. Ch., Niles, Ohio, 1997—, First Presbyn. Ch., Girard, 1997—. Perm. jud. commn. Eastminster Presbytery, Youngstown, Ohio, 1999—, mem. com. ministry, 2000—; commr. synod assembly Covenant Synod, Columbus, 1997—2001. Bd. dirs. Niles Cmty. Svcs., 1997—2002, WQLN Pub. TV & Radio, Erie, 1987—90. Avocations: reading, birdwatching.

DOCKSTEADER, KAREN KEMP, marketing professional; b. Salisbury, Md., Feb. 11, 1953; d. Robert George and Laverne (Briggs) Kemp; m. Gerald Hugh Docksteader, Apr. 3, 1997; children from previous marriage: Daniel Richard Arrington IV, James William Arrington. BS, Iowa State U., 1975; MEd, Salisbury U., 1979. Dir. horticultural project Chesapeake Rehab. Ctr., Easton, Md., 1975-76; mgr. greenhouses Bountiful Ridge Nurseries, Inc., Princess Anne, Md., 1976-77; instr. horticulture Dorchester Bd. Edn., Cambridge, Md., 1978-80, Fredrick (Md.) Bd. Edn., 1980-87; instr. agronomy Frederick C.C., 1985; treas. Kemp's Ltd., Inc., Martinsburg, W.Va., 1985-87, pres. Frederick, 1987—2001; mgr. U.S. retail sales Kord Products, Ltd., Brampton, 1995-98; sales and mktg. dir. Angelica Nurseries, Inc., Kennedyville, Md., 2001—. Keynote spkr. Vocat. Counseling Orgn., Md., 1980—88; cons. retail and comml. mktg. groups, 1977—91; dir. Russian-Georgian Rose Project, Tblissi, Georgia, 1993. Editor: (newsletter) The Spreader, 1990; featured narrator : (documentaries) Our Land, Our Future, 1980; exhibitor Assn. Nurserymen, Balt. and King of Prussia, Pa., 1986—2003. Coach 4-H, FFA, NJHA, and other youth orgns., 1977—98; state chair Soil Conservation Poster Competition, Md., 1990—91; judge horticulture county fairs, state and nat. 4-H and FFA activities, 1977—91; co-founder Windows of Oppotunity Found., 2000—. Named Conservation Tchr. of the Yr., State Soil and Water Conservation Svc., 1984. Mem.: DAR, Somerset Pa. Hist. Soc., Hackers Creek Hist. Soc., Md. Hist. Soc., New Market Grange, Md. Greenhouse Growers Assn. Avocations: geneaology and historical research, writing, needlepoint, gardening. Office: Kemp's Ltd Inc 26875 Mallard Rd Chestertown MD 21620 Office Phone: 410-810-7072. Personal E-mail: dock5153@earthlink.net. Business E-Mail: kkemp@angelicanurseries.com.

DODD, DARLENE MAE, nurse, retired military officer; b. Dowagiac, Mich., Oct. 11, 1935; d. Charles B. and Lila H. Dodd. Diploma in nursing, Borgess Hosp. Sch. Nursing, Kalamazoo, 1957; grad., USAF Flight Nurse Course, 1959, USAF Squadron Officers Sch., 1963, Air Command and Staff Coll., 1973; BS in Psychology and Gen. Studies, postgrad., So. Oreg. State Coll., 1987. Commd. 2d lt. USAF, 1959, advanced through grades to lt. col., 1975, staff nurse, 1959-60, Ladd AFB, Alaska, 1960-62, Selfridge AFB, Mich., 1962-63, Cam Rahn Bay Air Base, Vietnam, 1966-67, Seymour Johnson AFB, N.C., 1967-69, USAF Acad., Colorado Springs, Colo., 1971-72; flight nurse 22d Aeromed. Evacuation, Tenn., 1963-66; chief nurse USAF, Danang Air Base, Vietnam, 1968, flight nurse Yokota AFB, Japan, 1969-71, clin. coord. ob-gyn., flight nurse Elmendorf AFB, Alaska, 1973-76; clin. nurse coord. ob-gyn. and pediatric svcs. USAF Med. Ctr., Keesler AFB, Miss., 1976-79; ret., 1979; with Bear Creek Corp., Medford, Oreg. Decorated Bronze Star. Mem. DAV, VFW, Am. Legion (life), Soc. Ret. Air Force Nurses, Ret. Officers Assn., Vietnam Vets. Am., Uniformed Svcs. Disabled Retirees, Air Force Assn., Women of Moose, Psi Chi, Phi Kappa Phi. Home: 712 1st St Phoenix OR 97535-9787

DODD, GERALDA, metal products executive; children: T. Edward Sellers III, Madison Dodd Sellers., U. Toledo, Ohio. Receptionist Heidtman Steel, Toledo, 1978-79, various positions, 1979-88, dir. purchasing, 1988; vp HS Processing (subs. Heidtmann Steel), Balt., 1988-90; pres., CEO Thomas Madison Inc., Detroit. Bd. dirs. Detroit Regiional Chamber, Detroit Econ. Growth Corp., Workforce Devel. Music Hall, Nataki Talibath Sch., United Way Cmty. Svcs., Nat. Kidney Found. of Mich. and New Detroit, Inc. Mem. Womens Econ. Club, Nat. Assn. Women Bus. Owners, Nat. Assn. Black Automotive Suppliers, Assn. Women in Metals Industry, Greater Wayne County chpt. of The Links, Inc. Office: Thomas Madison Inc PO Box 20318 Ferndale MI 48220-0318 Fax: 313-273-8052.

DODD, LOIS, artist, art educator; b. Montclair, N.J., Apr. 22, 1927; d. Lawrence Dodd and Margaret Vanderhoff; m. William Dickey King (div.); 1 child, Eli Benjamin. Student, Cooper Union, 1945-48. Tchr. art Bklyn. Coll., 1971-92. One-woman shows include Tanager Gallery, N.Y.C., 1954—62, Green Mountain Gallery, 1969—76, Fischbach Gallery, 1978—2002, Washington (Conn.) Art Assn., 1977, Cape Split Pl., Maine, 1977—83, N.J. State Mus., Trenton, 1981, Lyman Allyn Mus., Conn., 1980, La. State U., Baton Rouge, 1984, Anne Weber Gallery, Maine, 1987, Caldbeck Gallery, 1990, 1995, 1998, 2001—03, Dartmouth (N.H.) Coll., 1990, Rider (N.J.) U., 1993, Montclair Art Mus., 1996, Farnsworth Art Mus., Rockland, Maine, 1996, Trenton City Mus., Alexandre Gallery, 2002—, Bowdoin Coll. Mus., Maine, 2004, Represented in permanent collections Colby Coll. Mus., Cooper Hewitt Mus., Farnsworth Mus.,

Kalamazoo Art Ctr., Montclair Art Mus., NAD, AT&T, Chase Manhattan Bank, Commerce Bancshares Inc., Met. Life Ins. Co., Readers Digest, R.V. Reynolds Security, Pacific Nat. Bank, First Nat. City Bank. Bd. govs. Skowhegan Sch. of Painting and Sculptures, 1980—. Recipient Disting. Alumni citation Cooper Union, 1987; Ingram Merrill Found. grantee, 1971. Mem. NAD, AAAL (award 1986). Home: 30 E 2d St New York NY 10003-8906

DODD, POLLY, nursing educator, recreational therapist; b. Zenda, Wis., Nov. 9, 1918; d. Jacob Polyock and Sarah McNeil; m. Jasper Messmore III, Dec. 17, 1943 (dec. Aug. 1944); 1 child, Jasper Messmore IV; m. Ronald Frank Dodd, June 11, 1955. RN, Mercy Sch. Nursing, Janesville, Wis., 1940; MA in Edn., DePaul U., 1952; MA in Human Devel., U. Chgo., 1972; MA in Dance/Movement Therapy, Columbia U. Chgo., 1990. RN Ga., Wis.; lic. profl. counselor Ga., registered therapist Acad. Dance Therapy. Head nurse, 2d lt. Army Nurse Corps, Orlando, Fla., 1942—44; clin. instr. St. Xavier Coll., Chgo., 1950—52, dir. edn., 1952—66; instr. psychiat. nursing South Suburban Coll., South Holland, Ill., 1966—87; therapist Dance/Movement Charter Peachford Hosp., Atlanta, 1990—93, Emory Eastside Med. Ctr., Snellville, Ga., 1996—. Adjudicator Nat. Dance Coun. Am., 1966—. Pres. Welcome Wagon Atlanta, 1990—91. Mem.: U.S. Terpsichore Assn., Nat. Assn. Dance Therapy, Imperial Soc. Tchrs. Dance, Freedom Alliance, Sigma Theta Tau. Avocations: reading, gardening, dance, travel, calligraphy. Office: Emory Eastside Med Ctr 1700 Medical Way Snellville GA 30078*

DODDS, LINDA CAROL, special education educator; b. Tucson, June 2, 1957; d. George A. and Bette R. (Bell) D. AA, U. Md., 1979; BA, Tex. Tech U., 1982; MBA, Our Lady of the Lake U., 1986, MEd, 2001. Svc. rep. USAA, San Antonio, 1982-84; portfolio asst. USAA-IMCO, San Antonio, 1984-85; sr. rep. USAA, San Antonio, 1985-86, asst. area mgr. Tampa, Fla., 1986-88, area mgr., 1988-92, dist. mgr., 1992-97, San Antonio, 1997-98; reading resource tchr. Boerne (Tex.) Ind. Sch. Dist., 1999—2002, head spl. edn. dept., 2000—02; resource tchr. N.E. Ind. Sch. Dist., San Antonio, 2002—. Treas. Forest Hills Homeowners Assn., Tampa, 1992-93; mem. Tex. Fedn. Rep. Women, San Antonio, 1985; co-chair United Way, 1995-96; active USAA Vol. Corp., Tampa, 1989—. Mem. Soc. CPCU, Delta Mu Delta, Sigma Iota Epsilon. E-mail: doddol@boerne-isd.net

DODERER, MINNETTE FRERICHS, retired state legislator; b. Holland, Iowa, May 16, 1923; d. John A. and Sophie S. Frerichs; m. Fred H. Doderer, Aug. 5, 1944 (dec. 1991); children: Dennis, Kay Lynn. BA, U. Iowa, 1948. Chair standing com. public health Iowa Ho. of Reps., 1965-66, mem., 1964-69, 81-01, minority whip, 1967-68, chairperson ways and means com., 1983-88, chair small bus. and commerce com., 1989-90, chair small bus., econ. devel. and trade com., 1991-92; mem. Iowa Senate, 1968-78, pres. pro tem, 1975-76; ret., 2001. Vis. prof. Stephens Coll., Iowa State Univ. (both 1979); vice-chairwoman Iowa Interstate Cooperation Commn., 1965-66; vice-chairwoman Democratic Party Johnson County, 1957-60; vice chairperson com. on budget and taxation Nat. Conf. State Legislatures, 1989-90; mem. Dem. Nat. Com., 1968-70, Dem. Nat. Policy Council Elected Ofcls., 1973-76; chairwoman Iowa del. Internat. Women's Yr. Del. Bd. fellows Iowa Sch. Religion; Senate activities: chair subcom. Election Law Revision, 1975-76, Legislative Census Liaison Commn., Legislative Interim Study of Juvenile Justice, Senate State Govt. Standing com., 1977-78; vice chair Legislative Coun., mem. Departmental Rules Review com., 1975-76, Interim Study com. on Prison Reform, Child Abuse Coun. Recipient Disting. Legis. Svc. award Iowa State Edn. Assn., 1969, Iowa Fedn. Bus. & Profl. Women's Clubs recognition, 1972, Iowa Civil Liberties award, 1978, Special award Midwest Race and Sex Desegregation Fed. Assistance Ctrs., 1979, Good Citizenship medal Sons of Am. Revolution, Friend of Edn. award Iowa City, 1986, Christine Wilson award for Equality and Justice Commn. on Status of Women, 1989, Gold Seal award Iowa Coalition Against Domestic Violence, 1995, Friend of Nursing award, 1996, citation Am. Acad. Pediat., 1996, Feminist of Yr. award, 1996, Friend of Nursing award, 1996, Woman of Achievement award Bus. and Profl. Women, 1997, Reproductive Rights Advocate award, 1998, medal of honor Vet. Feminists Am., 1999; named to Iowa Women's Hall of Fame, 1978, Woman of Yr. Iowa City Sr. Ctr., 1995. Mem. LWV, Pioneer Lawnmakers (pres. 1993-95), Delta Kappa Gamma (hon.). Democrat. Methodist.

DODGE, JUDITH C. musician; b. Florence, Ariz., Mar. 15, 1940; d. Natt Noyes and Mildred (Johnson) Dodge; m. David Worthy Breneman, June 10, 1962 (div. Dec. 1992); children: Erica Vernice Breneman, Carleton David Dodge Breneman. BME, U. Colo., 1962; MA, San Francisco State U., 1970. Asst. dir. San Francisco Boys Chorus, 1967-70; dir. music, organist St. Columba's Episcopal Ch., Washington, 1972-83; organist, choirmaster St. Lukes Episcopal Ch., Kalamazoo, 1987-889; adj. lectr. music Kalamazoo Coll., 1983-89; music dir., condr. Bach Festival Soc. Kalamazoo, 1985-89; dir. music, organist St. Philips in the Hills Ch., Tucson, 1989-93, St. Columba's Episcopal Ch., Washington, 1993—. Chair music and program bd. Cathedral Choral Soc., Washington, 1996-2003; mem. adv. bd., sacred circles Nat. Cathedral, Washington, 1998—; mem. standing commn. liturgy and music Nat. Epis. Ch., 2000—. Mem. editl. bd. Jour. Assn. Anglican Music; contbr. articles to profl. jours. Mem. task force Kalamazoo Pub. Schs., 1983-84; mem. selection com. New Yrs. Fest, Kalamazoo, 1986; mem. artistic adv. bd., trustee emeritus Gilmore Internat. Keyboard Festival, 1989-94. Named to Outstanding Young Women of Am., 1965. Mem. Am. Choral Dirs. Assn., Am. Guild Organists, Assn. Anglican Musicians (sec., pres., v.p. 1992-95), Royal Sch. Ch. Music, Am. Guild English Handbell Ringers, Kappa Delta Pi, Pi Kappa Lambda, Sigma Alpha Iota. Democrat. Avocations: tennis, opera, golf, travel, theatre. Office: St Columba's Episcopal Ch 4201 Albemarle St NW Washington DC 20016-2009

DODGE, KIRSTIN SUE, lawyer; b. N.Y.C., Apr. 23, 1966; BA in Polit. Sci., Yale U., 1988; postgrad. studies, U. Fribourg, Switzerland, 1988-89; JD, Harvard U., 1992. Bar: Wash., 1992. Law clk. Hon. Thomas S. Zilly U.S. Dist. Ct., Seattle, 1992-94; vis. lectr. Inst. for Civil Law U. Bern, Switzerland, 1994; assoc. Law Office Marilyn J. Endriss PS, Seattle, 1994-96, Perkins Coie, Bellevue, 1996—. Editor-in-chief Harvard Women's Law Jour., 1992; contbr. articles to profl. jours. Mem. outreach com. N.W. Women's Law Ctr., Seattle, 1996-98. Recipient Grad. Fellow scholarship Rotary Internat. Found., 1988-89. Mem. Wash. State Bar Assn., King County Bar Assn. (bd. trustees young lawyers divsn. 1996-98). Democrat. Office: Perkins Coie 10885 NE Fourth St Ste 700 Bellevue WA 98004-5579

DODGE ROBBINS, DOROTHY ELLIN, English educator; b. Aug. 16, 1958; MA, U. S.D., 1991; PhD, U. Nebr., 2000. Lectr. Tex. A&M, College Station, 1987-88; asst. prof. English Dakota Wesleyan U., Mitchell, S.D., 1995-99; instr. speech comms. La. Tech. U., Ruston, 1999-2000, asst. prof. English, 2000—. Co-editor: Christmas Stories from Louisiana, 2003, Christmas on the Great Plains, 2004. Office: PO Box 3162 Ruston LA 71272-0001 Office Phone: 318-257-2418. Business E-mail: drobbins@garts.latech.edu.

DODOHARA, JEAN NOTON, music educator; b. Monroe, Wis., Feb. 21, 1934; d. Albert Henry and Eunice Elizabeth (Edgerton) Noton; BA, Monmouth (Ill.) Coll., 1955; MS, U. Ill., 1975, adminstrv. cert., 1980, EdD, 1985; m. Laurence G. Landers, June 7, 1955 (div.); children: Theodore Scott, Thomas Warren, Philip John; m. Edward R. Harris, Nov. 27, 1981 (dec.); stepchildren: Adrianne, Erica; m. Takashi Dodohara, Aug. 7, 1988; 1 stepchild, Eve D. Dodohara. Tchr. music schs. in Ill. and Fla., 1955-76; tchr. ch. music for children, 1957-72; tchr. music Dist. 54, Schaumburg, Ill., 1976-93; teaching asst. U. Ill., 1979. Named Outstanding Young Woman of Yr., Jaycee Wives, St. Charles, Mo., 1968; charter mem. Nat. Mus. Women in Arts. Mem. NEA (life), AAUW, Music Educators Nat. Conf. (life), Ill. Educators Assn. (life), Elgin Area Ret. Tchrs. Assn., U. Ill. Alumni Assn. (life), Mortar Bd., Mensa, Delta Kappa Pi. Mem. United Ch. of Christ. Home: 1068 Hampshire Ln Elgin IL 60120-4905

DODSON, ALICEJEAN LEIGH, nursing administrator; b. S.I., N.Y., May 13, 1941; d. Wilbur Thomas Jr. and Beatrice Bertha (Beinert) Leigh; m. Robert Jean Olsen, Dec. 14, 1963 (div. Dec. 1969); 1 child, Aric Robert Olsen; m. Jonathan Boyd Dodson, June 1, 1988; stepchildren: Jacquelyn Nicole, Richard Lewis. BSN, Gustavus Adolphus Coll., 1963; postgrad., U. Puget Sound, 1977-78; M in Nursing, U. Wash., 1979. RN, Minn., Wash., Va. Head nurse ICU, nursing instr. Mary Bridge Children's Hosp., Tacoma, 1967-74; instr. Tacoma C.C., 1974-76, 77-78; instnl. nursing cons. State of Wash., Olympia, 1980-81; head nurse ICU Good Samaritan Hosp., Puyallup, Wash., 1981-83; spl. projects mgr. Puget Sound Hosp., Tacoma, 1983-88; program mgr. Frankfurt (Germany) Mil. Cmty., 1988-90; survey team adminstr. Health Mgmt. Strategies, Alexandria, Va., 1990-92; clin. practice specialist Am. Health Care Assn., Washington, 1992-95; DON Continence Care, Inc., Vienna, Va., 1995-97; project dir. marine new parent support program Quantico/Henderson Hall, 1998—. Reviewer on incontinence Agy. Health Care Policy & Rsch., Washington, 1994-95. Charter mem. Nat. Mus. Women in the Arts; mem. Tacoma Arts Commn., 1987-88; vice chairperson Pub. Arts Task Force, Tacoma, 1986. Lutheran. Avocations: travel, gardening, bicycling. Home: 6707 Kenmont Pl Springfield VA 22152-2424

DODSON, LOIS ALDERDICE, psychotherapist, consultant; b. Doylestown, Pa., Oct. 13, 1948; d. L.B. and Ruth E. (Fly) Alderdice; m. George L. Dodson (div. May 1996); children: Larissa Nicole, Erin Michelle. BA, Temple U., 1993, MEd, 1995. Cert. sch. counselor, Pa. Intensive cmty. counselor Penn Found., Sellersville, Pa., 1993-95, adolescent partial hosp. therapist, 1994-95, mobile therapist, behavior splst., sch. mental health cons., 1995—; psychotherapist Northampton County Children and Youth, Easton, Pa., 1995—; pvt. practice Sellersville, 1996—. Sec. bd. Vitalistic Therapeutic Ctr., Allentown, Pa., 1995—. Mem. Am. Counseling Assn., Am. Assn. Marriage and Family Therapists. Avocations: kayaking, hiking, reading, writing, gardening. Office: Penn Found 807 Lawn Ave Sellersville PA 18960-1594

DOEBLER, BETTIE ANNE, language educator, researcher, writer; b. Atlantic City; d. Willoughby Foster and Ann (Ratledge) Young; m. John W. Doebler, Sept. 1, 1954 (dec. Aug. 26, 1994); 1 child, Mark B. BA, Duke U., 1953, MA, 1955; PhD, U. Wis., 1961. From instr. to assoc. prof. Dickinson Coll., Carlisle, Pa., 1961-70; assoc. prof. Ariz. State U., Tempe, 1971, prof., 1975, prof. emeritus, 1994—, dir. interdisciplinary humanities program, 1989-94. Author: The Quickening Seed: Death in the Sermons of John Donne, 1974, Rooted Sorrow: Dying in Early Modern Eng., 1994; co-author: Book of the Mermaid: Poems by Doebler, Slotten, Thiem, 2001, Nine Waves: Poems by Doebler, Slotten, Thiem, 2003; co-editor: Funeral Sermons Publ. for Women (1600-1630), 6 vol., 1993—2004; contbr. East of Auden, South: An Anthology of the Southern Counties, Eng., 2002, poetry to Passages North, The Awakenings Rev., articles to profl. jour. Angier B. Duke Grad. fellow Duke U., 1954; recipient Faculty Rsch. award Ariz. State U., 1984. Episcopalian. Office Phone: 480-946-7460. E-mail: bettieadoebler@aol.com.

DOERING, DEBORAH ADAMS, artist, educator; d. Walter Haygood Adams; m. Glenn Nicholas Doering, Oct. 1, 1983. BA magna cum laude, Wheaton Coll., 1982; MA, Luth. Sch. Theology, Chgo., 1997; MFA, Sch. of Art Inst. Chgo., 2000. Prin. designer Bottega Design, Inc, Des Plaines, Ill., 1987—99; visual artist Fine Arts Bldg., Chgo., 1999—. Elder Presbyn. Ch. USA, Chgo., 1993—96. Recipient 1st prize, Chgo. Ho., 1990, Presdl. award, Nippon Steel, 1999, Internat. Young Art award, Sotheby's Artlink, 2000. Achievements include being one of first visual artists to incorporate digital media in the 1980s. Avocations: travel, journaling, cooking, color studies, healing arts. Home: 1708 S Crescent Ave Park Ridge IL 60068 Office: Fine Arts Bldg 410 S Michigan Ave Chicago IL 60605 Personal E-mail: bottega@aol.com.

DOERRIE, BOBETTE, secondary school educator; b. Albuquerque, June 22, 1944; d. Neill and Dorothy Madelyn (Jones) Patterson; m. Edward Lewis Horton, Aug. 21, 1966 (div. 1990); children: Leah, James, Carol, Neill; m. Jerome Lee Doerrie, July 28, 1991; children: Jennifer, Elena. BA, McMurry Coll., 1966; MEd, DePaul U., 1977. Cert. sec. broadfield sci. Tchr. physics and phys. sci. G/T coord. Perryton (Tex.) H.S.; tchr. Summit Sch., Dundee, Ill., 1974-77, Lamesa Middle Sch., 1980-85, Lamesa H.S., 1968-69, 85-91, Perryton High Sch., 1991—. Co-dir. Dawson County Sci. Fair, 1981-91; coach Odyssey of the Mind, 1988-91; mem. McMurry U. Ednl. Adv. Bd., 1991-97, engring. team faculty advisor, 1993—, sci. olympiad coach, 1998-2000, sci. bowl advisor, 2001—; mem. Mus. Bd. Dawson County, 1983-90; mem. Libr. Bd. Ochiltree County, 1993-95, v.p., 1994-95. Recipient Excellence in Teaching award Tex. State Assn. for Physics Tchrs., 1992, Tchr. of Yr., Region XVI Gifted and Talented Tchrs., 1994, Nat. Tchg. award RadioShack, 2001; NSF/Tex. Edn. Assn. Christa McAuliffe grantee, 1993, Outstanding Sci. Educator, Tex. Acad. Sci., 2002, Nat. Tchg. award Health Physics Soc., 2002. Mem.: Sci. Tchrs. of Tex. (treas. 1998—2001, Sci. Bowl Sponsor 2001—03), South Plains Sci. Soc. (pres. 1988, Sharon Christa McAuliffe Tchr. of Yr. 1987), Delta Kamma Gamma (pres.). Avocations: amateur radio, painting, archaeology, reading, writing. Home: 13925 CR B Booker TX 79005-9713 Office: Perryton High Sch 1200 S Jefferson St Perryton TX 79070-3700 E-mail: bdoerrie@yahoo.com.

DOESCHER, JILL TRAIN, lawyer; b. Schenectady, N.Y., June 20, 1956; d. Joseph Ernest and Dorothy Claire (Reinertsen) D.; m. Richard D. Train, July 21, 1978 (div. Dec. 1987); children: Colleen Doescher-Train, Nicole Doescher-Train. BS in Econs., U. Wis., 1978; JD cum laude, U. Minn., 1981. Rschr. State Wis. Gov.'s Manpower Planning Office, Madison, 1976-78; intern Hennepin County Atty., Mpls., 1979; atty. Johnson & Eastlund, Mpls., 1980-85, Am. Family, Mpls., 1985-88; litigation mgr. Progressive Ins. Co., Mpls., 1988-93; atty. Lommen Nelson Law Firm, Mpls., 1993-95; litigation atty. State Farm Ins. Co., St. Paul, 1995—. Co-author: Disposition of Unclaimed Property, 1983. Vol. atty. Chrysalis Women's Ctr., 1982—. Mem. Minn. Bar Assn., Ramsey County Bar Assn. Avocations: biking, skiing, scuba diving, canoeing, working out. Home: 2701 Princeton Ave # 20 Minneapolis MN 55416-1952 Office: 900 Norwest Tower 55 5th St E Saint Paul MN 55101-2701

DOETSCH, VIRGINIA LAMB, former advertising executive, writer; b. NYC, Oct. 12, 1920; d. Andrew Thomas and Cameola Weeden (Burns) Lamb; m. Gunter H. Doetsch, Oct. 12, 1953 (div. Feb. 1972); 1 child, Hugo. BS, Northwestern U., 1941; postgrad., Columbia U., 1943—44, postgrad., 1946—47. Writer, dir. pub. rels. J. Walter Thompson, Frankfurt, Germany, 1953-56; creative group head, v.p. to ptnr. Tatham-Laird & Kudner (now Euro RSCG Tatham Ptnrs.), Chgo., 1959—76; v.p. Needham Harper & Steers (now DDB Chgo.), Chgo., 1976-83; free-lance advt. writer and prodr. Chgo., 1983—; writer, rschr. OmniTech Cons. Group now Diamond Tech. Ptnrs., Chgo., 1992-99. Bd. dirs Chgo. Symphony Orch. Women's Assn., 2002—; bd. dirs. Better Bus. Bur., Chgo., 1973—76, Jr. Achievement, Chgo., 1973. With ARC, 1944—46, China, Burma, India. Decorated Bronze Star; named Woman of Yr., Am. Advt. Fedn., 1973. Mem. Women's Advt. Club Chgo. (Woman of Yr. award 1973), Chgo. Advt. Club (bd. dirs. 1973-76). Home: 400 E Randolph St Apt 828 Chicago IL 60601-7309

DOGANCAY, ANGELA, banker; b. Wetter/Marburg, Hesse, Germany, Jan. 9, 1950; Came to the U.S., 1969; d. Gerhard and Alice (Gruen) Hausmann; m. Burhan Dogancay, Dec. 11, 1978. BA, MA, CUNY, 1974; MA, U. Geneva, Switzerland, 1978. Public rels. officer UN, N.Y.C., 1974-76; sr. translator MHT Co., N.Y.C., 1976-78, credit analyst, 1978-80; credit analyst, asst. v.p. Christiania Bank, N.Y.C., 1986-89, v.p., head of loan adminstrn. dept., 1989—. Treas. Whispering Walls, Inc., N.Y.C., 1994—. Home: 220 E 54th St New York NY 10022-4837 Office: Nordea Bank 437 Madison Ave New York NY 10022

DOHERTY, SISTER BARBARA, religious institution administrator; b. Chgo., Dec. 2, 1931; d. Martin James and Margaret Eleanor (Noe) D. Student, Rosary Coll., 1949-51; BA in Latin, English and History, St. Mary-of-the-Woods Coll., 1953; MA in Theology, St. Mary's Coll., 1963; PhD in Theology, Fordham U., 1979; LittD (hon.), Ind. State U., 1990, Dominican U., Ill., 2002. Enter order of the Sisters of Providence. Tchr. Jr. and Sr. High Schs., Ind. and Ill., 1953-63; asst. prof. religion St. Mary-of-the-Woods Coll., Ind., 1963-67, 71-75, pres., 1984-98; provincial supr. Chgo. Province of Sisters of Providence, 1975-83; dir. Inst. of Religious Formation at Cath. Theol. Union, Chgo., 1999—. Summer faculty NCAIS-KCRCHE, Delhi, India, 1970. Author: I Am What I Do: Contemplation and Human Experience, 1981, Make Yourself an Ark: Beyond the Memorized Responses of Our Corporate Adolescence, 1984; editor: Providence: God's Face Towards the World, 1984; contbr. articles to New Cath. Ency. Vol. XVII, 1982, God and Me, 1988, Dictionary of Catholic Spirituality, 1993. Pres. Leadership Terre Haute, Ind., 1985-86; bd. regents Ind. Acad., 1987-98; bd. dirs. 8th Day Cen. for Justice, Chgo., 1978-83, Family Svcs., Swope Art Mus., Terre Haute, Ind., 1988-98. Arthur J. Schmidt Found. grantee, 1967-71. Mem. Women's Coll. Coalition (nat. bd. dirs. 1984-90), Ind. Colls. Ind., Ind. Colls. Found. (exec. bd.), Ind. Conf. Higher Edn. (chair), Leadership Conf. Women Religious of USA (program chairperson nat. assembly 1982-83, chair Neylan commn. 1993-97), Assn. Am. Colls. and Univs. Democrat. Roman Catholic. Avocations: walking, reading, traveling. Office: Cath Theol Union 5401 S Cornell Ave Chicago IL 60615-5664 E-mail: bdoherty@ctu.edu.

DOHERTY, BARBARA WHITEHURST, chemical purchasing manager; b. Charlotte, Jan. 18, 1935; d. Frank Joseph and Geneva Kathryn (Pease) Whitehurst; m. Martin William Doherty, Sr., June 23, 1956 (div. June, 1975); children: Martin William, Jr., Frank Whitehurst. BA in Religion magna cum laude, Duke U., 1956. Cert. notary pub., 1982-97. Rsch. asst., dept. sociology Duke U., Durham, N.C., 1953-56; sec. Pelham (N.Y.) Visiting Nurse & Family Svc., 1958-59, adminstrv. asst. Mecklenburg Times, Charlotte, N.C., 1972-73; bookkeeper Carolina Waterbed Co., Charlotte, N.C., 1972-74; mgr., purchasing and inventory control Reagents, Inc., Charlotte, N.C., 1974-97. Author: poems appear in: Southern Poetry Review, 1992, 1993, 1995, Charlotte Observer, 1993, Sparrowgrass Poetry Forum, 1997. Treas. Charlotte (N.C.) Fair Housing, 1968-70; mem. Charlotte-Mecklenburg Schs. Emergency Sch. Assistance Adv. Com., 1972; Co-chair Paul Leonard for City Council Campaign, Charlotte, 1970; friend of the ct. Swann vs. Bd. Edn., Charlotte, 1972; vol. Marylyn Huff for Sch. Bd., Charlotte, 1970, 74; founder ACLU, Charlotte, 1980 (sec., 1980-82, treas., 1982-84); vol. Harvey Gantt for Mayor campaign, Charlotte, 1983, 85; co-founder, treas. Parents and Friends of Lesbians and Gays, Charlotte, 1988-90; bd. mem. Metrolina Cmty. Svc. Project, Charlotte, 1990-93 (treas., 1992-93). Mem. Phi Beta Kappa, Sigma Delta Pi. Democrat. Avocations: politics, african travel. Home: 1419 Ferncliff Rd Charlotte NC 28211-2220

DOHERTY, EVELYN MARIE, data processing consultant; b. Phila., Sept. 26, 1941; d. James Robert and Virginia. Diploma, RCA Tech. Inst., Cherry Hill, N.J., 1968. Freelance data processing programmer, NJ, 1978-81; data processing cons., 1981—. Cons. collection agy., brokerage, banking, med., edn., transp., pub., food wholesaleing, utility systems, mfg.; reseller of PC's and software; lectr., mgr. data processing Camden County (N.J.) Coll. Contbr. articles to profl. jours.; author poems. Chair Collingswood (N.J.) Dems.; founder Babe Didrikson Collingswood Softball Team for Women; organizer Erlton South Town Watch (pub. cmty. notebook); mem. budget com. Cherry Hill Sch. Dist.; mem. Year 2000 Cherry Hill Schs. Technology Design Com.; adv. for vol. firefighters; vol. tech. lab learning ctr. Cherry Twp. Libr., vol. Cherry Hill Schs. Classroom Computer Learning Ctr.; alt. mem. Southampton Zoning Bd., 2004—. Mem.: Data Processing Mgmt. Assn. (chmn., mem. edn. com.). Roman Catholic. Avocations: tennis, bridge, chess, charitable activites.

DOHERTY, KAREN ANN, import company executive; b. Elizabeth, NJ, July 6, 1952; d. Eugene Nason Godfrey and Helen L. (Andersen) D.; m. Jonathan Kent Tillinghast, June 17, 1972 (div. Oct. 1978); 1 child, Robert. Account exec. John O'Donnell Co., N.Y.C., 1979-80; nat. conservation rep. Sierra Club, N.Y.C., 1980-81; dir. membership and top mgmt. programs Am. Mgmt. Assn., N.Y.C., 1981-97; program mgr. Am. Mgmt. Assn. Pres. Assn., N.Y.C., 1998-99; v.p. mktg. Internat. Inst. Learning, Inc., N.Y.C., 1999, Exaclair Inc., N.Y.C., 1999—. Bd. dirs. Old Mill Landowners Assn., 1994-98, Coop. Jamestown Tenants Assn., 1990-99. Mem. Trinity Coll. Alumnae Assn. (bd. dirs. Com. N.Y.C. group 1979-82), Women in Need (corp. adv. coun.). Democrat. Roman Catholic. Home: 138 71st St Apt F1 Brooklyn NY 11209-1141 Office: Exaclair Inc 143 W 29th St Ste 1000 New York NY 10001 Personal E-mail: karenadoherty@yahoo.com. Business E-Mail: kad@exaclair.com.

DOHERTY, KATHERINE MANN, librarian, writer; b. N.Y.C., July 11, 1951; d. Jack Howard Mann and Glenn (Ellis) Andrews; m. Craig A. Doherty, June 16, 1973; 1 child, Meghan Corinne. BA, U. N.Mex., 1973; MSLS, Simmons Coll., 1976. Cataloger Mass. Hist. Soc., Boston, 1976-79; libr. media specialist Zuni (N.Mex.) Pub. Sch.s, 1982-86; libr. dist. Zuni Pub. Schs., 1985-86; unified media specialist Nantucket (Mass.) Elem. Sch., 1986-87; dir. learning resources Fortier Libr., N.H. Cmty. Tech. Coll., Berlin, 1987—. Author: (children's books) Apaches and Navajos, 1989, Iroquois, 1989, (young adult books) Benazir Bhutto, 1990, The Zunis, 1993, Arnold Schwarzenegger, 1993, The Huron, 1994, The Narragansett, 1994, The Chickasaw, 1994, The Ute, 1994, The Chuilla, 1994, The Sioux, 1994, The Golden Gate Bridge, 1995, Hoover Dam, 1995, Mount Rushmore, 1995, Washington Monument, 1995, Gateway Arch, 1995, The Wampanoag, 1995, The Penobscot, 1995, The Astrodome, 1996, The Erie Canal, 1996, the Empire State Building, 1997, The Alaska Pipeline, 1997, Richard I and the Crusades, 2002; pub. Field Trial Mag. Office: NH Com Tech Coll Coll Libr 2020 Riverside Dr Berlin NH 03570-3717 Office Phone: 603-752-1113. E-mail: kdoherty@nhcte.us.

DOHERTY, LILLIAN EILEEN, classicist, educator; b. South Bend, Ind., Jan. 7, 1952; d. Thomas Henry Doherty, Rosemary (Jantzen) Doherty; m. Harvey Simon Luksenburg, Nov. 13, 1982. BA summa cum laude, Saint Mary's Coll., South Bend, 1974; MA, U. Chgo., 1977, PhD, 1982. Asst. prof. Classics U. Md., College Park, 1987—93, assoc. prof. Classics, 1993—. Author: Siren Songs, 1995, Gender and the Interpretation of Classical Myth, 2001; contbr. articles to profl. jours. Fellow Danforth Grad. fellow, Danforth Found., 1974—79. Mem.: Women's Classical Caucus (steering com. mem. 1993—96, membership officer 1996—, coord. mentoring initiative 1998—), Am. Philol. Assn., Am. Classical League. Roman Catholic. Avocations: travel, photography, family history. Office: Univ Md Dept Classics 2407 Marie Mount Hall College Park MD 20742

DOHERTY, PATRICIA ANNE, psychologist; b. Ottumwa, Iowa, May 25, 1947; d. Russell S. and Dorotha L. (Moehle) Cadwallader; m. Michael Doherty, Sept.6, 1969; 1 child, David M. BA in History, U. Iowa, 1969, MA, 1974, PhD in Counselor Edn., 1979. Lic. profl. counselor Wis., cert. Nat. counselor. Grad. asst. U. Iowa, Iowa City, 1974-78; counseling intern Colo. State U., Ft. Collins, 1978-79; sr. psychologist U. Wis., Stevens Point, 1979—. Co-author: Women, Power and Relationships; contbr. articles to profl. jour. Mem. Wausau (Wis.) Lyric Choir, 1995—, bd. dir., 1999-2003;

ofcl. Wis. Spl. Olympics, Stevens Point, 1989—. Mem. ACA, Am. Coll. Pers. Assn., Silvan Tomkins Inst., Nature Conservancy, Phi Delta Kappa, Phi Kappa Phi (exec.com. 2001--), Pi Lambda Theta. Avocations: singing, tennis, swimming, running, skiing. Office: U Wis Stevens Point Counseling Ctr 317 Delzell Hall Stevens Point WI 54481 Home: 9411 Woodland Cir [illegible]

DOHERTY, SHANNON, actress; b. Memphis, Apr. 12, 1971; d. Tom and Rosa D.; m. Ashley Hamilton, 1993 (div. 1994). Actor TV series Little House: A New Beginning, 1982-83, Our House, 1986-88, Beverly Hills, 90210, 1990-94, Charmed, 1998-2001, Scare Tactics, 2003; TV movies The Other Lover, 1985, Robert Kennedy and His Times, 1985, Obsessed, 1992, Rebel Highway: Jailbreakers, Showtime, 1994, A Burning Passion: The Margaret Mitchell Story, 1994, Gone in the Night, 1996, Sleeping with the Devil, 1997, The Ticket, 1997, Satan's School for Girls, 2000, Another Day, 2001, Hell on Heels: The Battle of Mary Kay, 2002, Nightlight, 2003; TV guest appearances include Father Murphy, 1981, Magnum, P.I., 1983, Airwolf, 1984, Highway to Heaven, 1985, 21 Jump Street, 1989, Life Goes On, 1989; films: Night Shift, 1982, (voice) The Secret of Nimh, 1982, Girls Just Want to Have Fun, 1985, Heathers, 1989, Blindfold: Acts of Obsession, 1993, Almost Dead, 1994, Mallrats, 1995, Nowhere, 1997, Striking Poses, 1999, The Rendering, 2002. Baptist.*

DOHMEN, MARY HOLGATE, retired primary school educator; b. Gary, Ind., July 28, 1918; d. Clarence Gibson and Margaret Alexander (Kinnear) Holgate; m. Frederick Hoeger Dohmen, June 27, 1964; children: William Francis, Robert Charles. BS, Milw. State Tchrs. Coll., 1940; M of Philosophy, U. Wis., 1945. Cert. tchr., Wis. Tchr. primary grades Baraboo (Wis.) Pub. Schs., 1940-43, Whitefish Bay (Wis.) Pub. Schs., 1943-64. Contbr. articles, story, poems to various pubs. Bd. dirs. Homestead H.S. chpt. Am. Field Svc., Mequon, Wis., 1970-80; mem. Milw. Aux. VNA, 1975—, 2d v.p., 1983-85, Milw. Pub. Mus. Enrichment Club, 1975—, Boys and Girls Club of Greater Milw., 1986—; vol. Reading is Fun program, 1987—, Milw. Symphony Orch. League, 1960—, Ptnrs. in Conservation, World Wildlife Fund, Washington, 1991—, Milw. Art Mus. Garden Club, 1979—, com. chmn., 1981-86; mem. Chancellor's Soc. U. Wis.-Milw., 1991—; travel lectr. various orgns., 1980—. Mem. AAUW, Milw. Coll. Endowment Assn. (v.p. 1987-90, pres. 1991-93), Bascom Hill Soc. (U. Wis.), Woman's Club Wis., Alpha Phi (pres. Milw. alumnae 1962-64), Pi Lambda Theta (pres. Milw. alumnae 1962-64), Delta Kappa Gamma. Republican. Presbyterian. Avocations: writing, travel, nature. Home: 3903 W Mequon Rd Mequon WI 53092-2727

DOI, DOROTHY MITSUE YANO, travel company executive; b. Honolulu, Feb. 21, 1934; d. Tokuju Yano and Hisayo Kashiwabara; children: Ken Kenichi, Claire Emiko, Garret Seitoku. BS in Edn., Phillips U., Enid, Okla., 1956; postgrad., UCLA, 1958, U. Hawaii, Honolulu, 1966-67, 72-74, Chaminade Coll. Honolulu, 1972-74, 77, LaVerne (Calif.) Coll., 1970-71. Cert. tchr., Hawaii. Tchr. L.A. City Schs., 1957-58, Hawaii, 1956-57, 65, 70-71; account exec. Catering, ind. contractor, Honolulu; skin care, health and beauty cons. Honolulu; travel agt., ind. contractor, dba Triple C Svcs., Honolulu, 1983—. Rschr. Manoa ethnic studies program U. Hawaii; account exec., cons. Royal Banquet, 1988-89. Active Kamuki Y-Teens, 1947-52; fund-raising co-chair Hui O'Hauolani Y-Teens Jesters Ball, Kaimuki HS, 1952; mem. World Wildlife Fund, 1991—, Hawaii Theatre Ctr., 1990—; vol. ARC, 1944-49, Salvation Army, 1945-50, bell ringer, 1989-98; translator Jal Honolulu Marathon Info. Booth Svc., 1995—. Mem. VFW Ladies Aux. (life), Am. Biograph. Rsch. Assn. (rschr., dep. gov.), NAFE, Nature Conservancy Local, Nat., Hawaii Fukuoka Kenjin Kai (gen. chair 35th anniversary and award ceremony 1992, com. chair, editor commemorative booklet, sec. 1988-91, 2d v.p. 1992-93, 1st v.p. 1993-95, pres. 1996, immediate past pres. 1997, vol. mayors and chamber pres. conf. Honolulu 1997, translation svc. registration desk rep. Hawaii Fukuoka Kenjn Kai), Smithsonian Instn., Kaimuki HS Alumni Assn. (charter, bd. dirs. 1988-2001, pub. rels. chair 1988-90, writer, rschr., editor, mng. editor Bulldogrowl newsletter), Okla. Sooners Club (Hon. Citizen of Okla. 1985), Japanese Cultural Ctr. Hawaii (hon. lifetime charter), Future Tchrs. Am. (treas. 1955-56), United Japanese Soc. Hawaii (sec. 1991-95, youth com. chair 1992—, gen. chair youth com. picnic Bunka Pikunikku 1994, culture day Bunka-no-Hi 1995, co-chair fundraising com. 1992-93, 95-96, mcee New Year luncheon 1993, 2d v.p. 1994-95, registration, score card analyzer Ganbare Golf Classics 1994-98, Mulligan sales co-chair 1995-97, program com. chair, lei com. chair Japan Festival 1996, chair welfare com. 1999-2001), Internat. Platform Assn., Honolulu Japanese C. of C. (ann. art exhbn. 1997-2000, ann. fundraising 1996-99). Avocations: commemorative postal stamp collecting, spectator sports, cooking and baking. Home: 1628 Kalakaua Ave #405 Honolulu HI 96826-2421

DOIG, BEVERLY IRENE, retired systems specialist; b. Bozeman, Mont., Oct. 21, 1936; d. James Stuart Doig and Elsie Florence (Andes) Doig Townsend. AA, Graceland Coll., 1956; BA, U. Kans., 1958; MS, U. Wis., 1970; cert. in Interior Design, UCLA, 1993, tng. classes Windows NT oper. sys., 1996, tng. classes in AUTOCAD, 1st level cert. AUTOCAD, 1998. Cert. NCIDQ 2001, lic. interior designer N.Mex., 2002. Aerodynamic technician II Ames Labs.-NACA, Moffett Field, Calif., 1957; real time systems specialist Dept. of Army, White Sands Missile Range, N.Mex., 1958-66; large systems specialist computing ctr. U. Wis., Madison, 1966-70; sr. systems analyst Burroughs, Ltd., Canberra, Australia, 1970-72; systems specialist Tech. Info. Office Burroughs Corp., Detroit, 1973-78; sr. systems specialist Burroughs Gmbh, Munich, 1978-79, Burroughs AB, Stockholm, 1979-80; networking cons. Midland Bank, Ltd., Sheffield, Eng., 1980-83; networking specialist Burroughs Corp. (now UNISYS), Mission Viejo, Calif., 1983-98; ret. Tchg. asst. Canberra (Australia) Coll., 1972; tchr. Wayne State U. Ext., Detroit, 1976-77; freelance interior designer, 1992-98; with Homeworks Decorating Showroom, Farmington, N.Mex., 1998—; part-time tchr. computer application San Juan Coll., Farmington, 1998—. Vol. youth groups and camps Reorganized LDS Ch., N.Mex., Wis., Australia, Mich., Calif., Germany, U.K.; inner youth worker, Detroit; mentor Saddleback H.S., Santa Ana, Calif. Scholar Mitchell Math., 1956-58, Watkins Residential, 1956-58. Mem. Assn. Computing Machinery (local chpt. chmn. membership 1969), Lambda Delta Sigma. Avocations: working with junior high, crafts, designing, gardening. Office: Homework Inc 115 W Main St Farmington NM 87401-6242

DOJKA, JENNIFER MIMI, art educator, artist; b. San Mateo, Calif., Nov. 5, 1959; d. Stanley Francis and Donna Gray Doyka; m. Harald Schlange, Dec. 31, 1996. BA Theatre Arts, Humboldt State Univ., Arcata, Calif., 1983; MA, San Francisco State Univ., Calif., 2001. Cert. tchng. elem. Humboldt State Coll., 1993. Theatre artist, designer mask maker Dell'Arte, Inc., Blue Lake, Calif., 1980—96; theatre artist Caravan Stage Co., Armstring, 1985—91; theatre artist, mask maker Caravan Stage Barge, St. Petersburg, Fla., 1996—2001; founder/dir. Artline, Arcata, Calif., 1993—. Lectr. art edn. Humboldt State Univ., Arcata, Calif., 2001—, San Francisco State Univ., Calif., 2002; art edn. cons. Edn. through Art Dell'Arte, Blue Lake, Calif., 1998—; designer/mask maker Kirby Arts Ctr. Green Party. Achievements include development of implemented successful arts edn. programming in rural and native Am. communities in No. Calif. and rural communities in El Salvador, Ctrl. Am. Avocations: gardening, hiking. Office: Art Dept Humboldt State Univ Arcata CA 95521

DOKKEN, AURORA DAWNE, music educator; b. Melfort, Sask., Can., Jan. 31, 1957; arrived in U.S., 1994; d. Maynard Howard Dokken and Aileen Marie Connelly; m. Carl Lawrence House, Aug. 14, 1984; children: Amy, Nealia, Frazer, Michael. MusB in Performance, U. Sask., Saskatoon, 1978, MusM in Theory/Composition, 1990; EdD, Tex. A&M U., 2002. Lectr. U. Sask., Saskatoon, 1978—98; prof. Tex. A&M U., Commerce, 1998—2001; prof., chair Minot (N.D.) State U., 2001—; prof. Queens U. Pres., founding mem. Acad. Musical Arts, Commerce, 1999—2001. Editor: (profl. jour.) Jour. Am. Hist. Keyboard Soc. Grantee, Szabo Found., 2001; Recommender grant, B.C. Arts Coun., 1995, Postdoctoral Rsch. grantee, Minot State U., 2003. Mem.: Coll. Music Soc., Am. Fedn. Musicians. Home: 790 Front Rd Kingst[illegible]

DOKMO, CYNTHIA J. state legislator; b. Pitts., May 24, 1946; m. Lew Dokmo; 3 children. BA, Gettysburg Coll., 1968; JD, U. Balt., 1978; cert., N.H. Coll., 1988. Bar: N.H., Md. Mem. Amherst (N.H.) planning bd. N.H. Ho. of Reps., 1984-94; vice-chair Amherst Sch. Bd., 1993—; mem. Nashua regional planning com. N.H. Ho. of Reps., 1993—; atty. Amherst. Mem. resources, recreation and develop. com. N.H. Ho. of Reps. Mem. exec. bd. Cub Scouts Am.; coord. Fish of Amherst. Republican. Address: 74 Christian Hill Rd Amherst NH 03031-3310 Office: PO Box 7483 Milford NH 03055-7483

DOLAMORE, JEANNE PORCINO, music educator; b. Peekskill, N.Y., Aug. 1, 1959; d. Cesar Bruno Porcino and Jane Patricia Jacobs; m. Michael John Dolamore, Sept. 2, 1984; children: Matthew Joseph, Christina Jane, Sophie Rose. BMus, SUNY, Potsdam, 1981; postgrad., Profl. Studio Kato Havas, Oxford, Eng., 1982; MS, L.I. U., 1990. Music tchr., string specialist William Floyd Schs., Mastic Beach, NY, 1982—83, Wellesley Sch. Music, St. Benedict's Secondary Sch., Landamere Music Sch., England, 1983—86, Poughkeepsie (N.Y.) City Schs., 1990—; founder, artistic and exec. dir. Flying Fiddlers String Chorale, Holy Cross Cmty. Outreach Program, Hudson Valley, NY, 1999—. Seminar presenter Am. String Tchrs. Assn. (ASTA) with NSDA Summer Music Conf., Albany, NY, 2002; counselor, coach, tchr. Fredonia (N.Y.) NYASTA-NSDA String Orch. Camp, 2003. Co-author: Flying Fiddles Book II, 2003. Music link tchr. Music Link Found., 2002—; bd. rep. Holy Cross Cmty. Outreach Program, Kingston, NY, 1999—; lay dir. Cornerstone Women's Conf., Woodstock, NY, 2000. Recipient Apple Gala award for vol. svc., Kingston City Sch. Dist., 1998; grantee Dutchess County Arts Coun., Poughkeepsie, 2001—. Mem.: Music Educators Nat. Conf., Kato Havas Assn. for New Approach, Am. String Tchrs. Assn., N.Y. State Sch. Music Assn. Roman Cath. Avocations: violin, reading, bicycling, cooking, geography. Home: 25 Beth Dr Kingston NY 12401 Office: Smith Magnet Sch Poughkeepsie City Sch Dist 11 College Ave Poughkeepsie NY 12601 Office Phone: 845-451-4720. E-mail: flyingfiddlers@hvc.rr.com.

DOLAN, DARIA, news correspondent; m. Ken Dolan. B in theater arts, Webster U.; D in comml. scis. (hon.), St. Thomas Aquinas Coll. V.p. NY Stock Exchange firm; contbr. CBS This Morning, CBS News Saturday Morning; co-host (with husband) CNBC news show; joined CNN, 2003; co-anchor (with husband) Dolans Unscripted, CNN Bus. News. Co-host (with husband) various money seminars. Co-author (with husband): five books on personal finance including Don't Mess with My Money, 2002. Office: CNN 5 Penn Plaza Fl 20 New York NY 10001-1810 Office Phone: 212-714-7800.*

DOLAN, JAN CLARK, former state legislator; b. Akron, Ohio, Jan. 15, 1927; d. Herbert Spencer and Jean Risk Clark; m. Walter John Dolan, Apr. 22, 1950 (dec. July 1986); children: Mark Raymond, Scott Spencer, Gary Clark, Todd Alvin. BA, U. Akron, 1949. Home svc. rep. East Ohio Gas Co., Akron, 1949-50; dietitian Akron City Hosp., 1950-51; tchr. Brecksville (Ohio) Sch. Dist., 1962-66; adminstr. Orchard Hills Adult Day Ctr., West Bloomfield, Mich., 1978-83; mem. Farmington Hills (Mich.) City Coun., 1975-88, Mich. Ho. of Reps., Lansing, 1989-96. Mayor City of Farmington Hills, 1978, 85; elder Presbyn. Ch. Republican. Home: 22587 Gill Rd Farmington Hills MI 48335-4037

DOLAN, KAY FRANCES, human resources administrator; Grad. with honors, U. Oreg. Dir. rsch. and demonstration divsn. Office of Personnel Mgmt., Washington, dep. asst. dir. Office of Retirement Programs, Honolulu area mgr.; dir. human resource mgmt. FAA; dep. asst. sec. human resources Dept. of Treasury, Washington, 1997—. Mem. Phi Beta Kappa. Office: Dept of Treasury Human Resources 15th and Pennsylvania NW 6113 Metro Sq Washington DC 20220-0001

DOLAN, LOUISE ANN, physicist; b. Wilmington, Del., Apr. 5, 1950; BA, Wellesley Coll., 1971; PhD in Physics, MIT, 1976. Jr. fellow in physics Harvard U., 1976-79; asst. prof. physics Rockefeller U., N.Y.C., 1979-82, assoc. prof., 1983-90, lab. head, 1990; prof. physics U. N.C., Chapel Hill, 1990—. Program dir. for theoretical physics NSF, 1995. Recipient Wellesley Alumna Achievement award, 2004; John Simon Guggenheim fellow, 1988. Fellow Am. Phys. Soc. (Maria Goeppert-Mayer award 1987). Office: U NC Dept Physics Chapel Hill NC 27599-0001

DOLAN, MARY ANNE, journalist, columnist; b. Washington, May 1, 1947; d. William David and Christine (Shea) D.. BA, Marymount Coll., Tarrytown, N.Y., 1968; HHD (hon.), Marymount Coll., %, 1984; student, Queen Mary, Royal Holloway colls., U. London, London Sch. Econs., Kings Coll., Cambridge U., 1966-68. Reporter, editor Washington Star, 1969-77; asst. mng. editor, 1976-77; mng. editor L.A. Herald Examiner, 1978-81, editor, 1981—, now commentator. Mem. Pulitzer Prize Journalism Jury, 1981—82; bd. selectors for Neiman Fellows Harvard U. Recipient Golden Flame award, Calif. Press Women, 1980, Woman Achiever award, Calif. Fed. Bus. and Profl. Women's Clubs, 1981. Mem.: Am. Soc. Newspaper Editors, NOW. Office: MAD Inc 1033 Gayley Ave Ste 205 Los Angeles CA 90024-3417

DOLAN, REGINA A. security firm executive; BS, St. John's U. With Ernst & Young, 1975—86, ptnr., 1986—92; sr. v.p. fin. and controls Paine Webber Group Inc., 1992—94, CFO, 1994—97, CFO, chief adminstrv. officer, 1997—2001; chief adminstrv. officer pvt. clients and asset mgmt. divsn. UBS Warburg, 2001—02; global head strategic planning and bus. devel. UBS Investment Bank, 2002—. Bd. dirs. Bus. Coun. Southwestern Conn. Office: Paine Webber Group Inc Ste 302 1285 Avenue Of The Americas Fl Sconc New York NY 10019-6096*

DOLAN, TERESA A. dean, educator, researcher; MPH, UCLA; BA Zoology, Rutgers U., 1979; DDS, U. Tex., 1983; cert. gen. practice, L.I. Jewish Med. Ctr., 1985; cert. geriatric dentistry, Vets. Adminstrn., 1989; cert. dental pub. health, U. Fla., 1991; grad., Pub. Health Leadership Inst. Fla., 1998; grad. cert., U. Fla., 2001. Diplomate Am. Bd. Dental Pub. Health, 1994. Resident in gen. dentistry dept. dentistry L.I. Jewish Med. Ctr., 1983—84, chief resident in gen. dentistry dept. dentistry, 1984—85; fellow geriatric dentistry Vets. Adminstrn. Med. Ctr., Sepulveda, Calif., 1987—89; asst. prof. U. Fla. Coll. Dentistry, 1989—93, assoc. prof. with tenure, 1993—98, acting assoc. dean acad. affairs, 1996—97, assoc. dean acad. affairs, 1997—2001, prof. with tenure, 1998—, assoc. dean edn., 2001—, interim dean, 2002—. Rschr., tchr., spkr. in field, lectr. various seminars; vis. asst. prof. U. Calif., 1985—87, adj. asst. prof., 1987—89; faculty discipline com. Fla. Dept. Edn., Statewide Course Numbering Sys., 1998—; reviewer grants in field; participant NIH Summer Inst. Rsh. on Minority Aging, 1991. Contbr. articles to profl. jours.; exec. prodr.: (ednl. satellite videoconf.) Dental Care for the Developmentally Disabled Patient, 1991, Challenges in Geriatrics: Moving on- Rehabilitation After Stroke, 1991, How Much is Enough? Dental Tretament Decisions for Older Adults, 1992; author (dir.): Five Steps to Improving the Oral Health of Your Older Patients: A Guide for Non-dental Health Professionals, 1994. Adv., treating dentist cmty. nursing homes, 1989—96; dentist to low income elderly participants U. Fla. Geriatric Dental Demonstration Project, Jacksonville, 1990—92; dir. dental svcs. to older and medically compromised patients U. Fla. Geriatric Dental Group, 1990—95. Named honorable mention AARP Healthy Order Adults, 2000 Recognition Programs Exemplary Contbns. to Healthy Aging, 1992; recipient numerous grants and awards; fellow Vets. Adminstrn. Geriatric Dentistry; scholar Rsch., Robert Wood Johnson Found. Dental Health Svcs., 1985—87, L.I. U., 1984—85. Mem.: APHA, Am. Coll. Dentists, Phi Beta Kappa, [illegible] (ad hoc reviewer Spl. Care in Dentistry 1992—93, judge Saul Kamen Sci. Report award competition 1993—, chmn. ann. sci. session 1996), Fla. Coun. Aging, Fla. Pub. Health Assn., Am. Assn. Pub. Health Dentistry (abstract reviewer 1987, co-chmn. local arrangements ann. meeting 1992, ad hoc reviewer Jour. Pub. Health Dentistry 1994, session co-chmn. ann. meeting 1996, judge grad. student merit award projects 1997, mem. at large exec. coun. 1997—2000, mem. awards and nominations com. 2000, Pres.'s award 1999), Am. Dental Assn. (com. G Coun. Dental Edn. and Licensure 1999—, Geriatric Dental Care award 1991), Internat. Assn. Dental Rsch. (v.p. abstract reviewer geriat. oral rsch. sect. 1992—93, dir. behavioral sci. and health svcs. rsch. sect. 1992—95, pres.-elect program chmn. geriat. oral rsch. sect. 1993—94, pres. symposium organizer geriat. oral rsch. sect. 1994—95), Am. Assn. Women Dentists (chmn. com. student and component chpts. 1986—88, trustee dist. XIII Calif. 1986—89, contbg. editor Chronicle 1986—91), Acorn Clinic (v.p., acting pres. 1996—97, pres. 1997—99, past pres. 1999—2000), Fla. Coun. Aging (bd. trustees 1993—95), U. Health Sci. Ctr., Edn. Task Force, U. Curriculum Com., Geriatric Rsch., Edn. and Clin. Ctr., ACORN Clinic, Internat. Assn. Dental Rsch. (session co-chmn., abstract reviewer geriat. oral rsch. sect. 1991—92, immediate past-pres., chmn. nominations com. geriat. oral rsch. sect. 1995—96, mem. awards com. geriat. oral rsch. sect. 1996—97, constn. and bylaws com. 1996—), Am. Bd. Dental Pub. Health (dir.-elect 2000—01), Am. Dental Edn. Assn. (chair-elect spl. interest group in geriatric dentistry 1991—92, editl. rev. bd. Jour. Dental Edn. 1991—94, chmn. spl. intertest group in geriatric dentistry 1992—93, immediate past chmn. sect. on gerontology and geriat. edn. 1993—94, abstract reviewer ann. session 1998—2000, ann. session planning com. 2002—), Beta Beta Beta, Omicron Kappa Upsilon (Xi Omicron chpt. 1998), Phi Beta Kappa. Office: U Fla Coll Dentistry 1600 SW Archer Rd D Box 100405 JHMH Gainesville FL 32610-0405

DOLAND, JUDY ANN, administrative assistant, retired financial rating company associate; b. Duluth, Minn., June 29, 1940; d. Burnham Oscar and Mary Katherine (Sederholm) D. Student, Mt. San Antonio Jr. Coll., Walnut, Calif., 1960. Subs. ledger acct. Pacific Intermountain Express, L.A., 1963-64; various positions Dun & Bradstreet, L.A., 1958-63, 64-80, state sales guide rep., 1980-83, payroll cashier Monterey Park, Calif., 1983-85, exec. sec. Long Beach, Calif., 1985-90, exec. sec. L.A. zone Van Nuys, Calif., 1990-92, exec. sec. Woodland Hills dist. Woodland Hills, Calif., 1992-93, ret., 1993; adminstrv. asst., office mgr. Sharpe Heating & Ventilating, Alhambra, Calif., 1995-96; office mgr. Air Blast Inc., Alhambra, 1996—. Avocations: environmental protection, science, art, music, tennis.

DOLCE, ANNE FRANCES, elementary school educator; b. Yonkers, N.Y., Mar. 31, 1964; d. William and Susan Chandler(Stepmother); m. Anthony Dolce, Aug. 24, 1996; children: Amelia, Christian. MusB in Edn., W.Va. U., 1987; MSc in Edn., Western Md. Coll., 1991. Permanent tchg. cert. N.Y. Tchr. Southampton Mid. Sch. and C. Milton Wright H.S., Bel Air, Md., 1987—88, High Point H.S., Calverton, Md., 1988—91. Dir. marching band color guard Mt. Vernon H.S., Alexandria, Va., 1991—92; mem. staff marching band Jamestown (N.Y.) H.S., 1992—97; tchr. Panama (N.Y.) Ctrl. Sch., 1992—; handbell choir dir. Saints Peter & Paul Ch., 2002—, dir. music ministries, 2002—; mem. staff marching band Jamestown (N.Y.) H.S., 2003—. Musician (french horn): (concert performances) Living Christmas Tree; musician: Bemus Bay Pops Chautaugua Concert Band; mellophone sect. leader W.Va. U. Marching Band (WVU Sect. Leader of the Yr., 1986). Vol. Jamestown Reps., 1998—2003. Mem.: NEA, N.Y. State Sch. Music Assn., Chautauqua County Music Tchrs. Assn., Panama Faculty Assn., Jamestown Musicians Local Union #134. Republican. Roman Catholic. Avocations: walking, softball, travel. Home: 38 Clyde Ave Jamestown NY 14701 Office: Panama Central School 41 North St Panama NY 14767 Personal E-mail: afdolce@yahoo.com. E-mail: adolce@pancent.org.

DOLCI, WENDY WHITING, government agency administrator; m. Robert Dolci. BS in Astronomy and Physics, U. Mass., 1980. Project mgr. airborne sci. missions and astrobiology NASA Ames Rsch. Ctr., 1987—. Avocations: reading, biking, walking, hiking. Office: NASA Ames Rsch Ctr Bldg 240 Rm 105 Moffett Field CA 94035

DOLE, ELIZABETH HANFORD, senator, former charitable organization administrator, former federal official; b. Salisbury, N.C., July 29, 1936; d. John Van and Mary Ella (Cathey) Hanford; m. Robert Joseph Dole (former U.S. Senator from Kans.), Dec. 6, 1975. BA with honors in Polit. Sci., Duke U., 1958; postgrad., Oxford (Eng.) U., summer 1959; MA in Edn. and Govt., Harvard U., 1960, JD, 1965. Bar: D.C. 1966. Staff asst. to asst. sec. for edn. HEW, Washington, 1966-67; practiced law Washington, 1967-68; assoc. dir. legis. affairs, then exec. dir. Pres.'s Com. for Consumer Interests, Washington, 1968-71; dep. asst. to Pres. The White House, Washington, 1971-73; commr. FTC, Washington, 1973-79; chmn. Voters for Reagan-Bush, 1980; dir. Human Services Group, Office of Exec. Br. Mgmt., Office of Pres.-Elect, 1980; asst. to Pres. for pub. liaison, 1981-83; sec. U.S. Dept. Transp., 1983-87; with Robert Dole Presdl. Campaign, 1987-88; participant 1988 Presdl. and Congl. campaigns; sec. U.S. Dept. Labor, 1989-90; pres. ARC, 1991-99; U.S. senator from N.C., 2003—; mem. armed services, agr., banking and aging coms., 2003—. Mem. nominating com. Am. Stock Exch., 1972, N.C. Consumer Coun., 1972. Trustee Duke U., 1974-88; mem. coun. Harvard Law Sch. Assocs., mem. vis. com. Harvard Sch. Pub. Health, 1992-95; mem. bd. overseers Harvard U., 1989-95. Recipient Arthur S. Flemming award U.S. Govt., 1972, Humanitarian award Nat. Commn. Against Drunk Driving, 1988, Disting. Alumni award Duke U., 1988, N.C. award, 1991, Lifetime Achievement award (Breaking The Glass Ceiling) Women Execs. in State Govt., 1993, North Carolinian of the Yr. award N.C. Press Assn., 1993, Radcliffe medal, 1993, Leadership award LWV, 1994, Maxwell Finland award Nat. Found. Infectious Diseases, 1994, Disting. Svc. award Nat. Safety Coun., 1989, Raoul Wallenberg award for Humanitarian Svc., 1995, Christian Woman of Yr. award, 1996; named one of Am.'s 200 Young Leaders, Time mag., 1974, one of World's 10 Most Admired Women, Gallup Poll, 1988, one of 10 most fascinating people 1996 Barbara Walter's Spl., most inspiring polit. figure 1996 MSNBC, 3d most admired woman in Am. Good Housekeeping, 1996, 98; selected for Safety and Health Hall of Fame Internat., 1993; inducted into Nat. Women's Hall of Fame, 1995. Mem. Phi Beta Kappa, Pi Lambda Theta, Pi Sigma Alpha. Office: Dirksen Sen Off Bldg Rm 34 Washington DC 20510

DOLEGOWSKI, DINA C. executive secretary; b. Jersey City, Oct. 17, 1965; d. Ludwig and Irma Weishaupt; m. Joseph A. Dolegowski, Nov. 14, 1992. Secretarial cert., The Berkeley Sch., 1987; Assocs. in Bus., Berkeley Sch. Bus., 1993. Sec. Prentice Hall, Paramus, NJ, 1988, Panasonic Indsl. Co., Secaucus, NJ, 1989—90; exec. sec. Panasonic Techs., Inc., Princeton, NJ, 1990—94; human resources sec. Mellon Finl. Svcs., Ridgefield Park, NJ, 1994; sales asst. Group W Prodns., L.A., 1994—96; exec. asst. Modern Videofilm, Inc., Burbank, Calif., 1996—. Avocations: wine tasting, travel, singing, bowling, cooking. Home: 23815 Laurelwood Ln Valencia CA 91354

DOLEZAL, RUTH ELLEN, resort owner; b. Frence Camp, Calif., Feb. 14, 1937; d. Irwin Graham and Mary Elizabeth (Rathbun) Erickson; m. LAurence E. Dolezal, Feb. 14, 1955; children: Larry John, Gary Ron (dec.). Grad. high sch., Napa, Calif. Owner, operator Sportsman's Resort, Ohio City, Colo. Sec., past pres. Quartz Greek Improvement Assn., Ohio City, 1973—; sec./treas. Cemetery Bd., Pitkin, Colo., 1991—, Vol. Fire Dept.,

Ohio City, 1976—; mem. Gunnison County hist. Preservation Bd. Mem. VFW (pres. 1995, Vol. of Yr. 1994), DAR (past regent), Am. Legion Aux., Top of the World Garden Club (v.p. 1994-96), Elks Ladies, UFW Auxilliary (past pres.), Am. Legion (past pres.), Top of the World. Democrat. Avocations: gardening, reading, bowling, family, quilting. Home: 158 County Rd 771 Ohio City CO 81237

DOLHANCYK, DIANA See **PAMIN, DIANA DOLHANCYK**

DOLIN, LONNY H. lawyer; b. Youngstown, Ohio, Jan. 24, 1954; d. Lawrence Joseph and Sonya (Sacks) Heselov; m. Gordon S. Black, Aug. 20, 1988; children: Nathaniel, Brooke, Aaron, Benjamin, Lindsay. AB, Georgetown U., 1976; JD, Cath. U., 1979. Bar: Vt. 1980, N.Y. State Bar 1984, U.S. Dist. Ct. (we. dist.) N.Y. 1984. Assoc. Downs, Rachlin & Martin, Burlington, Vt., 1979-81; pvt. practice Burlington, 1981-84; assoc., then ptnr. Harris, Beach, Wilcox, Rubin & Levey, Rochester, N.Y., 1984-90; ptnr. Harris, Beach & Wilcox, Rochester, N.Y., 1990-93; former of counsel to U.S. Congressman Fred J. Eckert, N.Y.; ptnr. Lonny H. Dolin and Assocs., Rochester, 1993—. Bd. dirs. Monroe County Legal Services Corp.; faculty mem. Nat. Adv. Inst.; co-chair 2d and 3d Ann. Nat. Inst. on Sexual Harassment; spkr. in field. Asst. editor ABA's Sect. of Labor and Employment Law Newsletter; contbr. chpts. and articles to profl. jours. Mem. Pittsford Town and County Com., N.Y., 1983—, Town of Pittsford Bd. of Zoning Appeals, N.Y., 1984—, vice chair 1990; chmn. Monroe County Comparable Worth Task Force, Rochester, 1985—, Fred J. Eckert Women's Adv. Council, Rochester, 1985—; del. The Jud. Dist. N.Y., Rochester, 1985—, chair 1990; bd. dirs. Nat. Council Jewish Women. Recipient Corpus Juris Secundum award West Pub. co., 1979. Fellow Coll. Labor and Employment Lawyers; mem. ABA (plaintiff's chair labor and employment law sect., co-chair nat. CLE/Inst. and Meetings Com., nat. co-chair employee's rights and responsibilities ethics subcom., nat. vice chair tort and ins. practice sect., spkr. ann. meetings), Nat. Employment Law Assn. (co-chair disabilities rights com.), Vt. Bar Assn., N.Y. Bar Assn., Monroe County Bar Assn. (mem. practice and perf. com.), Greater Rochester Women's Bar Assn. (treas. 1986), Assn. Trial Lawyers Am., N.Y. State Trial Lawyers Assn., Genesee Valley Trial Lawyers Assn. (treas. 1990). Republican. Avocations: golf, skiing, tennis. Home: 9 Hidden Springs Dr Pittsford NY 14534 2897 Office: Ste 130 135 Corporate Wood St Rochester NY 14623 Fax: 716-272-0574. E-mail: ldolin@dts.esg.com.

DOLL, LYNNE MARIE, public relations agency executive; b. Glendale, Calif., Aug. 27, 1961, d. George William and Carol Ann (Kennedy) D.; m. David Jay Lans, Oct. 11, 1986. BA in Journalism, Calif. State U., Northridge, 1983. Freelance writer Austin Pub. Rels. Systems, Glendale, 1978-82; asst. account exec. Berkhemer & Kline, L.A., 1982-83; pres. Rogers & Assocs., L.A., 1983—. Exec. dir. Suzuki Automotive Found. for Life, Brea, Calif., 1986-91; mem. strategic planning com. Gateway to Indian Am. Corp. for Am. Indian Devel., San Francisco, 1988-90. Pub. rels. cons., Rape Treatment Ctr., L.A., 1986—. Mem. Ad Club L.A. (bd. dirs., pres. 1994-95), Pub. Rels. Soc. Am. (L.A. chpt. Outstanding Profl. 1999), So. Calif. Assn. Philanthropy, Coun. on Founds., Internat. Motor Press Assn., Nat. Conf. for Cmty. and Justice (L.A. region bd. dirs. 1996—, nat. bd. dirs. 2002—). Democrat. Office: Rogers & Assocs 1875 Century Park E Ste 300 Los Angeles CA 90067-2504

DOLL, PATRICIA MARIE, marketing professional, public relations executive, consultant; b. Bryn Mawr, Pa., Apr. 13, 1960; d. Otello Louis (dec.) and Eleanor Caroline (De Pasquale) De Grandis; m. John Russell Doll, Oct. 5, 1985. BS in Speech Comms., Millersville (Pa.) U., 1982. Lic. radio operator. News reporter, dj, writer, promotions coord. WIXQ and WLAN Radio, Lancaster, Pa., 1978-82; prodr., writer, rschr. WGAL-TV, Lancaster, Pa., 1982; copywriter, advtsg.-mktg. coord. Strawbridge & Clothier, Phila., 1982-87; freelance writer, 1984—; mktg. dir. Rouse & Assocs., Internat. Developer, Phila., Pa., 1987-90; owner Publicity Works, Bowmansville, Pa., 1990—. Contbr. articles to newspapers and trade mags.; producer TV documentary, 1982. Mem. chambers, trade, local orgns.; registered alumni mentor Millersville U.; hospice vol. Named Internat. ATHENA Small Bus. Woman of Yr. award Berks County C. of C., 1996; recipient numerous regional and nat. awards for mktg. and cmty. work, SBA's Women's Bus. Advocate of Yr. award for Ea. Pa., 1997, MS Corp. Achievers award Nat. Multiple Sclerosis Soc., 1999; named 2 awards for outstanding fundraising Am. Heart Assn., 1987, 1 of Top 40 Under 40 Profls. in Ctrl. Pa., 1996, 1 of the Best 50 Women in Bus., Pa., Gov. of Pa., 1997. Mem. Am. Fedn. Musicians, Kappa Delta Phi. Roman Catholic. Avocations: writing, dance, professional violinist, modeling, community service. E-mail: info@publicity-works.com.

DOLORES, FIDISHUN, librarian, educator; b. East Stroudsburg, Pa., Dec. 7, 1955; d. John M. Fidishun, Dolores A. Fidishun; m. Albert J. Labonis. BS, Kutztown U., 1976; MS Libr. Sci., Drexel U., 1982; MEd, Widener U., 1993, EdD, 1996. Libr. Bensalem Sch. Dist., 1976—77; libr., media specialist Palisades Sch. Dist., Kintnersville, 1977—85; head audio-visual svcs. Montgomery County-Norristown Pub. Libr., Norristown, 1985—87, Widener U., Chester, 1987—95; head libr. Pa. State Great Valley Sch. Grad. Profl. Studies, Malvern, 1995—. Cons. Sch. Dist. of Borough of Morrisville, Computer Tng., 1997—. Recipient Library Sci. award, Kutztown U., Pa., 1976. Mem.: ALA, Libr. Info. and Tech. Assn., Libr. Adminstrn. and Mgmt. Assn., Assn. Ednl. Comm. and Tech., Assn. Coll. and Rsch. Librs. (women's studies sect. chair 2002), Phi Kappa Phi. Roman Catholic. Office: Pa State U Great Valley Libr 30 E Swedesford Rd Malvern PA 19355 Office Fax: 610-725-5223.

DOMAN, JANET JOY, professional society administrator; b. Phila., Dec. 16, 1948; d. Glenn J. and Hazel Katie (Massingham) D. Student, U. Hull, England, 1969-70; BA, U. Pa., 1971. Cert. tchr. Clinician Inst. Achievement Human Potential, Phila., 1971-74; dir. English Early Devel. Assn., Tokyo, 1974-75; dir. Evan Thomas Inst. Early Devel., Phila., 1975-77, Inst. Achievement of Intellectual Excellence, 1977-80; vice dir. The Inst. of Achievement and Human Potential, 1980-82, dir., 1982—. Internat. lectr. treatment of brain injured children and superiority. Chair Child Brain Devel., United Steelworkers Am., 1987. Recipient Gold medal Centro de Reabilitacion Nosa Senhora da Gloria, Rio de Janeiro, 1974, Brit. Star Brit. Inst. Achievement Human Potential, 1976, Sakura Korosho medal Japanese Inst. Achievement Human Potential, 1977, statuette with pedestal Internat. Forum Human Potential, 1980. Office: The Inst of Achievement and Human Potential 8801 Stenton Ave Glenside PA 19038-8319

DOMAN, MARGARET HORN, government policy and process consultant, civic official; b. Portland, Oreg., July 28, 1946; d. Richard Carl and Dorothy May (Teepe) Horn; m. Steve Hamilton Doman, July 12, 1969; children: Jennifer, Kristina, Kathryn. BA, Willamette U., 1968; postgrad., U. Wash., 1968-69, 72. Cert. tchr. Tchr. jr. high Bellevue (Wash.) Sch. Dist., 1969-70, subs. tchr., 1990-91; tchr. jr. high University City (Mo.) Sch. Dist., 1970-71; employment counselor Wash. State Dept. Employment Security, Seattle, 1971; planning commn. mem. City of Redmond, Wash., 1980-83, chmn., 1982-83, city coun. mem., 1983-91, pres., 1990-91; exec. dir. Eastside Human Svcs. Coun., Redmond, Wash., 1992; employment specialist Wash. State Dept. Employment Security, 1993; cons. land use planning & govt. process Redmond, 1993—. Redmond rep. Puget Sound. Coun. of Govt., Seattle, 1984-91, vice chmn., 1988, 90, chmn. transp., 1986-88, exec. bd., 1987, mem. standing com. on transp., 1986-91; bd. dirs., pres. Eastside Human Svcs. Coun., Bellevue, 1983-91, pres., 1990. Mem. state exec. com. Nat. History Day, Olympia, Wash., 1986; vol. Bellevue Sch. Dist., 1977—96; bd. dirs. Redmond YMCA, 1985—86, Youth Eastside Svcs., 1998—2001; bd. dirs. Eastside br. Camp Fire, Bellevue, 1992—94, Redmond Hist. Soc., 1999—2001. Mem. Redmond C. of C. (land use and transp. com. 1994-98), Bellevue Rotary (bd. mem. 2001—). Republican. Unitarian Universalist. Avocations: skiing, hiking, sailing, world travel. Home: 2104 180th Ct NE Redmond WA 98052-6032 E-mail: domanms@comcast.net.

DOMAR, ALICE DIANE, psychologist, educator; b. Balt., May 1, 1958; d. Evsey David and Carola Rosenthal Domar; m. David Allen Ostrow, Aug. 26, 1990; children: Sarah Domar Ostrow, Katherine Domar Ostrow. BA, Colby Coll., Waterville, Maine, 1980; MA, Yeshiva U., N.Y., 1984, PhD, 1986. lic. psychologist, Mass. Staff psychologist Deaconess Hosp., Boston, 1988-96; sr. scientist Mind/Body Med. Inst., Boston, 1994—2002, dir. ctr. women's health, 1994—2002; dir. Mind/Body Ctr. Women's Health, Boston IVF, 2002—. Asst. prof. Harvard Med. Sch., Boston, 1994—. Author: (book) Healing Mind, Healthy Woman, 1996, Self-Nurture, 2000, Conquering Infertility, 2002; co-author: Six Steps to Increased Fertility, 2000; adv. bd.: Parent's Mag., columnist: Health Mag. Mem. bd. experts Llumber. Recipient Young Investigators award, Mass. Dept. Pub. Health, 1993; grant Nat. Inst. Mental Health, 1990, 94. Mem. Mental Health Profl. Group (chair), 1997-98. Avocations: travel, cooking, reading. Office: 40 Second Ave Ste 300 Waltham MA 02451 E-mail: alice.domar@bostonivf.com.

DOMAR, CAROLA ROSENTHAL, social worker; b. Franfurt, Fed. Republic of Germany, Dec. 17, 1919; arrived in U.S., 1940; d. Siegfried and Betty (Warschauer) Rosenthal; m. Evsey David Domar, Apr. 16, 1946; children: Erica Domar Banderob, Alice Domar. BS, Carnegie Inst. Tech., 1947; MSW, Simmons Sch. Social Work, 1968. Cert. social worker; bd. cert. diplomate; lic. social worker, Mass. Social worker Burlington (Mass.) Pub. Sch. System, 1968-73; clin. social worker, dir. retardation svc. Eliot Community Mental Health Clinic, Concord, Mass., 1974-80; pvt. practice Concord, Mass., 1980—. Cons. Acton (Mass.) Pub. Health Nursing Svc., 1981-90, 97—, Nashoba Nursing Svc., Harvard, Mass., 1990-97. Pres. bd. Coun. for Children, Acton, 1975-78; v.p. bd. Dept. Mental Health and Retardation, Concord, Mass., 1985-88; bd. dirs. Dept. Mental Health, Arlington, Mass., 1988-91, Dept. Retardation, Arlington, 1988-95; mem. Acton Family Self-Sufficiency Com., 1997—; Coun. on Aging liaison to Affordable Housing Bd., 1997—. Recipient Cert. of Recognition, Gov. M. Dukakais, Boston, 1983, Cert. of Recognition, Office for Children, Boston, 1985; Ofcl. Citation, Ho. of Reps., Boston, 1983. Mem. NASW, Mass. Assn. Gerontology, Concord Mental Health Assn. (bd. dirs. 1988-89). Home and Office: 264 Heaths Bridge Rd Concord MA 01742-4921 E-mail: carola@ourconcord.net.

DOMBROWSKI, ANNE WESSELING, retired microbiologist, researcher; b. Cin., Jan. 26, 1948; m. Allan Wayne Dombrowski, Apr. 17, 1982; children: Amy, Alicia. BA summa cum laude, Xavier U., 1970; MS, U. Cin., 1972, PhD, 1974. Fellow Scripps Clinic & Rsch. Found., La Jolla, Calif., 1974-76; sr. rsch. microbiologist Merck & Co., Inc., Rahway, N.J., 1976-87, rsch. fellow, 1987 96, sr. rsch. fellow, 1996—2003, ret., 2003. Contbr. articles to profl. jours. Mem.: AAAS, Mycol. Soc., Am. Soc. Microbiology, Soc. Indsl. Microbiology (sec. 1982—85, dir. 1998—2001). Achievements include patents in field. Avocations: reading, gardening. Home: 51 Landsdowne Rd East Brunswick NJ 08816-4156 E-mail: annewd@aol.com.

DOMINGO, CORA MARIA CORAZON ENCARNACION, minister; b. Urdaneta City, Philippines, Mar. 25, 1917; d. Martin Cantaoe and Casimira Agbanlog Echalas; m. Nicanor Barrientos Domingo, Oct. 20, 1950; m. Teofilo Alonzo Manzano, July 8, 1935 (div. Sept. 26, 1950); children: Don Leonardo Manzano, Teddy Teofilo Manzano. BMin. and Practical Theology, Word of Faith Leadership & Bible Inst., Dallas, 1985. Ordained minister Ministry Salvation Ch., 1986. Tchr. Public Sch., Urdaneta City, Philippines, 1939—46; assoc. pastor The Assembly of the First Born, Kahului, Hawaii, 1993—; pres./founder Christ Tabernacle of Praise, Cabuloan, Philippines, 1999—; missionary pastor Cabuloan Village Chapel, Cabuloan, Philippines, 1971—99; child evangelist Child Evangelism Fellowship, Honolulu, 1980—92; pastor Maui Evang. Ch., Kahului, Hawaii, 1970—74; landlord and bus. woman Kahului, Hawaii, 1962—. Dir. of Filipino lang. radio program KNUI/KMVI, Kahului, Hawaii. Mem. Friendship Bible com., coord. Maui Christian Women's Club; pres., host Great Commn. Fellowship, 1980—95; mem. Maui Retarded Children's Assn., Big Bros./Big Sisters of Hawaii, Humane Soc.; treas., bd. dirs. Maui Adult Day Care Ctr., 1974—94; pres. Filipino Mins. Fellowship Maui, 1976—98; mem. Maui Christian Mins. Assn.; leader Girls Scout Am. Troop 78, 1953—63; bd. dirs. Status of Women, Com. on Aging, Wailuku, Hawaii. Recipient Outstanding Citizen of Filipino Ancestry, Maui Filipino Cmty. Assn., 1965, Worthy Matron of Order, Maui Chpt. 5 Order of the Ea. Star of Maui Hawaii, 1975, 1980, 1993, Conservative Patriotic award, Young Am. Found., 2003. Mem.: Maui Filipino Ladies Cir., Bus. & Profl. Women's Club (vp & chmn. 1965—69). R-Consevative. Christian. Avocations: reading, sewing, gardening, travel. Home and Office: 739 Iluna Pl Kahului HI 96732

DOMINGO, ESTHER, music educator; b. Havana, Cuba, July 13, 1954; d. Silverio and Esther (Benitez) D. MusB in Music Edn., MusB in Piano Performance, Mercer U., Atlanta, 1978; MusM in Piano Pedagogy, Ga. State U., 1985. Cert. Yamaha music edn. sys.; cert. Music in Edn. Nat. Tchr. Inst.; cert. ESOL; cert. tchr. grades K-12, Ga. Sec., Spanish/ESOL tchrs. asst. Atlanta Pub. Schs., 1978-81; pvt. piano and Yamah music edn. tchr. Atlanta Music Ctr., 1983-89; piano and music theory tchr. Mercer U., Atlanta, 1980-91; piano and group music classes tchr. The Children's Sch., Atlanta, 1989-92; ESL tchr. Internat. Edn. Ctr., Atlanta, 1991-92; piano, theory and group classes tchr. pvt. home music studio, Atlanta, 1976—; pvt. piano and music theory tchr. Ga. Acad. Music, Atlanta, 1992—; gen. music, choral tchr. Atlanta Pub. Schs., 1992—. Pianist Spanish Mission, Second-Ponce de Leon Bapt. Ch., Atlanta, 1970—; panelist Fulton County Art Coun., 1999; adjudicator for various music festivals in the state. Neighborhood rep. Hispanic cmty. Ga. Power Co., Atlanta, 1978-79; young artist performer DeKalb Coun. for the Arts; panelist Fulton County Arts Coun., 1999; pianist, handbell soloist; mem. handbell choir Second Ponce deLeon Bapt. Ch., 1985—. Recipient Excellence in Edn. award, BellSouth/Braves, 2002; Fine Arts grantee, Atlanta Pub. Schs., 1998. Mem. Music Tchrs. Nat. Assn. (cert.), Atlanta Music Tchrs. Assn. (cert., program chmn. 1990-91, membership chmn. 1991-92, v.p. 1992-93, pres. 1993-94), Ga. Music Tchrs. Assn. (cert.). Baptist. Avocations: handbell performer/choir, swimming, travel. Office: Morningside Elem Sch 1053 E Rock Springs Rd NE Atlanta GA 30306-3099 E-mail: edomingo@atlanta.k12.ga.us.

DOMINGUEZ, CARI M. government agency administrator; BA, MA, Am. U.; fellow Advanced Study Program in Pub. Mgmt., MIT; D in Humanitarian Svc. (hon.), Loma Linda U., 2003. Dir. exec. programs Bank Am. Corp.; partner Heidrick & Struggles; dir. Spencer Stuart, San Francisco; principal Dominguez & Associates, 1999; chair U.S. Equal Employment Opportunity Comm., 2001—. Named one of 80 Elite Hispanic Women, Hispanic Bus. mag., 100 Most Influential Hispanics in the Country; recipient Eagle Award, Bank America CEO, Chmns. 2002 award for excellence, Nat. Image, Inc. Mem.: Human Resources Planning Soc. (bd. mem.), Leadership Found. Internat. Women's Forum (bd. mem.). Office: Equal Employment Opportunity Comm 1801 L Street NW Washington DC 20507

DOMINGUEZ, KATHRYN MARY, political scientist, educator; b. Santa Monica, Calif., Nov. 26, 1960; d. Frederick A. and Margaret M. (McGauren) D. AB, Vassar Coll., 1982; MA, Yale U., 1984, M in Philosophy, 1985, PhD, 1987. Researcher Congl. Budget Office, Washington, summer 1984; rsch. scholar bd. of govs. FRS, Washington, 1985-86; asst. prof. pub. policy Kennedy Sch. Govt. Harvard U., Cambridge, Mass., 1987-91, assoc. prof. pub. policy, 1991-97; assoc. prof. pub. policy and econs. U. Mich., Ann Arbor, 1997—. Rsch. cons IMF, Washington, 1989; vis. asst. prof., asst. dir. internat. fin. sect. dept. econs. Princeton U., 1990-91; Nat. Bur. Econs. Rsch. Olin fellow, 1991-92. Author: (monograph) Oil and Money, 1989; Exchange Rate Efficiency and the Behavior of International Asset Markets, 1992; (with Jeff Frankel) Does Foreign Exchange Intervention Work?, 1993. Mem. Nat. Bur. Econ. Rsch. (rsch. assoc. 2000—), Am. Econ. Assn., Am. Fin. Assn., Phi Beta Kappa. Democrat. Office: U Mich Sch Pub Policy Lorch Hall 611 Tappan Ave Ann Arbor MI 48109-1220

DOMINGUEZ, MONICA RAYE, special education educator; b. Wichita, Kans., Oct. 9, 1976; d. Pete P. and Patricia A. Dominguez. B in Spl. Edn., U. Ctrl. Okla., Edmond, 2000; M in Ednl. Adminstr., Okla. State U., 2003. 6th/7th grade tchr. Tulsa Pub. Schs., 2000—01; 2nd grade spl. edn. tchr. Jenks (Okla.) Pub. Schs., 2002—. Mem.: Kappa Delta Phi (life). Conservative. Southern Baptist. Office: Jenks Public Schs 205 E B St Jenks OK 74037

DOMINIAK, GERALDINE FLORENCE, accounting educator, retired; b. Detroit, Sept. 28, 1934; d. Benjamin Vincent (dec.) and Geraldine Esther (Davey) D. BS, U. Detroit, 1954, MBA, 1956; PhD, Mich. State U., 1966. CPA, Mich. Audit supr. Coopers & Lybrand, 1958-63; asst. prof. U. Detroit, 1965-68; assoc. prof. Mich. State U., 1968-69; prof. acctg. Tex. Christian U., Ft. Worth, 1969-97, chmn. dept. acctg., 1974-83; Arthur Young prof. acctg. Fla. A&M U., 1977. Author: (with J. Edwards and T. Hedges) Interim Financial Reporting, 1972; (with J. Louderback) Managerial Accounting, 1975, 9th edit., 2000. Ford Found. fellow, 1964-65. Mem. AICPA, Am. Acctg. Assn., Inst. Mgmt. Accts., Am. Woman's Soc. CPAs, Tex. Soc. CPAs, AAUP, ACLU, Beta Alpha Psi, Beta Gamma Sigma. Roman Catholic. Home: 4401 Cardiff Ave Fort Worth TX 76133-3513

DOMINIAN, JULIE, human resources specialist; b. Bklyn., N.Y., Dec. 18, 1945; d. Armand and Belle (Baron) Dominian. BA, U. Stony Brrok, Stony Brook, N.Y., 1967. Cert. Tchg. N.Y., 1971. Assoc. staffing svcs. rep. N.Y.S. Dept. of Civil Svc., Albany, NY, 1983—98, mgr. of N.Y.S. employment record, 1998—2001; asst. dir. of pers. N.Y.S. Dept. of Transp., Albany, NY, 2001—. Actor: (plays) Various; contbr. articles to profl. jour. Vice. pres. for fin. NOW-NYS, Albany, NY, 1980—82. Scholar Fallsburg H.S. Tchr. Scholarship, 1963, Regents Scholarship, N.Y.S. Edn. Dept. 1963 - 1967. Achievements include development of cost effective position-specific testing for promotion for N.Y.S. employees. Avocations: science fiction, travel, writing, movies, music. Office: NYS Dept of Transp Harriman State Office Campus Bldg 5 Albany NY 12232 Personal E-mail: jdominian@prodigy.net.

DOMINIC, MAGIE, writer; 1 child, Heather Rose. Prodr./dir. Children's History Theatre, Woodstock, NY, 1978—84. Assoc. curator Caffe Cino Exhibit, Lincoln Ctr. Libr. for the Performing Arts, N.Y.C., 1985; actress N.Y.C. Off Off-Broadway movement, 1960s. Author: The Queen Of Peace Rm., 2002 (nominated ForeWord Mag. Book of Yr., 2003, nominated Judy Grahn award, 2003, CWSA award, 2003); editor, author: Belle Lettres/Beautiful Letters, 1995; author: (anthologies) Outrage, 1993, Pushing the Limits, 1996, Countering the Myths, 1996; Represented in permanent collections St. Vincent's Hosp., N.Y.C., The Malcolm Forbes Collection, prin. works include The Gown of Stillness Installation, Toronto, 1995, N.Y.C., 1996, UN, 1996; librettist: Symphony #2 - "Visions of a Wounded Earth", final movement, composer: (for voice and orchestra) Transformation of a Soul, 1997. Recipient Langston Hughes award Clark Ctr., 1968; grantee Dakota Found., Gottlieb Found., Am. The Beautiful Fund, Shaker Found., Artists fellowship New Sch. U. Faculty Devel. Fund. Mem. League of Can. Poets.

DOMINICK, LISA MARIE, elementary school educator; b. Las Vegas, Nev., July 24, 1973; BA, St. Josephs U., 1996; M in Mus. Edn., Tchg. Visual Arts, U. of The Arts, 1998. Elem. art tchr. Lower Merion Sch. Dist., 1998; adj. prof. St. Joseph's U., Philadelphia, 1998—99; art tchr. 7th-8th gr. Perkiomen Valley Sch. Dist., Collegeville, Pa., 1998—99; head visual arts dept./sr. tchr. Kid's Gallery Co., Ltd., Hong Kong, 1999—2001; art tchr. 3rd-5th gr. Pittston Area Sch. Dist., Pa., 2001—. Pres./CEO Coast Edn. Co., Inc., Pittston, Pa., 1999—. Exhibitions include Six Man Show, U. of the Arts Gallery, 1998, Juried Grad. Show, 1997, The Women of Kids Gallery, Hong Kong, 2001. Mem.: Pa. Art Edn. Assn., Nat. Art Edn. Assn. Democrat. Roman Catholic. Office Phone: 570-654-7176.

DOMINICUS, ADELE M. mathematician, educator; m. Anthony R. Dominicus, Aug. 0, 1994; children: Ariana, Alexis. BS in Elem. Edn., Iona Coll., 1989. Tchr. St. Anthony's Sch., Bronx, 1989—93, Bronx Pub. Schs., 1993—95; chmn. math dept. Melrose Sch., Brewster, NY, 2000—. Mem.: Nat. Coun. Math. Tchrs. Office: Melrose School 120 Federal Hill Rd Brewster NY 10509

DOMINIQUEZ, CARI M. federal agency administrator; BA, MA, Am. U. Ptnr. Heidrick & Struggles, Washington; dir. Spenser Stuart, San Francisco; prion. Diminiguez & Assocs., Md., 1999—2001; chair Equal Opportunity Commn., Washington, 2001—. Mem. leadership found. bd. Internat. Womens Forum, Hispanic Bus. Roundtable; bd. dirs. Holy Names Coll., Oakland, Calif., Human Resources Planning Soc. Fellow advanced study program pub. mgmt., MIT. Office: EEOC 1801 L St NW Washington DC 20507

DOMZELLA, JANET, retired library director; b. Marquette, Mich., Mar. 22, 1935; d. Jack Carl and Alice Margaret (Blom) Messenger; m. Theodore S. Wodzinski (div. 1974); children: Christopher, Joseph, Daniel; m. Perry Landon Domzella, July 15, 1977; stepchildren: Perry, Pamela. BS, No. Mich. U., 1973; MLS, U. Buffalo, 1979. Sch. libr. media specialist Niagara Falls (N.Y.) Bd. Edn., 1974-75, Iroquois Ctrl. Sch., Elma, N.Y., 1975-77; dir. Lewiston (N.Y.) Pub. Libr., 1977-2000, libr. emeritus, 2001—; ret., 2000. Mgr. LaSalle br. Niagara Falls Pub. Libr., NY, 2002. Co-author: Lewiston: Self Guided Tour, 1986. Vol. firefighter Upper Mountain Vol. Fire Co., Lewiston, 1980—90, treas., 1984—90; mem. Town of Lewiston Bur. Fire Prevention, 1988—90; mem. adv. bd. Documentary Heritage Program, 1991—93; mem. pub. libr. program Coll. of Charleston (S.C.) Conf., 1998, 2000, 2001. Democrat. Roman Catholic. Avocations: rosemaling, watercolor.

DON, AUDREY, clinical psychologist, neuropsychologist; BFA, Columbus (Ohio) Coll. Art and Design, 1990; MA, U. Windsor, Ont., 1994, PhD, 1997. Lic. clin. psychologist Wash. Postdoctoral fellow Children's Seashore Ho. of The Children's Hosp. of Phila., 1997—2000; pediat. psychologist, neuropsychologist Children's Therapy Unit, Good Samaritan Hosp., Puyallup, Wash., 2000—03; clin. psychologist, neuropsychologist The Ark Inst. Learning, Tacoma, 2003—. Exhibitions include Music on Paper paintings, drawings Scio Scio Gallery, Narbertha, Pa. Mem.: Wash. State Examining Bd. Psychology, APA, Nat. Acad. Neuropsychology, Chamber Music Am. Avocations: viola, chamber music, art. Office: The Ark Inst Learning 1916 S Washington St Tacoma WA 98405

DONAHOE, MAUREEN ALICE, accounting consultant; b. N.Y.C., June 9, 1959; d. William A. and Alice P. (O'Connor) D. BA in Acctg., Belmont Abbey Coll., 1982; MBA in Fin., Fordham U., 1992. CPA, N.Y.; cert. insolvency and reorgn. advisor. Staff acct. Bankers Trust Co., N.Y.C., 1982-85; sr. auditor Feldman Radin and Co., 1985—87; valuation svcs. mgr. Ernst & Young, 1987-91; sr. mng. dir. FTI Cons., Inc., 1991—2003; founder, ptnr. CCV Restructuring, Hackensack, NJ, 2003—. Dir. 417 E. 90th St. Corp., N.Y.C., 1995-2000. Mem. alumni bd. Belmont Abbey Coll., 1994-1997. Mem. AICPA, Assn. Insolvency Accts., N.Y. State Soc. CPAs (mem. insolvency and reorgn. com. 1993-94). Republican. Roman Catholic. Avocation: golf. Home: 12 Upper Mountain Ave Montclair NJ 07042-1814 Office: CCV Restructuring 411 Hackensack Ave 9th Fl Hackensack NJ 07601

DONAHOE, PATRICIA KILROY, surgeon; b. Boston, Apr. 12, 1938; MD, Columbia Coll. Physicians and Surgeons, 1964. Diplomate Am. Bd. Surgery with subspecialty in pediat. surgery. Intern Tufts-New Eng. Ctr. Hosp., 1964—65, resident in surgery, 1965—69; resident in pediat. surgery Children's Hosp., Boston, 1969—70, Mass. Gen. Hosp., Boston, 1970—71; pvt. practice in pediat. surgery Boston; chief surgeon Mass. Gen. Hosp. Mem.: Inst. of Medicine of NAS. Office: Massachusetts Gen Hosp Divsn Pediat Surgery 55 Fruit St Boston MA 02114-2696

DONAHUE, ANN M. television producer; Student, Ohio State U. Legal asst., Century City, Calif.; writer China Beach, Picket Fences, Murder One; prodr. 21 Jump St., Street Justice; writer CSI NBC, LA, 2000—. Author: (plays) Home Fires, (films) Those Beaumont Girls, Three Girls in the Air Force, Three Girls Pose for Playboy. Home: 1412 Warnall Ave Los Angeles CA 90024*

DONAHUE, ANNE DE LA BLANCHETAI, lawyer; b. Burlington, Vt., Mar. 20, 1956; d. John Clarke Jr. and Christiane (de Vitry) D. B.A., Boston Coll., 1978; J.D., Georgetown U., 1981. Bar: Mass. 1981, D.C. 1982, N.Y. 1982, N.J. 1983, U.S. Dist. Ct. N.J. 1983. News editor Times-Bull., Boonton, N.J., 1973-78; sr. staff atty. Covenant House, N.Y.C., 1981— . Recipient Advocacy award Internat. Acad. Trial Lawyers, 1981. Mem. ABA. Roman Catholic. Home: 3324 Perry Ave Bronx NY 10467-3215 Office: Covenant House 460 W 41st St New York NY 10036-6801

DONAHUE, DONNA CHARLENE, computer company executive, marketing professional; b. Dallas, June 25, 1974; d. Harold Charles and Jacqueline Lee Donahue. Grad. H.S., Chgo. Lic. real estate agt. N.Mex., 1996. V.p. mktg. Top Investment, Inc., Albuquerque, 1994—2000, spl. projects mgr. Albuquerque, 2002; v.p. Verix Tech. Group, Addison, Tex., 2000—02; tech. ptnr. Albuquerque Computer Innovations/Frost Mortgage, 2002—03; pres. DCD Consulting, Albuquerque, 2002—. Notary pub. State N.Mex., Albuquerque, 1996—2000; exec. com. sec. MDA N.Mex., Albuquerque, 1999—2000; vol. People for Pete, Albuquerque, 2002, Albuquerque Aquarium, 2003. Mem.: NAFE, Internat. Webmasters Assn., Am. Mktg. Assn. Republican. Episcopal Buddhist.

DONAHUE, JOAN ELIZABETH, elementary school educator; b. Middlesboro, Ky., Oct. 9, 1954; d. Calvin Coolidge and Cassie Marie (Harville) Whitaker; m. Andrew Lewis Donahue, Aug. 13, 1977; children: Timothy, Laura, Christopher. BS in Home Econs., U. Tenn., 1977; MS Edn., Ouachita Bapt., 1987. Cert. tchr., Ark. Home econs. tchr. Claiborne County Schs., Tazewell, Tenn., 1977-81; 2d grade tchr. Sparkman Schs., Arkadelphia, Sparkman, Ark., 1985, Arkadelphia Schs., 1985-87, Shelby County Schs., Memphis, 1987-89; 3d grade tchr. Mobile (Ala.) County Schs., 1989-91, 4th grade tchr., 1991-92, 3rd grade tchr., 1992-94; 4th grade tchr. Knox County Schs., Knoxville, Tenn., 1994-95, Green Magnet Math and Sci. Acad., Knoxville, 1995-96; 3d grade tchr. Shelby County Schs., Memphis, 1996—. Textbook cons. Walsworth Pub. Co., Marceline, Mo., 1991—; mem. supt. adv. bd. Mobile County Schs., 1991—. Active Woman's Club Am., New Tazewell, Tenn., 1977-81, v.p., 1981, Shelby County Govt. Bd. Commrs. (hon. commr. 1986), Memphis City Coun. (hon. commr. 1986). Classroom Edn. grantee Mobile Jr. League, 1989-90. Fellow Beta Sigma Phi (pres. 1986-878, Woman of Yr. 1987); mem. Joint Coun. on Econ. Edn. (2d place award 1987, 3d place award 1990), Ala. coun. on Econ. Edn. (1st place award 1990, 91, named Ala. Elem. Econs. Tchr. Yr. 1992). Republican. Methodist. Avocations: travel, crafts, basket-making, antiques, needlework. Home: 625 Kenrose St Collierville TN 38017-3704 Office: Highland Oaks Elem 5252 Annandale Dr Memphis TN 38125-4263 also: Highland Oaks Elem Sch 5252 Annandale Dr Memphis TN 38125-4263

DONAHUE, LAURA KENT, former state senator; b. Quincy, Ill., Apr. 22, 1949; d. Laurence S. and Mary Lou Kent; m. Michael A. Donahue, July 16, 1983. BS, Stephens Coll., 1971. Mem. Ill. State Senate, Quincy, 1981—2002. State senator; b. Quincy, Ill., Apr. 22, 1949; d. Laurence S. and Mary Lou (McFarland) Kent; m. Michael A. Donahue, July 16, 1983. B.S., Stephens Coll., 1971. Mem. Ill. State Senate, Quincy, 1981—. Mem. Lincoln Club of Adams County, Ill. Fedn. Republican Women. Mem. P.E.O. Lodge: Altrusa. Mem. Lincoln Club of Adams County, Ill. Fedn. Rep. Women. Mem. PEO, Altrusa Lodge.

DONAHUE, MARTHA, librarian, educator, retired; b. Danville, Ky., Jan. 5, 1936; d. Thomas E. and Mary Louise (Craig) D. BA, Centre Coll., 1958; MA, Ind. U., 1961; 6th Yr. Specialist's Cert., U. Wis., 1971. Tchr. Pompano Beach (Fla.) Jr. H.S., 1958-60; post libr. U.S. Army, Europe, Bad Tölz, Germany, 1961-65; instr. library Centre Coll., Danville, Ky., 1966-67, U. Wis., Whitewater, 1967-70; assoc. prof. library Mansfield (Pa.) U., 1971-93. Bd. dirs. Mansfield Free Pub. Libr., 1995-97, vol., 1998—; vol. Area Agy. on Aging, Towanda, Pa., 1993—, Sr. Citizen Meals Delivery, 1993—; mem. Parish Coun., Mansfield, 1994-97; bd. dirs. Ctr. Coll. Alumni Bd., 1996-98. Recipient Higher Edn. Act fellowship U. Wis., 1960. Mem. ALA, Pa. Libr. Assn. (chair various coms. 1971—), Friday Club of Wellsboro, Mansfield Garden Club, Columbia Lit. Exchange, The Book Group, Tioga County Hist. Soc., 1901 Soc. (pres. 2001-02). Roman Catholic. Avocations: reading, gardening, travel, cross-country skiing, bicycling. Home: 146 S Main St Mansfield PA 16933-1522

DONAHUE, MARY BETH, human services administrator; BA, Boston Coll., 1987; MPP, Georgetown U., 1992; grad. govt. program, Harvard U., 1997. Exec. asst. to Gov. Michael Dukakis, 1987-89; dir. scheduling for Tipper Gore 1992 Clinton-Gore Presdl. Campaign and Transition; with Office of the Asst. Sec. for Legislation Dept. Health and Human Svcs., 1993, dep. chief of staff, 1995-98, chief of staff, 1998—.

DONAHUE, SHIRLEY OHNSTAD, elementary school educator; b. Darlington, Wis., Aug. 29, 1937; d. Joseph and Edna L. (Peterson) Ohnstad; m. John V. Donahue, Aug. 20, 1960; children: Roger K., Jeffrey J. BS, U. Wis., Platteville, 1959; MS, No. Ill. U., 1978. Cert. tchr., Ill. Tchr. Freeport (Ill.) Sch. Sys., 1959-62, Belvidere (Ill.) Sch. Sys., 1962-64, Pecatonica (Ill.) Sch. Sys., 1964-66, Orangeville (Ill.) Sch. Sys., 1966-67, Rock Falls (Ill.) Sch. Sys., 1967-93; ret. Rock Falls (Ill.) Sch. System, 1993. Co-author gifted student curriculum materials. Mem. Liturgical com. St. Mary's Ch., Sterling, Ill., 1980-84, aux. min., 1980-94; mem. Friends of Sterling Pub. Libr., v.p. 1990-93, 96, pres. 1995; bd. dirs. YWCA, sec. bd. dirs., 1994-95, pres. bd. dirs. 1997-99; mem. Cmty. Gen. Hosp. Med. Ctr. Aux., 1993—, co-chair sr. health ins. program, 1994-2000, pres. 1995-99, v.p. ways and means, 1999--; pres. YWCA, 1997-99; bd. dirs. ARC, Lincolnland chpt., 1996-99. Recipient Western Ill. Master Tchr. award, 1991. Mem. NEA, Rock Falls Elem. Edn. Assn. (chmn. polit. action com. for edn. 1985-87), Ill. Edn. Assn. Roman Catholic. Avocation: bicycling. Home: 1720 Avenue E Sterling IL 61081-1124

DONALD, AIDA DIPACE, retired publishing executive; d. Victor E. and Bessie DiPace; m. David Herbert Donald; 1 child, Bruce Randall. AB cum laude, Barnard Coll.; MA, Columbia U.; PhD, U. Rochester. Instr. history dept. Columbia U., N.Y.C.; cons. and series editor Hill and Wang Pubs., N.Y.C.; editor Mass. Hist. Soc., Boston, 1960-64, Johns Hopkins U. Press, Balt., 1972-73; social sci. editor Harvard U. Press, Cambridge, Mass., 1973-79, exec. editor, 1979-89, editor in chief, 1989—2000, asst. dir., 1990—2000; ret., 2000. Editor: John F. Kennedy and the New Frontier, 1966, (with David Herbert Donald) Charles Frances Adams Diary, 2 vols., 1965. Columbia U. Dibblee fellow, 1952-53, U. Rochester fellow, 1953-55, 56-57, Oxford U. Fulbright fellow, 1959-60. Fellow AAUW; mem. Am. Hist. Assn., Orgn. Am. Historians. Avocations: writing, tennis, first editions, antique silver, coins.

DONALD, BERNICE B. judge; b. Miss., Sept. 17, 1951; d. Perry and Willie Bell (Hall) Bowie; m. W. L. Donald, Oct. 9, 1973. BA in Sociology, Memphis State Univ., 1974, JD, 1979; student, Nat. Judicial Coll., 1983, 84. Bar: Tenn. 1979, U.S. Fed. Ct. 1979, U.S. Supreme Ct. 1989. Clk. South Central Bell Telephone Co., 1971-75, mgr., 1975-80; staff atty. Memphis Area Legal Svcs., 1980, Shelby County Public Defenders Office, 1980-82; judge Gen. Sessions Criminal Ct. of Shelby County, Tenn., 1982-88; bankruptcy judge U.S. Bankruptcy Ct. (we. dist.) Tenn., Memphis, 1988-96; U.S. dist. judge U.S. Dist. Ct. (we. dist.) Tenn., 1996—. Mem. adv. com. on bankruptcy rules Jud. Conf., 1996—; faculty mem. Fed. Judicial Ctr., 1991—, Nat. Judicial Coll., 1992—; adj. prof. Shelby State C.C., 1980-84, Cecil C. Humphreys Sch. of Law, 1985-88; lectr., presenter in field. Featured in Essence mag., Ebony mag., Jet mag., Memphis mag., Dollars and Sense mag., Black Enterprise mag. Bd. dirs. Midtown Mental Health, 1990-92, 94-96, Memphis in May, 1994-97, Leadership Memphis, Inc., 1993-96, U. Memphis Alumni Bd., 1994—, Memphis Race Rels. and Diversity Inst., 1994—; former bd. dirs. numerous religious and civic orgns. including Calvary St. Ministry, Memphis Literacy Coun., YWCA. Recipient Cmty. Svcs. award Nat. Conf. on Christians and Jews, 1986, Martin Luther King Cmty. Svc. award, Young Careerist award State of Tenn. Raleigh Bureau of Profl. Women, plaques and certs.; named Citizen of Yr. Excelsior Chpt. of Eastern Star, Woman of Yr. Pentecostal Ch. of God in Christ. Mem. ABA (mem. standing com. on Gavel awards 1989-95, mem. adv. com. Ctrl. and Ea. European Law Initiative 1999—, mem. ho. dels. 1993-95, 99—, bd. govs. 1999—, liason labor and employment law sect. 1999—, Law Libr. Congress 1999—, Appellate Judges Conf. 1999-2000, Africa Legal Tech. Assistance Project 2000—, mem. legal opportunity scholarship com. 2000—, Mus.'s bd. dirs. 2000—, numerous jud. adminstrn. divsn. coms.), Nat. Assn. of Women Judges (treas. 1986-87, sec. 1987-88, v.p. 1988-89, pres. elect 1989-90, pres. 1990-91), Am. Judges Assn., Nat. Ctr. for State Cts., Am. Bar Assn., Nat. Bar Assn., Tenn. Bar Assn. (bd. dirs. 1997-98), Memphis County Bar Assn., Shelby County Bar Assn., Am. Trial Lawyers Assn., Assn. of Women Attys. (pres. 1991, bd. dirs.), Nat. Conf. of Bankruptcy Judges (bd. dirs. 1993-96), Nat. Conf. of Women's Bar Assn. (bd. mem.), Nat. Conf. of Spl. Ct. Judges (sec.), Leadership Memphis (pres. 1987, bd. dirs.), Internat. Women's Forum, Memphis Bar Assn. (bd. dirs. 1993), Zeta Phi Beta (Alpha Eta Zeta chpt.). Avocations: reading, crossword puzzles, music, bicycling, walking. Office: Federal Building 167 N Main St Ste 1111 Memphis TN 38103-1831

DONALDSON, LISA MILLER, city administration; b. Tallahassee, Fla., Aug. 8, 1963; d. Charles D. and Virginia Reynolds Miller; m. Gary E. Donaldson, July 24, 1993; 1 child, Haley. AA, Fla. State U., 1984; BA, Fla. Atlantic U., 1996. Asst. to CAO Cen. Corp., Ft. Lauderdale, Fla., 1987-88; planner Broward County Govt., Ft. Lauderdale, 1988-91, equal opportunity compliance analyst, 1991-94; cons. The Donaldson Group, Plantation, Fla., 1996-99, pres., 1999—; spl. projects coord. City of Oakland Park, Fla., 1999-2001; commn. adminstr. Ft. Lauderdale City Commn., 2001—. Chair Census 2000 adv. bd. City of Plantation, 1999. Bd. dirs. 1st United Meth. Ch. Adminstrv. Bd., Ft. Lauderdale, 1999; v.p. El Dorado Homeowners Assn., Plantation, 1998—; mem. fin. bd., bd. dirs. Oakland Park Main St. Orgn.; bd. dirs. Downtown Ft. Lauderdale TMA; trustee 1st United Meth. Ch. Mem. Am. Planning Assn., Am. Polit. Sci. Assn., LEAD Alumni (pres. 1993-94), Plantation Jr. Women's Club, Pi Sigma Alpha. Democrat. Methodist. Avocations: gardening, travel, history. Office: City Ft Lauderdale 100 N Andrews Ave Fort Lauderdale FL 33301 Home: 8862 Winged Foot Dr Tallahassee FL 32312-4058 Fax: (954) 581-6374. E-mail: Donaldsongroup@aol.com.

DONALDSON, MARCIA JEAN, lay worker; b. Wilmington, Del., June 20, 1925; C. Aubrey Smith and Marcia Allen (Hall) Whitman; m. Robert Donald Donaldson, Jan. 8, 1944; children: Robert Gary, Pamela Lynn, David Keith. Student pub. schs., Wilmington. Sunday Sch. tchr., Del., N.J., 1943-70; tchr. Child Evangelism Fellowship, Wilmington, 1943-55, tchr., bd. dirs., 1955-64, dir., 1964-73; pres., exec. dir. Christian Children's Assocs., Toms River, N.J., 1973—. Writer radio and TV syndicated programs worldwide for children; author: (booklet) A 30 Year Adventure; producer, hostess radio and TV program Adventure Pals. Mem. Nat. Religious Broadcasters Assn., Gideons Aux. Office: Christian Children's Assn Inc PO Box 446 Toms River NJ 08754-0446 Office Phone: 732-240-3003. E-mail: adventurepals@juno.com.

DONALDSON, MYRTLE NORMA, music educator, musician; b. Priddy, Tex., Feb. 9, 1923; d. Emil Otto and Brunhilda Eleanore (Riewe) Schneider; m. Fletcher William Donaldson, Feb. 12, 1943; children: Patricia Annette, Rebecca Joyce. BA, U. Ariz., 1970; MA, Middle Tenn. State U., 1982. Cert. profl. piano tchr. Tenn. Music Tchrs. Assn., profl. piano tchr.'s cert. Nat. Music Tchrs.' Assn. Organist Luth. chs., Aleman and Austin, Tex., 1937-42, 43-50, Kinston, N.C., 1943, Los Alamos, N.Mex., 1951-53; Ft. Worth, 1954-56; organist Tullahoma, Tenn., 1969-81; piano tchr., 1972-2001. Composer: sonata, 1981, theme and variations, 1980. Mem. Cmty. Concert Bd., Tullahoma, 1973-99; mem. Cmty. Concert Membership Ch., 1974-78, pres., 1978-80, 89-93. Mem. Music Tchrs. Nat. Assn. (coms. 1983-99, cert. 1991), Mid. Tenn. Music Tchrs. Assn. (sec. Murfreesboro chpt. 1975-77, chair membership state 1977-78, pres. Mid. Tenn. chpt. 1979-81, 87-89), Delta Phi Alpha. Republican. Lutheran. Avocations: knitting, sewing, creative memories album, national background of grandparents.

DONALDSON, SARAH SUSAN, radiologist; b. Portland, Oreg., Apr. 20, 1939; BS, RN, U. Oreg., 1961; MD, Harvard U., 1968. Intern U. Wash., 1968—69; resident in radiol. therapy Stanford (Calif.) Med. Ctr., 1969—72; fellow in pediatric oncology Inst. Gustave-Roussy, 1972—73; prof. radiol. oncology Stanford U. Sch. Medicine., 1973—. Mem.: NIH. Office: Stanford U Med Ctr Dept Radio/Oncology 875 Blake Wilbur Dr Stanford CA 94305-5847

DONALDSON, SUE KAREN, nursing educator, researcher; b. Detroit, Sept. 16, 1943; BSN, Wayne State U., 1965, MSN, 1966; PhD, U. Wash., 1973. Asst. assoc. prof. physiology and nursing U. Wash., Seattle, 1973-78; assoc. prof. physiology and nursing Rush U., Ill., 1978-84, dir. clin. nursing rsch. program, 1980-84; prof. physiology/nursing, former assoc. dean rsch. Sch. Nursing, U. Minn., Mpls., 1984—94; dean Sch. Nursing, Johns Hopkins U., Balt., 1994—2001, prof. physiology and nursing. Grantee, Wash. State Heart Assn., 1973—74, NIH, 1973—96, USPHS, 1980—, Muscular Dystrophy Assn., 1981—. Mem. ANA, AAN, IOM, NAS, Am. Heart Assn., APS, Biophysical Soc. Office: Johns Hopkins U Sch Nursing 525 N Wolfe St Baltimore MD 21205-2110

DONALDSON, WILMA CRANKSHAW, elementary school educator; b. Havre de Grace, Md., Aug. 28, 1942; d. John Hamilton and Wilma Chaffee (Thurlow) Crankshaw; m. James Neill Donaldson, Aug. 5, 1967. BA in Edn. cum laude, Westminster Coll., 1964; MA in Edn., Fairfield U., 1976. Educator Hurlbutt Elem. Sch., Weston, Conn., 1964-78, 92—, Weston Mid. Sch., 1979-91; tchr. Greek Mythology Elem. Sch., 1999—. Team leader Hurlbutt Elem. Sch., 1967—68, 1976—78, sci. rep., 1992—99, developer of curriculum; judge Odyssey of the Mind, Conn., 1995—2001; presenter of photography and Greek myth courses elem. sch., 2002—; tchr. pvt. student art courses; tchr. Music/Lit./Theater Workshop, 1997—; presenter in field; sci. cons. Greenwich Pub. Schs., 2002—. Author: (filmstrip script) Sci. Series, 1972, Metric Math Series, 1973. Chairperson fine arts New England Sch. Accreditation Com., Weston, 1990-91; trainer Project CHEM, Exxon Corp., 1991—; state planning com., program/site chmn. Conn. Elem. Sci. Day Conf., 1994—; organizer, advisor Student Elem. Sch. Environ. Orgn., 1992-2003, sci. cons. for Pub. Schs. Greenwich, Conn., 2002[00bf]; co-organizer, co-founder Elem. Family Sci. Night, Weston, 2000; dir./tchr. Camp Invention, Weston, 2002—, mem. Silvermine Arts Enrichment Com. Recipient Faculty Mem. Presdl. Recognition Sch. award U.S. Dept. Edn., 1987-88, Celebration of Excellence award State of Conn., 1989, 92, 95, 98. Mem. NEA, Nat. Sci. Tchrs. Assn. (workshop presenter Moscow 1991, NASA-NEWEST awardee 1997), ASCD, Conn. Edn. Assn., Conn. Alliance Arts Edn. (Weston Tchr. of Yr. 1994-95, Conn. Alliance for Art Edn. Disting. Tchr. of Yr. 1995), Coun. Elem. Sci. Internat. (com. chmn. 1991-98), Delta Zeta. Avocations: art, theater, photography, travel.

DONATH, THERESE, artist, author; b. Hammond, Ind., Dec. 14, 1928; Student, Monticello Coll., 1946-47; BFA, St. Joseph' Coll., 1975; additional study, Oxbow Summer Sch. Painting. Radio/TV personality, 1978-92; interviewer, prodr. Viewpoint Sta. WLNR-FM, Lansing, Ill., 1963-64; reporter, columnist N.W. Ind. Sentinel, 1965; freelance writer Monterey Peninsula Herald, 1981-85; contbg. author Monterey Life mag., 1981-85; asst. dir. Michael Karolyi Found., Vence, France, 1979. Creative cons. Aslan Tours and Travel, 1983-85; instr., lectr. Penland, N.C., 1970, Haystack Mountain Sch., Deer Isle, Maine, 1974, Sheffield Poly., Eng., 1978; bd. dirs., sec. Mental Health Soc. Greater Chgo., 1963-64; exec. dir. Lansing (Ill.) Mental Health Soc., 1963-64. One-woman shows include: Palos Verdes (Calif.) Mus., 1974, L.A. Inst. Contemporary Art, 1978, Mus. Contemporary Art, Chgo., 1975, Calif. State U., Fullerton, 1973, No. Ill. U., DeKalb, 1971, Bellevue (Wash.) Mus. Art, 1986-87; represented in permanent collections including Kennedy Gallery, N.Y.C., also pvt. collections; represented in the Mirror Book, 1978; author: Screams and Laughter, 1992; author, illustrator: Before I Die, A Creative Legacy, 1989; contbr. articles to profl. jours., newspapers; illustrator: Run Computer Run. Recipient awards No. Ind. Art Mus., 1966, 70, 71, 73; grantee Ragdale Found., Lake Forest, Ill. 1982.

DONEGAN, CHERYL, artist; b. New Haven, 1962; BFA in Painting, R.I. Sch. Design, 1984; MFA, Hunter Coll., 1990. Artist-in-residence Banff Ctr. Fine Arts, Alta., Canada, 1985. One-woman shows include Elizabeth Koury Gallery, N.Y.C., 1993, Studio Guenzani, Milan, Italy, 1994, All Girls, Berlin, 1994, Galerie Rizzo, Paris, 1994, Nice Fine Arts, France, 1994, Basilico Fine Arts, N.Y.C., 1996—97, Baumgartner Galleries, Washington, 1997, Lotta Hammer, London, 1998, exhibited in group shows at The Walter Philips Gallery, Banff, 1985, Jon Gerstadt Gallery, N.Y.C., 1986, P.S. 122, 1987, Althea Viafora Gallery, 1990, Simon Watson Gallery, 1990—91, 522 Lafayette St. Space, 1991, Dooley Le Cappelaine Gallery, N.Y.C., 1991, Kim Light Gallery, L.A., 1993, Mus. Contemporary Art, Chgo., 1994, Whitney Mus. Am. Art, 1995, Trans Hudson Gallery, Jersey City, N.J., 1996, 1998, Mus. Modern Art, N.Y.C., 1997, ACC Galerie Wiemar, 1998, Bard Ctr. Curatorial Studies, N.Y., 1999, numerous others; author: The Power of Feminist Art, 1994; contbr. articles to profl. jours. Recipient Grand Prix, 7th Internat. Festival of Saint-Gervais, Geneva, 1997. Office: DIA Ctr for the Arts 542 W 22nd St New York NY 10011-1108 Fax: 212-334-5187.

DONEHAM, SHAWNA ELYSE, set designer; b. Mar. 12, 1952; m. Michael Doneham, Dec. 24, 1977; 1 child, Andrew John. MFA, NYU, 1978. Stage mgr. Papermill Playhouse, Millburn, NJ, 1990—97; set designer Ford's Theatre, N.Y.C., 1998—2001, Meriks Performing Arts Ctr., Irving, Tex., 2002—. Avocations: acting, filmmaking. Office: Meriks Performing Arts Ctr 2601 DeWitt St Irving TX 75062-4139

DONEHEW, PAMELA K. reading specialist; b. Fairmont, W.Va., Sept. 24, 1949; d. Walter Hal Donehew and Eldora Jean (Eddy) Van Tol; m. E. William Ball, Sr., June 1, 1968 (div. Oct. 1993); children: E. William, Jr., Jennifer Catena, Geoffrey J.; m. Lawrence L. Lambert, Feb. 14, 1999; stepchildren: Leslie L., Laura M. AA, Ocean County Coll., Toms River, N.J., 1986; BA in English and Psychology, Monmouth U., 1989, MA, 1991, MSEd, 1992. Cert. reading specialist, tchr. psychology, English tchr., tchr. grades K-12, N.J. Dir. reading ctr. Monmouth U., West Long Branch, N.J., 1989-92; tchr. psychology Manasquan H.S., N.J., 1992-95; reading specialist West Ga. Tech., LaGrange, 1995—, SAT and ACT supr., 1996—. Learning cons. Georgian Ct. Coll., Lakewood, N.J., 1995; reader coll. bds. AP Psychology Exam, 1996—; GRE, GMAT Test administr., 1990-94. Author: Library Handbook, 1996; co-author: Learn to Tutor, 1990. Mem. APA, NEA, Nat. Coun. English Tchrs., Internat. Reading Assn., Phi Delta Kappa. Office: West Ga Tech 303 Fort Dr Lagrange GA 30240-5957 E-mail: pdonehew@westgatec.ga.tec.us.

DONEHEY, MARILYN MOSS, foundation administrator; b. Malad City, Idaho, Sept. 5, 1946; d. Ray Wesley and LaRue Camp Jones; m. Robert David Donehey, Apr. 15, 1966 (div. June 1989); children: Troy Robert, David Ray, Calli-Anne, Suzanne, Erin. AA, Elgin Cmty. Coll., 1987; BA, Judson Coll., 1992. Sec., receptionist Fox Valley Ctr. for Ind. Livng, Elgin, Ill., 1987-88, devel. dir., 1990-91; cmty. outreach specialist Tri-County Ind. Living Ctr., Akron, Ohio, 1993-94; program dir. Soc. of the Blind, Akron, 1997—2002. Subs. tchr. dispatcher, Ill. Sch. Dist. 300, Carpentersville, 1972-81. Precinct com. person Rep. Cen. Com., Kane County, Ill., 1977-90; pres. Consumer Advocacy coun., Akron, 2000-2002.; participant blindness adjustment program La. Ctr. Blind. Mem. Nat. Fedn. of the Blind (vice chair 1997-2001, sec. 2001-2002, scholar 1987). Republican. Mem. Lds Ch. Avocations: music, writing. Office: Soc of the Blind 325 E Market Akron OH 44304 E-mail: mmoss325@aol.com., Lynssom@aol.com.

DONELSON, ROSEMARIE QUIROZ CARVAJAL, human services professional, state official; b. San Antonio, Tex., Sept. 14, 1952; d. Frank Cordero Quiroz and Margaret Carvajal Quiroz; m. Dennis Michael Donelson, Oct. 7, 1972; 1 child, Alexandra (Sasha). Student, U. Tex., San Antonio, San Antonio Coll., 1976—. Assembly line worker Universal Bookbindery, San Antonio, 1971-73; day care instr., office mgr. Madison Sq. Presbyn. Ch., San Antonio, 1973-77; credit analyst Sears Roebuck and Co., San Antonio, 1976-85; adminstrv. tech. Tex. Dept. Human Svcs., San Antonio, 1985—. Video facilitator Pacific Inst., San Antonio, 1999. Active walks/runs Juvenile Diabetes Found., San Antonio, 1997—. Named Outstanding Women in Tex. Govt. Gov.'s Commn. for Women, 1998. Mem. San Antonio Conservation Soc., Nat. Hist. Preservation Soc., Victorian Soc. in Am. Democrat. Roman Catholic. Avocations: reading, antique collecting, history, personal/holistic fitness, working. Office: Tex Dept Human Svcs 11307 Roszell St San Antonio TX 78217-2511

DONG, MABEL H, music educator; d. Siu-tong Hau and Yim-ching Chan; m. Tony K Dong, Aug. 10, 1988; 1 child, Vanessa W. MusB, Hong Kong Bapt. U., 1977—81; MusM, SW Tex. State U., 1984—85; DMA in Progress, U. of Colo., 1986—88. Single Subject Tchg. Credential, Music Calif. Teacher's Credential Commn., 1997, Ill. Tchg. Cert., Music Chgo. Bd. of Edn., 1995. Music tchr. Tak Ngai Cath. Sch., Hong Kong, China, 1977—78, Alliance Elem. Sch., Hong Kong, China, 1981—83; job tng. coord. Chinese Mut. Aid Assn., Chgo., 1990—91; music dir. St. Barbara H.S., Chgo., 1991—94; piano/voice instr. Moraine Valley C.C., Palos Hill, Ill., 1992—95; music tchr. Florence Nightingale Sch., Chgo., 1995—96; chinese bilingual tchr. Glenview Elem. Sch., Oakland, Calif., 1996—97; music tchr. Jefferson Sch. Dist., Daly City, Calif., 1997—99, Berkeley Unified Sch. Dist., Berkeley, Calif., 1999—. Com. mem. Berkeley District-wide Music Curriculum Com., Berkeley, Calif., 2000—; music teacher's workshop presenter Jefferson Sch. Dist., Daly City, Calif., 1997—99. Recipient Second Pl. in Singing (Grad. Divsn.), Nat. Assn. of Teachers Singing, 1985. Mem.: Trinity Coll., London (licentiate LTCL 1983), Associated Bd. of Royal Schools of Music (licentiate LRSM 1981), Internat. Fedn. for Choral Music (assoc.), Chinese Music Tchr. Assn. of No. Calif. (assoc.), Am. Choral Dir. Assn. (assoc.), Music Educator Nat. Conf.

(assoc.). Office: Berkeley Unified School District 1500 Derby St Rm 509 Berkeley CA 94704 Personal E-mail: mabelhdong@sbcglobal.net.

DONIGER, WENDY, history of religions educator; b. N.Y.C., Nov. 20, 1940; d. Lester L. and Rita (Roth) Doniger; m. Dennis M. O'Flaherty, Mar. 31, 1964; 1 child, Michael Lester O'Flaherty. BA summa cum laude, Radcliffe Coll., 1962; PhD, Harvard U., 1968. Lectr. U. London Sch. Oriental and African Studies, 1968-75; vis. lectr. U. Calif., Berkeley, 1975-77; prof. history of religions Div. Sch., dept. South Asian langs., com. on social thought U. Chgo., 1978-85, Mircea Eliade prof., 1986—. Author: (under name of Wendy Doniger O'Flaherty) Asceticism and Eroticism in the Mythology of Siva, 1973, Hindu Myths, 1975, The Origins of Evil in Hindu Mythology, 1976, Women, Androgynes and Other Mythical Beasts, 1980, The Rig Veda: An Anthology, 1981, Karma and Rebirth in Classical Indian Traditions, 1980, Dreams, Illusion and Other Realities, 1984, Other Peoples' Myths, 1988, (under name of Wendy Doniger), The Laws of Manu, 1991, Mythologies, 1991, Purana Perennis, 1993, The Implied Spider, 1998, Splitting the Difference, 1999, The Bedtrick, 2000, The Kamasutra, 2002; editor Jour. Am. Acad. Religion, 1977-80, History of Religions, 1979—; mem. editl. bd. Ency. Britannica, 1987-98, Daedalus, 1990—. Recipient Lucy Allen Paton prize, 1961, Phi Beta Kappa prize, 1962; Jonathan Fay Fund scholar, 1962, Am. Inst. Indian Studies fellow, 1963-64, NEH summer stipend, 1980, Guggenheim fellow, 1980-81. Fellow: Am. Acad. Arts and Scis., Am. Philos. Soc.; mem.: Assn. Asian Studies (pres. 1998), Am. Acad. Religion (pres. 1984), Phi Beta Kappa. Home: 1319 E 55th St Chicago IL 60615-5301 Office: U Chgo Div Sch 1025 E 58th St Chicago IL 60637-1509

DONLEY, ROSEMARY, university official; Diploma in Nursing, Pitts. Hosp., 1961; BSN summa cum laude, St. Louis U., 1963; M in Nursing Edn., U. Pitts., 1965; postgrad. tng. in psychiatry, U. Pitts., Columbia U., 1967-69; PhD, U. Pitts., 1972; postgrad., Harvard U., 1986; LittD (hon.), Felician Coll., 1981, Villanova U., 1985; LLD (hon.), Loyola U., Chgo., 1988; HHD (hon.), Madonna Coll., 1988; Dr. Pub. Svc. (hon.), R.I. Coll., 1988, La Roche Coll., 1989. Staff nurse St. Mary's Hosp., St. Louis, 1961-63; instr. Pitts. Hosp. Sch. Nursing, 1963-71; cons. Vis. Nurses Assn. Allegheny County, Pitts., 1972; from instr. to assoc. prof. Sch. Nursing U. Pitts., 1971-79; dean and assoc. prof. Sch. Nursing Cath. U. Am., Washington, 1979-86, exec. v.p., 1986—. Bd. dirs. Ea. Mercy Health Care System, Forbes Health Care System, Nursing Econs. Found.; cons. in field; advisor internat. programs, lectr. various colls. and univs. Contbr. articles to profl. jours.; mem. editorial bd. Ednl. Record, 1985—, Jour. Contemporary Health Law and Policy, 1985—. Bd. dirs. Seton Hill Coll., 1991—. Recipient Hon. Recognition award Pa. League for Nursing, 1978, Alumni Merit award St. Louis U., 1980, Woman of Yr. award Pres.'s Commn. on Women, Cath. U. Am., 1984, McGrady award, Cath. Youth Assn. of Pitts. Inc., 1987, Medal of Distinction, U. Pitts., 1987; fellow Robert Wood Johnson Found. and Inst. Medicine, Nat. Acad. Sci., 1977-78; Disting. scholar in nursing NYU, 1994; Alumni fellows award U. Pitts., 1995. Fellow Am. Acad. Nursing; mem. Inst. Medicine, Nat. League for Nursing (pres. 1987-89), Sigma Theta Tau (sr. editor Image Jour. Nursing, 1st v.p. 1971-74, pres. 1975-81). Home: 7004 Riggs Rd Hyattsville MD 20783-2933 Office: Cath U Am Office Of Exec Vp Washington DC 20064-0001

DONLON, CLAUDETTE, performing company executive; Gen. mgr. Am. Ballet Theatre; exec. v.p. Kennedy Center for the Performing Arts. Office: Kennedy Center for the Performing Arts 2700 F St NW Washington DC 20566

DONLOU-RICHMOND, DORIS JULIA, scriptwriter; d. Gordon and Maria Donlou; m. Daniel Joseph Richmond, June 30, 2001. BA in English-Creative Writing with honors, Loyola Marymount U., Westchester, Calif., 1997; MFA in Screenwriting, U. So. Calif., L.A., 1999. Story analyst DeLine Pictures, L.A., 1999—2001, HSI Prodns., L.A., 1999—2001, Filmstew.com, L.A., 1999—2001. Author: (screenplays) Extra Virgin Olive Oil (USC Excellence in Screenwriting award, 1998, Austin Film Festival Quarterfinalist, 1999); asst. dir. : (plays) The Sun Dialogues; writer, rschr., co-editor: book Saint Katherine Greek Orthodox Church Consecration Commemorative Album. Greek Orthodox. Personal E-mail: ddonlou@aol.com.

DONNELL, JEAN DOWNEY, education educator; b. N.Y.C., Nov. 27, 1951; d. Chester Woodson and Deloris Sydnor Downey; m. Bennett Sr. Donnell, June 7, 1975; children: Joy, Bennett Jr. BS, Towson (Md.) U., 1995, MA, 1999; PhD in Comms. Design, U. Balt., 2003. Adj. prof. Exxex CC, Balt., 2001—03, U. Balt., 2003, Towson (Md.) U., 2003—. Author: (book) Sacred Circle Writing, 2003; dir.(exec.): Miss Am. Prelimenary Pageant, 1997—98, (creator) (documentary) Women in Ministry, Journeys of the Heart Creative Writing for Women. Home: 10500 Willow VIsta Way Cockeysville MD 21030 Office: RIver of Life Christian Ctr 5225 Hamilton Ave Baltimore MD 21206 E-mail: thebestview@aol.com.

DONNELLY, BARBARA SCHETTLER, retired medical technologist; b. Sweetwater, Tenn., Dec. 2, 1933; d. Clarence G. and Irene Elizabeth (Brown) Schettler; children: Linda Ann, Richard Michael. AA, Tenn. Wesleyan Coll., 1952; BS, U. Tenn., 1954; cert. med. tech., Erlanger Hosp. Sch. Med. Tech., 1954; postgrad., So. Meth. U., 1980-81. Med. technologist Erlanger Hosp., Chattanooga, 1953-57, St. Luke's Episcopal Hosp., Tex. Med. Ctr., Houston, 1957-58, 62; engring. R&D SCI Systems, Inc., Huntsville, Ala., 1974-76; cons. hematology systems Abbott Labs., Dallas, 1976-77; hematology specialist Dallas, Irving, Tex., 1977-81; tech. specialist microbiology systems Irving, Tex., 1981-83; coord. tech. svc. clin. chemistry systems, 1983-84; coord. customer tng. clin. chemistry systems, 1984-87; supr. clin. chemistry tech. svcs., 1987-88; supr. clin. chemistry customer support ctr., 1988-93; supr. clin. chemistry and x-systems customer support ctr., 1993-97; ret., 1997. Contbr. articles on cytology to profl. jours. Mem. Am. Soc. Clin. Pathologists (cert. med. technologist), Am. Soc. Microbiology, Nat. Assn. Female Execs., U. Tenn. Alumni Assn., Chi Omega. Republican. Methodist. Home: 204 Greenbriar Ln Colleyville TX 76034-8616

DONNELLY, CHRISTINA WOS, poet; arrived in U.S., 1951; d. Piotr and Marja Wos; m. Michael James Donnelly, June 24, 1973 (div. June 1993); children: Rebecca Anna, Melanie Margaret, Jessica Mary. BA magna cum laude, Daemen Coll., 1980. Pub. rels. intern The Am. Mus. of Natural History, New York, 1972; advt. copywriter Hens & Kelly, Buffalo, 1973—74, Wm. Hengerer Co., Buffalo, 1974—75; freelance writer and copyeditor Buffalo, 1975—93; lay min. Unity Ch. of Practical Christianity, Buffalo, 1990—93; poet Buffalo, 1993—. Featured reader in field. Copy-editor: Fan Engineering, 8th edition, 1982, contbr.: Off the Cuffs: poetry by and about the police, 2003, Common Roots, Common Ground, 2003, The Shadow's Imprint: Poetic Reflections on Death, 2002; author: Venus Afflicted, 2002; guest editor: online jour. Stirring, 2002—03; contbr. poetry to jours. and mags. Neighborhood rep. Com. for Reapportionment Compliance, Buffalo, 1982—82; vol. hosp. chaplain Pastoral Care Dept of Buffalo (N.Y.) Gen. Hosp., 1989—92; co-founder, co-dir. grassroots orgn. Greater Claremont Neighborhood Assn., Buffalo, 1980—82. Named Artvoice Artist of the Week, 2002. Mem.: Just Buffalo Lit. Ctr. (assoc.). Avocations: reading, films, dance, fitness.

DONNELLY, GLORIA FERRARO, university dean; b. Phila. Grad., Villanova U., U. Pa.; PhD in Human Devel., Bryn Mawr Coll., 1985. With Eastern Pa. Psychiat. Hosp., Inst. Pa. Hosp.; mem. faculty U. Pa. Sch. Nursing, Trenton (N.J.) State Coll., Villanova U.; founding dean of nursing La Salle U.; dean Sch. Nursing MCP Hahnemann U., Phila., 1996—98, Col. Nursing and Health Professions Drexel U., Phila., 1998—. Editor Holistic Nursing Practice Jour.; author 4 books. Recipient Am. Jour. Nursing Book of Yr. awards. Fellow Am. Acad. Nursing; mem. Nat. League for Nursing (bd. govs. 1995-97, chmn. coun. baccalaureate and higher degree programs, mem. exec. com.). Office: Drexel U Coll Nursing and Health Professions 245 N 15th St # 501 Philadelphia PA 19102-1192 Business E-Mail: gloria.donnelly@drexel.edu.

DONNELLY, SHARLOTTE K. B. NEELY, anthropology educator, author; b. Savannah, Ga., Aug. 13, 1948; d. Joseph Bowden and Kathleen Bell Neely; m. Thomas Christian C. Donnelly, June 21, 1980; 1 child, Bridgette. BA, Ga. State U., 1970; MA, U. NC, 1971, PhD, 1976. Prof. of anthropology No. Ky. U., Highland Heights, 1974—, anthropology coord., 1992—2000. Author: (book) Snowbird Cherokees, 1991; co-author: This Land Was Theirs, 1996, 1999; contbr. articles to profl. jours., chpts. to books. Pres. League for Animal Welfare, Cincinnati, Ohio, 1984—85. Recipient Strongest Influence Award, No. Ky. U. Alumni Assn., 1996. Fellow: Am. Anthrop. Assn.; mem.: Anthropologists and Sociologists of Ky. (pres. 1979—80). Democrat-Npl. Roman Catholic. Avocations: writing, travel. Office: No Ky U Nunn Dr Highland Heights KY 41099 Personal E-mail: donnelly@one.net. E-mail: neelys@nku.edu.

DONNEM, SARAH LUND, financial analyst, non-profit and political organization consultant; b. St. Louis, Apr. 10, 1936; d. Joel Y. and Erle Hall (Harsh) Lund; m. Roland W. Donnem, Feb. 18, 1961; children: Elizabeth Prince Donnem Sigety, Sarah Madison. BA, Vassar Coll., 1958. Tech. aide, computer programmer Bell Labs, Whippany, N.J., 1959-60; chmn. placement vol. opportunities N.Y. Jr. League, 1972-73, asst. treas., 1974-75, chmn. urban problems relating to mental health, 1967-69, mem. project rsch. com., 1967-70, chmn., 1973-74, mem. bd. mgrs., 1973-74. Chmn. cmty. rsch. Washington Jr. League, 1970-71, mem. bd. mgrs., 1970-71; mem. Stratford Hall (N.Y.) Com., 1970—; bd. dirs. East Side Settlement House, Bronx, N.Y., 1972—, v.p., 1975-76, chmn. Nat. Horse Show Benefit, 1976, winter antiques show com., 1994—, co-chmn. adv. com., 1991-94, chmn. VIP Day, 1999—, mem. nominating com., 1990—, mem. investment com., 1993—; bd. dirs. Stanley M. Isaacs Neighborhood Ctr., N.Y.C., 1973-76, v.p., 1975-76; bd. dirs. Presbyn. Home for Aged Women, N.Y.C., 1974-76, v.p., 1976; mem. exec. bd. N.Y. Aux. of Blue Ridge Sch., 1971-75, sec. 1965-67, pres., 1973-75; budget and benevolence com. Brick Presbyn. Ch., N.Y.c., 1973-76, mem. social svc. com., 1973-74, chmn. fgn. students com., 1963-64; bd. dirs. Search and Care, N.Y.c., 1973--76, Project LEARN, cleve., 1990-96, 2000—; chmn. Literacy Fund, 1991-95, mem., 1995—; mem. Friends of Project LEARN, 1986—, mem. Fedn. Cmty. Planning, Cleve., coun. on Older Persons, 1978-82, mem. future Planning task Force, 1980-81, commn. on social concerns, 1982-84; trustee Golden Age Ctrs. Greatr cleve., 1979-92, investment com., 1993, 1st v.p., 1980-81, pres. 1981-85, chmn. Western Res. Antiques show, 1979, 80; chmn. cleve. antiques Show Silver Anniv., 2000; mem. women's adv. coun. Westrn Res. Hist. Soc., 1977—, coord. sec., 1978; mem. women's com. Cleve. Orch., 1979-85, Vassar Coll. cleve. sec. 1980-82, v.p., 1983, pres. 1984-86; mem. AAVC Club Liaison com., 1986-89, chmn. regional program com., 1987-89; bd. dirs. Cleve. Ballet, 1980-2001, exec. com. 1981, fin. com. 1982-88, 95-98, nominating com., 1988-90, 95-2000, co-chmn. 1997-99; co-chmn. Yale Ball, 1983; bd. advisors Ret. Sr. Vol. Program, 1982, trustee, 1983-90, chmn. long range planning comm., 1986, sec. 1987-89; mem. Family Friends Adv. Coun., 1987-89; trustee Fairmount Presbyn. Ch., 1985-88; mem. long range planning com. United Way, Cleve., 1985-87; coord. Friends of Voinovich, 1987-89; womens adv. com. Voinovich for Governor, 1990, Voinovich for Senate, 1997-98, chmn. Voinovich Task Force on Aging, 1990-91, Ohio Adv. Coun. on Aging, 1991-2002, legis. com., 1994-2000; chmn.legis. com. Cuyahoga County Republican Party, 1994-2000, mem. policy com., mem. fin. com., 1999—, Plain Dealer adv. counsel for elderly coverage, 1991-93; chmn. Johns Hopkins Parents Fund, 1986-88, Project LEARN 15th Anniversary celebration (with Barbara Bush, hon. chmn.), 1989-90; coord. Decorative Arts Trust Cleve. Symposium, 1996; mem. Leadership Cleve. Class 1992; del. White House Conf. on Aging, 1995. Named Vol. of Yr. N.Y. Jr. League, 1975; recipient Sustainer Svc. award Jr. League Cleve., 1990. Mem. Nat. Inst. Social Scis. (membership com. 1972-92, trustee 1984-96), Nat. Soc. Colonial Dames, Colony Club (N.Y.C.), Chevy Chase Club (Washington), Intown club, Vassar Club, Kirtland Club (Cleve.). Address: 2945 Fontenay Rd Shaker Heights OH 44120 Home (Winter): 1 King St Apt 305 Charleston SC 29401

DONNESON, SEENA SAND, artist; b. N.Y.C. d. Max and Ann (Silber) S.; m. Sam Gershwin (dec.); children: Erika Donneson, Lisa Donneson. Attended, Pratt Inst., Art Students League. Art staff NYU, Nassau County Office Cultural Devel., New Sch. for Social Rsch., N.H. Coll.; guest artist Tamarind Lithography Workshop; vis. artist Clayworks, N.Y.C. One-woman shows include Lauren Rogers Mus. Art, Laurel, Miss., Greenville (N.C.) Mus. Art, Galerie #836, Sante Fe, N.Mex., Lehigh U., Princeton U., Portland (Maine) Mus. Art, Piertrantonio Gallery, N.Y.C., U. Calif., L.I. U., George Washington U., Danville (Va.) Mus. Fine Arts and History, others; exhibited in group shows at SUNY, N.Y.C., Quietude Sculpture Garden, N.J., Sculpture in Color, N.Y.C., Ft. Lauderdale (Fla.) Mus., Norfolk Mus. Arts and Scis., Bklyn. Mus., San Francisco Mus. Art, DeCordova Mus., Alternate Spac Mod Art Foundry, N.Y.C., fgn. traveling exhbns., USIS, Mcpl. Art Mus., Tokyo, also on tour throughout Japan, Musseo de Belles Artes, Buenos Aires, Argentina, Scotland, Eng.; represented in permanent collections Va. Mus. Fine Art, Bklyn. Mus., Doris Freidman Sculpture garden, Albright U., Reading, Pa., Norfolk Mus., USIA Art in Embassies, L.A. County Mus. Art, Mus. Modern Art, N.Y.C., Smithsonian Mus., Ft. Lauderdale Mus. Fine Art, Snug Harbor Cultural Ctr., N.Y.C., N.Y. Pub. Libr., Cornell Med. Sch., N.Y.C., others; also pvt. collections; revs. Newsday, The N.Y. Times, The N.Y. Post, Art News, Conran Octopus Ltd., others. Recipient numerous art awards; fellow Edward MacDowell Found., guest artist Tamarind Lithography Workshop, Creative Artists Pub. Svc. grant N.Y. State Coun. on Arts, 1983-84; grantee Mcpl. Art Soc., N.Y. Art in Park, 1974, Queens Coun. on Arts, 1992. Mem. Artists Equity, Nat. Assn. Women Artists (bd. dirs.), L.I.C. Artists (bd. dirs.). Studio: 43-49 10th St Long Island City NY 11101-6923 Fax: (718) 706-1342. E-mail: elaici@aol.com.

DONOGHUE, EILEEN M. former mayor; BA, U. Mass., 1976; JD, Suffolk U., 1979. Atty.; mayor City of Lowell, Mass., 1998—2001; city councilor Lowell, Mass., 2001—. Office: Office of the Mayor City Hall 375 Merrimack St Lowell MA 01852

DONOGHUE, MILDRED RANSDORF, education educator; b. Cleve. d. James and Caroline (Sychra) Ransdorf; m. Charles K. Donoghue (dec. 1982); children: Kathleen, James. EdD, UCLA, 1962; JD, Western State U., 1979. Asst. prof. edn. and reading Calif. State U., Fullerton, 1962-66, assoc. prof., 1966-71, prof., 1971—. Founder, dir. Donoghue Children's Lit. Ctr., Calif. State U., Fullerton, Calif., 2001—. Author: Foreign Languages and the Schools, 1967, Foreign Languages and the Elementary School Child, 1968, The Child and the English Language Arts, 1971, 75, 79, 85, 90, Using Literature Activities to Teach Content Areas to Emergent Readers, 2001; co-author: Second Languages in Primary Education, 1979; contbr. articles to profl. jours. and Ednl. Resources Info. Ctr. U.S. Dept. Edn. Mem. AAUP, AAUW, Nat. Network for Early Lang. Learning, Nat. Coun. Tchrs. English, Nat. Coun. Tchrs. Math., Nat. Coun. Social Studies, Nat. Sci. Tchrs. Assn., Am. Ednl. Rsch. Assn., Nat. Soc. for Study of Edn., Am. Assn. Tchrs. Spanish and Portuguese, Internat. Reading Assn., Nat. Assn. Edn. Young Children, Orange County Med. Assn. Women's Aux., Assn. for Childhood Edn. Internat., Phi Beta Kappa, Phi Kappa Phi, Pi Lambda Theta, Alpha Upsilon Alpha. Address: 800 State College Blvd Fullerton CA 92831

DONOHOE, CATHRYN MURRAY, journalist; b. Bronx, N.Y. d. Harry and Helen (Crowley) Murray; m. Thomas W. Donohoe, Dec. 1, 1962. BA cum laude in Am. Lit., Middlebury Coll., 1958; student in Russian lit., Columbia U., 1958—60; student in journalism, American U., 1983—84; cert. in Russian Lang. and Culture, Gornyi Inst., St. Petersburg, Russia, 1993. Rsch. and policy coord. Radio Liberty, N.Y.C., 1963—74; freelance journalist, 1977—84; reporter Potomac Almanac, Potomac, Md., 1985, Washington Times, Washington, 1985—94, deputy editor, features, 1994—. Recipient Nat. Mag. award for pub. svc., 1985. Office: Washington Times 3600 New York Ave NE Washington DC 20002-1996

DONOHOE, ANNE EMLEN, software engineer; b. Rome, N.Y., Mar. 2, 1967; d. Warren Metz and Carol (Taylor) Emlen; m. Brian Patrick Donohue, Sept. 8, 1990; children: Taylor Mae, Catharine Ruth. BA in Computer Sci., SUNY, Geseseo, 1989; ME in Software Engring., U. Colo., 1997. Software engr. BDM Internat., Boulder, Colo., 1989-97, Lucent Techs., Westminster, Colo., 1997-99, Level 3 Comm., Broomfield, Colo., 1999—. Mem. IEEE (assoc.), High Pointers Club (Summit of the States). Avocations: greyhounds, hiking.

DONOHUE, CLAIRE P. school librarian; b. Glen Cove, N.Y., Mar. 6, 1941; d. Hubert Aloysius Donohue and Catherine Teresa Scarlett; m. John T. Sexton, Aug. 30, 1975 (div. Apr. 1, 1983). BA, St. John's U., Jamaica, N.Y., 1965, MA, 1967; MLS, L.I. U., 1974. Cert. secondary English tchr. N.Y., 1967, sch. libr. media specialist N.Y., 1974, sch. dist. adminstr. N.Y., 1995. English tchr. St. Peter of Alcantara Sch., Port Washington, NY, 1966—68; adj. instr. N.Y.C. Tech. Coll., Bklyn., 1975—79; adj. instr., Palmer Sch. L.I. U., Greenvale, NY, 1991—95; libr. media dir. St. Agnes Acad. HS, College Point, NY, 1969—77; libr. media specialist Bethpage Union Free Sch. Dist., Bethpage, NY, 1977—91, libr. media chair, 1991—2003. Acting interim dir. Nassau BOCES Sch. Libr. Sys., Massapequa, NY, 2003. Mem.: ALA, Nassau Sch. Libr. SyS. Adv. Coun. (chair 1992—94), L.I. Sch. Media Assn. (bd. mem. 1991—93), N.Y. Libr. Assn. Home: 15 Tojan Dr East Islip NY 11730 Personal E-mail: clairedonohue@optonline.net.

DONOHUE, DIANE FRANCES, fine arts publisher, artist; b. Waterbury, Conn., Aug. 14, 1946; d. John Magee and Fannie Ada (Dawes) D. Student, New Haven & Hartford Bus. Sch., 1966, New Haven Acad. Bus., 1970, Yale U., 1981, Naugatuck Valley C.C., Waterbury, Conn., 1993-95. From data entry supr. to sys. coord. Data Pack, Inc., Waterbury, 1970-72; from computer operator to programmer Litchfield Farms Shops, Middlebury & Waterbury, 1973-74; from data entry I, II to programm/analyst list State of Conn., Hartford, 1975-77; from programmer to programmer/analyst Ind. Software Consulting, Conn., 1978-82; real estate developer, investor, founder Fanjack Properties, Waterbury, 1982-90; fine artist Artists Attic, Waterbury, 1996— Cons. artist, to student tchr. Western Conn. State U., Danbury, 1972; lectr. Naugatuck Valley Cmty.-Tech. Coll., Waterbury, 1996; restoration artist for pvt. collector, 1996. One woman show Naugatuck Valley Cmty.-Tech. Coll., 1994; works exhibited at The Berkshire Mus., Pittsfield, Mass., 1973, various other exhibits.; represented in pvt. collections. Vol. Women's Nat. Polit. Caucus for candidate, Prospect, Conn., 1996. Mem. Nat. Mus. Women in the Arts. Democrat. Roman Catholic. Avocations: horses, swimming, reading, advocate for women in the arts, working with the elderly. Home and Office: 47 Green Manor Thomaston CT 06787 Office Phone: 860-283-5889.

DONOHUE, MARY, lieutenant governor; b. Rensselaer County, N.Y. children: Sara, Justin. B.Edn., Coll. New Rochelle, 1968; MS in Edn., Russell Sage Coll., Troy, N.Y., 1973; JD, Union U., 1983. Bar: N.Y. 1983. Tchr. elem., jr. h.s. Rensselaer and Albany County (N.Y.) sch. dists., Albany, 1969-78; law clk., intern U.S. Atty.'s Office, Albany, 1980-83; assoc. O'Connell & Aronowitz, Albany, 1983-88; pvt. practice Troy, 1988-92; asst. county atty. Rensselaer County, 1990-92, dist. atty., 1992-96; justice N.Y. Supreme Ct., 3rd Jud. Dist., 1996-98; lt. gov. State of N.Y., Albany, 1998—. Chair Govs. Task Force on Sch. Violence, 1999—, Task Force on Quality Cmtys., 2000—, Govs. Task Force on Small Bus. Chair Capital Dist. Women's Adv. Coun., 1996; mem. Gov.-elect Pataki's Transition Team for Criminal Justice, 1994-96. Republican. Office: Office of Lt Governor State Capitol Rm 246 Albany NY 12224*

DONOHUE, PATRICIA CAROL, academic administrator; b. St. Louis, Jan. 11, 1946; d. Carroll and Juanita Donohue; m. James H. Stevens Jr., Aug. 27, 1966 (div. Mar. 1984); children: James H. Stevens III, Carol Janet Stevens. AB, Duke U., 1966; MA, U. Mo., 1974, PhD, 1982. Tchr. math. in secondary schs., Balt., St. Louis and Shawnee Mission, Kans., 1966-71; lectr. U. Mo., Kansas City, 1975-76, rsch. asst. affirmative action, 1976-79, coord. affirmative action, 1979-82, instl. rsch. assoc., 1982-84, acting dir. affirmative action and acad. pers., 1984; dir. instl. rsch. Lakeland C.C., 1984-86; asst. dean acad. affairs, math., engring. and tech. Harrisburg Area C.C., 1986-89, dean sch. bus., engring., and tech., 1989-93, dean Lebanon campus, v.p. cmty. devel. and external affairs, 1993; vice chancellor edn. St. Louis C.C., 1993—2002, acting pres. Florissant Valley campus, 1998-99; pres. Luzerne County C.C., 2002—. Active Pa. Coun. on Vocat. Edn., 1989—93; v.p. St. Louis Sch. to Work, Inc., 1994—96, pres., 1996—2002; chairperson Pa. Occupl. Deans, 1988—93; bd. dirs., chmn. edn. com. Humane Soc. Mo., 1997—2002; cons. evaluator North Ctrl. Assn., 2000—; bd. dirs. Diamond City Partnership, 2003, Greater Wilkes-Barre (Pa.) Chamber Bus. and Industry, 2004—. Bd. dirs., v.p. Am. Cancer Soc. Jackson County, 1975—84; mem. adv. coun. Ben Franklin Partnership, 1988—93; sec. Ctrl. Pa. Tech. Coun., 1992—93; mem. steering com. New Baldwin Corridor Coalition, 1991—93, chair edn. task force, 1992—93; mem. Leadership St. Louis, 1996—97, Exec. Leadership Wilkes-Barre, 2003; mem. strategic planning com. Penns Woods Girl Scout Coun.; bd. dirs. Hemlock coun. Girl Scouts U.S.A., 1986—93, PTA, 1975—77, Cmty. Lebanon Assocs., Ctrl. Pa. Tech. Coun., 1989—93, Mantec, 1988—93, Delta Gamma Ctr. for Children with Visual Impairments, 2001—02, Osterhout Libr., 2003—. Recipient Outstanding Service and Achievement award U. Mo. Kansas City, 1976, Outstanding Svc. award Ctrl. Pa. Tech. Coun., 1993; Jack C. Coffey grantee, 1978; named Outstanding Woman AAUW, 1989, one of Outstanding Leaders Nat. Inst. Leadership Devel., 1986, Exec. Leadership Inst., 1990. Mem.: Assn. Inst. Rsch., Women's Network, Nat. Assn. Student Pers. Adminstrs., Women's Equity Project, Soc. Mfg. Engrs. (chmn. 1989—90), Am. Assn. Women in Cmty. and Jr. Colls. (Pa. state coord. 1988, bd. dirs. Region 3 1989—91), Nat. Coun. for Occupl. Edn. (chairperson diversity task force 1991, chairperson job tng. 2000 task force 1992, v.p. programs 1992—93, bd. dirs. 1992—2000, v.p. membership 1993—94, pres. 1995—96, past pres. 1996—97), Am. Assn. Cmty. Colls. (coun. affiliated chairpersons 1994—2000, commn. on cmty. and workforce devel. 1995—97, chairperson coun. 1996—2000, commn. on cmty. and workforce devel. 1998—2001, acad. pres. 2003), Am. Vocat. Assn., Math. Assn. Am., Nat. Coun. Tchrs. of Math., ASCD, Delta Gamma (v.p., del. nat. conv. 1988, pres. 1989-91, bd. dirs. Delta Gamma Ctr. for Children with Visual Impairment 2001-) (del. nat. conv. 1988, pres. 1989—91, v.p., Cream Rose Outstanding Svc. award 1970), Pi Lambda Theta, Phi Kappa Phi, Phi Delta Kappa (pres. 1975, Read fellow 1989). Home: 40 Elmcrest Dr Dallas PA 18612 Office: Luzerne County C C 1333 S Prospect St Nanticoke PA 18634

DONOHUE, THERESE BRADY, artistic director, choreographer, designer; b. Washington, Jan. 13, 1937; d. John Bernard and Mary Catherine (Rupert) B.; m. Joseph W. Donohue Jr., June 13, 1959 (div. 1987); children: Sharon Marie, Maura Cathleen (dec.), Sheila Patricia. BA, Coll. of Notre Dame Md., 1958. Cert. tchr. ballet Royal Acad. Dance London. Advt. artist Kronstadt Advt. Agy., Washington, 1958; instr. art The Maret Sch., Washington, 1958-60, Princeton (N.J.) U., 1967-71; artist dir. Amherst (Mass.) Ballet Theatre Co., 1977—2000; founder, dir. Amherst Ballet

Centre, 1971—2000. Sch. adminstr. Amherst Ballet, 1999-; co-dir., founder Pioneer Valley Ballet, Northampton, Mass., 1972-77; dancer, tchr. Princeton Ballet, 1962-71; animal masks Charleston (S.C.) Ballet, 1985—; choreographer Roanoke (Va.) Ballet Theatre, 1983; chair N.E. Region Craft Choreography Conf., Amherst, 1979; artist/choreographer Nat. Gallery Art, [illegible] 1985, Hirshhorn Mus. & Sculpture Garden, 1993. Choreographer (ballets for children) Peter & the Wolf, 1973, One Thousand Cranes, 1974, Punch & Judy, 1975, Amherst Poets, 1977, Uncle Wiggily & the Duck Pond, 1979, (Springfield Symphony) History of Dance, 1983, (Project Opera) Hansel & Gretel, 1983, Sea Study (included in Aberdeen Internat. Youth Festival in Scotland), 1994, Peter Pan Amherst Cmty. Theater, 1995, Aida Commonwealth Opera, 1996, Flower Fairy Ballet, 1997, Ribbon Festival Ballet, 1997; rechoregraphed Matisse's Circus, Dancing with Dubuffet; toured Maui Hawaii Elem. Schs. (Amherst Ballet Theatre Co.), 1996; spl. projects dir. Amherst Ballet Spl., 2003-; prodr., Costumer Very Lonely Firefly, Russian Nat. Dances, 2003. Mem. Amherst Arts Coun., 1983-89. Recipient Town of Amherst Arts and Supplemental Edn. award, 1997, Mass. Senate Citation, 2002, C.C. Dakin Medallion award in edn., 2002. Mem. Amherst Club. Avocation: travel. Home: 17 Juniper Ln Amherst MA 01002-1227 Office: Amherst Ballet 29 Strong St Amherst MA 01002-1890

DONOVAN, ANN BURCHAM, medical office administrator; m. Gary Leonard Donovan, (div. June 1988); children: Leonard Matthew, William Marshall. Student, Baker U., 1970-71; Cert., Kansas City Sch. Med. Assts., 1973. Cert. med. practice exec. Med. asst. Penn Valley Med. Group, Kansas City, Mo., 1973-76, supr. accounts receivable, 1976-82; office adminstr. Heartland Hematology-Oncology Assn., Inc., Kansas City, Mo., 1982—. Cons. on cancer and AIDS patients for med. offices, Kansas City, Mo., 1982—. Contbr. articles to profl. jours. Mem. NAFE, Northland Med. Mgrs. Assn., Med. Group Mgrs. Assn., Adminstrs. of Oncology-Hematology Assn., Greater Kansas City Med. Mgrs. Assn. (recognition com.), Kansas City Sci. Fiction and Fantasy Soc. Avocations: painting, horseback riding, fishing, traveling. Office: Heartland Hematology Oncology Assn Inc 2000 NE Vivion Rd Kansas City MO 64118-6127

DONOVAN, ANNE, professional basketball coach, coach; b. Ridgewood, N.J., Nov. 1, 1961; Asst. coach Old Dominion U.; head coach women's basketball E. Carolina U., Greenville, 1995-98; head coach Phila. Rage, 1998-99, Indiana Fever, Indianapolis, 1999—. Recipient Naismith Player of Yr. award, 1983, Olympic Team Gold medal, 1984, 88, World Championship Team Gold medal, 1986. Mem. USA Basketball Com. (exec. bd. dirs. 1996—). Achievements include Three time All-Am. selection; led nation in rebounding, 1982; all-time leading scorer, blocker and rebounder Old Dominion Univ.; Olympian, 1980, 84, 88; World Championship team, 1983, 86. Address: Indiana Fever 125 S Pennsylvania St Indianapolis IN 46204-3610

DONOVAN, CAROL ANN, state legislator; b. Lynn, Mass., June 5, 1937; d. John B. and Virginia Mary (Pearce) D. AB, Regis Coll., Weston, Mass., 1959, MA, 1980. Tchr. home econs. Woburn (Mass.) Sch. System, 1959-74, spl. edn. tchr., 1974-84, spl. edn. liaison, 1984-90; mem. Mass. Ho. of Reps., Boston, 1991—; vice chair Post Audit and Oversight Com., Boston. Polit. cons. Mass. Tchrs. Assn., Boston, 1985-89. Mem. Mass. Caucus of Women Legislators, 1991—; mem. Nat. Women's Polit. Caucus, 1989—; bd. dirs. Ctrl. Middlesex Assn. Retarded Citizens, Woburn, 1984—, also past pres.; bd. dirs. Vis. Nurses Assn.-Middlesex East, 2003; sec. Woburn Dem. City Com., 1984—; mem. Gov.'s Commn. on Sexual and Domestic Violence; mem. Mass. Dem. State Com. Recipient Elder Advocacy award Minuteman Home Care, Burlington, Mass., 1993, Disting. Citizen award ARC Mass., Waltham, 1993, Legislator of Yr. award Mass. Disabilities Coun. and ARC, 1994, Disting. Svc. award to State Rep. of Yr., Silver Haired Legislature, 2003, Cert. of Appreciation, Head Start; named Friend of Yr., Mass. State Coll. Assn., 1999. Mem. Women's Legis. Lobby, Woburn Middlesex Lions Club. Roman Catholic. Avocation: travel. Office: State House Rm 473B Boston MA 02133

DONOVAN, DIANNE FRANCYS, journalist; b. Houston, Sept. 30, 1948; d. James Henry and Doris Elaine (Simerly) D.; m. Anthony Charles Burba; children: Donovan Anthony, James Donovan. Student, Trinity Coll., Dublin, Ireland, 1969; BA, Spring Hill Coll., 1970; MA, U. Mo., 1975, U. Chgo., 1982. Copy editor Chgo. Sun-Times, 1977-79; fgn./nat. copy desk supr. Chgo. Tribune, 1979-80, asst. editor for news/features, 1980-83, lit. editor, 1985-93, mem. editorial bd., 1993-99, sr. editor for recruitment, 2000—. Vis. prof. U. Oreg. Sch. Journalism, Eugene, 1983-85; adj. faculty Northwestern U. Sch. Journalism, 1980-81, 89-90; bd. dirs. Chgo. Tribune Found. Bd. dirs. Nelson Algren/Heartland lit. awards, Chgo., 1986-93; judge Nat. Headliners' Club Awards, Atlantic City, N.J., 1983. Recipient award for editl. writing Am. Soc. Newspaper Editors, 1999, Media award Chgo. Bar Assn., 1999. Episcopalian. Office: Chgo Tribune Co 435 N Michigan Ave Chicago IL 60611-4066

DONOVAN, DONNA MAE, newspaper publisher; b. Jersey City, Mar. 14, 1952; d. William Clayton and Elizabeth Dorothy (Hanley) Hagemann; m. Jerome Francis Donovan, Nov. 6, 1982; children: Matthew James, Andrew William, Erin Elizabeth. BA in Journalism, Syracuse U., 1974. Pub. Burlington (Vt.) Free Press, 1986-91, Utica (N.Y.) Observer-Dispatch, 1991—; v.p. East region Gannett Co., 1986-88. Bd. dirs. Chittenden County United Way, 1987-91, also chmn. cmty. svc. div.; bd. dirs. Leadership Champlain, 1987-91; bd. dirs. Leadership Mohawk Valley, 1992-98, pres., 1995-96, sec., 1997-98; bd. dirs. Ctrl. N.Y. Cmty. Arts Coun., 1994—, Downtown Utica Devel. Assn., 1992-98, sec., 1996-98; bd. dirs. Oneida County Indsl. Devel. Corp., 1993-97; bd. dirs. Oneida County EDGE, 1998—, Mohawk Valley C.C. Found., 1997—; mem. nat. adv. bd. Syracuse U. Sch. Journalism; mem. Our Lady of Lourdes Parents Adv. Bd., 1992-98; bd. dirs. Sch. & Bus. Alliance Oneida-Madison Boces, 2000—. Mem. Newspaper Assn. Am., N.Y. Newspaper Pubs. Assn. (bd. dirs. 1993-96, 2001—), Mohawk Valley C. of C. (bd. dirs. 1999-2000), United Way of Greater Utica (bd. dirs. 1999-00, 99—). Roman Catholic. Office: Observer-Dispatch 221 Oriskany Plz Utica NY 13501-1201 E-mail: ddonovan@utica.gannett.com.

DONOVAN, HELEN W. newspaper editor; Graduated from, Mount Holyoke Coll., 1969. Exec. editor Boston Globe, 1993—. Adv. bd., Nat. Arts Journalism Program. Office: Boston Globe Newspapers PO Box 2378 Boston MA 02107-2378*

DONOVAN, JOHANNAH L. state representative, educator; b. Burlington, Vt., Sept. 18, 1944; m. Thomas Donovan; 6 children. BA, Trinity Coll., 1967. Tchr.; state rep. State of Vt., 2001—. Bd. trustees Lund Family Ctr.; mem. Irish Heritage Com., Chittenden County Dem. Com., Burlington Dem. Com., Chirst the King Parish. Democrat. Office: 38 Bayview St Burlington VT 05401

DONOVAN, KATHLEEN A. water transportation executive, county official; b. Queens, N.Y., Sept. 3, 1952; d. Francis and Lillian Donovan; 1 child, Brendan. BA cum laude, Rutgers U., Newark, 1974; JD, Cleve. State U., 1977. Pvt. practice, N.J., 1977-94; staff atty. Bergen County (N.J.) Office Aging, 1983-88; pub. defender Twp. Lyndhurst, N.J., 1983-88; clk. County Bergen, Hackensack, N.J., 1988—; commr. Port Authority N.Y. and N.J., N.Y.C., 1994—. Pres., troop leader Girl Scouts Am. Bergen County, 1974—; former bd. dirs. Shelter Our Sisters; mem. for dist. 36 N.J. State Assembly, 1980-87; Rep. state chair, 1989-90; Rep. chair Legis. Reapportionment Com., 1990; mem., chair com. transition team Gov. Christine Whitman, 1994; Rep. candidate U.S. House Reps. 9th Dist., N.J., 1996. Mem. Bergen County Bar Assn. Roman Catholic.

DONOVAN, MARTHA ANDREWS, humanities educator; d. John Chauncey and Beatrice Florence Witter Donovan; m. Philip Cate Huckins, Aug. 20, 1988; 1 child, Sarah Donovan Huckins. BA, Williams Coll., 1980; MA, Bread Loaf Sch. English, 1989. Tchr. English Pingree Sch., South Hamilton, Mass., 1981—97; adj. [illegible] New Eng. Coll., Henniker, NH, 1998—99, instr. writing, 1999—2000, asst. prof. writing, 2000—. Author: (poem) Green Mountains Review, 1999—2000, Soundings East, 1989, Potpourri: A Magazine of the Literary Arts, 1999; co-author (with Marissa Walsh): (essay) English Jour. Mem., co-chair 6th ann. art & essay conf. Friends of H. Raymond Danforth Libr. New Eng. Coll., Henniker, NH, 2000—01. Recipient Charles P. Rimmer award excellence in tchg., Pingree Sch., 1991; fellow ind. study in humanities, Coun. for Basic Edn., NEH, 1991; New Eng. studies summer inst. fellow, Dartmouth Coll., 1983, Norm Christensen scholar, Bread Loaf Sch. English, Middlebury Coll., 1989. Mem.: Stone Bridge Poetry Project, N.H. Writers' Project. D-Liberal. Office: New England Col Bridge St Henniker NH 03242 E-mail: mdonovan@nec.edu.

DONOVAN, MAUREEN DRISCOLL, lawyer; b. N.Y.C., Dec. 2, 1940; d. Bartholomew Driscoll and Josephine (Keohane) Driscoll. AB, Coll. of New Rochelle, 1962; LLB with honors, Fordham U., 1966. Bar: N.Y. 1966, U.S. Supreme Ct. 1971, U.S. Ct. Appeals (2d cir.) 1975, U.S. Dist. Ct. (so. dist.) N.Y. 1976. Assoc. White & Case LLP, N.Y.C., 1966-75, ptnr., 1975—. Trustee St. Barnabas Hosp., Bronx, N.Y., 1992—, chair fin. com. 1997—, vice chair bd., 1998—; trustee N.Y. Urban Coalition, N.Y.C., 1990-94. Mem. ABA, Princeton Club (N.Y.), Coral Beach Club (Paget, Bermuda), Englewood (N.J.) Field Club. Office: White & Case LLP 1155 Avenue of the Americas New York NY 10036-2787 Office Phone: 212-819-8557.

DONOVAN, MAUREEN HILDEGARDE, librarian, educator; b. Boston, Dec. 13, 1948; d. Alfred Michael and Maureen Hildegarde (Murphy) D.; m. James Richard Bartholomew, Sept. 9, 1978; 1 child, Thomas Alfred Bartholomew. BA, Manhattanville Coll., 1970; MA in East Asian Langs. and Cultures, Columbia U., 1973, MS in Libr. Svc., 1974. Asst. editor R.R. Bowker Co., N.Y.C., 1973; librarian I Gest Oriental Libr. Princeton (N.J.) U., 1974-77, libr. II, 1977-78; instr., Japanese studies libr. Ohio State U., Columbus, 1978-88, asst. prof., Japanese studies libr., 1988-94, assoc. prof., Japanese studies libr., 1994—. Vis. lectr. Sch. Libr. and Info. Sci. Keio U., Tokyo, 1995-96; cons. U. Wis., Madison, 1991, McGill U., Montreal, Que., 1993, RMG, Inc., Chgo., 1993; webmaster East Asian Librs. Cooper WWW, 1994—; vis. rsch. scholar Internat. Rsch. Ctr. for Japanese Studies, Kyoto, 2003—; Japan specialist Digital Asia Libr., 1999-2002, Portal to Asian Internet Resources, 2002—. Editor mailing list Asian Database Online Cmty., 1993-97, editor electronic newsletter, 1998—. Fellow Japan Found., Tokyo, 1995-96; grantee U.S. Dept. Edn., 1994-96, Japan-U.S. Friendship Commn., 1994-96, Sun Microsystems, Inc., 1995; inductee Matignon H.S. (Cambridge, Mass.) Achievement Hall of Fame, 1999. Mem. ALA, Assn. for Asian Studies (chair com. on East Asian librs. 1991-94), Internat. Assn. Orientalist Librs. Home: 2372 Lytham Rd Columbus OH 43220-4640 Office: 328 Main Libr 1858 Neil Ave Columbus OH 43210-1225 E-mail: donovan.1@osu.edu.

DONOVAN, SHARON ANN, secondary school educator; b. Balt., Feb. 17, 1944; d. Jesse F. and Ruth Elizabeth (Keller) D. BA, U. Md., Balt., 1969. Cert. profl. tchr. Assoc. Coppin-Hopkins Humanities Program, Balt., 1986-91; asst. dean arts and humanities UMBC, Catonsville, Md., 1973-76; asst. to dean fine arts Towson (Md.) State U., 1977-85; tchr. Balt. City Schs., 1986—. Contbr. articles to publs.; founding mem., bd. dirs. The Feminist Press; founder "Herstory" MS Mag., 1976. Grantee Fund for Endl. Excellence. Mem. NCTE, MCTELA, Md. State Conf. on Women's Studies (chairperson, Tchr. of Yr. 1994, 95). Home: 2039 E Lombard St Baltimore MD 21231-1924 Office: 100 North Calhoun St Baltimore MD 21218-4837

DOODY, AGNES G. communications educator, management and communication consultant; b. New Haven; d. Daniel M. and Carrie Mae (Goodrich) D.; m. Arthur D. Jeffrey, Dec. 22, 1962 (dec. Sept. 1985); children: Andrew N., Jill; m. Ellis H. Maris, Jr., June 28, 1991. BA, Emerson Coll., 1952; MA, Pa. State U., 1954, PhD, 1961; cert. program on negotiation, Harvard U. Prof. communications U. R.I., Kingston, 1958—; pres. Arthur Assocs. Bd. dirs., co-chairperson PierBank, Narragansett, R.I., 1994. Mem. Soc. Profls. in Dispute Resolution, Internat. Comm. Assn., Nat. Comm. Assn., Ea. Comm. Assn. (pres. 1967-68), Rotary (newsletter editor Wakefield 1989-90). Avocations: photography, travel, gardening. Home: One Post Rd Wakefield RI 02879

DOODY, BARBARA PETTETT, computer specialist; b. Cin., Sept. 18, 1938; d. Philip Wayne and Virginia Bird (Handley) P.; 1 child, Daniel Frederick Reasor Jr. Attended Sinclair Coll., Tulane U., 1973-74. Owner, mgr. Honeysuckle Pet Shop, Tipp City, Ohio, 1970-76; office mgr. Doody & Doody, CPAs, New Orleans, 1976-77, computer ops. mgr., 1979—; office mgr. San Diego Yacht Club, 1977-79. Owner Hope Chest Linens, Ltd., 1994—2002. Mem. DAR, UDC, Jamestown Soc., Magna Charta, So. Dames, Colonial Dames of 17th Century, Nat. Soc. Daus. of 1812, Daus. Am. Colonists, Dames Ct. Honor, Colonial Order of the Crown, Societe Huguenot Nouvelle-Orleans, Huguenot Soc. Manakin, Soc. Knights of the Garter, Americans of Royal Descent, Plantaget Soc. Republican. Lutheran. Home: 36 Cypress Rd Covington LA 70433-4306 Office: 2525 Lakeway III 3838 N Causeway Blvd Metairie LA 70002-1767 E-mail: bdoody@bellsouth.net.

DOODY, MARGARET ANNE, English language educator; b. St. John, N.B., Can., Sept. 21, 1939; came to U.S., 1976; d. Hubert and Anne Ruth (Cornwall) D. BA, Dalhousie U., Can., 1960; BA with 1st class hons., Lady Margaret Hall-Oxford U., Eng., 1962, MA, 1965, D.Phil., 1968; LLD (hon.), Dalhousie U., 1985. Instr. English U. Victoria (B.C., Can.), 1962-64, asst. prof. English, 1968-69; lectr. Univ. Coll. Swansea, Wales, 1969-76; assoc. prof. English U. Calif.-Berkeley, 1976-80; prof. English dept. Princeton U., N.J., 1980-89; Andrew W. Mellon prof. humanities, prof. English Vanderbilt U., Nashville, 1989-99, dir. comparative lit. program, 1992-99; John and Barbara Glyn Family prof. lit. U. Notre Dame, 2000—, dir. PhD in Lit. program, 2001—. Author: A Natural Passion: A Study of the Novels of Samuel Richardson, 1974, The Daring Muse: Augustan Poetry Reconsidered, 1985, Frances Burney: The Life in the Works, 1988, The True Story of the Novel, 1996, Aristotle Detective, 1978, The Alchemists, 1980, Aristotle e la giustizia poetica, 2000, Aristotle and Poetic Justice, 2002, Aristotle and the Secrets of Life, 2003; author: (with F. Stuber) (play) Clarissa, 1984; editor (with Peter Sabor): Samuel Richardson Tercentenary Essays, 1989; co-editor (with Douglas Murray): Catharine and Other Writings by Jane Austen, 1993; co-editor: (with Wendy Barry and Mary Doody Jones) Anne of Green Gables, 1997; author: (novels) Aristotle and the Secrets of Life, 2003. Guggenheim postdoctoral fellow, 1979; recipient Rose Mary Crawshay award Brit. Acad., 1986. Episcopalian. Office: U Notre Dame PhD in Literature Program Notre Dame IN 46556 Office Phone: 574-631-0465. E-mail: mdoody@nd.edu.

DOOLEY, ANN ELIZABETH, freelance writers cooperative executive, editor; b. Mpls., Feb. 19, 1952; d. Merlyn James and Susan Marie (Hinze) Dooley; m. John M. Dodge, May 8, 1983; children: Christopher Dooley Dodge, Kathryn Dooley Dodge. BA in Journalism, U. Wis., 1974. Freelance journalist, 1974-75; photo editor C.W. Communications, Newton, Mass., 1975-77, writer, photographer, 1977-79; editor Computerworld O A, Framingham, Mass., 1979-83; editorial dir. Computerworld Focus, Framingham, 1983-92; pres. freelance writers coop. Dooley & Assocs., West Newbury, Mass., 1992—. Speaker, chmn. mem. editorial adv. bd. various computer confs. Mem. Pub. Relations Soc. Am., Women in Communications (sec. 1982-84). Democrat. Home and Office: 1 Old Parish Way West Newbury MA 01985-1222

DOOLEY, BETTY PARSONS, educational association administrator; Student, Tex. Inst. Tech., Tex. U. Lobbyist, Austin, Tex., 1969-70; dir. regional orgns. Health Security Action Coun., 1971-77, exec. dir. Congl. Caucus Women's Issues, 1977-79; pres. Women's Rsch. Edn. Inst., Washington, 19[illegible]. Mich. women's health adv. bd. Duke Med. Sch.; mem. adv. com. employment tng. Vets. Sec. Labor; mem. outreach com. Ctr. Cross Cultural Rsch. on Women, Oxford, Eng. Washington corr. Tex. Monthly Mag., 1974-75. Candidate Tex. State Legis., 1970, U.S. Congress, 1964. Mem. Nat. Coun. Rsch. Women (charter). Office: Womens Rsch Edn Inst 1750 New York Ave NW Ste 350 Washington DC 20006-5309

DOOLEY, GAYLE DARLENE, special education educator, consultant; b. Detroit, Nov. 14, 1967; d. Frank Roosevelt Owens Jr. and Beulah Julia Owens; m. John Earl Dooley Jr., Nov. 4, 2000; children: John Earl Dooley III, Andrew Justin. BA, Wayne State U., 1992; MA, U. of Detroit Mercy, 2002. Lic. tchr. Mich. Dept. of Edn., 2003. Dir. student affairs Sierra Leone Acad., Detroit, 1995—97; spl. edn. tchr. Detroit (Mich.) Pub. Schs., 1997—. Dir. Cyprian Annex, Detroit, 1994—95. Mem.: Coun. of Exceptional Children, Delta Sigma Theta (life; arts & letters com. 2002—03, round up com. 2002—03, scholarship 1987). Office: Howe Elementary School 2600 Garland Detroit MI 48219 Personal E-mail: gayledooleydst@hotmail.com.

DOOLEY, JO ANN CATHERINE, retired publishing executive; b. Cin., Nov. 24, 1930; d. Joseph Frank and Margaret Mary (Flynn) Dooley. Ed, U. Cin., 1966. Clk. Castellini Co., Cin., 1949-52; IBM operator Kroger Co., Cin., 1952; asst. acct. Gardner Publs., Inc., Cin., 1953-67, treas., sec., 1967-95, bd. dirs., 1983-99, v.p. fin., 1986-95, ret., 1995. Mem.: Am. Soc. Women Accts. (advt. mgr. Woman CPA 1979—81, nat. pres. 1982—83, exec. com., Achievement award), Mercy Hosp. Western Hills Aux. (treas. 2003—), Deaconess Hosp. Aux. (pres. 2003—). Roman Catholic.

DOOLEY, SHARON L. obstetrician, gynecologist; b. 1947; MD, U. Va. Mem. faculty Prentice Womens Hosp. Med. Sch. Northwestern U., Chgo., prof., dir. graduate med. edn. Office: Northwestern U Med Sch Prentice Womens Hosp 333 E Superior St Ste 410 Chicago IL 60611-3015

DOOLEY, WENDY BROOKE, vocalist, music educator; b. Paragould, Ark., Apr. 7, 1976; d. Garry Don and Nina Doris Dooley. MusB, U. Ctrl. Ark., 1999. Lic. tchr. Ark. Dept. Edn., 2000. Clk., employee trainer Crockett Oil Co., Rector, Ark., 1991—97; choral libr. U. Ctrl. Ark., Conway, 1997—99; music tchr. Cabot (Ark.) Jr. High North & South, 1999—2000, Eastside Elem. Sch., Cabot, 2000—01; tchr. Clarkton (Mo.) C-4 Pub. Schs., 2001—. Curriculum devel. com. Cabot Pub. Schs., 2000—01, Clarkton (Mo.) C-4 Pub. Schs., 2001—, cons., 2001—; caterer Simply the Best Catering, Little Rock. Entertainer C. of C., Rector, Ark., 1992—95; mem. Moark Gen. Bapt. Assoc., Campbell, Mo., 1989—2002. Mem.: Ark. Choral Dirs. Assn., Mo. Band Dirs. Assn., Clarkton Tchrs. Assn. (profl. devel. com. mem. 2002—03), Mo. State Tchrs. Assn., Music Educator's Nat. Conf. (sec. collegete chpt. 1998—99). Mem. Assembly Of God. Achievements include first to began a volunteer program to teach children music through the area libraries summer reading programs; started a traveling Vacation Bible School music program. During the summer I travel to different churches and handle all of the music for their VBS. This is a volunteer program without pay; entertain and lead group activities at area retirement centers; entertain at festivals, fair, and other special events. Avocations: travel, singing, reading, gardening. Home: 19 Deerwood Dr Conway AR 72034 Office: Clarkton C-4 Sch Hwy 162 Clarkton MO 63837 E-mail: the_singing_dooley@sbcglobal.net.

DOONE, MICHELE MARIE, chiropractor; b. Oak Park, Ill., Oct. 3, 1942; d. Robert Emmett and Tana Josephine (Alioto) D. Cert., Valley Coll. of Med. and Dental Careers, 1962; student, L.A. Valley Coll., 1960-63, Dallas County Community Coll., 1983-84; D in Chiropractic summa cum laude, Parker Coll. of Chiropractic, 1986. Lic. chiropractic, Calif., Tex.; cert. Nat. Bd. Chiropractic Examiners, impairment rater; diplomate Am. Acad. Pain Mgmt., Am. Bd. Disability Analysts. Med. asst. William Orlando M.D., Edwin Crost, M.D., 1962-65; nursing supr., chief radiologic technologist Vanowen Med. Group, North Hollywood, Calif., 1965-76; radiologic technologist/purchasing agt. Lanier-Brown Clinic, Dallas, 1976-83; faculty mem./ chief radiologic technologist Parker Coll. of Chiropractic, Irving, Tex., 1983-85; exam and X-Ray doctor Margolies Chiropractic Ctr., Richardson, Tex., 1986; clinic staff doctor, assoc. prof. Parker Coll. of Chiropractic, Irving, Tex., 1986-87; doctor/ mgr. contractor Accident Ctrs. of Am., Garland, Tex., 1987; clinic dir. Back Pain Chiropractic, Carrollton, Tex., 1988-91; assoc. in group practice Mullican Chiropractic Ctr., Addison, Tex., 1991-97; co-owner, COO, pres. Health North Chiropractic Rehab Ctr PC, Addison, Tex., 1997—2002; assoc. med. dir. Intracorp., Carrolton, 2002—. Adviser health-related matters Inner Devel. Inst., Dallas, 1977—; seminar com. Back Pain Chiropractic, Inc., Metairie, La., 1989-91, clinic dir., 1988-91. Mem.: Parker Chiropractic Rsch. Found., Metroplex Neurospinal Diagnostic Med. and Surg. Group (med. adv. com. 1989—95), Tex. Chiropractic Assn. (chmn. radiology com. 1990—94), Parker Coll. Alumni Assn. (bd. dirs. 1988—90, 1993—94, 1995—2000, 2001—03, Dr. of Yr. 1990), Pi Tau Delta. Home: 11083 Lockshire Dr Frisco TX 75035-3765 Office Phone: 214-763-0412. Personal E-mail: drbones1@msn.com.

DOONER, MARLENE S. communications executive; BA in Econs., St. Joseph's U.; MS in Fin., Drexel U. V.p. Comms. Lending Group PNC Bank; v.p. investor rels. Comcast Corp., Phila., with, 1995—. Office: Comcast 1500 Market St Philadelphia PA 19102*

DOORECK, LISA, special education educator, writer; b. N.Y.C., Jan. 30, 1974; d. Jay F. and Susan E. Dooreck. BA in Spl. Edn., L.I. U.; MS in Spl. Edn., Hunter Coll., N.Y.C. Tchr. Daytona Beach Pub. Schs., Fla.; ednl. evaluator N.Y.C.; spl. edn. therapist; mem. Com. on Spl. Edn., 1995—. Contbr. numerous poems to lit. pubs.; author: The Sound of Poetry, 2003, Calling You to the Throne, 2003; contbr. And So He Sends Your Soulmate, 1999.

DOORLEY, MATHILDA DOERSELN, chemist, educator; d. Martha B and Paul Doerseln; m. Peter Francis Doorley, Aug. 6, 1977; children: Carole Jeannette, John Francis, Stephen Michael. BA, William Paterson Coll., 1977; MS, U. of Ky., 1980. Coll. prof. SW TN C.C., Memphis, 2002—; sr. chemist Plough Inc., Memphis, 1980—82; adj. faculty State Tech. Inst. Memphis, 1993—96; corp. libr. Kraft Food Ingredients, Memphis, 1996—98; rsch. asst. KFI, Memphis, 1997—99; libr. specialist Memphis Pub. Libr., 1999—2002. Mem.: Am. Chem. Soc. Achievements include patents for coconut concentrate deflavoring process. Avocation: music.

DOORNINK, BARBARA, military officer; b. Prosser, Wash. BA in Polit. Sci., Wash. State U., 1973; MS in Info. Systems Mgmt., U. So. Calif.; grad., Army Command Gen. Staff Coll., Indsl. Coll. Armed Forces. Commd. 2d lt. U.S. Army, 1973, advanced through grades to brig. gen.; early assignments include platoon leader, protocol officer; chief of movements Region 1, 25th transp. control ctr., Seoul, korea, 1980; comdr. 100th transp. co., S3, exec. officer 6th transp. bn.; recorder for Dept. of Army Secretariat; co. grade assignments officer Transp. br.; divsn. transp. officer 9th infantry divsn. Ft. Lewis, Wash., 1987; comdr. 53d transp. bn. 37th TRANSCOM, Kaiserslautern, Germany, 1991-93; comdr. 507th corps support group Ft. Bragg, N.C., 1994-96; chief of jt. logistics ops. U.S. European Command, Stuttgart, Germany, 1996-98; comdr. Def. Distbrn. Ctr. U.S. Army, New Cumberland, Pa., 1998—. Decorated Def. Superior Svc. medal, Legion of Merit, Def. Meritorious Svc. medal, others. Master parachutist.

DOORY, ANN MARIE, lawyer, legislator; b. Yonkers, N.Y., Aug. 19, 1954; d. Gerard R. and Patricia M. Lowe; m. Robert Leonard Doory Jr., Sept. 29, 1979; children: Brian Robert, Elizabeth Lowe. BA in Polit. Sci., Towson State U., 1976; JD, U. Balt., 1979. Bar: Md. Counsel to majority leader Md. State Senate, 1981; vol., arbitrator Better Bus. Bur., 1984-86; chm. bd. York Woodbourne Action Area and York Rd. Planning Com. Md. Ho. of Dels., 1982—, zoning chairperson Homeland Assn., 1984-86, v.p. Homeland Assn., 1987—. Mem. Dem. State Cen. Com. 43d Legis. Dist., Baltimore City, 1982—, 3d Dist. Citizens for Good Govt., Baltimore City, issues and legis. com., Mayors Drug Abuse Adv. Council, Baltimore City, 1983-86. Mem. Women's Bar Assn., Md. Bar Assn. Democrat. Roman Catholic. Office: 112 Taplow Rd Baltimore MD 21212-3312 also: Md Ho of Dels State Capitol Annapolis MD 21401

DORAN, MAUREEN, sales executive; d. John and Patricia Doran. BA in Econs. and Fin., Rutgers U., 1982; MS in Dynamics of Orgn. with honors, U. Pa., 1995. From sales staff to v.p. conduit bus. leader GE Capital Mortgage Svcs., Cherry Hill, NJ, 1983—97; dir. internat. key accounts GE Capital Fleet Svcs., Brussels, 1997—98; v.p./mng. dir. bus. devel. GE Capital Real Estate, Stanford, Conn., 1998—2000; v.p. then sr. v.p., sales leader GE Comml. Equipment-Life Scis. Fin., Norwalk, Conn., 2000—03; mgr. At the Customer For the Customer GE Comml. Equipment Fin., Danbury, Conn., 2003—. Co-pres. Elfan chpt. GE Women's Network, Cherry Hill, NJ, 1996—97, co-chair social com., Stanford, Conn., 1999—. GE capt. United Way, Norwalk, 2001—02; vol. Elfan, 2000—, Spl. Olympics, 2000—, Best Buddies, 2000—. Mem.: Old Greenwich Yacht Club, Penn Club. Office: GE CEF 44 Old Ridgebury Rd Norwalk CT 06851

DORANTES DE FISCHER, DIANA L. language educator; b. Mexico City, July 12, 1944; arrived in U.S., 1999; d. Amado L. Dorantes and Leda Salas de Dorantes; m. Ramon Fischer Marquez, Jan. 19, 1971; children: Erica Fischer Dorantes, Edgar Fischer Dorantes, Oscar Fischer Dorantes. EdB, Inst. Am., Leon, Mexico, 1970; PhB in Edn., U. Exeter, Plymouth, Eng., 1994, EdM in TTELT, 2003. Lang. prof. U. Autonoma de BCS, La Paz, Mexico, 1988—99, asst. to dir. acad. affairs, head logistics dept., 1995—99; vis. prof. Spanish and WSL Valley City (N.D.) State U., 1994—99, vis. prof. Spanish and ESL, 1999—2001; vis. prof. Spanish Concordia Coll., Moorhead, Minn., 2001—04. Student tchr. supr. Concordia Coll., Moorhead, 2002—04, organizer Casa Hispana, 2002—04. Assoc. editor: Internat. Jour. of Learning, vol. 10. Bush grantee, Valley City State U., 2000, 2001. Mem.: Minn. Coun. on the Tchg. Langs. and Cultures. Office: Guaycura 204 Fracc Juarez La Paz 23090 Baja California Sur Mexico Home: 501 12th Ave S Moorehead MN 56560

DORCHAK, GLENDA, electronics company executive; Various positions IBM Canada, 1974—92; dir. sales and svc. AMBRA, 1993; various exec. positions in sales, mktg. and planning IBM US, 1993; pres. Value Am., Inc., Charlottesville, Va., 1998—99, chmn., CEO, 2000; v.p., COO Communications Group Intel Corp., v.p., Desktop Platforms Group, gen. mgr., Consumer Electronics Group. Named one of top 25 execs. of new millennium Computer Reseller News, 1999. Office: Intel Corp 2200 Mission College Blvd Santa Clara CA 95052-8119

DORE, KATHLEEN A. broadcast executive; m. Keith Jepsen. BA in Film and Broadcasting, U. Iowa, 1977, MBA 1984. Affiliate mktg. mgr. Rainbow Media Holdings, 1982—84, sales dir. Am. Movie Classics, 1984—86, regional dir. Am. Movie Classics, 1986, pres. Bravo Networks, 1996—2002, pres. Ind. Film Channel Cos., 2002—03, pres. Entertainment Svcs., 2003—. Named honoree, Girl Scouts Inc., 2002; named one of Fast 40, Fast Co., 100 Most Powerful Women in Hollywood, Hollywood Reporter, 2003; recipient Lee Salk Goodworks award, Theatreworks/USA, Disting. Alumni Achievement award, U. Iowa, 1998. Mem.: N.Y. Women in Film, Mktg. Soc. for Cable and Telecomm. Industry, Women in Cable and Telecomm. Found. (chair 2001—02, Woman of Yr. 2003). Office: Rainbow Media Holdings 200 Jericho Quadrangle Jericho NY 11753*

DORFMAN, CYNTHIA HEARN, government agency administrator; BA in English with honors, Skidmore Coll., 1970; M in English, Middlebury Coll. Sr. exec. fellow Kennedy Sch. Govt., Harvard U.; dir. OCRI Found.; mgr. Dept. Publs. and Outreach Programs and Projects U.S. Dept. Edn., Washington, dir. media and info. svcs. Office Ednl. Rsch. and Improvement, dir. comm. Office Innovation and Improvement. Office: US Dept Edn IES Capital Place 555 New Jersey Ave NW Washington DC 20208

DORFMAN, LISA ANN, nutritionist, consultant, educator; b. New Hyde Park, N.Y., Feb. 5, 1961; d. Walter and Melanie (Safane) Shapiro; m. Robert Alan Dorfman, May 1, 1982; children: Rebecca Elizabeth, Danielle Nicole, Joseph Charles. BS in Dietetics and Nutrition, Fla. Internat. U., 1983, MS in Dietetics and Nutrition, 1984; postgrad. in Clin. Psychology Miami Inst. Psychology. Registered dietitian, Fla.; lic./registered nutritionist; lic. psychotherapist, writer. Cons. Nutrition Assocs. of Am., Inc., Miami, Fla., 1983—, pres., 1983—, also bd. dirs.; nutritionist Doral Saturnia Internat. Spa Resort, Miami, 1987—; CEO Food Fitness Internat., Inc., 1985—. Adj. prof. dept. exercise sci. U. Miami, 2004—; sports nutritionist dept. athletics U. Miami, 2003—; spa cuisine cons. Sandals Resort Internat., 2001-2003, Butler End Resorts, BVI, 2003-; counselor, educator Anorexia and Bulimia Resource Ctr., Coconut Grove, Fla., 1983-87, Humana Hosp. Biscayne, North Miami Beach, Fla., 1984-86; clin. nutritionist Canteen Corps. of S. Fla. State Hosp., Hollywood, 1985-86; pub. health nutritionist U. Miami-Jackson Meml. Hosp., 1984-85; instr. Miami Dade Community Coll., 1986—; counselor, cons. Piedmont Airlines, Miami, 1986—; counselor, instr. Inst. of Eating Behaviors, Miami, 1986—. Author: The Tropical Diet, 1986, (curriculum guide) Close to You-Anorexia Nervosa and Bulimia, 1987, Vegetarian Sports Nutrition Guide, 2000, Tropical Diet; A Scientific Simple & Sexy Weight Loss Strategy for Health, Sport and Life, 2004; contbr. articles to profl. jours., chpts. to books; co-prodr., co-host TV series Dr. Green's Kitchen, 1986-87; co-host, co-prodr. Food Fitness, Sellkirk Communications, Inc., Hot Talk, Sta. WHQT, Miami. Mem. Am. Dietetic Assn. (nat. media spokesperson 2003—, dietetic practice group chmn. 1991-2000), Fla. Dietetic Assn., Miami Dietetic Assn., Soc. Nutrition Edn., South Fla. Cardiovascular and Sports Nutritionists (sec. 1985—), Am. Anorexia/Bulimia Assn. of Fla. (founder local chpt., pres., bd. dirs. 1984—), Am. Heart Assn. (com. mem. 1984-88); pub. relations chair, cons. Nutritionists Practice Group, 1988-89. Avocations: swimming, jogging, writing. Mailing: Food Fitness Internat 7000 SW 62 Ave Ste 350 Miami FL 33143

DORIGHI, NANCY S. computer engineer; BS in Math., U. San Francisco, 1974; MSEE, Stanford U., 1976. Mgr. air traffic control tower simulator Future Flight Ctrl., Ames Rsch. Ctr. NASA, Moffett Field, Calif., 1976—. Fellow: AIAA (assoc.); mem.: ASME (assoc. editor ASME jour.). Avocations: hiking, skiing, gardening.

DORLAND, BYRL BROWN, retired volunteer; b. Apr. 25, 1915; d. David Alma and Ethel Myrle (Petersen) Brown; m. Jack Albert Dorland, June 11, 1944; children: Lynn Dorland Ballinger, Lee Allison. Cert. AA, Snow Jr. Coll., Ephraim, Utah, 1936; tchg. cert., Brigham Young U., 1937; BA, Utah State Coll., Logan, 1940; BS, Family Inst. Vassar Coll., Poughkeepsie, N.Y., 1978; grad., John Robert Powers, Sch. Profl. Women, N.Y.C., 1980. Sch. tchr., Utah, 1937-39, 40-42. Restored Washington Irving's graveplot in Sleepy Hollow (N.Y.) Cemetery (named Nat. Hist. Landmark 1972); nat. dir. Washington Irving Graveplot Restoration Program, 1968—, designer landmark plaque for grave; mem. Nat. Coun. State Garden Clubs,1959—; pres. Potpourri Garden Club, Westchester, N.Y., 1966—; nat. chmn. for graveplot programs Washington Irving Bicentennial, 1983-84; dir. Dorland Family Graveyard Restoration, N.J. Hist. Landmark, 1983—. Named Miss Congeniality, World's Fair Golden Gate Internat. Exposition, Treasure Island, Calif., 1939—40; recipient May Duff Walters trophy, Nat. Coun. State Garden Clubs, 1974, Nat. Trophy, Nat. Historic Landmark Com., 1974, citation, Keep Am. Beautiful, 1974, Disting. Alumni award for Cmty. Svc. Snow Coll., 1989. Mem. Nat. Trust for Historic Preservation (assoc., Pres.'s award 1977), Nat. Historic Soc. Am., Gen. Soc. Mayflower Desc., Am. Mus. Natural History (hon.), Internat. Washington Irving Soc. (founder, pres. 1981-), Nat. Assn. for Gravestone Studies (hon.), Herb Soc. Am., DAR, Internat. Platform Assn., Old Dutch Churchyard Restoration Assn., Am. Mus. Natural History (hon.), Nature Conservancy (hon.), Girls and Boys Town (hon.). Home: 20802 N Cave Creek Rd Apt 60 Phoenix AZ 85024-4438

DORMAN, ANGELIA HARDY, writer; b. Moncks Corner, S.C., July 6, 1963; d. Dallas Mewborn Hardy and Jule Ann (Wyndham) Spencer; m. David Parris Dorman, July 4, 1983. BA in History, U. S.C., 1983, MA in Tchg., 1990; postgrad., U. Idaho, 1996—. Radio announcer Sta. WBER, Moncks Corner, 1980-81; radio announcer, writer WSCQ, Columbia, S.C., 1983; interlibr. loan libr. Thomas Cooper Libr., U. S.C., Columbia, 1989; asst. curator for edn. McKisick Mus., U. S.C., Columbia, 1989; tchr. Eau Claire H.S., Columbia, 1990, Alcorn Middle Sch., Columbia, 1990-92, Irving Jr. H.S., Pocatello, Idaho, 1992-96; adj. instr. Idaho State U., Pocatello, 1994-96; lead tchr. Moscow (Idaho) Alternative Sch. Ctr., 1996—2000, Warden (Wash.) HS, 2000—. Adj. prof. Big Bend (Wash.) C.C., 2000—; cons. in field. Author: 75th Anniversary History of Columbia YWCA, 1989, Martha Gellhorn and the Human Legacy of War, 1943-1945; contbr. articles to profl. jours. Mem. Martin Luther King Jr. Com., Pocatello, 1992—; com. mem. Women's Hist. Month com., Pocatello, 1992—; organizer Young women's Career Group, Pocatello, 1994—. Mem. U. S.C. Alumni Assn., Phi Alpha Theta.

DORMAN, HATTIE LAWRENCE, management consultant, trainer, former government agency official; b. Cleve., July 22, 1932; d. J. Lyman and Claire A. (Lenoir) Lawrence; m. James L. Dorman, May 16, 1959; children: Lydia, Lynda, James Lawrence. Student, Fenn Coll. (Cleve. State U.), part-time 1950-58, D.C. Tchrs. Coll., 1960-64, Dept. Agr. Grad. Sch., 1968-69; BA, Howard U., 1987. Clk., tax specialist, mgmt. analyst, supr., staff advisor IRS, Washington, 1954-79; spl. asst. to dep. asst. sec. adminstrn. Dept. Treasury, Washington, 1978-79; dep. dir. Interagy. Com. on Women's Bus. Enterprise SBA; Task Force on EEO Dept. Treasury, 1978-79; mem. Pres.'s Task Force on Women Bus. Owners, 1979; ret. Assoc. prof. continuing edn. U. D.C.; guest lectr. continuing edn. Howard U.; mem. cmty. rels. coun. Washington Hosp. Ctr., 1986-2000; chief of staff for Dept. Dir. Presdl. Transition Team, 1992-93; bd. dirs. Wider Opportunities for Women, 1993-2000; bd. dirs. Delta Housing Corp., 1997—; trainer and spkr. in field. Sec. Linton Hall Guild, 1978-80; chmn. trainer, cons., leader Girl Scout Svc. Unit, 1971-92; ofcl. observer Nat. Women's Conf., Houston, 1977; bd. dirs. YWCA, 1957-62; mem. planning com. Black Women's Summit, 1981; mem. Vestry Register, St. Paul's Episcopal Ch., 1981-86, Jr. Warden, 1992-94. Recipient spl. achievement award Commr. IRS, 1978, thanks badge Girl Scout Nation's Capital, 1977, recognition cert. for work in Christian edn. St. Paul's Episcopal Ch., 1976, Mary McLeod Bethune Centennial award Nat. Coun. Negro Women, 1975, other awards and certs. of appreciation. Mem. ASTD, Am. Soc. Pub. Adminstrs., Fed. Exec. Inst. Alumni Assn., Assn. Psychol. Type Inc., Howard U. Alumni Assn., Delta Sigma Theta. E-mail: hd3269@aol.com.

DORMAN, JO-ANNE, elementary school educator; b. Greenville, Miss. d. Joe Edward and Constance Bonita (Parks) D. BS, Delta State U., 1963. Cert. tchr., Fla. Tchr. Oakcrest Elem. Sch., Pensacola, Fla., 1963-93; ret., 1993; substitute tchr. Sch. Dist. Escambia County, Pensacola, Fla., 1993—. Traffic sch. instr., 1997—. Sunday sch. tchr. Methodist Ch., Pensacola, Fla., 1963, 65, 68; voter precinct clk. Escambia County, 1997—; vol. Sr. Friends, 2000—. Mem.: U. West Fla. Leisure Learners Soc., Pensacola Dog Fanciers Assn., Papillon Club Am., Five Flags Dog Tng. Club. Democrat. Methodist. Avocations: travel, reading, photography, theater, dogs. Home: 188 Talladega Trl Pensacola FL 32506-3202

DORMAN, MARGARET K. oil equipment manufacturer; BA in Econ. and Bus., Hendrix Coll. Sr. mgr. Ernst & Young; corp. contr. Landmark Graphics Corp.; v.p., contr. Smith Internat., Houston, 1995-2000, sr. v.p., CFO, treas., 2000—. Office: Smith Internat PO Box 60068 Houston TX 77205-0068

DORN, JENNIFER L. federal agency administrator; 2 children. Degree, Oreg. State U.; MPA, U. Conn. Dir. Office of Comml. Space Transp., 1983—85; assoc. dep. sec. transp. U.S. Dept. Transp., 1985—87; sr. v.p. Am. Nat. Red Cross, 1991—98; asst. sec. for policy U.S. Dept. Labor, 1988—90; adminstr. fed. transit adminstn. U.S. Dept. Transp., Washington, 2001—. Pres. Nat. Health Mus., 1998—2001. Office: US Dept Transp Fed Transit Adminstrn 400 7th St SW Washington DC 20590-0001

DORN, JENNIFER LYNN, charitable organization administrator; b. Grand Island, Nebr., Dec. 7, 1950; d. Harold Clarence and Ethel Agnes D. BA, Oreg. State U., 1973; MPA, U. Conn., 1977. Legis. asst. Senator M. Hatfield, Washington, 1977-81; com. staff Senate Appropriations, Washington, 1981-83; spl. asst. Sec. Elizabeth Dole, Washington, 1983-84; dir. Comml. Space Transp., Washington, 1984-85; assoc. dep. sec. U.S. Dept. Transp., Washington, 1985-87; asst. sec. policy U.S. Dept. Labor, Washington, 1989-91; sr. v.p. pub. support ARC, Washington, 1991-98; pres. Nat. Health Mus., 1998—. Mem. Washington Women's Forum, Cosmos Club. Republican. Lutheran. Home: 1155 NW 15th St # 810 Reston VA 20191-4842 Office: 1331 H St NW Ste 600 Washington DC 20005-4736 E-mail: nrodj@aol.com.

DORN, KATHIE LEE, medical/surgical nurse; b. Dallas, Aug. 8, 1948; d. Gordon Lee and Ruth Mae (Beadle) Cunningham; m. Gordon Lee Dorn, Oct. 30, 1969; Children: Scott Lee, Kelly Lee. Student, So. Methodist U., 1966-68; RN, Elcentro Coll., 1983. ADN, RN, CNOR, CPR Instr., ACLS; cert. plastic surgery nurse. Staff RN Parkland Meml. Hosp., Dallas, 1984-86, Peri-Op. Nurses of Dallas, 1986-87, Barton, Brown & Byrd Plastic Surgeons, Dallas, 1987-88, Mary Shiels Hosp., Dallas, 1988-95; PRN staff RN, CPR instr. Parkland Meml. Hosp., Dallas, 1986-95; scrub nurse, PRN D. Mark Jewell, Plastic Surgery, Eugene, Oreg., 1995-98; recovery room PRN, staff RN Sacred Heart Hosp., Eugene, 1996-97; cruise ship nurse Royal Caribbean Internat., 1998—. Item review bd. mem. Peri-Operative Nurses Inc., Denver, 1994; CPR instr. Dallas Community & Parkland Hosp., 1993-95; v.p. Dorn Microbiological Assocs., Eugene, 1986—. Contbr. various newsletters in field. Vol. Tex. flu step immunizations Tex. Vis. Nurses Assn., 1994, blood drives and fund raising Wadley Blood Bank Guild, 1986-91, clinics Dallas Ind. Sch. Dist., 1982-95, pub. clinics vital signs classes Am. Red Cross, 1980-95, nurse counselor Bolshoi Ballet Acad., Vail, Colo., 1990. Recipient Interlocking Circle of Caring award Delta Airlines, Dallas, 1986. Mem. AORN (nat. and Eugene chpts.), Am. Heart Assn. (mem. sci. coun. 1993—). Republican. Roman Catholic. Avocations: cross-country skiing, hiking, weight lifting, interior design, balletomine. Home and Office: 29323 Gimpl Hill Rd Eugene OR 97402-9054

DORN, MARY ANN, retired auditor; b. Overland, Mo., May 1, 1933; d. Bernard J. and Marie (Kunkler) Engler; children: Glennon (dec.), Pat Michael, Michelle; m. Donald Patrick Dorn, June 3, 2002. Student, Fontbonne Coll., 1951-52; AA, Sacramento City Coll., 1975; BS in Bus., Calif. State U., 1981. CPA, Calif.; cert. fraud examiner; cert. govt. fin. mgr. From asst. to acct. Mo. Rsch. Labs., Inc., St. Louis, 1953-55, adminstrv. asst., 1955-60; sec. western region fin. office Gen. Electric Co., St. Louis, 1960-62; credit analyst Crocker Nat. Bank, Sacramento, 1962-72; student tchr. Sacramento County Dept. Edn., 1979-81; acctg. technician East Yolo Community Services Dist., 1983; mgmt. specialist USAF Logistics Command, 1984; auditor Office Insp. Gen. U.S. Dept. Transp., 1984-92; auditor-in-charge Adminstrn. for Children and Families U.S. Dept. Health and Human Svcs., 1992—. Mem. Sacramento Community Commn. for Women, 1978-81, bd. dirs., 1980—; planning bd. Golden Empire Health Systems Agy. Mem. AARP (tax counselor), AAUW (fin. officer 1983—), AICPA, Nat. Assn. Accts. (dir., newsletter editor), Fontbonne Coll. Alumni Assn., Calif. State Alumni Assn., Assn. Govt. Accts. (chpt. officer), Calif. Soc. CPAs, German Geneological Soc. (bd. dirs. 1990—, publicity dir. 1994—), Sun City Lincoln Hills Assn., Beta Gamma Sigma, Beta Alpha Psi. Roman Catholic. Home: 815 Magnolia Ln Lincoln CA 95648-8429

DORN, SUE BRICKER, consultant, retired hospital administrator; b. Seattle, Apr. 1, 1934; d. Barney and Frances B. (Schnitzer) Bricker; m. Philip Henry Dorn, Dec. 31, 1955 (dec.); children: Charles, Martha Dorn. BA, Stanford U., Palo Alto, 1955; MA, Bank St. Coll., 1973. Cert. tchr., N.Y. Dir. promotion exec. compensation svc. Am. Mgmt. Assn., N.Y.C., 1956-58; tchr. spl. edn. N.Y.C. Bd. of Edn., 1969-77; assoc. dir. Yale U., New Haven, 1977-79; v.p. Bank St. Coll. of Edn., N.Y.C., 1979-81, Aspen Inst. for Humanistic Studies, N.Y.C., 1981-82; assoc. v.p. Yale U., New Haven, 1982-87; dep. dir. devel. and pub. affairs Mus. of Modern Art, N.Y.C., 1987-94; v.p., vice provost for devel. The N.Y. Hosp.-Cornell Med. Ctr., 1994—98. Mem. maj. gifts com. Stanford U.; cons. in field; bd. dirs. First Citicorp Life Ins. Co. Pres. LWV, Warren, Mich., 1962-65, Stanford Alumni Club of N.Y., N.J. and Conn., N.Y.C., 1968-70, 25 East 86th St. Corp., N.Y.C., 1989-93, 95—; mem. dirs. adv. bd. Yale Comprehensive Cancer Ctr., Yale U., 1990-94. Named Citizen of the Yr., Warren C. of C., 1962; recipient Citation, City of Warren, 1963, Gold Spike award and Cert. of Outstanding Achievement, Stanford U., 1976. Mem. Stanford Assocs., Univ. Club. Home: 25 E 86th St New York NY 10028-0553 E-mail: sdorn@nyc.rr.com.

DORN, VIRGINIA ALICE, artist, art gallery director; b. Mpls., June 22, 1916; d. Raymond Edwin and Ruth Virginia (Nylander) Henneman; m. John Emil Dorn, Feb. 22, 1937 (dec. Sept. 1971); children: John Robert, Michael Raymond. BS, U. Minn., 1937. Mgr. med. lab., Orinda, Calif., 1955-61; instr. art Orinda Civic Ctr., 1980-81; mgr., tchr. San Francisco Women Artists Gallery, 1984—. One woman shows include Lucien LaBaudt Gallery, San Francisco, 1975, St. Paul's Towers, Oakland, Calif., 1976, Contemporary Arts, Berkeley, Calif., 1977, 80, Trinity Gallery, Berkeley, 1982, Valley Arts Gallery, Walnut Creek, Calif., 1982, Univ. Club, San Francisco, 1983, Holy Names Coll. Gallery, Oakland, 1987, Wellness Cmty. Gallery, Walnut Creek, 1991, Vincent's Ear Gallery, Orinda, Calif., 1994, also many juried and invitational shows in Calif.; represented by San Francisco Women Artists Gallery and East Bay Royal Ground Gallery, Oakland, Calif. Recipient Lifetime Achievement award Women's Caucus for Art, 1996. Mem. San Francisco Women Artists (bd. dirs., fund raiser, mgr., instr., coord.), Oakland Art Assn., Valley Art Assn., Berkeley Art Ctr., East Bay Women Artists. Avocations: travel, music. Home: 95 Evergreen Dr Orinda CA 94563-3114

DORNER, DARLENE A. music educator; b. Green Bay, Wis., Apr. 24, 1951; d. Urban George and Marie Frances (Heim) Dorner. MusB, St. Norbert Coll., DePere, Wis., 1973; EdM, Viterbo Coll., LaCrosse, Wis., 2000. Tchr. Green Bay Pub. Schs., 1973—75, Oconto (Wis.) Unified Schs., 1976—78, tchr. music, choral dir., 1981—, tchr. Sheboygan (Wis.) Pub. Schs., 1978—79. Dir. musicals Oconto Cmty. Theater, 1999, 2002. Coach summer camp Green Bay Girls Choir, 1998; bd. appeals Oconto City Coun., 1995—96; choral dir. St. Joseph's Cath. Ch., Oconto, 1976—78, First Presbyn. Ch., Oconto, 1978—84; bd. dirs. Dudley Birder Chorale, DePere, 1994—96. Mem.: Wis. Choral Dirs. Assn., Am. Choral dirs. Assn. (5 star choir dir.), Music Educators Nat. Conf., Wis. Sch. Music Assn. (master adjudicator 1989—2003, state honors choir coach, 5 star choir dir.). Avocations: travel, theater, gardening, reading, piano. Home: 242 Michigan Ave Oconto WI 54153

DORR, ANN PIERCE, science educator; b. Tulsa, Aug. 11, 1918; d. Oscar Charles Pierce and Grace Esther Myers; m. John Van Nostrand Dorr II, Feb. 5, 1946; children: John Van Nostrand Dorr III, Charles Pierce Dorr, Katherine Grace Dorr. BA, U. Kansas City, 1939; MEd, Am. U., 1968. Geol. asst. Ark. Geol. Survey, Little Rock, 1942-43; asst. rsch. analyst Petroleum Adminstrv. for War, Washington, 1943-44; geol. asst. Great Lakes Carbon Corp., Wichita, Kans., 1943-46; earth sci. tchr. Fairfax County Pub. Schs., Va., 1964-75; co-instr. course for earth sci. tchrs. U. Va. Sch. of Continuing Edn., Fairfax County, 1974-76; cons. crustal evolution Nat. Assn. Geology Tchrs., Washington, 1977; author course guide and faculty materials Internat. Univ. Consortium, Md., 1982-83. Mem. coms. in field, including Nat. Sci. Resources Ctr.-Smithsonian Instn.-Nat. Acad. Sci. adv. com. for Middle Sch. Project "Catastrophic Events", 1997-2000. Author: Minerals: Foundations of Society, 3d edit., 2002, numerous other publs. in field. Mem. natural resources com. LWV, Montgomery County, Md., 1974—, chair 1974 78; cons. editor: Science Activities, 1982-85; bd. dirs. Mineral Info. Inst., 1984-98, v.p. Southeastern Region, MII, 1984-89; mem. energy and environ. task force Woman's Nat. Dem. Club, 1986—, chair 1992-96, co-chair 1987-92, 92-97, others. Recipient numerous awards in field, including Outstanding Earth Sci. Tchr. of Va., Nat. Assn. Geology Tchrs., 1974, Outstanding Earth Sci. Tchr. in S.E. U.S., Nat. Assn. Geology Tchrs. Mem. Women in Mining, Assn. Women Geoscientists, Am. Inst. Mining, Metallurgy, Petroleum Engrs., Population Ref. Bur. Democrat. Avocations: writing, backcountry travel, music. Home: 9707 Old Georgetown Rd Apt 2514 Bethesda MD 20814-1761

DORR, STEPHANIE TILDEN, psychotherapist; b. Orlando, Fla., Sept. 21, 1950; d. Luther Willis Tilden II and Lillian Murfee (Grace) Owen; m. Darwin Dorr, May 21, 1986. AA, El Camino Coll., 1975; BA, U. N.C., 1985; MA, Western Carolina U., 1991. Cons. psychologist Sylva (N.C.) Psychol. Assocs., 1991-92; staff psychologist Park Ridge Hosp., Naples, N.C., 1992, Blue Ridge Ctr., Asheville, N.C., 1991-93; pvt. practice psychology Asheville, 1991-93; project mgr. Sedgwick County Dept. Mental Health, Wichita, Kans., 1993-95; pvt. practice psychotherapy and psychol. assessment Counseling and Mediation Ctr., Wichita, Kans., 1995-98; therapist United Meth. Youthville Clinic, Wichita, 1998—2001; clin. therapist Wichita (Kans.) Pub. Schs. Greiffenstein Spl. Edn. Ctr., 2002—. Adj. faculty Kans. Newman Coll., Wichita, 1995—, Butler County (Kans.) Cmty. Coll., 1996-97; Assertive Cmty. Treatment (ACT) team clinician United Meth. Youthville, Wichita, 1997-98; presenter in field. Contbr. articles to profl. publs. Recipient Excellence in Tchg. award Butler County C.C., 1997, Outstanding Faculty Mem. award Butler County C.C., 1998. Mem. Soc. for Personality Assessment, Psychoanalytic Study Group (sec. 1989-93, award 1993), Western N.C. Psychol. Assn. (mem.-at-large 1985-93, pres.-elect 1993), Psi Chi, Pi Gamma Mu. Episcopalian. Avocations: sewing, rock collecting, gardening. Office: Wichita Pub Schs Greiffenstein Spl Edn Ctr 1221 E Galena Wichita KS 67216 E-mail: sdorr@usd259.net, stdorr@cox.net.

DORSEY, DOLORES FLORENCE, retired corporate treasurer, business executive; b. Buffalo, May 26, 1928; d. William G. and Florence R. D. BS, Coll. St. Elizabeth, 1950. With Aerojet-Gen. Corp., 1953—, asst. to treas., 1972-74, asst. treas., 1974-79, treas., 1979—2001. Mem. Cash Mgmt. Group San Diego (past pres.), Nat. Assn. Corp. Treas., Fin. Execs. Inst. (v.p.). Republican. Roman Catholic. Office: 10300 N Torrey Pines Rd La Jolla CA 92037-1020

DORSEY, DONNA BAGLEY, insurance agent; b. Macon, Ga., May 26, 1952; d. Clarence Henry and Sybil Audrey (Phillips) Bagley; m. David M.

Lewis, June 14, 1969 (div. May 1979); children: Scott D., Jeffrey A.; m. J. Larry Dorsey, July 1, 1980. Grad. high sch., Macon, Ga. Cert. ins. counselor; cert. profl. ins. woman. Rating clk. Bibb Underwriters Ins., Macon, 1977-80; book-keeper Wilson Typewriter, Macon, 1980-85; customer svc. rep. Ga. Ins. Agy., Macon, 1985; agt., customer svc. rep. Johnson and Johnson [illegible] Macon, 1985—. Recipient Outstanding Customer Svc. Rep. Ga. award Ind. Ins. Agts. Ga., 1993; Ruth Dupree Meml. scholar, 1987, Safeco Ins. Achievement award, 1995, 97; nominee T.J. Mims award of excellence, 1998. Mem. Profl. Ins. Agts. Ga. (bd. dirs. 1990-93, Eagle award 1989), Young Profl. Coun. Ga. (chmn. 1991-92), Ins. Women Macon (treas. 1991-92, v.p. 1992-93, pres. elect 1993-94, pres. 1994-95, Macon Ins. Woman of Yr. 1994, Ga. Ins. Woman of Yr. 1994, President's Vol. award 1994, Macon Ins. Profl. of Yr. 1995, Indivdual Edn. Achievement award 1996). Avocations: reading, water skiing, swimming. Office: Johnson and Johnson Ins Inc 420 Rogers Ave Macon GA 31204-2042

DORSEY, DONNA MORGAN, state agency administrator; b. Stroudsburg, Pa., Aug. 12, 1945; d. Lemuel James and Rose (Naegle) Morgan; m. Neil Dorsey, July 31, 1965; children: Kimberly Ann, Jennifer Lynn. BS in Nursing, East Carolina U., 1967; MS in Nursing, U. Md., 1975. Staff nurse Greenbelt (Md.) Convalescent Ctr., 1967-68; cmty. health nurse Montgomery County Health Dept., Rockville, Md., 1968-70; asst. prof. Sch. Nursing U. Md., Balt., 1972-81; asst. dir. staff devel. Ctrl. Md. chpt. Balt. Red Cross, 1981; exec. dir. Md. Bd. Nursing, Balt., 1981—. Adj. asst. prof. Sch. Nursing U. Md., Balt., 1985—; treas. Nat. Coun. State Bds. Nursing, Chgo., 1986-91; faculty assoc. Johns Hopkins U., Balt., 1990—. Mem. Gov.'s Commn. on Nursing, Balt., 1983, Gov.'s Commn. for Sch. Nursing, Balt., 1985; bd. dirs. Ctrl. Md. chpt. ARC, Balt., 1976—, chair, 1986-88, disatster nurse supr., 1990—; mem. nat. nursing com. ARC, Washington, 1992—; bd. dirs. Md. affiliate Am. Heart Assn., Balt., 1977-86. Recipient Silver Svc. award Md. Affiliate Am. Heart Assn., 1986, Ann Magnussen award ARC, 1992, John T. Menzies award Ctrl. Md. Chpt. ARC, 1993. Mem. ANA, Am. Assn. Exec. Women, Nat. League for Nursing, Md. Nurses Assn., Md. League for Nursing (pres. 1979-81), Profl. Nursing Orgn. East Carolina U. Avocations: travel, crafts. Home: 6391 Scarlet Petal Columbia MD 21045-4524 Office: Md State Bd of Nursing 4140 Patterson Ave Baltimore MD 21215-2254

DORSEY, MARY ELIZABETH, lawyer; b. Florissant, Mo., July 4, 1962; d. Richard Peter Jr. and Dolores Irene (McNamara) D. BA in Acctg., Benedictine Coll., 1984; JD, St. Louis U., 1987. Bar: Mo. 1989, U.S. Dist. Ct. (we. dist.) Mo. 1989, U.S. Dist. Ct. (ea. dist.) Mo. 1990, U.S. Supreme Ct. 1994, U.S. Ct. Appeals (8th cir.) 1997. Rschr. Ind. Legal Rsch., Florissant, 1987-89; atty. assoc. Deeba Sauter Herd, St. Louis, 1989-98; ptnr. Ahlheim & Dorsey, LLC, St. Charles, 1998—. Bd. dirs. North County, Inc. Merit badge counselor St. Louis Area coun. Boy Scouts Am., 1988—, mem. com. Troop 748, mem. Order of the Arrow, 1992, Brotherhood, 1994; corr. sec. Florissant Twp. Open Dem. Club, 1989-91, sgt. at arms, 1991-2000; treas. Friends of Rick Dorsey, St. Louis, 1988, 90, 92, 96; mem. Dem. Com., Florissant Twp., 1996—. Mem.: ATLA, ABA, St. Charles County Bar Assn., Bar Assn. Met. St. Louis (lectr. law related edn. com. 1988—96), Mo. Assn. Trial Attys., Mo. Jaycees (state legal counsel 1997—99, dist. dir. 1998—99, region dir. 2000, membership v.p. 2001, state legal counsel 2002—03), Florissant Valley Jaycees (dir. 1993—94, treas. 1994—95, state dir. 1995—97, v.p. 1997—98), U.S.Jaycees (regional coord. 2002, Nat. Resource Team 2003). Democrat. Roman Catholic. Avocations: golf, camping, theatre. Office: Ahlheim & Dorsey LLC 2209 1st Capitol Dr Saint Charles MO 63301-5809 E-mail: med@ahlheimdorsey.com.

DORSEY, RHODA MARY, retired academic administrator; b. Boston, Sept. 9, 1927; d. Thomas Francis and Hedwig (Hoge) D. BA magna cum laude, Smith Coll., 1949, LLD, 1979; BA, Cambridge (Eng.) U., 1951, MA, 1954; PhD, U. Minn., 1956; LLD, Nazareth Coll. Rochester, 1970, Goucher Coll., 1994; DHL (hon.), Mount St. Mary's Coll., 1976, Mount Vernon Coll., 1979, Coll. St. Catherine, 1983, Johns Hopkins U., 1986, Towson State U., 1987, Coll. Notre Dame of Md., 1995, Coll. of Notre Dame Md., 1995. Mem. faculty Goucher Coll., Balt., Md., 1954-94, prof. history, 1965-68, dean, v.p., 1968-73, acting pres., 1973-74, pres., 1974-94, pres. emeritus, 1994—. Lectr. history Loyola Coll., Balt., 1958-62, Johns Hopkins U., Balt., 1960-61; bd. trustee Roland Park County Sch., 1995—. Bd. dirs. Friends of Cambridge U., 1978—, sec., 1989-93; bd. dirs. Gen. German Aged Peoples Home, Balt., 1984—, Greater Balt. Med. Ctr., 1990—, Md. Humanities Coun., Baltimore County Landmarks Preservation Commn., 1994—; bd. dirs., chair Hist. Hampton, Inc., 1992—; trustee Loyola, Notre Dame Libr., Balt., 1994—, Roland Park Country Sch., 1995—; chair Gov.'s Commn. Svc., 1994—. Named Outstanding Woman Mgr. of 1984 U. Balt. Women's Program in Mgmt. and WMAR-TV, Woman of Yr. Balt. County Commn. for Women, 1993; recipient Outstanding Achievement award U. Minn. Alumni Assn., 1984, Andrew White medal Loyola Coll., Balt., 1985; named in peer survey as one of 100 Most Effective Coll. and Univ. Pres. in U.S., Chronicle of Higher Edn., 1986. Mem. Internat. Women's forum, Smith Club, Hamilton St. Club (Balt.), Cosmopolitan Club (N.Y.C.).

DORSHOW-GORDON, ELLEN, epidemiologist; b. St. Paul, May 16, 1946; d. Bennie and Goldie (Salita) Dorshow; m. Charles Gordon, May 15, 1977; 1 child, Gayle. BS in Med. Tech., U. Minn., 1968, MPH, 1983; postgrad., Western Mich. U., 2002—. Infection control coord. Samaritan Health Ctr., Detroit, 1980-83; cons Infection Control Resource Ctr., 1983-84; grad. rsch. asst. Rehab. Inst. Detroit, 1984-85; health and safety/mental health/nutrition coord. Renaissance Head Start, Detroit, 1984-86; infection control market specialist Calgon Vestal Labs., 1986-90; infection control coord. Sinai Hosp., Detroit, 1990-94; dir. quality svcs./infection control Great Lakes Rehab. Hosp., Southfield, Mich., 1994-95; epidemiologist Oakland County Health Divsn. Dept. Human Svcs., Pontiac, Mich., 1995-2000, Kalamazoo County Human Svcs. Dept., 2000—03, Jackson County Health Dept., Independence, 2003—. Mem. Nat. Sanitation Found. Task Group, 1997-99; mem. S.E. Mich. Epidemiology Com., 1995-2000, Coun. of State and Territorial Epidemiologists; mem. 5th Dist. Med. Response Coalition, 2002-03; presenter in field. Contbr. articles to profl. jours. Vol. B'nai Brith Women Twin Cities Coun., 1973-80, Hadassah, Am. Arab and Jewish Friends, 2002-03. U. Minn. Alumnae Freshman scholar, 1964; recipient Calgon Exec. Dir's. award, 1986, Calgon Vestal Lab. Pacesetter award, 1987. Fellow Mich. Pub. Health Leadership Inst., Wall of Tolerance; mem. NOW, ACLU, AARP, NAFE, Minn. Soc. Med. Tech. (bd. dirs. 1972-75), Minn. Alumnae Assn., Assn. Practitioners Infection Control and Epidemiology (edn. com. chair greater Detroit 1983-85, legis. liason greater Kansas City 2004—), Women and AIDS com., Am. Pub. Health Assn., Mo. Pub. Health Assn., So. Poverty Law Ctr, Greater Kansas City TB Coalition. Avocations: reading, net surfing, volunteering. Office: 313 S Liberty Independence MO 64050

DORTCH, CAROLE A. federal agency administrator; BS in Commerce Acctg., Rider U. Fin. cons. Parametric, Inc., Atlanta; fin. analyst, budge analyst City of Atlanta; dir. Bur. Budget Policy and Evaluation Mgmt. Audit Dept. Budget and Planning, 1979-83; commr., dir. Dept. Adminstrv. Svcs., Atlanta, 1983-93; regional adminstr. SE Sunbelt Region Gen. Svcs. Adminstrn., Atlanta, 1993—. Bd. dirs. YMCA; mem. cons. adv. bd. Coll. Architecture Ga. Tech.; active Fulton County Workforce Devel. Adv. Coun. Named to Nat. Black Coll. Alumni Hall of Fame. Mem. Internat. Facility Mgmt. Assn., Bldg. Owners and Mgrs. Assn. Office: Gen Svcs Adminstrn SE Sunbelt Region 401 W Peachtree St NW Atlanta GA 30308-3510

DORTON, LOUISE, library director; b. Oklahoma City, Mar. 6, 1936; d. Charles William Blatt and Beula O. (Williams) Nelson; m. Jack M. Dorton, Sept. 30, 1956 (div. 1985); children: Brenda, Kenneth, Janet, Dana. BA, Douglass Coll., 1973; MLS, Rutgers U., 1974. Dir. Pemberton (N.J.) Community Libr., 1974-79, Johnson City (Tenn.) Pub. Libr., 1979-89; br. dir. Chattanooga Libr.-Northgate, 1989-90; owner, mgr. Spoken Word Book Shop, Knoxville, Tenn., 1990-93; dir. Darlington County Libr., Darlington, S.C., 1991-96, Granville County Library System, Oxford, N.C., 1996—. Mem. North Johnson City Bus. Club, 1985-89; bd. dirs. Johnson City Girls' Club, 1986-89, pres., 1987-88. Grantee N.J. State Libr., 1975, 76, 77, N.J. Labor Dept., 1976, Tenn. State Libr., 1986, 87, U.S. Dept. Edn., 1987. Mem. ALA, AAUW (pres. 1984-85), Oxford C. of C. (Leadership 2000 1986-87). Office: Granville County Library System PO Box 339 210 Main St Oxford NC 27565-3321

DORTON, TRUDA LOU, medical, surgical and geriatrics nurse; b. Elkhorn Creek, Ky., Aug. 26, 1949; d. Clair Otis Parsons and Joyce Kidd; m. Eugene Anderson, Nov. 26, 1966 (dec. Apr. 1971); children: Gena Lynn, Richard Eugene; m. Leon Dorton, Dec. 15, 1972; children: Leondra Michelle, Jerald Thomas, Jonathan Layne. AS, student, Pikeville Coll., 1993. RN, Ky.; cert. ACLS, PALS. Instr. computer usage Lookout (Ky.) Elem. Sch., 1983; water/sewage technician McCoy & McCoy Environ. Cons., Pikeville, Ky., 1984; owner Signs of the Times, Elkhorn City, Ky., 1979-89; sec.'s asst. humanities and social scis. divsns. Pikeville Coll., 1989-92; nurse aide Mud Creek Clinic, Grethel, Ky., 1992-93; charge nurse Jenkins (Ky.) Cmty. Hosp., 1993-94; case mix coord. Parkview Manor Nursing Home, 1994-95, minimum data set and nursing care plan coord., 1995; acute care nurse Harrison Meml. Hosp., Cynthiana, Ky., 1996—2002; dir. nursing Robertson County Health Care Facility, Mt. Olivet, Ky.; long-term care charge nurse Trilogy Health Ctr. at Harrison Meml. Hosp., Cynthiana; med. inpatient svcs. Floyd Meml. Hosp., New Albany, Ind. Vol. nurse aide Mud Creek Clinic, Grethel, 1989-92. Founder free blood pressure clinic H.E.L.P.S. Community Action Program, Hellier, Ky., 1983; co-founder H.E.L.P.S. Community Action Group, Hellier, 1983; mem. Ellis Island Centennial Commn., N.Y., 1986. Appalachian Honors scholar Pikeville Coll., 1989-92. Mem. Nat. Geog. Soc., Ky. Nursing Assn., Order Ky. Cols. (Honorable Ky. Col. 1989), Smithsonian Inst., Nat. Trust Hist. Preservation, World Wildlife Fund, Pikeville Coll. Alumni Assn. Democrat. Mem. Worldwide Ch. of God. Avocations: creating indian jewelry and wall hangings, classical music. Home: RR 1 Box 80 Hwy 539 Mount Olivet KY 41064-9510

DORWARD, JUDITH A. business ordering customer service representative; b. Hazleton, Pa., Apr. 16, 1941; d. Eugene Joseph and Dorothy Cecelia (Shields) McNertney; m. Douglas Dean Owens, Apr. 15, 1961 (div. 1968); children: Kevin Patrick Owens, Kelly Shawn Owens. AA, Lehigh County Community Coll., 1979; BA, Muhlenberg Coll., 1984; grad. in statis. process control, Process Mgmt. Inst., Inc., Mpls., 1986. Customer svc. clk. Pa. Power & Light Co., Allentown, 1959-61; mgr. Merle Norman Cosmetic Studios, Allentown and Bethlehem, Pa., 1968-70; adminstrv. clk. Pillsbury Co., East Greenville, Pa., 1970-85, ops. prodn. mgr., 1985-87, mgr. distbn. and prodn. control, 1987-93, chair labor rels. com., 1987-91, customer svc., vender liaison mgr., 1993-94; Pillsbury customer svc. rep. Americold Corp., Fogelsville, Pa., 1994-95; exec. field rep. Better Bus. Bureau Ea. Pa., 1996—2001; nat. bus. ordering customer svc. rep. West Corp., Reno, 2001—. Held various offices Gen. Fedn. Women's Clubs; former voting machine operator Lehigh County, Slatington, Pa. Mem.: Exec. Women Internat. (dir. publs. 1991, dir. membership 1992—93, v.p., pres.-elect 1994, pres. 1995), Phi Beta Kappa. Democrat. Roman Catholic. Avocation: foreign travel. Home: 2830 Linden St Apt 3C Bethlehem PA 18017-3962 E-mail: JudyAD@aol.com.

DORWART, BONNIE BRICE, historian, retired rheumatologist; b. Petersburg, Va., Jan. 27, 1942; d. Gratien Bertrand and Myrtle Elizabeth (Houser) Brice; m. William Villee Dorwart, Jr., June 22, 1963; children: William Bertrand, Brice Burdan, Michael Walter. AB, Bryn Mawr Coll., 1964; MD, Temple U., 1968. Diplomate Am. Bd. Med. Examiners, Am. Bd. Internal Medicine, Am. Bd. Rheumatology. Intern then resident in internal medicine Lankenau Hosp., Jefferson Med. Coll., Phila., 1968-72; instr. medicine Hosp. U. Pa., Phila., 1972-74; fellow rheumatology U. Pa. Sch. Medicine, Phila., 1974; instr. medicine Jefferson Med. Coll., Phila., 1974-76, asst. prof., 1976-81, assoc. prof., 1981-95, clin. prof., 1995—2003; assoc. investigator divsn. rsch. Lankenau Hosp., Phila., 1978-88, chief arthritis clinic, 1982-86, chief connective tissue disorders, 1982-97; Civil War med. historian, writer, 2001—. Assoc. dir. Greater Delaware Valley Arthritis Control Program, 1975; mem. Gov.'s adv. bd. on Systemic Lupus Erythematosus, Phila., 1981-88. Author: Carson's Materia Medica of 1851: An Annotation, 2003; contbr. articles to med. jours., chpts. to books. Med. career advisor, active cells workshop Merion (Pa.) Elem. Sch., 1984-90; fund raiser Arthritis Found., Am. Cancer Soc., Phila., 1974-97; mem. resources com. Bryn Mawr Coll., 1985-90. Named Physician of Yr., 32 Carat Club, Phila., 1986; Janet M. Glasgow scholar Temple U. Sch. Medicine, 1968. Fellow ACP, Coll. Physicians Phila.; mem. AMA, Am. Coll. Rheumatology, Phila. Rheumatism Soc. (pres. 1981-82), Pa. Med. Soc., Philadelphia County Med. Soc. Lutheran. Avocations: wood-carving, cooking, gardening, embroidery, wood-carving. Home and Office: 124 Maple Ave Bala Cynwyd PA 19004-3031 Office Phone: 610-667-3849.

DOSAMANTES-BEAUDRY, IRMA, psychology educator; b. Mexico City; m. Walter A. Beaudry. BS, CUNY, 1959, MA, 1962; PhD, Mich. State U., 1967; postgrad., UCLA, 1972-73; grad. psychoanalyst, L.A. Inst./Soc. Psych. Studies, 1993. Assoc. dir., counselor SUNY, Stonybrook, 1968-71; assoc. prof. U. No. Colo., 1973-74, Calif. State U., L.A., 1974-77; prof. UCLA, 1977—. Dir. dance/movement therapy program UCLA, 1977—. Author: (book) Body-Image: A Cross-Cultural Perspective, 1993; editor-in-chief: (profl. jour.) The Arts in Psychotherapy Jour., 1998—, mem. editl. bd., 1986-87; mem. editl. bd. Am. Dance Therapy Jour., 1988-97. U. Calif. Pacific Rim Rsch. grantee, 1991-92. Mem. APA, Am. Dance Therapy Assn. (bd. dirs. 1974-84, pres. 1980-82, Chace Found. award 1997), Am. Assn. for Study of Mental Imagery (bd. dirs. 1982-86, pres. 1983-84), Internat. Psychoanalytic Assn., L.A. Inst. and Soc. for Psychoanalytic Studies. Avocations: tennis, gardening. Office: UCLA World Arts & Cultures Dept PO Box 951608 Los Angeles CA 90095-1608

DOSS-REED, HELEN GRIGSBY, writer; b. Sanderstead, Surrey, England, Aug. 9, 1915; (parents Am. citizens); d. Owen E. and Maude E. Grigsby; m. Carl M. Doss; adopted children: Don, Dorothy, Elaine, Ted, Lora, Susan, Tim, Rita, Diane, Alex, Richard(dec.), Greg(dec.) ; m. Roger W. Reed, 1986; stepchildren: John Reed, Jim Reed. Student, Santa Ana Coll., 1932—33, Eureka Coll., 1933—34; BA, U. Redlands, 1954; postgrad., UCLA, 1968. Author: The Family Nobody Wanted, 1954, 2001, A Brother the Size of Me, 1957, If You Adopt a Child, 1957, All the Children of the World, 1958, The Really Real Family, 1959, Friends Around the World, 1959, Jonah, 1964, King David, 1967, Where Can I Find God?, 1968, Young Readers Book of Bible Stories, 1970, All the Better to Bite With, 1976, Your Skin Holds You In, 1978, The U.S. Air Force, From Balloons to Space Ships, 1981. Mem.: AAUW. Methodist. Avocations: camping, reading. Home: 581 Scirocco Dr Yuba City CA 95991

DOSTAL, TAMARA, insurance company executive; b. San Francisco, Dec. 20, 1961; d. Vladimir Joseph Dostal and Rosalie Gerda Van Moppis. BA in Criminal Justice, Sacramento State U., 1984. Sr. claim specialist The Doctor's Co., Santa Monica, Calif., 1990—. Bd. dirs. Broadway Gymnastics, Venice, Calif., 2001—; vol. Westside Childrens Ctr., Culver City, Calif., 2003—. Mem.: So. Calif. Risk Mgmt. Assn. Avocations: travel, fitness, piano, gardening. Office: The Doctor's Co 100 Wilshire Blvd 5th Fl Santa Monica CA 90401

DOSTI, ROSE, newspaper columnist, author; b. N.Y.C., Feb. 6, 1931; Student, Hunter Coll., 1949-51, Ithaca Coll., 1952-53. Staff writer L.A. Times, 1964-92, columnist, 1992-01. Author: (cookbooks) Light Style, 1979, rev., 1991, New California Cuisine, 1986, Mid East Mediterranean, 1982, rev., 1993, Dear SOS, 1994, Dear SOS Desserts, 1996, Favorite Dear SOS Restaurant Recipies, 2001. Avocations: art, sculpture, piano, [illegible] exercise. E-mail: rosedosti@yahoo.com.

DOTSON, NANCY JEAN DAVIS, secondary school educator; b. Houston, Feb. 5, 1941; d. Willie and Callie D. (Morris) Davis; m. Earl Leslie Dotson, Oct. 2, 1964; children: Lisa Chandra, Leslie Chan, Lamar Cedric. BS, So. Univ., Baton Rouge, 1962; MS, Pepperdine U., 1974; postgrad., U. So. Calif., U. Calif., L.A. Cert. elem. tchr.; cert. secondary tchr.; cert. supervision K-12; cert. gen. adminstrn. Tchr. Houston Ind. Sch. Dist., 1962-64; math., sci. tchr. Gompers Jr. High Sch., L.A., 1964-70, math. tchr., coord., 1970-72; math. area advisor Area C, Title I Office, L.A. USD, 1972-76; compensatory edn. coord. Drew Jr. High Sch L.A. USD, 1976-88, categorical programs advisor, coord., 1988—. Owner, dir., cons. Agape Resource Ctr., Carson, Calif., 1988—. Contbr. instructional bulls. and aids and other writings for profls. local schs. V.p. Wheatley West Alumni, Inc., Carson, 1982—; sec. Good Neighbors Fariman Dr. Block Club, Carson, 1984—; vol. Harbor Christian Ctr. Libr., Wilmington, Calif., 1979—. Recipient edn. grants Pepperdine U., 1973, 74; Recipient Thank you for Sharing and Caring plaque Calif. Congress of Parents and Tchrs., 1969. Mem. ASCD, Nat. Coun. Tchrs. Maths., Internat. Alliance for Invitational Edn., Nat. Staff Devel. Coun., Calif. Math. Coun. (southern section pres., speaker), L.A. City Tchrs. Maths. Assn. (pres., speaker), Calif. Staff Devel. Coun., Calif. Assn. Supervision and Curriculum, Basic Coun. Edn., Assn. Tchr. Educators (pres., speaker, Nat. Mid. Sch. Assn., Calif. League Mid. Schs., Computer Using Educators, Inc., State Calif. Assn. Tchr. Educators, Secondary Coords. Assn. (pres. 1981—, Outstanding Svc. plaque, 1981-83, engraved gavel, 1981-83). Avocations: collecting quotations, collecting butterflies, travel, reading.

DOTT, NANCY ROBERTSON, geologist; b. Detroit, Sept. 20, 1929; d. James and Maud (Bignell) R.; m. Robert Henry Dott Jr., Feb. 1, 1951; children: James Robert, Karen Elizabeth, Eric Richard, Cynthia Elaine, Brian Russell. BS in Geology, U. Mich., 1951. Naturalist, guide U. Wis. Arboretum, Madison, 1972-94; naturalist Middleton (Wis.)/Cross Plains Sch. Dist., 1983—99. Presenter geology programs Rock Ladies of Madison, 1977—. Bd. dirs. Friends of Arboretum, Madison, 1993-96; leader Girl Scouts Am., 1966-75; mem. LWV, Madison, 1965-80; pres. Unitarian Universalist Womens Alliance, Madison, 1984-85, 93-94. Mem. Wis. Assn. Environ. Edn., Wis. Soc. of Sci. Tchrs., Audubon Soc. Avocations: hiking, camping, gardening, knitting. Home: 231 Durose Ter Madison WI 53705-3322

DOTY, GRESDNA ANN, theatre historian, educator; b. Oelwein, Iowa, Feb. 22, 1931; d. James William and Gresdna (Wood) D.; m. James G. Traynham, Nov. 28, 1980. AA, Monticello Coll., Alton, Ill., 1951; BA, U. No. Iowa, 1953; MA, U. Fla., 1957; PhD, Ind. U., 1967. Instr. S.W. Tex. State U., San Marcos, 1957—61, asst. prof., 1964—65, La. State U., Baton Rouge, 1967-73, assoc. prof., 1973-79, dir. theatre, 1973-77, 81-91, prof., 1979-84, alumni prof., 1984—, alumni prof. emeritus, 1996—, chair dept. theatre, 1991-93. Author: Anne Brunton Merry in the American Theatre, 1971; co-editor: (with Billy J. Harbin) Inside the Royal Court Theatre, 1956-81: Artists Talk, 1990; contbr. articles to profl. jours. Bd. dirs. Arts Coun. Greater Baton Rouge, 1987-92, pres., 1990-91; mem. exec. com. Swine Palace Prodns. Rsch. grantee Nat. Endowment Humanities, 1981, Exxon Edn. Found., 1981. Fellow S.W. Theatre Assn.; mem. Am. Theatre Assn. (bd. dirs. 1977-80), Am. Coll. Theatre Festival (nat. chmn. 1976-79), Am. Soc. Theatre Rsch. (mem. exec. com. 1988-91, v.p. 1994-97), Nat. Theatre Conf. (sec. 1999-02), Coll. of Fellows of Am. Theatre (dean-elect 2003-04, dean 2004—). Home: 122 Highland Trace Baton Rouge LA 70810-5061

DOUCETTE, MARY-ALYCE, computer company executive; b. Pitts., Feb. 12, 1924; d. Andrew George and Alice Jane (Sloan) Newland; m. Adrian Robert Doucette, Feb. 6, 1945 (dec. June 1983); children: David Robert, Regis Robert. BS cum laude, U. Pitts., 1945. Mgr. Newland Bros., Millvale, Pa., 1946-53; gen. mgr. Newland-Ludlo, Pitts., 1953-72; mgmt. cons. D3 Software, Garden City, N.Y., 1972-80, sec., corp. officer, 1980—. Fin. sec. Cerebral Palsy Assn., Garden City, Helen Keller Svcs. for Blind, Garden City; mem. Winthrop-U. Hosp. Aux., Mercy League, Friends of Adelphi Univ. Libr., Friends of Hist. St. George Ch. of Hempstead, N.Y., Adv. Coun. for Continuing Edn., Garden City Sch. Dist., 1988—. Mem. AAUW, L.I. Panhellenic, Univ. Club, Nassau County Hist. Soc. (life), Garden City Hist. Soc., Community Club Garden City-Hempstead, Woman's Club Garden City, Alpha Delta Pi, Pi Lambda Theta. Home: 146 Washington Ave Garden City NY 11530-3013 Office: D3 Software PO Box 8051 Garden City NY 11530-8051

DOUD, JACQUELINE POWERS, academic administrator; V.p. acad. affairs Woodbury U., L.A., until 1989, pres., 1989—. Office: Woodbury U 7500 N Glenoaks Blvd Burbank CA 91504-1099

DOUDNA, JENNIFER A. molecular biologist, educator; BA, Pomona Coll., 1985; PhD, Harvard U., 1989. Post-doctoral fellow Harvard Med. Sch., 1989-91, U. Colo., 1991-94; joined faculty Yale U., New Haven, 1994, Henry Ford II prof. molecular biophysics and biochemistry, assoc. investigator Howard Hughes Med. Inst. Contbr. articles to profl. jours. Recipient award for initiatives in rsch. NAS, 1999. Achievements include structure and function of ribozymes and RNA-protein complexes. Office: Yale Univ New Haven CT 06520-8114 Fax: 203-432-3104. E-mail: jennifer.doudna@yale.edu.

DOUDS, VIRGINIA LEE, elementary school educator; b. Pitts., Jan. 17, 1943; d. Leland Ray and Virginia Helen (Dodds) Frazier; m. William Wallace Douds, June 20, 1964; children: William Stewart Douds, Michael Leland Douds. BA in Elem. Edn., Westminster Coll., New Wilmington, Pa., 1964; MA (Master's Equivalency), Dept. Edn., State of Pa., 1990. Cert. elem. tchr., Pa. Elem. tchr./non-graded Good Hope Elem. Sch., Glendale-Riverhills, Wis., 1964-65; elem. tchr./1st grade Carlisle Elem. Sch., Delaware, Ohio, 1965-66; elem. tchr./3rd grade Meml. Elem. Sch., Bethel Park, Pa., 1973-74; elem. tchr./1st and 3rd grades Logan Elem. Sch., Bethel Park, 1974-91; elem. tchr./3rd grade Neil Armstrong Elem. Sch., Bethel Park, 1991-99, Ben Franklin Elem. Sch., Bethel Park, 1999—. Software cons. Coal Kids, U.S. Dept. Mines, 1993; mem. lang. arts, reading com. Bethel Park Schs., 1989-92, cooperating tchr., 1986—, mentor tchr. 1992-93, 95—, mem. instrnl. support team, 1988-91, integrated lang. arts com., 1999-2000; judge Ben Franklin Scholarship Comm., 2001-03; mem. Mid. States Accreditation com., 1993-94, strategic planning com., 1994-95; SIP scholarship com. Bethel Park Fedn. Tchrs., 1973—. Mem. alumni coun. exec. bd. Westminster Coll., 1979-83; mem. exec. bd. Parents Assn., 1985-89. Recipient mini grant/writing, publishing ctr. Bethel Park Schs., 1989, Gift of Time tribute Am. Family Inst., 1990, 91, All Star Educator award U. Pitts./Pitts. Post Gazette, 1996. Mem. Nat. Coun. Tchrs. of English (lang. arts/reading com. 2000-01), Bethel Park Fedn. Tchrs., PTO. Republican. Presbyterian. Avocations: reading, gardening, golf. Home: 2679 Burnsdale Dr Bethel Park PA 15102-2005

DOUGALL-SIDES, LESLIE K. lawyer; b. Washington, Sept. 5, 1953; d. George Malcolm Richardson and Kathleen (Cahill) Dougall; m. Kenneth Jacob Sides, Feb. 19, 1994. BA, New Coll., Sarasota, Fla., 1975; JD cum laude, Florida State U., Tallahassee, 1978. Bar: Fla. 1981, DC 1981, Oreg. 1986, cert.: in city, county and local govt. law 1996, cert. profl. human resources 2001, bar: U.S. Dis. Ct. (middle and southern dist.) Fla., U.S. ct. appeals (11th cir.). Staff atty. Ctrl. Fla. Legal Svcs., Cocoa, 1982—85, dir.

atty. Handicapped Law Ctr., 1985—87; asst. city atty., acting city atty. City of Key West (Fla.), 1987—95; asst. city atty. City of Clearwater (Fla.), 1995—; bd. dirs. IRRA, 2000—02; sec. West Ctrl. Fla. Chpt., Indsl. Rels. Rsch. Assn., 2003. Mem.: Indsl. Rels. Rsch. Assn. (sec. West Ctrl. Fla. chpt. 2003, bd. dirs. 2000—02), Soc. Human Resources, Clearwater Bar Assn., ABA. Avocation: sailing. Office: City of Clearwater City Atty's Office PO Box 4748 Clearwater FL 33758 Office Phone: 727-562-4010. Business E-Mail: lsides@clearwater-fl.com.

DOUGHERTY, BARBARA LEE, artist, writer; b. L.A., Apr. 25, 1949; d. Cliff and Muriel Tamarra (Rubin) Beck; m. Michael R. Dougherty, Feb. 10, 1970; children: Jessie, Luke, Elvi. BS in Fine Art, N.Y. State Coll., 1975; M of Orgnl. Mgmt., U. Phoenix, 2003; postgrad., Concord Law Sch. Staff writer South Coast Cmty. Newspapers, Santa Barbara, Calif., 1988-90; contbg. editor Art Calendar, Upper Fairmont, Md., 1991—, dir. mktg. Frenchtown, Md., 1993-96, publ., 1997-2001, Art and Info., Westover, Md., 2001—02; exec. dir. Art Inst. and Gallery, Salisbury, Md., 2002—. Instr. art programs, 1975—; mem. City Adv. Bd. on Art, Santa Barbara, 1979-89, chmn., 1991-94; producer KCTV, Santa Barbara, 1990-94; CEO Harvest Am. Publs., 1992-93; judge for art shows Va. Ctr. for the Arts, 1998, Arts Atlantica, 1998, others; pub. Art Calendar, 1997-2001. Author, artist: In Search of a Sunflower, 1992, Harvest California, 1990, Getting the Word Out, 1996, Getting Exposure, 1996; prodr. 4 videos on art, 1990—; contbr. articles to Mktg. Art, Sunshine Artists, 1996, Art Materials Today, 1999, The Pastel Jour.; contbr. book; one-woman show at Salisbury State U. Galleries, 1994. Fundraiser Boys and Girls Club of Am., Carpinteria, Calif., 1977-93; bd. dirs. Somerset County Art Coun., 1999. Recipient Best of Show award Hosp. Aux., Boulder, Nev., 1991, 1st place award Death Valley 49ers Club, 1989, 2d place award, 1990. Democrat. Roman Catholic. E-mail: barbdoug@dmv.com

DOUGHERTY, BETSEY OLENICK, architect; b. Guanatamo Bay, Cuba, Oct. 25, 1950; (parents Am. citizens); d. Everett and Charlotte (Kristal) Olenick; m. Brian Paul Dougherty, Aug. 25, 1974; children: Gray Brenner, Megan Victoria. AB in Architecture, U. Calif., Berkeley, 1972, MArch, 1975. Registered architect, Calif.; cert. Nat. Coun. Archtl. Registration Bds. Designer, drafter Maxwell Starkman, L.A., 1972-73, HO & K, San Francisco, 1975-76; job capt. Wm. Blurock & Ptnrs., Newport Beach, Calif., 1976-78; assoc. architect U. Calif., Irvine, 1978-79; arch. Dougherty & Dougherty Archs. LLP, Costa Mesa, 1979—. Author: Green Architecture, 1995; contbr. articles to profl. jours. Mem. Newport Beach Specific Area Plan Com., 1985, Career Edn. Adv. Com., Newport Beach, 1986; leader Orange County bd. Girl Scouts U.S.A., 1995-2001. Recipient Gold Nugget grand award Pacific Coast Builders Conf., 1998, Coalition for Adequate Sch. Housing award of excellence, 1992, 94, 96, Calif. Masonry award, 1992, So. Calif. Edison award of excellence, 1994, Disting. Svc. citation AIACC, 1994. Fellow AIA (pres. Orange County chpt. 1984, Calif. chpt. 1988, nat. bd. dirs. 1989-91, nat. sec. 1992-94, design awards Orange County chpt. 1981-86, 89-90, 98, Nathaniel Owings award Calif. Coun. 1997), Calif. Archtl. Found. (pres. 1995-97). Avocations: family, sailing, camping. Email: www.ddaia.com. Office: Dougherty & Dougherty Archs LLP 3194 Airport Loop Dr Ste D Costa Mesa CA 92626-3405

DOUGHERTY, JOCELYN, retired neurologist; b. Topeka, Kans., Oct. 10, 1934; d. Arthur McIntyre and Helen Marie (Olson) Dougherty; m. Fred Herzig. BS in Edn., U. Kans., 1956, MD, 1967. Diplomate Am. Bd. Quality Assurance. Intern Presbyn. Hosp., San Francisco, 1967—68, resident, 1968—70, U. Calif., Davis, Calif., 1970—71, fellow, 1971; fellow in neuro-ophthalmology Columbia Presbyn. Hosp., NY, 1972; neurologist Bronx VA Hosp., Bronx, NY, 1972; cons. Sydenham Hosp., NY, 1973—74, Fairview State Hosp., Calif., 1975—2000; ret., 2000. Cons. St. Barnebes Hosp., Bronx, 1972, Columbia-Presbyn. Harlem Divsn., 1974. Contbr. articles to profl. jours. Mem.: Am. Acad. Neurology. Home: 700 Malabar Dr Corona Del Mar CA 92625-1839

DOUGHERTY, JUNE EILEEN, librarian; b. Union City, N.J., Mar. 27, 1929; d. Robert John and Jane Veronica (Smith) Beyrer; m. Donald E. Dougherty, Dec. 2, 1946; 1 child, Glen Allan. BA in Edn., Peterson State Coll., 1967; postgrad., Rutgers U. Sch. Libr. Sci., 1959-69. With A. B. Dumont, Paterson, N.J., 1950-54; sch. libr. St. Paul's Elem. Sch., Prospect Park, N.J., 1957—. Dir. North Haledon (N.J.) Free Pub. Libr., 1957—92; sec.-treas. Dougherty & Dougherty, Inc., North Haledon, 1968—73. Den mother Boy Scouts Am., 1954-57; mem. Gov. N.J.'s Tercentenary Com., 1962-64. Mem. Am. Libr. Assn., N.J. Libr. Assn., North Haledon Libr. Assn., Cath. Libr. Assn., N.J. Librs. Roundtable, Bergen-Passaic LIbr. Club, Friends N. Haledon Publ. Libr., St. Paul's Social Club. Roman Catholic. Home: 155 Westervelt Ave Haledon NJ 07508-3074 Office: 129 Overlook Ave Haledon NJ 07508

DOUGHERTY, KARLA R. writer; b. Bklyn., Apr. 18, 1949; d. Harold H. Rosenberg and Irma Gertrude Ramm-Rosenberg; m. Donald J. Dougherty, Oct. 21, 1986. BS in Journalism, Boston U., 1971. Cert. spinning instr. YMCA. Co-founder, sr. writer HealthSouth Press, San Antonio, 1998—2003. Author: The Spark: The Revolutionary New Plan to Get Fit and Lose Weight, 2001, The Rules to Be Cool: Etiquette and Netiquette, 2001, The Baby Boomer's Guide to Women's Health: Living Great the Next 50 Years, 2002, (e-Book) The Ringing in Your Ears is Not All in Your Head, 2001, more than 35 others. Fundraising bicycle rider The AIDS Ride, Boston to New York, 1998, Leukemia Soc. Am.-Springfield chpt., NJ, 2000, Multiple Sclerosis Soc.-No. N.J. chpt., 2001—02; counselor Birch Family Camp for Families Living With AIDs, N.Y.C., 2001. Working scholar, Breadloaf Writers' Conf., 1983. Mem.: The Authors Guild. Avocations: bicycling, reading, travel. E-mail: Karladougherty@aol.com.

DOUGHERTY, PAMELA SUE See RZESZOTARSKI, PAMELA SUE

DOUGHERTY, URSEL THIELBEULE, communications and marketing executive; b. Rotenburg, Germany, July 30, 1942; naturalized U.S. citizen, 1965; d. Hugo and Margarete (Marquardt) Thielbeule; m. Erich A. Eichhorn, Jan. 3, 1979. BA in Polit. Sci. summa cum laude, Cleve. State U., 1971; MA in Polit. Sci., U. Wis., 1972; MBA in Fin., Case Western Res. U., 1982. Journalist maj. daily, women's mag., Germany, 1962-66; assoc. editor Farm Chems., 1967; publs. mgr. Trabon Sys., 1967-68; rsch. analyst Legis. Coun. State Wis., 1972; pub. rels. adminstr. to mgr. pub. info. Eaton Corp., Cleve., 1972-84; dir. pub. affairs Freightliner/Mercedes Benz Truck Co., Portland, Oreg., 1984-87; v.p. chmn.'s office Daimler Benz N.A. Holding Co., Inc., Washington, 1987-90; v.p. bus. devel., corp. affairs Penske Corp., Cleve., v.p. investor rels., 1990-97. V.p. investor rels. Detroit Diesel Corp., 1998—; founder, prin. USCH Internat. Fin. Comms. Firm; cons. small bus. Trustee Lake Erie coun. Girl Scouts U.S., 1975-82, Sr. Citizen Resources, 1978-81; amb. Jr. Achievement, 1979; steering com. YWCA Career Women of Achievement, 1981; adv. bd. Women's Career Networking, 1980-84; trustee, chair ad hoc planning com. Cleve. Music Sch. Settlement. Office: 1510 Crest Rd Cleveland OH 44121-1722

DOUGHERTY BUCHHOLZ, KAREN, communications executive; m. Carl Buchholz; 2 children. BS, Dickinson Collo.; MS, U. Pa. Mem. staff U.S. Sen. John Heinz, Gubernatorial candidate Barbara Hafer, 1990; supr. devel. Pyramid Club, Phila., 1991—93; sales exec. Comcast-Spectacor, 1993—97; pres. Phila. Host com. Rep. Nat. Convention, 1997—2000; v.p. corp. comms. Comcast Corp., Phila., 2000—03, v.p. adminstrn., 2003—. Bd. dirs. Phila. Convention and Vis. Bur.; trustee Crohn's and Colitis Found. Am.; bd. dirs. Millennium Phila.; bd. advisors Dickinson Coll.; bd. govs. Pyramid Club. Named PENJERDEL Coun. Citizen of Yr.; recipient Headliner award, Greater Phila. Hotal Assn., Take the Lead award, Girl Scouts U.S.A. Mem.: Nat. Assn. Women Bus. Owners (hon.). Office: Comcast 1500 Market St Philadelphia PA 19102

DOUGHTEN, MARY KATHERINE (MOLLY DOUGHTEN), retired secondary school educator; b. Belvidere, Ill., Apr. 26, 1923; d. Edwin Albert and Theora Teresa (Tefft) Loop; m. Philip Tedford Doughten, Oct. 15, 1947; children: Deborah Doughten Hellriegel, Susan Doughten Myers, Ann Doughten Fickenscher, Philip Tedford Jr., David, Sarah Doughten Wiggins. BA, DePauw U., 1945; MS, Western Res. U., 1947. Social worker Children's Svcs., Cleve., 1947, San Antonio, 1948-49; tchr. English Indian Valley High Schs., Gradenhutten, Ohio, 1962-66; tchr. English and sociology New Philadelphia (Ohio) High Sch., 1966-86. Mem. Tuscarawas County Juvenile Judges Citizen's Rev. Bd., 1980—2003, United Way, 1960—67, ARC, PTA, 1955—58, coun. pres., 1960—62, mental health chmn. state bd., 1963—65, libr. chmn., 1966—68; mem. Hospice, 1987—; founding com. Kent State U. Tuscarawas campus, 1961—62; v.p. Tuscarawas County U. Found., 1996—98, pres., 1998—2000; leader Girl Scouts, 1959—68; bd. mem. Tuscarawas County U. Found., 2000—; vol. Ohio Reads, 2000—; vol. reach for recovery Am. Cancer Soc., 2002—; mem. arts coun. Tuscarawas Philharmonic League; vol. Tuscarawas County Work and Family Svcs., 2003—; mem. Dem. Women, 1986—; bd. dir. Tuscarawas Valley Guidance Ctr., 1950—62, Cmty Mental Health Care, Inc., 1974—82, 1984—92, pres., 1979—81; bd. dir. Alcohol, Drug and Mental Health Svcs. bd., Tuscarawas-Carroll County, 1992—2001, v.p., 1996—98; bd. mem. State CC, 1965—68; founder, bd. dir. Ohio Cmty. Mental Health Svcs., Columbus, Ohio, 1970—80; bd. dir. Mobile Meals, 1992—. Recipient Mental Health award Community and Profl. Svcs., 1978; Martha Holden Jennings scholar, 1975-76; named WJER Woman of the Yr., 2002. Mem. AAUW (sec. 1962, v.p. 1996-98), Ohio Ret. Tchrs. (sec. 1987-89), New Philadelphia Edn. Assn., Friends of Libr., Chestnut Soc. (bd. dirs. 1987-89, 2001—), Tuscarawas County Med. Aux. (pres. 1959-60, 86-87, state bd. 1960-64), Union Hosp. Aux. (bd. dirs. 1986-98, editor 1986-98), DAR, Tuscarawas County Ret. Tchrs. Assn. (bd. dirs. 1999—), Coll. Club (scholarship chair 1989-91, 99-2001), Union Country Club, Atwood Yacht Club, Lady Elks, Mortar Bd., Phi Beta Kappa, Alpha Chi Omega, Theta Sigma Phi. Democrat. Presbyterian. Avocations: travel, golf, sailing, reading, photography. Home: 204 Gooding Ave NW New Philadelphia OH 44663-1727 E-mail: philmoll@tusco.net.

DOUGLAS, ASHANTI S. (ASHANTI), vocalist; b. Glen Cove, N.Y., Oct. 13, 1980; Singer: (albums) Ashanti, 2002 (Grammy award, 2002), Foolish/Unfoolish: Reflections on Love, 2002, Ashanti: The 7 Series, 2003 (nominated 2 Grammy awards, 2003), Chapter II, 2003, Ashanti's Christmas, 2003. Office: Murder Inc 825 8th Ave 20th Floor New York NY 10019

DOUGLAS, BONNIE, state representative; b. Ill., Aug. 26, 1948; m. Ronald Douglas; 2 children. BA, U. Ill., 1970; attending, U. Idaho. Lic. broker, ins. agt.; cons., bus. systems analyst various cos., 1970—82; office asst. Med. Office Ronald J. Douglas, 1982—; state rep. dist. 4A Idaho Ho. of Reps., Boise, 2002—. Leader La Leche League Internat., 1992—2002; treas. Kootenai County Dem. Cul. Com., 2000—02; bd. dirs. ICARE, 2002. Mem.: Internat. Soc. Tech. in Edn., Fernan Elem. PTO (sec. 1995—96). Democrat. Roman Catholic. Office: State Capitol PO Box 83720 Boise ID 83720-0081

DOUGLAS, CYNTHIA, executive administrative assistant; b. Park Ridge, Ill., Dec. 27, 1967; d.Lewis C. and Linda Douglas. Student, Northeastern Ill. U., 1996—. Office mgr. Douglas Contractors, Chgo., 1985-95; student aid Northeastern Ill. U., Chgo., 1996-97; asst. to pres. Caliber Data Tng., Chgo., 1997—. Computer lab. instr., Caliber Data Tng., 1997—. Home: 5500 N Bernard St Chicago IL 60625-4659

DOUGLAS, DIANE MIRIAM, museum director; b. Harrisburg, Pa., Mar. 25, 1957; d. David C. and Anna (Barron) D.; m. Steve I. Perlmutter, Jan. 23, 1983; 1 child, David Simon. BA, Brown U., 1979; MA, U. Del., 1982. Oral history editor Former Members of Congress, Washington, 1979-80; assoc. curator exhibitions John Michael Kohler Arts Ctr., Sheboygan, Wis., 1982-83; dir. arts ctr. Lill Street Gallery, Chgo., 1984-88; exec. dir. David Adler Cultural Ctr., Libertyville, Ill., 1988-91; dir. Bellevue (Wash.) Art Mus., 1992—. Program chair, exec. bd. nat. Coun. for Edn. in Ceramic Arts, Bandon, Oreg., 1990-93; nat. adv. bd. Friends of Fiber Art, 1992; artists adv. com. Pilchuck Glass Sch., 1993—; mem. bd. dirs. Archie Bray Found., Helena, Mont., 1995—. Office: Bellevue Art Mus 510 Bellevue Way NE Bellevue WA 98004-5014

DOUGLAS, FRANCES SONIA, minister; b. Stanaford, W.Va., May 12, 1931; d. Frank Gordon and Mary Celia Bradley; m. Paul Alexander Douglas, Jan. 6, 1949 (dec. Mar. 1993); children: Paul Jr., Sonia Paulette, Norton James, Mary Louise, Elizabeth Maria, Naomi Denise, Regina Michele, André(dec.). Doctorate(hon.), Christian Fellowship Ednl. Bible Coll., 1999. Housekeeper, 1955—70; sales rep. Amway Products, Niagara Falls, NY, 1970, Stuart McGuire Shoes, Niagara Falls, 1970, Finelle Products, Niagara Falls, 1980; founder, pastor True Deliverance Temple, Niagara Falls, 1974—. Chmn. Cleve. Ave. Sch. Parent Group, Niagara Falls, Harriet F. Abate Sch. Parent Group, Niagara Falls; vice chmn. Niagara Falls Faith Based Collaboration, 2000—01; former treas. Niagara Falls Ministerial Coun.; founder Emmanuel Temple No. 2 Ch., 1952; bd. dirs. Niagara Falls Faith Based Collaboration, 2001—. Recipient Cert. of Appreciation for Outstanding Cmty. Svc., Rainbow Sr. Citizens Inc., 1986. Avocations: embroidery, crocheting, sewing, travel. Office: True Deliverance Temple 1318 Niagara St Niagara Falls NY 14303

DOUGLAS, JANICE GREEN, physician, educator; b. Nashville, July 11, 1943; d. Louis D. and Electa Green. BA magna cum laude, Fisk U., 1964; MD, Meharry Med. Coll., 1968. Intern Meharry Med. Coll., 1968-71; NIH tng. fellow in endocrinology, instr. internal medicine Vanderbilt U., Nashville, 1971-73; sr. staff fellow sect. on hormonal regulation NIH, 1973-76; asst. prof. medicine Case Western Res. U. Sch. Medicine, Cleve., 1976-81, assoc. prof. medicine, 1981-84, prof. medicine, 1984—; dir. hypertension renal ambulatory care svc. Univ. Hosps. Cleve., 1976-80; dir. divsn. endocrinology and hypertension dept. medicine Univ. Hosps. Cleve. and Case Western Res. U., 1988-93, vice chair acad. affairs dept. medicine, 1991-99, dir. divsn. hypertension dept. medicine, 1993—. Mem. numerous grant rev. coms.; lectr., presenter in field; atteding physician in medicine and endicrinology U. Hosps., 1987; vis. prof. SUNY, Kings County Hosp. and Health Sci. Ctr., Bklyn., 1987, Med. U. S.C., 1989, Harlem Hosp., N.Y.C., 1993, N.Y. Med. Coll., Valhalla, 1994. Mem. editl. rev. bd. Jour. Clin. Investigation, 1990—, Am. Jour. Physiology, Renal Fluid and Electrolytes, 1989-91; editl. bd. Hypertension, 1994—, Am. Soc. Clin. Investigation, 1990—, Ethnicity and Disease, 1990—, Circulation, 1993—; guest editor Jour. Clin. Investigation, U. Calif., San Diego, 1992—; assoc. editor Jour. Lab. and Clin. Medicine, 1986-90; reviewer numerous manuscripts and abstracts.; contbr. numerous articles, abstracts to profl. publs., chpts. to books. Fellow High Blood Pressure Coun., Am. Heart Assn., 1993—. Mem. Assn. Am. Physicians, Cleve. Med. Assn., Am. Soc. Hypertension, Kidney Found. Ohio, Women in Endocrinology, Inter-Am. Soc. Hypertension, Women in Nephrology, Assn. for Acad. Minority Physicians, Am. Physiology Soc., Endocrine Soc., Ctrl. Soc. for Clin. Rsch., Internat. Soc. Hypertension in Blacks, Inst. Medicine of NAS, Internat. Soc. Nephrology, Am. Soc. Nephrology, Am. Soc. Clin. Investigation, Am. Fedn. Clin. Rsch., Am. Heart Assn., Phi Beta Kappa, Alpha Omega Alpha (pres. Meharry chpt. 1968), Beta Kappa Chi. Office: Case Western U Sch Medicine 10900 Euclid Ave # 165 Cleveland OH 44106-1712

DOUGLAS, MARY YOUNGE RILEY, retired secondary school educator; b. St. Louis, Dec. 4, 1930; d. Walter Archibald and Jerdie Lee (Bibb) Younge; m. John Samuel Riley Jr., Apr. 17, 1954 (dec. July 1973); children: John Samuel Riley III, Jerda Marie Riley, Joel Younge Riley; m. Walter Wadsworth Douglas, Jan. 14, 1989. Student, Fisk U., 1947-49; BS, Fontbonne Coll., 1951; Masters, U. Ill., 1953. Tchr. Sumner High Sch., St. Louis, 1953-55, Hadley Tech. Sch., St. Louis, 1956-57; subs. tchr. St. Louis C.C., 1975; tchr. Soldan High Sch., St. Louis, 1975-90, Roosevelt High Sch., St. Louis, 1990-93, Soldan-Internat. High Sch., 1993—2001. Past bd. dirs. Nursery Found., St. Louis, Met. YWCA, St. Louis, Mo. Assn. Social Welfare.

DOUGLAS, ROXANNE GRACE, secondary school educator; b. Orange, N.J., Dec. 17, 1951; d. Joseph Samuel and Mary (Ferro) Battista; m. Richard Joseph Douglas, June 26, 1982; 1 child, Regina Grace. BA cum laude, Montclair State Coll., 1973; student, Sorbonne U., Paris. Cert. French, social studies and elem. sch. tchr., N.J. Tchr. social studies West Orange (N.J.) Bd. Edn., 1973-74, Orange (N.J.) Bd. Edn., 1974-75; substitute tchr. various schs. N.J., 1975-76; supplemental tchr. Irvington (N.J.) Bd. Edn., 1976-80, tchr. govtl. programs, 1980—. Advisor 7th dist. NJSFWC-JM State Bd., 1991-93, 2002-04, membership chmn., 1994-96, 98—, pub. affairs chmn., 1996—, state membership task force, 1999—, edn. chmn., 2000-01, dist. asst., 2001—, 7th dist. v.p., 2002-04, state arts performing chmn., 2004-06. West Caldwell town columnist for local newspaper. Mem. West Caldwell Centennial Com., 2002—; cultural arts chmn. Caldwell/West Caldwell HSA League. Recipient Creative Writing awards NJSFWC-JM, Internat. Vol. of Yr. award, Citizenship award Am. Legion. Mem. Victorian Soc., N.J. Edn. Assn., Nat. French Hon. Soc., Nat. Edn. Hon. Soc., Jr. Women's Club of West Essex (co-pres., liaison internat. affairs chmn., pub. affairs chmn.), Coll. Club Orange-Short Hills, West Essex Women's Club (liaison to jr. woman's club, chmn. internat. affairs and pub. affairs dept. 1st night com. mem., pres., parent adv. coun.-bd. edn., pres., 1994—, internat. affairs chmn., centennial chmn., comm. chmn., performing arts chmn. 1996—), Verona Women's Club (membership chmn., v.p. 1998—, rec. sec. 2000—, twp. centennial com. mem., v.p. 2003-, mem. chmn. 2004-05), Willing Hearts and Cultural Arts (chmn.), Caldwell West Caldwell HSA League (corr. sec. 2003-04). Roman Catholic. Avocations: reading, antiques, walking, writing, travel.

DOUGLAS, SUSAN, data processing specialist, consultant; b. Chgo., Oct. 29, 1946; d. Lawrence and Phoebe Fern (Sibbald) D.; m. John D. Hauenstein, Dec. 21, 1972 (div. June 1975). BA, U. Iowa, 1972; postgrad., U. Wis., Whitewater, 1985, U. Wis., Madison, 1991—. Project coord. Westinghouse Learning Corp., Iowa City, Iowa, 1967-75; echocardiology technician Chgo. Osteo. Hosp., 1975-78; sys. programmer, analyst Household Fin. Corp., Prospect Heights, Ill., 1978-81; applications analyst Burdick Corp., Milton, Wis., 1981-84; cons. Edgerton, Wis., 1984—. Mem. Data Processing Mgmt. Assn. Episcopalian. Avocations: crafts, tree farming, skiing, sailing, hiking. Home and Office: 8203 County H Edgerton WI 53534-8887

DOUGLAS, VICTORIA JEAN, marketing professional, communications executive; b. Wilmington, Del., Sept. 1, 1972; d. Richard Otto and Genevieve Douglas. Student, U. Caen, France, 1993, Oxford (Eng.) U., 1995, NYU Paris, 1996; BA in English/French, U. Del., 1996, MA in French Lit., 1999. Dir. comm. Mayor's Office, Wilmington, 1993—2001; mktg. and comm. chief cons. Met. Wilmington Urban League, 2001—; CEO Barracuda Comm., Wilmington. Founder, chair Fgn. Lang. and Lit. Assn. Grad. Students, Newark, 1996—97; mem. mktg. com. Dept. Youth and Families, Wilmington, 1999—2000; supporting mem. Del. Ctr. for Contemporary Arts, Wilmington, 2001—; bd. mem. Kuumba Acad., Wilmington, 2001—; curriculum devel. staff, instr. English U. Caen Sch. Law, France, 1997—98; account supr. Saatchi and Saatchi, Rowland, NY, 2001. Organizer Nat. Night Out, Wilmington, 1993—95, Mayor's Breast Cancer Awareness Campaign, Wilmington, 2001; mem. ball com. Am. Diabetes Assn., 2002, mem. leadership coun., 2002—; v.p. sales Wilmington Drama League. Recipient Tomorrow's Leaders Today award, Pub. Allies, 1994, proclamation, City of Wilimington, 2000, Apex Award for Excellence in Mktg. and Pub. Rels. Brochures, 2002, APEX award Design & Layout, 2003, Comm. award, 2003. Mem.: AAUW, Pub. Rels. Soc. Am., Met. Wilmington Urban League, Pi Delta Phi, Golden Key Nat. Honor Soc., Phi Sigma Tau, Sigma Tau Delta. Office: Hagley Bldg Ste 104 3411 Silverside Rd Wilmington DE 19810 Business E-Mail: vdouglas@bcad.com.

DOUGLASS, DORRIS CALLICOTT, librarian, historian, genealogist; b. Nashville, Feb. 27, 1941; d. Claude Wilson and Catherine Hardy (Dorris) Callicott; m. George Patton Douglass, Aug. 28, 1965; children: George Archibald, Claudia Dorris Douglass James, Rebecca Rhodes Douglass Johnson. BA, Converse Coll., 1963; MLS, Vanderbilt U., 1965. Collator old newspapers Tenn. State Libr. and Archives, Nashville, 1963—64; cataloger Emory U. Theology Libr., Atlanta, 1965—67; clerical duties Ga. Hist. Commn., Atlanta, 1967; libr. Atlanta Hist. Soc., 1967—69; libr. circulation Columbia State C.C., 1993; asst. Williamson County Archives, 1993—94; libr., substitue in reference and genealogy Williamson County Pub. Libr., Franklin, Tenn., 1989—98, libr., head genealogy, 1998—. Contbr. articles to publs. Mem.: DAR (Tenn. state scrapbook chmn. 1974—76, chpt. chaplain 1984—86), U.S. Daus. War 1812 (chpt. v.p., program chmn. 1985—87, chpt. chaplain 1987—89, chpt. v.p., program chmn. 2003—). Presbyterian. Avocations: collecting pre-1900 school books, travel. Home: 2040 Old Hillsboro Rd Franklin TN 37064 Office: Williamson County Pub Libr 1314 Columbia Ave Franklin TN 37064 Office Phone: 615-595-1246 1.

DOUGLASS, ENID HART, educational program director; b. L.A., Oct. 23, 1926; d. Frank Roland and Enid Yandell (Lewis) Hart; m. Malcolm P. Douglass, Aug. 28, 1948; children: Malcolm Paul Jr., John Aubrey, Susan Enid. BA, Pomona Coll., 1948; MA, Claremont (Calif.) Grad. Sch., 1959. Research asst. World Book Ency., Palo Alto, Calif., 1953-54; exec. sec., asst. dir. oral history program Claremont Grad. U., 1963-71, dir. oral history program, 1971—, lectr. history, 1977—. Mem. Calif. Heritage Preservation Commn., 1977-85, chmn. 1983-85. Contbr. articles to hist. jours. Mayor pro tem City of Claremont, 1980-82, mayor, 1982-86; mem. planning and rsch. adv. coun. State of Calif.; mem. city coun. City of Claremont, 1978-86; founder Claremont Heritage, Inc., 1977-80; bd. dirs., 1986-95; bd. dirs. Pilgrim Pla., Claremont; founder, steering com., founding bd. Claremont Cmty. Found., 1989-95, pres., 1990-94. Mem. Oral History Assn. (pres. 1979-80), Southwest Oral History Assn. (founding steering com. 1981, J.V. Mink award 1984), Nat. Coun. Pub. History (founding com. 1980), LWV (bd. dirs. 1957-59, Outstanding Svc. to Cmty. award 1986). Democrat. Home: 1195 N Berkeley Ave Claremont CA 91711-3842 E-mail: enid.douglass@cgu.edu.

DOUGLASS, JANE DEMPSEY, theology educator; b. Wilmington, Del., Mar. 22, 1933; d. Hazell Brownlie and Ethel Katherine (Smith) Dempsey; m. Gordon Klene Douglass, Aug. 23, 1964; children: Alan Bruce, Anne Lorine, John Gordon. AB, Syracuse U., 1954; postgrad., U. Geneva, Switzerland, 1954-55; AM, Radcliffe Coll., 1961; PhD, Harvard U., 1963; ThD (hon.), U. Geneva, 1994; LHD (hon.), Franklin and Marshall Coll., 1992; DD (hon.), U. St. Andrews, Scotland, 1992; STD (hon.), MacMurray Coll., 2000. Assoc. dir. Presbyn. Student Ctr., Columbia, Mo., 1955-58; teaching fellow Harvard Divinity Sch., Cambridge, Mass., 1959-62; from instr. to prof. Sch. of Theology at Claremont and Claremont Grad. Sch., Claremont, Ca., 1963-85; Hazel Thompson McCord prof. hist. theology Princeton (N.J.) Theol. Sem., 1985-98, emerita, 1998—. Pres. Am. Soc. Ch. History, 1983; v.p. World Alliance of Reformed Chs., 1989-90, pres. 1990-97, hon. mem. exec. com., 1997-2004. Author: Justification in Late Medieval Preaching: A Study of John Geiler of Keisersberg, 1966, 2d edit.,

1989, Women, Freedom and Calvin, 1985; editor: (with Jack L. Stotts) To Confess the Faith Today, 1990, (with James F. Kay) Women, Gender and Christian Community, 1997, (with Páraic Réamonn) Partnership in God's Mission in the Middle East, 1998; contbr. articles to profl. jours. Presbyterian.

DOUGLASS, NERIA GAY, state legislator, lawyer; b. Boston, Mass., Nov. 16, 1952; d. James Elsworth and Neria Hockaday (Kohl) Ryder; m. Paul Stephen Douglass, Aug. 20, 1977; children: Ryan James, Nathan Paul, Neira Lauren. Student, U. Manchester, 1972-73; BA in Sociology with honors, Wellesley Coll., 1974; JD, Vanderbilt U., 1977. Bar: Maine, 1978, U.S. Dist. Ct. Maine 1978. Atty. Doyle and Nelson, Augusta, Maine, 1977, Platz and Thompson, Lewiston, Maine, 1978-80; asst. dist. atty. dist. III Androscoggin, Oxford and Franklin Counties, Auburn, Maine, 1980-82; atty. Isaacson and Raymond, Lewiston, Maine, 1985-88; mem. Auburn Sch. Comm., 1989-94, Bd. of Appeals, Lewiston, 1980-85; city councilor City of Auburn, Maine, 1994—98; mem. Maine Senate, Augusta, 1998-. Chmn. Lewiston Bd. of Appeals, 1985, vice-chmn. 1980-84; chmn. Gov.'s. adv. council Displaced Homemakers, Augusta, 1982-86. Mem. Maine State Dem. Com., Augusta 1980-82. Mem. Am. Trial Lawyers Assn., Maine Trial Lawyers Assn., Maine State Bar Assn., Androscoggin Bar Assn., LWV (dir. 1978-85). Home: RR 2 Box 588A Auburn ME 04210-9801 Address: Senate of Maine 3 State House Sta Augusta ME 04333-0003 Home: 465 West Auburn Rd Auburn ME 04210

DOUHOVNIKOVA, KAMELIA BORISSOVA, adult education educator; b. Sofia, Bulgaria, Jan. 30, 1941; arrived in U.S., 1998; d. Boris Nikolov Popov and Nena Petkova Popova; m. Todor Kolev Todorov, Dec. 31, 1963 (div. Sept. 1978); children: Radka Todorov, Nikolay Todorov; m. Hristo Iordanov Douhovnikov, Aug. 22, 1983; 1 child, Iordanka Hristova. MS in Civil Engring., U. Arch., Sofia, 1965. Cert. tchr. Sofia. Civil/structural engr. Energo Project, Sofia, 1965—72, Pharm Project, Sofia, 1972—73; tchr. Tech. Sch. Civil Engring. and Arch., Sofia, 1973—98, Adult Learning Ctr., Corpus Christi, Tex., 1999—. Author: Reinforced Concrete, 1985. Avocation: yoga. Home: 6702 Everhart #R105 Corpus Christi TX 78413 Office: Adult Learning Ctr 3902 Morgan Ave Corpus Christi TX 78405

DOUMLELE, RUTH HAILEY, communications company executive, broadcast accounting consultant; b. Nov. 6, 1925; d. Clarrie Robert Hailey and Virginia Susan Ferguson; m. John Antony Doumlele, May 8, 1943; children: John Antony, Jr., Suzanne Denise Doumlele Owen. Cert. in commerce, U. Richmond, 1968; BA, Mary Baldwin Coll., 1982. Sta. acct. Sta. WLEE-Radio, Richmond, Va., 1965-67, bus. mgr., 1967-73; area bus. mgr. Nationwide Cmms. Inc., Richmond, 1973-75; corp. bus. mgr. Neighborhood Comms. Corp., Inc., Richmond, 1978-86, asst. v.p., 1981-86; owner Broadcast Acctg. cons., Midlothian, Va., 1986-95; treas., dir. Guests of Honor, Ltd., Richmond, 1984-89; sec. Inner Light, Inc., 1984-96; docent Va.'s Gov.'s Mansion, 1997—. Contbr. articles to profl. jours., hist. and astrol. publs.; mem. editl. rev. bd. The Woman C.P.A., 1980—. Pres. Powhatan County Hist. Soc., 1999—. Mem. DAR, Am. Soc. Women Accts. (chpt. pres. 1974-76, contbg. editor The Coord. 1990, Chgo., Woman of Achievement award 1991), Broadcast Fin. Mgmt. Assn., Nat. League Am. Pen Women (br. pres. 1984-86), Am. Fedn. Astrologers, Va. Assn. Amateur Athletic Union (records chmn. 1959-62), Women's Club of Powhatan, Selective Svc. Sys. Local Bd., Powhatan Hist. Soc. (pres. 1999—). Episcopalian. Avocations: salt water fishing, civil war history, travel, astrology. Home and Office: 2510 Chastain Ln Midlothian VA 23113-9400

DOUTHAT, REBECCA ARLENE, secondary school educator; b. Norfolk, Va., Feb. 10, 1946; d. Thomas Alexander and Lena Faye Douthat. BS, Radford Coll., 1967, MA, 1974; MEd, Coll. of William & Mary, 1990, EdS, 1994. Lic. tchr. Commonwealth of Va. Tchr. Fincastle County Pub. Schs., Daleville, Va., 1967—68, Newport News Pub. Schs., Newport News, Va., 1968—72, York County Pub. Schs., Yorktown, Va., 1976—. Sponsor Students Against Drunk Driving, Tabb, Va., 1999—; sponsor food drive York County Social Svcs., York County, Va., 1995—2000. Mem.: Am. Counseling Assn., York Edn. Assn., Va. Edn. Assn., Nat. Edn. Assn., Colony Pines Residents Assn. (mem. membership drive 1995—), Kappi Delta Pi. Avocations: bowling, bicycling, reading, weightlifting. Home: 903 Belvoir Cir Newport News VA 23608 Office: Tabb HS 4431 Big Bethel Rd Yorktown VA 23693

DOUTHITT, SHIRLEY ANN, insurance agent; b. Mexia, Tex., Feb. 21, 1947; d. Othello Young and Hazel Lorene (Corley) Thompson; m. A. Dwane Douthitt, Nov. 24, 1966; 1 child, Steven Dwane. Student, Leonard's Tng Sch., Houston, 1979; student Tex. local recording agts. licensing course, Austin, Tex., 1980; student farmers ins. group tng. program, Austin, 1980; student life underwriters trng course, Tyler, Tex., 1987. Lic. ins. agt. Sec. Lindsey & Newsom Ins. Adjusters, Palestine, Tex., 1965-73, J. Herrington Ins. Agy., Palestine, 1973-76, Ramsey Ins. Agy., Palestine, 1976-79; agt. Farmers Ins. Group, Palestine, 1979—. Recipient Bus. Woman of Yr. Palestine Profl. Bus. Women, 1983. Mem. NAFE, Women's Club. Avocations: reading, gardening, concerts, home decorating. Office: Shirley Douthitt Ins Agy 3507 W Oak St Palestine TX 75801-8417 E-mail: douthit@risecom.net.

DOUTY, SHEILA, softball player; b. Diamond Bar, Calif., Feb. 26, 1962; Grad., UCLA; master's degree, U. So. Calif. Phys. therapist. Named to, UCLA Athletic Hall of Fame; recipient Silver medal, Pan Am. Games, 1983, Gold medal, Pan. Am. Games, 1987, 1991, 1995, ISF Women's World Championship, 1990, 1994, South Pacific Classic, 1994, Superball Classic, 1995, Atlanta Olympics, 1996, Gold medal, World Championships, 1998, Olympic Games, 2000, Intercontinental Cup, 1993. Office: Amateur Softball Assn Softball Fedn Internat 2801 NE 50th St Oklahoma City OK 73111-7203*

DOVAN, CAROL See VAN SCHENKHOF, CAROL

DOVE, RITA FRANCES, poet, English language educator; b. Akron, Ohio, Aug. 28, 1952; d. Ray A. and Elvira E. (Hord) D.; m. Fred Viebahn, Mar. 23, 1979; 1 child, Aviva Chantal Tamu Dove-Viebahn. BA summa cum laude, Miami U., Oxford, Ohio, 1973; postgrad., Universität Tübingen, Fed. Republic Germany, 1974-75; MFA, U. Iowa, 1977; LLD (hon.), Miami U., Oxford, Ohio, 1988, Knox Coll., 1989, Tuskegee U., 1994, U. Miami, Fla., 1994, Washington U., St. Louis, 1994, Case Western Res. U., 1994, U. Akron, 1994, Ariz. State U., 1995, Boston Coll., 1995, Dartmouth Coll., 1995, Spelman Coll., 1996, U. Pa., 1996, U. N.C., 1997, U. Notre Dame, 1997, Northeastern U., 1997, Columbia U., 1998, Washington & Lee U., 1999, SUNY, Brockport, 1999, Pratt Inst., 2001, Howard U., 2001. Asst. prof. English Ariz. State U., Tempe, 1981-84, assoc. prof., 1984-87, prof., 1987-89, U. Va., Charlottesville, 1989-93, Commonwealth prof. English, 1993—; U.S. poet laureate, cons. in poetry Libr. of Congress, Washington, 1993-95, spl. cons. in poetry, 1999-2000; columnist Washington Post, 2000—02. Writer-in-residence Tuskegee (Ala.) Inst., 1982; lit. panelist Nat. Endowment for Arts, Washington, 1984-86, chmn. poetry grants panel, 1985; judge Walt Whitman award Acad. Am. Poets, 1990, Pulitzer prize in poetry, 1991, Ruth Lilly prize 1991, Nat. Book award in poetry 1991, 98, Anisfield-Wolf Book awards, 1992—, Shelley Meml. award, 1997, Amy Lowell fellowship, 1997; poetry panel chmn. Pulitzer prize, 1997; final judge Brittingham and Pollack prizes, 1997; juror Christopher Columbus Fellowship Found., 1998—, Duke Ellington awards, 1999; bd. dirs. Poetry Daily, 2002. Author: (poetry) Ten Poems, 1977, The Only Dark Spot in the Sky, 1980, The Yellow House on the Corner, 1980, Mandolin, 1982, Museum, 1983, Thomas and Beulah, 1986 (Pulitzer Prize in poetry 1987), The Other Side of the House, 1988, Grace Notes, 1989 (Ohioana award 1990), Selected Poems, 1993 (Ohioana award 1994), Lady Freedom Among Us, 1994, Mother Love, 1995, Evening Primrose, 1998, On the Bus with Rosa Parks, 1999 (Ohioana award 2000), American Smooth, 2004; (verse drama) The Darker Face of the Earth, 1994 (W. Alton Jones Found. grant 1994, Kennedy Ctr. Fund for New Am. Plays award 1995, Geraldine Dodge Found. grant 1997) [illegible] edit., 1996, expanded 3d edit., 2000 (first performance Oreg. Shakespeare Festival 1996); (novel) Through the Ivory Gate, 1992 (Va. Coll. Stores Book award 1993); (short stories) Fifth Sunday, 1985 (Callaloo award 1986); (essays) The Poet's World, 1995, (song cycle) Seven for Luck (music by John Williams), 1st performance Boston Symphony Orch., Tanglewood, 1998; mem. editl. bd. Nat. Forum, 1984-89, Iris, 1989—; mem. adv. bd. Ploughshares, 1992—, N.C. Writers Network, 1992-99, Civilization, 1994-97; assoc. editor Callaloo, 1986-98; adv. and contbg. editor Gettysburg Rev., 1987—, TriQuarterly, 1988—, Ga. Review, 1994—, Bellingham Rev., 1996—, Internat. Quarterly, 1997—, Callaloo, 1998—, Mid-Am. Rev., 1998—; editor Best Am. Poetry, 2000. Commr. The Schomburg Ctr. for Rsch. in Black Culture, N.Y. Pub. Libr., 1987—; mem. Renaissance Forum Folger Shakespeare Libr., 1993-95, Coun. of Scholars Libr. of Congress, 1994—; mem. nat. launch com. AmeriCorps, 1994; mem. awards coun. Am. Acad. Achievement, 1994-2001; mem. adv. bd. Thomas Jefferson Ctr. Freedom of Expression, 1994—, U.S. Civil War Ctr., 1995-99, Va. Ctr. Creative Arts, 1995—, Student Achievement and Advocacy Svcs., 2002; The Poets Corner elector Cathedral Ch. St. John the Divine, N.Y.C., 1991-2002; bd. govs. Humanities Rsch. Inst. U. Calif., 1996-99; bd. dirs. Poetry Daily, 2004—. Presdl. scholar, 1970, Nat. Achievement scholar, 1970-73; Fulbright/Hays fellow, 1974-75, rsch. fellow U. Iowa, 1975, teaching/writing fellow U. Iowa, 1976-77, Guggenheim Found. fellow, 1983-84, Mellon sr. fellow Nat. Humanities Ctr., 1988-89, fellow Ctr. for Advanced Studies, U. Va., 1989-92, fellow Shannon Ctr. for Advanced Studies, U. Va., 1995—; grantee NEA, 1977, 89; recipient Lavan Younger Poet award Acad. Am. Poets, 1986, GE Found. award, 1987, Bellagio (Italy) residency Rockefeller Found., 1988, Ohio Gov.'s award 1988, Literary Lion citation N.Y. Pub. Libr., 1991, Women of Yr. award Glamour Mag., 1993, NAACP Great Am. Artist award, 1993, Golden Plate award Am. Acad. Achievement, 1994, Disting. Achievement medal Miami U. Alumni Assn., 1994, Renaissance Forum award for leadership in the literary arts Folger Shakespeare Libr., 1994, Carl Sandburg award Internat. Platform Assn., 1994, Heinz award in arts and humanities, 1996, Charles Frankel prize/Nat. Humanities medal Pres. of U.S. and NEH, 1996; inducted Ohio Women's Hall of Fame, 1991, Nat. Assn. of Women in Edn. Disting. Woman award, 1997, Sara Lee Frontrunner award, 1997, Barnes & Noble Writers for Writers award, 1997, Levinson prize Poetry mag., 1998, John Frederick Nims Translation prize, 1999, Libr. Lion award N.Y. Pub. Libr., 2000, Duke Ellington Lifetime Achievement award, 2001, Emily Couric Women's Leadership award, 2003; named Phi Beta Kappa poet Harvard U., 1993. Mem. PEN, ASCAP, Am. Philos. Soc., Poetry Soc. Am., Associated Writing Programs (bd. dirs. 1985-88, pres. 1986-87), Am. Acad. Achievement (mem. golden plate awards coun. 1994—2001), Phi Beta Kappa (senator 1994-2001), Phi Kappa Phi. Office: U Va Dept English 219 Bryan Hall PO Box 400121 Charlottesville VA 22904-4121

DOVIAK, INGRID ELLINGER, elementary school educator; b. New Britain, Conn., Feb. 10, 1971; d. John Leonard and Marjorie Chain Ellinger; m. Stephen Michael Doviak, June 8, 1996. BS, MA, So. Conn. State U., 1993. Tchr. head dept. enrichment grades k-8 Wntergreen Interdist. Magnet Sch., Hamden, Conn., 1998—. Adj. instr. deptl edn. Sacred Heart U., Fairfield, Conn., 2000—; adj. instr. So. Conn. State U., New Haven, 1998—; presenter Atomic Math Conf., 2001, 02, Conn. Assn. Math. Precocious Youth, 2000, 01, 02, Conn. Assn. Schs.

DOVRING, KARIN ELSA INGEBORG, writer, poet, playwright, media specialist; b. Stenstorp, Sweden, Dec. 5, 1919; arrived in US, 1953, naturalized, 1968; m. Folke Dovring, May 30, 1943. Grad., Coll. Commerce, Gothenburg, Sweden, 1936; MA, Lund (Sweden) U., 1943, PhD, 1951; Phil. Licentiate, Gothenburg U., 1947. Journalist several Swedish daily newspapers and weekly mags., 1940-60; tchr. Swedish colls.; rsch. assoc. of Harold Lasswell Yale U., New Haven, 1953-78; fgn. corr. Swedish newspapers, Italy, Switzerland, France and Germany, 1956-60; freelance writer, journalist, 1960—; rsch. prof. comms. and media studies U. Ill., Urbana, 2002. Vis. prof. Internat. U., The Vatican, Rome, 1958-60, Gottingen (W.Ger.) U., 1962; lectr. U.S. Army, Peace Corps, Yale U., U. Wis., McGill U., U. Iowa; rsch. assoc. U. Ill., Urbana, 1968-69, guest lectr., 2001-02; invited contbr. Social Sci. Rsch. Coun., 1988; speaker Conf. Law and Policy, Yale U. Law Sch., 1992-93, 99—; hon. mem. Profl. Women's Adv. Bd. Am. Biograph. Inst., Raleigh, N.C., 2003; adv. coun. Internat. Biographical Ctr., Cambridge, Eng.; interviewee radio and TV programs; writer Ill. Alliance to Prevent Nuclear War, radio, theater; hon. rsch. prof. comm. and media studies U. Ill. Coll. Comm., 2002—; moderator series U.S.A. Faces the World-Markets in Communications, 2004—; songwriter Hollywood and Nashville; plays for TV movies. Author: Songs of Zion, 1951, Land Reform as a Propaganda Theme, 3d edit., 1965, Road of Propaganda, 1959, Optional Society, 1972, Frontiers of Communication, 1975, English as Lingua Franca: Double Talk in Global Persuasion, 1997, (short stories) No Parking This Side of Heaven, 1982, Harold D. Lasswell: His Communication with a Future, 1987, 2d edit., 1988; (novel) Heart in Escrow, 1990; (poems) Faces in a Mirror, 1995, Changing Scenery, 2002, In the Service of Persuasion: English as Lingua Franca Across the Globe, 2001; contbr. articles to mags.; represented in several poetry anthologies in U.S. and Europe Recipient Swedish Nat. award for short stories Bonniers Pub. House Stockholm, 1951, Internat. Poet of Merit award Internat. Soc. Poets, 2002; named to Internat. Poetry Hall of Fame, 1996, Poet of Yr., 2000, 01, 02, 03. Mem. Soc. Jean Jacques Rousseau of Geneva (hon. life), Acad. Am. Poets. Democrat. Address: 613 W Vermont Ave Urbana IL 61801-4824

DOW, CHRISTINE DETSCHER, library assistant, educational consultant; b. Wolfeboro, NH, June 14, 1946; d. Richard William and Louise Hazel (Irish) Detscher; m. John Myrl Dow, Apr. 25, 1970; children: Matthew, Johanna, Bethany, Robin. BEd, Plymouth State Coll., 1968, MEd, 1993. Reality Therapy cert., Inst. for Choice Theory/ Reality Therapy & Quality Mgmt., 1992. 3d grade tchr. Hudson (N.H.) Sch. Dist., 1968-70; 2nd grade tchr. Inter-Lakes Sch. Dist., Meredith, N.H., 1972-73; tchr. Indian River Nursery Sch., Canaan, N.H., 1984-87, Cardigan Mt. Sch., Canaan, 1987-91; counselor Plymouth, N.H., 1993-94; sch. counselor Kearsarge Sch. Dist., Warner, N.H., 1994-97; libr. asst., guest svc. rep. Dartmouth Coll., Hanover, NH, 1997—. Practicum supr. Inst. for Choice Theory/ Reality Therapy and Quality Mgmt., Chatsworth, Calif., 1994-98; ednl. cons. Discovery Toys, 1997-99. Chair ann. fund raising Dinner Friends of Mascoma Schs., West Canaan, N.H., 1979-83; charter bd. dirs. Indian River Nursery Sch., 1979-84; town rep. Mascoma Sch. Bd., West Canaan, 1980-87; vice chmn. SAU #43 Sch. Bd., Lebanon, N.H., 1985-87; rider, mem. com. Pemiquaney Riding Club, Plymouth, 1989—. Recipient 10 Yr. Leader award 4-H Grafton County, 1995. Mem. Northeast Reality Therapists, Pemiquaney Riding Club, Appalachian Mountain Club, Mascoma Express Kayakers, Phi Delta Kappa, Order Ea. Star (N.H. chpt. Grand Electa 2002-03). Avocations: driving and riding horses, skiing, swimming, camping, water sports, crafts. Home: Box 1 C-2 Canaan NH 03741-9716 Office: Dartmouth Coll Hanover Inn Hanover NH 03755

DOW, LESLIE WRIGHT, communications company executive, photographer, writer; b. NYC, Apr. 28, 1938; d. Charles Leslie Kerr and Margaret Scott (MacArthur) Wright; m. William Arthur Dow, 1987; 1 child, John M. Haywood. AA, Colby-Sawyer Coll., 1957; cert., Katharine Gibbs Sch., 1958. Prodn. asst. Time Inc., N.Y.C., 1958-60; exec. asst. Jefferson-Standard Broadcasting Co., Charlotte, N.C., 1960-68, G.B. Wilkins Inc., Charlotte, 1981—82; pres., pub. relations cons. Wright Comm., Inc., Charlotte, 1982—. Contbr. photography to mags. and profl. jours.; contbr. articles to mags. Bd. dirs. Charlotte Symphony Women's Assn., 1964-71, Charlotte Symphony Orch., 1965; mem. Aux. of the Mint Mus., Charlotte, 1965—; bd. trustees Colby-Sawyer Coll., 1997—. Mem. NAFE, Am. Soc. Interior Designers (dir. [illegible] chpt. 1984-88), Am. Bus. Women's Assn., Am. Soc. Mag. Photographers, Profl. Photographers N.C., Profl. Photographers Am. Home and Office: 1954 Brawley School Rd Mooresville NC 28117-7083

DOW, MARTHA ANNE, biology educator; b. Little Rock, Jan. 3, 1939; d. Clarence Edgar and Gretchen Devron (Gable) Eudy; m. Gary Eugene Dow, Aug. 28, 1960; children: Julie, Kevin, Jerilyn. BS in Biology, No. Mont. Coll., 1961; MS in Microbiology, Mont. State U., 1969; PhD in Microbiology, U. Hawaii, 1989. Registered microbiologist. Prof., chair biology No. Mont. Coll., Havre, 1986-90, v.p. acad. affairs, 1990-92; provost Oreg. Inst. Tech., Klamath Falls, Oreg., 1992—. Dir. Mont. Environ. Tng. Ctr., EPA, No. Mont. Coll., 1989; pres. Nat. Environ. Tng. Assn., Phoenix, Oreg., 1990-92. Mem. Am. Soc. Microbiology, Am. Water Works Assn., Water Environment Fedn. Methodist. Office: Oreg Inst Tech 3201 Campus Dr Klamath Falls OR 97601-8801

DOW, MARY ALEXIS, auditor; b. South Amboy, N.J., Feb. 19, 1949; d. Alexander and Elizabeth Anne (Reilly) Pawlowski. BS with honors, U. R.I., 1971. CPA Oreg. Staff acct. Deloitte & Touche, Boston, 1971-74; sr. acct. Price Waterhouse, Portland, Oreg., 1974-77, mgr., 1977-81, sr. mgr., 1981-84; CFO Copeland Lumber Yards Inc., Portland, 1984-86; ind. cons. in field, 1986-94; elected auditor Metro, Portland, 1995—. Bd. dirs. Longview Fibre Co., Oreg. Health Sci. U. Med. Group. Contbr. articles to profl. jours. Past. chmn. bd. dirs., exec. com. Oreg. Trails chpt. N.W. Regional Blood Svcs. ARC; past. bd. dirs., exec. com., treas. Oreg. Mus. Sci. and Industry. Mem.: AICPA, Fin. Execs. Inst. (nat. exec. com., nat. treas., past pres. Portland chpt., past v.p. western area), Oreg. Soc. CPAs (past bd. dirs.), Am. Woman's Soc. CPAs, Pacific N.W. Intergovtl. Audit Forum (exec. com.), Multnomah Athletic Club (past treas., past trustee), City Club (past bd. govs.). Roman Catholic. Office: Auditor Office Metro 600 NE Grand Ave Portland OR 97232-2736 E-mail: dowa@metro.dst.or.us.

DOWBEN, CARLA LURIE, lawyer, educator; b. Chgo., Jan. 22, 1932; d. Harold H. and Gertrude Lurie; m. Robert Dowben, June 20, 1950; children: Peter Arnold, Jonathan Stuart, Susan Laurie. AB, U. Chgo., 1950; JD, Temple U., 1955. Bar: Ill. 1957, Mass. 1963, Tex. 1974, U.S. Surpeme Ct. 1974. Assoc. Conrad and Verges, Chgo., 1957-62; exec. officer MIT, Cambridge, Mass., 1963-64; legal planner Mass. Health Planning Project, Boston, 1964-69; assoc. prof. Life Scis. Inst. Brown U., Providence, 1970-72; asst. prof. health law U. Tex. Health Sci. Ctr., Dallas, 1973-78, assoc. prof., 1978-93; ptnr. Choate & Lilly, Dallas, 1989-92; head health law sect. Looper, Reed, Mark & McGraw, Dallas, 1992-95, of counsel, 1995-99. Adj. assoc. prof. health law U. Tex., 1993-95; cons. to bd. dirs. Mental Health Assn., 1958-86, Ft. Worth Assn. Retarded Citizens, 1980-90, Advocacy, Inc., 1981-85; dir. Nova Health Systems, 1975—, Tockwotton Home, 1994-98. Contbr. articles to profl. jours. Active in drafting helath and mental health legis., agy. regulation in several states and local govts. Mem. ABA, Tex. Bar Assn., Dallas Bar Assn., Am. Health Lawyers Assn., Hastings Inst. Ethics, Tex. Family Planning Assn. Mem. Soc. Of Friends.

DOWD, CAROLYN LAY, social worker; b. Hagerstown, Md., May 1, 1940; d. James S. Jr. and Emily Graham (Miller) Lay; m. William J. Dowd, Sept. 1, 1962 (dec.); children: William J. Jr., James P. AB, Meredith Coll., 1962; MSW, Catholic U., 1987. Cert. social worker, clin. social worker. Social work cons. Bethesda (Md.) Fellowship House, 1987-89; social worker Family Svcs. Agy., Gaithersburg, Md., 1987-98, dir. svcs. for srs., 1991-98, clin. dir., 1996-98; pvt. practice Gaithersburg, 1991-98; clin. care mgr. Falls Church, Va., 1998—. Presenter in field. Past mem. bd. dirs. Alzheimer's Assn. of Greater Wash. Mem. NASW (register of clin. social work, diplomate), Acad. Cert. Social Workers. Home: 21913 Foxlair Rd Gaithersburg MD 20882-1306 Address: 12369 C Sunrise Valley Dr Reston VA 20191 E-mail: cdowd@erols.com.

DOWD, FRANCES CONNELLY, retired librarian; b. Newburyport, Mass., Dec. 9, 1918; d. Martin Francis and Nelle Magdalen (Quinn) Connelly; m. James Reynolds Dowd, June 7, 1941 (dec. June 1944); children: James Reynolds Jr., Thomas Henry III. AB, Wellesley Coll., 1941; MLS, Columbia U., 1955. Cataloger Phillips Acad. Libr., Andover, Mass., 1955-57; asst. libr. Wheelock Coll. Libr., Boston, 1957-59; head of circulation U. R.I., Kingston, 1959-62; head libr. Ins. Libr., Boston, 1962-66; head bus. & sci. dept. Providence (R.I.) Pub. Libr., 1966-70; reference libr. Boston U. Libr., 1970-74; head libr. Mass. Horticulture Soc., Boston, 1974-79; reference libr. Haverhill (Mass.) Pub. Libr., 1979-89, Endicott Coll. Libr., Beverly, Mass., 1989—2001; ret., 2001. Lifelong learning instr. No. Essex C.C., 1997—. Editor: Whittier, 1992. Pres. Whittier Home Assn., Amesbury, Mass., 1989-96; treas. Macy-Colby House, 1979—; sec. Amesbury Carriage Mus., 1982—; reunion chmn. Wellesley Coll., 1971, 86. Mem. ALA, Abenaqui Country Club, Wellesley Coll. Club. Republican. Avocations: historic houses and gardens, travel, golf, gardening. Home: 3 Hillside Ave Amesbury MA 01913-2213

DOWD, JANICE LEE, foreign language educator; b. N.Y.C., Jan. 6, 1948; d. Edward H. and Mary A. (Vanek) D. BA, Marietta (Ohio) Coll., 1969; MA, Columbia U., 1971, MEd, 1979, EdD, 1984. Tchr. Teaneck (N.J.) Bd. Edn., 1970-99, supr. world langs., 1999—. Adj. asst. prof. Queens Coll., CUNY, 1984-94, Columbia U., N.Y.C., spring 1988, 93—; N.J. alternate route prof., 1990—; asst. prof. MA TESOL program in China, Changsha, 1986, Shanghai, 1987; SAT program adminstr. Teaneck H.S., 1978-83, yearbook sponsor, 1975-79, newspaper sponsor, 1984-92, co-chair Global/Multicultural Mgmt. Team, 1992-95. Contbr. articles to profl. jours. Mem. program com., v.p., pres. PEO, Teaneck, 1966—. Fellow Rockefeller Found., 1988. Mem. Am. Assn. Tchrs. French, Am. Assn. Tchrs. Spanish and Portuguese, Chinese Lang. Assn. for Secondary-Elem. Tchrs., Tchrs. English to Speakers Other Langs., N.Y. State Tchrs. English to Speakers Other Langs., N.J. Tchrs. English to Speakers Other Langs., Am. Assn. Applied Linguists, Am. Coun. Tchrs. Fgn. Langs., Fgn. Lang. Educators N.J., Nat. Assn. Dept. Heads and Suprs. of Fgn. Langs. Home: 56 Boulevard New Milford NJ 07646-1602 Office: Teaneck High Sch 100 Elizabeth Ave Teaneck NJ 07666-4798

DOWD, MAUREEN, columnist; b. Washington, D.C., Jan. 14, 1952; BA English Lit., Catholic U., Washington D.C., 1973. From editl. asst. to feature writer The Washington Star, 1974-81; from corr. to writer Time mag., 1981-83; metro reporter N.Y. Times, 1983-86, D.C. reporter, 1986-95, opinion-editl. columnist, 1995—. Finalist Pulitzer Prize for nat. reporting, 1992; named one of Glamour's Women of the Yr., 1996; recipient Breakthrough Award, "Women, Men and Media", Columbia U., 1991, Matrix Award, NY Women in Comm., 1994, Pulitzer Prize for commentary, 1999, Damon Runyon Award, Denver Press Club, 2000. Office: NY Times 1627 I St NW Washington DC 20006-4007*

DOWDELL, SHARONLYN SCOTT, accountant; b. Atlanta, Aug. 25, 1959; d. Joseph Sr. and Artie Bell Scott; m. Michael Grant Dowdell, Apr. 25, 1979 (div. Feb. 1989); children: Michael, Lanecia, Vanita. Tax agt. Dept. Revenue, Atlanta, 1984-95; reimbursement mgr. Dept. Cmty. Health., Atlanta, 1995-2000; owner Dowdell & Assocs, CPAs. Fellow AICPA, Ga. Soc. CPAs, Ga. Fiscal Mgmt. Coun.

DOWDY, VICKI J. music educator; b. Murray, Ky., Sept. 30, 1953; d. Noah William and Pauline Edwards; m. Craig Walters Ewing, Aug. 23, 1975 (div. Apr. 1990); 1 child, Megan Brooke. B of Music Edn., Murray

State U., 1975, M of Music Edn., 1985. Tchr. music Marshall County Schs., Benton, Ky., 1977—82; clk. Love's Jewelry, SC, 1982—83; sec., receptionist Black & Decker, Raleigh, NC, 1983—85; legal sec. Petree, Stockton & Robinson, Winston-Salem, 1985—88, Lovett & Johnson, Benton, 1990—91; tchr. music Marshall County Schs., 1991—2003. Singer: Paducah Symphony Chorus, 1989—2000. Mem.: Kt. Music Educations Assn., Ky. Edn. Assn. Avocations: walking, reading, sewing. Office: Calvert City Elem Sch 5th Ave PO Box 215 Calvert City KY 42029

DOWER GOLD, CATHERINE ANNE, music history educator; b. South Hadley, Mass., May 19, 1924; d. Lawrence Frederick Dower and Marie (Barbieri) Barber; m. Arthur Gold, Mar. 24, 1994 (dec. Oct. 1998). AB, Hamline U., 1945; MA, Smith Coll., 1948; B in Liturgical Music, U. Mont., Gregorian Inst. Am., 1949; PhD, The Cath. U. Am., 1968. New England rep. Gregorian Inst. Am., Toledo, 1948-49; tchr. music, organist St. Rose Sch., Meriden, Conn., 1949-53; supr. music Holyoke (Mass.) Pub. Schs., 1953-55; instr. music U. Mass., Amherst, 1955-56; prof. music Westfield (Mass.) State Coll., 1956-90, prof. emerita, 1991—; columnist and freelance writer Holyoke Transcript Telegram, 1991-93. Organist St. Theresa's Ch., South Hadley, 1937-41, St. Michael's Ch., N.Y., 1945-46; concert series presenter Westfield State Coll., 1987-91, rschr. tchr.; vis. scholar U. So. Calif., 1969; vis. assoc. prof. music Herbert Lehman Coll. CUNY, 1970-71. Author: Puerto Rican Music Following the Spanish American War, 1898-1910, 1983; (monograph) Yella Pessl, 1986, Alfred Einstein on Music, 1991, Yella Pessl: First Lady of the Harpsichord, 1992, Fifty Years of Marching Together, 2001; editor: (newsletter) Westfield State Coll., 2000—; presenter Irish Concert Springfield Symphony Orch., 1981 (plaque 1982); contbr. numerous pub. poems to anthologies. Pres. Coun. for Human Understanding Holyoke, 1981-83, Friends of Holyoke Pub. Libr., 1990-91; bd. dirs., chmn. nominating com. Holyoke Pub. Libr., 1987-89; bd. dirs. Holyoke Pub. Libr. Corp., 1991-94, Springfield Symphony Orch., 1992—94; bd. dirs. Fla. Philharm. Orch., 2000-03, trustee, 2002-03; presiding officer inauguration Dr. Irving Buchman pres. of Westfield State Coll.; ethics com. Holyoke Hosp., 1988-94; sec. Haiti Mission, 1982-94; bd. overseers Mullen U., 1993; hon. mem. bd. Coun. Human Understanding, 1994-; hon. mem. WSC Found., 1994-; co-chair United Jewish Appeal/Jewish Fedn. Boca Lago Women's Divsn., South Palm Beach County, 1996-97, 1st. v.p. fin. and adminstrn. Temple Beth El Women in Reformed Judaism, Boca Raton, 1997-99; active St. Patrick's Com., 1991—2004; bd. dirs. Friends of Music of Lynn U. Conservatory Music, 2003—. Recipient citation Academia InterAmericana de P.R., 1978, plaque Mass. Tchrs. Assn., Boston, 1984, medal Equestrian Order Holy Sepulchre of Jerusalem, Papal Knighthood Soc., Boston, 1984, Performance award Gov. Dukakis, Mass., 1988, award from Puerto Rican Jour. Al. Margens, 1992, Human Rels. award Coun. for Human Understanding, Holyoke, 1994; named Lady Comdr., Equestrian Order of the Holy Sepulche of Jerusalem, 1987, with star, 1990, Career Woman of Yr., Quota Internat. Holyoke, Mass., 1988; Westfield State U. concert series named Catherine A. Dower Performing Arts Series in her honor, 1991; recipient 1st prize in Raddock Eminent Scholar Chair Essay Contest, Fla. Atlantic U., 1996, Internat. Poet of Merit Silver Bowl award Internat. Libr. Poetry, 2002, First prize Essay Contest on World Peace by Brotherly Love Press, Mass. 2002, Outstanding Achievement in Poetry award Internat. Soc. of Poets, 2003. Mem. Nat. Soc. Arts and Letters, Am. Musicol. Soc., Coll. Mus. Soc., Ch. Music Assn. Am. (journalist), Acad. Arts and Scis. P.R. (medal 1977), Internat. Platform Assn., Friends of the Holyoke Pub. Libr. (pres. 1990-91), Irish Am. Cultural Inst. (chmn. bd. 1981-89), Holyoke Quota (v.p. 1976-79, pres. 1979-81, 90-92, chmn. speech and hearing com. 1987-94), B'nai B'rith of Boca Lago (sec. bd. dirs. 1994-1999, newsletter editor 1999-2000), Lifelong Learning Soc. Fla. Atlantic U. (life, sec. 1994-97, bd. dirs. 1994-98, 2003—), Westfield State Coll. Found., Women's Symphony League (life), Philharm. Assn. Boca (pres. 2002-03), Univ. Club Fla. Atlantic U. (parliamentarian 2003—), Nat. Soc. Art Letters, Phi Beta Kappa. Democrat. Home: 8559 Casa Del Lago Boca Raton FL 33433-2107 E-mail: cathig@juno.com.

DOWLING, DORIS ANDERSON, business owner, educator, consultant; b. Clover Valley, Minn., Sept. 24, 1917; d. Gustaf Axel and Amanda Sophia (Karlsson) Anderson; m. John Joseph Dowling, Jan. 8, 1943 (dec. Feb. 1953); 1 child, Mary Kathryn. Home econs. degree, U. Minn., Virginia, 1937. Fashion coord., lectr. Fair Store/Montgomery Ward, Chgo., 1939-65, Marshall Field's, Chgo., 1967-82; founder, owner Doris Anderson Sewing Schs., 1948—. Cons. colls., textile industry, retail stores, 1948—; lectr. retail stores, 1954-94. Author: Simplified Systems of Sewing and Styling, 1948. Career counselor, trainer, Chgo., 1948-82. Recipient Future Farmers Am. award Duluth C. of C. Coun. Agr., 1934. Mem. Nat. Needlework Assn., Fashion Group Internat. Inc., Assn. Crafts & Creative Industries, Chgo. Apparel Ctr., Merchandise Mart. Avocations: designing, gardening, writing, research. Home and Office: Doris Anderson Sewing Schs 222 E Pearson St Apt 1108 Chicago IL 60611-7356

DOWNES, PATRICIA ANN, minister; b. Sussex, N.J., Dec. 10, 1945; d. Leonard McGill and Violet McCarty; m. Randall Priest Jr., June 21, 1964 (div. May 20, 1988); children: Linda, Randall, Sarah-Elisabeth; m. Donald Downes, Oct. 17, 1994. AA, Brevard C.C., 1986; BSW, U. Ctrl. Fla., 1988; MDiv, Emory U., 1991; postgrad., So. Fla. Ctr. Theol. Studies, 2004—. Lic. practical nurse, Fla., 1965; ordained clergy, cert. in Christian edn. United Meth. Ch. Nurse Holmes Regional Hosp., Melbourne, Fla., 1965—67, therapeutic foster parent, 1967—88; pastor United Meth. Ch., Holly Hill, 1991—94, clergy mem. Miami, 1994—2001, Palm Beach, 2001—. Foster parent trainer Holmes Regional Hosp., Melbourne, 1980—88. Author: Foster Parent Manual, 1983. AIDS counselor, Melbourne, 1985—87; guardian ad litem GAL Program, Brevard County, 1981—86; bd. dirs. YMCA, Melbourne, 1975—79, Miami Urban Ministries, Miami, 1998—2000, Palm Bay Hosp., 2002—; grantwriter Foster Care Cmty. Edn., 1985. Named Child Advocate Yr., Children's Home Soc., 1983; recipient Cmty. Svc. award, Brevard C.C., 1986. Mem.: Dist. Bd. Ordained Ministry. Democrat. United Methodist. Avocations: writing, sewing, reading. Office: Palm Bay United Meth Ch 2100 Port Malabar Blvd Palm Bay FL 32905

DOWNEY, CHRISTINE, state legislator; b. Abilene, Kans., Mar. 26, 1949; children: Amy, Matthew, Erin. Elem. and mid. sch. tchr., 1975-93; mem. Kans. Senate from 31st. dist., Topeka, 1996—. Adj. prof. Bethel Coll., 1990-93; mem. edn. com. Kans. Senate, agriculture com., chldn's issues com., legis. ednl. planning com., ways and means com. Pres., bd. dirs. Newton Cmty. Children's Choir, 1991-92. Mem. Kans. Nat. Edn. Assn. (pres. 1990), Newton Nat. Edn. Assn. (pres. 1989). Home: 10320 N Wheat State Rd Inman KS 67546-8109

DOWNEY, DEBORAH ANN, systems specialist; b. Xenia, Ohio, July 22, 1958; d. Nathan Vernon and Patricia Jaunita (Ward) D. Assoc. in Applied Sci., Sinclair C.C., 1981, student, 1986—91; BA, Capital U., 1994. Jr. programmer, project mgr. Cole-Layer-Trumble Co., Dayton, Ohio, 1981-82; sr. programmer, analyst, project leader Systems Architects Inc., Dayton, 1982-84, Systems and Applied Sci. Corp. (now Computer Sci. Corp.), Dayton, 1984; analyst Unisys, Dayton, 1984-87; systems programmer Computer Sci. Corp., Fairborn, Ohio, 1987—. Cons. computer software M&S Garage/Body Shop, Beavercreek, Ohio, 1986-87. Mem. NAFE, Am. Motorcyclist Assn., Sinclair C. C. Alumni Assn., Cherokee Nation Okla., Cherokee Nat. Hist. Soc. Democrat. Mem. United Ch. Of Christ. Avocations: motorcycles, miniatures, sports, needlework.

DOWNEY, ROMA, actress; b. Northern Ireland, United Kingdom, May 6, 1963; m. David Anspaugh, 1995 (div. 1998); 1 child, Reilly Marie. BA in Fine Arts, Brighton Art Coll., England, 1983; diploma, London Drama Studio, 1985. Actress CBS Television, L.A. Appeared in Irelands Abbey Theatre, U.S. tour The Playboy of the Western World, 1991; on Broadway in The Circle; Off Broadway in Love's Labour's Lost, Tamara, Arms and the Man; TV appearances include A Woman Named Jackie, Touched by an Angel, 1994-2003, Borrowed Hearts, A Child is Missing; appeared in films including (TV series) A Woman Named Jackie, 1991, Devlin, 1992, A Child is Missing, 1995, Borrowed Hearts, 1997, Monday After the Miracle, 1998, A Test of Love, 1999, A Secret Life, 2000, Second Honeymoon, 2000, Sons of Mistletoe, 2001, Hairy Tale, 2003; exec. prodr. Borrowed Hearts, 1997, Monday After the Miracle, 1998, Second Honeymoon, 2000, Hairy Tale, 2003. Nominee Helen Hayes Best Actress award, 1991, Emmy award, 1997, 98, Golden Globe award, 1997-98; recipient TV Guide award for favorite actress in a drama, 1999. Office: Touched by an Angel care CBS/MTM Studios 4020 Radford Ave North Hollywood CA 91604-2101 Address: Gersh Agy 232 N Canon Dr Beverly Hills CA 90210-5302

DOWNEY-SARGENT, KATHRYN T. psychologist, researcher; b. Alexandria, Va., Oct. 11, 1969; BS, James Madison U., 1991; PhD, U. Vt., 2000. Survey rschr. Mathematica Policy Rsch., Washington, 1999—2001; sr. project leader Arbitron, Columbia, Md., 2002—04; rsch. psychologist U.S. Bureau Labor Statistics, Washington, 2004—. Mem.: APA, Am. Statis. Assn., Am. Assn. Pub. Opinion Rsch. Office: Postal Square Bldg #1950 2 Mass Ave NE Washington DC 20212 Office Phone: 202-691-7382. Personal E-mail: downeysargent@yahoo.com.

DOWNING, CYNTHIA HURST, therapist, addiction and abuse specialist; b. Fort Wayne, Ind., Sept. 10, 1942; d. James Dickson Hurst and Bernadette (Dygert) Lawyer; m. James S. Downing, Sept. 9, 1961 (div. 1979); children: David, Elizabeth, Jeffrey. BA in Psychology, Ursuline Coll., 1980; MA in Human Svcs., John Carroll U., 1982; PhD, Saybrook Inst., 1991. Lic. profl. clin. counselor; cert. chem. dependency counselor III-E Ohio, nat. cert. addiction counselor II, cert. master addiction counselor. Counselor United Meth. Alcohol and Chem. Counseling, Berea, Ohio, 1980-82; clin. dir. Earthrise Recovery Svcs., Inc., Chagrin Falls, Ohio, 1982—; clin. dir. chem. dependency Brentwood Hosp., Cleve., 1985; program coord. for recovery svcs. U. Hosp. & Health Sys.: Laurelwood Hosp. & Counseling Ctrs., 1998—2001. Coord. case study, instr. Ctr. Applied Scis. Corp. Nat. Relapse Prevention Cert. Sch., Chgo., 1988-98. Author: Triad: The Evolution of Treatment for Chemical Dependency, 1989; mem. editorial adv. bd. Behavioral Health Mgmt. mag., 1991—; contbr. articles to profl. jours. Mem. Nat. Assn. Alcoholism and Drug Abuse Counselors, Nat. Assn. Relapse Prevention Specialists (charter), Assn. Humanistic Psychology, Internat. Soc. for the Study of Dissociation.

DOWNING, JOAN FORMAN, editor, writer; b. Mpls., Nov. 16, 1934; d. W. Chandler and Marie A. (Forster) Forman; children: Timothy Alan, Julie Marie Downing Giesen, Christopher Alan. BA, U. Wis., 1956. Editl. asst. Sci. Research Assocs., Chgo., 1960-61, asst. editor, 1961-63, Childrens Press, Chgo., 1963-66, assoc. editor, 1966-68, mng. editor, 1968-78, editor-in-chief, 1978-81, sr. editor, 1981-95; propr. Downing Pub. Svcs., Evanston, Ill., 1995—. Dir. Chgo. Book Clinic, 1973-75, publicity chmn., 1973-74 Author: (with Eugene Baker) Workers Long Ago, 1968, Baseball Is Our Game, 1982, Junior CB Picture Dictionary, 1978; project editor: 15 vol. Young People's Story of Our Heritage, 1966 (Graphic Arts Council of Chgo. award), 20 vol. People of Destiny (Chgo. Book Clinic award 1967-68), 20 vol. Enchantment of South and Central America, 1968-70, 36 vol. Open Door Books, 1968, 42 vol. Enchantment of Africa, 1972-78, Hobbies for Everyone: Collecting Toy Trains, 1979 (Graphic Arts award Printing Industries Am.), (multi-vol.) World at War, 1980 87, (52 vol.) America the Beautiful, 1987-91, (52 vol.) From Sea to Shining Sea, 1991-95, (multi-vol.) Rookie Read-About Science, 1994-97, (multi-vol.) Cities of the World, 1995-2001, (multi-vol.) Encyclopedia of First Ladies, 1997-2000. Election judge, Cook County (Ill.), 1974— . Mem. Authors Guild, Authors League Am., Alpha Phi. Democrat. Home and Office: 2414 Brown Ave Evanston IL 60201-2526 E-mail: jd2414@aol.com.

DOWNING, JOHNETTE, musician, educator; b. Marrero, La., Jan. 19, 1962; BA in Theatre, Southeastern La. U., Hammond, 1984. Children's musician, New Orleans, 1988—. Preschool music tchr. Isidore Newman Sch., New Orleans, 1993—. Musician (singer/songwriter): (recordings) Music Time, Silly Sing Along (Parents' Choice award, 2002, Parenting Pubs. award, 2002), Wild and Woolly Wiggle Songs (Parents' Choice award, 2001, Parents' Guide to Children's Media award, 2001), From The Gumbo Pot (Parents' Choice Silver Honors award, 1999), The Second Line - Scarf Activity Songs. Mem.: Ind. Children's Artist Network (editor of applause (quar. newsletter) 2000—03, cofounder and v.p. 2000—), Children's Music Network, New Orleans Haiku Soc. (cofounder 2001—02). Office: Johnette Downing PO Box 13367 New Orleans LA 70185-3367 Personal E-mail: johnettemusic@aol.com. E-mail: johnettemusic@aol.com.

DOWNS, BETTY RATCLIFF, music educator; b. Scriba, N.Y., Nov. 8, 1915; d. Darius Mitteer and Ethel Lepine (Fulton) Ratcliff; m. Harry Joseph Downs, Sept. 5, 1941 (dec.); children: Richard Wayne, Joan Elizabeth. BA in Pub. Sch. Music, Houghton Coll., 1937; MA in Edn., La. State U., 1941. Cert. tchr. N.Y., La. Music tchr. Ctrl. Sch., Jasper, NY, 1937—38, Dalton, NY, 1938—40; substitute tchr. pub. schs., New Orleans, 1941—42; nursery sch. worker govt. nursery sch., New Orleans, 1942—45; music tchr. Crescent City Bapt. Sch., New Orleans, 1959—99; ch. organist Edgewater Bapt. Ch., New Orleans, 1967—77; ch. organist, choir dir. Chinese Presbyn. Ch., New Orleans, 1977—. Sec. New Orleans Music Tchrs. Assn., 1975—80. Mem.: New Orleans Music Tchrs., La. Fedn. Music Clubs. Republican. Baptist. Avocations: swimming, tennis, sewing. Home: 154 Lake Ave Metairie LA 70005

DOWNS, KATHLEEN ANNE, health facility administrator; b. Toledo, Sept. 20, 1951; d. Keith Landis and Cecelia Josephine Babcock; m. Michael Brian Thomas, July 17, 1971 (dec. Oct. 1973); m. David Michael Downs, Aug. 8, 1981. Student, San Diego Mesa Coll., 1968—70; BS, Union Inst., 1989. Cert. med. staff coordinator, provider credentialing specialist, profl. healthcare quality. Sec. Travelodge Internat., Inc., El Cajon, Calif., 1970-73; intermediate stenographer City of El Cajon, 1973-77; adminstrv. asst. MacLellan & Assocs., El Cajon, 1977-78; sr. sec. WESTEC Services, Inc., San Diego, 1978; adminstrv. sec. El Cajon Valley Hosp., 1978-80; asst. med. staff Grossmont Dist. Hosp., La Mesa, Calif., 1980-83, coord. med. staff, 1983-87, mgr., 1987-94; mgr. med. staff Sharp Meml. Hosp., San Diego, 1994; dir. med. staff svcs. Sharp HealthCare, San Diego, 1994-96, sr. specialist med. staff svcs., 1996; dir. med. staff svcs. Alvarado Hosp. Med. Ctr. and San Diego Rehab. Inst., San Diego, 1996-99; mgr. med. staff svcs. Kaiser Permanente Hosp., San Diego, 1999-2001, med. staff svcs. cons., 2001—; dir. med. staff svcs. Paradise Valley Hosp., National City, Calif., 2001—. Tchr. The Vogel Inst., San Diego, 1986; mem. med. staff svcs. adv. com. San Diego C.C. Dist.; adj. faculty Union Inst., 1991-96, Chemeketa C.C., 1991-95; credentials verification orgn. surveyor Nat. Com. Quality Assurance, Washington, 1996—. Mem. Nat. Assn. Med. Staff Svcs. (edn. coun. 1989-93, faculty 1990—, chmn. 1991-93, bd. dirs. 1991-93, editl. bd. Over View 1993-96), Calif. Assn. Med. Staff Svcs. (treas. San Diego chpt. 1984-86, pres. 1986-87, state sec. 1999-2001, pres.-elect 2001-03, pres. 2003-). Avocations: organic gardening, boating, gourmet cooking, yoga, reading, fitness walking.

DOXEY-TATE, SARAH ROLSTON, retired elementary school educator; b. Holly Springs, Miss., Mar. 13, 1933; d. Hindman and Mary Amis (Bitzer) Doxey; m. Lloyd O'Neil Tate, Dec. 25, 1960 (div. July 16, 1986); children: Katherine Bitzer Tate Guess, William Hindman Tate, Marisa O. Tate Stone, Frances Doxy Tate Johnson. MS, Belhaven Coll., 1951; BA in Art Edn., U. Miss., 1954, postgrad., 1981—83, Miss. So. U., 1986—89. Tchr. 2d and 4th grades Canton (Miss.) Pub. Schs., 1954—59; tchr. 3d grade Holly Springs Schs., 1959—60; art supr. 5 schs. Clarksdale (Miss.) Pub. Elem. Schs., 1961—62; art supr. 5 elem. schs. Tupelo (Miss.) Pub. Schs. ETV Art, 1962—69; tchr. kindergarten and pvt. sch. Playhouse, Tupelo, 1970—73; tchr. h.s. art and journalism Tupelo Pub. Schs., 1974—75, tchr. jr. high gifted edn., 1977—80; tchr. libr./media ctr. Lee County Schs., Tupelo, 1985—96. Pianist receptions, rehearsal dinners Tupelo Country Club, 1985—. Grand marshal Tupelo Christmas Parade, 2002; pres. bd. Friends of Lee County Libr., 2001—04; elder 1st Presbyn. Ch.; past pres., moderator Presbyn. Women, Tupelo; bd. dirs., past pres. Faith Haven, Inc. Home for Children, 1976—; head counselor Camp DeSoto Camp for Girls, Mentone, Ala., 1972—95; founder Ch. After Sch. Assn., Lee County, 1982—, civic chmn. Fortnightly Musicale, 1963—, pres., 1965; pianist Salvation Army Ch. Svcs., Tupelo. Named one of Mississippians Who Have Made a Difference, Miss. Mag., 1985, Outstanding Women of Am., 1967; recipient Freedom Found. Valley Forge Tchr.'s medal, 1969, Outstanding Citizen award, Tupelo Jr. Aux., Inc., 1999. Mem.: DAR (regent 1970), N.E. Miss. Ret. Tchrs. Assn. (dist. pres. 1997—99), Tupelo-Lee County Miss. Assn. Educators. Presbyterian. Avocation: playing piano. Home: 2611 Lakeshire Dr Tupelo MS 38804

DOYEL, CINDY M. information systems specialist; b. Stockton, Calif., Dec. 1, 1964; d. Nathan Cameron Doyel and Charlotte Blanche (Epler) Gezi. Student, Calif. State U., Sacramento, 1982-83; AA, MTI Bus. Coll., Sacramento, 1984. Supr. All Am. Mini Storage, Sacramento, 1988-89; mng. contr. The Royce Cos., Roseville, Calif., 1990-93; contr. Calif. Comml., Sacramento, 1993-95; gen. ptnr., operator Sierra Micro, Fair Oaks, Calif., 1995-98; help desk analyst Shared Med. Sys., Sacramento, Calif., 1998-99; info. tech. specialist Legis. Data Ctr., Sacramento, Calif., 1999—. Mem.: NAFE, NOW. Presbyterian. Avocations: writing, reading, waterpolo, swimming, softball. Office: Legis Data Ctr 1100 J St Ste 200 Sacramento CA 95814-2827

DOYEN, BARBARA J. literary agent; b. Laurens, Iowa; m. Robert Doyen. BA, Buena Vista U., 1972. Instr. art Ayrshire Pub. Sch., Iowa, 1971—75, Laurens Cmty. Sch., 1975—86; pres., CEO Doyen Lit. Svcs., Inc., Newell, 1988—. Author: Back to Protein, 2000, Everything Quick Meals, 2001, Growing a Great Garden, 2002, Fabulous Fruits & Berries, 2002. Office: Doyen Lit Svcs Inc 1931 660th St Newell IA 50568

DOYLE, CONSTANCE TALCOTT JOHNSTON, physician, educator, medical association administrator; b. Mansfield, Ohio, July 8, 1945; d. Frederick Lyman IV and Nancy Jean Bushnell (Johnston) Talcott; children: Ian Frederick Demsky, Zachary Adam Demsky. BS, Ohio U., 1967; MD, Ohio State U., 1971. Diplomate Am. Bd. Emergency Medicine; bd. cert. in emergency crisis response. Intern Riverside Hosp., Columbus, Ohio, 1971-72, resident in internal medicine Hurley Hosp., U. Mich., Flint, 1972-74; emergency physician Oakwood Hosp., Dearborn, Mich., 1974-76, Jackson County (Mich.) Emergency Svcs., 1975-95; cons. Region II EMS, 1978-79, disaster cons., 1983-95; St. Joseph Mercy Hosp., Ann Arbor, 1995—, med. flight physician helicopter life support svcs., 1996-2000; core faculty St. Joseph Merch Hosp./U. Mich. Emergency Residency, Ann Arbor, 1995—; survival flight physician helicopter rescue svc. U. Mich., 1983-91; course dir. advanced cardiac life support and chmn. advanced life support com. W.A. Foote Meml. Hosp., Jackson, 1979-95; dep. dir. emergency svcs. med. ctrl. bd. Washtenaw Livingston County, 2000—; core faculty St. Joseph Mercy Hosp., Ann Arbor, 1996. Clin. instr. emergency svcs., dept. surgery U. Mich., 1991—; faculty combined emergency medicine residency St. Joseph Mercy Hosp.-U. Mich., Ann Arbor, 1995—; asst. med. dir. Region 2 South Biodef. Network, 2002-03, co-med. dir., 2003—; instr. EMT refresher courses, Jackson County, Jackson C.C.; MedFlight physician, 1996-99; Washtenaw County Subcom. on Bioterrorism, 2000—; Washtenaw County Local Emergency Planning Com., 1998—; dep. med. dir. Washtenaw/Livingston County Med. Control Authority, 2000—. Contbg. author: Clinical Approach to Poisoning and Toxicology, 1983, 89, 97, May's Textbook of Emergency Medicine, 1991, Schwartz Principles and Practice of Emergency Medicine, 1992, Reisdorff Pediatric Emergency Medicine, 1993; contbr. articles to profl. jours. Mem. Disaster Med. Assistance Team, 2000—; served Ground Zero, 2001. Fellow Am. Coll. Emergency Physicians (pres. Mich. disaster com. 1987-88, bd. dirs. Mich. 1979-88, chmn. Mich. disaster com. 1979-85, mem. nat. disaster med. svcs. com. 1983-85, chmn. 1987-88, cons. disaster mgmt. course Fed. Emergency Mgmt. Agy. 1982, treas. 1984-85, emergency med. svcs. com. 1985, pres. 1986-87, councillor 1986-87, chair steering com. policy sect., 1994—, mem. disaster sect., 1995—, exec. com. disaster sect. 1997—, chair policy sect. disaster 1995—, vice chair sect. careers in emergency medicine 1997—, chair, 2000—), Nat. Am. Coll. Emergency Physicians (vice chair sect. of disaster med. svcs. 1990-92, nat. disaster subcom. 1989-90, chair subsect. psychol. rehab. svcs., disaster med. svcs. 1992-94, chair policy and legis. 1994-96, task force on hazardous materials 1993-97, steering com. sect. disaster medicine 1994-2002, exec. com. sect. disaster medicine 1995); mem. ACP, Am. Med. Women's Assn., Am. Assn. Women Emergency Physicians, Mich. Assn. Emergency Med. Technicians (bd. dirs. 1979-80), Mich. State Med. Soc., Washtenaw County Med. Soc., Sierra Club. Jewish. Office: 1251 King George Blvd Ann Arbor MI 48108 also: St Joseph Mercy Hosp Dept Emergency Medicine Ann Arbor MI 48109

DOYLE, DELORES MARIE, retired principal; b. Madison, S.D., July 24, 1939; d. Martin N. and Pearl M. (Anderson) Berkelo; m. Patrick J. Doyle; children: Kathleen, Shawn, Tamara, Timothy. AS, Dakota State Coll., Madison, 1959; BS, Mid. Tenn. State U., 1966, MEd, 1968, EdS, 1975; PhD, Peabody/Vanderbilt U., 1980. Cert. career ladder III tchr. Tchr. 4th grade Meriden-Cleghorn Schs., Meriden, Iowa, 1960-62; tchr. 1st grade Hanover (Ill.) Sch., 1963-66; tchr. 2d grade Hobgood Sch., Murfreesboro, Tenn., 1969-70; tchr. 1st grade Reeves-Rogers Sch., Murfreesboro, 1972-80, tchr. 2d grade, 1981-97, prin., 1997-2000; ret., 2000. Cooperating tchr. Mid. Tenn. State U. Student Tchrs., Murfreesboro, 1972—97, mem. task force edn., 1992—93; summer sch. dir. Murfreesboro City Schs., 1986—98; lead project tutor Reeves-Rogers Sch., Murfreesboro, 1987—90. Active Edn. 2000 Com., Murfreesboro C. of C., 1993; trustee Mid Tenn State U. Found., 1995—2001; bd. dirs. Grace Luth. Ch., Murfreesboro, 1991—93, 2001—03, mem. choir, 1975—. Named Career Ladder III Tchr., Dept. Edn., Nashville, 1984; named to Tenn. Tchrs. Hall of Fame, 2001; recipient Tenn. Tchr. of the Yr. award, Dept. Edn., Nashville, 1992, Murfreesboro City Tchr. of the Yr. award, Murfreesboro City Schs., 1991, Mid-Cumberland Dist. Tchr. of the Yr. award, Dist. Dept. Edn., 1991, Trailblazer award, 1995; Creative Tchg. grantee, State Dept. Edn., 1992, 1993. Mem.: Murfreesboro Edn. Assn. (pres. 1981—82), Tenn. Edn. Assn. (Disting. Classroom Tchr. award 1992, Disting. Adminstr. award 2000), Tenn. State Tchr. of Yr. Orgn. (v.p. 2000—), Nat. State Tchr. of Yr. Orgn., Delta Kappa Gamma. Democrat. Avocations: bridge, travel, reading, bicycling. Home: 1710 Sutton Pl Murfreesboro TN 37129-6513 Personal E-mail: pandddoyle@comcast.net.

DOYLE, EUGENIE FLERI, pediatric cardiologist, educator; b. Bklyn., Oct. 19, 1921; d. Paul Charles and Antoinette (Giovannetti) Fleri; m. Joseph Anthony Doyle, Aug. 19, 1944; children: Christopher, Stephen, Eugenie, Jane Marie, Richard. BS, Marymount Coll., Tarrytown, N.Y., 1943, DSc (hon.), 1993; MD, Johns Hopkins U., 1946; DSc (hon.), Coll. New Rochelle, 1975. Intern in pediatrics Johns Hopkins Hosp., Balt., 1946-47; pediatric resident Bellevue Hosp., N.Y.C., 1947-49; fellow pediatric cardiology NYU Med. Ctr., 1949-53, dir. pediatric cardiology, 1958-93; asst. prof. pediatrics NYU Sch. Medicine, 1953-58, assoc. prof., 1959-70, prof., 1970-92, prof. emerita, 1993—, clin. prof. pediatrics, 1994—. Mem. cardiac adv. com. N.Y. State Health Dept., 1983-92; dir. Vis. Nurse Svc., N.Y.C., 1984—. Editor: Pediatric Cardiology, 1985; contbr. articles to profl. jours. Trustee Marymount Coll., 1983-91, vice chair bd., 1988-91. Mem. Am. Acad. Pediatrics, Am. Pediatric Soc., Am. Coll. Cardiology, Am. Heart

Assn., N.Y. Heart Assn. (bd. dirs. 1977-84, pres. 1979-81), Cosmopolitan Club. Roman Catholic. Avocations: gardening, travel, ballet. Home: 32 Washington Sq W New York NY 10011-9156 Office: NYU Med Ctr 550 1st Ave New York NY 10016-6402

DOYLE, FLORENCE ELIZABETH, retired secondary school educator; b. Mayville, N.D., Oct. 30, 1920; d. Ole Matias and Petra (Ulland) Kjelsberg; m. Joseph Patrick Doyle, Aug. 12, 1952. BA, Concordia Coll., 1942; MA, St. Thomas U., 1967. Tchr. pub. sch., Odessa, Minn., 1942—43, Pine Island, Minn., 1943—44, 1944—47, Montevideo, Minn., 1947—52, Royalton, Minn., 1952—53, Mahnomen, Minn., 1953—59, Richfield, Minn., 1959—79. Docent gov.'s residence, St. Paul, 1985—. Mem.: AAUW, Minn. Hist. Soc. (pres. Women's Orgn. 1990—92). Republican. Roman Catholic. Home: 1377 Maynard Dr W # 161 Saint Paul MN 55116-2951

DOYLE, GILLIAN, actress; b. Maidenhead, Berkshire, Eng. came to U.S., 1977; d. John Joseph and Joan (Walker) D. BA in Theatre magna cum laude, Am. U., Washington, 1981. Appeared in (off Broadway) Ernest in Love, NYC, 1980; (plays) No Exit, Washington, 1985, Fefu and Her Friends, 1985, The Winters Tale, 1987, A Christmas Carol, 1987, Erpingham Camp, 1989, Turn of the Screw, 1989, Season's Greetings, 1986, Terra Nova, 1987, Mountain, 1990, Old Favorites, 1991, What the Butler Saw, 1993, Fawlty Towers, 1994, Last of the Red Hot Lovers, 1995, The Musical Comedy Murders of 1940, 1996, Move Over Mrs. Markham, 1997, Declarations: Love Letters of the Great Romantics, 1998, Present Laughter, 1999, Two, 1999, U.S.A., 2000, Blithe Spirit, 2002, A Midsummer Night's Dream, 2002, What The Butler Saw, 2003, Homebody, Kabul, 2003, Homebody/Kabul, 2003; (musical) The Cradle Will Rock, 2001; (films) Chances Are, 1989, Born Yesterday, 1993, North, 1993, Decade of Love, 1994, Wild Bill, 1994, The Tie That Binds, 1995, Independence Day, 1996, Play Me Again Sam, 1999, Love, 2000; (TV) Ancient Prophecies III, 1995, Friends, 1995, The Martin Short Show, 1995, Days of Our Lives, 1996, Love's Deadly Triangle: The Texas Cadet Murder, 1996, General Hospital, 1997, Port Charles, 1999, The Man Show, 1999, Titus, 2001; (music video) Johnny Sportcoat and the Casuals, 1987; (comml.) United Way, 1988. Mem. SAG, AFTRA, Actors Equity Assn., Phi Kappa Phi. Democrat. Roman Catholic. Avocations: equestrienne, golf, swimming, music, (cert.). E-mail: gilliandoyle@hotmail.com.

DOYLE, IRENE ELIZABETH, electronic sales executive, nurse; b. West Point, Iowa, Oct. 5, 1920; d. Joseph Deidrich and Mary Adelaide (Groene) Schulte; m. William Joseph Doyle, Feb. 3, 1956. RN, Mercy Hosp., 1941. Courier nurse Santa Fe R.R., Chgo., 1947-50; indsl. nurse Montgomery Ward, Chgo., 1950-54; rep. Hornblower & Weeks, Chgo., 1954-56; v.p. William J. Doyle Co., Chgo., 1956-80, Ormond Beach, Fla., 1980-88. Served with M.C., U.S. Army, 1942-46. Mem. Electronic Reps. Assn. Republican. Roman Catholic. Club: Oceanside Country (Ormond Beach).

DOYLE, JACQUELINE GRIFFITH LARCOMBE, psychologist; d. John Southey Larcombe, Jr. and Olive Kathleen Gallagher; m. Albert George Buehler, June 15, 1951 (div. Aug. 1958); 1 child, Jacqueline Elizabeth Buehler ; m. William Henri Doyle, Sept. 15, 1958 (div. Sept. 1968). Student, U. Md., 1951—53, student, 1956—57; BA in Speech Pathology and Psychology, MA in Psychology, U. N.Mex., 1959; postgrad., U. Calif., Berkeley, 1961—64. Lic. psychologist Mass., marriage and family therapist Calif., profl. clin. counselor N.Mex. Lectr. psychology U. Md., Seville, Spain, 1965—66; group coord., rsch. assoc. U. N.Mex., Albuquerque, 1967—69; dir. internat. program Esalen Inst., Big Sur, San Francisco, 1969—71; founder, dir. training Greenhouse, Inc., Boston, Cambridge, Mass., 1971—75; pvt. practice Cambridge, 1971—75, Belvedere, Calif., 1975—; clin. supr. Marin Treatment Ctr., San Rafael, Calif., 1978. Cons. Coca-Cola Co., US Social Security Adminstrn., Fed. Penitentiary Sys., Episcopal Dioceses, Mass. Dept. Mental Health. Co-founder, fellow Ctr. Coop. Global Devel., Am. U., Washington, 1981—85; trustee Planetary Citizens, 1982—89, Thornby Hall Project, 1982; gov. coun. Elmwood Inst., Berkeley, Calif., 1987; adv. com. Rollo May Ctr. Saybrook Inst., San Francisco, 1990—, trustee, 1991—2000. Rsch. fellow, NIMH, 1962—64. Democrat. Roman Catholic. Avocations: gardening, travel.

DOYLE, JENNIFER, surgical educator, scholar; b. Milw., Aug. 23, 1952; d. Sylvester Edward and Ethel Anna (Axmann) D. BA, Mt. Mary Coll., 1974; MA, U. Wis., Milw., 1979; postgrad., Brown U., 1979-84, Boston Coll., 2000—. Grad. tchg. asst. U. Wis., 1977-79; fellow Brown U., Providence, 1979-80, grad. teaching asst., 1981-84; adj. instr. Bryant Coll., Smithfield, R.I., 1985; adj. instr. history R.I. Coll., Providence, 1986-90; residency coord. dept. family medicine Brown U., Providence, 1986-87, edn. coord. dept. surgery, 1987-90; assoc. surgery Harvard Med. Sch., Boston, 1990-92, lectr. in surgery, 1992—; asst. dir. surg. edn. Deaconess Hosp., Boston, 1990-96; dir. ednl. devel. and evaluation Beth Israel Deaconess Med. Ctr., Boston, 1996—. Mem. instnl. assessment com. Sch. Medicine Brown U., 2000; inst. scholar Carl. J. Shapiro Inst. for Edn. and Rsch., Boston, 2000—. Dem. committeeman, Wauwatosa, Wis., 1976-78; mem. Big Sisters of R.I., Providence, 1980-88; co-organizer Providence Freeze Coalition, 1982; mem. instnl. assessment com. Brown U. Sch. Medicine, 2000-01. Recipient Charles Edison Meml. fellowship, 1974, Lucetta Bissell Meml. fellowship, 1978, univ. fellowship Brown U., 1979, Wayland Collegium fellowship Brown U., 1988. Mem. Am. Ednl. Rsch. Assn., Assn. Am. Med. Colls., Assn. Surg. Edn., Assn. Program Dirs. in Surgery (assoc.), Assn. of Women Surgeons (assoc.), Assn. for Study of Med. Edn. (U.K.), Generalists in Med. Edn., Am. Evaluation Assn., AAUW, Mass. Consort. on Faculty Devel. Home: 219 Willow St West Roxbury MA 02132-1326 Office: Beth Israel Deaconess Med Ctr Dept Surgery 110 Francis St Ste 3A Boston MA 02215-5501 Office Phone: 617-632-8632. E-mail: jdoyle@bidmc.harvard.edu., jennifer_doyle@hms.harvard.edu., jdoyle@bidmc.harvard.edu.

DOYLE, JUDITH MARIE, principal; d. William A. and Mary Alice Ryan; m. Mark F. Doyle, Aug. 1, 1980; children: Erin, Carleen, Keelin. BA, Ill. State U., 1980; M in Ednl. Adminstrn., St. Xavier U., 1988. Cert. type 10 cert., LD, EBD, EMH, TMH, type 75 ednl. adminstrn. Tchr. spl. edn. Sch. Dist. 103, Lyons, Ill., 1980—93, dir. spl. edn., 1993—2002, prin. home sch., 2002—. Mem. sch. bd. Our Lady of the Ridge, Chicago Ridge, Ill., 1993—2001, pres. sch. bd., 1999—2001. Mem.: ASCD, Ill. Spl. Found. Adminstrs., Ill. Prin. Assn. Avocations: reading, spending time with family, distance bike riding. E-mail: doylej@sd103.com.

DOYLE, JUDITH STOVALL, retired real estate executive; b. Dothan, Ala., Apr. 19, 1940; d. E. H. and Justine (Knowles) Stovall; m. John P. Doyle Jr., Aug. 22, 1964; children: John Patrick Doyle III, Michael D., Julie A. Boedicker. BS, Miss. State Coll. for Women, 1961. Tchr. math. Jr. H.S., Gulfport, Miss., 1961-62; asst. dir. dept. pub. rels. SUNY-Buffalo, 1962-64; tchr. math. Jr. H.S., Alexandria, Va., 1964-65, Auburn, N.Y., 1970-71; real estate agent Mosher Real Estate, Auburn, 1972-80, Doyle Real Estate, Auburn, 1991—. Active, past pres. Mercy Aux., Auburn; chairperson Owasco Township Bd. Assessment Rev., NY, 1976—98; com. person Dem. Com., Auburn, 1999—; v.p. coun. Sacred Heart Parish, Auburn, 1985—89; bd. dirs. Unity House, Auburn, 1985—87; bd. dirs. Cayuga County chpt. ARC, 1998—2001; bd. dirs. YMCA-WEIU, Auburn, membership com. mem., 1999—. Mem.: Ancient Order Hibernians (charter, ladies aux. #2 John F. Kennedy divsn.).

DOYLE, KRISTENE ANNE, psychologist, educator; b. N.Y.C., Oct. 5, 1972; d. Roger Christopher and Barbara Ann Doyle. BA, McGill U., 1994; MA with Distinction, Hofstra U., 1995, PhD, 1999. Lic. psychologist N.Y. Edn. Dept., 2000. Dir. clin. services Assn. Benefit Children, N.Y.C., 1999—2000; coordl. tng. and devel. Albert Ellis Inst., 2000—, dir. child and family svcs. clinic, 2000—, staff psychologist, 2000—, dir. clin. svcs., 2002—, assoc. exec. dir., 2003—. Adj. asst. prof. St. John's U., Jamaica, NY, 2000—. Co-author: Achieving Unconditional Self-Acceptance: Rational Emotive Behavior Therapy with a Depressed Woman, author: The Application of Rational Emotive Behavior Therapy In Women's Groups Therapy, My Idiosyncratic Practice of Rational Emotive Behavior Therapy, The Contribution of Social Psychology to Rational Emotive Behavior Therapy; mem. editl. bd.: Jour. Rational-Emotive and Cognitive-Behavior Therapy, 2002—. Fellow: Albert Ellis Inst.; mem.: APA, Assn. Advancement Behavior Therapy (chair inst. ann. psychol. conv. 2002—). Office: Albert Ellis Inst 45 East 65th St New York NY 10021 Personal E-mail: krisdoyle@msn.com. E-mail: krisdoyle@msn.com.

DOYLE, NANCY CAROLYN, writer; b. Taunton, Mass., Mar. 19, 1931; d. Herbert A. and Mildred (Sylvander) D. BA, Boston U., 1954; MA, Wellesley Coll., 1956. Rsch. and tng. asst. Wellesley (Mass.) Coll., 1954-56; press dir. United Fund Greater Boston, 1957-60; writer Mental Health Materials, N.Y.C., 1960-62, Nat. League Nursing, N.Y.C., 1962-65, Am. Lung Assn., N.Y.C., 1967-86; assoc. Am. Lung Assn. Greater Norfolk, Walpole, Mass., 1986-95. Author: The Dying Person and the Family, 1975, Smoking: A Habit to be Broken, 1979, Involuntary Smoking, 1987. Pres. Friends of Taunton (Mass.) Pub. Libr., 1993-95; bd. dirs. Star Players, Taunton, 1987-92. Mem. AAUW, Phi Beta Kappa, Sigma Xi. Avocations: tennis, travel, reading. Home: 20 Fairview Ave Taunton MA 02780-4413

DOYLE, NANCY HAZLETT, artist; b. Wilmington, Del., July 8, 1947; d. Theodore Jay and Catherine L. (Lynch) Hazlett; m. Michael Doyle, Nov. 20, 1982 (div. 1985). BS in Art Edn., Moore Coll. of Art, 1969; MFA in Painting, Pa. State U., 1975. Tchr. Chester County Juvenile Detention Home, Embreeville, Pa., 1972—73; instr. Pa. State U., State College, 1975—77; artist Chester County Art Assn., West Chester, Pa., 1977—78. One person shows include Pattee Meml. Libr., Pa. State U., University Park, 1974, Cygnet Framing Studio, West Chester, 1986, Va. Lippincott Gallery, Phoenixville, Pa., 1992, Agapè Gallery, Malvern, Pa., 1994; exhibited in group shows Coll. Arts and Arch., Zoller Gallery, Pa. State U., University Park, 1974-75, Erie (Pa.) Art Ctr., 1975, Corcoran Gallery, Washington, 1975, Juniata Coll., Huntingdon, Pa., 1976, Daisy Jamison Soroptomist Ann. Invitational Show, West Chester, 1979-82, Yellow Springs Ann. Art Show, Chester Springs, Pa., 1986-98, Chester County Art Assn. Invitational, 1986-88, Artworks Gallery, Kennett Square, Pa., 1992-95, Main Line Art Ctr., Haverford, Pa., 1994-96, Jun Gallery, Phila., 1994, Leslie Eadeh Art Gallery, Devon, Pa., 1995, Hardcastle Gallery, Wilmington, Del., 1996, Ctr. for Creative Arts, Hockessin, Del., 1997-2000, Del. Ctr. Contemporary Arts, Wilmington, 2001-03. Recipient grad. assistantships Pa. State U., 1973-75. Mem.: Del. Ctr. for Contemporary Arts, New Castle County Irish Soc. Democrat. Avocations: photography, crafts, reading, webmaster. Personal E-mail: ndoylebus@cs.com.

DOYLE, PATRICIA R. state representative; b. Sheridan, Wyo., Feb. 1, 1950; m. Daniel R. Doyle; four children. AA, Burlington Coll., 1970; BA, U. Vt., 1981. Commr. Chittenden Solid Waste Mgmt. Dist.; state rep. Vt. Ho. of Reps., 1996—. Chair Richmond Village Trustees, 1985-90; mem. Richmond Water and Sewer Commrs., 1985-93, Richmond Selectboard, 1990-93; mem. Vt. Health Policy Coun., 1990-93; bd. dirs. Chittenden County Child Care Resource. Home: PO Box 327 Richmond VT 05477-0327

DOYLE, REBECCA CARLISLE, state agency administrator; m. Ken Doyle; children: Eric, Ben. BS, U. Ill., 1975, MS, 1977. Pvt. practice, Ill.; dir. Ill. Agriculture Dept., Springfield, 1991—. Mem. Internat. Agriculture Mgmt. Assn., Nat. Assn. State Depts. Agriculture (officer), Mid-Am. Internat. Agri-Trade Council (officer), Women Execs. State Govt. Office: Illinois Dept Agriculture State Fairgrounds PO Box 19281 Springfield IL 62794-9281

DOZIER, ELEANOR CAMERON, computer company executive, writer; b. N.Y.C., May 20, 1939; d. Robert Paul and Marion Gill MacNeil; m. Norman Garlan Dozier, June 23, 1989; children: Karen Gonzales, Robert Bennett, Heidi Bennett, Julia, Ian, Jordan. Rep. to British Isles Max Factor, Inc., Hollywood, Calif., 1966—71; co-owner; also songwriter and poet MacNeil Dozier Pub. Co., Pembroke Pines, Fla., 1988—2002; v.p. Computer Dimensions Network Corp., N.Y.C., 1998—. Mktg. dir. Prometheus Devel., San Jose, Calif., 1986—87. Author: (book) O For The Love Of God!, 2003. Recipient commn., Stephen Ministry, Order St. Luke. Episcopalian. Avocations: bicycling, golf, tennis, travel. Business E-Mail: call4ecd1@hotmail.com.

DOZIER, KIMBERLY, reporter; BA in Human Rights and Spanish, Wellesley Coll., 1987; MA in Fgn. Affairs, U. Va., 1993. Reporter Energy Daily, Washington, 1988—91; reporter Christian Sci. Monitor, Cairo, 1993—95, Washington Post, Cairo, 1993, CBS News Radio and Voice of Am., Cairo, 1994—95, San Francisco Chronicle, Cairo, 1995; radio anchor BBC World Update, London, 1996—2001; reporter, bur chief CBS News, CBS Radio News, London, 1996—2001; chief corr. Jerusalem Bur. CBS 2. Recipient Alumnae Travel award, U. Va., 1993, Grand Gracie award, Am. Women in Radio and TV, 2000, Gracie award, 2000, 2001. Office: CBS 524 57th St New York NY 10019

DOZIER, THERESE KNECHT, educational association administrator, educator; BA in Social Studies Edn., U. Fla., 1974, MEd in Secondary Social Studies, 1976; EdD in Curriculum and Instrn., U. S.C., 1995; LHD (hon.), Winthrop Coll., 1985, U. S.C., 1985. Tchr. Lincoln Mid. Sch., Gainesville, Fla., 1974—76, Miami Edison Mid. Sch., Fla., 1976—77, Singapore Am. Sch., Singapore, 1986—89, Irmo H.S., Columbia, SC, 1977—85, 1989—90, 1992—93; instr. and coord. profl. devel. schs. U. S.C., Columbia, 1991—92; spl. advisor on tchg. to U.S. Sec. of Edn. Richard W. Riley U.S. Dept. Edn., Washington, 1993—97, sr. advisor on tchg. to U.S. Sec. of Edn. Richard W. Riley, 1997—2001; nat. tchr.-in-residence and assoc. prof., dir. ctr. tchr. leadership Sch. Edn. Va. Commonwealth U., Richmond, 2001—. Mem. Nat. Conf. State Legislatures Task-force on Sch. Leadership, Nat. Com. on Tchr. Mobility, Com. to Enhance K-12 Tchg. Profession in Va., Va. State Action for Ednl. Leadership Consortium; mem. adv. bd. Nat. Tchr. Recruitment Clearinghouse; mem. adv. panel SRI Internat.'s Study of Alt. Cert. of Tchrs.; mem. meritorious new tchr. com. Mid-Atlantic Regional Tchr. Project; advisor rural initiative Nat. Bd. Profl. Tchg. Stds.; mem. policy and planning coun. Met. Ednl. Rsch. Consortium; advisor DeWitt-Wallace Reader's Digest Found. Tchr. Leadership Initiative; mem. acad. coun. Nat. Inst. Cmty. Innovations Internat. Grad. Ctr.; sr. counsel on tchr. quality issues Widmeyer Comm.; cons. N. Ctrl. Regional Lab. Profl. Devel. Ctr., Asian-Pacific Econ. Coun. Tchr. Devel. Web Portal Project, NBPTS Prin.'s Initiative; presenter in field; bd. dirs. Coun. Basic Edn. Named Nat. Tchr. of Yr., 1985, S. Carolinian of Yr., 1985, Alumna of Outstanding Achievement, U. Fla., 1997; recipient Disting. Alumnus award U. Fla., 1985, Nat. Jefferson award for outstanding pub. svc. benefiting local communities, 1986, Hammer award for helping to make govt. more efficient and effective V.P. Gore, 1995; named to the Order of the Palmetto, 1985; Fulbright-Hays fellow to China, 1985; Holmes scholar U. S.C., 1991-93.

DRABINOWICZ, A. THERESA, state legislator; b. Nashua, N.H., Nov. 4, 1923; d. Raymond Harvey LaValley and Alice Jane Enright; m. Stanley Frank Drabinowicz, 1949 (div.); 1 child, John Michael. AB, Nashua, 1957; student, River Coll., 1997—. Chairwoman 4th Ward Dem. Com., Nashua, 1965-67; pres. Dem. Women's Club, Nashua, 1965-67; N.H. state rep. Dist. 17 4th Ward, 1969-72, Dist. 32, Hillsborough Dist. 36, 1993—; mem. labor, indsl. and rehab. coms. N.H. Ho. of Reps. Rep. to Gen. Ct. N.H., 1989—; mem. Ranking Dem. Legis. Svc. Commn.; computer disk coater Nashua Corp., 1974-89. Pres. Sports Award, Nat. Police Meml. Assn., 1993; active Crime Watch, Nashua Ward 4, F [illegible] 1993. Recipient Cert. of Appreciation, Am. Police Acad., 1983, Liberty and Justice award of merit, Am. Police Legion Honor medal Hall of Fame Mus., 1986; black belt Kenpo Karate, Ind. Karate Sch., 1989, black belt Enshudo Jyu jitsu, 1989. Mem. VFW Aux. (life, state pres. 1959-60), DAV Aux. (life, aux. comdr., state adjutant 1963-64), Nat. Law Enforcement Assn. (CB radio posse 1975-89), Nat. Assn. Physically Handicapped (life, nat. edn.). Office: State House 107 N Main St Concord NH 03301-4951

DRACUP, KATHLEEN ANNE, nursing educator; b. Santa Monica, Calif., Sept. 28, 1942; d. Paul Joseph and Lucy Elizabeth (Milligan) Molloy; children: Jeffrey, Jonathan, Joy, Jan, Brian. BS in Nursing, St. Xavier's Coll., Chgo., 1967; M of Nursing, U. Calif., L.A., 1974; D of Nursing Sci., U. Calif., San Francisco, 1982. Clin. nurse Little Co. of Mary Hosp., Chgo., 1967-70, UCLA Med. Ctr., 1970-74; asst. clin. prof. U. Calif., L.A., 1974-78, rsch. fellow dept. medicine, 1979-81, asst. prof. to prof., 1982-99; clin. nurse U. Calif. San Francisco Med. Ctr., 1979; pvt. practice psychotherapist, 1980—; dean, sch. nursing U. Calif., San Francisco, 2000-. Editor Heart and Lung Jour., 1981-91, Am. Jour. Critical Care, 1991—; editor Critical Care Nursing Series; contbr. chpts. to books, articles to profl. jours. Recipient Eugene Brunwald Acad. Mentorship award Am. Heart Assn., 2003; Disting. Practitioner Nat. Acad., Washington, 1987; Fulbright Sr. scholar, 1995. Fellow Coun. Cardiovascular Nursing, Am. Heart Assn., Am. Assn. Cardiopulmonary Rehab.; mem. Inst. of Medicine, Am. Nurses' Assn., Am. Assn. Critical Care Nurses (life), Sigma Theta Tau. Office: UCSF Sch Nursing 2 Koret Way Rm N319 San Francisco CA 94143-0604 E-mail: kathydracup@nursing.ucsf.edu.

DRAEGER, SUSANNE YARBROUGH, interior designer; b. Macon, Ga., July 16, 1950; d. Ceasar Augustus and Dorothy Anne (Patrick) Yarbrough; m. Charles Fred Newberry July 29, 1972 (div.); children: Catherine Neil, Charles Fred; m. Eric R. Stanley May, 1988 (div.); m. Lawrence William Draeger March 15, 1996. BSHE in Interior Design, U. Ga., 1972. Cert. ASID, IGD Am. Soc. Interior Designers, Inst. Bus. Designers. Interior designer Et Cetera, Inc., Athens, Ga., 1972-74; with Athens Federal Savings and Loan, Ga., 1974-77; co-owner, sr. designer Athens Interiors, Inc., Athens, Ga., 1974-77; independent interior designer Arlington, Va., 1978-82; interior designer Horizon Trading Co., Inc., Washington, 1983-84; pres., interior designer Nova Internat., Inc., Washington, 1984-94, Nova Europe, Inc., Washington, Paris, France, 1994-96; researcher Interior Design, 1996—. Selected NEA collection Nat. Endowment for the Arts, Am. Consulate Osaka, Japan, 1986. Significant projects with NOVA Europe include: Chevron Oil & Gas, Tengischevroil, Salans, Hertzfeld & Heilbronn, U.S. Agy. for Internat. Devel. in Budapest, Rabat, and Sofia, 1994-96; with NOVA Internat., Inc. U.S. consulate Bldg. Osaka, Japan, Am. consulate staff housing, Hong Kong, SATO for U.S. Mil. in Fed. Repub. West Germany, Mobil Oil, Aldwych House, London, UK, U.S. Dept. State staff housing worldwide, Turner Internat. Industries, N.Y., Peace Vector II Project, Beni Suef, Egypt, US Army Corps of Engrs., Transatlantic Divsn., Am. Internat. Contractors, Ins., Arlington, Va., Peace Vector IV Project, Sakara Egypt, 1984-94; others include Univ. Ga. Law Sch. Offices, Am. Embassies Cairo, Ankara, Islamabad, U.S. Consulate Building Osaka, Japan, Am. Consulate staff housing Hong Kong, Mobil Oil Aldwych House, London, Am. Embassies in Paris, Madrid, Islamabad, Minsk, Sofia and Athens. Vol. Alexandria Hosp., 1985-88. Episcopalian. Avocations: aerobic exercises, swimming, travel, oil painting. Home: 2409 Military Rd Arlington VA 22207-3907

DRAELOS, ZOE DIANA, dermatologist, consultant; b. Milw., Oct. 13, 1958; d. Dimitri Basil and Lorene June (Legan) Kececioglu; m. Michael Draelos, June 14, 1980; children: Mark, Matthew. BSME, U. Ariz., 1979, MD, 1983. Diplomate Am. Bd. Dermatology. Physician in solo dermatology practice, High Point, NC, 1988—. Cons., owner Dermatology Cons. Svcs., High Point, 1990—. Author: Cosmetics in Dermatology, 1995, Atlas of Cosmetic Dermatology, 2000. Rhodes scholar, Oxford, Eng., 1979. Office: Zoe Diana Draelos MD PA 2444 N Main St High Point NC 27262-7833 E-mail: zdraelos@northstate.net.

DRAGAN, ALEXANDRA, mechanical engineer, consultant, environmental engineer, researcher, engineering educator; d. Ioan and Arety Elena Dragan; 1 child, Miruna Roxanna. BME, MME, U. Bucharest Polytechnica, Romania, 1964; M in Environ. Engring., U. So. Calif., 1993; DEng, U. Constrn., Bucharest, 1998. Registered profl. engr., Calif., N.Y. From engr. to sr. engr. Designing Inst. for Wood Industry, Bucharest, 1967—73; cons. engr. FOREXIM/Technoforest, Bucharest, 1973—76; engr. Jack Stone Engrs., N.Y.C., 1978—81; from sr. engr. to group leader Haines Lundberg Waehler, N.Y.C., 1981—84; from sr. engr. to assoc. Syska and Hennessy, L.A., 1984—86; pvt. practice L.A., Calif., 1984—; chief engr. Donald Dickerson Assoc., L.A., 1986—88; dir. engring. Nat. Air Sys., L.A., 1988; from sr. engr. to supervising mech. engr. III County of L.A. Dept. Pub. Works, Alhambra, Calif., 1988—. Pres. Dragan Engring., L.A., 1984—98; prof. mech. engring. U. Politehnica of Bucharest, 2000—01, prof. emeritus, 2001—. Author: Thermal Processes and Power Generation in Wood Industry, 1973. Recipient Value Engring. award, County of L.A., 1986, Environ. Sci. and Engring. fellow, AAAS and US EPA, 1992. Mem.: ASHRAE (Cert. of Appreciation 1993—94, Symposium Paper award 2001), Internat. Soc. Indoor Air Quality and Climate, Am. Romanian Acad. for Arts and Scis. (exec. com. 2001). Republican. Avocation: singing. Home: 350 N Palm Dr Apt 402 Beverly Hills CA 90210 Personal E-mail: draganalexandra@yahoo.com.

DRAKE, ANN M. consumer products company executive; d. James and Mary Lou McIlrath; m. John Drake, II; stepchildren: Joanna, Tracy. B in English, U. Iowa, 1969; MBA, Northwestern U., 1984. Founder, prin. Camwilde Interiors; exec. v.p. DSC Logistics, DesPlaines, Ill., 1990—92, CEO, 1992—. Bus. adv. com. Northwestern U. Transp. Ctr. Mem.: Chgo. Network, Com. of 200. Office: DSC Logistics 1750 S Wolf Rd Des Plaines IL 60018*

DRAKE, CAROLYN A. administrative assistant; b. Lockwood, Mo., Jan. 13, 1943; d. Frenk Dirk and Abbie Dean (Cowan) Stolting; m. Stephen Dean Drake, Aug. 15, 1964; children: Eric Chadwick, Rachelle Alene. BS, N.W. Mo. State U., Maryville, 1964; student, U. Wyo., Laramie, Eastern Mich. U., Ypsilanti. Cert. h.s. tchr., Mich.; lic. travel agt. Tchr. King City (Mo.) H.S., 1964-67, Dept. Def. Schs., Clark AFB, Philippines, 1968-69; advt. rep. Seaway Rev., Glen Arbor, Mich., 1981-83; asst. Dennos Museum Ctr., Traverse City, Mich., 1991—. Co-dir. Sci./Math. Inst. Tchr., Traverse City, 1986-89, asst. to dir., 1982-86. Officer, PTO Traverse City; coach Odyssey of the Mind, Trverse City; directoress St. Anne's Altar Guild, Traverse City, 1990—. Recipient Margaret Morse Nice award Wilson Ornithol. Soc., Ann Arbor, Mich., 1988. Episcopalian. Avocations: reading, hiking, wood carving, photography, coin collecting/numismatics.

DRAKE, ELISABETH MERTZ, chemical engineer, consultant; b. N.Y.C., Dec. 20, 1936; d. John and Ruth (Johnson) Mertz; m. Alvin William Drake, July 31, 1957 (div. 1984); 1 child, Alan Lee. SB in Chem. Engring., MIT, 1958, ScD in Chem. Engring., 1966. Registered profl. engr., Mass. Staff engr. Arthur D. Little Inc., Cambridge, Mass., 1958-64, sr. staff, 1966-76, mgr. risk analysis, 1977-82, v.p. tech. risk mgmt., 1980-82, 86-89, cons., 1990-94; assoc. dir. new tech. MIT Energy Lab., 1990-2000, dir., 1994-95, cons., 2000—; lectr. U. Calif., Berkeley, 1971; vis. prof. MIT, Cambridge, 1973-74; chmn. chem. engring. dept. Northeastern U., Boston, 1982-86. Corp. mgr. MIT, 1981-86; mem. tech. pipeline safety stds. com. U.S. Dept. Transp., 1980-85; mem. mng. bd. AIChE, 1988-90; vice chair com. on rev. and evaluation on army chem. stockpile disposal program NRC, 1993-98, mem., 2002-2004, vice chair com. on chem. demil., 2004—. Contbr. articles to profl. jours.; inventor fractionation method and apparatus, 1972. Fellow AIChE (bd. dirs. 1987-90); mem. AAAS, NAE, Am. Chem. Soc., Sigma Xi. Home: 30F Inman St Cambridge MA 02139-2411 E-mail: edrake@alum.mit.edu.

DRAKE, EVELYN DOWNIE, secondary school educator; b. Longmont, Colo., Aug. 23, 1940; d. Milford West and Colette Dorothy (Mraz) Downie; m. Sherman Hoffman Drake, May 18, 1963 (div. 1971); children: Marcella Colette Drake-Bettis, Sherman Downie Drake; m. Robert Dale Mager, July 14, 1975 (div. 1981). BS, U. Wyo., 1962; MA, U. No. Colo., 1980; postgrad., U. Edinburgh, Scotland, 1982, Cambridge U., Eng., 1986. Cert. tchr./vocat. tchr., Colo. Sec./receptionist Barnard Realty, Casper, Wyo., 1959-61, Pure Oil Co. (now UNOCAL), Casper, 1961; coord., tchr. St. Mark's Pre-Sch., Casper, 1965; reporter, feature writer Casper Star-Tribune, Casper, 1970-71; instr., tchr. Casper Coll., 1964-69; tchr. home econs. Kelly Walsh High Sch., 1971-72; tchg. asst. U. No. Colo., Greeley, 1979-80; tchr. of English, journalism, art, home econs. Jefferson County R-1 Schs., Golden, Colo., 1972—97. Cons., tchr. Casper North Side Ctr., 1969-71. Artist: weaving exhibit, Pub. Libr., Casper, 1968, others. Ctrl. com. Jefferson County Democrats, Lakewood, Colo., 1989—; candidate bd. dirs. Green Mt. Townhouse Corp. #1 Lakewood, 1987; tchr. Lakewood Sister Cities Exch. Program to Miranda, New South Wales, Sutherlandshire, Australia, 1995. Nominated Colo. Tchr. of Yr., Evergreen (Colo.) Jr. High, 1989. Mem. Colo. Lang. Arts Soc., Nat. Coun. Tchrs. of English (planning com. nat. conf. 1989-90), NEA (faculty rep.), Colo. Educators Assn. (faculty rep.), JCEA Edn. Assn. (faculty rep.), Denver Press Club, Phi Delta Kappa (sec. 1995-96), Delta Kappa Gamma, others. Avocations: art, lit., writing, Western history

DRAKE, GRACE L. retired state senator, cultural organization administrator; b. New London, Conn., May 25, 1926; d. Daniel Harvey and Marion Gertrude (Wiech) Driscoll; m. William Lee Drake, June 9, 1946 (dec.); 1 child, Sandra Drake Sparber. With Am. Photographic Corp., N.Y.C., 1944-72; senator State of Ohio, Columbus, 1984—2001; dir. Ohio Ctr. Advancement Women in Pub. Svc., 2001—. Chairwoman Cuyahoga County Rep. Exec. Commn.; mem. Leadership Cleve., March of Dimes Metro and State Bd., HealthSpace Cleve. Bd., Masonic Learning Ctrs. Bd., Positive Edn. Program Bd., Coun. on Older Persons Bd., Northeast Ohio Nursing Initiative Bd. Named Legislator of the Yr., Rep. Legis.'s Assn., 1988; named to Ohio Women's Hall of Fame, 1995; recipient Meritorious Svc. award, Ohio State U., 2001, Ctr. for Health Affairs, 2001, Pub. Affairs award, March of Dimes, 2001. Roman Catholic. Avocations: bridge, golf. Home: 5954 Briardale Ln Solon OH 44139-2302 Office: Cleve State Univ 2121 Euclid Ave UR 140 Cleveland OH 44115 Business E-Mail: gdrake@urban.csuohio.edu.

DRAKE, JEANETTE WENIG, communications educator, public relations consultant, writer; b. Marion, OH, Mar. 14, 1963; d. Dwight L. and Mildred D. Wenig; m. Jeffrey P. Drake, Oct., 22, 1994. BA in Advt., Ohio State U., 1985, MA in Journalism, 1993; postgrad., Bowling Green State U., 1999—. cert. in pub. rels., Pub. Rels. Soc. of Am. Dir. advt. and pub. rels. The DeSantis Group, Columbus, OH, 1985-91; dir. comm. YMCA of Ctrl. Ohio, Columbus, 1991-93; co-founder, editor Perimeter Sun, Columbus 1993-95; marketing dir. The Prime Group, Washington C.H., OH, 1993 94; editor, mng. editor Ohio State U., Columbus, OH, 1994-98; asst. prof. U. Findlay, OH, 1998—. Pub. rels. cons., 1994—; bd. mem. Henry Co. Arts Coun., Napoleon, OH, 1999—, Campus Compact, Findlay, OH, 1999—; leader internat. exchange YMCA to Japan, 1992. Regional editor: Dialogue, 1999—; contbr. articles, essays to profl. pubs. Vol. Franklin Co. Children's Svcs., 1994—; cons. Concerned Citizens, OH, 1994—. Recipient Addy award campaign advt. fedn. YMCA, 1991, English award United Way, Columbus, 1993, Savvy award Retail Marketers Assn., 1994, Presdl. Things Gone Right award Ohio State U., 1998, Communicators award, 2001. Mem. Nat. Comm. Assn., Pub. Rels. Soc. of Am. (cert., v.p.), Ctrl. States Comm. Assn., Ohio State Alumni Assn. Avocations: traveling, glassblowing, poetry, writing, backpacking. Office: 1000 N Main St Findlay OH 45840-3653 E-mail: drake@findlay.edu.

DRAKE, MIRIAM ANNA, librarian, educator, writer; b. Boston, Dec. 20, 1936; d. Max Frederick and Beatrice Celia (Mitnick) Engleman; m. John Warren Drake, Dec. 19, 1960 (div. Dec. 1985); 1 child, Robert Warren. BS, Simmons Coll., Boston, 1958, MLS, 1971; postgrad., Harvard U., 1959-60; LHD (hon.), Ind. U., 1994; DLS (hon.), Simmons Coll., 1997. Assoc. United Rsch., Cambridge, Mass., 1958-61; with mktg. svcs. Kenyon & Eckhardt, Boston, 1963-65; cons. Boston, 1965-72; head rsch. unit libraries Purdue U., West Lafayette, Ind., 1972-76, asst. dir. libraries, prof. library sci., 1976-84; dean, dir. libraries, prof. Ga. Inst. Tech., Atlanta, 1984-2001, prof. emerita, 2001—. Trustee Online Computer Libr. Ctr., Inc., 1978-84, chair, 1980-83; trustee Corp. for Rsch. and Edn. Networking, 1991-94, U.S. Depository Libr. Coun., 1991-94, Simmons Coll., 1999-2004; trustee, corporator adv. bd. Engring. Info., 1997—. Author: User Fees: A Practical Perspective, 1981, Information Today, 2002; co-author: (with James Matarazzo) Information for Management, 1994; editor: Ency. Libr. Info. Sci., 2nd edit.; mem. editl. bd. Coll. and Rsch. Librs. Jour., 1985-90, Librs. and Microcomputers Jour., 1983-93, Sci. and Tech. Librs., 1989-98, Database, 1989-97; contbr. chpts. to books, articles to profl. jours. Recipient Alumni Achievement award Simmons Coll. Sch. Libr. and Info. Sci., 1985, Kent Meckler Media award U. Pitts., 1994. Fellow: Nat. Fedn. of Abstracting and Indexing Svs. (hon.); mem.: ALA (councilor at large 1985—89, Hugh Atkinson Meml. award 1992), Assn. Info. and Dissemination Ctrs. (pres. 2001—03), Spl. Librs. Assn. (pres.-elect 1992—93, pres. 1993—94, H.W. Wilson award 1983, John Cotton Dana award 2002), Am. Soc. Info. Sci., Am. Mgmt. Assn. Office: Ga Inst Tech Lib Info Ctr Atlanta GA 30332-0900 E-mail: mdrake@library.gatech.edu., mdrake@bellsouth.net.

DRAKE, PATRICIA EVELYN, psychologist; b. Lewiston, Maine, Feb. 9, 1946; d. Lewis and Anita (Bilodeau) D.; m. Colin Matthew Fuller, May 13, 1973 (div. Aug. 1983); children: R. Matthew, Meaghan Merry. Diploma, St. Mary's Sch. Nursing, 1967; BS, U. Nev., 1985; MA, Calif. Sch. Profl. Psychology, 1987, PhD, 1989. RN. Nurse Maine Med. Ctr., Portland, 1967-73, U. Calif. Sacramento Med. Ctr., 1973-78, Ben Taub Hosp., Houston, 1978-79; psychology intern Shasta County Mental Health Ctr., Redding, Calif., 1988-89, clin. psychologist, 1989-91, tng. dir., chief psychology, 1991—; psychologist pvt. practice, Redding, Calif., 1991—. Mem. AAUW, APA, Calif. Psychol. Assn., Shasta-Cascade Psychol. Assn., Phi Kappa Phi. Democrat. Roman Catholic. Avocations: swimming, cross-country skiing, crafts. Office: Shasta County Mental Health 2640 Breslauer Way Redding CA 96001-4246 Office Phone: 530-225-5980. E-mail: pdrake@co.shasta.ca.us.

DRAKE, ROBYN RENÉE (ROBYN FIELDER), writer, painter, equestrian; b. Carroll, Iowa, Jan. 9, 1964; d. Leslie Mac and Fern Marjorie (Schelldorf) Fielder. BA in Painting, BA in Drawing, BA in Art History, Drake U., Des Moines, 1997. Artist DeLaurent Fine Arts, Chgo., 1989-90; svc. mgr. Art Shuttle, Inc., Chgo., 1990-94; cons. Rita Bucheit Ltd., Chgo., 1994-96, Feigen Gallery, Chgo., 1995-98; cons., adminstr. Genesis Artists Village, Chgo., 1997—; cons., artist Kozan Studios, Chgo., 1998-99. Guest panelist Capricon Lit. Conv., Oak Brook, Ill., 1997-99, Windycon Lit. Conv., Schaumburg, Ill., 1997-99, World Fantasy Conv., Monterey, Calif., 1998, Providence, R.I., 1999. Author: The Wind at Tres Castillos, 1999; contbg. artist Ency. Living Artists, 11th edit., 1999. Recipient Cert. of Outstanding Achievement NASA, 1979, Open Five Gaited Champion Midwest, 1980, Midwest Saddleseat Equitation Runner-up, 1980. Mem. Degerberg Acad. Martial Arts (savate 1998, 99, Most Fit Female 1998, U.S. Savate Team nominee 2000). Avocations: horses, scuba diving, dance. Office: The Iff Theatre LLC PO Box 25786 Chicago IL 60625-0786 Home: 37375 N Hunt Club Rd Old Mill Creek IL 60083-9693 E-mail: savateuse@aol.com.

DRAKE, SYLVIE (JURRAS DRAKE), theater critic; b. Alexandria, Egypt, Dec. 18, 1930; came to U.S., 1949, naturalized, 1952; d. Robert and Simonette (Barda) Franco; m. Kenneth K. Drake, Apr. 29, 1952 (div. Dec. 1972); children— Jessica, Robert I.; m. Ty Jurras, June 16, 1973. M. Theater Arts, Pasadena Playhouse, 1969. Free-lance TV writer, 1962-68; theater critic Canyon Crier, L.A., 1968-72; theater critic, columnist L.A. Times, 1971-91, theater critic, 1991-93, theatre critc emeritus, 1993—; lit. dir. Denver Ctr. Theatre Co., 1985; pres. L.A. Drama Critics Circle, 1979-81, free lance travel writer, translator, book reviewer. Mem. Pulitzer Prize Drama Jury, 1994; adv. bd. Nat. Arts Journalism Program, 1994-97. Dir. publs. Denver Ctr. for the Performing Arts, 1994—; artistic assoc. for spl. projects Denver Ctr. Theatre Co., 1994—. Mem. Am. Theater Critics Assn. Office: Denver Ctr Performing Arts 1245 Champa St Denver CO 80204-2100

DRAKE, THELMA DAY, state legislator; b. Elyria, Ohio, Nov. 20, 1949; Grad. high sch. Mem. Va. State Legis., 1996—, mem. transp. com., mem. fin. com., mem. labor & commerce com., mem. claims com. Republican. Mem. United Ch. of Christ. Office: Gen Assembly Bldg POB ox 406 OFC# 717 Richmond VA 23218

DRAKEMAN, LISA N. biotechnology company executive; b. Boston, Oct. 30, 1953; d. Paul and Josephine (Covino) Natale; m. Donald L. Drakeman, Aug. 23, 1975; children: Cynthia Leigh Drakeman, Amy Elizabeth Drakeman. BA, Mt. Holyoke Coll., 1975; MA, Rutgers U., 1983, Princeton U., 1986, PhD, 1988. Chair, v. chair Monclair (N.J.) Redevelopment Agy., 1981-84; vis. scholar Dartmouth Coll., 1988-89; lectr. Princeton U., 1989-92; asst. dir. Alumni Coun. of Princeton U., 1991; dir. administrn. Medarex, Inc., Princeton, N.J., 1991-94, v.p. adminstrn., 1994-96, v.p., 1996-98, sr. v.p., head bus. devel., 1998-2000; CEO Genmab A/S, 1999—. Faculty fellow Grad. Coll. Princeton U., 1991-93, mem. adv. coun. dept. religion, 1996—; bd. dirs. Medarex Europe, B.V., GenPharm. Internat., Inc. Biopharm. adv. coun. Tech. Coun. Greater Phila., 1993-96; Gov.'s Biopharm. Task Force N.J. Econ. Master Plan Commn., Trenton, 1994-95; biotech. adv. com. The Franklin Inst., Phila., 1994-96; commr. Prosperity N.J., 1995-2000. Garden State grad. fellow State of N.J., 1981-85; named to N.J. High Tech. Hall of Fame, 2000. Mem. Soc. for Advancement of Women's Health Rsch. (steering com., corp. adv. coun. 1994-97), Biotech. Industry Orgn. (chair nat. capital formation task force 1995-98, Advocate of Yr. award 1995), Biotech. Coun. N.J. (v.p. 1996-2000, Outstanding Industry Woman of Yr. 1996). Home: 49 Rolling Hill Rd Skillman NJ 08558-2319 Office: 457 N Harrison St Princeton NJ 08540 also: Genmab A/S Toldbodgade 33 DK 1253 Copenhagen K Denmark

DRANTZ, VERONICA ELLEN, science educator and consultant; b. Chgo., Sept. 5, 1943; d. Albert William and Veronica Grace (Crowe) D. BS with high honors, U. Ill., Urbana, 1965, MS, 1969; PhD, De Paul U., Chgo., 1987. Biol. sci. forensic analytical chemist Chgo. Police Dept., Chgo., 1970-72, asst. head forensic analytical chemist, 1972-74; instr. Evanston Hosp. Sch. Anesthesia, Chgo., 1975—; Fort West Univ., Chgo., 1982-84, dir. biol. and phys. sciences, 1984—, asst. prof., 1987-88, assoc. prof., 1988-91, prof., 1991—, dir. electroneurodiagnostic technology program, 1988—; asst. prof. in MS of nursing DePaul U., Chgo., 1989—. Spkr. Ill. Assn. Nurse Anesthetists, 1978-80, Ill. Soc. Electroneurodiagnostic Tech., 1986—, Am. Soc. Electroneurodiagnostic Tech., 1994—; sci. cons., spkr. Chgo. Tchrs. Ctr., 1989; instr. Chgo. Heart Assn., 1989—. Co-author: Population Genetics A BSCS Self Instructional Prog., 1969 Recipient Rsch. assistantship NSF, U. Ill., 1965-66, Rsch. Fellowship NSF, U. Ill., 1966-70, Schmidt Acad. fellowship Schmidt Found., DePaul U., 1975-80, Cardiopulmonary Resuscitation award Chgo. Heart Assn., 1990. Mem. Phi Beta Kappa. Avocations: camping, hiking, nature study, photography, computers, gardening. Office: 4942 W School St Chicago IL 60641-4340 E-mail: drdrantz@msn.com.

DRAPALIK, BETTY R. volunteer, artist, educator; b. Cicero, Ill., July 4, 1932; d. Henry William and Jennie Margaret (Robbins) Degen; m. Joseph James Drapalik, Oct. 30, 1951; children: Betty Jennifer Drapalik Coryell, Joseph Henry. Grad., HS, Cicero. Sec., clk. Gt. Lakes (Ill.) Naval Base, until 1982; sect. to asst. dir. Arden Shore Boys' Home, Lake Bluff, Ill., 1984-87; substitute tchr. art Visual Art Ctr., Waukegan, Ill. Exhibited in group shows at Layson Gallery, Waukegan, Ill., 1993, Cmty. Gallery Art, Coll. Lake County, Grayslake, Ill., 1993—94, David Adler Cultural Ctr., Libertyville, Ill., 1994, Women's Works, Old Courthouse Art Ctr., Woodstock, Ill., 1994—95, Anderson Art Ctr., Kenosha, Wis., 1994—2002, one-woman shows include Jack Benny Ctr. Arts, 1995, exhibited in group shows at Cmty. Gallery Art, Coll. Lake County, Grayslake, Ill., 1996—2003, Lake County Mus., Wauconda, Ill., 1996—2003, Hardy Gallery, Ephraim, Wis., 1996—2002 (Purchase award, 1998), North Point Marina, Winthrop Harbor, Ill., 1996—2003 (1st pl. watercolor, 1996, 1999, 2d pl. watercolor, 1997, 1998, Best of Show, 1996, 1997, award of Merit watercolor, 1998, award of Excellence, 1999, 3d pl., 2001, 3d pl. watercolor, 2002), Truman State U., Kirksville, Mo., 1997, Moorehead (Minn.) State U., 1997, David Adler Cultural Ctr., Libertyville, Ill., 1997—2002, Kenosha Art Assn. and Lake County Art League Combined Art Event, 1997 (Best of Show, 1997), Hawthorne Hollow Art Festival, Kenosha, 1997—98, Deer Path Art League Festival, Lake Forest, 1997, N.W. N.Mex Arts Coun., Farmington, 1997, Dellora A. Norris Cultural Arts Ctr., St. Charles, Ill., 1998—2001, Waukegan Visual Arts Ctr., 1998, Kenosha Pub. Mus., 1998 (award of excellence), Spotlight Gallery, Kenosha, 1998—99, Monne's Gallery, 1998, Zion Chamber Orch. Concert and Art Contest, 1998 (Best of Show, 1st pl.), Clausen Art Shop, Wilmette, Ill., 1999, Deer Path Art League Festival, Lake Forest, 1999, Gull Lake Gallery, Richland, Mich., 1999—2002, Nippersink Gallery, Richmond, Ill., 1999—2001, Deer Path Gallery, Lake Forest, 1999—2003, Wauconda Pub. Libr., 1999, one-woman shows include Wauconda Area Pub. Libr., 1999, exhibited in group shows at Green Belt Cultural Ctr., North Chgo., 2000, Women's Works, Old Courthouse Art Ctr., Woodstock, Ill., 2000, Kenosha Art Assn. and Lake County Art League Combined Art Event, 2000 (3d pl., 2000), Kenosha Art Assn. Art Event, 2001—02 (Best of Show, 2001, 3d pl., 2002), City of Zion, Ill., 2001—02, Centennial Days Fine Art Show, 2001, Harring Galleries, Racine, Wis., 2001—03, Guenzel Gallery, Fish Creek, Wis., 2001—02, one-woman shows include Jack Benny Ctr. Arts, 2001, Invitational First Lady Hearts adn Flowers Art Exhbn., Ill., 2001—03, traveling exhbn., America the Beautiful, 2001—03; work published in book Celebrating Door Country's Wild Places, 2001; one-woman shows include Wauconda Area Pub. Libr., 2002, exhibited in group shows at Women's Works, Old Courthouse Art Ctr., Woodstock, Ill., 2002, Wauconda Pub. Libr., 2002, Jack Benny Ctr. Arts, 2003, Colo. Fine Art Ctr., 2003, one-woman shows include GreenBelt Cultural Art Ctr., North Chgo., 2003, Pikes Peak Watercolor Soc. Internat. Watermedia XIII/ Fine Art Ctr., Colo. Springs, 2003, exhibited in group shows at Dellora A. Norris Cultural Arts Ctr., St. Charles, Ill., 2003. Former leader, mem. pub. rels. com. Girl Scouts U.S.; visual arts cons. Green Belt Cultural Ctr. Lake County Forest Preserve Dist.; mem. outreach and evangelism missions bd. First Presbyn. Ch. Waukegan, 2000—02. Recipient Purchase award, Coll. Lake County, Grayslake, 1994, numerous courtesy awards. Mem.: Nat. Mus. Women in the Arts (charter), Bloomin' Artists, N.W. Area Arts Coun., Kenosha Art Assn., Red River Watercolor Soc., Deerpath Art League, Lakes Region Watercolor Guild (past rec. sec., co-program chair, exhibit chair), Lake County Art League (resource person, past pres., various bd. positions, fine arts cons. Green Belt Cultural Ctr. Lake County Forest Preserve), Midwest Watercolor Soc. (life), Internat. Starcraft Camper Club (Ill. chpt. sec./treas. 1975). Evangelical. Avocations: watercolor, photography, camping, gardening, hiking. Home: 2018 W Grove Ave Waukegan IL 60085-1607

DRAPEAU, SUZANNE EVA, art educator; b. Montpelier, Vt., Apr. 8, 1954; d. Norman Emile and Lucille Lorretta (LaBelle) D.; m. Gary William Moylen, Feb. 28, 1976 (div.); 1 child, Benjamin Patrick; m. David Gewanter, Dec. 24, 1988. BA in Visual Studies, Columbia U., 1989; MA in Studio Art, NYU, 1997. Cert. tchr., Conn. Self-employed title abstractor, N.J., 1980-86; title officer Chgo. Title Ins. Co., N.J., 1987; sr. title office mgr. Mountainside, N.J., 1988; art tchr. Master's Sch., West Simsbury, Conn., 1989-93, Hartford (Conn.) Pub. Schs., 1993-95, Avon (Conn.) Pub. Schs., 1996—. Programming coord. Artworks Gallery, Hartford, 1999, pres., 2000—; resident Contemporary Artists Ctr., North Adams, Mass., 1997; workshop leader Avon Continuing Edn., 1999—; presenter in field. One-woman shows at Women's Ctr., U. Hartford, 1993, 80 Washington Sq. East Galleries, N.Y., 1996, Fourwinds Ctr., Farmington, Conn., 1997, Artworks Gallery, Hartford, 1999; exhibited in group shows at Slater Mus., Norwich, Conn., 1992, 98, L'Instituto Universitario d'Architettura di Venezia, Venice, Italy, 1993, 94, Nat. Arts Coun. at Hartford, 1993, Farmington Art Guild, 1994, Casa Italia Zerilli-Marimo, NYU, N.Y.C., 1997, 98, 2000, Artworks Gallery, 1997, 99, 2000, South Windsor (Conn.) Pub. Libr., 1999. Mem. NEA, Nat. Art Edn. Assn., Conn. Art Educators Assn., Conn. Edn. Assn., Internat. Sculpture Ctr., Coll. Art Assn. Home: 6 Tamarack Ln Simsbury CT 06070-2432 Office: Avon Pub Schs 34 Simsbury Rd Avon CT 06001-3714

DRAPER, PENNY KAYE PEKRUL, music educator; b. Lansing, Mich., May 14, 1948; d. Edward Emil Pekrul and June Marie Piche-Fahlen; m. William Burle Draper III, June 13, 1970; children: Paige Lindsley, Josselin Bertrand. BA in Choral Edn. cum laude, Mich. State U., 1970, BA in Applied Piano Pedagogy cum laude, 1971, MA in Musicology, 1983, PhD in Musicology, 1997. Cert. tchr., Mich., continuing edn. tchr., Mich. Choral dir. Williamston (Mich.) H.S., 1970-78; dir. Renaissance Singers, East Lansing, Mich., 1979—, Jr. Renaissance Singers, East Lansing, Mich., 1990—; choral dir. East Lansing Schs., 1993-94; pvt. instruction East Lansing, 1993—. Mem. adj. faculty U. Mich., Flint, 1995—96; choral dir. Colonial Choir Plymouth Congl. Ch., 1995—, HOPE Acad., Lansing, Mich., 1996—2002; chair fine arts com. Plymouth Congl. Ch., 1997—2000, chair music sch. com., 1994, mem. organist search com., 2002, chair, dir. music search com. Author program notes MSU Symphony Orch., 1980-83, Lansing Symphony Orch., 1981, Elizabethan Musical Feast, 1983-92. Mem. Lansing Matinee Musicale, 1997—, chair performing arts students, 2002—; bd. deacons Plymouth Congl. Ch., 2002—; chair Performing Arts Students, 2002; mem. Lansing Matinee Musicale, 1997—; apptd. humanities profl. Mich. Humanities Coun., 2002—. Piano scholar Mich. State U., 1966-70, Lansing Matinee Musicale, 1965. Mem.: Capital Area Music Tchrs. Assn. (v.p. 1997—99, pres. 1999—2001, Tchr. of Yr. 2003), Mich. Music Tchrs. Assn. (awards chair 2002—, cert., bd. dirs.), Music Tchrs. Nat. Assn. (local chmn. state convention 2003), Pi Kappa Lambda, Sigma Alpha Iota. Home: 513 Woodland Dr East Lansing MI 48823-3273

DRAYSON, PAMELA K. library director; b. Windsor, Ont., Canada, Apr. 4, 1952; d. Douglas Alec and Alice Drayson. BA, NW Mo. State U., 1974; MLS, U. Mo., Columbia, 1977; M Mgmt., Ctrl. Mich. U., 1983; PhD, Kans. State U., 2001. Libr. dir. Midwest Rsch. Inst., Kansas City, Mo., 1985—88, Kansas City (Kans.) C.C., 1988—2000; dir. librs. ND State U., Fargo, 2000—. Bd. dirs. Biographic Ctr. for Rsch., Denver, 1995—2000; chmn. Kansas City Libr. Consortium, Kansas City Metro Libr. Network. Bd. dirs. Nat. Women's Jazz Festival, Kansas City, Mo.

DRAZIN, LISA, real estate and corporate investment banker, financial consultant; b. Washington, Nov. 26, 1953; d. Sidney and Bernice Ann (Jeweler) D. AB with honors, Wellesley Coll., 1976; MBA, George Washington U., 1980. Chartered fin. analyst. Securities analyst Geico, Inc., Chevy Chase, Md., 1982; mng. prin. Jefferson Securities Ltd., Bethesda, Md., 1983; chmn., CEO Drazin & Co., Inc., Bethesda, 1983-89, Drazin Properties, Inc., Bethesda, 1985-89, Drazin Securities, Inc., Bethesda, 1985-88, Woodmont Asset Mgmt. Inc., 1989—. Affiliate Montgomery County Bd. Realtors; real estate investment banker Restructuring Fed. Deposit Ins. Corp. Founder Ivy Connection, Washington, 1982; bd. dirs. Friends of Tel Aviv U., actine planning com. Jewish Nat. Fund; active Nat. Truste for Historic Preservation, UJA Fedn. of Greater Washington (young leadership divsn., Ruth Heritage Forum), Am. Friends Hebrew U., Jewish Inst. for Nat. Security Affairs, The Israel Project, Nat. Kidney Found., Shakespeare Theatre Guild. Fellow Wexner Heritage Found., Renaissance Inst., Friends for Life Benefit, Whitman Walker Clinic, Spiritual Ctr. Am., Assn. for Investment Mgmt. and Rsch., Turnaround Mgmt. Assn.; mem. Nat. Assn. Realtors, Comml. Investment Real Estate Coun., Relators Nat. Mktg. Inst., Wash. Soc. Investment Analysts, Inc., Wellesley Club (interns coord., recent grads. rep. 1981-84, Washington), Ben Gurion Club, Beta Gamma Sigma, Tau Zeta Epsilon. Office: Woodmont Asset Mgmt Inc 6403 Kirby Rd Bethesda MD 20817-5523 Personal E-mail: lisadrazin@verizon.net.

DREBEN, RAYA SPIEGEL, judge; b. Vienna, Dec. 3, 1927; came to U.S., 1928, naturalized, 1936; d. Shalom and Rose (Goldschmiedt) Spiegel; children: Elizabeth, Jonathan. AB magna cum laude, Radcliffe Coll., 1949; LL.B. cum laude, Harvard U., 1954. Bar: Mass. 1957, U.S. Supreme Ct. 1960. Law clk. to Judge Bailey Aldrich, U.S. Dist. Ct. for Mass., 1954-55; Bigelow fellow and instr. U. Chgo. Law Sch., 1955-56; asso. Firm Palmer & Dodge, Boston, 1964-71, partner, 1971-79; assoc. justice Mass. Appeals Ct., Boston, 1979—. Lectr. in copyright Harvard U. Law Sch., 1973-76; mem. adv. com. on copyright registration and deposit Libr. of Congress, 1993. Trustee Radcliffe Coll., 1981-89. Recipient 1st prize Nathan Burkan competition Harvard U. Law Sch., 1954, nat. winner, 1954 Mem. ABA (chmn. com. on authors 1977-79), Am. Law Inst. (adv. on restatement, property-donative transactions), Am. Bar Found., Copyright Soc. U.S.A. (trustee 1973-76, editorial bd. bull. 1974-85), Jud. Inst. Mass. Judiciary (chmn. adv. com. 1988-96). Office: Mass Appeals Ct 3 Center Plz Boston MA 02108-1701 Office Phone: 617-725-8556.

DRECHSEL, JOANNE J. writer, educator; b. Phila. m. Al Drechsel; children: Al, Robert. BA, Holy Family U., Phila., 1982; MA, Arcadia U., Glenside, Pa., 1984; CAS, U. of Pa., 1999. Part-time lectr. English Holy Family U., Phila., 1985—2000; lectr. English C.C. of Phila., 1986—87; prof. Bucks County C.C., Newtown, Pa., 1988—98; lectr. English Pa. State U., Abington. Freelance writer, rschr., Pa., 2000—. Contbr. articles to rsch. publs. Mem.: NOW, AAUW, Wellesley Ctrs. for Women. Personal E-mail: profjd@aol.com.

DREES, BETTY, dean, educator; Interim sect. chair in diabetes, endocrinology, and metabolism Truman Med. Ctr. Hosp. Hill, exec. assoc. dean; assoc. prof., docent U. Mo.-Kansas City Sch. Medicine, 1998, interim dean, 2001—. Office: 2411 Holmes Kansas City MO 64108

DREES, DOROTHY E. small business owner, real estate manager; b. Utica, N.Y., Oct. 12, 1953; d. Edward D. and Frances A. (Merritt) Drees; m. Richard D. Hulley. BA in Philosophy, SUNY, 1975; student, Bowman Tech. Sch., 1976, student, 1977. Engraver Appel & Weber, Lancaster, Pa., 1978—81; jeweler Crest Jewel, Fairfield, Iowa, 1982—85; sculptor Zimmerman Studios, Fairfield, 1986; jeweler Americus Diamond, Fairfield, 1987—88; prin., owner Dorothy Drees, Jewelry & Hand Engraving, Fairfield, 1985—; ptnr. Akashic Records & Tapes, Fairfield, 1995—, R&D Real Estate, Fairfield, 1997—. Ptnr.: Richard & Dorothy Jazz Duo, 2000, co-founder: Jivin' Mukti Rock Bhajan Band, 2002. Mem. Natural Resources Def. Coun. Mem.: Hand Engravers, NRDC, Maharishi U. Mgmt. Town Superradiance, Gen. Soc. Mayflower Descs. Avocations: singing, songwriting, piano, bass, dance. Home and Office: 104 South D St Fairfield IA 52556

DREHER, MELANIE CREAGAN, dean, nursing educator; BSN magna cum laude, L.I. U.; D in Anthropology, Columbia U. Mem. faculty Columbia U., N.Y.C.; dean Sch. Nursing, William Ryan disting. prof. U. Miami; dean Sch. Nursing, prof. U. Mass.; dean Coll. Nursing, prof. U. Iowa; now dean Univ. of Iowa Sch. of Nursing. Mem. editl. bds. various profl. jours. Recipient May A. Brunson award, CASE award. Mem. Sigma Theta Tau (pres. Beta Zeta chpt. 1995). Office: U Iowa Office Dean 101F NB Iowa City IA 52242

DREIZEN, ALISON M. lawyer; b. Bklyn., Sept. 14, 1952; d. Nathan Dreizen and Florence (Morgenstern) Barth. BA, Cornell U., 1974; JD, Harvard U., 1977. Assoc. White & Case, N.Y.C., 1977-85, ptnr., 1985-93, 95—, Moscow, 1993-95. Office: White & Case 40th Fl 1155 Avenue Of The Americas New York NY 10036-2787

DRENNAN, HEIDI MARIE, music educator; b. St. Charles, Mo., Nov. 15, 1973; d. Charles Herbert and Linda Kae Brunjes; m. Drennan William Andrew, Mar. 18, 2000. B Music Edn., Ctrl. Meth. Coll., 1996. Cert. K-12 vocal and instrumental tchr. Mo. Band dir. Wood Mid. Sch., Waynesville, Mo., 1996—98, Lebanon (Mo.) H.S., 1998—. Home: 345 Harrison Lebanon MO 65536 Office: 777 Brice Lebanon MO 65536

DRENNEN, JEAN COBBLE, retired public relations executive, linguist; b. Rome, Ga., Sept. 30, 1924; d. James Ernest and Vorus Frost (Ware) Cobble; m. Gaston Cliff Drennen, Nov. 21, 1948 (dec. Sep. 1994); 1 child, Cheryl Jen. BA, U. Tenn., 1946, MA, 1965. Publicist Curt Weinberg Assoc., N.Y.C., 1946-47; freelance columnist N.Y.C., 1947-49; ad copywriter Miller's Inc., Knoxville, Tenn., 1949-51; pub. rels. dir. United Fund, Knoxville, Tenn., 1955-58; instr. dialect studies Knox County Schs., Knoxville, Tenn., 1961-66; copy dir. Lavidge Assocs., Knoxville, Tenn., 1967-73; program devel dir. Medic Regional Blood Ctr., Knoxville, Tenn., 1974-89. Author, prodr. (video, poster) What Good Is A Blood Donor, 1984 (10th anniversary choice of Am. Blood Commn. 1985); (book, audio tape) Speaking English: A Sound Approach, 1965; author book: The Company Blood Drive Coordinator's Guidebook, 1987; contbr. articles to profl. jours. Adv. United Way; mem. nat. pub. rels. bd. United Funds of Am., 1956—. Recipient 36 1st place awards for TV and newspaper ads Greater Knox Ad Club, 1970-73. Mem. Am. Assn. Blood Banks (nat. pub. rels. bd. 1985—). Avocations: travel, writing. Home: 8101 Elderberry Dr Knoxville TN 37919-7033

DRENTEA, PATRICIA, science educator, researcher; b. Cleve., Sept. 20, 1967; d. Cornell and Dominique Drentea; m. Paul William Tybor, Dec. 28, 1996; 1 child, Hope Elena Drentea-Tybor. BA, U. Wis., 1989; MA, Ohio State U., 1994, PhD, 1999. Rschr. The Lerner PubIs. Co., Mpls., 1990—92; rsch. asst. The Ohio State U., Columbus, 1992—99; asst. prof. U. Ala., Birmingham, 1999—. Assoc. scholar Lister Hill Ctr. for Health Policy, Birmingham, 2000—; scientist Ctr. for Aging, Birmingham, 2000—. Contbr. articles to profl. jours. Grantee, U. Ala., Birmingham, 2002—03; Survey Rsch. fellow, The Ohio State U., 1998. Mem.: Sociologists for Women in Soc., Am. Sociol. Soc. Office: Univ Ala Birmingham U 239-I 1530 3rd Ave S Birmingham AL 35294-3350 E-mail: pdrentea@uab.edu.

DRESBACH, MARY LOUISE, state educational administrator; b. St. Paul, Feb. 17, 1950; d. Ernest Joseph and Kathryn Marion (Lauer) Mathes; m. David Philip Dresbach, Nov. 29, 1980. BA, Coll. St. Catherine, 1972; postgrad., U. St. Thomas, 1979-80; MA, Coll. of St. Catherine, 1995. Tchr. St. Paul Pub. Schs., 1974-78; dir. cmty. outreach, human resources and agy. svcs. Minn. Higher Edn. Svcs. Office, St. Paul, 1978—. Speaker Minn. Quality Conf., 1994, chair, 1996. Contbg. author Leading Edge Newsletter. Mem. exec. steering com. Minn. Quality Coll., 1998. Mem.: Assn. for Psychol. Type, Internat. Pers. Mgmt. Assn. (Minn. chpt.), Minn. Coun. Mgrs. (chair 1998), Minn. Ctr. for Women in Govt., Dakota County Quality Initiative, Dakota County Quality Coun., Minn. Quality Initiative, Am. Soc. for Quality, Nat. Assn. Exec. Women, Am. Bus. Womens Assn. (sec. 1979—80), Citizens League-Minn., Met. Mus. Art, Mpls. Inst. Arts, AAUW, Pi Gamma Mu, Phi Beta Kappa.

DRESCHER, FRAN, actress; b. Flushing, N.Y., Sept. 30, 1957; d. Mort and Sylvia D.; m. Peter Marc Jacobson, 1978. Co-creator, writer, prodr., actress in TV series The Nanny, 1993-99; appeared in feature films: Saturday Night Fever, 1977, American Hot Wax, 1978 (Five-Minute Oscar award Esquire mag.), Gorp, 1980, The Hollywood Knights, 1980, Ragtime, 1981, Young Lust, 1981, Dr. Detroit, 1983, This Is Spinal Tap, 1984, The Rosebud Beach Hotel, 1984, UHF, 1989, The Big Picture, 1989, It had to be You, 1989, Cadillac Man, 1990, Wedding Band, 1990, We're Talking Serious Money, 1992, Jack, 1996, Car 54, Where Are You:, 1996, The Beautician and the Beast, 1997, Picking Up the Pieces, 2000, Kid Quick, 2000; starred in TV series Charmed Lives, 1986, Princesses, 1991, Good Morning Miami, 2003-04; (TV film) Stranger in Our House, 1978, Rock 'n' Roll Mom, 1988, Love and Betrayal, 1989, What's Alan Watching?, 1989, Terror in the Towers, 1993, Beautiful Girl, 2003; guest appearances on TV programs Civil Wars, Alf, Night Court, Nine to Five, Fame, The Tracy Ullman Show; Spokesperson: Old Navy; Author: Enter Whining, 1995, Cancer Schmancer, 2002. Office: Gersh Agy Inc 232 N Canon Dr Beverly Hills CA 90210-5302*

DRESCHER, JUDITH ALTMAN, library director; b. Greensburg, Pa., July 6, 1946; d. Joseph Grier and Sarah Margaret (Hewitt) Altman; m. Robert A. Drescher, Aug. 10, 1968 (div. 1980); m. David G. Lindstrom, Jan. 10, 1981. AB, Grove City Coll., 1968; MLS, U. Pitts., 1971. Tchr. Hempfield Sch. Dist., Greensburg, 1968-71; children's libr. Cin. Pub. Libr., 1971-72, br. mgr., 1972-74; dir. Rolling Meadows (Ill.) Pub. Libr., 1974-79, Champaign (Ill.) Pub. Libr., 1979-85, Memphis/Shelby County Pub. Libr. and Info. Ctr., 1985—. Cons. Providence Assocs., Dallas, 1986-94; Tenn. del. White House Conf. on Librs. and Info. Svcs. Task Force, 1991-92; mem. Tenn. Sec. of State's Commn. on Tech. and Resource Sharing, 1991, 93, steering com. Tenn. Info. and Infrastructure, 1994-97, nat. adv. panel for assessment of role of sch. and pub. librs. U.S. Dept. Edn., 1995-98. Commn. on 21st century Rhodes Coll., Memphis, 1986-88, presdl. adv. com., 1992-2000; active Leadership Memphis, 1987—, selection com., 1992-96; active Memphis Arts Coun., 1989-94; bd. dirs. Literacy Coun., 1986-91, Memphis NCCJ, 1989-93, Memphis Grants Info. Ctr., 1992-97, sec., 1993-95; bd. dirs. Memphis Literacy Found., 1988-92, v.p., 1989-90; bd. dirs. Goals for Memphis, 1988-93, chair edn. com., 1989-91, chair nominating com., 1992, leadership acad., 1999—; bd. dirs. U. Memphis Soc., 1998—; bd. dirs. Cmty. Svcs. Agy., 2002-; exec. adv. bd. Children's Mus., 1988-94, exec. adv. coun. U. Memphis, 1989-99; allocations subcom. United Way, 1989-91, allocations com. Memphis Arts Coun., 100 for the Arts, 1989-91, Libr. Self-study Com. U. Memphis; pres. adv. coun. Lemoyne Coll.; search com. for dean librs. U. Memphis, 1999-2001; adv. com. Memphis Symphony Orch., 2003—. Paul Harris fellow Rotary, Memphis, 2002; recipient Govt. Leader award U. Ill. YWCA, 1981, Communicator of Yr. award Pub. Rels. Soc. Am., 1992, Humanitarian award NCCJ, Memphis, 2003, Charlie Robinson award Pub. Libr. Assn., 2003; named Libr. Coun. Libr. of Yr., 2002-. Mem.: ALA (chmn. intellectual freedom com. 1985—87, mem. coun. 1992—99, mem. nominating com. 2001—02), Assn. Pub. Adminstrs. (midsouth chpt., Adminstr. of Yr. 2002), Pub. Libr. Assn. (v.p., pres. 1994—95), Memphis Libr. Coun., Urban Librs. Coun., Tenn. Libr. Assn., Rotary (bd. dirs. 1992—94, sec. 1993—94, chair membership devel. com. 1994—95, bd. dirs. 2004—), Beta Phi Mu. Home: 1505 Vance Ave Memphis TN 38104-3810 Office: Memphis Shelby County Pub Libr & Info Ctr 3030 Poplar Ave Memphis TN 38111 Office Phone: 901-415-2748.

DRESCHER, KATHLEEN EBBEN, lawyer; b. Kaukauna, Wis., May 17, 1963; d. Willard Peter and Helen Mary (Joyce) Ebben; m. Park Morris Drescher, Aug. 12, 1989; children: John Park, William Morris. BA, Lawrence U., 1985; JD, Washington U. St. Louis, 1989. Bar: Mo. 1989, Wis. 1992. Assoc. Popkin & Stern, St. Louis, 1989-90; ptnr. Drescher & Drescher, St. Louis, 1990-92; shareholder Drescher & Drescher, S.C., Appleton, Wis., 1992—. Pres. bd. dirs. Emergency Shelters, Appleton, 1992—; bd. dirs. Child Care Resource and Referral, Appleton. Mem. ABA, Wis. Bar Assn., Mo. Bar Assn., Outagamie County Bar Assn. Avocation: tennis. Home: 4700 Hastings Ct Appleton WI 54913 Office: Drescher & Drescher SC 100 W Lawrence St Fl 3D Appleton WI 54911-5773

DRESCHHOFF, GISELA AUGUSTE MARIE, physicist, researcher; b. Moenchengladbach, Germany, Sept. 13, 1938; came to U.S., 1967, naturalized, 1976; d. Gustav Julius and Hildegard Friederike (Krug) D. PhD, Tech. U. Braunschweig (Ger.), 1972. Staff scientist Fed. Inst. Physics and Tech. Ger., 1965-67; research assoc. Kans. Geol. Survey, Lawrence, 1971-72; vis. asst. prof. physics U. Kans., 1972-74; dep. dir. radiation physics lab. Space Tech. Ctr., 1972-78, assoc. dir., 1979-84, co-dir., 1984-86, dir., 1996—; sr. sci. geology U. Kans., 1991, adj. assoc. prof. physics and astronomy, 1992. Assoc. program mgr. NSF, Washington, 1978-79. Patentee identification markings for gemstones and method of making selective conductive regions in diamond layers. Named to Women's Hall of Fame, U. Kans., 1978; recipient Antarctic Service medal U.S.A., 1979; recipient NASA Group Achievement award, 1983. Fellow Explorers Club; mem. AAAS, Am. Phys. Soc., Am. Geophys. Union, Am. Polar Soc. (pres. 2000-03), Antarctican Soc., Sigma Xi. Home: 2908 W 19th St Lawrence KS 66047-2301 Office: U Kans Dept Physics & Astronomy Lawrence KS 66045-7541 E-mail: giselad@ku.edu.

DRESHER, OLIVIA WHITAKER, publishing executive, writer; b. Washington, May 13, 1945; d. Melvin and Martha (Whitaker) Dresher. BA, U. of Wash., 1982—85. Editor, journalist, rschr. Various magazines and organizations, Los Angeles, 1967—72; music tchr. and performer self-employed, Los Angeles, 1972—79; program asst. U. of Wash., Seattle, 1982—90; founder, pub., editor of pub. co. Impassio Press, Seattle, 2001—. Founder/curator of the diaries, journals, and notebooks collection Richard Hugo Ho. Cmty. Ctr. for the Lit. Arts, Seattle, 1998—. Editor, contbr.: anthology Darkness and Light: Private Writing as Art; author: (book of poetry) A Candle in the Ice. Recipient First Prize Winner Interior Category in the Sixth Ann. Gt. Am. Home Awards, Nat. Trust for Hist. Preservation, 1994. Mem.: Small Publishers Assn. of N.Am., Pacific NW Booksellers Assn., Book Publishers NW, Hist. Seattle. Avocations: philosophical discussions, environmental issues, movies. Office: Impassio Press PO Box 31905 Seattle WA 98103 Personal E-mail: olivia@impassioned.net. E-mail: books@impassio.com.

DRESSELHAUS, MILDRED SPIEWAK, physics and engineering educator; b. Bklyn., Nov. 11, 1930; d. Meyer and Ethel (Teichteil) Spiewak; m. Gene F. Dresselhaus, Aug. 25, 1958; children: Marianne Dresselhaus Cooper, Carl Eric, Paul David, Eliot Michael. BA, Hunter Coll., 1951; DSc (hon.), CUNY, 1982, Hunter Coll., 1982; Fulbright fellow, Cambridge (Eng.) U., 1951—52; MA, Radcliffe Coll., 1953; PhD in Physics, U. Chgo., 1958; D Engring. (hon.), Worcester Poly. Inst., 1976; DSc (hon.), Smith Coll., 1980, Hunter Coll., 1982, N.J. Inst. Tech., 1984; DHC (hon.), U. Catholique de Louvain, 1988; DSc (hon.), Rutgers U., 1989, U. Conn., 1992, U. Mass., Boston, 1992, Princeton U., 1992; DEngring, Colo. Sch. Mines, 1993; D (hon.), Technion, Israel Inst. Tech., Haifa, 1994; DHC (hon.), Johannes Kepler U., Linz, Austria, 1993; DSc (hon.), Harvard U., 1995, Ohio State U., 1998; PhD (hon.), U. Paris, Sorbonne, 1999; DSc (hon.), Columbia U., 1999; DHC (hon.), Cath. U. Louvain, 2000; DSc (hon.), Northwestern U., 2003. NSF postdoctoral fellow Cornell U., 1958—60; mem. staff Lincoln Lab., MIT, Lexington, 1960—67; prof. elec. engring. MIT, Cambridge, 1968—, assoc. dept. head elec. engring., 1972—74, Abby Rockefeller Mauze chair, 1973—85, dir. Ctr. for Materials Sci. and Engring., 1977—83, prof. physics, 1983—, Inst. prof., 1985—; dir. Office of Science, U.S. Dept. of Energy, Washington, 2000—01. Vis. prof. dept. physics U. Campinas, Brazil, 1971, Technion, Israel, 1972, 90, Nihon and Aoyama Gakuin Univs., Tokyo, 1973, IVIC, Caracas, Venezuela, 1977; vis. prof. dept. elec. engring. U. Calif., Berkeley, 1983; Graffin lectr. Am. Carbon Soc., 1982; chmn. steering com. on evaluation panels Nat. Bur. Stds., 1978—83; mem. Energy Rsch. Adv. Bd., 1984—90; bd. dirs. Rogers Corp. Contbr. articles to profl. jours. Mem. governing bd. NRC, 1984—87, 1989—90, 1992—96; trustee Calif. Inst. Tech., 1993—2000; overseer Harvard U., 1997—2000; chmn. bd. Am. Inst. Physics, 2003—; bd. govs. Argonne Nat. Lab., 1986—89, Weizmann Inst., Rehovot, Israel, 1999—2000, 2001—. Named to Hunter Coll. Hall of Fame, 1972, Women in Tech. Internat. Hall of Fame, 1998; recipient Alumnae medal, Radcliffe Coll., 1973, Killian Faculty Achievement award, 1986—87, Nat. medal of Sci., 1990, Sigri Great Lakes Carbon award, 1997, Profl. Achievement award, Hunter Coll., CUNY, 1998, Nicholson medal, 2000, Karl T. Compton medal, 2001, Weizmann Woman and Sci. Millennial Lifetime Achievement award, 2000, Nat. Materials Advancement award, Fedn. Materials Socs., 2000. Fellow: AAAS (bd. dirs. 1985—89, pres. 1997—98, chair bd. dirs. 1998—99), IEEE, Am. Carbon Soc., Am. Acad. Arts and Scis., Am. Phys. Soc. (pres. 1984); mem.: NAS (coun. 1987—90, chmn. engring. sect. 1987—90, chmn. class III 1990—93, coun. 1992—96, treas. 1992—96), Am. Philos. Soc., Brazilian Acad. Sci. (corr.), Engring. Acad. Japan (fgn. assoc. 1993—), Soc. Women Engrs. (Achievement award 1977), Nat. Acad. Engring. (coun. 1981—87). Office: MIT 77 Massachusetts Ave Rm 13-3005 Dept Elec Engring Cambridge MA 02139

DRESSER, KAREN KERNS, state agency administrator; b. Urbana, Ohio, June 14, 1944; d. Edmund Howard and Kathryn Louise (Strapp) Kerns; m. David I. Dresser, Mar. 20, 1980 (dec. Feb. 1994). BA, Barat Coll., 1966; MA, Am. U., 1969. Mgmt. intern/program officer HUD, Washington, 1968-71; various positions Nat. League of Cities, Washington, 1971-82; v.p. Nat. Ctr. for Housing Mgmt., Washington, 1982-83; program dir. Ohio Dept. Devel., Columbus, 1983-84, asst. dep. dir., 1990—; exec. dir. Ohio Housing Fin. Agy., Columbus, 1984-88; pres. Nat. Affordable Housing Trust, Columbus, 1988-90. Treas. Devore-Dresser Devel., Columbus, 1986—. Author: City Council Training Series, 1975-76. Advisor, hon. trustee Ohio Cmty. Devel. Fin. Fund, Columbus, 1991—; bd. dirs. Coun. of State Housing Agys., Washington, 1986-88, Nat. Low-Income Housing Coalition, Washington, 1989-90; vol. German Village Soc., 1986—. Roman Catholic. Avocations: gardening, politics, travel, literacy tutoring. Home: 791 Mohawk St Columbus OH 43206-2112

DREW, ELIZABETH, television commentator, journalist, author; b. Cin., Nov. 16, 1935; d. William J. and Estelle (Jacobs) Brenner; m. J. Patterson Drew, Apr. 11, 1964 (dec. 1970); m. David Webster, Sept. 26, 1981 (dec. 2003). BA, Wellesley Coll., 1957; LHD, Hood Coll., 1976, Yale U., 1976, Trinity Coll., Washington, 1978, Reed Coll., 1979, Williams Coll., 1981, Georgetown U., 1981, George Washington U., 1994, Trinity Coll., Hartford, 2000. Writer, editor Congl. Quar., 1959-64; freelance writer, 1964-67; Washington editor Atlantic Monthly, 1967-73; host TV interview program Thirty Minutes With, 1971-73; commentator TV program Agronsky and Co. (now Inside Washington), 1973-92; Washington corr. New Yorker Mag., 1973-92; commentator Monitor Radio, 1992—95. Author: Washington Jour., 1975, Am. Jour., 1977, Senator, 1979, Portrait of an Election, 1981, Politics and Money, 1983, Campaign Jour., 1985, Election Jour., 1989, On the Edge: The Clinton Presidency, 1994, Showdown: The Struggle Between the Gingrich Congress and the Clinton White House, 1996, Whatever It Takes: The Real Struggle for Political Power in Am., 1997, The Corruption of Am. Politics, 1999, Citizen McCain, 2002; contbr. articles Washington Post, N.Y. Rev. of Books, [illegible] Recipient award for excellence Soc. Mag. Writers, 1971, Wellesley Alumnae Achievement award, 1973, DuPont award, 1973, Mo. medal, 1979, Sidney Hillman award, 1983, Amb. of Honor award Books Across the Sea, 1984, Lit. Lion award N.Y. Pub. Libr., 1985, Edward Weintal prize, 1988. Home and Office: 700 New Hampshire Ave NW Washington DC 20037

DREW, ELIZABETH HEINEMAN, publishing executive; b. Evanston, Ill., Aug. 26, 1940; d. Ben Harlow and Marion Elizabeth (Heineman) D. BA, U. Wis., 1961. With Doubleday & Co., Inc., N.Y.C., 1961-84, prodn. asst., 1961-63, personal asst. to editor-in-chief, 1963-66, adminstrv. asst. to editor-in-chief, 1966-69, editl. asst. to editor-in-chief, 1969-71, assoc. editor, 1971-74, editor, 1974-77, sr. editor, 1977-79, exec. editor, editl. dir., 1979-84; v.p., sr. editor William Morrow and Co., N.Y.C., 1984-92; v.p., pub. Lisa Drew Books/Macmillan Pub. Co., N.Y.C., 1993-94; v.p. pub. Lisa Drew Books/Charles Scribner's Sons, N.Y.C., 1994—. Tchr. NYU Sch. Continuing Edn., 1981-82. Bd. dirs. Barbara Bush Found. Family Literacy, 1995—, Am. Booksellers Found. for Free Expression, 2004-. Mem.: PEN, Assn. Am. Pubs. (internat. freedom to pub. com. 1978—, freedom to read com. 1988—, chmn. 1990—93, 1994—98, 2004—), Nat. Press Club, Women's Media Group (treas. 1982—84, pres. 1985—86, bd. dirs. 2000—02), First City Club (Savannah, Ga.), Century Assn. (N.Y.). Democrat. Episcopalian.

DREW, INA R. bank executive; BA, Johns Hopkins U., 1978; MA, Columbia U. Floor trader Bank of Tokyo, Manhattan, NY; with Chemical Bank, Springfield, NJ, 1982—96; mng. dir. Global Treasury Divsn. J.P. Morgan Chase & Co., N.Y.C., NY, 1996—. Mem. mgmt. com. J.P. Morgan Chase & Co., 1997—, mem. exec. com., 2003—. Named One of Most Powerful Women in Banking, U.S. Banker Mag., 2003. Office: JP Morgan Chase & Co 270 Park Ave New York NY 10017-2070*

DREW, K. financial advisor, management consultant; b. Freeport, N.Y. d. Harry P. and Kathleen (Isdal) Barton; children: Karen, Donna. BA, U. Ga., 1958; postgrad., U. Ill., 1960-61. Dir. YWCA, Corpus Christi, Tex., 1969-72, Dwoskin Nat. Wallcovering Co., Atlanta, 1974-76; dep. asst. fin. presdl. campaign, 1976-77; dir. fin. Presdl. Inaugural, Washington, 1976; dep. adv. for small bus. SBA, Washington, 1977-80, asst. to adminstr., 1980-82; v.p. Alpha Systems, Inc., Washington and Athens, Greece, 1980-85; human resource cons. MBA Mgmt., Inc., McLean, Va., 1982-84; bus. cons. Drew Cons., McLean, 1984—; cons. assoc. Walling, June & Assocs., Old Town Alexandria, Va., 1986-89; fin. advisor The Family Extended, Washington, 1990—; bus. rep. Nikken, Inc., Washington, 1996, KareMor Internat., Inc., Washington, 1996; cons. The B.O.W.L. Group, Washington, 1996—. Fin. advisor SAKA, Inc., Merrifield, Va., 1991—, Warrenton, Va., 1991-92, DeLeand Assocs., McLean, Va., 1991-92; fin. dir. Disting. Environments, Reston, Va., 1992-94. State rep. poverty program and suicide prevention bds. Corpus Christi Bus. Coun., 1969-71; bd. dirs. YWCA, Washington, 1983-85; head speaker's bur. Fairfax Symphony, 1979-85, mem. exec. devel. com., 1979-86; mem. Mental Health Exec. Bd. dirs., Washington, 1983-88; deacon Nat. Presbyn. Ch., Washington, 1988-90; asst. to exec. dir. T. Monk Found., Jazz Sch., Duke U., 1987-89; event dir. Easter Seal Soc., 1990-91; mem. Youth for Tomorrow devel. com. Joe Gibbs Charities, Washington, 1990-98; presdl. campaign team captain Va. and Ga. Inaugural Com., 1993; Ga. Ball host, Washington, 1993; host Presdl. Inaugural Gala, Washington, 1993; In Kind Svc. to White House Advance Office of Pres., 1993—; cons. advisor Battered Spouses & Their Children, Washington, 1995—; campa pres. team, 1996; pres. inaugural host, Washington, D.C., 1996; fin. mgr. Internat. Fellowship Family Extended, Washington, 1993-98; fin., mkgt. adv., mem. new bowl group Urban Prayer Breakfast, Washington, 1997—; job cons. Homeless Bd. and Symposium, Washington, 1997-98; pres. bd. dirs. WAR Against Broken Hearts, Atlanta, 1998—; hostess Christmas at the White House, Washington, 1999; chmn., newspaper editor Rotonda Pet, McLean, Va., 2000; chmn. Urban Prayer Breakfast for Homeless, Washington, 2000; v.p. Rotonda Assn., McLean, 2002-; pres. Su Casa Mi Casa Nat. Home Mgmt., McLean, Va., 2003. Mem. Nat. League Am. Pen Women (v.p., pres. Washington Capital chpt. 1987-89, nat. bd. dirs. 1987-90, nat. roster chmn. 1989—), Bus. and Profl. Women Washington, Nat. Platform Assn., Alpha Gamma Delta. Office: 8350 Greensboro Dr Ste 1-121 Mc Lean VA 22102-3533

DREW, KATHERINE FISCHER, history educator; b. Houston, Sept. 24, 1923; d. Herbert Herman and Martha (Holloway) Fischer; m. Ronald Farinton Drew, July 27, 1951. BA, Rice Inst., 1944, MA, 1945; PhD, Cornell U., 1950. Asst. history Cornell U., 1948-50; instr. history Rice U., 1946-48, mem. faculty, 1950—, prof. history, 1964—, Harris Masterson, Jr. prof. history, 1983-85, Lynette S. Autrey prof. history, 1985-96, prof. emeritus, 1996—, chmn. dept. history, 1970-80; editor Rice U. (Rice U. Studies), 1967-81, acting dean humanities and social scis., 1973, acting chmn. dept. art and art history, 1996-98. Author: The Burgundian Code, 1949, Studies in Lombard Institutions, 1956, The Lombard Laws, 1973, Law and Society in Early Medieval Europe, 1988, The Laws of the Salian Franks, 1991, also articles; editor: Perspective in Medieval History, 1963, The Barbarian Invasions, 1970; mem. bd. editors Am. Hist. Assn. Guide to Hist. Lit., 1987-94, Am. Hist. Rev. 1982-1985; contbr.: Life and Thought in the Middle Ages, 1967. Guggenheim fellow, 1959; Fulbright scholar, 1965; NEH Sr. fellow, 1974-75 Fellow Mediaeval Acad. Am. (coun. 1974-77, 2d v.p. to pres. 1985-87, del. to Am. Coun. Learned Socs. 1977-81); mem. Am. Hist. Assn. (coun. 1983-86), Am. Soc. Legal History, So. Hist. Assn. (vice chair, chair European sect. 1986-88, exec. com. 1989-91), Phi Beta Kappa. Home: 9333 Memorial Dr # 306 Houston TX 77024-5739 Office: Rice U Dept History MS 42 PO Box 1892 Houston TX 77251-1892 E-mail: kdrew@rice.edu.

DREWRY, JUNE E. information technology executive; Degree in math., Caldwell Coll. With Mut. Benefit Life Ins. Co., 1978—89; v.p. tech. Aetna Life Ins. and Annuity Co., Hartford, Conn., 1990, pres. of systematized benefits admstrs., 1991—96; sr. v.p. and chief knowlege and tech. officer Lincoln Nat. Corp., 1996—99; exec. v.p. and chief info. officer Aon Corp., Chgo., 2000—. Mem.: Soc. Info. Mgmt. (pres. (N.J. chapt.), at large mem. Internat. Bd. Dir., Internat. pres.). Office: Aon Corp 200 E Randolph St Chicago IL 60601*

DREXLER, JOANNE LEE, art appraiser; b. Washington, Mar. 21, 1944; d. Elias J. and Beatrice Charlotte (Goldberg) D.; m. James R. Cohen, May 31, 1965; children: Terri I., Brett F. Student, Louvre, Paris, 1963-64; BA, Tufts U., 1965; Diamond and Pearl Cert., GIA, N.Y.C., 1974. Tchr. of French Stuyvesant H.S., N.Y.C., 1965-66; decorator, art cons. Joanne Cohen Interiors, Mamaroneck, N.Y., 1967-69; assoc. prof. Hofstra U., L.I., N.Y., 1979-80; pres. Esquire Appraisals, N.Y.C. and Larchmont, N.Y., 1969—. TV appearances include CNN, Sept. 1991; cons., lectr. in field; art judge various contests, art dealer. Organizer, curator N.C. in N.Y. art show Nat. Arts Club, 1993, African Am. art show Nat. Arts Club, 1994; weekly columnist Gannett chain newspapers, 1980-86; contbr. articles to N.Y. Law Jour., Matrimonial Strategist. Mem. Am. Soc. Appraisers (sr.; v.p. Hudson Valley White Plains chpt. 1989, bd. dirs. 1997, pres. White Plains chpt. 1993-94, 97-98), Appraisers' Assn. Am. (cert.), Nat. Arts Club N.Y. (exhbn. com.). Avocations: travel, swimming, horseback riding. Home: 23 Trudy Ln Bedford NY 10506-1337 Office: Esquire Appraisals Inc 630 1st Ave New York NY 10016-3700 E-mail: leedrexler@esquireappraisals.com.

DREXLER, MARY SANFORD, financial executive; b. Pontiac, Mich., Apr. 19, 1954; d. Arthur H. and Kathryn S. (Sherda) Sanford; m. Brian Day, 1975 (div. 1978); m. York Drexler, 1980. BS, Ea. Mich. U., Ypsilanti, 1976,

MA, 1979; postgrad., Walsh Coll., Troy, Mich., 1983. CPA, Mich. Spl. edn. tchr. Oakland Schs., Pontiac, Mich., 1976-83; staff auditor Coopers & Lybrand, Detroit, 1983—84, sr. auditor, 1984—86; asst. contr. Webasto Sunroofs Inc., Rochester Hills, 1986-88; contr. Inalfa Roof Systems, U.S.A., Farmington Hills, Mich., 1988-92; v.p. fin., controller Inalfa Roof Sys., Farmington Hills, Mich., 1992-96, CFO, exec. v.p., 1997—. Bd. dirs. Inalfa Roof Systems, Inc., Inalfa Holding Inc. Bd. dirs. Neighborhood Civic Assn., Troy, 1986—, Coun. for Exceptional Children, Oakland County, 1976-83. Mem. Inst. Mgmt. Accts., Oakland County, Mich. Assn. CPA Mich., Forest Lake Country Club. Avocations: photography, painting, golf, swimming. Office: Inalfa Roof Systems USA 1370 Pacific Dr Auburn Hills MI 48326-1569

DREYER, LOIS HELENE GOODMAN, reading and language arts educator, researcher; b. N.Y.C., Aug. 26, 1944; d. Mac and Lilyan (Shulman) Goodman; m. Neil P. Dreyer, June 26, 1965; children: Jonathan, Peter. BS in Spanish and Elem. Edn., NYU, 1965; MA in Ednl. Psychology, Columbia U., 1978, EdM in Learning Disabilities, 1980, PhD in Ednl. Psychology, 1989. Cert. reading cons., Conn.; cert. reading tchr. K-12, N.Y.; cert. tchr. common br. subjects K-8, N.Y. Classroom tchr. P.S. 87, N.Y.C., 1965-68; reading and lang. arts cons. The Long Ridge Sch., Stamford, Conn., 1978-80; asst. supr. reading clinic Columbia U. Tchrs. Coll., N.Y.C., 1980-82, coord. reading svcs., 1982-90, adj. asst. prof., 1989-91; rsch. assoc. Haskins Labs., New Haven, 1989-93; dir. reading ctr. So. Conn. State U., New Haven, 1993—, prof. reading, 1991—. Rsch. assoc. Ctr. for Advanced Study in Edn., CUNY Grad. Sch., 2004—. Author Gates-MacGinitie Reading Teste, 4th edit.; contbr. articles to profl. jours., chpt. to book. Am. Ednl. Rsch. Assn., Internat. Reading Assn., Nat. Reading Conf., Orton Dyslexia Soc. (Outstanding Dissertation award 1990), Soc. for Scientific Study of Reading, Kappa Delta Pi. Avocation: photography. Home: 80 Sawmill Rd Stamford CT 06903-3106 Office: So Conn State U 501 Crescent St New Haven CT 06515-1330 E-mail: lgdreyer@optonline.net.

DREYER, MELANIE ANN, theater educator; d. Donald William Dittmar and Charlene Wells Glaze; m. Peter Dreyer-Lude, Dec. 27, 2001; 1 child, Cassidy James Dreyer Lude ; m. Jeffrey Mathes Dreyer, May 20, 1989 (div. Dec. 1994). BA in Theatre, U. Denver, 1983; MA in Dramatic Lit., Washington U., St. Louis, 1992; MFA in Directing, Northwestern U., 2000. Artist-in-residence Washington U., St. Louis, 1993—97; co-artistic dir., founder Shattermask Theatre, St. Louis, 1993—97; dir. performance French Theater, Northwestern U., Evanston, Ill., 1999—2000; head performance training U. Pitts., 2000—. Dir.: (plays) Endless Adventures of M.C. Kat, 1994, Old Times, 1994, Ozeanflug, 1999, Silent Spring, 2000, She Stoops to Conquer, 2002, Arabian Night, 2003. John J. McClay fellow, 2000, hewlett Small grantee, 2000, Hewlett Small grantee, 2003. Mem.: Am. Fedn. TV and Radio Artists, Actor's Equity Assn. Home: 421 Meridan St Pittsburgh PA 15211 Office: U Pitts 1617 Cathedral of Learning Pittsburgh PA 15211

DRIES, KATHLEEN MARIE, social worker; b. Beaver Dam, Wis., Feb. 21, 1946; d. Henry Frank and Eloise Marianne (Rake) D. BS in Sociology, No. Mich. U., 1969. Social worker Dept. Social Svcs., West Bend, Wis., 1969—. Social work cons. Group Home Elderly, Slinger, Wis., 1972-75. Mem. Labor Assn. of Wis., Cath. Knights Ins. Soc. (bd. dirs. 1979-94), Alpha Xi Delta. Roman Catholic. Avocations: tennis, spectator sports, theater, travel. Home: 601 Declark St Beaver Dam WI 53916-1309 Office: Dept Social Svcs 333 E Washington St Ste 3100 West Bend WI 53095-2585

DRIESSEN, CHRISTINE F. broadcast executive; m. Terry Driessen; 2 children. Contr. ESPN, 1985—90, v.p. fin. and planning, 1990—95, sr. v.p. and CFO, 1995—98, exec. v.p. and CFO, 1998—. Named one of Top 25 Women in Sports, St. & Smith's Sports Bus. Jour., 1999, Wonder Women in media, Multichannel News, 2003. Office: ESPN 935 Middle St Bristol CT 06010*

DRINKARD-HAWKSHAWE, DOROTHY LEE, historian, educator, writer; d. Junior Drinkard and Claudia Belle Ashe-Drinkard; m. Richard Ramsey Hawkshawe, Jan. 9, 1963 (dec. July 18, 1989); 1 child, Sharon Belle. BA, Howard U., Washington, D.C., 1960, MA, 1963; PhD, Cath. U. Am., Washington, D.C., 1974. Chair History Dept. East Tenn. State U., Johnson City, 1989—91, prof. of History, dir. of African and African Am. Studies, 1993—. Dir. of teen-age divsn. YWCA, Dayton, Ohio, 1960—61; Chair Dept. History and Politics Bowie (Md.) State U., 1979—82; liaison officer to colls. and univs. Nat. Endowment for the Humanities, Washington, 1983—85; assoc. dean of grad. sch. East Tenn. State U., Johnson City, 1992—95; exec. dir. and CEO Barnhardt & Ashe Pub., Inc., Miami, Fla., 2001—. Author: (book) Illinois Freedom Fighters: A Civil War Saga of the 29th Infantry United States Colored Troops, 1998; editor: The :Legacy of Reconstruction: 1865-1877, 1998. Candidate Howard County Sch. Bd., Columbia, Md., 1986. Named Citizen of the Yr., Theta Zeta chpt. Omega Psi Phi, 1994, Woman of the Year, Pro-to Club, Johnson City. Tenn., 1999; recipient Disting. Program award, Md. Assn. of Higher Edn., 1980. Mem.: AAUW, AAUP, Assn. Am. Publishers, Am. Hist. Assn., Assn. for Study of Afro-Am. Life and History. Liberal. Methodist. Avocations: music, travel, walking. Office: East Tenn State Univ Campus Box 70672 Johnson City TN 37614 Personal E-mail: dorodrink@aol.com. E-mail: DoroDrink@aol.com.

DRINNON, JANIS BOLTON, artist, poet, volunteer; b. Pineville, Ky., July 28, 1922; d. Clyde Herman and Violet Ethiele (Hendrickson) Bolton; m. Kenneth Cleveland Drinnon, June 13, 1948; 1 child, Dena Daryl. Student, Lincoln Meml. U., Harrogate, Tenn., 1947-48, Newspaper Inst. Am.; comml. art cert., Art Instrn. Sch., Mpls., 1968. Author: (poems) In HIS Care: A Book of Inspirational Poetry, 1998. Organizer, prodr., dir. religious plays drama dept. Alice Bell Bapt. Ch., Knoxville, Tenn.; mem. New Hopewell Bapt. Ch., Knoxville. Named to Internat. Poetry Hall of Fame, 1996; recipient Editors Choice award, Nat. Libr. Poetry. Mem.: Internat. Soc. Poets (disting. mem.). Republican. Avocations: arts, crafts, oil painting, composing poetry. Home: 7342 Hodges Ferry Rd Knoxville TN 37920-9732 E-mail: kcdrinnon@aol.com.

DRISCOLE, MELISSA REES, conductor, educator; b. Scranton, Pa., Jan. 2, 1971; d. William David and Sandra Irene Rees; m. Richard H. Driscole Jr., June 18, 1999; 1 child, Madison Sara. BA in Music Edn., Marywood U., 1992. Cert. instr. II Pa. Vocal coach Marywood U., Scranton, 1992—; dir. choral activities Dallas (Pa.) Jr. H.S., 1993—96; choral condr. Ch. of Epiphany, Clarks Summit, Pa., 1997—, Berwick (Pa.) Area Sr. HS., 1997—. Advisor Modernaires, Concert Choir, Berwick, 1997—, Student Coun., Berwick, 1997—; treas. Columbia-Montour County Chorus, Bloomsburg, Pa., 1997—. Recipient Voice medal, Marywood U., 1992. Home: PO box 280 Lake Winola PA 18625

DRISCOLL, COLLEEN MARY, writer, researcher, consultant; b. Endicott, N.Y., Apr. 1, 1937; d. Leo Xavier and Loretta Blanchette Driscoll; 1 child, Tara Colleen Maguire. PhD, Temple U., 1994. Dir. The Kurtz Inst. Peacemaking, Doylestown, Pa., 2000—03; assoc. dir. Common Heritage Inst., Swarthmore, Pa., 1978—2003; rsch. analyst Libr. of Congress, Washington; asst., adj. prof. Villanova U., Villanova, Pa., 1982—2001. Cons. various non-govtl. orgns., N.Y.C., 1981—2002; non-govtl. rep. U.N. Common Heritage Inst., N.Y.C., 1978—2003; member, bd. trustees Ctr. UN Reform Edn., N.Y.C., 1999—2003; rsch. asst. Nat. Planning Assn.; spkr. Congress European Space Program, 1992, UN Dept. of Pub. Info., 2002; free lance writer, 2003—; spkr. UN Dept. of Disarmament Affairs. Author: (monograph) Peaceful Uses of Outer Space, 1999, An International Satellite Monitoring Agency (ISMA), 1999, Outer Space for the Benefit of All Humanity, 2003; contbr. chapters to books, 1990, articles to profl. jours. Co.-chmn. McGovern Pres. Com., Philadelphia, 1972; chmn. New Dem. Coalition, Philadelphia, 1972—73; del. Dem. Nat. Con., Miami, 1972; co-chmn. CROP Walk of Chestnut Hill, Philadelphia; lect. Archdiocese Phila. Recipient Alt. scholar, Fulbright Scholars, 2000. Mem.: Intern. Inst. Space Law. Office: The Kurtz Inst Peacemaking PO Box 1330 Cheshire CT 06410 Office Phone: 203-272-0754. E-mail: kurtzinstitute@sbcglobal.net.

DRISCOLL, CONSTANCE FITZGERALD, education educator, writer, consultant; b. Lawrence, Mass., Mar. 29, 1926; d. John James and Mary Anne (Leecock) Fitzgerald; m. Francis George Driscoll, Aug. 21, 1948; children: Frances Mary, Martha Anne, Sara Helene, Maribeth Lee. AB, Radcliffe Coll., 1946; postgrad., Harvard U., U. Hartford, U. Bridgeport, U. Mass. Secondary sch. tchr., North Andover, Mass., 1946-48; book reviewer N.Y.C. and Boston pubs., 1955-64; asst. conf. edn. dir. U. Hartford, 1964-68; lectr. Pace U., N.Y.C., 1973-74; edn. commentary Radio WVOX, New Rochelle, N.Y., 1974-75; asst. ednl. adv. Nat. Girl Scouts, 1972-74; pres., owner, dir. Open Corridor Schs. Cons., Inc., Bronxville, N.Y., 1972-84; pres., dir. Open Corridor Schs., Inc., Oxford, Mass., 1984—2003, Sarasota and Jacksonville, Fla., 2003—, Bradenton, Fla., 2003—. Dir. assoc. grad. edn. program with U. Hartford, Bronxville, N.Y., 1975-82; dir. grad. edn. program Witt U. Bridgeport, Greenwich, Conn., 1975-82; creator in svc. edn. programs pub. schs., Norwalk, Conn., 1983-88; assoc. Worcester State Coll., 1984-85, Fitchburg State Coll., 1986-87; dir. assoc. grad. edn. for tchrs. Anna Maria Coll., Paxton, Mass., 1990-94; assoc. grad. tchr. edn. courses Fitchburg State Coll., 1995-99; English instr. grades 9-12, Bais Chana H.S. for Girls, Worcester, Mass., 2000—; provider long distance learning grad. edn. courses, Antigua and Anguilla, 1997—, U. Bridgeport, Conn., 1995—, assoc. agy. for grad. edn. courses for tchrs., 1995—; profl. devel. points provider Mass. State Dept. Edn., 1995—; tutor, cons. Worcester County Sch. Dists., 1989-95; CEU mgr. for Conn. Dept. Edn. O.C.S., Inc., Conn., 1989—; bi-lingual instr. for Indian and Vietnamese students in grades 5-12, 1988-91; freelance writer newspapers and small jours., 1991—; dir. grad. edn. courses for tchrs. Mass. Coll. Liberal Arts, North Adams, Mass., 1999—; cons. coll./univ. and grad. sch. placement, admissions procedures, 2000—; adviser, cons. Radcliffe Coll. Admissions Coun., 1946-48; summer dir. swim program ARC, North Andover, Mass., 1942-47; cons. Girl Scouts U.S., health guide multicultural program Greater Lawrence, Mass., 1946-48, holiday radio program, Thanksgiving 1774, Antigua and Barbuda; lectr., series for Girl Guides, Antigua, W.I., Nov., 1974. Author curriculum materials; contbr. poetry to Poetry Corner in The Patriot newspaper, 1994—, others. Recipient Educator award Nat. Coun. ARC, Washington, 1985, Edn. award Nipmuc Am. Indian Coun., Webster, Mass., 1985. Office: Open Corridor Schs Inc 3522 53d Ave W Ste 160 Bradenton FL 34210 also: Open Corridor Schs Inc 1015 Atlantic Blvd Ste 273 Atlantic Beach FL 32233

DRISCOLL, GENEVIEVE BOSSON (JEANNE BOSSON DRISCOLL), management and organization development consultant; b. Pitts., Mar. 26, 1937; d. George August and Emma Haling Bleichner; m. John Edwin Bosson, June 17, 1959; 1 child, Matthew Edwin; m. Frederick Driscoll, Oct. 7, 1972; stepchildren: Jennifer Locke, Cynthia Hall, Molly Davis, Julie Ann. BS cum laude, Fla. State U., 1959; postgrad., Nat. Tng. Labs., 1970. Planning asst. Ctr. Planning and Innovation, Dept. Edn. State of N.Y., 1967-71; planning cons. So. Tier Regional Office for Ednl. Planning, Elmira, N.Y., 1971-72; tng. dir. Neusteters, Inc., Denver, 1973-74; orgn. devel. specialist CONNECT, Inc., N.Y.C., 1975-77; cons. Robert H. Schaffer & Assocs., Stamford, Conn., 1977-80; ptnr. Driscoll Cons. Group, Williamstown, Mass., 1980-99; sales tng. mgr. Sheaffer Eaton, Pittsfield, Mass., 1983, mgr. human resources and orgn. devel., 1983-88; dir. human resources Canyon Ranch, Berkshires, 1989-95; dir. The Learning Inst., Bennington, Vt., 1997-99; ret., 1999. Office: 24 Lee Ter Williamstown MA 01267-2039

DRISCOLL, KATHLEEN J. writer; b. Boston, May 31, 1946; d. Frederick S. and Catherine T. McNamara D., one child, Catherine. Columnist, journalist The Patriot Ledger, Quincy, MA, 1979-84; editor The Pembroke Mariner, Pembroke, MA, 1984-86; acting pub., columnist South Shore News, Rockland, MA, 1986-94; columnist The Milton Times, Milton, MA, 1995—; feature writer Metro West Daily News, Framington, Mass., 1998—. Author, poetry, Dirty Woman's Rag, 1992, columns, features, NEPA, NFPW, Mass Media Women, etc. Vice pres., Natl. Org. for Women/MA, Mass., 1987-89. Mem., Natl. Writer's Union. Mailing: 451 Beech St Roslindale MA 02131

DRISCOLL, KIMBERLEE MARIE, lawyer; b. Binghamton, N.Y., July 17, 1961; d. Patrick Donald and Diane Cecile (Richmond) Lake; m. Matthew Victor Driscoll, Aug. 6, 1983; 1 child, John Patrick. BA, Colgate U., 1983; JD, Union U., 1986. Bar: N.Y. 1987, Mass. 1988. Asst. gen. counsel Oxbow Corp., Dedham, Mass., 1987-90; corp. counsel, sec. Putnam, Hayes & Bartlett, Inc., Cambridge, Mass., 1990-92; v.p., gen. counsel Merrill Internat. Ltd., Cambridge, 1992—. Mem. ABA (vice chair spl. com. internat. energy law 1993—), Am. Corp. Counsel Assn., Mass. Bar Assn., N.Y. Bar Assn. Home: 22 Battleflagg Rd Bedford MA 01730-2026 Office: Merrill Internat Ltd 200 Great Rd Ste 258 Bedford MA 01730-2750

DRISCOLL, LORRAINE EVA, obstetrician-gynecologist; b. Jersey City, Mar. 15, 1954; d. Anthony Edmunt and Albina Elizabeth (Kundracky) Zolnowski; m. Patrick Joseph Driscoll, Aug. 27, 1977; children: Kathrine Eva, Joseph Anthony Descours, Elizabeth Lucienne. BS in Biochemistry, St. Peter's Coll., Jersey City, 1976; MD, N.Y. Med. Coll., 1981. Diplomate Am. Bd. Obstetrics and Gynecology. Resident Lenox Hill Hosp., N.Y.C., 1981-85; pvt. practice N.Y.C., 1985-92, Rutherford, N.J., 1992—; staff physician Holy Name Hosp., Teaneck, N.J., St. Mary's Hosp., Passaic, N.J., Gen. Hosp. Ctr., Passaic, N.J., Hackensack (N.J.) U. Med. Ctr. Lectr. in field. Troop leader Girl Scouts U.S., Rutherford, 1995—, asst. scoutmaster Troop 166 Boy Scouts Am., Wood Badge, N.J. Fellow Am. Coll. Obstetricians and Gynecologists; mem. AMA, N.J. Med. Assn., Bergen County Med. Assn., Am. Med. Women's Assn., N.J. Med. Women's Assn., Lions Club. Roman Catholic. Avocations: needlework, camping, reading. Office: 9 Ridge Rd Rutherford NJ 07070-2020

DRISCOLL, VIRGILYN MAE (SCHAETZEL), retired art educator, artist, consultant; b. Fond du Lac, Wis., May 14, 1932; d. Edward William and Louise (Heider) Schaetzel; m. Patrick A. Driscoll, Aug. 13, 1955; children: Mark P., Craig A., Chris T. BS in Art Edn., Wis. State Coll., 1954; MS in Art, U. Wis., Milw., 1973. Tchr. elem. art Green Bay (Wis.) Pub. Schs., 1954-55, Elm-Brook Pub. Schs., Elm Grove, Brookfield, Wis., 1955-58, supr. elem. art, 1958-66; tchr. secondary art, dept. chair Greendale (Wis.) Pub. Schs., 1967—93; exec. dir. Wis. Alliance Arts Edn., 1993—2000; dir., co-founder Wis. Champions for Arts Edn. Bus. and Cmty. Advs., Inc., 2002—. Arts Edn. Cons., 2000—; art curriculum task force Wis. Dept. Pub. Instrn., 1981—85; mem. task force Wis. Plan Arts Edn., Arts in Sch.s Basic Edn. Grant, 1986—88; mem. State Supts. Commn. Arts Edn., 1988—89; coord. Student Art Exhibit Wis. Assn. Sch. Bd. Joint Conv., 1988—; mem. steering com. arts edn. Wis. Arts Bd., Wis. Alliance Arts Edn., Dept. Pub. Instrn., 1992—; chmn. Wis. Challenging Content Stds. in Arts, 1994—96; coord., facilitator State Supt.'s Blue Ribbon Commn. Arts Edn., 1999—2000; mem. task force Wis. Dept. Pub. Instrn. Integrated Curriculum Guide, 1999—2000; hon. bd. dirs. Wis. Alliance Arts Edn., 2000—. Mem. editl. bd. Spectrum: Jour. Wis. Art Edn., 1986—87, 1988—90; author: (handbook) National Year of Secondary Art, 1990. Named Educator of the Yr., Beloit (Wis.) Coll., 1986, Wis. Rep. Tchr. Inst., 50th Ann. Nat. Gallery Art, Washington, 1991; recipient Excellence in the Arts award, 2000, cert. of Recognition in the Arts and Art Edn., 2000, Disting. Alumnus award, U. Wis., 2001, Distinction award for Dance Edn., 2002. Mem.: NEA, Milw. Area Tchrs. Art (pres. 1982—83), Wis. Painters and Sculptors, Wis. Alliance Art Edn. (pres. 1991—, bd. dirs.), Wis. Art Edn. Assn. (mem. adv. bd. Young Artists Workshop 1982—99, pres. 1985—87, 1987—89, mem. coun., Wis. Art Educator of the Yr. 1989, Career award 2000—), Nat. Art Edn. Assn. (bd. dirs. 1984—89, secondary divsn. dir., mem. exec. com. 1989—91, We. Region Art Educator of Yr. 1990), U. Wis. Milw. Alumni Assn. (1st v.p. 1966—73, pres. 1968—69, pres., emeritus bd. trustee 1996—2000, emeritus trustee 2000—, co-chair Chancellor's Soc. 2000—03, bd. dirs. womens alumni). Avocation: running. Home: 1161 N Lost Woods Rd Oconomowoc WI 53066-8790

DRISKELL, LUCILE G. artist; b. N.Y.C., Dec. 20, 1924; d. Charles Albert and Clarice Dorothy (Jung) Gall; m. Richard O. Driskell, Sept. 4, 1946; children: Douglas G., Donald A., David O. AA, Finch Coll., 1945; student, La Jolla Art Ctr., Calif., 1956-63, Fratelli Da Prato Foundry, Pietra Santa, Italy, 1973-78, Art Students League, N.Y.C., 1984-88. Artist, San Diego, Calif., 1950-63, Cin., 1963-67, Aspen, Colo., 1967-72, Greve in Chianti, Italy, 1972-79, Wellsboro, Pa., 1979—, Phila., 1985—. Represented by Environment Gallery, N.Y.C., 1968—84, Rodger Lapelle Gallery, Phila., 1984—, Agora Gallery, NY, 1993—2002, Amsterdam Whitney Internat. Fine Arts, N.Y.C., 2002—. Sculptures, 1960—, wall reliefs, 1988—, prints, 1956—, Represented in permanent collections Woodmere Art Mus., Phila. Recipient Purchase award, Exxon, N.Y.C., 1978, Wachovia Bank, Wilmington, Del., 1996, Macy's, Washington, 1989, SAS Inst., Inc., Cary, N.C., 2001. Mem.: Nas. Assn. Women Artists, Washington Sculpture Group, Internat. Sculpture Ctr., Art Students League (life). Avocations: hiking, photography, travel. Home: 389 Fischler St Ext Wellsboro PA 16901-8925

DRIVER, MARTHA WESTCOTT, English language educator, writer, researcher; b. N.Y.C., Oct. 24; d. Albert Westcott and Martha Louise (Miller) D.; m. Thomas Edward Earl Rhodes, Aug. 4, 2001. BA, Vassar Coll., 1974; MA, U. Pa., 1975, PhD, 1980. Lectr. English Vassar Coll., N.Y.C., 1980-81; from asst. prof. to assoc. prof. Pace U., N.Y.C., 1981-95, prof. English, 1995—2003, Disting. prof. English, 2003—, dir. honors program, 1998-2000. Cons. N.Y. Pub. Libr., 1984; seminar participant Folger Inst., Folger Shakespeare Libr., 1994. Editor: Jour. of the Early Book Soc., 1998—2004; guest editor: Film & History: The Middle Ages, 1998—99, Literary and Linguistic Computing, 1999; contbr. 35 articles to profl. jours. Mem., lectr. St. John the Divine, N.Y.C., 1995. Recipient Dyson Achievement award, 2003; grantee Rsch. tools grantee, NEH, 1995, travel grantee, Am. Coun. Learned Socs., 1995, NSF, 2001—;, Houghton Libr. Harvard U. fellow, 1996—97. Mem. Early Book Soc. (chair 1988—), Coll. Art Assn., Medieval Acad. Am., Modern Humanities Rsch. Assn. (U.K.), Medieval Club of N.Y. (conf. coord. 1989-94. pres. 1987-89), Internat. Ctr. Medieval Art, Internat. Arthurian Soc., Medieval Feminist Art History Project, New Chaucer Soc. Episcopalian. Avocations: dance, museums, theater, concerts. Office: Pace U English Dept 41 Park Row New York NY 10038-1508 E-mail: mdriver@pace.edu.

DRIVER, SHARON HUMPHREYS, marketing executive; b. Staten Island, N.Y., Jan. 5, 1949, d. William Edward and Gloria (McCrave) Humphreys; m. William Weston Driver, Jr., June 3, 1972; children: Christopher John, Andrea Nicole. BA, Manhattanville Coll., Purchase, N.Y., 1970; MA, Coll. New Rochelle, N.Y., 1973. Lic. tchr., N.Y. Tchr. Somers (N.Y.) Ctrl. Sch. Dist., 1970-76, Ossining (N.Y.) Village Recreation Dept., 1983-87; media coord., bookkeeper Equation Comm., White Plains, N.Y., 1986-89; media dir. Sims Freeman O'Brien, Elmsford, N.Y., 1989-90; project dir. Rsch. Advantage, Hawthorne, N.Y., 1990-92; asst. v.p. Merson/Greener Assocs., Tarrytown, N.Y., 1992-94; pres. Decision Drivers, Briarcliff, 1994—. Sec. tng. liason, Jr. League, Westchester-on-Hudson, 1982-88; sustainer, trainer-facilitator, Jr. League, Tarrytown, 1988-96; past pres. St. Theresa's Parish Coun., Briarcliff Manor, N.Y.; sec. bd. dirs. Ossining Open Door Health Clinic, 1985-89. Mem. NAFE, Am. Mktg. Assn., Women in Comm. (bd. dirs.), Ad Club of Westchester (bd. dirs.), Qualitative Rsch. Cons. Assn., Sleepy Hollow Toastmasters (charter, sec. exec. com.). Roman Catholic. Avocations: boating, hiking. Home: 197 Macy Rd Briarcliff Manor NY 10510-1017

DRIVER-BARSTOW, SUSANNAH, editor; b. N.Y.C., Dec. 28, 1957; d. Tom Faw Driver and Anne Llewelyn Barstow. BA, Wesleyan U., 1979. Accounts payable clk. NYU Book Ctrs., N.Y.C., 1980-83; editl. staff St. Martin's Press, N.Y.C., 1983-85, Inst. Internat. Edn., N.Y.C., 1985; pub.'s asst., editl. staff The Feminist Press, CUNY, N.Y.C., 1985-90, sr. editor, fgn. rights mgr., 1990-95; freelance feminist editor Accord, N.Y., 1996—. Mem. Women in Scholarly Pub., Editl. Freelancers' Assn., Orgn. for the Study of Comm., Lang. and Gender.

DRIZIN, JULIE MERLE, public radio producer; BA in Comm., U. Pa., 1985. News dir. Pacifica Network News, Washington, 1993-96, bur. chief, 1996-98; producer Democracy Now, 1996-98; sr. prodr. "Justice Talking" Annenberg Pub. Policy Ctr., Washington, 1999—. Office: Annenberg Pub Policy Ctr Univ of Penn 320 Nat Press Bldg Washington DC 20045 Business E-Mail: jdrizin@appcpenn.org.

DROKE, EDNA FAYE, retired elementary school educator; b. Sylvester, Tex., Dec. 4, 1932; d. Ira Selle and Faye Emily (Seckinger) Tucker; m. Louis Albert Droke, June 2, 1951; children: Sherman Ray, Lyndon Allen, Lona Faye Droke Cheairs. BEd, Tarleton State U., Stephenville, Tex., 1983. Cert. ESL and 3d-8th lang. arts tchr., Tex. Tchr. ESL and lang. arts Wingate (Tex.) Ind. Sch. Dist., 1983-86; tchr. 2d grade and ESL Collidge (Tex.) Ind. Sch. Dist., 1986-88; tchr. 4th grade and ESL Peaster (Tex.) Ind. Sch. Dist., 1988-89; tchr. Chpt. I in 1st-6th grades, ESL in K-12th grades Ranger (Tex.) Ind. Sch. Dist., 1989-96, tchr. E.S.L. 3d grade, reading recovery tchr., 1996-98, ret., 1998; substitute tchr. I.S.D., Blanket, Tex.; E.S.L. tchr. 220th CSCD, Comanche, Tex. Tutor Hispanic probationers in English for 220th Dist. Ct., Comanche, Tex., Gustine (Tex.) Ind. Sch. Dist. Reading Improvement, 2000-2003. Mem. ASCD, Kappa Delta Pi, Alpha Chi. Baptist. Avocations: reading, quilting, knitting, playing piano, painting. Home: PO Box 44 Comanche TX 76442-0044

DROKE, MARILYN LOIS, music educator; b. Poplar, Mont., June 25, 1942; d. William Mark and Rose Agnes (Seed) Blankenship; m. Don R. Droke, Aug. 15, 1964; children: DeAnna Rae, Rhonda Lea, Dawn Michelle. MusB, Evangel Coll., Mo., 1964; MA, Southwest Mo. State U., 1981. Music instr. Sparta (Mo.) Pub. Schs., 1964—65, Galena (Mo.) Pub. Schs., 1965—68, Forsyth (Mo.) Pub. Schs., 1968—69, 1971—81, Hollister (Mo.) Pub. Schs., 1969—71, Branson (Mo.) Pub. Schs., 1981—2003; music educator Coll. of the Ozarks, Pt. Lookout, Mo., 1982—. Choir dir. Branson (Mo.) Bible Ch., First Bapt. Ch., Branson, Mo., 1984—86. Author: (articles in) Music Educators Jour., 1981—2001, Quarters Handbell Quar. Dir. Branson (Mo.) Arts Coun., 2002. Recipient Star Citizen, Branson Bus. Assn., 1993. Mem.: Mo. Music Educators, Mo. State Tchrs. Assn. (sec.). Avocations: sports, crafts.

DROLL, RUTH LUCILLE, missionary pastor; b. Peoria, Ill., Mar. 13, 1941; d. Elisha John Droll and Beulah Lorene West-Droll; 1 child, Ruth Lucille. BA in bible theology, No. Ctrl. Mpls., 1963. Missionary pastor Assemblies of God, Ariz., 1963—2003. Home: PO Box 3742 Milan NM 87021 Office: Assembly of God PO Box 402 Prewitt NM 87045-0402

DRONEN, LINDA-KAY, social worker; b. Wichite, Kans., Nov. 28, 1968; d. Sandra Jean Shaleen; m. Theodore Allen Dronen, Mar. 20, 1999; children: Bryce, Reina. BA, Antioch U., 1991; MSW, Calif. State U., 1993. LCSW Calif. Social worker Aspire, Turlock, Calif., 1993—96; inpatient social worker French Hosp., San Luis Obispo, Calif., 1996—99; hospice social worker Vis. Nurse Svc., Sante Marie, Calif., 1996—99, Hospice Inc.,

San Luis Obispo, 1999—2000; prin., owner Lattis Networks, Nipomo, Calif., 2000—03; pvt. practice mental health therapist Nipomo, 2003—. Cons. Lompoc (Calif.) Hosp., 1998—2000. Mem.: NASW. Avocations: reading, walking, music. Office: Lattis Networks 151 W Dana 206 Nipomo CA 93444 Home: 954 Vista Verde Ln Nipomo CA 93444-8959

DRONET, JUDY LYNN, elementary school educator, librarian; b. Kaplan, La., Dec. 9, 1946; d. Percy Joseph and Zula Mae (Harrington) D. BA in Elem. Edn., McNeese State U., 1968, MEd, 1971. Cert. tchr., libr., adminstr., La. Tchr. Shady Grove High Sch., Rosedale, La., 1968-69, Lake Arthur (La.) Elem. Sch., 1969-86, 88-90, Lake Arthur High Sch., 1986-88, 91-92, 1994-95; libr. Henry Heights Elem. Sch.; Lake Charles, La., 1992-93, Welsh Elem. Sch., 1993-94, West End Elm. Sch., 1995-96, Northside Jr. HS, 1996—; state assessor, 1997—; tchr. mentor, 1998—. Univ. supr. McNeese State U., Lake Charles, 1990-91, student tchr. supr.; dir. sch. musical prodns., Lake Arthur, 1976-85; judge sci. and social studies fairs, Lake Arthur, 1985-90, math fair, Jeff Davis Parish, 1993; parish com. Sch. Improvement Plan, 1999—; presenter workshops. Coach girls' softball Lake Arthur Jaycees, 1974; mem. Jeff Davis Parish Arts Coun., Jennings, La., 1990—; mem., hostess Friends of Zigler Mus., Jennings, 1990—; state 1st v.p. Bea Davis Leadership Devel., state com. mem. Mem. La. Assn. Educators, Jeff Davis Parish Assn. Educators (rep.), Calcasieu Parish Assn. Educators, Calcasieu Reading Coun., Women's Libr. Club, Cath. Daus. Am. (sec., regent 1968-93, Dau. of Yr. 1979-80, 93-94), La. Songwriters' Assn. (sec.-treas.), A Block Off Broadway Theater Group (actress, state/props mgr., bd. dirs., choreographer), Delta Kappa Gamma (dist. dir., state chmn., state music rep., state 2nd v.p., Alpha Kappa Golden Apple award, 1999, Epsilon State Achievement award, 2002). Democrat. Roman Catholic. Avocations: oil painting, needlepoint, songwriting, creative writing, singing. Home: PO Box 214 203 Pleasant St Lake Arthur LA 70549-4513

DRONSICK, MARGERY SUTTON, social worker; b. Sommerville, N.J., Oct. 13, 1942; d. Harold Robert and Grace Iona (Hamilton) Sutton; m. Lawrence Richard Dronsick, Jan. 11, 1964; children: Benjamin Michael, Daniel Lawrence. AAS, Wytheville C.C., 1987; BS, Radford U., 1988; MSW, Va. Commonwealth U., 1993. Lic. clin. social worker. Dir. cmty. diversion program Wythe County Cmty. Divsn., Wytheville, Va., 1988-91; crisis counselor Mt. Rogers Cmty. Svcs. Bd., Wytheville, Va., 1991-94; clin. social worker Blue Ridge Counseling Svcs., Bristol, Tenn., 1993-97, Columbia Lewis-Gale Clinic, Christiansburg, Va., 1997-98; psychiat. social worker Twin County Regional Hosp., Galax, Va., 1998—. Adj. faculty criminal justice Wytheville C.C., 1990-93; mem. bioethics com. Pulaski (Va.) Cmty. Hosp., 1997. Mem. NASW, Am. Assn. Christian Counselors. Home: RR 1 Box 123 Rural Retreat VA 24368-9744

DROST, MARIANNE, lawyer; b. Waterbury, Conn., Feb. 21, 1950; d. Albin Joseph and Henrietta Jean (Kremski) D. BA, Conn. Coll., 1972; JD, U. Conn., 1975. Bar: Conn. 1975. Assoc. Ritter, Tapper & Totten, Hartford, Conn., 1975-77; sr. atty. GTE Svc. Corp., Stamford, Conn., 1977-84, Chesebrough-Pond's Inc., Greenwich, Conn., 1984-85; corp. sec. GTE Corp., Stamford, Conn., 1985—; v.p., assoc. gen. counsel fin. GTE Svc. Corp., Stamford, Conn., 1991-97, v.p., dep. gen. counsel, 1997-2000; sr. v.p., dep. gen. counsel, corp. sec. Verizon Comm. Inc., NYC, 2000—. Tutor Lit. Vols., Stamford, 1985-90, bd. dirs. Lit. Vols. Am., 1988-94. Mem. ABA, Am. Soc. Corp. Secs. (former pres., bd. dirs. Fairfield-Westchester chpt.).

DROZ, ELIZABETH JANE, foundation administrator; b. Aug. 19, 1923; m. John J. Droz, May 26, 1945; 9 children. BS, Cornell U., 1944; M, Syracuse U., 1982. Founder, operator Kitchens by Elizabeth; exec. dir., sec., human resource chair Good News Found. Ctrl. N.Y. Inc., Utica, 1992—. TV comentator and fashion model; owner local real estate firm. Adult edn. advocate Eastern Vicariate, Diocese of Syracuse, N.Y.; pres. several sch. bds.; past mem. Cath. Charities Bd., St. Elizabeth's Hosp. Guild; mem. Fulton Chain of Lakes Assn., Adirondack Mus. Blue Mt. Lake, Arts Guild of Old Forge, Munson Williams Proctor Art Inst.; mem. edn. com. Deacon Cmty. of Syracuse Diocese; eucharistic min. Our Lady of Lourdes; trainer lectors at summer parish St. Bartholomew's Old Forge, lector and eucharistic min. Mem. Ballroom Dance Groups, Found. of Internat. Cooperation. Avocation: travel. Office: Good News Found Ctrl NY 2306 Genesee St Utica NY 13502-5810 E-mail: elizdroz@hotmail.com.

DROZD, PHYLLIS ANN, agricultural products supplier; b. Allegan, Mich., July 26, 1932; d. Edward and Wilma (Busfield) Moored; m. Thomas Drozd, June 20, 1953; children: Julie, T. Jon, Jay H. Sec. Cresent Machine Co., Allegan, Mich., 1949-55; farmer Tom & Phyllis Drozd, Allegan, Mich., 1953-85; co-owner Drozd Seed, Inc., Allegan, Mich., 1953—. Pres. Allegan County Sch. Dist., 1978—; treas., 1965-78; sec.-treas. Allegan County Sch. Bds. Assn., 1991-92; pres. Allengan Bus. & Profl. Women, 1986-87, 91-92, 1st sr. v.p., 1984-85; bd. dirs. Mich. Assn. Sch. Bds., 1993—, v.p., 1999-2000, pres.-elect, 2000-01, pres., 2001—; mem. various ednl. coms. Avocations: reading, collecting antiques, walking, travel. Home and Office: 537 32nd St # M40 Allegan MI 49010-9763 E-mail: pdrozd@accn.org.

DRUCKER, ANA BUENO, healthcare marketing and public relations executive, writer; b. N.Y.C., N.Y., Apr. 27, 1952; m. David M. Kreitzer, June, 1973 (div. Feb. 1979); 1 child, Anatol C. Kreitzer. Sr. writer healthcare Integral Sys., Inc., Walnut Creek, Calif., 1986-88; freelance writer L.A., 1989-92; cons. mktg. Health Net, L.A., 1992-96; pres. Bueno Healthcare Mktg., L.A., 1996-98; assoc. v.p. mktg. and creative svcs. City of Hope Cancer Ctr., L.A., 1998—. Spkr. on branding and healthcare. Author: Special Olympics: The First 25 Years, 1994; contbr. articles to profl. jours. Sponsor, vol. Spl. Olympics, Calif., 1988-96. Recipient Disting. Vol. Svc. award Spl. Olympics, 1992. Mem. AAUW, Jewish Bus. and Profl. Women, The Jewish Fedn. Jewish. Avocation: art collector.

DRUCKER, JACQUELIN F. lawyer, arbitrator, author; b. Celina, Ohio, Oct. 15, 1954; d. Jack Burton and Dorothea (Eckenstein) Davis; m. John H. Drucker, Sept. 8, 1990. BA with distinction and honors, Ohio State U., 1977, JD with honors, 1981. Bar: Ohio 1981, N.Y. 1992, U.S. Supreme Ct. 1989. Legis. asst. Speaker of Ohio Ho. of Reps., Columbus, 1974-78; lobbyist United Auto Workers, Columbus, 1978-81; labor and employment atty. Porter, Wright, Morris & Arthur, Columbus, 1981—84; gen. counsel Ohio Employment Rels. Bd., Columbus, 1984-86, exec. dir., 1986-88, vice chmn., 1988-90; pvt. practice arbitration of employment labor and comml. cases nationwide and the Caribbean, 1990—; dir. labor mgmt. programs sch. indsl. and labor rels. Cornell U., 1994-97. Dir. programs for neutrals Cornell U. Sch. of Indsl. and Labor Rels., 1996—; dir. for ednl. svcs. Cornell Inst. on Conflict Resolution, 1998—; cons. to W.J. Usery Ctr. for Workplace, Ga. State U.; counsel to Gov.'s Task Force on Collective Bargaining, Columbus, 1983-84; adj. prof. labor law Franklin U., Columbus, 1988-89; mem. panel of labor arbitrators Fed. Mediation and Conciliation Svc., Am. Arbitration Assn., AAA Employment Roster of Neutrals of Am. Arbitration Assn., N.Y. State Employment Rels. Bd.; mem. roster of neutrals N.Y.C. Office of Collective Bargaining; mem. panel V.I. Pub. Employment Rels. Bd., N.J. Pub. Employment Rels. Commn., N.Y. Pub. Employment Rels. Bd., Port Authority Employment Rels. Panel; mem. permanent arbitration panel United Mine Workers and Bituminous Coal Operators Assn., Am. Postal Workers Union, U.S. Postal Svc., Westchester Counth Health Care, Off-Track Betting Corp. and Local 32E, State of N.Y. and Pub. Employees Fedn., State of N.Y. and Civil Svc. Employees Assn., Consolidated Edison and Utility Workers Local 1-2, U. Cin. and Dist. 925, Beth Israel Med. Ctr. and 1199 Nat. Health and Human Svcs. Employees Union, Infineum and Teamsters Local 877, Orange County Sheriff and PBA; cons., lectr., spkr. in field. Author: Collective Bargaining Law in Ohio, 1993; editor L.I. Indsl. Rels. Quar., 1995-98, ADR in Employment Law; contbg. editor Pub. Sector Law and Employment Law supplement, 1995, Pub. Sector Labor and Employment Law, 2d edit.; assoc. editor Discipline and Discharge in Arbitration, 1998; editor in chief ADR in Employment Law; contbr. numerous articles to profl. jours. Fellow Coll. Labor and Employment Lawyers; mem. ABA (labor and employment law sect., neutral chmn. employment and labor law com. 2001—, co-chair tng. devel. sub-com. of ADR com. 1998-2001), Nat. Acad. Arbitrators, Ohio State Bar Assn., Assn. of Bar of City of N.Y., N.Y. State Bar Assn. (labor and employment law sect., chmn.-elect 2002-03, chmn. 2003, sec. 1997-98, co-chair ADR in employment com. 1998-2001, continuing legal edu. chair, 2001-2002), N.Y. County Lawyers Assn. (employment law and labor rels. com., chmn. 2003-04), Nassau County Bar Assn., Suffolk County Bar Assn., Indsl. Rels. Rsch. Assn. (N.Y. chpt., Cleve. chpt., L.I. chpt.), Soc. Fed. Labor Rels. Profls. Jewish. Office: 432 E 58th St Suite 2 New York NY 10022-2331 E-mail: jdrucker@aol.com.

DRUHE BRANDT, IRIS CLAIRE, retired elementary school educator; b. New Orleans, Oct. 28, 1935; d. Olivia Catherine Clair and Frederick George Druhe; m. Eugene Maximillian Brandt, June 11, 1960; children: Fred, Brenda, Philip. BA, So. La. U., 1956. Tchr. 2nd and 3rd grades, New Orleans, 1956-59; tchr. 2nd grade Pensacola, Fla., 1961; pre-sch. tchr. Escondido, Calif., 1984-89; clin. rschr. cancer U. Calif., Irvine, Calif., 2002—. Clin. cancer rschr. U. Calif., Irvine, 2002—. Vol. sec. Indian Wells Youth Football League; active Brownie and Cub Scouts Am.; vol. nutritional advisor, counselor Wellness Clinic, Morena Valley, Calif., 1998—2001; supporter D. Day Mus., New Orleans, 2003; mem. Episcopal Women St. Marks. Mem.: AAUW (chair ways and means com.), Humane Soc. U.S., San Diego North County Diabetes County Diabetes Support Group, Women's Assn. Commn. Officers Mess, Navy Relief Soc. (chmn. Lafayette chpt. 1961), Officers Wives Assn. (hospitality chmn., v.p., pres.). Home: 4527 Coronado Dr Oceanside CA 92057-4252

DRULINER, MARCIA MARIE, education educator; b. Dec. 18, 1946; M in Secondary Edn., U. Nebr., 1974; PhD, Marquette U., 1992. Assoc. prof. edn. Concordia Coll., Bronxville, N.Y., 1993-95; asst. prof. edn. Northwestern Coll., Orange City, Iowa, 1998-2000; instr. Spanish, Gretna (Nebr.) Pub. Schs., 2000—. Home: 20184 Glenmore Dr Apt 76 Gretna NE 68028

DRUM, ALICE, academic administrator, educator; b. Gettysburg, Pa., June 22, 1935; d. David Wentz and Charlotte Rebecca (Kinzey) McDannell; m. D. Richard Guise, June 15, 1957 (div. Aug. 1975); children: Gregory, Brent, Richard, Robert, Clay; m. Ray Kenneth Drum, Mar. 2, 1979; 1 child, Trevor. BA magna cum laude, Wilson Coll., 1957; PhD, Am. U., 1976. Adj. prof. gen. studies Antioch U., Columbia, Md., 1976-78; adj. asst. prof. English Gettysburg (Pa.) Coll., 1977-80; lectr. gen. studies Georgetown U., Washington, 1980-81; lectr. gen. honors U. Md., College Park, 1980-83; asst. prof. English Hood Coll., Frederick, Md., 1981-85, coord. writing program, 1981-83, assoc. dean acad. affairs, 1983-85; dean freshmen Franklin and Marshall Coll., Lancaster, Pa., 1985-88, v.p., 1988-2001, prof., chair womens studies, 2001—. Team mem. Mid. States Accreditation Assn., 1989-2003; cons. in field. Co-author: Funding A College Education, 1996; contbr. chpts. to books, articles and book revs. to profl. jours. Chair Lancaster County DA Commn., Lancaster, 1990-91; mem. Lancaster County Commn. on Youth Violence, Lancaster, 1990-91; bd. trustees Wilson Coll., 1997—, YWCA, Lancaster, Mellon grant, 1979; Davison Foreman fellow, 1975-76. Mem. MLA, N.E. MLA, Deans (pres. 1988-89), Coll. English Assn., Phi Beta Kappa (pres. chpt. 1990-91), Phi Kappa Phi. Democrat. Episcopalian. Avocations: hiking, reading, visiting art museums. Office: Franklin & Marshall Coll Lancaster PA 17604-3003

DRUM, JOAN MARIE MCFARLAND, federal agency administrator, educator; b. Waseca, Minn., Mar. 31, 1932; d. Leo Joseph and Bergetthe (Anderson) McFarland; m. William Merritt Drum, June 13, 1954; children: Melissa, Eric. BA in Journalism, U. Minn., 1962; MEd, Coll. William and Mary, 1975, postgrad., 1984-85. Govt. ofcl. fgn. claims br. Social Security Adminstrn., Balt., 1962-64; freelance writer Polyndrum Publs., Newport News, Va., 1967-73; tchr. Newport News (Va.) Pub. Schs., 1975-79; writer, cons. Drum Enterprises, Williamsburg, Va., 1980-82; developer, trainer communicative skills U.S. Army Transp. Sch., Ft. Eustis, Va., 1982-86; govt. ofcl. test assistance div. U.S. Army Tng. Ctr., Ft. Eustis, 1986, course devel. coord. distributed tng. office, 1992. Adj. faculty English dept. St. Leo Area Coll., Ft. Eustis, 1975-78; del. Communicative Skills Conf., Ft. Leavenworth, Kans., 1983; mem. Army Self-Devel. Test Task Force, 1991-92; task force mem. U.S. Army Tng. FAA; program developer multi-media electronic delivery prototype; tech. tng. facility trainer. Author: Ghosts of Fort Monroe, 1972, Travel for Children in Tidewater, 1974, Galaxy of Ghosts, 1992, Hampton's Haunted Houses, 1998, How to Feed a Ghost, 1998; editor: army newsletter for families, 1968-73, Social Services Resource Reference, 1970; contbr. articles to profl. jours. Chmn. Girl Scouts U.S., Tokyo, 1964-66, Army Cmty. Svc., Ft. Monroe, Va., 1967-68; chmn. publicity Hist. Home Tours, Ft. Monroe, 1971-73; chmn. adv. bd. James City County Social Svcs., 1989-95, chmn. adult svcs., 1989-90; mem. James City County Leadership Devel. Program Bd. Recipient numerous civic awards including North Shore Cmty. Svc. award, Hialeah, Hawaii, 1966, Home Bur. Svc. award, 1975, Svc. award Girl Scouts U.S., Tokyo, 1965, Comdrs. achievement award for civilian svc., 1995, 98. Mem.: Va. Writers Club. Home: 9 Bray Wood Rd Williamsburg VA 23185-5504 E-mail: wmd09@cox.net.

DRUM, SYDNEY MARIA, artist; b. Calgary, Alta., Can., Nov. 20, 1952; d. Ian Mondelet and Dorothy Mary (Weaver) D.; m. Frank DeSalvo, Nov. 7, 1987; 1 child, Christopher. BFA with distinction in art, U. Calgary, 1974; MFA, York U., 1976. Tchr. U. Ill., 1978-83, Govs. State U., 1983-84, Rutgers U., 1984-87. One-woman and 2 person exhibits include Art Gallery Ont., 1978, Condeso/Lawler Gallery, N.Y., 1981, Gallery Pascal, 1983, U. Pitts., 1984, Bau-Xi Gallery, Toronto, 1987, 90, 92, 95, 55 Mercer Gallery, N.Y., 1993, 96, Mus. am Ostwall, Dortmund, Germany, 1994, Hart House-U. Toronto, 1995; represented in pub. collections Can. Coun. Art Bank, U. Toronto, Toronto-Dominion Bank, Petro Can., Mus. Modern Art, N.Y., Phila. Mus. Art, Robert McLaughlin Gallery, Oshawa; commissions include Pope, Ballard, Shepard & Fowle, Chgo., 1983, Zimmerli Mus., Rutgers U., 1990; reviewer art exhibits New Art Examiner, Chgo., 1983-84. Can. Coun. grantee, 1978. Home: 138 W 120th St New York NY 10027-6401

DRUMHELLER, JANET LOUISE, librarian; b. Walton, W. Va., June 23, 1951; d. Nathan Earl and Edna Osial (Dye) Vineyard; m. Fred John Drumheller, Apr. 11, 1971; 1 child, Stephanie Katarina. BS in History, U. Tenn., 1974, MS in Libr. and Info. Scis., 1977. Mgr. Farragut br. Knox County Pub. Librs., Knoxville, Tenn., 1977—81, reference libr., 1983—96, reference svcs. mgr., 1996—. Bd. dirs. Tenn-Share. Bd. dirs. Knoxville-Oak Ridge Regional Network. Mem.: East Tenn. Libr. Assn., Tenn. Libr. Assn. Office: Knox County Libr System 500 W Church Ave Knoxville TN 37902

DRUMMOND, CAROL CRAMER, voice educator, singer, artist, writer; b. Indpls., Mar. 5, 1933; adopted d. Burr Ostin and L. Ruth Welch; m. Roscoe Drummond, 1978 (dec. 1983). Student, Butler U., 1951—53; studied voice with Todd Duncan, Frances Yeend, James Benner, Rosa Ponselle, Dr. Peter Herman Adler and John Bullock; studied drama with Adelaide Bishop, Washington, D.C. Original performer Starlite Musicals, Indpls., 1951; singer Am. Light Opera Co., Washington, Seagle Opera Colony, Schroon Lake, N.Y., 1963, 64; soloist St. John's Episcopal Ch., Lafayette Sq., Washington, 5th Ch. of Christ, Scientist, Washington, 1963-78; performer Concerts in Schs. Program, Washington Performing Arts Soc., 1967-99; soloist with Luke AFB band ofcl. opening Boswell Meml. Hosp, Sun City, Ariz., 1970; painter, artist, 1980—; pvt. tchr. voice, 1986—; voice tchr. Ellsworth H.S., Mt. Desert Island H.S., 1986—. Soloist numerous oratorio socs.; appearances with symphony orchs. including Nat. Symphony Orch., Fairfax (Va.) Symphony Orch., Buffalo Philharm. Orch., Concerts in the Pk., Arlington Opera Co., Lake George Opera Co., Glens Falls, NY, The Nat. Cathedral, Washington, Noye's Flood, Lufkin, Tex., 1965, Washington Opera; voiceover radio and TV commls., 1965—84; U.S. Govt. host The Sounding Bd. Sta. WGTS-FM, Washington, 1972—70, dir. ensembles, music/voice cons. Summer Festival of the Arts, S.W. Harbor, Maine, 1992—95, mem. adv. bd., 1986—; dri. Amahl and the Night Visitors, 1992; vocal solo concert The Smithsonian Instn., 1980. Former columnist: Animal Crackers, writer: newspaper and mag. articles and stories; one-woman shows include, Lemon Tree, Bangor, 1995, 1996, Grand Theater, Ellsworth, Maine, 1995, Southwest Harbor (Maine) Pub. Libr., 1997, U. Maine, 1999, Border's, Bangor, 2002; two-woman shows including, Am. Art League, Washington, 1997, two-woman show Cosmos Club, Wash., 1996, Arts Club, 1994, 1995, 1996, artist, owner Dream Come True Notecards, 1997—. Bd. dirs. Washington Sch. Ballet, 1978; life bd. dirs. Internat. Soundex Reunion Registry, Carson City, Nev. Recipient 1st pl. women's divsn. Internat. Printers Ink Contest, 1951. Mem.: Nat. League Am. Pen Women, Beta Sigma Phi, Kappa Kappa Gamma. Republican. Episcopalian. Avocations: cats, knitting, gardening, reading, travel. Home: PO Box 791 79 Clark Point Rd Southwest Harbor ME 04679 Office: 10802 Tradewind Dr Oakton VA 22124-1800 E-mail: ccdrummond@gwi.net.

DRUMMOND, WILLA HENDRICKS, physiology and medical educator; b. Harrisburg, Pa., Dec. 5, 1945; d. George Edson and Leah Clementine (Connelly) Hendricks; m. Thomas Weston Drummond, June 1966 (div. 1978). BA cum laude, Brown U., 1966; MD, U. Pa., 1970; MS in Med. Informatics, U. Utah, 1999. Resident in pediat. Children's Hosp. Phila., 1970-72, cardiology fellow, 1972-74; instr. pediat. U. Pa., Phila., 1973-74; rsch. fellow perinatology U. Oreg., Portland, 1974-75; staff pediatrician Kaiser-Permanente Clinics, Portland, 1975-76; instr. neonatology, fellow Cardiovasc. Rsch. Inst.-U. Calif., San Francisco, 1976-78; asst. prof. pediat. U. Fla., Gainesville, 1978-82, asst. prof. pediat. and physiology, 1981-82, assoc. prof. pediat. physiology and vet. med. scis., 1982-88, prof., 1988—. Cons. Baxter-Travenol Labs., Deerfield, Ill., 1986-88; co-chair Equine Neonatology Study Group, Gainesville, 1981-91; dir. Neonatology Fellowship Program U. Fla., Gainesville, 1981-85; cons., chief info. officer, chief med. officer, ICU DataSys., Inc., Gainesville. Contbr. numerous rsch. papers and abstracts to profl. jours.; poet: Carousel of Progress, 1979. Rsch. grantee (22) including Am. Heart Assn., NIH, Dept. of Def., 1976—; sr. fellow Med. Informatics, 1997-99. Mem. Am. Physiologic Soc., Soc. for Pediat. Rsch., Am. Pediat. Soc., Am. Acad. Pediat., Am. Med. Informatics Assn., Am. Heart Assn., So. Soc. Pediat. Rsch., Internat. Soc. Vet. Perinatology (bd. dirs., pres. 1995-97), Internat. Physicians for Prevention of Nuc. War (collective Nobel Peace Prize 1985), NOW, Sierra Club, other environ., women's and peace orgns. Democrat. Office: U Fla Coll Medicine PO Box 100296 Gainesville FL 32610-0296

DRUMMOND BORG, LESLEY MARGARET, clinical geneticist; b. Wellington, New Zealand, Oct. 26, 1948; came to U.S., 1986; d. Grant Allen and Yolanda Drummond; m. Kenneth Irvin Borg; children: Marc, Kyle. MBChB, Otago Med. Sch., New Zealand, 1971, MD, 1983; BSc, Auckland U., New Zealand, 1976. Diplomate Am. Bd. Pediatrics, Am. Bd. Med. Genetics; cert. clin. geneticist. Fellow in clin. genetics U. Auckland Med. Sch., 1974-77, med. geneticist, 1977-79; pediatric resident Hosp. Sick Children, Toronto, Ont., Can., 1980-82; gen. practitioner ARAMCO, Saudi Arabia, 1983-86; sr. fellow med. genetics U. Wash., Seattle, 1986-88; clin. geneticist Genetic Screening and Counseling Svc., Denton, Tex., 1988-95; dir., genetics divsn. Tex. Dept. of Health, Austin, Tex., 1995—. Clin. asst. prof. Tex. A&M U., College Station, 1991-98; cons. staff Odessa (Tex.) Women's Children's Hosp., 1991-96, Cook/Ft. Worth Children's Med. Ctr., 1991-98. Contbr. articles to profl. jours. Fellow Am. Acad. Pediatrics, Am. Coll. Med. Genetics (founder); mem. AMA, Am. Soc. Human Genetics. Avocations: jogging, swimming, hiking. Office: Tex Dept of Health Div Genetic Screening/Case Mgr 1100 W 49th St Austin TX 78756-3160

DRUSHAL, MARY ELLEN, education educator, former academic administrator; b. Peru, Ind., Oct. 24, 1945; d. Herrell Lee and Opal Marie (Boone) Waters; m. J. Michael Drushal, June 12, 1966; children: Lori, Jeff. B of Music Edn., Ashland Coll., 1969; MS, Peabody Coll., 1981; PhD, Vanderbilt U., 1986. Dir. music and spl. ednl. projects Smithville (Ohio) Brethren Ch., 1969-74; tchr. music Orrville (Ohio) Pub. Schs., 1969—70; seminar leader Internat. Ctr. for Learning, Glendale, Calif., 1974-76; dir. Christian edn. First Presbyn. and Christ Presbyn. Ch., Nashville, 1976-84; assoc. prof. Ashland (Ohio) Theol. Sem., 1984-91, acad. dean, 1991-95; provost Ashland U., 1995—2001, prof. edn., 2001—. Cons. in strategic planning for not-for-profit orgns. Author: On Tablets of Human Hearts: Christian Education with Children, 1991; co-author: Spiritual Formation: A Personal Walk Toward Emmaus, 1990; contbr. articles to profl. jours. Trustee Brethren Care Found., Ashland, 1989-99, Ashland Symphony Orch., 1986-87; pres., fundraiser Habitat for Humanity, Ashland, 1990-94; bd. dirs. JOY Day Care Ctr., 1988-90. Grantee Lilly Endowment Inc., 1991, 93, Brethren Ch. Found., 1989, 90. Mem. Assn. Theol. Schs. (com. underrepresented constituencies 1994-96), Am. Assn. for Higher Edn., Nat. Assn. Ch. Bus. Adminstrs., N.Am. Assn. Profs. of Christian Edn., Assn. Profs. and Rschrs. in Religious Edn., Nat. Assn. Evangelicals, Nat. Assn. Black Evangelical Assns., Epiphany Assn. (bd. dirs. 1994-98). Republican. Presbyterian. Avocations: reading, needlepoint. Office: Ashland U 401 College Ave Ashland OH 44805-3799 Office Phone: 419-289-5192. E-mail: medrusha@ashland.edu.

DRUSHELL, BARBARA JEAN, retired education educator; b. Jersey City, Nov. 20, 1941; d. Stephen and Jean Turzynski; m. Herbert Theophilus Drushell III, Sept. 9, 1967 (dec. June 1996); children: Andrea, Theo. BA summa cum laude, Douglass Coll., 1963; MA, Harvard U., 1964, PhD, 1971. Tchg. fellow Harvard U., Cambridge, Mass., 1964—66; instr. Ohio State U., Columbus, Ohio, 1967—68; lectr. Calif. State U., Bakersfield, Calif., 1984—92. Fellow Woodrow Wilson Fellowship, 1963—64. Mem.: AAUW, MENSA, Phi Beta Kappa. Democrat. Roman Catholic. Achievements include first to Determine new dates for Rhodian amphora handles, which are important dating tools in archeaol. excavations; spearheaded a successful fundraising campaign for a Tanzanian mission. Home: 2924 Waverly Dr Cameron Park CA 95682-9258

DRVAR, MARGARET ADAMS, vocational education educator; b. Morgantown, W.Va., Dec. 22, 1953; d. Lester Morris and Daun Collette (Benson) Adams; m. Marvin Lynn Drvar, July 29, 1978; children: Jacob Elias, Jared Nathaniel. BS in Family Resources, W.Va. U., 1977, MS in Family Resources, 1982. Cert. tchr., vocat. family and consumer scis. tchr., W.Va. Substitute tchr. Monongalia County Bd. Edn., Morgantown, 1983-86; tchr. vocat. family and consumer sci. Clay Battelle Jr.-Sr. H.S., Blacksville, W.Va., 1986-89, 91-92, South Mid. Sch., Morgantown, 1992—, treas. faculty senate, 1997—. Instr. culinary arts Monongalia County Tech. Edn. Ctr., Morgantown, 1989-91; youth group adv. Family, Career, Cmty. Leaders Am. (formerly Future Homemakers of Am.), 1986—. V.p. United Meth. Women, Brookhaven, W.Va., 1985-92; sec. bd. trustees Brookhaven United Meth. Ch., 1989-97; bd. dirs., sec. Morgantown AES Fed. Credit Union, 1989—; vol. 4-H leader Brookhaven Bulls 4-H Club, 1992—. Recipient Master Advisor award, Future Homemakers Am. Inc., 1996, Golden Apple Achiever award, Ashland Oil, 1996, Outstanding 4-H Leader Monongalia County award, 1996, Tchr. of Yr. award, W.Va. Family and Consumer Sci. Assn., 2002, Top 10 Tchrs. of the Yr., Am. Assn. of Family and Consumer Scis., 2002, 4-H All Star award for yrs. of cmty. svc., W.Va. 4-H, 2003. Mem.: NEA, Monongalia County 4-H Leaders Assn. (pres. 1998—99, 2001—03), W.Va. Vocat. Assn. (historian family and consumer sci. divsn. 1995—96), Assn. for Career and Tech. Edn., Monongalia County Assn. of Family and Consumer Scis., W.Va.Assn. Family and Consumer Scis., Monongalia County Edn. Assn., W.Va. Edn. Assn., Am. Assn. Family and Consumer Scis. (cert.) (Top 10 Tchr. of Yr. 2002), Gamma Phi Beta,

Alpha Upsilon Omicron. Avocations: travel, camping. Home: 3307 Darrah Ave Morgantown WV 26508-9187 Office: Monongalia County Schs South Mid Sch 500 E Parkway Dr Morgantown WV 26501-6839 E-mail: mdrvar@access.k12.wv.us.

DRY, JUDITH KALLEN, dental hygienist, cable producer, writer; b. Chgo., Apr. 5, 1952; d. Irwi Arthur and Marion (Silverman) Kallen; m .Fred Mark Dry, Aug. 14, 1973 (div. May 1985). BA, Northwestern U., 1980, student, 1982. Registered dental hygienist. Dental hygienist A.D.H.A., Chgo., 1982—; freelance dental cons. Chgo., 1982—. Prodr., writer standup comedy HBO, Comic Relief, Second City, Zanies, Politically Incorrect, The Improv; contbr. WGN-AM comedy routines. Avocations: design, dance, cooking, investing. Home: 4250 N Marine Dr Apt 602 Chicago IL 60613-1723

DRYDEN, MARY ELIZABETH, law librarian, writer, actress; b. Chgo., Oct. 18, 1952; d. James Heard and Hazel Anne (Potts) Rule; m. Ian Dryden, Nov. 22, 1975 (div. 1990, dec. 1993); m. Stephen Quadros, Sept. 12, 1992 (div. 1996); m. Larry Borkin, Jan. 3, 2003. Student, U. London, 1969, Bath U., 1970; BA, Scripps Coll., 1971; postgrad., U. Edinburgh, 1971-74. Libr. dir. Hahn, Cazier & Leff, San Diego, 1980, Fredman, Silverberg & Lewis, San Diego, 1980-83, Riordan & McKinzie, L.A., 1985—2003. Freelance photog. model, 1973-85. Theatrical appearances include Antony and Cleopatra, London, 1984, Table Manners, L.A., 1985, Julius Caesar, L.A., 1986, Witness for the Prosecution, L.A., 1987, Come and Go, L.A., 1988, The Actor's Nightmare, L.A., 1989, The Dresser, L.A., 1989, Absent Friends, Long Beach, Calif., 1990, Run For Your Wife!, Long Beach, 1991, The Hollow, Long Beach, 1992, Cock and Bull Story, Hollywood, 1993, Towards Zero, Long Beach, 1993, Angel Street, L.A., 1994, Bedroom Farce, L.A., 1995, Postmortem, L.A., A Weekend with Sam Beckett, L.A., 1997, Deathtrap, 1998, Angel Street, 1999, Fortinbras, L.A., 1999, Othello, Hollywood, 2000, Sweet Bird of Youth, 2000, Walt Whitman's Song of Myself, Edinburgh Festival, 2000, Richard III, 2002, Ancient Voices, 2004; (film) Private Collections, 1989, Eye Opener, 1992, A Situation, 1994, Porn Queens of the Seventies, 1994, The Nutty Professor, 1996, The Sophia Replacement, 1996; (TV) War Stories, 2002; also music videos and TV commls.; book critic L.A. Times; contbr. articles to newspapers. Mem. ABA, Brit. Equity, So. Calif. Soc. Law Librs., Brit. Assn. Film and TV Arts, SAG, Mensa, Phi Beta Kappa. Avocations: photography, wine, architecture, fine art, languages. Office: Riordan & McKinzie 300 S Grand Ave Ste 2900 Los Angeles CA 90071-3139

DRYER, BARBARA FERRELL, media specialist, educator; b. Norfolk, Va., July 21, 1948; d. Philip Earl and Bertha Buzzy Ferrell; m. Mark Steven Dryer, Jan. 25, 1968; 1 child, Elizabeth Anne ; 1 child, Jeffrey Lawrence. BSEE, Old Dominion U., Norfolk, Va., 1970, postgrad., 1999—. Media specialist Portsmouth Pub. Sch., Va., 1970—79, Norfolk Pub. Sch., 1988—89, Norfolk Collegiate Lower Sch., 1991—. Steering com. Norfolk Collegiate Sch., 2000—, sponsor writing club and newspaper, 1999—. Contbr. articles to profl. jours. Pres. Willard PTA, Norfolk, Va., 1991—93. Recipient Va. Reading Tchr. of Yr., Va. Reading Assn., 1978, Vol. of Yr., Willard Model Sch. PTA, 1989, 1990. Mem.: Va. Ednl. Media Assn. (workshop presenter 2001—), Va. Assn. Ind. Schs., Norfolk Reading Coun., Va. State PTA (life), Friends of the Norfolk Pub. Libr. Democrat. Avocations: reading, gardening, sewing, renovating our historic house. Home: 1514 Maury Cres Norfolk VA 23509 Office: Norfolk Collegiate Sch 5429 Tidewater Dr Norfolk VA 23509

DRZEWIECKI, DARLA RUTH, accountant; b. Pomona, Calif., Apr. 10, 1961; d. James Haywood Dabney, Sr. and Ruth Irene Dabney; m. David Adam Drzewiecki, Jan. 7, 1984; children: Brian Adam, Kenneth James. Posting clk. Scheu Mfg. Co., Upland, Calif., 1979—81; payroll clk. Data Electronics, Inc., San Diego, 1981—83; asst. acct. mgr. Elgar Corp., San Diego, 1983—84, Teledyne Micronetics Inc., San Diego, 1984—85; fin. acct. Teledyne Ryan Electronics, San Diego, 1985—87; sec. and acct. office mgr. Bethany Assembly of God, San Diego, 1990—. Spkr. in field. Youth group leader, Costa Rica, 1984—; vol. homeless teens, 2002—. Avocations: sports, stamp collecting. Home: 797 Monserate Ave Chula Vista CA 91910 Office: Bethany Assembly God 916 Hollister St San Diego CA 92154

DUANE, JEANNINE MORRISSEY, retired elementary school educator; b. Lancaster, Pa., Dec. 4, 1932; d. Frank Morrissey and Elsie Ebersole; m. W. Richard G. Duane, Jr., Apr. 15, 1963 (dec. 1996). BS in Elem. Edn., Millersville State U., 1954; MEd, Lehigh U., 1979, EdD, 1989. Cert. tchr. N.J., Pa., Hawaii, supr. N.J., supr. elem. tchr. Pa. Supr. elem. tchr. interns Lehigh U., Bethlehem, Pa.; tchr. Global Assocs., Kwajalein, Micronesia, U.S. Dept. Def., Bermuda, Chester (N.J.) Bd. Edn. Mem. Washington Twp. N.J. Bd. Edn., 1979—; edn. cons. EdPro Consulting; lectr. NASA, Delta Kappa Gamma Soc. Internat. workshop; rschr. in field. Author: (book) English-Marshallese Cookbook, Marshallese-English Phrase Book, The Education of Gifted Children, British and American Schools. Active CAP. Named N.J. nat. Finalist Tchr. in Space, Morris County N.J. Woman of the Yr., 1988. Mem.: NJSBA, ASCD, NEA, N.J. Edn. Assn., N.J. Reading Assn., Challenger Ctr., World Space Found., Lunar Planetary Inst., Phi Delta Kappa. Home: 390 Naughright Rd Long Valley NJ 07853-3847

DUARTE, GLORIA, chef; Student, Dumas Pere Culinary Sch., Glenview, Ill. Chef Ritz-Carlton Hotel, Chgo., The Drake hotel, Chgo.; wner, chef Las Bellas Artes, Elmhurst, Ill., 1987—. Host Mexico's Day of the Dead celebration James Beard Found.; guest chef Jalisco Culinary Arts resort, Mexico. Named one of Top Ten Restaurants, Chgo. Sun Times. Office: Las Bellas Artes 112 W Park Ave Elmhurst IL 60126

DUARTE, PATRICIA M. real estate and insurance broker; b. Truro, Mass., Feb. 23, 1938; d. Antone Jr. and Marjorie (Beckley) Duarte. Grad. H.S., Provincetown, Mass. Lic. ins. and real estate broker; constrn. supt. Sec. various ins. agys., Amherst, Mass., 1957-60; ins. and real estate agt. Duarte Ins. & Real Estate, Truro, 1960-66, owner, prin. agt., 1966-78; ins. risk mgr. J.L. Marshall & Sons, Inc., Pawtucket, R.I., 1979-92; owner, mgr. Patricia-Duarte Real Estate, Rockport, Maine, 1988-97. Restorer antique homes New Eng., Mass., 1979—. Mem., sec. Truro Planning Bd., 1965-72, chmn., 1974-78; mem. exec. com. Cape Cod Planning and Econ. Devel. Com., 1971-76; mem. Reelect Brawn for Senate Com., Camden, Maine, 1988; mem. Rockport Planning Bd., 1991-94, Rockport Comprehensive Plan Implementation Com., 1991-94; co-chmn. Rockport Capital Improvement Com., 1991-96; bd. dirs. Cape Cod chpt. Am. Heart Assn., 1963-70; mem. Opera House Commn., 1992-94. Mem. Penobscot Bay Bd. Realtors, Profl. Ins. Agts. New Eng. (bd. dirs. 1974-76), Gen. Fedn. Women's Clubs (2d v.p. Camden chpt. 1989), Hist. Preservation Assn. St. Thomas (arts coun. 1998-99, bd. dirs. 1998). Republican. Roman Catholic. Avocations: gourmet cooking, travel, photography, architectural and interior design. Address: PO Box 8 Port Clyde ME 04855 also: Cowpet Bay E St Thomas VI 00802

DUBACK, SALLY WOOD, artist, educator; b. St. Paul, Jan. 19, 1946; d. Thurston and Jane (Washburn) W.; m. Steven Rahr Duback, Aug. 6, 1966 (div. Dec. 1986); children: David, Peter, Andrew. Student, Vassar Coll., 1964; postgrad., U. Wis., Milw., 1969-75; BA, U. Mich., 1968. Tchr. U. Sch. Milw., 1988-93; owner, artist Spectrum 305 Studio, Grafton, Wis., 1983—. Designer, puppetmaster Marquette U. Theatre, Milw., 2000-01; tchr., artist-in-residence Milw. Pub. Schs., 1999-2000; theatrical designer Theatre X, Milw., 1996-98, Bialystock and Bloom, Milw., 1997-98. Author: Hand Papermaking, 1997; artist hand paper sculpture. Founder, The Truck Studio, Artists Working in Edn., Milw., 1999 (bd. dirs., co-pres., 2002-04); bd. dirs., officer Wild Space Dance Co., Milw., 1994-2000, Print Forum Milw. Art Mus., 1993-2002; bd. dirs., past pres. Theatre X, Milw., 1993-2002, bd. dirs. Riveredge Nature Ctr., 2003-; mem. North Suburban YMCA. Fellow Vt. Studio Ctr., 2001, 2002, 2004; recipient award Pub. Arts Commn., Wis. Arts Bd., 1996, Gov.'s award for Arts Artists Working in Edn., 2002. Mem. Wis. Acad. Scis., Arts and Letters, Cedarbury Artists Guild. Unitarian Universalist. Avocations: gardening, photography, writing, swimming, music. Office: Spectrum 305 Studio 1350 14th Ave Grafton WI 53024 E-mail: sally@sallyduback.com.

DUBÉ, SUSAN E. women's healthcare company executive; BA, Simmons Coll., 1969; MBA, Harvard U., 1981. V.p. ventures Brigham and Women's Hosp., Boston, 1985-91; exec. v.p., COO, v.p. bus. devel. Adeza Biomed., Inc., Sunnyvale, Calif., 1991-93; ind. cons. to numerous health cos., 1993-94; pres., CEO, BioIntervensions, Inc., Saratoga, Calif., 1994-95; cons. LifeSci. Econs., Inc., Menlo Park, Calif., 1995; v.p. mktg. and bus. devel., v.p. bus. devel. Imagyn Med., Inc., Laguna Niguel, Calif., 1996-97; sr. v.p. strategy and corp. devel. Imagyn Med. Techs., Inc., Newport Beach, Calif., 1997-98; jr. v.p., v.p. strategic planning and acquisitions Women First HealthCare, Inc., San Diego, 1998—. Office: Women First HealthCare Inc 12220 El Camino Real Ste 400 San Diego CA 92130-2091 Fax: 619-509-1353.

DUBLON, DINA, bank executive; b. Brazil; BA in Econs. and Math., Hebrew U.; MS, Carnegie Mellon U. Exec. v.p. corp. planning Chase Manhattan Corp., N.Y.C., 1996—2000; CFO, exec. v.p. J.P. Morgan Chase & Co., N.Y.C., 2000—. Bd. dirs. The Hartford Fin. Svc. Group, Inc., govWorks.com, N.Y. Mem. Carnegie Mellon U.'s Grad. Sch. Indsl. Adminstrn.'s Coun. on Finance; mem. adv. bd. St. John U.'s Grad. Sch. Bus. Office: JP Morgan Chase & Co 270 Park Ave New York NY 10260*

DUBOFSKY, JEAN EBERHART, lawyer, retired state supreme court justice; b. 1942; m. Frank Dobofsky; children: Joshua, Matthew. BA, Stanford U., 1964; LLB, Harvard U., 1967. Admitted to Colo. bar, 1967. Legis. asst. to U.S. Senator Walter F. Mondale, 1967-69; atty. Colo. Rural Legal Services, Boulder, 1969-72, Legal Aid Soc. Met. Denver, 1972-73; ptnr. Kelley, Dubofsky, Haglund & Harnsey, Denver, 1973-75; dep. atty. gen. Colo., 1975-77; counsel Kelly, Haglund, Garnsey & Kahn, 1977-79, 88-90, Jean E. Dubofsky, P.C., Boulder, 1991—. Justice Colo. Supreme Ct., Denver, 1979-87, vis. prof. U. Colo. Law Sch., Boulder, 1987-88. Office: 1000 Rosehill Dr Boulder CO 80302-7148

DU BOISE, KIM REES, artist, photographer, art educator; b. Hattiesburg, Miss., Apr. 7, 1953; d. Samernie and Margaret J. R.; divorced; children: Timothy L., M. Ashley (dec.). BA, U. So. Miss., 1986, M of Art Edn., 1988; postgrad., U. Ala., 1994-95. Art tchr. grades 7-12 Columbia (Miss.) Acad., 1975-76; with prodn./ad design Columbian-Progress/Sunday Mirror (News), Columbia, 1980-81; with advt. design/prodn. Washington Parish ERA-Leader (newspaper), Franklinton, La., 1981; art tchr. grades kindergarten 12 Hattiesburg Prep. Sch., 1984-85; instr. art Pearl River C.C., Poplarville, Miss., 1987-94; artist/photographer Dogwood Studios, 1988-97; artist, photographer PhotoArts Imaging Professionals, 1997—, PhotoArts Imaging Supply. Adj. instr. U. So. Miss., 1996-97, 98-2000; festival coord. Very Spl. Arts Festival, SE Dist., Poplarville, Miss., 1989-94; participant regional round-Table on discipline based art edn. Getty Ctr. for Edn. in Arts, Tulsa, 1988. Ann. Bi-State Competition, 1986, Exhibited in group shows at MSC/JCAIA Art Exhbn., 1991, Miss. Cmty. Jr. Coll. Art, 1991—92, Art by Art Teams. MAEA, 1992, Art Student League Exhibit, 1995, photography, U. N.Mex., 1995, So. Miss. Art Assn. Annual Juried Competitions, 1996—98, U. So. Miss., 1998, 2000, Hines C.C., Miss., 2000. Chmn. Troop 21 Dixie Com. Boy Scouts Am., Hattiesburg, 1989-93; mem. Miss. Jaycettes/Marion County Jaycettes, Columbia, 1976-84, U.S. Jaycee Women, 1976-84. Named one of Outstanding Young Women of Am., 1981-84, First Lady #83 (Life Mem.) Miss. Jaycettes, 1982, Winner Speak-Up Competition, Miss. Jaycettes, 1981. Mem. New Orleans Mus. of Art (assoc.), So. Miss. Art Assn., Nat. Mus. of Women in the Arts (charter), Nature Conservancy, U. So. Miss. Alumni Assn. (life), Walter Anderson Mus. Art. Episcopalian. Avocations: fishing, reading. Office Phone: 601-582-3686. E-mail: krd@photoartsstudio.com.

DUBOVSKY, EVA VITKOVA, nuclear medicine physician, educator; b. Prague, Czechoslovakia, 1933; MD, Charles U. Faculty Medicine, Prague, Czech Republic, 1957. Diplomate Am. Bd. Nuclear Medicine. Intern U. Hosp., Charles U., Prague, 1956-57, chief resident, 1961-63, fellow divsn. endocrinology & metabolism, 1963-65; rsch. fellow divsn. endocrinology U. Ala., Birmingham, 1968-70; clin. assoc. VA Med. Ctr., Birmingham, 1970-72; dir. nuc. medicine U. Ala. Hosp., Birmingham. From instr. to prof. U. Ala., Birmingham, 1954—; vis. prof. U. Cin., 1987, Cleve. CLinic, 1987, VA Med. Ctr., Portland, Oreg.,1988, Columbia Coll. Physicians & Surgeons, 1989, Dartmouth Med. Ctr., 1989, William Beaumont Hosp., 1992, 94, Charles U., 1994, Baptist Med. Ctr. Okla., 1994, U. Louisville, 1994. Editor: Nuclear Medicine Technology Continuing Education Review, 1976, 2d edit., 1981; co-editor: Nuclear Medicine in Clinical Urology and Nephrology, 1985, Atlas of Nuclear Medicine and Imaging; contbr. chpts. to books and articles to profl. jours. Mem. AMA, Am. Coll. Nuclear Physicians, Soc. Nuclear Medicine, Soc. Uroradiology. Office: U Ala Hosp Divsn Nuc Medicine 619 19th St S Birmingham AL 35233-0001

DUBREY, PATRICIA A. medical technician; b. Buffalo, Aug. 4, 1950; d. Lester Willard Wells and Rita Marie Duffney; m. Ronald Peter DuBrey, Oct. 3, 1970 (div. Sept. 21, 1983); children: Todd, Matthew. Registered cardiac sonographer Am. Registry Diagnostic Med. Sonographers. From EKG technician to supr. Ellis Hosp., Schenectady, NY, 1968—2003, supr. non-invasive cardiology, 2003—. Clin. instr. Hudson Valley CC. Active Am. Heart Assn., 2000—01; chairperson United Way, Schenectady, 1995. Mem.: Soc. Diagnostic Med. Sonographers. Home: 1027 W Claremont Ave Schenectady NY 12303 Office: Ellis Hosp Dept Cardiology 1101 Nott St Schenectady NY 12308 E-mail: dubreyp@ellishosp.org.

DUBROVSKY, GERTRUDE WISHNICK, journalist, researcher; b. N.Y.C., Mar. 10, 1926; d. Benjamin and Esther Raisa (Katz) Wishnick; m. Jack Dubrovsky, Feb. 24, 1946 (div. Sept. 1975); children: Richard, Steven, Benjamin; m. Sidney Gray, June 13, 1976 (div. June 1997). AB, Georgian Ct. Coll., 1956; MA, Rutgers U., 1959; EdD, Columbia U., 1974. Tchr. Keyport (N.J.) grammar sch., 1956-57, Point Pleasant (N.J.) H.S., 1959-61; asst. prof. Trenton (N.J.) State Coll., 1964-66; program dir. YIVO Inst. for Jewish Rsch., N.Y.C., 1975-81; freelance journalist, writer N.Y. Times, N.Y.C., 1979—; ind. scholar, rschr. Princeton, 1980—; rschr., writer,asst. to pres. Carnegie Found. for the Advancement of Tchg., Princeton, N.J., 1982-85; Yiddish instr. Ctr. Jewish Life Princeton U., 1974-95. Pres. Documentary III, Princeton, 1980—; specialist in field of Am. Jewish rural history. Author: The Land Was Theirs: Jewish Farmers, 1992, Six From Leipzig, 2004; Editor newsletter: Rural Roots: Jewish Farm History, 1988-95; translator: (poems) Kentucky, 1990 (Jewish Book Club selection); prodr., dir. documentary The Land Was Theirs, 1993 (1st Pl. award Berkeley Film Festival, 1994). Mcpl. committeeperson Dem. Party, Princeton, 1980—, chair, 1982-84; mem. Commn. on Aging, Princeton, 1980—, chair, 1991-93 Fellow Meml. Found. for Jewish Culture, 1975, Oxford (Eng.) Ctr. Hebrew & Jewish Studies, 1994; NEH grantee, 1976, 78. Mem. Assn. for Jewish Studies, Am. Jewish Hist. Soc., Am. Jewish Archives, Princeton Rsch. Forum, Clare Hall (life, fellow 2000-01). Avocations: swimming, walking, bridge, Scrabble, poetry reading. Home and Office: 244 Hawthorne Ave Princeton NJ 08540-3826 Office Phone: 609-924-7527. E-mail: gdubrovsky@aol.com.

DUBROW, HEATHER, English educator; b. San Antonio, Mar. 5, 1945; d. Hilliard and Helen (Volk) D.; m. Ian Ousby, June 21, 1969 (div. Dec. 1979). BA summa cum laude, Harvard/Radcliffe, 1966; PhD, Harvard U., 1972. Asst. prof. U. Mass., Boston, 1972-73; Leverhulme vis. fellowship U. Kent, Canterbury, Eng., 1973-74; lectr. U. Sussex, Brighton, Eng., 1974-75; from vis. asst. prof. to asst. prof. U. Md., College Park, 1975-80; from assoc. to prof. Carleton Coll., Northfield, Minn., 1980-90; from prof. to John Bascom prof. and Tighe-Evans prof. U. Wis., Madison, 1990—. External rev. team Oberlin Coll., Bryn Mawr Coll. Author: Genre, 1982, Captive Victors, 1987, A Happier Eden, 1990, Echoes of Desire, 1995, Transformation and Repetition, 1997, Shakespeare and Domestic Loss, 1999, Border Crossings, 2001; contbr. articles to profl. jours. Recipient Capt. Jonathan Fay award, Radcliffe Coll., 1966; sr. fellow Nat. Endowment for the Humanities, 1987—88, Guggenheim fellow, 2004. Mem. MLA (mem. editl. bd., exec. coun. 1996-2000), Milton Soc. of Am. (exec. com. 1997-99), Renaissance Soc. Am. (disciplinary rep. 2001-03), Spenser Soc., Phi Beta Kappa. Democrat. Avocations: architecture, art, cooking. Office: U Wis Dept of English 600 N Park St Madison WI 53706-1403 Office Phone: 608-263-2913.

DUBS, GLORIA L. artist, realtor; b. Hammond, Ind. d. Joseph and Mayme Gish; m. Jack H. Dubs, 1951; children: Jack R., David, Gary. BS, Purdue U., 1951. Lic. realtor, travel agt. Realtor Prudential Realty/Northside Realty, Atlanta. Exhibitions include Ocee Art Ctr., Duluth, Ga., 2001, 2002, 2003. Mem.: Ashford Club. Office Phone: 770-605-2046.

DUCAR, TRACY, former soccer player; b. Lawrence, Mass., June 18, 1973; m. Chris Ducar, 1997. BS in Biology, U. N.C., 1995. Mem. U.S. Nat. Women's Soccer Team, 1996—; including Nike Victory Tour, 1997; U.S. Women's Cup, 1997. Named Team Most Valuable Player, U. N.C., 1995. Mem.: Phi Beta Kappa. Office: US Soccer Fedn 1801-1811 S Prairie Ave Chicago IL 60616

DUCK, PATRICIA MARY, librarian; b. Bklyn., Jan. 22, 1951; d. Warren James and Virginia Susan (Noonan) Johnson; m. John Jacob Duck, Feb. 2, 1973; children: Michael, Jennifer, Matthew. BA, George Washington U., 1974; MLS, U. Pitts., 1980, PhD in Libr. Sci., 1992. Libr., serials cataloger U. Pitts., 1980-84, libr., coord., 1984-85, libr., project supr., 1985-86; dir. libr. U. Pitts. Greensburg, 1986—. Facilitator region 10 Gov.'s Conf. Libr. and Info. Svcs., Pitts., 1990. Contbr. articles to profl. jours. Leader troop 47 Girl Scouts U.S., 1990-91; trustee Penn Area Libr., Level Green, Pa., 1989-91. Mem. ALA, Beta Phi Mu. E-mail: pmd1@pitt.edu Avocations: art. Office: U Pitts Greensburg Campus 1150 Mount Pleasant Rd Greensburg PA 15601-5860

DUCKETT-WALLACE, BARBARA MONICA, hospital administrator; b. Jamaica, West Indies, Nov. 17, 1936; d. Owen Neville and Ellen Veta Duckett; m. Harold Lloyd Wallace, July 2, 1966; children: Gerald Downer, Traci. BA, Lehman Coll., Bronx, N.Y., 1995. Stenographer radiology dept. Bellevue Hosp., N.Y.C., NY, 1959—69, sec. radiology dept., 1959—69, personnel rep. human resources, 1969—76, sys. analyst dir.'s office, 1976—88, coord. mgr. exec. dir. office, 1988—96, coord. mgr. med. staff, 1996—99, coord. mgr. vol. dept., 1999—. Co-chair childcare com. Bellevue Daycare, Inc., N.Y.C., 1999—, founder and coord. vending program; sec., treas. Bellevue's Employees Adv. Coun., N.Y.C., 1972—; vol. notary to patients Bellevue Hosp. Mem. parish coun. Holy Family Ch., Bronx, NY, 1998—, eucharistic minister, 1998—. Recipient Martin Luther King Humanitarian award, NAACP, Bklyn., 2002, award, 100 Yr. assn., 2000, Unsung Hero award, Daycare Coun., 2002. Mem.: Managerial Employees Assn. (network rep 2001, Raymond E. Diana award 1998), Nat. Notary Assn. (ambassador, Notary of Yr. 2000). Roman Catholic. Avocations: painting, photography, gardening, writing, dancing. Office: Bellevue Hosp Ctr 27th St & 1st Ave New York NY 10016 Office Phone: 212-562-4858. E-mail: BABZ1117@aol.com.

DUCKWITZ, ERIKA, music educator; b. Mt. Pleasant, Utah, Sept. 18, 1978; d. Steven Parley and Kathy Frischknecht; m. Gregory Michael Duckwitz, Jan. 14, 2000; 1 child, Haley Ann. BA in music edn., choral emphasis, Brigham Young U., 2001. Choir tchr. Alpine Sch. Dist., Am. Fork, Utah, 2001—. Named Tchr. of the Month, Oak Canyon Jr. High, 2003. Mem.: Music Educators Nat. Conf., Am. Choral Dirs. Assn. Avocations: crafts, tennis, swimming, musicals.

DUCKWORTH, RUTH, sculptor; b. Hamburg, Germany, Apr. 10, 1919; arrived in US, 1964; d. Edgar Windmüller and Ellen Elise Strack. Student, Liverpool (Eng.) Sch. of Art, 1936—40, Hammersmith Sch. of Art, 1955, Ctrl. Sch. Arts & Crafts, London, 1956—58; D (hon.), DePaul U., 1982. Tchr. Ctrl. Sch. Arts & Crafts, London, 1959—64, U. Chgo., 1964—66, 1968—77; vis. artist Corsham Sch. of Art, England, 1965. Tchr. various workshops and seminars, 1972—93; lectr. in field, 1994—. One-woman shows include Appolinaire Gallery, London, 1953, Primavera, 1960, 1962, 1967, Arnolfini, Bristol, Eng., 1964, U. Chgo., 1965, Craftsmen's Gallery, Chgo., 1965, Agra Gallery, Washington, 1965, The Chgo. Pub. Libr., 1966, Gallery Mid-North, Chgo., 1966, Matsuya Dept. Store, Tokyo, 1967, Jacques Barach Gallery, Chgo., 1972, Kunstkammer Ludger Koster, Monchen-Gladbach, Germany, 1973, Calvary Sch. of Art, Alta., Can., 1974, Mus. fur Kunst und Gewerbe, Hamburg, 1976, Exhibit A, Evanston, Ill., 1977, Chgo., 1980, 1982, 1984, Hadler Gallery, N.Y.C., 1978, Mus. Boymans-Van Beuningen, Rotterdam, The Netherlands, 1979, Lake Forest (Ill.) Coll., 1984, Helen Drutt Gallery, Phila., 1986, Contemporary Art Ctr., London, 1986, Soc. of Art in Crafts, Pitts., 1987, Dorothy Weiss Gallery, San Francisco, 1989, 1992, 1994, Garth Clark Gallery, N.Y.C., 1990, 1996, 1999, 2002, L.A., 1991, Bellas Artes Gallery, Santa Fe, 1991, 1993, 1996, 2000, Pewabic Gallery, Detroit, 1992, Keramik-Galerie Bowig, Hannover, Germany, 1993, Schleswig-Holsteinische Landesmuseum, Rendsburg, Germany, 1994, galerie b15, Munich, 2000, exhibited in group shows at Art Inst. Chgo., 1969, Victoria and Albert Mus., London, 1972, Mus. Contemporary Art, Chgo., 1976, 1984, 1996, Milw. Art Mus., 1984, Am. Craft Mus., N.Y.C., 1987, Internat. Acad. Ceramics, Saga, Japan, 1996, Met. Mus. of Art, N.Y.C., 1999, L.A. County Mus. of Art, 2000, numerous others, prin. works include St. Joseph's Ch., New Malden, Eng., 1959—60, Solel Synagogue, Highland Park, Ill., 1965, Lab. for Geophys. Sci. Bldg., U. Chgo., 1967—68, Purdue U., Lafayette, Ind., 1972, Dresdner Bank, Bd. of Trade (moved to Options Exch. Bldg.), Chgo., 1976, Hodag Chem. Co. (transferred to Lewis & Clark Coll., Godfrey, Ill.), Skokie, Ill., 1978, Rozansky & Kay Co., Bethesda, Md., 1981, Sonnenschein, Carlin, North and Rosenthal Offices, Chgo., 1981, Main Bank of Chgo., 1982, Perkins & Will Arch. Offices, Chgo., 1982, Congregation Beth Israel, Hammond, Ind., 1982—83, Amcore Bank, Rockford, Ill., 1983, Teradyne Ctrl., Deerfield, Ill., 1984, Dr. R. Lee Animal Care Ctr. (commd. by Chgo. Coun. on Fine Arts 1/2% for the Arts Program), 1984, State of Ill. Bldg., Capitol Devel. Bd., Springfield, 1984—85, Unisys Offices, N.Y.C., 1986, St. Mary's Ch., Walsingham, Eng., 1987, Stowell, Cook, Frolichstein, Inc., Clearwater, Fla., 1988, Palm Beach (Fla.) Airport Terminal, 1990, State of Ill. Bldg., State Commn., Rockford, 1992, Chgo. Children's Mus., 1995, State of Ill. Commn., Lewis and Clark Coll., Godfrey, Ill., 1997—98, City of Chgo., Dept. Cultural Affairs, 1999, First Nat. Bank Collection, Columbia, Mo., 1999, Represented in permanent collections Windsor Castle, Eng., Nat. Mus. Modern Art, Japan, Smithsonian Instn., Washington, Mus. Contemporary Art, Chgo., St. Louis Art Mus., Boston Mus. Fine Arts, Art Inst. of Chgo., Phila. Mus. of Art, Fine Arts Mus. of San Francisco, Am. Craft Mus., N.Y.C., L.A. County Art Mus., Nat. Mus. Scotland, Edinburgh, Met. Mus. of Art, N.Y.C., numerous others. Recipient Gold medal, Ceramic Art of the World, Calgary, Can., 1973, Gold medal in craft arts category, Ill. Acad. Fine Arts, 1992, Lifetime Achievement in the Craft Arts Gold medal, Nat. Mus. of Women in the Arts, Washington, 1993, Gold medal, Nat. Soc. Arts and Letters, Washington, 1996, The Madigan prize for best sculpture in State of Ill., Springfield, 1999, Master of the Medium Gold medal, Renwick Alliance, Renwick Gallery, Washington, 2001, 3 Art award, Disting. Artist of Yr., 2003, Arts in Edn. award, 2003, 3 Arts award, 3Arts Club Chgo.,

2003, Visionary award, Mus. Arts and Design, NY, 2003, Beaux Arts Celebration award, Union League Club Chgo., 2003. Fellow: Am. Craft Coun. (award 1993, Gold medal 1997); mem.: Arts Club. Office: Thea Burger Assocs Inc 651 North Rd PO Box 68 Barnard VT 05031-0068 E-mail: BurgerThea@aol.com

DUCKWORTH, TARA ANN, insurance company executive; b. Seattle, June 7, 1956; d. Leonard Douglas and Audrey Lee (Limbeck) Hill; m. Mark L. Duckworth, May 16, 1981; children: Harrison Lee III, Andrew James, Kathryn Anne. AAS, Highline C.C., Seattle, 1976. From acctg. clk. to info. sys. supr. SAFECO Ins. Co., Seattle, 1977-90, rate sys. mgr., 1990-94; sys. mgr. SAFECO Mut. Funds, SAFECO Credit, PNMR, Seattle, 1994-97, mktg. comm. and incentives, quality assurance mgr., 1997-98, dir. comml. lines sys., 1998—2001, dir. quality assurance, 2001—03, dir. personal policy sys., 2003—. Mem. tech adv. com. for the computer info. svcs. program North Seattle Community Coll., 1984-96, chairperson tech. adv. com., 1988-90. Mem. Star Lake Improvement Club, 1988-94; mem. fellowship com. St. Lukes Luth. Ch., 1986—; mem. Boy Scouts Am., 1996-2003. Mem. NAFE, Nat. Assn. for Ins. Women, Soc. for State Filers, Nat. PTA. Office: SAFECO Ins Co Safeco Plz Seattle WA 98185-0001

DUCRAN, CLAUDETTE DELORIS, retired financial analyst; b. Trinityville, St. Thomas, Jamaica, July 23, 1941; came to U.S., 1962; d. Wellesley Provan and Hilda Maude (Beckford) DuC. Student, Corcoran Sch. Art, Washington, 1967; cert. of diploma, USDA Grad. Sch., Washington, 1972; student, Harvard U., 1976; BBA, George Washington U., 1982; postgrad., Columbia U., 1987. Adminstrv. asst. World Bank, Washington, 1964-75, fin. asst., 1975-85, ops. asst., 1985-88, disbursement asst., 1988-94, disbursement analyst, 1994-96; ret., 1996. Mem. adv. com. Very Spl. Arts Kennedy Ctr., Washington, 1990-93, Hands Across Hemisphere Craft Ctr., Washington, 1991; founder, pres. Let's Learn by Reading, Jamaica, 1990-2000. Author: Exhibitors Guidelines, 1989, 2d edit., 1990. Bd. dirs. Craft Ctr., Washington, 1991-99; panelist Career Week George Washington U., Washington, 1991, Women's Ctr., McLean, Va., 1991; founder, pres. The Claudette D. Ducran Found., Inc., Kingston, Jamaica, W.I., 1995-2001, Eureka Alliance, Inc., Washington, 1995—. Recipient 1st prize Writer's League, Washington, 1967, Internat. Order of Merit, 1994; named Internat. Woman of Yr., 1993-94. Mem.: World Bank 1818 Soc., World Bank Art Soc. (v.p. 1986—88, pres. 1988—93), Jamaica C. of C. (hon. Washington rep. 1997—). Avocations: performing and visual arts, children, travel, working with handicapped, international development. Home: The Brighton 2123 California St NW Apt B1 Washington DC 20008-1804

DUDASH, LINDA CHRISTINE, insurance company executive; b. Pitts. d. Andrew Daniel and Lillian (Reynolds) D. BA in English, Point Park Coll., 1969. Tech. writer Am. Insts. for Rsch., Pitts., 1968-69; claim svc. rep. Reliance Ins. Co., Pitts., 1969-70, claim rep., 1970-71, claim mgr. Jacksonville, Fla., 1971-73, Harrisburg, Pa., 1973-80, Chgo., 1980-86; maj. case unit mgr. Zurich Ins. Co., Schaumburg, Ill., 1986-88, asst. v.p., mgr. liability claims, 1988-91, asst. v.p., mgr. claims continuous improvement, 1991-92; v.p. dir. field ops. Zurich-Am. Ins., Schaumburg, Ill., 1992-95; sr. v.p. claims Casualty Ins. Co., divsn. Fremont Compensation Ins. Co., Chgo., 1995—2000; sr. v.p., chief claims officer Fremont Compensation Ins. Group, Glendale, Calif., 2000—. Office: Fremont Compensation Ins Group 500 N Brand Blvd Glendale CA 91203-3392 E-mail: ldudash@fremontcomp.com.

DUDDEN, ROSALIND F. librarian; b. New Haven, Nov. 4, 1944; d. George B. and Mary Ellen (Forgan) Farnam; m. Fred I. Dudden, June 20, 1970 (div. July 1993); 1 child, Laura Melissa. BA, Finch Coll., 1966; MLS, U. Denver, 1970. Dir. libr. svcs. Mercy Med. Ctr., Denver, 1971-86; health scis. libr. Nat. Jewish Med. and Rsch. Ctr., Denver, 1986—. Web site adminstr., 1995-2000; pres. Colo. Coun. Med. Librs., Denver, 1975-77. Vol. St. Francis Ctr., Denver, 1993—. Fellow Med. Libr. Assn. (pres. hosp. librs. sect. 1987-88, Frank Bradway Rogers award 1995, bd. dirs. 1998-2001, Pres. award 2003), mem. Acad. Health Info. Profs. (disting.). Office: Nat Jewish Med and Rsch Ctr 1400 Jackson St Denver CO 80206-2762

DUDDY, E. EILEEN, accountant; b. Chickasha, Okla., Dec. 28, 1934; d. William John and Minnie Ethel Hunteman; m. Laurence M. Duddy, Dec. 7, 1953; children: Margaret M., Michael L. Student, Okla. Ctrl. U., 1953; AS in Bus., Coll. Martin, 1974; AA in Data Process, Merced Coll., 1974; BA in Bus. Adminstrn./Acctg. with honors, Calif. State U., Stanislaus, 1976. CPA Calif. State Bd. Accountancy. Sec. inst. shop U.S. Civil Svc., Elmendorf AFB, Alaska, 1953-54; dist. official cashier, svc. rep. Mt. States Tel & Tel, Yuma, Ariz., 1956-57; sec. to dist. mgr. Am. Nat. Ins. Corp., Abilene, Tex., 1970; staff acct. Holman Accountancy Corp., Atwater, Calif., 1976-79; staff acct., auditor Robert C. Martin Accountancy Corp., Atwater, Modesto, Calif., 1979-80; CPA, staff acct. Ozenbaugh & Smith, CPAs, Merced, Calif., 1981; CPA, owner E. Eileen Duddy, Atwater, 1981—. Dir. Calif. Soc. CPAs, Redwood City, 1988-90; founder, chmn. Merced/Atwater CPA Discussion Group, 1982-86. V.p. Merced County Econ. Devel. Corp., 1998—; vice chmn., bd. dirs. Castle Joint Power Authority, Merced County, 1998—; mem. City Coun., Atwater, 1996—; mem. Calif. State Bd. Accountancy, 1992-97, long range planning com., legis. com., internat. reciprocity com, report quality monitoring com., liason to major case adv. com.; mem. City of Atwater Audit and Fin. Com.; chmn. City of Atwater Pub. Works Com., coun. liason; vice-chmn., rep. City of Atwater, 1998—; bd. dirs Atwater C. of C., 1996—, past pres. 1987-88, chamber bd. dirs, 1985-91; chmn. Atwater Econ. Devel. com.; mem. legis. com.; mem. Merced County Office Econ. and Strategic Devel. Task Force, 1987-88; alternate Assessment Appeals Bd. Merced County, 1988091, 91-94, Atwater citizens adv. com., 1994; Atwater Gen. Plan Review Com., 1991-92; active Girl Scouts Am., Brownie troop leader, Jr. troop leader, troop organizer, merit badge cons., 1963-71; den leader Cub Scouts Am., pack com. mem. 1970-72; troop cons. Boy Scouts Am., 1973-78; mem. wives clubs 516th TCW, past pres., Dyess AFB Waiting Wives Club, vol., 1963-71; active AF Handicapped Children's programs, Base Chapel Sunday Sch., tchr. Bible Sch, 1965-68; PTA and sch. vol. Dyess Elem. and Hamilton Elem. Schs., 1963-72; swimming instr. Dyess AFB Red Cross beginners classes, 1968-69. Mem. Am. Cancer Soc. (auditor ann. fund raising auction 1985-97), Am. Inst. CPAs, Calif. Soc. CPAs (bd. dirs., 1988-90, state discussion group com. 1987, past pres. San Joaquin chpt. 1989-90 v.p., chmn. chpt discussion group com. 1982-91, chpt. govt. rels. com. mem. chpt. profl. conduct com., acctg. prins. and auditing stds. com., taxation com., microcomputers user group), Calif. Firefighters Hist. Soc. (bd. dirs, life, treas. 1991—), Soroptimist Internat. Atwater (pres. 1989-90, fin. com. chmn. sierra Pacific region 1991-92, Soroptomist of Yr., 1992, Woman of Distinction, 1996), Merced Coll. Found (bd. dirs. 1992), Atwater Women's Club, Castle Air Mus. Found (life, Daughters of Air Mus.), Merced Trade Club (dir., bd. dirs. 1998—), Atwater C. of C. (dir., pres. 1987-88). Republican. Avocations: computers, home improvement projects, swimming, skiing, art. Office: PO Box 666 Atwater CA 95301-0666 E-mail: duddy@cyberlynk.com.

DUDICS-DEAN, SUSAN ELAINE, interior designer; b. Perth Amboy, N.J., Oct. 22, 1950; d. Theodore W. and Joyce M. (Ryals) D.; m. Rick Dean, Apr. 30, 1989; 1 child, Merissa Joyce. BS in Sociology, W.Va. U., 1972; postgrad., Rutgers U., 1975-78, U. Calif., Irvine, 1979-81, Can. Coll., 1981-89. Programmer Prudential Life, Newark, 1972-73; sr. sys. analyst Johnson & Johnson, New Brunswick, N.J., 1978-78, Sperry Univac, Irvine, 1978-80; sr. sys. analyst, project leader Robert A. McNeil, San Mateo, Calif., 1981-83; dist. design dir. TransDesigns, Woodstock, Ga., 1982-93; prin. Celestial Designs, 1980—; cons., dir. So. Living at Home, 2001—. Lectr., spkr. in the field of interior design, sales and Feng Shui, 1986—. Writer Drapery and Window Coverings, Design Lines, Window Fashions Mag., Designer Lines, Fine Furnishings Internat., Inspired House; guest on TV shows House Doctor, Marketplace Sta. KGO-TV; contbr. articles to profl. jours. High sch. mentor Directions, San Francisco, 1985-95. Recipient awards TransDesigns, Woodstock, 1984-87, 89-91, MoonRise Galleries, 1984-92, Mem. Women Entrepreneurs (membership [illegible] 1988-97), Romance Writers Am., Washington Romance Writers, Ctrl. N.J. Alumni Assn. Delta Gamma (assoc. sec., founder, pres.), Am. Soc. Interior Designers (allied mem. 1989-92), Profl. Bus. Women's Assn., Delta Gamma. Avocations: sewing, scuba diving, ballet, handcrafts.

DUDLEY, AMBER MARIE, music educator; b. Phoenix, Ariz., Mar. 4, 1976; d. David Walter and Jerilyn Whittaker; m. Christopher Neil Dudley, June 8, 2002. BA in Music Edn., BA in Viola Performance, No. Ariz. U., 1999, MA in Ednl. Leadership, 2004. Orch. dir. Mesquite H.S., Gilbert, Ariz., 1999—. Instr. music camp No. Ariz. U., Flagstaff, 1996—; violist Mesa (Ariz.) Symphony Orch., 1999—; pvt. tchr., 1996—. Recipient Catherine Adel scholarship, No. Ariz. U., 1999. Mem.: Suzuki Assn. Am., Am. String Tchr.'s Assn. Republican. Avocations: hiking, fiddling, reading, gardening, entertaining. Home: 1570 W Curry Dr Chandler AZ 85224 Office: Mesquite HS 500 S McQueen Rd Gilbert AZ 85233 Office Phone: 480-632-4750 4714.

DUDLEY, ELIZABETH HYMER, retired security executive, community volunteer; b. Hibbing, Minn., Mar. 12, 1937; d. Howard Golden and Esther Juliette (Wanner) Hymer; m. Richard Walter Dudley, 1962. BA, Brown U., 1959; postgrad., U. Calif., Berkeley. With AT&T Bell Labs., MurrayHill, N.J., 1959-89, systems programmer, personal info., 1965-67, systems analyst, personnel info., 1967-71, sr. systems analyst, mgmt. info. and adminstrv. systems, 1971-77, applications systems coord. mgmt. info./adminstrv. systems, 1977-78, group supr. affirmative action compliance and reports, 1978-81, group supr. service ops. system support group, 1982-84, mgr. security, 1984-85, mgr. govt. security, 1986-89, ret., 1989. Bd. dirs. Boca Ballet Theatre Co., 1994-2004, 1st v.p., 1998-2003; treas. Fla. Atlantic U. Vol. League, 1993-94; chmn. boutique Boca Ballet Guild, 1994, pres. 1994-97, v.p. membership, 1997-98, treas. 2000-02; treas. Boca Raton Hist. Soc. Gala, 2003; chair invitation com. Tri County Humane Soc. Gala., 2004. Recipient Boca Ballet Vol. of Yr. award, 2001. Mem. Humanitarian Soc., Nat. Soc. Arts and Lettters (2d v.p. 1998-99, v.p. 1999-2000, chair South Fla. ballet competition), Brown Nat. Alumni Sch. Coms., Nat. Security Indsl. Assn., Women's Rights Assn. (treas. 1977, v.p. 1978), Am. Soc. Indsl. Security, Nat. Classification Mgmt. Soc., Brown Network, Royal Palm Improvement Assn. (bd. govs., chair environ. inspection 1993-94, v.p., 1994, pres. 1994-96, chmn. security 1994), Friends of Boca Pops (governing coun.), Pembroke Coll. of N.J. Club (publicity chmn. 1965-69, v.p. 1969-70), U. Club Fla. Atlantic U. (corr. sec. 1999-2000), Lucia Chase Soc. (Am. Ballet Theatre).

DUDLEY, KATHRYN MARIE, anthropology and American studies educator; b. Dec. 9, 1958; BA in Psychology, U. Wis., Milw., 1984; MA in Anthropology, Columbia U., 1987, PhD in Anthropology, 1991. Adj. asst. prof. anthropology Columbia U., N.Y.C., 1991—93; from asst. prof. to assoc. prof. anthropology Yale U., New Haven, 1993—2002, prof. anthropology and Am. studies, 2002—. Author: The End of the Line: Lost Jobs, New Lives in Post-Industrial America, 1994, Debt and Dispossession: Farm Loss in America's Heartland, 2000. Recipient Harry Chapin Media award, 1995, Margaret Mead award, 2000. Mem. Phi Beta Kappa. Office: Yale U Dept Anthropology PO Box 208277 New Haven CT 06520-8277

DUDLEY-ESHBACH, JANET, university president; b. Balt. m. Joseph Eshbach; two children. BA in Spanish and Latin Am. Studies, Ind. U.; PhD in Latin Am. Lit., El Colegio de Mexico, Mexico City. Mem. faculty, instr. Spanish Allegheny Coll., Meadville, Pa., 1978-79; asst. prof., then assoc. prof. Spanish and Latin Am. Studies Goucher Coll., Towson, Md., 1979-88; chmn. dept. Modern Langs., then assoc. v.p. Acad. Affairs SUNY, Potsdam, 1988-92, dean Sch. Arts and Scis., then provost, 1992-96; pres. Fairmont (W.Va.) State Coll., 1996—. Mem. Sen. Jay Rockefeller's Trade Mission to Taiwan and Japan, 1997. Mem. MLA, Am. Assn. Higher Edn., Am. Assn. State Colls. and Univs. (internat. studies com.), N.Y. State Assn. Women in Higher Edn., Coun. Colls. of Arts and Scis., Latin Am. Studies Assn., Marion County C. of C., Phi Delta Kappa, Phi Beta Kappa Office: Fairmont State Coll Office of Pres 1201 Locust Ave Fairmont WV 26554-2451

DUDZIAK, EMMA M. cardiac sonographer; b. Buffalo, N.Y., July 27, 1957; d. Norman P. Koneski; m. Gregory D. Dudziak, Sept. 15, 1979; children: Keith G., Scott G. Diploma, Bryant & Stratton Bus. Inst., Buffalo, N.Y. Registered Diagnostic Cardiac Sonographer Am. Registry of Diagnostic Med. Sonographers, Rockville, Md., 2002. Supr., echo, stress, holter & EKG lab Erie County Med. Ctr., Buffalo, 1982—97; sr. cardiac sonographer Buffalo Heart Group, 1997—. Mem.: Am. Inst. of Ultrasound in Medicine, Soc. of Diagnostic Med. Sonography, ARDMS (assoc.). Roman Catholic. Avocations: travel, bowling, needlepoint, sewing, knitting. Office: Buffalo Heart Group 3435 Bailey Ave Buffalo NY 14215 Personal E-mail: thedudz@hotmail.com.

DUDZIAK, MARY LOUISE, law educator, lecturer; b. Oakland, Calif., June 15, 1956; d. Walter F. Dudziak and Barbara Ann Campbell; 1 child, Alicia. AB in Sociology with highest honors, U. Calif., Berkeley, 1978; JD, Yale Law Sch., 1984; MA, MPhil in Am. Studies, Yale U., 1986, PhD in Am. Studies, 1992. Adminstrv. asst. to dep. dir. Ctr. Ind. Living, Berkeley, 1978-80; law clk., nat. legal staff ACLU, N.Y.C., 1983; law clk. Judge Sam J. Ervin, III Fourth Cir. Ct. Appeals, Morganton, N.C., 1984-85; assoc. prof. coll. law U. Iowa, Iowa City, 1986-90, prof. coll. law, 1990-98. Vis. prof. U. So. Calif., 1997-98, prof. U. So. Calif., 1998-2002, Judge Edward J. and Ruey L. Guirado prof. law and history, 2002-; mem. faculty senate task force on faculty devel. U. Iowa, 1989-90, mem. faculty welfare com., 1990-92, mem. faculty senate task force on faculty spouses and ptnrs., 1991-92, mem. presdl. lecture com., 1992-95; v.p. rsch. adv. com. in social scis., 1992-94; fellow law and pub. affairs program Princeton U., 2002; presenter in field. Author: Cold War Civil Rights: Race and the Image of American Democracy, 2000; editor, co-author: September 11 in History: A Watershed Moment?, 2003; mem. bd. mng. editors Am. Quar., 2003—; contbr. articles to profl. jours. Bd. dirs. Iowa Civil Liberties Union, 1987-88; chairperson office svcs. for persons with disabilities program rev. com., U. Iowa, 1987-88, law sch. ombudsperson, 1991. Charlotte W. Newcombe Doctoral Dissertation fellow Woodrow Wilson Fellowship Found., 1985-86; Old Gold fellow U. Iowa, 1987, 88, 89, Moody Grant Lyndon Baines Johnson Fdn., 1998, Theodore C. Sorenson Fell., JFK Libr. Fdn., 1997, Orgn. Am. Historians-Japanese Assn. for Am. Studies fellow 2000; travel grantee Eisenhower World Affairs Inst., 1993; recipient Scholars Devel. award Harry S. Truman Libr. Inst., 1990. Mem. Am. Soc. Legal History (mem. com. on documentary preservation 1988-2000, mem. program com. for 1988 conf., mem. exec. com., bd. dirs. 1990-92, 95-97, chairperson program com. 1993, mem. nominating com. 1999-2001, chair nominating com. 2001), Am. Hist. Assn. (Littleton-Griswold rsch. grantee 1987), Am. Studies Assn. (mem. nominating com. 1999-2002, chair nominating com. 2002), Assn. Am. Law Schs. (sec.-treas. legal history sect. 1987, vice chair 1988, chair 1989), Law and Soc. Assn. (mem. Hurst prize com. 1992), Orgn. Am. Historians, Soc. Am. Law Tchrs., Soc. for Historians Am. Fgn. Rels. Democrat. Office: U So Calif Law Sch Los Angeles CA 90089-0001 E-mail: mdudziak@law.usc.edu.

DUE, JEAN MARGARET, agricultural economist, educator; b. Peterborough, Ont., Can., Sept. 19, 1921; d. Allan B. and Katherine Jean (Calder) Mann; m. John F. Due, Aug. 18, 1950; children— Allan Malcolm, Kevin John Burritt. B.Com., U. Toronto, 1946; MS, U. Ill., 1950, PhD, 1953. Economist Dept. Agr., Ottawa, Ont., 1946-49; research asso. in home econs. U. Ill., 1959-61, vis. prof., 1965-70, prof. dept. agr. econs., 1970-90. Contbr. articles to profl. jours. Mem. African Studies Assn., Am. Econ. Assn., Am. Agrl. Econs. Assn., Internat. Assn. Agrl. Econs., Assn. Women Internat. Devel. Home: 1208 Clark Lindsey Village 101 W Windsor Rd Urbana IL 61802 6663 Office: Univ Illinois 305MH 1301 W Gregory Dr # 305 [illegible] Urbana IL 61801-9015 E-mail: jdue@uiuc.edu.

DUENAS, LAURENT FLORES, health and nursing consultant; b. Yigo, Guam, Jan. 9, 1947; d. Joaquin Garcia and Maria Acosta (Calvo) Flores; m. Jimmy J. Duenas, Jan. 9, 1971; children: James Richard, Sherry Marie, Kenneth Ray. ADN, U. Guam, 1968; BSN, Mont. State U., 1969; MPH, U. Hawaii, Manao, 1984. RN, Guam, 1968, Mont., 1969; CNA, NLN; cert. SMDP trng., Internat. Pub. Health. Staff nurse Dept. Pub. Health and Social Svc., 1969—70, nurse supr. I, 1970—71, nurse supr. II, 1972—78, asst. adminstr. Bur. Cmty. Health and Nursing Svc., 1978—89, detailed adminstr., 1986—88, adminstr., 1989—95, ret., 1995. Health and nursing cons. Guam Legislature and U. Guam, 1996—,"HLATTE" project dir. U. GU, 2003-; adj. faculty health adminstrn., 1999-, bd. dir., chair Pacific Basin Maternal Child Health Resource Ctr., Mangilao, Guam, 1984-96, Pacific Basin MCH coord., Honolulu, 1984-95; mem. State and Territorial Dir. Nursing, 1987-98; mem. Interagy. Leadership Consortium for Individual's with Spl. Needs, 1990-98; mem. Maternal Child Health Task Force, 1996-98, Governor's Vision, 2000; Health Task Force, 1996-2000; chair Nurse Leaders Com., 1995-98, mem., 1998-2000; preceptor nursing students U.Guam, 1995—; bd. dir. Pacific Island Primary Care Assn., 2003-, bd. dir. Pacific Assn. Clin. Tng., 2003-; affiliate mem. Pacific Island Health Officers APNLC, 2003-; presenter in field. Author: Caring for Young Children, modified version, 1998. Recipient Centennial Award Nat. League of Nursing, 1994, Governor's Chief Gadao Disting. Award, 1995. Mem. ANA, APHA, Y'netnon Famaloan Dem. Women Leaders, Am. Pacific Nursing Leaders (coun. pres. 2001-, treas., 1986-92, vice mem. 1986—), Commn. on Licensure, Guam Bd. Nurses Examiners (bd. dir., chair 1981-90), Guam Nurses Assn. (bd. dir. 1992-94, Leadership Award 1988, Nursing Excellence Award 1990, Guam Nurse of Yr. 1993, Pub. Health Unit Award 1994, Guam Legis. Resolution 1995, 98), Orgn. Health and Med. Profl. Women (treas. 2003—), Pacific Island Health Officers Assn. Democrat. Roman Catholic. Avocations: crocheting, collecting recipes, baking, campaign strategies, visiting sick. Home: 3 N Cupa Perez Acres Yigo GU 96929-0142 Office: Univ Guam HLATTE Project UOG Sta Mangilao GU 96923

DUER, ELLEN ANN DAGON, anesthesiologist, general practitioner; b. Balt., Feb. 3, 1936; d. Emmett Paul and Annie (Sollers) Dagon; m. Lyle Jordan Millan IV, Dec. 21, 1963; children: Lyle Jordan V, Elizabeth Lyle, Ann Sheridan Worthington.; m. T. Marshall Duer, Jr., Aug. 23, 1985. AB, George Washington U., 1959; MD, U. Md., 1964; postgrad., Johns Hopkins U., 1965-68. Intern Union Meml. Hosp., Balt., 1964-65; resident anesthesiology Johns Hopkins Hosp., Balt., 1965-68, fellow in surgery, 1965-68; practice medicine specializing in anesthesiology Balt., 1968—; faculty Church Home and Hosp., Balt., 1969—; attending staff Union Meml. Hosp., Church Home and Hosp., Frankling Sq. Hosp., Children's Hosp., James Lawrence Kernan Hosp., Balt., 1982-94; co-chief anesthesiology James Kernan Hosp., 1983-94, med. dir. out-patient surgery dept., 1987-94. Mem. med. exec. com. Kernan Hosp., 1988-94; affiliate cons. emergency room Church Home and Hosp., Balt., 1969—, mem. med. audit and utilizaions com., 1970-72, mem. emergency and ambulatory care com., 1973-74, chief emergency dept., 1973-74; cons. anesthesiologist Md. State Penitentiary, 1971; fellow in critical care medicine Md. Inst. Emergency Medicine, 1975-76; mem. infection control com. U. Md. Hosp., 1975—; instr. anesthesiology U. Md. Sch. Medicine, 1975—; staff anesthesiologist Mercy Hosp., 1978—, audit com., 1979-80, 82; asst. prof. anesthegiology U. Md. Med. Sch., 1989-94; mem. med. exec. com. Kernan Hosp., 1990-94, v.p. 1990, chief of staff, 1992—; mem. Tappahannock Family Practice, 1994-96, Rappahannock Gen. Hosp. Family Practice, 1996—; active staff Rappahannock Gen. Hosp., 1996—, ethics com., 1997—; med. examiner No. Neck of Va., 1996—; mem. Commonwealth of Va. Med. Bd. Mem. AMA, Am. Coll. Emergency Physicians, Am. Acad. Gen. Practitioners, Met. Emergency Dept. Heads Am., Md. Soc. Anesthesiologists, Balt. County Med. Soc., Mid. Peninsula Med. Soc., No. Neck Med. Soc., Med. Soc. Va., Med. and Choir Faculty Med., Chiurgical Soc., Internat. Congress Anaesthesiologists, Internat. Anesthesia Rsch. Soc., Am. L'Hirondelle Club, Annapolis Yacht Club, Chesapeake Bay Yacht Racing Assn, Rappahannock River Yacht Club. Anglican. Address: 347 Coppedge Farm Rd White Stone VA 22578-2021 Office Phone: 804-435-2651.

DUERR, DIANNE MARIE, sports medicine consultant, educator; b. Buffalo, July 14, 1945; d. Robert John and Aileen Louise D. BS in Health and Phys. Edn., SUNY, Brockport, 1967; cert., SUNY, Oswego, 1982; postgrad., Canisius Coll., 1970-71. Cert. tchr., N.Y. Tchr. North Syracuse (N.Y.) Sch. Dist., 1967—; tchr. dept. orthopedic surgery SUNY Upstate Med. U., Syracuse, 1982—2003; creator Inst. for Human Performance SUNY Health Sci. Ctr., Syracuse, 1988. Coord. scholastic sports injury reporting system project SUNY, 1985-98; mem. com. on scholastic sports-related injuries NIH Inst. Arthritis, Musculoskeletal and Skin Diseases, 1993-96. Author: SSIRS Pilot Study Report, 1987, SSIRS Fall Study Report, 1988, SHASIRS Report, 1991; creator Scholastic Sports Injury Reporting System, 1985, Scholastic Head and Spine Injury Reporting System, 1989. Co-chmn. sports medicine USA Amateur Athletic Union, Nat. Jr. Olympic Games, Syracuse, NY, 1987; vol. sports medicine N.Y. State Sr. Games, 1990—95, sports medicine coord., 1990—95, U.S. Roller Skating Nat. Championships, 1995, N.Y. State Womens Lacrosse Championships, 1995, U.S. Nat. Precision Ice Skating Championships, 1997, Youth Basketball of Am., Northeast Regional Tournament, 1999; co-chmn. healthcare, security Empire State Games, Syracuse, 2002; mem. com. sports injury surveillance Ctrs. for Disease Control, 1995; cons. N.Y. Sci., Tech. and Soc. Edn. Project, 1995. Mem. AAUW, N.Y. State AAHPERD (pres. exercise sci. and sports medicine sect., 1994-98), Am. Coll. Sports Medicine, United Univ. Profs., Women's Sports Fedn., Am. Fedn. Tchrs., N.Y. United Tchrs., North Syracuse Tchrs. Assn., Phi Kappa Phi. Avocations: swimming, cycling, ice skating, reading, photography. Office: 418 Buffington Rd Syracuse NY 13224-2208 Office Phone: 315-449-9509. Business E-Mail: dmduerr@twcny.rr.com.

DUFER, MIRIAM DONYELLE, military officer, writer; b. Reform, Ala., Nov. 21, 1970; d. Albert Douglas Harris and Gradie Jean Bonner; m. David Alonzo Dufer, Apr. 16, 2002; 1 child, Youngsun Kim. BA in english, U. of Ala., 1995—98. Writer (poetry) Confession and Other Strange Impulses. Capt. U.S. Army. Decorated Army Commendation with oak leaf cluster U.S. Army, Army Achievement medal with oak leaf cluster, Good Conduct medal, Armed Forces Expeditionary medal, NATO medal. Mem.: Gamma Sigma Sigma (life). R-Conservative. Roman Catholic. Home: 2235 Willow Tree Grv Apt 201 Colorado Springs CO 80910-7105 Personal E-mail: miriamdufer@hotmail.com.

DUFF, HILLARY ANN, actress, singer; b. Houston, Sept. 28, 1987; d. Bob and Susan Duff. Actor: (TV films) True Women, 1997, Soul Collector, 1999; (TV series) Lizzie McGuire, 2001—03; (films) Human Nature, 2001, Cadet Kelly, 2002, Agent Cody Banks, 2003, The Lizzie McGuire Movie, 2003, Cheaper by the Dozen, 2003, (guest appearances on): (TV series) Chicago Hope, 2000, George Lopez, 2003, American Dreams, 2003, Frasier (voice), 2004; singer: (albums) Lizzie McGuire Television Soundtrack, 2001, Santa Claus Lane, 2002, The Lizzie McGuire Movie Soundtrack, 2003, (debut solo album) Metamorphosis, 2003 (charted #2 on Billboard 200 first week of release). Recipient Nickelodeon Kids Choice Award for Favorite Female Singer, 2004. Office: c/o PMK Public Relations 650 Fifth Ave 33rd Fl New York NY 10019*

DUFFEY, ROSALIE RUTH, elementary school educator; b. Randolph, Mo., July 4, 1938; d. Joseph Anthony and Katherine Ruth Spruytte; m. Robert Lee Duffey, Oct. 20, 1956; children: Susan, Carolyn, Janice, Maryann, Philip, David, Mark. AS in Early Childhood Edn., Ctrl. Mo. State U., 1973, BS in Edn., 1977, MS in Edn., 1980. Cert. tchr. elem. and spl. edn. Mo. Dir. ednl. ops. Head Start West Ctrl. Mo. Rural Devel. Corp., Appleton City, 1966—79; tchr. spl. edn. Butler (Mo.) Elem. Sch., 1979—87; tchr. Parents as Tchrs. Cass RIX Pub. Sch., Harrisonville, Mo., 1987—98; tchr. Marillac Sch., Kansas City, Mo., 1998—99, Trails West State Schs. for Severely Handicapped, Kansas City, 1999—. Mem. policy coun. Head Start, Appleton City; foster parent Divsn. of Family Svcs., Cass and Henry Counties, Mo., 1977—2000. Mem.: Ctrl. Mo. State U. Alumni Assn., Mo. State Ret. Tchrs. Assn., Assn. of Retarded Citizens, Coun. for Exceptional Children, Alpha Phi Delta, Kappa Delta Pi, Phi Kappa Phi, Alpha Phi Sigma. Roman Catholic. Avocations: quilting, gardening, walking.

DUFFY, ANNE M. artist; b. Fairbanks, AK, Sept. 26, 1974; d. Lawrence Kevin and Geraldine Antoinette D. BFA, Univ. Alaska, Fairbanks, AK, 1996; MFA, Pratt Inst., Brooklyn, NY, 1999. Exhibits asst. Univ. Alaska Mus., Fairbanks, AK, 1995-96; lectr. Univ. Alaska, Summer Fine Arts Grp., Fairbanks, AK, 1995, 97-98; advtg. creative cons. Coldwell Banker, Fairbanks, AK, 1996—; editl. asst., pub. rels. Univ. Wash., Seattle, 1999—. Adv. bd. of med., Univ. Wash., Seattle, WA, 1999—, art creative cons., Coldwell Banker, Fairbanks, AK, 1996—. Artist of fine arts, Phylum (show title), 1999, Linum, 1999, Tendere, 1999; contbr. conf. paper in field of libr. and info. sci. Mem. Amnesty Internat., Brooklyn, NY, 1996-99, Fairbanks, AK, 1992-96, Seattle, WA, 1999—. Recipient Bogardus Scholarship, Pratt Inst. Sch. of Libr. & Info. Sci., 1997, 98, 99, rsch. awd., ACRL, Blackwell's Book Svcs., 1999. Mem. Pratt Artists League, 1996—, Golden Key Honor Soc., 1995—, Pratt Inst. Alumni Assn., 1999—, Univ. Alaska Alumni Assn., 1996—, Friends of Univ. of Alaska Mus., 1994—, Phi Kappa Phi, 1996—. Avocations: architecture, writing, travel. Home: care Heather Hayworth 33212 124th St SE Sultan WA 98294-8674 E-mail: aduffy1475@washington.edu.

DUFFY, NANCY KEOGH, television broadcast professional; b. Washington, Nov. 24, 1947; d. William Francis and Gertrude K. (Keogh) D.; divorced; children: Peter Patrick, Matthew Michael. Student, St. Mary of the Woods Coll.; AB, Marywood Coll., 1967. News reporter Sta. WHEN TV and Radio, Syracuse, N.Y., 1967-70; press sec. City of Syracuse, 1970; news reporter Sta. WTVH, Syracuse, 1971-77; news anchorperson Sta. WIXT-TV, Syracuse, 1977—. Talk show host Syracuse New Channels, 1986-87; talk show host, producer Community Connections, 1987-89; instr. Syracuse U. Prodr. TV series Duffy's People, With Steve on Sunday. Founder Syracuse St. Patrick's Parade, 1983, pres., organizer, 1983-2001, hon. pres., 2002-; organizer Cooperstown 50th Ann. Baseball Hall of Fame Parade, 1989, opening ceremonies Empire State Games, 1990; co-organizer Save Our Syracuse Symphony, 1984—; organizer Bark-Out Against Rabies Paws Parade, 1995-98, Artist Eagle Faces Exhibits, 1999-2003; bd. dirs. Syracuse Symphony, 1992-98, The Media Unit, 1977-97; active Project children, Syracuse, YMCA; telethon hostess Muscular Dystrophy Assn.; organizer poetry workshops for children, 1995—; mem. Onondaga County Traffic Safety Bd., 1977-2002, Le Moyne Coll. Pres. Assocs.; honorary chair, Civil War Weekend, Peterborough, NY.; bd. dirs. Native Am. Svc. Agcy., 2002. Recipient Nat. Angel award Best Spl. Religion in Media, Post Std. Woman of Achievement award, 1st Downtown award for excellence, 1986, Mayor's Achievement award, 1985, Humanitarian award Project Children, 1993, N.Y. State Senate commendation, 1995; named Woman of Achievement N.Y. State Fair, 1994, NWCA Acad. Diversity Achievers, 2004. Mem. Am. Women in Radio and TV (nat. award 1973), Women in Comms. (Outstanding Communicator award 1985), Syracuse Press Club (bd. dirs. 1987—, v.p. 1990, 97, 98, pres. 1991-92, Bernard and Dorothy Newer Svc. award 1995, lifetime achievement award 2000), Syracuse Rotary (pub. rels. 1989-92), Am. Heart Assn. (hon. co-chair Ctrl. N.Y. 1997). Roman Catholic. Office: Sta WIXT-TV 5904 Bridge St East Syracuse NY 13057-2941

DUFFY, VIRGINIA, state representative, artist; b. Long Island, N.Y., May 16, 1939; m. Brant Duffy; 3 children. BA, U. Vt., 1961. Caseworker Nassau County Dept. Social Welfare, NY; realtor; state rep. State of Vt., 2001—. Republican. Roman Catholic. Office: 5 Newton St Rutland VT 05701

DUFNER, DONNA KANE, management information systems, project management educator; b. Greensburg, Pa., July 9, 1948; d. Clarence E. and Marie Anna Daniels; m. John Raymond Kevern, Dec. 23, 1995; 1 child, Kathleen Elizabeth. BA in Sociology cum laude, DePaul U., 1975; MBA, U. Chgo., 1977; MS in Computer and Info. Scis., N.J. Inst. Tech., 1995; PhD in Mgmt., Rutgers U., 1995. Cons. Planmetrics, Chgo., 1977-79; project mgr. AT&T, U.S. and Ireland, 1979-84; asst. v.p. Chem. N.Y. Corp., 1985-88; wireless networks project mgr. ARDIS (joint venture IBM and Motorola), 1991-94; asst. prof. Poly. U., NY, 1994-96, U. Ill., Springfield, 1996-00, U. Nebr., Omaha, 2000—03, assoc. prof., 2003—. Cons. proj. mgmt. Bell Atlantic/NYNEX, N.J., 1996, ICGS, 1999, Omaha/Douglas County, 2000-03; tchg. fellow Rutgers U., N.J., 1989-90; guest speaker NY Acad. Scis., 1995. Editl. bd. Comm. AIS; contr. articles to profl. jours. Docent Bahai House of Worship, Wilmette, Ill., 1979-82. Recipient Edna True Meritorious Svc. award Bahai Nat. Assembly, 1984, Univ. Scholar award U. Ill., 1998. Mem. IEEE (named Outstanding Referee 1998-99, sr. referee, 1998-), AIS, PMI, Beta Gamma Sigma. Bahai. Avocations: hiking, cross-country skiing, cooking, sculpture, pottery. Office: U Nebr Rm 117A Peter Kiewit Inst 110 South 67th St Omaha NE 68182-0392

DUFRESNE, ELIZABETH JAMISON, lawyer; b. Winter Haven, Fla., July 29, 1942; d. John W. and Thelma M. (Kinney) Jamison; 1 child, Brennan. BA, Vanderbilt U., 1964; JD, U. Fla., 1966. Bar: U.S. Dist. Ct. (so. dist.) Fla. 1967, U.S. Dist. Ct. (mid. dist.) Fla. 1968, U.S. Ct. Appeals (5th cir.) 1968, U.S. Supreme Ct. 1969, U.S. Ct. Appeals (11th cir.) 1981. Atty. So. Fla. Migrant Legal Svc., Miami, 1967-69; law reform chief Greater Miami Legal Svc., Miami, 1969-71; assoc. Tobias Simon P.A., Miami, 1971; ptnr. Tobias Simon & Elizabeth duFresne, P.A., Miami, 1971-77; sr. ptnr. duFresne & duFresne, P.A., Miami, 1977-82, duFresne & Bradley, P.A., Miami, 1982-86; equity ptnr. Steel, Hector & Davis, Miami, 1986—, bd. dirs., chmn. labor law divsn. adj. prof. law U. Miami, Coral Gables, Fla., 1977-93; mem. Civil Justice Adv. Group USDC, S.D. Fla., 1990—. Recipient Award of Honor ACLU, Dade, 1969, Award of Merit ACLU, Fla., 1970, 73. Mem. ABA, Fla. Bar Assn. (Pioneer award 1977), Dade County Bar Assn., Fed. Bar Assn., Assn. Trial Lawyers Am., Assn. Trial Lawyers Fla., Fla. Assn. Women Lawyers. Democrat. Roman Catholic. Avocations: cooking, reading, racquetball, cycling, sailing. Office: 200 S Biscayne Blvd Miami FL 33131-2310

DUGAN, JEAN BRODSHAUG, public relations consultant; b. Fargo, N.D., Oct. 11, 1959; d. Robert L. and Jacqueline Adelle (Qualley) Brodshaug; m. Joseph Robert Dugan, Sept. 14, 1991; children: Patrick Robert, Brian Joseph. BA, BS, U. N.D., 1981; MS, Boston U., 1984. Sr. copy editor Viewdata Corp., Miami, Fla., 1983-85; press sec. U.S. Senator Quentin Burdick, Washington, 1985-92, U.S. Senator Jocelyn Burdick, Washington, 1992-93; cons. Nat. Women's Polit. Caucus, Washington, 1993-96; comms. dir., dep. campaign mgr. Joan Kelly Horn for Congress, 1996—; sr. pub. rels. mgr. Osborn & Barr Comms., 1998—2002; instr. comm. U. Phoenix, 2001—. Author: Campaigning to Win, 1993. Chair Metro St. Louis Women's Polit. Caucus, 1997-98. Lutheran. Home and Office: 316 Oak Manor Ln Saint Louis MO 63119-1542

DUGAN, JOANN RUBINO, education educator; b. McKeesport, Pa., Dec. 31, 1953; d. Joseph Edward Rubino and Emma Jean Licht; m. William Allan Dugan, Feb. 23, 1973; children: Shannon Michael, Ryan James. BS in Elem. and Early Childhood Edn., California U. of Pa., 1979, MEd, 1993; PhD, U. Pitts., 1996. Cert. tchr. elem., early childhood, reading specialist Pa. Tchr. presch. Head Start Allegheny Intermediate Unit, Pitts., 1987—92; grad. asst. California U. of Pa., 1992—93; reading clinic dir., instr. U. Pitts., 1993—96; asst. prof. reading Tex. A&M U., Commerce, 1996—99, Clarion U., Pa., 1999—2003; assoc. prof. emergent literacy Ohio U., Athens, 2003—. Reading specialist, cons. Valley Grove Sch. Dist., 2000—; writing fellow Western Pa. Writing Project, Pitts., 1993—96; project dir. Clarion K-16 Reading Clinic, 2000—02, dir., 1999—2003. Editor: Coll. Reading Assn. yearbooks, 1997—; contbr. articles to profl. jours. Vol. reader Read Across America program Allegheny clarion Valley Sch. Dist., Foxburg, Pa., 2000—03. Recipient Elva Knight Rsch. award, Internat. Reading Assn., 1999, Dissertation award, Coll. Reading Assn., 1996; scholar Presdl. scholar, California U. Pa., 1996. Mem.: ACEI, Seneca Reading Coun. (v.p. 2002), Coll. Reading Assn. (editor 1995), Internat. Reading Assn., Ohio State Reading Assn. Democrat. Methodist. Achievements include research in in transactional model for encouraging thoughtful response to literature in the elementary classroom. Avocations: photography, painting, travel, writing. Office: Ohio Univ McCracken Hall Athens OH 45701

DUGAN, LYNN, communications company executive; BA in Mass Comm.-Journalism cum laude, Emerson Coll. Reporter, prodr. Sta. WERS-FM, Boston; asst. assignment editor Sta. WLVI-TV, Warner Bros. affiliate, Boston; prodn. asst. Sta. WHDH-TV, CBS affiliate, Boston; sta. rels. coord. Medialink Inc., N.Y.C., from 1995, dir. broadcast rsch. Office: Medialink Inc 708 3rd Ave Fl 9 New York NY 10017-4101 E-mail: ldugan@medialink.com.

DUGANIER, BARBARA J. corporate financial executive; Advisor to former U.S. Commerce Sec. William M. Daley; mng. ptnr. and CFO Andersen, Houston, 2001—. Office: 711 Louisiana St Houston TX 77002

DUGGAN, CAROL COOK, research director; b. Dillon, SC, May 25, 1946; d. Pierce Embree and Lillian Watkins (Eller) Cook; m. Kevin Duggan, Dec. 29, 1973. BA, Columbia Coll., 1968; MS, U. Ky., 1970. Reference asst. Richland County Pub. Libr., Columbia, S.C., 1968-69, asst. to dir., 1970, chief adult svcs., 1971-82; dir. Maris Rsch., Columbia, 1982—. Lectr. Greater Columbia (S.C.) Literacy Coun., 1973—75. Author: A History of the City of Forest Acres, S.C., 1998. Treas. Friends of S.C. Libr., 1995—2003; mem. zoning bd. appeals City of Forest Acres, 1999—; worship com. Washington St. United Meth. Ch., Columbia, SC, 1985—86, 1999—, mem. staff-parish rels. com., 1985—91, 2004—, chmn. staff-parish rels. com., 1993, trustee, 1995—98, mem. adminstr. bd., 1983—86, mem. adminstr. br., 1988—91, mem. adminstr. bd., 1993, mem. ch. coun., 2004—; exec. bd. United Meth. Women, 1983—2001, treas. unit 7, 1989—91, pres. unit 5, 1992—97, treas., 1998—; adminstrv. bd. Washington St. United Meth. Ch., Columbia, SC, 1988—91, 1993; del. S.C. Ann. Conf. of United Meth. Ch., 2004—. Recipient Sternheimer award, Columbia Coll., 1968. Mem.: PEO (pres. 1983—85, chmn. amendments and recommendations com. 1983—85, historian 1986—87, treas. state conv. 1987—88, historian 1990—92, v.p. 1998—99, del. internat. conv. 1999, historian 2002—), DAR, ALA (chmn. state membership com. 1979—83, councilor 1980—82), S.C. Pub. Libr. Assn. (pres. 1980—81), S.C. Libr. Assn. (sec. 1976, exec. bd. 1976, 1978—82), Columbia Coll. Alumnae Assn. (alumnae coun. spl. events com. 1996—, Columbia Coll. Commn. 150 2003), Beta Phi Mu. Methodist. Home: 2101 Woodmere Dr Columbia SC 29204-4341

DUGUID, DOROTHY ANN RAMSEYER, artist; b. Bloomington, Ill., Nov. 8, 1924; d. Roy Arthur and Ruth Frances (Bodell) Ramseyer; m. James Mitchell Duguid, mar. 31, 1947; children: John Robinson, Robert Mitchell, Carol D. Hootman, Barbara P. Ungs. Student, U. Ill., Champaign, Coe Coll., Ill. Wesleyan U., Chgo. Art Inst. Cert. tchr. Tchr. Jr. High Sch., San Antonio, Tex., Albuquerque, Urbana (Ill.) Jr. High; substitute tchr. Bloomington H.S. Mem. McLean County Weavers Guild, Bloomington - Normal Artists Guild, PEO, Margaret Fuller Club, Epsilon chpt. Kappa Kappa Gamma. Republican. Presbyterian. Avocation: piano.

DUHIG, SUSAN CAROLINE, writer; b. Atlanta, June 27, 1963; d. James Joseph and Kay Elizabeth (Hudgins) D. BA in English lit. summa cum laude, Emory U., 1985; MA in English lit., Cornell U., 1990, PhD in English lit., 1994. Rsch. and tchg. asst. Cornell U., Ithaca, NY, 1987—91, lectr., 1992—93, Ithaca Coll., 1993—94; asst. prof. cinema studies So. Ill. U., Carbondale, Ill., 1994—98; freelance writer, 1998—; med. writer Barnes-Jewish Hosp., St. Louis, 2001—03; rsch. assoc. ethical and social dimensions genetics Wash. U. Sch. Medicine, St. Louis, 2003—. Presenter in field. Harry S. Truman scholar, 1983, Robert T. Jones scholar, 1985-86; Sage fellow, 1986-87, Mellon fellow, 1991-92. Mem. Phi Beta Kappa. Home: 5118 Waterman # 101 Saint Louis MO 63108

DUHME, CAROL MCCARTHY, civic worker; b. St. Louis, Apr. 13, 1917; d. Eugene Ross and Louise (Roblee) McCarthy; m. Sheldon Ware, June 12, 1941 (dec. 1944); 1 child, David; m. H. Richard Duhme, Jr., Apr. 9, 1947; children: Benton (dec.), Ann, Warren (dec.). AB, Vassar Coll., 1939; DHL (hon.), Eden Theol. Sem., 2002. Tchr. elem. sch., 1939-41, 42-44; moderator St. Louis Assn. Congl. Chs., 1959—62; trustee 1st Congl. Ch., 1964—66; mem. ch. coun. St. Louis Assn. Congl. Ch., 1974-75, 84-85, 87-89, bd. deaconesses, 1978-81, bd. deacons, chmn. bd. Christian Edn., 1987-88. Former bd. dirs. Community Music Schs., St. Louis, Community Sch., Ch. Women United, John Burroughs Sch., St. Louis Bicentennial Women's Com., St. Louis Jr. League; pres. St. Louis Vassar Club; pres., bd. dirs. YWCA, St. Louis, 1973-76, chmn. ann. fund, 1989-90; bd. dirs. North Side Team Ministry, 1968-84, Chautauqua (N.Y.) Instn., 1971-79, mem. adv. coun. to bd., 1987—. Mem. adv. coun. Mo. Bapt. Hosp., 1973—89; mem. exec. com. bd. dirs. Eden Theol. Sem., 1981—95, presdl. search com., 1986—87, 1992—93, v.p., bd. dirs., 1991, chmn. 150th ann. com., 1996—2000; sec. bd. dirs. UN Assn., St. Louis, 1976—84, coun. advisors, 1993—, nat. coun., 1995—; mem. nat. coun. UN-USA, 1995—2001; pres. bd. dirs. Family and Children's Svc. Greater St. Louis, 1977—79; mem. chancellor's long range planning com. Wash. U., 1980—81, mem. Nat. Coun., Sch. Social Work, 1987—; chmn. Benton Roblee Duhme Scholar Fund; trustee Joseph H. and Florence A. Roblee Found., St. Louis, 1984—, pres., 1984—90; bd. dirs.; chmn. Chautauqua Bell Tower Scholar Fund, 1961—; bd. dirs. Nat. Inland Waterways Libr., St. Louis Merc Libr.; mem. corp. assembly Blue Cross Hosp. Svc. Mo., 1978—86; pres. Joseph H. and Florence A. Roblee Found., 2002. Recipient Mary Alice Messerley award for volunteerism Health and Welfare Coun. St. Louis, 1971, Vol. of Yr. award, YWCA, 1976, Woman of Achievement award St. Louis Globe Democrat, 1980, Outstanding Lay Women nomination Mo. United Ch. of Christ, 1991, Outstanding Alumna award John Burroughs Sch., 1992, Humanitarian award Planned Parenthood St. Louis, 2000. Home: 8 Edgewood Rd Saint Louis MO 63124-1817

DUITMAN, LOIS ROBINSON, artist; b. Green Bay, Wis. m. Rock Duitman; children: Christine M. Bomgardner, Brian R. Plog. Student, Art Student's League, N.Y., Women's U. of The Philippines, Manila, Baylor U., Waco, TX, Orange Coast Coll., Saddleback Coll., CA. Chief copywriter J.C. Penney's, L.A.; asst. editor Calif. Girl Mag., L.A. Tchr. art workshop Pepperdine U., Calif. One woman shows include Spearfish State Teachers' Coll., S. Dak., Roswell Art Mus., State Art Mus. of Santa Fe, Hawaii, 1984, Clearwater, Palm Harbor, Fla., Jacksonville, Dunedin, Sarasota, St. Petersburg, Fla., 1991-97, Rio Rancho (N.Mex.) Country Club, 1997, Albuquerque Little Theatre, 1999; exhibited in group shows at State Art Mus. of Santa Fe, (award), Natl. Art Gallery of The Philippines, Manila, Jehengir Art Gallery, Bombay, Roswell Art Mus., State Art Mus., Santa Fe, N.Mex., Art Encounter Gallery, Las Vegas, Nev., numerous others; painted in Spain, Portugal, France, Aden, Jamaica, The Bahamas, Africa, P.R., Germany, Singapore, Mozambique, others; artist (cookbook covers) Bon Appetit de Las Sandias, 1998, 99. Mem. Internat. Soc. Marine Painters, Fla. Watercolor Soc., West Mesa Woman's Club. Avocations: skiing, tennis, swimming, biking, bowling. Home: 64 Parkside Rd SE Rio Rancho NM 87124-3983

DUJON, DIANE MARIE, director, activist; b. Boston, Dec. 29, 1946; d. Alfred and Agnes C. (Hall) White; 1 child, Lisa M. Dujon. BA, U. Mass., 1983, MS, 1996. Asst. dir. assessment Coll. Pub. and Cmty. Svc. U. Mass., Boston, 1984-93, co-dir. assessment Coll. Pub. and Cmty. Svc., 1993-97, dir. experiential learning Coll. Pub. and Cmty. Svc., 1997—. Co-editor: For Crying Out Loud: Women's Poverty in U.S., 1996 (Myers Ctr. for the Study of Human Rights in N.Am. Outstanding Book award 1997); prodr. (radio documentary) Workfare: Anatomy of a Policy, 1982 (Alice award 1982), Nat. Commn. on Working Women; alternative radio (NPR) recorded speech, Women, Welfare and Poverty, 1998. V.p. Survivors, Inc., Boston, 1986—. Recipient Earl Douglas award City Mission Soc., 1987; named Unsung Heroine Rosie's Place, 1997. Mem. Nat. Welfare Rights Union, Mass. AFL-CIO (mem. exec. women's com. 1997-2001), U. Mass. Profl. Staff Union (bd. mem. chpt. Svc. Employees Internat. Union, Local 888). Baptist. Office: U Mass/Boston 100 Morrissey Blvd Boston MA 02125-3300

DUKAKIS, OLYMPIA, actress; b. Lowell, Mass., June 20, 1931; d. Constantine S. and Alexandra (Christos) D.; m. Louis Zorich; children: Christina, Peter, Stefan. BS, Boston U., 1952, MFA, 1957. Co-founder, artistic dir. Whole Theatre, Montclair, N.J., 1970-90; co-founder Charles Playhouse, Boston; master tchr. NYU, 1970-85. Appeared in over 125 prodns. for regional theatres, N.Y. Shakespeare Theatre, Circle Repertory Theatre, American Place Theatre and numerous Off-Broadway theatres; appearances on stage include King of America, Social Security; appearances in film include Lilith, 1964, Twice a Man, 1964, John and Mary, 1969, Made for Each Other, 1971, Death Wish, 1974, Rich Kids, 1979, The Wanderers, 1979, The Idolmaker, 1980, National Lampoon Goes to the Movies, 1982, Flanagan, 1985, Moonstruck, 1988 (Golden Globe, Academy Award Suppporting Actress), Working Girl, 1988, Steel Magnolias, 1988, Look Who's Talking, 1988, Dad, 1989, In the Spirit, 1990, Look Who's Talking II, 1990, Over the Hill, 1992, Look Who's Talking Now, 1993, The Cemetery Club, 1993, I Love Trouble, 1994, Digger, 1994, Jeffrey, 1995, Mighty Aphrodite, 1995, Mr. Holland's Opus, 1996, Dead Badge, 1995, Picture Perfect, 1997, Never Too Late, 1997, Jane Austen's Mafia!, 1998, A Life for a Life, 1998, Better Living, 2000, Brooklyn Sonnet, 2000, The Intended, 2002, The Event, 2003, Charlie's War, 2003, Jesus, Mary and Joey, 2003, ; (TV movies) Nicky's World, 1974, The Neighborhood, 1982, The Last Act is a Solo, 1990 (Ace award), Lucky Day, 1991, Fire in the Dark, 1991, Sinatra: The Mini-Series, 1992, Armistead Maupin's Tales of the City, 1994, A Century of Women, 1994, Young at Heart, 1995, A Match Made in Heaven, 1997, Scattering Dad, 1998, The Pentagon Wars, 1998, More Tales of the City (mini-series), 1998, Joan of Arc, 1999, Last of the Blonde Bombshells, 2000, And Never Let Her Go, 2001, Ladies and the Champ, 2001, Further Tales of the City (mini series), 2001, My Beautiful Son, 2001, Guilty Hearts (mini-series), 2002, Mafia Doctor, 2003, Babycakes, 2003. Del. Dem. Nat. Convention, 1988. Recipient 2 Obie awards, Los Angeles Film Critics award, 1988. Mem. Actor's Equity Assn., Screen Actors Guild, Am. Fedn. TV and Radio Artists. Office: William Morris Agy care Parseghian 1325 Avenue Of The Americas Fl 32 New York NY 10019-4702

DUKE, CAROL MICHIELS, b. Alexandria, La., Sept. 2, 1944; d. Leo A., Sr. and Elva L. (Wilson) Michiels; m. M. Carey Duke, Jr., Apr. 23, 1971; 1 child, Perrianne. Student in personnel mgmt. Nichols State U., 1974-77; grad. Dale Carnegie Inst., Realtors Inst. Officer mgr. Bayou Constrn. Co., Houma, La., 1974-76; mgr. Glynn & Assoc., Houma, La., 1976 79; owner, broker Century 21 Real Estate One, Houma, 1979-81; v.p., mgmt. cons. Century 21 of Tex. and La., Houston, 1981-82; v.p., gen. mgr. Doyle Stuckey, Houston, 1982-83; broker/mgr. Gary Greene Realtors, Better Homes and Gardens, Houston, 1983-85; regional mgr. Better Homes and Gardens, Des Moines, 1985-95; mgr., hearing instrument specialist Miracle Ear, Austin, Tex., 1995—; dist. mgr. Miracle Ear, Austin, Tex.; seminar condr.; chmn. conv. booth Realtors Nat. Home Builders, Houston, 1983. Editor Training and Policy Manual, 1982. Local chmn. Easter Seal Soc., Houma, 1979. Recipient Top Listing award, numerous Top Quarterly awards La. Dist. of Century 21, 1980, Yearly Top Goal award, Yearly Bottom Line award, Top Prodn. award, numerous Top Quarterly awards, Better Homes & Gardens, Houston, 1983, 84. Mem. Houston Bd. Realtors (edn. com. 1984-85), Tex. Assn. Realtors (realtor/builder, sec. 1983—), Nat. Assn. Realtors, Realtors Nat. Mktg. Inst., Jaycee Jaynes (state bd. dirs. 1976-77, sec. 1977-78). Democrat. Roman Catholic. Home: Apt #217 4201 Monterey Oaks Blvd Apt 217 Austin TX 78749-1025 Office: Miracle Ear Lakeline Mall Cedar Park TX 78613

DUKE, ELIZABETH (BETSY) A. bank executive; b. July 1952; BFA U. NC, Chapel Hill; MBA, Old Dominion U., Norfolk, VA; grad., Stonier Grad. Sch. Banking, Am. Bankers Assn. Sch. of Bank Investments, Va. Bankers Assn. Sch. Bank Mgmt. Pres., CEO Bank of Tidewater, 1991—2001; sr. v.p. govt. rels. SouthTrust Corp., Va. Beach, Va., 2001—03, exec. v.p. cmty. bank devel., 2003—. Nat. adv. coun. Fannie Mae, 2004—. Named One of 25 Women to Watch, U.S. Banker Mag., 2003. Mem.: Am. Bankers Assn. (chmn.-elect 2003—). Home: 301 Booty Lane Virginia Beach VA 23451-2030*

DUKE, ELIZABETH M. health facility administrator; B Polit. Sci., M Polit. Sci., Rutgers U.; M African Studies, Northwestern U.; PhD, George Washington U. Dir. gov. affairs inst. office exec. and mgmt. devel. Health Resources and Svcs. Adminstrn., HHS, 1978—84; dep. asst. dir., dir. policy and sys. office tng. and devel. U.S. Office Pers. Mgmt., 1984—86; dep. asst. sec. adminstrn. Adminstrn. Children and Families U.S. Dept. Health and Human Svs., CFO, mgmt. control officer, chief grants officer, chief info. officer Adminstrn. Children and Families, head grants policy, fin. mgmt. internal and state sys., human resources, other adminstrv. duties Adminstrn. Children and Families; acting adminstr. Health Resources and Svcs. Adminstrn., HHS, 2001—; adminstr. Health Resources and Svs. Adminstrn., HHS, 2002—. Rsch. writer Congressional Quarterly. Office: Health Resources and Svs Adminstrn US Dept Health & Human Svcs Parklawn Bld 5600 Fishers Ln Rockville MD 20857

DUKE, ELLEN KAY, planned giving administrator; b. Indpls., June 7, 1952; d. Richard Thomas and Ruby Mae (Wright) D. Student, Chapman Coll., Orange, Calif., 1972; BS in Pub. Affairs, Ind. U., Bloomington, 1975; postgrad., Portland State U., 1980—81; MPA, Calif. State U., 1998. Cert. playground safety specialist/inspector; cert. Dale Carnegie Pub. Speaking instr., 1987-93. Newsreporter Salem Statesman, Corvallis, Oreg., 1976-78; com. adminstr. Oreg. State Legislature, Salem, 1979-80; pub. involvement coord. Met. Regional Svc. Dist., Portland, 1981-82; account mgr. Thunder & Visions, Portland, 1982-83; project asst. Amdahl Corp., Sunnyvale, CAlif., 1983-84; spl. project coord. Computerland Corp., Hayward, Calif., 1984-89; prodr., lead facilitator Sage, Inc., Walnut Creek, Calif., 1982—; loan broker Capital Trust Mortgage, Campbell, Calif., 1994—. Co-author (ednl. film) Communication Skills, 1975. Pub. rels. dir. local YMCA; chairperson Corvallis Budget Commn., Oreg., 1978; commr. Hayward Libr., 1985—, Alameda County Consumer Affairs, Oakland, 1985; rep. Nat. Dem. Conv., N.Y.C., 1982. Named Able Toastmaster, Toastmasters Internat., 1981; grad. Leadership Oakland, 1991. Mem. NAFE, ASTD, Pub. Rels. Soc. Am., Nat. Planned Giving Coun., Nat. Soc. for Fund Raising Execs. (planned giving coun.), Kansas City Coun. on Philanthropy, Sierra Club (San Francisco). Office: Assn Unity Churches 401 SW Oldham Pkwy Lees Summit MO 64081-2747 Home: 1354 E Paul Ave Fresno CA 93710-4119

DUKE, ORA ELIZABETH, civic volunteer; b. Dec. 26, 1942; m. D. Mike Duke Sr. (dec.); children: Dawn Elaine, D. Mike Jr. Student, N.Mex. State U., 1963, San Juan Coll., 1969, Yavapai Extension Coll., Page, Ariz., 1975. Asst. reports editor Phys. Sci. Lab., N.Mex. State U., Las Cruces, 1964-67; reservation clk. Del Webb's Wahweap Lodge, Page, Ariz., 1970; [illegible] [illegible] System, 1971, mem. crew Sanderson Bros. River Expedition, Colo., 1972-75. Mem. John Wesley Powell Mus. Bd., program chmn. 1973-74, The Newcomers Club, 1986-87; wig chmn., Clacasieu Parish Extension Homemakers, 1988—; participant Calif. Conf. on Women, 1986, 87, La. Talent Bank of Women; Page, Ariz. Precinct West Dep. Registrar, Coconino County, 1974-75; sec., Page Recreation Assn., 1970-71, PTA, 1970-71; den mother, pack organizer Cub Scouts Am., 1972; den mother Cub Scout Latter Day Saints, 1971; chmn. Mayor's Commn. Pub. Sch. Expansion Research, Page, Ariz., 1974, Gov.'s com. Waste Disposal Alternatives for No. Ariz., 1975; vol. Titus Country Home Demonstration Office; adv. bd. Internat. Order Rainbow Girls, 1971-75, mother advisor 1974-75. Mem. Cactus Wrens Extension Homemakers Club (pres., organizer 1975-77), Red Sands Extension Homemakers Club (pres. 1973-74), Associated Country Women of the World, Country Women Council, Howard Ruff Discussion Forum (chmn. 1987-88), Nat. Assn. Women in Constrn. (program chmn. 1986-87), Hollywood Extension Homemakers Club (v.p. 1986-87, Vt. mem. 1993, 94), Mich. Extension Homemaker Club, Elks (ladies auxiliary 1999—), Order of the Eastern Star, Habitat for Humanity (nat. reg.) Xi Alpha Kappa (chmn., social chmn., program chmn. 1972-74), Beta Sigma Pi, Xi Beta Phi.. Clubs: Lake Powell Yacht (Lake Pals aux., charter); Glen Canyon Golf and Country (social com. 1971-72). Lodges: Order of Eastern Star, Order of The Rainbow for Girls (mother advisor 1974-75, adv. bd. 1971-75). Avocations: antique doll collecting, travel, genealogy. Home: # 760 13618 N 99th Ave Sun City AZ 85351-2813

DUKE, PHYLLIS LOUISE KELLOGG HENRY, school administrator, consultant; b. Mason City, Iowa, May 3, 1932; d. Wilbur Rhode and Dorothy Margaret (Bauer) Kellogg; children— Curtis Dean Henry, Catherine Rose Henry Jones, David Russell Henry. A.A. in Elem. Teaching, U. No. Iowa, 1953; B.A. Calif. State U.-Los Angeles, 1963, M.A., 1968. Cert. elem. tchr., cert. reading specialist, sch. adminstrn. credential. Tchr., Arlington pub. schs., Iowa, 1951-52, St. Louis Park pub. schs., Minn., 1953-55; tchr., supr. ABC Sch. Dist., Cerritos, Calif., 1963-69; cons. in reading State Dept. of Calif., Sacramento, 1969-70; cons. in edn. Orange County Dept. Edn., Santa Ana, Calif., 1970-75; sch. adminstr. Oakwood Acad., Long Beach, Calif., 1975— ; chmn. bd. dirs. New City Bank, Orange, Calif.; cons. in field. Author: Song of Sounds, 1969; (with others) Beginnings for Christian Schools, 1976. Conf. coordinator State Dept. Edn., Calif., Sacramento, Santa Barbara, 1970 (Outstanding Leadership award 1974-75). Mem. Nat. Ind. Pvt. Sch. (v.p. 1982-83, dir. seminars 1983), Pre-Sch. Assn. Calif. (legis. chair 1978-84), Reading Specialists Calif. (pres. 1970-73). Republican. Avocations: skiing; scuba diving; painting; photography; travel. Home: 1208 S Lemon Ave Walnut CA 91789-4822 Office: Oakwood Acad 2951 N Long Beach Blvd Long Beach CA 90806-1532

DUKE, ROBIN CHANDLER TIPPETT, retired public relations executive; b. Balt., Oct. 13, 1923; d. Richard Edgar and Esther (Chandler) Tippett; m. Angier Biddle Duke, May 1962; children: Jeffrey R. Lynn, Letitia Lynn, Angier Biddle Jr. Fashion editor N.Y. Jour. Am., N.Y.C., 1944-46; freelance writer N.Y.C., 1946-50; rep. Orvis Bros., N.Y.C., 1953-58; mem. pub. rels. staff Pepsi Cola Co., Internat., N.Y.C., 1958-62; amb. to UNESCO, Belgrade, 1980; amb. U.S. to Norway, 2000—01. Bd. dirs. Am. Home Products, N.Y.C., Internat. Flavors & Fragrances, N.Y.C., East River Bank, New Rochelle, NY; bd. dirs. emeritus Inst. Internat. Edn.; dir. Rockwell Corp., 1977—95. Co-chmn. Population Action Internat., N.Y.C., 1975-96; Met. Club Washington; bd. dirs. David Packard Found., U.S. Japan Found. Recipient Albert and Mary Lasker Social Svc. award, 1991, Margaret Sanger Woman of Yr. Valor award, 1995. Mem. Coun. on Fgn. Rels., Acad. Arts & Scis., World Affairs Coun. L.I. (co-chmn.), Colony Club, River Club. Democrat. Avocations: skiing, swimming. Home: 435 E 52nd St New York NY 10022-6445

DUKE, SARA WILLETT, curator; b. Schnectady, N.Y., May 26, 1963; d. Allen W. Duke and Sabina F. Hartley; m. Matthew Gregory Schneer, July 18, 1992; children: Sylvia Jane, Alexander Benjamin. BA, Bennington Coll., 1985; MA, SUNY, 1986, PhD, 1992; MLS, U. Md., 1997. Jr. fellow Prints and Photgraphs Divsn. Libr. Congress, Washington, 1991—92, cataloger Copyright Office, 1992—93, curatorial asst. Prints and Photographs Divsn., 1993—2000, asst. curator Prints and Photographs Divsn., 2000—. Author: Blondie Gets Married, 2000; co-author: Featuring the Funnies, 1995—; editor: Chromosome Deletion Outreach Newsletter, 2000—. Mem.: Libr. Congress Profl. Assn. Office: Prints and Photographs Divsn Libr Congress 101 Independence Ave SE Washington DC 20540-4730

DUKES, JOAN, state legislator; b. Tacoma, Wash., Oct. 1, 1947; 3 children. BA, Evergreen State Coll. Commissioner Clatsop County, 1983-87; mem. Oreg. Senate, Dist. 1, Salem, 1986-; senate dem. whip. Democrat. Office: Oreg State Senate 210 State St # S-318 Salem OR 97310-0001 Address: RR 2 Box 503 Astoria OR 97103-9617

DUKES, VANESSA JOHNSON, dietician; b. Charleston, S.C., Aug. 4, 1955; d. Rubin and Christena (Weston) Johnson; m. Warren L. Dukes, May 21, 1983. BS, S.C. State U., 1977, MEd, 1979. Registered and lic. dietitian. Grad. asst. in home econs. S.C. State Coll., Orangeburg, 1977-79; nutritionist Services Council Day Care Ctr., Aiken, S.C., 1980-83; food service supr. III S.C. Dept. Correction, Ridgeville, 1987—; tchr. emotionally handicapped Charleston County Sch. Dist., 1987-97; diet technician, dietitian Sodexho Mariott, Des Moines, 1997—; food svc. supr., diet tech., Mariott, Des Moines, 1997—. Dietary asst. S.C. Dept. Health and Environ. Control, Columbia, 1978; substitute tchr. Charleston County Sch. Dist., 1985—; nutritionist Franklin C. Fetter Health Clinic, Charleston, 1988—; companion, homemaker Med. Pers. Pool, Des Moines; asst. food svc. mgr. Fountain West Health Care Ctr., Des Moines, 1995—. Vol. Meals on Wheels, Aiken, 1976, Mercy House Diabetic Clinic, 1999—; vol. Project NOW Broadlawns Med. Ctr., 2001; alt. del. S.C. Dem. conv., 1980; voter registrar Aiken, SC, 1980—82. Recipient John H. Cromer Meml. scholarship S.C. Dietetic Assn., 1977. Mem. Am. Dietetic Assn., Ctrl. Iowa Dietetic Assn., Iowa Dietetic Assn., Kappa Omicron Phi. Avocations: reading, creative cooking, gardening, crafts. Home: 4046 Plainview Dr Des Moines IA 50311

DUKE-WHITAKER, LOIS, government and public relations educator, consultant, educator, researcher; b. Bessemer City, N.C., Feb. 13, 1935; d. Fred R. and Pearl (Kiser) Lovelace; married; children: Bruce F., Mary Louanne. BA, U. S.C., 1976, MA, 1979, PhD, 1986. Prof. Am. Govt. and polit. theory U. S.C., Auburn U., Mont., Ala., 1987—89; asst. prof. U. Ala., Tuscaloosa, 1989—90; assoc. prof. Clemson U., 1990—94, prof., 1994—96; prof., chmn. Ga. So. U., Statesboro, 1996—2000, prof., 1999—; cons. pub. rels. Pub. Rels./Mktg. Assocs., Charlotte, NC, 1982—85; chief, pub. info. and cmty. rels. officer Pub. Affairs Office, Fort Jackson, SC, 1973—82. Author: Women in Politics: Outsiders or Insiders; co-editor (book with James Burns, William Crotty, Lawrence Longley) The Democrats Must Lead: The Case for a Progressive Democratic Party; contbr. other pieces on women and politics and on U.S. nat. govt. Organist, choir dir. United Meth. Ch.; officer PTO; leader Indian Waters Coun. Boy Scouts Am., Congaree area Girl Scouts Am. Recipient Merit award distinctive contbns. to acad. profession, AAUP Clemson chpt., 1992. Mem.: Beta Sigma Phi, Pi Sigma Alpha, Sigma Delta Chi, Am. Women in Radio and TV (pres. Palmetto chpt.), Pub. Rels. Soc. Am. (pres.), Columbia Media, Columbia Advt., Gamma Tau Alpha. Achievements include research in mass media and politics and state and local govts. Home: 6106 Crabtree Rd Columbia SC 29206 Office: Dept Polit Sci Ga So U PO Box 8101 Statesboro GA 30460

DULANY, ELIZABETH GJELSNESS, university press administrator; b. Charleston, S.C., Mar. 11, 1931; d. Rudolph Hjalmar and Ruth Elizabeth (Weaver) Gjelsness; m. Donelson Edwin Dulany, Mar. 19, 1955; 1 son, Christopher Daniel. BA, Bryn Mawr Coll., 1952. Editor, R.R. Bowker Co., 1948-52; med. editor U. Mich. Hosp., Ann Arbor, 1953-54; editorial asst. E.P. Dutton & Co., N.Y.C., 1954-55, U. Ill. Press, Champaign, 1956-59, asst. editor, 1959-67, assoc. editor, 1967-72, mng. editor, 1972-90, asst. dir., 1983-90, assoc. dir., 1990—98, editor, 1998—. Democrat. Episcopalian. Home: 73 Greencroft Dr Champaign IL 61821-5112 Office: U Ill Press 1325 S Oak St Champaign IL 61820-6903 Office Phone: 217-244-0158. E-mail: edulany@uillinois.edu.

DULDNER, MARIANNE, director, educator; d. Kurt Paul and Ida Duldner. BA in Edn./Psychology, Kirkland Hamilton Coll., 1975; MS in Spl. Edn., So. Conn. State Coll., 1977. Ednl. therapist pvt. practice, N.Y.C., 1977—; head spl. learning St. Bernard's Sch., N.Y.C., 1987—93; asst. dir. Aaron Sch., N.Y.C., 2003—. Adj. reading instr. N.Y.C. C.C., Bklyn., 1977—80; adj. instr. reading Hunter Coll., N.Y.C., 1981—86. Mem.: CEC, Internat. Reading Assn., Internat. Dyslexia Assn. (presenter strategy workshops 1999—2001, events fund raiser). Office: Aaron Sch 309 E 45th St New York NY 10017

DULIN, MAURINE STUART, volunteer; b. Lonerock, Iowa, Feb. 16, 1919; d. Frank Meagher and Fern Adrienne (Wetzel) Stuart; m. William Carter Dulin, Oct. 5, 1940; children: Jacquelyn Dulin Wilson, Patricia F., Stuart M. AB in Polit. Sci./Econs., The Coll. of William and Mary, 1939. Coll. cons. Woodward and Lothrop, Washington, 1939-40; adminstr. asst. Sightler and Cox, Washington, 1942-43; acctg. dept. asst. The Am. U., Washington, 1964-69; corp. sec. Bittinger and Dulin, Arlington, Va., 1949-73; ptnr. 41 Limited Partnership, Bethesda, Md., 1979—, Montrose-270 Ltd. Partnership, Bethesda, 1979—. Mem. Rock Creek Womens Rep. Club, Bethesda, 1951-57; sgt.-at-arms Montgomery County Fed. of Rep. Women, Bethesda, 1952-53, State Fedn. of Womens Rep. Club, 1953-54; charter mem., com. chmn. Nat. Mus. of Women in the Arts; mem. Women's Bd.Cathedral Choral Soc. 1975—, com. chmn., 1988-90; mem. Women's Bd. George Washington U. Hosp., 1970—, Save Our Seminary at Forest Glen, Md., 1989—. Mem. The Town Club (pres. 1958-59), Pi Beta Phi (nat. com. chmn. 1971-75, province officer 1967-71). Episcopalian. Home: 9707 Old Georgetown Rd Apt 1416 Bethesda MD 20814

D'ULISSE-CALDWELL, MARYELLEN CECILIA, music educator; b. Darby, Pa., Mar. 26, 1955; d. Joseph Thomas and Margaret D'Ulisse; m. Douglas Lee Caldwell, 1986; 1 child, Mariah Elise-D'Ulisse Caldwell. BS in Music Edn., West Chester U., 1977. Dir. orchestras Arcola Intermediate Schoolmethacton Sch. Dist., Norristown, Pa., 1978—; dir. orch. Woodland Elem. Sch., Norristown, 1998—. Mem. Kennett Symphony Orch., Kennett Square, Pa., 1980—. Musician freelance, jazz, orchestral, folk. Grants com. chmn. PADESTA with NSOA, Pa. Mem.: Am. Fedn. Musicians (assoc.), Am. String Tchrs. Assn. (assoc.), Pa./Del. String Tchrs. Assn. (assoc.; grants chmn. 2002—03), Pa. Music Educators Assn. (assoc.; presenter annual conf. 2003). Office: Methacton School District Kriebel Mill Rd Norristown PA 19403 E-mail: mcaldwell@methacton.org.

DULO, DONNA ANN, computer scientist, consultant; b. Trenton, Nj, July 20, 1967; d. Joan Mary Barbieri and John Dulo. BS, USCG Acad., New London, Conn., 1993; diploma in Paralegal Studies, Blackstone Sch. of Law, Dallas, 1995; diploma in Arabic Langs., Def. Lang. Inst., Monterey, Calif., 1993; grad. diploma, Coll. Naval Command and Staff, Newport, R.I., 2002; MA in Mil. Studies in Strategic Intelligence, Am. Mil. U., 2003; MA in Nat. Security and Strategic Studies, US Naval War Coll., Newport, R.I., 2003; MS in Computer Info. Systems, Phoenix (Ariz.) U., 2003. Cert. Microsoft systems engr. 1999, A+ computer technician CompTIA, 2002. Computer engr. U.S. Army, Monterey, Calif., 1993—95; computer scientist Dept of Def., Monterey, Calif., 1995—. Specialist U.S. Army, 1991—95, Monterey. Mem.: Monterey Inst. for Rsch. in Astronomy (docent 1999—2003), IEEE Computer Soc. (assoc.), UN Assn. (bd. dirs. Monterey Bay chpt. 2003). Republican. Roman Catholic. Avocations: astronomy educator, karate instructor. Home: 1045 Scott Ct Marina CA 93933 Office: Dept of Defense Bldg 342 Rm 110 Presidio of Monterey CA 93944 E-mail: donna.dulo@monterey.army.mil.

DUMANIS, BONNIE M. prosecutor; Dist. atty., San Diego, 2003—; dep. dist. atty. San Diego Dist. Attys. Office. Instr. U. Calif. San Diego Sch. Law, Nat. and Calif. Jud. Colls. Recipient Tribute to Women award, YWCA, Calif. Women in Govt. Law and Justice award, Aux. award for women of dedication, Salvation Army, Belva Lockwood award, Lawyers Club. Mem.: San Diego Bar Assn. (bd. dirs.), Lawyers Club San Diego (past pres.). Office: Hall of Justice 330 W Broadway San Diego CA 92101

DUMAS, CHARLENE ANNE, music educator; b. Massena, N.Y., Aug. 25, 1954; d. Leon and Lucia Jean (Catanzarite) Johnson; m. Robert K. Dumas, July 28, 1979. MusB, State U. N.Y., 1975, MusM, 1987. Music tchr. Sacred Heart Sch., Massena, NY, 1976—77; carrier U.S. Postal Svc., Massena, 1977—82; music tchr. Trinity Cath. Sch., Massena, 1984—92, Salmon River Ctrl. Sch., Ft. Covington, NY, 1993—99, Massena Ctrl. Sch., Massena, 1999—2000, Salmon River Ctrl. Sch., 2000—. Composer: (songs) Land of Dreams, 1990. Mem.: N.Y. State Sch. Music Assn., Music Educator's Nat. Conf. Avocations: music performance, dance. Home: 5 Prospect Ave Massena NY 13662 Office: Salmon River Central School 637 County Route 1 Fort Covington NY 12937

DUMAS, JOYCE PENDLETON, social worker; b. Starville, Miss., July 24, 1951; d. Clifton and Beatrice Carr Sharp; m. Earnert Dumas, Aug. 2, 1991; children: Tiffany, Tianna. BA Social Work, Miss. State Univ., Miss., 1973; MA Social Work, Univ. Ala., Tucaloosa, Ala., 1975. LCSW Miss., lic. ACSW, BCD nationally. Family svc. worker Region 7 MH Ctr., Starkville, Miss., 1975—77; asst. prof. social work Miss. State Univ., Miss., 1977—79; program coord. Bobby Wright Mental Health, Chgo., 1979—83, Meth. Youth Ctr., Chgo., 1983—86; exec. dir. Big Brothers/Big Sisters, Columbus, Miss., 1989—92; social worker Lowndes County Sch., Columbus, Miss., 1989—92; owner, pvt. practice I Care Counseling, Starkville, Miss., 1992—. Sch. bd. mem. Starkville Sch. Dist., Miss., 1988—2000; bd. mem., pres. Safe Haven Domestic Shelter, Columbus, Miss., 1989—2003; bd. mem. Bd. of Examiners for Social Workers & MFT, Jackson, Miss., 1997—2003. Mem.: Am. Acad. of Cert. Social Workers (diplomate), Nat. Assn. Social Worker. Democrat. Pentacostal. Avocations: reading, antiques, interior decorating, coin and stamp collecting. Home: 1616 Churchill Cir Starkville MS 39759 Office: I Care Counseling 100 N Lafayette St Starkville MS 39759

DUMAS, RHETAUGH ETHELDRA GRAVES, university official; b. Natchez, Miss., Nov. 26, 1928; d. Rhetaugh Graves and Josephine (Clemmons) Graves Bell; m. A.W. Dumas, Jr., Dec. 25, 1950; 1 child, Adrienne. BS in Nursing, Dillard U., 1951; MS in Psychiat. Nursing, Yale U., 1961; PhD in Social Psychology, Union Grad. Sch., Union for Experimenting Colls. and Univs., Cinn., 1975; also various other courses; D Pub. Svc. (hon.), Simmons Coll., 1976, U. Cin., 1981; LHD (hon.), Yale U., 1989; LLD (hon.), Dillard U., 1990; LHD (hon.), U. San Diego, 1993, Georgetown U., 1996; DPub. Svc., Fla. Internat. U., Miami, 1996; DSc (hon.), Ind. U., Gary, 1996; JD (hon.), Bethune-Cookman Coll., 1997; LHD (hon.), U. Mass, 1997. Instr. Dillard U., 1957-59, 61; research asst., instr. Sch. Nursing Yale U., 1962-65, from asst. prof. nursing to assoc. prof., 1965-72, chmn. dept. psychiat. nursing, 1972; dir. nursing Conn. Mental Health Ctr., Yale-New Haven Med. Ctr., 1966-72; chief psychiat. nursing edn. br. Div. [illegible] and Tng. Programs, NIMH, Rockville, Md., 1972-76; dep. dir. Div. Manpower and Tng. Programs NIMH, 1976-79, dep. dir. alcohol, drug abuse and mental health adminstrn., 1979-81; dean, prof. U. Mich. Sch. Nursing, 1981-94; vice provost health affairs U. Mich., 1994-97, Lucille Cole prof. sch. nursing, 1994—, vice provost emerita, 1997—, dean emerita, 1997—. Dir. Group Rels. Confs. in Tavistock Model; cons., speaker, panelist in field; fellow Helen Hadley Hall, Yale U., 1972, Branford Coll., 1972; dir. Community Health Care Ctr. Plan, New Haven, 1969-72; mem. U.S. Assessment Team, cons. to Fed. Ministry Health, Nigeria, 1982; mem. adv. com. Health Policy Agenda for the Am. People, AMA, 1983-86; cons. NIH Task Force on Nursing Rsch., 1984; mem. Nat. Commn. on Unemployment and Mental Health, Nat. Mental Health Assn., 1984-85; mem. com. to plan maj. study of nat. long-term care policy Inst. Medicine, 1985; mem. adv. com. to dir. NIH, 1986-87; mem. Sec.'s Nat. Commn. on Future Structure of VA Health Care System, 1990-91; mem. coun. on grad. med. edn. Nat. Adv. Coun. on Nurse Edn. and Practice Workgroup on Primary Care Workforce Projection, Divsn. Nursing, 1994; mem. com. to rev. breast cancer rsch. program U.S. Army Med. Rsch. and Material Command, Inst. of Medicine, 1996-97; mem. Pres.'s Nat. Bioethics Adv. Commn., 1996—. Author profl. monographs; contbr. over 40 articles to profl. publs.; mem. editorial bd. Community Mental Health Rev., 1977-79, Jour. Personality and Social Systems, 1978-81, Advances in Psychiat. Mental Health Nursing, 1981. Bd. dirs. Afro Am. Ctr., Yale U., 1968-72; mem. New Haven Bd. Edn., 1968-71, New Haven City Demonstrations Agy., 1968-70, Human Rels. Coun. New Haven, 1961-63, Nat. Neural Circuitry Database Com., Inst. Medicine, Nat. Acad. Scis., mem. bd. scientific advisors, 1985—; mem. commn. on future structure of vets. health care U.S. Dept. Vets. Affairs, 1990; mem. Pres. Clinton's Nat. Bioethics Adv. Commn., 1996-01. Named Disting. Alumna, Dillard U., 1966; recipient various awards, including cert. Honor NAACP, 1970, Disting. Alumnae award Yale U. Sch. Nursing, 1976, award for outstanding achievement and service in field mental health D.C. chpt. Assn. Black Psychologists, 1980, Pres. 21st Century award The Nat. Women's Hall of Fame, 1994, Lifetime Achievement award, nat. Black Nurses Assn., 2000—. Fellow A.K. Rice Inst., Am. Coll. Mental Health Adminstrs. (founding), Am. Acad. Nursing (charter, pres. 1987-89); mem. Inst. Medicine NAS, Am. Nurses Assn., Nat. Black Nurses Assn., Am. Assn. Colls. Nursing (govtl. affairs com. 1990-93), Am. Pub. Health Assn., Nat. League Nursing (pres. 1997-99), Nat. Bioethics Adv. Commn., Sigma Theta Tau Internat. (mentor award 1989), Delta Sigma Theta. Office: U Mich 400 N Ingalls St Rm 4320 Ann Arbor MI 48109-2003

DUMAS, SANDRA KAY, music educator; d. Carroll Willis Formby and Annie Lee Dees; m. Lamah L. Dumas, June 4, 1961 (dec. Jan. 24, 1980); children: Lisa Kay, Stephen Lamah. BA in Edn. summa cum laude, La. Tech U., 1963; MusB in Edn. summa cum laude, So. Ark. U., 1980. Lang. arts educator Webster Parish Sch. Bd., Cotton Valley, La., 1965—68; music educator Taylor (Ark.) Pub. Schs., 1981—83; pvt. piano/organ tchr. Springhill, 1983—; elem. music educator White Hall (Ark.) Sch. Dist., 1987—. Organist First Bapt. Ch., Springhill, La., 1975—87, White Hall, 1990—; dir. Moody Singers, White Hall, 1998—. Named Dist. Elem. Tchr. of Yr., 1999; scholar, Sigma Alpha Iota, 1978. Mem.: NEA, Ark. Music Educators Assn., Music Educators Nat. Conf. (pres. So. Ark. U. chpt. 1978—79, Music award 1980), Alpha Chi, Phi Kappa Phi. Baptist. Avocations: writing family history, travel. Home: 112 Ruth Cove White Hall AR 71602 Office: Moody Elem Sch 700 Moody Dr White Hall AR 71602

DUMDUM, JOSEFINA MARTINEZ, chemist, researcher; b. Iloilo City, Iloilo, The Philippines, Aug. 4, 1944; d. Jose H. and Porferia (Martinez) D. BS in Chem. Engring., U. San José-Recoletos, Cebu City, The Philippines, 1965; MS in Chemistry, U. San Carlos, Cebu City, The Philippines, 1975. Registered profl. chem. engr., Philippines. Asst. prof. U. San José-Recoletos, Cebu City, Cebu, The Philippines, 1965-75; rsch. chemist Union Oil Co. of Calif., Brea, 1975-83, sr. rsch. chemist, 1983-88, rsch. assoc., 1988—. Contbr. articles to profl. jours. Pres. Filipino Cath. of St. Paul, Chino Hills, Calif., 1996-98, U. San Jose-Recoletos Alumni Assn., U.S.A., 1988-92. Fellow Nat. Lubricating Grease Inst. (chairperson subcom. on govt. regulations 1988-98, columnist Govt. Regulations Update mag. 1989-94); mem. ASTM. Republican. Roman Catholic. Achievements include patents for finding use of CeF3 as a suitable extreme pressure additive for lubricants, use of tetrathiocarbonates and trithiocarbonates of K as extreme pressure additives for lubricants. Office: 76 Lubricants 3611 S Harbor Blvd Ste 200 Santa Ana CA 92704-7949

DUMERER, LORRAINE JOANNE LORI, social studies educator, clinician, consultant; b. Providence, July 10, 1946; d. John and Edith (Flippin) Florio; m. James Edward Dumerer, Nov. 23, 1966; children: James, Marc, Jennifer, Matthew, Paul. Student, Seton Hill Coll., 1964-66, St. Louis U., 1966; AB, U. Ill., 1969, MAT, 1972; postgrad., Tex. Women's U., 1987-88, U. Tex., Dallas, 1993, So. Meth. U., 1999-2001. Cert. social studies tchr. talented and gifted Tex., coll. bd. endorsed Advanced Placement cons. Tchr. Dayton (Ohio) Pub. Schs., 1970—71, St. Benedicts Sch., San Antonio, 1979—80, Incarnate World H.S., San Antonio, 1980—81, Diocese of Dallas, 1981—88, Dallas Ind. Sch. Dist., 1988—97; tchr., chmn. social studies dept., dean of faculty Long Trail Sch., Dorset, Vt., 1997—98; tchr. govt. and politics, macro and microecons., law studies Carrollton-Farmer's Branch Ind. Sch. Dist., 1998—. Coach Fed Challenge econs. competition, 1998-2001, North Dallas H.S. CIS-site based team, 1996-97; mem. R.L. Turner H.S. CIC-site based team, 1999—; mem. train the writers program US Dept Edn. Nat. Coun. for Econ. Edn., Romania, 2003; coach model UN teams, 2000—; clinician Acad. Clin. Svc., Dallas, 1985—; coord. nat. history day Diocese of Dallas, 1985-87; coord. Jane Goodall CHIMP project, 1991; chmn. dept. social studies, student coun. advisor North Dallas H.S., 1993-97; ednl. cons., presenter Specialty Limited English Proficient Integration, 1990-96, Tex. Coun. Social Studies, Advanced Placement Reading Strategies, Cross-grade Level Curriculum Integration; Creating an Inclusive AP and Pre-AP Program, Integrating State Mandates in Pre-AP and AP Programs, Nat. Coun. for the Social Studies, AP Econ. Strategies, AP Govt., others; participant NEH Inst., 1995, Woodrow Wilson Inst., U. Tex., Dallas, 1993-1995, Congress in the Classroom Dirkson Ctr., Ill., 2003, Econs. for Leaders Found. for Tchg. Econs., So. Meth. U., 2000, Economic Forces in American History, Found. for Tchg. Econs.; reader Coll. Bd. Am. Govt., 2001-03; nat. endorsed Coll. Bd. cons.; selected for Tng. of Writers Project, Nat. Coun. Econ. Edn., U.S. Depts. of State and Edn., Bucharest, Romania, 2003; presenter in field Author: (essays) The Dilemma of Ethical Citizenship and the Political Outsider, 1995, numerous poems; contbr. chapters to books. Referee coord. N.E. Youth Soccer Assn., 1979-80, coach, 1979-80; coach, referee Mesquite Soccer Assn., 1981-86, referee liaison, 1981-82, sec., 1982-83, commr. of coaches, 1982-83. Mellon grantee, 1994; named Tchr. of Yr. Dallas Coun. for Social Studies, 1996, Outstanding HS Social Studies Tchr. of Yr., Tex. Coun. for Social Studies, 2002; named one of 50 Elite Tchrs., Tex. Coun. Econ. Edn., 2001. Mem. Nat. Coun. Social Studies, Tex. Coun. for Social Studies (sec. Peter's Colony Coun. for social studies 1998-99, v.p. 2000, pres. 2001-03, programs chair 2004—), North Tex. Women's Soccer Assn. (capt. 1989-95), Ctr. for Applied Linguistics (cons. World Culture Project 1996), Nat. Coun. Econ. Edn. Avocations: writing, soccer, travel. Home: 3535 Misty Meadow Dr Dallas TX 75287-6027 E-mail: dumererl@cfbisd.edu., dumererl@earthlink.net.

DUMITRESCU, CRISTINA M. intensive care nurse; b. Bucharest, Romania, Mar. 5, 1960; d. Mircea and Margareta Ispas; m. Gabriel N None, June 6, 1989. Degree in Biochem. Rsch. Mgmt., C.A. Rosetti, Bucharest,

Romania, 1980, BSc in Biochemistry, 1981; ADN, Walla Walla C.C., 1986; BS, U. Wash., 1988, studies in Psychiat. Social Nursing, 1987, studies in Family Analysis, studies in Cmty. Health Care Sys., U. Wash., 1988. RN Wash., 1986, lic. advance cardiac life support, Medic 7 Dist. Snohomish County, 1996. Biochem. rschr. Pharm. Co. Bucharest, Romania, 1981—82; registry relief nurse Kimberly Quality Care, Seattle, 1986—92; RN/charge nurse Swedish Med. Ctr., Seattle, 1988—93; home care ventilator nurse Nurse's Ho. Call, Seattle, 1989—94; registry relief nurse Amserv Western Med., Seattle, 1990—95; case mgr./mktg. dir. Vis. Nurse Svcs., Seattle, 1991—96; ICCU/CO RN Stevens Med. Ctr., Edmonds, Wash., 1996—. Marketer Vis. Nurse, Seattle, 1991—96; cmty. health care cons. Walla Walla DSHS, 1986; exec. sec./office mgr. Musica Romanica Inc., Seattle, 2000—; property mgmt. Dumitrescu Fourplex, Kent, Wash., 2002—; cmty. svc. dir. Seventh Day Adventist Ch., Seattle, 1992—. Contbr. articles to profl. jours. Dir. allocation of cmty. resources Cmty. Services Ctr., Seattle, 1992; project mgr. Helping Hands of Am., Seattle, 1993—94, Cmty. Services SDA, Snohomish, Wash., 1994—95. Mem.: NAFE (Excellence in Nursing award 2001), Walla Walla Businesswoman's Assn., U. Wash. Alumni Assn., Sigma Theta Tau Internat. Office: Musica Romanica Inc PO Box 5037 Kent WA 98064 Office Phone: 253-859-2870. Personal E-mail: musirom@earthlink.net.

DUMITRESCU, DOMNITA, Spanish language educator, researcher; b. Bucharest, Romania; came to U.S., 1984; d. Ion and Angela (Barzotescu) D. Diploma, U. Bucharest, 1966; MA, U. So. Calif., 1987, PhD, 1990. Asst. prof. U. Bucharest, 1966-74, assoc. prof., 1974-84; asst. prof. Spanish Calif. State U., L.A., 1987-90, assoc. prof., 1990-94, prof., 1995—. Author: Gramatica Limbii Spaniole, 1976, Indreptar Pentru Traducerea Din Limba Romana in Limba Spaniola, 1980; translator from Spanish lit. to Romanian; assoc. editor: Hispania, 1996—; contbr. articles to profl. jours. Fulbright scholar, 1993—. Mem. MLA, Linguistic Soc. Am., Internat. Assn. Hispanists, Linguistic Assn. S.W., Am. Assn. Tchrs. Spanish and Portuguese (past pres. So. Calif. chpt., Tchr. of Yr. award 2000), Sigma Delta Pi (v.p. West 1996—). Office: Calif State U 5151 State University Dr Los Angeles CA 90032-4226 Business E-Mail: ddumitr@calstatela.edu.

DUMITRU, MIRELA, accountant; b. Constanta, Romania, Dec. 3, 1959; d. Nicolae and Lucia Bradeanu; 1 child, Corina-Luiza. BS, St. Francis Coll., 2003. Acct. Robert Half Internat., Inc., N.Y.C., 1998—2002; acctg. supr. Display Sys., Inc., Maspeth, NY, 2002—. Cons. Descendent of Holy Spirit, Ridgewood, NY, 1991—2003. Scholar, St. Francis Coll., 2000. Christian Orthodox. Personal E-mail: mireladtru@aol.com. Business E-Mail: mirela@displaysystemsinc.com.

DUMLER, PATRICIA ANN, critical care nurse; b. San Antonio, Feb. 16, 1960; d. Raymond Lee and Ann Dell (Comer) Dumler; m. David Hastings Smith, Dec. 28, 1985. BSN, U. Md., Balt., 1983; student, James Madison U., Harrisonburg, Va., 1978-81. Staff nurse Bon Secours Hosp., Balt., 1983—85, Rockingham Meml. Hosp., Harrisonburg, Va., 1986—87; clin. nurse II Homewood Hosp. Ctr., Balt., 1987—91; clin. nurse Johns Hopkins Hosp., Balt., 1991—, performance improvement/utilization mgmt. specialist, 1991—.

DUMOULIN, DIANA CRISTAUDO, small business owner, writer; b. Washington, Jan. 5, 1939; d. Emanuel A. and Angela E. (Cogliano) Cristaudo; m. Philip DuMoulin, May 30, 1964; children: Joanmarie Patricia, John Philip. MA, U. Wis., 1967; BA, Rosary Coll., 1961; cert. in Creative Writing, Phoenix Coll., 2002. Project mgr. IDC Cons. Group, Framingham, Mass., 1982-84; sr. market analyst Cullinet, Inc., Westwood, Mass., 1984-86; prof. assoc. Ledgeway Group, Lexington, Mass., 1987-89; prin. Customer Mktg. Specialist, Brookline, Mass., 1989-93; pres. Customer Solutions Internat., Phoenix, 1994—2000. Adj. faculty Ulster County C.C. Stone Ridge, N.Y., 1967-74; lectr. Boston Coll., Chestnut Hill, Mass., 1976. Author:The Love Pad Dream Journal, 1996, Ourselves in the Garden, 1998; contbr. articles to profl. jours. Pres. LWV, Kingston, N.Y., 1973-74. Recipient Svc. to Young Adults award 70001 Career Assn., 1977, Honorable Mention award Writers Digest Writing Competition, 1996, 98; faculty fellow U. Wis., 1964-66 Mem. Am. Marketing Assn., Phoenix Composers Alliance, Nat. Writers Union Office: Create Music Poetry 8441 N 1st Dr Phoenix AZ 85021-5515 Office Phone: 602-371-0804.

DUMOVICH, LORETTA, real estate and transportation company executive; b. Kansas City, Kans., Sept. 29, 1930; d. Michael Nicholas and Frances Barbara (Horvat) D. Student public schs., Kansas City. Lic. real estate broker, Kans., Mo. Corp. sec., dir. Riss Internat. Corp., 1950-86, Riss Intermodal Corp., 1969-86, World Leasing Corp., 1969-86; pres., dir. Columbia Properties, Inc., 1969-86; v.p., dir. Republic Industries, 1969-86; corp. sec., dir. Comml. Equipment Co. Inc., Charlotte, N.C., 1980-93; v.p., corp. sec. Commonwealth Gen. Ins. Co., Kansas City, Mo., 1986-93, Heart of Am. Fire & Casualty Co., Kansas City, 1986-93. Mem. Kansas City (Mo.) Real Estate Bd., Bldg. Owners and Mgrs. Assn. of Kansas City (Mo.), Terminal Properties Exchange (founding mem.), Am. Royal Assn. (gov.) Office: 215 W Pershing Rd Kansas City MO 64108-4317

DUNAWAY, CAROLYN BENNETT, retired sociology educator; b. Atlanta, Mar. 3, 1943; d. Clarence Rhodes and Gay (McKenzie) Bennett; m. William Preston Dunaway, Aug. 26, 1967; 1 child, Robert Bennett Dunaway. BA in Social Scis., Auburn U., 1966, EdD, 1983; MA in Sociology, U. Ala., Tuscaloosa, 1967. Instr. sociology Jefferson State C.C., Birmingham, Ala., 1967-69; prof. Auburn U., Montgomery, Ala., 1970-71; prof. sociology and gerontology dept. Jacksonville (Ala.) State U., 1971-95, prof. emeritus, 1999—. Student counselor Jacksonville State U., Ala., 1971—. Contbd. articles to profl. jours. Cons., trainer Calhoun County Hospice Anniston, Ala., 1983—; presenter Calhoun County Gerontology, Anniston, 1985—; officer Jacksonville Book Club, Ala., 1984; elder, tchr. First Presbyn. Ch., Jacksonville, 1993. Recipient 100 Most Outstanding Women Alumna award Auburn U., 1991, U. Rsch. award Jacksonville State U., 1989. Mem. Ala.-Miss. Sociol. Assn. (v.p. 1975-76, Sociology Club, Inter-Se Study Club, Ala. Fedn. Womens Club (dist. sect.), Phi Kappa Phi, Kappa Delta Pi, Delta Delta Delta, Phi Delta Kappa. Democrat. Presbyn. Avocations: flower arranging, gardening, reading. Home: 902 11th St NE Jacksonville AL 36265-1230

DUNAWAY, FAYE (DOROTHY DUNAWAY), actress; b. Bascom, Fla., Jan. 14, 1941; d. John and Grace D.; m. Peter Wolf, Aug. 7, 1974 (div.); m. Terrence O'Neill; 1 son. Student, U. Fla., Boston U. Appearances include as original mem. Lincoln Ctr. Repertory Co., N.Y.C., off-Broadway in Hogan's Goat; also in (play) Curse of the Aching Heart, 1982; motion picture appearences include Bonnie in motion picture Bonnie and Clyde, 1967, Hurry Sundown, 1967, Puzzle of a Downfall Child, The Happening, 1967, The Thomas Crown Affair, 1968, A Place For Lovers, 1969, Little Big Man, 1970, Doc, 1971, La Maison Sous les Arbres, 1971, The Getaway, 1972, Oklahoma Crude, 1973, The Three Musketeers, 1973, Chinatown, 1974, The Towering Inferno, 1974, The Four Muscateers, 1975, Three Days of the Condor, 1975, Network, 1976 (Acad. award for Best Actress), The Voyage of the Damned, 1976, The Eyes of Laura Mars, 1978, The Champ, 1979, The First Deadly Sin, 1980, Mommie Dearest, 1981, The Wicked Lady, 1982, Ordeal by Innocence, 1985, Supergirl, 1984, Barfly, 1987, Burning Secret, 1988, La Partita, 1988, Midnight Crossing, 1988, The Gamble, 1989, In a Moonlit Night, 1989, Wait Until Spring, Bandini, 1989, The Handmaid's Tale, 1990, Three Weeks in Jerusalem, 1990, Scorchers, 1990, Arrowtooth Waltz, 1991, Double Edge, 1992, The Temp, 1993, Point of No Return, 1993, Even Cowgirls Get the Blues, 1994, Don Juan DeMarco, 1995, En brazos de la mujer madura, 1996, The Chamber, 1996, Albino Alligator, 1996, Dunston Checks In, 1996, Twilight of the Golds, 1997, Drunks, 1997, Fanny Hill, 1998 Love Lies Bleeding, 1999, Joan of Arc, 1999, The Thomas Crown Affair, 1999, The Yards, 2000, Stanley's Gig, 2000, Yellow Bird, 2001, Changing Hearts, 2002, Rules of Attraction, 2002, Mid-Century, 2002, The Calling, 2002, Blind Horizon, 2004, El Padrino, 2004, Jennifer's Shadow, 2004; TV movies: After the Fall, 1974, The Disappearance of Aimee, 1976, Evita Peron, 1981, 13 at Dinner, 1985, Beverly Hills Madame, 1986, Casanova, 1987, Cold Sassy Tree, 1989, Silhouette, 1990 (co-exec. prodr.), Columbo: It's All in the Game (Emmy award for Guest Actress in Drama 1994), Mother Love, 1995, A Family Divided, 1995, The People Next Door, 1996, Rebecca, 1997, Gia, 1998, A Will of Their Own, 1998, Running Mates, 2000, The Biographer, 2002; TV miniseries: Ellis Island, 1984, Christopher Columbus, 1985; TV series: It Had To Be You, 1993, A Will of Their Own, 1998. Recipient Most Promising Newcomer Award Brit. Film Acad., 1968 Address: c/o ICM attn Ed Limato 8942 Wilshire Blvd Beverly Hills CA 90211-1934

DUNBAR, BONNIE J. engineer, astronaut; b. Sunnyside, Wash., Mar. 3, 1949; d. Robert Dunbar; m. Ronald M. Sega. BS in Ceramic Engring., U. Wash., 1971, MS in Ceramic Engring. cum laude, 1975; PhD in Biomed. Engring., U. Houston, 1983. With Boeing Computer Svcs., 1971-73; sr. rsch. engr. space div. Rockwell Internat., Downey, Calif.; with NASA, 1978—, astronaut, 1981—, mission specialist flight STS 61-8, 1985, mission specialist flight STS-32, 1990, payload commander Shuttle Columbia Flight, 1992, spl. asst. to dep. assoc. adminstr., 1993. Vis. scientist Harwell Labs., Oxford, Eng., 1975; adj. asst. prof. mech. engring. U. Houston, mem. bioengring. adv. group; participant space missions, 1985, 90. Recipient Nat. Engring. award Am. Assn. Engring. Socs., 1992. Mem. AAAS, Am. Ceramic Soc. (life, Greaves-Walker award 1985, Schwalt Zwalder PACE award 1990), Soc. Biomed. Engring., Materials Rsch. Soc., Nat. Inst. Ceramic Engrs., Arnold Air Soc. and Angel Flight (bd. dirs.), Keramos, Tau Beta Pi. Address: NASA 300 E West Rd Houston TX 77060-5019

DUNBAR, MABLE CLEONE, counselor education, family; b. May 3, 1953; d. Byron Anderson and Ellen Elizabeth (Lynch) Douglas; m. Colin A. Dunbar, Aug. 13, 1972; children: Elrene Dunbar Perez, Elizabeth, Colin II. BA in Secondary Edn., West Indes Coll., Mandeville, Jamaica, West Indies, 1975; MA in Edn. and Counseling Psychology, Andrews U., 1990; PhD in Family Mediation, La Salle U., Mandeville, La., 1995. Lic. profl. counselor, Mich. Sec. Bermuda Conf. of S.DA, Bermuda, 1983 85; tchr. secondary sch. Bermuda Inst., 1986-88; dir. childrens' ministries Bermuda Conf. of S.DA, Bermuda, 1988; grad. asst. Andrews U., Berrien Springs, Mich., 1988-90; parent educator St. Joseph Med. Ctr., South Bend, Ind., 1989-90; exec. dir., counselor Safe Shelter, Inc., Benton Harbor, Mich., 1990-97; CEO, pres. Women In Renewal, Inc., Niles, Mich., 1997—. Founder Shelter Program for Christian Women in Crisis. Named Woman of Yr., Assn. of Adventist Women, Boston, 1997. Mem. Optimist Club. Seventh Day Adventist. Avocations: gardening, music, reading, walking, people. Office: Women In Renewal Inc PO Box 102 Berrien Center MI 49102-0102 Home: 5803 N Greenwood Blvd Spokane WA 99205-7538

DUNBAR, MARY ASMUNDSON, communications executive, investor and public relations consultant; b. Sacramento, Calif., Feb. 6, 1942; d. Vigfus Samundur and Aline Mary (McGrath) Asmundson; m. Robert Copeland Dunbar, June 21, 1969; children: Geoffrey Townsend, William Asmundson. BA in English Lit., Smith Coll., 1964; MA in Comm., Stanford U., 1967, MBA in Fin., Case Western Res. U., 1985. Cert. pub. rels. profl. Tchr. Peace Corps, Cameroun, Africa, 1964-66; writer, editor Ednl. Devel. Corp., Palo Alto, Calif., 1967-68, Addison-Wesley, Menlo Park, Calif., 1969-70; freelance writer, editor various cos., Cleve., 1970-85; account exec. Edward Howard & Co., Cleve., 1985-87, Dix & Eaton, Inc., Cleve., 1987-89, sr. account exec., 1990-92, v.p., 1992-96, sr. v.p., 1997—. Author publs. in field. Trustee Cleve. Coun. World Affairs, 1994—99. Smith Coll. scholar, Northampton, Mass., 1960-64; fellowship Stanford Univ., Palo Alto, Calif., 1967; recipient Internat. Assn. Bus. Comm. award, 1987, Women in Comm. award, 1987, Arthur Page award, 1990. Mem. Smith Coll. Club Cleve., Pub. Rels. Soc. Am. (Silver Anvil award 1997), Nat. Investor Rels. Inst. (past pres. Cleve.-No. Ohio chpt., elected to nat. bd. dirs. 2002), Cleve. Soc. Security Analysts. Republican. Episcopalian. Avocations: jogging, music. Home: 2880 Fairfax Rd Cleveland OH 44118-4014 Office: Dix & Eaton Inc 1301 E 9th St Ste 1300 Cleveland OH 44114-1820 E-mail: mdunbar@dix-eaton.com.

DUNBAR, SHIRLEY EUGENIA-DORIS, small business owner, writer; b. Haverhill, Mass., Apr. 26, 1930; d. Clement and Doris (Riel) Allard; m. Everett Allan Dunbar, Feb. 18, 1967; children: Linda, Andrew, Susan. BA magna cum laude, U. Mass., 1974; MA, U. N.H., 1975; EdD, Nova U., 1979. Cert. gemologist. From instr. to prof. comm. Bunker Hill C.C., Boston, 1975-89, prof. emeritus, 1989—; owner Treasure Coast Gem Lab. Dir. tchg. tng. program, Taipei, Taiwan, 1983—84; owner Dunbar Enterprises, St. Lucie, Fla., 1988—96, Treasure Coast Gem Lab., Port St. Lucie, 1996—; cons. in field. Author: Heisey Glass: The Early Years, 1896-1924, 2000. Dir. Learn to Read, Port St. Lucie County, 1989—91; judge Young Floridian awards St. Lucie County, 1998—. Recipient Pub. Svc. award, Ministry of Edn., Taiwan, 1982—83, citation for outstanding performance, Gov. Michael Dukakis, 1985, Nat. Competition Non-Fiction award, 2001, 1st pl. award, Mid-Adminstrn. Congress, Non-Fiction Pub. Adult Book 1st pl. award, Fla. State, 2001, Best in Show award, Rock and Gem Club, 2003; CAEL fellow, U. Ohio, 1984. Mem.: AAUW (founding br. pres.), Nat. Assn. Jewelry Appraisers, Nat. Assn. Jewelry (cert. appraiser), Nat. League Am. Pen Women, Fla. Women's Consortium. Avocations: silversmithing, goldsmithing, writing. Home: 2002 SE Isabell Rd Port Saint Lucie FL 34952-8864 E-mail: shirley400@aol.com.

DUNCALFE HOLT, LUCINDA BROMWYN, marketing executive; b. Kingston, N.Y., Jan. 16, 1963; d. Walter John Douglas and Marjory Edith (Merritt) D.; m. Jamal Malik Benin, Oct. 16, 1989. BA, U. Pa., 1985; MBA, Wharton Sch. Mktg. mgr. Automated Call Processing Corp., San Francisco, 1985-89; managing dir., Assest Management Group SEI Corp.; prod. mgr. Infonautics; CEO and pres. Destiny Web Solutions, Inc., Conshohoken, Pa., 1996—. Avocation: shotokan karate (black belt). Office: Destiny Web Solutions PO Box 276 Lafayette Hill PA 19444-0276

DUNCAN, ALLYSON K. federal judge; b. Durham, NC, Sept. 5, 1951; BA, Hampton U., 1972; JD, Duke U., 1975. Bar: N.C. 1975, D.C. 1977. Assoc. editor Lawyers Coop. Publ. Co., 1976—77; law clk. to Hon. Julia Cooper Mack DC Ct. Appeals, 1977—78; appellate atty., asst. to dep. gen. counsel, asst. to chmn. EEOC, 1978—86; assoc. prof. NC Ctrl. U. Sch. Law, 1986—90; assoc. judge NC Ct. Appeals, 1990; commr. NC Utilities Commn., 1991—98; ptnr. Kilpatrick Stockton LLP, Raleigh, NC, 1998—2003; judge US Ct. Appeals (4th cir.), 2003—. Mem.: Wake County Bar Assn. (pres. 2002—03), N.C. Bar Assn. (pres.-elect 2002). Office: Kilpatrick Stockton LLP Ste 400 3737 Glenwood Ave Raleigh NC 27612

DUNCAN, CAROL LYNN, English language and literature educator; b. Jellico, Tenn., June 15, 1948; d. Billy Gene and Vivian Alberta (Stanfill) Whited; m. Jackie Leland Duncan; children: Jennifer Lynn, Cresta Leigh, Jana Layne. BA, Cumberland Coll., 1971; MA in Edn., Eastern Ky. U., 1987. English tchr. Scott County Schs., Huntsville, Tenn., 1983-85; instr. English Alice Lloyd Coll., Pippa Passes, Ky., 1985-89; prof. English Jefferson C.C., Louisville, 1990—. Coach, evaluator Carroll County Schs., Carrollton, Ky., 1994—. Mem. Nat. Coun. Tchrs. English, Libr. Congress. Avocations: needlework, antiques. Home: 106 Delaware Way Carrollton KY 41008-9621 Office: Jefferson CC 324 Main St Carrollton KY 41008-1025 Office Phone: 502-732-4846.

DUNCAN, CLEO, state legislator; m. John Duncan. BS, Ball State U.; MS, Purdue U. Sales rep. Gray & Gray Specialties; mem. Ind. State Ho. of Reps. Dist. 67, mem. edn., pub. policy, ethics and vet. affairs com., mem. roads and transp. com., vice-chmn. environ. affairs com. Councilman Greensburg, Ind.; pres. Decatur County Solid Waste Bd.; mem. Greensburg City Planning Commn., Decatur County Coun. Youth; founder Project HELP. Mem. Greensburg C. of C., Decatur County Found.

DUNCAN, CONSTANCE CATHARINE, psychologist, educator, researcher; b. Watertown, Wis, Nov. 2, 1948; d. Howard Burton and Mary Elizabeth (Fagan) Duncan; m. R.E. Johnson, Jr., 1974 (div. 1984); m. Allan Franklin Mirsky, July 4, 1986. BA, Northwestern U., 1970; AM, U. Ill., 1973, PhD, 1978. Sr. rsch. analyst Adolf Meyer Mental Health Ctr., Decatur, Ill., 1971-73; asst. in rsch. and tchg. dept. psychology U. Ill., Champaign, 1974-78; NIMH postdoctoral fellow in neurosis. Stanford U. Sch. Medicine, Palo Alto, Calif., 1978-81; rsch. psychologist VA Med. Ctr., Palo Alto, 1978-81; sr. staff fellow Lab. Psychology and Psychopathology, NIMH, 1981-88; chief unit on psychophysiology NIMH, Bethesda, Md., 1982-89, rsch. psychologist, 1988-89, rsch. specialist, 1989-93; pvt. practice Bethesda, Md., 1981—. Adj. assoc. prof. Johns Hopkins Sch. Hygiene and Pub. Health, Balt., 1987—; guest rschr. Lab. Psychology and Psychopathology NIMH, 1993—97, Sect. on Clin. and Exptl. Neuropsychology NIMH, 1997—; rsch. assoc. prof. Uniformed Svc. Univ. Health Sci., 1993—. Assoc. editor Psychophysiology, 1987-91; mem. editl. bd. Internat. Jour. Psychophysiology, 2002—; cons. editor numerous sci. jour.; contbr. articles to profl. jour., chpt. to books. Found. assoc. Nat. Women's Econ. Alliance; mem. NIMH/NINCDS Assembly of Sci. Coun., 1982-84. Recipient Nat. Rsch. Svc. award, NIMH, 1978-81, Golden Anniversary Scholarship award, AAUW, 1974; NIMH fellow, 1970-74. Fellow: APA (mem. awards com. 2001—), Internat. Orgn. Psychophysiology (mem. world congress com. 2004), Am. Psychol. Soc.; mem.: EEG and Clin. Neurosci. Soc., Am. Psychopathol. Assn., Internat.Neuropsychol. Soc., Soc. for Neurosci., Soc. for Rsch. in Psychopathology (bd. dirs. 1986—88, membership com. 1987—88), Soc. for Psychophysiol. Rsch. (program com. 1979, 1980, nominating com. 1981, chmn. early career award com. 1981—84, program com. 1982, bd. dirs. 1982—85, nominating com. 1983, chmn. conv. com. 1983—87, program com. 1986, chmn. program com. 1987, program com. 1988, nominating com. 1989, Blue Ribbon Panel on state of soc. in Yr. 2000 1990—93, chmn. enhancement com. 1992—93, chmn. early career award com. 1994—96, conv. com., sec.-treas. 1996 99, com. governance and ops. 2000—01, program com. 2001, sr. award com. 2001—, chair sr. award com. 2002—03, pres. 2002—03, Early Career Contbn. award 1980), Phi Beta Kappa, Pi Mu Epsilon, Alpha Lambda Delta, Phi Kappa Phi, Sigma Xi, Shi-Ai, Mortar Bd. Achievements include electrophysiological and neuropsychological research on normal and disordered attn. and cognition. Office: Uniformed Svc U Health Sci Dept Psychiatry Clin Psychophysiology and Psychopharm Lab 4301 Jones Bridge Rd Bethesda MD 20814-4799 E-mail: connieduncan@mail.nih.gov.

DUNCAN, DEBORAH L. finance company executive; BA in Econs., Smith Coll.; MS in Acctg., NYU. With Chase Manhattan, N.Y.C., 1979—2000; numerous positions including corp. treas., co-head global markets, We. Hemisphere treas., treas. Chase Tokyo, others; sr. v.p. Chase Manhattan, N.Y.C., 1991-94; exec. v.p. markets, We. Hemisphere treas., treas. Chase Tokyo, others, 1994—; CEO, mng. dir. Freemont Investment Advisors, 2001—03, chmn., 2003—. Bd. dirs. Investment Co. Inst. Bd. dirs. United Way of Tri-State, YMCA of Greater N.Y., Ronald McDonald House. Office: Freemont Investment Advisors 333 Market St Ste 2000 San Francisco CA 94105-2127

DUNCAN, DIANNE WALKER, elementary school educator; b. Altavista, Va., Nov. 15, 1954; d. Robert and Catherine Forte. BS in History and Govt., Longwood Coll., 1977; MEd in Curriculum and Instrn., Va. Commonwealth U., 1993. Cert. tchr. social studies. Social studies tchr. Stonewall Jackson Mid. Sch., Mechanicsville, Va., 1977—98; civics tchr. John Witherspoon Mid. Sch., Princeton, NJ. Cmty. svc. coach John Witherspoon Mid. Sch. Do Something, N.Y.C.; mem. Character Edn. Partnership, Washington; character edn., citizenship presenter N.J. Edn. Assn. Conf., Atlantic City, 2001; mentor jr. level presvc. tchrs. Rider U., Lawrenceville, NJ, Princeton U., NJ. Mem. So. Poverty Law Ctr., Mont., Ala., 2001—; sponsor, coord. of food dr. John Witherspoon and Crisis Ministry Trenton and Princeton, 1999—2003; sponsor, supervise mid. sch. tutors Princeton Young Achievers After Sch. Programs, Princeton, 2000—03. Recipient John Marshall award for excellence in tchg. the Constn., Va. Ctrl. Region, 1995, Best Practices award in citizenship, character edn., N.J., 2000. Mem.: N.J. Edn. Assn., N.J. Coun. Social Studies, Nat. Coun. Social Studies, ASCD. D-Liberal. Avocations: gardening, reading. Office: Princeton Regional Schs 217 Walnut Ln Princeton NJ 08540 Office Phone: 609-806-4270.

DUNCAN, DONNA JEAN, librarian, educator; b. Arkadelphia, Ark., Apr. 6, 1946; d. Buford L. and Mildred Teresa Prince; m. Robert Lewis Duncan, May 18, 1968; children: Laura Elizabeth Lockhart, Lisa Ruth Barron. BS in Edn., Ouachita Bapt. U., Arkadelphia, Ark., 1968; MLS, Tex. Woman's U., Denton, 1986. First grade tchr. Aledo Ind. Sch. Dist., Aledo, Tex., 1968—70; mid. sch. libr. Lake Worth Ind. Sch. Dist., Lake Worth, Tex., 1977—87, Ft. Worth Ind. Sch. Dist., Tex., 1987—92; jr. high libr. Hurst-Euless-Bedford Ind. Sch. Dist., Bedford, Tex., 1993—95; dir. libr. svcs. Mesquite Ind. Sch. Dist., Mesquite, Tex., 1995—2002; adj. prof. Tex. A&M U., Commerce, Tex., 2000—. Libr. cons./author, Mesquite, 2002—. Author: (professional books for educators) I Search, You Search, We All Learn to Research, The I Search Connection: Linking Standards, Tests, and Evidence-Based Practice, 2004. Workshop chairperson Young Writers Workshop, Mesquite, Tex., 1996—2002; mem. libr. sci. adv. coun. Tex. Woman's U., Denton, Tex., 1998—2000. Mem.: Tex. Assn. of Sch. Libr. Administrs. (chair 2000—01), ASCD, ALA, Tex. Libr. Assn. (mem. centennial com. 1998—2002), Delta Kappa Gamma (pres. 1988—89). Democrat. Baptist. Avocations: reading, interior decorating, travel. Home: 2305 Penrose Mesquite TX 75150 Personal E-mail: bandddduncan@msn.com.

DUNCAN, DORIS GOTTSCHALK, information systems educator; b. Seattle, Nov. 19, 1944; d. Raymond Robert and Marian (Onstad) D.; m. Robert George Gottschalk, Sept. 12, 1971 (div. Dec. 1983). BA, U. Wash., Seattle, 1967, MBA, 1968; PhD, Golden Gate U., 1978. Cert. data processor, systems profl., computer profl., data educator. Comm. cons. Pacific N.W. Bell Tel. Co., Seattle, 1968-71; mktg. supr. AT&T, San Francisco, 1971-73; sr. cons., project leader Quantum Sci. Corp., Palo Alto, Calif., 1973-75; dir. co. analysis program Input Inc., Palo Alto, 1975-76; lectr. acctg. and info. systems Calif. State U., Hayward, 1976-78, assoc. prof., 1978-85, prof., 1985—, coord. computer info. sys., 1994-97; dir. info. sci. dept. Golden Gate U., San Francisco, 1982-83, mem. info. systems adv. bd., 1983-85, co-advisor grad. program Computer Inf. Sys., e-bus. programs, 1999—. Cons. pvt. cos., 1975—; vis. prof. U. Wash., Seattle, 1997-98; internat. spkr. profl. groups and confs. Author: Computers and Remote Computing Services, 1983; contbr. articles to profl. jours.; mem. editl. rev. bd. Jour. Info. Systems Edn., 1992-97, Jour. Informatics Edn. Rsch., 2000-02, assoc. editor, 2003--. Loaned exec. United Good Neighbors, Seattle, 1969; nat. com. woman bd. dirs. Young Reps., Wash., 1970-71; advisor Jr. Achievement, San Francisco, 1971-72; mem. nat. bd. Inst. for Certification of Computer Profls. Edn. Found., 1990-93; bd. dirs. Computer Repair Svcs., 1992-94, mem. adv. bd. Ximnet Corp., 2000-02. Recipient Disting. Rsch. award Allied Acads., 1999; named Computer Educator of Yr., Internat. Assn. Computer Info. Systems, 1997. Mem. Data Processing Mgmt. Assn. (Meritorious Svc. award, Bronze award 1984, Silver award 1986, Gold award 1988, Emerald award 1992, Diamond award 1994, Double Diamond award 1999, Triple Diamond award 2001, Nat. grantee, 1984, dir. edn. chmn. San Francisco chpt. 1984-85, sec. and v.p.

1985, pres. 1986, assn. dir. 1987, by-laws chmn. 1987, chair awards com. 1992-95, nat. bd. dirs. spl. interest group in edn. 1985-87), Am. Inst. Decision Scis., Western Assn. Schs. and Colls. (accreditation evaluation team 1984-85), Assn. Computing Machinery, Jr. Club of Seattle (Beautiful Home award Foster City 1994, 95, winner Tournament of Christmas Lights 1996, 2001) [illegible] include development of Information systems (information science), curriculum development, professional certification, industry standards, computer literacy and user education, system analysis and design, design of databases and data banks, electronic commerce. Office: Calif State U Sch Bus & Econs Hayward CA 94542

DUNCAN, ELIZABETH CHARLOTTE, retired marriage and family therapist, educational therapist, educator; b. L.A., Mar. 10, 1919; d. Frederick John de St. Vrain and Nellie Mae (Goucher) Schwankovsky; m. William McConnell Duncan, Oct. 12, 1941 (div. 1949); 1 child, Susan Elizabeth Duncan St. Vrain. BA, Calif. State U., Long Beach, 1953; MA, UCLA, 1962; PhD, Internat. Coll., 1984. Cert. marriage and family therapist; cert. clin. psychopathologist, Wash. Dir. gifted program Palos Verdes (Calif.) Sch. Dist., 1958-64; TV tchr., participant ednl. films Los Angeles County, 1961-64; dir. U. So. Calif. Presch., L.A., 1965-69, Abraham Maslow rsch. assoc., 1962-69; pvt. practice family counseling Malibu, Calif., 1979—2003, Ventura, 1979—2003, Eastsound, 1979—2003, Seattle, 1979—2003; pvt. practice psychotherapy West Seattle, 1994—2003; ret., 2003. Psychotherapist Children's Program North Sound Regional Support Network, 1992; resident psychologist for film series Something Personal, 1987—; mem. Rsch. Inst. of Scripps Cliic, La Jolla, Calif.; charter mem. Inst. Behavioral Medicine, Santa Barbara, Calif.; pub. spkr., lectr. comm.; cons. in field. TV performer in documentary The Other Side, 1985; creator: Persephone's Child, 1988. Active Chrysalis Ctr., L.A., 1984-86; mem. Ventura County Mental Health Adv. Bd., 1985-86, United Way, L.A., 1985-92; mem. Menninger Found. San Juan County, Wash., 1992; mem. adv. bd. North Sound Regional Support Network, 1992, Amb.'s People to People, San Juan County Network, 1998-00. Recipient Emmy award for best documentary Am. Acad. TV Arts and Scis., 1976; named Child Adv. of Yr., Calif. Mental Health Adv. Bd., 1987. Mem. AACD (Disting. Svc. award 1990), Transpersonal Psychol. Assn., Calif. State Orgn. Gifted Edn. (sec. 1962-64), Internat. Platform Assn., Am. Assn. for Marriage and Family Therapy (supr. licenses). Democrat. Avocations: swimming, plays, concerts, boating, political issues, especially women and child abuse. Home: 4455 Providence Point Pl SE Issaquah WA 98029 Office Phone: 425-427-8003.

DUNCAN, FRANCES MURPHY, retired special education educator; b. Utica, N.Y., June 23, 1920; d. Edward Simon and Elizabeth Myers (Stack) Murphy; m. Lee C. Duncan, June 23, 1947 (div. June 1969); children: Lee C., Edward M., Paul H., Elizabeth B., Nancy R., Frances B.(dec.), Richard L.(dec.). BA, Columbia State U., 1942; MEd, Auburn U., 1963, EdD, 1969. Head sci. dept. Arnold Jr. H.S., Columbus, Ga., 1960-63; tchr. physiology, Spanish Jordan H.S., Columbus, Ga., 1963-64; tchr. spl. edn. mentally retarded Muscogee County Sch. Sys., Columbus, Ga., 1964-65; instr. spl. edn. Auburn (Ala.) U., 1966-69; assoc. dir. Douglas Sch. for Learning Disabilities, Columbus, 1969-70; prof. edn. and spl. edn. Columbus Coll., 1970-85, ret., 1985. Past dir. Columbus Devel. Ctr.; past sec. exec. bd. Muscular Dystrophy Assn., 1968-70; 73-74; mem. Gov.'s Commn. on Disabled Georgians; past trustee Listening Eyes Sch. for Deaf; past mem. Mayor's Com. on Handicapped; mem. team for evaluation and placement of exceptional children Columbus Pub. Schs. Vol. Med. Ctr. Columbus Regional Healthcare Sys., Ga., Achievement Acad., Columbus, Ga., Columbus Hospice, Columbus, Ga. Fellow Am. Assn. Mental Retardation; mem. AAUP, AAUW (pres. 1973-75, divsn. rec. sec. 1975—), Coun. Exceptional Children (legis. chmn. 1973-74), Psi Chi, Phi Delta Kappa. Roman Catholic. Home: 1811 Alta Vista Dr Columbus GA 31907-3210 Business E-Mail: duncanf@knology.com.

DUNCAN, HOLLY H. foundation executive; b. Cleve., July 8, 1946; d. Martin Luther and Jean Righter Hecht; m. Richard David Duncan, Dec. 23, 1967 (dec. Apr. 19, 2003); children: Darby Hecht, Whitney Duncan Ribonson. BA in Govt. summa cum laude, Ohio U., 1968; MA in Polit. Sci. magna cum laude, Miami U., Ohio, 1970. Grad. asst. Miami U., Oxford, Ohio, 1968-69; jr. officer, polit. sect. U.S. Dept. State, U.S. Fgn. Svc., Bonn, Germany, 1969-70; dir. devel. Fla. Orch., Tampa, 1980-85, Lowry Park Zoo, Tampa, 1985-87; dir. major gifts Eckerd Coll., St. Petersburg, 1987-88; v.p. devel. Ruth Eckerd Hall, Clearwater, 1988-93, Fla. Aquarium, Tampa, 1993-96; pres., CEO Morton Plant Mease Found., Clearwater, 1996—. Panelist Fla. Arts Coun., Tallahassee, 1988—93; pres. Jr. League Clearwater, 1985; chmn. Clearwater Regional C. of C., 2004; pres. Fla. Dance Assn., Tallahassee, 1988—93. Mem.: Assn. Health Philanthropy, Nat. Soc. Fundraising Execs., Bellear Country Club, Countryside Country Club, Phi Beta Kappa, Kappa Kappa Gamma (nat. devel. com. 1988—92). Democrat. Episcopalian. Avocations: current events, sports, wellness consulting. Home: 2724 Burning Tree Ln Clearwater FL 33761-3001 Office: Morton Plant Mease Found 1200 Druid Rd S Clearwater FL 33756-1995 E-mail: holduncan@msn.com.

DUNCAN, JENNIFER R. secondary school educator; d. Michael and Janet Duncan. M in Sch. Adminstrn., Murray (Ky.) State U., 2003. Lang. arts tchr. Madisonville-North Hopkins H.S., 1997—; Upward Bound instr. Madisonville C.C., 2003. Mem.: NEA. Baptist. Avocations: reading, home improvement, antiques.

DUNCAN, LINDSAY VERE, actress; b. Edinburgh, Scotland, Nov. 7, 1950; m. Hilton McRae; 1 child, Cal. Attended, Ctrl. Sch. Speech and Drama, London. Actor: (films) Loose Connections, 1983, Prick Up Your Ears, 1987, Manifesto, 1988, Body Parts, 1991, The Reflecting Skin, 1991, A Midsummer Night's Dream, 1996, City Hall, 1996, An Ideal Husband, 1999, Mansfield Park, 1999, Star Wars: Episode 1 - The Phantom Menace, 1999; (TV series) Just William, 1977—78, Ace of Spies, 1983, Dead Head, 1986, Traffik, 1989 (FIPA Golden award, Cannes Internat. Film Festival, 1990), Jake's Progress, 1995, Get Real, 1998; (TV miniseries) A Year in Provence, 1993, The History of Tom Jones, 1997, Oliver Twist, 1999; (Broadway plays) Les Liaisons Dangereuses (award, 1987, Tony award nomination, 1987, Theatre World award, 1987), Top Girls (Obie award, 1982), A Midsummer Night's Dream, Ashes to Ashes (Drama Desk nomination), Celebration, The Room, Private Lives (winner Tony award for Best Performance by a Leading Actress in a Play, 2002, Drama Desk Best Actress award, 2002); (films) Under the Tuscan Sun, 2003; (TV miniseries) Shooting the Past, Perfect Strangers. Office: ICM Oxford House 76 Oxford St London W1D 1B5 England

DUNCAN, LYN M. pathology educator; MD, Washington U., 1986. Bd. cert. pathology, dermatopathology. Resident anatomic pathology Barnes Hosp., 1990; fellow dermatopathology Mass. Gen. Hosp., 1991; clin. faculty anatomic pathology; asst. prof. pathology, dir. dermatopathology tng. Harvard Med. Sch. Achievements include research in melanoma, lymphoma, pregnancy associated skin disease, pigmented lesions. Office: Mass Gen Hosp WRN 827 55 Fruit St Boston MA 02114-2696 Fax: 617-726-8711. E-mail: duncan@helix.mgh.harvard.edu.

DUNCAN, MARGARET CAROLINE, physician; b. Salt Lake City, June 9, 1930; d. Donald and Margaret Aileen (Eberts) D.; m. N. Paul Arceneaux, Dec. 26, 1958; children: David Paul, Eleanor Anne, Stephen Louis, Andre. BA, U. Tex., 1952, MD, 1955. Intern Kings County Hosp., Seattle, 1955-56; resident in pediat. John Sealy Hosp., Galveston, Tex., 1956-58; resident in neurology Charity Hosp., New Orleans, 1958-60; fellow child neurology Johns Hopkins Hosp., Balt., 1960-61; mem. faculty La. State U. Med. Ctr., New Orleans, 1961—, prof. neurology and pediat., 1973-2000, prof. neurology emeritus, 2000—. Chmn. La. Com. Epilespy and Cerebral Palsy, 1976-79. Fellow Am. Acad. Neurology, Am. Acad. Pediat.; mem. Child Neurology Soc., Profs. Child Neurology, Alpha Omega Alpha. Episcopalian. Office: 1542 Tulane Ave New Orleans LA 70112-2825

DUNCAN, MARY ELLEN, academic administrator; b. N.Y.C., NY, Aug. 29, 1941; d. Harry and Mary (Laveglia) Fielder; 1 child, Kathryn Mary Dickens. BS, St. John's U., 1963; MA, U. Conn., 1973, PhD, 1982. Grad. rsch. asst. U. Conn., Storrs, 1971-75; instr. English and Grad. West Islip Pub. Schs., N.Y.C., 1963-71; instr. Tri-County Tech. Coll., Pendleton, S.C., 1975-76, instrnl. assoc. ACCTion Ctr., 1976-82, dir. ea. region, 1980-82, dir. instnl. devel., 1982-83, dean, 1987-88; dean planning and devel. Catonsville Community Coll., Balt., 1988-89, 90-91, interim pres., 1989-90; pres. Tech. Coll. SUNY, Delhi, 1991—. Author: Indicators of Institutional Effectiveness, 1989. Recipient Merit award S.C. women in Higher Edn., 1985. Mem. Am. Assn. Community and Jr. Colls. (fed. rels. task force 1990-91, Merit award 1982, John Fry award 1981), Am. Assn. Women Community and Jr. Colls., Nat. Coun. Resource Devel. (legis. liaison 1990—). Avocation: golf. Home: 1236 Crows Foot Rd Marriottsville MD 21104-1445 Office: SUNY Coll Tech Delhi Delhi NY 13753

DUNCAN, SHIRLEY A. portfolio manager; b. Greenville, Ga., Jan. 14, 1949; d. Crawford Lee and Mary Elizabeth Duncan; m. Francis LLoyd Lasenby, Aug. 31, 1968 (div. Oct. 1996); 1 child, Cynthia Diane Lasenby Acosta. Grad., Fla. Bankers Assn. Trust Sch., 1976; student, Fla. C.C., 1982, Jones Coll., 1987—88. Sec. Atlantic Bancorp, Jacksonville, Fla., 1970—82; portfolio mgr. Atlantic Bancorp/First Union, 1982—90, First Union Corp., Tampa, 1990—96; regional investment dir. First Union/Wachovia, Jacksonville, 1996—2003; sr. v.p. Wachovia Corp., Jacksonville, 2003—. Mem.: Assn. Investment Mgmt. & Rsch., Jacksonville Fin. Analysts Soc. (membership chmn. 1986). Avocations: tennis, golf. Office: Wachovia 214 N Hogan St 2d Fl Jacksonville FL 32202

DUNDON, MARGO ELAINE, museum director; b. Cleve., July 3, 1950; d. Elmer Edward and Ruth Ann (Dreger) Buckeye. BS in Comm. cum laude, Ohio U., 1972; postgrad. in Mus. Studies, U. Okla, 1987. Mem. gen. staff Grout Mus. History and Sci., Waterloo, Iowa, 1974-75, coord. edn., 1976-78, co-dir., 1979-87, dir., 1988-90; exec. dir. Mus. Sci. and History, Jacksonville, Fla., 1990-99, pres., 1999—. Apptd. grievance com. Fla. Bar 4th Jud. Cir., 2002—. Chairperson Waterloo Hist. Preservation Commn., 1987—88; cultural com. Visitors and Conv. Bur., Waterloo, 1988—90, My Waterloo Days, 1982, 1983; mem. Jacksonville Women's Network, Non-Profit Execs. Round Table, 1990—95; bd. dirs. Resource Plus, Waterloo-Cedar Falls, Iowa, 1986—88, CJI, Girls Inc. of Jacksonville, 1994—95, Ritz Theater & LaVilla Mus., 1998—2000, Jacksonville and the Beaches Conv. and Vis. Bur., 2001—. Am. Law Inst.-ABA scholar, 1979, 86; recipient Mayor's Vol. Performance award, Waterloo, 1983, Vol. award Gov. of Iowa, 1990. Mem.: Iowa Mus. Assn. (pres. 1984—86), Fla. Attractions Assn. (bd. dirs. 1997—98), Fla. Assn. Mus. (pres. 1995—96), Southeast Mus. Conf., Midwest Mus. Conf. (pres. 1988—90), Am. Assn. Mus. (site surveyor mus. assessment program 1982—, site examiner mus. accreditation commn. 1987—, regional councilor 1988—90, Peer Reviewer award 2000), Jacksonville C. of C., Quota Club (pres. 1982), Rotary. Avocations: snorkeling, scuba diving, travelling, gardening. Office: Mus Sci & History 1025 Museum Cir Jacksonville FL 32207-9053 Office Phone: 904-396-7062.

DUNEVANT, CAROL DARY, music educator, conductor; b. Wichita Falls, Tex., May 11, 1959; d. David Archie and Carolyn Sue Dary; m. David Lynn Dunevant; 1 child, Cristian Pennington. BMusEd, U. Kans., Lawrence, 1982, MMusEd, 1992—92; Post Grad. Studies, Coll.Conservatory of Music, U. Com., 1992—95. Dir. of bands. Chanute (Kans.) H.S., 1984—88, No. Ky. U., Highland Heights, 1995—2002; music dir., condr. Frank Simon Band, 2002. Mgr. festival Ky. Music Educators, Calvert City, 1995—2002. Musician (guest conductor): (music concert) Philharmonic Orch., 2000. Named Outstanding Univ. Tchr., Dist. VI, 1999. Mem.: Internat. Conductors Guild, World Assn. of Symphonic Bands and Ensembles, Women Band Dirs. Internat., Coll. Band Dirs. Assn., Sigma Alpha Iota (advisor 1995—2002), Tau Beta Sigma, Kappa Kappa Psi (hon.), Pi Kappa Lambda. Avocations: boxing, golf, camping, reading. Home: 849 Shawnee Trace Court Cincinnati OH 45255 Office: 849 Shawnee Trace Ct Cincinnati OH 45255 Business E-Mail: franksimonband@earthlink.net.

DUNHAM, ANNE, educational institute director; Exec. dir. Youth Sci. Inst., 1995—. Office: Youth Sci Inst 296 Garden Hill Dr Los Gatos CA 95032-7669

DUNHAM, CHRISTINE, dancer; b. Dallas; Studies with Myrtha Rosello; student, Sch. of Am. Ballet. Mem. Dallas Ballet, Am. Ballet Theatre, 1985-87, soloist, 1987-89, prin. dancer, 1989—. Guest artist, Australian Ballet, 1991—. Lead dancer ballet Imperial, La Bayadere, Variation Six, Birthday Offering, Bouree Frantasque, Don Quixote (Kitire's Wedding), Fall River Legend, Giselle, Sleeping Beauty, Swan Lake, Firebird, Raymonda, Etudes; featured role in The Leaves are Fading, La Bayadere, Drink to Me Only With Thine Eyes, Les Sylphides; leading role in Nine Sinatra Song, Symphonie Conertante, Three Virgins and a Devil, Paquita, Manon; solo role in Paquita, Raymonda, Requiem, The Sleeping Beauty, Swan Lake. Scholar Sch. of Am. Ballet. Office: Am Ballet Theatre 890 Broadway New York NY 10003-1211

DUNHAM, JOAN ROBERTS, administrative assistant; b. Dayton, Ohio, Jan. 25, 1933; d. Harold Hathaway and Lydia Roberts Dunham. BA, U. Colo., 1954; postgrad., U. Pa., 1959-65, U. Chgo., 1971-72. Office clk. Daniels & Fisher Stores, Denver, 1954-56; clk., stenographer Dept. of State, Madras, India, 1957-59; clk. admissions office Temple Buell Coll., Denver, 1969—71; typist, adminstrv. clk. State of Colo., Denver, 1987-99; ret., 1999. Fgn. lang. fellow U.S. Dept. Health, Edn. and Welfare, U. Pa., 1961-62. Republican. Christian Scientist. Home: 1350 Josephine St Unit 210 Denver CO 80206-2243

DUNHAM, KATHERINE, choreographer, anthropologist, dancer; b. Glen Ellyn, Ill., June 22, 1909; d. Albert Millard and Fanny June (Taylor) Dunham; m. Jordis McCoo (div.); m. John Thomas Pratt, July 10, 1941 (dec. Jan. 1986); 1 child, Marie Christine Pratt. BA in Anthropology, U. Chgo., 1936, MS; PhD, Northwestern U.; LhD (hon.), MacMurray Coll., 1972. Dir., tchr. of own schs. of dance, theatre and cultural arts, Chgo., N.Y.C., Haiti, Stockholm and Paris, from 1931; profl. dancer, from 1934; choreographer for theatre, opera, motion pictures and TV; mem. Chgo. Opera Co., 1935-36; supv. Chgo. City Theatre Project on cultural studies, 1939; dance dir. Labor Stage, 1939-40; prodr., dir. Katherine Dunham Dance Co., from 1945; established dance sch. Port-au-Prince, Haiti, 1961; advisor to First World Festival on Negro Art U.S. Dept. State, 1966; artistic and tech. advisor to Pres. of Senegal, 1966-67; cultural counselor and dir. Performing Arts Tng. Ctr., So. Ill. U., East St. Louis, from 1967; prof. So. Ill. U., Edwardsville, from 1968. Choreographer concerts Tropics, 1937, Schulhoff Tango, 1937, Madame Christoff, 1937, Primitive Rhythms, 1937, Biguine-Beguine, 1937, Florida Swamp Shimmy, 1937, Lotus Eaters, 1937, Haitian Suite, 1937, Peruvienne, 1938, Le Jazz Hot (Boogie-Woogie), 1938, Saludade da Brazil, 1938, Spanish Earth Suite, 1938, Island Songs, 1938, Mexican Rhumba, 1938, L'Ag'Ya, 1938, A Las Montanas, 1938, Bre'r Rabbit an' de Tah Baby, 1938, Bahiana, 1939, Cuidad Maravillosa, 1939, Concert Rhumba, 1939, Cumbancha, 1939, Plantation Dances, 1940, Babalu, 1941, Haitian Suite II, 1941, Honky-Tonk Train (added to Le Hot Jazz), 1941, Rites de Passage, 1941, Tropical Revue, 1943, Callaco, 1944, Choros Nos. 1-5, 1944, Flaming Youth 1927, 1944, Para Que Tu Veas, 1944, Havana 1910/1919, 1944, Carib Song, 1945, Bal Negro, 1946, Motivos, 1946, Haitian Roadside, 1946, Nostalgia (Ragtime), 1946, Batacada, 1947, Bolero, 1947, C'Est Lui, 1947, Rhumba Trio, 1947, Floor Exercises, 1947, La Valise, 1947, Octaroon Ball, 1947, Angelique, 1948, Blues Trio, 1948, Macumba, 1948, Missouri Waltz, 1948, [illegible] 1948, [illegible], 1948, Adeus Terras, 1949, Afrique, 1949, Jazz in Five Movements, 1949, Brazilian Suite, 1950, Los Indios, 1950, Frevo, 1951, Rhumba Jive, 1951, Rhumba Suite, 1951, Spirituals, 1951, Caymmi, 1952, Ramona, 1952, La Blanchisseuse, 1952, Southland, 1952, Afrique du Nord, 1953, Samba, 1953, Cumbia, 1953, Dora, 1953, Honey in the Honeycomb, 1953, Incantation, 1953, Carnaval, 1955, Floy'd Guitar Blues, 1955, Jazz Finale, 1955, Just Wild About Harry, 1955, New Love, 1955, Banana Boat, 1957, Plating Rice, 1957, Sister Kate, 1957, Ti'Cocomaque, 1957, A Touch of Innocence, 1959, Bamboche, 1962, Diamond Thief, 1962, Anabacoa, 1963, theatre The Emperor Jones, 1939, with George Balanchine Cabin in the Sky, 1941, theatre Pins and Needles, 1940, Tropical Pinafore, 1939, Les Deux Anges, 1965, (films) Carnaval of Rhythum, 1939, Pardon My Sarong, 1942, Star Spangled Rhythum, 1942, Stormy Weather, 1943, Casbah, 1948, Boote e Risposta, 1950, Mambo, 1954, Green Mansions, 1958, The Bible, 1966, (Operas) Aida, 1963; author: Katherine Dunham's Journey to Accompong, 1946, Katherine Dunham's Journey to Accompong, rev. edit., 1972; author: (autobiography) A Touch of Innocence, 1959, A Touch of Innocence, rev. edit., 1980; author: Island Possessed, 1969, Kasamance: A Fantasy, 1974; co-author: (plays) Ode to Taylor Jones, 1967—68; author: TV scripts, produced in Mexico, Australia, France, Eng., Italy; contbr. short stories sometimes under pseudonym Kaye Dunn to mags. Pres. Dunham Fund for Rsch. and Devel. Cultural Arts Inc.; founder Found. Study of Arts and Scis. of Vodun; v.p. Found. Devel. and Preservation Cultural Arts Inc.; bd. dirs. Nat. Inst. Aging, Ill. Arts Coun.; mem. Ill. com. JFK Ctr. Alliance Arts Edn., Am. Coun. Arts in Edn., Arts Worth/Intercultural Coun.; cons. Interamerican Inst. Ethnomusicology and Folklore, Caracas, Venezuela, NEH; mem. rev. com. OAS; mem. adv. bd. Modern Orgn. Dance Evolvement. Decorated Legion of Honor Haiti; named Cmdr., Grand Officer, Hon. Citizen, Port-an-Prince, Haiti, 1957; recipient Merit Chevalier, Haiti, Dance Mag. award, 1968, Eight Lively Arts award, 1969, Disting. Svc. award, So. Ill. U., 1970, East St. Louis Monitor award, 1970, Dance Divsn. Heritage award, AAHPERD, 1972, Nat. Ctr. Afro-Am. Artists award, 1972, Black Merit Acad. award, 1972, Am. Dance Guild award, 1975, 6th Kennedy Ctr. Honors award, 1983, Profl. Achievement award, U. Chgo., Samuel M. Scripps/Am. Dance Festival award, 1986, Nat. Medal Arts, 1989, Capezio Dance award, 1991, Key to City, East St. Louis, Ill., 1968; Julius Rosenfeld Travel fellow, 1936—37, Fulbright fellow, State Dept. Internat. Edn., Mather scholar, Case We. Res. U., 1973. Mem.: AEA, SAG, ASCAP, Lincoln Acad., Royal Anthrop. Soc., Negro Actors Guild, Inst. Black World (bd. dirs.), Black Acad. Arts and Scis., Writers Guild, Am. Fedn. Radio Artists, Am. Guild Music Artists, Am. Guild Variety Artists (bd. govs. 1943—49), Sigma Epsilon. Avocations: horseback riding, cooking, painting, walking, steam baths. Office: Katherine Dunham Mus 532 N 10th St East Saint Louis IL 62201-1946

DUNHAM, LAURA, elementary school educator; b. Highland Park, Mich., June 2, 1947; d. Clement and Joy C. Harland; m. Roger W. Dunham, Feb. 14, 1969; children: Chad Roger, Craig William. B in Music Edn. cum laude, U. Miami, 1969; BA in Edn. magna cum laude, Fla. Atlantic U., 1979. Music tchr. grades K-5 Hollywood (Fla.) Park Elem., 1969-70; substitute tchr. grades K-5 Otis AFB Elem. Sch., Falmouth, Mass., 1970-71; music tchr. grades 6-9 Olsen Mid. Sch., Dania, Fla., 1971—74; music tchr. grades 6-12 Westminster Acad., Ft. Lauderdale, Fla., 1979-83; art tchr. Ft. Lauderdale Christian Sch., 1983—2002, chmn. developing tchr. program for new educators, 1993—2002; art tchr. Sunrise Mid. Sch., 2002—. Cons. scholarship and award writer graduating srs. Ft. Lauderdale Christian Sch., 1993-95; sponsor Nat. Art Honor Soc. at Ft. Lauderdale Christian Sch., 1995-2002, Nat. Honor Soc., 2001-02; host Internat. Children's Art Exhbn., 1996; entourage mem. Broward County Ctr. for the Performing Arts, 1996—; com. mem. Broward County Nat. Week of the Ocean, 1996-2002; nat. mem. The Smithsonian Instn., 1998-99; presenter Christian Schs. Fla. Seminar, 1999. Profl. flautist, 1969—. Vol. hosp. surg. suite; Sunday sch. tchr., mem. ch. choirs, handbell choirs, vacation Bible sch. tchr., vol. classroom arts and crafts, deacon, pastor nominating com.; vol. for badges, cub scout leader Boy Scouts Am., 1984—, Habitat for Humanity, 2001-03; active Fla. Rep. Party, 1993—. Named H.S. Tchr. of Yr., Broward County Fair, 1996. Mem. ACA, Nat. Art Edn. Assn., Fla. Art Edn. Assn., Nat. Mus. Women in the Arts, Assn. Ind. Schs. Fla. (accreditation team 1999), Am. Assn. Christian Counselors, Am. Sch. Counseling Assn., U. Miami Alumnae Assn., U. Miami Band of the Hour Club, Mortar Bd., Alpha Tau Omega (little sister), Delta Zeta (alumnae pres., Woman of Yr. Broward County Gold Coast Area Alumnae 1996), U. Miami Alumnae Delta Zeta (area chair), Rho Lambda, Chi Sigma Iota (sec.), Tau Beta Sigma, Alpha Theta Kappa, Sigma Alpha Iota (pres., Province award), Phi Delta Kappa, Phi Kappa Phi, Kappa Delta Pi, Chi Sigma Iota (sec.). Republican. Methodist. Home: 301 Lake Dr Coconut Creek FL 33066-1840 Office: Sunrise Middle Sch Fort Lauderdale FL 33304

DUNHAM, VIVIAN L. state legislator; b. Palmer, Mass., Apr. 29, 1946; m. Jay Spencer Dunham, 2 children. Student, Conn. State Coll., 1964-66; grad., Katherine Gibbs Sch., 1968. Mem. corrections and criminal justice com. N.H. Ho. of Reps., mem. dist. 29. Republican. Home: 12 Wallace Cir Londonderry NH 03053-2871

DUNION, CELESTE MOGAB, consultant, business manager, township official; b. Atlantic City, Mar. 6, 1932; d. Cyril Joseph and Lavina Edna (Bolen) Mogab; m. John Joseph Dunion, May 8, 1954 (dec. Apr. 1978); children: Dana, John, Robert, Denise. Tech. degree, Am. Acad. Dramatic Arts, N.Y.C., 1951; grad. advanced govt. fin. inst., Georgetown U., 1986. Cert. govt. fin. mgr.; lic. notary pub., Pa. Asst. to bus. mgr. Rose Tree Media Sch. Dist., Media, Pa., 1969-78; dir. fin., tax collector, treas. Twp. of Middletown, Glen Riddle, Pa., 1978-98; bus. mgr. Rocky Run YMCA, 2003—. Profl. model, NYC, Phila., Atlantic City; mem. Christy Modeling Agy., Phila. Models Guild, Atlantic City Models Guild, Atlantic City Press Bur.; cons. in fin. mgmt. peer-to-peer program Pa. Dept. Cmty. Affairs, Harrisburg, 1988-96; treas., bd. dir. Pa. Mcpl. Investment Program, 1990-98. Past sec. Wyncroft Civic Assn.; former committeewoman Middletown Twp; treas. Middletown Rep. Women, 1998-2003; treas. Rep. Women of Western Delaware County, 2003-; bd. dirs. Darlington Woods, 2001—. Recipient Dedicated Pumper award Lenni Fire Co., 1983, Pres.'s award Lima Fire Co., 1985, Outstanding Leadership award Pa. East Govt. Fin. Officers Assn., 1986, Cmty. Svc. award Middletown Fire Co., 1996. Mem. Govt. Fin. Officers Assn. (Pa. rep., nat. cash mgmt. com., women's fin. network, Mid-Atlantic rep.), Assn. Govt. Acct., Pa. Govt. Fin. Officers Assn. (past pres., sec., S.E. bd.), MidAtlantic Govt. Fin. Officers Assn. (Pa. rep., mem. legis. com.), Women's Fin. Officers Network (chmn. membership), Delaware County Tax Collectors Assn. (v.p. 1984-85, pres. 1986), Pa. Tax Collectors Assn., Pa. Assn. Notaries. Republican. Roman Catholic. Avocations: silk flower arranging, tap dancing, country western dancing, writing poetry, cooking. Office: CMD/CGFM Darlington Woods 153 Kingswood Ct Glen Mills PA 19342-2016 also: Rocky Run YMCA 1299 W Baltimore Pike Media PA 19063 E-mail: cmdcgfm@msn.com.

DUNIPHAN, J. P. state legislator, small business owner; b. Aug. 31, 1946; Mem. S.D. Ho. of Reps., Pierre, 1995—, mem. commerce com., judiciary com., chair local govt. com. Republican. Fax: 605 342 6399.

DUNKELMAN, LORETTA, artist; b. Paterson, N.J., June 29, 1937; d. Samuel and Rae (Gutkin) D. BA, Rutgers U., 1958; MA, Hunter Coll., 1966. Lectr. Hunter Coll., N.Y.C., 1966-67; vis. artist U. Cin., 1974; asst. prof. U. R.I., Kingston, 1974-75, Cornell U., Ithaca, N.Y., 1977-80; vis. artist Ohio State U., Columbus, 1984; asst. prof. Va. Commonwealth Univ., Richmond, 1986-88; vis. artist The Sch. of the Art Inst. of Chgo., 1990; vis.

prof. art U. Calif., Berkeley, 1993-94. One woman shows include A.I.R. Gallery, N.Y., 1973-74, 78, 81, 83, 87, Douglass Coll., New Brunswick, 1973, U. Cin., 1974, U. R.I., Kingston, 1975, 1708 E. Main Gallery, Richmond, 1987; exhibited in group shows at Whitney Mus. Am. Art, N.Y., 1973, N.Y. Cultural Ctr., N.Y., 1973, Newark Mus., 1973, Cranbrook Acad. Art Mus., Bloomfield Hills, Mich., 1974, Grand Rapids (Mich.) Art Mus., 1974, Johnson Mus., Cornell U., Ithaca, N.Y., 1977, Inst. Art and Urban Resources, Pub. Sch. 1, N.Y.C., 1978, McIntosh/Drysdale Gallery, Washington, 1980, Douglass Coll., Rutgers U., New Brunswick, 1981, Kulturhuset, Stockholm and Lunds Konsthall, Sweden, 1981-82, Picker Art Gallery, Colgate U., Hamilton, N.Y., 1983, Hopkins Hall Gallery, The Ohio State U., 1984, Kenkeleba Gallery, N.Y., 1985, A.I.R. Gallery, 1985, 91, Bernice Steinbaum Gallery, N.Y., 1986, Anderson Gallery, Va. Commonwealth U., Richmond, Va., 1987, Rabbet Gallery, New Brunswick, N.J., 1989, Michael Walls Gallery, 1989, 148 Duane St., N.Y.C., 1992, Contemporary Art Inst., N.Y.C., 1994, Mason Gross Sch. of the Arts Galleries, Rutgers U., New Brunswick, N.J., 1996, A.I.R. Gallery, N.Y.C., 1997, Kingsborough C.C., Bklyn., 1998, Yaddo Centennial Arts Festival, N.Y.C., 2000; represented in permanent collections Bellevue Med. Ctr., N.Y.C., The Chase Manhattan Bank, N.Y.C., City Univ. Grad. Ctr., N.Y.C., The Picker Art Gallery, Dana Art Ctr., Colgate U., Hamilton, N.Y., U. Cin., Gene Swenson Collection at U. Kansas Art Mus., Lawrence, Bristol-Myers, Squibb, Lawrenceville, N.J., Hunter Coll., N.Y.C. CAPS fellow N.Y. State Coun. Arts, 1975; Visual artist fellow Nat. Endowment for the Arts, 1975, 82, 93, AAUW fellow, 1976-77, Artist fellow N.Y. Found. for the Arts, 1991; grantee Adolph & Esther Gottlieb Found., 1991. Home and Office: 151 Canal St New York NY 10002-5033

DUNKER, AMY MELISSA, sales manager; b. Dallas, Sept. 10, 1967; d. Max Albert Derden, Jr. and Barbara Dianne (Henry) Stiff; m. Michael Paul Dunker, Apr. 28, 1990 (div. Jan. 1998). BBA in Fin./Econs., Baylor U., 1989. Fin. analyst Leprino Foods, Denver, 1989-90; customer svc. rep. Integrated Payment Systems/Amex, Englewood, Colo., 1990-91, tng. specialist, 1991-92; dist. account mgr. Integrated Payment Systems/First Data Corp., Houston, 1992-93, dist. sales mgr., 1994-97, nat. account mgr. Austin, 1997, nat. sales mgr., 1997—; sales rep. Moore Bus. Forms, Houston, 1993-94; dir. sales First Data Corp., 1998—99; v.p. bus. devel. Western Union Money Lap, 2000—01; CEO AME Enterprises, Inc., 2002—. Vol. Tex. Spl. Olympics, Austin, 1988, 89, 93, 95, 96, 97, Mental Health Mental Retardation, Denison, Tex., 1993-97. Mem. Baylor U. Alumni, Kappa Alpha Theta. Avocations: reading, boating, snow skiing. Office: First Data Corp 6200 S Quebec St Englewood CO 80111-4729

DUNKINS, BETTY, wedding coordinator, publisher; b. St. Louis, July 16, 1933; d. William and Rose Marie (Vaughn) McPherson; m. Bruce Washington Dunkins, Mar. 19, 1966; children: Bruce, Eric. BS in Med. Record LS, St. Louis U., 1955. Registered med. record adminstr. Med. records adminstr. St. Louis City Govt., 1955-56; chief med. records adminstrn. Good Samaritan Hosp., Dayton, Ohio, 1956-59, HEW-St. Elizabeths Hosp., Washington, 1959-67, pers. staffing specialist, 1967-79; pers. mgmt. specialist HHS, Rockville, Md., 1979-89; owner, mgr. Tying The Knot Wedding Svc., Silver Spring, Md., 1989—; pub. Gray, McPherson Pub. Co., Silver Spring, 1993—. Cons. on weddings to local and nat. TV, Washington and Md., 1990—; advisor on wedding sites to local and nat. TV, Washington and Md., 1991—. Author, editor pub.: The Perfect Choice, 1994, 98; contbr. numerous articles on weddings to mags. and newspapers. Mem. membership and freedom fund com. NAACP, Washington, 1965-69; cultural chmn. Stonegate Elem. Sch., Silver Springs, 1977-78; mem. membership com. Stonegate Citizen Assn., silver Spring, 1975, area leader, dir. publ., 1976, security officer, 1983-84. Mem. Assn. Bridal Cons. (accredited, honor award 1998), Assn. Wedding Profls. (membership chmn. 1997-98), Alpha Kappa Alpha Sorority (Theta Omega Omega 3rd grade mentor, 1994, 1998-99, Hon. award 1999). Avocations: reading, travel, aerobics. Office: PO Box 6080 Silver Spring MD 20916-6080

DUNKIS, PATRICIA B. school system administrator; Prin. C.R. Streams Elem. Sch., Upper St. Clair, Pa., 1982-97; dir. elem. edn. Upper St. Clair Sch. Dist., 1997—. Recipient Elem. Sch. Recognition award U.S. Dept. Edn., 1989-90. Office: 1820 Mclaughlin Run Rd Upper Saint Clair PA 15241 E-mail: pdunkis@uscsd.k12.pa.us.

DUNKLIN, BETSY D. state legislator; b. Goshen, Va., Oct. 9, 1949; m. Charles F. Cole; 1 child, Kate. BA in English, Newberry Coll., 1971; postgrad., U. S.C., 1972-73; MSW, U. Md., Balt., 1981. Svcs. coord. Families Forward, Boise, 1986, dir., 1986-87, Women's and Children's Crisis Ctr., Boise, 1987-89; bd. pres. Idaho Women's Network, Inc., Boise, 1989-90, exec. dir., 1990-94; pub. affairs coord. Planned Parenthood of Idaho, Boise, 1995-96; mem. Idaho Senate, Dist. 19, Boise, 1996—. Mem. edn. and judiciary and rules com.; adj. faculty, Boise State U., 1988-89. Mem. Idaho Coun. Tech. and Learning, Hispanic Commn. Idaho, Baltimore City Tenants' Assn., United Farm Workers. Mem. Idaho Women's Network (founding mem.; Opal Brooten award), Idaho Rivers United, WCA of Boise (pres. we. states ctr.). Democrat. Unitarian-Universalist. Office: State Capitol PO Box 83720 Boise ID 83720-3720

DUNLAP, BARBARA J. music educator; b. Beaver Falls, Pa., May 22, 1947; d. Henry and Henrietta Podbielski; m. Douglas Keith Dunlap, June 29, 1985; 1 child, Rebecca Marie. M in Music Edn., Duquesne U., 1975. Music tchr. Valley Grove Sch. Dist., Franklin, Pa., 1969—86, Big Beaver Falls Area Sch. Dist. Mem. Beaver County Wind Ensemble, 2000—03. Mem.: Pa. State Edn. Assn. (licentiate), Music Educators Nat. Conf. (life). Home: 349 Ridgemont Dr Midland PA 15059 Personal E-mail: bjd522@yahoo.com.

DUNLAP, CONNIE, librarian; b. Lansing, Mich., Sept. 9, 1924; d. Frederick Arthur and Laura May (Robinson) Robson; m. Robert Bruce Dunlap, Aug. 9, 1947. AB, U. Mich., 1946, AM in Libr. Sci., 1952. Head acquisitions dept., then head grad. library U. Mich. Libr., 1961-75, dep. assoc. dir., 1972-75; univ. libr. Duke U., 1975-80; cons., 1981—. Contbr. articles to publs. in field, chpts. in books. Forewoman Grand Jury U.S. Dist. Ct. 13th Dist. Mich., 1967-68; bd. dirs. U. Mich. Libr. Friends, v.p., 1997-2000, officer at large, 2000-02, bd. dirs. A.B. Bach, 1999—, v.p., 2002, chair, 2003; treas. Ann Arbor Hist. Found., 1998—. Recipient Disting. Alumnus award U. Mich. Sch Libr. Sci., 1977 Mem. ALA (mem. coun. 1974-83, mem. exec. bd. 1978-83, pres. resources and tech. svcs. divsn. 1972-73), AAUP, Assn. Coll. and Rsch. Librs. (bd. dirs. 1975-78, pres. 1976-77), Assn. Rsch. Librs. (bd. dirs. 1976-80, pres. 1979-80). Address: 1570 Westfield Ave Ann Arbor MI 48103-5740

DUNLAP, ELLEN ROE, music educator; b. Savannah, Ga., June 1, 1966; d. George Ryburn and MarySue Littlewood Roe; 1 child, William David. MusM in Edn., Ga. So. U., 1994. Gen. music tchr. Savannah (Ga.) Chatham Bd. Of Edn., 1989—94, strings orch. dir. Fine and Performing Arts Academies, 1994—. Founder, dir. Savannah (Ga.) Summer Strings, 2003—; founder, coord. String Fling, Savannah, 2000—; adj. prof. Armstrong Atlantic State U., Savannah, 1999—; music min. Baptist Ch., Savannah, 1994—99. Author: Rodeo; Discipline Based Music Education unit of study, 1994, Little Train of Cipira: Disciplined Based Music Education unit of study, 1994. Youth choir dir. Wilmington Is United Meth. Ch., Savannah, 1994—95. Mem.: Ga. Music Educators Assn. (assoc.; dist. one orch. chair 2003). Office: Savannah Chatham County Public Schools 208 Bull St Savannah GA 31401

DUNLAP, ELLEN S. library administrator; b. Nashville, Oct. 12, 1951; d. Arthur Wallace and Elizabeth (Majors) Smith; m. Arthur H. Dunlap, Jr., Dec. 27, 1972 (dec. 1977); m. Frank Armstrong, May 11, 1979; 1 child, Libbie Sarah. BA, U. Tex., Austin, 1972, MLS, 1974. Rsch. assoc. Humanities Rsch. Ctr. U. Tex., Austin, 1973-76, rsch. libr., 1976-83; exec. dir. Rosenbach Mus. and Library, Phila., 1983-92; pres. Am. Antiquarian Soc., Worcester, Mass., 1992—. Bd. dirs. Rsch. Librs. Group, Inc., Mountain View, Calif.; dir. 18th Century Short Title Catalogue/N.Am., 1992—. Mem. acad. affairs com. Winterthur Mus., 1995—; dir. Worcester Mcpl. Rsch. Bur., 1993—; mem. fin. com. Town of West Boylston, Mass., 1997—, chmn., 2001—; corporator Greater Worcester Cmty. Found., Mass., 1997—; pres. Mass. Found. for Humanities, 2002—; bd. dirs. Rare Books Sch., U. Va., 1994—. Mass. Found. for Humanities, 1996—. Mem. Am. Antiquarian Soc., Mass. Hist. Soc., Colonial Soc. Mass., Grolier Club (N.Y.C.), Worcester Club. Office: Am Antiquarian Soc 185 Salisbury St Worcester MA 01609-1636

DUNLAP, KAREN F. BROWN, academic administrator; BA, Mich. State U.; MS, Tenn. State U.; PhD Mass Comm., U. Tenn. Dean reporting, writing and editing faculty The Poynter Inst., St. Petersburg, Fla., pres., 2003—. Bd. trustees Poynter; reporter Nashbille Banner, Macon News, St. Petersburgs Times. Co-author: The Effective Editor: How to Lead Your Staff to Better Writing and Better Teamwork, The Editorial Eye. Office: The Poynter Inst 801 3rd St S Saint Petersburg FL 33701

DUNLAP, PATRICIA C. state legislator; b. Rochester, N.H., Nov. 6, 1926; Grad. h.s. Mem. N.H. Ho. of Reps., mem. comm., small bus., consumer affairs, econ. devel. coms., also mem. com. environment and agr. Ward clk., Rochester, NH, 1991—92; supr. checklist, 1992; bank customer rels. rep., 90. Treas. Gafney Home for Aged Mgmt. Bd., 1992—; asst. treas. 1st Ch. Congl., 1992-95, fin. sec., 1996—. Mem. DAR (asst. treas. Mary Torr chpt. 1992-94), OWLS (treas. 2001—). Office: NH House of Reps 107 N State St Concord NH 03301-4334

DUNLOP, DOROTHY D. statistician; BS, Wheaton Coll., 1972; MHS, Johns Hopkins U., 1974; PhD, Northwestern U., 1990. Statistician Northwestern U., Evanston, Ill., 1991—. Author: (book) Statistics and Data Analysis, 2000. Mem.: Am. Statis. Assn. (pres. Northeastern Ill. chpt. 2000—00, Chpt. Svc. award 2002).

DUNLOP, KAREN OWEN, lawyer; b. 1966; BS, Georgetown U., 1987; MA, U. Va., 1989, JD, 1992. Bar: Ill. 1992. With Sidley Austin Brown & Wood, Chgo., 1992—, ptnr., 2001—. Mem.: Am. Health Lawyers Assn. (vice chair health sys. transactions com.). Office: Sidley Austin Brown and Wood Bank One Plz 10 S Dearborn St Chicago IL 60603*

DUNLOP, MARIANNE, retired English as second language educator; b. Niobrara, Nebr, Mar. 14, 1933; d. Harvey Wesley LaBranche and Karen Sanna Arneson; m. Richard Campbell Dunlop, Apr. 26, 1959; 1 child, Christopher Campbell. BA, Vt. Coll., 1985, MA, 1989, Bd. dir./bd. mem. The Sargent House Mus., Gloucester, Mass., 1992-96; ESL educator Penasquitos Laubach Literacy Ctr., San Diego, 1999—2002; ret., 2002. Author: (book) Judith Sargent Murray: Champion of Social Justice, 1993; editor: (book) Judith Sargent Murray: Her First 100 Letters, 1995; writer, contbr.: (book) Standing Before Us: Unitarian Universalist Women and Social Reform 1776-1936, 1999; spkr., contbr. (documentary) Judith Sargent Murray: 18th Century Feminist. Officer, bd. dirs. Sargent House Mus., Gloucester, Mass., 1992—96, mem. adv. bd., 1996—; ESL educator Penasquitos Laubach Literacy Ctr., San Diego, 1999—2002, mem. Sargent House Mus. Mem. Virginia Woolf's Outsider Soc., Unitarian Universalist Women's Heritage Soc. Unitarian Universalist. Avocation: honoring otherness. Home: 11032 Ipai Ct San Diego CA 92127-1382

DUNMEYER, SARAH LOUISE FISHER, retired health care consultant; b. Ft. Wayne, Ind., Apr. 13, 1935; d. Frederick Law and Jeanette Blose (Stults) Fisher; m. Herbert W. Dunmeyer, Sept. 9, 1967; children: Jodi, Lisa. BS, U. Mich., 1957; MS, Temple U., 1966; EdD, U. San Francisco, 1983. Lic. clin. lab. technologist, Calif. Instr. med. tech. U. Vt., Burlington, 1966-67, Northeastern U., Boston, 1967-68, instr. lab. asst. program, 1968-70; educator, coord. sch. med. tech. Children's Hosp., San Francisco, 1970-73; dir. course devel. for continuing edn. program Pacific Presbyn. Med. Ctr., San Francisco, 1974-82; project mgr., cons. Peabody Mktg. Decisions, San Francisco, 1983-87; sr. rsch. assoc. Inst. for Health and Aging, U. Calif., San Francisco, 1986-89; rsch. analyst student acad. svcs. U. Calif., San Francisco, 1991-94; external cons. Health Care Consulting Svcs., San Francisco, 1986-97; clin. lab. scientist Kaiser Hosp., San Francisco, 1989—2002, ret. Seminar presenter Am. Assn. Blood Banks, San Francisco, 1976, Am. Soc. Clin. Pathologists, Miami Beach, Fla., 1977, Ann. Meeting of Am. Soc. Med. Technology, Atlanta, 1977; site surveyor Nat. Accrediting Agy. for Clin. Lab. Scis., Chgo., 1974-80. Contbr. articles to profl. jours.

DUNN, ANNE YVONNE, advocacy organization executive; b. Detroit, Feb. 15, 1948; d. Reginald King and Gwendolyn Leah (Reynolds) Hawkins; divorced; 1 child, James Jay Dunn II. BA, Calif. State Coll., L.A., 1985. Coun. dep. 1st Dist., L.A., 1980-85; mgr. Cmty. Devel. Dept. Pacoima Enterprise Zone, L.A., 1985-90; asst. exec. dir. Commn. on the Status of Women, L.A., 1990—. Singer Jubilee Singers, 1968—. Founding mem. L.A. County Women's Caucus, 1991, L.A. City Domestic Violence Task Force, 1995, Women Against Racism, L.A., 1995; mem., co-chair L.A. County Domestic Violence Coun., 1992-97. Recipient certs. of appreciation L.A. City Coun. and Mayor, 1981, 82, 90, 91, plaque L.A. City Coun., 1996, commendation U.S. Assembly State of Calif., 1990, L.A. County Bd. Suprs., 1995, 96. Mem. Women's Legis. Coaliation, Nat. Assn. Commns. on Women, Albert McNeil Jubilee Singers, William Grant Still Performing Arts Soc. (v.p. 1989—). Avocations: performing arts, creative arts, travel, reading, saltwater aquariums. Office: Commn on Status of Women 200 N Main St CHE 7th Fl Los Angeles CA 90012

DUNN, BONNIE BRILL, chemist; b. Bethesda, Md., Mar. 10, 1953; m. William H Dunn, July 13, 1974 (div.); children: Daniel Brill, Vanessa Thompson; m. Ronald G Manning, Aug. 2, 1996. AA, Montgomery Coll., 1972; BS in Food Sci., U. Md., 1974, MS in Food Chemistry and Stats., 1978, PhD in Food Chemistry, 1982. Rsch. asst. U. Md., College Park, 1976-79, tchg. asst., 1977-80; rschr. divsn. chemistry and physics U.S. FDA, Washington, 1979; statistian USDA, Beltsville, Md., 1980, rschr., 1980-82; radiochemist Positron Emission Tomography; head quality assurance NIH, Bethesda, 1984-93; rev. chemist FDA, Rockville, Md., 1993-95, expert scientist, 1996, dep. dir. divsn. new drug chemistry, 1996—2003; scientfic review admintsr. NIH, Bethesda, Md., 2003—. Contbr. articles to profl jours. Secy, vpres PTA, 1988—94; mem PTA Forest Knolls Elem, Montgomery County, Md., 1988—94; mem exec bd dirs PTA Eastern Mid Sch, Montgomery County, Md., 1992—94; leader Girl Scouts US, 1988—91; bd dirs Olney Children Ballet Theater, 1996—99. Recipient Performance Award, NIH, 1987—92, USPHS, 1993—96; fellow Nat Leadership, 1997—98. Mem.: Soc Nuclear Med, Am Chemistry Soc. Home: 9901 Indian Ln Silver Spring MD 20901-2521 Office: NIH 6707 Democracy Blvd Bethesda MD 20892-5469 Business E-Mail: dunnbo@mail.nih.gov.

DUNN, CAROLA, writer; b. London, Eng., Apr. 1946; d. Margaret and Max Brauer; 1 child, Joseph. BA, U. Manchester, Eng., 1967. Author: (novels) Toblethorpe Manor, 1981, Lavender Lady, 1983, (novel) Angel, 1984, The Miser's Sister, 1984, Lord Iverbrook's Heir, 1986, The Man in the Green Coat (aka Gabrielle's Gamble), 1987, Smugglers' Summer, 1987, Miss Hartwell's Dilemma, 1988, Black Sheep's Daughter, 1989, A Poor Relation, 1990, Lady in the Briars, 1990, A Susceptible Gentleman, 1990, Two Corinthians, 1990, A Lord for Miss Larkin, 1991, Byron's Child, 1991, Polly and the Prince, 1991, The Fortune Hunters, 1991, The Frog Earl, 1992 (Reviewer's Choice Best Regency Comedy Award of Excellence, 1992), The Road to Gretna, 1992, Miss Jacobson's Journey, 1992, My Lord Winter, 1992, Thea's Marquis, 1993, Ginnie-Come-Lately, 1993, His Lordship's Reward, 1994, The Captain's Inheritance, 1994, Death at Wentwater Court, 1994, The Lady and the Rake, 1995, The Winter Garden Mystery, 1995, The Tudor Secret, 1995, Requiem for a Mezzo, 1996, Damsel in Distress, 1997, The Babe and the Baron, 1997, Mayhem and Miranda, 1997, Murder on the Flying Scotsman, 1997, Dead in the Water, 1998, The Improper Governess, 1998, Crossed Quills, 1998, Styx and Stones, 1999, Rattle His Bones, 2000, To Davy Jones Below, 2001, The Case of the Murdered Muckraker, 2002, Mistletoe and Murder, 2002 (IMBA bestseller), (novels) Die Laughing, 2003, A Mourning Wedding, 2004, numerous others. Reader SMART, Eugene, 1998—2003. Mem.: Sisters in Crime. Avocations: gardening, reading, walking, travel, dogs. Personal E-mail: carola@sinc-ic.org.

DUNN, DEBRA L. computer company executive; B.Comparative Econs., Brown U., Providence; M.Bus., Harvard U. Exec. devel. mgr. corp. tng. divsn. Hewlett-Packard Co., Palo Alto, Calif., 1983—86, various devel. and mfg. mgmt. positions, 1986—92, mfg. mgr., 1992—93, mktg. mgr., 1993—96, gen. mgr. video comm. divsn., 1996—98, gen. mgr. exec. com., 1998, v.p., 1999—2000, v.p. strategy and corp. ops., 2000—02, sr. v.p. corp. affairs, 2002—. Mem. UN Info. and Comm. Tech. Task Force; bd. dirs. Opportunities Industrialization Ctr. West, BayCat. Office: Hewlett Packard Co 3000 Hanover St Palo Alto CA 94304*

DUNN, DORIS MARJORY, retired educator, volunteer; b. Chgo., Jan. 7, 1921; d. William Christian and Mary Esther (Hoffman) Rose; m. Jack Harold Wheeler Dunn, Sept. 19, 1945 (dec. June 1978); children: Randall L., Jon G., Bonham. BS in Edn., Ind. U., 1942; postgrad., Northwestern U., 1943-44; MS, Valparaiso U., 1973. Life lic. in teaching, Ind. Tchr. Crown Point (Ind.) High Sch., 1963-74, Lowell (Ind.) High Sch., 1942-45; sch. tchr., jr. coll. tchr., 1976-78. Asst. to engring.libr. U. Tex., Austin, 1947-49. Pres. LWV, Crown Point, 1974; pres.-elect Good Samaritan Hosp. Aux., v.p., 1988-89, pres., 1989-90; buyer Good Samaritan Gift Shop, 1989—; chmn. ways and means Assistance League, 1988-89, regional coun. rep., 1990-91, mem. resource devel. nat. bd., 1991-98; pres. Luckiamute Water Bd., 1988—; mem. Republican Senatorial Inner Circle, State of Oreg., 1997-98. Mem. P.E.O. (pres. 1989-90), Corvallis Country Club. Ladies Orgn. (pres. 1989-90), Kappa Kappa Kappa (pres. 1975), Delta Kappa Gamma. Methodist. Avocations: wood carving, golf, flying, stained glass creation, travel. Home: 12260 Rolling Hills Rd Monmouth OR 97361-9758

DUNN, GAIL PEDERZOLI, English language educator; b. Springfield, Mass., July 28, 1947; d. Eugene A. and Ruth E. (Eaton) Pederzoli; m. John H. Dunn, Nov. 19, 1982. BA in English, Elmira Coll., 1969; MA in English, U. Wis., 1970; MEd in Guidance Psych. Svcs., Springfield Coll., 1976. Prof. English Springfield Tech. C.C., 1970—. Recipient Excellence in Teaching award Nat. Inst. for Staff and Orgn. Devel., 1995-96, Joseph J. Deliso Endowed Chair award for excellence in tchg. Springfield Tech. C.C., 1998. Mem. NEA, Nat. Mus. Women in Arts (charter), Mass. Tchrs. Assn., Nat. Women's History Mus. (charter). Democrat. Roman Catholic. Avocations: reading, film, gardening, cooking, antiquing. Home: 102 Lakeside Dr Monson MA 01057-9735 Office: Springfield Tech CC 1 Armory Sq Springfield MA 01105-1204

DUNN, GLORIA JEAN, artist; b. Detroit, Apr. 21, 1927; d. Donald Stanton and Etta Florence (Barber) Hopkins; m. Eugene Oliver Dunn, Dec. 28, 1944; children: Michael Eugene, Patricia Ann. Student, Wayne County C.C., Taylor, Mich., 1987-90. Instr. arts and crafts YWCA, Wyandotte, Mich., 1963-86; instr. painting and calligraphy, adult edn. Lincoln Park (Mich.) Sch. Sys., 1982-90; owner, mgr. Pen, Brush and Anvil Studio, Southgate, Mich., 1975-95, Gloria Hopkins Dunn Studio of Fine Art, Wyandotte, 1995—; represented by Home Gallery, Taylor, Mich., Swann Gallery, Lincoln Park, Mich., Fuenteo Gallery, Wyandotti. Mem. adv. bd. Wyandotte St. Art Fair, 1962—, organizer, co-chair, 1962-81. One-woman shows include Taylor (Mich.) Cmty. Libr., Southgate (Mich.) City Hall, Swann Gallery, Detroit, Taylor (Mich.) City Hall, Trenton (Mich.) City Hall. Mem. Southgate Cultural Commn., 1974-82, 91-99. Recipient Cmty. Svc. award City of Southgate, 1978, Hon. Tribute, City of Wyandotte, 1982, 20 Yrs. Dedication to Art award City of Wyandotte, 1991, Salute to Excellence award Downriver Coun. for the Arts, 2003. Mem. Acanthus Art Soc. Wyandotte (pres. 1994—), Downriver Arts and Crafts Guild (exhibit chair 1995, 96, 97, 98, 99, 2000, jury chair 2000-01), Art Ambience (historian 1993—, bd. dirs., v.p. 1999—, pres. 2001-02, Downriver Coun. Arts Salute to Excellence award, 2003), Nat. Assn. Fine Arts. Avocations: swimming, photography, gardening, riding. Office: 2930 Biddle St Wyandotte MI 48192-5214

DUNN, GRACE VERONICA, retired executive secretary; b. Bklyn. d. Richard William and Grace Veronica (Mason) D. BA, Our Lady of the Lake U., 1940; postgrad., Columbia U., 1958. Sec. Hunt Oil Co., Dallas, 1947-48, Standard Oil Co. (N.J.), N.Y.C., 1955-59, Pan Am. Health Orgn., Washington, 1964-76. Mem., Vol. Stephanie Roper Com., Upper Marlboro, Md., 1987-92, Friends of the Kennedy Ctr., Washington, 1991—; soprano soloist Holy Trinity Cath. Ch., Dallas, 1945-47, Ch. of the Incarnation Episcopal Ch., Dallas, 1945-47; soloist White House Christmas Tree, 1988. Grad. fellow Karl Schultz Found., 1940; pvt. scholar Elisabeth Schumann, N.Y.C., 1948-52. Roman Catholic.

DUNN, JENNIFER BLACKBURN, congresswoman; b. Seattle, Wash., July 29, 1941; d. John Charles and Helen (Gorton) Blackburn; div.; children: Bryant, Reagan. Student, U. Wash., 1960-62; BA in English Lit., Stanford U., 1963. Sys. engr. IBM, 1964-69; with King County Dept. of Assessments, 1979-80; former chmn. Rep. Party State of Wash., 1981-92; mem. U.S. Congress from 8th Wash. dist., Washington, 1993—. Bd. dirs. Nat. Endowment Democracy; mem. ways and means com., homeland sec. com., econ. com.; mem. adv. bd. Internat. Rep. Inst.; participant Preparatory Commn. World Conf. Status of Women, Nairobi, 1985, World Econ. Forum, Davos, Switzerland, 2000. Del. Rep. Nat. Conv., 1980, 84, 88; presdl. apptd. adv. coun. Historic Preservation, adv. coun. volunteerism SBA; apptd. presdl. commn. on debates; N.W. Regional Dir. Met. Operal Regional Auditions; mem. Jr. League of Seattle Named one of 25 Smartest Women in Am., Mirabella mag., one of 10 Most Powerful Women in Wash., Washington Law and Politics mag. Mem. Internat. Women's Forum (Wash. chpt.), Gamma Phi Beta. Republican. Office: US Ho Reps 1501 Longworth Ho Office Bldg Washington DC 20515-4708*

DUNN, JERI R. food products executive; Grad., Edinboro State U. With Parker White Metal Co., Curtis Industries; assoc. dir. application systems Stouffer's Hotels; asst. v.p. tech. and standards Nestle SA, Switzerland; v.p., chief info. officer Nestle USA; with Tyson Foods, Inc., Springdale, Ark., 2001—02, sr. v.p., chief info. officer, 2002—. Office: Tyson Foods Inc 2210 W Oaklawn Dr Springdale AR 72762-6999*

DUNN, LIN, professional basketball coach; b. Nashville, May 10, 1947; BS in Health and Phys. Edn., U. Tenn., Martin, 1969; MS in Phys. Edn., U. Tenn., 1970. Women's basketball coach Austin Peay State, 1970-76, U. Miss., Oxford, 1977-78, U. Miami, 1979-87, Perdue U., W. Lafayette, Ind., 1987-96; head coach Portland Power, Oreg., 1996-98; draft consultant & assist. coach Houston Comets, 1998-99; head coach & gen. mgr. Seattle Storm, 1999—. Asst. coach silver-medal winning Select Team, 1986, gold-medal winning Pam Am. Games, 1987, Select Team, 1989, gold-medal winning Goodwill Games, gold-medal winning World Championship teams, 1990, Olympic bronze-medal winning team, Barcelona, Spain, 1992; head coach bronze-medal winning R. Williams Jones Cup team, Taipei,

Taiwan, 1995; mem. Player Selection Com. that overseas the selection of players for all U.S.A. basketball teams. Achievements include being the first Big Ten coach to serve on an Olympic staff. Office: Seattle Storm 351 Elliott Ave W Seattle WA 98119-4101 E-mail: info@portlandpower.com.

DUNN, LINDA KAY, physician; b. Grand Rapids, Mich., Jan. 11, 1947; d. Roger John and Mary Kathryn (Bouwer) Kloote; m. Jeffrey Marc Dunn, June 3, 1972; children: David Alan, Kathryn Ann. AB in Chemistry, Hope Coll., 1968; MD, U. Mich., 1972. Diplomate Am. Bd. Ob-Gyn, Am. Bd. Maternal-Fetal Medicine, Am. Bd. Med. Genetics. Resident in ob-gyn. U. Mich., Ann Arbor, 1972-75, fellow in maternal-fetal medicine, 1975-77; hon. rsch. registrar St. Mary's Hosp., London, 1977-78; dir. of perinatology Temple U. Sch. Medicine, Phila., 1978-79, assoc. prof. ob-gyn, 1991-97; dir. subsect. on genetics Pa. Hosp., Phila., 1980-90; pres Medigen, Inc., Phila., 1987-90; dir. maternal-fetal medicine and genetics Abington (Pa.) Meml. Hosp., 1991-97. Med. dir. Comprehensive Maternal and Infant Svcs., Phila., 1987-90; pres. Abington Perinatal Assocs., P.C., 1993-97; dir. maternal-fetal medicine, chair dept. ob-gyn. Allegheny U., 1997-99; pres., CEO Allegheny U. Hosp. at City Ave.; chair dept. ob-gyn. Chestnut Hill Hosp., Phila., 1999—. Fellow Am. Coll. Ob-Gyn.; mem. AMA, Soc. Maternal Fetal Medicine, Am. Soc. Human Genetics, Am. Coll. Med. Genetics, Pa. State Med. Soc., Phila. Obstet. Soc., U. Mich. Med. Ctr. Alumni Soc. (chair 1996), Norman Miller Gynecologic Soc. (pres. 1996). Mem. Soc. Of Friends. Avocations: travel, piano. Office: Chestnut Hill Hosp 8835 Germantown Ave Philadelphia PA 19118-2765 E-mail: dunnl@chh.org.

DUNN, LORETTA LYNN, lawyer; b. Owensboro, Ky, Dec. 3, 1955; d. John Edwin and Arnetta Mae (Trunnell) D.; m. Herbert S. Lunenfeld, Oct. 18, 1985; 1 child, Jack W. BA, U. Ky., 1976, JD, 1979; LLM, Georgetown U., 1983. Bar: Ky. 1979, D.C. 1984. Staff atty. U.S. Senate Com. Commerce, Sci. and Transp., Washington, 1979-86, minority counsel, 1982-86, sr. trade counsel, 1987-93; asst. sec. for legis. and intergovernmental affairs Dept. Commerce, 1993-95; v.p. govt. affairs Hughes Electronics, Arlington, Va., 1995—. Named Order of Coif. Mem. D.C. Bar Assn., Ky. Bar Assn., Washington Internat. Trade Assn., Women Internat. Trade, Trade Policy Forum, Phi Beta Kappa. Office: Hughes Electronics Ste 810 555 11th St NW Washington DC 20004-1310

DUNN, M. CATHERINE, college administrator, educator; b. Chgo., Mar. 26, 1934; d. John and Catherine (Donovan) Dunn BA, Ariz. State U., 1968, MA, 1970, PhD, 1977. Cert. tchr., Iowa, Ariz. Tchr. St. Mathew Sch., Phoenix, 1956-60; tchr. St. Vincent Sch., Chg., 1960-68; asst. prin. Carroll Sch., Lincoln, Ill., 1970-73; mem. faculty Clarke Coll., Dubuque, Iowa, 1973-79, v.p. devel., 1979-84, pres., 1984—. Bd. dirs. Am. Trust Bank, Dubuque, 1989—; cons. in field. Bd. dirs. Internat. Student Leadership, Notre Dame, Ind., 1975—, Med. Assocs. HMO, Dubuque, 1980—, Jr. Achievement, 1982—; mem. Iowa Dept. Transp. Commn., Ames, 1989—. Named One of Ten Outstanding Leaders in Dubuque Telegraph Herald newspaper, 1987, 88, 89. Mem. Am. Coun. Edn., Coun. Ind. Colls. (bd. dirs.), Am. Assn. Cath. Colls., Iowa Assn. Coll. Pres. (bd. dirs. 1984—), Ariz. State Alumni Assn., Dubuque C. of C. (mem. coun. 1973—, bd. dirs. 1986—, Outstanding Civic Leader award 1974, Civic Svc. award 1993), Coun. Advancement and Support Edn. (bd. dirs.), Phi Delta Kappa, Pi Lambda Theta. Avocations: cooking; music; walking; traveling. Home: 2350 Clarke Crest Dr Dubuque IA 52001-3125 Office: Clarke Coll 1550 Clarke Dr Dubuque IA 52001-3117

DUNN, MARGARET M. general surgeon, educator, university official; b. Freeport, N.Y., Sept. 8, 1954; d. Howard James and Evelyn Ann (Madden) D.; m. William Anthony Spohn, July 4, 1982; children: Christopher, Marie. BS, Pa. State U., 1974; MD, Jefferson Med. Coll., 1977. Diplomate Am. Bd. Surgery. Resident in surgery Montefiore Hosp., Bronx, N.Y., 1977-82; prof. surgery Wright Sch. Medicine, Dayton, Ohio, 1982—, assoc. dean for faculty and clin. affairs, 1999—. Fellow ACS; mem. Assn. Women Surgeons, Am. Med. Women's Assn., Ctrl. Surg. Assn., Soc. Surgery Alimentary Tract. Office: Wright State U Sch Medicine 3640 Col Glenn Hwy Dayton OH 45435

DUNN, MARY MAPLES, former university dean; b. Sturgeon Bay, Wis., Apr. 6, 1931; d. Frederic Arthur and Eva (Moore) Maples; m. Richard S. Dunn, Sept. 3, 1960; children— Rebecca Cofrin, Cecilia Elizabeth. BA, Coll. William and Mary, 1954, LHD (hon.), 1989; MA, Bryn Mawr Coll., 1956, PhD, 1959; LLD (hon.), Marietta Coll., 1987, Amherst Coll., 1987, Brown U., 1989; LittD (hon.), Lafayette Coll., 1988, Haverford Coll., 1991; LHD (hon.), Transylvania U., 1991, U. Pa., 1995, Mt. Holyok Coll., 1996, Smith Coll., 1998, U. Mass., 1998, U. South, 1999. Faculty Bryn Mawr Coll., 1958-85, prof. history, 1974-85; acting dean Undergrad. Coll. Bryn Mawr (Pa.) Coll., 1978-79, dean, 1980-85; pres. Smith Coll., Northampton, Mass., 1985-95; Carl and Lily Pforzheimer Found. dir. Arthur and Elizabeth Libr. Radcliffe Coll., 1995-99; acting pres., acting dean Inst. for Advanced Study Harvard U., 1999—2000. Author: William Penn: Politics and Conscience, 1967; editor: Political Essay on the Kingdom of New Spain (Alexander von Humboldt), 1972, rev., 1988, (with Richard S. Dunn) Papers of William Penn, vols. I-IV, 1979-87. Trustee The Clark Sch. for the Deaf, 1988-95, Acad. Mus., 1985-95, Hist. Deerfield, Inc., 1986—, Bingham Fund for Teaching Excellence at Transylvania U., 1987—, John Carter Brown Libr., 1994-99, NOW/Legal Def. and Edn. Fund., 1996—, Marlboro Music, 1996—. Recipient Disting. Tchg. award Lindbeck Found., 1969, Radcliffe medal Radcliffe Assn., 2001; fellow Inst. Advanced Study Princeton U., 1974. Mem. Berkshire Conf. Women Historians (pres. 1973-75), Coordinating Com. Women Hist. Profession (pres. 1975-77), Am. Hist. Assn., Am. Philos. Soc. (co-exec. officer), Inst. Early Am. History and Culture (chmn. adv. council 1977-80), Mass. Hist. Soc., Phi Beta Kappa. Office: American Philosophical Society Exec Office 104 S Fifth St Philadelphia PA 19106-3287

DUNN, MELANIE LEA, information technology manager; d. Hal Clayton and Diane Kiel Klopfer; m. Bradley Stuart Dunn, Oct. 21, 2000; 1 child, Jordan Stuart. AA, Fla. C.C., Jacksonville, 1995; BA in Psychology, U. Ctrl. Fla., 1998. Customer svc. staff SunTrust Banks, Inc., Orlando, Fla., 1995—98; project mgr. Hewitt Assocs., Inc., Orlando, 1998—. Methodist. Avocations: exercising, creative memories.

DUNN, PATRICIA ANN, school system administrator, English language educator; b. Englewood, N.J., Mar. 17, 1942; d. Thomas Joseph and Rosanna Valerie (Cummings) D.; m. James Edward Egan, 1963 (div. 1974); 1 child, Deirdre Tracy. BA in English Edn., William Paterson U., 1963, MA in Communication Arts, 1974; postgrad., Montclair (N.J.) State U., 1986—. Cert. tchr., N.J., N.Y.; cert. prin., supr., N.J. Tchr. English, Intermediate Sch. Dist. 218, Bklyn., 1965-66, tchr. English and humanities, 1966-67, co-chmn. dept. humanities, 1967-68; tchr. English Midland Park (N.J.) Schs., 1969-91, staff devel. coord., 1987—, dir. curriculum, instrn., staff devel., 1991—. Coord. bus. workshops Women in Bus., 1983, Stress, 1983. Editor N.J. Staff Devel. Coun. Newsletter, 1988-91; contbr. articles to profl. publs. Co-founder, coord. Ministry for Separated and Divorced Caths., Montclair, 1983-86. Recipient N.J. Woman of Distinction award World of People. Mem. ASCD, AAUW, N.J. Prins. and Suprs. Assn., Nat. Staff Devel. Coun., N.J. Staff Devel. Coun. (co-founder, dir. 1991-94, pres. 1995-96, trustee 1997—, editor Exchange 1996—98), N.J. Ctr. for Achievement of Sch. Excellence, N.J. Coalition Essential Schs. (del. to nat. congress 1996—98, co-chair exec. bd. 1995-2002), Nat. Coun. Tchrs. English, Midland Park Adminstrs. and Suprs. Assn. (pres. 1996—), Dramund Springs Club. Democrat. Roman Catholic. Avocations: dance, reading. Office: Midland Park High Sch 250 Prospect St Midland Park NJ 07432-1398

DUNN, PATRICIA C. investment company executive; AB in Journalism and Econ., U. Calif., Berkeley. With Barclays Global Investors, N.A., San Francisco, 1976—, chmn. Bd. dirs. Hewlett-Packard Co. Contbr. articles to profl. jours. Mem. new media bd., U. Calif. Sch. Journalism, Berkeley. Office: Barclays Global Investors 45 Fremont St San Francisco CA 94105-2204

DUNN, REBECCA JO, state legislator; d. Francis G. and Eldred (Wagner) D. BA, U. S.D., 1967; MA, U. Hawaii, 1972. Senator S.D. State Senate Dist. 15, 1993—2001, asst. minority leader, mem. legis. exec. bd., mem. corrections com. Motivational spkr. Author: The Pearl of Potentiality, Co-A, 1979. Bd. dirs. S.D. Humanities Found. Mem. PEO, Downtown Rotary, Hawaii Yacht Club, Kappa Alpha Theta. Home: 320 N Summit Ave Sioux Falls SD 57104-2933

DUNN, REBECCA M. telecommunications industry executive; b. Selma, Ala. BS in Math., Auburn U., 1970. Asst. engr. South Ctrl. Bell, 1970, engrng. assoc., staff engr., asst. engrng. mgr. costs, dist. mgr. capital recovery, 1975, ops. mgr. regulatory, asst. v.p. pub. affairs, 1984, gen. mgr. bus. mktg. for Ala. and Miss. ops., 1987—89; v.p. corp. affairs BellSouth Corp., Atlanta, 1989—91, v.p. human resources and corp. svcs., 1991—99, v.p. shared svcs., sr. v.p. corp. compliance, corp. sec., 2001—. Mem. adv. coun. Coll. of Bus., Auburn U.; vol. United Way; bd. dirs. Atlanta History Ctr., Homeward Inc., Ctrl. Atlanta Progress. Office: BellSouth Corp 1155 Peachtree St NE Atlanta GA 30309-3610

DUNN, SANDRA E. insurance agent; b. Asheville, NC, Mar. 10, 1959; d. Riley Jefferson Wells and Margaret (Worley Wells) Bates; Cert. ins. counselor, profl. ins. woman. File clk. then personal ins. sales BB & T Insurance, Asheville, NC, 1977-80, office and agy. mgr., 1980-84, asst. v.p., 1992, v.p., MIS dir., 1996-99, v.p., dir. agy. svcs., 1999—, sr. v.p., 2002—. Computer systems trainer and data conversion specialist BB & T Ins., Charlotte, NC, 1994—96; design rev. and product devel. chair AMS Users Group, 1997—2000, bd. dirs., 2000, exec. bd., 04. Mem. Nat. Assn. Insurance Profls., Charlotte Assn. Insurance Women, Cert. Profl. Ins. Women. Avocations: snow skiing, reading, power walking, golf, baking. Home: 125 Clearwater Ln Mooresville NC 28117-7529 Office: BB & T Insurance Svcs 5925 Carnegie Blvd Ste 400 Charlotte NC 28209-4659

DUNN, SHANNON, Olympic athlete; b. Steamboat Springs, Colo., Nov. 26, 1972; Mem. U.S. Olympic Snowboarding Team. Named 4th pl., World Championships, 1997, 1st pl., World Cup, 1996, 5th pl., 1995, 4 time winner, U.S. Snowboard Grand Prix; recipient Bronze medal Snowboarding Halfpipe, Nagano Olympics, 1998. Achievements include one of the dominant halfpipe competitors in the world; key athlete in the progression of women's snowboarding. Office: c/o US Ski and Snowboarding Assn PO Box 100 Park City UT 84060-0100

DUNN, VIRGINIA, artist, community volunteer; b. Long Island, N.Y., Dec. 11, 1951; d. James Joseph and Margaret Virginia Dunn. Student, Lynn U., 1970—71, SUNY, Purchase, 1972-75, Propersie Sch. of Art, 1975-76, Lynn U., Boca Raton, Fla. Nurse's aide St. Joseph's Hosp., Stamford, Conn., 1967-70; with advt. dept. Cuisinart, Greenwich, Conn., 1977-89. One-woman shows include Greenwich Hosp., 2002, Garden Cafe, Greenwich, 2002, Nathaniel Witheral, exhibitions include Hurlbutt Gallery, Greenwich (Conn.) Libr., various yrs., Gertrude White Gallery, Greenwich, 1998—2002, Greenwich Garden Ctr., Cos Cob, Conn., 1989—2002 (honorable mention, 2002, 2d place, 2 honorable mentions), Ferguson Libr., Stamford, Conn., 1993—2002, Hammond Mus. & Japanese Stroll Garden, North Salem, N.Y., 1993—2001, Whitby Sch., Greenwich, 1994, Rush-Holley House, Cos Cob, 1994, Wilton (Conn.) Libr., 1995—96, E.C. Potter Gallery, Greenwich, 1996—2002, The Coffee Shoppe, Greenwich Hosp., 1997, Stamford Art Assn., 1999 (3d Pl. award), Greenwichart, Stamford, 1999, Art Soc. Old Greenwich Sidewalk Shows, 1999—2002, Stamford Art Assn., 2001, Westfield Ct., 2001, Greenwich Libr., Flinn Gallery, 2001, 2002, Landson Park, Katona, N.Y., 2001, Flynn Gallery, Greenwich Libr., 2001—02, Landson Park, Katona, N.Y., 2002, St. Raphael's Hosp., New Haven, 2002, Hammond Mus., 2002, Circe d'Art Gallery, Rowayton Art Ctr. Recipient Honorable Mention award Greenwich Art Soc., 1999, other awards for art. Mem. Oriental Brush Artist Guild (mailing com. 1993-2002), Eastern Arts Connection, The Greenwich Art Soc. (mailing com. 1988-89, Second Place award 2000), The Art Soc. of Old Greenwich (hostess 1988-89, 2d place award 2002, numerous honorable mentions), Conn. Graphic Art Ctr., Greenwich Arts Coun., The Stamford Art Assn., The Hammond Mus., Women in the Arts, Rowayton Art Assn. Avocations: art, music, travel, cats, American Indian flute. Home: 12 Newton Rd Gaylordsville CT 06755

DUNNAM, MARIE MCCLURE, social worker; b. Spartanburg, S.C., July 6, 1945; d. Harold Gordon and Martha Elizabeth (Lynch) McC.; m. Charles Eugene Smith, Oct. 1, 1988. BA in Journalism, La. State U., 1967; MSW, U. S.C., 1979. Case mgr. I Spartanburg (S.C) County Dept. Social Svcs., 1967-73, case mgr. II, 1973-74, adult svcs. supr., 1974-78; nursing home ombudsman Ombudsman Office-Gov.'s Office, Columbia, S.C., 1978-79; social svcs. program dir. II S.C. Dept. Social Svcs., Columbia, 1979-81; county social svcs. dir. I Oconee County Dept. Social Svcs., Walhalla, S.C., 1981-85; dir. adult svcs. S.C. Dept. Social Svcs., Columbia, 1985-88; county social svcs. dir. III Aiken (S.C.) County Dept. Social Svcs., 1988-93; dir. Office Cmty. Resource Devel. S.C. Dept. Social Svcs., Columbia, 1993—. Bd. dirs. Infant Mortality Task Force and Rev. Team, Aiken, 1989-93, Hitchcock Rehab. Ctr., Aiken, 1988-93; sponsor Coop. for Nat. Svc., Columbia, 1994-96; state govt. divsn. chair United Way of the Midlands, Columbia, S.C., 1997; United Way campaign coord. S.C. Dept. Social Svcs., 1996-97; sec., treas. Seneca Jr. Women's Club, 1983-85. Recipient Spirit of the Midlands award United Way of Midlands, 1997, Pres.'s award S.C. Social Welfare Forum 1987, resolution S.C. Ho. Reps., 1991, 93. Mem. NASW, S.C. Assn. Vol. Adminstrns., S.C. State Employee Assn. (bd. dirs. 1986—), S.C. Dirs. and Suprs. Assn. (v.p. 1983-85), Nat. Assn. Child Welfare Adminstrns. (regional rep. 1984-86), Nat. Bus. and Profl. Womens Club (chairperson spl. needs com. 1975-78). Office: SC Dept Social Svcs 1535 Confederate Ave Columbia SC 29201-1915

DUNNE, DONNALEE, artist, educator, writer; d. Joseph Waldemar Nelsen and Minnie Rebecca Hanson; m. Ralph Fred Dunne, Dec. 10, 1954; children: Kathy Ritscher, Michael, Randy, Tina Williams. BA in Art, Calif. State U., Fresno, 1993, MA in English, 1996, MA in Art, 1999. Instr. Calif. State U., Fresno, 1999—, Fresno City Coll., 1999—2003, Reedley (Calif.) Coll., 2000—. Webmaster Arts-Network.org, Fresno, Win Win Writers Group, Fresno; juror various art exhbns. Author: Quiet Electricity, 1999; contbr. articles to jours.; one-woman shows include, Fresno, 1999, 2003, Mill Valley, 2000, Paris, 2001, Barcelona, Spain, 2002, 2003, Madrid, 2002, 2003, Valencia, Spain, 2002, Toulouse, France, 2003, Florence, Italy, 2003. Mem.: Arts Network (founder), Golden Key, Phi Kappa Phi. E-mail: donnalee@cvip.net.

DUNNE, JUDITH DOYLE, information scientist, educator; b. Mineola, NY, Dec. 17, 1962; d. James Macdonnel and Lois Hart Doyle; m. Michael John Dunne, May 28, 1989. BS, North Adams State Coll., 1984. Elem. edn., art tchr. Rosary Acad., Watertown, Mass., 1985—86; 3d and 6th gr. math. tchr. St. Patrick's Sch., Watertown, Mass., 1986—91: art tchr. Holy Name, West Roxbury, Mass., 1991—96; Tech. coord. computer, art and math. tchr. Good Shepherd Sch., Perryville, Md., 1997—. Mem.: Nat. Cath. Edn. Assn. Avocations: crafts, skiing, ice skating, in-line skating. Office: Good Shepherd Sch 810 Aiken Ave Perryville MD 21903

DUNNE, LINDA, museum administrator; b. London, Jan. 26, 1953; arrived in U.S., 1953; d. James and Anita (Hodgson) Dunne; m. John Egner, Dec. 24, 1983. Adminstrv. asst. Cranbrook Acad. of Art/Mus., Bloomfield Hills, Mich., 1971—77, mus. adminstr., 1977—83, adminstrv. officer Cooper-Hewitt Mus., N.Y.C., 1983—, dep. dir., 1988—. Recipient Merit award, Smithsonian Instn., 1984; scholar, J. Paul Getty Trust, 1985. Home: 25 Mercer St Apt 2A New York NY 10013-5811 Office: Cooper-Hewitt Mus 2 E 91st St New York NY 10128-0669

DUNNE, MARY MAGUIRE, federal agency administrator, lawyer; BA, Coll. of New Rochelle, 1963; JD, St. John's U., Jamaica, N.Y., 1966. From asst. U.S. atty. to spl. asst. U.S. atty. So. Dist. N.Y. Dept. Justice, Bklyn., 1966-67, chief atty. examiner bd. immigration rev. Falls Church, Va., 1977-95, vice chmn. bd. immigration appeals, 1995—; dep. assoc. adminstr. for major sys. and policy Ofice Mgmt. and Budget, Washington, 1980-82. Editor St. John's Law Rev., 1965-66. Office: Dept Justice Exec Office Imm Rev Bd Immigration Apls 5107 Leesburg Pike Ste 2400 Falls Church VA 22041-3234

DUNNE, NANCY ANNE, retired social services administrator; b. Ionia, Mich., Aug. 5, 1929; d. Warner Kingsley and Hazel Fern (Alliason) McSween; m. James Robert, Oct. 28, 1952; children: James Robert Jr., Stephen Michael. BA, Albion (Mich.) Coll., 1951. Tchr. Oakdale Elem., Grand Rapids, Mich., 1951-53, Lakeside Sch., East Grand Rapids, Mich., 1953; clk. Office of Naval Rsch., Washington, 1954-55; dir. pub. rels. Diocesan Office Health and Social Svcs., Albany, N.Y., 1971-74; dir. vol. action dept. Coun. of Human Resources, Schenectady, N.Y., 1974-76; pers. asst. Am. Soc. Assn. Execs., Washington, 1977-78; adminstrv. asst. N.Y. Soc. Cons. Engrs., N.Y.C., 1978-79, Assessment Designs, Inc., Orlando, Fla., 1980-82, Catholic Social Svcs., Orlando, Fla., 1982-84, ret., 1984. Active NY State Comm. Cultural Resources, Albany, 1970-73, Anna Maria Island Cmty. Ctr., 2000-01; bd. dirs. Coalition for the Homeless, Orlando, 1983-87; tutor Anna Maria Island Elem. Sch., Fla.; vol. Blake Hosp., Bradenton, Fla., 1999-2003, Imagine Manatee Task Force, Bradenton, 2003; 1st v.p. Performing arts Downtown Manatee County, Inc., 2003. Mem. AAUW (pres. Manatee County br. 2001-03), Jr. League of Schenectady (Vol. of Yr. award 1965-66), Schenectady Symphony Orch. (pres. 1969-70), Ladies of Charity (pres. Albany chpt. 1970-72, pres. Orlando chpt. 1984-86, nat. pres. 1990-94, nat. bd. dirs. 2001-02, v.p. internat. 1990-94, bd. dirs. 1994-2000). Roman Catholic. Avocations: reading, traveling, golfing, bridge, entertaining friends. Home: 6400 Flotilla Dr Apt 31 Holmes Beach FL 34217-1425

DUNNING, LISA ANNE, marriage and family therapist; BA, U. Calif., Irvine, 1992; MA, Philips Grad. Inst., 1994. Lic. marriage and family therapist Calif., 1999. Foster care social worker Hollygrove Foster Care, Glendora, Calif., 1994—97, Ettie Lee Foster Homes, Baldwin Park, Calif., 1997—98; program coord. Robert F. Kennedy Inst., Wilmington, Calif., 1998—99; pvt. practice lic. marriage/family therapist Hermosa Beach, Calif., 1999—. Lectr. in field. Author: Good Parents Bad Parenting; contbr. articles to profl. jours. Bd. mem. edn. Palos Verdes Hills Nursery Sch., Rolling Hills, Calif., 2003—. Mem.: Calif. Assn. Marriage and Family Therapists, Am. Assn. Marriage and Family Therapists. Avocations: tennis, acting.

DUNN KELLY, RUTH EMMA, management consultant; b. Tuskegee, Ala., Apr. 26, 1945; d. Moses and Annie Virgia Dunn; m. Bernard Kelly, June 2, 2001. BS, Wayne State U., 1985; MS, Ctrl. Mich. U., 1989. Analyst Gen. Motors, Detroit, 1969—99; test adminstr. Aon Cons., Finley, Ohio, 1998—; counselor Macomb County Crisis Ctr., Warren, Mich., 1994—95.

DUNPHY, MAUREEN MILBIER, reading educator; b. Springfield, Mass., Feb. 25, 1949; d. Donald J. and Mary C. Milbier; m. Terrence Michael Dunphy. BS in Edn., Westfield State Coll., 1971, MEd, 1975, Cert. Advanced Grad. Study, 1988; cert. paralegal, 1996. Tchr. Thornton Burgess Intermediate Sch., Hampden, Mass., 1971-75; reading specialist, reading dept. head West Springfield Jr. H.S., 1975—2002; reading supr. K-12 Westfield (Mass.) Pub. Schs., 2002—. Acting asst. prin. W. Springfield Jr. HS, 1989; cons. Nat. Evaluations Systems, Amherst, Mass. Mem. editl. bd.: MRA Primer, 1999—. Mem. Long Range Bldg. Needs Com., Westfield, 1986-87, 2000-02. Mem. Pioneer Valley Reading Coun. (pres. 1977-79), Mass. Reading Assn. (dir. 1977-81), West Springfield Edn. Assn. (negotiations sec.), Mass. Tchrs. Assn., Hampden County Tchrs. Assn. Home: 282 Steiger Dr Westfield MA 01085-4934 Office: North Mid Sch 350 Southampton Rd Westfield MA 01085 E-mail: m.dunphy@mail.ci.westfield.ma.us.

DUNST, KIRSTEN, actress; b. Point Pleasant, N.J., Apr. 30, 1982; d. Klaus and Inez Dunst. Appeared in films Bonfire of the Vanities, 1990, High Strung, 1991, Greedy, 1994, Interview with the Vampire, 1994, Little Women, 1994, Jumanji, 1995, Wag the Dog, 1997, (voice) Anastasia, 1997, Drop Dead Gorgeous, 1999, Dick, 1999, The Virgin Suicides, 1999, Bring It On, 2000, crazy/beautiful, 2001, The Cat's Meow, 2001, Spider-Man, 2002, Levity, 2003, Mona Lisa Smile, 2003, Eternal Sunshine on the Spotless Mind, 2004; appeared on TV in Storytime, 1994, Darkness before Dawn, 1993, Saturday Night Live, others. Recipient Golden Globe Award nomination for best supporting actress, 1995, Boston Soc. of Film Critics Award for best supporting actress, 1994, Chicago Film Critics Assn. Award for most promising actress, 1994. Office: c/o Iris Burton Agy 8916 Ashcrof Ave Los Angeles CA 90069-1327*

DUNWICH, GERINA, writer, magazine editor, astrologer; b. Chgo., Dec. 27, 1959; d. W.E. Novotny (dec.) and Teri Enies (LoMastro) D. Ordained min. Univ. Life Ch., 1998. Freelance writer, 1975—; editor, pub. Golden Isis mag., 1980—. Guest spkr. Craftwise Pagan Gathering, Waterbury, Conn., 1996, The Real Witches' Ball, Columbus, Ohio, 1997, Pagan Day Festival, Westwood, Calif., 2000, West Hollywood, Calif., 2001, 02; spokesperson Wiccan/Neo-Pagan Cmty. Author: Candlelight Spells, 1988, The Magick of Candleburning, 1989, Circle of Shadows, 1990, The Concise Lexicon of the Occult, 1990, Wicca Craft, 1991, Secrets of Love Magick, 1992, The Wicca Spellbook, 1994, The Wicca Book of Days, 1995, The Wicca Garden, 1996, The Wicca Source Book, 1996, Wicca Love Spells, 1996, Wicca Candle Magick, 1996, Everyday Wicca, 1997, A Wiccan's Guide to Prophecy and Divination, 1997, Wicca A to Z, 1997, Magick Potions, 1998, The Wicca Source Book, rev. 2d edit., 1998, Your Magickal Cat: Feline Magick, Lore and Worship, 2000, The Pagan Book of Halloween, 2000, Exploring Spellcraft, 2001, The Cauldron of Dreams, 2002, A Witch's Guide to Ghosts and the Supernatural, 2002, Dunwich's Guide to Gemstone Sorcery, 2003; editor, pub. Aquarius Anthology, 1986, The Liberated Voice, 1987, Coven, 1987, Evil Genius Poetry Jour., 1987-88; appeared on numerous radio talk shows across U.S. and Can.; contbr. articles to profl. jours.; contbr.: Circles, Groves and Sanctuaries, 1992, Llewellyn's Witches' Calendar, 1999, 2000, 2001, Witches' Datebook, 1999, 2000, 2001, Llewellyn's Magical Almanac, 1999, 2000, 2001, Llewellyn's Spell-A-Day Calendar, Llewellyn's Herbal Almanac, The Cat Book of Lists, 2001, A Witch Like Me, 2002, Haunted Northern New York, 2002, The Action Hero's Handbook, 2002. High Priestess and founder Circle of the Old Ways (formerly Coven Mandragora); founder North Country Wicca, 1996; founder Wheel of Wisdom Sch.; bd. advisors Am. Biog. Inst. Mem. Pagan Poets Soc. (founder), Circle, The Fellowship of Isis, The Authors Guild, The Authors League Am. Office: Golden Isis Press PO Box 4263 Chatsworth CA 91313-4263 E-mail: witchywoman13@paganpoet.com.

DUNWOODY, SHARON LEE, journalism and communications educator; b. Hamilton, Ohio, Jan. 24, 1947; d. Walter Charles and Fanchon (Kapp) D. MA, Temple U., 1975; PhD, Ind. U., 1978. Asst. prof. journalism Ohio State U., Columbus, 1977-81; from asst. prof. to prof. Sch. Journalism and Mass Comm. U. Wis., Madison, 1981—, dir. Sch. Journalism and Mass Comm., 1998—2003, assoc. dean Grad. Sch., 2003—. Instr. Inst. Environ. Studies U. Wis., Madison, 1985—, head acad. programs, 1995-98. Co-editor: Scientists and Journalists, 1986, Communicating Uncertainty, 1999. Mem. AAAS (chair sect. on gen. interest in sci. and Eng. 1992-93), Soc. for Social Study of Sci., Midwest Assn. for Pub. Opinion Rsch. (pres. 1989-90). Home: 1306 Seminole Hwy Madison WI 53711-3728 Office: Univ Wis Sch Journalism & Mass Comm 821 University Ave Madison WI 53706-1412

DUNYE, CHERYL, artist, film maker; b. Phila. BA, Temple U.; MFA, Rutgers U. Part-time instr. dept. media studies Pitzer Coll., Calif. Film maker (short film films) Greetings from Africa, 1994, (video films) The Potluck and the Passion, creator (films) The Watermelon Woman, contbr. articles to profl. jours. Recipient Major Artists award, MARMAF Pa., 1993; fellow, Rutgers U., 1990, 1991, Art Matters, Inc., 1992, grantee, Astrea Found., 1992, Frameline, 1992, NEA, 1995. Office: c/o Media Studies Pitzer Coll Scott Hall Basement 1050 N Mills Ave Claremont CA 91711-3908

DUPEY, MICHELE MARY, communications specialist; b. Bronx, NY, Feb. 26, 1953; d. William B. and Sandra Nancy (Raia) D.; m. Daniel Michael Gieser, July 14, 1980 (div. May 1991). BA, Montclair State Coll., 1975; cert. in copywriting, NYU, 1988. Sec. DDB Needham Worldwide Inc. Advt. (formerly Doyle Dane Bernbach Advt. Co.), N.Y.C., 1985—88; asst. pub. info. officer Hudson County (N.J.) Bd. Chosen Freeholders, 1988-2000; media specialist Englewood (NJ) Hosp. and Med. Ctr., 2000—01; freelance copywriter Jersey City, 1988—; pub. info. officer Jersey City Free Pub. Libr., 2004—. Creator ann. Hudson County Women's History Month Program; in-house planning chair 150th Anniversary Celebration of Hudson County; participant Comm. Gay Games IV, N.Y.C., 1991—94; mem. planning com., pub. rels. Hudson County Am. Heritage Festival, 1994—95; program prodr. pub. rels. 1996 Olympic Torch Relay Hudson County, 1996; developer Hudson County ADv. Commn. on Women; developer seminars, prodr. video What is a Freeholder?; spkr. in field. Contbr. articles to profl. publs. Recipient Gov.'s award, Hudson County Am. Heritage Festival, 1995; fellow Leadership N.J., 1995. Democrat. Roman Catholic. Home and Office: Copy on Target 206 Washington St Apt 3A Jersey City NJ 07302-4566 Office Phone: 201-547-4579. Business E-Mail: mdupey@jclibrary.org. E-mail: wittywoman@aol.com.

DUPLANTIER, DAWN ELIZABETH, communications executive; b. New Orleans, May 1, 1970; d. Dennis Paul and Judith Dawn (Hepburn) D. BBA, U. Tex., 1991, MA in Journalism/Pub. Rels., 1994. Accredited in pub. rels. Pub. rels. asst. Nat. Wildflower Rsch. Ctr., Austin, Tex., 1993; comms. dir. Travis County Bar Assn., Austin, 1993—95, Tex. Bankers Assn., Austin, 1995—99; sr. v.p. Nat. Child Identification Program, 1999—2000; regional pub. rels. mgr. GM RxWorks, Dallas, 2000—. Mem. Austin Postal Customer Coun., 1992-95. Editor: (mags.) Austin Lawyer, 1993-95, Tex. Banking, 1995—. Vol. Am. Heart Assn., Austin, 1995, Goodwill Industries, Austin, 1995, bd. dirs. Dallas County affiliate Susan G. Konen Breast Cancer Found., 2000-02, pres., 2002; grad.Banking Leadership Tex., 1998. Scholar Nat. Assn. Bar Execs. Mem. Pub. Rels. Soc. Am., Phi Kappa Phi. Avocations: running, skiing, politics. Office: Gen Motors RxWorks 130 E John Carpenter Foy Dallas TX 75062

DUPLESSIS, SANDRA WALSH, librarian, educator; b. N.Y.C., Mar. 14, 1945; d. Maurice David and Helen Rose (Flynn) Walsh; m. Dwight Charles Duplessis, July 11, 1970; children: Anton, Laura, James. BA in Edn., U. La., Monroe, 1966; MLS with honors, La. State U., 1984. Libr., tchr. Chapelle H.S., Metairie, La., West Jefferson H.S., Harvey, La.; libr., cataloger Jefferson Pub. Libr., Metairie, La.; libr., tchr. St. Rita Sch., Harahan, La. Chair Regina Medal Selection Com. Recipient Sister Mary Aquin award/Libr. of the Yr. Mem.: ALA, Greater New Orleans Libr. Assn., La. Libr. Assn., Greater New Orleans Cath. Libr. Assn. (v.p., pres., newsletter editor), Cath. Libr. Assn. (children's sect., mem. at large, sec., v.p., pres.), Beta Phi Mu. Home: 138 Miami Pl Kenner LA 70065

DUPONT, NICOLE, artist; b. Wilmington, Del., July 24, 1957; d. Henry E.I. duPont and Deborah (Eldredge) duPont Hogan. Artist, CEO Visionary Art Studios, Novato, Calif., 1989-93, Creative Light Prodns., Kapa'a, Hawaii, 1993—. Artist; creator Hawaiian Legend Leis; leis collected in museums including Bishop Mus., Honolulu. Adminstrv. for cmty. classes in Hawaiian culture, Kapa'a, 1994-95. Winner 1st Place award Mokihana Festival Lei Contest, 1997, 98. Mem. Kaua'i Soc. Artists, Garden Island Arts Coun., Kaua'i C. of C. Office: Creative Light Prodns 1191 Kuhio Hwy 116 Kapaa HI 96746 E-mail: hnd@aloha.net.

DUPREE, NATHALIE, chef, television personality, writer; b. Dec. 23, 1939; m. Jack Bass. Advanced Cert., Cordon Bleu. Founder Rich's Cooking Sch., Atlanta, 1975; guest PM Mag., Atlanta; host New So. Cooking with Nathalie Dupree, 1986—. Bd. dirs. So. Foodways Alliance, 2000—02. Author: Cooking of the South, 1984 (Tastemaker award), New Southern Cooking, 1986, Nathalie Dupree's Matters of Taste, 1990, Nathalie Dupree Cooks Great Meals for Busy Days, 1994, Nathalie Dupree Cooks Everyday Meals from a Well-Stocked Pantry, 1995, Nathalie Dupree's Comfortable Entertaining: At Home with Ease and Grace, 1998 (Crystal Whisk award IACP, 1999), Savoring Savannah: Feasts from the Low Country, 2001. Recipient Tastemaker award. Office: Box 1197 Social Circle GA 30025

DUQUETTE, DIANE RHEA, library director; b. Springfield, Mass., Dec. 15, 1951; d. Gerard Lawrence and Helen Yvette (St. Marie) Morneau; m. Thomas Frederick Duquette Jr., Mar. 17, 1973. BS in Sociology, Springfield Coll., 1975; MLS, Simmons Coll., 1978. Libr. asst. Springfield City Libr., 1975-78; reference libr. U. Mass., Amherst, 1978-81; head libr. Hopkins Acad., Hadley, Mass., 1980; instr. Colo. Mountain Coll., Steamboat Springs, 1981-83; libr. dir. East Routt Libr. Dist., Steamboat Springs, 1981-84; agy. head Solono County Libr., Vallejo, Calif., 1984; dir. libr. svcs. Shasta County Libr., Redding, Calif., 1984-87; dir. librs. Kern County Libr., Bakersfield, Calif., 1987—. Chmn. San Joaquin Valley Libr. System, 1988. Contbr. articles to profl. jours. Recipient John Cotton Dana Spl. Pub. Rels. award, H.W. Wilson and ALA, 1989. Mem. ALA, Calif. Libr. Assn. (mem. coun. 1987—), Calif. County Librs. Assn. (pres. 1990). Democrat. Roman Catholic. Avocations: golf, skiing, bicycling, reading, gardening. Home: Pine Mountain Club PO Box 6595 Frazier Park CA 93222-6595 Office: Kern County Libr 701 Truxtun Ave Bakersfield CA 93301-4800

DURAN, DIANNA J. state legislator; b. Tularosa, 1956; Dep. chief clk. County; mem. N.Mex. Senate, Dist. 40, Sante Fe, 1992—; mem. edn. com., mem. ways and means com. N.Mex. Senate. Republican. Office: 909 8th St Rm 423 Tularosa NM 88352-2221 E-mail: dduran@state.nm.us.

DURAN, LOIS JANINE, lawyer; b. Lima, Ohio, Dec. 2, 1952; d. John William and Eileen Marie (Jettinghoff) Freyer; m. Luis Thomas Duran, Aug. 14, 1975; children: Alex Jason, Chelsea Marie. Student, Miami U., Oxford, Ohio, 1971-73; BA, Ohio State U., 1974, JD, 1978. Bar: Ohio 1978, Tex. 1979, U.S. Dist. Ct. (no. dist.) Tex. 1979. Mgr. legal collections Tex. Utilities Electric Co., Dallas, 1978—. Mem. Dallas area Labor Law Group, 1986-87; tchr. legal asst. program U. Tex., Arlington, 1988-89. Mem. Leadership Arlington, 1991-92, Accent Arlington, 1992—. Mem. ABA, Fed: Bar Assn., Tex. Bar Assn., Dallas Bar Assn. (sec. environ. law sect. 1986-87), Coll. State Bar Tex. (cert. 1984-86), Dallas Assn. Young Lawyers (com. mem. 1985-88), Assn. Women Execs. (com. mem. 1985-87), Dallas C. of C. (com. mem. 1985-87). Home: 2204 Rockbrook Ct Arlington TX 76006-5752 Office: Tex Utilities Electric Co 200 W Carpenter Fwy Ste 128 Irving TX 75039-2003

DURAND, BARBARA, dean; Dean Coll. Nursing, prof. Ariz. State U., Tempe. Office: Ariz State U PO Box 872602 458 Nursing Bldg Tempe AZ 85287-2602

DURAND, SYDNIE MAE M. state legislator; b. Lafayette, La., Apr. 30, 1934; d. Sidney August and Hattie Ann (Belaire) Maraist; m. Alcee J. Durand, Oct. 16, 1955; 1 child, Alcee J. (Chip). Student, U. Southwestern La., 1952-55. Landman Sohio Pet, Lafayette, 1955-60; acct. Austral Oil, Lafayette, 1960-79; environ. coord. Mobil Oil, Lafayette, 1979-91; police juror St. Martin Parish, Baton Rouge, 1979-91; mem. La. Ho. of Reps., Baton Rouge, 1991—. Recipient Conservation award Woodman of the World, 1988, Bishop's medal Diocese of Lafayette, 1989. Mem. Nat. Assn. Counties, La. Policy Jury Assn. (exec. bd. 1982-92), Evangeline Econ. Bd. (v.p. 1985-92). Democrat. Roman Catholic. Avocations: photography, fishing, hunting, making friends. Address: PO Box 2840 Parks LA 70582-2840

DURDAHL, CAROL LAVAUN, psychiatric nurse; b. Crookston, Minn., Jan. 18, 1933; d. Elmer Oliver and Ovidia (Olson) Durdahl; m. Hans A. Dahl, May 22, 1956 (div. 1983); children: Hana Sorensen-O'Neill, Carla Pederson. RN, St. Lukes Hosp., Duluth, Minn., 1953; BA in Human Svcs., Met. State U., St. Paul, 1982. Staff nurse various hosps., Minn., 1953-59; human svcs. tech. Willmar (Minn.) State Hosp., 1970-74, supplemental tchr., 1974-83; staff nurse Rice Meml. Hosp., Willmar, 1983-86; utilization rev. various nursing homes, Willmar, 1985-86; tchr. Willmar Area Vocat. Tech. Inst., 1986; dir. nurses Glenmore Recovery Ctr., Crookston, Minn., 1986-88; shift supr. Golden Valley (Minn.) Health Ctr., 1988-92, with crisis dept. Hennepin County Med. Ctr., 1988—; managed care of psychiat. and substance abuse MCC Managed Behavioral Care, Mpls., 1992. Contbr. articles to profl. jours. Mem. AAUW, Bus. and Profl. Women, League Women Voters (pres. and state bd.), Federated Women, Does. Republican. Lutheran. Avocations: reading, walking, crafts. Home: 3720 Independence Ave S Apt 41 Minneapolis MN 55426-3767 Office: Hennepin County Med Ctr 701 Park Ave Minneapolis MN 55415-1623 Office Phone: 612-873-3170. E-mail: cdurdahl@aol.com.

DUREGGER, KAREN MARIE, health facility administrator; b. Des Moines, Jan. 16, 1952; d. Francis William and Luella Marie (Smith) Moore; m. Michael Steven Duregger, Feb. 26, 1972; children: Chadwick Michael, Joshua William (dec.), Francis Steven. Secretarial diploma, Am. Inst. Bus., Des Moines, 1971; cert. health care adminstr., Des Moines Area Community Coll., 1985. Sec. Harry Rodine Co., Des Moines, 1970, Iowa State Assn. Secondary Sch. Prins., Des Moines, 1971-72; asst. adminstr. Hancock County Care Facility, Garner, 1973-74, adminstr., 1974-89, Duncan Heights, Inc., Garner, 1989—, bd. dirs., recording sec., 1989—. Mem., sec. Mental Health, Mental Retardation and Devel. Disabled Adv. Bd., Garner, 1983-93. Mem. Cmty. Edn. Bd., Garner, 1989-2000; mem. ch. choir, 1993—; mem. Hancock County Little Theatre, 1994—, v.p., 1999—. Mem. County Care Facility Adminstrs. (dist. pres. 1985-87, treas. 1989-91), Human Svcs. Tng. Network, Tng. Planning Group Health Task Force; mem. Bell Choir, 1995. Republican. Lutheran. Avocations: making porcelain and vinyl dolls, remember me dolls, fishing, ballroom and country western dancing, family. Home: 145 W Lyons St Garner IA 50438-1920 Office: 1465 Highway 18 Garner IA 50438-8621

DUREK, DOROTHY MARY, retired English language educator; b. Pitts., Jan. 23, 1926; d. Joseph Adam and Helen Barbara (Ondich) D. BS in Edn., Youngstown State U., 1962; MS in Edn., Westminster Coll., 1969. Cert. English tchr., Ohio, comprehensive English cert., Pa. Tchr. English Brookfield (Ohio) Schs., 1962-64, Sharon (Pa.) City Schs., 1964-88. Mem., pres. Coll. Club Sharon, 1993-94. Charter mem., bd. dirs. LWV Mercer County, Pa., 1993—97; docent Butler Inst. Am. Art, Youngstown, 1988—; mem. Shenango Valley Women's Interfaith Coun., Jewish-Christian Dialogue Group, Sharon; charter mem. Mus. Women's Art, Washington, Nat. Mus. of the Am. Indian, Washington; mem., bd. dirs. Christian Assocs. Shenango Valley. Mem.: AAUW, NEA, Read and Discuss Group, Sharon Lifelong Learning Coun. (bd. dirs. 1995), Cath. Collegiate Assn., Sharon Tchrs. Assn., Pa. State Educators Assn., Prospect Heights Lit. Club. Roman Catholic. Home: Apt 302 Victory Terrace 9440 Newbridge Dr Potomac MD 20854

DURGIN, DIANE, arbitrator, lawyer, mediator; b. Albany, N.Y., May 17, 1946; BA, Wellesley Coll., 1970; JD magna cum laude, Boston Coll., 1974. Assoc. Shearman & Sterling, N.Y.C., 1974-83; corp. sec. Ga.-Pacific Corp., Atlanta, 1983-92, v.p. law, dep. gen. counsel, 1986-89, sr. v.p. law, gen. counsel, 1989-93; arbitrator, mediator Atlanta, 1993—; dep. exec. dir. legal and non-profit affairs Atlanta Housing Authority, 1994-98. Bd. dirs. Atlanta Symphony Orch., 1991-97, Am. Arbitration Assn., 1991-97, Met. Atlanta chpt. ARC, 1988-94, Actor's Express, 2000—, Atlanta Women's Found., 1999—; bd. dirs., mem. exec. com. Alliance Theatre Co., 1985-97; mem. bd. sponsors Georgian Chamber Players, Inc., 1986-92, 97-2002. Mem.: ABA, Am. Law Inst., Ga. State Bar, Bd. Dirs. Network, Nature Conservancy (bd. dirs. Ga. chpt. 1989—96), 191 Club, Order of Coif.

DURHAM, BETTY BETHEA, therapist; b. SC, Jan. 27, 1933; d. Liston Fenton and Rosalie (Bracey) Bethea; m. John Lewis Cottrell, June 8, 1952 (div. June 1972); children: John Lewis Jr., Gregory Bethea; m. John I. Durham, Apr. 29, 1988. BS, U.N.C. at Pembroke, 1974; MSW, U. Ga., 1981. Psycho-social specialist Dublinaire Nursing Care, Dublin, Ga., 1979-80; med. social worker C. Vinson V.A. Med. Ctr., Dublin, 1982-86; therapist Raleigh (N.C.) employee's assistance program Raleigh Cmty. Hosp., 1987-88; pastoral counselor Greenwich (Conn.) Bapt. Ch., 1988-94; therapist Big Island, Va., 1995—. Marriage and family counselor Bapt. Ch., Greenwich, 1988-94; supr. grad. studies U. Ga., Fla. State U., Dublin, 1982-86. Editor Hospital Social Svc. manuals, 1982-86. Mem. Laurens County Ga. Mental Health Bd., 1975-76, Ga. Grand Jury and Gov. Com. on Drug Abuse, 1977; survey and coord. of nursing home svcs., 52 counties in Ga., 1982-86. Recipient Citation for Developing Nursing Home Fund Drive Nat. Heart Assn., 1979, Hands and Heart award VA, 1984. Mem. AAUW, Nat. Mus. of Women in the Arts (tour leader Europe and Mid. East 1988—), Nat. Women's History Mus. (charter). Mem. United Meth. Ch. Avocations: needlepoint, painting, horticulture, reading the classics. Home: 1509 Tolley Meadow Rd Big Island VA 24526-2977 Personal E-mail: johnandbettyd@aol.com.

DURHAM, BETTY LOUISE, poet; b. Hamilton, Ohio, Sept. 11, 1944; d. Gertrude Durham, Ralph Durham. Author: (poetry) Place in the Sun, 1992, Passages-An Anthology of Contemporary Lit., 1992, Reflections-The Poetry Ctr., 1992, The Best Poems of the 90's, 1992, Great Poems of Our Time, 1993, Treasured Poems of Am., 1993. Sgt. USMC, 1967—70. Recipient Songwriter award, I.M.X Recording Co., 1995; scholar Golden Poet scholar, World Of Poetry, 1990—93. Avocations: reading, gardening, writing poetry. Home: 355 E School St #B Covina CA 91723 Personal E-mail: bettyd24@juno.com.

DURHAM, CHRISTINE MEADERS, state supreme court chief justice; b. L.A., Aug. 3, 1945; d. William Anderson and Louise (Christensen) Meaders; m. George Homer Durham II, Dec. 29, 1966; children: Jennifer, Meghan, Troy, Melinda, Isaac. AB, Wellesley Coll., 1967; JD, Duke U., 1971. Bar: N.C. 1971, Utah 1974. Sole practice law, Durham, N.C., 1971-73; instr. legal medicine Duke U., Durham, 1971-73; adj. prof. law Brigham Young U., Provo, Utah, 1973-78; ptnr. Johnson, Durham & Moxley, Salt Lake City, 1974-78; judge Utah Dist. Ct., 1978-82; assoc. justice Utah Supreme Ct., 1982—2002, chief justice, 2002—. Pres. Women Judges Fund for Justice, 1987-88. Fellow Am. Bar Found.; mem. ABA (edn. com. appellate judges' conf.), Nat. Assn. Women Judges (pres. 1986-87), Utah Bar Assn., Am. Law Inst. (coun. mem.), Nat. Ctr. State Courts (bd. dirs.), Am. Inns of Ct. Found. (trustee). Office: Utah Supreme Ct PO Box 140210 Salt Lake City UT 84114-0210

DURHAM, JO ANN FANNING, artist; b. Sulphur Springs, Tex., May 31, 1935; d. William Jeffress and Merle Jo (Barrett) Fanning; m. William E. Durham (dec.); children: William, John Lee (dec.). BS, Tex. A&M U., 1956; postgrad., U. Tex., Austin, 1953-55, Tex. Woman's U., Denton, Tex., 1953-55; docteur honoris causa in arts, 1994. Exhibited in group shows at Galerie Jean Lammelin, Paris, 1991, Salon D'Automne Grand Palais, Paris, 1992, 93, Vanderbilt Museum, Long Island VIU, N.Y., 1995, Lever House, VIU, N.Y., 1995, Pen and Brush Club, 1995,96, VIU, N.Y., 1996, Templeton, Fort Worth Artists and Co., Fort Worth, 1996, Sumner Art Museum, Washington, 1996, Belgium Grand Prix, De Paadestallen Van Het Park Van Enghien, Belgium, 1996, Soc. Internat. Des Beaux Arts, Paris, 1996,97, Southwestern Watercolor Soc., D-Art, Dallas, 1996, 97, Anthology Art Gallery, Lebanon, 1997, Longboat Key Art Ctr., North Tex. Health Sci. Ctr., 1997, Atrium Gallery, Fort Worth, 1998, Laura Knott Gallery, Bradford Coll., Mass., 1998, Lee Scarfone Gallery, U. Tampa, Fla., 1998, Fort Mason, San Francisco, 1998, Yale Med. Sch. Libr., 2000, La Chapelle des Penitents, Gordes, France, 2000, Columbia U., 2000, Huntsville (Ala.) Mus. Art, 2001, Salmagundi Club, 2002, 03, ISEA, Chgo., 2003 and Aberdare, Wales, 2004; The Artist's Magazine, Dec. 2001, Nautilus Fellowship, Internat. Soc. of Experimental Artists, Oct. 2001, Encaustic Works Biennial, 2001, Internat. Soc. of Experimental Artists, Dennos Museum, Traverse City, 2001, Minetrista Cultural Ctr, Muncie, 2002, Salmagundi Club, N.Y.C., 2002, 03, Internat. Soc. Exptl. Artists, Beverly Arts Ctr., Chgo., 2003, WALES, Aberdare, 2003,-04 Splash 8, 2004. Recipient Gold medal Belgium Grand Prix, 1993, Best of Show, Internat. Soc. of Experimental Artists, 2003. Mem. Soc. Watercolor Artists (signature), Internat. Soc. Exptl. Artists (signature; pres. 1999), Soc. Layerists in Multimedia (signature), Allied Artists, Tex. Fine Arts Assn. (past pres., regional dir., exec. bd.), D Art, Dallas Women's Caucus for the Arts, Dallas Artists Rsch. and Exhbn., Southwestern Watercolor Soc. (signature), Tex. Visual Artists Assn., Fort Worth Woman's Club Art Dept., Templeton Art Ctr., Nat. League of Am. Pen Women, Contemporary Art Ctr., Christians in the Visual Arts, Nat. Coll. Soc., Salmagundi Club. Home: 4300 Plantation Dr Fort Worth TX 76116-7607 Home Fax: 817-737-6520.

DURHAM, NANCY RUTH, elementary school educator, music educator; b. Cushing, Okla., Aug. 28, 1947; d. Edward Fowler and Margaret Mailine Albritton; m. Dale Leonard Durham, Aug. 8, 1970. B in Music Edn., Okla. State U., 1969. Vocal music tchr. grades 3-12 Okeene (Okla.) Pub. Schs., 1969—70; elem. music tchr. grades K-6 Choctaw (Okla.) Pub. Schs., 1970—76; pvt. bus. owner Mayo-Durham Clothing, Wagoner, Okla., 1977—86; bus. owner Bartlesville/Tulsa, Okla., 1986—88; elem. music tchr. Wagoner Pub. Schs., 1988—. Sec. Wagoner Assn. Classroom Tchrs., 1991—93, bldg. rep., 1994—95. Christmas parade chmn. Wagoner C. of C., 1979—80, v.p., 1979—81, pres., 1982; chmn./co-chmn. Tartan Day Celebration State of Okla., 2000—01. Mem.: Okla. Music Educators Assn. (choir dir. grades 5 and 6 elem. choir state honor group 1974, 1976), United Scottish Clans Okla., Scottish Club Tulsa (pres. 1997—2000). Republican. Mem. Ch. Of Christ. Avocations: sewing, embroidery, gardening, fitness, Scottish heritage activities. Home: 1505 Berkley Wagoner OK 74467

DURHAM, SUSAN B. state legislator; b. Portsmouth, Va., Nov. 15; d. J.C.G. Wilson and Irene Leona Jones; m. Frank Conrad Durham, July 26, 1958; children: Kimberly, Alison, Elizabeth, George. Student, U. Hawaii, 1957-58, U. Mich., 1963. Mem. dist. 22 N.H. Ho. of Reps., Concord. Mem. edn. com. N.H. Ho. of Reps., 1991-94. Walk leader Beaver Brook Conservation Land, Hollis, N.H., 1980—; nature educator Soc. for Protection of N.H. Forest, Concord, 1985-90; mem. Hollis Sch. Bd., 1980-86, v.p., 1984-86; mem. Hollis Planning Bd., 1986-90; trustee Beaver Brook Assn., v.p. 1988-90, pres. 1990-91. Mem. LWV (bd. dirs. Milford area 1978-80). Republican. Unitarian-Universalist. Avocations: gardening, sailing, reading. Home: 70 Hayden Rd Hollis NH 03049-6289

DURHAM, SUSAN F. music educator; b. Nashville, Mar. 25, 1956; d. Charles Dean and Ethelyn Dodd Fuqua; m. David H. Durham, Nov. 3, 1978; children: Philip Charles, Laurelyn Leigh. B of Music Edn., Samford U., 1979; MusM, Southwestern Bapt. Theol. Sem., 1981. Choral dir. Coosa High Sch., Rome, Ga., 1994—2001; adminstrv. asst. to theatre dir. Northeast Ala. C.C., Rainsville, Ala., 2002—03; choral dir. Durant High Sch, Brandon, Fla., 2003—. Republican. Baptist. Home: 818 Sandcastle Cir Brandon FL 33511-6155 Office: Durant High Sch 4748 Cougar Path Plant City FL 33567

DURHAM, SUSAN K. research scientist; b. Stafford, Kans., May 18, 1957; d. Rolla Evern and Betty Florence Durham. BS, Kans. State U., 1979, MS, 1981; PhD, Iowa State U., 1991. Postdoctoral fellow Mayo Clinic, Rochester, Minn., 1991-94, Baylor Coll. Medicine, Houston, 1994-98, rsch. assoc., 1998—; tech. svcs. coord. Diagnostic Systems Lab. Inc., Webster, Tex., 1999—. Mem. Endocrine Soc., Women in Endocrinology (travel award 1993), Am. Soc. Animal Sci. Avocations: reading, antiques, animals. Office: Baylor Coll Medicine 6621 Fannin St Houston TX 77030

DURHAM, THENA MONTS, microbiologist, researcher, management executive; b. Bradenton, Fla., July 10, 1945; d. Turner and Silverrene (Taylor) M.; m. Millard Durham, Aug. 30, 1969 (dec. 2001); children: Bryce Vincent-Barnard, Brittanie Yvonne. BS, Fisk U., 1966; MS, Purdue U., 1968. Rsch. microbiologist Ctrs. for Disease Control, Atlanta, 1968-86, assoc. dir. for programs Nat. Ctr. for Prevention Svcs., 1988-95; program analyst Office Dir., Ctr. for Health Promotion and Edn., 1986-88; dir. exec. secretariat Ctrs. for Dis. Control and Prevention, Atlanta, 1995—2001; dep. dir. for policy Nat. Ctr. for HIV, STD, and TB Prevention for CDC, Atlanta, 2001—. Cons. FDA. Author numerous tech. papers; contrb. articles to profl. jours. Mem. NAACP, Neighborhood Planning Unit. Recipient Sec.'s award for Disting. Svc., Dept. HHS, 2001. Mem. AAAS, Sci. Rsch. Soc., Am. Soc. Microbiologists, CDC Assn. Exec. Women (founder, co-chmn.), Women in Sci. and Engring., Sigma Xi. Democrat. E-mail: tmd1@cdc.gov.

DURKIN, DIANE L. nurse; b. Youngstown, Ohio, Feb. 1, 1952; d. Harold Henry and Helen Michelle Durkin. Diploma, St. Elizabeth Sch. Nursing, Youngstown, 1973. RN; cert. in neonatal intensive care nursing. Staff nurse St. Christopher Children's Hosp., Phila., 1979-80, Jackson Meml. Hosp., Miami, Fla., 1973-79, 80-81, assoc. head nurse newborn intensive care, 1981—, neonatal transport nurse, 1975-79, 80—. Contbr. articles to profl. jours. Mem. comty. adv. com. WPBT Pub. Broadcast, Miami, Fla., 1999. Mem.: Fla. Assn. Flight Nurses, S.E. Fla. Assn. Neonatal Nurses (steering com. 1993—94, treas. 1994—96, v.p. 1996—98, pres. 1999, co-founder), Nat. Assn. Neonatal Nurses (NANN pages editor 2000, Central Lines editor 2002—03, chair comms. com., corres. mem. newsletter com.). Republican. Roman Catholic. Avocations: reading, walking. Office: U Miami/Jackson Meml Hosp 1511 NW 12th Ave Miami FL 33136 Personal E-mail: plemented@aol.com.

DURKIN, DOROTHY ANGELA, university official; b. Glen Cove, NY, June 23, 1945; d. Frank Vincent and Rose Marie Durkin; 1 child, David Francis. BA, SUNY, Stony Brook, 1968; MA, NYU, 1974. Adminstrv. asst. SUNY, Stony Brook, 1965-67; prodn. editor Holt, Rinehart & Winston, Inc., Stony Brook, 1967-69; editor Hill & Wang Pub., Inc., NYC, 1969-70;

asst. dir. pub. info. NYU Sch. Continuing Edn., 1970-72; assoc. dean pub. affairs and student svc. Sch. Continuing and Profl. Studies NYU Sch. Continuing Edn. and Profl. Studies, 1983—. Cons. NYC Ctr. for Lifelong Learning, 1974; producer TV series Continuum, Sta. WNYC, 1974. Editor: NSF student mag., 1961. Recipient Merit award Andy Advt., 1972, [illegible] Big Apple award NY Radio Broadcasters Assn., 1985, Admissions Mktg. Report awards, 1987-88, 98-2001, Catalog Age awards, 1988, 93, Silver and Bronze award in Print Advt., 2004, Gold and Silver award in Print Advt., 2004. Mem. Univ. Continuing Edn. Assn. (chair info. svc. 1980-81, nat. award chair, chair mktg. adv. com. 1989-98, group leader Learn From Success series 1989-90, bd. dir. 1991-93, membership com. 1994-95, mktg. conf. planning com. 1993-00, presenter, Bronze, Silver and Gold awards 1978, 81-2002, Internat. Leadership in Continuing Edn. award 1999, Gold award in publications, 2002, Gold and Bronze award in Electronic Marketing Communications, 2002, Silver award in Mixed Media: Publications, Advertising, PR and Web), Am. Coll. Pub. Rels. Assn. (nat. award 1973), Coun. for Advancement and Support of Edn. (awards 1982-83, 85-87, 89-90, 92-94), Women in Comms. (job chair), Pub. Rels. Soc. Am. (Am. demographics adv. bd. 1989-90), Direct Mktg. Assn. (Echo Leadership award 1987, 88), Internat. Direct Mktg. Assn., SUNY Alumni Assn. (bd. dir.), The College Bd. (speaker, cons.), Learning Resources Network. Office: NYU Sch Continuing Edn 25 W 4th St Rm 203 New York NY 10003-4475 E-mail: dorothy.durkin@nyu.edu.

DUROCHER, FRANCES A. retired physician, educator; b. Woonsocket, R.I., Mar. 11, 1943; d. Armand D. and Teresa (Leverone) DuRocher. BA with honors, Trinity Coll., 1964; MS, Brown U., 1966; postgrad., Woman's Med. Coll., 1970. Med. resident Phila. VA Hosp. and Med. Coll. Pa., 1971-73; assoc. in internal med. Guthrie Clinic Ltd., Sayre, Pa., 1973-79; assoc. in internal medicine Annandale (Va.) Group Health Assocs., 1979-87; assoc. chair internal medicine Annandale Group Health Assocs., 1986-87; pvt. practice Fairfax, Va., 1987—2004; ret., 2004. Clin. asst. prof. med. and health svcs. George Washington U. Med. Sch., Washington, 1994—. Bd. dirs. Fairways of Penderbrook Homeowners Assn., 1993—, sec., 1995-96, pres., 1996—. Mem. AMA, ACP-Am. Soc. Internal Medicine, Am. Med. Women's Assn. (exec. bd. br. I, 1985-91, pres. 1987-88), Med. Soc. Va., Fairfax County Med. Soc. Avocations: reading, traveling.

DURRANT, M. PATRICIA, diplomat; BA, Diploma in Internat. Rels., U. W.I.; Diploma in Overseas Devel. Studies, U. Cambridge, Eng. With Jamaica Fgn. Svc., 1971—, minister, dep. permanent rep. to UN, 1983—87, amb. to Germany, 1987—92, non-resident amb. to Israel, the Netherlands, Switzerland and the Holy See, 1987—92; dir.-gen. Min. of Fgn. Affairs and Fgn. Trade, 1992—95, permanent rep. of Jamaica to UN, 1995—, rep. for Jamaica on Security Coun. UN, 2000—01, vice chair Open-Ended Working Group on the Reform of UN Security Coun. Chair consultative com. UN Devel. Fund for Women; pres. High Level Com. on Tech. Coop. Among Developing Countries, 1999—2001; vice chair preparatory com. spl. session on population and devel. UN Gen. Assembly, 1999. Named Disting. Grad., U. W.I., 1998; recipient Order of Distinction in the rank of Comdr., 1992, Order of Jamaica, 2000, Disting. Achievement award, World Assn. of Former UN Interns and Fellows. Office: Permanent Mission of Jamaica to UN 767 Third Ave 9th Flr New York NY 10017

DURRANT, RITA DELORES, poet, educator; b. Chgo., July 4, 1919; d. Walter Carl Hilger and Marian Elizabeth George; m. John Merdidith Durrant, Feb. 24, 1945; children: Michael S., Julie Anne. BA, Gov.'s State U., 1977; MA, Gov.'s State, 1980. Freelance writer, Chgo., 1970—82; instr. lit. Holy Family Coll., Phila., 1983—87; instr. poetry Coll. William & Mary, Williamsburg, Va., 1994—99, Williamsburg Libr., 1997—2003. Author: College After 30, 1981. Recipient 2d pl. poetry award, The Parts Domain, Va., 1997. Mem.: Va. Poetry Soc. (v.p. 1995—98, 1st pl. Sonnet award 1997), Williamsburg Poetry Guild (founder, pres. 1995—2003), Nat. League Am. Pen Women (life; v.p. 1975, treas. 1985, 1st pl. award 1993, 1994, 1995). Avocations: reading, travel, swimming. Home: 3800 Treybrun Dr Williamsburg VA 23185

DURRETT, NANCY KASHNER, health science association administrator; BSN, Va. Commonwealth U., 1958, MSN, 1972. Instr. Lewis-Gale Hsop., Roanoke, Va., 1958-61; staff nurse Med. Coll. Va., Richmond, 1962-65, St. Mary's Hosp., Richmond, 1965-69, part-time staff nurse, 1976-79; from asst. instr. to asst. prof. Va. Commonwealth U., Richmond, 1969-76; asst. prof. Petersburg (Va.) Gen. hosp., 1977; asst. prof., coord. med.-surg. nursing John Tyler C.C., Chester, Va., 1977-80, program head nursing, asst. prof., 1980-84; asst. exec. dir. Va. Bd. Nursing, Richmond, 1984-95, exec. dir., 1995—. Mem. nursing svc./edn. coun. Richmond Area Nursing Dirs. Group, 1980-84; mem. long-range planning com. Nat. Coun. State Bds. Nursing, 1989-93, bd. dirs., 1993—. Mem. ANA, Va. Commonwealth Alumni Assn., Sigma Theta Tau, Sigma Zeta. Office: Va Bd Nursing 6606 W Broad St Fl 4 Richmond VA 23230-1717

DURST, CAROL GOLDSMITH, food studics educator; b. Bklyn., Mar. 1, 1952; d. Hyman and Florence (Weisblatt) Goldsmith; m. Marvin Ira Durst, June 18, 1972 (div. Sept. 1977); m. Leslie Mark Wertheim, Apr. 1, 1984; 1 child, William David. BA, Hamilton Kirkland Coll., 1973; MA, Columbia U., 1974; postgrad., Union Inst., 2004. Career counselor Hofstra U., Hempstead, N.Y., 1974-75, Ocean County C.C., Toms River, N.J., 1975-76; rsch. assoc. Catalyst, N.Y.C., 1975-77; coord. displaced homemakers program N.Y. State Dept. Labor, N.Y.C., 1977-79; dir. N.Y. restaurant sch. New Sch. Social Rsch., N.Y.C., 1979-83; owner New Am. Catering Corp., N.Y.C., 1983-98; tchr., career counselor Peter Kump's N.Y. Cooking Sch., N.Y.C., 1988-98. Adj. prof. food studies dept. NYU, 1997—, Westchester C.C., 2001—, Kingsborough C.C., 2003. Author: I Knew You Were Coming So I Baked a Cake, 1997. Mem. AAUW, N.Y. Women's Culinary Alliance (new mem. chair 1995-96), Women Chefs and Restaurateurs (co-chair mentoring program 2003-2004), Nat. Mus. Women in the Arts, Am. Mus. Natural History, Met. Mus. Art. Avocations: fine arts, piano, opera, ice skating. Home and Office: PO Box 270 Millwood NY 10546-0270

DURST, JO, artist, educator; b. Wendell, Idaho, Mar. 23, 1948; d. Lewis Cleveland Ross, Ida Mae Ross; m. Robert Wayne Durst, May 26, 1973; children: Tristan, Jefferson. BA, Albertsons Coll., 1970; MA, Idaho State U., 1972. Instr. Miss. State U., Starkville, 1978—. Artist, Starkville, 1998—; dir. performance art Miss. State U., Starkville, 1998—. Mem.: N.Y. Artists Equity Assn., Southeast Theatre Assn., Miss. Alliance for Arts Edn., Miss. Theatre Assn. (Best Dir. 2000), Nat. Oil and Acrylic Painters Soc. Avocations: art, theater, reading, philosophy, women's studies. Home: 799 Pine Cir Starkville MS 39759 Office Phone: 662-325-3205. Business E-Mail: bdurst@comm.msstate.edu.

DURST, KAY HORRES, physician; b. Charleston, SC, Feb. 11, 1967; d. George Gardner Durst and Virginia Kay Horres-Durst. Degree(hon.), U. L'Inst. de Tours, France, 1988; student, U. SC, 1989, MD, 1998. Diplomate Am. Bd. Family Medicine. Asst. Durst Family Medicine, Charleston, SC, 1989—90; rsch. asst. MIND Works, Charleston, 1990; tchr. Berlitz Sch. Langs., San Juan, PR, 1991—92; sci. lab. asst. St. John's H.S., San Juan, 1991—92, tchr., 1991—92; intern family medicine U. Fla. Family Medicine, Coral Springs, Fla., 1998—99; resident U. Miami Family Medicine, Miami, Fla., 1999—. Mem.: AMA, Am. Acad. Family Physicians, So. Med. Assn., Philharmonic Assn., Petset, Jr. League. Avocations: sailing, scuba, boating, golf, travel. Home: 2508 NE 21st Ct Fort Lauderdale FL 33305-3516

DUSA, JOAN ELIZABETH, history educator; b. Rochester, Pa., Sept. 4, 1949; d. Dan and Agnes (Kayden) D. BA, U. Pitts., 1971; MA, UCLA, 1974, PhD, 1988. Educator adult divsn. L.A. Unified Sch. Dist., 1988-96; educator juvenile ct. and cmty. schs. L.A. County Office Edn., 1994-96. [illegible] Adult Sch., L.A., 1990-92, co-chair leadership coun. Wilson-Lincoln Cmty. Adult Sch., L.A., 1995-96; chair site based coun., Central Juvenile Hall, 1996—2002, mem. law related edn. project Ctrl. Juvenile Hall, L.A., 1996; mem. bd. dirs. Alethos Found., 1998—, Power Sharing, 1998-2002; co-founder Parents in Crisis, 2002. Author: Medieval Dalmatian Episcopal Cities, 1991. Mem. Wildlife Waystation, L.A., 1991—; mem. Family Sch. Community Partnership 2000, L.A. County Office Edn., 1997—. Recipient Purrs of Praise award Wildlife Waystation, 1992, Outstanding Staff award Sylmar Juvenile Hall, 1995, Disting. Svc. award Los Angeles County Office of Edn., 2000, Family, Sch., Cmty. Partnership Tchr. of Yr. award, 2001, Tchr. of the Yr. award L.A. County Office of Edn., 2002. Mem. Am. Hist. Assn., United Tchrs. L.A. (chpt. chair 1994-96), Orgn. History Tchrs., Haskins Soc., Mediterranean Studies Assn., Sierra Club. Office: Ctrl Juvenile Hall 1605 Eastlake Ave Los Angeles CA 90033-1009

DUSENBURY, MARY MCCLINTOCK, arts scholar, farmer, rancher; b. N.Y.C., Aug. 22, 1942; d. John Thomas and Mary Bedinger (Mitchell) McClintock; m. Jerry Kenneth Dusenbury, July 25, 1964; 1 child, Kenneth Stuart. BA, Radcliffe/Harvard Coll., 1964; MA, U. Kans., 1992, PhD, 1999. Ind. scholar, 1984—; instr. Wichita (Kans.) Ctr. for Arts, 1985-89; curatorial assoc. Spencer Mus. Art, Lawrence, Kans., 1992-95. Contbr. articles to jour., ency., catalog; contbr. chpts. to book. Elder Presbyn. Ch. U.S.A., Freeport, Kans., 1994—. Mombusho fellow Japanese Ministry of Edn., Tokyo, 1974-76. Mem. AAUW, Coll. Art Assn., Textile Soc. Am. (pres.). Democrat. Avocations: reading, music, photography, hiking, riding. Home: 1238 NW 100 Rd Attica KS 67009-9305 Office: Spencer Mus Art U Kans Lawrence KS 66045-0001

DUSK, BROOKE, meteorologist; BS in Meteorology, Iowa State U., 2000. Weekend meteorologist NewsCenter 13 WEAU-TV, Eau Claire, Wis., 2001—. Avocation: golf. Office: WEAU-TV Po Box 47 Eau Claire WI 54702

DUSSAULT, NANCY, actress, singer; b. Pensacola, Fla., June 30, 1936; d. George Adrian and Sarah Isabel (Seitz) D.; m. James D. Travis, Oct. 4, 1958. MusB, Northwestern U., 1957; studies with Alvina Kraus, Lotte Lehmann. Actress: (stage prodns.) Guys and Dolls, 1955, Street Scene, 1959, The Mikado, 1959, The Cradle Will Rock, 1960, Do Re Mi, 1960 (Theatre World award 1960), The Sound of Music, 1962 (Kit Kat Club award), Apollo and Miss Agnes, 1963, What Makes Sammy Run, 1964, Phoebe, 1965, Carousel, 1966, Finian's Rainbow, 1967, Fiorello!, 1968, On a Clear Day You Can See Forever, 1968, South Pacific, 1969, Trelawny of the Wells, 1970, The Last of the Red Hot Lovers, 1972, Detective Story, 1973, Irene, 1975, Winter Interludes, 1976, Side by Side by Sondheim, 1977, (TV series) The New Dick Van Dyke Show, 1971, Too Close for Comfort, 1980-83, (TV spls.) Alan King Looks Back in Anger: A Review of 1972, 1973, Burt and the Girls, 1973, The Many Faces of Comedy, 1973, The Lily Tomlin show, 1973, Night of 100 Stars, II, 1985; solo vocalist Chgo. Symphony Orch., 1957 (Young Artists award Soc. Am. Musicians 1957); other mus. performances include Broadway Answers Selma, 1965, ASCAP Salute, 1967, The Magic of Cole Porter, 1967, The Heyday of Rodgers and Hart, 1969, A Salute of Rudolph Friml, 1969, A Hammerstein Salute, 1972, The Revue of Revues, 1973, A Salute to Jules Styne, 1974; host Good Morning, America, 1975, The Shape of Things, 1982; guest various talk shows including The Tonight Show, The Mike Douglas Show, The Merv Griffin Show. Mem. Actors' Equity Assn., AFTRA, Screen Actors Guild, Am. Guild Mus. Artists, AGVA, Delta Delta Delta. Avocations: needlework, cooking, reading, music. Office: 8500 Wilshire Blvd Ste 506 Beverly Hills CA 90211-3121

DUSTMAN, ELIZABETH, art educator, designer; b. Detroit, June 25, 1919; d. John Anthony and Frances (Brade) Kreuzer; m. Edward Anthony Matula, May 13, 1950 (dec. June 1976); children: Maura, Janet; m. Herman C. Dustman, Aug. 25, 1979 (dec. May 5, 1999); stepchildren: Herman, Karl. BFA, Mundelein Coll., 1940; MEd, Loyola U., Chgo., 1964. Artcraft instr. Chgo. Pk. Dist., 1941-44; art educator Mundelein Coll., Chgo., 1945-46, 1955-81, assoc. prof. emeritus, 1982—; package designer Walgreen Co., Chgo., 1946-51. Instr. U.S. Mil. Recreation Pers. Ind. U., 1942; workship tchr. in field. Mem. adv. bd. Northbrook (Ill.) Park Dist., 1983-85; bd. dirs. Northbrook Hist. Soc., 1983-90, North Shore Sr. Ctr., Northfield, 1990-92. Recipient Outstanding Educator award Outstanding Educators Am., 1972; Am. textiles rsch. grantee Kellogg Found., 1974-75. Avocations: travel, research, lecturing, painting.

DUSTMAN, PATRICIA (JO) ALLEN, public school educator, educational consultant, researcher; b. Salem, Ohio, Mar. 22, 1947; d. Alton Davis Allen and Mary Evaline Allen (Iler); m. George Bird Dustman, June 10, 1972; 1 child, Mary Elizabeth Wastchak. BS, Kent State U., 1967—69, MA, 1970—71; EdD, Ariz. State U., 1998. Cert. Teacher AZ. Tchr. Ashtabula City, Ravenna City, N. Ridgeville City Sch. Districts, Ohio, 1969—75; prin. North Ridgeville City Schools, Ohio, 1975—80; asst. supt. Madison Local Schools, Ohio, 1980—82; supt. of schools St. Clairsville-Richland City Schools, Ohio, 1982—85; dist. and bldg. adminstr. Scottsdale Pub. Schools, Ariz., 1985—94; supt. of schools Queen Creek Unified Sch. Dist., Ariz., 1994—98; rschr., cons. SW Interdisciplinary Rsch. Consortium, Ariz. State U., Tempe, Ariz., 1999—; ednl. cons. The Dustman Group, Scottsdale, Ariz., 1999—. Mem. Bel-Tech Adv. Bd., St. Clairsville, Ohio, 1982—85; academic standards design team mem. Ariz. Dept. of Edn., Phoenix, 1996—98; mem. East Valley Think Tank, Mesa, Ariz., 1994—98, Mesa C.C. Adv. Bd., Ariz., 1997—98; mentor SPR-Early Career Preventionist Network, Washington, 2003—; mem., cmty. adv. bd. for student services Osborn Elem. Sch. Dist., Phoenix, 2000—; mem., acad. profls. Sch. of Social Work, Ariz. State U., 2003—. Contbr. articles to profl. jours. Mem. C. of C., St. Clairsville, Ohio, 1982—85; founding mem. and chair Scottsdale Prevention Inst., Ariz., 1985—87; mem. Scottsdale Ednl. Enrichment Services, Ariz., 1985—2003; donor Kent State U. Alumni Assn., The Wilson Conf. of the Coll. of Edn., The Bowman Fellowship Fund, Ariz. State U. Alumni Assn. Founders' Day, 1990—2003. Recipient Key to the City, Mayor and City Coun. of St. Clairsville Ohio, 1985; Tech. grant, Olin Charitable Trust, 1995—98, Saturday Sch., Rural Metro Corp., 1998, Summer Acad. scholarships, MGC Pure Chemicals Am., 1997—98, grant, Key Pers.: Drug Resistance Strategies Project, NIH/NIDA, 1999—, grant, Key Pers.: Assoc. Dir.: SW Interdisciplinary Rsch. Consortium, 2002. Mem.: Belmont- Harrison Superintendents' Assn. (chair 1983—85), Soc. for Prevention Rsch., Ariz. Sch. Administrators (life), Phi Delta Kappa (program chair 1978—80). Avocations: reading, writing, travel, skiing. Office: Southwest Interdisciplinary Research Con P O Box 873711 Tempe AZ 85287-3711 Office Phone: 480-945-5485. Personal E-mail: dustmangroup@yahoo.com. Business E-Mail: patricia.dustman@asu.edu.

DUTCHER, JANICE JEAN PHILLIPS, oncologist; b. Bend, Oreg., Nov. 10, 1950; d. Charles Glen and MayBelle (Fluit) Phillips; m. John Dutcher, Sept. 8, 1971 (div. 1980). BA with honors, U. Utah, 1971; MD, U. Calif., Davis, 1975. Diplomate Am. Bd. Internal Medicine, Am. Bd. Med. Oncology. Intern Rush-Presbyn. St. Luke's Hosp., Chgo., 1975-76, resident, 1976-78; clin. assoc. Balt. Cancer Rsch., Nat. Cancer Inst., 1978-81, sr. investigator, 1981-82; asst. prof. U. Md., Balt., 1982, Albert Einstein Coll. Medicine, N.Y.C., 1983-86, assoc. prof., 1986-92, prof., 1992-98, course co-dir. Advances in Cancer Treatment Rsch. Manhattan, 1984-96; prof. medicine N.Y. Med. Coll., 1998—; assoc. dir. for clin. affairs Comprehensive Cancer Ctr., Our Lady of Mercy Med. Ctr., 1998—. Chmn. biol. response mod. com. Ea. Coop. Oncology Group, Madison, Wis., 1989-95, mem. exec. com., 1995-97, chair renal subcom., 1998—; mem. data safety com. Nat. Heart Lung Blood Inst., Bethesda, Md., 1990-95; mem. biologic response modifier study sect. Nat. Cancer Inst., Bethesda, 1988, 90, 94, 96, mem. NIH [illegible] mem. FDA Oncology Drug Adv. Bd., 1995-99, chair FDA-ODAC, 1996-99, NCI subcom. D for program project rev., 1995-98, mem. subsplty. med. oncology bd. Am. Bd. Internal Medicine, 1997-2003; mem. NCI subcom. A for Cancer Ctrs., 1998-2002; mem. faculty AACR/ASCO Workshop on Clin. Trials Devel., 1996-2002, NIH Progress Rev. Group on Kidney Cancer, 2001. Editor: Handbook of Hematology/Oncology Emergencies, 1987, Modern Transfusion Therapy, 1990; sect. editor: Neoplastic Diseases of the Blood, 3d edit., 1996, 4th edit., 2003; mem. editl. bd. Jour. Immunotherapy, Med. Oncology, Jour. Clin. Oncology, Jour. Clin. Pharm., Ann. Intern. Med.; sect. editor Current Treatment Options in Oncology, 2000-, Chronic Leukemia, 2000—; contbr. articles to Blood, Leukemia, Jour. Clin. Oncology, Jour. Immunotherapy, Clin. Cancer Rsch., Soc. Am. Cancer Jour. Recipient Beecham award in Hematology So. Blood Club, 1983, Henry C. Moses Clin. Rsch. award Montefiore Med. Ctr., 1989, Outstanding Alumnus award U. Calif., Davis, 1989; named Outstanding Young Investigator Ea. Coop. Oncology Group, 1993; recipient numerous grants. Internat. Soc. Biol. Therapy (exec. com.). Achievements include findings related to management of alloimmunization to platelet transfusions, intensive maintenance of patients with acute leukemia, studies of new biologic response modifiers as antitumor drugs, management of renal cell cance, melanoma and breast cancer, study and treatment with biologic antitumor agents. Address: Our Lady of Mercy Med Ctr Comprehensive Cancer Ctr 600 E 233rd St Bronx NY 10466-2604

DUTCHER, JUDI, state auditor; b. MI, Nov. 27, 1962; married; two children. BA, U. of MN, 1984, JD, 1987. Asst. atty. City of Minneapolis, MN, 1987-88; atty. Lang, Pauly & Gregerson, Ltd, Minneapolis, MN, 1988-94; state auditor Minn. State, Saint Paul, 1995—. Bd. dirs. State Bd. of Investment, State Exec. Coun., Land Exch. Bd., Pub. Employees Retirement Assoc. Bd., MN Housing Fin. Agy., Rural Fin. Adminstrn. Bd., Bd. of Govt. Innovation and Cooperation. Office: Minn State Auditor Off 525 Park St Ste 300 Saint Paul MN 55103-2197 Fax: 651-206-4755. E-mail: stateduditor@osa.state.mn.us.

DUTTA, MITRA, physicist, educator; b. Patna, Bihar, India, July 3, 1953; came to U.S., 1976; d. Dhiren N. and Aruna (Ray) D.; m. Sudhin Datta, Apr. 26, 1983. BS, U. Delhi (India), MSc, 1973; PhD, U. Cin., 1981. Lectr. Coll. Arts, Sci. and Tech., Kingston, Jamaica, 1973-76, U. West Indies, Kingston, 1973-76; rsch. assoc. Purdue U., West Lafayette, Ind., 1981-83; sr. rsch. assoc. CCNY, N.Y.C., 1983-86; rsch. engr. Systematic Gen. Corp., Eatontown, N.J., 1986-88; rsch. physicist and leader optoelectronics team Army Rsch. Lab. Electronics and Power Sources Directorate, Ft. Monmouth, NJ, 1988—2001, coord. NSF, 1990—2001; prof. U. Ill., Chgo., 2001—, head, electrical & computer engring. dept., 2001—. Mem. JDL Reliance Sub-Sub Panel on Photonic Devices, 1991—, tech. adv. com. on narotechnology Univ. Rsch. Iniative, 1992—, condensed matter adv. group, ARO, 1993—. Contbr. approximately 60 articles to Phys. Rev., Applied Physics Letters, IEEE Jour. Quantum Electronics. Nat. Merit scholar Govt. of India, 1968-71, Univ. Grants scholar Univ. Grants Commn., Delhi, India, 1971-73, R & D Achievement award, U.S. Army, 1990, 92, 94, ETDL Narold Jacobs award, 1991, Nat. Achievement award, Soc. for Women Engrs., 2003. Mem. IEEE (sr. mem.), Am. Phys. Soc., Optical Soc. Am., Sigma Xi. Achievements include 2 patents in field. Office: U Ill at Chgo 851 S Morgan M/C 154 Chicago IL 60607 E-mail: dutta@ece.uic.edu.

DUTTON, CHRISTINA PARKER, interior designer, event planner; b. Washington, Mar. 30, 1968; d. Frederick Gary and Nancy (Hogan) D.; m. Paul Thomas Fucci, Oct. 3, 1998. BA, Occidental Coll., 1991. Spl. asst. Clinton for Pres., Washington, 1992, Inaugural Com., Washington, 1992-93; pres., owner Christina Dutton Interiors, LLC, Washington, 1995—. Cons. spl. events Dem. Nat. Com., Washington, 1992, 96. Mem. Jr. League of Washington. Episcopalian. Home: 4839 Reservoir Rd NW Washington DC 20007-1543 Office: Christina Dutton Interiors 5017 Tilden St NW Washington DC 20016-2333 E-mail: DuttonDC@aol.com.

DUTTON, DIANA CHERYL, lawyer; b. Sherman, Tex., June 27, 1944; d. Roy G. and Monett D.; m. Anthony R. Grindl, July 8, 1974. BS, Georgetown U., 1967; JD, U. Tex., 1971. Bar: Tex. 1971. Regional counsel U.S. EPA, Dallas, 1975-79, dir. enforcement div., 1979-81; ptnr., head firm-wide environ. practice, mem. Dallas practice com. Akin, Gump, Strauss, Hauer & Feld, L.L.P., Dallas, 1981—. Bd. dirs. Dallas Nature Ctr., 2001-02, Girls Inc.; chair Greater Dallas Chamber Environ. Com., 2001. Named One of Best Lawyers in Dallas D Mag., 2001, Ams. Leading Bus. Lawyers Chambers USA, 2003, Tex. Super Lawyer and among Top 50 Tex. Women Attys., Tex. Monthly Mag., 2003. Mem. ABA, Tex. Bar Assn. (chmn. environ. and natural resources law sect. 1985-86), Dallas Bar Assn. (chmn. environ. law sect. 1984), Dallas Bar Found.. Episcopalian. Office: Akin Gump Strauss Hauer & Feld LLP 1700 Pacific Ave Ste 4100 Dallas TX 75201-4675 Office Phone: 214-969-2855. E-mail: ddutton@akingump.com.

DUTTON, JO SARGENT, education educator, researcher, consultant; b. L.A., Calif., Oct. 26, 1940; d. Paul and Jayne (O'Toole) Sargent; m. Ted W. Dutton, Nov. 15, 1979; children: Brooks, Berndan, Mark; step-children: Robert, William, Jeanne, Jerry. BS, U. So. Calif., 1962, MS, 1966; PhD, U. Calif. Riverside, 1996. Cert. elem. tchr., Calif.; corp. paralegal cert.; preliminary adminstrv. svcs. credential. Elem. sch. tchr. 6th grade Lawndale Unified Sch. Dist., 1963-64; reading instr. Culver City (Calif.) Unified Sch. Dist., 1964; prof. edn. U. So. Calif., 1964-65; remedial reading instr. Santa Monica (Calif.) Unified Sch. Dist., 1965-66; dist. remedial reading instr. San Marino Unified Sch. Dist., 1967-70; real estate broker Calif., 1972-96; adj. prof. English Chaffey C. C., Rancho Cucamonga, Calif., 1991-93; rsch. fellowCalif. Ednl. Rsch. Coop. U. Calif., Riverside, 1993-95. Prof. Calif. Bapt. Coll., 1997; dir. rsch. Calif. Virtual U., 1997; dir. devel. U. Calif. Riverside, Sch. Edn., 1997-2000. Contbr. articles to profl. jours. Mem. exec. com. Inland Empire Cultural Found., 1980-83, Sister Cities Internat., Ontario, Calif., 1980-82; chair steering com. San Bernardino County Arts League, 1983-84; commr. San Bernardino County Mus.; mem. bd. Inland Empire Symphony; survey and assessment conductor Calif. Arts Coun. Mem. Am. Ednl. Rsch. Assn., Chaffey Cmty. Arts Assn., Calif. Ednl. Rsch. Assn. Home: PO Box 2960 Blue Jay CA 92317-2960 Office: U Calif Riverside Sch of Edn Riverside CA 92502-9874

DUVALL, BERNICE BETTUM, artist, exhibit coordinator, jewelry designer; b. Washington, Mar. 17, 1948; d. William A. and Bergny (Farovig) Bettum; m. Donald Dunn Duvall, Oct. 5, 1968; children: Gregory Thomas, Peter Brian. Grad. high sch., Washington, 1966; art edn. pvt. study, 1970-74. Artist watercolor, acrylic, needlework design, Chevy Chase, Md., 1972—; exhibit coord. Discovery Channel, Learning Channel, Discovery Comms., Inc., Bethesda, Md., 1993—, N.Y.C., Miami, L.A., 2000—, Your Choice TV, Bethesda, Md., 1995-97, Discovery Com., Inc., Chgo., 2001—, Charlotte, NC, 2003—. Pub. rels. and publicity Town Ctr. Gallery, Rockville, Md., 1986-89; banner designer St. Paul's Luth. Ch., Washington, 1985—; sch. art project coord. Am. Speech-Lang.-Hearing Assn., Rockville, Md., 1998-99; spkr. in field. Exhbns. include Capricorn Gallery, Bethesda, 1982, Westmoreland Mus. Art, Greensburg, Pa., 1982, 87, Hull Gallery, Washington, 1983, 85, Butler Inst. Am. Art, Youngstown, Ohio, 1983, DeLand (Fla.) Mus., 1984, Springfield (Mo.) Art Mus., 1988, 95, 98, Newberry Gallery, Pa., 1989, Broadway Gallery, Va., 1989, Watergate Gallery, Washington, 1990, Fine Art Mus. of South, Mobile, Ala., 1990, Images Internat. Gallery, Bethesda, 1991-93, So. Watercolor Soc., 1993, 99, Charles Sumner Sch. Mus., Washington, 1994, Sugar & Frichtl Gallery, Kensington, Md., 1994, Univ. Club, Washington, 1995, NIH, Bethesda,

1995, Margaret Smith Gallery, Ellicott City, Md., 1995, Office Gov. State of Md., Balt., 1996, Md. State House, Annapolis, 1996, Fine Arts Invitational, Oxford, Md., 1996-97, 99-02, Hughes Network Sys., Germantown, Md., 1996, Arlington County Sch. Bd., Arlington, Va., 1997, Delaplaine Visual Art Ctr., Frederick, Md., 1998, Mt. St. Mary's Coll., Emmittsburg, Md., 1998, Howard County Pub. Sch. Adminstrn. Gallery, Ellicott City, Md., 1999; one-woman shows include Wash. County Mus. Art, Hagerstown, Md., 1999; exhibited in group shows at Internat. Artists in Watercolor, London, 1981, Glenview Mansion Civic Ctr. Art Gallery, Rockville, Md., 2000, Dorchester Art Ctr, 2001, Sandy Spring (Md.) Mus., 2003; prin. works represented in pub. and pvt. collections including Montgomery County Contemporary Art Acquisitions, New Eng. Life Ins. Co., Pelavin Assocs., Inc., Capricorn Gallery, Univ. Club Washington; contbr. articles to Am. Artist, Watercolor, The Artist mag. Vol. artist Nat. Zoo, Washington, 1985-91; art judge Art in Schs., Parks, Pub. Places, Montgomery County, Md., 1988-90. Recipient Award of High Commendation Internat. Artists in Water Colors, 1981, Arthur Alexander award So. Water Color Soc., 1981, Award of Merit Md. Fedn. Art, 1980, Liquitex award Adirondacks Am. Watercolorists, 1989, Bendann Gallery award Balt. Water Color Soc., 1990, Washington Water Color Assn. award, 1993, Patron's award Watercolor U.S.A., 1995, First Place award Fed. Reserve, 1995. Mem. Pa. Watercolor Soc., Art League (bd. dirs. 1982-86), Washington Water Color Assn. (bd. dirs. 1986-87, award 1993), Town Ctr. Gallery (bd. dirs. 1986-89), Potomac Valley Watercolorists (bd. dirs. 1993—), Artists Equity, Arts Coun. Montgomery County, So. Watercolor Soc. (co-chmn. ann. juried exhibit 1993), Balt. Watercolor Soc., Strathmore Arts Found., Women's Club Chevy Chase. Lutheran. Avocations: gardening, horseback riding, needlework. Home: 3414 Taylor St Chevy Chase MD 20815-4024 E-mail: bbduvall.art@starpower.net.

DUVALL, DEBRA, school system administrator; Asst. supt. elem. edn. Mesa Pub. Sch., Ariz., 1987—95, asst. supt. curriculum and instrn., 1987—95, acting assoc. supt., 1995—2000, supt., 2000—. Chair Mesa Cmty. Coll. Commn. on Excellence in Edn., 2001—03. Recipient Disting. Adminstr. award (Supt. Divsn.), Ariz. Sch. Adminstrs. Assn., 2003. Office: Mesa Pub Sch #101 63 E Main St Mesa AZ 85201-7400 Office Phone: 480-472-0000. E-mail: dlduvall@mpsaz.org.

DUVALL, FLORENCE MARIE, software engineer; b. Malden, Mass., Aug. 4, 1953; d. George Perry Jr. and Florence Mary D. BS in Biology-Wildlife Ecology, U. Ariz., 1975; Global MBA, Nat. U., 2000. Chemistry rsch. lab. tech. Burr Brown Rsch. Corp., Tucson, 1975-77; supr. Transamerica Occidental Life, L.A., 1977-79; owner The Post Sta., Tucson, 1980-82; programmer analyst First Capital Life Ins., San Diego, 1982-94; sys. cons. Pacific Life Ins. Co., Newport Beach, Calif., 1994—, Yr. 2000 project mgr., 1996-2000. Vol. cons. patient database genetic counseling dept. Sharps Perinatal Ctr., San Diego, 1993-94; dir. tech. comms. Gospel Light COGIC, 2000—. Webmaster Gospellight Church.org, 1999—. Mem. foster parent program Orange County Social Svc., Orange, Calif., 1999; mem. Gospellight Ch. God in Christ, mem. usher bd. and women's coun., 1999—. Mem. IEEE, Data Processing Mgmt. Asn., Akbash Dogs Internat. (sec. 1998—), Project Mgmt. Inst. Office: Pacific Life Ins Co 700 Newport Center Dr Newport Beach CA 92660-6307 E-mail: fduvall@pacificlife.com.

DUVALL, HOLLIE JEAN, music educator; b. Greensburg, Pa., Dec. 8, 1953; d. William Gilbert Smail and Betty Jane Rygiel; m. Charles Timothy Duvall, Feb. 18, 1977; children: Charles Timothy, Renee Jean. B in Music Edn., Seton Hill Coll., 1995; MA, Ind. U. of Pa., 1997. Pa. instrnl. cert. in music edn. Music dir. Ch. of God (Holiness), Greensburg, Pa., 1970—; wedding and fashion show cons. Greensburg, 1982-98; interior designer, 1982—; freelance pianist, 1985—; instr. piano and voice Pvt. Studio, Greensburg, 1985—; prof. music Westmoreland County C.C., Youngwood, Pa., 1996—, music coord., 1998—; prof. music C.C. of Allegheny County, West Mifflin, Pa., 1999—, Pa. State U., Fayette, Pa., 2002—. Judge-fine arts Keystone Christian Edn. Assn., Pa., 1989—, Ea. Nazarene Regional Div., Greensburg, Pa., 1990, Am. Fedn. Women's Clubs, Greensburg, 1995-97. Reviewer in field. Sunday sch. tchr. Ch. of God (Holiness), Greensburg, 1975—. Recipient scholarship award AAUW, 1993, scholarship award PEO Sisterhood, 1994. Mem. Profl. Music Educator's Assn., Alpha Sigma Lambda (Scholarship award 1992). Republican. Avocations: reading, floral arranging, decorating. Office: Westmoreland County CC 400 Armbrust Rd Youngwood PA 15697-1801 E-mail: hjd11@psu.edu., hollie_duvall@yahoo.com.

DUVALL, LORRAINE, recreation center owner; b. Hamilton, Ohio, Jan. 31, 1925; d. Saul and Martha Jane (Huff) Baker; m. Ray DuVall, June 12, 1951; children: Sharon DuVall Keese, Deborah D. Velchoff, Steve, Annette. BA, U. Cin., 1951; MA, Tex. A&I U., 1963; postgrad., Miami U., Oxford, Ohio, 1958, U. Toledo, 1959, U. Tex.-Austin, 1968. Elem. tchr., Larkmoor, Lorain, Ohio, 1956-60; tchr. math Incarnate Word High Sch., Corpus Christi, 1964-70; owner, instr. Aerobic Fitness, Corpus Christi, 1973-93; owner, coach Corpus Christi Marlin Swim Team, 1972—. Mgr. Corpus Christi Country Club Pool, 1973-88; pres., mgr. Club Estates Pool Chems., Corpus Christi, 1980-89, Club Estates Recreation, Corpus Christi, 1977—. Vol. psychiat. ward Meml. Hosp., Corpus Christi, 1966-70, U.S. Swimming Club Devel., 1993-97; harpist First Bapt. Ch. Orch., 1995—; adminstrv. gen. chair South Tex. Swimming, 1996-99; liaison to U.S. Swimming Club Devel. Com, 1995; bd. dirs. vol. YWCA, Corpus Christi, 1970-77; water safety trainer ARC, Corpus Christi, 1975-82; CPR instr. Am. Heart Assn., Corpus Christi, 1980-84; vol. children's choir dir. St. John Methodist Ch., Corpus Christi, 1966-78, Asbury United Meth. Ch., 1980-93; vol. harpist 1st Bapt. Ch., 1995—. NSF grantee U. Tex.-Austin, 1968. Mem. Am. Swim Coaches Assn., Am. Harp Soc. Avocations: music, swimming, tennis, skiing, backpacking. Home: 6709 Pintail Dr Corpus Christi TX 78413-2337 Office: 4902 Snowgoose Dr Corpus Christi TX 78413-2328 E-mail: l-r-duvall@prodigy.net.

DUVALL, MARJORIE L. English and foreign language educator; b. Lehighton, Pa., Dec. 2, 1958; d. Charles Jacque and Carole Faye (Eckhart) Lusch; m. Glenn Edward Duvall, July 26, 1954. BA in German, Lafayette Coll., 1980; MA in German, U. Fla., 1998; postgrad., East Stroudsburg U., 1982, Ga. So. U., Middlebury Coll., 1988, Augusta State U., U. Pa., 1994, U. S.C., 1993; student, Goethe-Inst., Germany, 2003, Accord Lang. Sch., Paris, France, 2003. German and French tchr. Evans (Ga.) Mid. Sch., 1987-89, Harlem (Ga.) Mid. Sch., 1989-92; ESOL tchr. Lakeside Mid. and H.S.'s, Evans, Ga., 1992-97; ESL tchr. Davidson & Murphy H.S.'s, Mobile, Ala., 1997-99; German tchr. Brookwood H.S., Snellville, Ga., 1999-00; tchr. ESOL and lang. arts for gifted Freedom Middle Sch., Stone Mountain, Ga., 2000—03; tchr. English, Dunwoody H.S., Ga., 2003—. Contbr. articles to profl. jours. Recipient scholarship Profl. Assn. Ga. Educators, 1994. Mem.: TESOL, Fgn. Lang. Assn. Ga., Ga. Assn. Gifted Children, Nat. Coun. Tchrs. English, Am. Assn. Tchrs. of French, Am. Assn. Tchrs. of German, Friends of Goethe, DeKalb County Supporters of the Gifted, Mensa. Lutheran. Avocations: choral music, piano, swimming, baton twirling, dance. Home: 4809 Leeds Ct Dunwoody GA 30338 Office: Dunwoody HS 5035 Vermack Rd Dunwoody GA 30338 E-mail: pardette80@aol.com.

DUVALL, SHELLEY, actress; b. Houston, July 7, 1949; d. Robert Duvall and Bobbie Crawford. Founder Armadillo Prodns. Actress: films (debut) Brewster McCloud, 1970, McCabe and Mrs. Miller, 1971, Thieves Like Us, 1974, Nashville, 1975, Buffalo Bill and the Indians, 1976, Three Women, 1977 (Cannes Film Festival Best Actress award, L.A. Film Critics' Best Actress award, 2d pl. N.Y. Film Critics), Annie Hall, 1977, Popeye, 1981, The Shining, 1981, Time Bandits, 1981, Roxanne, 1987, Suburban Commando, 1991, Changing Habits, 1996, The Portrait of a Lady, 1996, Alone, 1997, Home Fries, 1997, Space Cadet, 1997, Tale of the Mummy, 1998, Big Monster on Campus, 2000, Dreams in the Attic, 2000, Manna From Heaven, 2003, (TV movies) Bernice Bobs Her Hair, 1977, Lily, 1986, (TV episode) Twilight Zone, 1986; creator, exec. producer, on-camera host Faerie Tale Theatre; exec. producer: video and pay TV series Faerie Tale Theatre, (Peabody award, Golden Ace award, others), Shelley Duvall's Bedtime Stories, Shelley Duvall's Tall Tales and Legends, The Strange Case of Dr. Jekyll and Mr. Hyde, 13 episode children's series Mrs. Piggle-Wiggle. Founder, Think Entertainment prodn. co., 1988. Mem. Nat. Acad. Cable Programming (bd. govs.). Office: care The Gersh Agency 232 N Canon Dr Beverly Hills CA 90210-5302

DUVAL-PIERRELOUIS, JEANNE-MARIE, educational association executive; b. Chgo., June 5, 1953; d. Paul A. and Virginia (Bertsch) Duval; m. Claude Pierrelouis, Apr. 4, 1982; 1 child, Eryc Pierrelouis. BA, Bryn Mawr Coll., 1977; MEd, Temple U., 1982. Acad. coord. internsive English program Temple U., Phila., 1979-84; asst. dir. coop. grants program Nat. Assn. Fgn. Studnet Affairs, Assn. Internat. Educators, Washington, 1984-86; dir. coop. grants program NAFSA, Assn. Internat. Educators, Washington, 1986-89, sr. dir. ednl. program, 1989-96, assoc. exec. dir., 1996-99; mng. dir. higher edn. programs Am. Couns. Internat. Edn., Washington, 2000—02, v.p. higher edn., 2002—. Cons. Fund Improvement Post Secondary Edn., Washington, 1995-97; mem. exec. com. Alliance Internat. Ednl. and Cultural Exch., Washington, 1997-99. Mem. edn. com. Barrie Sch., Silver Spring, Md., 1998-99. Fulbright grantee Bd. Fgn. Scholarships, 1988. Avocations: weaving, photography. Office: Am Couns Internat Edn ACTR/ACCELS 1776 Mass Ave NW Ste 700 Washington DC 20036 Fax: 202-833-7523.

DUVEEN, ANNETA, artist; b. Bklyn., May 21, 1924; d. Julius and Shirley (Klugman) Applebaum; m. Charles J. Duveen Jr., Dec. 21, 1942 (div. 1954); children: Wendy, Charles III, Peter; m. Benjamin Duveen, Nov. 24, 1976. Student, U. Iowa, 1941, Adelphi Acad., 1941, Columbia U., 1941, 42, 56; HHD, St. Francis Coll., 1986. Founder, pres. Duveen Internat. Ltd., Port Chester, N.Y., 1987—. Lectr. Westchester Arts Coun., White Plains, N.Y., 1993-94. Prin. works exhibited in group and retrospective and one-woman shows including Pacem in Terris Gallery, N.Y.C., 1970, The Signs of God in the World, Santa Croce Basilica Grand Cloister, Florence, Italy, 1985, Marymount Manhattan Coll., 1986, Artiste 86, Rome, 1986; commd. sculptures include heroic meml. busts of Ella T. Grasso, Robert F. Kennedy, St. Maximilian Kolbe and the Papal Family, The Child: Moments in Bronze, Our Lady of the Eucharist, Tabernacle: Our Lady of the Grain of Wheat, many others; also 49 stained glass window designs of St. Anthony; also collage Alas, She Died in Childbirth; co-author: Essentials of Astronomy, 1976. Mem. exec. com. Franciscans Internat., Bklyn., 1989-99; internat. rep. for justice, peace and ecology Secular Franciscan Order, Rome, 1990-92; tchr., dir., ednl. specialist, proposal designer, rschr., cons. Fellow Royal Astron. Soc.; mem. AAAS, AAUW, Sede di Dante, N.Y. Acad. Scis., Inst. for Theol. Encounter with Sci. and Tech., Nat. Fedn. Press Women, Portchester Coun. for Arts, Westchester Arts Coun. Home and Office: 3 Rye Rd Port Chester NY 10573-5313

DUVO, MECHELLE LOUISE, oil company executive, consultant; b. East Stroudsburg, Pa., Apr. 25, 1962; d. Nicholas and Arlene Birdie (Mack) D. AS, Lehigh County C.C., 1982. Rehab. counselor Phoenix Project, Bakersfield, Calif., 1982-84; nat. sales mgr. Olympia Advt., L.A., 1984-85; oil exploration cons. Cimmaron Mgmt., Nashville, 1985-86; exec. sec. Pueblo Resources Corp., Bowling Green, Ky., 1986-87; nat. oil cons. El Toro, Inc., Bowling Green, 1986-87; founder, pres. and CEO Majestic Mgmt. Corp., Glasgow, Ky., 1987—; nat. oil cons. Impact Oil, Inc., Glasgow, 1987—. Lease procurator El Toro, Inc., 1986-87; spkr. Nat. Investment Seminars, 1994—. Editor, pub.: (newsletter) The Majestic Field Copy, 1994—. Fundraiser Am. Cancer Soc., LA, 1984-85; vol. Humane Soc., Nashville, 1985-86, Humane Soc., Bowling Green, 1986-87, Boy Scouts Am., 2001-02; counselor Salvation Army, Bakersfield, 1982-84; vol. mgr. Food Pantry Outreach Program, 1999-2001, Relay for Life, 2001—. Mem. NAFE (exec. program), Internat. Platform Assn., Ky. Oil & Gas Assn. Avocations: house plants, gardening, music, gourmet cooking. Home and Office: Majestic Mgmt Corp 1202 S Green St Glasgow KY 42141-2014 E-mail: majestic-mgmt-corp@glasgow-ky.com.

DUYCK, KATHLEEN MARIE, poet, musician, retired social worker; b. Portland, Oreg., July 21, 1933; d. Anthony Joseph Dwyer and Edna Elisabeth Hayes; m. Robert Duyck, Feb. 3, 1962; children: Mary Kay Boeyen, Robert Patrick, Anthony Joseph. BS, Oreg. State U., 1954; MSW, U. Wash., 1956. Cert. NASW, Oreg. Adoption worker Cath. Svcs., Portland, 1956-61, Cath. Welfare, San Antonio, 1962; musician Tucson Symphony, 1963-65; prin. cellist Phoenix (Ariz.) Coll. Orch., 1968-78, Scottsdale (Ariz.) Symphony, 1974-80; poet, 1993—. Author: (poetry cassettes) Visions, 1993 (Contemporary Series Poet 1993), Visions II, 1996 (Contemporary Series Poet 1996); author numerous poems. Rep. worker Maricopa County Reps., Phoenix, 1974; mem. Scottsdale Cultural Coun.; NASW bd. Cath. Charities Rep., Portland, 1959-61. Recipient Golden Poet award World of Poetry, 1991, 92, Editor's Choice awards Nat. Libr. Poetry, 1993-2003, Sec. gift Phoenix Exec. Bd., 1976. Recognition award Archbishop Howard, 1961, 5-Yr. Kathleen Duyck award Cello Congress V, 1996, Internat. Poet of Merit award Internat. Soc. Poets, 2003. Mem. Internat. Poetry Hall Fame, Ariz. Cello Soc., Nat. Libr. Poetry, Internat. Soc. Poets, Phoenix Symphony Guild (exec. bd. 1970-80). Republican. Roman Catholic. Avocations: piano, photography, poetry, artistic collections, concerts. Home: 4545 E Palomino Rd Phoenix AZ 85018-1719

DVORAK, KATHLEEN S. business products company executive; married; 2 children. BS in Edn., No. Ill. U., 1978; MBA in Fin., DePaul U., 1988. Tchr. math. Conrady Jr. H.S., 1977-82; dir. investor rels./corp. comms. United Stationers Inc., Des Plaines, Ill., 1982-97, v.p. investor rels., 1997-2000, v.p. investor rels. and fin. adminstrn., 2000—. Recipient Howard Beasley Managerial Excellence award. Mem. Nat. Investor Rels. Inst. Home: 1032 Oakwood Dr Westmont IL 60559-1040 Office: United Stationers Inc 2200 E Golf Rd Des Plaines IL 60016-1257

DWINELL, ANN JONES, retired special education educator; b. Lowell, Mass., Oct. 28, 1934; d. George Hubert and Bridget Jones; m. Roland A. Dwinell, Dec. 23, 1956; children: Theresa, Joseph, Richard, John. BA, Framingham State Coll., 1972; MEd, Lesley Coll., 1974; PhD, Boston Coll., 1991. Cert. Eng. tchr., moderate spl. needs instr., Mass., adminstr., supt., spl. edn. adminstr., R.I. Spl. edn. tchr., adminstr. Marlborough (Mass.) Pub. Sch., 1972-78; core chairperson Malden (Mass.) Pub. Schs., 1978-80, spl. edn. specialist, 1980—2001. Contbr. articles to profl. jours. Mem. NEA, Mass. Tchrs. Assn. (rep. 1983-85, liaison 1987—), Phi Delta Kappa. Roman Catholic. Avocations: dance, music, boating, reading.

DWORIN, MICKI (MAXINE DWORIN), automobile dealership executive; widowed; children: Judy, Diane. V.p. Dworin Chevrolet, Inc., East Harford, Conn., 1955-83, Dworin Auto Leasing. Pres. Eastern Auto Ins., Conn. Chevrolet Dealers Assn., Tarrytown Zone Dealer Coun., Atlantic Coast Region Dealer Coun., Boulevard, Inc. Sec. BBB, Hartford, Conn.; vol. coord. Vol. Broward, 1998-99, Children's Diagnostic and Treatment Ctr., 1996-98, Am. Cancer Soc., 1994-96, Kids in Distress, 1991-95; hon. trustee Hartford Coll. for Women; sec., bd. govs. Point of Am. Condominium; coord. Trinity Coll.; bd. dirs. Combined Health Appeals; chmn. King David Soc., 1995-96. Mem. Advt. Assn. Grtr. Hartford. Fax: 954-522-6770. E-mail: volbrow@safari.net.

DWORSKY, CLARA WEINER, lawyer, former merchandise brokerage executive; b. N.Y.C., Apr. 28, 1918; d. Charles and Rebecca (Becker) Weiner; m. Bernard Ezra Dworsky, Jan. 2, 1944; 1 child, Barbara G. Goodman. BS, St. John's U., N.Y.C., 1937, LLB, 1939, JD, 1968. Bar: N.Y. 1939, U.S. Dist. Ct. (ea. dist.) N.Y. 1942, U.S. Dist. Ct. (so. dist.) Tex. 1993, U.S. Ct. Appeals (9th cir.) 1994, U.S. Ct. Appeals (5th cir.) 1995, U.S. Supreme Ct. 2003. Pvt. practice, N.Y.C., 1939-51; assoc. Bessie Farberman, N.Y.C., 1942; clk., sec. U.S. Armed Forces, Camp Carson, Colo., Camp Claiborne, La., 1944-45; abstractor, dir. Realty Title, Rockville, Md., 1954-55; v.p. Kelley & Dworsky Inc., Houston, 1960—. Appeals agt. Gasoline Rationing Appeals Bd., N.Y.C., 1942; bd. dirs. Southlan Sales Assocs., Houston. Vol. ARC, N.Y.C.; vice chmn. War Bond pledge drive, Bklyn.; vol. Houston Legal Found., 1972-73; pres. Women's Aux. Washington Hebrew Acad., 1958-60, v.p. bd. trustees, 1959-60; co-founder, v.p. S. Tex. Hebrew Acad. (now Hebrew Acad.), Houston, 1970-75, hon. pres. women's divsn., 1973. Recipient Cert. award Treas. of U.S., 1943; Commendation Office of Chief Magistrate of City N.Y., 1948; Pietas medal St. Johns U., 1985. Mem.: ABA (chmn. social security com., sr. lawyers divsn. 1989—93, mem. sr. lawyers divsn. coun. 1989—95, chairsubcom. 1993—95, chmn. social security com., sr. lawyers divsn. 1995—, mem. editl. bd. sr. lawyers divsn. pub. Experience), Nat. Assn. Women Lawyers (chmn. organizer Juvenile Delinquency Clinic N.Y. 1948—51), Houston Bar Assn. (sec. social secutiry sect. 1995—96), Fed. Bar Assn. (vice chair programs, sr. lawyers divsn. 1994—96, dep. chair 1996—97, chmn. 1997—98, chair sr. lawyers com. south Tex. chpt. bd. 1998—, co-editor sr. citizens handbook, 2d printing 2002—03, chmn. soc. sec. com., sen. lawyers divsn.), N.Y. State Bar Assn., St. Johns U. Alumni Assn. (coord. Houston chpt. 1983—, pres. 1986), Amit Women Club, Delphians Past Pres.'s Club, Hadassah. Jewish. Home: 9726 Cliffwood Dr Houston TX 77096-4406

DWORSKY, MARY, interior designer; b. Mpls., Feb. 17, 1948; d. Zollie and Lucille Dworsky. Attended, U. Minn., 1966-71. Cert. interior designer Minn. Interior designer Creative Furniture, Mpls., 1974-79, Mr. Furniture, Mpls., 1980-82, Dorothy Collins Interiors, Edina, Minn., 1982-89, Interior Design Ptnrs., Edina, 1989-92, The Design Studio of Gabberts, Edina, 1992-2000, Mary Dworsky Interior Design Ltd., Mpls. Decorations chair Mpls. Crisis Nursery, 1996. Mem.: ASID (Minn. chpt. pres. 2000—01, dir., sec., pres. 2000—01, Presdl. Citation 1994, 1996, 1999, 2000), Rotary (com. chair 1991—99). Home: #121 3720 Independence Ave S Minneapolis MN 55426-3781 Office: Mary Dworsky Interior Design Ltd 275 Market St Ste 451 Minneapolis MN 55405

DWYER, JOHANNA TODD, nutrition research scientist, clinical nutritionist, educator; b. Syracuse, N.Y., Oct. 20, 1938; d. M. Harold and Frances (Markey) D. BS with distinction, Cornell U., 1960; MSc, U. Wis., 1962; MS, Harvard Sch. Pub. Health, Boston, 1965, DSc, 1969. Asst. prof. Harvard Sch. Pub. Health, 1969-73; home economist Procter & Gamble, Cin., 1962-64; rsch. asst. U. Wis., Madison, 1960-62; assoc. prof. Tufts Med. Sch., 1974, prof. medicine and nutrition, 1984—; sr. scientist human nutrition rsch. USDA, Boston, 1988—, asst. adminstr. for human nutrition Agrl. Rsch. Svc. Washington, 2001—02; sr. nutrition rsch. scientist Office of Dietary Supplements, NIH, 2003—. Dir. Frances Stern Nutrition Ctr., New Eng. Med. Ctr., Boston, 1974—; adj. prof. Harvard Sch. Pub. Health, 1988—. Author of 3 books, 1979, 83; contbr. 300 articles to profl. jours. Mem. Mass. Nutrition Bd., Boston, 1980—; cons. Exec. Office of Pres., Washington, 1970, mem. bd. sci. counselors Nat. Cancer Inst., 1985-89; com. mem. and nuitrition work study Am. Cancer Soc., 1990-94. Recipient Lenna Frances Cooper award/Lydia Roberts lectr., Am. Dietetic Assn., 1995, Medallion award Am. Dietetic Assn., 2002; Robert Wood Johnson Health Policy fellow, 1980-81, John Stalker award Am. Sch. Food Svc. Assn., 1990. Fellow: Am. Soc. Nutrition Scis., Soc. for Nutrition Edn. (bd. dirs. 1975—77, J. Harvey Wiley award 1983); mem.: APHA (program devel. bd. 1990—92), Dannon Inst. (sci. adv. bd. 2003—), Internat. Life Scis. Inst. (bd. dirs. 1999—), Food and Drug Law Inst. (bd. dirs. 1980—95), Am. Inst. Food and Wine (bd. dirs. 1991—95), Nutrition Screening Initiative (tech. and sci. rev. com. 1990—), Am. Inst. Nutrition (pres. 1994—95, bd. dirs.), Am. Soc. Clin. Nutrition (sec. 1990—93), Inst. Medicine of NAS (food and nutrition bd. 1990—2000, councilor 2001—03), Am. Dietetic Assn. (legis. and pub. policy com. 1998—), Am. Soc. Parenteral and Enteral Nutrition (adv. bd. 1978—). Office: New Eng Med Ctr 750 Washington St PO Box 783 Boston MA 02102-0783 Office Phone: 617-636-5273. E-mail: jdayer1@tufts.nemc.org.

DWYER, JUDITH A. marriage and family therapist; b. Phila., Apr. 15, 1956; d. Arthur William and Virginia Arlene (Courter) Crouthamel; m. John Adam Dwyer, Dec. 15, 1979; children: Allison Michelle, Kimberly Virginia, Matthew John. BS in Elem. Edn., Millersville U., 1978; MA in Pastoral Counseling, La Salle U., 1994. Cert. marriage and family therapist. Intern La Salle Family Studies Clin., Phila., 1992-93, Wayne Counseling Ctr., Wayne, Pa., 1994-95; marriage and family therapist N.E. Career Ctr., Princeton, N.J., 1995-96, Counseling Ctr. at St. Luke U., Glenside, Pa., 1996—. Dir. Support Police Immediate Response Intervention Team, Glenside, Pa., 1996—; vol. Second Alarmes Rescue Squad, Willow Grove, Pa., 1986—. Mem. Am. Assn. Marriage and Family Therapists, Pa. Assn. Marriage and Family Therapists. Republican. Presbyterian. Avocations: church choir, swimming, hiking, reading.

DWYER, KATHERINE, cosmetic company executive; With Revlon, 1993—; pres. Revlon Cosmetics USA; sr. v.p. Revlon, Inc., apptd. pres. consumer products, 1999—. Office: Revlon Inc 625 Madison Ave Fl 8 New York NY 10022-1894 Fax: 212-527-4995.

DWYER, MAUREEN E. lawyer; BA, Smith Coll., 1973; JD, Cath. U. Am. Columbus Sch. Law, 1978. Shareholder Wilkes Artis, Wash., DC; law ptnr. real estate group Shaw Pittman, Wash., DC. Named one of 100 Most Powerful Women in Wash., Washingtonian mag., 2001. Mem.: DC C. of C., Urban Land Inst., Greater Wash. Bd. Trade, DC Bldg. Industry Assn. Office: Shaw Pittman LLP 2300 N St NW Washington DC 20037-1128 Office Phone: 202-663-8000. Office Fax: 202-663-8007.*

DWYER, RUTH E. music educator; b. Kokomo, Ind., Oct. 25, 1955; d. William Dwyer and Sarah Carothers; m. Dean Spenner, June 10, 1993. B in Music Edn., Ind. U., 1978, MS in Edn., 1982. Music tchr. Seymour (Ind.) Cmty. Schs., 1978—93, MSD Wayne Twp., Indpls., 1993—97; assoc. dir. Indpls. Children's Choir, 1988—, dir. edn., 1997—. Adj. prof. Butler U., Indpls., 1998—. Author: Prepatory Program-Theory and Solfage, 2001; composer, arranger, editor: Ruth Dwyer Choral Series, contbg. author: Colla Voce Publishers, Hal Leonard Choral Publs. Named Music Educator of Yr., Ind. Music Educators Assn., 1996. Mem.: Music Educators Nat. Conf., Orgn. Am. Kodaly Educators (guest condr. 2000), Am. Choral Dirs. Assn. (life). Office: Indpls Childrens Choir 4600 Sunset Ave Indianapolis IN 46208

DWYER, THERESA, utilities executive; b. 1935; Pvt. practice; dir. The Dwyer Group, 1994—, chair bd. dirs., 1995—; majority stockholder, pres. Worldwide Cabinet Sys., Inc., Worldwide Refinishing Sys., Inc., Worldwide Whirlpool Sys., Inc., Worldwide Franchise Cons., Ltd., Aames Auto Leasing, Inc., Sun Screen of Austin, Inc., 1994—; v.p. Worldwide Supply, Inc.; sec. Dwyer Real Estate and Devel., Inc.; mng. ptnr. Dwyer Investments, Ltd. Office: The Dwyer Group Inc 1010 N University Parks Dr Waco TX 76707

DWYER SOUTHERN, KATHY, museum administrator; m. Hugh Southern; 1 child. BA in Mktg., U. Wis., 1968, MA in Arts Adminstrn., 1972. Exec. dir. Nat. Cultural Alliance, 1990—94, Montpelier, Va., 1994—96;

pres., CEO Port Discovery, Balt., 1996—2001, Capital Children's Mus., Washington, 2001—. Arts mgmt. prof. Am. U., Va. Commonwealth U., Shenandoah Conservatory Music; bd. dirs. Am. Assn. Mus., Coun. Children's Mus. Office: Capital Childrens Mus 800 Third St NE Washington DC 20002*

DY-ANG, ANITA C. pediatrician; b. Cavite, The Philippines, Feb. 21, 1943; came to U.S., 1970; m. Raymundo Ang., May 1, 1977; children: Aileen Ang, Audrey Ang. MD, U. East Ramon Magsaysay, Quezon City, Philippines, 1967. Diplomate Am. Bd. Pediatrics. Pediat. resident Tulane U. Charity Hosp. New Orleans, 1973; pvt. practice Warsaw, N.Y. Mem. attending staff Wyoming County Cmty. Hosp. Mem. Wyoming County Med. Soc. Office: 78 N Main St Warsaw NY 14569-1329

DYAR, KATHRYN WILKIN, pediatrician; b. Colquitt, Ga., Feb. 20, 1945; d. Patrick McWhorter and Virginia (Wilkin) Dyar; m. James Ansley Patten, Jan. 1, 1985. BS in Biology, Emory U., Decatur, Ga., 1966; MD, Med. Coll. Ga., Augusta, 1970. Resident in pediatrics Eugene Talmadge Meml. Hosp., Augusta, Ga., 1970-72, Georgetown U. Hosp., Washington, 1972-73; pediatrician Children's Clinic, Tifton, Ga., 1973-74, Children and Youth Project, Norfolk, Va., 1974-83, 90-95, dir., 1990-94; pediatrician Hampton (Va.) Health Dept., 1983-90. Fellow Am. Acad. Pediatrics.

DYBELL, ELIZABETH ANNE SLEDDEN, clinical psychologist; b. Buffalo, Sept. 25, 1958; d. Richard Edward and Angela Brigid (Scimone) Sledden; m. David Joseph Dybell, Nov. 30, 1985. BA in Psychology summa cum laude, U. St. Thomas, Houston, 1980; PhD in Psychology, Tex. Tech. U., 1986. Lic. clin. psychologist, Tex. Rsch. asst. health sci. ctr. Tex. Tech. U., Lubbock, 1983-84, psychol. cons. health sci. ctr. neurology dept., 1982-84; psychology intern U. N.Mex. Med. Sch., Albuquerque, 1984-85; psychotherapist Katz & Assocs. P.C., Houston, 1985-88, Meyer Ctr. for Devel. Pediatrics Tex. Children's Hosp., Houston, 1988-92; pvt. practice Houston, 1990—. Author: (monograph) When Will Life Be Normal?, 1989, Myths of the Super Parent: Finding the Power of Real Parenting, 2003; contbr. articles to numerous publs. Choir mem. St. Thomas More Ch., Houston, 1974-87. Mem. APA, Md. Psychol. Assn., Assn. for the Care of Childrens Health, Nat. Ctr. Clin. Infant Programs, Soc. Pediatric Psychology, Southwestern Psychol. Assn., Tex. Psychol. Assn., Houston Psychol. Assn., Am. Psychol. Soc. (charter). Roman Catholic. Avocations: water gardening, horticulture, nature studies, ornamental koi raising, ecology. Home and Office: PO Box 609 Jefferson MD 21755-0609

DYBVIG, MARY MCILVAINE, educational consultant, psychologist; b. Chgo., Feb. 23, 1936; d. John Harmon and Mildred Petrina McIlvaine; m. Noel Tyl, June 13, 1958 (div. Apr. 1976); 1 child, Kimberly Tyl ; m. Paul Dybvig, Mar. 21, 1978 (div. Feb. 1999); m. Melvin Leonard Sward, Apr. 7, 2002; stepchildren: Alyssa Quanbeck, Mary Eide, Mark Sward, Paul Sward, Natalie Nutting, Carole Sward. BA cum laude, Radcliffe/Harvard U., 1958; MA in Ednl. Psychology, NYU, 1968; PhD in Ednl. Adminstrn., U. Minn., 1992. Tchr. Kinkaid Sch., Houston, 1958—60, Dalton Sch., N.Y.C, 1960—63, Packer Collegiate Inst., Brooklyn, NY, 1963—68, Am. Army Sch., Munich, 1968—69, Düsseldorf (Germany) Internat. Sch., 1969—72, Heinrich-Heine Gymnasium, 1972—73, St. Paul Acad., 1973—77; sch. psychologist St. Paul (Minn.) Schs., 1977—94, prin., 1994—2001; pvt. practice cons./sch. psychologist St. Paul/Mpls., 2001—. Instr. St. Thomas U., St. Paul, 1990—94; cons. in field; presenter in field. Active St. Luke Luth. Ch., St. Paul, 1996—. Mem.: Minn. Assn. Sch. Psychologists, Nat. Assn. Sch. Psychologists, Alpha Delta Kappa. Avocations: travel, golf, cooking. Home: 1640 Mackubin St Saint Paul MN 55117

DYDEK, MARGO, professional basketball player; b. Poland, Apr. 28, 1974; Profl. basketball player Huragan Wolomin, Poland, 1986—91, Poznan Olympia, Poland, 1991—94, Valenciennes Ochies, France, 1994—96, Pool Getafe, Madrid, 1996—98, VBW Clima Gdynia, Poland, 1998—, Utah Starzz, 1998—2002, San Antonio Silver Stars, 2003—; mem. Polish Nat. Team, 1992—. Mem. Polish Nat. Team. Named MVP, Polish League Finals, 1999—2000, Best Basketball Player, Italian Sports Mag., La Gazetta dello Sport, Sport's Woman of Yr., Poland. Avocations: billiards, reading, videos, movies. Office: 301 W South Temple Salt Lake City UT 84101

DYE, LINDA KAYE, elementary school educator; b. Shelbyville, Tenn., Dec. 26, 1962; d. John William Dye and Adeline Stewart Dye Adams. BS, David Lipscomb Univ., Nashville, 1985; postgrad., Middle Tenn. State U. Title I reading tchr. Bedford County Bd. Edn., Shelbyville, Tenn. Mem. NEA, Tenn. Edn. Assn., Nat. Coun. Tchrs. English, Bedford County Edn. Assn.

DYE, NANCY SCHROM, academic administrator, historian, educator; b. Columbia, Mo., Mar. 11, 1947; d. Ned Stuart and Andrea Elizabeth (Ahrens) Schrom; m. Griffith R. Dye, Aug. 21, 1972; children: Molly, Michael. AB, Vassar Coll., 1969; MA, U. Wis., 1971, PhD, 1974. Asst. prof. U. Ky., Lexington, 1974—80, assoc. prof., 1980—88, prof., 1988, assoc. dean arts and scis., 1984—88; dean faculty Vassar Coll., Poughkeepsie, NY, 1988—92, acting pres., 1992—94; pres. Oberlin Coll., Oberlin, Ohio, 1994—. Author: As Equals And As Sisters, 1981; contbr. articles to profl. jours. Bd. mem. Pomona Coll. Mem.: Coun. Colls. of Art and Scis. (bd. dirs. 1980—91). Office: Oberlin Coll Cox Admin Bldg, Room 201 70 N Professor St Oberlin OH 44074-1090

DYE, REBECCA FEEMSTER, legislative counsel; b. Charlotte, N.C., May 8, 1952; BA, U. N.C., 1974, JD, 1977. Spl. counsel Broughton (N.C.) Psychiat. Hosp., 1977-78; atty. project coord. Legal Svcs. N.C., 1978-79; atty. office of chief counsel USCG, 1979-83; law instr. USCG Acad., 1983-85; atty. office of chief counsel Fed. Maritime Adminstrn., 1985-87; minority counsel Com. Merchant Marine & Fisheries, Washington, 1987—. Office: Com Merchant Marines & Fisheries 538 Ford House Office Bldg Washington DC 20515-0001

DYER, ARLENE THELMA, retail company owner; b. Chgo., Oct. 23, 1942; d. Samuel Leo Sr. and Thelma Arlene (Israel) Lewis; m. Don Engle Dyer, July 3, 1965 (div. 1970); 1 child, Artel Terren. Cert. in mgmt. effectiveness, U. So. Calif., 1987; cert. Ryan Designated Subjects, UCLA, 2000. Cmty. resource rep. Calif. State Employment Devel. Dept., L.A., 1975-76, spl. projects rep., 1976; employment services rep. Culver City, Calif., 1977; contract writer L.A., 1976-80; employment program rep., 1980—; pres. Yabba and Co., L.A., 1981-83; pres., designer, cons. Spiritual Ties Custom Neckwear, L.A., 1985—; pres. Dyer Custom Shirts, Blouses and Suits, Beverly Hills, Calif., 1988—; contr. writer L.A. Watts Times, 2002—03; designer Sweet Thoughts & Inspirations, 2003—. Founder self-evaluation seminar; pres. MYSELF, Inc., 1998. Author: Who Are You and What Are You All About?, 1994, Escaping to the Workplace, 1996, I Got the Job!. . .Now What?, 1998, You Got the Job?...Now What?, 1999; exhibited in fashion shows, Calif., 1984—; radio personality, 1995 Vol. Big Sister Gwen Bolden Found., L.A., 1986, Juvenile Hall, 1996; mem. Operation PUSH, Chgo., 1983, Mahogany Cowgirls & Co.; program chair Black Advs. in State Svc., 1987—; leader Girl Scouts U.S., L.A., 1982, L.A. Urban League; spirit team leader Calif. Special Olympics; mem. Big Sisters of L.A. Recipient IRWIN award, 1998. God's Leading Ladies, 2002. Mem. NAACP (Beverly Hills-Hollywood chpt.), Nat. Alliance Homebased Businesswomen (v.p., program chair 1987), NAFE, Nat. Spkrs. Assn. (Grtr. L.A. chpt.), Calif. State Employees Assn., Greater L.A. C. of C., Kiwanis Club (dir.), U. So. Calif. Alumni Assn., L.A. Urban League, Black Women's Forum. Democrat. Avocations: traveling, reading, bicycling, roller skating. E-mail: arlenedyer@ugotthejob.com.

DYER, BARBARA F. retired accountant, writer; b. Rockland, Maine, May 19, 1924; d. Milton Earl and Elizabeth Ayoube Dyer. Grad., LaSalle Ext. U., 1967; student, U. Maine, Thomaston, 2001. Office mgr., acct. Camden Shipbuilding Co., 1942—86; tchr. Adult Edn. Sch. Adminstrv. Dist #28, Camden, 1987 [illegible] 1984, 2004—; writer Village Soup.com, Village Soup Times. Author: Grog Ho, 1984, Vintage Views, 1987, History 1st Congregational Church, 1991, Images Camden-Rockport, 1995, Home Sweet Home, 1996, Vessels of Camden, 1998, More Memories of Camden, 1997; contbr. articles to publs. Bd. selectmen Town of Camden, 1992—95; ind. commr. Camden Pub. Libr., 1998—2002; mem. Camden War Meml. Com., 2003—; budget com. Town of Camden, 2003—; deacon First Congl. Ch., Camden, 1970—74, historian, 1985—2002, 2003—, 200th ann. com., 2003—. Named Paul Harris fellow, Rotary Internat., Camden, 1995, Townsperson of Yr., Camden, Lincolnville, Rockport C. of C., Camden, 1996; recipient Disting. Personal Enrichment award, Maine Adult Edn. Assn., 1993, first place/weekly award, Maine Press Assn., 1993. Mem.: Camden H.S. Alumni Assn. (com.), Camden Women's Club (charter, past pres.), Phi Theta Kappa. Republican. Avocations: knitting, crocheting, oil painting, swimming, dancing. Home: 11 Highland Ave Camden ME 04843-2119

DYER, DORIS ANNE, nursing consultant; b. Washington, Jan. 14, 1944; d. William Edward and Helen Gertrude (Smith) Swain; m. Robert Francis Dyer, Jr., June 27, 1970; children: Robert Francis, William Edward, Anne-Marie Helen Sallie, Scott Robertson McGavin. RN cum laude, Sibley Nursing Sch., Washington, 1964; BS, Am. U., 1966, MEd, 1969. Mem. staff emergency medicine dept. George Washington U. Hosp., 1960-69, emergency specialist protective svcs. clinic, 1967-70, adminstrv. asst. to dir. clinic, 1970-78, nurse. cons., 1987—. Author: Say Ah, 1971; contbr. articles to profl. jours. Patron Sibley Meml. Hosp. Chapel, 1992. Trinity Coll. scholar, 1960; Lucy Webb Hayes scholar, 1964; recipient Martha Washington award Md. Soc. SAR, 1977, Cmty. Leaders award, 1979, Washington medal, 1984, disting. women of Washington award 1987; decorated Comdr. Order of St. Lazarus, 1984, medal of merit, 1989; created dame Order of Sovereign Mil. Order, 1980, dame comdr., 1992; named Dame Grand Cross, 1984, Dame Grand Officier, 1992. Mem. ANA, D.C. Nurses Assn., Am. Acad. Ambulatory Nursing Adminstrs., Washington Med.-Surg. Soc. Aux. (pres.), U. U. Grads. Assn., DAR, Washington Assembly, Colonial Hist. Soc., Washington Club, Annapolis Yacht Club, Kenwood Golf and Country Club. Address: 5608 Albia Rd Bethesda MD 20816-3303

DYER, KAREN MARIE, education educator; b. Berkeley, Calif., Mar. 11, 1954; d. Shelley and Bennie Eloise Dyer. AB, U. Calif., Berkeley, 1975; MEd, Holy Names Coll., Oakland, Calif., 1983; EdD, U. of the Pacific, Stockton, Calif., 1996. Tchr. St. Louis Bertrand Sch., Oakland, 1976—77, Fairfield (Calif.)-Suisun Unified Sch. Dist., 1977—85, prin., 1985—89; exec. dir. North Bay Sch. Leadership Ctr., Santa Rosa, Calif., 1989—93, Bay Area Sch. Leadership Ctr., San Rafael, Calif., 1993—96, Chgo. Acad. Sch. Leadership, 1996—2000; mgr. edn. sector Ctr. Creative Leadership, Greensboro, NC, 2000—. Mem. conf. planning com. Nat. Staff Devel. Coun., 2002. Co-author: (book) The Intuitive Principal, 2000. Mem.: Links, Inc. (v.p. 2003—), Alpha Kappa Alpha. Roman Catholic. Office: Ctr Creative Leadership 1 Leadership Pl Greensboro NC 27410

DYER, STEPHANIE JO, anesthesiologist; b. Oxnard, Calif., Jan. 25, 1957; d. Donald Eugene and Sharron Lee (Brown) Dyer; m. William J. Carpenter, June 1996 (div. Jan. 2002). BSN, U. N.Mex., 1980; MD, U. Nev., Reno and Las Vegas, 1991. RN, N.Mex., Nev. Intern U. Ariz. Affiliated Hosps.; staff nurse Lovelace Med. Ctr., Albuquerque, 1980-82, U. N.Mex. Hosp., Albuquerque, 1982-83; charge nurse St. Mary's Hosp., Roswell, N.Mex., 1983-84; staff nurse Washoe Med. Ctr., Reno, 1984-91; resident in anesthesiology U. N.Mex., Albuwquerque; assoc. prof. anesthesiology U. Tex. Health Sci. Ctr., San Antonio. Cons. Legis. Com. Health-Health Care, Nev. Legislature, Carson City; rschr. Robert Wood Johnson Found. Study, 1987—88; dir., pres. Armadillo Anes Inc.; v.p. health policy Town Hall Comm., Inc. Author: (proposal) Prevention of Adolescent Pregnancy, 1989. Recipient Don Mello award for Community Svc., 1991. Mem. AMA, Am. Med. Women's Assn. (student coord. Reg. XI 1987-88), Physicians for Social Responsibility (chmn. 1988-89), Am. Soc. Anesthesiologists, Soc. Cardiovasc. Anesthesiologists, Tex. Soc. Anesthesiologists. Republican. Roman Catholic. Avocations: gardening, yoga, running, biking, poetry, writing short fiction stories. Office: Alice Regional Hosp 2500 E Main St Alice TX 78332 Home: 12436 FM 1960 Rd W #164 Houston TX 77065-4809

DYER-COLE, PAULINE, school psychologist, educator; b. Methuen, Mass., Aug. 20, 1935; d. E. Dewey and Rose Alma (Des Jardins) Dyer; m. Richard Grey, Aug. 1, 1964 (dec. 1977); children: Douglas Richard, Christopher Lachlan, Heather Judith; m. Malcolm A. Cole, July 23, 1983. BS in Edn. and Music, Lowell State Coll., 1957; MEd, Boston State Coll., 1961; EdD, Clark U., 1991. Lic. ednl. psychologist, Mass.; cert. sch. psychologist, Mass.; nat. cert. sch. psychologist. Supr. music and art Merrimac and W. Newburg (Mass.) Pub. Schs., 1957-59; music editor textbooks Allyn & Bacon, Inc., Boston, 1959-64; prof. music West Pines Coll., Chester, N.H., 1969-72; sch. psychologist Nashoba Regional H.S., Bolton, Mass., 1979—2001, chair SPED dept., 1995—2001, dir. SPED dept., 1998—2001; child study dept. Worcester (Mass.) Pub. Schs., 2001—. Vis. lectr., then vis. prof. Framingham (Mass.) State Coll., 1980—; dir. psychol. testing Nashoba Regional Sch. Dist., Bolton, Mass., 1980-94. Author: The Play Game Songbook, 1964. V.p., bd. dirs. Timberlane Devel. Ctr., Plaistow, N.H., 1970-73; founder Friends of Kimi Nichols Devel. Ctr., Plaistow, N.H., 1973; chmn. human svcs. St. Ann Parish, Southborough, Mass., 1974-77, active, 1973-85; citizen amb. del. People to People, China, 1995; active The Regional Lab., Andover, Mass., 1993-2001. Fellow Frances L. Hyatt fellow, Clark U., 1977—79. Mem. Nat. Assn. Sch. Psychologists (cert.), Mass. Assn. Sch. Psychologists, Mass. Tchrs. Assn., People to People Internat. Roman Catholic. Avocations: music, boating, swimming, reading, creative writing. Home: 43 Crowningshield Dr Paxton MA 01612-1253 Office: Child Study Dept 24 Chatham St Worcester MA 01609 Office Phone: 508-799-3075. E-mail: dyercole@charter.net.

DYESS, KIRBY A. computer company executive; BS in Physics, U. Idaho, 1968. Human resource staffing mgr. Intel Corp., Oreg., 1979-81, with computer info. svc. orgn., 1981-87, mktg. mgr. Pers. Computer Enhancement Divsn., 1987-89, bus. unit mgr., 1989-92, v.p., dir. human resources, 1992, mem. exec. staff, 1993-96, corp. v.p., 1996, v.p., dir. With ICN Med. Labs., Inc., Portland. Office: Intel Corp 2111 NE 25th Ave Hillsboro OR 97124-5961 E-mail: kirby.dyess@intel.com.

DYKEMAN, ALICE MARIE, public relations executive; b. Fremont, Nebr., May 18; d. Cecil Victor and Dorothy Lillian (Sillik) Jansen; divorced; children: David Clair, Cinda Cecille Dykeman Nordgren. Pub. relations dir. Meth. Hosp., Dallas, 1961-72; regional pub. info. officer Small Bus. Adminstrn., Dallas, 1972-74; owner Dykeman Assocs. Inc., Dallas, 1974—. Adj. prof. U. Dallas Grad. Sch. Mgmt., Irving, Tex. 1972-78; guest lectr. numerous Univs., and seminars; mem. pub. rels. com. Dallas/Ft. Worth Fed. Exec. Bd., 1973, mem. minority bus. opportunity com., 1974; mem. Gov.'s Coun. on Small Bus., Tex., 1980-81, 500, Inc., 1982-90; chmn. export coun. pub. affairs task force U.S. Dept. Commerce, 1980-83. Contbr. articles to bus., health care and pub. rels. jours. Mem. fgn. visitors com. Dallas Coun. on World Affairs, 1962-98, Dallas Pub. Health Bd., 1972-74, Dallas Urban Rehab. Stds. Bd., 1981-83, Econ. Devel. Adv. Bd., City of Dallas, 1983-86; pres. Concerned Citizens for Cedar Springs, 1982—; bd. dirs. Oak Lawn Forum, 1983-92; mem. exec. com. Oak Lawn Com., 1983-95. Recipient Matrix award Women in Comm., Dallas, 1968, 88, Lifetime Achievement award Dallas chpt. Religion Communicators Coun., 2004. Fellow Pub. Rels. Soc. Am. (accredited, chmn. S.W. dist. 1971-72, bd. dirs. North Tex. chpt. 1966-72, pres. 1969, assembly del. 1970-73, 91); mem. North Dallas Fin. Forum (pres. 1991), Nat. Assn. Women Bus. Owners, S.W. Venture Forum, North Dallas C. of C. (bd. dirs. 1980-82, chmn. networking [illegible] 1990—), co-founder [illegible] 1994—, religion comm. coun. 1997—), Press Club Dallas (bd. dirs. 1981-83, headliner 4 times), SMU Mustang Club (bd. dirs. 1996-99), also others. United Methodist. Office: Dykeman Assocs Inc 4115 Rawlins St Dallas TX 75219-3661 E-mail: adykeman@airmail.net.

DYKERS, CAROL REESE, communications educator; b. Cherry Point, N.C., Nov. 30, 1946; d. Charles Lawrence and Eleanor Zahniser Reese; m. Newton Adnair Collyar, Feb. 4, 1968 (div. Dec. 1979); m. John Reginald Dykers Jr., May 12, 1984. BA, U. North Tex., 1968; MA, U. N.C., 1992, PhD, 1995. Advt. copywriter WBEU AM-FM Radio, Beaufort, S.C., 1968; reporter Longview (Tex.) Daily News, 1968-69; tchr. Beaufort H.S., 1970; reporter Savannah (Ga.) Morning News, 1970-73; hist. planning and pub. rels. dir. Lowcountry Coun. Govts., Yemessee, S.C., 1973; editor Hilton Head news Savannah Morning News, 1973-74; editor Longview (Tex.) Morning Jour., 1974-76; editor, then editl. writer Charlotte (N.C.) Observer, 1976-86; asst. metro editor Greensboro (N.C.) News and Record, 1986-88; asst. prof. comms. Salem Coll., Winston-Salem, N.C., 1995—. Contbr. chpt. to book: Assessing Public Journalism, 1998. Mem. Assn. for Edn. in Journalism and Mass Comm. (rsch. chair civic journalism 1997-99), Internat. Comm. Assn. (rsch. paper reader), N.C. Cattlemen's Assn. (past bd. dirs.), Am.-Internat. Charolais Assn., Chatham County Cattlemen's Assn. (past bd. dirs.), Kappa Tau Alpha. Democrat. Episcopalian. Avocations: farming, photography. Home: 1783 Alston Bridge Rd Siler City NC 27344-9581 Office: Salem Coll Main Hall 601 S Church St Winston Salem NC 27101-5318 E-mail: dykers@salem.edu.

DYKES, VIRGINIA CHANDLER, occupational therapist, educator; b. Evanston, Ill., Jan. 10, 1930; d. Daniel Guy and Helen (Schnedier) Goodman; children: Ron Lee, Chuck Lee Chandler, james R., Jr. BA in Art and Psychology, So. Meth. U., 1951; postgrad. in occupl. therapy, Tex. Women's U., 1953. Occupl. therapist Beverly Hills Sanitarium, Dallas, 1953-55; dir. occupl. and recreational therapy Baylor U. Med. Ctr., Dallas, 1956-60, 68-89; pvt. practice Dallas, 1989-92; dir. occupl. and recreational therapy Fla. Hosp., Orlando, 1962-65; staff therapist Parkland meml. Hosp., Dallas, 1965-68. Cons. Arthritis Found., 1974-89, benefactor; Fanny B. Vanderkodi lectr. Tex. Women's U., 1993—. Author: (manual) Lightcast II Splints, 1976; Adult Visual Perceptual Evaluation, 1981; contbr. articles to profl. jours. Sponsor Kimball Art Mus.; mem. coord. bd. allied health adv. com. Tex. Coll. and Univ. Sys., 1980—88; bd. dirs. Tex. Arthritis Found., chmn. patient svcs. com., 1985—89, exec. bd. sec.; bd. dirs. Dallas Opera, also women's bd.; bd. dirs. Dallas Arboretum, Theatre III, Fort Worth Opera, Baylor U. Med. Ctr. Found.; found. bd. Tex. Women's U.; chmn. adv. bd. healing environment program Baylor Med. Ctr.; pres. Diana Dean Head Injury Guild, 1992—93. Named Tex. Occupl. Therapist of Yr., 1985, Annual Virginia Dykes Leadership award named in her honor, Tex. Women's Univ. Mem. Tex. Occupl. Therapy Assn. (life mem. award), Am. Occupl. Therapy Assn. 9del. Fla. 1964, Tex. 1980-88), World Fedn. Occupl. Therapists (participant 8th Internat. Congress, Hamburg, Germany, 1982, del. to 10th European Congress on Rheumatology, Moscow 1983), Boomerang Club (dir. 1971-88), Les Femmes du Monde, Pierian Lit. Club. Home: 3203 Alderson St Dallas TX 75214-3059

DYKSTRA, GAIL SULLIVAN, information scientist, consultant; 1 child, Matthew R. BA, Alma (Mich.) Coll., 1965; MS in Info. Sci. and Librarianship, U. of Wash., 1969. Dir. pub. legal edn. programs and policy Can. Law Info. Coun., Toronto, Canada, 1977—89, sr. dir. programs and policy, 1989—92; dir. pub. and govt. rels. Micromedia Ltd., Toronto, 1992—97; sr. dir. IHS-Micromedia Ltd., Toronto, 1997—99; rsch. mgr., info. svcs. Microsoft Corp., Redmond, Wash., 1999—2000; prin., owner Dykstra Rsch., Bellevue, Wash., 2001—; software tech. mgr. tech. transfer digital ventures U. Wash., 2003—. Program com. Puget Sound Bus. Intelligence Group, Seattle. Home and Office: Dykstra Research 10550 NE 29th Street Suite E Bellevue WA 98004 E-mail: gail.dykstra@dykstraresearch.com.

DYKSTRA LYNCH, MARY ELIZABETH, library and information science educator; b. Philadelphia, Pa., May 21, 1939; arrived in Canada, 1964; d. Edward and Marietta R. (Kuiper) Heerema: m. Michael F. Lynch, Aug. 12, 1995; children from previous marriage: Mark Edward, Jeffrey Garth. BA, Calvin Coll., 1960; MLS, Dalhousie U., Halifax, N.S., 1970; PhD, Sheffield (Eng.) U., 1986. Head cataloguer Dalhousie U. Libr., 1970-74; asst. prof. Sch. Libr. Svc. Dalhousie U., 1974-78, assoc. prof., 1978-82, assoc. prof. Sch. Libr. and Info. Studies, 1983-86, prof., 1987-97, prof. emeritus, 1997—, dir. Sch. Libr. and Info. Studies, 1986-95. Sr. audiovisual libr. Nat. Film Bd. of Can., Montreal, 1982-83, cons. 1977-83; cons. Coun. Mins. Edn., Toronto, Ont., 1984-85, art history info. program J. Paul Getty Trust, Williamstown, Mass., 1988-94; mem. adv. bd. Sch. Health Records Sci., Halifax Infirmary, 1984-97, Libr. Technician Programme, Kings Regional Vocat. Sch., N.S., 1987-90; mem. Can. Commn. on Cataloguing, 1986-94; mem. working group on stds. for subject access Nat. Archives of Can., 1987-93; mem. Can. Adv. Com. for Internat. Orgn. for Standardization, Tech. Commn., Info. and Documentation, 1991—; mem. nat. info. highway adv. coun. of Can., 1994-95, 96-97; rsch. officer U. Sheffield (Eng.), 1996-97. Author: Access to Film Information, 1977, Precis: A Primer, 1985; editor 2 books, several film catalogues; editl. bd. Film Canadiana, 1982-84, Cataloging and Classification Quar., 1980-86, Expert Sys. for Info. Mgmt., 1990-93, Libr. and Info. Sci. Rsch., 1992-96; series editor, occasional papers Sch. Libr. and Info. Studies Dalhousie U., 1986-94; contbr. articles to profl. jours. Pres. Citadel North Neighbourhood Assn., Halifax, 1988; bd. dirs. CANARIE (Canadian Network for Advancement of Rsch., Industry & Edn.), 1996-98, internat. consultants com. World Info. and Comm. Report, UNESCO, Paris, 1998-99, Biblioteca nazionale centrale, Florence, Italy, 2001. Rsch. grantee Dalhousie U., 1976, 80, 90, 96, Social Scis. and Humanities Rsch. Coun., Ottawa, 1987-90. Mem. Can. Libr. Assn. (rep. Can. com. on cataloguing 1986-94), Nova Knowledge, Internat. Soc. for Knowledge Orgn. Office: Dalhousie Univ Sch Libr & Info Studies Halifax NS Canada B3H 4H8 E-mail: m.lynch@sheffield.ac.uk.

DYLAG, HELEN MARIE, healthcare administrator; b. Cleve., Oct. 14, 1950; d. Stanley John and Helen Agnes (Jarkiewicz) D. BSN, St. John Coll., Cleve., 1971; MS, Ohio State U., 1973. RN, Ohio. Nurse V.A. Adminstrn. Hosp., Brecksville, Ohio, 1971-72; clin. specialist, psychiat.-mental health nursing Marymount Hosp./Mental Health Ctr., Garfield Heights, Ohio, 1973-78, dir. consultation and edn. dept., 1978-84, dir. Ctr. for Health Styles, 1984-88; adminstrv. dir. Women's Healthcare Ctr./St. Luke's Hosp., Cleve., 1988-90; adminstrv. dir. dept. of psychiatry MetroHealth Sys, Cleve., 1990-97; pres. FarWest Ctr., Westlake, Ohio, 1997—. Contbg. author: Nursing of Families in Crisis, 1974, Distributive Nursing Practice: A Systems Approach to Community Health, 1977; producer and host "Health Styles" TV Talk Show, 1987-88; contbr. articles to profl. jours. Trustee The Stroke Assn. of Ohio, Cleve., 1990-91; mem. Women of Achievement com., Women's City Club, Cleve., 1989-91. Recipient award Greater Cleve. Hosp. Assn., 1981, Innovator award Am. Hosp. Assn./Ctr. for Health Promotion, 1985, Disting. Women Healthcare award Healthcare Monitor and Vis. Nurse Assn. Cleve., 2000. Mem. Assn. Mental Health Adminstrs., Am. Coll. Healthcare Execs., Healthcare Adminstrs. Assn. of Northeast Ohio, Sigma Theta Tau. Avocations: interior design, gardening, jazz, aerobic exercise, travel. Office: FarWest Ctr 29133 Health Campus Dr Cleveland OH 44145-5256

DYMAN, KATHLEEN ELEANOR, medical association administrator; b. Port Jervis, N.Y., Aug. 16, 1950; BS in Health Sys. Mgmt., SUNY, Utica, 1980. Pres. Profl. Career Sys., Utica, 1990-94; exec. dir. Med. Socs. Oneida, Herkimer, Madison, Chenango & Oswego Cos., New Hartford, N.Y.,

1994—, Ctrl. N.Y. Acad. Medicine, 1994—. Mem. adv. bd. Oneida County Medicaid Managed Care, Utica, 1990—; bd. dirs. United Way. Mem. budget panel United Way, 1990; bd. dirs. United Cerebral Palsy, 2000—, Cmtys. That Care, 2002—; mem. exec. com. Herkimer County Rural Health Network, 2000—. Mem. Am. Assn. Med. Soc. Execs., N.Y. Assn. Long Term Care Adminstrs., Cosmopolitan Ctr. (bd. dirs. 1989—). Office: Med Socs 4311 Middle Settlement Rd New Hartford NY 13413 Home: 68 6 White St Clinton NY 13323

DYNEK, SIGRID, corporate lawyer, retail executive; b. 1949; BS, JD, Marquette U. Bar: Wis. 1973. V.p., gen. counsel Kohl's Dept. Stores, Inc., Menomonee Falls, Wis. Office: Kohl's Dept Stores Inc N56w17000 Ridgewood Dr Menomonee Falls WI 53051-5660

DYRSTAD, JOANELL M. former lieutenant governor, consultant; b. St. James, Minn., Oct. 15, 1942; d. Arnold A. and Ruth (Berlin) Sletta; m. Marvin Dyrstad, 1965; children: Troy, Anika. BA, Gustavus Adolphus Coll., St. Peter, Minn., 1964; MA, Hamline U., 1996. Mayor City of Red Wing, Minn., 1985-90; lt. gov. State of Minn., 1991-94; now independent bus. and govt. cons. Ptnr. Corner Drugstore, Red Wing, 1968—; v.p. League Minn. Cities, 1990-91, Minn. Mayors Assn., 1989-90; mem. Nat. Conf. Lt. Gov.'s, 1991-94, chair, 1993-94. Trustee Gustavus Adolphus Coll., 1989-98, U. Minn. Found., 1993-99; dir. corp. bd. Fairview Health Sys.; dir. Fairview Red Wing Health Svcs., chair, 2002; dir. Minn. Hosp. Health Care Partnership, 1999—. Mem. AAUW (Citizen of yr. award 1985), LWV.

DYSON, ANNE HAAS, English language educator; BS in Elem. Edn., U. Wis., 1972; MEd in Curriculum and Instrn. (Reading), U. Tex., 1976, PhD in Curriculum and Instrn. (Lang. Arts/Reading), 1981. Elem. tchr. 2d grade El Paso Cath. Diocese, Tex., 1972-73; adult educator Crawford English Acad., El Paso, Tex., 1973; substitute tchr. Austin Ind. Sch. Dist., Tex., 1974-75, presch. tchr. for 4 yr olds, 1975, elem. tchr. 1st grade, 1977-79; dir., staff coord. learning abilities ctr. materials lab., tutoring coord. learning abilities ctr. U. Tex., Austin, 1975-76, teaching asst., 1975-77, instr., 1979-80, rsch. asst., 1981, grad. fellow, 1980-81; head tchr., coord. summer lang. arts/reading program Alamo Heights Ind. Sch. Dist., San Antonio, 1978; asst. prof. dept. lang. edn. U. Ga., 1981-85, grad. faculty, 1984-85, vis. asst. prof. divsn. lang. and literacy sch. of edn. U. Calif., Berkeley, 1984-85, asst. prof. divsn. lang. and literacy sch. of edn., 1985-87, assoc. prof. divsn. lang. and literacy sch. of edn., 1987-91, prof. divsn. lang. and literacy sch. of edn., 1991—2002, co-dir. Ctr. for the Study of Writing and Literacy, 1990—2002; prof. tchr. edn. Mich. State U., 2002—. Author: Multiple Worlds of Child Writers: A Study of Friends Learning to Write, 1989; co-author: Language Assessment in the Early Years, 1984; editor: Collaboration Through Writing and Reading: Exploring Possibilities, 1989; contbr. articles to profl. jours., contbr. chpts. to books; editor, adv. bd. mem. Early Childhood Yearbook, 1990—; mem. editl. bd. Research in the Teaching of English, 1992—, Language and Literacy, 1989—; co-editor rsch. currents dept. Language Arts, 1983-90; editor Newsletter of the Spl. Interest Group in Language Devel. Am. Ednl. Rch. Assn., 1984-86; speaker in field. Recipient Annual Human Rights award Oakland Baha'is, 1991, Lois Gadd Nemec Disting. Alumni award U. Wis., 1990, Promising Rechr. award Nat. Coun. Tchrs. of English, 1982, award for Excellence in Ednl. Journalism Ednl. Press Assn. Am., 1982.

DYSON, ESTHER, publisher, editor; b. Zurich, Switzerland, July 14, 1951; d. Freeman John and Verena Esther (Huber) D. BA in economics, Harvard U., 1972. Reporter Forbes Mag., N.Y.C., 1974-77, columnist, 1987—; v.p. New Ct. Securities, N.Y.C., 1977-80, Oppenheimer & Co., N.Y.C., 1980-82; editor Rosen Electronics Letter, 1982; founder, owner, chmn. EDventure Holdings, Inc. (acquired by CNET Networks 2004), 1983—. Founder, past chmn. ICANN; past dir. Electronic Frontier Found. Author: Release 2.0: A Design for Living in the Digital Age, 1997; columnist Release 3.0, N.Y. Times syndicate; moderator ann. Personal Computer Forum; contbr. articles to profl. jours. Mem. Women's Forum N.Y., Assn. Data Processing Svc. Orgns., Software Pubs. Assn. Avocation: swimming. Office: EDventure Holdings 104 5th Ave Fl 20 New York NY 10011-6987*

DZAMBA, ANNE O. history and women's studies educator; b. N.Y.C., Oct. 18, 1938; d. Stephen Andrew and Barbara (Dressler) D.; m. Ronald Jay Miller, June 19, 1987. BA, Swarthmore Coll., 1960; PhD, U. Del., 1973. Instr. history Widener U., Chester, Pa., 1967-68; from asst. prof. to prof. history and women's studies West Chester (Pa.) U., 1968—2002, chairperson dept. history, 1995—99, prof. emeritus. Author: Richard Wagner and the English, 1979; contbr. to books.

DZIEWANOWSKA, ZOFIA ELIZABETH, neuropsychiatrist, pharmaceutical executive, researcher, educator; b. Warsaw, Nov. 17, 1939; came to U.S., 1972; d. Stanislaw Kazimierz Dziewanowski and Zofia Danuta (Mieczkowska) Rudowska; m. Krzysztof A. Kunert, Sept. 1, 1961 (div. 1971); 1 child, Martin. MD, U. Warsaw, 1963; PhD, Polish Acad. Sci., 1970. MD recert. U.K., 1972, U.S., 1973. Asst. prof. of psychiatry U. Warsaw Med. Sch., 1969-71; sr. house officer St. George's Hosp., U. London, 1971-72; assoc. dir. Merck Sharp & Dohme, Rahway, N.J., 1972-76; vis. assoc. physician Rockefeller U. Hosp., N.Y.C., 1975-76; adj. asst. prof. of psychiatry Cornell U. Med. Ctr., N.Y.C., 1978—; v.p., global med. dir. Hoffmann-La Roche, Inc., Nutley, N.J., 1976-94; sr. v.p. and dir. global med. affairs Genta Inc., San Diego, 1994-97; sr. v.p. drug devel. and regulatory Cypros Pharms. Corp., Carlsbad, Calif., 1997-99; pres., med. dir. New Drug Assocs., La Jolla, Calif., 1999—; sr. v.p. clin. and regulatory Maxia Pharms, San Diego, 2001—02; v.p. clin. rsch. Ligand Pharm, Inc., San Diego, 2002—. Lectr. in field. Contbr. articles to profl. publs. Bd. dirs Royal Soc. Medicine Found.; mem. alumni coun. Cornell U. Med. Ctr. Recipient TWIN Honoree award for Outstanding Women in Mgmt., Ridgewood (N.J.) YWCA, 1984. Mem. AMA, AAAS, Am. Soc. Pharmacology and Therapeutics, Am. Coll. Neuropsychopharmacology, N.Y. Acad. Scis., PhRMA. (vice chmn. steering com. med. sect., chmn. internat. med. affairs com., head biotech. working group), Royal Soc. Medicine (U.K.), Drug Info. Assn. (Woman of Yr. award 1994), Am. Assn. Pharm. Physicians. Roman Catholic. Achievements include original research on the role of the nervous system in the regulation of respiratory functions, research and development and therapeutic uses of many new drugs, pharmaceutical medicine and biotechnology; molecular biology derived as well as conventional products including antisense, interferon efficacy in cancer, virology and AIDS and drugs useful in cardiovascular, immunological, neuropsychiatric, infectious diseases, and others; impact of different cultures on medical practices and clinical research; drug evaluation and development management strategies of pharmaceutical industries; treatments against cardiac and brain ischemia, cytoprotection; speaker in field.

EACHO, ESTHER MACLIVELY, special education educator; b. Springfield, Mass., Feb. 28, 1943; d. Charles James and Mary Eileen (May) MacL.; m. Robert Lee Eacho, Sept. 11, 1971; 1 child, Carla Eileen. BS in Edn., Westfield (Mass.) State Coll., 1964; MA in Edn., Am. Internat. Coll., 1969; M in Learning Disabilities, Am. U., 1990; postgrad., Harvard U., 1998. Cert. tchr., Va., Md., Conn. Classroom tchr., Conn., Md., 1964-71; pres. Eileen-Lee Assocs., McLean, Va., 1979-83; v.p. ops. Fabulous Foodstuffs, Ltd., Alexandria, Va., 1983-89; dir. of learning disabilities program Seton Cts., Falls Church, Va., 1989-92; learning disabilities specialist Fairfax County Pub. Schs., Va., 1992—; edn. specialist, cons. Va., 1998—. Bd. dirs. Gourm-E-Co Imports, Sterling, Va. V.p., sec. Jr. Woman's Club, McLean, 1972-79. Mem. ASCD, ASTD, CEC. Avocations: reading, travel, cooking, creative design.

EADENS, DANIELLE MAYA, gifted and talented educator; b. Miami, Fla., Apr. 26, 1980; d. Talbot and Jayne Ginkus Pratt; m. Daniel Wayne Eadens, June 22, 2002; 1 child, Joshua James. BA in Mass. Comm., U. South Fla., 2001, MA in Spl. Edn., postgrad., U. South Fla., 2003—. Cert. tchr. exceptional student edn. and journalism Fla. Staff Sam Seltzer's Steakhouse, Clearwater, Fla., 1998—2001; retail mgr. Bentley's Luggage, Tampa, Fla., 1999—2000; substitute tchr. Pinellas County Schs., Largo, Fla., 2001, inclusion tchr. exceptional student edn. St. Petersburg, Fla., 2001—02, Supported Varying Exceptionalities/Trainable Mentally Handicapped tchr. exceptional student edn., 2002—. Yearbook tchr. Azalea Mid. Sch., St. Petersburg, 2002—, tech. trainer, 2003—. Mem.: Coun. for Exceptional Children, Golden Key, Phi Kappa Phi. Avocations: photography, technology. Office: Azalea Mid Sch 7855 22nd Ave North Saint Petersburg FL 33710

EAGAN, SUSAN LAJOIE, finance educator, consultant; b. Worcester, Mass., Oct. 31, 1951; d. Alexander George Lajoie, Jr. and Nora Lajoie; m. Patrick L. Eagan; 1 child, Nora Elizabeth. BA summa cum laude, U. Mass., 1973; M Pub. Policy, Harvard U., 1975, PhD Pub. Policy, 1978. Exec. dir. Mardel Ctr. for Nonprofit Orgns. Case Western Reserve U., Cleve., 2001—; Mandel prof. Case Western Reserve U., Cleve., 2001—. Instr. U. Mass., Boston, 1977—78. Exec. v.p. Cleve. Found., 1999—2001, assoc. dir., 1990—99, asst. dir., 1986—90, program officer, 1982—86, program analyst, 1980—82, cons., 1978—80; co-chair Ohi Cts. Futures Commn., Columbus, 1996—2000; mem. Ohio Commn. on the Pub. Svc., 1992—93, Cleve. Bicentennial Legacy Com., 1993—94; trustee Inst. Ednl. Renewal. Recipient Woman of Influence award, Crain's Cleve. Bus., 1997, Carrer Woman of Achievement award, YWCA, Cleve., 2000. Mem.: Ohio Assn. Nonprofit Orgns., Women's Cmty. Found., Found. Ctr., Phi Kappa Phi, Phi Beta Kappa. Avocations: reading, hiking, music, gardening. Office: Case Western Reserve U 10900 Euclid Ave Cleveland OH 44106 Business E Mail: sle7@po.cwru.edu.

EAGLEEYE-LORD, AMY S. editor; d. Jack W. and Lynn C. Eagleeye; m. William N. Lord; 1 child, Daisy R. Lord. BA, U. Toledo, 1988—93. Tech. editor Am. Prep. Inst., Killeen, Tex., 1998—2000; copy editor Pro ED Comm., Inc., Beachwood, Ohio, 2001—. Mem.: Am. Med. Writers Assn. Office: Pro ED Comm Inc 25101 Chagrin Blvd Ste 230 Beachwood OH 44122

EAKER, SHERRY ELLEN, entertainment newspaper editor; b. N.Y.C., Nov. 30, 1949; d. Ira and Lee (Eisenberg) E. BA, Queens Coll., 1971, MS, 1976. Tchr. art, English N.Y.C. Bd. Edn., 1971-76; editor-in-chief Back Stage, The Performing Arts Weekly, N.Y.C., 1977—. Editor, compiler: Handbook for Performing Artists: The How-to and Who-to-Contact Reference for Actors, Singers, Dancers, 1989, rev., 1991, 95, 2004, The Cabaret Artist's Handbook-Creating Your Own Act in Today's Liveliest Theatre Setting, 2000. Mem. Drama Desk (sec. 1984-87, v.p. 1987-91), Am. Theatre Critics Assn., Nat. Theatre Conf., League Profl. Theatre Women, N.Y. Coalition Profl. Women in Arts and Media (spl. adv.), advisory coun. Inst. of Outdoor Drama, Manhattan Assn. Cabarets. Avocations: theatre, cabaret. Office: Back Stage 770 Broadway New York NY 10003-9595

EALY, CYNTHIA PIKE, artist, realtor; b. Eveleth, Minn., Apr. 13, 1932; d. Robert Sheldon Pike and Lila Mary Saari; m. Donald Rae Ealy, Dec. 14, 1952; children: Elizabeth, Dennis, Jonathan, Richard. Student, Coll. of Ams., Mexico City, 1950-52, U. So. Calif., 1952-53. Actress, Mexico City, 1950-52; owner Woodland World Travel, Tarzana, Calif., 1965-70; decorator Ridgewood, N.J., 1970-71; artist, 1972—; realtor, 1987—. Bd. dirs., pres. Rep. Women's club, Woodland Hills, Calif., 1964-69; active Internat. Sch. of Brussels, 1975-80; co-chmn. Reps. Abroad, Europe, 1978-82. Recipient Outstanding Svc. award Am. Women's Club of Brussels, 1984. Mem. Sierra Artists Network, Niguel Art Assn. of Orange County. Avocations: instructing French lang. and cuisine. Home: PO Box 6534 467 Driver Way Incline Village NV 89450 also: 27142 Paseo Del Este San Juan Capistrano CA 92675-4927

EANES, JANET TERESA, elementary school educator, music educator; b. Panama City, Fla., Sept. 26, 1955; d. Kenneth O. and Arthalia Claggion Brown; m. Ralph Derwin Eanes, Jr., June 10, 1982; children: Krystle Meggan, Kimberly Miriam. Student, St. Augustine's Coll., 1974—75, Tidewater C.C., Portsmouth, Va., 1975—76; BS in Music, Norfolk State U., 1981. Cert. collegiate profl. edn. K-12 music Va. Piano instr. YMCA, Raleigh, NC, 1974—75; recreation aide Portsmouth (Va.) Pks. and Recreation, 1976—77; youth choir dir. Mt. Calvery Bapt., Portsmouth, 1978—80; pharmacy technician Farmco Pharmacy, Norfolk, 1983—85; adminstrv. asst. Langley AFB, Hampton, Va., 1986—88, Army Corp Engr., Norfolk, 1985; data entry clk. Hampton Social Svcs., 1989—90; pharmacy technician VA Hosp., Hampton, 1990, Revco Pharmacy, Hampton, 1990—91; elem. music tchr. Newport News (Va.) Pub. Sch., 1991—. Sunday sch. tchr. Sixth Mount Zion Bapt., Hampton, 1999. Mem.: NEA (lobbyist 1999—2000), Music Educators Nat. Conf., Alpha Kappa Alpha (rec. sec. 1977—79). Avocations: piano, computers, gardening, cooking, bowling. Office: Newport News Pub Schs Newport News VA 23606

EARHART, EILEEN MAGIE, retired child and family life educator; b. Hamilton, Ohio, Oct. 21, 1928; d. Andrew J. and Martha (Waldorf) Magie; m. Paul G. Earhart; children: Anthony G., Bruce P., Daniel T. BS, Miami U., Oxford, Ohio, 1950; MA in Adminstrn. and Enrl. Services, Mich. State U., 1962, PhD in Edn., 1969; H.H.D. (hon.), Miami U., Oxford, Ohio, 1980. Tchr. home econs. W. Alexandria (Ohio) Schs., 1950-51; elementary tchr. Waterford Twp. Schs., Pontiac, Mich., 1958-65, reading specialist, 1965-67; prof., chmn. family and child ecology dept. Mich. State U., East Lansing, 1968-84; prof., head dept. home and family life Fla. State U., Tallahassee, 1984-89; ret., 1989. Author: Attention and Classification Training Curriculum; co-editor spl. issue of Family Relations, 1984; contbr. chpts. to profl. jours., books. Mem. adv. bd. Lansing Com. on Children's TV, Family/Sch./Cmty. Partnership Project, Tallahassee; bd. dirs. Women's Resource Ctr., Grand Rapids, Mich., Wesley Found., Fla. State U., 1989-99; mem. campus ministries bd. Fla. A&M U., 1995-98; Sunday sch. tchr. Haines City United Meth. Ch., 2001-; mem. Mich. Gov.'s Task Force on Youth. Mem. Nat. Coun. Family Rels. (pres. Assn. of Couns. 1987-88, bd. dirs. 1986-88, chair nat. meeting local arrangements 1992), Fla. Coun. Family Rels. (pres. elect 1985-86, pres. 1986-87), Nat. Assn. Edn. Young Children, Assn. Childhood Edn. Internat., Am. Home Econs. Assn. (named AHEA leader at 75th Ann. of Assn. 1984), Internat. Fedn. Home Econs., Mich. Home Econs. Assn. (pres. 1980-82), Fla. Home Econs. Assn. (chmn. scholarship com. 1986-88, dist. chmn. 1990-91, chmn. nominating com. 1991-92, co-chair ann. meeting 1995), Ednl. Rsch. Assn., Killearn United Meth. Ch., United Meth. Women (cir. chair 1993-97, pres. 1994), Phi Kappa Phi (pres. Fla State U. chpt. 1988-89), Delta Kappa Gamma, Omicron Nu, others. Home (Summer): 22 Oak Tree Ct Franklin NC 28734 Home: 2973 Chickasaw Dr Haines City FL 33844-8419 E-mail: emearhart@aol.com.

EARL, MARTHA FRANCES, librarian, researcher; b. Washington, Aug. 18, 1956; d. Jefferson Davis Earl, Ruby Smith; m. Walter Robert Gawryla; 1 child, Frank Gawryla ; m. Stephen Jack Cobert (div. Aug. 6, 1984). BS, U. Tenn., 1978, MS in Libr. Sci., 1985. Cert. secondary edn. Sci. tchr. First Assembly Christian Sch., Memphis, 1979—80; libr. clk. Memphis State U., 1980—81; sr. libr. asst. U. Tenn., Knoxville, 1981—87; reference libr. Meharry Med. Coll., Nashville, 1987—90; head of reference East Tenn. State U., Coll. Medicine Libr., Johnson City, Tenn., 1990—97; reference coord. U. Tenn. Med. Ctr., Knoxville, 1997—. Cons. Indian Path Hosp., Kingsport, 1990—94, N.E. Tenn. Rehab. Hosp., Johnson City, 1992—97, Morristown Hamblen Hosp., 1993—97, N.E. Tenn. Area Health Edn. Ctr., Greeneville, 1994—98, East Tenn. State U., Johnson City, 2001—; mem. adv. bd. Tenn. Adv. Coun. on Librs., Nashville, 1998—99. Author: (book) Bibkit #9: Managed Care: A Guide to Information Sources, 2000; contbr. chapters to books, revs. to publs., articles to profl. jours. Organizer Tenn. Libr. Legislative Day, 1999—2001; historian Alpha Phi Omega Svc. Fraternity, Knoxville, 1976—78; comm. team Ebenezer United Meth. Ch., Knoxville, 1998—2001; libr. First United Meth. Ch., Bristol, 1994—97, Holston Chapel United Meth. Ch., Knoxville, 1973—78, Sunday sch. tchr., 1972—78. Recipient Rsch. award, South Ctrl. Chpt. Med. Libr. Assn., 2001; grantee Grateful Med. Outreach grant, Nat. Libr. Medicine, 1990—92, Exhibit grant, Nat. Network Librs. Medicine, 1994, 1996, 2003—04, Internet Tng. grant, Nat. Libr. Medicine, 1997—98, Access to Electronic Info. for the Pub. grant, NIH, 2001—02, Physicians Med. Edn. Resource Fund, 2001—04; scholar Nat. Alumni scholar, U. Tenn. Nat. Alumni Found., 1974—78, Roddy Mfg., 1974, 1978. Mem.: ALA (chpt. rels. coun. 1998—99), Med. Libr. Assn. (Brodman com. for excellence in acad. health scis. libr. 1995—97, So. chpt. rsch. com. chair 1997—98, So. chpt. sec. 1999—2000, program com. leadership and mgmt. sect. 2000—01, R&D and demonstration project jury chair 2000—01, Kronick jury chair 2001—02, So. chpt. comm. com. 2001—04), Assn. Coll. and Rsch. Librs. (state affiliate chair 1995—96), Knoxville Area Health Scis. Librs. Consortium (pres. 2001—02), East Tenn. Libr. Assn. (pres. 2003—), Tenn. Adv. Coun. on Librs. (Tenn. electronic libr. subcom. 1998—99), Tenn. Health Scis. Librs. Assn. (membership chair 1998—2000), Tri-Cities Health Scis. Librs. Consortium (chair 1994), Tenn. Libr. Assn. (coll. and univ. librs. sect. chair 1996—97, Tenn. libr. editl. rev. bd. 1996—2000, pres. 1998—99, conf. com. program chair 1998—2000, assoc. pres. 1999, ad hoc com. on staffing 2000—01, chair strategic planning 2000—03, publs. bd. chair 2003—, Appreciation award 1999, 2002), Tennshare (chmn. long range planning 2002—, TELII steering com. 2002—), U. Tenn. Sch. Info. Sci. Alumni Bd. (mentoring subcom. and mem.-at-large 2001—03). Methodist. Avocations: reading, walking, swimming, movies, travel. Office: Univ Tenn Med Ctr 1924 Alcoa Hwy Knoxville TN 37920 Office Phone: 965-544-9525. Office Fax: 865-544-9527. Personal E-mail: earlmartha@yahoo.com. Business E-Mail: mearl@utk.edu.

EARLE, EUGENIA, music educator; b. Birmingham, Ala., May 2, 1922; d. Paul Hamilton Earle and Rosa Munger; m. Jere Butler Faison, Nov. 26, 1969 (dec.). BA, Birmingham So. Coll., 1943; MA, Columbia U., 1956, PhD, 1979. Instr. Mannes Coll. Music, N.Y.C., 1946—63, Union Theol. Sem. Sch. Sacred Music, N.Y.C., 1963—73, Manhattan Sch. Music, N.Y.C., 1963—73; adj. assoc. prof. Columbia U. Tchrs. Coll., N.Y.C., 1969—. Harpsichordist concerts throughout U.S. Composer: Conversation Pieces, 1972, 18th Century Dances: How to Add Melodic Ornamentation, 1973. Mem.: Coll. Music Soc., Am. Bach Soc., Am. Musicol. Soc. Democrat. Presbyterian. Avocations: hiking, attending concerts, theatre. Home: 15 W 84st (9D) New York NY 10024

EARLE, JEAN BUIST, financial officer; b. Newton, N.J., Oct. 5, 1951; d. Richardson and Jean (Mackerly) Buist; m. Terry Dean Earle, Mar. 4, 1989; children: Morgan, Abigail. AB, Cornell U., 1973, MEd, Coll. William and Mary, 1974; MBA, U. Pa., 1987. Mgr. The Korman Corp., Jenkintown, Pa., 1975-77; v.p. ops. Community Assn. Mgmt. Co., Havertown, Pa., 1977-78; adminstrv. asst. Albert Einstein Med. Ctr., Phila., 1978-83; assoc. adminstr. Meml. Hosp. Burlington County, Mt. Holly, N.J., 1983-87; v.p. Overlook Hosp., Summit, N.J., 1987-95; exec. dir. Summit (N.J.) Child Care Ctrs., Inc., 1995-96; owner, ptnr. Computer Edn. Inst., Kenilworth, N.J., 1996—; CFO ECLC of N.J., Chatham, 1998—. Past pres. Family Link of Union and Essex Counties, 1994-96; chmn. Kirby Ctr. YMCA Family Coun., 1996-98. Fellow Am. Coll. Healthcare Execs; mem. Am. Hosp. Assn., U. Pa. Wharton Sch. Alumni Assn., Cornell Club, Ctr. for Enabling Tech. (trustee 1997—, treas. 1999—). Home: 37 Rose Ter Chatham NJ 07928-1826 Office: ECLC NJ 21 Lum Ave Chatham NJ 07928 Office Phone: 973-635-1705. E-mail: jbearle@hotmail.com.

EARLE, MARY MARGARET, marketing executive; b. Newberry, Mich., June 26, 1947; d. William Loren and Naida Theresa (Ward) E. Student, St. Mary's Coll., Notre Dame, Ind., 1965—67. Cert. employment cons. Receptionist Western Girl World, San Francisco, 1968-69; receptionist, sec. Advanced Memory Systems, Sunnyvale, Calif., 1969-71; career cons. Qualified Pers., Madison, Wis., 1972-75; VIP asst. Summit Sports Arena Grand Open, Houston, 1975, S. Petroleum Gp/OTC, Houston, 1976, Astrodomain Assn., Houston, 1976-77; bus. mgr. Mobile Colo TV Prodn., Houston, 1977-80; broadcast bus. affairs dir. G.D.L. & W. Adv., Houston, 1980-90; broadcast talent cons. Willis, Tex., 1990-93; mktg. cons., pvt. practice Marquette, Mich., 1993-95; pres. IXL Creative-Mktg. Excellence, Marquette, 1996—; cable mktg. cons. Bresnan Comm., Marquette, 1998-2000, Charter Media, 2000—02. Modeling judge Page Parks Sch. Modeling, Houston, 1988-91; cons. industry/union rels. AFTRA/SAG, Houston, 1985-92. Houston mem. Fashion Group, 1989-90; sec. Bluebell Estates Assn., Willis, 1991, pres. 1992; pub. rels. vol. Women's Ctr. seminars, Houston, 1984-85; co-chair/treas. Art on the Rocks, 1999—; bd. dirs. Big Bros./Big Sisters; mem. exec. com. domestic Violence Coalition of Marquette County; bd. dirs. Marquette County Humane Soc. Named Disting. Salesman of Yr. Sales and Mktg. Execs., Madison, 1973, 74. Mem. Adminstrv. Mgmt. Soc. (cons. ofcl. panel 1974), Pers. Adminstrs. Soc., Am. Assn. Advt. Agys. (so. broadcast policy com.), Lake Superior Art Assn. (bd. dirs. 1996—), Ishpeming Art Faire Assn. (pres. 2000—), Rotary (pres. Ishpeming, Mich. 2002-03). Avocations: walking, raising dogs. Home and Office: 612 County Road 480 Marquette MI 49855-9411 E-mail: mmearle@chartermi.net.

EARLE, PATRICIA NELSON, artist; b. West Point, NY, Dec. 18, 1942; d. Wilton Haynsworth and Patricia Ann (Nelson) Earle; m. James Edward Lipscomb III, 1970 (div. 1998); 1 child, Drayton Earle; stepchildren: James E. Lipscomb IV, Claude Benjamin Lipscomb. AA, Mt. Vernon Coll., 1963; BS, Furman U., 1986. One-woman shows include Furman U., Greenville, SC, 1993, exhibited in group shows at Taos Art Assocs., N. Mex., 1994, Art in the Park, Greenville, 1996—97, one-woman shows include Barnes and Noble, Greenville, SC, 1997, Cafo Ristretto, 1997, exhibited in group shows at Carolina, Ga. Blood Ctr., Greenville, 1998, Art in the Park, Greenville, SC, 2003, Represented in permanent collections Liberty Life Corp., NYC, Carolina First Bank, Greenville, SC, Summit Nat. Bank, Erskine Coll., SC, Laurel Creek Gallery . Mem.: Upstate Visual Arts, Jr. League of Greenville. Democrat. Episc. Avocation: travel. Home: 925 Cleveland St #210 Greenville SC 29601 E-mail: TEarleArt@aol.com.

EARLE, SYLVIA ALICE, research biologist, oceanographer; b. Gibbstown, N.J., Aug. 30, 1935; d. Lewis Reade and Alice Freas (Richie) E. BS, Fla. State U., 1955; MA, Duke U., 1956, PhD, 1966, PhD (hon.), 1993, Monterey Inst. Internat. Studies, 1990, Ball State U., 1991, George Washington U., 1992, U. R.I., 1996, Plymouth State Coll., 1996; DSc (hon.), Ripon Coll., 1994, U. Conn., 1994. Resident dir. Cape Haze Marine Lab., Sarasota, Fla., 1966-67; research scholar Radcliffe Inst., 1967-69; research fellow Farlow Herbarium, Harvard U., 1967-75, researcher, 1975—; research assoc. in botany Natural History Mus. Los Angeles County, 1970-75; research biologist, curator Calif. Acad. Scis., San Francisco, from 1976; research assoc. U. Calif., Berkeley, 1969-75; fellow in botany Natural History Mus., 1989—; chief scientist U.S. NOAA, Washington, 1990-92, advisor to the adminstr., 1992-93; founder, pres., CEO, bd. dirs. Deep Ocean Engrs., Inc., Oakland, Calif., 1981-90; founder, chmn., CEO Deep Ocean Exploration and Rsch., Oakland, 1992—, bd. dirs., 1992—; advisor SeaWeb, 1996—. Bd. dirs. Dresser Industries, Oryx Energy, Inc.; explorer-in-residence Nat. Geog., 1998; dir., Natl. Geographic Suatainable Seas Expedition, 1998—. Author: Exploring the Deep Frontier, 1980, Sea Change, 1995; editor: Scientific Results of the Tektite II Project, 1972-75; contbr. 100 articles to profl. jours. Trustee World Wildlife Fund U.S., 1976-82, mem. coun., 1984—; trustee World Wildlife Fund Internat., 1979-81, mem. coun., 1981-95; trustee Charles A. Lindbergh Fund, pres.,

1990-95; trustee Ctr. Marine Conservation, 1992—, Perry Found., chmn., 1993-95; mem. coun. Internat. Union for Conservation of Nature, 1979-81; corp. mem. Woods Hole Oceanographic Inst., trustee, 1996—; mem. Nat. Adv. Com. on Oceans and Atmosphere, 1980-94. Recipient Conservation Svc. award U.S. Dept. Interior, 1970, Boston Sea Rovers award, 1972, 79, Nogi award Underwater Soc. Am., 1976, Conservation Svc. award Calif. Acad. Sci., 1979, Order of Golden Ark Prince Netherlands, 1980, David B. Stone medal New Eng. Aquarium, 1989, Gold medal Soc. Women Geographers, medal Radcliffe Coll., 1990, Pacon Internat. award, 1992, Dirs. award Natural Resources Coun. Am., 1992, Washburn award Boston Mus. Sci., 1995, Charles A. and Ann Morrow Lindbergh award, 1996, Julius Stratton Leadership award, 1997, Kilby award, 1997, Bal de la Mar Found. Sea Keeper award, 1997, Sea Space Environment award, 1997; Environmental Global Zoo Awd., 1998; U.S. Environmental Hew Awd., 1998; named Woman of Yr. L.A. Times, 1970, Scientist of Yr., Calif. Mus. Sci. and Industry, 1981. National Women's Hall of Fame, 2000. Fellow AAAS, Marine Tech. Soc. (Compass award 1997), Calif. Acad. Scis., Calif. Acad. Sci., Explorers Club (hon., bd. dirs. 1989-94, Lowell Thomas award 1980, Explorers medal 1996); mem. Internat. Phycological Soc. (sec. 1974-80), Phycological Soc. Am., Am. Soc. Ichthyologists and Herpetologists, Am. Inst. Biol. Scis., Brit. Phycological Soc., Ecol. Soc. Am., Internat. Soc. Plant Taxonomists. Home and Office: 12812 Skyline Blvd Oakland CA 94619-3125

EARLL, JANE, state legislator, lawyer; b. Aug. 10, 1958; d. Howard G. and Ruth Earll. BA, Allegheny County Coll., 1980; JD, Ohio No. U., 1985. Mem. Pa. Senate, Dist. 49, Harrisburg, 1996—; vice chmn. cmty. and econ. devel. com. Pa. Senate, Harrisburg, mem. aging and youth com., mem. intergovtl. affairs com., mem. jud. com., mem. transp. com., mem. urban affairs and housing com. Bd. dirs. Salvation Army, Polish Sharpshooters Club Aux.; past pres., bd. dirs. YWCA, Rape Crisis Ctr. of Erie. Mem. Pa. Bar Assn., Erie County Bar Assn., Pa. Dist. Attys. Assn., Bus. and Profl. Women, S.O.N.S. of Lake Erie, Nat. Coun. Rep. Women, Erie Coun. Rep. Women. Office: 200 W 11th St Erie PA 16501-1702

EARLS, IRENE ANNE, art history educator; d. William Thomas and Constance Ellen (Yanalavage) O'Connor; m. Walter Edward Earls, June 21, 1958. BA, U. Miami, Coral Gables, Fla., 1959; MA, U. Colo., 1968; PhD, U. Ga., 1975. Tchr. advanced placement history of art, English lang. and composition, advanced placement English lit. and composition Orlando (Fla.) Pub. Schs.; prof. classics dept. U. Fla., Gainesville, 1994—. Author: Book Renaissance Art, 1987, Napoléon III l'Architecte et l'Urbaniste de Paris, 1991, Baroque Art, 1997, Young Musicians in World History, 2003, Artists of the Renaissance, 2004; contbr. articles to profl. jours. Named Tchr. of Yr., 1987-88, Nat. Honor Soc. Tchr. of Yr., 1987-88, also others. Mem. Western Soc. French History (officer of program com.), Soc. for French Hist. Studies, Consortium on Revolutionary Europe. Avocation: writing. Office: 1625 Beulah Rd Winter Garden FL 34787-4407

EARLY, DELOREESE PATRICIA See REESE, DELLA

EARNEY, MARY K. writer, educator; b. Marfa, Tex., Mar. 2, 1920; d. Hunter Orgain and Fletcher (McKennon) Metcalfe; m. William Harvey Earney (dec. Dec. 1993); children: Craig M., Robert Franklin, John Fletcher, Ann Elizabeth Curtis. BA, U. Tex., 1941; MA, Sal Ross State U., 1969. Clk. West Tex. Utilities, Marfa, 1941, USN, San Diego, 1942-44, O.P.A. Civil Svc., Marfa, 1944-45; newspaper corr., photographer El Paso Times, Ft. Worth Star Telegram, San Angelo Std., El Paso and Ft. Worth, 1953—; tchr. Marfa Ind. Sch. Dist., 1963-73; columnist Big Bead Sentinel, Marfa, 1993-2000. Author: First Find the Courthouse, 1997, Woolgathering, Life in a Little West Texas Town, 2000, For God and Texas, Life of Dr. Francis Asbury Mood, 2001. Mem. NEA, Tex. State Tchrs., Classroom Tchrs. Assn., Retired Tchrs., San Gabriel Writers League, Alpha Phi. Methodist. Home: 1105 S Church St Georgetown TX 78626-6830

EARNHARDT, TERESA, race team owner; m. Dale Earnhardt, 1982 (dec.); 1 child, Taylor Nicole stepchildren: Kerry, Dale Jr. CEO, team owner Dale Earnhardt Inc., Mooresville, NC, 1982—. Named Outstanding Mother of Yr., Nat. Mother's Day Com., 2002. Office: Dale Earnhardt Inc 1675 Coddle Creek Hwy Mooresville NC 28115-8245

EASLEY, CHERYL EILEEN, nursing educator, department chairman; b. Huntington, W.Va., July 15, 1946; d. Paul Allen and Koneta Seona (Phillips) E. BS, Columbia Union Coll., Takoma Park, Md., 1967; AM, NYU, 1970, PhD, 1989. Pub. health nurse Yonkers (N.Y.) Pub. Health Dept., 1967-68; home care coord. N.Y. Infirmary, N.Y.C., 1969-70; instr. nursing Herbert H. Lehman Coll., CUNY, Bronx, 1971-74; asst. prof. Andrews U., Berrien Springs, Mich., 1974-78, U. Mich. Sch. Nursing, Ann Arbor, 1978-79, interim chmn., grad. program dir. community health nursing, 1980-82, interim asst. dean undergrad. studies, 1983-86; King-Chavez-Parks vis. prof. in women's studies U. Mich., Ann Arbor, 1990; asst. prof. pub. health U. Ill. Coll. Nursing, Chgo., 1989-90; assoc. prof., chmn. dept. community health nursing Coll. Nursing Rush U., Rush-Presbyn. St. Luke's Med. Ctr., Chgo., 1990—, interim assoc. dean ednl. program Coll. Nursing., 1992-93; dir. utilization mgmt. Rush-Presbyn. St. Luke's Med. Ctr., 1993; DON Rush Primary Care Inst., 1994—. Mem. peer rev. panel for advanced nursing edn. program USPHS, Rockville, Md., 1991—; cons. Nat. League for Nursing, N.Y.C., 1988-89. Mem. editorial bd. Jour. Rural Health, 1991-93; contbr. articles to profl. jours., chpts. to books. Chmn. bd. dirs. All Nations Inst. for Social and Econ. Change Inc., Berrien Springs, 1990—; mem. Southwestern Mich. Women's Polit. Coalition, Berrien Springs, 1991—. Grantee HERS Summer Inst. for Women in Higher Edn. Adminstrn., U. Mich., 1981. Mem. APHA (governing coun. pub. health nursing sect. 1980-83, sect. coun. 1986), ANA (cons. 1984-86), Ill. Nurses Assn., Ill. Pub. Health Assn., Sigma Theta Tau, Phi Delta Kappa, Pi Lambda Theta. Adventist. Avocations: reading, handiwork, birding. Home: 8380 Kephart Ln Berrien Springs MI 49103-9570 Office: Rush U Coll Nursing Rush-Presbyn-St Luke's Med Ctr 1743 W Harrison St Chicago IL 60612-3823

EASLEY, CHRISTA BIRGIT, nurse, researcher; b. Berlin, Apr. 30, 1941; came to U.S., 1966; d. Albert and Marianne (Uhlmann) Baldauf; m. Loyd Allen Easley, Oct. 23, 1964 (widowed Dec. 1993). Degree in nursing, Pawlow Coll. of Nursing, Aue, Fed. Republic of Germany, 1959; BS, NYU, Albany, 1978; MBA, Cen. Mich. U., 1979; EDS, Ctrl. Mo. U., 1983; PhD, Kensington U., Glensdale, Calif., 1983. With placement sect. Sembach, A.B., Fed. Republic of Germany, 1972-73, suggestion program mgr., 1973-74; adminstrv. clk. Lajes Field, A.B., Terceira, Acores, Portugal, 1975-78, incentive awards and suggestion program mgr., 1978-79; intern Cen. Mo. State U., Warrensburg, 1980-81; instr. in bus. overseas campus Cen. Tex. Coll./Yokota, A.B., Japan, 1983; instr. Tokyo Ctr. for Lang. and Culture, 1981-83; tchr. dept. of def. Yokota Dept. of Def., Yokota AFB, Japan, 1981-84; tax examiner IRS, Austin, Tex., 1984-86; sr. clin. rsch. coord. HealthQuest Rsch., Austin, 1987-96; v.p. Austin Clin. Rsch., 1996—. Treas. Am. Sch. System PTA, Acores, 1978-79; precinct chmn. Austin Rep. Com., 1988-96. Mem. Am. Acad. Allergy & Immunology, Am. Assn. Translators, AAUW, Sigma Tau Delta. Methodist. Avocations: rock hunting, flower gardens. Home: 12422 Deer Trak Austin TX 78727-5746 Office: Austin Clin Rsch Inc 12885 Research Blvd # 109 Austin TX 78750-3220

EASLEY, JUNE ELLEN PRICE, genealogist; b. Chgo., June 7, 1924; d. Fred E. and Bernadette (Mailloux) Price; m. Raymond Dale Easley, Dec. 24, 1945. Student, McCormack Sch. Commerce, Englewood Jr. Coll., Chgo. Lic. genealogist Assn. Profl. Genealogists. Statis. clk. Arthur Andersen & Co., Chgo., 1968-74; corr. sec. ICG R.R., Chgo., 1974-86; self-employed genealogist-computers Arlington Heights, Ill., 1986-94, Mountain Home, Ark., 1994—2001, Springfield, Mo., 2001—. Editor, typist genealogical books, 1996—. Contbr. religion articles to Daily Herald, 1991; editor romance stories, 1990—, genealogy books, 1996—. Sec. Citizens for Clean Water, Mountain Home, Ark., 1996-98. Mem. AARP (sec. 1997-98), DAR (auditor-treas. Chgo. chpt. 1981-82, rec. sec. Chgo. chpt. 1982-88, Mountain Home ROTC 1995-97, publicity chmn. 1996-97), Huguenot Soc., Nat. Soc. R.R. Bus. Women (newsletter editor 1991-2002), Northwest Suburban Coun. Genealogists (pres. 1988-90, corr. sec. 1990-94), Daus. of War 1812, Daus. of Union Vets. (Civil War). Republican. Avocations: genealogy, writing, antiques, computers, travel. Home and Office: 2315 E Lark St Springfield MO 65804 E-mail: juneeasley@alltel.net.

EASLEY, MARY, retired elementary school educator, state representative; b. Cassville, Mo. m. Truman Easley; children: Michael, Kevin, Lisa Gage. BA in Lang. Arts and Bus., Friends U., Wichita, Kans.; MA, Northeastern Okla. State U., Tahlequah. Rep. Ho. Reps., State of Okla., Okla. City, 1997—. Asst. majority fl. leader Okla. Ho. Reps., Okla. City., 1997—, chair banking and fin. com., 1997—, vice chair subcom. on edn. to appropriations and budget com., 1997—, mem. common edn., energy and utility regulation, and pub, safety and homeland security coms., 1997—. Democrat. Office: 2300 N Lincoln Blvd Rm 302-A Oklahoma City OK 73105 Home and Office: 1360 S 99thE Ave Tulsa OK 74128 E-mail: easleyma@lsb.state.ok.us.

EASON, ELEANOR WILSON, realtor; b. Hartselle, Ala. d. Joseph Franklin and Ophelia Ethel (Lee) Wilson; m. George Echols Eason, Sept. 17, 1946; children: George William, Susan Rebecca. BS, Athens Coll., 1940; postgrad., U. N.C., 1956. Grad. Realtors Inst.; cert. realtors specialist. Math tchr., Red Bay, Ala., 1940-43; math and biology tchr. Ponce de Leon, Fla., 1943-44; office mgr. Montgomery, Ala., 1944-46; pvt. realtor, broker owner Kingsport, Tenn., 1966—. State pres. Womens Coun. Realtors, 1979; dir. Nat. Assn. Realtors, 1986-95. Trustee Emory and Henry Coll., 1989—, Va., First Broad St. United Meth. Ch., Kingsport, Sunday sch. tchr.; pres. Kingsport Downtown Assn., 1992. Mem. Tenn. Assn. Realtors (regional v.p. 1984), Kingsport Bd. Realtors (life, pres. 1978, Realtor of Yr. 1978), Kingsport C. of C. Democrat. Methodist. Avocations: art, golf. Home: 100 Northerland Ln Apt 327 Kingsport TN 37660-7249

EASON, LINDA LEE, music educator; b. Denver, Colo., Nov. 20, 1946; d. M. Verne and Elma Iris Eason. BA in Music Edn., Colo. State Coll., 1968; MA in Music Edn., U. No. Colo., 1973. Tchr. music, band Window Rock Pub. Schs., Ft. Defiance, Ariz., 1968—69; tchr. orch. Kearney (Nebr.) Pub. Schs., 1969—76, Albany County Pub. Schs., Laramie, Wyo., 1976—, chmn. Dept. Music, 1984—. Pres. site coun. Laramie (Wyo.) Jr. HS, 2000—01. Docent Laramie (Wyo.) Plains Mus., 1989—; bd. dirs. Friends of the Libr., Laramie, 1986—. Mem.: NEA, Wyo. Edn. Assn., Music Educators Nat. Conf., Am. String Tchrs. Assn., Wyo. Am. String Tchrs. Assn. (state pres. 1985—86), Alpha Delta Kappa (pres. Zeta chpt. 1986—88, state sec. 1990—92, pres. Zeta chpt. 1996—98). Independent. Avocations: needlecrafts, gardening, reading, travel.

EASON-WATKINS, BARBARA JUNE, principal; b. Detroit, June 1, 1952; d. Ceroy Alfred and Glady Mabel (Rush) Hollis; m. Laras Edred Eason, June 29, 1974 (div. 1978); 1 child, Marques Eason; m. Irvin B. Watkins, July 22, 1990. BA, U. Mich., 1973; MA, Chgo. State U., 1982; postgrad., U. Chgo., 1983—. Tchr. Highland Park (Mich.) Pub. Schs., 1973-74, Chgo. Pub. Schs., 1974-85, prin., 1985—. Recipient Whitman award Whitman Corp., 1988, Kizzy award Revlon Corp., 1988, Community Svc. award Chgo. Intervention Network, 1988, 91; Urban Partnership grantee Ill. State Bd. Edn., 1990, Sci. Literacy grantee Ill. State Bd. Edn., 1990, Joyce Found. grantee, 1990. Mem. Chgo. Prins. Assn., Samuel Stratton Assn. PTA, Prin.'s Coalition for the Arts. Methodist. Avocations: reading, aerobics.

EAST, JANETTE DIANE, marketing consultant; b. Phoenix, Jan. 5, 1950; d. Henry Melvin Clatterbuck and Dorothy (Eakin) Newman; m. John L. East, III, 2003. Student World Campus Afloat, Chapman Coll., 1967-68; BA in Anthropology and Archeology, Ariz. State U., 1972. CNA. Owner, mgr., buyer Walls Galore and Bath Decor, Corvallis, Oreg., 1977-84; mgr., trainer, buyer Bloomingdales, Dallas, 1984-85; mgr. Frederick and Nelson, Seattle, 1986-87; mgr., buyer The Bon Marché, Seattle, 1987-89; mktg. cons. Kinder-Harris, 1989-93; lectr., cons. merchandising and display, 1993—. Intern trainer Oreg. State U., 1981-83. Contbr. articles to profl. jours. Mem. Downtown Mchts. Assn., Corvallis, 1977-84, Oreg. Homebuilders Assn., Corvallis, 1977-84; vol. Make-A-Wish Found., Bailey-Boushay Hospice. Mem. Am. Business Woman's Assn. (Corvallis chpt.); award winning portrait painter. Democrat.

EAST, LEETTA JOYCE, elementary school educator, music educator; b. Springfield, Mo., Dec. 2, 1949; d. James Harold Young and Loretta Alice (Heard) Young Bruton; m. John Edgar East, June 5, 1971 (dec. Nov. 1999). BS in Music Edn., Southwest Mo. State U., 1971, MS in Music Edn., 1993. Cert. tchr. Mo., master level Orff cert. Memphis Univ., 1995. Tchr. vocal, instrumental music Sparta Pub. Sch., Mo., 1972—73; tchr. vocal music Hartville Pub. Sch., 1974—76, Willow Springs Pub. Sch., 1976—77, substitute tchr., 1977—80, Cabool Pub. Sch., 1977—80, Mountain Grove Pub. Sch., 1977—80, West Plains Pub. Sch., 1977—80; tchr. elem. math., reading aide Willow Springs Pub. Sch., 1980—81, tchr. elem. music, 1981—. Dir. choir Trinity Bapt. Ch., Willow Springs, 1980—81. Mem.: NEA, Mtn. Orff-Schulwerk Assn., Am. Orff-Schulwerk Assn., Music Educators Nat. Conf., Delta Kappa Gamma. Home: 721 Trimble Dr Willow Springs MO 65793 Office: Willow Springs Elem Sch 214 W 4th St Willow Springs MO 65793 E-mail: eastl@wpsgs.k12.mo.us.

EAST, MARY ANN HILDEGARDE, vocalist; b. Summit, N.J., July 7, 1976; d. Thomas Patrick and Jacqueline Marie McKavitt; m. Joseph Andrew East, Nov. 17, 2001. MusB in Edn., Ind. U., 1999; MusM in Vocal Performance, MusM in Choral Conducting, George Mason U., 2002. Cert. tchr. Va. Gen. music tchr. Sunrise Valley Elem. Sch., Reston, Va., 1999—2000; choral dir. Wash. Irving Mid. Sch., Springfield, Va., 2000—01, George C. Marshall H.S., Falls Church, Va., 2001—. Sect. leader Washington Women's Chorus, 2002—; mem. Nat. Women's Honor Choir, 2003. Mem.: NEA, Va. Music Educators Assn., Fairfax County Choral Dirs. Assn., Am. Choral Dirs. Assn., Music Educators Nat. Conf., Ind. U. Alumni Assn. (life). Avocation: piano. Office: George C Marshall HS 7731 Leesburg Pike Falls Church VA 22043

EASTABROOK, DIANNE, news correspondent; Grad., Northwestern U., 1982. Weekend prodr., anchor Sta. WSAN-TV, Wausau, Wis.; contbr. consumer news Sta. WEEK-TV, Peoria, Ill.; money editor Sta. WNYT-TV, Albany, N.Y.; Midwest corr., bur. chief Nightly Bus. Report, Chgo. Office: NBR 100 S Sangamon St Chicago IL 60607-2614

EASTERDAY, SHANDA HANSMA BLUE, language educator, writer; m. Robert William Easterday, Nov. 23, 2001; children: Danyi Hansma Heckaman, Graydon Courtney Blue, Morgan Genevieve Blue, Kerry Easterday Olvera, Eric William. Post grad., Western Mich. U., Kalamazoo, 1994—; BA in English, Women's Studies, 1997; MFA in Creative Writing, Western Mich. U., Kalamazoo, 2000; PhD in English creative writing, 2004. Master of Fine Arts in Creative Writing Western Mich. U., 2000. Doctoral assoc. in English Western Mich. U., Kalamazoo, 2000—, tchg., 1998—. Editor Third Coast magazine. Mem. Syracuse Ind. Town Coun., 1990—93. Fellow, Western Mich. U., 2000, 2001, 2002, 2003—04. Mem.: MLA, MMLA, Phi Beta Kappa. Office: Western Michigan U W Michigan Kalamazoo MI

EASTIN, DELAINE ANDREE, foundation administrator; b. San Diego, Aug. 20, 1947; d. Daniel Howard and Dorothy Barbara Eastin. BA in Polit. Sci., U. Calif., Davis, 1969; MA in Polit. Sci., U. Calif., Santa Barbara, 1971. Instr. Calif. Community Colls., various locations, 1971-79; asst. mgr. Pacific Bell, San Francisco, 1979-84; corp. planner Pacific Telesis Group, San Francisco, 1984-86; assemblywoman Calif. State Legis., Sacramento, 1986-95; supt. of public instruction Calif. Edn. Dept., Sacramento, 1995—2003; exec. dir. Nat. Inst. Sch. Leadership, 2003—. Ex officio mem. bd. regents U. Calif., 1995—2003; ex officio mem. bd. trustees Calif. State U., 1995—2003. Bd. dirs. CEWAER, Sacramento, 1988-2003, Pence Gallery, 2003—, Internat. Assn. Fgn. Students Found., 2003—; commr. Commn. on Status of Women, Sacramento, 1990-2003; mem. coun. City of Union City, Calif., 1980-86; chair Alameda County Libr. Commn., Hayward, Calif., 1981-86; planning commr. City of Union City, 1976-80; mem., pres. Alameda County Solid Waste Mgmt. Authority, Oakland, Calif., 1980-86. Named Outstanding Pub. Ofcl. Calif. Tchrs. Assn., 1988, Cert. of Appreciation Calif. Assn. for Edn. of Young Children, 1988-92, Legislator of the Yr. Calif. Media Libr. Educators, 1991, Calif. Sch. Bd. Assn., 1991, 94, Ednl. Excellence award Calif. Assn. Counseling and Devel., 1992. Mem. Am. Bus. Women's Assn. (Outstanding Bus. Woman 1988), The Internat. Alliance (21st Century award 1990), World Affairs Coun., Commonwealth Club. Democrat. Avocations: photography, hiking, reading, theater. Home: 4228 Dogwood Pl Davis CA 95616-6066

EASTMAN, DONNA KELLY, composer; b. Denver, Sept. 26, 1945; d. Donald Lewis and Frances Marie (Smith) Kelly; m. John Bernard Eastman, July 1, 1973; children: Jonathan Kelly, James Alan; stepchildren: Barbara Kathleen, Sally Toye. B Music Edn., U. Colo., 1967; MA, U. Md., 1973, D in Mus. Arts, 1992. Pvt. studio tchr., coach, 1960—; choral dir. Dept. Def. Overseas Sch., Okinawa, Japan, 1970-72; dir. Choraleers Choral Ensemble, Stuttgart, Germany, 1974-76, Bangkok Music Soc. Ensemble and Madrigal Singers, Thailand, 1982-84; instr. in music No. Va. C.C., Alexandria, 1986-89. Creator, pianist, vocalist Am. Music Programs for U.S. Mission, Thailand, 1981-84; vis. asst. prof. Ill. Wesleyan U., Bloomington, 1994; vis. composer Sweet Briar (Va.) Coll., 1998, Grinnell (Iowa) Coll., 1999. Composer choral, orchestral, opera, vocal/instrumental solo and chamber, and electronic works; recs. include Capstone Records-Soc. of Composers, Inc. Series CPS 8632, 1996, and New Music for Flute and Piano, CPS 8664, 1999; Living Artist Recs.-Music from the Setting Century Series, Vol. 2, 1996; New Ariel Recordings-Contemporary American Eclectic Music for the Piano Series, AE002, 1996; Columbine Chorale Recs.--European Tour, 1999, Blue House Productions--Alone Into the Crowd, 2002; contbr. to jours. Recipient 6 Internat. Composition awards, Composer Guild, 1991—, Internat. Piano Composition award, Roodeport Internat. Eisteddfod, South Africa, 1991, Glad-Robinson-Youse Composition award, Nat. Fedn. Music Clubs, 1992, Internat. Choral Composition award, Florilège Vocal Tours, France, 1995, Keyboard award, Delius Composition Competition, 1997, Margaret Fairbank Jory Copying Assistance award, Am. Music Ctr., 1999, Nat. Music Composition Competition award, Nat. League of Am. Pen Women, 2000; fellow, Charles Ives Ctr. for Am. Music, 1990; grantee, 1993, Ragdale Found., 1991, Va. Ctr. for Creative Arts, 1991—2002. Mem. Soc. for Electro-Acoustic Music in the U.S., Internat. Alliance for Women in Music, Soc. of Composers, Inc. (life), Nat. Mus. Women in Arts (charter), Broadcast Music, Inc., Am. Composers Forum, Southeastern Composers League (pres.), Friday Morning Music Club Washington, Phi Kappa Phi, Pi Kappa Lambda, Sigma Alpha Iota. Avocations: travel, handicrafts, photography. Home: 15253 W Morningtree Dr Surprise AZ 85374-4619 Personal E-mail: dkeastman@cox.net.

EASTON, KELLY ANNE, writer, educator; b. Arcadia, Calif., Sept. 3, 1960; d. Robert William and Marilyn Eleanor Easton; children: Isabelle Easton Spivack, Isaac Robert Easton Spivack. MFA, U. Calif., San Diego, 1991. Lectr. U. N.C., Wilmington, 1994—2000; guest artist U. R.I., Kingstown, 2000—01; adj. prof. Roger Williams U., RI, 2002—, Rhode Island Coll., 2003—. Author: (novels) The Life History of a Star, 2001 (Golden Kite Honor award, 2002, listed in Book Sense 76 Top Ten Books for Teens., 2002, ALA Popular Paperbacks for Teens), Trouble at Betts Pets, 2002, Canaries and Criminals: Trouble at Betts Pets, 2003, Walking on Air, 2004; contbr. articles to profl. jours. Democrat. E-mail: eastonka@hotmail.com.

EASTON, LORY BARSDATE BARSDATE, lawyer; b. 1962; BA in Linguistics summa cum laude, Yale U., 1983, JD, 1988. Bar: Pa. 1990, Conn. 1990, Ill. 1991. Clk. to Jose A. Cabranes, U.S. Dist. Ct. for Conn., 1988-89; clk. to Hon. Ralph K. Winter, U.S. Ct. Appeals for 2d Cir., 1989-90; assoc. Sidley & Austin, Chgo., 1990-96, ptnr., 1996—. Mng. editor Yale Law Jour., 1987-88. Office: Sidley & Austin Bank One Plz 425 W Surf St Apt 605 Chicago IL 60657-6139 Fax: 312-853-7036. E-mail: leaston@sidley.com.

EASTON, MICHELLE, foundation executive; b. Phila., Aug. 12, 1950; d. Glenn H. Jr. and Jeanne (Mulhall) Easton; m. Ron Robinson, Sept. 14, 1974; children: Ronald Jr., Daniel, Thomas. AA, BA, Briarcliff Coll., 1972; JD, Am. U., Washington, 1980. Bar: Va. 1981. Asst. to exec. dir. Young Ams. for Freedom, Sterling, Va., 1973-78; asst. to dir. pub. rels. Nat. Right to Work Com., Springfield, Va., 1978; legal asst. Nat. Right to Work Legal Def. Found., 1979; transition team mem. Office of Pres.-Elect, Equal Employment Opportunity Commn., Washington, 1980-81; atty. U.S. Dept. Justice, Washington, 1981; spl. asst. to gen. counsel U.S. Dept. Edn., Washington, 1981-83; pvt. vol. orgns. liaison officer, Africa Bur. Agy. for Internat. Devel., 1984; dir. Missing Children's Program Office of Juvenile Justice and Delinquency Prevention, U.S. Dept. Justice, 1985-87; dir. intergovtl. affairs U.S. Dept. Edn., Washington, 1987-88, dep. under sec. for intergovtl. and interagy. affairs, 1988-91; dir. Office Pvt. Edn., Washington, 1991-93; pres. Clare Boothe Luce Policy Inst., 1993—. Apptd. by Gov. Allen to Va. State Bd. Edn., Richmond, 1994-98, bd. pres. 1996; bd. dirs. The Family Found., Richmond, Va., 1998-99; sec. Nat. Conservative Campaign Fund, 2000—. Mem.: Phila. Soc. (trustee 2000—02). Republican. Episcopalian.

EASTWOOD, KATHLEEN J. medical/surgical nurse; b. Wichita, Mar. 17, 1960; d. Robert A. and Kathleen A. Eastwood; m. Bradford A. Brinkopf, May 25, 1985 (div. Nov. 2001); children: Katrina K. Brinkopf, Amanda M. Brinkopf. Diploma in nursing, 1981, BSN, 1985. RN Mo., Kans., Tenn., Tex. Surg. nurse St. John's Med. Ctr., Mo., 1981—86, Memphis Surgery Ctr., 1986—88, West Houston Med. Ctr., 1988—89, St. Joseph Med. Ctr., Kansas City, Mo., 1989—91, Kans. U. Med. Ctr., Kans., 2001—. Asst. leader Girl Scouts Am., Kans., 1993—94; mem. com. Jr. League, Kansas City, 1992—96. Avocations: gardening, swimming.

EATON, DORLA DEAN See KEMPER, DORLA DEAN EATON

EATON, EMMA PARKER, special education educator; b. Conway, N.C., June 21, 1945; BS in Special Edn., Norfolk State Coll., 1978; MA, Norfolk State U., 1995. Spl. edn. educator Norfolk Pub. Schs., Va.

EATON, MAJA CAMPBELL, lawyer; b. 1955; BA, U. Iowa, 1977, JD, 1984. Bar: Ill. 1984, U.S. Dist. Ct. (no. dist.) Ill. 1984, U.S. Dist. Ct. (no. dist.) Calif. 1993. With Sidley Austin Brown & Wood, Chgo., ptnr., 1993—. Former adj. prof. law Chgo.-Kent Coll. Law. Mem.: Def. Rsch. Inst. Office: Sidley Austin Brown and Wood Bank One Plz 10 S Dearborn St Chicago IL 60603*

EATON, NANCY RUTH LINTON, librarian, dean; b. Berkeley, Calif., May 2, 1943; d. Don Thomas and Lena Ruth (McClellan) Linton; m. Edward Arthur Eaton III, June 19, 1965 (div. 1980) AB, Stanford U., 1965;

MLS, U. Tex., 1968, postgrad., 1969. From cataloger to asst. to dir. U. Tex. Libr., Austin, 1968-74; automation libr. SUNY, Stony Brook, 1974-76; head tech. svcs. Atlanta Pub. Libr., 1976-82; dir. libr. U. Vt., Burlington, 1982-89; dean libr. svcs. Iowa State U., Ames, 1989-97; dean univ. librs. Pa. State U., University Park, Pa., 1997—. Bd. dir. Ctr. for Rsch. Libr., 1988-92, chair, 1989-90; del. user's coun., mem. exec. com. Online Computer Libr. Ctr., Inc., Dublin, Ohio, 1980-82, 86-88, trustee, 1987-2002, chair bd. trustees 1992-96; mgr. Nat. Agrl. Text Digitalizing Project, 1986-92; bd. dir. New Eng. Libr. Network, 1987-89; chair steering com. Digial Libr. Fedn., 2000-2002; mem. adv. bd. Nat. Digital Info. Infrastructure and Preservation Program, 2001-2002. Co-author: Optical Information Systems: Implementation Issues for Libraries, 1988.; co-editor: A Cataloging Sampler, 1971, Book Selection Policies in American Libraries, 1972; contbr. articles to profl. jours. U.S. Office of Edn. post-master's fellow, 1969; Dept. Edn. Title II-C grantee, 1985, 87-88, Title II-D grantee, 1992-96. Mem. ALA, Libr. and Info. Tech. Assn. (pres. 1984-85, bd. dirs. 1980-86), Assn. Rsch. Librs. (bd. dirs. 1994-97), Digital Libr. Fedn. (exec. com. 1997-2003), Coalition for Networked Info. (steering com. 1999—). Democrat. Avocations: tennis, walking. Home: 441 Homan Ave State College PA 16801-6337 Office: Pa State Univ 510 Paterno Library University Park PA 16802-1812

EATON, PAULINE, artist, educator; b. Neptune, N.J., Mar. 20, 1935; d. Paul A. and Florence Elizabeth (Rogers) Friedrich; m. Charles Adams Eaton, June 15, 1957; children: Gregory, Eric, Paul, Joy. BA, Dickinson Coll., 1957; MA, Northwestern U., 1958. Lic. instr. Calif. Instr. Mira Costa Coll., Oceanside, Calif., 1980-82, Idyllwild Sch. Music and Arts, Calif., 1983—; instr. dept. continuing edn. U. N.Mex. Juror, demonstrator numerous art socs. One-woman shows include Nat. Arts Club, N.Y.C., 1977, Designs Recycled Gallery, Fullerton, Calif., 1978, 1980, 1984, San Diego Art Inst., 1980, Spectrum Gallery, San Diego, 1981, San Diego Jung Ctr., 1983, Marin Civic Ctr. Gallery, 1984, R. Mondayi Winery, 1987, exhibited in group shows at Am. Watercolor Soc., 1975, 1977, Butler Inst. Am. Art, Youngstown, Ohio, 1977—79, 1981, NAD, 1978, N.Mex Arts and Crafts Fair, 1994 (Best in Show award), Corrales Bosque Gallery, Originals: N.Mex. Women in the Arts, 2003, Represented in permanent collections Butler Inst. Am. Art, St. Mary's Coll., Md., Mercy Hosp., San Diego, Sharp Hosp., Redlands Hosp., Riverside; work featured in: book Watercolor, The Creative Experience, 1978, Creative Seascape Painting, 1980, Painting the Spirit in Nature, 1984, Exploring Painting (Gerald Brommer); author: Crawling to the Light, An Artist in Transition, 1987; author: (with Mary Ann Beckwith) Best of Watercolor Texture, 1997; contbr. chapters to books. Trustee San Diego Art Inst., 1977—78, San Diego Mus. Art, 1982—83. Recipient award, Hollywood (Calif.) Form Arts, 1986, Grumbacker award, Conf. 96 Hill Country Art Ctr., 2d award, Tex. Friends and Neighbors, Irving, 2000, award of excellence, Ariz. Aqueous, 2002, Originals award, N.Mex. Women in Arts, Albuquerque Mus., 2003. Mem.: Soc. Layerists Multi-Media (bd. dirs. 1992—), Eastbay Watercolor Soc. (v.p. 1988—90), West Coast Watercolor Soc. (exhbns. chmn. 1983—86, pres. 1989—92), Western Fedn. Watercolor Socs. (chmn. 1983, 3d prize 1982, Grumbacher Gold medal 1983), N.Mex Watercolor Soc. (Grumbacker award, Wingspread award 1999), San Diego Artists Guild (pres. 1982—83), Artists Equity (v.p. San Diego 1979—81), San Diego Watercolor Soc. (pres. 1976—77, workshop dir. 1977—80), Marin Arts Guild (instr. 1984—87), Internat. Soc. Exptl. Artists (Nautilus Merit award 1992, 1998), Watercolor West (Strathmore award 1979, Purchase award 1986), Rocky Mountain Watermedia Soc. (Golden award 1979, Mustard Seed award 1983), Nat. Watercolor Soc., Watercolor USA Soc. (hon. Veloy Vigil Meml. award 1986), Nat. Soc. Painters Acrylic and Casein (hon.). Democrat. Home: 68 Hop Tree Trl Corrales NM 87048-9613 E-mail: pfeaton@earthlink.net.

EATON, SHIRLEY M. medical/surgical nurse; d. Benjamin W. Randall Sr. and Rena B. Randall; children: Everett Kennedy, Eran Margret Eaton Parker. MPH, So. Conn. U., 1997. RN Conn. Nurse, SC and Conn., 1960—; mem. staff ombudsman program Norwalk (Conn.) Social Svcs., 1996—. Mem. adv. coun. Area of Nursing, Norwalk, 1997—. Author: Handbook for Caregivers to the Elderly, 1998. Presbyterian. Avocations: singing, sewing, writing, travel, designing.

EATON, STEPHANIE, state legislator; b. Littleton, N.H., July 22, 1936; BA, Middlebury Coll., 1958, MA, 1967; JD, Franklin Pierce Law Ctr., 1990. N.H. state rep.; mem. pub. works and hwys. com. N.H. Ho. of Reps.; cartographer; mem. sci. & tech. com. N.H. Ho. of Reps. Mem. Glenwood Cemetery Com., 1990-94; trustee Littleton Trust Funds, 1992-94. Mem. LWV, Profile Women's Club. Address: 243 Pleasant St Littleton NH 03561-4917

EATON ADAMS, ELIZABETH SUSAN, retired middle school educator, jazz musician; b. Norfolk, Va., Apr. 13, 1947; d. Russell Samuel and Miriam Kathleen (Kindermann) E.; m. Robert F. Adams, May 24, 1998. BA, Marquette U., 1970; MS, U. Wis., Milw., 1973; PhD equivalency, Wis. Coll. Conservatory Music, 1979. Cert. tchr. grades 1-6, Wis., reading tchr. grades 1-8, Wis. Reading tchr. grades 1-6 Garfield Elem. Sch., Milw., 1973-77, reading tchr. grades 6-8 King Mid. Sch. Gifted & Talented, Milw., 1979-82; 2d grade tchr. Elm Creative Arts Elem. Sch., Milw., 1983-84; English & social studies tchr., jazz studies tchr. Roosevelt Mid. Sch. Creative Arts, Milw., 1984-89; reading tchr. grades 6-8 Morse Mid. Sch. Gifted & Talented, Milw., 1979-82, English tchr., 1990-94, yoga tchr., 1993-95, reading tchr., 1994-96; asst. to head libr. Marquette U. and Wis. Coll. Conservatory of Music, 1996—2000; English, study skills and curriculum coord. Northshore C.C., 1999, Wellspring House, 1999; reading tchr. Rockport (Mass.) Mid. Sch., 2000, ret., 2001. Chmn., advisor Nat. Jr. Honor Soc., Milw., 1991-94; co-dir. Morse Drama Club, 1991-93, advisor, mem., performer Fin Arts Week Morse com., 1991-96. Prodr., vocalist, lyricist, arranger (CD and cassette recs.) It's Time Now, 1995. Bd. trustees Hist. Pabst Theatre, Milw., 1972-79; dir. asst., vol. Summerfest World Festivals, Inc., Milw., 1969-71; vol., fund raiser Sta. WYMS Jazz Radio, 1995. Mem. Siddha Yoga, Inc. (ctr. host, 2002, 03), Wis. Arts and Music, Inc., Pi Lambda Theta. Avocations: travel, antique & art collecting, genealogy. Home: 7 Doctors Run Rockport MA 01966-1357 Office: Morse Mid Sch Gifted & Talented 4601 N 84th St Milwaukee WI 53225-4958

EAVES, DOROTHY ANN GREENE, music educator; b. Pinson, Ala., Feb. 27, 1938; d. Albert Anderson Greene and Dorothy Elizabeth McCool; m. Richard Glen Eaves, June 19, 1959; 1 child, Lisa Michelle Eaves Stooksbury. MusB magna cum laude, Miss. State Coll. for Women, 1959; student, Peabody Coll., 1959, U. Ala., 1960-65; MEd, Auburn U., 1970. Tchr. piano and organ Clarke Coll., Newton, Miss., 1959-62; min. of music Bay Springs (Miss.) Bapt. Ch., 1960-62; ind. piano tchr. Clinton, Miss., Tuscaloosa and Auburn, Ala., 1963-86; adj. tchr. music edn. Auburn U., 1971-72; adj. tchr. piano and ch. music Miss. Coll., Clinton, 1984-89; pianist Woodville Heights Bapt. Ch., Jackson, Miss., 1985-86. Music accompanist Auburn U., 1968-70; piano competition judge, recitalist, Ala., Miss., La., 1970—; instr. piano and music history Hinds C.C., Raymond, 1986—. Mem. faculty Miss. Piano Camp, Raymond, 1988, 90, 95—. Faculty devel. grantee Hinds C.C., Raymond, 1995, 98. Mem. Music Tchrs. Nat. Assn. Republican. Baptist. Avocations: travel, reading, walking, church projects. Home: 8246 Jade Tree Ln Knoxville TN 37938-3186

EAVES, MARIA PERRY, realtor; b. Cluj, Romania; d. Nicholas Brudan and Ema (Filipescu) Perry; m. John Eaves, June 16, 1951; children: Bryan Perry, Susan Eaves Clark. BA, MA, UCLA, 1945; postgrad., Columbia U., 1947-51, U. London, 1953-54. Lic. realtor, Md., Va.; rev. appraiser. Advt. and market analyst Foote, Cone & Belding, N.Y.C., 1948-49; fgn. affairs officer U.S. Dept. State, N.Y.C., 1950-53; dir. rsch. Radio Free Europe Press, N.Y.C., 1955-56; info. officer, media reaction analyst USIA, Washington, 1956-58, rsch. cons., 1958-61; market and pub. opinion cons., Washington, 1969-72; realtor Colquitt Carruthers Inc., Bethesda, Md., 1972-81, Long & Foster Real Estate Inc., Potomac, Md. and McLean, Va., 1982—. One-woman paintings show at Nicosia, Cyprus; group shows include New Delhi (India), White Plains, N.Y., Bethesda, Md.; also pvt. collections. Vol. Gov. Nelson Rockefeller's Com. to Welcome UN Diplomats, N.Y.C., 1968, 69; mem. World Affairs Coun. Washington; Woodrow Wilson Info. Ctr. for Scholars, Washington; charter mem. Nat. Mus. Women in the Arts, Washington, Nat. Mus. Am. Indian. Mem. NAFE, LWV, AAUW, NARFE, FIAPCI, Internat. Fedn. Realtors, Internat. Real Estate Inst. (registered), Nat. Assn. Realtors, Nat. Assn. Rev. Appraisers and Mortgage Underwriters, Md. Assn. Realtors, No. Va. Assn. Realtors, Women's Coun. Realtors, Greater Capital Area Assn. Realtors, Woman's Nat. Dem. Club (Washington), Tournament Players Club (Potomac, Md.), Diplomatic and Officers Club Ret., Columbia U. Club (Wash.), Mil. Dist. of Washington Club. Democrat. Episcopalian. Avocations: bridge, painting, classical music, reading, computers. Home: 11312 Coral Gables Dr North Potomac MD 20878-3803 Office: Long & Foster Realtors 9812 Falls Rd Potomac MD 20854-3996

EAVES, SALLY ANN, military career officer; b. Salt Lake City, Feb. 25, 1945; d. Frank C. and Magdalene (Buller) Winslow; m. Stephen Douglas Eaves, Apr. 27, 1974; children: Trevor Bernard, Lindsay Douglas, Christian Francis. BA in English, Gonzaga U., 1967; postgrad., Utah State U., 1980, U. So. Calif., 1985. Individual mobilization asst. to dir. of logistics U.S. Forces Korea, 1983-87; individual mobilization asst. to chief of transp., dir. distbn., dir. commodities Ogden (Utah) Air Logistics Ctr., 1987-93; individual mobilization asst. to dir. logistics N.Am. Aerospace Def. Command and U.S. Space Command, Peterson AFB, Colo., 1993-95; mobilization asst. to commdr. Okla. Air Logistics Ctr., Oklahoma City, 1995-98; mobilization asst. to dir. logistics Air Combat Command, Langley AFB, Va., 1998—; v.p. N.W. Rsch. Inst., Las Vegas, 1996—. V.p., bd. dirs. The Pond Homeowners Assn., Arvada, Colo., 1992-95; ednl./comty. vol. Jeffco Pub. Schs., 1992-95; ch. vol. Spirit of Christ Cath. Ch., Arvada, 1989—, career devel. counselor Adams County Sch. Dist. 50, Westminster, Colo., 1989—. Brig. gen. USAFR, 1967—. Decorated Def. Meritorious Svc. medal, Meritorious Svc. medal. Mem. Nat. Def. Transp. Assn., Soc. Logistics Engrs., Air Force Assn., Res. Officers Assn. (v.p. Okla. chpt. 1996-97), Logistics Officers Assn. Home: 8708 Independence Way Arvada CO 80005-1247

EBBESON, KAREN ANN, retired social worker; b. Wayne, Nebr., Mar. 19, 1937; d. Elwin Alva and Blanch Alene (Buchanan) Fels; m. Gordon Frank Wedel, Sept. 3, 1964 (div. 1978); children: Rodrick, Terry Lynn, Michelle Marie, Kimberly; m. James Otto Ebbeson, June 16, 1979; stepchildren: Christy, Frida, Erika, Jeffery. BS, U. Wis., 1960; postgrad., U. Wis., Milw. and Madison, 1970's. Cert. social worker, Wis. Social worker Dane County Dept. Social Svcs., Madison, Wis., 1960-61, Outagamie County Dept. Social Svcs., Appleton, Wis., 1961-64, Milwaukee County Dept. Social Svcs., Milw., 1964-66, Waukesha County Dept. Social Svcs., Waukesha, Wis., 1972-77, Door County Dept. Social Svcs., Sturgeon Bay, Wis., 1977-87, Door County Counseling Svcs., Sturgeon Bay, 1987-91, 1991-97; pvt. practice social worker Family Bridges-Social Work Svcs. for All Ages, Sturgeon Bay, 1994-97. Mem. Teen Pregnancy Task Force, 1993-96; organizer Grief Support Task Force, Door County, Wis., 1995-97; organizer HELP of D.C., 1978, bd. dirs., 1978-83, chair, 1983. Pres. Local Planned Parenthood Assn., 1989—97, Wis. Inter Profl. Com. on Div., 1988—97, chairperson, 1990—90; active Peninsula Chamber Choir, 1988—; bd. mem. Birch Creek Assn., Door County, 1990—92; chair family selection com. Habitat for Humanity, 1991—96, 2000—; mem. allocation com. United Way, 1997—98; chairperson local Habitat for Humanity, 1999—; founding mem. domestic violence program, bd. dirs. Door County Help, Inc., Wis., 1978—82; active Meth. Ch. Choir; mem. pastor parish com. Meth. Ch. Coun., 1999; chair pastor parish rels. com. Meth. Ch., 2002—. Mem. LWV (state bd. mem. 1980-92, bd. dirs. D.C. chapt. 1980-88, pres. 1986-88, com. chair children at risk study 1995-96, prodn. publ. 1998, v.p. 1999-2002, pres. 2002—). Democrat. Methodist. Avocations: art, skiing, sailing, singing, golf. Home: 3280 Lake Forest Park Rd Sturgeon Bay WI 54235-9148

EBELING, VICKI, marriage and family therapist, psychotherapist, writer; b. Detroit, Nov. 18, 1948; d. Paul F. and Constance Jean Ebeling; m. James Robert Marchese, 1983; 1 child, Drew Ebeling Marchese. BA, Mich. State U., 1969; M of Sci., Marriage, Family & Child Counseling, Calif. State U., Dominguez Hills, 1990; PhD in Human Behavior, Newport U., 1999. Diplomate Am. Psychotherapy Assn.; cert. youth effectiveness tng. instr.; bd. cert. ednl. therapist., Assn. Ednl. Therapists. With various TV and radio prodn. cos., Detroit, Lansing, Mich., 1969-74; TV and film prodn. cos. L.A., 1974-90; psychotherapist/marriage, family and child therapist Torrance, Calif., 1990—; ednl. therapist, 1994—. Author: Educating America in the 21st Century, 2002. Counselor South Bay Rape Crisis Ctr., 1988-92; mem. orientation team St. Peter's by Sea Presbyn. Ch., Palos Verdes Estates, Calif., 1993-95; vol. cons. 1736 Family Crisis Ctr., 1988, Calif. Spl. Olympics, 1990-91, pediat. ward UCLA-Harbor Hosp., 1991-92, Child Shelter Care, Los Angeles County Children's Ct., 1992-93, ARC Disaster Svc., 1995—. Named Adult Amateur Horsemanship Champion, Los Serranos Award Circuit, Rolling Hills, Calif., 1993. Mem. Calif. Assn. Marriage and Family Therapists (South Bay newsletter editor 1992-94), Assn. Ednl. Therapists. Office: 24586 Hawthorne Blvd # 7 Torrance CA 90505-6807

EBERHARDT, MARTY LAMPERT, botanical garden administrator; b. Albuquerque, Aug. 6, 1952; d. Charles Lampert and Mary Elizabeth (Marty) E.; m. Thomas George Schramski, Mar. 19, 1977 (div. May 1986); children: Paul, Sam; m. Philip Alan Hastings, Dec. 12, 1987. BA, Prescott Coll., 1974; MEd, U. Ariz., 1978. Program dir. Tumamoc Hill Environ. Edn. Ctr., Tucson, 1978-79; tchr. Cmty. Psychology and Edn. Svcs., Tucson, 1985-87; asst. dir./edn. coord. Tucson Bot. Gardens, 1986-88, exec. dir., 1988—. Reviewer grants Inst. Mus. and Libr. Svcs., Washington, 1994—; mem. adv. bd. Registree, 1993—. Mem. steering com. Nat. and Cultural Heritage Alliance of Pima County, 1996—; mem. exec. com. Intercultural Ctr. for Study of Deserts and Oceans, Puerto Peñasco, Mex., 1998—, Tucson Cmty. Found., 1997-99, Tucson Origins Project, 1999—. Recipient Women on the Move award YWCA, Tucson, 1993, various grants from corps. and founds., 1988—. Mem. Exec. Women's Coun., Strategic Leadership in Changing Environ., Am. Assn. Bot. Gardens and Arboreta (regional coord.), Am. Assn. Museums (reviewer grants 1994-98), Native Seeds/SEARCH. Avocations: hiking, backpacking, reading, gardening. Office: Tucson Bot Gardens 2150 N Alvernon Way Tucson AZ 85712-3153

EBERLE, MARY U. state legislator; b. St. Louis, June 6, 1949; m. James T. Graha; 3 children. BA, St. Louis U., 1971; JD, U. Mich., 1976. Mem. Dist. 15 Conn. Ho. of Reps., 1993—; pvt. practice Bloomfield. Mem. Bloomfield (Conn.) Bd. Tax Rev., 1983-85; chmn. Bloomfield Bd. Edn., 1985-91, mem., 1992. Mem. Bloomfield C. of C. Office: Ct State Legislature Legislative Ofc Bldg Rm 3900 Hartford CT 06106-1591

EBERLEY, HELEN-KAY, opera singer, classical record company executive, poet; b. Sterling, Ill., Aug. 3, 1947; d. William Elliott and P. (Conneely) E. MusB, Northwestern U., 1970, MusM, 1971. Chmn., pres., artistic coord. Eberley Inc., Evanston, Ill., 1973-92; founder H.K.E. Enterprises, 1993—, pres., 1993—; circulation libr. Evanston Pub. Libr., 1995-98. Founder EB-SKO Prodns., 1976-92, tchr., coach, 1976—; exec. dir., performance cons. E-S Mgmt., 1985-92; featured artist Honors Concert, Northwestern U., 1970, Alumni Concert, 1999, Master Class and guest lectr. various colls. and univs.; host Poetry in Process monthly seminar Barnes & Noble; music lectr. rep. Harvard Club, Chgo.; numerous TV and radio talk show appearances and interviews. Operatic debut in Peter Grimes, Lyric Opera, Chgo., 1974; starred in: Cosi Fan Tutte, Le Nozze Di Figaro, Dido and Aeneas, La Boheme, Faust, Tosca, La Traviata, Falstaff, Don Giovanni, Brigadoon, others; jazz appearances with Duke Ellington, Dave Brubeck and Robert Shaw; performing artist Oglebay Opera Inst., Wheeling, W.Va., 1968, WTTW TV/PBS, Chgo., 1968; solo star in: Continental Bank Concerts, 1981-89, United Airlines-Schubert, Schumann, Brahms, Mendelssohn, Faure, Mozart, Duparc/Wolf, Supersta. WFMT Radio, Chgo., 1982-90; featured artist with North Shore Concert Band, 1989; starring artist South Bend Symphony, 1990, Mo. Symphony Soc., 1990, Milw. Symphony, 1990; spl. guest artist New Studios Gala Sta. WFMT, 1995, West Valley Fine Arts Concert Series, Phoenix, 1999; prodr.-annotator Gentlemen Gypsy, 1978, Strauss and Szymanowski, 1979, One Sonata Each: Franck and Szymanowski, 1982; starring artist-exec. prodr. Separate But Equal, 1976, All Brahms, 1977, Opera Lady, 1978, Eberley Sings Strauss, 1980, Helen-Kay Eberley: American Girl, 1983, Helen-Kay Eberley: Opera Lady II, 1984; performed Am. and Can. nat. anthems for Chgo. Cubs Baseball Team, 1977-83, Chgo. Bears Football, 1977; also starred in numerous concert recital and symphony appearances, Europe, Can., U.S.; author: Angel's Song, 1994, The Magdaleva Poems, 1995, ChapelHeart, 1996, Desert Dancing, 1997, Canyon Ridge, 2000, Rivervoice, 2002. Docent, new mem. tour guide Art Inst. Chgo.; spl. events hotline vol. Art Inst. Chgo. Christian Indsl. League, St. Joseph's Table of St. Peter's in the Loop, Chgo.; vol., facilitator City Yr. Chgo.-Urban Peace Corps; Chgo. Humanities Festival VIII of Ill. Humanities Coun., Evanston Shelter for Battered Women, Rape Victim Adv., Habitat for Humanity; Midwest Vol. Facilitator 1st Indsl. Realty Trust; mem. Mayor's founding com. Evanston Arts Coun., 1974-75; judge Ice-Skating Competition, Wilmette (Ill.) Park Dist., 1974-77, bd. dirs., 1973-77; bd. dirs. Ctr. for Voice, Chgo., 1994-96; vol. Saints-Usher Corps of Chgo., 1998-99. Recipient Creative and Performing Arts award Ind. Jr. Miss. and South Bend Jr. Miss, 1965, Milton J. Cross award Met. Opera Guild, 1968; prize winner Met. Opera. Nat. Auditions, 1968, 1st pl. prize for The Pond, Chicagoland Poetry Contest, 1997, 1st pl. prize and Best of the Best award for The Rose Garden, 1999; F.K. Weyerhauser scholar Met. Opera, 1967. Mem. People for Ethical Treatment of Animals, Am. Soc. for Prevention of Cruelty to Animals, Assisi Animal Found., Am. Guild Mus. Artists, Internat. Platform Assn., Whale Adoption Project, Amnesty Internat., Environ. Def. Fund, Doris Day Animal Found., Poets and Patrons, Humane Soc., Greenpeace, Physicians Com. for Responsible Medicine, Notre Dame Alumni Club, St. Mary's Acad. Alumnae Assn., Delta Gamma. Office: HKE Enterprises 1726 Sherman Ave Evanston IL 60201-5619

EBERSOLE, ANDREE D. finance company executive, consultant; d. Carl M. and Didine A. Ebersole. BS in Chemistry, Coll. of William & Mary, 1998. Cons. PricewaterhouseCoopers, N.Y.C., 1998—2000; v.p. ops. Quantum Bus. Solutions, Annandale, NJ, 2000—03. Personal E-mail: aebersole@mail.com.

EBERSOLE, HELEN BROWNSBERGER, elementary school educator; b. Glendale, Ariz., Nov. 23, 1916; d. Albert Joseph Brownsberger and Estella Simmons; m. Walter Jennings Ebersole, Aug. 17, 1941; children: Brian, Susan, Joan. BA, LaVerne Coll., 1938; cert., UCLA. Tchr. Azusa Ctr., 1938—42, Bonita Unified Sch. Dist., LaVerne, Calif., 1956—77. Spkr. on traveling. Vol. ministries disaster child care Red Cross & Ch. of Brethren, 1980—90; vol., dir. song leader Camp LaVerne, Ch. Brethren, 1926—60. Mem.: DAR, AAUW, Traveler's Century Club. Republican. Protestent. Avocations: art, travel, reading, sports. Home: 2765 Mountain View Dr Apt 208 La Verne CA 91750

EBERSOLE, PATRICIA SUE, advertising executive, design educator; b. Poughkeepsie, N.Y., Nov. 6, 1952; d. Edward and Virginia Mae (Vanderof) E. AAS, Dutchess Community Coll., Poughkeepsie, 1974; student, Art Ctr. Coll. of Design, 1976-77; BS, SUNY, 1981; MA, Syracuse U., 1993. Graphic artist So. Dutchess News, Wappingers Falls, N.Y., 1974; asst. illustrator Jarvis Studio, Westwod, Calif., 1975-78; freelance illustrator Poughkeepsie, N.Y., 1978—; graphic dir. Ulster County Coun. for the Arts, Kingston, N.Y., 1979; art dir. Diversified Creative Svcs., Kingston, 1979-80; graphic designer Advertiser's Graphic Svcs., Poughkeepsie, 1981-82; pres. Ebersole Graphiks, Poughkeepsie, 1982—. Adj. instr. Dutchess C.C., 1980-87. Recipient Recognition award IBM Corp., 1987, Cert. of Excellence Silver award Strathmore Graphics Gallery, 1988, 90, Desi award Graphic Design, 1984, 88, Excellence award Printing Industries of Am., 1988, Activities award Nat. Assn. for Campus Activities, 1985, Gold, Silver and Bronze awards Hudson Valley Area Mktg. Assn., Inc., 1989, 94, 95, 96, 97, Merit awards, 1994, Nat. Calendar Bronze award, 1991, Bronze award, 1995, Big Apple award, 1996, Communicator award of distinction, 1996, award of Excellence Am. Econ. Devel. Coun., 1992, Notable Merit award FPG Internat., 1992, Gold award Advt. Club of Westchester, 1996, Bronze award, 1997, Bronze award Westchester chpt. Women in Comms., Clarion award, 1997, 99, Bronze award Neenah Paper, 1998, Best of Show award Profl. Trade Shows, Inc., 1998, award of distinction, award of excellence, hon. mention The Communicator, 1999, 2000, cert. of merit Printing Industries Am. Inc., 2000, Gold award, Advertising Club of Westchester, 2001, Bronx Award, Advt. Club of Westchester, 2002, Cert. Distinction Hon. Mention Printing Industries Am. Inc., 2002. Mem. Greater So. Dutchess C. of C. Avocations: hunter equitation, scuba diving, photography, illustration. Office: Ebersole Graphiks 308 Old Kings Hwy Stone Ridge NY 12484

EBERT, DOROTHY ELIZABETH, retired county clerk; b. Beaver Dam, Wis., Apr. 16, 1941; d. Merlin Herman and Gertrude Elizabeth (Hupke) E. Grad. high sch., Beaver Dam. Sec., receptionist Household Fin. Corp., Beaver Dam, 1958—67; dep. county clk. Dodge County, Juneau, Wis., 1967—82, county clk., 1983—2003; ret., 2003. Past bd. dirs. Dodge County chpt. Am. Cancer Soc. Mem. Wis. County Clks. Assn. (historian 1994-95, treas. 1995-96, sec. 1996-97, v.p. 1997-98, pres. 1998-99). Republican. Lutheran. Avocations: bowling, golf, calligraphy, singing, bell choir.

EBERT, LESLIE, artist; b. Oregon City, Oreg., Sept. 20, 1962; d. Larry Dwayne Ebert and Carol Kay Bino; m. Paul Ian Boundy, May 2. BArch, U. Oreg., 1987. Archtl. intern, Portland, Oreg., 1986—99; studio apprentice Debra Olsen, Portland, 1990—91; owner Leslie Ebert Studio, Portland, 1994—. Exhbn. artist Celebration of Am. Paper Arts, Crane Mus. Papermaking, Mass., 2003, Landmarks in Paper, Friends of Dard Hunter, St. Paul, 2003, Crossing Boundaries, Internat. Symposium of Print Arts, Portland, 2000. Contbr. artwork to book The Artful Greeting, 2003, artwork to mag. Somerset Studio, 2000, artwork Am. Mus. Papermaking, 2003; Represented in permanent collections Crane Papermaking Mus. Founding bd. dirs. Art in the Pearl, Portland; mem. curatorial adv. bd. Am. Inst. Archs., Portland, 1992; publicity chair Waterstone Gallery, Portland, 1994. Mem.: N.W. Paint Coun., Am. Craft Coun., Soc. Layerists in Multimedia. Avocations: travel, photography, gardening, reading. Office: Leslie Ebert Studio PO Box 68604 Portland OR 97268 E-mail: leslie@leslieebert.com.

EBIN, CYNTHIA REBECCA, artist, sculptor; d. Leo Ebin and Ruth Ann Shapiro; children: David Marc Taub, Ari Jason Taub. Student, Boston U., 1960—63; BA in Fine Art, Calif. State U., Northridge, 1981, MA in Sculpture, 1983; MFA in Sculpture, Calif. State U., Long Beach, 1989; fine art credential, UCLA, 2001. Artist in residence Glendale (Calif.) Art Forum, 1978—79; pvt. instr. Ebin Studio, Woodland Hills, Calif., 1990—. Adj. prof. Calif. State U., Northridge, 1983; lectr., workshop instr. Calif. State Summer Sch. for the Arts, 1989; art instr. Pepperdine U., Malibu, Calif., 1992, Malibu, 2001, Pierce Coll., Woodland Hills, 1997—2000, L.A. Unified Sch. Adult, Woodland Hills, 2001—; lectr. in field. Solo and two person exhbns., Calif. State U., Northridge, 1983, Udinotti Gallery, Scottsdale, Ariz., 1984, Warner Ctr. Art Gallery, Woodland Hills, 1987, Calif. State U., Long Beach, 1988, OverReact Gallery, 1988, The Platt Gallery, U. Judaism, L.A., 1988, 2003, Finegood Art Gallery, West Hills, Calif., 1988,

14 Sculptor's Gallery, SoHo, N.Y., 1990, Brand Libr. Art Gallery, Glendale, Calif., 1991, L.A. County Mus. Rental, 1999—2001, exhibited in group shows at Orlando Gallery, L.A., 1989, Artworks Gallery, Santa Barbara, Calif., 1989, Long Beach Art Gallery, 1989, exhibited in group shows at Gallery of Functional Art, Santa Monica, Calif., 1989, Momentum Gallery, Ventura, Calif., 1990, L.A. City [illegible] and Rotunda, 1990, Pierce Coll. Art Dept., Woodland Hills, 1992, Carnegie Art Mus., Oxnard, Calif., 2000, Mats Bergman Gallery, Stockholm, 2000—04, 2002—03, Sulkin-Secant Gallery at Bergamont Sta., Santa Monica, 2001, Cultural Affairs Studio Tour, Woodland Hills, 2002, 2003, Finegood Gallery, West Hills, 2003, many others, Represented in permanent collections Hebrew Union Coll. Skirball Mus., French Consulate, Avignon, France, TietoEnator Art Club, Sweden, many others. Avocations: hiking, nature, animals. Office: El Camino Real Adult Sch Mulholland Dr Woodland Hills CA 91367

EBINGER, LINDA ANN, nurse; b. North Attleboro, Mass., Apr. 6, 1944; d. Donat Leo Deshetres and Muriel Francis Mumford; m. Carl R. Ebinger, Jr. (dec. Apr. 1994); children: Carl R. III, Eric Edward. Diploma in practical nursing, Lindsay Hopkins Nursing Sch., Miami, 1978. LPN, Fla.; cert. LPN IV therapy cert. ECG technician Sturdy Meml. Hosp., Attleboro, Mass., 1962-65, with radiology dept., 1968-69; stewardess TWA, 1965; clin. lab. technician Wrentham State Sch., Mass., 1965-71, EKG dept. mgr., 1965-70; rental property owner, mgr., 1973—; orthopedic/med.-surg. unit nurse Bapt. Hosp. Miami, 1978-81, oncology unit nurse, 1981-82, ob-gyn. unit, 1982—84, with Joslin Diabetes Care Ctr., 1984-93, orthop./neurol. nurse, 1993-99, nurse short stay overnight unit, 1999—2001; vol. Domestic Violence Abuse Ctr., Punta Gorda, Fla., 2002—. Mem. LWV (sec. Dade County 1995-98, bd. dirs. 1998-2001, Port Charlotte, Fla. chpt., Freeman House Soc. (sec. 2002-), Bimini Bay Condo Assn. (sec., bd. dirs. 2002-). Republican. Roman Catholic.

EBINGER, MARY RITZMAN, pastoral counselor; b. Reading, Pa., Nov. 23, 1929; d. Michael Erwin and Daisy Mae (Shaeffer) R.; m. Warren Ralph Ebinger, Aug. 11, 1951; children: Lee, Lori, Jonathan. BA, North Cen. Coll., Naperville, Ill., 1951; MS, Loyola Coll., Balt., 1981; grad. student, Wesley Theol. Sem., 1976, Cath. U., 1977. Cert. nat. counselor Dept. of Md. Health and Mental Hygiene, cert. nat. counselor Am. Assn. Pastoral Counselors; cert. in marriage inventory. Elem. tchr. Naperville Washington Sch., 1952-54; dir. adult work Millian Ch., Rockville, Md., 1974-76; pastoral counselor Washington Pastoral Counselors, 1976-81; assoc. dir. Balt. Washington Conf. Pastoral Care and Counseling, Balt., 1990-95; marriage retreat co-leader. Mem. adj. faculty psychology Frederick (Md.) C.C., 1982-87, Anne Arnold (Md.) C.C., 1988-90; pres. Wesley Guild Wesley Theol. Seminary, Washington, 1987-89; del. gen. conf. U. Meth. Ch., 1988, 92; leader marriage retreats and premarriage and marriage inventoppea; marriage and spiritual life retreat co-leader, 1990—. Author: I Was Sick and You Visited Me, 1976, 2d edit., 1995, enlarged and translated into Spanish, 1996, Does Anybody Care, 1978, (with husband Warren) Do-It-Yourself Marriage Enrichment, 1998; contbr. chpt. to book. Growing in Love, 2001, Meditations for Families, 2001, Dimensions for Living, 2001. Pres. Ch. Women United, Springfield, Ill., 1969-71; chmn. Episcopacy com. United Meth. Ch., Balt., 1988-90; del. gen. and jurisdictional conf. United Meth. Ch., 1988, 92. Recipient Disting. Alumnus award North Cen. Coll., 1990, Loyola Coll., 1991, Two Thousand Women of Achievement award Dartmouth Eng. Mus., 1969. Mem. Am. Assn. Counseling and Devel., Am. Assn. Pastoral Counseling (cert., Atlantic region chmn. theol. and social concerns 1988-92). Avocations: writing, reading, swimming. Home: 308 Forbes St Apt J Annapolis MD 21401-8122 E-mail: MREWRE@aol.com.

EBISUZAKI, YUKIKO, retired chemistry educator; b. Mission City, B.C., Can., July 25, 1930; came to U.S., 1957; d. Masuzo and Shige (Kusumoto) E. BS with honors, U. Western Ont., London, Can., 1956, MS, 1957; PhD, Ind. U., 1962. Postdoctoral U. Pa., Phila., 1962-63; faculty rsch. assoc. Ariz. State U., Tempe, 1963-67; acting asst. prof. UCLA, 1967-75; assoc. prof. N.C. State U., Raleigh, 1975-99, assoc. prof. emeritus, 1999—. Contbr. articles to profl. jours. Ont. Rsch. Found. fellow Ont. Rsch. Coun., 1957-60, Gerry fellow Sigma Delta Epsilon, 1977-78. Mem. Am. Chem. Soc., Sigma Xi.

EBLER, MARILYN ANN, graphic designer, educator; b. Socorro, N.Mex., Mar. 9, 1955; d. Robert Gerald Ebler and Mary Eulala (Castillo) Barber; children: Manuel Anthony Anaya, Josephine Lynn Duke. Cert. Cosmetology, Lea County Beauty Coll., 1977; AAS, N.Mex. Jr. Coll., 1992; BS with honors, Ea. N.Mex. U., 1995; MS in Edn., Capella U., Mpls., 2001. Cosmetologist Glamour House, Hobbs, N.Mex., 1977—85, Linda's Styling Salon, Hobbs, N.Mex., 1985—91; staff graphic arts dept. N.Mex. Jr. Coll., Hobbs, 1991—92; computer lab. asst., office asst. Ea. N.Mex. U., 1993—94; graphic arts asst. N.Mex. Jr. Coll., Hobbs, 1994—95, prof. comml. graphic design, 1995—. Mem. faculty senate N.Mex. Jr. Coll., 1995—; attendee numerous confs. Contbr. graphic designs to profl. jours. Recipient numerous awards. Mem. Vocat. Indsl. Clubs Am. (advisor 1995-97), Kappa Pi (sec. 1993-94). Avocations: photography, water color, cross stitch, walking, crochet. Home: 1009 W Cain St Hobbs NM 88240-5612 E-mail: maebler@3dinet.com.

EBRAHIM, ADA, special education educator; d. Hamad and Rosa Rivera Ebrahim. BS in Spl. Edn., Fla. Internat. U., 1991, MS in Diagnostic Tchg., 1993. Prof. educators cert. Fla. Exceptional student edn. tchr. Miami-Dade County Pub. Schs., Miami, Fla., 1991—97, staffing specialist, 1997—. Sponsor and co-coach Spl. Olympics, Miami, 1993. Mem.: United Tchrs. of Dade, Coun. for Exceptional Children, Kappa Delta Pi, Phi Sigma Sigma.

EBY, MARLENE JEAN, retired secondary school educator; b. Montgomery County, Ohio, June 12, 1944; d. Emerson Leroy and Eileen Phyllis Eby. BS in Edn., Bowling Green State U., 1966, MA, 1970. Cert. tchr., Ohio. Grad. asst. Bowling Green (Ohio) State U., 1969-70; tchr. Gt. Valley Schs., Malvern, Pa., 1970-71; from tchr. math. to ret. Huber Heights (Ohio) City Schs., 1966—2003, ret.; instr. Wright State U., 2003—. Charter mem. math. com. Alliance for Edn., Dayton, Ohio; renaissance tchr. Wayne H.S., Huber Heights, 1996. Vol. Good Samaritan Hosp., Dayton, Ohio, 1972-90, Victoria Theater, Dayton, 1991—. Mem. Nat. Coun. Tchrs. Math. (manuscript reader 1994—), Ohio Coun. Tchrs. Math. Avocations: travel, reading. Office: Wright State U 201 MM 3690 Colonel Glenn Hwy Dayton OH

EBY, PATRICIA LYNN, music educator; b. Chgo., Aug. 11, 1946; d. Chester Arthur Eby and Ann Elaine Daley; m. David Martin Thompson, Sept. 18, 1976 (div. Dec. 1994); children: Robert Chester, Paul Hendrix, Katherine Elaine, Mark Andrew. BS in Music Edn., Chgo. State U., 1968; M in Music, Kent State U., 1976, postgrad. Tchr. music Lourdes H.S., Chgo., 1968—73; dir. music First Christian Ch., Stow, Ohio, 1975—86, Sacred Heart Ch., Fond du Lac, Wis., 1990—; chair arts and humanities Marian Coll., Fond du Lac, 1986—95; chair music program U. Wis., Fond du Lac, 1995—. Prodr. and dir.: CD Unity, 1999, A Christmas Wish, 2001, HFCC "Live", 2003; dir.: (CD) "Grande Musica in Chiesa" concerto di musica sacra in Roma, 2003. Mem.: Music Educators Nat. Conf., Am. Choral Dirs. Assn. Roman Catholic. Avocations: home improvement projects, gardening, tai chi. Home: 185 N Park Ave Fond Du Lac WI 54935

ECCLES, JACQUELYNNE S. psychology educator; BA in social psychology, U. Calif. Berkeley, 1966; PhD, U. Calif. Los Angeles, 1974. HS math sci. tchr. US Peace Corps, Ghana, 1966—68; asst. prof. Smith Coll., 1974—76; asst. to assoc. to full prof. U. Mich., 1974—92, asst. v.p. rsch., 1987—88; prof. U. Colo., 1988—92. Chair Internat. Doctorate Program, Life Span Devel. with Max Planck, Berlin, 2002—; mem. Psychology Dept. Exec. Com., U. Mich., 1981—86; Chair U. Mich., Edn., Psychology, 1992—2002; mem. U. Mich., Rackham Exec. Com., 1993—95, Pres. Adv. Com. on Women's Issues, U. Mich., 1993—98; interim chair U. Mich., Dept. Psychology, 1998—99. Mem.: NSF, Nat. Acad. Edn., Pathways to Coll. Network Rsch. Scholars Panel, Adv. Com. for Jossey-Bass Series on new Directions for Youth Devel., Coun. for [illegible] Coun. for Soc. for Psycho. Study of Social Issues, Am. Psycho. Assn. Office: U Mich Inst Rsch on Women and Gender 204 S State St Ann Arbor MI 48109 Home: 1109 Pearl St Ypsilanti MI 48197 E-mail: jeccles@umich.edu.

ECCLES, MARY, writer; b. Urbana, Ill., Dec. 23, 1950; d. Robert and Edith Eisner; m. Robert Norris Eccles, Dec. 27, 1974; children: Robert W., Claire, Nora. BA in History, Harvard U., 1971, MA in Pub. Policy, 1973, PhD in Pub. Policy, 1976. Staff writer The New Republic, Washington, 1973, Congl. Quar., Washington, 1976—78; legis. asst. Office of Rep. Stanley Lundine, Washington, 1978—80; sr. economist Joint Econ. Com., Washington, 1980—85; legis. asst. Office of Senator John D. Rockefeller IV, Washington, 1985—87; legis. dir. Office of Senator Kent Conrad, Washington, 1987—91; assoc. dir. Office of Congl. Rels., cons. to Sec. of Labor U.S. Dept. Labor, Washington, 1993—95; writer Chevy Chase, Md., 1995—. Author: (children's book) By Lizzie, 2001. Mem.: The Writer's Ctr., Women's Nat. Book Assn., Soc. Children's Book Writers and Illustrators (grantee 1997). Home: 3407 Raymond St Chevy Chase MD 20815

ECHAVESTE, MARIA, government official, lawyer; b. Tex. BA in Anthropology, Stanford U.; JD, U. Calif., Berkeley. Wage and hour adminstr. Dept. Labor, Washington, dir. pers., 1993; asst. to Pres., dir. pub. liaison White House, Washington, 1997-98, asst. to Pres., dep. chief staff, 1998—. Office: The White House Office Dep Chief Staff 1600 Pennsylvania Ave NW Washington DC 20502-0001

ECHOLS, IVOR TATUM, retired educator, assistant dean; b. Oklahoma City, Dec. 28, 1919; d. Israel E. and Katie (Bingley) Tatum AB, U. Kans., 1942; postgrad., U. Nebr., 1945-46; MS in Social Work, Columbia U., 1952; postgrad., U. So. Calif., 1961-62, DSW, 1968. Tchr. social studies h.s., Holdenville, Okla., 1942-43, Geary, Okla., 1943-45; caseworker ARC, Chgo., 1946-47; resident group worker Dosoris House for Teen-Age Girls Cmty. Svcs. Soc., N.Y.C., 1950-51; supr. group work Walnut Grove Ctr. Neighborhood Clubs, Oklahoma City, 1948-51; program dir. Camp Lookout YWCA, Denver, 1951; dir. program svcs. Presbyn. Neighborhood Svcs., Detroit, summer 1960; supr. group work Merrill-Palmer Inst., Detroit, 1951-70; asst. dir. Merrill-Palmer Camp, Dryden, Mich., 1951-59; prof. Sch. Social Work U. Conn., West Hartford, 1970-89, also asst. dean, ret., 1989. Del. Inter-Univ. Consortium of Social Devel., Nairobi, Kenya, 1974, Hong Kong, 1980; mem. Conn. adv. com. U.S. Commn. Civil Rights. Mem. ad hoc com. Citizens Concerned with Equal Ednl. Opportunity, Detroit, 1964—; cons. to NEA Conf. Family Camping Washington, 1959, ednl. film Scott Paper Co., Phila., 1963, 64; summer study skills project Presbyn. Ch. Bd. Nat. Missions, Knoxville, Tenn., 1965—; nat. sec. United Neighborhood Ctrs. Am., N.Y.C.; pres. Protestant Cmty. Svcs., Detroit, 1969-70; trustee Conn. Energy Found., 1987-92; commr. Conn. Hist. Commn., 1986-96, ret., 1996. ARC scholar; fellow Nat. Urban League, Porter R. Lee fellow, fellow NIMH; recipient Educator Human Rights award UN Assn., 1987, Sojourner Truth award Detroit chpt. Nat. Assn. Negro Bus. and Profl. Women, 1969, UN Assn. award for Edn. and Women's Rights, 1987, Maria R. Stewart Women's Rights award Conn. Women's Ednl. and Legal Found., 1991, Outstanding Women award U. Conn., 1991, Achievement award Assn. Advancement Soc. Groupwork, 1994, 1st Truth award Capitol C.C. Hartford, 1999; named Conn. Social Worker of Year NASW, 1979; Ivor J. Echols Endowment Fund named in her honor U. Conn. Found., 1990. Mem. Nat. Assn. Colored Women's Clubs (participant White House conf. on Children and Youth 1960), A.M.E. Ministers Wives, Acad. Certified Social Workers (hon.), Nat. Assn. Black Social Workers (honored as founding mem. 1968), Nat. Trust for Hist. Preservation, Delta Sigma Theta (Delta Dear recognition 1998). Mem. A.M.E. Ch. Office: U Conn 1798 Asylum Ave Ste 1 West Hartford CT 06117-2603 Home: PO Box 1642 Georgetown KY 40324-6642

ECHOLS, MARY EVELYN, travel consultant; b. LaSalle, Ill., Apr. 5, 1915; d. Francis Ira and Mary Irene (Coleman) Bassett; m. David H. Echols, Aug. 31, 1951 (dec.); children: Susan Echols O'Donnell, William. Grad. high. sch., Chgo. Founder Internat. Travel Tng. Courses, Inc., Chgo., 1962—; pres. Evelyn Echols Cons. Ltd., 1998. Bd. dirs. Conv. and Tourism Bur.; past pres. Pres. Reagan's Adv. Com. for Women's Bus. Ownership; v.p. United Cerebral Palsy Assn., Prevent Blindness in Am.; bd. dirs. Am. Cancer Soc., Gus Geordiano Jazz Dance Chgo., Little Sisters of the Poor; mem. Women's Internat. Forum. Named Entrepreneur of Yr. Women Bus. Owners N.Y., 1985, Bus. Woman of Yr. Nat. Assn. Women Bus. Owners, 1985, Crain's Chgo. Bus., 1993; named to Chgo.'s Hall of Fame, 1992. Mem.: Soc. Am. Travel Agts., Acad. TV Arts and Scis., Chgo. Execs. Club.

ECK, DOROTHY FRITZ, state legislator; b. Sequim, Wash., Jan. 23, 1924; d. Ira Edward and Ida (Hokanson) Fritz; m. Hugo Eck, Dec. 16, 1942 (dec. Feb. 1988); children: Laurence, Diana. BS in Secondary Edn., Mont. State U., 1961, MS in Applied Sci., 1966. Mgr. property mgmt. bus., 1955—; conf. coord. Am. Argl. Econs. Assn., 1967-68; state-local coord. Office of Gov. Mont., Helena, 1972-77; mem. Mont. State Senate, 1981—, Mont. Environ. Quality Coun., 1981-87. Bd. dirs. Meth. Youth Fellowship, 1960-64, Mont. Coun. for Effective Legislature, 1977-78, Rocky Mountain Environ. Coun., 1982—; del. Western v.p. Mont. Constl. Conv., 1971-72; chmn. Gov.'s Task Force on Citizen Participation, 1976-77; mem. adv. com. No. Rockies Resource and Tng. Ctr. (now No. Lights Inst.), 1979-81. Recipient Outstanding Alumna award Mont. State U., 1981, Centennial Faculty award, 1989. Mem. LWV (state pres. 1967-70), Common Cause, Nat. Women's Polit. Caucus. Democrat. Home: 10 W Garfield St Bozeman MT 59715-5602 Office: State Senate State Capitol Helena MT 59620

ECKARDT, ADELAIDE CAMPBELL, state legislator, psychiatric nurse; BS, U. Md., 1978, MS, 1981. RN, Md. Clin. psychiat. specialist nurse Eastern Shore Hosp. Ctr., Cambridge, Md., 1973—; state del. dist. 37B Md. Ho. of Dels., Md. Mem. econ. matters com., health ins. subcom., spl. task force on drug and alcohol abuse Md. Ho. of Dels. Republican. Home: 12 Nanticoke Rd Cambridge MD 21613-1012

ECKHARDT, LAUREL ANN, biologist, researcher, educator; b. Palo Alto, Calif., Sept. 4, 1951; d. Joseph Carl Augustus Eckhardt and Ada Jane Williams Smith; m. Michael Warren Young, Dec. 27, 1978; children: Natalie Alice Eckhardt Young, Arissa Caroline Eckhardt Young. BA summa cum laude, U. Tex., 1974; PhD in Genetics, Stanford (Calif.) U., 1980. Damon Runyon-Walter Winchell postdoctoral fellow Albert Einstein Coll. Medicine, Bronx, 1980-83; asst. prof. Dept. Biol. Sci., Columbia U., N.Y.C., 1984-88, assoc. prof., 1989-92; prof. Dept. Biol. Sci., Hunter Coll. of CUNY, 1992—, Marie Hesselbach prof. biology, 1999—. Reviewer immunobiology study sect. Dept. Rsch. Grants, NIH, Bethesda, Md., 1993-96; reviewer grand rev. com. Am. Heart Assn., N.Y.C., 1990-93, sci. rev. Immunological Sciences peer rev. com., Dept. of Def. Breast Cancer Rsch. Program, 1998, 2000, 03, rev. panelist for rsch. tng. fellowships for med. students, Howard Hughes Med. Student, Howard Hughes Med. Inst., 2002-. Assoc. editor Jour. Immunology, 1997-2001; contbr. articles to profl. jours. Rsch. grantee NIH-Inst. Allergy and Infectious Diseases, 1984-90, 90—, Am. Cancer Soc., 1990-95, NIH-Nat. Cancer Inst., 1994-99. Mem. Am. Assn. Immunologists (program com. mem. 1995-99), N.Y. Acad. Scis., Harvey Soc. Democrat. Avocations: tennis, gardening, dance. Office: Hunter College of CUNY Dept Biol Sci 695 Park Ave New York NY 10021-5085

ECKHOFF, KRISTINE KAY, mental health therapist; b. Killen, Tex., Dec. 2, 1968; d. Dennis John Eckhoff and Patricia Marie (Cronin) Pearson. BS, U. S.D., 1991, MA in Counseling, 1994. Cert. AIDS counselor. Mental health counselor U. S.D., Vermillion, 1993-94; family therapist Luth. Social [illegible], Spearfish, S.D., 1994-95; therapist Turning Point Vols. of Am., Sioux Falls, SD, 1995—. Mem. ACA. Roman Catholic. Avocations: volleyball, weightlifting. Home: 1308 S Annway Dr Sioux Falls SD 57103-3539 Office: Turning Point Volunteers of America PO Box 89306 Sioux Falls SD 57109-9306

ECKLES, MARY ANN, state legislator; b. Tallahassee, Fla., July 22, 1947; d. Joseph P. and Ann T. (Bandorf) Jones; m. George Love Eckles; children: George Love Eckles, Ryan Allen. BS in Edn., U. Memphis, 1969. Elem. sch. tchr., Fayetteville, Tenn., 1969-73; real estate broker Jack Dayton Real Estate, Winchester, Tenn., 1984-87; bus. owner Murfreesboro, Tenn., 1987-98; mem. Tenn. Gen. Assembly, Nashville, 1994—. Sec. health, human resource com., chair mental health subcom. Tenn. Gen. Assembly, Nashville, 1997. Bd. dirs. Boys and Girls Club, Murfreesboro, Tenn., 1991—, Am. Cancer Soc., 1992—, foundation Middle Tenn. State U., Murfreesboro, 1995—. Named Legis. of Yr. Assn. Retarded Citizens, 1997, Cmty. Rehab. Assn., 1997. Mem. Tenn. Med. Assn. (legis. chmn. 1994—, Legis. of Yr. 1997), Civilian Police Acad., Noon Rotary, Stones River Garden Club. Democrat. Episcopalian. Avocations: flying, tennis. Home: 2811 Windsong Pl Murfreesboro TN 37129-6558 Office: Tenn Gen Assembly Ste 25 Legis Plz Nashville TN 37243

ECKLES, SUSAN, former management executive; b. St. Louis, Oct. 8, 1939; Dir. Resource Mgmt., Dept. of Defense, Washington, 1998-99. Office: Dept of Def Command Control Comm & Intelligence 6000 Defense Pentagon Washington DC 20301-6000

ECKLUND, CONSTANCE CRYER, French language educator; b. Chgo., Nov. 20, 1938; d. Gilbert and Electra (Papadopoulos) Cryer; m. John E. Ecklund, Mar. 22, 1975. BA magna cum laude, Northwestern U., 1960; PhD, Yale U., 1965. Asst. prof. Ind. U., Bloomington, 1964-66; asst. prof. French, So. Conn. State U., New Haven, 1967-70, assoc. prof., 1970-76, prof., 1976—2002. Spkr. in field. Contbr. articles to profl. jours. Named Tchr. of Yr., So. Conn. State U., 2002. Mem. AAUP, MLA, Am. Coun. Tchg. Fgn. Langs., Am. Assn. Tchrs. French, Phi Beta Kappa. Republican. Avocations: piano, gardening, cooking, travel, graphic art. Home: 27 Cedar Rd Woodbridge CT 06525-1642

ECKMAN, FERN MARJA, journalist; b. N.Y.C., Aug. 27; d. Isidor Peter and Zara Nettie (Sloate) Friedman; m. Irving Eckman, June 21, 1957. BA, N.Y. U., 1957. Reporter N.Y. Post, 1944-78; assigned to UN, 1945-49, 60-65. Author: The Furious Passage of James Baldwin, 1967; contbg. editor Working Mother, 1981-91; feature writer for nat. publs., 1965-90. Recipient George Polk Meml. award for distinguished met. reporting, 1951, 55; Page One award for community service N.Y. Newspaper Guild, 1955, for best feature reporting, 1961; citation for community service Council Puerto Rican and Spanish-Am. Orgns., 1955; Lasker award for med. journalism, 1960; Front Page award for distinguished feature writing, News Women's Club N.Y., 1949, 51, 56, 64; for distinguished series (co-recipient), 1970; Cultural News award Newspaper Reporters Assn., N.Y.C., 1967; Empire State award for excellence in med. reporting, 1968 Home: 749 W End Ave New York NY 10025-6224

ECKSTEIN, MARLENE R. vascular radiologist; b. Poughkeepsie, N.Y., Sept. 6, 1948; d. Marc and Lola (Charm) E. AB, Vassar Coll., 1970; MD, Albert Einstein Coll. Medicine, 1973. Diplomate Nat. Bd. Med. Examiners; cert. Am. Bd. Radiology. Intern in medicine Yale-New Haven Med. Ctr., 1973-74, resident in diagnostic radiology, 1974-77; asst. radiologist, chief vascular radiology sect. South Nassau Cmtys. Hosp., Oceanside, N.Y., 1977-78, assoc. radiologist, chief vascular radiology sect., 1978-81, asst. dir. dept. radiology, chief vascular radiology sect., 1981-83; asst. radiologist Mass. Gen. Hosp., 1983-87, assoc. radiologist, 1987—. Asst. prof. clin. radiology SUNY-Stony Brook Med. Sch., 1980-83; instr. radiology, Harvard Med. Sch., 1983-84, asst. prof., 1984—. Mem. exec. com. and hosp. chmn. United Jewish Appeal of Physicians and Dentists of Nassau County, N.Y., 1981-83. Fellow Am. Coll. Angiology, Soc. Cardiovasc. and Interventional Radiology; mem. AMA, Am. Coll. Radiology, Am. Inst. Ultrasound in Medicine, Am. Assn. Women Radiologists, Am. Med. Women's Assn., Mass. Radiol. Soc., Mass. Med. Soc., New Eng. Soc. Cardiovasc. and Interventional Radiology (pres. 1985-86), Radiol. Soc. N.Am. Achievements include design and development of line of vascular catheters. Home: 141 Fulton Ave Apt 312 Poughkeepsie NY 12603-2841 Office: Mass Gen Hosp Vascular Radiology Sect Boston MA 02114 E-mail: mreckstein@alum.vassar.edu.

ECKSTUT, ARIELLE, literary agent, writer; b. N.Y.C., Aug. 25, 1970; d. Stanton and Joann Eckstut; m. David Henry Sterry, July 5, 2002. BA, U. Chgo., 1992. Pastry chef Tribeca Bakery, N.Y.C., 1992—93; lit. agt. Levine Greenberg Lit. Agy., N.Y.C., NY, 1993—2003. Spkr. numerous orgns., 1999—; instr. Stanford U., Palo Alto, Calif., 2003—. Author: (book) Pride & Promiscuity, Satchel Sez, Putting Your Passion Into Print. Vol., instr. writing Sage, San Francisco, 2002—03. Richter Fund Grant, U. Chgo., 1991. Office: Levine Greenberg Literary Agy 307 7th Ave Ste 1906 New York NY 10001 E-mail: aeckstut@levinegreenberg.com.

ECONOMOS, KATHERINE, oncologist; b. Bklyn., Jan. 4, 1961; MD, State U. NY Bklyn. Health Sci. Ctr., 1986. Cert. ob-gyn 1996, gynecologic oncology 1998. Intern Maimonides Med. Ctr., Bklyn., 1986—87, resident, 1986—90; fellowship U. Tex. Med. Ctr., SW, Dallas, 1990—93; asst. attending physician NY Presbytn. Hosp., N.Y.C., 1993—; assoc. attending physician NY Meth. Hosp., N.Y.C., 1993—2000; asst. prof. to assoc. prof. Cornell Med. Coll., OB-GYN Dept., N.Y.C., 1993—; assoc. attending physician NY Meth. Hosp., Oncology, Gynecology, N.Y.C., 2000—. Office: Cornell U 525 East 68th St Ste J130 New York NY 10021

ECTON, DONNA R. management consultant, retired food products executive; b. Kansas City, Mo., May 10, 1947; d. Allen Howard and Marguerite (Page) E.; m. Victor H. Maragni, June 16, 1986; children: Mark, Gregory. BA (Durant Scholar), Wellesley Coll., 1969; MBA, Harvard U., 1971. V.p. Chem. Bank, N.Y.C., 1972-79, Citibank, N.A., N.Y.C., 1979-81; pres. MBA Resources, Inc., N.Y.C., 1981-83; v.p. adminstrn., officer Campbell Soup Co., Camden, N.J., 1983-89; chmn. Triangle Mfg. Corp. subs. Campbell Soup Co., Raleigh, N.C., 1984-87; sr. v.p., officer Nutri/System, Inc., Willow Grove, Pa., 1989-91; pres., CEO Van Houten N.Am., Delavan, Wis., 1991-94, Andes Candies Inc., Delavan, 1991-94; chmn., pres., CEO Bus. Mail Express, Inc., Malvern, Penn., 1995-96; COO PETsMART, Inc., Phoenix, 1996-98; chmn., pres., CEO EEI Inc., Phoenix, 1998—. Bd. dirs. H&R Block, Kansas City, Mo.; commencement spkr. Pa. State U., 1987. Bd. Overseers Harvard U., 1984-90; mem. Coun. Fgn. Rels., N.Y.C., 1987—; trustee Inst. for Advancement of Health, 1988-92. Named One of 80 Women to Watch in the 80's, Ms. mag., 1980, One of All Time Top 10 of Last Decade, Glamour mag., 1984, One of 50 Women to Watch, Bus. Week mag., 1987, One of 100 Women to Watch, Bus. Month mag., 1989; recipient Wellesley Alumnae Achievement award, 1987; Fred Sheldon Fund fellow Harvard U., 1971-72; Margaret Rudkin scholar Harvard U., 1969-71. Mem. Harvard Bus. Sch. Assn. (pres. exec. council 1983-84), Harvard Bus. Sch. Club Greater N.Y. (pres. 1979-80, lifetime bd. dir.), Wellesley Coll. Nat. Alumnae Assn. (bd. dirs., 1st v.p. 1977-80). Avocations: public speaking, art, gardening, reading, bicycling.

EDDLEMAN, DIAN P. music educator; b. Union City, Tenn., Feb. 1, 1961; d. Otis Dean and Mary Gray Pritchett; m. Phillip Roy Eddleman, May 10, 1980; children: Jeremiah Phillip, Jessica. BA in Music Edn., Harding U., 1981. Tchr., choir dir. Jackson (Tenn.) Christian Sch., 1982—90, Jackson-Madison County Schs., Jackson, 1991—. Performer Jackson Theatre Guild, Jackson Symphony, Jackson Opera and Choral Soc. Mem.: NEA, Am. Choral Dirs. Assn., Music Educators Nat. Conf., Jackson-Madison County Edn. Assn., West Tenn. Vocal Music Educators Assn. (chmn. regional honor choir 2001), Tenn. Music Educators Assn. (chmn. all-state chorus 2003). Republican. Church Of Christ. Home: 196 E Hughes Rd Jackson TN 38305 Office: North Side H S 3066 N Highland Ave Jackson TN 38305

EDDY, COLETTE ANN, aerial photography studio owner, photographer; b. Sept. 14, 1950; d. William F. and Jeanne (Valeski) Trump; m. Robert K. Eddy, Aug. 21, 1976 (div. Sept. 1992). AA, St. Petersburg (Fla.) Jr. Coll., 1970; BA, U. South Fla., 1973; MS, Nova U., 1988. Yacht caretaker The Sundowner, St. Petersburg, 1972-73; mgr. Aunt Hattie's Restaurant, St. Petersburg, 1973-79, Johnathan Jones, Inc., St. Petersburg, 1979-80; photographer, sales rep. Smith Aerial Photos, Tampa, Fla., 1980—; owner, aerial photographer Aerial Innovations, Inc., Tampa, 1987—; owner Havanna Connection Inc., Carribean. Mem. Tampa Mus. Art. Named Winner Tampa Chamber Small Bus. of Yr., 1998. Mem. Profl. Photographers Am. (30 Merit awards), Fla. Profl. Photographers (22 Merit awards 1987-90), Profl. Aerial Photographers Assn., Tampa C. of C., Emerging Bus. Coun. Republican. Home: 198 Ceylon Ave Tampa FL 33606-3330 Office: Aerial Innovations Inc 3703 W Azeele St Tampa FL 33609-2807

EDDY, DARLENE MATHIS, poet, educator; b. Elkhart, Ind., Mar. 19, 1937; d. William Eugene and Fern (Paulmer) Mathis; m. Spencer Livingston Eddy, Jr., May 23, 1964 (dec. May 1971). BA, Goshen Coll., 1959; MA, Rutgers U., 1961, PhD, 1967. Instr., lectr. Douglass Coll. and Rutgers U., 1962-64, 66-67; asst. prof. English Ball State U., Muncie, Ind., 1967-70, assoc. prof., 1971-75, prof., 1975-99, poet-in-residence, 1989-93, prof. emerita, 1999. Whitinger lectr. Honors Coll., 1998-99; tchr., cons. numerous creative writing workshops; adj. prof. core program U. Notre Dame, 2001-, adj. prof. Eng. Goshen Coll., 2002-. Author: The Worlds of King Lear, 1968, Leaf Threads, Wind Rhymes, 1985, Weathering, 1991, Portraits, 1992; poetry editor Forum, 1985-89; contbg. editor Snowy Egret, 1988-89; cons. editor Blue Unicorn, 1995—; founding editor The Hedge Row Press, 1995; contbr. articles to English Lang. Notes, Am. Lit., other jours.; contbr. poetry to various publs. Mem. commn. on the status of women in the profession, Nat. Coun. of Teachers of English, 1976-79; coord. Women's Studies program, 1976-82. Woodrow Wilson Nat. fellow, 1959-62, Notable Woodrow Wilson fellow, 1991, Rutgers U. grad. honors fellow, 1964-65; recipient numerous rsch., creative teaching and creative arts grants. Mem. AAUW, DAR, Soc. Mayflower Descs., Nat. League Am. Pen Women, League Women Voters. Home: 1840 Cobblestone Blvd Elkhart IN 46514

EDDY, NANCY C. counselor; BS in Elem. Edn., EdM in Sch. Counseling, U. Ark.; JD, U. Ark., Little Rock. Counselor Clinton Elem., Sherwood, Ark., 1984—. Treas., bd. dirs. S.W. Ednl. Lab., 2003—. Chmn. Pulaski Fedn. Tchrs. Cmty. Svcs.; co-chmn. Ctrl. Ark. Jobs With Justice; vol. United Way; pres. Ctrl. Ark. Labor Coun., 1999. Office: Clinton Elem 142 Hollywood Ave Sherwood AR 72120

EDDY, WANDA CRIGER, music educator; b. Sidney, Mont., Feb. 24, 1947; d. Ralph D. and Marian (Mangan) Criger; m. Roger Eugene Eddy, June 26, 1971 (div. Apr. 27, 1981); children: Colin Arkan, Shannon Lee. MusB, U. Mont., Missoula, 1968, MA, 1969; MusD, U. Oreg., Eugene, 1987. Lic. tchr. Oreg. Instr. music Great Falls Coll., Mont., 1970—71, Mount Royal Coll., Calgary, Canada, 1971—72, Alberta Coll., Edmonton, Canada, 1972—73; grad. tchg. fellow (summers) U. Oreg., Eugene, 1980—85; elem. music specialist Winston Dillard Schs., Dillard, Oreg., 1981—87, Roseburg (Oreg.) Schs., 1987—. Dir. music First United Meth. Ch., Roseburg, Oreg., 1982—; sec. bd. dirs. Umpqua Symphony Assn., Roseburg, 1987—91; dir. Umpqua Youth Choir, Roseburg, 1992—2001. Contbr. articles to Oreg. Music Jour. Vol. campaign worker Roseburg Cmty. Concerts, 1997—; lay mem. to ann. conf. First United Meth. Ch., Roseburg, Oreg., 2001—04. Mem.: Music Educators Nat. Conf., Oreg. Music Educators Assn. (state elem. rep. 2000—02). Methodist. Avocations: crossword puzzles, reading, quilting, travel. Office: Green Elem Sch 4498 SW Carnes Rd Roseburg OR 97470

EDEAWO, GALE SKY, publishing company executive, writer; b. Detroit, Mar. 22, 1946; d. John Bryd Martin and Minerva Lee Dubrey; m. Robert Judkins, Jan. 23, 1965 (div. Jan. 1979); children: Consuella Judkins. AA, L.A. City Coll., 1977; student, Calif. State U., L.A., 1977-78. Telecom. PBXtra Placement, L.A., 1979-98; owner, mgr., writer Sky Publs., Savannah, Ga., 1998—; pvt. real estate investor, 2000—. Travel cons. Alwayz Travel, Inglewood, Calif., 1989-92. Peer counselor Rosa Parks Rape Crisis Ctr., L.A., 1990—98, Rape Crisis Ctr., Savannah, Ga., 1999—2001, bd. dirs., 2000—; jail, prison activist, 2000—; AIDS activist, contbg. writer Project Azuka, Savannah, 1998—2000, AIDS Project L.A., 1997—; cmty. outreach, spkr. Alzheimer's Assn., L.A., 1996—97; bd. dirs. Alcoholism Ctr. Women, L.A., 1992—94; leader writer's workshops for youth at risk Dept. Family and Children's Svcs., Savannah, 1999—; founder re-entry program for incarcerated women Project Welcome Home, 2001—; mem. adv. bd. Regional Youth Detention Ctr., 2001—; local storyteller, 2001—. Mem. Am. Legion Women's Aux. (mem. pub. rels. 1986, historian 2000), Am. Corrections Assn., Nat. Coun. Negro Women, Fraternal Order Police. Democrat. Methodist. Avocations: traveling, writing, cats, reading, researching the south. Office: Sky Publs 12511 Largo Dr Savannah GA 31419-2601 Fax: 912-961-9076.

EDELMAN, BARBARA J. cancer registrar; b. S.I., N.Y., June 18, 1943; d. Samuel J. and Edith Rose (Kovner) E. Sec. pathology dept. Richmond Meml. Hosp., S.I., 1961-62; pvt. sec. Nestle Le Mur Co., N.Y.C., 1962-65; tumor registrar Beekman Downtown Hosp., N.Y.C., 1965-68; exec. sec. UCLA Med. Ctr., 1968-71; office mgr. NYU Med. Ctr., 1971-74; exec. sec. S.I. Med. Group, 1974-77; tumor registrar J.F. Kennedy Med. Ctr., Edison, N.J., 1977-80; adminstrv. asst. UCLA Med. Ctr., 1980-83; exec. sec. Children's Hosp. L.A., 1984-88; cancer registrar Children's Hosp., L.A., 1989—. Vol. Westside Spl. Olympics, Santa Monica, Calif., 1981-97, head bowling coach, 1983-97, mem. adv. bd., 1984-89. Named Sec. of Month Profl. Sec. Internat., 1978. Mem. Nat. Cancer Registrars Assn. (cert. 1990, founder pediat. group), Calif. Cancer Registrars Assn., So. Calif. Cancer Registrars Assn. Democrat. Jewish. Home: 15445 Cobalt St Spc 13 Sylmar CA 91342-0572 Office: Childrens Hosp 4650 W Sunset Blvd Los Angeles CA 90027-6062 Office Phone: 323-669-4654. E-mail: bjectr@aol.com.

EDELMAN, BARBARA JANE, writer, educator; d. Milton Tobias and Esther Leav Edelman. BA in English, Colgate U., 1975; MA in English Lit., Calif. State U., Northridge, 1992; MFA in Poetry, U. Pitts., 1995. Freelance actor theatrical and TV prodns., L.A., 1978—85; instr. English as 2d lang. L.A. Unified Sch. Dist., L.A., 1995—2000; part-time instr. U. Pitts., 1995—2000, Carnegie Mellon U., Pitts., 1996—98; writer in residence Waynesburg (Pa.) U., Waynesburg, 1997—98; poet in residence Ellis Sch., Pitts., 1997—2001; vis. lectr. U. Pitts., 2001—; playwriting instr. Bennington (Vt.) Coll., 2002. Mem. poetry selection com. Pitts. Post-Gazette, 1996—2002; freelance editor. Author: (poetry chapbook) A Girl in Water, 2001; contbr. poetry and short stories to anthologies. Recipient Pa. Coun. on Arts grant for poetry, 2000, award, New Works Festival, Pitts. Festival of 1-Act Plays, 0199. Office: U Pitts Dept English CL 526 Pittsburgh PA 15260 E-mail: edelman@pitt.edu.

EDELMAN, JUDITH H. architect; b. Bklyn., Sept. 16, 1923; d. Abraham and Frances (Israel) Hochberg; m. Harold Edelman, Dec. 26, 1947; children: Marc, Joshua. Student, Conn. Coll., 1940-41, NYU, 1941-42; BArch, Columbia U., 1946. Designer, drafter Huson Jackson, N.Y.C., 1948-58; Schermerhorn traveling fellow, 1950; pvt. practice, 1958-60; ptnr. Edelman & Salzman, N.Y.C., 1960-79, Edelman Partnership (Architects), N.Y.C., 1979—2002, Edelman, Sultan, Knox, Wood /Architects LLP, N.Y.C., 2002—. Adj. prof. Sch. Architecture CUNY, 1972-76, vis. lectr. grad. program in environ. psychology, 1977, 77; vis. lectr. Washington U., St. Louis, 1974, U. Oreg., 1974, MIT, 1975, Pa. State U., 1977, Rensselaer Poly. Inst., 1977, Columbia U., 1979; First Claire Watson Forrest Meml. lectr. U. Oreg., U. Calif., Berkeley, U. So. Calif., 1982. Prin. works include Restoration of St. Mark's Ch. in the Bowery, N.Y.C., 1970-82, Two Bridges Urban Renewal Area Housing, 1970-96, Jennings Hall Sr. Citizens Housing, Bklyn., 1980, Goddard Riverside Elderly Housing and Cmty. Ctr., N.Y.C., 1983, Columbus Green Apartments, N.Y.C., 1987, Chung Pak Bldg., N.Y.C., 1992, Child Care Ctr., Queens, N.Y., 1999. Recipient Bard 1st honor award City Club N.Y., 1969, Bard award of merit, 1975, 82, award for design excellence HUD, 1970, 1st prize Nat. Trust for Hist. Preservation, 1983, award of merit Mcpl. Art Soc. N.Y., 1983, Pub. Svc. award Settlement Housing Fund, 1983, Women of Vision award NOW, 1989, 1st prize for design excellence C. of C., Borough of Queens, N.Y., 1989, Best in Srs.' Housing award Nat. Assn. Home Builders, 1993, Hamilton-Madison House Cmty. Svc. award, 1997. Fellow AIA, dir. N.Y. chpt., chmn. commn. on archtl. edn. 1971-73, chmn. nat. task force on women in architecture 1974-75, v.p. N.Y. chpt. 1975-77, chmn. ethics com. 1975-77, Residential design award 1969, Pioneer in Housing award 1990, N.Y. State Assn. Architects-AIA Honor award 1975); mem. Alliance of Women in Architecture (founding, mem. steering com. 1972-74), Architects for Social Responsibility (mem. exec. com. 1982-85), Columbia Archtl. Alumni Assn. (bd. dirs. 1968-71). Home: 37 W 12th St New York NY 10011-8502 Office: Edelman Sultan Knox Wood 100 Lafayette St 6th Fl New York NY 10013 E-mail: judithedelman@mac.com., jedelman@edelmansultan.com.

EDELMAN, MARIAN WRIGHT, not-for-profit organization administrator, lawyer; b. Bennettsville, S.C., June 6, 1939; d. Arthur J. and Maggie (Bowen) Wright; m. Peter B. Edelman, July 14, 1968; children: Joshua, Jonah, Ezra. Merrill scholar, Univs. Paris, Geneva, 1958-59, BA, Spelman Coll., 1960; LLB (J.H. Whitney fellow 1960-61), Yale U., 1963, LLD (hon.), Smith Coll., 1969, Lowell Tech. U., 1975, Williams Coll., 1978, Columbia U., U. Pa., Amherst Coll., St. Joseph's Coll.; DHL (hon.), Lesley Coll., 1975, Trinity Coll., Washington, Russell Sage Coll., 1978, Syracuse U., Coll. New Rochelle, 1979, Swarthmore Coll., 1980, SUNY Old Westbury, Northeastern U., 1981, Bard Coll., 1982, U. Mass., 1983, Hunter Coll., U. So. Maine, SUNY, Albany, 1984, Columbia U., U. Pa., Yale U., 1985, Rutgers U., Bates Coll., Maryville Coll., Bank St., 1986, Claremont Grad Sch., Lincoln U., Georgetown U., Chgo. Theol. Coll., 1987, Wheaton Coll., Tulane U., Grinnell Coll. Brandeis U., Wheelock Coll., Dartmouth Coll., U. S.C., U. N.C., Grad. Ctr. CUNY, U. Wis. Milw., 1988, Interdenom. Theol. Ctr., Hofstra U., Tufts U., Borough Manhattan Community Coll., Wesleyan U., Calif. State U. L.A., Dillard U., U. Md., U. Miami, 1989, Howard U., Beloit Coll., Queens Coll., Am. U., New Sch. of Social Rsch., Coll. of Notre Dame, DePaul U., 1990, Beaver Coll., Fordham U., Simmons Coll., Hamline U., Clark U., Harvard U., Union Coll., 1991, Tuskegee U., Washington U. St. Louis, Hood Coll., Duke U., Mercy Coll., 1992, Princeton U., U. Ill., Calif. State U. San Francisco, Wittenberg (Ohio) Coll., Shaw U., So. Meth. U., 1993, Brown U., U. Balt., Ea. Conn. State U., U. Notre Dame, 1994. Bar: D.C., Miss., Mass. Staff atty. NAACP Legal Def. and Ednl. Fund, Inc., N.Y.C., 1963-64, dir. Jackson, Miss., 1964-68; Congl. and fed. liaison Poor People's Campaign, summer 1968; partner Washington Research Project of So. Center for Pub. Policy, 1968-73; dir. Harvard U. Center for Law and Edn., 1971-73; pres., founder Children's Def. Fund, 1973—. Author: The Measure of Our Success: A Letter To My Children and Yours, 1992, Families in Peril, 1987. Mem. exec. com. Student Non-Violent Coordinating Com., 1961-63; mem. adv. coun. Martin Luther King Jr. Meml. Libr.; mem. adv. bd. Hampshire Coll.; mem. Presdl. Commn. on Missing in Action, 1977, Presdl. Commn. on Internat. Yr. of Child, 1979, Presdl. Commn. on Agenda for 80's, 1980; bd. dirs. NAACP Legal Def. and Ednl. Fund; trustee Spelman Coll., Carnegie Coun. on Children, 1972-77, Martin Luther King Jr. Meml. Ctr.; mem. Yale U. Corp., 1971-77, Aetna Found., Nat. Commn. on Children, 1989—; bd. dirs. Aetna Life Casualty Found., Citizens for Constitutional Concerns, US. com. UNICEF, Robin Hood Found., Aaron Diamond Found., Nat. Alliance Business, City Lights, Leadership Conf. Civil Rights, Skadden Fellowship Found., Parents as Tchrs. Nat. Ctr., Inc.; U.S. rep. UNICEF; active U.S. Olympic Com. Named one of Outstanding Young Women of Am., 1966; recipient Mademoiselle mag. award, 1965, Louise Waterman Wise award, 1970, Washington of Yr. award, 1979, Whitney M. Young award, 1979, Profl. of Yr. award Black Ent., 1979, Leadership award Nat. Women's Polit. Caucus, 1980, Black Womens Forum award, 1980, medal Columbia Tchrs. Coll., Barnard Coll., 1984, Eliot award Am. Pub. Health Assn., John W. Gardner Leadership award of Ind. Sector, Pub. Svc. Achievement award Common Cause, Compostela award Cathedral St. James, 1987, MacArthur prize fellow, 1985, Albert Schweitzer Humanitarian prize Johns Hopkins U., 1987. Philip Hauge Ahelson award AAAS, 1988, Hubert Humphrey Civil Rights award, AFL-CIO award, 1989, Radcliffe Coll. medal, 1989, Fordham Stein prize, 1989, Gandhi Peace award, 1990, M. Carey Thomas award, Robie award for humanitarianism, Essence award, numerous others; hon. fellow U. Pa. Law Sch. Mem. Phi Beta Kappa (hon.), Inst. Medicine. Address: Children's Def Fund 25 E St NW Washington DC 20001-1522

EDELSBERG, SALLY COMINS, physical therapy educator and administrator; b. Rowno, Poland, Aug. 6, 1937; came to U.S., 1949; d. Joseph Luria and Chana (Bebczuk) Comins; m. Warde C. Pierson, Oct. 8, 1968 (div. 1978); m. Paul Edelsberg, Feb. 2, 1979; 1 child, Tema. BS in Phys. Medicine, U. Wis., 1963; MS, Northwestern U., 1972. Lic. phys. therapist. Staff and supervisory phys. therapist Hines VA Hosp., Maywood, Ill., 1963-67; program dir. Health Careers Council of Ill., Chgo., 1967-70; instr., clin. edn. coord. Programs in Phys. Therapy, Northwestern U. Med. Sch., Chgo., 1970—72, dir., assoc. prof., 1972—99, dir. devel. and alumni rels., 1999—2003. Pres. Phys. Therapy Ltd., Chgo., 1986-95; v.p. World Confedn. Phys. Therapy, 1995-99, exec. com., 1991-95. Mem.: Am. Phys. Therapy Assn. (bd. dirs. 1975—78, 1979—82, Ill. pres. 1972—76, Catherine Worthingham fellow 1999). E-mail: s-edelsberg@northwestern.edu.

EDELSON, MARY BETH, artist, educator; b. East Chicago, Ind. d. Albert Melvin and Mary Lou (Young) Johnson; children: Lynn Switzman, Nick. Student, Art Inst. Chgo., 1953-54; BA, DePauw U., 1955; MA, NYU, 1959; DFA (hon.), DePauw U., 1993. Instr. Corcoran Sch. Art, Washington, 1970-75; artist in residence U. Ill., Chgo., 1982, 88, U. Tenn., Knoxville, 1983, Ohio U., Columbus, 1984, Md. Inst. Art, Balt., 1985, Kansas City Art Inst., Mo., 1986, Cleve. Art Inst., 1991, U. Colo., 1993, Clemson U., 1994, McMullen Mus. of Art, Boston Coll., 1997, Danish Royal Acad., Copenhagen, 2000—02. Lectr. at various art gatherings. Solo exhbns. include Nicole Klagsburn Gallery, N.Y.C., 1993, A/C Project Rm., N.Y.C., 1993, Creative Time, N.Y.C., 1994, Nicolai Wallner, Copenhagen, Denmark, 1996, Halle für Kunst, Berlin, 1997, Agency Gallery, London, 1998, Malmö Mus., Sweden, 2000, traveling solo exhbn. to 8 sites in U.S., 2000-2002 30 yr. survey of Edelson's work with 200 page book, full color book, The Art of Mary Beth Edelson; group exhbns. include Internat. Feministiche Kunst, Stichting de Appel, Amsterdam, The Netherlands, 1980, Mendel Gallery, Mus. du Que., Phillips Gallery, Can., 1986-88, Corcoran Gallery Art, Washington, 1989, Mus. Modern Art, N.Y.C., 1988-89, Walker Art Ctr., Mpls., 1989, W.P.A., Washington, 1989, A.C. Project Room, N.Y.C., 1991-97, Phillippe Rizzo, Paris, 1992, P.P.O.W., N.Y.C., 1992, Fawbush Gallery, N.Y.C., 1992, Amy Lipton Gallery, N.Y.C., 1992, David Zwirner Gallery, N.Y.C., 1993, Turner/Krail Galleries, L.A.,o1993, Mercer Union, Toronto, 1996, The Agency, London, 1995, Lombard/Freid, N.Y.C., 1995, Chaisse Post gallery, Atlanta, 1996, Linda Kirkland Gallery, N.Y.C., 1996, Boston Mus. Art, McMullen, 1997, Magasin Ctr. National D'Art Contemporain, Grenoble, France, 1997, Dorfman Projects, N.Y.C., 1998, Internat. Ctr. Photography, N.Y.C., 1997, Neubergher Mus., Purchase, N.Y., 1999, Nicolai Wallner, Copenhagen, 1999, Postmasters, N.Y.C., 1999, New Mus., N.Y.C., 2000, 2001, Tate Gallery, London, Gallerie LeLong, N.Y.C., 2002, Guild Hall, East Hampton, 2002; Chelsea Mus., NYC, 2003; ShedHalle Space, Zurick, 2003, Mumok Museum, Vienna, 2003, Internat. Art Festival, Lofoten, Norway, 2004; represented in permanent collections: Walker Art Ctr., Nat. Mus. Am. Art, Washington, Nat. Collection, Washington, Nat. Mus. Women in the Arts, Washington, Guggenheim Mus. Art, N.Y.C., Mus. Contemporary Art, Chgo., Malmo Mus., Sweden, and others; subject of 15-yr. retrospective travelling to numerous art and ednl. instns. throughout U.S., 1988-91, Survey of Edelson's Work Rescripting the Story, various locations, 2000-02; author: Seven Cycles: Public Rituals, 1981, To Dance: Painting with Performance in Mind, 1985, Seven Sites, 1988-90, Shape Shifter: Seven Mediums, 1990; author/photographer: Firsthand, 1993, The Art of Mary Beth Edelson, 2002; contbr. articles to profl. jours.; included numerous books including The Power of Feminist Art, 1994, Lone Visions, Crowder Frames, 1994, The Pink Glass Swan, 1995, Art and Propaganda, 1997, Saffrages and She-Devils, 1997, Where is Ana Mendiata, 1999, Picturing the Modern Amazon, 2000, Feminist Art-Theory; An Anthology, 1968-2000, Art and Feminism, 2001, The Artists Body, 2000, Sex Politik, 2001, Alternative Art N.Y., 2002, The End of Art, 2004. Recipient Visual Arts grant NEA, 1981, Creative Artists Pub. Svc. grant State of N.Y., 1982, Andy Warhol Found. grant NEA, Pollack/Krasner Found., Florsheim Found., 2000 Mem. Conf. Women in Visual Arts (founding mem.), Women's Action Coalition, Heresies Mag. Collective (founding mem.). Home: 110 Mercer St New York NY 10012-3865

EDELSON, ZELDA SARAH TOLL, retired editor, artist; b. Phila., Oct. 18, 1929; d. Louis David and Rose (Eisenstein) Toll; m. Marshall Edelson, Dec. 27, 1952; children: Jonathan Toll Edelson, Rebecca Jo Edelson, David Edelson Tolchinsky. BA, U. Chgo., 1949, postgrad., 1949-52. Editor-writer Consol. Book Pubs., Chgo., 1953-56; social worker Balt. City Dept. Pub. Welfare, 1956-57; pub. rels. writer Md. Dept. Employment Security, Balt., 1958-59; mus. editor Yale Peabody Mus., New Haven, 1970-76, head publs., 1976-95, editor mus.'s Discovery mag., 1983-95; lectr. in sci. writing Yale U., 1983—84. Author (and illustrator): Apologies for a Nightingale: Images of Turkey, 1997; editor: numerous publs. including The Great Dinosaur Mural at Yale: The Age of Reptiles, 1990. U. Chgo. scholar, 1947-51. E-mail: zstedelson@worldnet.att.net.

EDELSTEIN, BARBARA A. radiologist; b. N.Y.C., NY, 1952; MD, NYU Sch. Medicine, 1977. Cert. diagnostic radiology 1983. Intern Lenox Hill Hosp., N.Y.C., 1977—78; resident Montefiore Hosp., N.Y.C., 1979—82; radiologist Women's Radiology, N.Y.C., 1983—. Office: Womens Radiology 1045 Pk Ave New York NY 10028-1030

EDELSTEIN, JEAN, artist, performance artist; b. N.Y.C., Mar. 18, 1927; d. Jack Silvers and Sarah Glassman; m. Seymour Edelstein, June 23, 1949; children: Bruce, Barbara. Cert., Pratt Inst., 1947; student, Art Students League, 1947-48, UCLA, 1952. One-person shows include Laguna Beach (Calif.) Mus. Art, 1973, Jacqueline Anhalt Gallery, L.A., 1974, Bird's Eye View Gallery, Newport Beach, Calif., 1978, Karl Bornstein Gallery, Santa Monica, Calif., 1981, Gallery Newz, Tokyo, 1985, Ruth Bachofner Gallery, Santa Monica, 1985, 87, 89, Sherry Frumkin Gallery, Santa Monica, 1992, U. Judaism, L.A., 1993, Nemiroff-Deutsch Gallery, Santa Monica, 1994; exhibited in group shows Otis Art Inst., L.A., 1967, Mt. St. Mary's Coll., L.A., 1975, L.A. County Mus. Art, Rental Gallery, 1978, LACE Gallery, L.A., 1980, Eason Gallery, Santa Fe, 1983, San Francisco Mus. Art, 1985, Korean Cultural Gallery, L.A., 1989, Sherry Frumkin Gallery, Santa Monica, 1991, Valerie Miller Gallery, Palm Desert, Calif., 1992, Art Space Gallery, N.Y.C., 1992; represented in pub. collections and commns. Robert Civitas Pub., Sao Paolo, Brazil, Sheraton Inner Harbor Hotel, Balt., Focus Lexington Hotel, Tulsa, Lloyds Bank, L.A., Toyota Corp., Torrance, Calif., Revoltella Mus., Trieste, Italy; performances at Ruth Bachofner Gallery, L.A., 1985, 93, Pacific Asian Mus., Pasadena, Calif., 1990, Exploratorium Mus., San Francisco, 1992, Revoltella Mus., Trieste, 1993, Nat. Mus. Women in Arts, Washington, 1994; works published in L.A. Times, Artweek, Images and Issues, ArtScene, Visions Mag., Flash Art. Recipient scholarship Art Students League, 1947, fellowship NEA Midatlantic, 1996. Home: # 5A 48 Brooks Ave Venice CA 90291-3226 Office Phone: 310-399-3592.

EDELSTEIN, ROSEMARIE (ROSEMARIE HUBLOU), medical/surgical nurse, educator, medical and legal consultant; b. Drake, N.D., Mar. 3, 1935; d. Francis Jerome and Myrtle Josephine (Merbach); m. Harry George Edelstein, June 22, 1957 (div.); children: Julie, Lori, Lynn, Toni Anne. BSN, St. Teresa of Avila Coll., Winona, Minn., 1956; MA in Edn., Holy Names Coll., Oakland, Calif., 1977; EdD, U. San Francisco, 1982, postgrad., 1987, U. Ariz., 1985—; cert. pub. health nurse, U. Calif., Berkeley, 1972. Dir., clin. supr. San Francisco Sch. for Health Professions, 1971-74, Rancho Arroyo Sch. of Vocat. Nursing, Sacramento, 1974-75; intensive care nurse Kaiser-Permanente Hosp., San Rafael, Calif., 1976-77; dir. insvc. edn. Ross Hosp., Calif., 1977-78; dir. nursing edn. St. Francis Meml. Hosp., San Francisco, 1978-85; med.-legal nursing cons., med.-surg. staff nurse met. hosps., San Francisco, 1985-90, St. Luke's Hosp., Duluth, Minn., 1990-91, St. Charles Hosp., New Orleans, 1992, U. Tex. Med. Br., Galveston, 1992—94; staff nurse St. Anthony of Padua Hosp., Oklahoma City, 1994—95, med.-surg. nurse, 1994-95; nurse Northgate Conv. Hosp., San Rafael, 1995—. Night charge nurse Creekside Conv. Hosp., Santa Rosa, Calif., 1996; charge nurse medications, treatment and Alzheimer's Unit Fallon Conv. Ctr., Nev., 1996; charge nurse Medicare unit White Pine Conv. Ctr., Ely, Nev., 1997; emergency rm., ICU nurse Battle Mt. Gen. Hosp., Nev., 1997; nurse supr. Medicare-Med. Seaview Care Ctr. Sun Corp., Eureka, Calif., 1997—98; mem. staff Walker Post Manor Oxford, NE Lantis Corp., 1998, The Lincoln Ambassador, 1999, Rapid City (S.D.) Care Ctr. Beverly Enterprises, 2000—01, Houghton County Med. Care Facility, Hancock, Mich., 2000—, Norlite Nursing Ctr., Marquette, Mich., 2001—02, Whidbey Island Manor, Oak Harbor, Wash.; mem. staff Medicare unit Everett (Wash.) Rehab. and Care Ctr., 2002, St. Joseph Care Ctr., Spokane, 2003, Idaho Falls (Idaho) Care Ctr., 2003—; invited mem. People to People Nursing Edn. and Adminstrn.; candidate to East Asia Philosophy, 1985; postgrad. candidate U. Zurich, Switzerland, 1988. Author: The Influence of Motivator and Hygiene Factors in Job Changes by Graduate Registered Nurses, 1977; Effects of Two Educational Methods Upon Retention of Knowledge in Pharmacology, 1981; co-author: (with Jane F. Lee) Acupunture Atlas, 1974. Candidate U.S. Senate Inner Circle, 1988, 89. Lt. col. USAR Med. Res. Mem. Am. Heart Assn., Calif. Nurses Assn., Sigma Theta Tau. Roman Catholic.

EDELSTEIN, TERI J. art history educator, art administrator, small business owner; b. Johnstown, Pa., June 23, 1951; d. Robert Morten and Hulda Lois (Friedhoff) E. BA, U. Pa., 1972, MA, 1977, PhD, 1979; cert., NYU, 1984. Lectr. U. Guelph, Ont., 1977-79; asst. dir. for acad. programs Yale Ctr. Brit. Art, New Haven, 1979-83; dir. Mt. Holyoke Coll. Art Mus., South Hadley, Mass., 1983-90, Skinner Mus., 1983-90, mem. faculty dept. art., 1983-90; dir. Smart Mus. Art U. Chgo., 1990-92, sr. lectr. dept. art, 1990-2000; prin., owner Teri J. Edelstein Assocs., Chgo., 1999—. Dep. dir. Art Inst. Chgo., 1992—99; pres. Teri J. Edelstein Assocs. Museum Strategies, 1999—; mem. adv. bd. Sculpture Chgo., 1991—96, Mus. Loan Network, Knight and Pew Founds., 1994—96. Office: 1648 E 50th St # 6B Chicago IL 60615-3207 Fax: 773-241-9992. Office Phone: 773-241-9991.

EDEN, BARBARA JANIECE, commercial and residential interior designer; b. Inpls., Oct. 14, 1951; d. Justin January and Marjorie May (Miller) E.; m. Stephen A. Bowman, Oct. 25, 1975; children: Christopher Eden Bowman, Jessica Eden Bowman. BA, Purdue U., 1973. Interior design dir. Bohlen, Meyer, Gibson & Assoc., Indpls., 1973-78; interior designer, sole propr. Barbara Eden Design, Indpls., 1978-85; pres., prin. designer Eden Design Assocs., Inc., Carmel, Ind., 1985-97, Carson Design Assocs. Design/Project Mgmt./ Mktg., Carmel, Ind., 1997—. Past mem. accreditation team Found. for Interior Design Edn. Rsch. (FIDER); past mem. adv. bd. Purdue U. Interior Design Dept.; bd. dirs. Hamilton County Intercultural Svcs. Prin. projects include wheelchair accessible bathroom Kohler (Wis.) Design Ctr., United Airlines, Indpls. Maintenance Ctr., N.Am. hdqrs. Brightpoint, Inc., Plainfield, Ind., Peabody Retirement Ctr., North Manchester, Ind., Oakwood Inn, Syracuse, Ind., Resort Condominiums, Internat., Carmel, Ind., Merchants' Pointe, Carmel, restaurant, retail & office devel., arch., interior design; also corp., healthcare, schs., univs., librs., sr. living and residential interior design, space planning and project mgmt. Mem. Internat. Facility Mgrs. Assn., Internat. Interior Design Assn., Illuminating Engring. Soc., Carmel Clay C. of C. (mem. exec. bd., chair edn. com., Small Bus. Person of Yr. 1993). Avocations: hiking, horseback riding, traveling. Office: Carson Design Assocs 11590 N Meridian St Ste 104 Carmel IN 46032-6955 E-mail: edenbj@carsondesign.com.

EDEN, BARBARA JEAN, actress; b. Tucson, Arizona, Aug. 23, 1934; d. Harrison Connon and Alice Mary (Franklin) Huffman; 1 child, Matthew Michael Ansara; m. Jon Trusdale Eicholtz, Jan. 5, 1991. Student, San Francisco City Coll., San Francisco Conservatory of Music, Elizabeth Holloway Sch. of Theatre. Pres. Mi-Bar Productions; bd. dirs. Security First Nat. Bank of Chgo. Films include Voyage to the Bottom of the Sea, 1961, Five Weeks in a Balloon, 1962, Wonderful World of the Brothers Grimm, 1963, Seven Faces of Dr. Lao, 1964, Harper Valley PTA, 1978, also The Brass Bottle, Ride the Wild Surf, The New Interns, The Girls in the Office, 1979, Condominium, 1980, Return of the Rebels, 1981, Chattanooga Choo Choo, 1984, A Very Brady Sequel, 1996, Mi Casa, Su Casa, 2003, Carolina, 2003; TV debut on series West Point, 1956; numerous other TV appearances; starred in TV series I Dream of Jeannie, 1965-69, Harper Valley P.T.A., 1980-82; appeared in several TV movies including The Feminist and the Fuzz, 1971, A Howling in the Woods, 1971, The Woman Hunter, 1972, Guess Who's Sleeping in My Bed, 1973, The Stranger Within, 1974, Let's Switch, 1975, How to Break Up a Happy Divorce, 1976, Stonestreet: Who Killed the Centerfold Model, 1977, The Stepford Children, I Dream of Jeannie: 15 Years Later, Secret Life of Kathy McCormick, 1989, Your Mother Wears Combat Boots, 1989, Brand New Life, 1989, Her Wicked Ways, 1990, Hell Hath No Fury, 1991, I Still Dream of Jeannie, 1991, Visions of Murder, 1993, Eyes of Terror, 1994, Dead Man's Island, 1995, Nightclub Confindential, 1996, Gentlemen Prefer Blondes, 1998; also stage and club appearances. Office: William Morris Agy c/o Gene Schwam 151 S El Camino Dr Beverly Hills CA 90212-2775*

EDEN, BECKY DESPAIN, dental educator; b. Oklahoma City, July 14, 1948; children: Brian Thomas, Meredith Lynn. BS in Dental Hygiene, Baylor U., 1970; MEd, Cen. State U., Okla., 1982. Registered dental hygienist. Pvt. practice clin. dental hygienist, Oklahoma City, 1970-73; instr. Coll. Dentistry, Okla. U. Health Scis. Ctr., Oklahoma City, 1973-82, asst. prof., 1982-85, acting chair dept. dental hygiene, 1984-85, clin. dental hygienist faculty practice, 1977-85; assoc. prof., dir. Caruth Sch. Dental Hygiene Baylor Coll. Dentistry, Dallas, 1985-93, assoc. prof. dept. pub. health scis., 1993—; clin. dental hygienist Drs. Israelson, Plemons & Jaynes, Richardson, Tex., 1995-97. Clin. instr. Rose Jr. Coll., Midwest City, Okla., 1972; mem. affil. staff Okla. Children's Meml. Hosp., Oklahoma City, 1977-85; clin. dental hygienist North Tex. Periodontal and Implant Assn., Richardson, 1988-91; mem. test constrn. com. Nat. Bd. Dental Hygiene, ADA, Chgo., 1987-91, dental hygiene cons. Commn. on Dental Accreditation, 1989-96; investigator grants and contracts HHS, NIH; bd. dirs. Childrens Oral Health Ctr. Dallas. Editorial rev. bd.: Jour. Dental Hygiene, Chgo., 1982-2000, Jour. Practical Hygiene, 2002—; contbr. abstracts and articles to profl. jours. Spkr. sch. vols. program Oklahoma City Pub. Schs., 1976-85; project dir. Oral Healthlink: Dallas-Ft. Worth Coalition for Oral Health 2000; bd. dirs. Dallas chpt. ACLU of North Tex., pres., 1996-97; Tex. coord. nat. spit tobacco edn. program, Oral Health Am., 1996-97; bd. dirs. So. Methodist U. YWCA, 1997-98. Recipient small grant award Rsch. Coun., OUHSC, Oklahoma City, 1985, Dental Hygiene Rsch. grant Oral-B Labs., Redwood City, Calif., 1985. Mem. APHA, Am. Assn. Dental Schs., Am. Assn. Dental Rsch., Am. Dental Hygienists Assn. (del. 1980-84), Am. Assn. Pub. Health Dentistry (editor), Tex. Dental Hygienists Assn., Tex. Dental Hygiene Dirs. Assn. (sec. 1990-92), Dallas Dental Hygienists Soc. (v.p. 1994, pres.-elect 1995, pres. 1996), The Woman's Ctr. of Dallas (chair health care task force, bd. dirs. 1994-96, health com. Women's Coun. of Dallas County 1995-97), Sigma Phi Alpha, Kappa Delta Pi. Office: Baylor Coll Dentistry PO Box 660677 Dallas TX 75266-0677

EDEN, F. BROWN, artist; b. Jericho Center, Vt., Oct. 10, 1916; d. Arthur Castle and Eva Merita (Lowrey) Brown; m. Edwin Winfield Eden, Sept. 4, 1937; m. Allan L. Day, July 11, 1994; children: Donna Jean, Sandra Elizabeth, Kathy Lynn. Student, U. Fla. Extension, 1955-59, U. Mich., 1963. Art instr. Ann Arbor (Mich.) City Club, 1962-63; tchr., oil painting, printmaking Jacksonville (Fla.) Art Mus., 1963-68. One-woman shows include The Fox Galleries, Atlanta, 1986, Harmon Galleries, Sarasota, 1987, 1989—90, 1992—93, Gallery Contemporanea, Jacksonville, Artist Assocs. Gallery, Atlanta, 1965—90, The Hodgell Gallery, Sarasota, 1997—2002, The Center, Ponte Vedra, Fla., 1998, Kent Campus Gallery, Fla. C.C., Jacksonville, 1999, Represented in permanent collections Fed. Res. Bank Atlanta, Bank Am., Coca-Cola, So. Bell, Sheraton Corp., AT&T, Trust Co. Ga., Shell Oil Co., Touche Ross, Cooper and Lybrand, Delta Airlines "Crown Rm.", 5th Dist. Ct. Appeals Bldg., Daytona Beach, Fla., Edwin and Ruth Kennedy Mus. Am. Art, U. Ohio, Athens, exhibited in group shows at Ala. Nat. Watercolors, Fla., Ga., nationally, exhibitions include Am. Painters in Paris, 1975—76, Painters in Casein and Acrylics, N.Y.C. Chmn. area VI Fla. artist group Jacksonville Mus. Art, 1979—89. Recipient Painting of Yr. award, Mead Co., 1962—63, First award, Fla. Artist Group, 1971, 1979, Fla. Artists, 1969, The Painting award, Maj. Fla. Artists, 1979, others. Mem.: Fla. Crown Treasures, Fla. Artists Jacksonville, Jackson Coalition of Visual Artists, Ala. Watercolor Soc., Ga. Watercolor Soc., Fla. Watercolor Soc. (Signature artist), So. Watercolor Soc., Nat. Mus. of Women in Arts (charter), Am. Women Artists. Avocation: playing organ. Home: 5375 Sanders Rd Jacksonville FL 32277-1333

EDEN-FETZER, DIANNE TONI, nurse, project coordinator; b. Washington, Mar. 1, 1946; d. Lawrence Antonio Laurenzi and Eleanor Charlotte (Sparrough) Watson; m. William Earle Eden, Aug. 5, 1967 (div. 1982); 1 child, Christopher Lance; m. John Thompson Fetzer, Sept. 2, 1987. AA in Nursing, SUNY, Farmingdale, 1978; BS in Nursing, Towson (Md.) State U., 1990; MS in Nursing Informatics, U. Md., 1999. RN, N.Y., Md. Charge nurse dept. neurosurgery U. Md. Hosp., Balt., 1978-79, nurse clincian I, 1979-84, dept. nursing and neurology project coord. Nat. Stroke Data Bank, 1984-90, nursing edn. cons. dept. neurology and neurosurgery, 1984-99, sr. ptnr. neuro intensive care unit, 1990-99; sys. analyst clin. info. sys. U. Md. Med. Ctr., Balt., 1999—. Mem. AACN, Am. Heart Assn. (fellow stroke coun.), Sigma Theta Tau. Democrat. Roman Catholic. Office: Univ Md Hosp 22 S Greene St Baltimore MD 21201-1544

EDENS, BETTY JOYCE, reading recovery educator; b. Hillsboro, Tex., Oct. 20, 1944; d. Edward Alton and Mary Alma (Pendley) Harbin; m. Eugene Cliett Edens, May 29, 1964; children: Michael Eugene, Anne-Marie DeWitt, Kristen Babovec. BEd, Ind. U., 1985; MS, Tex. A&M of Commerce, 1995. Cert. elem. tchr., reading tchr., Tex. 1st grade tchr. Monday Primary, Kaufman, Tex., 1986-93, Franklin Elem., Hillsboro, Tex., 1993-96, reading recovery tchr., 1994-98, 99-00, 2nd grade tchr., 1998-99; reading recovery tchr. Hillsboro Elem. Sch., 1999—. Mem. early literacy com. TSRA, 1998, Susan G. Komen Found. Mem. Reading Recovery Coun. of N.Am., Internat. Reading Assn., Tex. Reading Assn., Monday Rev. Club. Republican. Mem. Ch. of Christ. Avocations: recreational reading, walking, computers.

EDGAR, JANELLE DIANE WARD, financial services executive; b. Albany, Ga., Aug. 27, 1955; d. John David and Margaret Irene (Curtis) Ward; m. James Curtis Edgar, July 7, 1973; children: Lauren Marie, William Robert. BA, Marymount U., 1989. Treas. specialist Fed. Home Loan Mortgage Corp., Washington, 1977-81; mgr. cash acctg. Pentagon Fed. Credit Union, Alexandria, Va., 1981-84; mgr. bus. devel. Fin. Technologies, Inc., Alexandria, 1984-85; v.p. ops. Continental Fed. Savs. Bank, Fairfax, Va., 1985-88; v.p. corp. ops. and info. svcs. Md. Nat. Bank/Am. Security Bank, Washington, 1988-89; dir. mktg. NRC, McLean, Va., 1990-91; dir. mktg. cash mgmt. div. Fin. Mgmt. Svcs. Dept. U.S. Treasury, 1991-98; dir. bus. devel. Diversinet Corp., McLean, Va., 1998—. Mem. tech. and ops. com. Internet, Inc., Reston, Va., 1986-88. Adv. The Women's Ctr. of No. Va., Vienna, 1987; deacon Little Falls Presbyn. Ch. Mem. Washington Cash Mgmt. Assn., Mid-Atlantic Clearing House Assn. (rep. Va. League Savs. to bd. dirs. 1987-88), Bank Adminstrn. Inst. (bd. dirs. 1989-90), Nat. Corp. Cash Mgmt. Assn., Nat. Automated Clearing House Assn. (rules and ops. com.). Republican. Presbyterian. Avocations: ice skating, reading, kayaking, kick-boxing. Office: Diversinet Corp 8201 Greensboro Dr Ste 1000 Mc Lean VA 22102-3840 also: 322 6th St Oakmont PA 15139-1715

EDGAR, RUTH R. retired elementary school educator; b. Great Falls, S.C., Jan. 7, 1930; d. Robert Hamer and Clara Elizabeth (Ellenberg) Rogers. AA, Stephens Coll., Columbia, Mo., 1949; BS, So. Meth. U., 1951; MA, Appalachian State U., Boone, N.C., 1977; postgrad., Limestone Coll., Gaffney, S.C., 1971. Lic. real estate salesman, broker. Home economist Lone Star Gas Co., Dallas, 1951-53, So. Union Gas Co., Austin, Tex., 1953-56, Southwestern Pub. Svc. Co., Amarillo, Tex., 1956-57; with Peeler Real Estate, 1970-71, Burns High Sch., Lawndale, N.C., 1971-73, Cen. Cleveland Mid. Sch., Lawndale, 1973-77, Burns Jr. High Sch., Lawndale, 1977-88; resource tchr. South Cleveland Elem. Sch., Shelby, N.C., 1988-90, Elizabeth Elem. Sch., Shelby, 1990-94, Washington Elem. Sch., Waco, N.C., 1990-92; ret., 1994. Mem. supts. adv. coun., Cleveland County, 1971-75, Cleveland County Art Soc., 1972-73, Cen. United Meth. Ch. Home: 401 Forest Hill Dr Shelby NC 28150-5520

EDGE, CHARLENE L. writer; b. Salisbury, Md., Mar. 26, 1952; d. Joseph Albert and Anne Rochefort Lamy; m. Hoyt L. Edge, Apr. 19, 2002; 1 child from previous marriage, Rachel Bishop. BA summa cum laude, Rollins Coll., Winter Park, Fla., 1994. Tech. writer Bisk-Totaltape, Tampa, 1996—98; documentation writer Sungard HTE Inc., Lake Mary, Fla., 1998—2001, proposal writer, 2001—. Proposal specialist Sungard HTE Inc., 1998—. E-mail: crlamy@attglobal.net.

EDGE, LARA, editor; m. Robert Benz. B in Journalism, U. Ala. Copy editor Rocky Mountain News, Colo., Albuquerque Tribune, Birmingham (Ala.) Post Herald; with Scripps, 1985; dir. online graphics E.W. Scripps Co., Knoxville, Tenn., 1997—98; asst. mng. editor Knoxville News-Sentinel, 1998—99, mng. editor, 1999—. Office: Knoxville News-Sentinel 23332 News Sentinel Dr PO Box 59038 Knoxville TN 37950-9038*

EDGELL, ISABEL JULIE HOFF, hospice nurse; b. Portland, Maine, June 30, 1959; d. Lydia Henriette and Peter Carl Hoff; children: Thomas, Catherine, Sarah. BA, Tufts U., 1981; BSN, No. Mich. U., 2000. Cert. hospice & palliative care. Practice mgr. Northern Neurosurgery, Marquette, Mich., 1991—93, Columbus Neurosurgery, Columbus, Ind., 1993—94; network svc. rep. Southeastern Ind. Health Care Org., Columbus, 1994—96; owner, artistic dir. BalletWorks, Ironwood, Mich., 1996—98; hospice nurse U.P. Home Health and Hospice, Negaunee, Mich., 2001—. Bd. trustees Marquette Area Pub. Schs. Bd. Edn., Marquette, 1999—2002; bd. dirs. Domestic Violence Escape, Inc., Ironwood, 1996—98, Grandview Health Sys. Clinic, Ironwood, 1996—97; sec. Marquette City Commn. Arts and Culture Com., 1995—96. Recipient Outstanding Academic award, Nom Michm U., Sch. Nursing, 2000. Mem.: Sigma Theta Tau. Avocations: running, skiing, bicycling, triathlons, snowboarding. Office: Lake Superior Hospice W Fair Ave Marquette MI 49855

EDGELL, KARIN JANE, reading specialist, special education educator; b. Rockford, Ill., July 17, 1937; d. Donald Rickard and Leona Marquerite (Villard) Williams; m. George Paul Edgell III, May 6, 1960; 1 child, Scott. Student, Rollins Coll., 1955-57; BS, U. Ill., 1960, MEd, 1966; MA, Roosevelt U., 1989; adminstrv. endorsement, U. Va., 2001. Tchr. Alexandria (Va.) City Pub. Schs., 1963-79; asst. to dir. Reading Ctr. George Washington U., Washington, 1979-80; tchr. Winnetka (Ill.) Pub. Schs., 1982-89, Arlington County (Va.) Pub. Schs., 1989—. Mem. NEA, ASCD, Nat. Coun. Tchrs. Eng., Internat. Reading Assn., Va. Edn. Assn., Va. Reading Assn., Greater Washington Reading Coun., Coun. Exceptional Children, Phi Delta Kappa. Presbyterian. Home: Landmark Mews 6275 Chaucer View Cir Alexandria VA 22304-3546 Office Phone: 703-228-5820. Personal E-mail: Karinedgell@mindspring.com.

EDGERTON, DEBRA, artist, educator; b. Junction City, Kans., Mar. 15, 1958; d. Hughes and Tamie E.; m. Terry Baxter, Apr. 13, 1991; children: Noah Hunter, Jesse Dylan. Student, Am. Acad. Art, Chgo., 1979; BFA, U. Kans., 1980. Artist Hallmark Cards, Kansas City, Mo., 1981-86; freelance artist Flagstaff, Ariz., 1986—. Instr's. asst in printmaking U. Kans., Lawrence, 1987, instr. painting Lawrence Art Ctr., 1991-93, Sr. Citizen Ctr., Lawrence, 1992, No. Ariz. U., Flagstaff, 1993—. Exhibited in group shows Tex. Watercolor Soc., Ann. Allied Artists of Am. 86th Ann. Exhbn., Midwest Watercolor Soc. Ann. Transparent Exhbn., Am. Watercolor Soc.'s Ann. Exhbn., Nat. Watercolor Soc.'s Ann. Exhbn. Mem. Round Table for Arts, Lawrence, 1991-92; mayoral appointee Lawrence Art Commn., 1992-93; pres. Lawrence Art Guild Assn., 1992. Recipient Excellence award Geary County Sch. Dist., 1991, Merit award Ariz. Aqueous, 1994; Profl. Devel. grantee Kans. Art Commn., 1992, Tech. Asst. grantee Lawrence Arts Commn., 1992; Dolan Found. scholar, 2001; San Francisco Art Inst. Grad. fellow, 2001. Mem. Am. Watercolor Soc., Nat. Watercolor Soc., Allied Artists Am., Midwest Watercolor Soc. (life). Office: No Ariz U PO Box 6020 Flagstaff AZ 86011-0001

EDGEWORTH, EMILY, retired insurance agency executive, retired small business owner; b. Brilliant, Ala., July 12, 1927; d. James Allen and Cara Margie (Mayes) Addison; m. Billy Pate, Oct. 8, 1947 (div. July 1968); m. William Edgeworth, Sept. 24, 1972. Student, Ala. Bus. Coll., 1952; grad. life underwriters tng. coun., U. Ala., 1976. Med. aide, receptionist Office Dr. A.M. Walker, Tuscaloosa, Ala., 1952-58; credit mgr. Busch Jewelry Co., Tuscaloosa, 1958-66; purchasing clk. Avco Fin. Corp., Tuscaloosa, 1966-71; sec. Ala. Farm Bur. Ins. Co., Tuscaloosa, 1971-73; multilines saleswoman Farm Bur. Ins. Co., Tuscaloosa, 1973-76; owner, salesman Emily Edgeworth Ins. Co., Tuscaloosa, 1976-86; owner, mgr. Rural Relics, Tuscaloosa, 1986-89, ret., 1989. Contbr. poetry and short stories to various publs., including Best Poems of 1996 and 1997, Journey of the Mind, 1994, Growing Up on a Two Mule Farm, 1996. Active Heritage Found., Washington, Meals on Wheels, Tuscaloosa, 1980's, Unity Bapt. Ch., Tuscaloosa; active Tuscaloosa Rep. Com., Nat. Rep. Com. Mem. Internat. Soc. Poets (disting. mem.). Avocations: writing poetry and short stories, collecting depression era farm items. Home: 6103 41s St Tuscaloosa AL 35401

EDIGHOFFER-MURRAY, ANNA BARBEL, procurement officer, political scientist, pharmacist; b. Annweiler, Germany, Apr. 9, 1956; came to U.S., 1988; d. Kurt and Irmgard (J.) Edighoffer; m. Peter Ian Murray, Apr. 6, 1996. Diploma in Polit. Sci., Freie Universität Berlin, 1985, Cert. in Internat. and European Law, 1987; Cert. pharmacist asst. Germany. With pharm. bus., until 1977; editl. asst. Der Tagesspiegel, Berlin, 1980-81; rsch. asst. Freie U., Berlin, 1984-86; JPO UN, N.Y.C., 1988-89, procurement, adminstrv. officer, 1989—. Mem. Nat. Assn. Procurement Mgmt., Gewerkschaft Oeffentlicher Transport und Verkehr. Office: UNTSO/Chief Gen Svcs PO Box 490 91004 Jerusalem Israel

EDINGER, REBECCA TATE, retired property manager, volunteer; b. Tulsa, Okla., Aug. 6, 1946; d. Leo Edward and Della Mildred (Howard) Tate; m. Robert Scholl Edinger, Nov. 20, 1993; stepchildren: Christopher, Jennifer Edinger Johnson, Andrew; m. Cecil Gray Sholar, July 18, 1969 (div. Oct. 31, 1978); 1 child, Bryan Lee Sholar ; m. Sherrell Addison Hester, Aug. 14, 1964 (div. Aug. 14, 1967); 1 child, Timothy Allen Hester. At, Brazosport Coll., Clute and Lake Jackson, Tex., 1977—78. Co-chair crafts and hobbies Brazoria County Fair Assn., Angleton, Tex., 1972—73, adminstr. antiques divsn., 1974—80, bd. dirs., 1976—80; sec. and pres. Brazoria County Battlefield Relic Club, Lake Jackson, Tex., 1974—76; S.W. region coord. and newsletter editor Nat. Fedn. of Hist. Battle Clubs, 1974—75; vol. hostess Brazosport Mus. of Nat. Sci., Clute, Tex., 1994—. Vol. Dem. Hdqs., Lake Jackson, Tex. Recipient Svc. cert. and pin, Brazosport Mus. of Nat. Sci., 2002. Democrat. Baptist. Avocations: antiques, genealogy, webmaster. Home: 211 Huisache Lake Jackson TX 77566 Personal E-mail: tategeneology@cs.com.

EDMANDS, SUSAN BANKS, consulting company executive; b. New Rochelle, N.Y., Oct. 7, 1944; d. George Dixon and Marian (Lepied) Banks; children: Whatleigh Winthrop, Benjamin Bruce II. BS, Boston U., 1966; cert. in libr. sci., Northeastern U., Boston, 1974. Tchr. project head start Office Econ. Opportunity, Washington, 1966; English tchr. Wattana Sch., Bangkok, 1969-71; market researcher Pauline Rendell Assocs., Somerville, Mass., 1971-72; food info. specialist FIND/SVP Inc., N.Y.C., 1977-80; mgr. tech. and indsl. group Find/SVP, Inc., N.Y.C., 1980-90, dir. consulting svcs. divsn., 1990—2003, v.p. corp. quality svcs., 2003—. Pres. Packer Collegiate Parents Orgn., Bklyn. Heights, N.Y., 1987-89, trustee, 1987-89. Mem. Soc. Chimie Industrielle (v.p. Am. sect. 1985-93), Chemists Club (trustee 1984-93), Am. Soc. Info. Sci., Spl. Librs. Assn. Avocations: antique collecting and restoration, travel, cooking, bicycling, gardening. Home: PO Box 1655 New Canaan CT 06840 Office: Find/SVP Inc 625 Avenue Of The Americas New York NY 10011-2095

EDMO, JEAN UMIOKALANI, artist, poet; b. L.A., Apr. 12, 1942; d. Lemuel Kanekikawaiola Cutter and Nancy James Watson; m. Edward McCleary Edmo, Mar. 17, 1984 (dec. Mar. 1996); 8 stepchildren. Grad., Comml. Art Sch., San Francisco, 1963. Author: (poetry) Songs of Life and Love, 2000, rev. edit., 2002, (short stories) Some Passions Never Die, 2002; one-woman shows include nine oil, acrylic and mixed media landscapes., Photographs in One Woman Shows, Chile, 1962; Nat. Photo Book. Nominee Poet of Yr., Internat. Poetry Guild, 2001; recipient Editors award, 2002, Outstanding Achievment cup, Internat. Soc. Poets, Merit Award medal. Green Party. Episcopalian. Avocation: walking, gardening, making craft wreaths, birdwatching.

EDMONDS, ANNE CAREY, librarian; b. Penang, Malaysia, Dec. 19, 1924; d. William John and Neil (Carey) E. Student, U. Reading, England, 1942-44; BA, Barnard Coll., 1948; MSLS, Columbia U., 1950; MA, Johns Hopkins U., 1959; postgrad., Western Res. U., 1960-61; LHD, Mount Holyoke Coll., 1994. With War Damage Commn., London, 1944-46; children's asst. Enoch Pratt Free Libr., Balt., 1948-49; reference libr. Sch. Bus. Adminstrn., CCNY, 1950-51; reference libr. then asst. libr. readers' svcs. Goucher Coll., Balt., 1951-60; exchange reference libr. European svcs. libr. BBS, London, 1955; instr. Sch. L.S., Syracuse U., summer 1960; libr. Douglass Coll., Rutgers U., New Brunswick, N.J., 1961-64, instr., summer 1962, fall 1963; libr. Mt. Holyoke Coll., 1964-94. Vis. libr. U. North, Turfloop, South Africa, 1976-77; mem. libr. vis. com. Wheaton Coll., Norton, Mass., 1978-92; mem. local systems adv. group Online Computer Libr. Ctr., Inc., 1984-87, mem. adv. com. on coll. and univ. librs., 1988-89. Author: A Memory Book: Mount Holyoke College, 1834-1987, 1988 (with Gai Carpenter and others) Computing Strategies in Liberal Arts Colleges, 1992. Mem. South Hadley (Mass.) Bicentennial Com., 1975—76; mem. accreditation teams Middle State Assn. Colls. and Secondary Schs., 1963—94, New Eng. Assn. Schs. and Colls., 1986—94; exec. com. New Eng. Libr. Info. Network, 1974—76, 1979—85, chmn., 1982—84; mem. Adv. Commn. Historic Deerfield, 1975—81, 1986—94; trustee Ctr. for Maine Contemporary Art, Rockport, Maine, 2001—; bd. dirs. U.S. Book Exch., 1973—76, 1980—83. Mem. AAUW (bd. dirs. main chpt. 1998—), ALA, Assn. Coll. Rsch. Librs. (pres. 1970-71, chmn. constn. and bylaws com. New Eng. chpt. 1975-76, pres. New Eng. chpt. 1983-84). E-mail: ACE13@midcoast.com.

EDMONDS, BETH A. state legislator; m. Dan Nickerson. Children's libr. Freeport Cmty. Libr.; mem. Maine Senate from 23d Dist., Augusta, 2001—, chair labor com., 2001—, mem. marine resources com., 2001—. Mem. Freeport Housing Trust, 1987-95, chair, 1991-95; chair Freeport Mcpl. Employee Labor Com., 1996-97. Home: 122 Hunter Rd Freeport ME 04032 Office: State House 3 State House Sta Augusta ME 04333 Office Fax: (207) 287-1585. E-mail: edmonds@gwi.net.

EDMONDS, EILEEN CELESTE, music educator, musician, composer; b. Hampton, Va., July 8, 1963; d. Thomas Bruce, Sr. and Laetitia Williams Edmonds. BA in Music Edn., Va. CC, Richmond, 1988. Lic. instr. U.S. Sailing Assn. Artist in residence Va. Arts Commn., Middlesex, Va., 1990—91; tchr. Manchester HS, Chesterfield, Va., 1993—94, New Kent (Va.) Sch. Bd., 2000—. Mem. music curriculum com. New Kent Schs., 2000—; mem. character edn. com. New Kent elem. sch, 2000—; pres. Edmonds Music, BMI. Composer and producer: cd's Time to Heal, 1992, Eileen Edwards, 1996, performer at benefits. Mem.: MENC, Va. Elem. Music Edn. Assn. (dist. rep. 2001—), U.S. Sailing Assn. Avocations: gardening, sailing, fishing.

EDMONDS, MARIA NIEVES, college administrator; b. Arecibo, P.R., July 7, 1945; came to U.S., 1965; d. Giobel and Cruz Maria (Montes) Nieves; 1 child, Maria Elizabeth Ries; m. David C. Edmonds, Mar. 1, 1997. BA cum laude, U. P.R., 1965; MS, Fla. State U., 1967; Hon. Degree, Baoji Coll. Arts and Scis., China, 1995. Disability adjudicator Vocat. Rehab., Tallahassee, 1968-71; vocat. rehab. counselor State of Fla. Vocat. Rehab. Office, Clearwater, 1971-73; instr. psychology St. Petersburg Jr. Coll., Clearwater, 1973-76, dir. women on the way program, 1980-85, dir. exptl. learning and coop. edn. programs, 1985-88, coord. Ctrl. Am. Scholarship Program, 1988-94, asst. provost internat. edn., 1994—. Co-dir. Fla.-Japan Inst., State of Fla.; bias reviewer for coll. level acad. skills project State of Fla.; mem. adv. bd. Educators in Industry, Pinellas County, Fla.; chair Clearwater Job Svc. Employer's Com.; sponsor, coord. numerous topical seminars and workshops with cmty. colls.; seminar presenter cultural transition P.R., Ecuador, Costa Rica, China, Guatemala, Honduras, Nicaragua, Dominican Republic, 1988—. V.p., pres. Leadership Pinellas, Clearwater; vice-chair Pinellas Assn. Children and Adults with Learning Disabilities, Clearwater; founder, mem. Bay Area Assn. for Women, Tampa; treas., sec. Found. for Quality Pub. Svc., Pinellas County. Recipient Susan B. Anthony award NOW, 1980, Women Honoring Women award Soroptimjist Internat., Pinellas County, 1981, Twin award Tribute to Women in Industry, YWCA, 1988, Disting. Leadership award Nat. Assn. Cmty. Leadership, 1990. Mem. Univ. Women's Assn., Cmty. Colls. for Internat. Devel., Women in Edn. Assn., Fla. Women's Alliance, Pinellas County

Assn. Children and Adults with Learning Disabilities (v.p. 1988), Fla. Assn. Cmty. Colls. Avocations: avid walking, travel, antique collecting. Office: St Petersburg Jr Coll 2465 Drew St Clearwater FL 33765-2816

EDMONDS, MARY PATRICIA, biological sciences educator; b. Racine, Wis., May 7, 1922; d. Millard Samuel and Sarah (Gibbons) E. BA, Milw.-Downer Coll., 1943; MA, Wellesley (Mass.) Coll., 1945; PhD, U. Pa., 1951; DSc (hon.), Lawrence U., 1983. Instr. Wellesley Coll., 1945-46; postdoctoral fellow U. Ill., Urbana, 1950-52, U. Wis., Madison, 1952-55; rsch. assoc. Montefiore Hosp., Pitts., 1955-65; asst. prof. U. Pitts., 1965-71, assoc. prof., 1971-76, prof., 1976—92, prof. emeritus, 1992—. Mem. molecular biology study sect. NIH, Bethesda, Md., 1974-78. Contbr. articles to profl. jours. Recipient Woman of Yr. in Sci. award Chatham Coll., 1986; Rsch. Career Devel. award NIH, 1962-71, rsch. grantee, 1962-91. Mem.: NAS, Am. Soc. Biochemistry and Molecular Biology. Office: U Pitts Dept Biol Sci Pittsburgh PA 15260

EDMONDSON, MARY ELLEN, artist; b. McLean, Va., Nov. 8, 1919; d. William Grant and Mary Pauline (Neff) E. Student, George Washington Jr. Coll., Washington, 1938-39; degree in art, Abbott Art Sch., 1943. Artist, illustrator Fed. Govt. Petroleum Adminstrn. for War, 1942-46, Bur. Reclamation, 1946-49. Exhibited in group shows Art League, Alexandria, Va., 1972-87, Miniature Soc. Washington, 1974-96 (awards 1978, 89, 91), Royal Miniature Soc., London, 1995. Mem. Ga. Miniature Soc. (1st place graphics 1996), Miniature Soc. N.J. (2d place in fine prints, 1977, 3d place, 1994). Democrat. Avocations: reading, walking, art with children. Home: 1927 Franklin Ave Mc Lean VA 22101-5310

EDMUNDS, JANE CLARA, communications consultant; b. Chgo., Mar. 16, 1922; d. John Carson and Clara (Kummerow) Carrigan; m. William T. Dean, Aug. 30, 1947 (div. 1953; dec. July 1984); 1 son, John Charles; Edmund S. Kopacz, Sept. 24, 1955 (div. 1973); children: Christine Ellen, Jan Carson. Student in chemistry and math., Northwestern U. Chemist Mars Inc., Oak Park, Ill., 1942-47; with Cons. Engr. Mag., Maujer Pub. Co., St. Joseph, Mich., 1953-58, 69-74; sr. editor Cons. Engr. Mag. Tech. Pub. Co., Barrington, Ill., 1975-77, exec. editor, 1977-82, editorial dir., 1983-86; asst. editor women's pages rewrite desk News-Palladium, Benton Harbor, Mich., 1967-68; freelance journalist St. Joseph, 1959-68; communications cons. Schaumburg, Ill., 1987—. Chmn. Berrien County (Mich.) Nat. Found. March of Dimes, 1968; mem. campaign com. Rep. Party, 1954. Recipient award Bausch & Lomb, 1940, award Nat. Found. Service, 1969, Silver Hat award Constrn. Writers Assn., 1986, honor mem. 2000, Chmn.'s award Profl. Engrs. in Pvt. Practice div. NSPE, 1987; grantee AID, 1979 Assoc. fellow Soc. Tech. Communication (chmn. St. Joseph chpt. 1972 Disting. Tech. Communication awards); mem. Am. Soc. Bus. Press Editors (past bd. mem.), Constrn. Writers Assn., Smithsonian Instn., Chgo. Art Inst. Assocs., Field Mus. Assocs. Republican. Episcopalian.

EDMUNDS, NANCY GARLOCK, federal judge; b. Detroit, July 10, 1947; m. William C. Edmunds, 1977. BA cum laude, Cornell U., 1969; MA in Teaching, U. Chgo., 1971; JD summa cum laude, Wayne U., 1976. Bar: Mich. 1976. With Plymouth Canton Public Schools, 1971-73; law clk. Barris, Sott, Denn & Driker, 1973-75; law clk. to Hon. Ralph Freeman U.S. Dist. Ct. (ea. dist.) Mich., 1976-78, with Dykema Gossett, Detroit, 1978-84 ptnr. litigation sect., 1984-92; apptd. judge U.S. Dist. Ct. (ea. dist.) Mich., 1992—. Commr. 21st Century Commn. on Cts., 1990; mem. faculty, bd. mem. Fed. Advocacy Inst., 1983-91. Editor in chief Wayne Law Review. Mem. com. of visitors Wayne Law Sch., Detroit; mem. com. on defender svcs. Nat. Jud. Conf.; mem. Nat. Coun. Jewish Women; bd. gov.'s Cranbrook Schs.; bd. dirs. Mich. Mems. of Stratford Festival; bd. trustees Stratford Shakespearean Festival of Am., Temple Beth El, 1990-97, Hist. Soc. U.S. Dist. Ct. (ea. dist.) Mich., 1993-98. Mem. ABA, FBA (exec. bd. dirs. 1989-92), Am. Judicature Soc., Fed. Judges Assn., State Bar Mich. (chair U.S. cts. com. 1990-91). Avocations: skiing, reading. Office: US Dist Ct US Courthouse #211 231 W Lafayette Blvd Detroit MI 48226-2700 E-mail: karen_hillebrand@mied.uscourts.gov.

EDMUNDSON, LORNA DUPHINEY, academic administrator; b. Sept. 6, 1942; MEd, Boston Coll., 1969; EdD, Columbia U. Tchrs. Coll., 1975. Continuing edn. program dir. Am. U. Paris, 1976-77; asst. dean dir. Columbia U., New York, N.Y., 1978-84; acad. v.p. Marymount Coll., Tarrytown, N.Y., 1984-92; acting pres. v.p. Colby Sawyer Coll., New London, N.H., 1993-96; pres. Trinity Coll. Vt., Burlington, Vt., 1996-98, Assoc. Vt. Colls., Shelburne, Vt., 1998—. Office: # 307-309 29 Ethan Allen Ave Colchester VT 05446-3305

EDSON, MARGARET, playwright; b. Washington, July 4, 1961; life ptnr. Linda Merrill. BA, Smith Coll., 1983; MA, Georgetown U., 1992. Tchr., elementary D.C. public schools, 1992—98; tchr. kindergarten John Hope Elem. Sch., Atlanta, 1998—. Author: (play) Wit, 1999. Recipient Drama League of NY playwright award, 1993, LA Drama Critics Circle award, 1996, Berrilla Kerr Found. playwrights award, 1998, Fellowship of Southern Writers drama award, 1999, Pulitzer prize for drama, 1999. Home: 6201 Trolley Sq Xing NE Atlanta GA 30306-3791*

EDSTROM, PAM, public relations executive; b. 1954; Pvt. practice, 1968-74; with Fred Meyer Savings and Loan, Portland, Oreg., 1974-77, Tektronix, Inc., Beaverton, Oreg., 1977-81, Microsoft Corp., Redmond, Wash., 1982—84; sr. v.p. Waggener Edstrom, Inc., Portland, 1984—2000, exec. v.p., 2000—. Office: Waggener Edstrom Inc 3 Center Pointe Dr Ste 300 Lake Oswego OR 97035

EDWARD, G. GAIL, investment company executive, theater operator; BS in Math., U. Western Ont. With Ernst & Ernst, Hamilton, Ont., Can., Price Waterhouse, Toronto, Ont.; sr. mgr. Can. Imperial Bank of Commerce, Toronto; with Del. North Cos., 1989—; pres., COO, CFO, v.p., treas. GC Cos., Inc., Chestnut Hill, Mass., 1996—. Office: GC Cos Inc 1280 Goylston St Chestnut Hill MA 02467 Fax: (612) 264-8206.

EDWARDS, ARDIS LAVONNE QUAM, retired elementary education educator; b. Sioux Falls, S.D., July 30, 1930; d. Norman and Dorothy (Cade) Quam; m. Paul Edwards, Apr. 18, 1953 (dec. Sept. 1988); children: Kevin (dec. 1980), Kendall, Erin, Sally, Kristin, Keely. Tchg. credentials, Augustana Luth. Coll., Sioux Falls, 1949; provisional tchg. credentials, San Jose State Coll., 1953, student, 1953-57. Lic. pvt. pilot, FAA, 1984. Mgr. The Cottage Restaurant, Sioux Falls, 1943-50; one-room sch. tchr. Whaley Sch., Colman, S.D., 1949-50; one-room sch. tchr. 8 grades East Sioux Sch., Sioux Falls, 1950-51; recreation dir. City of Albany, Calif., 1951-52; first grade tchr. Decoto (Calif.) Sch. Dist., 1952-58; ret., 1958. Author Health Instrn. Unit Study Packet for Tchrs. Treas. PTA, Hayward, Calif., 1959; chmn. Our Savior Luth. Ch. Blood Bank, 1968—; officer Healthy Cmtys., Healthy Youth; mem. Am. Heart Assn., March of Dimes, Am. Cancer Soc., Arthritis Found.; rm. mother Chadbourne Grammar Sch.; team mother Fremont Little League; Brownie leader, den mother; bible sch. tchr., Sunday sch. tchr. East Side Luth. Ch., Sioux Falls, SD, 1945—51; charter mem. Our Savior Luth. Ch., Fremont, Calif., 1964—, mem. choir, transition task force, Christian Week Day Sch. tchr., 1970, 1987, ch. historian, 1986—; other offices; pres. Luth. Women's Missionary League, 1976; edn. officer, fraternal communicator, respecteen officer Luth. Brotherhood. Recipient Spl. Svc. award Girl Scouts U.S., 1971, Arthritis Found., Fremont, 1974-75, Spl. Commendation March Fong Eu, 1954. Mem. NAFE, AARP, Republic Airlines Ret. Pilots Assn., Ret. Airline Pilots Assn., N.W. Airlines Ret. Pilots Assn., Aircraft Owners and Pilots Assn., S.W. Airways Pilots Wives Assn., Concerned Women for Am., World Affairs Coun., Philomathian Lit. Soc., Tri-Cities Assn. Evangelicals, Washington Twp. Hist. Soc., Mission Highlands Swim Club. Republican. Avocations: bible study, grandchildren, flying, history, antiques.

EDWARDS, BARBARA ANN, county official; b. Kingsport, Tenn., Jan. 16, 1940; d. Kermit Ezra and Nina Lee (McConnell) Quillen; m. Kenneth Gray Edwards, Nov. 9, 1962; children: Randall Scott, Shannon Patrick. AAS, Mountain Empire C.C., Big Stone Gap, Va., 1988. Sec. Dept. Agr., Washington, 1957-58, Holston Defense Corp., Kingsport, Tenn., 1958-62; tchr. Neighborhood Youth Corps, Gate City, Va., 1972-74; sec. Scott County, Gate City, 1974-96, dep. coord. emergency svcs., 1975—, asst. county adminstr., 1997, 99—, acting county adminstr., 1997-98, asst. county adminstr., 1999—. Mem. adv. bd. Mountain Empire C.C., Big Stone Gap, Va., 1989—. Mem. Va. Mcpl. Clks. Assn. Baptist. Avocations: reading, japanese bunka, crafts. Home: PO Box 1553 Gate City VA 24251-1553 Office: 112 Water St Ste 1 Gate City VA 24251

EDWARDS, CAROLYN MULLENAX, public relations executive; b. French Camp, Calif., Dec. 3, 1943; d. Charles Harold and Jessie Jewel Mullenax; m. Helton Pressley (div.); m. Dennis D. Edwards, May 29, 1993. BFA, U. Tulsa, 1967; MEd, Ea. N.Mex. U., 1976. Artist Wessels Agy., Spokane, Wash., 1968-70; pub. rels. dir. Spokane (Wash.) Symphony Soc., 1970-72; advt. coord. Crescent Dept. Store, Spokane, 1972-73; art dir., copywriter Sta. KMTY Radio, Clovis, N.Mex., 1976; news editor Clovis News Jour., Clovis, 1976-77; promotion and art dir. Sta. KENW-TV, Portales, N.Mex., 1977-78; coord. alumni affairs and pubs. Ea. N.Mex. U., Portales, 1978-80, dir. pubs., TV and pub. info. Clovis, 1985-90, asst. dir. alumni affairs Portales, 1998-00, dir. pubs., 2000—; devel. and pub. info. dir. Mental Health Resources Inc., Portales, N.Mex., 1980-85; dir. mktg. & pub. info. Clovis Community Coll. (formerly Ea. N.Mex. U.-Clovis), 1990-98; producer pub. affairs program Sta. KMCC-TV, Clovis, 1981-84. Bd. dirs. N.Mex. Outdoor Drama Assn., San Jon, 1986-95, Univ. Symphony League, Clovis, 1984-88. Named N.Mex. Press Women Communicator of Acheivement, 1999. Mem. N.Mex. Press Women (scholarship chair 1994-99, comm. awards 1981-2002, treas. 2000-2001, v.p. 2001—), Nat. Fedn. Press Women (comm. awards 1984-97), Am. Women in Radio and TV, Clovis C. of C. (bd. dirs. 1984-89), Jr. League (Lubbock, Tex.), Coun. for Advancement and Support Edn. (sec.-editor dist. IV 1990 92, design award 1991, 99), Nat. Coun. for Mktg. and Pub. Rels. (dist. IV award 1989-91, 93-97, 99, nat. award 1993-98), Altrusa Club, Nat. Assn. of Vocational and Tech. Edn. (awards 1995-96), Delta Delta Delta (former dist. alumnae officer, chair Delta Century Fund, graphics cons.). Republican. Episcopalian. Avocations: reading, classical music, free lance art, volunteer work, dance. Office: Ea NMex Univ Univ Rels Sta # 6 Portales NM 88130 E-mail: carolyn.edwards@enmu.edu.

EDWARDS, CHARLOTTE ANN, elementary school educator; b. Jasper, Tex., Sept. 16, 1948; d. Delois and geraldine L. (McNeill) Dominy; m. Charles Ray Dorgan, Apr. 5, 1969 (div. Feb. 1985); m. William Lee Edwards, Nov., 1997. BS, Lamar U., 1981; MEd, SFASU, Nacogdoches, Tex., 1991. Lab. technician Tex. Animal Health Commn., Austin, 1968-69; tchr. Brookland (Tex.) Ind. Sch. Dist., 1982-85; tchr. math., sci. and art Jasper (Tex.) Ind. Sch. Dist., 1985—. PTA scholar, 1990. Mem. Tex. Assn. for Advancement of Math. Skills, Conf. Advancement Math. Tech., Tex. Art Edn. Assn., VFW Ladies Aux., Assn. Tex. Profl. Educators (pres. 1989, 91, 93, 97). Ch. of christ. Office: J H Rowe Intermediate Sch 100 Park Ln Jasper TX 75951-3466

EDWARDS, CHRISTINE ANNETTE, retired lawyer, securities firm executive; b. Ft. Monmouth, N.J., Aug. 30, 1952; d. Harry W. Jr. and Elizabeth Power; m. John H. Edwards, Aug. 24, 1974; children: Lindsey, John. BA, U. Md., College Park, 1974; JD with honors, U. Md., Balt., 1983. Bar: Md. 1983, D.C. 1984, Ill 1990. With Sears, Roebuck and Co., Md., 1971-81, sr. paralegal, staff asst., 1981-83, atty. govt. affairs, 1983-87; asst. v.p., dir. govt. affairs Dean Witter Fin. Svcs. Group, Washington, 1987-88, v.p., gen. counsel Lincolnshire, Ill., 1988-89, sr. v.p., 1989-91, exec. v.p., sec., chief legal officer N.Y.C., 1991-97; exec. v.p., chief legal officer, corp. sec. Morgan Stanley Dean Witter & Co. (merger Dean Witter Discover & Co. with Morgan Stanley & Co. Inc.), N.Y.C., 1997—99; legal dept. ABN AMRO, 1999—2000; v.p., gen. counsel Bank One Corp., 2000—03. Mem. bd. Fin. Svcs. Coun., Washington, 1990—; bd. trustees Nat. Found. for Consumer Credit Counseling Svcs., Silver Spring, Md., 1990-92; mem. Women in Housing and Fin., Washington, 1982—, SAI Letigation Com., 1995—, N.Y. Stock Exchange Legal Adv. Com., 1992-95; bd. dirs. Chgo. Bd. of Options Exchange, SPS Transaction Svcs. Inc.; exec. v.p., chief legal officer, corp. sec. CLO Roundtable, 1995—. Recipient Disting. Mem. award Women in Housing and Fin., Washington, 1988; named 1 of 50 Top Women Lawyers Nat. Law Journal, 1998. Mem. ABA, Securities Industry Assn. (mem. fed. regulation com. 1990—).

EDWARDS, CHRISTINE UTLEY, social services administrator, consultant; b. Key West, Fla., Nov. 12, 1951; d. Samuel Tracy and Shirley (White) Utley; m. Lester G. Edwards, Aug. 11, 1973. B in Eng., U. Southwestern La., Lafayette, 1974; MPA, Syracuse U., 1980. Rsch. asst. So. Mut. Help Assn., Abbeville, La., 1974; dir. women's options Oneida Co. Coop. Extension, New Hartford, N.Y., 1975-76; planning specialist Oneida Co. Community Action, Utica, N.Y., 1980-81; dir. crisis services YWCA, Utica, N.Y., 1981-89; dir. edn. and community affairs Planned Parenthood Mohawk Valley, Utica, N.Y., 1989-95; exec. dir. YWCA Mohawk Valley, 1995-98; mgmt. cons. Computer Connection of Ctrl. N.Y., 1999-2000; exec. dir. Chenango Health Network, 2001—. Mem. com. for rape crisis ctrs. N.Y. State Dept. Health, Albany, 1984-89; cons./trainer Pvt. Devel. Orgn., Domestic and Sexual Violence Related Topics, Ilion, N.Y., 1986-93; adj. faculty mem. Mohawk Valley C.C., Utica, 1989; cons./trainer domestic violence unit N.Y. State Dept. Social Svcs., 1989-92; owner Tiger Lily Antiques, 1995. Founding mem. Rape Crisis Svcs., Utica, 1975; bd. dirs. Mohawk Valley Com. Against Child Abuse, 1985-88; mem. Mt. Markham Family Life Edn. Adv. Com., West Winfield, N.Y., 1988-90; mem. adv. com. rape crisis svcs. YWCA, Herkimer, N.Y., 1989—; bd. dirs. Canine Working Companions, Inc., 1990—, pres. 1993-95; bd. dirs. Metro Utica BPW, sec., 1993-95; master gardener Oneida County Cooperative Extension, 1993-95; mem. N.Y. State AIDS Inst. Statewide Prevention Planning Group, 1994-98; mem. steering com. Cen. N.Y. HIV Care Network, 1993-98; mem. Oneida County Domestic Violence Coalition, 1995-98. Recipient Women of Merit award Mohawk Valley Women's History Project, Utica, N.Y., 1985, Kirkland Art Ctr. Color Photography award, 1989. Mem. N.Y. Coalition Against Sexual Assault (founding mem., pres. 1988-90), Nat. Coalition Against Sexual Assault (bd. dirs. 1985-87). Democrat. Avocations: photographer, cross country skier, hiker, birder, gardener. Home: 140 Elizabethtown Rd Ilion NY 13357-3700

EDWARDS, CLAUDETTE LECOQ, speech pathology/audiology services professional; b. Lafayette, La., Sept. 29, 1959; d. Nolan Joseph LeCoq and Dorian Virginia Aronson; m. John Henry Edwards, May 15, 1981; 1 child, John Henry. BS, U. of So. Miss., 1981, MS, 1982. Cert. clin. competence Am. Speech-Language-Hearing Assn., 1983, lic. Ms State Bd. of Health, 2003. Speech-lang. pathologist Richton (Miss.) Sch. Dist., 1982—; speech-lang. pathologist, part-time Perry County Nursing Home and Hosp., Richton, Miss., 1987—2003. Mem.: Miss. Speech-Lang.-Hearing Assocation, Am. Speech-Lang.-Hearing Assn. (award 1997), Internat. Assn. Method Task Force (continuing edn. chairperson 1995—98), Richton Home and Garden Club (pres. 1986—), Richton Women's Club (pres. 1991—2000). Republican. Southern Baptist. Avocations: golf, skiing, travel, reading, church. Office: Richton Sch Dist 701 Elm Ave PO Box 568 Richton MS 39476 Office Phone: 601-788-6975. Personal E-mail: speech929@aol.com.

EDWARDS, DORIS PORTER, computer specialist; b. Lambert, Miss., Jan. 18, 1962; d. Willie Morris and Carrie Mae (Tillman) E.; 1 child, Stacy Nicole. AA in Computer Sci., Draughons Coll., Memphis, 1981. Counselor French Riviera Spa, Memphis, 1989-90; pvt. practice, computer application developer Memphis, 1990—; owner, fin. cons., fund locator Developing Processing in Comm., Memphis, 1998—. Bus. owner Developing Processing in Comms.; fin. cons., cream developer. Developer cosmetic cream. Jehovah's Witness. Avocations: mathematics, reading. Home and Office: 2638 Burns Ave Memphis TN 38114-4913

EDWARDS, ESTHER G. museum administrator, former record, film and entertainment company executive; b. Oconee, Ga. d. Berry and Bertha Ida (Fuller) Gordy; m. George H. Edwards, Apr. 12, 1951 (dec.); 1 son (by previous marriage), Robert Berry Bullock. Ed., Howard U., Wayne State U. Sr. v.p., sec., dir. Motown Record Corp., Detroit, 1959-1988; with Jobete Music Pub. Co., Inc., 1959—; sr. v.p., corporate sec. Motown Industries, Hollywood, Calif., 1973-88; founder, chmn., CEO Motown Hist. Mus., Detroit, 1985—. Dir. Bank of the Commonwealth, 1972-79 Bd. dirs. Detroit Econ. Growth Corp.; founder, exec. dir. Gordy Found., 1968—; chmn. Wayne County Dem. Women's Com., 1956; Mich. del.-at-large Dem. Nat. Conv., 1960; bd. dirs. Martin Luther King Ctr. for Non-Violent Social Change; former trustee Detroit Inst. Arts; mem. corp. Lawrence Tech. U., Southfield, Mich.; commr. Mich. Hist. Commn., 1989-95. Mem. Greater Detroit C. of C. (treas., exec. bd. 1973-79), Met. Detroit Conv. and Visitor's Bur. (dir.), Econ. Club Detroit (dir.), African Am. Heritage Assn. (founder, chmn.), Alpha Kappa Alpha, Gamma Phi Delta. Office: Motown Hist Mus 2648 W Grand Blvd Detroit MI 48208-1237

EDWARDS, FRANCES LAVINIA, city official; b. Phila., Sept. 12, 1948; d. Harry Donaldson and Anna Louise (McColgan) Edwards; children: Frances Lavinia Papapietro, David Allen Winslow Jr. BA, Drew U., 1969, MA, 1971; M Urban Planning, NYU, 1974, PhD, 1978. Cert. hazardous material mgmt. U.C. Irvine, 1991. Adminstrv. asst. Borough of Florham Park, N.J., 1970-73; instr. Kean Coll., Union, N.J., 1973-75; adminstrv. analyst Irvine (Calif.) Police Dept., 1984-86; coord. emergency svcs. City of Irvine, 1986-91; dir. emergency svcs. City of San Jose, Calif., 1991—, acting asst. fire chief, 1993—94; dir. San Jose Met. Med. Task Force, 1997—, San Jose Urban Area Security Interactive, 2003—. Instr. U. Calif., Irvine, 1990—91, Berkeley, 1996—98, Santa Cruz, 1997—2001; adj. prof. San Jose State U., 1999, 2004, Santa Clara U., 2002; mem. Calif. Seismic Safety Commn., 1991—95, Calif. Hosp. Bldg. Safety Bd., 1994—95; mem. exec. session on domestic preparedness Kennedy Sch., Harvard U., 1999—2003; vice chair Collaborative for Disaster Mitigation, 2000—; met. med. response sys. rev. com. NAS/Inst. Medicine, 2000—02; rsch. assoc. Mineta Transp. Inst., San Jose, 2001—, adj. prof., 2004; mem. U.S.-Germany Counter Terrorism project Stanford U., 2002—, biol. warfare working group, 1998—; mem. air monitoring project NAS, 2002; mem. radiol. edn. project CDC, 2003—; mutual aid com. Calif. Met. Med. Task Force, 2003—; radiol. working group NATO, 2003—; cons. in field. Editor: NCEER Workshop Procs., 1990, 1992, others; contbr. chapters to books, articles to profl. jours.; panelist BioWar series on Nightline, 1999, guest (TV series) Live Response, 2001, columnist ASPA On-Line, 2001—. Vice pres. San Diego Chaplain's Wives, 1976-79; treas. Girl Scouts U.S.A., Yokohama, Japan, 1980-81, Camp Pendleton Officer's Wives Club, 1982-83, pres., 1983-84; vice-chmn. curriculum ARC Disaster Acad., 1989-90, chmn., 1991; cmty. disaster preparedness com. ARC, 1992-97; del. Internat. Assn. Emergency Mgrs., 1990—; cert. emergency mgr. 1998—; bd. dirs. Calif. Earthquake Safety Found., 1997—, vice-chair, 2003—; bd. dirs. Vol. Ctr. Silicon Valley, 2002—, emergency svc. com., 2002—; mem. Cupertino Gen. Plan Task Force, 2003—, chair public safety commn. Recipient Vol. Svc. award Navy Relief Soc., 1984; Lasker Found. fellow, 1972; named one of Women of Distinction, Soroptimists Internat., 1991; named Pub. Adminstr. of Yr., Governing Mag., 2002; named to Silicon Valley Power 100, San Jose Mag., 2002. Mem. ASPA (program chmn. Orange County 1984-85, chmn. criminal justice sect. award com. 1988-92, Santa Clara County bd. dirs., 1992—, co-chmn. mini-conf. 1993, sec. 1994-95, pres. 1995-98, bd. dirs. 1993—, chair sect. emergency mgmt. 1999-2002, nat. policy com. 1995-99, nat. membership chair 1996-97, nat. coun. 1998-2000, chpt. awards chair 1993-98, 2000-01, mem. editl. bd. Pub. Adminstrn. Rev. 2003—), Am. Planning Assn. (regional conf. planning com. 1989-90), Internat. City Mgrs. Assn., Assn. Police Planning and Res. Officers (past ec., v.p. Orange County 1984-90), Creekers Club (pres. 1985-88), San Jose Mgmt. Assn. (bd. dirs. 1992-98), Portofino Villas Homeowners Assn. (v.p. 1995-2001, 2003—, bd. dirs. 1995—), Calif. Emergency Svcs. Assn. (conf. program com. 1992, 95, 98, 2001, legis. chair 1997-98, Platinum award 1998, Gold award 1998, John Fetz Meml. award 2000), Santa Clara County Emergency Mgrs. Assn. (sec. 1995, v.p. 1996, pres. 1997), Yokohama Internat. Women's Club (v.p. for social svcs. 1979-81). Republican. Methodist. Avocations: amateur radio, music, reading, biking, swimming. Home: PO Box 2753 Cupertino CA 95015-2753 Office: City of San Jose OES 855 N San Pedro St # 404 San Jose CA 95110-1718 Personal E-mail: kc6thm@yahoo.com. Business E-Mail: frances.winslow@sanjoseca.gov.

EDWARDS, GLORIA TAYLOR, public relations executive; b. Richmond, Va., Sept. 17, 1955; d. Albert Taylor and Nina Spain Wallace; m. Larie D. Edwards Sr., Mar. 15, 1975; 1 child, Larie D. Edwards Jr. AAS, J. Sargeant Reynolds C.C., Richmond, 1985; diploma, Inst. Children's Lit., W. Redding, Conn., 1995. Pub. rels. officer Commonwealth of Va., Richmond, 1990—2003. Author: The Proclamation, 1992, Stories from Ancient Africa, 1995, Death Will Pay the Debt, 1999, Sins of the Parents, 2003; news prodr. and talk show host WCLM-AM Radio, Richmond, 1996—. Legis. comm. adv. Va. Citizens United for Rehab. of Errants, Arlington, 1991—; mem. So. Poverty Law Ctr., Montgomery, Ala., 2001—. Recipient Cert. of Appreciation, Va. Citizens United for Rehab. of Errants, 1994. Mem.: Nat. Law Enforcement Officers (bd. dirs. 2001—), Nat. Assn. Women Writers, Va. Writers Club. Avocations: writing, book collecting. Office: Voices From the Drum PO Box 27504 Richmond VA 23261-7504 E-mail: vftdgte@aol.com.

EDWARDS, HELEN THOM, physicist; b. Detroit, May 27, 1936; d. Edgar Robertson and Mary (Milner) Thom; m. Donald A. Edwards. BS in Physics, Cornell U., 1957, MA in Physics, 1963, PhD in Physics, 1966. Rsch. assoc. Cornell U., Ithaca, N.Y., 1966-70; assoc. head booster Fermi Nat. Accelerator Lab., Batavia, Ill., 1970-71, staff physicist, M.R., 1971-75, head switchyard extraction group, 1975-78, leader tevatron design group, 1978-79, dep. head saver div., 1980-81, dep. head accelerator div., 1981-86, head accelerator div., 1987-88; head accelerator constrn. div. SSC/URA, Dallas, 1989-90, tech. dir., 1990-91. Recipient Achievement in Accelerator Physics and Tech. U.S. Summer Sch. on Particle Accelerator Prize, 1985, Ernest O. Lawrence award Dept. of Energy, 1986, Nat. Medal Tech., 1989; MacArthur Found. Chgo. fellow, 1988. Fellow Am. Phys. Soc.; mem. NAE.

EDWARDS, IRENE ELIZABETH (LIBBY EDWARDS), dermatologist, educator, medical researcher; b. Winston-Salem, N.C., Mar. 17, 1950; d. Robert Dixon Edwards and Irene Octavia (Temple) Fisher; m. Clayton Samuel Owens, Apr. 19, 1985; 1 child, Sarah Tay. BS magna cum laude, Wake Forest U., 1972; MD, Bowman Gray Sch. Medicine, 1976; postgrad., N.C. Bapt. Hosp., 1979, U. Ariz., 1981, 84. Diplomate Nat. Bd. Med. Examiners, Am. Bd. Internal Medicine, Am. Bd. Pediatrics, Am. Bd. Dermatology. Intern N.C. Bapt. Hosp., Winston-Salem, 1976-78, resident in pediatrics, 1978-79; resident in internal medicine U. Ariz. Health Scis. Ctr., Tucson, 1979-81, resident in dermatology, 1982-84; instr. dermatology U. Ariz. Coll. Medicine, Tucson, 1984-85, asst. prof. dermatology, 1985-90; clin. rschr., chief sect. dermatology Tucson VA Med. Ctr., 1984-90; chief dermatology Carolinas Med. Ctr., Charlotte, N.C., 1990—; clin. assoc. prof. dermatology, clin. rschr. Wake Forest U., Winston-Salem, 1993—, U. N.C., Chapel Hill, 1993—. Nat. lectr. in field. Author: Dermatology in Emergency Care, 1997; co-author: Genital Dermatology, 1994; contbr. chpts. to books, numerous articles to profl. jours. Reynolds scholar, 1969-72. Fellow Am. Acad. Dermatology, Am. Acad. Pediatrics; mem. Soc. Pediatric Dermatology, Internat. Soc. Tropical Dermatology, Women's Dermatologic Soc., Internat. Soc. for Study of Vulvovaginal Disease (pres.-elect), Charlotte Dermatological Soc., Phi Beta Kappa, Alpha Epsilon Delta. Home: 2409 Cuthbertson Rd W[illegible] NC [illegible]

EDWARDS, JANINE C. educational administrator; b. Sept. 2, 1943; 1 child, Amanda. BA in English cum laude, St. Mary's Dominican Coll., 1967; MEd in Ednl. Adminstrn. and Supervision, Tulane U., 1970; PhD in Instrnl. Systems, Fla. State U., 1979. Instr. English, St. Bernard Parish C.C., Chalmette, La., 1971-75; tchr., chmn. lang. arts dept. Chalmette H.S., 1969-75; rsch. asst. NSF Curriculum Project, Tallahassee, Fla., 1977; sr. curriculum analyst St. Charles Parish Pub.Schs., Luling, La., 1979-80; instrnl. design cons. Pan-Am. Video, New Orleans, 1980; asst. prof. dept. family medicine La. State U. Sch. Medicine, New Orleans, 1981-86, rsch. assoc. prof. dept. medicine, dept. ob-gyn., 1987-89, coord. Office Ednl. Devel. and Evaluation, 1983-89; dir. rsch. in med. evaluation, assoc. prof. dept. surgery St. Louis U. Sch. Medicine, 1989-92; adj. assoc. prof. dept. psychology St. Louis U., 1990-92; assoc. dean Student Affairs, assoc. prof. family medicine Med. Coll. of Wis., Milw., 1992-95, assoc. prof. family and cmty. medicine, 1995-96; assoc. dean Student Affairs and Admissions, assoc. prof. Tex. A&M Univ. Health Sci. Ctr. Coll. Medicine, College Station, 1996-98, vice chair acad. affairs, 1998—, vice chair family medicine dept., 1999—. Cons. med. schs., Am. Podiatric Med. Assn., U. Va. Sch. Medicine, U. Conn. Sch. Nurisng, Coll. of Medicine and Dentistry of N.J., U. Alta. Sch. Medicine, others; vis. prof. admissions McMaster Univ. Health Scis., 1994, vis. prof. U. Ariz. Sch. Medicine, Tucson, 1989; adj. prof. dept. edn. Tulane U., 1981, U. New Orleans dept. curriculum and instrn., 1981; coord. Med. Women's Conf., La. State U. Sch. Medicine, 1981, chmn. steering com. for accreditation, 1982-83. Editor: A Handbook for Residents and Medical Students, 1995; co-editor: A Manual for Attending Physicians and Residents, 1992, Clinical Teaching for Medical Residents: Roles, Techniques and Programs, 1988; assoc. editor Academic Medicine, 1990, reviewer, 1992—; reviewer Teaching and Learning in Medicine, 1988—, Ednl. Evaluation and Policy Analysis, 1986-88; contbr. articles to profl. jours., chpts. to books. Active Metairie Park Country Day Parents' Club, New Orleans, 1982-89, Tulane U. Cath. Ctr., New Orleans, 1977-89, Clayton Sch. Dist. PTO, St. Louis, 1989-92, Washington U. Newman Ctr., St. Louis, 1989-92, Holy Family Cath. Ch., Milw., 1992-96, Univ. Sch. of Milw. Parents' Assn., 1992-96, Bryn Mawr Coll. Parents' Assn., 1996—, St. Mary's Cath. Student Ctr., Tex. A&M U., 1996—; dir. ann. Notre Dame Union-Mgmt. Conf., 1953—. Recipient Meritorious Svc. award Nat. War Labor Bd., 1945, Dir.'s award for Outstanding Achievement in Indsl. Rels., Fed. Mediation and Conciliation Svc., 1992. Mem. Am. Edn. Rsch. Assn. (v.p. divsn. edn. in professions 1997-99, program com. chmn. 1992), Assn. Am. Med. Colls., Cognitive Sci. Soc., Soc. Tchrs. Family Medicine, Assn. for Profs. of Ob-Gyn., Soc. Surg. Edn., Delta Epsilon Sigma (pres. New Orleans chpt. 1973-75). Office: Tex A&M U Health Sci Ctr Coll Medicine 152 Reynolds Med Bldg College Station TX 77843-0001

EDWARDS, JOELLEN BECKETT, dean, community health nurse educator; b. Alliance, Ohio, May 25, 1951; d. Russell M. and Lois Myers Burrier. ADN, Kent State U., 1974; BSN, Ohio U., 1979, PhD in Interpersonal Comm., 1988; MSN in Primary Care, W.Va. U., 1982. RN, Tenn. From staff nurse obstet. to house supr. emergency rm. Twin City Hosp., Dennison, Ohio, 1974-78; instr. maternity nursing Muskingum Area Joint Vocat. Sch., Zanesville, Ohio, 1978-79; instr. maternal-child health nursing Belmont Tech. Coll., Clairsville, Ohio, 1979-81; staff devel. coord. maternity unit Bethesda Hosp., Zanesville, 1981-82; asst. prof. cmty. health nursing Ohio U., Athens, 1982-85; asst. prof. family and cmty. nursing Clemson U., SC, 1985-89; assoc. prof., chmn. dept. family and cmty. nursing East Tenn. State U., Johnson City, 1989-93, assoc. dean, rsch., 1993-94, dean, prof. Coll. Nursing. Apptd. to Gov. Roundtable on TennCare, 1995; presenter in field. Contbr. articles to profl. jour. Kellogg Cmty. Partnerships post-doctoral leadership devel. fellow, 1992-94. Mem. ANA, APHA, Tenn. Nurses Assn., Phi Kappa Phi, Sigma Theta Tau. Office: East Tenn State U Coll Nursing Family and Cmty Nursing Johnson City TN 37614-0002

EDWARDS, JUDITH ELIZABETH, advertising executive; b. St. Louis, May 22, 1933; d. Archie Earl and Ivy Elizabeth (Jones) Hector; m. George N. LaMont Jr., Jan. 9, 1960 (div. Oct. 1965); m. Gary W. Edwards, Nov. 25, 1966 (dec. Feb. 14, 2001); stepchildren: Michael Brent, David Reed. Grad. high sch., St. Louis, 1951; student, Brown's Bus. Coll., St. Louis. Exec. sec., asst. to chmn. Rep. Nat. Com., Washington, 1958-60; dep. to county clk. Vanderburgh County, Evansville, Ind., 1972-76; sec.-treas. Edwards Outdoor Advtg., Carmi, Ill., 1979-2000, ret., 2000. Mem. Evansville Health Planning Coun., 1974-76. Pres. White County Rep. Women's Club, Carmi, 1989—, White County Hosp. Aux. Named Ky. Col. Mem. Carmi Bus. and Profl. Women's Club (past pres.), Carmi C. of C., Kiwanis, Order Ea. Star, Sigma Alpha. Methodist. Avocation: music (vocalist for ch., civic and fraternal groups). Home: PO Box 260214 Saint Louis MO 63126-8214

EDWARDS, KASSANDRA BENNETT, psychotherapist, consultant; b. Richmond, Va., June 13, 1944; d. Edward Joseph and Jane Jeffery Stephani; m. Scott Odell Edwards, Nov. 20, 1988; m. Robert Nelson Dills, June 18, 1966 (div. June 1979). BA Psychology, Pitzer Coll., Claremont, Calif., 1966; MA, Univ. Redlands, Calif., 1982; MSW, San Francisco State Univ., Calif., 1985. Lic. marriage, family, and child therapist 1987, LCSW 1988. Social worker San Mateo County, Calif., 1970—84; counselor, parent edn. instr. Family Svc. Agy., Burlingame, Calif., 1980—86, clin. supr., 1986—93; trainer., cons. Golden Gate Trg., San Francisco, 1986—; oral examiner State of Calif., Bd. Behavioral Scis., Sacramento, 1999—2003, subject matter expert, 2002—; psychiat. social worker Kaiser Child Psychiatry Clin., San Francisco, 1996—. Contbr. scientific papers, 2002. Mem.: NASW. Achievements include co-founder San Mateo county's child sexual abuse treatment program; development of intensive outpatient program for treatment of emotionally disturbed adolescents Kaiser SSF child psychiatry clinic. Avocations: travel, bicycling, opera. Office: Kaiser Child Psychiatry Clin 801 Traeger San Bruno CA 94066 Office Phone: 650-742-2746. E-mail: scott.kassandra@sbcglobal.net.

EDWARDS, KATHLEEN, real estate broker, former educator; b. Grundy, Va., Nov. 13, 1929; d. Cornelius and Vallie Mae (Wallace) Lester; m. George Perry Bailey, July 18, 1950; children: Shearer, George, Craig; m. Richard C. Edwards, June 10, 1967; 1 child, Richard Cornelius; stepchildren: Randall, Mark, Ashley. BA, Radford (Va.) U., 1950; MEd, U. Va., 1965. Cert. tchr., Va.; lic. real estate broker. Tchr. pub. elem. schs., Va., 1950-71, 1971-73; dir., owner Fireside Sch., Va., 1973-81; real estate broker, pres., owner View Properties Inc., Va., 1977—. Mem.: DAR (regent Harmony Hall chpt. 1999—2001), Nat. Assn. Realtors. Avocations: oil and pastel painting, travel, grandchilren.

EDWARDS, KATHRYN INEZ, educational technology consultant; b. L.A., Aug. 26, 1947; d. Lloyd and Geraldine E. (Smith) Price; 1 child, Bryan. BA in English, Calif. State U., L.A., 1969; supervision credential, 1974, adminstrn. credential, 1975; MEd in Curriculum, UCLA, 1971; PhD, Claremont Grad. Sch., 1979. Tchr. L.A. Pub. Schs., 1969—78, adv. specially funded programs, 1978—80, advisor librs. and learning-resources program, 1980—81, instructional specialist, 1981—84; cons. instructional media L.A. County Office of Edn., Downey, Calif., 1984-90; coord. ednl. media and tech. Pomona (Calif.) Unified Sch. Dist., 1990-92; cons. edn. tech. Apple Computer, Inc., 1992-96; client mktg. rep. IBM; sales devel. mgr. SUN Microsys., 1999—2000; dir. mktg. Vinendi Universal Interactive Pub., 2000—02; mgr. strategic urban initiatives Apple Computer, 2002—. Cons. Walt Disney Prodns., Alfred Higging Prodns., others; mem. distance lng. think tank U.S. Office Edn., 1997. Author guides and curriculum kits. Apptd. by assembly spkr. Willie Brown to Calif. Ednl. Tech. Com., 1990-92, Calif. State Assembly Resolution from Gwen Moore, 1988, Edn. Coun. for Tech. in Learning 1993-96[illegible] Corp. co-owners, 1991-92. Recipient cert. commendation Senator Diane Watson, 1988, Mabel Wilson Richards scholar, 1968, Calif. Congress Parents and Tchrs. scholar, 1968, UCLA fellow, 1968; named Outstanding Woman of Yr. L.A. Sentinel, 1987. Mem. ASCD, Nat. Assn. Minority Polit. Women, Internat. Reading Assn. (spkr. nat. conv. 1988), L.A. Reading Assn. (pres.), Calif. Assn. Tchrs. of English (conf. del. 1982), Calif. Media and Libr. Educators Assn. (state conf. co-chair 1989, v.p. legal divsn. 1992—), Nat. Assn. Media Women (Media Woman of Yr. 1987), Alpha Kappa Alpha. Democrat. Roman Catholic. Avocations: reading, gardening, travel. Office: IBM Corp 400 N Brand Blvd Glendale CA 91203-2311 E-mail: Kathryne1@attbi.com.

EDWARDS, LINDA L. former elementary education educator; Tchr. Highland Park Elem. Sch., Lewistown, Mont.; ret., 1999. Named Mont. State Elem. Tchr. of Yr., 1993. Office: Highland Park Elem Sch 1312 7th Ave N Lewistown MT 59457-2112

EDWARDS, LORI, state legislator; b. Jersey City, N.J., Apr. 7, 1957; Student, Mercer U., 1975-78; BA in Bus. Adminstrn., Warner So. Coll., 1992. Mem. Fla. Ho. of Reps., Tallahassee, 1992—; mem. acad. excellence, econ. impact justice couns. Mem. bd. dirs. Winter Haven Cmty. Girls' Clubs, 1983-85; mem. adv. bd. Fla. Lng. Diagnosite Resource Ctr., 1984, Polk C.C. New Beginnings, 1990-94; publicity chair Fla. Spl. Olympics, 1986; active United Way, Polk County. Recipient Spl. Recognition award Fraternal Order of Police, 1993, 100 Percent Voting Record award Polk Edn. Assn., 1993, Legislator of Yr. award Fla. Pub. Libr. Assn. Cmty. Svc. Recognition award Landmark Christian Elem. Sch., 1994. Mem. Rotary Internat. Lutheran. Avocations: water sports, reading. Office: Fla Capitol 402 S Monroe St Rm 1401 Tallahassee FL 32399-6526 also: 201 S Main St Auburndale FL 33823

EDWARDS, LYDIA JUSTICE, state official; b. Carter County, Ky., July 9, 1937; d. Chead and Velva (Kinney) Justice; m. Frank B. Edwards, 1968; children: Mark, Alexandra, Margot. Student, San Francisco State U. Began career as acct.; then Idaho state rep., 1982-86; treas. State of Idaho, 1987-99. Legis. asst. to Gov. Hickel, Alaska, 1967; conf. planner Rep. Gov.'s Assn., 1970-73; mem. Rep. Nat. Commn., 1972, del. to nat. conv., 1980, 96. Mem. Rep. Womens Fedn. Congregationalist.

EDWARDS, LYNN A. retired school system administrator; b. Cicero, IL, Apr. 1, 1923; d. Calvin S. Yakley and Linda Olson; m. Edward M. Edwards; children: Dean, Dyke, Elizabeth. BA, U. Ill., 1944; MEd, U. Toledo, 1975. Secondary tchr. Sylvania Schs., Sylvania, Ohio, 1968—70, media specialist, 1971—83, sch. adminstr., 1984—86. Named Ironman Triathlon World Champion, 1992—93; recipient Olympic Distance World Triathlon Champion, Can., 2001, Long Course World Champion, Ind., 1997, numerous championships in marathons and running events.; fellow Fulbright scholar to India, U.S. Congress, 1980 and, 1984. Avocation: participating in numerous running events.

EDWARDS, MARIE D. social services administrator; b. Cin., Sept. 17, 1943; d. George Junior Denning and Lola Dortheia Jackson; children: Daniel J., Grayson G.; m. Terrance Anthony Edwards Sr., July 24, 1982; stepchildren: Terrance A. Edwards, Troy Edwards, Heather Kraus. Owner, mgr. Greendale Grill, Lawrenceburg, Ind., 1980-86, M.E. & Assocs. Realtors, Vevay, Ind., 1986-93; mgr. Coldwell Banker, Lawrenceburg, 1993-98; exec. dir. Dearborn Adult Ctr., Lawrenceburg, 1998—. Bd. dirs. Southea. Ind. Econ. Opportunity Ctr., 1995—; chairperson I Love Lawrenceburg com., 1999—, Bicentennial City of Lawrenceburg, 2001—. Named Cmty. Leader 2000, Lawrenceburg C. of C., 2001; recipient Dearborn County award for svc. and humanitarian effort, 2001. Mem. Dearborn County C. of C. (gov.'s com. transp., Cmty. Leader of Yr. 2001, 02), Southea. Women's Network (pres. 2000-2001), Southea. Bd. Realtors (treas. 1990), Order Ea. Star (assoc. matron). Democrat. Methodist. Avocation: gardening. Office: Dearborn Adult Ctr Inc 311 W Tate St Lawrenceburg IN 47025 E-mail: maedwards@seidata.com.

EDWARDS, MICHELLE DENISE, professional basketball player; b. Mar. 6, 1966; Degree in gen. studies, Iowa State U., 1988. Basketball player, Faenza, Italy, 1989-90, Pistoia, Italy, 1990-93, Ferrara, Italy, 1993-95, Pavia, Italy, 1995-97; basketball player Cleveland Rockers Women's NBA, Cleve., 1997—. Mem. Olympic Festival Team, 1985; recipient Bronze medal Pan Am. Games, 1991; named MVP Italian League All-Star team, 1997. Office: Cleveland Rockers Gund Arena One Center Ct Cleveland OH 44115

EDWARDS, PATRICIA BURR, small business owner, counselor, consultant; b. Oakland, Calif., Feb. 19, 1918; d. Myron Carlos and Claire Idelle (Laingor) Burr; m. Jackson Edwards, Nov. 14, 1942; children: Jill Forman-Young, Jan Kurzweil. AB, U. So. Calif., 1939, MSEd, 1981. Prin. Constructive Leisure, L.A., 1968—. Spkr. in field; writer, prodr. counseling materials for career, leisure, life planning including computer software, audio cassettes and assessment surveys. Author: You've Got to Find Happiness: It Won't Find You, 1971, Leisure Counseling Techniques: Individual and Group Counseling Step-by-Step, 1975, 3d edit., 1980; (software) Leisure PREF, 1986, Over 50: Needs, Values, Attitudes, 1988, Adapting to Change: The NVAB Program, 1997; contbr. articles to profl. jours., mags. and books. Chmn. L.A. County Foster Families 50th Anniversary, 1962-64, L.A. Jr. League Sustainers, 1964-65, Hollywood Bowl Vols., L.A., 1960-61, Hollywood Bowl Patroness com., 1961—. Mem. Am. Counseling Assn., Calif. Assn. for Counseling and Devel., Nat. Recreation and Park Assn., Assn. for Adult Devel. and Aging, Trojan League, Travellers Aid Soc. L.A., Jr. League L.A., First Century Families of L.A., Delta Gamma. Republican. Episcopalian. Avocations: family activities, singing, dance, pets, learning.

EDWARDS, PATRICIA KLOBUS, former dean, architecture/urban studies educator; m. John N. Edwards; children: John, Michael, Christine, David, Richard, Jay. BS in Mus. Edn., SUNY, Potsdam, 1957; MS in Sociology, Va. Tech., 1970, PhD in Sociology, 1974. From asst. prof. to prof. urban affairs and planning Va. Poly. Inst. and State U., Blacksburg, 1974-99, asst. dean, 1989-92, dean, 1993-97. Co-chair Internat. Conf. on Housing in the 21st Century, Alexandria, Va., 1997. Co-editor: SUNY Series in Urban Public Policy, 1989—; cons. editor Jour. Applied Behavioral Sci., 1984-89; founding editor Jour. Urban Affairs, 1980-85, mem. editl. bd., 1985-90; contbr. more than 50 articles to profl. publs. on program evaluation and pub. policy analysis for internat., fed., state, and local govt. agys. Recipient numerous grants. Mem. Internat. Sociol. Assn. (sec.-treas. rsch. com. for housing and the built environment 1994-98, v.p. 1999—). Office: Va Poly Inst and State U Architecture & Urban Study 201 Architecture Annex Blacksburg VA 24061-0205

EDWARDS, PRISCILLA ANN, paralegal, business owner; b. Orlando, Fla., Sept. 28, 1947; d. William Granville and Bernice Royster; m. Charles R. King, Apr. 2, 1981. Paralegal cert., U. Calif., Berkeley, 1994. Paralegal Charles R. Garry Esquire, San Francisco, 1989-90; owner, mgr. Fed. Legal Resources, San Francisco, 1991—. Speaker Sonoma State U., Santa Rosa, Calif., 1993. Publisher: (book) Zero Weather, 1981. Recipient Wiley W. Manuel award for pro bono legal svcs. Bd. Govs. State Bar of Calif., 1994, 95, 96, 97, 98. Episcopalian. Avocations: horseback riding, mountain biking. Home: 2173 Francisco Blvd E Ste K1 San Rafael CA 94901-5523

EDWARDS, ROBIN MORSE, lawyer; b. Glens Falls, N.Y., Dec. 9, 1947; d. Daniel and Harriet Morse; m. Richard Charles Edwards, Aug. 30, 1970; children: Michael Alan, Jonathan Philip. BA, Mt. Holyoke Coll., 1969; JD, U. Calif., Berkeley, 1972. Bar: Calif. 1972. Assoc. Donahue, Gallagher, Thomas & Woods, Oakland, Calif., 1972—77, ptnr., 1977—89, Sonnenschein, Nath & Rosenthal, San Francisco, 1989—, mgmt. com., 1998—. Bd. dirs. Temple Sinai, 1997-2002. Mem. ABA, Calif. Bar Assn., Alameda County Bar Assn. (bd. dirs. 1978-84, v.p. 1982, pres. 1983), Alameda County Bar Found. (bd. dirs. 1998-2000). Jewish. Avocations: skiing, cooking. Office: Sonnenschein Nath Rosenthal 685 Market St 6th Fl San Francisco CA 94105-4202 E-mail: redwards@sonnenschein.com.

EDWARDS, SARAH ALEXANDER, minister, educator; b. N.Y.C., Feb. 17, 1921; d. James S. and Hortense Clapp (Heywood) Alexander; m. Robert L. Edwards, Sept. 6, 1947; children: Edith Heywood, James Deane. AB cum laude, Bryn Mawr (Pa.) Coll., 1943; MDiv, Union Theol. Sem., 1950; STM, Hartford Sem., 1966, PhD, 1974. Ordained to ministry Congregational Ch., 1951. Interim pastor various chs., 1951-61; v.p. Ct. Fellowship of Congrl. Christian Women; adj. prof. bibl. studies Hartford Sem., 1976—. Coauthor: Christological Perspectives, 1984, Christology in Dialogue, 1993. Bd. dirs. Union Theol. Sem., N.Y.C., 1962-77. Democrat. Avocations: skiing, hiking, swimming, canoeing. Home: 275 Steele Rd West Hartford CT 06117-2716

EDWARDS, SARAH ANNE, radio, cable TV personality, clinical social worker; b. Tulsa, Jan. 7, 1943; d. Clyde Elton and virginia Elizabeth Glandon; m. Paul Robert Edwards, Apr. 24, 1965; 1 son, Jon Scott. BA with distinction, U. Mo., Kansas City, 1965; MSW, U. Kans., 1974. Cmty. rep. OEO, Kans. City Regional Office, 1966-68; social svc./parent involvement and resource specialist Office of Child Devel., HEW, Kansas City, Kans., 1968-73; dir. tng. social svcs. dept., children's rehab. unit U. Affiliated Facility, U. Kans. Med. Ctr., Kansas City, 1975-76; co-dir. Cathexis Inst. S., Glendale, Calif., 1976-77; pvt. practice psychotherapy, tng. and cons. personal and interpersonal, orgnl. behavior, Sierra Madre, Calif., 1973-80; sys. operator CompuServe Info. Svc., 1983-98. Prodr., co-host radio show Working From Home, on Bus. Talk Radio, 1988-01; co-host cable show Working from Home Scripp's Howard Home and Garden Cable TV Network, 1995-97; commentator CNBC, 1996-99, NPR Marketplace, 1996-97. Columnist for Home Office Computing Mag., 1988-97, Your Home Office, L.A. Times Syndicate, 1997-99, Entrepreneur's Home Office, 1998—, Price CostCo Connection, 1994—, Inc-Com., 2000—; co-author: How to Make Money with Your Personal Computer, 1997, Getting Business to Come to You, 1998, Working From Home, rev. edit., 1999, Secrets of Self-Employment, 1996, Finding Your Perfect Work, 1996, Teaming Up, 1997, Home Businesses You Can Buy, 1997, Cool Careers for Dummies, 1998, Making Money in Cyberspace, 1998, Best Home Business for the 21st Century, 1999, Working From Home, 1999, The Practical Dreamer's Handbook, 2000, Home-Based Business for Dummies, 2000, Changing Directions without Losing Your Way, 2001, Entrepreneurial Parent, 2002, Sitting with the Enemy, A Novel, 2002, Why Aren't You Your Own Boss?, 2003. Dir. nature-guided counseling programs Pine Mountain Inst., 2001. Address: Box 6775 2624 Teakwood Ct Frazier Park CA 93222 Office Phone: 661-242-2624. E-mail: sedwards@frazmtn.com.

EDWARDS, SARAH R. state representative; b. Ft. Lauderdale, Fla., Jan. 1, 1953; m. Blake Ross; 2 children. BS in Biology and Ecology, Marlboro Coll., 1978; MS in Orgn. and Mgmt., Antioch U., 1996; grad. in govt., Vt. Leadership Inst., 2002. State rep. State of Vt., 2003—. Vice chair Brattleboro Selectboard; chair Town fin. com.; mem. Planning Commn., Econ. Develop. Subcom., Agrl. Adv. Com., Capital Grant Rev. Bd., Rental Housing Improvement Program, Town Com. Alternative Revenue Sources, Town Meeting Rep., Cities for Climate Protection; pres. bd. dirs. Brattleboro Food Coop.; bd. dirs. Brattleboro Area Hospice, Green Mountain Tng. Ctr. for Healthy Schs. and Communities, Media Knowledge; project dir. NSF Found. Rsch. Project, Boston; pres. bd. dirs. Belle of Brattleboro. Home: 44 Chapin St Brattleboro VT 05301 Office: 28 Loomis St 05602 E-mail: sedwards@let.state.vt.us.

EDWARDS, SHARON MARIE, minister, educator; b. Akron, Ohio, Jan. 28, 1944; d. Michael Robert Batche and Kathleen Marie Austin; m. Ronald Payne Edwards, Apr. 4, 1970; children: Carrie JoAnn, Suzanne Kathleen. BA, Malone U., 1971. Lic. pastor Ohio, 1977. Pastor Abundant Life Ministries, Akron, Ohio, 1977—78; founder and sr. pastor Harvest Christian Ctrs., Internat., North Canton, Ohio, 1978—. Adv. bd. Living Water Tchg., Internat., Caddo Mills, Tex.; fin. sec. Living Water Ch., Akron; mem. fin. bd. Sherwood Pk. Baptist, Akron; spkr. in field. Author bible studies materials, (corr. course) Foundations Series, 1999—2003. Recipient Voices award, Nat. Campaign Influential Women USA, 2003. Mem.: Women's Missionary Union (mem. state bd. 1972—74). Avocations: travel, bible studies. Office: Harvest Christian Ctrs Internat 116 9th St NW North Canton OH 44720 Office Phone: 330-499-5683.

EDWARDS, SHEILA M. banker, educator; b. Arab, Ala., Aug. 10, 1960; d. Raymond O'Neal and Nellie Marie Moody; m. Justion Kyle Edwards, Dec. 17, 1976; children: Melissa LaAnn, Justina Marie. AS, Jefferson State U., Pinson, Ala., 1982; student, Am. Inst. Banking, Birmingham, Ala., 1992, 93. Asst. head teller Leeth Nat. Bank, Cullman, Ala., 1982-83; loan asst. v.p. Regions Bank, Oneonta, Ala., 1987-93; br. mgr. Valley Fin., Guntersville, Ala., 1993-95; adminstrv. mgr. Lowe's, Cullman, 1995-96; comml. lending SouthTrust Bank, Guntersville, 1996-99; v.p. EvaBank, Cullman, 1999—; tchr. fin. Am. Inst. Banking-Wallace State, Cullman, 1999—; br. mgr. Colonial Bank, Locust Fork, Ala., 2001—03; v.p., trainer, security officer Cmty. Bank, Blountsville, Ala., 2003—. Trainer/spkr., pres. trainer/seminars in fin., career success, customer svc. Edwards Profl. Svc. Troop leader Girls Scouts U.S., Blountsville, Ala., coord., 1984—91. Mem.: Bount W Bus. and Profl. Women (pres. 2002—), Cullman Bus. and Profl. Women (pres. 2001—), Ala. Bus. Women (bd. dirs.), Bus. and Profl. Women (v.p. 2000, pres. 2001—), Fin. Women Internat. (pres. Mountain Valley group 1999—2000, state officer 2001—, Ala. v.p. 2002—03, Ala. state officer of edn., tng., state pres. 2003—), C. of C. Office: PO Box 1000 Blountsville AL 35031 E-mail: jsedward@urisp.net.

EDWARDS, SUSAN M. hotel executive; b. Bristol, Eng., Jan. 2, 1953; Student in English lit., 1970. Office mgr. Godfrey Davis Internat., San Francisco, 1970's; dir. sales Karageorgis Cruises, San Francisco, 1980's; regional sales dir., then nat. sales dir. Aston Hotels and Resorts, Hawaii, 1981-91, assoc. v.p., 1981-91; pres. Delfin Hotels & Resorts, Santa Cruz, Calif., 1991—. Avocation: dogs. Office: 2840 College Ave Ste A Berkeley CA 94705-2148

EDWARDS, SYLVIA ANN, artist; b. Boston, Jan. 30, 1937; d. Junius Griffiths and Sylvia Emma (Mailloux) E.; m. Sadredin M. Golestaneh (div.); children: Shirin, Nader, Leila. Diploma, Mass. Coll. of Art, Boston, 1957, Boston Mus. of Fine Arts, 1958; postgrad., Modern Art Studies, London, 1980-81. One-woman shows include CCA Gallery, Oxford, Eng., 1996, Munson Gallery, Chatham, Mass., 1992, Jaeshke Gallery, Braunschweig, Germany, 1991, Natalie Knight Gallery, Johannesburg, South Africa, 1991, Bankamura, Tokyo, 1991, Gallery K. Hyazaki Perfecture, 1991, The Berkeley Sq. Gallery, London, 1991, CCA Gallery, 2003, numerous others, exhibited in group shows at Cadogan Contemporary Art, London, 1996, Berkeley Sq. Gallery, Korea Art Expo, Seoul, 1996, 2002, N.Y. Art Expo, N.Y.C., 1994, Lond Internat. Contemporary Art Fair, 1989, The Bath Arts Festival, Eng., 1988, Paris Art Salon, 1986, 1987, 1988, Sarasota Visual Art Ctr., numerous others, Represented in permanent collections Nat. Mus. for Women in the Arts, Washington, Boston U. Spl. Collections, Cape Mus Fine Arts, Dennis, Mass, Mus. Fine Arts, Alexandria, Egypt, Governorate of Alexandria, Mass. Gen. Hosp., Boston, Chelsea Westminster Hosp., London, Midwest Mus. Am. Art, Elkhart, Ind., Tate Gallery, London, publs., Valley of Sils, Lithograph, 1982, N.Mex. Watch, lithograph, 1982, covers, Arts Rev., 1982, 1985, others, numerous, UNICEF cards, Greenpeace publs., World Wildlife/U.K., book covers, reference and art books, others, monograph, Pallas Athere, London, 2003. Mem. U.K. UNICEF Com. Mem. London Royal Acad., World Watercolor Soc., Chelsea Arts Club/London. Avocations: writing, theatre, travel, swimming, reading. Studio: 14 Cadogan Square London SW1X 0JU England

EDWARDS-LEBOEUF, RENEE CAMILLE, public relations professional, logistics engineer; b. Falls Church, Va., Aug. 6, 1961; d. Walter Thomas and Elizabeth Ann Holt. BS, George Mason U., Fairfax, 1983; MS, Central Mich. U., Merrifield, 1988; grad. program mgmt. course, Def. Systems Mgmt. Coll., 1990. Cert. contracting officer's rep. Logistics analyst The BDM Corp., McLean, Va., 1983-85; deputy program mgr. COMARCO/IBS, Arlington, Va., 1985-88; logistics mgr., speaker, briefer SWL, Inc., Arlington, Va., 1988-89; mem. profl. staff Def. Systems Mgmt. Coll., Ft. Belvoir, Va., 1989-92; dir. computer-aided acquisition and logistics support tng. and edn. Office Asst. Sec. of Def. Prodn. and Logistics, Falls Church, Va., 1992-93; dir. pub. affairs U.S. Dept. Commerce, Nat. Tech. Info. Svc., Springfield, Va., 1993—. Co-chmn. computer aided acquisition Logistics Systems Rsch. Group. Contbr. articles to profl. jours. Bd. dirs. Woodwalk Condominium, Burke, Va., 1987-96, mem. indsl. tech. adv. com., 1997-99. Named Best Speaker Toastmasters, McLean, 1985, Best Evaluator Toastmasters, McLean, 1985; recipient Excellence award Dept. Def., 1993, Outstanding Svc. award Dept. Commerce, 1996. Mem. Soc. of Logistics Engrs., Pub. Rels. Soc. Am. Republican. Avocations: racquetball, cycling, embroidery, guitar. Office: US Dept Commerce NTIS 5285 Port Royal Rd Springfield VA 22161-0001

EDWARDSON, SANDRA, dean, nursing educator; Dean Sch. Nursing, U Minn., Mpls. Office: U Minn Twin Cities Sch Nursing 6-101 Weaver-Densford Hall 308 Harvard St SE Minneapolis MN 55455-0353

EFFEL, LAURA, lawyer; b. Dallas, May 9, 1945; d. Louis E. and Fay (Lee) Ray; m. Marc J. Patterson, Sept. 19, 1992 (dec. July 30, 2002); 1 child, Stephen Patterson. BA, U. Calif., Berkeley, 1971; JD, U. Md., 1975. Bar: N.Y. 1976, U.S. Dist. Ct. (so. and ea. dists.) N.Y. 1976, U.S. Ct. Appeals (2d cir.) 1980, U.S. Supreme Ct. 1980, D.C. 1993, N.C. 1998, Va. 2001. Assoc. Burns Jackson Miller Summit & Jacoby, N.Y.C., 1975-78, Pincus Munzer Bizar & D'Alessandro, N.Y.C., 1978-80; v.p., sr. assoc. counsel Chase Manhattan Bank, N.A., N.Y.C., 1980-96; counsel Baker & McKenzie, N.Y.C., 1996-99; gen. counsel Garban Cos., 1999-2000; counsel Flippin Densmore Morse & Jessee, Roanoke, Va., 2000—02, ptnr., 2002—. Bd. dirs. Blue Ridge Pub. TV, 2001—. Mem. Workforce Devel. Com., New Century Tech. Coun.; bd. dirs. Bklyn. Legal Svcs. Corp. A, 1992-2000. Mem.: ABA (com. pretrial practice 2000—03, litig. sect. co-chair, subcom. atty. client privilege), Roanoke Bar Assn., Va. Bar Assn., NC Bar Assn., Am. Corp. Counsel Assn. (dir. emeritus, pro bono svc. award 1989). Office: Flippin Densmore Morse & Jessee Drawer 1200 Roanoke VA 24006 Office Phone: 540-510-3026.

EFROS, ELLEN ANN, lawyer; b. N.Y.C., Jan. 18, 1950; d. Edwin David and Judith (Breitman) E.; m. Fritz R. Kahn, June 26, 1983. BA, Case Western Res. U., 1971; MA, St. John's U., 1973; JD, Hofstra U., 1978. Bar: D.C. 1978, N.Y. 1979, Md. 1990, U.S. Ct. Appeals (5th cir.) 1978, U.S. Ct. Appeals (2d, 7th and D.C. cirs.) 1979, U.S. Ct. Appeals (Fed. cir.) 1993, U.S. Dist. Ct. D.C. 1981, U.S. Ct. Claims 1986, U.S. Supreme Ct. 1989. Trial atty. ICC Gen. Counsel, Washington, 1978-79; assoc. Verner & Liipfert, Washington, 1979-81; ptnr. Vorys, Sater, Seymour & Pease, Washington, 1981-97; hearing officer, office dispute resolution NASD Regulation, Inc., Washington, 1997-2000; ptnr. Rader, Fishman & Grauer, Washington, 2000—. Asst. editor Antitrust Law Jour., 1987-90. Mem. ABA (sects. intellectual property and litigation), D.C. Bar Assn., N.Y. Bar Assn., Md. Bar Assn. Office: Rader Fishman & Grauer 1233 20th St NW Ste 501 Washington DC 20036-2365 E-mail: eae@raderfishman.com.

EGAN, LORA RAE, music educator; b. St. Cloud, Minn., Aug. 8, 1973; d. Charles Dean and Wanda Lou Anderson; m. Sean Christopher Egan, Sept. 23, 2000; 1 child, J.J. B Music Edn., S.D. State U., 1997. Dir. instrumental music Marion (S.D.) Pub. Schs., 1998—2002; instrumental dir. Sioux Falls Pub. Schs., 2002—03; owner pvt. percussion studio, 2003—. Pvt. percussion instr. with area schs. Performer: (percussionist) Swiss Chorale, Schmeck Fest Pit Orch., 2001—; band dir. Marion City Band, 1999—2002; photographer (book) Sketches of the Eye, 2001. Recipient Outstanding Svc. as an Educator award, Congl. Youth Leadership Coun., 2001. Mem.: Music Educators Nat. Conf., Marion Tchrs. Assn. (pres. 2001—02), Women Band Dirs., Percussive Arts Soc. Avocations: music, tennis. Home: 5500 W 44th St Apt 1 Sioux Falls SD 57106 Office: Sioux Falls Pub Schs Sioux Falls SD E-mail: drummergirl1@moose-mail.com.

EGAN, MARSHA CHRISTINE, school psychologist; b. Schenectady, N.Y., Oct. 8, 1946; d. Edwin G. and Doris (Brownell) E.; m. Kurt Patrick Riesenberg. BA in Liberal Arts and Social Scis., Buffalo State Coll., 1968; MS in Elem. Edn., Syracuse U., 1981, postgrad.; MS, cert. advanced study sch. psychology, SUNY, Oswego, 1988. Cert. in edn. and sch. psychology, N.Y. Tchr. elem. edn. Liverpool (N.Y.) Schs., 1968-69, St. Rose of Lima Sch., North Syracuse, N.Y., 1981-83; tchr. Tappan (N.Y.) Elem. Sch., South Orangetown Sch. Dist., 1969-71; sch. psychologist Liverpool Ctrl. Schs., 1988—. Cons., evaluator Learning Disabilities Assn., Syracuse; presenter Nat. Coun. for Family Rels. Conf., Milw., 1998, Ann. Conf. Nat. Assn. for Edn. of Young, Rochester, N.Y., 1999. Columnist Ptnrs. in Parenting, Syracuse Herald Jour., 1998—. Avocations: stained glass work, newspaper writing on children and families. Home: 6050 Bannister Dr Cicero NY 13039-8309 Office: Liverpool Ctrl Schs Donlin Drive Elem Sch Liverpool NY 13039

EGAN, MARTHA AVALEEN, history educator, archivist, consultant; b. Kingsport, Tenn., Feb. 26, 1956; d. Jack E. and Opal (Pugh) E. BS in Comm., U. Tenn., 1978; MA in History, East Tenn. State U., 1986; postgrad., U. Ky., 1986-89, Milligan Coll., 1990. Cert. tchr., Tenn.; cert. Am. Acad. Cert. Archivists. News reporter, anchor WJCW-AM/WQUT-FM, Johnson City, Tenn., 1980-82; staff asst. 1st Dist. Office U.S. Senator Jim Sasser, Blountville, Tenn., 1982-84; instr. history East Tenn. State U., Johnson City, 1984-86; tchg. asst. dept. history U. Ky., Lexington, 1986-89; rschr./writer history project Eastman Chem. Co., Kingsport, 1991; adj. faculty history and humanities N.E. State Tech. C.C., Blountville, 1992—93, adj. faculty humanities, 2000—03; archivist Kingsport Pub. Libr. and Archives, 1993—2002; adj. asst. prof. history King Coll., Bristol, Tenn., 1994-99; adj. faculty history Emory and Henry Coll., Emory, Va., 2002—. Author: Images of America: Kingsport, 1998; rschr., writer: Eastman Chemical Company: Years of Glory, Times of Change, 1991; contbr. Ency. of Appalachia, Tenn. Ency. History and Culture, Ency. of the Harlem Renaissance, Ency. of Am. Indsl. History, Dictionary of Am. History. Vice chair Sullivan County Dem. Party, 1992-93; rec. sec. Sullivan County Dem. Women's Club, 1992, corr. sec., 1994; mem. Kingsport Symphony Chorus, sec.-treas., 1994-95; mem. East Tenn. Camerata, Johnson City Civic Chorale; mem. flute choir First Broad St. Meth. Ch.; mem. St. Christopher's Episcopal Ch. Mem. AAUW (Kingsport chpt.), Orgn. Am. Historians, Appalachian Studies Assoc., Soc. Am. Archivists, Tenn. Archivists, Kingsport Music Club (corr. sec. 1995-97), Sullivan County Hist. Soc. (bd. dirs.), Nat. Flute Assn., Phi Alpha Theta, Pi Gamma Mu, Sigma Delta Chi. Avocations: flute, photography. Home: 544 Rambling Rd Kingsport TN 37663

EGAN, MOIRA, poet, educator; b. Baltimore, Md., July 21, 1962; d. Michael and Betty Egan. B.A., Bryn Mawr Coll., 1980—85; M.A., Johns Hopkins U., 1993—94; M.F.A., Columbia U., 1990—92. Tchr., english & creative writing Catonsville H.S., Catonsville, Md., 2002—; lectr. in english Morgan State U., Balt., 2002—02, Towson U., Towson, Md., 2001—01; instr., ib english Anatolia Coll., Thessaloniki, Greece, 1998—2001; cmty. rels. mgr. Barnes & Noble, NYC, 1997—98; cons. curricular outreach U. Md. Ctr. Visual Arts and Culture, 2003—. Poetry editor Link: A Critical Jour. on the Arts, Balt., 2002—; host, readings for reading benefit series The Learning Bank, Balt., 2002; mem.; contbr. to pedagogical papers sessions Associated Writing Programs, 2001—. Author: (poems) The Garden of Her Choosing (Spl. Merit award, Mayor's Adv. Com. on Arts & Culture, 1994), Poetry, Boulevard, American Letters & Commentary, Laurel Review, Smartish Pace, West Branch, Poems & Plays, Poet Lore, and in numerous other journals., nominated for the Pushcart Prize, 1994, 2002, anthology, Kindled Terraces: American Poets in Greece, Cleave (First Book award, 2004); multi-media visual piece, Elegy. Vol. Com. to Re-elect the Mayor, Balt., 2003. Recipient David Craig Austin Prize, The Writing Divsn., Columbia U., 1992, Campbell Corner Poetry Prize, 2nd Pl., Campbell Corner, 2002; Grad. Writing fellowship, Columbia U., 1990—92, Grad. Tchg. fellowship, Johns Hopkins U., 1993—94. Mem.: Assoc. Writing Programs. Avocations: yoga, travel, reading. Personal E-mail: moirae333@earthlink.net.

EGBERT, DONNA, elementary school educator; b. Evansville, Ind., Mar. 3, 1947; d. Arthur Ralph and Helen Daphine E. BME, Murray State U., 1969; MAE, Western Ky. U., 1979. Jr. high school band dir. Marion County Public Schs., Lebanon, Ky., 1969-79; teacher Catholic Schs., Louisville, 1979-85, Breckinridge County Schs., Hardinsburg, Ky., 1988—. Teacher rep. Site Based Decision Making Coun., Custer, Ky., 1994—, elementary academic team Custer Elementary, 1988—. Mem. Delta Kappa Gamma Soc. Internat. (2nd. v.p., 1998—), Sigma Alpha Iota-Womens Music Fraternity (life, chaplain, 1968-69). Avocations: walking, singing in choral groups. Home: 408 Natalie Dr Elizabethtown KY 42701-9423 Office: Custer Elementary Sch PO Box 9 Custer KY 40115-0009 E-mail: egbertd@excite.com.

EGEN, MAUREEN MAHON, publishing executive; BA, Trinity Coll., 1964. Editl. trainee and numerous other positions Doubleday & Co., Inc., 1964; mng. dir. Doubleday Book Clubs, 1979, pub., editl. dir., 1981; editor-in-cheif Warner Hardcover Books Time Warner Book Group, 1990—98, pres., chief oper. officer, 1998—. Co-chair ann. book fair Goddard Riverside Cmty. Ctr.; mem. diversity steering com. Time Warner Book Group. Bd. dirs. The Ctr. Ind. of Disabled, N.Y.C. Mem.: Assn. Am. Pubs. (mem. freedom to read com.), Women's Media Group. Office: Time Warner Book Group 1271 Ave of Ams New York NY 10020

EGER, DENISE LEESE, rabbi; b. New Kensington, Pa., Mar. 14, 1960; d. Bernard D. and Estelle (Leese) E. BA in Religion, U. So. Calif., 1982; MA in Hebrew Letters, Hebrew Union Coll., L.A., 1985; Rabbi, Hebrew Union Coll., N.Y.C., 1988. Ordained rabbi, 1988. Chaplain Rabbi Beth Chayim Chadashim, L.A., 1988-92; founding rabbi Congregation Kol Ami, West Hollywood, Calif., 1992—. Columnist Edge mag., Lesbian News; contbr. articles to religious publs., chpts. to anthologies. Mem. cmty. adv. bd. Shanti Found.; treas. So. Calif. Bd. Rabbis; chair Task Force on Gays and Lesbians in the Rabbinate. Recipient Rainbow Key award City West Hollywood, L.A.C.E. Spirituality award L.A. Gay and Lesbian Ctr., Angel Amidst award City of West Hollywood. Mem. Cen. Conf. Am. Rabbis, Interfaith Clergy Assn. (past chair gays and lesbians bd.). Avocation: guitar. Office: 1200 Larrabee St West Hollywood CA 90069-2060

EGGEN, BELINDA LAY, education educator; b. Albemarle, NC, Sept. 17, 1952; d. Bobby Grier and Elizabeth White Lay; m. David Paul Eggen, Dec. 31, 1993; children: Jennifer Hackenholt Tillman, Charity Suzanne. BA in English, U. N.C., Charlotte, 1973, MEd in Curriculum and Instrnl. Supervision, 1988; PhD in Edn., U. S.C., 2001. Cert. early childhood edn. S.C., 1973, reading recovery Clemson U., 1991, curriculum and instrnl. supervision N.C., 1988, elem. edn. N.C., 1973, elem. prin. S.C., 1989. K-2 multiage classroom tchr. Charlotte-Mecklenburg Schs., Charlotte, NC, 1973—75; instr., advancement studies dept. Ctrl. Piedmont C.C., Charlotte, NC, 1978—81; tchr., grades 4-5 Charlotte Cath. Schools, Charlotte, NC, 1981—83; chpt. 1 reading tchr., grades 2-6 Union County Schs., Monroe, NC, 1984—86; chpt. 1 after sch. coodinator Charlotte-Mecklenburg Schs., Charlotte, NC, 1986—88; dist. office math coord. Horry County Schs., Conway, SC, 1988—93, asst. prin. Myrtle Beach, 1993—99; asst. prof. edn. W.Va. State Coll., Institute, W.Va., 1999—2001; coord. mater of arts in tchg. program U. of SC, Columbia, SC, 1999—2001; program dir., early childhood edn. U. S.C., Beaufort, 2003—. Contbr. articles to profl. jours., chapters to books. Fellow: S.C. Coun. Tchrs. of Math. (assoc.; sec. 1996—98), Horry-Georgetown Math. Advancement Coun. (assoc.; pres. 1989—91), Internat. Reading Assn. (assoc.; v.p. 1981—83); mem.: S.C. Assn. of Tchr. Educators, Reading Recovery Assn., Nat. Coun. of Teachers of English (assoc.), Assn. of Am. Colleges of Tchr. Edn. (assoc.), Nat. Assn. for the Edn. of Young Children (assoc.). Roman Catholic. Avocations: boating, African safaris, tutoring students. Office: U SC 801 Carteret St Beaufort SC 29902 Office Phone: 843-521-3128. E-mail: bleggenØ@gwm.sc.edu.

EGGERSMAN, DENISE, computer engineer, educator; b. Orange, Calif., Feb. 22, 1954; d. Arthur Fred and Margaret Frances Eggersman. BS, Kennesaw State U., 1998; MS, U. Phoenix, Ariz., 2002; PhD, U. Phoenix, 2002—. Systems adminstrn. Smallwood, Reynolds, Stewart & Stewart, Atlanta, 1983—89; trainer/adminstr. Ctrl. Health, Atlanta, 1989—91; cons. Software Assist, Duluth, Ga., 1991—97; LAN adminstrn. IBM, Atlanta, 1997; project mgmt. Hewlett-Packard, Atlanta, 1998; sales/network engr. Verizon Comm., Alpharetta, Ga., 1999—2001; coll. prof. Chattahoochee Tech. Coll., Marietta, Ga., 2003, Capella U., Mpls., 2003—. Vol. Hands on Atlanta, 2003. Mem.: IEEE (assoc.), Women in Tech. (assoc.), Tech. Assn. Ga. (assoc.). Home: PO Box 965452 Marietta GA 30066 Office: Chattahoochee Tech Coll 980 South Cobb Dr Marietta GA 30066 also: Grad Sch of Tech Copella Univ Minneapolis MN 55402 Personal E-mail: deggersman@prodigy.net. E-mail: deggersman@chat.tec.com.

EHDE, AVA LOUISE, librarian, educator; b. Buffalo, Feb. 11, 1963; d. Louise and Robert Andrew Kinn(Stepfather), Henry Emil Nonnenberg. BA in History and German cum laude, SUNY, Buffalo, 1995, MLS, 1997. Cert. pub. libr. N.Y. Intern libr. Niagara Falls (N.Y.) Pub. Libr., 1996—97, local history libr., 1997—98; reference libr. Trocaire Coll., Buffalo, 1998—99, libr. dir., 1999; libr. Buffalo & Erie County Pub. Libr., 1999—2002; head reference, sys. coord. D'Youville Coll. Libr., Buffalo, 1999—2002; adj. faculty SUNY Sch. Informatics, Buffalo, 2001—; Island Branch supr. Manatee County Pub. Libr. Sys., Bradenton, Fla., 2002—. Co-chair Western N.Y. Reference Discussion Group, Buffalo, 2000—02; mem. Regional Automation Com., Buffalo, 2000—02, TBLC Continuing Edn. Com., 2003—. Co-author: (workshop) Networking and Operating Systems for Librarians, 2001—; author: Implementing New Libr. Technologies, 2003—. Reader Niagara Frontier Radio Reading Svc., Cheektowaga, NY, 1999—2002. Named Alberta Riggs Meml. scholar, Sch. Info. and Libr. Studies, 1997; recipient Dr. Marie Ross Wolcott Meml. award, 1997; grantee, NYLA Reference and Adult Svcs. Sect. Continuing Edn., 2002; Profl. Devel. grant, Western N.Y. Libr. Resources Coun., 2001—02. Mem.: AAUP (v.p., exec. com. 2001—02), ALA, Assn. Coll. and Rsch. Librs., Libr. and Info. Tech. Assn., Beta Phi Mu. Avocations: bicycling, hiking, reading, scuba diving, cooking. Home: 401 Clark Lane Holmes Beach FL 34217 Office: Libr Sys Island Branch 5701 Marina Dr Holmes Beach FL 34217 Office Phone: 941-778-1721. E-mail: librarianava@hotmail.com., ava.ehde@co.manatee.fl.us.

EHLERS, KATHRYN HAWES (MRS. JAMES D. GABLER), physician; b. Richmond Hill, N.Y., Aug. 22, 1931; d. Albert and Edna (Hawes) E.; m. James D. Gabler, Dec. 5, 1959; children— Jennifer K., Emily E. AB, Bryn Mawr Coll., 1953; MD, Cornell U.; MD (Hannah E. Longshore Meml. Med. scholar 1953-57, Elsie Strang L'Esperance scholar 1956-57), 1957. Diplomate: Am. Bd. Pediatrics, Am. Bd. Pediatric Cardiology. Intern N.Y. Hosp., 1957-58, asst. resident pediatrics, 1958-60; fellow in pediatric cardiology Cornell U. Med. Coll., N.Y.C., 1960-64, instr. pediatrics, 1964-66, asst. prof., 1966-70, asso. prof. pediatrics, 1970-75, prof., 1975-96, prof. emeritus, 1996—, vice-chmn. pediat., 1988-96; practice medicine specializing in pediat. cardiology N.Y.C., 1958-96. Contbr. articles to profl. jours. Research trainee N.Y. Heart Assn., 1960-62, Am. Heart Assn., 1962-64. Fellow Am. Coll. Cardiology; mem. N.Y. Heart Assn., Am. Heart Assn., Harvey Soc., Am. Pediatric Soc., Am. Acad. Pediatrics, Alpha Omega Alpha. Home: 102 Wilderness Dr Apt 2116 Naples FL 34105-2603

EHLIG-ECONOMIDES, CHRISTINE A. petroleum engineer; BA cum laude, Rice U., 1971; MAT, U. Kans., 1974, MS in chem. engring., 1976; PhD in petroleum engring., 1979. Rsch. asst. petroleum engring. dept. Stanford U., 1976—78, prog. mgr. geothermal prog., 1979—80, acting asst. prof. petroleum engring, 1979—80; head petroleum engring. dept. U. Alaska, Fairbanks, 1981—83; section head dynamic reservoir description Flopetrol Johnston Schlumberger, Melun, France, 1983—86; section head layered reservoir testing Schlumberger Perforating and Testing, Houston, 1986—88; section mgr. reservoir engring. Schlumberger Well Service, 1988—90; project leader reservoir dynamics Etudes et Productions, Schlumberger, Clamart, France, 1990—92; tech. advisor Schulumberger Internat. Coordination, Houston, 1993—95, Anadrill Schulumberger, Sugar Land, Tex., 1995—96; tech. and mktg. mgr., production enhancement Schulumberger Oilfield Services, 1996—97; area mgr. Latin Am. North Schulumberger Reservoir Tech., Caracas, Venezuela, 1997—99; global account mgr. Schulumberger Global Client Accounts, Houston, 1999—; adj. prof. U. Houston, 2000—. Vis. prof. U. Houston, 1994, Stanford U., 1995. Grantee Standard Oil of Calif. Fellowship, Stanford U. Mem. Soc. Petroleum Engrs. (disting., Europe steering com. 1992, chmn. cultural diversity com. 1993-95, Disting. Achievement award for Petroleum Engring. Faculty, 1982, Formation Evaluation award 1995, Lester C. Uren award 1997, disting. lectr. 1997-98), Phi Kappa Phi, Sigma Xi. Achievements include contributions to analytical models for well-test analysis, development of practical methodology for well-test interpretation, design of testing procedures; evaluation of testing hardware and pressure-transient data quality. Office: Dept Chem Engring U Houston 4800 Calhoun Ave Houston TX 77204-4004 E-mail: ceconomides@uh.edu.

EHLKE, NANCY JO, agronomist; Assoc. prof. U. Minn., St. Paul, 1986—. Recipient CIBA GEIGY award in Agronomy Am. Soc. of Agronomy, 1995. Office: U Min Dept of Agronomy and Plant Genetics 411 Borleug Hall 1991 Buford Ave Saint Paul MN 55108-1013

EHRENBERG, MAUREEN, management consultant; Pres. Grubb & Ellis Mgmt. Svcs., Inc., Northbrook, Ill., 1999—. Office: Grubb & Ellis Mgmt Svcs Inc 2215 Sanders Rd Ste 400 Northbrook IL 60062-6114

EHRENFELD, ELLIE (ELVERA EHRENFELD), health science association administrator; b. Phila., Mar. 1, 1942; m. Donald F. Summers. BA cum laude, Brandeis U., 1962; PhD in Biochemistry, U. Pitt., 1967; postdoctoral student, Albert Einstein Coll. Medicine, 1967—74. Asst. to assoc. prof. dept. cell biology Albert Einstein Coll. Med.; from assoc. prof.to prof. biochemistry and biology U. Utah, 1974—92; dean sch. biol. scis. U. Calif., Irvine, 1992—97; dir. ctr. scientific rev. Dept. Health and Human Svcs., Bethesda, Md., 1997—2003. Mem. various coms. including rsch. adv. panel Walter Reed Army Inst. Rsch., exptl. virology study sect. NIH; mem. bd. sci. counselors Nat. Inst. Allergy and Infectious Diseases; cons. immunopathology lab. Scripps Inst. Med. Rsch. Recipient Bill Joklik Lectureship award, Am. Soc. Virology; scholar Nat. Sci., Brandeis U. Office: NIAID Bldg 50 Rm 6120 50 South Dr Bethesda MD 20892-8011

EHRET, JOSEPHINE MARY, microbiologist, researcher; b. Roswell, N.Mex., Feb. 26, 1934; d. Edward and Glenna (Memmer) E. BS, U. N.Mex., 1955. Med. technologist U. Colo. Health Scis. Ctr., Denver, 1956-75, rsch. microbiologist, 1956—, Denver Dept. Health and Hosps., 1980—; instr. sch. medicine U. Colo., 1985—. Contbr. articles to profl. publs. Mem. Am. Soc. for Microbiology, Am. Soc. Med. Technologists (cert.), Am. Venereal Disease Assn., Calif. Assn. Continuing Med. Lab. Edn. Democrat. Avocations: reading, birding. Home: 1344 S Eudora St Denver CO 80222-3526 Office: Denver Pub Health Dept 605 Bannock St Denver CO 80204-4505

EHRHARDT, MARGARET WRIGHT, retired librarian; b. Orangeburg, S.C., Sept. 17, 1918; d. Harry Alison and Florence Olive (Black) Wright; B.A., Duke U., 1939; B.A.L.S., Emory U., 1949; postgrad. Furman U., 1970, U. S.C., 1978, U. Pitts., 1978; m. Benedict Groseclose Ehrhardt, Oct. 27, 1951; 1 son, Benedict Glen. High sch. librarian, library supr. Orangeburg (S.C.) Public Schs., 1945-51; children's librarian Richland County (S.C.) Public Library, Columbia, 1952-58; asst. order librarian U. S.C., Columbia, 1960-64; order librarian Wofford Coll., 1964-65; library cons. S.C. Dept. Edn., Columbia, 1965-87. Mem. ALA, Southeastern Library Assn., S.C. Library Assn. (sec. 1971-72, pres. 1977), Delta Kappa Gamma. Lutheran. Editor: Media Services Newsletter, 1965-77, contbr. articles, revs. to S.C. Librarian, Media Center Messenger. Home: 5005 Mahncke Rd Longbranch WA 98351

EHRKE, MINDY JO, minister; d. Herbert H. and Jean E. Dietz; m. Gregory B. Ehrke, June 30, 1979; children: Christopher, Sara, Daniel. BA in English, Augutang Coll., 1978; MDiv, Luther Nahwestern Sem., 1985. Ordained minister Am. Luth. Ch., 1985. Pastor St. Johns & Crocker Luth. Ch., Bradley, SD, 1985—89, St. Paul Luth. Ch., Bowdle, SD, 1990—96, Bethany Luth. Ch., Viberg, SD, 1996—. Chmn. standing com. for assembly planning S.D. Synod Evang. Luth. Ch. Am., Sioux Falls, SD, 1998—. Co-author: The Embroydered Word, 1989, The Embroydered Word II, 1995, Creative Worship 2, 2003. Mem.: S.E. Conf. Pastors (sec. 2000—), Viborg Ministerial Assn. (chmn. 1996—, chmn. Turner county thrievent chpt. 2003). Avocations: singing, guitar, cooking, reading. Home: PO Box 202 Viborg SD 57070 Office: Bethany Lutheran Church PO Box 195 Viborg SD 57070

EHRLICH, ANNE HOWLAND, research biologist; b. Des Moines, Nov. 17, 1933; d. Winston Densmore and Virginia Lippincott (Fitzhugh) Howland; m. Paul Ralph Ehrlich, Dec. 18, 1954; 1 child: Lisa Marie Daniel. Student, U. Kans., 1952-55; LLD (hon.), Bethany Coll., 1990; doctorate (hon.), Oreg. State U., 1999. Technician Dept. Entomology U. Kans., Lawrence, 1955; rsch. asst. Dept. Biol. Scis. Stanford (Calif.) U., 1959-72, rsch. assoc., 1972-75, sr. rsch. assoc., 1975—; assoc. dir. Ctr. for Conservation Biology Stanford U., 1987—. Bd. dirs. Pacific Inst., Ploughshares Fund. Author: (with others) Ecoscience: Population, Resources, Environment, 1977, The Golden Door, 1979, Extinction, 1981, Earth, 1987, The Population Explosion, 1990, Healing the Planet, 1991, The Stork and the Plow, 1995, Betrayal of Science and Reason, 1996; contbr. articles to profl. jours. Named to Global 500 Roll of Honour for Environ. Achievement, UN, 1989, UNEP-Sasekawa prize, 1994, Heinz award, 1995, Tyler prize, 1998. Fellow Am. Acad. Arts & Scis., Calif. Acad. Scis. (hon.); mem. Am. Humanists Assn. (hon. life, Disting. Svc. 1985, Raymond B. Bragg award 1985). Avocations: flyfishing, hiking, reading. Home: Pine Hill Stanford CA 94305 Office: Stanford U Dept Biol Scis Stanford CA 94305

EHRLICH, AVA, television executive; b. St. Louis, Aug. 14, 1950; d. Norman and Lillian (Gellman) Ehrlich; m. Barry K. Freedman, Mar. 31, 1979; children: Alexander Zev, Maxwell Samuel. BJ, Northwestern U., 1972, MJ, 1973; MA, Occidental Coll., 1976. Reporter, asst. mng. editor Lerner Newspapers, Chgo., 1974-75; reporter, news editor Sta. KMOX, St. Louis, 1976-79, [illegible]; exec. producer Sta. KSDK-TV, St. Louis, 1985—. Guest editor Mademoiselle mag., N.Y.C., 1971; freelance writer, coll. prof. Detroit, Chgo., St. Louis, 1987; adj. faculty mem. Washington U., St. Louis, 1994—. Trustee CORO Found., St. Louis, 1976-77, 86—, St. Louis Jewish Light, 1999—, Crown Ctr., 2000; bd. dirs. Nat. Kidney Found., St. Louis, 1987, Crowne Ctr., 2000—. Named Outstanding Woman in Broadcasting, Am. Women in Radio & TV, 1983, Among 18 Most Influential Women in the Region St. Louis Dispatch, 2000; recipient Journalism award Am. Chiropractic Assn., 1989, AP award Ill. UPI, 1989, Illuminator award AMC Cancer Rsch., 1994, Women in Comms. Nat. award, 1988, Emmy award, 1995, Virginia Betts award for Contbns. in Journalism, 1999; CORO Found. fellow in pub. affairs, 1975-76. Mem. NATAS (com. mem. 1986—, bd. dirs. 1994—, 18 local Emmy awards 1986—), Women in Comms., Inc. (sec. 1978-79, Clarion award 1989, Best in Midwest Feature award 1989), Soc. Profl. Journalists. Democrat. Jewish. Home: 8002 Walinca Ter Saint Louis MO 63105-2565 Office: Sta KSDK-TV 1000 Market St Saint Louis MO 63101-2011 E-mail: aehrlich@ksdk.gannett.com.

EHRLICH, GERALDINE ELIZABETH, management consultant; d. Joseph Vincent and Agnes Barbara (Campbell) McKenna; m. S. Paul Ehrlich, Jr.; children: Susan Patricia, Paula Jeanne, Jill Marie. BS, Drexel Inst. Tech. Nutrition cons. hypertension rsch. team U. Calif. Micronesia, 1970; regional sales mgr. Marriott Corp., Bethesda, Md., 1976-78; dir. sales and profl. svcs. Coll. and Health Care divsn. Macke Co., Cheverly, Md., 1978-79, v.p. ops. divsn., 1979-80, pres. Health Care divsn., 1980-81; regional v.p. Custom Mgmt. Corp., Alexandria, Va., 1981-83, v.p. mktg., 1983-87; v.p. mktg. and healthcare sales Morrison's Custom Mgmt., Mobile, Ala., 1987-88; v.p. sales ARA Svcs., Phila., 1988-93; v.p. bus. devel. ARAMARK, Phila., 1993-95; exec. dir. The Resource Group, Phila., 1995—2001; healthcare mktg. cons., 2001—. Cons. mktg. The Green House, Tokyo, 1987-88; chmn. bd. Mktg. Matrix, Falls Church, Va., 1984—. Mem. Health Systems Agy. No. Va., 1976-77; chmn. Health Care Adv. Bd., Fairfax County, Va., 1973-77; vice chmn. Fairfax County Cmty. Action Com., 1973-77; treas. Fairfax County Dem. Com., 1969-73; trustee Fairfax Hosp., 1973-77; bd. dirs. Tennis Patrons, Washington, 1984-88, Phila. Singers, 1993-98, Physicians for Peace, 1993-98; mem. adv. bd. Nat. Mus. Women in the Arts, 2000—. Mem. NAFE, AAUW, Internat. Women's Assn., Am. Mgmt. Assn., Soc. Mktg. Profls., Gulfstream Club, Rotary Club. Home: 1132 Seaspray Ave Delray Beach FL 33483 E-mail: gehrlich@profserve.com.

EHRLICH, MARGARET ISABELLA GORLEY, systems engineer, mathematics educator, consultant; b. Eatonton, Ga., Nov. 12, 1950; d. Frank Griffith and Edith Roy (Beall) Gorley; m. Jonathan Steven Ehrlich. BS in Math., U. Ga., 1972; MEd, Ga. State U., 1977, EdS, 1982, PhD, 1987; postgrad., Woodrow Wilson Coll. of Law, 1977-78. Cert. secondary tchr., Ga. Tchr. Dekalb County Bd. Edn., Decatur, Ga., 1972-83; chmn. dept. math. Columbia H.S., Decatur, Ga., 1978-83; with product development Chalkboard Co., Atlanta, 1983-84; math. instr. Ga. State U., Atlanta, 1983-92, lectr., dir. of mentoring, 2001—; pres. Testing and Tech. Svcs., Atlanta, 1983—. Course specialist Ga. Pacific Co., Atlanta, 1984-86; sys. engr. Lotus Devel. Corp., 1986-89; rsch. assoc. SUNY-Stony Brook, 1976; modeling instr. Barbizon Modeling Sch., Atlanta, 1991; instr. Ga. State Coll. for Kids, 1984-85; test-taking cons., hon. mem. Comm. Workers of Am. Local 3204, Atlanta, 1985—. Author: (software user manual) Micro Maestro, 1983, Music Math, 1984; (test manual) The Telephone Company Test, 1991, AMI Pro Advanced Courseware, 1992, A Study Guide for the Sales and Service Representative Test, 1993, A Study Guidy for the Technical Services Test, 1995; (book) Philadelphia Methodist Church 1860-90: Members and History, 1998, Mrs. Beall's Mill, 1999; mem. editl. bd. CPA Computer Report, Atlanta, 1984-85. Tchr. St. Phillips Ch. Sch., Atlanta, 1981-88; mem. Atlanta Preservation Soc., 1985, Planned Parenthood, St. Phillips welcome com., 1988-96, drug and alcohol counseling HOPE, 1988-96; sponsor Fair Test 1991—, Ctr. Fair and Open Testing, parish choir St. Phillips Ch., 1995-96; team leader guest svcs. Atlanta Com. Olympic Games, 1996; vol. Atlanta Hist. Soc. Archives and Libr., 2000—/ Named State Tchr. Achievement Recognition Tchr. DeKalb County Bd. Edn., 1979, 80, 81, Most Outstanding Tchr., Barbizon Sch. of Modeling, 1980, Colo. Outward Bound, 1985, Disting. Educator, Ga. State U., 1987; recipient Jefferson Davis Gold Medal, United Daughters of Confederacy, 1999. Mem.: DeKalb Personal Computer Instr. Assn. (pres. 1984), Assn. Women in Math. (del. to China Sci. and Tech. Exch. 1989—90), Math. Assn. Am., Ga. Coun. Tchrs. Math., Nat. Coun. Tchrs. Math., Math. Assn. Am., DAR, Hamilton Nat. Geneal. Soc. (treas. 1998—), First Families of Ga. (sec.), Ga. Hist. Soc., N.Y.C. Track Club, Atlanta Track Club. Democrat. Episcopalian. Avocations: piano, pilates, fashion, skiing, harp. Home: 240 Cliff Overlook Atlanta GA 30350-2601 Office: PO Box 500173 Atlanta GA 31150-0173

EHRLICH, STACY WHEELER, school fundraiser, administrator; b. Austin, Tex., May 30, 1969; d. Robert Green and Sandria Eberhardt Wheeler; m. James Charles Ehrlich, June 11, 1994; 1 child, Megann Simms. BS in Advt., U. Tex., 1991; postgrad., U. Tex. Pan Am., Edinburg, 1995; MA in Human Svcs., St. Edwards U., 1996. Cert. fund raising exec. Asst. account exec. Meyer, Griffin and Wright, Houston, 1992-93; dir. devel., pub. rels. With Love Found., Houston, 1993; freshman counselor U. St. Thomas, Houston, 1993-94; dir. corp. found. giving Marine Mil. Acad., Harlingen, Tex., 1994-95; devel. assoc. major gifts U. Tex., Austin, 1995-96; dir. devel. Austin Waldorf Sch., Austin, 1996—. Cons. Non-Profit Mgmt. Assistance Program, Austin, 1997. Oscar night sponsor party co-chair Child and Family Svc., Austin, 1997. Mem. Jr. League of Austin, Nat. Soc. of Fund Raising Execs. (v.p. membership 1998-99), U. Tex. Ex-Students Assn., Zeta Tau Alpha. Roman Catholic. Avocations: volunteer work, church activities, self development tasks. Office: Austin Waldorf Sch 8700 S View Rd Austin TX 78737-1241

EHRMAN, LEE, geneticist, educator; b. N.Y.C., May 25, 1935; m. Richard Ehrman, 1955; children: Esther, Judith. BS, Queens Coll., 1956; MS, Columbia U., 1957, PhD in Genetics, 1959; DSc (hon.), CUNY, 1989. Mem. faculty Barnard Coll., 1956-58; postdoctoral fellow in genetics Columbia U., N.Y.C., 1959-61, assoc. seminar on population biology, 1981—; mem. faculty SUNY-Purchase, 1970—, prof. div. natural scis., 1972—; Disting. prof. biology SUNY, Purchase, 1995—; mem. spl. study sect. NIH, NIMH, 1979-80. Vis. disting. prof. U. Miami, Coral Gables, Fla., 1981; vis. lectr. U. Puerto Rico, Rio Piedras, 1987; coordinator, panelist workshops, programs in field; mem. panels NIH, 2003—. Author: Behavior Genetics and Evolution, 2nd edit., 1981; assoc. editor Evolution; assoc. editor for genetics and cytology Am. Midland Naturalist; co-editor: Behavior Genetics; assoc. editor, exec. com. Soc. Am. Naturalists, 1977-85, pres.-elect 1990; contbr. more than 500 articles to profl. jours. Recipient Lit. Soc. Found. medal in German, 1956; Shirley Farr postdoctoral fellow, 1961-62; USPHS postdoctoral fellow, 1959-61; faculty exch. scholar, 1974—; NSF grantee, 1979-84; Sr. Scientist awardee Whitehall Found., 1987, 93; NIH gen. med. scis. grantee, 1987—; SUNY travel grantee, 1988, 93, 96; Merck rsch. support grantee, 2000—. Fellow AAAS (Rsch. Support award Merck/AAAS, 2001), Inst. Soc. Ethics and Life Scis; mem. AAUW (life), Am. Soc. Naturalists (pres. 1990), Behavior Genetics Assn. (pres. 1978, Dobzhansky award for lifetime resch. 1988), Soc. for Study of Evolution (exec. council 1986), Phi Beta Kappa, Sigma Xi Home: 2 Jennifer Ln Rye Brook NY 10573-1916 Office: SUNY Div Natural Scis Purchase NY 10577 Fax: (914) 251-6635. Office Phone: 914-251-6671.

EICH, SUSAN, public relations executive; Dir. corp. pub. rels. Target Corp. (formerly Dayton Hudson Corp.), Mpls., 1995—. Office: Target Corp 33 S 6th PO Box 1392 Minneapolis MN 55440-1392

EICHEL, BEVERLY, apparel company executive; [illegible] (formerly Ernst & Whinney), 1980-84; dir. acct. MGM/UA Home Video, 1984-87; corp. contr. Danskin, Inc., 1987-92, CFO, exec. v.p., 1992-98, DonKenny, Inc., N.Y.C., 1998—. Office: Donn Kenny Inc 1411 Broadway 10th Fl New York NY 10018

EICHENLAUB, ROSEMARY WARING, music educator; b. Saratoga Springs, N.Y., Dec. 1, 1949; d. Edward Joseph and Marion Hewitt Waring; m. Ed J. Eichenlaub, July 10, 1982; children: Brian, Julie. MusB Cum Laude, Nazareth Coll., 1971, MS Elem. Edn., 1976. Tchr. vocal, gen. music Rochester City Sch. Dist., NY, 1971—. Music mentor Rochester City Sch. Dist., NY, 1996—; presenter All Children Are Children First Conf., 1997; presenter in field, 1994—2004; liaison Eastman Sch. Music, 1992; chairperson Arts Enrichment Com. Sch. 1, 1990—2004, Character Edn. Program Sch. 1, 1995—. Author: (article in) The Orff Echo, 1996. Com. mem. St. Margaret Mary Ch., Rochester, 1983—2001. Recipient Outstanding Music Educator award, Rochester Philharmonic Orch., 1998. Mem.: Music Educators Nat. Conf., Greater Rochester Chpt. Am. Orff Schulwerk Assn. (pres. 1990), Am. Orff Schulwerk Conf. (fundraising chair 2000). Roman Catholic. Avocations: reading, theater, skiing, tennis. Office: Sch 1 Rochester City Sch Dist 85 Hillside Ave Rochester NY 14610

EICHINGER, MARILYNNE HILDEGARDE, museum administrator; children: Ryan, Kara, Julia, Jessica, Talik. BA in Anthropology and Sociology magna cum laude, Boston U., 1965; MA, Mich. State U., 1971. With emergency and outpatient staff Ingham County Mental Health Ctr., 1972; founder, pres., exec. dir. Impression 5 Sci. and Art Mus., Lansing, Mich., 1973-85; pres. Oreg. Mus. Sci. and Industry, Portland, 1985-95; bd. dirs. Portland Visitors Assn., 1985-95; pres. Informal Edn. Products Ltd., 1995—, 1995—. Bd. dirs. N.W. Regional Edn. Labs., 1991-97; instr. Lansing (Mich.) C.C., 1978; ptnr. Eyrie Studio, 1982-85; condr. numerous workshops in interactive exhibit design, adminstrn. and fund devel. for schs., orgns., profl. socs. Author: (with Jane Mack) Lexington Montessori School Survey, 1969, Manual on the Five Senses, 1974; pub. Mich. edit. Boing mag. Founder Cambridge Montessori Sch., 1964; bd. dirs. Lexington Montessori Sch., 1969, Mid-Mich. South Health Sys. Agy., 1978-81, Cmty. Referral Ctr., 1981-85, Sta. WKAR, 1981-85; active Lansing "Riverfest" Lighted Boat Parade, 1980; mem. state Health Coordinating Coun., 1980-82; mem. pres.'s adv. coun. Portland State U., 1986—90, mem. pres.' adv. bd., 1987-91; bd. dirs. Portland Visitors Assn., 1994-97, Friends of Tryon Creek State Pk., 2001—. Recipient Diana Cert. Leadership, YWCA, 1976-77, Woman of Achievement award, 1991, Community Svc. award Portland State U., 1992. Mem. Am. Assn. Mus., Oreg. Mus. Assn., Assn. Sci. and Tech. Ctrs. (bd. dirs. 1980-84, 88-93), Mus. Store Assn., Direct Mktg. Assn., Zonta Lodge (founder, bd. dirs. East Lansing club 1978), Internat. Women's Forum, Portland C. of C. Office: Informal Edn Products Ltd 2517 SE Mailwell Dr Milwaukie OR 97222

EID, CYNTHIA ANN, metalsmith, jeweler, designer, educator; b. Madison, Wis., May 22, 1954; d. Richard O. and Ann E. (Henning) E.; m. David S. Reiner; children: Andrew Eid Reiner, Eric Eid Reiner. BS, U. Wis., 1977; MFA, Ind. U., 1980. Designer/goldsmith Joel Bagnal, Goldsmith, Concord and Wellesley, Mass., 1980-81; jewelry designer/goldsmith Neal Rosenblum, Goldsmith, Worcester, Mass., 1981; modelmaker, designer, supr. Verilyte, Inc., Brookline, Mass., 1982-85; tchr. metalsmithing Lexington (Mass.) Arts and Crafts Soc., 1992-94; instr. advanced silversmithing and jewelry DeCordova Mus. Sch., Lincoln, Mass., 1995—; freelance metalsmith/jeweler Lexington, 1985—. Illustrator: Anthology of Fiddle Styles, 1976, Anthology of Jazz Violin Styles, 1981; metalwork featured: (Women in Design, Internat.) Compendium, 1981 (Outstanding Achievement award), (by Michael Wolk) Designing for the Table, 1992, Metalsmith, 1997, American Silversmith, 1997, 1998 Metalsmith Exhbn. in Print, (by B.S. Rabinoritch) Contemporary Silver, 2000, (by K. Morton) Judaiz Artizans Today, 2002, (by D. Meilach) Art Jewelry Today, 2003, (by Lark) 1,000 Rings, 2004; exhibited at Soc. of Arts and Crafts, Boston, 1992—. Recipient Best in Show award Wis. Union Craft Exhbn., 1975, metal award Beaux Arts Designer Craftsman, 1979, flatware award Sterling Silver Design competition, 1980, award winner SAVE Jewelry Design competition, 1996, jewelry and metals award Silverhawk Nat. Fine Crafts Competitions, 1996, 97, jurors award Crafts Nat. 31, 1997, Winning Desinger of SNAG Hon. Membership award, 2003; Ford Found. fellow, 1978. Mem. Soc. Am. Silversmiths (artisan mem., hon., Silverhawk award 1996, 97, 98, Metalsmithing New Millenium 1998, Millennium medal 2001, Niche award 1999), Soc. N.Am. Goldsmiths, Soc. Arts and Crafts (artist mem.). Avocations: tennis, swimming, biking, skiing, playing banjo in reiner family band. Office Phone: 781-863-0140. E-mail: ceid@cynthiaeid.com.

EIDE, TRACEY J. state legislator; m. Mark Eide; children: Joanna, Matthew. Mem. Wash. Ho. of Reps., Olympia, 1993-98, asst. majority whip, 1993-94, chair Federal Way Human Svcs. Commn., 1997-98; vice chair edn. com.; vice chair environ. quality and water resources com.; mem. Puget Sound Coun.; mem. transp. com.; majority asst. whip; mem. joint com. on children's oversight; co-chair commute trip reduction task force; mem. Wash. Senate, Dist. 30, Olympia, 1998—. Mem. Puget Sound. Coun.; alt. mem. Coun. State Govt., Western Water Policy Com.; mem. Wash. State Recycling Task Force. Recipient Disting. Leadership in Edn. award Fed. Way Sch. Dist., Emerging Leader award Nat. Conf. State Legislatures. Democrat. Office: 410 Legis Bldg Olympia WA 98504-0430

EIGEL, MARCIA DUFFY, editor; b. Denver, July 15, 1936; d. Eugene and Margaret (Foley) Duffy; m. Edwin G. Eigel Jr., May 30, 1959; children: Edwin III, Mary. BA, Webster U., 1958. Editor, writer corp. hdqrs. GE, Fairfield, Conn., 1985-92, copy editor, 1996-2000; dir. comms. Girl Scouts of Housatonic Coun., Bridgeport, Conn., 1994-97; editor Blue Cross of Northeastern Pa., 2001—. Instr. in bus. writing So. Conn. State U., New Haven, 1986, U. Bridgeport, 1990. Writer, editor newsletter Customer Fin. Svcs. News, 1987-92, Woman Traveler, 1990—; contbr. articles and poetry to profl. jours. Bd. trustees Greater Bridgeport (Conn.) Symphony, 1998—. Mem.: AAUW, U. Bridgeport Women's Forum. Home and Office: 33 Pepperbush Ln Fairfield CT 06424-4036

EIMERS, JERI ANNE, retired therapist; b. Berkeley, Calif., Jan. 20, 1951; d. Alfred D. Wallace and Marjorie E. (Nordheim) Stevens; m. Roy A. Neiman, June 12, 1969 (div. Aug. 1977); children: Lorien, Arwen; m. Richard A. Eimers, Mar. 2, 1996. AA, Palomar Jr. Coll., 1977; BA in Psychology with distinction, Calif. State U., Long Beach, 1979, MA in Psychology with distinction, 1981; postgrad. Human Sexuality Program, UCLA, 1991-92. Lic. marriage, family, child therapist, Calif.; cert. community coll. instr., counselor; cert. sex therapist. Rsch. asst. Calif. State U., 1978-82; tchr. Artesia (Calif.)-Bellflower-Cerritos Unified Sch. Dist., 1982-83; dir. Am. Learning Corp., Huntington Beach, Calif., 1983-85; social worker Los Angeles County Children's Protective Svcs., Long Beach, 1986-88; sr. social worker Orange County Social Svc. Agy., Orange, Calif., 1988-90; therapist Cypress Mental Health, Cypress, Calif., 1988—, cons., 1990—. Cons., 1990—; group chair, leader Adults Abused as Children, Los Altos Hosp., Long Beach, 1991—, Coll. Hosp., Cerritos, 1993—; speaker, presenter in field. Mem. Child's Sexual Abuse Network, Orange, 1988—; mem. legis. com. Child Abuse Coun. of Orange County, 1988. Women's League scholar, 1980-81. Mem. AAUW, Am. Assn. Marriage, Family Therapists, Calif. Assn. Marriage, Family Therapists, Am. Profl. Soc. for Abused Children, Calif. Profl. Assn. for Abused Children, Phi Kappa Phi, Psi Chi. Republican. Methodist. Avocations: writing, theater, classical and jazz music, swimming.

EINBINDER, SUSAN LESLIE, literature educator, rabbi; b. Ridgewood, N.J., Dec. 9, 1954; d. Seymour K. and Julia M. (Morrison) E. BA in Math. magna cum laude, Brown U., 1976; MHL, Hebrew Union Coll., 1983; MA in English and Comparative Lit., Columbia U., 1978, MPhil, 1986, PhD in [illegible] rabbi, 1983. Vis. lectr., chaplain to Jewish students Colgate U., Hamilton, N.Y., 1987-88; adj. prof. gen. studies NYU, N.Y.C., 1990-92; adj. prof. Manhattan Sch. Music, N.Y.C., 1991-92; vis. lectr. U. Md., College Park, 1992-93; asst. prof. Hebrew lit. Hebrew Union Coll., Cin., 1993-96, assoc. prof., 1996—2001, prof., 2001—. Fellow Davis Ctr., 1999, Nat. Humanities Ctr., 2000. Translator: (novella) IYA (Shimon Ballas), 1995; author: Beautiful Death, 2002; contbr. articles to profl. jours. and confs. Bd. dirs. Prospect House, Cin., 1995-2002; spkr. at cmty. orgns. Fellow Fulbright Found., 1986-87, Nat. Found. for Jewish Culture, 1988-89. Mem. MLA, AHA, Cen. Conf. of Am. Rabbis, Nat. Assn. Profs. of Hebrew, Assn. for Jewish Studies, Medieval Acad.. Office: Hebrew Union Coll Jewish Inst Religion 3101 Clifton Ave Cincinnati OH 45220-2404

EINODER, CAMILLE ELIZABETH, retired secondary school educator; b. Chgo., June 15, 1937; d. Isadore and Elizabeth T. (Czerwinski) Popowski; m. Joseph X. Einoder, Aug. 5, 1978; children: Carl Frank, Mark Frank, Vivian Einoder, Joe Einoder, Tim Einoder, Sheila Einoder, Jude Einoder. Student, Fox Bus. Coll., 1954; BEd in Biology, Chgo. Tchrs. Coll., 1964; MA in Analytical Chemistry, Gov.'s State U., 1977; MA in Adminstrn. and Supervision, Roosevelt U., 1986; postgrad., 1992—. Sec., Chgo., 1955-64; tchr. biology Chgo. Bd. Edn., 1964-1975, tchr. biology and agr., 1975-81, tchr. biology, agr. and chemistry, 1981-2000, ret., 2000. Human rels. coord. Morgan Park High Sch., Chgo., 1980—, tchr. biology Internat. Studies Sch., 1983—, adv. bd., 1989—; owner Einoder Masonry, 1997—, Einoder Antiques, 1996—; career devel. cons. for agr. related curriculum; internat. baccalaureate tchr., Chgo. pub. schs. consulting tchr., 1997; edn. cons. Neighborhood Coun., 1974; rep. Chgo. Tchrs. Union, 1969; exec. bd. dir. The Lira Ensemble, 1996—; mem. Renaissance Circle, DePaul U.; edn. com. Polish-Am. Initiative of Chgo. Cmty. Trust, 1999—; owner Einoder Masonry, 1986—; antique dealer, 1995—. Bd. dirs., founding mem., author constn. Cmty. Coun., 1970—; bd. dirs., edn. cons. Neighborhood Coun., 1974; rep. Chgo. Tchrs. Union, 1969; exec. bd. dirs. The Lira Ensemble, 1996—; mem. Chums Giving Club Com.; charter mem. Humanists Cir. Chgo. Humanities Festival, 2003—. Mem. AAAS, NSTA, Polish Inst. for Arts and Sci., Am. Chem. Soc., Am. Biology Tchrs. Assn., Nat. Assn. Women Bus. Owners, Found. Women Contractors, Copernicus Found., Kosciuszko Found., Polish Arts Club, Phi Delta Kappa, Iota Sigma Pi. Home: 512 N McClurg Ct #4210 Chicago IL 60611 E-mail: camilleein@aol.com.

EINREINHOFER, NANCY ANNE, art gallery director; b. Paterson, N.J., Sept. 8, 1944; d. John Edward and Nora (Niland) Gleason; m. Robert Einreinhofer, Nov. 26, 1966; 1 child, Robert. BA in Art, William Paterson Coll., 1976, BA in English, 1977, MA in Visual Arts, 1978; cert. in supervisory mgmt., Rutgers U., 1986; PhD in Mus. Studies, Leicester U., England, 1993. Art critic N.J. News, 1973-76; gallery curator O.K. Harris Works of Art, N.Y.C., 1978; dir. gallery William Paterson U., Wayne, N.J., 1979—. Bd. dirs. Mus. Council of N.J., 1984—; cons. Sussex County Arts Council, N.J., 1987. Author: The American Art Museum: Elitism and Democracy, 1997; contbr. articles to profl. jours. Recipient grant Nat. Endowment for Arts, 1979, NEH, 1984-85, 87-88, N.J State Ccouncil Arts, 1984-85, 85-86, 87-88, 2000—. Mem. Am. Assn. Mus., Internat. Council Mus., Mid Atlantic Assn. Mus., Assn. Coll. and U. Mus. Galleries, Mus. Council of N.J. (exec. bd. 1984-88). Home: 1 Cheyenne Trl Sparta NJ 07871-2924 Office: William Paterson U Ben Shahn Galleries Wayne NJ 07470 E-mail: EinreinhoferN@WPUNJ.edu.

EIRICH, MICHELLE A. editor, writer; b. Sheboygan, Wis., Nov. 7, 1968; 1 child, Karina A. Curi. BA, U. Wis.-Parkside, Kenosha, 1991. Mktg. writer Arthur Andersen LLP, Milw., 2000—01; pub. rels. editor Covenant Healthcare, Milw., 2001—. Contbr. articles to newspapers. Mem.: Pub. Rels. Soc. Am. Unitarian Universalist. Home: 1126 S 70th St Milwaukee WI 53214 Office: Covenant Healthcare 1126 S 70th St Milwaukee WI 53154 Personal E-mail: write2michelle@earthlink.net. Business E-Mail: maeirich@covhealth.org.

EIS, RUTH SUSANNE, museum curator, artist; b. Mainz, Germany, Feb. 6, 1920; came to U.S., 1937; d. Sali and Margaret (Weissmann) Levi; m. Max Eis, Jan. 4, 1942 (dec. 1991); children: Regina, Steven. Student, Fashion Design Sch. Feige, Berlin, Fashion Design Sch. Traphagen, N.Y.; AA, Oakland Jr. Coll., 1956; BA, U. Calif., Berkeley, 1958; MA, Lone Mountain Coll., 1975. Curator ceremonial art J.L. Magnes Mus., Berkeley, 1960—. Author: (mus. catalogs) Hanukkah Lamps, 1977, Torah binders, 1979, Ornamented Bags, 1994, 25 Years Magnes Museum, 1987, (book) Poems of an Immigrant, 1995; retrospective art exhbn., 1997. Home: 5401 Belgrave Pl Oakland CA 94618-1743

EISENBERG, CAROLA, psychiatry educator; b. Buenos Aires, Sept. 15, 1917; came to U.S., 1945; d. Bernardo and Teodora (Kahan) Blitzman; m. Manfred Guttmacher, Oct. 11, 1946 (dec. 1966); m. Leon Eisenberg, Aug. 31, 1967; children: Laurence, Alan. M of Social Work, Liceo de Senoritas; MD, U. Buenos Aires, 1945. Resident in psychiatry U. Md., 1946-48; fellow in child psychiatry Johns Hopkins Hosp., 1948-50, asst. prof. psychiatry and pediatrics, 1960-67; psychiatrist MIT, Boston, 1967-72, dean of students, 1972-78; dean student affairs Harvard Med. Sch., Boston, 1978-90, dir. internat. programs for students, 1990-92, lectr. psychiatry, 1970-92, lectr. social medicine, 1992—. Co-chmn. women in biomed. careers workshop Office on Women's Health, NIH, 1992, mem. adv. com. on rsch. and women's health, 1995-98; mem. com. on human rights ACP; mem. com. on women in sci. and engring. NAS, 1992-95. V.p. Physicians for Human Rights, Boston, 1987—; pres. Examiners Club, Boston, 1993-2003. Recipient Morani Renaissance Woman award, Found. for History of Women in Medicine, 2003. Fellow Am. Psychiat. Assn. (Disting. life fellow 2003, mem. Coun. Internat. Affairs, com. on human rights), Am. Orthopsychiat. Assn. (life); mem. AAUP. Avocations: traveling, music, reading. Home and Office: 9 Clement Cir Cambridge MA 02138-2205

EISENBERG, DOROTHY, federal judge; b. 1929; LLB, Bklyn. Law Sch., 1950. Bar: N.Y. 1951, U.S. Dist. Ct. (ea. and so. dists.) N.Y., U.S. Ct. Appeals (2nd cir.), U.S. Supreme Ct. Assoc. Otterbourg, Stiendler, Houston & Rosen, N.Y.C., 1950-51, Goldman, Horowitz & Cherno, Mineola, N.Y., 1970-80; pvt. practice Garden City, N.Y., 1981; ptnr. Shaw, Licitra, Eisenberg, Esernio & Schwartz, P.C., Garden City, 1981-89; bankruptcy judge ea. dist. U.S. Bankruptcy Ct., N.Y., 1989—. Mem. Com. on Character and Fitness, Appellate divsn, 2nd Dept., 1983-89; panel trustee U.S. Bankruptcy Ct. (so. dist.) N.Y., 1979-89, U.S. Bankruptcy Ct. (ea. dist.) N.Y., 1975-89. Fellow: Am. Bar Found.; mem.: ABA, Nassau Suffolk Women's Bar Assn. (former pres.), Bar Assn. Nassau County, Am. Bankruptcy Inst., N.Y. State Women's Bar Assn. (Nassau County chpt.), Nat. Assn. Women Judges, Theodore Roosevelt Am. Inn of Ct. (former pres.). Office: PO Box 9013 290 Federal Plz PO Box 9013 Central Islip NY 11722-4437

EISENBERG, KAREN SUE BYER, nurse; b. Bklyn., Mar. 11, 1954; d. Marvin and Florence (Beck) Byer; m. Howard Eisenberg, May 11, 1974; children: Carly Beth, Mariel Bryn. Diploma, L.I. Coll. Hosp. Sch. Nursing, 1973; BS in Nursing, L.I. U., 1976, M in Profl. Studies, 1977. Nurse recovery room and surg. ICU Downstate Med. Ctr., Bklyn., 1973-75; utilization rev. analyst Bezallel Health Related Facility, Far Rockaway, N.Y., 1975-76; utilization rev. analyst, RN supr. Seagirt Health Related Facility, Far Rockaway, 1976; staff nurse neurosurg. and rehab. nursing Downstate Med. Ctr., Bklyn., 1978, nurse ICU, 1978-79; asst. nursing dir. pathology, clin. rsch. assoc. Rsch. Found., Bklyn., 1979-90; instrl. support specialist pathology SUNY Health Sci Ctr., Bklyn., 1990-92; nurse practitioner pathology SUNY Rsch. Found., Bklyn., 1992-95; nurse rsch. coord. trauma surgery SUNY Health Sci. Ctr., Bklyn., 1995—. Clin. rsch. assoc. dept. urology SUNY Health Sci. Ctr., Bklyn., 2001—. Contbr. articles to profl. jours. Mem.: ANA, NY State Nurses Assn., L.I. Coll. Hosp. Alumnae Assn. Office: 450 Clarkson Ave Brooklyn NY 11203 E-mail: karenb.eisenberg@verizon.net.

EISENBERG, PATRICIA LEE, medical/surgical nurse; b. Benton, Ky., Aug. 25, 1952; d. James and Katherine (Bolton) Goodman; m. Paul Eisenberg, Apr. 24, 1982; 1 child, Jamie. BSN, Murray (Ky.) State U., 1974; MSN, St. Louis U., 1981. RN; cert. med.-surg. clin. specialist. Charge nurse Mayfield (Ky.) Community Hosp., 1974-75; staff nurse surg. step-down unit Med. U. S.C., Charleston, 1975; charge nurse ICU North Trident Hosp., Charleston; staff nurse ICU VA Hosp., Memphis, 1977-79, staff nurse surg. ICU St. Louis, 1979; staff nurse ICU various hosps., St. Louis, 1979-80; clin. nurse specialist surgery Jewish Hosp. at Washington U., St. Louis, 1981-88, nutritional support clin. nurse specialist, 1989-98; clin. nurse specialist Community Hosp., Indpls., 1998—. Cons. Resource Applications/Mosby Year Book, Inc., 1991-98; cons. Am. Healthcare Inst., Silver Spring, Md., 1990, Sheryl A. Fuetz, Atty., Kansas City, Mo., 1984-86; cons. enteral products Argyle div. Sherwood Med., St. Louis, 1984-2000; clin. faculty Sch. Nursing U. Mo., 1989-93; adj. clin. instr. Grad. Sch. Nursing, St. Louis U., 1982-88; advisor Ross Labs., 1989; contr. NCLEX-RN Exam. Nat. Coun. State Bds. of Nursing, Inc., 1998; speaker in field. Reviewer Concept Media, Inc., 1989-90; reviewer, editor Clin. Specialist Jour., 1986—, Nutrition, 1988, Intravenous Nurses Soc., 1999-; contbr. articles to profl. jours. Vol. Ladue Jr. High Sch., 1987-89, Coun. Girl Scouts, St. Louis, 1984-86, March of Dimes, 1984-85; active children and youth com. Jewish Community Ctr. Assn., 1983-85, Family Fair West County Shopping Ctr., 1984; coord. St. Louis Model Health Fair ARC, 1984, 83, Emerson Electric Health Fair, 1984. Capt. USAR, 1981-87. Recipient Mo. Tribute to Nursing Rsch. award, 1991, Jewish Hosp. Nursing Rsch. award, 1995, Commitment to Evidence-Based Practice Nursing Excellence award, 2003, Comm. Health Network. Mem. ANA (coun. clin. nurse specialist, program planning com. 3d dist. 1984-85, hostess state bd. nursing test 1984, proctor state bd. nursing 1984), Mo. Nurses Assn. (chmn. awards com. 1986-88, dir. at large 1988-90, achievement in clin. practice award 1987), Am. Soc. Parenteral and Enteral Nutrition (nat. nurses com. 1986, 87, nursing rep. pub. policy com. 1987-89), Am. Heart Assn. Coun. Cardiovascular Nursing, Midwest Nursing Rsch. Soc., St. Louis Nursing Rsch. Consortium, Am. Nurses Credentialing Ctr., Clin. Specialist in Med. Surgical Nursing Content Expert Panel, Commn. on Collegiate Nursing Edn., Bd. of Commr. Practicing Nurses Rep., Am. Soc. of Parenteral and Enteral Nutrition Publication Review Bd. E-mail: peisenberg@attglobal.net., peisenberg@ecommunity.com.

EISENBERG, PHYLLIS ROSE, author; b. Chgo., June 26, 1924; d. Lewis Rose and Frances (Remer) Rose Blossom; m. Emanuel M. Eisenberg; 1 child, Bart. BA, UCLA, 1946. Writing instr. L.A. Valley Coll., Van Nuys, Calif., 1975-78, L.A. Pierce Coll., Woodland Hills, Calif., 1983-85, UCLA, 1986; jour. writing instr. Everywoman's Village, Van Nuys, 1987-92; writing instr. Calif. State U., Northridge, 1996—, L.A. Valley Coll., 2003—04. Lit. cons., 1975—; presenter in field. Author: A Mitzvah Is Something Special, 1978 (one of 12 outstanding works of fiction of yr. Yearbook Ency. 1979), Don't Tell Me A Ghost Story, 1982 (All Choice Book Internat. Children's Exhbn., Munich 1983), You're My Nikki (NCSS-CBC Notable 1992 Children's Trade Book award, Children's Book of Yr. Bank St. Coll.); contbr. fiction, poetry and non-fiction to numerous newspapers and periodicals; creator Author in the Classroom program, 1986-88. Exec. sec. Founder's Guild of San Fernando Valley Child Guidance Clinic, Studio City, Calif., 1985; writing instr. Sophia Myers Sch. for Visually Handicapped, Van Nuys, 1987; reading instr. remedial program for children YMCA, Van Nuys, 1990; exec. sec. Valley Jewish Cmty. Ctr., North Hollywood, Calif., 1982. Mem. PEN, Soc. Children's Book Writers and Illustrators, Soc. Children's and Young People's Literature. Avocations: folk dancing, textile painting, yoga.

EISENBERG, ROBIN LEDGIN, religious education administrator; b. Passaic, N.J., Jan. 10, 1951; d. Morris and Ruth (Miller) Ledgin. BS, West Chester State U., 1973; M Edn., Kutztown State U., 1977. Administrv. asst. Keneseth Israel, Allentown, Pa., 1973-77; dir. edn. Cong. Schaarai Zedek, Tampa, Fla., 1977-79, Kehilath Israel, Pacific Palisades, Calif., 1979-80, Temple Beth El, Boca Raton, Fla., 1980-99, 2003—, Levis Jewish Cmty. Cen., Boca Raton, 1999—2003. Contbr. Learning Together, 1987, Bar/Bat Mizvah Education: A Sourcebook, 1993, The New Jewish Teachers Handbook, 1994. Chmn. edn. info., Planned Parenthood, Boca Raton Fla. 1989. Recipient Kamiker Camp award Nat. Assn. Temple Educators, Pres.'s award for adminstrn., 1990; Mandel fellow in Jewish Edn., Levis Jewish Cmty. Ctr., 2001-2003. Mem. Nat. Assn. Temple Educators (pres. 1990-92, chair UAHC-CCAR-NATE commn. on Jewish edn. 1997-99, accreditation chair 2000—), Coalition Advancement of Jewish Edn. (chair strategic planning com. 2003—), Assn. Jewish Ctr. Profls. (Profl. of Yr. award 2003). Avocation: photography. Home: 2428 NW 35th St Boca Raton FL 33431 Office: Temple Beth El 333 SW 4th Ave Boca Raton FL 33432 Office Phone: 561-391-9092. E-mail: robledeise@aol.com, reisenberg@bocatemplebethel.org.

EISENBERG, SONJA MIRIAM, artist; b. Berlin, June 10, 1926; arrived in U.S., 1938, naturalized, 1947; d. Adolf and Meta Cecilie (Bettauer) Weinberger; m. Jack Eisenberg, Mar. 31, 1946; children: Ralph, Lynn, Lauren. Student, Queens Coll., 1943—46, Middlebury Coll., 1945, NYU, 1952—54, BA, 1954; postgrad., Nat. Acad. Sch. Fine Arts, 1961. Artist-in-residence Cathedral of St. John the Divine, N.Y.C.; apptd. art dir. Hermes Media B.V., Amsterdam, 1992. One-woman shows include Bodley Gallery, N.Y.C., 1970, 1973, 1975, 1980, Galerie Art du Monde, Paris, 1973, Buyways Gallery, Sarasota, Fla., 1973—75, 1978, Galerie de Sfinx, Amsterdam, Netherlands, 1974, Huntsville (Ala.) Mus. Art, 1974, Anglo-Am. Art Mus., Baton Rouge, 1974, Comara Gallery, L.A., 1974, Palm Spring (Calif.) Desert Mus., 1975, Fordham U., N.Y.C., 1976, Omega Inst., New Lebanon, NY, 1979, Am. Mus., Hayden Planetarium, N.Y.C., 1980, Avila Graphics, Ltd., 1981, YWCA, N.Y.C., 1981, Cathedral of St. John the Divine, 1983, 1985, The Millbrook Gallery, NY, 1989, 1994, Christopher Leonard Gallery, N.Y.C., 1993, Park Hotel, Vitznau, Switzerland, 1994, The Burgenstock (Switzerland) Hotels, 1995, Wainscott Gallery, NY, 1997, Galerie Dussmann, Kulturkaufhaus, Berlin, 1998, Horton Gallery, Phila., 2001, exhibited in group shows at Mus. Fine Arts, St. Petersburg, Fla., 1973, Am. Watercolor Soc., 107th, 108th Exhbn., 1974—75, Galerie Frederic Gollong, St. Paul de Vence, France, 1978, Betty Parson's Gallery, N.Y.C., 1981, Foster Harmon Galleries of Am. Art, Sarasota, Fla., 1988, Tokyo Met. Art Mus. 14th Internat. Art Friendship Exhbn., 1989, Galerie Herbert Leidel, Munich, Germany, 1991, Park Ave. Armory, N.Y.C., 1996, Akim-USA, 1996, Represented in permanent collections Archives Am. Art, Smithsonian Inst., Jewish Mus., N.Y.C., Fordham U. Mus., Palm Springs Desert Mus., Omega Inst., Cathedral of St. John the Divine; designer WFUNA cachet for UN Water Power Conf., 1977, UN Internat. Yr. of Disabled Persons, 1981, commd. commemorative painting Crystal Night for Telecom Telefon Karte, Munich, 1993, completed project Seeing the Gospel According to St. John (text and 41 paintings) for Cathedral of St. John, 1987; author: From Here to There and Back Again, 2001, Poems and Paintings, 2002, The Red Painted House, 2002. Regent Cathedral of St. John the Divine, 1990. Recipient Gold medal for artistic merit, Internat. Parliament for Safety and Peace, 1983, Palma D'Oro Europe, 1986. Mem.: Accademia Italia delle Arti e del Lavoro (Gold medal 1981). Home and Office: 1020 Park Ave New York NY 10028-0913

EISENHAUER, GAYLE ANN, elementary school educator, secondary school educator; d. Marshall William and Shirley Elizabeth Morton; m. Dale Edward Eisenhauer, Mar. 3, 1984. BS, U. Ctrl. Okla., 1981, MA in Instrnl. Media, 1985. Tchr. Depew (Okla.) Pub. Sch., 1981—84; tchr. music Wickliffe Sch., Salina, Okla., 1984—91, libr., 1984—91; media specialist Salina (Okla.) Sch., 1991—93; tchr. music Hardesty (Okla.) Sch., 1993—2002, media specialist, 1993—2002; tchr. Newkirk (Okla.) Sch., 2002—. Named Tchr. of Today, Masons, 1995—96. Mem.: NEA, Okla. Music Edn. Assn. (judge 1999—2003), Okla. Edn. Assn., Nat. Music Edn. Assn. Democrat. Avocations: piano, singing, camping, travel, reading. Office: Newkirk Public School 701 W South St Newkirk OK 74647

EISENHAUER, LINDA ANN, volunteer; b. Logansport, Ind., Dec. 3, 1937; d. Donald Johnson and Isabel Owens (Murdock) Grube; m. Ronald George Eisenhauer, Aug. 12, 1961; 1 child, Donald Johnson. BS, Northwestern U., 1959. Tchr. Devonshire Sch., Skokie, Ill., 1959-61; tchr. 6th grade Atlanta Sch. Dist., 1961-62; tchr. 5th grade Marquette Sch., Gary, Ind., 1962-65. Elected adv. bd. Winfield Twp., Ind., 1987—, sec. adv. bd., pres. 1987—; vol. coun. bd. Am. Symphony Orch. League, Washington, 1975-82; pres. Calumet Parliamentary Unit, 1991-92; bd. dirs. Hospice of Calumet area, 1992—, Northwestern U. Alumnae, 1993—, Legacy Found. Grants, 1994—, Women's Assn. Chgo. Symphony Orchestra, 1999—; founder Greater Gary Heights Arts Coun. and Lake Area Arts Coun.; regional chmn. Indian Advocates for the Arts; bd. dirs. Am. Cancer Soc., chmn. breast cancer clinic. Named Outstanding Young Woman, Ind., 1967; recipient svc. award Northwestern U., 1993. Fellow AAUW (pres. Gary-Merrillville br. 1975-77); mem. N.W. Ind. Symphony (v.p. 1981-85, bd. dirs. 1968—), Women's Assn. N.W. Ind. Symphony (pres. 1972-74, bd. dirs. 1965—), Soc. 600 of Internat. Violin Competition (v.p. 1991, bd. dirs. 1988—), Northwestern U. Alumni Assn. (v.p. 1986-88), Northwestern Alumni Club N.W. Ind. (pres. 1976-96), Kappa Kappa Kappa (pres.), Alpha Chi Omega (pres. alumni chpt.). Republican. Episcopalian. Avocations: travel, golf, health. Address: 1736 Beachview Ct Crown Point IN 46307-9411

EISENHOWER, LAURIE, performing company executive; BA in Dance, MFA in Dance, Arizona State U. Faculty Oakland U., Rochester, 1986—, full professor & head of dance; founder, artistic dir. Eisenhower Dance Ensemble, Rochester Hills, Mich., 1991—. Recipient Oakland U Faculty Recognition Award, 1997. Office: Eisenhower Dance Ensemble 1541 W Hamlin Rd Rochester Hills MI 48309*

EISENSTADT, PAULINE DOREEN BAUMAN, investment company executive, state legislator; b. N.Y.C., Dec. 31, 1938; d. Morris and Anne (Lautenberg) Bauman; m. Melvin M. Eisenstadt, Nov. 20, 1960; children: Todd Alan, Keith Mark. BA, U. Fla., 1960; MS, U. Ariz., 1965; postgrad., U. N.Mex. Tchr., Ariz., 1961—65, 1972—73; adminstrv. asst. Inst. Social Rsch. U. N.Mex., 1973—74; founder, 1st exec. dir. Energy Consumers N.Mex., 1977—81, chmn. consumer affairs adv. com. Dept. Energy, 1979—80; v.p. tech. bd. Nat. Ctr. Appropriate Tech., 1980—; pres. Eisenstadt Enterprises, investments, 1983—; mem. N.Mex. Ho. of Reps., 1985—92, chairwoman majority caucus, chair rules com., 1987—, chair sub. com. on children and youth, 1987; mem. N.Mex. State Senate, 1996—2000; mem. senate fin. com., com. higher edn., com. econ. devel., sci. & tech., water & natural resources, electric deregulation com., chair conservation co; mem. senate fin. com., com. higher edn., com. econ. devel., sci. & tech., water & natural resources, electric deregulation com.; chair conservation com. Mem. exec. com., vice chair pvt. coun. Nat. Conf. State Legislators, 1987, vice chmn. Sandoval County (N.Mex.) Dem. Party, 1981—; mem. N.Mex. Dem. State Ctrl. Com., 1981—; N.Mex. del. Dem. Nat. Platform Com., 1984, Dem. Nat. Conv., 1984. Host (TV program) N.Mex. Today and Tomorrow, 1992—, exec. prodr., host Tech Talks, 2001—; author: Corrales, Portrait of a Changing Village, 1980. Pres. Anti Defamation League, N.Mex., 1994—95; mem. N.Mex. First; pres. Sandoval County Dem. Women's Assn., 1979—81; vice chmn. N.Mex. Dem. Platform Com., 1984—; mem. Sandoval County Redistricting Task Force, 1983—84, Rio Rancho Ednl. Study Com., 1984—. Recipient Gov.'s award Outstanding N. Mex. Women, Commn. on the Status of Women and Gov. Bruce King, 1992; grantee, NSF, 1965. Mem.: Rio Rancho Rotary Club (pres. 1995—, Rotarian of Yr. 1995), Kiwanis (1st woman mem. local club). Home: PO Box 658 Corrales NM 87048-0658 E-mail: peisenstad@aol.com.

EISENSTEIN, ELIZABETH LEWISOHN, historian, educator; b. N.Y.C., Oct. 11, 1923; d. Sam A. and Margaret V. (Seligman) Lewisohn; m. Julian Calvert Eisenstein, May 30, 1948; children: Margaret, John (dec.), Edward. AB, Vassar Coll., 1944; MA, Radcliffe Coll., 1947, PhD, 1953; LittD (hon.), Mt. Holyoke Coll., 1979. From lectr. to adj. prof history Am. U., Washington, 1959-74; Alice Freeman Palmer prof. history U. Mich., Ann Arbor, 1975-88, prof. emerita, 1988—. Scholar-in-residence Rockefeller Found. Ctr., Bellagio, Italy, June 1977; mem. vis. com. dept. history Harvard U., 1975-81, vice-chmn., 1979-81; dir. Ecole des Hautes Etudes en Sciences Sociales, Paris, 1982; guest spkr., participant confs. and seminars; I. Beam vis. prof. U. Iowa, 1980; Mead-Swing lectr. Oberlin Coll., 1980; Stone lectr. U. Glasgow, 1984; Van Leer lectr. Van Leer Fedn., Jerusalem, 1984; Hanes lectr. U. N.C., Chapel Hill, 1985 first resident cons. Ctr. for the Book, Libr. of Congress, Washington, 1979; mem. Coun. Scholars, 1980-88; pres.'s disting. visitor Vassar Coll., 1988; Pforzheimer lectr. N.Y. Pub. Libr., 1989, Lyell lectr. Bodleian Libr., Oxford, 1990, Merle Curti lectr. U. Wis., Madison, 1992, Jantz lectr. Oberlin Coll., 1995, Clifford lectr. Austin, Tex., 1996; vis. fellow Wolfson Coll., Oxford, 1990; sem. dir. Folger Inst., 1999. Author: The First Professional Revolutionist: F. M. Buonarroti, 1959, The Printing Press as an Agent of Change, 1979, 2 vols. paperback edit., 1980 (Phi Beta Kappa Ralph Waldo Emerson prize 1980), The Printing Revolution in Early Modern Europe, 1983 (reissued as Canto Book, 1993), Grub Street Abroad, 1992; mem. editorial bd. Jour. Modern History, 1973-76, 83-86, Revs. in European History, 1973-86, Jour. Library History, 1979-82, Eighteenth Century Studies, 1981-84; contbr. articles to profl. jours., chpts. to books. Bd. dirs. Folger Shakespeare Libr., 2000—. Belle Skinner fellow Vassar Coll., NEH fellow, 1977, Guggenheim fellow, 1982, fellow Ctr. Advanced Studies in Behavioral Scis., 1982-83, 92-93, Humanities Rsch. Ctr. fellow Australian Nat. U., 1988. Fellow Am. Acad. Arts and Scis., Royal Hist. Soc.; mem. Soc. French Hist. Studies (v.p. 1970, program com. 1974), Am. Soc. 18th Century Studies (nominating com. 1971), Soc. 16th Century Studies, Am. Hist. Assn. (com. on coms. 1970-72, chmn. Modern European sect. 1981, coun. 1982-85, Scholarly Distinction award 2003), Renaissance Soc. Am. (coun. 1973-76, pres. 1986), Am. Antiquarian Soc. (exec. com., adv. bd. 1984-87), Phi Beta Kappa. Office: U Mich Dept History Ann Arbor MI 48109 E-mail: eisenst@mindspring.com.

EISENSTEIN, TOBY K. microbiology educator; b. Phila., Sept. 15, 1942; d. Edward and Sylvia (Mandel) Karet; m. Bruce A. Eisenstein, Sept. 8, 1963; children: Eric, Andrew, Ilana. BA, Wellesley Coll., 1964; PhD, Bryn Mawr Coll., 1969. Instr. Med. Sch. Temple U., Phila., 1969-71, asst. prof., 1971-79, assoc. prof. microbiology and immunology Med. Sch., 1979-84, prof., 1984—, acting chair, 1990-92, co-dir. Ctr. Substance Abuse Rsch., 1992—. Mem. bacteriology and mycology study sect., NIH, 1976-80, 88-92, Drugs of Abuse and AIDS study sect., 1994—. Contbr. articles to profl. jours. Recipient Rsch. prize Temple U., 2003; NIH fellow, 1965-69; USPHS grantee, 1971—. Fellow Am. Acad. Microbiology; mem. AAAS, Am. Soc. Microbiology (pres. Ea. Pa. br. 1983-86, coun. policy com. 1993-96, chair membership bd. 2003—), Am. Assn. Immunologists, Soc. Leukocyte Biology (sec. 1998-2000), Internat. Endotoxin Soc., Soc. Neuroimmune Pharmacology (Jospeh Wybran award), Psychoneuroimmunology Rsch. Soc., Coll. on Problems of Drug Dependence, Sigma Xi, (pres. Temple U. chpt. 1981-83). Office: Temple U Sch Medicine Dept Microbiology and Immunology 3400 N Broad St Philadelphia PA 19140-5104 Office Phone: 215-707-3585. E-mail: tke@temple.edu.

EISLER, SUSAN KRAWETZ, advertising executive; b. N.Y.C., Aug. 18, 1946; d. Aaron and Bertha (Platt) Krawetz; m. Howard Irwin Eisler, June 8, 1980; 1 stepchild, Robin Joy; 1 adopted child, Joseph. BA, U. Pitts., 1967; MA, New Sch. for Social Rsch., 1971. Analyst Marplan, Inc., N.Y.C., 1968-69; project dir. Market Facts, Inc., N.Y.C., 1969-70; assoc. rsch. mgr. Gen. Foods, Inc., White Plains, N.Y., 1970-75, product mgr., 1975-80; rsch. dir. Elizabeth Arden, N.Y.C., 1980-81; v.p., assoc. rsch. dir. Lintas: N.Y. (formerly SSC&B: Lintas Worldwide), N.Y.C., 1981-87, sr. v.p., assoc. rsch. dir., 1987-92, exec. v.p., dir. strategic planning and rsch., 1992-94, Gotham, Inc., 1995—, mng. ptnr., dir. rsch. and info. svcs. Named Woman of Yr., YWCA Acad. Women Achievers, 1989. Mem.: Advt. Rsch. Found. (copy rsch. coun.), Am. Mktg. Assn. Office: Gotham Inc 100 5th Ave Fl 16 New York NY 10011-6996

EISNER, CAROLE SWID, artist; b. N.Y.C., Oct. 30, 1937; d. David and Selma (Claar) Swid; m. Richard Alan Eisner, May 7, 1961; children: Joseph, Susan, Michael, Douglas, Hallie. AB, Syracuse U., 1958; studies with Schwabacher, N.Y.C., 1963; studies with Marge Walzer, Westport, Conn., 1969-78; postgrad., Internat. Sch. Photography, 1976-78. Solo shows include Silvermine (Conn.) Ctr. for Arts, 1977, 84, Lubin House Gallery, N.Y.C., 1979, 82, Segal Gallery, N.Y.C., 1984-85, 86, Jill Youngblood Gallery, L.A., 1985, Jack Gallery, N.Y.C., 1987, 88, First Women's Bank, N.Y.C., 1988, New Inst. of Contemporary Art, London, 1988, David Findlay Galleries, N.Y.C., 1990, Gallery Tanishima, Tokyo, 1992, Gallery Sagan, Tokyo, 1992; group shows include Segal Gallery, N.Y.C., 1985, 86, Guggenheim Mus., N.Y.C., 1986, Images Gallery, Norwalk, Conn., 1986, Jack Gallery, N.Y.C., 1987, Inst. of Contemporary Art, London, 1988, many others; represented in permanent collections at Guggenheim Mus., Syracuse U., Nat. Assocs., Inc., S.E. Banking Corp., Northstar Reins. Co., Knoll Internat., FMC Corp., Skadden, Arps, Meager & Flom, Orion Bank, Ltd., Goldmark Ptnrs., Inc., MBS Multi Mode, Inc., Bill Silver Assocs.; sculptures exhibited at The River Park Atrium, Norwalk, Conn., 1997-98, Chesterwood, Stockbridge, Mass., 1998, Burlington County Coll. Sculpture Garden, Pemberton, N.J., 1998, Veterans Park, Norwalk, 1999, Peninsula Park, Jersey City, 1999, Cranbury Park, Norwalk, 1999, City Hall, Norwalk, 1998-99, Fordham U., 2000, Lock Bldg., Norwalk, 2001, Heritage Park, Norwalk, 2002, Silvermine Guild, Norwalk; created stage design for four Off-Broadway plays at Theater XII, 1978. Recipient Award for Sculpture Merchants Bank and Trust Co., 1975, Champion Internat. Corp., 1980, Rosenthal Award for Outdoor Sculpture, 1978; named among ten outstanding young women Mademoiselle Mag., 1962; finalist Nat. Sculpture Competition, 1980. Home and Office: 1107 5th Ave New York NY 10128-0145 Fax: 212-828-4415.

EISNER, DIANA, pediatrician; b. Houston, May 7, 1951; d. Elmer and Edith (Dubow) E. BA in Biology cum laude, Brandeis U., 1973; MD, Southwestern Med. Sch., 1977. Diplomate Am. Bd. Pediatrics. Intern, resident Baylor Coll. Medicine, Houston, 1977-80; pvt. practice Houston, 1981—. Chmn. dept. pediat. Meml. N.W. Hosp., Houston, 1990. Recipient Commendation award Children's Protection Com. Tex. Children's Hosp., 1978, Physician's Recognition award AMA, 1983. Mem. Am. Acad. Pediatrics, Tex. Med. Assn., Tex. Pediatric Soc., Houston Pediatric Soc. (treas. 2001-02, sec. 2002-), Harris County Med. Soc. Avocations: ballet, swimming, walking. Office: 2030 North Loop W Ste 123 Houston TX 77018-8132 Office Phone: 713-688-8393.

EISNER, GAIL ANN, artist, educator; b. Detroit, Oct. 17, 1939; d. Rudolph and Florence (White) Leon; m. Marvin Michael Eisner, June 14, 1959 (dec. Feb. 1993); 1 child, Alan. Student, Art Student League of N.Y.; BFA, Wayne State U. Alan prof. Pace U., N.Y.C. (one-woman shows) The Starkweather Art Cultural Ctr., Romeo, Mich., Shiawassee Arts Ctr., Owosso, Mich., Worthington Art Ctr., Ohio, OK Harris/David Klein Gallery, Birmingham, Mich., Sinclair Coll., LRC Gallery, Dayton, Ohio, U. Mich. Hosps., Ann Arbor, Collin County Coll., Plano, Tex., 1997, Art Ctr. Mt. Clemens, (group shows) Islip Art Mus., East Islip, N.Y., Columbia (Mo.) Coll., Tubac (Ariz.) Ctr. of Arts, Ft. Wayne (Ind.) Mus. of Art, C.W. Post Coll., Brookville, N.Y., NAWA, Jacob K. Kavits Ctr., N.Y.C., Schoharie County Coun. of Arts, Cobbleskill, N.Y., ARC Gallery, Chgo., McPherson (Kans.) Coll., Med. Coll. Ga., Augusta, Heckscher Mus. Art, Huntington, Nassau County Mus. Art, Roslyn, N.Y., Guild Hall, East Hampton, N.Y., Castle Gould, Sands Point, N.Y., Pastel Soc. Am., N.Y.C., Carrier Found., Belle Meade, N.J., Hill Country Arts Found., Ingram, Tex., Cunningham Meml. Art Gallery, Bakersfield, Calif., Henry Hicks Gallery, Bklyn. Hts., U. N.D., Grand Forks, Nassau C.C., Garden City, N.Y., Trenton (N.J.) State Coll., Wenatchee Valley (W.Va.) Coll., Del Mar Coll., Corpus Christi, Tex., Minot (N.D.) State U., Ctrl. Mo. State U., McNeese State U., Lake Charles, La., Worthington Art Ctr., Ohio, Art Ctr., Mt. Clemens, Mich., Oakland C.C., Krasl Art Ctr., St. Joseph, Mich., Fontana Concert Soc., Kalamazoo, Mich., Art Ctr. Battle Creek, Mich., Ctrl. Mich. U., Mt. Pleasant, Birmingham (Mich.) Bloomfield Art Assn., Cmty. House, Birmingham, Sch. Art Inst., Chgo., Cheekwood Mus. Art, Nashville, Grand Rapids (Mich.) Mus. Art, Flint (Mich.) Inst. Arts, Ariana Gallery, Royal Oak, Mich., Judith Paul Gallery, Medford, Oreg., The Art Collector, San Diego, Gwenda Jay Gallery, Chgo., Columbia Greens Coll., Hudson, N.Y., Worthington (Ohio) Art Ctr., Holland Area Arts Coun., Mich., The Art Source, Santa Barbara, Calif., Outside The Line Gallery, Grosse Ile, Mich., (permanent collections) Rabobank, Chgo., Resurrection Hosp., Kanai (Hawaii) Hotel, Jules Joyner Designs, Royal Oak, Mich., The Lumber Store, Chgo., others, (also pvt. collections). Recipient Adriana Zahn award Pastel Soc. Am., Heckscher Mus. award, Our Visions: Women in Art award Oakland C.C., 1995, Beatrice G. Epstein meml. award, 1997. Mem. Nat. Assn. Women Artists (Sara Winston Meml. award 1992), N.Y. Artist Equity Assn., Art Student League N.Y. (Sidney Dickinson Meml. award), Birmingham Bloomfield Art Assn. Studio: Ste 108 27600 Farmington Rd Farmington Hills MI 48334-3365

EISNER, SISTER JANET MARGARET, college president; b. Boston, Oct. 10, 1940; d. Eldon and Ada (Martin) E. AB, Emmanuel Coll., 1963; MA, Boston Coll., 1969; PhD, U. Mich., 1975; LHD (hon.), Northeastern U. Joined Sisters of Notre Dame de Namur, Roman Cath. Ch. Dir. admissions Emmanuel Coll., 1967-71; lectr., teaching asst. U. Mich., Ann Arbor, 1971-73; dir. Emmanuel Coll. and City of Boston Pairings, 1976-78, asst. prof. English, 1976-78, chmn. dept., 1977-78, acting pres., 1978-79, pres., 1979—. Mem. Mass. Bd. Regents, chmn. regents planning com., 1980-86; mem. adv. bd. Ctr. for Religious Devel., 1983—; mem. exec. com. Boston Higher Edn. Partnership, 1991—. Trustee Trinity Coll., 1979-85, mem. adv. coun. on enrollment planning, 1981-82; adv. coun. pres. Assn. Governing Bds., 1982-88; mem. commn. on women in higher edn. Am. Coun. on Edn., 1985-87; mem. adv. bd. Synod of Archdiocese of Boston, 1988, Anti-Defamation League Dinner Com., 1988-89; chair four-yr. coll. div. United Way Campaign, 1989; mem. NAICU/NIIC joint task force Minority Participation in Ind. Higher Edn., 1989; mem. govs. award com. Carballo Scholarships, 1989; bd. dirs. Med. Area Svc. Corp., 1989—; trustee Boston Cath. TV Ctr., 1990—. Rackham prize fellow, Ford Found. fellow, 1973-75. Mem. Nat. Assn. Ind. Colls. and Univs. (commn. on policy analysis 1991—), Assn. Ind. Colls. and Univs. in Mass. (chair 1991—), Women's Coll. Coalition (exec. com. 1991—). Office: Emmanuel Coll Office of the President 400 Fenway Boston MA 02115-5725

EISNER, REBECCA SUZANNE, lawyer; b. Wheeling, W.Va., Aug. 27, 1962; d. Paul and Marilyn June (Muffeny) Redosh; m. Craig George Eisner, Dec. 30, 1988. BA, Ohio State U., 1984; JD, U. Mich., 1989. Assoc. Mayer, Brown & Platt, Chgo., 1989-92; assoc. group counsel, asst. v.p. Equifax,

Inc., Atlanta, 1993—. Exec. vol. United Way of Metro Atlanta, 1994; vol. fund raiser Atlanta Women's Fund, 1994. Mem. ABA. Avocations: running, golf. Office: Equifax Inc 1600 W Peachtree St NE Atlanta GA 30309-2642

EIZENBERG, JULIE, architect; BArch, U. Melbourne, Australia, 1978; [illegible] II, UCLA, 1981. Lic. architect, Calif., reg. architect, Australia. Principal, architect Koning Eizenberg Architecture, Santa Monica, Calif., 1981—. Instr. various courses UCLA, MIT, Harvard U.; lectr. in field; jury member P/A awards. Exhbns. incl. Koning Eizenberg Architecture 3A Garage, San Francisco, 1996, "House Rules" Wexner Ctr., 1994, "The Architect's Dream: Houses for the Next Millenium" The Contemporary Arts Ctr., 1993, "Angels & Franciscans" Gagosian Gallery, 1992, Santa Monica Mus. Art, 1993, "Broadening the Discourse" Calif. Women in Environmental Design, 1992, "Conceptional Drawings by Architects" Bannatyne Gallery, 1991, Exhbn. Koning Eizenberg Projects Grad. Sch. Architecture & Urban Planning UCLA, 1990; prin. works include Digital Domain Renovation and Screening Room, Santa Monica, Lightstorm Entertainment Office Renovation and Screening Room, Santa Monica, Gilmore Bank Addition and Remodel, L.A., 1548-1550 Studios, Santa Monica, (with RTA) Materials Rsch. Lab. at U. Calif., Santa Barbara, Ken Edwards Ctr. Cmty. Svcs., Santa Monica, Peck Park Cmty. Ctr. Gymnasium, San Pedro, Calif., Sepulveda Recreation Ctr., L.A. (Design award AIA San Fernando Valley 1995, Nat. Concrete and Masonry award 1996, AIA Calif. Coun. Honor award 1996, L.A. Bus. Coun. Beautification award 1996, AIA Los Angeles Chpt. Merit Award, 1997), PS # 1 Elem. Sch., Santa Monica, Farmers Market, L.A. Additions and Master Plan (Westside Urban Forum prize 1991), Stage Deli, L.A., Simone Hotel, L.A. (Nat. Honor award AIA 1994), Boyd Hotel, L.A., Cmty. Corp. Santa Monica Housing Projects, 5th St. Family Housing, Santa Monica, St. John's Hosp. Replacement Housing Program, Santa Monica, Liffman Ho., Santa Monica, (with Glenn Erikson) Electric Artblock, Venice (Beautification award L.A. Bus. Coun. 1993), 6th St. Condominiums, Santa Monica, Hollywood Duplex, Hollywood Hills (Record Houses Archtl. Record 1988), California Ave. Duplex, Santa Monica, Tarzana Ho. (Award of Merit L.A. chpt. AIA 1992, AIA Calif. Coun. Merit Award, 1998, Sunset Western home Awards citation 1993-94), 909 Ho., Santa Monica (Award of Merit L.A. chpt. AIA 1991), 31st St. Ho., Santa Monica (Honor award AIACC 1994, Nat. AIA Honor award 1996), others. Recipient 1st award Progressive Architecture, 1987; named one of Domino's Top 30 Architects, 1989. Mem. L.A. County Mus. Art, Westside Urban Forum, Urban Land Inst., Architects and Designers for Social Responsibility, Mus. Contemporary Art, The Nature Conservancy, Sierra Club. Office: Koning Eizenberg Architecture 1454 25th St Santa Monica CA 90404-3008

EKANGER, KARIN L. educational consultant; b. Boise, Idaho, Apr. 8, 1954; d. Bernard Olaf and Mary Louise E.; m. Mitchell Durand, June 3, 1978 (div. Oct., 1980). BA in English with honors, U. Mont., 1976; MEd, Mont. State U., 1983; adminstrv. endorsement, U. Nev. Las Vegas, 1993—98; EdD, Nova Southeastern U., 2003. Cert. K-12 reading splst., 7-12 English, K-12 adminstr. Reading lab tchr. Powell County High Sch., Deer Lodge, Mont., 1976-77; reading lab tutor, substitute tchr. Billings (Mont.) Sch. Dist. # 2, 1977-78; tchr. remedial reading, English Lincoln Jr. High Sch., 1978-79; lang. arts tchr. Castle Rock Jr. High Sch., 1979-84; reading improvement splst. George Dewey High Sch. U.S. Dept. Def. Dependents Schs., Subic Bay, Philippines, 1984-87; reading improvement splst. Grafenwoehr Am. Ele. Sch. Grafenwoehr, Germany, 1987-88; tchr. reading, English Vilseck (Germany) Am. High Sch., 1988-89; reading tchr. Joe Walker Middle Sch. Westside Union Sch. Dist., Lancaster, Calif., 1989-90; tchr. English Highland High Sch. Antelope Valley High Sch. Dist., Palmdale, Calif., 1990-92; reading tchr. J.D. Smith Middle Sch. Clark County Sch. Dist., Las Vegas, 1993-96; tchr. English Las Vegas Acad. Internat. Studies, Performing and Visual Art, 1996-97; tchr. on spl. assignment, 1996—97; tchr. on spl. assignment sys. design, staff devel., 1997; dean of students Valley High Sch., 1998—; adminstr. on spl. assignment Adminstrv. Tng. Dept., 2000—; secondary cons. Pearson Learning Group, Henderson, Nev., 2001—. Summer sch. dean intern Bonanza High Sch., 1997; grant writer; presenter in field; attendee numerous confs. Recipient Cert. Appreciation ARC, 1986-87, Achievement award DoDDS, 1987. Mem. Nat. Coun. Tchrs. English, Internat. Reading Assn., Nev. Assn. Sch. Adminstrs., Clark County Assn. Secondary Sch. Prins., So. Nev. Coun. Tchrs. English and Lang. Arts (exec. bd. dirs. 1997, planner, host Poetry Alive! performance 1997), Assn. Supervision and Curriculum Devel., Phi Delta Kappa. Home: 185 Ruidoso Ln Henderson NV 89074

EKANGER, LAURIE, retired state official, retired contractor; b. Salt Lake City, Mar. 4, 1949; d. Bernard and Mary (Dearth) E.; m. William J. Shupe, Nov. 6, 1973; children: Ben, Robert. BA in English, U. Oreg., 1973. Various pos. Mont. State Employment & Tng. Divsn., Helena, 1975-80, dep. adminstr., 1980-82; adminstr. Mont. State Purchasing Divsn., Helena, 1982-85, Mont. State Personnel Divsn., Helena, 1985-93; labor commr. Mont. Dept. Labor & Ind., Helena, 1993-97; dir. Mont. Dept. Pub. Health and Human Svcs., 1997-2000. Council chair State Employee Group Benefits Coun., 1985-93; bd. dirs. Pub. Employee Retirement Bd., 1988; mem. various state adv. couns. for health and human svcs. Home: 80 Pinecrest Rd Clancy MT 59634-9505

EKBATANI, GLAYOL, language educator, director, writer; b. Tehran, Iran; d. Saed and Parvin (Sohai) E. PhD, U. Ill., 1981. Dir., prof. English 2d lang. program U. Maine, Orano, 1987-90; dir. English 2d lang., bilingual programs C.C. Phila., 1990-92; dir., prof. English 2d lang. programs St. John's U., Jamaica, N.Y., 1992—. Rschr. Georgetown U., Washington, 1986-87. Author: Learner Directed Assessment, 1999; contbr. articles to profl. jours. Mem. Nat. Assn. Fgn. Students Washington, Tchrs. English to Spkrs. of Other Langs. (pres. 1991-92). Home: 301 E 79th St Apt 16 New York NY 10021-0951 Office: St John's U 8000 Utopia Pkwy Rm 377 Jamaica NY 11432-1343

EKELCHIK, JODI, management consultant; BSBA, U. of Del., 1989; M in Pub. Fin., NYU, 1995. Cert. Coll. Bus. Mgmt. Inst. SACUBO - Ky., 2000. Sales assoc. Alex Brown LLP, N.Y.C., NY, 1989—93; mgmt. cons. BearingPoint (formerly KPMG Consulting), N.Y.C., NY, 1996—2003, applications and ops. cons., ind. contractor London, 2003—. Personal E-mail: jekelchik@sugob.com.

EKSTROM, LISA MARIE, special education educator; b. Gary, Ind., Sept. 8, 1956; d. Casmir and Sally Deane (Liedtke) Tokarz; m. Edward Jay Ekstrom, Oct. 3, 1987; children: Melody Dawn, Justin Edward. BS, Ball State U., Muncie, Ind., 1978; MA, Ball State U., Muncie, Ind., 1983; continued edn., Purdue Univ.-Calumet, Hammond, Ind., 1980, Ind. Wesleyan U., Marion, Ind., 2000—02. Cert. Therapeutic Crisis Intervention Cornell U., 2000, Mentally Handicapped Ind., 1978, Learning Disabled Ind., 1983. Spl. edn. tchr. South Newton Mid. Sch., Kentland, Ind., 1978—. Summer sch. spl. edn. tchr. (mentally handicapped) Benton Ctrl. Sch. Corp., Oxford, Ind., 1981; elem. summer sch. tchr. South Newton Sch. Corp., Kentland, Ind., 1987; jr. class sponsor South Newton Jr. Sr. H.S., Kentland, Ind., 1980—82, Kentland, 1989—90; student coun. sponsor South Newton Mid. Sch., Kentland, Ind., 2000—, building-level discussions com., 2000—01; actress in The Music Man and State Fair South Newton Drama Dept., Kentland, Ind., 2001—, publicity chairperson, make-up crew for Grease, 2001—; chaperone for nat. conv. South Newton H.S. FBLA, Washington, 1986; chaperone 8th grade student trip South Newton Mid. Sch., Washington, 1996. Mem. of Live 'n Learn Newton County Ext. Homemakers, Kentland, Ind., 2000; alumni Psi Iota Xi, Brook, Ind., 1987—90; vacation bible sch. staff United Meth. Ch., Brook, Ind., 1997—2000; pastor parish com. Brook United Meth. Ch., Brook, Ind., 2001. Recipient 20th Yr. of Tchg. Pin/cert., South Newton Sch. Corp. supt. and Bd. of Trustees, 1998, 25th Yr. of Tchg. Pin/cert./pen Set, 2003. Mem.: South Newton Faculty Orgn. (sec. 1983—85), South Newton Classroom Tchrs. Assn., Ind. State Tchrs. Assn., Nat. Edn. Assn., Coun. for Exceptional Children (assoc. 2 time nominee for Tchr. of Yr.). United Meth. Achievements include greatest accomplishment [illegible] remain in the spl. edn. classroom for 26 yrs. with the "burn out" factor with spl. educators, I am very proud I'm still helping kids be the best they can be. Avocations: scrapbooks, travel, theater, reading. Office: S Newton Mid Sch 13100 S 50 E Kentland IN 47951 Office Phone: 219-474-5167 229. Personal E-mail: ekstrom4@sugardog.com. E-mail: ekstroml@newton.k12.in.us.

ELCANO, MARY S. lawyer; BA cum laude, Lynchburg Coll., 1971; JD, Cath. U., Washington, 1976. Litigation atty. Balt. Legal Aide Bur., 1976; staff atty. Office Solicitor Dept. Labor, 1979; gen. trial and appellate atty. Office Labor Law U.S. Postal Svc., 1982, exec. dir. Office EEO, 1984, regional dir. human resources N.E. region, 1987, sr. v.p., gen. counsel, 1992-99, exec. v.p., gen. counsel, 1999-2000; ptnr. Sidley Austin Brown & Wood LLP, Washington, 2000—03; gen. counsel, corp. sec. ARC, Washington, 2003—. Office: ARC 2025 E St NW Washington DC 20006 Office Phone: 202-303-5422. E-mail: ElcanoM@usa.redcross.org.

ELCIK, ELIZABETH MABIE, fashion illustrator; b. Bklyn., Sept. 16, 1933; d. Cornelius Peter and Anna Julia (Cunningham) Mabie; m. John Joseph Elcik, Apr. 20, 1963. Grad., Jamesine Franklin Sch. Profl. Arts, N.Y.C., 1954; student in painting, NYU; student life class, Art Students League, N.Y.C., Alliance of Queens Artists, 2003. Fashion illustrator Vogue patterns Conde Nast Publs., 1954-59; freelance illustrator various clients, N.Y.C., 1960-74; fashion illustrator Butterick Fashion Mktg. Co., N.Y.C., 1974-82, McCall Pattern Co., N.Y.C., 1982—2001. Monitor profl. sketch classes, N.Y.C., 1962—79. Exhibitions include Cedar House Gallery, 2004. Scholar N.Y.C Art, 1951, Jamesine Franklin Sch., 1952. Mem.: Women's Studio Ctr. Inc., Nat. Mus. Women in Arts. Roman Catholic. Avocation: travel.

ELDEFRAWI, AMIRA TOPPOZADA, medical educator, toxicologist, pharmacologist, neuroscientist; b. Giza, Cairo, Egypt, Feb. 10, 1937; came to U.S., 1968; d. Hussein Khairy Toppozada and Fadila Arif; children: Mosen M., Mona D. Hoff, Mohab M. BS, U. Alexandria, Egypt, 1957; PhD, U. Calif., Berkeley, 1960. Asst. prof. U. Alexandria, 1960-68; rsch. assoc. prof. Cornell U., Ithaca, N.Y., 1968-76; from rsch. assoc. prof. to rsch. prof. U. Md. Sch. Medicine, Balt., 1976-88; prof. U. Md., Balt., 1988—. Cons. U.S. State Dept., U.S. Environ. Protection Agy., Washington, 1982—, Nat. Inst. Environ. Health Sci. Rev. Com., Research Triangle Park, N.C., 1987-91, ad-hoc, 1991—, EPA Sci. Adv. Panel, 1997—; scholar-in-residence Queen's U. Sch. Medicine, Kingston, Ont., Can., 1985. Author: Resistance of Insects to Insecticides, 1966; editor Myasthenia Gravis, 1983; assoc. editor Membrane Biochemistry, 1987-93; mem. editorial bd. Pesticide Biochemistry & Physiology, 1987-99, Jour. Toxicology and Environ. Health, 1987—, Environ. Rsch., 1995—, Jour. Pesticide Management and Environ., 1996—; publ. scientific papers and revs. in field. Grantee NIH, 1975—, NATO, 1986-89, U.S. Army, 1995-98. Mem. Am. Soc. Pharmacology and Exptl. Therapeutics, Soc. Toxicology (pres. neurotoxicology splty. sect. 1996-97). Office: U Md Sch Medicine 655 W Baltimore St Baltimore MD 21201-1509 E-mail: aeldefra@umaryland.edu.

ELDER, AMY HOPE, psychotherapist, counselor; b. Ann Arbor, Mich., June 16, 1970; d. Robert Gordon and Martha Key (Rock) Ause; m. Bobby Van Elder, Dec. 3, 1994. Student, Regensburg (Germany) U., 1990-91; BA in Psychology, Vanderbilt U., 1992; MA in Counseling, Denver Sem., 1995. Counselor InCare Inc., Knoxville, Tenn., 1996; therapist Genesis Treatment Ctr., Kansas City, Mo., 1996-97; career counselor for substance abusing offenders Maryville (Mo.) Treatment Ctr., 1997—2000; counselor Northwest Mo. State U., 2000—01; contractor Warrenville, Ill., 2001—. Big sister Doulos Ministries/Shelterwood, Branson, Mo., 1992-93. Mem. ACA, Am. Assn. Christian Counselors, Chi Omega, Psi Chi. Avocations: cooking, sports, singing. Home: 25467 Choice Drive Warrenville IL 60555

ELDER, IRMA, retail automotive executive; b. Xicotencalt, Mex., 1934; m. James Elder, 1963 (dec.); 3 children. Owner, CEO Elder Automotive Group, 1983—. Mem. VIP panel 36th Annual Northwood U. Internat. Auto Show; founder Woman's Automotive Assn. Internat. Bd. dirs. Northwood U., Coll. Creative Studies, Oakland Family Svcs., Econ. Club Detroit. Named Woman Yr., Woman's Automotive Assn. Internat., 2001; named one of 100 Most Influential Women, Crain's Detroit Bus., 100 Leading Women, Automotive News, 2000; recipient Automotive Hall Fame Svc. Citation award, 2000, Pres. award, Ford Motor Co., 2000, 2001, Pride of Jaguar award, 1999, 2000. Achievements include frequently honored for many charitable assn; first woman to own Ford dealership in metropolitan Detroit market; successfully expanded co. from one dealership to eight after death of husband, founder of Elder Automotive; number one Saab dealership in US in volume of automobile sales (Saab of Troy); number one Jaguar dealership in N. Am. in volume of automobile sales (Jaguar of Troy); Elder Automotive consistently ranks top ten of Hispanic Bus. mag. top 500 Hispanic owned co. Office: 777 John R Rd Troy MI 48083 Office Fax: 248-583-0815.*

ELDER, MARY LOUISE, librarian; b. Ann Arbor, Mich., Sept. 7, 1937; d. John Dyer and Elsie (Phelps) E. BA, St. Louis U., 1959; MA, U. Chgo., 1962; postgrad., U. Calif., Berkeley, 1965-69. Libr. U. Chgo., 1961-63; rare book cataloger U. Kans., Lawrence, 1963-65; rare books libr. St. Louis Pub. Libr., 1969-74; rare book cataloger Duke U., Durham, N.C., 1979-84, Smithsonian Inst., Washington, 1984-91, Libr. Congress, Washington, 1991—2002; ret. Mem. ALA, Am. Printing History Assn., Bibliog. Soc., Bibliog. Soc. Am., Cath. Libr. Assn., Soc. History Authorship, Reading and Publishing, Alpha Sigma Nu.

ELDERKIN, HELAINE GRACE, lawyer; b. New Rochelle, N.Y., Sept. 18, 1954; d. EllsworthJay and Madelyn A. (Roberts) E.; m. Stefan Shrier, Feb. 23, 1985. BA, Fla. Atlantic U., 1975; JD, George Mason U., 1985. Bar: Va. 1985, U.S. Ct. Appeals (4th cir.) 1985, U.S. Ct. Fed. Claims 1994. Aide Carter/Mondale Presdl. Campaign Com., Atlanta, 1976, Presdl. Transition Staff, Washington, 1976-77; spl. asst. Agy. Internat. Devel. U.S. Dept. State, Washington, 1977; spl. asst. U.S. Dept. Def., Washington, 1977-79; mem. tech. staff System Planning Corp., Arlington, Va., 1980-83; dir. corp. rsch. Analytics, Inc., McLean, Va., 1983-85, v.p., gen. counsel Fairfax, Va., 1985-91; of counsel Feith and Zell, P.C., Washington, 1986-91; dep. gen. counsel Computer Scis. Corp., 1991—. Mem. Army Sci. Bd., 1994-98. Fellow Mil. Ops. Rsch. Soc.; mem. ABA (mem. coun. sect. pub. contract law 2001--). Democrat. Home: 624 1/2 S Pitt St Alexandria VA 22314-4138 Office: Computer Scis Corp 3170 Fairview Park Dr Falls Church VA 22042-4516

ELDREDGE, LINDA GAILE, psychologist; b. Tex., 1959; BS, Howard Payne U., 1980; MA, Tex. Woman's U., 1981; EdD, Baylor U., 1989. Lic. psychologist, Tex.; cert. tchr. hearing impaired, sch. counselor, spl. edn. counselor, Tex.; cert. verbal self def. trainer. Tchr. hearing impaired Waco (Tex.) Ind. Sch. Dist., 1982-85, spl. edn. sch. counselor, cons. hearing impaired, 1986-87; doctoral teaching fellow Baylor U., Waco, 1985-87; dir. regional alcohol and drug abuse svcs. Heart of Tex. Coun. Govts., Waco, 1987; psychotherapist Houston, 1989-91; psychologist, 1991—, Tex. Sch. for the Deaf, Austin, Tex., 1993-95. Mem. APA, Am. Deafness and Rehab. Assn., Am. Assn. of the Deaf-Blind, Gentle Art of Verbal Self-Defense Trainers Network, Internat. Soc. for the Study of Subtle Energies and Energy Medicine. Avocations: collecting minerals and seashells, world music, reading, art, water sports. Office: Bldg 4 Ste 200 4601 Spicewood Springs Rd Austin TX 78759

ELEAZER, NILA KAY LANKFORD, speech pathology/audiology services professional; b. Shelby, N.C., May 9, 1956; d. Dwight and Jessie Lankford; m. Carl B. Eleazer, Oct. 6, 1990. BSc in Edn., We. Carolina U., 1978, MA in Edn., 1985; student, U. S.C., 1987—98, Converse Coll., 2001. [illegible] speech pathologist S.C., 1989. Speech therapist Rutherford County Sch. Dist., Spindale, NC, 1978—83, Spartanburg County Sch. Dist., Campobello, SC, 1985—. Speech therapist Appalachian III Home Health Svcs., Spartanburg, SC, 1990—93; tchr. evaluator Spartanburg County Dist. One, Campobello, 1999—2000, 2002—03, speech rep. leadership team, 2000—03. Capt. Inman Elem. relay for life Am. Cancer Soc., Inman, SC, 2001—03. Named Grad. Student of Yr., We. Carolina U., 1985; grantee, Jr. League, 1994—95, 1997—98. Mem.: Nat. Stuttering Assn., S.C. Speech, Lang. and Hearing Assn., Am. Speech, Lang. and Hearing Assn. Avocations: jogging, gardening, reading, camping. Home: PO Box 127 Lyman SC 29365 Office: Inman Elementary School 25 Oakland Ave Inman SC 29349

ELECTRA, CARMEN, actress; b. Sharonville, Ohio, Apr. 20, 1972; m. Dennis Rodman, 1998 (div. 1999); m. Dave Navaro, 2003. Actor(co-host): (TV series) Singled Out, 1997, Baywatch, 1997—98, Til' Death Do Us Part: Carmen & Dave, 2004; (TV films) Christmas in Malibu, 1999, Baywatch Hawaiian Wedding, 2003; (films) An American Vampire Story, 1997, Starstruck, 1998, The Mating Habits of the Earthbound Human, 1999, Scary Movie, 2000, The Great White Dope, 2000, Perfume, 2001, Get Over It, 2001, Sol Goode, 2000, Whacked, 2002, Rent Control, 2002, Uptown Girls, 2003, My Boss' Daughter, 2003, Starsky & Hutch, 2004, (guest voice): (TV series) The Simpsons. Office: 149 44 15th Ave Flushing NY 11357*

ELEWSKI, BONI ELIZABETH, dermatologist, educator; b. Cleve., Aug. 7, 1953; d. John Stanley and Alberta (Gulish) E.; married. BA summa cum laude, Miami U., Oxford, Ohio, 1975; MD cum laude, Ohio State U., 1978. Intern U. N.C., Chapel Hill, 1978-79, resident, 1979-82; staff dermatologist Akron (Ohio) Clinic, 1982-88; prof. dermatology Univ. Hosps. of Cleve., Case Western Res. U., 1988-99; prof. U. Alabama, 1999—. Author chpts. to books; editor: Cutaneous Fungal Infections, 1992, 2d edit., 1998; contbr. articles to profl. jours. Fellow Cleve. Dermatology Soc. (sec. bd. dirs., chair skin cancer screening program 1988—, pres. 1994), Am. Acad. Dermatology (bd. dirs. 1996-2000, v.p. elect, 2000, v.p. 2001, pres.-elect 2003-04, pres. 2004); mem. Am. Dermatol. Assn., Women's Dermatology Soc. (sec.-treas., pres.-elect 1999, pres. 2000), Dermatology Found. (trustee 1987-91). Roman Catholic. Home: PO Box 430037 Birmingham AL 35243 Office: U Alabama Birmingham Dept Derm 700 18th St S Birmingham AL 35233-1856 Fax: 205-934-5766. E-mail: BEElewski@aol.com.

ELFERVIG, LUCIE THERESA SAVOIE, ophthalmic consultant; b. Donaldsonville, La., Oct. 15, 1948; d. Charles Clarence Sr. and Ursula Marie (Prados) Savoie; m. John Lars Elfervig, May 19, 1972; children: John Lars II (dec.), Martye Elizabeth, Michelle Karene, Taylor Anders. BSN, U. Southwestern La., 1972, postgrad., 1979-80; MSN, Northwestern State U., 1975; D Nursing Sci., La. State U., 1996. RN, Utah, Ga., Ark., Ariz., Miss., Tenn., La., Mo.; cert. ophthalmic nurse, advanced practice RN, CNS, Tenn., La., Utah; cert. of fitness with prescription privile, Tenn. Nurse's aide St. Elizabeth's Hosp., Paincourtville, La., 1969, Charity Hosp., New Orleans, 1971; staff nurse Confederate Meml. Med. Ctr., Shreveport, La., 1972-73; staff nurse med./surg. dept. Dr.'s Hosp., Shreveport, 1973; pediatric clin. nurse specialist La. State U. Med. Ctr., Shreveport, 1975-76; instr. in nursing U. Southwestern La., Lafayette, 1980; pediatric clin. nurse specialist, emergency staff nurse LeBonheur Children's Med. Ctr., Memphis, 1984-85; pediatric clin. nurse specialist, agy. nurse emergency dept. So. Health Sys., Profl. Health Care, Memphis, 1985-90; ophthalmic clin. nurse specialist Hamilton Eye Clinic, Memphis, 1990-91; ind. ophthalmic cons. Memphis, 1992—. Pediatric instr. Stanley Kaplan Ednl. Ctr., Memphis, 1986; ophthalmic clin. nurse specialist Mid-South Retina Assocs., Memphis, summer 1988, Albany (Ga.) Retinal Eye Ctr., summer 1989; cons. Rea & Assocs., Inc., Med. Mgmt. and Fin. Svcs., Memphis, 1992-94, Ridge Lake Ambulatory Surg. Ctr., Memphis, 1992-95, Vitreo-Retinal Found., Memphis, Van Dyck Eye Ctr., Paris, Tenn., So. Eye Assocs., Jonesboro, Ark., Physicians Surg. Ctr. Eye Clin., Jackson, Tenn.; lectr., cons., ophthalmic clin. nurse cons. People to People Citizen Ambassador Program. Contbr. articles to profl. publs.; mem. editl. bd. Insight Jour., 1997; jr. reviewer JAGS. Vol. blood pressure screening program La. Heart Assn., Shreveport, 1974; vol. Holy Rosary Sch., Memphis, 1981-92; tchr. math. Head Start of Memphis, 1986; track meet ofcl. Germantown (Tenn.) Track Club, 1988-92; vol. ophthalmic nurse specialist South Am. Mission/World Lens Project, Pupalla, Peru, 1991, Marantha Mission, Cadereyta, Mex., 1993; campaign vol. Gov.-Elect Don Sundquist, 1994; team leader silent auction bldg. fund benefit Christian Bros. H.S., Memphis, 1993, 94; mem. health ministry Our Lady of Perpetual Help Ch., 1996—. Recipient Endowment, Rep. Congl. Order of Liberty, 1993, Congl. Cert. of Appreciation U.S. Congress, 1993, Edna Ashy award for contbns. to ophthal. nursing. Fellow Am. Acad. Nursing; mem. ANA (coun. nurses in advanced practice), Am. Soc. Ophthalmic RNs (mem. peer rev. com. jour. 1994—, nominating com. 1996—, approver com. 1998, Honor award 1998, pres. mid-south chpt. 1997, editl. bd. 1997, awards com. 2000), Tenn. Nurses Assn., NLN (coun. for nursing practice), West Tenn. League Nurses (chpt. chair 1994-95), Am. Geriatrics Soc. (jr. reviewer jour.), Nat. Assn. CNS, Am. Nurses Found., Nat. Assn. Pro-Life Nurses, Mid. Tenn. Advanced Practice Nurses, Nat. Assn. Cert. Nurse Specialists, Vision Group of U. Tenn. Memphis, Memphis Eye Soc., Greater Memphis Advanced Practice Nursing, Am. Acad. Ophthalmology, Am. Acad. Nurse Practitioners, Sigma Theta Tau. Avocations: cooking, reading, travel, hunting, family. Office: Vitreo-Retinal Found 825 Ridge Lake Blvd Ste 310 Memphis TN 38120-9411

ELG, ANNETTE, food products executive; b. Culdesac, Idaho; d. Ralph and Shirley Steigers; m. Brad Elg, 1977; 2 children. B in Acctg., U. Idaho, 1978. With Arthur Andersen LLP; corp. contr. J.R. Simplot Co., Boise, Idaho, 1990, CFO, 2002—. Office: JR Simplot One Capital Ctr 999 Main St PO Box 27 Boise ID 83707-0027

ELGAVISH, ADA, molecular and cellular biologist; b. Cluj, Romania, Jan. 23, 1946; came to U.S. 1979; d. David and Malca (Neuman) Simchas; m. Gabriel A. Elgavish, Dec. 28, 1968; children: Rotem, Eynav. BSc, Tel-Aviv U., 1969, MSc, 1972; PhD, Weizmann Inst. Sci., Rehovot, Israel, 1978. Postdoctoral vis. fellow NIH, Balt., 1979-81; instr. U. Ala. Sch. Medicine, Birmingham, 1981-82, rsch. assoc., 1982-84, rsch. asst. prof. pharmacology, 1984-89, asst. prof. comparative medicine, 1989—92, assoc. prof. comparative medicine, 1992—2002, assoc. prof. genetics, 2002—. Scientist Cell Adhesion and Matrix Rsch. Ctr., Birmingham, 1995—, Clin. Nutrition Rsch. Ctr., 2001—, Ctr. Metabolic Bone Disease, Ctr. for Aging, 1996; mem. Cancer Ctr.; founder Diacell, Inc., 1998. Grantee Cystic Fibrosis Found., 1986—90, Am. Lung Assn., 1987—92, NIH, 1989—2000, Interstitial Cystitis Assn., 1998, Am. Inst. Cancer Rsch., 2000, Pfizer, 2000—03. Mem.: Am. Assn. Cancer Rsch., Soc. for Basic Urol. Rsch., Am. Physiol. Soc., Sigma Xi. Office: U Ala Sch Medicine Dept Genetics Birmingham AL 35294-0019 Office Phone: 205-934-6547.

ELIAS, MERLE, writer, consultant; b. N.Y.C., June 1, 1958; d. Pincus and Helen Elias. Student, SUNY, Stony Brook, 1977—79, NYU, 1980—83. Exec. asst. to Dustin Hoffman, N.Y.C., 1982—85, Billy Joel, N.Y.C., 1986—89, Quincy Jones, L.A., 1992—94, Michael Crichton, L.A., 1994—96; freelance project mgr., writer Merle Elias Inc., L.A., 1996—. Author: Los Angeles First Class, 2001. Mem.: Ind. Writers So. Calif., PEN West. Home and Office: 11044 Ophir Dr # 503 Los Angeles CA 90024

ELIAS, ROSALIND, mezzo-soprano; b. Lowell, Mass., Mar. 13, 1931; d. Salem and Shelahuy Rose (Namy) E.; m. Zuhayr Moghrabi. Student, New

Eng. Conservatory Music, Accademia di Santa Cecilia, Rome; studies with, Daniel Ferro, N.Y.C. Singer New Eng. Opera, 1948-52, Met. Opera, 1954—; artistic dir. Am. Lyric Theatre. Debut with Boris Goldowsky, Boston, 1948; appeared in numerous roles including Cherubino, Dorabella, Rosina, Hansel, Cenerentola, Carmen, Amneris and Azucena (Verdi), Charlotte and Giulietta (Massenet), Herodias, 1987; originated role of Erika in Vanessa (Samuel Barber) and Cleopatra in Antony and Cleopatra (Barber); also appeared with Scottish Opera, Vienna Staatsoper, Glynbourne Festival, many others; prodr. Carmen, Cin., 1988, Il Barbiere di Siviglia, Opera Pacific, Costa Mesa, Calif., 1989; recs. for RCA and Columbia records include La Gioconda, La Forza del Destno, Il Trovatore, Falstaff, Madama Butterfly, Rigoletto, Der fliegende Holländer. Mem. Sigma Alpha Iota.

ELIASON, BONNIE MAE, county treasurer; b. Stanley, N.D., Jan. 10, 1947; d. Melvin Otis and Mabel Isabel (Borst) Howell; m. Murrey Allen Eliason, June 23, 1971; 1 child, Christal Medora. BA, Minot (N.D.) State Coll., 1970. Clk. N.D. Personal Property Tax Collector, Bismarck, summer 1965, Mountrail County Auditor, Stanley, 1970-74; dep. Mountrail County Treas., Stanley, 1974-77, treas., 1979—. Vice pres., mem. Am. Legion Aux., Stanley, 1980. Mem. Stanley Women's Bowling League (sec., treas. 1973-74, v.p. 1976-77, pres. 1977-78), Stanley Women's Bowling Assn. Presbyterian. Avocations: reading, crossword puzzles, sewing. Home: 7915 70th NW Stanley ND 58784-9013 Office: PO Box 69 Stanley ND 58784-0069

ELIASON, PAMELA PARKER, minister, social worker; b. Wilmington, Del., Jan. 10, 1952; d. James T. and Barbara R. Eliason. BA, Catawba Coll., 1974; MSW, Washington U., 1978; MDiv, Union Theol. Sem., N.Y.C., 1990; D in Ministry, Columbia Theol. Sem., 2003. Ordained min. Presbyn. Ch., 1991; LCSW N.C., 1996. Social worker Watkins Ctr. Human Devel., Charlotte, NC, 1979—84; program coord. Calkins Hall-Florence Crittenton Svcs., Charlotte, 1984—85; chaplain resident Carolinas Med. Ctr., Charlotte, 1990—91; assoc. pastor First Presbyn. Ch., Morehead City, NC, 1993—95; clin. social worker Charlotte (N.C.) Inst. Rehab., 1991—93, 1995—2002; stated supply Johnston Meml. Presbyn. Ch., Charlotte, 1997—2001; pastor First Presbyn. Ch., Dunbar, W.Va., 2002—. Co-founder Inter-Faith Clergy Women, Charleston, W.Va., 2002 ; mem. Charlotte Jr. League, 1984—86; bd. dir. Charlotte (N.C.) SANE, 1984—85, Charlotte (N.C.) Organizing Project, 1984—85. Recipient Golden Screw award, Blue Masque Drama Club, 1974. Mem.: Presbytery W.Va., Dunbar Ministerial Assn. Avocations: reading, dance, birdwatching, children. Office: First Presbyn Ch 1414 Myers Ave Dunbar WV 25064

ELIASOPH, JOAN, radiologist, educator; b. N.Y.C. AB, Hunter Coll., 1946; MD, NYU, 1949. Diplomate Am. Bd. Radiology. Intern Mt. Sinai Hosp., N.Y.C., 1949-50, Heineman fellow pathology, 1950-51, resident in radiology, 1951-53, fellow radiology, 1955-56; radiology Columbia U., N.Y.C., 1953-55, instr., 1953-55; asst. attending radiologist Mt. Sinai Hosp., N.Y.C., 1955-70, attending radiologist, 1982-85, 90; clin. asst. prof. Mt Sinai Med. Sch., N.Y.C., 1970-77; assoc. prof. radiology U. So. Calif., L.A., 1977-82, columbia U., 1982-85, Coll. of Physicians and Surgeons; attending radiologist Dartmouth-Hitchcock Med. Ctr., 1990-92; attending radiologist gastrointestinal/critical care imaging Kingsbridge VA Med. Ctr., 1992—. Cons. Silver Hill Found., Conn., 1965-77, Stamford Hosp., Conn., 1970-77, White River Junction VA Hosp., 1990-92. Contbr. articles to profl. jours. Mem. Friends of Ballona Wetlands, Los Angeles, 1977-82. Heineman pathology fellow Mt. Sinai Hosp., 1950-51, Radiology fellow, 1955-56. Fellow Am. Coll. Radiology, Am. Coll. Gastroent.; mem. Am. roentgen Ray Soc., Am. Gastroent. Soc., Radiol. Soc. N.Am., Soc. Gastrointestinal Radiologists, N.Y. Roentgen Soc., Assn. Univ. Radiologists, Ukiyo-E Soc. of Am. Avocations: environment, birding, japanese prints. Office: Kingsbridge Vets Adminstrv Med Ctr Dept Radiology 130 W Kingsbridge Rd Bronx NY 10468-3904

ELIZABETH, HER MAJESTY, II, (ELIZABETH ALEXANDRA MARY), Queen of United Kingdom of Great Britain, Northern Ireland and Canada, and her other Realms and Territories, head of the Commonwealth, Defender of the Faith; b. Apr. 21, 1926; d. King George VI (formerly Duke of York) and Queen Elizabeth (formerly Duchess of York); m. Prince Philip, Duke of Edinburgh, Nov. 20, 1947; children: Charles Philip Arthur George (now The Prince of Wales), 1948, Anne Elizabeth Alice Louise (now The Princess Royal), 1950, Andrew Albert Christian Edward (now The Duke of York), 1960, Edward Antony Richard Louis (now The Earl of Wessex), 1964. Succeeded to throne following death of father, Feb. 6, 1952; crowned Queen, June 2, 1953. Address: Buckingham Palace London SW1A 1AA England*

ELKIN, LOIS SHANMAN, business systems company executive; b. Cin., Oct. 31, 1937; d. Jerome David and Mildred Louise (Bloch) Shanman; m. Alan I. Elkin, May 6, 1962; children: Karen A., Jeffrey R. BA in Math., Goucher Coll., 1959. Sys. engr. ea. region IBM, Balt. and Columbia, S.C., 1959-61, mgr. Computer Test Ctr. ea. region, 1961-64; exec. v.p. Advance Bus. Sys., Balt., 1964—, A&L Real Estate, Balt., 1970—; pres. Our World Gallery, Inc., Balt., 1995—. Mentor for math. and bus. Goucher Coll., Balt., 1982—86; co-owner ATMS, Balt., 1994—2002; guest lectr. MBA program Loyola Coll. Md., Balt., 1993—94, Towson U., 1999; steering com. Loyola Ctr. Closely Held Cos., Balt., 1993—; conducted seminars Towson U. Leadership Group, 1999; bd. dirs. Hunt Valley Bus. Forum, Balt.; ptnr. Enable Technologies, Balt., 2001—. Vol. House of Ruth, Balt., 1990—, Image Recovery Ctr., Union Meml. Hosp., Balt., 1995—96; exec. bd. dirs. Pride of Balt. II, 1994—2000; co-chair Multiple Sclerosis Class of '98 fundraiser, 1998; exec. bd. Md. chpt. Nat. Multiple Sclerosis Soc., 2000—; sponsor maj. fundraising event Johns Hopkins Children's Ctr., Balt., 2002; chair Gala, Balt. Zoomerang!, 2004; bd. dirs. Hearing and Speech Agy., Balt., 1996—2001. Named Entrepreneur of Yr., Ernst and Young, 2001; named one of Top 500 Women-Owned Businesses in U.S., Working Woman Mag., 1998—2001, Md.'s Top 100 Women, 1999, 2001; named to, Circle of Excellence, 2004; recipient AAA Torch award for ethics in bus., 1997, Champion of Children award, Casey Cares Found., 2004, honoree, Chimes Ann. Hall of Fame Tribute, 2002. Mem.: Women's Bus. Club (founder 2002—), Nat. Assn. Women Bus. Owners (Woman of the Yr. award Balt. chpt. 1985). Avocation: collecting art. Office: Advance Bus Sys 10755 York Rd Cockeysville Hunt Valley MD 21030-2114

ELKINS, JENI L. MCINTOSH, webmaster; b. Chgo., Sept. 23, 1967; d. Glen Reed McIntosh and Cherie Lee Whybrew; m. Robert Lloyd Elkins Jr., Apr. 23, 1994. BA Orgnizational Comm. & Spanish, Ind. U., 1991, MBA Mktg., 1998. Sr. libr. asst. Ind. U., Gary, 1994—97, webmaster, 1997; mgr. Net Nitco, Hebron, 1997—98; webmaster Citizens Fin. Svcs., Munster, 1999—. Author: Bub's Glasses, 1998. Vol. instr. ESL Gavit High Sch., Hammond, Ind., 1993; founding mem. AUSA, Ind., 1990—91. Lutheran. Home: PO Box 44 Lowell IN 46356 E-mail: jelkins@alumni.indiana.edu.

ELKOWITZ, SHERYL SUE, radiologist; b. N.Y.C., Apr. 20, 1962; BS in Biology summa cum laude, Adelphi U., Garden City, N.Y., 1982; MD, Wayne State U., Detroit, 1986. Diplomate Am. Bd. Radiology; lic. physician, N.Y. Intern internal medicine L.I. Jewish Hillside Med. Ctr., New Hyde Park, N.Y., 1986-87, resident diagnostic radiology, 1987-91; fellow pediatric radiology, chief fellow L.I. Jewish Hillside Med. Ctr., Schneider Children's Hosp., New Hyde Park, 1991-92; staff attending dept. diagnostic radiology L.I. Jewish Hillside Med. Ctr., New Hyde Park, 1992-96; asst. prof. radiology Albert Einstein Coll. Medicine, Yeshiva U., Bronx, N.Y., 1992—. Presenter various orgns. Contbr. articles to profl. jours. Mem. AMA, Soc. Pediatric Radiology, Radiol. Soc. N.Am., Am. Coll. Radiology, Am. Roentgen Ray Soc., Am. Assn. Women in Radiology (bylaws com. 1995), N.Y. Met. Pediatric Radiology Group, Neuhauser Soc., N.Y. State Radiol. Soc. Home: 3 Phaeton Dr Melville NY 11747-2019 Office: Good Samaritan Hosp Med Ctr 1000 Montauk Hwy West Islip NY

ELLEDGE, GLENNA ELLEN TUELL, journalist; b. Welch, W.Va., Aug. 2, 1931; d. William Jackson and Ellen Annabelle (Jackson) Tuell; div.; children: Carl Gene, Jerry Elwood, Ernest Everett. Certificate in comptometer, Capital City Coll., 1949; student, Wytheville (Va.) C.C., S.W. Va. C.C., Richlands, Va. Intermont Coll. Accounts clk. Household Fin. Corp., Charleston, W.Va., 1951-52; with incest divsn. FBI, Washington, 1953; asst. bookkeeper and acctg. clk. Ft. McNair Officers Open Mess, Washington, 1953-54; stat. analyst Office Strategic Intelligence, Washington, 1954-55; stock control 836th Supply Squadron, Langley AFB, Va., 1957-59; acct., office asst. Comml. Contracting, Troy, Mich., 1970-71; office svcs. asst. Southwestern State Hosp., Marion, Va., 1971-95; staff writer, photographer Saltville (Va.) Progress, 1977-81, Saltville News-Messenger, 1981-93, Family Cmty. Newspapers, Marion, 1993-2000, Saltville Progress, 2000—. Fire brigade Southwestern State Hosp., Marion, 1986-93, instr. CPR, 1986-89, adv. bd., 1986-93. Editor, keyboardist Grandma's Favorite Recipes, 2000, Lucy's Secret, 2001-02. Vol. Air Force Family Svcs., 1956-69, den mother Cub. Scouts Am., 1962-67; bd. dirs. Smyth County Crisis Ctr., Marion, 1971-81; sec., pres. Smyth Coun. Santa's Elves, Marion, 1974-78, Family Oriented Group Home parent Group Home Juveniles 28th Juvenile Domestic Rels. Ct., Abingdon, Va., 1978-81; EMT, instr. Am. Heart Assn., Smyth, Wise, Grayson Counties, 1986-89; mem. and former sunday sch. tchr., supr. Laural Springs United Meth. Ch.; chairperson Mayor's promotional com., Marion, 1994-95; mem. Surry County (N.C.) Hist. Soc., Grayson County (Va.) Hist. Soc. Mem. Nat. Fedn. Press Women (del. 1978, awards), Va. Press Women (del. 1978, awards), Va. Press Assn. (awards), Nat. Press Assn., Nat. Soc. DAR, Nat. Soc. Col. Dames XVII Century. Jamestowne Soc. Republican. Avocations: writing, reading, travel. Office: PO Box 901 Marion VA 24354-0901 Personal E-mail: ellglen@hotmail.com.

ELLEMAN, BARBARA, editor; b. Coloma, Wis., Oct. 20, 1934; d. Donald and Evelyn (Kissinger) Koplein; m. Don W. Elleman, Nov. 14, 1970. BS in Edn., Wis. State U., 1956; MA in Librarianship, U. Denver, 1964. Sch. libr. media specialist Port Washington (Wis.) High Sch., 1956-59, Homestead High Sch., Thiensville-Mequon, Wis., 1959-64; children's libr. Denver Pub. Libr., 1964-65; sch. libr. media specialist Cherry Creek Schs., Denver, 1965-70, Henry Clay Sch., Whitefish Bay, Wis., 1971-75; children's reviewer ALA, Chgo., 1975-82, children's editor, 1982-90, editor Book Links, 1990-96. Vis. lectr. U. Wis., 1974-75, 81-82, U. Ill., Circle Campus, 1983-85; Disting. scholar children's lit., Marquette U., 1996—; cons. H.W. Wilson Co., 1969-75; mem. Libr. Congress Adv. Com. on selection for children's books for blind and physically handicapped, 1980-88, Caldecott Calendar Com., 1986; judge The Am. Book Awards, 1982, Golden Kite, 1987, Boston Globe/Horn Book, 1990; mem. faculty Highlights for Children Writers Conf., 1985-90; mem. orgn. com. MidWest Conf. Soc. Children's Books Writers, 1974-76; chair Hans Christian Andersen Com., 1987-88; advisor Reading Rainbow, 1986-96, Ind. R.E.A.P. project, 1987-93; jury mem. VI Catalonia Premi Children's Book Exbhn., Barcelona, Spain, 1994; adv. bd. Parent's Choice, Cobblestone Publ., Georgia Pub. TV's 2000, The New Advocate mag., 20th Century Children's Writers, Encyclopedia of Children's Literature, Cooperative Children's Book Ctr., U. Wis., Madison, Riverbank Rev., 1998—, Ency. of Children's Lit., 1998—; lang. arts com. NCTE Notable Books, 1997—; spkr. in field. Author: Reading in a Media Age, 1975, 20th Century Children's Writers, 1979, rev. edit., 1984, What Else Can You Do With a Library Degree?, 1980, Popular Reading for Children, 1981, Popular Reading II, 1986, Children's Books of International Interest, 1984, Tomie dePaola, His Art and His Stories, 1999, Virginia Lee Burton: A Life in Art, 2002; contbr. articles to profl. jours. Publicity chair Internat. Bd. Books for Young People Congress, Williamsburg, Va., 1990. Recipient Jeremiah Ludington award Ednl. Paperback Assn., 1996, Hope S. Dean award Found. Children's Lit., 1996. Mem. ALA (2000 Caldecott Com. 1999—), Soc. Children's Book Writers (mem. orgn. com. MidWest Conf. 1974-76), Internat. Bd. Books for Young People (U.S. assoc. editor Bookbird 1978-86, chair nominating com., 1985, bd. dirs. 1990-92), Children's Reading Round Table Chgo. (award 1987), Nat. Coun. Tchrs. English (bd. dirs. children's lit. assembly 1986-88, mem. editl. adv. bd. CLA bull. 1989-91, mem. using nonfiction in classroom com. 1990-96, 2000 Caldecott com., Laura I. Wilden com. 2001--). Office: 20 Bayon Dr Apt 5 South Hadley MA 01075-3338*

ELLEN, JANE, composer, music educator, researcher; b. San Pedro, Calif., May 11, 1956; d. Annabel M. Quesnel. BA, U. N.Mex., 1992, postgrad., 1992-93. Cert. music tchr., N.Mex. Freelance composer, Albuquerque, 1986—. Parish organist Our Lady of Annunciation, Albuquerque, 1994—98; nat. dir. Signa Alpha Iota Am. Composers Bur., 1999—2003; contract prof. ElderHostel, U. N.Mex., 1996—2001; resident instr. OASIS, 1996—. Composer (more than 300 works including): Dancing in Deep Heaven for chamber orch., 1991; composer: Elegy for the Children of Sarajevo, woodwind quintet, 1992; composer: (with text by Ann Cragg) Phantom Lost for voice, oboe and piano, 1999; composer: Images of Rome for piano, 2000; composer: (with text by Claire Roth) The Eternal Ring for SATB choir, 2001; : commns. include NEA/NMAD; composer: MTNA state composer New Music Across Am., Canossian Daus. of Charity, Am. Guild Organists Dist. VII Conf., 1993, 2003, N.Mex. Quincentenary Commn., N.Mex. Women Composers Guild, (with text by Roth) Per La Grazia di Dio for SATB choir, 2001, (with text by Roth) Hearts and Hands United for SATB choir, 2002. Recipient 1st place award Nat. League Am. Pen Women, 1996, 1st, 2d and 3d place awards, 1998. Mem. ASCAP (grantee 1990—), Music Tchrs. Nat. Assn. (profl. cert.), N.Mex. Music Tchrs. Assn. (cert.), Albuquerque Music Tchrs. Assn.(1st v.p. 1998-2000, 2003-04), Phi Beta Kappa, Phi Kappa Phi, Sigma Alpha Iota (Ruby Sword of Honour award 1992). Roman Catholic. Avocations: reading, studying italian, writing poetry and prose, watching old films, researching civil war music. Home: 2226 B Wyoming NE 182 Albuquerque NM 87112-2620 E-mail: Jane@JaneEllen.com.

ELLENBERGER, DIANE MARIE, nurse, consultant; b. St. Louis, Oct. 5, 1946; d. Charles Ernst and Celeste Loraine (Neudecker) E. RN, Barnes Hosp., St. Louis, 1970; BSN, St. Louis U., 1976; MSN, U. Colo., 1977. Bd. cert. legal nurse cons.; cert. clin. nurse specialist. Staff nurse hosps., clin. nurse, St. Louis, 1973-76; nurse clinician Sedalia, Mo., 1977-78; nurse clinician, educator Bothwell Hosp., Sedalia, 1977-78; clin. nurse specialist, coord. perinatal outreach edn. Cardinal Glennon Meml. Hosp. Children, St. Louis, 1978-80; instr. McKendree Coll., Lebanon, Ill., 1980; asst. prof. Maryville Coll., St. Louis, 1982-85; nurse cons. Carr, Korein, Tillery, Attys. at Law, East St. Louis, Ill., 1986—97; owner, nurse cons. The Med-Legal Advantage, San Anselmo, Calif., 1997—. Owner, operator Diane Designs Needlepoint, St. Louis, 1981-96. Contbr. articles to profl. jours. Mem. Divine Sci. Ch. With Nurse Corps, USAF, 1970-72. Mem. ANA (Calif. affiliate bd. dirs. 1998-2002), AACN, Am. Assn. Legal Nurse Cons. (Bay Area bd. dirs. 1999-2003), Nat. Perinatal Assn., Assn. Women's Health, Obstetric and Neonatal Nurses, Mo. Nurses Assn. (bd. dirs. 1995-97, bylaws chair 1990-2001, del. to ANA 1996, 3d dist. pres. 1993-96), Mo. Perinatal Assn. (v.p. 1980), Sigma Theta Tau. Office: PO Box 1638 San Anselmo CA 94979-1638 E-mail: mladvntg@pacbell.net.

ELLENBOGEN, ELISABETH ALICE, retired accountant; b. Lemberg, Ukraine, Sept. 10, 1940; d. Joseph and Leah Karolina (Wiener) Ellenbogen. B in Humanities, cert. in acctg., Pa. State U.; student, Elizabethtown Coll. Cert. civil servant. Buyer McCrory Corp., York, Pa., 1959-65; account mgr. WT Grant Co., York, Pa., 1965-70; various acctg. civil svc. positions Commonwealth of Pa., Harrisburg, 1970-89. Contract mgr. health and human svcs. Commonwealth of Pa., 1989—99. Author: Bill of Rights for Citizens Facing the End of Life, 1997, (bulletin) Out Cry!, 1975, (policies/procedures) Constitutional Rights for Handicapped Citizens, 1975—. Bd. dirs. ACLU, Pa., 1978—2003, disability rights adv., 1978—; convenor Ecumenical Coalition to Abolish the Penalty of Death, Pa., 1985—2003; activist Harrisburg Rape Crisis, 1973—77; counselor Women's Ctr., Harrisburg, 1975—79. Mem.: NOW, Prime Time Group (mem. women's consciousness raising support 1973—77). Democrat. Jewish. Home and Office: 298 Colonial Rd # 4 Harrisburg PA 17109-1556 E-mail: handicaprights@webtv.net.

ELLENBOGEN, MARJORIE, elementary school educator; b. N.Y.C., Oct. 28, 1936; d. Franklyn and Molly (Berman) E. BA, Vassar Coll., 1958; MA, Columbia U., 1959. Cert. elem. tchr., N.Y. Tchr. Bd. Edn. N.Y.C. Allen-Stevenson Sch., N.Y.C., 1959-60, Ethical Culture Sch., N.Y.C., 1960-65, Columbia Grammar Sch., N.Y.C., 1965-67, UN Internat. Sch., N.Y.C., 1967—97. Avocations: swimming, travel. Home: 45 Sutton Pl S New York NY 10022-2444 Office: UN Internat Sch 24-50 FDR Dr New York NY 10010-4046

ELLENBROOK, CAROLYN KAY, religious organization administrator; b. Denton, Tex., Sept. 2, 1943; d. Herman and Winnie Louise (Garrett) Baker; m. Edward Charles Ellenbrook, Jr., Apr. 13, 1968; 1 child, Margaret. A, Cameron Jr. Coll., 1963; BS in Edn., Okla. State U., 1965. Child welfare caseworker State of Okla., Lawton, 1965—68; religious edn. sec. Comanche-Cotton Bapt. Assn., Lawton, 1981—. Contbr. chapters to books Heart Call-The Call to Prayer, 1998; co-author: (book) Comanche-Cotton Baptist Association A Centennial History, 1902-2002, 2002. Area adv. City PTA, Lawton, 1977—80, mem., 1973—86; treas. Eisenhower H.S. PTA, 1984—86; pres. So. Bapt. Women's Missionary Union, Okla., 1993—98. Named Ch. Women of Yr., DAR, 2000. Mem.: Nat. So. Bapt. Sec. Orgn., Okla. So. Bapt. Sec. Orgn., So. Bapt. Assoc. Religious Educators (pres. 2002). Avocations: hiking, history, writing, travel, working with children. Home: 1603 Keystone Dr Lawton OK 73505 Office: Comanche-Cotton Baptist Assoc 2612 E Ave Lawton OK 73505 Office Phone: 580-353-2701. E-mail: ecebrook@sirinet.net.

ELLERBACH, SUSAN, editor; Reporter Tulsa World, 1985, bus. editor, state editor, Sunday editor, 1994—95, mng. editor. Office: Tulsa World 315 S Boulder PO Box 1770 Tulsa OK 74103*

ELLERMAN, LINDA ANN, music educator; b. Decatur, Ill., Aug. 26, 1978; d. George Charles and Chong Suk Carter. BMus, Millikin U., 2001. Cert. tchr. Ill. Asst. band dir. Greater Decatur (Ill.) Youth Band, 1998—99; band dir. Meridian Ctrl. Unified Sch. Dist., Decatur, 2000—02; grad. asst., 2002—. Mem.: Am. Coll. Personal Assoc. (ACPA), Phi Kappa Phi. Home: 1102 E Van Buren St Clinton IL 61727

ELLERT, LUCINDA JOAN, musician, educator; b. Holland, Mich., Apr. 18, 1953; d. Ernest Edwin and Lois Vander (Meulen) Ellert; life ptnr. Daniel Robert Walker; 1 child, Amelia Harper. BA in Theatre, Grinnell Coll., 1976; M in Jazz Composition, New Eng. Conservatory, 1989, M in Music Edn., 1997. Music dir. Happy Feet Dance Orch., Boston, 1986—; musical dir. Clef Club Syncopators, Reading, Mass., 1990—; dir. bands Austin Prep. Sch., Reading, 1997—. Pvt. music tchr., Reading, 1985—; drum maj. Natick (Mass.) Am. Legion Band, 1996—; music dir. Says You Sta. WGBH-FM, Boston, 1997—98; cons. Scoreworks, Reading, 2000—. Transcriber 1925-1935 jazz band works, arranger: 1925-1935 jazz band music, dir., arranger, pianist, vocalist: albums Lucinda Ellert and Her Happy Feet, Hop Off, The River and Me. Mem.: AFM Local 9, Music Educators Nat. Conf., New Eng. Found. Arts (mem. touring roster 1989), Phi Delta Kappa. Independent. Congregationalist. Avocations: gardening, needlepoint, furniture restoration. Office: Happy Feet Dance Orch 31 Longwood Rd Reading MA 01867 Personal E-mail: lellertwithhappyfeet@comcast.net. E-mail: lellertwithhappyfeet@comcast.net.

ELLERY, TRACEY, internet company executive; Student, Deakin U. Mng. editor; pvt. cons. practice; CEO Student Svc. Australia; co-founder, pres. LookSmart, Inc., San Francisco. Office: LookSmart Ltd 625 Second St San Francisco CA 94107

ELLIE, BETH JOY, writer; b. Bloomer, Wis., 1968; m. David Ellie; children: Rachel, Madeline. BA in English & Journalism, U. of Wis., Eau Claire, 1990. English tchr. Siping Tchr.'s Coll., Siping, China, 1990—92; editor Augusta Area Times/The Tri-County News, Osseo, Wis., 1995—97; freelance writer Eau Claire, 1997—; editor Wis. West Mag., Eau Claire, 1998—99. Mem.: We. Wis. Christian Writers Guild (v.p. 2001—). Avocation: painting.

ELLIN, NAN, architecture educator, writer; b. Balt., July 10, 1959; d. Morton and Carole Beerman Ellin; 1 child, Theodora Ellin Ballew. BA, Bryn Mawr Coll., 1981; MA, Columbia U., 1983, MPhil, 1993, PhD, 1994. Instr. NYU, N.Y.C., 1986—90; vis. asst. prof. U. So. Calif., L.A., 1991—92; mem. faculty So. Calif. Inst. Arch., L.A., 1993—95; asst. prof. Ariz. State U., Tempe, 1996—97, assoc. prof., 1999—. Author: (book) Postmodern Urbanism, 1996; editor: (anthology) Architecture of Fear, 1997. Recipient Fulbright award, 1985. Fellow: Inst. Urban Design. Office: Ariz State U Sch Arch Tempe AZ 85287-1605 Business E-Mail: nan.ellin@asu.edu.

ELLINGER-LABULIS, KATHLEEN MARIE, application developer, consultant; b. Syracuse, N.Y., Apr. 7, 1961; d. Thomas Donald Ellinger and Jeanette June LaPluer; m. Edward James Labulis, July 31, 1982; children: Bradley James, Stephanie Marie. AAS, CCBI, 1998; BS in Bus. and Distributive Edn., SUNY, Oswego, 1991, MS in Edn., 1996. Cert. Pub. Sch. Tchr. State of N.Y. Corp. office sys. trainer CIS Corp., Syracuse, NY, 1986—89; desktop pub. inst. OCM BOCES Adult Edn., Liverpool, NY, 1992—95, bus. careers inst., 1995—2001; graphic comm. tchr. OCM BOCES Workforce Prep H.S., 2001—. Curriculum devel. OCM BOCES, Liverpool, NY, 1992—. Recipient Mary Lynch Award, CCBI Coll., 1986. Mem.: Printing Industires of Am., Graphic Arts Tech. Found., Visual Comm. Consortium (sec. 2001—03). Cath. Avocations: golf, bowling, cross country skiing, jogging, bicycling. Home: 2946 Weller Rd Weedsport NY 13166

ELLINGSEN, SUSAN P. music educator; b. Watertown, S.D. m. Michael O. Ellingsen; children: Andrew M., Katherine S. BA, Hamline U., 1974. Cert. tchr. Minn. Band dir. Blue Earth (Minn.) Area Pub. Schs., 1974—. Office: Blue Earth Area Pub Schs 315 E 6th St Blue Earth MN 56013-2006

ELLINGTON, JANE ELIZABETH, experimental psychologist; b. Little Rock, Jan. 23, 1946; d. Julian Buril and Dorothy (Davidson) Priddy; m. Edward Lee Stephens, May 22, 1982. AB, Washington U., St. Louis, 1968; MA, Abilene Christian U., 1971; PhD, U. North Tex., 1984. Staff psychologist West Tex. Rehab. Ctr., Abilene, 1971-75; tchg. fellow U. North Tex., Denton, 1981-84; asst. prof. psychology Austin Coll., Sherman, Tex., 1987-92, assoc. prof. psychology, 1992—, chair dept. psychology, sociology & anthropology, 1995-2000. Mem. APA, Am. Name Soc., Southwestern Psychol. Assn. Mem. Ch. of Christ. Avocation: quiltmaking. Office: Austin Coll 900 N Grand Ave Ste 61575 Sherman TX 75090-4440

ELLINGTON, KAREN RENAE, secondary education resource specialist; b. Turlock, Calif., Oct. 19, 1965; d. Edward Ray and Barbara Janet (Rafatti) E. BS, Calif. Poly., 1989; postgrad., Chapman U., 1994-96. Tchg. credentials include multiple subject, agr., bus., spl. edn.-learning handicapped; cert. resource specialist; cert. crosscultural, lang. and acad. devel.

specialist. Asst. mgr. House of Fabrics, San Luis Obispo, Calif., 1985-88, Macy's, Sacramento, 1988-90; clk. Raley's, Modesto, Calif., 1990-93; substitute tchr. Merced & Stanislaus Counties, Calif., 1993; resource specialist Los Banos (Calif.) H.S., 1994—. Computer instr. ARBOR, Modesto and Merced, 1994-97. Leader 4-H, Merced County, 1990—, dir. 1998—; mem. Calif. [illegible] Mem. NEA, Calif. Tchrs. Assn., Los Banos Tchrs. Assn., Coun. for Exceptional Children, Calif. Ag. Tchrs. Assn. (assoc.), Internat. Dyslexia Assn. Avocations: traveling, stitchery, photography, athletics. Office: Los Banos HS 1966 S 11th St Los Banos CA 93635-4812 E-mail: karenellington@hotmail.com., kellington@losbanosusd.k12.ca.us.

ELLINGTON, MILDRED L. librarian; b. Marion, Ohio, June 7, 1921; d. Edward J. and Julia Ellen (Oiler) E. BA, Olivet Nazarene Coll., Kankakee, Ill., 1943; MA in French, Ohio State U., 1952; MA in English, Bowling Green (Ohio) U., 1964; MLS, Rosary Coll., River Forest, Ill., 1976. English and French tchr. Morral (Ohio) High Sch., 1944-49, Reddick (Ill.) High Sch., 1949-55; English tchr. Bremen Community High Sch., Midlothian, Ill., 1955-58, Bloom Twp. High Sch., Chicago Heights, Ill., 1958-60, Willowbrook High Sch., Villa Park, Ill., 1960-66; English tchr., then library dir. Addison (Ill.) Trail High Sch., 1966-82; reference librarian Maywood (Ill.) Pub. Library, 1982—. Sunday sch. supt. Elgin (Ill.) Ch. of the Nazarene, 1985-92. Mem. Ill. Library Assn. Democrat. Mem. Ch. of the Nazarene. Avocations: opera, singing, genealogy, travel. Office: Maywood Pub Libr 121 S 5th Ave Maywood IL 60153-1307

ELLIOT, GERRI, information technology executive; married; 2 children. BA in Polit. Sci., NYU. V.p. distbn. sector IBM, Tokyo, IBM Americas Group; corp. v.p. industry solutions group Microsoft, Redmond, Wash. Avocations: restoring homes, coaching & playing basketball, step aerobics, travel. Office: One Microsoft Way Redmond WA 98052-6399

ELLIOT, JANET LEE, occupational medicine physician; b. Hannibal, Mo., Aug. 6, 1955; d. Bobby Neal and Mary Elizabeth (Ford) Vandiver; m. Roger Larry Elliot, July 26, 1986. Student, U. Mo., 1979, MD, 1981; MPH, Med. Coll. Wis., 1999. Lic. family practitioner, surgeon, breath alcohol tech.; diplomate Am. Acad. Pain Mgmt., Am. Bd. Forensic Examiners. Resident Truman Med. Ctr., Kansas City, Mo.; with occupational gen. Landmark Med. Ctr., Kansas City, Mo., 1982-84, North Indsl. Clinic, Kansas City, 1984-88; aviation med. examiner N.J., 1985; with mini residency occupational medicine Robert Wood Johnson Med. Sch., U. of Medicine and Dentistry of N.J., 1987; dir. of occupational medicine Suburban Heights Med. Ctr., Chicago Heights, Ill., 1988—. Mem. Am. Occupational Medicine Assn., Am. Acad. Family Practice, Am. Assn. Ry. Surgeons, Norfolk and Western Ry. Assn., Am. Coll. Forensic Examiners, Am. Acad. Pain Mgmt., VFW. Republican. Roman Catholic. Avocations: skiing, football, dance, movies.

ELLIOT, KATHLEEN ANN, school system administrator; b. Kew Gardens, N.Y., Sept. 27, 1942; d. Thomas Peter Jr. and Ann D'oilé (Jenkins) Rothwell; m. Lee Elliot, May 23, 1980 (div. Feb. 1999); 1 child, Laurie Ann. BFA, Syracuse (N.Y.) U., 1964. Tchr. N.Y. Pub. Sch. Sys., Seaford, 1964-65; advt. account exec., supr. various agys., N.Y.C., 1966-86; tchr. N.Y. Pub. Sch. Sys., Cornwall, 1986-90; dir. recreation Pine Lakes C.C., North Ft. Myers, Fla., 1991-94, Seven Lakes Assocs., Ft. Myers, Fla., 1994—99, S.W. Fla. Coll., 2002—. Sec. bd. dirs. Country Pines Condominium Assn. North Ft. Myers 1997-98. Mem. AAUW (sec. 1997—), Syracuse U. Alumni Club Ft. Myers, Resort and Comml. Recreation Assn. Republican. Roman Catholic. Avocations: reading, recreational writing, swimming, boating. Home: 1200 Hall Rd Fort Myers FL 33903-5718

ELLIOT, TAMMY, newscaster; B Comms., U. Wis., 1991. Anchor WFRV-TV, Green Bay, Wis.; morning co-host Murphy in the Morning WIXX, Green Bay, Wis.; news anchor WISN, Milw. Office: WISN PO Box 402 Milwaukee WI 53201-0402

ELLIOTT, BARBARA STEVENS, music educator; d. Harvey Nathaniel and Hattie Nowlin Stevens; m. Alvin Douglas Elliott, Mar. 29, 1986; children: Jessica Latisia, Maya Simone. BA, Lynchburg Coll., 1978, MEd. Cert. tchr. Music tchr. CTl. Va. Tng. Ctr., Madison Heights, 1978—84, spl. edn. tchr., 1985, Laurel Regional Program, Lynchburg, Va., 1985—90; music tchr. R. S. Payne Elem. Sch., Lynchburg, 1990—93, Kizer Elem., Lynchburg, 1990—94, Linkhorne Mid. Sch., Lynchburg, 1994—2002; choral dir. Heritage HS, Lynchburg, 2002—. Baptist. Avocations: reading, bowling. Home: 204 Westburg Dr Lynchburg VA 24502

ELLIOTT, CANDICE K. interior designer; b. Cedar Rapids, Iowa, Aug. 29, 1949; d. Charles H. and Eunice A. (Long) Goodrich; m. John William Jr. Elliott, Jan. 27, 1973 (div.); 1 child, Brandon Christian; m. Timothy G. Kling, Sept. 14, 2002; 3 stepchildren, John William III, Andrew Timothy, Nathan David. BA, U. Iowa, 1971. Interior designer Dayton's, Mpls., 1971-76, Candice Interior Space Planning and Design, Guilford, Conn., 1981-87; owner, interior designer Sofa Works, King of Prussia, Pa., 1987-90; interior designer Jerrehians's Home Furnishings, West Chester, Pa., 1990-92; dir. sales and visual merchandising Sheffield Furniture, Malvern, Pa., 1992-95; owner Candice Interior Space Planning and Design, Wayne, Pa., 1996-97, Mt. Vernon, Iowa, 1997-2000, Kill Devil Hills, NC, 2000—01, Kitty Hawk, NC, 2001—. Bd. dirs. The Old Capitol Restoration Com., Iowa City, 1970-76; curator Guilford Keeping Soc., 1983-88; cons. Zion Episcopal Ch., North Branford, Conn., 1985-88; mem. planning and zoning bd. City of Mt. Vernon, Iowa, 1997-99. Mem. Am. Soc. Interior Designers (bd. dirs. Conn. chpt., profl. mem.). Republican. Avocations: golf, needlepoint, gardening. Home and Office: 1016 Creek Rd Kitty Hawk NC 27949

ELLIOTT, CAROL C. career officer; BS in Internat. Rels. and Polit. Sci., Iowa State U., 1972; disting. grad., Officer Tng. Sch., 1973, Squadron Officer Sch., 1977; MBA in Aviation, Embry-Riddle Aero. U., 1984; disting. grad., Air Command and Staff Coll., 1987; student, Nat. War Coll., 1992. Commd. 2d lt. USAF, 1973, advanced through grades to brig. gen., 1998; intelligence analyst 432d Tactical Fighter Wing, Udorn Royal Thai AFB, Thailand, 1974-75, USAF, Clark Air Base, The Philippines, 1975-76; chief target intelligence br. 388th Tactical Fighter Wing, Hill AFB, Utah, 1976-79, 52d Tactical Fighter Wing, Spangdahlem Air Base, W. Germany, 1979-82; target intelligence officer Armed Forces Air Intelligence Ctr., Lowry AFB, Colo., 1983; chief target devel. br. then target studies br. Hdqs. USAF Europe, Ramstein Air Base, W. Germany, 1983-86, directorate intelligence applications, dep. chief staff intellegence, 1983-86; various assignments Hdqs. USAF, Pentagon, Washington, 1987-91, 97, vice dir. intelligence J2 joint staff, 1997—; chief collection mgmt. div., asst. chief staff intelligence Hdqs. U.S. Forces Korea, Yongsan, S. Korea, 1992-94; dep. dir. intelligence Air Combat Command, Langley AFB, Va., 1994-95; comdr. 692d Intelligence Group, Hickam AFB, Hawaii, 1995-96; dir. intelligence Hdqs. Pacific Air Force Base, Hickam AFB, 1996-97; dep. dir. intelligence, surveillance and reconnaissance Hdqs. USAF, Washington, 1997, dep. chief staff for Air & Space Ops., 1997; vice dir. intelligence J2 Joint Staff, Washington, 1997-99; vice comdr. Air Intelligence Agy., Kelly AFB, Tex., 1999—. Decorated Legion of Merit. Office: Kelly AFB SAALC / CV 100 Moorman Ste 1 Kelly A F B TX 78241-5800

ELLIOTT, CINDY SUE, academic administrator; b. Ontario, Calif., Jan. 23, 1958; d. Harvey Charles and Mary Alice (Doherty) Wilkin. AS, Richland Community Coll., Dallas, 1982; BA in Psychology, U. Tex., Dallas, 1982, MA in Teaching, 1983. Cert. tchr., Tex. Teaching asst. The Willows Montessori Sch., Dallas, 1979-80; tchr. Richland Childrens Ctr., Richardson, Tex., 1981-82, Palisades Childrens Ctr., Plano, Tex., 1981-82; sec. student govt. U. Tex.-Dallas, Richardson, 1982, rsch. asst. tchr. edn., 1982-87, sec. admissions office, admissions asst., 1987, admissions counselor, 1987-93; instrnl. aide Victor Primary Sch., Victorville, Calif., 1993-96; tutor Sylvan Learning Ctr., Victorville, 1993-96, now dir. edn., ctr. dir., 1999—. Tchr. [illegible] Apple Valley, Calif., 1999—. Mem. AAUW, Assn. Metroplex Internat. Educators, Nat. Assn. Fgn. Student Affairs, North Tex. Coun. Coll. and Univ. Admissions Officers, Order Eastern Star. Republican. Christian Scientist. Avocations: tennis, reading, walking, ceramics.

ELLIOTT, DOLORES, disabilities advocate, film producer; b. N.Y.C., Nov. 13, 1950; d. Thomas Augustus Elliot and Vera A. Burll. BFA, NYU, 1972; MEd, Hunter Coll., 1996. Prodr. Ctr. for Study Music, N.Y.C., 1988—; assoc. prodr. Stanley Nelson Prodns., N.Y.C., 1990-93, Search-Light, San Francisco, 1993; tng. dir. Achilles Track Club, N.Y.C., 1994—. Mentor Networking project, N.Y.C., 1993—. Mem. Manhattan Soc., 1994—. Teens, N.Y.C. Artworks, YWCA, 53rd St. Membership Com. Mem. Soc. Disability Studies. Roman Catholic. Achievements include completing 3 N.Y.C. marathons, 1993, 94, 95. Home: 535 W 110th St New York NY 10025-2086

ELLIOTT, DONNA LOUISE, artist; b. Oak Park, Ill., Sept. 2, 1931; d. Carl and Sarah Louise (Shelton) Reinecke; m. Gerald Morris Elliott, June 24, 1950. BS in Art Edn., U. Wis., Milw., 1966. Art tchr. Grafton H.S., Wis., 1969—70; instr. art Cardinal Stritch U., Fox Pt., Wis., 1990—95; leader workshop Wauwatosa Woman's Club, Wauwatosa, Wis., 1996; instr. workshop West Bend Art Mus., Wis., 1999, Peninsula Sch. Fine Arts, Fish Creek, Wis., 2002—03; represented Art Elements Gallery, Mequon, Wis. One-woman shows include Firehouse Gallery, Cedarburg, Wis., 1972, Milw. Athletic Club, 1974, 1982, 1993, Sistermoon Gallery, Milw., 1978, Marine Bank, Fox Pt., 1987, Concordia Coll. Gallery, 1988, Firestation Gallery, Milw., 1989, one-woman shows include Alexian Village Gallery, 1994, Metrix Co., Waukesha, Wis., 1997, one-woman shows include The Andersen Arts Ctr., Kenosha, Wis., 1999, exhibitions include League of Milw. Artists Show, 1970—, Wis. Watercolor Soc., 1989—, Wis. Women in Arts, Milw., 1990 (award of Excellence, 1982), Wis. Painters and Sculptors (various shows), 1995— (1st place, 1998, Exhbn. award, 1999), Wustum Mus., Racine, Wis., 2002—03, Art League of Bonita Springs, Fla., 2004, Represented in permanent collections Am. Internat. Supply Co., SBC-Wis. Telephone Co., Coopers & Lybrand, Milw., others, exhibitions include Midwest Biennial, New Visions Gallery, 2003, Northwestern Mutual Ins. Co. Vol. watercolor instr. North Shore Sch. Srs., United Meth. Sch., Whitefish Bay, Wis., 2001. Recipient Best of Show award, League of Milw. Artists, 1982, 1994. Mem.: AAUW, Wis. Artists in All Media, Wis. Painters and Sculptors (chair S.E. chapter 2001—), Midwest Watercolor Soc. Methodist. Avocations: swimming, walking, gardening. Home: 9102 Windswept Dr Bonita Springs FL 34135-8187

ELLIOTT, DOROTHY GAIL, music educator writer; b. Kennard, Ind., Oct. 23, 1918; d. Clyde Harrison and Hazel Uvah (Houk) Copeland; m. Robert E. Elliott, Aug. 22, 1948 (dec. Mar. 1997); children: R. Bruce, Marla Beth, John H. BS in Edn., Ball State Tchrs. Coll., 1940; student Chgo. Theol. Sem., U. Chgo., 1944—47. Tchr. music and math. New Castle (Ind.) Jr. H.S., 1940-43; dir. religious edn. Bethany Union Ch., Chgo., 1945-47; dir. youth activities Hillfields Congl. Ch., Coventry, Eng., 1947-48; music tchr. grades 4, 5, 6 and 7 Silberstein Elem. Sch., Dallas, 1967-70; dir. H.S. choir Singapore Am. Sch., 1970-71; music tchr. grades 4, 5, 6 and 7 Degolyer Elem. Sch., Dallas, 1971-72; music edn. writer J. Weston Walch, Pub., Portland, Maine, 1973—; proprietor Noteman Press, Dallas, 1982—. Author (three books, two tapes) Harmonious Recorder, 1969-2004, (book, worksheets, tapes) ZOUNDS!, 1973-2003, (book, worksheets) Sight-Singing for Young Teens, 1981-97, (reproducible book) Rediscovered Songs, 1991, (historical musical) G.T.T. (Gone to Texas), 1984-2004; author, editor: JUBILEE!, 1987-2004; editor: Dancing with Cancer, 1995-2003; contbg. author: Music and You, 1991. Named Music Alumni of Yr., Ball State U., Muncie, Ind., 1979. Mem. Am. Recorder Soc., Music Educators Nat. Conf., Am. Orff-Schulwerk Assn. Democrat. Avocations: gardening, crafts, theatre, concerts. Home and Office: 2603 Andrea Ln Dallas TX 75228-3503 Office Phone: 214-327-4466.

ELLIOTT, ELEANOR THOMAS, foundation executive, civic leader; b. N.Y.C., Apr. 26, 1926; d. James A. and Dorothy Q. (Read) Thomas; m. John Elliott, Jr., July 27, 1956. BA, Barnard Coll., 1948; DHL (hon.), Duke U., 2002. Assoc. editor Vogue mag., 1948-52; asst. dir. research and speech writing div. N.Y. State Republican Com., 1952; social sec. to Sec. of State and Mrs. John Foster Dulles, 1952-55; dir. James Weldon Johnson Community Centers, N.Y.C., 1955-60; bd. dirs. Celanese Corp., 1974-87, CIT Fin. Corp., 1978-81, INA Life Ins. Co. of N.Y., 1983-1998. Author: Glamour Magazine Party Book, 1966. Trustee Barnard Coll., 1959—, chmn. bd., 1973-76; bd. dirs. Maternity Center Assn., 1960-70, pres., 1965-69; bd. govs. N.Y. Hosp., 1972—, v.p., 1979— ; bd. dirs. Found. for Child Devel., N.Y.C., 1969—, chmn., 1972-79, 1973— ; bd. dirs. United Way Greater N.Y., 1977-86, NOW Legal Def. and Edn. Fund, 1983-90, Catalyst Inc., 1978-83, Am. Women's Econ. Devel. Corp., 1980-86, Woodrow Wilson Nat. Fellowship Found, 1983—, chmn. 1993-1999, co-chair, Nat. Adv. Coun., 2000—, Edna McConnell Clark Found., 1984-93, Coun. on Women's Studies, Duke U.; overseer Cornell U. Med. Coll., 1995—. Recipient Alumni medal, Columbia U., 1977, medal of distinction, Barnard Coll., 1979, Red Cross Humanitarian award, 1986, Extraordinary Woman of Achievement award, NCCJ, 1978, Disting. Trustee award, United Hosp. Fund., 1991, Disting. Cmty. Svc. award, 1994, award for disting. svc. to City of New York, St. Nicholas Soc., 2002. Mem.: Colony Club of N.Y.C. Episcopalian. Home: 1035 5th Ave New York NY 10028-0135 Fax: (212)472-6506.

ELLIOTT, ERIC S, insurance company executive; B in mgmt. and fin., MBA, Temple U. Sr. v.p. managed care/pharmacy services Rite Aid Corp., 1989; CEO Eagle Managed Care (Rite Aid); with Mellon Bank; sr. v.p. pharmacy mgmt. CIGNA, 2000—03; sr. v.p. bus. mgmt. PCS Health Systems; v.p. pharmacy mgmt. Aetna Inc., 2003—. Office: Aetna Inc 151 Farmington Ave Hartford CT 06156

ELLIOTT, FRANCES CARANO, lawyer, educator; b. Carovilli, Italy, Aug. 17, 1950; d. Remo Marino and Angelia (Elia) Carano; m. G. Mark Elliott, Sept. 23, 1972; children: Cara, Adrienne. BS in Phys. Therapy, Ohio State U., 1972; JD cum laude, U. Akron, 1983; postgrad., John Marshall Sch. Law, Chgo., 1998—. Bar: Ohio, U.S. Dist. Ct. Ohio; cert. phys. therapist. Dir. phys. therapy Ohio Rehab. Clinic, Columbus, 1972-76; rsch. asst. U. Akron Sch. Law, 1980, adj. prof., 1984-85; prodr., legal advisor Feedback Series: Legal Questions, WEAO Pub. TV, Kent, Ohio, 1989-94; ind. contractor West Group, Inc., 1998—; sole practitioner Hudson, Ohio, 1983—. Legal advisor WEAO Pub. TV, 1989-94; lectr. in field. Pres., Hudson Music Assn., 1990-94; mem. cabinet, legal divsn. United Way, Akron, 1987; publicity dir. Hudson Bicentennial Comm., 1995-97. Mem. Ohio State Bar Assn., Ohio Bar Coll., Akron Bar Assn. (publicity dir.), Hudson C. of C. (bd. dirs. 1986-88). Republican. Roman Catholic. Avocations: gardening, trading in the stock market, reading, travel. Home: 83 Sussex Rd Hudson OH 44236-1650 Office: Law Offices of Frances Elliott 118 W Streetsboro St # 140 Hudson OH 44236-2711 E-mail: eeefce@yahoo.com.

ELLIOTT, INGER MCCABE, designer, textile company executive, design consultant; b. Feb. 23, 1933; arrived in U.S., 1941, naturalized, 1946; d. David and Lova (Katz) Abrahamsen; m. Osborn Elliott, Oct. 20, 1963; children from previous marriage: Kari McCabe, Alexander McCabe, Marit McCabe. AB in History with honors, Cornell U., 1954; postgrad., Harvard U., 1955; AM, Radcliffe Coll., 1957. Photographer Photo Rschrs., 1960—98; pres. China Seas, Inc., N.Y.C., 1972—80, Gifted Textile Collection to L.A. County Mus. Art, 1991—. Textile Exhibit L.A. County Mus. Art, 1996—96; cons. Sotheby's Inc., 1992—; mem. Coun. Fgn. Rels. Author: A Week in [illegible] A Week in Henry's World, Exteriors, 1992; contbr.: photographic essays to Esquire, Vogue, Life, Newsweek, N.Y. Times, Infinity, House & Hargen; author: Batik: Fabled Cloth of Java, 1985, 2004. Mem. East Asia vis. com. Harvard U.; trustee The Asia Soc., Am. Scandinavian Found. Recipient Roscoe awards, 1978—. Mem.: Am. Women's Econ. Devel. Corp., Am. Soc. Mag. Photographers, Com. of 200, Ellis Island Yacht Club (lt. comdr.), Cosmopolitan Club, Phi Beta Kappa. Home: 84 Water St Stonington CT 06378

ELLIOTT, JEAN ANN, librarian emeritus; b. Martinsburg, W.Va., Jan. 18, 1933; d. Howard Hoffman and Dorothy Jean (Horn) E. AB in Edn., Shepherd Coll., Shepherdstown, W.Va., 1954; MS in Libr. Sci., Syracuse U., 1957; MS, Shippensburg (Pa.) U., 1974. Asst. libr. Fairmont (W.Va.) State Coll., 1957-60; reference asst. U. Pitts., 1960-61; acting libr. Shepherd Coll., 1961-62, coord. libr. sci., 1962-97. Compiler Jefferson County Hist. mag., 1990. Nat. treas. Palatines of Am., Columbus, Ohio, 1986-88. Mem. ALA, AAUW, DAR (W.Va. treas. 1980-83, 86-89, 95-98, state regent 1998-2001, hon. state regent 2001—), W.Va. Libr. Assn. (election chmn. 1988-90), Jefferson County Hist. Soc., Nat. Soc. Daus. Am. Colonies (nat. libr. 1991-94, hon. state regent 1991—), Nat. Soc. Daus. 1812 (nat. libr. 1994-96), W.Va. Soc. Daus. 1812 (state pres. 1991-94, hon. state pres. 1994—), Nat. Soc. Daus. Colonial Wars (state pres. 2001—), Alpha Beta Alpha (nat. exec. sec. 1968-76), Phi Kappa Phi. Presbyterian. Avocations: genealogy, travel, knitting, computers. Home: PO Box 1649 Shepherdstown WV 25443-1649

ELLIOTT, KIMBERLY ANN, economist; Adj. prof. Johns Hopkinst U.; adv. Coun. Fgn. Rels., Carnegie Commn. Task Force Preventing Deadly Conflict, Carter Ctr. Author: Auction Quotas and United States Trade Policy, 1987, Economic Sanctions Reconsidered, 2d edit., 1990, Measuring the Costs of Protection in the United States, 1994, Reciprocity and Retaliation in US Trade Policy, 1994, Corruption and the Global Economy, 1997; contbr. articles to profl. jours. Rsch. fellow Inst. Internat. Econs. Office: Inst Internat Econs 11 Dupont Cir NW Washington DC 20036-1207 also: Johns Hopkins U Sch Advanced Internat Study 1740 Massachusetts Ave NW Washington DC 20036-1903

ELLIOTT, LEE ANN, company executive, former government official; b. June 26, 1927; BA, U. Ill. V.p. Bishop, Bryant amd Assocs., Inc., 1979-81; mem. Fed. Election Commn., Washington, 1981-2000, chmn., 1884, 90, 96; pres. Form Meets Function Enterprises, Inc., Chandler, Ariz., 2000—. Lectr., author and inventor in field. Bd. dirs., pres. Chgo. Area Pub. Affairs Group; bd. dirs. Kids Voting, USA. Mem. Am. Med. Polit. Action Com. (asst. dir. 1961-70, assoc. exec. dir. 1970-79), Am. Assn. Polit. Cons. (bd. dirs.), Nat. Assn. Mfrs. (award of excellence), U.S. C. of C. (pub. affairs com.). Office: Form Meets Function Enterprises Inc 820 W Warner Rd Ste 123 Chandler AZ 85225-2940

ELLIOTT, MARIAN KAY, real estate manager; b. Wheatland, Wyo., Aug. 29, 1950; d. James Beal Jr. and Marian L. Angle; m. William Paul Elliott, June 1, 1978; children: Kenneth James Judd, L.R. Dedee Judd, William Paul, Joseph G., Christina Hope, Denise Faith. Cert. Mont. Comml. Credit Mgmt. Assn.; therapeutic foster parenting Dept. Family Svcs.; lic. real estate agt. Wyo. Comml. credit mgr. Pacific Steel, Mills, Wyo., 1978—79; mgr. investment real estate Casper, Wyo., 1981—; real estate assoc. Associated Brokers, Casper, 1982—85. Local reporter National Voter; editor: (newsletter) Wyoming Recycler. Chair fundraising com. Casper Jaycee Jinx, 1974—76; Wyo. scholastic pageant judge Casper Jaycees, 1993; amb. Casper Area C. of C., 1995—96; guardian Youth in Crisis and Mentally Disabled Adults, Casper, 1996—2002; ct. apptd. spl. advocate for abused and neglected children CASA of Natrona County, Casper, 2002—03; vol. Blue Envelope Health/ Elem. Strep Prevention Program, Casper, 1975—78; vol. resource class aide Elem. Sch., Casper, 1975—76, PTA bd. mem., 1979—83; foster parent Dept. Family Svcs., Casper, 1986—96, spkr. new foster parent tng., 1987—91; advocate, lobbyist foster children's rights Foster Parents of Natrona County, Casper, 1989—91; v.p. St. Christopher's Presch. Guild, Casper, 1976; confirmation class tchr. St. Mark's Episcopal Ch., Casper, 1975—78. Mem.: Hat Club/ Resources for Women in Spl. Circumstances (pres. 1997—2001), Big Bros./ Big Sisters Ctrl. Wyo. (adv. coun. 2002—03). Democrat. Achievements include sued for and won the right to sue elected officials in the State of Wyoming; helped change Wyoming laws to allow earlier adoption of foster children. Avocations: gardening, fire arms. Home: 1434 S Beech St Casper WY 82601 Personal E-mail: willelliott1@bresnan.com.

ELLIOTT, MISSY, musician; b. Portsmouth, Va., July 1, 1971; d. Ronnie and Pat Elliott. Grad., Manor H.S., Portsmouth, 1990. With Elektra Entertainment, 1996—; owner Gold Mind. Musician: Supa Dupa Fly, 1997 (Platinum), Da Real World, 1999 (Platinum), Miss E...So Addictive, 2001 (Platinum), Under Construction, 2002 (2 times Platinum), This Is Not A Test!, 2003. Nominee 3 Grammy awards, 2002, 2 Grammy awards, 2003; named Best Female Hip-Hop Artist, BET, 2002, 15th of 50 Greatest Hip Hop Artists, VH1, 2003; recipient Best Video of Yr. for The Rain, Rolling Stone, 1997, Soul Train Lady of Soul award for Best R&B/Soul or Rap Music Video for Get Ur Freak On, 2001, Grammy award for Best Rap Solo for Get Ur Freak On, 2002, Soul Train Lady of Soul award for Best R&B/Soul or Rap Music Video for One Minute Man, 2002, Grammy award for Best Female Rap Solo Performance for Scream aka Itchin, 2003, Soul Train Music award for Best R&B/Soul or Rap Music Video for Work It, 2003, Soul Train Lady of Soul awards for Best Song and Best Music Video for Work It, 2003, Video of Yr., Best Hip Hop Video for Work It, 2003, Favirote Rap/Hip-Hop Female Artist, Am. Music Awards, 2003. Office: Elektra Entertainment 75 Rockefeller Plz New York NY 10019*

ELLIOTT, SUSAN AUGUSTE, psychologist, psychotherapist, consultant; b. Mt. Shasta, Calif., Aug. 24, 1951; d. Cecil Edwin and Edith Ruth (Holland) E.; m. Richard Martinez, 1973 (div. 1975); 1 child, Lorin Wade Alder; m. Mark Johnson, 1999. AB, U. Calif., Berkeley, 1973; postgrad., Calif. State U., San Francisco, 1975-76, Towson (Md.) State U., 1984-85; MA, Goddard Coll., 1988; doctoral student, Fielding Inst., 2000—. Lic. psychologist-master, Vt. Co-founder, crisis worker, fundraiser, project dir. Humboldt Women for Shelter and Umbrella Project, Arcata, Calif., 1976-81; devel. coord. House of Ruth, Balt., 1984; orgnl. cons., Balt., 1984-85; counselor Tri-County Youth Svcs., Charlotte Hall, Md., 1985-86; sexual assault clinician Walden Counseling Ctr., California, Md., 1986-87; coord., organizer SAFELINE, Chelsea, Vt., 1987-88; clinician Orange County Mental Health Svcs., Randolph, Vt., 1988-92; psychologist, psychotherapist, Montpelier & Barre, Vt., 1989—. Founding co-dir. Our House, Barre, Vt., 1989; conf. coord. Women and Therapy, Plainfield, Vt., 1988; supr., trainer Vt. Dept. Corrections, Vt. Dept. Mental Health, 1988-91, World Congress Mental Health, Washington, 1983; dir. programs Prevent Child Abuse-Vt., 1998-99; clin. supr. family support program and Allenbrook Homes for Youth, Easter Seals, 1993—; creator outdoor retreats for sexually abused and abusive youth, 1997—; bd. dirs. Vt. Partnership for Abuse Free State, 1993-99. Contbg. author: Politics of the Heart, 1987; guest reviewer Women and Therapy, 1987; co-editor Vt. Psychologist, 1990; author sexual abuse-free environment for teans curriculum for jr. high schs. Lobbyist Md. Food Com., Balt., 1982. Recipient appreciation award Humboldt Easter Seal Soc., 1981, Svc. to Children and Families award Ct. Vt. Social Workers Assn., 1991; grantee Reader's Digest, 1976, Jenny McKean Moore Fund for Writers, 1984; Charlotte Newcombe scholar Towson State U., 1985. Mem. APA (assoc.), Assn. for Treatment and Tng.

in the Attachment of Children, Intenat. Soc. for Traumatic Stress Studies. Avocations: gardening, swimming, cross-country skiing, writing. Address: RR 1 Box 152 East Calais VT 05650-9513 E-mail: sabinpond@aol.com.

ELLIOTT, SUSAN DONISE, secondary school educator; b. Newport Beach, Calif., Sept. 21, 1968; m. Raymond Hevey, Jr., Oct. 18, 1996. AAS in Bus. Adminstrn., Pima C.C., 1990; BA in Polit. Sci. and Comm., U. Ariz., 1994, tchr. cert., 1996. Cert. substance abuse counselor Ariz. Bd. Behavioral Health Examiners; cert. tchr. social studies, Ariz., Calif.; cert. in cross-cultural lang. acquisition and devel. Behavioral health technician LaPaloma Family Svcs., Tucson, 1992-95; substance abuse counselor Gateway Found., Tucson, 1995, Project PPEP, Tucson, 1996; history tchr. Pueblo H.S./U. Ariz., Tucson, 1996; spl. edn. tchr. Calexico Unified. Sch. Dist., 1996-97; social studies tchr. Azusa Unified Sch. Dist., Calif., 1997—. Author: Lyrical Poetry, 1991; contbg. author: Joruney Between Stars, 1997. Elected site rep., mem. sch. site coun., Azusa Unified Sch. Dist., 2002. Avocations: geneology, mexico, history, family, education. Home: 1340 N Enid Covina CA 91722 Office: 1415 Skyway Ln Pomona CA 91768-1258

ELLIOTT, SUSAN SPOEHRER, information technology executive; b. St. Louis, May 4, 1937; d. Charles Henry and Jane Elizabeth (Baur) Spoehrer; m. Howard Elliott Jr., Sept. 2, 1961; children: Kathryn Elliott Love, Elizabeth Elliott Niedringhaus. AB, Smith Coll., 1958. Systems engr. IBM, St. Louis, 1958-66; founder, chmn., CEO, SSE (Sys. Svc. Enterprises, Inc.), St. Louis, 1966—; systems analyst Mo. State Dept. Edn., Jefferson City, Mo., 1967-70; systems coord. Bank of Am. (formerly Boatmen's Nat. Bank), St. Louis, 1979-83. Bd. dirs., exec. com. Mo. Automobile Club; class C dir., dep. chmn. Fed. Res. Bd., St. Louis, 1996-98, chmn., 1999-2000; bd. dirs. Ameren Corp., Angelica Corp., Regional Bus. Coun., St. Louis Regional Commerce and Growth Assn., sec. bd. dirs., 1991-94; bd. dirs. AAA Mo. Trustee, vice-chmn. Mary Inst., St. Louis, 1976-89, Webster U., 1987-96; commr., vice-chmn. St. Louis Civil Svc. Commn., 1985-86, Mo. Lottery Commn., Jefferson City, 1985-87; bd. dirs. St. Louis Zoo, 1990-96, St. Louis Sci. Ctr., 1995—; pres.'s adv. coun. area coun., tech. com. Girl Scouts U.S.; chair women bus. owner's com. United Way, 1996-97. Mem. Internat. Women's Forum. Republican. Presbyterian. Avocations: golf, fitness. Office: SSE (Sys Svc Enterprises Inc) 77 West Port Plz Ste 500 Saint Louis MO 63146 3126 E-mail: sselliott@SSEinc.com.

ELLIOTT, TERESA J. music educator; b. Winchester, Ky., Oct. 29, 1955; d. Harold H. and Marjorie G. Crawford; m. George R. Elliott, July 19, 1980; 1 child, Robert Michael. B of Music Edn., Morehead State U., 1977; M of Music Edn., U. Ky., 1978, MusM, 1979. Educator New Philadelphia (Ohio) City Schs., 1980—85, Paoli (Ind.) Comty. Schs., 1980—85, Lafayette (Ind.) Sch. Corp., 1985—87, Plainfield (Ind.) Comty. Schs., 1987—90, Jefferson County Pub. Schs., Louisville, 1990—94, Fayette County Pub. Schs., Lexington, 1994—; adj. prof. clarinet Transylvania U. Facilitator Bands of Am., Indpls., 1984—94, Attitude Concepts for Today, Bluffton, Ind., 1984—96. Recipient Middle Sch. Tchr. Yr., Ky. Music Educators, 2004. Mem.: Women Band Dirs. Internat. (Scroll of Achievement nat. chpt. 1997), Music Educators Nat. Conf. Home: 769 Malabu Dr Lexington KY 40502 Office: Beaumont Mid Sch 2080 Georgian Way Lexington KY 40504

ELLIOTT, VIRGINIA F. HARRISON, retired anatomist, publisher, educator, investment advisor; b. St. Louis, Mar. 15, 1918; d. George Benjamin and Florence Gertrude (McManus) H.; m. William Hector Marsh, Dec. 1, 1963 (dec. Dec. 1986); m. George William Elliott, Oct. 27, 1991; stepchildren: Carolyn Frances Roberts, George William II, Robert Bonner (dec. Apr. 1995), Cathrine Susan Dimino. BS, U. Wis., 1940, PhD, 1959; MA, Columbia U., 1944. Lectr. Columbia U., N.Y.C., 1943-46; asst. prof. Mary Washington U., Fredericksburg, 1946—48, Oreg. State U., Corvallis, 1948-50, assoc. prof., 1950-59; instr. Army Med. Acad./Brooks Army Med. Ctr., San Antonio, 1959-60, assoc. prof., 1960-64; lectr. Hadassah Med. Sch., Hebrew U. of Jerusalem, 1965; pub. stock market letter Washington, 1969-84; ret., 1984. Fashion model, 1936-47, with John Robert Powers Schs., Phila., Pitts., N.Y.C., 1943-47; cons. U. Tex. Med. Sch., 1962-64, U.S. Pentathlon Team, San Antonio, 1960-64, Dentists for Treatment of Pain from Muscular Tension, San Antonio, 1960-64; vis. prof. grad. sch. U. Wash., Seattle, 1961; lectr. in field. Contbr. articles to profl. jours. Mem. bd. visitors Sch. Edn., U. Wis., Madison, 1992-95, now emeritus; mem. Washington com. Nat. Coun. on Women's Giving. Recipient Civilian Meritorious Svc. award U.S. Civil Svc., 1965; Amy Morris Homans fellow, 1958; hon. fellow U. Wis., 1956, 58, 59. Fellow AAHPERD, Tex. Acad. Sci.; mem. Am. Alliance Health, Phys. Edn., Recreation and Dance, Am. Assn. Anatomists divsns. Fedn. Am. Socs. for Exptl. Biology (emeritus), Cosmos Club (emeritus). Presbyterian. Avocations: designing clothing, furniture, landscaping and boats, sculpting, painting. Home: 6333 Cavalier Corridor Falls Church VA 22044-1301

ELLIOTT-MOSKWA, ELAINE SALLY, psychologist, researcher; b. St. Louis; d. Walter Leonard and Helen (Krelo) E.; m. Alexander Moskwa Jr.; 1 child, Katherine. BA in Psychology, U. Mo., 1973; MA in Psychology, San Diego State U., 1977; PhD in Psychology, U. Ill., 1980. Vis. rsch. assoc. Lab. Human Devel., Harvard U., Cambridge, Mass., 1980-81; lectr. dept. psychology Brandeis U., Waltham, Mass., 1981; fellow Ctr. for Cognitive Therapy, U. Pa., Phila., 1982-83; cons. Presbyn. U. Pa. Med. Ctr., Phila., 1984-85; pvt. practice Newton Centre, Mass., 1985-92; dir. Ctr. for Cognitive Therapy Greater Boston, Newton Centre, 1988-92; pvt. practice Princeton, N.J., 1992—. Instr. Med. Sch. Harvard U., 1989-99; asst. dir. tng., cognitive therapy and rsch. program Mass. Gen. Hosp., 1991-92, cons. depression rsch. program, 1992-99. Author: chpt. Carmichael's Handbook of Child Psychology, 1983, Advances in Psychology, 1989. Nat. Inst. on Aging grantee Brandeis U., 1988. Mem. Am. Psychol. Assn., Assn. for Advancement Behavior Therapy. Office: 20 Nassau St Ste 507 Princeton NJ 08542-4505

ELLIOTT-ZAHORIK, BONNIE, nurse, administrator; b. Algona, Iowa; AAS, Coll. Lake County, Grayslake, Ill., 1979; student, U. Iowa; BS, U. St. Francis, Joliet, Ill., 1988; MS, Nat. Louis U., Evanston, Ill., 1989; grad., Northwestern U., 2001. Cert. nurse adminstr.-advanced; cert. critical incident stress debriefing provider. Chair coordinating coun. Vista Health, Waukegan, Ill., 1998, chair managerial coun., 1998—2002; dir. med./surg. oncology, inpatient pediat., adolescent and outpatient units across the life span Vista Health/Victory Meml. Hosp., 2000—. Preceptor/mentor Graceland U., Parkside and St. Xavier U.; fellow, doctorate pgm, adminstrn Walden U., 1995—96. Contbr. articles to profl. jours. Co-chair Victory Healthcare Svcs. Combined Appeal Campaign, 1997; mem. combined appeal com., vol. Am. Heart Assn., 1995—2003; designer and vol. Festival of Trees fundraiser, 1992—2001. Mem.: AACN, Ill. Orgn. Nurse Leaders (bd. dirs. 1991—, pres. 1998, past pres., state chmn. bylaws com. 1998—99, pres.-elect region 2-B 2000, strategic planning com. 2000—, pres. IONL region 2-B 2001), Ill. Coalition Nursing Resources (legis. funding com. 2001—, pres. 2004, exec. bd. dir. 2000—), Ill. Coun. Nurse Mgrs. (past pres. Region 2B), Am. Orgn. Nurse Execs.

ELLIS, ANNE ELIZABETH, fundraiser; b. Orngestad, Aruba, Aug. 21, 1945; d. Thomas Albert and Anne Elizabeth (Belis) Wolfe; m. Earl Edward Ellis, Feb. 14, 1970. BS, La. State U., 1967. Fashion coord., Baton Rouge, 1962-67; textile researcher La. State U., Baton Rouge, 1965-67; buyer I.H. Rubensteins., Baton Rouge, 1967-68; fashion distbr. J.C. Penney, Inc., Arlington, Tex., 1969-70, asst. buyer Dallas, 1970-73; exec. dir. Nassau County Mus. Fine Art Assn., Roslyn, N.Y., 1985-88. Speaker C.W. Post U., Greenvale, N.Y., 1988—; cons. in field. Chmn., editor: (cookbook) Specialities of the House, 1981-83. Bd. dirs., com. chmn. Congregational Ch., Manhasset, N.Y., 1975-96; exec. v.p., bd. dirs., com. chmn. Jr. League Internat.; benefit gala chmn., com. chmn. Grenville Baker Boys & Girls Club, Locust Valley, N.Y., 1983-91; pres. bd., vice-chmn. cmty. outreach, benefit gala chmn. Tilles Performing Art Ctr. L.I. U., Greenvale, N.Y., 1985—; bd. dirs., benefit co-chmn. Nassau County Family Assn. Svcs., Hempstead, 1988-96; benefit vice-chmn. Glen Cove/North Shore Cmty. Hosp., 1989-93; mem. exec. bd., exec. v.p., trustee WLIW, L.I. Pub. TV, 1990-2001, chmn. bd. dirs., 1997-99; trustee Cmty. Found. of Oyster Bay, 1991-94; trustee Dowling Coll., Oakdale, N.Y., 1993-98, exec. bd., 1997-98; adv. bd. Westbury (N.Y.) Gardens, 1993-97; chmn. adv. bd. Long Island chpt. Save the Children, 1995-2001; trustee L.I. U., 1998—. Recipient Vol. of Yr. award Jr. League L.I., 1984, 85, Outstanding Vol. Svcs. and Commitment award County of Nassau, 1989, Juliette Low award Nassau County Girl Scouts, L.I., 1991, Disting. Leadership award, L.I., 1991, Outstanding Community Vol. award Jr. League of L.I., 1991-92, Disting. Svc. medal L.I. State Parks Found., 1999, Women of Achievement award Jr. League L.I., 2000. Mem. P.E.O. (pres. 1985-87), The Creek Inc., Meadowbrook Club Inc., Nat. Arts Club, Lost Tree Club, Forest Creek Club, Kappa Kappa Gamma (alumna pres. 1971-72). Republican. Congregationalist. Avocations: golf, gardening, needlepoint.

ELLIS, BERNICE, financial planning company executive, investment advisor; b. Bklyn. d. Samuel and Clara H.; m. Seymour Scott Ellis; children: Michele, Wayne. BA, Bklyn. Coll.; MS, Queens Coll., 1970. Cert. fin. planner, N.Y. 1987, elem. educator, N.Y.C. Elem. tchr. L.I. Sch. Dists., Merrick, N.Y.; tchr. reading N.Y.C. Bd. of Edn., Bklyn., 1972-73; coordinator Reading is Fundamental, Lawrence, N.Y., 1973-75; pres., founder N.Y. State Assn. for the Gifted and Talented, Valley Stream, N.Y., 1974-87; pres. Ellis Planning, Valley Stream, N.Y., 1984—. Cons. Nassau County Bd. Coop. Ednl. Svcs., Westbury, N.Y., 1973-74; adminstrv. intern region II U.S. Office Edn., 1977-78; adj. asst. prof. Nassau C.C., Garden City, N.Y., 1975-91, adj. assoc. prof., 1991-94, adj. full prof., 1995—; fin. commentator Money Talk radio program WHPC FM; arbitrator NASD, 1996. Contbr. articles to profl. jours and fin. newsletters. Mem. adv. com. Ams. for Ams. for Hope, Growth and Opportunity, 1998; mem. Nat. Rep. Party, Valley Stream Rep. Party, N.Y. State Rep. Party. Recipient Ednl. Professions Devel. Act fellow CUNY Inst. for Remediations Skills for Coll. Pers., Queensborough C.C., 1970-73; named Business Person of Yr. Nat. Rep. Congl. Com., 2003. Mem. AAUW (North Shore bd., chmn. Money Talk 1991—), Nat. Assn. Securities Dealers (arbitrator 1996), Nat. Alliance of Sales Execs., Inst. for CFPs, Inst. for CFPs of L.I. (bd. dirs.), Internat. Assn. Fin. Planners (legis. com. L.I. chpt. 1986-87), N.Y. State Reading Assn., Adj. Faculty Assn. Nassau C.C., L.I. C. of C., Rotary, Womens Nat. Republic Club. Avocations: reading, swimming. Office: Ellis Planning Inc 628 Golf Dr Valley Stream NY 11581-3594

ELLIS, BETTY GRAHAM, radiographer, sonographer; b. Jefferson, N.C., July 20, 1963; Registered radiologic technologist, diagnostic med. sonographer, vascular technologist. Chief sonographer WRMC, N. Wilkesboro, NC, 1984—, adj. faculty mem., 1984—; clin. instr. Caldwell Cmty. Coll., 1984—, adv. bd., 1984—.

ELLIS, CARLENE, computer company executive; children: Stephanie, Jason. BS in Maths., U. Ga., 1969. Electrical engr. Western Electric; computer programmer U. Ga.; info. sys. officer City of Jacksonville; with Fairchild Camera & Instrument; mgr. planning and control corp. info. sys. Intel Corp., 1980-83, dir. sales and mktg. adminstrn., 1983-85, dir. corp. info. svcs., 1985-87, v.p. corp. info. sys., 1987-89, corp. officer, 1989, v.p. fin. and adminstrn., 1988-90, v.p. human resources, 1990-93; v.p. info. tech., 1993-98; v.p., dir. edn., 1999—. Dir. Merix Corp., fellow Am. Leadership Forum. Recipient Bus. Month's Corp. Women on the Move award, 1989, CIO 100 awrad, 1994, 96, 97, Bay Area's Most Powerful Corp. Women award San Francisco Chronicle, 1995. Mem. Delta Gamma. Office: Intel Corp PO Box 58119 2200 Mission College Blvd Santa Clara CA 95052-8119 E-mail: carlene.ellis@intel.com.

ELLIS, CAROLYN TERRY, lawyer; b. N.Y.C., Apr. 20, 1949; D. Francis Martin and Sarah Baker (Ames) E. m. H. Lake Wise, Feb. 27, 1982; children: Carolyn Campbell Wise, Burke Ames. BA, U. Chgo., 1971; JD, NYU, 1974. Bar: N.Y. 1975. Rsch. analyst Dept. Justice, N.Y.C., 1973-74; from assoc. to ptnr. Lord, Day & Lord, N.Y.C., 1974-86; ptnr. Coudert Bros., N.Y.C., 1986-98; pres., gen. counsel Bklyn. (N.Y.) Cmty. Housing & Svcs., Inc., 1998—2003; asst. atty. gen. Charities Bur. N.Y. State Office Atty. Gen., 2003—. Instr. Bklyn. Law Sch., 1980-82. Mem. Assn. of Bar of City of N.Y. (antitrust and trade regulation com. 1989-92, internat. trade com. 1993-95).

ELLIS, CYNTHIA BUEKER, musician, educator; b. Santa Monica, Calif., Dec. 3, 1958; d. Robert Arthur and Patricia June Bueker; m. Tony Lyle Ellis, June 18, 1983. B Music, Calif. State U., 1981, M Music, 1983. 2nd flutist Pasadena (Calif.) Chamber Orch., 1981—84; piccoloist Pacific Symphony Orch., Santa Ana, Calif., 1979—; prin. flutist Opera Pacific Orch., Costa Mesa, Calif., 1995—; lectr. Calif. State U., Fullerton, 1985—; applied flute instr. Pomona Coll., Claremont, Calif., 1990—92. Adj. faculty Claremont Grad. Sch., 1996—97; mem. faculty Pacific Symphony Inst., 1993—; flute instr. Pomona Coll., 1990—92. Contbr. articles to profl. jours.; musician: (songs) (for motion pictures) Twilight, 1998, Kissing a Fool, 1998, Pentagon Wars, 1998, She's So Lovely, 1997, First Time Felon, 1997, Campfire Tales, 1996, Breaking Commandments, 1996, Baby's Day Out, 1994, Pochahontas, 1994, Stayed Tuned, 1992, Wind, 1992; numerous others. Family coord. Southern Calif. Labrador Retriever Rescue, 1999—. Mem.: Music Tchrs. Assn. Calif., Nat. Flute Assn. (chamber music competition 1st place award 2000), Mu Phi Epsilon, Phi Kappa Phi, Pi Kappa Lambda. Republican. Methodist. Avocations: fitness, cooking. Home: 1192 Beechwood Dr Brea CA 92821

ELLIS, DEBORAH MARIE, art educator; d. Deborah Marie Ellis. Minor Spanish, Universidad de Alcala de Henares, Spain, 1997; BFA in Art Edn., Bowling Green State U., 1998; MA in Art Edn., Kent State U., 2003. Cert. K-12 visual art edn. Ohio. Visual art tchr. Cleve. Mcpl. Sch. Dist., 1998—. Aux. police officer Lakewood City Police, Ohio, 2001—03; mem. reunion com. Lakewood H.S., 2002—03. Grantee, ICARE, 1999—2002. Mem.: Ohio Art Edn. Assn., Nat. Art Edn. Assn., Westshore Orchid Soc., Phi Delta Kappa. Avocations: growing orchids, art. Home: 1477 Westwood Lakewood OH 44107 E-mail: dellis19@juno.com.

ELLIS, E. SUSAN, library director, lay mminister; b. Louisville, Sept. 22, 1954; d. William Stanley and Elizabeth Mae Ellis. B Music in Vocal Performance, Eastern Ky. U., Richmond, 1977; MS in LS, U. Ky., 1988. Lic. lay minister Christian Ch. Disciples of Christ. Libr. faculty Ky. State U., Frankfort, 1988-91; libr. dir. Cynthiana-Harrison County Pub. Libr., Cynthiana, Ky., 1991—; music dir. Rep. Christian Ch. Disciples of Christ, Cynthiana, 1997—2000. Mem. ALA, Ky. Libr. Assn. Office: Cynthiana-Harrison County Pub Libr 104 N Main St Cynthiana KY 41031-1205 E-mail: sellis@harrisonlibrary.org.

ELLIS, HARRIETTE ROTHSTEIN, editor; b. Memphis, Feb. 29, 1924; d. Samuel and Edith (Brodsky) Rothstein; m. Manuel J. Kaplan, June 1, 1944 (div. Jan. 1970); children: Deborah Elise Kaplan-Wyckoff, Claire Naomi Kaplan, Amelia Stephanie Kaplan; m. Theodore J. Ellis, Aug. 22, 1971 (div. Jan. 1992). Student, Memphis State U., 1941—43, Memphis Art Acad., 1940-43; BA, U. Ala., Tuscaloosa, 1944; postgrad., UCLA, 1949-50, Chouinard Art Inst., L.A., 1948. Advt. art/copy retail industry, New Orleans, Albuquerque, L.A., 1944-49; writer, graphic artist for newspapers and mags., L.A., 1944-49; editor Jewish Fedn. News, Long Beach, Calif., 1969-81; editor, writer Calif. Fashion Publs., L.A., 1982-86; editor Valley Mag., Granada Hills, Calif., 1987; pub. rels. Joan Luther & Assocs., Beverly Hills, Calif., 1988-90; editor Jewish Cmty. Chronicle, Long Beach, 1990—; dir. corp. comms. Startel Corp., Irvine, Calif., 1981-82. Mem. com. implementation flouridation city water sys., Long Beach, Calif.; cmty. interfaith com.; bd. dirs. Hillel, 1999—, Camp Komaroff, 1994—2001, Jewish Cmty. Ctr., Long Beach, Temple Israel, Long Beach. Named Woman of Yr., Temple Israel, Pioneer Women; recipient awards, Coun. Jewish Fedns. Mem.: AAUW, Am. Jewish Press Assn. (exec. com.), Calif. Media Profls. (pres. 1997—2002, bd. dirs., treas., v.p., Newspaper awards), Women of Reform Judaism (bd. dirs.), Nat. Fedn. Press Women (Newspaper awards), Sierra Club. Avocations: theater, music, travel, archaeology. Office: 3801 E Willow St Long Beach CA 90815-1734 E-mail: jchron@surfside.net.

ELLIS, J. RENEE ELEY, special events administrator; b. Mobile, Ala., June 8, 1959; d. Howard and Barbara (Mallett) Eley; m. Larry Ellis, Mayy 28, 1994. BS in Leisure Svcs., U. South Ala., 1981, MPA, 1991. Activities therapist II Charter Hosp., Mobile, 1981-84; cmty. activities coord. Cmty. Activities Program, Mobile, 1984-86; program supr. City of Mobile Recreation Dept., 1986-91; spl. events mgr. City of Mobile, 1991—. Sec. First Night Mobile, 1991—; bd. dirs. BayFest, Inc., Mobile; sec.,v.p., pres. Pub. Employees Tng. Coun., Mobile, 1988-90. Bd. dirs. U. South Ala. Leisure Svcs. Adv. Com., Mobile, 1986-87, Children's Musical Theatre, Mobile, 1987-91; mem. children's shopping spree Mobile Jaycees, 1988; mem. quality coun. City of Mobile, 1995—; mem. Leadership Mobile, 1996—. Recipient Recreation Program award Mobile Assn. for Retarded Citizens, 1989, Ala. Assn. for Retarded Citizens, 1990; named Career Woman of Yr., Gayfers Career Club, 1993, Jaycee of Month, Mobile, 1988. Mem. Nat. Soc. Fund Raising Execs., Internat. Festival Assn., Southeastern Festival and Events Assocs. (treas. 1995—), Art Patrons League. Republican. Avocations: skiing, travel, crafts, reading, gardening.

ELLIS, JANICE RIDER, nursing educator, consultant; b. Sioux City, Iowa, Mar. 13, 1939; d. Evert Alvin and Lillian June (Hanson) Rider; m. Ivan R. Ellis, Aug. 3, 1959; children: Mark Allen, Anne Grace Ellis Wiley. BSN, U. Iowa, 1960; MN, U. Wash., 1971; Phd, U. Tex., 1990. RN, Wash. Staff nurse various hosps., Wash., Oreg., Iowa; prof., dir. nursing edn. Shoreline C.C., Seattle. Rschr. in field. Author textbooks; contbr. to profl. jours.; cons. in field. Mem. ANA, Nat. League Nursing, Wash. State Nurses Assn., Sigma Theta Tau, Phi Kappa Delta. Office: Shoreline C C 16101 Greenwood Ave N Seattle WA 98133-5667

ELLIS, JULIET S. bank executive; b. Washington, Ind., Feb. 23, 1959; d. John Topping Simpson; widowed; children: Christian, John. BA, Ind. U., 1981. CPA; chartered fin. analyst. Field cons. Merrill Lynch, Houston, 1981-87; sr. v.p. investment mgmt. group, sr. portfolio mgr. Chase Bank, Houston, 1987—. Methodist. Office: Chase Asset Mgmt 600 Travis St Houston TX 77002-3002

ELLIS, KAY CROSBY, fundraiser; b. Dallas, Sept. 5, 1945; d. Albert S. and Frances B. (Rowland) Crosby; m. Frank C. Ellis, Jr., May 27, 1972; children: Sarah Elizabeth, Mary Katherine. BA, Tex. Christian U., 1967. Reporter, feature writer Dallas Morning News, 1967-74; free-lance writer/publicist Dallas, 1974-94; v.p. devel. Juliette Fowler Homes, Dallas, 1994—. Contbr. articles to mags. including Archtl. Digest, So. Accents, Dallas-Ft. Worth Home and Garden, Texas Homes. Bd. dirs. Greater Dallas Cmty. of Chs., 1991-93, v.p. bd. dirs., 1994. Recipient Matrix award Woman in Comm., Dallas, 1974. Mem. Assn. Fundraising Profls. Mem. Christian Ch. (Disciples Of Christ). Office: Juliette Fowler Homes Inc 1234 Abrams Rd Dallas TX 75214-4824 Office Phone: 214-827-0813.

ELLIS, MARGARET BOLAND, editor, publisher; b. Meridian, Miss., Dec. 30, 1925; d. Leo Paul and Ethel Nelson Boland; m. Wesley Crosby Ellis, May 12, 1957; children: Leslie Ellis Sharbel, Margaret (Peggy) Nelson, John Howard. BA, U. Miss., Oxford, 1946. Cert.: U. South Ala. (Para Legal) 1995. Traffic and sales agt. Ea. Air Lines, Atlanta, 1947—58; pub. rels./camp dir. Girl Scouts of the USA, Mobile, Ala., 1967—72; pub. rels. dir., instr. St. Paul's Episcopal Sch., Mobile, 1969—97; pub., editor Magnolia Mansions Press, Mobile, 1996—. Author: (autobiography) Be Good Sweet Maid, 1984, (fiction novel) The Shamrock Diary, 1998, (novel) A Brief Garland, 2004. Named to Hall of Honor, St. Paul's Episcopal Sch., 2002; recipient Newton Cox Tennis award, Mobile Tennis Club, 1975, M.O. Beale Scroll of Merit, City of Mobile, 1979. Mem.: Press Club Mobile, Soc. Profl. Journalists (sec. 1978—79), Pub. Rels. Coun. Ala. (bd. dirs. 1984—86). Episcopalian. Avocations: tennis, golf. Office: Magnolia Mansions Press 4661 Pinewood Dr East Mobile AL 36618 E-mail: magnoliamansions@aol.com.

ELLIS, MARY LOUISE HELGESON, retired insurance company executive, business consultant; b. Albert Lea, Minn., May 29, 1943; d. Stanley Orville and Neoma Lois (Guthier) Helgeson; m. David Readinger, Nov. 5, 1994; children from previous marriage: Christopher, Tracy. BS in Pharmacy, U. Iowa, 1966; MA in Pub. Adminstrn., Iowa State U., 1982, postgrad., 1982—83. Faculty Duquesne U., Pitts., 1977; cons. in pharmacy Colville, Wash., 1978—79; dir. pharmacy Mt. Carmel Hosp., Colville, 1978—79; clin. pharmacist Iowa Vets. Home, Marshalltown, Iowa, 1980—81; instr. Iowa Valley C.C., Marshalltown, 1981—83; dir. Iowa Dept. Substance Abuse, Des Moines, 1983—86, State of Iowa Pub. Health; dir. Iowa Dept. Pub. Health, Des Moines, 1986—90; spl. cons. health affairs Blue Cross/Blue Shield of Iowa, 1990—91; v.p. Blue Cross/Blue Shield of Iowa and S.D., 1991—2000; ret., 2000; bus. cons., 2001—. Chair Iowa Health Data Commn., Des Moines, 1986—90; bd. dirs. Health Policy Corp. Iowa, 1986—90; adj. asst. prof. U. Iowa, Iowa City, 1984—; commd. officer U.S. FDA, 1989—90; mem. alumnae bd. dirs. U. Iowa Coll. of Pharmacy, 1989—; chair Nat. Commn. Accreditation of Ambulance Svcs., 1992—97. Mem. Iowa State Bd. Health, 1981—83, v.p., 1982—83; mem. adv. coun. Iowa Valley C.C., 1983—85. Recipient Woman of Achievement award, Des Moines YWCA, 1988. Mem.: APHA, Iowa Pub. Health Assn. (bd. dirs., Henry Albert award 1990), Iowa Pharmacists Assn., Pi Sigma Alpha, Phi Kappa Phi, Alpha Xi Delta. Republican. Home: 2912 Caulder Ave Des Moines IA 50321-2637

ELLIS, PATRICIA WEATHERS, small business owner, retired electronic technician; b. Shelby, N.C., June 21, 1941; d. William Roy and Lucille Elzora (Allen) Weathers; m. Donald Eugene Ellis, Nov. 16, 1957; children: Dana Michelle, Lisa Maria. Student, Gaston Coll., Gastonia, N.C., 1970, 82. Tel. operator So. Bell, Greensboro, N.C., 1959-61, Gastonia, N.C., 1961-63, dial clk., 1963-68, frame technician, 1968-79, test technician, 1980-84, maintenance adminstr., 1984-85, toll test technician, 1985-87; electronic technician BellSouth, Gastonia, 1987-91, Charlotte, N.C., 1991-2000, electronic technician toll rm. Gastonia, 2000—02; store mgr. Ellis Carpet and Floor Ctr., Inc., 2002—, 2002—. Store mgr. Ellis-Bowen Carpet Svc., Gastonia, 1969-70. Commr. Gaston County, Gastonia, 1992-96; bd. dirs. Gaston County Health Dept., Airport Com., Gaston Mus. Art and History, 1992-96, Gaston County Dept. Social Svcs.; alt. Ctrl. Lina Coun. Govts., 1994-95; mem. dedication com. Gaston Good Neighbor; com. mem. Right-Sizing County Govt. Mem. Tel. Pioneers Am., Home Builders Assn. Gaston County, Inc., Woman's Aux. Fedn. Postal Clks. (charter; pres. Gastonia 1966, State v.p. 1966-69). Republican. Avocations: art, writing poems and songs, collecting dolls and stamps.

ELLIS, ROSS, non-profit organization executive; Co-owner Visions & Images; founder, event planner Elegant Events; v.p., dir. corp. affairs and events pharm. comm. co.; dir. resource devel. child abuse prevention group; founder, CEO Love Our Children, USA, 1999—. Active with Starlight Children's Found.; mem Phillip Morris Domestic Violence Coun. Mem.: NY Women's Agenda, NY Women in Comm. (bd. dirs.). Achievements include created and ran programs Dreams Come True and NY Cares at Mt. Sinai Med. Ctr. Office: Love Our Children USA 220 E 57th St New York NY 10022 Office Phone: 212-629-2099. Business E-Mail: rellis@loveourchildrenusa.org.*

ELLIS, SHARON ALSTON, lawyer, political organization worker; b. Jackson, Tenn., July 10, 1950; d. Thomas Parmer Aycock Jr. and Joy Anne Vallier; m. Mark Siegfried Henne, Aug. 22, 1987. JD, Thomas Cooley Law Sch., 1980. Bar: Mich., cert.: (mediator). Atty. Law Office Sharon Alston Ellis, Mich., 1983—; campaign, polit. cons. pvt. practice, Williamston, 1990—. Nat. spkr. Pfizer, Inc., 2000—; polit. commentator Mich. Talk Radio Network, Mich., 2001—02. Past pro bono gen. counsel Lansing Area AIDS Network; elected twp. clk. Williamstown Twp., Mich., 2000—02; past pres. Thomas Cooley Law Sch. Alumni Assn.; chair fund devel. Lansing affiliate Susan B. Komen Breast Cancer Rsch. Found., Mich., 2004; past pres. Mich. Festival, Inc., Lansing Art Gallery, Capital Area Women's Network; past v.p. Capital Area Humane Soc.; past mem. Mich. Capital Girl Scout Coun. Named Woman of Yr., Capital Area Women's Network. Mem.: ACLU, State Bar Mich., Sierra Club. Democrat. Episcopalian. Avocations: jazz, art. Office: Law Office Sharon Alston Ellis 5070 Barton Rd Williamston MI 48895

ELLIS, SHARON HENDERSON, arbitrator, mediator; b. Wenatchee, Wash., May 31, 1944; d. Marvin T. and Nola Henderson; m. Alfred D. Ellis, Aug. 1972. BA, U. Wash., 1967; JD, Suffolk U., 1975. Adminstrv. law judge Mass. Labor Rels. Commn., Boston, 1978-81; arbitrator, mediator Brookline, Mass., 1982—. Adj. prof. New Eng. Sch. Law, 2002—. Contbg. author: (book) Labor and Employment Arbitration, 1988. Vol. II, tchr. U.S. Peace Corps, Tunisia, 1967-69. Mem. Am. Arbitration Assn., Nat. Acad. Arbitrators (regional chair 1997-99), Mass. Bar Assn. (sect. co-chair 1999-2000), Assn. for Conflict Resolution. Home: 36 Salisbury Rd Brookline MA 02445-2105 E-mail: sharonhendersonellis@rcn.com.

ELLIS, STACI ELAINE, psychotherapist, actress; d. Horace Lenwood and Elaine Vance Ellis; m. Phillip Sydney Ihlenfeld. AA, Pa. State U., Lima, 1992; BA, Temple U., 1994; MS in Psychology, St. Joseph's U., Phila., 2000. Support aide and vol. Bala Cynwyd Convalescent Home, Bala Cynwyd, Pa., 1991—92; rsch. asst., Dr. Aaron Beck Ctr. for Cognitive Therapy, Phila., 1993—94; rsch. asst., Dr. Howard Hoffman Bryn Mawr (Pa.) Coll., 1996—97; mobile therapist and behavior specialist Holcomb Behavioral Health Systems, Exton, Pa., 1995—; actress (many commericals, newspaper's mag. adds) and model Expressions Model and Talent Agy., Phila., 1982—. Actor: (plays) The Dining Room, 1986; (plays, theater) Greater Tuna, 1987; (films) Philadelphia, 1993, Twelve Monkeys, 1995; (plays) others; singer: (various pub. performances with a band) My Friend Jack, 1998—2000. Com. mem., fundraiser Am. Cancer Soc., Pa., 2000—03; fundraiser, proponent Am. Autism Soc., Pa., 2003; vol. various children, women's, and elderly orgns., Pa., 1994—2003. Mem.: APA (assoc.), Psi Chi (reocognition of honor status 1996). Avocations: training llamas, home rehabilitation and interior decorating, hiking, camping, art. Office: Holcomb Behavioral Health Sys 930 East Lancaster Ave Suite 220 Exton PA 19341 Personal E-mail: staciellis1@aol.com.

ELLIS, TERESA EILEEN, real estate appraiser; d. Everett D. Pitts and Velma L. Climenhaga; m. Luther W. Ellis, Nov. 5, 1966; children: Sara Elizabeth, Jonathan Grant. BA, U. of Tex., 1966. Cert. appraiser Internat. Soc. of Appraisers, 2001, Am. Quilters' Soc., 1995. Prin., owner Mistletoe Estate Sales and Appraisals, Ft. Worth, 1991—. Vice chmn. Ft. Worth (Tex.) Zoning Commn., 1992—97; mem. MHMR Visions, Ft. Worth, 2003—, Women's Policy Forum, Ft. Worth, 2002—. Mem.: Mental Health Mental Retardation, Am. Collectors and Dealers Assn., Tarrant Antique Dealers Assn. (pres. 1996—97), Internat. Soc. of Appraisers, PA of Appraisers of Quilted Textiles (sec. 1999—2002), N. Tex. Chpt., Internat. Soc. of Appraisers (pres. 2002—), Nat. Quilters Assn., Am. Quilters' Soc., Am. Quilt Study Group, Internat. Quilters Assn. Home and Office: Mistletoe Estate Sales and Appraisals 1205 Mistletoe Dr Fort Worth TX 76110

ELLIS, TERRY, vocalist; b. Austin, Tex., Sept. 5, 1966; Vocalist En Vogue, Acto/Eastwest Records, N.Y.C., 1988—. Albums include Born to Sing (Platinum 1990), Funky Divas, Remix to Sing, Runaway Love, The Best of En Vogue, 1999. Recipient Soul Train Music award, 1991; nominated Grammy award. Office: care En Vogue Atco/Eastwest Records 75 Rockefeller Plz New York NY 10019-6908

ELLISON, BETTY D. retired elementary school educator; b. Meriwether County, Ga., Jan. 28, 1950; d. Haywood Sr. and Mary Susan (Green) Daniel; m. Darthus Ellison, Jr., June 25, 1972; children: Darthus III, Keith Brandon. BA, Morris Brown Coll., 1972; MA, Atlanta U., 1975. Cert. tchr. Tchr. Meriwether County Bd. Edn., Greenville, Ga.; reading specialist Talbot County Bd. Edn., Talbotton, Ga. Advisor Nat. Jr. Honor Soc.; owner, operator Ellison's Tutorial Svc. Ga. State Tchrs. scholar; named County Star Tchr., 1991. Mem. NEA, Internat. Reading Assn., Ga. Assn. Educators, Zeta Phi Beta, Pi Delta Phi. Home: 88 Johnson Ave Manchester GA 31816-1602

ELLISON, PAMELA ION, secondary school educator, consultant; b. Copiaque, N.Y., Sept. 14, 1957; d. James Monroe and Ruby Louise (Miles) E.; divorced; 1 child, Bravetta Elizabeth. BS in Elem. Edn. and Spl. Edn., Hampton U., 1980; MA in Elem. and Secondary Adminstrn., George Washington U., 1992. Cert. tchr., Va. Elem. tchr. Fairfax County Pub. Schs., Alexandria, Va., 1980—, mid. sch. tchr. sci., 1993—. Peer observer performance evaluation program Fairfax Co. Pub. Schs., Fairfax, 1988—, writer sci. curriculum, 1987, 90, 93, 94, sci. lead tchr., 1985—; coord. elem. sch. sci. Hayfield Elem. Sch., Alexandria, 1987-93; cons. on sci. curriculum Nat. Sci. Resource Ctr., Washington, 1994; sci. lead tchr., cons. Va. Quality Edn. in Scis. and Tech., Blacksburg, 1994; workshop presenter in field. Telethon vol. United Negro Coll. Fund, Washington, 1995; vol. Girl Scouts U.S.A., Alexandria, 1992, 93; mem. PTA. Scholar Fairfax Edn. Assn., 1991, Columbian Women scholar George Washington U., 1991. Mem. ASCD, NEA, FEA, AAUW, Nat. Coun. of Negro Women, Inc. Baptist. Avocations: writing, improving science education, crafts, painting, bowling. Home: PO Box 15419 Alexandria VA 22309-0419

ELLIS-SCRUGGS, JAN, theater arts educator; b. Phila., Apr. 7, 1951; d. Roger C. and Greta M. Ellis; m. William Marquis Scruggs, Aug. 8, 1970; children: William Marcus Jr., Christopher Michael. BA, Cheyney U., 1987; MA, Villanova U., 1991. Lectr., instr. U. Conn., Storrs, 1989-90; theatre arts instr. Delaware County C.C., Media, Pa., 1994-95; asst. prof. theatre arts Cheyney (Pa.) U., 1993-94, 97—; actor, singer, dir., theater educator, adminstr. U.S. and London. Assoc. prodr., Citeaux, Inc., London, 1979-83; dir. Cheyney U., 1997—. Mem. editl. adv. bd., Collegiate Press, San Diego, 1999—. Missionary, Mother Bethel African Meth. Episc. Ch., Phila., 1994—. Mem. AFTRA, SAG (Screen Actors Guild), Actors Equity Assn., Alpha Psi Omega. Home: 7942 Cedarbrook Ave Philadelphia PA 19150 Office: Cheyney U of Pa Marian Anderson Music Ctr Cheyney PA 19319 E-mail: jebs267@aol.com.

ELLMANN, SHEILA FRENKEL, investment company executive; b. Detroit, June 8, 1931; d. Joseph and Rose (Neback) Frenkel; m. William M. Ellmann, Nov. 1, 1953 (dec. Jan. 16, 2002); children: Douglas Stanley, Carol Elizabeth, Robert Lawrence. BA in English, U. Mich., 1953. Dir. Advance Glove Mfg. Co., Detroit, 1954—78; v.p. Frome Investment Co., Detroit, 1980—96, pres., 1996—. Mem. U. Mich. Alumni Assn., Nat. Trust Hist. Preservation, VFW Aux. Home: 28000 Weymouth Dr Farmington Hills MI 48334

ELLNER, CAROLYN LIPTON, not-profit organization executive, retired dean, consultant, dean, consultant; b. Jan. 17, 1932; d. Robert Mitchell and Rose (Pearlman) Lipton; m. Richard Ellner, June 21, 1953; children: D. Lipton, Alison Lipton. AB cum laude, Mt. Holyoke Coll., 1953; AM, Columbia Tchrs. Coll., 1957; PhD, [illegible]. Tchr., prof., administr. N.Y. and Md., 1957-62; prof. dir. tchr. edn., assoc. dean Claremont Grad. Sch., Calif., 1967-82; prof., dean sch. edn. Calif. State U., Northridge, 1982-98, dean emerita, 1998—. Pres., CEO On-the-Job Parenting. Co-author: Schoolmaking, 1977, Studies of College Teaching, 1983 (Orange County Authors award 1984). Trustee Ctr. for Early Edn., L.A., 1968-71, Oakwood Sch., L.A., 1972-78, Mt. Holyoke Coll., South Hadley, Mass., 1979-84; commr. Economy and Efficiency com., L.A., 1974-82, Calif. Commn. Tchr. Credentialing, 1987-90, 93—, vice chair, 1995-96, chair, 1996-98; bd. dirs. Found. for Effective Govt., L.A., 1982, Calif. Coalition for Pub. Edn., 1985-88, Valley Hosp. Found., 1992-94, Mt. Holyoke Alumnae Assn. Bd., 1993-96; founding dir. Decade of Edn., 1990; assoc. dir. New Devel. in Sci. Project NSF, 1985-94; bd. dirs., chair edn. com. Valley Industry and Commerce Assn., 1990-93, v.p. 1993-94; co-prin. dir. Mid South Calif. Arts Project, 1991-98; mem. coun., trustees L.A. Alliance for Restructing Now (LEARN), 1992-2000; bd. dirs. Inner City Arts Found., 1993-96; involved with L.A. Annenberg Met. Project (LAAMP); exec. bd. DELTA, 1995—, Calif. Subject Matter Projects, 1998—. Ford Found. fellow 1964-67, fellow Ednl. Policy Fellowship Program, 1989-90; recipient Office of Edn. award U.S. Office of Edn., 1969-72, Alumnae medal of honor Mt. Holyoke Coll., 1998; W.M. Keck Found. grantee, 1983, 94. Mem. ASCD, Am. Edn. Rsch. Assn., Am. Assn. Colls. for Tchr. Edn., Nat. Soc. for Study of Edn. E-mail: ellner@otjp.org.

ELLSWORTH, JULIE, state representative; b. Boise, Idaho, Dec. 8, 1961; m. Maurice Ellsworth; children: Rachel, Chapman. BS in Edn., Brigham Young U. Former tchr.; state rep. dist. 18B Idaho Ho. of Reps., Boise, 1996—, vice chair state affairs com., mem. environ. affairs, judiciary, rules and adminstrn. coms. Republican. Office: State Capitol PO Box 83720 Boise ID 83720-0038

EL MALLAKH, DOROTHEA HENDRY, editor, publishing executive; b. Emmett, Idaho, July 16, 1938; d. David Lovell Parker and Lygia Teressa (Dalton) Hendry; m. Ragaei William El Mallakh, Aug. 26, 1962 (dec. Mar. 1987); children: Helen Alise, Nadia Irene. BA in Modern Langs., Lewis and Clark Coll., 1960; MA in History, U. Colo., 1962, PhD in History, 1972; postgrad., Georgetown U., 1962-63. Exec. adminstr., treas. Internat. Rsch. Ctr. Energy & Econ. Devel., Boulder, Colo., 1973-87, exec. dir., 1987—. Assoc. editor Jour. Energy & Devel., Boulder, 1975-87, mng. editor, 1987—; bd. dirs. Rocky Mountain Eye Found., Boulder. Author: The Slovak Autonomy Movement, 1979; author (with others): The Genius of Arab Civilization, 1983; editor: The Energy Watchers I-IX, 1990-98; author and editor: Saudi Arabia, 1982. Perrine Meml. fellow, U. Colo., 1960-61, Rare Lang. fellow, U.S. Govt., U. Colo., 1961-62, Rotary Internat. fellow, Boise, Idaho, 1962. Mem. Internat. Assn. Energy Econs. (v.p. internal affairs 1989-91, sec. 1988-89). Office: ICEED 850 Willowbrook Rd Boulder CO 80302-7439 E-mail: iceed@stripe.Colorado.EDU.

ELMAN, NAOMI GEIST, artist, producer; b. Chgo. d. Harry and Rita (Goldstein) Geist; m. Murray Elman, May 29, 1946 (dec. Dec. 1965); 1 child, Margaret (Peggy) Gillespie. Student, Hamilton Inst. for Girls, Nat. Acad. of Design, Art Students League. Personal mgr. in performing arts, prodr. concerts in, N.Y.C. and Hawaii, N.Y., 1968-80. One-woman shows include Churchill Gallery, 1962, Pen and Brush Club, 1986, Neuwirth Gallery, Phoenix, 1994; exhibited in group shows; represented in a permanent collection Tchrs. Coll. N.Y.C. Alumni Assn. Vol. nurses aid pvt. and army hosps., ARC, 1939-45; v.p. N.Y. Diabetes Assn., 1955-58; mcpl. chmn. Dem. Club, Tenafly, N.J., 1958; Dem. com. woman, 1959-61; bd. dirs. Nat. Children's Cardiac Home, N.Y.C., 1940-49, Bergen County Dem. Club, 1958-60. Recipient Margareet Sussman award, 1985, Salamagundi award, 1987, Julia Lucille award, 1988. Mem. Internat. Platform Assn., Soc. Mil. Widows, Retired Officers Club (life), Disabled Am. Vets., Artists Equity, Kent Art Assn. Democrat. Address: PO Box 1278 Amherst MA 01004-1278

ELMENDORF-LANDGRAF, MARY LINDSAY, retired anthropologist; b. Ruby, S.C., Apr. 13, 1917; d. James Calvin Lindsay and Ana Eugenia MacGregor; m. John van Gaasbeek Elmendorf, Dec. 27, 1937 (dec. Feb. 1980); children: Calvin Lindsay, Susan Elmendorf Roberts; m. John L. Landgraf, Nov. 27, 1981. AB in Psychology, U. N.C., 1937, MA in Social Work and Pub. Adminstrn., 1940; PhD in Anthropology, Union Grad. Sch., 1972, U. N.C., 1987, PhD (hon.), 1994. Rsch. fellow Ford Found., N.Y.C., Mex., 1972-73; cons. anthropologist UNITAR/AAAS, Washington, 1975—, USAID, Washington, 1980-85, Internat. Devel. Rsch. Ctr., Ottawa, Calif., 1980-90, World Bank, Washington, 1975-95; ret., 1996—. Instr. Putney (Vt.) Sch., 1941—43; dir. AFSC Spanish Refugee Program, France, 1945—46; dir. CARE de Mex., 1952—60; coord. off-campus studies Brown U., 1962—65, New Coll., U. Fla., 1965—69; vis. assoc. prof. anthropology Hampshire Coll., Amherst, Mass., 1973, Semester at Sea, 1974—75; mem. part-time faculty Goddard Coll., Vt., 1973; adj. prof. anthropology U. Fla., 1992—; mentor New Coll., U. Fla., 1987—; advisor Union Inst., 1990—; cons. World Bank/UNDP Water and Sanitation Program, 1978—96, UNICEF, WHO, FAO, IDRC, others, IRC, WASH; lectr. in field. Author: The Mayan Woman and Change, 1972, La Mujer Maya y el Cambio, 1973, Nine Mayan Women: A Village Faces Change, 1976, The Socio-Cultural Aspects of Excreta Disposal, 1980, The International Drinking Water and Sanitation Decade and Women's Involvement, 1990, Priorities, Challenges and Strategies: A Feminine Perspective, Women, Water and UNIFEM, 2001, Water is Life at Hannover, Germany, 2002, Rights, Resources, Culture and Conservation in Maya Communities of Yucatan, Mexico: Studies Inspired by the Work of Mary Elmendorf, 2003; contbr. numerous articles to profl. jours.; collection papers Smathers Libr., U. Fla., Nat. Anthrop. Archives, Smithsonian Instn. Recipient with other Quaker vols. Nobel Peace Prize, 1947; recipient Margaret Mead award, 1982, Disting. Alumna award U. N.C., 1997. Fellow: Soc. Applied Anthropology, Am. Anthrop. Assn.; mem.: UNIFEM, AAUW, Sister Cities, AAAS, UN Assn./USA, Internat. Drinking Water Commn. (Ad Hoc Com. 2003—). Democrat. Mem. Soc. Of Friends. Avocations: gardening, swimming, enjoying grandchildren. Home: 535 S Blvd Of Presidents Sarasota FL 34236-2014 also: San Miguel Allende Mexico E-mail: maryelmendorf17@aol.com.

ELMES, MARTHA L. art educator; b. Ft. Wayne, Ind., June 25, 1951; d. Edward and Maxine R. Leitz; m. Robert B. Elmes, Feb. 2, 1974; children: Anna Elizabeth Elmes-Spalding, Conor Michael. A, Green Mountain Coll., 1971; BA, St. Lawrence U., 1973; EdM, Lesley Coll., 1999. Art tchr. Lyndon Town Sch., Lyndonville, Vt., 1989—2003; adj. prof. Lyndon State Coll., 2003—. Coord. arts in sch. Burklyn Arts Coun., Burke, Vt., 1975—2003. Editor: Wings. Pres. PATT Parent Group, Lyndonville, 1980—86. Named Vt. Tchr. of Yr., Dept Edn., 1980. Mem.: NEA. Home: 258 Sherburne Pl Lyndonville VT 05851

EL-MOSLIMANY, ANN PAXTON, paleoecologist, educator, writer; b. Fullerton, Calif., Aug. 2, 1937; d. Donald Dorn and Sarah Frances (Turman) Paxton; m. Mohammed Ahmad El-Moslimany, May 31, 1962; children: Samia, Ramsey, Rasheed. BS, N.Mex. State U., 1959; MS, Am. U., Beirut, 1961; PhD, U. Wash., 1983. Tchr. various schs., 1959-83, Kuwait U., 1984-86, Seattle Ctrl. C.C., 1986-90; prin., tchr. Islamic Sch. Seattle, 1989-99, curriculum coord., 1999—. Paleoecological rschr. Palynological Consultants, 1987—. Author: Zaki's Ramadan Fast, 1994; contbr. articles to sci. jours.; mem. adv. bd. Sisters Aziah mag. Mem. Amnesty Internat., Am. Quaternary Assn., Geog. Alliance of Wash. Home: PO Box 367 Seahurst WA 98062-0367 Office: Islamic Sch Seattle 720 25th Ave Seattle WA 98122-4902 E-mail: annelmoslimany@yahoo.com.

ELROD, LINDA DIANE HENRY, lawyer, educator; b. Topeka, Kans., Mar. 6, 1947; d. Lyndus Arthur Henry and Marjorie Jane (Hammel) Allen; divorced; children: Carson Douglas, Bree Elizabeth. BA in English with honors, Washburn U., 1969, JD cum laude, 1971. Bar: Kans. 1972. Instr. U. S.D., Topeka, 1970-71; research atty. Kans. Jud. Council, Topeka, 1972-74; asst. prof. Washburn U., Topeka, 1974-78, assoc. prof., 1978-82, prof. law, 1982-93, disting. prof., 1993—, dir. Children and Family Law Ctr. Vis. prof. law U. San Diego, Paris Summer Inst., 1988, 90, Washington U. Sch. Law, St. Louis, 1990, 98, summer 1991, 93, Fla. State U. Law Sch., spring, 2000; bd. dirs. Appleseed. Author: Kansas Family Law Handbook, 1983, rev. edit., 1990, supplement, 1993, Child Custody Practice and Procedure, 1993, supplements, 1994-97, 99, 2000, 01, 03; co-author: Principles of Family Law, 1999, 5th edit., 2003, Kansas Family Law Guide, 1999, supplement, 2000, 01, 02; editor Family Law Quar., 1992—; mem. NCCUSL joint editl. bd. on uniform family law; contbr. articles to profl. jours. Pres. YWCA, Topeka, 1982-83; vice-chair Kans. Commn. on Child Support, 1984-87, Supreme Ct. Commn. on Child Support, 1989—; chair Kans. Cmty. Svc. Orgn., 1986-87; adv. bd. CASA, 1997—; bd. dirs. Appleseed, 2000—. Recipient Disting. Service award Washburn Law Sch. Assn., 1986; named YWCA Woman of Distinction, 1997. Mem. ABA (coun. family law sect. 1988-92, sec. 1998, vice-chair, 1999, chair-elect 1999-2000, chair 2000-01, chair Schwab Meml. Grant Implementation 1984-87, co-chair Amicus Curiae com. 1987-92, ch-chair pro bono child custody project adv. bd. 2001—, steering com. on unmet legal needs of children 2002—), Topeka Bar Assn. (sec. 1981-85, v.p. 1985-86, pres. 1986-87), Kans. Child Support Enforcement Assn. (bd. dirs. 1988—, Child Support Hall of Fame 1990), Kans. Bar Assn. (sec.-treas. 1988-89, com. ops. and fin. 1988, pres. family law sect. 1984-86, Disting. Svc. award 1985), NONOSO, Phi Kappa Phi, Phi Alpha Delta Alumni Assn. (justice 1976-77), Phi Beta Delta, Kappa Alpha Theta (pres. alumnae chpt. 1995-97). Presbyterian. Avocations: bridge, reading, quilting. Office: Washburn U Law Sch 17th and College Topeka KS 66621 Office Phone: 785-231-1010. E-mail: linda.elrod@washburn.edu.

ELROD, LU, music educator, actress, author; b. Chattanooga, Apr. 23, 1935; d. John C. Elrod and Helen Pauline (Kohn). MusB, Ga. State U., 1960; M in Music Edn., U. Ga., 1970, EdD, 1971; PhD, U. London, 1975. Prof. music, music coach U. Md., Balt., 1972-78, Calif. State U., L.A., 1978—. Singer with Dallas Opera, 1957. Appeared in movies Charly, 1969, Brewster's Millions, 1986, Major Pettigrew and Me, 1976, Seduction of Joe Tynan, 1977, Atlanta Child Murders, 1985, Children Don't Tell, 1986, For Love or Money, 1986, High School High, 1996, Wag the Dog, 1997, The Big Lebowski, 1998, Primary Colors, 1998, Lloyd the Ugly Kid, 1999, Beautiful, 1999, Glory Days, 2001, Freaky Friday, 2003, Kicking and Screaming, 2004; appeared on TV in Lazarus Syndrome, 1980, Hill Street Blues (Emmy award), 1988, Superior Court, 1988, TV Bloopers, 1989, Beakman's World (Emmy award), Dream On, 1993, Misery Loves Company, 1995, Caroline in the City, 1995, Louie, 1996, George and Alana, 1996, Maggie, 1998, Two Guys and a Girl, 2000, Glory Days, 2001; appeared in TV commls. Recipient Leadership Devel. award Ford Found., 1967, Leadership Fellows award Ford Found., 1968, Tift Coll. voice scholar, 1953, Baylor U. voice scholar, 1956; Lu Elrod scholarship named at Calif. State U., L.A., 1989; named to Calif. State U., L.A. Wall of Fame, 1993. Mem. AAUP, AFTRA, SAG, Am. Guild Variety Artists, Calif. Faculty Assn., Coll. Music Soc. Avocations: philanthropy, fundraising. Office: Calif State Univ 5151 State University Dr Los Angeles CA 90032-4226 E-mail: lelrod@calstatela.edu.

ELROD, MIMI COBB MILNER, academic administrator; b. Atlanta, Jan. 30, 1944; d. Benjamin Charles and Eleanor Wuerpel (O'Beirne) Milner; m. John William Elrod, Jan. 21, 1940; children: Adam Milner, Joshua O'Beirne. BS, Oglethorpe U., 1966; MS, Iowa State U., 1977, PhD, 1980; DHL (hon.), Washington and Lee U., 2002. Tchr. Cooper jr. high N.Y.C. Pub. Schs., 1966-69, after sch. care provider, 1967-68; tchr. asst. Iowa State U., Ames, 1976-78, 79-80, instr., 1978-79, 80-81, asst. prof., 1982-84, Dabney Lancaster C.C., Clifton Forge, Va., 1985-86; asst. dir. admissions Washington and Lee U., Lexington, Va., 1986-90, asst. dir. spl. programs, 1990-91, assoc. dir. spl. programs, dir. summer scholars, 1991—. Child/family devel. cons., 1984-90. Contbr. articles to profl. jours. Vol./hotline adv. Project Horizon, Lexington, 1985—, bd. dirs., pres., 1989-97, pres., 1999-2002; vol. parent adv. com. Lylburn Downing Sch., Lexington, 1985-86; vol., adv. bd. mem. Total Action Against Poverty, Lexington, 1991—; bd. dirs., pres. Rockbridge Mental Health Assn., 1985-88; bd. dirs. Assn. for Retarded Citizens, 1985-88, Yellow Brick Rd. Child Day Care Ctr., 1997—; bd. dirs., pres. Rockbridge Area Cmty. Svc. Bd., 1989-94; mem., elder Lexington Presbyn. Ch., 1991—; mem. adv. bd. Shepherd Poverta Program, 2002; mem. Lexington (Va.) City Coun., 2003—; mem. State Coun. of Higher Edn. for Va., 2003—. Recipient Women and Leadership award Washington and Lee U., 1996; Iowa Home Econs. Assn. scholar Iowa State U., Ames, 1977-78; Pearl Swanson Grad. fellow Iowa State U., Ames, 1978-79; grantee Home Econs. Rsch. Inst., 1980-82, Iowa State U. Rsch. Found., 1982. Mem. Soc. for Rsch. in Child Devel., Nat. Assn. for the Edn. of Young Children, Va. Assn. for the Edn. of Young Children, Nat. Head Start Assn., So. Assn. on Children Under Six, Omicron Nu, Phi Kappa Nu, Phi Kappa Phi. Democrat. Avocations: tennis, gardening, sewing, traveling, playing piano. Office: Washington and Lee Univ Spl Programs/Summer Scholars 218 W Washington St Lexington VA 24450-2122 Home: 207 White St Lexington VA 24450-1934

ELSE, CAROLYN JOAN, retired library director; b. Mpls., Jan. 31, 1934; d. Elmer Oscar and Irma Carolyn (Seibert) Wahlberg; m. Floyd Warren Else, 1962 (div. 1968); children: Stephen Alexander, Catherine Elizabeth. BS, Stanford U., 1956; MLS, U. Wash., 1957. Cert. profl. libr. Wash. Libr. Queens Borough Pub. Libr., N.Y.C., 1957—59, U.S. Army Spl. Svcs., France, Germany, 1959—62; info. libr. Bennett Martin Libr., Lincoln, Nebr., 1962—63; br. libr. Pierce County Libr., Tacoma, 1963—65, dir., 1965—94; ret., 1994. Wellness cons. Nikken, Inc., 1994—. Mem. Higher Edn. Coun., South Puget Sound, 1988—92; mem. study commn. Wash. State Local Governance, 1985—88; bd. dirs. Campfire, Tacoma, 1984—92, Cmty. Health Care, 1997—2003. Mem.: Pacific N.W. Libr. Assn. (sec. 1969—71), Wash. Libr. Assn. (v.p. 1969—71), ALA, Tacoma Rotary #8 Club (bd. dirs. 1995—97), City Club (Tacoma). Office Phone: 253-565-9635. Personal E-mail: carolyn.else@stanfordalumni.org.

ELSHTAIN, JEAN BETHKE, social and political ethics educator; b. Windsor, Colo., Jan. 6, 1941; d. Paul G. and Helen L. Bethke; m. Errol L. Elshtain, Sept. 3, 1965; children: Sheri, Heidi, Jenny, Eric. BA in History, Colo. State U., 1963; MA in History, U. Colo., 1965; PhD in Politics, Brandeis U., 1973; LLD (hon.), Gonzaga U., 1996; DHL (hon.), Valparaiso U., 1996, Grinell Coll., 1997, Maryville U., 1997, Messiah Coll., 1999, Carthage Coll., 2000, Lake Forest Coll., 2001, Siena Coll., 2002, North Park Coll., 2002. Prof. polit. sci. U. Mass., Amherst, 1973-88, Vanderbilt U., Nashville, 1988-94; vis. prof. Harvard U., Cambridge, Mass., 1994; prof. ethics U. Chgo., 1995—. Author: Public Man, Private Woman: Women in Social and Political Thought, 1982, 2d edit., 1992 (Top Choice acad. book), Czech transl., 1999, Ukrainian transl., 2002, Women and War, 1987, Japanese translation, 1994, Power Trips and Other Journeys, Essays on Feminism as Civic Discourse, 1990, Meditations on Modern Political Thought: Masculine/Feminine Themes Luther to Arendt, 1992, Democracy on Trial, 1995 (N.Y. Times Notable Book 1995), Augustine and the Limits of Politics, 1996; co-author: But Was It Just? Reflections on the Morality of the Gulf War, 1992; editor: The Family in Political Thought, 1982, Just War Theory, 1991; co-editor: Women, Militarism and War, 1990, Politics and the

Human Body, 1995, Promise to Keep, Decline and Renewal of Marriage in America, 1996, Real Politics, Political Theory and Everyday Life, 1997, New Wine in Old Bottles: International Politics and Ethical Discourse, 1998 (Top Choice acad. book), Who are We? Critical Reflection, Hopeful Possibilities, 2000 (Named Best Acad. Book, Am. Theol. Booksellers Assn. 2000), Jane Addams and the Dream of American Democracy, 2002; editor: The Jane Addams Reader, 2002, Just War Against Terror: The Burden of American Power, 2003 (named One of Best Non-Fiction Books of 2003, Publishers Weekly). Trustee Inst. for Advanced Study, 1994-99, Nat. Humanities Ctr., N.C., 1996—; chair Coun. on Civil Soc., N.Y.C. and Chgo., 1995—, Coun. on Families in Am., N.Y.C., 1995—; bd. dirs. Nat. Endowment for Democracy, 2002--. Fellow AAAS; mem. Am. Polit. Sci. Assn. (v.p. 1998-99, Maguire chmn. ethics at Libr. of Congress 2003—2004, Goodnow award for lifetime svc. 2002), Am. Soc. Polit. and Legal Philosophy (v.p. 1996-97). Avocations: movies, reading. Home: 4010 Wallace Ln Nashville TN 37215-2308 Office: U Chgo Div Sch 1025 E 58th St Chicago IL 60637-1509 E-mail: jbelshta@uchicago.edu.

ELSON, SUZANNE GOODMAN, community activist; b. Memphis, Oct. 17, 1937; d. Charles F. and Isabel (Ehrlich) Goodman; m. Edward Elliott Elson, Aug. 24, 1957; children: Charles Myer, Louis Goodman, Harry II. Student, Randolph-Macon Women's Coll., Lynchburg, Va.; BA, Agnes Scott Coll., 1959. Sec. Nat. Coun. Jewish Women, N.Y.C., 1977-79; pres. Nat. Mental Health Assn., 1980-82; trustee emeritus Randolph Macon Women's Coll., 1988-98, 99. Chmn. Am. Craft Coun., 1989-92, hon. chmn., 1992-94, hon. trustee, 1994-; bd. dirs. Rosalynn Carter Inst., 1990-, Nat. Coun. Medicine Emory U., 1990-95; trustee Va. Mus. of Fine Art., 1992-96, High Mus. Fine Art, 1972-92, Am. Craft Mus., 1999-; bd. regents U. System of Ga., 1993-97; adv. bd. Breast Cancer Rsch. Found., 1998-; bd. dirs. Friends of Art and Preservation in Embassies, 1999- (trustee 1998); bd. govs. Mus. of Art and Design, 1998-; trustee Soc. for the Fine Arts, 2003-, Preservation Soc. of Palm Beach, 2004-; bd. dirs. Armory Art Ctr. Home: 180 Cocoanut Row Palm Beach FL 33480-4121

ELWELL, BARBARA LOIS DOW, community organizer; b. Purcell, Okla., Feb. 15, 1933; d. Henry Kenneth and Leah Maude (Caldwell) Dow; m. Robert G. Elwell, Apr. 7, 1956 (div. July 1977); children: David Robert, Kenneth Dow. Student, Endicott Coll., 1950-51, Jackson Von Ladau Sch. Design, 1952-54. Dir. Alternative House, Inc., Lowell, Mass., 1976-84; mem. staff Encode Tech., Inc., Nashua, NH, 1984-87; staff asst. Harvard Smithsonian Ctr. Astrophys., Cambridge, Mass., 1987-99; pvt. asst. Smithsonian Astrophys. Obs., 1999—. Founder Alternative House, Lowell, 1978; founding mem. Mass Coalition of Battered Women Svc. Groups, Boston, 1976, steering com., 1976-84, adv. bd. 1978-80. Recipient Outstanding Achievement award, Mass. Coalition of Battered Women Svc. Groups, 1976. Avocations: woodworking, antique collecting, miniatures, gardening, painting. Home: 142 Graniteville Rd Chelmsford MA 01824-1122

ELWOOD-AKERS, VIRGINIA EDYTHE, retired librarian, archivist; b. L.A., Nov. 9, 1938; d. George Henry and Eileen Edythe Elwood; m. Roy Stanley Akers, Apr. 12, 1980 (widowed May 2003). BA, UCLA, 1964; MLS, U. Oreg., 1972; MA in Mass. Comm., Calif. State U., Northridge, 1981. Editor UCLA, L.A., 1970-71, writer, 1971-72; libr., archivist Calif. State U., Northridge, 1972—2001, ret., 2001. Reader Huntington Libr., San Marino, Calif., 1990—. Author: Women War Correspondents in the Vietnam War, 1988, contbr. articles to profl. jours. Calif. State U. Found. grantee, Northridge, Calif. State U. Libr. grantee. Mem. Calif. Acad. & Rsch. Librs., Western Assn. Women Historians, Soc. Calif. Archivists. Democrat. Episcopalian. Avocations: travel, musical theater.

ELY-RAPHEL, NANCY, diplomat; b. N.Y.C, Feb. 4, 1937; d. Thomas Clarkson and Margaret (Merritt) Halliday; widowed; children: John Duff Ely, Robert Duff Ely, Stephanie Joyce Raphel. AB, Syracuse U., 1957; JD, U. San Diego, 1968. Bar: Calif. 1968, U.S. Supreme Ct. 1976. Dep. city atty. City of San Diego, 1969—70; asst. U.S. atty. So. Dist. Calif., 1970—71; assoc. Tyler, Cooper, Grant, Bowerman and Keefe, New Haven, 1971—72; from asst. to assoc. dean Sch. Law Boston U., 1972—75; atty.-advisor U.S. Dept. State, Washington, 1975—77; spl. atty. Boston Strike Force U.S. Dept. Justice, 1977—78; asst. legal advisor African Affairs U.S. Dept. State, Washington, 1978—87, asst. legal advisor Nuclear Affairs, 1988—89; dep. asst. Sec. of State Bur. Democracy, Human Rights and Labor Affairs, Washington, 1878—83, prin. dep. asst., 1993—95; Balkan coord. Bur. European and Can. Affairs, Washington, 1995—98; U.S. amb. to Slovenia, Am. Embassy, Ljubljana, 1998—2001, sr. advisor to sec., 2001—03; counselor on internat. law, 2003; v.p. Save the Children, Washington, 2003—. Mem. Coun. on Fgn. Rels., 1990—. Recipient Outstanding Alumni award U. San Diego Law Sch., 1979, Superior Honor award U.S. Dept. State, Washington, 1983, 84, Presdl. Meritorious Svc. award U.S. Govt., Washington, 1986, 94, 98, Presdl. Disting. Svc. award, 1992, Author Hughes Career Achievement award, 2001. Home: 1304 30th St NW Washington DC 20007-3343 Office: Save the Children 2000 M St NW Ste 500 Washington DC 20036 E-mail: nelyraphel@dc.savechildren.org.

EMANUEL-SMITH, ROBIN LESLEY, special education educator; m. Allen Weston Smith, Apr. 14, 1983; children: David, Ariel, Weston. BS in Engring., U.S. Mil. Acad., 1981; BS in Health-Phys. Edn. summa cum laude, Cameron U., Lawton, Okla., 1992; M Spl. Edn., Coll. of St. Rose, Albany, 1995. Cert. spl. edn., health and phys. edn. tchr., N.Y. Enlisted U.S. Army, 1974-76, commd. 2d lt., 1981, advanced through grades to capt., 1984, resigned, 1990; tchr. spl. edn. Ulster County Bd. Coop. Ednl. Svcs., Port Ewen, N.Y., 1992—. Roman Catholic. Avocations: weightlifting, coaching and officiating youth soccer, softball and baseball. Office: Ulster County Bd Coop Ednl Svs Rt 32 New Paltz NY 12561

EMBER, CAROL R. anthropology educator, author; b. Bklyn., July 7, 1943; d. Hy and Elsie (Kardonsky) Ruchlis; m. Lawrence Baldwin, 1963 (div. 1969); m. Melvin Ember, Mar. 21, 1970; children: Katherine Ann, Julie Beth. BA, Antioch Coll., 1965; postgrad., Cornell U., 1965-66; PhD, Harvard, 1971. Lectr. Hunter Coll. CUNY, 1970-71; from asst. prof. to assoc. prof. CUNY, 1971-80; prof. Hunter Coll., 1981-97; exec. dir. Human Rels. Area Files Yale U., New Haven, 1997—. First author (sr author/editor): Anthropology, 1973, 11th edit., 2004, Cultural Anthropology, 1973, 11th edit., 2004, (with M. Ember) Marriage, Family, and Kinship: Comparative Studies of Social Organization, 1983; sr. co-author: Anthropology: A Brief Introduction, 1991, 5th edit., 2003, (with Burton Pasternak and M. Ember) Sex, Gender, and Kinship: A Cross-Cult Perspective, 1997; sr. co-author: Cross-Cultural Research Methods, 2001; co-editor: Cross-Cultural Research for Social Science, 1998, Portraits of Culture, 1998; sr. co-editor: Encyclopedia of Medical Anthropology, 2004, Encyclopedia of Sex and Gender, 2004; sr. co-author: Research Frontiers in Anthropology, 1998; co-author: Countries and Their Cultures, 2001, Encyclopedia of Urban Culture, 2002; sr. co-author: New Directions in Anthropology, 2003. Woodrow Wilson Fellow, 1965-66, predoctoral fellow NIMH, 1969-70; rsch. grantee NSF, 1983-84, 86-98, U.S. Inst. Peace, 1990-92. Mem. Am. Anthrop. Assn., Soc. for Cross-Cultural Rsch. (pres. 1985), Soc. for Psychol. Anthropology, Human Behavior and Evolution Soc. Office: Yale U Human Rels Area Files 755 Prospect St New Haven CT 06511-1225

EMBERGHER, MARY LOUISE, elementary school educator; b. Bklyn., July 22, 1943; d. Joseph and Anna Buonfiglio E. BS in Elem. Edn., St. John's U., 1964; MS in Elem. Edn., Bklyn. Coll. U. of N.Y., 1966. Cert. elem. tchr., Fla. Tchr. N.Y.C. Pub. Schs., Ozone Park, 1964-68, Broward County Pub. Schs., Pembroke Pines, Fla., 1968—. Adminstr. summative for master tchr. program State of Fla., Pembroke Pines, 1984-87; mem. tchr. rep. Broward county Quality Incentive coun. Broward County Pub. Sch. Bd., Ft. Lauderdale, 1983-84, peer tchrs., coach for new tchrs. Broward County Pub. Schs., Pembroke Pines, 1980-98; supr. tchr. for intern tchrs., 1970-98. Publicity chmn. Greater Hollywood Young, Fla., 1969; sec. Reps., 1970. Named Outstanding Young Educator Pembroke Pines Jaycees, 1973, Fla. Master Tchr. State of Fla., 1984-87; recipient Achievement in Edn. award Pembroke Pines Optimist Club. Mem. Women Educators (chpt. pres. 1980-82), Delta Kappa Gamma (yearbook chair 1972-73, chpt. 1st v.p. 1978-80). Republican. Roman Catholic. Avocations: traveling, reading, music, politics, working with children. Office: Lakeside Elem Sch 900 NW 136th Ave Pembroke Pines FL 33028 Office Phone: 754-323-6400.

EMEK, SHARON HELENE, risk management consultant; b. Bklyn., Oct. 23, 1945; d. Hyman Sampson and Cynthia Gertrude (Roth) Rabinowitz; children: Aleeza Judith, Joshua Michael, Elana Yael. BA, CCNY, 1967; MA, Bklyn. Coll., 1970; EdD, Rutgers U., 1977. Cert. ins. counselor. Dir. preliminary program for small coll. Bklyn. Coll., 1969-71, 73-74; dir. Am. Ctr. Reading Skills, Tel Aviv, 1972; asst. prof. Brookdale C.C., Lincroft, N.J., 1975-77, Rutgers U., New Brunswick, N.J., 1977-82; pres. The Emek Group, Inc., N.Y.C., 1980-98, CEO Metro Ptnrs., Inc., N.Y.C., 1998—2001; dir. CBS Coverage Group, Inc., 2001—. Spkr. profl. meetings. Author: Answers for Managers, 1986, Dealing Successfully with Key Management Issues, 1986; contbr. articles to profl. jours. Mem. Mayor's Small Bus. Adv. Bd., N.Y.C., 1998—2001, Small Bus. Rsch. and Tech. Adv. Coun. IBM, 1998—2000, Ctr. for Women's Bus. Rsch. adv. bd., 2000—; mem. adv. coun. Women's Fin. Network at Siebert, 2000—02; founding bd. dirs. Nat. Mus. Women's History, 1997—2002; bd. dirs. Family Bus. Coun. Greater N.Y., 1997—98; bd. dirs., v.p. N.Y. Women's Agenda, 2000—; chair bd. dirs. Inst. for Student Achievement, N.Y.C., 1999—; bd. dirs. Women's Econ. Devel. Task Force, N.Y.C., 1999—2001; mem. Women's Leadership Exch. adv. bd., 2002—. Recipient Promising Rsch. award Nat. Coun. Tchrs. English, 1978, Woman of Power and Influence award NOW, N.Y.C., 1999, Mem. Profl. Ins. Agts. Assn., Nat. Assn. Women Bus. Owners (bd. dirs., pres. 1997-98, Mem. of Yr. 1997), Ind. Ins. Agts. and Brokers of Am. (bd. dirs. 2000—), Ins. Fedn. N.Y., Ins. Brokers Assn. N.Y., Coun. Ins. Brokers Greater N.Y., Nat. Assn. Ins. Women (Helen Garvin Outstanding Achiever in Ins. Industry award 1999), Assn. Profl. Ins. Women, Women's Pres. Orgn., Emily's List (majority coun.), Coun. Ins. Brokers Greater N.Y. Avocations: writing, reading, jogging, tennis, travel. E-mail: semek@cbsinsurance.com.

EMELY, MARY ANN, association executive; b. Bridgeport, Conn., Aug. 10, 1947; d. John and Stefanie Maria (Hutta) Horvath; m. Timothy Vellrath, Sept. 7, 1968 (div. Mar. 1975); 1 child, Wendy Amethyst Vellrath Delbrook; m. Charles H. Emely, Sept. 1, 1979. BA, U. Conn., 1969; postgrad., U. Bridgeport, 1975-76, Ohio U., 1982-83. Adminstrv. asst. ARC, Bridgeport, 1973-78; dir. mem. svcs. Comprehensive Assn. Cons., Ft. Washington, Pa., 1978-81; exec. dir. Muskingum County Respiratory Disease, Zanesville, Ohio, 1981-83; assoc. exec. dir. The Vol. Ctr., Syracuse, N.Y., 1984-86; dir. mem. programs NEA, Rockville, Md., 1986-91; dir. mem., mktg. Am. Geophys. Union, Washington, 1991-93; sr. dir. membership Coun. for Exceptional Children, Reston, Va., 1993-94; dep. exec. dir. Spl. Librs. Assn., Washington, 1994-95; exec. dir. Fedn. Govt. Info. Processing Couns., Fairfax, Va., 1995-99; mng. dir. Nat. Assn. Profl. Employer Orgns., Alexandria, Va., 2000—01; v.p. ops. Am. Coun. Engring. Cos., 2001—. Cons. Comprehensive Assn. Cos., Garrisonville, Va., 1991—. Editor Husky P.A.W. Print, 1995-96, Fedn. Facts, 1995-99; columnist Female Exec., 1994-95. Bd. dirs. Pub. Employees Roundtable, Washington, 1995-00; mem. Nat. Rep. Coalition for Choice, Washington, 1993—, Jr. League of Washington, 1986—. Mem. NAFE, Am. Soc. Assn. Execs. (cert., mentor diversity programs 1994-95), Am. Radio Relay League, Greater Washington Soc. Assn. Execs., Found. for Internat. Meetings, Mercedes Benz Club of Am., U. Conn. Alumni Assn. (Washington chpt., pres. 1996-99, nat. bd. dirs. 2002-, nat. fundraising com. 2001-), Kappa Alpha Theta. Methodist. Avocations: gardening, flower arranging, reading, travel. Home: PO Box 96 Garrisonville VA 22463-0096 Office: 1015 15th St NW Washington DC 20005

EMERICH, SUZAN MARIE, art educator, artist; d. Frank Lawrence Nicklas and Evon Evelyn Elway; m. Michael Andrew Emerich, Oct. 31, 1981; 1 child, William Michael. BA in Art Edn., Saginaw Valley State U., 2002. Cert. secondary art edn. (LX) K-12, Psychology (CE) 7-12 Mich. Dept. Edn. Provisional Cert., 2003. With Ea. Mich. Bank, Deckerville, Mich., 1989—97, Sanilac County Probate Ct., Sandusky, Mich., 1997—98; substitute tchr. Sanilac County Intermediate Sch. Dist., Mich., 1999—, East China Sch. Dist., St. Clair, Mich. Treas. Port Sanilac Fine Arts Assn., 1992—99; grief support facilitator St. Mary's Cath. Ch., Port Sanilac, 1999. Exhibitions include Art in the Park, Port Sanilac, Mich., 1999, one-woman shows include Sanilac Dist. Libr., Port Sanilac, 2001. Mem. McKenzie Hosp. Devel. Com., Sandusky, Mich. Recipient Pres.'s Leadership award, Marygrove Coll., 1999, Cert. of Recognition, St. Clair County C.C., 2001; Theodore Beard scholar, 2001. Mem.: Mich. Edn. Assn. (assoc.), Mich. Art Edn. Assn. (assoc.), Nat. Art Edn. Assn. (assoc.), Phi Theta Kappa. Roman Catholic. Avocations: herbal and botanical gardening, painting, hiking, studying nature. Address: PO Box 80 Port Sanilac MI 48469

EMERLING, CAROL G(REENBAUM), consultant; b. Cleve., Sept. 13, 1930; d. Bernard and Florence A. Greenbaum; m. Norton Harvey Noll, Oct. 1, 1950 (dec. July 1951); m. Stanley Justin Emerling, May 2, 1953 (div. Aug. 1971); children— Keith S., Susan C.; m. Jerrold A. Fadem, Aug. 24, 1974 (div. Oct. 1977). Student, Vassar Coll., 1948-49, Case Western Res. U., 1949-50; LL.B. summa cum laude, Cleve. State U., 1955. Bar: Ohio 1955, Calif. 1975, N.Y. 1982, U.S. Supreme Ct. 1975. Instr. Cleve. Coll., 1956-59; from staff atty. to atty.-in-charge Legal Aid Defenders Office, Cleve., 1962-70; regional dir. FTC, Cleve., 1970-74, L.A., 1974-78; sec. Am. Home Products Corp., N.Y.C., 1978-96; chmn. bd. Global Health Coun., 1998—2002. Adv. com. criminal rules Supreme Ct. Ohio, 1970-73; chmn. Cleve. Fed. Exec. Bd., 1973; internat. health policy cons.; mem. nat. adv. com. Cleve. State U. Law Sch. Co-author: The Allergy Cookbook, 1969; contbr. articles to legal jours. Founder Pepper Pike (Ohio) Civic League, 1959; sec. Pepper Pike Charter Commn., 1966. Recipient Claude E. Clarke award Legal Aid Soc., 1967, Disting. Service award FTC, 1972. Mem. State Bar Calif., State Bar Ohio.

EMERSON, ALICE FREY, political scientist, educator emerita; b. Durham, N.C., Oct. 26, 1931; d. Alexander Hamilton and Alice (Hubbard) Frey; divorced; children: Rebecca, Peter. AB, Vassar Coll., 1953; PhD, Bryn Mawr Coll., 1964; LLD (hon.), Wheaton Coll., 1986, Middlebury Coll., 1998; DHL (hon.), Trinity Coll., 1992. Tchr., Newton (Mass.) High Sch., 1956-58; mem. faculty Bryn Mawr (Pa.) Coll., 1961-64, U. Pa., Phila., 1966-75, asst. prof. polit. sci., 1966-75, dean of women, 1966-69, dean of students, 1969-75; pres. Wheaton Coll., Norton, Mass., 1975-91, pres. emerita, 1991—; sr. fellow Andrew Mellon Found., N.Y.C., 1991-98, sr. advisor, 1998—2002. Bd. dirs. AES Corp.; mem. bd. Edna McConnell Clark Found., HERS Mid-Am. Mem. World Resources Inst., Szburg Seminar, Nantucket Hist. Assn., MGH-IHP. Address: PO Box 206 Siasconset MA 02564-0206 E-mail: afe@alum.vassar.edu.

EMERSON, ANNE DEVEREUX, museum administrator; b. Boston, Oct. 6, 1946; d. Kendall and Margaret (Drew) E.; (div. 1980); children: Josephine, Hannah; m. Peter Alexander Altman, 1992. BA magna cum laude, Brown U., 1968; MA, Fletcher Sch. Law and Diplomacy, Tufts U., 1969; MBA, Boston U., 1990. Exec. asst. to v.p. adminstrn. Boston U., 1977—85, dir. adminstrn., program devel., 1985—88; exec. dir. Ctr. for Internat. Affairs Harvard U., Cambridge, 1988—98, acting exec. dir. David Rockefeller Ctr. for L.Am. Studies, 1995—96; pres. Bostonian Soc., Boston, 1998—2002; exec. dir. The Boston History Ctr. and Mus., Inc., 1999—, pres., 2004—. Bd. dirs. Integrated Foster Care, Cambridge, 1985-89; trustee Winsor Sch., 1989-91, Internat. Honors Program, 1995-2003; bd. dirs. World Affairs Coun., Boston, 1991-94, Urban Edge, 2003-; mem. exec. com. Boston Com. Fgn. Affairs, 1997-99. Mem. Phi Beta Kappa. Office: The Boston Mus Project 55 Court St Boston MA 02108

EMERSON, DONNA LUCILLE, social worker, educator; b. Pasadena, Calif., May 12, 1944; d. Ralph Ernest and Doris Lucille Rhodes; m. Gregory Lynn Colvin, Mar. 27, 1994; children: Jared, Chris, Juliet Belle. BA in Sociology and Psychology, U. Calif., Berkeley, 1966, MSW, 1968. LCSW. Social worker spl. edn. unit San Francisco Unified Sch. Dist., 1968—79; pvt. practice Sonoma, San Francisco, Mendocino, Calif., 1973—; coord. spl. edn. unit San Francisco Unified Sch. Dist., 1978—79; supr. dept. social svcs. Lighthouse for the Blind, San Francisco, 1979—81; dir. social svcs. Novato (Calif.) Cmty. Hosp., 1981—84; cons. Headstart Program, Ukiah, Calif., 1984—86; med. social worker Hospice Petaluma (Calif.), Petaluma Valley Home Care, Petaluma Valley Hosp., 1987—93; team bldg. specialist Clarke Home Nursing, Novato, 1992—97, med. social worker, 1993—94. Instr. Santa Rosa Jr. Coll., 1988—; photographer. Author: (chpt.) Low Vision, 1981; contbr. articles to profl. jours. Democrat. Avocations: piano, gardening.

EMERSON, JO ANN, congresswoman; b. Sept. 16, 1950; d. Ab and Sylvia Hermann; m. Bill Emerson, 1975 (dec.); children: Victoria, Katharine; m. Ron Gladney, 2000; stepchildren: Elizabeth, Abigail, Alison, Jessica, Stephanie, Sam. BA in Polit. Sci., Ohio Wesleyan U., 1972; DHL (hon.), Westminster Coll., Fulton, Mo. Mem. 105th-108th Congress from 8th Mo. dist., 1997—; appropriations com. 106th Congress, 1998—. Sr. v.p. Am. Ins. Assn.; dir. state rels. and grassroots programs Nat. Restaurant Assn.; dep. dir. comm. Nat. Rep. Congl. Com.; mem. Sub-Com. Agriculture, Transp. Energy & Water Devel. Mem. PEO Womens's Svc. Group (FY chpt.), Cape Girardeau; mem. adv. com. Children's Inn, NIH; mem. adv. bd. Arneson Inst. Practical Politics and Pub. Affairs, Ohio Wesleyan U.; trustee, Harry Truman Scholarship Found.; hon. and life trustee Westminster Coll. Mem. Copper Dome Soc. Republican. Presbyterian. Office: 2440 Rayburn HOB Washington DC 20515-2508

EMERSON, KIRK, government agency administrator; BA in Psychology, Princeton U.; M in City Planning, Mass. Inst. Tech.; PhD, Indiana U. Dir. U.S. Inst.. for Environmental Conflict Resolution, 1998—. Mem.: Am. Political Science Assoc. (William Anderson Award 1998), Am. Inst. of Certified Planners, Am. Planning Assoc., Am. Arbitration Assoc., Arizona's Dispute Resolution Assoc., Am. Bar Assoc. Dispute Resolution Sec., Assoc. for Conflict Resolution. Office: 130 S Scott Ave Tucson AZ 85701-1922*

EMERSON, MIA DIANE, English educator; b. Balt., June 20, 1969; d. Philip Henry and Constance Diane Scharper. BA, Coll. Notre Dame, Balt., 1991; MA, Johns Hopkins U., 1993. Adj. instr. Johns Hopkins U., Balt., 1993—, Coll. Notre Dame, Balt., 1993—. Freelance tutor and writer. Contbr. poetry to small jours. Mem. Delta Epsilon Sigma, Eta Sigma Phi, Sigma Tau Delta, Kappa Gamma Pi. Avocations: reading, writing. Office: 4701 N Charles St Baltimore MD 21210-2404

EMERSON, SHARON B. biology researcher and educator; b. Santa Monica, Calif., July 14, 1945; BA, U. Calif., Berkeley, 1966, MS, U. So. Calif., 1968, PhD, 1971. Rsch. assoc. Field Mus. Natural History, Chgo.; rsch. prof. Dept. Biology U. Utah. Recipient excellence in environ. health rsch., Lovelance Inst., Albuquerque, 1995; fellow John D. and Katherine T. Mac Arthur fellowship, 1995. Mem.: Am. Soc. Zoology (chair divsn. vertebrate morphology). Office: U Utah Dept Biology 257 S 1400 E Salt Lake City UT 84112-0840

EMERSON, SUSAN, oil company executive; b. Bryan, Tex., Nov. 2, 1947; d. Joseph Nathanial and Lorraine Parks; m. John S. Emerson, June 5, 1970 (div. 1984); children: John H., Christopher P.; m. Gerald W. Parker, May 4, 1985. Owner Emerson Ins. Agy., San Antonio, 1970-84, Emerson Oil Co., San Antonio, 1970—; mem. N.H. Ho. of Reps. Bd. dirs. Washington Hosp. Ctr.; elected state rep., dist. 13, N.H. Mem. Washington Hosp. Ctr. Women's Aux., 1988-95; mem. D.C. Rep. Com., 1991-95, alt. del. Rep. Nat. Conv., Washington, 1992, 4th ward committeewoman, 1992; commr. Adv. Neighborhood Commn., Washington, 1990-95; 2d v.p. 4D Commn., Washington, 1990-95; founder Boarder Baby Project, 1991-95; Rep. candidate for D.C. del. to Congress, 1992; vice chmn. Cheshire County Rep. Com., Cheshire County Rep. Womens Club; hmn. Rindge Rep. Com.; Justice of the Peace, Notary Pub.; elected N.H. State Rep; state rep. HHS com. New House. Recipient Sr. Adv. Silver Fox award Wash. Hosp. Women's Aux., 1989-95, Vol. award, 1990. Mem. LWV, DAR (state credentials, publicity chmn. Ashuelot chpt., 2d vice chpt. regent), D.C. Hosp. Assn. (trustee 1989-95), Am. Hosp. Assn. (D.C. del. 1990-92), Vis. Nurses Assn. (bioethic com. 1991-95), Rindge Hist. Soc. (life), Tex. Breakfast Club, Rindge Womens Club, Rindge Garden Club, Daughters of Am. Revolution (pub. chmn.). Lutheran. Avocations: travel, gourmet cooking, gardening, needlepoint. Home: 571 Route 119 Rindge NH 03461 E-mail: susan.emerson@leg.state.nh.us., semerson435@aol.com.

EMERY, CAROLYN VERA, non-commissioned officer; d. Earl Woodrow and Joan Ruth Emery. AA, Ctrl. Tex. Coll., 1988. Commd. 2d. lt. U.S. Army, 1982, advanced through grades to master sgt., noncommissioned officer in charge force protection br. HHC U.S. Army Pacific, 1999—. Office: HHC US Army Pacific Fort Shafter HI 96858

EMERY, JANE DAILEY, English literature and language educator; b. Omaha, Aug. 27, 1917; d. Charles Edward and Alice Jane (Atkinson) Dailey; m. Tabor Robert Novak, Mar. 30, 1940 (dec. Jan. 1984); children: Nana Alice, Tabor Robert Jr., Kay Douglass, Clare Christine; m. Clark Mixon Emery, May 25, 1986. BA summa cum laude, Carleton Coll., 1934; MA in English, U. Miami, 1964; PhD in English Lang. and Letters, U. Chgo., 1970. Asst. editor Millar's Chgo. Letter, 1940-42; grad. asst. English dept. U. Miami, Coral Gables, Fla., 1962-64; instr., then asst. prof. U. Ill., Chgo., 1966-73; Leverhulme Found. vis. fellow U. East Anglia, Norwich, Eng., 1973-74; sr. lectr. U. Queensland, Brisbane, Australia, 1974-82, George Watson vis. fellow, 1986; from vis. scholar to lectr. continuing studies Stanford (Calif.) U., 1982—91, lectr. continuing studies, 1991—, mem. editl. bd. Notes in the Margins, 1993—. Author: (under name Jane Novak) The Razor Edge of Balance: Study of V. Woolf, 1975; (under name Jane Emery) Rose Macaulay: A Writer's Life, 1991. Vol. numerous orgns. Mem. MLA, Am. Assn. for Australian Lit. Studies, Virginia Woolf Soc., Phi Beta Kappa. Democrat. Episcopalian. Avocation: travel. Home: 3351 Alma St Apt 321 Palo Alto CA 94306-3510 Office: Stanford U Dept Continuing Studies Stanford CA 94305

EMERY, LIN, sculptor; d. Cornell and Jean (Weill) E.; m. Shirley Brooks Braselman, Aug. 17, 1962, 1 child, Brooks. Certificat, Sorbonne U., Paris, 1949; studies with Ossip Zadkine, Paris, 1949-50; LHD (hon.), Loyola U., 2004. Vis. critic architecture Tulane U., New Orleans, 1969-70; vis. artist Newcomb Sch. Art, New Orleans, 1980; lectr., vis. artist various including U. Tex., Ga. Coll., Art Acad. Cin., U. New Orleans, LaGrange Coll., 1980-86; vis. artist U. Maine, 1988. Adv. New Orleans Art com., 1987-88, Nat. Sculpture Conf.; Works by Women, Cin., 1986-87; chair studio sessions Coll. Art Assn., N.Y.C., 1979, conf. Nat. Sculpture Ctr., Lawrence, Kans., 1976; chair Internat. Sculpture Conf., Phila., 1992. Prin. works include meml. column, fountain New Orleans Civic Ctr., 1966, 70, kinetic sculptures Lawrence Civic Ctr., 1982, fed. bldg. Houma, La., 1977, state library, Baton Rouge, 1982, various pub., corp. commns. Singapore, Chgo., Osaka (Japan), Washington, various pub. art commns. City of Va. Beach, 1988, Oxnard, Calif., 1989, Melbourne, Fla., 1990, Tallahassee, Fla., 1990, Hofstra U., 1992, Daytona Airport, 1993, Sterling Drug Rsch. Ctr., Pa.,

1993; one-woman shows include New Orleans Mus. Art, 1962, 64, Sculpture Ctr., N.Y.C., 1962, 67, Tenn. Fine Arts Ctr., Nashville, 1962, Mus. N.Mex., Santa Fe, 1966, Centennial Art Mus., Corpus Christi, Tex., 1967, Lauren Rogers Mus., Laurel, Miss., 1977, Hunter Mus., Chattanooga, 1985; solo gallery exhibits Max Hutchinson, Kouros, N.Y.C., Arthur Roger, New [illegible] Sculpture Ctr., Hamilton, NJ, 2000—; bd. mem. NY Sculpture Ctr., New York, NY, 1990—92, Contemporary Arts Ctr., New Orleans, La., 1994—2000; advisor Arts Coun., New Orleans, La., 1997—2003. Va. Ctr. Creative Art fellow, 1981; recipient mayor's award City of New Orleans, 1980, "Sweet-art" award Contemporary Arts Ctr., New Orleans, 1987, Lazlo Aranyi Honor award for Pub. Art, 1990, Gov.'s Arts award, La., 2001; named Woman of Achievement, State of La., 1984, Disting. La. Artist, New Orleans Ctr. for Creative Arts, 1988. Mem. Internat. Sculpture Ctr. (bd. dirs. 1973-79, 88-89), Sculptors Guild, New Orleans PerCent for Art Com., N.Y. Sculpture Ctr. (bd. mem. 1989-91), Nat. Acad. Design. Democrat. Achievements include 22 museum collections:National Collection of American Art; Walter Chrysler Museum; Sofia Museum of Foreign Art; etc; 52 solo exhibitions: U.S.; Kyoto, Paris, London, Canada. Avocations: archaeology, metallurgy. Home: 7520 Dominican St New Orleans LA 70118-3738 E-mail: lin@linemery.com.

EMERY, MARGARET ROSS, elementary school educator; b. Columbus, Ohio, May 21, 1923; d. Galen Starr and Stella May (Albright) Ross; m. Richard Clayton Emery, Oct. 27, 1943 (dec. June 1988); children: Richard C. Jr., Margaret Elizabeth Chapman. BA in Edn., U. Mich., 1944; MS in Elem. Guidance, U. Notre Dame, 1967. Life lic. in edn., Ind. 1st grade tchr. Grosse Ile (Mich.) Schs., 1944-45; 2nd grade tchr. Rumson (N.J.) Pub. Schs., 1945-46; homebound tutor Schenectady (N.Y.) Pub. Schs., 1946-48; tutor Hinsdale (Ill.) Pub. Schs., 1948-50; substitute tchr. South Bend (Ind.) Pub. Schs., 1951-53, 93—; head lower sch., guidance couns., 1st grade tchr. The Stanley Clark Sch., South Bend, 1958-88. Mem. St. Joseph County Rep. Women, South Bend, 1958-96; election day clk. Election Bd., South Bend, 1986-96; docent No. Ind. Hist. Soc., South Bend, 1990—. Mem. AAUW, Panhellenic Assn. (pres. South Bend Mishawaka 1993-95), Zonta Internat. (historian, bd. mem. 1994—), Delta Kappa Gamma (pres. Nu chpt. 1992-94). Republican. Presbyterian. Avocations: reading, needlework, golf, volunteer tutoring, bridge. Home: 322 Rue Flambeau Apt 403 South Bend IN 46615-2827

EMERY, NANCY BETH, lawyer; b. Shawnee, Okla., July 9, 1952; d. Paul Dodd Finefrock and Kathryn Jo (Saling) Hutchens; m. Lee Monroe Emergy, May 18, 1974. BA with highest honors, U. Okla., 1974; JD, Harvard U., 1977. Bar: D.C. 1981. Atty. advisor Office Gen. counsel, USDA, Washington, 1977-79; legal advisor Fed. Energy Regulatory Commr. Matthew Holden, Jr., Washington, 1979-81; assoc. Pierson, Ball & Dowd and predecessor Sullivan & Beauregard, Washington, 1981-83, Paul Hastings, Janofsky & Walker, Washington, 1983-87, ptnr., 1987-93, Sutherland, Asbill & Brennan, Washington, 1993-97; v.p., gen. counsel, corp. sec. Calif. Ind. Sys. Operator Corp., 1997-99; ptnr. Hopkins & Sutter, Washington, 1999-2001, Ballard, Spahr, Andrews & Ingersoll, LLP, Washington, 2001—. Nat. adv. bd. USAID Tng. Program, 1994—98. Bd. dirs., sec. Park Place Condominium Assn., Inc., Washington, 1982—84; page Continental Congress DAR, 1978—82, chpt. del., 1981, 1984; bd. dirs. New Hope Housing, Inc., Alexandria, Va., 2001—, chmn. strategic planning com., 2002—. Mem.: ABA (natural resources energy and eviron. law sect. 1990—98, bd. editors Natural Resources & Environment 1990—98, pub. utility law sect., vice chmn. electricity com. 1998—, chmn. program com. 2000—01, chmn. mem. com. 2001—02, chmn. strategic planning com. 2001—02, chmn. cmty. outreach com. 2002—, mem. coun. 2002—, chmn. cmty. involvment 2002—), Soc. Profl. Journalists, Fed. Energy Bar Assn. (chair tax com. 1986—87, chair FERC ops. and adminstrn. com. 1991—93, chair elec. utility regulation com. 1995—97, chair program com. 1997—98), Mortar Bd., Phi Beta Kappa. Democrat. Office: Ballard Spahr Andrews & Ingersoll LLP 601 13th St NW Washington DC 20005 also: Sr VP and Gen Counsel City Pub Svc PO Box 1771 San Antonio TX 78296-1771 E-mail: bemery@ballardspahr.com.

EMERY, VICKI MORRIS, school library media administrator; b. Kansas City, Mo., Sept. 7, 1948; d. Arthur Paul and Merna Alva (Powell) Morris; m. Harvey William Emery Jr., July 19, 1974. BS in Edn., Emporia (Kans.) State U., 1970; M in Urban Affairs, Va. Poly. Inst. and State U., 1980; MS in Libr. Sci., Cath. U. Am., 1995; postgrad. student in ednl. leadership, U. Va., 1997—. Tchr. St. Pius X Sch., Mission, Kans., 1970-72, Shawnee Mission (Kans.) Pub. Schs., 1973-74; editing supr. CTB/McGraw-Hill, Monterey, Calif., 1975-76; sch. libr. media specialist Fairfax County (Va.) Pub. Schs., 1995-99, sch. libr. adminstr., 1999—. Mem. adv. bd. Fairfax County Sch. Bd., 1996-99. Contbr. revs. and articles to profl. jours. Pres. PTA Sangster Sch., Springfield, Va., 1994-95, 96-98, scholarship chair Fairfax County Coun. PTAs, 1995-99; pres., bd. dirs. Spring-Mar Coop. Presch., Springfield, 1989-90. Recipient Outstanding Svc. award Va. Coop. Presch. Coun., 1991. Mem. ALA, Am. Assn. Sch. Librs. (mem. pres.'s program com. 1998), Assn. Supervision and Curriculum Devel., Va. Ednl. Media Assn., Va. Soc. Tech. Edn., Va. Congress Parents and Tchrs. (hon. life mem.), Beta Phi Mu (local chpt. sec. 2000—). Office: Lake Braddock Secondary Sch 9200 Burke Lake Rd Burke VA 22015-1682

EMERY, VIRGINIA OLGA BEATTIE, psychologist, researcher; b. Cleve., Apr. 9, 1938; d. W. Joseph P. and Antoinette Pauline (Misjak) Kennick; m. Paul Hamilton Beattie Sr., 1960 (div. 1975); children: Tamsan Beattie Tharin, Paul Hamilton Beattie Jr.; m. Paul E. Emery, 1979. BA, U. Chgo., 1962, PhD, 1982; MA, Ind. U., 1973. Diplomate Am. Bd. Disability Analysts, Am. Acad. Traumatic Stress; lic. psychologist, N.H., Ohio; cert. brief therapist Nat. Acad. Brief Therapists; cert. cognitive therapist Nat. Bd. Behavioral Therapists, cert. domestic violence counselor endorsement; cert. expert traumatic stress, cognitive therapist. Asst. prof. psychology Case Western Res. U., Cleve., 1986-89, asst. clin. prof. psychiatry, 1986-89; sr. faculty assoc. Ctr. on Aging and Health, Concord and Hanover, N.H., 1986-89, dir., 1989—; adj. clin. asst. prof. psychiatry Dartmouth Med. Sch., Lebanon, 1983-85, clin. assoc. prof., 1989—. Mem. com. human devel. NIMH, Adult Devel. & Aging Traineeship, U. Chgo., 1974-76; sub-project dir. Case Western Res. U. Sch. Medicine, 1986-90; sec. women's faculty assn. Case Western Res. U., 1987-89; cons. Vets. Affairs Med. Ctr., Manchester, N.H., 1989—; sub-project dir. NIMH Mental Health Clin. Rsch. Ctr. Grant, Case Western Res. U. Sch. Medicine, 1986-90; mem. Dartmouth Coll. and Dartmouth Med. Sch. Neurosci. Group, 1990—; lectr. on medicine Harvard U. Faculty of Medicine, 1996—; Paul Janssen lectr. U. Goteberg, Sweden, 1997; invited lectr. Inst. for Health of Elderly, Newcastle-upon-Tyne, Eng., 1999. Author: Language and Aging, 1985, Pseudodementia: A Theoretical and Empirical Discussion, 1988, Language Impairment in Dementia of the Alzheimer Type: A Hierarchical Decline, 2000, Interface between Vascular Dementia and Alzheimer Syndrome: Nosologic Redefinition, 2000, Retrophylogenesis of Memory in Dementia of the Alzheimer Type: A New Evolutionary Memory Framework, 2003, Noninfarct Vascular Dementia and Alzheimer Syndrome Spectrum, 2003; editor: Dementia: Presentations, Differential Diagnosis, and Nosology, 1994, 2d edit., 2003; contbr. chapters to books, articles to profl. jours. Bd. dirs. Frontiers of Knowledge Civic Trust, Concord, N.H., 1990—, pres. 1990-95. Recipient Adult Devel. and Aging grant/traineeship NIH/NIMH, 1974-76, Rsch. prize Am. Aging Assn., 1983, Havighurst prize for aging rsch. U. Chgo., 1984, N.H. Hosp. award for outstanding rsch. in dementia, 2003; named Frontiers of Knowledge Atlee Zellers lectr., 1994, Paul Janssen Med. Inst. lectr., 1997; rsch. grantee Western Res. Coll., 1986-87, NIMH Mental Health Clin. rsch. grantee, 1986-89. Fellow Gerontol. Soc. Am. (Disting Creative Contbn. award 1989; clin. medicine membership com. state liaison 1998—; lectr. Boston, 2002), Am. Psychol. Assn., N.H. Psychol. Assn. (bd. dirs. 1991-93, chair com. acad. rsch. interests 1992-94, sec. 1994—, Riggs Disting. Contbn. award 1991, chmn. Women and Minorities com. 2001—), APA (student rsch. award 1984), Am. Acad. Experts in Traumatic Stress; mem. AAAS, AAUW, Internat. Psychiat. Rsch. Soc., Internat. Psychogeriatric Assn. (Pfizer lectr. 1997, 2d place award for rsch. paper 1995, 2nd Pl. Rsch. award in psychogeriatrics for paper 1995, IPA/Bayer Rsch. award in [illegible]), Boston Soc. Gerontol. Psychiatry, Acad. Psychosomatic Medicine, N.Y. Acad. Scis., Am. Acad. Experts in Traumatic Stress, Assn. Alzheimer's Disease Scientists, Am. Mensa Ltd. Home: 15 Buckingham Dr Bow NH 03304-5207 Office: Dartmouth Med Sch Dept Psychiatry Box HB 7750 Lebanon NH 03756 E-mail: vobemeryphd@aol.com.

EMIG, CAROL A. music educator, musician; d. Clifford R. Sterner and Violet E. Knechel; m. Thomas E. Emig, Aug. 16, 1980; children: Elizabeth A., Andrew T. BS in Music Edn., Mansfield (Pa.) U., 1978; MusM in Music Edn., West Chester (Pa.) U., 2003. Instrnl. cert. II Pa. Dept. Edn. Organist, choir dir. Little Zion Luth. Ch., Telford, Pa., 1985—97; elem. music educator Quakertown (Pa.) Cmty. Sch. Dist., 1998—. Dir. Pennridge Cluster Choir, Perkasie, Pa. Mem.: Am. Guild Organists, Am. Choral Dirs. Assn., Nat. Assn. Music Edn. Avocation: travel. Home: 22 Longview Rd Perkasie PA 18944 Office: Richland Elem Sch Quakertown Cmty Sch Dist 500 Fairview Rd Quakertown PA 18951 Personal E-mail: temig@comcat.com.

EMME, model, apparel designer; b. N.Y.C. Degree in speech comm., Syracuse U. Reporter, Flagstaff, Ariz.; morning anchor NBC affiliate Sta. KNAZ-TV; spokesperson Revlon and numerous fashion houses; clothing designer Emme; supermodel. Lectr. in body image and self-esteem at h.s. and univs.; first model invited to speak to a congressional subcom. on eating and body-image disorders, Washington. Host Fashion Emerency, E! Entertainment TV; author: True Beauty-Positive Attitudes & Practical Tips from the World's Leading Plus Size Model; columnist: Ask Emme. Hon. bd. dirs. Eating Disorders & Awareness Prevention, Am. Anorexia & Bulimia Assn.; ambassadors Mutiple Sclerosis Soc. Named Woman of Yr., Glamour Mag., 1997; named one of 50 Most Beautiful People, People Mag., 1994, 1999, Most Fascinating Woman of Yr., Ladies Home Jour., 1997, Most Important Women in Am., 1999; named to Orange Plus Hall of Fame, Syracuse U.; scholar Full athletic scholar, Syracuse U., Rowing Team. Studio: William Morris Agency Brian Dubin 1325 Ave of Americas Flr 15 New York NY 10019

EMMERICH, CONSTANCE, musician; b. Stamford, Conn., Nov. 25, 1935; d. Bernard Charles Marantz and Sadye R. (Rubin) Lee; m. André Emmerich, Aug. 25, 1958 (div. June 1994); children: Adam, Toby, Noah. BA, Smith Coll., 1950, MA, 1951; MEd, Bank St. Coll., 1956. Concert pianist, soloist, 1939-46; founder, pianist An Die Musik, N.Y.C., 1976—. Trustee Bank St. Coll., N.Y.C., 1959, Chamber Music Am., N.Y.C., 1986-90, Elaine Kaufman Cultural Ctr., N.Y.C., 1995—. Contbr. articles to profl. jours. Recipient Merkin Concert Hall Artistic Achievement award Elaine Kaufman Cultural Ctr., N.Y.C., 1995. Democrat. Avocation: collecting americana and old master drawings and historic decorative arts. Home: 1060 5th Ave New York NY 10128-0104

EMMERICH, KAROL DENISE, foundation executive, daylily hybridizer, former retail executive; b. St. Louis, Nov. 21, 1948; d. George Robert and Dorothy (May) Van Houten; m. Richard James, Oct. 18, 1969; 1 son, James Andrew. BA, Northwestern U., 1969; MBA, Stanford U., 1971. Nat. divsn. account officer Bank of Am., San Francisco, 1971-72; fin. analyst Dayton Hudson Corp., Mpls., 1972-73, sr. fin. analyst, 1973-74, mgr. short term financing, 1974-76, asst. treas., 1976-79, treas., 1979—, v.p., 1980-93; exec. fellow U. St. Thomas Grad. Sch. Bus., 1993—; pres. Emmerich Found., Edina, Minn., 1993—. Bd. dirs. Slumberland; co-owner Springwood Gardens. Bd. dirs. Hemerocallis Soc. Minn. Mem. Minn. Women's Econ. Roundtable. Home and Office: 7302 Claredon Dr Edina MN 55439-1722

EMMICH, LINDA L. private school educator; b. Cin., Feb. 8, 1949; d. Jack C. and Edna E. (Wiese) Emmich. BS, U. Cin., 1971, MA, 1986. Cert. secondary edn. tchr., permanent sch. counselor. Permanent counselor Friars Club, Cin., 1986-89; with Archdiocese of Cin., 1971—, tchr., counselor Nativity Sch., 1986—, mem. curriculum com., 1983, tch. Purcell Marian HS summer program, 1991-95; tutor, facilitator Lang. and Learning Ctr. No. Ky., 1996-98; tchr., counselor Navitity Sch., Cin. Ednl. resource Creative Therapy Assocs., Cin., 1989, Cin., 90; participant E-CASE best schs. program Xavier U. Grantee Fed. Study, 1978—79, 2002—03. Mem.: Ohio Cath. Edn. Assn. (conv. spkr. 1987), Nat. Cath. Edn. Assn. Office: Nativity Sch 5936 Ridge Ave Cincinnati OH 45213-1699

EMMONS, ALICE M. state legislator; b. Springfield, Vt., Feb. 14, 1955; BS, U. N.H., 1977. State rep. Windsor dist. 6 Vt. Ho. of Reps., 1983—. Owner, operator Lamp and Shades by Alice. Chmn. Windsor County Dem. Com.; mem. Springfield Bd. Civil Authority, Springfield Planning Commn. Home: 318 Summer St Springfield VT 05156-2829 Office: Vt House of Reps Drawer 33 115 State St Montpelier VT 05633-0001

EMMONS, JOANNE, state legislator; b. Big Rapids, Mich., Feb. 8, 1934; d. Ray J. and Emma M. (Von Glahn) Gregory; m. John Francis Emmons, June 9, 1956; children: Sarah, Dorothy. BS, Mich. State U., 1956; degree in pub. svc. (hon.), Ferris State U., 1992. Tchr. Mecosta (Mich.) High Sch., 1956-58; treas. Big Rapids Twp., 1976-86; state rep. State of Mich., Lansing, 1987-91; mem. Mich. Senate from 23rd dist., Lansing, 1991—. Chair Mecosta County Rep. Com., 1976-80; vice chair 10th dist. Rep. Com., 1984-86; bd. dirs. Luth. Child and Family Svcs., 1990-96; chair Senate fin. nat. conf. of state legis. exec. com., 1993—. Named Nat. Rep. Legislator of Yr., Nat. Assn. State Legislators, 1993, Legislator of Yr., Mich. Twp. Assn., 1993. Mem. Am. Legion Aux., Mich. Farm Bur. (legis. com. 1970-96), Milk Haulers Assn. (Legislator of Yr. 1995), Omicron Delta Kappa. Avocations: reading, sewing. Home: PO Box 30036 Lansing MI 48909-7536 Office: Mich State Senate State Capitol Lansing MI 48909

EMMONS, VICTORIA ANN, hospital administrator, marketing consultant; b. Carmel, Calif., Sept. 27, 1950; d. Herbert Glen and Miriam Box; m. Daniel Richard Stober, June 24, 1972 (div. July 1982); 1 child, Katharine Evans Stober; m. John Louis Emmons, May 16, 1987. BA in French, Fla. State U., 1972; student, U. Strasbourg, France, 1970-71; postgrad., U. South Fla., 1978-80, U. San Francisco, 1999—, student. Thcr. French and journalism Brookside Jr. H.S., Sarasota, Fla., 1974-79, St. Stephen's Sch., Bradenton, Fla., 1980-81, dir. devel., 1982-84; comms. specialist Manatee Meml. Hosp., Bradenton, 1984-85; sr. dir. cmty. rels. Washington Hosp., Fremont, Calif., 1985-93; exec. dir. Washington Hosp. Found., Fremont, 1993-96; pres., owner E2 Cons., Los Altos, Calif., 1994—; v.p. mktg. and devel. El Camino Hosp., Mountain View, Calif., 1997—. Bd. dirs. Mid-Peninsula Home Health and Hospice, Inc., Mountain View, 1997—, Fremont Healthy Start, 1992-94. Contbr. articles to Vim and Vigor Mag., Health Signs, others. Bd. dirs., chair pub. rels. Spl. Olympics of Alameda County, Fremont, 1995-96; mem. Jr. League of Manatee County, Fla., 1976-79; bd. dirs. Manatee County Cancer Soc., Bradenton, 1984-85, Ctr. for Cmty. Dispute Settlement, Livermore, Calif., 1996; chair March of dimes Walk-a-Thon, 1999. Recipient YWCA Tribute to Women and Industry award, San Jose, 1998; Bradenton Herald/Knight-Ridder journalism scholar, 1979. Mem. Healthcare Profls. of No. Calif., Women in Comms., Commonwealth Club, Assn. for Healthcare Philanthropy, No. Calif. Soc. for Healthcare Pub. Rels. and Mktg. (bd. dirs.), Fremont C. of C., Newark C. of C., Rotary Club (pres. Warm Springs chpt. 1993-94, L.A. chpt.), Kappa Alpha Theta (bd. dirs., chair pub. rels. of alumni club). Democrat. Episcopalian. Avocations: golf, reading, piano, speaking french, travel. Office: El Camino Hosp 2500 Grant Rd PO Box 7025 Mountain View CA 94039-7025

EMPERADO, MERCEDES LOPEZ, librarian; b. Manila, Aug. 9, 1941; came to U.S., 1969; d. Evaristo Villasor and Marina (Gallardo) Lopez; m. Conrado Emperado, June 30, 1968; children: Joshua Caleb, Marita Eve. BS in Elem. Edn., Philippine Normal Coll., 1963; MLS, Cath. U. Am., 1974. Libr. math. and computation lab. Fed. Preparedness Agy., Washington, 1976-79; libr. Fed. Emergency Mgmt. Agy., Washington, 1979—. Mem. ALA, Am. Soc. Info. Sci., Spl. Librs. Assn., Nat. Coordinating Coun. on Emergency Mgmt. Baptist. Home: 6303 Elm Way Clinton MD 20735-3928 Office: Fed Emergency Mgmt Agy Libr 500 C St SW Washington DC 20024-2523 Office Phone: 202-646-3771.

EMPSON, HEATHER LEIGH (PARMANN), elementary school educator; b. Coos Bay, Oreg., Jan. 16, 1976; d. David Albert and Judy Lynn Parmann; m. Shane Clifton Empson, June 15, 2002. BA, Concordia Coll., Ann Arbor, Mich., 1996—98; MA tchr., reading, lang. arts, Oakland U., Rochester, Mich., 1999—2002. Cert. tchg., k-8 all subjects, 6-8 English, 6-8 Psyc. State of Mich., 1998, Tchg., Reading Specialist K-12 State of Mich., 2003. Kindergarten through second grade tchr. St. Paul Luth. Sch., Sterling Heights, Mich., 1998—. Volleyball coach St. Paul Luth. Sch., Sterling Heights, Mich., 1999—. Mem.: Mich. Reading Assn. (assoc.), Internat. Reading Assn. (assoc.). Office: St Paul Lutheran School 42681 Hayes Road Sterling Heights MI 48313 Personal E-mail: emp615@comcast.net.

EMRICH, JEANNE ANN, poet, artist; b. Mpls. d. George Jacob Emrich and Janis Virginia (Elstone) Emrich Erickson; m. Glenn Merle Eriksen, Jan. 17, 1981; children: Stephanie, Anthony. BA in Art History, U. Minn., 1969. Pub., founder Lone Egret Press, Mpls., 1996—2003; founder. first editor HAIGA Online, Mpls., 1998—2001; tchr. The Loft Lit. Ctr., Mpls., 1998—2000. Author (editor): (book) The Haiku Habit, 1996, Barely Dawn, 1999, Berries and Cream: Contemporary Haiga in North America, 2000, Reeds: Contemporary Haiga, 2003. Bd. dirs. Bloomington Art Ctr., 1994—98. Recipient H.G. Henderson award, Haiku Soc. Am., 1995, 2001. Mem.: Nat. League of Am. Penwomen (pres. br. and state assn. Minn. chpt. 1998-2000), Minn. Artists Assn. (pres. 1988-90), Minn. Watercolor Soc. (co-founder, first pres. 1983-86), Minn. Haiku Soc. (co-founder 2003), Rendezvous Minn. (co-founder, first pres. 1993-94). Avocations: nature study, painting. E-mail: jemrich@aol.com.

ENDERS, ELIZABETH MCGUIRE, artist; b. New London, Conn., Feb. 18, 1939; d. Francis Foran and Helen Cuseck (Connolly) McGuire; m. Anthony Talcott Enders, June 9, 1962; children: Charles Talcott, Alexandra Eustis, Camilla, Ostrom II. BA, Conn. Coll., 1962; MA, NYU, 1987. Trustee Artists Space, N.Y.C., 1986-95, Conn. Coll., New London, 1988-93; assoc. dept. prints and illustrated books Mus. Modern Art, 1993—, Lyman Allyn Art Mus., 1994—. One-woman shows include Paul Schuster Gallery, Cambridge, Mass., 1966, Ulysses Gallery, N.Y.C., 1992, 94, Lyman Allyn Art Mus., New London, Conn., 1994, Charles Cowles Gallery, N.Y.C., 1995, Norbert Considine Gallery, Princeton, N.J., 1997, Artists Space, N.Y.C., 2001; exhibited in group shows at Boston Symphony Orch., 1982, NYU, 1983, Conn. Conn., 1988, Bronx Coun. on Arts, 1990-91, Addison Gallery Am. Art, 1993, Angel Art, L.A., 1993, Lyman Allyn Art Mus., New London, Conn., 1994-95, 98, 99, So. Alleghenies Mus. Art, Loretto, Pa., 1994, Artists Space Multiple, 1995, New Mus. Contemporary Art, N.Y.C., 1995, Denise Bibro Fine Art, N.Y.C., 1995, 99, N.Y. Studio Sch., N.Y.C., 1995, 2002, Divine Design '95, L.A., Spring Benefit Raffle, Sculpture Ctr., N.Y.C., 1996, 97, 98, 2000, 03, Charles Cowles Gallery, N.Y.C., 1996, 98, 2000, 01, 02, 03, Fax Art Week, Copenhagen, Assn. Danish Graphic Artists, 1996, Open Studio, Downtown Arts Festival, N.Y.C., 1997, 98, Dieu Donne Papermill, 1997, 99, 2001, Robert Brown Gallery, Wash. D.C., 1999, 2001, 02, New York Acad. of Art Benefit Auction, 1999, Cooley Gallery, Old Lyme, Conn., 1999, 2002, (Benefit for the Nature Conservancy), Nielsen Gallery, Boston, 2001, Artwalk, Coalition for the Homeless, 2001; traveling group show Artists Space, 1992, 94, Southeastern Ctr. Contemporary Art, Winston-Salem, N.C., 1993, Allentown (Pa.) Art Mus., 1994, Cleve. Ctr. Contemporary Art, 1994, Salt Lake Art Ctr., Salt Lake City, 1995, Kemper Ctr. Contemporary Art and Design, Kansas City, Mo., 1996, Bass Mus. of Art, Miami Beach, Fla., 1997, Flint (Mich.) Inst. Arts, 1998, Blaffer Gallery, U. Houston, TX, 1998, Contemporary Art Ctr., Va. Beach, 1998, Tampa Mus. of Art, 1998-99, Art Mus. of Southeast Tex., 1999, Fresno Metropolitan Mus., Calif., 2000, www.sfnbotanicalart.com, 2003; represented in permanent collections at Addison Gallery of Am. Art, Andover, Mass., Graham Gund, Cambridge, Dow Jones, N.Y.C., Agnes Gund, N.Y.C., Lyman Allyn Art Mus., Conn. Coll., New London. Recipient Citation of Appreciation, Conn. Coll., 1990, medal, 1993. Mem. The Bklyn. Mus., Contemporary Art Coun. Home: 530 E 86th St New York NY 10028-7535

ENDICOTT, JENNIFER JANE REYNOLDS, education educator; b. Oklahoma City, Oct. 17, 1947; d. M. Ector and Jessie Ruth (Carter) Reynolds; m. William George Endicott, June 2, 1969 (dec. Sept. 1976); 1 child, Andrea A. BA History, U. Okla., 1969, MEd Adminstrn., 1975, PhD, 1987. Cert. secondary edn. tchr.: history, govt., geography, econs., adminstr., Okla. Mid. sch. tchr. Norman (Okla.) Pub. Schs., 1970-77, adminstr. elem. edn., 1977-80; grad. asst. U. Okla., Norman, 1984-88; adj. lectr. U. Ctrl. Okla., Edmond, 1988-90, asst. prof., 1990-94, assoc. prof., 1995-98, prof., 1999—. Mem. adv. bd. The Annual Editions Series, Guilford, Conn., 1994—; editor Okla. Assn. Tchr. Educators Jour., 1997-2001, mem. editl. bd., 2002—; reviewer Action in Teacher Education ATE Jour.; contbr. articles to profl. jours. Bd. dirs. Cleveland County Hist. Soc., Norman, 1980-88, Arts and Humanities Coun., Norman, 1982-88; bd. dirs. Jr. League, Inc., Norman, 1982-90; bd. dirs. Assistance League, Norman, 1982-90, pres. 1988-89. Recipient Harriet Harvey Meml. award U. Okla. Found., 1984; named Norman Cmty. Family of the Yr. Finalist, LDS Ch., Norman, 1985; named to The Educator's Leadership Acad., The Outstanding Profs. Acad., 1999-2000. Mem. ASCD, Okla. Assn. for Supervision and Curriculum Devel., Okla. Assn. Tchr. Educators (bd. dirs. 1994-2003, pres. 1996-97, exec. sec. 2001-03), Am. Assn. Tchr. Educators, Soc. for Philosophy and History of Edn., Nat. Soc. Study of Edn., Am. Ednl. Rsch. Assn., Philosophy of Edn. Soc., Kappa Delta Pi (univ. sponsor 1991-96), Phi Delta Kappa (bd. dirs. Mid. State chpt. 1993-99, v.p. 1997-99, Svc. Key 1998). E-mail: jendicott@ucok.edu.

ENDRES, ELEANOR ESTELLE, speech pathology/audiology services professional; b. Balt., Dec. 11, 1953; d. Thomas Edward and Elizabeth Jane Donatt; m. Charles Jeffrey Knickman, Feb. 1974 (div. Mar. 1981); m. Gregory Scott Endres, Apr. 1119; children: Meghan, Graciela, Daniel. BS, Towson State U., Md., 1976; MS, Towson State U., 1989. Speech pathologist Anne Arundel Pub. Schs./Infant Toddlers Program, Glen Burnie, Md., 1989—. Asst. county exec. campaign TAAAC, 2001; religious edn. tchr. Holy Trinity Ch./Archdiocese of Balt., Glenn Burnie, 1998—. Recipient ACE award, Am. Speech and Hearing Assn., 2003. Mem.: Speech and Lang. Assn. of Anne Arundel County (exec. bd. 1999), Md. Speech and Hearing Assn. (exec. bd. 2000—, Svc. award 2000). Democrat. Roman Catholic. Avocation: dogs. Home: 17 Proctor Ave Glen Burnie MD 21061 Office: AACO Infant Toddlers Program Point Pleasant Elem Sch Glen Burnie MD 21060

ENDRESEN, LISA CASTRO, curatorial assistant; b. Ft. Hood, Tex., Oct. 31, 1969; d. Albert Charles Castro and Sandra Lynne Moore-Pope. BA in Art History, U. Md. European Divsn., Heidelberg, Germany, 1997; postgrad., U. Tex., San Antonio, 2002—. Adminstrv. asst. U. Md. Euorpean Divsn., Heidelberg, 1988-93, adminstv. asst. grad. programs, 1993-98; art auction coord. Sta. KLRN Pub. TV, San Antonio, 1998-99; curatorial asst.

McNay Art Mus., San Antonio, 1999—. Advisor Predls. Scholarship Com., Heidelberg, 1995-98. One-woman shows include Hanau Exhbn., 1996. Elected advisor Dems. Abroad, Heidelberg, 1995-97. Mem. Urban 15, Art History Webmasters Assn. Democrat. Avocations: painting, writing, dance, travel. Office: McNay Art Mus 6000 N New Braunfels Ave San Antonio TX 78209-4618 Fax: 210-824-0218.

ENDRUSICK, ROSE MARIE, educator; b. Creighton, Pa., Feb. 11, 1929; d. Paul Anthony and Ann Catherine Fricioni; m. Stanley Endrusick, June 19, 1950; children— Anne, Scott. B.S., Drexel Inst. Tech., 1950; M.A., Calif. State U.-Los Angeles, 1970; cert. Culinary Inst. Am., 1973. Tchr. home econs., Springdale, Pa., 1950-53, Glendale, Calif., 1953-55, Arcadia (Calif.) Unified Sch. Dist., 1955-83; designer antique doll clothes. Named Outstanding Tchr. in Arcadia, So. Calif. Industry-Edn. Council, 1968. Mem. Am. Home Econs. Assn., Calif. Tchrs. Assn., NEA, Arcadia/San Gabriel PTA (hon. life), Doll Collectors Gallery Calif. (v.p. 1981-83). Republican. Roman Catholic. Office: 301 S 1st Ave Arcadia CA 91006-3802

ENDYKE, DEBRA JOAN, data communications marketing professional; b. Manchester, N.H., July 24, 1955; d. Paul Ronald and Theresa Joan (Smith) Cote; m. Michael Thomas Pidgeon, May 15, 1976 (div. Aug. 1984); m. Thomas Allen Endyke, Sept. 21, 1985. BS in Computer Sci., N.H. Coll., 1984. Mktg. specialist Bedford (N.H.) Computer Corp., 1981-84; sales and mktg. dir. electronic services program First Software Corp., Lawrence, Mass., 1984-86; account exec. Genesys Software Systems, Inc., Lawrence, 1986-87; group sales mgr. N.E. data communications div. Panasonic Co., Secaucus, N.J., 1987-88; sr. account exec. Bus. Systems Sales Group Gen. DataComm, Inc., Middlebury, Conn., 1988-89; sr. cons. Hollis (N.H.) Info. Assocs., 1989-90; applications engr. Octocom Systems, Inc., Wilmington, Mass., 1989-94; sr. sys. product mgr. Microcom Inc., Norwood, Mass., 1995-99; sr. product line mgr. Nortel Networks, Billerica, Mass., 1999—; dir. product mgmt. voice divsn. Unisphere Solutions, Burlington, Mass., 1999—. Republican. Roman Catholic. Avocations: golf, fishing, reading, theatre. Home: 41 Naticook Ave Litchfield NH 03052-8036 Office: Unisphere Solutions 10 Technology Park Dr Westford MA 01886-3140

ENG, CATHERINE, health care facility administrator, physician, medical educator; b. Hong Kong, May 20, 1950, came to U.S., 1953; d. Doi Kwong and Alice (Yee) E.; m. Daniel Charles Chan; 1 child, Michael B. BA, Wellesley Coll., 1972; MD, Columbia U., 1976. Diplomate Am. Bd. Internal Medicine, Am. Bd. Gastroenterology; cert. added qualifications geriatrics. Intern in internal medicine Presbyterian Hosp./Columbia, Presbyterian Med. Ctr., 1976-77, resident in internal medicine, 1977-79; fellow in gastroenterology/hepatology N.Y. Hosp./Cornell U. Med. Coll., 1979-81; instr. medicine Cornell U. Coll. Medicine, N.Y.C., 1980-81; staff physician On Lok Sr. Health Svcs., San Francisco, 1981-86, supervising physician, 1986-91, med. dir., 1992—. Asst. clin. prof. dept. family and cmty. medicine U. Calif., San Francisco, 1986-95, asst. clin. prof. dept. medicine, 1992-95; assoc. clin. prof. dept. medicine, U. Calif., San Francisco, 1995-2001, clin. prof. medicine, 2001—; primary care specialist Program of All-inclusive Care for the Elderly, San Francisco, 1987-94; asst. chief dept. medicine Chinese Hosp., San Francisco, 1993-98, chmn. com. credentials, 1994—. Instr. BLS Am. Heart Assn., San Francisco, 1988-92; mem. nominating com. YWCA of Marin, San Francisco, San Mateo, 1991-95; mem. mgmt. com. YWCA-Chinatown/North Beach, San Francisco, 1989-95; bd. dirs. Chinatown Cmty. Children's Ctr., San Francisco, 1987-90. Durant scholar Wellesley Coll., 1972. Fellow ACP; mem. Am. Geriatrics Soc., Am. Soc. Aging, Am. Gastroent. Assn., Calif. Med. Assn. (assoc.), San Francisco Med. Soc. (assoc.), Sigma Xi, Alpha Omega Alpha. Avocations: reading, hiking. Home: 130 Dorchester Way San Francisco CA 94127-1110 Office: On Lok Sr Health Scvs 1333 Bush St San Francisco CA 94109-5691 E-mail: cathy@onlok.org.

ENGEL, BARBARA ALPERN, history educator; BA in Russian Studies, CCNY, 1965; MA in Russian Studies, Harvard U., 1967; PhD in Rusian History, Columbia U., 1974. Part-time instr. Drew U., Madison, NJ, 1972—73; instr. Columbia U., N.Y.C., 1974; asst. prof. Sarah Lawrence Coll., 1974—76, U. Colo., Boulder, 1976—82, assoc. prof., 1982—92, prof., 1992—, dir. Ctrl. and Ea. European studies, 1993—95, chair dept. history, 1995—98. Author, co-editor: Five Sisters: Women Against the Tsar, 1975; author: Spanish transl., 1980, new edit., 1992, Mothers and Daughters: Women of the Intelligentsia in Nineteenth Century Russia, 1983; author, co-editor: Russia's Women: Accomodation, Resistance, Transformation, 1991; author: Between the Fields and the City: Women, Work and Family in Russia, 1861-1914, 1994, paperback edit., 1996; co-editor: A Revolution of their Own. Voices of Women in Soviet History, 1998; cons. editor Feminist Studies, 1979—98, mem. editl. bd. Frontiers, 1980—86, Slavic Rev., 1996—2001; contbr. articles. Recipient Heldt Article award, 1991, cert. tchg. excellence, Mortar Bd. Sr. Honor Soc., 1994, Heldt prize for Outstanding Achievement in Slavic Studies, AWSS, 1996, numerous other awards, grants; Wallenberg fellow, Rutgers Ctr. Hist. Analysis, 1995, fellow, John Simon Guggenheim Meml. Found., 2003, Sr. Exch. grant with the Soviet Union, IREX, 1985, 1987, 1991, Fulbright-Hays tng. grant, Faculty Rsch. Abroad program, 1987, Woodrow Wilson fellow, 1991, John D. and Catherine T. MacArthur Found. grantee, 1993—95, NEH fellow, 2003—. Mem.: Am. Assn. for Advancement of Slavic Studies, We. Assn. Women Historians (book prize com. 1990), Internat. Fedn. Socs. Rsch. Women's History (mem. U.S. com. 1988—91), Am. Hist. Assn. (com. on women historians 1987—89, mem. profl. divsn. 1990—92, mem. program com. 1994—95), Phi Beta Kappa. Office: U Colo Dept History Boulder CO 80309-0234

ENGEL, CAROL LOUISE, music educator; b. Tracy, Minn., Sept. 1, 1948; d. Elmer Roy Johnson, Frances Lucille Johnson; m. John Robert Engel; children: Christopher, Benjamin. BS in Music, Minn. U.-Mankato, 1970. Pianist, organist, Balaton, Minn., 1962—66, East Grand Forks, Minn., 1975—; supr. United Day Nursery, Grand Forks, ND, 1977—92; tchr. piano East Grand Forks, Minn., 1980—97; accompanist musicals, ensembles, solos, concerts East Grand Forks Pub. Schs. #595, 1987—; pianist Valley Meml. Homes, Grand Forks, ND, 1991—; tchr. elem. music East Grand Forks Pub. Schs. #595, 1992—. Accompanist Cmty. Theaters, Grand Forks, ND, 1975—80. Musician (CD): Piano by Carol, 1991, Piano by Carol 2, 1994, Forever Yours, 2000, In My Heart There Rings A Melody, 2001. Pianist, entertainer VFW Conv., Grand Forks, 2001, First Night, Grand Forks, 1992—97. Mem.: Music Boosters, Music Educators Nat. Conf., Sigma Alpha Iota (life; President - local chapter 1968—69). Republican. Lutheran. Avocations: painting, reading, travel, crafts. Home: 616 8th St SE East Grand Forks MN 56721 Office: East Grand Forks Public Schools - #595 1900 13th St SE East Grand Forks MN 56721 Personal E-mail: cengel@gra.midco.net.

ENGEL, SUSAN E. retail executive; Degree Indsl. and Labor Rels., Cornell U., 1968; MBA, Harvard U., 1976. With mgmt. and mktg. dept. J.C. Penney, N.Y.C., 1968-77; v.p. Booz, Allen and Hamilton, 1977-91; pres., CEO Champion Products, Inc., 1991-94; pres., COO Dept. 56, Inc., Eden Prairie, Minn., 1994-96, CEO, 1996—, also bd. dirs. Bd. dirs. Wells Fargo & Co., SuperValu Inc. Mem. pres. coun. Cornell Women, Cornell U.; bd. overseers Carlson Sch. Mgmt.; bd. dirs. Mpls. Guthrie Theater. Mem. Mpls. LWV. Avocations: sailing, tennis, collecting antiques, classical music and theater. Office: Dept 56 Inc One Village Pl 6436 City West Pkwy Eden Prairie MN 55344-7728

ENGEL, TALA, lawyer; b. NYC; d. Volodia Vladimir Boris and Risia (Modelevska) E.; m. James Colias, Nov. 22, 1981 (dec. Nov. 1989). AA, U. Fla., 1952; BA in Russian and Spanish, U. Miami, 1954; JD, U. Miami, Coral Gables, 1957; postgrad., Middlebury Coll., 1953. Bar: Fla. 1957, D.C. 1982, U.S. Dist. Ct. (so. dist.) Fla. 1957, Ill. 1962, U.S. Dist. Ct. (no. dist.) Ill. 1962, U.S. Supreme Ct., 1965. Pvt. practice, Miami, Fla., 1957—61, Chgo., 1966—86, Washington, 1987—89, Chgo., 1990—93, Washington, 1993—2002, Miami, Fla., 2002—. Atty. Immigration and Naturalization Svc., Chgo., 1961-62; parole agt. Ill. Youth Commn., Chgo., 1963-66. Editor The Lawyer, 1956; mem. editl. bd. Miami Law Quar., 1955-57, 10 ML Q 110 Criminal Law, 10 ML Q 608 Ins. Law, 1955-56. Bd. dirs. Cordi-Marian Settlement, Chgo., 1977-93. Named One of 2000 Outstanding Women of 20th Century, Dictionary Internat. Biography, 2000. Mem.: Fla. Bar Assn., Fed. Bar Assn., Chgo. Bar Assn. (devel. of law com. 1985—87, entertainment com. 1971—72), Ill. Bar Assn. (gen. assembly 1984—86), Chgo. Bar Found. (life), Nu Beta Epsilon, Alpha Lambda Delta. Avocations: travel, theater, singing, computers, Russian and Spanish languages. Home: 601 Three Islands Blvd #215 Hallandale FL 33009

ENGEL, WALBURGA See VON RAFFLER-ENGEL, WALBURGA

ENGELBREIT, MARY, art licensing entrepreneur; b. St. Louis, 1952; m. Phil Delano, 1977; 2 children. Illustrator greeting card cos., 1983; founder, pres. Mary Engelbreit Studios Retail and Pub. Cos., St. Louis, 1983—; founder, head The Mary Engelbreit Store; founder, creator Mary Engelbreit's Home Companion mag., 1996—. Syndicated columnist At Home with Mary Engelbreit. Illustrator The Snow Queen, 1993, The Night Before Christmas, 2001. Office Phone: 314-726-5646.

ENGELHARDT, CATHERINE, elementary school educator; b. Willimantic, Conn., Nov. 13, 1951; d. Clarence Silver and Marjorie Marie Grant; m. Frederick William Engelhardt, June 30, 1979 (div. Feb. 2, 1994); adopted children: Danielle, Gregory, Tabitha. BS, Springfield Coll., 1972; MA, U. Conn., 1980. Cert. elem. tchr. K-8, tchr. math. K-12. Educator Toms River (N.J.) Intermediate Sch., 1973—74, Toms River (N.J.) Intermediate West, 1974—76, Pine Beach (N.J.) Elem., 1976—87, South Toms River (N.J.) Elem., 1988—. Regional admissions rep. Springfield (Mass.) Coll., 1973—; facilitator math. implementation Toms River Schs., 2002—03, co-facilitator family tools and tech. program; coord. contest Top 10 Sci-Con, 2002—. Author: (in-dist. booklet) Grade 6-Word Finds, 1970—80. Vol. various orgns.; educator C.C.D. Bible Sch., St. Luke's Ch., Toms River, 1990. Mem.: Ocean County Edn. Assn., NEA, Toms River Edn. Assn., N.J. Edn. Assn., South Toms River Elem. Sunshine Club (treas. 2000—). Roman Catholic. Avocations: swimming, racquetball, computers, reading, exploring. Home: 23 S Gateway Toms River NJ 08753 Office: Toms River Schs 1144 Hooper Ave Toms River NJ 08753 E-mail: cath13ardt@juno.com., cengelhardt@trschools.com.

ENGELHARDT, REGINA, cosmetologist, artist, small business owner; b. Kiwerce, Poland, Oct. 1, 1928; came to U.S., 1949; d. Marian and Maria (Wardach) Engelhardt; m. Gerard Edward Twardon, May 30, 1953 (div. 1961); children: Miriam Teresa Twardon Bielski, Elizabeth Maria Twardon Israel, Renee Marie Twardon Gilchrist. Grad., Laski Inst. Tech., 1951; lic. cosmetologist, Hamtramck Beauty Sch., 1960; art student, Mercy Ctr., 1980-84. Sec. Am. Savs., Detroit, 1950-55; cosmetologist Magic Touch Salon, Oak Park, Mich., 1960—. Owner Regina's Fine Arts, Detroit, 1986—, Art Restorations, 1986—; art tchr. Farmington Activity Ctr., Farmington Hills, Mich., 1993—; spkr. in field. Artist lithographs; represented in permanent collection at Althorp Mus., Eng., 1998, also pvt. collections in U.S., Can., Poland, Eng., India, The Philippines. Mem. Dem. Nat. Com., 1996—; mem. nat. com. to preserve social security and medicare, 1993—. Recipient Gold and Silver medals Internat. Art Challenge, 1987-88, 90, Kubinski award Friends of Polish Arts, 1989, First and Fourth awards Mich. State Exhibit, 1988. Mem. Sculptores Guild of Mich., Four Octave Club, Farmington Artists Club (6 Popular Vote awards 1985, 86, 97, merit award local art exhibit 1997, two merit awards 1998), Sierra Club, Internat. Platform Assn., Nature Conservancy. Roman Catholic. Avocations: music, needlework, dance, reading. Home: 17345 Wildemere St Detroit MI 48221-2722 E-mail: reginaart@webtv.net.

ENGELHARDT, SARA LAWRENCE, organization executive; b. Phila., Aug. 23, 1943; d. Ruddick Carpenter and Barbara (Dole) Lawrence; m. Dean Lee Engelhardt, June 20, 1970; children: Barbara Elizabeth, Margaret Ann. BA, Wellesley Coll., 1965; MA, Tchrs. Coll., Columbia U., 1970. Staff asst. Carnegie Corp., N.Y.C., 1966-70, asst. sec., 1972-74, assoc. sec., 1974-75, sec., 1975-87; exec. v.p. Found. Ctr., N.Y.C., 1987-91, pres., 1991—. Free-lance editor and writer, Storrs, Conn., 1970-72. Bd. dirs. Nat. Charities Info. Bur., 1984-2000, chair, 1987-91; trustee Found. Ctr., 1984-87; bd. dirs. Trust for Philanthropy AAFRC, 1989-98; trustee Consortium for Advancement of Pvt. Higher Edn., 1989-93, chair, 1992-93; mem. bd. overseers Ctr. Rsch. on Women, Wellesley Coll., 1979-88; nat. bd. dirs. Girls Inc., 1992-98, Ind. Sector, 1992-98, Coun. Ind. Colls., 1993-94; bd. dirs. NOW Legal Def. and Edn. Fund, 1994-2001, Amigos de las Americas, 1995-2001, Nat. Coun. for Rsch. on Women, 2001—, Rsch. Found. of Metro N.Y. Better Bus. Bur., 2002—. Home: 173 Riverside Dr New York NY 10024-1615 Office: Foundation Ctr 79 5th Ave Fl 2 New York NY 10003-3076

ENGELKING, ELLEN MELINDA, textiles executive, manufacturing executive, real estate broker; b. Columbus, Ind., May 12, 1942; d. Lowell Eugene and Marcella (Brane) E.; children: Melissa Claire Fairbanks John David Prohaska, Ellen Margaret Brunner. Student, Sullins Coll., 1961, Franklin Coll., 1961-62, Ind. U., 1963. Chmn., CEO Engelking, Inc., Columbus, Ind. Founder The FlexCell Group. Sec. Bartholomew County Rep. Party, 1976-80; chmn. bd. dirs. Jr. Achievementm 1996—; chmn. Pvt. Industry Coun. South Ctrl. Ind.; protocol hostess Pan Am. Games X, Indpls., 1987. Bd. dirs. Ind. Humanities Coun., 1997—, United Way, 2000—. Recipient Franklin Coll. Alumni Citation, 1994, Athena award Oldsmobile Inst. Am. Bank C. of C., 1995. Mem. Columbus Area C. of C. (vice chmn. bd. dirs. 1990, bd. dirs. 1997—), Centra Credit Union (bd. dirs.), Delta Delta Delta. Roman Catholic. Avocation: study and present adaptation of shaker work ethic. Office: Engelking Inc PO Box 607 Columbus IN 47202-0607

ENGELMAN, MARJORIE JECKEL, retired higher education administrator; b. Delavan, Ill., Oct. 9, 1927; d. John B. and Reka M. (Hellman) Jeckel; m. Kenneth L. Engelman, Mar. 26, 1949; children: Ann K., Barth B. BA, Ill. Wesleyan U., 1945-49; MA, Northwestern U., 1953; MS, U. Wis., 1965, PhD, 1977. Dir. outreach/ext. U. Wis., Green Bay, 1973-85, dir. equal opportunity, 1974-79; asst. to chancellor affirmative action U. Wis. ext., Madison, 1985-89. Part-time instr. U. Wis., Madison, 1991-93. Author: Aerobics of the Mind: Keeping the Mind Active in Aging, 1996; contbr. articles to ch. publs. Bd. trustees Garrett-Evangel. Sem., Northwestern U., Evanston, Ill., 1975-96; bd. Meriter Retirement Svcs., Meriter Health, Madison, 1985-96; bd. dirs. Madison Campus Ministry, 1994-96; del. to White House Conf. on Aging, 1995. Kramer Found. grantee, 1985, Wis. Humanities grantee, 1980. Mem. Alumni Assn., Assn. Aging Groups in Wis., Phi Delta Kappa, Phi Kappa Phi. Democrat. United Methodist. Avocations: hiking, biking, birding, canoeing, reading. Home: 738 Seneca Pl Madison WI 53711-2918

ENGELS, BEATRICE ANN, retired real estate company executive, poet, artist; b. N.Y.C., Oct. 1, 1925; d. Sydney and Marguerite Agnes (Carroll) Jonap; m. James J. Engels, May 10, 1944 (dec.); children: James J. Jr.(dec.), Edward R., Marguerite Mary McHale. Brokers degree, Dowling Coll., Oakdale, N.Y., 1970. Real estate sales agt. Kathleen Hart Real Estate, Bayport, NY, 1969—70; real estate broker, pres. Beatrice A. Engels Realty, Patchogue, NY, 1970—76, Blue Point, NY, 1976—95; dir., pres. Beatrice A. Engels Art Gallery, Patchogue, 1970—76, Petite Pallette Art Gallery, Bayport, 1989—91; ret., 1995. Mem. real estate bd. Suffolk County, 1970—80; ecology adv., Blue Point, 1974—94; columnist LI Advance, Patchogue, NY, 1971—75, Suffolk County News, Sayville, NY, 1971—75. Author: Morning Song, 1996 (Editor's Choice award, 1996), Sea Sonnets and Other Poems, 1997, Endless Skies of Blue (Editor's Choice award, 1997), Best Poems of 1997, Celebration of Poets, 1997, Outstanding Poets of 1998 (Editor's Choice award, 1998), Best Poems of 1998; author, illustrator: Marguerite, The Story of a Dolly, 2003, songwriter: Best Christmas Present, 1998; artist numerous mediums. Mem. Blue Point Rep. Club, 1970—88. Mem.: Rosary Soc. (pres.), Internat. Soc. Poets (life), Wet Paints Studio Group (life). Roman Catholic. Achievements include ecological efforts that helped to save the wetlands near Blue Point, N.Y. E-mail: beabysea@bellsouth.net.

ENGELS, PATRICIA A. communications executive; BA, U. Minn. Assoc. market mgr. United Airlines, Chgo., 1981—88, v.p. market devel., 1988—90; pres., bd. dirs. Mileage Plus, Chgo., 1990—93; several exec. positions Ameritech Corp., Chgo., 1993—2000; pres. bus. process mgmt., mem. exec. ops. team EDS Corp., 2001—02; v.p. wholesale mktg. group Qwest Comm. Internat., Inc., Denver, 2002—03, exec. v.p., 2003—. Mem. U. Ill. Bus. Adv. Coun., Chgo. Named Achiever, YWCA Acad. Women Achievers, 1987. Mem.: Chgo. Network. Office: Qwest Comms Internat Inc 1801 California St Denver CO 80202

ENGEN, REBECCA LYNN, music educator; b. Marengo, Iowa, July 6, 1964; d. Charles Edward and Janet Elizabeth Fillman; m. Steven Brent Engen, May 23, 1987. MusB, U. Iowa, 1987, MA, 1997, PhD, 2003. Bd. cert. music therapist Certification Bd. for Music Therapists, 1990. Music therapist Luther Pk. Health Ctr., Charter Cmty. Hosp. and Children's Habilitation Ctr., Des Moines & Johnston, Iowa, 1988—88, Richard Young Luth. Hosp., Omaha, 1988—91, Broadlawns Med. Ctr., Des Moines, 1991—95, U. Hosps. and Clinics, Iowa City, 1995—96; pvt. music therapist Iowa City, 1995—98; tchg. asst., instr. U. Iowa, Iowa City, 1995—2001; asst. prof. music, music therapy Queens U. Charlotte, NC, 2001—. Cons. Children and Families Iowa, Des Moines, 1993—95; artist ArtShare, Iowa City, 1998—2001. Founder/dir. A Cabella!, North Liberty, Iowa, 1995—2001; musician Mission, North Liberty, 1997—2001; sr. high youth facilitator First United Meth. Ch., North Liberty, 1999—2001; singer Oratorio Singers of Charlotte, Charlotte, 2002—, Oratorio Chamber Singers, Charlotte, 2002—. Mem.: Music Therapy Assn. N.C. (pres. elect 2003—), Am. Music Therapy Assn. (assembly del. 1996—98), Am. Guild English Handbell Ringers, PEO (guard, jk-ia 1994—95). Achievements include first to explore vocal music techniques to develop breath control and symptom management in elderly persons with chronic obstructive pulmonary disease. Avocations: music, reading, hiking, volleyball, home improvement projects. Office: Queens University of Charlotte 1900 Selwyn Ave Charlotte NC 28274 E-mail: engenr@queens.edu.

ENGERRAND, DORIS DIESKOW, business educator; b. Chgo., Aug. 7, 1925; d. William Jacob and Alma Willhelmina (Cords) Dieskow; m. Gabriel H. Engerrand,Oct. 26, 1946 (dec. June 1987); children: Steven, Kenneth, Jeannine. BS in Bus. Adminstrn., N. Ga. Coll., 1958, BS in Elementary Edn., 1959; M. Bus. Edn., Ga. State U., 1966, PhD, 1970. Tchr., dept. chmn. Lumpkin County H.S., Dahlonega, Ga., 1960-63, 65-68; tchr. Gainesville, Ga., 1965; asst. prof. Troy (Ala.) State U., 1969-71; asst. prof. bus. Ga. Coll. and State U., Milledgeville, 1971-74, assoc. prof., 1974-78, prof., 1978-90, chmn. dept. info. sys. and comms., 1978-89; retired, 1990. Contbr. articles on bus. edn. to profl. publs. Named Outstanding Tchr. Lumpkin County Pub. Schs., 1963, 66; Outstanding Educator bus. faculty Ga. Coll., 1975, Exec. of Yr. award, 1983. Fellow Assn. for Bus. Communication (v.p. S.E. 1978-80, 81-84, 89-92, bd. dirs.), Nat. Bus. Edn. Assn., Ga. Bus. Edn. Assn. (Postsecondary Tchr. of Yr. award 10th dist. 1983, Postsecondary Tchr. of Yr. award 1984), Am. Vocat. Assn., Ga. Vocat. Assn. (Educator of Yr. award 1984, Parker Liles award 1989), Profl. Secs. Internat. (pres. Milledgeville chpt. 1996-97), Ninety-nines Internat.. (chmn. N. Ga. chpt. 1975-76, named Pilot of Yr. N. Ga. chpt. 1973). Methodist. Home: 1674 Pine Valley Rd Milledgeville GA 31061-2465

ENGFER, SUSAN MARVEL, zoological park executive; b. Mpls., Dec. 6, 1943; d. Frederick Paul and Dorothy M. Engfer. BS, Albion Coll., 1965; MS, U. Wyo., 1968; postgrad., U. Calif., Santa Barbara, 1975-76; dipl., Sch. Profl. Mgmt. Devel. for Zoo and Aquarium Pers., 1981. Ranger, naturalist Grand Teton Nat. Park, Moose, Wyo., 1967; cancer rsch. technician U. Calif., Santa Barbara, 1967-68; zoo keeper Santa Barbara Zool. Gardens, 1968-70, edn. curator, 1970-72, asst. dir., 1972-88; pres., CEO Cheyenne Mountain Zool. Park, Colorado Springs, Colo., 1988—. Cons. oiled bird rehab. Union Oil and Standard Oil Co., 1968-70; master plan cons. Moorpark (Calif.) Coll., 1986-88; instr., bd. regents Sch. Profl. Mgmt. Devel. Zoo and Aquarium Pers., Wheeling, W.V., 1984-87. Author: North American Regional Studbook, Asian Small-Clawed Otter (Aonyx cinerea), 1987—. Fellow Am. Assn. Zool. Pks. and Aquariums (profl., bd. dirs. 1987-90, mem. accreditation commn. 1990—, chmn. accreditation commn. 1994-95); mem. Internat. Union Dirs. Zool. Gardens, Internat. Union Conservation of Nature and Natural Resources (mem. otter specialist group), Soc. Conservation Biology, Colo. Women's Forum, Rotary. Office: Cheyenne Mountain Zool Pk 4250 Cheyenne Mountain Zoo Rd Colorado Springs CO 80906-5755

ENGLAND, JULIE SPICER, computer company executive; BS in Chem. Engring., Tex. Tech. U., 1979. First line engr. Tex. Instruments, sr. mem. tech. staff, quality mgr. Semiconductor Group, v.p. Semiconductor Group; bus. mgr. Computer and Imaging Sys. Tex. Instruments Worldwide Application Specific ProductsUnit. Bd. dirs. Fed. Res. Bank, Dallas. Recipient Women of Achievement award Richardson Tex. YWCA, Hall of Fame award Women in Tech. Internat. Mem. IEEE (sr.), Soc. Women Engrs. (life), Dallas C. of C. (mem. exec. women's roundtable), Dallas Women's Found. (circle of honor award). Office: Tex Instruments Inc 8505 Forest Ln Dallas TX 75243-4136 Fax: 972-995-4360.

ENGLAND, LYNNE LIPTON, lawyer, speech pathologist, audiologist; b. Youngstown, Ohio, Apr. 11, 1949; d. Sanford Y. and Sally (Kentor) Lipton; m. Richard E. England, Mar. 5, 1977. BA, U. Mich., 1970; MA, Temple U., 1972; JD, Tulane U., 1981. Bar: Fla. 1982, U.S. Dist. Ct. (mid. dist.) Fla. 1982, U.S. Ct. Appeals (11th cir.) 1982; cert. clin. competence in speech pathology and audiology. Speech pathologist Rockland Children's Hosp., N.Y., 1972-74, Jefferson Parish Sch., Gretna, La., 1977-81; audiologist Rehab. Inst. Chgo., 1974-76; assoc. Trenam, Simmons, Kemker, Scharf, Barkin, Frye & O'Neill, Tampa, Fla., 1981-84; asst. U.S. atty. for Middle Dist. Fla. Tampa, 1984-87; asst. U.S. trustee, 1987-91; ptnr. Stearns, Weaver, Miller, Weissler, Alhadeff & Sitterson, P.A., 1991-94, Prevatt, England & Taylor, Tampa, Fla., 1994-99; pvt. practice Brandon, Fla., 1999—. Editor Fla. Bankruptcy Casenotes, 1983. Recipient clin. assistantship Temple U., 1972-74. Mem. ATLA, Comml. Law League, Am. Speech and Hearing Assn., Tampa Bay Bankruptcy Bar Assn. (dir. 1990-95), Am. Bankruptcy Inst., Fla. Bar Assn., Hillsborough County Bar Assn., Order of Coif. Jewish. Avocations: tennis, golf, playing french horn and piano. Office: 1463 Oakfield Dr Ste 125 Brandon FL 33511-0802

ENGLE, CAROLE RUTH, aquaculture economics educator; b. Harrisburg, Pa., July 7, 1952; d. Morris Mumma Engle and Mildred Evelyn (Orris) Wambold; m. Nathan Mayhew Stone, May 30, 1981; children: Reina, Eric, Cody. BA, Friends World Coll., 1975; MS, Auburn U., 1978, PhD, 1981. Vis. prof. U. Centroamericana, Managua, Nicaragua, 1981-83; fisheries economist Inter-Am. Devel. Bank, Santiago, Panama, 1984-85; asst. prof. econs. Auburn U., Montgomery, Ala., 1985-88; assoc. prof. aquaculture econs. U. Ark., Pine Bluff, 1988-94, prof., 1994—; dir., Aquacultural Fisheries Ctr., U. Ark., Pine Bluff, 1989—. Aquaculture coord. U. Ark., Pine Bluff, 1989—; cons. FAO, Rome, 1986, 88. Contbr. articles to profl. jours.; editor conf. proceedings. Mem. World Aquaculture Soc., Am.

Fisheries Soc., Am. Assn. Agriculture Econs., So. Agriculture Econs. Assn., Ark. Acad. Scis. Avocations: gardening, reading, swimming. Office: U Ark PO Box 108 1200 University Dr Pine Bluff AR 71601-2799

ENGLE, CYNTHIA LOUISE, art educator; b. Hannibal, Mo., May 17, 1952; d. Charles Robert and Betty Lou Hayes; m. Hugh Blanton Engle, June 29, 1974 (div. Jan. 15, 1987); children: John Robert, Jacob Blanton. BS in Edn., Truman U., 1974; M in Curriculum and Instrn., Cen. Mo. State U., 2000. Tchr. art K12, English 7-10 Madison (Mo.) Sch. Dist., 1975—76; tchr. art K-12, English 7-9 Chilhowee (Mo.) Sch. Dist., 1987—98; art tchr. 9-12 Knob Noster (Mo.) Sch. Dist., 1998—. Mem.: Mo. Art Educators Assn., Nat. Art Educators' Assn. Avocations: creating works of art, working out, gardening, travel. Home: 304 E Benton Windsor MO 65360 Office: Knob Noster HS 504 S Washington St Knob Noster MO 65336

ENGLE, JEANNETTE CRANFILL, medical technologist; b. Davie County, N.C., July 7, 1941; d. Gurney Nathaniel and Versie Emmaline (Reavis) Cranfill; m. William Sherman Engle (div. 1970); children: Phillip William, Lisa Kaye. Diploma, Dell Sch. Med. Tech., 1960; BA, U. N.C., Asheville, 1976; MS in Biomed. Sci.-Genetics, Marshall U., 1999. Instr. Dell Sch. Med. Tech., Asheville, 1960-67; rotating technologist Meml. Mission Hosp., Asheville, 1967-68, asst. supr. hematology, 1968-71; supr. Damon Subs. Pvt. Clinic Lab., Asheville, 1971-73; chemistry technologist VA Med. Ctr., Durham, N.C., 1973-74, 75-76, supr., 1974-75, asst. supr. microbiology Salem, Va., 1976-79; supr. rsch. Med. Svc. Lab., Salem, 1979-90; flow cytometrist VA Med. Ctr., Huntington, W.Va., 1990-92, cons. to clin. lab. flow cytometry dept., 1992—. Reviewer Jour. Club, Roanoke-Salem, Va., 1980-90. Author: (poem) Reflections on a Comet, 1984; contbr. numerous articles and abstracts on med. tech. to profl. jours., 1982—. Mem. The Acting Co. Ensemble. Democrat. Episcopalian. Avocations: reading, flower arranging, interior design, art, music. Home: 4775 Green Valley Rd Huntington WV 25701-9793 E-mail: jeaengle@aol.com.

ENGLE, KATHLEEN FAYE, elementary education educator; b. Rapid City, S.D., July 8, 1958; d. Frank Denton and Marie Lucille (Coffield) Packard; m. Steven S. Engle, June 1, 1984; children: Kirstin Marie, Kalin Kathleen. BS in Edn., Black Hill State Coll., 1980. Tchr. physical edn. Campbell County Sch. Dist., Gillette, Wyo., 1980-84, Weston County Sch. Dist., Newcastle, Wyo., 1985—. Mem. evaluatin team Conestiga Rep., Gillette, 1982-83; mem. adv. team Newcastle Mid. Sch., 1981—, evaluation team, 1992—. Middle Sch. Physical Edn. Teacher or the Year, Nat. Assn. for Sport & Phys. Edn., 1995. Mem. Wyo. Edn. Assn., Wyo. Alliance Physical Edn. Health Recreation and Dance, Wyo. Coaching Assn., Newcastle Edn. Assn., Delta Kappa Gamma. Avocations: aerobics instr., weightlifting, family. Office: Newcastle Mid Sch 116 Casper Ave Newcastle WY 82701-2705

ENGLE, MARY ALLEN ENGLISH, physician; b. Madill, Okla., Jan. 26, 1922; d. Russell C. and Vera (Apperson) English; m. Ralph Landis Engle, Jr., June 7, 1945 (dec. Oct. 2000); children: Ralph Landis III (dec.), Marilyn Elizabeth. AB cum laude, Baylor U., 1942; MD, Johns Hopkins U., 1945; D.Sc. (hon.), Iona Coll., 1982. Diplomate: in pediatric cardiology Am. Bd. Pediatrics. Intern pediatrics Johns Hopkins Hosp., 1945-46, asst. dir. pediatrics out-patient dept., 1946-47, fellow pediatric cardiology, 1947-48; instr. pediatrics Johns Hopkins U., 1946-48; asst. resident Sydenham Hosp. Contagious Diseases, Balt., 1946, N.Y. Hosp., 1948-49, asst. attending pediatrician, 1952-60, assoc. attending pediatrician, 1960-62, attending pediatrician, 1962-92, hon. staff, 1992—; fellow in pediatrics Cornell U., N.Y.C., 1949-50, mem. faculty, 1950-92, prof., 1969-92, prof. emeritus, 1992—, Stavros S. Niarchos prof. pediatric cardiology, 1979-92, emeritus, 1992—. Med. dir. Insts. in Care Premature Infant, 1952-55, dir. pediatric cardiology, 1963-92. Recipient Spence-Chapin award for contbns. to pediatrics, 1958, award of merit Philoptochos Soc. N. and S. Am., 1978, Woman of Conscience award Nat. Council Women, 1979, citation Nat. Bd. Med. Coll. Pa., 1979, Disting. Achievement award Baylor U., 1981, Disting. Alumna award Baylor U., 1988, Maurice Greenberg Disting. Svc. award N.Y. Hosp.-Cornell Med. Ctr., 1991; hon. fellow Cornell U. Med. Coll. Alumni, 1984; Mary Allen Engle Div. Pediatric Cardiology, N.Y. Hosp.-Cornell U. Med. Coll. dedicated in her honor, 1992, Johns Hopkins U. Soc. Scholars award, 1992, Alumni Assoc. Detlev Bronk award, 1993, Disting. Alumna award, 2002. Mem. Am. Acad. Pediat. (charter mem. sect. cardiology, Founder's award cardiology sect. 1983), Am. Clin. and Climatological Assn. (recorder 1992-2000, pres. 2003-04), Am. Heart Assn. (bd. dirs. 1975-78, award of merit 1975, Helen B. Taussig award 1976), N.Y. Heart Assn. (bd. dirs. 1980-86), N.Y. Acad. Medicine, N.E. Pediatric Cardiology Soc., Harvey Soc., Soc. Pediatric Rsch., Assn. European Pediatric Cardiologists (corr.), Royal Soc. Medicine (bd. dirs. Found. 1983-92, hon. bd. dirs. 1992-2000), Am. Coll. Cardiology (master tchr. 1969, 73, 76, trustee 1974-79, bd. govs. 1990-94, pres. N.Y. State chpt. 1991-92, Theodore and Susan Cummings Humanitarian award 1973, 76), Am. Pediatric Soc., Pediatric Cardiology Soc. Greater N.Y., N.Y. Cardiology Soc. (bd. dirs., pres. 1986-87), Soc. Scholars, Phi Beta Kappa, Alpha Omega Alpha. Presbyterian. Home: 2451 Brickell Ave Ph A Miami FL 33129-2472 also: 27213 Baileys Neck Rd Easton MD 21601-8503

ENGLE, MARY ELIZABETH, dietician, educator; b. Nowata, Okla., July 28, 1914; d. Charles Levi and Vena Ethel Engle. BS, So. Mo. State U., 1934; MS in Instn. Mgmt., Kans. State U., 1945; postgrad., Iowa State U., 1939, 40, 48, U. Wis., 1965-66. Tchr. home econs. Forsyth (Mo.) H.S., 1934-38; tchr. vocat. home econs. Richland (Mo.) H.S., 1938-43, Aurora (Mo.) H.S., 1943-44; grad. asst. instn. mgmt. Kans. State U., Manhattan, 1944-45, U. Wis., Madison, 1965-66; assoc. prof. Ctrl. Mo. State U., Darrensburg, 1967-80. Mem. NEA, AAUW (pres.), Mo. Tchrs. Assn., Delta Kappa Gamma, Sigma Kappa, Kappa Omicron Phi. Methodist. Avocations: bridge, travel, cooking. Home: 37 Timberline Dr Warrensburg MO 64093-2906

ENGLE, MOLLY, program evaluator, preventive medicine researcher, medical educator; b. Ft. Leavenworth, Kans., Apr. 12, 1947; d. Robert Thomas and Phyllis Adele (Germann) E. BSN, U. Ariz., 1971, MS, 1973, PhD, 1983. RN, Ariz. Rsch. assoc. U. Ariz., Tucson, 1979-82; program assoc. Am. Coll. Testing, Iowa City, 1982-84; instr. Sch. Medicine U. Ala., Birmingham, 1984-87, asst. prof. Sch. Medicine, 1987-94; dir. rsch. and evaluation Health East, Mpls., 1992-93; assoc. prof. dept. medicine Sch. Medicine U. Ala., Birmingham, 1994-98; assoc. prof. extension svc., dept. pub. health Oreg. State U., Corvallis, 1998—. Co-dir. Geriat. Edn. Ctr., U. Ala., Birmingham, 1990-91; evaluation cons. Am. Soc. Aging, San Francisco, 1990-94, USPHS Health Resources and Svcs. Adminstrn., Bur. of Health Professions, Rockville, Md., 1996-98; cons. health svcs. rsch. and evaluation HealthEast, 1993-94. Prodr. (video series) Substance Abuse and the Pregnant Woman: A Series, 1994. Co-chair Adam Elem. Sch. Parent Tchr., Corvallis, 1999—2001. Recipient fellowship NIMH, 1972-73, fellowship Health Scis. Consortium, 1989, Postdoctoral fellowship Gerontol. Soc. Am., 1990. Mem.: Am. Evaluation Assn. (health topical interest group program chair 1986—2001, bd. dirs. 1992—94, pres.-elect 2001, pres. 2002—03, sec. 2003, health topical intreest group program chair 2004, Svc. Recognition award 1994). Avocations: reading, travel, violin. Office: Oreg State U Extension Svc 307 Ballard Extension Hall Corvallis OR 97331-8538

ENGLEHART, JOAN ANNE, consultant; b. Susquehanna, Pa., Sept. 15, 1940; d. George Louis and Muriel Elois (Washburn) Wanatt; m. Dale John Englehart, Nov. 24, 1958. AAS, Broome C.C., 1981; BS in Cultural Studies, Empire State Coll., 1984; postgrad., SUNY, Binghamton, 1984; PhD in Bus. Adminstrn., Century U., 1994. Office mgr., coord. sales Bush Transformer Corp., Endicott (N.Y.), Boston, 1959-65; mgr., cons. Snelling & Snelling, Binghamton, Endicott, 1965-71; mgr., tchr. Can. Acad., Kobe, Japan, 1971-72; owner Typewriting, Endicott, 1980-85; exec. v.p. Tioga County C. of C., Owego, N.Y., 1985-87, pres., 1988-99; exec. v.p. Chamber Found., 1987-99. Cons. specializing in non-profit orgns., 1999—. Mem. scholarship com. Civic Club Binghamton, 1984-87; adv. bd. Broome and Tioga County Health Fairs, 1985-87; sec.-treas. Tioga County C. of C. Found., 1987-99, chmn. sustaining membership com. Broome United Way, Binghamton, 1986-87; planning process com. Broome-Delaware-Tioga BOCES vocat. edn. coms., 1989, 92; bd. dirs. NYPENN Health Sys. Agy., 1989-91, Pvt. Industry Coun., 1994-99, Sch. to Careers, 1997-98, Tioga County Rural Ministry, 1992-97, chmn., 1993-97; pres. Tioga County divsn. Am. Heart Assn., 1994-99; active Tioga County Tourism Coun., 1994-99, County Comprehensive Plan, 1994-97; v.p. Tioga County Revitalization Task Force, 1997-98; adv. com. So. Tier Rail, 1997; active Binghamton Met. Transp. Study, 1997; media and pub. rels. specialist So. Tier chpt. Alzheimer's Assn., 1999-2000; pub. rels. coord. So. Tier SeniorNet, 2002-2003, ch. coun. v.p and pub. rels. coord., Holy Nativity Luth. Ch., 2003-. Recipient award Boy Scouts Am., 1979, Evening Student Assn., 1991, Friends Binghamton Libr., 1982, ATHENA award C. of C., 1986; named Woman of Achievement Broome County Status of Women Coun., 1978. Mem. AAUW (life, pres. 1986-87), So. Tier World Commerce Assn. (bd. dirs. 1992-99), Nat. Assn. Women in C. of C.'s (charter mem., Nat. Achievement award 1993, com. chmn. 1994-96), Am. C. of C. Execs., N.Y. State C. of C. Execs. (bd. dirs. 1991), Zonta (pres. Tioga County area club 1985-89, mem. internat. bd. dirs., gov. dist. II 1982-84, Woman of Achievement 1985-88). Republican. Lutheran. Avocations: reading, interior design, music, photography, sports car activities. Home and Office: 4 Lancaster Dr Endicott NY 13760-4320 E-mail: jenglehar@stny.rr.com.

ENGLEMAN, ELLEN G. federal agency administrator; BA in Eng. and Comm., Ind. U., 1983, JD, 1987; MPA, Harvard U., 1993. Bar: Ind. 1987, U.S. Dist. Ct. (no. and so. dists.) 1987. Pub. affairs exec. GTE, 1987—92; pres., CEO Electricore, Ind., 1994—2001; adminstr. rsch. and spl. programs adminstrn. U.S. Dept. Transp., Washington, 2001—03; mem., chmn. Nat. Transp. Safety Bd. (NTSB), Washington, 2003—. Dir. Corporate & Govt. Affairs, Direct Relief Internat., 1993—94. Bd. dirs. Direct Relief Internat., dir. corp. & govt. affairs. With USNR, 2000. Mem.: Pub. Rels. Soc. Am. (cert. pub. rels.). Office: NTSB Headquarters 490 L'Enfant Plaza SW Washington DC 20594

ENGLER, EVA KAY, dental and veterinary products company executive; b. Czechoslovakia, May 7, 1927; m. Alfred Engler (dec. 1979); children: Raya, Michael David. Pres., founder med. and dental mfg. co. Engler Engrng. Corp., Hialeah, Fla., 1964—. Avocations: languages, painting. Office: Engler Engrng Corp 1099 E 47th St Hialeah FL 33013-2139 Fax: 305-685-7671.

ENGLER, RENATA JOHANNA MARTHA, allergist, immunologist, internist, educator; b. Frankfurt, Germany, 1949; MD, Georgetown U., 1975. Diplomate Am. Bd. Internal Medicine, Am. Bd. Allergy and Immunology (bd. dirs.). Intern Nat. Naval Med. Ctr., Bethesda, Md., 1975-76, resident in internal medicine, 1978-80; fellow in allergy and immunology Walter Reed Army Med. Ctr., Washington, 1980-82, mem. staff, 1982—, chief allergy & immunization svcs. Assoc. prof. Uniformed Svcs. U. Health Sci., Bethesda. Mem. ACP, Am. Acad. Allergy and Immunology, Am. Coll. Allergy, Am. Fedn. Clin. Rsch. Home: 1900 Wallace Ave Silver Spring MD 20902-1302 Office: Sair Hosp and Clinic Allergy-Immunology Dept Walter Reed Army Med Ctr Washington DC 20307-0001

ENGLERT, HELEN WIGGS, writer; b. Nashville, June 1, 1927; d. Lawrence Raymond and Frances Eloise (Smith) Wiggs; m. Roy Theodore Englert Sr., Sept. 25, 1948; children: Lee Ann Englert Regan, Roy Theodore Jr. AA, Ward Belmont Coll., Nashville, 1948; AB, George Washington U., Washington, 1954, postgrad., 1969-71. Lectr. Weight Watchers, Washington & Va., 1972-84. Author: Hey, Wait a Minute! Dealing with Feelings and Weight Control, 1992, We Hold These Values...What is Uniquely American about Being an American, 2002. Elder Old Presbyn. Meeting House, Alexandria, Va., 1982—; bd. mem. Sr. Citizens Employment & Svcs. Inc., Alexandria, 1994-97. Mem. George Washington U. Club, Campagna Ctr. (Alexandria), Nat. Mus. Women in Arts, Phi Theta Kappa. Avocations: walking, travel, tennis, grandchild, geneology. Home: 12183 Cathedral Dr Woodbridge VA 22192-2227

ENGLERT, PHYLLIS ANN, psychology educator; b. Richmond, Calif., Oct. 15, 1961; d. Donald Carmen and Lenora Marie (Cardoza) McCrocklin; m. Paul Michael Englert, Mar. 20, 1985; children: Ryan Paul, Margarete Aislim. BA, U. Va., 1982; MA, U. Calif., Riverside, 1987, PhD, 1993. Mktg. coord. Am. Assn. Med. Transcription, Modesto, Calif., 1983-84; rsch. asst. U. Calif., Riverside, 1984-87, teaching asst., 1985-88; instr. Whittier (Calif.) Coll., 1989, Calif. State U., Fullerton, 1990, Chaffey Coll., Alta Loma, Calif., 1994—. Mem. Ontario (Calif.) PTA, 1994-95. Mem. AAUW (corr. sec. 1988-90), Am. Psychol. Assn., Western Psychol. Assn., Phi Beta Kappa. Avocations: gardening, swimming. Home: PO Box 182 Cedar Glen CA 92321-0182 Office: Calif State Poly U 3801 W Temple Ave Pomona CA 91768

ENGLISH, EVONNE KLUDAS, artist; b. Cherokee, Iowa, Dec. 31, 1934; d. Earl Philip and Ruby Jacqueline (Whiting) Kludas; m. John Cammel English, July 29, 1966. BFA, Drake U., 1957; postgrad., U. No. Iowa, 1958—59; MFA, U. Iowa, 1962. Instr. h.s. & jr. h.s. art Sycamore Cmty. Unit Sch. Dist. 427, Sycamore, Ill., 1959-61; instr. art Wis. State U., Whitewater, 1962-63; asst. prof. art Stephen F. Austin State U., Nacogdoches, Tex., 1963-66. Instr. adult edn. Lawrence (Kans.) Arts Ctr., 1976; presenter in field. One woman shows include Sanford Mus., Cherokee, 1958, Cmty. Ctr., Cherokee, 1966, Baker U., Baldwin, Kans., 1971, 76, 7 East 7th Gallery, Lawrence, 1975-79, Unitarian Gallery, Kansas City, Mo., 1980, Kansas City Kans. Pub. Libr., 1984, Kans. U. Med. Ctr. Gallery of Art, Kansas City, Kansas, 1986, Lawrence Pub. Libr., 1986, 91, Baldwin State Bank, 1988, Lawrence C. of C., 1988, Galesburg (Ill.) Civic Art Ctr., 1988, Park Coll., Parkville, Mo., 1991, Sta. KSHB-TV, Kansas City, Mo., 1993, Art Affair, Baldwin, 1997; group exhbts. include Santa Fe Connection, Kansas City, 1979, Baker U., 1980, Kansas City Kansas Pub. Libr., 1995, Iowa Art Salon, 1957-59, 61-62, 65, Gallery Arkep, N.Y.C., 1965, George Walter Vincent Smith Art Mus., Springfield, Mass., 1965, Soc. Am. Graphic Artists, 1966, Galesburg Civic Art Ctr., 1983, Lawrence Arts Ctr., 1983, 97, Carrier Fine Arts Show, Belle Mead, N.J., 1984-85, 88, 90, 92, Gallery Lawrence, 1986, Hays (Kans.) Arts Coun., 1990, Hunterdon Art Ctr., Clinton, N.J., 1991, Wis. State U., Whitewater, 1962, Park Ctrl. Gallery, Springfield, Mo., 1976, Crown Ctr., Kansas City, Mo., 1979, Kellas Gallery, Lawrence, 1980-82, 84, Santa Fe Depot Ctr., 1985, Baldwin City Pub. Libr., 1993-95, Art Affair, Baldwin, 1996-98, 2002-03, Carnegie Ctr. for Arts, Dodge City, Kans., 2001, Carnegie Bldg., Lawrence, Kans., 2002, others; represented in permanent collections at Baker U., Baldwin, Spencer Mus. Art, U. Kans., others; designer bicentennial plate Baldwin City ofcl. seal, 1976. Panelist Spencer Mus. Art, Lawrence, 1978. Grantee State Wis. Bd. Regents State Colls., 1963, Lawrence Lithography Workshop 1988; recipient award Atchison Art Assn., 1997. Mem. AAUW (sec. Baldwin chpt. 1977-79, hospitality chair 1985—), Kansas City Artists Coalition, Baldwin Cmty. Arts Coun. (sec. 1988-90, exhibit com. chair 1988-90), Delta Phi Delta. Unitarian Universalist. Avocation: photography. Studio: PO Box 537 Baldwin City KS 66006-0537

ENGLISH, LAUREN JACKSON, media specialist, secondary school educator; EdM, Ga. Coll. and State U., 1999. Cert. media specialist Ga. Profl. Stds. Commn., French tchr. Ga. Profl. Stds. Commn. French tchr. Monroe County Bd. Edn., Forsyth, Ga., 1991—99, media specialist, 1999—. Merit badge counselor Boy Scouts Am., Forsyth, 1997—2003; vacation Bible sch. dir. Forsyth United Meth. Ch., 2001—03. Named Tchr. of the Yr., Peer Tchrs., 2000—01. Mem.: Geogia Libr. Assn. (assoc.), PA of Ga. Educators (assoc.), Alpha Chi Omega (life; treas. 1983—85). Avocations: reading, travel.

ENGLISH, MARLENE CABRAL, management consultant; b. Lawrence, Mass., Apr. 28, 1954; d. Amick John and Mary Rose (Vasconcelos) Cabral; m. Richard Gayle English, June 24, 1978. BBA, U. Mass., 1976. Acct. mgr. Revlon, Inc., N.Y.C., 1977-79; tech. rep. Rapidata, Inc., N.Y.C., 1979-80; mgr.acctg. systems group Pannell, Kerr, Forster, Dallas, 1980-83; mgmt. cons. Blythe/Nelson, Dallas, 1983-84, Prism Cons., Arlington, Tex., 1984—. Sec., treas. Highland-Avery Industries, Inc., Dallas, 1988-95. Author: And God Created Woman, 1995. Tech. systems procurement & installation Rep. Nat. Conv., Dallas, 1984; dir. Faith Harvest Ministries, Inc., Dallas, 1990-95; sys. cons. Van Cliburn Internat. Piano Competition, Ft. Worth, 1985. Roman Catholic. Avocations: Victorian studies, antique linen restoration, gardening, Christian writing, classical piano. Home and Office: Prism Cons 4320 Rambling Creek Dr Arlington TX 76016-3418 E-mail: jicky@sbcglobal.net.

ENGLISH, MICHELA, entertainment company executive; married; 2 children. BA in Internat. Affairs, Sweet Briar Coll.; M Pub. and Pvt. Mgmt., Yale U. Policy analyst Fed. Energy Adminstrn.; sr. mgr. McKinsey & Co.; v.p. corp. planning and bus. devel. Marriott Corp.; sr. v.p. Nat. Geog. Soc.; pres. Discovery.com, Bethesda, Md. Bd. dirs. Riggs Nat. Corp., Washington; cons. in field. Bd. dirs. Sweet Briar (Va.) Coll. Mem. Nat. Found. for Improvement of Edn. (bd. dirs.). Office: Discovery.com 7700 Wisconsin Ave Fl 5 Bethesda MD 20814-3557 Fax: 301-986-4826.

ENGLISH, MILDRED OSWALT, retired nurse supervisor; b. Moberly, Mo., May 28, 1916; d. Oscar and Lulu (Street) Oswalt; m. Deaver English, Apr. 9, 1955. RN, Jewish Hosp. St. Louis Sch. Nursing, 1942; BS, U. N.C., 1952. RN, Tex. Pub. health nurse supr. Mo. Div. Health, Jefferson City, Mo., 1946-56; supervising pub. health nurse L.A. County Health Dept., 1957-67; sch. nurse Bonita Unified Sch. Dist., San Dimas, Calif., 1967-72; quality assurance coord. Moberly (Mo.) Regional Med. ctr., 1973-83; ret., 1983. Cmdr. Nurse Corps, USNR Ret., active duty 1943-46. Home: 1163 Fox Run Cir New Braunfels TX 78130-7200

ENGLISH-ANDERSON, SAN DEI, minister; b. Jacksboro, Tex., Aug. 27, 1945; d. Robert March English and Ressie English; m. Donald Loren Anderson, Dec. 19, 2001; children: Traci Dixon, Tiara Cunningham, Joshua English. AA, Jarvis Christian Coll., Hawkins, Texas, 1965. Minister, assoc. pastor New Creation Outreach, Anaheim, Calif., 2001—02; producer/host Sonic Cable TV, San Luis Obispo, Calif., 1982—86; CEO Tiara Prodns., Mission Viejo, Calif., 1987—2002. V.p. ways & means Laguna Niguel Rep. Women Federated, 2000—01. Served USAF, 1964—65. Named Model of Yr., Foxes and Hares Model Assn., 1967, Ms. Royal Ambassador 2002, Mrs. Orange County Am., 2003. Mem.: Ctr. Stage/ Performing Arts Guild, Phenomenal Women Orgn. (treas.). Avocation: writing, sewing, reading, dancing, meditating. Business E-Mail: strongmeat@cox.net.

ENGLUND, GAGE BUSH, dancer, educator; b. Sept. 7, 1931; d. Morris Williams and Margaret Wallace (Gage) Bush; m. Richard Bernard Englund, Dec. 1, 1959; children: Alixandra Gage, Rachel Rutherford. Student, Sch. Am. Ballet, 1960. Founder Birmingham Civic Ballet, 1952; mem. Robert Joffrey Ballet, N.Y.C., 1957-60, soloist, 1959-60; mem. Am. Ballet Theatre, N.Y.C., 1960-63, Huntington Dance Ensemble, L.I., N.Y., 1968-69; soloist Dance Repertory Co., 1969-72; tchr. ballet, assoc. chmn. Friends of Am. Ballet Theatre, N.Y.C., 1972—. Dir. Ala. By-Products Corp., 1971—77; rehearsal coach Am. Ballet Theatre II, 1973—85; mem. scholarship com. Am. Ballet Theatre Sch., N.Y.C., 1974—; rehearsal coach Joffrey Ballet II, 1985—95, Am. Ballet Theatre Studio Co., 1995—. Trustee Ballet Theatre Found., 1974—87, v.p., 1980—81; trustee Chapin Sch., 1982—2003, Animal Med. Ctr., N.Y.C., 1982—, Cancer Rsch. Inst., 1984—, Episcpoal Sch. N.Y., 1979—83; bd. dirs. Children's Hosp. Clinic, Birmingham, 1955—57, Spoleto Festival, U.S.A., 1980—83, Ala. State Ballet, 1967—, Birmingham Civic Ballet, 1952—67. Named Queen, Birmingham Festival Arts, 1957; recipient Silver Bowl award, 1957, Lucia Chase award for svcs. to Am. Ballet Theatre, Soc. Fine Arts U. Ala., 2001, Patron of the Arts award, 2002; scholar Ford Found., 1960. Mem.: Am. Guild Mus. Artists, Jr. League N.Y.C., Colonial Dames Ala., Colony Club, Lakewood Country Club. Episcopalian. Home: PO Box 469 17367 Scenic Hwy 98 Point Clear AL 36564

ENGSTROM, STEPHANIE CLOES, wildlife artist, small business owner; b. L.A., Nov. 1, 1943; d. John Augustus Cloes and Margaret Virginia Gerlach; m. Jean-Claude Louis Engstrom, Sept. 1, 1962 (div. 1967); children: Dominique Yvette Lubow, Denise Collette Engstrom. Student, UCLA, U. Md., USDA Grad. Sch. licensee MMDS. Adminstrv. mgr. Microband Corp. Am., Washington, 1972-74; sr. mgmt. cons. various, 1976—; licensee Microwave MMDS, various, 1983—. Tchr. Fairfax County Adult Edn., Vienna, Va., 1991-92, creativity workshop Guild Natural Sci. Illustrators Internat. Conf., Evora U., Portugal, 2000, Coll. of the Atlantic, Bar Harbor, Maine, 2001, Palos Verdes (Calif.) Art Ctr., 2001—, Univ. of Kans., Lawrence, 2002; cofacilitator Artist's Way Sems. Borders Books & Music, Torrance, Calif., 1998; workshop tchr. in field. Cover artist: (book) International Studbook, Cheetah, Acinonyx jubatus, 1988; artist, writer Endangered Species Note Cards, 1986-90, Internat. Wildlife Rancher, 1989; juried group show Palos Verdes Art Ctr., 2000, 01, 02, 03, 04 (People's Choice award 2000); solo show, The Distinctive Edge, 2001. Pres. PTA, Hermosa Beach, Calif., 1971-72; vol. Smithsonian, Washington, 1982-94; keeper aide Nat. Zool. Pk., Washington, 1985-90. Mem. Guild Nat. Sci. Illustrators (artist, writer newsletter 1988-89, 99—, pres. So. Calif. chpt. 2000-02, v.p. 2003), Artists Open Group Palos Verdes Art Ctr (v.p., 2003—). Avocations: amateur naturalist, amateur animal behaviorist, writing poetry. Home and Office: 500 Avenue G Apt 25 Redondo Beach CA 90277-6002 Office Phone: 310-540-9867.

ENGVALL, EVA, biochemist; b. Stockholm, Mar. 11, 1940; BSc, U. Stockholm, 1964, PhD in Immunology, 1975. Rsch. assoc. biochemistry Rsch. Lab. LKB, Stockholm, 1965-66, KABI AB, Stockholm, 1966-69; jr. rsch. sci. immunology U. Stockholm, 1969-75; fellow immunology U. Helsinki, 1975-76; fellow City Hope Med. Ctr., 1976-77, asst. rsch. sci. immunology, 1977-79; fellow European Molecular Biol. Orgn., 1975-77; scientist La Jolla (Calif.) Cancer Rsch. Found., 1979-96, Burnham Inst., La Jolla, 1996—. Recipient Biochemical Analysis award Ger. Soc. Clin. Chemistry 1976, Scientific Achievement award Edmund & Mary Shea Family Found., 1994. Mem. Am. Assn. Cancer Rsch., Am. Assn. Immunologists. Achievements include research in molecular interactions of extracellular matrix components. Office: Burnham Inst 10901 N Torrey Pines Rd La Jolla CA 92037-1062

ENLOE, LORAINE ALEXANDER DAVIS, music educator; b. Owensboro, Ky., Aug. 17, 1954; d. Howell Jeffries Davis and Evelyn Nell Winfries; m. Ben L. Clark, May 19, 1978 (div. May 12, 1979); m. Joe B. Enloe, Jr., Mar. 22, 1985. BA in Music Performance and Music Edn., Transylvania U., Lexington, Ky., 1976; MusM in Music Edn., U. N.C., Greensboro, 2002. Cert. travel cons., lic. tchr. K-12 music. Dir. bands W. Hardin HS, Stephensburg, Ky., 1976—78, Chatham Ctrl. HS, Bear Creek, NC, 2002—; travel agent, 1979—99; owner Dunfaire, Inc., 1999—2003. Woodwind tchr., Siler City, NC, 2000—; profl. woodwind player, 2000—; woodwind clinician, 2000—. Dir. instrumental music 1st Bapt. Ch., Siler City, 1997—. Recipient Disting. Sales award, Sales and Mktg. Execs., 1986. Mem.: Nat. Assn. Coll. Winds and Percussions Instrs., Coll. Music Soc., Music Educators Nat. Conf. Republican. Avocations: dressage, yachting, golf. Home: 1660 Coleridge Rd Siler City NC 27344 Office: Chatham Ctrl HS 14950 NC Hwy 902 Bear Creek NC 27207 Office Phone: 336-558-4130. Personal E-mail: lenloe@direcway.com.

ENNIS, JILL ANN, medical/surgical nurse, educator; b. Morgantown, W.Va., Feb. 3, 1970; d. Noah Perry and Marie Louise Fletcher; m. Donald Allen Ennis, July 11, 1997; children: Donald Jr., Christopher; children from previous marriage: Andrew Lovejoy, Courtney Lovejoy, Kasey Lovejoy. BSN, Marshall U., 1984; postgrad., Frontier Sch. Midwifery and Family Nursing. RN W.Va.; cert. vocat. edn. tchr. W.Va., PALS Am. Heart Assn., basic life support Am. Heart Assn. RN Charleston (W.Va.) Area Med. Ctr., 1994—95, 1996—97, 2000—03; clin. assessment coord. Riverside Nursing and Rehab. Ctr., St. Albans, W.Va., 1995—96; home health staff nurse Kanawha Charleston Health Dept., 1997—98; dir. nursing Valley Health Village, South Charleston, W.Va., 1998, Quarry Manor Personal Care Home, Charleston, 1998—2000; practical nursing instr. Kanawha County Schs., Charleston, 2000—. Facilitator Insvc., Cultural and Religion Edn. Day. Mem.: Kanawha Fedn. Tchrs., Assn. Career and Tech. Edn., Am. Coll. Nurse Midwives, Nat. Assn. Childbearing Ctrs. Democrat. Avocations: reading, walking, computers. Home: 36 Lee Dr Saint Albans WV 25177

ENOS, KELLY D. telecommunications company financial executive; V.p. Sutro & Co., 1991-94, Oppenheimer & Co., Inc., 1994-95, Fortune Fin., 1995-96; ind. cons. mcht. banking field, 1996; CFO, Telecom., Inc., Santa Barbara, Calif., 1996—, treas., 1997—. Office: STAR Telecom Inc 223 E De La Guerra St Santa Barbara CA 93101-2206 Fax: 805-899-2972.

ENOS, MINDY See PARSONS, MINDY

ENRIGHT, CYNTHIA LEE, illustrator; b. Denver, July 6, 1950; d. Darrel Lee and Iris Arlene (Flodquist) E. BA in Elem. Edn., U. No. Colo., 1972; student, Minn. Sch. Art and Design, Mpls., 1975-76. Tchr. 3d grade Littleton (Colo.) Sch. Dist., 1972-75; graphics artist Sta. KCNC TV, Denver, 1978-79; illustrator No Coast Graphics, Denver, 1979-87; editorial artist The Denver Post, 1987—. Illustrator (mag.) Sesame St., 1984, 85; illustrator, editor "Tiny Tales" The Denver Post, 1991-94. Recipient Print mag. Regional Design Ann. awards, 1984, 85, 87, Phoenix Art Mus. Biannual award, 1979. Mem. Mensa. Democrat. Home: 1210 Ivanhoe St Denver CO 80220-2640 Office: The Denver Post 1560 Broadway Denver CO 80202-5177 Personal E-mail: leeenright@aol.com.

ENRIQUEZ, CAROLA RUPERT, museum director; b. Washington, Jan. 2, 1954; d. Jack Burns and Shirley Ann (Orcutt) Rupert; m. John Enriquez, Jr., Dec. 30, 1989. BA in History cum laude, Bryn Mawr Coll., 1976; MA, cert. in mus. studies, U. Del., 1978. Pers. mgmt. trainee Naval Material Command, Arlington, Va., 1972-76; tchg. asst. dept. history U. Del., Newark, 1976-77; asst. curator/exhibit specialist Hist. Soc. Del., Wilmington, 1977-78; dir. Macon County Mus. Complex, Decatur, Ill., 1978-81, Kern County Mus., Bakersfield, Calif., 1981—. Pres. Kern County Mus Found., 1991—2002; advisor Kern County Heritage Commn., 1981-88; chmn. Hist. Records Commn., 1981-88; sec.-treas. Arts Coun. of Kern, 1984-86, pres., 1986-88; county co-chmn. United Way, 1981, 82; chmn. steering com. Calif. State Bakersfield Co-op Program, 1982-83; mem. cmty. adv. bd. Calif. State U.-Bakersfield Anthrop. Dept., 1986-88; bd. dirs. Mgmt Coun., 1983-86, v.p., 1987, pres., 1988; bd. dirs. Calif. Coun. for Promotion of History, 1984-86, v.p., 1987-88, pres., 1988-90; mem. cmty. adv. bd. Calif. State U.-Bakersifled Sociology Dept., 1986-88; mem. women's adv. com. Girls Scouts U.S., 1989-91; bd. dirs. Greater Bakersfield Conv. and Visitors Bur., 1993-95; co-chair 34th St. Neighborhood Partnership, 1994—. Hagley fellow Eleutherian Mills-Hagley found., 1977-78; Bryn Mawr alumnae reg. scholar, 1972-76. Mem. Calif. Assn. Mus. (regional rep. 1991—2002, v.p. legis. affairs 1992—2002), Am. Assn. State and Local History (chair awards com. Calif. chpt. 1990, regional vice chair 1999—2002). Presbyterian. Office: Kern County Museum 3801 Chester Ave Bakersfield CA 93301-1345

ENROTH-CUGELL, CHRISTINA ALMA ELISABETH, neurophysiologist, educator; b. Helsingfors, Finland, Aug. 27, 1919; came to US, 1956, naturalized, 1962; d. Emil and Maja (Syren) E.; m. David W. Cugell, Sept. 5, 1955. MD, Karolinska Inst., 1948, PhD, 1952; Hon. Doctors Degree, U. Helsinki, Finland, 1994. Resident Karolinska Sjukhuset, 1949-52; intern Passavant Meml. Hosp., 1956-57; with Northwestern U., Evanston, Ill., 1959-91, prof. emeritus, 1991—, prof. dept. neurobiology and physiology and dept. biomedical engring., 1974—; mem. vision rsch. program com. Nat. Eye Inst., 1974-78, mem. nat. adv. eye coun., 1980-84. Contbr. articles to profl. jour. Recipient Ludwig von Sallman award Internat. Assn. Rsch. in Vision and Ophthalmology, 1982. Fellow Am. Inst. Med. and Biol. Engring., Am. Acad. Arts and Sci.; mem. Am. Assn. Rsch. in Vision and Ophthalmology (co-recipient Friedenwald award 1983, recipient W.H. Helmerich III award 1992), Soc. Neurosis., Am. Physiol. Soc., Physiol. Soc. (U.K.) Office: Northwestern U McCormick Sch Engring Technl Inst 2145 Sheridan Rd Evanston IL 60208-0834 E-mail: enroth@northwestern.edu.

ENSEKI, CAROL, museum director; Deputy dir. N.Y. Brooklyn Children's Mus., dir. programs, dir. exhbn. & collections, exhibit devel., 1989—96, pres., 1997—. Mem.: Assn. Children's Mus., Arts & Bus. Coun., Am. Assn. Mus. Office: Bklyn Children's Mus 145 Bklyn Ave Brooklyn NY 11213

ENSEY, SUZANNE CLINTON GORMAN, volunteer; b. Waco, Tex., Mar. 23, 1922; d. Harry Bernard and Fay Hardeman (Clinton) Gorman; m. John Hanson Ensey, II, Nov. 2, 1946; children: John Hanson, III, Kathleen Gorman. BA, U. Tex., 1942. Cert. tchr., Tex. Sch. newspaper tchr., social studies tchr. Lamar Jr. H.S., Bryan, Tex., 1943-45; responder letters to editor Life Mag., N.Y.C., 1945-46. Pres. Waco Symphony Women's Coun., 1965-66; first lady Dumbarton House, Washington, 1980-82, hon. bd. dirs., 1996; mem. Tex. com. Nat. Mus. Women in Arts, Washington, 1987-89. Named to Roll of Honor Nat. Soc. Colonial Dames Am., 1988. Mem. Woman's Club Waco (pres. 1979-81). Episcopalian. Avocations: music, travel, books, bridge.

ENSLEY, RENNÉ WHITAKER, secondary school educator, artist; b. May 1, 1977; d. DEmpsey Vaughn and Lores McBee Whitaker; m. Steve E. Ensley, May 1, 1977; children: Matthew Whitaker, Tucker Gilbert. BA, Mars Hill Coll., N.C., 1976. Cert. tchr. N.C., 1977. Tchr. Buncombe County Schs., Asheville, NC, 1978—. Office: CA Erwin HS 60 Lees Creek Rd Asheville NC 28806

ENTEEN, VICKI L. public relations executive; b. N.Y.C., Oct. 8, 1946; d. Harry and Pauline Arons; m. Robert Enteen, Dec. 22, 1968; children: Lauren, Alexandra. BFA, Pratt Inst., N.Y.C., 1968; MBA, NYU, 1981. Dir. pub. rels. Footwear Coun., N.Y.C., 1985—86; v.p. Brooks Rogers Pub. Rels., N.Y.C., 1986—89; pres. Enteen & Rosen Pub. Rels., N.Y.C., 1990—91; dir. pub. rels. Laura Ashley N.Am., N.Y.C., 1991—96; v.p. pub. rels. Gilbert Whitney & Johns, Whippany, NJ, 1996—97; dir. pub. rels. Waverly divsn. F. Schumacher, N.Y.C., 1997—99; dir. pub. rels., creative svcs. Stroheim & Romann, N.Y.C., 1999—. Editor (and writer): (book) Shawls of the East from Kashmir to Kerman, 2003; contbr. articles to internat. newsletters. Activist NOW, 1970—; vol. Planned Parenthood, NY, 1981; vol. ESL Lit. Vols. Am, 2002—. Mem.: Internat. Furniture and Design Assn. (bd. dirs. 1994—2003, chpt. advisor 2000—01, pres. 1999, nat. bd. dirs. 2001—03). Avocations: theater, antiques, literature, historic sights, foreign travel. Home: 408 Rutland Ave Teaneck NJ 07666

ENTESSAR, TAHMINEH, political scientist, educator; b. Tehran, June 22, 1953; arrived in U.S., 1972; d. Fatollah and Azar Entessar; m. Robert Beller Weisenfeld, Aug. 18, 1984; 1 child, Aryan Entessar Weisenfeld. BA cum laude, Webster U., 1975; MA, So. Ill. U., Edwardsville, 1977; PhD, St. Louis U., 1983. Tchr. secondary sch. Springboard to Learning, St. Louis, 1978—83; adj. prof. Webster U., St. Louis, 1983—2001, lectr., grad. adviser, 2001—. Guest commentator Sta. KTVI-TV, St. Louis, 1991, World News Report, St. Louis, 1984—97; guest analyst St. Louis Post Dispatch, 1990. Mem.: AAUP, Pi Sigma Alpha. Avocations: classical music, jogging, piano. Office: Webster U 470 E Lockwood Ave Saint Louis MO 63119 E-mail: entessar@webster.edu.

ENTWISLE, DORIS ROBERTS, sociology educator; b. Wilbraham, Mass., Sept. 28, 1924; d. Charles Edwin and Helen (McMenigall) Roberts; m. George Entwisle, Aug. 31, 1946; children: Barbara, Beverly, George H.; m. 2d Donald Roberts, Nov. 12, 1993. BS, U. Mass., 1945; MS, Brown U., 1946; PhD, Johns Hopkins U., 1960. Postdoctoral fellow Social Sci. Research Council Johns Hopkins U., Balt., 1960-61, research assoc. edn. and elec. engring., 1961-64, part-time asst. prof., 1964-67, assoc. prof., 1967-71, prof. sociology and engring. sci., 1971-98, prof. emerita, 1998—2003, rsch. prof., 2003—. Mem. com. on child devel. and pub. policy NRC, 1982-87. Harvard vis. com. for sociology dept., 1986-91. Author: (with S.G. Doering) The First Birth, 1981, (with L.A. Hayduk) Early Schooling, 1982, (with K.L. Alexander and Susan Dauber) The Success of Failure, 1984, 2d edit., 2002, (with K.L. Alexander, L.S. Olson) Children, Schools and Inequality, 1997; editor: Sociology of Education, 1975-78; assoc. editor Am. Sociol. Rev., 1972-75, 95-98; co-editor Jour. Rsch. in Adolescence, 1990-94. Guggenheim fellow, 1976-77 Fellow APA, Am. Sociol. Assn. (chair sect. children); mem. Am. Ednl. Rsch. Assn., Soc. Rsch. in Child Devel. (pub. com. 1987-93, chair 1989-91, governing coun. 1993-99). Office: Johns Hopkins U 530 Mergenthaler Baltimore MD 21218 E-mail: entwisle@jhu.edu.

EPHRON, NORA, writer; b. N.Y.C., May 19, 1941; d. Henry and Phoebe (Wolkind) E.; m. Dan Greenburg (div.); m. Carl Bernstein (div.); children: Jacob, Max; m. Nicholas Pileggi. BA, Wellesley Coll., 1962. Reporter N.Y. Post, 1963-68; free-lance writer, 1968—; contbg. editor, columnist Esquire mag., 1972-73, sr. editor, columnist, 1974-78; contbg. editor N.Y. mag., 1973-74. Author: Wallflower at the Orgy, 1970, Crazy Salad, 1975, Scribble Scribble, 1978, Heartburn, 1983, Nora Ephron Collected, 1991; screenwriter: (with Alice Arlen) Silkwood (nominated Acad. award for best original screenplay), 1983, Heartburn, 1986, Cookie, 1989, When Harry Met Sally (nominated Acad. award, BAFTA award for best screenplay), 1989, My Blue Heaven, 1990; dir., screenwriter (with Delia Ephron) This Is My Life, 1992, Mixed Nuts, 1994, Michael, 1996, You've Got Mail, 1998; co-screenwriter, dir. Sleepless in Seattle (nominated Acad. award for best original screenplay), 1993; prodr., dir. Lucky Numbers, 2000; screenwriter, prodr. Hanging Up, 2000; playwright Imaginary Friends, 2002. Mem. Writers Guild Am., Authors Guild, Dirs. Guild of Am., Acad. Motion Picture Arts and Scis.

EPP, DIANNE NAOMI, secondary educator; b. Yankton, S.D., Oct. 1, 1939; d. Willard H. and Florence A. (Leigh) Waltner; m. Anthony R. Epp, Aug. 18, 1964; children: Alain René Epp Weaver, Rachel Epp Buller. BA in Chemistry, Bethel Coll., 1961; MA, U. Mo., 1963; cert. etudes, L'Ecole d'Administration, Brussels, 1965. Chemistry instr. Bethel Coll., North Newton, Kans., 1963-64; sci. tchr. Ecole Secondaire, Sundi-Lutete, Zaire, 1965-67; rsch. chemist FMC Glass Lab., Golden, Colo., 1967-70; vis. instr. Nebr. Wesleyan U., Lincoln, 1973-74, 77-79, 1980-81; chemistry tchr. East High Sch., Lincoln, 1982-93, 94—; vis. scholar Miami U., Oxford, Ohio, 1993-94. Cons. NSF Doing Chemistry Videodisc, 1988; cons. small scale CD ROM Synapse Corp., Lincoln, 1993. Author: Chemical Manfacturing: The Process of Mixing, 2000, Experimental Design: The Chemistry of Adhesives, 1998, Product Testing: The Chemistry of Ice Cream, 1998; cons. editor: Starting at Ground Zero, 1989; author: (monograph series) A Palette of Color, 1995; contbr. articles to profl. jours. Recipient Excellence in Teaching award Cooper Found., 1990, Excellence in High Sch. Chemistry Teaching award Am. Chem. Soc., 1990, 91, Presdl. award for Excellence in Sci. and Math. Teaching NSF, 1994, Kiewit Found. Tchg. award, 1997, 01. Mem. Nat. Sci. Tchrs. Assn. Office: East High Sch 1000 S 70th St Lincoln NE 68510-4297

EPPERSON, SHARON, television correspondent; B in Govt. and Sociology, Harvard U.; M in Internat. Affairs, Columbia U. Journalist Time Mag., Time Inc., 1993-96, corr. Time New Media; corr. Bus. News, CNBC, Ft. Lee, N.J. Contbr. The News Hour with Jim Lehrer, N.Y. One News. Recipient award Nat. Assn. Black Journalists, 1994. Office: CNBC 2200 Fletcher Ave Fort Lee NJ 07024-5005

EPPERSON, STELLA MARIE, artist; b. Oakland, Calif., Nov. 6, 1920; d. Walter Peter and Martha Josephine (Schmitt) Ross; m. John Cray Epperson, May 10, 1941; children: Therese, John, Peter. Student, Calif. Coll. Arts & Crafts, 1939, 40-41, 56; postgrad., Art Inst., San Miguel d'Allende, Mex., 1972. Portrait artist Oakland Art Assn., 1956—, San Francisco Women Artists, 1962—, Marin Soc. Artists, Ross, Calif., 1971—. Art docent Oakland Mus., 1969-71, mem. women's bd., 1971—, art chmn. fund raiser, 1971-89, art guild chmn., 1965-69, chmn. exhbt. Japanese artists in Brazil, Kaiser Ctr., Oakland, for honoring artist Xavier Martinez, event honoring Neil Armstrong, Calif. Coll. Arts and Crafts. One-woman shows include Oakland Mus. Auction, 1993, Univ. Club, San Francisco, 1994; exhbns. include Women's Art Gallery, San Francisco, Kaiser Ctr., St. Mary's Coll. Hearst Gallery, numerous others; commd. portrait Mrs. Evangelina Macapagal, Malacalang Palace. Recipient San Francisco Women Artists, 1989, Oakland Art Assn., 1991, 1997, 2000, Marin Soc. Artists, 1992, Figurative Subject First award, Oakland Art Assn. Mem. Oakland Art Assn. (1st award in small format show 1998, 1999 Artistic award in Kaiser Ctr. Gallery Exhibit, Merit award 2000, Artistic award 2001), San Francisco Women Artists, Marin Art Assn., U. Calif. Berkeley Faculty Club, Orinda Country Club. Republican. Roman Catholic. Avocations: dress design, gourmet cooking, tennis. Home: 31 Valley View Rd Orinda CA 94563-1432

EPPLEY, FRANCES FIELDEN, retired secondary education educator, writer; b. Knoxville, Tenn., July 18, 1921; d. Chester Earl and Beulah Magnolia (Wells) Fielden; m. Gordon Talmage Cougle, July 25, 1942; children: Russell Gordon Eppley, Carolyn Eppley Horseman; m. Fred Coan Eppley, Mar. 8, 1953; 1 child, Carolene Eppley Sellers. BA in English, Carson Newman Coll., 1942; MA, Winthrop U., 1963. Tchr. East Corinth (Maine) Acad., 1942-43, pub. schs., Charlotte, N.C., 1950-53, 59-83, Greenville, S.C., 1954-56, Spartanburg, S.C., 1957-58; Head Start tchr., summers 1964-68. Author: First Baptist Church: Its Heritage, 1982, Flint Hill Church, 1984, Religion and Astrology, 1991, Astrology and Prophecy, 1992, Sammy's Song, Jericho, Aunt Lillian's Sea Foam Candy, The First Astrologer, 1993, The Story of William Fielden, 1998, Search for an Ancestor, 1999, Christmas Magnus, Stella and the Sitting Stone, Messiah, An Immediate Family, 1999, The Signs of Your Life, 2000, Another Mary, 2000, The Winter Solstice, 2001, Of Course Your Child Can Read!, 2002, Columbus: The Race Home, 2003, Canada Trilogy, 2003; : To A Japanese Friend, 2002, Wacky Kings and Mystic Things, 2003, The Yellow River, 2003, To A Japanese Friend, 2004. Mem. hist. com. N.C. Bapt. Conv., 1985-88. Alpha Delta Kappa Grantee, 1970. Mem. NEA, N.C. Social Studies Conf., Writers Assn., Alpha Delta Kappa, Pi Kappa Delta, Alpha Psi Omega. Baptist. Mailing: 251 N Highway 16 Apt 1 Denver NC 28037

EPPS, MARY ELLEN, state legislator; b. Copperhill, Tenn., Dec. 25, 1934; Student, Regis Coll.; BS, Colo. Christian U. Former bus. owner; nurse/physician asst.; owner, founder Future Visions Video Prodn. Co.; mem. Colo. Ho. of Reps., Dist. 19, 1986-98, Colo. Senate, Dist. 11, Denver, 1998—; chair health, environment, welfare and instns. com.; mem. judiciary com., mem. transp. com. Edn. com. chair Am. Legis. Exch. Coun., Criminal Justice Task Force; leader Girl Scouts; active El Paso County Planning Commn.; vice-chair Social Svcs. Consumer Rev. Bd. Mem. AARP, VFW, Nat. Conf. State Legislatures (arts and tourism com.), Security Lioness Club, Optimists Club, Fountain Valley Lions Club, Am. Legion Aux., ENT Aero Club, Fountain Valley Teen Club. Republican. Home: 825 S Union Blvd Colorado Springs CO 80910-3466 Office: State Capitol 200 E Colfax Ave Ste 346 Denver CO 80203-1716

EPPS, ROSELYN ELIZABETH PAYNE, pediatrician, educator; b. Little Rock, Dec. 11, 1930; d. William Kenneth and Mattie Elizabeth (Beverly) Payne; m. Charles Harry Epps, Jr., June 25, 1955; children: Charles Harry III (dec.), Kenneth Carter, Roselyn Elizabeth, Howard Robert. BS, Howard U., 1951, MD, 1955; MPH, Johns Hopkins U., 1973; MA, Am. U., 1981. Intern Freedmen's Hosp., Howard U., Washington, 1955-56, pediatric resident, 1956-59, chief resident, 1958-59; practice medicine specializing in pediatrics Washington, 1960; med. officer, pediatrics D.C. Dept. Pub. Health, Washington, 1961-64, dir. Clinic for Retarded Children, 1964-67, chief Infant and Pre-Sch. div., 1967-71, dir. children and youth project, 1970-71, dir. maternal and crippled children services, 1971-75; chief Bur. Clin. Services D.C. Dept. Human Services, Washington, 1975-80, acting commr. pub. health, 1980; instr., asst. research investigator Howard U. Coll. Medicine, Washington, 1960-61, prof. Dept. Pediatrics and Child Health, 1980-98, chief divsn. child devel., dir., 1985-89, dir. Child Devel. Ctr., 1985-89; rsch. assoc., vis. scientist smoking tobacco and cancer program, div. cancer prevention and control Nat. Cancer Inst. NIH, Washington, 1989-91; expert Nat. Cancer Inst. NIH, Pub. Health Applications Br., Bethesda, Md., 1991-97; scientific program adminstr. Nat. Cancer Inst. Pub. Health Applications Branch, Bethesda, Md., 1997-98; med. pub. hlth cons., 1998—; sr. program advisor for women's health programs Women's Health Inst., Howard U., Wash., 1999—. Chmn. task force to prepare comprehensive child care plan for D.C. Dept. Human Services, 1973-74, mem. nat. task force on pediatric hypertension Heart, Lung and Blood Inst., NIH, 1975; chmn. rsch. grants rev. com. maternal and child health and crippled children's svcs. HEW, Rockville, Md., 1978-80; sec. Commn. Licensure to Practice Healing Arts, Washington, 1980; trustee med. svc. D.C. Blue Shield Plan Nat. Capital Area, 1980; chmn. sec.'s adv. com. on rights and responsibilities of women HEW, Washington, 1981; dir. high-risk young people's project Howard U. Hosp., 1981-85; Washington coord. Know Your Body Program Am. Health Found., N.Y.C., 1982-91; mem. bd. advs. Coll. Home Econs. Ohio State U., Columbus, Ohio, 1983-87; adv. com. Nat. Ctr. for Edn. in Maternal and Child Health Georgetown U., Washington, 1983-89; nat. steering com., subcom. chmn. Healthy Mothers, Healthy Babies Coalition, Washington, 1983-90, mem. nominating com., 1991; cons. sickle cell disease NIH, 1984-88, Govt. Liberia and World Bank, 1984, UN Fund for Population Activities, N.Y. and Caribbean, 1984, filmstrip Miriam Berg Varian/Parents Mag. Films, 1978; bd. dirs. Vis. Nurse Assn., Inc., Washington, 1983-89; pres. bd. dirs. Hosp. for Sick Children, Washington, 1986-90, bd. dirs., 1984-94; frequent guest lectr. Weekly columnist Your Child's Health, Afro-Am. Newspaper, Washington, 1960-63; contbr. articles syndicated column Nat. Newspaper Pubs. Assn., 1982, Nat. Newspaper Assn., 1986-87; co-author audiocassettes; exhibitor sci. program; contbr. more than 90 articles to profl. jours. US trustee Children's Internat. Summer Villages, Casstown, Ohio, 1969—76, pres., 1974—75; trustee nat. bd. Palmer Meml. Inst., Sedalia, NC, 1969—71, Ford's Theater, Washington, 1973—79; bd. mgrs. YWCA of DC, 1970—83, vice chmn., 1975—76; v.p. Jack and Jill of Am., Inc., Washington, 1970—71; nat. bd. dir. Ctr. Population Options, Washington, 1980—86, Alexander Graham Bell Assn. for Deaf, Washington, 1974—78; bd. dir. Washington Performing Arts Soc., DC, 1971—81, v.p., 1979—81, hon. dir., 1981—. Recipient Leadership and Meritorious Service in Medicine award Palmer Meml. Inst., 1968, 14th Ann. Fed. Women's award CSC, Washington, 1974, Superior Performance award D.C. Govt., 1975, Meritorious Community Service award Howard U. Sch. Social Work Alumni Assns. and vis. com., 1980, Cert. Commendation Mayor of D.C., 1981, Roselyn Payne Epps M.D. Recognition Resolution of 1983 Council D.C., 1983, Disting. Vol. Leadership award March of Dimes Birth Defects Found., 1984, Community Svc. award D.C. Hosp. Assn., 1990, Physician of Yr. award Women's Med. Assn. N.Y.C., 1990, 91; named Outstanding Vol. in Leadership category YWCA Nat. Capital Area, 1983; inducted into D.C. Women's Hall of Fame D.C. Commn. for Women, 1990; grantee Robert Wood Johnson Found., Princeton, N.J., 1982, div. maternal and child health HHS, Rockville, Md., 1986; honored Tribute Resolution of 1981 declaring Feb. 14 Dr. Roselyn Payne Epps Day, Council of D.C., 1981; recipient Ophelia Settle Egypt award Planned Parenthood of Met. Washington, 1991, Advocacy award Soc. Advancement Women's Health, 1996, Horizon award Nat. Assn. Negro Bus. and Profl. Women's Clubs, 1999, Dorothy I Height award, Nat. Coun. of Negro Women, 2001, Lifetime Achievement award, Girls Inc., 2003. Fellow Am. Acad. Pediatrics (alt. state chmn. D.C. 1973-75, exec. com. D.C. chpt. 1983-94, pres. D.C. chpt. 1988-91, sec. cmty. pediatrics sect. 1973-75, cert. appreciation 1979, mem. coun. of child and adolescent health, cmty. and internat. health sect., charter mem., exec. com. 1992-94); mem. Acad. Medicine, AMA (alt. del. Nat. Med. Assn. 1983 85), Am. Med. Women's Assn. (chmn. pub. health com. 1973-75, pres. br. 1 1974-76, sec. 1988, v.p. 1989, pres-elect nat. 1990, pres. 1991, found. founding pres. 1992, bd. dirs. 1992-97, chmn. nominating com. 1993, Physician of Yr. award 1991, Cmty. Svc. award 1990, Elizabeth Blackwell award 1992), Women's Forum Washington, Med. Soc. D.C. (exec. bd. 1990, sec. 1990, pres.-elect 1991, pres. 1992, chair exec. bd. 1993, ann. Cmty. Svc. award 1982), Am. Pediatric Soc., D.C. Hosp. Assn. (Cmty. Svc. award 1990), Am. Pub. Health Assn. (action bd. 1977-79, joint policy com. 1978-79, gov. council 1978-81), Met. Washington Pub. Health Assn. (gov. council 1975-78, 81-83, ann. award 1981), Nat. Med. Assn. (chmn. pediatric sect. 1977-79, Ross Labs. award 1979, Outstanding Svcs. to Children during Internat. Yr. of Child award 1979, Meritorious Service Appreciation award 1979, W.M. Cobb co-lectr. 1985, mem. Coun. on Maternal and Child Health, 1974-92, chmn. 1979-89, ann. Roselyn Payne Epps Symposium 1994—, Grace Marilyn James award for Disting svc. Pediatric sect. 1991, Achievement award 1993, ann. Roselyn Payne Epps symposium 1994—), Am. Hosp. Assn. (maternal and child health sect. governing coun. 1989, 1992-94, maternal and child health nominating com. 1991), Soc. for the Advancement of Women's Health Rsch. (award for advocacy 1996), The Women's Forum of Washington, Alpha Omega Alpha, Delta Omega, Alpha Kappa Alpha. Mem. United Ch. of Christ. Clubs: Pearls (pres. 1984-86), Carrousels (corr. sec. 1978-80), Links (pres. Met. chpt. 1986-89) (Washington), Cosmos. Lodge: Zonta, Internat. Women's Forum. Home and Office: 1775 N Portal Dr NW Washington DC 20012-1014

EPSTEIN, BARBARA, editor; b. Boston, Aug. 30, 1929; d. Harry W. and Helen (Diamond) Zimmerman; children: Jacob, Helen. BA, Radcliffe Coll., 1949. Editor N.Y. Rev. Books, N.Y.C., 1963—. Office: NY Rev of Books 1755 Broadway Fl 5 New York NY 10019-3743 E-mail: bepstein@nybooks.com.

EPSTEIN, BARBARA MYRNA ROBBIN, language educator; b. Chgo., Oct. 15, 1939; d. Jack M. and Angeline Delores (Benzuly) Robbin; m. Erwin Howard Epstein, Sept. 3, 1961; children: Jack R., Eric M., M. Avi. BS, U. Wis., 1961; MA, U. Chgo., 1964. Bilingual assessment, transitional bilingual, secondary English, elem. tchr. Ill. Tchr. Sch. Dist. 65, Evanston, Ill., 1963—64, Waynesville R-IV Schs., Ft. Leonard Wood, Mo., 1980—82, Am. Sch. Found., Monterrey, Mexico, 1982—83; instr. U. PR, Rio Piedras, 1964; cons., tchr. Colegio Ingles, Monterrey, 1979—80; English tchr. Rolla (Mo.) Pub. Schs., 1983—92, Pickerington (Ohio) Local Schs., 1992—98; bilingual tchr. Schaumburg (Ill.) Sch. Dist., 1998—, bilingual assessment liaison, 2003—. Pres. Rolla Cmty. Tchrs. Assn., 1991—92; pres. Ozarks chpt. Phi Delta Kappa, Rolla, 1986; state pres. Ptnrs. of the Americas

(Brazil-U.S.), Mo., 1987—88; bd. dirs. South Ctrl. Mo. Arts Coun., 1991—92. Recipient Kemper Knapp scholarship, U. Wis., 1957—61, humanities fellowship, U. Chgo., 1962—64, tchr. recognition, U. Kans., 1991. Mem.: NEA, AAUW (sec. Glenview chpt. 2001—), Ill. Assn. Multilingual-Multicultural Educators, Nat. Coun. Tchrs. of English, Nat. Assn. Bilingual [illegible] of Chgo. (v.p. 1999—). Jewish. Avocations: movies, theater, reading, travel, cooking. Home: 135 Rutgers Ct Glenview IL 60025 Office: Sch Dist 54 524 E Schaumburg Rd Schaumburg IL 60194 Office Phone: 847-885-6520. E-mail: bmepstein@ameritech.net.

EPSTEIN, ELAINE MAY, lawyer; b. Phila., May 29, 1947; d. Sidney and Helen (Brill) Epstein; m. James A. Krachey, July 25, 1987; stepchildren: Ross Krachey, Anna Krachey. BA, U. Pa., 1968; MA, Yale U., 1971; JD, Northeastern U., 1976. Assoc. Law Offices of P.J. Piscitelli, Brockton, Mass., 1975-78; ptnr. LoDolce & Epstein, Brockton, 1978-94, Todd & Weld, Boston, 1994—. Mem. Bd. Bar Overseers, Boston, 1984-88; trustee Mass. Continuing Legal Edn., Boston, 1991-93. Mem. editl. bd. Mass. Lawyers Weekly, 1993-98. Fellow Mass. Bar Found. (trustee 1993-98); mem. ABA, Mass. Bar Assn. (pres. 1992-93), Women's Bar Assn. (pres. 1979-80). Democrat. Jewish. Home: 4 Manns Hill Cres Sharon MA 02067-2267 Office: Todd & Weld 28 State St Fl 31 Boston MA 02109-1775

EPSTEIN, MARSHA ANN, public health administrator, physician; b. Chgo., Feb. 4, 1945; 1 child, Lee Rashad Mahmood. BA, Reed Coll., 1965; MD, U. Calif., San Francisco, 1969; MPH, U. Calif., Berkeley, 1971. Diplomate Am. Bd. Preventive Medicine. Intern French Hosp., San Francisco, 1969-70; resident in preventive medicine Sch. Pub. Health, U. Calif., Berkeley, 1971-73; fellow in family planning dept. ob-gyn. UCLA, 1973-74; med. dir. Herself Health Clinic, L.A., 1974-79; pvt. adult gen. practitioner L.A., 1978-82; dist. health officer L.A. County Pub. Health, L.A., 1982—2001, area med. dir., 2001—. Part-time physician U. Calif. Student Health, Berkeley, 1970-73; co-med. dir. Monsenior Oscar Romero Free Clinic, L.A., 1992-93. Mem.: APHA, Calif. Acad. Preventive Medicine, So. Calif. Pub. Health Assn., L.A.-Am. Med. Women's Assn., Am. Med. Women's Assn., Am. Coll. Physician Execs. Democrat. Jewish. Avocations: dance, native plants, meditating. Office: Tucker Health Ctr 123 W Manchester Blvd Inglewood CA 90301 E-mail: mepstein@dhs.co.la.ca.us.

EPSTEIN, SUSAN BAERG, librarian, consultant; b. Chgo., Feb. 28, 1938; d. Philip William and Alice (Mackenzie) Ruppert; m. William Baerg, 1960 (div. 1971); children: Elisabeth Baerg, William Philip Baerg, Sara Margaret Baerg; m. A. H. Epstein, 1977 (div. 1981). BA in Econs., Wellesley Coll., 1960; MLS, Immaculate Heart Coll., 1972. Sys. analyst IBM, San Jose, Calif., 1960-63, Control Data Corp., Palo Alto, Calif., 1963-64; dir. tech. and automation svcs. Huntington Beach (Calif.) Pub. Libr., 1972-74, asst. city libr., 1974-78; spl. asst. to county libr. Los Angeles County Pub. Libr., L.A., 1978-81, chief tech. svcs., 1979-81; pres. Susan Baerg Epstein, Ltd., Costa Mesa, Calif., 1981—. Columnist: Libr. Jour., 1984—. Mem.: ALA (chair com.), Calif. Libr. Assn. (councilor 1973—80). Office: 1992 Lemnos Dr Costa Mesa CA 92626-3534 Personal E-mail: sbepstein@aol.com.

EPSTEIN-SHEPHERD, BEE, mental skills golf coach, hypnotist, professional speaker; b. Tubingen, Germany, July 14, 1937; came to U.S., 1940; naturalized, 1945; d. Paul and Milly (Stern) Singer; m. Leonard Epstein, June 14, 1959 (div. 1982); children: Bettina, Nicole, Seth; m. Frank Shepherd, 1991 (dec. 1992). Student, Reed Coll., 1954-57; BA, U. Calif., Berkeley, 1958; MA, Goddard Coll., 1976; PhD, Internat. Coll., 1982; DCH, Am. Inst. Hypnotherapy, 1999. Bus. instr. Monterey Peninsula Coll., 1975-85; owner, mgr. Bee Epstein Assocs., 1977—; cons. to mgmt. Carmel, Calif., 1977—; pres. Success Tours Inc., Carmel, 1981—; founder, prin. Monterey Profl. Spkrs., 1982. Instr. Monterey Peninsula Coll., Golden Gate U., U. Calif., Santa Cruz, Am. Inst. Banking, Inst. Ednl. Leadership, Calif. State Fire Acad., U. Calif., Berkeley, Foothill Coll., U. Alaska; pres. Becoming Media Inc., 2002; sr. v.p. TheHoundIsLoose.com Inc. Author: How to Create Balance at Work, at Home, in Your Life, 1988, Stress First Aid for the Working Woman, 1991, Free Yourself From Diets, 1994, Mental Management for Great Golf, 1996, Mental Mastery System, 2001; contbr. articles to newspapers and trade mags. Rsch. grantee, 1976. Mem. NAFE, Nat. Spkrs. Assn., Peninsula Profl. Women's Network Assn. for Advancement Applied Sports Psychology, Nat. Guild of Hypnotists. Democrat. Jewish. Office: PO Box 221383 Carmel CA 93922-1383 E-mail: DrBeeMM@aol.com.

ERB, BETTY JANE, retired real estate agent, activist; b. Balt., July 10, 1930; d. Edgar Smith Shanks and Delora Hickman Cockrum; m. William Cornelius Smith, Oct. 14, 1950 (div. Aug. 11, 1966); children: Stephen Cole Smith, Scott Douglas Smith, Cindy Lynn Smith; m. George Lewis Erb, Apr. 30, 1982. Grad., Manchester (Md.) H.S., 1948. Mainframe computer operator Svc. Bur. Corp., Balt., 1974—86; real estate agt. Carroll County Assn. Realtors, Westminster, Md., 1988—2002. Mem.: Carroll County Coin Club (pres., v.p., sec., bd. dirs.). Baptist. Home: 402 Barnes Ave Westminster MD 21157

ERDELY, BEATRICE, musician; m. Stephen Erdely. Artist diploma, Am. Conservatory Music, Chgo. Mem. faculty Am. Conservatory Music, Chgo., Cleve. Inst. Music, Hiram Coll., Ohio, Ohio State U., Toledo, Brandeis U., New England Conservatory Music, Boston Conservatory Music. Lectr in field. Performer: (recital) Orch. Hall, Town Hall, Severance Hall, Jordan Hall, Kresge Auditorium, (concerts and radio programs) with Erdely Duo; editor: (book) From Children To Children, Johann Christian Bach--Francesco Pasquale Ricci: Introduction to the Piano; musician: (albums) Educo; musician: (piano soloist) Chgo. Symphony, Grant Pk. Symphony Orch., Chgo. Orch., Cleve. Orch., WQXR Orch., various cmty. and univ. orchs. Recipient First prize, Young Pianist of Midwestern States, Soc. Am. Musicians, Young Artists Competition. Mem.: Music Tchrs. Nat. Assn., European Piano Tchrs. Assn., New England Piano Tchrs. Assn. Home: 21 Hillcrest Rd Concord MA 01742

ERDMAN, BARBARA, visual artist; b. N.Y.C., Jan. 30, 1936; d. Isidore and Julia (Burstein) E. Postgrad., Chinese Inst., 1959-60; BFA, Cornell U., 1956. Visual artist, Santa Fe, 1977—. Guest critic Studio Arte Centro Internat., Florence, Italy, 1986; guest lectr. Austin Coll. Sherman, Tex., 1986; mem. Oracle Conf. Polaroid Corp., nationwide, 1986-88. One-woman shows include Aspen Inst., Baca, Colo., 1981, Scottsdale (Ariz.) Ctr. for Arts, 1988, AAAS, Washington, 1994; exhibited in group shows, 1959—, including AAAS, 1994, Wichita Falls Art Mus., Tex., 1996, San Bernardino County Mus., 1998; represented in permanent collections N.Mex. Mus. Fine Arts, Santa Fe, IBM, N.Y.C.; author: New Mexico USA, 1985. Bd. dirs. N.Mex. Right to Choose, Santa Fe, 1981-87, Santa Fe Ctr. for Photography, 1983, pres. bd. 1985-89; mem. N.Mex. Mus. Found., Albuquerque Mus. Found. Mem. Art Student's League (life), Soc. for Photographic Edn. (guest lectr. 1987), Santa Fe Ctr. for Photography (pres., bd. dirs. 1984-89), Am. Coun. Arts. Avocations: ceramics, textiles, cats. Home and Office: 1070 Calle Largo Santa Fe NM 87501-1090

ERDRICH, LOUISE (KAREN ERDRICH), fiction writer, poet; b. Little Falls, Minn., June 7, 1954; d. Ralph Louis and Rita Joanne (Gourneau) E.; m. Michael Anthony Dorris, Oct. 10, 1981 (dec. Apr. 1997); children: Abel (dec.), Sava, Madeline, Persia, Pallas, Aza. BA, Dartmouth Coll., 1976; MA, Johns Hopkins U., 1979. Vis. poet, tchr. N.D. State Arts Council, 1977-78; tchr. writing Johns Hopkins U., Balt., 1978-79; communications dir., editor Circle-Boston Indian Council, 1979-80; textbook writer Charles Merrill Co., 1980. Author: (textbook) Imagination, 1981; (poetry) Jacklight, 1984, Baptism of Desire, 1989; (novels) Love Medicine, 1984 (Nat. Book Critics Circle award for fiction 1984, Virgina McCormick Scully prize 1984, L.A. Times award for best novel 1985, Sue Kaufman prize for first fiction Am Acad. and Inst. of Arts and Letters 1985), The Beet Queen, 1986, Tracks, 1988, (with Michael Dorris) The Crown of Columbus, 1991 (with Dorris) Route 2, 1991, The Bingo Palace, 1994, The Blue Jay's Dance: A Writer's Year with Baby, 1995, Tales of Burning Love, 1996, The Antelope Wife, 1998; (children's) Grandmother's Pigeon, 1997, The Birchbark House, 1999; contbr. short stories, essays and poems to popular mags., other publs. Johns Hopkins U. teaching fellow, 1979; Macdowell Colony fellow, 1980; Yaddo Colony fellow, 1981; vis. fellow Dartmouth Coll., 1981; Guggenheim fellow, 1985-86; recipient numerous awards for profl. excellence including Nelson Algren award, 1982, Pushcart prize, 1983, Nat. Mag. Fiction award, 1983, 87, First prize O. Henry awards, 1987. Mem. PEN (exec. bd. 1985-90),, Am. Acad. Arts and Letters, Authors Guild, Western Lit. Assn. Address: c/o Andrew Wylie Agy 250 W 57th St Ste 2114 New York NY 10107-2199 Office: PO Box 476 Cornish Flat NH 03746*

EREKSEN, CHRISTA ANN, social worker, marriage and family therapist; b. Manville, N.J., Oct. 19, 1973; d. Paul Erek Ereksen and Chris Anntoinette Bladzinski; m. Marshall Chandler McCoy, July 2, 1996 (div. Jan. 2001). Cosmetology lic., Richards Beauty Coll., San Bernardino, Calif., 1994; A in Liberal Arts, Victor Valley Coll., 1999; B in Psychology, Calif. State U., San Bernardino, 2002; postgrad., Calif. Bapt. U., 2004. Cosmetologist Fantastic Sams, Apple Valley, Calif., 1995—99; eligibility worker San Bernardino County, 1999—2000, social worker II, 2000—. Intern marriage and family therapy Foothills AIDS Project, San Bernardino, 2003—, MFI Recovery, Riverside, Calif., 2003—. Mem.: APA (student affiliate divsn. 29), Calif. Assn. Marriage and Family Therapists, Calif. State Alumni Assn., Phi Kappa Phi. Democrat. Roman Catholic. Avocations: reading, writing, poetry. Office: San Bernardino County 799 E Rialto Ave San Bernardino CA 92415

EREM, SUZAN, writer; b. Hackensack, N.J., Sept. 13, 1963; d. Nejat Hussein Erem and Elaine Gloria Dinallo; m. Robert Timothy Yeager, Apr. 25, 1987 (div. Dec. 1997); 1 child, Ayshe Rezan. B in Journalism/English, U. Iowa, 1985. Field mgr. Ill. Pub. Action Coun., Rock Island, 1985-86; union rep. Iowa United Profls., Des Moines, 1987-89; editl. asst. The Town Jour., Saddle River, N.J., 1989; organizer Local 32B-32J Svc. Employees Internat. Union, N.Y.C., 1989-90; rsch. asst. Labor Coalition on Pub. Utilities, Chgo., 1991; comms. dir. Local 73 Svc. Employees Internat. Union, Chgo., 1993-2000. Mem. adv. com. U. Ill. Labor Edn. Program, Chgo., 1999. Author: Labor Pains: Stories from Inside America's New Union, 2001; contbr. articles to Am. Anthropologist, Sojourners Mag., N.Am. Review, Iowa Woman; editor/designer The Jour., 1993-2000. Field organizer Jesse Jackson for Pres., Cedar Rapids, Iowa, 1988; founding mem. Rainbow Coalition of Iowa, Des Moines, 1989; area coord. Jesus Garcia for Sen., Chgo., 1992; steering com. mem. Oak Park Cmty. Action, Oak Park, Ill., 1991-93; del. Chgo. Fedn. of Labour, 1993-2000; co-chair Nat. Writers Union Local 12, 1999, nat. del., 1999, 2001. Mem. Ill. State Labor Press Assn. (v.p. 1998-99). Avocations: hiking, travel, rollerblading. Home: 1114 Outer Dr State College PA 16801-8239

ERGEN, VIOLA S. accountant; b. Mpls., Sept. 10, 1915; d. Otto and Anna Katherine (Matikainen) Siebenthal; m. William Krasny Ergen, Feb. 5, 1944 (dec. Feb. 1971); children: Anne Katherine, John Arnold Krasny, Frederick Julien Krasny, Charles William Krasny, Mary Elizabeth. BBS, U. Minn., 1939. Sr. acct. U. Minn., Mpls., 1938—45; various duties Gallop Poll, Princeton, NJ, 1945—46; bus. mgr. Children's Mus. Oak Ridge, Tenn., 1973—2004. Bd. dirs., fin. chmn. Girl Scouts U.S., Knoxville, Tenn. (Thanks badge 1982); treas. U. Tenn. Arboretum Soc., Oak Ridge, 1984-91. Recipient Vol. Youth Svc. award Rotary Club Oak Ridge, 1984-85. Mem. AAUW (treas. 1990-92, 1994-2002). Episcopalian. Avocations: girl scouts, hiking, gardening. Home: 103 Orkney Rd Oak Ridge TN 37830-3806

ERICKSON, ANN FLORIN, recreational facility executive, realtor; b. Missoula, Mont., Jan. 24, 1953; d. Henry James and Catherine Catherine M. Florin Florin; m. Robert W. Erickson, May 31, 1951. Cert. profl. ski instr. Profl. Ski Instrs., Idaho, 1977. Supr. Sun Valley (Idaho) Ski Sch., 1976—. Sec. Joan Leidy Found., Hailey, Idaho, 1993—. Mem.: Profl. Ski Instructors of Am. (life). Democrat. Avocations: swimming, skiing, dog showing, inline skating, hiking. Home: PO Box 2396 Hailey ID 83333 Office: Sun Valley Ski School Sun Valley Resort Sun Valley ID 83353 Personal E-mail: copperhill@cox-internet.com.

ERICKSON, ELAINE MAE, composer, poet; b. Des Moines, Iowa, Apr. 22, 1941; d. Iver Carl and Ruth Eloise (Johnson) E. MusB, Wheaton Coll., 1964; MusM, Drake U., 1967. Pvt. piano tchr., Des Moines, 1964—; music libr. Main Pub. Library, Des Moines, 1965-67; composer-in-residence Ford Found. Fellowship, Ft. Lauderdale, Fla., 1967-68; tchr. piano music theory Drake U., Des Moines, 1969-72; pianist Ctr. for New Music State U. Iowa, Iowa City, 1974-76; piano tchr. Waxter Ctr., Balt., 1988-89, Church Lane Elem. Sch., Balt., 1989-90; tchr. music composition Ctrl. Coll., Pella, Iowa, 1993-96; composer-in-residence Charles Ives Ctr. Am. Music, New Milford, Conn., 1981—83, 1993. Guest composer Meet the Composer, Saranac Lake, NY, 1987; touring artist Very Spl. Arts Iowa, 1994—. Author (poetry) Separate Trains, 1988, A Visit Home, 1990, Solo Drive, 1992, Portraits and Selected Poems, 1994, The Cottage, 2001; writer 5 operas, 3 performed at Peabody Conservatory, Balt., 1986-91; contbr. poetry to numerous jours. Pianist various retirement homes, Balt., Des Moines, 1978—, music appreciation tchr., Balt., 1991-93, Des Moines, 1993—; organist Divinity Luth. Ch., Towson, Md., 1987-88. Recipient Pyle Commn. award Iowa Composers Forum, Des Moines, 1997, composition award Nat. League Am. Pen Women, 1992; touring grantee Iowa Arts Coun., 1974-75, 81-82. Democrat. Avocation: photography. Home and Office: 3700 Hillsdale Dr Des Moines IA 50322-3947

ERICKSON, KIM, consumer products company executive; Sr. v.p. fin. SuperValu Inc., Eden Prairie, Minn., sr. v.p. strategic planning, treas., 1998—. Office: SuperValu Inc 11840 Valley View Rd Eden Prairie MN 55344-3691

ERICKSON, LINDA RAE, elementary school educator; b. Huron, S.D., Aug. 17, 1948; d. Robert Emil and Esther (Schorzman) E. BS, U. Nebr., 1966; MA, U. No. Colo., Greeley, 1970; cert., U. Denver, 1990. Cert. elem. tchr., adminstr., prin. Spl. edn. resource tchr., Ignacio, Colo., 1983-85; elem. tchr. Woodland Park, Colo., 1985-86; tutor spl. edn. Am. Sch. London, 1987; elem. tchr. Borough of Brent, London, 1987, Internat. Sch. Hampstead, London, 1987-88; tchr. spl. edn. Carronhill Sch. for Handicapped, Stonehaven, Scotland, 1988-89; elem. tchr. Littleton (Colo.) Pub. Schs., 1970-83, 89-01; staff developer Pub. Edn. Bus. Coalition, 2001—; affiliate faculty Regis U., 2001—. Enrichment program coord. Sandburg Sch., 1991; co-chair Alternative Authentic Assessment Com., 1991—2001, Sandburg Parent Adv. Com., 1993—96; facilitator Littleton Pub. Schs., 1977—83, 1990—2001; workshop presenter Nat. Coun. Tchrs. English, Nat. Coun. Social Studies, WNET-TV Sta.; mem. Littleton Dist. Assessment Com., 1997—2001; chair Mother/Daughter Book Club, 1997—; affiliate faculty, supr. student tchrs. Regis U., 2001—; presenter in field. Active Fawcett Soc., London, 1987-89, NEA-Colo. Edn. Assn. Women's Caucus, 1979-01; mem. Sandburg Sch. mother/daughter book club, 1996—; founder mother/son book club, 1999-2000. Woman of Yr. nominee Littleton Jaycees, 1982; fed. grantee Use of Group Paperbacks in the Elem. Classroom, 1978. Mem. ASCD, NEA (women's leadership tng. cadre 1978-85), NOW, Colo. Edn. Assn., Littleton Edn. Assn. (bd. dirs., chair unit-bargaining team 1976-85), Internat. Reading Assn. (chair Pikes Peak 1986, Colo. coun. children's books award com. 1993-97, workshop presenter, reader meets writer com. co-coun. 1996—, tutor comitis crisis ctr. for homeless 1995-97, conf. presenter), Nat. Coun. Tchrs. English (co-lang. arts soc. exec. bd. dirs. 1995-97, co-chair storytelling contest 1997-98, mem. editl. bd. 1997-2001, presenter state conf. 1997), Planned Parenthood, Sierra Club, Alpha Delta Kappa, Phi Delta Kappa. Democrat. Lutheran. Avocations: skiing, water skiing, scuba diving, mountain biking, gardening. Home: 439 Saddlewood Cir Highlands Ranch CO 80126-2284

ERICKSON, NANCY CAROLYN, dean; b. Roseau, Minn., Dec. 28, 1948; d. Harold Raymond and Ellen Amelia Fichter; m. Gary Stephen Erickson, Sept. 13, 1970; children: Stephen, Catherine. PhD in German Lang. and Lit., U. Minn., 1989. Instr. German, dept. chair Bemidji (Minn.) State U., 1981—85, prof. German, dept. chair, 1985—97, dean Coll. Arts and Letters, 1997—. Contbr. articles to profl. jours. Pres. North Country Arts Coun., Bemidji, 1979—81; chair statewide modern lang. competency com. Minn. State Univs., 1989—91; bd. dirs. Minn. Humanities Commn., St. Paul, 1997—, exec. bd., 2001—03; bd. dirs., exec. bd. Minn. Coun. for Tchg. of Fgn. Lang., 1984—89. Mem.: MLA, Am. Coun. Colls. and Univs. Avocations: travel, reading, hiking, outdoor activities. Office: Bemidji State U 1500 Birchmont Dr Bemidji MN 56601

ERICKSON, PHYLLIS TRAVER, marketing executive; b. N.Y.C., Mar. 31, 1952; d. Harold August and Barbara Lucille (Seifert) T.; m. C. Carl Muscari, June 30, 1979 (div. Nov. 1982); m. Roger C. Erickson, July 8, 1995. BA, Northwestern U., 1974; MBA, Harvard U., 1978. Dir. rsch. Staub, Warmbold and Assocs., N.Y.C., 1974-75; dir. rsch., assoc. cons. Coopers and Lybrand, N.Y.C., 1975-76; asst. product mgr. Nestle Food Corp., White Plains, N.Y., 1978-79, product mgr., mktg. mgr., 1979-83, bus. dir. Purchase, N.Y., 1983-90; pres. PT Ventures, 1990—, Barrier Systems, Inc., Greenwich, Conn., 1991-92; v.p. mktg. Homeview, Inc., Needham, Mass., 1992-94, Media One, Boston, 1995-99. Pres. Erickson Cons., 1999—. Contbr. articles to mktg. jours. Named to Acad. Women Achievers YWCA. Mem. Harvard U. Bus. Sch. Club. Republican. Episcopalian. Home and Office: 133 Washington St Duxbury MA 02332-4520 E-mail: perickson@adelphia.net.

ERICKSON, RUTH ALICE, poet, artist; b. Green Bay, Wis., Apr. 9, 1933; d. Walter Byron and Verona Ann (Giese) Kottke; m. Clyde Gordan Hansen, Oct. 15, 1949 (dec. Dec. 1965); children: Gary Hansen, Gloria Hansen, Debora Hansen, Dale Hansen; m. Norton M. Erickson, July 31, 1977. Nursing asst., Nursing Acad. Green Bay, 1966. Choir dir. St. John's Luth. Ch., Green Bay, 1954—66; nurse Nursing Home, Hosp., DePere, Wis., 1966—79; poet Green Bay, 2001—. Author: Spiritual Lyrics and Poems, 2001, Hidden Haven, 2003. Recipient Merit Silver Bowl award, Internat. Soc. Poets, 2002, Two Bronze Medallions, 2003, Silver Cup award, 2003. Home: 2139 Packerland Dr Green Bay WI 54304*

ERICKSON, SHERYL LARAINE, education educator; b. Wichita, Kans., Sept. 8, 1957; m. Larry Lynn Erickson; 1 child, Jacob Heath. BA, Wichita State U., 1979, MA, 1990, EdD, 1998. Cert. tchg. and adminstrv. cert. Kans. Tchr. Unified Sch. Dist. 402, Augusta, Kans., 1979—90, bldg. prin., 1990—2001; tchr. of gifted Unified Sch. Dist. 259, Wichita, 2001—. Adj. prof. Baker U., Wichita, 1999—, Wichita State U., 2000—03. Mem. Augusta City Coun., 1998—2002; mem. park bd. City of Augusta, 1998—2002; mem. play park steering team Ptark Park, Augusta, 2001—02; mem. libr. improvement com. Augusta Pub. Libr., 1999—2000. Recipient Good Apple award, Unified Sch. Dist. 259, 2003. Mem.: ASCD. Office: Baker Univ 3450 N Rock Rd Wichita KS 67226

ERICSSON, SALLY CLAIRE, not-for-profit organization administrator; b. Madison, Wis., Jan. 16, 1953; d. William H. and JoAnn (Finnell) E.; m. Thomas A. Garwin, Oct. 7, 1979; children: Rachel, Benjamin. B in Urban and Regional Planning, U. Ill., 1976; M in Pub. Policy, Harvard U., 1981. Legis. analyst Dem. Steering and Policy Com, Washington, 1982-87; adminstr. asst. Rep. Sam Geidenson U.S. Ho. Reps., Washington, 1987-89; legis. asst. to Sen. John F. Kerry U.S. Senate, Washington, 1989-90; asst. to pres. for policy and rsch. Svc. Employees Internat. Union, Washington, 1990-93; assoc. under sec. for econ. affairs U.S. Dept. Commerce, Washington, 1993-96, dep. chief of staff, 1996-97; assoc. dir. for natural resources Coun. on Environtl. Quality, Exec. Office of the Pres., 1997-99; dir. outreach Pew Ctr. on Global Climate Change, Arlington, Va., 1999—. Home: 1805 Monroe St NW Washington DC 20010-1014 Office: Pew Ctr on Global Climate Change 2101 Wilson Blvd Ste 550 Arlington VA 22201-3038

ERIKSEN, BEVERLY MORGAN, retired primary school educator; b. Newark, Ohio, May 14, 1937; d. William Thomas and Geraldine Mae (Marsh) Morgan; m. Harold Eugene Eriksen, Nov. 11, 1961; children: Linda, Janet. BA, Wayne State U., 1959; postgrad., So. Conn. State U., 1969-71; cert. in elem. edn., Fla. So. Coll., 1985. Cert. elem. tchr., educator spkrs. of other langs. endorsement, Fla. Paraprofl. tchr. kindergarten Medulla Elem. Sch., Lakeland, Fla., 1979-85; tchr. kindergarten Scott Lake Elem. Sch., Lakeland, 1985-89, Sikes Elem. Sch., Lakeland, 1989-95, Walsingham Elem. Sch., Largo, Fla., 1995—99, ret., 1999. Mem. Fla. Ret. Educators Assn., Heisey Collectors Am. (donator to Nat. Heisey Glass Mus.). Democrat. Avocations: reading, family genealogy, travel. Home: 1575 Eunice Ln Clearwater FL 33756-3220

ERION, CAROL ELIZABETH, music educator; b. Quincy, Ill., Jan. 16, 1943; d. Alva Eugene and Margaret Althea (Kaempfer) McKenney; m. David F. Erion, June 19, 1965; children: Elizabeth Celia Erion Matthews, Paul Frederick. MusB, Oberlin Coll., 1965; MusM, New England Conservatory Music, 1982; cert., U. Toronto, Ont., Can., 1978, Mozarteum Acad. Music, Salzburg, Austria, 1979. Music tchr. Montessori Sch. No. Va., Annandale, 1972-84, St. Agnes Episcopal Sch., Alexandria, Va., 1984-85, The Sidwell Friends Sch., Washington, 1985-87; music and fine arts tchr. Arlington (Va.) Pub. Schs., 1988-00; supr. arts edn. Arlington Pub. Schs., 2000—. Music dir. All Saints Episcopal Ch., Alexandria, 1983-90; workshop clinician various music edn. orgns. in U.S., 1980—; adj. instr. George Mason U., Fairfax, Va., 1983-2001; cons. WETA-TV, Washington, 1987. Author: Tales to Tell, Tales to Play, 1982; contbr. articles to profl. jours. Humanities fellow Coun. Basic Edn., 1989. Mem. NEA, AAUW, ASCD, Am. Recorder Soc., Am. Orff Schulwerk Assn. (pres. 1993-95), Arlington Edn. Assn. (pres. 1998-2000). Democrat. Episcopalian. Home: 19 W Linden St Alexandria VA 22301-2621 E-mail: cerion@arlington.k12.va.us.

ERLA, KAREN, artist, painter, collagist, printmaker; b. Pitts., Nov. 17, 1942; d. Jack and Lenore (Kamons) Franklin; children: Stephanie, Joan. BFA, George Washington U., 1965; postgrad., Parsons Sch. Design, 1979-81, Carnegie Inst., 1958-59, Boston U., 1960-62, Pratt Inst., 1980-82, NYU, 1982. Solo exhbns. include Phoenix Gallery, N.Y.C., 1985, E.L. Stark Gallery, N.Y.C., 1988, Bertha Urdang Gallery, N.Y.C., 1986, Bennett and Siegel Gallery, 1989, 90, U. of South, Sewanee, Tenn., Manhattanville Coll., Purchase, N.Y., 1982, Printmaking Council of N.J., 1982, Bennet Siegel Gallery, N.Y.C., 1990, Bryant Gallery, N.Y.C., 1990, Queens Coll., N.Y.C., 1991; group shows include Herbert Johnson Mus. Art, Atlanta Coll. Art, Van Straaten Gallery, Chgo., Greene Gallery, Guilford, Conn., Nat. Mus. of Am. Art, Washington, D.C., Fine Arts Museum of L.I., N.Y., Zimmerli Mus., New Brunswick, N.J., Printmaking Council of N.J., Somerstown Studios and Gallery, Somers, N.Y., Cork Exhbn. in Lincoln Ctr., Fay Gold Gallery, Atlanta, 1984, Boston Printmakers 37th Nat. Exhbn., 1985, The Print Club's 61st Internat. Juried Exhbn., Phila., Schering-Plough Corp. Gallery, Madison, N.J., New Brunswick, N.J., Australian Nat. Gallery, 1989, E.L. Stark Exhbn., 1990, Am. Embassy, 1990, others; represented in permanent collections at Balt. Mus. of Art, Herbert F. Johnson Mus., Cornell U., Bklyn. Mus. Art, Huntsville Mus. Art, Ala., L.A. County Mus. Art, Met. Mus. Art, N.Y., Nat. Museum Am. Art, Australian

Nat. Gallery, Smithsonian Inst., New Orleans Mus. Art, Phila. Mus. Art, Tampa Mus., Fla.; featured in Monograph of Karen Erla (text by Ronnie Cohen) 1988, Monoprints Karen Erla (text by Dr. Mary Lee Thompson), Paintings: Karen Erla (text by Bertha Urdang and E.L. Stark); featured in Newsday as New Yorker mag.; solo exhibitions E.L. Stark Gallery, Bertha Urdang Gallery, N.Y.C., Harrison Library, Harrison, N.Y. Manhattanville Coll., Purchase, N.Y., Sound Shore Gallery, N.Y.C., The Print Club 62d Internat., Phila. Recipient Nat. Art award, Pa., 1959, Herbert F. Johnson Mus., Cornell U.; Mamroneck Artists Guild award, 1983. Mem. World Print Council, Printmaking Council N.J., Artists Equity, Pratt Graphic Ctr., L.A. Printmaking Soc. Avocations: music, reading, traveling. Address: PO Box 202 White Plains NY 10603-0202

ERLEBACHER, ARLENE CERNIK, retired lawyer; b. Chgo., Oct. 3, 1946; d. Laddie J. and Gertrude V. (Kurdys) Cernik; m. Albert Erlebacher, June 14, 1968; children: Annette Doherty, Jacqueline. BA, Northwestern U., 1967, JD, 1973. Bar: Ill. 1974, U.S. Dist. Ct. (no. dist.) Ill. 1974, U.S. Ct. Appeals (7th cir.) 1974, Fed. Trial Bar 1983, U.S. Supreme Ct. 1985. Assoc. Sidley & Austin, Chgo., 1974-80, ptnr., 1980-95, ret., 1996. Fellow Am. Bar Found.; mem. Order of Coif. E-mail: Erlebacher@comcast.net.

ERLEBACHER, MARTHA MAYER, artist, educator; b. Jersey City, Nov. 21, 1937; d. Desiderius and Mary Mayer; m. Walter Erlebacher, June 26, 1961 (dec. Aug. 1991); children: Adrian Immanuel, Jonah Daedalus. Student, Gettysburg (Pa.) Coll., 1955-56; B of Indsl. Design, Pratt Inst., 1960, MFA, 1963. Indsl. designer, illustrator Arthur Wagner Assocs., N.Y.C., 1956-61; tchr. anatomy and figure drawing U. of Arts, Phila., 1978-94. Tchr. Phila. Coll. Art, 1966-68, 78-94; tchr. anatomical drawing and painting Grad. Sch. Figurative Art, N.Y. Acad. Art, N.Y.C., 1992—, others; guest lectr. Grad. Sch. Art Yale U., 1974, Vassar Coll., Poughkeepsie, N.Y., 1975, Phila. Coll. Art, 1976, U. Conn., Storrs, 1977, Tyler Sch. Art Temple U., 1978, Med. Coll. Pa., Phila., 1987, N.Y. Acad. Art, 1990, others; vis. artist colls. and univs. including U. Wis., Oshkosh, 1979, Syracuse U., 1986-87, U. Mich., 1988, Calif. State U., 1989, 91, Tulane U., New Orleans, 1992, Kalamazoo Inst. Arts, 1989; panelist arts shows, 1978—; juror U. Del., 1979, N.Y. Statewide Bi-Annual, Trenton, 1984, Moss Rehab. Hosp., Phila., 1985, Tex. Nat. '98, Nacogdoches. Exhibited in one-person shows at Robert Schoelkopf Gallery, N.Y.C., 1973, 75, 78, 80, 82, 85, Dart Gallery, Chgo., 1976, 78, 83, Koplin Gallery, L.A., 1989, 91, Kalamazoo Inst. Arts, 1989, Fischbach Gallery, N.Y.C., 1993, 95, The More Gallery, Phila., 1993, 97, 2000, Hackett-Freedman Gallery, San Francisco, 1999, 2002, Arnot Mus., Elmira, NY, 2001, Forum Gallery, N.Y.C., 2003, others; exhibited in group shows Bklyn. Mus., 1960, Phila. Art Alliance, 1967, Suffolk Mus., Stony Brook, N.Y., 1971, Pratt Manhattan Ctr., 1971, Am. Acad. Arts & Letters, N.Y.C., 1973, 76, 87, Yale U. Art Gallery, 1973, Phila. Civic Ctr., 1974, Mus. Art, Penn. State U., 1974, 76, N.Y. Cultural Ctr., 1975, Libr. Congress, 1975, U. Notre Dame, 1976, Ringling Mus. Art, Sarasota, Fla., 1976, Fogg Art Mus. Harvard U., Cambridge, Mass., 1976, Art Gallery Boston U., 1977, Penn. Acad. Fine Arts, 1978, 81, 82, Phila. Mus. Art, 1979, Centro Colombo Americano, Bogota, Colombia, 1979, Fendrick Gallery, Washington, 1980, Print Club, Phila., 1980, 88, Albright-Knox Gallery, Buffalo, 1981, Woodmere Art Gallery, Phila., 1982, Univ. Art Mus., Santa Barbara, Calif., 1983, N.J. State Mus., Trenton, 1984, Hudson River Mus., Yonkers, N.Y., 1986, [illegible] Fine Arts Gallery Ind. U., 1987, Sherry French Gallery, N.Y.C., 1988, 91, 92, Jack Wright Gallery, Palm Beach, Fla., 1992, Contemporary Realist Gallery, San Francisco, 1993, 94, Gerald Peters Gallery, Sante Fe, 1993, Fletcher Gallery, Sante Fe, 1994, Arnot Mus., Elmira, 2000, many others; represented in pvt. and pub. collections including Cleve. Mus. Art, Ball State U., Muncie, Ind., AT&T Co., Inc., Chgo., U. Notre Dame, Art Inst. Chgo., Fogg Mus. of Art, Fed. Reserve Bank, N.Y.C., Penn. Acad. Fine Arts, Phila., Valparaiso U., Phila. Mus. Art, Libr. Congress, Flint Inst. Arts, N.J. State Mus., others. Recipient Bertha Shay award Cheltenham Art Ctr., 1967, Netsky-Sernaker Meml. prize, 1973, Vivian and Meyer P. Potamkin prize, 1974; Yaddo fellow, 1966, 73, sr. fellow Nat. Endowment for Arts, 1982, fellow Pa. Coun. on Arts, 1988; grantee Ingram Merrill Found., 1978, Mellon Venture Fund, 1987; also other grants and awards. Home: 7733 Mill Rd Elkins Park PA 19027-2708 E-mail: mmayererlebacher@aol.com.

ERLENMEYER-KIMLING, L. psychiatrist, researcher; b. Princeton, N.J. d. Floyd M. and Dorothy F. (Dirst) Erlenmeyer; m. Carl F. E. Kimling. BS magna cum laude, Columbia U., 1957, PhD, 1961; DSc (hon.), SUNY, Purchase, 1997. Sr. rsch. scientist N.Y. State Psychiat. Inst., N.Y.C., 1960-69, assoc. rsch. scientist, 1969-75, prin. rsch. scientist, 1975-78, dir. div. devel. behavioral studies, 1978—, chief med. genetics, 1991—; asst. in psychiatry Columbia U., 1962-66, rsch. assoc., 1966-70, from asst. prof. to assoc. prof. psychiatry and genetics, 1970—78, prof., 1978—. Vis. prof. psychology New Sch. Social Rsch., 1971—97; mem. peer rev. group NIH, 1976—80; mem. work group guidance and counseling Congl. Commn. Hungtinton's Disease, 1976—77; mem. task force intervention Pres.'s Commn. Mental Health, 1977—78; mem. initial rev. group NIMH, 1981—85; mem. adv. bd. Croatian Inst. Brain Rsch., 1991—93. Editor: (book) Life-Span Research in Psychopathology, 1986; issue editor: Differential Reproduction, Social Biology, 1971, Genetics and Mental Disorders, Internat. Jour. Mental Health, 1972, Genetics and Gene Expression in Mental Illness, Jour. Psychiat. Rsch., 1992, Measuring Liability to Schizophrenia: Progress Report, 1994; mem. editl. bd. Schizophrenia Bull., 1978—; issue editor: Schizophrenia Bull., 1994; mem. editl. bd. Social Biology, 1970—79, Jour. Preventive Psychiatry, 1980—84, Croatian Med. Jour., 1991—, Neurology/Psychiatry/Brain Rsch., 1991—, Neuropsychiat. Genetics, —, Am. Jour. Med. Genetics, 1992—. Recipient Disting. Investigator award, Merit award, NIMH, 1989—96, William K. Warren Schizophrenia Rsch. award, Internat. Congress Schizophrenia Rsch., 1995, Lifetime Achievement award, Internat. Soc. of Psychiatric Genetics, 2002; grantee, NIMH, 1966—69, 1971—, Scottish Rite Com. Schizophrenia, 1970—74, 1984—87, 1989—94, W. T. Grant Found., 1978—86, MacArthur Found., 1981, Stnaley Found., 1995—, NARSAD, 1996—2000. Fellow: APA, Am. Psychol. Soc., Am. Psychopath. Assn.; mem.: AAAS, Soc. Study Social Biology (bd. dirs. 1969—84, 1992—96, sec. 1972—75, pres. 1975—78), N.Y. Acad. Scis., Internat. Soc. Psychiat. Genetics (Lifetime Achievement award 2002), Behavior Genetics Assn. (mem.-at-large 1972—74, Theodosius Dobzhansky award 1985), Am. Soc. Human Genetics, Sigma Xi, Phi Beta Kappa. Office: NY State Psychiat Inst Dept Med Genetics 1051 Riverside Dr Mail Unit 6 New York NY 10032-2603 Office Phone: 212-543-5475. E-mail: le4@columbia.edu.

ERLICHSON, MIRIAM, fundraiser; b. Bronx, NY, July 26, 1948; d. Jack and Bess (Hyatt) E.; m. Walter Forman, Sept. 26, 1970 (div. 1975); m. Victor Petrusewicz, July 17, 1980. BA in English, CCNY, 1969, MA in English, 1976; postgrad., Hunter Coll., 1970-71; JD, Pace U., 1993. Cert. secondary tchr., N.Y. Tchr. English Intermediate Sch. 84, Bronx, 1972-78; coord. ann. and planned giving N.Y. Hosp.-Cornell Med. Ctr., N.Y.C., 1979-90; sr. devel. assoc. I.H. Found., Inc., N.Y.C., 1996-98, assoc. dir. N.E. region, 1998—2002; devel. comms. mgr. G.H. Ednl. Found., Inc., N.Y.C., 2002—03; dir. ann. fund Marymount Manhattan Coll., 2003—. Bd. dirs. 77 Settler Corp. Mem. N.Y. County Lawyers Assn., Jane Austen Soc. (Eng.), N.Y.S. Bar, Phi Beta Kappa.

ERNEST, PAMELA KAY, business consultant; b. St. Petersburg, Fla., Nov. 8, 1950; d. C.W. Bill and Marian June (Ford) Young; m. Harvey F. Ernest, Jr., Jan. 1, 1989. Grad. high sch., St. Petersburg. Press sec. to co-chmn. Rep. Nat. Com., Washington, 1971-74; sec., adminstrv. asst. to minority sgt.-at-arms U.S. Ho. of Reps., Washington, 1974-77; pub. affairs rep. NAM, Mpls., 1977-80; advanced person to Mrs. Bush, Reagan-Bush for Pres. Campaign, Washington, 1980; pub. affairs rep. Honeywell Inc., Washington, 1981-83, mgr. internat. policy, 1984-89, dir. fed. affairs, 1989-96; v.p. River Group, Falls Church, Va., 1996—. Avocations: skiing, biking, reading, gardening. Fax: (703) 237-2519.

ERNI, CORINNE, writer, cultural projects manager; b. Sursee, Lucerne, Switzerland, May 21, 1962; d. Mireille Edith Erni-Carron and Johannes Alfred Erni. MA in journalism, NY U., 1996—97. N/A N/A. Project mgr. Swiss Peaks, NYC, 2001—03; dep. cultural attache Consulate Gen. of Switzerland, NYC, 1999—2001; writer NY @ Night, NYC, 1998—99; communication asst. UN, NYC, 1991—97; arts program coord. Swiss Peaks, N.Y.C., 2003—. Organizer Swiss festival, N.Y.C., 2003. Editor: (magazine) Altitude. Personal E-mail: corinnee1@aol.com.

ERRECART, JOYCE HIER, lawyer; b. Vergennes, Vt., July 1, 1950; d. Lloyd Maurice and Lillian Adela (Jay) Hier; m. Michael Terry Errecart, Mar. 30, 1971; children: Michael Jay, Jacqueline Marie. BA, Wellesley Coll., 1972; JD, Am. U., 1976; LLM in Taxation, Georgetown U., 1981. Bar: Md. 1976, U.S. Tax Ct. 1977, Vt. 1984, U.S. Dist. Ct. Vt. 1984. Law clk. to spl. trial judge U.S. Tax Ct., Washington, 1975-76; trial atty. dist. counsel IRS, Washington, 1976-83; assoc. Dinse, Erdmann & Clapp, Burlington, Vt., 1983-86; sole practice Burlington, 1986-91; commr. Vt. Dept. of Taxes, Montpelier, Vt., 1991—. Mem. ABA (tax sect.), Vt. Bar Assn. (tax sect.). Republican. Avocation: quilting. Home: 149 Harbor Xing Shelburne VT 05482-7588 Office: Vt Dept Taxes Pavilion Office Bldg Montpelier VT 05602

ERSKINE, KALI (WENDY COLMAN), psychoanalyst; b. Flushing, N.Y., July 6, 1950; d. Leo M. and Ray (Fine) Colman BS, Tufts U., 1972; MA, NYU, 1977, PhD in Occupational Therapy, 1984; postgrad., Phila. Sch. of Psychoanalysis, 1988-92. Cert. psychoanalyst. Occupational therapist Extended Family Ctr., San Francisco, 1973-74; cons. child abuse San Francisco, 1974-75; sr. occupational therapist Roosevelt Hosp., N.Y.C., 1975-77; adj. instr. occupational therapy dept. NYU, N.Y.C., 1977-80; asst. prof. occupational therapy dept. Boston U., 1980-83; dir. grad. edn. occupational therapy, dept. assoc. prof. Temple U., Phila., 1984-87; cons. curriculum design Kean Coll. N.J., Union, 1985-88; cons. spl. projects, vice provost for rsch.- grad. studies Temple U., Phila., 1987-88; evaluation rsch. coord. Nat. Inst. Adolescent Pregnancy, Phila., 1986-90; pvt. practice psychotherapy and psychoanalysis, 1988—. Tng. and supervising analyst Phila. Sch. of Psychoanalysis. Editor VAPS Aviso newsletter, 1998-2000; contbr. articles to profl. jours. and texts in occupl. therapy and psychoanalysis (under names Wendy Colman and Kali Erskine). Fellow Am. Occupl. Therapy Assn.; mem. APA (Divsn. psychoanalysis), Nat. Assn. Advancement Psychoanalysis, Vt. Assn. for Psychoanalytic Studies, Soc. Phila. Sch. Psychoanalysis. Achievements include being first person to earn doctorate in occupational therapy. Office: Montpelier Psychoanalytic Group 201 Kildrummy Way Montpelier VT 05602 Office Phone: 802-223-6465. E-mail: ccpsygal.ke@verizon.net.

ERTEN, DUYGU, civil engineer, project manager, educator; b. Gazlantep, Turkey, Oct. 3, 1965; came to U.S. 1988; d. Dogan Mehmet and Fatos E. BS, Bogazici U., Istanbul, Turkey, 1988; MS engineering, Rutgers U., New Brunswick, 1990, PhD engineering, Rutgers U., 1994. Registered Professional Engineer. Rsch. staff Princeton U., N.J., 1988-89; asst. engineer Parsons & Brinkerhoff, Princeton, 1989-90; rsch., tchg. asst. Rutgers U., New Brunswick, N.J., 1990-94, staff engineer Lockwood Singh & Assoc., L.A., 1994-95; sr. staff engineer Earth Tech., Inc., Long Beach, Calif., 1995-96; project mgr. Daniel, Mann, Johnson & Mendenhall, L.A., 1996-2000; part time faculty mem. U. Southern Calif. Com. mem. Transp. Rsch. bd.; cons. in field. Contbr. articles to profl. jours. Mem. Kader-organization to support women legislators in Turkey, bd. mem. Women's Transportation Seminar, 1998—. Mem. Am. Soc. Civil Engineers. Avocations: hiking, biking, reading, skiing. Home: 13210 Fiji Way Un D Marina Del Rey CA 90292-7069 E-mail: derten@dellnet.com.

ERTING, CAROL JEAN, special education educator, researcher, anthropologist; b. St. Louis; MA, Northwestern U., 1972, BS, 1970; PhD, Am. U., 1982. Tchr. St. Louis (Mo.) County Spl. Sch. Dist., 1970—71, Atlanta Area Sch. for the Deaf, Clarkston, Ga., 1972—74; rschr. Linguistic Rsch. Lab. Gallaudet U., 1974—76, rschr. Kendall Demonstration Elem. Sch., 1977—79, rschr. Gallaudet Rsch. Inst., 1979—87, dir. culture and comm. studies program, 1987—96, prof. Dept. Edn., 1996—2003. Author: Deafness, Communication, Social Identity: Ethnography in a Preschool for Deaf Children, 1994; editor: From Gesture to Language in Hearing and Deaf Children, 1990, The Deaf Way, 1994 (Choice Outstanding Academic Book award, 1995), The Deaf Child in the Family and at School, 2000; contbr. articles to profl. jours. Bd. mem. Adams Morgans Lofts Condominium Assn., Washington, 2002—03. Fellow, NSF, 1974—77, 1985—86. Fellow: Soc. for Applied Anthropology; mem.: Internat. Soc. Lang. Studies (mem. exec. bd.), Coun. of Am. Instructors of the Deaf, Am. Assn. for Applied Linguistics, Coun. on Anthropology and Edn., Soc. for Rsch. in Child Devel., Am. Ednl. Rsch. Assn., Am. Anthrop. Assn., Cosmos Club. Office: Dept Education Gallaudet University 800 Florida Ave NE Washington DC 20002 E-mail: carol.erting@gallaudet.edu.

ERWIN, BARBARA F. school system administrator; b. Chgo. married; 2 children. BS in Spl. Edn., Ind. U., Bloomington; MS in Sch. Adminstrn., Purdue U., West Lafayette, Ind.; PhD in Sch. Adminstrn., Ind. U., Bloomington. Mid. sch. spl. needs tchr.; Title IV-C cons. Ind. Dept. Pub. Instrn.; spl. edn. diagnostician; tchr.; elem. sch. prin.; supt., Allen (Tex.) Ind. Sch. Dist., 1994—2000, Scottsdale (Ariz.) Pub. Sch., 2000—. Nominee Nat. Supt. of Yr., 1999; named Supt. of Yr., Tex. Assn. of Sch. Bds., 1997, Tex. Assn. Sch. Adminstrs., 1998; recipient Top Suburban Supt. Leadership Learning award, Am. Assn. of Sch. Adminstrs., 1996. Office: Scottsdale Pub Sch Edn Ctr 3811 N 44th St Phoenix AZ 85018-5420*

ERWIN, BETTY, bank executive; b. Charlotte, N.C., Nov. 11, 1945; d. John and Lula Bell Erwin; children: Wanda E. Dae, Johnny Maurice. BTh, Teamers Sch. of religion, 1989; BD, Teamers Sch. of Religion, 1991; BA, Shaw U., 1996; M in Christian Edn., Pheiffer U., 1998; Doctorate of Min., New Life Theol. Sem., 2000. Asst. buyer First Union, Charlotte, NC, 1986—97; courier specialist First Union Nat. Bank, Charlotte, 1997—2001. Mem.: Alpha Chi. Home: 3045 La Salle St Charlotte NC 28216

ERWIN, JUDITH ANN (JUDITH ANN PEACOCK), writer, photographer, lawyer; b. Decatur, Ga., Jan. 4, 1939; d. Milo Eugene and Lucy Isabelle (Simpson) Peacock; m. William Wofford Erwin, Sept. 5, 1959 (div. Mar. 1982); children: William Wofford Jr., Allison Sheridan (Norton). AA, Fla. C.C., 1987; BA summa cum laude, Jacksonville U., 1989; JD, U. Fla., 1993. Cert. mediator, custody evaluator. Photography instr., freelance writer, Jacksonville, Fla., 1986-91; freelance dance photographer, 1984-91; theater and dance critic Folio Weekly, Jacksonville, Fla., 1987-89; writer dance VUE mag.; founder On Our Own, 1991; pvt. practice lawyer. Pres. Ballet Guild, Jacksonville, 1973—75, Ballet Repertory Jacksonville, 1979—80; freelance costume designer, Jacksonville, 1981—86; mem. grand rev. dance panel Fla. Dept. Cultural Affairs, 1996—97, 2002; seminar spkr. in field; child custody evaluator. Mem. editorial staff Kalliope, Jour. Women's Art, 1989-91; editor-in-chief U. Fla. Jour. of Law and Pub. Policy, fall 1993; editor Jacksonville Trial Lawyers Newsletter. Mem. del.'s council Art's Assembly Jacksonville, 1979-80. Mem. AAUW, Fla. Bar Assn., Phi Kappa Phi, Phi Theta Kappa. Republican. Episcopalian. Office Phone: 904-733-2645. E-mail: jerwinatt@aol.com.

ERWIN, JUDY, state legislator; b. Detroit, 1950; BS, U. Wis.; MA, Nat. Coll. Edn., Evanston, Ill.; postgrad., Kennedy Sch. Govt., 1987. Formerly tchr. pub. schs.; mgmt. cons. Grant Thornton LPP; formerly dir. comms. staff Senate Dem. Staff; mem. from 11th dist. Ill. Ho. of Reps. Former del. Dem. Convs.; mem. Gov.'s Human Resource Task Force. Home: 1545 N Wells Chicago IL 60610-1307 Office: Ill Ho of Reps State Capitol Springfield IL 62706-0001

ERWIN, LINDA MCINTOSH, librarian, consultant; b. Austin, Tex., June 22, 1939; d. William Erwin and Martha (Ferguson) McIntosh; m. Kenneth James Erwin, June 7, 1962 (div. Feb. 1986); 1 child, Jason Emerson. BA magna cum laude, U. Tex., 1961, MLS, 1968. Tchr. Spanish, Victoria (Tex.) H.S., 1961-62, El Campo (Tex.) H.S., 1962-63, Del Valle (Tex.) H.S., 1963-66; libr. U. Tex., Austin, 1968-69, Corpus Christi Pub. Librs., 1981-89; cons. South Tex. Libr. Sys., Corpus Christi, 1989-99, asst. coord., 1999—. Ford Found. scholar, 1966-67. Mem. ALA, Tex. Libr. Assn., Pub. Libr. Assn., Phi Beta Kappa, Alpha Phi, Sigma Delta Pi. Office: South Tex Libr Sys 805 Comanche St Corpus Christi TX 78401-2715

ERZINGER, KATHY MCCLAM, nursing educator; b. Lake City, S.C., July 14, 1951; d. Curtis Brown and Parneace Ora (Timmons) McClam; m. Dennis Eugene Erzinger, Sr., June 22, 1974; children: Amberlyn Marie, Dennis Eugene Jr. AA, Brevard C.C., 1971; BS in Vocat. Edn., Carson-Newman Coll., 1974; degree in Vocat. Nursing, Simi Career Inst., 1994. Lic. vocat. nurse, Calif., 1994, cert. intravenous therapy and blood withdrawal, Calif., 1997; staff devel. Calif., 2001, tchr. Calif., 2001. Tchr. First Bapt. Acad., Thousand Oaks, Calif., 1988—90, Hillcrest Christian Sch., Thousand Oaks, 1990—93; charge nurse Victoria Care Ctr., Ventura, Calif., 1994—95, Thousand Oaks (Calif.) Health Care, 1995—2001; dir. staff devel. Westlake Healthcare Ctr., Westlake Village, Calif., 2001—02; instr. Simi Career Inst., Simi Valley, Calif., 2000—. Vol. Am. Cancer Assn., Simi Valley, 2003. Mem.: Calif. Vocat. Educators, Calif. Coun. for Adult Edn., Simi Educators Assn., Calif. Tchrs. Assn., Health Occupations Student Assn. Republican. Avocations: painting, baking, walking, music, gardening. Office: Simi Valley Adult School 3192 Los Angeles Ave Simi Valley CA 93065

ESCALLON, ANA MARIA, museum director, writer, curator; b. Columbia; Dir. Art Mus. of the Ams., Washington, 1996—. Author: Gerchman, 1994, Mejia-Guinand, 2002. Office: Art Mus of the Americas 1889 F St NW Washington DC 20006*

ESCARRA, VICKI B. airline company executive; b. Atlanta; married; 2 children. Grad., Ga. State U.; exec. mgmt. program, Columbia U.; exec. leadership program, Harvard U. Joined, in-flight svc. div. Delta Airlines Inc., Atlanta, 1973—92, dir. in-flight svc. ops., 1992—94, v.p. reservation sales, 1994-96, v.p. reservation sales and distribution planning, 1996, v.p. airport customer svc. to sr. v.p. airport customer svc., 1996—98, exec. v.p. customer svc., 1998—2001, exec. v.p., chief mktg. officer, 2001—. Serves on Women Build Steering Coun. of Habitat for Humanity, Internat.; bd. dirs. AG Edwards, Atlanta C. of C., Woodward Acad., Atlanta Convention and Visitors Bur., chair elect, 2003—05. Named Women of Year, Women Looking Ahead mag.; named one of 200 Most Powerful Women in Travel, Travel Agent mag., 1997, 1999, 2000, 2001; recipient Nat. Aviation and Space Exploration Wall of Honor certificate, Nat. Air & Space Mus. of Smithsonian Institution, 2000, YWCA Women of Achievement award, 2002. Mem.: Com. of 200, Internat. Women's Forum, Wings Club, Women in Aviation Internat. Office: Air Lines Inc 1040 Delta Blvd Dept 640 Atlanta GA 30354-1989

ESCHETE, MARY LOUISE, internist; b. Houma, La., Feb. 8, 1949; d. Marshall John and Louise Esther (Davis) E.; m. Lorphy Joseph Bourque, July 7, 1979. BS, La. State U., 1970; MD, La. State U. Med. Ctr., Shreveport, 1974. Diplomate, Am. Bd. Internal Medicine. Resident in internal medicine La. State U. Med. Ctr., Shreveport, 1974-77, staff instr., 1979, fellow in infectious disease, 1979; pvt. practice Houma, 1980-83; staff, dept. internal medicine South La. Med. Assocs., Houma, 1983—. Chmn. infection control Terrebonne Gen. Hosp., 1981—2000, 2002—, mem. performance improvement, 2000—; chmn. infection control S. La. Med. Ctr., 1983—; pub. health dir. Region III, 1993—98, pub. health infectious disease cons., 1998—. Contbr. articles to med. jours. Bd. dirs. Houma Battered Women's Shelter, 1983-87, Houma YWCA, 1987-94; mem. Roche Nat. AIDS Adv. Bd., 1993; Triparish vol. activist, 1994. Named Citizen of Yr. Regional and State Social Workers, 1992, Outstanding Dr. in South East. Mem. ACP, AAAS, AMA, Infectious Disease Soc., Am. Soc. Microbiology, So. Med. Assn. (grantee 1978), N.Y. Acad. Sci., La. State Med. Soc., Terrebonne Parish Med. Soc. (sec. 1982-83, treas. 1988-89, 98—, v.p. 1993-94, pres. 1994-95), Krewe of Hyachinthians (pres. 1989-90, 94-95, bd. dirs. 1990-96), Houma Jr. Women's Club (reporter 1988-89, rec. sec. 1989—, pres.-elect 1991-93, pres. 1993-95, chaplain 1998—2002), Alpha Epsilon Delta. Democrat. Roman Catholic. Avocation: gardening. Home: 3984 Highway 311 Houma LA 70360-8115 Office: Chabert Med Ctr 1978 Industrial Blvd Houma LA 70363-7055 Office Phone: 985-873-1800.

ESCOBAR, DEBORAH ANN, gifted and talented education educator; b. Schenectady, NY, Aug. 21, 1952; d. Richard H. and Rose Marie (Denny) Quay; m. Jorge Escobar, Oct. 25, 1975; children: Rosana, Michael, Jorge R. AA, Schenectady County C.C., NY, 1988; BA, Russell Sage Coll., Troy, NY, 1990; MA, State Univ. Albany, NY, 1995. Lic. tchr. social studies, secondary edn., N.Y. Asst. editor, legis. liaison Internat. Assn. Fire Chiefs, Washington, 1972-76; tchr. gifted and talented Guilderland Sch. Dist., NY, 1991—. Author: Answering the Call, 1993, Teaching the History of the Albany Internat. Airport, 2000, Creating Hist. Documentaries, 2001, From Africa to NY: Slavery in NY State, 2001, (website) NYS Archives Legacies, 2003. Named Outstanding New Tchr. Sally Mae and Am. Assn. Sch. Adminstrs., Washington, 1992, NYS Hist. Day Tchr. of the Yr., 2001; Nat. Hist. Day Richard T. Ferrell Tchr. of Merit, 2001. Mem. NY State Hist. Assn. (Yorker advisor 1992-94), NY State Coun. Social Studies, Capital Dist. Coun. Social Studies, Phi Alpha Theta, Phi Kappa Phi, Phi Theta Kappa. Democrat. Avocations: writing, dance, genealogy. Office: Farnsworth Mid Sch State Farm Rd Guilderland NY 12084

ESCOTT-RUSSELL, SUNDRA, state legislator; b. Birmingham, Feb. 21, 1954; 1 child, David Russell, Jr. BS in Bus., Ala. State U., 1976. Legis. liaison Gov. Bob James, 1976-81; ins., real estate broker; mem. Ala. Ho. of Reps., Montgomery, 1981-93, Ala. State Senate, Montgomery, 1993—. Chairperson Violent Acts Against the Elderly and Domestic Violence subcom. Judiciary Com., Land, Air, and Water subcom. Conservation, Environment, and Natural Resources Com.; mem. Waterways and Coastal Waters subcom. Conservation, Environment, an Natural Resources Com., Banking subcom. Banking and Ins. Com. Mem. Met. Dem. Women, Jefferson County Coalition; mem. Israel Ind. Meth. Ch. Democrat. Avocation: reading. Home: 1500 Hibernian St Birmingham AL 35214-5232 Office: Ala State House 11 S Union St Rm 731 Montgomery AL 36130-2103 also: PO Box 8343 Birmingham AL 35218-0343

ESCUTIA, MARTHA, state senator; b. East Los Angeles, Calif. m. Leo Briones; 2 children. BA in Pub. Adminstrn. with honors, U. So. Calif; JD, GEorgetown U.; postgrad., Nat. Autonomous U., Mexico City. Sr. rsch. atty. Los Angeles County Superior Ct.; pvt. practice with law firm specializing in civil litigation, L.A.; mem. Calif. State Assembly, 1992-98, Calif. State Senate, 1998—, chmn. health and human svcs. com. V.p. govt. affairs and pub. policy United Way of L.A. Recipient numerous awards for pub. svc. Democrat. Office: Calif State Senate State Capitol Rm 5080 Sacramento CA 95814 also: Ste 125 12440 E Imperial Hwy Norwalk CA 90650

ESFANDIARY, MARY S. physical scientist, operations consultant; b. Passaic, N.J., June 27, 1929; d. Peter J. and Veronica R. (Kida) Nieradka; m. Mohsen S. Esfandiary; children: Homayoun Austin, Dara S. BS in Chemistry, St. John's U., 1951; postgrad., Polytechnic Inst. N.Y., 1955-56. Research chemist Picatinny Arsenal, Dover, N.J., 1951-56; supr. phys. sci. Bur. Mines, Washington, 1956-61; asst. to dir. research Nat. Iranian Oil Co., Tehran, 1961-64; lectr. U. Tehran and Aryamehr Inst. Tech., Tehran, 1961-64, 69-73; dir. internat. affairs Acad. of Scis., Tehran, 1977-79; chief geog. names br. Def. Mapping Agy., Washington, 1981-86, chief prodn. mgmt. office, 1986-87, chief support div., chief inventory mgmt. div., 1987-90, chief product mgmt. dept., 1990-92, dep. dir. distbn. mgmt. ops. Combat Support Ctr., 1993, chief, co-prodn. mgmt. divsn., 1993-94, chief divsn. internat. ops. coprodn. mgmt., 1993-96; ops. mgmt., 1996; dir. MS svcs., 1997—. Contbr. papers and articles to tech. jours., 1952-78. Pres. UN Delegations Women's Club, N.Y.C., 1967-69, v.p., program dir., 1964-67; pres. Diplomatic Corps. Com. for Red Cross, Bangkok, Thailand, 1974-76; v.p., bd. dirs. Found. for Blind of Thailand, Bangkok, 1973-77. Recipient Badge of Honor for Social Service, Thailand, 1975, 1st Class medal Red Cross, Thailand, 1976. Home and Office: 4401 Sedgewick St NW Washington DC 20016-2713

ESHLEMAN, DIANE VARRIN, bank executive; b. Jan. 1956; d. Robert D. Varrin; m. Gregory V. Eshleman, Sept. 6, 1980. Grad., Princeton U., 1978. With Chemical Banking Corp.; exec. v.p. Chase Manhattan bank; mng. dir., chief procurement officer info. tech. JP Morgan Chase, N.Y.C. Named one of 25 Women to Watch, US Banker Mag., 2003. Office: JP Morgan Chase 270 Park Ave New York NY 10017-2070*

ESHOO, ANNA GEORGES, congresswoman; b. New Britain, Conn., Dec. 13, 1942; d. Fred and Alice Alexandre Georges; children: Karen Elizabeth, Paul Frederick. AA with honors, Canada Coll., 1975. Chmn. San Mateo County Dem. Ctrl. Com., Calif., 1978-82; chair Human Rels. Com., 1979-82; mem. U.S. Congress from 14th Calif. dist., 1993—; at-large minority whip; mem. energy and commerce com., intelligence com. Chief of staff Calif. Assembly Spkr. Leo McCarthy, 1981; regional majority whip No. Calif., 1993-94. Co-founder Women's Hall of Fame; chair San Mateo County (Calif.) Dem. Party, 1980; active San Mateo County Bd. Suprs., 1982-92, pres., 1986; pres. Bay Area Air Quality Mgmt. Dist., 1982-92; mem. San Francisco Bay Conservation Devel. Commn., 1982-92; chair San Mateo County Gen. Hosp. Bd. Dirs. Democrat. Roman Catholic. Office: US Ho Reps 205 Cannon Ho Office Bldg Washington DC 20515-0001*

ESKRIDGE, CAROLE FAY, artist; b. Port of Spain, Trinidad, July 3, 1947; came to U.S., 1948; d. Woodrow Wilson and Lyda Mae (Blanchard) E.; m. Harold Sherman Frye, Aug. 6, 1966 (div. Aug. 1976); children: Sarah Mae Frye, Rebecca Jane Frye. Grad. magna cum laude, Ala. A&M; photography cert., U. Ala., Huntsville, 1981. Founder Visionary Artists Guild for Mentally Ill Artists, Huntsville, 1991—. Mural painter History of Mental Health, 1992. Recipient Disting. Svc. award Huntsville-Madison County Mental Health Bd., 1992, Consumer of Yr. award Ala. Alliance Mentally Ill, 1993, Creativity award Mental Health Consumers Ala., 1995, cert. Spl. Congrl. Recognition, 1996. Mem. Docents of Hunsville Mus. Art. Roman Catholic. Avocations: sailing, writing, pub. speaking. Studio: 115 Clinton Ave Apt 805 Huntsville AL 35801 Office: Visionary Guild Mentally Ill Artists Huntsville AL 35801 Office Fax: 256-539-4161. E-mail: eskridgec@bellsouth.net.

ESKRIDGE, JUDITH ANN, secondary school educator; b. Tuscola, Ill., July 15, 1941; d. Reed Warren and Marjorie May (Reeder) Blain; m. Donald R. Henderson, July 10, 1966 (div. Dec. 1977); m. Howard Dean Eskridge, June 29, 1986; children: Kendra Eskridge Chriss, Jodi Henderson Samsa. BA, MacMurray Coll., 1963; MEd, U. Ill., 1968. Title I tchr., dir. Arcola (Ill.) Cmty. Unit #306, 1978—. Recipient Cert. of Appreciation Ea. Ill. Area Spl. Edn., 1988. Mem. NEA, Internat. Reading Assn., Ill. Reading Coun., Title I Dirs., Arcola Edn. Assn. Methodist. Avocations: reading, gardening, exercising, traveling. Home: 424E E County Road 1250 N Tuscola IL 61953-7074 Office: Arcola High Sch 351 W Washington St Arcola IL 61910-1120

ESLER, BARBARA HART, accountant, consultant; d. Gordon Clifford and Dorothy Marguerite (Hart) Allen; m. Dale Clement Ulrich, Nov. 7, 1953 (div.); children: David Allen Ulrich, Rebecca Anne McAllister. A, Mich. State U., 1953. Asst. contr. Liggett Sch., Grosse Pointe, Mich., 1960—67; acting contr. Robinson Furniture Co., Warren, Mich., 1967—73; contr. Taylor-Thompson Machinery Co., Troy, Mich., 1973—81; acctg. mgr. MotivAction, Inc., Southfield, Mich., 1981—83; fin. mgr. Associated Photographic Industries, Royal Oak, Mich., 1983—85; acct. Peterson Window Corp., Ferndale, Mich., 1983—91, SHOWTECH Presentation Systems, Inc., Wixom, Mich., 1998—2002; v.p. adminstrn. Image Network, Inc., Southfield, 1984—, Classic Body Fashion, Ltd., Livonia, Mich., 2002—; office mgr., acct. Concept Tech., Inc., Birmingham, Mich., 1992—; owner Esler Acctg. Svcs., Troy, Mich., 1983—. Sec., mem. adv. bd. YWCA Camp Cavell, Lexington, Mich., 1990—. Named Outstanding Jr. Mem., Mich. Soc. DAR, 1967. Mem.: Paint Creek Folklore Soc. (treas. 2002—), Zeta Tau Alpha (life; various local alumnae orgn. offices 1957—62). Avocations: cooking, needlecrafts, reading, music, travel. Office: Esler Acctg Svcs P O Box 1552 Troy MI 48099-1552 Personal E-mail: barbarae@sprynet.com.

ESMAELI, BITA, ophthalmologist; b. Tehran, Iran, Mar. 6, 1963; came to U.S., 1978; d. Mohammed T. Esmaeli and Nahid Hidaji; m. Howard Gutstein (div.); 1 child, Brett Ferdosi Gutstein. BS in Biology, Rhodes Coll., 1984; MA in Cell Physiology, U. Calif., Santa Barbara, 1984; MD, Chgo. Med. Sch., 1990. Bd. cert. Am. Bd. Ophthalmology; lic. physician, Calif., Mich., Tex. Intern Ill. Masonic Med. Ctr., Chgo., 1990-91; resident in ophthalmology U. Mich., Ann Arbor, 1991-94; fellow in ophthalmic plastic and reconstructive surgery U. Toronto, Ont., Can., 1995-96; staff ophthalmologist St. Joseph Mercy Hosp., Ann Arbor, 1994-98; asst. prof., chief ophthalmology sect. M.D. Anderson Cancer Ctr., Houston, 1998—. Adj. asst. prof. ophthalmology Baylor Coll. Medicine, 1998—. Contbr. numerous articles to profl. jours. Recipient Janet M. Glasgow Meml. citation Am. Med. Women's Assn., 1990, Muscular Dystrophy Assn. Med. Student Rsch. award, 1987; Rhodes Coll. Sci. scholar, 1980-84. Fellow Am. Acad. Ophthalmology; mem. AMA, Am. Soc. Ophthalmic Plastic and Reconstructive Surgery (Merril Reeh Pathology award 1997), Assn. for Rsch. in Vision and Ophthalmology, Assn. for Women in Ophthalmology, Am. Acad. Ophthalmology, Alpha Omega Alpha. Avocations: live classical concerts, persian rugs (history and collection), wine tasting, international ophthalmology. Home: 2324 Bolsover St Houston TX 77005-2612 Office: MD Anderson Cancer Ctr Box 62 1515 Holcombe Blvd Houston TX 77030-4009

ESNES, VALERIE JUNE, music educator; b. Bayshore, N.Y., Dec. 29, 1957; d. Charles George Gilliam and June Carol Nobile; m. Thomas Chester Esnes, Aug. 9, 2003; stepchildren: Michael, Karen, Christopher. B in Music Edn., SUNY, Fredonia, 1980; MFA, SUNY, Stony Brook, 1986. Band dir. Bellport (N.Y.) Mid. Sch., 1982—. Mem.: Suffolk County Music Educators, N.Y. State Tchrs. Assn., N.Y. State Sch. Music Assn., Internat. Clarinet Assn. Avocations: exercise, reading, travel. Home: 10 Ashley Ln Shoreham NY 11786 Office: Bellport Mid Sch Kreamer St Bellport NY 11713

ESPARZA, KACIE LYNNE, military officer; b. Atlantic, Iowa, June 27, 1980; d. Stanton Farrell Campbell and Lisa Luanne Flowers; m. Andrew Arthur Esparza, II, Nov. 3, 2001; 1 child, Andrew Arthur III. Student, CC Air Force, Davis-Monthan AFB, Ariz., 2000—. Asst. mgr. Hy-Vee Food Stores, Souix Falls, SD, 1999—2000; enlisted USAF, 2000; maintenance prodn. mgr. 358 Amu 355 Amxs 355 Wing, Davis-Monthan AFB, 2001—. Dormitory coun. pres. 355 Wing, Davis-Monthan Air Force Base, Ariz., 2001. Republican. Lutheran. Avocations: writing, vocal music, art, softball, dance. Home: 6639 E Broadway # 149 Tucson AZ 85710 Personal E-mail: kacie.esparza@americanamicable.com Business E-Mail: kacie.esparza@dm.af.mil.

ESPENLAUB, MARGO LINN, women's studies educator, writer, artist; b. Decorah, Iowa, May 1, 1944; d. Lloyd Wilson and Margaret Mary (Seegmiller) Ruid; children: Arn R. Johnson, Cara C. Johnson. BA in Philosophy, U. Colo., 1983, M in Humanities, 1985; PhD in Women's Studies, The Union Inst. Grad. Sch., 1995. Assoc. dir. student devel., mem. faculty U. Denver, The Women's Coll. Mem. faculty senate Inst. for Ethics, Ctr. for Teaching and Learning, faculty coord. TWC Student Writer's Club U. Denver; colloqium coord. Front Range Feminist Scholars, 1991-98. Co-author: Women's Studies: Thinking Women, 1993; gen. editor Voices of the Women's Coll. Mem. biomed. ethics com. Kaiser Permanente, Denver, 1986-96. Mem. Nat. Mus. Women in the Arts. E-mail: mespenla@du.edu.

ESPINOZA, DORIS LOIDA, music educator, minister; b. Albuquerque, Oct. 9, 1950; d. Jose Leandro and Abedulia (Martinez) Padilla; m. Bernardino Pedro Espinoza Jr., Aug. 11, 1972; children: Eunice Dina, Eli Jose. Student, L.Am. Bible Inst., El Paso, Tex., 1969-72; BA in Christian Edn., S.W. Assemblies of God U., 1987. Ordained to ministry Assemblies of God Ch., 1986. Sec.-treas. Women's Ministries Gulf L.Am. Dist., 1972-75, 88—, dist. youth choir dir., 1980-85, choir dir., 1988-98; exec. sec. Straus-Frank, San Antonio, 1973-75; sect. missionette coord. Villa Del Sol, Crystal City, Tex., 1985-88; music tchr. Wintergarden Christian Acad., Crystal City, Tex., 1990-96; home sch. tchr. Crystal City, Tex., 1985-91, 97—. Cons., counselor; musical group dir. Composer; author numerous poems. Coord. Missionette Girls Club, Crystal City, 1985-88; mem. drug free com. Crystal City, 1988-94; exec. sec. Assembly God Gulf Latin Am. Dist., 1976-82 Mem. L.Am. Bible Inst. Alumni Assn. (pres. 1982-86), Religious Conf. Mgmt. Assn. Avocations: walking, jogging, handcrafts, singing, playing the piano. Office: Womens Ministries GLAD PO Box 313 Crystal City TX 78839-0313

ESPOSITO, BONNIE LOU, marketing professional; b. Chgo., July 20, 1947; d. Ralph Edgar and Dorothy Mae (Groh) Myers; m. Frank Merle Esposito, Aug. 15, 1969 (div. Sept. 1985); children: Mario Henry, Elizabeth Ann. BA, George Williams Coll., 1969. Caseworker Little Bros. of the Poor, Chgo., 1969-72; dir. Little Bros.-Friends of the Elderly, Mpls., 1972-78; organizer Community Crime Prevention, Mpls., 1978-81; owner Espo Inc./Mario's Ristorante, Mpls., 1978-85; mktg. mgr. City of Mpls. Energy Office, 1981—; dir. mktg. and tng. The Energy Collaborative, 1987-93; dir. mktg. Ctr. for Energy and Environment, Mpls., 1989-95; dir. WINGS program Employment Action Ctr., Mpls., 1995-97; dir. Minn. Office Citizenship and Vol. Svcs., Mpls., 1997—2002; exec. dir. Account Ability Minn., 2002—. V.p., bd. dirs. Resource Alternatives, Inc.; sec. bd. dirs. Golden Girl Homes, 2002—. Bd. dirs. Vital Aging Network, 2002; bd. dir. Golden Girls Homes, 2002—. Recipient Disting. Leadership award, Minn. Assn. Vol. Adminstrn., 2002. Mem. NAFE (bd. dirs. Monday Night Network 1988), Midwest Direct Mktg. Assn., Minn. Multi-Housing Assn., Nat. Apt. Assn., Profl. Assn. for Consumer Energy Edn. (bd. dirs. 1993—97, chmn. fin. com.). Office: Office Accountability Minn 2300 Myrtle Ave Ste 180 Saint Paul MN 55114

ESQUIVEL, MARY, agricultural products company executive; b. 1945; Homemaker, 1976; ct. interpreter State of Calif., Salinas, 1976-83; sec., treas. Adobe Packing Co., Salinas, 1983—. Office: Adobe Packing Co PO Box 4940 Salinas CA 93912-4940

ESSA, LISA BETH, elementary school educator; b. Nov. 19, 1955; d. Mark Newyla and Elizabeth (Warda) Essa. BA, U. Pacific-Stockton, 1977, MA in Curriculum and Instrn. Reading, 1980. Cert. tchr. elem., multiple subject and reading specialist Calif. Libr. media specialist Delhi (Calif.) Elem. Sch. Dist., 1978-80; reading clinic tutor San Joaquin Delta C.C., Stockton, Calif., 1980; libr. media specialist Hayward (Calif.) Unified Sch. Dist., 1980—. Chair curriculum coun. Hayward Unified Sch. Dist., 2000—01; support provider Beginning Tchr. Support Assessment, 2000—01. Supr. San Francisco host com. Dem. Nat. Conv., 1984. Named Master Tchr., Intel Teach to the Future; recipient Hon. Svc. award, 1999. Mem.: Hayward Unified Tchrs. Assn., Calif. Tchrs. Assn., Jr. League San Francisco. Episcopalian. E-mail: chalktalk1@aol.com.

ESSANDOH, HILDA BRATHWAITE, kindergarten educator; b. N.Y.C., Feb. 19, 1925; d. Charles Christopher and Millicent Marian (Boxill) Brathwaite; m. Samuel O. Essandoh, June 11, 1959; children: Millicent Efua, Yvonne Araba, Dorothy Esi. BA, Hunter Coll., 1959; MS, Bank Street Coll. Edn., 1976, profl. diploma in supervision-adminstrn., 1980. Cert. nursery, kindergarten, 1st-6th grades, sch. adminstrn. and supervision. Tchr. kindergarten N.Y.C. Bd. Edn., 1962-91. Recipient Ely Trachtenberg award. Home: 548 W 165th St New York NY 10032-4942

ESSEX, LAUREN S. women's health care company executive; BA in Psychology and Bus., U. Rochester; MS in Mgmt., Northwestern U. Various brand mgmt. positions Helene Curtis, 1984-94, br. mgr., 1991-94; v.p. personal care products, sales and customer svc. La Costa Products Internat., 1994-96; v.p. mktg. Cosmederm Tech.s, Inc., 1996-98; v.p. mktg. self-care products Women First HealthCare, Inc., San Diego, 1998—. Office: Women First HealthCare Inc 12220 El Camino Real Ste 400 San Diego CA 92130-2091 Fax: 619-509-1353.

ESSICK, CAROL EASTERLING, elementary school educator; d. Woodrow Wilson and Laura Byrd Easterling; m. Irving Louis Essick, Mar. 26, 1994. MusB, Berry Coll., 1980. Cert. performance based tchr. Ga. Profl. Stds. Commn. Elem. music specialist McDuffie County Schs., Thomson, Ga., 1980—81, Waycross (Ga.) City Schs., 1981—93, Ware County Schs., Waycross, 1993—98, Glynn County Schs., Brunswick, 1998—. Vice-chairperson Goodyear Elem. Sch. Coun., Brunswick, 2001—02, sec., 2002—. Mem.: NEA, Music Educators Nat. Conf., Sigma Alpha Iota (life Sword of Honor 1979). Methodist. Avocations: golf, photography, coin collecting. Office: Goodyear Elem Sch 3000 Roxboro Rd Brunswick GA 31520 Personal E-mail: cessick@adelphia.net. Business E-Mail: cessick@glynn.k12.ga.us.

ESSIEN, FRANCINE B. geneticist, educator; BA in Biology, Temple U.; PhD in Genetics, Yeshiva U.; postgrad., U. Conn. Prof. dept. biol. scis. Rutgers U., New Brunswick, N.J., 1997—. Dir. Minority Undergrad. Sci. Programs, Rutgers U., 1988—, founder, co-founder Success in the Scis., Biomed. Careers Program, Rsch. Apprentice Program, ACCESS-MED, mem. adv. bd. Douglass Project for Rutgers Women in Math, Sci. and Engring.; mem. rev. panel NSF/NIH; cons. CUNY, Atlanta U.; lectr. in field. Contbr. articles to profl. jours. Fulbright scholar; recipient Spina Bifida Assn. Am. award, N.J. Women of Achievement award Woodrow Wilson Found. Instns.; named Black Achiever in Sci., Chgo. Mus. Sci. and Industry, U.S. Prof. of Yr. for Rsch. and Doctoral Univs., Carnegie Found. Advancement of Teaching.; Disting. Black Scholar-in-Residence, U. Cin., 1988; CASE Professor of the Yr. 1994-95; recipient W.E.B. DuBois award for edn. NAACP of Cen. N.J., 1997. Office: Rutgers U Nelson Lab/Busch Campus 604 Allison Rd Piscataway NJ 08854-8000

ESSIG, KATHLEEN SUSAN, university official, management consultant; b. Denver, July 5, 1956; d. Robert and Ethel Essig. BS in BA, Colo. State U., 1979, MS, 1987. CPA, Colo. Personal fin. planner, v.p. fin. Successful Money Mgmt., Ft. Collins, Colo., 1987-88; accts. payable technician Colo. State U., Ft. Collins, 1980-81, supr. comml. accts. receivable, 1981-83, gen. acct. II, 1983-85, supr. student loans, 1985-87, supr. accts. receivable, acct. II, 1988-89, cost acct. III, 1989-94, univ. ofcl., contr., 1994; univ. mgmt. cons. KPMG Peat Marwick, Denver, 1994-97, 1995-97; mgr. prin. cons. Oracle Corp., Redwood Shores, Calif., 1998—. Mem. Am. Bus. Women's Assn. (v.p. 1985, Woman of Yr. 1985), Nat. Assn. Accts. Avocations: photography, golf, skiing, scuba diving.

ESSIG, NANCY CLAIRE, publishing executive; b. Canton, Ohio, Oct. 4, 1939; d. Atlee L. and Bernice (Bowen) E. AB, Ohio U., 1962. Publicity asst. Charles Scribner's Sons, N.Y.C., 1962-64, Dell Pub. Co., N.Y.C., 1965-66; publicity dir. Columbia U. Press, N.Y.C., 1966-73; sales mgr. Johns Hopkins U. Press, Balt., 1973-74, mktg. dir., 1974-83, asst. dir., mktg. dir., 1983-88; dir. U. Press of Va., Charlottesville, 1988—. Mem. Assn. Am. Univ. Presses (bd. dirs. 1981-83), Women in Scholarly Publishing (pres. 1982-83), Women's Nat. Book Assn. (pres. 1980-81), Colonnade Club-(Charlottesville). Office: University Press of Va PO Box 400318 Charlottesville VA 22904-4318

ESSINGER, SUSAN JANE, special education educator; b. Paris, Ill., Oct. 7, 1952; d. Rex Milburn and Virginia Ellen (White) E. BS in Edn., Ea. Ill. U., Charleston, 1973; MS in Edn., Ind. State U., 1981, postgrad. Cert. learning disabilities, elem., educationally mentally handicapped with early childhood endorsement. Elem. tchr. Havana (Ill.) Sch. Dist., 1973-74; tchr. early childhood spl. edn. Paris Sch. Dist. 95, 1974—. Mem. APA, NEA, IDEC, CEC, Assn. for Edn. Young Children, Ill. Edn. Assn., Paris Tchrs. Assn. Avocations: dollmaking, gardening, collecting coins and stamps. Home: 1104 S Main St Paris IL 61944-2823 Office: Paris Sch Dist 95 S Main St Paris IL 61944 E-mail: sessinger@comwares.net.

ESSMAN, SAUNDRA CAROL, music educator; b. Memphis; d. John and Mable Hill; m. James Timothy Essman, Feb. 11, 1967; children: Caroline, Sheridan, Jimmy. BMusE, Ark. State U., Jonesboro, 1968, MMusE, 1972. Music tchr., K-6 Walnut Ridge (Ark.) Pub. Sch., 1968—72; choral music and humanities tchr., 9-12 Mt. St. Mary's Acad., Little Rock, 1972—73; music tchr., K-6 Carlisle (Ark.) Pub. Sch., 1973—78, Walnut Ridge Pub. Sch., 1984—. Mem.: Ark. Choral Dirs. Assn., Ark. Elem. Music Educators Assn. (award 2003), Music Educators Nat. Conf. Avocations: collecting alabaster boxes, miniature pianos, old textile spools, travel.

ESTABROOK, ALISON, breast surgeon; b. N.Y.C., Oct. 29, 1951; d. Edwin Burke and Shirley (Butler) E.; m. William Harrington, June 12, 1982. BA, Barnard Coll., 1974; MD, NYU, 1978. Resident in surgery Columbia-Presbyn. Med. Ctr., N.Y.C., 1978-81, 82-84, fellow in surgery, onocology, 1981-82, asst. prof. surgery, 1984—, dir. Breast Clinic, 1985—97, Florence Irving asst. prof., 1989-92, chief breast surgery, 1991-97, assoc. prof. surgery, 1992-95, prof. clin. surgery, 1995—; chief breast surgery St. Luke's Roosevelt Hosp., N.Y.C., 1998—. Mem.: Am. Soc. Breast Disease (bd. dirs. 1996—2001), Soc. Surg. Oncology, N.Y. Surg. Soc., N.Y. Met. Breast Group, Assn. Women Surgeons, Am. Soc. Clin. Oncology, Sigma Xi (Kappa chpt.). Office: St Lukes Roosevelt Hosp 425 W 59th St New York NY 10019-1104 Office Phone: 212-523-7500.

ESTABROOK, IRIS W. state representative; b. N.Y.C., June 28; married; two children. BS, Cornell U., 1972; MST, U. Chgo., 1973. Former tchr. and ednl. rschr.; past dir. U. N.H. Child Care Resource and Referral; mem. dist. 8 N.H. Ho. of Reps., Concord, 1996—. Adv. com. N.H. Child Day Care. Mem. Oyster River Sch. Bd., N.H., 1991-94; past bd. dirs. Seacoast Assn. Child Care. Democrat. Home: 8 Burnham Ave Durham NH 03824-3011

ESTELL, DORA LUCILE, retired educational administrator; b. Ft. Worth, Mar. 3, 1930; d. Hugh and Hattie Lucile (Poole) E. BA, East Tex. Bapt. U., 1951; MA, U. North Tex., 1959; EdD, East Tex. State U., 1988. Tchr. Mission (Tex.) Ind. Sch. Dist., 1951-53; tchr., adminstr. Marshall (Tex.) Ind. Sch. Dist., 1953-68; dep. dir. Region VII Edn. Svc. Ctr., Kilgore, Tex., 1968-94, ret., 1994. Contbr. articles to profl. jours. Bd. dir. South Milan County United Way, Richards Meml. Hosp. Named Rockdale Citizen of Yr., 2001. Mem. Rockdale C. of C. (bd. dirs.), Phi Delta Kappa. Baptist. Avocations: photography, gardening. Home: 611 W Bell Ave Rockdale TX 76567-2809

ESTEP, MYRNA LYNNE, systems analyst, philosophy educator; b. Whitesville, W.Va., Jan. 7, 1944; d. Modest Schaeffer and Mary Magdalene E.; m. Richard Keith Schoenig, June 5, 1971; 1 child, Debora Lynne. BA, Ind. U., 1970, MS, 1971, PhD, 1975; postgrad., U. Tex., 1993. Assoc. instr. Ind. U., Bloomington, 1972-75; asst. prof. U. Tex., San Antonio, 1975-78; rsch. edn. specialist Acad. Health Scis., San Antonio, Tex., 1979-84; program systems analyst, field researcher USMC, U.S. Navy, Quantico, Va., 1984-87; grad. faculty, advisor U. Zimbabwe, 1987-89; rsch. systems analyst San Antonio, 1990—; adj. faculty in philosophy U. of Incarnate Word, San Antonio, 1996-99, Our Lady of the Lake U., San Antonio, 1996-98. Grad. faculty U. Zimbabwe, Harare; advisor to ministries of higher edn. and labour, manpower planning and social welfare, Zimbabwe, 1987-89. Author: The Relation Between Theoretical and Procedural Knowing, 1975, A Theory of Immediate Awareness: Self-Organization and Adaptation in Natural Intelligence, 2003; co-editor (with E.S. Maccia and others): Women and Education, 1975; reviewer (for jours.); contbr. articles to profl. jours. including Applied Sys. and Cybermetics, Pergamon, Feminista: The On-Line Jour. of Feminist Reconstrn. Recipient Best Paper award U. Vienna, Austria, 1992. Mem. AAAS, Internat. Soc. Gen. Systems Rsch., Austrian Soc. Cybernetics, Math. Assn. Am., N.Y. Acad. Sci., Phi Kappa Phi. Home: 16022 Oak Grove Dr San Antonio TX 78255-1128 E-mail: emathematica@aol.com.

ESTERLY, NANCY BURTON, physician; b. N.Y.C., Apr. 14, 1935; d. Paul R. and Tanya (Pasahow) Burton; m. John R. Esterly, June 16, 1957; children: Sarah Burton, Anne Beidler, John Snyder, II, Henry Clark, II. AB, Smith Coll., 1956; MD, Johns Hopkins U., 1960. Intern, then resident in pediatrics Johns Hopkins Hosp., 1960-63, resident in dermatology, 1964-67; instr. pediatrics Johns Hopkins U. Med. Sch., 1967-68; instr., trainee La Rabida U. Chgo. Inst.; also dept. pediatrics U. Chgo. Med. Sch., 1968-69; asst. prof. Pritzker Sch. Medicine, U. Chgo., 1969-70, assoc. prof., 1973-78; asst. prof. dermatology Abraham Lincoln Sch. Medicine, U. Ill., 1970-72, assoc. prof. dermatology and pediatrics, 1972-73; dir. div. dermatology, dept. pediatrics Michael Reese Hosp. and Med. Ctr., Chgo., 1973-78; prof. pediatrics and dermatology Northwestern U. Med. Sch., 1978; head div. dermatology, dept. pediatrics Children's Meml. Hosp., Chgo., 1978-87; prof. pediatrics and dermatology Med. Coll. Wis., Milw., 1987—; head div. dermatology, dept. pediatrics Children's Hosp. Wis., Milw., 1987—. Editor-in-chief Pediatric Dermatology, 1983—; contbr. numberous articles to profl. jours. Recipient David Martic Carter award, Am. Skin Assn., 2002, Lifetime Career Educator award, Dermatology Found., 2002, Disting. Svc. award, Med. Coll. Wis., 2004. Mem.: Wis. Pediat. Soc., Women's Dermatol. Soc., Soc. Pediat. Dermatology (1st Lifetime Achievement award 1998), Soc. Pediat. Rsch., Am. Acad. Pediatrics, Soc. Investigative Dermatology, Wis. Dermatol. Soc., Am. Dermatol. Assn., Am. Acad. Dermatology, Internat. Soc. Pediat. Dermatology, Sigma Xi. Office: 9200 W Wisconsin Ave Milwaukee WI 53226-3522 Office Phone: 414-805-5304.

ESTES, CARROLL LYNN, sociologist, educator; b. Fort Worth, May 30, 1938; d. Joe Ewing and Carroll (Cox) E.; 1 child, Duskie Lynn Gelfand Estes. AB, STanford U., 1959; MA, So. Meth. U., 1961; PhD, U. Calif., San Diego, 1972; DHL (hon.), Russell Sage Coll., 1986. Rsch. asst., asst. study dir. Brandeis U. Social Welfare Rsch. Ctr., 1962-63, rsch. assoc., 1964-65, project dir., 1965-67; vis. lectr. Florence Heller Grad. Sch., 1964-65; rsch. dir. Simmons Coll., 1963-64; asst. prof. social work San Diego State Coll.,

1967-72; asst. prof. in residence dept. psychiatry U. Calif., San Francisco, 1972-75, assoc. prof. dept. social and behavioral scis., 1975-79, prof., 1979-92, chair dept. social and behavioral scis., 1981-93, coord. human devel. tng. program, 1974-75; dir. Aging Health Policy Rsch. Ctr., 1979-85, Inst. for Health and Aging, 1985-99. Faculty rsch. lectr. U. Calif., 1993. Author: The Decision-Makers: The Power Structure of Dallas, 1963; co-author: Protective Services for Older People, 1972, U.S. Senate Special Committee on Aging Report, Paperwork and the Older Americans Act, 1978, The Aging Enterprise, 1979 Fiscal Austerity and Aging, 1983, Long Term Care of the Elderly, 1985, Political Economy, Health and Aging, 1984, The Long Term Care Crisis, 1993, The Nation's Health, 2001, 7th edit., 2003, Critical Gerontology, 1999, Social Policy and Aging, 2001, Social Theory, Social Policy and Aging, 2003, Health Policy, 4th edit., 2004; contbr. articles to profl. jours. Mem. Calif. Commn. on Aging, 1974-77; cons. U.S. Senate Spl. Com. on Aging from 1976, Notch Commn. U.S. Commn. Social Security, 1993-94; bd. dirs. Nat. Com. to Preserve Social Security and Medicare, 2002—. Recipient Matrix award Theta Sigma Phi, 1964, award for contbns. to lives of older Californians, Calif. Commn. on Aging, 1977, Helen Nahm Rsch. award U. Calif., San Francisco, 1986, Woman Who Would Be Pres. League of Women Voters, 1998. Mem. Inst. Medicine of NAS, ACLU, Am. Sociol. Assn. (Disting. Scholar award Aging and Life Course 2000), Assn. Gerontology in Higher Edn. (pres. 1980-81, recipient Beverly award 1993, Tibbitts award 2000), Am. Soc. on Aging (pres. 1982-84, Leadership award 1986), Gerontol. Soc. Am. (Kent award 1992, pres. 1995-96), Older Women's League (v.p. 1994-97), Soc. Study Social Problems, Alpha Kappa Delta, Pi Beta Phi. Democrat. Office: U Calif San Francisco Inst Health & Aging 3333 California St Ste 340 San Francisco CA 94118-1944

ESTES, ELAINE ROSE GRAHAM, retired librarian; b. Springfield, Mo., Nov. 24, 1931; d. James McKinley and Zelma Mae (Smith) Graham; m. John Melvin Estes, Dec. 29, 1953. BSBA, Drake U., 1953, tchg. cert., 1956; MSLS, U. Ill., 1960. With Pub. Libr. Des Moines, 1956-95, coord. ext. svcs., 1977-78, dir., 1978-95, ret., 1995. Lectr. antiques, hist. architecture, librs.; mem. conservation planning com. for disaster preparedness for librs. Author bibliographies of books on antiques; contbr. articles to profl. jours. Mem. State of Iowa Cultural Affairs Adv. Coun., 1986—94, Nat. Commn. on Future of Drake U., 1987—00, chmn. Des Moines Mayor's Hist. Dist. Commn.; mem. nominations review com. Iowa State Nat. Hist. Register, 1983—89; chmn. hist. subcom. Des Moines Sesquecentennial Com., 1993, Iowa Sister State Commn., 1993—95; mem. com. 40th Anniversary Drake U. Alumni Weekend, 50 Yr. Drake Alumni Weekend, 2003, mem. July 4 com. Iowa Sesquecentennial; nat. exch. dir. Friendship Force, 1997; mem. nat. adv. bd. Cowles Libr., 1998—; mem. Gov.'s Iowa Centennial Meml. Found., 1998—; mem. acquisition com. Salisbury House; mem. cultural ctr. task force African Am. Hist. Mus., 1999; mem. Iowa author com. Pub. Libr. Des Moines Found., 2001—03; mem. Terrace Hill Commn., 2001—; bd. dirs. Des Moines Art Ctr., 1972—83, hon. mem., 1983—; bd. dirs. Friends of Libr. USA, 1986—92, Henry Wallace House Found., Iowa Libr. Centennial Com., 1990—91. Recipient Recognition award Greater Des Moines, YWCA, 1975, Disting. Alumni award Drake U., 1979, Woman of Achievement award YWCA, 1989, Excellence in Hist. Preservation award City of Des Moines, 1994, Contbn. to Cmty. award Connect Found., 1995, Friend of Literacy award Pub. Libr. of Des Moines Found., 2003; named Textbook Project in her honor, Forest Libr., 2002; named to Wall of Fame, YWCA, 2003. Mem.: ALA (50th Anniversary Honor Roll for Intellectual Freedom 1999), Iowa Soc. Preservation Hist. Landmarks (bd. dirs. 1969—97), Libr. Assn. Greater Des Moines Metro Area (chmn. 1992, pres.), Iowa Urban Pub. Libr. Assn., Iowa Libr. Assn. (life; pres. 1978—79), Iowa Antique Assn., Terrace Hill (Gov.'s Mansion) Soc. (bd. dirs. 1972—, v.p. 1991—93, pres. 1993—96), Links Inc. (40th ann. com. 1997), Drake U. 50 Yr. Club, Questers Inc. Club (pres. 1982, state 2d v.p. 1984—86, 1st v.p. 1990—2000, pres. 1997, state pres. 2000—03, pres. 2001—03), Rotary (history com. 2001), Proteus (pres. 2003—04).

ESTES, PAMELA JEAN, pastor; b. Topeka, Oct. 14, 1953; d. Jack E. and Bonita A. (Hatfield) E. BA, Bin Music Edn., Ouachita U., 1974, M in Music Edn., 1976; MLS, Vanderbilt U., 1983; MDiv, Boston U., 1988, MST, 1989. Tchr. Thayer (Mo.) Schs., 1976-79; libr. Pochontas (Ark.) H.S., 1979-82; libr. intern Vanderbilt U., 1982-83, libr., 1983-85; cataloger Boston U. Sch. Theology, 1985-89; pastor Union Congl. Ch., Walpole, Mass., 1987-88; pianist East Walpole (Mass.) United Meth. Ch., 1988-89; pastor First United Meth. Ch., Camden, Ark., 1989-92, Stamps (Ark.) Charge, 1992-93, St. James United Meth., Little Rock, 1993-96, St. Luke United Meth. Ch., Little Rock, 1996—2000, First United Meth. Ch., Blytheville, Ark., 2000—. Pvt. musician, 1970—; cataloger Ouachita, summer, 1976-82; chair Commn. on the Status and Role of Women, 1989-95, Ark. Del. to White House Conf. on Librs., 1991, Sexual Harrassment Task Force United Meth. Ch., Ark., 1992-95. Editor: United Methodist Women's Day Reference, 1991; author of poetry. Debate moderator LWV, Camden, Ark., 1989-92; vol. Friends of the Libr., Little Rock, 1993-95. Oxnam scholar Boston U. Sch. Theology. Mem. DAR, P.E.O., Rotary Club (Paul Harris fellow), Sigma Alph Iota, Delta Kappa Gamma. Democrat. Avocations: music, reading, children, poetry, travel. Home: 608 Ridgeway N Blytheville AR 72315 Office: First United Meth Ch 701 W Main Blytheville AR 72315 E-mail: pjestes@missconet.com.

ESTES, VALERIE, independent consultant; b. Inglewood, Calif., Apr. 9, 1941; d. Warren Clough and Mary Katherine (Pray) E.; m. Robert Burns Morrill, May 26, 1963 (div. 1969). BS in Home Econs., U. Nev., 1962; AB in Anthropology, U. Calif., Berkeley, 1973, MA in Anthropology, 1975, PhD in Anthropology, 1984. Adminstrv. asst. Office of Sen. Howard W. Cannon, Washington, 1962-63; asst. pub. rels. Calif. Wine Inst., San Francisco, 1963-64; pvt. practice tutor English pvt. practice, Greece, Turkey, Libya, Italy, 1964-67; editl. asst. Grey Fox Press & Grove Press, San Francisco, 1968-75; dir. women, work & family project U. Calif., Berkeley, 1984-85, lectr. Hayward, 1985-86; dir. women & work and 3d world Am. Higher Edn. Consortium for Urban Affairs, Berkeley, 1986-88; co-dir. minority edn. project U. Calif., Berkeley, 1988-90; gender & socioeconomic analyst Devel. Strategies for Fragile Lands Project, Washington, 1991-93; sr. social analyst Gender in Social and Econ. Systems Project, Washington, 1993-94; creator, coord. Gender and Environ. Network, Washington, 1991-94; ind. cons. U.S. Agy. Internat. Devel. & Inter-Am. Devel. Bank, Washington, 1994-96; gender analyst U.S. Agy. Internat. Devel., 1996—. Grad. fellow Danforth Found., U. Calif., 1974-80, rsch. fellow Inter-Am. Found., La Paz, Bolovia, 1977-80, Ford Found., 1981-83; Robert Lowie Grad. scholar U. Calif., 1983-84, vis. scholar, 1990-91. Mem. Am. Anthropology Assn., Consortium Women in Devel. Home and Office: 1600 N Oak St Apt 1526 Arlington VA 22209-2768

ESTHER, QUEEN, playwright, scriptwriter, songwriter, solo performer, actor, musician; d. James Monroe and Ivory Boone Pooser. BA in Screenwriting, The New Sch., 1994. Performer: (plays and musicals) Whoa, Jack!, Harlem Song (Audelco Award nomination for best supporting actress, 2002), RENT, Stagedoor Canteen (NY Drama Desk Award for Tribeca Playhouse, 2002); solo performer, vocalist, playwright: one person shows The Moxie Show, Queen Esther: Unemployed Superstar; vocalist, songwriter (recordings) Mighty (as blues duo Hoosegow with guitarist Elliot Sharp), 1996, featured vocalist No Escape from the Blues: The Electric Lady Sessions (featured vocalist w/guitarist James "Blood" Ulmer) (Named one of the Top 50 CD's of 2003 by Rolling Stone Magazine); performer: (Documentary TV Series) The It Factor, 2001, (movie) Marcy X, 2001. Recipient Governor's Honor's Program, State of Ga., 1982, Arts Recognition and Talent Search (Merit award), Nat. Found. for the Arts, 1983; Scholarships in Acting, The U. of Tex. at Austin, 1983. Mem.: Go Girls Music, Women In Music. Born Again Christian. Achievements include performing at White House for the President, First Lady, various Cabinet members, and Dignitaries in honor of Black History Music Month in June, 2003; started a label, EL Recordings, debut solo CD of Black Americana released in 2004. Avocations: apologetics, travel, writing, reading. Personal E-mail: info@queen-esther.com.

ESTILETTE, KATHLEEN C. music educator; b. Ft. Worth, Oct. 6, 1955; d. Thomas William and Norma Dean Crenshaw; m. Randall Bryan Harper, Oct. 1973 (div. 1980); children: Thomas Randall Harper, Stephen Bryan Harper; m. Michael Estilette, Mar. 31, 1989 (div. Apr. 2001). Grad., Jasper (Tex.) H.S., 1973; student in Piano Studies, 1996—. Sec. Jasper Meml. Hosp., 1980—83, Jasper Title and Abstract, 1983—86, Lawyers Title, Carrollton, Tex., 1986—89, Richard Jackson and Assoc., Dallas, 1989—92; sec., office mgr. Law Firm of Bill Reppeto, Dallas, 1992—96; owner, tchr. Piano Studio, Carrollton, 1995—. Asst. tchr. Piano Studio of Dr. Mary Humm, McKinney, Tex., 1997—98; singer and composer Step By Step, Dallas. Editor (scale book): Scale Technique, 1998. Mem., sponsor James Group-A Christ Centered 12-Step Program, Dallas, 1988—. Mem.: Carrollton Music Tchrs. Assn. (pres. 1999—2000, Tchr. of Yr. 1999—2000). Ch. Of Christ. Avocations: piano playing, singing, reading, cross stitching. Home: 3139 Barton Rd Carrollton TX 75007

ESTIN-KLEIN, LIBBYADA, advertising executive, medical writer; b. Newark, July 13, 1937; d. Barney and Florence B. (Tenkin) Straver; m. Harvey M. Klein, Sept. 9, 1984. Student, Syracuse U., 1955-57; BS, Columbia, 1960; RN, Columbia-Presbyn. Med. Ctr., 1960; cert., N.Y. Sch. Interior Design, 1962. Med. rsch. tech. writer, N.Y.C., 1960-62; pres. Libbyada Estin Interiors, N.Y.C., 1962-65; v.p. advt. and pub. relations Behrman/Estin Inc., N.Y.C., 1965-67; account exec., dir. pub. rels. J.S. Fullerton, Inc., N.Y.C., 1968-69, Kallir Philips Ross Inc., N.Y.C., 1969-71; copy supr. William Douglas McAdams Inc., N.Y.C., 1971-75, Sudler & Hennessey Inc., N.Y.C., 1975-80; v.p., exec. adminstr., creative dir. Grey Med. Advt. Inc., N.Y.C., 1980-84; founder, ptnr. Estin Sandler Comm. Inc., N.Y.C., 1984; v.p. Barnum Comm. Inc., N.Y.C., 1984-86; sr. v.p. ICE Comm., Inc., Rochester, N.Y., 1986-87; pres. Estin-Klein Comm. Inc., Rochester and Pittsford, N.Y., 1987—. Dir. health group Robert Comm., Inc., East Rochester, N.Y., 1993-95; bd. dirs., Perinatal Network of Monroe County. Pathways to Health. mem. PRSA Health Acad. Mem. Pub. Rels. Soc. Am., Advt. Women N.Y., Am. Advt. Fedn., Advt. Coun. of Rochester, Rochester Sales and Mktg. Execs. Club, Mktg. Communicators of Rochester, Am. Med. Writers Assn., Women in Comm., Healthcare Mktg. and Comms. Coun., Healthcare Bus. Women's Assn., Am. Nurses Assn., Allied Bd. Trade, Columbia-Presbyn. Hosp. Alumnae Assn., Columbia U. Alumnae Assn., Syracuse U. Alumnae Assn., Sigma Theta Tau, Delta Phi Epsilon. Home and Office: 289 Garnsey Rd Pittsford NY 14534-4540 Personal E-mail: libbyada@aol.com.

ESTOK, ROSEMARIE DENORSCIO, educational administrator; b. Newark, Apr. 26, 1946; d. John F. and Theresa (Tordilio) DeNorscio; m. Louis G. Estok, July 25, 1981. BA, William Paterson Coll., 1967; MA, Kean Coll., 1974. Elem. tchr. Woodbridge (N.J.) Twp. Sch. Dist., 1967-79, learning disabilities tchr. cons., 1979-90, spl. edn. curriculum specialist, 1990-93, supr. spl. edn., 1993—. Instr. acrobics YMCA, Metuchen, N.J., 1981-94, Middlesex County Coll., 1990. Named Outstanding Elem. Tchr. Am., 1973. Mem. N.J. Assn. Learning Cons. (treas. 1987-89, pres.-elect 1991-92, pres. 1992-93), N.J. Schoolwomen, Alpha Delta Kappa (charter pres. Alpha Epsilon chpt. 1975-78, state sec. 1989-91, state historian 1991-93, state treas. 1993-96). Avocations: tennis, golf, travel. Office: Woodbridge Twp Sch Dist PO Box 428 School St Woodbridge NJ 07095

ESTRIN, JUDITH, computer company executive; m. Bill Carrico. BS in Maths. and Computer Sci., UCLA; MSEE, Stanford U. Co-founder Bridge Comms.; pres., CEO Network Computing Devices; chief tech. officer, sr. v.p. Cisco Sys., Inc., San Jose; chmn. Packet Design, Palo Alto, 2002—. Bd. dirs. Fed. Express, Sun Microsystems, Walt Disney Co. Named to, Women in Tech. Internat. Hall Fame. Office: Packet Design Inc 3400 Hillview Ave Bldg 3 Palo Alto CA 94304 Fax: 408-526-4100.

ESTRIN, JUDY ANN, human resources consultant; b. Los Angeles, Mar. 17, 1952; d. Sam and Dorothy (Levinson) Estrin; m. Christopher Stanley Martin, July 21, 1974 (div. Mar. 1976). BA in English, Calif. State U., Northridge, 1973; MA, George Washington U., 1987. Personnel and tng. officer First City Bank, Pasadena, Calif., 1976-79; human resource devel. cons. First Interstate Bank Calif., Los Angeles, 1979-82; sr. tng. advisor Superior Oil Co., Houston, 1982-85; sales and mktg. tng. specialist Bank Boston, 1985-86; mgr. career resource cen. Drake, Beam, Morin Inc., Houston, 1986; cons. tng. and devel. First City Bank Corp. Tex., Houston, 1986-88; mgr. career ctr. Fuchs, Cuthrell & Co. Inc., South San Francisco, Calif., 1988—. Mem. Am. Inst. Banking, Am. Soc. Tng. and Devel. Democrat. Jewish. Office: Fuchs Cuthrell & Co Inc 501 Hilltop South San Francisco CA 94080

ESTRIN, THELMA AUSTERN, retired electrical engineer; b. N.Y.C., Feb. 21, 1924; d. I. Billy and Mary (Ginsburg) Austern; m. Gerald Estrin, Dec. 21, 1941; children: Margo, Judith, Deborah. BSEE, U. Wis., Madison, 1947, MSEE, 1948, PhD, 1951; DSc. (hon.), U. Wis., 1990. Cert. clin. engr. Research engr. UCLA Brain Research Inst., 1960-70, dir. data processing, 1970-80; prof. computer sci. UCLA, 1980—; dir. div. electronics, computer and systems engring. NSF, Washington, 1982-84; dir. extension dept. engring. and sci., asst. dean Sch. Engring. and Applied Sci., UCLA, 1984-89; ret. Trustee Aerospace Corp., 1979-82; mem. biomed. tech. resources com. NIH, 1981-86; mem. U.S. Army Sci. Bd., 1982-84; mem. energy engring. bd. NRC, 1985-88. Contbr. articles to tech. jours. Mem. Los Angeles Women in Bus. Recipient Disting. Contbn. to Engring. Edn. award NSPE, 1985, Achievement award Soc. Women Engrs. 1981, Disting. Svc. citation U. Wis., 1976. Fellow Soc. Women Engrs., AAAS (fellow, chair engring. sect. 1989), IEEE (fellow, bd. dirs. 1979-80, exec. v.p. 1982, recipient Centennial medal 1984, pres. Engring. in Medicine and Biology Soc. 1977, Haraden Pratt Svc. award 1991). Jewish.

ETEFIA, FLORENCE VICTORIA, school psychologist; b. Alton, Ill., Feb. 13, 1946; d. Esau and Pearl (Taylor) Anthony. BA, Mich. State U., 1968; MAT, Oakland U., Rochester, Mich., 1972; EdS, Wayne State U., 1977, MA, 1987, postgrad. Cert. tchr. mentally impaired, Mich.; spl. edn. supr., Mich.; cert. tchr. mentally impaired, learning disabled, K-8 gen. edn., psychology, Mich. Special edn. tchr. Sch. Dist. of Pontiac, Mich. Mem. NEA, Mich. Edn. Assn., Pontiac Edn. Assn., Delta Sigma Theta. Home: 3035 Debra Ct Auburn Hills MI 48326-2044

ETEROVICH MAGUIRE, KAREN ANN, actress, writer; b. Cleve., Feb. 24, 1961; d. Anthony William and Alice (Troyan) Eterovich; m. John Gordon Maguire. BA, U. Akron, Ohio, 1983; MFA, U. S.C., Columbia, 1989. Actress ArtReach Touring Theatre, Cin., 1983—85; actress, office mgr. Indpls. Shakespeare Co., 1984—86; grad. tchg. asst. U. S.C., Columbia, 1986—89; acting intern Shakespeare Theatre, Washington, 1987—88; resident profl. tchg. assoc. Cornell U., Ithaca, NY, 1991—92; actress Ind. Repertory Theater, Indpls., 1993; actress, producer, dir. Love Arm'd Productions, N.Y.C., 1993—. Producer Cosmic Leopard Productions, N.Y.C., 1994—2002; publicity cons. Fertile Ground Inc., N.Y.C., 1995—97. Actor: (Multi-Media Play) Love Arm'd, Aphra Behn & Her Pen, 1997 (Listed in Grants & Awards). Recipient Juliet Hardtner Endowment for Women in the Arts, McNeese State U., 2000, NEH Endowment for Faculty Devel., Albertson Coll.of Idaho, 2000, N.Y. State Coun. on the Arts Decentralization Program, Keuka Coll., 2001. Avocations: skiing, swimming, tennis. Office: Love Arm'd Productions P O Box 2668 Times Sq Station New York NY 10108-2668 Personal E-mail: karen_eterovich@hotmail.com. Business E-Mail: karen_eterovich@hotmail.com.

ETGEN, ANN, ballet educator, artistic director, choreographer; b. Dallas; d. Eddy R. Etgen and Myrtle (Applegate) Etgen; life ptnr. Bill Atkinson, Aug. 16, 1961. Dance, active Arts Magnet Sch., 1980, 81, 82, 83. Dancer Met. Opera Ballet, N.Y.C., 1958—60. Artistic dir. Etgen-Atkinson Sch. of Ballet, Dallas, 1962—, Dallas Met. Ballet, 1964—; dance panel Tex. Fine Arts Com., 1978—79. Dancer (Broadway musicals) Brigadoon, Carousel; guest dancer Omnibus History of Dance for Agnes De Mille, 1957, host S.W. Regional Ballet Festival, 1973, Creator (ballets) Dallas Met. Ballet. Recipient choreography plan award, Nat. Assn. Regional Ballet, 1983; grantee NEA choreography grantee, 1976, Tex. Fine Arts Commn., 1973, 1976—77, Mobile Oil, 1979, 500 Inc., 1978—79. Mem.: S.W. Regional Ballet Assn. (membership chmn. 1986—87), Nat. Assn. Regional Ballet. Presbyterian. Office: Etgen Atkinson Ballet School 6815 Hillcrest Ave Dallas TX 75205-1308

ETGETON, CASSANDRA ZEHNTNER, mathematician, educator; d. Melvin Keith and Mary Joe Zehntner; m. Robert John Etgeton, Jr., Mar. 21, 1974; children: Robert John III, Bonita Elizabeth. BS in Math. Edn., Fla. State U., Tallahassee, 1972; EdM Adminstrn. and Supervision, Fla. Atlantic U., Boca Raton, 1981; post grad., U. Ctrl. Fla., Orlando, 2003—. Cert. tchr. Fla., 1972. Math. tchr. Hernando County Sch. Bd., Brookesville, Fla., 1972—73, Hendry County Sch. Bd., LaBelle, 1973—75, Clewiston, 1978—81; CFO Silver Lake Amusements, LaBelle, 1976—93; math. tchr. Hendry County Sch. Bd., LaBelle, 1992—; adj. prof. Edison C.C., Ft. Myers, 2002—. Pres. Am. Bus. Women's Assn., Labelle, Fla., 1983. Mem.: AFT, NEA, Fla. Music Educators Assn., Music Educators Nat. Conf., Fla. Bandmaster's Assn., Fla. Edn. Assn., Nat. Coun. of Teachers of Math., Pi Mu Epsilon, Phi Delta Kappa, Kappa Delta Pi, Phi Kappa Phi. Avocation: reading. Home: 990 Silver Lake Rd LaBelle FL 33935 Office: LaBelle HS 4050 Cowboy Way LaBelle FL 33935

ETHAN, CAROL BAEHR, psychotherapist; b. N.Y.C., May 30, 1920; d. Irving and Sadie (Goldman) Baehr; m. Sy Ethan, Mar. 18, 1955; children: Willa Capraro, Barbara. Trained, Greenwich Inst. Psychoanalytic Studies, 1965-70; BA in Psychology with honors, NYU, 1978; MA in Psychology, New Sch. Social Rsch., 1981. Tchr. Queens Coll., 1956-57; consumer psychology rschr., cons., 1950-70; staff psychotherapist Fifth Ave. Ctr. Counseling & Psychotherapy, 1965-70; psychotherapist pvt. practice, N.Y.C., 1967—. Vol. social rehab. program Queens County Mental Health Soc., 1965—66; Dem. committeewoman Queens County, 1960. Recipient Founders Day award, NYU, 1978; Internat. Coun. Sex Edn. and Parenthood fellow, Am. U. Fellow: Am. Orthopsychiat. Assn.; mem.: APA, Nat. Assn. Advancement of Psychoanalysis, Am. Psychotherapy Assn. (cert. diplomate), N.Am. Assn. Masters in Psychology (cert.), Internat. Acad. Behavioral Medicine, Counseling and Psychotherapy (clin. mem.), Family and Divorce Mediation Coun. N.Y., Am. Mental Health Counselors Assn., N.Y. State Assn. Practising Psychotherapists (cert.). Address: 235 W 76th St New York NY 10023-8210 E-mail: cethan@nyc.rr.com.

ETHERIDGE, DIANA CAROL, internet business executive; b. Alliance, Nebr., Mar. 18, 1940; d. Elvon Lynn and Enola Nadene Howe; m. Brian Newman Etheridge, May 30, 1940; children: Melissa Ann, Juliana Lynn. Student, U. Geneva, Switzerland, 1960-61; BA, U. Denver., 1962; MA, Simmons Coll., 1981. Cert. tchr., Colo., Fla.; real estate lic., Fla., 1995, Va., 1982; cert. internatl property specialist, Nat. Assn. of Realtors, 1994-00. Tchr. French, science, English Denver Pub. Schs., 1962-63, 64-68; tchr. 7th grade, French tchr. preK-7th grade St. Anne's Episcopal Sch., Denver, 1974—76; tchr. 6th grade, French tchr. k-8th grade Collegiate Sch., Denver, 1976—80; real estate broker Merrill Lynch, Prudential, Long & Foster, Treder Realty, Potomac, Md. and Titusville, Fla., 1982—, Keenan Realty, Cocoa Beach, Fla., Metro Referrals, Fairfax, Va. Mem. No. Va. Coun. Comml. Realtors, Fairfax, Va., 1993—95, Govtl. Internat. and Info. Svcs. Coms., Fairfax, Internat. Real Estate Inst., Alexandria, Minn., 1996—2001, World Trade Ctr. Inst., Balt., 1995; cert. internat. property specialist Nat. Assn. Realtors, 1994—2000, judge Who is Today's Realtor, 1995; pres., founder e-dea, Inc., Merritt Island, Fla., 1997—, Cybernastics, Inc., Merritt Island, 1999—, Flexystema/Flexhome, Inc., Merritt Island, 2000—. House bill proofreader Colo. State Legislature, Denver, 1970; campaign staff mem. U.S. Congressman Dave Weldon, Melbourne, Fla., 1996, 1998, 2000; hon. chmn. Fla. bus. adv. coun. Nat. Rep. Congl. Com., 2003. Recipient Lifetime award Prudential Preferred Properties, 1990. Mem.: Md. Assn. Realtors, Fla. Bus. Adv. Coun., Montgomery Assn. Realtors (Lifetime award), Nat. Assn. Realtors, Nat. Assn. Home Builders, Nat. Assn. Women in Constrn., Hospitality and Info. Svcs. Internat. Club, Long and Foster Pres.'s Club (life), Optimists Club (past pres. Capital City), Brevard County Newcomer's Club, Welcome to Washington Internat. Club, Phi Beta Kappa, Pi Beta Phi. Achievements include patents for building construction. Avocations: skiing, swimming, scuba diving, hiking, aerobics. Office Phone: 321-453-7665. Business E-Mail: info@e-dea.com.

ETHERIDGE, MELISSA LOU, singer, songwriter; b. Leavenworth, Kans., May 29, 1961; d. John and Elizabeth Etheridge; m. Tammy Lynn Michaels, Sept. 22, 2003; children: Bailey, Beckett. Student, Berklee Coll. of Music, Boston, 1970. Wrote songs for the film, Weeds; albums include Melissa Etheridge, 1988, Brave and Crazy, 1989, Never Enough, 1992, Yes I Am, 1993, Your Little Secret, 1995, Breakdown, 1999, Skin, 2001, Lucky, 2004. Named Entertainer of Year Can. Acad. Recording Arts and Scis., 1990; Grammy award, Best Female Rock Vocal for "Aint It Heavy," 1993, Female Rock Vocal Performance for "Come to My Window," 1994. Address: MEIN PO Box 884563 San Francisco CA 94188-4563*

ETHERINGTON, CAROL A. medical association administrator; b. Tenn. married. MSN in Psychology and Mental Health. RN Tenn. With Internat. Med. Corps, Bosnia-Herzegovina, 1994; pres., bd. dirs. U.S. sect. Doctors Without Borders, 1999—; asst. prof. nursing Vanderbilt U. Med. Ctr., Nashville. Founder Victims Intervention Program, Nashville Police Dept., 1975—95; mem. internat. com. ARC, 1980, vol. for disaster relief. Recipient Internat. Achievement award, Florence Nightingale Internat. Found., Geneva, 2003, Florence Nightingale medal, Internat. Red Cross, 1997—98. Office: Vanderbilt Univ 336 First Hall 461 21st Ave S Nashville TN 37240

ETHERN, ABERDEEN, music educator; b. LaBelle, Mo., June 1, 1917; d. Richard and Stella Mae Butler Range; m. Luceluits Ethern, July 30, 1938 (dec. Feb. 1986); children: James R., Stella L. BA, Drake U., 1936; M of Music, U. Mo. Kansas City, 1992. Piano accompanist Kansas City Sch. Dist., 1965-76; music tchr. Upbound Rockhurst Coll., Kansas City, 1970-71; pianist, organist Friendship Bapt. Ch., Kansas City, Mo., 1946-86; music tchr. Ethern Sch. of Music, Kansas City, 1975-92. Recipient Spl. Recognition award Friendship Bapt. Ch., 1996. Mem. NAACP, Kansas City Organ Guild (sec. 1991-92), Music Tchrs. Nat. Assn., Kansas City Music Tchrs. Assn. Home: 900 E Armour Blvd Apt 608 Kansas City MO 64109-2366

ETHERTON, JANE, retired sales executive, marketing professional; b. Sevierville, Tenn., Oct. 11, 1953; d. Arthur B. (Jack) and Grace Etherton; m. Randy King, Aug. 18, 1974; 1 child, Kevin King. Student, Abbey Dale Grange, Eng., 1971-72, U. Tenn., 1972-74, U. South, 1994-98, Tusculum Coll., 1999—. Lic. funeral dir. Funeral dir. Holly Hills Funeral Home, Knoxville, Tenn., 1973-86; pre-arrangement trust dir. Berry's Morticians, Knoxville, 1987-89; gen. mgr. Southpointe Mortgage Co., Sevierville,

1989-91; dir. ops. Southpointe Fin. Svcs., Knoxville, 1991-92; pres., chief profl. officer United Way of Sevier County, Sevierville, 1993-2000; dir. sales and mktg. Collier Foods, Knoxville, Tenn., 2000—01, Aberdeen Mktg., Sevierville, Tenn., 2001—. Recipient Pres. citation Sevier Sunrise Rotary 1995. Mem. Smoky Mountain Hist. Soc., Smoky Mountain Toast- [illegible] Episcopalian. Home: 1208 Tara Ln Sevierville TN 37862-2963 Office: Aberdeen Mktg Sevierville TN 37862

ETHRIDGE, BRENDA KAY, advertising employee; b. Hugo, Okla., July 27, 1967; d. Lee Washington Boyd and Jeanne (Bass) Rowe; m. Larry Charles Ethridge, Jan. 11, 1992. BS, E. Cen. U., 1990. Account exec. Cen. Telephone, Bartlesville, Okla., 1990, supr. Cape Girardeau, Mo., 1990-91; account exec. Sch. Supplies Advantage, Oklahoma City, 1991-92; asst. mgr. Pepsico, Oklahoma City, 1992; telemktg. adminstr. Southwestern Bell, Oklahoma City, 1993-94, sales rep., 1994. Mem. Nat. Assn. Investment Clubs, Tycoons In Training Club (treas. 1997—). Avocations: reading, kick-boxing, ju-jitsu, theatre.

ETHRIDGE, SALLY ANNETTE, music educator; b. Lebanon, Oreg., June 1, 1951; d. J. A. and Ferne Large Ethridge. AA, Dawson C.C., Glendive, Mont., 1982; B in Music Edn., Mont. State U., 1988. Studio instr., 1971—99; tchr. Columbus (Mont.) Pub. Schs., 1988—90, Colstrip (Mont.) Pub. Schs., 1990—93; choir dir. Hellgate Middle Sch., Missoula, Mont., 1993—95; tchr. Loyola Sacred Heart H.S., Missoula, 1994—99; music dir. Rancho Cotate H.S., Rohnert Park, Calif., 2000—. Cmty. choir dir. Colstrip Cmty. Choir, 1991—93; singer, sec., bd. dirs. Occidental (Calif.) Cmty. Choir, 2001—; subst. pianist Moonlighters Swing Band, Santa Rosa, Calif., 2000—. Mem.: Calif. Music Educators Assn., No. Calif. Band Dirs. Assn., Music Educators Nat. Conf. Avocations: travel, reading, gardening. Office: Cotati-Rohnert Park Unified Sch Dist 5450 Snyder Ln 94928

ETHRIDGE, VEREE KEPLEY, economist, educator; b. Princeton, Ind., May 31, 1945; d. Vance Ivan and Georgia C. (Smith) Kepley; m. James I. Ethridge, Aug. 18, 1973; children: Kersten, Karee. BS, U. Ill., 1967, MS, 1971, PhD, 1978. Residential rep. Ill. Power Co., Danville, 1967-68; food svc. adminstrn. U. Ill., Urbana, 1968-71, asst. prof., 1978-81; instr. U. Nev., Reno, 1971-73; prof. bus. adminstrn. U. St. Francis, Joliet, Ill., 1984—. Contbr. articles to profl. jours. Pres. Troy Sch. Bd., Shorewood, Ill., 1982-86. Mem. Am. Econ. Assn., Midwest Bus. Econ. Assn. (v.p., pres. 1993-95), Delta Kappa Gamma (rsch. chair 1993, fin. chair 1994—). Office: Univ of St Francis 500 Wilcox St Joliet IL 60435-6188

ETIENNE, MICHELE, financial consultant; b. Cap Haitien, Haiti, Oct. 16, 1946; d. Raymond and Claudia (Prophete) Kersaint; m. Ernst Etienne, Mar. 2, 1967; children: Patrick, Bernard. BBA, Baruch Coll., 1976. Dir. fin. Martha Graham Ctr., N.Y., 1973-98; fin. adv. Lee Strasberg Theatrical Inst., N.Y., 1999—. Pres. Primevere Club; mem. Casegha. Home: 84-15 168th St Jamaica NY 11432 Office: Lee Strasberg Theatrical Inst 115 E 15th St New York NY 10003-2188 E-mail: metienne16@aol.com.

ETTEL, ZITA MOAK, nursing administrator, food services executive; b. Blythewood, S.C., Feb. 11, 1922; d. George Washington and Ophelia Louise (Halstead) Moak; m. James Hughlon Lylos, Oct. 24, 1949 (dec. June 1960); 6 children ; m. James Phillip Ettel, Dec. 25, 1995. RN, Elizabeth Buxton Sch. Nursing, 1941. Carpenter Blythewood Shop, S.C., 1938; RN Elizabeth Buxton, Va., 1942; armament electrician, welder Columbia, SC, 1943; aircraft mechanic Army Air Base, Columbia, 1944; charge nurse Providence Hosp., Columbia, 1945; decorator Macy Dept. Store, N.Y.C., 1947; auto mechanic, 1948; food svc. supr. Columbia Hosp., 1959; psychoanalyst Hall Inst., Columbia, 1964; RN Valley Meml. Hosp., Grand Forks, N.D., 1965; beautician Columbia, 1970—76; orthop. nurse Vet. Hosp., Columbia, 1973, 1980-85. Author: My Abused Childhood, Tommy Turtle, 1955, (poems) Farewell, The Christmas Promise, Too Many; inventor. Nurse Am. Red. Cross, Ft. Monroe, Va., 1942, Ft. Jackson, 1943; driver Blind Assn., Columbia, S.C., 1970; former ch. organist, Sunday Sch. tchr., sec. Luther League. With U.S. Air Force, 1943. Recipient Editor's Choice award Nat. Libr. Poetry, 1996, Golden Poet award World of Poetry, 1989, 91 Mem. N.Y. Acad. Scis. Home: 1001 Confederate Ave Columbia SC 29201

ETTENGER, DEBORAH JEAN, music educator; b. Denver, Sept. 7, 1947; d. John Richard and Grace Spencer Bond; m. James Francis Ettenger, July 14, 1984; 1 child, Devon Christopher. BA in Music Edn., U. Wyo., 1970; BA in Gen. Edn., Loretto Heights Coll., Denver, 1988. Lic. gen. music tchr. K-12 Colo., instrumental music tchr. 3-12 Colo., classroom tchr. K-6 Colo., cert. Carl Orff method tchg. music. Gen. music tchr. grades 7-9 Harrison Sch. Dist. # 2, Colorado Springs, Colo., 1971—72; gen. music tchr. grades K-5 Aurora (Colo.) Pub. Schs., 1972—. Mem.: Rocky Mountain Orff Schulwork Assn., Colo. Music Educators Assn., Music Educators Nat. Conf., Colo. Hunter-Jumper Assn., Delta Omicron, Gamma Phi Beta. Methodist. Avocations: gardening, singing in church choir, singing in musicals and light opera, Boy Scouts, competing in horse shows.

ETTER, FAYE MADALYN, interior design company executive; b. Boston, Dec. 19, 1951; d. Charles Gaines and Rosemarie (Verlinde) E. BS in Design and Merchandising, Drexel U., 1973, MS in Interior Design, 1987. Staff designer Bloomingdale's, Jenkintown, Pa., 1980-83, design dir. Chestnut Hill, Mass., 1983-85; pres. Etter Interiors, Newton, Mass., 1985—. Contbr. articles to interior design mags. Mem. Am. Soc. Interior Designers (sec. 1988, chair designers auction 1990, bd. dirs. 1988, 90, 91, Presdl. Citation 1988, 90). Office: Etter Interiors 8 Varick Rd Waban MA 02468-1319

ETZEL, DEBORAH ANNE, computer technician, consultant; b. Cornwall, N.Y., Apr. 24, 1953; d. Tyler Adrian and Lorraine Etzel; m. Joseph Paul Ausikaitis; 1 child, Ashley Etzel Ausikaitis. BS, William Smith Coll., 1974; MS, SUNY, Stony Brook, 1976. Statis. programmer to mgr. Gen. Foods Corp., Tarrytown, NY, 1976—88; self-employed computer cons. Barrington, Ill., 1988—; devel. coord. Gender Equity Fund, Ill., 1999—2000. Mem. Dist. 220 Sch. Bd., Barrington, 2001; chair for equity in edn. AAUW, Barrington, 1998; program chair Choices for Success, Schaumburg, Ill., 2000; pres. BMS Prairie Campus PTO, Barrington, 2000—01, sec., 1998—2000; mem. Bd. of Edn., Barrington, 2003—, pres., 2003—; bd. dirs. Barrington Youth Svcs., Barrington, 2000, District 220 Ednl. Found., Barrington, Ill., 2001, Gender Equity Fund, 2000—01.

ETZEL, RUTH ANN, pediatrician, epidemiologist, educator; b. Milw., Apr. 6, 1954; d. Raymond Arthur and Marian Dorothy Etzel. Student, St. Olaf Coll., 1972-73; BA in Biology summa cum laude, U. Minn., 1976; MD, U. Wis., 1980; PhD, U. N.C., 1985. Resident in pediat. N.C. Meml. Hosp., Chapel Hill, 1980-83; adj. asst. prof. pediat. Emory U. Sch. Medicine, Atlanta, 1985-87; epidemic intelligence svc. officer Ctr. Environ. Health Ctrs. Disease Control, Atlanta, 1985-87, med. epidemiologist Ctr. Environ. Health and Injury Control, 1987-90, chief air pollution and respiratory health br., 1991-96, asst. dir. preventive medicine residency program, 1992-97; dir. divsn. epidemiology and risk assessment Office Pub. Health and Sci., Food Safety and Inspection Svc., USDA, Washington, 1998—2001; adj. prof. environ. and occupl. health George Washington U., Washington, 2000—. Mem. preventive medicine and pub. health test com. Nat. Bd. Med. Examiners, 1992—94; mem. U.S. Med. Licensing Exam. Step 2 Preventive Medicine and Pub. Health Test Material Devel. Com., 1992—94; mem., trustee Am. Bd. Preventive Medicine, 1992—2001, vice chair pub. health and preventive medicine, 1997—2001. Contbr. articles to profl. publs.; editor: book Handbook of Pediatric Environmental Health, 1999—. Recipient Arthur S. Flemming award, DC Jaycees, 1991; Robert Wood Johnson Clin. scholar, U. N.C., 1983—85, MacPherson scholar, 1972. Fellow: Am. Coll. Preventive Medicine, Am. Acad. Pediats. (Ctrs. Disease Control and Prevention liaison 1986—92, chmn. sect. epidemiology 1988—92, ex-officio 1993—94, chmn. com. environ. health 1995—99, editor Handbook Pediatric Environmental Health 1999—2003, mem. com. environ. hazards, mem. com. on native Am. [illegible] Internat. Soc. Environ. Epidemiology, Soc. Pediatric Epidemiol. Rsch., Ambulatory Pediatric Assn. (mem. rsch. com. 1987—, comms. dir. 2002—), Delta Omega, Phi Beta Kappa. E-mail: retzel@earthlink.net.

EU, MARCH FONG, ambassador; b. Oakdale, Calif., Mar. 29, 1929; d. Yuen and Shiu (Shee) Kong; children by previous marriage: Matthew Kipling Fong, Marchesa Suyin Fong; m. Henry Eu, Aug. 31, 1973; stepchildren: Henry, Adeline, Yvonne, Conroy, Alaric. Student, Salinas Jr. Coll.; BS, U. Calif.-Berkeley, 1943; MEd, Mills Coll., 1947; EdD, Stanford U., 1956; postgrad., Columbia U., Calif. State Coll.-Hayward; LLD, Lincoln U., 1984; LLB (hon.), Western U., 1985; DHL (hon.), Northrup Coll., 1991; LLB (hon.), Pepperdine U., 1993. Chmn. divsn. dental hygiene U. Calif. Med. Center, San Francisco, 1948-56; dental hygienist Oakland (Calif.) Pub. Schs., 1948-56; supr. dental health edn. Alameda County (Calif.) Schs.; lectr. health edn. Mills Coll., Oakland; mem. Calif. Legislature, 1966-74, chmn. select com. on agr., foods and nutrition, 1973-74; mem. com. natural resources and conservation, com. commerce and pub. utilities, select com. med. malpractice; chief of protocol State of Calif., 1975-83, sec. of state, 1975-94; amb. to Federated States of Micronesia, Am. Embassy, Pohnpei, 1994—. Chmn. Calif. State World Trade Commn., 1983-87; ex-officio mem. Calif. State World Trade Commn., 1987—; spl. cons. Bur. Intergroup Relations, Calif. Dept. Edn.; ednl., legis. cons. Sausalito (Calif.) Pub. Schs., Santa Clara County Office Edn., Jefferson Elementary Union Sch. Dist., Santa Clara H.S. Dist., Santa Clara Elementary Sch. Dist., Live Oak Union H.S. Dist.; mem. Alameda County Bd. Edn., 1956-66, pres., 1961-62, legis. adv., 1963, Assembly Retirment Com., Assembly Com. on Govtl. Quality Com., Assembly Com. on Pub. Health; pres. Alameda County Sch. Bds. Assn., others; U.S. advisor Shenzhen Internat. Ent. Co., Ltd., Shenzhen, Guangzhou, China, 1997; internat. hon. advisor 4th World Chinese Entrepreneurs Conv., Vancouver, B.C., 1997; hon. chmn. Sino-Am. Inst. Human Resources, L.A., 1997; U.S. advisor Internat. Hort Exposition for 1999, Kunming, Yunnan, 1997; exec. adv. bd. Asian Am. Policy Rev. Bd., Washington, 1998, others; adj. prof. on regional and continuing edn. Calif. State U., Sacramento, 2000; S.E. Asia advisor Startec Global Telecomm., Inc.; bd. dirs. East L.A. Coll. Found.; adv. bd. for canonization of Blessed Junipero Serra, Santa Barbara, Calif., 2000-01; hon. advisor Internat. Leadership Found., Sacramento, Calif., 2000; adj. prof., sr. adv. Calif. State U. Coll. Continuing & Regional Edn., Sacramento, 2000; sr. advisor S.E. Asia, Startec Global Oper. Co., Bethesda, Md., 2000; bd. regents presdl. adv. com. So. Calif. U. Health Scis., Whittier, Calif., 2002. Mem. adv. bd. for canonization of Father Junipero Sierra, Franciscan Fathers, Santa Barbara, Calif., Internat. Leadership Found. Recipient Citizen of Yr. award Chinese-Am. United for Self Employment, 1996, Govt. Svc. award friends of Mus. of Chinese Am. History, L.A., 1997, Cmty. Svc. award Coll. of San Mateo, Ann. Humanitarian award Women's Ctr., Coll. of Law, San Diego, Asian Am. on the Move award for politics L.A. City Employees Asian Am. Assn., Outstanding Svc. to Cmty. award Irish-Israeli Italian Soc. San Francisco, Disting. C.C. Alumni award Calif. C.C. and Jr. Coll. Assn., Outstanding Woman award Nat. Women's Polit. Caucus, Daisy award Calif. Landscape Contrs. Assn., 1980, Milton Shoong Hall of Fame Humanitarian award, 1981, Citizen of the Yr. award Coun. for Civic Unity of San Francisco Bay Area, 1982, Woman of the Yr., Dems. United, San Bernardino, 1986, Woman of Achievement Award of Distinction, San Gabriel Valley YWCA, 1987, Disting. svc. award Rep. of Honduras, 1987, Woman of the Yr. award Santa Barbara County Girls Club Coalition, 1987, Polit. Achievement award Calif. Dem. Party, Black Caucus, 1988, 1989, JFK Am. Leadership award Santa Ana Dem. Club, 1989, Cmty. Leadership award Torat-Haijun Hebrew Acad., 1990, Mother of the Yr. award No. Am. TV Corp., 1999, Lifetime Achievement award Orgn. Chinese Ams. Inc., 1999, Outstanding Overseas Chinese award San Francisco Chinese Benevolent Assn. and Chinese Consol. Women's Assn. San Francisco, 2001, Outstanding Citizen award Chinese Am. Citizens Alliance, 2002, Spirit of Am. award Chinese Am. Citizen's Alliance, 2003, numerous others; March Fong Eu ann. achievement award named in her honor Nat. Notary Pub. Assn. Fellow Internat. Coll. Dentists; mem. Navy League (life), Am. Dental Hygienists Assn. (pres. 1956-57), No. Calif. Dental Hygienists Assn., Oakland LWV, AAUW (area rep. in edn. Oakland br.), Calif. Tchrs. Assn., Calif. Agrl. Aircraft Assn. (hon.), Calif. Sch. Bd. Assn., Alameda County Sch. Bd. Assn. (pres. 1965), Alameda County Mental Health Assn., Calif. Pub. Health Assn. Northern Divsn. (hon.), So. Calif. Dental Assn. (hon.), Bus. and Profl. Women's Club, Soroptimist (hon.), Hadassah (life), Ebell Club (L.A.), Chinese Retail Food Markets Assn. (hon.), Chinese Women's Assn. Singapore, Am. Assn. Singapore, Pilot Club Internat., Clara Barton Soc. Am. Red Cross (L.A. chpt.), Delta Kappa Gamma, Phi Alpha Delta (hon.), Phi Delta Gamma (hon.), others. Democrat. Avocation: painting. E-mail: marcheu@aol.com.

EUBANKS-POPE, SHARON G. real estate company executive, entrepreneur; b. Chgo., Aug. 26, 1943; d. Walter Franklyn and Thelma Octavia (Watkins) Gibson; m. Larry Hudson Eubanks, Dec. 20, 1970 (dec. Jan. 1976); children: Rebekah, Aimée; m. Otis Eliot Pope, June 7, 1977; children: O. Eliot Jr., Adrienne. BS in Edn., Chgo. Tchrs. Coll., 1965; postgrad., Ill. Inst. Tech., 1967, John Marshall Law Sch., 1970, Governor's State U., 1975-76. Educator, parent coord. Chgo. Bd. Edn., 1965-77; owner, ptnr. Redel Rentals, Chgo., 1977—. Bd. dirs. Jack and Jill of Am. Found. Adminstrv. bd. St. Mark United Meth. Ch., Chgo., 1967, bd. trustees, 1988; com. chair Englewood Urban Progress Ctr., Chgo., 1973; coord., educator LWV, 1975-76; chair comms. Marian Cath. H.S., 1999—, adv. bd.. Named Outstanding Sch. Parent Vol., Chgo. Bd. Edn., 1977; recipient Outstanding Cmty. Law Class award LWV, 1975-76, Christian Leadership award United Meth. Women, Chgo., 1985. Mem.: NAACP, NAFE, Nat. Assn. Realtors, Am. Soc. Profl. and Exec. Women, St. Mark Cmty. Devel. Corp., Jack and Jill Am., Inc. (Chgo. chpt. journalist 1989—91, Midwestern region sec./treas. 1993—95, nat. treas. 1998—2000, founder Parents for Parity in Edn. 1992, pres. Eubanks-Pope Devel. Co., Inc. 1993, parliamentarian of Parity 1991), Jack & Jill of Am. Found. (bd. dirs. 1995—2000), Links, Inc., Alpha Beta Gamma (female exec. del. to China People to People Amb. program 1998). Office: Redel Rentals 4338 S Drexel Blvd Chicago IL 60653-3536

EUDALY, OLIVIA COGGIN, not-for-profit executive, educator; b. Dec. 23, 1945; BA, Tex. Christian U., 1967; MA, Southwestern Bapt. Theol. Sem., Ft. Worth, 1972. Spl. events mgr. Rafter Seven Ranch, Ft. Worth, 1970-99; tchr. Western Hills H.S., Ft. Worth, 1992-94; adj. prof. Tex. Christian U., Dallas Bapt. U., Tarrant City Coll., 1989—; dep. dir. Tarrant Area Food Bank, Ft. Worth, 1996—. Bd. dirs. Happy Hill Farm. Committeewoman State Rep. Exec. Com., Tex., 1994-98; candidate U.S. Ho. of Reps., 1995-96; trustee Hardin Simmons U.; mem. Leadership Ft. Worth. Recipient Gt. Women of Tex. award, 2001. Mem.: Assn. Fundraising Profls. (v.p.), Leadership Ft. Worth (v.p.). Office: Tarrant Area Food Bank 2600 Cullen St Fort Worth TX 76107-1302

EURICH, NELL P. education educator; b. Norwood, Ohio, July 28, 1919; d. Clayton W. and Adah (Palmer) Plopper; m. Alvin C. Eurich, Mar. 15, 1953 (dec. 1987); children: Juliet Ann, Donald Alan; m. Maurice Lazarus, 1988. AA, Stephens Coll., 1939; BA, Stanford U., 1941, MA, 1943; PhD, Columbia U., 1959. Dir. student union U. Tex., 1942-43; resident counselor Barnard Coll., 1944-46; asst. to pres. Woman's Found., 1947-49; officer charge pub. relations State U. N.Y., 1949- 52; acting pres. Stephens Coll., 1953-54; asst. prof. English NYU, 1959-64; academic dean New Coll., Sarasota, Fla., 1965; dir. project to reorganize curriculum Aspen (Colo.) Pub. High Sch., 1966; dean faculty, prof. English Vassar Coll., 1967-70; provost, dean faculty, prof. English, v.p. acad. affairs Manhattanville Coll., N.Y., 1971-75; sr. cons. Internat. Council for Ednl. Devel., 1975-82, Acad. for Ednl. Devel., 1982-88. Mem. nat. selection com., chmn. Rocky Mountain regional com. Nat. Endowment Humanities, 1966-67, cons. [illegible] mem. Middle States Commn. Marshall Scholarships, 1967-68; chmn. Northeastern region, 1969-71; mem. U.S. Commn. on Ednl. Tech., HEW, 1968-69; mem. overseer's vis. com. on summer sch. and univ. extension Harvard, 1969-75; mem. panel of judge's Fed. Woman's award, 1969; cons. Acad. for Ednl. Devel., 1970-71; mem. career minister rev. bd. U.S. Dept. State, 1972; participant Ditchley Conf. V, 1973; mem. Rhodes Scholarship Selection Com., 1976; moderator exec. seminar Aspen Inst. for Humanistic Studies, 1977, 79, 80; dir. Adult Learning Project Carnegie Found. for Advancement Teaching, 1985-90; advisor Nat. Acad. of Engring., 1987-88; vis. com. Neuro Scis., Mass. Gen. Hosp. Author: Science in Utopia, 1967, Higher Education in Twelve Countries: A Comparative View, 1981, (with B. Schwenkmeyer) Great Britain's Open University, 1971, Corporate Classrooms, 1985, The Learning Industry, 1991; contbg. author: (Alvin Toffler) Learning for Tomorrow, 1974, From Parnassus: Essays for Jacques Barzun, 1976; contbr. articles to profl. jours. Past trustee Bank Street Coll., Salisbury Sch., Hudson Guild Neighborhood House, Colo. Rocky Mountain Sch., Bennington Coll.; trustee Carnegie Coun. on Policy Studies in Higher Edn., 1977—80, Carnegie Found. for Advancement of Teaching, 1978—84; trustee emeritus New Coll. Found., 1964—2001. Mem. MLA, Am. Assn. Colls. (spl. com. on liberal studies 1966-70), World Soc. Ekistics, Nat. Coun. Women (hon.), Century Assn. N.Y.C. Home: 144 Brattle St Cambridge MA 02138-2202

EUSTER, JOANNE REED, retired librarian; b. Grants Pass, Oreg., Apr. 7, 1936; d. Robert Lewis and Mabel Louise (Jones) Reed; m. Stephen L. Gerhardt, May 14, 1977; children: Sharon L., Carol L., Lisa J. Student, Lewis and Clark Coll., 1953-56; BA, Portland State Coll., 1965; MLibrarianship, U. Wash., 1968, MBA, 1977; PhD, U. Calif., Berkeley, 1986. Asst. libr. Edmonds C.C., Lynnwood, Wash., 1968-73, dir. libr.-media ctr., 1973-77; libr. Loyola U., New Orleans, 1977-80; libr. dir. J. Paul Leonard Libr., San Francisco State U., 1980-86, Rutgers State U. N.J., New Brunswick, 1986-89, v.p. info. svcs., 1989-91, v.p. univ. librs., 1991-92; libr. dir. U. Calif., Irvine, 1992-97; ret., 1997. Cons. Coll. S.I., Union Ejidal, La Penita, Nayarit, Mexico, 1973, Univ. D.C., 1988; co-cons. Office of Mgmt. Svcs. Assn. of Rsch. Librs., 1979—; bd. regents, Kansas; mem. adv. coun. Hong Kong U. Sci. and Tech. Librs., 1988—, Princeton U. Libr., 1988-92, U. B.C., Can., 1991—. Author: Changing Patterns of Internal Communication in Large Academic Libraries, 1981, The Academic Library Director, Management Activities and Effectiveness, 1987; columnist Wilson Libr. Bull., 1993-95; contbr. articles to profl. jours. Pres. Seattle Repertory Orgn.; trustee Seattle Repertory Theatre. Mem. ALA, Calif. Libr. Assn., Assn. Coll. and Rsch. Librs. (pres. 1987-88), Rsch. Librs. Group (chair bd. dirs. 1991-92).

EUSTICE, ESTHER, elementary school educator; b. Portland, Oreg., June 1, 1947; d. Orin Rudolph and Helen Marian Karges; m. David Edward Eustice, Dec. 31, 1969; children: David Dean, Kimberly Anne. AA, Miltonvale Wesleyan Coll., Miltonvale, Kans., 1969; BS, Mary Coll., Bismarck, N.D., 1984; MS, Univ. Mary, Bismarck, N.D., 1991. Cert. elem. tchr., K-8 N.D., reading specialist, K-8 N.D. Preschool tchr. Warner Christian Acad., South Daytona, Fla., 1974—76; instr. (summers) Univ. Mary, Bismarck, 1992—94; title I tchr. K-5, elem. tchr. K-4 Hazen Pub. Sch., ND. Mem. ch. bd. Faith Cmty Nazarene Ch., Beulah, ND, 1983—, children's ch. dir., 2001—03, Sunday sch. tchr., 1983—; bd. dirs. Concert Series, Hazen, ND. Mem.: Delta Kappa Gamma (2nd v.p. 1999—2001, 1st v.p. 2001—03, state pres. 2003—, Golden Gift Seminar 2002). Avocations: gardening, walking, bicycling, reading, cake decorating. Home: 302 6th Ave NW Hazen ND 58545 Office: Hazen Pub Sch 519 1st Ave NE Hazen ND 58545

EUSTIS, JENNIFER MARIE, language educator; b. Glendale, Calif., Oct. 21, 1970; d. Mathew Carl Wargat and Cecily Hills Robinson. BA, U. San Diego, 1991; maitrise, diplome d'etudes app., U. Burgundy, Dijon, France, 1995; MA, St. John's U., Santa Fe, 2001. Cert. TEFL Cambridge. Tchr. English Le Greta, Dijon, 1998—99; English tchr., translator, libr. Linguarama, Dijon, 1998—99; French lang. asst. St. John's Coll., Santa Fe, 2000; pvt. French/English tutor-tchr. Santa Fe, 2000—. Vol. L'Arche, Dijon, 1993—99, Literacy Am., Santa Fe, 2000—. Recipient Gold Medal, Alliance Francaise, 1991. Mem.: AAUW, Am. Philos. Assn., Soc. of Anthropology for Consciousness, Math Club of U. San Diego. Green Party. Roman Catholic. Avocations: hiking, movies, music, travel, ancient Greek. Personal E-mail: jeneustis@yahoo.com.

EUTEMEY, KAREN DENISE, art educator, sculptor; b. Bklyn., July 1, 1950; d. Kenneth D. and Helen Barnes Eutemey; children: Lucien Spencer Bayless, Eliot Drew Bayless. BFA, Boston U., 1972. Cert. tchr. Mass. H.S. art tchr. Boston Pub. Schs., 1972—73; art instr. Elma Lewis Sch. Fine Arts, Dorchester, Mass., 1973—75; sculpture instr. pre-college program Mass. Coll. Art, Boston, 1977—77; art instr. Rockland (Mass.) Youth Commn., 1989—96; art specialist The Chestnut Hill (Mass.) Sch., 1992—. Prin. works include sculpture Woman Stretching, Rise (Edward Ingersoll Browne Fund, 1998), prin. works include sculpture-13 reliefs Accomplishments of Paul Robeson. Small group leader Internat. Churches of Christ, Boston, 2001—03. Finalist, Betty Brazil Meml. Fund award Competition for Career Devel. in Sculpture, 1981; recipient Second prize Afro-Am. Impressions Africa, Black Dimensions in Art, 1984, The Power of Art award, The Robert Rauschenberg Found., 2003. Mem.: Nat. Art Edn. Assn. Avocations: dance, tai chi. Office: The Chestnut Hill School 428 Hammond St Chestnut Hill MA 02467-1229 E-mail: keutemey@tchs.org.

EVANGELISTA, ANITA LORETTA, freelance writer, psychologist, nurse, publishing executive; b. L.A., Nov. 9, 1952; d. Carl A. and Etta L. (Erickson) Anderson; m. Nick F. Evangelista, 1979; children: Jamie, Justin. Student, Pepperdine U., 1970-71, U. So. Calif., 1972; BSN, S.W. Mo. State U., Springfield, 2001; MSN, MS in Psychology, S.W. Mo. State U., 2004; postgrad., Duquesne U., 2004—. RN, APN; cert. clin. hypnotherapist. Asst. to dir. internat. fin. Max Factor, L.A., 1972-73; asst. to 2d mgr. steel dept. Sumitomo Shoji, L.A., 1973-75; freelance writer, 1975—; columnist Mo. Farm Mag., Clark, 1984-87; adminstr. West Plains (Mo.) Coun. on Arts, 1986-91; editor Ranch Dog Trainer mag., West Plains, 1990-92; mng. editor Fencers Quar., 1999—. Spkr., lectr. Mid West Hypnosis Conv., Chgo., 1983; cons. film dir. R. Wise, Hollywood, Calif., 1977; reader Llewellyn Pub., 1997—. Author: Hypnosis-A Journey into the Mind, 1980, Dictionary of Hypnotism, 1991, How to Develop a Low-Cost Family Food Storage System, 1995, How To Live Without Electricity and Like It, 1997, Backyard Meat Production, 1997, (with N. Evangelista) Blood Lust Chickens and Renegade Sheep: A First Timer's Guide to Country Living, 1999, (with N. Evangelista) Country Living is Risky Business, 2000, (with N. Evangelista) The Women Fencer, 2001; indexer: Tikkum Olam, 1996; contbr. articles to mags., periodicals including Mother Earth News, Sci. Digest, Reason, Chronicles, Backwoods Home, Small Farmers Jour., Practical Farmer of Iowa, Fate, Maine Organic Gardner, Dairy Goat Jour., numerous others. Vol. Ozark Med. Ctr., West Plains, 1995-98, ARC, 1999. Recipient TZ 1st prize Twilight Zone Mag., 1989, 1st place Fine Arts Heart of the Ozarks Fair, 1989. Mem.: Advanced Practice Nurses of the Ozarks, Parapsychology Assn., Mo. Psychol. Assn., Cath. Med. Assn., Ozark Area Psychol. Assn., Am. Psychol. Soc., Internat. Assn. Clin. Hypnotherapists, Calif. Profl. Hypnotist Assn. (chpt. pres. L.A. 1976—82), Am. Soc. Clin. Hypnosis, Am. Holistic Nurses Assn., Am. Soc. Psychical Rsch., Sigma Theta Tau, Psi Chi, Alpha Sigma Lambda, Phi Theta Kappa. Roman Catholic. Achievements include research in apolipoprotein E4 in Alzheimer's linguistic expression; Parkinson's disease and visual scanning;

Alzheimer's disease and divorce; assessing single-question screening tool for problem drinking; learning hypnotizability; nurse license disciplinary actions. E-mail: evangel@atlascomm.net.

EVANGELISTA, LINDA, model; b. St. Catherine's, Ont. m. Gerald Marie (div.). Model Elite Model Mgmt. Corp. Appearances include Gianni Versace shows, (video) George Michael's Freedom, Unzipped, 1995, Catwalk, 1995, The Loss of Sexual Innocence, 1999, New Kid on the Block, 1999. Recipient Spl. Lifetime Achievement award VH1 Fashion and Music Awards, 1997. Office: Wilhamenas Womens Divsn # 532 295 Greenwich St New York NY 10007-1049

EVANS, BEVERLY ANN, state legislator, school system administrator; b. Tod Park, Utah, Jan. 26, 1944; d. Elias Wilbur and Geraldine Vilate (Rigby) Cook; m. Stephen R. Evans, July 31, 1965; children: Lorie Ann, James. BS, Utah State U., 1965, MS, 1974. Tchr. Duchesne (Utah) Sch. Dist., 1965-70; instr. Utah Basin Applied Tech. Ctr., Roosevelt, Utah, 1970-73, adminstr., 1973—; instr. Utah State U., Logan, 1968—; mem. Utah Ho. of Reps., Salt Lake City, 1986-98, Nat. Nuclear Waste Task Force, 1987-88, Utah Senate, Dist. 26, Salt Lake City, 1998—. Cons. Utah State U., 1980—. Recipient Award of Merit, Nat. Safety Coun., Chgo., 1985-87, Alumni award Nat. 4-H, 1989, Bus. Woman of Yr award Utah BPW, 1990, Pub. Servant award Duchesne County C. of C., 1993. Mem., Amer. Vocational Assoc., Uintah Basin Education Ctr., Chamber of Commerce,Wasatch & Duchesne Counties. Republican. Mem. Lds Ch. Avocations: computers, outdoor activities, writing. Home: HC 65 Box 36 Altamont UT 84001-9704 Office: State Capitol Salt Lake City UT 84111

EVANS, BONITA DIANNE, adult education educator; b. N.Y.C., Jan. 14, 1940; d. Roy Simon and Verna (Ashton) Evans; m. Robert John Watts, Aug. 1981 (div 1996); 1 child, Helena Watts. BA, U. Canberra, Australia, 1990; MDS, Monash U., Melbourne, Australia, 1992; PhD, Walden U., Minn., 1996. With Dept. of Prime Minister and Cabinet, Australian Dept. Fgn. Affairs, Canberra, 1986—88; devel. rsch. officer Aboriginal Hostels, Canberra, 1986—88; cultural affairs asst. U.S. Embassy, Canberra, 1988—90; mem. Diplomatic Corps UN Mission to Nambia, S.W. Africa, 1978; field officer Israeli/Egyptian border UN Peacekeeping Forces, 1979—80, adj. prof. English Montclair State U., NJ, 1996—2000; vis prof Rutgers U., Newark, 1999—2000; mem. internat. adv. bd., literacy; faculty African and African-Am. studies and Women's Studies depts. William Paterson U.; tchr. bilingual dept. Essex County Coll., 2003—. Author: Youth in Foster Care, 1997, Kijani, 2002, New Hope Rising, 2002.

EVANS, CAROL ROCKWELL, nursing administrator; b. New Orleans, Jan. 8, 1953; d. Daniel Raymond Sr. and Helen (Fischer) Rockwell; divorced; children: Nikki Elizabeth, Mimi Michelle. ADN, La. State Med. Ctr., 1990. RN, La.; cert. ACLS, BLS, cert. case mgr.; lic. life and health ins. agent. Life and health ins. agt. La. Ins. Agts. Assn., New Orleans, 1975-95; dir. case mgmt. and utilization rev. Associated Med. Rev. Svcs., Metairie, La., 1986-95; charge nurse med-surg. telemetry unit Elmwood Med. Ctr., Jefferson, La., 1990—; RN specialist III ICU dept. St. Charles Gen. Hosp., New Orleans, 1993—; dir. med. mgmt. Nat. Health Resources, Inc., Metairie, La., 1995-99, Med. Care Solutions, Inc., 1999—2002; owner Case Mgmt. Svcs., Metairie, 2002—. Lobby La. Health Care, Baton Rouge, 1991. Mem. ANA, NAFE, Case Mgmt. Soc. Am., Individual Case Mgmt. Assn., Assn. Respiratory Care, New Orleans Community Care, La. Managed Healthcare Assn. (Great Nurses award 1997). Republican. Roman Catholic. Avocations: sports, dance, swimming, traveling, theater. Home: 6316 York St Metairie LA 70003-3557 Office: Case Mgmt Svcs PO Box 74137 Metairie LA 70033-4132 E-mail: CRocky108@aol.com.

EVANS, CAROLE CLINTON, special education educator; b. Logansport, Ind., Feb. 21, 1946; d. Charles M. and Norma (Collins) Clinton; m. Richard Martin Evans, Feb. 18, 1967; children: Nathaniel C., Ashley E. BS in Edn., U. Tenn., 1969, MS, 1973. Lic. tchr., career ladder III, Tenn.; professionally recognized spl. educator. Tchr. Tenn. Sch. for Deaf, Knoxville, 1969-70; tchr. spl. edn. Bryan (Tex.) Pub. Schs., 1971-72; grad. asst. dept. spl. edn. U. Tenn., Knoxville, 1972-74; tchr. spl. edn. Oak Ridge (Tenn.) Schs., 1980—. Follow-up course facilitator, vol. summer workshop Ctr. for Innovation, Oak Ridge, 1990-97; site coord. Reading Is Fundamental Program, Oak Ridge, 1986-2002. Leader Girl Scouts U.S.A., Oak Ridge, 1985-87, Camp Fire, Oak Ridge, 1986—; vol. Spl. Olympics, Knoxville, 1986-95; vol. Very Spl. Arts Festival, Oak Ridge, 1984-89. Grantee Oak Ridge Tchrs. Ctr., 1985, Tenn. Dept. Edn., 1991, Lifetouch Nat. Sch. Studios, Inc., 1993, Youth Garden, 1997. Mem. NEA, Coun. for Exceptional Children, Tenn. Edn. Assn., Oak Ridge Edn. Assn. (team leader 1995—, sch. rep. 1994-96), Assn. for Retarded Citizens, Learning Disabilities Assn., Ctr. for Innovation in Edn. (life), Phi Delta Kappa. Methodist. Home: 901 S Illinois Ave Oak Ridge TN 37830-8032

EVANS, C(AROLINE) SUE, social sciences educator; b. Bethel, Ohio, July 14, 1948; d. Raymond George Brown and Relva Olive Spears-Brown; m. Gary W. Evans, June 18, 1966; children: Rhonda Fannin, Gary Lee, Daniel Ray, Rebekah Sue, David Jonathan. Assoc. of Applied Bus., So. State C.C., Hillsboro, Ohio, 1989; BS, Wilberforce U., 1999. Leader, lectr. Weight Watchers, Inc., West Union, Ohio, 1974-80; lab. asst. So. State C.C., Sardinia, Ohio, 1989-92, 93-99, coord., instr., 1999—; project sec. Ford Motor Co., Batavia, Ohio, 1992-93, coord./instr., 1999—. Adv. bd. mem. Your Place Bd., Sardinia, Family/Cons. Sci., Seaman, Ohio. Author: Broken Wings Fly, 2003. Bd. dirs. United Ch. of God, South Portsmouth, Ohio, Adam Brown Counties Econ. Opportunities Inc., 2001—. Mem.: Take Off Pounds Sensibly (leader). Home: 1525 Moores Rd Seaman OH 45679 Office: So State CC 12681 US 62 Sardinia OH 45171 Office Phone: 937-695-0307. E-mail: sevans@sscc.edu.

EVANS, CHARLOTTE MORTIMER, communications consultant, writer; b. Newton, NJ, Nov. 26, 1933; d. Karl Otto and Wilhelmina (Otterbach) Pfau; m. John Atterbury Mortimer, Nov. 20, 1964; children: Meredith Elizabeth, Mandy Leigh; m. G. Robert Evans, Sept. 4, 1982. Student, Douglass Coll., 1952—54; BS, RN, Columbia U. Presby. Hosp., 1957; postgrad., Columbia U. Presbyn. Hosp., 1957—59, NYU, 1959—60; MPA, Coll. of Notre Dame, 1979. Spl. assignment nurse Columbia-Presbyn. Med. Center, N.Y.C., 1957—59; med. advt. copywriter Paul Klemtner & Co., N.Y.C., 1959—61, William Douglas McAdams Agy., N.Y.C., 1961—62; account exec. Arndt, Preston, Chapin, Lamb & Keen, N.Y.C., 1962—63; Rocky Mountain corr. Med. World News, Denver, 1963—64; owner Publicite, Denver; gen. mgr. Center Mktg. Assn., Palo Alto, Calif., 1964—66; freelance writer, pub. rels. and mgmt. cons. Woodside, Calif., 1966—85; pres. Communications for Youth, 1979—. Mem. Palo Alto-Stanford Hosp. Aux., 1968—72; pub. rels. assistance Peninsula Children's Ctr., Palo Alto, 1968—73, Triton Mus. Art, San Jose, Calif., 1966—70; health component Early Childhood Com. Woodside Elem. Sch. Dist.; past chair, mem., bd. dirs. ct.-apptd. spl. advocate program CASA-Kane County, 1989—96; mem. San Mateo County Mental Health Adv. Bd., Friends of Woodside Libr. Bd., 1983—85, Nat. CASA advocate program, 1989; vol. Nat. Com. for Prevention Child Abuse and Neglect, 1987—96; acting chair, founder Chicagoland Media & Children Com., 1993—96; adv. com Our Children's Place, Kane County, 1995—98; mem. Rep. Senatorial Inner Cir., 1982—86; chmn. citizens adv. com. San Mateo County Juvenile Social Svcs.; mem. adv. com. South County Youth and Family Svcs. Program; mem. Statewide Citizens Adv. Com. on Child Abuse and Neglect, Ill. Dept. Children and Family Svcs., 1987-1999, 1987—99; chair adv. com. to Congressman Dennis Hastert on Family and Child Legis., 1990—92; bd. dirs. N.J. Jr. C. of C./UNICEF/African Project, 1960—61, Natividad Ranch, first-time offenders program, 2001—, Friends of the Monterey Symphony, 2000—. Home and Office: PO Box 223380 Carmel CA 93922-3380

EVANS, EILEEN, music teacher; b. Rochester, N.Y., Apr. 12, 1960; d. Helmut Kurt and Ingrid Elisabeth Jung; m. Ken Davis Evans, July 30, 1980; children: Jennifer, Jason, Jesse. AA, Wstn. Wyo. C.C., 1984; BMus, Brigham Young U., 1998. Pvt. piano tchr., Green River, Wyo., 1980—. Mem. Nat. Wyo. Music Tchr. Assn., Nat. Guild Piano Tchrs. Mem. Lds Ch. Home: 1590 Nebraska St Green River WY 82935-5953

EVANS, ELIZABETH ANN WEST, retired real estate agent; b. Xenia, Ohio, Mar. 28, 1933; d. Millard Stanley and Elizabeth Denver (Johns) West. BA, Ohio U., 1966, MA, 1968. Cert. GRI, 1993. Sec. various orgns., Ohio, 1952-61; tchr. Ohio U., Athens, 1966-67, Zanesville, 1968-72, Collier County Pub. Schs., Naples, Fla., 1972-77; sales Helen's Hang Ups, Naples, 1978-79; mgr. pvt. practice Wilmington, Ohio, 1979-87; adminstrv. asst. Powell Assocs., Cambridge, Mass., 1987-90; real estate agt. Bill Evans Realty, Inc., Naples, 1989-90, Howard Hanna Real Estate Svcs., Naples, 1991-93, Downing-Frye Realty, Inc., Naples, Fla., 1993-97, Downing-Frye Referral Network Realty Inc., Naples, 1997—2002, ret., 2002. Fellow: Phi Beta Kappa; mem.: DAR (chaplain 1988—90, chmn. Motion, Picture, Radio and TV 1992—94, asst. chaplain 1994—96, chaplain 2000—01, chmn. pub. rels. 2003—), Kappa Alpha Theta (50-yr. mem.), Phi Kappa Phi, Phi Sigma Iota. Republican. Presbyterian. Avocation: leading group discussions. Home: 182 Cape May Dr Wilmington OH 45177 E-mail: eevans5@cinci.rr.com.

EVANS, FAITH, singer; b. June 10, 1973; m. Christopher Wallace (The Notorious B.I.G.), 1995 (dec.); 1 child, Christopher Wallace Jr., 1996. Student, Fordham U. Singer: (albums) Faith, 1995, Keep The Faith, 1998 (Grammy award for best rap performance, 1998), Faithfully, 2001; singer: (background vocals) (Mary J. Blige) My Life, 1994, Ballads, 2001, (Hi-Five) Keep it Goin On, 1992, (Frankie) My Heart Belongs to You, 1997, (LSG) Levert, Sweat, Gill, 1997 (also assoc. prodr.), (The Notorious B.I.G.) Life After Death, 1997, (Eric Benet) Day in the Life, 1999, (Jon B.) Pleasures U Like, 2001, (Kelly Price) Priceless, 2003, and others. Office: c/o Bad Boy Records 1440 Broadway, 16th Fl New York NY 10018

EVANS, GAIL HIRSCHORN, television news executive; b. N.Y.C., Dec. 17, 1941; d. David Louis and Violet Ideta (Burkart) Hirschorn; m. Robert Mayer Evans, Mar. 13, 1966; children: Jason, Jeffrey, Julianna. BA, Bennington Coll., 1963. Aide to rep. William Fitts Ryan U.S. Congress, Washington, 1960-63, aide to rep. James Roosevelt, 1963-64; exec. asst. senator Harrison Williams U.S. Senate, Washington, 1964-65; legis. asst. The White House, Washington, 1965-66; owner, ptnr. Global Rsch. Svcs., Atlanta, 1976-80; prodr. CNN, Atlanta, 1980-87, v.p., 1987-91, sr. v.p., 1991-97, exec. v.p., 1997—. Trustee Radio TV News Dirs. Found., Washington, 1993—; adj. faculty Emory U. Bus. Sch., Atlanta, 1994—; bd. advisors Ga. State U. Law Sch., Atlanta, 1995—. Mem. Citizens Rev. Panel of Juvenile Ct. Atlanta, 1995—, Com. 200, 1996—; participant Leadership Atlanta, 1978-79; bd. dirs. Atlanta Clean City Commn., 1976-79, Ga. Endowment for Humanities, Atlanta, 1976-80, chairperson, 1980-81; bd. govs. Atlanta Press Club, 1994—; commr. Pres.'d Commn. on White House Fellowships, 1996—. Selected Mem. of 1995, YWCA Acad. Women Achievers. Mem. Am. Women in Radio and TV (Com. of 200). Democrat. Jewish. Home: 886 E Rock Springs Rd NE Atlanta GA 30306-3044 Office: CNN One CNN Center Atlanta GA 30303

EVANS, GAYE LOIS, comptroller; b. Washington, Jan. 8, 1957; d. Verne and Marion Lois (Van Horn) E. BS in Acctg. and Mgmt., Radford U., 1978; postgrad., Am. U. From acct. to budget analyst Naval Air System Command, Washington, 1978-85; budget analyst Navy Comptr., Washington, 1985-93, budget analyst supr., 1993-96; dep. fin. mgmt. Marine Corps Sys. Command, Quantico, Va., 1996—. Mem. Am. Soc. Mil. Comptr. Episcopalian. Home: 6132 Roxbury Ave Springfield VA 22152-1624 Office: Marine Corps Sys Command Quantico VA 22134-5001

EVANS, GENE M. publishing executive; b. N.Y.C., Dec. 30, 1946; d. Murray and Ruth (Lederer) Weintraub; m. Garry Arthur Evans, May 11, 1974 (div. Feb. 1980). AA in Journalism, Miami (Fla.)-Dade C.C., 1972; BA in English, Fla. Internat. U., 1974. Sales rep. Holt-Saunders Ltd., London, Eng., 1975-79; publs. mgr. Internat. African Inst., London, 1979-81; edtl. dir. Update Publs., London, 1981-83; mng. dir. Excerpta Medica UK, London, 1983-84; pub. dir. Medicom UK and Internat., London, 1984-86; mng. dir. Merit Pub. Internat., Inc., Basingstoke, Hants., Eng., 1986—; pres. Merit Pub. Internat., INc., Coral Springs, Fla., 1992—. Adv. cons. Meducom Internat., Guelph, Can., 1992—, Stone & Bender, Basingstoke, 1992—. Avocations: internet, cycling, traveling, reading, aerobics. E-mails. E-mail: meritpi@aol.com, merituk@aol.com.

EVANS, GERALDINE ANN, academic administrator; b. Zumbrota, Minn., Feb. 24, 1939; d. Wallace William and Elda Ida (Tiedemann) Whipple; m. John Lyle Evans, June 21, 1963; children: John David, Paul William. AA, Rochester Community Coll., 1958; BS, U. Minn., 1960, MA, 1963, PhD, 1968. Cert. tchr., counselor, prin. and supt., Minn. Tchr. Hopkins (Minn.) Pub. Schs., 1960-63; counselor Anoka (Minn.) Pub. Schs., 1963-66; cons. in edn. Mpls., 1966-78; policy analyst Minn. Dept. Edn., St. Paul, 1978-79; dir. personnel Minn. Community Coll. System, St. Paul, 1979-82; pres. Rochester (Minn.) Community Coll., 1982-92; chancellor Minn. C.C. System, St. Paul, 1992-94; exec. dir. Ill. C.C. Bd., Springfield, 1994-96; chancellor San Jose (Calif.) Evergreen C.C. Dist., 1996—. Mem. San Jose Workforce Investment Bd., 2000—; mem. legis. and adv. com. Calif. C.C. League, 1998-2002. Mem. Gov.'s Job Tng. Coun., St. Paul, 1983—94, chair, 1992—94; mem. Silicon Valley Pvt. Industry Coun., 1997—2000, Workforce Silicon Valley, 1998—2002; trustee Golden Gate U., 1997—; chair Rochester (Minn.) United Way, 1985—86; mem. campaign cabinet United Way of Silicon Valley, 2003—; moderator Mizpah United Ch. Christ, Hopkins, 1982; mem. complete count com. U.S. Census, Santa Clara County, 2000; vice chair, bd. dirs. Wayzata (Minn.) Sch. Bd., 1980—83; bd. dirs. Minn. Tech. Ctr., Rochester, 1991—92; bd. mem. Boy Scouts San Clara Coun., 2004—; sec.-treas. Coun. North Ctrl. Cmty. and Jr. Colls., 1990—92; mem. ACE Commn. on Edn. Credit and Credentials, 1992—96. Winner Rochester C. of C. Athena award, 1990, San Jose YWCA Exec. award, 1998; Inst. Ednl. Leadership fellow, Washington, 1978-79. Mem. Nat. League Nursing (bd. assoc. degree accreditation rev. 1990-93, exec. com. 1993-96), Am. Assn. Cmty. Colls. (workforce commn. 2000-03), Am. Assn. Cmty. Jr. Colls. (bd. dirs. 1984-87), North Ctrl. Assn. Cmty. and Jr. Colls. (evaluator 1985-96), Silicon Valley C. of C. (bd. dirs. 2001-04), La Raza Roundtable, Rotary. Congregationalist. Avocations: travel, gardening. E-mail: geraldine.evans@sjeccd.org.

EVANS, HELEN RUTH, music educator, pianist; b. Grant City, Mo., May 26, 1913; d. John Larkin and Inez (Florea) Hall; m. Donald Maurice Mathias, Oct. 7, 1934 (div.); m. Thomas Claude Evans, Sept. 1. Student, No. Colo. U., 1968-69. Piano tchr., Colo., 1940-50, 1950-96; ret., 1996. Mem. AAUW, N.Mex. Music Tchrs. Assn., Delta Kappa Gamma. Republican. Presbyterian. Avocations: pianist, reading, cooking. Home: 400 N Locke Ave Farmington NM 87401-5857

EVANS, JANET, former Olympic swimmer; b. Placentia, Calif., Aug. 28, 1971; Degree in comms., U. So. Calif., 1994. Competed Atlanta Olympic Games, 1996; swimming coach U. So. Calif., host Janet Evans Invitational. Named U.S. Swimmer of Yr., 1987, USOC Sportswoman of the Yr.; recipient 4 Gold medals, 400m Freestyle, 800m Individual Medley, Seoul Olympic Games, 1988, 3 Gold medals, 800m Freestyle, 400m Freestyle, 400m Individual Medley, Barcelona Olympic Games, 1992, Silver medal, 400m Freestyle, 1992, Wubber 40th Nat. Title-400m Freestyle, Phillips 66 Nat. Swimming Championships, Indpls., 1994. Office: US Swimming Inc One Olympic Plaza Colorado Springs CO 80909-5724

EVANS, JEANNE CAROL, retired military officer; b. Santa Monica, Calif., Feb. 2, 1952; d. Virgil Drennan Comee and Mary Arline Duquette. AA in Art, L.A. Pierce Coll., Woodland Hill, Calif., 1972; BS in Commercial Media/Graphic Design and Photography, Fitchburg State Coll., 2002; post Baccalayreate, Sch. Mus. of Fine Arts, 2003. Enlisted U.S. Army, 1974, advanced through grades to master sgt., 1989, ret., 1994. Exhibited in group shows at Limner Art Gallery, N.Y., 2003, mag. layout, Direct Art Mag., 2004. Master sgt. US Army, 1974—94, Texas. Decorated NCO Profl. Devel. Ribbon with number 3, Army Achievement medal with oak leaf cluster, Nat. Def. Svc. Medal, Army Commendation medal with oak leaf cluster, Meritorious Svc. medal with oak leaf cluster. Home: 94 Barre Rd Templeton MA 01468 Personal E-mail: jcevans@net1plus.com.

EVANS, JO BURT, communications executive, rancher; b. Kimble County, Tex., Dec. 18, 1928; d. John Fred and Sadie (Oliver) Burt; m. Charles Wayne Evans II, Apr. 17, 1949; children: Charles Wayne III, John Burt, Elizabeth Wisart. BA, Mary Hardin-Baylor Coll., 1948; MA, Trinity U., 1967. Owner, mgr. Sta. KMBL, Junction, Tex., 1959-61; real estate broker Junction, 1965-74; staff economist, adv. on 21st Congl. Dist., polit. campaign Nelson Wolff, 1974-75; asst. mgr., bookkeeper family owned ranches/rental property Junction, 1948—; gen. mgr. TV Translator Corp., Junction, 1968—, sec.-treas., 1980—. Treas., asst. to coord. Citizens for Tex., 1972; historian Kimble Hist. Soc.; mem. Com. of Conservation Soc. to Save the Edwards Aquifer, San Antonio, 1973; homecoming chmn. Sesquicentennial Yr., Junction; treas., asst. coord. New Consitution, San Antonio, 1974; legis. chair Hill Country Women, Kimble County, 1990—; cashier Texan Theatre; campaign chmn. for Challenge U. Mary Hardin, Baylor, 2000. Named an outstanding Texan, Tex. Senate, 1973. Mem. AAUW (scholarship named in honor 1973), Nat. Translator Assn., Daus. Republic Tex., Tex. Sheriffs Assn., Nat. Cattlewomens Assn., Internat. Platform Assn., Bus. and Profl. Women (pres. 1981-82). Republican. Mem. Unity Ch. Home: PO Box 283 Junction TX 76849-0283 Office: 618 Main St Junction TX 76849-4635

EVANS, JOY, foundation administrator; b. Waterbury, Conn., Feb. 15, 1940; 4 children. Student, Hartford Coll. for Women, 1959. Weekly radio personality Young Stars on Parade Sta. WBRY, Waterbury, 1951-58; exec. sec. dir.'s office Discover Am. Travel Orgns., Washington, 1962-71; exec. sec. adminstr.'s office Nat. Ctr. for Housing Mgmt., Washington, 1971-72; exec. sec. mgr.'s office Nat. Visitor's Ctr. Nat. Park Svc. Dept. Interior, 1972-73; staff asst. divsn. pub. programs Nat. Endowment for Humanities, Washington, 1973-81, pub. info. officer, office of the chair, 1981—. Founding chair fed. woman's com. Nat. Endowment for Humanities, 1980-82, liaison White House task force on the humanities and arts 1981-82; spkr. commencement address Nat. Coll. Bus. and Tech., Charlottesville, Va., 2002, 04. Staff newsletter editor Not Hardcopy Newsletter, 1996-98. Mem. Annandale Homeowner's Assn. (pres. Terrace Townhouses 1989-92, TTA newsletter editor 1988-92), Soc. Govt. Meeting Planners (D.C. chpt. 1991-92). Roman Catholic. Avocations: music, art, dance, photography, theater, feng shui. Office: Nat Endowment for Humanities Rm 402 1100 Pennsylvania Ave NW Washington DC 20506-0001

EVANS, JUDITH P. music educator; b. Akron, Ohio, May 29, 1945; d. Clyde J. and Margie M. Petersen; m. Frederick F.D. Evans, Dec. 27, 1969. B in Music Edn., Baldwin Wallace Coll., 1967; M in Music Edn., Fla. Atlantic U., 1971. Elem. string tchr. Alliance (Ohio) Pub. Schs., 1967—68, Fremont (Ohio) Pub. Schs., 1968—70; orch. dir. Margate (Fla.) Mid. Sch., 1970—79, Pine Ridge Mid. and Barron Collier High, Naples, Fla., 1979—. Pres. Fla. Am. String Tchrs. Assn., 1976; clinician United Musical Instruments, Elkhart, Ill., 1982—; chair Am. Tchrs. Edn. Found., Naples, 1998. Editor: (mag.) Nat. Sch. Orch. Assn. Bull., 1990—95. Dir. Collier County Chamber Strings, Naples, 1998—. Named Fla. Music Educator of Yr., Fla. Music Edn. Assn., 1994—95; recipient Golden Apple award, Edn. Found. Collier County, 1996, Alumni Achievement award, Baldwin Wallace Coll., 1997. Mem.: Collier County Music Tchrs. Assn. (pres. 1984—86, treas.), Fla. Orch. Assn. (pres. 1981—83), Am. String Tchrs. Assn. (nat. sec. 1994—96, Svc. award 1996). Home: 191 Oakwood Ct Naples FL 34110-1145

EVANS, JUDY ANNE, health center administrator; b. Elmira, N.Y., Mar. 29, 1940; d. Hugh Kenneth and Mary (Faul) Leach; m. Nolly Seymour Evans, Feb. 18, 1965; children: Samantha, Meredydd, Clelia, Nolly III. BS, Cornell U., 1962; MBA, Syracuse U., 1992. Fin. analyst Morgan Guaranty Trust Co., N.Y.C., 1962-66; bus. adminstr. SUNY Health Sci. Ctr., Syracuse, 1983-89, adminstr. dept. pediatrics, 1990-99; adminstr. Biomed. Engring. Inst. Johns Hopkins U., Balt., 1999—. Mem. allocations com. Children Miracle Network, Syracuse, 1990-99; children's hosp. steering com. Crouse Irving/Univ. Hosp., Syracuse, 1990-99; bd. dirs. Syracuse Friends of Chamber Music, 1983-89, Syracuse Camerata, 1982-88; adminstr. Johns Hopkins Biomed. Engring., 1999—. Mem. Assn. Adminstrs. of Acad. Pediatrics. Avocations: sailing, cooking. Home: 647 W University Pky Baltimore MD 21210-2907 Office: 720 Rutland Ave Baltimore MD 21205-2109

EVANS, LINDA, actress; b. Hartford, Nov. 18, 1942; m. John Derek (div.); m. Stan Herman, 1976 (div.). Appearances include (films) Twilight of Honor, 1963, Those Calloways, 1964, Beach Blanket Bingo, 1965, The Klansman, 1974, Avalanche Express, 1979, Tom Horn, 1980, Dead Heat, 1988; (TV series) The Big Valley, 1965-69, Wonder Woman, Hunter, 1977, Dynasty, 1980-88 (Emmy award nominee 1983); (TV movies) Nakia, 1974, The Big Ripoff, 1975, Nowhere to Run, 1978, Standing Tall, 1978, Bare Essence, 1982, I'll Take Romance, 1983 (also exec. prodr.), Dynasty Reunion, 1991, The Gambler Returns: The Luck of the Draw, 1991, Dazzle, 1995, The Stepsister, 1997; (TV mini-series) include Bare Essence, 1982, North and South Book II, 1986, The Last Frontier, 1986; sr. prodr.: Yanni in Concert: Live at the Acropolis, 1994; author: Linda Evans Beauty and Exercise Book, 1983. Office: 9696 Culver Blvd Ste 203 Culver City CA 90232-2700*

EVANS, LINDA KAY, publishing company executive; b. Tipton, Ind., June 16, 1945; d. Walter K. and Helen S. (Fakes) E. BA in English, Purdue U., 1968. Asst. to mng. editor Random House Pubs., N.Y.C., 1969-71; asst. to dir. editorial svcs. Sch. div. McGraw-Hill Book Co., N.Y.C., 1971-75, mgr. state contracts and inventory dept., 1975-88; bookstore owner, pres. The Literary Bookshop, N.Y.C., 1988-93; prodn. mgr. trade div. Simon & Schuster, N.Y.C., 1994—. Pub. cons. for sch. textbooks Prentice-Hall Book Co., Englewood Cliffs, N.J., 1992-93. Recipient Holiday Window Display award to Lit. Bookshop, Greenwich Village C. of C., 1990. Avocations: reading, antique collecting, furniture making, travel. Office: Simon & Schuster Trade Div 1230 Ave of the Americas New York NY 10020-1586

EVANS, LINDA PERRYMAN, foundation adminstrator; b. Dallas, Apr. 25, 1950; d. Walter Lewis Perryman Jr. and Betty Lou (Slaughter) Williams; married, 1990. BS, U. Tex., 1972; postgrad., E. Tex. State U., 1975, So. Meth. U., 1976. Press asst. Pres. Ford Com., Washington, 1976; press asst. Connally for Pres. Com., Washington, 1977-79; adminstrv. asst. Am. Enterprise Inst., Washington, 1980-81; staff asst. The White House, Washington, 1981-83; exec. dir. Dallas Welcoming Com., 1984-85; pres. Linda Perryman & Assocs., Dallas, 1985-87; vice chmn. Stern, Nathan & Perryman, Dallas, 1987-90; v.p., dir., trustee Meadows Found., Dallas, 1987-96, pres., COO, 1996—. Active Charter 100, Dallas; bd. dirs. Tex. Bus. Hall of Fame Found., YWCA Dallas, Equest, Dallas Citizens Coun.; mem. Cattle Baron's Ball com. Jr. League of Dallas, mem. Crystal Charity Ball com.; appointee Coll. Opportunity Act Com. Gov. Bill Clements, 1989; mem. Dallas Assembly. Office: Meadows Foundation Inc Wilson Historic Block 3003 Swiss Ave Dallas TX 75204-6049

EVANS, LISBETH, business networking executive, political party official; b. Clarkton, N.C. m. James T. Lambie; 3 stepchildren. BS, MBA, Wake Forest U. Tchr.; with Alex, Brown & Sons Inc., Merrill Lynch, Pierce Fenner & Smith; pres. Health Equity Properties; CEO, bd. dirs. BizNexus; CEO, bd. dirs., sole shareholder West 3d St. Mgmt. Co. Chair N.C. Dem. Party; mem. Dem. Nat. Com.; Dem. chair Women's Campaign Fund. Presbyterian. Office: 8 W 3d Ste 400 Winston Salem NC 27101

EVANS, MARGARET A. volunteer; b. N.Y.C., Jan. 20, 1924; d. Bernard J. and Katherine (Walsh) Markey; m. John Cullen Evans, Jr., Nov. 24, 1951. BA, Coll. Mt. St. Vincent, 1944; postgrad., Columbia U. Rep. N.Y. Telephone Co., 1944; pers. office Sak's 34th, N.Y.C., 1944-45, tng. supr. selling and non-selling depts., 1945-49, spl. assignment for store mgr., 1949-50; non-selling tng. supr. Gimbel Bros. and Saks 5th Inc., 1950-51; rep. Gimbels and Sak's 34th at NCCJ Retail Group meeting, 1949-50; instr. textile painting for ARC Chelsea Navy Hosp., 1952-54. ARC vol., 1980-92. Bd. dirs. Marblehead Hosp. Aid Assn., 1954, pres. 1955-58; sec. Mass. Hosp. Assn. Coun. of Hosp. Auxilliaries, 1957-59, chmn. North Shore region, 1959-61, chmn.-elect 1961-62, state chmn., 1962-64; exofficio trustee Salem Hosp.; trustee Mary A. Alley Hosp., 1956-79, chmn. bd. 1974-79; mem. Welcome Wagon of Fairfield/Easton (Conn.), 1979-83; chmn. Fairfield/Easton Theatre Group, Fifth Wheel Club of Fairfield, 1983-85. Mem. Alumnae Assn. Coll. Mt. Saint Vincent, Arrangers of Marblehead (chmn. garden therapy 1967-79), Marblehead Women's Newcomers (pres. 1953). Home: 108 Cedarwood Ln Fairfield CT 06825-1308

EVANS, MARGARET ANN, human resources administrator, business owner; b. Great Bend, Kans., Dec. 26, 1947; d. Freddy Florence and Peggy (Hawkins) Green; m. Carl Evans, Aug. 13, 1972 (dir.); children: Carl André, Christopher Dion. B in Psychology, U. Mo., 1971, MPA, 1972. Pers. specialist Met. Jr. Coll., Kansas City, Mo., 1972-73; employee rels. specialist Amoco Oil Co., Kansas City, 1973-74; classification specialist Richards-Gebaur AFB, Mo., 1974-75; employee rels. officer Govt. Employee Hosp. Assn., Kansas City, 1977-84, mgr. pers., 1984-87, dir. human resources, 1987—. Mem. pers. com. Sta. KKFI, Kansas City, 1989—; mem. cert. bd. Human Resource Inst., exam devel. dir., 1994-95, sec.-treas., 1995-96. Sec. and v.p. Booster Club, Hickman Mills High Sch., Kansas City, 1989—; bd. dirs. Saturday Scholars, 2000-02. Ford Found. fellow U. Mo., 1971; recipient Contbr. of Yr. award Human Resource Mgmt. Assn., 1992, Pres. award 1993, 1995; named One of Kansas City's 100 Most Influential Kansas Citians KC Globe Most Influential African Ams. of Kansas City, 1993, 95, 96, 97. Mem. NAFE, Soc. Human Resources Mgmt. (pers. rsch. com. Kansas City chpt. 1989—, nat. com. 1990—, sec.-treas. Mo. state coun. 1992-93, bd. dirs., v.p. at large 1999-2000, v.p. Area IV 2000, 02, 03), Pers. Mgmt. Assn. (co-chmn. coll. rels. 1981), Urban League, NAACP, Links, Inc., ASTD, Alpha Kappa Alpha (chair midwestern regional conf., 1996, Outstanding Grad. Soror). Home: 10216 E 96th St Kansas City MO 64134-2309 Office: Govt Employee Hosp Assn 17306 E Us Highway 24 Independence MO 64056-1808

EVANS, MARGARET UTZ, secondary school educator; b. Gladwyne, Pa. d. Joseph H. and Marion Irwin (Laughead) Utz; m. James Irvin Evans. BA, King's Coll., Briarcliff Manor, N.Y.; MA, Ea. Bapt. Theol. Sem., Wynnewood, Pa. Tchr. Menaul High Sch., Albuquerque, Haverford Sch. Dist., Havertown, Pa., Penn-Delco Sch. Dist., Aston, Pa. Recipient Wilbor T. Elmore prize in history, James A. Barkley award in history. Mem. NEA. Home: 820 Montico Rd Wilmington DE 19803-4007

EVANS, MARI, art educator; b. Olympia, Wash., Aug. 2, 1947; B of Art Edn., Wash. State U., 1975; M of Edn., Leslie U., 1990. Cert. cert. tchr. Wash., 1978. Adj. prof. U. Puget Sound, Tacoma, 1983—93, Western Wash. State U., Bellingham, 1998—2002, City U., Bellevue, 1995—; visual art specialist Yelm Cmty. Schs., Wash., 1975—. Mem.: Nat. Art Edn. Assn. (Pacific Region Art Educator 2003, Pacific Region Elem. Art Educator 1994), Wash. Art Edn. Assn. (Wash. State Art Educator 2002), Beth Theta. Home: PO Box 3514 Lacey WA 98509

EVANS, MARIWYN, periodical editor; Exec. editor Jour. Property Mgmt., Chgo. Office: Jour Property Mgmt 430 N Michigan Ave Chicago IL 60611-4011

EVANS, MARSHA JOHNSON, non-profit association administrator, former career officer; b. Springfield, Ill., Aug. 12, 1947; d. Walter Edward Johnson and Alice Anne Field; m. Gerard Riendeau Evans, June 30, 1979. AB, Occidental Coll., 1968; MA, MA in Law & Diplomacy, Fletcher Sch., 1977; postgrad., Nat. War Coll., 1988-89. Commd. ensign USN, 1968, advanced through grades to rear admiral, 1993; mideast policy officer Commander-in-Chief, U.S. Naval Forces, Europe, London, 1977-79; spl. asst. to sec. treasury U.S. Treasury Dept., Washington, 1979-80; staff analyst Office of Chief Naval Ops., Washington, 1980-81; dep. dir. Pres. Commn. on White House Fellowships, Washington, 1981-82; exec. officer Recruit Tng. Command, San Diego, 1982-84; commanding officer Naval Tech. Tng. Ctr., San Francisco, 1984-86; battalion officer, sr. lectr. polit. sci. U.S. Naval Acad., Annapolis, Md., 1986-88; chief of staff San Francisco Naval Base, 1989-91, Naval Acad., Annapolis, Md., 1991-92; exec. dir. of the standing com. on mil. and civilian women Dept. of the Navy, 1992-93; comdr. Navy Recruiting Command, Washington, 1993-95; supt. Naval Postgrad. Sch., Monterey, Calif., 1995-97; CEO, nat. exec. dir. Girl Scouts U.S.A., N.Y.C., 1998—2002; president American Red Cross, 2002—. Interim dir. George C. Marshall European Ctr. Security Studies, Garmisch Partenkirchen, Germany, 1996-97; nat. exec. dir. Girl Scouts. Am., 1998—. White House fellow, 1979; Chief Naval Ops. scholar, 1976. Mem. Mortar Bd., Phi Beta Kappa. Office: Am Red Cross 430 17th St NW Washington DC 20006-5307

EVANS, MELINDA DIANNE, elementary school educator; b. Lubbock, Tex., Nov. 28, 1967; d. Ernie DeWayne and Judith Kay (Shuler) Christie; m. John Robert Evans, June 3, 1989. BS in Edn., U. Mary Hardin Baylor, 1991; postgrad., Tarleton State U. Tchr. 3d grade Abilene (Tex.) Ind. Sch. Dist., 1991-94, tchr. 4th grade, 1994-95; tchr. 3d grade Birdville Ind. Sch. Dist., Ft. worth, 1995-97. Mem. Assn. Tec. profl. Educators, Tex. Coun. Tchrs. English, Big Country Coun. Tchrs. English (newsletter editor 1994-95). Republican. Mem. Ch. of Christ. Avocations: reding, crafts, camp counselor. Office: Wichita Christian Schs 4729 Neta Ln Wichita Falls TX 76302 Home: 1528 Celia Dr Wichita Falls TX 76302-4127

EVANS, MICHELLE T. county official; b. Elizabeth City, N.C., June 4, 1959; d. Kirby Lee and Carrol (Owens) Tillett; m. George Hunter Evans, June 19, 1977; 1 child, Stella Asia. Grad., Manteo (N.C.) H.S., 1977. Gift buyer Fearings Inc., Manteo, 1977-79; dental asst. Randal Latta, DDS, Manteo, 1979-80; with Dare County, Manteo, 1984—, tax collector, 1993—. Bd. dirs. Munis Computer Group, Raleigh, N.C., 1999—. Vol., Dept. Social Svcs., Manteo. Mem. N.C. County and Mcpl. Tax Collectors (dir. Dist. I, 1999—). Democrat. Avocations: running, biking, swimming. Office: Dare County Tax Dept 211 Budleigh St Manteo NC 27954

EVANS, ORINDA D. federal judge; b. Savannah, Ga., Apr. 23, 1943; d. Thomas and Virginia Elizabeth (Grieco) E.; m. Roberts O. Bennett, Apr. 12, 1975; children: Wells Cooper, Elizabeth Thomas. BA, Duke U., 1965; JD with distinction, Emory U., 1968. Bar: Ga. 1968. Assoc. Fisher & Phillips, Altanta, 1968-69, Alston, Miller & Gaines, Atlanta, 1969-74, ptnr., 1974-79; judge U.S. Dist Ct. (no. dist.) Ga., Atlanta, 1979—, chief judge. Adj. prof. Emory U. Law Sch., 1974-77; counsel Atlanta Crime Commn., 1970-71 Recipient Disting. award BBB, 1972. Mem. Atlanta Bar Assn. (dir. 1979) Democrat. Episcopalian. Office: US Dist Ct 1988 US Courthouse 75 Spring St SW Atlanta GA 30303-3309

EVANS, PAMELA R. sales and marketing executive; b. Hoisington, Kans., Aug. 25, 1957; d. John Roy and Sarah Mace (Alder) E. BS in Bus., U. Kans., 1980. Sales rep. Home & Automotive Products div. Union Carbide Corp., Seattle, 1981, dist. sales mgr. Syracuse, N.Y., 1981-82; from mktg mgr. to assoc. product mgr. [illegible] Products divsn. Union Carbide Corp., Danbury, Conn., 1982—84; from asst. product mgr. to product mgr. Grocery Products divsn. Ralston Purina, St. Louis, 1984—86; from product mgr. to group dir. mktg. Eveready Battery Co. subs. Ralston Purina, St. Louis, 1986—90; dir. mktg. Consumer Products div. Esselte Pendaflex, 1990-91; dir. new bus. devel. Olympus Am., Inc., Woodbury, NY, 1991—94; v.p. mktg. consumer products group Olympus Am., Woodbury, NY, 1994—2001; pres. blueprints, inc., New Hope, Pa., 1994—2000, SJI Cos., St. Louis, 1998—2000; sr. v.p. sales and mktg. Sentry Group, Rochester, NY, 2000—03; pres. Evans Cons., Rochester, NY, 2003—. Bd. advisors Electri-Cord Mfg. Co.; bd. dirs. Humane Soc., Rochester, NY, The Little Theatre, Rochester. Avocations: music, sports, reading, photography. E-mail: pamalert@aol.com.

EVANS, PAT, mayor; b. Abilene, Tex., Feb. 12, 1943; m. Chuck Evans, 1964; 3 children. BA, U. Tex., Austin, 1964; JD, Southeastern Meth. U., 1991. Atty. Gay & McCall, Inc., 1991—95; family law instr. Southeastern Paralegal Inst., 1996—97; atty., 1991—; dep. mayor pro-tem, 2000; mayor, 2002—. Tchr. Richardson Ind. Sch. Dist., 1964—70; owner landscape design co. Mem. Preston & Pk. Task Force; county rep. Fed. Emergency Mgmt. Agy.; mem. Jr. League of Plano, Plano C. of C., Plano Planning and Zoning Commn.; past appointee Plano City Coun., 1998—2001; staff Christ United Meth. Parish Commn. Office: City of Plano 1520 Avenue K Plano TX 75074 E-mail: mayorevans@plano.gov.*

EVANS, PATRICIA MARIE, sales executive; d. Frank and Evelyn Francis Logandice; m. Larry Earl Evans, Feb. 19, 1971; children: Dana Lynn, Kim Marie Evans-Meyer. Student, Riverside (Calif.) C.C., 1993. Cert. new home sales Profl. Bldg. Industry Assn., 1996. Loan officer RP Fin. Svcs., Riverside, 1993—94; hostess Pacific Greystone Homes, Corona, Calif., 1994—95; jr. sales asst., sr. sales agt. Lewis Homes Mgmt. Corp., Upland, Calif., 1995—99; sr. sales agt. Lennar Homes/U.S. Home, Anaheim, Calif., 1999—2002, Citation Homes, Irvine, Calif., 2002—03, Centex Homes, Corona, 2003—. Mem. adv. com. Lennar Homes, Anaheim, 2002. Recipient three Outstanding Sales Achievement plaques, Nat. Assn. Homebuilders, 1997. Mem.: Sales and Mktg. Coun. Orange County. Republican. Avocations: gardening, cooking, wine tasting, travel, reading.

EVANS, PATRICIA MCCORMICK, clinical therapist; b. Cheraw, S.C. d. Foris Linsley and Mary Lucille Jackson; children: Robert, Antonio, Ronnie Jr. BA in Sociology, Coker Coll., 1996; MA in Counseling, Webster U., 1999; postgrad., Walden U., 2000—. Cashier Wal-Mart, Cheraw, SC, 1996—97; instr. South Piedmont C.C., Polkton, SC, 1997—2001; social worker Richmond County Dept. Social Svcs., Rockingham, SC, 2000—01; facilitator grief counseling group Richmond County Hospice. Founder, dir. Edn. Mentoring/Tutoring Program, Chesterfield, S.C., 2000—; founde,r pres. Maknadifrens, Inc. Author of poems. Vol. Richmond County Hospice. Mem.: Am. Correctional Assn., Am. Counseling Assn. Democrat. Baptist. Home: PO Box 882 Cheraw SC 29520 Office: Carolina Behavioral Svcs LLC Divsn Mentor Network 1219 Rockingham Rd Ste 12 Rockingham NC 28379 E-mail: cateyes@peedeeworld.net.

EVANS, PAULINE D. physicist, educator; b. Bklyn., Mar. 24, 1922; d. John A. and Hannah (Brandt) Davidson; m. Melbourne Griffith Evans, Sept. 6, 1950; children: Lynn Janet Evans Hannemann, Brian Griffith. BA, Hofstra Coll., 1942; postgrad., NYU, 1943, 46-47, Cornell U., 1946, Syracuse U., 1947-50. Jr. physicist Signal Corps Ground Signal Svc., Eatontown, N.J., 1942-43; physicist Kellex Corp. (Manhattan Project), N.Y.C., 1944; faculty dept. physics Queens Coll., N.Y.C., 1944-47; teaching asst. Syracuse U., 1947-50; instr. Wheaton Coll., Norton, Mass., 1952; physicist Nat. Bur. Standards, Washington, 1954-55; instr. physics U. Ala., 1955, U. N.Mex., 1955, 57-58; staff mem. Sandia Corp., Albuquerque, 1956-57; physicist Naval Nuclear Ordnance Evaluation Unit, Kirtland AFB, N.Mex., 1958-60; programmer Teaching Machines, Inc., Albuquerque, 1961; mem. faculty dept. physics Coll. St. Joseph on the Rio Grande (name changed to U. Albuquerque 1966), 1961—, assoc. prof., 1965—, chmn. dept., 1961—. Mem. AAUP, Am. Phys. Soc., Am. Assn. Physics Tchrs., Fedn. Am. Scientists, Sigma Pi Sigma, Sigma Delta Epsilon. Achievements include patents on mechanical method of conical scanning (radar), fluorine trap and primary standard for humidity measurement Home: 730 Loma Alta Ct NW Albuquerque NM 87105-1220

EVANS, R. MARLENE, social welfare administrator, educator; b. Riverside, Calif., Apr. 15, 1950; d. Donald R. Evans and Minnie L. Taylor; m. David Franklin Eldridge, Jr., June 23, 1987 (div. June 1992); children: Kymberlie Renee Neal, Kahshanna Almani Evans Eldridge. BA in Sociology, Calif. State U., San Bernardino, 1987, MSW, 1996; PhD, LaSalle U., Mandeville, La., 1999. Eligibility worker San Bernardino County DPSS, Redlands, Calif., 1986-88; assessment and referral counselor United Way, Inc., Ontario, Calif., 1988-90; intake assessment and referral counselor Charter Hosp., Redlands, 1990-91; eligibility worker Dept. Pub. Social Svcs., Redlands, 1991—96; social svc. practitioner San Bernardino County CPS, San Bernardino, 1996-97, San Bernardino County Adoptions, San Bernardino, 1997-99, supervising social svc. practitioner, 1999—. Kaiser Found. grantee, 1995. Mem.: NASW, AAUW (Career Devel. grantee 1993), North Rubidoux Women's Club (sec., v.p., pres.). Democrat. Roman Catholic. Avocations: sewing, contemporary jazz, reading, mentoring. Home: PO Box 6941 San Bernardino CA 92412-6941 Office: San Bernardino County Dept Children's Svcs San Bernardino CA 92408-0021

EVANS, SUE HOLLIS, journalist, public relations executive; b. Louisville, Ky., Aug. 14, 1942; d. Raymond Myers Evans and Elizabeth Allene Bales; m. Jack Tomlinson Rodgers, Dec. 30, 1965 (div. Aug. 1976); children: Blair, Hollis. BFA, U. Ala., 1964. Asst. to gen. mgr. Ky. News Network, 1978—79; news dept. asst., pub. svc. coord., public/media rels. coord., writer/prodr. WAVE-TV, 1979—85; pub. rels. and promotions mgr. Ky. Derby Mus., 1988—91; various positions to asst. to v.p., corp. comms. and to dir. of comty. rels. Churchill Downs, Inc., Louisville, 1988—97; editor The Writing Factory, Inc., Louisville, 1994—95; assoc. editor Louisville Sports Report, Inc., Louisville, 1997—. Editor: Tennis in Ky., 1994—2002. Named Ky. Col., Gov. Julian M. Carroll, Ky., 1978; recipient Media award, Ky. Tennis Assn., 2000. Office Phone: 502-636-4330. Personal E-mail: sue@cardinalsports.com.

EVANS, SUSAN A. chemist; Postdoctoral and rsch. fellow Edsel B. Ford Inst. for Med. Rsch. and dept. pathology Henry Ford Hosp., Detroit; v.p. rsch., devel. and engring. LifeScane, Inc., a Johnson and Johnson Co., Milpitas, Calif. Fellow: Nat. Acad. Clin. Biochemistry; mem.: NCCLS (fin. com., nominating com., strategic planning com., area com. on clin. chemistry and toxicology), Internat. Fedn. Clin. Chemistry (sec. and corp. rep. edn. and mgmt. divsn.), Am. Assn. Clin. Chemistry (sec. 2002—, exec. com. bd. dirs., fin. com., ex-officio mem. ho. of dels. steering com., chair program coord. commn., sec., chair, councilor Fla. sect., vice chair San Diego sect. 1993, recording sec. Chgo. sect. 1997, founding mem., treas. industry divsn., mem. long range planning com. 1985—89, mem. coun. steering com. 1987—88, co-chair ann. meeting 1988). Achievements include research in has focused on immunodiagnostic methods. Office: LifeScan Inc 1000 Gilbralter Dr MS-3D Milpitas CA 95035-6312

EVANS, THELMA JEAN MATHIS, internist; b. East St. Louis, Ill., Jan. 29, 1944; d. Clemmie and Catherine (Rose) Mathis; m. Timothy Charles Evans, June 29, 1968; children: Cynthia Marie, Catherine Elizabeth (twins). BS in Zoology with honors, U. Ill., 1967; MD, U. Ill., Chgo., 1969. Intern, then resident U. Ill. Hosp., Chgo., 1969-71, fellow in pulmonary medicine, 1971-73; med. dir., acute care unit Presbyn.-St. Luke's Hosp., Chgo., 1973-75, asst. to dir. emergency svcs., 1975-77, staff physician Health Specialists, S.C., Chgo., 1977-80, AT&T (Western Electric), Cicero, Ill., 1980-85, Health First, Inc., Chgo., 1985-89, Michael Reese Health Plan, Chgo., 1989-98; mem. adv. bd. Advocate Profl. Group, Chgo., 1998—; bd. dirs. Advocate Health Care Network, Chgo., 2000—. Instr., Rush Med. Coll., Chgo., 1973-84; tuberculosis control officer, infectious disease sect. Chgo. Dept. Health, 1976-77. V.p., Com. to Elect Timothy C. Evans, Chgo., 1989. Grantee, Chgo. Lung Assn., 1972-73. Fellow ACP; mem. Am. Soc. Internal Medicine, NAACP, AMA. Democrat. African Methodist Episcopal. Avocations: photography, gardening, collecting thimbles, bells and music boxes. Office: Advocate Health Ctrs 9831 S Western Ave Chicago IL 60643-1791

EVANS, V. FAYE, postmaster; b. Laurel, Miss., Feb. 20, 1956; Fin. and acct. clerk USPS, Hattiesburg, Miss., 1989, postmaster, 1998. Home: 24 Lakeview Dr Purvis MS 39475

EVANS-FREED, NANCY JANE, secondary school educator; d. Evan Francis and Anna Arminda (May) Evans; m. Robert M. Freed, Aug. 17, 1980 (dec. May 1993); 1 stepchild, Kristina Leigh Freed Gerhling. BS in Home Econs. Edn., Ohio State U., 1964, MA in Higher Edn., 1969; postgrad., Cornell U., Ohio State U., Miami U., Oxford, Ohio. Cert. tchr. home econs., vocat. home econs., counseling and guidance. Home econs. tchr. West Geauga H.S., Chesterland, Ohio, 1964—65; vocat. home econs. and home arts instr. Reynoldsburg City Schs., Ohio, 1967—94. Compiler, pub. Favorite Recipes of Our Best Cooks, 1978. Pres. Women of the Ch., Parkview Presbyn. Ch., Reynoldsburg, Ohio; mem. Christian edn. com. Parkview Presbyn. Ch.; ruling elder on the session Presbyn. Ch. Grantee, Martha Holden Jennings Found. grantee, 1982. Mem.: NEA, Am. Home Econs. Assn. (hostess internat. reception nat. conv., nat. consumers week organizer 1990—93), Ohio Home Econs. Assn., Ohio Edn. Assn., Reynoldsburg Edn. Assn., West Geauga Edn. Assn., Geauga County Home Economists, Phi Delta Kappa, Mortar Bd., Pi Lambda Theta, Omicron Nu, Phi Upsilon Omicron. Avocations: sewing, reading, bicycling, swimming, gardening.

EVANSON, BARBARA JEAN, middle school education educator; b. Grand Forks, N.D., Aug. 15, 1944; d. Robert John and Jean Elizabeth (Lommen) Gibbons; m. Bruce Carlyle Evanson, Dec. 27, 1965; children: Tracey, John, Kelly. AA, Bismarck State Coll., 1964; BS in Spl. and Elem. Edn., U. N.D., 1966. Tchr. spl. edn. Winship Sch., Grand Forks, 1966-67, Simle Jr. High, Bismarck, 1967-70; tchr. Northridge Elem. Sch., Bismarck, 1980-86, Wachter Middle Sch., Bismarck, 1986—. Cons. Dept. Pub. Instrn., Bismark, 1988—, Chpt. I, Bismark, 1989—, McRel for Drug Free Schs., Denver, 1990-95. Co-founder The Big People, Bismarck, 1978-95; mem. task force Children's Trust Fund, N.D., 1984; senator N.D. Legislature, Bismarck, 1989-94; mem. N.D. Bridges Adv. Bd., 1991-97, DPI English Adv. Com., 1993—; co-facilitator Lead Mid. Sch. for Carnegie, 1994-97, N.D. Health Adv. Coun., 1993-94, N.D. Tchr.'s Fund for Retirement, State Investment Bd. 1996—; co-founder, bd. dirs. Neighbors Network, 1983—. Recipient Gold Award Bismark Norwest Bank, 1985; named Tchr. of Yr., N.D. Dept. Pub. Instrn., 1989, Legislator of Yr., Children's Caucus, 1991, Outstanding Alumnae, Bismarck State Coll., 1991, Milken Nat. Tchr. of Yr., 1995-96, KX Golden Apple award, 1999. Mem. N.D. Reading Assn., N.D. Coun. of Tchrs. of English., NEA, N.D. Edn. Assn., Bismarck Edn. Assn. Avocations: clown, walking, reading, travel, remodeling. Office: Wachter Middle Sch 1107 S 7th St Bismarck ND 58504-6533

EVDOKIMOVA, EVA, prima ballerina assoluta, choreographer, director, producer, actress; b. Geneva, Dec. 1, 1948; parents Am. citizens; m. Michael Gregori, 1982. Student, Munich State Opera Ballet Sch., Royal Ballet Sch., London; studied privately with Maria Fay (London), Vera Volkova (Copenhagen), Natalia Dudinskaya (Leningrad), 1964-66; student in Music Studies, Guild Hall Sch. Music, London, 1964—66, Juilliard Sch., 1998—2000; student in Drama Studies, H.B. Studio, N.Y.C., 1997—2000. Pres. of jury Rudolf Nureyev Internat. Ballet Competition, Budapest, 1994, 96, 98; chm. Jury Varna Internat. Ballet Competition, Bulgaria, 1996; ballet mistress Boston Ballet, 2002-03; ballet coach; drama performances 5 off off Broadway drama prodns., 1997-2002; contemporary dance performances created for her by Igal Perry, Henning Rübsam, Angela Jones; simultaneous translation and interpretation between English, French, German, Russian, Italian, Danish. Latin Studies. Debut Royal Danish Ballet, Copenhagen, 1966; Prima Ballerina Assoluta, Deutsche Oper Berlin, 1969-90; frequent guest artist with numerous major ballet cos. worldwide including London Festival Ballet, English Nat. Ballet, Am. Ballet Theatre, Paris Opera Ballet, La Scala, Kirov Ballet, Tokyo Ballet, Teatro Colon, Nat. Ballet of Can., Stuttgart Ballet, Royal Danish Ballet, and all other major nat. ballet cos.; premiered roles in Rudolf Nureyev's classical ballet prodns. (ptnr. over 15 years); appeared in over 16 classical and modern ballets with Rudolf Nureyev across the world; repertoire of more than 130 roles includes Swan Lake, Giselle, La Sylphide, Sleeping Beauty, Romeo and Juliet, Don Quixote, La Bayadere, Onegin, Raymonda; created roles in many contemporary ballets for stage, film and TV; film appearances include The Nutcracker, La Sylphide, Cinderella, A Family Portrait, The Romantic Era, Invitation to the Dance, Portrait of Eva Evdokimova, and others. Recipient Diploma, Internat. Ballet Competition, Moscow, 1969; winner Gold medal Varna Internat. Ballet competition, 1970; awarded title Prima Ballerina Assoluta, Berlin Senate, 1973, Berlin Critic's Prize, 1974; first fgn. mem. Royal Danish Ballet, first Am. and Westerner to win any internat. ballet competition, first Am. to perform with Kirov Ballet, 1976, first Am. to perform in Peking after the Cultural Revolution, 1978, first and only Am. dancer with portrait in permanent collection, Mus. Drama and Dance, Leningrad, St. Petersburg, Russia, only Am. performer ever to be honored in a German opera house, Grand Défilé ceremony, 1990 Deutsche Oper Berlin; recipient letter for meritorious svc. from Pres. Bush, 1990, numerous other awards; holder world record for 67 curtain calls with 40 minute standing ovation, Berlin, 1990. Achievements include world record performing in two different Gisells, two full length Prokofiev Ballets and eight other works with three companies; at Lincoln Center, New York, in three debuts with three different companies within a three month period.

EVE, (EVE JIHAN JEFFERS), rap artist, actress; b. Phila., Nov. 10, 1978; Formed female rap duo EDGP; former mem. DMX's Ruff Ryders posse; signed one-yr. deal with DMX's new label Aftermath. Performer: (albums) Let There Be Eve...Ruff Rider's First Lady, 1999, Scorpion, 2001, Eve-Olution, 2002; musician: (songs) "Eve of Destruction", 1998; musician: (with Gwen Stefani) "Let Me Blow Ya Mind", 2001 (Grammy award best rap/sung collaboration, 2001); musician: (with The Roots) "You Got Me"; musician: (with Blackstreet & Janet Jackson) "Girlfriend/Boyfriend"; musician: (with Missy Elliott) "Hot Boyz"; actor: (films) XXX, 2002, Barbershop, 2002, The Woodsman, 2003, Barbershop 2: Back in Business, 2004; (TV series) Eve, 2003; co-exec. prodr. (TV series) Eve, 2003; actor(guest appearances): (TV series) Third Watch, 2003, One on One, 2004, (voice): (video game) XIII, 2003. Office: Interscope Records 2220 Colorado Ave Santa Monica CA 90404*

EVELEIGH, ARLENE, marine business owner, county commissioner; b. Lakin, Kans., Dec. 10, 1931; d. Herbert and Elva T. (Brown) W.; m. Leon Eveleigh, Aug. 15, 1950; children: Lavon, Curtis, Patricia. Grad. h.s., Lakin, Kans.; student, Kansas City Secretarial Sch., Mo., 1949-50. Owner marine bus., Ellis, Kans. Sec. Cedar Bluff Lake Assn., Ellis, Kans., 1990—; bd. mem. Cedar Bluff Tech. Adv. Com., Ellis, 1995. Bd. dirs. 7th Dist. Kans. Fedn. of Women, 1957-60, 6th Dist. Kans. Fedn. of Women, 1964-66, Smoky-Hill-Saline River Basin Com., Kans., 1993—, Trego County Commission, WaKeeney, Kans., 1995—, chmn. 1997; vice chmn. Reps. of Trego County, 1993-96, comitteewoman Reps. of Riverside Twp., 1991—. Avocations: camping, fishing, pleasure boating, reading. Home: RR 2 Box 76 Ellis KS 67637-9413

EVELETH, JANET STIDMAN, law association administrator; b. Balt., Sept. 6, 1950; d. John Charles and Edith Janet (Scales) Stidman; m. Donald P. Eveleth, May 11, 1974. BA, Washington Coll., 1972; MS, Johns Hopkins U., 1973. Counselor Office of Mayor, Balt., 1973-75; asst. dir. Gov. Commn. on Children, Balt., 1975-78; lobbyist Balt., 1978-80; comm. specialist Med. Soc., Balt., 1980-81; dir. pub. affairs Mid-Atlantic Food Dealers, Balt., 1981-84; dir. comm. Home Builders Assn., Balt., 1984-87, Md. Bar Assn., Balt., 1987—. Contbr. articles to profl. jours. Recipient Gov. citation State of Md., 1993, Citizen citation City of Balt., 1993. Mem.: NAFE, Nat. Assn. Bar Execs. (chmn. pub. rels. sect. 1994—95, Achievement award 1995, E.A. Wally Richter award 1997, Luminary award 1999, 2001, 2003), Md. Soc. Assn. Execs. (pres. 1992—93), Am. Soc. Profl. Women, Pi Lambda Theta, Alpha Chi Omega. Office: Md Bar Assn 520 W Fayette St Baltimore MD 21201-1781 E-mail: jeveleth@msba.org.

EVERETT, CHERYL ANN, music educator, pianist; b. Crawfordsville, Ind., July 7, 1945; d. Howard Dennis and Thelma Louise (Rutledge) P. Student, DePauw U., 1975. Church organist Christian Sci. Ch., Methodist Ch., Presbyn. Ch., Crawfordsvill, Ind., 1958—; celeste player Indpls. Philharmonic Orch., 1994—; accompanist Wabash Coll. Glee Club, Crawfordsville, 1997—; adj. instr. piano Wabash Coll., 2003—. Chmn. Ind. Jr. Festival Nat. Fedn. Music Clubs, 1984-94, Indpls Jr. Festival Nat. Fedn. Music Clubs, 1984-94, Indpls. West Festival, 2000—; chmn. Indpls. West Festival, 2000—; performed in recitals and master classes of Internat. Workshops in Italy, Eng., France, Can., Switzerland, 1986-89, with Internat. String Orch. in workshops in Eisenstadt, Austria, 1989; adjudicator Tippecanoe Piano Tchrs. Lafayette, Ind, 1993-97, Logansport (Ind.) Piano Tchrs., 1993-97, Stickley Meml. Competition, South Bend, Ind., 1989, Ind. State Fair Young Hoosier Pianists Competition. Founder, dir. Presbyn. Artists Concert Series, Crawfordsville, 1991; founder, organizer Montgomery County Multi-keyboard Extavaganza featuring 170 players, Crawfordsville, 1995-97. Chosen 15 times Ideal Lady, Sunshine Soc. Girls, 1977-97. Mem. Indiana Music Tchrs. Assn. (chair monster concert 1998, Tchr. of Yr. 1999), Nat. Music Tchrs., Indpls. Piano Tchrs. (pres. 1986-88), Nat. Guild of Piano Tchrs., Crawfordsville Music Club (pres. 1989), Ind. Fedn. Music Clubs, Nat. Fedn. Music Clubs. Avocations: sewing, needlework, quilting. Home: 207 S Water St Crawfordsville IN 47933-2536 E-mail: ceverett@link2000.net.

EVERETT, DONNA RANEY, finance educator; b. Corpus Christi, Tex., May 30, 1939; d. Donald Wayne and Zora Lee (Wynne) Raney; div.; 1 child, Donna Melinda. BA, Phillips U., Enid, Okla., 1961; MS, U. Houston, 1983, EdD, 1988. Various positions various orgns., Tex., 1965-80; adj. prof. U. Houston, 1983-88; asst. prof. bus. Tex. Tech U., Lubbock, 1988-89, Lamar U., Beaumont, Tex., 1989-90; asst. prof. bus. edn. Tex. Tech U., Lubbock, 1990-93; assoc. prof. bus. and mktg. edn. Ea. N.Mex. U., Portales, 1993-94; asst. prof. bus. edn. U. Mo., Columbia, 1994-96, Morehead State U., Morehead, Ky., 1996—. Sponsor Zeta Kappa chpt. Pi Omega Pi, Phi Beta Lambda; co-sponsor Gamma Chi, Delta Pi Epsilon undergrad. mentor, 1996. Troop leader Girl Scouts U.S., Ft. Worth and Lake Jackson, Tex., 1964-80, dir. tng. Lake Jackson coun., 1980-82. Recipient curriculum devel. award Tex. Higher Edn. Coordinating Bd., 1987-88, outstanding article award Nat. Assn. Bus. Tchrs. Edn. Rev., 1992, Outstanding Paper award Orgn. Systems Rsch. Assn., 1997, Dean's Excellence in Tchg. award Coll. Bus./Morehead State U., 1999; named Outstanding Faculty Mem., Tex. Tech U., 1991. Mem. Am. Ednl. Rsch. Assn. (bus. edn. and inf. sys. spl. interest group), Internat. Soc. Tech. in Edn., Tex. Bus. Edn. Assn. (editor 1988-93, Collegiate Bus. Tchr. of Yr. dist. 4 1988, dist. 17 1992), Nat. Bus. Edn. Assn. (mem. computer enrichment task force), Tex. Computer Edn. Assn., Ky. Bus. Edn. Assn., S.W. Fedn. Adminstrv. Disciplines (Disting. Paper award 1989, 93, 2000), Am. Vocat. Assn. (com. mem. 1990-95), Delta Pi Epsilon (pres. Alpha Gamma chpt. 1988-89), Phi Delta Kappa (sec. Alpha Mu chpt.). Avocations: travel, reading.

EVERETT, KAREN JOAN, retired librarian, genealogist, educator; b. Cin., Dec. 12, 1926; d. Leonard Kelly and Kletis V. (Wade) Wheatley; m. Wilbur Mason Everett, Sept. 25, 1950; children: Karen, Jan, Jeffrey, Jon, Kathleen, Kerry, Kelly, Shannon. BS in Edn. magna cum laude, U. Cin., 1976, postgrad., 1982-85, Coll. Mt. St. Joseph, 1981-86, Xavier U., Cin., 1985-87, U. Cin., 1982-85, Miami U., 1987. Libr. S.W. Local Schs., Harrison, Ohio, 1967-97, dist. media coord., 1980-97, dist. vol. dir., 1980-97, ret., 1997; instr. genealogy U. Cin., 1998—. Tchr. genealogy U. Cin., 1997—; cons. in field; bd. dirs. U. Cin. ILR; lectr. in field. Contbr. articles to profl. jours. Pres. Citizens Adv. Coun., Harrison, Ohio, 1981-84, 88—, Citizens Adv. Coun., 1989; state chmn. supervisory div. Ohio Ednl. Libr./Media Assn.; mem. Ohio Ambulance Licensing Bd., 1991—. Named Woman of the Yr., Cin. Enquirer, 1978, Xi Eta Iota, 1979; named PTA Educator of the Yr., 1981, others. Mem. NEA, Ohio Ednl. Libr./Media Assn. (chair supervisory div. 1990—, bd. dirs. 1993-94), Ohio Edn. Assn., S.W. Local Classroom Tchrs. Assn., Hamilton County Geneal. Soc. (bd. dirs. 1992—). Avocations: flying, travel, genealogy. Office: U Cin PO Box 210146 Cincinnati OH 45221-0146

EVERETT NOLLKAMPER, PAMELA IRENE, legal management company executive, educator; b. L.A., Dec. 31, 1947; d. Richard Weldon and Alta Irene (Tuttle) Bunnell; m. James E. Everett, Sept. 2, 1967 (div. 1973); 1 child, Richard Earl; m. Milton Nollkamper, Dec. 20, 2000. Cert. Paralegal, Rancho Santago Coll., Santa Ana, Calif., 1977; BA, Calif. State U.-Long Beach, 1985; MA, U. Redlands, 1988. Owner, mgr. Orange County Paralegal Svc., Santa Ana, 1979—; pres. Gem Legal Mgmt. Inc., Fullerton, Calif., 1986—; co-owner Bunnell Publs., Fullerton, Calif., 1992-96. Instr. Rancho Santiago Coll., 1979-96, chmn. adv. bd., 1980-85; instr. Fullerton Coll., 1989-2002, Rio Hondo Coll., Whittier, Calif., 1992-94; advisor Saddleback Coll., 1985—, North Orange County Regional Occupational Program, Fullerton, 1986-99, Fullerton Coll. So. Calif. Coll. Bus. and Law; bd. dirs. Nat. Profl. Legal Assts. Inc., editor PLA News. Author: Legal Secretary Federal Litigation, 1986, Bankruptcy Courts and Procedure, 1987, Going Independent--Business Planning Guide, Fundamentals of Law Office Management, 1994. Republican. Avocation: reading. Office: 940 Manor Way Corona CA 92882 E-mail: 2Pan@attbi.com.

EVERETT-THORP, KATE, digital marketing executive; Grad. in Journalism, San Diego State U., 1991. TV reporter; media planner J. Walter Thompson U.S.A., San Francisco; v.p.-crusader advt. programs CNET, 1993; chmn. media measurement task force Internet Advt. Bur.; pres., CEO Lot21, San Francisco, 1998; chmn. Carat Interactive, 2002. Office: 548 4th St San Francisco CA 94107-1621

EVERHART, ANGIE, model; b. Akron, Ohio, 1969; d. Bobby and Ginnie E. Model Seventeen, 1985—. Appeared in Glamour, Sports Illustrated Swimsuit Edition, (film) The Last Action Hero, 1993, Bordello of Blood, Jade. Address: 11726 San Vicente Blvd Ste 368 Los Angeles CA 90049-5075

EVERHART, DOROTHY L. music educator; b. Chicago, IL, May 4, 1919; d. Harvey William Lindaman and Alice Leishman; m. Donald Lough Everhart; children: Mary Ellen, Lawrence C., Gregory W., Douglas L. AB, BMus, Denison U., 1940. Music instr. Glouster (Ohio) H.S., 1940—41, Jackson (Ohio) Mid. Sch., 1941—42; piano and cello instr. Wheatridge, Colo., 1954—59, Arlington Heights, Ill., 1960—77. Home: 3203 North 15th St Unit 304 Grand Junction CO 81506-5268 Office Phone: 970-245-5165. E-mail: dondorhart@aol.com.

EVERIST, BARBARA, state legislator; b. Sioux Falls, S.D., July 6, 1949; d. F. M. and H. M. (Kobb) McBride; m. Thomas Stephen Everist Jr., 1968; children: Thomas Stephen III, Michael Clayton, Lacey Elizabeth. BA, U. Santa Clara, 1971; JD, U. S.D., 1990. Bar: S.D. 1990, U.S. Dist. Ct. S.D. 1990. Law clk. S.D. 2d Cir., 1990-91; state rep. S.D. Ho. Reps. Dist. 14, 1993-94; mem. S.D. Senate Dist. 14, 1995—; mem. state affairs and judiciary coms. S.D. State Senate Dist. 14, chmn. edn. com. Mem. Commerce, Judiciary and Taxation Coms.; atty., Sioux Falls, 1990—. Mem. S.D. State Bar Assn., Assn. Gifted and Talented (pres. 1985), Jr. League Sioux Falls (pres. 1980-81), Phi Alpha Delta, Pi Beta Phi. Home: 709 E Tomar Rd Sioux Falls SD 57105-7053 Office: SD Senate 500 E Capitol Ave Pierre SD 57501-5070

EVERITT, ALICE LUBIN, labor arbitrator; b. Dec. 13, 1936; d. Isador and Alice (Berliner) Lubin. BA, Columbia U., 1968, JD, 1971. Assoc. Amen, Weisman & Butler, N.Y.C., 1971-78; spl. asst. to dir. Fed. Mediation and Conciliation Svc., Washington, 1978-81; pvt. practice labor arbitration Washington, N.Y.C., 1981-87, Petersburg, Va., 1987—. Mem. various nat. mediation and arbitration panels including Fed. Mediation and Conciliation Svc., U.S. Steel and United Steelworkers, Am. Arbitration Assn. Editor Dept. Labor publ., 1979. Mem. Am. Arbitration Assn., Soc. Profls. Dispute Resolution, Indsl. Rels. Rsch. Assn., Civil War Roundtable of Richmond, Petersburg Planning Commn. Office: 541 High St Petersburg VA 23803-3859

EVERITT, ELIZABETH M. school system administrator; d. William Stith; m. Tom Everitt; 1 stepchild, Brian. BS, MA, East Carolina U.; PhD in Spl. Edn., U. N.Mex., 1983. Asst. prin. Mark Twain Elem. Sch., Northeast Heights, prin.; dir. spl. svcs. Albuquerque Pub. Schs., 1995—97, asst. supt. for curriculum and instrn., 1997—98, assoc. supt., 1998—2002, one of 4-person superintendency team, 2002—03, supt., 2003—. Office: Albuquerque Pub Schs 725 University Blvd SE Albuquerque NM 87106*

EVERITT-NEWTON, KATHERINE EVELYN, international management consultant; b. Cleve., Sept. 2, 1957; BS, Bowling Green State U., 1979, MBA, 1981. Sci. systems analyst Eli Lilly & Co., Indpls., 1981-83, systems tng. cons., 1983-84; customer liaison mgr. Ind. U., Bloomington, 1985, prodn. ops. mgr. Indpls., 1985-86; prin. systems cons. Wang Labs., Inc., Carmel, Ind., 1986-93; mgmt. cons. AMT-Sybex (I) Ltd., Dublin, 1994 99; sr. cons. mgr. AMT-Sybex, Ltd., U.K., Letchworth, 1999—. Cons. Ind. Univ., Bloomington, 1984-85, Allied Irish Bank, Dublin, Ireland, 1990-91. Contbr. (book) Introduction to Business, 1980, Introduction to Accounting, 1981, Computers and Data Processing, 1981. Republican. Presbyterian. Avocations: scuba diving, photography, biking, crafts, horseback riding. Office: AMT-Sybex Ltd Spirella Bldg Bridge Rd Letchworth SG6 4ET England Home: 2 Beaulieu Close Bracknell, Berkshire RG12 9QL England E-mail: Katherine_everitt-newton@amt-sybex.com.

EVERSON, JEAN WATKINS DOLORES, librarian, media consultant, educator; b. Forest City, N.C., Feb. 14, 1938; d. J.D. Watkins and Hermie Roberta (Dizard) Watkins; children: Curtis Bryon, Vincent Keith. BS Elem. Edn., U. Cin., 1971, M Secondary Edn., 1973. Cert. X-ray technician. Educator Cin. Pub. Schs., Cin., 1965—2002, classroom tchr., parent/school coord., 1965—2002; work study coord. Butler County Edn. Ctr., Fairfield, Ohio, 1997—98; long term sub. Brown County -Georgetown Sch. Sys., Gerogetown, Ohio, 1993; sr. staff asst., cpc/alcohol substance abuse, inc. Cin. Pub. Schs., Cin., 1992—93; libr. tech. media; libr. media tech. asst. langsam libr. University of Cin.cinnati-Langsam Library, Cincinnati. Dir. and coord. tutoring program So. Baptist Ch., Cincinnati, 1990—91. Author: (booklet) Gospel Music: Copywrite Laws, 1987 (1987). Prodr./dir./coord. city music festival in music hall Cin. Pub. Schs., 1972—77. Mem.: Ohio Assn. Suprs. and Work Study Coords., Music Educator Nat. Conf. Baptist. Avocations: travel, walking. Home: PO Box 8337 West Chester OH 45069 Office: Cin City Pub Schs-Woodward 7001 Reading Rd Cincinnati OH 45237 Home Fax: 513-858-6880; Office Fax: 513-758-1279. Personal E-mail: jeanwatkinseverson@msn.com. Business E-Mail: eversoj@cpsboe.k12.oh.us.

EVERS-WILLIAMS, MYRLIE, cultural organization administrator; b. Vicksburg, Miss., Mar. 17, 1933; m. Medgar Evers (dec. June 1963); 3 children; m. Walter Edward Williams (dec. 1995). Student, Alcorn State U.; BA in Sociology, Pomona Coll., 1968, honorary degree; cert., Simmons Coll.; honorary degree, Medgar Evers Coll., Spelman Coll., Columbia Coll., Chgo., Bennett Coll., Tougaloo Coll., Pomona Coll. Mem. staff, sec. NAACP; dir. planning Claremont (Calif.) Colls., 1968-70; v.p. advt. & publicity Seligman & Latz, N.Y.C., 1973-75; dir. consumer affairs Atlantic Richfield Co.; commr. Pub. Works Bd., L.A., 1987-95; chmn. NAACP, 1995-98. Civil rights leader, lectr. Author: For Us the Living, 1967, Watch Me Fly, 1999; contbg. editor Ladies Home Jour. Candidate for Congress in Calif., 1970; candidate for L.A. City Coun., 1987; head So. Calif. Dem. Women's Divsn.; convener Nat. Women's Polit. Caucus; founder, chmn. Medgar Evers Inst. Named Woman of Yr., Glamour Mag., 1995, Ms. Mag., 1995, one of Women of Yr., Ladies Home Jour., 1996; recipient Mary Church Terrell award Delta Sigma Theta, 1996, Althea T.L. Simmons Social Action award, 1998; recipient Spingarn award, NAACP, Atlanta, 1998; recipient Trumpeter's award, Nat. Consumers League, New Orleans, 1998; named one of 200 most influential women, Vanity Fair mag., Jan. 1999. Office: MEW Assocs Inc 15 SW Colorado Ave Bend OR 97702-1150

EVERT, CHRIS (CHRISTINE MARIE EVERT), retired professional tennis player; b. Ft. Lauderdale, Fla., Dec. 21, 1954; d. James and Colette Evert; m. John Lloyd, Apr. 17, 1979 (div.); m. Andy Mill, July 30, 1988; children: Alexander James, Nicholas Joseph, Colton Jack. Amateur tennis player, until Dec. 1972; profl. tennis player, 1972-89; ret. from tennis, 1989; owner Evert Enterprises/IMG, Boca Raton, Fla., 1989—; Olympics commentator CBS Sports, 1992. Commentator NBC Sports tennis events; winner numerous tournaments including U.S. Jr. Championship, 1970, 71, U.S. Open, 1975, 76, 77, 78, 80, 82, Wimbledon Singles, 1974, 76, 81, doubles, 1976, Australian Open, 1982, 84, French Open Singles, 1974, 75, 79, 80, 83, 85, 86, Virginia Slims, 1972, 73, 75, 77, 87, European Women's Open, Geneva, 1987, Eckerd Open, 1987; spl. advisor to U.S. Nat. Tennis Team by U.S. Tennis Assn.; bd. dirs. Internat. Tennis Hall of Fame; trustee Womens Sports Found. Corp. spokesperson and rep., appearing in TV commls. and print advertisements; host and organizer Chris Evert Pro-Celebrity Tennis Classic, 1989, 90, 92, 93, 94, 95, 96, 97, 98, 99. Founder Chris Evert Charities, Inc., Healthy Start. Recipient Lebair Sportsmanship trophy, 1971; named Female Athlete of Yr. AP, 1974, 75, 77, 80, Athlete of Yr. Sports Illustrated, 1976, Greatest Woman Athlete of Last 25 Years Women's Sports Found., 1985, Flo Hyman award Women's Sports Found., 1990, Providencia award Palm Beach County Conv. and Visitors Bur., 1991; named one of Top 10 Romantic People of 1989, Korbel; inducted Madison Sq. Garden Walk of Fame, 1993, inductee, Internat. Tennis Hall of Fame, 1995. Mem. U.S. Lawn Tennis Assn. (Top Women's Singles Player award 1974), Nat. Honor Soc., Fla. Sports Found. (bd. dirs.), Women's Tennis Assn. (pres. 1982-91, exec. com., Sportsmanship award 1979, Player Svc. awards 1981, 86, 87).*

EVERT, MARGARET JANE, principal; b. Chgo., July 27, 1947; d. George and Margaret Mary (Hussey) Brown; m. Robert Lawrence Evert, Oct. 4, 1969; 1 child, Elizabeth Anne; m. Christopher Deutscher, May 30, 1997. BA in Elem. Edn., Northeastern U., 1969; MA in Ednl. Adminstrn., Dominican U., 1997. Cert. elem. tchr., elem. adminstr., Ill. Tchr. St. Leonard Sch., Berwyn, Ill., 1969-70, St. Edmund Sch., Oak Park, Ill., 1971-93, acting prin., 1993-96, prin., 1996—. Mem. adv. bd. I Search Program, Oak Park, 1993—. Bd. dirs. Rochetta-Wessies Scholarship Found., 1993—; mem. MADD. Mem. ASCD, NAESP, Nat. Cath. Edn. Assn. Avocations: piano, travel, reading. Office: Saint Edmund School 200 S Oak Park Ave Oak Park IL 60302-3299

EWELL, MIRANDA JUAN, journalist; b. Beijing, Apr. 25, 1948; d. Vei-Chow and Hsien-fang Yolanda (Sun) J.; m. John Woodruff Ewell Jr., Feb. 20, 1971; children: Emily, David, Jonah. BA summa cum laude, Smith Coll., 1969; postgrad., Princeton U., 1971, U. Calif., Berkeley, 1981-82. Staff writer The Montclarion, Oakland, Calif., 1982-83; with San Jose (Calif.) Mercury News, 1984-99, staff writer; now correspondent San Jose (Calif.) Mercury News, San Francisco Bureau, 1990-95; correspondent in bus. San Jose Mercury News, 1997-99. Recipient Elsa Knight Thompson award Media Alliance, San Francisco, 1984, George Polk award L.I. U., N.Y., 1989, Heywood Broun award Newspaper Guild, Washington, 1989; Knight fellow Stanford U., 1995. Mem. Asian-Am. Journalists Assn.

EWEN, PAMELA BINNINGS, lawyer; b. Mar. 22, 1944; d. Walter James and Barbara (Perkins) Binnings; m. Jerome Francis Ayers, Aug. 22, 1965 (div. July 1974); 1 child, Scott Dylan Ayers ; m. John Alexander Ewen, Dec. 13, 1974 (div. Feb. 2003); m. James Craft Loft, Dec. 27, 2003. BA, Tulane U., 1977; JD cum laude, U. Houston, 1979. Bar: Tex. 79, U.S. Dist. Ct. (so. dist.) Tex. 81, U.S. Ct. Appeals (5th cir.) 81. Law clk. Harris, Cook, Browning & Barker, Corpus Christi, Tex., 1977—79; assoc. Kleberg, Dyer, Redford & Weil, Corpus Christi, 1979—80; atty. law dept. Gulf Oil Corp., Houston, 1980—84; assoc. Baker & Botts, L.L.P., Houston, 1980—84, ptnr., 1988—. Author: Faith On Trial, 1999. La. Legis. scholar, New Orleans, 1976—77. Mem.: ABA (forum com. on franchising 1983—85, law practice mgmt. sect., subcom. Women Rainmakers Assn.), Tex. Assn. Bank Coun., Tex. State Bar (bd. dirs. 1994—97), Am. Petroleum Inst. (com. on product liability 1982—85, spl. subcom. to gen. com. on law), Order of Barons, Jr. Achievement S.E. Tex. (bd. dirs. 1997—2001, bd. dirs. Inprint, Inc. 2002—). Office: Baker & Botts 3000 1 Shell Plz Houston TX 77002 Office Phone: 713-229-1126.

EWERS, ANNE, opera company director; Gen. dir. Boston Lyric Opera, 1984—89, Utah Opera, Salt Lake City, 1990—2002; CEO, gen. dir. Utah Symphony & Opera, Salt Lake City, 2002—. Bd. trustees OPERA Am.; panelist NEA. Dir.: (60 productions for more than 25 opera cos.); (Operas) Dreamkeepers, The Seven Deadly Sins of the Petite Bourgeoisie, 2003. Founder Utah Opera Young Artist Program, 1992. Office: Utah Symphony & Opera 123 W South Temple Salt Lake City UT 84101-1403 Office Phone: 801-533-5626.

EWERS, MARLA ROUSE, voice educator; b. Charleston, Ill., Dec. 11, 1952; m. John M. Ewers; children: John Robert, Meridith Anne. MusB, Ea. Ill. U., 1975; MSEd, U. Ill., 1995, student in Edn., 1996—98. Music specialist grades K-8 Decatur (Ill.) Pub. Schs., 1979—94, 1997—98; grad. asst. U. Ill., Urbana, 1994—97; choral dir. Stephen Decatur H.S., 1998—2000, Eisenhower H.S., Decatur, 2000—. Adjudicator Ill. H.S. Assn., Bloomington, 1993—. Mem.: Music Educators Nat. Conf., Assn. Supervision and Curriculum Devel., Am. Choral Directors Assn., Phi Delta Kappa, Sigma Alpha Iota (treas. 1988—92, Sword of Honor 1993). Home: 881 S Oakland Ave Forsyth IL 62535 Office: Eisenhower HS 1200 S 16th St Decatur IL 62521 Personal E-mail: Marla881@msn.com.

EWERSEN, MARY VIRGINIA, retired school system administrator, poet; b. Van Wert County, Ohio, June 7, 1922; m. Herbert Ewersen (dec.); 2 children. BS in Elem. Edn., Bowling Green, 1966, Toledo and Ohio State U. Cert. tchr. K-12, reading, Ohio. Remedial reading tchr. Port Clinton (Ohio) City Schs., 1966-70, reading tchr. chpt. I/coord., 1970-94; ret. Lyrics writer Hilltop Records. Author: Keepsakes and Celebrations!, 1997, (activity card set)) From Hyperactive to Happy-Active in Limited Spaces, 1979, The Lures of Pan, 2001. Mem. Internat. Reading Assn., Sandusky Choral Soc., Acad. Am. Poets, Internat. Soc. Poets, Kappa Delta Pi. Home: 1786 S Hickory Grove Rd Port Clinton OH 43452-9637 Office: 431 Portage Dr Port Clinton OH 43452-1724

EWING, ELISABETH ANNE ROONEY, priest; b. San Bernardino, Calif. m. James E. Ewing. Student, Mt. San Antonio Coll., 1978. Ordained priest Communion Evang. Episcopal Ch., 1998, ordained to ministry Meth. Ch. Pastor, gen. overseers, CEO St. Matthew's Nationwide Chs., N.Y.C. Mem. Rand Rsch. Corp.; mem. diplomat cir. L.A. World Affairs Coun. Co-editor: (book) Church History, 1996—98, The Church Visible, 1996—98, Life After Death, 1996—98, Bible Lessons, 1996—98; head pub. rels., assoc. editor Pinnacle Today Internat. Mag.; assoc. editor: St. Matthew Tribune. Recipient St. Augustine cross, Archbishop of Canterbury. Mem.: Knights of Malta (dame).

EWING, MARILYN, English educator; b. Rochester, N.H., Oct. 19, 1940; d. Thomas Kirby and Ida Maryann (Scala) McKee; m. Richard Edwin Ewing, June 29, 1963 (div. Nov. 1974); 1 child, Julie E. BA cum laude, U. N.H., 1962; MA, U. No. Colo., 1974; PhD, U. Colo., 1982. Tchr. Portsmouth (N.H.) H.S., 1962-63, Green Springs (Ohio) Local Sch., 1964-66; tchg. asst. U. No. Colo., Greeley, 1973-77; tchg. asst., part-time instr. U. Colo., Boulder, 1977-82; from asst. prof. to assoc. prof. English, Eastern Oreg. U., La Grande, 1982—. Translator poems by Pablo Neruda, Colo.-North Rev., 1976; columnist The Longmont (Colo.) Ledger, 1971; author essays and article. Recipient Svc. award Oreg. Women in Higher Edn., 1999. Mem. NOW, MLA, Nat. Coun. Tchrs. English, Oreg. Writing Project (mem. steering com. 1994—), Lambda Pi. Office: Eastern Oreg U 1 University Blvd La Grande OR 97850-2807

EWING, ROBYN, writer, educator; d. Robert Alexander Ewing and Nancy Moore Powers. BFA, Cornell U., 1982; MFA in Poetry, U. Iowa, 2001; MA in Fiction, Johns Hopkins U., 2002. Freelance art dir./designer, N.Y.C., 1985—97, L.A., 1985—97; fellow and instr. Iowa Writer's Workshop, Iowa City, 2000—01; poet-in-residence Carver Ctr. Art and Technology, Towson, Md., 2001; instr. Johns Hopkins Ctr. Talented Youth, Balt., 2001—02; lectr. Johns Hopkins Writing Seminars, Balt., 2002—03; fellow in writing Vt. Studio Ctr., Johnson, 2003. Author: Chemical Wedding, 2002 (Colorado prize); contbr. articles to profl. jours. Named to Athletic Hall of Fame, Cornell U., 1998; recipient prize, Acad. Am. Poets, 1998.

EWING, SUSAN R. art educator, artist; b. Lawrenceville, Ill., 1955; AA in Music, Stephens Coll., 1974; BA in Jewelry, Metalsmithing, Ind. U., 1976, MFA in Jewelry, Metalsmithing, 1980. Head metals program Miami (Ohio) U., 1981—. One-person shows include Hans Hansen Sølv, Copenhagen, Denmark, Nat. Tech. Mus., Prague, Czech Republic, Phoenix Mus. Art, Ohio Craft Mus., Columbus, Ork. Art Ctr., Little Rock; group shows include Aspects Gallery, London, Park Ryu Sook Gallery, Seoul, Korea, Schweizerisches Landesmuseum, Zurich, Switzerland, Cercle Mcpl. Galerie Oféo, Luxembourg, Mus. Kunsthandwerk, Frankfurt, Germany, Deutsches Klingenmuseum, Solingen, Germany, Schmuckmuseum, Pforzheim, Germany, Galerie Matter, Cologne, Germany, Galerie Ende, Cologne, Mathildenhohe Mus., Darmstadt, Germany, Galerie Spectrum, Munich, Germany, Galerie Ventil, Munich, Fortunoff's N.Y.C., Urban BobKat Gallery, N.Y.C., Lever House, N.Y.C., Seventh Regiment Armory, N.Y.C., Am. Craft Mus., N.Y.C.; represented in permanent collections White House. Recipient Dolibois Faculty Devel. award, disting. Lifetime Achievement award Ohio Designer

Craftsmen; Summer Rsch. fellow Miami U., Ohio Arts Coun. Individual Artist fellow, 1987, 89, 91, Fulbright grantee, 1997, 98; Rsch. Challenge grantee Ohio State Bd. Regents. Office: Sch Art Fine Arts Dept Miami U Oxford OH 45056

[illegible], music educator; b. Summit, N.J., July 20, 1956; d. Martin Francis and Lillian Virginia Dress; m. Stephen Robert Exley, Mar. 18, 1988; children: Alicia Sarah, Stephen Jr. Robert. MEd, Coll. of N.J., Ewing, 1986. Cert. adminstrv. prin. Mont., 2002, music tchr. Mont., 2002, N.J., 1978, supr. music N.J., 1986. Choir, orch., band, and world drumming music tchr. Bozeman (Mont.) Sch. Dist., 1998—; choir dir. and gen. music tchr. Yellowstone Acad. at Yellowstone Boys and Girls Ranch, Billings, Mont., 1997—98; band dir. Belvidere (N.J.) Sch. Dist., 1987—93; gen. music, choir, band, and orch. dir. Allamuchy Sch., NJ, 1983—87; band dir. Trenton Pub. Schools, 1980—83, Iselin Jr. HS, 1978—79. Freelance french horn player Bozeman Symphony, Mont., 1998—2002; guest artist, french horn Jamaica Syphony. Dir.: (orchestra, choir and band); watercolors;, singer. Worship leader and singer First Presbyn. Ch., Billings, Mont., 1996—98; musician Grace Bible Ch., Bozeman, Mont., 2001—03. Mem.: Music Educator's Nat. Conf. Avocations: watercolor painting, french horn, nature travel, photography, camping. Home: #3 1602 W Koch Bozeman MT 59715 Office: Sacajawea Mid Sch 3525 S 3rd Bozeman MT 59715 Personal E-mail: mexley@imt.net. E-mail: mexley@bozeman.k12.mt.us.

EXPOSITO, DAISY, advertising executive; b. Cuba; arrived in U.S., 1964; Creative dir. Bravo Group, N.Y.C., 1981—85, sr. v.p., gen. mgr., 1985—90, CEO, chmn., 1990—. Named one of N.Y.'s Top 100 Top Minority Execs., Crain's N.Y. Bus., 100 Outstanding Hispanic Women in Comm., Hispanic Mag.; recipient Corp. Achiever of the Yr. award, Nat. Hispanic Acad. Media Arts & Scis., Salute to Model award, Am. Advt. Fedn. Dist. 2. Mem.: Assn. Hispanic Advt. Agys. (pres.), Internat. Arts Rels., Am. Assn. Advt. Agys. Found., Inc. (bd. dirs.), Nat. Coun. La Raza, Hispanic Fedn., New Am.'s Alliance. Office: Bravo Group 20 Cooper Sq New York NY 10003

EYRE, PAMELA CATHERINE, retired career officer; b. Chgo., Nov. 3, 1948; d. Francis Thomas and Jane (Burd) E. BA, Ctrl. State U. Okla., 1972; MPA, U. Okla., 1976; postgrad., U. Tex., 1998—. Commd. 2d lt. U.S. Army, 1973, advanced through grades to lt. col., 1991, test and evaluation officer, 1982-85, R&D coord. Ft. Monmouth, N.J., 1985-88, with army gen. staff Pentagon Washington, 1988-91, acquisition policy staff officer Army Secretariat Pentagon, 1991-94, asst. project mgr. Def. Telecom. Svc., 1994-95, test and evaluation officer Army Secretariat Pentagon, 1995-96; ret., 1996; program mgr. unmanned aerial vehicles Mission Techs., Inc., San Antonio, 2000—. Home: 200 PR 4660 Castroville TX 78009 E-mail: eyre@texas.net.

EYRING, MAXINE LOUISE, small business owner, esthetician; b. Baltimore, MD, Sept. 17, 1946; d. William Charles Whippo and Catherine Marie Bennett; m. William John Eyring (div.). Student, Catonsville C.C., Baltimore, 1964. Lic. esterician Md., 1979. Owner Maxime's Skin and Nail Care, Annapolis, Md., 1980—88; with Salon West, Annapolis, 1988—89, Lord's and Lady's Salon, Annapolis, 1989—91; esthetician Robert Andrew Day Spa, Gambills, Md., 1991—97, Vincent's Masterpiece Internat. Day Spa, Annapolis, 1997—2000, Rumors of Annapolis, 2000—02; mgr. Esthencian Vincent's Masterpiece Internat. Day Spa, 2002—. Democrat. Lutheran.

EZAKI-YAMAGUCHI, JOYCE YAYOI, dietician; b. Kingsburg, Calif., Mar. 18, 1947; d. Toshikatsu and Aiko (Ogata) Ezaki; m. Kent Takao Yamaguchi, Oct. 28, 1972; children: Kent Takao, Jr., Toshia Ann. AA, Reedley Coll., 1967; BS in Foods and Nutrition, U. Calif., Davis, 1969. Dietetic intern Henry Ford Hosp., Detroit, 1969-70, staff dietitian, 1970-71; renal dietitian Sutter Meml. Hosp., Sacramento, 1971-72; therapeutic dietitian Mt. Sinai Hosp., Beverly Hills, Calif., 1972-73; clin. dietitian Pacific Hosp., Long Beach, Calif., 1973-77; consulting dietitian Doctor's Hosp., Lakewood, Calif., 1976-77; clin. dietitian Mass. Gen. Hosp., Boston, 1977-78, Winona Meml. Hosp., Indpls., 1978-80; renal dietitian Fresno (Calif.) Community Hosp., Calif., 1980—. Author: (computer program) Dialysis Tracker, 1987; author: (with others) Cultural Foods and Renal Diets for the Dietitian, 1988, Standards of Practice Guidlines for the Practice of Clinical Dietetics, 1991. Religious chair Fresno Dharma Sch. Fresno Betsuin Buddhist Temple, 1994—; sec. Japanese Lang. Sch., 1997-01. Mem. Nat. Kidney Found. (exec. com. coun. renal nutrition 1991-98, region V rep., nutrition editor, chair patient and pub. edn. com. 1992-93, chair elect comms. chair 1994-95, chair 1995-96, past chair 1997-98, chair nominations com., chair rsch. grant com., Disting. Svc. award 1996, Nat. Kidney Found./Coun. on Renal Nutrition Recognized Renal Dietitian award 1999), Am. Dietetic Assn. (bd. cert. renal nutrition specialist, renal practice group 1993-98, renal practice group nominating com. chair 1999), No. Calif/No. Nev. chpt. Nat. Kidney Found. (disting. achievement award coun. on renal nutrition 1993, co-chair-elect 1993-94, co-chair 1994-95, co-past chair 1995-96, treas., corr. sec.). Buddhist. Avocations: computers, cross stitch. Office: Cmty Med Ctrs CAPD Fresno & R Sts Fresno CA 93715-2094

EZELL, MARGARET J. language educator; John Paul Abbott prof. of liberal arts Tex. A&M U., College Sta., 1997—; dir. Rsch. Inst. Inner Asian Studies. Author: The Patriarch's Wife: Literary Evidence and the History of the Family, Writing Women's Literary History, Social Authorship and the Advent of Print; editor: (series) Women Writers in English, 1350-1830. Fellow, John Simon Guggenheim Meml. Found., 2003. Office: Tex A&M U Dept English 243D Blocker Bldg (MS 4227) College Station TX 77843

EZENWA, JOSEPHINE NWABUOKU, social worker; b. Oct. 20, 1959; d. Igwe Silas O. and H.R.H. Veronica A. Ezenwa. BA in Psychology and Human Svc.(hon.), Fontbonne Coll., St. Louis, 1980; MSW, Washington Univ., St. Louis, 1981; postgrad., St. Louis U., 1991—93. Diplomate Am. Coll. Profl. Mental Health Practitioners, 2002. Rsch. dir. Nat. Benevolent Assn., St. Louis, 1981-89; tchr. U. City Sch. Dist., St. Louis, 1989-94; therapist Presbyn. Children's Home, St. Louis, 1994-95; social worker St. Louis Regional Med. Ctr., 1995-97; founder, chair St. Louis Regional Med. Ctr. Dialysis Support Group, 1995-97; social worker St. Louis U. Hosp., 1997; CEO, pres. BBS Care U.S.A., Inc., St. Louis, 1997—; pres. BBS Charities, Inc., St. Louis, 2000—; chair Bus. Adv. Coun. Nat Rep. Congl. Com., St. Louis, 2002—. Founder and chair St. Louis Regional Med. Ctr. Dialysis Support Group, 1995-97; chair long range planning com. Washington U.; co-chair Bus. Adv. Coun., 2002; presenter in field. Chair bus. adv. coun. Nat. Rep. Congl. Com., 2002—. Named Businesswoman of Yr., Nat. Rep. Congl. Com., 2003; recipient Nat. Leadership award, St. Louis Regional Med. Ctr. Dialysis Support Group, 2002, Gold Medal award, Nat. Rep. Congl. Com., 2003. Mem. NASW, NAFE, Coun. Nephrology Social Workers; Nat. Assn. Forensic Counselors; Nat. Assn. Cognitive Behavioral Therapists, Washington U. Sch. Social Work Alumni Assn. (bd. dir.); Creve Coeur-Olive C. of C.; Lions Club. Avocations: choreography, fashion cons., event coord., design, travel. Office: St Louis U Hosp 3536 Vista Grand Saint Louis MO 63110 also: BBS Care USA Inc 8420 Delmar Blvd Ste 505 Saint Louis MO 63124-2180

EZRATI, SUSAN GRAHAM, investment company executive, economist; b. Denver, Dec. 29, 1945; d. Earl Ellis and Winona (Davidson) Graham; m. Milton J. Ezrati, June 19, 1976; 1 child, Isabel Diana. BA, Pomona Coll., 1968; MA, Denver U., 1970; MPhilD, Columbia U., 1985. CFA, Va. Sr. analyst Citibank, N.Y.C., 1970-73, economist, 1973-78; instr. Rutgers U., Newark, 1978-81; economist GM Corp., N.Y.C., 1982-88; mgr. internat. divsn. GMIMCo, N.Y.C., 1989-95, dir. internat. strategy, 1995-99; chief investment officer Client Affiliates, 1999—2003; v.p. Client Rels. Adv. bd. LA Corp. Bond Fund, London, 1996, Advent Internat., Boston, 1997; bd. dirs. GMAC Ins., 1999—2003. Author: Michigan Yearbook of International Legal Studies, 1984, The Experience of the Automotive Industry in Industrial Policies of [illegible] Fort Washington, N.Y., 1997-2000; bd. dirs. NY-Conn. Found. United Meth. Ch., 2001—. Mem. Am. Econ. Soc., Assn. for Investment Mgmt. and Rsch., N.Y. State Securities Analysts. Democrat. Methodist. Avocations: choir, gardening. Office: GMIMCo 767 5th Ave New York NY 10153-0023

FAATZ, JEANNE RYAN, councilperson; b. Cumberland, Md., July 30, 1941; d. Charles Keith and Elizabeth (McIntyre) Ryan; children: Kristin, Susan. BS, U. Ill., 1962; postgrad., Harvard U., 1984; MA, U. Colo., Denver, 1985. Instr. speech dept. Met. State Coll., Denver, 1985-98; sec. to majority leader Colo. Senate, 1976-78; mem. Colo. Ho. Reps. from Dist. 1, 1979-98; dir. Colo. Sch.-to-Career, 1999—2001; councilwoman City of Denver, 2003—. Former ho. asst. majority leader. Past pres. S.W. Denver YWCA Adult Edn. Club; former mem. bd. mgrs. S.W. Denver YMCA; past pres. Harvey Park (Colo.) Homeowners Assn. Gates fellow, Harvard U., 1984. Home: 2903 S Quitman St Denver CO 80236-2208

FABE, DANA ANDERSON, state supreme court justice; b. Cin., Mar. 29, 1951; d. George and Mary Lawrence (Van Antwerp) F.; m. Randall Gene Simpson, Jan. 1, 1983; 1 child, Amelia Fabe Simpson. BA, Cornell U., 1973; JD, Northeastern U., 1976. Bar: Alaska 1977, U.S. Supreme Ct. 1981. Law clk. to justice Alaska Supreme Ct., 1976-77; staff atty. pub. defenders State Alaska, 1977-81; dir. Alaska Pub. Defender Agy., Anchorage, 1981—. Judge Superior Ct., Anchorage; justice Alaska Supreme Ct., Anchorage, 1996—, chief justice, 2000-03. Named alumna of yr. Northeastern Sch. Law, 1983, alumni pub. svc. award, 1991. Office: Alaska Supreme Ct 303 K St Fl 5 Anchorage AK 99501-2013

FABENS, SALLY FISHER, communications executive, consultant; b. Marlborough, Mass., Sept. 9, 1964; d. Benjamin Henry and Barbara L. (Myles) Fabens; life ptnr. Lori L. Morris. BA magna cum laude, Wells Coll., 1986; MA, Cornell U., 1989. Tchr. St. James Sch., Arlington, Mass., 1986—87; mng. dir. Dance Projects, Inc./Beth Soll & Co., Boston, 1990—94; devel. dir. Artists Found., Boston, 1991—94; assoc. dir. devel. AIDS Action Com., Boston, 1994—99; dir. comm. and devel. VSA Arts Mass., Boston, 1999—2001; dir. comm. United Way Schenectady (N.Y.) County, 2002—. Cons. Sally Fabens Consulting, Delmar, NY, 2001—. Chairperson Triangle Theater Co., Boston, 1994—2000. Grad. fellow, Cornell U., 1988. Mem.: Am. Mktg. Assn., Phi Beta Kappa. Avocations: theater, reading, cooking, entertaining. Office: United Way of Schenectady County Ste 102 650 Franklin St Schenectady NY 12054 E-mail: fabens@uwschdy.org.

FABER, SANDRA MOORE, astronomer, educator; b. Boston, Dec. 28, 1944; d. Donald Edwin and Elizabeth Mackenzie (Borwick) Moore; m. Andrew L. Faber, June 9, 1967; children: Robin, Holly. BA, Swarthmore Coll., 1966, DSc (hon.), 1986; PhD, Harvard U., 1972; DSc (hon.), Williams Coll., 1996. Asst. prof., astronomer Lick Obs., U. Calif., Santa Cruz, 1972-77, assoc. prof., astronomer, 1977-79, prof., astronomer, 1979—; Univ. Prof. U. Calif., Santa Cruz, 1996—. Mem. astronomy adv. panel NSF, 1975-77; vis. prof. Princeton U., 1978, U. Hawaii, 1983, Ariz. State U., 1985; Phillips visitor Haverford Coll., 1982; Feshbach lectr. MIT, Cambridge, Mass., 1990; Darwin lectr. Royal Astron. Soc., 1991; Marker lectr. Pa. State U., 1992; Bunyan lectr. Stanford U., 1992; Tomkins lectr. U. Calif., San Francisco, 1992; Mohler lectr. U. Mich., 1994; mem. Nat. Acad. Astronomy Survey Panel, 1979-81Nfat. Acad. Com. on Astronomy and Astrophysics 1993-1995; chmn. vis. com. Space Telescope Sci. Inst., 1983-84; co-chmn. sci. steering com. Keck Obs., 1987-92, leader DEIMOS spectrograph team, 1993—; mem. Wide Field Camera team Hubble Space Telescope, 1985-97, user's com., 1990-92, mem. advanced radial camera selection team, 1995,co-chmn. TAC review comm., 2002; mem. treas. pgm. advis. comm. 2002-; mem. Calif. Coun. on Sci. and Tech., 1989-94,; Com. on Future Smithsonian Instn., 1994-95; mem. White House Space Sci. Workshop, 1996, Waterman Awards Com., NSF, 1997-99, Nat. Medal of Sci. selection com., 1999-2001; mem. Plumian Prof. selection com. Cambridge U., 1998—. Assoc. editor: Astrophys. Jour. Letters, 1982-87; editorial bd.: Ann. Revs. Astronomy and Astrophysics, 1982-87; contbr. articles to profl. jours. Trustee Carnegie Instn., Washington, 1985—; bd. dirs. Ann. Revs., 1989—, SETI Inst., 1997—; editl. affairs com. Ann. Revs., 1996—; exec. com. Ann. Revs., 1998—; Scripps Instn. Oceanography Coun., 2000--; bd. overseers Fermilab, 2002--. Recipient Bart J. Bok prize Harvard U., 1978, Director's Distinguished Lectr. award Livermore Nat. Lab., 1986; NASA Group Achievement award, 1993, DeVaucouleurs medal U. Tex., 1997; Carnegie Lectr. Carnegie Inst. Washington, 1988, 99; NSF fellow, 1966-71; Woodrow Wilson fellow, 1966-71; Alfred P. Sloan fellow, 1977-81; listed among 100 best Am. scientists under 40, Sci. Digest, 1984, listed among 50 best Am. Women scientists, Discover Mag., 2002; Tetelman fellow, Yale U., 1987. Fellow Calif. Coun. on Sci. and Tech.; mem. NAS (vice chair adv. panel on cosmology 1993, rsch. in astronomy commn. on orgn. and mgmt. astrophysics 2001, co-chmn. TAC rev. commn. 2002, mem. treas. program adv. commn. 2002--), Am. Philos. Soc. Am. Acad. Arts and Scis., Calif. Acad. Scis., 1998—, Am. Astron. Soc. (councilor 1982-84, Dannie Heineman prize 1986), Internat. Astron. Union, Am. Philos. Soc., Phi Beta Kappa, Sigma Xi. Office: U Calif Lick Obs Santa Cruz CA 95064 E-mail: faber@ucolick.org.

FABICH, PENELOPE JANE, humanities educator; b. Medina, Ohio, Dec. 22, 1952; d. Charles Edward Swingle, Margaret Helen Swingle; m. Ronald William Fabich, Aug. 1, 1980; children: Nathaniel, Emmaline, Abigail. BA in History, Latin, U. Akron, 1975, M in Multicultural Edn., 1994, postgrad. Cert. permanent tchg. lic. History, Latin, English Ohio. Tchr. Latin/History Brunswick H.S., Brunswick, Ohio, 1976—81; tchr. Govt./History Polaris Vocat. Sch., Berea, Ohio, 1982—83, Our Lady of Elms H.S., Akron, Ohio, 1983—84; tchr. Latin/History Brunswick H.S., 1986—. Levy com. mem. Buckeye Local Schs., Medina, Ohio, 2000. Mem.: Am. Classical Leagu. Democrat. Roman Catholic. Home: 6800 Wolff Rd Medina OH 44256 Office: Brunswick High Sch 3581 Center Rd Brunswick OH 44212-3695

FABING, SUZANNAH, museum director; b. Cin., Oct. 1, 1942; d. Howard Douglas John and Esther Clare (Maring) F.; m. Peter B. Doeringer, June 19, 1965 (div. June 1981); 1 child, Eric Atchley; m. James Alexander Muspratt, Aug. 21, 1993. AB in Art History with hons., Wellesley Coll., 1964; AM, Harvard U., 1965. Asst. to curator of Ancient art to dep. dir. mus. Fogg Art Mus./Harvard U., 1965-83; curator of records Nat. Gallery of Art, Washington, 1983-84, mng. curator of records and loans, 1984-91, head Divsn. of Rsch. on Collections, 1991-92; dir., chief curator Smith Coll. Mus. of Art, Northampton, Mass., 1992—. Overview panel NEA, 1993-94; reviewer NEH, 1992-94; surveyor AAM Mus. Assessment Program, 1991—; mem. Art Info. Task Force, Getty Art Info. Program, 1990-94; vis. com. Wellesley Coll. Mus., 1988—, Fitchburg Art Mus., chmn. 1983-88, others; trustee Fitchburg Art Mus., 1975-82, Revels, Inc., 1981-82, 88-92), others. Contbr. articles to profl. jours. Mem. New Eng. Mus. Assn. (panelist), Mus. Computer Network (bd. dirs. 1984-90, sec. 1988, v.p. 1988-89, pres. 1989-90), Phi Beta Kappa. Avocations: various langs. including French, German, Italian, Latin, ancient Greek. Office: Smith Coll Mus Of Art Northampton MA 01063-0001

FABYANSKI, MARY IRENE, nursing administrator; b. Bayonne, NJ, July 14, 1952; d. Edward John and Rose Virginia (Mulhern) F. AAS in Nursing, Felician Coll., Lodi, N.J., 1977; student, Jersey City (N.J.) State Coll., 1970-72. RN NJ. Nurse St. Francis Hosp., Jersey City, 1971-77, 1977-83, Children's Specialized Hosp., Mountainside, NJ, 1984-88; asst. dir. nursing Manor Care of Mountainside, N.J., 1988-89; dir. nursing Morrishills Multicare Ctr., Morristown, N.J., 1989-90; asst. adminstr., dir. nursing Berkeley Hall Nursing Home, Berkeley Heights, N.J., 1990-93; dir. nursing [illegible] Franciscan Home and Rehab. Ctr., Jersey City, 1998; pres., cons. long term care Quality Care Cons., Union, N.J., 1996—; dir. ops. Future Care Cons., BHCC, Irvington, N.J., 1998-99; regional adminstrv. nurse mgr. Genesis Eldercare, 1997—. Bd. adv. Hudson County C.C., Jersey City, N.J., 1996-98. Recipient Award for Excellence Bd. Dirs., Berkeley Hall, Berkeley Heights, 1991, Award of Recognition, Bd. Dirs., Hudson City Coll., Jersey City, 1997, 98. Mem. NAACP, N.J. Long Term Care Nursing Assn., Nat. Assn. Long Term Care. Democrat. Roman Catholic. Home: 147 Jockey Hollow Way Union NJ 07083-4158 Office: Quality Care Consultants 147 Jockey Hollow Way Union NJ 07083-4158

FADDEN, SISTER R. PATRICIA, academic administrator, nun; b. Canonsburg, Pa. d. Gerald and Ruth Fadden. AB in Math., Immaculata Coll.; MA in Edn., Ohio State U.; EdD in Edn., Immaculata Coll. Tchr. elem. sch., 1960—68; tchr. West Cath. H.S. Girls, 1968—77; dir. of studies Cardinal O'Hara H.S., 1977—85; prin. Archbishop Prendergast H.S., Upper Darby, Pa., 1985—90; dir. secondary curriculum and instr. Office of Edn. Archdiocese of Phila., 1991—99; prin. Villa Maria Acad., Malvern, Pa., 1999—2002; pres. Immaculata U., Immaculata, Pa., 2002—. Mem. bd. trustees Immaculata Coll., 1991—2000, adj. faculty, 1991—2000; vice chair exec. com. Commn. on Secondary Schs. Mid. States Assn., mem. strategic planning com., mem. com. on instn.-wide accreditation, mem. com. to restructure; chair IHM Profl. Devel. Com., 1995—2000. Office: Immaculata Coll 1145 King Rd Immaculata PA 19345*

FADEN, RUTH R. medical educator, ethicist, researcher; BA, U. Pa., 1970; MA, U. Chgo., 1971; MPH, U. Calif., Berkeley, 1973, PhD, 1976. Sr. rsch. scholar Kennedy Inst. Ethics, Georgetown U., 1978—; prof. health policy and mgmt. Johns Hopkins U., Balt., 1986—, joint appointment in medicine, Sch. of Medicine, 1992—, prof., Philip Franklin Wagley chair in biomed. ethics, 1995—, exec. dir. Phoebe R. Berman Bioethics Inst., 1995. Chair pres.'s adv. com. on human radiation expts., 1994—95; chmn. adv. panel on reproductive hazards in workplace Office Tech. Assessment, 1984—85; mem. com. on risk perception and comm. NAS, 1987—88; mem. panel on confidentiality and data access om. on Nat. Stats. and Social Sci. Rsch. Coun., 1989—91; mem. Alcohol, Drug Abuse, and Mental Health Adminstrn., AIDS Adv. Com., 1990—92; mem. Workshop on Biomed. Ethics in U.S. Pub. Policy Office Tech. Assessment, 1992; mem. adv. bd. Finding Common Ground Project: The Reproductive Rights and Needs of Women and the Emerging Conflict in Maternal and Child Health, 1992—93; mem. Adv. Panel on Prospects for Health Tech. Assessment Office Tech. Assessment, 1992—93; co-chair com. on legal and ethical issues relating to inclusion of women in clin. studies Inst. Medicine, 1992—93, mem. com. on clin. rsch. in pub. interest, 1996—97, mem. bd. on health scis. policy, 1995—, mem. com. on battlefield radiation exposure criteria, Med. Follow-Up Agy., 1996—98, mem. adv. com. on strategies to protect health of deployed U.S. forces, 1998—99; chmn. acv. com. on human radiation expts. Human Radiation Expts., 1996; mem. nat. adv. coun. for human genome rsch. NIH, 1996—97; mem. adv. bd. to nat. info. resource on ethics and human genetics Kennedy Inst. Ethics, 1996—99; mem. privacy law adv. com. Ctrs. for Disease Control and Prevention, Coun. State and Territorial Epidemiologists, Assn. State and Territorial Epidemiologists, and Nat. Coun. State Legislators, 1998—; mem. genetics adv. com. Genetics Legis. Project, 1999—2001. Author (with T.L. Beauchamp, J. Wallace and L. Walters): Ethical Issues in Social Science Research, 1982; author: (with T.L. Beauchamp) A History and Theory of Informed Consent, 1986; author: (with G. Geller, M. Powers) AIDS, Women and the Next Generation, 1991; author: (with A.C. Mastroianni, D. Federman) Women and Health Research: Ethical and Legal Issues of Including Women in Clinical Studies, vol. I, 1994, vol. II, 1994; author: (with N. Kass) HIV, AIDS and Childbearing: Public Policy, Private Lives; mem. editl. bd.: The Millbank Quarterly, 2000—. Fellow: APA, Hastings Ctr. (fellow's coun.); mem.: APHA, Am. Soc. for Bioethics and Humanities, Forum on Bioethics (co-founder, former chmn.), Am. Assn. Bioethics (organizing com.), Inst. Medicine. Office: Phoebe R Berman Bioethics Inst Hampton House 352 624 N Broadway Baltimore MD 21205-1996 E-mail: rfaden@jhsph.edu.

FADER, SHIRLEY SLOAN, writer; b. Paterson, N.J. d. Samuel Louis and Miriam (Marcus) Sloan; m. Seymour J. Fader; children: Susan Deborah, Steven Micah Kimchi. BS, MS, U. Pa. Writer, journalist, author, Paramus, N.J. Chmn., coord. ann. writers seminar Bergen C.C., 1973-76. Author: (books) The Princess Who Grew Down, 1968, From Kitchen to Career, 1977, Jobmanship, 1978, Successfully Ever After, 1982 (Brit. edit. 1985), Wait a Minute: You Can Have It All, 1993, paperback edit., 1994; (columns) Jobmanship, People and You, Family Weekly mag., 1971-82, How to Get More From Your Job, Glamour mag., 1978-81, Start Here, Working Woman mag., 1980-88, Work Strategies, Working Mother mag., 1987-88, Women Getting Ahead, Ladies Home Jour., 1980-90, How Would You Handle It, New Idea mag., 1984—, Moving Up, Woman mag., 1989-90, Career Expert "Ask the Experts", Woman's World mag., 1992-95; contbg. editor Family Weekly, 1971-82, Glamour mag., 1978-81, Working Woman mag., 1980-88, Working Mother mag., 1987-88, Ladies Home Jour., 1980-90, Woman mag., 1989-90; contbr.: (book) Foundations of English, 2002; contbr. articles on career, relationships and travel to mags. worldwide.. Mem. Authors Guild, Am. Soc. Journalists and Authors (moderator ann. writer's conf. 1971-2000, nat. v.p. 1976-77, mem.-at-large nat. exec. coun. 1976-78, 83-86, nat. sec., mem. exec. coun. 1995-96), Nat. Press Club, Newswomen of N.Y. Address: 377 Mckinley Blvd Paramus NJ 07652-4725

FADIMAN, ANNE, writer, editor; b. N.Y.C., Aug. 7, 1953; d. Clifton and Annalee Whitmore (Jacoby) F.; m. George Howe Colt, Mar. 4, 1989; children: Susannah, Henry. BA, Harvard U., 1975. Contbr. editor Harvard Magazine, Cambridge, Mass., 1973-75; instr. Nat. Outdoor Leadership Sch., Lander, Wyo., 1975-76; columnist Country Journal, Manchester, N.H., 1978-79; asst. sci. editor Life, N.Y.C., 1979-81, columnist, 1986-87, staff writer, 1981-88; columnist, editor-at-large Civilization, Washington, 1994—97; editor The Am. Scholar, Washington, 1997—2004. Bd. incorporators Harvard Magazine, Cambridge, Mass., 1985— (bd. dirs., 1985-91), vis. lectr. Smith Coll., 2000-02. Author: The Spirit Catches You and You Fall Down, 1997 (Nat. Book Critics Circle award for nonfiction, 1997, LA Times Book Prize for Current Interest, 1997, Ann Rea Jewell Non-Fiction Prize, Boston Book Rev., 1997), Ex Libris: Confessions of a Common Reader, 1998. Recipient Nat. Magazine award for Reporting Am. Soc. Magazine Editors, 1987; named John S. Knight fellow in Journalism Stanford (Calif.) U., 1991-92. Mem. Phi Beta Kappa (hon.).*

FADLEY, ANN MILLER, retired literature educator, literature educator; b. Ft. Worden, Wash., Nov. 22, 1933; d. Albert Delmar and Helen Elizabeth (Bush) Miller; m. Mit Rowley White, June 19, 1953 (div. Apr. 1977); children: Don M., Sharon L. White Patterson, Barbara A. White Salzman, Brian A.; m. John Lewis Fadley, Oct. 13, 1979 (dec. Jan., 1996). Student, Denison U., 1951-53; BA cum laude, Ohio State U., 1974, MA, 1976, PhD, 1986. Lectr. Ohio State U., Columbus, 1981-84; instr. Ohio Dominican Coll., Columbus, 1984-87; asst. prof. English, Marshall U., Huntington, W.Va., 1987-88; assoc. prof. English, Fla. So. Coll., Lakeland, 1988-99; ret., 1999. Adj. prof. Ohio U., Ironton, 1988; panelist pub. TV, Columbus, 1985; chmn. Nat. Poetry Day, 1991-97; chmn. vis. creative writers Fla. So. Coll., Lakeland, 1990-99. Author: (fiction and poetry) Onionhead, 1989, 95, (poetry) Birmingham Poetry Review, 1992, Heartbeat, 1994, pre-concert lecture for Nat. Shakespeare Co.'s As You Like It, Fla. So. Coll. Festival of Arts, Feb. 18, 1997; poetry readings Lakeland Choral Soc. Concert, Apr., 1997, Nat. Humanities Ctr., 1998, and many others; also articles and lit.

criticisms; asst. editor Ohio Jour., 1975-76; founder, editor Cantilever Jours., 1989-96; vis. poet Fla. So. Coll., 1998, guest poet Cantilevers, 1999. Organizer, pres. Tri-Village Jr. C. of C. Wives Club, Columbus, 1959-60; awards chmn. Young Musician's competition; chair Ruth Flower Brown Scholarship, Huntington, 1988; contest supr., mem. com. SCORE, 1988; judge VFW Voice of Democracy contest, Lakeland, 1990, 91, Fla. state judge, 1992; trustee Christ United Meth. Ch., Lakeland, 1991-96, sec. trustees, 1991-93, 95, mem. bldg. com., organ fund task force, 1993-94, chairperson status and role of women, 1996-98, adminstrv. bd., 1996-98, women's exec. com., 2003—; judge short fiction contest Nat. League Am. Pen Women Fla. State Assn. 1996, 98, short fiction and poetry contest, 1997, creative writing Polk County Citrus Festival, 1993, poetry contest Nat. League Am. Pen Women, Lakeland, Fla., 2000. Grantee Fla. Endowment Humanities, 1991, Jessie Ball duPont Found.Nat. Humanities Ctr., 1998; recipient Merit award Fla. Poets Competition, WORDART Soc., 1990, 96, 98, Distinction award, 1991, 97, recipient hon. mention Nat. League Am. Pen Women, Lakeland, 1993, 94, award hanging poetry Arts in the Park, Lakeland, 1993, 94, hanging poetry display Lake Morton Libr., 1994. Mem. Fla. State Poets Assn. (head Lakeland workshop 1991, 92), Delta Delta Delta. Republican. Avocations: gardening, swimming, fishing, decorating, travelling.

FAERBER, ABIGAIL HOBBS, physician; b. Columbus, Ohio, Aug. 30, 1943; d. Theodore Caleb and Olliffe Elizabeth (Litchfield) Hobbs; m. George Oswald Faerber, Feb. 19, 1966; children: Rachel, Peter, George. BA, Ohio Wesleyan U., 1964; MS, U. Ill., 1966; DO, Ohio U., 1985. Bd. cert. in family practice, 1992. Physician, mgr. Dist. Physicians Inc., Columbus, Ohio, 1986-97; physician Asian Am. Health Initiative Clinic, 2000—02, Sr. Friendship Clinic Inc., Ft. Myers, Fla., 2004—. Adj. clin. faculty Ohio U. Coll. Medicine, Athens, Ohio, 1986-96; physician DH Family Practice VIII, Columbus, Ohio, 1995-96; mgr. Scioto Cliff Farms, Delaware, Ohio, 1995—; bd. dirs. Nat. Alumni Ohio U., Athens, 1989-92; medicine adv. bd. Ohio U. Coll. Osteo., 1994—. Bd. dirs. Columbus Chamber Music Soc., 1977-83; mem. Beaux Art Columbus Mus. Art, 1971-82. Recipient Cmty. Svc. award Ciba Geigy, 1986. Mem. Am. Osteo. Assn., Ohio Osteo. Assn., Ohio State Med. Assn., Franklin County Med. Soc., (chair of credentials com., 1991-93). Republican. Lutheran. Avocations: sailing, hiking, reading, travel. Home and Office: Dist Physicians Inc 2411 Sierra Ln Punta Gorda FL 33950

FAGIN, CLAIRE MINTZER, nursing educator, nursing administrator; b. NYC; d. Harry and Mae (Slatin) Mintzer; m. Samuel Fagin, Feb. 17, 1952; children: Joshua, Charles. BS, Wagner Coll., 1948; MA, Tchrs. Coll. Columbia, 1951; PhD, NYU, 1964; DSc (hon.), Lycoming Coll., 1983, Cedar Crest Coll., 1987, U. Rochester, 1987, Med. Coll. Pa., 1989, U. Md., 1993, Wagner Coll., 1993, Loyola U., 1996, Case Western Res. U., 2002; LLD (hon.), U. Pa., 1994, U. Toronto, 2003; DHL (hon.), Hunter Coll., 1993, Rush U., 1996, Johns Hopkins U., 2003. Staff nurse, clin. instr. Sea View Hosp., S.I., NY; clin. instr. Bellevue Hosp., N.Y.C.; psychiat. nurse cons. Nat. League for Nursing, N.Y.C.; asst. chief psychiat. nursing svc. clin. ctr. NIH; rsch. project coord. dept. psychiatry Children's Hosp., Washington; instr., assoc. prof. psychiat.-mental health nursing NYU, N.Y.C., dir. grad. programs in psychiat. mental health nursing, 1965—69; chmn. nursing dept., prof. Herbert H. Lehman Coll., CUNY, N.Y.C., 1969—77; dir. Health Professions Inst., Montefiore Hosp. and Med. Ctr., 1975—77; Margaret Bond Simon dean sch. of nursing U. Pa., Phila., 1977—92, Leadership chair prof., 1992—96, interim pres., 1993—94, dean emeritus, prof. emeritus, 1996—. Dir. program bldg. acad. geriatric nursing John A. Hartford Found.; bd. dirs. Provident Mut. Ins. Co., chmn. audit com., 1985—96, exec. com., 1986—96, adv. com., 1996—2003; mem. audit com. Salomon, Inc., 1994—97; bd. dirs. Vis. Nurse Soc. N.Y., 1998—, N.Y. Acad. Medicine, 1998—; bd. dirs., chair audit com. Van Ameringen Found., 1996—2004; spkr., cons. in field. Contbr. articles to profl. jours. Named Disting. Dau. Pa., 1994; recipient Achievement award, Wagner Coll., 1956, Tchrs. Coll., 1975, Disting. Alumna award, NYU, 1979, Founders award, Sigma Theta Tau, 1981, Hon. Recognition award, ANA, 1988, Woman of Courage award, Women's Way, 1990, Alumni Merit award, U. Pa., 1991, Leadership award, Trustee Coun. Pa. Women First, 1991, Caring award, Phila. Vis. Nurses Assn., 1994, Lillian Wald award, N.Y. Vis. Nurses Assn., 1994, Hildegard Peplau award outstanding contbn. psych-nursing, 1994, Pres. medal, NYU, 1998, Nightingale Lamp award, Am. Nurses Found., 2002; disting. scholar, 1984, hon. fellow, Royal Coll. Nursing, 2002. Mem.: Nat. League for Nursing (pres. 1991—93), Am. Orthopsychiat. Assn. (bd. dirs. 1972—75, exec. com. bd. dirs. 1973—75, pres. 1985—86), Am. Acad. Nursing (governing coun. 1976—78, Living Legend award 1998), Inst. Medicine of NAS (governing coun. 1981—83, chmn. bd. health promotion and disease prevention 1991—94, mem./chair Lienhard Com. 1999—2004). Address: 200 Central Park S Apt 12E New York NY 10019-1415 Office: U Pa Sch Nursing 354 Neb Bldg Philadelphia PA 19104-6096 E-mail: cfagin@att.net.

FAGUNDO, ANA MARIA, creative writing and Spanish literature educator; b. Santa Cruz de Tenerife, Spain, Mar. 13, 1938; came to U.S., 1958; d. Ramón Fagundo and Candelaria Guerra de Fagundo. BA in English and Spanish, U. Redlands, 1962; MA in Spanish, U. Wash., 1964, PhD in Comparative Lit., 1967. Prof. contemporary lit. of Spain and creative writing U. Calif., Riverside, 1967—. Vis. lectr. Occidental Coll., Calif., 1967; vis. prof. Stanford U., 1984. Author 10 books of poetry including Invention de la Luz, 1977 (Carbala de Oro Poetry prize Barcelona 1977), Obra Poetica: 1965-90, 1990, Isla En Si, 1992, Antologia, 1994, El Sol, la Sombra En El Instante, 1994, La Miriada de Los Sonambulos, 1994, Trasterrado Marzo, 1999; founder, editor Alaluz, 1969—. Grantee Creative Arts Inst., 1970-71, Humanities Inst., 1973-74; Summer faculty fellow U. Calif., 1968, 77; Humanities fellow, 1969. Mem. Am. Assn. Tchrs. Spanish and Portuguese, Sociedad Gen. de Autores de Espana. Roman Catholic. Avocations: tennis, jogging, walking. Home: 5110 Caldera Ct Riverside CA 92507-6002 Office: U Calif Spanish Dept Riverside CA 92521-0001

FAHERTY, ANNALEE, social worker, nun; b. Perryville, Mo., Mar. 16, 1936; d. Lynn Henry and Catherine Faherty. BA in English, Marillac Coll., 1964; MSW, St. Louis U., 1966. Joined Daus. of Charity religious order 1954; North Ctrl. accreditation for tchr. edn. Mo. Sch. Bd. Edn., 1964. Houseparent, tchr., bookkeeper St. Mary's Home for Girls, Mobile, Ala., 1956—60; elem. and secondary tchr. Daus. of Charity Schs., Mobile, 1956—64, St. Louis, 1956—64; caseworker families, day care, adoption St. Louis Cath. Charities, 1966—70; prof. social work, dept. chair Marillac Coll., St. Louis, 1967—74; rural social worker, interdisciplinary team Springfield-Cape Girardeau Diocese, West Plains, Mo., 1974—78; adminstr., CEO, social svcs. dir. Marywood Maternity and Adoption Agy., Austin, Tex., 1978—89; social svcs. dir. Guardian Angel Settlement, St. Louis, 1989—2001, dir. spl. programs and program assessment, 2001—. Field placement supr. St. Louis U. Sch. Social Work, 1968; assoc. prof. social work Marillac Coll., St. Louis, 1973; mem. planning com. St. Louis Cath. Charities, 1971—75; governing bd. mem., chair DePaul Social Ctr., San Antonio, 1975—80. Trustee Providence Hosp., Waco, Tex., 1980—90; mem. program com. Pillar Place, St. Louis, 1994—2000. Mem.: NASW (cert. social worker 1982, advanced clin. practitioner 1982, diplomate clin. social worker 1987, lic. clin. social worker 1989), Mo. Assn. Social Workers. Republican. Avocations: Cardinal and Rams fan, reading, statistics. Home: 12407 McKelvey Rd Saint Louis MO 63146 Office: Guardian Angel Settlement PO Box 2055 Saint Louis MO 63158

FAHEY, BARBARA STEWART DOE, public agency administrator; b. Chgo., Aug. 9, 1950; d. William Bethel and Doris (Charn) Doe. BA, U. Colo., 1972; MA, Sangamon State U., 1975. Dir. Wilderness Study Project, Springfield, Ill., 1973-75, Environ. Ctr., Boulder, Colo., 1976-79; natural resource specialist U.S. Bur. Reclamation, Denver, 1977-78; rsch. assoc. Nat. Conf. State Legislatures, Denver, 1979-80; asst. to transp. dir. City of Boulder, 1980-81, project mgr., 1981-85, parking coord., 1985-90, open space planner, 1991-92; interpretive park naturalist Jefferson County, Golden, Colo., 1992, adminstr. Nature Ctr., 1993-95; county dir. Colo. State U. Coop. Extension in Jefferson County, 1995—. Vice chmn. Boulder County Energy Adv. Com., Boulder, 1987; bd. mem. County Bd. Rev., Boulder, 1984-86, Historic Boulder, 1991-92. Bd. mem. Colo. Open Space Coun., Denver, 1979-80; mem. Leadership Boulder C. of C., 1986. Named Young Career Woman Colo. Bus. and Profl. Women's Fedn., Denver, 1981; recipient Innovation award Denver Coun. Govts., 1985, State Dir.'s Merit award, 1997, Nat. Program Leadership award Assn. Natural Resources Ext. Profls., 2002. Mem. Nat. Assn. Interpretation, Denver Botanic Gardens, Denver Mus. Sci. and Nature, Colo. Native Plant Soc., Boulder Bus. and Profl. Women (treas. 1983-84, v.p. 1987-88, pres. 1989-90, winner speech contest 1985), Sierra Club (bd. mem. Sangamon Valley Group 1973-75). Avocations: cross-country skiing, backpacking, hiking, classical and folk music. Office: 15200 W 6th Ave Ste C Golden CO 80401-6588 E-mail: bfahey@co.jefferson.co.us.

FAHEY, ELLEN MCKENNEY, recreation director; b. Boston, June 26, 1925; d. John J. Devine and Margaret Roche; m. Joseph W. McKenney, May 22, 1948 (dec. July 1970); children: William McKenney, Brian McKenney, Mari-An Kathleen McKenney; m. Richard S. Fahey, Sept. 26, 1976. BS in Edn., Tchrs. Coll. Boston, 1946. Pres. Executours of Boston, The Network, Boston. Author: Twenty Five Years on the Freedom Trail, 1998. Republican. Roman Catholic. Avocations: painting, cooking. Home and Office: 36 Hurd Rd Belmont MA 02478*

FAHNESTOCK, JEAN HOWE, retired civil engineer; b. Pitts., May 22, 1930; d. James Murray and Hazel Margaret (Alberts) F. AA, Stephens, 1950; BS in Civil Engring., Carnegie-Mellon, 1955. Registered profl. engr., Ill., Mich., Iowa. Sr. project mgr. De Leuw, Cather & Co., Chgo., 1955-92. Design mgr. De Leuw, Cather & Co., Kuwait, 1978-81, Abu Dhabi, 1981-85, Kennedy Expy. and Elgin-O'Hare Expy., Chgo., 1985-92. Fellow ASCE (life); mem. NSPE, Ill. Soc. Profl. Engrs. (life). Republican. Presbyterian. Avocations: bridge, travel, politics. Home: 4606 W Bryn Mawr Ave Chicago IL 60646-6632 E-mail: jhf4606@aol.com.

FAHRBACH, RUTH C. state legislator; b. N.Y.C. Grad. high sch., East Meadow, N.Y. Mem. Dist. 61 Conn. Ho. of Reps., 1981—, minority whip. Appropriations com., pub. health com., legis. mgmt. com., select com. inquiry. Active Windsor Rep. Town Com., Order Women Legislators; mem. Windsor Bd. Edn., 1977-81, v.p., 1979-80; bd. dirs. Celebrate Windsor!, Inc., 2001--. Mem. First Dist. Rep. Womens Club, Fedn. Rep. Women, Civitan Club Windsor (past pres), Nat. Order of Women Legislators, Conn. Order of Women Legislators (sec.), Conn. Fedn. of Rep. Women, Nat. Fedn. of Republican Women, St. Casimir's Lithuanian Club Women's Aux. Home: 592 Poquonock Ave Windsor CT 06095-2204 Office: Legis Office Bldg Rm 4200 Hartford CT 06106-1591 E-mail: ruth.fahrbach@housegop.po.state.ct.us.

FAHRINGER, CATHERINE HEWSON, retired savings and loan association executive; b. Phila., Aug. 1, 1922; d. George Francis and Catherine Gertrude (Magee) Hewson; m. Edward F. Fahringer, July 8, 1961 (dec.); 1 child, Francis George Beckett. Grad. diploma, Inst. Fin. Edn., 1965. With Centrust Bank (formerly Dade Savs. and Loan Assn.), Miami, 1958-85, v.p., 1967-74, sr. v.p., 1974-82, sec., 1975-79, head savs. personnel and mktg. divsn., 1979-83, exec. v.p. office of chmn., 1984, dir., 1984-90, co-chmn. audit com. of bd. dirs., 1990; referral assoc. Referral Network Inc. subs. Coldwell Banker, 1990—. Pub. arbitrator NASD, 1999—. Contbr. articles to profl. jours. Trustee United Way of Dade County (Fla.), 1980-87, chmn. audit com. 1982-84, trustee, Pub. Health Trust, Dade County, 1974-84, sec. 1976, vice chmn., 1977-78, chmn. bd., 1978-81; mem. adv. coun. Women's Bus. Devel. Ctr., Fla. Internat. U., 1993-95; mem. spl. steering com. Breast Cancer Task Force, Jackson Meml. Hosp., 1991; hon. bd. govs. U. Miami, Soc. for Rsch. in Med. Edn.; trustee South Fla. Blood Svc., Miami, 1979-84, vice chmn., 1980, chmn., 1981-84; trustee Dade County Vocat. Found., 1977-81; trustee Fla. Internat. U. Found., 1976-90; trustee emeritus, 1990, v.p. bd., 1978-81, pres. 1982-84; bd. dirs. Sta. WPBT-TV, 1984-2002, founding lifetime dir., 1995, chmn. budget and fin. com., 1986, mem. exec. com. 1985-92, sec. 1987, investment com., 1988-90, vice chmn. 1988-92, mem. fin. com., 1992, chmn. audit and control com., 1994, 2000, 2001, mem., 1997-98; bd. dirs., mem. nominating com. Girl Scout Coun., Tropical Fla., 1985-89, chmn. 1988-89, mem. long range planning com., 1986-88; citizens oversight com. Dade County Pub. Sch. System, 1986-90, chmn. 1988-90; bd. dirs. New World Sch. of Arts, 1987-90, chmn. devel. com., 1987-90, chair New World Sch. of Arts Gala, 1990; mem. Disaster Relief Com., chair Hurricane Disaster Relief Distbn. Ctr., 1992; mem. fin. commn., chmn. capital improvement fund com. Coral Gables Congrl. Ch., summer concert series com., chmn. refreshment sub com.; commd. Stephen min., 1995—; mem. grievance com. 11th Jud. Cir. Fla. Bar, 1988-92; bd. trustees United Protestant Appeal, 1994-96; mem. parking adv. bd. City of Coral Gables, 1997-98, bd. of adjustments, 1998—, vice chmn., 2001—2003, chmn.2003—; mem., 3rd v.p. Bush chpt. Women's Cancer Assn. U. Miami, 1997-99, 2nd v.p., treas. and parliamentarian, 1999-2001, chmn. meml. fund, 1998-2003, 3rd v.p., 2002-03. Named Women of Yr. in fin., Zonta Internat., 1975, amb., Air Def. Arty., 1970, U.S. Army Air Def. Command, 1970, Woman of Yr. in Sports, Links Club, 1986, First Lady of Athletics, Fla. Internat. U., 2003; recipient Trail Blazer award, Women's Coun. of 100, 1977, Cmty. Headliner award, Women in Comm., 1983, Outstanding Citizen of Dade County award, 1984, Honors and Recognition award, Golden Panthers Club of Fla. Internat. U., 1989, Disting. Svc. and Leadership award, Fla. Internat. U., 1991, appreciation, New World Sch. of the Arts, 1990, Meritorious Pub. Svc. award, Fla. Bar, 1991, Outstanding Svc. award, Country Club Coral Gables, 2001, hon. BA, U. Hard Knocks Alderson-Broaddus Coll., 1987, Key to City of Coral Gables for Cmty. Svc., 2000, Dedicated Svc. award, Women's Cancer Assn. of U. Miami, 2001, Outstanding Svc. Award, 2001. Mem.: LWV, Women's Union of Russia, Fla. Women's Alliance (bd. dirs. 1983—91, pres. 1987—89), Internat. Women's Alliance, Savs. and Loan Pers. Soc. South Fla., Savs. and Loan Mktg. Soc. South Fla. (past pres.), Inst. Fin. Edn. (life; nat. dir., past pres. Local Greater Miami chpt.), Greater Miami Women's Golf Assn. (social dir. 1999—2001), Greenway Women's Golf Assn. (treas. 1988—89), Biltmore Women's Golf Assn., Fla. Internat. U. Athletics Club, Golden Panther Club (bd. dirs. 1988—, v.p. 1991, pres. 1992—94), Links Fla. Internat. U. Club (v.p. 1992, bd. dirs., sec.), Country Club of Coral Gables (treas. women's golf assn 1988—89, sec., bd. dirs., found. trustee 1993, v.p. bd. dirs. 1994, pres. 1995, chmn. bldg. restoration, capital improvement and maintenance com. 1995—99, bd. advisor 1996—99, liaison City of Coral Gables 1997—99, rear commodore The Fleet, vice-commodore 1998, commodore 1999, publicity chmn. woman's bd. 2000—01, pres. women's golf assn. 2001—02, mem. adv. bd. govs. 2003—, historian 2004, advisor/directory chair 2004), Dade Bus. and Profl. Women's Club (past pres.). Democrat.

FAHY, NANCY LEE, food products marketing executive; b. Schenectady, N.Y., Aug. 15, 1946; d. Christopher Mark and Frances (Lee) F.; m. Steven Neil Wohl, June 8, 1968 (div. Apr. 1978). BS cum laude, Miami (Ohio) U., 1968. Educator Palatine (Ill.) Pub. Schs., 1968-70, Glencoe (Ill.) Pub. Schs., 1970-78; sales rep. Keebler Co., Elmhurst, Ill., 1978-80, dist. mgr., 1980-82, account mgr., 1982-83, zone mgr., 1983-85, account mgr., 1985-89, regional mktg. mgr. Coll. Pk., Ga., 1989—. Vol. Lincoln Park Zool. Soc., Chgo., 1975-78. Mem. Food Products Club, Merchandising Execs. Club (bd. dirs. 1984-85), Grocery Mfgs. Sales Execs. Club (bd. dirs. 1984-85, asst. sec. 1987, treas. 1988, 1st v.p. 1989), Phi Beta Kappa. Avocations: gardening, literature, skiing, antiques. Office: Keebler Co 4751 Best Rd Ste 140 College Park GA 30337-5616 E-mail: Nancy_Fahy@keebler.com.

FAILLA, SOPHIA LYNN, artist, educator; b. Bronx, Oct. 23, 1928; d. Joseph John and Lucy (Iaia) F.; divorced; 1 child, Lynn. Student, Brevard C.C., 1968-75. Asst. designer Vogue Patterns/Conde Nast, Old Greenwich, Conn., 1948-51; owner The Sewing Box, Darien, Conn., 1953-55; draftsman C.B.F., Stamford, Conn., 1957-58; outreach tchr. Brevard (Fla.) C.C., 1969-75; missionary, founder Honduran Christian Crafts, Honduras, 1975-79; owner, founder Fashions of Love, Lompoc, Calif., 1983-89; artist, tchr. Especially for You Gallery, Melbourne, Fla., 1989—. Founder Amigos de Jesus. Recipient Excellence award Manhattan Art Internat., cert. of merit Stockholm Internat. Art Show, 1st prize Internat. Art League, 1998; winner 1998 Internat. Art competition (pub. in Art Times). Mem. AAUW, Nat. Mus. Women in Arts. Avocations: teaching, painting, travel, black choir music. Studio: Especially for You Gallery 909 E New Haven Ave # 5-67 Melbourne FL 32901-5478

FAIN, CHERYL ANN, translator, editor; b. Providence, May 16, 1953; d. Harry and Pearl (Friedman) F. Student, U. Salzburg, Austria, 1973-74; BA with high distinction, U. R.I., 1975; MA, postgrad. cert. Eng.-German Transl., Monterey Inst. Internat. Studies, 1978. Cert. translator German-English, French-English Am. Translators Assn. Freelance German and French transl. various govt. agys., transl. burs., record co., pvt. clients, Washington, Balt. and Monterey, Calif., 1976—; in-house German and French med. translator Social Security Adminstrn., Balt., 1984-94; German/French trans., sci. and tech. specialist Embassy of Switzerland, Washington, 1994—. Mem. Swiss delegation to the European Space Agy. Internat. Space Sta. Working Group, Washington, D.C., 1994-2003. Translator: Perspectives on Mozart, 1978, also various articles and liner notes, program notes, U.S., Switzerland. Mem.: Nat. Capital Area Am. Translator's Assn. (spkr.seminar on translating for fgn. govts. 2004), Am. Translators Assn., Sci. Diplomats' Club of Washington, Phi Kappa Phi. Avocations: international travel, performance in operas, choral concerts and plays. Home: 2401 Calvert St NW Apt 421 Washington DC 20008-2667 Office: Embassy of Switzerland 2900 Cathedral Ave NW Washington DC 20008-3499

FAIR, MARCIA JEANNE HIXSON, retired educational administrator; b. Scobey, Mont. d. Edward Goodell and Olga Marie (Frederickson) Hixson; m. Donald Harry Mahaffey (div. Aug. 1976); 1 child, Marcia Anne (dec.); m. George Justin Fair, Mar. 26, 1997. BA in English, U. Wash.; MA in Secondary Edn., U. Hawaii, 1967. Cert. secondary and elem. tchr., adminstr. Tchr. San Lorenzo (Calif.) Sch. Dist., 1958-59, Castro Valley (Calif.) Sch. Dist., 1959-63, vice prin., 1963-67, Sequoia Union High Sch. Dist., Redwood City, Calif., 1967-77, asst. prin., 1977-91, ret., 1991. Tchr. trainer Project Impact Sequoia Union Sch. Dist., Redwood City, 1986-91; mem. supr.'s task force for dropout prevention, 1987-91, Sequoia Dist. Goals Commn. (chair subcom. staff devel. 1988) chair, Sequoia Union H. S. Dist. Grading Com., 1976-1984; mentor tchr. selection com., 1987-91; mem. Stanford Program Devel. Ctr. Com., 1987-91; chairperson gifted and talented Castro Valley Sch. Dist.; mem. family svcs. bd., San Leandro, Calif. Vol. Am. Cancer Soc., San Mateo, Calif., 1967, Castro Valley, 1965; chair Carlmont H.S. Site Coun., Belmont, Calif., 1977—91; active Nat. Trust for Hist. Preservation; Neighborhood Beautification project dir. Bridle Trails Cmty. Club, 1999—2001; mem. Golden Grads. scholarship com. Roosevelt H.S., Seattle, 2000—; Sunday sch. tchr. Hope Luth. Ch., San Mateo, 1970—76. Recipient Life Mem. award Parent, Tchr., Student Assn., Belmont, 1984, Svc. award, 1989, Exemplary Svc award Carlmont High Sch., 1989, 92; named Woman of the Week, Castro Valley, 1967, Outstanding Task Force Chair Adopt A Sch. Program San Mateo (Calif.) County, 1990. Mem. ASCD, AAUW, DAR, Assn. Calif. Sch. Adminstrs. (Project Leadership plaque 1985), Sequoia Dist. Mgmt.Assn. (pres. 1975, treas. 1984-85), Met. Mus. Art, Smithsonian Instn., Libr. of Congress Assocs. (charter), Am. Heritage - The Soc. of Am. Historians, Internat. Platform Assn., Animal Welfare Advocacy, Woodrow Wilson Internat. Ctr. Scholars, Am. Mus. Natural History (charter mem.), Delta Kappa Gamma, Alpha Xi Delta (Order of Rose award 1997). Avocations: oil painting, travel, tap dancing, redecorating, writing poetry.

FAIR, NANCY HAZEN, media specialist, educator; d. Lewis Arthur and Katherine Krementz Hazen; m. Terrence William Fair, Sept. 24, 1966; 1 child, Katherine Emily. BS, U. Rochester, 1965; MLS, So. Conn. State U., 1988. Tchr. elem. sch. Gibsonia (Pa.) Bd. Edn., 1965—66, Bloomfield (Conn.) Bd. Edn., 1966—70; media specialist mid. sch. Granby (Conn.) Bd. Edn., 1989—. Named Tchr. of Yr., Cable Television, 1990. Mem.: Beta Phi Mu, Delta Kappa Gamma. Avocations: reading, kayaking. Office: Granby Meml Mid Sch 321 Salmon Brook St Granby CT 06035

FAIRBAIRN, JOYCE, Canadian government official; b. Lethbridge, Alta., Can., Nov. 6, 1939; m. Michael Gillan (dec.). BA in English, U. Alta., 1960; B Journalism, Carleton U., 1961. Mem. news staff Ottawa (Ont., Can.) Jour., 1961; mem. staff parliamentary press gallery UPI, Ottawa, 1962-64; mem. staff parliamentary bur. F.P. Publs., 1964-70; legis. asst., sr. legis. advisor Prime Minister of Can. Pierre Elliott Trudeau, 1970-84, comms. coord., 1981-83; mem. Senate for Province of Alta., 1984—, appt. to privy coun., leader govt., 1993-97, minister with spl. responsibility for literacy, 1993-97, spl. advisor for literacy, 1997. Mem. Spl. Senate Com. on Youth, Senate Standing Coms. on Transp. and Comm., Legal and Constl. Affairs, Fgn. Affairs, Agr. and Forestry, mem. senate social affairs com.; founding mem. standing com. on Aboriginal peoples; chair spl. com. on Anti-Terrorism, 2001, Friends of the Can. Paralympics, Can. Paralympic Found.; vice chair Nat. Liberal Caucus and Western and No. Liberal Caucus, 1984-91; co-chair nat. campaign com. Liberal Party of Can., 1991. Past mem. senate U. Lethbridge; mem., pres. Kainai Cheiftanship; chmn. Friends of Can. Paralympics, 1998-2003; chmn. bd. dirs. Can. Paralympic Found., 2003—. Inducted into Kainai Chieftainship, Blood Nation; Hon. col. 18th Air Def. Regt., Royal Can. Army. Office: Can Senate 571-S Centre Block Ottawa ON Canada K1A 0A4

FAIRBAIRN, KRISS, newscaster; 1 child. News anchor WDSU News Channel 6, New Orleans, 1990—97; media rels. Ochsner Hosp.; spokesperson FBI, La.; news anchor WDSU News Channel 6. Coach basketball team; sub. tchr. Avocation: riding her Harley Davidson motorcycle. Office: WDSU Nes Channel 6 846 Howard Ave New Orleans LA 70113

FAIRBAIRN, URSULA FARRELL, human resources executive; b. Newark, Feb. 5, 1943; d. Henry C. and Clara J. (Ziefle) Otte; m. William Todd Fairbairn III, May 14, 1978; children: W. Todd, Mary. BA, Upsala Coll., 1965; MAT in Math., Harvard U., 1966. Instr., numerous mktg. positions IBM, N.Y.C., 1966-78; exec. asst. to sec., White House fellow U.S. Treasury Dept., Washington, 1973-74; exec. asst. to chmn. bd., group dir. IBM, Armonk, N.Y., 1978-79, v.p. mgmt. svcs., then v.p. mktg. ops. west, 1980-84, dir. pers. resources, 1984-87, dir. bus. and mgmt. edn., 1987, dir. edn., 1987-89, dir. edn and mgmt. devel., 1989-90; sr. v.p. human resources Union Pacific Corp., Bethlehem, Pa., 1990-96; exec. v.p. human resources and quality Am. Express Co., N.Y.C., 1996—. Bd. dirs. VF Corp., Greensboro, N.C., Air Products Corp., Allentown, Pa., Sunoco Corp., Phila. Contbg. author: Managing Human Resources in the Information Age, 1991. Mem. Com. of 200, Catalyst, N.Y.C.; vice-chair Nat. Acad.-HR; chair Pers. Round Table. Mem. Bus. Roundtable, Employee Rels. Com., Labor Policy Assn. (bd. dirs., mem. exec. com.). Avocations: gardening, art, reading, walking, travel. Office: Am Express Co 35 N Moore St New York NY 10013

FAIRBANK, JANE DAVENPORT, editor, civic worker; b. Seattle, Aug. 21, 1918; d. Harold Edwin and Mildred (Foster) Davenport; AB magna cum laude, Whitman Coll., 1939; postgrad. U. Wash., 1940-42; m. William Martin Fairbank, Aug. 16, 1941; children: William Martin, Robert Harold, Richard Dana. Sci. staff mem. Radiation Lab. Mass. Inst. Tech., Cambridge, 1943-45; [illegible] Careers for Women, Stanford, Calif., 1970-75; chmn. annual continuing edn. program Whitman Coll. Sr. Alumni Coll., 1986-96; founding mem. Bay Area Consortium on Ednl. Needs of Women. 1971; mem. Canada Coll. Citizens Adv. Com. for Community Edn., 1968; mem. organizing com. for conf. on frontiers of physics Stanford U., 1982; tchg. asst. U. Wash., 1940-42. Mem. Whitman Coll. Alumni Assn. (bd. dirs. 1986-96), Calif. Congress Parents and Tchrs. (hon. life), Mortar Bd., Phi Beta Kappa. Alpha Chi Omega. Mem. United Ch. of Christ. Mem. Stanford Univ. Women's Club (pres. 1975-76). Editor: Radar Maintenance Manual (2 vols.), 1945; co-editor Near Zero: New Frontiers of Physics, 1988; Second Careers for Women: A View from the San Francisco Peninsula, 1971; Second Careers for Women, vol. II: A View of Seven Fields from the San Francisco Bay Area, 1975. Office: 1712 Clearview Ct Fort Collins CO 80521-4330

FAIRCHILD, SHARON ELAINE, corrections administrator; b. Little Rock, Sept. 10, 1947; d. Robert Roscoe Fairchild and Mable Tyler Fleming. BA, So. U., Baton Rouge, La., 1972; MS, Tex. So. U., Houston, 1984. Psychologist Mo. Dept. Corrections, St. Louis, 1987-91, corrections supt. Kansas City, 1991—. Mem. criminal justice adv. bd. Penn Valley C.C., Kansas City, Mo., 1997—; bd. dirs. Springfield (Mo.) Pub. TV, 1992-93. Tutor, mentor Youth Friends, North Kansas City Pub. Schs., 1995—. Mem Am. Correctional Assn., Mo. Correctional Assn. (bd. dirs. 1993-95), Nat. Assn. Blacks in Criminal Justice (chair women's task force 1995—, Mary Terrell Church award 1995), Delta Sigma Theta. Methodist. Avocations: reading, skating. Office: Kansas City Cmty Release Ctr 651 Mulberry St Kansas City MO 64101-1235

FAIRCLOTH, MARY WILLIAMS, minister, educator; d. Willie Sylvester and Katie Ruth Williams; m. Alonzo Vernon Faircloth, Nov. 23, 1978. BS in Mgmt., Rutgers U., 1978; MDiv, New Brunswick Theol. Sem., 1995. Mgmt. staff Port Authority N.Y. and N.J., N.Y.C., 1967—95, adminstrv. asst., 1978—84; clin. chaplain Ctr. for Hope, Linden, NJ, 1995—96, Dobbs Youth Devel. Ctr., Kinston, NC, 1997—2000; pastor Anderson Chapel AME Ch. AME Ch., Inc., Greenville, NC, 1998—; prof. ethics/religion/philosophy Shaw U., Raleigh/Greenville, NC. Ch. growth and devel. AME Ch., Greenville, 1999—. Tchr., organizer, youth leader Dobbs Youth Devel. Ctr., Kinston, 1998—2002. Recipient Cert. of Achievement, Pitt County Meml. Hosp., 1997, 1998, 1999. Mem.: Assn. Seminarians (life; pres./v.p. 1992—94, Cert. of Achievement 1995). Methodist. Avocations: travel, reading, writing, antiques, cooking. Home: 208 Buckingham Dr Winterville NC 28590-9418 Office: Anderson Chapel AME Church PO Box 30791 3788 Ivan Harris Rd Greenville NC 27833 Office Phone: 252-746-8724. Personal E-mail: andersonchapame@aol.com.

FAIRFAX, KATHLEEN M, director; d. William Marvin and Rose Mary Fairfax; m. Mark S Luebker, Dec. 30, 1989; children: Rose Marie Luebker, Emily Jean Luebker, Sarah Elisabeth Luebker. BA, DePauw U., 1980—84; MA, Ind. U., 1984—86. Coord. of off-campus study DePauw U., Greencastle, Ind., 1986—89; fgn. svc. officer U.S. Info. Agy., Washington, 1989—90, U.S. Embassy - Mex., Mex. City, 1990—93; dir. of study abroad Southwestern U., Georgetown, Tex., 1993—95; dir., programs for study abroad Purdue U., West Lafayette, Ind., 1995—2001; dir., office of study abroad Mich. State U., 2001—. Girl scout leader Girl Scouts of Sycamore Coun., Lafayette, Ind., 1998—2001, Girl Scouts of Mich. Capital Coun., Holt, Mich., 2001. Recipient Mary Patterson award, Girl Scouts of Sycamore Coun., 2000. Mem.: NAFSA (chair, region vi 2000—01). Catholic. Avocations: camping, softball, travel. Office: Michigan State University 109 International Ctr East Lansing MI 48824 E-mail: kfairfax@msu.edu.

FAIRHURST, MARY E. judge; BA in Polit. Sci. cum laude, Gonzaga U., 1979, JD magna cum laude, 1984. Jud. clk. to Hon. William H. Williams Wash. Supreme Ct., 1984, jud. clk. to Hon. William C. Goodloe, 1986; chief revenue, bankruptcy and collections divsn. Wash. Atty. Gen.'s Office, 1986—2002; justice Wash. State Supreme Ct., Olympia, 2003—. Mem. Supreme Ct.'s Gender and Justice Commn., Access Justice Bd. Com.; mem. bd. advisors Gonzaga Law Sch. Recipient Myra Bradwell award, Gonzaga U., 1999. Mem.: Wash. Women Lawyers (pres., Passing the Torch award 1999), Wash. State Bar Assn. (pres., mem. bd. govs.). Office: Wash Supreme Ct PO Box 40929 415 12th Ave SW Olympia WA 98504-0929 Business E-Mail: J_M_Fairhurst@courts.wa.gov.

FAIRLEY, DARLENE, state legislator; m. Michael Fairley; 1 child, Andrew. BA in Polit. Sci., U. Wash. Owner Fairlook Antiques; mem. Wash. Senate, Dist. 32, Olympia, 1995—; chair labor and workforce devel. com.; mem. energy, tech. and telecom. com.; mem. ways and means com.; mem. adv. com. on minority and women's bus. enterprises; mem. water supply adv. com.; mem. joint com. on abstinence edn.; mem. organized crime adv. com. Mem. Lake Forest City Coun., 1992-95; vol. Cath. Relief Svcs.; mem. adv. bd. Lake Forest Park Stewardship Found.; vol. victim advocate Seattle Police Dept.; spl. advocate for abused children Snohomish County Juvenile Ct.; co-chair legis. com. Human Svcs. Roundtable of King County; founder Cuc Family Med. Clin., Vietnam; co-chair Lake Forest Park Telecom. and Electronic Access Com. Democrat. Office: 425 John Cherberg Bldg Olympia WA 98504-0001

FAIRLIE, CAROL HUNTER, artist, art educator; b. White Plains, NY, Dec. 14, 1952; d. Robert Fairlie; m. Jiri Dolezal, Sept. 18, 1988. MFA, U. North Tex., 1990—93. Four Year Cert., Painting Penn. Acad. Fine Arts, 1974. Lectr. U. North Tex., SOVA, Denton, Tex., 1993; assoc. prof. art Sul Ross State U., Alpine, Tex., 1996—. Newsletter editor, Nat. Watercolor Soc., Los Angeles, Calif., 2002—. Exhibitions include Plate Glass, West Tex. Signature Watercolor Exhbn., Nat. Competition, FAC Contemporary Artists, Nat. Competition, Laredo Internat. Watercolor Exhbn., Ariz. Aqueous, IX/94, Nat. Competition, WASH Internat. Juried Exhbn., Watercolor USA, Nat. Competition, Pa. Acad. Fellowship Exhbn., Pa. Watercolor Soc. Nat. Exhbn., Noyes Museum, Oceanville, NJ, Side By Side NWS/PWCS Watercolor Exhbn. (Barnett Meml. Award, 2002), Watercolor Mo. Nat. Works on Paper Exhbn., La. Nat. Watercolor Exhbn., Western Colo. Watercolor Exhbn., Krasdale Gallery Corp. Exhbn., Krasdale Galleries, Pa. Watercolor Soc., Nat. Competition, Pa. Acad. Fellowship Exhbn., one-woman shows include Enclosure, Irving Arts Assn., Brno-Dallas Sister City Exch., Ivancice Cultural Ctr., Laredo Ctr. for the Arts, Alpine Gallery Night, Salon 109. Co dir. Desert Islander Tahitian Dance Troupe, Alpine, Tex., 1996—2003; costume and programs Big Bend Players, Theatrical Group, Alpine, Tex., 2002—03; juror Region 18 H.S. Art programs, All area, west Tex., Tex., 1999—2003; newsletter editor Nat. Watercolor Soc., LA, 2002—03; treas. Alpine Family Crisis Ctr., Alpine, Tex., 2001—03, Alpine Pub. Libr., Alpine, Tex., 1998—2003; v.p. Purple Sage Women's Club, Alpine, Tex., 2000—02; treas. Alpine Women's Club, Alpine, Tex., 1998—99. Fellow: Pa. Acad. Fine Arts; mem.: The Midland Arts Assn., Nat. Watercolor Assn. (assoc.), Mid Am. Print Alliance. Office: Dept of Fine Arts & Comm SRSU Box C-90 Alpine TX 79832

FAISON, HOLLY, state official; b. Sherman, Tex., Aug. 11, 1953; d. Ronald Miller and Ann (LaRoe) F. BA, Tex. A&M U., 1976. Dispatcher College Station (Tex.) Police Dept., 1976-77; police comm. operator Tex. Dept. Pub. Safety, Bryan, 1977-83; supr. police comm. cations, facility, Tex. Dept. Pub. Safety, Austin; supr. police comm. facility Tex. Dept. Pub. Safety, Victoria, 1985-87, Bryan, 1987-92, regional supr. police comm., 1993—. Mem. Brazos County Emergency Mgmt./CD Coun., Bryan, 1987-92; chmn. adv. group S.E. Tex. Crime Info. Ctr., 1998. Prodr. video tng. tapes. Bd. dirs. Houston Regional Amber Plan, 2001—. Mem. Assoc. Pub. Safety Comms. Ofcls. (2d v.p. Tex. chpt. 2003—), Exec. Women in Tex. Govt. (chmn. Houston chpt. 1998), Dept. Pub. Safety Officers' Assn. [illegible] collecting. Home: 6304 Rumford Ln Houston TX 77084-2052 Office: Tex Dept Pub Safety 12230 West Rd Houston TX 77065 Office Phone: 281-517-1316.

FAISON, LUGENIA MARION, special education educator; b. Bklyn., Apr. 17, 1954; d. Jerry Faison and Marion Braxton-Faison. BA in Elem. Edn., U. V.I., St. Croix, 1982; MA in Learning Disabilities and Reading, U. Fla., Coral Gables, 1989; MA in Counseling and Guidance, Point Loma Nazarene U., 2002. Profl. clear multiple tchg. credential, profl. clear spl. edn. credential, profl. clear pupil pers. svcs. credential. Elem. tchr., St. Croix, 1976—93; spl. edn. tchr. Pasadena, Calif., 1994—. Mem.: ASCD, NAACP. Democrat.

FAIZ, ALEXANDRIA, nonfiction writer, researcher; d. Robert Lee and Eileen Helen (Wagner) F. BA in English with honors, Fairfield U., 1993; postgrad., Columbia U., 1993-94. Intern to writer Thirteen/Sta. WNET, N.Y.C., 1995—; founder, coord. environ. assocs. program Fairfield (Conn.) U., 1994—; news and pub. affairs writer Sta. WPKN Radio, Bridgeport, Conn., 1994—. Mem. editl. bd. Columbia: A Magazine of Poetry and Prose, 1993; author, editor: In Honor of the Earth, 1997. Advocate Literacy Vols. Am., Fairfield County, Conn., 1988—; founding mem. Alumnae Forum, Fairfield, 1995; trustee Alfred Adler Inst. N.Y., treas., sec., 1997—. Mem. Nat. Writers Union (Conn. organizer 1995—), Philosophy of Sci. Assn., History of Sci. Soc., UN Assn. Conn. (treas. 1997—), Nature Conservancy, Am. Mus. Natural History, Libr. Congress Assocs. (charter), Gt. Books Found. Roman Catholic. Avocations: linguistics, logic and mathematics, issues concerning intellectual property and freedom of expression, professional ethics.

FAJARDO, SARAH ELIZABETH JOHNSON, financial consultant; b. Montgomery, Ala., July 27, 1956; d. Robert Kellogg and Mary Loretta (Franks) Johnson; m. Thomas Ronald Fajardo, Sept. 5, 1987; children: Emilia Katherine, Roberto Thomas. BA in Anthropology, U. Ariz., 1979; postgrad., Inst. Fin. Edn., Tucson, 1985-87. Resident advisor Tucson Job Corps, 1980-81; felony release specialist Pretrial Release of Pima County, Tucson, 1981-82; dir. retention counseling Tucson Coll. Bus., 1982-84; teller, new account rep. Western Savs., Tucson, 1984-86; stockbroker Western Savs./Invest, Tucson, 1986-87; fin. planner Boucher, Oehmke & Quinn, Tucson, 1987-89, Consolidated Investment Svcs., 1989-92; registered rep. Plan Am., 1992—93; designed and developed investment dept. Nat. Bank Ariz., 1993—95; fin. cons. pvt. client svcs. Wells Fargo Investment (formerly Norwest), 1995—. Mgr. telemarketing dept. Ariz. Theatre Co., Tucson, 1988-89. Contbr. articles to profl. jours. Mem. com. Tucson Tomorrow, 1988; founding mem. Brewster Ctr. for Victims of Family Violence, Tucson, 1982-86; vol. Peace Corps, Senegal, Africa, 1979; chair ann. awards banquet events YWCA Women on the Move, 1991, grad. leadership tng. program, 1990; mem. investment adv. and fin. com. So. Ariz. Ctr. Against Sexual Assault, 2002-03; bd. dirs. Ariz. Children's Assn.; chair fin. com. Planned Parenthood So. Ariz., 1993—, bd. dirs., 2001—. Mem. Resources for Women (group leader of money talks 1987), NAFE, Successful Bus. Referral Club, Indsl. Recreation Coun. (treas. 1986-87), Greater Tucson Econ. Coun. (small bus. task force 1992-93). Democrat. Avocations: gourmet cooking, bicycling, weight training, running, gardening. Office: Wells Fargo Investments Wells Fargo Pvt Client Svcs 2195 E River Rd Ste 105 Tucson AZ 85718

FAJT, KAREN ELAINE, art educator; d. E. Albert and Angeline Louise DeLuca; m. Henry Gervase Fajt, Jr., June 22, 1974; children: Merritt Lynn, Holly Elizabeth. BA, Seton Hill U., 1970; MEd, U. Pitts., 1973. Art educator Hempfield Area Sch. Dist., Greensburg, 1970—. Bd. trustees Laurel Ballet Theatre, Greensburg, 1989—93; mem. St. Lucy's Aux. to the Blind., Pitts., 1994—, Frick Art and Hist. Ctr., 2001—, Westmoreland Mus. Am. Art, 1985—; bd. dirs. Lawyers' Aux., Greensburg, 1978—. Recipient Sullivan award, Seton Hill U., 1970. Mem.: NEA, Hempfield Area Edn. Assn., Pa. State Edn. Assn., Nat. Art Edn. Assn., Greensburg Coll. Club (bd. trustees 1970—, parliamentarian 1970—, chmn. scholarship com.), Univ. Club. Avocations: painting, travel, reading, gardening, shopping. Office: Hempfield Area Sch Dist RD # 6 Greensburg PA 15601

FALBERG, KATHRYN E. pharmaceutical executive; B in Econs., UCLA, 1981, MBA in Fin. and Acctg., 1984. CPA. Various positions Applied Magnetics, 1984-93, v.p., CFO, treas., 1993-94; treas. Amgen, Inc., Thousand Oaks, Calif., 1995-96, asst. contr. sales and mktg., 1996, v.p. investor rels. dept. and corp. tax dept., 1996-98, sr. v.p. fin., CFO, 1998—. Edward Carter scholar UCLA, 1984. Office: Amgen Inc 1 Amgen Center Dr Thousand Oaks CA 91320-1799

FALCAO, VERONICA GRACE, midwife; b. Washington, July 12, 1957; d. John Moniz and Phyllis Margaret Falcao. BA, Coll. of Holy Cross, 1979; MS, Stanford U., 1984; cert., Midwifery Inst. Calif., Windsor, 1995. Lic. midwife, Calif., 1997. Programmer Evans, Griffiths & Hart, Inc., Lexington, Mass., 1979-82; tchg. asst. Stanford U., Palo Alto, Calif., 1983-84; tech. staff mem. Acorn Rsch. Ctr., Palo Alto, 1984-86, Olivetti Rsch. Ctr., Menlo Park, Calif., 1987-90; sr. software engr. Metaphor, Inc., Mountain View, Calif., 1990-94; asst. midwife Tender Vigil Birthing Svc., East Palo Alto, Calif., 1995; intern Casa de Nacimiento, El Paso, 1996. Homebirth midwife, 1997—. Editor: Midwife Archives. Mem. Midwives Assn. N.Am., Assn. Pre- and Perinatal Psychology and Health, Calif. Assn. Midwives, Phi Beta Kappa, Pi Mu Epsilon. Avocations: classical piano, singing, gardening, bicycle commuting, feminist studies. Home and Office: 286 Vincent Dr Mountain View CA 94041-2210 Office Phone: 650-961-5475. E-mail: ronnie@gentlebirth.org.

FALCO, EDIE, actress; b. Northport, NY, July 5, 1963; BFA, SUNY, Purchase, NY, 1986. Appeared in films Sweet Lorraine, 1987, The Unbelievable Truth, 1990, Trust, 1990, Time Expired, 1992, Laws of Gravity, 1992, I Was on Mars, 1992, Bullets Over Broadway, 1994, Backfire!, 1995, The Addiction, 1995, Layin' Low, 1996, The Funeral, 1996, Breathing Room, 1996, Firehouse, 1997, Cost of Living, 1997, Cop Land, 1997, Trouble on the Corner, 1997, A Price Above Rubies, 1998, Hurrican Streets, 1998, Judy Berlin, 1999, Random Hearts, 1999, Overnight Sensation, 2000, Death of a Dog, 2000, Sunshine State, 2002 (Best Supporting Acress award LA Film Critics Assn. 2002, Golden Satellite award best supporting actress 2003); appeared in TV movies The Sunshine Boys, 1995, Jenifer, 2001; appeared in TV series Oz, 1997-99, The Sopranos, 1999- (Golden Globe award best actress in a drama 2000, 03, Emmy for best actress 1999, 2001, 2003, Actor of Yr., Am. Film Inst. 2001, Golden Satellite award 2002, SAG award 2003); TV guest appearances include Homicide: Life on the Street, 1993-94, 97, Law & Order, 1993-94, 97, New York Undercover, 1995; film dir. Rift, 1993; TV prodr. Stringer, 1999; theater appearances include Side Man, 2000, The Vagina Monologues, 2001, Frankie and Johnny in the Clair de Lune, 2002. Office: c/o Sandra Marsh Mgmt 9150 Wilshire Blvd Ste 220 Beverly Hills CA 90212-3429

FALCONE, PATRICIA JEANNE LALIM, investor, foundation administrator; b. Montevideo, Minn., Oct. 12; d. Clarence I. and Eva (Corneliusen) Lalim; m. Alfonso Benjamin Falcone, Oct. 22; children: Christopher Lalim Falcone, Steven Lalim Falcone. BS, U. Minn.; MS, PhD, U. Wis. Former libr. asst. U. Minn., St. Paul; former singer/performer Mpls.; former asst. prog. dir. U. Wis. Meml. Union, Madison; former instr. U. Wis., Madison; medical executive A.B. Falcone, M.D., Ph.D., Fresno, Calif.; pres. Dr. A.B. Falcone Meml. Found., U. Calif., Berkeley Coll. of Chemistry. Pvt. investor lectr. in field Patricia Lalim Falcone; contbr., presenter various confs. and seminars. Contbr. articles to profl. jours.;, author various ednl. and profl. pamphlets; former artist/craftsman (textile designs) U. Wis. [illegible] Action Com., Medical Soc., 1985-89, 1990, treas. 1997-2001, Philip Lorenz Meml. Keyboard Concert, (bd. dirs. 1988—); mem. Supts. Roundtable, Fresno Unified Sch. Dist., 1989; chmn. U. Calif., Fresno com. to bring UC campus to Fresno area, 1987—; chmn. Parent Adv. Com. for Gifted and Talented, Fresno Unified Sch. Dist., 1985, mem. 1984—; citizens adv. coun. U. Calif., San Joaquin, 1991—. Fellow U. Wis.; scholar. Mem. AAUW, Med. Alliance of Fresno/Madera County Med. Soc. (exec. bd. 1989—), Assn. for Acad. Excellence (chmn. 1988-91), Edison Computech Assn., Am. Scandinavian Found., U.S. English, Sharada Sangeet Sadan, Kappa Omicron Nu, Pi Lambda Theta, Phi Delta Gamma (pres. Alpha Beta chpt.), Pacific Legal Found., Fresno/Verona, Italy Sister City (com. 2001-), St. George Greek Orthodox Church Cmty. Lutheran Brotherhood, Sharada Sangest Sadan. Avocations: genealogy, swimming, travel, cross country skiing. Office: PO Box 14030 Pinedale CA 93650-4030 also: Riverview Tower # 1707 1920 First St South Minneapolis MN 55454-1055

FALCONER, KAREN ANN See **DAVIS, KAREN ANN**

FALCONER, MARGUERITE ELIZABETH, artist; b. Boston, July 5, 1919; d. Edward Henry and Marguerite Marie (McCarthy) Walsh; m. Charles Bowman Falconer, July 7, 1942 (dec. Apr. 1975); children: Charles Edward, Susan Jane Falconer; m. Frederick Cyrille Cuthbertson, Jan. 12, 1991 (dec. Mar. 1999). Student, Mus. Fine Arts, Boston, De Cordova Mus., Lincoln, Mass. Artist, proprietess McElwain-Falconer Gallery, Chatham, Mass., 1969—, sole propr., 1987-92, Falconer's, Chatham, 1992—. Co-founder Chatham Creative Arts Ctr. Represented in permanent collections at Cape Mus. Fine Arts. Mem. Archtl. Rev. Bd., Chatham, 1979-87; bd. dirs. Lower Cape Arts Lottery Coun.; mem. vestry St. Christopher's Episcopal Ch., Chatham, Mass. Mem. Am. Artists Profl. League, Nat. Mus. Women in Arts Archives, Women Painter's West, Copley Soc. Boston, Cape Mus. Fine Arts, Cape Cod Conservatory Music and Arts, Nat. Gallery Am. Art Smithsonian Inst. Archives, L.a. Contemporary Art Assn., Lower Cape Arts and Humanities, Copley Soc., Salmagundi Club. Episcopalian. Avocations: swimming, writing, music, travel, reading.

FALETTO, KIMBERLY ELIZABETH, art educator; b. Norfolk, Va., Nov. 20, 1964; d. Edmund Andrew Niec and Neva Lucille Ward; children: Andrew Moore, Devin. BFA with tchg. cert., Edinboro U., 1987. Art educator Shelby County Schs., Memphis. Ceiling tile painter LeBonbuer Children's Hosp.; mission trip participant on ch. constrn. to Nicaragua Bellevue Bapt. Ch., 2001, mission trip participant on ch. constrn. to El Salvador, 2002, mission trip participant on ch. constrn. to Nicaragua, 2001. Mem.: Tenn. Educators Assn., Nat. Art Educators Assn., Shelby County Educators Assn.

FALGUIERE, SHARON ELLEN, costume designer; b. White Plains, N.Y., Jan. 31, 1968; d. Joel Albert Falguiere and Barbara Jean (Bruns) Meeker. Student, Western Carolina U., 1985-88; cert. in filmmaking and costume, Valencia C.C., 1989. Stylist numerous commls., 1989—2002, costume designer, 1991—2002. Costume designer: Unsolved Mysteries, 1989, 93, What Would You Do?, 1991, 92, Clarissa Explains It All, 1992, HBO-One Night Stands, 1992, Fortune Hunter, 1994, Bermuda Triangle, 1995, Shootfighter II, 1995, The Good Life, 1996, Good Guys, Bad Guys, 2000, In the Shadows, 2000; designer feature film Emmett's Mark, 2001; asst. designer, buyer: The Adventures of Superboy, 1990-91, Automatic Avenue, 1997, Wild Things, 1997, Holyman, 1997, Gone in 60 Seconds, 2001, Assassination Tango, 2001 (filmed in Argentina); set costumer: The Grand Pardon, 1992, Extralarge II, 1992-93, Drop Zone, 1994, Two Much, 1995, Rosewood, 1996, The Pest, 1996, Armaggedan, 1997, Something About Mary, 1998, Any Given Sunday, 2000, Gone in Sixty Seconds, 2000; stylist: Disney World Co., Pepsi, Sears, Maxwell House Coffee, Labott's Beer, Publix, Craven Cigarettes, Timotei Shampoo, Disney Cruise Lines, Italian Vogue, T.J. Maxx, Bacardi Rum, Delta Airlines, Am. Express, and numerous others. Fundraiser Dem. Party, Orlando, Fla. 1996—. Mem. Women of the Motion Picture Industry, Mus. Art and Scis. (Miami), IATSE, Costume Designers Guild. Roman Catholic. Avocations: politics, boating, traveling, photography, paintings. E-mail: ellefab@aol.com.

FALK, BARBARA HIGINBOTHAM, music educator; b. Grindstone, Pa., May 22, 1950; d. Warren Charles and Erma Lou (Randolph) Higinbotham; m. Helmut Falk, July 7, 1973; children: Gregory Brock, Jennifer Arlene. BA in Music Edn., Western Ky. U., 1972; postgrad., Jersey City State Coll., 1974, postgrad., 1997, Montclair State Coll., 1990—91, Yale U., 1993; MA in Creative Arts Edn., Rutgers U., 1994; postgrad., Caldwell Coll., 1996, St. Peter's Coll., Jersey City, 1996—98. Cert. music tchr. N.J., Orff cert. tchr. N.J. Band dir. Bridgeton (N.J.) Jr. H.S., 1972—73; instrumental music tchr. Hopewell Twp. Sch., Bridgeton, 1972—73; gen. music tchr. Marlboro (N.J.) Twp. Schs., 1973—79; music dir. S. Br. Ref. Ch. Nursery Sch., Somerville, NJ, 1987; vocal and gen. music tchr. Washington Twp. Schs., Long Valley, NJ, 1988—. Youth choir dir. First Bapt. Ch., Freehold, NJ, 1981—83, Bridgewater Bapt. Ch., 1987—89; mem. master tchr. governing com. N.J. Symphony Orch., 1993—; cons. to N.J. Dept. Edn. State Arts Curriculum Framework Writer, Trenton, NJ, 1997; mem. Morris County profl. devel. bd. N.J. Dept. Edn., 1999—; chair Morris County Profl. Devel. Bd., 2002—03; presenter in field. Bible sch. music dir. Jackson (N.J.) Bapt. Ch., 1977—79, 1st Bapt. Ch., Bridgeton, 1980—86. Recipient Master Tchr. award, N.J. Symphony Orch. and Dodge Found., 1993; grantee Creating Original Opera grant, N.Y. Met. Opera Guild, 1993. Mem.: N.J. Edn. Assn. (profl. devel. bd. 2001—), Music Educators Nat. Conf., Washington Twp. Edn. Assn. (exec. com. 1993—, pres. 2001—), Kappa Delta Pi. Baptist. Avocations: golf, gardening. Home: 645 Case Rd Neshanic Station NJ 08853 Office: Old Farmers Rd Sch 51 Old Farmers Rd Long Valley NJ 07853 Home (Summer): 30 Garfield Pl Ocean City NJ 08826

FALK, DIANE M. research director, librarian, editor, writer; b. N.Y.C. d. Leon H.E. Falk and J. Constance Moorehead (Lilienthal) Stephenson. BA in English and World Lit., Columbia U., 1973, MLS, 1979. Text editor, bibliog. enhancement N.Y. Times Info. Svc., Inc., N.Y.C., 1980—; rsch. libr., documents analyst Atlantis Energy and Minerals, N.Y.C., 1980-81; project coord. legal dept. GAF Corp., N.Y.C., 1981-82; cataloger Exxon Edn. Found., N.Y.C., 1982; indexer, fact-checker H. W. Wilson & Co., Bronx, N.Y., 1982; bibliog. orgn. The Rockefeller Found., N.Y.C., 1983; rsch. info. specialist Harkavy Info. Svc., N.Y.C., 1983-84, Newsworld Comm., N.Y.C., 1985, features writer, 1977—78, rsch. (clippings) libr., 1985; dir. rsch., head libr., editl. rsch. specialist The World & I: The Mag. for Lifelong Learners, Washington, 1986—. Copy editor, rsch. mgr. HSA-UWC, N.Y.C. and Washington, 1974-75, 86; reference asst. Lehman Libr., Columbia U., N.Y.C., 1978; rsch. libr., documents analyst UN Ctr. for Transnational Corps., 1979; coord., conf. participant Ambs. for Peace, 2001--, Svc. for Peace. Editor-in-chief FOCUS, 1979-80; contbr. articles to profl. jours. English and comms. prof., vol. United to Serve Am., Washington Saturday Coll., Howard U., Washington, 1992-94; ofcl. tour guide Washington Times Found. and Corp.; conf. coord. Internat. Acad. Arts, World Media Assn., Literary, Bus., Legal and Polit. Groups and Issues, 1991—; instr., conf. demonstrator for internet and other knowledge mgmt. tech. rsch. resources; vol. Ambs. for Peace Seminars, 2001-03; sponsor, participant Svc. for Peace, 2002. Recipient Corp. award Washington Times Corp., 1997, cert. appreciation Intellectual Freedom Com. D.C. Libr. Assn., 1996-97, 2002-03. Mem. ALA, World Media Assn., Spl. Libr. Assn., D.C. Libr. Assn. (cert. of appreciation chair Intellecutal Freedom com., 2002-03), Intellectual Freedom Interest Group (chairperson 1996-97, com. chair 2002-03), Rsch. and Reference Interest Group, Women's Fedn. for World

Peace (sec. D.C. chpt. 1993—), Internat. Leadership Seminars (staff vol. 1991—), Internat. Fedn. for World Peace (signature campaign staff 1990-91, vol. 1990—, acting sec. 1993—), The Prosperity Coun. (editor newsletter 1991), Inst. Mus. and Libr. Svcs., World Assn. Non-Govtl. Orgns. Avocations: photography, arts, travel, writing. Home: 508 Columbia Rd NW Washington DC 20001-2904 Office: The World & I: The Mag for Lifelong Learners Libr and Rsch Dept 3600 New York Ave NE Washington DC 20002-1947 Office Phone: 202-635-4059. E-mail: dmfalk@worldandimag.com., research@worldandimag.com., library@worldandimag.com.

FALK, ELLEN STEIN, media specialist, educator; b. Mobile, Ala., Aug. 19, 1942; d. Louis James and Elizabeth Jeffers Stein; m. Michael Marc Falk, July 3, 1968; 1 child, Rachel Mara. BS in Fine Arts, Spring Hill Coll., 1964; student, St. Thomas Aquinas, 1981—85, William Paterson U., 2001—. Cert. tchr. N.J., 1986. Flight attendant United Airlines, N.Y.C., 1965—68, flight ops. office Newark, 1968—73; tchr. Meml. Sch., Montvale, NJ, 1986—2001, media specialist, 2001—. Del. People To People Amb. Program, China, 1994, New Zealand, Australia, 2001. Named Tchr. of Yr., Govs. Tchr. Recognition Program, 1994. Mem.: Ednl. Media Assn. N.J., Nat. Coun. Tchrs. English, Internat. Reading Assn., Friends of Libr., Parent Tchr. Orgn., Pi Lambda Theta. Home: 77 Akers Ave Montvale NJ 07645 Office: Memorial School 53 West Grand Avenue Montvale NJ 07645

FALK, JULIA S. linguist, educator, dean; b. Englewood, N.J., Sept. 21, 1941; d. Charles Joseph and Stella Sableski; m. Thomas Heinrich, Jan. 20, 1967; 1 child, Tatiana Prentice. BS, Georgetown U., 1963; MA, U. Wash., 1964, PhD, 1968. Instr. linguistics Mich. State U., East Lansing, 1966-68, asst. prof., 1968-71, assoc. prof., 1971-78, prof., 1978-2001, asst. dean Coll. of Arts and Letters, 1979-81, assoc. dean Coll. Arts and Letters, 1981-86, prof. emerita, 2001—. Vis. scholar U. Calif., San Diego, 2000—; cons. on lang. and law, lang. and gender, bias-free communication. Author: Linguistics and Language, 1973, 2d revised edit., 1978, Women, Language and Linguistics, 1999; contbr. articles on history of linguistics to profl. jours. Fellow Woodrow Wilson Found., 1963, NDEA Title IV, 1963-66, NSF, 1965; recipient Paul Varg Alumni award for Tchg., 1993, Faculty Profl. Women's Assn. Outstanding U. Woman Faculty award, 1999. Mem.: N.Am. Assn. History of Lang. Scis. (pres. 2000), Linguistic Soc. Am. Home: 8939 Caminito Verano La Jolla CA 92037-1606

FALK, MELANIE KAY, art director; b. O'Neill, Nebr., Feb. 28, 1978; d. James Ruben and Sharon Kay Falk. BFA, U. Nebr., 2001. Intern graphic design U. Nebr. Found., Lincoln, 1999—2001; freelance designer Doc's Place, Lincoln, 1999—2003, J. Finnegan's Steak & Seafood, Lincoln, 2001—03, Island Distributing, Lincoln, 2001—03; art dir. Nebr. Wesleyan U., Lincoln, 2001—03. Mem. Gallery 9 Profl. Artist Affiliation, Lincoln, 2001—03, co-coord., 2003. Exhibitions include U. Nebr., Lincoln, 2001 (Vreeland award, 2001, Faulkner award, 2001), Mus. Nebr. Art, Kearney, 2003. Mem.: Am. Inst. Graphic Arts (Silver Gold Poster Design award 2001, Silver Poster Design award 2002). E-mail: melaniefalk@hotmail.com.

FALKENBERG, MARY ANN THERESA, realtor; b. Dec. 8, 1931; d. Joseph and Catherine (Bausch) Haselsteiner; m. Charles V. Falkenberg Jr., Apr. 9, 1955; children: Catherine, Grace Ann, Susan Marie, Charles V., Robert, Thomas, Martin, Mary Elizabeth, Joseph. Student, Barat Coll., 1953. Cert. home protection cons. Piano tchr., 1946—73; organist St. Thomas of Villanova Ch., 1960—, choir dir., 1960—; sales staff Quinlan & Tyson, Realtors, Inc., Palatine, Ill., 1970—77; pres., co-owner, broker, mgr. Assoc. Realty Corp., Palatine, 1978—91; mgr. Prudential Preferred Properties, 1991—, Coldwell Banker, 1998—. Named Palatine Woman of Yr., Suburban Press Found., 1962. Mem.: NAFE, Women in Sales, Women in Sales, N.W. Suburban Bd. Realtors (edn. com. 1977—78, non-resident com. 1982, broker-lawyer com. 1986—91, grievance com. 1988—), Nat. Assn. Realtors (accredited profl. residential appraiser, cert. real property appraiser), Ill. Assn. Realtors (life mem. five million dollar club, mem. seven million dollar club, Gold award 1980, leading edge award), Am. Mgmt. Assn., Women in Mgmt., Barat Coll. Alumni Assn., Multiple Listing Orgn. (bd. dirs. 1986—2003, sec. 1988—90, treas. 1990—91, v.p. 1991—92, pres. 1993—96), Women's Club. Republican. Roman Catholic. Home: 517 Warwick Ave Palatine IL 60074-3875 Office: 792 E Rand Rd Arlington Heights IL 60004-4006

FALKOWSKI, BRENDA LISLE, business executive, consultant; b. Lexington, Ky., July 2, 1943; d. Edward Spencer and Evelyn (Wright) Lisle; m. Edward John Falkowski, Oct. 19, 1963; children: Brenda June Falkowski-Ashway, Richard Spencer, Lance Edward. AA in Liberal Studies, Neumann Coll., Aston, Pa., 1994, BS in Liberal Studies, 1998. Pres., v.p. Tokyo Am. Club Women's Group, Tokyo, 1981-85; assoc. Webb Jewelers and Silversmiths, West Chester, Pa., 1986-89; realtor Fox and Lazo Realtors/Prudential Preferred Properties, West Chester, 1990-92; internat. cons. corp. svcs. Fox and Lazo Relocation Mgmt., Paoli, Pa., 1993-95; pres. Touch of Glass Inc., Mt. Pleasant, SC, 1993—2000; v.p. Brenlan Assocs. Inc., Mt. Pleasant, 1995—; exclusive buyers agt. The Real Buyers Agt., Mt. Pleasant, SC, 2001—. Bd. govs. Tokyo Am. Club, 1981—85; cons. cross-cultural relocation, West Chester, Pa., 1996—98; internat. cons. Chamness Relocation, Mt. Pleasant, SC, 2002—. Monthly contbr. newspaper column The Tokyo Am., 1983-95. Membership chair Reps. Abroad, Tokyo, 1984; neighborhood vol. Am. Cancer Soc., Am. Heart Assn., Am. Kidney Found. Mem.: NAFE, AAUW, Nat. Assn. of Exclusive Buyers Agts., Nat. Assn. Realtors, Nat. Assn. Bus. Coaches (E. Cooper Prof. Women), Adult Women's Network, Internat. Women's Club. Methodist. Avocations: breeding of rare dogs, personal fitness training, retirement home pet therapy. Home: 3527 Stockton Dr Mount Pleasant SC 29466-6990

FALKOWSKI, THERESA GAE, chemistry educator; b. El Paso, Tex., Mar. 19, 1958; d. Chester Doan and Patricia Ann Harman; m. Henry Steven Falkowski, May 16, 1981. AA, Potomac State Coll., 1978; BA, W.Va. U., 1980. Lab. asst. Potomac State Coll., Keyser, W.Va., 1977-78, gen. chem. prep rm. mgr., 1986—, chem. lab. instr., 1995-99; chem. lab. tchg. asst. W.Va. U., Morgantown, 1981-83, chem. lab. tech., 1981-85, adj. instr. chemistry, 1999—. Cons. USS N.C. Battleship Meml., Wilmington, 1981—; mem. haz-mat response team Potomac State Coll., 1993—. Author: Clark Hall of Chemistry: A Pictorial History, 1996, Laboratory Manual for Chemistry 112, 1996; illustrator: Laboratory Manual for Chemistry 115/116, 1991. Mem. Am. Chem. Soc., W.Va. Acad. Sci., Carnegie Mus. Natural History and Sci. Ctr., The Nat. Maritime Ctr., The N.C. Aquarium Soc., The Mote Marine Lab. Avocations: model building, world war ii history, aircraft identification, science fiction. Office: Potomac State Coll Fort Ave Keyser WV 26726

FALL, DOROTHY, artist, art director, administrator; b. Rochester, N.Y., Apr. 7, 1930; d. Isadore and Esther Paula (Rudman) Winer; m. Bernard B. Fall, dec. Feb. 1967; children: Nicole Francoise, Elisabeth Anne, Patricia Madeleine Marcelle. BFA, Syracuse U., 1952; postgrad., Am. U., 1956-58, 66; student, Acad. de la Grande Chaumiere, Paris, 1961, Acad. Julian, 1965. Dep. art dir. AMERIKA Mag. U.S. Info. Agy., Washington, 1956-80; owner, art dir. Fall Design Comms., Washington, 1980-88; dir. Gallery 10, Washington, 1994—. Bd. dirs. Pyramid Atlantic, Riverdale, Md. Editor: Last Reflections on a War, 1967, 2d edit., 2000; art dir., designer Space Science Comes of Age, 1981; one-woman shows include Mickelson Gallery, Washington, 1969, 73,79, 84, Plum Gallery, Kensington, Md., 1989, O St. Studio, Washington, 1989, 92, AVA Gallery, Lebanon, N.H., 1990, Covington & Burling, Washington, 1990, Am. Hort. Soc., Alexandria, Va., 1993, Gallery 10, Washington, 1996, 2000, Cosmos Club, 2000, Galerie Internationale, N.Y.C., 1968, Maison de France, Phnom Penh, Cambodia, 1962; group shows include Hanoi (Vietnam) Fine Arts Coll., 2000, Assioma Gallery, Prato, Italy, 2000, 01, Marino Marini Mus., 2001, Pistoia, Italy, Venezia Viva, Venice, 2001, UN, N.Y.C., 2001; represented in permanent collections and by Verve Art Gallery, Leuven, Belgium, Gallery 10, Washington, AVA Gallery, Lebanon, N.H., Aries East, Brewster, Mass. Recipient gold medal award Art Dirs. Club of Met. Washington Exhibits, 1965, 66, 69, 79, distinctive merit Art Dirs. Club of N.Y. Exhibits, 1969, 74, 77, 78, 79, 81, 82, 83, silver medal N.Y. Soc. Illustrators, 1969. Mem. Women's Caucus on Arts, Washington Sculptors Group, Artists Equity, Cosmos Club. Home: 4535 31st St NW Washington DC 20008-2130

FALLAR, GAIL M. state representative, town clerk; b. Rutland, Vt., Mar. 3, 1954; m. Richard Fallar; 3 children. Grad., C.C. Vt. Town clk.-treas. Town of Tinmouth; state rep. State of Vt., 2003—. Editor: Tales of Tinmouth. Zoning adminstr.; 911 coord.; sec. Tinmouth Cmty. Fund; past mem. Rutland Regional Planning Com.; past chair Rutland Natural Resource Conservation Dist.; sec. Tinmouth Cmty. Ch. Mem.: Tinmouth Hist. Soc. (sec.), Vt. League of Cities and Towns (v.p.). Office: 515 N End Rd Tinmouth VT 05773

FALLER, RHODA, lawyer; b. N.Y.C., Dec. 21, 1946; d. Benjamin and Marion (Mediasky) Sragg; m. Stanley Grossberg, Apr. 12, 1973 (div. Oct. 1983); children: Joseph Seth, Daniel Benjamin; m. Bernard Martin Faller, May 31, 1987. BS, SUNY, Stony Brook, 1967; MS, Pace U., 1973; JD, N.Y. Law Sch., 1978. Bar: N.Y. 1979, N.J. 1979, U.S. Dist. Ct. N.J. 1979, Fla. 1980, U.S. Dist. Ct. (ea. and so. dists.) N.Y. 1982, Ky. 1996, U.S. Dist. Ct. (ea. dist.) Ky. 1997. Assoc. Fuchsberg & Fuchsberg, N.Y.C., 1982-91, DeBlasio & Alton, P.C., N.Y.C., 1991-95, Rhoda Grossberg Faller, Esq., Teaneck, 1995-96, Becker Law Office, Louisville, Ky., 1997-2000; pvt. practice Louisville, 2000—. Mem.: Women Lawyers Assn., Louisville Bar Assn., Fla. Bar Assn., N.Y. State Bar Assn., Ky. Bar Assn., Ky. Acad. Trial Attys., Nat. Assn. Women Bus. Owners, Assn. Trial Lawyers Am., Million Dollar Advocates Forum. Democrat. Jewish. Home: 213 Mockingbird Gardens Dr Louisville KY 40207-5718 Office: Law Office of Rhoda Faller PLLC 455 S 4th St Ste 310 Louisville KY 40202

FALLER, SUSAN GROGAN, lawyer; b. Cin., Mar. 1, 1950; d. William M. and Jane (Eagen) Grogan; m. Kenneth R. Faller, June 8, 1973; children: Susan Elisabeth, Maura Christine, Julie Kathleen. BA, U. Cin., 1972; JD, U. Mich., 1975. Bar: Ohio 1975, Ky. 1989, U.S. Dist. Ct. (so. dist.) Ohio 1975, U.S. Ct. Claims 1982, U.S. Ct. Appeals (6th cir.) 1982, U.S. Supreme Ct. 1982, U.S. Tax Ct. 1984, U.S. Dist. Ct. (ea. dist.) Ky., 1991. Assoc. Frost & Jacobs, Cin., 1975-82; ptnr. Frost & Jacobs LLP, Cin., 1982-2000; mem. Frost Brown Todd LLC, Cin., 2000—. Assoc. editor Mich. Law Rev., 1974-75; contbg. author: MLRC 50-State Survey of Media Libel and Privacy Law, 1982-93, MLRC 50-State Survey of Media Libel Law, 1999-, MLRC State Survey of Employment Libel and Privacy Law, 1999-. Bd. dirs. Summit Alumni Coun., Cin., 1983-85; trustee Newman Found., Cin., 1980-86, Cath. Social Svc., Cin., 1984-93, nominating com., 1985-88, sec., 1990; mem. Class XVII Leadership Cin., 1993-94; mem. exec. com., def. counsel sect. Media Law Resource Ctr., 1998-2002, chmn. membership com., 2003-04; pres., def. counsel sect. Libel Def. Resource Ctr., 2001; mem. parish coun. St. Monica St. George Ch., 1996-2000. Recipient Career Women of Achievement award YWCA, 1990. Mem. ABA (co-editor newsletter media litig. 1993-97), FBA, Ky. Bar Assn., No. Ky. Bar Assn., No. Ky. Women's Bar Assn., Ohio Bar Assn. (chair media law com. 2001-02), Cin. Bar Assn. (com. mem.), Potter Stewart Inn of Ct., U. Cin. Alumni Assn., Arts & Scis. Alumni Assn. (bd. govs. U. Cin. Coll. 1988-2000), U. Mich. Alumni Assn., Mortar Bd., Leland Yacht Club, Coll. Club, Clifton Meadows Club, Phi Beta Kappa, Theta Phi Alpha. Roman Catholic. Home: 5 Belsaw Pl Cincinnati OH 45220-1104 Office: Frost Brown Todd LLC 2200 PNC Ctr 201 E 5th St Cincinnati OH 45202-4182 Office Phone: 513-651-6941. E-mail: sfaller@fbtlaw.com.

FALLETTA, JO ANN, conductor; b. N.Y.C., Feb. 27, 1954; d. John Edward and Mary Lucy (Racioppo) F.; m. Robert Alemany, Aug. 24, 1986. BA in Music, Mannes Coll. Music, N.Y.C., 1976; MA in Music, Juilliard Sch., N.Y.C., 1983, PhD in Musical Arts, 1989; doctorate (hon.), Marian Coll., Wis., 1988, Old Dominion U., 1996, Canisius Coll., 2000. Music dir. Queens Philharmonic, N.Y.C., 1978-91, Den. Chamber Orch., Colo., 1983-92; assoc. condr. Milw. Symphony, Wis., 1985-88; music dir. Women's Philharmonic, San Francisco, 1986-96; music dir., condr. Long Beach Symphony, Calif., 1989-00; music dir. Va. Symphony, Norfolk, 1991—, Buffalo Philharm., 1999—. Over 30 recordings with the London Symphony, the Buffalo Philharmonic, the Virginia Symphony, the English Chamber Orchestra, the New Zealand Symphony, the Long Beach Symphony, the Czech National Symphony and the Women's Philharmonic. Stokowski Conducting Competition, Toscanini Conducting award, John S. Edwards Award, Am. Symphony Orchestra League, Seaver/Nat. Endowment for the Arts Conductors Award, 2002. Office: ICM Artists LTD 40 W 57th St Fl 16 New York NY 10019-4098*

FALLIN, BARBARA MOORE, human resources director; b. Paducah, Ky., Nov. 12, 1939; d. James Perry Moore and Margaret Arminta (Winn) Kastner; m. Jon Ball, Jan. 21, 1961 (div. July 1963); m. Ralph Daniel Fallin, May 23, 1965; children: Wade, Cathi, Cindy Pergrim, Danielle. Student, Fla. Christian Coll., 1957-58. Cert. sr. profl. in human resource mgmt. Exec. asst. to contr. The Borden Co., Tampa, Fla., 1958-65; mktg. asst. Martin-Marietta Corp., Shalimar, Fla., 1965-71; asst. to pres. Browning-Marine, Ft. Walton Beach, Fla., 1973; pers. coord. Keltec Fla., Shalimar, 1974-78; pers. mgr. Metric Systems Corp., Ft. Walton Beach, 1979-87, pers. dir., 1987-92; dir. human resources Metric Sys. Corp., Ft. Walton Beach, 1992—. Mem. Job Svc. Employer Com., Ft. Walton Beach, 1985—; mem. adv. bd. Bay Area Vocat.-Tech. Ctr., Ft. Walton Beach, 1988-92; mem. adv. bd. Okaloosa Applied Tech. Ctr. Sch. Adv. Coun., 1995-98, chmn., 1997-98; bd. dirs. Pvt. Industry Coun., 1996—, vice chmn., 1998-99, chmn. 2000—. First mistress Krewe of Bowlegs, Ft. Walton Beach, 1983-84, first lady to Cap'n Billy Bowlegs XXXII, 1986-87; mem. citizens adv. com. U. West Fla., Pensacola, 1991-97; mem. funds distbn. com. Okaloosa County United Way, 1990-93; mem. BNA's Pers. Policies Forum, 1995-96; mem. Pacesetters fund raiser team Salvation Army Capital Campaign, 1996-97. Mem. NAFE, Soc. Human Resource Mgmt. (Emerald Coast chpt. pres. 1986-88, bd. dirs. 1988-92), Nat. Mgmt. Assn., Ft. Walton Beach C. of C. (hosts com. 1991—), Laureate Gamma Phi (exec. bd. dirs. 1996-97, sec. 1997-98, Valentine queen 1997, v.p. 2000-2001). Republican. Presbyterian. Avocations: collecting penquins and camels, making scrapbooks. Office: Metric Sys Corp 645 Anchors St NW Fort Walton Beach FL 32548-3803

FALLIN, MARY COPELAND, lieutenant governor; b. Warrensburg, Mo., Dec. 9, 1954; d. Jospeh Newton and Mary (Duggan) Copeland; children: Christina, Price. BS, Okla. State U., 1977. Bus. mgr. Okla. Dept. Securities, Oklahoma City, 1979-81; state travel coord. Okla. Dept. of Tourism, Oklahoma City, 1981-82; sales rep. Associated Petroleum, Oklahoma City, 1982-83; mktg. dir. Brian Head (Utah) Hotel & Ski Resort, 1983-84; dir. sales Residence Inn Hotel, Oklahoma City, 1984-87; dist. mgr. Lexington Hotel Suites, Oklahoma City, 1988-90; real estate assoc. Pippin Properties, Inc., Oklahoma City, 1990-94; state rep. Okla. Ho. of Reps., Oklahoma City, 1990-94; lt. gov. State of Okla., Oklahoma City, 1995—. Chmn. Nat. Conf. Lt. Govs. Mem., del. Okla. Fedn. Rep. Women; mem. Am. Legis. Exch. Coun., Nat. Conf. State Legislatures; former bd. mem. United Way Oklahoma City, YWCA; mem. adv. bd. Trail of Tears; former hon. chair Organ Donor Network; former hon. co-chair Indian Territory Arts and Humanities Coun.; former co-chair Festival of Hope Named Woman of Yr., Ladies in Comm., 1998, Girl Scouts Am., 1998, Nat. Legislator of Yr., Okla. Ladies in the News, Disting. Former Student, U. Ctrl. Okla.; recipient Bi-liner award, 1997, Guardian of Small Bus. award, Small Bus. Adv. award, Nat. Fedn. Ind. Small Bus., Women in the News award, Women in Comm. Mem.: Aerospace States Assn. (chmn. 2003—). Republican. Presbyterian. Office: State Capitol Rm 211 Office of Lt Governor Oklahoma City OK 73105*

FALLON, PAT, artist, educator; b. Cartagena, Colombia, Nov. 2, 1939; (parents Am. citizens); d. Carlos Fallon and Maureen (Bryne) Fallon Laird; m. Ronald Patrick Conner, Dec. 26, 1960 (div. June 1976); children: Haldey Kathryn Conner, Kenneth Fallon Conner. BA, Antioch Coll., 1962; BFA, Cleve. Inst. Art, 1980; MFA, Kent State U., 1982. Prof. Ursuline Coll., Cleve., 2001—. Exhibitions include nat. and internat., U.S., Ireland, Germany. Vol. N.E. Ohio Coalition Homeless, Cleve. Fellow, Ohio Humanities Coun., 1986—94. Mem.: Mus. Contemporary Art Cleve., So. Poverty Ctr. Democrat. Roman Catholic. Home: 3300 Kenmore Rd Shaker Heights OH 44122-3462 Office: Ursuline Coll 2550 Lander Rd Cleveland OH 44124-4318

FALLON, RAE MARY, psychology educator, early childhood consultant; b. N.Y.C., Apr. 13, 1947; d. Frank J. and Santa A. T.; m. John J. Fallon, 1972; children: Sean, Christopher. BA, CUNY, 1968, MA, 1971; PhD, Fordham U., 2001. Cert. N-6 tchr., spl. edn. tchr., N.Y. Elem. tchr. Pub. Sch. 1, Bronx, NY, 1968—72; pre-sch. tchr. Valley Nursery Sch., Walden, NY, 1972—73; tchr. spl. edn. Orange-Ulster Bd. Coop. Edn. Svcs., Goshen, NY, 1973—75, early childhood specialist, 1982—89; instr. edn. Mt. St. Mary Coll., Newburgh, NY, 1989—93, asst. prof., 1993—2001, assoc. prof. psychology, 2001—. Early childhood cons., Montgomery, N.Y., 1989—; mem. early childhood com. Valley Ctrl. Sch. Sys., Montgomery, 1994. Mem. West Street Sch. Cmty. Sch. Bd., Newburgh, 1990—; mem. early intervention com. Orange County Health Dept., Goshen, 1993—; chmn. program com. Montgomery Rep. Club, 1990-94. Mem. ASCD, Coun. for Exceptional Children, Assn. for Edn. Young Children (regional coord. 1991-92), Kiwanis, Delta Kappa Gamma (pres. Alpha chpt. 2002-04), Phi Delta Kappa. Roman Catholic. Office: Mt St Mary Coll 330 Powell Ave Newburgh NY 12550-3412 Office Phone: 845-569-3169.

FALLON, SALLY, writer; b. Santa Monica, Calif., June 22, 1948; d. Harry Herman and Margaret Kirkpatrick Wetzel Jr.; m. William Byron Holt, May 19, 1970 (dec. Sept. 1970); m. John R. Fallon, Mar. 24, 1972; children: Sarah, Nicholas, James, Davidson. BA in English with honors, Stanford U., 1970; MA in English with high honors, UCLA, 1972. Pres. Weston A. Price Found., Washington, 1999—. Author: Nourishing Traditions, 1996; editor jour. Price Pottenger Nutritional Found., 1997-98; contbr. articles on nutrition and health to profl. publs. V.p. Price Pottenger Nutrition Found., San Diego, 1997-98; founder A Campaign for Real Milk, Washington, 1997. Office: Weston A Price Found PBM 106-380 4200 Wisconsin Ave NW Washington DC 20016-2143 E-mail: safallon@aol.com.

FALLON, TINA K. state legislator; b. Goldsboro, N.C., Sept. 16, 1917; d. George Peele and Lillian (Langston) P.; m. James D. Fallon Jr., 1938 (dec.); children: George P., James D. III, William N., Howard F. AB, Meredith Coll., 1938; MEd, U. Del., 1956; postgrad., Coll. of William & Mary, Northwestern U., Am. U., U. Md. Mem. Dist. 39 Del. Ho. of Reps., 1978—, past chmn. edn. and agr. com., past state task force on edn. for econ. growth, mem. state edn. com., vice chmn. edn. com., nat. conf. state legis., mem. grant for higher order thinking task force; former tchr. Seaford. Past mem. Gov. Peurpich's Exec. Bd., Del. Recipient Second Mile award and Excellence in Edn. award, U. Del. Mem. AAUW, Del. State Edn. Assn. (exec. bd. dirs. 1973-74), Bus. and Profl. Women, Del. Ret. Tchrs. Assn., Seaford Edn. Assn. (v.p., pres. 1971-73), Seaford C. of C., Rotary Club (hon.), Del. Adv. Scout Coun., Alpha Beta Phi. Home: RR 4 Box 219 Seaford DE 19973-9612 Office: Del House of Reps State Capitol PO Box 1401 Dover DE 19903-1401

FALLS, KATHLEENE JOYCE, photographer; b. Detroit, July 3, 1949; d. Edgar John and Acelia Olive (Young) Haley; m. Donald David Falls, June 15, 1974; children: Daniel John, David James. Student, Oakland Community Coll., 1969-73, Winona Sch. Profl. Photography, 1973-80, postgrad., 1988, 90. Lic. ham radio-technician class. Printer Guardian Photo, Novi, Mich., 1967-69; printer, supr. quality control N.Am. Photo, Livonia, Mich., 1969-76; free lance photographer Livonia, 1969-76; owner, pres. Kathy Falls, Inc., Carleton, Mich., 1976—2001; instr. digital imaging Monroe County (Mich.) C.C., 1994-95. Instr. continuing edn. Monroe County C.C., 1981-83; nat. artisan judge Congl. H.S. Art Competition, 1985-2000; owner Picture Perfect, Carleton, 1987; co-owner Haleys Gift Shoppe, Dundee, Mich., 1989; pub. info. officer Am. Radio Relay League, 1998-2000. Author: (booklet) Emergency Photo-Retouching for Photographers, 1988; editor The Hertzian herald, 1998; contbr. articles to profl. jours.; represented in spl. categories in the Nat. Loan Collection, Profl. Photographers Am., 1980, 81, 83, 87, 2002; represented in permanent Collections Monroe County Hist. Mus., Archives Notre Dame; newsletter editor Hertzian Herald. Active Big Bros. and Big Sisters, Monroe, 1986—87; corr. sec. Monroe Women's Ctr., 1986—88; mem. Amateur Radio Emergency Svc., pres. Our Lady of Knock divsn. Laoh Adrian, Laoh State Bd., 2001—; Catechist St. Parick's Ch., Carleton, 1984—87, mem. parish coun., 1998—2000; bd. dirs. Ladies Ancient Order of Hibernians. Recipient Photographic Craftsman degree, 1989, numerous awards granted by profl. photographic orgns.; editor: Hertzian Herald. Mem.: NAFE, Nat. Orgn. Women Bus. Owners, Monroe C. of C. (chmn. council women bus. owners), Monroe County Fine Arts Coun. (pres. 1998—2000), Am. Photog. Artisans Guild (bd. dirs. 1987—, Photog. Artisan degree 1989, Artisan Laurel degree 1991, pres. 1992, exec. sec. 2001—, editor Palette Page 2001—, exec. dir. 2002, coun. mem.), Profl. Photographers Am. (photographic specialist degree 1988, cert. profl. photog. specialist, Photog. Craftsman degree 1990, cert. electronic imager), Profl. Photographers Mich. (artisan chair 1982—83, bd. dirs. 2000—, dir. 2001—, Best of Show award 1976, 1981, 2001, Artist of Yr. 1980, 1991), Detroit Profl. Photographers Assn. (artisan chmn. 1981—82, bd. dirs. 1987—, Best of Show award 1981, 1983), Am. Soc. Photographers, Hillsdale Art Guild, Toastmasters, Monroe County Radio Comms. Assn., Ladies Ancient Order of Hibernians (bd. dirs. 1998—99), Monroe Camera, Hillsdale County Amateur Radio Club, Scarab Club Detroit, Internat. Club. Republican. Roman Catholic. Avocations: guitar, piano, drawing, travel, camping. Home and Office: 14940 Carpenter Rd Camden MI 49232 E-mail: katfalls@tdi.net.

FALUDI, SUSAN C. journalist, scholarly writer; Formerly with West Mag., San Jose, Calif., Mercury News; with San Francisco Bur., Wall St. Jour. Spkr. in field. Author: Backlash: The Undeclared War Against American Women, 1991 (National Book Critics Circle award for general non-fiction 1992); contbr. articles to mags. Recipient Pulitzer Prize for explanatory journalism, 1991. Office: care Sandra Dijkstra Literary Agy 1155 Camino Del Mar PMB 515 Del Mar CA 92014-2605

FALWELL, CAROL, school librarian, real estate broker; b. Searcy, Ark., Apr. 14, 1953; d. Carl William and Adred Verda Frances Siler; m. Lendol Kent Falwell Jr., Aug. 15, 1975; children: Vanessa, Amelia D. BSE in Phys. Sci., Ark. State U., 1975; MS in Ednl. Media/Libr. Sci., U. Ctrl. Ark., 1992. Office worker Smith Clinic, Bradford, Ark., 1969-71; chemistry tchr. Newport (Ark.) H.S., 1975-81, chemistry and physics tchr., 1986-92, libr. media specialist, 1992—; jr. high sci. tchr. Bradford H.S., 1983-84; assoc. broker Sink Realty Co., Newport, 1977—. Cons. Mary Kay Cosmetics, Dallas, 1980—. Leader 4-H, Jackson County, 1991—; Sunday sch. tchr. First Bapt. Ch., Newport, 1994-98. Recipient Jackson County Young Careerist award Bus. and Profl. Women, 1979. Avocations: reading, roller skating. Home: 2800 Lynn St Newport AR 72112-4905 Office: Newport HS 406 Wilkerson Dr Newport AR 72112-3949

FANN, MARGARET ANN, counselor; b. Pasco, Wash., July 16, 1942; d. Joseph Albert David and Clarice Mable (Deaver) Rivard; m. Jerry Lee Fann, June 13, 1986; children: Brenda Heupel, Scott Sherman, Kristin Johnson, Robert Lack III. AA, Big Bend C.C., Moses Lake, Wash., 1976; BA in Applied Psychology magna cum laude, Ea. Wash. U., 1977, MS in Psychology, [illegible] dependency counselor II, nat. cert. addictions counselor II, cert. in chronic psychiat. disability. Intern counselor Linker House Drug Rehab., Spokane, Wash., 1976-78; drug counselor The House drug program, Tacoma, Wash., 1978-80; exec. dir. Walla Walla (Wash.) Commn. Alcohol, 1980-82; dir. Cmty. Alcohol Svcs. Assn., Kennewick, Wash., 1982-86; primary care coord. Carondelet Psychiat. Care Ctr., Richland, Wash., 1986-90; part-time instr. Ea. Wash. U., Cheney, 1981-88; instr. Columbia Basin Coll., Pasco, 1990-93; adminstr. Action Chem. Dependency Ctr., Kennewick, 1993—. Bd. dirs. Benton-Franklin County Substance Abuse Coalition, Pasco, Kennewick, Richland, 1990—. Vol. Pat Hale for Senator, Kennewick, 1994. Mem. Am. Counselors Assn., Nat. Mental Health Counselors Assn., Wash. State Mental Health Counselors Assn., Tri-Cities Counselors Assn., Phi Theta Kappa. Avocations: swimming, bicycling, running. Office: Action Chem Dependency Ctr 552 N Colorado St Ste 5525 Kennewick WA 99336-7779 also: Benton-Franklin County MICA Detoxification Ctr 1020 E 7th Ave Kennewick WA 99336-5936

FANNIN, JOSEPHINE JEWELL, social services administrator; b. Wayne, W.Va., Feb. 12, 1944; d. Edgar James and Beatrice Hall (Watkins) Jewell; m. Michael Dorsey Fannin; 1 child, Michelle René. Student, Davis Coll., Am. Inst. Banking, L.A., 1962-65, Nat. Floral Inst., 1966-68; lic., Bucks Coll., Newtown, Pa., 1984; AAS in Human Svcs., Ariz. Western Coll., 1994. Women's program dir. for Europe, USN, Rota, Spain, 1976-77; with mktg. svcs. dept. Bank of Am., Fairfield, Calif., 1962-65; comml. accounts specialist Commerce Bank, St. Charles, Mo., 1970-73, 75-76, comml. accounts rep., 80-82, Pa. Nat. Bank, Phila., 1978-81; info. and referral field nurse Upjohn Health Care, Newtown, 1982-85, info. and referral specialist Jacksonville, Fla., 1985-89; dir. vol. and ret. sr. vol. program Western Ariz. Coun. Govts., Yuma, 1992-94; sr. program adminstr. Mid East Area Agy. on Aging, Brentwood, Mo., 1994-99; exec. dir. Hosp. Hospitality Ho., Huntington, W.Va., 1999—. Spkr. Internat. Platform Assn., 1985-95. Bd. dirs. Ch. Women United, Bucks County, Pa., 1980-85, Yuma Regional Med. Ctr., 1992-94; bd. dirs., mem. fin. com. Jacksonville and Yuma hospices, 1985-94; ombudsman adv. Western Ariz. Coun. Govts., 1989-94; mem. adv. bd. vol. clearing house and human svcs. program St. Charles C.C., 1995, bd. dirs., 1997; exec. dir. Hosp. Hospitality House, 1999—; bd. dirs. St. Charles Cmty. Coun., 1997, City of Huntington Found., 2000. Recipient Outstanding Employee award Western Coun. Govts., 1994. Mem. AAUW, Assn. Fundraising Profls., Nat. Soc. Fund Raising Execs., Zonta (past bd. dirs. and program dir. Yuma), Rotary Internat. (bd. dirs.), Phi Theta Kappa (Alumni award 1994). Avocations: travel, writing, speaking on current events and senior advocacy and volunteer programs. Office: Hosp Hospitality House 2801 S Staunton Rd Huntington WV 25702 also: O'Fallon Sr Programs 410 E Elm St O Fallon MO 63366-2608 Home: 1661 Washington Blvd Huntington WV 25701 E-mail: huntingtonhhh@aol.com.

FANNING, DAKOTA, actress; b. Conyers, Ga., Feb. 23, 1994; d. Steve and Joy Fanning. Actor: (films) Tomcats, 2001, I Am Sam, 2001, Father Xmas, 2001, Trapped, 2002, Sweet Home Alabama, 2002, Hansel & Gretel, 2002, Uptown Girls, 2003, The Cat in the Hat, 2003, Man on Fire, 2004, (voice): (TV films) Kim Possible: A Stitch in Time, 2003, : (TV miniseries) Taken, 2002, (guest appearances): (TV series) ER, 2000, Ally McBeal, 2000, Strong Medicine, 2000, CSI: Crime Scene Investigation, 2000, The Practice, 2000, Spin City, 2000, Malcolm in the Middle, 2001, The Fighting Fitzgeralds, 2001, The Ellen Show, 2001, Friends, 2004, (guest appearances, voice) Family Guy, 2001. Office: Osbrink Talent Agy 4343 Lankershim Blvd Ste #100 North Hollywood CA 91602 Office Phone: 818-760-2488.*

FANOS, KATHLEEN HILAIRE, osteopathic physician, podiatrist; b. Bremerhaven, Germany, Aug. 18, 1956; came to U.S., 1957; d. Homer Dantangelo and Ilse Helmar (Ochs) F. AAS in Music, Nassau C.C., Garden City, N.Y., 1976; BS in Music Edn., Hofstra U., 1978, postgrad., 1978-79; D Podiatric Medicine, Coll. Podiatric Med. and Surg., Des Moines, 1987; DO, Coll. Osteo. Med. and Surg., Des Moines, 1994. Diplomate Am. Bd. Internal Medicine. Tchr. music McKenna Jr. H.S. and Eastlake Elem. Sch., Massapequa, N.Y., 1978-79; musician numerous profl. orgns., N.Y., Iowa, 1979—; preceptorship in podiatry Bayshore, N.Y., 1987-88; pvt. practice podiatry Hyde Park, West Roxbury and Brookline, Mass., 1988-91; resident in internal medicine Winthrop U. Hosp., Mineola, N.Y., 1994-97; internist Cmty. Med. Assocs., Jackson, NJ, 1997-2000, Ocean County Family Care, Jackson, 2000—03, Hinds Interna l Medicine, Jackson, 2003. Ins. med. examiner Portamedic, Burlington, Mass., 1988-91. Mem. AMA, ACP, Am. Bd. Internal Medicine, Am. Soc. Internal. Medicine, Am. Osteo. Assn., Am. Coll. Osteo. Family Physicians, N.Y. State Internal Medicine Soc., Phi Theta Kappa, Pi Kappa Lambda, Sigma Sigma Phi, Phi Delta Epsilon. Avocations: music, tennis, bowling, skiing, travel. Office Phone: 601-372-2616. E-mail: kmozartf@bellsouth.net.

FANSELOW, JULIE RUTH, writer; b. Springfield, Ill., July 26, 1961; d. Byron and Ruth Leona (Neumann) F.; m. Bruce Edward Whiting, Apr. 25, 1992; 1 child, Natalie. BS in Journalism, Ohio U., 1982. Reporter Salem (Ohio) News, 1982-85; editor Vindicator, Youngstown, Ohio, 1985-89; reporter Times-News, Twin Falls, Ohio, 1989-91; pvt. practice writer Twin Falls, 1991—. Co-founder Guidebookwriters.com. Author: Traveling the Oregon Trail, 1993, new edit., 2001, Traveling the Lewis and Clark Trail, 1994, 3d edit., 2003, Idaho Off The Beaten Path, 1998, new edit., 2002, Texas (Lonely Planet), 1999, 2d edit., 2002, British Columbia (Lonely Planet), 2001; contbr. articles to nat. publs. Recipient 1st place for mag. writing Idaho Press Club, 1992, 1st place for guidebook Nat. Assn. for Interpretation, 1993. Mem. Am. Soc. Journalists and Authors, Soc. Am. Travel Writers, Lewis and Clark Trail Heritage Found., Oreg.-Calif. Trail Assn. Unitarian Universalist. Avocations: kayaking, travel, reading, arts, hiking. Home and Office: Fanselow Comm 1511 9th Ave E Twin Falls ID 83301-6611

FANTIN, ARLINE MARIE, state legislator; b. Hammond, Ind., Sept. 26, 1937; Ill. state rep. Dist. 29, 1995-99; twp. assessor Thornton Twp., South Holland, Ill., 1994—. Address: Fantin State Rep 109 Foresdale Park Calumet City IL 60409-5309

FANTOZZI, PEGGY RYONE, geologist, environmental planner; b. Providence, Feb. 2, 1948; d. Eugene Baker and Cynthia (Bragg) Ryone; m. Thomas Allen Collins, Jan. 4, 1969 (div. 1985); children: Christin, Cindi; m. Thomas Edward Fantozzi, Mar. 22, 1985 (div. 1989); 1 child, Amy. BA in Earth Scis., Bridgewater State Coll., 1969; MS in Geology, Franklin and Marshall Coll., 1971. Registered sanitarian, Mass.; cert. wastewater treatment operator grade 4-M; cert. soil evaluator. Project mgr. Coastal Zone Mgmt. Grant, Eastham, Mass., 1980-81; geologist, project mgr. BSC Group/Cape Cod, Barnstable Village, Mass., 1982-88; sr. environ. scientist A.M. Wilson Assocs., Osterville, 1988-94, Daylor Consulting Group, Braintree, Mass., 1994-97. Instr. earth scis. and geology Bridgewater (Mass.) State Coll., 1972-74, Cape Cod C.C., West Barnstable, Mass., 1979-82; cons. conservation and health bds. Town of Bourne, Mass., 1984-85; mem., chair State Comm. for the Conservation of Soil, Water and Related Resources, 1996—; mem. Nat. Resources Conservation and Devel. Coun., 1998. Bd. dirs., v.p. Assn. for Preservation of Cape Cod, Orleans, Mass., 1979-85; bd. trustees Cape Cod Mus. Natural History, Brewster, 1982-85; advisor Barnstable County Marine Resources program, 1980-82; chmn. Eastham Conservation Commn., 1978-82, Selectmen's Task Force on Local Pollution, Bourne, 1985-87; del. Barnstable County Water Resources Adv. Coun., 1979-89, Bourne Shore and Harbor Com., 1989-92; rep. Tri-Town Septage treatment Facilities Planning Commn., Eastham, Orleans, citizen's adv. com. groundwater discharge program Mass. Dept. EPA, 1987-88, Surface Water Quality, 1990, 93, Mass. Bays Program [illegible] Com., [illegible], pres. Mass. Assn. Conservation Dists., 1995-98; chair Mass. State Commn. for the Conservation of Soil, Water and Related Resources, 1998—. Grantee USDA-Natural Resources Conservation Svc., 1997-98. Mem. Nat. Assn. Conservation Dists. (dir.), Mass. Health Officers Assn., Mass. Water Works Assn., Monument Beach Civic Assn. Home: 25 Shore Rd Buzzards Bay MA 02532-5425 Office: Land Use Permitting 25 Shore Rd Bourne MA 02532-5425

FANUS, PAULINE RIFE, librarian; b. New Oxford, Pa., Feb. 14, 1925; d. Maurice Diehl and Bernice Edna (Gable) Rife; m. William Edward Fanus, June 20, 1944; children: Irene Weaver, Larry William, Daniel Diehl. BS, Pa. State U., 1945; MLS, Villanova U., 1961; postgrad., Temple U., 1986—. Periodical libr. Tex. Coll. Arts Industries, Kingville, 1945; tchr. nursery sch. Studio Sch., Wayne, Pa., 1953-55; libr. circulation, reference Franklin Inst., Phila., 1963-66; asst. libr. Ursinus Coll., Collegeville, Pa., 1966; catalog libr., instr. Eastern Coll., St. Davids, Pa., 1967-71; head libr. Agnes Irwin Sch., Rosemont, Pa., 1971-93, head libr. emeritus, 1993—. Book reviewer The Book Report. Mem. AAUP (chpt. sec. Eastern Coll. 1970-71). Home: 78 Holly Dr New Holland PA 17557-9476

FARACI, DIANA, social worker, department chairman; b. Glen Cove, N.Y., June 4, 1957; d. William George and Violet Ann (Germano) Faraci, Albert Kenyon (Stepfather). MS in Biology, C.W. Post Coll., Greenvale, N.Y., 1984; MSW, Adelphi Sch. Social Work, Garden City, N.Y., 1987; BS in Metaphysics, Am. Inst. Holistic Theology, Youngstown, Ohio, 1997, MS in Metaphysics, 1999. Diplomate Am. Psychotherapy Assn., 1998, RCSW 1994. Rsch. asst., biology Sch. Nursing, Balt., 1984—86; clin. social worker Epilepsy Found. DTP, Garden City, NY, 1987—90, Social Svc. Dept., Assn. Help of Retarded Children (Article 16), Nassau County, NY, 1990—94, Assn. Help of Retarded Children (Article 16), Nassau County, NY, 1994—98, dept. head, 1998—. Sexuality educator Association for Help of Retarded Children, Nassau County chpt., Brookville, Freeport, Plainview, NY, 1995—, orientation trainer, 1995—; presenter, sexuality and mentally retarded population, NY, 1998—; co-author, instr. Sexuality Assessment Questionnaire, 1995, Sexuality Consent Determination, 1998; author, instr. Healthy Boundaries tng. curriculum, 2001. Mem., supporter Teach Tolerance Program Southern Poverty Law Ctr., Montgomery, Ala., 1995—, Hale House, N.Y.C., 1995—. Mem.: NASW, Am. Psychotherapy Assn., Nat. Assn. Devel. Disabilities. Avocations: photography, travel, metaphysics. Office: AHRC 230 Hanse Ave Freeport NY 11520

FARBER, JACKIE, editor; b. Jersey City, Apr. 16, 1927; d. Herman B. and Pauline (Birnbaum) Levine; m. Samuel Farber, June 25, 1950 (div. 1981); children: Thomas Adam, John David; m. 2d Jay Topkis, Sept. 27, 1981. BA, Smith Coll., 1949. Editor Bernard Geis Assocs., N.Y.C., 1963-72; sr. editor Delacorte Press, N.Y.C., 1972-74, exec. editor, 1980-81, editor-in-chief, 1981-89, fiction editor, 1989—; sr. editor William Morrow, N.Y.C., 1974-78, Random House, N.Y.C., 1978-80; fiction editor Delacorte Press div. Bantam Doubleday Dell Pub. Group, 1980-91; v.p., fiction editor Delacorte Press divsn. Bantam Doubleday Dell Pub. Group, 1991—. Mem. Women's Media Group, Columbia Golf and Country Club. Jewish. Home: 155 E 72nd St New York NY 10021-4371 Office: Bantam Doubleday Dell Pub Co 1540 Broadway Ste 9E New York NY 10036-4040

FARBER, ROSANN ALEXANDER, geneticist, educator; b. Charlotte, N.C., Nov. 21, 1944; d. J. Wilson Jr. and June Adell (Childs) Alexander; m. Gerald Lee Farber, July 28, 1966 (div. Jan. 1969); m. Thomas Douglas Petes, July 20, 1973; children: Laura Elizabeth Petes, Diana Christine Petes. AB in Biology, Oberlin Coll., 1966; postgrad., U. Pitts., 1967-68, Albert Einstein Coll. Medicine, 1969; PhD in Genetics, U. Wash., 1973. Diplomate in clin. cytogenetics and clin. molecular genetics Am. Bd. Med. Genetics. Postdoctoral fellow Nat. Inst. for Med. Rsch., London, 1973-75; rsch. assoc. Children's Hosp. Med. Ctr., Boston, 1975-77; from asst. prof. to assoc. prof. U. Chgo., 1977-88; assoc. prof. dept. pathology and lab. medicine, program molecular biology and biotechnology, curriculum genetics and molecular biology U. N.C., Chapel Hill, 1988-97, prof., 1997—, prof. dept. genetics, 2001—. Mem. U. N.C. Lineberger Comprehensive Cancer Ctr., 1996—. Contbr. articles to profl. jours. NIH grantee, 1978—. Mem. AAAS, Am. Soc. Human Genetics. Achievements include research in human molecular genetics, somatic cell genetics, cancer genetics. Home: 612 Morgan Creek Rd Chapel Hill NC 27517-4928 Office: U N C CB 7525 Brinkhous-Bullitt Bldg Chapel Hill NC 27599

FARBMAN, RUTH ELLEN, lawyer; b. N.Y.C., July 1, 1935; d. Leon and Clara (Gersman) Shacknow; divorced; children: Leon Edward, Caroline Barbara, S. Peter. BA magna cum laude, Smith Coll., 1956; MA, Northwestern U., Evanston, Ill., 1972; JD, Northwestern U., Chgo., 1987. Claims rep., field rep. supr. Social Security Adminstrn., U.S. Dept. HEW, N.Y.C., 1957-63; assoc. Eich & Franklin, Chgo., 1987-95. Cert. arbitrator Cook County Arbitration Bd., Chgo., 1993—; mem. social security disability project Northwestern U. Law Sch., Chgo., 1986-87. Pres. bd. dirs. Probation Support Sys., Evanston. Mem. AAUW, Chgo. Bar Assn., Woman's Bar Assn. Democrat. Jewish. Avocations: trekking, camping, cycling, theater, reading. Home: 2 E Oak St Apt 3604 Chicago IL 60611-6203

FARCI, PATRIZIA, medical educator, researcher; b. Villasimius, Italy, Feb. 2, 1954; came to U.S., 1989; d. Miniato and Eleonora (Scuda) F.; m. Paolo Lusso; 1 child, Emanuele. MD, U. Cagliari, Italy, 1979, cert. infectious diseases, 1983, cert. gastroenterology, 1987. Intern in internal medicine U. Cagliari, 1979-83, asst. prof., 1984-92, head hepatology sect., 1985—, assoc. prof. medicine, 1992—2000, prof. medicine, 2000—. Vis. scientist Free Hosp., London, 1983-85, Lab. of Infectious Diseases/NIAID/NIH, Bethesda, Md., 1989-96; adj. investigator LID/NIAID/NIH, Bethesda, 1997—. Contbr. more than 145 articles to profl. jours. Mem. Am. Assn. for the Study of Liver Diseases. Roman Catholic. Avocations: music, reading, travel. Office: LID NIAID/NIH Bldg 50 Rm 6531 9000 Rockville Pike Bethesda MD 20892-0001 also: Dept Med Scis U Cagliari ss 554 Bivio Sestu 09042 Cagliari Italy Fax: +39-070-510064. E-mail: farcip@pacs.unica.it.

FARENTHOLD, FRANCES TARLTON, lawyer; b. Corpus Christi, Tex., Oct. 2, 1926; d. Benjamin Dudley and Catherine (Bluntzer) Tarlton; children: Dudley Tarlton, George Edward, Emilie, James Doughterty, Vincent Bluntzer (dec.). AB, Vassar Coll., 1946; JD, U. Tex., 1949; LLD, Hood Coll., 1973, Boston U., 1973, Regis Coll., 1976, Lake Erie Coll., 1979, Elmira Coll., 1981, Coll. Santa Fe, 1985. Bar: Tex. 1949. Pvt. practice, 1949-65, 67-76, 80—; mem. Tex. Ho. of Reps., 1968-72; dir. legal aid Nueces County, 1965-67; pres. Wells Coll., Aurora, N.Y., 1976-80; asst. prof. law Tex. So. U., Houston, Thurgood Marshall disting. vis. prof., 1994-95. Lawyer; b. Corpus Christi, Tex., Oct. 2, 1926; d. Benjamin Dudley and Catherine (Bluntzer) Tarlton; children: Dudley Tarlton, George Edward, Emilie, James Doughterty, Vincent Bluntzer (dec.). AB, Vassar Coll., 1946; JD, U. Tex., 1949; LLD, Hood Coll., 1973, Boston U., 1973, Regis Coll., 1976, Lake Erie Coll., 1979, Elmira Coll., 1981, Coll. of Santa Fe, 1985. Bar: Tex. 1949. Pvt. practice, 1949-65, 67-76, 80—; mem. Tex. Ho. of Reps., 1968-72; dir. legal aide Nueces County, 1965-67; asst. prof. law Tex. So. U., Houston; pres. Wells Coll., Aurora, N.Y., 1976-80; disting. vis. prof. Thurgood Marshall Tex. So. U., Houston, 1994-95. Mem. Human Relations Com., Corpus Christi, 1963-68, Corpus Christi Citizen's Com. Community Improvement, 1966-68; mem. Tex. adv. com. to U.S. Commn. on Civil Rights, 1968-76; mem. nat. adv. council ACLU; mem. Orgn. for Preservation Unblemished Shoreline, 1964—; Dem. candidate for Gov. of Tex., 1972; del. Dem. Nat. Conv., 1972, 1st woman nominated to be candidate v.p. U.S., 1972; nat. co-chmn. Citizens to Elect McGovern-Shriver, 1972; chmn. Nat. Women's Polit. Caucus, 1973-75; mem. Dem. platform com., 1988; trustee Vassar Coll., 1975-83; bd. dirs. Fund for Constl. Govt., Ctr. for [illegible] Policy, [illegible] Mexican Am. Legal [illegible] chmn. Inst. for Policy Studies, 1986-91; mem. bd. dirs. Rothko Chapel, 1997—. Recipient Lyndon B. Johnson Woman of Year award, 1973. Mem. State Bar Tex. Mem. Human Rels. Com., Corpus Christi, 1963-68, Corpus Christi Citizens Com. Cmty. Improvement, 1966-68; mem. Tex. adv. com. to U.S. Commn. on Civil Rights, 1968-76; mem. nat. adv. coun. ACLU; mem. Orgn. for Preservation Unblemished Shoreline, 1964—; Dem. candidate for Gov. of Tex., 1972; del. Dem. Nat. Conv., 1972, 1st woman nominated to be candidate v.p. U.S., 1972; nat. co-chair Citizens to elect McGovern-Shriver, 1972; chmn. Nat. Women's Polit. Caucus, 1973-75; mem. Dem. Platform Com., 1988; trustee Vassar Coll., 1975-83; bd. dirs. Fund for Constl. Govt., Ctr. for Devel. Policy, 1983—, Mexican Am. Legal Def. and Ednl. Fund, 198--83; chmn. Inst. for Policy Studies, 1986-91; bd. dirs. Rothko Chapel, 1997—, chmn., 2001—. Recipient Lyndon B. Johnson Woman of Yr. award, 1973, Lifetime Svc. award Dem. Party of Tex., 1998. Mem. State Bar Tex. Office: 2929 Buffalo Speedway Apt 1813 Houston TX 77098-1710

FARGO, HEATHER, mayor; b. Oakland, Ca, Dec. 12, 1952; m. Alan Moll. BS in environmental planning and mgmt., U. Cal-Davis, 1975. Mem. Sacramento City Coun., 1989—98; mayor City of Sacramento, Calif., 2001—. Office: City Hall 730 I St Ste 321 Sacramento CA 95814 E-mail: hfargo@cityofsacramento.org.

FARGO, SUSAN C. state legislator; BA, Northwestern U.; MAT, MPA, Harvard U. Mem. 5th Dist. Mass. Senate, Boston, 1997—, mem. senate ethics com., mem. edn., arts, and humanities, mem. election laws com., chairperson local affairs com. Selectman Town of Lincoln; mem. adv. bd. Town of Middlesex, exec. com.; bd. dirs. Mass. Housing Partnership, Low-Level Radioactive Waste Mgmt. Bd. Mem. Mass. Aubudon Soc., LWV, Phi Beta Kappa. Democrat. Office: Mass Senate State House Rm 504 Boston MA 02133

FARHATT, KENDRA, travel company executive; b. Belleville, Ill.., May 3, 1981; d. Charles Kenneth and Sherrill Dustine Worley; m. Anthony Thomas Farhatt, Aug. 6, 2003; 1 child, Wesley. BA in Mktg. with departmental honors, Webster U., 2003. Sales and mktg. Intrav/USAA, St. Louis, 2003—. Avocations: photography, poetry, camping. Office: USAA Cruise Travel Westline Industrial Saint Louis MO 63146

FARINA, LAURA, lawyer; b. Trenton, N.J., Aug. 29, 1961; d. Charles Anthony and Regina Rose (Alvino) F. BA, Georgetown U., 1983; postgrad., NYU, 1985; JD, Rutgers U., 1988. Bar: N.J. 1988, N.Y. 1990, D.C. 1991, U.S. Dist. Ct. N.J. 1988, U.S. Dist. Ct. (so. and ea. dists.) N.Y. 1990. Law clk. to Hon. Justice Gary S. Stein N.J. Supreme Ct., Hackensack, 1988-89; assoc. Paul, Weiss, Rifkind, Wharton & Garrison, N.Y.C., 1989-91; dep. atty. gen. Office of N.J. Atty. Gen., Trenton, 1991-92; assoc. Crummy, Del Deo, Dolan, Griffinger & Vecchione, Newark, 1992-95; pvt. practice Princeton, N.J., 1995—. Barrister Am. Inn. of Ct., New Brunswick, N.J., 1993-94, 97—. Articles editor Rutgers Law Rev., 1986-88. V.p. Princeton Day Sch. Alumni Bd., 1993—; alumni interviewer Alumni Admissions Program, Georgetown U., Princeton, 1984—. N.J. Bar Found. scholar, 1987-88. Avocations: running, tennis, music, skiing.

FARINELLI, JEAN L. public relations executive; b. Phila., July 26, 1946; d. Albert J. and Edith M. (Falini) F. BA, Am. U., Washington, 1968; MA, Ohio State U., Columbus, 1969. Asst. pub. relations dir. Dow Jones & Co., Inc., N.Y.C., 1969-71; account exec. Carl Byoir & Assocs., Inc., N.Y.C., 1972-74, v.p., 1974-80, sr. v.p., 1980-82; pres. Tracy-Locke/BBDO Pub. Relations, Dallas, 1982-87, Creamer Dickson Basford, Inc., N.Y.C., 1987-88, chmn., chief exec. officer, 1988-98; pres., chief exec. officer Eurocom Corp. & PR (U.S.), 1991, Corp. Graphics, Inc., 1992; pres. Farinelli Cons. Group, LLC, 1999—. Dir. The Cologne Life Reinsurance Co., 1997-99. Recipient PR CaseBook, PR Reporter, N.H., 1984, Silver Spur, Tex. Pub. Rels. Assn., Dallas, 1985, Matrix award Women in Comms., 1993. Mem.: Nat. Found. for Infectious Diseases (former trustee), Arthur W. Page Soc. (treas., v.p. adminstrn. and fin.), Internat. Pub. Rels. Assn. (pub. rels. seminar), Nat. Investor Rels. Inst., The Women's Forum (bd. dirs.), Women in Comms. (chmn. 1995, dir. 1999—, Matrix award 1993), Pub. Rels. Soc. Am. (Silver Anvil awards chmn. 1987, acad. exec. bd. 1990—91, trustee found., Silver Anvil award 1980—81, 1985, Excalibur award Houston chpt. 1985, Best of Show Silver Anvil award 1998). Office: 20 Sutton Pl S New York NY 10022-4165

FARKAS, NANCY A. realtor; b. Chgo., Sept. 4, 1944; d. James and Lillian Cafouros; m. Charles B. Farkas, Oct. 20, 1972 (div. June 25, 1981). BA, Vassar Coll., 1966. Leadership tng. grad., cert. residential specialist, grad. Real Estate Inst., accredited buyer rep., E cert., cert. USAA. Asst. buyer, buyer Carson Pirie Scott, Chgo., 1971—80; buyer, divisional merchandise mgr. Marshall Fields, Chgo., 1981—89; divisional merchandise mgr. Rich's, Atlanta, 1990; v.p., divisional merchandise mgr. Robinson's, L.A., 1991; v.p. Duty Free Shoppers, San Francisco, 1992—96; v.p., divisional merchandise mgr. Elder Brerman, Dayton, Ohio, 1997; realtor Prudential Residenz, Realtors, Dayton, 1998—. Trustee Dayton Pub. Radio, 1998—2003; mem. consumer adv. bd. Dorothy Lane Markets, Dayton, 1999—2002; mem. adminstrv. bd. Normandy United Meth. Ch., Dayton, 1999—2003; bd. dirs. Dayton Opera Guild, 2003, Am. Inst. Food and Wine, Dayton, 1999—2003. Recipient Award of Excellence, Ohio Assn. Realtors, 1999—2002. Mem.: Dayton Area Bd. Realtors (mem. grievance com. 2002—03, Award of Excellence 1999—2002), Women's Coun. Realtors (pres. 2003—04). Methodist. Avocations: travel, theater, ballet, opera, gourmet food and wine. Home: 1623 Olde Haley Dr Dayton OH 45458 Office: Prudential Residenz Realtors 7265 Far Hills Ave Dayton OH 45459 E-mail: nancyfarkas@realtor.com.

FARLEY, CAROLE, soprano; b. Le Mars, Iowa, Nov. 29, 1946; d. Melvin and Irene (Reid) F.; m. Jose Serebrier, Mar. 29, 1969; 1 dau., Lara Adriana Francesca. MusB, Ind. U., 1968. Fulbright scholar Hochschule für Musik, Munich, 1968-69. (Musician of Month, Musical Am./Hi Fidelity 1977), Am. debut at Town Hall, N.Y.C., 1969, Paris debut, Nat. Orch., 1975, London debut, Royal Philharmonic Soc., 1975, S.Am. debut, Teatro Colon, Philharmonic Orch., Buenos Aires, 1975; soloist with, major Am. and European symphony orchs., 1970—, soloist, Welsh Nat. Opera, 1971, 72, Cologne Opera, 1972-75, Phila. Lyric Opera, 1974, Brussels Opera, 1972, Lyon Opera, 1976, 77, Strasbourg Opera, 1975, Linz Opera, 1969, N.Y.C. Opera, 1976, New Orleans Opera, 1977, Cin. Opera, 1977, Met. Opera Co., N.Y.C., 1977—, Zurich Opera, 1979, Chgo. Lyric Opera, 1981, Can. Opera Co., 1980, Düsseldorf Opera, 1980, 81, 84, Palm Beach Opera, 1982, Theatre Mcpl. Paris, 1983, Theatre Royale dela Monnaie Brussels, 1983, Teatro Regio, Turin, Italy, 1983, Nice Opera (France), 1984, 86, 87, 88, Cologne Opera, 1985, Teatro Comunale, Florence, Italy, 1985, BBC Opera, 1987, TeatroColon, Buenos Aires, 1987, 88, 89, Opera de Montpellier (France), 1988, 94, Theatre des Champs Elysees, Paris, 1988, Helsinki Festival, 1989, Tchaikovsky Opera Arias Pickwick/IMP Records, 1993, Met. Opera Premiere Shostakovich Opera Lady Macbeth of Mtzensk, 1994, Theatre Capitole de Toulouse Wozzeck, 1994, internat. tour with Nat. Chamber Orchestra of Toolouse, 2003; on New Zealand Broadcasting Commn. Orchestral Tour, 1986; TV film for ABC Australia La Voix Humaine, also co-producer compact disc and video for BBC, London, 1990; co-producer compact disc and video The Telephone, 1990; recorded compact disc Weill, 1992, Metro. Opera Shostakovich: "Lady Macbeth", 1994, Strausslieder with Czech Philharmonic, 1995, Les Soldats Morts, 1995 (Grand Prix du Disque); recorded for Deutsche Gramophone (Diapason d'or prize 1997), Chandos, CBS, BBC, ASV, RCA, Ricercar and Varese-Sarabande records, London/Decca Records, IMP Masters, Pickwick; new CD Naxos: Selected Songs Ned Rorem, 2001, The Songs of Ernesto Lecuona For Bis Records, 2003; Argentine premier Bomarzo by Alberto Finastera, Teatro Colón Buenos Aires, 2003. Recipient Abiati prize for her role as Lulu, Italy, 1984, Deutsche Schallplatten award for recording Carole Farley Sings French Songs, 1988; named Alumni of Year, U. Ind., 1976. Mem. Am. Guild Mus. Artists. Home: 270 Riverside Dr New York NY 10025-5209 E-mail: caspi123@aol.com.

FARLEY, CAROLYN JUANITA, music educator; b. Cleve., Oct. 25, 1963; d. Christopher and Minnie (Zell) Phillips; m. Sam Winkfield, Nov. 27, 1987 (div. July 15, 1992); m. Michael Alan Farley, June 22, 1996; children: Marilyn, Michael Alan Jr.; 1 stepchild, Arline. MusB, Cleve. State U., 1988, MusM in Choral Conducting, 1994. Cert. tchr. music K-12 Ohio, Orff I music tchr., Kodaly I music tchr. Piano tchr. Rainey Inst. Music, Cleve., 1977—96, Murtis Taylor, Cleve., 1982—90, E. End Neighborhood House Settlement Music Sch., Cleve., 1988—95; music tchr. K-6 Elyria (Ohio) Bd. Edn., 1989—90; minister of music Cornerstone Bapt. Ch., Cleve.; coord. music Mt. Pleasant United Meth. Ch., Cleve., 2000—; music tchr. 7-12, k-3 Beachwood (Ohio) Bd. Edn., 1990—. Workshop clinician Annointed Ministries, Cleve., 1990—94. Composer: (songs) Prince of Peace, 1994 (Anointed, 1994). Mem. Dem. Nat. Com., 1990—2000. Recipient Creative award, Annointed Ministries, 1994. Mem.: Kindermusik Internat., Musicians United to Stay in Contact, Black Gospel Musicians' Exchange (birthday coord. 1999—). Democrat. Methodist. Avocations: guitar, bass, flute, composing. Home: 2782 Richmond Rd Beachwood OH 44122 Office: Beachwood Bd Edn 24601 Fairmont Blvd Beachwood OH 44122 E-mail: cjf@bw.beachwood.k-12.ohio.us.

FARLEY, MARGARET WILHELMINA, librarian; b. Hallam, Nebr., June 29, 1919; d. Benjamin Wilhelm Buhrmann and Wilhelmina Talena Asseln-Buhrmann; m. Cecil Morgan McClouston, July 9, 1945 (dec. Jan. 1951); m. Robert Laverne Farley, Apr. 29, 1954 (dec. Sept. 9, 1992). Student, U. Nebr., 1936—39; diploma, Pepin Acad. Fashion, 1940; student, Mt. San Antonio Coll., 1986, Calif. State U., 1986—90. Spl. diets State Mental Hosp., Lincoln, Nebr., 1939—40; sewing, alterations Dayton Dept. Store, Mpls., 1940—41; inspector (WWII) New Brighton Cartridge, 1941—43; art dir. Internat. Inst., St. Paul, 1943—45; libr. L.A. County Libr., Downey, 1959—80; children's libr. in charge cataloging La Crecenta (Calif.) Pub. Libr. Mem.: Rep. Women Federated, Antelope Valley Allied Arts Assn., Rep. Women, Palmdale Women's Club, Newcomers Club. Avocations: art, gardening, sewing. Home: 4326 Avoca Ave Palmdale CA 93552

FARLEY, PEGGY ANN, finance company executive; b. Phila., Mar. 12, 1947; d. Harry F. and Ruth (Lloyd) F.; m. Reid McIntyre, Dec. 31, 1985 (div.); 1 child, Margaret Ruth Farley. AB, Barnard Coll., 1970; MA with honors, Columbia U., 1972. Admissions officer Barnard Coll., N.Y.C., 1973-76; adminstr. Citibank NA, Athens, Greece, 1976-77; cons. Orgn. Resources Counselors, N.Y.C., 1977-78; sr. assoc. Morgan Stanley and Co. Inc., N.Y.C., 1978-84; mng. dir., CEO AMAS Securities Inc., N.Y.C., 1984-90, also bd. dirs. AMAS Securities Inc., N.Y.C.; pres., CEO Ascent Asset Mgmt. Adv. Svc., Inc., N.Y.C., 1998-99. Pres., CEO, bd. dirs. Ascent/Meredith Asset Mgmt. Inc., N.Y.C., 1999—, Ascent/Meredith Portfolio Mgmt. Inc., N.Y.C., 1999—; bd. dirs. Robert R. Meredith & Co. Inc., N.Y.C.; partner Ascent Med. Tech. Fund, 1999-; mng. dir. Ascent Pvt. Equilty, 1999-, Ascent Capital Adv., 2001-. Author: The Place Of The Yankee And Euro Bond Markets In A Financing Program For The People's Republic of China, 1982, Ascent Quar. Rev. Mem. Columbia U. Seminar on China-U.S. Bus. Mem. China Inst., Fgn. Policy Assn., Met. Club, Econ. Club of N.Y. Republican. Presbyterian. Avocations: gardening, film, swimming. Home: 908 Owassa Rd Newton NJ 07860-4015 Office: Ascent/Meredith Asset Mgmt Inc 712 5th Ave New York NY 10019-4108 E-mail: pfarley@amam.net.

FARMER, ANN DAHLSTROM, English language educator; b. South Gate, Calif., June 18, 1934; d. Merrill Xanthus and Marcia Hazel (Ross) Dahlstrom; m. Roger Lee Chandler, Aug. 19, 1956 (div. 1960); 1 child, Mark Walton Chandler; m. Malcolm French Farmer, Oct. 25, 1963. BA, Whittier Coll., 1956, MA, 1971, Calif. State U., Fullerton, 1976. Prof.'s asst. Whittier (Calif.) Coll., 1960-62, gen. studies instr., 1963-70, English instr., 1970-72, dir. freshman English, 1972-87, dir. English lang. prog. for internat. students, 1978-86, asst. prof. English, 1983-95, assoc. prof. English, 1995—99. Author: Jessamyn West, rev. edit., 1996; co-author: Jessamyn West: A Descriptive and Annotated Bibliography, 1998, Creative Analysis, rev. edit., 1978. Mem.: Linguistic Soc., Western Lit. Assn., AAUW (gift honoree 1995, Las Distinguidas award 2003), Whittier Hist. Soc. (sec. 2000—), Friends of the Shannon Ctr. at Whittier Coll. (Bookfaire co-chair 2000—, v.p. 2002—, Dorothea S. Boyd award 2001), Phi Kappa Phi, Delta Kappa Gamma (Star in Edn. 1990). Democrat. Mem. Soc. Of Friends. Avocations: dollhouse miniatures, rubber stamps, antiques, family history, cats. E-mail: Farmer6146@yahoo.com.

FARMER, CORNELIA GRIFFIN, lawyer, consultant, hearings official; b. NYC, Mar. 3, 1945; d. John Bastin and Elizabeth McCue (Sussman) Griffin; m. William Paul Farmer, Jan. 8, 1972; children: Suzanne Elizabeth, John Paul. BA, Mt. Holyoke Coll., 1967; M in Regional Planning, Cornell U., 1970; JD, Marquette U., 1978. Bar: Wis. 1978, Pa. 1981, Minn. 1996, Oreg. 1999, Ill. 2002. Planner Frederick P. Clark Assoc., Rye, N.Y., 1970-71, Tri State Regional Planning Com., N.Y.C., 1971-72, State of Wis. and City of Milw., 1973-75; assoc. Friebert & Finerty, Milw., 1978-80, Baskin & Sears, Pitts., 1981-82; cons. County of Allegheny, Pitts., 1983; adj. faculty U. Pitts., 1986-94; jud. law clk. Commonwealth Ct. of Pa., Pitts., 1992-95; pvt. practice Mpls., 1996—99; staff atty., hearings ofcl. Lane Coun. Govts., Eugene, Oreg., 1999—2001. Vic-chmn. loan monitoring com. Pitts. Countywide Corp., 1981—87; child adv. Allegheny County Pro Bono Program, Pitts., 1986—92; mediator Dispute Resolution Ctr., St. Paul, 1998—99; adj. faculty U. Wis., Milw., 1978—79. Book reviewer, referee books and articles. Vol. polit. campaigns Milw., Pitts., Mpls., Chgo., and Eugene, 1972-2004; trustee Falk Sch. Fund; v.p. PTA Falk Lab. Sch. U. Pitts., 1985-89; ct. monitor abuse cases WATCH, Mpls., 1996-99; vol. WITS tutoring and mentoring program, 2002-, SMART, Eugene, Oreg. Mem. ABA, APA, Chgo. Bar Assn., Silver Bay Assn. Coun., Mt. Holyoke Coll. Alumnae Assn. (alumnae vol.). Mt. Holyoke Club Pitts. (past pres., treas.).

FARMER, JANENE ELIZABETH, artist, educator; b. Albuquerque, Oct. 16, 1946; d. Charles John Watt and Regina Mortimere (Brown) Kruger; m. Michael Hugh Bolton, Apr. 1965 (div.); m. Frank Urban Farmer, May 1972 (div.). BA in Art, San Diego State U., 1969; postgrad., U. San Diego, San Diego State U., U. Calif., San Diego, 1983—85. Owner, operator Iron Walrus Pottery, 1972-79. Tchr. Cath. schs., San Diego, 1983—86, Ramona Unified Sch. Dist., 1986—, mentor tchr., 1994—98, cons. tchr., 2001—03; tchr. environ. art San Diego Natural History Mus., 1996—97, San Diego Wild Animal Park, 1996; resident artist, instr. ext. dept. U. Calif., San Diego, 2003. Exhibited in group shows at San Diego Mus. Art, San Diego City Adminstrn. Bldg., Univ. City Libr., San Diego, Art Scene Gallery, Kauai, Hawaii, Am. Soc. Interior Designers, San Diego, Sierra Club Bookstore, Quail Bot. Gardens, Encinitas, Calif. Mem. Coronado Arts and Humanities Coun., 1979—81; mem. edn. adv. com. La Jolla (Calif.) Playhouse, 1996; mem. edn. com. Calif. Wolf Ctr., 1999—2001. Grantee, Calif. Arts Coun., 1980—81. Roman Catholic. Home: # 35 4435 Nobel Dr San Diego CA 92122-1559 Office Phone: 858-450-3041. E-mail: farmerj4@earthlink.net.

FARMER, MARTHA LOUISE, retired college administrator; b. Cin. d. William S. and Genevieve (Fye) Farmer. BA, Wheaton Coll., 1935; postgrad., Wellesley Coll., 1936; MA, Columbia U., 1937, EdD, 1956. Assoc. prof. Manhattanville Coll. Sacred Heart, 1936-43, 46-48; adminstr. dept. student life City Coll., CUNY, 1948-69, prof., coord. dept. student pers. svcs., 1969-75, cons. student pers. svcs. for adults in higher edn., 1975—. Vis. prof. Grad. Sch. Edn., N.Y. U., 1967-69; cons. student personnel services for adults in higher edn., 1975— . Editor: Student Pers. Svcs. For Adults in Higher Edn., 1967, Counseling Svcs. for Adults in Higher Edn., 1971. Mem. mgmt. com. Emma Ransom YWCA, N.Y.C., 1958, mem. resident com., 1956-58; mem. jr. high teens com. YWCA, Ridgewood, N.J., 1962-75; mem. N.J. com. U.S. Commn. on Civil Rights, trustee Hispanic Commn. on Alcoholism in N.J. Served as lt. USNR (W), 1943-46. Recipient Bernard Reed award, 1963, 85-86, Winifred Fisher award, 1974. Mem. Am. Coll. Pers. Assn. (program com. 1960-62, mem. com. I, 1963-65, chmn. Com. XIII 1965-67, mem. Com. IV 1968-72), Am. Pers. and Guidance Assn., Assn. U. Evening Colls. (coms. 1961-72), U.S. Assn. Evening Students (chmn. bd. trustees 1970-71, hon. life trustee 1975—), Evening Student Pers. Assn. (pres. 1962-63), Adult Student Pers. Assn. (chmn. bd. trustees 1968-71, hon. life trustee 1975—). Home: 348 Lake St Upper Saddle River NJ 07458-1750

FARMER, NANCY, state official; b. Jacksonville, Ill., 1956; m. Darrell Hartke. Grad., Ill. Coll., 1979. Exec. dir. Skinker-DeBaliviere Cmty. Coun.; state rep. dist. 64 Mo. Ho. of Reps., 1993—2001; asst. treas. State of Mo., 1997—2001, treas., 2001—. Mem. Woman's Polit. Caucus Mo. Ho. of Reps.; dir. intergovernmental affairs City of St. Louis, 1997. Active Woman's Com. Forest Park, Rosedale Neighborhood Assn., mem. exec. com.; active West End Arts Coun.; cand. for Mo. U.S. Senator, 2004. Mem. Ctrl. West End Assn., Women Legislators Mo. Office: PO Box 210 Jefferson City MO 65102

FARMER, SUSAN LAWSON, broadcasting executive, former secretary of state; b. Boston, May 29, 1942; d. Ralph and Margaret (Tyng) Lawson; m. Malcolm Farmer, III, Apr. 6, 1968; children: Heidi Benson, Stephanie Lawson. Student, Garland Jr. Coll., 1960-61, Brown U., 1961-62. Mem. Providence Home Rule Charter Commn., 1979-80; sec. of state State of R.I., Providence, 1983-87; pres., CEO Sta. WSBE-TV R.I. PBS, Providence, 1987—. Spl. adv. R.I. Family Ct., 1978-83; mem. nat. voting stds. panel Fed. Election Commn. co-chmn. Nat. Voter Edn. Project; mem. electoral coll., 1984; chmn. Gov.'s Com. on Ethics in Govt., 1985-86; mem. teaching facility and adv. panel Internat. Ctr. on Election Law and Adminstrn.; mem. nat. edn. adv. com. Pub. Broadcasting System, 1987-89; trustee Eastern Ednl. TV Network, 1987-95; mem. R.I. Task Force on Tech., 1995—, R.I. Info. Mgmt. Commn., 1997; bd. dirs., mem. exec. com. Program Resources Group, 1993-2001; mem. Gov.'s Telecom. Task Force, 2000—; mem. nat. media adv. com. WomenFuture, 2002--. Bd. dirs. Justice Resources Corp., Marathon House, Inc., R.I. Council Alcoholism, R.I. Hist. Soc., Planned Parenthood (R.I. chpt.), R.I. Rape Crisis Ctr., The Newport Inst.; mem. Mayor's Task Force on Child Abuse, R.I. Film Commn.; v.p. Miriam Hosp. Found.; mem. adv. com. Women in Polit. and Govtl. Careers Program, U. R.I., 1985—; mem. adv. bd. Com. for Study of Am. Electorate-Ford Found. Project-Efficacy in State Voting Laws, 1986; mem. Commn. to Study Length of Election Process, 1985-87; steering com. Nat. Fund for America's Future, Project Vote R.I.; bd. dirs. Dawn for Children Tng. Thru Placement; pres. R.I. PBS Found.; bd. dirs. R.I. Anti-Drug Coalition Exec. Com., Nat. Forum for Pub. TV Execs., 1998-2004, chmn., 1999. Named Woman of Yr., Nat. Women's Polit. Caucus, 1980. Mem. LWV, NATAS (bd. govs. New Eng. chpt. 1995—), N.E. Assn. Schs. and Colls. (com. on tech. and course instns.), So. Ednl. Comms. Assn. (bd. dirs. 1993-96), R.I. Women's Polit. Caucus (Woman of Yr. 1980), Bus. and Profl. Women (Woman of Yr. 1984), Common Cause, Save the Bay, Providence Preservation Soc., Orgn. State Broadcasting Execs, Agawam Hunt Club, Mill Reef Club (Antigua, West Indies), Nat. Assn. of Ams. Pub. TV Stas. (trustee 1996-2002), Nat. Acad. TV Arts and Scis. (bd. govs. N.E. chpt. 1995-2001), Nat. Ednl. Telecomms. Assn. (bd. dirs. 1997—, Nat. Forum Pub. TV Execs. (bd. dirs. 1998—, chmn. 1999). Home: 147 Lloyd Ave Providence RI 02906-1552 Office: RI PBS 50 Park Ln Providence RI 02907-3124 E-mail: sfarmer@RIpbs.org.

FARNATH, DOROTHY WHITMYER, recruitment company executive; b. Hammonton, N.J., Mar. 3, 1942; d. Theodore George and Dorothy Priest Whitmyer; children: Melissa Scott Ciliberti, Theodore George. BS in Med. Tech., U. Pa., 1964. Med. tech. Thomas Jefferson U. Medicine, Phila., 1966-69; supr. South Jersey Urology Assocs., Cherry Hill, N.J., 1977-84; supr., mgr. 227 Labs., Phila., 1984-88; pres. Dorothy Whitmyer Farnath & Assocs., Inc., Marlton, N.J., 1988—. Pres. Championship Family Restaurant, Trenton, N.J., 1995—; gen. mgr. GDV Enterprises, Trenton, 1995—; owner Hair Sta., Haddon Heights, N.J., 1994—; co-owner Hardshell Cafe, Marlton, N.J., 2000—. Mem. Rep. Nat. Com., Washington, 1994—. Mem. U.S. C. of C. Avocations: reading, genealogy. Office: 104 Centre Blvd Ste B Marlton NJ 08053-4130

FARNELL, MARY ANN, minister; b. Cambridge, Md., Oct. 18, 1935; d. William Elwood Murphy and Mary Elizabeth Brannock-Murphy; m. Robert Emmett Farnell III, July 20, 1934; children: Christopher Robin, Mark William. AA, Chesapeake Coll., 1992; postgrad., Wesley Seminary, 1994. Min. United Meth. Ch., Wingate, Md., 1987—94, Vienna, Md., 1994—. Chaplain Ruritan, Vienna, 1994—, Vienna Fire Co., 1994—, Md. State Fireman's Assn., Vienna, 2001—. Avocations: singing, reading, gardening. Home and Office: 2009 Rhodesdale Vienna Rd Vienna MD 21869

FARNEY, CHARLOTTE EUGENIA, musician, music educator; b. Long Beach, Calif., Jan. 06; d. Charles Thomas and Eugenia Moody (Fisher) Dalton; m. John Nathan Pierce, Aug. 1972 (div. 1978); m. Raymond C. Farney, June 30, 1990; stepchildren: Anna Louise, Paul Jerrod. AA, Orange Coast Coll., Costa Mesa, Calif., 1959; MusB, U. Redlands, 1962; MusM, Yale U., 1966; D of Musical Arts, U. Ariz., 1983. Std. secondary cert. tchg. music K-12 and Spanish Ariz. Cellist Denver Symphony Orch., 1966—69; instr. faculty trio West Tex. State U., Canyon, 1969—71; grad. tchg. asst. cello U. Ariz., Tucson, 1977—81; string orch./gen. music tchr. Tucson Unified Sch. Dist., 1979—90; string orch. tchr. Scottsdale (Ariz.) Unified Sch. Dist., 1995—2001, Washington Elem. Sch. Dist., Phoenix, 2001—; cellist Tucson Symphony Orch., 1977—90, Symphony of the West Valley, Sun City, Ariz., 1990—, String Sounds, Phoenix, 1994—99. Pvt. cello tchr., Denver, 1966—69; prin. first chair cellist Amarillo Symphony, Tex., 1969—71; cellist Symphony Orch., Toluca, Mexico, 1974—77; cello soloist Tucson Civic Orch., 1982; cons. in field. Author music revs. Asst. Sunday sch. tchr. Scholar, Yale U., 1963—66, Denver Symphony Guild, 1968, Tchrs. Performance Inst./Oberlin Coll., 1969, Blossom Music Sch., 1970. Mem.: Am. String Tchrs. Assn. (coach String Fling Phoenix chpt. 2000—02, coach Cellobration 2001—03), Sigma Alpha Iota (chaplain U. Redlands chpt 1960—61, Phoenix chpt. v.p. membership 1995—2001, Sword of Honor 1998, Rose of Honor 2000). Avocations: travel, swimming. Home: 6202 E Aster Dr Scottsdale AZ 85254

FARNHAM, KATHERINE A, music educator, vocalist; d. Dean A and Betty L Farnham; m. Pamir Kiciman. MusB summa cum laude, Berklee Coll. of Music, 1993—96; MusB, U. of Cin. Coll.-Conservatory of Music, 1991—93; MusM, U. of Miami Sch. of Music, 2002. Voice & piano faculty Boston Music Co., 1997, Sdoia-Satz Music Inst., Miami, Fla., 1997—2000; voice faculty Creative Workshops, Aventura, Fla., 2000—01; music theatre voice faculty New World Sch. of the Arts, Miami, Fla., 2001—03; dir. The Miracles of Hope Sch. for the Performing & Healing Arts, Hollywood, Fla., 2003—. Songwriter (albums) For the Love of it All, Songs from the Troubadour; singer (also songwriter and co-producer): (original words & music) Mosaic, Miami's theme song; songwriter (original words & music) Destiny (South Fla. Songwriter of the Yr., 2003); composer (producer): (contemporary musical) Age of the Jaguar. Recipient Performer/Songwriter Competition Winner, Berklee Coll. of Music, 1995; Mortar Bd. Scholarship for Leadership, U. of Cin. Coll.-Conservatory of Music, 1993. Mem.: Nat. Acad. of Rec. Arts & Sciences, NAFE, Am. Soc. of Composers, Authors & Publishers. Christian. Avocations: reading, movies, swimming, yoga, travel. Personal E-mail: kathfarnham@earthlink.net. E-mail: manager@katherinefarnham.com.

FARNSWORTH, ELIZABETH, broadcast journalist; b. Mpls., Dec. 23, 1943; d. H. Bernerd and Jane (Mills) Fink; m. Charles E. Farnsworth, June 20, 1966; children: Jennifer Farnsworth Fellows, Samuel. BA, Middlebury Coll., 1965; MA in History, Stanford U., 1966; LLD (hon.), Colby Coll., 2002. Reporter, panelist PBS World Press, KQED, San Francisco, 1975-77; reporter InterNews, Berkeley, Calif., 1977-80; freelance TV and print reporter, San Francisco, 1980-91; fgn. corr. MacNeil/Lehrer News Hour, San Francisco, 1991-95; chief corr., prin. substitute anchor News Hour with Jim Lehrer, Arlington, Va., 1995-97, San Francisco, 1997-99, sr. corr., 1999—. Co-author: El Bloqueo Invisible, 1974; prodr., dir. documentary Thanh's War, 1991 (Cine Golden Eagle award); contbr. articles to various publs. Mem. adv. bd. Berkeley Edn. Found., 1990-95, U. Calif. Sch. Journalism, Berkeley; mem. nat. adv. bd. Ctr. Investigative Reporting, 2001-; bd. dirs. Data Ctr., Oakland, Calif., 1993-95. Recipient Golden Gate award San Francisco Film Festival, 1984, Best Investigative Reporting award No. Calif. Radio, TV News Dirs.' Assn., 1986, Blue Ribbon, Am. Film and Video Festival, 1991, Silver World medal N.Y. Film Festivals, 2001; nominee Emmy award, 2002. Mem. AFTRA, NATAS, World Affairs Coun. No. Calif. (bd. dirs. 1998—), Nat. Adv. Writers Corps, Phi Beta Kappa. Presbyterian. Avocations: gardening, hiking, writing poetry.

FARON, FAY CHERYL, private investigator, writer; b. Kansas City, Mo. d. Albert David and Geraldine Fay (Morgan) F. Student, Glendale (Ariz.) C.C., 1967-68, Ariz. State U., 1968-71, U. Ariz., 1971-72. Lic. pvt. investigator, Calif. Owner Monogramation, San Francisco, 1976-80; assoc. prodr. Sta. KGO-TV, San Francisco, 1980-81, Power/Rector, San Francisco, 1982-83; owner Office in the City, San Francisco, 1982-83, The Rat Dog Dick Detective Agy., San Francisco, 1983—. Lectr., spkr. San Francisco U., 1984—, San Francisco Assn. Legal Assts., 1984—, Commonwealth Club San Francisco, 1987, Calif. Collectors Coun., San Francisco, 1992—. Book Passage Mystery Writers Conf., 1997-99. Author: A Private Eye's Guide to Collecting a Bad Debt, 1991, Missing Persons, 1997; author/editor: The Instant National Locator Guide, 1991, 2nd edit., 1993, 3rd edit, 1996, Rip-Off, 1998; columnist Ask Rat Dog, 1993—; host, writer: (Court TV Crime Story Spl.) Rip-Offs and Scams, 2000. Co-founder, pres. bd. ElderAngels, San Francisco. Subject of Jack Olsen's book, Hastened to the Grave, 1998. Mem. Nat. Assn. Investigative Specialists, Nat. Assn. Bunco Investigators (asst.), Profls. Against Confidence Crimes (asst.), Sisters in Crime. Avocations: biking, camping, horseback riding, river rafting, travel.

FARQUHAR, MARILYN GIST, cell biologist, pathologist, educator; b. Tulare, Calif., July 11, 1928; d. Brooks DeWitt and Alta (Green) Gist; m. John W. Farquhar, June 4, 1952; children: Bruce, Douglas (div. 1968); m. George Palade, June 7, 1970. AB, U. Calif., Berkeley, 1949, MA, 1952, PhD, 1955. Asst. rsch. pathologist Sch. Medicine U. Calif., San Francisco, 1956-58, assoc. rsch. pathologist, 1962-64, assoc. prof., 1964-68, prof. pathology, 1968-70; rsch. assoc. Rockefeller U., N.Y.C., 1958-62, prof. cell biology, 1970-73, Sch. Medicine Yale U., New Haven, 1973-87, Sterling prof. cell biology and pathology, 1987-90; prof. pathology cell molecular medicine U. Calif., San Diego, 1990—, chair divsn. cellular and molecular medicine, 1991-99, prof. cellular & molecular medicine, chair dept. cellular & molecular medicine, 1999—. Mem. editorial bd. numerous sci. jours.; contbr. articles to profl. jours. Recipient Career Devel. award NIH, 1968-73, Disting. Sci. medal Electron Microscope Soc., 1987, Gomori medal Histochem. Soc., 1999, A.N. Richards award Internat. Soc. Nephrology, 2003. Mem.: NAS, Internat. Soc. Nephrology (A.N. Richards award 2003), Am. Soc. Nephrology (Homer Smith award 1988, Gottschalk award 2002), Am. Assn. Investigative Pathology (Rous Whipple award 2001), Am. Soc. Cell Biology (pres. 1981—82, E.B. Wilson medal 1987), Am. Acad. Arts and Scis. Home and Office: U Calif San Diego Sch Med 12894 Via Latina Del Mar CA 92014-3730

FARQUHARSON, PATRICE ELLEN, primary school educator; b. West Haven, Conn., Feb. 10, 1956; d. Robert Douglas and Margaret Ellen (Dietle) Farquharson; children: Julia, Elena. BS in Edn., U. Conn., 1978; MS in Edn., So. Conn. State U., 1984; EdD, Nova Southeastern U., 1995. Cert. tchr., adminstr., Conn. Asst. dir. West Haven (Conn.) Child Devel. Ctr., 1978-82, exec. dir., 1982-96, 97—; edn. cons. dept. pediatrics div. child and family studies U. Conn., 1993-95; mgmt. cons. West Haven Child Devel. Ctr., Inc., 1996—; asst. prof. early childhood, dir. early childhood programs Teikyo-Post U., Waterbury, Conn., 1996—. Adj. prof. U. Conn. Inst. Pub. Policy, 1996; cons. early childhood edn., workshop presenter, internat. and New Eng., 1987—; profl. cheerleader The New Eng. Patriots football team, 1980; dir., ptnr. New Eng. Cheerleading Camp, West Haven, 1982-84; cheerleading coach U. New Haven, 1982-90; textbook webguide developer Thomson Pub., 2001; online course developer Teikyo Post U., Charter Oak State Coll. Conn. Early Childhood Edn. Coun. scholar, 1993-96. Mem. AAUW, Nat. Assn. Edn. Young Children, Conn. Assn. Edn. Young Children, Dirs. Forum, Gov. Adv. Coun. Early Childhood Edn., South Ctrl. Conn. Agy. on Aging (adv. coun.), West Haven Rotary Club. Avocations: ballet, jazz dancing, horseback riding, reading, traveling. Home: 5 Sunflower Cir West Haven CT 06516-6229 Office: West Haven Child Devel Ctr 201 Noble St West Haven CT 06516-6047

FARR, CARLA LAKE, therapist; d. Carl and Beulah (Mansker) Hamilton; m. Merritt Michael Lake, Aug. 19, 1972 (div.); children: Kyle Merritt Lake, Ansley Hamilton Lake; m. John Mitchell Farr, Apr. 7, 1988 BS in Psychology, Murray State U., 1971, MA, 1975; PhD, So. Ill. U., 1993. Cert. psychometrist; lic. real estate sales counselor, marriage and family therapist. Juvenile counselor Dept. Child Welfare, Paducah, 1971-73; vocat. evaluator West Ky. Easter Seal Ctr., Paducah, 1973-78; real estate sales counselor Park Ave ERA, Paducah, 1977—; supr. rehab. svcs. West Ky. Easter Seal Ctr., Paducah, 1978-89; vocat. expert Dept. Health & Human Svcs., Paducah, 1982-83; grad. asst. So. Ill. U., Carbondale, 1989-91; therapist Christian Counseling Ctr., Paducah, 1991; pvt. practice, 1995—; host radio show Psych Talk with Dr. Carla Farr, 2000. Project reviewer West Ky. Pvt. Industry Coun., Mayfield, 1984—; mem. Art Guild; pres. Paducah Symphony League, 1994-95; bd. dirs. Paducah Symphony Orch., 1994-, Workforce Investment Bd., 1984-, Rape Crisis Ctr., 2000-03, Women Aware, 2003—. Mem.: AACD, Ky. Assn. Marriage Family Therapists, Am. Assn. Marriage Family Therapists, Ky. Assn. Realtors, Nat. Assn. Realtors, Phi Theta Kappa, Phi Kappa Phi. Avocation: travel. Office: 1924 Kentucky Ave Paducah KY 42003

FARR, IVANNE ESTELLE, small business owner, consultant, artist, sculptor; b. Texarkana, Ark., Feb. 7, 1940; d. Franklin Lynnwood and Leone Faye (Seedig) F.; m. William D. Alsup, Aug. 27, 1960 (div. Aug. 1975); children: Joe Farr, Mark De Witt, Lara LeAnne. Attended, S.W. Tex.U.; cert. diamond, Gemological Inst. Am., 1979. Founder, owner Ivanne et Cie, Inc., Corpus Christi, Tex., 1976—; v.p. Internat. Agri-Ventures, Inc., Corpus Christi, 1985—89; owner Bosque River Valley Breeders, Ltd., Emu prodn. facilities, Meridian, Tex., 1990—97. Cons. C.I.C.C., Inc., Montreal, Can., 1985, Mexican Jewelers Assn., Mexico City, 1988, Jireh Resources, Inc., Paris, 1988, CEI, St. Thomas, 2003—; co-founder, charter pres. Bosque County Tourism Coun., Inc., 1992; co-founder Farr Rsch. Internat.; cons. Bibl. Archaeology Mus., Springfield, Mo., 1997; co-founder, chmn., chair Odyssey of Flight, 1991-94; chmn. John A. Lomax Gathering Trading Post Silent Auction, 1991-94; bd. dirs. Econ. Opportunities Advancement Corp.,

Region XI, 2002—. Mem. Mus. Oriental Culture; bd. dirs. Chem. Dependency Unit South Tex., Coastal Bend Youth City, Palmer Drug Abuse Program; bd. of govs., chmn. membership com. Art Mus. South Tex.; chmn. bd. govs., co-founder Alliance for Justice Found., Inc., 1988—; docent Fossil Rim Wildlife Ctr., Glenrose, Tex.; pres. Bosque County Tourism [illegible] co-founder Bosque County Chisholm Trail Cowboy Gathering Trail Ride and Rendezvous, 2000-01, Tex. Chisholm Trail Heritage Celebration, 2002-2003, co-chmn., 2003; founding pres. Tex. Chisholm Trail Assn., Inc., 2003. Mem. Gemological Inst. Am., Coast Conservation Assn., Inst. Tex. Cultures (amb.), Jewelers Assn. Am., Marine Mil. Acad. Parents Assn., Navy League (bd. dirs.), Norwegian Soc. Tex., PTA, Scandinavian Soc. South Tex. (co-founder), Tex. Jewelers Assn., Internat. Group (co-founder), Corpus Christi C. of C. (bd. dirs.), Corpus Christi Area Econ. Devel. Corp. (internat. com.), Am. Emu Assn., Tex. Emu Assn., Emu Coop., Am. Assn. Museums, Ducks Unltd., Mid-Morning Group (co-founder), Daus. of the King Internat., S.W. Tex. U. Alumni Assn. Republican. Episcopalian. Avocations: water skiing, snow skiing, travelling, sailing, opera. E-mail: farrlands@hotmail.com., ifarr@pardners.org.

FARR, JUDITH BANZER, writer, literature educator; b. N.Y.C., Mar. 13, 1937; d. Russell John and Frances Anna (Wissell) Banzer; m. George F. Farr, Jr., June 30, 1962; 1 child, Alec Winfield. BA, Marymount Manhattan Coll., 1957, LHD, 1992; MA, Yale U., 1959, PhD, 1965. Instr. in English Vassar Coll., Poughkeepsie, N.Y., 1961-63; asst. prof. St. Mary's Coll., Moraga, Calif., 1964-68; assoc. prof. SUNY, New Paltz, 1968-77, Georgetown U., Washington, 1978-90, prof. of English and Am. Lit., 1990-99, prof. emerita, 1999—. Vis. assoc. prof. Georgetown U., 1977-78. Author: The Life and Art of Elinor Wylie, 1983, The Passion of Emily Dickinson, 1992, I Never Came to You in White: A Novel, 1996; editor: Twentieth Century Interpretations of Sons and Lovers, 1970, New Century Views: Emily Dickinson, 1995; contbr. articles, poems, short stories to profl. and comml. publs. Am. Philos. Soc. fellow, 1983, Morgan-Porter fellow Yale U., 1960-61; grantee Am. Coun. Learned Socs., 1984, 86, N.Y. State Rsch. FOund., 1974, Georgetown U. Ctr. German Studies, 1992; recipient Alumnae award for Distinction in Arts and Letters, Marymount Manhattan Coll., N.Y.C., 1976, Alpha Sigma Nu Best Book award, 1993. Mem. AAUP, Modern Lang. Assn., Cosmos Club. Avocations: antiques, especially 18th century china, gardening, american painting. Home: 5064 Lowell St NW Washington DC 20016-2616 Office: Georgetown U 330 New North Hall 37th St and O Washington DC 20057

FARR, SHEILA G. critic, poet; b. Seattle, Mar. 29, 1951; d. Sheldon Grant and Helen Balich Farr; m. W. Paul Heald (div.). Student, Cornish Coll. Arts, U. Wash.; MA, Western Wash. U. Art critic Bellingham (Wash.) Herald, 1989—94, Seattle Weekly, 1995—98; freelance art critic Seattle, 1998—2000, The Seattle Times, 2000—. Author: The Snake Song, 1994, Leo Kenney: A Retrospective, 2000, Fay Jones, 2000, James Martin: Art Rustler at the Rivoli, 2001. Recipient Leslie Hunt Poetry awards, 1990, 1994, Wash. State Poetry awards, 1992, Excellence in Journalism-Arts/Criticism award, Soc. for Profl. Journalists, 1996, 1998, 1999, Feature Stories award, Wash. Press Assn., 1996, Arts Criticism award, 1997, C.B. Blethen Meml. award, 2003, George Polk award, 2004. Office: The Seattle Times PO Box 70 Seattle WA 98111

FARRAGHER, CLARE M. state legislator; b. Richmond Hill, N.Y., Dec. 11, 1941; m. Liam; children: Irene, Anne Marie, Kathleen, Mary Clare. Student, St. John's U. Mem. N.J. Assembly, Trenton, 1987—. Asst. minority whip, 1990-91, dep. spkr., 1989-90, 96—, mem. Legis. Svcs. Commn., 1990-95, vice-chair ins. com., mem. trans. and comm. com.; mem. Am. Legis. Exch. Coun., 1987—, N.J. chmn., 1990-2003, chmn., Telecom and Info. Tech. Task Force, 2003-; mem. Nat. Conf. Ins. Legislators, 1992—, v.p., 1998, pres.-elect, 1999, pres. 2000—; mem. Joint Commn. on Auto Ins. Reform, 1998-99, Appropriations Commn., 2000—, Banking & Ins. Commn., 2000-, Assembly Budget Com. (current). Past sr. citizen liaison Freehold Twp., committeewoman, 1982-91, police commr., 1984; dep. mayor, 1984, 88, mayor, 1985; mem. Monmouth County Rep. Com., 1978—; treas. Freehold Twp. Rep. Club; exec. com. Rep. Women of 90's. Named Ins. Legislator of Yr., Am. Legis. Exch. Coun., 1995. Mem. Nat. Order Women Legislators, Nat. Coun. Ins. Legislators (v.p.), N.J. Assn. Elected Women Ofcls. (bd. dirs.). Home: 2606 Strawberry Patch Ct Freehold NJ 07728 Office: 3rd Fl 400 W Main St Freehold NJ 07728-2539

FARRAND, LOIS BARBARA, pharmaceutical company administrator; b. Chgo., Oct. 5, 1935; d. Harold Everett Peel, Ethel Barbara Rizer; m. Michael MacNaughton Farrand, June 12, 1954; children: David Everett, Jill, Jon Michael. Student, U. Colo., 1953—55, Western Mich. U., 1961—62; AA, LaSalle U., Chgo., 1969. Ins. agt. Ins. Investors Diversified, Kalamazoo, 1971—73; floor covering salesperson, mgr. Montgomery Ward, Kalamazoo, 1973—82; real estate agt. Perry Realtors, Kalamazoo, 1982—83; floor covering salesperson, office mgr. N.Y. Carpet World, Portage, 1982—2000; sec. Quantum Resources, Portage, 2001—. Mem.: UN, DAR (vice regent 2001—), Schoolcraft Hist. Soc. Democrat. Avocations: genealogy, music, presenting historical programs. Home: 720 Flamingo Ln Portage MI 49024

FARRAR, DONNA BEATRICE, hospital official; b. Ayer, Mass., Feb. 4, 1950; d. Raymond H. and Shirley E. (Perham) F. B Music Edn., U. Mass., Lowell, 1971; MDiv, Bangor Theol. Sem., 1979; D Ministry, Christian Theol. Sem., 1987; M Family Studies, U. Ky., 1997. Tchr. music Billerica (Mass.) Pub. Schs., 1971-76; chaplain intern various hosps., Bangor, Maine, 1979; assoc. pastor Emanuel United Ch., Hales Corners, Wis., 1980-82; chaplain resident Ind. U & Meth. Hosp., Indpls., 1982-85; assoc. chaplain Ohio State U. Hosp., Columbus, 1985-87; assoc. dir., dir. Ind. U. Med. Ctr., Indpls., 1987-92; dept. dir. U. Ky. Hosps., Lexington, 1992—. Mem.: Am. Assn. Marriage and Family Therapists (lic. marriage family therapist). Democrat. Mem. Christian Ch. Avocations: reading, felines, dance, travel, art. Office: U Ky 800 Rose St # H-118 Lexington KY 40536-0293

FARRAR, ELAINE WILLARDSON, artist; b. L.A. d. Eldon and Gladys Elsie (Larsen) Willardson; children: Steve, Mark, Gregory, JanLeslie, Monty, Susan. BA, Ariz. State U., 1967, MA, 1969, PhD, 1990. Tchr. Camelback Desert Sch., Paradise Valley, Ariz., 1966-69; mem. faculty Yavapai Coll., Prescott, Ariz., 1970-92, chmn. dept. art, 1973-78, instr. art in watercolor, oil, acrylic painting, intaglio, 1971-92, instr. art relief intaglio and monoprints, 1971-92; grad. advisor Prescott Coll. Master of Arts Program, 1993-97. (one-woman shows) R.P. Moffat's, Scottsdale, Ariz., 1969, Art Ctr., Battlecreek, Mich., 1969, The Woodpeddler, Costa Mesa, Calif., 1979, (group shows) Prescott (Ariz.) Fine Arts Assn., 1982, 1984, 1986, 1989, 1990—95, 1996, 1997, (invitational group shows) The Elements, 2001, Collage & Works on Paper, 2002, (group shows) N.Y. Nat. Am. Watercolorists, 1982, Ariz. State U. Women Images Now, 1986, 1987, 1989, 1990—92, Prescott Fine Arts Assn., 1999, 2001; Exhibited in group shows at Prescott Fine Arts Assn., 1999, 2001; (group shows) Prescott Fine Arts Assn., 2002. Mem., curator Prescott Fine Arts Visual Arts com., 1992-97, Works on Paper, 2002; mem. exec. com., 1996-98; bd. dirs. Prescott Fine Arts Assn., 1995-98, Friends Y.C. Art Gallery Bd., 1992-97. Mem. Northern Ariz. Watercolor Assn., Mountain Artists Guild (past pres.), Women's Nat. Mus. (charter Washington chpt.), mus. of North Ariz. and Phoenix Art Mus., Kappa Delta Pi.

FARRAR, MARY CAROLINE, speech and language pathologist; b. Cleve., Ohio, June 10, 1945; d. Charles Joseph and Mary Hennessy Clinton; m. James Charles Farrar, Aug. 2, 1969; children: James Patrick, Mary Kathleen, Daniel Clinton, Amy Hennessy. BS, Marquette Univ., Milw., Wis., 1967; MEd, John Carroll Univ., Cleve., Ohio, 1976; MA, Cleve. State Univ., Cleve., Ohio, 1990; post grad., Notre Dame Coll., Cleve., Ohio, 1997. Cert. clin. competence Am. Speech & Hearing Assn., Ohio, lic. Ohio. Speech/lang. pathologist Cleve. Bd. Edn., 1967—71, Cleve. Heights/Univ. Heights Bd. Edn., Univ. Heights, Ohio, 1972—. Named Support Person of the Yr., Cleve. Assn for the Edn. of Young Children, 2000. Mem.: Northeast Ohio Speech and Hearing Assn., Ohio Speech and Hearing Assn., Am. [illegible] Roman Catholic. Avocations: reading, tennis, golf, family.

FARRAR, RUTH DORIS, reading and literacy educator; b. Freeport, N.Y., June 11, 1943; d. Frederick and Ruth Harriet (Pagington) F.; m. David Conrad Farrar. BA, Ea. Nazarene Coll., 1965; MS in Edn., Hofstra U., 1975, EdD, 1989. Cert. cons. tchr. of reading and supr. reading programs, tchr. English 7-12. Tchr. English Newport (R.I.) Pub. Schs., 1965-66; tchr. reading and English Norwin Pub. Schs., North Huntingdon, Pa., 1966-67; kindergarten tchr. USN Base, Somerset, Bermuda, 1967-68; clin. diagnostician Brookwood Child Care, Bklyn., 1972-76; instr. reading Nassau C.C., Garden City, N.Y., 1974-76; reading specialist Cambridge (Mass.) Sch. Dept., 1976-80; reading coord. Brookwood Sch., Manchester, Mass., 1980-90; asst. prof. Bridgewater (Mass.) State Coll., 1990-92, assoc. prof., 1998—2003, prof., 2003—; asst. prof. Rivier Coll., Nashua, N.H., 1992-93. Dir. The Reading Ctr. Bridgewater State Coll., Am. Reads, Bridgewater State Coll.; vis. lectr. Salem (Mass.) State Coll., 1987—; adj. prof. Hofstra U., Hempstead, NY, 1989—; mem. Mass. Consortium for Media Literacy Edn., 1994—; sponsor summer reading enrichment program Bridgewater-Raynham Regional Pub. Schs., 1994—; coord. grad. programs reading, coord. curriculum leadership ctr. Bridgewater State Coll., co-chair student affairs com., 1998—, convener Resources for Reading Specialists; univ. rep., mem. Curriculum Team for English Lang. Arts Salem Pub. Schs., Canton, Mass., Pub. Schs. PALMS Leadership Team, LEAD Program; mem., curriculum cons. Brockton Pub. H.S.; grant dir. after-sch. reading enrichment program Brockton Pub. Schs., 1998—, grant dir. Sat. morning reading enrichment program; presenter Assn. Am. Colls. Tchr. Edn., 2000; ptnr., trainer, cons. John F. Kennedy Sch., Brockton, 2000—; lectr. U. Natal at Pietermaritzburg, Kwazulu, South Africa, 2002—; co-sponsor UN Literacy Day, 2003; mem. cmty. coordinating coun. Rockland Regional Adult Learning Ctr.; cons. Houghton-Mifflin Co., McGraw Hill, Allyn & Bacon, Bay State Readers Initiative Tng. Modules, Bay State Readers Initiative Higher Edn. Editor The Massachusetts Primer, 1991-94; reviewer Mass. Dept. of Edn. Baystate Readers Initiative. Sr. warden St. Peter's Episcopal Ch., Beverly, Mass., chair spiritual formation com., 2000—01. Grantee Ctr. for Advancement Rsch. and Tchg., Bridgewater State Coll., 1993-94; fellow reading dept. Hofstra U., Hempstead, N.Y., 1985-86; Continuing Edn. Faculty Award, New England Region of the Univ. Continuing Edn. Assn., 2003. Mem. ASCD, Am. Edn. Rsch. Assn., Internat. Reading Assn. (presenter, chair publs. spl. interest group), Internat. Listening Assn. (presenter), Assn. Tchr. Edn. (presenter, curriculum, assessment com.), Nat. Coun. Tchrs. English (presenter), Mass. Reading Assn. (bd. dirs.), Mass. Assn. Coll./Univ. Reading Educators (bd. dirs. 1993—, pres. 1998-99), Kappa Delta Pi. Home: 16 Herrick Street Ext Beverly MA 01915-2731 Office: Bridgewater State Coll Sch Edn 133 Hart Hl Bridgewater MA 02325-0001 E-mail: rfarrar@bridgew.edu.

FARRELL, DONNA MARIE, photographer, graphic artist; b. Hackensack, N.J., Jan. 24, 1968; d. Raymond Patrick and Rosemarie Farrell. BFA, Va. Commonwealth U., 1991. Freelance artist Murals in Motion, 1991—; photographer/graphic artist McFarlane Design Group, Bloomingdale, NJ, 1999—. Capt. The Rave, Montclair, NJ, 1998—2002; photographer Goodwill Games, New York, 1998—98, Paraylmic Games, Atlanta, 1996—96; adj. prof. William Paterson U., Wayne, NJ, 1991—92. Prin. works include mural Olympic Athlete Commemorative Mural Project. Vol., photographer Revlon Run/Walk, New York, 2002—02, Goals for Life, Montclair, 2000—02. Named Women of Distinction World of Art, Lenni Lenape Girl Scout Coun., 1993; recipient Gold medal, Ga. Games, 1994, 1995, 1997; grantee Art & Photography grant, Summer Olympics, 1992, 1996, Winter Olympics, 1994, 1998. Mem.: N.J. Club Printing Ho. Craftsmen, Nat. Mus. Women in Arts, U.S. Soccer Found., Women's Sport Found., Sportfriends Soccer Club. Roman Catholic. Office: McFarlane Design Group 15 Hamburg Turnpike Bloomingdale NJ 07403 Office Phone: 973-709-0943. Personal E-mail: donnamarie.farrell@att.net. E-mail: dfarrell@mcfarlane.com.

FARRELL, MARGARET, magazine publisher; BA, Fordham U. With Time Inc., 1975—90; assoc. pub. Reader's Digest, 1990—92; pub. Marie Claire, 1994-97; v.p., pub. Country Living Gardens, N.Y.C., 1997—2000; sr. v.p. Family Cir. G+J USA, 2000—, pub. Family Cir., 2000—. Office: G+J USA Publishing 375 Lexington Ave New York NY 10017-5514

FARRELL, MARGARET DAWSON, lawyer; b. Bellingham, Wash., July 23, 1949; d. Sterling Jacob and Irene Hegg; m. David S. Farrell, June 10, 1972; children: Lindsay S., Charles D. BA cum laude, Smith Coll., 1971; postgrad., Georgetown U., 1971-72; JD, U. Cin., 1974. Bar: Ohio 1974, U.S. Dist. Ct. (so. dist.) Ohio 1974, R.I. 1976, U.S. Dist. Ct. R.I. 1976. Assoc. Frost & Jacobs, Cin., 1974-76; from assoc. to ptnr. Tillinghast, Collins & Graham, Providence, 1976—81; ptnr. Hinckley, Allen & Snyder LLP, Providence, 1981—. Lectr. Bryant Coll., 1979-80; dir., sec. Bank R.I., 1996—, Bancorp R.I., Inc., 2000—. Trustee Women and Infants Hosp., Providence, 1981—, sec., 1982-96, vice chair, 1996—2003, chair 2004-; bd. dirs. Women and Infants Corp., Providence, 1989—2003, chair 2004-, sec., 1989-96, vice chair, 1996—; trustee, sec. Providence Preservation Soc. Revolving Fund, 1982-88; trustee Butler Hosp., 1995—, Care New England Health Sys., 1996—, R.I. Hist. Soc., 1980-85, Gordon Sch., East Providence, R.I., 1990-95; trustee Hosp. Assn. R.I., 1989-2003, mem. exec. coun., 1998-2003; trustee, sec., pres. Found. for Repertory Theatre, R.I., 1978-84; R.I. del. Am. Hosp. Assn. Congress Hosp. Trustees, 1993-98; mem. R.I. Bd. Regents for Elem. and Secondary Edn., 1987-90. Mem. ABA, R.I. Bar Assn. Avocations: golf, sailing, skiing, horseback riding. Office: Hinckley Allen & Snyder LLP 1500 Fleet Ctr Providence RI 02903-2319 Office Phone: 401-274-2000.

FARRELL, PATRICIA ANN, psychologist, educator, writer; b. N.Y.C. d. Joseph Alexander and Pauline Farrell. BA, Queens Coll.; MA, PhD, NYU. Lic. psychologist, N.J., Fla.; cert. online computer instr. Assoc. editor Pubs. Weekly Mag., N.Y.C.; editor Bestsellers Mag., N.Y.C.; assoc. editor King Features Syndicate, N.Y.C.; staff psychologist, intake coord. Mid-Bergen Cmty. Mental Health Ctr., Paramus, NJ; instr. Bergen C.C., Paramus, 1978-94; prof. clin. psychology Walden U., 1995—2001. Resident clin. psychology Am. Inst. for Counseling, N.J., 1990-91; cons. Family Counseling Svc. of Ridgewood, N.J., 1984; clin. psychology intern Marlboro (N.J.) Psychiat. Hosp., 1984-85, staff psychologist, 1985-87; rsch. analyst Mt. Sinai Sch. Medicine, 1987-88; account exec., sr. med. writer Manning, Selvage and Lee, N.Y.C., 1988-90; sr. clin. psychologist, mem. med. staff Greystone Pk (N.J.) Psychiat. Hosp., 1990-96; pvt. practice psychology, Englewood, N.J.; health sci. editor Time Warner Cable, Channel 10 News, 1995-2000; med. specialist N.J. Divsn. Disability Determination, 1997—; police surgeon Boro Ft. Lee, N.J., 1998—; psychiatry preceptor U. Medicine and Dentistry N.J. Med. Sch.; cons. pharm. clin. protocols; psychologist, expert moderator on anxiety and panic WebMD, 2000—. Guest radio and TV shows including The Today Show, Nat. Geog. TV, MSNBC, Hollywood at Large, The View, The O'Reilly Factor, ABC Sports Spl., ABC World News Tonight, Court TV, CNN Radio, Newsweek-on-Air, Voice of Am., Family Talk, Up Front Tonight, Pros and Cons, Local Live, USA Radio Network, Ken Hamblin Show, KNU Radio, Fox Beyond the News, Real Talk, Jay Thomas Radio Show, Sally Jessy Raphael, Montel Williams, Gordon Elliott Show, Inside Edit., Am. Jour., Joan Rivers Show, Fox Cable News, Good Day N.Y., Mark Walberg, Am. After Hours, Dini, The Shirley Show, Camilla Scott, USA Live, Alive and Wellness with Carol Martin, News Talk, Maury Povich, Caucus N.J., It's Your Call, One-on-One, The Carnie Wilson Show, AP Newswire, Judge for Yourself TV Show, N.Y.C. 10 O'Clock News, Cosmo, Redbook, Self, Fitness, Latina, Maxim, Good Housekeeping, AARP, Cooking Light, Smart Money, Woman's World, In Touch, Achieve Solutions, First for Women, Washington Post, [illegible] Detroit News, Chgo. Tribune, Home Office Computing, Working Woman, N.Y. Post, Boston Globe, NY Daily News, New Woman, Phila. Enquirer, WPIX-TV, N.Y., UPN 9 News, WWOR-TV News, WNRR-TV, In Your Interest, LTV, Channel 10 News, On Campus, Sta WTTM, WSNJ, WHSI-TV, Bloomberg News, UPI News, KGAB, WSAR, Don Weeks Show, Common Concerns, WHSE-TV, Alan Nathan's Battle Lines, Dirk Van NBC radio, Ruth Koscielak Show, Voice of Am., WTOP, Redbook, Ramp, Fox & Friends, Eyewitness News, Cork Talks Back, TalkSport, The Week, Reuters TV, Bev Smith Show, Fitness, The Oregonian, Arnie Arneson Show, Talk Am., Real Simple, Marie Claire, Seventeen, Parents, Shape, Physical, Christian Single, Mental Health Law Report; author: (manual) Alzheimer's Disease Assessment Scale test, How To Be Your Own Therapist, 2002, 04; contbr. book chpt. to Innovations in Clin. Practice: A Source Book, 15th edit., 2000; contbr. articles to Writer's Digest, Real World, Postgrad. Medicine, newspapers. Bd. dirs., chmn. med. liaison com. liaison to dept. psychiatry Bergen Pines County Hosp., Paramus, 1994-95. McDonald's rsch. grantee, 1994-95; recipient Sci. award Rotary Club. Avocations: fitness, racquetball, kite-flying. Office: PO Box 1525 Englewood Cliffs NJ 07632-0283 E-mail: pfarrell@ix.netcom.com.

FARRELL, SHARON ELAINE, retired real estate broker; b. Boston, Nov. 8, 1941; d. Winston Cushman and Evelyn (Murphy) Lawson; m. James E. Waldron, Oct. 15, 1961 (div. Apr. 1987); children: Peter M., Kathleen M.; m. Richard J. Farrell, May, 1994. Grad., Realtors Inst., 1987; BS, Stonehill Coll., 1998. Cert. residential specialist. Den mother Cub Scouts Boy Scouts Am., East Bridgewater, 1972-76, den leader, coach, 1976-78; mem. com., 1978-79. Mem. Am. Soc. Notaries (life), Green Key Soc., Beta Xi, Theta Alpha Kappa. Roman Catholic. Avocations: reading, travel. Home: 10 Colewood Rd East Bridgewater MA 02333-1687

FARRELL, SUZANNE, ballerina; b. Cin., Aug. 16, 1945; d. Robert Ficker and Donna (Von Holle) Holly; m. Paul Mejia, Feb. 21, 1969. Studies with Marian LaCour, Cin. Conservatory Music; LHD (hon.), Georgetown U., 1984, Fordham U., 1987; DFA (hon.), Yale U., 1988; LLD (hon.), U. Notre Dame, 1990; D of Performing Arts (hon.), U. Cin., 1990; ArtsD (hon.), Middlebury Coll., 1992; LHD (hon.), Coll. Mt. St. Vincent, 1995. Hon. lectr. dance U. Cin.; guest tchr. Sch. Am. Ballet., Kennedy Ctr. for Performing Arts. With N.Y.C. Ballet, 1961-69, 75-89, became featured dancer, 1962, prin. dancer, 1965-69, 75-89; appeared in film version Midsummer Night's Dream, Bejart Ballet of 20th Century, Brussels, 1971-75, as Juliet in Romeo and Juliet, N.Y.C. Ballet in New Ravel Festival, Tzigane, in G Major, 1976, (documentary) Elusive Muse, 1996; created roles in other ballets Ah, Vous Dirais Je, Maman?, the young girl in Rose in Nijinsky, Clown of God, 1971, Laura in I Trionfi; featured in TV show: Balanchine Dance in Am., Parts I-IV; author: (autobiography) Holding on to the Air, 1990; repetiteur for George Balanchine Trust. Vice chmn. bd. trustees Profl. Children's Sch., N.Y.C.; mem. sr. adv. bd. N.Y. chpt. Arthritis Found.; mem. arts adv. bd. Princess Grade Found.-USA. Recipient Merit award Mademoiselle mag., 1965, Dance mag. award, 1976, award of honor for arts and culture N.Y.C., 1979, Spirit Achievement award Albert Einstein Coll. Medicine, 1980, Merit award Brandeis U., Emmy award, 1985, Golden Plate award Am. Acad. of Achievement, 1987, N.Y. State Gov.'s Arts award, 1988, Nat. Medal of Arts, 2003.*

FARRER, CLAIRE ANNE RAFFERTY, anthropologist, educator, folklorist; b. N.Y.C., Dec. 26, 1936; d. Francis Michael and Clara Anna (Guerra) Rafferty; 1 child, Suzanne Claire. BA in Anthropology, U. Calif., Berkeley, 1970; MA in Anthropology and Folklore, U. Tex., 1974, PhD in Anthropology and Folklore, 1977. Various positions, 1953-73; fellow Whitney M. Young Jr. Meml. Found., N.Y.C., 1974-75; arts specialist, grant adminstr. Nat. Endowment for Arts, Washington, 1976-77; Weatherhead resident fellow Sch. Am. Research, Santa Fe, 1977-78; asst. prof. anthropology U. Ill., Urbana, 1978-85; assoc. prof., coord. applied anthropology Calif. State U., Chico, 1985-89, prof., 1989—2001, dir. Multicultural and Gender Studies, 1994, prof. emerita, 2002—. Cons. in field, 1974—; mem. film and video adv. panel Ill. Arts Coun., 1980-82; mem. Ill. Humanities Coun., 1980-82; vis. prof. U. Ghent, Belgium, 1990; vis. prof. Southwestern studies Colo. Coll., Colorado Springs, 2002—, Hulbert chair in Southwestern studies, 1997; bus. mgr. Calif. Folklore Soc., 1994-99; NEH and Harry J. Gray disting. vis. prof. in humanities U. Hartford, Conn., 2002-03. Author: Play and Inter-Ethnic Communication, 1990, Living Life's Circle: Mescalero Apache Cosmovision, 1991, Thunder Rides a Black Horse: Mescalero Apaches and the Mythic Present, 1994, 96, others; co-founder, co-editor Folklore Women's Commn., 1972; editor spl. issue Jour. Am. Folklore, 1975, 1st rev. edit., 1986; co-editor: Forms of Play of Native North Americans, 1979, Earth and Sky: Visions of the Cosmos in Native North American Folklore, 1992; contbr. numerous articles to profl. jours., mags. and newspapers, chpts. to books. Recipient J. Gordon prize in S.W. Studies, Colo.Coll., fellowships and grants. Fellow Am. Anthrop. Assn.; mem. Authors Guild, Am. Ethnol. Soc., Am. Folklore Soc., Am. Soc. Ethnohistory, Astronomy in Culture Office Phone: 719-389-6649. E-mail: clairerfarrer@aol.com., clairefarrer@aol.com.

FARRINGTON, BERTHA LOUISE, retired nursing administrator; b. Poteet, Tex., Jan. 20, 1937; d. Leonard Gilbert and Janie (Hernandez) Lozano; m. James Charles Farrington, Jan. 30, 1965; children: Mark Hiram, Robert Lee. BSN, Tex. Women's U., 1960; NP, U. Tex., 1984. RN, Tex. Charge nurse emergency rm. Parkland Meml. Hosp., Dallas; head nurse emergency rm./day surgery Bapt. Meml. Hosp., Pensacola, Fla.; asst. dir. health svcs. U. Tex. Southwestern Med. Ctr., Dallas, dir. student health svcs., ret., 2002. Cons. Student Health Com. E-mail: j.bfarrington@sbcglobal.net.

FARRIS, CHARLYE OLA, lawyer; b. Wichita Falls, Tex., 1930; d. James and Roberta Farris. Bachelor's Degree, Prairie View A&M Coll.; postgrad., U. Denver; JD, Howard U., 1953. Bar: Tex. 1953. Pvt. practice, Wichita Falls, 1955—. Office: 921 7th St Wichita Falls TX 76301*

FARRIS, VERA KING, former college president; b. Atlantic City, July 18, 1940; BA in Biology magna cum laude, Tuskegee Inst., 1959; MS in Zoology, U. Mass., 1962, PhD in Zoology/Parasitology, 1965; LHD (hon.), Marymount Manhattan Coll., 1985; LLD (hon.), Monmouth Coll., West Long Branch, N.J., 1987; DSc honoris causa, Johnson and Wales Coll., 1988. Dean spl. programs, assoc. prof. pathology and biology SUNY, Stony Brook, 1968-72, vice provost acad. affairs, prof. biological sci. Brockport, 1973-80; v.p. acad affairs, prof. biological sci. Kean Coll. N.J., Union, 1980-83; pres. Stockton State Coll., Pomona, NJ, 1983—2003. Contbr. articles to profl. jours. Founding mem. Gov.'s Pride award acad., 1986—, Gov.'s adv. coun. Holocaust Edn. in N.J., 1982—. Recipient Golden Trefoil award, Delaware Valley Coun. Girl Scouts Am., 1987,Chancellors Medal for Exemplary and Extraordinary Svc., U. Mass., 1986, Honor Roll Ednl award Wash. Ctr. for Internships and Acad. Seminars, Commendation for Outstanding Achievement in Edn., N.J. Assembly, 1993, others; named Lifetime Honorary citizen of Atlanta, 1984, N.J. Woman or Yr. N.J. Woman's Mag. Mem. Am. Coun. Edn. (bd. dirs. 1988-91), Coun. Post-Secondary Accreditation (bd. dirs. 1988—), Middle States Assn. Colls. and Secondary Schs. (pres. bd. trustees), Am. Assn. State Colls. and Univs. (nominating com.), N.J. State Bd. Examiners, N.J. State Coll. Pres. (chair 1987-89), B'naiB'rith (life hon.), Cosmos Club (Washington). Home: 689 St Andrews Dr Egg Harbor City NJ 08215-5119

FARROW, MARGARET ANN, former state official; b. Kenosha, Wis., Nov. 28, 1934; d. William Charles and Margaret Ann (Horan) Nemitz; m.

John Harvey Farrow, Dec. 29, 1956; children: John, William, Peter, Paul, Mark. Student, Rosary Coll., 1952-53; BS in Polit. Sci. and Edn., Marquette U., 1956, postgrad., 1975-77. Tchr. Archdiocese of Milw., 1956-57; trustee Elm Grove Village, Wis., 1976-81, pres., 1981-86; mem. Wis. Assembly, Madison, 1986-89, Wis. Senate from 33rd dist., Madison, 1989—2001; lt. gov. State of Wis., 2001—03; dir. local govt. affairs Whyte Hirshboeck Dudek Govt. Affairs, 2003—. Chair govt. effectiveness, 1998-2001, asst. majority leader, 1998; mem. joint com. on audit, 1993-97, mem. joint survey com. on tax exemptions, 1993-97, chair Wis. women's coun., 1991—, Rep. caucus chair, 1996, 99, mem. coun. on workforce excellence, 1995—, mem. Wis. glass ceiling commn., 1993—; mem. Senate Com. on edn., 1999, Senate com. on labor, 1999. Republican. Home: W 262 # 2402 Deer Haven Dr Pewaukee WI 53072-4572

FARSHEE, MARLENA W. title company executive; b. Prattville, Ala., Sept. 30, 1964; d. Albert G. Wallace Jr. and Mary Margaret Gray; m. Charles Morgan King, Feb. 6, 1981 (dec. Jan. 1985); 1 child, Candice King ; m. William B. Farshee, Jr., Aug. 8, 1999; children: Carly, Anna, William. Legal sec. Sasser & Littleton, PC, Mont., Ala., 1992—94; mgr. Closing Assocs., Prattville, 1994—98; pres. Flagship Closing Svcs., Mont., 1998—2004; owner Advantage Closing, LLC, Mont., 2004—. Mem.: Greater Montgomery Homebuilders Assn. (assoc. com. chair 2001—02, Assoc. of Yr. 2002), Women's Coun. Realtors, Real Estate Assn. Ala. (affiliate com. 2000—03). Republican. Methodist. Avocations: gardening, reading, boating. Home: 120 Huckleberry Dr Deatsville AL 36022 Office: Advantage Closing LLC 6767 Taylor Cir Montgomery AL 36117 Office Phone: 334-558-0166. Office Fax: 334-558-0213.*

FARUQUE, CATHLEEN JO, social worker, educator; b. Winona, MN, May 27, 1958; d. Richard John Cieminski, Lorraine Norma Cieminski; m. Syed M. Faruque. PhD, North Ctrl. U., 2000; MSW, San Diego State U., 1991; BS in Sociology, Winona State U., 1982. Diplomat APA, 1998, lic. Ind. Clin. Social Worker 1997, cert. Cert. Care Mgr. 1996. Assoc. Prof. Winona State U., Winona, Minn., 1997—; dir. Sr. Svcs. Cmty. Svcs. Assn., Mountain View, Calif., 1992—97; instr. San Jose State U., San Jose, Calif., 1995—97; instr. Psychology Master's Inst., San Jose, 1996—97; cons. Social Svcs. Family Svcs. Assn., San Jose, 1997—97; ins. rep. AARP Hartford, San Diego, 1987—89; case mgr. Cmty. Counseling Ctr., Oklahoma City, 1983—87. Dir. Social Work Program Winona State U., 1998—2001; allocations bd. mem. United Way, Winona, 2001; treas. Olmsted County Migrant Worker's Coun., Rochester, Minn., 1998—2000; county commr. Human Svcs. Social Svcs. Adv. Bd., San Jose, 1995—97; cons. Santa Clara County Geriatric Consultation Team, Mountain View, 1993—97; mem. adv. bd. Churches on Homelessness, Mountain View, 1993—96; cons. Mental Health Consortium, Oklahoma City, 1984—87. Author: (Journal Article) Diversity in the Elderly, 2000 (1999 Minnesota Governer's Commendation - Partnership America, 1999); contbr. chpts. in books, articles to profl. jours.; author: Migration of Hmong to the Midwestern United States, 2002. Mem.: NASW, Am. Psychoterapists Assn., Coun. on Social Work Edn. Democrat. Roman Catholic.

FARWELL, NANCY LARRAINE, public relations executive; b. Sellersville, Pa., May 2, 1944; d. Warren Gregory and Mary Rita (Zaniboni) F. BA, Pa. State U., 1966. Asst. TV rep. H.R. TV Reps., Phila., 1966-68; various positions Hawthorne Advt. Inc., Phila., 1968-73; dir. employee rels. Colonial Penn Group Inc., Phila., 1973-75, mgr. press rels., 1976-78, mgr. pub. rels., 1978-82; dir. comm. Provident Mut. Life Ins. Co., Phila., 1982-83, asst. v.p., comm., 1983-87; pres. Nancy Farwell Assocs., Phila., 1987-90; v.p. Anne Klein & Assocs., Inc., Mt. Laurel, NJ, 1990-92, sr. v.p., 1992-97, sr. v.p., COO, 1998-2001, sr. v.p. strategic planning, 2001—03, sr. councilor, 2003—. Adv. bd. City of Phila. Century IV Tall Ships, 1982. Author: (photo essay) Philadelphia, 1976; contbr. chpt. to home health care mktg. book. Founder, co-chair Portico Row Neighborhood Assn., Phila., 1989-92; bd. dirs. Washington Sq. West Project Area Com., Phila., 1990-92, Boys and Girls Clubs of Metro Phila. Adv. Coun., 1991—; adv. com. Phila. 6th Police Dist., 1990-92. Mem. Pub. Rels. Soc. Am. (9 Pepperpot awards, Award of Excellence, Silver Anvil award of Excellence), Phila. Pub. Rels. Assn. Office: Anne Klein & Assocs Inc Three Greentree Ctr Ste 200 Marlton NJ 08053

FASCIALE, YVONNE M. art educator, musician; b. Jersey City, N.J., Feb. 5, 1954; d. Patrick A and Elvira Fasciale; children: Jessica Napolitano, Toni Marie Napolitano. BFA magna cum laude, Kean Coll., 1991—95. Tchr. of Art Edn. K-12 New Jersey, 1996 Va., 2002, 1996. Tchr. of art Woodbridge Bd. of Edn., NJ, 1997—, home instr.-tutor, 2000—; tchr. of art Bedford County Bd. of Edn., Bedford, Va., 2001—02; tchr. Slyvan Learning Ctr., South Plainfield, NJ, 2002—; musician Ind., Middlesex County, NJ. Mem.: Woodbridge Arts Coalition. Catholic. Avocations: painting, music, reading, yoga, photography. Home: 47 Victory Ct Metuchen NJ 08840 Office Phone: 732-602-8600. Personal E-mail: AKOOSTX@aol.com.

FASEL, IDA, English language educator, writer; b. Portland, Maine, May 9, 1909; d. I.E. Drapkin and Lilian Rose Harwich; m. Oscar A. Fasel, Dec. 24, 1946 (dec. Apr. 1973). BA summa cum laude, Boston U., 1931, MA, 1945; PhD, U. Denver, 1963. Mem. faculty English U. Conn., New London, Midwestern U., Wichita Falls, Tex., Colo. Woman's Coll., Denver; prof. English U. Colo., Denver, 1962-77, prof. emerita of English, 1977. Presenter in field; contest judge. Translator from French and Italian, editl. cons.: Baroque and Renaissance Lyrics, 1962; author (poetry): On the Meanings of Cleave, 1979 (Nortex Publ. award); author: The Study of Writing Poetry, 1983; author: (poetry) Where Is the Center of the World?: Selections From Seven Chapbooks, 1981-1991, 1999 (U. Fla. and Before the Rapture Press prize chapbooks), All Real Living Is Meeting, 1999, The Difficult Inch, 2000, Journey of a Hundred Years, 2002, Air, Angels and Us, 2002, Waking to Light, 2002 (Best Chapbook Angels Without Wings Found. 2003), Aureoles, 2002; translator: Renaissance and Baroque Lyrics, 1962; contbg. author: The Study and Writing of Poetry, 1983; contbr. articles to profl. jours., chpts. to books, poetry to anthologies and jours. Faculty Rsch. fellow U. Colo., 1979; recipient Disting. Alumni honor Boston U., 1979, Alumni Poetry prize, 1983, 85, Before the Rapture Chapbook prize, 1985, Colo. Poet Honor, Friends of Denver Pub. Libr., 1991, Panhandler Chapbook prize, U. West Fla., 1991, Prize Poems award Colo. Authors League, 1993-94. Mem. Milton Soc. Am. (life), Friends of Milton's Cottage (charter), Assn. Literary Scholars and Critics, Conf. on Christianity and Lit., Poetry Soc. Tex., Colo. Ctr. for the Book, Denver Woman's Press Club, Phi Beta Kappa. Avocations: ballet, Star Trek, collecting angels, piano, translating French poetry. Home: 165 Ivy St Denver CO 80220-5846

FASH, VICTORIA R. healthcare company executive; Sr. v.p. bus. strategy Dun & Bradstreet Corp., 1995-96; exec. v.p., CFO Cognizant, 1996—; exec. v.p., chmn., CEO IMS Internat., Westport, Conn., 1999—. Bd. dirs. Orion Capital Corp. Office: IMS Health Inc 1499 Post Rd Fairfield CT 06430-5940

FASICK, ADELE MONGAN, information services consultant; b. N.Y.C., Mar. 18, 1930; d. Stephen Leo and Florence (Geary) Mongan; m. Frank Fasick, Aug. 14, 1955 (div. 1986); children: Pamela, Laura, Julia. BA, Cornell U., 1951; MA, Columbia U., 1954, MSLS, 1956; PhD, Case Western Reserve U., 1970. Libr. N.Y. Pub. Libr., 1955-56, L.I.U., Bklyn., 1956-58; asst. prof. Rosary Coll., River Forest, Ill., 1970-71; prof. U. Toronto, 1971-96, dean Faculty of Libr. and Info. Sci., 1990-95. Adj. prof. San Jose State U., 1999—, U. .C., 2002—. Author: Managing Children Services in Public Libraries, 1991, 2d edit., 1998, Beauty Who Would Not Spin, 1987; co-author: ChildView, 1987; editor: Lands of Pleasure, 1990; editor International Research Abstracts: Youth Library Services, 1993—. Mem. ALA (com. on accreditation 1990-92), Assn. Libr. Svc. to Children (exec. bd. 1980-84), Assn. Librs. and Info. Sci. Edn. (pres. 1992), Internat. Fedn. Libr. Assn. (sec./treas. sect. on reading 1997—). E-mail: amfasick@earthlink.net.

FASKE, DONNA See KARAN, DONNA

FASSE, JANE ELLEN, art educator; b. Beaver Dam, Wis., Mar. 24, 1953; d. William Herman and Ellen Mae Fasse; m. Thomas Gregory Moss, Aug. 24, 1984. BS, U. Wis., 1978, MFA, 1994. Mgr. gift shop and installation Madison (Wis.) Art Ctr., 1984—88; prodn. asst. Wildwood Art Prodns., Madison, 1988—91; instr. (summer) Peninsula Art Sch., Fish Creek, Wis., 1998, Rhinelander (Wis.) Sch. of Art, 1998; instr. Outreach for Arts, U. Wis., Madison, 1994—2001; tchg. asst. U. Wis., Madison, 1992—94; instr., prof. Madison Area Tech. Coll., 1994—, Edgewood Coll., Madison, 2000—. Juror, judge Wis. Regional Arts Program, 1998; guest printmaker U. Dallas, Irving, Tex., 1999. Contbr. artwork Love: A Day Book, 1989, Best of Printmaking Internat. Collection, 1999. Mem.: Nat. Mus. Women in the Arts. Avocations: reading, writing, cooking, gardening. Office: Edgewood Coll Edgewood Coll Dr Madison WI 53705

FASSETT, FRANCES NICHOLAS (KITTY FASSETT), pianist, record producer; b. Louisville, Sept. 15, 1933; d. Charles and Frances (Allen) Nicholas; m. Richard Ashford Lee, Aug. 27, 1955 (div. 1975); children: Frances Lee Davis, Edward Ashford Lee, Maria Catalina Ryan; m. Stephen Bryant Fassett, Dec. 4, 1975 (dec. Mar. 1980). BA with honors, Vassar Coll., 1955; BMus, P.R. Conservatory of Music, San Juan, 1965, MMus, 1966. Founder, dir. Waldo Theatre, Inc., Waldoboro, Maine, 1990—. Home and Office: 3630A Brownsboro Rd # 300 Louisville KY 40207-1861

FASSLER, CRYSTAL G. marketing consultant; b. Marion, Ohio, Mar. 15, 1942; d. Lloyd C. and Iola M. (Runkle) Mahaffey; student public schs., Prospect, Ohio; m. Donald D. Fassler, May 6, 1960; 1 son, Curtis A. Media buyer H. Swink Advt., Marion, 1968-73; media buyer and planner Tracey Locke Advt., Columbus, Ohio, 1973-74, Lord, Sullivan & Yoder Advt., Marion, 1974-82; youth conselor State of Ohio Employment Services, Marion, 1982-83; nat. mktg. consultant WMRN-AM and FM, Marion, 1983-84, gen. mgr., 1985; gen. sales mgr. WRFD Radio, Columbus, 1986-90; gen. sales mgr. Stas. WMAN-AM and WYHT-FM, Mansfield, Ohio, 1990-92, media cons., Dimension Media Svcs., Marion, Ohio, 1992-93, cons., Credit Bur. Co., Marion, 1993-94, ptnr. Media Mktg. Strategies, 1994-1998, Vizual Express, Marion, 2001—. Home and Office: Vizual Express Ptnr Ctr St Marion OH 43302-7352 E-mail: fishal1@aol.com.

FAST, BETTY BLOCKMAN, travel agency owner; b. Memphis, Oct. 12, 1929; d. Morris David Arthur and Sadie (Shefsky) Blockman; married, Dec. 1962. BA, Southwest Coll., 1952; MA, Memphis State U., 1960. Owner Betty Fast Travel Svc. Commr. Safety bd., Miami Beach, 1971. Mem. Am. Soc. Travel Agts., Women's Zionist Orgn. (pres. 1970-72), Cruise Line Industry Assn., Airline Reporting Corp.

FASTIGE, NELLIE MARSHALL, elementary school educator; b. Balt., May 10, 1961; d. Carmen Jr. and Gloria (Schmidt) Fastige. BA, Hood Coll., Frederick, Md., 1983; MA, Hood Coll., 1989. Advanced profl. tchg. cert. Md. Kindergarten tchr. Quarterfield Elem. Sch., Glen Burnie, Md., 1983—84; kindergarten, 2d grade Tyler Hts. Elem. Sch., Annapolis, Md., 1984—90; tchr. 2d grade Sunset Elem. Sch., Pasadena, Md., 1990—97; tchr. 1st grade Woodside Elem. Sch., Glen Burnie, 1997—98; tchr. 2d grade Ferndale Elem. Sch., Md., 1998—2001, High Point Elem. Sch., Pasadena, 2001—. Presenter fall conf. Md. Assn. Sci. Tchrs., Urbana, 1998. Recipient Ednl. Excellence award, No. Anne Arundel County C. of C., 2001. Mem.: NEA, Tchrs. Assn. of Anne Arundel County, Md. State Tchrs. Assn. Democrat. Presbyterian. Avocations: travel, reading, crafts. Home: 302 Christy Rd Pasadena MD 21122 Office Phone: 410-222-6454. E-mail: nfastige@comcast.net.

FATTMAN, ANNE CARILYN, elementary school educator; b. York, Pa., Apr. 21, 1938; d. Otto and Carrie Myrtle Scheib; m. E. George Fattman, Apr. 26, 1937; children: George, Laura, Stephen. BA, Juniata Coll., 1960. Tchr. elem. sch. West York Sch. Dist., Pa., 1960—61, Westmont Hilltop Dist., Johnstown, 1961—63, homebound instr., 1992—98. Treas., tutor Cambria County Lit. Coun., Johnstown, 1997—2003; pres. Johnstown Day Care Ctr., 1976—78. Mem.: AAUW (pres. 1992—2003, v.p. 1992—2003, treas. 1992—2003). Lutheran. Home: 1408 Coventry Ct Johnstown PA 15905

FAUCETTE, GLORIA MARIE, accountant, educator; b. Burlington, N.C., Aug. 29, 1948; d. Jesse Graham and Mildred Kathryn Faucette. BA in Social Scis., Elon Coll., 1982; BS in Acctg., N.C. A&T State U., 1991; MBA, Elon Coll., 1993. Social worker Alamance County Dept. Social Svcs., Burlington, NC, 1974-89; instr. acctg. and bus. N.C. A&T State U., Greensboro, NC, 1991-99, N.C. AT&T State, Greensboro, NC, 2000—01; acct. Cobb Ezekiel Brown and Co., Graham, NC, 1999—2000; bus. tchr. Hawfields Mid. Sch., 2001—. Mem. acad. rels. com. Inst. Internal Auditors, Greensboro, 1996-97; cons. bus. ednl. career decisions mid/secondary sch. students; small bus. cons. Contbr. articles to profl. jours. Mem. AICPA, N.C. Assn. CPA (mem. acctg. edn. com. 1995-97; chair careers in acctg. com. 1999), Beta Alpha Psi, Beta Gamma Sigma Democrat. Methodist.

FAUCETTE, MERILON COOPER, retired secondary school educator; b. Washington, Ark., Oct. 17, 1931; d. Andrew and Narciss (Tyus) Cooper; m. Clarence William Faucette, Jr., May 17, 1958 (dec. 1982); children: Billie Reneé, Gwenevere Yvetta. BS, Ark. Bapt. Coll., Little Rock, 1953; MEd, Henderson State U., Arkadelphi, Ark., 1975. Tchr. Searcy (Ark.) Sch. Dist., 1953-61, Pulaski County Spl. Sch. Dist., Searcy, 1961-86; ret., 1986. Mem.: Telephone Pioneers Am. (assoc.).

FAUGHT, BRENDA DORMAN, health sciences educator; m. Jesse Albert Faught. AA, Phoenix Coll., 1970—73. Master Tchr. Tex. State PTA, 1998. Testing clk. Midland Coll., Tex., 1998—2000, health sciences continuing edn. specialist, 2002—. Tchr., kids coll. Midland Coll., Tex., 1992—97; store mgr. Connie's Fashion, Midland, Tex., 1993—94; owner Party Pizazz, Midland, Tex., 1993—95; substitute tchr. Midland Ind. Sch. Dist., 1994—95; part-time testing clk. Midland Coll., Tex., 1995—98. Pres. Volunteers In Pub. Schools, Midland, Tex., 1988—89, Midland City Coun. of PTA, Tex., 1989—90, Goddard Jr. H.S., Midland, Tex., 1990—91, Midland Freshman H.S., Tex., 1991—92, Midland H.S. PTA, Tex., 1993—94; mem. Midland Symphony Guild, Tex., 1992—99; parade of homes chmn./treas. Jr. Woman's Club, Midland, Tex., 1985—90; pres. Opportunity Ctr. Aux., Midland, Tex., 1983—84, Santa Rita Elem. Sch. Parent, Tchr. Assn., Midland, Tex., 1986—87; by-laws com. mem. Alamo Heights Bapt. Ch., Midland, Tex., 1990—93, spl. events com. chmn., 1989—92, vacation bible sch. chmn., 1989—90, parliamentarian, 1998—99; pres. & mem. Youth Centers, Midland, Tex., 1992—93; pres., treas. Greater Midland Football Cheerleader Bd., Tex., 1989—92; mem. Midland Coll. 25th Anniversary, Tex., 1998—99; pres. Cert. Pub. Accountants Wives Club, Midland, Tex., 1975—81. Recipient Nat. Dean's List, Ednl. Comm., Inc., 1997—98, 1998—99. Mem.: Tex. Administrators of Continuing Edn. for Cmty./Jr. Colleges (assoc.), Tex. PTA (hon.; life mem.), Phi Theta Kappa Hono Soc. (life), Sigma Kappa Nat. Social Sorority (life; pres. of Midland alumnae 1975—80, Ernistine Duncan Collins Pearl Ct. Award 1989). R-Consevative. Southern Bapt. Avocations: ceramics, party decorating, needlecrafts, crewel, tennis. Office: Midland Coll 3600 N Garfield - DHS #228 Midland TX 79705 Personal E-mail: bdfmidtx@aol.com. E-mail: bfaught@midland.edu.

FAUL, MAUREEN PATRICIA, healthcare and research consultant; d. Michael M and Margaret A Faul; life ptnr. Stacey Citrin. BSN, Wheeling Jesuit U., W.Va., 1983. RN Pa., 1983. V.p. Heart Ctr. of Excellence North Broward Hosp. Dist., Ft. Lauderdale, Fla., 1998—2003; pres. The Resh Group, Inc, Coral Springs, Fla., 2003—. Bd. dirs. Am. Heart Assn., Ft. Lauderdale, Fla., 1998—2003. Office: The Resh Group Inc 477 NW 118th Ave Coral Springs FL 33071 E-mail: maureen@thereshgroup.com.

FAULES, BARBARA RUTH, retired elementary education educator; b. Austin, Tex., Mar. 10, 1940; d. Milton Friedrich Hausmann and Ruth Elizabeth Hornbuckle; m. John Wilson Faules, May 30, 1967. BA cum laude, Harding U., 1962; MA in Curriculum and Instrn., U. Mo., Kansas City, 1995. Cert. elem. tchr., Mo. Tchr. 4th grade Searcy Grammar Sch., Ark., 1962-64, Pulaski County Spl. Sch., Little Rock AFB Elem., Jacksonville, Ark., 1964-67; tchr. grades 3, 4, and 6 Butcher Greene Elem. Consol. Sch. Dist. #4, Grandview, Mo., 1967-98, ret., 1998. Contbr. (poetry) Sunrise and Soft Mist, 1999 (Editor's Choice 1999). Mem. Nat. Congress Parents and Tchr. (hon. life mem.). Mem. Ch. of Christ. Avocations: freelance photography, writing, gardening, reading, traveling. Home: 305 Valley Ct Smyrna TN 37167-5509 E-mail: Tchow1101@aol.com.

FAULKNER, DEBORAH KAY, school system administrator, principal; b. Compton, Calif., June 26, 1951; d. Dwight Eugene and Blondie (Seeger) Lister; m. Edmond Paul Fawaz, Aug. 18, 1973 (div. May 2001); children: Brandon Paul Fawaz, Ryan Matthew Fawaz; m. Jack Taylor Faulkner, June 23, 2001. BA, Calif. State U., Long Beach, 1973; spl. edn. credential, Calif. State U., Chico, 1992, resource specialist credential, 1993, MA. Classroom tchr. Bellflower (Calif.) Unified Sch. Dist., Calif., 1974—83, Ft. Jones (Calif.) Elem. Sch. Dist., 1987—89, resource specialist, 1989—91, Montague (Calif.) Elem. Sch. Dist., 1991—93; supt., prin. Delphic Elem. Sch. Dist., Montague, 1993—. CTAP instr. Calif. Tech. Assistance, Calif., 1994—2000. Bd. mem. Siskiyou County Adv. Bd., Yreka, Calif., 1998—2001. Mem.: AAUW (pres., Woman of Yr. 1992). Home: 15308 N Hwy 3 Fort Jones CA 96032 Office: Delphic Elem Sch Dist 1402 Delphic Rd Montague CA 96064

FAULKNER, JANICE H. state official; BS in English, MA in English, East Carolina U., PhD (hon.), 1997; postgrad., Breadloaf Sch. English, Vt. English prof., dir. alumni affairs, dir. Regional Devel. Inst., assoc. vice chancellor regional devel. East Carolina U.; revenue sec. State of N.C., Raleigh, 1993-96, sec. of state, 1996-97; commr. N.C. Divsn. Motor Vehicles, Raleigh, 1997—. Dir. N.C. Dem. Party; mem. Univ. Found., former chair bd. visitors East Carolina U., former mem. Pitt County Indsl. Devel. Commn.; past pres. N.C. World Trade Assn.; past chair bd. dirs. N.C. Inst. Polit. Leadership; trustee Fedn. Tax Adminstrs. Recipient Disting. Alumnae award East Carolina U., 1993. Mem. Am. Assn. Motor Vehicle Adminstrs. (Region II bd. dirs.). Office: Divsn Motor Vehicles Office of the Commr 1100 New Bern Ave Raleigh NC 27697-0001

FAULKNER, JULIA ELLEN, opera singer; b. St. Louis, Nov. 1, 1957; d. Seldon and Dona Leah (Clark) F. MusB cum laude, Ind. U., 1980, MusM, 1983. Instr. voice No. Ariz. U., Flagstaff, 1984, Iowa State U., 1984-85; solo artist San Francisco Opera Ctr., 1985-86, Wolftrap Opera Co., Vienna, Va., 1986, Bavarian State Opera, Munich, 1987-91, Vienna (Austria) State Opera, 1991-97, Metropolitan Opera, N.Y.C., 1997—; studio voice tchr., 1998—2002; mem. faculty U. Wis. Sch. Music, 2003—. Solo performances with opera cos. and theaters at La Scala, Carnegie Hall, N.Y.C., Met. Opera, N.Y.C., L.A. Philharm., San Francisco Philharm., also in Miami Fla., Berlin, Hamburg, Germany, Lyon, Jerusalem, Bordeau, Stockholm, Amsterdam and Genoa; dir. Oklahoma and Old Maid and the Thief, Flagstaff, 1984; rec. artist Elektra, 1990, Der Rosenkavalier, 1991, Rossini, Semiramide, Schumann, Genoveva; recorded Pergolese Stabat Mater Deutsche Grammophone Das Paradis und die Peri, Verdi's Falstaff. Recipient award Met. Opera, N.Y.C., 1985, 3d prize Whitaker Internat. Voice Competition, 1985, Festspiel prize Bavarian State Opera, 1988. Democrat. Office: Sch of Music Univ Wis Madison WI 53703

FAULKNER, MELANIE E. music educator; d. Miles and Erin Mauldin; m. Rick Faulkner; 1 child, Lindsey Meadows. MusB in Edn., Lee U., Cleveland, Tenn., 1978. Cert. tchr. Fla. Music tchr. Lexington County Sch. Dist. 5, Columbia, SC, 1978—84, Gwinnett County Schs., Lawrenceville, Ga.; music specialist Hillsborough County Schs., Fla., 1989—. Fine arts festival chair Hillsborough County Elem. Music Educators Coun., Tampa, Fla. Named Tchr. of the Yr., N.W. Elem., Tampa, FL, 1997, Hunter's Green Elem., Tampa, FL, 2003. Mem.: Hillsborough County Elem. Music Educators Coun., Fla. Elem. Music Educators Assn., Fla. Music Educators Assn., Music Educators Nat. Conf. Church Of God. Avocations: gardening, piano. Office: Hillsborough County Schs Tampa FL E-mail: melanie.faulkner@sdhc.k12.fl.us.

FAUNCE, LORI, marketing professional, graphics designer; BS in Mktg., West Chester U., 1999. Mktg. mgr. Ednl. Directories Unlimited, Chester, Pa., 1999—. Cons. Design by Mktg., Phila., 2003—. Mem.: Am. Mktg. Assn. Personal E-mail: lorifaunce@yahoo.com.

FAUNCE, SARAH CUSHING, former museum curator; b. Tulsa, Aug. 19, 1929; d. George Jr. and Helen Pauline (Colwell) F. BA, Wellesley Coll., 1951; MA, Washington U., St. Louis, 1959; postgrad., Columbia U., 1960-63. Tchr. history Hartridge Sch., Plainfield, N.J., 1954-56; tchr. art Mary C. Wheeler Sch., Providence, 1958-59; instr. art history Barnard Coll., N.Y.C., 1962-64; sec. adv. council art history Columbia U., 1963-70, registrar, curator, 1965-70; exhbn. cons. Jewish Mus., N.Y.C., 1968-70; curator paintings and sculpture Bklyn. Mus. Art, 1970-98, curator emeritus, project dir. Courbet Catalogue Raisonné project, 1998—. Author: Courbet, 1993; exhbn. catalog author: Anne Ryan Collages, 1974, Carl Larsson, 1982; author, editor: Belgian Art 1880-1914, 1980, Courbet Reconsidered, 1988, In the Light of Italy: Corot and Early Plein Air Painting, 1996; editor: Northern Light: Realism and Symbolism in Scandinavian Painting 1880-1910, 1982. Travel grantee Columbia U., 1963 Mem. AAM-ICOM, Coll. Art Assn., Phi Beta Kappa. Democrat. Home: 28 E 92nd St New York NY 10128-0616 Office: Courbet Catalogue Raisonne Project 28 E 78th St New York NY 10021

FAUNTLEROY, ANGELA COLLEEN, music educator; b. Phila., Dec. 16, 1956; d. Rudolph Simmons and Marlyn Fauntleroy. MusB in applied piano, Boston Conservatory Music, 1978; MusB in music edn., U. of the Arts, 1989; MusM in edn. admin., Cheyney U., 1994. Cert. secondary educator Pa., 1996. Music tchr. Sch. Dist. of Phila., 1980—. Mem.: Nat. Assoc. Female Execs., The Schoolmen's Club of Phila., Sigma Alpha Iota, Kappa Delta Pi, Nu Theta Chpt., Internat. Honor Soc. in Edn. Avocations: travel, dance. Home: 4533 Sansom St Philadelphia PA 19139-3624 Office Phone: 215-299-7000. E-mail: afauntleroy@phila.k12.pa.us.

FAUST, DREW GILPIN, historian, educator; b. N.Y.C., Sept. 18, 1947; d. McGhee Tyson and Catharine (Mellick) G.; m. Stephen Faust, Dec. 28, 1968 (div. 1976); m. Charles E. Rosenberg, June 7, 1980; 1 child, Jessica Rosenberg. BA magna cum laude, Bryn Mawr Coll., 1968; MA, U. Pa., Phila., 1971, PhD, 1975. Asst. prof. Am. civilization U. Pa., Phila., 1976-80, assoc. prof., 1980-84, prof., 1984-89, Stanley I. Sheerr prof. history, 1988-89, Annenberg prof. history, 1989—2000; dean Radcliffe Inst. for Advanced Study at Harvard U., 2000—; Lincoln prof. history Harvard U., 2001—. Walter Lynwood Fleming lectr. La. State U., 1987; mem. ednl. adv. bd. Guggenheim Found., 1988—; cons. Before Freedom Came: African American Life in the Antebellum South, exhbn. at Mus. Confederacy, 1988-91; NEH panel Interpretive Rsch. Program, 1987; mem. Pulitzer Prize History Jury, 1986, 90; lectr. various colls. and univs. Author: A Sacred

Circle: The Dilemma of the Intellectual inthe Old South, 1977, paperback edit., 1986, James Henry Hammond and the Old South: A Design for Mastery, 1982, The Creation of Confederate Nationalism: Ideology and Identity in the Civil War South, 1988, Southern Stories; Slaveholders in Peace and War, 1992, Mothers of Invention: Women of the Slaveholding South in the American Civil War, 1996 ([illegible] prize 1996); mem. editl. bd. Jour. Am. History, 1991—, Pa. Mag. History and Biography, 1986-89, Jour. So. History, 1981-86; contbr. articles to profl. jours. Recipient Jules F. Landry award James Henry Hammond and the Old South, 1982, Charles Sydnor award, Prize Soc. Historians of Early Am. Republic, 1983, article prize Berkshire Conf. Women's Historians, 1991; U. Pa. Rsch. Found. grantee, 1982; assoc. fellow Stanford Humanities Ctr., Stanford U., 1983-84, Am. Coun. Learned Socs. fellow, 1986, Guggenheim fellow, 1987, Mass. Hist. Soc. fellow, 2002, Elizabeth Hall fellow Concord Acad., 2003. Mem. So. Hist. Assn. (chair nominating com. 1993, exec. coun. 1987-90, Frank L. Owsley prize com. 1987, pres. 1999-2000), Am. Hist. Assn. (v.p. profl. divsn. 1992-95, coun. mem. 1992—), Orgn. Am. Historians (chair Avery Craven Prize Com. 1991, chair program com. 1987, mem. coun. 1999-2002), Am. Studies Assn. (mem. coun. 1988-90), Hist. Soc. Pa. (mem. bd. 1988-91), So. Assn. Women Historians (membership com. 1988—, pres. 1998-99). Office: Radcliffe Inst Adv Study Harvard Univ Cambridge MA 02139

FAUST, MARILYN B. middle school principal; Prin. Little Oak Mid. Sch., Slidell, La., 1983—. Recipient Elem. Sch. Recognition award U.S. Dept. Edn., 1989-90. Office: Little Oak Mid Sch 59241 Rebel Dr Slidell LA 70461-3713

FAUST, NAOMI FLOWE, education educator; b. Salisbury, N.C. d. Christopher Leroy and Ada Luella (Graham) Flowe; m. Roy Malcolm Faust, Aug. 16, 1948. AB, Bennett Coll; MA, U. Mich., 1945; PhD, NYU, 1963. Elem. tchr. Pub. Schs. Gaffney (S.C.); tchr. English, French, phys. edn. Atkins H.S., Winston-Salem; instr. English Bennett Coll. and So. U., Scotlandville, La., 1944-46; prof. English Morgan State Coll., Balt., 1946-48; tchr. English Greensboro (N.C.) Pub. Schs., 1948-51, N.Y.C. Pub. Schs., 1954-63; prof. edn. Queens Coll. of CUNY, Flushing, 1964-82; writer, lectr., poetry readings, 1982—. Lectr. in field. Author: Discipline and the Classroom Teacher, 1977; (poetry) Speaking in Verse, 1974, All Beautiful Things, 1983, And I Travel by Rhythms and Words, 1990; contbr. poetry to jours. Named Tchr.-Author of 1979, Tchr.-Writer; recipient Cert. of Merit for Poem Cooper Hill Writers Conf., 1970, Achievement award L.I. br. AAUW, 1985, Poet of the Millennium award Internat. Poets Acad., Excellence in World Poetry award Internat. Poets Acad., 2002; named Internat. Eminent Poet, Internat. Poets Acad. Mem. AAUP, AAUW, Acad. Am. Poets, Nat. Coun. Tchrs. English, Nat. Women's Book Assn., Nat. Assn. Univ. Women (L.I. br.), World Poetry Soc. Intercontinental, N.Y. Poetry Forum, Poetry Soc. Am., NAACP, United Negro Coll. Fund, Alpha Kappa Alpha, Alpha Kappa Mu., Alpha Epsilon. Home: 11201 175th St Jamaica NY 11433-4135

FAUSTMAN, DENISE L. immunologist; b. Royal Oak, Mich., 1958; BS in Zoology and Chemistry, U. Mich., Ann Arbor, 1978; PhD in Transplantation Immunology, Washington U., St. Louis, 1982, MD, 1985. Intern and resident in medicine Mass. Gen. Hosp., Boston; rsch. assoc. Harvard Med. Sch., 1996—; dir. Immunology Lab., Mass. Gen. Hosp., Boston. Sr. editor: Jour. Women's Health. Recipient Arnold B. Zetcher award for excellence in rsch., Bay State chpt. Juvenile Diabetes Found., 1997, Lily Found. award, award, Am. Soc. for Reproductive Medicine, 2000; selected as part of, NIH's "Changing the Face of Medicine" exhbn., 2003. Mem.: AAAS, Diabetes Rsch. Internat. Network (co-founding mem.), Cell Transplant Soc. (founding mem.), Soc. for Women's Health Rsch. (chair bd. dirs. 1998—). Achievements include head of study that cured type I diabetes in mice, 2003. Office: Mass Gen Hosp E Bldg 149 13th St Charlestown MA 02129*

FAVARO, MARY KAYE ASPERHEIM, pediatrician, writer; b. Edgerton, Wis., Sept. 30, 1934; d. Harold Wilbur and Genevieve Catherine (Hyland) Asperheim; m. Biagino Philip Favaro, May 31, 1969; children: Justin Peter, Gina Sue. BS, U. Wis., 1956; MS, St. Louis Coll. Pharmacy, 1965; MD, U. Wis., 1969. Instr. pharmacology St. Louis U. and St. Mary's Hosp. Sch. Practical Nurses, 1959-64; staff pharmacist U. Hosps., Madison, Wis., 1964-65; intern Albany (N.Y.) Med. Center, 1969-70; resident, 1970-71; resident in pediatrics U. S.C., Charleston, 1971-72, asst. prof. pediatrics, 1973-75; pvt. practice pediatrics, 1974-99; ret. Author: Pharmacology, an Introductory Text, 2001; The Pharmacologic Basis of Patient Care, 1985. Mem. AMA. Roman Catholic. Home: 1407 Southwood Dr Surfside Beach SC 29575

FAVOR-HAMILTON, SUZANNE MARIE, track and field athlete, Olympian; b. Stevens Point, Wis., Aug. 8, 1968; m. Mark Hamilton, May 1991. BS, U. Wis., 1991. Track and field athlete Nike. Winner 4 indoor NCAA mile titles, 4 outdoor 1,500m titles; winner 9 NCAA titles and 21 individual Big Ten championships, 6 time nat. champaion; 3 time Olympian; former Am. record holder 1,000 meters; current Am. record holder in indoor 800 meters. Achievements include Am. Record Holder in 1,000m 1995 and indoor 800m, 1999. Office: USA Track and Field PO Box 120 Indianapolis IN 46206-0120

FAVORULE, DENISE, publishing executive; Advt. dir. Stagebill Mag., 1993—96; advt. mgr. Prevention Mag., 1996—98, nat. advt. dir., 1998—99, assoc. pub., 1999—2000, v.p., pub., 2000—. Office: Rondale Press Inc 33 E Minor St Emmaus PA 18098-0099

FAWCETT, FARRAH LENI, actress, model; b. Corpus Christi, Tex., Feb. 2, 1947; d. James William and Pauline Alice (Evans) F.; m. Lee Majors, July 28, 1973 (div. 1982); 1 son, Redmond James. Student, U. Tex. at Austin. Works as model. Movie debut in Myra Breckenridge, 1970; other film appearances include Love is a Funny Thing, 1970, Logan's Run, 1976, Somebody Killed Her Husband, 1978, Sunburn, 1979, Saturn 3, 1980, Cannonball Run, 1981, Extremities, 1986, See You in the Morning, 1989, Man ofthe House, 1995, The Apostle, 1997, The Love Master, 2000, Dr. T and the Women, 2000; TV movie appearances include Charlie's Angels, 1976, Murder in Texas, 1981, The Red Light Sting, 1984, The Burning Bed, 1984, Between Two Women, 1986, Nazi Hunter: The Beate Klarsfeld Story, 1986, Margaret Bourke-White, 1989, The Substitute Wife, 1994, Dalva, 1996, Silk Hope, 1999, Baby, 2000, Jewel, 2001, Hollywood Wives, 2003; regular on TV series Charlie's Angels, 1976-77, Good Sports, 1991, Spin City, 2001, The Guardian, 2001-02; other TV appearances include Harry O, McCloud, The Six Million Dollar Man, Marcus Welby, M.D., Apple's Way; N.Y.C. Stage debut (off-Broadway) Extremities, 1983; TV miniseries appearances include Poor Little Rich Girl: The Barbara Hutton Story, 1987, Small Sacrifices, 1989, Children of the Dust, 1995; Posed for Playboy, 1995. Mem. Delta Delta Delta.*

FAWCETT, GAYLE P. bank executive; m. Ken Fawcett; 2 children. Degree, Mass. Sch. Fin. Studies; student in Fin. Studies, Fairfield U. Cert. para-planner. Joined Berkshire Bank, Pittsfield, Mass., 1977, sr. v.p. Retail Banking and Ops. Bd. dirs. EastPoint Tech. Users Group. Bd. dirs. St.Mark's Ch. Fin. Com. Named One of 25 Women to Watch, U.S. Bankers Mag., 2003. Office: Berkshire Bank 24 North St PPO Box 1308 Pittsfield MA 01202-1308*

FAWCETT, JOY LYNN, professional soccer player; b. Inglewood, Calif., Feb. 8, 1968; m. Walter Fawcett; children: Katelyn Rose, Carli, Madilyn Rae. Degree in phys. edn., U. Calif., Berkeley, 1990. Women's soccer coach UCLA, 1993-97, 1993—97; mem. U.S. Nat. Women's Soccer Team, 1987—; profl. soccer player San Diego Spirit, 2001—03. Named 3-time All-Am., 1987—89, Most Valuable Player, So. Calif., L.A. Times, 1987, World Cup Champion, 1991, 1999, MVP, WUSA, 2002, Defender of Yr., 2002; named to, U. Calif. Berkeley Hall of Fame, 1997; recipient Silver medal, Sydney Olympics, 2000. Achievements include 1995 FIFA World Cup, Sweden; 1994 CONCACAF Qualifying Championship, Montreal, U.S. Olympic Festival, Denver, 1995, FIFA Women's World Cup, Sweden, 1995; gold medal U.S. Olympic Team, 1996; mem. Ajax of Manhattan Beach Club Soccer Team (champions U.S. Women's Amateur Nat. Cup, 1992, 93). Office: US Soccer Fedn 1801-1811 S Prairie Ave Chicago IL 60616

FAWSETT, PATRICIA COMBS, federal judge; b. 1943; BA, U. Fla., 1965, MAT, 1966, JD, 1973. Pvt. practice law Akerman, Senterfitt & Edison, Orlando, Fla., 1973-86; commr. 9th Cir. Jud. Nominating Commn, 1973-75, Greater Orlando Crime Prevention Assn., 1983-86; judge U.S. Dist. Ct. (mid. dist.) Fla., Orlando, 1986—. Trustee Legal Aid Soc., 1977-81, Loch Haven Art Ctr., Inc., Orlando, 1980-84, U. Fla. Law Sch., 2001—; hon. trustee Reago Spiritual Scholarship Found., 1999—; commr. Orlando Housing Authority, 1976-80, Winter Park (Fla.) Sidewalk Festival, 1973-75; bd. dirs. Greater Orlando Area C. of C., 1982-85. Mem. ABA (trial lawyers sect., real estate probate sect.), Am. Judicatures Soc., Assn. Trial Lawyers Am., Fla. Bar Found. (bd. dirs. grants com.), Commn. on Access to Cts., Fla. Coun. Bar Assn. Pres.'s (pres., bd. dirs. 9th cir. grievance com.) Osceola County Bar Assn., Fla. Bar (bd. govs. 1983-86, budget com., disciplinary rev. com., integration rule and bylaws com., com. on access to legal system, bd. of cert., designation and advt., jud. adminstrn., selection and tenure com., jud. nominating procedures com., pub. rels. com., ann. meeting com., appellate rules com., spl. com. on judiciary-trial lawyer rels., chairperson midyr. conv. com., bd. dirs. trial lawyers sect.), Orange County Bar Assn. (exec. coun. 1977-83, pres. 1981-82), Order of Coif, Phi Beta Kappa. Office: US Dist Ct Federal Bldg 80 N Hughey Ave Ste 611 Orlando FL 32801-2231

FAY, CATHARINE C. aerospace engineer; BS in Chemistry, Va. Tech. U.; MS in Applied Sci. Polymer Chemistry, PhD, Coll. William & Mary. Aerospace technologist, chem. engr., polymetric mats. rschr. NASA Langley Rsch. Ctr., Hampton, Va. Contbr. articles to profl. jours.; patentee in field. Avocations: mountain biking, hiking, swimming, volleyball, water skiing. Office: NASA Langley Rsch Ctr 100 Nasa Rd Hampton VA 23681-2199

FAY, SISTER MAUREEN A. university president; BA in English magna cum laude, Siena Heights Coll., 1960; MA in English, U. Detroit, 1966; PhD, U. Chgo., 1976. Tchr. English, speech, moderator student newspaper, student council St. Paul High Sch., Grosse Pointe, Mich., 1960-64; chairperson English dept., dir. student dramatics, moderator student publs. Dominican High Sch., Detroit, 1964-69; co-dir. Cath. student ctr. Adrian (Mich.) Coll., 1969-71; instr. English Siena Heights Coll., Adrian, 1969-71; evaluators inst. criminal justice execs. U. Chgo., 1971-73; instr. English U. Ill., Chgo., 1971-74; dir. evaluation sch. new learning DePaul U., Chgo., 1974-75; fellow in acad. adminstrn. Saint Xavier Coll., Chgo., 1975-76, dean. grad. studies, 1979-83, dean continuing edn., 1976-83; asst. prof. No. Ill. U., Dekalb, 1980-83; pres. Mercy Coll. Detroit, 1983-90, U. Detroit Mercy, 1990—. V.p. VAUT Corp, bd. dirs. four inner city high schs., Archdiocese Chgo.; mem. exec. com. Assn. Mercy Colls.; adv. com. Adult Learning Svcs., The Coll. Bd., Met. Affairs Corp. of Detroit and S.E. Mich., cons. Nat. Assn. for Religious Women, 1974-75, North Cen. Assn. Colls. and Schs., evaluator commn. on higher edn.; trustee Rosary Coll., River Forest, Ill., New Detroit, Inc., 1993; emeritus mem. div. bd. Mercy Hosps. and Health Svcs. of Detroit; bd. dirs. Nat. Bank of Detroit., Detroit Econ. Growth Corp., 1992; mem. Nat. Commn. Ind. Higher Edn.; commr. North Centrl Assocs., Commn. on Instns. of Higher Edn., 1993. Asst. editor: (book rev.): Adult Education, A Journal of Research and Theory, 1971-74. Bd. dirs. United Way SE Mich., 1991, Assn. Catholic Colls. and Univs., 1992; Steering com. Metro Detroit GIVES; exec. com., edn. task force Detroit Strategic Planning com., 1987; trustee Mich. Opera Theatre; bd. dirs. Greater Detroit Interfaith Round Table Nat. Conf. Christians and Jews, Inc., The Detroit Symphony; mem. Nat. Bipartisan Commn. on Ind. Higher Edn. in U.S., 1993. Mem. Am. Assn. Higher Edn., North Cen. Assn. (cons., evaluator commn. on higher edn.), Nat. Assn. Ind. Colls. and Univs. (bd. dirs.), Assn. Ind. Colls. and Univs. of Mich. (exec. com., chairperson), Am. Assn. Cath. Colls. and Univs., AAUW, Pi Lambda Theta. Office: U Detroit Mercy Office Pres PO Box 19900 4001 W McNichols Rd Detroit MI 48219-0900

FAY, TONI GEORGETTE, communications executive; b. N.Y.C., Apr. 25, 1947; d. George E. and Allie C. (Smith) Fay. BA, Duquesne U., Pitts., 1968; MSW, U. Pitts., 1972, MEd, 1973; cert., Yale U. Drug Dependence Unit, 1973. Caseworker N.Y.C. Dept. Welfare, 1968-70; regional commr. Gov. Pa. Coun. Drugs and Alcohol, 1973-76; dir. social svcs. Pitts. Drug Abuse Ctr., 1972-73; dir. planning and devel. Nat. Coun. Negro Women, 1977-79; exec. v.p. D. Parke Gibson Assocs., 1979-82; mgr. cmty. rels. Time Inc. (now AOL Time-Warner Inc.), N.Y.C., 1982-83; dir. corp. cmty. rels. and affirmative action Time Inc. (now Time-Warner Inc.), N.Y.C., 1983-93, v.p., corp. officer, 1993-2001; pres. TGF Assocs., Englewood, N.J., 2001—. Bd. dirs. UNICEF, Congl. Black Caucus Found., NAACP Legal Def. Fund Bd., Franklin and Eleanor Inst., Apollo Theatre Found.; apptd. bd. advs. Nat. Inst. Literacy, 1996—, Corp. for Nat. and Cmty. Svc., 2000. Named Woman of Yr., Pitts. YWCA, 1975, N.Y. Women's Forum; recipient Twin award YWCA of USA, 1987; named one 100 Top Women in Bus., Dollars and Sense Mag., 1986. Office: TGF Assocs 233 W Hudson Ave Englewood NJ 07631 Fax: 201-568-5157. E-mail: tonigfay@aol.com.

FAYE, THALIA GARIN, retired microbiologist, educator; b. Jerusalem, June 9, 1938; came to U.S., 1965; d. Joseph and Esther (Wengroviz) Garin; m. Allan Faye, Aug. 17, 1967; children: Howard, Scott. BSc, Tel-Aviv U., 1960, MSc, 1962. Specialist in clin. microbiology and pub. health. Microbiologist pediat. rsch. Kaplan Hosp., Rehovot, Israel, 1962-64, Biosci. Lab., Van Nuys, Calif., 1966-69; supr. microbiologist Biochem. Lab. Procedure, North Hollywood, Calif., 1969-76; mgr., microbiologist Olive View Med. Ctr., Sylmar, Calif., 1977—2003; ret., 2003—. Mem. NA'AMAT USA (life mem., club pres. 1976-78, coun. pres. 1982-84, nat. bd. dirs. 1987-93, coord. Western area 1997-2001), Am. Soc. Microbiology. Democrat. Jewish. Avocations: reading, computing, solving crossword puzzles. Office: Olive View Med Ctr 14445 Olive View Dr Sylmar CA 91342-1437

FAZIO, EVELYN M. publisher; b. Hackensack, N.J. BA in History, U. Bridgeport, 1975; MA in History, U. Conn., 1977. Cert. social studies tchr., N.J. Tchr. social studies Cedar Grove (N.J.) High Sch., 1977-79; prodn. editor Prentice-Hall, Inc., Englewood Cliffs, N.J., 1980-82, devel. editor, l982-83, acquisitions editor, l983-85; sr. acquisitions editor P-H/Simon & Schuster, Inc., Englewood Cliffs, 1985-88; mng. editor Random House, Inc., N.Y.C., 1988—; exec. editor polit. sci., internat. rels. and policy studies Paragon House Pubs., Inc., N.Y.C., 1989-91; editorial dir. Marshall Cavendish Pubs., N. Bellmore, N.Y., 1992-95; v.p., pub. M.E. Sharpe, Armonk, N.Y., 1995-00; v.p. e-content acquisition Baker & Taylor, Bridgewater, NJ, 2001—03; cons. and lit. agt. ISMF Agy., Hackensack, NJ, 2003. Mem.: Am. Soc. Pubs., ALA (panelist Charleston conf. 2000).

FEARRINGTON, ANN PEYTON, writer, illustrator, newspaper reporter, portraitist; b. Winston-Salem, N.C., Aug. 25, 1945; d. James Cornelius Pass Fearrington and Florence Moore (McCanless-Fearrington) Blackwood; m. Hege Hill Russ, Sept. 1967 (div. 1984); children: James Pass Fearrington Russ, Joseph Peyton Fearrington Russ; m. Vance Edwin Cox, Jr., June 17, 1985; 1 stepson, Charles Jonathan Cox. BA in Secondary Edn. and English, U. N.C., 1967; MS in Life Scis., Botany & Horticulture, N.C. State U., 1972. Mid. sch. tchr. Wake County Sch. Sys., Raleigh, 1967-71; landscape designer pvt. practice N.Y.C., Winston-Salem, N.C., 1972-83; corr. Raleigh News & Observer, 1993—. Writer/artist-in-residence Raleigh-Wake County Pub. Schs., 1997-2000. Author, illustrator: Christmas Lights, 1996, Little Green Book, 18 Keys to Your Child's Reading [illegible], 1999 ([illegible] Newspaper Assn. Literacy award 1999), Teacher and Librarian Guide for the Little Green Book, 2000, Pequeño Libro Verde, 2000, Who Sees the Lighthouse?, 2002. Sch. libr. vol. Wake County Sch. Sys., Raleigh, 1985—; Sunday Sch. tchr. Highland United Meth. Ch., Raleigh, 1986-90. Recipient Literacy award, Southeastern Newspaper Assn., 1999. Mem.: N.C. Reading Assn. (James B. Hunt Literacy award 2001), Internat. Reading Assn., Soc. Children's Book Writers and Illustrators, Beatrix Potter Soc., N.C. State Univ. Club. Avocations: gardening, reading, sketching.

FEATHERMAN, SANDRA, academic administrator, political science educator; b. Phila., Apr. 14, 1934; d. Albert N. and Rebe (Burd) Green; m. Bernard Featherman, Mar. 29, 1958; children: Andrew Charles, John James. BA, U. Pa., 1955, MA, PhD, U. Pa., 1978. Asst. prof. dept. polit. sci. Temple U., Phila., 1978-84, assoc. prof., 1984-91, asst. to pres., 1986-89, pres. faculty senate, 1985-86, dir. Ctr. Pub. Policy, 1986-91; vice chancellor acad. adminstrn., prof. polit. sci. U. Minn., Duluth, 1991-95; pres. U. New Eng., Biddeford, Maine, 1995—. Commr. New Eng. Assn. Schs. and Coll. Higher Edn. Commn., 2002—. Author: Jews, Black and Ethnics, 1979, Race and Politics at the Millenium, 2000; contbr. articles to profl. jours. Nat. bd. Girls Inc., 1971—74; pres. Pa. Fedn. C.C., Girls Inc.; sec. Maine Women's Forum, 2002—; active Maine Compact for Higher Edn., 2003—; bur. osteo. edn. Am. Osteo. Assn., 2004—; nat. bd. dirs. Women and Founds.-Corp. Philanthropy, 1986—91; bd. dirs. Citizens Com. Pub. Edn. Phila., 1977—89, pres., 1979—81; trustee C.C. Phila., 1970—92, chmn. bd. trustees, 1984—86; life trustee, v.p. Samuel Fels Found., 1978—; bd. dirs. United Way SE Pa., 1977—89, United Way Pa., 1981—84, U. New Eng., Gulf of Maine Aquarium, Kennebec Girl Scout Coun., Va. Gildeslove Internat. Fund., 2003—, Vis. Nurse Assn., 2002—03; chair Assembly Pres. Am. Assoc. Coll. Osteopathic Medicine; chmn. Maine Commn. on the State Ceiling on Tax-exempt Bonds, 1999—2000. Recipient Brooks Graves award, Pa. Polit. Sci. Assn., 1982, Cmty. Svc. award, City of Phila., 1984, Women's Achievement award, YWCA, 1989, Adminstr. of Yr. award, Minn. Women in Higher Edn., 1994, Champion of Econ. Growth award, Maine Devel. Found., 2002. Mem.: AAUW (bd. dirs. Phila. chpt. 1975—78, 1980—91, pres. 1984—86, nat. chair internat. fellowships panel 1987—91, nat bd. dirs. 1993—, Outstanding Woman award 1986), Am. Coun. Edn. (commn. on advancement racial and ethnic equality 2001—), Maine Ind. Colls. Assn. (pres. 1998—2000), Greater Portland Alliance Colls. and Univs. (pres. 1997—98), Nat. Assn. Ind. Colls & Univs. (com. policy analysis & pub. rels. 2001—), Am. Polit. Sci. Assn., Maine Ind. Colls. Assn. Office: U New Eng Hills Beach Rd Biddeford ME 04005-9526

FEATHERS, GAIL M. WRATNY, social worker; b. Gowanda, NY, Nov. 19, 1958; d. Frank John and Elinor Louise (Miller) Wratny; m. Donald James Feathers, May 24, 1980; children: Ryan James, David John, Rachel Marie. BA in English, SUNY, Geneseo, 1982; MSW, Syracuse U., 1992. Cert. social worker. Staff U. Rochester (N.Y.) Med. Ctr., 1992; social worker cmty. of caring program Cath. Family Ctr., Rochester, 1993-95, Cath. Charities of Livingston County, Mt. Morris, N.Y., 1995-97; dir. social work Nicholas H. Noyes Meml. Hosp., Dansville, N.Y., 1997—. Social svcs. adv. com. Livingston County Dept. Social Svcs., Mt. Morris, 1993—, chair, 2000—01; social worker early intervention program Livingston County Dept. Health, 1996—2000; mem. Livingston County Teen Pregnancy Prevention Task Force, Mt. Morris, 1993—99, Livingston County Cmty. Resource Network, Mt. Morris, 1993—, chair, 1994—98; family and consumer edn. com. Cornell Coop. Ext., 1999—2002, bd. dirs.; mem. Wayland Cmty. Chest, 1997—2003, sec., 2001—03. Mem. Livingston-Wyoming Assn. Retarded Citizens, 1986—96, bd. dirs., 1987—96, chairperson advocacy com., 1988—92, children's svcs. com., 1988—91; organizer, mem. parents panel on children who have disabilities SUNY Geneseo and Livingston-Wyoming-Steuben Bd. Coop. Ednl. Svcs., 1988—94; mem. adv. coun. N.Y. State Senate Select Com. for the Disabled, NY, 1990—92; mem. Rochester Sch. Deaf Task Force, 1996; mem. deaf awareness panel SUNY Geneseo and Nat. Tech. Inst. for the Deaf, 1998—99. Mem.: NASW. Avocations: golf, reading. E-mail: gfeathers@noyes-hospital.org., rdfthr3307@aol.com.

FEATHERSTONE, DIANE L. utilities executive; B in Econs. and History, Towson U.; M in Econs., U. Va. CPA. Joined Constellation, 1976; pres. Constellation Energy Source; v.p. mgmt. consulting and auditing Constellation Energy Group, Balt.; v.p., gen. auditor Edison Internat., Rosemead, Calif., 2002—, v.p., gen. auditor So. Calif. Edison subs., 2002—. Office: Edison Internat 2244 Walnut Grove Ave Rosemead CA 91770

FEBO, DIANA LUCILE, counseling administrator; b. Columbus, Ohio, June 26, 1947; d. Lawrence W. and Lucile Waddell; m. Paul Richard Febo; children: Laurie Johnson, Leandra Thompson, Lawrence. BS in Edn., Miami U., Oxford, Ohio, 1968; MS in Edn., U. Dayton, Ohio, 1985. Cert. tchr. Ohio, counselor Ohio. Counselor So. State C.C., Ohio, 1990—2001, instr. English and speech, 1986—2001, mgr., 2001—. Trainer, counselor, corp. and cmty. svc. So. State C.C., Washington Court House, 1998—2003. Mem.: Fayette County WIA Youth Coun., Fayette County Youth Asset Builders, Nat. Employment Coun. Assn., Am. Coun. Assn. Lutheran. Avocations: genealogy, gardening, mosaic/stained glass crafting. Home: 3721 US 62 SW Washington Court House OH 43160 Office: So State Cmty Coll 1270 US 62 SW Washington Court House OH 43160 Business E-Mail: dfebo@sscc.edu.

FEDER, JUDITH, dean; BA in Polit. Sci., Brandeis U., 1968; MA in Polit. Sci., Harvard U., 1970, PhD in Polit. Sci., 1977. Author: Medicare: The Politics of Federal Hospital Insurance, 1977; author: (with John Holahan) Financing Health Care for the Elderly: Medicare, Medicaid and Private Health Insurance, 1979; author: (with Jack Hadley and John Holahan) Insuring the Nation's Health: Market Competition, Catastrophic and Comprehensive Approaches, 1981; editor (with John Holahan and Theodore Marmor): National Health Insurance: Conflicting Goals and Policy Choices, 1980; editor: (with Diane Rowland and Anita Salganicoff) Medicaid Financing Crisis: Balancing Responsibilities, Priorities and Dollars, 1993; contbr. articles to profl. jours., chapters to books. Mem.: Inst. Medicine. Office: Georgetown Pub Policy Inst 3600 N St NW Ste 200 Washington DC 20007*

FEDERMAN, SIMONE, theater educator, theater director; b. Santa Barbara, Calif., Dec. 7, 1962; d. Raymond and Erica Federman. BA, Oberlin Coll., 1984; MFA, Harvard U., 1994. Edn. specialist C.A.M.B.A., Bklyn., 1988; dir., counselor, outreach coord., teen specialist N.Y. Women Against Rape, 1988—92; instr. Harvard U., Cambridge, Mass., 1992—94; lectr. Bowdoin Coll., Brunswick, Maine, 1996—99; asst. prof. SUNY New Paltz, 1999—. Acting coach, cons., N.Y.C., 1994—; educator, actor AIDS Prevention Project Reality Theater, N.Y.C., 1990—92; instr. Philajob Arts and Culture Program, Phila., 1990; coord. Youth Devel. Program The Friendly Place-El Sitio Simpatico, Harlem, NY, 1989—90; asst. tchr. Children's Storefront Sch., Harlem, 1988. Dir.: (plays) N.Y.C., New Paltz, N.Y., Portland, Maine, Cambridge, Mass., Oberlin, Ohio; actor: N.Y.C., Portland, Maine, Bread and Puppet Theatre. Home: 138 Ludlow St #24 New York NY 10002*

FEDOR, TERESA, state senator; b. Toledo, May 2, 1956; BS in Edn., U. Toledo. State rep. Ohio Ho. of Reps., Columbus, 2000—02; state sen., dist. 11 Ohio State Senate, Columbus, 2003—, ranking minority mem., pub. utilities com., mem. edn., ins., commerce and labor, judiciary criminal justice, and rules coms. Named Legislator of Yr., Ohio Environ. Coun., Second Harvest Food Banks; recipient award, Internat. Reading Assn., 1990. Mem.: Women's Legis. Network, Nat. Caucus Women in Govt., Nat. Caucus Environ. Legislators, Nat. Conf. State Legislators, Ohio Fedn. Tchrs. Democrat. Office: Senate Bldg Rm # 226, 2d fl Columbus OH 43215

FEDOROFF, NINA VSEVOLOD, research scientist, consultant, educator; b. Cleve., Apr. 9, 1942; d. Vsevolod N. and Olga S. (Snegireff) Stacy; children: Natasha, Kyr, James. BS, Syracuse U., 1966; PhD, Rockefeller U., 1972. Asst. mgr. transl. bur. Biol. Abstracts, Phila., 1962-63; flutist Syracuse (N.Y.) Symphony Orch., 1964-66; acting asst. prof. UCLA, 1972-74; postdoctoral fellow UCLA and Carnegie Inst. Washington, Los Angeles and Balt., 1974-78; staff scientist Carnegie Inst. Washington, Balt., 1978-95; dir. Biotechnol. Inst., Pa. State U., 1995—, Willaman prof. of life scis., 1995—, Evan Pugh prof., 2002—; external faculty Santa Fe Inst., 2003—. Dir. Life Scis. Consortium, Pa. State U., 1996—2002; prof. dept. biology John Hopkins U., 1979-95; mem. devel. biology panel NSF, Washington, 1979-80; sci. adv. panel Office of Tech. Assessment, Congress, Washington, 1979-80; recombinant DNA adv. com. NIH, Bethesda, Md., 1980-84; sci. adv. com. Japanese Human Frontier Sci., 1988; sci adv. com. Competitive Rsch. Grants Office, USDA; mem. commn. on life scis., basic biology bd. NRC, NAS, 1984-90; bd. dirs. Genetics Soc. Am.; mem. bd. overseers Harvard U., 1988-91; trustee BIOSIS, Phila., 1990-96; mem. NAS Coun., 1991-94; dir. Internat. Sci. Found., 1992-93; mem. adv. com. Directorate for Biol. Scis., 1994-97; chmn., bd. dirs. Sigma-Aldrich Corp., 1996—. Editor: Gene, 1981—84, Perspectives in Biology and Medicine, 1991—2001, Procs. Nat. Acad. Sci., 1996—2000; editor, bd. rev. editors: Sci., 1985, mem. sci. adv. bd.: The Plant Jour., 1991—98, book editor: various publs.; contbr. chapters to books articles to profl. jours. Recipient Merit award, NIH, 1990, Howard Taylor Ricketts award, U. Chgo., 1990, Arents Pioneer award, Syracuse U., 2003; grantee, NSF and USDA, 1979—84, NIH, 1984—, NSF, 1992—, NASA, 1997—. Mem.: AAAS, NAS (editor procs. 1995—), AAAS (bd. dirs. 2000—03), Am. Acad. Arts and Scis., Nat. Sci. Bd., Sigma Xi (McGovern Sci. and Soc. medal 1997, 1997), Phi Beta Kappa (vis. scholar 1984—85, vis. scholar 1984—85), Sigma Xi, Phi Beta Kappa. Avocations: chamber music, gardening, skiing, tennis, flying. Home: 2398 Shagbark Ct State College PA 16803-3367 Office: Huck Insts Life Scis Pa State U University Park PA 16802

FEEBACK, CYNTHIA ANN, corporate financial executive, accountant; b. Hinton, Okla., Aug. 30, 1957; d. Billy Vernon Warden and Mary Ann Findley; m. Daniel Lee Feeback, May 1, 1981; 1 child, Shauna Lee. BS in Accountancy, U. Ill., Urbana, 1977—79. CPA Ill., 1979, reciprocal lic., Okla., 1981. Staff auditor Arthur Andersen & Co., Okla. City, 1979—81; contr. Hoover Oper. Co., 1981—88; acctg. mgr. Plains Resources Inc., Okla. City, 1988—90, contr., 1990—91, Houston, 1991—93, contr. and prin. acctg. officer, 1993—99, v.p. - acctg. & asst. treas., 1999—2001; v.p. acctg. and treas. Plains All Am. Pipeline, L.P., Houston, 2000—01; sr. v.p. - acctg. and treas. Plains Resources Inc., Houston, 2001—02, Plains Exploration & Prodn. Co., 2002—. Mem.: AICPA. Office: Plains Exploration & Prodn Co Ste 700 500 Dallas Houston TX 77059

FEEBACK, LORETA DOTALINE KREEGER, artist; b. Omaha, July 7, 1938; BFA, Kansas City Art Inst., 1960; MA, U. Mo., Kansas City, 1993. Sales/designer Keeshan's Frame & Gallery, Kansas City, Mo., 1991—95; sales cons. Keith Coldsnow Artist Materials, Overland Park, Kans., 1995—98; art tchr. Johnson Co. C.C., Overland Park, 1998—2001, Johnson County Parks and Recreation, Overland Park, 1992—. Pastel Artist Internat., 1999, book, The Best of Pastels, 1996, mag., Pastel Artist Internat., 2001; actor:. Recipient Patron award, Kans. Pastel Soc., 1988—89, Juror's award, Degas Pastel Soc., 1990, Nat. Art Competition, City of Merriam, Kans., 1998—2003. Mem.: Nat. Oil and Acrylic Painters Soc., MidAm. Pastel Soc.

FEENEY, JOAN N. judge; BA in French and Govt., Conn. Coll., 1975; MA, Amherst Coll.; JD, Suffolk Univ. Law Sch., 1978. Law clk. to Judge Harold Lavien U.S. Bankruptcy Ct. Mass., 1978-79, law clk. to Judge James N. Gabriel, 1978-79, 82-86; assoc. Feeney & Freeley, Boston, 1979-82; assoc., then ptnr. Hanify & King P.C., Boston, 1986-92; bankruptcy judge U.S. Bankruptcy Ct. Mass., Boston, 1992—. Mem. Suffolk Univ. Law Review, 1976-78; editor Suffolk Transnational Journal, 1977-78, Suffolk Voluntary Defenders, 1977-78, Volunteer Lawyer's Project. Mem. Mass. Assn. of Women Lawyers, Am. Bankruptcy Inst. Office: Thomas O'Neill Federal Bldg 10 Causeway St Rm 1101 Boston MA 02222-1009

FEENEY, KENDALL GREER, art director, music educator; b. Pomona, CA, Apr. 26, 1958; d. John Francis Feeney, Carol McEuen Feeney; m. Anthony Michael Flinn. Bachelor of Music, University of Southern California, Los Angeles, California, 1978—80, Masters of Music, 1981—84. Artistic dir. ZEPHYR, Spokane, Wash., 1991—; faculty assoc. Ea. Wash. U., Cheney, 1990—. Guest spkr. Wash. State Music Tchrs Assn., 1987—; faculty mem. Taubman Inst. Piano, Williamstown, Mass., 1997—. Musician: (Concert performer) Bellingham Music Festival, 2000, Round Top Festival Inst., 1983—84, New Coll. Festival, 1981, author essay writer for Clavier magazine. Board Member Hanford Education and Action League, Spokane, WA, 1986—99. Recipient Artist of the Yr. award, Spokane, Wash., 1997. Mem.: Music Teachers National Association. Avocation: Reading, gardening, animals, equestrian work, outdoors. Home: 1230 East 14th Ave Spokane WA 99202 Office: Eastern Washington University Music Department Cheney WA 99004 Personal E-mail: kgfeeney@earthlink.net. Business E-Mail: kfeeney@ewu.edu.

FEENEY, MARYANN MCHUGH, not-for profit professional; b. Bklyn., July 9, 1948; d. Michael Daniel and Mary Bridget (Hourican) McH.; m. Brian Francis Feeney, Sept. 21, 1974 (dec. Mar. 1992); 1 child, Michael. BA, Marymount Manhattan Coll., 1980; MA, Bklyn. Coll., 2002. Human resources mgr. Muir Cornelius Moore, Inc., N.Y.C., 1977-84; human resources dir. Statue of Liberty-Ellis Island Found., N.Y.C., 1984—95; pres. The Taft Inst., N.Y.C., 1995—97; dir. nat. fundraising Girls Scouts U.S.A., N.Y.C., 1997—99; exec. dir. Bklyn. Tech. H.S. Alumni Assn., 2003—. Exec. producer Your Vote Video, 1991 (nominated ACE and Emmy awards 1991). Bd. dirs. Bklyn. Conservatory of Music, 1992-94, SFX-Prospect Park Baseball, Bklyn., 1986—; pres. emeritus, trustee The Taft Inst. at Queens Coll., 1997—; trustee Park Slope Civic Coun. Recipient Cmty. Svc. award SFX-Prospect Park Baseball, 1992, 95, 97. Mem. Ireland House at NYU, Park Slope Civic Coun. Democrat. Roman Catholic. Avocations: reading, history, gardening. Office Phone: 718-797-2285. E-mail: mfeeney3@aol.com.

FEHIR, KIM MICHELE, oncologist, hematologist; b. Chgo., Aug. 31, 1947; d. William Frank and Beatric Mae (Mc Glaughlin) Debelak; m. John Stephen Fehir, Dec. 24, 1974. BS, Mich. State U., 1969; MS, U. Ill., Chgo., 1973, PhD, 1975; MD, Rush Med. Sch., Chgo., 1978. Diplomate Am. Bd. Internal Medicine. Intern, resident John Hopkins Hosp., Balt., 1978-81; fellow in oncology Meml. Sloan Kettering Cancer Ctr., N.Y.C., 1981-83; dir. med. oncology Stehlin Oncology Clin., Houston, 1983—. Asst. prof. medicine Bayler Coll., Houston, 1983-98. Contbr. to profl. jours. Mem. AMA, Am. Med. Soc. Hematologist, Am. Med. Soc. Clin. Oncology. Republican. Avocations: running, climbing, skiing. Office: Med Assocs of Johnson County 497 W Lott St Buffalo WY 82834-1609 E-mail: kfehir@wyoming.com.

FEHR, LOLA MAE, health organization administrator; b. Hastings, Nebr., Sept. 29, 1936; d. Leland R. and Edith (Wunderlich) Gaymon; m. Harry E. Fehr, Aug. 15, 1972; children: Dawn, Cheryl, Michael. RN, St. Luke's Hosp., Denver, 1958; BSN magna cum laude, U. Denver, 1959; MS, U. Colo., Boulder, 1975. Dir. staff devel. Weld County Gen. Hosp., Greeley, Colo., 1972-76, dir. nursing, 1976-80; exec. dir. Colo. Nurses Assn., Denver, 1980-89; dir. membership Assn. Oper. Rm. Nurses, Inc., Denver, 1989-90, exec. dir., 1990-99; pres. Fehr Cons. Resources, Frisco, Colo., 1999—; exec. dir. Am. Soc. Bariatric Physicians, 2000—01; program dir. Colo. Ctr. for Nursing Excellence, 2003; exec. dir. N.Y. State Nurses Assn., 2003—. Editor Colo. Nurse, 1980-89. Recipient U. Colo. Alumni award, Colo. Nurses Assn. Profl. Nurse of Yr. award. Mem. Am. Acad. Nursing, Nat. Assn. Parliamentarians, Am. Soc. Assn. Execs., Colo. Nurses Assn., Sigma Theta Tau.

FEHRING, MARY ANN, secondary school educator; Secondary tchr. Bishop Noll Inst., Hammond, Ind. Named Outstanding High Sch. tchr. Inland Steel Ryerson Found., 1992. Office: Bishop Noll Inst 1518 Hoffman St Hammond IN 46327-1769

FEIDNER, MARY P. retired speech and language pathologist; b. Cin., Jan. 24, 1933; d. Paul Francis and Rosemary (Witte) Thesing; m. Edward Joseph Feidner, Aug. 27, 1955; children: Julie Marie, Elizabeth Ann, David Mark, Eric Joseph, Jon Edward. BS in Secondary Edn., U. Dayton, 1954; MS in Speech Pathology, U. Vt., 1971; cert. advanced grad. study, St. Michael's Coll., 1987. Elem. tchr. Holy Angels Sch., Dayton, Ohio, 1954-55, Norfolk (Va.) Sch. Dist., 1955-56; speech instr. U. Vt., Burlington, 1965-66; speech therapist Ctr. for Disorders of Comm., Burlington, 1966-69; speech-lang. pathologist So. Burlington (Vt.) Sch. Dist., 1971-95. Clin. supr. U. Vt., Burlington, 1990-95. Lister Town of Hinesburg, Vt., 1995-2000; coord. Friends of Families, Hinesburg, 1998—2000 project dir. Vt. Coun. Humanities, Hinesburg, 1999-2000; chmn. Hinesburg Dem. Com., 1997-2000; docent Park-McCullough Historic House, North Bennington, Vt. Mem. Am. Speech, Lang., and Hearing Assn., Vt. Speech, Lang., and Hearing Assn., Lions, Delta Kappa Gamma (state pres. 1999-2001, pres. chpt. 2001-03). Democrat. Avocations: piano, reading, attending plays and concerts, playreading group, writing group. Home: 26 College Rd North Bennington VT 05257 E-mail: maryfeidner@earthlink.net.

FEIGENHOLTZ, SARA, state legislator; b. Chgo., Dec. 11, 1956; d. Bernard and Florence (Buky) F. Student, Northeastern Ill. U. Ill. state rep. Dist. 12, 1995—. Chmn. human svcs. com. Ill. Ho. of Reps., co-chair tobacco settlement proceeds distribution, vice-chair health care availabity com., mem. state govt. adminstrn. and appropriations human svcs. coms.; exec. dir. Cen. Lakeview Merchants Assn., 1993-94; former cons., Chgo. Mem. NOW, Nat. Coun. Jewish Women, Am. Jewish Coun. (gov. coun. 1994-95), Conf. Women Legislators, Phi Theta Kappa. Office: 1051 W Belmont Ave Chicago IL 60657-3327

FEIGIN, BARBARA SOMMER, marketing consultant; b. Berlin, Nov. 16, 1937; arrived in US, 1940, naturalized, 1949; d. Eric Daniel and Charlotte Martha (Demmer) Sommer; m. James Feigin, Sept. 17, 1961; children: Michael, Peter, Daniel. BA in Polit. Sci., Whitman Coll., 1959; cert. of Bus. Adminstrn., Harvard-Radcliffe Program Bus. Adminstrn., 1960. Mktg. rsch. asst. Richardson-Vick Co., Wilton, Conn., 1960-61; market rsch. analyst SCM Corp., N.Y.C., 1961-62; group rsch. supr. Benton & Bowles, Inc., N.Y.C., 1963-67; assoc. rsch. dir. Marplan Rsch. Co., N.Y.C., 1968-69, exec. v.p. worldwide strategic svcs., mem. agy. policy coun. Grey Advt. Inc., N.Y.C., 1969-99, cons., dir. Bd dirs VF Corp, Circuit City Stores, Inc. Contbr. articles to profl jours. Overseer emeritus Whitman Col; past bd advisors Catalyst. Recipient Women Achievers Award, YWCA, 1987. Mem.: Advert Research Found (past chmn, bd dirs). Office: 777 3d Ave 36th Fl New York NY 10017

FEIGL, DOROTHY MARIE, chemistry educator, university official; b. Evanston, Ill., Feb. 25, 1938; d. Francis Philip and Marie Agnes (Jacques) F. BS, Loyola U., Chgo., 1961; PhD, Stanford U., 1966; postdoctoral fellow, N.C. State U., 1965-66. Asst. prof. chemistry St. Mary's Coll., Notre Dame, Ind., 1966-69, assoc. prof., 1969-75, prof., 1975—, chmn. dept. chemistry and physics, 1977-85, bd. regents, 1976-82, acting v.p., dean faculty, 1985-87, v.p., dean faculty, 1987-99, Denise DeBartolo York prof. of chemistry, 2003—. Author: (with John Hill and Erwin Boschmann) General Organic and Biological Chemistry, 1991, (with John Hill and Stuart Baum) Chemistry and Life, 1997; contbr. articles to chem. jours., chpts. to texts. Recipient Spes Unica award St. Mary's Coll., 1973, Maria Pieta award, 1977 Mem. Am. Chem. Soc., Royal Soc. Chemistry, Internat. Union Pure and Applied Chemistry, Sigma Xi, Iota Sigma Pi. Democrat. Roman Catholic. Office: Dept Chemistry Saint Mary's College Notre Dame IN 46556

FEIGON, JUDITH TOVA, ophthalmologist, surgeon, educator; b. Galveston, Tex., Dec. 2, 1947; d. Louis and Ethel Feigon; m. Nathan C. Goldman; children: Michael G., Miriam G. AB, Barnard Coll., Columbia U., 1970; postgrad., Rice U., U. Houston, 1970-71; MD, U. Tex., San Antonio, 1976. Diplomate Am. Bd. Ophthalmology. Intern Mt. Auburn Hosp., Cambridge, Mass.; intern, clin. tchg. fellow Harvard U. Med. Sch., 1976-77; resident in ophthalmology Baylor Coll. Medicine, Houston, 1977-80, fellow in retina, 1980-82, clin. faculty, 1982-95; asst. prof. ophthalmology U. Tex. Med. Br., Galveston, 1982-85, clin. asst. prof., 1985-91, clin. assoc. prof., 1992—; pvt. practice medicine specializing ophthalmology, vitreoretinal diseases, surgery, Houston, 1983—. Physician advisor to Houston br. Tex. Soc. to Prevent Blindness, 1987-89, also bd. dirs.; mem. staff Meth., St. Lukes, Tex. Children's, St. Joseph's Hosp.; clin. faculty Baylor Coll. Medicine, 1992-95. Contbr. articles to profl. publs. Mem. Assn. Am. Physicians and Surgeons, Am. Acad. Ophthalmology, Tex. Med. Assn. Houston Ophthal. Soc., Harris County Med. Soc., U. Tex. San Antonio Alumni Assn., Am. Soc. Retina Specialists, Tex. Ophthalmol. Assn. Office: 7515 Main St Ste 650 Houston TX 77030-4599

FEILER, JO ALISON, artist; b. LA, Apr. 16, 1951; d. Alfred Martin (dec.) and Leatrice Lucille Feiler. Student, UCLA, 1969, Art Ctr. Coll. Design, L.A., 1970-72; BFA, Calif. Inst. Arts, 1973, MFA, 1975. Asst. dir. Frank Perls Gallery, Beverly Hills, Calif., 1969-70; photography editor Coast Environ. mag., L.A., 1970-72; art dir. Log/An Inc., L.A., 1975-82. One-woman shows Inst. Contemporary Art, London, 1975, Calif. Inst. Arts, Valencia, 1975, NUAGE, L.A., 1978, Susan Harder Gallery, N.Y.C., 1984; exhibited in numerous group shows, 1975—; represented in permanent collections including Nat. Portrait Gallery, London, Victoria and Albert Mus., London, Met. Mus. Art, N.Y.C., Mus. Modern Art, N.Y.C., Los Angeles County Mus. Art, Internat. Mus. Photography, Rochester, N.Y., Santa Barbara Mus. Art, Oakland Mus., Mus. Fine Arts, Houston, Bibliotheque Nat., Paris, Musee D'Art Moderne De La Ville De Paris, Fondation Vincent Van Gogh, Arles, France, others. Recipient cert. art excellence Los Angeles County Mus. Art, 1968, award Laguna Beach Mus. Art, 1976; Calif. Inst. Arts scholar, 1974. Mem. Royal Photog. Soc. Gt. Britain, Friends of Photography. Democrat. Avocations: cross-country skiing, tennis, collecting art and books, music. Address: Manoir de Clairefontaine Chemin Fontaine Marie 14910 Benerville-Sur-Mer France E-mail: feiler77@aol.com.

FEIN, LEONA MOSS, artist; b. N.Y.C., Apr. 6, 1930; d. Leo and Pauline (Binnick) Moss; m. Harris Abraham Fein, May 25, 1952 (dec. Oct. 25, 1988); children: Ellen Beth Fein Shapiro, Scott Martin, Eric Bruce. BA in Studio Art, Queens Coll., 1980. Instr. The Craft Students League, N.Y.C., 1972-87; owner Leona M. Fein Ltd., Nassau County, N.Y., 1982—. Lectr. Met. Mus. of Art, N.Y.C., 1970-80; cons., tchr. N.Y. Coun. Arts, N.Y.C., Elder Craftsman, N.Y.C. One-woman show Queens Coll., N.Y.C., 1981; gallery show Nabisco Internat. and more, 1986; artist-in-residence Queens Mus., N.Y.C.; represented in collection of Pres. Bill Clinton. Recipient Woman of Distinction award, 2004. Mem. Nat. Assn. Women Artists, Nat. Guild Decoupeurs, Guild Judaic Artists. Avocation: travel. Home and Office: 125 Knickerbocker Rd Plainview NY 11803-2629 E-mail: LeonaMFein@aol.com.

FEIN, LINDA ANN, nurse anesthetist, consultant; b. Cin., Dec. 10, 1949; d. Joseph and Elizabeth P. (Kannady) Stofle; m. Thomas Paul Fein, Dec. 11, 1971. Nursing diploma, Miami Vly. Hosp. Sch. Nursing, Dayton, Ohio, 1971, Wright State U., 1969; postgrad., U. Cin. Med. Ctr., 1978. Nursing asst. Miami Vly. Hosp, 1969-71; staff nurse operating rm. Cin. Children's Hosp. & Med. Ctr., 1971, 73, Peninsula Hosp., Burlingame, Calif., 1972-73; staff nurse operating rm., emergency rm. Doctor's Hosp., San Diego, 1972; staff nurse emergency rm. Ohio State U. Hosps., Columbus, 1973-75, head nurse operating rm., 1975-76; staff nurse anesthetist Bethesda Hosps., Cin., 1978-86, Mercy Hosp. Fairfield, Cin., 1986-95; locum tenens anesthetist Fort Hamilton-Hughes Hosp., Hamilton, Ohio, 1994—95, staff anesthetist, 1995—, Butler County Surgery Ctr., Hamilton, 2000—. Childbirth educator psychoprophylactic method, 1975—; critical care nursing cons. Med. Communicators & Assocs., Salt Lake City, 1985-89; ind. nursing cons., 1989—; co-owner Exec. Shops, Cin., 1982-85; spkr. in field. Search com. Cin. Gen. Hosp. Sch. Anesthesia for Nurses, 1981-82; bd. dirs. YWCA, 1988-91, Children's Diagnostic Ctr., 1989-95, pres. bd. dirs., 1994, Planned Parenthood, 1992-95. Recipient recognition award for profl. excellence First Nurse Anesthesia Faculty Assocs., 1982, Florence Nightingale awards, 1995. Mem. Miami Vly. Hosp. Sch. Nursing Alumni Assn., Cin. Gen. Hosp. Sch. Anesthesia for Nurses Alumni Assn., Nurse Anesthetists Greater Cin., Ohio Assn. Nurse Anesthetists, Am. Assn. Nurse Anesthetists, Am. Assn. Critical Care Nurses, Nat. Registry Cert. Nurses in Advanced Practice (cert.), Ohio Coalition Nurses with Specialty Cert., Am. Soc. Critical Care Medicine, Am. Trauma Soc., NAFE, Altrusa Internat. (officer 1985-92), Order Eastern Star. Republican. Methodist. Avocations: antiques, gourmet cooking, african violets, roses, swimming. Home: 650 History Bridge Ln Hamilton OH 45013-3659

FEINBERG, GLENDA JOYCE, restaurant chain executive; b. Louisville, Feb. 8, 1948; d. Harold and Winnie Esther (McIntosh) F.; divorced; 1 child, Anthony John. Student, Purdue U., 1967-68, Ind. U., 1977-79. Cert. in restaurant and personnel mgmt. Beverage mgr. Don Ce Sar Beach Hotel, St Petersburg Beach, Fla., 1979-80; catering dir. Best Western-Skyway Inn, St. Petersburg, Fla., 1980-83; gen. mgr. Village, Inc., St. Petersburg Beach, 1983-86; banquet mgr. Tradewinds Resort Hotel, St. Petersburg Beach, 1986-87; exec. mgr. Ponderosa, Inc., Clearwater, Fla., 1987-90; food and beverage dir. Days Inn Island Beach Resort, St. Petersburg Beach, 1990-92; owner, mgmt. cons., pvt. caterer G.F. Sans Inc., 1992—. Bd. dirs. AIDS Coalitions Pinellas, 1990. Mem. NOW, World Wildlife Fedn., Nat. Geog. Soc., Greenpeace, Amnesty Internat., Environ. Def. Fund, Nat. Audubon Soc., Nat. Arbor Day Found. Democrat.

FEINBERG, WENDIE, producer; BS in Journalism, U. Fla.; MS in Journalism, Boston U. Sr. prodr. Nightly Bus. Report, Miami, Fla. Office: NBR Enterprises 14901 NE 20th Ave Miami FL 33181-1121

FEINER, ARLENE MARIE, librarian, researcher, consultant; b. Spring Green, Wis., Mar. 23, 1937; d. Herman Joseph and Cecelia Margaret (Meixelsperger) F. BA in History, Alverno Coll., 1959; MA in Libr. Sci., Rosary Coll., 1971; MA in Orgnl. Devel., Loyola U., Chgo., 1985. Gen. office worker USIA, Washington, 1959-60; adminstrv. sec. Nat. Coun. Cath. Women, Washington, 1960-62; asst. libr. U. Md., Munich, 1962-64; preliminary cataloger, 1st editor MARC Pilot Project Libr. of Congress, Washington, 1965-67; head libr. Acad. Holy Cross, Kensington, Md., 1967-70, Jesuit Sch. Theology Libr., Chgo., 1971-79; coord. serial activities, women's studies bibliographer Loyola U., Chgo., 1979-86; tech. svcs., collection devel. cons. DuPage Libr. Sys., Ill., 1986-91; contract adminstr. Wabash Nat. Fin., Arlington Heights, Ill., 1992-99; founder, dir. Women's Inst. and Gallery, New Harmony, Ind., 2000—. Editor: (bibliography) Current Serials, 1980-85; compiler: (bibliography) Guide to Women's Studies Sources, 1985; author poems; contbr. articles to profl. jours. Bd. dirs. Women's World Ctr., Chgo., 1985—88. Grantee Assn. Theol. Schs. in U.S. and Can., 1976. Mem. ALA, Nat. Mus. Women in Arts, C.G. Jung Inst. Chgo. Roman Catholic. Avocations: poetry, hiking, music. Home: PO Box 373 New Harmony IN 47631-0373

FEINER, AVA SOPHIA, public affairs and management consultant, economist; b. Bklyn., Feb. 13, 1950; d. Ignace and Lola (Pasternak) F.; m. Clifford Douglas Stromberg, June 25, 1972; children: Kimberly Greta, Eric George. BA summa cum laude, Yale U., 1971; MA, Harvard U., 1974, PhD in Govt., 1978. Legis. asst. to U.S. Senator Bill Bradley, Washington, 1979-82; dir. internat. trade policy U.S. C. of C., Washington, 1982-83, mgr. internat. policy dept., 1983-85; corp. program dir. IBM, Washington, 1985-87, corp. dir. pub. affairs, trade and investment, 1987; pres. Feiner Pub. Affairs Cons., Washington, 1988—; co-founder, dir. Washington Alive! Inc., 1989-90, pres. Washington Networks, 1990—; mem. campaign and transition team Ehrlich for Gov., 2002; mem. Md. State Ethics Commn., 2003—. Tchg. fellow Harvard U., Cambridge, Mass., 1972-74; lectr. nat. and internat. politics and econs., 1978—; bd. dirs. World Trade Forum, Washington, 1987-89. Co-author: American Excellence in A World Economy, 1987; contbr. articles on econs., trade, fgn. policy to various publs. Del. to Atlantic Coun. Young Leadership Program, Wis. and Can., 1978, 80, Aspen Inst. Exec. Seminar, 1982, Germany-U.S. Young Leadership Conf., San Francisco, 1982, Harbor Sch. Bd., 1992-93; co-chair Holton-Arms Sch. Silent Auction, 1995-96; mem. adv. com. Cmty. Homeowners, 1999—, chmn., 2001—; 1st v.p. Potomac Women's Rep. Club., 2002-03. Fgn. Policy fellow Brookings Instn., 1975-76, guest scholar, 1976-77; Carnegie Endowment for Internat. Peace fellow, 1975-76; finalist Photographer's Forum Mag. Mem.: Trade Policy Forum, Coun. Fgn. Rels. (task force on women 1988—91, term membership com. 1988—91, internat. affairs fellows com. 1991—95, Washington program adv. com. 1995—98), Phi Beta Kappa. Avocations: photography, Karate, swimming, bicycling, tennis.

FEINSTEIN, DIANNE, senator; b. San Francisco, June 22, 1933; d. Leon and Betty (Rosenburg) Goldman; m. Bertram Feinstein, Nov. 11, 1962 (dec.); 1 child, Katherine Anne; m. Richard C. Blum, Jan. 20, 1980. BA History, Stanford U., 1955; LLB (hon.), Golden Gate U., 1977; D Pub. Adminstrn. (hon.), U. Manila, 1981; D Pub. Service (hon.), U. Santa Clara, 1981; JD (hon.), Antioch U., 1983, Mills Coll., 1985; LHD (hon.), U. San Francisco, 1988. Fellow Coro Found., San Francisco, 1955-56; with Calif. Women's Bd. Terms and Parole, 1960-66; mem. Mayor's com. on crime, chmn. adv. com. Adult Detention, 1967-69; mem. Bd. Suprs., San Francisco, 1970-78, pres., 1970-71, 74-75, 78; mayor City of San Francisco, 1978-88; senator from Calif. U.S. Senate, Washington, 1992—. Mem. exec. com. U.S. Conf. of Mayors, 1983-88; Dem. nominee for Gov. of Calif., 1990; mem. Nat. Com. on U.S.-China Rels.; mem. judiciary com., appropriations com., rules and adminstrn. Com., energy and natural resources com. Mem. Bay Area Conservation and Devel. Commn., 1973-78; mem. Senate Fgn. Rels. Com. Recipient Woman of Achievement award Bus. and Profl. Women's Clubs San Francisco, 1970, Disting. Woman award San Francisco Examiner, 1970, Coro Found. award, 1979, Coro Leadership award, 1988, Pres. medal U. Calif., San Francisco, 1988, Scopus award Am. Friends Hebrew U., 1981, Brotherhood/Sisterhood award NCCJ, 1986, Comdr.'s award U.S. Army, 1986, French Legion of Honor, 1984, Disting. Civilian award USN, 1987; named Number One Mayor All-Pro City Mgmt. Team City and State Mag., 1987. Mem. Trilateral Commn., Japan Soc. of No. Calif. (pres. 1988-89), Inter-Am. Dialogue, Nat. Com. on U.S.-China Rels. Democrat. Office: US Senate 331 Hart Senate Office Bldg Washington DC 20510-0001*

FEINSTEIN, ROCHELLE, artist, educator; BFA, Pratt Inst., 1975; MFA, U. Minn., 1978. Represented by Max Protetch Gallery, N.Y.C.; tchr. Bonnington Coll., 1979—94; assoc. prof. painting, printmaking Yale U., 1994—98, prof. painting and printmaking, 1998—. Participant pub. arts project CETA/N.Y. Artists Program, 1978—79. Represented in permanent [illegible] Mus. Modern Art. Nat. Endowment for the Arts grantee, 1990, Joan Mitchell Found. grantee, 1994, John Simon Guggenheim Meml. Found. fellow, 1996. Office: Yale U Sch Art PO Box 208339 New Haven CT 06520-8339

FEIR, DOROTHY JEAN, entomologist, physiologist, educator; b. St. Louis, Jan. 29, 1929; d. Alex R. and Lillian (Smith) F. BS, U. Mich., 1950; MS, U. Wyo., 1956; PhD, U. Wis., 1960. Instr. biology U. Buffalo, 1960-61; mem. faculty St. Louis U., 1961—, prof. biology, 1967-99, prof. biology emeritus, 1999—. Mem. tropical medicine and parasitology study sect. NIH, 1980-84 Editor Environ. Entomology, 1977-84; mem. editl. bd. Jour. Med. Entomology, 1995-99, chair editl. bd., 1999. Fellow Entomol. Soc. Am. (hon.; pres. 1989, Riley Achievement award north ctrl. br. 1993), Mo. Acad. Sci. (v.p. 1987-88, pres.-elect 1988-89, pres. 1989-90, Most Disting. Scientist award 1995); mem. AAAS, Am. Physiol. Soc., N.Y. Acad. Sci., Phi Beta Kappa, Sigma Xi. E-mail: feirdj@slu.edu.

FELBAB, AMANDA JANE, marketing professional, consultant; b. Harvard, Ill., Oct. 12, 1972; d. Michael and Elizabeth Palmer; m. Jeff Edward Felbab, June 23, 2000. MS, U. Wis., Milw., 1998, PhD, 2002. Project asst. U. Wis., Milw., 1996—99, lectr., 1998—2003; rsch. analyst Marquette U., Milw., 2000—02; mktg. rsch. specialist Northwestern Mut., Milw., 2002—. Rsch. and statis. cons., Milw., 1997—. Scholar, Robert B. Ingle Found., 1999. Mem.: Am. Statis. Assn., Am. Mktg. Assn., Phi Kappa Phi. Office: Northwestern Mutual 720 E Wisconsin Ave Milwaukee WI 53202 Personal E-mail: amanda@felbab.com.

FELD, CAROLE LESLIE, marketing executive; b. L.A., Nov. 12, 1955; d. Harold Brenman and Phyllis Pearl (Fishman) F.; m. David C. Levy; 1 child, Alexander Wolf Levy. BA, U. Calif., Berkeley, 1979; MBA, U. So. Calif., 1982. Mgr. rsch. Columbia Pictures, L.A., 1982-83; dir. promotion and field pub. Tri-Star Pictures, N.Y.C., 1983-86; dir. promotion and retention mktg. Home Box Office, N.Y.C., 1987-92; v.p. promotion and advt. Pub. Broadcasting Svc., Washington, 1992-97, sr. v.p. advt., promotion and corp. communications, 1995-99, sr. v.p. comms. and brand mgmt., 1999-2000; v.p. brand mktg. The Motley Fool, Washington, 2000—01, mktg. cons., 2002—03; prin. Giving Tree Group, Washington, 2003—. Pres. CINE; cons. New Sch. Beacons in Jazz Program, N.Y.C., 1990—. Named one of Mktgs. Top 100 Advertising Age, 1995. Avocations: skiing, travel, art, film.

FELD, KAREN IRMA, columnist, journalist, broadcaster, public speaker; b. Washington, Aug. 23; d. Irvin and Adele Ruth (Schwartz) F. BA, Am. U. Columnist, reporter Roll Call Newspaper, Washington; nat. pub. rels. coord. Ringling Bros./Barnum & Bailey Circus, Washington; publicist Twentieth Century Fox, L.A.; pub. rels. account exec. Harshe, Rotman & Druck, L.A.; freelance writer, broadcaster; corr. People mag., Washington, 1980-85; adj. instr. Kent State U. Pol. Campaign Mgmt. Inst., 1981; broadcaster Voice of Am., 1984; columnist, contbg. editor Capitol Hill mag., Washington, 1980-89; columnist Washington Times, 1986-87, Universal Press Syndicate, 1988-89, Creators Syndicate, 1989-90; syndicated columnist Capital Connections, 1990—; Prodigy polit. columnist, 1990-93. Radio/TV commentator syndicated radio segment Radio America, 1993—; syndicated columnist Nat. Post, 1998-99; Washington editor Delta Shuttle Sheet, 2000—; lectr. in field, 1990—. Contbr. articles to Parade mag., People mag., Money mag., Time mag., Vogue mag., George, USA Weekend, Family Circle, others. Recipient Health Journalism award Am. Chiropractic Assn., 1991. Mem. AFTRA/SAG, Nat. Fedn. Press Women (Excellence in Journalism award 1984-2003), Capital Press Women (v.p. 1985-91, Excellence in Journalism award 1984-2003, Entrepreneur/Communicator of Yr. 1995), Am. Soc. Journalists and Authors (award), N.Am. Travel Journalists Assn. (Best Mag. Feature award 2003), Nat. Press Club, Capitol Hill Club, Woodmont Country Club (Rockville, Md.), U.S. Senate Press Gallery, White House Corr. Assn., Soc. Profl. Journalists (bd. dirs.). Jewish. Office: 1698 32nd St NW Washington DC 20007-2969 Office Phone: 202-337-2044. E-mail: news@karenfeld.com.

FELDER, SHEILA KAY, music educator; b. Rockford, Ill., Jan. 11, 1965; d. Frederick L. and Jean Ardis Kennerly; m. Thomas Anthony Felder, June 15, 1991; children: Madeleine Kay, Natalie Jean. MusB in Edn., Morningside Coll., 1983—87; M of music edn., VanderCook Coll. of Music, 1993—95. Cert. Tchr. Ill., 1987, Iowa, 1987. Pvt. studio tchr., Rockford, Ill., 1987—; orch. dir. Freeport Pub. Schools, Ill., 1987—2001; sect. cellist Dubuque Symphony Orch., Dubuque, Iowa, 1988—; orch. dir. Highland C.C., Freeport, Ill., 1989—91; sect. cellist Rockford Pops Orch., Ill., 1992—; orch. dir. Rockford Luth. Schools, Ill., 2001—. Editor Ill. Am. String Teachers Assn., 1999—; dist. viii orch. chairperson Ill. Music Educators Assn., 1989—. Worship & music com. chair Westminster Presbyn. Ch., Ill., 2002, deacon, 1999—2002; sec. Blackhawk Bicycle & Ski Club, Ill., 1998—2002. Recipient Grammy Signature Music Dept., The Rec. Acad., 2000, 2001, Guest Condr. for North Ctrl. Jr. Conf. Music Festival, Colleagues, 2002. Mem.: Luth. Educators Assn., Freeport Edn. Assn., Ill. Edn. Assn., NEA, Nat. String Orch. Assn., Ill. Music Educators Assn. (dist. viii orch. chairperson 1989), Ill. Am. String Teachers Assn. (editor 1999), Am. String Teachers Assn., Blackhawk Bicycle & Ski Club (sec. 1998—2002), Tandem Club of Am. Presbyterian. Avocations: tandeming, camping, bicycling, hiking. Home: 4299 Windswept Way Loves Park IL 61111 Office: Rockford Lutheran Schools 3411 N Alpine Rd Rockford IL 61114 E-mail: www.rockfordlutheran.com.

FELDER-HOEHNE, FELICIA HARRIS, librarian; b. Knoxville, Tenn. d. Henry Thomas and Luvilla Tate Harris. BS in English, Knoxville Coll., 1958; MS in Libr. Sci., Atlanta U., 1966; postgrad., U. Tenn., 1972—78. English tchr. McMinn County Schs., J.L. Cook Sch., Athens, Tenn., 1958—60; adminstrv. asst. Adminstrv. Offices Knoxville (Tenn.) Coll., 1960—63, adminstrv. asst. to the dir. pub. rels., 1963—65; grad. libr. asst. Trevor Arnett Libr., Atlanta U., 1965—66; head circulation and reserve svcs. Alumni Libr. Knoxville Coll., 1966—69; tchr., libr. summer study skills program United Presbyn. Ch., Bd. Nat. Missions, Knoxville Coll., 1967—68; prof., reference libr. John C. Hodges Libr. U. Tenn., Knoxville, 1969—. Founder, dir. LARKS: Librs. Linking with At-Risk Students, Knoxville, 1997—. Author: A Subject Guide to Basic Reference Books in Black Studies; co-author: (online ency.) Project TAPP: Tennessee Authors Past and Present, 1999—; contbr. Notable Black American Women, Book I, Notable Black American Women, Book II, Behavioral & Social Sciences Librarian;, author poems; contbr. articles to profl. jours. Notary pub. at-large State of Tenn., Nat. Notary Assn., 1992—; adv. bd. Mentoring Acad. for Boys, Knoxville, 1997—; sec. to bd. Ctr. for Neighborhood Devel., Knoxville, 2000—02; dir. pub. rels. Concerned Assn. Residents East, Knoxville, 1988—90; active Tenn. Valley Energy Coalition, Knoxville, 1988—90, Town Hall East, Knoxville, 1988—, Save Our Cumberland Mountains, Tenn., 1988—; mem. religious task force World's Fair, Knoxville Internat. Energy Exposition, 1982; pres. Spring Place Neighborhood Assn., Knoxville, 1980—; others; pk. vol. Knox COunty Pk. Vol. Corps., 2003—; bd. dirs. Ctr. for Neighborhood Devel., Knoxville, 1998—2002, Knoxville Opera Co., 1999—, UT Fed. Credit Union, Knoxville, 1984—89; adv. bd. dirs. Bd. Probation and Parole State of Tenn., Knoxville Office, 2003—; bd. dirs. Knox County Parks Recreation, 2004—. Named one of Outstanding Young Women of Am., 1967; named to Tenn. African Am. Hall Fame, 1994; recipient Cert. of Merit for Contbns. to Edn., Jack and Jill, Inc., 1976, Plaque of Appreciation, Interdenominational Concert Choir, 1976, Religious Svc. award, Nat. Conf. Christians and Jews, 1976, Citizen of the Yr. award, Order of the Ea. Star Prince Hall Masons, 1979, Cert. of Appreciation, Knoxville's Internat. Energy Exposition, 1982, Pub. Svc. award, U. Tenn. Nat. Alumni Assn., 1984, Habitat for Humanity award, 1992, The Humanitarian Libr. Spirit award, 1994, The Miles 500 Libr. Spirit award, 1994, Cit[illegible] Knoxville Police Dept., 1998, The Knoxville News-Sentinel Cmty. Cornerstone award, 1998, Harold B. Love Outstanding Cmty. Involvement award, 2003, The Vol. Spirit award, U. Tenn., 2003, Merit award for Outstanding Achievement, City of Knoxville, Mayor Ashe, 1994, Plaque of Appreciation, Utah Fed. Credit Union. Mem.: YWCA, YMCA, ALA, NAACP, Nat. Mus. Women in the Arts (charter), East Tenn. Libr. Assn., Tenn. Libr. Assn., Citizens Police Acad. Alumni Assn., Beck Cultural Exch. Ctr. (charter), Met. Opera Guild, Knoxville (Tenn.) Opera Guild, Alpha Kappa Alpha. Avocations: community service, music, drama, writing poetry. Office: 145 John C Hodges Libr 1015 Volunteer Blvd Knoxville TN 37916-3109 Office Phone: 865-974-0018.

FELDHOUSE, LYNN, automotive company executive; m. Bob Feldhouse; 1 child, Katherine. Grad., Wayne State U.; postgrad., Oakland U. V.p., sec. Chrysler Corp. Fund, 1982—. Immediate past chair Nat. Contbns. Coun., The Conf. Bd., N.Y.C., bd. trustee Coun. Mich. Founds., Grand Haven, Citizens' Scholarship Found. of Am., St. Peter, Minn.; bd. trustees, treas. Mich. Womens' Found., Lansing; mem. nat. corp. com. Philanthropic Adv. Svc., Coun. of BBBs, Washington; mem. exec. com. Detroit Funders' Collaborative. Active vol. United Way Comty. Svcs. Southeastern Mich., Mich. Corp. Vol. Coun., Wayne State Alumni Assn. Office: Chrysler Fund Detroit MI 48231

FELDHUSEN, HAZEL JEANETTE, elementary school educator; b. Camp Douglas, Wis., Feb. 20, 1928; d. Vincent O. and Helen (Johnson) Artz; m. John F. Feldhusen, Dec. 18, 1954; children: Jeanne V., Anne M. B, U. Wis., 1965; M, Purdue U., 1968; postgrad., U. Wis. Tchr. Suldal Sch., Mauston, Wis., 1947-50, Lake Geneva (Wis.) Schs., 1950-55, West Lafayette (Ind.) Schs., 1965-91. Presenter World Conf., Hamburg, 1985, Juneau (Alaska) Schs., 1986, Vancouver (B.C., Can.) Schs., 1990, Norfolk (Va.) Schs., 1991, Taiwan Nat. U., 1992, U. New South Wales, Sydney, Australia, 1993, New Zealand Schs., Auckland, 1993; 2d Nat. Conf. Gifted, Taiwan, 1992, Sarasota, Fla., 1998. Author: Individualized Teaching of the Gifted, 1993, 2d edit., 1997; contbr. articles to profl. jours., chpts. to books, 1981-2002. Mem. Tchr. of Yr. Com., West Lafayette, 1988. Recipient Outstanding Tchr. award Elem. Tchrs. Am., 1974, Appreciation award U. Stellenbosch, 1984, Appreciation award Australian Assn. for the Gifted, 1987; winner Golden Apple Tchg. award Greater Lafayette C. of C., 1989, Disting. Alumnus award Purdue U., 1996. Mem. NEA, Ind. State Tchrs. Assn., West Lafayette Edn. Assn. (Outstanding Achievement award 1984), Phi Delta Kappa, Delta Kappa Gamma (v.p 1983-85). Avocations: reading, interior decorating. Home: Sarasota Bay Club 1301 N Tamiami Apt 205 Sarasota FL 34236 E-mail: feldhusenjf@aol.com.

FELDMAN, ARLENE BUTLER, aviation industry executive; BA cum laude in Polit. Sci., U. Colo., 1975; JD, Temple U. Sch. Law, 1978. Supervising atty. U.S. Railway Assn., Phila., 1977-82; dir. divsn. aeronautics N.J. Dept. Transp., Trenton, 1982-84; from acting dir. to dep. dir. tech. ctr. FAA, Atlantic City, N.J., 1984-86, dep. dir. Western-Pacific region Exec. Sch. L.A., 1986-87, dep. dir. Western-Pacific region, 1986-87, regional adminstr. N.Eng. Region Burlington, Mass., 1988-94, exec. sch., 1986-87, eastern regional adminstr. Jamaica, N.Y., 1994—. Panelist, guest spkr. Women in Aviation Conf., 1992, 93; vice-chair N.Y. Fed. Exec. Bd.; chairperson regional airport sys. planning adv. com. Delaware Valley Regional Planning Commn.; founder rotorcraft R&D forum FAA. Chairwoman Boston Federal Exec. Bd. Saving Bond, 1993; mem. adv. bd. U. So. Calif. Recipient Presdl. Meritorius Rank award Sr. Exec. Svc., Disting. Svc. award N.J. Aviation Hall of Fame, Amelia Earhart medal; inducted N.J. Aviation Hall of Fame, 1997. Mem. ABA, Ninety-Nines Internat. Orgn. (Earhart medal), Lawyer/Pilot Bar Assn., Air Traffic Control Assn. (dir., exec. bd., conf. panel moderator 1993, 91, spkr. 1993, chmn. bd. 1996, chmn. elect 1997), Am. Assn. Airport Execs., Am. Assn. State Hwy. and Transp. Ofcls., Am. Helicopter Soc., Helicopter Assn. Internat. (hon.), Nat. Assn. State Aviation Ofcls., Nat. Coun. Women in Aviation Aerospce, Internat. Aviation Women's Assn., Profl. Women Contrs., Inc. (1st hon. mem.), Wings Club N.Y.C. (bd. govs. 1996), Pi Sigma Alpha. Office: FAA 1 Aviation Plz Jamaica NY 11434

FELDMAN, CLARICE ROCHELLE, lawyer; b. Milw., Dec. 2, 1941; d. Harry and Beatrice (Hiken) Wagan; m. Howard J. Feldman, July 11, 1965; 1 child, David Lewis. BS, U. Wis., 1963, LL.B., 1965. Bar: Wis. 1965, D.C. 1969, Md. 1984. Appellate atty. NLRB, Washington, 1965—69; co-counsel to Joseph A. Yablonski, Washington, 1969; atty. Washington research project Clark Coll., 1970-72; asso. gen. counsel United Mine Workers Am., Washington, 1972-74; partner Becker, Channell, Becker & Feldman, Washington, 1974-76, Becker & Feldman, 1976-77; gen. counsel Ams. for Energy Independence, Washington, 1978-80; atty. Office of Spl. Investigations, Dept. Justice, 1980-84; pvt. practice law Washington, 1984-98; atty. pro bono, 1999—. Trustee Washington Internat. Sch., 1987-98; advisor Assn. Union Democracy. Mem. Wis., D.C., Md. bar assns. Democrat. Jewish. Home: 4455 29th St NW Washington DC 20008-2307

FELDMAN, DEDE, state legislator; b. West Chester, Pa., Mar. 10, 1947; m. Mark M. Feldman. BA, U. Pa., 1968, MA, 1969. Tchr. pub. h.s., 1970-75; journalist, 1975-82; owner Dede Feldman & Co., Pub. Rels., 1985—; adj. coll. prof., 1980-92; comm. cons.; mem. N.Mex. Senate, Dist. 13, 1996—; mem. conservation com., mem. pub. affairs com. N.Mex. State Senate. Past chair Albuquerque Cmty. Adv. Group; mem. Shared Vision Land Use and Transp. Caucus; mem. N.Mex. for Open Govt.; mem. North Valley Neighborhood Coalition; former precinct chair, ward chair Dem. Party, also former mem. state ctrl. com. Mem. N.Mex. Press Women (past pres. Albuquerque chpt.), N.Mex. Pub. Rels. Soc. Democrat. Office: 1821 Meadowview Dr NW Albuquerque NM 87104-2511 E-mail: dfeldman@state.nm.us.

FELDMAN, ELAINE BOSSAK, medical nutritionist, educator; b. N.Y.C., Dec. 9, 1926; d. Solomon and Frances Helen (Fania) Nevler Bossak; m. Herman Black, Dec. 23, 1951 (div. 1957); 1 child, Mitchell Evan; m. Daniel S. Feldman, July 19, 1957; children: Susan, Daniel S. Jr. AB magna cum laude, NYU, 1945, MS, 1948, MD, 1951. Diplomate Am. Bd. Internal Medicine, Nat. Bd. Med. Examiners; cert. in Clin. Nutrition. Rotating intern Mt. Sinai Hosp., N.Y.C., 1951-52, resident in pathology, 1952, asst. resident, 1953, fellow in medicine, resident in metabolism, 1954-55, rsch. asst. in medicine, 1955-58, clin. asst. physician Diabetes Clinic, 1957; asst. vis. physician Kings County Hosp., Bklyn., 1958-66, assoc. vis. physician, 1966-72; asst. attending physician Maimonides Hosp., Bklyn., 1960-68; spl. fellow USPHS Dept. of Physiol. Chemistry U. of Lund, Sweden, 1964-65; attending physician Eugene Talmadge Meml. Hosp., Augusta, Ga., 1972-92, Univ. Hosp., Augusta, 1972-92, cons., 1973; prof. medicine Med. Coll. Ga., Augusta, 1972-92, prof. emeritus, 1992—, chief sect. of nutrition, 1977-92, chief emeritus, 1992—, acting chief sect. of metabolic/endocrine disease, 1980-81, prof. physiology and endocrinology, 1988-92, prof. emeritus physiology and endocrinology, 1992—; instr. medicine SUNY Downstate Med. Ctr., 1957-59, asst. prof. medicine, 1959-68, assoc. prof. medicine, 1968-72. Tchg. fellow edn. zoology U. Wis. Grad. Sch., 1945-46, dept. biology NYU Grad. Sch., 1946-47; cons. N.Y.-N.J. Regional Ctr. for Clin. Nutrition Edn., 1983-92; vis. prof. and Harvey lectr. Northeastern Ohio Sch. Medicine, Youngstown, 1985; cons., vis. prof. U. Nev. Sch. Medicine (NCI grant), 1989-94; mem. nat. adv. com. nutrition fellowship program Nat. Med. Fellowship Inc., 1988-95; dir. Ga. Inst. Human Nutrition, 1978-92, dir. emeritus, 1992—; dir. Clin. Nutrition Rsch. Unit, 1980-86; mem. med. nutrition curriculum initiative adv. bd. U. N.C., Chapel Hill, 1992-2001; advisor ednl. materials Am. Inst. Cancer Rsch., 1997—. Author: Essentials of Clinical Nutrition, 1988; (with others) Conference on Biological Activities of Steroids in Relation to Cancer, 1969, Nicotinic Acid, 1964, The Menopausal Syndrome, 1974, Hyperlipidemia, Medcom Special Studies, 1974, Medcom Famous Teaching in M[illegible], Harrison's Principles of Internal Medicine, 1980, Health Promotion: Principles and Clinical Applications, 1982, The Encyclopedic Handbook of Alcoholism, 1982, The Climacteric in Perspective, 1986, Selenium in Biology and Medicine, Part A., 1987, Medicine for the Practicing Physician, 1988, Clinical Chemistry of Laboratory Animals, 1989, Ency. Human Biology, 1991, Laboratory Medicine: The Selection and Interpretation of Clinical Laboratory Studies, 1993, Modern Nutrition in Health and Diseases, 1994, Nutrition Assessment-A Comprehensive Guide for Planning Intervention, 1995, The Women's Complete Healthbook, 1995, The American Medical Women's Association's Guide to Nutrition and Wellness, 1996, Normal Nutrition and Therapeutics, 1996, Handbook of Nutrition and Food, 2001; editor: Nutrition and Cardiovascular Disease, 1976, Nutrition in the Middle and Later Years, 1983 (paperback edit. 1986), Nutrition and Heart Disease, 1983, Handbook of Nutrition and Food, 2001, Human Nutrient Needs in the Life Cycle, 2001; mem. editl. adv. bd. Contemporary Issues in Clin. Nutrition, 1980-92; mem. edit. bd. Am. Jour. Clin. Nutrition, 1983-91, 92-98, Jour. Clin. Endocrinology and Metabolism, 1984-88, MidPoint: Counseling Women through Menopause, 1984-85, Jour. Nutrition, 1985-89; cons. editor Jour. Am. Coll. Nutrition, 1982-94; mem. edit. bd. Complementary Med. for the Physician, 1996-2000; contbg. editor Nutrition Rev., 1997-2002; mem. editl. bd. Nutrition Today, 1999—; reviewer Jour. Lipid Rsch., Biochm. Pharmacology, Sci., The Physiologist, Jour. Am. Acad. Dermatology, Israel Jour. Med. Scis., N.Y. State Jour. Medicine, Jour. of Nutrition Edn., Jour. Am. Dietetic Assn., Am. Jour. Medicine, Am. Jour. Med. Sci., So. Med. Jour., Jour. AMA, Jour. NCI; contbr. more than 175 articles to profl. jours; presenter in field. Mem. tech. adv. com. for sci. and edn. Rsch. Grants Program, Human Nutrition Grants Peer Panel, USDA, 1982, mem. bd. sci. counselors human nutrition; Community Svc. Block Grant Discretionary Program Panel; vice chmn. Urban and Rural Econ. Devel. Panel, Dept. HHS, 1982, grant reviewer, 1983; mem ad hoc and spl. rev. coms. and groups NIH, 1979-93, mem. nutrition study sect., 1976-80; mem. Rev. Panel Nat. Nutrition Objectives, Life Scis. Rev. Office, Fed. Am. Socs. Exptl. Biology, 1985-86; mem. subcom. Women's Health Trial Nat. Cancer Inst., 1987, mem. bd. sci. counselors cancer prevention and control program, 1990-94; mem. adv. com. Clin. Nutrition Rsch. Unit, U. Ala., 1986-94, Ga. Nutrition Steering Com., 1974-75, Ctrl. Savannah River Area Nutrition Project Coun. 1974-75, ednl. adv. com. Health Central, 1980; mem. geriatrics and gerontology rev. com. Nat. Inst. on Aging, 1986-90; breast cancer initiative peer rev. Dept. of Def., 1997, 98. N.Y. Heart Assn. rsch. fellow, 1955-57. Fellow Am. Heart Assn. Coun. on Atherosclerosis (nominating com. 1978, chmn. nominating com., mem. exec. com. 1979-80, Spl. Recognition award 1995), Am. Inst. Nutrition (grad. nutrition edn. com. 1980-83, 89-93); mem. Am. Coll. Nutrition (chmn. com. pub. affairs), Am. Soc. for Clin. Nutrition (com. on nutrition edn. 1982, chmn. subcom. on nutrition edn. in med. schs. 1983-84, chmn. com. on med./dental residency edn., 1985-87, com. on subsplty. tng. 1988-92, nominating com. 1982, 90, chair nominating com. 1994, com. on clin. practice issues in health and disease 1989-92, Nat. Dairy Coun. award 1991, rep. coun. acad. socs. 1990-96, membership com. 1996—, chair 1999, 2000), Fedn. Am. Socs. Exptl. Biology. Am. Oil Chemists Soc., Am. Physiol. Soc., Endocrine Soc., Soc. Exptl. Biology and Medicine, So. Soc. Clin. Investigation, Am. Diabetes Assn., Am. Fedn. Clin. Rsch., Am. Gastroent. Assn., AMA (Joseph B. Goldberger award 1990), Am. Med. Women's Assn. (profl. resources com. 1975-76, med. edn. and rsch. fund com. 1976-79, chmn. 1978-90, chmn. student liaison subcom. of membership com. 1981-84, pres. Br. 51, Augusta 1977-80, treas. 1980-97, Calcium Nutrition Edn. award 1991, CSRA Girl Scout Women of Excellence award 1994), Am. Soc. Parenteral and Enteral Nutrition, Am. Heart Assn. (Ga. affiliate, nutrition com., chmn. sci. session for nutritionists, 1978, chmn. nutrition com. 1979-90, mem. long range planning com. 1980-81, rsch. com. 1980-83, bd. dirs. 1987-90, profl. edn. task force, 1988-89), Richmond Country Med. Assn., Augusta Opera Assn. (bd. dirs. 1973—, recording sec. 1973-74, pres. 1974-75, coord. audience devel. 1975-77, at-large exec. com. 1994-96, chair nominating com. 1994-96, corr. sec. 1998-99, 1st v.p. 1999-2000, chair search com., gen. dir. 2002), Augusta Sailing Club (women's com. 1973), Greater Augusta Arts Coun. (Arts Festival Collage 1982 chmn. promotion and publicity com., Festival coms. 1983-86, 89-93, 95, 96, 98, 99, bd. dirs. 1984-94, Vol. of the Yr., 2001), Gertrude Herbert Inst. Art (bd. dirs. 1987-92), Authors Club Augusta, Philomathic Club (sec. 1999—2001), Phi Beta Kappa, Sigma Xi (chpt. sec. 1982-83, pres. elect 1983-84, pres. 1984-85), Alpha Omega Alpha. Avocations: opera, wine tasting, travel. Home: 2123 Cumming Rd Augusta GA 30904-4333 E-mail: efeldman7@comcast.net.

FELDMAN, EVA LUCILLE, neurology educator; b. N.Y.C., Mar. 30, 1952; d. George Franklin and Margherita Enriceta (Cafiero) F.; children: Laurel, Scott, John Jr. BA in Biology and Chemistry, Earlham Coll., 1973; MS in Zoology, U. Notre Dame, 1975; PhD in Neurosci., U. Mich., 1979, MD, 1983. Diplomate Am. Bd. Neurology; lic. med. practitioner, Mich. Instr. dept. neurology U. Mich., Ann Arbor, 1987-88, asst. prof. neurology, 1988-94, mem. faculty Cancer Ctr., 1992-2000, assoc. prof. neurology, 1994-2000, prof., 2000—. Mem. faculty neurosci. program U. Mich., Mich. Diabetes Rsch. and Tng., Ann Arbor, 1988—; dir. JDRF Ctr. for the Study of Complications in Diabetes. Contbr. chpts. to books, articles to profl. jours. Grantee, NIH, 1989, 1994, 1997, 1998, 2001, 2003, Juvenile Diabetes Rsch. Found., 1994, 1997, 1999, 2001. Achievements include research on the elucidation of the role of growth factors in the pathogenesis of human disease. Office: Dept Neurology U Mich 200 Zina Pitcher Pl Rm 4144 Ann Arbor MI 48109-2205 Office Phone: 734-763-7274.

FELDMAN, HARRIET RUTH, dean; b. Bklyn., May 5, 1945; d. Mickey and Florence (Gordon) Martin; m. Ronald M. Feldman, Dec. 22, 1973; children: Craig, Jaime. Diploma in nursing, L.I. Coll. Hosp., 1965; BS, Adelphi U., 1968, MS, 1971; PhD, NYU, 1984. Asst. dean Adelphi U., Garden City, N.Y., 1984-87; prof., chairperson dept. nursing Fairleigh Dickinson U., Teaneck, N.J., 1987-93; dean Lienhard Sch. Nursing Pace U., 1993—. Pres. Deans and Dirs. of Nursing Greater NY, 2001—, Strategies for Nursing Leadership, 2001; accreditation site visitor Commn. on Collegiate Nursing Edn., 1999—. Editor: Nursing Leadership Forum, 1998—, Nursing Leaders Speak Out: Issues and Opinions, 2001; co-author: Nurses in the Political Arena: The Public Face of Nursing, 2000; contbr. articles to profl. jours. Fellow: Am. Acad. Nursing; mem.: Am. Assn. Colls. Nursing (mentor Leadership for Acad. Nursing program 1999—2002). Home: 2243 Brody Ln Bellmore NY 11710-5101 E-mail: hfeldman@pace.edu.

FELDMAN, LILLIAN MALTZ, early childhood education consultant; b. N.Y.C. d. Jacob and Ida (Burko) Maltz; m. Harry A. Feldman (dec. Jan. 1985); children: Ronald, Donna Feldman Weisman, Jeffrey, Robert. AB, George Washington U., 1937, MA, 1939; EdD in Early Childhood Edn., Syracuse U., 1987; HLD (hon.), SUNY, 1993. Cert. tchr., guidance counselor, sch. adminstr., N.Y. Elem. sch. guidance counselor Syracuse (N.Y.) Sch. Dist., 1963-65, Kindergarten tchr., 1957-63, dir. early children edn., 1965-83; dir. Syracuse Head Start, summers 1968-70; cons. early childhood edn. Syracuse, 1985—. Adj. instr. child, family and community studies Syracuse U., 1988-89, adj. prof. child and family studies, 1990-91. Author invited papers in early child devel. and care, 1988, 89, 95, 96. Adv. com. network adv. bd. Dr. Martin Luther King Jr. Cmty. Sch., Syracuse, 1988—. Named Woman of Achievement in Edn., Post-Standard, Syracuse, 1969; recipient Hannah G. Solomon Award Nat. Coun. Jewish Women, Syracuse, 1979, Honoree Na'amat USA 1988, Friend of Children award Women's Commn. Task Force on Children, 1992. Mem. Syracuse Assn. for Edn. Young Children (Outstanding Early Childhood Educator award 1984),

Consortium for Children's Svcs. (Silver Dove award 1985, Friend of Family award 1992), Onondaga County Child Care Coun. (Community Svc. award 1983, Friend of Children award 1992), Delta Kappa Gamma, Phi Delta Kappa. Democrat.

FELDMAN, NANCY JANE, health organization executive; b. Green Bay, Wis., July 6, 1946; d. Benjamin J. and Ellen M. Naze; m. Robert P. Feldman, Aug. 24, 1968; 1 child, Sara J. BA, U. Wis., 1969, MS, 1974. Supr. EPSDT program Minn. Dept. Human Svcs., St. Paul, 1974-80, supr. healthcare programs, 1980-84; team leader human resources budget Minn. Dept. Fin., St. Paul, 1984-87; asst. commr. Minn. Dept. Health, St. Paul, 1987-91; team leader CORE program Minn. Dept. Adminstrn., St. Paul, 1991-93; dir. state pub. programs Medica, Allina Health Sys., Mpls., 1993-95; CEO UCare Minn., St. Paul, 1995—. Mem. Minn. Coun. Health Plans, Mpls., 1995—; bd. dirs. Stratis Health. Bd. dirs. Vols. Am. Health Nat. Svcs., 1994—; vice chair bd. dirs. Ctr. for Victims of Torture, 1997-2003, chair, 2004. Mem. Women's Health Leadership Trust. Avocations: distance swimming, bicycling, travel. Home: 4124 Burton Ln Minneapolis MN 55406-3638 Office: UCare Minn PO Box 52 Minneapolis MN 55440-0052 E-mail: nfeldman@ucare.org.

FELDMAN, SANDRA, labor union executive; b. N.Y.C., Oct. 14, 1939; m. Arthur Barnes. B, Brooklyn Coll., 1960; M in English Lit., NYU, 1965. Tchr. Pub. Sch. 34, N.Y.C.; field rep. United Fedn. Tchrs., 1966-83, exec. dir., 1983-86, sec., 1983-86, pres., 1986-97, Am. Fedn. Tchrs., 1997—. Exec. com. Edn. Internat., v.p.; exec. coun. AFL-CIO, 1997—. Active Coun. on Competitiveness, Internat. Rescue Com., Freedom House, A. Philip Randolph Inst., Jewish Labor Com., Coalition Labor Union Women, Nat. Coun. Ams. to Prevent Handgun Violence, N.Y. Urban League, Women's Forum, Women's Commn. on Refugee Children; co-chair Child Labor Coalition; nat. bd. mem. Profl. Tchg. Stds.; chair AFL-CIO Com. on Social Policy; mem. U.S. com. UNICEF Named one of N.Y.C. 75 Most Influential Women, Crain's New York Bus.; recipient Disting. Labor Leadership award, Nat. Urban Coalition, 1989, Labor award, Nat. Jewish Congress, 1997, Robert F. Kennedy-Martin Luther King Jr. award, Coalition to Stop Gun Violence, 2001, Not For Ourselves Alone Outstanding Leadership award, N.Y. State United Tchrs., 2002. Avocations: collecting African art, jazz, reading. Office: Am Fedn Tchrs 555 New Jersey Ave NW Washington DC 20001-2029 E-mail: online@AFT.org.*

FELDMANN, SHIRLEY CLARK, psychology educator; b. Niagara Falls, N.Y., Apr. 14, 1929; d. Franklin T. and Mildred L. (Payne) Clark; m. Robert Feldmann, June, 1952 (dec.); m. Horace S. Bush (dec.). BA, Barnard Coll., 1951; MA, Columbia U., 1952, PhD, 1961. Asst. prof. edn. SUNY, Fredonia, 1958-60; asst. research prof. psychiatry N.Y. Med. Coll., N.Y.C., 1960-63; prof. sch. edn. City Coll., CUNY, N.Y.C., 1963-98; prof., PhD program in cdnl. psychology CUNY Grad. Sch., N.Y.C., 1974-98, exec. officer, 1976 85; ret., 1998. Contbr. articles to prof. jours. Mem. APA. Home: 11 Cedar Lake Rd Chester CT 06412-1009

FELDSHUH, TOVAH S. actress; b. N.Y.C., Dec. 27, 1952; d. Sidney and Lillian (Kaplan) F.; m. Andrew Harris-Levy, Mar. 20, 1977. BA, Sarah Lawrence Coll., Bronxville, N.Y.; McKnight fellow, Guthrie Theatre-U. Minn. Broadway debut in: Cyrano de Bergerac, 1973; starring role in Yentl, N.Y.C., 1974, Yentl Goes to Broadway, 1975; leading lady Am. Shakespeare Festival, Stratford, Conn., 1976, 80, 81, TV appearances include: The Amazing Howard Hughes, 1976, Holocaust, 1977, The Triangle Factory Fire Scandal, 1979, Beggarman-Thief, 1980, The Women's Room, 1980, Citizen Cohn, 1992, Love and Betrayal: The Mia Farrow Story, 1995; CBS pilot Murder Inc, 1981, ABC series Mariah, 1987, L.A. Law, 1987; off-Broadway appearance in Three Sisters, 1977; nat. tour in Peter Pan, 1978; starring role in Broadway musicals Sarava, 1978, Lend Me A Tenor, 1989, Golda's Balcony, 2003 (Tony nom. best actress in a play, 2004); films include: The Idolmaker, 1980, Cheaper to Keep Her, 1980, Daniel, 1983, Brewster's Millions, 1985, Blue Iguana, 1988, En Dag I Oktober, 1992, Trouble, 1995, Hudson River Blues, 1997, A Walk on the Moon, 1999, Happy Accidents, 2000, Kissing Jessica Stein, 2001, Noon Blue Apples 2002, Tollbooth, 2004; one-woman show, Guthrie Theater, 1980, 81. Recipient Theatre World award, Outer Critics Circle award, Drama Desk award, Israeli Govt. Friendship award, Eleanor Roosevelt Humanitarian award. Address: William Morris Agency Inc 151 S El Camino Dr Beverly Hills CA 90212-2704*

FELDT, GLORIA A. social service administrator; b. Temple, Tex., Apr. 13, 1942; m. Alex Barbanell; 3 children; 3 stepchildren. BA in Sociology and Speech with honors, U. Tex. Permian Basin, 1974; postgrad., Ariz. State U., Western Behavioral Scis. Inst., La Jolla, Calif. Broadcast operator Sta. KOIP-FM, Odessa, Tex., 1965-67; substitute tchr. Ector County Ind. Sch. Dist., Odessa, Tex., 1967-68; tchr., spl. projects dir. head start Greater Opportunities of the Permian Basin, Odessa, Tex., 1968-73; exec. dir. Planned Parenthood of West Tex., Odessa, 1974-78; exec. dir., CEO Planned Parenthood Ctrl. and Northern Ariz., Phoenix, 1978-96; pres. Planned Parenthood Fedn. Am., Planned Parenthood Action Fund, N.Y.C., 1996—; also bd. dirs. Planned Parenthood Fedn. Am. Mem. steering com. Pro-Choice Ariz.; founder Planned Parenthood Fedn. Am. Leadership Inst.; cons. in leadership and strategic planning for non-profit orgns. Spkr. in field; Author: Behind Every Choice Is a Story, 2003. Mem. exec. bd. Ariz. Affordable Health Care Found.; bd. dirs. Pro-Choice Resource Ctr., Hospice of the Valley; mem. cmty. adv. bd. Jr. League of Phoenix; mem. adv. bd. UN Assn.; charter mem. Ariz. Women's Town Hall; active Charter 100, World Affairs Coun., Ariz. Acad. Town Halls. Recipient Women of Achievement award, 1987, Ruth Green award Nat. Exec. Dirs. Coun., 1990, award Women Helping Women, 1989, 94, Golden Apple award Sun City chpt. NOW, 1995, City of Phoenix Martin Luther King, Jr. Living the Dream award City of Phoenix Human Rels. Commn., 1996. Mem. APHA, Nat. Family Planning and Reproductive Health Assn., Ariz. Pub. Health Assn. Office: Planned Parenthood Fedn of Am 434 W 33rd St #12 New York NY 10001-2601*

FELIOUS, ODETTA, vocalist; b. Ala., Dec. 31, 1930; d. Reuben and Flora (Sanders) Holmes; m. Don Gordon (div. 1959); m. Gary Shead, 1960; m. Iversen Minter, 1977. Degree in Classical Music/Musical Comedy, L.A. City Coll. Singer Turnabout Theater, Hollywood, Calif. Recs. My Eyes Have Seen, Newport Folk Festival, Ballad for American, 1959, Odetta at Carnegie Hall, Odetta Sings Christmas Spirituals, 1960, Odetta and the Blues, Odetta at Town Hall, Sometimes I Feel Like Crying, 1962, Odetta Sings Folk Songs, Odetta, Fantasy, One Grain of Sand, 1963, It's A Mighty World, Odetta Sings of Many Things, 1964, Odetta Sings Ballads and Blues, Odetta Sings Dylan, 1965, Odetta in Japan, At the Gate of Horn, 1966, Odetta at Carnegie Hall, 1967, Odetta Sings the Blues, 1968, The Essential Odetta, 1973, Odetta, Verve/Folkways, Odetta, Archive of Folk and Jazz, 1974, Ballad for American/Lonesome Train, 1976, Odetta and the Blues, Movin' It On, 1987, Christmas Special, 1998, To Ella, Best of the Vanguard Years, Blues Everywhere I Go, 1999, appeared Carnegie Hall, Newport Folk Festival, New Orleans Jazz Festival, Ann Arbor Folk Festival;, performer films, (TV series) including The Autobiography of Miss Jane Pittman. Recipient Sylvania award for excellence, 1959, Key to the City of Birmingham, Ala., 1965; Duke Ellington fellow Yale U. Office: Douglas A Yeager Prodns 300 W 55th St # 15 New York NY 10019-5138 Fax: 212-245-6576.

FELLER, MILLICENT (MIMI) A. newspaper publishing executive; BA cum laude, Creighton U., 1970; JD, Georgetown U. Asst. dir. congl. rels. Gen. Svcs. Adminstrn., 1975-77; legis. asst. Environ. and Pub. Works Com. U.S. Senate, 1977-81; from legis. dir. to Washington chief of staff Sen. John Chafee (Rep.), R.I., 1981-83; dep. asst. sec. legis. affairs U.S. Dept. Treasury, 1983-85; from v.p. to sr. v.p. pub. affairs and govt. rels. Gannett Co., 1985—. Bd. dirs. Nat. Ct. Apptd. Spl. Advs. Assn. Bd. dirs. Creighton U. Recipient Disting. Alumnus award Creighton U., 1987. Office: Gannett Co Inc 7950 Jones Branch Dr Mc Lean VA 22107*

FELLIN, OCTAVIA ANTOINETTE, retired librarian, historical researcher; b. Santa Monica, Calif. d. Otto P. and Librada (Montoya) F. Student, U. N.Mex., 1937-39; BA, U. Denver, 1941; BA in L.S., Dominican U., River Forest, Ill., 1942. Asst. libr. instr., libr. sci. St. Mary-of-Woods Coll., Terre Haute, Ind., 1942-44; libr. U.S. Army, Bruns Gen. Hosp., Santa Fe, 1944-46, Gallup (N.Mex.) Pub. Libr., 1947-90; post libr. Camp McQuaide, Calif., 1947; freelance writer mags., newspapers, 1950—. Libr. cons.; N.Mex. del. White House Pre-conf. on Librs. & Inof. Svcs., 1978; dir. Nat. Libr. week for N.Mex., 1959. Author: Yahweh the Voice that Beautifies the Land; A Chronicle of Mileposts a Brief History of the University of New Mexico, Gallup Campus. Chmn. Red Mesa Art Ctr., 1984—88; pres. Gallup Area Arts Coun., 1988; mem. Western Health Found. Century Com., 1988; mem. cultural bd. Gallup Multi-Model Cultural Com., 1988—95; organizer Gt. Decision Discussion groups, 1963—85; co-organizer, v.p. chair fund raising com. Gallup Pub. Radio com., 1989—95; mem. McKinley County Recycling Com., 1990—; mem. local art selection com. N.Mex. Art Dirs., 1990; mem. Gallup St. Naming Com., 1958-59, Aging Com., 1964-68; chmn. Gallup Mus. Indian Arts and Crafts, 1964—78; mem. Eccles. Conciliation and Arbitration Bd., Province of Santa Fe, 1974; mem. publicity com. Gallup Inter-Tribal Indian Ceremonial Assn., 1966—68; mem. Gov.'s Com. 100 on Aging, 1967—70, U. N.Mex.-Gallup Campus Comty. Edn. Adv. Coun., 1981—82; N.Mex. organizing chmn. Rehoboth McKinley Christian Hosp. Aux., pres., 1983, chmn. aux. scholarship com., 1989—, chmn. comty. edn. loan selection com., 1990—, bd. dirs., corr. sec., 1991—94; mem. N.Mex. Libr. Adv. Coun., 1971—75, vice chmn., 1974—75; chmn. adv. bd. Gallup Sr. Citizens, 1971—73; mem. steering com. Gallup Diocese Bicentennial, 1975—78, chmn. hist. com., 1975; chmn. Trick or Treat for UNICEF, Gallup, 1972-77, Artists Coop, 1985-89; chmn. pledge campaign Rancho del Nino San Huberto Empalme, Mexico, 1975—80; active Network: Nat. Cath. Social Justice Lobby; bd. dirs. Gallup Opera Guild, 1970—74; bd. dirs., sec., co-organizer Gallup Area Arts Coun., 1970—78; mem. N.Mex. Humanities Coun., 1979, Gallup Centennial Com., 1980-81, Cathedral Parish Coun., 1980—83, v.p., 1981; mem. N.Mex. Coalition to End the Death Penalty, 1999—; active Gallup Multi-Model Cultural Com. Comty. Concerts Assn., 1957—78; com. mem. Rio Grande Hist. Collection, NMSU, 1991—96; mem. 35th anniversary com. U. N.Mex., Gallup, 2001—02. Recipient Dorothy Canfield Fisher $1,000 Libr. award, 1961, Outstanding Cmty. Svc. award for mus. svc. Gallup C. of C., 1968, 70, Outstanding Citizen award, 1974, Benemerenti medal Pope Paul VI, 1977, Celibrate Literarcy award Gallup Internat. Reading Assn., 1983-84, Woman of Distinction award Soroptimists, 1985, N.Mex. Disting. Pub. Svc. award, 1987, Edgar L. Hewitt award Hist. Soc. N.Mex., 1992, Gov.'s award as Outstanding N.Mex. Woman, 1988, Cmty. Svc. award U. N.Mex., 1993; Octavia Fellin Pub. Libr. named in her honor, 1990. Mem.: NAACP, LWV (v.p. 1953—56), AAUW (v.p. co-organizer Gallup br., chmn. com. on women), ALA, N.Mex. Gallup Film Soc. (v.p. 1950—58, co-corgnizer), N.Mex. Mcpl. League (pres. libr.'s div. 1979), Gallup C. of C. (organizing chmn. women's div. 1972, v.p. 1972—73), N.Mex Architectural Found., Plateau Scis. Soc, N.Mex. Libr. Assn. (hon.; chmn. hist. materials com. 1964—66, pres. 1965—66, chmn. com. to extend libr. svcs. 1969—73, chmn. local and regional history roundtable 1978, v.p., sec., salary and tenure com., nat. coord. N.Mex. Legis. com., Libr. of Yr. award 1975, life, Cmty. Achievement award 1990, Lifetime Membership award 1994), N. Mex Foklore Soc., N.Mex. Women's Polit. Caucus, Women's Ordination Conf. Network, Gallup Hist. Soc., Hist. Soc. N.Mex., Pax Christi U.S.A., Call to Action Nat. Ca. Renewal Org., Habitat for Humanity, Alpha Delta Kappa (hon.). Roman Catholic. Home and Office: 513 E Mesa Ave Gallup NM 87301-6021

FELLINGER-BUZBY, LINDA, interior and industrial designer; b. Altoona, Pa., Oct. 1, 1952; d. John and Louise (Reighard) Fellinger; m. Gordon Buzby, June 21, 1975 (div. 1987); 1 child, Sarah. BFA, Moore Coll. Art and Design, Phila., 1975; M Indsl. Design, Domus Acad., Milan, 1990. Project mgr., designer Interspace Inc., Phila., 1972-78; cons. interior residential design and indsl. pub. design Smith Kline Corp., Phila., 1978-79; interior designer, Phila., 1979—; prof. interior design Moore Coll. Art and Design, Phila., 1986-90; prof. interior design and architecture Phila. Coll. of Textile and Sci., Phila., 1996-98. Mem. Am. Soc. Interior Designers, Interior Design Council (exec. com. 1987—), Phila. Mus. Art (collaborative com.). Republican. Episcopalian. Achievements include patents for modular wall washer light fixture with moveable lens, environmentally sensitive postcard Earthly Greetings, portable pocket phones for personal communications system, Dupont corianbathroom sink design, eyeglasses, child's safety vest. Home: 703 Polo Cir Bryn Mawr PA 19010-3841

FELLOWS, ALICE COMBS, artist; b. Atlanta, Sept. 14, 1935; d. Andrew Grafton III and Wilhelmina Drummond (Jackson) Combs; m. Robert Ellis Fellows Jr., Aug. 20, 1957 (div. 1978); children: Ariadne Elisabeth Fellows-Mannion, Kara Suzanne Fellows. BFA, Syracuse U., 1957; M in Clin. Psychology, Antioch U., 1992. Guest artist Yaddo, Saratoga Springs, N.Y., 1991; artist-in-residence Dorland Colony, Temecula, Calif., 1983; guest lectr. psychology seminar UCLA, 1990. Exhibited works in numerous group and one-woman shows including Au Naturel, di Rosa Preserve, Napa, 2003, diRosa Preserve, Napa, Calif., 2003, Hiromi Gallery, Santa Monica, Otis Gallery, Otis Coll. Art and Design, L.A., 2000, L.A. Mcpl. Art Gallery, C.O.L.A. Fellows Exhbn., 1998, El Camino Coll., 1997, Hunsaker-Schlesinger Gallery, 1996, The Armory Ctr. at Pasadena, 1996, Barnsdall Mcpl. Gallery, 1995, Claremont Grad. Sch. Gallery, 1991, Saxon-Lee Gallery, L.A., 1989, Santa Monica Coll. Gallery Art, 1988, J. Rosenthal Gallery, Chgo., 1986, The Biennial at the Hirshhorn Mus. and Sculpture Garden, Washington, 1986, Kirk de Gooyer Gallery, L.A., 1984, 85, many others; works represented in numerous collections including The Norton Collection, Santa Monica, Broad Found., Santa Monica, Mint Mus., Charlotte, N.C., N.C. Mus. Raleigh, N.C., Security Pacific Corp., L.A., Ft. Lauderdale Mus.; others. Arts commr. City of Santa Monica Arts Commn., 1995—99; mem. Pub. Art Com., Santa Monica, 1996—2000; mem. artists adv. bd. L.A. Mcpl. Art Gallery at Bransdall, 1998—2001. Recipient Durfee Found. award; grantee Dale Chihuly grant for Srs. Making Art Workshops, 1996; painting fellow Western States Arts Fedn./NEA, 1990, painting fellow Getty Trust, 1990, NEA fellow in painting, 1991, City of L.A. Individual Artist's fellow, 1998. Home: 18880 Melvin Ave Sonoma CA 95476 E-mail: alicefellows@earthlink.net.

FELLOWS, ESTHER ELIZABETH, musician, music educator; b. Miami, Ariz., Nov. 5, 1952; d. John Wilmont and Flora Elizabeth (Eyestone) Walker; m. James Michael Fellows, Aug. 20, 1976; children: Joy Christine, Rachel Lindsay, Daniel Matthew, Jessica Grace. B in Music Edn., U. Colo., 1975. Co-dir. Children's Piano Lab. U. Colo., Boulder, 1975-76; instr. So. Calif. Conservatory Music, Sun City, 1976-78; pvt. instr. Ft. Lauderdale, 1978-84; instr. Ft. Lauderdale Christian Sch., 1981-83; sect. violinist Signature Symphony Tulsa Ballet, 1984—, Bartlesville (Okla.) Symphony, 1990—; pvt. instr. Broken Arrow, Okla., 1984—. Pvt. instr. Ft. Lauderdale, 1978-84. Mem. Music Tchrs. Nat. Assn. (cert. piano, violin and viola), Am. String Tchrs. Assn., Am. Viola Soc., Okla. Music Tchr. Assn., Suzuki Assn. Am., Hyechka Music Club Tulsa, Tulsa Accredited Music Tchrs. Assn. (chair scholarship com.). Avocation: biking. Home: 19821 S Harvard Ave Mounds OK 74047-5049

FELSTED, CARLA MARTINDELL, librarian, writer, editor; b. Barksdale Field, La., June 21, 1947; d. David Aldenderfer Martindell and Dorthe (Hetland) Horton; m. Robert Earl Luna, Aug. 24, 1968, (div. 1972); m. Hugh Herbert Felsted, Nov. 2, 1974. BA in English, So. Meth. U., 1968, MA in History, 1974; MLS, Tex. Woman's U., 1978. Cert. secondary tchr., Tex.; cert. learning resources specialist, Tex. Tchr. Bishop Lynch High Sch., Dallas, 1968-72, Lake Highlands Jr. High Sch., Richardson, Tex., 1973-75; instr. Richland Coll., Richardson, Tex., 1973-76; library asst. So. Meth. U., Dallas, 1977-78; librarian Tracy-Locke Advt., Dallas, 1978-79; corp. librarian Am. Airlines, Inc., Ft. Worth, 1979-84; research librarian McKinsey & Co., Dallas, 1984-85; reference librarian St. Edward's U., Austin, Tex., 1985—2002, assoc. prof., 1994—2002; libr. Sedona (Ariz.) Pub. Libr., 2003—. Ptnr. Southwind Info. Svcs. and Southwind Bed-Breakfast, Wimberley, Tex., 1985-92. Editor, compiler: Youth and Alcohol Abuse, 1986; co-editor Mexican Meanderings, 1991-99; contbr. Frommer's travel guides, 1991-96. Mem. adv. bd. Sch. Libr. and Info. Scis., Tex. Women's U., Denton, 1982-84; mem. curriculum com. Wimberley Ind. Sch. Dist., 1986; bd. dirs. Hays-Caldwell Coun. on Alcohol and Drug Abuse, San Marcos, Tex., 1986-88, Inst. Cultures for Wimberley Valley, 1989-91, Tex. Alliance Human Needs, 1992-96; Tex. Team Survivor, Danskin Triathlon, 1998-2002, co-capt. 1997-99; vol. Breast Cancer Resource Ctr., 1998-2000, Sedona Cultural Pk., 2003—, Sedona Pub. Libr., 2003, Sedona Gt Decisions, 2004-. Grantee St. Edward's U., 1986-89, 96. Mem. ALA, Tex. Libr. Assn. (dist. program com., membership com. 1986-88, Tex.-Mex. rels. com. 1992-2002), REFORMA, Wimberley C. of C. (bd. dirs. 1987-88). Unitarian Universalist. Avocations: health issues research and advocacy, regional and ethnic cooking, physical fitness, art history, travel. Home: 205 Sunset Dr 23 Sedona AZ 86336

FELTENSTEIN, MARTHA, lawyer; b. Kansas City, Mo., 1954; BA, Princeton U., 1975; MPhil, U. London, 1977; JD, Columbia U., 1981. Bar: N.Y. 1982. Ptnr. Skadden, Arps, Slate, Meagher & Flom, N.Y.C. Office: Skadden Arps Slate Meagher & Flom 4 Times Sq Fl 24 New York NY 10036-6595

FELTON, CYNTHIA, educational administrator; b. Chgo., Apr. 1, 1950; d. Robert Lee Felton Sr. and Julia Mae (Cheton) Felton-Phillips. BA, Northeastern, 1970; MEd, National Coll., 1984; MA, DePaul U., 1988; PhD, Loyola U., Chgo., 1992. Cert. tchr, adminstrv., Ill. Tchr. Chgo. Pub. Schs., 1971-86, adminstr., 1986-89, asst. prin., 1989-92, prin., 1992-97; dir. Chgo. Acad. for Sch. Leadership, 1997—. Mem. ASCD, Nat. Staff Devel. Coun., Nat. Coun. Tchrs. Math, Nat. Coun. Suprs. Math, Ill. Coun. Tchrs. Math (bd. dirs. 1992-95). Office: Chgo Acad Sch Leadership 221 N Lasalle St Chicago IL 60601-1206

FELTON, DOROTHY, state legislator; m. J. Jerome Felton Jr.; children: Jethro J. III, F. Bryan. BA in Journalism, U. Ark. Sect. editor Tulsa Tribune; mem. profl. staff So. Regional Edn. Bd.; pub. rels. cons.; rep. 43d dist. Ga. Ho. of Reps., 1975—. Mem. house appropriations com., house state planning and cmty. affairs com., house ways and means com. Ga. Ho. of Reps. Chair Rep. caucus Ga. Ho. of Reps., 1988-92, Gen. Assembly Election Com., 1982; vice chair tech. com. Nat. HUD Manufactured Home Adv. Coun., 1982, Fulton County Pers. Bd., 1972-74; del. Rep. nat. conv., 1984; co-chair Women for Reagan-Bush, 1984; Ga. chair So. Rep. Leadership Conf., 1983; chair adv. com. Fulton County Schs.; bd. dirs. Atlanta Girls' Club, Protestant Radio and TV Ctr., Inc., Sandy Springs Art and Heritage Soc., Sandy Springs Found., Nat. Conf. State Legislators, 1993-96; founding bd. dirs. Leadership Sandy Springs; past bd. dirs. Campbell-Stone Retirement Homes, Coll. of Health Edn. Ga. State U., Riverwood H.S. PTA, Ga. Soc. to Prevent Blindness; mem. adv. bd. DeKalb Juvenile Ct.; mem. Fulton County Task Force of Gov.'s Conf. on Edn., Leadership Atlanta, LWV; past pres. North Springs H.S. PTA; named to regional leadership inst. Atlanta Regional Commn., 1992. Recipient Disting. Svc. award Med. Assn. Ga., 1980, 88, Ga. Agribus. Coun., award for dedication to children Am. Acad. Pediat. Ga. chpt., Movers and Shakers award Atlanta Jour.-Constn./North Fulton Extra, Outstanding Cmty. Svc. award Delta Gamma, Outstanding Legislator award NAACP, Outstanding Pub. Svc. award Atlanta Alumnae Panhellenic Coun.; named Outstanding Legislator for 1993 in U.S., Nat. Rep. Legislator's Assn., one of Ten Most Powerful People in North Fulton, Atlanta Bus. Chronicle, Woman of Yr., St. James United Meth. Ch. Home: 465 Tanacrest Dr NW Atlanta GA 30328-2838 Office: Legis Office Bldg Rm 404 Atlanta GA 30334

FELTS, REBECCA NANCY, elementary school educator; b. Tulsa, June 8, 1954; d. Frank Barry Dayton and Nancy Ann Parker; m. Merrill Bryce Felts, May 23, 1973; children: Rebecca Katharine, Andrew Bryce. BS in Elem. Edn., North Ea. State U., Tahlequah, Okla., 1976; MS in Elem. Adminstrn., North Ea.State U., Tahlequah, Okla., 1982. Tchr. Peggs (Okla.) Sch. Dist., 1976—82, Tahlequah (Okla.) Pub. Schs., 1982—2003. Commr. Okla. Commn. Tchr. Preparation, 2001—03. Del. Nat. Dem. Conv., L.A., 2000. Grantee, Tahlequah Pub. Sch. Found. Mem.: NEA (bd. dirs. 1997—2002), Tahlequah Edn. Assn., AAUW, Okla. Edn. Assn. (v.p. 2003—), Leadership Okla. Class XVII, Delta Kappa Gamma. Democrat. Methodist. Avocations: oil painting, needlecrafts, stained glass work. Home: 20010 Stick Ross Mountain Rd Tahlequah OK 74464 Office: Oklahoma Education Association 323 E Madison Oklahoma City OK 73154 E-mail: bfelts@okea.org.

FELTY, SHARON J. elementary school educator; b. Birmingham, Ala., Oct. 6, 1949; d. W.E. and Marjorie Johnson; m. Daniel O. Felty, July 22, 1972; children: Chris, Brian. MusB Edn., Evangel Univ., Sprinfield, Mo., 1972; grad. studies, Univ. Okla., Norman, Okla., 1988, The Julliard Sch., N.Y., 2001. Cert. tchg. Nat. Bd. of Profl. Tchg. Standards, 2002. Tchr. Dekalb County Sch., Decatur, Ga., 1972—74, Jenks Pub. Sch., Okla., 1988—2003. Dept. chmn. Jenks Pub. Sch., Okla., 1988—93, arts coord., 1998—99, dist. music coord., 2002—. Contbr. articles to profl. jour. Vol. Am. Cancer Society, 2000, 2003. Recipient Okla. Tchr. of the Yr., V.F.W., 2002—03; grantee funds for tchrs., Houston, Tex., 2001—02; scholar Fulbright Meml., Fulbright Meml. Fund, Tokyo, Japan, 2003. Mem.: Nat. EducatorsmAssn., Jenks Classroom Tchrs. Assn., Music Educators Nat. Conf. Achievements include The Eagle student recording selected for the Millennium Capsule in Washington, Clinton Adminstrn. Avocations: walking, interior decorating, fitness. Office Phone: 918-299-4411.

FENDERSON, CAROLINE HOUSTON, psychotherapist; b. East Orange, N.J., June 17, 1932; d. George Cochran and Mary Bullard (Saunders) Houston; m. Kendrick Elwell Fenderson, Jr.; 1 child, Karen Sibley. BA, Vassar Coll., 1954; MA, U. So. Fla., 1973. Lic. mental health counselor, Fla.; diplomate Am. Bd. Cert. Managed Care Providers, diplomate Am. Psychotherapy Assn.; cert. Nat. Bd. for Cert. Clin. Hypnotherapists, Inc.; cert. trainer, devel. of human capacities Found. for Mind Rsch.; ordained to ministry of edn. Unitarian Universalist. Dir. of religious edn. Unitarian Universalist Ch., St. Petersburg, Fla., 1960-80, min. of religious edn. Clearwater, Fla., 1981-83; counselor and staff devel. cons. Pinellas County (Fla.) Schools, 1973-83; pvt. practice Clearwater and Palm Harbor, Fla., 1983—. Author: Life Journey, 1988; (with Kendrick Fenderson Jr.) Magnets, 1961, Southern Shores, 1964; (with others) Man the Culture Builder, 1970, U.U. Identity, 1979; contbr. articles to profl. jours. Pub. affairs chmn. St. Petersburg Jr. League, 1960; founder Childbirth and Parent Edn. League of Pinellas County, 1960-70, pres., v.p., com. chair, tchr.; v.p. Child Guidance Clinic, St. Petersburg, 1960. Mem. ACA, Liberal Religious Edn. Dirs. Assn. (v.p. 1980-81), Assn. Transpersonal Psychology, Assn. Humanistic Psychology, Internat. Transpersonal Assn., Unitarian Universalist Assn. (com. mem. 1975-79), Phi Beta Kappa, Kappa Delta Pi. Home: 29 Freshwater Dr Palm Harbor FL 34684-1106 Office: 25 400 US 19 N Ste 172 Clearwater FL 33763 Office Phone: 727-797-7211.

FENIGER, SUSAN, chef, television personality, writer; Former mem. staff Le Perroquet, Chgo., Ma Maison, L.A., L'Oasis, France; formerly chef, co-owner City Cafe, L.A.; chef, co-owner CITY, L.A., 1985—94, Border Grill, L.A., 1985—91, Santa Monica, 1990—. Co-host (TV series) Too Hot Tamales, 1995—, Tamales' World Tour, (radio show) Good Food; co-author: City Cuisine, 1989, Mesa Mexicana, 1994, Cantina, 1996, Cooking with Too Hot Tamales, 1997. Active Scleroderma Rsch. Found., Named Chef of Yr., Calif. Restaurant Writers, 1993. Mem.: Chef's Collaborative 2000, Women Chefs and Restaurateurs. Office: Border Grill 1445 4th St Santa Monica CA 90401

FENN, SANDRA ANN, programmer, analyst; b. Sugar Land, Tex., Oct. 31, 1953; d. William Charles and Helen Maxine (Kyle) F.; m. Jimmie Dan Watts, May 21, 1973 (div. June 1988); children: Gabriel Nathaniel Watts, Lindsay Nichelle Garza. AA in Gen. Studies summa cum laude, Alvin (Tex.) C.C., 1994; BS in Computer Info. Sys., U. Houston, Clear Lake, 2000. Shampoo asst. LaVonne's Salon of Beauty, Houston, 1972-73; coding clk. Prudential Ins. Co., Houston, 1974-75; word processing operator MacGregor Med. Assn., Houston, 1983-85; computer applications analyst Computer Scis. Corp., Houston, 1987-92; program support adminstr. Sci. Applications Internat. Corp., Houston, 1992-95, programmer/analyst, 1995-98; software developer astronaut office Johnson Space Ctr., 1998-2000; info. tech. analyst El Paso Corp., Houston, 2000—03. Mem. Am. Bus. Women's Assn. (newsletter chair 1995-2001, 1999 Woman of Excellence), Phi Theta Kappa. Avocations: horseback riding, camping, biking, volleyball, reading. Home: 1619 Newcomb Way Houston TX 77058 E-mail: safenn@orbitworld.net.

FENNEL, MELODY H. federal agency administrator; Grad., Vassar Coll. Legis. rep. Nat. Coun. State Housing Agys., 1988—90; legis. dir. Nat. Assn. Home Builders, 1990—95; profl. staff mem., chief housing advisor to Senator Phil Gramm U.S. Senate Com. on Banking, Housing and Urban Affairs, 1995—2001; asst. sec. for congl. and intergovernmental rels. Dept. HUD, Washington, 2001—. Office: Dept HUD Congl and Intergovernmental Rels 451 7th St SW Washington DC 20410-9000

FENNELL, DIANE MARIE, marketing professional, process engineer; b. Panama, Iowa, Dec. 11, 1944; d. Urban William and Marcella Mae (Leytham) Schechinger; m. Leonard E. Fennell, Aug. 19, 1967; children: David, Denise, Mark. BS, Creighton U., Omaha, 1966. Process engr. Tex. Instruments, Richardson, 1974-79; sr. process engr. Signetics Corp., Santa Clara, Calif., 1979-82; demo lab. mgr. Airco Temescal, Berkeley, Calif., 1982-84; field process engr. Applied Materials, Santa Clara, 1984-87; mgr. product mktg. Lam Rsch., Fremont, Calif., 1987-90; dir. sales and mktg. Ion & Plasma Equipment, Fremont, Calif., 1990-91; pres. FAI, Half Moon Bay, Calif., 1990-96; v.p. mktg. Tegal Corp., Petaluma, Calif., 1997-99; v.p. mktg. and sales Semicaps, Inc., Santa Clara, Calif., 1999—2001; exec. dir. Ctr. for Internat. Devel., Santa Clara, 2001—. Founder, coord. chmn. Plasma Etch User's Group, Santa Clara, 1984-87; tchr. computer course Adult Edn., Half Moon Bay, Calif., 1982-83. Founder, bd. dirs. Birth to Three program Mental Retardation Ctr., Denison, Tex., 1974-75; fund raiser local sch. band, Half Moon Bay, 1981-89; community rep. local sch. bd., Half Moon Bay, 1982-83. Mem. Am. Vacuum Soc., Soc. Photo Instrumentation Engrs., Soc. Women Engrs., Material Rsch. Soc., Commonwealth Club. Avocations: hiking, reading, gardening. Home: 441 Alameda Ave Half Moon Bay CA 94019-5337

FENNELL ROBBINS, SALLY, writer; b. Greensburg, Pa., Feb. 17, 1950; d. Clifford Seanor and Charlotte Louise (Hoffman) Fennell; m. John W. Robbins, Sept. 22, 1984. BS in Journalism cum laude, Ohio U., 1972; MA in Journalism magna cum laude, Marshall U., 1974. Intern, reporter Tribune-Rev., Greensburg, Pa., 1972; prodn. asst. Harper's Bazaar, N.Y.C., 1972; reporter UPI, Birmingham, Ala., 1972-73; reporter, dept. editor Home Furnishings Daily, Fairchild Pubs., N.Y.C., 1974-77; acct. exec. supr., client svc. mgr., v.p. Burson-Marsteller, N.Y.C., 1977-83; group mgr., v.p. pub. rels. divsn. Ketchum Comm., 1983-84; freelance writer, editor, 1984-89; dir. comm. Deloitte & Touche Retail Svcs. Group, NY, 1989-93; writer and author, 1993—; grad. teaching asst. Sch. Journalism/Reporting, Marshall U., Huntington, W.Va., 1973-74. Home and Office: 237 E 20th St New York NY 10003-1805 E-mail: sally.robbins@att.net.

FENNELLY, JANE COREY, lawyer; b. N.Y.C., Dec. 12, 1942; d. Joseph and Josephine (Corey) F. BA, Cornell U., 1964; MLS, UCLA, 1968; JD, Loyola U., L.A., 1974. Bar: Calif. 1974, U.S. Dist. Ct. (ctrl. and so. dists.) Calif. 1974, U.S. Dist. Ct. (ea. dist.) Calif. 1977, U.S. Dist. Ct. (no. dist.) Calif. 1980, N.Y. 1982, Colo. 1993, Ariz. 1995. Ptnr. Graham & James, 1976-83; with legal dept. Bank of Am., L.A., 1973-76, Wyman, Bautzer, Kuchel & Silbert, L.A., 1983-87, Dennis, Shafer, Fennelly & Creim (merged with Bronson & McKinnon), L.A., 1987-96; with Squire, Sanders & Dempsey, Phoenix, 1996—98; prin. Jane C. Fennelly, P.C., Phoenix, 1998—; of counsel Creim, Macias & Koenig LLP, L.A., 1999—. Mem. ABA, Am. Bankruptcy Inst., Calif. Bankruptcy Forum, L.A. County Bar Assn. (bd. dirs., mem. exec. com. comml. law and bankruptcy sect. 1989-92), Maricopa County Bar Assn., Fin. Lawyers Conf. (pres. bd. dirs. 1983-84, mem. bd. govs. 1984—). Home: 15356 W Pasadena Dr Surprise AZ 85374 Office: #610 Ste 101 15508 W Bell Rd Surprise AZ 85374 E-mail: jane.fennelly@azbar.org.

FENNER, SUZAN ELLEN, lawyer; b. Grand Junction, Colo., Dec. 5, 1947; d. Harry J. and Louise (Bain) Shaw; m. Michael Lee Riddle, Apr. 24, 1969 (div. Feb. 1976); m. Peter R. Fenner, Nov. 24, 1978; children: Laura Elizabeth, Adam Kyle. BA, Tex. Tech U., 1969, JD, 1971. Bar: Tex. 1972, U.S. Dist. Ct. (no. dist.) Tex. 1972. Assoc. Smith & Baker, Lubbock, Tex., 1971-72; law clk. to presiding judge U.S. Dist. Ct., Dallas, 1972-73; assoc. Gardere Wynne Sewell LLP, Dallas, 1973-78, ptnr., 1978—, chair retirement com., 1973—, chair tax practice., 2001—, mem. ptnrs. bd., 1991—94. Bd. dirs. Tex. Lawyers Ins. Exch., 1985—, S.W. Benefits Assn. (formerly S.W. Pension Conf.), 1987—92, pres., 1990—91. Bd. dirs. East Dallas Devel. Ctr., 1982—91; Lone Star coun. Camp Fire USA, 1995—2001, v.p. outdoor programs, 1996—98, pres.-elect, 1997, pres., 1998—2000; bd. dirs. Episcopal Ch. Women of the Diocese of Dallas, 1992—, pres., 1996—2000; del. to triennial nat. conv. Episcopal Diocese of Dallas, 1994, 1997, 2000, asst. chancellor, 1994—, exec. coun., 1995—2000, standing com., 2001—; pres. Episcopal Ch. Women for Episcopal Ch. of Ascension, 1992, bd. dirs., 1992—94; pres. Province VII Episcopal Ch. Women, bd. dirs., 1999—2002; exec. coun. Province VII of the Episcopal Ch., 1999—2002. Mem. ABA, Tex. Bar Assn. (chmn. bar. jour. com. 1982-88), Dallas Bar Assn. (treas. employee benefits com. 1998, sec. 1999, v.p. 2000, pres. 2001), Dallas Bus. League (pres. 1986). Episcopalian. Avocation: sailing. Home: 600 Goodwin Dr Richardson TX 75081-5603 Office: Gardere Wynne Sewell LLP 1601 Elm St Ste 3000 Dallas TX 75201-4761 Office Phone: 214-999-4576. E-mail: sfenner@gardere.com.

FENNING, LISA HILL, lawyer, mediator, former federal judge; b. Chgo., Feb. 22, 1952; d. Ivan Byron and Joan (Hennigar) Hill; m. Alan Mark Fenning, Apr. 3, 1977; 4 children. BA with honors, Wellesley Coll., 1971; JD, Yale U., 1974. Bar: Ill. 1975, Calif. 1979, U.S. Dist. Ct. (no. dist.) Ill., U.S. Dist. Ct. (no., ea., so. & cen. dists.) Calif., U.S. Ct. Appeals (6th, 7th & 9th cirs.), U.S. Supreme Ct. 1989. Law clk. U.S. Ct. Appeals 7th cir., Chgo., 1974-75; assoc. Jenner and Block, Chgo., 1975-77, O'Melveny and Myers, L.A., 1977-85; judge U.S. Bankruptcy Ct. Cen. Dist. Calif., L.A., 1985-2000; mediator JAMS, Orange, Calif., 2000-01; ptnr. Dewey Ballantine LLP, L.A., 2001—. Bd. govs. Nat. Conf. Bankruptcy Judges, 1989-92; pres. Nat. Conf. of Women's Bar Assns., N.C., 1987-88, pres.-elect, 1986-87, v.p., 1985-86, bd. dirs.; lectr., program coord. in field; bd. govs. Nat. Conf. Bankruptcy Judges Endowment for Edn., 1992-97, Am. Bankruptcy Inst., 1994-2000; mem., bd. advisors Nat. Jud. Edn. Program to Promote Equality for Women and Men in the Cts., 1994—. Mem., bd. advisors: Lawyer Hiring & Training Report, 1985-87; contbr. articles to profl. jours. Durant scholar Wellesley Coll., 1971; named one of Am's. 100 Most Important Women Ladies Home Jour., 1988, one of L.A.'s 50 Most Powerful Women Lawyers, L.A. Bus. Jour., 1998. Fellow Am. Bar Found., Am. Coll. Bankruptcy (bd. regents 1995-98); mem. ABA (standing com. on fed. jud. improvements 1995-98, mem. commn. on women in the profession 1987-91, Women's Caucus 1987—, Individual Rights and Responsibilities sect. 1984—, bus. law sect. 1986—, bus. bankruptcy com.), Nat. Assn. Women Judges (nat. task force gender bias in the cts. 1986-87, 93-94), Nat. Conf. Bankruptcy Judges (chair endowment edn. bd. 1994-95), Am. Bankruptcy Inst. (nominating com. 1994-95, bd. steering com. stats. project 1994-96), Calif. State Bar Assn. (chair com. on women in law 1986-87), Women Lawyers' Assn. L.A. (ex officio mem., bd. dirs., chmn., founder com. on status of women lawyers 1984-85, officer nominating com. 1986, founder, mem. Do-It-Yourself Mentor Network 1986-96), Phi Beta Kappa. Democrat. Office: Dewey Ballantine LLP 333 S Grand Ave 26th Fl Los Angeles CA 90071 E-mail: Lfenning@deweyballantine.com.

FENOGLIO-PREISER, CECILIA METTLER, pathologist, educator; b. N.Y.C., Nov. 28, 1943; d. Frederick Albert and Cecilia Charlotte (Asper) Mettler; m. John Fenoglio Jr., May 27, 1967 (div. 1977); 1 child, Timothy; stepchildren: Johanna, Andreas, Nicholas; m. Wolfgang F.E. Preiser, Feb. 16, 1985. Ach, Coll. St. Elizabeth, 1965; MD, Georgetown U., 1969. Diplomate Am. Bd. Pathology. Intern Presbyn. Hosp., N.Y.C., 1969-70; dir. Central Tissue Facility Columbia-Presbyn. Med. Ctr., N.Y.C., 1976-83; co-dir. div. surg. pathology Presbyn. Hosp., N.Y.C., 1978-82, div. dir. surg. pathology, 1982-83; dir. Electron Microscop. Lab. Internat. Inst. Human Reprodn., 1978-85; assoc. prof. pathology Coll. Physicians and Surgeons, Columbia U., 1981-82, prof., 1982-83, attending pathologist, 1982-83; dir. lab. services Albuquerque VA Med. Ctr., 1983-90; prof. pathology U. N.Mex. Sch. Medicine, Albuquerque, 1983-90, also vice-chmn. dept. pathology; MacKenzie prof., chmn. dept. pathology and lab. medicine U. Cin. Sch. Medicine, 1990—, dir. cancer programs, 2001—. Mem. com. gastrointestine cancer WHO. Author: General Pathology, 1983, Gastrointestinal Pathology, An Atlas and Text, 1999, 2nd edit., 1999, Tumors of the Large and Small Intestine, 1990; editor: Advances in Pathobiology Cell Membranes, 1988-92, Advances in Pathobiology: Aging and Neoplasia, 1976, Progress in Surgical Pathology, vols. I-XIV, 1980-87, Advances in Pathology, vols. I-V, 1988-89. Grantee NIH, 1973, 79-82, 84-87, 85-2003, Cancer Rsch. Ctr., 1975-83, Population Coun., 1977-83, Nat. Ileitis and Colitis Found., 1979-80, Am. Cancer Soc., 1987-94. Fellow AAAS (life); mem. U.S. and Can. Acad. Pathology (edn. com. 1980-85, coun. 1984-87, exec. com. 1987-91, v.p. 1987, pres.-elect 1988, pres. 1989, fin. com. 1998-2001), Internat. Acad. Pathology (N.Am. v.p. 1990-94, pres. 1996-98, exec. com. 1990-2000, edn. com. 1998—), Nat. Surg. Adj. Breast Project (sci. adv. bd.), Am. Assn. Pathologists, Armed Forces Inst. Pathology (sci. adv. bd. 1990—), N.Y. Acad. Sci., N.Y. Acad. Medicine, Fedn. Am. Scientists for Exptl. Biology, Gastrointestinal Pathologist Group (founding mem. edn. com. 1983-85, sec.-treas. 1993-96, pres.-elect 1996, pres. 1997), S.W. Oncology Group (chmn. GI tumor biology com., chmn. pathology com., chmn. correlative sci. com.), Arthur Purdy Stout Soc. (coun. 1987-90). Office: U Cin Sch Medicine 231 Bethesda Ave Cincinnati OH 45229-2827 E-mail: cecilia.fenogliopreiser@uc.edu.

FENSELAU, CATHERINE CLARKE, chemistry educator; b. York, Nebr., Apr. 15, 1939; d. Lee Keckley and Muriel (Thomas) Clarke; m. Allan Herman Fenselau, 1962 (div. 1980); children: Andrew Clarke, Thomas Stewart; m. Robert James Cotter, 1984. AB, Bryn Mawr Coll., 1961; PhD, Stanford U., 1965. Research scientist U. Calif.-Berkeley, 1965-67; instr. to prof. Johns Hopkins U., Balt., 1967-87; chmn. chemistry, biochemistry U. Md., Balt. County, 1987-98, prof. dept. chemistry and biochemistry College Park, 1998—; chmn. dept. chemistry and biochemistry, 1998-2000. Cons. NIH, NSF, USDA, U.S. Army, FDA, others. Editor: Biomed. Environ. Mass Spectrometry, 1973—89; editor: (assoc. editor) Analytical Chemistry, 1990—; contbr. articles to profl. jours. Fellow: AAAS; mem.: Am. Soc. Pharmacology and Exptl. Therapeutics, Am. Chem. Soc. (Garvan medal 1985, Md. Chemist award Md. sect. 1989), Am. Soc. Mass Spectrometry (pres.). Office: U Md Dept Chemistry Biochemistry College Park MD 20742-0001

FERBER, LINDA S. museum curator; b. May 17, 1944; BA cum laude, Barnard Coll., 1966; MA, Columbia U., 1968, PhD in Art History, 1980. Curator Am. Painting and Sculpture The Bklyn. Mus. Art, 1970-97, chief curator, 1985-99, Andrew W. Mellon Curator Am. Art, 1997—. Author: William Trost Richards (1833-1905): American Landscape and Marine Painter, 1980, Tokens of a Friendship: Miniature Watercolors by William T. Richards, 1982, (with others) The New Path: Ruskin and the American Pre-Raphaelites, 1985, Never at Fault: The Drawings of William T. Richards, 1986, (with others) Albert Bierstadt: Art and Enterprise, 1991, (with others) Masters of Color and Light: Homer, Sargent and the American Watercolor Movement, 1998, Pastoral Interlude: William T. Richards in Chester County, 2001, (with others) In Search of a National Landscape: William T. Richards in the Adirondacks, 2002; contbr. articles on 19th and 20th century Am. art history. Wyeth Endowment for Am. Art fellow, 1976-77; recipient Disting. Alumna award Barnard Coll., 2001, Fleischman award Smithsonian Archives of Am. Art, 2002. Mem. Coll. Art Assn., Am. Assn. Mus., Am. Studies Assn., Assn. Art Mus. Curators, Century Assn., Phi Beta Kappa. Office: Brooklyn Mus Art 200 Eastern Pkwy Brooklyn NY 11238-6052 E-mail: linda.ferber@brooklynmuseum.org.

FERDERBER, JUNE H. state legislator; children: Deven Armeni, Adrien. Student, Youngstown State U. Mem. Ohio Ho. of Reps., 1986—, mem. energy and environment, judiciary and criminal justice coms. Mem. adv. com. ohio child support guidelines, women's policy and rsch. Com.; ranking minority mem. family svcs. com. Contbr. articles to Warren Tribune Chronicle. Active Animal Welfare League. Named Woman of Yr., Coalition Labor Union Women, YWCA, 1988. Mem. NOW (Trumbull County chpt.), LWV, Ohio Bus. and Profl. Women, Ohio Farm Bur., Mosquito Creek Devel. Assn., Farmer's Union, Sierra Club. Democrat. Home: 1435 Locust St Mineral Ridge OH 44440-9721 Office: Ohio House of Reps Office of House Mems Columbus OH 43215

FERDINAND, LISA G. psychotherapist; d. Louis Jerome and Anna Marie Ferdinand. BA in Am. Studies, West Chester U., 1979; MSW, U. Ga., 1989; MA in Clin. Psychology, postgrad., Ga. State U., 2001—. Vol. tchrs. aide Bull Learning and Rsch. Ctr. West Chester (Pa.) U., 1975—76, group facilitator, peer counselor, 1977, 1978, 1979; undergrad. writing intern Childton Pub. Co., Radnor, Pa., 1978—79; undergrad. intern Martin Luther King Ctr. for Nonviolent Social Change, Atlanta, 1979; with team def. project Vols. in Svc. to Am., Atlanta, 1980—82; resource devel. coord. Atlanta Legal Aid Soc., 1982—86; vol. Ga. Mental Health Inst., Atlanta, 1986—87; devel. coord. The Bridge, Atlanta, 1986—88, lic. clin. social worker, psychotherapist, 1994—98, 2002; program dir./developer United Cerebral Palsy, Atlanta, 1988—89; social work intern Jewish Family Svcs., Atlanta, 1988—89; lic. clin. social worker, child and adolescent specialist Fayette Counselign Ctr., Fayetteville, Ga., 1989—92; lic. clin. social worker, psychotherapist Laurel Heights Hosp., Atlanta, 1992—94; pvt. practice lic. clin. social worker, psychotherapist Atlanta, 1993—; lic. clin. social worker, psychotherapist Hillside Hosp., Atlanta, 1998—2002. Grad. rsch. asst. Couples' Rsch. Project psychology dept. Ga. State U., Atlanta, 1999—, grad. tchg. asst. psychology dept., 2001—02, Atlanta, 2002, Atlanta, 2003—; with Ga. Regents Ctr. for Learning Disorders Assessment Practicum, Atlanta, 2000; with Psychology Clinic Therapy Practicum Ga. State U., Atlanta, 1999—; presenter in field. Contbr. articles to profl. jours. Scholar, AAUW. Mem.: NASW, APA (student), Am. Assn. for Marriage and Family Therapy (student), Psi Chi, Golden Key. Office: PO Box 5329 Atlanta GA 31107

FERENCZ, CHARLOTTE, pediatrician, epidemiology and preventive medicine educator; b. Budapest, Hungary, Oct. 28, 1921; came to U.S., 1954; d. Paul Ferencz and Livia deFekete. BSc, McGill U., 1944, MD, CM, 1945; MPH, Johns Hopkins U., 1970. Cert. pediatrics Royal Coll. Physicians and Surgeons, Can., pediatric cardiology Am. Bd. Pediatrics. Demonstrator McGill U., Montreal, 1952-54; asst. prof. pediatrics Johns Hopkins U., Balt., [illegible]; U. Chi., 1959-60, asst. prof. SUNY, Buffalo, 1960-66, assoc. prof., 1966-73; assoc. prof. epidemiology and preventive medicine U. Md. Sch. Medicine, Balt., 1973-74, prof., 1974-98, prof. pediatrics, 1985—, prof. emeritus, 1998—. Prin. investigator population based study Etiology of Congenital Heart Disease, 1981-89; mem. epidemiology and disease control study sect. NIH, 1984-88; pres. Delta Omage Alpha chpt. Pub. Health Soc., 1990-92. Recipient M.E.S. Abbott scholarship McGill U., 1943-45, M.E.R.I.T. award Nat. Heart, Lung & Blood Inst., 1987, Fogarty Internat. Ctr. Health Sci. Exchange award NIH, 1988, Helen B. Taussig award Am. Heart Assn. Md. Affiliate, 1991, Achievement award Univ. Ctr. Life Scis., Balt., 1993, Johns Hopkins U. Disting. Alumnus award, 2001. Fellow Am. Acad. Pediatrics (Spl. Achievement award Md. chpt. 1994), Am. Coll. Cardiology; mem. Teratology Soc. Democrat. Office: U Md Sch Medicine 660 W Redwood St Baltimore MD 21201-1541

FERGUS, PATRICIA MARGUERITA, English language educator, writer, editor; b. Mpls., Oct. 26, 1918; d. Golden Maughan and Mary Adella (Smith) Fergus. BS, U. Minn., 1939, MA, 1941, PhD, 1960. Various pers. and editing positions U.S. Govt., 1943-59; mem. faculty U. Minn., Mpls., 1964-79, asst. prof. English, 1972-79, coord. writing program conf. on writing, 1975, dir. writing centre, 1975-77; prof. English and writing, dir. writing ctr., assoc. dean Coll. Mt. St. Mary's Coll., Emmitsburg, Md., 1979-81; dir. writing seminars Mack Truck, Inc., Hagerstown, Md., 1979-81; writer, 1964—. Editor, 1997—; vocal soloist, 1997—; editl. asst. to pres. Met. State U., St. Paul, 1984—85; coord. creative writing, writer program notes for Coffee Concerts The Kenwood, 1992—94; dir. Kenwood Scribes Presentation, 1994; spkr., cons. in field; dir. 510 Groveland Assocs.; bus. mgr. Eitel Hosp. Gift Shop; freelance manuscript editor, 1997—99; writer, reviewer Whittier Pubs., Long Beach, NY, 1997; instr. Elderlearning Inst., 1999—2000, Univ. Coll., U. Minn., 1999—2000; poetry and prose reading, retirement cmtys., 2002—04; pres., resident coun. Walker, Tree Tops, Mpls., 2003—05. Author: Spelling Improvement, 5th edit., 1991; contbr. to Downtown Cath. Voice, Mpls., Mountaineer Briefing, ABI Digest, Women in the Arts The Penletter; contbr. poems to Minn. English Jour., Women in the Arts, Decatur Area Arts Coun. Newsletter, Mpls. Muse, The Moccasin, Heartsong and Northstar Gold, The Pen Woman, Midwest Chaparral, Rhyme Time, The Best of Rhyme Time, 1998, Fantasy, 1998; contbr. short stories to anthologies, including Seeking the Muses, Inspired Works of Creativity, 2000; musical works performed at St. Olaf Ch., 1997, Nat. League Am. Pen Women, 1998. Mem. spl. vocal octet St. Olaf Ch. Choir, 1977-79, 81-92, St. Olaf Parish Adv. Bd., 1982-84, Windmore Found. for the Arts., 1996. Recipient Outstanding Contbn. award U. Minn. Twin Cities Student Assembly, 1975, Horace T. Morse-Amoco Found. award, 1976; Golden Poet award World of Poetry, 1992; Edml. Devel. grant U. Minn., 1975-76, Mt. St. Mary's Coll. grant, 1980; 3d prize vocal-choral category Nat. Music Composition Contest, Nat. League Am. Pen Women, poetry prize No. Dist. Women's Club, Va., 1996. Mem.: Midwest Fedn. Chaparral Poets (poetry judge, numerous poetry prizes including 1st prize 1998, 1999, 2001, 2003), Mpls. Poetry Soc. (pres. 2000—02, numerous poetry prizes including 1st prize 1999, 2d prize 2003), World Lit. Acad., Nat. League Am. Pen Women (Minn. br. past pres., 1st pl. Haiku nat. poetry contest 1992), Minn. Coun. Tchrs. English (chmn. career and job opportunities comm., spl. com. tchr. licensure, sec. legis. com.), Nat. Coun. Tchrs. English (regional judge 1974, 1976—77, state coord. 1977—79), Mpls. Woman's Club (critic writers group). Roman Catholic. Home and Office: # 612 3535 Bryant Ave S Minneapolis MN 55408-4134

FERGUSON, AUDREY DIANE, elementary school educator; b. St. Louis, June 28, 1946; d. Goldie Walter and Muriel Lee (Quarles) Buford; m. Chavis Edward Ferguson, Sr., Sept. 4, 1965; children: Chavis Edward II, Kevin, Robin. AB in Edn., Harris-Stowe Tchrs. Coll., St. Louis, 1968; MA in Teaching, Webster U., St. Louis, 1984. Cert. elem. edn., mid. schs., learning disabled, behavior disorders, emotionally handicapped, reading, Mo. Classroom tchr. St. Louis Pub. Schs., 1969-76, remedial math. tchr., 1976—, chpt. I supt. adv. com., 1984-85, elem. math. cons., 1982—. Chairperson INROADS Parent Support Group, St. Louis, 1992-93; mem. INROADS, 1989—. Recipient Parent of Yr. award INROADS, St. Louis, 1994; inducted into Mid-Am. Edn. Hall of Fame, 2003. Mem. Nat. Coun. Tchrs. Math., Internat. Reading Assn., Harris-Stowe Alumni. Mem. Ch. of God. Avocations: music, crafts, reading, church work. Home: 16735 Stanford Place Dr Florissant MO 63034-3214

FERGUSON, CHRISTINE C. lawyer, state agency administrator; b. East Lansing, Mich., Oct. 28, 1958; d. George and Claire Ferguson; m. Fred Glomb; 1 child, Gregory. BA, U. Mich., 1980; JD, Am. U., 1986. Staff asst. Hon. John H. Chafee, U.S. Senate, Washington, 1981-88, legis. dir., 1988-92, dep. chief of staff, 1992-94; dir. R.I. Dept. Human Svcs., 1995—. Recipient awards Nat. Assn Community Health Care Ctrs., Nat. Downs Syndrome Congress, Nat. Family Planning and Reproductive Health Assn., Sec. Health and Human Svcs.; named one of 100 Most Influential Attys., Nat. Law Jour., 1994, one of 25 Most Influential Working Mothers, Working Mother Mag., 2000. Avocations: sailing, outdoor sports. Office: Dept Human Svcs 600 New London Ave Cranston RI 02920-3050

FERGUSON, CYNTHIA CLAIRE, music educator, consultant; b. LaCrosse, Wis., Feb. 3, 1947; d. Harold Loren Hauge and Esther Irene Mattison - Hauge; m. John Franklin Ferguson, June 21, 1969; children: Klaus Edmund, Erik Nels, Scott Nathan. B in Music Edn., U. Idaho, 1969; MS in Elem. Edn., Western Oreg. U., 1994. Lic. tchr. Oreg. Tchr. Stds. and Practices Commn., 2001. Band and choir dir. Glide (Oreg.) Sch. Dist., 1970—72; pvt. music educator Roseburg, Oreg., 1972—83; music specialist South Umpqua Sch. Dist., Tri City, Oreg., 1983—84; elem. music specialist Roseburg (Oreg.) Pub. Schs., 1985—. Music curriculum cons. Oreg. Dept. Edn., Salem, 2002; presenter in field. Author: (music curriculum) ROADMAPS - Roseburg Public Schools; actor: (umpqua actors community theater) Nunsense II, Mikado, Quilters, Nuncrackers; musician (soloist): Roseburg Cmty. Band; singer: Vintage Singers. Musician Faith Luth. Ch., Roseburg, 1998—2003. Mem.: Oreg. Music Educators Assn., Music Educators Nat. Conf., Sigma Alpha Iotat. Protestant. Avocations: gardening, reading, cultural events, boating - fishing, travel. Home: 128 W Bodie St Roseburg OR 97470 Office: Fullerton Elementary School 2560 W Bradford Dr Roseburg OR 97470 Personal E-mail: mtnhigh@mcsi.net. E-mail: cferguson@roseburg.k12.or.us.

FERGUSON, DIANA S. food products executive; b. 1963; M in Mgmt., Northwestern U.; Bachelor's, Yale U. With Eaton, Fannie Mae, First Nat. Bank Chgo., IBM, US Fort James Corp.; v.p., treas. Sara Lee Corp., 2001—. Fellow: Leadership Greater Chgo. Office: Sara Lee Corp 3 First Nat Plaza Chicago IL 60602-4260*

FERGUSON, ESTHER B. philanthropist; b. Sumter, S.C., Jan. 24, 1943; d. Norwood Fleming Baskin and Nan Richardson Rickenbaker; m. George William Moore (div.); m. James Larnard Ferguson. BA in Polit. Sci./Art History, U. S.C.; LLD, William Penn Coll., 1983; DHL, Dominican Coll., 1987, U. Pacific, 1990, Johnson and Wales U., 1996, Coker Coll., 1996. Founder Nat. Drop-Out Prevention Fund & Ctr., Clemson U., 1985—, Study Abroad Program, Trujillo, Spain, 1995; bd. dirs. Charleston Symphony Orchestra, S.C., 1990-2000; vice-chmn. Young Concert Artists, N.Y.C., 1982-2000; bd. dirs. Spoleto U.S.A., Charleston, 1983-2000, Internat. Found. for Edn. and Self-Help, Phoenix, 1980—, Monmouth (N.J.) Coll., 1985-89, Coke Coll., Hartsville, S.C., 1993-96; founder, chair Am. Mental Health Resources, 1999—. Contbr. articles to profl. publs. and newspapers. Episcopalian. Republican. Avocations: reading, skiing, shooting, internat. travel. Office: PO Box 1457 Charleston SC 29402

FERGUSON, JEAN KENNAN, psychotherapist; b. Maui, Hawaii, Sept. 22, 1940; d. Robert McCormack and Mary Violet (Judy) Kennan; m. Richard C. Ferguson, June 8, 1963; children: Kennan, Rona. BA cum laude, Whitman Coll., 1962; MA, UCLA, 1963; MS, U. So. Calif., 1985. Life gen. secondary tchg. and jr. coll. tchg. credentials, Calif.; lic. marriage, family and child counselor, Calif.; lic. profl. counselor, Wyo. Tchr. English secondary sch., Thousand Oaks, Calif., 1963-93, peer counseling tchr., 1990-95; pvt. practice psychotherapy, Westlake Village, Calif., 1985-97; pvt. practice psychotherapy Jackson Hole, Wyo., 1997—. Dir. Be Free substance abuse recovery program Woodland Hills (Calif.) Adult Group, 1983-88. Mem. Calif. Assn. Marriage and Family Therapists, Phi Beta Kappa. Democrat. Avocations: hiking, travel.. Home: PO Box 4443 Jackson WY 83001-4443 Office: 290 E Kelly Ave Jackson WY 83001

FERGUSON, LISA BERYL, accountant; b. L.A., Apr. 17, 1958; d. Harry Alfred Abramson and Dolores Gloria Cohen; m. Jeffrey Monroe Ferguson, June 23, 1984 (div. Oct. 1992); children: Kate Emily, Colin James; m. Michael Jonathan Miqdadi, May 17, 2003. BSBA, U. Phoenix, 1997. CPA Calif., 2000; notary pub. Calif., 1979. Acct. Neal Levin and Co., Beverly Hills, Calif., 1978—2002; acct., mng. ptnr. Premier Bus. Mgmt. Group, 2003—. Democrat. Office: Premier Bus Mgmt Group 15260 Ventura Blvd # 1700 Sherman Oaks CA 91403 Office Phone: 818-933-2600.

FERGUSON, MARGARET ANN, tax consultant; b. Steuben County, Ind., Mar. 24, 1933; d. Leo C. and Ruth Virginia (Engle) Wolf; m. Billy Hugh Ferguson, Feb. 15, 1955 (dec. Oct. 1971); children: Theresa Ruth, Scott Earl, Wade Leo, Luke, Angela, Cynthia, Brenda. AA in Psychology/Social Svs., Palomar Coll., San Marcos, Calif., 1977; BA in Behavioral Sci., Nat. U., Vista, Calif., 1980. Enrolled agt. Office mgr., adminstr. asst. Better Bus. Bur., San Diego, 1979-82; tax technician IRS, Oceanside, Calif., 1982-84, problem resolution tax specialist, 1985-87, revenue agt., 1987-90; pvt. cons. Vista, Calif., 1991—. Instr. adult edn. Vista Unified Sch. Dist., 1990-99; mem. adv. com. of nat. cemetery sys. Dept. Vet. Affairs, 1991-98, adv. coun. IRS, 1999-2001. Mem. AAUW (treas.), Calif. Assn. Ind. Accts., Calif. Soc. Enrolled Agts. (dir. Palomar chpt. 1993-95, 2000-01, 1st v.p. 1998-2000), Inland Soc. Tax Cons., Assn. Homebased Bus., Gold Star Wives Am., Inc. (regional pres. 1989-90, chpt. pres. 1992-93, 96-97, nat. pres. 1993-95). Avocations: lace making, needle work, gardening, writing. Home and Office: 1161 Tower Dr Vista CA 92083-7144 E-mail: gswtax@aol.com.

FERGUSON, MARGARET GENEVA, writer, publisher, real estate broker; d. James B. and Dollie (McCloud) F. Student, Kansas City Jr. Coll., 1949, YMCA Real Estate Inst., 1960, Bryant and Stratton Bus. Coll., 1962, Ill. Inst. Tech., 1969, 70, 72; postgrad. in sociology, Chgo. State U. pub. spkr. Sec. Cook County Grand Jury, 1979; acting mgr. internal svc. dept. Xerox Corp., 1985-86, fin. specialist, 1984-87. Tutor reading and math., 1988; instr. sociology Chgo. State U., 2001-2002; host Black Image Prodn. Cable 19, 1989; interviewed on various TV shows, including PM Mag., 1983; active pub. rels. newspapers, Chgo., Detroit, Kansas City, St. Louis, 1970-91; conductor workshops in field, participant Pan Meth. Pilgrimage to Eng., 1984, World Meth. Conf., Nairobi, Kenya, 1986; spkr. in field. Author, pub.: The History of St. Paul CME Church 1907-1988, 1989, Books in Print, 1989-90, This Is Your Life Dr. Owens, 1991. Co-treas. fund raiser Citizens for Mayor Harold Washington, Chgo., 1987; treas. St. Paul Mortgage Fund, 1984; vol. Am. Cancer Soc., Salvation Army, Lighthouse for the Blind, 1982, Dem. Nat. Conv., 1996, Olympic Torch, Nat. Coun. State Legis.; dist. pres. Christian Methodist Episcopal Ch. Nat. Women's League, 1980-86, nat. fin. sec., 1980-92; officer St. Paul Christian Methodist Episcopal Ch., 1983—; v.p. lay ministry, 1987-92, pres. 1992-99; 2d v.p. Ann. Conf. Lay Ministry, 1996-99; sec. Christian Methodist Episcopal Long Range Planning Commn., 1982-86; mem. Chgo. State Street Women's Coun.; judge Chgo. City Elections Bur., 1997; mem. State Street Woman's Coun., 1976, Du Sable Mus., 1990. Recipient PUSH Prison Min. award, 1970, Vol. of Yr. award Chgo. Lighthouse, 1982, Gold Coaster award Kiwanis Club, 1983, Black on Black Love award, 1988, History Writing award Christian Meth. Episcopal Ch., 1990, 1st Lady award V-103FM, 1991, Key to City, Ft. Smith, Ark., 1992, Lifetime Achievement Culture Ctr. award, Citizens award V-103FM, 1994, Bishop's award C.M.E. Ch., 1996; named to Cultural Citizens Found. Hall of Fame, 1990. Mem. NAACP, Nat. Coun. Negro Women, People United to Serve Humanity (prison ministry award 1991, Fred Davis award 1994, Steward of Yr. award 1999), Chgo. Bd. Realtors, S.W. Suburban Bd. Realtors, Hyde Park Co-op Soc. (bd. dirs. 1994-95), Internat. Platform Assn., Am. Assn. Ret. Persons (55 Alive instr. 1996—), DuSable Mus., Lambda Kappa Mu. Home: 727 E 60th St Apt 808 Chicago IL 60637-2592

FERGUSON, NANCY L. psychotherapist, social worker; b. Milw., Jan. 8, 1947; d. Earl Wayne and LaVerne Caroline Ferguson; children: Nathan J. Rosnow, Katherine Ann Rosnow. BA, U. Wis., Madison, 1971; MSW, U. Wis., Milw., 1983. Lic. clin. social worker; cert. alcohol and drug counselor. Adminstr. McMahon Residential Ctr., Milw., 1973-79; children's program coord. Horizon House, Milw., 1980-84; family therapist Elmbrook Meml. Hosp., Brookfield, Wis., 1984-97; sch. social worker Greendale (Wis.) Schs., 1987—2002; psychiat. social worker Greenbriar Hosp., Milw., 1991-95; psychotherapist Acacia Clinic, White-Leonard Clinic, Lighthouse Clinic, Milw., 1993—; asst. prof. Cardinal Stritch U., Milw., 1997—. Cons., trainer, spkr. Nancy L. Ferguson & Assocs., LLC, Milw., 1997—. Co-author: Community Living Guide, 1976; author: Adolescent Post-Treatment Support: A High School Substance Recovery Course, 2001. Mem. NASW. Unitarian Universalist. Home: 2424 S Wentworth #6 Milwaukee WI 53207 Office: 2577 N Downer Ave #215 Milwaukee WI 53211 Business E-Mail: nfergus@execpc.com.

FERGUSON, PAMELA ANDERSON, mathematics educator, educational administrator; b. Berwyn, Ill., May 5, 1943; d. Clarence Oscar and Ruth Anne (Stroner) Anderson; m. Donald Roger Ferguson, Dec. 18, 1965; children: Keith, Amanda. BA, Wellesley Coll., 1965; MS, U. Chgo., 1966, PhD, 1969. Asst. prof. Northwestern U., Evanston, Ill., 1969—70, U. Miami, Coral Gables, Fla., 1972—77, assoc. prof., 1978—81, prof. math., 1981—91, dir. honors program, 1985—87, assoc. provost, dean Grad. Sch., 1987—91; pres. Grinnell Coll., Iowa, 1991—97, prof. math., 1991—2003, Breid McFarland prof. of sci., 2003—. Mem. Nat. Sci. Bd., 1998—2004; vis. com. phys. scis. divsn. U. Chgo., 1996—. Contbr. articles to profl. jours. Mem. Iowa Rsch. Coun., 1993—97. Grantee NSF grantee. Mem.: Am. Women in Math., Am. Math. Soc., Wellesley Club, Phi Beta Kappa, Omicron Delta Chi, Sigma Xi. Lutheran. Avocations: hiking, reading, skiing. Office: Grinnell Coll Dept Math PO Box 805 Grinnell IA 50112-0805

FERGUSON, PATRICIA ANNE, language educator; b. Kansas City, Mo., Nov. 14, 1973; d. Robert Lewis and Deborah Ellen Lawrence; m. Eric Neil Ferguson, Nov. 20, 1997; children: Jordan Blake Lawrence, Cole Ashton. BA, West Tex. A&M U., 2003; AA, Frank Phillips Coll., 1994. Tchg. Cert. Tex., 2003. Staff writer, lifestyle editor Borger News-Herald, Tex., 1996—99; corr., sec. Borger Ind. Sch. Dist., 1999—2002, mid. sch. tchr., 2002—. Author: (news articles) Borger Ind. Sch. Dist. Series (NEA Nat. Schoolbell Award, 1999). Wrote articles, fundraising United Way, Borger, 1997—98; wrote articles promoting HOPE, Borger, 1997; wrote articles, designed cover pages Borger C. of C., 1996—99. Mem.: NEA. Avocations: writing, reading, research.

FERGUSON, PAULA IRENE, nursing administrator; b. Worcester, Mass., Aug. 7, 1954; d. Richard R. and Patricia I. (Gilbert) Wood; children from previous marriage: Andrew, Brian. Diploma summa cum laude, David Hale Fanning Sch., 1974; BS in Computer Sci. summa cum laude, Clark U., 1986; AAS summa cum laude, SUNY, Albany, 1988; BSN, Barry U., 1996, MSN summa cum laude, 1998; PhD summa cum laude, Columbus U., 1999. Cert. nursing adminstrn. ANA, dir. nurses Nat. Assn. Dirs. Nursing Adminstrn./Long Term Care, nursing adminstrn. Head nurse Seven Hills Adolescent Program, Worcester, 1985-88; coord. utilization rev. Worcester County Hosp., 1988-90, 45th St. Mental Health Ctr., West Palm Beach, Fla.; nurse mgr. N.Medico Neurol. Rehab. Ctr. of Palm Beach (Fla.), 1990-91; dir. nurses Edgewater Pointe Estates, Boca Raton, Fla., 1991-93; DON Empathy Care, Boca Raton, 1993-96; owner Traditional Home Health Svcs., Inc., Lake Worth, Fla., 1996-99; nurse mgr. Genesis Eldercare Network, Laconia, N.H., 1998-99; DON Hollywood Hills Nursing Home, 1999-2001; adminstr. Physician's Choice Home Health Svcs., 2001—; case mgr. OASIS Home Care, 2003—. Trustee Fla. Nurse Found., 2003—; mem. content expert panel ANCC Nurse Adminstrn., 2002—. Trustee Fla. Nurse Found. Mem.: ANA, Nat. Assn. Dir. Nursing Adminstrn. (chairperson home health coun., cert.), Fla. Nurses Assn. (Quality and Unity in Nursing coun. mem., dist. XI bd. mem.), Fla. Orgn. Nursing Execs., Sigma Theta Tau. E-mail: docpaula54@yahoo.com.

FERGUSON, RENEE, news correspondent, reporter; m. Ken Smikle; 1 child, Jason. B Journalism, Ind. U. With Sta. WLWI-TV, Indpls.; reporter Sta. WBBM-TV, Chgo., 1977—81; news corr. CBS Network, N.Y.C., Atlanta; gen. assignment reporter Sta. WMAQ-TV, Chgo., 1987—, investigative reporter, 1997—. Recipient 6 Chgo. emmys, AWRT Gracie Allen award, Columbia-duPont award; fellow Benton fellowship in Journalism, U. Chgo., 1991. Office: NBC 454 N Columbus Dr Chicago IL 60611

FERGUSON, SARAH, The Duchess of York; b. London, Oct. 15, 1959; d. Ronald Ivor Ferguson and Susan Mary (Fitzherbert Wright) Barrantes; m. Andrew, Duke of York, July 23, 1986 (div. 1996); children: Beatrice Elizabeth Mary, Eugenie Victoria Helena. Student, Hurst Lodge, Sunningdale, Eng., Queen's Secretarial Coll., London. Author: Budgie the Little Helicopter, 1989, Budgie at Bendick's Point, 1989, Budgie Goes to Sea, 1991, Budgie and the Blizzard, 1991, Victoria and Albert-Life at Osborne House, Travels with Queen Victoria, My Story, 1996. Recipient Mother Hale award, 1996. Address: Simon & Schuster Publicity Dept Ste C3A 1230 Avenue Of The Americas Fl Conc1 New York NY 10020-1586

FERGUSON, SARAH ANN, music educator; b. Marshalltown, Iowa, June 4, 1978; d. William Robert and Patricia Ann Blakesley; m. Christopher John Ferguson, Aug. 3, 2002. MusB, St. Olaf Coll., Northfield, Minn., 2000. Cert. tchr. K-12 Music Ind. Music educator, band dir. Shakamak Jr./Sr. H.S., Jasonville, Ind., 2000—. Mem.: Music Educators Nat. Conf., Ind. Music Educators Assn. (1st yr. music educators panel 2002). Democrat. Presbyterian. Avocations: cooking, gardening, history, literature. Home: 2268 Sweetbriar Ct Bloomington IN 47401

FERGUSON, SHARON C. community relations and planning specialist; b. Little Rock, Oct. 17, 1942; d. Herman H. and Eleanor Beatrice (Fulmer) Scates; m. C. Anthony Ferguson, June 10, 1961; children: Lisa Ferguson Hirschman, Dana Ferguson Silaski, C. Anthony II. Cert. meeting planner. Owner, exec. dir. North Little Rock (Ark.) Jr. Cotillion, 1969—; asst. to pres. Fed. Home Loan Bank, Little Rock, 1978-85; exec. asst. to pres. Fairfield Resorts, Little Rock, 1988—, dir. incentive programs and cmty. rels., 1998—. Staff mem. Ark. Ho. of Reps., 1974-81; mem. exec. com. Nat. Vol. Health Agys. Ark., Little Rock, 1988—; vol. Ark. Cancer Rsch., 1988—, F.L.A.M.E., Stewpot for the Homeless, 1980—, Alter Soc.-Cathedral of St. Andrew, 1980—; bd. dirs. United Way. Named Woman of Yr., North Little Rock C. of C., 1975, Ark. Outstanding Young Woman, 1976; recipient Outstanding Svc. to Youth award Mayor of North Little Rock, 1995. Mem. Jr. League of North Little Rock (bd. dirs., chmn. 1994-95, Mem. of Yr. 1995), Exec. Women Internat. Roman Catholic. Avocations: tennis, bridge, walking, family activities, grandchildren.

FERGUSON, TAMARA, clinical sociologist; b. The Hague, Netherlands; came to U.S., 1955; d. Simon and Sonia (Pokrowska) Van den Bergh; m. John D.A. Ferguson, Sept. 12, 1958. MA in Sociology, Columbia U., 1962, PhD, 1970. Asst. prof. U. Detroit, 1960-71; from asst. prof. to assoc. prof. U. Windsor, Ont., Can., 1971-78; adj. assoc. prof. sociology Wayne State U. Med. Sch., Detroit, 1978-99; assoc. med. staff dept. psychiatry Harper Hosp., Detroit, 1982-99. Co-author: The Young Widow: Conflict and Guidelines, 1981; contbg. author: Clinical Sociology in Mental Health Setting, 1991, Qualitative Analysis in Human Sciences: New Perspectives in Methodology, 1996. 2d lt. Free French armed forces, 1944-45, ETO. Mem. Am. Sociol. Assn., Found. Thanatology, Sociol. Practice Assn. (bd. dirs. 1990-96). Avocations: reading, music, swimming. Office: UPC Jefferson 2751 E Jefferson Ave Detroit MI 48207-4166

FERGUSON, TAMELA, management consultant, educator; b. Man, W.Va., May 9, 1960; d. Emory S. and Aileen R. Browning; m. William L. Ferguson; children: Lindsey, Christopher, Brandon. AS Acctg., Pikeville Coll., 1980; BBA Fin., Marshall U., 1982, MBA Econs., 1989; PhD Strategic Mgmt., La. State U., 2000. Asst. prof. Marshall U., Huntington, W.Va., 1990—97, Colo. State U., Ft. Collins, 1999—2000; asst. prof., dept. of mgmt. U. of La., Lafayette, 2000—. Cons., 1990. Troop/pack committees, den mother Boy Scouts of Am., 1990; vol. W.Va. Spl. Olympics, Huntington, 1994—95; judge W.Va. State Social Studies Fair, Huntington, 1993—95; youth program com. vol. Episcopal Ch. of the Ascension, Lafayette, 1997. Mem.: We. Risk and Ins. Assn., Asia-Pacific Risk and Ins. Assn., Western Decision Sciences Inst., Strategic Mgmt. Assn., Acad. of Mgmt. Episcopalian. Avocation: travel. Office: U La PO Box 43570 Lafayette LA 70504-3570 Business E-Mail: tferguson@louisiana.edu.

FERGUSON, WENDELL, private school educator; b. Sandersville, Ga., May 6, 1954; d. Isadore and Willie Mae (Roberts) Jordan; m. Larry Brown Sr., May 28, 1971 (div. Dec. 1985); children: Larry Brown Jr., Dwyne Lamont Brown, Anthony Patrick Brown; m. Jerry Lang Ferguson, Sept. 28, 1992 (div.). Diploma, Alphena C.C., 1972; student, Ga. State U., 1983-87. Sales clk. U.S. NAS, Albany, Ga., 1972-74, 76-77; substitute tchr. Ga. Dept. Edn., Houston County, 1976-77; nutritionist (nursery) Howard AFB, Panama Canal, 1980; joined Sweet Adelines, Inc., Tulsa, 1981; data entry operator dept. budget mgmt. Atlanta City Hall, 1982; mgr., operator Atlanta Connections, 1982-83; asst. supr. micro-film Ga. Dept. Revenue, Atlanta, 1986-88; promotional sales rep. RG Clothier/L.B. Holyfield, Atlanta, 1992-95; substitute tchr. Old Nat. Christian Acad., College Park, Ga., 1995—; loan broker Cherokee Funding Inc., Thomaston, Ga., 1989—; owner, wholesale dist. Dells' Clevor Enterprises, 2000. Libr. YWCA, Rochester, N.Y., 1999; co-prodr., writer, owner Jeri-Del Prodns., Atlanta. Actress, singer, dancer various prodns. (Irving Berlin award 1982); author: Times In Life, 1996. Vol. persona bus. broker Asst. Sec. of State, Atlanta, 1994, J.D. Sims Recreation Ctr., 2000, Atlanta; Gospel Fest judge, 1995, coord. nominees judgeship position Fayette, Pike, Upson & Spaulding Counties, Ga., 1992; surveyor for st. lights, Atlanta, 1982; vol. Fulton County Dept. Parks and Recreation, Burdett Gym, 1996—; active We Are Today and Tomorrow; founder Steadfast Children Learning Systems Atlanta Coalition of Chs., 1997. Recipient Gold Citizens Acheivement award Mayor William Campbell, 1997, Outstanding People of 20th Century, Internat. Biog. Assn. Democrat. Avocations: horseback riding, chess, painting, cooking, tennis. Home: Fergusons' Entertainment PO Box 492383 College Park GA 30349 E-mail: dellthangs@aol.com.

FERGUSSON, FRANCES DALY, college president, educator; b. Boston, Oct. 3, 1944; d. Francis Joseph and Alice (Storrow) Daly. BA, Wellesley Coll., 1965; MA, Harvard U., 1966, PhD, 1973; DLitt, U. Hartford, 2000, U. London, 2001. Asst. prof. Newton Coll., Mass., 1969—75; assoc. prof. U. Mass., Boston, 1974—82, asst. chancellor, 1980—82; provost, prof. Bucknell U., Lewisburg, Pa., 1982—86; pres. Vassar Coll., Poughkeepsie, NY, 1986—. Bd. dirs. HSBC Bank N. Am. Bd. overseers Harvard U., 2002—; trustee Mayo Found., 1988—2002, chair, 1998—2002; trustee Ford Found., 1989—2001, Historic Hudson, 1990—99, Isamu Noguchi Found., 2004—. Recipient Founder's award Soc. Archtl. Historians, 1973, Eleanor Roosevelt at Val-Kill medal, 1998, Centennial medal Harvard Grad. Sch. of Arts and Scis., 1999. Fellow: Am. Acad. Arts and Scis.; mem.: Fgn. Policy Assn. (bd. dirs. 2003—). Avocation: piano. Office: Vassar Coll PO Box 1 Poughkeepsie NY 12604-0001

FERHOLT, J. DEBORAH LOTT, pediatrician; b. New Rochelle, N.Y., Aug. 27, 1942; d. Sidney and Rose Lott; m. Julian Ferholt, June 19, 1963; children: Beth, Sarah. BS in Biology, U. Rochester, 1963, MD, 1967. Diplomate Am. Bd. Pediatrics. From instr. to assoc. prof. Yale Sch. Nursing, New Haven, 1969-90, lectr., 1990—, clin. assoc. prof. pediatrics, 1987—2003; pvt. practice pediatrics New Haven, 1982—. Author: (book) Health Assessment of Children, 1980 (Best Pediatric Book award 1981). Fellow Am. Acad. Pediatrics. Office: 303 Whitney Ave New Haven CT 06511-7204

FERLAND, BRENDA L. state representative; b. Lebanon, N.H., Oct. 23, 1949; d. Wilbur Fred Snelling and Lorraine Latouche; m. Daniel Edward Ferland; children: Lisa Marie, James Daniel. State rep. N.H. Ho. of Reps., Concord, 1997-98, 2001—. Treas. Charlestown (N.H.) Econ. Assn. Tourism, 1996-, Jesse Farwell Sch. Trust, 1990-95; mem. Charlestown Bd. of Select, 2000—, N.H. Traffic Safety Commn., 1998-, VFW Ladies Aux., 1999. Office: NH State Legis State House Concord NH 03301

FERLAND, DARLENE FRANCES, management consultant; b. Pawtucket, R.I., Feb. 11, 1955; d. Stephen William and Frances Grace (Masterson) Regula; m. Edward Oscar Ferland, Nov. 22, 1973; 1 child, Francesgrace. AS in Criminal Justice, Salve Regina U., 1975, BA in History and Polit. Sci., 1976; MA in History, Providence Coll., 1980; PhD in Human Resource Mgmt., Clayton U., 1991. Dir. Barbizon Sch. R.I., Providence, 1979-82, Barbizon Agy. R.I., Providence, 1980-81; tchr. Bay View Acad., Riverside, R.I., 1982-84; v.p. Edward Ferland Constrn. Co., Pawtucket, R.I., 1983—; pres. Enterprising Images Inc., Pawtucket, 1985—. Guest lectr. Providence Coll., 1980—. Nat. judge numerous scholarship pageants, 1978—. Mem. Bay View Alumnae Assn. (pres. 1981-84, Outstanding Alumna award 1983, 94), Arrive Alive Am. (nat. bd. 1986—), Salve Regina Alumni Assn. (pres. 1986—), AAUW (Providence chpt. pres. v.p. 1983-86, legis. chair 1982-83). Democrat. Roman Catholic. Avocations: reading, travel, music, theater, voluntary services. Home and Office: 225 Greenslitt Ave Pawtucket RI 02861-3231 also: Cabrita Point St Thomas VI 00802 also: Swan's Nest 34 Dory Ct Wakefield RI 02879-5922

FERM, LOIS ROUGHAN, religious organization administrator; b. Buffalo, Feb. 5, 1918; d. Laurence Francis and Bertha Margaret Lucy (Jopp) R.; m. Robert O. Ferm, June 28, 1941 (dec. Mar. 1994); children: Lois Esther, Rebecca Ann, Paul Robert, Stephen John. BA, Houghton Coll., 1939; MA, U. Mich., 1955; PhD, U. Minn., 1972. Cert. tchr., N.Y. Tchr. Rushford (N.Y.) Cen. Sch., 1939-41; instr. library, sociology John Brown U., Siloam Springs, Ark., 1949-51; librarian Cuba (N.Y.) Cen. Schs., 1953-55; chmn. dept. edn. Houghton (N.Y.) Coll., 1955-57; instr. edn. U. Minn., Mpls., 1959-61, mgr. Coll. Edn. Library, 1961-64; personal asst. rsch., resource coord. Billy Graham Evangel. Assn., Mpls., 1973—. Pres. Riceville Property Owners Assn., Asheville, N.C., 1982, 83, 87, 88; bd. dirs. N.C. Arboretum, 1992-96. Mem. Soc. Am. Archivists, Oral History Assn. Pi Lambda Theta. Republican. Baptist. Avocations: sewing, gardening, walking. Home: 27 Patriots Dr Asheville NC 28805-9730 Office: Billy Graham Evang Assn PO Box 1270 Charlotte NC 28201-1270

FERNANDER, KAREN GENEINE, secondary school educator; b. Ft. Lauderdale, Fla., Feb. 18, 1957; d. Wilbur Franklin and Gloria Elaine (Chunn) Fernander. BA, Wesleyan Coll., Macon, Ga., 1978; MS, Nova U., Ft. Lauderdale, Fla., 1987. Cert. tchr. Fla. Author: (book) Hired Help, 1996. Charter mem. Dem. Women's Club of Ctrl. Broward, Ft. Lauderdale, 1990—91; mem. Dem. Exec. Com., Broward County, 1995—96; bd. dirs. Gwen Cherry Polit. Caucus, Ft. Lauderdale, 1988—90. Recipient Plaque for Svc./MAC chair, Broward Tchrs. Union, Tamarac, Fla., 1990. Mem.: Fla. Edn. Assn. (minority leadership cert. trainer 2001—), Broward Tchrs. Union (area v.p. 1985—, mem. exec. bd. 1985—). Democrat. Baptist. Avocations: travel, snorkeling, theater. Home: 27 SW 7th Ave Dania FL 33004

FERNANDEZ, GISELLE, newscaster, journalist; b. Mex. Former student, Sacramento State U. Past journalist, Pueblo, Colo.; past anchor WCIX-TV, Miami; past anchor Today (weekend edit.), NBC Nightly News (Sunday edit.) NBC-TV, now co-host Access Hollywood. Guest anchor CBS This Morning, CBS Evening News, CBS Weekend News; contbr. (TV) Eye On America, CBS Sunday Morning News, Face the Nation, 48 Hours. Recipient 5 Emmy awards. Avocations: hiking, running. Office: Skinny Hippo Prodns 1305 N Beverly Dr Beverly Hills CA 90210-2309

FERNANDEZ, HAPPY CRAVEN (GLADYS FERNANDEZ), academic administrator; b. Scranton, Pa., Mar. 3, 1939; d. Orvin William and Florence (Waite) Craven; m. Richard Ritter Fernandez, June 10, 1961; children: John Ritter, David Craven, Richard William. BA, Wellesley Coll., 1961; MA in Teaching, Harvard U., 1962; MA, U. Pa., Phila., 1970; EdD, Temple U., 1984. Social studies tchr. various pub. schs., 1961-64; from vis. asst. prof. to prof. Sch. Social Adminstrn. Temple U., Phila., 1974—92; exec. dir. Parents Union for Pub. Sch., Phila., 1980-82; dir. The Child Care and Family Policy Inst., Phila., 1988-92; city councilwoman Phila., 1992-98; candidate for mayor City Phila., 1998-99; pres. Moore Coll. of Art and Design, Phila., 1999—. Cons. Nat. Com. for Citizens in Edn., Columbia, Md., 1982—87, Phila. Youth Study Ctr., 1988—90; commr. Phila. Gas Commn, 1992—97; trustee Edn. Law Ctr., Phila., 1983—; bd. dirs. Cultural Fund, 1996—98; chair Select Com. on Bus. Taxes, 1992—98, Select com. on Land Reuse, 1997—98; pres. Delaware Valley Child Care Coun., 1988—90. Author: Parents Organizing to Improve Schools, 1976, The Child Advocacy Handbook, 1980, Elder Care and Child Care Policies of Philadelphia Area Businesses, 1991. Chair bd. dirs. Am. for Dem. Action, Phila., 1980—92; chair Children's Coalition, 1982—86; bd. dirs. Phila. Citizens for Children and Youth, 1986—93; Greater Phila. Cultural Alliance, 2000—; Rock Sch. Ballet, 2000—01; Pa. Women's Forum, 2000—; founder Parents Union for Pub. Schs., 1972—, chair, 1972—75, 1978—80; del. Dem. Nat. Conv., Atlanta, 1988, N.Y.C., 1992, Chgo., 1996. Recipient Women in Edn. award Womens Way, 1989, Pub. Citizen of Yr. award NASW, 1991, Local Elected Ofcl. award Pa. Citizens for Better Librs., 1993, Pub. Svc. award Homeowners Assn. Phila., 1994 Phila. Op. Smile award, 1999, Woman of Yr.-Ivy Willis award, 2000, Fleisher Art Meml. Founders award 2001; named Outstanding Adv., Health Promotions Coun., 1994, 2002, Dist. Daughter of Pa., 2002; Wellesley Coll. scholar, 1961. Fellow: Nat. Assn. Orthopsychiatry; mem.: Nat. Assn. Ind. Colls. and Univs. (bd. dirs. 2003—), Greater Phila. C. of C., Assn. Ind. Schs. of Art and Design (nat. sec. 2001—, nat. bd. dirs.). Mem. United Church of Christ. Avocations: tennis, gardening. Home: 3400 Baring St Philadelphia PA 19104-2076 Office: Moore College 20th & Parkway 4 Philadelphia PA 19103 E-mail: hfernandez@moore.edu.

FERNANDEZ, HELEN AGNES, municipal official; b. Mansfield, La., Jan. 15, 1944; d. Arthur and Tommie Lee (Sabbath) Brown; m. Lamar Green (div. Nov. 2, 1973); 1 child, Marla elena Green McNear ; m. David C. Fernandez, Dec. 9, 1995. BA in Edn., Ariz. State U., 1968; doctoral postgrad., Arizona State Univ. Sch. of Pub. Affairs, 1992—2003; MEd, No. Ariz. U., 2001. Cert. coll. tchr. Ariz. Jr. H.S. tchr., Phoenix, 1968—76; math. tchr. Job Corps, Phoenix, 1976—78; retail buyer Broadway S.W.,

Mesa, Ariz., 1978—84; real estate adminstr. City of Phoenix, 1984—91, elections administr., 1991—; tchr. Glendale (Ariz.) C.C., 1997. Candidate Valley Leadership Inst., Phoenix, 2003; tchr., chmn. vacation bible sch. Bapt. Ch.; campaign worker Terry Goddard for Mayor, Phoenix, 1982; chmn. Bapt. Women's Day. Mem.: Nat. Forum for Black Pub. Adminstrs [illegible] City County Mgmt. Assn., Toastmasters, Delta Sigma Theta. Avocations: collecting dolls, biographies, skiing, study of Black History, genealogy, travel. Office: City of Phoenix City Clk Dept 200 W Washington St Phoenix AZ 85003

FERNANDEZ, KATHLEEN M. cultural organization administrator; b. Dayton, Ohio, Oct. 8, 1949; d. Norbert Katzen and Yenema Vermeda (Bermingham) F.; m. James Robert Hillibish, Oct. 1, 1977. BA, Otterbein Coll., 1971. Edn. asst. Ohio Hist. Soc., Columbus, 1971, vol. coord., 1971-74, interpretive specialist Zoar, 1975-88, site mgr., 1988—. Author: A Singular People: Images of Zoar, 2003. Bd. dirs., newsletter editor Ohio & Erie Canal Corridor Coalition, Akron, 1989—. Mem. Am. Assn. State and Local History, Nat. Trust Hist. Preservation, Zoar Cmty. Assn., Communal Studies Assn. (pres. 1981, editor newsletter 1981-86, 97—, bd. dirs. 1995—), Am. Assn. Mus. (surveyor mus. assistance program 1999—). Office: Zoar Village State Meml PO Box 404 221 W 3d St Zoar OH 44697

FERNANDEZ, LISA, softball player; b. Long Beach, Calif., Feb. 27, 1971; Grad., UCLA, 1997. Winner Silver medal Super Classic, Columbus, Ga., 1997; mem. Calif. Commotion Amateur Softball Assn. Recipient Gold medal Pan Am. Games, 1991, ISF Women's World Championship, 1990, 94, Women's World Challenger Cup, 1992, Intercontinental Cup, 1993, South Pacific Classic, 1994, Superball Classic, 1995, Atlanta Olympics, 1996, Honda award, 1991-93; named All-Am. Amateur Softball Assn., Sports Woman of Yr., 1991-92. Office: USA Softball 2801 NE 50th St Oklahoma City OK 73111-7203 also: TPS Hbg care Lisa Fernandez PO Box 35700 Louisville KY 40232-5700

FERNANDEZ, YOLANDA, newscaster; married; 2 children. BA in Broadcast Journalism, Music and Modern Lang., Troy State U. Reporter WKAB-TV, Montgomery, Ala., WTOG, St. Petersburg, Fla.; gen. assignment reporter WCIX-TV, Miami, Fla.; from gen. assignment news reporter toanchor WFLA-TV, Tampa, Fla., 1989—. Named Miss Ala., 1982, 3d runner-up to Miss Am., 1982. Office: WFLA-TV PO Box 1410 Tampa FL 33601

FERNANDEZ-LEVIN, ROSA, language educator; Student, U. Md., 1976—77; BA in Spanish magna cum laude, BA in Psychology magna cum laude, U. Colo., Colorado Springs, 1980; MA in Spanish, U. Colo., 1983, PhD, 1989. Assoc. prof. Grand Valley State U., Allendale, Mich.; ESL advisor Seoul Internat. Sch., 1976—78; ESL program coord., advisor Sch. Dist. 5, Colorado Springs, 1983—86; grad. fellow U. Colo., Boulder, 1983—86, instr. Spanish lang. and lit. Colorado Springs, 1984—89; asst. prof. Spanish lang. and lit. Grand Valley State U., Allendale, Mich., 1990—96, assoc. prof. Spanish lang. and lit., 1997—. Author: Trapped in a Guilded Cage: Guadalupe Loaeza's Unhappy Women, 1999, El autor y el personaje femenino en dos novelas del siglo veinte, 1997; contbg. editor: Books for College Libraries: Iberian Nineteenth and Twentieth Century Literature, 1998; contbr. articles to profl. jours. Recipient Pres. award, Assn. Borderland Scholars, 1994, Thomas F. McGann award, 1995. Mem.: So. Coun. for L.Am. Studies, L.Am. Studies Assn., Pacific Coast Coun. for L.Am. Studies, Spanish Semiotics Assn., Hispanic Inst. Culture, Assn. Literary Scholars and Critics, Mich. Acad. Arts and Letters, Sigma Delta Pi, Psi Chi, Phi Beta Kappa. Home: 2522-6 Woodlake Rd SW Grand Rapids MI 49509 Office: Dept Modern Langs and Lit Grand Valley State Univ Allendale MI 49401-9403

FERNBACH, LOUISE OFTEDAL, physician, educator; b. Fargo, N.D., Dec. 24; d. Sverre and Agnes Lenore (Halland) Oftedal; children: Bertram, Olinda, David, Pamela, Theodore, Robert; m. Alfred Philip Fernbach. BA, Wellesley (Mass.) Coll.; MD, George Washington U. Gen. practice medicine and obstets., Fishersville, Va., 1954-59; psychiatry resident UCLA, 1960; psychiatry fellow Johns Hopkins U., Balt., 1972; dir. mental health U. Fla., Gainesville, 1961-64, U. Ariz., Tucson, 1965-68; asst. prof. psychiatry Sch. Medicine Johns Hopkins U., Balt., 1972-74; dir. Washington Acupuncture Ctr., 1974-81; dir. Orthomolecular Med. Ctr. Linus Pauling Inst., Palo Alto, Calif., 1981-85; pvt. practice of neuropsychiatry and geriatrics Charlottesville, Va., 1985—. Lectr. Physicians for Social Responsibility, 1980—. Author: Acupuncture in Medical Practice, 1980. Fellow Am. Geriat. Soc.; mem. AAAS, AMA (com. on acupuncture), Am. Med. Women's Assn. (Va. state dir. 1991—, Cmty. Svc. award 1994), Am. Psychiat. Assn., Am. Acad. Psychosomatic Medicine, N.Y. Acad. Scis., Am. Acad. Pain Mgmt., World Fedn. for Mental Health. Unitarian Universalist. Avocations: tennis, cooking, painting, writing, golf, swimming. Home and Office: 250 Pantops Mountain Rd Apt 5221 Charlottesville VA 22911

FERRANTE, JOAN MARGUERITE, language educator, literature educator, writer; b. N.Y.C., Nov. 11, 1936; d. Nicholas Henry and Josephine (Pisacane) Ferrante; m. R. Carey McIntosh. Student, Brearley Sch., 1950-54, Radcliffe Coll., 1954-55; BA, Barnard Coll., 1958; MA, Columbia U., 1959, PhD, 1963. Asst. prof. English and comparative lit. Columbia U., N.Y.C., 1966-70, assoc. prof., 1970-74, prof., 1974—, chmn. English and comparative lit., 1988-91, dir. Ctr. Italian Studies, 1977-80. Lectr. modern langs. Swarthmore (Pa.) Coll., 1968; lectr. medieval studies Fordham U., N.Y.C., 1976; Andrew Mellon prof. humanities Tulane U., 1984. Author: (book) The Conflict of Love and Honor, 1973, Guillaume d'Orange, Four Twelfth Century Epics, 1974, Woman as Image in Medieval Literature from the Twelfth Century to Dante, 1975; author: (with Robert Hanning) The Lais of Marie de France, 1978; author: The Political Vision of the Divine Comedy, 1984, To the Glory of Her Sex: Women's Roles in the Composition of Medieval Texts, 1997; editor (with George Economou): In Pursuit of Perfection, Courtly Love in Medieval Literature, 1975; editor: (with Robert hanning) The Challenge of the Medieval Text, 1985; editor: Database: Epistolae, Correspondence of Medieval Women, Texts and Translations; mem. adv. bd. Spectrum, 1975—78, cons. editor Records of Civilization, 1975—. Am. Coun. Learned Socs. fellow, 1969—70, NEH fellow, 1980—81. Fellow: Medieval Acad. Am. (councillor, 2d v.p. 1998—99, 1st v.p. 1999—2000, pres. 2000—01); mem.: MLA (exec. coun. 1986—90), Internat. Courtly Lit. Soc., Internat. Arthurian Soc., Dante Soc. Am. (councillor, v.p. 1978—83, pres. 1985—91), Phi Beta Kappa (senator 1979—97, v.p. 1988—91, pres. 1991—94). Office: Columbia U 614 Philosophy Hall New York NY 10027

FERRANTE, OLIVIA ANN, retired educator, consultant; b. Revere, Mass., Nov. 9, 1948; d. Guy and Mary Carmella (Prizio) F. BA, Regis Coll., 1970; MEd, Boston Coll., 1971, postgrad., 1977-81, Middlebury Coll., 1974, Lesley Coll., 1982. Cert. history tchr., tchr. of blind. Chmn. Braille dept. Nat. Braille Press, Boston, 1971-74; tchr. of visually impaired, spl. needs dept. Revere H.S., 1974-92. Steven J. Rich scholarship com., 1993—; cons. Revere PTA, 1984—. Contbr. articles to profl. jours. Vol. Morgan Meml., Boston, 1983—, tchr. braille, 1993—, tchr. literacy program, 1993—; mem. Revere Com. for Handicapped Affairs, 1985—, Everett (Mass.) Chorus, 1974-76, Adult Music Ministry, 1989, Revere First Com., 1993, publicist; soloist Revere Music Makers, 1977-79; mem. partnership com. Internat. Year Disabled, 1980-81; mem. adult choir Immaculate Conception Ch., 1966—, lectr., 1995—, cantor, 1997; publicist Revere Commn. on Disabilities, 1985—, Revere Hist. Commn., 1996—, Cath. Daus., SHARE, 1995—, A Woman's Concern, 1996; mem. adv. bd. Mass. Commn. of Blind, 1988—, governing bd. on ind. living, 1989; access monitor Mass. Orgn. on Disability, 1988—; mem. adv. bd. Radio Reading Svc. for Blind, 1989; mentor Nat. Braille Literacy Project, 1992, Braille Lib., 1995—; mem. Friends of the Sick Children's Trust, 1992; vol. Birthright, 1992, ProLife Office, 1992; active Arts Coun. Coop, 1992—; mentor Vision Found., 1993—; friend Wang Ctr., 1993—, Boston Pub. Garden and Common, 1993—, Boston Pops, 1992—; mem. mobility adv. bd. Mass. Com. for Blind, 1994—; mem. Historic Mass., 1994—, Cath. League, 1994—, Friend Paul Revere House, [illegible] 1994—, Ctr. for Marine Preservation, 1994—; sponsor Rite of Cath. Initiation for Adults, 1995—; publicist Next Door Theater Group, 1996, Animal Umbrella Cat Shelter, 2003—; mem. access task force Revere Pub. Libr., 1996; mem. Revere 2000 Com., 1998-99. Mem. NEA, Internat. Soc. for Endangered Cats, Mass. Tchrs. Assn. Revere Tchrs. Assn., Nat. Space Soc., Nat. Cath. Assn. for Persons with Visual Impairment, Cath. Daus. of Am. (publicist), Soc. Bl. Kateri Tekakwitha, 1997, Friends of Revere Pub. Libr., Friends of Librs. for Blind, Friends of Boston Symphony Orch., Nat. Writers Union, Amnesty Internat., Soc. Creative Anachronism, Women Affirming Life, Michael Crawford Internat. Fan Assn., Revere Soc. for Cultural and Hist. Preservation (publicist, life mem., v.p. 1998—, chmn. grants com. 1998, 2000 com., 1998), Chelsea Hist. Soc., Mass. Aviation Hist. Soc., Brian Boitano Fan Club, Barry Manilow Fan Club, Michael Feinstein Fan Club, Feregrine Fund, Paul Revere House, Greater Lynn Arts and Crafts Soc.. Roman Catholic. Avocations: travel, music, swimming, ice skating, crafts. Home: 115 Reservoir Ave Revere MA 02151-5826 Office: Revere High Sch Spl Needs Dept 101 School St Revere MA 02151-3099

FERRARA, DONNA, state legislator; b. N.Y.C., June 22, 1959; m. Robert Gregory; children: Kathleen Lillian, Brendan Baron. BA, Albany U.; JD, St. John's U. Rep. Dist. 15 N.Y. State Assembly, 1992—. Office: NY Assembly Legis Office Bldg Rm 322 Albany NY 12224 also: 150 Post Ave Westbury NY 11590-3172

FERRARI, DONNA MAE, retired autobody shop owner; b. Grants Pass, Oreg., Oct. 21, 1931; d. Clyde Willis and Lorene Margaret (Hart) Brewer; m. William Dominic Ferrari, June 2, 1956 (div. May 1977), remarried Nov. 24, 1977 (div. June 1987); children: Julie Ann Leasure, Jennifer Lynn Tuomi. Student, Humboldt State Coll., 1949-50. Optician Dr. Ferdinand Shaw, San Francisco, 1951-57; co-owner Superb Auto Reconstrn., San Francisco, 1966-77; optician Dr. Donald Schulz, San Francisco, 1977-84; owner Superb Auto Reconstrn., San Francisco, 1987-98; ret., 1998. Presbyterian. Avocations: photography, physical fitness, gardening, foreign travel.

FERRARI, L. KATHERINE, speaker, consultant, entrepreneur; b. Chgo. d. August and Aurora (Lenzi) Puccinelli; m. Charles Wasserman; children: Michael John, Alexandra Marie; m. Gordon Wharton Holt Jr. MA in Architecture, MS in Engring., Stanford (Calif.) U., 1972; BA in Polit. Sci., Northwestern U.; M in Hypnotism, Hypnotism Tng. Sch. L.A., 1989. Educator Moreland Sch. Dist., San Jose, Calif., 1961-65; pres. Ferrari Design, Los Gatos, Calif., 1970—; project dir. AIA Energy Conservation Retrofit, San Jose, Calif., 1978—81, AIA/N.A.S.A. tech. house of future, Moffet Field, 1982—85; pres. Internat. Laughter Soc. Inc., Los Gatos, 1983—, Ferrari Communications, Los Gatos, 1989—. Bd. dirs. Pacific We. Bank, San Jose; bldg. cons. & design in field; product designer Internat. Laughter Soc. Inc., Los Gatos, 1983—; trainer non-profit groups. Contbr. articles to profl. jours. Mem. Advanced Tech. Advancement Com., Moffett Field, Calif., 1977-89; pres., v.p. League of Eastfield Children's Ctr., Campbell, Calif., 1964-66; pres., treas. Triton Mus. of Art, Santa Clara, Calif., 1979-81; bd. dirs. Coun. Environ. & Econ. Improvement, San Jose, Calif., 1976-79. Art Inst. scholar. Mem. AIA (hon. assoc., bd. dirs. San Jose chpt.), A.S.I.D., Nat. Speakers Assn., Am. Coun. Hypnotists, Nat. Guild Hypnotists. Avocations: travel, reading. Office: Ferrari Communications 16000 Glen Una Dr Los Gatos CA 95030-2911

FERRARI, TAMARA W. benefits compensation analyst; b. Chula Vista, Calif., Mar. 8, 1966; d. Paul Henry and Deirdre Teresa (Salers) F.. AA, Pierce Jr. Coll., Woodland Hills, Calif., 1996. Policy rep. State Compensation Ins. Fund of Calif., San Francisco, 1989—91, payroll auditor, underwriter, 1991—93, sr. payroll auditor, 1993—96, claims adjuster, 1997—2000, bus. analyst, 2000—. Vol. Rotary Club, Hayfork, Calif., 1993—. Avocations: travel, movies, needlepoint, photography, mentoring. Office: 7901 Fall Creek Rd Apt 203 Dublin CA 94568-3803

FERRARO, BETTY ANN, former state senator; b. Newport, Vt., Mar. 3, 1925; d. Clarence John and Mauretta Rowena (Potter) Morse; m. Dominic Thomas Ferraro, Oct. 8, 1964; children: Deborah, David, Susan, Barbara. Student, Mary Hitchcock Hosp. Sch. Nursing, Coll. St. Joseph, Rutland, Vt. Exec. sec. to asst. treas. Ctrl. Vt. Pub. Svc. Corp., Rutland, 1943-44; sec. to dean N.Y. Med. Coll., N.Y.C., 1944-46; model G. Fox Co., Hartford, Conn., 1947; corp. sec., office mgr. John Russell Corp., Rutland, 1970-80; exec. dir. Rutland Area Coordinated Child Care Com., Washington, 1977-79; adminstrv. asst. Hilinex of Vt., Rutland, 1981-83; owner Classic Connection Gift Shop, Rutland, 1983-87; adminstr. Vicon Recovery Sys., Inc., Rutland, 1987-90. Owner, operator nursery sch., 1973—77; mgr. Day Care Ctr., 1978—80; mem. Rutland City Bd. Aldermen, 1984—86, 2001—03; resource dir. Rutland City Emergency Mgmt. Team for State of Vt., 1984—90; mem. Vt. State Cmty. Devel. Commn., 1986. Chmn. Rutland City Rep. Com., 1991-93; county committeewoman State Rep. Com., 1984-86, rep.; rep. Rutland County Rep. Com.; state del. Rep. Nat. Conv., 1992; Rep. campaign coord. State of Vt., 1997-98; county co-chair Jim Douglas for Gov., 2001-02; mem. Vt. Ho. Reps., 1990-92; mem. Vt. Senate, 1992-94, 95-97; mem. jud. nominating bd. Human Resource Investment Com., 1995-96, Vt. Student Assistance Corp. Bd.; mem. Amtrak Study Commn., 1995-96; bd. dirs. Vt. Physicians Coun., 1997—, Coll. St. Joseph, 1996-2000, Marble Valley Transit, 1996—; mem. adv. bd. Paramount Theatre, 1997—; sec., receptionist Orton Family Found., 1999-2000; sec., receptionist Eddy Enterprises, Inc., 2000-01; county co-chair Jim Douglas for Gov., 2002; mem. Vt. State Transp. Bd, 2003—; devel. coord. Rutland West Neighborhood Housing Svcs., Inc. Fleming Inst. fellow, 1995; named Woman of Yr. Green Mt. Coun. of Boy Scouts Am. Mem. Nat. Assn. Women in Constrn. (chartered, past pres.), Rutland County Rep. Women. Republican. Roman Catholic. Avocation: flower arranging. Home and Office: Condo 17 155 Dorr Dr Rutland VT 05701-3853 Office Phone: 802-438-2303 ext. 224. E-mail: b.m.ferraro@verizon.net.

FERRARO, GERALDINE ANNE, lawyer, former congresswoman; b. Newburgh, N.Y., Aug. 26, 1935; d. Dominick and Antonetta L. (Corrieri) F.; m. John Zaccaro, 1960; children: Donna, John, Laura. BA, Marymount Manhattan Coll., 1956, hon. degree, 1982; JD, Fordham U., 1960; postgrad., NYU Law Sch., 1978, hon. degree, 1984, Hunter Coll., 1985, Plattsburgh Coll., 1985, Coll. Boca Raton, 1989, Va. State U., 1989, Muhlenberg Coll., 1990, Briarcliffe Coll. for Bus., 1990, Potsdam Coll., 1991. Bar: N.Y. 1961, U.S. Supreme Ct. 1978. Pvt. practice, N.Y.C., 1961-74; asst. dist. atty. Queens County, N.Y., 1974-78; chief spl. victims bur., 1977-78; mem. 96th-98th Congresses from 9th N.Y. Dist., 1979—85; sec. House Democratic Caucus; 1st woman vice presdl. nominee on Democratic ticket, 1984; fellow Harvard Inst. of Politics, Cambridge, Mass., 1988—92; mng. ptnr. Keck Mahin Cate & Koether, N.Y., 1993-94. Appointed Amb. to UN Human Rights Commn., 1994-95; co-host Crossfire, CNN, 1996-97; pres. G&L Strategies Golin Harris Internat., 1999—, Fox News Nightly, 1999—. Author: Ferraro, My Story, 1985, Changing History: Women, Power, and Politics, 1993, Framing a Life, 1998. Chair Dem. Platform Com., Bertarelli Found.; Dem. candidate U.S. Senate, 1992, 98; U.S. President Clinton's appointee to UN Human Rights Commn. Conf., Geneva, 1993, World Conf., Vienna, Austria, 1993, World Conf. on Women, 1995; bd. dirs. Fordham Law Sch. Bd. Visitors; bd. advocates Planned Parenthood Fedn. Am.; bd. dir. Nat. Women's Health Rsch. Ctr., Nat. Dem. Inst. Mem. Queens County Women's Bar Assn. (past pres.), Coun. Fgn. Rels., Internat. Inst. Women's Polit. Leadership (former pres.), Assn. Bar City NY. Roman Catholic.

FERRARO, MARIE, dental hygienist; b. Jamaica, West Indies, Mar. 12, 1937; arrived in U.S., 1964; d. Louis Ezekel and Uta Doreen Ferraro; m. Lionel Cunningham, Dec. 13, 1957; children: Sonia Francis, Karel. AS, N.Y.C. Tech. Coll., 1970; BS, Lehman Coll., 1986; MS, Columbia U., 1988. [illegible] Dental hygienist Montefiore Med. Ctr., Bronx, NY, 1970—. Dental health coord. N.Y.C. Pub. Schs., Bronx, 1970—87. Mem.: Am. Dental Hygienists Assn., Columbia Alumni Assn. Democrat. Baptist. Home: 2030 SE 16 Ave Homestead FL 33035

FERREE, CAROLYN RUTH, radiation oncologist, educator; b. Liberty, N.C., Jan. 29, 1944; d. Numer Floyd and Mary Isabel (Glass) Black; m. Richard C. Sanders, June 5, 1999. BA, U. N.C., Greensboro, 1966, DSc (hon.), 1998; MD, Bowman Gray Coll., Winston-Salem, N.C., 1970. Diplomate Am. Bd. Radiation Oncology. Intern medicine N.C. Bapt. Hosp., Winston-Salem, 1970-71, resident in radiation oncology, 1971-74; instr. radiation oncology Bowman Gray Sch. Medicine, Winston-Salem, 1974-75, asst. prof., 1975-80, assoc. prof., 1980-87, prof., 1987—. Contbr. articles to profl. jours. Mem., v.p. County Bd. of Pub. Health, Winston-Salem, 1985-92; bd. dirs. U. N.C.-Greensboro Excellence Found., 1988-94; med. dir. Forsyth County chpt. Am. Cancer Soc., 1975-90; bd. dirs. Hospice, 1998—. Recipient Disting. Svc. award U. N.C.-G Alumni, 1997, Disting. Achievement award Wake Forest U. Sch. Medicine, 1999; named Disting. Woman of N.C. in Professions, Gov.'s award, 1998, Patient Advocate award Cancer Svcs., 2002; voted Top Dr. by peers, 2000-03. Fellow Am. Coll. Radiology; mem. AMA (N.C. del. to AMA), Pediat. Oncology Group (radiotherapy coord.), N.C. Med. Soc. (2d v.p. 1990-91, sec.-treas. 1991-95, pres.-elect 1996, pres. 1997), Am. Soc. Therapeutic Radiologists Orgn. Office: Wake Forest U Sch Medicine Med Center Blvd Winston Salem NC 27157-0001 Office Phone: 336-713-3600. E-mail: cferree@wfubmc.edu.

FERRELL, CONCHATA GALEN, actress, performing arts educator; b. Charleston, W.Va., Mar. 28, 1943; d. Luther Martin and Mescal Loraine (George) F.; m. Arnold A. Anderson; 1 dau., Samantha. Student, W.Va. U., 1961-64, Marshall U., 1967-68. Actor: (NY theater appearances) The Hot L Baltimore, 1973, The Sea Horse, 1973—74 (OBIE award and Drama Desk award, 1974), Battle of Angels, 1975, (L.A. plays) Getting Out, 1978, Here Wait, 1980; (TV series) The Hot L Baltimore, 1975, B.J. and the Bear, 1979, McClain's Law, 1981, E.R., 1984, A Peaceable Kingdom, 1989, L.A. Law, 1991, Hearts Afire, 1993—94, Townies, 1996, Teen Angel, 1997, Push, Nevada, 2002, Two & 1/2 Men, 2003—, (movies) Network, 1975, Dangerous Hero, 1975, Heartland, 1981, Where the River Runs Black, 1986, For Keeps, 1987, Mystic Pizza, 1987, Witches of Eastwick, 1987, Chains of Gold, 1990, Edward Scissorhands, 1990, Family Prayers, 1993, True Romance, 1993, Samurai Cowboy, 1993, Heaven and Earth, 1993, Freeway, 1995, Touch, 1996, My Fellow Americans, 1996, Erin Brokovich, 2000, Crime and Punishment-High School, 2000, Stranger Inside, 2001, K-Pax, 2001, Mr. Deeds, 2002, (TV movies) A Girl Called Hatter Fox, 1977, A Death in Canaan, 1977, The Orchard Children, 1978, Before and After, 1979, Bliss, 1979, Reunion, 1980, The Rideout Case, 1980, The Great Gilley Hopkins, 1981, Life of the Party, 1982, Emergency Room, 1983, Nadia, 1984, Miss Lonely Hearts, 1985, Samaritan, 1986, Northbeach and Rawhide, 1986; actor, actor: Picnic, 1986, Eye on the Sparrow, 1987, Runaway Ralph, 1987, Goodbye Miss Liberty (Disney Channel), 1988, Running Mates, 1990, Deadly Intentions, Again, 1990, Back Field in Motion, 1991, 120 Volt Miracle, 1992, Forget Me Not, 1996, Sweetdreams, 1996, Amy and Isabelle, 2001. Recipient Wrangler award Nat. Cowboy Hall of Fame, 1981, Most Promising Newcomer award Theatre World, 1974, Emmy award nomination, 1991-92. Mem. AFTRA, ACLU, NOW, Actors Equity Assn., Screen Actors Guild, Women in Films, Circle West. Democrat. Office: Paradigm 10100 Santa Monica Blvd Los Angeles CA 90067-4003

FERRELL, DENISE MOORE, music educator; b. South Boston, Va., Aug. 28, 1958; d. Jesse James and June Walker Moore; m. L. T. Ferrell, Jr.; children: Jason T., Michael L. B in Music Edn., East Carolina U., 1980; MS in Edn., Longwood Coll., 1985. Music tchr. Mecklenburg County Pub. Schs., Boydton, Va., 1980—85, Halifax (Va.) County Pub. Schs., 1985—. Music dir. Main St. United Meth. Ch., South Boston, 2000—. Participant Jump Rope for Heart, Virgilina, Va., 2000—02, Relay for Life, South Boston, 2002—03. Named Region VIII Tchr. of Yr., Va. Dept. Edn., 2003. Mem.: NEA, Am. Guild English Handbell Ringers, Halifax Edn. Assn., Va. Edn. Assn., Delta Kappa Gamma (pres. 1998—2002). Methodist. Avocations: reading, sports, camping, gardening. Home: 3120 Harmony Rd Alton VA 24520 Office: South of Dan Elem Sch 1011 South of Dan Rd South Boston VA 24592

FERRERE, RITA L. band director, music educator; b. Grove City, Pa., Feb. 19, 1965; d. Regis R. and Anna F. Ferrere. BS summa cum laude in Edn., Clarion U., 1987; M in Music Edn., Dana Sch. Music, Youngstown State U., 1992. Cert. instrnl. level II tchg. Pa., 1991. Instrumental music /band tchr. Elk County Christian H.S., St. Marys, Pa., 1988—94; instrumental music/band dir. Kane Area Sch. Dist., 1994—95, Brookville Area H.S., Pa., 1995—2001; instrumental music tchr. Chartiers Valley Intermediate Sch., Pitts., 2001—02; instrumental music/band dir. Moniteau Sch. Dist., West Sunbury, Pa., 2002—. Jazz band dir./founder Jazz Transitions Big Band, Pa., 1990—95; band dir. Harrisville Cmty. Band, Pa., 1994—98. Recipient Band Dir. Distinction award, Fiesta-Val Band Festival, Va. Beach, 2001. Mem.: Phi Beta Mu (Nu chpt.), Pa. Music Educators Assn. (life), Women Band Director's Internat. Assn. (life), Music Educators Nat. Conf. (life). Avocation: music. Home: 272 Boyers Rd PO Box 55 Forestville PA 16035 Office: Moniteau HS 1810 West Sunbury Rd West Sunbury PA 16061 Personal E-mail: rferrere@moniteau.k12.pa.us.

FERRIER, MARIA HERNANDEZ, federal official, educator; BA in Speech, MEd in Gidance and Counseling, Our Lady of the Lake U.; EdD in Ednl. Adminstrn., Tex. A&N U. Dir. ESL San Antonio Norteast Ind. Sch. Dist. Cmty. Edn. Program, Tex.; dir. Office Bilingual Edn. and Minority Langs. Affairs, Washington, 1992; exec. dir. City Year; host and exec. prodr. City Spirit; dir. office English Lang. Acquisition U.S. Dept. Edn., Washington, 2002—. Founding mem., creator Comty. Edn. Leadership Program; mem. San Antonio Literacy Commn.; nat. bd. dirs. City Yr.; San Antonio Air Force Comty. Named United Way Vol. of Yr.; recipient Minority Leadership award, Nat. Comty. Edn. Assn., Imagineer award, Mind Sci. Found., Edn. award, Hispanic Heritage Month. Mem.: Rotary Club San Antonio (bd. dirs.). Office: 400 Maryland Ave SW Washington DC 20202 E-mail: maria.ferrier@ed.gov.

FERRINGER-BURDICK, SUSAN, elementary school educator; b. Titusville, Pa., Apr. 16, 1959; d. Robert Gerald Ferringer I and Donna H. Ferringer; m. Douglas K. Burdick, Sept. 13, 1980; children: Andrew, Benjamin, Jonathon. BA in Elem. Edn., Grove City Coll., 1981. Asst. dir. Cambridge Springs (Pa.) Pub. Libr., 1990—91; tchr. Penncrest Sch. Dist., Saegertown, Pa., 2001—03. State contact NTL Osteoporosis Found., Washington, 1998—. Sec., past prodr. Cmty. Theatre, Cambridge Springs, 1978—; cer. exercise instr. Arthritis Found., Erie, Pa., 1998—. Mem.: GAM SAC MAH. Home: 420 Venango Ave Cambridge Springs PA 16403-1134

FERRIS, RITA BERNADETTE, social worker; b. New Haven, Aug. 9, 1918; d. John B. and Olympia (D'Orio) Affinito; m. Edward A. Ferris, Aug. 8, 1942 (dec. Jan. 1987); 1 child, Miles. AB, Albertus Magnus Coll., 1940; postgrad., McGill U., 1940-41; MS, Fordham U., 1942; postgrad., Yale U., 1945. Caseworker Cath. Family Agy., Norfolk, Va., 1944, sr. caseworker New Haven, 1944-46, 50-52; social worker Psychiat. Clinic VA, Hartford, Conn., 1947-48; case workers, sr. citizen coord. Asnuntuck C.C., Enfield, Conn., 1978-79; tutor young children primary grades Broward County, Fla., 1983—. Vol. adult handicapped and retarded, 1986; v.p. Rep. Women's Club, Suffield, Conn., 1985, Ch. Guild Orgn., Suffield, 1986, Newcomers

Club; pres. Coll. Alumnae, Milford, Conn., 1970; chief checker polls, Suffield, Conn.; vol. I'm a Listener program. Mem. NASW, AAUW (v.p. Fla. Broward Count. 1992—), All Wars Veterans Club. Republican. Roman Catholic. Avocations: singing in a choral group, western line dancing, bocci, art courses, political discussion groups. Home: Garfield Bldg A208 1601 SW 128th Ter Pembroke Pines FL 33027-2149

FERRIS-WAKS, ARLENE SUSAN, compliance officer; b. N.Y.C., Apr. 4, 1954; d. Jack Charles and Marcia (Berman) Ferris; m. Robert Gilman Waks, Sept. 20, 1981; 1 child, Jason Lowell. BA cum laude, SUNY, Buffalo, 1977; M. of Libr. and Info. Sci., CUNY, 1981. Rsch. analyst Zimmerman & Assocs., Washington, 1981-83; sr. mkt. analyst Am. Stock Exch., N.Y.C., 1983-84; prin. market analyst N.Y. Stock Exch., N.Y.C., 1984-97; sr. compliance officer J.W. Genesis Securities Corp., Boca Raton, Fla., 1996-99; assoc. dir. compliance Dalton Kent Securities Group, Inc., N.Y.C., 1999—2001; cons. J.B. Hanauer, Parsippany, NJ, 2001—02; fin. advisor Morgan Stanley Dean Witter, 2003—04; supervisory investigator N.J. Bur. of Securities, 2004—. Lectr./demonstrator N.Y. Stock Exch., 1989-96; cons. in compliance bus. info., 2001-02. Mem. Nat. Soc. Compliance Profls. Home: 601 Kensington Dr Westfield NJ 07090-3604 Office: NJ Bur of Securities PO Box 47029 Newark NJ 07101 E-mail: afwaks@lycos.com.

FERRO, ELIZABETH KRAMS, lawyer; b. Cheverly, Md., Oct. 14, 1948; d. Harry Francis and Jeanne Elizabeth (Edwards) Krams; children: Stephen Christopher, Elizabeth Juliet, Alexander Eli; m. Jose M. Ferro, Oct. 7, 1994. BS magna cum laude, U. Md., 1977; JD, George Washington U., 1982. Bar: D.C. 1983. Adminstr. Raleigh Stores Corp., Washington, 1973-83; atty. Lansfam Mgmt. Corp., Balt., 1983-2000, corp. sec., 1986-2000. V.p., dir. Sidney Lansburgh III Found., 1989—; bd. dirs. Debel Foods Corp., Elizabeth, N.J., 1986. Mem.: D.C. Bar Assn., Phi Kappa Phi, Alpha Sigma Lamda. Roman Catholic. Home: 10210 Riggs Rd Hyattsville MD 20783-1213 Office: Elizabeth K Ferro Esq 300 E Lombard St Ste 1800 Baltimore MD 21202-6739 Office Phone: 410-528-5851. E-mail: eferro1048@aol.com.

FERRO, NANCY JOHNSTON, secondary school educator, artist, art educator; b. Wichita Falls, Tex., Oct. 26, 1944; d. James Alfred and Ellen Morganstern Johnston; m. Samuel James Ferro, Aug. 19, 1967 (div. Oct. 27, 1992); 1 child, Stephen James. BA in Elem. Ednl. Art, Stephen F. Austin State U., 1966; MA in Printmaking, U. Dallas, 1986, MFA in Drawing and Printmaking, 1988. Art instr. Dallas (Tex.) Ind. Sch. Dist., 1966—67, 1969—74; kindergarten instr. Sturgeon (Mo.) Ind. Sch. Dist., 1967—68; pre-k instr. Children's Ctr., Dallas, 1979—86; art instr. Dallas Mus. Art, 1990, Garland (Tex.) Ind. Sch. Dist., 1992—95, Highland Park Ind. Sch. Dist., Dallas, 1996—. Guest lectr. Meadows Mus., Dallas, 2002; presenter Tex. Art Educators Assn. Conf., Lubbock, 1991—2001; sponsor Nat. Art Honor Soc., 1995—2003. Exhibitions include, D-Art Visual Ctr., Dallas, 1985, City Hall Open, Dallas, 1986, Warehouse for the Living Arts, Corsicana, Tex., 1987, Tex. Cultural Alliance Invitational, Dallas, 1987, Northlake Coll., Irving, Tex., 1987, Mark Twain Gallery, St. Louis, Mo., 1987, Dallas Women's Caucus for Art, 1987, one-woman shows include Conduit Gallery, Dallas, 1988, exhibitions include Locus Gallery, St. Louis, 1988, Art in the Metroplex, Tex. Christian U., Ft. Worth, 1988, Dallas Women's Caucus for Art, Dallas, 1989, Conduit Gallery, 1990, 1990, one-woman shows include, Dallas, 1991, The Hockaday Sch., 1991, exhibitions include Minot (N.D.) Art Gallery, 1993, Northlake Coll., Irving, 1995, Dallas Women's Caucus for Art, 1995, The Mckinney Ave. Contemporary, 1995, Warehouse for the Living Arts, Corsicana, 1996, Upstairs, Dallas, 1998, U. Tex. Dallas, Richardson, Tex., 1998, The Assemblage Art Awards, Irving, 1999, Highland Park H.S., 2000, Bath House Cultural Ctr., 2000, 2001, White Rock Artist's Studio Tour, 2001, Northlake Coll., 2001. Cub scout leader, 1964—66; dir. children's bible classes Sst. Patricks, Dallas, 1976—78; dir. Vacation Bible Sch. St. Patricks; pres.-sch. mother's pres. St. Thomas and St. Patricks, Dallas, 1975—78. Mem.: Highlang Park Art Tchrs. Assn. (pres. 2001—02), Dallas Visual Arts Ctr., Tex. State Tchrs. Art Assn., Nat. Art Edn. Assn., Delta Kappa Gamma. Avocations: gardening, traveling. Home: 624 Northlake Dr Dallas TX 75218 Office: Highland Park HS 4220 Emerson Ave Dallas TX 75205

FERRY, JOAN EVANS, school counselor; b. Summit, N.J., Aug. 20, 1941; d. John Stiger and Margaret Darling (Evans) F. BS, U. Pa., 1964; cert., Coll. of Preceptors, London, 1966; EdM, Temple U., 1967; postgrad., Villanova U., 1981. Cert. elem. sch. tchr., elem. sch. counselor; cert. vol. Dale Carnegie; cert. cash flow cons. Indsl. photographer Bucksco Mfg. Co., Inc., Quakertown, Pa., 1958-59; math. and German tutor St. Lawrence U., Canton, N.Y., 1959-61; research asst. U. Pa., Phila., 1963; tchr. elem. sch. Pennridge Schs., Perkasie, Pa., 1964—77, elem. sch. counselor, 1981—2001; pvt. practice counselor, real estate partnership Perkasie, 1981—; chair child study team Perkasie Elem. Sch., 1988-94; editor Princeton (NJ) Pub. Group, 2000—; self-employed as cash flow cons., 2004—. Tutor math., German, St. Lawrence U., Canton, N.Y., 1959-61; supervisory tchr. East Stroudsburg U., Pennridge Schs., 1971-74; research asst. U. Pa., Phila., 1963; mem. acad. coms. for Pennridge Schs.; adj. faculty Bucks County Community Coll., 1983—; instr. Am. Inst. Banking, 1982—; notary pub., 1986—; mcpl. auditor, sec. bd. auditors, 1984-90, mcpl. auditor 1990—, chmn. bd. auditors 1990—; cons. in field. Author (with others) Life-Time Sports for the College Student: A Behavioral Objective Approach, 1971, 3d rev. edit. 1978, Elementary Social Studies as a Learning System, 1976. Vol. elem. sch. counselor Perkasie, 1979-81; mem. Hilltown Civic Assn., 1965-70, 92—; chair exec. com. Hilltown PTO, 1965-73; soloist Good Shepherd Episcopal Ch. Choir, Hilltown, 1964-77, mem. choir, 2000—; mem. steering com. Perkasie Sch., 1989-95; poll watcher, 1993; med. vol. Olympics, Atlanta, 1996; vol. Dublin Ambulance Squad, 1996—, House Rabbit Soc., Chadds Ford, Pa., 1998—, Spl. Olympics World Games, Summer, N.C., 1999, Silverdale Quick Response Med. Svc., 1999-2001, Chalfont Ambulance Squad, 2000—; mem. Dublin Vol. Fire and Ambulance Co., Silverdale (Pa.) Fire Co.; mem. prin.'s round table Perkasie (Pa.) Sch., 1997; vol. House Rabbit Soc. Southeastern Pa./Del. Foster Home and Sanctuary, Chadds Ford, Pa., 1998—; vol. marshal First Union US Pro Championship Cycling Race, Phila., 1999-2003; vol. spl. driver Bush Family and Friends at Rep. Nat. Conv., Phila., 2000, Bucks County Crisis Response Team, 2001—; mem. Chalfont Chem. Fire Engine Co. No. 1; mem. Nat. Arbor Day Found., Best Friends Animal Sanctuary. NSF grantee, Washington, 1972-73, Philanthropic Edn. Orgn. grantee, Doylestown, Pa., 1982; recipientJudith Netzky Meml. Fellowship award B'nai B'rith, Phila., 1979; Durning scholar Delta Delta Delta, Arlington, Tex., 1981, Am. Mgmt. Assns. scholar, N.Y.C., 1983, Achievement award Women's Inner Circle, 1990, Golden Acad. award for lifetime achievement, 1991; named to Women's Internat. Hall of Fame, 2003, Internat. Tennis Hall of Fame, 2000, Cmty. Leaders of Am. Hall of Fame, 1990, Internat. Bus. and Profl. Women's Hall of Fame, 1994, Millennium Hall of Fame, 1999; recipient Lifetime Achievement Acad. Humane Soc. U.S., Internat. Honor Soc. In Edn., Cert. of appreciation Atlanta Olympics Med. Team, 1997, Hon. Educator cert. St. Joseph's Indian Sch., 1996, ARC, 1986, Cert. Achievement in Recognition of Contbn. as Med. Svcs. Vol. at Centennial Olympic Games, 1996, Honor Award for Svc. to Edn. and Tchg. Profession, 1996, 99, award for Outstanding Svc. to Edn. Pennridge Schs., 1999, Cert. of appreciation Spl. Olympics World Summer Games, 1999, World Lifetime Achievement award, Raleigh, 2003, 21st Century award for Achievement, Internat. Bio. Ctr., 2004. Mem. AAUW, NEA, NAFE, Humane Soc. U.S., Pa. State Edn. Assn. (polit. action com. for edn., chair Pennridge Schs. 1986—, del. leadership conf. 1987, 89, Honor award for svc. to edn. and tchg. profession, 1996, 99), Pennridge Edn. Assn. (faculty rep. 1986-88, exec. coun. 1986—, negotiations resource com. 1987-89, 1990-93, steering com. Perkasie Sch. 1989-95, chair Child Study Team, 1988-94, Instructional Support Team, 1992—), Am. Inst. Banking (chair 1987), U.S. Tennis Assn. (hon. life), Pa. and Mid. States Tennis Assn. (hon. life), U.S. Profl. Tennis Registry, Mid. States Profl. Tennis Registry, Women's Internat. Tennis Assn., Nat. Ski Patrol (Svc. Recognition award 1994), Spring Mountain Ski Patrol, Pa. Elected Women's Assn., Bucks County Assn. Twp. Ofcls., Bucks County Sch. Counselors Assn., Pa. Sch. Counselors Assn., Pa. Assn. Notaries, Am. Soc. Notaries, Internat. Fedn. Univ. Women, Internat. Platform Assn., Rails-to-Trails Conservancy, World Wildlife Fund, Bucks County Sch. Counselors Assn., Highpoint Athletic Club, Pennridge Cmty. Rep. Club. (rec. sec. 1986-91, publicity chmn. 1991-92, Pen care chmn. 1992—), Assn. Tennis Profls. Tour Tennis Ptnrs., Sierra Club, The Nature Conservancy, Nat. Wildlife Fedn., John Wayne Found., Mediterranean Club, Phila. Sports Club, Delaware Valley Jaguar Club, Jaguar Clubs N.Am., Nockamixon Boat Club, Peace Valley Yacht Club, Kappa Delta Pi. Episcopalian. Avocations: land and water sports, flying, music, parasailing, photography. Home and Office: 834 Rickert Rd Perkasie PA 18944

FERSHTMAN, JULIE ILENE, lawyer; b. Detroit, Apr. 3, 1961; d. Sidney and Judith Joyce (Stoll) F.; m. Robert S. Bick, Mar. 4, 1990. Student, Mich. State U., 1979-81, James Madison Coll., 1979-81; BA in Philosophy and Polit. Sci., Emory U., 1983, JD, 1986. Bar: Mich. 1986, U.S. Dist. Ct. (ea. dist.) Mich. 1986, U.S. Ct. Appeals (6th cir.) 1987, U.S. Dist. Ct. (we. dist.) Mich. 1993. Assoc. Miller, Canfield, Paddock and Stone, Detroit, 1986-89; assoc. Miro, Miro & Weiner P.C., Bloomfield Hills, Mich., 1989-92; pvt. practice, Bingham Farms, Mich., 1992—; of counsel Zausmer, Kaufman August & Caldwell, P.C., Farmington Hills, Mich., 2002—. Adj. prof. Schoolcraft Coll., Livonia, Mich., 1994—; lectr. in field. Author: Equine Law & Horse Sense, 1996, More Equine Law and Horse Sense, 2000; contbr. article to Barrister Mag. Bd. dirs. Franklin Cmty. Assn., 1989-92, sec., 1991-92; mem. Franklin Planning Commn., 1993-94; bd. dirs. Am. Youth Horse Coun., 2003—. Recipient Nat. Ptnr. in Safety award Assn. for Horsemanship Safety and Edn., 1997, Outstanding Achievement award Am. Riding Instrs. Assn., 1998, Catalyst award, 2002; named one of Crain's Detroit Bus. "40 Bus. Leaders Under 40", 1996. Mem. ABA (planning bd. litigation sect. young lawyers divsn., FBA (courthouse tours com. Detroit chpt., featured in Barrister mag. in 21 Young Lawyers Leading US into 21st Century 1995), State Bar Mich. (exec. coun. young lawyers sect. 1989-96, chmn. 1995-96, bd. commrs. 1994-96, 1999-2002, 03—, grievance com. 1997-99, structure and governance com. 1997-98, strategic planning action group 2001, rep. assn. 1997-2002, chmn. rep. assembly 2001-02), Oakland County Bar Assn. (profl. com. 1995—, chmn. 1998-99 Inns of Ct. com. 1995—, chair 1998-99, bd. dirs. 2001—, Professionalism award 2000), Mich. State Bar Found. (trustee 2003—), Markel Equestrian Safety Bd., Women Lawyers Assn., Soc. Coll. Journalists, Phi Alpha Delta, Omicron Delta Kappa, Phi Sigma Tau, Pi Sigma Alpha. Avocations: horse showing, writing, music, art. Bus. Office: 31700 Middlebelt Rd Ste 150 Farmington Hills MI 48334 Home: 31700 Briarcliff Franklin MI 48025 Office Phone: 248 851-4111. Personal E-mail: fershtman@aol.com.

FERTEL, RUTH U. restaurant owner; b. 1927; Pres. Ruth's Chris Steak House, New Orleans, 1965-97, chmn., founder, 1997—. Office: 711 N Broad St New Orleans LA 70119-4206

FESSLER, DIANA M. state representative; b. Huber Heights, Ohio; m. Rob Fessler; children: Angela, Aaron, Anne-Marie, Andrew, Elizabeth, Olivia. Attended, Sinclair C.C., Wright State U. Sec. various cos., 1963—72; owner Leiter Fabrics, 1972—74; founder Home Birth of Dayton, 1978; midwife, 1978—90; editor Legal-Legislative News, 1989—94; state rep. dist. 79 Ohio Ho. of Reps., Columbus, 2000—, mem. county and twp. govt., edn., health, homeland security engring. and archtl. design, and ins. coms., vice chair vets. affairs subcom. and human svcs. and aging com. Mem. Ohio State Bd. Edn., 1995—2000, Miami County Rep. Ctrl. Com., 1992—; co-founder Edn. Action Coun. Recipient Eagle award, Eagle Forum, 1998, award, Pro-Family Constnl. Conv., 1998. Mem.: Nat. Assn. State Bds. Edn., Miami County Twp. Assn., Edn. Writers Assn., Tippecanoe Hist. Soc., NRA, United Conservatives of Ohio, Ohio Family Assn., Citizens for Cmty. Values, Ohio Roundtable Exec. Com., Farm Bur.., Right to Life, Huber Heights Rep. Club, Miami County Rep. Women's Club. Republican. Baptist. Office: 77 S High St 13th fl Columbus OH 43215-6111

FEST, MARIA, educational association administrator, educator; b. Pitts., June 2, 1943; d. Joseph Foch Fest and Jennie Palmieri. BS, La Roche Coll., Pitts., 1965; MS, U. Notre Dame, South Bend, Ind., 1974; ArtsD, Lehigh U., Bethlehem, Pa., 1984. Mid. sch. tchr. Pitts. Diocese St. Mary's Sch., Glenshaw, 1965—66; HS tchr. Divine Providence Acad., Pitts., 1967—71, prin., 1971—77; fin. aid dir. La Roche Coll., Pitts., 1977—81, assoc. prof. natural scis., 1984—90; exec. dir. Providence Connections, Inc., Pitts., 1998—. Leadership team Sisters of Divine Providence, Allison Park, Pa., 1991—2001; trustee Pitts. Mercy Health Sys., Pitts., 1992—96, La Roche Coll., Pitts., 1994—. Author: (jour. article) Nat. Assn. Nurse Anesthetistis Jour., 1989. Roman Catholic. Avocations: reading, gardening, wellness activities. Home: 63 N Euclid Ave Pittsburg PA 15202 Office: Providence Connections Inc 3113 Brighton Rd Pittsburg PA 15202 Office Phone: 412-635-5411. E-mail: mariafest@juno.com.

FETNER, SUZANNE, small business owner; b. Fowlerville, Mich., May 4, 1929; d. Clayton Charles and Ferne Marie (Abbey) Fenton; m. William Clyde Peters, June 1950 (div. Aug. 1971); children: Randall Ray, Gregory Kim, Melinda Jane Peters Jones, Kelly Sue Peters Raymond; m. Eugene Macelee Fetner, Apr. 10, 1977. BS, Ea. Mich. U., 1967. Cert. early childhood edn., Fla. Tchr. kindergarten Fowlerville (Mich.) Pub. Schs., 1949-50, Horsebrook Sch., Lansing, Mich., 1950-51, Grand Ledge (Mich.) Pub. Schs., 1951-52, Manchester (Mich.) Pub. Schs., 1952-56, Holy Trinity Episcopal Sch., Melbourne, Fla., 1967-72; owner, tchr. Country Adventure, Inc., Melbourne, 1973-77; owner, dir. Woodlake Wonderland, Inc., Palm Bay, Fla., 1978-89, Country Beginnings, Inc., Palm Bay, 1985-93. Mem. Presch. Adminstrv. Cons., Palm Bay, 1985-96; mem. adv. bd. Dist. Interagy. Coun. for Early Childhood Svcs., Brevard County, 1990-96, South Brevard H.S. Child Care, Melbourne, 1980-93. Author: (booklet) Stepping Stones, 1984. Founder, coord. Read to Your Child Week, Melbourne, Palm Bay, 1988-92. Named Unforgettable Lady of 80's Soroptomist Club, Melbourne, 1989. Mem. Nat. Assn. Child Care Profls., Brevard Assn. Children Under Six (pres. 1981-82), Fla. Assn. Children Under Six, So. Assn. Children Under Six. Republican. Methodist. Home and Office: 567 Birch St West Melbourne FL 32904-2541 E-mail: genesue6@juno.com.

FETT, DEBRA, adaptive music specialist; b. Manitowoc, Wis., Dec. 30, 1959; d. Clark and Estelle Johnson; m. David Fett, July 26, 1986; children: Leah, Erin. MusB, Silver Lake Coll., 1983. Cert. music tchr. DPI, 1983. Adaptive music specialist Coop. Ednl. Svc. Agy. 6, Oshkosh, Wis., 1990—. Scholar, Orv Clark Found., Ltd., 2002. Mem.: Music Educators Nat. Conf. (assoc.). E-mail: dfett@cesa6.k12.wi.us.

FETTERLY, MARY E. counseling administrator; b. Wenatchee, Wash., Aug. 9, 1960; d. Jesus Gonzalez Pliego, Anita Maria Castillo; m. Roger Dale Fetterly, Aug. 14, 1982 (div. Nov. 20, 2000). Grad. H.S., Burien, Wash. Cert. completion fgn. credentials analysis. Internat. admissions evaluator U. Wash. Office Grad. Admissions, Seattle, 1980—91, internat. admissions counseling svcs. coord., 1991—. Recipient Cert. Appreciation to Region 1 Conf., Nat. Assn. for Fgn. Student Affairs, 1997. Mem.: Nat. Assn. for Fgn. Student Affairs (nat. com. on edn. and tng. 2001—), Nat. Assn. Grad. Admissions Profls., Assn. Wash. State Internat. Student Affairs, Seattle Athletic Club. Roman Catholic. Avocations: Karate, travel, collecting thimbles, bicycling, skiing. Office: U Wash Grad Admissions #301 Loew Hall Box 352191 Seattle WA 98195-2191 Home: Apt B 4124 214th St SW Mountlake Terrace WA 98043-6517

FEUERMAN, CAROLE A. sculptor, artist; b. Hartford, Conn., Sept. 21, 1945; d. Milton and Doris Sue Ackerman; div.; m. Ron Cohen; children: Lauren, Craig, Sari Gibson; stepchildren: Adam, Aurielle, Leah Cohen. Student, Hofstra U., 1963, Temple U., 1964, Sch. Visual Arts, 1967. Pres. Feuerman Studios, Inc., N.Y.C., 1967—. One-woman shows include Art 10 '79 Basel Art Fair, Switzerland, 1979, O.K. Harris, Scottsdale, Ariz., 1982, Ackland Art Mus., Chapel Hill; N.C., 1985, Queens Mus., Flushing, N.Y., 1987, Arnesen Gallery, Vail, Colo., 1990, Internat. Swimming Hall of Fame, Ft. Lauderdale, Fla., 1993, So Alleghenies Mus. Art, Loretto, Pa., 2000, Lobby Gallery The Durst Orgn., N.Y.C., 2001, Queensborough C.C. Mus. and Art Gallery, CUNY, Bayside, N.Y., 2003, Frederick R. Weisman Mus. Art, Malibu, Calif., 2003, Pepperdine U., 2003, exhibited in group shows at The State Hermitage, St. Petersburg, Russia, Isetan Mus. Art, Tokyo, ACA Gallery, Harkone Open-Air Mus., Parrish Art Mus., Whitney Mus. Am. Art, Nat. Sculpture Soc., Riverside Art Mus., West Chelsea Arts Festival, N.Y.C., 1998, Frederick R. Weisman Mus. Art, Pepperdine U., Malibu, Calif., 1998, Biennale Internat. dell'ARTE Contemporanea, Florence, Italy, 2001 (Lorenzo di Medici award, 2001), So. Alleghenies Mus. Art, 2002, Queensborough C.C. Mus. and Art Gallery, 2002, Nat. Biennale fur Bildende Kunst, 2002 (Honor prize), Austria Biennale (Honor prize, 2002), Boca Raton (Fla.) Mus., Chelsea (Mass.) Art Mus., Bass Art Mus., Represented in permanent collections Lowe Art Mus., Fla., Tampa Mus. Art, So Alleghenies Mus. Art, Brandeis U., Queensborough Cmty. Coll. at CUNY, Bayside, NY, Bass Mus., Miami, Fla., Sen. Hilary Rodham Clinton, Pres. Bill Clinton, Dr. Henry Kissinger, Bass Mus., Fla., Ft. Lauderdale (Fla.) Mus. Art, Boca Raton Mus., Fla., Caldic Collection, Rotterdam, The Netherlands, Pres. Mikael S. Gorbachov, Moscow, Lowe Art Mus., U. Miami, Tampa Mus. Art, Apollon Art Rsch. Found., various individuals. Recipient Betty Parsons Sculpture award 1970, Charles D. Murphy Sculpture award 1981, Amelia Peabody award for sculpture 1982, 1st prize U.S. Nat. Fine Arts Competition 1984. Mem.: Internat. Women's Forum (N.Y.), Solomon R. Guggenheim Mus., Met. Mus. Art, Mus. Modern Art, Internat. Sculpture Ctr., Nat. Assn .Women Artists, Am. Women's Econ. Devel. Corp., Pro Arts, Nat. Women Caucus for Art, SVA Alumni Assn., UNESCO. Home: 200 Mercer St Apt 1F New York NY 10012-1510 Studio: Feuerman Studios Inc 350 Warren St 8th fl Jersey City NJ 07302-1101 Business E-Mail: caroljf@mindspring.com.

FEUERSTEIN, PENNY, artist; b. Chgo. d. Charles Gustin and Edith Reich; m. Jay Feuerstein; children: Lina, Alexa. BS, So. Ill. U., 1982; MFA, Sch. Art Inst. Chgo., 1999. Keyline design Feldkamp Malloy, Chgo., 1983-84; package design Lipson & Assocs., Northbrook, Ill., 1984-86; freelance textile designer, artist Chgo., 1986—. Mem. Leukemia Rsch. Found., 1985—. Mem. Contemporary Art Soc.

FEURTADO, RHONDA ELIZABETH, minister; d. Henry Durham and Mary Elizabeth Feurtado. BA in Biology, U. New Orleans, 1987; MDiv, Asbury Theol. Sem., 1991. Cert. ordained elder United Meth. Ch., La., 1994. Vol. lab technician (summers) Utila (Honduras) Cmty. Clinic, 1983—85; lab asst. U. New Orleans, 1984—86; file clk. Berrigan, Danielson, et.al. Law Firm, New Orleans, 1986—87; student chaplain summer Valley Bapt. Med. Ctr., Harlingen, Tex., 1990—90; pastor La. Conf. of the United Meth. Ch., 1991—, 2000—. Dist. bd. of ordained ministry United Meth. Ch., Alexandria, La., 1993—94, mem. conf. com. on hispanic ministries, Baton Rouge and New Orleans, La., 1994—, mentor to persons exploring ministry or entering the ordained ministry conf., 1997—, dist. bd. of ch. ext., 1999—2000, spiritual dir. New Orleans area cursillo, Metairie, 2001—03. Author poetry. Mem., (local unit chaplain for 2 years) Lion's Club Internat., 1998—; ESL tchr. Rapides Parish, Forrest Hill, La., 1999—2000; steering com. Shreveport (La.)-Bossier Svc. Coalition, 1995—98; mem. South Rapides Svc. Orgn., Lecompte, La., 1998—2000, Lecompte Pie Festival Organizing Com., 2000—00; participant David Vitter's Innagural Women's Leadership Forum, Metairie, 2002—02; participant, co-coord. Garden of Memories Ecumenical Cmty. Easter Sunrise Svc., Metairie, 2001—03; mem. bd. dirs. Friends of Families, New Orleans; vol. Superbowl XXXVI Host Com., New Orleans, 2002—02. Mem.: Am. Assn. Christian Counselors, Lion's Club Internat. (chaplain 1999—2000). Republican. Methodist. Avocations: writing poetry and song lyrics, stamp collecting, mug collecting, travel, computer. Home: 5613 Ruth St Metairie LA 70003 Office: Metairie United Methodist Church 3741 Pontiac St Metairie LA 70002 Personal E-mail: utila675@aol.com. E-mail: metairieumc@aol.com.

FEUSS, LINDA ANNE UPSALL, lawyer; b. White Plains, N.Y., Dec. 9, 1956; d. Herbert Charles and Edna May (Hart) Upsall; m. Charles E. Feuss, Aug. 16, 1980; children: Charles Herbert, Anne Hart. BA, Colgate U., 1978; JD, Emory U., 1981. Bar: Ga. 1981, S.C. 1981, Minn. 2000. Assoc. Rainey, Britton, Gibbes & Clarkson, Greenville, S.C., 1981-83; counsel Siemens Energy & Automation, Atlanta, 1983-91, Siemens Corp., Atlanta, 1991-93, sr. counsel, 1993-94, assoc. gen. counsel, 1994-98; v.p., gen. counsel Pillsbury Co., 1998-2000, Demstar Inc., 2001—. Rep. law coun. II Mfr.'s Alliance, Washington, 1995-98; rep. law com. Nat. Elec. Mfr.'s Assn., Washington, 1995-98. Bd. dirs. Am. Heart Assn., Greenville, 1981-83, Success with Children, 1999, CityLights, 1999; mem. leadership com. Woodruff Arts Ctr. Campaign, Atlanta, 1985-90; vol. High Mus. Art, Atlanta, 1993-99, Ga. 100 Mentor Exch., 1998. Mem. ABA, Am. Corp. Coun. Assn. (dir. Ga. chpt. 1995-98, v.p. Ga. chpt. 1996, pres. 1997), State Bar Ga., S.C. Bar, Minn. Bar Assn., Colgate Club Atlanta (pres. 1986-88, bd. dirs. 1989-98). Office: Pillsbury Co MS 19F3 200 S 6th St Ste 200 Minneapolis MN 55402-6005 E-mail: linda.Feuss@pemstar.com.

FEY, TINA, actress; b. Upper Darby, Penn., May 18, 1970; BA in drama, U. Va., 1992. Head writer Saturday Night Live, 1997—. Writer: TV series Saturday Night Live: 25th Anniversary, 1999, The Colin Quinn Show, 2002—, NBC 75th Anniversary Special, 2002, films Mean Girls, 2004; actor: (films) Mean Girls, 2004; (TV series) Saturday Night Live, 2000—, (guest appearances) The Real World/Road Rules Extreme Challenge, Upright Citizens Brigade. Mailing: 30 Rockefeller Plaza New York NY 10112*

FICCA, RHONDA LEE, music educator; b. Rochester, Pa., Sept. 9, 1959; d. Alfred and Filamena (Sarracino) Ficca. B of Music Edn., Wittenberg U., Springfield, Ohio, 1981; masters equivalent, Dept. Edn., Harrisburg, Pa., 1992. Music tchr./choral dir./coach Ansonia (Ohio) Area Sch. Dist., 1981—82; music tchr./choral dir. New Carlisle (Ohio) Mid. Sch., 1982—86; elem. music tchr./choral dir. New Brighton (Pa.) Area Sch. Dist., 1986—; choral dir. United Hosanna Min., 1996—98. In-svc. presenter New Brighton Area Sch. Dist., 1995—, Beaver Valley Intermediate Unit, Aliquippa, Pa., 2000—; cooperating tchr. Geneva Coll. Edn. Dept., Beaver Falls, Pa., 1991—; grade chair practical and fine arts depts. New Brighton Elem. Sch., 1986—; co-chair New Brighton Caring Team for Children, 1996—. Dir. music New Brighton Adult Cmty. Choir, 1997—; mem. New Brighton PTA; pres. Dorcas Women's Ministries Beaver Falls Christian Assembly, 1991—, choir dir., 1986—, bd. mem., sec., 2000—, sound sys. mgr., 2000—, children's ch. tchr., 1986—. Recipient Founder's Day award, New Brighton PTA, 1995, Random Acts of Kindness award, Blue Cross/Blue Shield of We. Pa., 2000, Beaver County Peace Links award, 2001, Beaver County Sheriff's Dept. award, 2003, Lee Canter's Assertive award, 1995—. Mem.: NEA, Pa. Music Educator's Assn., Music Educator's Nat. Conf., New Brighton Edn. Assn. (sec., pub. rels. chair 1991—), Pa. State Edn. Assn., Beaver Valley Cmty. Concert Assn. (vol. 1995—), Delta Kappa Gamma (music chair 2000—02, social chair 2002—, Woman of Distinction award 2000, 2001, ATHENA award nominee 2002). Home: 617 21st St Beaver Falls PA 15010 Office: New Brighton Elem Sch 3200 43rd St New Brighton PA 15066 Office Phone: 724-843-1194 161. Personal E-mail: rficca@access995.com. Business E-Mail: rficca@nbsd.k12.pa.us.

FICHANDLER, ZELDA, director; m. Thomas C. Fichandler (separated); children: Hal, Mark. BA in Russian Lang. and Lit., Cornell U., 1945; MA in Theater Arts, George Washington U., 1950, Doctor in Humane Letters (hon.), 1974, Smith Coll. Co-founder, producing dir. Arena Stage, Washington, 1950—90. Former vis. prof. U. T[illegible] Boston U.; former artistic cons. Huntington Theater Co.; former artistic dir. The Acting Co.; chmn. grad. acting program Tisch Sch. of the Arts, NYU. Dir. at Arena Stage: (plays) A Doll House, The Three Sisters, Death of a Salesman, An Enemy of the People, Six Characters in Search of an Author, Duck Hunting, Ascent of Mt. Fuji, Screenplay, Inherit the Wind, After the Fall, The Crucible. Recipient Artistic Founder award Cultural Alliance of Greater Washington, 1989, Common Wealth award, John Houseman award The Acting Co., The Margo Jones award, Washingtonian of the Yr. award, Brandeis U. Creative Arts award, Tony award, 1976, Nat. Medal of Arts award, 1997;Inducted to The Theatre Hall of Fame, 1999.

FICHTHORN, FONDA GAY, gifted and talented educator, retired principal; b. Jamestown, Ohio, Sept. 4, 1949; d. Robert William and Evelyn Elizabeth (Schmitt) Fichthorn. BS, Otterbein Coll., 1970; MEd, Wright State U., 1983. Cert. tchr., prin., supr., elem. music, gifted edn. Ohio. Elem. tchr. Groveport (Ohio) Madison Schs., 1970-71, Miami Trace Schs., Washington Court House, Ohio, 1971-92, prin., 1992-2000, ret., 2000. Part-time gifted coord. Clark County Schs., Ohio; part-time intervention coord. Miami Trace Schs., Ohio. Bd. dirs. Scioto Paint Valley Mental Health Ctr., crisis vol. Recipient Class Act award Sta. WDTN-TV, 1990. Mem. AAUW, Phi Delta Kappa, Delta Kappa Gamma. Republican. Avocations: piano, flute, travel, gardening. Home: 7313 State Route 729 NW Washington Court House OH 43160-9526

FICHTNER, MARGARIA, journalist; b. Lakeland, Fla., May 4, 1944; d. August Albert and Margaret Louise (Kelly) Fichtner. BA, Fla. So. Coll., 1966. Sr. feature writer Miami Herald, 1968—. Recipient First Pl. Criticism Green Eyeshade award, Am. Assn. Sunday and Feature Editors, 1996, First Pl. Criticism award, Fla. Soc. Newspaper Editors, 1997, First Pl. Criticism Green Eyeshade award, Soc. Profl. Journalists, 2000, First Pl. Criticism Sunshine State award, 2002, 2003. Office: The Miami Herald Pub Co One Herald Plz Miami FL 33132-1693 E-mail: mfichtner@herald.com.

FICKLER, ARLENE, lawyer; b. Phila., Apr. 21, 1951; BA cum laude, U. Pa., 1971, JD cum laude, 1974. Bar: Pa. 1974, D.C. 1980, U.S. Supreme Ct. 1989. Ptnr. Hoyle Fickler Herschel & Mathes LLP, Phila. Staff atty. Commn. on Revision of Fed. Ct. Appellate System, 1974-75; exec. asst. Bicentennial Com. Jud. Conf. of U.S., 1975-76. Comment editor U. Pa. Law Rev., 1973-74; contbr. articles to law jours. Pres. U. Pa. Law Sch. Alumni Bd. Mgrs., 1997-99; trustee Jewish Fedn. of Greater Phila., 1981-88, 89-93, 94-98, 99—, Phila. Bar Found., 1993-98, Jewish Cmty. Rels. Coun. Greater Phila., 1983-94, 98-00; trustee Jewish Cmty. Ctrs. of Phila., 1997—, chair, 2003—; trustee HIAS Immigration Svcs. Phila., 1998—, treas., 1999-2003; mem. United Jewish Appeal Nat. Young Women's Leadership Cabinet, 1982-87; v.p. Phila. chpt. Am. Jewish Congress, 1995-2001; co-chmn. Phila. Maccabi Games, 2001. Recipient Mrs. Isidore Kohn Young Leadership award Jewish Fedn. Greater Phila., 1981, Next Generation Leadership award Jewish Cmty. Ctrs. Assn., 2000, award of merit U. Pa. Law Sch. Alumni, 2001. Mem. ABA, Am. Law Inst., Am. Bar Found., Pa. Bar Assn., D.C. Bar, Phila. Bar Assn. (chmn. fed. cts. com. 1992), Fed. Bar Coun. of Second Cir., U. Pa. Am. Inn of Ct. Office: Hoyle Fickler Herschel & Mathes LLP One South Broad St 1500 Philadelphia PA 19103 Business E-Mail: afickler@hoylelawfirm.com.

FIDEL, RAYA, library science educator; b. Tel Aviv, Jan. 18, 1945; came to U.S., 1977; BSc, Tel Aviv U., 1970; MLS, Hebrew U., Jerusalem, 1976; PhD, U. Md., 1982. Tchr. Adult Edn. Ctr., Jerusalem, 1971-72; br. libr. Hebrew U., Jerusalem, 1972-77; asst. prof. libr. sci. U. Wash., Seattle, 1982-87, assoc. prof. libr. sci., 1987-2000, prof. Info. Sch., 2000—, head Ctr. Human-Info. Interaction The Info. Sch., 2003—. Vis. libr. Duke U. Libr., Durham, N.C., 1992-93. Author: Database Design, 1987; editor Advances in Classification, 1991-94 (award 1992-94); contbr. articles to profl. publs. Recipient Research award Am. Society for Information Science, 1994 Mem. AAUP (chair U. Wash. chpt. 1990-92, pres. state conf. 1992-97), Assn. Computing Machinery, Am. Soc. Info. Sci. (dir.-at-large 2000-02). Home: 5801 Phinney Ave N Seattle WA 98103-5862

FIDLER, SHELLEY N. legislative director; b. Bklyn., Jan. 19, 1947; d. Jay William and Rhoda H. (Wander) F.; m. Curtis B. Gans, Sept. 23, 1979; 1 child, Aaron. BA, Brown U., 1968. Legis. asst. Rep. Philip Sharp, 1976-80; asst. to chmn. Subcom. Fossil and Synthetic Fuels Ho. Com. Energy and Commerce, 1980-86, asst. to chair Subcom. Energy and Power, 1987-94, staff dir., 1994-96; chief Staff Coun. on Environ. Quality, 1996—. Office: Old Executive Bldg Rm 360 Washington DC 20501-0001

FIDONE, LAURA PEEBLES, social worker; b. Little Rock, Nov. 30, 1962; d. L.M. and Tish (Maynard) Peebles; m. Jeff W. Fidone, Sept. 9, 1989. BA, Harding U., 1985, MSW, 1987. Lic. social worker, Ark., Tex., lic. cert. social worker, bd. cert. social worker., advanced clin. practitioner. Intern Ark. State Dept. Health, Little Rock, 1985-86; social worker intern Youth Home Inc., Little Rock, 1986-87; med. social worker VA Med. Ctr., Little Rock, 1987-91, Shreveport, 1991-94; med. social worker, discharge planning team leader Specialty Hosp., Tyler, Tex., 1994-97. Co-chair Nat. Celebration of Social Work Monty, Little Rock, 1988, 91, co-chair enrichment com., 1989-91; co-chair La. Celebration of Social Work Monty, 1991, group therapist Cancer Support Group, 1990-91, Intensive Care Support Group, 1988-89, neurology multidisciplinary team leader, 1989-91, acute care medicine multidisciplinary team leader, 1991-94, vol. and student supr., 1991-94. Vol. bereavement group therapist Shiloh Ch. of Christ, tchr. boundaries and parenting seminars, motherhood seminar, 2000, group leader woman's Bible class and women's ministries, 2001—. Fellow NASW; mem. Tex. Med. Alliance, Smith County Med. Alliance Soc. Mem. Ch. Christ.

FIEDLER, JOHANNA, writer; b. Boston, Mass., Sept. 17, 1950; d. Arthur and Ellen Bottomley Fiedler. BA, Sarah Lawrence Coll., Bronxville, NY, 1967. Program editor NY Phillearmonic, New York, NY, 1972—75; gen. press dir. Met. Opera, New York, NY, 1975—90; exec. dir. NY Chamber Symphony, New York, NY, 1990—97. Avocation: animal assisted therapy.

FIEGEN, KRISTIE K. state legislator; State rep. S.D. Dist. 11, 1992-2000. Mem. Health and Human Svc. and Local Govt. Coms., S.D. Ho. Reps. Home: 6832 W Westminster Dr Sioux Falls SD 57106-3234 Office: SD House of Reps State Capitol Pierre SD 57501

FIEL, MAXINE LUCILLE, journalist, behavior analyst, educator; d. William Jack and Rowena (Burton) Stempel; m. David H. Fiel; children: Meredith Susan, Lisa Beth. Student in psychology and humanities, NYU. Nat. columnist, contbg. editor Mademoiselle Mag., N.Y.C., 1972—2001; nat. columnist Womens World, Englewood, N.J., 1979-89; contbg. editor Overseas Promotions, N.Y.C., 1979—; articles and features editor Japanese Overseas Press, 1976—; feature editor N.Y. Now, N.Y.C., 1980-91; contbg. editor Woman's World mag., 1979-89, Bella mag., Eng., 1987-89; nat. columnist First mag. for women, 1989-91; founder Starcast Astrological Svcs., Floral Park, NY, 1993—; columnist Borderland Mag., Japan, 1995—2000, IM Mag., Japan, 1997—2000; pres. GemEssence Co., 2002—. Cons. legal profession jury selection, 1984—; mktg. cons. Imperial Enterprises, Tokyo and Princeton, N.J., 1983—; cons. spokesperson Rowland Co., N.Y.C., 1972-81, Allied Chem. Co., N.Y.C., 1972-75; lectr., cons. Atlanta and Fla. Bar Assns., 1986—; creator Touch Game Parker Bros., Salem, Mass., 1971-76; behavior analystand communications advisor multi-nat. bus. corps.; cons. Chesebrough-Ponds, Footwear Coun., Grand Marnier Liquor; founder Starcast Astrological Svcs., 1993; pres. Interglobal Mktg. Co., 1999. Pioneer field of polit. body lang., 1969; author: Lovescopes, 1998, The Little Book of Body Language, 1998; contbr. articles [illegible] Tim., L.A. Times, Newhouse News Svc., Newspaper Enterprise Assocs., King Features, Borderland Mag.; adv. bd. mem. Writers Digest Mag., 2002; TV appearances on morning and afternoon shows including A Current Affair, The Regis Philbin Show, Eyewitness News, Cable News Networks, Tonight Show, Today Show, Good Morning Am., Joan Rivers Show, Jenny Jones, Entertainment Tonight, Hard Copy, Inside Edition, BBC Breakfast Show, Good Morning Japan, Fox News Channel, MSNBC, many others; appears in daily segment Good Morning Japan; own daily TV show on Nippon Network, Japan, 1989—. Active Sister Cities, Tokyo and N.Y.C.; charter mem. Elem. Sch. Cultural Exchange, Toyko and N.Y.C., Ctr. Environ. Edn.; bd. dirs. Periwinkle Prodns. Anti-Drug Abuse, N.Y.C., Adirondacks Save-A-Stray. Recipient Achievement award field behavioral sci. and photojournalism, Tokyo, 1974, Outstanding Rsch. award field psychology of gesture, Tokyo, 1976, Outstanding Achievement award Internat. Conf. Soc. Para-Psychology, 1974-75; honored guest at award dinner for involvement and support in the merging of Eye Rsch. Inst. Boston and Harvard Med. Sch., 1991. Mem. AFTRA, Internat. Found. Behavioral Rsch. (past v.p.), Nat. Writers Assn. (profl.), Profl. Writers Assn., Authors Guild, Authors League, World Wildlife Fund, Whale Protection Fund, Environ. Def. Soc., Nature Conservancy, Greenpeace, People for Ethical Treatment Animals, Humane Assn. U.S., Sea Shepherd Conservation Soc., Defenders of Wildlife, Guiding Eyes for Blind, Braille Camps for Blind Children, Save the Children, Lotos Club (N.Y.C.), East End Yacht Club (Freeport, N.Y.). Office: 338 Northern Blvd Ste 3 Great Neck NY 11021-4808 Office Phone: 516-482-3700.

FIELD, BARBARA STEPHENSON, small business owner; b. San Raphael, Calif., Dec. 10, 1958; d. Thomas David and Shirley Anne (Rowe) Stephenson; m. Frederick W. Field, Nov. 25, 1985 (div. Sept. 1987); 1 child, Chantelle Nicole. Student, Grossmont C.C., La Jolla, Calif., Bishops Coll., La Jolla. Internet retail exec. Have2Have.com, L.A., 1998—. Active supporter of missing children and terminal illness charities. Democrat. Home and Office: 6456 Lunita Rd #119 Malibu CA 90265-2629

FIELD, CAROL HART, writer, journalist, foreign correspondent; b. San Francisco, Mar. 27, 1940; d. James D. and Ruth (Arnstein) Hart; m. John L. Field, July 23, 1961; children: Matthew, Alison. BA, Wellesley Coll., 1961. Contbg. editor, assoc. editor, asst. editor City Mag., San Francisco, 1974-76; contbg. editor New West/Calif. Mag., San Francisco, L.A., 1975-80, San Francisco Mag., 1980-82; fgn. corr. La Gola, Milan, Italy, 1990-94, Il Sole 24 Ore, Milan, 2000—. Lectr. Smithsonian Inst., Washington, 1991, 95, Schlesinger Libr., Radcliffe Coll., 1995; TV appearances with Lorenza de Medici, 1992, Julia Child, 1995. Author: The Hill Towns of Italy, 1983 (Commonwealth Club award 1984), new edit., 1997, The Italian Baker, 1985 (Internat. Assn. Culinary Profls. award 1986), Celebrating Italy, 1990 (Commonwealth Club award Internat. Assn. Culinary Profls. award 1991), paperback edit., 1997, Italy in Small Bites, 1993 (James Beard award), new edit., 2004, Focaccia: Simple Breads from the Italian Oven, 1994, In Nonna's Kitchen: Traditional Recipes and Culture from Italian Grandmothers, 1997 (main selection Good Food Club, Book of the Month Club), Mangoes and Quince, 2001, paperback, 2002; contbr. articles to profl. jours. Mem. lit. jury Commonwealth Club Calif., San Francisco, 1987, 88, 92; bd. dirs. Women's Forum West, San Francisco, 1990-92, Bancroft Libr. U. Calif., Berkeley, 1991-97, Headlands Inst., San Francisco, 1992-93; bd. dirs. Mechanics' Inst., San Francisco, 1987-92, pres., 1990-92, Arion Press/Lyra Corp., 1998—; mem. Food Runners, San Francisco, 2000—. Recipient Internat. Journalism prize Maria Luigia Duchessa di Parma, Italy, 1987, Barbi Colombini prize Tuscany, 1991, Nat. Journalism prize Vanghetto d'Oro, 1997, Gold Medal World Media awards Australia, 1999; named Alumna of Yr. Head Royce Sch, Oakland, Calif., 1991, Honoree of Yr. Bread Bakers Guild of Am., 1999. Mem. Accademia Italia della Cucina, Authors Guild, Les Dames d'Escoffier, Internat. Assn. Culinary Profls., Pen Ctr. USA West. Home and Office: 2561 Washington St San Francisco CA 94115-1818

FIELD, DEBBIE, state representative; b. Rexburg, Idaho, Jan. 26, 1955; m. Mike Field; children: Jeremy, Chad, Bryn. AA in Bus., Ricks Coll. Campaign cons.; state rep. dist. 18A Idaho Ho. of Reps., Boise, 1995—, vice chair, judiciary, rules and adminstrn. com., mem. revenue and taxation com. Mem. Ada County Ctrl. Com., 1992—94; Bannock County Rep. chair, 1985—86; co-chair Idaho Inaugural Celebration, 1995. Recipient Disting. Svc. award, Idaho Rep. Party, 1992. Republican. Office: State Capitol PO Box 83720 Boise ID 83720-0038

FIELD, FRANCES, state representative; b. Albion, Idaho; children: Bill, Jean, Terry, Howard, Mike, Janet, Julie, Pat. Grad., Albion State Normal Tchrs. Coll. Ret. tchr. Joint Sch. Dist. 365; ret. bus. mgr.; state rep. dist. 23A Idaho Ho. of Reps., Boise, 1996—, vice chair appropriations com., mem. agrl. affairs and resources and conservation coms. Owyhee County Rep. chair; former mem. sch. bd. Mem.: FFA (hon. State Farm degree 1994), Idaho Sch. Bus. Ofcls. (former pres.), Idaho Weed Control Assn., Leadership Idaho Agr. Found. (bd. dirs.), Owyhee County Cowbelles, Ea. Owyhee Libr. Bd., Owyhee County Farm Bur., Mountain Home C. of C. Republican. Office: State Capitol PO Box 83720 Boise ID 83720

FIELD, KAREN ANN (KAREN ANN SCHAFFNER), real estate broker; b. New Haven, Conn., Jan. 27, 1936; d. Abraham Terry and Ida (Smith) Rogovin; m. Barry S. Crown, 1954 (div. 1969); children: Laurie Jayne, Donna Lynn, Bruce Alan, Bradley David; m. Michael Lehmann Field, 1969 (div. 1977); m. Ronald E. Schaffner, Apr., 1998. Student, Vassar Coll., 1953-54, Harrington Inst. Interior Design, 1973-74, Roosevelt U., 1987—. Cert. residential specialist. Owner Karen Field Interiors, Chgo., 1970-86, Karen Field & Assocs. Realtors, Chgo., 1980-81; pres., ptnr. Field-Pels & Assocs. Realtors, Chgo., 1981-86; with top sales volume Sudler-Marling, Inc., Chgo., 1989; sales broker Koenig & Strey GMAC, Chgo., 1992—. Mem. Women's Coun. Camp Henry Horner, Chgo., 1960; bd. dirs., treas. Winnetka Pub. Sch. Nursery (Ill.), 1961-63; pres. Jr. Aux. U. Chgo. Cancer Rsch. Found., 1960-66, mem. exec. com. women's bd., 1965-66; bd. dirs., sec. United Charities, Chgo., 1966-68, Victory Gardens Theatre, Chgo., 1979; co-founder, pres. Re-Entry Ctr., Wilmette, Ill., 1978-80; mem. br. Child Abuse Svcs., Chgo., 1981-89; Stop AIDS Real Estate Divsn., 1988, AIDS Walkathon Com., 1990; bd. dirs. The Chgo. Ctr. for Self-Taught Art, 1993-96. Recipient Servian award Jr. Aux. of U. Chgo. Cancer Rsch. Found., 1966, Margarite Wolf award Women's Bd., U. Chgo. Cancer Rsch. Found., 1967, Founder's award, 1997, WAIT Woman of Day. Mem. Chgo. Real Estate Bd., Chgo. Assn. Realtors, Chgo. Coun. Fgn. Rels., English Speaking Union (jr. bd. 1958-59), Art Inst. Chgo., Field Mus., Union League Club, Pres.'s Club, Founders Club, Confrerie de la Chaine des Rotisseurs (Dame de la Chaine), Fulton River Dist. Assn. Office: Koenig & Strey GMAC 900 N Michigan Ave Chicago IL 60611-1514 Office Phone: 312-893-3556.

FIELD, PATRICIA, apparel designer; Fashion designer. Costume designer (TV series) Crime Story, 1986, L.A. Takedown, 1989, Spin City, 1996—2002, Sex and the City, 1998—2004, Big City Blues, 1999. Recipient Award for Excellence for Costume Design for TV (contemporary), Sex in the City, Costume Designers Guild, 2000, 2004, Emmy Award for Outstanding Costumes for Series, Sex and the City, 2002. Office: Hotel Venus 382 W Broadway New York NY 10012*

FIELD, PHYLIS SHARON, consulting director; b. Huntington, N.Y., Apr. 28, 1960; d. Richard Del and Jean (Sharp) F. BA, BS, U. Pa., 1981; MBA, UCLA, 1990. Bus. adminstr. TRW, San Diego and L.A., 1984-88; mem. staff UCLA, 1989-90; sr. cons. Deloitte & Touche Consulting, L.A., 1990-92, mgr., 1992-94; consulting dir. Deloitte & Touche Consulting Group, Santa Ana, Calif., 1995—. Office: Ledgent 1111 [illegible] CO [illegible] E-mail: phylisf@ledgent.com.

FIELD, SALLY, actress; b. Pasadena, Calif., Nov. 6, 1946; m. Steve Craig, Sept. 1968 (div. 1975); children: Peter, Eli; m. Alan Greisman, Dec. 1984 (div. 1994); 1 son, Samuel. Student, Actor's Studio, 1973-75. Starred in TV series Gidget, 1965, The Flying Nun, 1967-69, The Girl With Something Extra, 1973; film appearances include The Way West, 1967, Stay Hungry, 1976, Heroes, 1977, Smokey and the Bandit, 1977, Hooper, 1978, The End, 1978, Norma Rae, 1979 (Cannes Film Festival Best Actress award 1979, Acad. award 1980), Beyond the Poseidon Adventure, 1979, Smokey and the Bandit II, 1980, Back Roads, 1981, Absence of Malice, 1981, Kiss Me Goodbye, 1982, Places in the Heart, 1984 (Acad. award for best actress 1984), Murphy's Romance (also exec. producer), 1985, Surrender, 1987, Punchline, 1987 (also prodr.), Steel Magnolias, 1989, Soapdish, 1991, Not Without My Daughter, 1991, Homeward Bound: The Incredible Journey, 1993 (voice only), Mrs. Doubtfire, 1993, Forrest Gump, 1994; TV movies include Maybe I'll Come Home In the Spring, 1971, Marriage: Year One, 1971, Home for the Holidays, 1972, Bridges, 1976, Sybil, 1976 (Emmy award 1977), A Woman of Independent Means, 1994; prodr. Dying Young, 1991, Eye for an Eye, 1995, Homeward Bound II: Lost in San Francisco, 1996, Merry Christmas George Bailey, 1997, From The Earth to the Moon, 1998, A Cooler Climate, 1999.

FIELDING, ELIZABETH M(AY), public relations executive, writer; b. New London, Conn., May 16, 1917; d. Frederick James and Elizabeth (Martin) F. AB, Conn. Coll. for Women, 1938; MA in Pub. Adminstrn., Am. U., 1944. Dollar-a-year cons. Census Bur., 1938-39; rsch. writer Rep. Nat. Com., Washington, 1940, acting dir. rsch., 1944, asst. dir. rsch., 1948-53; govt. statistician, personnel clk., economist, 1941-42; civil def. dir., 1943-46; rsch. writer Rep. Nat. Com., 1942-48; staff writer, spl. cons. to several U.S. congressmen, 1944-52; exec. sec., legis. asst. to Senator Alexander Wiley of Wis., 1953-54; assoc. dir. rsch. Rep. Nat. Com., 1954-57; rschr., speech writer, 1960-61; staff aide Rep. Nat. Platform Coms., 1944, 48, 52, 56, 60; legis. analyst, newsletter editor Nat. Assn. Electric Cos., 1957-60; pub. rels. dir. Nat. Fedn. Rep. Women, 1961-68; spl. asst. to asst. postmaster gen. U.S. Post Office Dept., 1969-71; pub. affairs dir. Pres.'s Coun. on Youth Opportunity, 1970-71; asst. adminstr. for pub. affairs Nat. Credit Union Adminstrn., 1971-75; pres. Profl. Enterprises, 1975—; editl. asst. U.S. Ho. of Reps., 1976-82. Author numerous party publs. including: A History of the Republican Party, 1854-1944. Editor Rep. Clubwoman, 1961-68; dir. spl. activities women's div. United Citizens for Nixon-Agnew, 1968; fin. coordinator Inaugural Com., 1968-69; Grievance Commn., State of Md., 1980-89; auxiliary policewoman Met. Police Dept., Washington, 1942-45. Recipient Achievement medal for outstanding govt. service Conn. Coll., 1971; Disting. Service award Nat. Fedn. Rep. Women, 1964, 67; named Hon. Citizen, several U.S. cities. Mem. AAAS, NAFE, Am. Polit. Sci. Assn., Am. Acad. Polit. and Social Sci., Am. Soc. for Socio-Econs., Soc. for Scholarly Pub., Nat. Press Found., Washington Ind. Writers, Soc. for Tech. Communication, Nat. Mus. of Women in Arts, Nat. Fedn. Press Women, HALT-Ams. for Legal Reform, Pemaquid Watershed Assn., Treasure Cove Citizens Assn. (pres. 1976-78, 92-93), Washington Nat. Cathedral, Phi Beta Kappa. Clubs: Nat. Press, Am. News Women's, Capital Press Women, Capitol Hill, Congl. Staff, Senate Staff, Antique Auto of Am. Home: 1312 Thornton Pkwy Fort Washington MD 20744-6869

FIELDS, DAISY BRESLEY, human resources specialist, writer; b. Bklyn., 1915; m. Victor Fields, Aug. 2, 1936; 1 child, Barbara Fields Ochsman. Student, Hunter Coll., 1932-35, Am. U., 1949-53. Pers. officer USAF Base, Norfolk, Va., 1942-45; asst. pers. officer Dept. Agr., Phila., 1945-47; asst. dir. pers. Smithsonian Instn., Washington, 1954-60; chief spl. programs NASA, Washington, 1960-67; spl. asst. Fed. Womans Program VA, Washington, 1967-70; sr. program assoc. Nat. Civil Svc. League, 1971-72; cons. Equal Employment Opportunity/Affirmative Action, 1978—90; exec. dir. Federally Employed Women, Washington, 1975-77. Pres. Fields Assocs., Silver Spring, Md., 1978—2000; exec. dir. The Womens Inst., Am. U.; instr. Mt. Vernon Coll., 1979-80, Am. U., 1982; cons. USAID, 1990-93; freelance writer. Author: A Woman's Guide to Moving Up in Business and Government, 1983; editor: Winds of Change: Korean Women in America, 1991; contbr. articles to profl. jours. Chair Montgomery County (Md.) Pers. Bd., 1972-78; chair legis. com. Comm. for Women in Pub. Adminstrn., 1976-79; commr. Md. Commn. for Women, 1973-77, commr. Montgomery County Commmn. for Women, 1979-82; editor newsletter, past pres. Clearinghouse on Womens Issues; v.p., mng. editor Womens Inst. Press; bd. dirs. Nat. Womans Party, 1989-97. Reciipent UN Assn. U.S.A. award, 1980, Vet. Feminists Am. medal, 1998. Mem. NAFE, Nat. Coun. Career Women, Womens Equity Action League (pres. Md. 1972-74, award 1978), Federally Employed Women (pres. 1969-71, editor newsletter 1972-77, award 1974, 78), Nat. Press Club, Am. News Womens Club, Internat. Womens Writing Guild, Washington Ind. Writers, Capital Press Women, Fedn. Orgns. Profl. Women (exec. coun. 1976-77, 80-82), Nat. Assn. Women Bus. Owners, Freelance writer. Home and Office: #404 3005 S Leisure World Blvd Silver Spring MD 20906-8305 E-mail: dbresley@aol.com.

FIELDS, DEBBI, cookie franchise executive; m. Randy Fields (div.); 5 children; m. Michael Rose. Founder Mrs. Fields Original Cookies, Salt Lake City. Office: Mrs Fields Original Cookies 2855 Cottonwood Pkwy Ste 400 Salt Lake City UT 84121-7050

FIELDS, HARRIET GARDIN, counselor, educator, consultant; b. Pasco, Wash., Feb. 25, 1944; d. Harry C. and Ethel Jenell (Rochelle) Gardin; m. Avery C. Fields; 1 child, Avery C. BS in Edn., S.C. State U., Orangeburg, 1966; MEd, U. S.C., 1974. Lic. profl. counselor and supr.; nat. bd. cert. counselor and career counselor. Tchr. Richaldn Sch. Dist., Columbia, S.C., 1966-67 73-76; counselor supr. S.C. Dept. Corrections, Columbia, 1971-73; counselor Techinal Edn. System, West Columbia, S.C., 1967-70; exec. dir. Bethlehem Community Ctr., Columbia, 1976-79; human rels. cons. Calhoun County Schs., St. Matthews, S.C., 1979-82; admission counselor Allen U., Columbia, 1982-83; pres., cons. H.G. Fields Assn., Columbia, 1973—. Exec. dir. Big Bros./Big Sisters, Columbia, 1984-87 Mem. Richland County Coun., Columbia, 1989-97, chair, 1993, 94, 95, 96, 97; 2d vice chair Richland County Dem. Party, Columbia, 1984-88; sec. Statewide Reapportionment Com., 1990-97; mem. Richland Lexington Immunization Com., Hope for Kids, The Lifeline: Mission to Families; commr. Midlands Tech. Coll., 2001—. Recipient inaugural Woodrow Wilson award Greater Columbia C. of C., 1994, Pres.'s Disting. Svc. award Nat. Orgn. Black County Ofcls., 1996, numerous human rels. and outstanding svc. awards. Mem. ACA (resolutions chair So. br. 1993-94, parlimentarian 1998, 99-2000), SC Counseling Assn. (chair govt. rels. 1985-97, 98-99, pres. 1982-83), Assn. Multicultural Counseling Devel. (v.p. for African Am. concerns 1999-2000, rep. to Am. governing coun. 2000-2003), SC Coalition Pub. Health, Nat. Assn. Counties (d. dir. 1996, bylaws and election cm. 1996, 97, employment steering com. 1997), Nat. Assn. Counties (employment steering com. 1993-97, chair youth subcom. employment steering 1995-97, vice chair 1993-94), Am. Bus. Women's Assn. (pres. Midlands chpt. 1998-99), Columbia C. of C. Democrat. Methodist. Avocations: travel, reading. Home and Office: HG Fields and Assocs 412 Juniper St Columbia SC 29203-5055

FIELDS, JANICE L. food service executive; From crew mem. to regional v.p. Pitts. McDonald's Corp., 1978—94, v.p Pitts. region, 1994—2000, sr. v.p. ctrl. divsn., 2000—03, pres. ctrl. divsn., 2003—. Recipient WON award, Women's Operator Network, 1988, Women's Leadership award, Women's Network, 2002. Office: McDonald's Corp McDonald's Plz Oak Brook IL 60523

FIELDS, JERRI LYNN, foundation administrator; b. Sept. 1965; d. Larry and Janice Fields; m. David Burgess. B in English, M in Coll. Student Pers. Adminstrn., Western Ill. U. Positions at De Paul U., Chicago; dir. youth svcs. Horizons Cmty. Svcs., Chicago, anti-violence project dir., dir. programs; exec. dir. Rape Victim Adv., Chicago, 1998—2001; devel. and comm. dir. Fund for City of N.Y., 2001, V-Day: Until the Violence Stops, N.Y.C., 2001—02, exec. dir., 2002—. Past pres. Ill. Coalition Against Sexual Assault; mem. leadership com. Rape Victim Advs.; mem. adv. coun. RAINN Nat. Sexual Assault Hotline.*

FIELDS, RUTH KINNIEBREW, secondary and elementary educator, consultant; b. Notasulga, Ala. d. Lee Wesley and Olivia S. (Scruggs) Kinniebrew; m. Benjamin Belton Fields, Dec. 24, 1950; children: Ivan W., Benjamin B. Jr. BS, Tuskegee Inst., 1949, MEd, 1954, postgrad., 1971—75. Cert. vocat. home econs. tchr., Ala.; cert. supt. edn., Ala. Prin., tchr. Choctaw County Bd. Edn., Butler, Ala., 1950-56; dietician, tchr. home econs. Hale County Bd. Edn., Greensboro, Ala., 1957-62; prin., tchr. Tuscaloosa (Ala.) County Bd. Edn., 1962-64, tchr. home econs., 1964-67, home sch. worker, 1967-76, tchr. kindergarten, early childhood edn., 1976-85. Supervising tchr. of students Ala. A&M U., Normal, U. Ala., Tuscaloosa, 1976-85; sec./treas. Dist. II Attendance Suprs., Ala., 1974-75. Bd. dirs. ARC, Tuscaloosa, 1967-73, Girl Scouts, Tuscaloosa, 1967-73, Am. Red Cross, Tuscaloosa, 1968-74, LWV, Tuscaloosa; treas. Planned Parenthood, Tuscaloosa, 1967-76, Cmty. Svc. Programs, Tuscaloosa, 1968-74; advisor Chpt. 2/Title II Adv. Coun., Tuscaloosa, 1985-89. Recipient Presdl. Assoc. award Tuskegee U., 1990; named to Nat. Women's Hall of Fame, 1995. Mem. NEA, AAUW, LWV (dir. Greater Tuscaloosa chpt. 2003), Ala. Edn. Assn. (Excellence in Edn. 1982), Tuscaloosa County Edn. Assn., Nat. Women's History Mus., The Links, Inc., Delta Kappa Gamma, Alpha Kappa Alpha, Gamma Sigma Sigma. Democrat. Baptist. Avocations: reading, working puzzles, walking, cooking, traveling. Home: PO Box 1755 Tuscaloosa AL 35403-1755

FIELDS, SARA A. travel company executive; Sr. v.p. onboard svc. UAL Corp., Elk Grove Village, Ill. Office: UAL Corp 1200 E Algonquin Rd Arlington Heights IL 60005-4712 also: PO Box 66100 Chicago IL 60666-0100 Fax: 847-700-4899.

FIELDS, SUZANNE BREGMAN, syndicated columnist; b. Washington, Mar. 7, 1936; d. Samuel Holiday and Sadie (Hurwitz) Bregman; m. Theodore Martin Fields, June 16, 1957; children: Alexandra, Miriamne, Tobias. BA, George Washington U., 1957, MA, 1964; PhD, Cath. U., 1971. Freelance writer, Washington, 1965-71; editor Innovations Mag., Washington, 1971-79; columnist Vogue mag., Washington, 1982; author Like Father, Like Daughter (Little Brown), 1983; columnist Washington Times, 1984—; syndicated columnist L.A. Times Syndicate, Washington, 1988-2001, Chgo. Tribune Media Svcs., 2001—. TV commentator, regular panelist CNN & Co. Mem. Phi Beta Kappa. Jewish. Home: 1934 Biltmore St NW Washington DC 20009-1510 Office: The Washington Times 3600 New York Ave NE Washington DC 20002-1996

FIELDS, VELMA ARCHIE, medical/surgical nurse; d. Charles and Ella Ruth Archie; m. Herrell Lee Fields Sr., July 29, 1972; children: Sherri Debnam, Herrell Jr., LaShonda Hairston. BSN, Winston-Salem State U., 1968. Cert. N. C. State Bd. Nursing. Nurse, oper. rm. nurse N.C. Bapt. Hosp., Winstom-Salem, 1969—90; nursing instr. Forsyth Tech. Coll., Winston-Salem, 1990—93; client coord. Sr. Svcs. Meals-on-Wheels, Winston-Salem, 1993—96; nurse Nursefinders, Winston-Salem, 1997—. Based on story of Velma Field's hat and her daddy (off-Broadway play) Crowns, 2002—03. Vol. cardiopulmonary instr. ARC, Winston-Salem, NC, 1980; vol. Nurse Database for Bioterrorism Response Team Forsyth County Dept. Pub. Health, 2003—; deacon Emmanuel Bapt. Ch., Winston-Salem, NC. Recipient Race Progress Promotors Achievement award in healthcare, Effort Club, New Bethel Bapt. Ch., Winston-Salem, N.C., 2001. Baptist.

FIELDS, WENDY LYNN, lawyer; b. N.Y.C., Sept. 22, 1946; d. Sidney and Helen (Silverstein) F. BA, George Washington U., 1968, JD, 1976. Bar: D.C. 1976. Assoc. Arent, Fox, Kintner, Plotkin & Kahn, Washington, 1976-78; ptnr. Weissbard & Fields, Washington, 1978-83, Wilkes, Artis, Hedrick & Lane, Washington, 1983-86, Foley & Lardner, Washington, 1986-97, Katten Muchin Zavis Rosenman, Washington, 1997—. Mem. George Washington Law Rev., 1973-75. Mem. D.C. Bar Assn. Office: Katten Muchin Zavis Rosenman 1025 T Jefferson St NW East Lobb Ste 700 Washington DC 20007-5214

FIELDS-GOLD, ANITA, retired dean; b. Amarillo, Tex., Oct. 29, 1940; d. Dera and Mamie Maureen (Craig) Bates; m. Maurice Gold; 1 child, William Kyle. Grad. nursing, Jefferson Davis Hosp., 1962; BSN, Tex. Christian U., 1966; MSN, Northwestern State U. La., 1974; PhD, Tex. Women's U., 1980. C.E. coord., asst. prof. Northwestern State U., Shreveport; prof., dean McNeese State U., Lake Charles, La., ret., 2000. Gov.'s appointee, chmn. S.W. La. Hosp. Dist. Commn., 1989—91. Mem. allocations com. and loaned exec. United Way, 1991—92, Am. Heart Assn.; Am. Cancer Soc.; ARC. Recipient Ben Taub award, 1962, Ann Magnussen award, ARC, 1977. Mem.: ANA (del.), Lake Charles Dist. Nurses Assn. (bd. dirs., Nurse of Yr. award 1972, 1980), La. Nurses Assn. (past pres. and 1st v.p., Spl. Recognition award 1993, Nightingale Hall of Fame award 2002), Phi Kappa Phi, Delta Kappa Gamma, Sigma Theta Tau (Image of Nursing award 1993). Home: 2339 21st St Lake Charles LA 70601-7946 E-mail: amgold@cox-internet.com.

FIELO, MURIEL BRYANT, interior designer; b. Bklyn., Dec. 11, 1921; d. Harry and Minnie (Dick) Bryant; m. Julius Fielo, June 17; 1 child, Michael Kenneth. Student, CCNY, 1938-41, Rutgers U., 1965-69; cert., N.Y. Sch. Interior Design, 1970. Gen. mgr. Fidelity Discount Corp., Irvington, NJ; advt. supr. Lincoln Loan Co., Essex County, NJ, 1941-49; interior designer Alex Fielo Interior Decorators, Newark, 1942-49, prin., 1949-69, owner, 1969—. Designer, cons. space engr. MUDGE Interior Design Studios, East Orange, N.J., 1969—; mem. adv. panel Interior Design mag., 1977—. Clk. Essex County Bd. Freeholders, 1972-76; commr. East Orange Bus. Devel. Authority, 1977-86; mem. U.S. adv. coun. SBA-Region II, 1980-811 active LWV, 1950-55; organizer, 1st pres. South Orange chpt. Women's Am. ORT, 1952-54, mem. nat. spkrs. bur., 1952-65, parliamentarian No. N.J. coun., 1955-65; pres. Amity chpt. B'nai B'rith, Newark, 1946-48, v.p. No. N.J. coun., 1948-49, various nat. and state positions, 1948-80; mem. nat. com. on sect. fund raising Nat. Coun. Jewish Women, 1979-81, nat. tour chmn., 1979-81; trustee cmty. svcs. coun. Oranges and Maplewood, United Way Essex and West Hudson, 1981-83; bd. dirs. East Orange Central Avenue Mall Assn., 1979-83, chmn. new voter registration drive East Orange 2d Ward, 1955, entire city, 1969; pres. East Orange Dem. Club, 1957-58, campaign coord. for Dem. mayoral candidate, 1969; calendar coord. Essex County Dem. Com., 1970-76; mem. N.J. Bipartisan Coalition for Women's Appts., 1981. Named Outstanding Entrepreneur of 1984, Gov. of N.J., Outstanding Orgn. Pres., Kean Coll. Profl. Women's Assn., 1985, Wonder Woman of 1986, Bus. Jour. N.J., One of 8 Women To Watch, Jersey Woman mag., 1987, Bus. Person of Yr., East Orange C. of C., 1988; recipient various awards for civic svc. Mem. Internat. Soc. Interior Designers (bd. dirs. 1981-85), Nat. Home Fashions League (N.J. membership chmn. N.Y. chpt. 1981-82), Interior Design Soc., Internat. Interior Design Assn. (charter), N.J. Assn. Women Bus. Owners (state bd. dirs. 1979-82), Women Entrepreneurs N.J. (pres. 1981-85, CEO 1987—), N.J. Home Furnishings Assn. (bd. dirs. 1981-84, 86—), Constrn. Specifications Inst., N.J. Soc. AIA profl. affiliate), Guild Designer Woodworkers, Women Bus. Ownership Ednl. Coalition (N.J. pres. 1985-87, CEO 1987—, mem. steering com. interior designers for licensing in N.Y. 1985—), East Orange C. of C. (bd. dirs. 1977—, v.p. 1981-85), Bus. and Profl. Women's Club Oranges (bd. dirs. 1958-66). Jewish. Home and Office: Mudge Interior Design Studio 185 S Clinton St East Orange NJ 07018-3099 Fax: (973) 672-7287. Office Phone: 973-673-6008.

FIERRO, MARCELLA FARINELLI, forensic pathologist; b. Buffalo, May 24, 1941; d. Marcello Francis and Lena Louise (Luppino) Farinelli; m. Robert J. Fierro, May 30, 1966. BA in Biology cum laude, D'Youville Coll., 1962; MD, SUNY, Buffalo, 1966. Cert. Am. Bd. Pathology. Deputy chief med. examiner, city med. examiner State of Va., Richmond, 1975-92, chief med. examiner, 1994—; designated med. exam. and forensic pathologist Med. Exam Sys., N.C., 1992-94; prof. forensic pathology Sch. of Medicine East Carolina U., Greenville, N.C., 1992-94. Mem. UP/MP files task force FBI, Washington; chmn. forensic pathology com. CAP, 1996—. Mem. Am. Med. Women's Assn., Med. Soc. Va., Richmond Acad. Medicine, Va. Soc. Pathology, Nat. Assn. Med. Examiners (bd. dirs. 1993-95, mem. exec. com. 1995, pres. 1991), Am. Soc. Clin. Pathologist (mem. forensic pathology coun. 1992-96), Am. Acad. Forensic Sci. Office: Office Chief Med Examiner 400 E Jackson St Richmond VA 23219

FIERSTIEN, NANCY LOUISE, writer; b. Muskegon, Mich., Aug. 18, 1953; d. Carl Wilson Sircher, Martha Elizabeth Sircher; m. John Frederick Fierstien; children: Steven, Ryan. BA, Ctrl. Mich. U., 1975. Reporter The Advisor Newspaper, Utica, Mich., 1978—80, The Okla. Jour., Midwest City, 1980—80; pub. info. officer Met. Libr. Sys., Oklahoma City, 1980—83; info. specialist Tex. Natural Resource Conservation Commn., Austin, 2000—01; writer, calendar editor, assoc. editor United Parenting Pubs., Austin, 2001—03. Author: (poem) Going Home, 1997, Chalk Talk, 1998, This Turkey Gets His Wish, 2000, Restrictions, 2002. Founding pres. Friends of the Dripping Springs Cmty. Libr., 1998—2000, bd. advisor, 2000—02; active Dripping Springs Mid. Sch. PTA, Hays County Aggie Moms Club. Recipient Dist. Svc. award, Utica (Mich.) Edn. Assn., 1978—79, Best Ann. Report Nat. Achievement award, Libr. Pub. Rels. Coun., 1983. Mem.: Writer's League of Tex., Friends of Salmon Poetry Press, Mothers Against Drunk Drivers, Internat. Soc. Poets, Friends of the Spring Br.-Meml. Libr. Houston (life; newsletter editor 1988—91). Lutheran. Avocations: photography, reading, music. Home: 517 Stonegate Ln Dripping Springs TX 78620

FIFER CANBY, SUSAN MELINDA, library administrator; b. Stockton, Calif., Jan. 23, 1948; d. Reginald Dekovan and Shirley Rae (Canaday) Fifer; m. Thomas Yellott Canby, Oct. 9, 1982. BS, U. Nebr., 1970; MLS, U. Md., 1974. Circulating libr. Nat. Geog. Soc., Washington, 1975-81, asst. libr., 1981-83, dir. libr., 1983-94, dir. libr. & indexing, 1994-99, dir. librs., 1999—, v.p. librs. and info. svcs., 2002—. Mem. mems. coun. OCLC, Dublin, Ohio, 1997-2003; literacy tutor; bd. dirs. Washington Lit. Coun., 1999-2001. Bd. dirs. tech. com. D.C. Coun. Govts., 1985-88, D.C. Libr. Coun., 1997-2003, Capital Area Libr. Network, 1989-95, 98—, chair, 1994-95; bd. dirs. Sandy Spring Mus., 2002—. Named Alumna of Yr., U. Md., 2004. Mem.: ALA (John Cotton Dana award 1985, 1989), Spl. Librs. Assn. (pres. DC Spl. Librs. 2003—, Innovations and Tech. award 2001). Avocations: gardening, reading. Home: 6855 Haviland Mill Rd Clarksville MD 21029-1308 Office: Nat Geog Soc Library 1145 17th St NW Washington DC 20036-4701 Office Phone: 202-857-7787. E-mail: sfiferca@ngs.org.

FIFFIE PROCTOR, JOANN, media and technology specialist; b. New Orleans; d. Joseph Paul Sr. and Elouise Marie Fiffie. BA in Comm., U. Southwestern, Lafayette, La., 1980; EdM, Minot State U., 1992; M of Libr. and Info. Sci., U. So. Miss., 1997. Tchr. St. James Sch. Bd., Lutcher, La., 1992-93, tchr. computers, 1994-96; spl. edn. tchr. Calif. Sch. Dist., Sacramento, 1993-94; instr. Southwestern U., Lafayette, La., 1997-98; media/tech. specialist St. John Sch. Bd., Reserve, La., 1998—; rschr. Lyndon Baines Johnson Presdl. Libr., 1996—2000. Dir. sta. WJLO-TV Magnet Sch., LaPlace, La., 2000. Founder mag. Tender Times, 2000. Active Parent-Tchr., St. James, La., 1994-96; pres./CEO House Hands & Hugs, Vacherie, La.; mem. adv. bd. Big Brothers & Sisters, Lafayette. Houma-Terabone grantee, 1998; Metrovision Sch.-To-Career grantee, 2002. Mem. ALA, AAUW, NEA, Libr. Info. Tech. Assn., Nat. Assn. Female Execs., Mothers of 21st Century Leaders. Office: John L Ory Magnet Sch 182 W 5th St La Place LA 70068-4501

FIGG-CURRIER, CINDY, professional golfer; b. Mount Pleasant, Mich., Feb. 23, 1960; 1 child, Kaitland Elizabeth. Degree in mktg., U. Tex., 1982. Golfer LPGA, 1984—; winner State Farm Rail Classic, 1997. Achievements include 1 LPGA career hole-in-one. Office: c/o LPGA 100 International Golf Dr Daytona Beach FL 32124-1082

FIGLAR, ANITA WISE, retired bank executive; b. Camas, Wash., Oct. 7, 1950; d. William Hulon and Mary Wise (Adkisson) Ward; m. Richard Bould Figlar, Aug. 7, 1976; children: Richard Bould II, David Wise. Student, U. Wash., 1968-70; BA in Intercultural Studies, Ramapo Coll., 1974. Mktg. coord. power and control ops. Gen. Cable Corp., Union, N.J., 1975-76, mktg. analyst power and control ops., 1976-78; various positions Potters Industries, Inc., Hasbrouck Heights, N.J., 1971-75, with highway safety programs dept. Parsippany, N.J., 1981-82, mgr. highway safety programs dept., 1982-84, mgr. bus. devel., 1985-86, industry mgr. Highway Products div., 1986-89; with customer svc. United Jersey Bank, Hackensack, N.J., 1989, fin. svc. rep., 1989-90, asst. br. mgr., bank officer, 1990-91, bank officer retail sales, 1991-92, bank officer retail sales mgr., 1992-94; v.p., mgr. retail sales Summit Bank (formerly United Jersey Bank), Hackensack, N.J., 1994-97, market mgr., 1997-98, sr. regional mgr. New Canaan, Conn., 1998-99; v.p., dist. mgr. Summit Bank, New Canaan, Conn., 1999-2000; v.p., regional sales mgr. The Bank of N.Y., Nanuet, 2000—02, ret., 2002. Contbr. articles to many profl. and govtl. publs.

FIGUEROA, LIZ, state senator; b. San Francisco; children: AnaLisa, Aaron. Ed., Coll. San Mateo. Owner, oeprator Figueroa Employment Cons., 1981-98; mem. Union Sanitary Dist., pres., 1985; mem. Calif. State Senate, 1998—, mem. bus. and professions com. Mem. Hispanic Cmty. Affairs Coun.; mem. Fermont Adult Sch. Adv. Bd.; bd. dirs. Legal Assistance for Srs.; local bd. dirs. Selective Svc. Sys.; mem. adv. bd. Peninsula Coll. Law. Named Outstanding Legislator by several orgns. Mem. Calif. Elected Women's Assn. for Edn. and Rsch. (bd. dirs.). Democrat. Office: Calif State Senate State Capitol Rm 2057 Sacramento CA 95814 also: 43271 Mission Blvd Fremont CA 94539-5826

FIGURES, VIVIAN DAVIS, state legislator; b. Mobile, Ala., Jan. 24, 1957; m. Michael A. Figures; Akil Michael, Shomari Coleman, Jelani Anthony. BS in Mgmt. Sci., U. New Haven (Conn.). Mem. Mobile City Coun., Ala. State Senate, 1997—. Mem. Judiciary Com., Edn. Com., Constitution, Campaign Fin., Ethics, and Elections Com., Tourism and Mktg. Com., Fin. and Taxation Gen. Fund, Local Legislation No. 3 Com. Mem. Ala. Dem. Exec. Com., Ala. New South Coalition; bd. dirs. Big Bros., Big Sister Program Met. Mobile YMCA, mem. exec. com., Homeless Coalition of Mobile, Inc. Democrat. Baptist. Avocations: reading, tennis, travel, physical fitness. Home: Clemente Ct Mobile AL 36617 Office: Ala State House 11 S Union St Rm 732 Montgomery AL 36130-2103 also: PO Box 40536 Mobile AL 36640-0536 E-mail: vdfigures@aol.com.

FIJALKOWSKI, ISABELLE, professional basketball player; b. May 23, 1972; d. Tadeusz and Leokadia Fijalkowski. Student, U. Colo., 1995, U. d'Orleans, 1997—. Basketball player Euroleague, 1996-97; forward Cleveland Rockers, (WNBA), 1997—. Office: Cleveland Rockers Gund Arena One Center Ct Cleveland OH 44115

FILARDO, JANET BECHERER, lobbyist; b. Chgo., Aug. 18, 1938; d. Adam Jacob and Agnes Evelyn (Baker) Becherer; m. Joseph Michael Filardo, May 24, 1986; children: Elizabeth Allison O'Hamill, Andrea Leigh O'Hamill. BA, Washington U., 1966; MSW, Denver U., 1968. Exec. dir. Mental Health Assn. Hamilton County, Chattanooga, Tenn., 1968-70; dir. pub. info. and vol. svcs. Pa. Bd. Probation and Parole, Harrisburg, 1970-71; exec. dir. Pa. chapt. Nat. Assn. Social Workers, Carlisle, 1971-73; asst. prof. social sci. Shippensburg (Pa.) U., 1971-73; legis. liaison Pa. Dept. Health and Welfare, Harrisburg, 1973-79; exec. dir. Ctrl. Pa. Youth Ballet, Carlisle, 1979; asst. dir. govt. rels. Pa. State Edn. Assn., Harrisburg, 1980—. Cons. PSEA Internat. Edn. com., 1993-98. Founder, pres. Mid-Susquehanna Arts in Edn. Coun., Harrisburg, 1977-80; co-founder, sec. Citizens for the Arts in Pa., 1978-79; founder Unity Summer Day Camp, Mechanicsburg, Pa., 1997; exec. dir. Pa. chapt. Nat. Assn. Social Workers, 1971-73; mem. Fgn. Affairs Com., Harrisburg, 1997. Avocations: meditation, ufo's, painting, wreath-making, cross-stitching. Office: Pa State Edn Assn 400 N 3rd St Harrisburg PA 17101-1346

FILARSKI HASSELBECK, ELIZABETH, television host/personality; b. Cranston, RI, May 28, 1977; d. Kenneth J. Filarski and Elizabeth A. DelPadre; m. Tim Hasselbeck, July 6, 2002. Degree in Art, Boston Coll., 1999. Tchr., Belize, 1997; contestant, finished fourth Survior: The Australian Outback, 2001; judge Miss Teen USA Pageant, 2001; shoe designer Puma; host The Look for Less, The Style Network, 2001—; co-host The View, ABC, 2003—. Office: The View ABC 320 W 66th St New York NY 10023 6304 also: Babette Perry Internat Creative Mgmt 8942 Wilshire Blvd Beverly Hills CA 90211*

FILCHOCK, ETHEL, education educator; BS in Edn., Kent State U. Tchr. Cleve. Pub. Schs.; with EFC Creations, Solon, Ohio. Author: Voices in Poetics: Vol. 1, 1985 (Merit award), Hall of Fame, Ethel Filchock, Vol. 1, 1991, (book of poetry) Softer Memories Across a Lifetime, 1989, (poetry chapbook) A Glimpse of Love, 1991; composer: Praise God, The Lord is Coming; lyricist (numerous songs including most recently) (Harmonious Honor award, Award for Excellence, 2000), (songs) Beautiful Lady of Medugorje, 1993, This Holy Morning, 1998, Theatre of the Mind, 2003, Only The Faces Change, 2003, Amerecord, 2003, My Beautiful America, 2003, this Holy Child, 2003, What About Tomorrow, 2003, Rolling On For Freedom, 2003, Something About You, 2003, Santa's Ho-Ho-Ho, 2003, Hilltop, 2003, Holiday Blues Circle of Life, 2003 (named into Nat. Lib. Poetry, 03). Chmn. sch. United Way, 1985-86. Recipient Cert. of Achievement N.Y. Profl./Amateur Song Jubilee, 1986, Editor's Choice award Disting. Poets of Am., Outstanding Achievement in Poetry, Nat. Libr. of Poetry, 1993, Outstanding Poets of 1994, Interregnum Nat. Libr. of Poetry, Best Poets of 1995, Transformation, Nat. Libr. of Poetry, Editor's Choice award Outstanding Achievement in Poetry, 1996, 2000, 01, 02, Nat. Libr. of Poetry, 1995, 96, 2001, Outstanding Poets of 1998 for Magnanimous Beauty, Nat. Libr. of Poetry, 1998, Editor's Choice award for outstanding achievement in poetry, 1998. Mem. NAFE, Am. Fedn. Tchrs. Clubs: Akron Manuscript. Roman Catholic. Avocations: painting, traveling, dance, fishing.

FILI-KRUSHEL, PATRICIA, media company executive; b. Nov. 12, 1953; BA, St. John's U., Jamaica, NY, 1975; MBA, Fordham U., Bronx, NY, 1982. Various positions including program contr. ABC Sports ABC, 1975—79; dir. sports adminstrn. HBO, 1979—80, dir. sports and spls. program budgeting, 1980—81, dir. of prod., 1981—83, v.p. business affairs, 1984—88; senior v.p. programming & prod. Lifetime Television, 1988—89; group v.p. Hearts/ABC-Viacom Entertain. Services, 1990—93; pres. of ABC Daytime Walt Disney Co., 1993—98, pres., ABC TV, 1998-2000; pres., CEO Web MD, 2000—01; exec. v.p., admin. AOL Time Warner Inc. (now Time Warner Inc.), 2001—. Bd. dirs. Oxygen Media, Inc. Co-chair child care initiative Mayor Bloomberg's Commn. on Women's Issues; bd. dirs. Second Stage Theater, The Ctrl. Pk. Conservancy; mem. bd. comm., trustee Fordham U. Named Woman of Yr., Police Athletic League; recipient Muse award, Women in Film, 1993, Vision award, 1996, Women of Achievement award, Women's Project and Prodns., 1999, Matrix award, N.Y. Women in Comm., Inc., Crystal Apple award, City of N.Y. Mem.: Acad. TV Arts and Scis. (exec. com., bd. govs.), N.Y. Women in Film (past pres.). Office: Time Warner Inc 75 Rockefeller Plz New York NY 10012

FILIPIAK, DEBRA ANN, speech pathology/audiology services professional; b. Milw., Mar. 17, 1958; d. Barbara Ann Filipiak and Donald Max Filipiak. BS, Marquette U., 1980, MS, 1981. Cert. Clinical Competency Am. Speech Lang. and Hearing Assn., 1983. Speech pathologist Coop. Ednl. Svc. Agy. 18 (now Coop. Ednl. Svc. Agy. 2), Milton, Wis., 1982—84, Randall Consol. Sch., Bassett, Wis., 1984—. Leadership team mem. CESA 2/WSEA, Salem, Wis., 1986—, spl. edn. adv. com., 1990—2002. Blockwatch capt. Milw. Police Dept., 1993—. Recipient Randall Tchr. of the Yr., Randall Consol. Sch., 1996—97, Poland's Millenium Achievement award, 1980, Poland's Millenium Orgn. of Milw. award, 1980, Am. Speech Lang. and Hearing Assn. award for Continuing Edn., Am. Speech Lang. and Hearing Assn., 1990—, Nat. Disting. Svc. Registry: Speech, Lang., Hearing, 1989, Outstanding Young Women of Am., 1987, Polanki- Michael and Maria Laskowski Coll. Achievement award, Polanki Orgn. of Milw., 1981, Polanki Michalak Coll. Achievement award, 1980; U.S. Office of Edn. Grad. fellowship in Speech Pathology, U. S. Office of Edn., 1980, Partial Tuition scholarship, Marquette U., 1981, Marquette Woman's Club fellowship, 1980. Mem.: Randall Teacher's Assn. (assoc.), Wis. Speech Lang. and Hearing Assn. (assoc.), Am. Speech Lang. and Hearing Assn. (assoc.). Catholic. Avocations: swimming, camping, reading. Home: 3362 S 19th St Milwaukee WI 53215 Office: Randall Consolidated Sch PO Box 38 Bassett WI 53101 E-mail: filideb@randall.k12.wi.us.

FILIPPOVA, DARIA VLADIMIROVNA, private school educator; b. Chelyabinsk, Russia, Sept. 15, 1969; d. Vladimir Konstantinovich Filippov and Elina Yakovlevna Filippova; m. J. Gordon Wade, Sept. 23, 2000; 1 child, Margarita Filippova. BS, St. Petersburg (Russia) State U., 1991, MS, 1993; PhD, Bowling Green State U., 2001. Math. tchr. pub. schs., St. Petersburg, 1991; math. instr. boarding sch., St. Petersburg, 1991—93, Bowling Green (Ohio) State U., 1996—2001; math. tchr. Maumee Valley Country Day Sch., Toledo, 2001—. Mem.: Math. Assn. Am., Nat. Coun. Tchrs. Math. Home: 318 Leroy Ave Bowling Green OH 43402

FILKINS, SUSAN ESTHER, small business owner; b. McCloud, Calif., Dec. 21, 1958; d. Donald Gene Ragan and Sandra Esther (Lange) Heron; m. Timothy John Filkins, Oct. 10, 1987; children: Erin Sue, Ann Lauren, Eric Timothy. Degree in Office Adminstrn., Moore's Bus. Coll., Sacramento, 1978; AS in Studio Art and Design summa cum laude, Cayuga C.C., Auburn, N.Y., 2001. Lic. real estate, broker. Adminstrv. asst. Sacramento Blood Ctr., 1979—83; convention coord. Calif. State Blood Banking Sys., Sacramento, 1982; supr. radiology Mercy Gen. Hosp., Sacramento, 1983—87; owner, pres. Rose Sparrows Agy., Skaneateles, NY, 1988—. Radiology computer software specialist Mercy Gen. Hosp., Sacramento, 1986; cons. Syracuse U. Ctr. Career Svcs., 2002—03. Photographer N.Y. State Fair Exhbn., 1996, 1997, 2002. Mem. planning bd. Village of Elbridge, 1990—91; team leader Jordan-Elbridge Site-Base Mgmt. Jordan-Elbridge Ctrl. Sch. Dist., 1993—; mem. Cayuga County Arts Coun.,

2000—; alumni program coord. Syracuse U.; com. person Rep. Com., Elbridge, NY, 1998—. Mem.: Phi Theta Kappa. Baptist. Avocations: theater, writing, photography. Office: Rose Sparrows Agy PO Box 645 Skaneateles NY 13152

FILLEMAN, TERESA ELLEN, technical writer; b. Columbus, Ohio, Aug. 19, 1952; d. Marion Denver and Doris Audrey (Freeland) Grow; m. John Jay Filleman, June 4, 1977; children: John Wesley, Scott Ashley. AA in Geology, Glendale C.C., 1973; BS in Geology, No. Ariz. U., 1975, postgrad., 1975-77. Hydrologist Ariz. Dept. Water Resources, Phoenix, 1977-82, 84-85; computer cons., bd. dirs. Cross Roads Presch., Ltd., Phoenix, 1984-89; computer cons. Geraghty & Miller, Inc., Phoenix, 1987-88; tech. writer Digital Equipment Corp., Phoenix, 1989-92; documentation designer ASI Solution Integrators, Phoenix, 1994-95, pres., 1994-2000; client svcs. rep., Web master Ref. Pathology Svcs., 1997-98; office mgr., adminstrv. asst., ops. mgr., IQ/OQ documentation designer, webmaster CapPlus Techs., Glendale, Ariz., 1999—. Tech. writer, cons. Mt. Shadows Elem. Sch., Glendale, 1987-91, Desert Sage Elem. Sch., 1991-94. Co-author: A Study of Global Sand Seas, 1979, also various sci. studies and publs.; performer mus. CD and taps Wings Like Eagles, 1994; newsletter editor Mt. Shadows and Desert Sage Elem. Schs., 1987-94; prodr., performer on cassette tape Jammin' for Jesus, 1997, Drummin' to Beat Hell, 1998, Sizzlin' Steel, 2000, Steel Wonderland, 2001; featured in video Leading in the Spirit. Edn. coord. Dove of the Desert United Meth. Ch., Glendale, Ariz., 1990-94, dir. steel band, 1991—; parent rep. Deer Valley Unified Sch. Dist., Phoenix, 1993; chmn. parents' adv. bd. Mt. Ridge H.S. Band, 1999-2001. Recipient Giant Slayer award Dove of the Desert United Meth. Ch., 1991, 93, Chmn.'s award City of Phoenix Electric Light Parade, 1993, Judges award for Best Theme Entry, City of Phoenix Electric Light Parade, 1994. Mem. Percussive Arts Soc., Phi Theta Kappa. Republican. Avocations: steel drums, piano, nutrition, walking, volleyball.

FILLINGANE, JOEY, lawyer, state representative; b. Hattiesburg, Miss., Jan. 10, 1973; BS, U. So. Miss., 1994; JD, Miss. Coll. Sch. Law, 1998. Clk. Miss. Supreme Ct., 1998—99; lawyer Dist. Atty's Office, Lamar County, Miss., 1999; assoc. Law Office William J. Gamble III, Sumrall, Miss., 1999—; rep. Ho. of Reps., State of Miss., Jackson, 1999—. Mem. Edn., Judiciary B, Juvenile Justice, Oil, Gas and other Minerals, and Penitentiary coms. Miss. Ho. Reps., Jackson, 1999—. Mem. choir, Oral Bapt. Ch., Sumrall, Miss., tchr. Sunday Sch. and Discipleship. Republican. Bapt. Home: 241 Fillingane Rd Sumrall MS 39482 Office: Miss Ho of Reps PO Box 1018 Jackson MS 39215-1018 E-mail: jfillingane@mail.house.state.ms.us.

FILLOON, KAREN, radio personality; BS Meteorology, Fla. State U. With Nat. Weather Svc.; on-air meteorologist TV Tallahassee; meterologist Sta. KSTP-TV, Sta. KSTP-FM; staff meteorologist Sta. WCCO Radio, Mpls., 1989—. Instr. meteorology U. St. Thomas. Co-chair ann. golf tournament Am. Heart Assn. Mem.: Minn. Multiple Sclerosis Soc. (mem. strategic bd. devel. com., bd. trustees). Office: WCCO 625 2nd Ave S Minneapolis MN 55402

FILOMENO, LINDA JEAN HARVEY, elementary school educator; Bilingual tchr. Phila. Pub. Sch. Sys., 1976-79, Woodrow Wilson Elem. Sch., Trenton, N.J., 1979-83; head presch. tchr. YWCA Greater R.I., Central Falls, 1984-88; tchr. in language, culture William D'Abate Elem. Sch., Providence, 1988-95; tchr. lang. and culture dept. Providence Pub. Schs., 1995—; coord. literacy and profl. devel. Woonsocket Edn. Dept. Named R.I. State Tchr. of Yr., 1993, 94; recipient Milken Family Educator award, 1995.

FILTER, E. MARGIE, business equipment manufacturing executive; b. Teaneck, N.J., Sept. 19, 1940; BA in Econs., CCNY, 1966. Security analyst Morgan Guaranty Trust Co. N.Y., 1966-70; sr. tech. analyst G.A. Saxton & Co., N.Y.C., 1970-73; mgr. Xerox Corp., Stamford, Conn., 1973-79, dir. investor rels., 1979-84, v.p., corp. sec., 1984—, treas., 1990—. Bd. dirs. Baker Hughes, Inc., Houston, Briggs & Stratton, Milw., LaBranche & Co., N.Y.C. Chmn. bd. trustees Wells Colls., Aurora, N.Y., 1990-2001; bd. dirs. United Way Tri-State, N.Y.C., 1989-93, Westport-Weston (Conn.) United Way, 1989-93. Recipient Graham & Dodd award Fin. Analysts Fedn., N.Y.C., 1971; named to Acad. of Women Achievers YWCA of N.Y.C., 1981. Mem. Fin. Execs. Inst. (com. on corp. fin. 1994—), Investor Rels. Assn. of N.Y. (pres. 1984-85), Nat. Investor Rels. Inst., Nat. Assn. Corp. Treas., Am. Soc. Corp. Secs., Fin. Women Assn. of N.Y., The Conf. Bd. - Coun. of Corp. Treasurers. Office: Xerox Corp 800 Long Ridge Rd Stamford CT 06902-1288

FINAURI, GRACIELA MARIA, foreign service professional; b. Buenos Aires, June 18, 1956; d. Gerardo and Norma Mercedes (Burich) F. Student in law, Cath. U. Buenos Aires, 1985. Adminstr. protocol dept. Ministry of Fgn. Affairs, Buenos Aires, 1979-85, pvt. sec. min., 1985-87; pvt. sec. amb. Embassy of Argentina, Rome, 1987-91; pvt. sec. min. Ministry of Internal Affairs, Buenos Aires, 1993-95; chief of protocol Senate of Argentina, Buenos Aires, 1995-98; pvt. sec. to v.p. Argentine Republic, Buenos Aires, 1995-98; attaché Mission of Argentina to UN, N.Y.C., 1998—2003; attache Promotion Ctr. and Consulate Gen. of Argentine Republic in N.Y., N.Y.C., 2003—. Named Cavalier of Hon. and Merit, Haiti Republic, 1983, Officer of Order of Merit, Italian Republic, 1985; recipient Insignia award, Mex. Order of Aztec Eagle, 1984. Roman Catholic. Office: Promotion Ctr and Consulate Gen of Argentine Republic NY 12 W 56th St New York NY 10019 Office Phone: 212-603-0412. E-mail: gmf@mrecic.gov.ar.

FINBERG, BARBARA DENNING, not-for-profit developer; b. Pueblo, Colo., Feb. 26, 1929; d. Rufus Raymond and Velma Aileen (Hopper) Denning; m. Alan R. Finberg, June 21, 1953 (dec. 1995). BA, Stanford U., 1949; MA, Am. U. Beirut, Lebanon, 1951. Intern U.S. Dept. State, Washington, 1949-50, fgn. affairs officer, Tech Coop. Adminstrn., 1952-53; program specialist, area chief Inst. Internat. Edn., N.Y.C., 1953-59; editorial assoc., program officer Carnegie Corp. N.Y., N.Y.C., NY, 1959-80, v.p. program, 1980-88, exec. v.p., 1988-97; v.p. MEM Assocs., Inc., 1997—. Vis. fellow Woodrow Wilson Nat. Fellowship Found., 1998. Bd. dirs. Parent Child Home Program, 2002—, Nat. Coun. Rsch. on Women, 2003—; trustee Stanford U., 1976—86, v.p. bd. dirs., 1981—85, vis. com. Stanford U. Librs., 1984—90, 1993—96, chmn., 1986—88; trustee N.Y. Found., 1979—91, vice chmn. bd. dirs., 1983—85, chmn., 1985—89; bd. dirs. Bard Musical Festival, 1995—, vice chair, 2003—; bd. dirs. Ednl. Equity Concepts., 2003—, U. Cape Town (South Africa) Fund, 1997—, High/Scope Ednl. Rsch. Found., 1998—, vice chair, 2003—; mem. adv. com. to govtl. studies program Brookings Instn., 1996—2000; bd. govs. New Sch. U., Eugene Lang Coll., 1997—2001; nat. adv. panel Inst. for Rsch. on Women and Gender, Stanford U., 1991—, Humanities and Scis. Coun., Stanford U., 1996—, chair, 2002—; nat. adv. com. Ctr. for the Comparative Study of Race and Ethnicity, Stanford U., 2001—; mem. Stanford in Washington Coun., 1998—, chmn., 2002—; bd. dirs. Hole in the Wall Gang Camp Fund, 1987—. Recipient Women of Vision award, N.Y. Women's Found., 1995, John Dewey award for disting. pub. svc., Bard Coll., 1998; fellow Rotary Found., 1950—51. Mem.: Coun. Fgn. Rels., Soc. Rsch. Child Devel., Century Assn., Cosmopolitan Club NY. Home: 165 E 72nd St Apt 19L New York NY 10021-4351 Office: MEM Assocs Inc 521 5th Ave 17th Fl New York NY 10175-0088

FINCH, CATHERINE ANN, firework display artist, aromatherapist; b. Guildford, Surrey, Eng., Jan. 17, 1963; m. Robert Sherman Finch, Nov. 16, 1997; 1 child, Titanya Zoe. Student, Eastleigh Coll., Southampton, Eng., 1996. Dental nurse, Guildford, 1980-81; trainne Pain's Fireworks, Sailsbury, Eng., 1981-92; chief pyrotechnician, owner Big Bang Co., Southampton, 1992-97. Candidate for local coun., Southampton, 1994. Mem. NOW. Avocations: aromatherapy, making beaded jewelry, antique collecting, Web surfing. Home: 7600 Schomburg Rd Ste L Columbus GA 31909-1853

FINCH, DIANE SHIELDS, retail sales executive; b. Detroit, Aug. 25, 1947; d. Earl Arthur and Carrie (Steele) Shields; m. Glenn A. Finch III, Oct. 5, 1968; 1 child, Jennifer Lynn. AA, U. Houston, 1969; student, Rice U., 1980. Ter. mgr. Plough Sales, Houston, 1979-80, area mdse. mgr., 1980-84, dist. sales mgr., 1984-86; dist. mdse. mgr. Schering-Plough Healthcare Product, Houston, 1986-92; dist. retail merchandising mgr. McNeil Consumer Products, Houston, 1992-95; dist. sales mgr. Walt Disney Home Video, Houston, 1995—. Area chmn. Assn. Cmty. TV, Houston, 1985-87; mem. Friends of Ronald McDonald House; mem. Citizens Animal Protection. Mem.: NAFE, Women on the Move (chair 2000, 2001), Houston Fedn. Profl. Women, Tex. Exec. Women (pres. 2003, bd. dirs.), Am. Mgmt. Assn. Avocations: aerobics, cross country skiing, sailing. Office: Walt Disney Home Video 5020 Longmont Dr Houston TX 77056-2416

FINCH, EVELYN VORISE, financial planner; b. Marietta, Ohio, Jan. 20, 1930; d. Richard Raymon Juantzee and Oreatha Fay (Carnes) Metcalf; m. Herman Frederick Ahrens, May 13, 1948 (div. Nov. 1957); children: Erick K.F. Ahrens, Hilda Kate Ahrens(dec.), Nicole Schwartz; m. James Derwood Finch, June 29, 1973 (dec. Oct. 1993). BS in Music Edn., Concord Coll., 1961; postgrad., U. Md., Am. U., Northeastern U., 1990. Registered Health Underwriter, Boston. Music tchr. Prince George's County (Md.) pub. schs., 1961—72; pvt. piano tchr. Washington, 1961—73; china and crystal sales rep. Quality Products Co., Washington, 1973—80; ins. agt. Mut. of Omaha Cos., Washington, 1980—92, Memphis, 1992—94; pvt. practice Alamo, Tenn., 1994—; tax assoc. H&R Block Inc., Jackson, Tenn., 2002—. Ind. assoc. Pre-Paid Legal Svcs., Inc., 2000—. Supporting mem. Nat. Mus. Women in Arts, Washington, 1990—, Women's Philharm., San Francisco, 1993—. Mem.: LWV (Memphis br.), AAUW (br. pres. 1994-96, Tenn. chair ednl. found. 1996-98, Nat. Diversity Resource Team 1997-2000), Internat. Assn. Fin. Planners, Nat. Assn. Health Underwriters (registered health underwriter), Nat. Assn. Ret. Fed. Employees, Chesapeake Bay Yacht Clubs Assn. (commodore 1982), Prince George's Yacht Club (commodore 1978), Potomas River Yacht Clubs Assn. (legis. chair 1978-87), Nat. Boating Fedn. (pres. 1985), Kappa Delta Pi, Pi Mu. Home and Office: 208 Finch Rd Alamo TN 38001-5923 E-mail: EvelynFinch@msn.com.

FINCH, SHEILA, writer; b. London, 1935; 3 children. Postgrad., Ind. U. Faculty creative writing El Camino Coll., Torrance, Calif. Author: (novels) Infinity's Web, 1985, Triad, 1986, The Garden of the Shaped, 1987, Shaper's Legacy, 1988, Shaping the Dawn, 1989, Tiger in the Sky, 1999, Reading the Bones, 2003, Birds, 2004, (short fiction including) The Confession of Melakos, 1977, The Man Who Lived On The Queen Mary, 1983, Babel Interface, 1988, Rembrandts of Things Past, 1989, Firstborn Seaborn, 1995, The Falcon and the Falconer, 1997, Nor Unbuild the Cage, 2000, Forkpoints, 2002, Reach, 2003, Confessional, 2004. Winner 1998 Nebula award for short fiction: Reading the Bones. Avocations: travel, tai chi, hiking, 4-wheeling in the desert. Office: c/o Avon Books Harper Collins 10 E 53rd St New York NY 10022-5244*

FINCHER, RUTH MARIE EDLA, medical educator, dean; b. Hartford, Conn., Dec. 16, 1949; d. Wilber Roe and Hannah Camilla (Andersen) Griswold; m. Michael Edward Fincher, June 26, 1977. BA, Colby Coll., 1972; BMS, Dartmouth U., 1974; MD, Emory U., 1976. Diplomate Am. Bd. Internal Medicine. Intern then resident internal medicine Emory Hosps., Atlanta, 1976-79; practicing internist Pub. Health Svc., Ludowici, Ga., 1979-81; pvt. practice internal medicine Hinesville, Ga., 1981-82; staff physician Am. Lake VA Med. Ctr., Tacoma, Wash., 1982-84; asst. prof. medicine Med. Coll. Ga., Augusta, 1984-89, assoc. prof., 1989-94, prof. medicine, 1994—, vice dean acad. affairs, 1994—. Pres. Clerkship Dirs. in Internal Medicine, Washington, 1992—93; com. chair Nat. Bd. Med. Examiners, Phila., 1995—96; co-chair rsch. in med. edn. com. Assn. Am. Med. Colls., Washington, 1995—96, chair group on ednl. affairs, 1996—97. Co-editor: Clinical Medicine 2nd Edit., 1995; contbr. articles to profl. jours.; editl. bd. Am. Jour. Medicine, Birmingham, Ala., 1994-98, Jour. Gen. Internal Medicine, 1998—. Fellow: ACP (gov. Ga. chpt. 2003—, J. Willis Hurst Tchg. award 1994, Disting. Tchg. award 1996); mem.: ACP, Alpha Omega Alpha (bd. dirs. 2003—, Robert J. Glaser Disting. Tchg. award 1996, Daniel S. Tostesen award for leadership in med. edn. 2003). Avocations: woodworking, gardening, running. Office: Med Coll Ga CB 1843 1457 Laney Walker Blvd Augusta GA 30912 E-mail: rfincher@mail.mcg.edu.

FINDLEY, MILLA JEAN, nutritionist; b. Dallas, Aug. 14, 1934; d. Houston Henry and Juanita Imogene (Lisenbe) Shaw; m. Jack Stacy, may 29, 1952; children: Jere, David. Diploma, Rutherford Bus. Sch., Dallas, 1959; student, Mountain View C.C., 1978, El Centro C.C., 1976, Cedar Valley C.C., 1985. File clk. Texaco Oil Co., Dallas, 1952-53; sales assoc. Toys R Us and Sears, Dallas, 1970s; nutrition specialist Cedar Hill Ind. Sch. Dist., Tex., 1983-87, Duncanville Ind. Sch. Dist., Tex., 1996—. Active cradle roll Cedar Hill Ch. of Christ, 1996. Recipient nutrition award Tex. Sch. Food Svcs. Assocs., Lewisville Ind. Sch. Dist., 1987. Mem. NAFE, Assn. Tex. Profl. Educators. Avocations: foods, grandchildren, church, parks, books. Home: 510 Meadow Ridge Dr Cedar Hill TX 75104-1977

FINDLEY-LILES, SHANNON MARIE, sales executive; b. Oakland, Calif., Oct. 4, 1955; d. Bobby and Shirley Liles; m. Robert Wayne Liles, Apr. 10, 2003; 1 child, Mathew Jameson Liles. Ins. agt. ind. and various orgns., Columbia, Mo., 1981—99; v.p. sales and mktg. The Alliance Companies, Columbia, Mo., 1999—. Mem.: NAFE (dir. Columbia chpt. 2002—), Women's Network (steering com. 2000—), Columbia C. of C. (coms. 1999—). Office: The Alliance Cos 111 E Broadway Ste 340 Columbia MO 65203 E-mail: shannon@alliancecompanies.info.

FINE, ANDREA JOINER, writer; b. Bartow, Fla., Aug. 19, 1950; d. Ann Joiner Brewster and Miller V. Joiner(Stepfather); life ptnr. Pamela Gabell. BA, U. Fla., 1972. Phila. corr. People Mag., 1986—95; contbg corr. Chgo. Tribune, Chgo., 1997—99, Christian Sci. Monitor, Boston, 1997—99; editl. dir. Nutri/Sys., Inc., Horsham, Pa., 1999—2002; freelance writer Phila., 2002—. Contbr. chapters to books. Home and Office: 325 E Allens Lane Philadelphia PA 19119 Personal E-mail: a.fine@verizon.net.

FINE, ANNE, author; b. Leicester, Eng., Dec. 7, 1947; d. Brian and Eileen Mary (Baker) Laker; m. Kit Fine, Aug. 3, 1968 (div. 1991); children: Ione, Cordelia. BA with honors, U. Warwick, Eng., 1968. Tchr. Cardinal Wiseman Secondary Sch., Coventry, U.K., 1968-69; info. officer Oxfam, Oxford, England, 1969-71; tchr. Saughton Prison, Edinburgh, Scotland, 1971-72. Author: (children's fiction) The Summer-House Loon, 1978, The Other Darker Ned, 1979, The Stone Menagerie, 1980, Round Behind the Ice House, 1981, The Granny Project, 1983, Scaredy-Cat, 1984, Anneli the Art Hater, 1986, Madame Doubtfire, 1987, Crummy Mummy an Me, 1987, A Pack of Liars, 1988, Goggle-Eyes, 1989, Bill's New Frock, 1989, The Book of the Banshee, 1991, Flour Babies, 1992, Step By Wicked Step, 1995, The Tulip Touch, 1996, Charm School, 1999, Bad Dreams, 2000, Up on Cloud Nine, 2002, The True Story of Christmas, 2003, others; (adult fiction) The Killjoy, 1986, Taking the Devil's Advice, 1990, In Cold Domain, 1994, Telling Liddy, 1998, All Bones and Lies, 2001, STories of Jamie and Angus, 2002. Decorated Order Brit. Empire; named Children's Author of Yr., Brit. Book Awards, 1990, 1993, U.K. nominee for Hans Christian Anderson Author award, 1998, Children's Laureate, 2001—03; recipient Children's Lit. award, The Guardian, 1990, Carnegie medal, Brit. Libr. Assn., 1990, 1993, Whitbread Children's Novel award, 1993, 1996, Horn Book award, Boston Globe, 2003; fellow, Royal Soc. Lit., 2003. Avocations: reading, walking. Office: David Higham Assocs 5-8 Lower John St Golden Sq London W1R 4HA England

FINE, DEBORAH, publishing executive; V.p., advt. dir. Family Cir. Mag., 1991—93; v.p., assoc. pub. Mary Emmerling's Country, 1993—94; advt. dir. Glamour, 1994—95, assoc. pub., 1995—96; pub. Bride's Mag., 1996—99; v.p., pub. Glamour, 2000—01; pres. Avon Future, 2001—. Office: Avon Future 1345 Avenue of the Americas New York NY 10105-0196

FINE, ELSA HONIG, editor, publishing executive; b. Bayonne, N.J., May 24, 1930; d. Samuel M. and Yetta (Susskind) Honig; m. Harold J. Fine, Dec. 23, 1951; children: Erika S., Amy Fine Collins. BFA, Syracuse U., 1951; MEd in Art, Tyler Coll. Fine Arts, 1967; EdD in Art History, U. Tenn., 1970. Asst. prof. art Knoxville (Tenn.) Coll., 1970—75; adj. prof. various univs. and coll., Knoxville, 1975—80; founding editor Woman's Art Jour., Glenside, Pa., 1980—, pub., 1980—. Author: The Afro-American Artist: A Search for Identity, 1973, Women and Art: A History of Women Painters and Sculptors from the Renaissance to the 20th Century, 1978. Recipient Woman of Achievement award, Woman's Caucus for Art, 1996, Status of Women award, Coll. Art Assn., 2001, Alumni award, Tyler Coll., 2002. Home and Office: Woman's Art Jour 1711 Harris Rd Glenside PA 19038-7208

FINE, MARJORIE LYNN, lawyer; b. Bklyn., Aug. 14, 1950; d. Percy and Sylvia (Bernstein) F.; m. John Kent Markley, May 6, 1979; children: Jessica Paige Markley, Laura Anne Markley. BA, Smith Coll., 1972; JD, U. Calif., 1977. Bar: Calif. 1977. Assoc. to ptnr. Donahue Gallagher Woods, Oakland, Calif., 1977-87; sr. counsel Bank of Am., San Francisco, 1987-89; assoc., gen. counsel Shaklee Corp., San Francisco, 1989-90; gen. counsel, v.p. Shaklee U.S., Inc., San Francisco, 1990-94, Shaklee U.S., Shaklee Technica, 1995-99, 1999—, Yamanouchi Pharma Techs., Inc., 1999-2001; gen. counsel, sr. v.p. Shaklee Corp., 2001—. Judge pro tem Oakland Piedmont Emeryville Mcpl. Ct., 1982-89; fee arbitrator Alameda Co. Bar Assn., 1980-87. Mem. ABA, Calif. Bar Assn., Calif. Employment Law Coun. (bd. dirs. 1993-2003). Jewish. Office: Shaklee Corp 4747 Willow Rd Pleasanton CA 94588-2740

FINE, MIRIAM BROWN, artist, educator, poet, writer; b. Vineland, N.J., Mar. 8, 1913; d. Abraham and Katie (Walidarsky) Brown; m. Irvin Fine, Nov. 3, 1935; children: Ruth Eileen Fine, Adele Aviva Fine Gross. BFA, The U. the Arts (formerly Indsl. Sch. Arts) and U. Pa., 1935; postgrad., Cheltenham (Pa.) Art Sch., 1968-77, Temple U., 1976-91. Tchr. art and watercolor painting Phila. Pub. Schs., 1953-60; lectr., watercolor tchr. Assn. Ret. Profls. Temple U., 1976-92. Pvt. tchr. art, Phila., 1952-77; geriatric poster contest judge and program cover design Pa. Podiatric Med. Assn., 1984-95; tchr., vis. artist Abington Friends Com., 1989-90; tchr. watercolor N.E.-Cultural Art Coun. Phila., 1987-90; tchr. watercolor, speaker poetry forum David G. Neuman Sr. Ctr., Jewish Community Ctr. Phila., 1991—. Executed 7 murals at Spruance Elem. Sch., Phila., 1951, Holocaust oils and watercolors displayed in Temple Sholom Synagogue, Oxford Cir. Synagogue, UN Women's Conf., Nairobi, Kenya, 1985—, Libr. Nat. Mus. Women in Arts, Washington, 1992—; 16 one-person exhbns. John Wanamaker's Fine Art Gallery, The Hahn Gallery, Cida Art Gallery, First Pa. Bank, Revsin Art Gallery, Frankford Trust Co., Temple U. Ctr. City, Northeast Regional Libr., Phila., 1996, Spring Art Exhbn. N.E. Regional Libr., 1997, Printmaking Gallery U. of Arts, Phila., 1998; group shows include: U.N. Women's Conference, Nairobi, Phila. Art Show, Provident Nat. Bank, Cheltenham Art Ctr., Art Alliance, Pa. Acad. Fine Arts, Phila. Mus. Art, Camden County Hist. Soc., Rutgers Coll., Frankford Women's Art League, Pennock Art & Flower Show, Nat. Coun. Jewish Women, Immaculata Coll., Ocean City Art League, Artist Equity, Cape May Art Ctr.; author: (poetry and illustrations) Word and Drawings, 1984, (in braille) 1996, Mom I Didn't Know It Was Like That, Family History, 1984, The Full Moon Energises My Creativity, 1988, You Are in My Galaxy, 1990, That's Life, 1992, Flowers I, 1993 (Nat. Mus. Women in Arts, Washington), Treasures of Miriam Brown Fine for You, 1993; author, illustrator: My Bible, 1994; contbr. watercolor paintings on boxes and book covers Continental Box Co., 1995, Flower Book VII, 1996, Flower Book VIII, 1996, Flower Book IX, 1997, Flower Book X, 1998, Flower Book XI, 1999, Flower Book XII, 2000-02, cover (Passover prayer book) The Haggadah, 1998 (honored by Am. Jewish Congress, Pa. region, 1998); author: Poetry from My Soul, 1998. Did benefit for St. Christopher's Children's Hosp., Phila., 1984-87; mem. Torch of Life chpt. City of Hope, Phila., 1935—, mem. Herman chpt., 1992—; vol. Overbrook Sch. for the Blind, Phila., 1991—. Recipient Phila. Art Tchrs. award, 1956, Chapel of Four Chaplains Humanitarian award Torch of Life chpt. City of Hope, 1964, Nat. Synagogue Women's League award, Frankford Women's League award, 50 Yr. Svc. award 1981, 60 Yr. Svc. award 1991, Solomon Schector Illustrated Book award, City Coun. Citizen award City of Phila., 1996, award City of Hope, 1996; Bd. Edn. Art scholar, 1931; Citation in honor of Miriam Brown Fine for her artistic and literary contbn. to the life of the City of Phila. and N.E. Regional Libr., 1996. Mem. NOW, Artists Equity Inc., Phila. Watercolor Club (hon.), Women's Caucus for Art, Univ. Arts Alumni Assn., Acad. Am. Poets, Nat. Fedn. State Poetry Socs., Writers Cadence Crafters, Poets Study Group, Nat. Mus. of Women in Arts (charter mem.), Temple U. Assn. Ret. Profls. (pres. emeritus, award), Pa. State Poetry Socs., Fight for Sight. Republican. Jewish. Avocations: music, teaching, sharing knowledge, learning. Home: Brith Sholom House 3939 Conshohocken Ave Apt 820 Philadelphia PA 19131-5470

FINE, PAMELA B. newspaper editor; Grad., U. Fla. With Atlanta Journal-Constitution, 1982—94; mng. editor, v.p. Mpls. Star Tribune, 1994—2002; mng. editor The Indianapolis Star, 2003—. Office: The Indianapolis Star PO Box 145 Indianapolis IN 46206-0145

FINE, RANA ARNOLD, chemical and physical oceanographer; b. N.Y.C., Apr. 17, 1944; d. Joseph and Etta (Kreisman) Arnold; m. Shalle Stephen Fine, June 20, 1965 (div. 1979); m. James Stewart Mattson, Jan. 5, 1983. BA, NYU, 1965; MA, U. Miami, 1973, PhD, 1975. Systems analyst Svc. Bur. Corp. subs. IBM, Miami, 1965-69; rsch. assoc. Rosenstiel Sch. U. Miami, 1976-77, rsch. asst. prof., 1977-80, rsch. assoc. prof., 1980-84, assoc. prof., 1984-90, prof. marine and atmospheric chemistry, 1990—, chair divsn. marine and atmospheric chemistry, 1990-94; assoc. program dir. NSF, Washington, 1981-83. Mem. div. polar programs adv. com. NSF, Washington, 1987-90; mem. geophys. study com. NAS, Washington, 1989-92, mem. ocean studies bd., 1992-98; mem. adv. panel Tropical Ocean/Global Atmosphere Program, 1990-93, chair adv. panel major ocean programs, 1996-98. Contbr. articles to profl. jours. Vol. guide Vizcaya Mus., Miami, 1967-78, adv. panel mem. methane hydrade rev. 2003-. Grantee NSF, 1977—, NOAA, 1986—, Office of Naval Rsch., 1983-88, NASA, 1990-97. Fellow: AAAS (chair-elect atm card and hydrospheric sci. sect. 2001—04), Am. Meteorol. Soc. (coun. mem. 2001—), Am. Geophys. Union (sec.oceanography sect. 1986—88, pres.-elect oceanography sect. 1994—96, pres. 1996—98); mem.: Oceanography Soc. Avocations: sailing, scuba diving, fishing, tennis, reading. Office: RSMAS/MAC/U Miami 4600 Rickenbacker Cswy Miami FL 33149-1031 Office Phone: 305-361-4722. E-mail: rfine@rsmas.miami.edu.

FINE, SALLY SOLFISBURG, artist, educator; b. Aurora, Ill., July 20, 1948; d. Roy John Jr. and Edith Warrick (Squires) Solfisburg; m. Philip Clark Fine, May 5, 1973 (div. 1997); children: Alexander, Arielle. BFA, Ohio U., 1970; postgrad., Boston U., 1978-82, MFA, 1985. Graphic designer Mus. of Sci., Boston, 1970-72; teaching fellow Boston U., 1980-81; instr., lectr. U. Mass., North Dartmouth, 1993-95; sr. lectr.

Bradford Coll., 1995-96, asst. prof., 1996-2000; assoc. prof. art. Regis Coll., Weston, Mass., 2000—. Prin. S.S. Fine Design, Boston, 1970—. Solo shows include Viridian Gallery, N.Y.C., Bradford Coll., Chapel Gallery; exhibited in group shows at DeCordova Mus., Lincoln, Mass., Danforth Mus. of Art., Framingham, Mass., Brockton (Mass.) Art Mus., Newport (R.I.) Art Mus., A.I.R. Gallery, N.Y.C., Cité Internationale Gallerie, Paris. Bd. dirs. Kendall Ctr. for the Arts, 1983-86. Visual Artists grantee Mass. Coun. for the Arts, 1995, Sculpture fellow New Eng., Found. for the Arts, 1995, others. Mem. AAUP, Coll. Art Assn. Avocations: swimming, gardening, biking. Office: Regis Coll 235 Wellesley St Weston MA 02493-1571 E-mail: sally.fine@regiscollege.edu.

FINE, VIRGINIA O. psychologist; b. Great Falls, Mont., Apr. 18, 1921; d. Jesse Thomas and Helen (Hanner) Owens; m. Robert D. Kemble, Oct. 29, 1944 (div. 1968); children: Stephen B. Kemble; Brian S. Kemble, David B. Kemble, Maricia J. Kemble, Janet Kemble Onopa; m. Jules Fine, July 6, 1969 (dec. 1983). BA, Okla. A & M, 1943; postgrad., Columbia U., 1945; MEd, U. Hawaii, 1964, PhD, 1975. Lic. psychologist, Hawaii. Psychologist U. Hawaii, Honolulu, 1964-74; pvt. practice Honolulu, 1974—, Kailua, Hawaii, 1994—. Cons. Family Ct., Honolulu, 1978-85, Dept. of Edn., Honolulu, 1994-95. Mem. APA, Hawaii Psychol. Assn., Assn. Humanistic Psychology, Assn. for Transpersonal Psychology, Assn. for Advancement of Psychology. Democrat. Unitarian Universalist. Avocations: bed and breakfasts, lace making, family. Home: 1042 Maunawili Loop Kailua HI 96734-4621

FINEGOLD, AMY BETH, elementary school educator, consultant; b. Bklyn., June 10, 1968; d. Ira and Barbara May Finegold. BA, Univ. Miami, 1990; MA, Ind. State U., 1992, N.Y.U., 1999. Cert. tchr. N.Y. Tchr. ESL N.Y. Bd. Edn., N.Y.C., 1997—. New tchr. staff devel. tchr.; elem. lang. trainer; geography cons. N.Y. Geographic Alliance; mem. spl. interest group N.Y. State Tchrs. Eng. to Spkrs. Other Langs., 1997—2001; presenter in field. Contbr. articles to newsletters. Vol., chair events for entertainment United Jewish Appeal Fedn. Young Leadership, 1995—98; mem. Make A Wish Found., NY, 1997. Grantee, Excell, N.Y., 1998, United Fedn. Tchrs., 1998; scholar, NYU, 1996—97. Mem.: Manhattan Soc., Kappa Delta Pi, Pi Lambda Theta (membership chair, historian). Republican. Jewish. Avocations: reading, dance. Home: 309 East 49th St Apt 5B New York NY 10017

FINELSEN, LIBBI JUNE, lawyer; b. Encino, Calif., Apr. 14, 1968; BA in Polit. Sci. summa cum laude, U. Nev., 1990; JD magna cum laude, Lewis and Clark Coll., 1993. Bar: D.C. 1996, U.S. Ct. Appeals (9th, 11th and D.C. cirs.) 1996, U.S. Ct. Appeals (4th cir.) 1999, U.S. Ct. Appeals (fedl. cir.) 2001, Ct. Fed. Claims 2001. Jud. law clk. Gen. Svcs. Bd. Contract Appeals, Washington, 1993-94; assoc. McAleese & Assocs. P.C., McLean, Va., 1994-96, atty. USDA, Washington, 1996-99; trial atty. U.S. Dept. Air Force, Wright Patterson AFB, Ohio, 2000—01; atty./adv. U.S. Dept. Air Force, L.A. AFB, 2001—. V.p. edn. Hadassah Young Profls. Group, Washington, 1998-99; mem. hospitality com. Kesher Israel Synagogue, Washington, 1998-99. Mem. ABA, Phi Alpha Delta, Phi Kappa Phi. Avocations: cooking, handicrafts, travel, art exhibitions.

FINEMAN, GERALDINE GOTTESMAN, artist; b. Phila., Mar. 8, 1920; d. Harry and Bessie Gottesman; m. Al I. Fineman, Nov. 28, 1943 (dec. Nov. 2002); children: Samuel, Lawrence. BS in Edn., N.J. State Tchrs. Coll., 1941; MEd, Temple U., 1949. Tchr. elem., Blackwood, NJ, 1941—43, Phila., 1943—45; tchr. deaf, 1960—70; watercolorist, 1970—. Tchr. sign lang., Boca Raton, Fla., 2000—. Represented in permanent collections Gallaudet U., Kellogg, Battle Creek, Mich., Nat. Deaf Inst., Fla. Mem. bd. assocs. Jewish Found. for Group Homes, Rockville, Md., 1992—; aux. mem. bd. assocs. Gallaudet U., Washington, 1985—2002; established program for developmentally disabled deaf adults Rockville. Fellow: Artist Guild Boca Mus. (numerous awards), Palm Beach Watercolor Soc. (numerous awards), Women in Visual Arts (numerous awards). Avocations: swimming, sewing, travel, reading. Home: 900 NE Spanish River Blvd Boca Raton FL 33431*

FINESTONE, SHEILA, former legislator; b. Montreal, Que., Can., Jan. 28, 1927; d. Monroe and Minnie Abbey; m. Alan Finestone, June 9, 1947; children: David, Peter, Maxwell, Stephen. BS in Edn., McGill U. M.P. to Ho. of Commons for Mount Royal, 1984, 88, 93-99; critic for commn. and culture, 1985-93; Sec. of State Multiculturalism and the Status of Women, 1993-96; appt. Senate of Can., Ottawa, Canada, 1999—. Advisor to Parliament on eliminating anti-personal land mines; mem. transp. and comm., statutes and regulations; vice chair human rights; mem. spl. com. custody and access in divorce, constitution amendments edn.; past pres. La Fed. des Femmes du Quebec; vice chair Amendment Equality Rights Can. Constn., 1985; leader Can. Delegation Beijing World Conf. on Women's Rights, 1995. Pres. (hon.) Young Men and Young Women's Hebrew Assn.; ret. sec. Parliamentarian Assoc.; v.p. Canadian Mus. of Civilization; pres. World Exec. of Inter Parliamentary Union; mem. Nat. Coun. Jewish Women; hon. gov. Jewish Gen. Hosp.; mem. exec. com. Orgn. Jewish Parliament. Named Person of the Yr., McGill U., 2001; recipient Jackie Robinson Leadership award, 1996, Samuel Bronfinan Leadership award, 1995, O.R.T. Sophie Benett award, 1996. Mem. Orgn. Rehab. and Tng. Liberal.

FINGER, IRIS DALE ABRAMS, elementary school educator; b. Ironton, Ohio, Jan. 22, 1939; d. Frank Abrams and Pearl (Moore) Schwab; m. Robert James Roderick Sr., July 20, 1957 (div. Nov. 1971); children: Robert James Roderick Jr., Elizabeth Ann Roderick Travis; m. Henry Waterman Bromley Jr., May 14, 1972 (div. June 1987); child: Henry Waterman Bromley III; m. Grover Cleveland Finger III, Apr. 1, 1989. Degree in early childhood and elem. edn., U. South Fla.; degree in design, Jackson Coll., Honolulu. Cert. middle sch. math. tchr.; cert. TESOL; cert. gifted edn. Children's libr. Ft. Myers (Fla.) Pub. Libr., 1955-57; workmen's compensation payroll adminstr. San Diego, 1964-66; permanent substitute tchr. Sigsbee Elem. Sch., Key West, Fla., 1968-70; part-time libr. Danielson (Conn.) Libr., 1970-71; residential design Bateman Homes, Leigh Acres, Fla., 1971-72; structural steel designer So. Machine and Steel, Ft. Myers, 1972-73; dir. Ft. Myers Bus. Coll., 1973-77; structural prestress concrete designer Southland Prestress, Dean Steel and Kirby MaCumber Steel, 1977-83; tchr. Lee County Sch. Bd., Ft. Myers, 1983—, team leader, math. coach, 1983, 94-95; with Bonita Spring Mid. Sch., 1994-96, equity coord., 1995-96. Pres. PTA, Key West, 1966-68, Fla. Art League, Ft. Myers, 1984-86; dir. Ft. Myers Bus. Coll., 1973-77; hosp. nurse ARC, 1964-66; med. evacuation for Vietnam wounded Philippine Islands Subic Hosp.; mem. Treasury of Island Coast Uni-Serve; rep. to Lee County Safety Com. Recipient Pres. Regan Achievement award, 1976, Pres. Johnson People to People award and plank award for sch. constrn. at San Meguel, the Philippines, 1960; named to Wall of Tolerance, 2004, Wall at Justice Ctr., Montgomery, Ala., 2004. Mem.: Am. Legion, VFW Aux., Navy Wives and Navy Relief Soc., Pioneer Club Ft. Myers, Lee County Math. Coun., Fla. Math. Coun., Rep. Assembly, Tchrs. Assn. Lee County, Fla. Tchrs. Profession, NEA, Phi Beta Kappa (program chmn., treas.), Alpha Delta Kappa. Republican. Methodist. Avocations: arts and crafts, reading, vacationing at the beach, family socials, swimming. Home: 186 Price St Naples FL 34113

FINGERHUT, MARILYN ANN, federal agency administrator; b. Bklyn., Oct. 3, 1940; d. Robert Vincent and Marion (Carroll) F.; m. David W. Haartz, May 14, 1988; children: Margot, D. Bradley. BS in Cell Biology, Coll. of St. Elizabeth, Convent Station, N.J., 1964; PhD in Cell Biology, Cath. U. Am., 1970; MS in Occupational Health, Harvard U., Boston, 1981. Tchr. elem. schs., Jersey City, 1961-62, East Orange, N.J., 1964-65; instr. Coll. of St. Elizabeth, 1970-71; rsch. assoc. N.J. Coll. Medicine and Dentistry, Newark, 1971-72; asst. prof. to assoc. prof. St. Peter's Coll., Jersey City, 1973-80; researcher St. Joseph Med. Ctr., Paterson, N.J., 1977-80; predoctoral fellow USPHS, 1966-69, commd. capt., 1989; epidemiologist Nat. Inst. for Occupational Safety and Health, Cin., 1981-88, br. chief, 1988-94, sr. scientist office of dir. Washington, 1994-95, asst. dir. ops., 1995-96, chief staff, 1996—99; coord. occup. and environ. health WHO, Geneva, 2000—02; internat. coord. NIOSH, Washington, 2003—. Contbr. articles to sci. jours. Founding mem. Women's R&D Ctr., Cin., 1987-95. Recipient disting. svc. medal, 2000, commendation medal USPHS, 1989, 92. Mem. APHA, Soc. for Epidemiologic Rsch. Democrat. Roman Catholic. Office: NIOSH 200 Independence Ave SW Washington DC 20201

FINK, ALMA, retired elementary education educator; b. Missoula, Mont., Sept. 2, 1934; d. Frederick James and Annabelle (Pearson) Gariepy; m. Millard Allen Fink, June 18, 1955 (dec. Sept. 1980); children: Melanie Ann, Laurie Jean. Diploma, Western Mont. Coll., Dillon, 1954; BA, U. Mont., 1968, MA, 1992. Cert. elem. and reading tchr., Mont. Tchr. 1st grade Granite County Elem. Sch., Phillipsburg, Mont., 1954-55, Missoula County Pub. Schs., Missoula, 1955-56, 68-99; ret. Mem. Five Valleys Reading Coun., MIssoula. Editor state newsletter Chit Chat. Named Gold Star Tchr., KECI-TV, 1998. Mem. NEA (life), Missoula Elem. Edn. Assn. (polit. action com. for educators, mem. exec. bd.), Alpha Delta Kappa (Mont. state pres. 1988-90, pres. chpt., regional chmn., Violet award). Roman Catholic. Avocations: sewing, crafts, sports, reading, travel.

FINK, CATHY DEVITO, small business owner; b. Jacksonville, Fla., Dec. 23, 1957; d. Pasquale and Kay Francis (Mentry) DeVito; m. Robert Thomas Fink, May 5, 1984; 1 child, Christopher DeVito Fink. AAS, Canton (N.Y.) Agrl. & Tech., 1978. Adminstv. asst. MPR Assocs., Washington, 1978-84; owner, dir. CDF Svcs., Falls Church, Va., 1984—. PAC mgr. Neece, Cator & Assocs., Inc., Washington, 1987—. Tchr. computers Haycock Elem. Sch., Fairfax, Va., 1986-87, pres. PTA; v.p. Capital Boys Hockey Club, Washington, 1987-89; bus. mgr. Women in Housing and Fin. Mem. NAFE, Nat. Economists Club (bus. mgr. 1988—), Nat. Economists Ednl. Found. (bus. mgr. 1988—), Bus. Network Internat. (pres. Falls Church chpt.). Republican. Roman Catholic. Avocations: raquetball, computer technology, bicycling, teaching children, business management. Office: CDF Svcs 6712 Fisher Ave Falls Church VA 22046-1820

FINKEL, MARION JUDITH, internist, pharmaceutical administrator; b. N.Y.C., Nov. 2, 1929; d. Israel and Bella (Stillman) Finkel; m. Simon V. Manson, Sept. 12, 1954. Student, L.I. U., 1945-48; MD (Howard Sloan Meml. scholar), Chgo. Med. Sch., 1952. Intern Jersey City Med. Ctr., 1952-53; resident in internal medicine Bellevue Hosp., N.Y.C., 1954-56; med. editor Merck and Co., 1957-61; pvt. practice specializing in internal medicine, N.Y.C., 1956-57, 1961-63; with FDA, 1963-85, dir. divsn. metabolic and endocrine drugs, 1966-70, dep. dir. bur. drugs, 1970-71, 72-74, dir. office new drug evaluation, 1971-72, 74-82, dir. office orphan products devel., 1982-85; exec. dir. R&D Berlex Labs., Inc., 1985-88; v.p. drug registration and regulatory affairs Sandoz Pharms., Inc., 1988-94, v.p. corp. regulatory compliance, 1994-95, cons. regulatory affairs, clin. R&D, 1995—. Contbr. chpts. to books, numerous articles to profl. jours. Recipient award of merit FDA, 1972, Superior Svc. award USPHS, 1976, 84, Fed. Woman's award Fed. Govt., 1976, Meritorious Exec. award, 1980; named Disting. Alumnus, Chgo. Med. Sch., 1977, L.I. U., 1980. Office: 21 Squirrel Run Morristown NJ 07960-6411

FINKELSTEIN, BARBARA, education educator; b. Bklyn., Mar. 22, 1937; d. Joseph and Helene (Gutter) Eisenberg; m. James D. Finkelstein; children: Donna Ilene, Laura Helene. BA, Barnard Coll., 1959; MA, Columbia U., 1960, EdD, 1970. Asst. prof. U. Md., College Park, 1970-74, assoc. prof., 1974-83, dir. Internat. Ctr. for Study of Edn., Policy and Human Values, 1979—, mem. East Asian com., 1980—, prof. edn., 1983—. Dir. Mid-Atlantic Region Japan-in-the-Schs. Program, 1985—, Internat. Ctr. for Study of Edn. Policy and Human Values, 1979—, Nat. Intercultural Edn. Leadership Inst. Author, editor: Regulated Children, Liberated Children, 1979 (Critic's Choice award 1981), Governing the Young: Teacher Behavior in Primary Schools in Nineteenth-Century United States, 1988, Experiencing Education and Culture inJapan: Transcending Stereotypes, 1990, Discovering Culture in Education: An Approach to Program Design and Evaluation, Education Historians as Mythmakers, 1992, A Crucible of Contradictions: Historical Roots of Violence Against Children, 2001, Is Adolescence Here to Stay? 2002; editor Reflective History series Tchrs. Coll. Press; exec. editor Pedagogica historica, Jour. Edn. Policy; contbr. articles to profl. jours. Grantee U.S.-Japan Found., 1985-88; NEH fellow, 1976-77, fellow U. of Tokyo, 1992. Mem. Am. Ednl. Studies Assn. (pres. 1979-82), History of Edn. Soc. (bd. dirs. 1980-82, v.p. 1998, pres. 1998-99), Am. Ednl. Rsch. Assn. (v.p. 1989—). Home: 3916 Garrison St NW Washington DC 20016-4220 Office: U Md Dept Edn Policy College Park MD 20742-0001 E-mail: bf6@umail.umd.edu.

FINKELSTEIN, NANCY R. lawyer; BA, Hunter Coll. Bar: N.Y. Law clk. N.Y. State Ct. Appeals, N.Y.C.; sssoc. Kaye, Scholer, Fierman, Hays & Handler, LLP, N.Y.C., ptnr., Schulte, Roth & Zabel LLP, N.Y.C. Mem. ABA (comml. fin. svcs. com.), Assn. Bar City N.Y., Turnaround Mgmt. Assn. (bd. dirs. N.Y. chpt., mem. nominating com.). Office: Schulte Roth & Zabel LLP 900 3d Ave New York NY 10022 E-mail: nancy.finkelstein@srz.com.

FINLEY, DOROTHY HUNT, beverage distribution company executive; b. Douglas, Ariz. d. John P. and Salley E. (Stewart) Hunt; m. Harold Walter Finley, June 29, 1946 (dec. 1983); 1 child, John H. BA, MEd, U. Ariz. Cert. tchr., sch. adminstr., Ariz. Tchr. Tucson Unified Sch. Dist., 1943-46, 55-58, supervising tchr., 1958-60, sch. prin., 1960-80; pres., dir. Finley Distbg. Co., Inc., Tucson, 1983—. Bd. dirs. Tucson YWCA, 1984, Tucson area Girl Souts U.S., 1985, Tucson chpt. Planned Parenthood, 1987; founder, pres. Women's Studies Orgn. U. Ariz., Tucson, 1986; chair Met. Tucson Conv. and Visitors Bur. Mem. Ariz. Whgolesale Beer and Liquor Assn., Pima County Wholesale Beer and Liquor Assn., Tucson Key Club, U. Ariz. Alumni Club, Pi Lambda Theta, Delta Kappa Gamma. Republican. Episcopalian. Avocations: golf, cards, needlepoint, travel. Office: Finley Distbg Co Inc 2104 S Euclid Ave Tucson AZ 85713-3653

FINLEY, GLENNA, writer; b. Puyallup, Wash., June 12, 1925; d. John Ford and Gladys De Ferris (Winters) F.; m. Donald MacLeod Witte, May 19, 1951; 1 child, Duncan MacLeod. BA cum laude, Stanford U., 1945. Prodr. internat. divsn. NBC, 1945-49; film libr. March of Time, 1949; with news bur. Life Mag., 1950; publicity and radio writer Seattle, 1950-51; freelance writer, 1951-57; contract writer New Am. Libr. Inc., N.Y.C., 1970—. Author numerous books including Master of Love, 1978, Beware My Heart, 1978, The Marriage Merger, 1978, Wildfire of Love, 1979, Timed for Love, 1979, Love's Temptation, 1979, Stateroom for Two, 1980, Affairs of Love, 1980, A Business Affair, 1983, Wanted for Love, 1983, A Weekend for Love, 1984, Love's Waiting Game, 1985, A Touch of Love, 1985, Diamonds for My Love, 1986, Secret of Love, 1987, The Marrying Kind, 1988, Island Rendezvous, 1990, Stowaway for Love, 1992, The Temporary Bride, 1993. Named Matrix Table Woman of Achievement, 1976. Mem.: Women's Univ. Club (Seattle). Republican. Anglican. Home: 7868-F Rea Rd #312 Charlotte NC 28277

FINLEY, JULIE HAMM, political party official; Nat. co-chmn. Fin. Dole for Pres., 1995—96; asst. secy. 1996 Rep. Nat. Conv.; co-chmn. D.C. Republican Party, Team 100, 1997—; nat. committeewoman D.C. Republican Com., 1999—. Founding bd. mem. US Com. on NATO. Office: DC Rep Comm 1275 K St, NW Washington DC 20005

FINLEY, KATHERINE MANDUSIC, professional society administrator; b. Mansfield, Ohio, Nov. 8, 1954; d. Sam and Ann Julia (Konves) Mandusic; m. Edwin D. McDonell, Aug. 18, 1979 (div. Dec. 1994); m. Jeffrey A. Finley, June 12, 1999. BA, Ohio Wesleyan U.; MA in History and Mus. Studies, Case Western Res.; MBA, Ind. U. Rschr. Conner Prairie Mus., Fishers, Ind., 1978-82; exec. dir., rsch. historian Ind. Med. History Mus./Ind. Hist. Soc., Indpls., 1982-91; asst. dir. comm. and mktg. Ind. U. Ctr. Philanthropy, 1991-93; exec. dir. Roller Skating Assn. Internat., Indpls., 1993-2000, Assn. Rsch. Nonprofit Orgns. and Voluntary Action (ARNOVA), 2000—; mem. faculty philanthropic studies Ind. U.-Purdue U., Indpls., 2001—. Author: (book) The Journals of William A. Lindsay, 1989; contbg. editor: The Encyclopedia of Indianapolis, 1994; contbr. articles to profl. jours. Pres. Altrusa Internat. Indpls., 1995—97, treas., 1998—99, chmn. svc. com., 1999—2000; pres. Altrusa Found. Indpls., 2001—03; bd. dirs. Nat. Mus. Roller Skating, Lincoln, 1994—2000. Mem.: Assn. Fund Raising Profls. (bd. dirs. Ind. chpt. 2003—), Ind. Soc. Assn. Execs. (chair edn. com. 1997—98, chair conv. com. 1999—2000, bd. dirs. 1999—2001, chair found. 2000), Nat. Soc. Fund Raising Execs. (cert.), Am. Soc. Assn. Execs. (cert., Assn. Exec. of Yr. 2002), MINI Cooper Car Club Ind. (club advisor), Toastmasters (v.p. edn. 1998—99, v.p. pub. rels. 2000, v.p. edn. 2000—02, gov. area 18 2001—02), Rotary Internat. of Indpls., Phi Beta Kappa, Sigma Iota Epsilon, Beta Gamma Sigma. Avocations: reading, walking, gourmet cooking. Office: ARNOVA Ste 301 550 W North St Indianapolis IN 46202 E-mail: kmfinley@iupui.edu.

FINLEY, KERRY A. lawyer; b. Iowa CIty, Iowa, June 15, 1965; d. Thomas A. and Diane Deckard F.; m. Roger A. Dahl, Dec. 14, 1996; children: Beckett, Deckard. BA, Dartmouth Coll., 1987; JD, U. Iowa, 1990. Bar: N.Y. 1991, Iowa 1993. Assoc. Willkie, Farr & Gallagher, N.Y.C., 1990-93; ptnr., shareholder Finley, Alt, Smith, Scharnberg, Craig, Hilmes & Gaffey, Des Moines, 1993—. Mem. ABA, Iowa Bar Assn., Polk County Bar Assn., C. Edwin Moore Am. Inn of Ct. (barrister). Democrat. Office: Finley Alt Smith Scharnberg Craig Hilmes & Gaffey 604 Locust St Des Moines IA 50309-3705 Home: 475 N Shore Dr Clear Lake IA 50428-1374

FINLEY, MARGARET MAVIS, retired elementary school educator; b. Jackson, Mich., Dec. 2, 1927; d. Allen Aaron and Minnie Mavis (Graham) Lincoln; m. Duane Douglas Finley, Aug. 23, 1952; 1 child, Linda Louise. BS, Ea. Mich. U., 1960; postgrad., Pepperdine U., 1968-72. Cert. tchr., Mich., Calif. Tchr. Jackson Sch. Dist., 1960-67, Pomona (Calif.) Sch. Dist., 1967-88. Editor Calif. Ret. Tchrs. Assn. Divsn. 82 Newsletter; contbr. poetry and articles to profl. jours. Mem. AAUW, Calif. Ret. Tchrs. Assn., Calif. Tchrs. Assn. (life), DAR. Avocations: writing, reading, hiking, travel, theater. Home: 1072 Cypress Point Dr Banning CA 92220-5404

FINLEY, MARLYNN HOLT, elementary educator consultant; b. Columbia, Mo., Oct. 19, 1936; d. Robert McDonnnell and Lorraine Isabelle (Miller) Holt; husband dec. BS in Edn., U. Mo., 1958, MS in Edn., 1965, PhD in Spl. Edn., 1978. Cert. elem. educator, elem. adminstr., spl. educator. Elem. tchr. Ferguson (Mo.)/Florissant Schs., 1958-59, 60-61; elem., jr. high tchr. Anniston (Ala.) Schs., 1959-60; univ. instr. U. Mo., Columbia, 1961-64; elem. tchr. Riverview (Mo.) Gardens Schs., 1964-65; lang. arts cons. St. Charles (Mo.) Schs., 1966-69, Parkway Schs., Chesterfield, Mo., 1969-73, reading specialist, 1973-95; ednl. cons. self-employed Town & Country, Mo., 1995—. Jefferson Club trustee chmn. Devel. Coun., U. Mo., Columbia, 1991—. Grantee, 1967-69, 70-71. Alumni adv. chmn. Coll. Edn. Alumni, U. Mo., 1969-89; Sunday sch. tchr. Ladue Chapel Presbyn., St. Louis, 1960-61, deacon, 1999—. Recipient Carter award U. Mo., 1965, Life Saving award, 1980. Mem. AAUW, Internat. Reading Assn. (treas. 1970-72), St. Louis Suburban Reading Assn. (Svc. award 1982), Order of Ea. Star (grand rep. of B.C. and Yukon 1999-00, assoc. conductress 1982, conductress 1983, assoc. matron 1984, worthy matron 1985, 00, sec. 1987-95), PEO, Pi Lambda Theta, Zeta Tau Alpha. Republican. Avocations: reading, swimming, walking, skating, bridge, travel. Home: 12 Summerhill Ln Chesterfield MO 63017-8408

FINLEY, PATRICIA ANN, psychologist, artist; b. Phoenix, Oct. 30, 1936; d. Richard Edward and Ethel Buck Finley; m. William M. Larson, Aug. 31, 1957 (div. June 5, 1978); children: Sabin Lynne Larson, Shura Lee McGraw, Sean William Larson. BFA Graphic Design, Univ. Ariz., Tucson, Ariz., 1958; MS Art Edn., Univ. Oreg., Eugene, Oreg., 1981, PhD Art Edn., 1984; PhD Psychology, Walden Univ., Mpls., 2002. Cert. basic tchg. Oreg., 1982, lifetime tchg. in C.C. Ariz., 1987. Coll. instr. Ariz. State Univ./Columbia Coll., Phoenix, 1985—95; psychotherapist Sexual Assault Recovery Inst., Phoenix, 1990—94, Westside Social Svc., Phoenix, 1994—97; clin. specialist ProtoCall Crisis Line, Portland, 1997—2000; sex offender therapist New Horizons Wellness Svc., Portland, Oreg., 2000—01; Psychologist, owner, dir. Lake Oswego (Oreg.) Counsel Ctr., 2001—. Exec. dir. Phoenix Festivals, Phoenix, 1987—90; bd. cert. expert Am. Acad. Trauma Svc., Portland, Oreg., 1997—. Media coord. John Denver Ariz. Windstar Connection Group, Phoenix, 1989; mem., planning com. Very Spl. Arts, Scottsdale, Ariz., 1993. Fellow: Kappa Kappa Gamma; mem.: Milton H. Erickson Found., Eye Movment Desensitisation & Reprocessing, Am. Psychol. Assn., Am. Mental Health Assn. (Oreg. chpt.), Psi Chi. Independent. Unitarian. Avocations: running, swimming, reading, cooking, antiques. Office: Lake Oswego Counseling Ctr Inc 15110 SW Boones Ferry Rd #248 Lake Oswego OR 97035 Office Phone: 503-675-2830.

FINLEY, SARA CREWS, medical geneticist, educator; b. Lineville, Ala., Feb. 26, 1930; m. Wayne H. Finley; children: Randall Wayne, Sara Jane. BS in Biology, U. Ala., 1951, MD, 1955. Diplomate Am. Bd. Med. Genetics; cert. clin. geneticist; cert. clin. cytogeneticist. Intern Lloyd Noland Hosp., Fairfield, Ala., 1955-56; NIH fellow in pediatrics U. Ala. Med. Sch., Birmingham, 1956-60; NIH trainee in med. genetics Inst. Med. Genetics, U. Uppsala, Sweden, 1961-62; mem. faculty U. Ala. Med. Sch., 1960-96, co-dir. lab. med. genetics, 1966-96, prof. pediatrics, 1975-96, occupant Wayne H. and Sara Crews Finley chair med. genetics, 1986-96, prof. emeritus, 1996—; Disting. Faculty lectr. Med. Ctr., U. Ala. at Birmingham, 1983; mem. staff Univ. U. Ala. Hosp., Children's Hosp. Ala. Mem. ad hoc com. genetic counseling Children's Bur., HEW, 1966; mem. ad hoc rev. panel for genetic disease and sickle cell testing and counseling programs, 1980; mem. genetic diseases program objective rev. panel Bur. Maternal and Child Health and Resources Div., HHS, 1989, mem. adv. group on lab. quality assurance, 1989. Birmingham Author papers on clin. cytogenetics, human congenital malformations, human growth and devel. Mem. White House Conf. Health, 1965; mem. rsch. manpower rev. com. Nat. Cancer Inst., 1977-81; mem. Sickle Cell Disease Adv. Com., NIH, 1983-87; chairperson physician's campaign bd. dirs. United Way, 1993-95. Recipient Disting. Alumna award U. Ala. Sch. Medicine Alumni Assn., 1989, Med. award Ala. Assn. for Retarded Children, 1969, Turlington award Planned Parenthood of Ala., 1982, Nat. Outstanding Alumnae award Zeta Tau Alpha, 1992, Disting. Alumna award U. Ala. Nat. Alumni Assn., 1994, Brother Bryan Prayer Point award Birmingham Women's Com., 2001, Gardner award Ala. Acad. Sci., 2002, Lifetime Achievement award Birmingham Bus. Jour., 2003; co-recipient Will Holmes award Children's Aid Soc. Birmingham, 1999; named Top Ten Women in Birmingham, 1989, Top 31 Most Outstanding Alumnae U. Ala., Tuscaloosa, 1993, Ala. Health Hall of Fame, 2001, named to Birmingham Bus. Jour. Healthcare Hall of Fame, 2002, Finley-Compass Bank Genetics Conf. Ctr. with portrait opened, 2001. Fellow AMA (founding), Am. Coll. Med. Genetics; mem. Am. Soc. Human Genetics, Med. Assn. Ala. (Samuel Buford Word award 2003), Ala. Assn. Retarded Children (Ann. Med. awad 1969), Ala. Acad. Sci., Jefferson County Med. Soc. (pres. 1990), Jefferson County Pediatric Soc., Rotary Club of Birmingham, Phi Beta Kappa, Sigma Xi, Alpha Omea Alpha, Alpha Epsilon Delta, Omicron Delta Kappa, Phi Kappa Phi, Zeta Tau Alpha. Office: U Ala Kaul Bldg 210E Birmingham AL 35294

FINLEY, SARAH MAUDE MERRITT, social worker; b. Atlanta, Nov. 19, 1946; d. Genius and Willie Maude (Wright) Merritt; m. Craig Wayne Finley, Aug. 10, 1968; children: Craig Wayne Jr., Jarret Lee. BA, Spelman Coll., 1968; postgrad., Atlanta U., 1968-69. Cert. GPS/MAPP leader 2001. Job placement advisor Marsh Draughton Bus. Coll., Atlanta, 1971-72; child attendant Fulton County Juvenile Ct., Atlanta, 1972; social worker Fulton County Dept. Family and Children Svcs., Atlanta, 1972-2000, casework supr., 1976-98, Title VI customer svc. coord. Ctrl. City/North Area office, 1990-98; RTD Fulton County Govt., 1996—; counselor/asst. to the project dir. Right Way Home Project N.W. Area Office, 1998-99; social svcs. case mgr. Placement Resource Devel. N.W. Area Office, 2000; social worker Clayton County Dept. Family and Children Svcs., Jonesboro, Ga., 2000—; co-leader GPS/MAPP, 2001—. Supr. Count on Me video Ga. Dept. Human Resources, 1987. Vol. coord. family support program Family Support Group of Atlanta Detachment of 2d Army Maneuver Tng. Command.; vol. family support coun. 87th Maneuver Area Command (now 4th Brigade, 87th Divsn.), 1991-93; del. Ft. McPherson (Ga.) Army Family Symposium, 1992, 3d ann. worldwide USAR Family Support Conf., St. Louis, 1992. Mem.: Fulton County Ret. Employees Assn., Nat. Assn. Counties, Ga. County Welfare Assn., Nat. Alumnae Assn. Spelman Coll., Womens Aux. Ga. VFW. Baptist. Avocations: poetry, reading, volunteer work, stress mgmt. Office: Clayton County Dept Family & Children Svcs 877 Battlecreek Rd Jonesboro GA 30236

FINLEY-MORIN, KIMBERLEY K. secondary school educator; b. San Angelo, Tex., Nov. 23, 1954; d. James Griffith Jr. and Imogene (Powers) Finley; m. Michael Morin, Feb. 15, 1986. BA cum laude, Pan Am. U., 1982; MA, Endicott Coll., 2004. Cert. Acupressuriest. Tchr. Dallas Theatre Ctr., Greenfield (Mass.) Child Care Ctr.; site coord., tchr. Greenfield Girls Club; tchr. theatre/acting Shea Theatre, Turners Falls, Mass.; prof. theatre/speech Greenfield Com. Coll., 1996—. Resident dir. Fellowship Players of South Deerfield, 1996—. Pres. Arena Civic Theatre, 1992—. With USN, 1976-80. Mem. Tex. Ednl. Theatre Assn., Alpha Omega. Home: 62 High St Turners Falls MA 01376-1709

FINN, ANGE DICKSON, freelance/self-employed writer; b. Memphis, Jan. 20, 1957; d. Robert Malcolm and Rose Wilkerson Dickson, Emi Dickson (Stepmother); m. David Samuel Finn, Apr. 3, 1981; 1 child, Dareth Anne. BA magna cum laude, Angelo State U., 1978. Gen. mgr. Theatre Under Stars, Houston, 1982—85; dir. spl. projects Jewish Nat. Fund, Houston, 1985—87; pub. info. officer City of Houston Housing Authority, 1987—88; exec. dir. Theater Dist., Houston, 1988—93; dir. corp. comm., theater devel. project mgr. Pace Entertainment, Houston, 1993—98; cons. Houston, 1998—; freelance writer, 2002—. Author: (book) The In-Gate: A Complete Guide for Novice Horse Show Parents; columnist (website) Horse Show Parenting; contbr. articles to newspapers, to magazines. Bd. dirs. Theater Dist. Assn., Houston, 1993—2003, treas., 1993—98; pres. Longfellow Elem. PTA, Houston, 1997—98; mem. design com. Hobby Ctr. Performing Arts, Houston, 1997—2000; tech. advisor, mem. planning and design com. Houston Downtown Mgmt. Dist., 1998—99; mem. of the bd. dirs Houston (Tex.)Downtown Alliance, 2003—. Avocation: equestrian events. Personal E-mail: angefinn@aol.com.

FINN, FRANCES MARY, biochemistry researcher; b. Pitts., May 6, 1937; d. Stephen B. and Geraldine H. (Weber) F.; m. Klaus Hofmann, Feb. 26, 1965 (dec. Dec. 25, 1995); m. Eric Reichl, July 19, 1999. BS in Chemistry, U. Pitts., 1959, MS in Biochemistry, 1961, PhD in Biochemistry, 1964. Asst. rsch. prof. biochemistry U. Pitts., 1969-73, assoc. rsch. prof., 1973-80, assoc. prof. medicine, 1980-88, prof., 1988-99, prof. emerita, 1999—. Mem. Am. Chem. Soc., Endocrine Soc., Am. Soc. for Biochemistry and Molecular Biology, Am. Peptide Soc., Protein Soc. Home: 150 Brooks Bnd Princeton NJ 08540-7545 E-mail: ffreichl@patmedia.net.

FINNBERG, ELAINE AGNES, psychologist, editor; b. Bklyn., Mar. 2, 1948; d. Benjamin and Agnes Montgomery (Evans) Finnberg; m. Rodney Lee Herndon, Mar. 1, 1981; 1 child, Andrew Marshal Herndon. BA in Psychology, L.I. U., 1969; MA in Psychology, New Sch. for Social Rsch., 1973; PhD in Psychology, Calif. Sch. Profl. Psychology, 1981. Diplomate Am. Bd. Forensic Examiners, Am. Bd. Forensic Medicine, Am. Bd. Med. Psychotherapists and Psychodiagnosticians, Am. Bd. Disability Analysts (profl. adv. coun.), Am. Bd. Psychol. Specialties, Prescribing Psychologists Register (fellow), lic. psychologist Calif. Rsch. asst. in med. sociology Cornell U. Med. Coll., N.Y.C., 1969-70; med. abstractor USV Pharm. Corp., Tuckahoe, N.Y., 1970-71, Coun. for Tobacco Rsch., N.Y.C., 1971-77; editor, writer Found. of Thanatology Columbia U., N.Y.C., 1971-76, cons. family studies program cancer ctr. Coll. Physicians & Surgeons, 1973-74; dir. grief psychology and bereavement counseling San Francisco Coll. Mortuary Scis., 1977-81; rsch. assoc. dept. epidemiology and internat. health U. Calif., San Francisco, 1979-81, asst. clin. prof. dept. family and cmty. medicine, 1985-93, assoc. clin. prof., dept. family and cmty. medicine, 1993—; active med. staff Natividad Med. Ctr., Salinas, Calif., 1984—2002, chief psychologist, 1984-96. Asst. chief psychiatry svc. Natividad Med. Ctr., 1985—96, acting chief psychiatry, 1988—89, vice-chair medicine dept., 1991—93, sec.-treas. med. staff, 1992—94; cons. med. staff Salinas Valley Meml. Hosp., 1991—2003, Mee Meml. Hosp., 1996—97; dir. tng. Monterey Psychiat. Health Facility, 1996—97, chief clin. staff, 1996—97; expert cons. Calif. Bd. Psychology; cons. psychologist Calif. Forensic Med. Group, 1984—, Calif. Dept. Mental Health Sexually Violent Predator Program, 1996—. Editor: Jour. Thanatology, 1972—76, Cahtexis, 1976—81, Calif. Psychologist, 1988—95. Mem. Gov.'s adv. bd. Agnews Devel. Ctr., San Jose, Calif., 1988—96, chair, 1989—91, 1994—95. Mem.: APA, Internat. Soc. Police Surgeons, Internat. Rorschach Soc., Soc. Personality Assessment, Assn. Treatment Sexual Abuses, Am. Med. Writers Assn., Assn. Advancement Behavior Therapy, Western Psychol. Assn., Forensic Mental Health Assn. Calif., Mid-Coast Psychol. Assn. (sec. 1985, treas. 1986, pres. 1987, Disting. Svc. to Psychology award 1993), Soc. Behavioral Medicine, Calif. Psychol. Assn. (Disting. Svc. award 1989), Nat. Register Health Svc. Providers Psychology. Office Phone: 831-772-0158. Personal E-mail: finnberg@sbcglobal.net.

FINNEGAN, SARA ANNE (SARA F. LYCETT), publisher; b. Balt., Aug. 1, 1939; d. Lawrence Winfield and Rosina Elva (Huber) F.; m. Isaac C. Lycett, Jr., Aug. 31, 1974. BA, Sweet Briar Coll., 1961; MLA, Johns Hopkins U., 1965; exec. program, U. Va. Grad. Sch. Bus., 1977. Tchr., chmn. history dept. Hannah More Acad., Reisterstown, Md., 1961-65; redactor Williams & Wilkins Co., Balt., 1965-66, asst. head redactory, 1966-71, editor book div., 1971-75, assoc. editor-in-chief, 1975-77, v.p., editor-in-chief, 1977-81, pres. book div., 1981-88, group pres., 1988-94; editor Kalends, 1973-78, 89-92; exec. sponsor jour. Histochemistry and Cytochemistry, 1973-77. Dir. Passano Found., 1979-91. Editor Visions, Friends of Art of Sweet Briar Coll. Mag., 2001—. Trustee St. Timothy's Sch., Stevenson, Md., 1974—83; mem. adv. bd. Balt. Ind. Schs. Scholarship Fund, 1977—81; mem. adv. coun. grad. study Coll. Notre Dame of Md., 1983; mem. bd. overseers Sweet Briar Coll., 1987—88, bd. dirs., 1988—2000, chmn.-elect, 1994, chmn., 1995—2000, dir. emerita, 2003—; docent The Walters Art Mus., 1994—; v.p. The Walters Art Mus. Docents, 2000—01, pres., 2001—02; bd. trustees The Walters Art Mus., 2001—02; bd. dirs. The Woman's Indsl. Exch., Balt., 1997—2000, v.p., 1998—2000; bd. dirs. Friends of Art of Sweet Briar Coll., 2000—, The Hamilton St. Club, 2003—, The Art Seminar Group, 2004—. Mem. Assn. Am. Pubs. (exec. coun. profl. and scholarly pub. divsn. 1984-85), Internat. Sci., Tech. and Med. Pubs. Assn. (group exec. 1986-93, chmn.-elect 1988, chmn. 1989-92). Republican. Lutheran. E-mail: sendike@aol.com.

FINNERAN, KATIE, actress; b. Chgo., Jan. 22, 1972; Actor: (Broadway plays) On Borrowed Time, 1991—92, Two Shakespearean Actors, 1992, My Favorite Year, 1992—93, In the Summer House, 1993, The Heiress, 1995, Neil Simon's Proposals, 1997—98, The Iceman Cometh, 1999, Cabaret, 2000—01, Noises Off, 2001—02 (Tony award for Best Performance by a Featured Actor in a Play, 2002, Outer Critics Circle award, Drama Desk award nomination); (films) You've Got Mail, 1998, Liberty Heights, 1999, Night of the Living Dead; (TV series) Sex and the City, 1998, Frasier, 1999, Oz, 2001, Bram and Alice, 2002, Wonderfalls, 2003—. Office: CBS Studios May West Bldg Ste 30 5555 Melrose Ave Los Angeles CA 90023

FINNERTY, ISOBEL, Canadian senator; b. Timmins, ON, Can., July 15, 1930; m. Leslie Finnerty; children: Lorne, John. Grad., Timmins Bus. Coll., 1948. Med. sec., Timmins, 1948—58; internat. trainer Nat. Dem. Inst. for Internat. Affairs, Benin, 1994; senator The Senate of Can., Ottawa, 1999—. Bd. dirs. YMCA, Stratford, 1970—72; mem. fundraising com. Burlington Art Ctr. Liberal. Office: 457-S Centre Block The Senate of Canada Ottawa ON Canada K1A 0A4

FINNERTY, LOUISE HOPPE, beverage and food company executive; b. Alexandria, Va., Jan. 19, 1949; d. William G. and Ruth A. (Ehren) Hoppe; m. John D. Finnerty, May 21, 1988; 1 child, William Patrick Taylor. BA, Va. Commonwealth U., 1971; postgrad., Am. U., 1972—73. Staff asst. to Dr. Henry Kissinger NSC, Washington, 1971-73; adminstrv. asst. Nat. Petroleum Coun., Washington, 1973-75; profl. staff mem. Senate Armed Svc. Com., Washington, 1976-81; spl. asst. Office Legis. Affairs, U.S. Dept. State, Washington, 1981-84, dep. asst. sec. of state, 1984-88; mgr. govt. affairs PepsiCo, Inc., Purchase, NY, 1988-91; dir. govt. affairs PepsiCo Foods and Beverages Internat., Somers, NY, 1991-95; v.p. internat. govt. affairs PepsiCo., Inc., Purchase, 1995—2003, v.p. global health and wellness policy, 2004—. Mem. Nat. Fgn. Trade Coun. (bd. dirs. 1991—), Spring Lake Bath and Tennis Club. Republican. Lutheran. Avocations: reading, gardening, cooking. Home: 400 Park Ave Rye NY 10580-1213 also: 506 2nd Ave Spring Lake NJ 07762-1107 Office: PepsiCo Inc 700 Anderson Hill Rd Purchase NY 10577-1444 E-mail: louise.finnerty@pepsi.com.

FINNEY, ANN JUNG, bank executive; b. Arlington Heights, Ill., June 26, 1936; d. Erich Herman and Miriam Webb Jung; 1 child, Sarah Elizabeth Hernandez. BA, Knox Coll., Galesburg, Ill., 1954—58. Dir. of Pub. & Patient Rels. N.W. Cmty. Hosp., Arlington Heights, 1973—81; docent Robert McCormick Mus., Cantigny, Wheaton, Ill.; v.p. & sr. relationship mgr. Harris Trust & Savs. Bank, Chgo., 1994. V.p. & asst. corp secy Suburban Bancorp, Inc., Palatine, Ill., 1981. Mem.: Inst. for Continued Edn., Univ. (u.). Achievements include Spearheaded campaign to get the Bell Sys. to list paramedic numbers with fire & police listings; member of team taking corp. public & team making hostile takeover bid. Home: 1296 Old Mill Lane Elk Grove Village IL 60007-4089

FINNEY, KATHRYN REBECCA, music educator; b. Nashville, Mar. 13, 1960; d. William Penn and Carol Jane (Binkley) Finney. MusB, BME, Murray State U., 1983; MusM, La. State U., 1984. Tchr. Trigg County Schs., Cadiz, Ky., 1985—91, Glasgow Mid. Sch., Alexandria, Va., 1991—2001, Luther Jackson Mid. Sch., Falls Church, Va., 2001—. Pvt. flute instr., Springfield, Va., 1991—. Dir., dir.: Sch. Band. Recipient Outstanding Svc. award, Am. Philharmonic Youth Orch. Mem.: MENC, Women Band Dirs. Internat., Va. Band and Orch. Dirs. Assn., Fairfax (Va.) Edn. Assn. Office: Luther Jackson Middle School 3020 Gallows Rd Falls Church VA 22042

FINNEY, LYNNE DRATLER, writer, educator, retired psychotherapist, lawyer; b. June 29, 1941; BA cum laude, U. Calif., Berkeley, 1962; JD magna cum laude, Loyola U., L.A., 1967; MSW with honors, U. Utah, Salt Lake City, 1989. Bar: Calif. 1968, D.C. 1975, U.S. Supreme Ct. 1976, UT 1986. With Loeb & Loeb, L.A., 1967—70; asst. county counsel County of Santa Cruz, Calif., 1970—71; counsel U.S. Senator Mike Gravel, Washington, 1973—75; atty. spl. subcom. on investigations of ho. interstate and fgn. commerce com. U.S. Ho. of Reps., Washington, 1973—75; ptnr. Gailor & Elias, Washington, 1975—75; dir. Office of Industry Devel., Washington, 1977—79, Fed. Home Loan Bank Bd., Washington, 1977—79; pres. Internat. Fin. Svcs., 1980—89; atty.-adv. UN policy advisor AID, 1982—83; cons. to dean, adj. prof. U. Utah, Salt Lake City, 1984—89; therapist Adolescent Residential Treatment and Edn. Ctr., Salt Lake City, 1987—88, Sexual Abuse Treatment Ctr., Salt Lake City, 1988—89, pvt. practice, Pk. City, Utah, 1989—96; tchr., trainer Salt Lake City C.C., 1998—2000; motivational spkr.; cons. to law firms and therapists; expert witness; trainer, 1989—. Adj. prof. Loyola U., L.A., 1969—70; asst. prof. U. Santa Clara, 1971—73, dir. law clinic, 1971—73; adj. prof. Wash. Coll. Law Am. U., Washington, 1974—75; adv. bd. exec. women's divsn. Nat. League of Savs. and Loan Assns., 1975—77; mem. Fed. Interagency Task Force on Deregulation, Washington, 1977—79, Fed. Interagency Task Force on Elect. Funds Transfer, Washington, 1977—79, Fed. Interagency Task Force on Cmty. Reinvestment, Washington, 1977—79, Fed. Interagency Task Force on Minority Fin. Insts., Washington, 1977—79; steering com. White Ho. Interagency Task Force on Women, Washington, 1977—79; mem. Pres.'s Task Force on Women Bus. Owners, Washington, 1977—79, Pres.'s Task Force on Small Bus., Washington, 1977—79, Caribbean Basin Devel. Task Force, Washington, 1981—84, U.S. Telecommunications Task Force, Washington, 1982—84; U.S. del. UN Devel. Program Conf., Geneva, 1982; U.S. rep. Diplomatic Mission to evaluate Housing Guarantee Program, Israel, 1983; chair and U.S. rep. Internat. Conf. on Alternative Energy Sources, Thailand, 1984; motivational speaker and trainer for corps, U.'s, women's orgns., spiritual and religious orgns., state and fed. agys., hosps. and gen. pub., 1990—. Co-author: (U.S. Govt. report) A.I.D.'s Housing Investment Guaranty Program in Israel, Project Impact Evaluation, 1983; author: (books) Reach for the Rainbow, 1990, Reach for the Rainbow (2d edit.), 1992, Reach for the Rainbow (Chinese edit.), 2003, Reach for Joy, 1995, Clear Your Past, Change Your Future, 1997, Clear Your Past, Change Your Future (Spanish edit.), 2000, Clear Your Past, Change Your Future (Russian edit.), 2001, Clear Your Past, Change Your Future (Indian edit.), 2001, Windows to the Light, 2001, Train the Trainer Guide, 1997, (CD) Connecting with the Universe, 2004; contbr. chapters to books, articles to profl. jours.; presenter and keynote spkr. (at govt. and profl. confs.). Founder and chair The Network, 1975—84; sponsor Women's Campaign Fund, Washington, 1979—80, adv. bd., 1977—84; bd. dirs. Mexican-Am. Legal Def. Fund, L.A., 1969—70, Legal Aid Soc. Santa Clara County, Calif., 1971—73. Recipient Chmn.'s award for Outstanding Performance, Fed. Home Loan Bank Bd., Washington, 1978, First pl. for Best Pub. Svc. Radio Program, Utah Broadcasters Assn., 1987, Key to City, Mayor of Selma, Ala., 1991; rcognized for creating minority-owned savs. and loan assn. program, Pres. Jimmy Carter, 1978. Mem.: ABA, Utah Bar Assn., Calif. Bar Assn., D.C. Bar Assn., Pk. City Writers. Achievements include overcoming childhood abuse and helping others overcome it. Avocations: helping people lead fulfilling lives, walking in the mountains with my dog and others, snowshoeing, reading, swimming with dolphins. Home and Office: PO Box 681539 Park City UT 84068-1539 Office Phone: 435-649-2378. E-mail: lynnefinney@yahoo.com.

FINNIE, DORIS GOULD, investment company executive; b. Mpls., Sept. 2, 1919; d. Earl Chester and Marie Ethelee (McGulpin) Gould; m. Donald Johnstone Finnie, May 23, 1939; children: Dianne Elaine Boggess, Denise Finnie-Pascento. BA in Journalism, U. Denver, 1941. Office mgr. K&P, Inc., Golden, Colo., 1965-82; exec. dir. Rocky Mountain Coal Mining Inst., Lakewood, 1982—2000; conf. coord. Colo. Mining Assn., 2000—. Editor Procs. of Rocky Mountain Coal Mining Inst., 1982-2000. Founder City of Lakewood, 1968; dir. Alzheimer and Kidney Found., Denver, 1970-72. Recipient Ernest Thompson Seton award Camp Fire, Inc., 1963, St. Barbara's Day medal Colo. Mining Assn., 1999; named Woman of Yr. Denver Area Panhellenic, 1977, Paul Harris fellow Rotary Internat., 1998. Mem. Colo. Soc. Assn. Execs., Meeting Planners Internat. (Humanitarian award 1992), Profl. Conv. Mgmt. Assn., Mortar Board (Disting. Lifetime Mem. Achievement award 2001), Kappa Delta (Outstanding Alumnae award 1959, 74, Order of Emerald 1987). Avocations: gourmet cooking, playing bridge. Office: 11701 W 21st Pl Lakewood CO 80215-1101

FINNIGAN, CLAIRE MARIE, media specialist, librarian; b. Putnam Valley, N.Y., Sept. 4, 1923; d. William Edward and Rose Ann (Crowell) F. BS, SUNY, Geneseo, 1945; MS, Columbia U., N.Y.C., 1952; postgrad., Columbia U., 1963, Westchester C.C., 1994-95. Sch. libr. Eden (N.Y.) Cen. Sch., 1945-47, New Paltz (N.Y.) High Sch., 1947-48, Peekskill (N.Y.) Elem. Schs., 1948-90, ret.; libr. U.S. Naval Air Sta., Atlantic City, N.J., summer 1948; assoc. prof. Queens Coll., Flushing, N.Y., summer 1955. Cons. N.Y. State Edn. Dept., Albany, 1953-57, Franciscan H.S., Lake Mohegan, N.Y., 1984-86. Contbr. articles to profl. jours. Dir. RIF program, Peekskill, 1972-87; sec., bd. dirs. City Libr., Peekskill, 1991-03, sec., 1993-03; bd. dirs. City Mus., Peekskill, 1982-87, sec., 1984-85; vol. Westchester Lighthouse for the Blind, 1992-03, Peekskill Paramount Ctr. for the Arts, 1993-95. Recipient Svc. award Home-Sch. Coun., 1984, Leadership award Bd. of Edn., 1987. Mem. Internat. Reading Assn. (award 1982), Women's Club of Peekskill (sec., treas., bd. dirs. 1962-87), Delta Kappa Gamma, Alpha Omicron (v.p. No. Westchester, N.Y. chpt. 1988-90, pres. 1990-92, treas. 1994-03, comms. state com. 1991-93, travel and study state com. 1993-95). audit com. 1999-03. Avocations: drama, opera, reading, handcrafts, travel. Home: 1 Lakeview Dr Apt 6L Peekskill NY 10566-2238

FINS, ILENE, theater educator, director; b. Bklyn., Apr. 19, 1962; d. Caroline Rothstein Fins. BA, Clemson U., 1984; MFA, U. N.C., Greensboro, 1987. Sr. faculty mem. Seattle Children's Theatre Drama Sch., Seattle, Wash., 1993—; tchg. artist Book-It Repertory, Seattle, Wash., 1996—. Mem.: Soc. Am. Fight Directors, Actors Equity Assn. Democrat. Jewish. Avocation: culinary pursuits.

FINSTER, MARY RUTH, deacon, retired elementary school educator, cosmetics executive; b. Ft. Wayne, Ind., Nov. 3, 1922; d. Charles Madison Pfeiffer and Mary Ruth Marshal; m. Wallace Finster, Mar. 28, 1953 (div. June 1976). BS, Manchester Coll., 1944; MA, Colo. State U., Greeley, 1949; cert. deacon, Sch. Faith Ministry, S. Bend, Ind., 1990. Tchr. Kokomo Ctr. Sch., Ind., 1946—85; deacon St. Andrew Episcopal, Kokomo, 1990—. Cons. Mary Kay, Kokomo, 2003—. Cons. Mayors Task Force for Handicap Issues, Kokomo, 1999—; mem. adv. bd. St. Margaret's House, S. Bend, 1989—; bd. dirs. Am. Cancer Soc., Kokomo, Big Sister, Kokomo, 1977—80, YWCA, Kokomo, 1982—85, ARC, Kokomo, 1996—2000. Mem.: Phi Beta Psi (sec. 1963—2003). Avocations: watercolor painting, travel, reading, water aerobics. Home: 1817 W Monroe Kokomo IN 46901

FINTA, FRANCES MICKNA, secondary school educator; b. Stafford Springs, Conn., June 17, 1927; d. John Joseph Mickna and Mary Frances Breslin; m. Quinn Finta, Aug. 21, 1951; children: John Wright, Susan Frances Finta Phillips. BA in Math., Boston U., 1949; postgrad., U. Va., 1963—69, Prince George's C.C., Largo, Md., 1982, No. Va. C.C., Alexandria, 1982—84, postgrad., 1994, U. Va., Fairfax, 1988—89; MEd in Guidance and Counseling, George Mason U., 1975. Cert. tchr. Va. Food prodn. mgr., dining rm. mgr., waitress, field ops. rep., liaison to airlines Marriott Corp., Marriott In-Flight Svcs., Inc., Washington, 1950—62; tchr., guidance counselor Arlington (Va.) Pub. Schs., 1963—. Substitute tchr. Fairfax (Va.) Pub. Schs., 1972—73; 'substitute tchr. Arlington (Va.) County Pub. Schs., 1972—. Mem. Arlington County Scholarship Fund for Tchrs., Inc., 1995—, sec., 1996—2001, treas., 2002—; mem. Friends of Arlington Parks, 1995—, Maywood Cmty. Assn., 1966—; treas. Washington-Lee H.S. Band Booster Club, 1979—81, Evelyn Staples for County Bd., 1991; vol. coord. David Foster for Sch. Bd., 1994, 2003; Maywood del. Arlington County Civic Fedn., 1982—; mem. Arlingtonians for a Better County, 1999—; membership chmn. Arlington County Civic Fedn., 1984—, treas., 2000—; mem. Arlington County Rep. Com., 1994—, chmn. hdqrs., 2000—, mem. fin. com., 1994—95, canvass chmn., 2000—04, chmn. nominations com., 2000—01; mem. steering com. John Hager for Gov., 2000; del. to state conv. Rep. Party Va., 1996, 1998, 2000, Va. Fedn. Rep. Women, 1996—; mem. credential com. Va. 8th Dist. Rep. Conv., 1998; sec.'s adv. com. Commonwealth of Va., 1998—2002; mem. Organized Women Voters of Arlington, 1997—, mem. nominating com., 2000, treas., 2000—. Recipient Hon. Guardian of Srs.' Rights award, 60 Plus Assn., 1999, Vol. Svc. award, Arlington County Rep. Com., 1995—99, Hilda Griffith Lifetime Achievement award, 1999, Leon Delyannis Cmty. Involvement award, 1997, Cert. of Appreciation, Arlington County Civic Fedn., 1988, 1997, Jour. Newspapers trophy, 2001, Parent Vol. award, Washington-Lee H.S. Band Boosters Club, 1979, Appreciation award, 1981, Parent Vol. award, Woodmont Elem. Sch., 1975, Patrick Henry award, Commonwealth of Va., 2001, Disting. Meritorious Svc. award, Arlington County Civic Found., 2003, Vol. Svc. award, Arlington County Rep. Com., 2003. Mem.: AAUW (del. to Arlington County Civic Fedn. 1994—, co-1st v.p. programs 2001—03, co-1st programs exec. com. 2001—03, exec. com. 2001—, 1st v.p. programs 2002—03, policy chair 2003—), NEA, Arlington Ret. Tchrs. Assn., 1st V.P. Programs, Arlington Edn. Assn., Va. Edn. Assn., Va. Ret. Tchrs. Assn. (life), Arlington County Taxpayers' Assn., Arlington Rep. Women's Club (auditor 1996, asst. treas. 1997, pres. 1998—99, newsletter editor 1998—99, chmn. achievement awards 2000, chmn. bylaws com. 2000, chmn. Barbara Bush literacy com. 2000, dir. 2000—01, chair fin. com. 2002—, auditor 2002—03, fin. chmn. 2003—04). Republican. Roman Catholic. Avocations: civic and political activities, reading. Home: 3317 23d St N Arlington VA 22201-4310

FINUCANE, ANNE M. communications and marketing executive; married; 4 children. BA with honors, U. N.H. Pub. info. officer Mayor of City of Boston; dir. creative svcs. Sta. WBZ-TV, Boston; head creative svcs. Hill, Holliday, Connors, Cosmopulos, Inc., Boston, dir. account mgmt., dir. corp. devel.; prin. Anne Finucane Mktg. and Telecomm., Boston; sr. v.p., dir. corp. mktg. and comm. Fleet Fin. Group, Boston, 1995—. Bd. dirs. Internat. Ctr. for Journalists. Bd. dirs. Urban Improv, Emerson Coll., New Eng. Coun., Mass. Women's Forum; co-chmn. tech. divsn. United Way of Mass. Bay Campaign, 1995, 96; mem. adv. coun. Children's Defense Fund, Washington, Conservation Law Found. Office: Fleet Fin Group Corp Mktg & Comm One Federal St Boston MA 02110 Fax: 617-346-4740.

FIOCK, SHARI LEE, not-for-profit developer; b. Weed, Calif., Oct. 25, 1941; d. Webster Bruce and Olevia May (Pruett) Fiock; children from previous marriage: Webster Clinton Pfingsten, Sterling Curtis. Cert., Art Instrn. Sch., Mpls., 1964. Copywriter Darron Assocs., Eugene, Oreg., 1964-66; staff artist Oreg. Holidays, Springfield, 1966-69, 71; co-owner, designer Artre Enterprises, Eugene, 1969-74; design entrepreneur Shari & Assocs., Yreka, Calif., 1974-99; exec. dir. Siskiyou County Econ. Devel. Coun., Yreka, Calif., 1999—. Cons., devel. sec. Cascade World Four Season Resort, Siskiyou County, Calif., 1980—86; owner Coyote pub., 1991—99; adminstrv. asst., coord. regional catalog Gt. Northern Corp. U.S. Dept. Commerce and Econ. Devel., 1994—96; local cons. CalEnergy Co., Inc., 1998—99. 5 ton chain saw sculpture, Oreg. Beaver, 1967, Holiday Fun Book, 1978; author, illustrator: Family Reunions and Clan Gatherings, 1991, Blue Goose Legend, 1995, Blue Goose Legend, rev. edit., 1998; editor: Choo and Moo Cookbook, 1998. Counselor Boy Scouts Am., 1983—91; co-creator Klamath Nat. Forest Interpretive Mus., 1979—91; residential capt. United Way, Eugene, 1972; rschr. Beaver Ofcl. State Animal, Eugene, 1965—71. Mem.: Siskiyou Writers Club (co-founder, pres. 1986—). Home: 406 Walters Ln Yreka CA 96097-9704 Office Phone: 530-842-1638. E-mail: sharifiock@snowcrest.net.

FIORI, PAMELA, publishing executive, magazine editor, writer; b. Newark, Feb. 26, 1944; d. Edward and Rita (Rascati) F.; m. Colton Givner. BA cum laude, Jersey City State Coll., 1966. Tchr. English Gov. Livingston High Sch., Berkeley Heights, N.J., 1966-67; assoc. editor Holiday Mag., N.Y.C., 1968-71, Travel & Leisure Mag., N.Y.C., 1971-74, sr. editor, 1974-75, editor-in-chief, 1975-80; editor-in-chief, exec. v.p. Am. Express Pub. Corp. (Travel & Leisure/Food & Wine), N.Y.C., 1980-89, editorial dir., exec. v.p., 1989-93; editor-in-chief Town & Country, N.Y.C., 1993—. Columnist: Travel & Leisure, 1976—89, Town & Country, 1993—; contbr. articles to periodicals. Bd. dirs. Jazz at Lincoln Ctr., East Side Houses Settlement. Recipient Chevalier de l'Ordre du Merite, 1985, Melva C. Pederson award for disting. travel journalism Am. Soc. Travel Afts., 1992, Outstanding Woman of the 90s award Found. for Neurosurg. Rsch., 1994, Bus. award Nat. Italian Am. Found., 1996. Office: Town & Country 1700 Broadway New York NY 10019-5905

FIORINA, CARLETON S. (CARLY FIORINA), computer company executive; b. Austin, Tex., Sept. 6, 1954; married, Frank Fiorina. BA in Medieval History and Philosophy, Stanford U., 1976; MBA, U. Md., 1980; MSc, MIT, 1989; postgrad., UCLA. Account exec. Long Lines AT&T, 1980, sr. v.p. Global Mktg., pres., AT&T network systems, N. Am., 1994—95; exec. v.p. corp. ops. Lucent Technologies, Murray Hill, NJ, 1995—96, pres., consumer products bus., 1996—97, group pres. Global Svc. Provider bus., 1997—99; pres. Hewlett-Packard, Palo Alto, 1999—2000, CEO, 1999—, chmn. bd. dirs., 2000—. Bd. dirs., PowerUp, Hewlett-Packard, 1999-, Merck & Co. Inc., 1999-2001, Cisco Sys., 2001-, N.Y. Stock Exch., 2004-; mem., U.S. China Bd. Trade. Named one of Fortune Mag. Most Powerful Women in Am. Bus., Hon. Fellow London Bus. Sch., 2001. Office: Hewlett-Packard 3000 Hanover St Palo Alto CA 94304-1181

FIOTI, JEAN K. pharmacist; b. Wilkes-Barre, Pa., Dec. 4, 1959; d. William Raymond and Jean (Welebob) Kustis; m. Vito Joseph Fioti, Oct. 24, 1987; children: Christoper Joseph, Maria Celesta. BS in Pharmacy, Duquesne U., 1982; PharmD, U. Md. at Baltimore, 2000. Registered Pharmacist, 1982. Pharmacy mgr. Rite Aid Corp., Wilkes-Barre, Pa., 1982—90; cons. pharmacist Beverly Enterprises, Wilkes-Barre, 1995; v.p. Precision Mgmt. Cons., Inc., Wilkes-Barre, 1995—97; pharmaceutical sales rep. Bayer, Inc., West Haven, Conn., 1990—95; market devel. assoc. Merck, Inc., West Point, Pa., 1995—96; sr. clin. hosp. rep. Genentech, Inc., S. San Francisco, 1996—98; mid-atlantic regional cons. cardiology svcs. Schering-Plough, Kenilworth, NJ, 1998—99; immunology specialist Centocor, Inc., Malvern, Pa., 1999—2001, clin. info. scientist, med. affairs-immunology, 2001— Instr. SAT Princeton Review, 1996-98. Mem. Lackawanna Co. Pharmaceutical Assn. (v.p. 1996-97). Avocations: music, archaeology, tutoring. Office: Centocor Inc 550 Lantern Hill Rd Shavertown PA 18708-9451

FIRCHOW, EVELYN SCHERABON, German language and literature educator, writer; b. Vienna; came to U.S., 1951, naturalized, 1964; d. Raimund and Hildegard (Nickl) Scherabon; m. Peter E. Firchow, 1969; children: Felicity (dec. 1988), Pamina. BA, U. Tex., 1956; MA, U. Man., 1957; PhD, Harvard U., 1963. Instr. coll. math. Balmoral Hall Sch., Winnipeg, Man., Can., 1960-61; tchg. fellow in German Harvard U., Cambridge, Mass., 1957-58, 61-62; lectr. German U. Md. in Munich, 1961; instr. German U. Wis., Madison, 1962-63, asst. prof., 1963-65; assoc. prof. German U. Minn., Mpls., 1965-69, prof. German and Germanic philology, 1969—; vis. prof. U. Fla., Gainesville, 1973; Fulbright rsch. prof. Iceland, 1966-67, 80, 94; vis. rsch. prof. Nat. Cheng Kung U., Tainan, Taiwan, 1982-83; permanent vis. prof. Jilin U., Changchun, China, 1987—. Vis. prof. U. Graz, Austria, 1989, 91, 2002-03, U. Vienna, Austria, 1995, U. Bonn, 1996, Nat. U. Costa Rica, 2000. Editor and author: (under name E.S. Coleman) Taylor Starck-Festschrift, 1964, Stimmen aus dem Stundenglas, 1968, (under name E.S. Firchow) Studies by Einar Haugen, 1972, Studies for Einar Haugen, 1972, Was Deutsche lesen, 1973, Deutung und Bedeutung, 1973, Elucidarius in Old Norse Translation, 1989, The Old Norse Elucidarius: Original Text and English Translation, 1992, Notker der Deutsche von St. Gallen: De interpretatione, 1995, Categoriae, 2 Vols., 1996, De nuptiis Philologiae et Mercurii, 2 Vols., 1999, Notker der Deutsche von St. Gallen (950-1022): Ausführliche Bibliographie, 2000, De consolatione Philosophiae, 3 vols., 2003, Reluctant Modernists, Festschrift Peter Firchow, 2002, Gottfried von Strassburg: Tristan und Isolde, 2004; translator: Einhard: Vita Caroli Magni, Das Leben Karls des Grossen, 1968, 84, 95, Einhard: Vita Caroli Magni, The Life of Charlemagne, 1972, 85, Icelandic Short Stories, 1974, 87, East German Short Stories, 1979, (with P.E. Firchow) Alois Brandstetter, The Abbey, 1998; dir., editor Computer Clearing-House Project for German and Medieval Scandinavian, to 2000; assoc. editor Germanic Notes and Revs., Am. Linguistics, Germanic Linguistics; contbr. articles and book revs. to profl. jours. Fulbright scholar Tex., 1951-52; fellow Alexander von Humboldt-Stiftung, Munich, 1960-61, Tuebingen, 1974, Marburg, 1981, Goettingen, 1985, Tokyo, 1991, Marburg and Berlin, 1993, Bonn, 2001, Fulbright Found., Iceland, 1967-68, 80, 94, Austrian Govt., 1977, NEH, 1980-81, Am. Inst. Indian Studies, 1988, BUSH fellow, 1989, Thor Thors fellow, 1994, Mc Knight summer fellow, 1995, 96, 99, 2004, Deutscher Akademischer Austausdienst (DAAD) rsch. fellow, 2000; elected hon. mem. Multilingual Rsch. Ctr., Brussels, 1986. Mem. AAUP, MLA (chmn. divsn. German lit. to 1700 1979-80, 93-96, vice chmn. pedagogical seminar for Germanic philology 1979-86, 91-93, chair 1994), Medieval Acad. Am., Soc. German-Am. Studies (chair Linguistics I 1992), Internat. Comparative Lit. Assn., Soc. for Advancement Scandinavian Studies (chmn. Germanic philology 1979, text editing 1980, linguistics 1984, computers and Old Norse 1985), Assn. for Lang. and Linguistic Computing (founding mem.), Am. Comparative Lit. Assn., Midwest Modern Lang. Assn. (chmn. German I 1965-66, chmn. Scandinavian 1979), Am. Assn. Tchrs. German, Mediävisten Verband, Soc. for Germanic Philology, Österreichische Germanisten-Gesellschaft, Assn. Lit. Scholars and Critics. Office: U Minn Dept German Minneapolis MN 55455 E-mail: firch001@umn.edu.

FIREBAUGH, FRANCILLE MALOCH, university official; b. El Dorado, Ark., July 15, 1933; d. Delton Verdis and Dorothy Lucille (Measeles) Maloch; m. John David Firebaugh, Dec. 28, 1970. BS, U. Ark., 1955; MS, U. Tenn., 1956; PhD, Cornell U., 1962. Instr. U. Tex., Austin, 1956-58; asst. prof. home econs. Ohio State U., Columbus, 1962-65, assoc. prof., 1965-69, prof., 1969-88; dir. Sch. Home Econs., 1973-82; acting v.p. agrl. adminstrn.; exec. dean of agr., home econs., natural resources, 1982-83; assoc. provost Office Acad. Affairs, 1983-84; vice provost for internat. affairs, 1984-88; acting provost, v.p. acad. affairs, 1985-86; dean coll. human ecology Cornell U., Ithaca, NY, 1988-99, dir. spl. projects office of pres. and provost, 2000—01, vice provost for land grant affairs, spl. asst. to the pres., 2001—. Mem. joint com. on agrl. research and devel. Bd. Internat. Food and Agr., 1982-87. Author: Home Management: Context and Concepts, 1975, Family Resource Management, 1981, 88. Bd. dirs. Columbus Coun. on World Affairs, 1987-88, Boyce Thompson Inst. for Plant Rsch., 1991-97; moderator First Baptist Ch., 1981-83; bd. dirs. Cayuga Med. Ctr., 1992-2001, Panamerican Agr. Sch., Zamorano, Honduras, 1994—, Kendal at Ithaca, 1995-2003; Families and Work Inst., N.Y.C., 1995—; trustee Ithaca (N.Y.) Coll., 2000—, Cmty. Found. of Tompkins County, 2000-02. Mem. Nat. Coun. Family Rels., AAAS, Am. Home Econs. Found. (bd. dirs. 1987-90), Am. Assn. of Family and Consumer Scis., Ohio State U. Faculty Club (pres. 1988), Assn. Women in Devel. (sec. 1988-89), Sigma Xi, Sigma Delta Epsilon, Kappa Omicron Nu, Phi Upsilon Omicron, Gamma Sigma Delta, Phi Kappa Phi, Epsilon Sigma Phi. Office: Cornell U Office of Provost 449 Day Hall Ithaca NY 14853-2801 Office Phone: 607-255-1256. E-mail: fmfl@cornell.edu.

FIREHOCK, BARBARA A. interior designer; b. Alexandria, Va., Feb. 2, 1944; d. George W. Jr. and Geraldine Tinsley (Wallin) Sickler; m. Scott Walton Ripley, Dec. 27, 1966 (div.); m. Raymond B. Firehock, Jr.; 1 child, Christopher Francis. BA, U. N. Tex., 1966; postgrad., U. Md., 1976-77. Vol. Peace Corps, Colombia, 1967-69; owner Walnut Hill Interiors, 1981—; instr. in interior design Charles County C.C., LaPlata, 1990; site supr./interior design internship U. Md., College Park, 1992. Program com. Matawoman Creek Arts Ctr., Charles County, Md., 1995-96; fundraiser The Gallery Com. of Charles County, 1988-94; interior designer Fredericksburg Area Svc. League Decorator Showhouse, 1997—, So. Md. Decorator Showhouse, 1998. Design work featured in Town and Country, 1997, Community Carousel Weekly Show/Prestige Cable, Fredericksburg, The Maryland Independent, 1991, The Maryland House and Garden Pilgrimage, 1995-96, Traditional Home, 1999. Spl. events chair Charles County Garden Club of Md.; chair Christ Ch. Concert Series, LaPlata, 1995; charter mem. Blaetsfriars Theater, Staunton, Hist. Staunton Found. Recipient Residential Restoration award Hist. Staunton Found., 2003; named Woman of Yr. Bus. and Profl. Women, Charles County, 1982. Fellow Nat. Trust for Hist. Preservation (nat. capitol area fellow, design assoc.); Mem. ASID, Interior Design Soc. (pres. Md. chpt.), AAUW (pres., v.p., cultural chair Charles County chpt.), Chi Omega (rush info. chair for So. Md. 1993-98). Democrat. Episcopalian. Avocations: horseback riding, gardening, needlework, genealogy. also: 330 Vine St Staunton VA 24401-4354 Office Phone: 540-886-5898.

FIRESTONE, NANCY B. federal judge; b. Manchester, N.H., Oct. 17, 1951; d. Albert and Bernice (Brown) F. BA, Washington U., St. Louis, 1973; JD, U. Mo., 1977. Bar: Mo. 1977, U.S. Ct. Appeals (2nd, 4th, 5th, 6th, 9th, 8th and 10th cirs.). Trial atty. U.S. Dept. Justice, Washington, 1977-84, asst. chief, 1984-85, dep. chief environ. enforcement, 1985-89, dept. asst. atty. gen., environment & natural resources div., 1995—98; assoc. dep. adminstr. EPA, 1989-92, adminstrv. judge, 1992-95; judge U.S. Ct. of Fed. Claims, 1998—. Adj. prof. Georgetown U. Law Ctr., 1986—. Mem. ABA.*

FIRESTONE, SUSAN PAUL, artist; b. Madison, Wis., Nov. 13, 1946; d. John Robertson and Sue Hadaway Paul; m. John D. Firestone, Nov. 30, 1943 (div.); children: Mary, Lucy. BA, Mary Baldwin Coll., 1968; MFA, Am. U., 1972; MA in Art Therapy, NYU, 2002. Mem. Art Table, N.Y.C., Mus. bd. Corcoran Gallery, Washington, collectors com. Nat. Gallery, Washington; trustee Skowhegan Sch., N.Y.C.; mem. faculty Corcoran Coll. Art & Design. Artist/author: Armour-Amour, 1992; solo exhbns. include Gallery K, Washington, 1983-95, Harmony Hall, Washington, Md., 1993, NIH, Bethesda, Md., 1992, Peat Marwick Inaugural Show, Washington, 1988, Covington and Burling, Washington, 1985, others; group exhbns. Inst. of Contemporary Art, Boston, 1995, San Diego Art Inst., 1995, Nat. Mus. of Women in Arts, 1994, Drawing Ctr., N.Y., 1993, Ctr. for Visual Arts, U. Toledo, 1993, Coll. of Notre Dame, Md., 1993, Minot (N.D.) Art Gallery, 1993, Art Works Gallery, Green Bay, Wis., 1993, others; various pub. and pvt. collections. Resident Pyramid Atlantic, Riverdale, Md., 1993; cultural exch. student USIS/Morocco, 1994. Office: Redstone Studio 59 Wooster St New York NY 10012-4349 E-mail: rubilite@aol.com.

FIRSTENBERG, JEAN PICKER, film institute executive; b. N.Y.C., Mar. 13, 1936; d. Eugene and Sylvia (Moses) Picker; m. Paul Firstenberg, Aug. 9, 1956 (div. July 1980); children: Debra, Douglas BS summa cum laude, Boston U., 1958. Assoc. producer Altman Prodns., Washington, 1965-66; media advisor J. Walter Thompson, N.Y.C., 1969-72; asst. for spl. projects Princeton (N.J.) U., 1972-74, dir. publs., 1974-76; program officer Markle Found., N.Y.C., 1976-80; dir., CEO Am. Film Inst., L.A., Washington, 1980—. Bd. dirs. Trans-Lux Corp.; former chmn. nat. adv. bd. Peabody Broadcasting Awards; bd. dirs. Trans-Lux Corp. Former trustee Boston U.; mem. adv. bd. Will Rogers Inst., N.Y.C.; chmn., bd. advisors Film Dept. N.C. Sch. of Arts. Recipient Alumni award for disting. service to profession Boston U., 1982; seminar and prodn. chairs at directing workshop for women named in her honor Am. Film Inst., 1986 Mem. Women in Film (Crystal award 1990), Trusteeship for Betterment of Women, Acad. Motion Picture Arts and Scis. Office: Am Film Inst 2021 N Western Ave PO Box 27999 Los Angeles CA 90027-0999

FISCHBACH, MICHELLE L. state legislator; b. Nov. 3, 1965; m. Scott Fischbach; 2 children. BA, St. Cloud State U. Mem. Minn. Senate from 14th dist., St. Paul, 1996—. Home: 416 Burr St Paynesville MN 56362-1110 Office: 149 State Office Bldg 100 Constitution Ave Saint Paul MN 55155-1232

FISCHBACH, RUTH LINDA, ethics educator, social scientist, researcher; b. NYC, June 7, 1940; d. Edward Joseph and Bess (Wolsk) Zeitlin; m. Gerald David Fischbach, July 8, 1962; children: Elissa, Peter, Mark and Neal (twins). Attended, Mt. Holyoke Coll., 1958-60; BS, RN, Cornell U., 1963; MS, Boston U., 1975, PhD, 1983; MPE, Washington U., 1990. Dir. patient edn. Beth Israel Hosp., Boston, 1978-80; postdoctoral fellow Washington U. Sch. Medicine, St. Louis, 1983-86, asst. rsch. prof., 1986-90, asst. dean, 1989-90; asst. prof. Harvard Med. Sch., Boston, 1990-98; sr. advisor for biomed. ethics Office of Dir. for Extramural Rsch./NIH, Bethesda, Md., 1998—2001; prof. bioethics Coll. Physicians and Surgeons, Mailman Sch. Pub. Health Columbia U., NYC, 2001—, dir. Ctr. Bioethics, 2001—. Dir. Program for Humanities in Medicine Washington U. Sch. Medicine, 1988—90, Program in Practice of Sci. Investigation Harvard Med. Sch., 1990—98; bd. dir. Pub. Responsibility in Med. and Rsch., Boston, 1992—; reviewer Univ.-wide AIDS Rsch. Program State Calif., 1995; adv. bd. Beth Israel Clin. Investigator Tng. Program, Boston, 1995—; vice chmn. bd. dirs. Pub. Responsibility in Med. and Rsch., Boston, 2002—. Producer: (dramatization) Miss Evers' Boys, 1993; editl. bd. Sci. & Engring. Ethics, 1994—; contbr. articles to profl. jours., chpts. to books. Pres. Lincoln Sch. PTA, Brookline, Mass., 1978—80; vol. Mass. Coalition of Battered Women Svc. Groups, Boston, 1993—98; trustee Penzance Point, 1998—, Parc Somerset Condo., Chevy Chase, Md., Morris Jumel Mansion, 2002—; med. and profl. adv. coun. Gold Found., 2002—; bd. dirs. Joint Com. on Status of Women, Boston, 1990—97. Fellow Exec. Inst. of Advanced Study, St. Louis, 1988; recipient Disting. Alumna award Cornell U., 2003. Mem. Applied Rsch. Ethics Nat. Assn. (bd. dirs. 1994—), Mass. Bioethics Forum (bd. dirs. 1994—), Md. Mothers of Twins (pres. 1969-70), Sigma Theta Tau. Avocations: horticulture, travel, music. Home: 100 Riverside Dr # 3A New York NY 10024

FISCHBARG, ZULEMA F. pediatrician, educator; b. Buenos Aires, Mar. 22, 1937; arrived in U.S., 1962; d. Naun and Esther (Pollner) Fridman; m. Jorge Fischbarg; children: Gabriel Julian, Victor Ernesto. MD, U. Buenos Aires, 1960. Pediatric intern Children's Hosp., Louisville, 1962-63, resident in pediatrics, 1963, chief resident in pediatrics, 1964; fellow hematology Michael Reese Med. Ctr., Chgo., 1964-66, Presbyn. St. Lukes Hosp., Chgo., 1966-67; fellow pediatric hematology Children's Meml. Hosp., Chgo., 1967-68; asst. clin. pediatrician U. Chgo., 1968-69; instr. in pediatrics Cornell U. Med. Sch., N.Y.C., 1970-72, asst. prof. in pediatrics, 1972-76; assoc. prof. clin. pediatrics Weil Med. Coll., Cornell U., N.Y.C., 1978—; assoc. attending pediatrician N.Y. Hosp., Queens, N.Y.C., 1978—; attending in pediatrics St. John's Hosp./Cath. Med. Ctr., N.Y.C.; med. specialist, sch. health Dept. Health, N.Y.C., 1994—. Assoc. in pediat. Lenox Hill Hosp., N.Y.C.; instr. in medicine Ill. U., Chgo., 1967—68; assoc. attending physician N.Y. Hosp., N.Y.C., 1972—. Fellow: Am. Acad. Pediat. Democrat. Jewish. Home: 175 E 62nd St # 6D New York NY 10021-7626 Office: 37-51 72d St Jackson Heights NY 11372 Fax: 718-651-8225.

FISCHER, COLLEEN THERESA, music educator; b. Arlington, Minn., Jan. 11, 1966; d. Gerald and Jeanne Catherine Kreger; m. David Alan Fischer, Aug. 14, 1993; 1 child, Andrea Lauren. BS, Mankato State U., 1984—88. Lic. Tchr. Dept. of Children, Families, and Learning, Minn., 2002, cert. Music Contest Judge Minn. State H.S. League, Minn., 2003. Camp dir. Lake Wash. Band Camp/Mankato State U., Minn., 1989—97; band dir. Pine River Pub. Schools, Minn., 1988—89, Richfield Jr. H.S., Minn., 1989—97, Centennial Mid. Sch., Cir. Pines, Minn., 1997—98, Richfield Sr. H.S., Minn. Guest condr. Madelia Jr. H.S. Band Festival, Minn., 2002; presenter Minn. Collegiate MENC, 1998; guest condr. Sibley East Pub. Schools Elem. Band Festival, Arlington, Minn., Mankato State U. Jr. H.S. Honor Band Festival, Minn., 1996—97. Recipient Richfield H.S. Nat. Honor Soc. Tchr. Appreciation award, Richfield H.S. Nat. Honor Soc., 2003, Disting. Svc. award, Lake Wash. Band Camps/Mankato State U., 1997, Richfield Pub. Schools Gold Helmet award, Richfield Pub. Schools Dedicated Fund, 2003; Tau State Recruitment grant, Delta Kappa Gamma, 1988. Mem.: Edn. Richfield (v.p. 1994—97), Edn. Minn., Minn. Band Directors Assn., Minn. Music Educators Assn., Music Educators Nat. Conf. Dfl. Catholic. Avocations: music, travel, sewing, woodwinds. Office: Richfield Pub Schools 7001 Harriet Ave So Richfield MN 55423

FISCHER, DALE SUSAN, judge; b. East Orange, N.J., Oct. 17, 1951; d. Edward L. and Audrey (Tenner) F.D. Student, Dickinson Coll., 1969-70; BA magna cum laude, U. So. Fla., 1977; JD, Harvard U., 1980. Bar: Calif. 1980. Ptnr. Kindel & Anderson L.L.P., L.A., 1980-96; spl. counsel Heller Ehrman White & McAuliffe, L.A., 1996-97; judge L.A. Mcpl. Ct., 1997, L.A. Superior Ct., 2000; dist. judge U.S. Dist. Ct. Ctrl. Dist. Calif., L.A., 2003—. Faculty Nat. Inst. Trial Advocacy; lawyer in classroom Constl. Rights Found.; moderator, panelist How to Win Your Case with Depositions. Recipient Lawyer in Classroom award Constl. Rights Found. Mem. Nat. Assn. Women Judges, Am. Judicature Soc., Calif. Assn. Judges, So. Calif. Litigation Inn of Ct. (past pres.). Office: US Dist Ct 255 E Temple St Rm 830 Los Angeles CA 90012 Office Phone: 213-894-7115. E-mail: Dale_Fischer@cacd.uscourts.gov.

FISCHER, ELIZABETH (BETSY), television producer; b. New Orleans, Feb. 17, 1970; d. George Julius and Sally (Ford) Fischer; m. Gene Robert Raineri, Oct. 21, 1995; 1 child, Ella Elizabeth Raineri. BA cum laude, Am. U., 1992, MA, 1996. Polit. rschr. NBC News Meet the Press and Polit. Unit, Washington, 1992-94, assoc. prodr., 1995-96, prodr., 1997, sr. prodr., 1998—2002, exec. prodr., 2002—. Mem. Jr. League Washington. Nominee Emmy, Nat. Acad. TV Arts and Scis., 1997; recipient Walter Cronkite/USC Annenberg award. Mem.: Am. Women Radio and TV, Radio and TV News Dirs. Assn., Nat. Press Club, Am. New Women's Club, Delta Gamma. Presbyterian. Avocations: racquetball, genealogy, reading, tennis. Home: 6525 Orland St Falls Church VA 22043-1865 Office: NBC News Meet the Press 4001 Nebraska Ave NW Washington DC 20016-2733

FISCHER, ELLEN E. art gallery director; b. Oak Park, Ill., Aug. 17, 1956; parents Ralph F. and Edith V. Fischer. BFA, Ind. U.-Purdue U., 1978; MFA, Sch. Art Inst. Chgo., 1981. Curator Greater Lafayette Mus. Art, Lafayette, Ind., 1989—97; curator exhbns. and collections Ctr. for Arts, Vero Beach, Fla., 1997—2000; dir. The Littleton Collection, Fort Pierce, Fla., 2001—. Grant panelist Fla. Dept. State, Tallahassee, 2000. Author: (exhbn. catalog) Broken Silences: The Collages of Paul Jenkins, 2000; editor: The Bryna Collection of Mexican Art, 2000; contbr. articles to profl. jours. Sec. Cultural Coun. Indian River County, 2002—. Scholar, Skowhegan Sch. Painting and Sculpture, 1978. Mem.: Ind. U. Alumni Assn. Office: Littleton Collection 3890 N US 1 Fort Pierce FL 34946 Office Phone: 772-595-0845 Business E-Mail: hkl@tctg.com.

FISCHER, EMILY CHRISTINA, primary school educator; b. St. Louis, Mar. 26, 1979; d. James Edward and Anne Marie Fischer. BA in Deaf Edn., Fontbonne Coll., Clayton, Mo., 2001. Asst. mgr. The Magic Ho., St. Louis Children's Mus., St. Louis, 1996—2001; 3rd grade tchr. St. Ambrose Cath. Sch., St. Louis, 2002—. Recipient Nina Shavers Award for outstanding leadership, John F. Kennedy HS Pom Squad, 1997, trophy, Bellarmine Speech League, 1993, Dancing awards, various dance competitions. Roman Catholic. Office: St Ambrose Catholic Sch 5110 Wilson Ave Saint Louis MO 63110

FISCHER, IRENE KAMINKA, geodesist, researcher, retired mathematician; b. Vienna, July 27, 1907; came to U.S., 1941; d. Armand and Clara (Loewy) Kaminka; m. Eric Fischer, Dec. 21, 1930; children: Gay A., Michael M.J. MA, U. Vienna/Vienna Inst. Tech., 1931; postgrad., U. Va., Georgetown U., 1950-57; D. in Engring., U. Karlsruhe/Tech. Inst., Karlsruhe, Fed. Republic Germany, 1975. Tchr. secondary schs., Vienna, 1931-38; tchr. secondary schs. and colls. Washington, D.C., Mass., N.Y., Mass, 1941-45; rschr. MIT, Cambridge, Mass., 1942-44; rsch. geodesist Army Map Svc., Def. Mapping Agy., Washington, 1952-77. Author: Geometry, 1965, Basic Geodesy, 1972, The Geoid--What's That?, 1973, Geodesy-What's That?, 1988; contbr. hundreds of articles to profl. jours. Recipient medals Dept. Army, 1957, 66, 67, Dept. Def., 1967, Def. Mapping Agy., 1971, Nat. Civil Svc. League Career award, 1976; named Fed. Retiree of Yr. Nat. Assn. Retired Fed. Employees, 1978. Fellow Am. Geophys. Union, Internat. Assn. Geodesy (sec. sect. V 1963-71, chmn. study groups 1963-75); mem. Nat. Acad. Engring. Home: 50 Sutherland Rd #403 Brighton MA 02135

FISCHER, LUCY ROSE, gerontologist, researcher, artist; b. Wilmington, Del., Sept. 15, 1944; d. Henry Rose, Helen Rose; m. Mark Samuel Fischer; 1 child, Jeremy (Yirmi). PhD, U. Mass., 1979. Asst. prof. U. of Minn., Mpls., 1979—87; assoc. prof. St. Olaf Coll., Northfield, Minn., 1987—89; sr. rsch. scientist Wilder Rsch. Ctr., St. Paul, 1989—92; sr. rsch. investigator HealthPartners Rsch. found., Mpls., 1992—2002. Author: Linked Lives: Adult Daughters and Their Mothers, 1986, Older Volunteers, 1993 (NSFRE Research Prize, 1994); editor: Healthy Outcomes, 1994—2003; contbr. over 90 articles to profl. jours.; in one-woman and group exhbns., exhibitions include Creating and Connecting, Coll. of St. Catherine, 1997, Minn. State Fair Art Pavillion, 1999, 2003 (hon. mention), Phipps Ctr. for Arts, 1999. Chair Aging Panel-Jewish Fedn, Minneapolis, 1983—86. Grantee Rsch. grant, Blandin Found., 1988, Nat. Inst. Aging, 1999—2002, MacArthur Found., 1999—2001. Fellow: Gerontol. Soc. Am. (chair qualitative interest group 1995—98).

FISCHER, MARY ELIZABETH, library director; b. Buffalo, N.D., Feb. 14, 1935; d. Patrick Francis and Elizabeth Sarah (Laufenberg) Killoran; m. Clair Arthur Fischer, Sep. 27, 1952 (dec. Aug. 1967); children: Judith, Barbara, Veronica, Theresa, Ruth, Raymond, Linda, Rudolph; m. Donald Edward Anderson, Apr. 17, 1995 (dec. Oct. 2002). BS in Edn. summa cum laude, Valley City (N.D) State U., 1978. Librn. Valley City Barnes County Pub. Libr., 1978-88, libr. dir., 1988—, ADA promotor, 1990—. Instrumental in completion of handicapped-accessible addition to VCBC Pub. Libr., providing internet access to libr. users, card catalog to patrons and collection automation, more internet computers, 2002, web catalog, 2002, libr. col. Libr. on Web! Columnist Valley City Times Record, 1978—; contbr. poetry to anthologies, stories to collections. Active St. Catherine's Ch., Valley City, 1970-79; 4H leader Hobart Honeydews (5 yr. leadership pin 1975), Valley City, 1960-79; active local PTA, 1960-79; club and orgn. spkr.; active bible study, prayer groups; mem. Friends of the Libr. (facilitator, 1988—); mem. Art Coun.; contbr. Cmty. Planning; mem. Cath. Daus. of Am., 2003. Recipient various poetry awards, 1990—, Universal Access award Mayor's Com. on Employment of People with Disabilities, 1999; named Famous Poet, Famous Poetry Soc., 2000. Mem. N.D. Libr. Assn. Democrat. Roman Catholic. Avocations: bird watching, gardening, cooking, handicrafts. Home: 3420 113th Ave SE Valley City ND 58072-9430 Office: Valley City Barnes County Libr 410 Central Ave N Valley City ND 58072-2949 E-mail: mafische@ictc.com.

FISCHER, MICHELLE K. lawyer; BA in Econs. magna cum laude with distinction, Yale U., 1986; JD with honors, U. Chgo., 1989. Bar: Ohio 1989, D.C. 1991. With Jones Day, Cleve., 1989—, ptnr., 1999—. Mem.: ABA (antitrust law sect.), Cleve. Bar Assn., Ohio State Bar Assn. (bd. govs. antitrust law sect.). Office: Jones Day North Point 901 Lakeside Ave [illegible]

FISCHER, PAMELA SHADEL, public relations executive; b. Harrisburg, Pa., Feb. 28, 1959; d. Richard Lee and Pauline Louise (Nies) S.; m. Charles J. Fischer Jr., June 11, 1983; 1 child, Zachary Joseph. BA in English, Lebanon Valley Coll., Annville, Pa., 1981. Cert. child passenger safety technician AAA. Pub. rels. coord. Pa. Optometric Assn., Harrisburg, 1981-83; pub. rels. dir. Morris Ctr. YMCA, Cedar Knolls, NJ, 1983-85; pub. rels. coord. Delta Dental Plan of N.J., Parsippany, 1985-86; pub. rels. mgr. AAA N.J. Automobile Club, Florham Park, NJ, 1986-91, mgr. mem. svcs. and pub. affairs, 1991-94, asst. v.p. pub. rels. & safety, 1994-96, asst. v.p. pub. affairs and fin. svcs., 1996—2002, v.p. pub. affairs and fin. svcs., 2002—. Corp. capt. United Way of Morris County, Cedar Knolls, 1985—90, chmn. publs. com., 1989—90, chmn. mktg. com., 1991—95, v.p. mktg., 1996, mem. women's leadership initiative exec. com., 1999—, vice chmn., 2002—03, chmn., 2003—; career counselor Lebanon Valley Coll., 1983—90, bd. dirs. of exec. com., vol. v.p. mktg., 1996—99, alumni amb., 2004—; mem. hwy. traffic safety policy adv. com. Gov.'s Office, 1998—; chair legis. com. Gateway Tourism Coun., 1997—2000; mem. Driver Edn. Commn. N.J., 1999—; bd. dirs. First Night of Morris County, 1999—2002, chmn., 2003—04; mem. NJ Motor Vehicle Commn., 2003—, vice chmn., 2004; bd. dirs. Morris Ctr. YMCA, 1992—94, Hist. Morris Visitors Ctr., 1999—2003, bd. pres., 2001—04. Rotary Found. scholar, 1981; recipient Gold award United Way of Morris County, 1988. Mem. Pub. Rels. Soc. Am. (bd. dirs. 1995), N.J. Press Assn., N.J. Travel Industry Assn., Internat. Assn. Bus Communicators, Y's Club of Cedar Knoll (pres. 1986-91), Long Valley Ice Hockey Club (dir. media rels. 2003—). Republican. Roman Catholic. Avocations: stenciling, reading, writing, photography. Office: AAA NJ Automobile Club 1 Hanover Rd Florham Park NJ 07932-1888 Office Phone: 973-245-4858.

FISCHER, VIOLETA PÈREZ CUBILLAS, Spanish literature and linguistics educator; b. Havana, Cuba, Nov. 20, 1923; came to U.S., 1959; d. Josè M. and Carmen (Reyes Pizey) Pèrez Cubillas; m. Rolando F. Fischer, Dec. 27, 1947 (dec. May 1994); 1 child, Violet Fischer Pack. PhD in Law, U. Havana, 1949; postgrad., U. N.C., 1967-68, MA in Romance Langs., 1975. Prin. Spl. Ctr. for English Teaching, Havana, Cuba, 1945—59; lawyer Havana, Cuba, 1949—59; asst. prof. East Carolina U., Greenville, NC, 1962—66; prof. Spanish lit. and linguistics Coastal Carolina Community Coll., Jacksonville, NC, 1970—96; ret., 1996. Speaker various civic, mil., ednl. assns., and community colls., 1963—. Bd. dirs. Onslow County Community Concerts, Jacksonville, N.C., 1987; chmn. CCCC Women's Assn., 1972-73. Recipient Josè de la Luz y Caballero award Cruzada Educativa Cubana Assn., 1987, Juan J. Remos award Cruzada Educativa Cubana, 1987, N.C. State Svc. award for 30 yrs. of svc., 1994; Paul Harris fellow Rotary Internat., 1996. Mem. MLA, Nat. Assn. Cuban Lawyers, Havana Bar Assn. in Exile, Nat. Cuban Tchrs. Assn., Nat. Assn. Cuban-Am. Educators, Count of Galvez Hist. Soc., Sigma Delta Mu (co-founder, state rep.), Delta Kappa Gamma (chmn. world fellowship com. 1982-84, 96-98, Wreath of Excellence ednl. award 1989, 2d v.p. Upsilon chpt. Jacksonville 1994-96). Roman Catholic. Home: 2107 Perry Dr Jacksonville NC 28546-1642

FISCHMAN, MYRNA LEAH, accountant, educator; d. Isidore and Sally (Goldstein) Fischman. BS, Coll. City N.Y., 1960, MS, 1964; PHD, NYU, 1976. CPA N.Y. Asst. to contr. Sam Goody, Inc., N.Y.C.; tchr. accounting Ctr. Comml. H.S., N.Y.C., 1960—63, vicat. adviser, 1963—66; instr. acctg. Borough of Manhattan C.C., N.Y.C., 1963—66; self-employed acct. N.Y.C., 1960—; chief acct. investigator rackets Office Queens Dist. Atty., 1969—70, cmty. fels. coord., 1970—71; adv. prof. L.I. U., 1970—79, prof. acctg. taxation and law, 1979—, coord. grad. capstone courses, 1982—86, dir. Sch. Profl. Accountancy Bklyn. Campus, 1984—, dir. Ctr. Acctg. and Tax Edn., 1986—, chmn. acctg. dept. Editor: Ea. Bus. Educators Jour., 1988. Rsch. cons. pre-tech. program N.Y.C. Bd. Edn., mem., 1992—; acct.-advisor Inst. for Advancement of Criminal Justice; acct.-cons. Coalition Devel. Corp., Interracial Coun. for Bus. Opportunities; treas. Breakfree Inc., Lower East Side Prep. Sch.; mem. ednl .task force Am. Jewish Com., 1972—; mem. Chancellor Com. Against Discrimination in Edn., 1976—97; chmn. supervisory com. Fed. Credit Union # 1532, N.Y.C., 1983—; chmn. consumer coun. Astoria Med. Ctr., 1980—92; mem. subcom. on bus. edn. to the econ. devel. and mktg. com. Bklyn. C. of C., 1984—; mem. adv. bd. acctg. dept. burough of Manhattan C.C., 1997—; mem. Bus. Edn. Adv. Coun.; mem. steering com., youth div. N.Y. Dem. County Com., 1967—68; del. to Nat. Conv. Young Dems. Am., 1967, rep. assigned to women's activities com., 1967; mem. legis. adv. bd. N.Y. State Assemblyman Dennis Butler, 1979—97. Recipient award for meritorious svc., Cmty. Svc. Soc., 1969, Lifetime Achievement award, Soroptimist Internat. Bklyn., 1997. Mem.: NEA (bus. edn. assns.), AAUP, AICPA, Inst. Mgmt. Accts. (dir. N.Y. chpt. 1983—, dir. profl. devel. 1986—87, dir. pub. rels. 1987—88, dir. manuscripts 1991—92, dir. univ. rels. 1993—94), Tax Inst. L.I. U. (dir. Blyn. chpg. 1984—), N.Y. State Soc. CPAs (mem. com. on recruitment for CPA careers 1981—, auditing com. 1991—, gen. com. on edn. in colls. and univs. 1991—, pub. rels. com. 1992—, pres. Bklyn. chpt. 2001—02, Dr. Emanuel Saxe Outstanding CPA in Edn. award 1994—95), Fed. Credit Union (chmn. supervisory com. # 1532 n.Y.C. 1983—), Young Alumni Assn., Am. Assn. Jr. Colls., Doctorate Assn. N.Y. Educators (v.p. 1975—97), Assn. Govt. Accts. (dir. N.Y. chpg. 1983—, pres. elect n.Y. chpg. 1989—90, pres. N.Y. chpt. 1990—91), Fin. Execs. Inst., Grad. Students Orgn. NYU (treas. 1971—73), Internat. Soc. Bus. Edn., Nat. Eastern (co-chmn. ann. meeting 1967), Am. Acctg. Assn., Govt. Accts. (v.p. 1973—74, dir. rsch. and manuscripts 1985—, pres. elect N.Y. chpt. 1989—90, pres. 1990—91, bd. dirs. N.Y. chpt. 1994—), Emanu-El League Congregation Emanu-El, N.Y. (chmn. cmty. svcs. com. 1967—68), Jewish Guild for Blind, Jewish Braille Inst., Cmty. Welfare Com. Assn., Friends Met. Mus. Art, Friends Am. Ballet Theatre, Women's City Club (N.Y.), Delta Pi Epsilon (treas. 1976). Democrat. Jewish. Achievements include development of new bus. machine course and curriculum Borough Manhattan Bus. C.C. Office: LI U Sch Bus 1 University Plz Rm 700 Brooklyn NY 11201-5301

FISH, JANET ISOBEL, artist; b. Boston, May 18, 1938; d. Peter and Florence (Voorhees) F. BA, Smith Coll., 1960; postgrad., Skowhegan (Maine) Art Sch., summer 1961; BFA, MFA, Yale U., 1963; DFA (hon.), Lyme Acad., 2000. Represented by D.C. Moore Gallery, N.Y.C. One-woman shows D.C. Moore Gallery, N.Y.C., Columbus (Ga.) Mus., also others; represented in permanent collections Whitney Mus. Am. Art, N.Y.C., Met. Mus. Art, N.Y.C., Cleve. Mus. Art, Dallas Mus. Fine Arts, Am. Fedn. Arts, Am. Acad. Inst. Arts and Letters, Art Inst. Chgo., Kemper Mus., Kansas City,, Albright-Knox Gallery, Buffalo, N.Y., Newark Mus., Mpls. Mus. of Art, Nat. Gallery of Victoria, Melbourne, Australia, Powers Inst., Sydney, Australia, Colby Coll., Waterville, Maine, Mus. of Fine Arts, Houston Art Ctr., RISD, Providence, Mus. Art, Providence, Va. Mus. Fine Arts, Richmond, Yale U., New Haven, Smith Coll. Mus. Art, Northampton, Mass., Albrecht Art Mus., St. Joseph, Mo., Milw. Art Mus., Hunter Mus. Art, Chattanooga, others. Bd. govs. Skowhegan Sch. Painting and Sculpture, Marie Walsh Sharpe Art Found. Recipient Harris award Chgo. Bienale award, 1974, Outstanding Woman Artist award Aspen Mus., 1992, Am. Acad. of Arts and Letters award, 1994, Henry Ward Ranger Purchase prize Nat. Acad. Design, N.Y., 2001; MacDowell fellow, 1968, 69, 72; Yale scholar, Australian Coun. for Arts grantee, 1975. Mem. Am. Acad. and Inst. of Arts and Letters (assoc.). Office Phone: 212-966-0616. E-mail: jfcp1@earthlink.net.

FISH, MARY MARTHA, economics educator; b. Albert Lea, Minn., July 17, 1930; d. Charles H. and Olga (Stennes) Thomassen; m. Donald C. Fish, Oct. 1954 (dec.); children: Jill S., Lynn M., Jason M. BBA, U. Minn., 1951; MBA in Econs, Tex. Tech. Coll., 1957; PhD (AAUW fellow 1960), U. Okla., 1963. [illegible], pub. health analyst State of Calif., 1953-54; analytical statistician 46th Med. Gen. Lab., U.S. Army Forces, Tokyo, 1954-57; instr. econs. and bus. Odessa (Tex.) Coll., 1957-58; asst. prof., then assoc. prof. West Tex. State U., 1961-66; prof. econs. U. Ala., 1966-99, prof. emeritus, 1999—; prof. econs. Landegg Internat. U., Wienacht, Switzerland, 2000—02. Fulbright lectr. U. Liberia, 1974-75, Gambian Govt., 1978-79; cons. in field. Co-author: Convicts, Codes and Contraband, 1974; contbr. articles to profl. jours. Grantee U. Ala., 1967-68, 87-89, Dept. Labor, 1978-79; Fulbright rsch. fellow, Taiwan, 1995; Phifer Faculty Scholar, 1998. Mem. Am. Econ. Assn., So. Econ. Assn. Mem. Baha'i faith. Home: 1405 High Forest Dr N Tuscaloosa AL 35406-2153 Business E-Mail: mfish@cba.ua.edu.

FISHBURN, JANET FORSYTHE, university dean; m. Peter Clingerman Fishburn, 1958; children: Susan, Katherine, Sally. BA magna cum laude, Monmouth Coll., 1958, LHD (hon.), 1984; PhD, Pa. State U., 1978. Ordained to ministry Presbyn. Ch., U.S., 1988. Dir. Christian edn. 1st United Presbyn. Ch., Cleveland Heights, Ohio, 1958-60; lectr. Pa. State U., 1977-78; asst. prof. Christian edn. Theol. Sch., Drew U., Madison, N.J., 1978-83, assoc. prof., 1983-90, asst. prof. Am. ch. history, 1982-83, assoc. prof., 1983-95, prof. tchg. ministry, 1990-95, prof. emeritus, 1995—, acting dean Theol. Sch., 1994-95. Parish assoc. Mt. Freedom Presbyn. Ch., 1991—94; manuscript reviewer Scholars Press, Fairleigh Dickinson Press, U. Pa. Press; lectr. in field, 1982—; panelist, spkr. profl. confs. and religious orgns.; cons. books for Pastors Series Abingdon Press, 1987; mem. social justice com. Newton Presbytery, 1989—95, mem. coun., 1995—2001, mem. com. on ministry, 2001—. Author: (book) The Fatherhood of God and the Victorian Family: The Social Gospel in America, 1982, Confronting the Idolatry of Family: A New Vision for the Household of God, 1991, Parenting is for Everyone: Living Out Our Baptismal Covenant, 1996; editor: Drew Gateway, 1989—93; contbr. articles and revs. to profl. jours., clergy jours. and encys; editor: People of a Compassionate God: Creating Welcoming Congregations, 2003. Leader weekly bible study Madison Presbyn. Ch., 1985—89, mem. chancel choir, 1982—90, Morristown United Meth. Ch., 1992—96, co-leader spiritual growth group, 1990—; spkr. clergy confs. Mem.: Am. Soc. Ch. History, Presbyn. Profs. Social Witness Policy (panel coord. 1994), United Meth. Assn. Scholars Christian Edn. (chmn. rsch. com. 1995—97). E-mail: jfishbur@drew.edu.

FISHBURNE, LILLIAN E. career officer; b. Md., 1949; BA in Sociology, Lincoln U., 1971; MA in mgmt., Webster Coll., 1980; MS in Telecomms. Systems Mgmt., Naval Postgrad. Sch., Monterey, Calif., 1982; Grad., Indsl. Coll. of Armed Forces, Washington, 1993. Commd. ensign USN, 1973, advanced through grades to rear adm., 1998—; personnel and legal officer Naval Air Test Facility, Lakehurst, N.J., 1973-74; various to officer-in-charge Naval Telecomms. Ctr., Great Lakes, Ill., 1977-80; various to spl. projects officer Command, Control, Comms. Directorate/Chief of Naval Opers., 1987-90; commanding officer Naval Computer and Telecomms. Sta., Key West, Fla., 1990-92; various to chief Command and Control Systems Support divsn./Joint Staff, Washington, 1994-95; various to dir. Navy Sapce, Info. Warfare, Command and Control Directorate, Washington, 1995—. Decorated Def. Superior Svc. medal, Legion of Merit, Meritorious Svc. medal (2 times), Navy Commendation medal (2 times), Navy Achievement medal.

FISHEL, RACHEL THERESE, principal, elementary school educator; b. Prairie du Chien, Wis., May 8, 1969; d. Michael Francis and Victoria Lynn Ott; m. Vance Jared Fishel, Nov. 29, 2003; children: Katelyn, Meredith. BS in Elem./Mid. Edn., Viterbo U., 1991. Tchr. kindergarten St. Anastasia, Hutchinson, Minn., 1991—92; tchr. 5th grade Harmony (Minn.) Elem., 1992—93; tchr. grades 7-8 St. Peter's Sch., Hokah, Minn., 1993—, prin., 2000—. Avocations: fishing, scrapbooks, piano. Home: Houston MN 55943 Office: St Peters Sch PO Box 357 Hokah MN 55941

FISHER, ADA MARKITA, physician, health services administrator, writer, poet; b. Durham, N.C., Oct. 21, 1947; d. Miles Mark and Ada Virginia (Foster) Fisher; children: Shevin Michael, Charles Malvern. BA, U. N.C., Greensboro, 1970; MD, U. Wis., 1975; MPH, Johns Hopkins U., 1981. Resident in family medicine U. Rochester (N.Y.), Highland Hosp., 1975-78; chief med. officer, med. dir. Plain View Health Svcs., Inc., Greenevers, N.C., 1978-80; residency supr., employee health supr., physician, program dir. Alcohol Detoxification Unit John Umstead Hosp., Butner, N.C., 1981-85; indsl. physician Martin Marietta Energy Sts., Inc., Oak Ridge, Tenn., 1985-89; dir. occupl. medicine, med. dir., mgr. med. policies and practices Amoco Corp., Chgo., 1989-95; assoc. program dir. occupl. and environ. medicine program Healthline Corp. Health Svcs., St. Louis, 1995-96; occupl. health physician, OWCP cons. VA Hosp., Salisbury, N.C., 1996—, chief occupl. health, safety and wellness, Office Workers Compensation Program cons., 1996—. Participant, med. rep. Am. Petroleum Inst.; lectr. in field. Author: How to Survive a Terrorist Attack Citizens Advisory, 2003. Mem sch. reform/local sch. coun. Chgo. Pub. Schs., 1989-94; treas. Alliance of Black Jews, 1995—; bd. dirs. Salisbury Rowan Symphony Soc., Inc.; trustee Barber Scotia Coll., Concord, N.C., 1997-99; mem. Rowan Salisbury Bd. Edn., 1998-2002, bd. Preservation N.C., Salisbury Symphony bd.; candidate U.S. Senate, 2002, U.S. 12th Congl. Dist. for 2004; mem. NMA, NRA, ACOEM; advocate children at-risk. Named one of Ten Outstanding Young Women in Am., 1984, Outstanding Alumni, Hillside High Sch.; recipient Alumni Disting. Svc. award U. N.C. Greensboro Alumni Assn., 1985. Mem. AAUW, NAFE, AMA, APHA, NAACP (life), APA (occupl. heath psychology adv. bd.), Rowan County C. of C. (bd. dirs. 1997—). Jewish. Avocations: restoring buildings and furniture, student recruitment for black colleges and universities. Home: PO Box 777 Salisbury NC 28145-0777

FISHER, ANITA JEANNE (KIT FISHER), language educator; b. Atlanta, Oct. 22, 1937; d. Paul Benjamin and Cora Ozella (Wadsworth) Chappelear; m. Kirby Lynn Fisher, Aug. 6, 1983; 1 child from previous marriage, Tracy Ann. BA, Bob Jones U., 1959; postgrad., Stetson U., 1961, 87, U. Fla., 1963, 87, 90; MAT, Rollins Coll., 1969; PhD in Am. Lit., Fla. State U., 1975; postgrad., U. Ctrl. Fla., 1978, NEH Inst., 1979, U. Ctrl. Fla., 1987, Disney U./U. Ctrl. Fla., 1996, Jacksonville U., 1996; student, Agnes Scot Coll. AP Inst., 1998, Duke Univ. AP TIP Summer Inst., 1999. Cert. English, gifted and adminstrn. supr., in ESOL. Chairperson basic learning improvement program secondary sch. Orange County, Orlando, Fla., 1964-65; chmn. composition Winter Park (Fla.) HS, 1978-80; chmn. English depts. Orange County Pub. Schs., Fla., 1962, 71; reading tchr. Woodland Hall Acad., Reading Rsch. Inst., Tallahassee, 1976; instr. edn., journalism, reading, Spanish, thesis writing Bapt. Bible Coll., Springfield, Mo., 1976-77; prof. English S.W. Mo. State U., Springfield, 1980-84, instr. continuing edn. music and creative writing, 1981-82, editor LAD Leaf; tchr. Volusia County Schs., Fla., 1984-88, 95-97, gifted students, 1986-88; tchr. Lee County Schs., 1988-95; gifted students Lake Mary HS, 1997; tchr. Seminole Pub. Schs., 1997—. Instr. Seminole CC; adj. prof. Edison CC, 1989—95, U. So. Fla., 1990—95, Barry U., 1993; mem. steering com. So. Assn. Colls. and Schs.; active Fla. Coun. Tchrs. English; assessor tchr. performance Nat. Bd. Profl. Tchg. Stds.; panel mem. PSAT/NMSQT Descriptive Score Report Ednl. Testing Svc.; spkr. in field.; chair advanced placement vertical team Lake Mary HS, 2000—01, chair dept. English, chair vertical team curriculum implementation, 2001—. Contbr. writings to publs. in field, papers to nat. profl. confs.; co-editor: Fla. English Jour., 1998—2000. Vol. Green County Action Com., 1977, Heart Fund, 1982; book reviewer Voice Youth Advs. Writing Program fellow U. Ctrl. Fla., 1978; mem. Rep. Nat. Com., 1994—; active Rep. Presdl. Task Force, 1998—2000. Named Lee County Tchr. of Distinction, 1994—95. Mem.: Seminole County Tchrs. English (chartered, pres. 1998—2000), Volusia Coun. Tchrs. English (pres. 1997), Fla. Coun. Tchrs. English (chair commn. ESL 1997—99, sch. adv. coun.), [illegible] Kappa (historian). Presbyterian.

FISHER, ANN BAILEN, lawyer; b. N.Y.C., Oct. 15, 1951; d. Eliot and Elise (Thompson) Bailen; m. John C. Fisher, Apr. 6, 1980. BA magna cum laude, Radcliffe Coll., 1973; JD, Harvard U., 1976. Bar: N.Y. 1977. Assoc. Sullivan & Cromwell, N.Y.C., 1976-80, 82-84, ptnr., 1984—, assoc. Paris, 1980-82. Mem. ABA, N.Y. State Bar Assn. Clubs: Cosmopolitan, Harvard (N.Y.C.). Episcopalian. Office: Sullivan & Cromwell 125 Broad St Fl 32 New York NY 10004-2400

FISHER, ANNA LEE, physician, astronaut; b. N.Y.C., Aug. 24, 1949; m. William Frederick Fisher; children: Kristin Anne, Kara Lynne. BS in Chemistry, UCLA, 1971, MD, 1976, MS in Chemistry, 1987. Physician, 1976-78; astronaut NASA Johnson Space Ctr., Houston, 1978—, mission specialist STS, 51-A, 1984. Office: NASA Johnson Space Ctr Astronaut Ofc Houston TX 77058

FISHER, BARBARA, broadcast executive; m. Michael Scott; children: Kyle, Zachary. BA, Oberlin Coll., Ohio. Publicist A&M Records; prodr. Dave Bell Assoc.; v.p. creative affairs New World Pictures; dir. movies and miniseries Universal TV Entertainment; v.p. creative affairs MCA TV Entertainment; pres. Universal TV Entertainment, 1991—99, Universal Studios Network Programming, 1999—2002; exec. v.p. Lifetime Entertainment Svcs., 2002—. Office: Lifetime Entertainment Svcs 2049 Century Park E Ste 840 Los Angeles CA 90067 Office Phone: 310-556-7504.

FISHER, CARLYN FELDMAN, artist, writer; b. Atlanta, Nov. 5, 1923; d. Abrom Lewis and Jennie (Saul) Feldman; m. Ted V. Fisher, 1944 (div. 1972); m. Morris Berthold Abram, Jan. 22, 1975 (div. May 1987); 1 child, Eve Fisher Shulmister. BS in Fine Art, Skidmore Coll., 1945; postgrad., Atelier 17, Paris, 1964, Pembroke Coll., Oxford, Eng., 1984. Founder, pub. Abstract Arts Festival of Atlanta, 1955-67; art editor Atlanta Mag., 1966-72; dir., writer, rschr. NEA, 1967-68; writer, dir. TV documentaries PBS, Channel 8, 1974-75; exec. prodr. Cape Cod/Sta. WGBH, Cape Cod, Boston, 1986-87. Co-founder, exec. Arts Festival Atlanta, 1953-62; chair bd. Hambidge Ctr., Rabun Gap, Ga., 1992-96; trustee adv. bd. Mus. Art, U. Ga., Athens, 1983—; artist-in-residence Hambidge Ctr. for Arts and Scis., Rabun Gap, 1987, 92-95, Mishkenot Sha'ananim, Jerusalem, 1987. One-person shows include Alexander Gallery, Atlanta, 1965, Heath Gallery, Atlanta, 1971, 88, Oglethorpe Gallery, Atlanta, 1973, Elaine Starkman Gallery, N.Y.C., 1982, Signature Shop Gallery, 1990, Dorothy Berge Gallery of Contemporary Art, Stillwater, Minn., 1993, Studio Exhbn., Atlanta, 1995; exhibited in group shows Atlanta High Mus. Art Shop, 1962, Ga. Artists Exhbn., 1967, Skidmore Coll., Saratoga Springs, N.Y., 1970, Lighting Assocs., Inc., N.Y.C., 1977, Ga. Artists Working in N.Y., N.Y.C., 1982, Cape Mus. Fine Arts, Dennis, Mass., 1985, Sen. Wyche Fowler Jr. Ga. Exhbn., Washington, 1991, Trinity Gallery, Atlanta, 1992; commd. murals installed Cobb Galleria Conv. Ctr., Atlanta, 1994; included in Exhbn. of Ga. Artists, Washington, 1992-93, The Great Frame Up Gallery, 1998; commd. sculpture installed in front of The Jewish Comty. Ctr., Atlanta, 1989; murals at the Westin Hotel Ballroom, Savannah, 1999,designer, executor commemorative poster for Piedmont Park Centennial Celebration, 1995; rschr., author: The Arts in Georgia, 1967-68; writer, co-dir. (TV documentaries) The Image Makers, 1974 (Emmy award); exec. prodr. (TV documentary) Art In Its Soul, 1987 (Silver Apple award). Bd. dirs. Richard Allen Ctr., N.Y.C., 1977-79; bd. dirs., exec. com. Ga. chpt. Nat. Mus. Women, Washington, 1987-95. Grantee Nat. Endowment for Arts, 1967-68; Ga. Women in the Visual Arts award State of Ga., 1997. Mem. Mensa, bd. mem. U. Georgia, Georgia Mus. Art, Atlanta History Ctr. Archives Avocations: travel, swimming, hiking, mountain climbing, teaching art. Home: 62 Forrest Pl NE Atlanta GA 30328-4868

FISHER, CARRIE FRANCES, actress, writer; b. Beverly Hills, CA, Oct. 21, 1956; d. Eddie Fisher and Debbie Reynolds; m. Paul Simon, 1983 (div. 1984); 1 child, Billie Catherine. Ed. high sch., Beverly Hills, Calif.; student, London Cen. Sch. Speech and Drama. Mem. chorus in Broadway musical Irene, 1972, also in Broadway prodn. Censored Scenes from King Kong; appeared in films Shampoo, 1975, Star Wars, 1977, Mr. Mike's Mondo Video, 1979, The Blues Brothers, 1980, The Empire Strikes Back, 1980, Under the Rainbow, 1981, Return of the Jedi, 1983, Garbo Talks, 1984, The Man with One Red Shoe, 1985, Hannah and Her Sisters, 1986, Hollywood Vice Squad, 1986, Amazon Women on the Moon, 1987, Appointment With Death, 1988, When Harry Met Sally..., 1989, The 'Burbs, 1989, Loverboy, 1989, She's Back, 1989, Sibling Rivalry, 1990, Drop Dead Fred, 1991, Soapdish, 1991, This Is My Life, 1992, Austin Powers: International Man Of Mystery, 1997, Scream 3, 2000, Famous, 2000; TV movies include Come Back, Little Sheba, (spl.) 1977, Leave Yesterday Behind, 1978, Liberty, Sunday Drive, 1986, Sweet Revenge, 1990; TV series Leaving L.A., 1997; author: Postcards from the Edge, 1987, (also screenplay, 1990), Surrender the Pink, 1990, Delusions of Grandma, 1994.

FISHER, CHRISTINE LYNNE, art educator, artist; d. Mack Bement and Sally Elizabeth MacKellar; m. Larry Sherman Fisher, June 10, 1976 (div.); children: Kenneth Eastment, Lori Lynn Tripp, Sarah Austin. BS in Edn., Ctrl. Mich. U., Mt. Pleasant, 1981. Cert. permanent tchng. Mich., 1986. Office supr. Ctrl. Mich. U., Mt. Pleasant, 1976—86; tchr. Cadillac Area Pub. Schools, Mich., 1986—88, Clare Area Pub. Schools, 1988—98, Cadillac Area Pub. Schools, 1998—. Exhibitions include From Women's Hands Gallery, 2003, Beaver I. - A Retrospective, Ctrl. Mich. U., 2003; developer: web site www.chrisfisherart.com. Events coord. Susan G. Komen Found. and Nat. Lee Denim Day, Cadillac, Mich., 1998—2003, Cadillac H.S., 1998—2003. Mem.: NEA (life), Nat. Art Edn. Assn. (assoc.), Mich. Art Edn. Assn. (assoc.), Mich. Edn. Assn. (life), Cadillac Area Artists Assn. (assoc.). Avocations: jewelry, lampwork, pottery, gardening, rock hound. Office: Cadillac Area Pub Schs 400 Linden Cadillac MI 49601 Personal E-mail: clf4855@chrisfisherart.com.

FISHER, COLLEEN M. trade association administrator; b. Pitts., Sept. 29, 1954; d. C. Francis and Dolores Rita (Darby) Fisher. BA, Georgetown U., 1976; MA, George Washington U., 1980. Legis. asst. Senator Richard S. Schweiker, Washington, 1976-81; profl. staff mem. U.S. Senate Appropriations Com., Washington, 1981-83; sr. v.p. govt. rels. Nat. Apt. Assn., Washington, 1983-91; indsl. rels. mgr. Resolution Trust Corp., Washington, 1991-95; exec. dir. Coun. for Affordable and Rural Housing, Alexandria, Va., 1996—; ptnr. Stuart-Fisher Meeting Mgmt. LLC, Fredericksburg, Va., 1999—. Mem. Fredericksburg Rep. Com., 1995—. Roman Catholic. Home: 803 Sylvania Ave Fredericksburg VA 22401-4736 Office: CARH 121 N Washington St Ste 301 Alexandria VA 22314-3022

FISHER, DEBRA A. communications executive, educator; b. Muncie, Ind., May 23, 1957; d. David A. Hampton and Janet L. Valencia; 1 child, Amy Lynn. BA summa cum laude, Grand Canyon U., Phoenix, Ariz., 2002. Devel. dir. Sojourner Ctr., Phoenix, 1991—95; prin. Bapt. Mgmt. Svcs., Phoenix; pres., owner Vision Treks Cons., Phoenix, 1998—2002, Castle Bridge Comms., Phoenix, 2002—. Editor Canyon Inst. Advanced Studies, Phoenix, 2000—. Mem. Ariz. Town Hall, Phoenix, 2001—03; bd. dirs. Cancer Ctr. Phoenix Children's Hosp., 1989—91, founder Michael Fisher Meml. Fund, 1984. Ray-Maben scholar, Grand Canyon Univ., 2002. Mem.: Sloan Consortium, Alpha Chi (chpt. pres. 2001—02), Pi Lambda Theta. Avocations: hiking, travel, reading. Office: Castle Bridge Comms 4949 W Wescott Dr Glendale AZ 85308

FISHER, DEENA KAYE, social studies education administrator; b. Elk City, Okla., Dec. 20, 1950; d. Earl Dean and Rosa Lee (Stone) Music; m. Mike Fleck, May 29, 1970 (div. June 1988); children: DeeAnna Michelle, Carrie Denise, William Michael; m. Tom Fisher, Nov. 13, 1993; 1 stepchild, Eleni. BA in Edn.-Social Sci., Southwestern Okla. State U., 1979, MEd in Social Sci., 1983, MEd in Sch. Counseling, 1987; postgrad., U. Okla., 1999. Instr. in social sci. Cordell (Okla.) H.S., 1979-85, El Reno (Okla.) C.C., 1985-88, Upward Bound guidance and career counselor, instr., 1987-89; instr. Am. History Yukon (Okla.) H.S., 1986-87; instr. polit. sci. and Am. history Southwestern Okla. State U., 1987-89; chair dept. Am. history, instr. Am. govt. Woodward (Okla.) H.S., 1989-96; instr. social studies Northwestern Okla. State U., Alva, 1989—, dir. Woodward campus, 1996—. Author ednl. materials in field. Del. Dem. Nat. Conv., Okla. Dem. Party, Chgo., 1996; law day coord. Okla. Bar Assn., Woodward, 1990-96; regional coord. Citizen Bee, Tulsa World, 1994-97; panelist U.S. History Nat. Assessment of Ednl. Progress, St. Louis, 1994. Recipient Outstanding Am. History Tchr. award Okla. Soc. DAR, 1993, Tchr. of Yr. award Okla. Supreme Ct., 1992; Bill of Rights Edn. Collaborative grantee, 1991. Mem. Nat. Coun. for Social Studies (ho. dels., co-chmn. resolution com. 1996), Okla. Social Studies Suprs.' Assn. (membership bd. 1997), Okla. Coun. for Social Studies (del.-at-large 1996, pres. 1994-96), Woodward Edn. Assn. (pres. 1996), Woodward C. of C. (mem. edn. com. 1997), Delta Kappa Gamma (pres. Psi chpt. 1996-98), Phi Delta Kappa. Mem. Christian Ch. (Disciples Of Christ). Avocations: reading, chess. Home: 3308 Bent Creek Dr Woodward OK 73801-6931 Office: Northwestern Okla State U Woodward Campus PO Box 1046 Woodward OK 73802-1046

FISHER, ELLEN ROOP, retired librarian, educator; b. Washington, Dec. 16, 1944; d. Robert Wendell and Katherine (Booth) Roop; m. Allan Campbell Fisher, June 14, 1969; children: Bradford Booth, Katherine Thayer. BA, Smith Coll., Northampton, Mass., 1966; MA, U. Chgo., 1974. Cert. library sci. edn., Pa. Rsch. asst. Indsl. Rels. Ctr. Library, U. Chgo., 1967-68; asst. sys. libr. U. Chgo. Libraries, 1968-71; reference asst. Toledo (Ohio) Pub. Libr., 1972; libr. Cleve. Orch. Chorus Library, 1973-74; reference libr. Harford County Library Sys., Bel Air, Md., 1975; computer tchr. Lawrence Twp. Sch. Dist., Indpls., 1982-84; music tchr. Hegvik Sch. of Music, Wayne, Pa., 1984-86; libr. Edn. Resource Ctr., Cabrini Coll., Wayne, Pa., 1986—87; libr. Radnor Twp. Sch. Dist., Wayne, Pa., 1987—94, head libr., 1994—2001. Author: Sources and Nature of Errors in Transcribing Bibliographic Data into Machine Readable Form, 1974; co-author: The University of Chicago Bibliographic Data Processing System, 1970. Singer St. Cecilia Chamber Choir, Newcastle, Maine, Tapestry Singers. La Verne Noyes scholar U Chgo., 1966. Mem.: ALA, Am. Recorder Soc. Unitarian Universalist. Avocations: travel, genealogy. Home: 13 Pilot Circle PO Box 134 Nobleboro ME 04555-0134

FISHER, FRANCES, actress; b. Milford-on-Sea, Eng., May 11, 1952; d. William I. and Olga (Moen) F.; 1 child, Francesca Ruth Fisher-Eastwood. Student, Lee Strasberg, Stella Adler, Marilyn Fried, Sandra Seacat, HB Studios. Appearances include (films) Can She Bake a Cherry Pie?, 1985, Tough Guys Don't Dance, 1986, Patty Hearst, 1987, Lost Angels, 1988, Pink Cadillac, 1989, Welcome Home Roxy Carmichael, 1989, L.A. Story, 1991, Unforgiven, 1992, Baby Fever, 1992, The Stars Fell on Henrietta, 1994, Molly and Gina, 1992, Female Perversions, 1993, Striptease, 1995, Wild America, 1996, Titanic, 1997, True Crime, 1998, The Big Tease, 1998, The Rising Place, 2002, Gone in 60 Seconds, 2000, (TV) Elysian Fields, 1987, Sudie & Simpson, 1988, Cold Sassy Tree, 1989, Promises to Keep, 1990, Lucy & Desi: Before the Laughter, 1991, Devlin, 1987, Crime and Punishment, 1989, Law and Order, 1990, Praying Mantis, 1992, Attack of the 50 Foot Woman, 1993, The Other Mother, 1994, Strange Luck, 1995, Becker, 2000, Audrey Hepburn, 1999, Titus, 2001, Jackie, 2000, Glory Days, 2001, (theater) Cat on a Hot Tin Roof, 1981, Hay Fever, 1981, The Chain, 1983, Desire Under the Elems, 1982, Still Life, 1983, Ruffian on the Stair, 1979, A Midsummer Night's Dream, 1981, Hunchback of Notre Dame, 1981, Orpheus Descending, 1986, The Hitchhikers, 1985, Crackwalker, 1987, Fool for Love, 1985, Three More Sleepless Nights, (Drama Logue award 1996), 1996, 1984, 1984, Jammed, 1997. Mem. Actors Studio. Office: Nevin Dolcefino Innovative Artists 1505 10th St Santa Monica CA 90401*

FISHER, GAIL FEIMSTER, epidemiologist, researcher, government agency administrator; d. Maurice Blake and Sarah Estelle (Abell) Feimster; m. Eugene Joseph Fisher, Dec. 2, 1950 (dec.); children: Laurence Eugene, Robert Maurice. BA, U. Md., 1949, MA, 1951; PhD, U. N.C., 1976. Rsch. analyst Bur. of State Svcs., Dept. HHS, 1956-66; evaluation officer Bur. Health Svcs., Dept. HHS, 1966-68; planning officer Nat. Ctr. Health Stats.-Ctr. for Disease Control-Dept. HHS, Rockville, Md., 1968-93, assoc. dir. Hyattsville, Md., 1973-98; cons. epidemiologist, 1998—. Contbr. rsch. reports to profl. jours. and presentations. Avocation: antique vehicle restoration and preservation. Office: DHHS-CDC-Nat Ctr Hlth Stats PO Box 234 9685 Johnsontown Rd La Plata MD 20646 E-mail: gailfisher@aol.com.

FISHER, JANET WARNER, secondary school educator; b. San Angelo, Tex., July 7, 1929; d. Robert Montell and Louise (Buckley) Warner; m. Jarek Prochazka Fisher, Oct. 17, 1956 (div. May 1974); children: Barbara Zlata Harper, Lev Prochazka, Monte Prochazka. BA, So. Meth. U., 1950, M of Liberal Arts, 1982; student various including, Columbia U., U. Dallas, U. Colo., U. London and others. Cert. English, German and ESL tchr., K-12, Tex., N.Y. Bd. dirs., sec. Masaryk Inst., N.Y.C., 1968-71; with orphan sect. Displaced Persons Commn., Washington, 1950; fgn. editor Current Digest of the Soviet Press, N.Y.C., 1953-55; cable desk clk. Time, Inc., N.Y.C., 1955-56; tchr. of English and reading, langs. Houston Ind. Sch. Dist., 1975-80; tchr. Carmine Ind. Sch. Dist., Round Top, Tex., 1980-82; tchr. German Region IV Interactive TV, 1983-85; adj. prof. English U. Houston, 1983-87; tchr. Royal Ind. Sch. Dist., Brookshire, Tex., 1989-92, Hempstead Ind. Sch. Dist., Waller County, Tex., 1992-94. Adj. prof. English, U. Houston, Houston C.C., 1983-87, 1997—; tchr. Amnesty Program, Houston, 1988-90; adj. prof. English Blinn Coll., Brenham, Tex., 1995-97. Candidate sch. bd., South Orangetown, N.Y., 1962, state rep., Houston, 1980; del. Houston Tchrs. Assn., 1975-80; officer LWV, Nyack, N.Y., 1960-62; trustee, chair adminstrn. bd. Shepherd Drive United Meth. Ch., Houston, 1994-2003; del. Tex. ann. conf. United Meth. Ch., 1994-2001; del. Tex. State Dem. Conv., 1996, 2000, 02. Recipient award for Svc. to Missions, United Meth. Ch., Houston, 1985. Mem. AAUW, NOW, WILPF, Harris County Women's Polit. Caucus. Avocations: Russian and German literature, real estate development. Home: PO Box 66067 Houston TX 77266-6067 E-mail: jsufish@aol.com.

FISHER, JEWEL TANNER (MARY FISHER), retired construction company executive; b. Port Lavaca, Tex., Oct. 31, 1918; d. Thomas M. and Minnie Frances (Dunks) Tanner; m. King Fisher, Aug. 13, 1937; children: Ann Fisher Boyd, Linda Fisher LaQuay. A in Bus., Tex. Luth. Coll., 1937. Sec. treas. King Fisher Marine Svc., Inc., Port Lavaca, 1959-82, dir., cons., 1958-98; artist, poet. Trustee Meml. Med. Ctr., 1976-81, 90-94, Golden Crescent Coun. Govts., 1980-81, Crisis Hotline Calhoun County, 1985-93; pres. bd. trustees Meml. Med. Ctr., 1992-93; trustee Golden Crescent Coun. Govts., 1980-81. Lic. pvt. pilot. Mem. DAR (regent Guadalupe Victoria chpt. 1986-88), Daus. Republic Tex., 99's, Internat. Orgn. Women Pilots. Home: PO Box 166 Port Lavaca TX 77979-0166

FISHER, JIMMIE LOU, state official; b. Delight, Ark., Dec. 31, 1941; Student, Ark. State U.; grad. John F. Kennedy Sch. Govt., Harvard U., 1985. Treas. Greene County, Ark., 1971-78; auditor State of Ark., Little Rock, 1979, treas., 1981—. Sec. Ark. State Bd. Fin. Trustee, ex-officio mem. Ark. Pub. Employees Retirement System, Ark. Tchr. Retirement System; trustee Ark. State Hwy. Retirement System; former vice chair Dem. State Com.; former mem. Dem. Nat. Com.; del. Dem. Nat. Conv., 1988; past pres. Ark. Dem. Women's Club; mem. Ark. Devel. Fin. Authority. Mem. State Bd. Fin. (sec.), State Bd. Election Commrs., Nat. Assn. State Treas. (pres.). Office: Treasury Dept 220 State Capitol Little Rock AR 72201-1059

FISHER, JO ANN, television technical director; b. Mpls., Sept. 14, 1957; d. Philip and Rita Blossom (Joss) F.; m. Steven William Koeln, Oct. 29, 1983; children: Nathan Ross Fisher-Koeln, Gertrude Rose Fisher-Koeln. BA, U. Minn., 1981. Floor dir. KSTP-TV, Mpls., 1979-82, duty dir., 1982-85, tech. dir., 1985-88, occasional dir., 1987-88; freelance dir., tech. dir. IDS/Amex Fin. Advisors, Mpls., 1987—, Met. Sports Commn., Mpls., 1989—, IVL Post, Mpls., 1990—, KTCA Pub. TV, St. Paul, 1990—, ESPN, 1993—, Juntunen Media Group, 1995—, Juntunen Mobile TV, 1998—, N.W. Mobile TV, 1992-99. Mem. com. J.C.C. Childcare, St. Paul, 1989-93; vol. St. Paul Pub. Schs., 1991—; mem. com. Shir Tikvah Synagogue, Mpls., 1992-93, chair com., 1994-95. Recipient I.D.E.A. award, 1993. Democrat. Jewish. Avocations: jewelry making, miniatures, reading mysteries.

FISHER, KATHLEEN V. lawyer; b. Aug. 9, 1948; AB, UCLA, 1971; JD, U. Calif., Davis, 1976. Bar: Calif. 1976. Extern to Hon. Raymond Sullivan Calif. Supreme Ct., 1975; mem. Morrison & Foerster, San Francisco. Mem. Order of Coif. Office: Morrison & Foerster 425 Market St San Francisco CA 94105

FISHER, LINDA ALICE, physician; b. Plainfield, N.J., Dec. 27, 1947; d. Alvin Edwin and Bertha Sophie (Steigmann) F. BA, Douglass Coll., New Brunswick, N.J., 1970; M in Med. Sci., Rutgers U., 1972; MD, Harvard U., 1975; MPH, St. Louis U., 1996. Diolomate Am. Bd. Internal Medicine, Am. Bd. Preventive Medicine. Intern, then resident Jewish Hosp. St. Louis, 1975-78; dir. ambulatory care St. Luke's Hosp., St. Louis, 1978-84; chief med. officer St. Louis County Dept. Health, Clayton, 1984-97, dir. rsch., 1997-2000; project dir. St. Louis STD/HIV Prevention Tng. Ctr., 1995-2000. Chief physician St. Louis Met. Police Dept., 1978-88; clin. instr. medicine Washington U., St. Louis, 1978-94, asst. clin. prof., 1994-2000; asst. clin. prof. medicine St. Louis U., 1979-95, assoc. clin. prof., 1996-2000; adj. faculty health svcs. mgmt. U. Mo., Columbia, 1996, St. Louis U. Sch. Pub. Health, 1993-2000; bd. overseers St. Louis Regional Med. Ctr., 1985-95, cons. Ill. Local Govtl. Law Enforcement Officers Tng. Bd., 1988; dir. Fairfax County Health Dept., 2000-2001. Contbr. articles to profl. jours.; author of short stories. Chmn. licensure com. Mo. Bd. Registration for Healing Arts, 1983-86; adv. coun. Greater St. Louis Coun. Girl Scouts U.S., 1986-2000. Recipient Disting. Alumni award Douglass Coll., 1992, Publ. award Mo. Pub. Health Assn., 1994, St. Louis Woman of Achievement award KMOX Radio and Suburban Jours., 1995. Fellow ACP; mem. AMA, APHA, Am. Med. Women's Assn. (chpt. pres. 1982-85, Cmty. Svc. award 1992), Am. Med. Writers Assn., Nat. Assn. Med. Communicators (Ken Alvord Cmty. Svc. award 1998), St. Louis Met. Med. Soc. (councilor 1982-84, sec. 1986, editor 1989-90), Med. Soc. No. Va., Internat. Women's Forum, Assn. Documentary Editing. Lutheran. Office: Box 3927 Fairfax VA 22038-3927 Office Phone: 571-212-0497. E-mail: lfisher2@cox.net.

FISHER, LINDA J. federal agency administrator; b. Saginaw, Mich., June 26, 1952; BA, Miami U., Oxford, Ohio, 1974; MBA, George Washington U., 1978; JD, Ohio State U., 1982. Legis. asst. to Hon. Clarence J. Brown, Ohio, 1974-75, Hon. Ralph S. Regula, Ohio, 1976-80; special asst. to asst. adminstr. solid waste and emergency response EPA, 1982-84, chief staff to adminstr., 1985-87, asst. adminstr. policy and evaluation, 1988, asst. adminstr. pesticides and toxic substances, 1989—93, dep. adminr., 2001—03; of counsel Latham & Watkins, 1993—95; v.p. govt. and pub. affairs Monsanto, 1995—2000.

FISHER, LUCY, film producer; b. N.Y.C., Oct. 2, 1949; d. Arthur Bertram and Naomi (Kislak) F.; m. Douglas Z. Wick, Feb. 16, 1986; children: Sarah, Julia, Tessa. BA, Harvard U., 1971. V.p. prodn. 20th Century Fox, L.A., 1979-80; v.p. worldwide prodns. Zoetrope Studios, Burbank, Calif., 1980-81; v.p., sr. prodn. exec. Warner Bros. Pictures, Burbank, 1981-87, sr. v.p., 1987-89, exec. v.p. prodn., 1989-96; vice chmn. Columbia Tristar Motion Picture Co., Culver City, Calif., 1996-2000; producer Red Wagon Productions, Culver City, Calif., 2000—. Office: Red Wagon Entertainment Hepburn West 10202 Washington Blvd Culver City CA 90232-3119

FISHER, NANCY, writer, producer, director; b. Oct. 21; d. Seymour and Tema Fisher; 1 child, Sarah Olivia. BA, Barnard Coll. Head creative group Doyle, Dane, Bernbach Advt., London; creative group head Benton & Bowles Advt., London, McCann Erickson Advt., N.Y.C.; creative dir. Norman, Craig & Kummel Advt., N.Y.C.; pres. Nancy Fisher Inc., N.Y.C., 1981—2002, Creative Programming Inc., N.Y.C., 1981-89. Author: Vital Parts, 1993, Side Effects, 1994, Special Treatment, 1996, Code Red, 1998, Code Blue, 2000; creator, writer, prodr. (TV series) Womanwatch, 1982—89, Celebrity Chefs, 1983—89, (numerous home video cassettes including) Look Mom, I'm Fishing (Parents Choice award), The Annapolis Book of Seamanship Video Series (Cindy award), The Christmas Carol Video, Video Dog, Video Cat, Video Baby; prodr.: (TV series) The Real Bottom Line. Sr. v.p., dir. comm. The Ch. Pension Group, N.Y.C., 2000—. Recipient 5 broadcast awards Network Documentary Series. Mem. Dirs. Guild Am., Authors Guild.

FISHER, NANCY DEBUTTS, library director; b. Pitts., Apr. 10, 1945; d. Jacob John DeButts and Marie Christine Grills; m. Bruce C. Fisher, May 29, 1971. BS, Cleve. State U., 1968; MSLS, Case Western Res. U., 1973. Reference libr. Cleveland Heights-University Heights Pub. Libr., 1968-79; mgr. Beachwood (Ohio) br. Cuyahoga County Pub. Libr., 1980-90; dir. Wickliffe (Ohio) Pub. Libr., 1990—. Mem. adv. coun. Wickliffe United Way, 1991—2001; key communicator Wickliffe City Schs., 1992; mem. comm. com. Lake County United Way, 2002—, mem. cabinet, 2003—04; mem. Wickliffe Cmty. Adv. Panel, 1995—; grad. Leadership Lake County, 2003; bd. dirs. Wickliffe Civic Ctr., Inc., 1999—; mem. adv. com. Holden Aboretum Warren H. Corning Libr., 1999—2002; mem. alumni planning com. Case Western Res. U. Libr. Sci., 1997—; mem. Lake Hosp. Sys., women's health adv. bd., 1999—. Mem.: ALA, Cleve. Area Met. Libr. Sys. (bd. dirs. 1994—96, mem. pers. com. 2003—), Ohio Libr. Coun., Lake County C. of C. Bd., Wickliffe C. of C. (v.p. 1998—99, pres. 2001—03, Civic Leader of Yr. 1999), Rotary (pres. 1992—94, chair charity ball 2002—03). Home: 939 Stuart Dr South Euclid OH 44121-3425 Office: Wickliffe Pub Libr 1713 Lincoln Rd Wickliffe OH 44092-2499 E-mail: nfisher@wickliffe.lib.oh.us.

FISHER, NANCY LOUISE, pediatrician, medical geneticist, former nurse; b. Cleve., July 4, 1944; d. Nelson Leopold and Catherine (Harris) F.; m. Larry William Larson, May 30, 1976 (div. Oct. 2000); 1 child, Jonathan Raymond. Student, Notre Dame Coll., Cleve., 1962-64; BSN, Wayne State U., 1967; postgrad., Calif. State U., Hayward, 1971-72; MD, Baylor Coll. of Medicine, 1976; M in Pub. Health, U. Wash., 1982, certificate in ethics, 1993. Diplomate Am. Bd. Pediatrics, Am. Bd. Med. Genetics. RN coronary care unit and med. intensive care unit Highland Gen. Hosp., Oakland, Calif., 1970-72; RN coronary care unit Alameda (Calif.) Hosp., 1972-73; intern in pediatrics Baylor Coll. of Medicine, Houston, 1976-77, resident in pediatrics, 1977-78; attending physician, pediatric clinic Harborview Med. Ctr., Seattle, 1980-81; staff physician children and adolescent health care clinic Columbia Health Ctr., Seattle, 1981-87, founder, dir. of med. genetics clinic, 1984-89; maternal child health policy cons. King County div. Seattle King County Dept Pub. Health, 1983-85; dir. genetic svcs. Va. Mason Clinic, 1986-89; dir. med. genetic svcs. Swedish Hosp., 1989-94; pvt. practice Seattle, 1994-97; med. cons. supr. office of managed care Wash. State Dept. Social and Health Svcs., Olympia, 1996-97; med. dir. Medicaid Dept. of Social and Health Svcs., Wash., 1997-99; assoc. med. dir. Govt. Programs Regence Blue Shield, 1999; med. dir. Regence Blue Shield, 2000—02; chief med. officer Wash. State Health Care Authority, 2003—. Nurses aide psychiatry Sinai Hosp., Detroit, 1966-67; charge nurse Women's Hosp., Cleve., 1967; research asst. to Dr. Shelly Liss, 1976; with Baylor Housestaff Assn., Baylor Coll. Medicine, 1980-81; clin. asst. prof. grad. sch. nursing, U. Wash., Seattle, 1981-85, clin. asst. prof. dept. pediatrics, 1982-92, clin. assoc. prof. dept. pediatrics, 1992—; com. appointments include Seattle CCS Cleft Palate Panel, 1984-97; bd. dirs., first v.p. King County Assn. Sickle Cell Disease 1985-86, acting pres. 1986, pres. 1986-87; hosp. affiliation include Childrens Orthopedic Hosp. and Med. Ctr., Seattle, 1981—, Virginia Mason Hosp., Seattle, 1985-89, Harborview Hosp., Seattle, 1986—. Contbr. articles to profl. jours. Active Seattle Urban League, 1982-96, 101 Black Women, 1986-94; bd. dirs. Seattle Sickle Cell Affected Family Assn., 1984-85, Am. Heart Assn., 2001—; mem. People to People Citizen Ambassador Group; sec. Health and Human Svcs. Com. on Infant Mortality, 1993—2003; mem. Twins Com. Inst. of Medicine, 1995-2000; Evaluation, Rsch. and Planning Group Ethical Legal and Social Implications Nat. Human Genome Rsch. Inst., 1997-2000. Served to lt. USN Nurse Corps, 1966-70. Fellow Am. Coll. Medicine Genetics (founder); mem. Am. Acad. Physician Execs., Student Governing Body and Graduating Policy Com. Baylor Coll. Medicine (founding mem. 1973-76), Loans and Scholarship Com. Baylor Coll. Medicine (voting mem. 1973-76), Am. Med. Student Assn., Student Nat. Med. Assn., Admission Com. Baylor Coll. Medicine (voting mem. 1974-76), AMA, Am. Med. Women's Assn., Am. Acad. Pediatrics, Am. Pub. Health Assn., Am. Soc. Human Genetics, Nat. Speakers Assn., Wash. State Assn. Black Providers of Health Care, Soc. Health and Human Values, Wash. State Soc. Pediatrics, Seattle C. of C. (mem. Leadership Tomorrow 1988—), Wash. State Med. Assn. (women in medicine com., interspecialty coun., fin. com.), Sigma Gamma Rho, Phi Delta Epsilon. Office: Wash State HCA 676 Woodland Sq Loop SE MS-42701 Olympia WA 98504-2701 Office Phone: 360-923-2709. E-mail: nfis107@hca.wa.gov.

FISHER, NANCY M. educator, poet; b. New Bern, N.C., May 10, 1934; d. Malcolm H./ and Nannie Bynum McWhorter; m. William D. Fisher, Mar. 31, 1956; children: Karen Davenport, Karl. BA, U. N.C., 1956; MA, Fla. State U., 1959; PhD, U. Tenn., 1969. Prof. Coppin State Coll., Balt., 1969—70, Knoxville Coll., 1970—71, Roane State C.C., Harriman, 1971—91, Tenn. Wesleyan Coll., Athens, 1991—. Author: Vision at Delphi, 1995. Mem.: Lions Club. Democrat. Methodist. Office: Tenn Wesleyan Coll College St Athens TN 37303

FISHER, ROBYN ANGELA, music educator; d. Robert Floyd and Jo Angela Fisher. MusB in Violin Performance, Cen. Mo. State U., 1995; B of Music Edn. in Instrumental Music Edn., Ariz. State U., 1999. Cert. tchr. K-12 music edn. Ariz. Pvt. violin and viola tchr., various locations, Ariz., 1995—; violinist duo with guitarist Tempe, Ariz., 1996—2000; freelance violinist Phoenix, 1996—; elem./mid. sch. orch. tchr. Laguna Elem. and Mountainside Mid. Sch., Scottsdale Unified Sch. Dist., 1999—2003; violinist Sun City (Ariz.) Symphony, 2000—03, Scottsdale (Ariz.) Bible Ch., 2002—; elem. orch. tchr. Laguna Elem. and Anasazi Elem., Scottsdale Unified Sch. Dist., 2003—; lk. Condr. asst. Ariz. All-State Elem. Orch., 2003; condr., arranger elem. performance group Laguna All-Star Strolling Strings, 1999—; condr. mid. sch. performance group Mountainside Honor Orch., 1999—2002; founder, dir. Mountainside Orch. Boosters, Scottsdale, 2002. Composer: (violin solo) Sunrise over the Hills, 2002. Grantee, Pepsi Notes-Share the Joy with Music, 2001. Mem.: Amnesty Internat., Ariz. Music Educators Assn., Am. String Tchrs. Assn., Sigma Alpha Iota (grad. adviser Phoenix alumnae chpt. 1996—99). Democrat. Avocations: sailing, painting, reading, dance, exercising. Office: Laguna Elem Sch 10475 E Lakeview Dr Scottsdale AZ 85258 E-mail: rfisher@susd.org.

FISHER, RUTH E. lawyer; b. Frankfurt, Germany, Dec. 12, 1955; BA, Scripps Coll., 1976; JD, UCLA, 1980. Law clk. to Judge Malcolm M. Lucas U.S. Dist. Ct. (cen. dist.) Calif., 1980—82; with Munger, Tolles & Olson LLP, L.A., 1982—87, corp. ptnr., 1987—. Lectr. in field. Mem.: ABA (chair subcom. of bus. law sect.), Women Lawyers' Assn., L.A. County Bar Assn. Office: Munger Tolles & Olson LLP 35th Fl 355 S Grand Ave Los Angeles CA 90071

FISHER, SALLIE ANN, chemist; b. Green Bay, Wis., Sept. 10, 1923; BS in Chemistry, U. Wis., 1945, MS, 1946, PhD, 1949. Instr. Mt. Holyoke Coll., South Hadley, Mass., 1949-50; asst. prof. U. Minn., Duluth, 1950-51; group leader Rohm & Haas Co., Phila., 1951-60; assoc. dir. rsch. Robinette Rsch. Labs., Berwyn, Pa., 1960-72; v.p. Puricons, Inc., Malvern, Pa., 1972-76, pres., 1976—. Mem. adv. bd. Internat. Water Conf., Pitts., 1976-91, Reactive Polymers, Netherlands, 1982-88. Contbr. chpts. to books and over 100 articles to profl. jours. Recipient award of merit Engring. Soc. Western Pa., Pitts., 1984. Fellow ASTM (vice-chmn. D-19 1972-78, award of merit 1974, Max Hecht award com. D-19 1975); mem. Soc. Chem. Industry (Ion Exchg. award, separations sci. sect. 2000), Am. Chem. Soc., Am. Waterworks Assn. Achievements include patent for regeneration of anion resins; research in process for the concentration and recovery of uranium; devel. of methodology for analyis of resins for nuclear industry. Office: Puricons Inc 101 Quaker Ln Malvern PA 19355-2480

FISHER, SHARON MARY, musician; b. Orange, N.J., Sept. 29, 1944; d. Stanley and Veronica Shirley (Conway) Cozza; m. Andrew Fisher IV, Aug. 16, 1969. B Music Edn., Westminster Choir Coll., 1966; postgrad., Acad. Vocal Arts, 1966-67, Temple U., 1967-69. Cert. music tchr., N.J. Chorister Westminster Choir, Princeton, N.J., 1964-66; music tchr. Phila. Pub. Schs., 1967-69; sect. leader Phila. Boys' Choir, 1969; performer Manhattan Light Opera Co., N.Y., 1969-70; soprano soloist St. Peter's Ch., Morristown, N.J., 1975-79; organist Ch. of the Saviour, Denville, N.J., 1981-84; performer, lectr., 1986—. Performer Scottish Games, Millington, N.J. Albums include Concert Memories, 1991, Ireland: Land of Harp and Song, 1998. Grand marshal Holiday Parade, Denville C. of C., 1991. Recipient Marietta MacLeod award An Comunn Gaidhealach, 1989, Scots award Scottish Club of Twinstates, 1988-89, Harp/Voice trophy O'Carolan Harp Festival, Keadue, Ireland, 1988, Merit award Passaic County Irish Am. Cultural Soc., 1995. Mem. Clarsach Soc. (Edinburgh), Scottish Harp Soc. Am. (Ellice MacDonald grantee 1987), Am. Harp Soc., Nat. Assn. Tchrs. Singing, Nat. Assn. Pastoral Musicians, Internat. Soc. Folk Harpers and Craftsmen, Comhaltas Ceoltoiri Eireann. Avocations: gardening, language study, study of pain management through music. Home: 46 W Shore Rd Denville NJ 07834-1520 E-mail: harpvoice@msn.com.

FISHER, VIRGINIA CAROLYN, music educator, director; b. Cinn., Nov. 5, 1943; d. William and Elizabeth Mark; m. Forrest E. Fisher, June 15, 1974; children: Aaron, Paul. MusB, Coll. Conservatory Cinn., 1966; BS in music edn., U. Cinn., 1967; M in music edn., Miami U., 1974. Trumpet soloist Cincinnati Symphony Orch., 1958—60; band dir., tchr. Clermont Northeaster Schs., Owensville, Ohio, 1967—76; tchr. Lamplighter Ednl. Ctr., Terrace Park, Ohio, 1980—85; band dir., tchr. Bethel-Tate Schs., Bethel, Ohio, 1985—. Sec. Land of Grant Honor Band, Bethel, Ohio, 1986—88. Contbr. articles The Sch. Musician Mag., 1972. News corr. Cmty. Press, Loveland, Ohio, 1993; advisor Clermont County 4H Club, Owensville, Ohio, 1996—2001. Recipient OMEA 25 Yr. Dist. Svc. award, Ohio Music Edn. Assoc., 2002. Mem.: Mu Phi Epsilon Music Sorority (hostess 1990—2003). Republican. Baptist. Avocations: camping, sewing, travel, performing. Home: 1785 Clermontville Laurel Rd New Richmond OH 45157 Office Phone: 513-734-2261. E-mail: fisher-v@bethelrate.org.

FISHGRAB, BARBARA JEANNE, school psychologist, mental health services professional; b. Fredonia, Kans., Dec. 13, 1950; d. William Jr. and Geraldine Lee (Dalton) Parks; m. Donald Ray Fishgrab, Aug. 9, 1974 (div. Nov. 1990); children: Philip, Charity, Tabitha. BS in Elem. Edn., Baptist

Bible Coll., 1975; MA in Psychol. Counseling, Liberty U., 1991, BS in Multidisciplinary Studies, 2000; postgrad., Argosy U., Phoenix, 2001—. Cert. crisis prevention trainer. Elem. sch. tchr. Hilltop Christian Sch., Tse Bonito, N.Mex., 1986-88, Gallup- McKinley County Schs., Gallup, N.Mex., 1990-91, guidance counselor, 1991-92, student assistance counselor, 1992-94, sch. psychologist, 1994—2001; mental health counselor Mesilla Valley Four Corners Resource Ctr., Gallup, N.Mex., 1994-95, Our Lady Mt. Carmel Home for Girls, Gallup, N.Mex., 1995—2001; sch. psychologist Deer Valley Sch. Dist., Phoenix, 2001—02, Saddle Mountain Sch. Dist., 2002—. Mem. adv. bd. Drug Free Schs., Gallup-McKinley, 1995—2001. Mem.: ACA, Am. Assn. Christian Counselors, Nat. Assn. Sch. Psychologists, World Congress Martial Artists Assn., Phi Delta Kappa. Avocations: swimming, hiking, racquet ball, tae-kwondo. Office: Saddle Mountain Sch Dist Ruth Fisher Sch 38201 W Indian Sch Rd Tonopah AZ 85354 Personal E-mail: brunettestarfish@cox.net.

FISHMAN, ELLEN BETH, lawyer; b. Bklyn., May 19, 1953; d. Stanley Irving and Elizabeth Flynn Fishman. BA summa cum laude, MA, Tufts U., 1974; JD, U. Pa., 1978. Bar: N.Y. 1979. Asst. corp. counsel N.Y.C. Law Dept., 1978—86, asst. chief. appeals divsn., 1986—2000, sr. coun. appeals divsn., 2000—03; appellate coun. Martin Clearwater & Bell LLP, N.Y.C., 2003—. Pres. Epiphany Parish Coun., N.Y.C., 1988—89. Mem.: N.Y. Cir. Translators, N.Y. County Lawyers Assn., N.Y. State Bar Assn. (chair com. on appellate cts. 1992—94). Democrat. Roman Catholic. Office: Martin Clearwater & Bell LLP 220 E 42nd St New York NY 10017 Office Phone: 212-697-3122.

FISHMAN, HELENE BETH, social worker; b. Portchester, N.Y., Oct. 23, 1937; d. Henry William and Hortense (Baumblatt) Sandground; B.A., Mt. Holyoke Coll., 1959; M.S. in Social Work, Columbia U., 1961; m. Bernard Fishman, Feb. 14, 1959; children: Kara Jo, Charles Lee. Psychiat. social worker Children's Village, Dobbs Ferry, N.Y., 1961, 1965-66; asst. dir. Afro-Am. Cultural Found., White Plains, N.Y., 1968-78; mental health technician tchr., White Plains, 1970-71; cons. social worker, Hartsdale, N.Y., 1978—; cons. edn./research Oceanic Soc., Stamford, Conn., 1985-86. Chmn. cottage program Greenburgh Dist. 7; active PTA. Mem. Assn. for Children with Learning Disabilities (chmn. dist. 7). Jewish. Home: 6 Old Farm Ln Hartsdale NY 10530-2204

FISK, DORIS ROSALIE SCANLAN, volunteer; b. Mpls., Aug. 20, 1915; d. Arthur William and Lea Marie (Beauchaine) Scanlan; m. Ellsworth William Fisk, Aug. 31, 1942; children: Gregory, Janine, Marilyn, Kathleen. Student, Mpls. Bus. Coll., 1935, U. Minn., 1940, San Antonio Jr. Coll., 1964. Hosp. vol. ARC, 1940-71; vol. Audie Murphy Vets. Hosp., 1972—; med. transcriber Radiology Assocs., San Antonio, 1962-64; nurse office mgr. for surgeon San Antonio, 1964-77; vol. Sr. Svc. Orgn., San Antonio, 1970—; vol., fund raiser Vis. Nurse Assn. S.W. San Antonio, 1992-97; vol. Quantum Brookhollow Med. Ctr., 1999—. Sec. vol. Demo-Ne Demos, San Antonio, 1960-64; pres. YWCA Wives, San Antonio, 1964-65, Espada Mission Aux., San Antonio, 1965-66; chair March of Dimes, San Antonio, ARC, 1940-1971, chmn. of vols.; vol. usher and seamstress Harlequin Theatre, from 1971; treas. altar soc. St. Mary's Cath.Ch., 1984-92; pres. flu shot prog. VNA, vol. Brookhollow Libr., 1995-96; chmn. Brooke Gen. Hosp. Vols. Recipient Golden Globe award Vol. Vis. Nurse of the Yr., San Antonio, 1993, Gold Key ring J.C. Penney; Letter of Congratulation, Pres. Clinton. Mem. AAUW, La Societé Francaise Canadian, Ret. Sr. Vols. (bd. mem. 1970—), Officers Wives Club (tour guide 1996-97, tel. chairperson 1999-2000, 2000-2001), Smithsonian Instn., Williamsburg, Met. Mus., Beta Sigma Phi (life), Kappa Kappa Gamma. Democrat. Roman Catholic. Avocations: travel, reading, sewing. Home: 7709 Beckett Rd Apt 1174 Austin TX 78749-1174

FISKE, SANDRA RAPPAPORT, psychologist, educator; b. Syracuse, N.Y., Sept. 25, 1946; d. Sidney Saul and Helen (Lapides) Rappaport; m. Jordan J. Fiske, June 22, 1974. BS, Cornell U., 1968; M.Ed., Tufts U., 1969; MA, Columbia U., 1971, PhD., 1974. Supervising sch. psychologist St. Elizabeth's Sch., N.Y.C., 1971-76; instr. clin. psychology Tchrs. Coll. Columbia, N.Y.C., 1973, clin. asst. dept. psychology, 1975-76; adj. prof. Syracuse U., 1976; sch. psychologist Syracuse Bd. Edn., 1976-77; prof. psychology Onondaga Community Coll., Syracuse, 1976-87, prof., 1988—, chair social sci. dept., 1993-99; pvt. practice psychology Syracuse, 1976—. NIMH fellow, 1969-72. Mem. APA, Ctrl. N.Y. Psychol. Assn., Sigma Xi, Psi Chi. Home: 2 Signal Hill Rd Fayetteville NY 13066-9674 Office: Onondaga Community Coll Dept Psychology Syracuse NY 13215 E-mail: sanjor@prodigy.net.

FITCH, JANET, writer; b. L.A. Grad., Reed Coll. Mng. editor Am. Film mag.; editor The Mancos Times Tribune; book reviewer Speak mag., San Francisco. Author: Kicks, 1996, White Oleander, 1999, short stories. Office: c/o Heather Rizzo Little Brown and Co 1271 Avenue of the Americas New York NY 10020*

FITCH, LINDA BAUMAN, elementary school educator; b. Elmira, N.Y., Jan. 6, 1947; d. Floyd Theodore Bauman and Wilma Mildred Rennie; m. H. Taylor Fitch, Feb. 15, 1969; children: Trevor Andrew, Matthew Taylor. BS, Keuka Coll., Keuka Park, 1969. Elem. tchr. Penn Yan (N.Y.) Ctrl. Sch. Dist., 1972-73, tchg. asst. K-5, 1999—; computer coord. Fitch Auto Supply, Penn Yan, 1973-99. Com. chmn. troop 48 Boy Scouts Am., Branchport, N.Y., 1986-92; v.p. Penn Yan Cen. Sch. Bd., 1984-92, 95-97, pres., 1992-95; chmn. pub. rels. Yates Day Care Ctr., Penn Yan, 1980-82; mem. Bd. Coop. Ednl. Svcs., 1992-99. Mem. AAUW, Nat. Sch. Bds. Assn. (fed. rels. network 1988-99), N.Y. State Sch. Bds. Assn. (state legis. network 1991-99), Four County Sch. Bds. Assn. (legis. chmn., 2d v.p., 1st v.p., pres., mem. commr.'s adv. coun. sch. bd. mems. 1995). Republican. Presbyterian. Avocations: needlework, reading, swimming. Home: 3120 Kinneys Corners Rd Bluff Point NY 14478-9752 E-mail: tnlfitch@adelphia.net.

FITCH, MARY KILLEEN, human resources specialist; b. Carroll, Iowa, July 15, 1949; d. Michael Francis and Mildred (Pauley) Killeen; m. David Paul Fitch, July 3, 1971; 1 child, Emily Grace. BS, Iowa State U., 1971, MS, 1975; postgrad., U. Minn., 1982—. Pers. adminstr. Control Data Corp., Roseville, Minn., 1976-77; sr. compensation analyst/employee rels rep. Honeywell, Inc., Mpls., 1977-80; human resource mgr./compensation and benefits mgr. No. Telecom, Inc., Minnetonka, Minn., 1980-82; compensation cons. Gen. Mills, Wayzata, Minn., 1984-85; mgr. compensation Northwestern Nat. Life Ins., Mpls., 1985-87; prin. compensation specialist Comml. Bldgs. Group, Honeywell, Inc., Mpls., 1987-89; dir. compensation, HRIS, benefits, incentive design Nat. Car Rental Sys., Inc., Mpls., 1989—98; dir. compensation, HRIS, benefits, and pay system N.Am. Rental Group (combined Alamo and Nat. Car), Mpls., 1998—99; v.p. compensation, HRIS ANC Rental Corp., Ft. Lauderdale, Fla., 1999—2003. Cons. human resources compensation, Fitch, Fitch Assoc., 1986—, cons. human resources Les Kraus & Assocs., Edina, Minn., 1984; pres. Personnel Mgmt. Services of Twin Cities, St. Paul, 1983—; adj. instr., tchg. asst. Lakewood Cmty. Coll./U. Minn., Mpls., 1982-84. Author: (with Paul Muchinsky) Organization Behavior and Human Performance, 1975; (with John Fossum) Personnel Psychology, 1985. Former chmn., bd. dirs. Kathadin, United Way Agy., Mpls., 1985-89; curriculum com. U. Minn., 1983-84. George Catt Iowa State U. scholar, 1970. Mem. AAUW, Assn. Human Resources Systems Profls., Am. Compensation Assn., Psi Chi, Phi Kappa Pi. Avocations: dressage, Karate. Home: 18660 Clifton Rd NW Anoka MN 55303 Office: 12230 Forest Hill Rd Ste 110V Wellington FL 33414 Office Phone: 612-384-2401. Personal E-mail: mfitch@hotmail.com. Business E-Mail: fitchm@ancrental.com.

FITCH, NANCY ELIZABETH, historian, educator; b. White Plains, N.Y., June 17, 1947; d. Robert Franklin and Nancy Elizabeth (Harvey) F. BA in Polit. Sci./English Lit., Oakland U., Rochester, Mich., 1969; MA in History, U. Mich., 1971, PhD in History, 1981. Danforth tchg. intern dept. history U. Mich., Ann Arbor, 1970, asst. prof. history and lit. Sangamon State U., Springfield, Ill., 1972-74; sr. social sci. rsch. analyst The Congl. Rsch. Svc. of Libr. of Congress, Washington, 1975-78; asst. to the chmn./historian U.S. EEO Commn., Washington, 1982-89; asst. prof. history Lynchburg Coll. of Va., 1989-91; asst. prof. African Am. studies Temple U., Phila., 1991-92; Jesse Ball Dupont vis. scholar Randolph-Macon Woman's Coll., Lynchburg, Va., 1992-93; assoc. prof. history U. N.C. at Asheville, 1993-95; assoc. prof. history and English Coll. New Rochelle, NY, 1995—, chair dept., 1999—2003. Chmn.'s rep. White House Inst. on Hist. Black Colls. and Univs., U.S. Dept. Edn., 1985-89, EEO com.; pub. rels. vol. S. Africa Exhibit Project, Washington, 1986-88; mem. adv. com. DuPont Vis. Scholars Project, Va. Found. Ind. Colls., 1990-91; adj. prof. in history Shaw U., Asheville, 1994; lectr. Jesse Ball DuPont Found. Coll. Confs. on Diversity, The Aspen Inst., Queenstown, Md., 1995, 96; participating historian, spkr. Schomburg Ctr. for Rsch. in Black Culture, N.Y.C., 1994, Booker T. Washington Jr. Anniversary Commemoration. Anthology Editor: How Sweet the Sound: The Spirit of African American History, 1999; editl. assoc.: Jour. South Asian Lit., 1969-79; co-editor: Diversity: A Jour. of Multicultural Issues, 1995-98; mem. editl. adv. bd. Kente Cloth: African Am. Voices in Tex.; book reviewer Jour. African Am. History, Jour. South Asian Lit., Lit. East and West, The Historian, Jour. Asian Studies; author: (series) Essays on Liberty, 1988; contbr. articles to profl. jours. Organizer, producer Ann. Dr. Martin Luther King Jr. Celebration prog., Washington, 1986-88; guest lectr. on history of Am. music Blue Ridge Music Festival, Lynchburg, 1991; participant Radio America African-Am. contbrs. to art and lit., 1990; vol./cons. The Holiday Project, Washington, 1986-88; mem. Widening Horizons Prog. of D.C. Pub. Schs., 1986-88; trustee Sister to Sister Internat. Recipient Achievement award Mt. Vernon Day Care Ctr., 1983, Spl. Commendation, U.S. EEO Commn., 1985-89, Ft. Drum Sgt. Maj.'s medal for svc. 10th Mountain div. Light Inf., Ft. Drum, N.Y., 1992; fellow Ford Found., 1971-72, Nat. Def. Fgn. Lang., 1970, U. Mich., 1970-71, 78-79, John Hay Whitney Found., 1969-70; Faculty summer seminar fellowship Nat. Endowment for the Humanities, U. Kans., Lawrence, 1996; Alden B. Dow creativity fellow Northwood U., 1998; Millennium writer Westchester Libr. Sys. Inc., 2000. Fellow Soc. Values in Higher Edn.; mem. Assn. for Study African Am. Life and History, Orgn. Am. Hists., Phi Alpha Theta (faculty advisor 1990-91). Republican. Episcopalian/Buddhist. Avocation: photography. Home: 267 Bedford Ave Mount Vernon NY 10553-1517 Office: Coll New Rochelle 29 Castle Pl New Rochelle NY 10805-2338

FITCH, RACHEL FARR, health policy analyst; b. July 27, 1933; d. Allen Edward and Rosie Leola (Jones) Farr; m. Coy Dean Fitch, Mar. 31, 1956; children: Julia Anne, Jaquelyn Kay. Student, Little Rock U., 1965-67; BS, St. Louis U., 1974, MS, 1976, PhD, 1983. RN, Mo. Psychiat. staff nurse VA Ft. Root Hosp., North Little Rock, Ark., 1954-57; surg.-med. staff nurse St. Vincent Infirmary, Little Rock, Ark., 1957-65; acute care nurse Georgetown U. Hosp., Washington, 1968-69; pub. health nurse to adminstr. South office Vis. Nurse Assn. Greater St. Louis, 1970-73; cons. in edn. St. Louis City Health Dept., 1977-80; rsch. specialist Sen. John C. Danforth, St. Louis, 1980; owner RFF Assocs., 1983-86. Project dir. study of infant mortality in city of St. Louis, 1978. Mem. community health edn. com. Am. Heart Assn., 1977-87; bd. dirs. LWV of Mo., 1984-2001, editor newspaper, 1984-87, dir. health issues, 1987-99, 1st v.p. 1999-2001, 2003—; chmn. Mo. Consumer Health Care WATCH, 1996-2002; mem. adv. com. Mo. Medicaid Consumer, 1996-97; mem. Mo. Welfare Coord. Com., 1997-99; mem. healthcare mgmt. and policy adv. com. Maryville U., 2002—; mem. Mo. Found. for Health Advocates steering com., 2003—. Mem. Am. Pub. Health Assn., Healthcare Mgmt. Policy Adv. Com., Acad. Polit. Sci., Grand Jury Assn. St. Louis (bd. dirs.), Woman's Club (St. Louis U. Sch. Medicine, past pres.), Jr. League St. Louis, Sigma Theta Tau. Address: 23 Lenox Pl Saint Louis MO 63108-1901 E-mail: rachel.farr.fitch@sbcglobal.net.

FITTS, CATHERINE AUSTIN, investment advisor; b. Phila., Dec. 24, 1950; d. William Thomas Jr. and Barbara Kinsey (Willits) Fitts. AA, Bennett Coll., 1970; student, Chinese U., Hong Kong, 1971; BA, U. Pa., 1974, MBA, 1978; postgrad., MIT. With Dillon, Read & Co., Inc., N.Y.C., 1978-89, sr. v.p., 1984-86, mng. dir., 1986-89, also bd. dirs.; asst. sec. housing, urban devel., fed. housing commr. HUD, Washington, 1989-90; pres., chmn. Hamilton Securities Group, Inc., Washington, 1990-97, Solari, Inc., Tenn., 1998—. Bd. dirs. Student Loan Mktg. Assn. Sallie Mae, 1991—94; mem. adv. bd. Fedn. Nat. Mortgage Assn. Fannie Mae, 1992—93, Sanders Rsch., London; mem. emerging markets adv. com. SEC, 1990—93. Columnist: The Real Deal, Scoop Media. Mem. grad. adv. bd. Wharton Sch., U. Pa., Phila., 1986—95.

FITZ-CARTER, ALEANE, elementary school educator, composer; b. Council Bluffs, Iowa, July 24, 1929; d. Andrew Wilburt and Beatrice Mildred (Maddox) Fitz; m. James Benny Carter, Dec. 10, 1958 (wid. Aug. 1964); children: Angel Beatrix, Angel Sherrie. BSEd, U. Nebr., 1956. Elem. sch. tchr. Omaha Pub. Schs., 1956-69; instr. Black history and music U. Nebr., Omaha, 1970-74; nat. faculty mem. Gospel Music Workshop Am. Inc., 1986; music tchr. Ascension Luth. Sch., L.A., 1990-94; min. music Messiah Luth. Ch., L.A., 1996—2003; church musician Tamarind Seventh Day Adventist Ch., Compton, Calif., 1997—2003; performing artist Nebr. Arts Coun., Omaha, 1980—, Iowa Arts Coun., Des Moines, 1998—; tchr. adult edn. L.A. Unified Schs., 1998—; ednl. cons. Torrance (Calif.) Unified Schs., 1997—99; min. of music Olivet Luth. Ch., Hawthorne, Calif., 2003—. Program prodr. KETV TV, Omaha, 1970-73; radio talk show host, KOWH Radio, Omaha, 1973-74; comms. cons. Mayor's Human Rels. Bd., Omaha, 1970-73; midwest bd. rep. Nat. Black Media Coalition, Washington, 1973-76, others; tchr. Black Awareness Opportunities Industrialization Ctr., 1969-74; instr. history of jazz, Oasis, L.A., 1997-2001; arranger, librettist, lyricist, elocutionist, storyteller, lectr. in field. Founder, dir. Omaha Gospel Choir, 1965—68, recs. include I Love Jesus, 1965, A Mighty Fortress, 1986; performer: (one-woman show) Rosa Parks, 1979—, Omaha Junior Theater, 1980—85; actress appearing in I Elvis, Hard Copy, 1992, Ice Cube video Dead Homie MTV, 1990, (films) A Man Apart, 2003, music dir. (stage show) One Last Look, Marla Gibbs Theater, 1990; contbr. articles to profl. jours.; composer: One Child, 1993, (sacred hymns) Psalm 91, 1993—97, Children's TV workshop, Strawberry Square II: Take Time, NETV, 1983; invitee South African churches of KwaZulu Natal and African Enterprises to do a piano performance for country's celebration of 1st yr. anniversary freedom, Durban, S. Africa, 1995. Presentation vis. with Huell Howser, KCET; rschr. soul food history and cooking. Nominee Best Supporting actress, Great White Hope Ctr. Stage, Omaha, Nebr., 1982; recipient Cmty. Christian Leadership award, Salem Baptist Ch., Omaha, Nebr., 1987, Woman in Fine Arts award, Alyce Wilson Womens Ctr., Omaha, 1987, 5 yr. ACT-SO award, NAACP, Omaha, 1986, Outstanding Songwriter award, 1987—88, Psalm 91 Song of Yr. award, Thurston Frazier Chorale, 1987, Nebr. Chpt. GMWA award, 1987—88, Fine Arts award, Bethesda Seventh Day Adventist Ch., 1988, Cmty. Guest Day, Bethesda Seventh Day Ch., Omaha, Nebr., 1988, Outstanding Svc. award, L.A. Union Seventh Day Acad., 1992, Creativity in music award, Thurston Frazier Chorale, GMWA, 1993, Svc. cmty. award, Salem Baptist Mission, Norfolk, Nebr., 1995; grantee, L.A. Dept. of Cultural Affairs. Mem.: ASCAP, SAG, Rec. Acad., Profl. Musicians Union - Local 47, Nebr. Congress of Parents and Tchrs. (hon. life), Gold Star Wives Am., L.A. Pianist Club, VFW Ladies Aux., Sigma Gamma Rho (Gamma Beta Sigma chpt.). Seventh Day Adventist. Avocations: walking, swimming, cooking. Mailing: PO Box 90087 Los Angeles CA 90009 Home: 200 E Hyde Pk Blvd #1 Inglewood CA 90302 Personal E-mail: Psalm91@mymailstation.com.

FITZGERALD, HELEN TERESA, grief therapist, writer; b. Jackson, Minn., Nov. 12, 1938; d. John Raymond and Mayme Mary (Benes) Cihak; m. Richard Carl Olson; stepchildren: Mark Albert Olson, Thomas Parker Olson, Jeffrey Paul Olson, Melissa Karen Franger; m. Jerald Charles Fitzgerald (dec. Apr. 1, 1974); children: Patti Ann Rauld, Sarah Jane Turosak, Charles Edwin, Mary Elizabeth. Diploma, Jackson HS, Jackson, MN, 1956. Cert. in thanatology Assn. for Death Edn. and Counseling, 2003. Creative therapist Fairfax Hosp., 1972—82; coord. grief program Mt. Vernon Ctr. for Cmty. Mental Health, Alexandria, Va., 1977—2000; dir. tng. Am. Hospice Found., Washington, 1996—. Mem. adv. bd. Haven of No. Va., Annandale, Va. Author: (Book) The Grieving Child, 1992, The Mourning Handbook, 1994, The Grieving Teen, 2000, (tng. manual) Grief At School, 1998, Grief At Work, 1999. Recipient Outstanding Performance award, Cmty. Svcs. Bd. Fairfax County, 1998, Cmty. Svc. award, Social Work Assn. Fairfax County, 1999. Mem.: Assn. for Death Edn. and Counseling (bd. dirs. 1993—96, Clin. Practices award 1999). Avocation: painting. Home: 3601 Devilwood Ct Fairfax VA 22030 Office: Am Hospice Found Ste 200 2120 L St NW Washington DC 20037 Personal E-mail: helen38@cox.net.

FITZGERALD, JANET ANNE, philosophy educator, academic administrator; b. Woodside, N.Y., Sept. 4, 1935; d. Robert W. and Lillian H. (Shannon) F. BA magna cum laude, St. John's U., 1965, MA, 1967, PhD, 1971, LLD (hon.), 1982. Joined Sisters of St. Dominic of Amityville, Roman Catholic Ch., 1953; NSF postdoctoral fellow Cath. U. Am., summer 1971; prof. philosophy Molloy Coll., Rockville Centre, NY, 1969—, pres., 1972-96, pres. emerita, 1996—. Trustee L.I. Regional Adv. Coun. on Higher Edn., 1972-96, chmn., 1981-84; trustee Commn. on Ind. Colls. and Univs., 1981-84, 89-92, Cath. Charities, Diocese of Rockville Centre, 1979-82; trustee Fellowship of Cath. Scholars, 1977—, v.p., 1977-80; invited expert peritus Vatican Internat. Conf. on Cath. Higher Edn., Rome, 1989; prof. S. John Neumann, Archdiocese of N.Y.; invited auditor St. Thomas Aquinas Pontifical U., Rome, 1999. Author: Alfred North Whitehead's Early Philosophy of Space and Time, 1979. Mem. bd. advisors Sem. of Immaculate Conception, 1975-80; mem. adv. bd. pre-theology program Dunwoodie Sem., Archdiocese of N.Y.; mem. pub. policy com. N.Y. State Cath. Conf., 1992-94; mem. N.Y. State Edn. Dept.-Blue Ribbon Panel on Cath. Schs., 1992-93; 1st woman grand marshal St. Patrick's Day Parade, Glen Cove, 1992. Recipient Disting. Leadership award L.I. Bus. News, 1988, plaque of recognition L.I. Women's Coun. for Equal Edn. Tng. and Employment, 1989, Pathfinder award Town of Hempstead, 1990, Disting. Long Islander in Edn. award Epilepsy Found. L.I., 1991, Educator of Yr. award Assn. Tchrs. N.Y., 1980, Spl. award for arts in edn. L.I. Arts Coun., 1994; honored by L.I. Cath. League for Religious and Civil Rights, 1989; named L.I.'s 100 Influentials, L.I. Bus. News, 1992, 93, 94, 95, 96. Mem. Soc. Cath. Social Scis. (bd. advisors). Office: Molloy Coll PO Box 5002 Rockville Centre NY 11571-5002 E-mail: jfitzgerald@molloy.edu.

FITZGERALD, JOAN, principal; Prin. Xavier Coll. Prep. Sch., 1975—. Recipient Blue Ribbon Sch. award 1990-91. Office: Xavier Coll Prep Sch 4710 N 5th St Phoenix AZ 85012-1738

FITZ-GERALD, JOAN, state senator; Dem. senator dist. 13 Colo. State Senate, 2000—. Mem. edn. com. Colo. State Senate, chair bus., labor and fin. com. Office: Colo State Senate 200 E Colfax Rm 330 Denver CO 80203 Fax: 303 526-2052.

FITZGERALD, JUDITH KLASWICK, federal judge; b. Spangler, Pa., May 10, 1948; d. Julius Francis and Regina Marie (Pregno) Klaswick; m. June 5, 1971 (div. Dec. 1982); 1 child; m. Barry Robert Fitzgerald, Sept. 20, 1986; 1 child. BSBA, U. Pitts., 1970, JD, 1973. Legal rschr. Assocs. Fin., Pitts., 1972-73; law clk. to pres. judge Beaver County (Pa.) Ct. Common Pleas, 1973-74; law clk. to judge Pa. Superior Ct., Pitts., 1974-75; asst. U.S. atty. U.S. Dist. Ct. (we. dist.) Pa., Pitts. and Erie, 1976-87, U.S. bankruptcy judge Pitts., Erie and Johnstown, 1987—, U.S. Dist. Ct. (ea. dist.) Pa., U.S. Dist. Ct. Del., 1997. Adj. prof. law U. Pitts., 1997. Co-author: Bankruptcy and Divorce, Support and Property Division, 1991; editor: Pennsylvania Law of Juvenile Delinquency and Deprivation, 1976; contbr. articles to profl. jours. Mem. Pitts. Camerata, 1978-80, Allegheny County Polit.-Legal Edn. Project, 1980, Mendelssohn Choir Pitts., 1982—; mem. coun. Program to Aid Citizen Enterprise, 1985-87. Recipient Spl. Achievement awards Dept. Justice, Spl. Recognition award Pittsburgh mag., Operation Exodus Outstanding Performance award Dept. Commerce, 1986. Mem. Internat. Women's Insolvency and Restructuring Conf., Allegheny County Bar Assn., Women's Bar Assn. of Western Pa., Nat. Conf. Bankruptcy Judges, Am. Bankruptcy Inst., Nat. Conf. Bankruptcy Clks., Comml. Law League of Am., Fed. Criminal Investigators Assn. (Spl. Svc. award 1988), Zonta. Republican. Lutheran. Avocations: singing, reading, traveling. Office: US Bankruptcy Ct 600 Grant St Ste 5490 Pittsburgh PA 15219-2805

FITZGERALD, LAURINE ELISABETH, university dean, educator; b. New London, Wis., Aug. 24, 1930; d. Thomas F. and Laurine (Branchflower) F. BS, Northwestern U., 1952, MA, 1953; PhD, Mich. State U., 1959. Instr. English, dir. devel. reading lab., head resident-dir. Wis. State Coll., Whitewater, 1953-55; area dir. residence and counseling Ind. U., 1955-57; teaching grad. asst. guidance and counseling, then instr., counselor Mich. State U., East Lansing, 1957-59; asst. prof. psychology and edn., assoc. dean students U. Denver, 1959-62; asst. prof. counseling psychology, staff counselor for Carnegie Found. project U. Minn., 1962-63; assoc. dean, assoc. prof. Mich. State U., 1963-70, assoc. dean students. prof. adminstrn. and higher edn., dir. divsn. edn. and rsch., 1970-74; dean Grad. Sch., prof. counselor edn., dir. N.E. Wis. Coop. Regional Grad. Ctr. U. Wis.-Oshkosh, 1974-85; dean, dir. Ohio State U.-Mansfield, 1985-87, prof. edn. policy and leadership, 1985-93, dir. student pers. asst. program, edn. policy and leadership, 1989-92. Adj. prof. edn. policy and leadership Ohio State U., 1992-93; vis. lectr. U. Okla., Norman, 1961; vis. prof. Oreg. State U., 1977; cons. in field; vocat. expertwitness, 1962-95. Contbr. numerous articles to profl. jours.; co-author monographs, texts. Adv. bd. Mansfield Gen. Hosp., 1986-94; bd. dirs. Renaissance Theatre, 1986-87, New Beginnings, 1986-94; exec. com. Ohio Consortium on Tng. and Planning, 1985-87; trustee Mt. Carmel Coll. Nursing, chmn. acad. affairs com., 1988-96. Recipient Higher Edn. Rocky Mountain coun. Girl Scouts U.S., 1961, Evelyn Hosmer U. Denver, 1962, Merit award Northwestern Alumni Assn., 1993; named Old Master Purdue U., 1979, Most Disting. Women in Edn., Mich., 1973; Elin Wagner Found. fellow, 1963-64. Mem. AAUW, AAUP (chpt. treas. 1955-56), NEA, Am. Psychol. Assn., Mich. Psychol. Assn., Am. Pers. and Guidance Assn., Am. Coll. Pers. Assn. (sec. 1965-67, exec. bd. 1968-70, chmn. women's task force 1970-71, editor jour. 1976-82, Disting. Scholar award 1985, sr. scholars com. 1985-90, historian 1982-95, chmn. scholars com. 1986-87, sr. scholars diplomate 1990, awards and commendations com. 1988-89, pres.-elect 1989-90, pres. 1990-91, past pres. 1991-92, Esther Lloyd-Jones Disting. Svc. award 1997), Assn. Counselor Edn. and Supervision, Am. Assn. Higher Edn., Nat. Assn. Women Deans, Adminstrs. and Counselors (rsch., ednl. by-laws programs, publs., univ. coms. 1959-72, v.p. 1972-74, KSP Trust Commn. 1979-81, pres. 1980-81, editl. bd. 1991-2000), Mich. Assn. Women Deans, Adminstrs. and Counselors (pres. 1967-69), Ohio Assn. Women Deans, Adminstrs. and Counselors, Mich. Coll. Pers. Assn., Wis. Coll. Pers. Assn., Midwest Assn. Grad. Schs. (pres. 1980-82), Intercollegiate Assn. Women Students (editorial bd., nat. advisor), Women's Equity Action League (past pres. Mich., nat. sec.-treas. legal and edn. def. fund), Bus. and Profl. Women's Club (chpt. pres. 1980, state officer 1981, Lena Lake Forest fellow 1966-67), Wis. Soc. for Higher Edn. (Achievement award 1985, Pres. award 1982), Altrusa Internat. (mem. bd. dirs. 1986-94), Mortar Bd., Shi-Ai, Beta Beta Beta, Psi Chi, Alpha Lambda Delta, Delta Kappa Gamma, Zonta (pres. Lansing club, chmn. internat. status of women com. 1960-85). Home: 812 Wyman St New London WI 54961-1771

FITZGERALD, MARY EILEEN, museum program director; b. Dayton, Ohio, Dec. 21, 1944; d. William McAvoy and Irene Ann (Dougherty) F. BA in Studio Art, U. Dayton, 1966; MA in Art History, Ohio State U., 1970; PhD in Humanities, Syracuse U., 1986. Lectr. Colgate U., Hamilton, N.Y., 1984-85; asst. prof. Ithaca (N.Y.) Coll., 1987-89, Syracuse (N.Y.) U., 1989-90, Roanoke Coll., Salem, Va., 1990-96; curator of edn. Maier Mus. of Art, Lynchburg, Va., 1996—2002; head of edn. Art Mus. Western Va., Roanoke, 2002—. Vis. prof. Ohio U., Athens, 1986-87; adj. asst. prof. Sweet Briar (Va.) Coll., 2001—. Mem. editl. bd. Artemis, 1994-95. Grantee St. James Ch. (Italy), 1983, NEH, 1994; Mednick fellow Va. Found. Ind. Coll., 1991, Florence fellow Syracuse U., 1977-79. Mem. Artemis (pres. bd. dirs. 1994-98). Avocations: photography, hiking, yoga. Home: 2571 Brambleton Ave SW Roanoke VA 24015-4303 Office: Art Mus Western Va Roanoke VA 24011-1436 E-mail: mfitzgerald@artmuseumroanoke.org.

FITZGERALD, MAURA, public relations executive; b. 1949; Former freelance writer AP, UPI, Electronic Bus., Boston Globe, USA Today; former reporter Ft. Lauderdale News, Quincy Patriot Ledger; v.p. Sterling Hager, Inc.; sr. account exec. Miller, 1986, account supr., 1986-88, v.p., 1988-89, sr. v.p., 1990-91; ptnr. Cunningham Comm., Santa Clara, Calif., 1991-93; founder, pres. Fitzgerald Comm., Cambridge, Mass., 1993—. Office: Fitzgerald Comm Inc 2 Seaport Ln Boston MA 02210-2001

FITZGERALD, NORMA ANNE, emergency nurse; b. San Francisco, Mar. 6, 1951; d. Craig Clayton and Margaret Carol Chandler; m. John David Fitzgerald, Oct. 13, 1973 (div. May 1989); children: Constance St. Claire, Patricia S., David D. Diploma, Washington Hosp. Ctr. Sch. Nursing, Washington, 1972. RN. Nurse Brooke Army Med. Ctr., Ft. Houston, Tex., 1972—74; RN, emergency dept., ICU San Antonio, 1974—76; RN, emergency dept. Watonga, Okla., 1976—78; dir. long range planning, mktg. and devel. Humana Hosp., San Antonio, 1978—84; med. mktg. cons. San Antonio, 1984—90; emergency rm./flight nurse Pa. and N.Y., 1990—2003; lead infusion nurse Apria Home Care, Syracuse, NY, 2001—. Foster parent, San Antonio, 1973—85. 2d lt. Nurse Corps U.S. Army, 1968—74, Ft. Houston, Tex. Named to Warren (Pa.) County Sports Hall of Fame, 1989; recipient U.S. Nat. 1 meter, 3 meter and Tower Nat. Champion (Diving), Masters Competition, 48 World and Nat. Springboard and Tower Diving Championship titles (Masters). Democrat. Episcopalian. Avocations: writing poetry, community theater, athletics, art. Home: 917 Madison St Unit 112 Syracuse NY 13210 Office: Apria Healthcare 12 Petra Ln Albany NY 13210 E-mail: annefitz@twcny.rr.com.

FITZGERALD-VERBONITZ, DIANNE ELIZABETH, healthcare executive; b. Tampa, Fla., July 11, 1943; d. James Gerald and Bernice Elizabeth (Creel) F.; children: Deborah Elizabeth Guilbault Starr, Fred Anthony Guilbault Jr. AA, Montgomery Coll., 1979; BS in Health Svcs. summa cum laude, No. Ariz. U., 1985, MEd, 1987. Nurse in Washington Internship, Advanced Internship. Pvt. practice counselor, Phoenix; mem. faculty C.V. Mosby Co., St. Louis; nurse clinician in orthopedics; mgr. orthopedic program Kimberly Quality Care; adminstr. Staff Builders Health Svcs., Phoenix, Cypress Health Care Svcs.; now exec. dir. Ariz. Psychol. Assn., Scottsdale. Bd. dirs. Valley of Sun Sch. and Rehab. Ctr., Arthritis Found.; mem. Am. Vol. Med. Team; med. vol. Habitat for Humanity. Named one of Top Ten Bus. Women in Managed Health Care, Today's Ariz. Woman 1998. Mem.: State and Provincial Psychol. Assns., Am./Ariz. Soc. Assn. Execs. (bd. dirs.), Nat. Assn. Orthopedic Nurses (pres. 1989—90), Rotary, Phi Kappa Phi (life).

FITZGIBBON, KATHERINE LENORE, music educator, director; b. Indianapolis, Ind., July 25, 1976; d. Joan Meltzer and Daniel Harvey FitzGibbon. BA in music, Princeton U., 1994—98; MusM in conducting, U. of Mich., 1999—2002. Dir. of choirs Duxbury Schools, Duxbury, Mass., 2002—; chorusmaster Windsor Symphony Orch., Windsor, Canada, 1999—2002; choral condr. U. of Mich., Ann Arbor, Mich., 1999—2002; dir. of vocal music Noble and Greenough Sch., Dedham, Mass., 1998—99; voice and conducting faculty Berkshire Choral Festival, Sheffield, Mass., 2001—; soprano, asst. condr. Boston Secession, Boston, Mass., 2002—. Conducting fellowship, U. of Mich., 1999—2001. Mem.: Boston Singers Resource, Coll. Music Soc., Music Educators Nat. Conf., Am. Choral Directors Assn., Phi Beta Kappa. Home: 9 Appleton Street Apt 200 Boston MA 02116

FITZMORRIS, PAMELA S. music educator; d. Charles Harmon Fitzmorris and Betty June Fingland; m. Richard J. Russnow, Oct. 14, 1978. BS in Music Edn. and Performance, Nazareth Coll. of Rochester, Pittsford, N.Y., 1978; MA in Liberal Studies, SUNY Coll., Brockport, N.Y., 1985; post grad., U. Ctrl. Fla., Lake Buena Vista, 1992, Fla. State U., Orlando, 1996. Permanent tchr. cert. N.Y. Vocal music tchr. Frankfort - Schuyler Consol. Sch. Dist., Frankfort, NY, 1980—82, Rome (N.Y.) City Sch. Dist., 1982—84, Spencerport Consol. Sch. Dist., 1985—, tchr. leader music k - 12, 1987—. Bd. mem Monroe County Sch. Music Assn., Rochester, NY, 1995—, choral coord.; dir. Spencerport Theatre Arts Group Experience, 1987—. Grantee Expression Through the Arts, N.Y. Coun. of the Arts, 1990—99. Mem.: Music Educators Nat. Conf., N.Y. State Music Assn., Assn. Supervision and Curriculum Design, Am. Choral Dirs. Assn. Democrat. Episcopalian. Home: 52 Glencross Cir Rochester NY 14626

FITZPATRICK, JANE, entrepreneur; b. Cuttingsville, Vt., Nov. 18, 1923; m. John H. Fitzpatrick, Sept. 7, 1944; children: Nancy Jane, JoAnn Fitzpatrick Brown. HHD (hon.), N. Adams State Coll., Mass., 1978; LHD (hon.), U. Mass., 1987, Am. Internat. Coll., Springfield, Mass., 1994. Co-founder, chmn. bd. Country Curtains, Stockbridge, Mass., 1956—. Life trustee Boston Symphony Orch., trustee, 1982—96; trustee emerita The Norman Rockwell Mus., Stockbridge, Mass. Chmn. Berkshire Theatre Festival, Stockbridge, Mass, (bd. pres. 1977-98). Office: PO Box 954 Stockbridge MA 01262-0955

FITZPATRICK, JOYCE J. nursing educator, former dean; BSN, Georgetown U., LHD (hon.), 1990; MS in Psychiatric-Mental Health Nursing, Ohio State U.; PhD in Nursing, NYU; MBA, Case Western Reserve U., 1992. Dean Frances Payne Bolton Sch. Nursing Case Western Reserve U., Cleve., 1982—97, Elizabeth Brooks Ford prof. nursing, 1998—. Dir. WHO Collaborating Ctr. for Nursing, Bolton Sch. Editor: Applied Nursing Rsch.; co-editor: Annual Rev. Nursing Rsch.; contbr. articles to profl. jours. Recipient Book of Yr. awards, Am. Jour. Nursing, Disting.Contbn. to Nursing Rsch. award, Midwest Nursing Rsch. Soc.; fellow USPHS Primary Care Policy fellow, 1995; scholar Inst. Medicine/Am. Acad. Nursing/Am. Nurses Found. scholar, 1994—95. Fellow: Am. Acad. Nursing; mem.: N.Am. Nursing Diagnosis Assn. (chair taxonomy com.). Office: Case Western Res U F P Bolton Sch Nursing 2121 Abington Rd Cleveland OH 44106-4904

FITZPATRICK, LOIS ANN, library administrator; b. Yonkers, N.Y., Mar. 27, 1952; d. Thomas Joseph and Dorothy Ann (Nealy) Sullivan; m. William George Fitzpatrick, Jr., Dec. 1, 1973; children: Jennifer Ann, Amy Ann. BS in Sociology, Mercy Coll., 1974; MLS, Pratt Inst., 1975. Clk. Yonkers Pub. Libr., 1970-73, libr. trainee, 1973-75, libr. I, 1975-76; reference libr. Carroll Coll. Libr., Helena, Mont., 1976-79, acting dir., 1979, dir., 1980—; asst. prof. Carroll Coll., Helena, 1979-89, assoc. prof., 1989-99, prof., 2000—. Bd. dirs. Mont. Shares; chmn. arrangements Mont. Gov.'s Pre White House Conf. on Libraries, Helena, 1977-78; mem. steering com. Reference Point coop. program for librs., 1991; mem. adv. com. Helena Coll. of Tech. Libr., 1994—; adv. coun. Mont. Libr. Svcs., 1996-2000; mem. Networking Task Force, 1998-2003, Laws Revision Task Force, 1998-2001; pres. elect Helena Area Health Sci. Libraries Cons., 1979-84, pres., 1984-88; bd. dirs. Mont. FAXNET. Co-chmn. interst group OCLC; chmn. local arrangements Mont. Gov.'s Pre White House Conf.; mem. Mont. Race for the Cure; bd. dirs. ACLU-MT, 1999—; mem. adv. com. Am. Cancer Soc. Lewis and Clark County. Mem. Mont. Libr. Assn. (task force for White House conf. 1991, chair govt. affairs com. 1997-2003, EdLINK-MT 1997-99, 2000-01), Soroptimist Internat. of Helena (2d v.p. 1984-85, pres. 1986-87). Home: 1308 Shirley Rd Helena MT 59602-6635 Office: Carroll Coll Jack & Sallie Corette Libr 1601 N Benton Ave Helena MT 59625-0001 Business E-Mail: lfitzpat@carroll.edu.

FITZPATRICK, M. LOUISE, dean, nursing educator; b. South River, N.J., May 24, 1942; d. John Francis and Bettina (Galassi) F. Diploma in nursing, Johns Hopkins U., 1963; BSN, Cath. U. Am., 1966; MA, Columbia U., 1968, MEd, 1969, EdD, 1972; cert., Harvard U., 1985. Former assoc. prof., dept. nursing edn. Tchrs. Coll., Columbia U., N.Y.C.; dean, prof. Villanova (Pa.) U. Coll. Nursing, 1978—. Cons. Mid. States Assn., Phila.; cons. to numerous univs., also univs. in Morocco, Egypt, Jordan, West Bank, Sultanate of Oman; cons., reviewer USPHS; bd. dirs. Nurses Ednl. Funds, Inc., N.Y.C. Author: The National Organization for Public Nursing, Development of a Practice Field, 1975; editor: Present Realities/Future Imperatives, 1977, Historical Studies in Nursing, 1978, Nursing in Society: A Historical Perspective, 1983; also 21 articles in profl. jours. Recipient Disting. Alumni award Columbia U. Tchrs. Coll., 1966, Cath. Univ. McManus medal, 1992; WHO fellow, Scandinavia and U.K., 1974; Am. Acad. Nursing fellow, 1978. Mem. Am. Nurses Assn. (past chmn. cabinet on nursing edn.), Am. Assn. Colls. Nursing, Nat. League for Nursing (bd. of govs.). Democrat. Roman Catholic. Avocations: music, theater, cooking, international travel. Home: 80 Woodstone Ln Villanova PA 19085-1425 Office: Villanova U Coll Nursing Villanova PA 19085

FITZPATRICK, NANCY HECHT, editor; b. Dec. 29, 1942; d. Ira Youngwood and Bettie Jane (Van Cleave) Hecht; m. Alan Rush Fitzpatrick, Dec. 15, 1973 (dec.); m. Thomas H. Gervais, May 17, 2003. Student, Upsala Coll., 1960-62, New Sch. Social Rsch., 1962-64, Johns Hopkins U., summer 1987, Bennington Coll., summer 1988, Union Inst., 2002—. Asst. copyeditor Am. Home mag., N.Y.C., 1964-68; v.p. Creative Comms. Assocs., Newark, 1968-70; sr. editor Family Circle mag., N.Y.C., 1970-77; corp. sec., v.p. mktg. Alternative Telecom. Corp., N.Y.C., 1977-92; exec. editor Meeting News mag., N.Y.C., 1993-95; assoc. news editor, book and art reviewer The Vineyard Gazette, 1997—2001; archivist and publs. editor Wampanoag Tribe of Gay Head/Aquinnah, 2002—. Editor various publs. Mem.: LWV, NOW, Eastern Bedford Environ. Assn. (treas.), Empire women in Telecom. (pres.), N.Y. Women in Comms.

FITZPATRICK, SUSAN, biochemist, neurologist, foundation executive; married. Grad., St. John's U.; PhD in Biochemistry and Neurology, Cornell U. Postdoctoral tng. Yale U., New Haven; dir. edn. Miami Project To Cure Paralysis, Miami, Fla., assoc. exec. dir.; adminstr. grants program Brain Trauma Found., Miami; program dir. James S. McConnell Found., St. Louis. Office: James S McDonnell Found Ste 1850 1304 S Brentwood Blvd Saint Louis MO 63117

FITZROY, NANCY DELOYE, engineering executive, mechanical engineer; b. Pittsfield, Mass., Oct. 5, 1927; d. Jules Emile and Mabel Winifred (Burr) deLoye; m. Roland Victor Fitzroy, Jr., Mar. 24, 1951. BChemE, Rensselaer Poly. Inst., Troy, 1949; DEng (hon.), Rensselaer Poly. Inst., 1990, DSc (hon.), N.J. Inst. Tech., 1987. Registered profl. engr., N.Y. Heat transfer engr. corp. R & D GE, Schenectady, NY, 1950-71, mgr. heat transfer consulting, 1971-74, strategy planner, 1974-76, mgr. program devel. gas turbine divsn., 1976-82, mgr. energy and environ. program, 1982-87. Dir. West Hill Devel. Corp., Rotterdam, NY, 1955—65; mem. adv. com. rsch. NSF, Washington, 1972—75; mem. transp. rsch. bd. coordinanting com. rsch. and tech. NRC, 1996—99; cons. in field; bd. dirs. ASME Found., 1989—95, 1997—, trustee, 1998—. Author, editor: book Heat Transfer and Fluid Flow, Data Books, 1955—75. Charter mem. Rensselaer Poly. Inst. Coun., 1972—. Named to Rensselaer Poly. Inst. Hall of Fame, 1999; recipient Demers medal, Rensselaer Poly. Inst., 1975, Achievement award, Fedn. Profl. Women, 1984, Disting. Alumna medal, Rensselaer Poly. Inst., 1996. Fellow: ASME (1st woman nat. pres. 1986—87, trustee Gear Rsch. Inst. 1987—89), Soc. Women Engrs. (Outstanding Achievement award 1972), Instn. Mech. Engrs. London (hon.); mem.: Assn. Engrings. Socs. (gov. 1987—89), Nat. Acad. Engring., Coral Ridge Yacht Club (Ft. Lauderdale, Fla.), Mohawk Golf Club, Whirly-Girls Club, Ninety-Nines Club. Republican. Episcopalian. Achievements include patents in field. Home: 2125 Rosendale Rd Niskayuna NY 12309-5418

FITZSIMMONS, ELLEN MARIE, lawyer; Sr. gen. counsel CSX Corp., Richmond, asst. gen. counsel, 1995-97, gen. counsel, 1997—. Office: CSX Corp One James Ctr PO Box 85629 901 E Cary St Richmond VA 23285-5629

FITZSIMMONS, TERRI KATHLEEN, career consultant, educator; b. Vancouver, B.C., Can., June 1, 1949; came to the U.S., 1975; d. Boyce William and Rose (Stangle) Banner; m. Charles Russell Fitzsimmons, Sept. 3, 1989; stepchildren: Charles, Richard. AS, Mt. San Jacinto Coll., 1989; BA, Calif. State U., San Bernardino, 1991, MS in Pupil Pers. Svcs.-Counseling, 1994; tchg. credential, Chapman Coll., 1995; postgrad., Asuza Pacific U. Clk. admissions and records, registration clk. Mount San Jacinto (Calif.) Coll., 1988-91; career counselor Calif. State U., San Bernardino, 1992—; substitute tchr. Hemet (Calif.) Sch. Dist., 1993—; spl. edn. tchr. Nueview Sch. Dist., Nuevo, Calif., 1994-95; substitute tchr. San Jacinto (Calif.) Sch. Dist., 1995—. Instr. grad. studies Calif. State U., San Bernardino; sociology tchr., tutor, trainer instr., coord. for welfare reform Mt. San Jacinto (Calif.) Coll.; pvt. practice career cons., Hemet, 1992—. Vol. Valley Resource, San Jacinto, 1994-95. Scholar Mount San Jacinto Coll., 1988, CACD, 1993. Mount San Jacinto Coll. scholar, 1988; mem. Univ. Assn. Women, Calif. Assn. Counselors (scholar 1993). Home: 27189 Roger St Hemet CA 92544-8311

FITZSIMONS, MARJORIE KITCHEN, art consultant; b. Cin., Apr. 8, 1946; d. John Milton and Jane Rauch Kitchen; m. Michael John FitzSimons, Aug. 8, 1970; children: Kelly, Colin, Ellie, Libby. BA, Wellesley Coll., 1967; MAT, Harvard U., 1970. Cert. women bus. owner Majority Bus. Initiative. Rschr. Frick Art Reference Libr., N.Y.C., 1968-69; tchr. Univ. Liggett Sch., Grosse Pointe, Mich., 1980-85; corp. cons. Joy Emery Gallery, Grosse Pointe, 1988-90; art cons., owner Art Cons. Svcs., Grosse Pointe, 1991—. Vol. Detroit Artists Market, 1980-99; mem. Altar Guild, Christ Ch., Grosse Pointe, 1985—; bd. dirs. Garden Club Mich., Grosse Pointe, 1989—, Friends Modern Art, Detroit Inst. Arts, 1997—. Mem. Women's Dist. Golf Assn., Women's Econ. Club. Episcopalian. Avocations: golf, sailing. Home and Office: 2727 N Ocean Blvd #6 Gulf Stream FL 33483-7357

FITZSIMONS, SHARON RUSSELL, international consumer goods, financial and treasury executive; b. Toronto, Ont., Can., June 25, 1945; d. Leslie Alfred and Winifred Marjorie (Williston) Russell; m. John Henry Fitzsimons, Jan. 4, 1969; children: Luke Edward, Michael Russell. BA, U. So. Calif., 1968; MA, Calif. State U., 1971; MS in Bus. Adminstrn., U. Calif., Irvine, 1978; grad. internat. sr. mgmt. program, Harvard Bus. Sch., 1990. Mgr. rsch. William Pereira Assocs., Newport Beach, Calif., 1970-71; asst. mgr. interior design Concept Environment Inc. subs. Ford Motor Co., Orange County, Calif., 1971-72; v.p. Urban Interface Group, Orange County, 1972-74; cons. in field, 1975-76; mgr. strategic planning Mission Viejo Co., Orange County, 1976-80; mgr. fin. Philip Morris Internat., N.Y.C., 1980-82, asst. treas., 1983-84, ops., strategic mktg. and logistics exec. PM Australia Ltd., Melbourne, 1984-86, dir. U.S. export logistics and customer svc., N.Y.C., 1987-90, fin. dir., treas., N.Y.C., 1990—; chmn., CEO, Internat. Intrigues, 1997—, pres., CEO, co-trustee Pamco Preservation Mgmt. Co., Phoenix, Ariz. Mem. Harvard Women's Alumnae Network Assn. (bd. dirs.), Women in Mgmt., Harvard Club Greater N.Y., The Internat. Alliance.

FITZWATER, KATHERINE SAUTER, elementary school educator; b. Summerville, SC, Jan. 23, 1974; d. Harold Charles and Lorna Jesine Sauter; m. William Ryan Fitzwater, June 19, 1999. BS in Edn., Cumberland Coll., 1997; MEd in Early Edn. & Spl. Edn., Tenn. State U., 2001. Boating instr. YMCA, Manchester, NH, 1995—97; spl. edn. tchr. Nashville (Tenn.) Pub. Schs., 1997—2001, kindergarten tchr., 2001—03. Cancer rsch. contact Nat. Cancer Rsch., Nashville, 2001—03. Mem.: Internat. Reading Assn., Metro Nashville Edn. Assn. Avocations: reading, hiking, gemology. Office: Bordeaux Enhanced Option Elem 1910 S HamiltonRd Nashville TN 37218 E-mail: ksfitzh20@comcast.net.

FIX, CAROLYN ELIZABETH, retired geologist, writer, editor; b. Utica, N.Y., Nov. 28, 1922; d. William Anthony and Evelina Marie F. BA in Biology cum laude, Utica Coll. of Syracuse U., 1951; MS in Geology, Syracuse U., 1953. Registered radiology technician, N.Y.; registered pub. health sanitarian, Va. Geologist U.S. Geol. Survey, Denver, 1953-58, Washington, 1958-60; writer, editor U.S. Army and Navy, Washington, 1960-63; reporter, editor Free Press Newspapers, Falls Church, Va., 1964; pub. health sanitarian Fairfax (Va.) County Health Dept., 1971-77; indexer, editor (database) Am. Geol. Inst., Alexandria, Va., 1980—2000, ret., 2001. Author: (U.S. Geol. Survey Book) Annotated Bibliography of Uranium in Marine Black Shales in the U.S., 1958; artist wood carving, painting, Vol. demonstrator Fairfax County Park Authority, 1980—; hist. demonstrator U.S. Nat. Park Svc., Jamestown (Va.) Festival, 1990 (awd. 1990), Mt. Vernon, Va., 1993; bd. dirs. Vienna (Va.) Comty. Band, 1993—; mem. at large Mayor's Adv. Com., Vienna, 1993—. Staff sgt, WAC, WWII, 1943-51. Recipient Fulbright scholarship U.S. Govt. Fulbright Program, U. Queensland, Australia, 1954; recipient many awards for photography; named 1st woman Fairfax (Va.) County Health Dept., 1971-77. Mem. Organ Hist. Soc. (sec.-treas. Hilbus chpt. 1971-77), Am. Guild of Organists, Nat. Geneal. Soc., Am. Legion, D.A.V., WAC Vets Assn. Avocations: music, natural history, genealogy, archaeology, art.

FLACK, ROBERTA, singer; b. Black Mountain, N.C., Feb. 10, 1939; d. Laron and Irene F.; m. Stephen Novosel, 1966 (div. 1972). BA in Music Edn., Howard U., 1958. Tchr. music and English lit. pub. schs., Farmville, N.C., Washington, 1959-67; rec. artist Atlantic Records, 1968—. Star ABC TV spl. The First Time Ever, 1973; composer: (with Jesse Jackson and Joel Dorn) Go Up, Moses; albums include: First Take, 1969, Chapter Two, 1970, Quiet Fire, 1971, Killing Me Softly, 1973, Feel Like Makin' Love, 1975, Blue Lights In The Basement, 1977, Roberta Flack, 1978, The Best of Roberta Flack, 1981, I'm The One, 1982, Born To Love, 1983, Hits and History, 1984, Roberta Flack, 1985, Oasis, 1989, Set the Night to Music, 1991, Roberta, 1994; writer TV theme song Valerie. Recipient Gold Record for The First Time Ever I Saw Your Face, 1972; Grammy awards for best record, best song (The First Time Ever I Saw Your Face), 1972, best record, best female vocalist (Killing Me Softly With His Song), 1973, best pop vocal duo (Where Is The Love), 1972, winner Downbeat's reader poll as best female vocalist, 1971-73; City of Washington celebrated Roberta Flack Human Kindness Day, 1972; Star on the Hollywood Walk of Fame,2000. Mem. Sigma Delta Chi. Office: care Atlantic Records 75 Rockefeller Plz New York NY 10019-6908

FLACK, TERESA HOPPER, music educator; b. Rutherfordton, N.C., Apr. 12, 1954; d. Charles William Hopper and Mae Guffey Johnson; m. Geary Michael Flack, June 25, 1977; children: Michael Ellis, Lauren Elizabeth. B in Music Edn., Converse Coll., 1976; MusM in Piano Pedagogy, So. Meth. U., 1982. Pvt. piano tchr., 1974—94; elem. music tchr., choral dir. Wesleyan Christian Acad., High Point, NC, 1995—. Mem.: Am. Choral Dirs. Assn., Music Educators Nat. Conf., Am. Orff Schurlwerk Assn. (historian/sec. Pedmont, N.C. chpt. 1999—2000). Republican. Methodist. Home: 2507 Burch Pt High Point NC 27265 Office: Wesleyan Christian Acad 1917 N Centennial St High Point NC 27262

FLAGG, HELEN CLAWSON, writer; b. Netcong, N.J., May 27, 1921; d. Clyde Leroy and Rose Ann (Wood) Wilgus; m. Raymond E. Clawson, Feb. 7, 1942 (dec. May 1988); children: Lana Hope (Mrs. Dale Hope), Rory Zane; m. Allen Macomber Flagg, Nov. 16, 1991. Student, Rutgers U., 1941-42. CEO, ATS Corp., nat. placement co., Ft. Collins, Colo., 1976-80; pres. Status Unltd., pub. rels., Ft. Collins, 1982-90; fin. planner Waddell & Reed, Ft. Collins, 1984-90; stockbroker Dean Witter, Clearwater, Fla., 1990-91; fin. planner, ins. rep. Walnut Street Securities, Clearwater, 1992-95. Former pub. spr. on fin. and religious subjects. Author: Joy in the Morning, 1995; contbr. numerous articles to newspaper and mags., including Fortune mag. Cons., historian Presbyn. Ch., Clearwater, 1995-99; supporter numerous civic orgns, sec. Altrusa, Ft. Collins, 1976-80. Mem. NAFE. Republican. Avocations: writing, poetry, reading history. Home: PO Box 8041 Radnor PA 19087-8041

FLAGG DAVIS, VIVIAN ANNETTE, librarian, researcher, public policy consultant; b. Milledgeville, Ga., July 18, 1960; d. Rufus and Sandra Ann (Seals) F.; m. Joe H. Davis Jr., Jan. 16, 1993. BA, Ga. State U., 1982, MPA, 1988. Purchasing and sales clk. Reed Drugs, Atlanta, 1980-81; libr. assoc. Atlanta Jour. & Constn., 1981-84, libr. asst., 1984-89, assoc. libr., rsch. supr., 1989-91, systems libr., 1991—. Tutor Lit. Action, Atlanta, 1981-83, Alonzo Herndon Elem. Sch., 1999-2001; bd. dirs. Odyssey Family Counseling Ctr., Hapeville, Ga., 1983-85; mem. adv. coun. Vol. Atlanta, 1984-87, pres., 1983-85; vol. spl. projects Changed Living Recovery, 1994—; mem. svc. coun. Youth Devel. Allocations and Evaluation Com., Atlanta, 1987—, planning and allocations com. United Way, Atlanta, 1987—, co-chair Task Force for Homeless and Hungry, 1992—; chmn. social action com. social svcs. and human resources dir. Greater Piney Grove Bapt. Ch.; mem. Atlanta Ballet Assocs.; bd. dirs. Higher Plain Ministries, 1994—, chair adminstrn. com., 2003; co-chair edn. com. AJC in Action; founder reading program Will You Read To Me?, 2003. Recipient Outstanding Leader award Vol. Ga., 1984. Mem. ASPA, Nat. Young Profls. Forum, NAACP, Am. Soc. Info. Sci., Spl. Librs. Assn. Democrat. Avocations: piano, sewing, tennis, gardening, travel. Home: 3735 Landgraf Cv Decatur GA 30034-4775 Office: Atlanta Jour Constn 72 Marietta St NW Atlanta GA 30303-2804

FLAHARTY, GERALDINE, state representative; b. Parsons, Kans., Mar. 4, 1936; BS, Wichita State U., 1962, MEd, 1971. Elem. tchr. Wichita Pub. Schs., 1956—57; reading tchr. Oaklawn Elem., 1966—; mem. Kans. Ho. of Reps., 1995—. Precinct woman, 1988—. Mem.: AAUW, Kans. Nat. Edn. Assn., Internat. Reading Assn., Wichita State U. Alumni Assn. Democrat. Office: 279-W State Capitol 300 SW 10th Ave Topeka KS 66612 Address: 1816 Fernwood Wichita KS 67216-8039

FLAHERTY, ANNE H. advocate; b. Boston, Dec. 24, 1960; children: Sarah, Matthew. BS in Health Promotion/Edn., Bridgewater State Coll., Mass., 1991; postgrad., Boston U. Media cons. Greenworks, Cambridge, Mass., 1989—92; owner Star Struck Enterpriser DJ and Karaoke Co., Newton, Mass., 1992—97; founder, CEO Social Justice Today Orgn., Framington, Mass., 1999—. Cons. Empower Us, Nashville, 2000—03. Mem. ACLU; contbg. writer Sojourner Feminist Inst., Boston, 1999—2002. Recipient Internat. Poet of Merit award, Internat. Poetry Soc., 2002. Libertarian. Christian Ch. Avocations: singing, fitness, songwriting, music. Office: Social Justice Today PO Box 1033 Los Alamos NM 87544

FLAHERTY, EMALEE GOTTBRATH, pediatrician; b. LaGrange, Ky., May 24, 1944; d. Frank Herman and Katherine Lee (Carothers) Gottbrath; m. Joseph Flaherty, Apr. 28, 1973 (div.); children: Joshua, Megan. BS, Purdue U., W. Lafayette, Ind., 1966; MD, Ind. U., Indpls., 1970. Resident, pediatrics U. Ill. Hosp., 1970-72, Columbus Hosp., 1972-73, med. dir. outpatient dept., 1984-96, med. dir. Columbus-Maryville Reception Ctr., Chgo., 1986-95; dir. ambulator pediatrics Columbus Hosp., Chgo., 1979-96, project dir. pediatric primary care tng. grant, 1989-95; med. dir. protective svc. team Children's Meml. Hosp., Chgo., 1996—; asst. prof. pediatrics Northwestern U. Sch. Medicine, Chgo., 1997—. Mem. Am. Acad. Pediat. (chpt. treas.), Pediatric Primary Care Rsch. Grp. (steering com.), Pediatric Rsch. Office Setting (dist. coord.), Columbus Hosp. Woman's Bd. (exec. bd. 1988-96). Office: Children's Hosp 2300 N Childrens Plz # 16 Chicago IL 60614-3363

FLAHERTY, LOIS TALBOT, editor, psychiatrist, educator; b. Nashville, Apr. 28, 1942; BA, Wellesley Coll., 1963; MD, Duke U., 1968. Diplomate Nat. Bd. Med. Examiners. Intern D.C. Gen. Hosp., 1968-69; resident in psychiatry Georgetown U. Hosp., 1969-71; resident in child psychiatry Johns Hopkins Hosp., 1971-73; pvt. practice Cross Keys, Md., 1973-81; dir. tng. divsn. child and adolescent psychiatry U. Md., 1981-89, assoc. prof. med. sch. divsn. child and adolescent psychiatry, 1982-93, dir. divsn. child and adolescent psychiatry, 1984-92, adj. assoc. prof., 1994—; clin. assoc. prof. psychiatry U. Pa., 1997-2000; pvt. practice Blue Bell, Pa., 1994-99; editor Adolescent Psychiatry, 2000—. Instr. depts. psychiatry and pediatrics Johns Hopkins U. Sch. Medicine, 1973-92; attending staff psychiatrist family, child and adolescent divsn. Sinai Hosp. Balt., 1974-77; staff child psychiatrist Walter P. Carter Ctr., 1977-78, dir. child and adolescent svcs., 1978-92, acting dir. impatient adolescent unit, 1979-80; clin. asst. prof. U. Md., 1977-81; lectr. psychiatry Harvard U., 2002—; cons. Northwest Drug Alert Sinai Hosp. Balt., 1971-72, St. Vincent's Child Care Ctr., 1973-78, Children's Guild, Inc., 1975-82, SSA, Balt., 1985, many others. Contbr. chpts. to books and articles and book revs. to profl. jours. NIMH grantee, 1983-86. Fellow: Am. Soc. for Adolescent Psychiatry (disting.), Am. Psychiat. Assn.; mem.: Group for Advancement of Psychiatry, Am. Coll. Psychiatrists, Am. Acad. Child Psychiatry. Office: 4 Charlesgate East #605 Boston MA 02215-2369 E-mail: lflaher770@aol.com.

FLAHERTY, SISTER MARY JEAN, dean; Dean, prof. Sch. Nursing, Cath. U. Am., Washington. Office: Cath U Am Sch Of Nursing Washington DC 20064-0001

FLAHERTY, PAMELA POTTER, bank executive; b. Jefferson City, Mo., July 1, 1944; d. Reese H. and Mary Jane (Stagg) Potter; m. Peter A. Flaherty, Nov. 28, 1970; children: Jonathan Peter, David Alexander. BA, Smith Coll., 1966; MA in internat. rels., Johns Hopkins U., 1968. Various positions internat. banking Citicorp, N.Y.C., 1968-76, various position consumer banking, 1976-85, head of human resources, 1985-89, head of consumer banking in N.E., 1989—95, senior v.p., dir. community rels., 1995—98; senior v.p., global community rels. Citigroup Inc. (formerly Citicorp), N.Y.C., 1998—. Bd. dirs. Rockefeller Fin. Svcs., Inc., N.Y.C.; mem. adv. coun. Bass plc U.S., 1990—; bd. dirs., mem. exec. com. Am. Women's Econ. Devel. Corp., N.Y.C., 1987—. Bd. trustees Johns Hopkins Medicine, 2000—. Named one of Women Who Make a Difference by Smith Coll. Club of N.Y., 1991. Mem. Com. of 200. Office: Citigroup 399 Park Ave New York NY 10043

FLAHERTY, SERGINA MARIA, ophthalmic medical technologist; b. Düsseldorf, Germany, Nov. 22, 1958; came to U.S., 1962; d. Austin W. and Evelyn (Kähl) F. Cert. ophthalmic med. technologist. Ophthalmic asst. U.S. Army, Ft. Rucker, Ala., 1978-82; ophthalmic technician Wiregrass Total Eye Care Clinic, Enterprise, Ala., 1983-86, Straub Hosp. and Clinic, Honolulu, 1986-90; ophthalmic technologist Eye Cons. of San Antonio, San Antonio, 1993-96, Stone Oak Ophthalmology, San Antonio, 1996—. Founder, owner, CEO Ophthalmic Seminars of San Antonio, 1996—. Mem. Assn. Tech. Pers. in Ophthalmology, Ophthalmic Photographer Soc., Hawaii Ophthalmic Assts. Soc. (founding mem., sec. 1987-89, pres. 1989-90), Ophthalmic Pers. Soc. San Antonio (program dir. 1994-95, 2001—, pres. 1996-2000). Avocation: shin shin toitsu aikido. Office: Stone Oak Ophthalmology 540 Madison Oak Dr Ste 450 San Antonio TX 78258-3932 Office Phone: 210-490-6759.

FLAHERTY, TINA SANTI, corporate communications executive, writer; b. Memphis; d. Clement Alexander and Dale (Pendergrast) Santi; m. William Edward Flaherty, Feb. 22, 1975. BA, U. Memphis, 1961; hon. doctorate, St. John's U., 1979. Commentator host interview program Sta. WMC-TV, Memphis, 1960-61; newscaster, commentator Sta. WHER, Memphis, 1961-62; cmty. rels. specialist Western Electric Co., N.Y.C., 1964-66; v.p. pub. rels. divsn. Grey Advt., N.Y.C., 1966-72; dep. dir. corp. rels. Colgate-Palmolive Co., N.Y.C., 1972-75, dir. corp. rels., 1975-76, corp. v.p., v.p. in charge of communications, 1976-84; v.p. pub. affairs GTE Corp., Stamford, Conn., 1984-86; pres., chief exec. officer Image Mktg. Internat., N.Y.C., 1986—. Author: The Savvy Woman's Success Bible, 1997 (one of Top Motivational Books of Yr., Books for a Better Life 1997), Talk Your Way to the Top, 1999, What Jackie Taught Us. Lessons from the remarkable Life of Jacqueline Kennedy Onassis, 2004. Former chmn. Bus. Coun. of UN Decade for Women; bd. dirs. Nat. Jr. Achievement, 1978—; mem. The White House Pub. Affairs Advisors, 1981-84; nat. bd. dirs. Animal Med. Ctr. Recipient Jr. Achievement Meml. award, 1984; named One of N.Y.C.'s Outstanding Women of Achievement, NCCJ, One of 100 Top Corp. Women, Bus. Week, One of 73 Women Ready to Run Corp. Am., Working Woman, Woman of Distinction, Birmingham So. Coll., One of 100 Amazing Ams., Am.'s Elite, 2000. Mem. DAR, Com. of 200, Internat. Women's Forum. Home and Office: Image Mktg Internat 1040 Fifth Ave New York NY 10028-0137 Office Phone: 212-535-0025. E-mail: imi1040@aol.com.

FLAKES, SUSAN, playwright, screenwriter, director; b. San Diego, July 9, 1943; d. Herbert Franklin and Dorothy Jean (Loafman) Barrows; m. Donald Lewis Flakes, Dec. 31, 1964; 1 child, Daniel Keith. BA, U. N.Mex., 1965; MA, San Diego State U., 1969; PhD, U. Minn., 1973. Asst., then assoc. prof. Tisch Sch. Arts NYU, 1973-76, dept. chair Tisch Sch. Arts, 1973-76; founder, artistic dir. Blue Tower Theatre, Stockholm, 1977-80, Strindberg's Intima Teater, Stockholm, 1981-83, Source Prodns., N.Y.C., 1984-90. Instr. U.S. Internat. Univ., San Diego, 1972-73; founder, artistic dir. 1st Strindberg Festival, Stockholm, 1977; mem. Women's Project and Prodns., N.Y.C., 1984-90; v.p. Ibsen Soc. Am., N.Y.C., 1986-99; coord. writers unit W. Coast Ensemble Theatre, Hollywood, Calif., 1991-93. Author plays, 1977, 92, 95-97, 98, 99, 2001, 2003, The Woman Will Play Strindberg's Christina, Laura, Silent Star, And Immortality, Marilyn's Rose, Portrait of Psyche, Daddy's Eyes, To Take Arms, Cafe L.A., (with Shirl Hendryx) 4F; (libretto with Galt MacDermot) Take It Higher, Maid of Lorraine, Any Saints Out There? (with Gabe Green), It Girls; (screenplays) To Take Arms, Stand the Storm, Hometown, Inc., Café L.A., Francois Poet/Thief, Lifetime Achievement, Immortality Daddy's Eyes; dir. Hughie, 1989, Mother Love, 1994; author: (book) Sing The Person; contbr. articles to profl. jours. and books in U.S., Russia, and Sweden; creator Exptl. Theatre Wing U.G. Drama Tisch Sch. Arts, NYU, 1975-76; contbr. play And Immortality to Baltic Seasons Mag., Russia, 2003. Ensign USN, 1965-67. Recipient honorable mention Writers Digest Writing Competition, 1999, winner 10-minute play festival, Fire Rose Productions, 2004, Fullerton Coll. Playwriting Festival, Resident Theater Co., 2004, Lamia Ink Internat. competition, 1991; fellow Am. Film Inst., 1990; grantee Nat. Endowment for Arts, 1972; travel grantee Am. Scandinavian Found., Norwegian and Swedish Govts., 1985, 86, 89, 94, 2001; finalist Susan Smith Blackburn prize, 1996-97, Nat. Playwrights Conf., 2000. Mem. Dramatists Guild, Actor's Studio (playwright/dirs. unit), Am. Film Inst. (finalist directing workshop for women 2003), Phi Beta Kappa. Address: 7552 Amazon Dr #1 Huntington Beach CA 92647 E-mail: sflakes@socal.rr.com.

FLANAGAN, AILEEN MARY, special education educator; b. Berwyn, Ill., July 17, 1976; d. John James and Marianne C. Flanagan. BS, Bradley U., 1998; MS in Edn., No. Ill. U., 2003. Cert. tchr. Ill. Tchr. Burbank (Ill.) Sch. Dist. #111, 1999—2000, Lincoln-Way H.S. #210, Frankfort, Ill., 2000—. Com. mem. North Ctrl. Accreditation, 2002—. Mem.: Coun. for Exceptional Children, Kappa Delta Pi. Home: 3338 Thomas Hickey Dr Joliet IL 60431 Office: Lincoln Way East HS 201 Colorado Ave Frankfort IL 60423

FLANAGAN, BARBARA, journalist; b. Des Moines; d. John Merrill and Marie (Barnes) F.; m. Earl S. Sanford, 1966. Student, Drake U., 1942-43. With promotion dept. Mpls. Times, 1945-47; reporter Mpls. Tribune, 1947-58; women's editor, spl. writer Mpls. Star and Tribune, 1958-65; columnist Mpls. Star, 1965—. Author: Ovation, Minneapolis. Active Junior League Mpls., Womans Club Mpls. Mem. Mpls. Soc. Fine Arts (life), Mpls. Inst. Arts (founding mem. Minn. Arts Forum), Mpls. Club, Minikahda Club, Kappa Alpha Theta, Sigma Delta Chi. Episcopalian. Home: 3200 W Calhoun Pky Apt 301 Minneapolis MN 55416-4650 Office: Mpls Star Tribune 5th And Portland Sts Minneapolis MN 55488-0001

FLANAGAN, DEBORAH MARY, lawyer; b. Hackensack, N.J., Sept. 17, 1956; d. Joseph Francis and Mary Agnes (Fitzsimmons) F.; m. Glen H. Koch, Aug. 27, 1983. BA summa cum laude, Fordham U., 1978, JD, 1981; LLM in Taxation, NYU, 1987. Bar: N.Y. 1982 and U.S. Dist. Ct. 1988. V.p., assoc. tax counsel The McGraw-Hill Inc. Cos., N.Y.C., 1981—. Mem. Assn. Bar City N.Y., Fordham U. Law Alumni Assn., NYU Law Alumni Assn. Home: 201 Chestnut Ridge Rd Saddle River NJ 07458-2812 Office: The McGraw-Hill Companies 1221 Avenue Of The Americas 48th Fl New York NY 10020-1095

FLANAGAN, FIONNULA MANON, actress, writer, theater director; b. Dublin; came to U.S., 1968; d. Terence Niall and Rosanna (McGuirk) F.; m. Garrett O'Connor, Nov. 26, 1972. C.I.H.E., U. Fribourg, Switzerland, 1962; student, Abbey Theatre Sch., Dublin, 1964-66. Pres. The Rejoycing Co., 1978—. Stage appearances include: Ulysses in Nighttown, N.Y.C., 1974, Lovers, 1968, Ghosts, 1989, Happy Days, 1991, Unfinished Stories, 1992, Countess Cathleen, 1992, Summerhouse, 1994; author, actress one-woman shows: James Joyce's Women, 1977 (L.A. Drama Critics award, San Francisco Theatre Critics award, Drama-Logue award); films include: Ulysses, 1967, In the Region of Ice, 1980, Mr. Patman, 1980, James Joyce's Women, 1984, Reflections, 1984, Chain Reaction, 1985, Death Dreams, 1992, Mad at the Moon, 1992, Money for Nothing, 1993, Some Mother's Son, 1996, Waking Ned Devine, 1998, With or Without You, 1999, The Others, 2000, Divine Secrets of the Ya-Ya Sisterhood, 2001; TV appearances include: The Picture of Dorian Gray, 1973, The Legend of Lizzie Borden, 1975, Rich Man Poor Man, 1976 (Emmy award for most outstanding support role 1976), How the West Was Won, 1977-79 (Emmy nominee 1978), A Winner Never Quits, 1986, White Mile, 1994, Kings in Grass Castles, 1998, To Have and To Hold, 1998; dir. Freedom of the City, Theatre West L.A., 1988 (Dramalogue award), Faith Healer, 1989, Away Alone, Court Theatre, L.A., 1991, Abbey Theatre, Dublin, 1992, A Secret Affair, 1999, Havana Nocturne, 2000. Mem. AFTRA, Actors' Equity, Screen Actors' Guild, Irish Actors Equity. Office: Don Buchwald & Assocs 6500 Wilshire Blvd Ste 2200 Los Angeles CA 90048-4942

FLANAGAN, JUDY, special events professional, entertainment and marketing specialist, professional public speaker; b. Lubbock, Tex., Apr. 28, 1950; d. James Joseph II and Jean (Breckenridge) F. BS in Edn., Memphis State U., 1972; postgrad., Disney U., 1975-81, Valencia C.C., 1977-79, Rollins Coll., 1979; MS in Comm., U. Tenn., 2004. Area/parade supr. entertainment divsn. Walt Disney World, Orlando, Fla., 1972—81; parade dir. Gatlinburg (Tenn.) C. of C., 1981-85; entertainment prodn. mgr. The 1982 World's Fair, Knoxville, 1982; cons. Judy Flanagan Prodns./Spl. Events, Gatlinburg, 1982—, Miss U.S.A. Pageant, Knoxville, 1983; prodn. coord. Nashville Network, 1983; dir. sales River Terr. Resort, Gatlinburg, 1985-86; account exec. Park Vista Hotel, Gatlinburg, 1986-88; project coord. Universal Studios, Fla., 1988-90; dir. spl. events U. Tenn., Knoxville, 1990—. Dir. Neyland Stadium Expansion Dedication, 1996—; U. Tenn. Bicentennial Events, 1994, 21st Century Campaign Major Events; prodn. mgr. 1984 World's Fair Parades and Spl. Events, New Orleans, Neil Sedaka rock video, Days of Our Lives daytime soap opera. Recipient Gatlinburg Homecoming award, 1986, World Lifetime Achievement award, 1993. Mem.: ASPCA, Tenn. Festivals and Events Assn. (bd. dirs.), Internat. Festivals and Events Assn. (cert. festival and events exec., found. bd.), Internat. Spl. Events Soc., Doris Day Animal League, Defenders of Wildlife, Humane Soc. U.S., U. Tenn. Soc. Pres. Club. Roman Catholic. Home: 350 Bruce Rd Gatlinburg TN 37738-5612 Business E-Mail: judy-flanagan@utk.edu.

FLANAGAN, MARIANNE, music educator; d. William James and Catherine Theresa Flanagan. B in Music Edn., N.E. La. U., 1984; M in Music Edn., U. So. Miss., 1998. Band dir. Bastrop (La.) Jr. HS, 1988—89; dir. band Bastrop HS, 1989—91, Lakeview MS, Winter Garden, Fla., 1991—92, Colonial HS, Orlando, Fla., 1992—. Mem.: Internat. Assn. Jazz Educators, Music Educators Nat. Conf., Fla. Bandmasters Assn. (adjudicator 1995—, mem. profl. resource com. 1996—). Office: Colonial HS 6100 Oleander Dr Orlando FL 32807 Business E-Mail: flanagan@ocps.net.

FLANAGAN, MARTHA LANG, publishing executive; BS in Fine Arts, U. Cin., 1978. Various exec. secretarial positions, 1960-75; corp. sec., asst. to pres. Cin. Enquirer, 1973—. Mem. comms. adv. com. to Cin. Police Chief, 1976-85; mem. Cin. Music Hall Centennial Com., 1976-78; mem. adv. bd. U. Cin. Coll. Design, Art, Architecture and Planning, 1988-91; trustee Neediest Kids of All, 1980—, Women's Fund Greater Cin. Found., 2000—, St. Ursula Acad., 2002—. Office: The Cincinnati Enquirer 312 Elm St Fl 20 Cincinnati OH 45202-2739 Office Phone: 513-768-8094. E-mail: mflanagan@enquirer.com.

FLANAGAN, NATALIE SMITH, state representative; b. Bradford, Mass., Aug. 6, 1913; d. Forrest Van Zandt and Blanche (Robbins) Smith; m. John Frances Flanagan, Sept. 20, 1944 (dec.). Grad. high sch., Vassalboro, Maine. Mem. N.H. Ho. of Reps., Concord, 1973—, chmn. constl. and statutory com., 1987—. Pres. Mass. chpt. Young Reps., 1930—; pres. bd. dirs. Haverhill (Mass.) Girls Club, 1940—; founder Rockingham (N.H.) Nutrition Program, 1979; mem. N.H. Bicentennial Commn., 1983—; mem. Commn. for the Smithsonian Festival of Am. Folklife for N.H., 1996—. Recipient Meritorious Pub. Svc. medal Sec. State, 1990. Congregationalist. Avocation: reading. Home: PO Box 959 Atkinson NH 03811-0959 Office: NH State Legis Legis Office Bldg Rm 302 Concord NH 03301

FLANAGAN, SUSAN MARIE, special education educator; d. John Bresnahan Flanagan and Marguerite McKenna; m. Norman Christian Kristoff, 1981 (div. 1983). MS, Johns Hopkins U., 2001; BS, Wheelock Coll., 1979. Meyers Briggs Cert. Md., 1990, cert. State Dept. Edn. Md., 1997, Pvt. Pilot Fla., 1995. Dir. pediat. play therapist Dartmouth Hitchcock Med. Ctr., Hanover, NH, 1979—81; pediat. play therapist Meml. Sloan Kettering Hosp., New York City, 1981—83. Recruiter Cosmopolitan, New York, 1983—88; real estate developer Foxmoore Assocs. Ltd. Partnership, Annapolis, Md., 1988—97; child adv.- entrepreneur Susan Flanagan, M.S., LLC, Annapolis, 1997. Author (designer): Phlanagan Phonics Reading Program (Amb. Award, 2003). Bd. mem. Jr. League of Annapolis, 1988—2003. Clara E. Cade Scholarship, Quincy Sch., 1974. Mem.: Learning Disabilities Assn., Coun. For Exceptional Children, Johns Hopkins Alumni Assn., Pvt. Pilots Assn. (pvt. pilot). Achievements include design of Created a remedial reading program for students with disabilities. Avocations: collector of movie memorabilla, fitness training, long distance runner, gourmet cook. Office: Susan Flanagan MS LLC 2315 Forest Drive Annapolis MD 21401

FLANAGAN, SYLVIA, editor; b. Chgo., June 26, 1952; BA in Journalism, Chgo. State U.; MS in Journalism, Roosevelt U. Various to sr. editor Jet newsmag. Johnson Pub. Co., Chgo., 1972-85. Mem. The Chgo. Bd. Rossevelt Univ., 2000. Former bd. govs. Roosevelt U.; bd. trustees LaRabida Children's Hosp. and Rsch. Ctr., Chgo. Mem. Nat. Assn. Black Journalists, Chgo. Assn. of Black Journalists. Office: Johnson Pub Co 820 S Michigan Ave Chicago IL 60605-2103

FLANAGAN, THERESA, quality assurance professional; BA in Econs., MBA in Mktg., Rutgers U. With Total Rsch. Corp., Princeton, N.J., 1983—, divn. pres. quality mgmt. Office: 5 Independence Way # Cn5305 Princeton NJ 08540-6627

FLANDERS, ELEANOR CARLSON, community volunteer; b. Spearville, Kans., Mar. 27, 1916; d. Carl Edward and Laura Rebecca (Pine) Carlson; m. Laurence Burdette Flanders, Jr., June 6, 1941; children: Laurel F. Umile, John C., Lynette F. Moyer, Paul L. BA, cert. journalism, U. Colo., 1938; family inst. cert., Vassar Coll., 1958. Examiner of credits U. Colo., Boulder, 1938-41; stock market analyst trust dept. First Nat. Bank, Longmont, Colo., 1970-85; landlady Historic Library Hall Apt. House. Pres. St. Vrain Hist. Soc., 1954—; v.p. St. Vrain Valley Sch. Bd., 1978—84. Contbr. articles to profl. jours. Precinct worker, del. Rep. Party, Longmont and Boulder, 1941—; club leader 4-H Boulder County, 1947-63; pres., charter mem. Boulder County Mental Health Clinic, 1947-60; mem. PEO Sisterhood, 1948—; trustee, investment com. First Congl. Ch., Longmont, 1960-2001; North Colo. area rep. Am. Field Svc., Longmont, 1965-70; coord. tutoring program Boulder County Juvenile Ct., 1965-81; trustee, farm mgr. Carl and Laura Carlson Trust, Oberlin, Kans., 1971-85; trustee, dir. Colo. 4-H Youth Fund, Ft. Collins, 1973-86; trustee, investment counsel Am. Mothers Endowment Fund, N.Y.C., 1979-90; founder, pres. St. Vrain Edn. Found. Endowment Fund, Longmont, 1985—; trustee, bd. dirs. Longmont Cable Trust, 1986-88; nat. treas. Am. Mothers, N.Y., 1988-90; elected 2-term dir. St. Vrain Valley Sch. Bd., 1978-86. Mem.: AAUW (charter), St. Vrain Edn. Found. (founder, dir., pres. 1984—), St. Vrain Hist. Soc. (dir., pres. 1970—), Sunshine Club, U. Colo. Alumni Assn. (dir., sec. 1950—58), Delta Kappa Gamma (hon.). Avocations: gardening, travel, duplicate bridge, reading, writing. Home: 917 W 3rd Ave Longmont CO 80501-5413

FLANDERS, JANET HUESSY, travel company executive; b. Denver, Sept. 8, 1949; d. Hans R. Huessy and Ellen Nora West; m. Stephen Nathaniel Flanders, Dec. 27, 1969. MusB, Boston U., 1971. Owner, mgr. Janet Flanders Travel, Norwich, Vt., 1980—. Treas. Cantabile women's choir. Mem.: Internat. Airline Transport Assn., Travelsavers, Airline Reporting Corp., Am. Soc. Travel Agts. Avocations: cooking, gardening, running, soprano small choral groups. Office: Janet Flanders Travel Inc PO Box 250 Norwich VT 05055-0250

FLANIGEN, EDITH MARIE, materials scientist, consultant; Rsch. fellow materials sci. UOP Tarrytown (N.Y.) Tech. Ctr., ret.; cons. White Plains, N.Y. Recipient Perkin medal, Soc. Chem. Ind., 1992, Francis P. Garvan-John M. Olin medal, Am. Chem. Soc., 1993. Home: 502 Woodland Hills Rd White Plains NY 10603-3136

FLANNELLY, LAURA T. mental health nurse, nursing educator, researcher; b. Bklyn., Nov. 7, 1952; d. George A. Adams and Eleanor (Barragry) Mulhearn; m. Kevin J. Flannelly, Jan. 10, 1981. BS in Nursing, Hunter Coll., 1974; MSN, U. Hawaii, 1984, PhD in Ednl. Psychology, 1996. RN, N.Y., Hawaii. Psychiat. nurse Bellevue Hosp., N.Y.C., 1975, asst. head nurse, 1975-77; psychiat. nurse White Plains (N.Y.) Med. Ctr., 1978-79; community mental health nurse South Beach Psychiat. Ctr., N.Y.C., 1979-81; psychiat. nurse The Queen's Med. Ctr., Honolulu, 1981-83; crisis worker Crisis Response Systems Project, Honolulu, 1983-86; instr. nursing U. Hawaii, Honolulu, 1985-92, asst. prof., 1992—, assoc. grad. faculty, 1998—; adj. instr. nursing Hawaii Loa Coll., Honolulu, 1988; assoc. prof. Am. Samoa Community Coll., Honolulu, 2000—, adj. instr. nursing, 1987, 89, 90. Mem. adv. bd., planning com. Psychiat. Day Hosp. of The Queen's Med. Ctr., Honolulu, 1981-82; program coord. Premenstrual Tension Syndrome Conf., Honolulu, 1984; dir. Ctr. Psychosocial Rsch., Honolulu, 1987—; program moderator 1st U.S-Japan Health Behavioral Conf., Honolulu, 1988; faculty Ctr. for Asia-Pacific Exch., 1995-99, Internat. Conf. on Transcultural Nursing, Honolulu, 1990; mem. bd. dirs. U. Hawaii Profl. Assembly, 1994-97; mem. Hawaii State Coun. Mental Health, 1997—. Contbr. articles to profl. jours. N.Y. State Bd. Regents scholar, 1970-74; NIH nursing trainee, 1983-84; grantee U. Hawaii, 1986, 91, Hawaii Dept. Health, 1990. Fellow Internat. Soc. Rsch. on Aggression; mem. AAAS, APA, Am. Ednl. Rsch. Assn., Am. Psychol. Soc., Am. Psychiat. Nurses Assn., Am. Statis. Assn., Nat. League for Nursing, N.Y. Acad. Scis., Sigma Theta Tau (rec. sec. chpt. 1995-97). Achievements include research on aggressive behavior, educational testing, learning styles, problem-based learning, cross-cultural differences, statistical modeling. Office: U Hawaii Sch Nursing Webster Hall Honolulu HI 96822 E-mail: flannel@hawaii.edu.

FLANNERY, ELLEN JOANNE, lawyer; b. Bklyn., Dec. 13, 1951; d. William Rowan and Mary Jane (Hamilla) Flannery. AB cum laude, Mount Holyoke Coll., 1973; JD cum laude, Boston U., 1978. Bar: Mass. 1978, D.C. 1979, U.S. Ct. Appeals (D.C. cir.) 1979, U.S. Dist. Ct. D.C. 1980, U.S. Ct. Appeals (4th cir.) 1981, U.S. Supreme Ct. 1983. Spl. asst. to commr. of health Mass. Dept. Pub. Health, Boston, 1973-75; law clk. U.S. Ct. Appeals D.C. cir., Washington, 1978-79; assoc. Covington & Burling, Washington, 1979-86, ptnr., 1986—. Lectr. ins. U. Va. Sch. Law, 1984—90, Boston U. Law Sch., 1993; bd. visitors Boston U. Sch. Law, 1995—; lectr. ins. U. Md. Sch. Law, 1994; mem. Nat. Conf. Lawyers and Scientists, AAAS-ABA, 1989—92; chair Fellows Adv. Rsch. Commn., 2002—. Contbr. to articles to profl. jours. Fellow: Am. Bar Found. (chair fellows adv. rsch. com. 2002—); mem.: ABA (chmn. life scis. divsn. 1982—84, chmn. com. med. practice 1987—88, chmn. life scis. divsn. 1988—91, vice chair food and drug law com. 1991—97, chmn. sect. sci. and tech. 1992—93, del. of sci. and tech. sect. to ho. of dels. 1993—, chmn. coordinating group on bioethics and the law 1998—2000, vice chair Ho. Tech. Com. 2002—, chmn. conf. sect. and divsn. dels. 2003—), Cosmos Club. Office: Covington & Burling 1201 Pennsylvania Ave NW Washington DC 20004-2401 Office Phone: 202-662-5484.

FLANNERY, SUSAN MARIE, library administrator; b. Newark, Feb. 18, 1953; d. John Patrick Flannery and Assunta (Lardieri) Ege; m. Stephen A. Coren, Oct. 6, 1984. BA in History of Art, U. Pa., 1974; MLS, Simmons Coll., 1975. Dir. of libr. Newton Country Day, 1975-77, Am. Sch. in Switzerland, Montagnola, 1977-78; young adult libr. Somerville (Mass.) Pub. Libr., 1979-81; reference libr. Cary Meml. Libr., Lexington, Mass., 1981-83; asst. dir. Lucius Beebe Libr., Wakefield, Mass., 1983-87; dir. Reading (Mass.) Pub. Libr., 1987-91; assoc. dir. Cambridge (Mass.) Pub. Libr., 1991-1993, dir., 1993—. Steering com. Mass. delegation to White Ho. Conf. on Librs., 1990; corporator East Cambridge Savs. Bank. Reviewer Sch. Libr. Jour.; contbr. articles to profl. jours. Incorporator Cambridge (Mass.) Family YMCA, 1991—93; bd. dirs. Guidance Ctr., Inc., Cambridge, 1994—2000, sec., 2001—. Mem. ALA (Mass. councilor 1993-97, John Cotton Dana award 1989, Outstanding Libr. Adv. 20th Century 2000),

ACLU Mass. (adv. bd. 1994-96, bd. dirs. 1996—2004), Mass. Libr. Assn. (pres. 1985-87, v.p. 1983-85), Rotary (bd. dirs. Cambridge 1993-99, v.p. 1995-96, pres. 1997-98, pres. Reading club). Office: Cambridge Pub Libr 449 Broadway Cambridge MA 02138-4125 Office Phone: 617-349-4032. E-mail: sflannery@ci.cambridge.ma.us.

FLANNIGAN, SANDRA F. secondary school educator; b. Mt. Pleasant, Pa., Dec. 22, 1946; d. James and Esther Pauline (Jordan) F. BS in Edn., Taylor U., Upland, Ind., 1968. Tchr. English, Mentor (Ohio) High Sch., 1968-70; tchr. speech Glenbrook High Sch., Glenview, Ill., 1970-71; tchr. English, Batavia (Ill.) High Sch., 1971—, chair English dept., 1996—. Cons. Chgo. Area Writing Project, Evanston, 1979-81; dir. The Writing Exch., Lombard, Ill., 1987—. Editor, author: The Writing Exchange, 1987, Network, 1987-89. Chgo. Area Writing Project fellow, 1979, Christa McAuliffe Found. fellow/grantee, Washington, 1987, Nat. Humanities Ctr. fellow, Research Triangle Park, N.C., 1989, NEH Tchr.-Scholar fellow, 1992-93. Mem. Nat. Coun. Tchrs. English, Ill. Assn. Tchrs. English. Republican. Avocations: needlework crafts, travel, creative writing, attending plays and concerts. Home: 1342 S Finley Rd Apt 1P Lombard IL 60148-4321 Office: Batavia High Sch 1200 W Wilson St Batavia IL 60510-1628

FLANTROY, TAMMY L. financial analyst; d. Charles Flantroy and Sherley A. Jackson. AA, Fla. C.C., Jacksonville, 1993; BA, U. Wis., Eau Claire, 1997. Benefit analyst Walkspring Resources, Jacksonville, 1998—99; tester Citistreet, Jacksonville, 1999—2001, implementation analyst, 2001—.

FLATTAU, PAMELA EBERT, research psychologist, consultant; b. Chgo., Dec. 24, 1946; d. Raymond Clarence and Sylvia Anne (Jones) E.; m. Edward Samuel Flattau, Feb. 1, 1977; children: Jeremy Paul, Victoria Celeste. BSc with honors, U. Leeds, Eng., 1969; MS, U. Ga., 1972, PhD, 1974. Congrl. sci. fellow AAAS-APA, Washington, 1974-75; staff officer NAS/NRC, Washington, 1975-81, sr. staff officer, 1985-90, unit dir., 1990-95; policy analyst NSF, Washington, 1981-85; mgr. Flattau Assocs. LLC, Washington, 1995—. Mem. exec. com. Coun. Profl. Assns. for Fed. Stats., Washington, 1986-87. Editor: Research Doctorate Programs in U.S., 1995; author, editor series Biomed and Behavioral Research Personnel 1975-80, 1994; author, contbr.: Science and Engineering Indicators Series, 1981-85. Bd. dirs. Assn. Advancement Psychology, Washington, 1980-82. Mem. AAAS, APA (NSF travel grantee 1992, 2000, Young Psychologist travel award 1976), Am. Psychol. Soc., Soc. for Social Studies of Sci., Human Resources Planning Soc., Sigma Xi. Office: Flattau Assocs LLC 5335 Wisconsin Ave NW Ste 440 Washington DC 20015-2052 E-mail: pflattau@flattau.com.

FLAVIN, NANCY ANN, state legislator; b. Northampton, Mass., June 6, 1950; d. James Edward and Margaret (Leveille) F.; divorced. Student, Northampton Comml. Coll., 1968-69; certificate, Tufts U., 1985; BA, U. Mass., 1987. Sec. sch. nursing U. Mass., Amherst, 1969-87; adminstrv. asst. State Rep. Shannon P. O'Brien, Mass., 1987-92; mem. Mass. Ho. of Reps., 1993—; vice chair ways & means com.; mem. ethics com.; mem. redistricting com. Bd. dir. Riverside Industries; chmn. com. on ins.; mem. com. on long-term debt. Officer Univ. Staff Assn., 1977-86; mem. adv. task force Easthampton Pub. Sch.; bd. dirs. Easthampton Cmty. Ctr., 1991—, mem. Mass. Women's Polit. Caucus, Pascommuck Conservation Trust. Mem. Five Coll. Fed. Credit Union. Office: Mass Ho of Reps State Capitol Rm 239 Boston MA 02133 E-mail: repnancyflavin@state.hou.ma.us.

FLAVIN, SONJA, artist; b. Southampton, NY, Sept. 25, 1936; m. Daniel N. Flavin Jr., Oct. 28, 1961. MFA, Rochester Inst. Tech., 1982; BA in Art History, Washington Sq. Coll., 1978. Advisor Dan Flavin Catalogue Raisonné, 1998—. One-woman shows include LA Nightlights and other natural forces, San Juan Capistrano Libr. Gallery, 1997; Group exhbns: Elaine Benson Gallery, Bridgehampton, N.Y., 1990, Internat. Textile Fair Exhbn., Kyoto, Japan, 1994, Craft Art Western N.Y., Burchfield-Penney Art Ctr., Buffalo, N.Y., 1996-97, Chamot Gallery, Jersey City, N.J., 1998; co-curator Weltge Exhbn., 1987, Bauhaus Weaving Workshop, Phila. Catalogued George Eastman archives, Rochester, N.Y., 1981-82, Bauhaus textiles, Busch-Reisinger Mus./Harvard U., Cambridge, 1980; workshops for L.A. Unified Sch. Sys. Park Program, 1996. Recipient Grand Prize 3rd Am. Crafts awards, N.Y., 1990, fellowship N.Y. Found. Arts, 1986.

FLECHNER, ROBERTA FAY, graphic designer; b. N.Y.C., June 7, 1949; d. Abraham Julius and Evelyn (Medwin) F. BA, CCNY, 1970; MA, NYU, 1972; cert., Printing Industries Met., N.Y., N.Y.C., 1974, 75, 79. Researcher, asst. editor Arno Press, N.Y.C., 1970-73; free-lance editor Random House, N.Y.C., 1973-74, graphic designer/compositor coll. dept., 1984-88; graphic designer Core Communications in Health, N.Y.C., 1974-76; prodn. mgr. Heights-Inwood News, N.Y.C., 1976-77; art dir., graphic designer Jour. Advt. Research, N.Y.C., 1976-81; prin., graphic designer/compositor W.W. Norton & Co., Inc., N.Y.C., 1977—, McGraw Hill, Inc., N.Y.C., 1990-94, 2000—; graphic design, layout artist, compositor R. Flechner Graphics, 1976—. Graphic designer, layout artist, compositor R. Flechner Graphics, 1976—; mech. artist Fawcett, N.Y.C., 1979-80; graphic designer Avon Internat., N.Y.C., 1982; art dir., compositor, layout artist Source: Notes in the History of Art, N.Y.C., 1982—; graphic designer John Wiley & Sons, Inc., N.Y.C., 1985. Designer stationery, 1979 (Art Direction mag., Creativity-cert. distinction 1979). Art dir. enviroNews, N.Y. State Atty. Gen.'s Environ. Protection Bur., N.Y.C., 1977-78. Mem. Graphic Artists Guild, NOW, Women's Nat. Book Assn. (cons.), NAFE, Women's Caucus for Art, Am. Inst. Graphic Arts, CCNY Alumni Assn., NYU Alumni Assn. Office: 10615 Queens Blvd Flushing NY 11375-4365

FLECK, LISA C. physician assistant, dietician; b. Ft. Wayne, Ind., Aug. 8, 1970; d. Louis Leroy and Norma Emily Fleck. BS with distinction in Dietetics, Purdue U., 1992; MS with honors, Baylor U., 1996. Cert. physician asst.; registered dietitian. Dietetic intern Edward Hines Jr. VA Hosp., Hines, Ill., 1993—94; physician asst. Cabarrus Family Medicine-Concord, 1997—. Physician asst. Cabarrus County Schs., Concord, 1997—, Barber Scotia Coll. Infirmary, Concord, 1998—. Fellow: Ctrl. Carolina Assn. Physician Assts., N.C. Acad. Physician Assts., Am. Acad. Physician Assts.; mem.: N.C. Med. Soc., Metrolina Assn. Physician Assts., Phi Beta Kappa. Methodist. Avocations: travel, reading, rollerblading, hiking. Office: Cabarrus Family Medicine-Concord 270 Copperfield Blvd Ste 102 Concord NC 28025 Office Phone: 704-786-6521.

FLEESLER, FAITH B. writer; b. N.Y.C., June 13, 1973; d. Zachary and Barbara F. BA in English, Binghamton, U., 1995; MA in English, Carnegie Mellon U., 1996; postgrad., Tchrs. Coll., Columbia U. Libr., Binghamton, N.Y., 1991-95; instr. 92nd St. YM-YWHA, N.Y.C., 1993-97, 2000—; teaching asst. Binghamton U., 1994-95; instr., tutor Tchrs. Coll., Columbia U. Writing Skills Ctr., N.Y.C., 1996-98; corp. comm. & technical writer CSI Complex Syss., N.Y.C., 1997-98; product coord., technical writer Info. Builders, Inc., N.Y.C., 1998—. Adj. prof. Hofstra U., Hempstead, N.Y., 1996-97; story coord. King World Prodns., N.Y.C., 1997; mem. Rhetoric Colloqium, Pitts., 1995-96; mentor, instr. Pitts. Cmty. Literacy Ctr., 1995; rsch. asst. profl. writing project English dept. Carnegie Mellon U., Pitts., 1995; participant in program for future faculty Carnegie Mellon U. Teaching Ctr., Pitts., 1995. Co-developer/co-editor: (textbook) Rhetoric 242 Handbook: Writing and Discourse, 1994, (manual) Rhetoric 242 Teaching Assistant Manual, 1995; co-editor, staffwriter mag. Wordplay: Mag. Creative Non-fiction, 1994, Tchr.'s Coll. Columbia U.: Non-fiction Workshop Mag., 1996; asst. editor Offcl. Jour. Conf. English Edn., 1997; staff writer mag. World: Bristol-Meyers Squibb Co., 1997. Carnegie Mellon U. scholar, 1995-96. Mem. Soc. Technical Comm. Avocations: travel, fitness, water-skiing, theater, movies. Home: 350 1st Ave Apt11c New York NY 10010-4905

FLEETWOOD, M. FREILE, psychiatrist, educator; b. Valparaiso, Chile, Nov. 20, 1915; d. Alfonso Larrea and Berta (Cordovez) Freile; children: Harvey Blake, Francis Freile. MD, U. Chile, 1941; PhD, Pedagogic Inst., Santiago, Chile, 1947; MD, U. of State of N.Y., 1950. Instr. biochemistry to asst. in pub. emergencies U. Chile, Santiago, 1937-41, resident in neurology at neurol. clinic, 1941-42, head of rsch. lab. in psychiatry, 1944-48; resident in psychiatry Henry Phipps Clinic, John Hopkins U., Balt., 1942-44; provisional asst. in psychiatry to out-patient psychiatrist N.Y. Hosp., N.Y.C., 1948-61; attending psychiatrist Gracie Square Hosp., N.Y.C., 1961—; clin. asst. prof. psychiatry Cornell Univ., N.Y. Hosp., N.Y.C., 1970-88, emeritus status, 1988—. Instr. psychiatry, Payne Whitney Clinic, Cornell U., N.Y. Hosp., N.Y.C., 1950-63; cons. Family Svc. of Patterson, N.J., 1955-56, East Harlem Project Community Svc. Soc., N.Y.C., 1960-61, Manhattan Family Svc. Ctr. Community Svc. Soc., N.Y.C., 1960-61; asst. psychiatrist NYU, U. Hosp., Bellevue Med. Ctr., N.Y.C., 1954, psychiatrist 1954-55, and others. Contbr. articles to profl. publs. Recipient Rockefeller Found. grantee, 1942-43, 43-44, 44-45, Sagin Fund grantee, 1952-53, Squibb Fund grant, 1952-53. Mem. AAAS, Med. Soc. State and County of N.Y., Am. Med. Soc. on Alcoholism and Other Drug Dependencies, Am. Psychiat. Assn. (N.Y. county dist. br.), N.Y. Acad. Sci., Spanish Am. Med. Soc., Pan Am. Med. Soc., N.Y. Soc. for Adolescent Psychiatry, The N.Y. County Review Orgn., Women's Med. Assn. N.Y., Am. Med. Women's Assn. Office: PO Box 1955 28 Central Ave Amagansett NY 11930 also: 69 W 83rd St New York NY 10024-5248

FLEEZANIS, JORJA KAY, violinist, educator; b. Detroit, Mar. 19, 1952; d. Parios Nicholas and Kaliope (Karageorge) F.; m. Michael Steinberg, July 3, 1983. Student, Cleve. Inst. Music, 1969-72, Cin. Coll.-Conservatory Music, 1972-75. Violinist Chgo. Symphony Orch., 1975-76; concertmaster Cin. Chamber Orch., 1976-80; violinist Trio D'Accordo, Cin., 1976-80; asst. prin. 2d violinist San Francisco Symphony Orch., 1980-81; assoc. concertmaster San Francisco Sympony Orch., 1980-89; acting concertmaster Minn. Orch., Mpls., 1988-89, concertmaster, 1989—; violinist Fleezanis-Ohlsson-Grebanier Piano Trio, San Francisco, 1984—; faculty mem. San Francisco Conservatory of Music, 1983-89, U. Minn., 1989—. Founder Chamber Music Sundaes, San Francisco, 1980-89, The Am. String Project, 2002; artist-in-residence U. Calif., Davis, 1995—; radio host St. Paul Sunday Show, Minn. Pub. Radio, 1998-2000; guest concertmaster, London Classical Players, L.A. Philharmonic, Sydney Symphony, Balt. Symphony. Performer World Premiere John Adams Violin Concerto with Minn. Orch., 1994, Nicholas Maw, Sonata for Solo Violin, commd. by Minn. Pub. Radio, 1997, Sir John Taverner's Ikon of Eros, commd. for her by Minn. Orch., 2002; commd. by Pub. Radio Internat. and Minn. Pub. Radio for world premiere of Nicholas Maw Sonata for Solo Violin, 1998; soloist Am. premier Benjamin Britten Double Concerto, 1998; rec. artist Reference CRI, Koch, Cypre's Records. Democrat. Avocations: photography, cooking. Office: Minn Orch 1111 Nicollet Mall Minneapolis MN 55403-2406

FLEHARTY, MARY SUE, state government staff member; b. Lincoln, Nebr., Aug. 13, 1962; d. Joseph Patrick and Joy Lou (Harnish) Huntley; m. Bradley Doyle Osborne, Mar. 26, 1983 (div. June 1988); m. Terry Lester Fleharty, Aug. 13, 1990. Student, Lincoln Sch. Commerce, 1996-97; student in sign lang., S.E. C.C., 2003—. Loan processor Am. Charter Fed. Savings and Loan, Lincoln, 1981-84; pub. broadcast exchange operator, sec. Lincoln Clinic, P.C., 1989-91; PBX operator, sec. Woods Park Med. Mgmt. Inc., Lincoln, 1991-93; data reporting asst. Harris Tech. Group, Lincoln, 1993; lease coord. Progressive Lease, Inc., Lincoln, 1993; PBX comms. specialist Branker Buick, Lincoln, 1994-97; sec., receptionist Reel Quick, Inc., Lincoln, 1997-98; case mgmt. sec. Madonna Rehab. Hosp., Lincoln, 1998-2000; exec. adminstrv. asst. Nebr. Heart Inst., Lincoln, 2000; office clk. Nebr. Dept. Labor, Lincoln, 2000—01, staff asst. I, 2001—. Sec. Lincoln Police Citizen Acad., 2001—. Vol. ARC, Lincoln, 1977—, chmn., 1983-84, pres. Lincoln Fire Dept. Aux., 1993; cert. EMT; notary public Nebr., 1993. Named Outstanding Vol. ARC, 1985. Mem. NAFE, Benevolent Patriotic Order of Does (inner guard 1999, sec. 2000-01, chaplain 2000-02, flag bearer 2002), Lancaster County Emergency Mgmt., Internat. Assn. Workforce Profls. Republican. Presbyterian. Avocations: church handbell ringing, shuffleboard, playing pool, bowling, gardening. Office: Nebr Dept Labor 550 S 16th St Lincoln NE 68508 E-mail: mfleharty@aol.com.

FLEISCHER, REBECCA, federal agency administrator; Degree in Secondary Edn. cum laude, Ball State U. Chief of staff Greater Ednl. Opportunities Found., Indpls.; exec. assoc. dir. White House Office Mgmt. and Budget; dir. outreach and planning Office Innovation and Improvement U.S. Dept. Edn., Washington. Office: US Dept Edn 400 Maryland Ave SW Washington DC 20202

FLEISCHER-RIEVESCHL, ELLEN LEE, real estate agent; b. Cin., Dec. 15, 1945; d. Leo Simon and Janet Fleischer; m. George Rieveschl, Jr. BA in Mgmt. Econs., U. Cin., 1968. Pub. rels. Cin. Gas and Electric CO., 1968-71; campaign coord. Taft for Senate, Cin., 1971-72; new bus. devel. profl. Fifth Third Bank N.A., Cin., 1973-77; mktg. mgr. Williamsburg Mgmt., Cin., 1984-86; real estate agt. Sibcy Cline Realtors, Ft. Mitchell, Ky., 1986-91, Re/Max Affiliates, Ft. Mitchell, 1992—. Artist, Cin., 1978-85; mem. Kenton Boone Bd. Realtors, Northern Ky. Exhibitor watercolor abstracts various galleries in Cin., Naples and Coral Gables, Fla., N.Y.C.; author essay, Congl. Record, 1st pl. award, 1968. Mem. steering com. Emery Soc. Childrens Hosp.; bd. dirs. Carnegie Arts Ctr. Mem. Ky. Assn. Realtors, Nat. Assn. Realtors, Million Dollar Club, Friends of Covington, No. Ky. Heritage League, Cin. Art Mus., Cin. Symphony Com., Forward Quest of Covington, Omicron Delta Epsilon. Avocations: horseback riding, walking, swimming, travel, painting. Home: 100 Riverside Pl Covington KY 41011-1718

FLEISCHMAN, BARBARA GREENBERG, public relations consultant; b. Detroit, Mar. 20, 1924; d. Samuel J. and Theresa (Keil) Greenberg; m. Lawrence A. Fleischman, Dec. 18, 1948; children: Rebecca, Arthur, Martha. BA, U. Mich., 1944. Tchr. Detroit Pub. Schs., 1944-45; psychoanalyst's sec., 1947-49; sec. Greenberg Ins. Agy., 1947-49; customer/pub. rels. cons. Kennedy Galleries, N.Y.C., 1976—. Bd. dirs. Detroit Artists Market, 1958-66, Planned Parenthood, N.Y.C., 1990-96, Am. Craft Coun., 1980-83, Friends of Channel 13, 1968-80, pres., N.Y.C., 1975-79, chmn. auction, 1975, trustee, 1975-84; mem. women's com. Detroit Inst. Arts, 1957-66; pres. Friends of N.Y. Pub. Libr., 1979-84, trustee, 1980—, v.p., bd., 1987—; trustee The Acting Co., 1986-89, pres., 1988-89; mem. gov. bd. Off the Record Luncheons, Fgn. Policy Assn., 1978-85; assoc. prodr. Channel 13 Auction, 1978-80; trustee Mus. TV and Radio, 1988-92, Archives of Am. Art, 1997—, caryatids chmn., 1998-2003; vis. com. Am. Wing, Met. Mus., 1998—; commr. Art Commn. of the City of N.Y., 1995-98; hon. patron Brit. Mus., 1996—, Caryatids com., pres., 1998—2003, chmn.; v.p. Archives of Am. Art, pres.; mem. trustees com. Libr. Mus. Modern Art, 1998—; pres. Archives of Am. Art, 1998—; mem. Coun. Am. Mus. Nat. History, 1999—; mem. devel. trust Brit. Mus., 1999—2003; treas. Friends of the Art Commn., 1999—; trustee The J. Paul Getty Trust, 2000—. Mem. Cosmopolitan Club. Office: Kennedy Galleries 730 5th Ave New York NY 10019-4105 E-mail: bgf324@aol.com.

FLEISCHMAN, FRANCINE D. elementary school educator; b. Bklyn., N.Y., Jan. 28, 1951; d. Alvin and Lillian Rachel Moskowitz; m. Herman Israel Fleischman, Feb. 3, 1973; children: Meredith, Brandon, Gary. BS, West Conn. State Coll., 1973; MS, Bklyn. (N.Y.) Coll., 1975. Tchr. Bd. Edn., Bklyn., 1973—. Prof. Nassau C.C., Garden City, NY, 1994—; v.p. United Mutual Industries, Inc., Merrick, NY, 1987—. Home: 2970 Hewlett Ave Merrick NY 11566

FLEISHMAN, SUSAN NAHLEY, film company executive; b. Charlottesville, Va., Sept. 26, 1960; d. Richard and Mary Daniels Nahley; m. Eric Philip Fleishman, Dec. 28, 1995; 1 child, Henry Richard. BA Am. Lit., Middlebury Coll., Middlebury, Vt., 1978—82. Copywriter Macy's, New York, NY, 1984—86; dir. Interbrand, New York, NY, 1986—87; asst. v.p. Continental Ins., New York, NY, 1987—93; dir., pub. affairs Sony Corp. of Am., New York, NY, 1993—95; v.p. corp. comm. & pub. affairs Universal Studios, Los Angeles, Calif., 1995—2000, sr. v.p. corp. comm. & pub. affairs, 2000—. Bd. mem. Workplace, Hollywood, Los Angeles, Calif., 2001—, St. Joseph's Hosp., Burbank, Calif., 2002—. Office: Universal Studios LRW-14 100 Universal City Plaza Universal City CA 91608*

FLEKKE, MARY MURIEL, instructional services librarian; b. Mpls., Oct. 21, 1956; d. John Morris and Muriel Marie Flekke. BA in History, St. Cloud (Minn.) State U., 1980, BA in English, MS in Libr. Sci., 1982. Instrnl. svcs. libr. Roux Libr. Fla. So. Coll., Lakeland, 1982—. Author: Telling Our Stories, Oral and Family History, 4th edit., 1999. Comms. dir. Polk County Br. Trivent Fin. for Luths., 2003—; chair Lake Conf., Fla.-Bahamas Synod Evang. Luth. Ch. in Am., Polk/Highlands Counties, Fla., 2001—; archivist Fla.-Bahamas Synod Evang. Luth. Ch. Am., 1995—; bd. dirs., sec. James R. Crumley, Jr. Archives, Evang. Luth. Ch. in Am., Columbia, SC, 1995—. Mem.: AAUW (pres. 2001—03), Polk County Libr. Assn. (past pres., other offices, pres. 2002—), Fla. Libr. Assn. (past caucus chair), Soc. Fla. Archivists (v.p. 2001—03, pres. 2003—). Democrat. Lutheran. Avocations: reading, writing, cross stitch, oral history, genealogy. Office: Roux Libr Fla So Coll 111 Lake Hollingsworth Dr Lakeland FL 33801-5698 E-mail: mflekke@flsouthern.edu.

FLEMING, ALICE CAREW MULCAHEY, writer; b. New Haven, Dec. 21, 1928; d. Albert Leo and Agnes (Foley) Mulcahey; m. Thomas J. Fleming, Jan. 19, 1951; children: Alice, Thomas, David, Richard. Author: The Key to New York, 1960, A Son of Liberty, 1961, Doctors in Petticoats, 1964, Great Women Teachers, 1965, The Senator from Maine: Margaret Chase Smith, 1969, Alice Freeman Palmer: Pioneer College President, 1970, Reporters At War, 1970, General's Lady, 1971, Highways into History, 1971, Pioneers in Print, 1971, Ida Tarbell, The First of the Muckrakers, 1971, Nine Months, 1972, Psychiatry, What's it All About?, 1972, The Moviemakers, 1973, Trials that Made Headlines, 1974, Contraception, Abortion, Pregnancy, 1974, New on the Beat, 1975, Alcohol: The Delightful Poison, 1975, Something for Nothing, 1978, The Mysteries of ESP, 1980, What to Say When you Don't Know What to Say, 1982, The King of Prussia and a Peanut Butter Sandwich, 1988, George Washington Wasn't Always Old, 1991, What, Me Worry?, 1992, P.T. Barnum: The World's Greatest Showman, 1993, A Century of Service, 1997, Frederick Douglass From Slave to Statesman, 2003; editor: Hosannah the Home Run!, 1972, America Is Not all Traffic Lights, 1976; contbr. articles to mags. Nat. bd. dirs. Medic Alert Found. U.S., 1991-97, vice chmn., 1996-97, past chmn. N.Y. regional bd.; mem. pres.'s coun. United Hosp. Fund. Recipient Nat. Media award, Family Svc. Assn. Am., 1973, Alumnae Achievement award, Trinity Coll., 1979, Nat. Vol. of Yr. award, Medic Alert Found., 1991, 1993. Mem. PEN, Authors Guild. Address: 315 E 72nd St New York NY 10021-4625 E-mail: Fleming315@aol.com.

FLEMING, BLANCHE MILES, educational administrator; d. William Alford and Mary Blanche (Cottman) Miles; m. Daniel Edward Fleming II, Apr. 12, 1952 (dec. Mar. 1970); 1 child, Daniel Edward III. BS, Del. U., 1939; MA, Columbia U., 1947; PhD, Union Grad. Sch., Yellow Springs, Ohio, 1976. Cert. profl. edn., Del.; lic. bus. cert., Del. Tchr. English Wilmington (Del.) Bd. Edn., prin. Bayard Jr. H.S., supr. social studies, intern to supt. of schs., 1974-75; coord. undergrads. Del. State U., Dover, 1971; exec. dir. Nat. Tchr. Corps U. Del., Newark, 1970-72; dir. secondary edn. Del. Bd. Edn., Wilmington, 1980-83; pres. B.M. Fleming & Assocs. Charter mem. Helping Hands Cmty. Svc., Inc., Wilmington, 1996—; bd. dirs. Common Cause of Del., Wilmington, 1984—, Housing Opportunity of No. Del., Wilmington, 1987—, Del. state adv. com. U.S. Commn. on Civil Rights, Washington, 1991—; chair housing com. LWV, Wilmington, 1997—. Recipient Legacy from Del. Women award Chesapeake Bay Girl Scouts, Wilmington, 1987. Mem. Nat. Assn. Univ. Women (pres. 1990-94, cert. of appreciation 1994), Wilmington Women in Bus. (bd. dirs. 1983-85), Delta Kappa Gamma Internat. (corr. sec. 1991-93), Phi Delta Kappa, Kappa Delta Pi, Pi Beta Lambda. Avocations: photography, painting, poetry. Office: Fleming & Assocs 2806 W 5th St Wilmington DE 19805-1824

FLEMING, CAROLYN ELIZABETH, religious organization administrator, interior designer; b. Sept. 24, 1946; d. Jerry J. and Mary Josephine (Korten) Maly; m. Roger Earl Fleming, May 26, 1974; children: Karl Joseph, Briana Danika. Student, Texarkana Jr. Coll., 1963-65, Okla. State U., 1965-66; BS in Interior Design, U. Tex., 1970. Asst. to designer Planning/Design Cons., Inc., Tulsa, 1970-72; pvt. cons. Texarkana, Tex., 1972-73; with Anchorage Neuro-Spinal Clinic, 1987-90, 91-96; sec. Nat. Tchg. Com. Bahais of Alaska, Anchorage, 1976—84, mem., 1989-92, Baha'i materials promotion com., Anchorage, 1987-89, Nat. Spirituality Assembly, Bahais of Alaska, 1992-97, sec. gen., CEO, 1994-96; chmn. Anchorage Bahais Local Spiritual Assembly, 1990-92; mem. Texarkana Bahai Local Spirituality Assembly, 1985, Oceanview (Alaska) Bahai Local Spiritual Assembly, 1986-87; rec. sec. Chena Valley (Alaska) Local Spiritual Assembly Bahais, 1997; mem. internat. goals com. Nat. Spiritual Assembly Bahais of Alaska, Inc., 1997-2000; adminstrv. asst. to treas. in corp. offices Alaska Comm. Sys. Group, Inc., 2000—, adminstrv. asst. to treas. and v.p., 2000, adminstrv. asst. to v.p. investor rels., 2000-2001, adminstrv. asst. to CFO and treas., 2001—, v.p. investor rels., 2001—, v.p. sales and mktg.-Corp. office, 2001—. Coord. Interdenominational Cultural Unity Conf. for Anchorage Area, 1986. Vol. Rural Comty. Action Program, 1986-87, Alaska Coun. on Prevention Alcohol and Drug Abuse, 1987, Spirit Days, 1987-88; trainee Parent and Youth Mediation Program, 1990; mem. Anchorage Local Spiritual Assembly, 1998; asst. aux. bd. for Bahai Oceanview Comty., 1989-92; mem. Arts Coun., Valdez, Alaska, 1974-76, Beyond Beijing Coalition, Anchorage, 1995-96. Mem. ACS (contbns. and donations com. 2000-2001), Assn. Interior Designers, Alaska Women's Network (chmn. 2001-02, vice-chmn. 2000-01, v.p. 2000—), Internat. Assn. of Adminstrv. Profls., Bus. and Profl. Women's Orgn., Beta Sigma Phi. Mem. Baha'I Faith. Office: PO Box 101997 Anchorage AK 99510-1997

FLEMING, JANE WILLIAMS, retired educator, writer; b. Bethlehem, Pa., May 26, 1926; d. James Robert and Marion Pauline (Melloy) Groman; m. George Elliott Williams, July 2, 1955 (div. July 1965); children: Rhett Dorman, Santee Stuart, Timothy Cooper; m. Jerome Thomas Fleming, Sept. 25, 1980 (dec. 2002). BS, UCLA, 1951; MA, Calif. State U., Long Beach, 1969. Tchr. San Diego Unified Sch Dist., 1951-55, Costa Mesa (Calif.) Sch. Dist., 1955-56, Long Beach (Calif.) Sch. Dist., 1956-58, 62-87, 90-92; ret. Author: Why Janey Can't Teach, 2001. Mem. Phi Kappa Phi, Ret. Tchrs. Assn., UCLA Alumni Assn., Planetary Soc. (charter), Mus. of Tolerance. Avocations: theater, travel. Address: PO Box 13053 Long Beach CA 90803-8053 E-mail: jwilli5687@aol.com.

FLEMING, JUANITA WILSON, nursing educator, academic administrator; BS, Hampton Inst., 1957; MA, U. Chgo., 1959; PhD, Cath. U. Am., 1969; D Pub. Svc., Berea Coll., 1994. From staff nurse to head nurse med.-surg. pediat. unit Children's Hosp., Washington, 1957-58; pub. health nurse Bur. Pub. Health Nursing, 1959-60; instr. nursing children Sch. Nursing Freedmen's Hosp., Washington, 1962-65; cons. pub. health nursing dept. pediat. Child Devel. Clin., Howard U., 1965-66; from asst. prof. to assoc. prof. U. Ky. Coll. Nursing, Lexington, 1969-73; prof. U. Ky., Lexington, 1973—, spl. asst. to pres. for acad. affairs, 1991—2001, prof. emeritus, 2001—03; interim v.p. acad. affairs Ky. State U., Frankfort, 2003—. Mem. grad. faculty Coll. Nursing, U. Ky, 1971—, asst. dean grad. edn., 1975-81, assoc. dean dir. grad. edn., 1982-86; prof. C[illegible] Edn. Policy Studies and Evaln., 1979—; assoc. vice-chancellor acad. affairs Med. Ctr., 1984-91; prin. investigator nursing care high risk infants State Maternal and Child Health Divsn., 1972; project dir. advanced nurse tng. grant divsn. nursing Dept. Health Edn. and Welfare, 1977-80, prin. investigator high tech home care chronically ill children Bur. Maternal Child Health, 1989-93; prin. investigator healthcare and devel. status Children and Their Families MIRT Fogarty Ctr., 2001-2002; vis. prof. Case We. Res. U., Cleve., 1984, West Chester U., 1997; Martin Luther King/Rosa Parks/Cesar Chavez vis. prof. U. Mich., Ann Arbor, 1989, Elizabeth Carnegie endowed vis. prof. Howard U., 1995; Houston Endowed Minority Health and Rsch. Disting. vis. prof. Prairie View U., 1998; prin. investigator Am. Nurses Found., 1970-71; Faville lectr. Wayne State U., 1998. Recipient Ky. Nurses Assn. award, Marion E. McKenna leadership award, 1988, Disting. Svc. award ANA, 1994; Olhson scholar U. Ill., 1999, Robert A. Zumwinkle Student Rights award U. Ky. Student Govt. Assn., 2001. Mem. Am. Acad. Nursing, Nat. Acad. Scis., Inst. Medicine. Office: Interim VP for Acad Affairs Ky State Univ Frankfort KY 40601

FLEMING, MARCELLA, journalist; b. Paoli, Ind., Oct. 14, 1955; d. Kenneth Gale and Neva Louise (Thomas) F.; m. Brian D. Smith. AB in Journalism and English, Ind. U., 1978. Cert. tchr. Reporter Wabash Plain Dealer, 1978-80, Marion Chronicle-Tribune, 1980-83, city editor, 1990-91; city reporter, feature writer, copy editor, Sunday editor Ft. Wayne (Ind.) Jour.-Gazette, 1983-88; editor pubs. Children's Mus. Indpls., 1988-90; freelance writer Indpls. Monthly, 1989-91; nat. editor Indpls. CEO, Columbus (Ohio) CEO mags., 1991-92; writer state desk Indpls. Star & News, 1992—. Judge Thomas R. Keating Writing Competition, 1990. Recipient award of Excellence Nat. Down Syndrome Congress, 1988, Best Newsletter, Best Feature Story and Best News Story awards Editor's Forum, 1990, Best Ann. Report award Internat. Assn. Bus. Communicators, 1990. Mem. Ednl. Press Assn. (Breaking News Story Disting. Achievement award 1994). Office: Indpls Star 307 N Pennsylvania St Indianapolis IN 46204-1819

FLEMING, MARJORIE FOSTER, freelance writer, artist; b. Phila., Sept. 12, 1920; d. Major Bronson and Helen Margaret (Vertner) Foster; m. John Joseph Hundermark, Sept. 24, 1949 (div. Sept. 1955); children: John Foster Hundermark, David Laurence Hundermark; m. Paul Stewart Fleming, May 6, 1961. BA, Ursinus Coll., 1942; studied painting with Morris Blackburn, Pa. Acad. Fine Arts and Cheltenham Ctr. for Arts; with Robert Goldman, Cheltenham Twp. Ctr. Arts; studied painting with Paul Wieghardt, Chgo. Art Inst. and Cheltenham Twp. Ctr. for Arts. Cert. tchr. Cost acct. Philco Corp., Phila., 1942-43; asst. bank auditor Liberty Title and Trust, Phila., 1943-44; asst. dept. spl. events Phila. Evening Bulletin, 1945-47; asst. stage TV and radio show prodr. Phila., 1947-49; dir. dept. art. Phila. Pub. Schs. Appeared on Wit's End (live pilot TV show), 1948, guest Poetry Today, Sta. WRTN radio, N.Y.C., 1997; adult edn. studies Temple U. Pierce Business Coll, Cheltenham H.S., Oak Ln. Co. Day Sch., Cheltenham Adult Sch., Arthur Murray Dance Sch. Author: (poetry) Whispers of Escaped Thoughts, 2003; contbr. poetry to local newspapers. Vol. occupl. therapist ARC; spl. duty hostess for Purple Heart and Stage Door Canteen, WWII. Mem. Internat. Poetry Mus., Internat. Libr. Poetry, Internat. Soc. Poets (inducted into Hall of Fame Mus.), Poetry Guild, Am. Diabetes Assn., Cheltenham Ctr. Arts, Kappa Chi Delta, Omega Chi. Republican. Methodist. Avocations: sculpture, photography, creative needlework, pianist, collecting sheet music. Home: 82 Holly Dr Crystal Lake IL 60014-5022

FLEMING, PATRICIA STUBBS, artist; b. Phila., Mar. 17, 1936; d. Fredrick Douglass Stubbs and Marion Turner Stubbs Thomas; m. Harold S. Fleming, June 1958 (div. Feb. 1971); children: Douglass, Craig, Gordon. BA, Vassar Coll., 1957; postgrad., NYU, 1958-60, U. Pa., 1957-58, Pa. Acad. Fine Arts, 1957-58. Legis. asst. to reps. U.S. Ho. of Reps., Washington, 1971-77; asst. to sec. HEW, Washington, 1977-78, dir. intergovtl. and legis. affairs Office Civil Rights, 1979-80; asst. to sec. U.S. Dept. Edn., Washington, 1979-80, dep. asst. sec. legis., 1980-81; sr. pub. policy assoc. James H. Lowry & Assocs., Washington, 1981-83; chief staff Rep. Ted Weiss U.S. Ho. of Reps., Washington, 1983-86, profl. staff mem. subcom. human resources & intergovtl. rels, 1986-93; spl. asst. to sec. HHS, Washington, 1993-94; dir. Office Nat. AIDS Policy The White House, Washington, 1994-97, cons. on govt. rels. and AIDS policy and programs, 1997—. Washington rep. Joint Co-sponsored UN Programme on HIV/AIDS, 1997-99, Prevention Works Needle Exch. Program in the Nation's Capitol. One-person shows NYU, Foundry Gallery, Washington; exhibited in group shows in N.Y.C., Washington and St. Petersberg, Russia; mem. Foundry Gallery, Washington.. Democrat. Episcopalian. Avocations: travel, music, reading. Home and Studio: 6009 Massachusetts Ave Bethesda MD 20816-2041

FLEMING, RENÉE L. opera singer; b. Indiana, Pa., Feb. 14, 1959; d. Edwin Davis Fleming and Patricia (Seymour) Alexander; m. Richard Lee Ross, Sept. 23, 1989 (div. 2000). BM in Music Edn., Potsdam State U., 1981; MM, Eastman Sch. Music, 1983; student, Juilliard Am. Opera Ctr., N.Y.C., 1983—84, Juilliard Am. Opera Ctr., 1985—87; PhD (hon.), The Julliard Sch., 2003. Rec. artist Decca Records, London, 1995. Debut engagements include Spoleto Festival, Charleston and Italy, 1986-90, Houston Grand Opera & N.Y.C. Opera, 1988, 89, San Francisco Opera, 1991, Met. Opera, Paris Opera at the Bastille, 1991, Covent Garden, London, 1989, Teatro Colon Buenos Aires, 1991, La Scala, 1993, Lyric Opera of Chgo., 1993, Paris Opera at Palais Garnier, 1996. Winner Met. Opera Nat. Auditions, 1988; recipient George London prize, 1988, Richard Tucker award, 1990, Solti prize l'Acad. du Disque Lyrique, 1996, Prize l'Acad. du Disque Lyrique, 1998; Fulbright scholar, Frankfurt, Germany, 1984-85; named Vocalist of Yr. Mus. Am., 1997; nominated 8 Grammy awards, 1997-99; recipient Grammy award, 1999, 2003, 3 gramophone awards, 1999, record of yr., opera award, recital award, Gift of Music award Orch. of St. Luke's, 2000; named one of top 10 classical singers of the 90s, AP, 2000; La Diva Renée dessert named in her honor by chef Daniel Boulud, 1999; Renee Fleming iris introduced, 2004; named Commandeur de l'Ordre des Arts et des Letters Republic of France, 2002. Office: care ML Falcone Pub Rels 155 W 68th St Apt 1114 New York NY 10023-5817

FLEMING, RHONDA, actress, singer; b. LA; d. Harold Cheverton and Effie (Graham) Louis; m. Ted (dec.); 1 child, Kent Lane. Student, pub. and pvt. schs., L.A., Beverly Hills. Appeared in 40 motion pictures, including Spellbound, 1945, Spiral Staircase, 1945, Out of the Past, 1947, A Connecticut Yankee in King Arthur's Court, 1949, The Great Lover, 1949, The Eagle and the Hawk, 1950, Cry Danger, 1951, Last Outpost, 1951, Hong Kong, 1952, Tropic Zone, 1953, Tennessee's Partner, 1955, Gunfight at OK Corral, 1956, Slightly Scarlett, 1956, Home Before Dark, 1958, Pony Express, 1953, The Nude Bomb, 1980; Broadway debut in The Women, 1973; appeared in musical and plays, including The Boyfriend, 1975, Marriage Go Round, 1960, Bell, Book and Candle, 1962, Kismet at Music Center, 1976; sang Gershwin concert in; 10-week tour, 1963; starred in Las Vegas, Nev., 1959, one-woman concert at Hollywood Bowl, 1964, numerous guest appearances on TV series and talk shows including MacMillan and Wife, Love Boat; TV movies include The Last Hours Before Morning, 1975; NBC's Legends of the Screen, 1980, Metromedia Spl. Road to Hollywood, 1983, Wildest West Show of the Stars, 1986. Founder Rhonda Fleming Mann Clinic and Resource Ctr. for Women's Comprehensive Care at UCLA, PATH (People Assisting the Homeless) Rhonda Fleming Family Ctr.; benefactor Music Ctr.; supporter Childhelp USA, Achievement Rewards Coll. Scientists; life assoc. Pepperdine U.; founding mem. French Found. for Alzheimer Rsch.; adv. bd. Olive Crest Treatment Ctrs. for Abused Children; supporter Freedoms Found. at Valley Forge, City of Hope, Excellence in Media, SPCA, Humane Soc. USA; patron of the arts Music Ctr. Blue Ribbon; bd. dirs. World Opportunities Internat., St. John's Med. Ctr. [illegible] Hood; Gold Angel award Excellence in Media, Woman of the World award Childhelp, USA, Eve award Mannequins of the Assistance League, 1986, Our Lady of Perpetual Inspiration award; named Woman of Year City of Hope, Oper. Children, 1991, honoree of the Music Ctr. Club 100, 1992, UCLA Alumni Assn. Disting. Contbns. award to UCLA Cmty., 2000; Rhonda Fleming Rsch. fellowship for women's cancer established at City of Hope, 2000.

FLEMING, SUZANNE MARIE, academic administrator, freelance/self-employed writer; b. Detroit, Feb. 4, 1927; d. Albert T. and Rose E. (Smiley) F. BS, Marygrove Coll., 1957; MS, U. Mich., 1960, PhD, 1963. Joined Congregation of Sisters Servants of Immaculate Heart of Mary, Roman Catholic Commn. for Cmty., 1945. Chmn. natural sci. div. Marygrove Coll., Detroit, 1970-75, v.p., dean, 1975-78, acad. v.p., 1978-80; asst. v.p. acad. affairs Eastern Mich. U., Ypsilanti, 1980-82, acting assoc. v.p. acad. affairs, 1982-83; provost, acad. v.p. Western Ill. U., Macomb, 1983-86; vice chancellor U. Wis., Eau Claire, 1986-89; freelance writer, 1989—. Vis. scholar U. Mich., 1989-2001; pres. Mich. Coll. Chemistry Tchrs. Assn., 1975; councilor Mich. Inst. Chemists, 1973-77; bd. dirs. Nat. Ctr. for Rsch. to Improve Postsecondary Teaching and Learning, 1988-90. Contbr. articles to profl. publs. NIH research grantee, 1966-69 Home and Office: 2888 Cascade Dr Ann Arbor MI 48104-6659 E-mail: res4atf@comcast.net.

FLEMING, TERRI, newspaper editor; b. 1955; BS in Comm. Journalism, So. Ill. U., 1979. Copy editor, features writer Colorado Springs (Colo.) Sun, 1979-81; news editor, copy editor, designer The Gazette Telegraph, Colorado Springs, 1982-87, design dir., 1987-91, dep. mng. editor, 1991-96; mng. editor The Gazette, Colorado Springs, 1996-2000, acting editor, 2000—. Various editor positions Auckland (New Zealand) Herald, Christchurch (New Zealand) Press, Fiji times, 1980-81; copy editor Thousand Oaks (Calif.) News chronicle, 1981-82. Mem. Am. Soc. Newspaper Editors, Soc. Newspaper Design, Soc. Profl. Journalists, Associated Press Mng. Editors. Avocations: mountain biking, gardening, dance, travel, voluntarism. Office: The Gazette 30 S Prospect St Colorado Springs CO 80903-3671

FLESHER, MARGARET COVINGTON, communications consultant, writer; b. San Angelo, Tex., July 29, 1944; d. Charles C. and Helen Irene (Little) F.; m. Alexander Ribaroff, Dec. 11, 1976 (div. June 1988). BA in Polit. Sci., Vassar Coll., 1966. Assoc. editor Harcourt Brace Inc., N.Y.C., 1966-74; prodr. Guidance Assocs. subsidiary of Harcourt Brace, N.Y.C., 1974-76; freelance writer, editor London, 1976-81; sr. editor Franklin Watts, Inc., N.Y.C., 1981-85; pres. The Westport (Conn.) Pub. Group, 1985-89; coord. cmty. rels. Texaco Inc., White Plains, N.Y., 1989-91, sr. coord. media rels., 1991-93, contbg. editor, 1993-97; pursuit. cons. Deloitte & Touche, Wilton, Conn., 1998—. Author: Mexico and the United States Today: Issues Between Neighbors, 1985, New Leaves: A Journal for the Suddenly Single, 1987. Mem.: Internat. Women's Writing Guild, Fairfield County Pub. Rels. Assn. (bd. dirs. 1991—92), The Assn. for Women in Comm. (Fairfield County chpt. pres. 1986—88, v.p. profl. devel. 1994—95, Westchester chpt. bd. dirs., Clarion award 1995), Conn. Women's Forum (chair comm. com.), Conn. Press Club (v.p. programs 1998—99). Avocations: hiking, yoga, photography, gardening. Office: Deloitte & Touche 10 Westport Rd Wilton CT 06897-4522

FLESKES, CAROL LYNN, environmental engineer; b. Yakima, Wash., Aug. 4, 1946; d. Victor Leo and Margaret Ann (O'Neill) Rabung; m. Hubert William Fleskes, Oct. 24, 1972; children: Susan Carol, Brett William. BSCE, U. Wash., 1969. Registered profl. engr., Wash., Oreg., Calif. City engr. City of Albany, Oreg., 1970-72; design engr. John Sharrah & Assocs., Red Bluff, Calif., 1973-74; solid waste engr. Butte Co., Oroville, Calif., 1974-75; project engr. Ringel & Assocs., Oroville, 1975-77; environ. engr. Wash. Dept. Ecology, Olympia, 1978-88, program mgr. toxic cleanup program, 1988-94, program mgr. water resources, 1994-97, adminstrv. svcs. mgr., 1997—. Bd. mem Bd. of Registration for Profl. Engrs. and Land Surveyors, 1993-2003; chair Town of Bucoda (Wash.) Planning Commn., 1983-93; vol. firefighter Town of Bucoda, 1978-85; emergency med. technician Town of Bucoda Fire Dept., 1979-83. Recipient Disting. Mgrs. award Gov. of Wash., 1991. Mem. NSPE, Wash. Soc. Profl. Engrs. (Environ. Engr. of Yr. award 1991). Avocations: camping, crafts. Home: 502 S Wright St Bucoda WA 98530 Office: Wash Dept Ecology PO Box 47600 Olympia WA 98504-7600 Fax: (360) 407-6989. E-mail: cfle461@ecy.wa.gov.

FLETCHER, BETTY BINNS, federal judge; b. Tacoma, Mar. 29, 1923; BA, Stanford U., 1943; LLB, U. Wash., 1956. Bar: Wash. 1956. Mem. firm Preston, Thorgrimson, Ellis, Holman & Fletcher, Seattle, 1956—79; judge U.S. Ct. Appeals (9th cir.), Seattle, 1979—, sr. judge, 1998—. Mem.: ABA (Margaret Brent award 1992), Fed. Judges Assn. (past pres.), Am. Law Inst., Wash. State Bar Assn., Phi Beta Kappa, Order of Coif. Office: US Ct Appeals 9th Cir 1010 5th Ave Ste 1000 Seattle WA 98104-1196

FLETCHER, CATHY ANN, auditor; b. Barnesville, Ga., Aug. 23, 1949; d. John James and Dorothy Lee (Banks) Fletcher; 1 child, Lisa Faye. Student, Ohio State U., 1969—70; AS, Mass. Bay C.C., 1982; BS, AS, Northeastern U., 1984; MA in Human Resources Mgmt., Emmanuel Coll., Boston, 1993. Mail clk. Fed. Res. Bank, Boston, 1971-72; office mgr. Breckenridge Sportswear, Boston, 1973-74; asst. dir. Whittier Street Health Ctr., Boston, 1974-81; sec. to dir. Northeastern U., 1981-84; auditor Def. Contract Audit Agy. N.E. Region, Boston, 1984—. Sec., bd. dirs. Boston Tenant Policy Coun., 1977-79; mgr. northeastern region Fed. Women's Program, 1989—, mgr. northeastern region Black Employment program, 1999—; mem. adv. bd. DCAA EEO, 1989—. Author: Softball Team Book, 1975. V.p., bd. dirs. Bromley Heath Tenant Mgmt. Corp., Jamaica Plain, Mass., 1976-91, bd. dirs., 1997-2000; apptd. fed. women program coord. State of Mass., 1988; mem. women's opportunity com. Boston Fed. Exec. Bd., 1990—, mem. women's coun., 1994—, mem. diversity com., 1997—; with Women's Ednl. Indsl. Union, 1993-99; mem. Fed. Spl. Emphasis Program Coalition, 2000—. Mem. NAFE, Profl. Coun., Nat. Tenants Orgn., Assn. Govt. Accts. (cert. govt. fin. mgr.), Federally Employed Women (treas. Greater Boston chpt. 1992-93, pres. 1994—, New Eng. Regional mgr. 1995—, rep. 1996—), Hawkettes Social (pres., past. mem. profl. coun.), Blacks in Govt., Sigma Epsilon Rho. Avocations: reading, bible studies, cooking, walking, travel. Office: Def Contract Audit Agy Boston Br Office 101 Merrimac St Ste 820A Boston MA 02114-4724

FLETCHER, DENISE KOEN, strategic and financial consultant; b. Istanbul, Turkey, Aug. 31, 1948; came to U.S., 1967, naturalized, 1976; d. Moris and Kety (Barkey) Koen; m. Robert B. Fletcher, Nov. 11, 1969; children— David, Kate. AB (Coll. scholar), Wellesley Coll., 1969; M in City Planning, Harvard U., 1972. Analyst Ea. div. Getty Oil Co., N.Y.C., 1972-73, sr. analyst, 1973-74, cash mgmt. and bldg. supr., 1974-76, Getty Oil Co. (Eastern), 1976; asst. treas. N.Y. Times Co., N.Y.C., 1976-80, treas., 1980-88; pres. Fletcher Assocs. Inc., Larchmont, N.Y., 1988-96; CEO Comm. Venture Group, Ltd., N.Y.C., N.Y., 1989-90; v.p., CFO Bowne & Co., 1996-98, sr. v.p., CFO, 1998—2000; exec. v.p., CFO Mastercard, 2000—03. Bd. dirs. Software, Etx. Stores, Inc., 1991-94, Unisys Corp., 2001—, Orbitz, Inc., 2004—. Bd. dirs. Overseas Edn. Found. Internat., 1989-90, Boy Scouts Am., Exploring, 1991-93; bd. dirs., trustee and v.p. bd. dirs., exec. com. YWCA, N.Y., 1987—; mem. budget com. City of Larchmont, N.Y., 1981-83, chmn. zoning bd. appeals, 1987—, mem. selection com., 1985-87; mem. alumni exec. coun. Harvard U. Sch. Govt., 1982-87. Mellon scholar, 1970 Mem. Academy of Women Achievers, The Business Leadership Coun., Fin. Execs. Internat., Fin. Women's Assn., Women's Forum, Treasurers Club N.Y., Harvard Club (N.Y.C.), Phi Beta Kappa.*

FLETCHER, LOUISE, actress; b. Birmingham, Ala., 1936; d. Robert Capers F. BA, U. N.C., 1957; student acting with Jeff Corey; LHD (hon.), Gallaudet U., 1982, Western Md. Coll., 1986. Films include Thieves Like Us, 1973, Russian Roulette, 1974, One Flew Over the Cuckoo's Nest, 1975 (Acad. award as best actress), Exorcist II: The Heretic,, 1976, The Cheap Detective, 1977, The Magician, 1978, Natural Enemies, 1979, The Lucky Star, 1979, The Lady in Red, 1979, Strange Behavior, 1980, Brainstorm, 1981, Strange Invaders, 1982, Once Upon a Time in America, 1982, Firestarter, 1983, Overnight Sensation, 1983, Invaders from Mars, 1985, The Boy Who Could Fly, 1985, Nobody's Fool, 1986, Flowers in the Attic, 1987, Two Moon Junction, 1987, Blue Steel, 1988, Best of the Best, 1989, Shadowzone, 1989, Blind Vision, 1990, The Player, 1991, Return to Two Moon Junction, 1993, Tollbooth, 1993, Virtuosity, 1995, Mulholland Falls, 1995, 2 Days in the Valley, 1995, Edie & Pen, 1995, High School High, 1995, Girl Gets Moe, 1996, Heartless, 1996, Love Kills, 1998, A Map of the World, 1999, More Dogs than Bones, 1999, Cruel Inventions, 1999, Time Served, 1999, Very Mean Men, 2000, Silver Man, 2000, Seeing in the Dark, 2000, Big Eden, 2000; TV appearances include Maverick, Wagon Train, The Law-Man, Playhouse 90, The Millionaire, Alfred Hitchcock, Thou Shalt Not Commit Adultery, 1978, A Summer to Remember, 1984, Island, 1984, Second Serve, 1985, Hoover, 1986, The Karen Carpenter Story, 1988, Nightmare on the 13th Floor, 1988, Twilight Zone, 1988, Final Notice, 1989, The Hitchhiker, 1990, Tales from the Crypt, 1991, In a Child's Name, 1991, Boys of Twilight, 1991, The Fire Next Time, 1992, Civil Wars, 1993, Deep Space Nine, 1994, 95, 96, 97, 98, 99, The Hawunting of Cliff House, Dream On, 1994, Someone Else's Child, 1994, VR5, 1994, 95, Picket Fences, 1996, Stepford Husbands, 1996, Twisted Path, 1997, Breastmen, 1997, Married to a Stranger, 1997, Profiler, 1997, The Practice, 1998, Brimstone, 1998, Devil's Arithmetic, 1999. Bd. dirs. Deafness Rsch. Found., 1980—. Mem. Nat. Inst. Deafness and Other Communicable Disorders (adv. bd.).

FLETCHER, MARIS, literature educator; b. Ark., Aug. 10; d. C. W. and Annie Tolbert; m. Orville Fletcher; children: Ken, Mark. MA in English, Sul Ross State U., 1980; MA in Comp. Lit., U. Ark., 1995, PhD in Comp. Lit., 1996. Master gardener. Instr. U. Ozarks, Clarksville, Ark., 1980—90, U. Ark., Fayetteville, Ark., 1990—97; asst. prof. Ark. State U., Beebe, Ark., 1997—. Instr. Upward Bound, Fayetteville, 1990—97. Contbr. columns in newspapers Spiro News, 1970. Judge White County Creative Writers, Searcy, Ark., 1998—. Methodist. Avocation: gardening. Office: Ark State Univ 1000 Iowa St Beebe AR 72012 Home: 221 N Cypress Beebe AR 72012 E-mail: mjfletcher@asub.edu.

FLETCHER, MARJORIE AMOS, librarian; b. Easton, Pa., July 10, 1923; d. Alexander Robert and Margaret Ashton (Arnold) Amos; A.B., Bryn Mawr Coll., 1946; m. Charles Mann Fletcher, May 14, 1949; children: Robert Amos, Elizabeth Ashton, Anne Kennard. Asst. to dir. rsch., then rsch. asst. to pres. Penn Mut. Life Ins. Co., 1946-49; officer A.R. Amos Co., Phila., 1949-66; part-time tchr., 1965-68; librarian Am. Coll., Bryn Mawr, Pa., 1968-77, archivist, 1973—, dir. oral history collection, 1975—, lectr. on archives, 1975—, asst. prof. edn., 1973-87, dir. archives and oral history, 1977—; curator art collection Am. Coll., 1981-; pres. pub. rels. MAF Enterprises, 1987—. Author articles in field. Recipient awards Phila. Flower Show, 1965—; bd. dirs. Emergency Aid Found.. Mem. Spl. Librs. Assn. (pres. Phila. 1977-78), Soc. Am. Archivists (chairperson oral history sect. 1981-87, award of merit 1987), Oral History Assn., Hist. Soc. Pa., U.S. Pony Club, D.A.R., Nat. Soc. Colonial Dames in Commonwealth of Pa., Emergency Aid Pa. Found., Phila. Skating Club, Davis Creek Yacht Club, Bridlewild Pony Club (sponsor), Bridlewild Trails Club (Gladwyne). Republican. Episcopalian. Home: 1135 Norsam Rd Gladwyne PA 19035-1419 Office: Am Coll Bryn Mawr PA 19010

FLETCHER, ROBIN MARY, health care administrator; b. Waco, Tex., May 24, 1952; d. Arthur Hale Fletcher and Bersha Pauline (King) Gardner; 1 child, Jonathon Potter. AAS in Nursing, Tarrant County Jr. Coll., 1973; B of Liberal Studies in healthcare adminstrn. summa cum laude, St. Edwards U., 1996; M of Pub. Health in Cmty. Health, U. Tex., Houston, 1997. Staff/charge RN St. Joseph Hosp., Ft. Worth, 1973-75; staff RN/asst. head nurse Tarrant County Hosp. Dist., Fort Worth, Tex., 1975-76; staff/charge RN/asst. patient care coord. Med. Plaza Hosp., Ft. Worth, 1977-80; home health nurse Upjohn Health Care and Med. Pers. Pool, Fort Worth, 1981; med. care analyst, rev. supr. and mgr., dir. rev. Tex. Med. Found., Austin, 1981-83, 84-96; TQI coord. VA North Tex. Health Care Sys., Dallas, 1998-99; project dir. Tex. Med. Found., Austin, 1999—2002, dir. physician and hosp. quality improvement, 2002—. Bd. dirs., adv. bd. for med. record program Tex. Women's U., Dallas, 1989-90. Mem. ANA, Tex. Nurses Assn., Tex. Pub. Health Assn., Am. Diabetes Assn. (bd. dirs. local chpt. 1996-98), Health Care Compliance Assn., Alpha Sigma Lambda Nat. Honor Soc. Avocations: antiques, jogging, volkssports, rollerblading, travel. Office: Tex Med Found Barton Oaks Plz Two 901 Mopac Expy S Ste 200 Austin TX 78746

FLETCHER, SARAH LEE, retired elementary school educator; b. Webb, Ala., May 7, 1925; d. James Harvey and Emma Freddie (Scarborough) Lee; m. Gaston Maurice Fletcher, June 24, 1948; children: S. Daphne, Lee Maurice, Timothy J. Student, Bob Jones Coll., 1943-44, assoc. bus. cert., 1947; student, Calhoun Coll., 1968-70, Troy State U., 1970-72; BRE, Bethany Theol. Seminary, 1995, MRE, 1996. With Atlanta and St. Andrews Bay Rwy. Co., 1944-46; sec. to pub. Dothan (Ala.) Eagle, 1947-48; tchr. Morgan County Schs., Decatur, Ala., 1967-69, Newton (Ala.) Pub. Schs., 1969-72, Trinity Christian Schs., Oxford, Ala., 1972-73, Berachah Christian Acadamy, Huntsville, Ala., 1973-75; sec. Dominion Textile, Yarmouth, Nova Scotia, 1975-76; tchr. Mueller Christian Sch., Miami, 1976-79, Berean Christian Sch., Dothan, 1979-86, Grace Bible Acad., Dothan, 1987-90, Clinton Christian Acad., Upper Marlboro, Md., 1990-91. Cons. Mary Kay Cosmetics, 1982-99. Author: To Love Again, 1996, Love in Bloom, 2001; compiler, contbg. author: (book of short stories) The Set of the Sails, 1997; contbr. articles to Christian papers and mags. Active in ch. Mem. Troy State U. Creative Writing Club, Dothan Creative Writing Group. Baptist. Avocations: helping the elderly, writing, walking, speaking. Home: 1119 Garden Ln Dothan AL 36301-3407 E-mail: Aleph@aol.com.

FLETCHER, SUZANNE WRIGHT, epidemiologist, medical educator, editor; b. Jacksonville, Fla., Nov. 14, 1940; d. Robert Dean and Helen (Selmer) Wright; m. Robert H. Fletcher; children: John Wright, Grant Selmer. BA, Swarthmore Coll., 1962; MD, Harvard Med. Sch., 1966; MSc, Johns Hopkins U., 1973. Diplomate Nat. Bd. Med. Examiners, Am. Bd. Internal Medicine. Intern Stanford (Calif.) U. Med. Ctr., 1966—67, resident, 1967—68; physician 22nd med. detachment U.S. Army, New Ulm, Germany, 1969—70; asst. prof. epidemiology and health Mc Gill U., Montreal, Canada, 1974—77, assoc. prof., 1977—78, asst. prof. medicine, 1973—78; dir. med. clinic dept. medicine NC Meml. Hosp., 1978—82; assoc. prof. medicine U. NC, 1978—83, co-chief divsn. gen. medicine and clin. epidemiology dept. medicine, 1978—86, rsch. assoc. health svcs. rsch. ctr., 1978—90, vice chmn. clin. svcs., 1981—90, prof. medicine, clin. prof. epidemiology, 1983—90, program dir. faculty devel. gen. medicine and gen. pediatrics, 1985—90, co-dir. internat. clin. epidemiology network program Rockefeller Found., 1986—90; prof. ambulatory care and prevention Harvard Med. Sch., 1994—; editor Annals of Internal Medicine, Phila., 1990—93. Adj. prof. medicine U. Pa., Phila., 1990—93, Jefferson Med. Coll., 1991—93, U. NC, 1994—; physician internal medicine; chmn. NIH Tech. Assessment Conf., 1992, Nat. Cancer Inst. Internat. Workshop, 1993;

active World Bank Seminar on Preventive Strategies in Med. Edn., Hangzhou, China, 1986, Ad Hoc NCI Com. on BSE Cancer Detection Rsch. and Applications, 1986. Author: Clinical Epidemiology—The Essentials, 1982, 3d edit., 1995; contbr. chpts. to books, articles to profl. jours. Named rsch. grantee, Conseil de la Recherche en Sante du Quebec, 1975—77; recipient Can. Nat. Health Rsch. Scholar award, Can. Govt., 1975—78; grantee, Health and Welfare Can., 1976—78, Robert Wood Johnson Teaching Hosp. Gen. Medicine Group Practice Program, 1980—84, Nat. Ctr. Health Scis. Rsch. and Health Tech., 1985—89, Rockefeller Found. Clin. Epidemiology Resource and Tng. Ctr., 1986—90, NIH, 1987—90, 1997—. Master: ACP (med. knowledge self assessment program 1984—85, clin. practice subcom. 1987, pub. policy subcom. 1988—89); fellow: Coll. Physicians Phila., Am. Coll. Epidemiology (bd. dirs. 1990—93, chmn. pub. com. 1992—94); mem.: APHA, Am. Bd. Internal Medicine (bd. govs. 1981—87), NCI Bd. Sci. Advisors, World Assn. Med. Editors (v.p. 1997—2001), Internat. Clin. Epidemiology Network (bd. dirs.), Inst. Medicine (coun. 1993—96, exec. com. 1993—96), Soc. Gen. Internal Medicine (counsellor 1978—81, pres.-elect 1982—83, pres. 1983—84, co-editor Jour. Gen. Internal Medicine 1984—89, mem. publs. com. 1990—, chmn. Glaser award com. 1991). Unitarian Universalist. Office: 208 Boulder Bluff Chapel Hill NC 27516 Business E-Mail: Suzanne_Fletcher@hms.harvard.edu.

FLETCHER, WINONA LEE, theater educator emeritus; b. Nov. 25, 1926; m. Joseph Grant; 1 child, Betty. BA, Johnson C. Smith U., 1947; MA, U. Iowa, 1951; PhD, Ind. U., 1968. Prof. speech and theatre Ky. State U., Frankfort, 1951-78; prof. theatre and afro-Am. studies Ind. U., Bloomington, 1978-94, prof. emeritus, 1994; assoc. dean COAS, 1981-84. Costumer, dir. summer theatre, U. Mo., Lincoln, 1952-60, 69. Sr. editor: Community Memories: A Glimpse of African American Life in Frankfort, Ky., 2003. Recipient Lifetime Achievement award, 1993; Am. Theatre fellow, 1979. Mem. Am. Theatre for Higher Edn., Black Theatre Network, Ky. Hist. Soc., Nat. Assn. Dramatic and Speech Arts, Nat. Theatre Conf., Alpha Kappa Alpha. Home: 317 Cold Harbor Dr Frankfort KY 40601-3011

FLETTNER, MARIANNE, opera administrator; b. Frankfurt, Germany, Aug. 9, 1933; d. Bernhard J. and Kaethe E. (Halbritter) F. Bus. diploma, Hessel Bus. Coll., 1953. Sec. various cos., 1953-61, Pontiac Motor Div., Burlingame, Calif., 1961-63, Met. Opera, N.Y., 1963-74, asst. co. mgr., 1974-79; artistic adminstr. San Diego Opera, 1979—. Avocations: travel, hiking, swimming, cooking. Home: 4015 Crown Point Dr San Diego CA 92109-6270 Office: San Diego Opera 1200 Third Ave 18th Fl San Diego CA 92101-4112 E-mail: marianne.flettner@sdopera.com.

FLEXNER, JOSEPHINE MONCURE, musician, educator; b. Marion, Va., Oct. 11, 1919; d. Walter Raleigh Daniel and Harriet Ashby (Ogburn) M.; m. Kurt Fisher Flexner, Dec. 20, 1942; children: Thomas Moncure, Peter Wallace. BA, Univ. Richmond, 1941; tchr. cert. in piano, Peabody Conservatory, 1945; MS in piano, Juilliard Sch. Music, 1950. Class piano tchr. Balt. Pub. Sch., 1945-46; mem. piano faculty Peabody Conservatory Prep., Balt., 1945-46, Pius X Sch. Manhatanville Coll. Sacred Heart, N.Y.C., 1946-50, Henry Street Settlement Sch., N.Y.C., 1949-50; piano tchr. Bronxville, N.Y., 1950-54; mem. piano faculty Rhodes Coll., Memphis, Tenn., 1970-82; piano tchr. St. Mary's Episcopal Sch., Memphis, 1982-87. Judge for Tenn. piano auditions, 1980-85, judge in Tenn. Nat. Guild Auditions, 1983-84. Contbr. articles to profl. jours. Den mother Boy Scouts Am., 1963-65, vice chmn., 1964-65; precinct worker, capt. Nat. Elections, Memphis, 1972, 74; mem. Memphis Arts Coun., 1977-79; area chmn. Westchester Soc. Performing Arts, 1964-66, chmn. cultural activities Sch. No. 8, Yonkers, N.Y., 1963-66; vice chmn. music dept. Bronxville Women's Club, 1964-66; pres. chancel choir Dutch Reformed Ch., Bronxville, 1963-66; program chmn. Seoul Internat. Women's Assn., Seoul, Korea, 1967-68, chmn. cultural activities Seoul Am. Schs., 1966-68, chmn. culutral seminars Am. Women's Club, Seoul, 1967-68; treas., pres. Greater Memphis Music Tchrs. Assn., 1975-79; bd. dirs. Young Peoples Piano Concerto Competition, 1979-85, Tenn. Music Tchrs. Assn., 1977-79. Named Tchr. of Yr., Greater Memphis Music, 1983, Tchr. of Yr., Tenn. Music Tchrs. Assn., 1985. Democrat. Presbyterian. Avocations: writing, reading, playing piano. Home: The Fountains at Millbrook 17 Crestview Rd Millbrook NY 12545

FLICK, CAROL J. middle school educator; b. Denver, Dec. 13, 1944; d. David Marshall and Eleanore Francis (Jones) Brewer; m. Leland Gene Johnson, Aug. 4, 1965 (div. Feb. 1975); children: Teri Lynn Johnson Flick Key, Troy Lee Johnson; m. Wayne A. Flick, Mar. 29, 1975; children: Patrick Allen, Pamela Kay. BA, Mesa State Coll., Grand Junction, Colo., 1976; MA, U. No. Colo., Greeley, 1990; postgrad., Colo. State U., 2000—. Cert. tchr., Colo. Asst. mgr. Safeway Stores, Grand Junction, 1975-84; tchr. Sch. Dist. 51, Grand Junction, 1989—. Assessment liaison Sch. Dist. 51, 1996—. Mem. Nat. Staff Devel. Coun., Nat. Coun. Tchrs. English, Colo. Edn. Assn., Colo. Staff Devel. Coun., Mesa Valley Edn. Assn. (area dir. 1989-99, polit. action com. 1995-99, Outstanding Tchr. 1995 96), Beta Sigma Phi, Phi Delta Kappa (Outstanding Tchr. award 1995), Delta Kappa Gamma (v.p. 1995-99). Avocations: reading, continuing education, singing, writing, hiking. Home: 3026 Cline Ct Grand Junction CO 81504-5612

FLICK, CONNIE RUTH, real estate agent, real estate broker; d. Hugh D and Lenore Violet Myers; children: Kendra A Merriman, Tonya L Moore, Charity I Risley. Lic. Ind. Real Estate Broker Ind. Profl. Licensing Agy., 1968. Plant mgr. USPS, Terre Haute, Ind., 1993—, quality specialist Lafayette, Ind., 1986—93; owner, realtor, broker Flick Realty, Crawfordsville, Ind., 1968—; ins. agt. Met. Ins. Co., Lafayette, Ind., 1981—82; supr. mail processing USPS, Lafayette, Ind., 1985—86; hq test team mem. USPS, Equipment Devel., Merrifield, Va., 1989—92. Priority mail improvement team USPS, Indpls., 1995—96, activation coord., Inpls., Ind., 2000—02, mgr., air mail facility, 1995—96, acting postmaster (officer in charge), Lafayette, Ind., 1995—96, internat. svc. ctr. activation coord., Chgo., 1999—2000. Mem. Sch. Bd. Nominating Com., Crawfordsville, Ind., 1983—85; fund raising chmn. Hose PTO, Crawfordsville, Ind., 1980—81; vice precinct committeeman Rep. Party, Crawfordsville, Ind., 1980—85. Recipient Gold Sales award, Met. Ins. Co., 1981, Cert. of Appreciation, US Postal Svc., 1991, U.S. Postal Svc., 2001. Mem.: MIBOR, Past Presidents Bus. and Profl. Women (pres. 1979—80), Nat. Assn. of Realtors, Montgomery County Bd. of Realtors (sec. 1969—72), Ind. Realtors Assn., Ea. Star, Faternal Order of Women of the Eagles, Women of the Moose. Independent-Republican. Baptist (Brownsvalley Missionary Baptist Church). Avocations: swimming, reading, birdwatching, puzzles, genealogy. Home: 300 Covington St Crawfordsville IN 47933-1332 Office: United States Postal Service 150 West Margaret Dr Terre Haute IN 47802-9997 Office Phone: 812-231-4011. Personal E-mail: cflick@tctc.com. E-mail: cflick@usps.gov.

FLINN, MARY AGNES, artist, educator; b. Balt., July 31, 1962; d. Eugene Aloyisious and Rose Flora F. BFA, Swain Sch. Design, New Bedford, Mass., 1985; MFA, CUNY, 1991. Art handler, conservation technician NAD Mus., NYC, 1992—. Tchr. Kundalini Yoga, dir./tchr. training program in Yoga at the Energy Ctr., NYC, 2003-2003, Yoga tchr. Hunter Coll., NYC, 2000-2003, Yoga tchr. Pratt Inst., NYC, 2002-2003; tchr. art Melrose Cmty. Ctr., Bronx, N.Y., 1993, Saraswati Prodns., Bklyn., 1996; vis. artist Fairleigh Dickinson Coll., N.J., 1994. One-woman shows include Prince St. Gallery, N.Y.C., 1995, 1997, 1999, two person show, Dartmouth Coll., N.H., 2001, exhibited in group shows at Balt. City Hall, 1995, Prince St. Gallery, 1996, also pvt. collections, restored mural, Grand Ctrl. Sta., N.Y.C.; featured: article (Mary's Loft) Ascent mag., 2001. Vol. Meth. Hosp., Bklyn., 1995-96. Fellow Vt. Studio Ctr., 1987. Mem. Women's Mus., Amnesty Internat. Avocations: yoga, healing arts.

FLINN, ROBERTA JEANNE, management, computer applications consultant; b. Twin Falls, Idaho, Dec. 19, 1947; d. Richard H. and Ruth (Johnson) F. Student, Colo. State U., 1966-67. Cert. Novell netware engr. Ptnr. Aqua-Star Pools & Spas, Boise, Idaho, 1978—, mng. ptnr., 1981-83. Ops. mgr. Polly Pools, Inc., Canby, Oreg., 1983-84, br. mgr. Polly Pools, Inc., A-One Distributing, 1984-85; comptr., Beaverton Printing, Inc., 1986-89; mng. ptnr. Invisible Ink, Canby, Oreg., 1989—. Mem. Nat. Appaloosa Horse Club, Oreg. Dressage Soc., NetWare Users International (Portland chpt.). Home: 24687 S Central Point Rd Canby OR 97013-9743 E-mail: rjflinn@invisibleink.net.

FLINSPACH, URSULA R. pharmacy technician, mathematics educator; b. Washington, Pa., Jan. 22, 1950; d. Albert M. Sr. and Rose K. Jackson; m. Donald A. Flinspach, Jr., May 20, 1972; 1 child, Donald A. III. BS in Math., So. Ill. U., Carbondale, 1975; AA in computer sci., John Wood C.C., Quincy, Ill., 1985; cert. in pharmacy tech., Harcourt Learning Direct, 2001. Cert. tchr. math., sci., computer sci. Ill., 1974, Mo., 1975, pharmacy technician Ill., 1997, Nat. Bd. Pharmacy Technician Cert., 1998, Mo., 2000. Math. instr. Highland HS, Ewing, Mo., 1975—76; math. and computer sci. instr. Notre Dame HS, Quincy, Ill., 1977—85; math. instr. Homer HS, 1986—88; math./physics instr. Mt Zion HS, 1989—92; math. instr. Routt HS, Jacksonville, 1993—95, Unity HS, Mendon, 1995—98; cert. pharmacy technician ShopKo Stores, Inc., Quincy, 1998—. Golf coach Notre Dame HS, Quincy, Ill., 1978—85; coach Mt Zion HS, 1989—92, Unity H.S., Mendon, 1996—98. Neighborhood chairperson Mother's Mar. of Dimes, Quincy, Ill., 2003—03; vol. runner Hannibal Regional Hosp., Hannibal, Mo., 1996—2003; vol. coach Little People's Golf Tournament, Quincy, 1979—85; team leader Shopko store #2139 United Way, 1999—99; mayoral candidate Ind. Party, Quincy, Ill., 1995—96. Tradesman 2d class WAVES USN, 1969—72. Decorated Nat. Def. Medal USN; nominee Hero of the Year award, Champaign County, 1989; recipient Above and Beyond Tchg., Homer Cmty. Consol. Sch. Bd., 1986—88, 5-10k Bronze medal, Hannibal Regional Hosp., 2001. Mem.: Quincy Soc. Fine Arts, Pharmacy Technician Certification Bd., Am. Pharmacists Assn. Roman Catholic. Achievements include first female from 1967 Trinity High School to enlist in the military WAVES during Vietnam; first female Mayoral candidate Quincy Illinois. Avocations: reading, continued education, walking/hiking, music, biking. Home: 1608 Madison Quincy IL 62301 Office: ShopKo Stores Inc 3200 Broadway Quincy IL 62301 Personal E-mail: uflin@hotmail.com.

FLIOTSOS, ANNE, theater educator; b. Fort Wayne, Ind., Mar. 19, 1964; d. George V. and Marilynn E. Fliotsos. BA, Purdue U., 1982—86; MLS, Ind. U., 1987—89; PhD in theater, U. of Md., 1993—97. Reference librarian & online search coord. Winthrop U., Rock Hill, SC, 1990—93; vis. prof. of theatre U. of Mo., Columbia, Mo., 1997—99; asst. prof. of theatre Purdue U., West Lafayette, Ind., 1999—. Dir.: (musical theatre) The Fantasticks, (also choreographer, co-author, co-lyricist) Oedipus! A New Musical Comedy (Jim Henson award for projects related to puppetry, 1996, artistic achievement for playscript and meritorious achievement in directing, Kennedy Ctr./Am. Coll. Theatre festival, 1996), : (plays) Don Quixote de La Jolla, Anton in Show Business, The Events of 9/11, Inspecting Carol, That Homo Play, The Yellow Dwarf, Cheese? (meritorious achievement award for direction, Kennedy Ctr./Am. Coll. Theatre festival, 1995), Chocolate Cake, (also writer, costume designer) Snow White; editor: (book) Teaching Theatre Today, 2004; contbr. articles to jours. Social dir. Greater Lafayette Ambassador's Club, Lafayette, Ind., 2003—. Recipient Tchg. award, Dept. of Visual & Performing Arts, Purdue U., 2002, Libr. Scholar's grant, Purdue U. Libraries, 2001;, 2000, Purdue Rsch. Found. Summer Faculty grant, Purdue Rsch. Found., 2002, Dean's Rsch. Incentive grant, Sch. of Liberal Arts, Purdue U., 1999. Mem.: Popular Culture/Am. Culture Assn., Theatre Commuications Group, Assn. for Theatre in Higher Edn. (co-director of task force on promotion & tenure 2000—01). Office: Purdue Theatre 128 Memorial Mall West Lafayette IN 47907

FLIPPO, KAREN FRANCINE, social welfare administrator; b. Chgo., Nov. 19, 1947; d. Irving Albert and Ruth Goldie Feuerstadt; m. Charles Wayne Flippo, Aug. 6, 1978; 1 child, Ian David. BA in Govt., Am. U., 1969; M in Rehab. Adminstrn., U. San Francisco, 1981. Legis. aide Calif. Senate Subcom. on the Disabled, San Francisco, 1980-81; membership svcs. coord. Calif. Life Underwriters Assn., Oakland, 1981-84; project dir. U. San Francisco, 1984-90; sr. rsch. analyst InfoUSE, Berkeley, Calif., 1990-91, 2000; tng. assoc. Va. Commonwealth U., Richmond, 1991-96; dir. best practice initiative United Cerebral Palsy Assn., Washington, 1996-99, COO, 1999; rehab. program specialist Nat. Inst. on Disability and Rehab. Rsch., Dept. Edn., Washington, 2000; v.p. Brain Injury Assn., Alexandria, Va., 2001—03; exec. dir. Nat. Assn. Couns. on Devel. Disabilities, Washington, 2003—. Adv. bd. mem. InfoLines, St. Augustine, Fla., 1995—; bd. mem. Va. Coun. on Assistive Tech., Richmond, 1996-2001, CARF-The Accreditation Commn., Tucson, 1998-2000; dir. spl. projects Assn. for Persons in Supported Employment, Richmond, 1997-98. Lead editor: Assistive Technology: A Resource for School, Home and Community, 1995. Mem. Rehab. Engring. and Assistive Tech. Soc. N.Am., Assn. for Persons in Supported Employment (v.p. bd. dirs. 1993-95). Avocations: travel, reading, golf, community service. Office: Assn Couns on Devel Disabilities 1234 Massachusetts Ave NW Washington DC 20005 E-mail: kfflippo@aol.com.

FLOCKHART, CALISTA, actress; b. Freeport, Ill., Nov. 11, 1964; d. Ronald and Kay F. BA in acting, Rutgers U. Actress Ally McBeal Twentieth Century Fox, L.A. Appeared in Broadway plays, including The Glass Menagerie, The Three Sisters; television work includes; The Guiding Light, 1978, Darrow, 1991, Ally McBeal, 1997-2002; film work includes; Quiz Show, 1994, Getting In, 1994, Naked in New York, 1994, Pictures of Baby Jane Doe, 1996, The Birdcage, 1996, Milk and Money, 1997, Drunks, 1997, Telling Lies in America, 1997, A Midsummer Night's Dream, 1999, Like a Hole in the Head, 1999, Jane Doe, 1999. Recipient Best Actress award Golden Globes, 1998 for her work on Ally McBeal. Office: Ally McBeal c/o David E Kelly Productions c/o Twentieth Century Fox 10201 W Pico Blvd Bldg 80 Los Angeles CA 90064-2606

FLODEN, ROBERTA B. librarian, columnist; b. Chgo., Aug. 23, 1936; d. Hymen Bresloff and Edith Naomi Rosenbloom; 1 child, Laural Floden Reid. BA, U. Ill., 1958; postgrad., Northwestern U., 1963—64. English/drama tchr. various pub. H.S., Chgo., 1960—70; libr. Marin Librs., Marin County, Calif., 1971—. Theatre/art critic Marin Newspapers, Marin County, 1982—93; garden columnist Marin & San Francisco Chronicle, 1991—, Marin/Ind. Jour., 1991—99, San Francisco Chronicle, 2001—; tchr. gardening workshops Coll. Marin, Kentfield, Calif., 1995—; mem. adv. bd. Marin Arts Coun., Marin County, 1991—. Author: Growing Herbs, 1993; editor: (mus. catalog) Beyond the Obvious, 1999. Mem.: Bay Area Theatre Critics Conf. (newsletter editor 1991—93), Garden Writers Am., Marin Arts Coun. (life). Home: PO Box 494 Forest Knolls CA 94933

FLOERSCH, SHIRLEY PATTEN, dietician, consultant; b. Fayette, Ala., Mar. 22, 1924; d. Thomas Warren and Virgie Lee (Shirley) Patten; m. Joseph Paul Floersch, Aug. 5, 1950; children: Shirley Anne, Mary Jo, Paula. BS in Home Econs., Miss. State Coll. for Women, 1946. Cert. dietitian. Dietetic intern Vanderbilt U., Nashville, 1947; asst. adminstrv. dietitian St. Thomas Hosp., Nashville, 1947-48; adminstrv. dietitian Midstate Bapt. Hosp., Nashville, 1948-51; clin. dietitian St. Elizabeth's Hosp., Washington, 1953-56, VA Hosp., Houston, 1956; therapeutic dietitian Our Lady of the Lake Hosp., Baton Rouge, 1956-59; clin. dietitian USPHS, New Orleans, 1961-78; cons. dietitian New Orleans Home and Rehab. Ctr., 1980-92; retired. Recipient, Dan Forth fellow, 1945, Sr. Citizen Cert. of Merit, Archdiocese of New Orleans, 1998. Mem. Am. Dietetic Assn., 1947—, La. Dietetic Assn., New Orleans Dietetic Assn. (past. pres., treas, com. chmn. 1961—), Nutrition Today Soc., Nat. Assn. Retired Federal Employees (pres.), pres. St. Ann. Over Fifty CLub, 1995-97. Clubs: Chapelle Parents (Metaine, La.) (corr. sec., parliamentarian 1982—). Democrat. Roman Catholic. Avocation: sewing. Home: 1901 Elizabeth Ave Metairie LA 70003-2137

FLOETER, VALERIE ANN, music educator; b. Davenport, Iowa; d. Russell Michael Krebs and Jean Antonia Luerman; m. Alan Dale Floeter, Aug. 21, 1976; children: Sean, Jessi. BA in Math., Alverno Coll., 1976; MusM, Concordia U., 2002. Computer programmer Northwestern Mut. Life, Milw., 1976; software engr. Midwest Analog & Digital, New Berlin, 1977—78, GE Corp., Waukesha, 1978—81; freelance cons., 1981—98; organist Mt. Calvary Luth. Ch., Waukesha, 1986—; tchr. piano pvt. practice, 1989—. Adj. prof. music Wis. Luth. Coll., Milw., 1998—; pres. Software Experience, Waukesha, 1985—; treas. Soli Deo Gloria Inst. Arts, 2003—. Musician: (albums) In the Fullness of Time, 1998, In Three Days, 1999, In Joyful Hope, 2000, In Our Hearts, 2003. Mem.: Hymn Soc., Assn. Luth. Ch. Musicians. Avocation: genealogy. Home: S33 W30212 St David Dr Waukesha WI 53189

FLOOD, ANGELA, interior designer, artist; b. N.Y.C., Jan. 22, 1945; d. Americo Montes and Candace M. Hansen; m. Oscar William Rocafort, June 2, 1963 (div.); 1 child, Angélique Rocafort-Ward ; m. Steven Arthur Flood, June 12, 1988. Student, NYU, 1965—66, Pace U., 1973—76; AAS, Suffolk C.C., 1992. Artist, curator F.O.R.E., Bedford, NY, 1976—86; owner, designer A&S Interiors, Westhampton Beach, NY, 1992—; owner design and art exhbns. Exhibitions include Easthampton (N.Y.) Town Hall, 2001, Westhampton Beach Libr., 2002, Southampton RML Gallery, 2003, Easthampton Guild Hall Mus., 2004. Counselor ARC, White Plains, NY, 1974—77. Republican. Avocations: horseback riding, kayaking, canoeing, sailing, skiing. Office: A&S Interiors PO Box 413 Westhampton Beach NY 11978 E-mail: lilly11967@yahoo.com.

FLOOD, DOROTHY GARNETT, neuroscientist; m. Paul David Coleman, Feb. 26, 1983. BA cum laude, Lawrence U., 1973; student, U. Ill., 1972-73; MS, PhD, U. Rochester, N.Y., 1980. Sr. instr. in anatomy U. Rochester, 1980-83, asst. prof. neurology, neurobiology and anatomy, 1984-90, assoc. prof. neurology, neurobiology and anatomy, 1990-94; sr. sci. Cephalon, Inc., West Chester, Pa., 1994—. Contbr. to book chpts. and articles in field; mem. editl. bd. Neurobiology of Aging, 1989—. Recipient Fenn award U. Rochester, 1980; grantee NSF, NIH, Office of Naval Rsch., 1979-94. Mem. Soc. Neurosci. Office: Cephalon Inc 145 Brandywine Pkwy West Chester PA 19380-4249 E-mail: dflood@cephalon.com.

FLOOD, H(ULDA) GAY, editor, consultant; b. Plainfield, N.J., Aug. 14, 1935; d. William Edward and Lucy (Dycker) Flood. BA, Smith Coll., 1957. With picture dept. Sports Illustrated, Time Inc., N.Y.C., 1957-58, with letters dept., 1958-59, reporter, 1959-60, writer-reporter, 1960-71, assoc. editor, 1971-85, sr. editor, 1985-90. Mem. Greater Consistory First Reformed Ch., Nyack, NY. Mem.: Smith Coll. Students Aid Soc., Alumnae Assn. Smith Coll., Garden Club Nyack (chair cmty. flower show 2001), Smith Coll. Club N.Y. Office: 7 Sampson Commons Plymouth MA 02360

FLOOD, JOAN MOORE, paralegal; b. Hampton, Va., Oct. 10, 1941; d. Harold W. and Estalena (Fancher) M.; 1 child by former marriage, Angelique. B.Mus., North Tex. State U., 1963; postgrad., So. Meth. U., 1967-68, Tex. Women's U., 1978-79, U. Dallas, 1983-86. Clk. Criminal Dist. Ct. Number 2, Dallas County, Tex., 1972-75; reins. libr. Scor Reins. Co., Dallas, 1975-80; corp. ins. paralegal Assocs. Inc. Group, 1980-83; corp. securities paralegal Akin, Gump, Strauss, Hauer & Feld, 1983-89; asst. sec. Knoll Internat. Holdings Inc., Saddle Brook, N.J., 1989-90, 21 Internat. Holdings, Inc., N.Y.C., 1990-92; dir. compliance Am. Svc. Life Ins. Co., Ft. Worth, 1992-93; v.p., sec. Express Comm., Inc., Dallas, 1993-94; fin. transactions paralegal Thompson & Knight, Dallas, 1994-96; corp. transactions paralegal Jones, Day, Reavis & Pogue, Dallas, 1996-97, Weil, Gotshal & Manges, LLP, 1998—99; corp. paralegal PennCorp. Fin. Group, Inc., Dallas, 1999-2001; debt trade mgr. Patton Boggs LLP, 2001—03, sr. paralegal bus. transactions, 2003; corp. paralegal Carrington, Coleman, Sloman & Blumenthal, LLP, Dallas, 2003—. Mem. ABA, Tex. Bar Assn. Home: PO Box 190165 Dallas TX 75219-0165 Business E-Mail: jflood@ccsb.com.

FLOR, HERTA, psychology educator; b. Schnaittenbach, Germany, Apr. 23, 1954; d. Georg and Maria (Reitinger) F. BS, U. Würzburg, Germany, 1977; diploma, U. Tübingen, Germany, 1981, PhD, 1984. Postdoctoral fellow Yale U., New Haven, 1983-84; asst. prof. U. Bonn, Germany, 1984-85; vis. asst. prof. U. Pitts., 1985—87; asst. prof. U. Tübingen, 1987—90; vis. prof. U. Marburg, Germany, 1990-91; Heisenberg fellowship U. Tübingen, 1991-93; assoc. prof. Humboldt U., Berlin, 1993-94, prof., 1995; prof. neurosci. U. Heidelberg Ctrl. Inst. Mental Health, Mannheim, Germany, 2000—. Author: Psychobiology of Pain, 1991. Recipient Pain Rsch. prize German Pain Soc., 1992, 2000, prize for clin. rsch., Smithkline Beecham Found., 1996, Sertürner award for pain rsch., 1999, Max-Planck Rsch. prize, 2000, Muscle Pain Rsch. award, 2001, German Psychology prize, 2002; fellow Deutsche Forschungsgemeinschaft, 1987-90. Mem. AAAS, Internat. Assn. Study of Pain, Soc. for Psychophysiol. Rsch., Soc. for Neurosci. Achievements include research in psychophysiology and behavioral treatments of chronic pain; role of cortical reorganiztion in chronic pain, especially phantom limb pain. Office: U Heidelberg Dept Neuropsy Ctrl Inst Mental Health J5 68159 Mannheim Germany E-mail: flor@zi-mannheim.de.

FLORA, KATHLEEN M. state representative; b. Dearborn, Mich., Nov. 10, 1952; m. James A. Flora; two children. BA, Mich. State U., 1975, MA, 1977. State rep. N.H. Ho. of Reps., 1996—. Mem. Bedford Rep. Com., 1996— Vol. adv. bd. VNA Hospice, 1996-97. Mem. ASTD. Office: NH State Legis State House Concord NH 03301

FLORENDO, ANDREA OLIVA, art director, artist, educator; b. Manila, Philippines, May 16, 1949; arrived in U.S, 1988; d. Nestor Sobreviñas Oliva and Melita Velisano; m. Romulo Buccat Florendo; children: Johann Giovanni, Michaelangelo Paulo, Gian Paulo. BA in English and Journalism, St. Paul Coll., Manila, 1971; BSc in Childhood Edn., St. Joseph Coll., Manila, 1974; assoc. in interior design, Philippine Sch. Interior Design, 1977; diplomate in decorative arts, N.Y. Sch. Interior Design, 1985; rsch. fellow Sch. Divinity, Yale U., 2002. Tchr. art kindergarten to 8th grade St. John's Chrysostom/Archdiocese N.Y., Manhattan, 1988—89; head tchr. Hilltop Early Childhood Ctr., Queens, NY, 1989—91. Prodr. (pub. TV) Sta. QP-TV, 1996—, (TV how-to-art program) Where Flowers Bloom: An Artist's Odyssey, 1996; author: (children's story book) Potpourri of Tales, 1987, (art and history book) The Liturgy of Flowers in a Mary Garden, 2003; feature, consulting editor (art mag.) Arts for the Millennium, 1998—; editor: (cmty. newspaper) St. Nick's Today, 2001—; pub. (57 designs cards, 18x24 lithographs) Promise of a Garden, Fresh Meadows collection, Woodland Sonata, prodr. (art-related documentary films). Harpist Queen's Ensemble, Fresh Meadows, NY, 1998—; mem. pastoral coun. St. Nicholas Tolentine Pastoral Coun., Queens, 1999—. Grantee, Cmty. Outreach and Art Edn. Cultural Affairs, Manhattan, 1997, 1998; pub. art edn. grantee, N.Y. State Senate Initiative, Albany, N.Y., 2001—03, 2003. Mem.: Am. Harp Soc., Hunt Inst. Bot. Documentation, Am. Soc. Bot. Artists. Democrat. Roman Catholic. Achievements include creator of Mary: the Masterpiece Baroque and Renaissance-inspired altar pieces, retables and icons on wood panels. Avocations: piano, harp, gardening, painting, poetry. Home: 162-10 78 Rd Fresh Meadows NY 11366 Office: Nat Mus Cath Art & History 443 East 115th St New York NY 10029 E-mail: olivaflorendo@hotmail.com.

FLORES, LINDA, state representative; m. Armando Flores; 5 children. Legal technician Fed. Hwy. Adminstrn.; legal asst. Rober M. Mercer; ptnr. contracting bus.; ptnr. yard maintenance bus.; mem. Oreg. Ho. of Reps., 2002—. Vice chair Oreg. Rep. Party, 2002—. Mem.: Oreg. Fedn. Rep. Women (pres. 1999—2003). Republican. Office: 900 Court St North East H-287 Salem OR 97301

FLORES, MARION THOMAS, advertising executive; b. Bradford, Pa., Mar. 8, 1946; d. Charles Gordon and Marion Eleanor (Hoffman) Thomas; m. I.D. Flores III, Aug. 31, 1968; 1 child, Whidden. BA magna cum laude, Wellesley Coll., 1968; MBA, Columbia U., 1971. Trainee Citibank, N.Y.C., 1971-72; officer First Nat. Bank, Dallas, 1972-74; cons. Booz, Allen & Hamilton, Dallas, 1974-77, assoc., 1977-80, prin., 1980-82; sr. v.p., chief fin. officer The Bloom Cos., Inc., Dallas, 1983-85; exec. v.p., CFO, dir. Publicis/Bloom Inc., Dallas, 1985-94; exec. v.p. Brierley and Ptnrs., Dallas, 1995-96, WCM Holding, Dallas, 1997—98; CFO Mirage Sys., 2000—02, Vistas Unltd., 2002—. Bd. dirs., exec. com. North Tex. Corp. for Pub. Broadcasting, 1988-98; pres. U. Tex. Southwestern Pres.' Rsch. Coun., 1998-2000. Trustee, pres. Non-Profit Loan Fund, Dallas, 1987-90; bd. dirs. YWCA, Dallas, 1984-89, Ctr. Non-Profit Mgmt., 1988-92; trustee Dallas Opera Found., 1997, chmn., 2002-; trustee Alliance for Higher Edn. Mem. Tex. Coun. Advt. (treas., bd. dirs. 1984-94), Wellesley Coll. Alumnae Assn. (treas., bd. dirs. 1989-91), Charter 100, Dallas Forum, Fin. Execs. Inst. Home: 4218 Fairfax Ave Dallas TX 75205-3025 Office: 2901 Dallas Pkwy #350 Plano TX 75093

FLORES, ROBIN ANN, social worker, social services administrator; b. Allentown, Pa., Oct. 6, 1949; d. Norman Henry and Ann May (Huff) F. BS in Edn., Kutztown U., 1971; MS in Adminstrn., U. Scranton, 1983. Exec. dir. Lehigh County Aging and Adult Svcs., Allentown, 1996—. Lectr. cmty. svcs., family care giving and on aging process, utilization cmty. resources, Lehigh County. Mem. adv. bd. Cmty. Acting Com. Lehigh Valley, 1979-82, Elder Well, 1987-90; Pa. del. White House Conf. on Aging, Hershey, Pa., 1981; bd. dirs. Vis. Nurse Assn. Lehigh County, 1982-98, Women Inc., 1983-87; mem. adv. bd. Homecare, Inc., 1982-91, Geriatric Edn. Modules, Allentown Osteo. Hosp., 1979; mem. profl. adv. com. Lehigh Valley Hospice, 1984-98; mem. utilization and rev. bd. Vis. Nurse Assn., 1979-98; consumer rep. Pa. Power and Light Co.; co-chmn. Human Svcs. Tng. Coop., 1975-81; bd. assocs. Lehigh Valley Hosp.; bd. trustees, Ethics Inst, Inc, Leigh County, TRIAD. Mem.: NAFE, United Way Alliance Aging, Pa. Assn. Area Agys. on Aging, Nat. Assn. Area Agys. on Aging, Am. Soc. Aging, Allentown Art Mus., Quota Internat. Home: 2206 Overlook Ln Fogelsville PA 18051-1812 Office: Lehigh County Aging & Adult Svcs Govt Ctr 17 S 7th St Allentown PA 18101-2401 Office Phone: 610-782-3036. E-mail: robina6@msn.com.

FLORESTANO, PATRICIA SHERER, state official; b. Washington, Mar. 15, 1936; d. Wilbur L. and Virginia M. (Moriconi) F.; m. Thomas Florestano, Nov. 29, 1959; children: Leslie C., Thomas. BA in Am. Civilization, U. Md., 1958, MA in Govt. and Plitics, 1970, PhD in Pub. Adminstrn. and Am. Govt., 1974. Rsch. staff State Legis. Com. on Intergovt. Cooperation, 1972-75, State Gov.'s Commn. on Functions of Govt., 1973-75; staff ast. to pres. Md. Senate, 1975-78; asst. prof. Inst. Urban Studies, U. Md., College Park, 1974-79, dir. Inst. Govtl. Svc., 1979-85, vice chancellor govtl. rels., 1985-91; prof. govt. Schaefer Ctr. Pub. Policy, U. Balt., 1991-95, pub. adminstr., sr. fellow; sec. Md. Higher Edn. Commn., Annapolis, 1995-2000; mem. bd. regents Univ. Sys. of Med., 2001—. Cons. ednl. evaluation, mgmt. and survey rsch. Author: (with other) The States and Metropolitan Areas, 1981; Attitudes of Special Interest Groups and the Public on Chesapeake Bay Areas, 1980; also articles. Lector St. Elizabeth Ann Seton Ch., 1970-92; dir. Crofton (Md.) Gynmastics Program, 1972-74; vice chmn. Anne Arundel County (Md.) Commn. on Women, 1975; mem. Transition Exec. Com. for Gov.-Elect of Md., 1994-95; mem. Anne Arundel County Schs. Adv. Corum, 1975-76, chmn. nominations com., 1976-78. Recipient Outstanding Tchg. award Students Assn. of U. Md., 1979. Mem. Am. Soc. Pub. Adminstrn. (pres. 1983-84, conf. fellow), Am. Polit. Sci. Soc., So. Polit. Sci. Assn., Urban Affairs Assn. (past chmn. governing bd.), So. Consortium Univs., Pub. Svcs. Orgns. (former editor). Democrat. Roman Catholic. Home: 1 Compromise St Unit D Annapolis MD 21401-1824 Office: Md Higher Edn Commn 16 Francis St Annapolis MD 21401-1714

FLOREZ, DIANE O. county clerk; b. Pecos, Tex., Oct. 22, 1954; d. Leandro Tapia and Angelita Martinez (Carrasco) Orona; m. Margarito B. Florez, June 8, 1974 (div. June 1990); children: Bryan Gabriel, Jessica Ann. Student, Odessa (Tex.) Coll., 1972, 84-86. Adult probation officer 143d Jud. Dist. Probation Dept., Pecos, 1984-91; sec. Randall Reynolds, Atty., Pecos, 1992; dep. tax assessor Tax Office, Pecos, 1993; sec. Walter M. Holcombe, Atty., Pecos, 1994; pharmacist Reeves County Hosp., Pecos, 1994-95; county clk. Reeves County Clk.'s Office, Pecos, 1995—. Local registrar Reeves County, 1998—; spkr. in field. Bd. dis. X-Mas in April, 1995—; Cmty. Coun., 1997—, Lamar Elem. Sch. Improvement Campus Program, 1998—. Mem. Assn. County and Dist. Clks., Pecos C. of C. (bd. dirs. 1998—) Lions Club (bd. dirs. 1997—). Avocations: volleyball, swimming, dance, singing, coaching soccer. Home: 923 S Hickory St Pecos TX 79772-4910 Office: Reeves County Clk's Office PO Box 867 Pecos TX 79772-0867

FLORI, ANNA MARIE DIBLASI, nurse anesthetist, educational adminstrator; b. Amsterdam, N.Y., Oct. 29, 1940; d. Tony and Maria (Macario) DiBlasi; children: Tammy, Tina, Toni; m. Gilberto Flori, May 24, 1986. Grad., Albany Med. Ctr. Sch. Nursing, 1962, Fairfax Hosp. Sch. Nurse Anesthetists, Va., 1972; BS in Anesthesia, George Washington U., 1979; M. in Bus. and Pub. Adminstrn., Southeastern U., Washington, 1982; PhD, Columbia Pacific U., 1983. Cert. registered nurse anesthetist. Staff nurse West Seattle Gen. Hosp., 1962-64; office nurse Filmore Buckner, M.D., Seattle, 1964-66; staff nurse anesthetist Fairfax Hosp., 1972-73; staff nurse anesthetist Potomac Hosp., Woodbridge, Va., 1973, chief nurse anesthetist, 1973—; dir. Potomac Hosp. Sch. for Nurse Anesthetists and Sch. for Nurse Anesthesia; faculty mem. Columbia Pacific U., 1973-90; chief nurse anesthetist No. Va. Anesthesia Assn., 1988—; guest lectr. No. Va. Community Coll., Inservice Potomac Hosp., George Washington U.; coord. Free Clinic Prince William County, Woodbridge, Va. Contbr. books on anesthesia. Mem. Am. Assn. Nurse Anesthetists, Va. Nurse Anesthesia Assn., Nat. Italian Am. Found. Home: 12954 Pintail Rd Woodbridge VA 22192-3831

FLORIAN, MARIANNA BOLOGNESI, civic leader; b. Chgo.; d. Giulio and Rose (Garibaldi) Bolognesi; BA cum laude, Barat Coll., 1940; postgrad. Moser Bus. Sch., 1941-42; m. Paul A. Florian III, June 4, 1949; children: Paul, Marina, Peter, Mark. Asst. credit mgr. Stella Cheese Co., Chgo., 1942-45; With ARC ETO Clubmobile Unit, 1945-47; mgr. Passavant Hosp. Gift Shop, 1947-49; pres., Jr. League Chgo., Inc., 1957-59; pres. woman's bd. Passavant Hosp., 1966-68; bd. dirs. Northwestern Meml. Hosp., 1974-81, mem. exec. com., 1974-79; pres. Women's Assn., Chgo. Symphony Orch., 1974-77, founder WFMT/CSO Radiothon, 1976; chmn. Guild Chgo. Hist. Soc., 1981-84, trustee Chgo. Hist. Soc., 1981-84; life trustee Orchestral Assn., v.p. 1978-82, vice chmn. 1982-86, mem. exec. com. 1978-87; mem. women's bd. U. Chgo.; mem. vis. com. dept. music U. Chgo., 1980-90; pres. bd. dirs. Antiquarian Soc. of Art Inst., 1989-91. Recipient Citizen Fellowship, Inst. Medicine Chgo., 1975, Presdl. Commendation for leadership and svc. Barat Coll., 1990. Clubs: Friday (pres. 1972-74), Contemporary; Winnetka Garden. Home and Office: 123 Melrose Ave Kenilworth IL 60043-1248

FLORIAN-LACY, DOROTHY, therapist, educator; b. Dearborn, Mich., Oct. 27, 1958; d. Raymond Joseph and Dorothy Mae Florian; m. Bill George Lacy, July 25, 1981; children: Jason M., Miles, Anderson. BS in Psychology and Edn., Eastern Mich. U., 1978, MA in Guidance and Counseling, 1979; EdD in Counselor Edn., Tex. Southeastern U., 1998. Lic. profl. counselor, Tex. Realtor Century 21, Ann Arbor, Mich., 1978-79; tchr. Adult Exception Ctr., Compton, Calif., 1979-81; owner, dir. Village Learning & Play Ctr., Houston, 1982-94; dept. chair spl. edn. Milby Sr. High, Houston, 1994-2000, therapist Houston Achievement Place, 1998—. Author: Fundamentals of Mathematics I, Fundamentals of Mathematics II, Consumer Math; co-author: Reference Manual for Special Education Department Chairpersons. Vol. Child Abuse Prevention, Houston, 1989-91, vol. coach YMCA, Houston, 1987-90. Recipient Adaptor grant Impact II, 1997, Study Group grant Impact II, 1998. Mem. Am. Counseling Assn., Children's Mus. Avocation: golf coach. Office: Houston Achievement Place 236 W 17th St Houston TX 77008-4002 E-mail: dflorian@houstonisd.org.

FLORIN, JULIE A. music educator; b. Abingdon, Pa., Feb. 5, 1965; d. Roberta Ely and C. Thomas Lechner; m. Gregory A. Florin, Aug. 6, 1988. BS in Music Edn., Pa. State U., 1987; MusM in Ch. Music, E. Carolina U., 1996; cert. in ch. music, Shenandoah U., 1999; BA in Theatre Edn., N.C. Ctrl. U., 2001. Music tchr. Godwin Mid. Sch., Dale City, Va., 1988—92, Jordan HS, Durham, NC, 1992—93; drama/music tchr. Athens Dr. HS, Raleigh, NC, 1993—97, S.E. Raleigh HS, 1996—2000; co-dir. music and worship Grace Cmty. Ch., Raleigh, NC, 2000—. Piano tchr., Raleigh, 1992—2003; musical dir. Burning Coal Theatre Co., Raleigh, 2000—03; musical dir. univ. theater N.C. State U., Raleigh, 2002—03. Musician: Colossal Nerve. Organist Aquia Episcopal Ch., Stafford, Va., 1990—92, St. Andrews Presbyn. Ch., Raleigh, 1994—2000. Recipient Collegiate award, Acad. All-Am., 1987, N.C. Tchr. of the Yr., Coun. for Exceptional Children, 1993—94, Wake County Tchr. of the Yr., 1993—94. Mem.: NEA, Theatre Comm. Group, Music Educators Nat. Conf., Am. Guild Organists (sec. Ctrl. N.C. chpt. 2003—), Pi Kappa Lambda, Alpha Psi Omega. Home: 1112 Berwyn Way Raleigh NC 27615

FLORY, MARGARET K. state representative, lawyer; b. Colchester, Vt., Aug. 2, 1948; m. Joseph J. Flory; 3 children. A, So. Vt. Coll., 1968, Champlain Coll., 1990. Law clk. under Richard A. Pearson, 1992—95; atty.; state rep. State of Vt., 1999—. Chair Pittsford Selectboard; mem. Rutland Region Transp. Coun., Joint Steering Com. on Transp., Rutland County Diversion Rev. Bd. Mem.: ABA, Rutland County Bar Assn., Vt. Bar Assn., Toastmasters (pres.), Rotary. Roman Catholic. Home: 3011 US Rt 7 Pittsford VT 05763

FLOTEN, BARBARA JEAN, educational dean; b. Mount Clemens, Mich., Aug. 21, 1946; d. Joseph Michael and Dorothy Winston (Bowles) Sarto; m. William Frederick Floten, Sept. 10, 1971. M.S., Portland State U., 1970, B.A., 1968. Social worker Multnomah County, Portland, Oreg., 1970-71; instr. Mount Hood Community Coll., Gresham, Oreg., 1971-74; dir. student programs Edmonds Community Coll., Lynnwood, Wash., 1974-77, dean students, 1977— ; chair or member of various profl. groups, 1971— . Bd. dirs. Planned Parenthood, Snohomish County, 1978; mem. Joint Action Council Edn., Seattle, 1979. Named Honorary Triton ASEdCC, 1975-78; recipient numerous profl. recognitions. Mem. Wash. Community Coll. Adminstrs. (founder, exec. council), Nat. Assn. Student Personnel Adminstrn., League of Women Voters, American Association of University Women, Club: Wash. Athletic (Seattle). Office: Edmonds Community Coll 20000 68th Ave W Lynnwood WA 98036-5912 also: Bellevue Community Coll 3000 Landerholm Cir SE Bellevue WA 98007-6406

FLOTT, CARMAN MARIE, mobile intensive care technician, instructor; b. Topeka, Kans., Jan. 12, 1957; d. Charles Eugene and Dixie Ann (Deines) F.; m. Randall Joe Petty, Jan. 14, 1977 (div. May 1980); children: Karra Marie, Dallas Joe, Dustin Albert; m. Terry Arnold Hackney, Dec. 31, 1983 (div. Aug. 1986); m. Durwin Dale Dallinga, Aug. 31, 1991 (div. Dec. 1997); 1 adopted child, Jason Edward. Cert. first responder, emergency med. technician, tng. officer I, II, mobile intensive care technician, emergency med. technician instr., coord., mobile intensive care technician instr., coord., Kans.; advanced cardiac life support, pediatric advanced life support, Am. Heart Assn., neonatal resuscitation provider Am. Acad. Pediatrics. Vol. 1st responder Riley County Emergency Med. Svcs., Manhattan, Kans., 1991-93, emergency med. technician, 1993-94, mobile intensive care technician, 1994-97; adminstrv. sec. Region IV Emergency Med. Svcs. Coun., Riley, Kans., 1993-98; mayor City of Riley, Kans., 1995-97; emergency med. technician instr./ coord. Barton County C.C., Junction City, Kans., 1996-97; emergency med. technician instr., coord. Butler County C.C., Coun. Grove, Kans., 1997—; mobile intensive care technician, dir. Morris County Emergen Med. Svc., Council Grove, Kans., 1997—. Affiliate faculty BLS, Am. Heart Assn., Topeka, Kans. 1994—; dir. Morris County Emergency Med. Svc., Council Grove, Kans., 1997—; paramedic instr. Barton County C.C., 1999—, Flinthills Tech. Coll., 1999—. Founder North Riley County Self Help and Resource Exch., Riley Kansas, 1992; lead advisor Boy Scouts Am. Explorer Post 911, Riley, Kans., 1993-96, mem. adv. bd. Explorer Post 611, Manhattan, Kans., 1993-96; pres. Riley City Promotional Assn., 1994; vol. KHaSEC/AmeriCorps, Manhattan, Kans., 1995; youth farm safety instr., KHaSEC, Manhattan, Kans., 1995; vol. Spl. Olympics, Manhattan, Kans., 1995 Named First Responder of Yr., 1994, Riley County Emergency Med. Svc., Manhattan, Kans., 1994. Mem. NAFE, Kans. Emergency Med. Svc. Assn., Kans. Emergency Med. Technicians Assn. (Outstanding Attendant 1998). Avocations: motorcycle riding, leather clothing design, winemaking, tattoos. Office: Morris Cty EMS 606 N Washington St Council Grove KS 66846-1422 Home: 1524 Road 90 Hartford KS 66854-9269

FLOURNOY, LINDA WESLEY, minister, educator; b. Minden, La., Aug. 29, 1957; d. John Henry and Lillie Anderson Wesley; m. Connell Flournoy, Feb. 14, 1975; children: Adrian Connell, Amber Nicole. AA, La. Tech. U., 1994, BA, 1996, postgrad., 1998. Ordained elder 1995. Prescription tutor Eckerd Drug Stores, Minden, 1982—84; accounts receivable clk. City of Minden, 1984—90; office mgr. Custom Windows and Glass, Shreveport, La., 1991; pastor, tchr. Christian Meth. Ch., Shreveport, 1991—, Hattiesburg, Miss., 1998—2002. Established youth and young adult outreach ministry, Bassfield, Miss., 1999. Recipient Devoted and Invaluable Svc. award, Webster Parish Penal Farm Ministry, Minden, 1992, 1994—95, Invaluable Svc. award, Town & Country Nursing Home Ministry, Minden, 1992. Democrat. Avocations: interior decorating, homebuilding, reading. Home: 137 Flournoy Dr Minden LA 71055 Office: Christian Meth Ch Holcomb Dr Shreveport LA 71103

FLOURNOY, NANCY, statistician, educator; b. Long Beach, Calif., May 4, 1947; d. Carr Irvine Flournoy and Elizabeth Flournoy-Rivera; m. Leonard B. Hearne, Aug. 28, 1978. BS, UCLA, 1969, MS, 1971; PhD, U. Wash., 1982. Dir. clin. stats. Fred Hutchinson Cancer Rsch. Ctr., Seattle, 1974-86; dir. stats. and probability NSF, Washington, 1986—; prof. stats. American U., Washington, 1988—2002; chmn., prof. stats. U. Mo., Columbia, Mo., 2002—. Mem. of corp. Nat. Inst. Statis. Scis., Research Triangle Park, N.C., 1990-97. Editor Multiple Stats. Integration, 1991, Adaptive Designs, 1995, New Developments and Applications in Experimental Designs, 1998; assoc. editor Jour. Statis. Planning and Inference, 1998—. Grant reviewer AAUW, NSF, NIH, Nat. Security Agy. USPHS fellow, 1969-71; Nat. Cancer Inst. grantee, 1975-86, NSF grantee, 1989-90, 96-2001, Am. Math. Soc./Inst. of Math. Stats./Soc. of Indsl. Applied Math. grantee, 1989, 92, EPA grantee, 1994-2000; recipient Elizabeth Scott award Com. of Pres. of Statis. Socs., 2000. Fellow AAAS, Inst. Math. Stats., Am. Statis. Assn. (chair coun. sects. 1994), World Acad. Art & Sci., Washington Acad. Sci.; mem. AAUW, Caucus for Women in Stats., Internat. Stats. Inst., Internat. Biometric Soc., Internat. Assn. for Statis. Computing, Assn. Women in Math. Democrat. Achievements include development of new statistical procedures for clinical trials and response-driven experimental designs; research on bone marrow transplantation, on graft versus leukemia, on infectious diseases in immuno-compromised hosts, on information management. Office: U Mo Dept Stats 146 Middlebush Columbia MO 65211-4100

FLOWE, CAROL CONNOR, lawyer; b. Owensboro, Ky., Jan. 3, 1950; d. Marvin C. Connor and Ethel Marie (Thorn) Smith; children: Samantha Kathleen, Andrew Benjamin. BME magna cum laude, Murray State U., 1972; JD summa cum laude, Ind. U., 1976. Bar: Ohio 1977, D.C. 1981, U.S. Dist. Ct. (so. dist.) Ohio 1977, U.S. Dist. Ct. Md. 1983, U.S. Dist. Ct. D.C. 1981, U.S. Supreme Ct. 1987, U.S. Ct. Appeals (2d, 3d, 4th, 5th, 7th, 9th and D.C. cirs.). Assoc. Baker & Hostetler, Columbus, Ohio, 1976-80, Arent Fox Kintner Plotkin & Kahn, Washington, 1980-87; dep. gen. counsel Pension Benefit Guaranty Corp., Washington, 1987-89, gen. counsel, 1989-95; ptnr. Arent Fox, PLLC, 1995—. Mem. ABA, D.C. Bar Assn., Order of Coif, Alpha Chi, Phi Alpha Delta. Avocations: computers, reading. Home: 8608 Aqueduct Rd Potomac MD 20854-6249 Office: Arent Fox Kintner Plotkin & Kahn 1050 Connecticut Ave NW Ste 500 Washington DC 20036-5339 Office Phone: 202-857-6054. E-mail: flowe.carol@arentfox.com.

FLOWER, JEAN FRANCES, art educator; b. Schenectady, N.Y., Apr. 12, 1936; d. Francis Tunis and Marjorie (Colcord) Fort; m. Wesley Allen Flower, Aug. 23, 1958; children: Kimberly Lynn, Kristina Kathleen. BA, Syracuse U., 1958; BFA cum laude, Western Mich. U., 1984, MFA magne cum laude, 1989. Free-lance artist, 1981-86; tech. grad. asst. Western Mich. U., Kalamazoo, 1988, grad. asst. early mgmt., 1989, instr. art, 1989-93, Kalamazoo Inst. Art, 1993—. One-woman shows include Peoples Ch., Kalamazoo, 1991; exhibited in group shows Kalamazoo Area Art Show, 1992, 94 95, 97, Nat. Art Show, Dallas, 1993, Libr., Parchment, Mich., 1993, EAA Aviation Internat. Art Show, 1992, 95; murals executed Kalamazoo Valley Pub. Mus., 1995, Kalamazoo Aviation History Mus., 1996. Pres., mem. Anna Cir. 1st United Meth. Ch., Kalamazoo, 1980—, mem. communications commn., 1994—; sec.-treas. Airward, Plainwell, Mich., 1986—. Mem. Am. Assn. Aviation Artists, Plainwell Pilots Assn., Kalamazoo Aviatrix Assn. (past v.p.). Avocations: flying, painting, golf, tennis, cross-country skiing. Home: 8745 Marsh Rd Plainwell MI 49080-8818

FLOWER, JOANN, state legislator; b. May 6, 1935; m. Paul Flower. BS, Johns Hopkins U. Kans. state rep. Dist. 47, 1996—; nurse, 1996—. Home: PO Box 97 Oskaloosa KS 66066-0097 Office: Kans State Ho of Reps State Capital Topeka KS 66612

FLOWERS, CYNTHIA, investment company executive; b. N.Y.C., May 29, 1951; d. Bernard and Pearl (Davis) Heller; m. Robert Flowers, June 3, 1973; children: Perry, Lindsey. BS summa cum laude, Boston U., 1973; MBA with honors, NYU, 1976. Sr. mgr. portfolios Citibank NA, N.Y.C., 1973-82; v.p. Nat. Securities Corp., N.Y.C., 1982-87; pres. Stillrock Mgmt. Inc., N.Y.C., 1987-90; founder, pres. Flowers Capital Mgmt. Inc., N.Y.C., 1990—. Mem.: Westside Tennis Club, Beta Gamma Sigma. Avocations: tennis, antiques. Office: Flowers Capital Mgmt Inc 97 Groton St Forest Hills NY 11375-5956

FLOWERS, MARY E. state legislator; b. July 31, 1951; married. Ed., Kennedy-King C.C., U. Ill. Mem. from 21st dist. Ill. Ho. of Reps., 1985—, chair com. on health care availability access, vice chair com. appropriations-elem. and secondary edn. com., mem. commerce and bus. devel. com., mem. human svcs. com. Co-chmn. Il. Conf. Women Legis.; spokesperson Com. on Ins.; mem. Healthcare and Human Svcs. Com., Fin. Instns. Com., Consumer Protection Com. Recipient Black Rose award League of Black Women, 1988, Kizzy award Black Women Hall of Fame Found., 1990, Friend of Labor award AFL-CIO, 1990. Office: Ill Ho of Reps 251-E Stratton Bldg Springfield IL 62706-0001 also: 2525 W 79th St Chicago IL 60652 E-mail: state.repflowers@comcast.net., mflowers@hdsmail.state.il.us.

FLOWERS, VONETTA, Olympic athlete; b. Birmingham, Oct. 29, 1973; d. Jimmie and Barbara Jeffery; m. Johnny Mack Flowers. Olympic athlete, mem. U.S. bobsled team; grad. asst., men's track team U. Ala., 1997—99, asst. track coach, 1999—; placed 13th at the summer olympic trials Sacramento, 2000. Mem. U.S. Olympic Festival Team; chosen to compete in the World U. Games. Named U.S. push champion and record holder for boblsed start, 2002 Winter Olympics, 7-time NCAA All-Am.; named one of 50 most inspiring African-Am., 2002, 57 of the most intriguing blacks, Ebony Mag., 2002; recipient 4 World Cup medals, 2002 Winter Olympics, Gold medal for long jump, 1994 Olympic Festival, Citizen through Sports Alliance award, 2002, U.S. Olympic Spirit award, 2002, Victor award, 2002, Live the Dream award, 2002, 50 most beautiful people, People Mag., 2002, Wilma Rudolph Athlete of the Yr. award, 2002, Dodge Nat. Athletic Olympian award, 2003, U.S. Olympic Com. Team of the Yr. award, 2003. Achievements include 1st African-Am. to win a gold medal in the winter olympics, 1st person from Ala. to win a gold medal in the winter olympics, 2002 olympic champion. Office: U Ala-Birmingham 701 20th St S Birmingham AL 35294-010

FLOYD, ANN R. elementary school educator; b. Mullins, S.C., June 29, 1951; d. Harry Theodore and Mary Elizabeth (Winburn) Richardson; m. Larry Dwight Floyd, Sr., Feb. 20, 1971; 1 child, Larry Dwight Jr. Student, Coastal Carolina, 1969-71; BA in Early Childhood Edn., Clemson U., 1981; MEd in Reading, Francis Marion U., 1990. Cert. early childhood edn., elem. edn. Fourth grade tchr. McKissick Elem., Easley, S.C., 1981-82; first grade tchr. Concrete Elem., Easley, 1983-84, third grade tchr., 1984-85; fourth grade self contained tchr. Royall Elem., Florence, S.C., 1985-91, sixth grade sci./health tchr., 1991-93, sci. specialist, 1993—99; 3rd grade tchr. Red Bank Elem., Lexington, SC, 1999—. Mem. Supts. Faculty Adv. Bd., 1993-99. Loyalty fund mem. Clemson U., 1981—, mem. Iptay, 1981—; active Friends of the Mus., S.C. State Mus., Columbia, 1988—, S.C. Wildlife Orgn., 1990—, Supt.'s Adv. Bd., Florence, 1993. Recipient Presdl. award for excellence in sci. tchg. NSF, 1995; grantee Pee Dee Edn. Found., 1995. Mem. NSTA, Internat. Reading Assn., S.C. Ednl. TV Endowment, S.C. Sci. Coun., S.C. Middle and Elem. Sch. Sci. Coun. (bd. dirs., charter mem.), S.C. Children's Sci. Coun. (exec. bd. 1995—), Nat. Wildlife Assn., Nat. Geographic Soc. Office: Red Bank Elem Sch 246 Community Dr Lexington SC 29073

FLOYD, LINDA SMITH, principal; b. Hamilton, Ohio, Dec. 9, 1959; d. Willis and Billie Jeanette Smith; m. Joey Brian Floyd, Feb. 11, 1984; 1 child, Lindsay Jo. BS in Bus. Adminstrn. & Office Adminstrn., Union Coll., 1982; MA in Bus. Edn., Ea. Ky. U., 1985. Paralegal Cunnagin Law Offices, London, Ky., 1982—85; assoc. prof. Sue Bennett Coll., London, 1984—88; tchr. Laurel County State Vo-Tech. Sch., London, 1988—98; prin. Ky. Tech.-Knox County Area Tech. Ctr., Barbourville, Ky., 1998—, Ea. Ky. U., 1998—. Assoc. prof. Ea. Ky. U., Richmond, Ky., Somerset C.C., Somerset, Ky. Mem. State Mktg. Team, Ky., 1999—. Recipient Outstanding Adminstrv. Staff award, Ky. Workforce Devel. Cabinet Dept. Tech. Edn., 2001. Avocations: boating, reading, time with family. Home: 736 Keithshire Drive London KY 40744 Office: Ky Tech Knox County ATC 210 Wall Street Barbourville KY 40906

FLOYD, ROSALYN WRIGHT, pianist, accompanist, educator; b. Charleston, S.C., Oct. 22, 1956; d. Reginald Abram and Dorothy (Brunson) Wright; m. Hernan Augustus Floyd, Nov. 27, 1987. BA, Talladega (Ala.) Coll., 1977; MusM in Piano Performance/Pedagogy, U S.C., 1981; D Musical Arts in Piano Performance, U. S.C., 1990. Music tchr. Charleston County Dist. 20, Charleston, 1977-78; grad. asst. U. S.C., Columbia, S.C.,

1978-85; asst. prof. dept. music Benedict Coll., Columbia, SC, 1985—88; rehearsal accompanist Columbia Lyric Opera, 1983-86; prof. dept. fine arts Augusta (Ga.) State U., 1988—; rehearsal accompanist Augusta Choral Soc., 1994—. Bd. dirs. Augusta Choral Soc. Performer lectures and recitals; accompanist for Martina Arroyo and Myrtle Hall in their performances for Pope John Paul II, 1987. Evaluator, Arts Infusion program Greater Augusta Arts Coun., 1992, Music panel Ga. Coun. for the Arts, 1997-98. Black Am. Music Symposium scholar, 1985; Ambrose Headen scholar Talladega Coll., 1973-77. Mem. Augusta Music Tchrs. Assn. (v.p. for membership 1998-2000), Ga. Music Tchrs. Assn., The Links Inc. (v.p. Augusta chpt. 1999-2001, pres. 2001-03), Ctr. for Black Music Rsch. (pres. 2001-03). Baptist. Avocations: crocheting, sewing, gardening, computing. Home: 2503 Larchmont Ct Augusta GA 30909-6567 Office: Augusta State U 2500 Walton Way Augusta GA 30904-4562 E-mail: rfloyd@aug.edu.

FLOYD, SHELLY L. computer company executive; b. Oklahoma City, 1950; Grad., Grinnell Coll., 1972, U. London, 1974; MBA, Stanford U., 1977. Contbg. editor Technologic Ptnrs.; v.p. Salomon Bros.; spl. limited ptnr. L.F. Rothschild, Unterberg, Towbin; with Intel Corp., Santa Clara, Calif., 1997—, v.p. fin. Office: Intel Corp PO Box 58119 2200 Mission College Blvd Santa Clara CA 95052-8119 E-mail: shelly.floyd@intel.com.

FLOYD, STACY Y. retail executive; Grad., East Tex. State U. CPA, Tex. Acct., Texarkana, Tex., 1988-90; asst. contr. E-Z Mart Stores, Texarkana, 1990, now CFO. Bd. dirs. Easter Seals, Wadley Hosp. Guild. Mem. AICPA, Tex. Soc. CPA's, Texarkana CPA's. Office: E-Z Mart Stores 602 Falvey Ave Texarkana TX 75501-6677

FLOYED, CHERYL W. web site designer; b. Texas City, Tex., July 23, 1963; d. John Sexton and Judy Davis; m. H. Scott Floyed, May 15, 1993; children: Tommy J. White, Jessica Louise. Cert. IT Specialist Harris County CC, 2000. Owner Talica Designs, Katy, Tex., 1997—. Ind. cons., Houston, 1996—98. Editor: (online newspaper) Ctrl. Tex. News. Coord. Girl Scouts of Am., Katy, Tex., 2002—; amb. Katy Area C. of C., Tex., 2002—03. Mem.: Am. Bus. Women's Assn. (assoc.; membership chmn. 2003—, dir. 2003—). Office: Talica Designs 20738 Park Bend Dr Katy TX 77450 E-mail: cheryl@talica.com.

FLUCK, MICHELE M(ARGUERITE), biology educator; b. Geneva, Aug. 5, 1940; came to U.S., 1972; d. Wilhelm and Henriette Alice (Delaloye) F. MS, U. Geneva, 1964, 66, PhD, 1972. Rsch. assoc. N.Y. Pub. Health Rsch. Inst., N.Y.C., 1972-73; instr. Harvard Med. Sch., Boston, 1973-78, asst. prof., 1978-79; assoc. prof. Mich. State U., East Lansing, 1979-86, prof., 1986-90, disting. prof., 1990—. Contbr. articles to profl. jours. Recipient Young Investigator's award, Nat. Cancer Inst.; grantee Nat. Cancer Inst., 1979—, Am. Cancer Soc. grantee, 1987—. Fellow Leukemia Soc. Am. (scholar 1979-85); mem. AAAS, Am. Assn. virologists. Avocations: music, feminism, social issues. Office: Mich State U Microbiology Dept Giltner Hall East Lansing MI 48824-1101

FLUG, JANICE, librarian; b. Mpls., Oct. 19, 1949; d. Albert William and Elberta Edna (Kimball) F.; m. William Raymond LeFevre, Jan. 2, 1982 (dec. June 1986). BA, Hamline U., St. Paul, 1971; MLS, U. Md., 1975; MPA, Am. U., 1980. Acquisitions searcher Am. U. Libr., Washington, 1972-75, asst. to the univ. libr., 1975-91, acquisitions libr., 1991—. Chmn. U. Libr. Faculty Coun., 1999—2003; mem. faculty senate Am. U., chmn. com. on instrl. budget and benefits, 2003—. Mem. bd. editors The Pub. Mgr., 1996—. Mem. exec. bd. LOMS, 1997—99. Mem.: ALA, Libr. Orgn. Mgmt., Libr. Adminstrn. Mgmt. Assn. (mem. exec. bd. 1997—99, mem. leadership devel. com. 1999—2003, chmn. leadership devel. com. 2001—03, budget and finance com. 2003—), Am. Soc. Pub. Adminstrn. (pres. Md. chpt. 1994—95, nat. coun. 1995—99, chair policy issues com. 1998—99, fin. com fin. vice chair 1999—2000, chair 2000—01, bd. ins. trustees 2001—, vice chair steering group 2002—03, chmn. steering group 2003—04, past chair 2004—). Democrat. Lutheran. Avocations: swimming, church activities. Home: 2927 Mozart Dr Silver Spring MD 20904-6802 Office Phone: 202-885-3211. E-mail: jflug@american.edu.

FLUGGER, PENELOPE ANN, banker; b. Chgo., June 26, 1942; d. William and Florence Bernadette (Brongiel) Grabos; m. Robert John Flugger, July 11, 1970. BS, U. Ill., 1964; MBA, Baruch Coll., 1971. CPA, N.Y., Ill. Sr. mgr. Price Waterhouse Co., N.Y.C., 1964-75; with Morgan Guaranty Trust Co., 1975-98, auditor, 1982-94, sr. v.p., 1982-94, mng. dir., 1994-98. Mem. N.Y.C. Audit Com., Fin. Exec. Inst. Mem. AICPAs, Inst. Mgmt. Accts., Fin. Execs. Inst., N.Y. State Soc. CPAs, Ill. State Soc. CPAs. E-mail: flugger1@juno.com.

FLUKE, LYLA SCHRAM (MRS. JOHN M. FLUKE SR.), publisher; b. Maddock, N.D. d. Olaf John and Anne Marie (Rodberg) Schram; m. John M. Fluke, June 5, 1937; children: Virginia Fluke Gabelein, John M. Jr., David Lynd. BS in Zoology and Physiology, U. Wash., Seattle, 1934, diploma tchg., 1935. H.S. tchr., 1935-37; tutor Seattle schs., 1980-84; pub. Portage Quar. mag. Hist. Soc. Seattle and King County, 1980-84. Author articles on history. Co-founder N.W. chpt. Myasthenia Gravis Found., 1953, pres., 1960-66; obtained N.W. artifacts for Navy destroyer Tender Puget Sound., 1966; mem. Seattle Mayor's Com. for Seattle Beautiful, 1962; sponsor Seattle World's Fair, 1962; charter and founding mem. Seattle Youth Symphony Aux., 1974; bd. dirs., Cascade Symphony, Salvation Army, 1981-87; benefactor U. Wash., 1982-01, nat. chmn. ann. giving campaign, 1983-84; benefactor Cascade Symphony, Salvation Army, Sterling Cir. Stanford U., MIT, 1984, Seattle Symphony, 1982-2003, Wash. State Hist. Soc., Pacific Arts Coun., Pacific Sci. Ctr. Twenty-Twelve Club, 1962-2002; mem. condr.'s club Seattle Symphony, 1978—; mem. U. Wash. Campaign Exec. Com., 2003—, hon. mem. Campaign Com. NSF Grant to Nat. Nanotechnology Infrastructure Network. Recipient Crystal plaque Coll. Engring. U. Wash., 2002; Seattle Pacific U. fellow, 1972. Mem. IEEE Aux. (chpt. charter mem., pres. 1970-73), Wash. Trust for Hist. Preservation, Nat. Trust for Hist. Preservation, N.W. Ornamental Hort. Soc. (benefactor, life, hon.), Nat. Assn. Parliamentarians (charter mem., pres. N.W. unit 1961-64), Wash. Parliamentarians Assn. (charter), Seattle C. of C. (women's divsn. 1965-66), Seattle Symphony Women's Assn. (life, charter, sec. 1982-84, pres. 1985-87), Hist. Soc. Seattle and King County (exec. com. 1975-78, pres. women's mus. league 1975-79, pres. Moritz Thomsen Guild of Hist. Soc., 1978-80, 84-87), Highlands Orthopedic Guild (life), Wash. State Hist. Soc., Antiquarian Soc. (v.p. 1986-88, pres. 1988-90, hon. mem. John Fluke Mfg. Co. 20 Year Club 1987—), Rainier Club, Seattle Golf Club, Seattle Tennis Club, U. Wash. Pres.'s Club. Republican. Lutheran. Achievements include sponsorship of the Fluke Chair in Coll. of Engring. U Wash. Address: 1206 NW Culbertson Dr Seattle WA 98177-3942 also: Vendovi Island PO Box 703 Anacortes WA 98221-0703

FLYNN, CANDY RUTH, music educator; b. Chattanooga, Oct. 3, 1962; d. J. Ralph and Mary Sue McIntyre; m. Matt O. Flynn, Dec. 27, 1983; children: Adison Rivers, Aaron Clay, Abigail Elizabeth. MusM, Ea. Ky. U., 2000, MA in Tchg., 2003. Music tchr. Richmond (Ky.) Area Arts Coun., 1995—; freelance voice tchr. Richmond, 1996—; min. of music Gt. Crossing Bapt. Ch., Georgetown, Ky., 2000—02; music tchr. Berea (Ky.) Bd. of Edn., 2001—. Dir. family hospitality Ky. Spl. Olympics, Frankfort, 1994—2003; local dir. Fellowship of Christian Athletes, Berea, 2001—03. Mem.: Ky. Music Edn. Assn., Delta Omicron. Office: Berea Bd Edn 1 Pirate Pkwy Berea KY 40403

FLYNN, CAROL, state legislator; b. Aug. 7, 1933; m. Richard L. Flynn; 2 children. Mem. Minn. State Senate, 1990—. Mem. Democratic Farm Labor Party. Office: Minn Senate 120 State Capitol 75 Constitution Ave Saint Paul MN 55155-1606

FLYNN, ELIZABETH ANNE, advertising and public relations company executive; b. Washington, Aug. 21, 1951; d. John William and Elizabeth Goodwin (Mahoney) F. AA, Montgomery Coll., Rockville, Md., 1972; BS in Journalism, U. Md., 1976; postgrad., San Diego State U., 1976. Writer, researcher Sea World, Inc., San Diego, 1977-79; sr. writer Lane & Huff Advt., San Diego, 1979-80; account exec. Kaufman, Lansky, Baker Advt., San Diego, 1980-82; mng. dir. Excelsior Enterprises, Beverly Hills, Calif., 1983-84; sr. account exec. Berkhemer & Kline, Inc., L.A., 1985; pres. Flynn Advt. & Pub. Rels., L.A., 1985—; pub. info. dir. Dept. Neighborhood Empowerment City LA, 2001—02; cons. 1736 Family Crisis Ctr., 2003—. Cons. Coca-Cola Bottling Co. L.A., 1982-84; U.S. corr. Aeronovum mag., 1990-98; v.p. mktg. Graffiti Prevention Systems, L.A., 1990-91; acct. supr. new bus. devel. BBDO Hispanica, L.A., 1992-93; pub. rels. dir. Regional Organ Procurement Agy. So. Calif., UCLA Med. Ctr., 1994-97, pub. info. officer/cons. Cmty. Devel. Dept. City of L.A., 1998-2000. Bd. dirs. Friends of Reconstructive Surgery, Beverly Hills, 1983-89, Nat. Kidney Found., 1994, Nat. Orgn. for Renal Disease, L.A., 2000-2002, So. Calif. Coalition on Donation, 1994-97, also mem. steering com., 1995-97; sec. Nat. Coun. Local Coalitions, 1995-97; comms. com. Assn. Organ Procurement Orgns.; cons. Rotary Internat. Give of Yourself program, 1993-2002; media cons. divsn. transplantation HHS, 1994-98; found. rels. mgr. Juvenile Diabetes Rsch. Found. Internat., 2000. Mem. Nat. Orgn. Women Bus. Owners, Women in Film. Address: Flynn Advt & Pub Rels 1440 Reeves St Ste 104 Los Angeles CA 90035-2950

FLYNN, ELIZABETH E. bank executive; m. Andy Flynn; children: Spencer, Grace. BA in Math., Providence Coll.; MBA, NYU. With Chase Manhattan Corp., 1982-1994, sr. v.p., 1994-97; exec. v.p. Chase Manhattan Corp. JP Morgan Chase, 1997—. Integration and support exec. Chase Nat. Consumer Svcs. businesses, 1996—; bd. dirs. Providence House. Office: The Chase Manhattan Corp 270 Park Ave Fl 12 New York NY 10017-2036

FLYNN, GARY L. pharmaceutical executive; b. Columbus, Ohio, Oct. 8, 1949; BBA, Franklin U. Various fin. and mgmt. positions Abbott Labs., Abbott Park, Ill., 1971—, divisional v.p., contr. Ross Products divsn., 1993, v.p., contr., sr. v.p. Ross Products, 2001—. Mem. bd. dirs. Columbus Children's Hosp. Rsch. Inst.; bd. trustees Franklin U. Office: Abbott Labs 100 Abbott Park Rd Abbott Park IL 60064-6400

FLYNN, LAURIE M. social worker; Exec. dir. Nat. Alliance for the Mentally Ill, Arlington, Va., 1984—. Bd. trustees Found. for Accountability; mem. adv. com. Johns Hopkins U. Health Svcs. Ctr., interdisciplinary adv. bd. Jour. Psychiat. Svcs., Am. Psychiat. Assn.; apptd. by Pres. Clinton to White House Nat. Bioethics Adv. Commn.; past co-chair Md. Commn. Women's Health; past mem. Nat. Task Force on Homelessness and Mental Illness; past bd. dirs. Child Welfare Inst.; mem. nat. adv. bd. Ctr. Rsch. Orgn. and Financing of Care for the Severely Mentally Ill, Rutgers U. Co-author: Care of the Seriously Mentally Ill: A Rating of State Programs, Criminalizing the Seriously Mentally Ill: The Abuse of Jails as Mental Hospitals; co-editor: Using Clinet Outcomes Information to Improve Mental Health and Substance Abuse Treatment; mem. editl. bd. Assn. Health Svcs. Rsch.; contbr. articles to profl. jours., chpts. to books. Recipient Presdl. Commendation award Am. Psychiat. Assn., 1994, Patient Advocacy award, 1995, Mental Health Sect. award APHA, McLean Hosp. award, Disting. Svc. award NAPHS and Am. Hosp. Assn., Pub. Svc. award Am. Assn. Psychosocial Rehab., 1996; Hon. fellow Academia, Medicnae & Psychiatric Found. Office: Nat Alliance for the Mentally Ill Ste 300 2107 Wilson Blvd Arlington VA 22201-3042

FLYNN, MARGARET ALBERI, nutritionist, dietitian; b. Hurley, Wis., Nov. 22, 1915; d. Bernard and Anna (Chiado) Alberi; m. May 31, 1938 (dec. 1960); children: Phoebe, Timothy. BS, Coll. St. Caterine, St. Paul, 1937; MS, U. Iowa, 1938; PhD, U. Mo., 1960. Registered dietitian, diplomate Am. Bd. Nutrition, lic. dietitian Mo. Instr. Coll. St. Catherine, St. Paul, 1937-38; rsch. asst. pediatrics U. Iowa, Iowa City, 1939-40; instr. dietetics Levi Meml. Hosp., Hot Springs, Ark., 1942-46; teaching dietitian Holy Name Hosp., Teaneck, N.J., 1950-54; rsch. asst. pediatrics U. Mo., Columbia, 1961-63, asst. prof. nutrition and dietetics, 1966-69, assoc. prof. medicine, 1969-75, prof. medicine, 1975-86, prof. emeritus medicine, 1986—. Contbr. articles to profl. jours. Nat. Cancer Inst. grantee, 1977; Nat. Meat Bd./Wallace Genetic Found. grantee, 1978—; named Sesquicentennial Prof. U. Mo., 1989, Disting. Faculty awardee, 1988, Faculty Alumni award, 1976. Fellow Am. Coll. Nutrition; mem. Am. Soc. Clin. Nutrition, Am. Inst. Nutrition. Office: U Mo Sch Medicine 1 Hospital Dr Columbia MO 65201-5276 Home: 300 Kildaire Woods Dr Apt 233 Cary NC 27511-7715

FLYNN, MARIE COSGROVE, portfolio manager, corporate financial executive; b. Honolulu, Jan. 1, 1945; d. John Aloysius and Emeline Frances Cosgrove; m. John Thomas Flynn, Jr., June 3, 1968; children: Jamie Marie, Jacqueline Elizabeth. BA, Trinity Coll., 1966. CFP, CFA. Analyst U.S. Govt., Washington, 1967-70; coord. nat. reading coun. F.X. Doherty Assocs., N.Y.C., 1970-71; security analyst Corinthian Capital Co., N.Y.C., 1971-73; portfolio mgr. Clark Mgmt. Co., Inc., N.Y.C., 1973-78; 1at v.p., sr. portfolio mgr. Lexington Mgmt. Corp., Saddle Brook, NJ, 1978-96; pres. Corinthian Capital Mgmt. Co., Inc., Morristown, NJ, 1996-99; 1st v.p., mng. dir., sr. portfolio mgr. Glenmede Trust Co., 1999—. Bd. dirs., v.p. First Call for Help, 1996—2000; bd. trustees N.J. Pension and Annuity Fund, 1996—; elected mem. Somerset County Rep. Com., 1994—98; treas. Bernardsville Rep. Com., 1996—98, Bernardsville Planning Bd., 1996—98; elected to Bernardsville Borough Coun., 1998—; mayor Bernardsville, 2002; police commr. Bernardsville Police Commn., 2000—; pres. Women's Polit. Caucus N.J., 2001—03; bd. dirs. Soc. Women's Health Rsch., 2004. Recipient Tribute to Women award, Patriots' Path Coun., 2002. Mem. Fin. Analysts Fedn., Inst. Chartered Fin. Analysts, N.Y. Soc. Security Analysts. Home: 50 Pickle Brook Rd Bernardsville NJ 07924-1909 Office: Carriage Ct II 264 South St Morristown NJ 07960-6078

FLYNN, PATRICIA M. director, special education educator, gifted and talented educator; b. East Cleveland, Ohio, Sept. 11, 1952; d. Harry L. and Eleanore (Mahon) Flynn. BS in Edn. magna cum laude, St. John Coll., Cleve., 1974, MS in Edn., 1975; cert., Notre Dame Coll., 1992, Ursuline Coll., 2001. Cert. elem. edn., prin., edn. handicapped Ohio Detp. Edn. Reading specialist East Cleveland City Schs., 1974—98, reading coord., 1998—2000, curriculum specialist, 2000—01; dir. pupil svcs. Fairview Park (Ohio) Schs., 2001—. Local coord. Reading Is Fundamental Project, East Cleveland, 1996—2000; coord. East Cleveland Elem. Acad., East Cleveland, 1999. Scholar, St. John Coll., 1974. Mem.: Nat. Assn. Fed. Edn. Program Adminstrs., Internat. Reading Assn., Ohio Assn. Adminstrs. State and Fed. Edn. Programs, Ohio Assn. Pupil Svcs. Adminstrs., Irish Am. Club, City Club Cleve., Kappa Gamma Pi. Roman Catholic. Office: Fairview Park City Schs 20770 Lorain Rd Fairview Park OH 44126

FLYNN, PATRICIA MARIE, economics educator; b. Lynn, Mass. BA in Econs., Emmanuel Coll., 1972; MA in Econs., Boston U., 1973, PhD in Econs., 1980. Rsch. assoc. Inst. for Employment Policy, Boston U., 1975-83; prof. econs. Bentley Coll., Waltham, Mass., 1976—; sr. rsch. fellow New Eng. Bd. Higher Edn., Boston, 1980-82; vis. sch. Fed. Res. Bd., Boston, 1983-84; exec. dir. Inst. for Rsch. & Faculty Devel., Bentley Coll., Waltham, 1986-90; assoc. dean faculty Bentley Coll., Waltham, Mass., 1991-92, dean grad. sch., 1992—2002, Trustee prof. econs. and mgmt., 2002—. Mem. faculty Inst. in Employment and Tng. Adminstrn. Harvard U., Cambridge, Mass., summers, 1979-81; cons. U. Mo., Columbia, 1983-84, First Security Svcs. Corp., Boston, 1985, Devel. Alternatives, Inc., Jakarta, Indonesia, summer, 1987, ABT Assocs., Cambridge, 1987-89; bd. dirs. Fed. Savs. Bank, Waltham, Mass. Author: Technology Life Cycles and Human Resources, 1993; co-author: Turbulence in the American Workplace, 1991; contbr. articles to profl. jours. Adv. panel mem. Office Tech. Assessment, U.S. Congress, Washington, 1989-91; accreditation team mem. New Eng. Assn. Schs. and Colls., 1985—; mem. Newton (Mass.) Econ. Devel. Commn., 1984-87; bd. dirs. Big Sisters Assn., US Trust, 1998-2000, Boston Fed. Savs. Bank, 2000—, BostonFed Bancorp, Inc., 2000—; trustee Mass. Taxpayers Found., Sloan Found., 1995-98. Grantee Dept. Labor, 1982-84, 88-89, Nat. Inst. Edn., 1982-83, NSF, 1990-93, Sloan Found., 1995-98; recipient Gregory H. Adamian award for tchg. excellence Bentley Coll., 1986, Scholar of Yr., 1991, New Eng. Woman's Leadership award, 1998. Mem. Fin. Womens Assn., Am. Econ. Assn., Com. on the Status of Women in Econs. Professions, The Boston Club, The Boston Econ. Club. Office: Bentley Coll 175 Forest St Waltham MA 02452-4713

FLYNN-CONNORS, ELIZABETH KATHRYN, editor; b. Chgo., Aug. 17, 1939; d. Timothy Carver Flynn and Elizabeth Eleanor (Tait) Scanlon; m. Gerald Martin Connors, Dec. 30, 1978; children: Andrew, Kathryn, Elizabeth. Student, Monmouth Coll., Ill., 1957-59; BA in Journalism, U. Wis., 1961, postgrad., 1965-66. Cityside reporter Mpls. Tribune, 1961-62, Chgo. Daily News, 1962-66, UN/N.Y. corr., 1966-75, Washington corr., 1968; writer, press officer UN, N.Y.C., 1975-82; sr. writer UN Chronicle, N.Y.C., 1982-85, editor-in-chief, 1985-96; chief editor Yearbook of UN, N.Y.C., 1996-99; chief UN pubs., N.Y.C., 1999—. Troop leader Girl Scouts U.S., Tarrytown, N.Y., 1993-95. Russell Sage fellow U. Wis., 1965-66; recipient Investigative Reporting award Sigma Delta Chi, 1962, 1st Pl. Spot News award AP, 1970. Mem. UN Corrs. Assn. (alumni), Phi Beta Kappa, Kappa Delta. Avocations: reading, watching old movies. Home: 238 Hunter Ave Sleepy Hollow NY 10591-1317

FLYNN SCHNEIDER, DANA, psychologist; b. Hannibal, Mo., Nov. 22, 1969; d. Larry R. and Nancie P. Flynn; m. Patrick Schneider, Mar. 23, 2000. D. of Clin. Psychology, Ill. Sch. Profl. Psychology, 2001; EdS of Counseling and Guidance, Marriage and Family Emphasis, U. Mo. Kansas City, 1995, MA in Counseling and Guidance, Mental Health Emphasis, 1994; BA in Psychology/Sociology, Birmingham-So. Coll., 1992. Primary counselor Aletheia Ho., Birmingham, Ala., 1996—97; asst. site dir., postdoctoral fellow Shared Vision Inc. Cicero West Sch., Ill., 2001—02, clin. site dir. Shared Vision Inc., 2002—03; clinical coord. Pediat. Psychology Assocs., Oak Brook, Ill., 2002—. Mem.: APA (assoc.), Ill. Psychol. Assn. (assoc.). Home: 1171 Gunderson Ave Oak Park IL 60304 Office Phone: 708-790-8619.

FOARD, SUSAN LEE, editor; b. Asheville, N.C., Aug. 1, 1938; d. Carson Cowan and Anne (Brown) F. AB, Salem Coll., 1960; MA, William and Mary Coll., 1966. Asst. editor Inst. Early Am. Hist. and Culture, Williamsburg, Va., 1961-66, assoc. editor, 1966; editor U. Va. Press, Charlottesville, 1966—. Office: PO Box 400318 Charlottesville VA 22904-4318

FOCH, NINA, actress, creative consultant, film director, educator; b. Leyden, The Netherlands, Apr. 20, 1924; came to U.S. 1927; d. Dirk and Consuelo (Flowerton) F.; m. James Lipton, June 6, 1954; m. Dennis de Brito, Nov. 27, 1959, 1 child, Dirk de Brito; m. Michael Dewell, Oct. 31, 1967 (div.). Grad., Lincoln Sch., 1939; studies with Stella Adler. Adj. prof. drama U. So. Calif., Grad. Sch. Cinema & TV, L.A., 1966—68, 1978—80, adj. prof. film, 1987—; creative cons. to dirs., writers, prodrs. of all media. Artist-in-residence U. N.C., 1966, Ohio State U., 1967, Calif. Inst. Tech., 1969-70; mem. sr. faculty Am. Film Inst., 1974-77; founder, tchr. Nina Foch Studio, Hollywood, Calif., 1973—; founder, actress Los Angeles Theatre Group, 1960-65; bd. dirs. Nat. Repertory Theatre, 1967-75. Motion picture appearances include Nine Girls, 1944, Return of the Vampire, 1944, Shadows in the Night, 1944, Cry of the Werewolf, 1944, Escape in the Fog, 1945, A Song to Remember, 1945, My Name Is Julia Ross, 1945, I Love a Mystery, 1945, Johnny O'Clock, 1947, The Guilt of Janet Ames, 1947, The Dark Past, 1948, The Undercover Man, 1949, Johnny Allegro, 1949, An American in Paris, 1951, Scaramouche, 1952, Young Man with Ideas, 1952, Sombrero, 1953, Fast Company, 1953, Executive Suite, 1954 (Oscar award nominee), Four Guns to the Border, 1954, You're Never Too Young, 1955, Illegal, 1955, The Ten Commandments, 1956, Three Brave Men, 1957, Cash McCall, 1959, Spartacus, 1960, Such Good Friends, 1971, Salty, 1973, Mahogany, 1976, Jennifer, 1978, Rich and Famous, 1981, Skin Deep, 1988, Sliver, 1993, Morning Glory, 1993, 'Til There Was You, 1996, Hush, 1998, Shadow of Doubt, 1998, How to Deal, 2003; appeared in Broadway plays including John Loves Mary, 1947, Twelfth Night, 1949, A Phoenix Too Frequent, 1950, King Lear, 1950, Second String, 1960; appeared with Am. Shakespeare Festival in Taming of the Shrew, Measure for Measure, 1956, San Francisco Ballet and Opera in The Seven Deadly Sins, 1966; also many regional theater appearances including Seattle Repertory Theatre (All Over, 1972 and The Seagull, 1973); actress on TV, 1947—, including Playhouse 90, Studio One, Pulitzer Playhouse, Playwrights 56, Producers Showcase, Lou Grant (Emmy nominee 1980), Mike Hammer; series star: Shadow Chasers, 1985, War and Remembrance, 1988, LA Law, 1990, Hunter, 1990, Dear John, 1990, 91, Tales of the City, 1993, Dharma and Greg, 1999, Just Shoot Me, 2000, recurring role Bull, 2000-01, State of Grace, 2003; many other series, network spls. and TV films; TV panelist and guest on The Dinah Shore Show, Merv Griffin Show, The Today Show, Dick Cavett, The Tonight Show; TV moderator: Let's Take Sides, 1957-59; assoc. dir. (film) The Diary of Anne Frank, 1959; dir. (nat. tour and on-Broadway) Tonight at 8:30, 1966-67, Family Blessings, 1997; assoc. producer re-opening of Ford's Theatre, Washington, 1968. Hon. chmn. Los Angeles chpt. Am. Cancer Soc., 1970. Recipient Film Daily award, 1949, 53. Mem. AAUP, Acad. Motion Picture Arts and Scis. (co-chair exec. com. fgn. film award, membership com., chair foreign lang. award com., 1998-99), Hollywood Acad. TV Arts and Scis. (bd. govs. 1976-77). Avocation: work. Office: PO Box 1884 Beverly Hills CA 90213-1884

FOCHT, SANDRA JEAN, elementary school educator; b. Santa Monica, Calif., Aug. 1, 1944; d. George Allen and Pauline Estella De Bra; m. R. Duane Focht, Feb. 1, 1964; children: Jeremy D., Jennifer R. BS in Edn., Wright State Univ., 1969, MEd in Ednl. Media, 1981, cert. in Gifted Edn. 1-12, 1985. Cert. elem. tchr. Ohio, tchr. gifted Ohio. Tchr. Parkwood Elem., Beavercreek, Ohio, 1970—99, Ankeney Middle Sch., Beavercreek, 1999—2004. Pres., dir. Beavercreek (Ohio) Cmty. Theatre, 1994—99; adv. Muse Machine, Dayton, Ohio, 1995—2004; founder Jr. Thespian Chpt. at Ankeney Middle Sch. Co-author: (textbook) Writing Step By Step, 1986. Recipient Golden Apple Achievement award, Ashland Oil, 1996; Jennings scholar, 1975. Mem.: NEA, Ednl. Theatre Assn., Ohio Edn. Assn., Nat. Coun. Tchrs. English, Phi Delta Kappa. Avocations: writing, directing plays, directing musicals, photography. Home: 224 Cleek Springs Ct Dayton OH 45440 Office: Ankeney Middle Sch 4085 Shakertown Rd Beavercreek OH 45430 Office Phone: 937-429-7567.

FODOR, SUSANNA SERENA, lawyer; b. Tg-Mures, Romania, Apr. 24, 1950; came to U.S., 1963; d. Bela Akos and Rachel (Rafira) F.; 1 child, Brooke Alexandra Bodoki-Fodor. BS, U. Wis., Milw., 1969; JD, U. Wis., Madison, 1972. Bar: Wis. 1972, N.Y. 1974. In ho. counsel Wis. Dept. Devel. Natural Resources, Madison, 1972-73, U.S. EPA, N.Y.C., 1973-74, Urban Devel. Corp., N.Y.C., 1975-77; assoc. Schulte, Roth & Zabel, N.Y.C., 1977-79; ptnr. Weil, Gotshal & Manges, N.Y.C., 1979-85, Shea & Gould, N.Y.C., 1985-89, Jones, Day, Reavis & Pogue, N.Y.C., 1989—. Editor chpt. to book; contbr. articles to profl. publs., chpt. to book. Mem. ABA (real property, probate and trust constrn. form com.), Am. Coll. Real Estate Lawyers, Profl. Women in Constrn., Real Estate Bd. N.Y. (owner labor coordinating com.), Am. Coll. Constrn. Lawyers, Am. Arbitration Assn. (large complex case panel), Comml. Real Estate Women N.Y. (editl. bd.), Urban Land Inst., CoreNet Global; CoreNet Learning Advisory Bd.; Wis. State Bar Assn., N.Y. State Bar Assn., Hungarian-Am. C. of C. of N.Y./N.J. Avocations: sports, art, languages. Home: 200 E End Ave Apt 14F New York NY 10128-7887 Office: Jones Day Reavis & Pogue 599 Lexington Ave Fl C1A New York NY 10022-6030 E-mail: ssfodor@jonesday.com.

FODREA, CAROLYN WROBEL, educational researcher, publisher, consultant; b. Hammond, Ind., Feb. 1, 1943; d. Stanley Jacob and Margaret Caroline (Stupeck) Wrobel; m. Howard Frederick Fodrea, June 17, 1967 (div. Jan. 1987); children: Gregory Kirk, Lynn Renee. BA in Elem. Edn., Purdue U., 1966; MA in Reading and Lang. Devel., U. Chgo., 1973; postgrad., U. Colo., Denver, 1986-87. Cert. [illegible] various schs., Ind., Colo., 1966-87; founder, supr., clinician Reading Clinic, Children's Hosp., Denver, 1969-73; pvt. practice in reading and lang. rsch. clinic Denver, 1973-87; pvt. practice in reading rsch. ctr. Deerfield, Ill., 1973—; creator of pilot presch.-kindergarten lang. devel. program Gary, Ind. Diocese Schs., 1987—, therapist lang. and reading disabilities, 1987—; pres. Reading Rsch. Ctr., Arlington Heights, Ill., 2000—. Conducted Lang. Devel. Workshop, Gary, Ind. 1988; tchr. adult basic edn. Dawson Tech. Sch., 1990, Coll. Lake County, 1991, Prairie State Coll., 1991—, Chgo. City Colls., 1991, R.J. Daley Coll., 1991, Coll. DuPage, 1991—; condr. adult basic edn. workshops for Coll. of DuPage, R.J. Daley Coll., 1992, Ill. Lang. Devel. Literacy Program; tchr. Korean English Lang. Inst., Chgo., 1996, Lang. Devel. Program for Minorities, 2000; dir. pilot study Cabrini Green Tutoring Ctr., Chgo., 2000; presenter in field. Author: Language Development Program, 1985, Presch. Kindergarten Lang. Devel. Program, 1988, A Multi-Sensory Stimulation Program for the Premature Baby in Its Incubator to Reduce Medical Costs and Academic Failure, 1986, Predicting At-Risk Babies for First Grade Reading Failure Before Birth A 15 Year Study, A Language Development Program, Grades 1 to Adult, 1988, 92; editor, pub.: ESL For Native Spanish Speakers, 1996, ESL For Native Korean Speakers, 1996. Active Graland Country Day Sch., Denver, 1981-83, N.W. Ind. Children's Chorale, 1988—; Ill. state chair Babies and You com. March of Dimes, 1999—. Mem. NEA, Am. Ednl. Rsch. Assn., Internat. Reading Assn., Am. Coun. for Children with Learning Disabilities, Am. Acad. Environ. Medicine (presenter pilot study at conf. 2002), Assn. for Childhood Edn. Internat., Colo. Assn. for Edn. of Young Children, Infant Stimulation Edn. Assn., Art Inst. Chgo., U. Chgo. Alumni Club (Denver area ann. fund, Pres. fund com. 1988—, numerous positions Denver area chpt. 1974-87). Roman Catholic. Avocations: sports, health and nutrition, literary and cultural activities, sewing. Office Phone: 888-296-7633. Personal E-mail: cfodrea1@aol.com. Business E-Mail: cfodrea@readingresearch.com.

FOGARASSY, HELEN CATHERINE, writer; b. Gyula, Hungary, Oct. 30, 1949; arrived in U.S., 1957; d. Janos and Ilona (Skerl) Fogarassy; m. Karl Matlin, Aug. 23, 1972 (div. Aug. 1978). BA in Comparative Lit., Ind. U., 1972. Editor Scholastic Mag., N.Y.C., 1974—76, Sloan-Kettering Cancer Ctr., N.Y.C., 1976—79; owner, mgr. On Paper Office Svcs., N.Y.C., 1979—88. Author: Mix Bender, 1987, Mission Improbable: The World Community on a UN Compound in Somalia, 1999; contbr. Voices Unabridged.com. Mem.: Internat. Womens Writing Guild, Poets & Writers, Pen & Authors Guild. Democrat. Home and Office: 44 E 74th St #3D New York NY 10021 E-mail: helfog@aol.com.

FOGEL, JENNIFER LYNN, technical associate, researcher; b. L.A., Apr. 15, 1976; d. Kenneth L. and Marcia Fogel. BS in Zoology, U. Tex., 1998; postgrad., Calif. State U., Northridge. Tech. assoc. US Borax Inc., Valencia, Calif., 1999—. Spkr. in field. Contbr. rsch. papers to profl. jours. Mem. AAAS, Internat. Rsch. Group, Forest Products Soc., U.S. Olympic Assn. Avocations: running, travel, reading, playing piano, singing. Office: US Borax Inc 26877 Tourney Rd Valencia CA 91355-1847 Office Fax: 661-287-6014. E-mail: jennifer.fogel@borax.com.

FOGG, JANET, architectural firm executive; Prin. OZ Arch., Denver, mng. ptnr., CFO, dir. human resources Boulder (Colo.) Studio, bd. dirs. Chmn. Downtown Boulder (Colo.), Inc., bd. dirs. Office: OZ Architecture Inc 3012 Huron St Ste 100 Denver CO 80202

FOGGIN, BRENDA FRAZIER, retired state agency administrator, volunteer; b. Bogalusa, La., Jan. 24, 1942; d. Joseph Wiley Frazier and Virginia Mary Holmes; m. Joseph Jimes, Feb. 23, 1963 (div. May 1989); children: Jeffery, Joel, Christina; m. Howard Francis Foggin, Dec. 23, 1992. AA, La. Tech. U., 1998, BA, 1999. Cert. master gardener, La.; notary public. Supr. Dept. of Health, Bossier City, La., 1967-76; motor vehicle officer Dept. Pub. Safety, Bossier City, 1976-87; supr. State Employees Group Benefits, Shreveport, La., 1987-96. Author, editor: (short stories) Collage of Memories, 1998, poems. Mem. Citizens Leadership Acad. The Polit. Tng. Inst., Shreveport, 1998; mem. Highland Area Partnership, 1993-99, Nat. Trust Historic Preservation, 1997-99; sec. Profl. Rep. Women's Club, Shreveport, La., 2001-02. Mem. Highland Historic Preservation Assn., Golden Key, Krewe of Highland. Republican. Roman Catholic. Avocations: reading, writing, gardening, historic preservation. Home: 857 Robinson Pl Shreveport LA 71104-3029

FOGLIA, MICHELLE LYNN, psychologist; b. Poughkeepsie, N.Y., Oct. 26, 1971; d. John Joseph and Diane Marie (Gunn) F. AA, Dutchess Cmty. Coll., Poughkeepsie, 1991; BA in psychology, Marist Coll., 1993; MA in counseling, Webster Univ., 1997. Hab tech./tchr. asst. Astor Home for Children, Rhinebeck, N.Y., 1992-93; sales assoc. Limited Express, Poughkeepsie, 1993-95, sales mgr. Charleston, S.C., 1995-96; support team mem. Cmty. Living of Wilmington, Wilmington, N.C., 1996-97; family & group therapist Oaks Pscyhiatric Hosp., Wilmington, N.C., 1996-97; CAP case mgr. Southeastern Ctr. for Mental Health, Wilmington, N.C., 1997—; child psychologist Beckman Mental Health Clinic, Greenwood, S.C., 1998. Mem. adv. com. Southeastern Mental Health, Wilmington, 1997—. Tutur, tchr. Cape Fear Literacy Coun., Wilmington, 1996; sponsor Christian Children's Fund, N.Y., 1991. Mem. Am. Counseling Assn., Young Men's Club of Am., Alzheimers Assn., Humane Soc. Avocations: exercise, jazz, ballet dance, yoga, gardening, spending time with my dogs. Home: 119 E Laurel Ave Greenwood SC 29649-1637 Office: Southeastern Mental Health Ctr 5041 New Centre Dr Ste 200 Wilmington NC 28403-1624

FOISY, RENÉE THÉRÈSE, financial consultant; b. Nashville, Sept. 5, 1966; d. Hector Bernard and Joanne Theresa (Fleury) F. AB in French Lit., Dartmouth Coll., 1988; postgrad., U. Paris V, 1988-89; MBA, So. Meth. U., 1994. English asst. Lycée Victor Duruy, Paris, 1988-89; tchr. French and Spanish, Greenhill Sch., Dallas, 1989-91; tchr. French, Spanish and German, Hurst Tex.)-Euless-Bedford Ind. Sch. Dist., 1992; grad. asst. So. Meth. U., Dallas, 1992; fin. analyst Am. Airlines Corp., Dallas-Ft. Worth Airport, 1994-95, sr. fin. analyst corp. devel., 1995-96, mgr. internat. treasury, assoc., prin., mgr., 1996—98; mgr. internat. planning AMR, 1998—2000; CFO Adventure Tours, 2001; fin. cons. SOS Consulting, 2002—. Vol. Girls' Inc. Met. Dallas, 1994; bd. dirs. ARTS for People, 2001-03; fin. com. Dallas Women's Found., 1998-2002, grant com., 2002. Dean's scholar Southern Meth. U., 1992-94, Tate scholar, 1993-94, Tex. KT scholar, 1993-94. Mem. Dallas-Ft. Worth Cox Alumni Club (v.p. 1994-96). Unitarian Universalist.

FOK, AGNES KWAN, retired cell biologist, educator; b. Hong Kong, Dec. 11, 1940; came to U.S., 1962; d. Sun and Yau (Ng) Kwan; m. Fok, June 8, 1965; children: Licie Chiu-Jane, Edna Chiu-Joan. BA in Chemistry, U. Great Falls, 1965; MS in Plant Nutrition and Biochemistry, Utah State U., 1966; PhD in Biochemistry, U. Tex., 1971. Asst. rsch. prof. pathology U. Hawaii, Honolulu, 1973-74, Ford Found. postdoctoral fellow, anatomy dept., 1975, asst. rsch. prof., 1975-82, assoc. rsch. prof., 1982—96, rsch. prof. Pacific Biomed. Rsch. Ctr., 1988-96, grad. faculty, dept. microbiology, 1977—2003, dir., 1994-96, dir., prof. biology program, 1996—2003, prof. emeritus, 2003—. Contbr. articles to profl. jours. Mem. Am. Soc. for Cell Biology, Soc. for Protozoologists, Sigma Xi (treas. Hawaii chpt. 1979-2002). Avocations: reading, gardening, hiking, sewing. Office: U Hawaii Biology Program Honolulu HI 96822

FOLAND, SARA, geologist, association executive; b. Anderson, Ind., May 6, 1956; d. James Phillip and June Irene (DeWood) F. BS in Chemistry, Ind. U., Ft. Wayne, 1978, BS in Geology, 1979; MS in Geology, U. Mont., 1982; Exec. MBA, Ind. U., Bloomington, 1994; postgrad., U. Calif., Santa Cruz, 1998—. Cert. petroleum geologist. Physician asst. Ft. Wayne, 1974-80; [illegible] Illinois Nat. Lab., 1982; geologist, mgr. Amoco Prodn. Co., Denver, 1982-98; CEO, pres. Farallon Energy Group Ltd., Denver, 1998-99; CEO Geol. Soc. Am., Boulder, Colo., 1999—. Nat. corp. sec. Amoco Corp., Houston, 1996-98; chair Denver Outreach Com. for Elem. Edn., 1990-96; mem. adv. bd. Amoco Women's Employee Network, 1990-94. Contbr. more than 30 articles to profl. jours. Vice chair Colo. AIDS Inst. Found., Denver, 1998—; chair planning com. of bd. trustees U. Mont. Found., Missoula, 1996—. Assn. Western Univs. grantee, 1982. Mem. AAUW, Am. Geophys. Union (life), Am. Assn. Petroleum Geologists, Geol. Soc. Am., Sigma Xi. Avocations: skiing, golf, flying, fly fishing. Office: Geol Soc Am 3300 Penrose Pl Boulder CO 80301-1806 Home: 41205 Juniper Springs Ct Steamboat Springs CO 80487-9469

FOLBRE, NANCY, economics educator; BA in Philosophy, U. Tex., 1971, MA in Lat. Am. Studies, 1973; PhD in Econs., U. Mass., 1979. Trainee Nat. Inst. Child Health Care and Devel. Population Rsch. Ctr. U. Tex., 1974-75; postdoct. rsch. fellow Econ. Growth Ctr. Yale U., New Haven, Conn., 1979-80; asst. prof. econs. Bowdoin Coll., 1980-83, New Sch. Social Rsch., N.Y.C., 1983-85; assoc. prof. econs. U. Mass., Amherst, 1984-91, prof. econs., 1991—. Cons. Maine Commn. for Women, 1981, Beijer Inst. Author: A Field Guide to the U.S. Economy, 1988, Who Pays for the Kids? Gender and the Structures of Constrint, 1994, The New Field Guide to the U.S. Economy, 1995, War on the Poor: A Defense Manual, 1996, De la différence des sexes en économie politique, edit. des femmes, 1997; editor: The Economics of the Family, 1996; co-editor: Issues in Contemporary Economics, vol. 4, 1991; mem. editl. bd.: Explrations in Economic History, 1995—); contbr. numerous articles to profl. jours., newspapers, chpts. to books. Co-chair rsch. network on families in the economy The MacArthur Found., 1997. Tchg., rsch. fellow French-Am. Found., 1995-96; MacArthur fellow John D. and Catherine T. MacArthur Found., 1998; faculty rsch. grantee U. Mass., 1987, Healey Pub. svc. Endowment grantee U. Mass., 1989, grantee NSF, 1989. Mem. Am. Econs. Assn. (presenter), Internat. Assn. Feminist Econs. (bd. dirs. 1992—, program chair Ctr. Popular Econs. 1979—, presenter, spkr.). Office: U Mass Dept Econs Amherst MA 01003 Fax: 413-545-2921. E-mail: folbre@econs.umass.edu.

FOLCH-PI, WILLA BABCOCK, romance language educator; b. Milw., June 22, 1925; d. Charles Whitney and Helen Gertrude (Robinson) Babcock; m. Jordi Folch-Pi, June 23, 1945 (dec. Oct. 1979); children: Raphael, Diana, Frederic. BA, Barnard Coll., 1945; MA, Harvard U., 1963, PhD, 1969. Lectr. in English Pembroke, Brown U., Providence, 1945-46; teaching fellow Harvard U., Cambridge, Mass., 1968-69; curator of manuscripts Harvard Med. Sch., Boston, 1971-75; assoc. acad. dean, asst. prof. romance langs. Tufts U., Medford, Mass., 1975-85, assoc. dean, asst. prof. emerita, 1985—. Vis. lectr. MIT, Cambridge, fall 1973; seminar lectr. Radcliffe, fall 1975; coord. program abroad Tufts U., 1975-82, prelaw advisor, 1975-85. Author rsch. papers in field. Pres. Sandwich Woman's Club, Center Sandwich, N.H., 1990-92, N.E. Assn. Pre-law Advisors, 1984; mem. Squaw Lakes Assn., Holderness, N.H., 1962—, Friends of Sandwich Libr., Center Sandwich, 1985—, Sandwich Hist. Soc., Center Sandwich, 1985—. Travel grantee Am. Philos. Soc., 1967, Tufts Mellon Found., 1982; fellow Bunting Inst., Radcliffe, 1969-71. Mem. MLA, Medieval Acad. Am., Societe Internationale Arthurienne, Societe Rencesvals, N.Am. Catalan Soc., Harvard Club. Avocations: painting, sewing, reading. Home: 909 Holderness Rd Center Sandwich NH 03227-3108

FOLCO, ANGELIKA, secondary school educator; b. Germany, Feb. 6, 1949; arrived in U.S., 1952; d. Heinrich Karl and Christel Heise; m. Glen Frank Folco, Apr. 3, 1971; children: Brian Glen, Bradley Jason. BA, Lakeland Coll., 1971; MA, Ind. U., 1982. Tchr. Woodview Jr. High Sch., Indpls., 1972—74, Creston Jr. High Sch., 1972—74, Stonybrook Jr. High Sch., 1975—82, Warren Ctrl. High Sch., 1982—83, Stonybrook Jr. High Sch., 1983—93, Warren Ctrl. High Sch., 1993—, dept. chair fgn. lang., 2002—. Presenter Staff Devel. Best Practices, Indpls., 1998. Mem.: Assn. Curriculum Devel., Ind. Fgn. Lang. Tchrs. Assn., Ind. State Tchrs. Assn. Avocations: reading, gardening, travel. Office: MSD Warren Twp Warren Ctrl High Sch 9500 E 16th St Indianapolis IN 46229 Office Phone: 317-532-6323.

FOLEY, ANN, broadcast executive; BA, Mount Holyoke Coll., 1976. Exec. v.p. programming Showtime Networks, Inc., N.Y.C., 1988—96, exec. V.P. east coast programming, 1996—. Mem.: FCC Oversight Monitoring Bd., TV Parental Guidelines Monitoring Bd. Office: Showtime Networks Inc 1633 Broadway Fl 17 New York NY 10019-6708*

FOLEY, BRIANA, music educator, consultant; b. Jersey City, N.J., Sept. 23, 1958; d. Daniel Joseph and Jane Catherine Moriarty; m. Gregory Howard Foley, Oct. 12, 1980; 1 child, Elizabeth Ann. Student, Fla. State U., 1978; B of Music Edn., Westminster Choir Coll., Princeton, N.J., 1981. Cert. music edn.K-12 Fla. Voice and piano instr. pvt. home studio, Clearwater, Fla., 1981—83; choral dir. N.W. Presbyn. Ch., St. Petersburg, Fla., 1981—94; music specialist Mildred Helms Elem. Sch., Largo, Fla., 1982—90, Garrison-Jones Elem. Sch., Dunedin, Fla., 1990—. Cons. profl. edn. music dept. Pinellas County Schs., Largo, 1986—2003; mem. Pinellas County Student Achievement Grant. Author: (study guide) The Florida Orchestra Youth Concert Series Guide, 1986—2003. Vol. Clearwater Jazz Holiday, 1984—87; coord. Adopt-a-Grandparent Program, Largo, 1985—89. Recipient grantee, Fla. Dept. Edn., 1989. Mem.: Music Educators Nat. Conf., Pinellas Classroom Tchrs. Assn. Achievements include development of first music inclusion program in Pinellas County School District. Avocations: yoga, walking, playwriting, reading, travel. Office: Garrison-Jones Elem Sch 3133 Garrison Rd Dunedin FL 34698

FOLEY, CHERYL M. company executive; V.p., gen. counsel PSI Energy, Inc., Ind., 1989-91; v.p., gen. counsel, corp. sec. PSI Energy, Inc. and PSI Resources Inc., Ind., 1991-94; v.p., sec., gen. counsel Cinergy Corp., Cin., 1994-99, v.p., sec., 1999—; pres. Cinergy Global Resources subs. Cinergy Corp., Cin. Office: Cinergy Corp 221 E 4th St # 30 Cincinnati OH 45202-4124

FOLEY, CORNELIA MACINTYRE, retired artist; b. Honolulu, Jan. 31, 1909; d. Malcolm and Florence (Hall) M.; m. Paul Foley Jr., June 4, 1936 (dec. July 1990); children: Jean Drake, John Malcolm, Mark Lincoln. Student, U. Hawaii, 1926-27, Slade Art Sch., London, 1929-31; BA in Fine Arts, U. Wash., Seattle, 1932. One-woman shows at Honolulu Art Acad., Long Beach (Calif.) Pub. Libr., Army-Navy Club, Long Beach, Newport (R.I.) Art Assn., Hofstra U. Libr., Mallette Gallery, Garden City, N.Y., also 6 banks in L.I.; 3 woman show at Manhasset Pub. Libr.; exhibited in numerous group shows, including Hofstra U., L.I. Fedn. Women Artists, Rockefeller Center, N.Y., Seattle Art Mus., Corcoran Gallery of Art, Washington, Nat. Art Gallery of NSW, Australia, Honolulu Acad. Arts, Mfrs. Hanover Trust, N.Y.C., Glen Cove Boy's Club, Lever House, N.Y.C., Equitable Life Assurance, N.Y.C., Nassau F.A. Mus., Manhasset Libr., Great Neck Libr., Post Coll., Great Neck House, others; represented in permenent collections at Libr. of Congress, Washington, Honolulu Printmakers Assn., Castle Collection, Honolulu, Harold Mertz Collection, L.I., Whitney Mus. of Am. Art, N.Y.C., Honolulu Acad. of Arts, Mitchell Wolfson Collection, Miami, Fla., also many pvt. collections; works reproduced in Islands, Discover Am. travel book, Island Home.. Recipient Purchase prizes and Best in Show award Honolulu Printmakers, 1st and 2d prize Jr. League Regional Shows, 1st prize Nat. Jr. League Frontespiece Contest, Grand prize and Hon. Mention award Honolulu Artists, 4th prize L.I. Fedn. Women Artists, numerous 1st, 2d, 3d, and hon. mention awards Manhasset Art Assn., 1st prize Nassau County Cerebral Palsy, Molly M. Canaday Meml. prize Nat. Assn. Women Artists, Grumbacher Gold medal Nat. Assn. Women Artists, award of excellence Ind. Art Soc., Hon. Mention [illegible] Art League. Mem. Manhasset Art Assn. (past pres.), Nat. Assn. Women Artists. Avocations: needlecraft, creative writing. Home: 141 Chapel Rd Manhasset NY 11030-3635

FOLEY, JANE DEBORAH, foundation executive; b. Chgo., May 30, 1952; d. Colin Gray Stevenson and Bette Jane (Cullenbine) Coleman; m. George Edward Foley, Jan. 29, 1972; children: Sy Curtis, Shelly. BA, Purdue U., 1973, MS, 1977, PhD, 1992. Cert. elem. adminstr., Ind., cert. elem. adminstrn. and supervision. Tchr. phys. edn. and health Lafayette (Ind.) Jefferson H.S., 1973-74; tchr. music and phys. edn. Valparaiso (Ind.) Cmty. Schs., 1974-79, tchr. elem. phys. edn., 1979-90; prin. South Ctrl. Elem. sch., Union Mills, Ind., 1990-93, Flint Lake Elem. Sch., Valparaiso, 1993-98; v.p. Milken Family Found., Santa Monica, Calif., 1998—2003, sr. v.p., 2003—. Mem. panel of experts The Master Tchr., 1996-98, Nat. Endowment for the Humanities; key note spkr., presenter state and nat. confs. Contbr. articles to profl. jours. and books; author: Technology Integration: A School Administrator's Guide, Success in Restructuring: A Road Map for Administrators, The Administrator's Technology Training Booklet. Mem. Valparaiso Sch. Sys. PTA, mem. exec. bd., 1993-98; bd. dirs. Hold Onto Your Music, Wings Inc. Recipient Hoosier Sch. award, 1992, Ind. 2000 Designation award 1994, Outstanding Dissertation award Internat. Soc. Ednl. Planning, 1993, Nat. Educator award, Milken Family Found., 1994, Ind. Bell Ringer award Ind. Dept. Edn., 1994, Ind. 4 Star Sch. award, 1995, 96, 97, 98, Internat. Tech. Edn. Assn. award, 1995, Cmty. Improvement award Valparaiso C. of C., 1994, NCREL Pathways to Improvement Pilot Site, 1995, Ind. Sch. Improvement award, Ind. Dept. Edn., 1998, others; Ind. 2000 Planning grantee, 1993, Milken Educator Tech. Project leader, 1997, other grants. Mem. ASCD (assoc.), NAESP, Ind. Assn. Sch. Prins., Valparaiso Tchrs. Assn. (treas. 1989-90), Phi Kappa Phi. Avocations: running, reading, writing, computers. Office: Milken Family Found 1250 4th St Santa Monica CA 90401-1350 E-mail: jfoley@mff.org.

FOLEY, KATHLEEN M. neurologist, educator, researcher; b. Flushing, N.Y., Jan. 28, 1944; d. Joseph Cyril and Catherine (Cribbin) Maher; m. Charles Thomas Foley, Aug. 10, 1968; children: Fritz, David. BA in Biology magna cum laude, St. John's U., N.Y.C., 1965; MD, Cornell U., 1969; DSc (hon.), St. John's U., N.Y.C., 1992. Diplomate Am. Bd. Psychiatry and Neurology (examiner 1980-), lic. physician N.Y. Intern, then resident in neurology The N.Y. Hosp., N.Y.C., 1969—74; asst. attending neurologist, neuology dept. Meml. Sloan-Kettering Cancer Ctr., N.Y.C., 1974—79, assoc. attending neurologist, 1979—88, chief-pain svc., 1982—, attending neurologist, 1988—, Manhattan (N.Y.) Eye & Ear Hosp., 1974—83; instr. in neurology, Med. Coll. Cornell U., N.Y.C., 1974—75, asst. prof., 1975—79, assoc. prof., 1979—89, assoc. prof. pharmacology, 1979—89, prof. neurology and neuroscience, 1989—, prof. clin. pharmacology, 1990—; rsch. assoc. lab. neuro-oncology Sloan-Kettering Inst. Cancer Rsch., N.Y.C., 1981—84. Vis. asst. physician, cons. in neurology Rockefeller U. Hosp., 1975—79, vis. assoc. physician, 1979—; cons. Calvary Hosp., 1982—; assoc. mem. Meml. Sloan-Kettering Cancer Ctr., 1985—88, mem., 1988—. Editor: Clin. Jour. Pain, 1985—87, Jour. Pain and Symptom Mgmt., 1987—, Palliative Medicine Jour., 1993—. Patient svcs. adv. group Am. Cancer Soc. Named Outstanding Woman Scientist, Women in Sci. Met. N.Y. chpt., 1987, A. Soriano Jr. Meml. Lectr., The Andres Soriano Cancer Rsch. Found. Inc., 1992; recipient Jr. Faculty award, Disting. Svc. award, Am. Cancer Soc., 1975—78, Disting. Svc. award, 1992, Nat. Bd. award, The Med. Coll. Pa., 1986, William M. Witter award, U. Calif. San Francisco, 1987, Annie Blount Storrs award, Calvary Hosp., 1988, Balfour M. Mount award, Am. Jour. Hospice Care, 1988, Disting. Oncologist award, Dayton Oncology Soc., 1990, Tenth Barbara Bohen Pfeifer award, Am. Italian Found. for Cancer Rsch., 1993; fellow Neuro-Oncology spl. fellow, Meml. Sloan-Kettering Cancer Ctr., 1975—78; grantee Genetic Tng. grantee, NIH, 1970—71, Program for Pain Rsch. grantee, Bristol-Myers, 1988—92. Mem.: NAS (Inst. Medicine), AMA (ad hoc adv. panel mgmt. chronic pain, DATTA reference panel), AAAS, Inst. Medicine NAS, Soc. for Neurosci., N.Y. Acad. Scis. (USP adv. panel on neurology 1990—), Internat. Assn. Study Pain (councilor 1984—90, edn. com. 1986—93, various other coms.), Harvey Soc., Eastern Pain Assn. (John J. Bonica award 1986), Assn. Rsch. in Nervous and Mental Diseases, Am. Soc. Clin. Pharmacology and Therapeutics, Am. Soc. Clin. Oncology (program com. 1991—92, com. on care at the end of life 1993—, other coms., David Karnosky award), Am. Pain Soc. (bd. dirs. 1980—82, pres. 1984—85, bylaws com. 1986—87, long range planning task force 1989—), Am. Neurol. Assn. (com. 1984—85, councilor 1984, 1994), Am. Med. Womens Assn., Am. Fedn. Clin. Rsch., Am. Acad. Neurology (chmn. long range planning com. 1990—, sci. program com. 1990, other coms.), Acad. Hospice Physicians, Cornell U. Med. Coll. Alumni Assn. (bd. dirs., nominating com.), Children's Hospice Internat., Children's Hospice, Alpha Omega Alpha. Office: Meml Sloan-Kettering Cancer Ctr Box 52 1275 York Ave New York NY 10021-6094

FOLEY, MARY E. medical association administrator, nursing administrator; Diploma in nursing, New Eng. Deaconess Hosp., 1973; BSN, Boston U., 1976; MS in Nursing Adminstn. and Occupl. Health, U. Calif., San Francisco, 1994. RN. Asst. dir. ambulatory care rev. N.Y. County Health Svcs. Rev. Orgn.; med.-surg. nurse St. Francis Meml. Hosp., San Francisco, dir. nursing and chief nurse exec.; pres. ANA, Washington. Part-time clin. faculty San Francisco State U. Sch. Nursing; lectr. in field. Contbr. articles to profl. jours. Mem. Calif. Tuberculosis Elimination Task Force Dept. Health Svcs., 1993—94; mem. Mayor's HIV Task Force, San Francisco, 1989, Calif. RN Spl. Adv. Com. on Nursing Shortage, Dept. Consumer Affairs, 1989; project cons. tng. for devel. of innovative control tech. project Trauma Found. at San Francisco Gen. Hosp., 1990. Mem.: ANA (2d v.p. 1994—96, 1st v.p. 1996—2000, chair constituent assembly, ofcl. rep. to Internat. Coun. Nurses 1997, 1999, chair legis. com., mem. polit. action com. bd. dirs.), Calif. Nurses Assn. (pres., treas.). Office: American Nurses Assn 600 Maryland Ave SW #100W Washington DC 20024-2571

FOLEY, PATRICIA JEAN, accountant; b. Bridgeport, Conn., Jan. 12, 1956; d. John Edward and Louise (Caselli) F. AA, Housantonic C.C., 1978; BS, Cen. Conn. State Coll., 1980; MBA, U. Hartford, 1996. CPA, Conn. Staff acct. Spitz, Sullivan, Wachtel & Falcetta, Hartford, Conn., 1981-82, client acct., 1982-85, sr. acct., 1985-87, supr., mgr., 1987-97; mgr. Falcetta Wachtel & Knochenhauer LLC, Bloomfield, Conn., 1997-98; prin. Patricia J. Foley, CPA, Newington, Conn., 1998—. Mem. Acctg. Del. to Russia, Ukraine & Estonia Citizens Amb., 1993. Pres. Woodsedge Condominium Assn., Newington, Conn., 1989—92, treas., 1985—92; bd. dirs. Friends of the Lucy Robbins Welles Libr., 1996—, membership co-chair, 2000—, v.p., 2001, pres., 2002—04. Mem. AICPA (mgmt. adv. svc. com. 1987—, info. tech. divsns., 1992—), Conn. Soc. CPAs, Am. Women Soc. CPAs, Cmty. Assn. Inst. (membership chair Conn. chpt. 1991-92), Nat. Assn. Women Bus. Owners (treas. 2001-03, mem. pub. policy com. 2000—). Home: 35 Woodsedge Dr Apt 1B Newington CT 06111-4271 Office: 35-1B Woodsedge Dr Newington CT 06111-4271 Office Phone: 860-667-1504. E-mail: pattyjfoley@pattyjfoley.com.

FOLEY, RUTH IONA, music educator; d. John and Jolan Elizabeth Szakacs; m. Chris Charles Foley; children: Jonathan, Caralise. BA, BEd, U. Winnipeg, Man., Can., 1982; MMus, U. N.D., Grand Forks, 1989; DMA, U. Nebr., 2000. Assoc. prof. music Liberty U., Lynchburg, Va., 1992—; organist-choir master Bethlehem Luth. Ch., Lynchburg, Va., 2002—. Mem.: Choristers Guild, Am. Guild Organists, Nat. Assn. Tchrs. Singing. Home:

112 Westridge Circle Lynchburg VA 24502 Office: Liberty U Dept Fine Arts 1971 University Blvd Lynchburg VA 24502 Personal E-mail: rifoley@peoplepc.com. E-mail: rifoley@liberty.edu.

FOLEY, VIRGINIA SUE LASHLEY, counselor, international training consultant; b. Richmond, Ind., May 1, 1942; d. Robert E. and Flora Rose (Johnson) Lashley; m. Laurence Michael Foley Sr., Jan. 28, 1968 (dec. 2002); children: Megan Leigh, Jeremie Beth, L. Michael Jr. BA, Hanover Coll., 1964; MS, San Francisco State U., 1969. Cert. profl. counselor and internat. mental health tng. cons.; nat. bd. cert. hypnotherapist; Myers Briggs Type indicator cert. specialist. Vol. Peace Corps, Danao City, The Philippines, 1964-66; counselor, tng. cons. In Touch Found., U.S. Peace Corps., Asian Devel. Bank, Manila, 1981-85, Internat. Sch., 1981-85; counselor, tng. cons. to Overseas Briefing Ctr. U.S. Dept. of State, Washington, 1988-90; counselor, mental health cons. U.S. State Dept./U.S. Peace Corps, La Paz, Bolivia, 1990-92; mental health coord. U.S. Embassy, Lima, Peru, 1992—96; counselor, preferred provider Aetna/HAI, Lima, Peru, 1994-96, mental health cons., internat. tng. cons. Harare, Zimbabwe, 1996-2000; preferred provider AETNA-HAI, Peru, 1994—96; mental health cons., internat. tng. cons. Aetna/HAI, Amman, Jordan, 2000—02; cons. USAID, U.S. State Dept., Washington, 2002—. Archiving specialist USAID, Jordan, 2001—02. Author: Leisure Time Activities for Families in Manila, 1983; (manuals) Career Development Manual, 1984; writer mags. What's On in Manila, 1983-85, Off Duty Mag., 1985, USAID Frontlines, 1991-94, Lima Times, 1994, Fgn. Svc. Jour., 1996; contbr. articles to mags. Mem. U.S. Embassy Mental Health Com.; chair Cmty. Morale Com. Recipient award of recognition Bukidnon State Coll., The Philippines, 1985. Mem.: ACA, Assn. Boliviana de Psicologia Humanista (founding), Internat. Assn. Marriage and Family Counselors (chair cmty. morale com.), Royal Soc. for Conservation of Nature, Am. Women's Assn. of Amman, Friends of Archeology, Am. Women's Club. Avocations: instrumental music, art, crafts, hiking, literature. Address: 509 Thayer Ave Silver Spring MD 20910 E-mail: virfoley@hotmail.com.

FOLEY MULLANEY, ELLEN MADALINE, journalist; b. Chgo., Apr. 13, 1952; d. Thomas Jennings and Joan Ellen (Murphy) F.; m. Thomas Foley Mullaney, June 30, 1984; children: Kaitlin, Maura. BA in Polit. Sci., U. Wis., 1974, MA in Journalism, 1988. Mng. editor Menominee (Mich.) Herald Leader, 1976-78; copy editor The Milw.-Sentinel, 1978-79, The Detroit News, 1979-80; reporter, copy editor The Star-Tribune, Mpls., 1980-91, asst. features editor, food editor, 1991-93; features editor The Kansas City (Mo.) Star, 1993-96, asst. mng. editor/features, 1996—98; mng. editor The Phila. Daily News, Phila., 1998—2004; editor Wis. State Jour., Madison, 2004—. Mem. Jr. League of Mpls., 1980—, bd. dirs., 1989; founder Violence Against Women Coalition, Mpls., 1988-93. Recipient Third Pl. award Minn. Chpt. Soc. Profl. Journalists, 1982, Minn. Page One award, 1987, Vol. of Distinction award Assn. Jr. Leagues Internat., 1996. Mem. Am. Assn. Sun. & Feature Editors (bd. dirs., conf. host. 1996-98). Avocations: reading, hiking, family adventures. Office: Wis State Jour 1901 Fish Hatchery Rd PO Box 8058 Madison WI 53708*

FOLGATE, CYNTHIA A. social services administrator; b. Chgo., Jan. 27, 1950; d. William C. and Cassie Edna (Sisemore) F. BA, No. Ill. U., 1974, MA, 1983. Cert. domestic violence profl. Ill. Sec. No. Ill. U., DeKalb, 1974—80, 1980—91, instr., 1981—92; outreach coord. Safe Passage, DeKalb, 1992—96, crisis intervention/outreach coord., 1996—97, systems advocacy coord., 1997—2002, cmty. edn. and tng. coord., 2002—. Instr. Waubonsee C.C., Sugar Grove, Ill., 1990—; mem. DeKalb County Domestic Violence Forum, 1990-91; family violence coord. coun. Ill. 16th Jud. Cir.; mem. adv. bd. Coop. Edn. Internship Office No. Ill. U. Speech cons. for various election campaigns DeKalb County, 1988—90; coord. DeKalb County Domestic Violence Initiative, 1998—2000; mem. bd. deacons 1st Congregational United Ch. of Christ, DeKalb, 1989—92. Mem.: Friends of Barb City Manor. Office: Safe Passage PO Box 621 Dekalb IL 60115-0621

FOLKERTS, LINDA JO, publishing executive; b. Fayetteville, N.C., Oct. 28, 1960; d. James Cole and Leona B. Edwards; m. David Dempse Folkerts, Oct. 13, 1988; children: Ginda Dawn, Zachary Cole. BS in Elem. Edn., So. Adventist U., Collegedale, Tenn., 1982. Cert. tchr. Tenn., Fla. Tchr. elem. edn. Tenn. Dept. Edn., Oakland, 1982—83, Somerville, 1987—88, Fla. Dept. Edn., Avon Park and Haines City, 1988—92, N.Am. divsn. Office of Edn. of Seventh-Day Adventists, various locations, 1992—99; instructional tech. specialist Tenn. Spl. Tech. and Resource Ctr., Jackson, 2000—02; staff writer/photographer The Courier, Savannah, Tenn., 2002—. Contbr. articles to profl. jours. Tutor children and adults in reading and math; mem. sml. schs. adv. bd. Ga.-Cumberland Conf. Seventh-Day Adventists, Lakeland, 1993—95. Recipient Zapara award for recognition for excellence in tchg., Gen. Conf. SDA Office Edn., 1995. Seventh-Day Adventist. Avocation: photography. Office: The Courier 801 Main St Savannah TN 38372

FOLLIT, EVELYN V. retail executive; b. 1947; BA in Math., MBA in Fin. and Info. Sys.; degree in Exec. Planning and Tech., Cornell U., MIT. With Dunn & Bradstreet; v.p. ops. and engring. AC Nielson; from v.p. human capital to v.p., COO RadioShack Corp., Fort Worth, Tex., 1997—99, v.p., 1999—, COO, 1999—, sr. v.p. orgnl. enabling svcs., 2003—. Bd. dir. Catalina Mktg. Corp., chmn. audit com., mem. fin. com.; chmn. CIO Coun. Nat. Retail Fedn., 2000—; mem. adv. bd. Ctr. Values Based Leadership, 2002—. Bd. visitors Tex. Christian U., Fort Worth. Named one of Top 10 CIOs in Retailing, Retail Tech. Mag., 1999, Top 10 CIOs Across Am., Info. Week, 1999, 100 Premier IT Leaders in Country, Computerworld, 2001, 25 Most Influential People in Retail, Retail Info Sys. News, 2001, Pioneering Women in Tech., Am. Friends Jerusalem Coll. Tech., 2002; recipient Leadership and Innovation award, Exec. Tech. Mag./Compaq Computer, 2002. Office: RadioShack Corp 100 Throckmarton Ste 1900 Fort Worth TX 76102

FOLLMER, HELENE GREENE, retired museum administrator, civic worker; b. Mitchell, S.D., Apr. 13, 1931; d. Walter Thomas and Frances Ellen (Spangler) Greene; m. Hugh Crawford Follmer, Aug. 27, 1954; children: Anne Frances Follmer DeMartini, Walter Crawford, Bruce Spangler. Student, Colo. Coll., 1949-51; BA, U. Nebr., Lincoln, 1953. Tech. artist U. Nebr. Coll. Medicine, Omaha, 1953-55; project dir. Discovery, The Children's Mus., Las Vegas, Nev., 1984-86, asst. dir., 1986-88; acting dir. Lied Discovery Mus., Las Vegas, 1991, mktg. and membership assoc., 1992-94, mem. adv. bd., 1994—; ret., 1994. Mem. com. City Spirit Project, Las Vegas, 1979-80; mem. Allied Arts Coun. So. Nev., 1975—, also past pres.; mem. adv. com. Las Vegas Master Plan, 1983; mem., sec. Nev. Coun. on Arts, 1981-89; mem. adv. coms. Clark County (Nev.) Sch. Dist., 1980, 81, 83; mem. steering com. Las Vegas Valley Cultural Plan, 1993; com. chmn. Jr. League Las Vegas, 1972—, Assistance League Las Vegas, 1985—; vestrywoman All Saints Episcopal Ch., 1996—. Recipient Carnation Cmty. Svc. award Vol. Action Ctr., 1979, gov.'s arts award State of Nev., 1981. Mem. PEO (past pres.), Kappa Alpha Theta (past pres. alumna club). Republican. Avocations: travel, bridge, reading, aerobics, grandchildren.

FOLSOM, VIRGINIA JEAN, music educator; b. Oakland, Calif., Mar. 26, 1944; d. John Dixon Vincent and Marjorie Estelle Toothaker; d. Virginia J. Hansen; m. Robert Bruce Folsom, Oct. 19, 1970; children: Paul Dixon, Colleen Marie, Katherine Anne. BFA cum laude, U. Utah, 1973. Piano recitalist, 1960—; tchr. music, 1968—; lectr. music, 1972—; instr. piano U. Utah, Salt Lake City, 1982-83. Vol. Utah Pub. Schs., Salt Lake City, 1970-98. Mem. Music Tchrs. Nat. Assn. (chpt. v.p., Tchr.'s Enrichment grantee 2000), United Fedn. Music Clubs (chpt. treas.), Mu Phi Epsilon. Democrat. Mem. Lds Ch. Avocations: music, reading, cooking. E-mail: gfols@yahoo.com.

FOLTZ, KATRINA MARIE, music educator; b. Dubois, Pa., Feb. 10, 1976; d. John Max and Mary Linda Foltz. MusB in Edn., Mercyhurst Coll., 1998, MA in Ednl. Leadership, 2001. Pvt. music tchr., Erie, Pa., 1995—; music tchr. Our Lady of Peace Sch., Erie, 1998—2001, Jamestown (N.Y.) Pub. Schs., 2001; choral dir. Woodrow Wilson Mid. Sch., Erie, 2001—03, N.W. Pa. Collegiate Acad., Erie, 2003—. Organist, pianist Sacred Heart Cath. Ch., Erie, 1998—2001; accompanist A Canterbury Feast Dinner Theatre, Erie, 2001—; organist, pianist St. Jude's Cath. Ch., Erie, 2002—; music dir. Our Lady of Peace Playhouse, Erie, 1998—, bd. dir.; music dir. Erie (Pa.) Playhouse, 2003, condr., 03. Musician: St. Peter's Cathedral, 2001, St. Patrick's Cathedral, 2002, St. Peter's Basilica. Mem.: Pa. State Educators Assn., Music Educators Nat. Conf. (v.p. 1996), Kappa Gamma Pi. Office: NW Pa Collegiate Acad 2825 State St Erie PA 16508

FONDA, JANE, actress; b. N.Y.C., Dec. 21, 1937; d. Henry and Frances (Seymour) F.; m. Roger Vadim (div.); 1 child, Vanessa; m. Tom Hayden, Jan. 20, 1973 (div.); 1 child, Troy; m. Ted Turner, Dec. 21, 1991 (div. 2001). Student, Vassar Coll. Appeared on Broadway stage in There Was a Little Girl, 1960, The Fun Couple, 1962; appeared in Actor's Studio prodn. Strange Interlude, 1963; appeared in films Tall Story, 1960, A Walk on the Wild Side, 1962, Period of Adjustment, 1962, Sunday in New York, 1963, In the Cool of the Day, 1963, The Love Cage, 1963, La Ronde, 1964, Cat Ballou, 1965, The Chase, 1966, Any Wednesday, 1966, The Game Is Over, 1967, Hurry Sundown, 1967, Barefoot in the Park, 1967, Barbarella, 1968, Spirits of the Dead, 1969, They Shoot Horses, Don't They?, 1969, Klute, 1970 (Acad. award best actress), Steelyard Blues, 1973, A Doll's House, 1973, The Blue Bird, 1976, Fun with Dick and Jane, 1976, Julia, 1977, also producer Coming Home, 1978 (Acad. award best actress), California Suite, 1978, Comes a Horseman, 1978, also producer The China Syndrome, 1979, Electric Horseman, 1979, Nine to Five, 1980, On Golden Pond, 1981, Rollover, 1981, The Dollmaker, 1984 (ABC-TV, Emmy award best actress), Agnes of God, 1985, The Morning After, 1986 (Acad. award nomination best actress), Old Gringo, 1988, Stanley and Iris, 1990, producer Lakota Woman, 1994; (TV miniseries) A Century of Women, 1994; author: Jane Fonda's Workout Book, 1981, Women Coming of Age, 1984, Jane Fonda's New Workout & Weight-Loss Program, 1986, Jane Fonda's New Pregnancy Workout & Total Birth Program, 1989, Jane Fonda Workout Video, 12 additional videos. Recipient Golden Apple prize for female star of yr. Hollywood Women's Press Club, 1977, Golden Globe award, 1978; rated no. 1 heroine of young Ams., U.S. News Roper Poll, 1985, 4th most admired woman in Am., Ladies Home Jour. Roper Poll, 1985. Office: Creative Artists Agy care Kim Hodgert 9830 Wilshire Blvd Beverly Hills CA 90212-1804

FONG, BERNADINE CHUCK, academic administrator; BA, MA, PhD, Stanford U. Psychology and child devel. prof.; pres. Foothill Coll., Los Altos Hills, Calif., 1994—. Vis. prof., scholar Stanford U. Sch. Edn.; vice-chair Univ. Bd. Trustees Minority Alumni Rels. Task Force; bd. mem. Nat. Ctr. for Postsecondary Improvement Bd. Sr. Scholars, SCT Corp. Exec. Adv. Coun., Am. Inst. for Fgn. Study Bd. Acad. Advisors; trustee Stanford U., Menlo Coll., Am. Assn. C.C., CEO's of Calif. C.C., Assn. for Calif. C.C. Adminstrs., ACE Leadership Devel. Commn., Coun. for Internat. Edn. and Exch. Recipient Phenomenal Woman award, Harold Washington Coll. Chpt., Am. Assn. Women in C.C., 2002. Mem.: Carnegie Found. for Advancement Tchg. (bd. mem.). Office: Foothill Coll 12345 El Monte Rd Los Altos CA 94022

FONG, HEATHER J. protective services official; b. San Francisco; BA, MA in social work, U. San Francisco. With San Francisco Police Dept., 1977—, deputy chief police, 2000—03, acting asst. police chief, 2003, asst. chief police, 2003—04, acting chief police, 2004. Recipient Officer Yr. award, 1979, Outstanding Pub. Svc. award, Asian Pacific Am. Cmty. Ctr., 2003. Office: Hall of Justice 850 Bryant St Rm 549 San Francisco CA 94103*

FONG, PHYLLIS KAMOI, federal agency administrator, lawyer; b. Phila., Oct. 16, 1953; d. Bernard W.D. and Roberta (Wat) F.; m. Paul E. Tellier, Nov. 25, 1978. BA, Pomona Coll., 1975; JD, Vanderbilt U., 1978. Bar: Tenn. 1978, D.C. 1982. Atty. U.S. Commn. on Civil Rights, Washington, 1978-81; asst. gen. counsel Legal Svcs. Corp., Washington, 1981-83; assoc. counsel to the insp. gen. U.S. Small Bus. Admin., Washington, 1983-88, asst. insp. gen. for mgmt. and policy, 1988-94, asst. insp. gen. for mgmt. and legal counsel, 1994-99, insp. gen., 1999—. Mem. ABA, Tenn. Bar Assn., D.C. Bar Assn. Office: Small Bus Admin Off of Insp Gen 409 3rd St SW Washington DC 20416

FONTAINE-WHITE, BARBARA FRANCES, art educator; b. Watervliet, NY, Aug. 31, 1955; d. Raymond Leo Fontaine and Caroline Elenor Harnish; m. William Daniel IV White, Jan. 9, 1981; children: Justin William White, Aaron Daniel White. BA, SUNY, Albany, 1978, MA, 1981; MFA, So. Meth. U., 1984. Cert. tchr. Tex. Adv. art instr. Eastfield Coll., Mesquite, Tex., 1984—96; continuing edn. art instr. So. Meth. U., Dallas, 1984—96, adj. art instr., 1985—87; art specialist, ESL tchr. Dallas Ind. Sch. Dist., 1993—96; asst. prof. art U. Mary-Hartin Baylor, Belton, Tex., 1997—. Exhibitions include Cultural Activities Ctr., 2000, Hermanas en Arte Exch. Show, 2001, Temple Coll. Downtown Ctr., 2003. Membership chmn. Dallas Area Educators of Art, 1993—96; col. Outback Steakhouse Cmty. Outreach, Killeen, Tex., 1997—. Recipient Meadows fellowship, So. Meth. U., 1982—84. Mem.: Tex. Interacholastic Press Assn. (award for yearbook 2001, 2002, 2003), Coll. Art Assn., Killeen C. of C. Roman Catholic. Avocations: art history, fitness, reading. Home: 506 Impala Killeen TX 76548 Office: U Mary Hardin Baylor 900 College St Box 8012 Belton TX 76513

FONTANA, SANDRA ELLEN FRANKEL, special education educator; b. N.Y.C., July 12, 1951; d. Robert Lowell and Mildred (Tropan) Sharoff; m. Jay Tommy Frankel, May 25, 1973 (div. 1993); children: Austin, Lauren; m. David Fontana, July 27, 2002; stepchildren: Troy, Tara. BS in Med. Tech., Rochester (N.Y.) Inst. Tech., 1973; MA in Linguistics, Gallaudet U., 1984. Cert. comprehensive permanent S.I.G.N. Nat. Assn. Deaf SIGN Instr. Guidance Network, 1985, profl. Am. Sign Language Tchr. Assn. (ASLTA), 1986. Coord. bus. affairs/sign lang. program dept. bus. affairs Gallaudet U., 1980-83; coord. dept. sign communication faculty retreat N000, winter 1981; instr. dept. interpreter/translator instruction Gallaudet U., 1981-84, instr. in sign lang. dept. sign communication, spring 1982, ASL instr. dept. sign communication, 1982-84, coord. NDC sign lang. program dept. sign communication, 1984-88, instr. dept. sign communication, 1984-88, head instr./trainer, ASL instr. dept. sign communication, 1988-89, ASL instr. Coll. Continuing Edn. extension/summer programs, 1988; assoc. prof. interpreting preparation program C.C. Balt. County, 1990—2002, Riverside (Calif.) C.C., 2002—. Evaluator Sign Instr. Guidance Network, Indpls., 1989-90; mem. Sign Instr. Guidance Network; bd. dir. State Md. Office Govr. Assistive Tech. Guaranteed Loan Program, 1999-2002. Mem. Am. Sign Lang. Tchr. Assn. (evaluator 1990-), Nat. Assn. of the Deaf, Metro. Wash. Assn. of the Deaf, Md. Assn. of the Deaf. Home: 1540 Highridge Rd Riverside CA 92506 Office: Riverside CC 4800 Magnolia Ave Riverside CA 92506

FONTENOTE-JAMERSON, BELINDA, museum director; Pres. Mus. African Am. Art, L.A. Office: Mus African Am Art 4005 S Crenshaw Blvd Fl 3 Los Angeles CA 90008-2534

FONTES, PATRICIA J. educational psychologist; b. Providence, Dec. 10, 1936; d. Manuel William and Conceicao Elizabeth (Sousa) F. BS in Edn., Boston U., 1957; MEd, Boston Coll., 1965, PhD, 1968. Tchr. Warwick (R.I.) pub. schs., 1957-59; religious sister/superior Sisters of Our Lady of Providence, 1959-65; asst. prof. U. R.I., Kingston, 1968-69; asst./assoc. prof. Salve Regina Coll., Newport, R.I., 1969-72; cons. psychologist Girl Scouts of R.I., Inc., Providence, 1972-73; research fellow Ednl. Research Ctr., St. Patrick's Coll., Dublin, Ireland, 1973-88; cons. psychologist Girl Scouts R.I., Providence, 1989-92; prof. CEFOPE, U. Minho, Braga, Portugal, 1992—. Lectr. in field. Author: Equality in Primary Teaching 1985, As Crianças, como Agentes de Mudança Ambiental; contbr. articles to profl. jours. Boston U. scholar, 1953-57; Boston Coll. fellow, 1965-68; Inst. for Portuguese Lang. and Culture grantee, 1982. Mem. APA, Am. Ednl. Rsch. Assn., Nat. Coun. on Measurement in Edn., Internat. Coun. Psychologists (sec.-gen. 1991-94), Internat. Assn. Applied Psychology. Roman Catholic. Avocations: biking, mountain walking, travel, gardening, reading, cooking.

FOOTE, EVELYN PATRICIA, retired military officer; b. Durham, N.C., May 19, 1930; d. Henry Alexander and Evelyn Sevena (Womack) Foote. BA summa cum laude, Wake Forest U., 1953, LLD (hon.), 1989; student, U.S. Army Command & Gen. Staff Coll., Leavenworth, Kans., 1971-72, U.S. Army War Coll., Carlisle, Pa., 1976-77; MS in Govt. and Pub. Affairs, Shippensburg State U., 1977; student, U. Va. Sch. Bus. Adminstrn., 1980. Commd. 1st lt. U.S. Army, 1960, advanced through grades to brig. gen., 1986, platoon officer WAC, 1960-61, selection officer 6th recruiting dist. Portland, Oreg., 1961-64; comdr. WAC Co. U.S. Army Engr. Brigade, Ft. Belvoir, Va., 1964-66; student Adj. Gen. Officer Advanced Course, Ft. Benjamin Harrison, Ind., 1966; exec. officer, chief adminstrv. div. pub. affairs office U.S. Army, Vietnam, 1967; exec. officer, office personnel ops. WAC, Washington, 1968-71, plans and programs officer OFC, dir., 1972-74; personnel mgmt. officer U.S. Army Forces Command, Ft. McPherson, Ga., 1974-76; comdr. 2d basic tng. bn. U.S. Army Tng. Brigade and Military Police Sch., Ft. McClellan, Ala., 1977-79; faculty mem. U.S. Army War Coll., 1979-82; student Fgn. Service Inst., Dept. of State, Washington, 1982-83; comdr. 42d Mil. Police Group, Mannheim, Fed. Republic of Germany, 1983-85; spl. asst. to comdg. gen. 32d Army Air Def. Command Hdqrs., Darmstadt, Fed. Republic of Germany, 1985-86; dep., insp. gen. for inspections Hdqrs. Dept. of the Army, Washington, 1986-88; dep. comdg. gen. Mil. Dist. Washington, comdr. Ft. Belvoir, Va., 1988-89; ret. U.S. Army, 1989, recalled to active duty Sr. Rev. Panel, 1996-97, ret., 1997. Lectr. various U.S. Army and civilian groups. Contbr. articles to mil. jours. and books. Mem. Am Battle Monuments Commn., 1994—2001; bd. visitors Wake Forest U., 1991—2003, chmn. bd. visitors, 2001—03; trustee Fund for Peace, 2002—; bd. dirs. U.S. Army Women's Mus. Found., 1995—. Decorated DSM, Legion of Merit with oak leaf clusters, German Cross of Svc. 1st class; named Spokesperson of the Yr., Dept. Army, 1997—98; named to Disting. Fellows Hall of Fame, U.S. Army War Coll., 1996, Regimental Hall of Fame, U.S. Army MP Corps, 1998; recipient Disting. Pub. Svc. award, Wake Forest U., 1987, DSM, Am. Battle Monuments Commn., 2001. Mem.: Zonta. Democrat. Lutheran. Avocations: music, reading, hiking.

FOOTE, JILL, film producer, educator, investment banker; b. Covington, La., Nov. 1, 1964; d. Richard Quentin and Jo Lynn F.; m. Adiel Jacob Eshkenazi, Sept. 2, 2001. BA in Econ. and Managerial Studies, Rice U., Houston, 1987; MA in Econ., NYU, 1992; PHD in Econ., Fordham U., Bronx, N.Y., 2002. Fixed income sales assoc. Goldman Sachs & Co., N.Y.C., 1987—93, v.p., 1993—99; founder, mng. mem. Jillybean Prodns., LLC, L.A., 2000—02. Cons. Net.Univ., L.A., 2001—02; mem. Ind. Film Project/West; asst. prof. Rice U., 2002—. Bd. dirs. Rice U. Alumni, 1998—2002. Mem.: Assn. Investment Mgmt. and Rsch. Avocations: reading, backgammon, dogs, movies, music. Office: Jones Grad Sch 6100 Main St Houston TX 77005 Home: 5011 Jackwood St Houston TX 77096-1506

FOOTE, SHERRILL LYNNE, retired manufacturing company technician; b. Marshalltown, Iowa, Apr. 19, 1940; d. Howard Raymond and Lois Ellen Ellis; m. Terry D. Downey, July 27, 1958 (div. 1978); children: Patrick L., Holly L. Harrelson; m. Frank H. Foote, Nov. 17, 1979 (div. 1989); stepchildren: Lauri K., Christopher R. Student, Marshalltown C.C., 1981—. Receptionist Drs. Long & Clawson, Marshalltown, 1958-59; clk. Fisher Controls, Marshalltown, 1963-73, cost estimating analyst, 1974-82, sr. cost estimator, 1982-95. Contbr. limericks Des Moines Register (Contest Winner), 1976, Marshalltown Times Rep., 1986. Mem. Mensa (contbr. Bull. Wordplay 1981—, limerick editor M-Pressions Ctrl. Iowa newsletter 1989-91, local sec. 1991-93). Democrat. Methodist. Avocations: games, reading, movies, plays. Home: 702 Ratcliffe Dr Marshalltown IA 50158-3453

FOOTE-KRAGBE, MARILYN, elementary school educator; b. Buffalo, Nov. 2, 1952; d. Lonnie Charles Foote and Mary Ellen Dryer; children: Lisa Monique Kragbe, Tatchy Benny Kragbe. BS in Elem. Edn., Rosary Hill Coll., 1974; MS in Elem. Edn., SUNY, 1989. Tchr. kindergarten Guardian Angel Day Care, Buffalo, 1974—76; tchr. elem. sch. Intrnat. Sch. Abidjan, 1976—88; tchr. presch. Early Childhood Rsch. Ctr., Amherst, NY, 1988—89; tchr. elem. sch. Buffalo Pub. Schs., 1989—. Sci. facilitator Buffalo Pub. Schs., 1995—99, tchr., mentor Deamen Coll., Amherst, 1999—. Contbr. articles to profl. jours. Mem.: NAACP, African Am. Hist. Western N.Y. State. Avocations: poetry, walking, Bible study, volleyball. E-mail: foote52@localnet.com.

FORBES, SARAH ELIZABETH, gynecologist, real estate corporation officer; b. Currituck, N.C., May 4, 1928; d. Dexter and Mary (Brock) Forbes. BA, U. Rochester, 1949; MD, Med. Coll. of Va., 1954. Diplomate Am. Bd. Ob-Gyn. Intern Norfolk (Va.) Gen. Hosp., 1954-55; resident ob-gyn Johnston-Willis Hosp., 1955-56, Norfolk Gen. Hosp., 1956-57, chief resident, 1957-58; pvt. practice gynecologist Newport News, Va., 1958—; pres., real estate investor Mary B. Forbes Land Corp., Newport News, 1972—; pres. Sebrof Corp., Newport News, 1978—, Haras, Inc., Newport News, 1984—, S.S. U.S., Inc., Newport News, 1984—. Bd. dirs. Family Planning Coun.; mem. teaching staff ob-gyn dept. Riverside Hosp. Pres. Peninsula Soc. for Prevention Cruelty to Animals, 1966—; mem. adv. bd. Peninsula chpt. Parents without Ptnrs.; bd. dirs. Newport News chpt. Am. Cancer Soc., pres., 2d v.p., 1971-72, 1st v.p., 1972-73, pres., 1973-74, chmn. rsch., 1961-69; candidate for Newport News City Coun., 1986; bd. dirs. Va. Peninsula Boys and Girls Club, 1991-99, 1st v.p., pres. Va. Peninsula Boys and Girls Club, 2000—. Recipient AMA Physicians Recognition award for Continuing Edn., 1973-76, Twin award Va. Peninsula YWCA, 1987, Medallion award Peninsula Boys and Girls Club, 1993; named Woman of Yr. for Peninsula Area, 1975. Mem. Va. Peninsula Acad. Medicine (pres. 1973-74, v.p. 1972-73, sec., treas. 1971-72); fellow AMA, Va. Med. Soc., Newport News Med. Soc. Am. Coll. Ob-Gyn, Tidewater Ob-Gyn Soc. Office: 12420 Warwick Blvd Newport News VA 23606-3001

FORBES, SHARON ELIZABETH, software engineer; b. Lynn, Mass., Nov. 23, 1960; d. Leland James Brown and Vail (Wilkinson) Bartelson. BSChemE, U. Mass., 1983. Software engr. K&L Automation div. Daniel Industry, Tucson, 1983-86, 1986-87, asst. mgr. software systems, 1987; software mgr. Daniel Automation, Houston, 1987-91; sr. software engr. Praxis Instruments, Inc., Houston, 1991-93, Dresser Measurement, Houston, 1993-97, Dresser Roots Instruments Operation, Houston, 1997-98, Roots Meters and Instruments, Houston, 1999-2001, Dresser Inc., Houston, 2001; sr. softward engr. Omni Flow Computers, Inc., Stafford, Tex., 2002—. Republican. Avocations: church, contemporary jazz, computers. Home: 5735 Henniker Dr Houston TX 77041-6589 Office: Omni Flow Computers Inc 10701 Corporate Dr Ste 300 Stafford TX 77477 E-mail: sforbes@omniflow.com.

FORBES JOHNSON, MARY GLADYS, retired secondary school educator; b. Bend, Oreg., June 19, 1929; d. Percy Lloyd and Bertha May

(Gettman) F.; married, 1996 BA in Edn. magna cum laude, Cascade Coll., 1951; BS in Edn., Western Oreg. State Coll., Monmouth, 1951, MS in Edn., 1968. Cert. tchr., Oreg. Tchr. Christian & Missionary Alliance, Mamou, Guinea, West Africa, 1952-54, Bend (Oreg.)-Redmond Christian Day Sch., 1954-56, Dalat Sch., Asia, 1956-76, Bend-LaPine Sch. Dist. 1, Bend, [illegible], administr., tchr., 1981-87, tchr. kindergarten Thompson Sch., 1989-99. Cons. Chpt. I Program in Spl. Edn., 1976-88; supt. Sunday sch. Christian and Missionary Alliance, 1976-80, Faith Fellowship Four Sq., Madras, Oreg., 1981-88. Mem. Citizens for the Republic, Washington, 1989; mem. Rep. Nat. Com., 1990—. Recipient cert. of appreciation Hale Found., 1986, 87, Skyhook II Project, 1987, Concerned Women Am., 1987, Nat. Law Enforcement Officer Meml., 1991, Am. Indian Relief Coun., 1992. Mem. Am. Def. Inst., Nat. Right to Life Com., Coun. for Inter-Am. Security, Nat. Assn. for Uniformed Svcs., Concerned Women for Am., Capitol Hill Women's Club, Christian Coalition, Am. Ctr. for Law and Justice, Am. Life League, Oreg. Citizens Alliance, Heritage Found., Delta Kappa Gamma. Avocations: gardening, cycling, hiking, farming. Home: PO Box 107 Bend OR 97709-0107 Office: Bend LaPine Sch Dist 1 520 NW Wall St Bend OR 97701-2608

FORBUSH, SANDRA M. artist, educator; b. Garden City, N.Y., Jan. 14, 1940; d. John Herbert Jr. and Mary Elizabeth (Keeler) Mears; m. Wade Hampton Massie III, Mar. 27 (div. Aug. 1980); 1 child, Nancy Massie Wiley; m. Lloyd Augustus Forbush, Sept. 6, 1982. Student, Md. Inst. Art, Balt., 1957-59. Fashion model Garfinckel & Co., Washington, 1960-65; fashion freelance model, commls. and TV Washington, Balt., N.Y.C; ballet tchr. Wakefield Country Day Sch., Huntly, Va., piano tchr.; profl. portrait artist, art tchr. self-employed, Flint Hill, Va. Ofcl. artist The Va. Gold Cup, Great Meadow, 2002, $100,000 Grand Prix Jumper Classic, Great Meadow, 2002. One-woman shows include Montpelier, Va., Middleburg Libr., Fifth St. Gallery; exhibited in shows at Am. Acad. Equine Art, 1999, The Dog Mus., St. Louis, Farmington Hunt Club, Beresford Gallery, Saratoga Springs, N.Y., Mus. of Hounds and Hunting, At the Dog Show, Wichita, Kans., Somoza Gallery, Houston, 2000, others; offl. artist Va. Gold Cup, 2002, Grand Prix, Gt. Meadow, 2002; works include sporting art in oil, numerous portraits in oil; contbr. articles to profl. jours. Mem.: Am. Acad. Equine Art (assoc.). Episcopalian. Home: Foxhall Farm Box 149 Flint Hill VA 22627 E-mail: sforbush@rmaonline.net.

FORCE, CHRISTINE, small business developer; b. Brockton, Mass., Dec. 11, 1948; d. James Louis Force and Miriam Jesse Carter; m. Richard Gregory Mraz, Aug. 21, 1999; m. Richard Hill-Rowley, Mar. 17, 1978 (div. Sept. 15, 1995); 1 child, Trevor Hill-Rowley. BA, U. Mass., 1971; postgrad., Mich. State U., 2001—. Cert. cartography Mich. State U., 1974. Cartographer Met. Area Planning Commn., Boston, 1977, Camp Dresser and McKee, 1977—78; econ. devel. specialist State of Mich., Lansing, 1982—2000; licensing assoc./small bus. devel. Mich. State U., East Lansing, 2000—. Author: The Preservation Directory; asst. cartographic editor Atlas of Michigan. Chair Hist. Dist. Study Com., East Lansing, 1987—89. Janet Loria Grad. Student scholar, Mich. State U., Coll. Human Ecology, 2002. Mem.: The Textile Mus., Assn. U. Tech. Managers, Am. Assn. Mus., Costume Soc. Am. Avocations: fiber arts, travel. Home: 1858 Linden St East Lansing MI 48823 Office: Michigan State U 246 Adminstrn Bldg East Lansing MI 48824 Personal E-mail: forcec@msu.edu.

FORCE, ELIZABETH ELMA, retired pharmaceutical executive; b. Phila., Sept. 6, 1930; d. Harry Elgin and Loretta G. (Werner) Force. BA, Temple U., 1952; postgrad., U. Pa., 1965-67; MPh, George Washington U., 1972, PhD, 1973. Cons. sr. scientist Booz-Allen Hamilton, Bethesda, Md., 1967-68; rsch. cons. scientist GEOMET, Inc., Rockville, Md., 1968-70; profl. assoc. div. med. scis. NAS-NRC, Washington, 1970-74; mgr. clin. adminstrn. dept. clin. rsch. and devel. Wyeth Labs., Radnor, Pa., 1974-77; exec. dir. regulatory affairs Merck Sharp and Dohme Rsch. Labs., West Point, Pa., 1977-88; cons. Clin. Regulatory Systems, Sarasota, Fla., 1988-91. Asst. prof. epidemiology and environ. health Sch. Medicine George Washington U., Washington, 1972—74; vis. assoc. prof. cmty. health and preventive medicine Med. Coll. Jefferson U., Phila., 1981—83. Editor: Clin. Rsch. Practice and Drug Regulatory Affairs, 1983—85, Drug Info. Jour., 1984—88; contbr. articles to profl. jours. Chmn. adv. coun. bd. trustees Ringling Mus. Art, 1991—95; pres. bd. dirs. Siesta Tower Condominium Assn., Sarasota, 1990—92; vice chmn. Com. Minotiry Contracts, Sarasota County, 1991; pres. Women's Resource Ctr., Sarasota, 1992—94; chmn. adv. coun. bd. trustees Coun. Violence, Sarasota County, 1994; pres. Sterling Lakes Owners Assn., Boynton Beach, 1996—98; mem. steering com. Harid Conservatory Music, Lynn U., Boca Raton, 1999—2000; chmn. resident coun. Abbey Delray S., 2004—. Pub. Health fellow, U. Pa. Sch. Medicine, 1965—67, Ruhland Pub. Health fellow, George Washington U. Sch. Medicine, 1971—73. Mem.: AAUW, Durg Info. Assn. (pres. 1986—87, Outstanding Dir. award 1985), Heritage Soc. George Washington U., Torch Club Boca Raton. Avocation: collecting oriental antiques. Home: 1717 Homewood Blvd Apt 247 Delray Beach FL 33445-6801

FORCE, JILL L. health facility executive; BA in Polit. Sci., Miami U.; MSA, Georgetown U.; JD, U. Louisville. Acct. Coopers & Lybrand; atty. Greenebaum, Doll & McDonald, Louisville, Hirn, Reed & Harper, Louisville; sr. v.p., gen. counsel Vencor, Inc., Louisville, 1989—. Bd. dirs. Healthcare Recoveries, Inc. Trustee J.B. Speed Art Mus., Spirit of Louisville Found. Office: Vencor Inc 680 S 4th St Ste 1 Louisville KY 40202-2412

FORCIER, TERESA ELAINE, state legislator; b. Oct. 6, 1953; d. Waid Stanley and Elaine Agusta (Swift) Fosburg; children: Christopher, Delaine. Student, Alliance Coll., Edinboro U. Legis. aide 6th Legis. Dist., Meadville, Pa., 1979-86, 5th Legis. Dist., Meadville, 1987; per diem employee Crawford County, Meadville, 1988-89, asst. dir. tax claim bur., 1989-90; mem. Pa. Ho. of Reps., Titusville, 1991—; mem. appropriations com., transp. com. Sec. Legis. Office for Rsch. Liaison; co-chmn. Emergency Svcs. Outreach Group; active Fire Fighters Caucus, Task Force on Jobs and Bus. Expansion, Task Force on Environ., Task Force on Welfare Reform, Anti-gambling Caucus. Former editor Crawford County GOP Newsletter. Former asst. coord. Cambridge Springs (Pa.) Little League and Little Griddlers; former mem. Miss Crawford County Pageant Scholarship Exec. Bd., Cambridge Springs Presbyn. Food Pantry; mem. adv. bd. U. Pitts., Titusville; past dist. leader GOP Cambridge Dist.; active Cambridge Springs Presbyn. Ch., also former mem. bd. deacons; active Meadville Med. Ctr. Aux., Pa. Ag Reps., Craford County GOP Exec. Bd., Northwest Coun. Rep. Women, Capitol Area Coun. Rep. Women in Govt. Mem. NRA, Bus. and Profl. Women, Meadville Sportsmen Club, Pa Ruffled Grouse Soc., Kiwanis Club of Cambridge Springs. Home: 629 State St Meadville PA 16335-2262 Office: 401 S OFC PO Box 202020 Harrisburg PA 17120-2020

FORD, ALMA REGINA, union official, educator; b. Owings, W.Va., Oct. 4, 1939; d. Charles Feathers and Pearl (Costello) Ford. AB, Fairmont State Coll., 1960; MA, W.Va. U., 1964, Ball State U., 1984; postgrad., Sorbonne. Cert. counselor. Tchr., Ohio, 1961—78, 1961—78, 1961—78, 1961—78, 1961—78, 1961—78, 1961—78; v.p., dep. rep. Dept. Def. Dependents Schs.-Europe; negotiator Overseas Fedn. Tchrs., 1978—80; tchr. Zweibrucken, Germany, 1980—, counselor, 1997; ret., 1999—2003. Del. various internat. meetings. Recipient Sustained Superior/Performance award, Dept. Army, 1972—76, Exceptional Performance award, 1984; NDEA fellow, 1968. Mem.: LWV, AARP, AAUW, Marion County Ret. Tchrs. Assn., W.Va. Sheriff's Assn., Overseas Fedn. Tchrs., Am. Fedn. Tchrs., Speech Assn. Am., Nat. Assn. Ret. People, Nat. Coun. Tchrs. English, Nat. Assn. Ret. Fed. Employees, Zweibrucken Alumnus Assn., Fairmont State Coll. Alumnus Assn., Ret. Eagles Club, W.Va. Travelers Club, Moose, Elks, Eagles Ladies Aux., Am. Legion Ladies Aux., VFW Ladies Aux., Alpha Psi Omega, Phi Delta Kappa. Home: 13 Eldora St Fairmont WV 26554-7967

FORD, ANABEL, research anthropologist, archaeologist; b. LA, Dec. 22, 1951; d. Joseph B. Ford and Marjorie Henshaw; m. Michael A. Glassow, May 4, 1974. BA in Anthropology, U. Calif., Santa Barbara, 1974, MA in Anthropology, 1976, PhD in Anthropology, 1981. Teaching asst. dept. anthropology & environ. studies U. Calif., Santa Barbara, 1975-80, rsch. asst. archaeologist office of pub. archaeology, 1980-81, lectr. dept. archaeology, 1982—, asst. rsch. archaeologist Social Process Rsch. Inst., 1982-87, founding dir. MesoAmerican Rsch. Ctr., 1987, asst. rsch. archaeologist Community Orgn. Rsch. Inst., 1987-91, assoc. rsch. archaeologist, 1991-98, dir. MesoAm. Rsch. Ctr., 1991-98, rsch. archeologist Inst. Social, Behavioral and Econ. Rsch., 1998—; assoc. rsch. archaeologist Inst. Social, Behavioral and Econ. Rsch., 1991-98, rsch. archaeologist, 1998—. Vis. asst. prof. dept. anthropology UCLA, 1987-89; co-participant USIA, 1995-96; active commn. Centroamericana de Ambiente Y Desarrollo, 1996, Mac Arthur World Environment and Resources Program, 1997, Inst. for Internat. Edn., 1998; program initiator Ford Found., 1998; co-dir. Rsch. Across Disciplines, 1999; lectr., presenter in field. Contbr. over 50 articles to profl. jours. Supr. Vol. Lab. and Field Program, 1978—; pres. Exploring Solutions Past-the Maya Forest Alliance. Humanities fellow U. Calif., Santa Barbara, 1989-91; Fulbright rsch. scholar, 1986, 90; grantee U. Calif., Santa Barbara, L.S.B. Leakey Found., NSF, NEH, Heinz Found., Wenner-Gren, CIRMA, CIES/USIS, Univ. Rsch. Expeditions Program, Ford Found., Fulbright-Hays Found; recipient Rolex award for Enterprise, 2000, Outstanding Cmty. Svc. award U.S. Senate, 2000, certificate of recognition Amigos de El Pilar Belize/Guatemala, 2000; named Educator of Yr. Goleta Chamber, 2000, Calif. State Assembly, 2000, Calif. State Senate, 2000, Alumna of Yr., U. Calif., Santa Barbara, 2003. Mem. AAAS, Am. Anthropol. Assn., Soc. for Am. Archaeology, Assn. for Field Archaeology, Sociedad Mexicana de Antropologia, So. Calif. Mesoamerican Network, UCSB Affiliated Faculty Women, Assn. for Belizean Archaeology, Belize Ctr. for Environ. Studies, Sigma Xi. Office: U Calif Inst Social Behav & Econ Rsch Santa Barbara CA 93106-2150 E-mail: ford@marc.ucsb.edu., elpilar@btl.net.

FORD, ANN SUTER, family nurse practitioner, health planner; b. Mineola, N.Y., Oct. 31, 1943; d. Robert M. and Jennette (Van Derzee) Suter; m. W. Scott Ford, 1964; children: Tracey, Karin, Stuart. RN White Plains Hosp., Sch. Nursing (N.Y.), 1964; BS in Nursing with high distinction, U. Ky., 1967; MS in Health Planning, Fla. State U., 1971, PhD, 1975, MSN, 1992. Nurse U. Ky. Med. Ctr., 1964-65, Tallahassee Meml. Hosp., 1968-69; guest lectr. health planning dept. urban/regional planning Fla. State U., Tallahassee, 1973-76, health planner and research assoc., 1974-76, vis. asst. prof., 1976-77, asst. prof. and dir. health planning splty., 1977-83, assoc. prof., 1982-83, health care analyst and policy cons., 1983-86; med., health program analyst Aging and Adult Svcs. for State of Fla., 1986-90; coordinator Fla. Alzheimer's Disease Initiative, 1986-90; family nurse practitioner Capital Area Physicians' Svcs., 1993-94; assoc. prof. nursing Fla. A&M U., 1994—2002; clin. nurse Tallahassee Meml. Regional Ctr., 1990—. Bd. dirs. Regional Fla. Lung Assn., 1986-91; mem. exec. com. human services and social planning tech. dept. Am. Inst. Planners, 1977-83. Author: The Physician's Assistant: A National and Local Analysis, 1975; contbr. numerous articles on health edn. and health planning to profl. jours.; contbr. chpts. to books; author rsch. reports. USPHS grantee, 1965-67; HEW grantee, 1978; Univ. fellow Fla. State U., 1971-72; recipient Am. Inst. Planners' Student award, 1975. Mem. Am. Planning Assn. (charter mem. human services and social planning tech. dept. 1976-83, chmn. health planning session Oct. 1978, 79, health policy liaison 1979-83, author assn. health policy statement), Am. Health Planning Assn., Fla. Nurses Assn., Phi Kappa Phi, Sigma Theta Tau. Address: 2602 Cline St Tallahassee FL 32308-0810

FORD, ANNA MARIA, language educator; b. Starachowice, Poland, Aug. 17, 1940; arrived in U.S., 1954; d. Antoni Niedzwiedzki and Wanda Gluszkiewicz; married; 1 child, Alexandra Johanna Paszowski. BA, Wayne State U., 1963, MA, 1970. Cert. secondary edn. tchr. French, Spanish, English Mich., S.C., advanced placement French tchr. S.C., 1999, nat. cert. tchr. adolescence/young adulthood English lang. arts 2001. Tchr. French and Spanish Ford Mid. Sch., Highland Park, Mich., 1965-66; tchr. fgn. lang. dept. Highland Park Cmty. HS, 1966-97, head fgn. lang. dept., 1968-70, 73-78, lang. arts facilitator, 1991-94; owner, founder Horizons-Internat., Grosse Pointe Park, Mich., 1993-97; dist.-wide lang. cons./coord. Highland Park Pub. Schs., 1994-97; Spanish, French and English lang. tchr. Georgetown (S.C.) County Sch. Dist., 1997—. Ind. contractor, cons. Langs. and Svcs. Agy., 1993—; assessor, field study, tchr. performance lang. arts Nat. Bd. Profl. Tchg. Stds., Mich., 1994; scorer writing proficience assessments Mich. Dept. Edn., 1994—97, trainer of tchrs., 1995, trainer of trainers, 1995—97, mem. elem. and secondary content literacy com., 1995—; instrnl./profl. devel. task force Mid. Cities Assn., Lansing, Mich., 1995—97; mem. North Ctrl. Accreditation Evaluation Teams, 1970—97; cons. Coastal Area Writing Project, SC, 1998—; TEAM evaluator, asst. tng. evaluator, SC, 1999—; advisor H.S. yearbook Polar Bear, 1985—86. Editor: (newsletter) Happenings, 1977—79, Mich. Writing Assessment News, 1994—97. Bd. dirs. Friends of Polish Art, Mich., 1995—97, French Inst. Mich., Southfield, 1985—97. Recipient Big E award, Josten's Printing Divsn., 1986, cert. appreciation for participation in Classrooms of Tomorrow program, Mich. Gov., 1990. Mem.: AAUW, Alliance Francaise (Detroit/Grosse Pointe/Charleston), Alpha Mu Gamma. Roman Catholic. Avocations: travel, sailing, skiing, literature, music. Home: 38 Wexford Ln River Club Pawleys Island SC 29585-7614 Office: Horizons Internat 38 Wexford Ln Pawleys Island SC 29585-7614

FORD, BARBARA JEAN, library studies educator; b. Dixon, Ill., Dec. 5, 1946; BA magna cum laude with honors, Ill. Wesleyan U., 1968; MA in Internat. Rels., Tufts U., 1969; MS in Libr. Sci., U. Ill., 1973. Dir. Soybean Insect Rsch. Info. Ctr. Ill. Natural History Survey, Urbana, 1973-75; from asst. to assoc. prof. U. Ill., Chgo., 1975-84, asst. documents libr., 1975-79, documents libr., dept. head, 1979-84, acting audiovisual libr., 1983-84; asst. dir. pub. svcs. Trinity U., San Antonio, 1984-86, assoc. prof., assoc. dir., 1986-91, acting dir. librs., 1989, 91; prof., dir. univ. libr. svcs. Va. Commonwealth U., Richmond, 1991-98; asst. commr. Chgo. Pub. Libr., 1998—2002; dir., disting. prof. Mortenson Ctr. Internat. Libr. Programs, U. Ill., Urbana, 2003—. Mem. women's re-entry adv. bd. U. Ill., Chgo., 1980-82, student affairs com., 1978-80, student admissions, records, coll. rels. com., 1981-84, univ. senate, 1976-78, 82-84, chancellor's libr. coun. svcs. com. 1984, campus lectrs. com. 1982-83; admissions interviewer for prospective students Trinity U., 1987-91, reader for internat. affairs theses, 1985-91, libr. self-study com., 1985-86, internat. affairs com., 1986-91, inter-Am. studies com., 1986-91, faculty senate, 1987-90; with libr. working group U.S./Mex. Commn. Cultural Coop., 1990. Contbr. articles to profl. pubs., papers to presentations. Bd. dirs. Friends of San Antonio Pub. Libr., 1989-91; adv. com. chair Office for Libr. Pers. Resources, 1994-95; mem. steering com. Virtual Libr. Va., 1994-98, chair user svcs. com., 1995-96. Celia M. Howard fellow Tufts U., 1969; sr. fellow UCLA Grad. Sch. Libr. and Info. Sci., 1993. Mem. ALA (conf. program com. 1985-91, libr. edn. assembly 1983-84, membership com. 1978-79, status of women in librarianship com. 1983-85, exec bd., 1996-99, Lippincott Award Jury 1979-80, Shirley Olofson Meml. award 1977), ALA Coun. (at-large councilor 1985-89, chpt. councilor Ill. Libr. Assn. 1980-84, com. on coms. 1987-88, spl. coun. orientation com. 1982-83, ALA exec. bd., 1996-99, pres.- elect 1996-97, pres. 1997-98), Assn. Coll. and Rsch. Librs. (bd. dirs. 1989-92, pres.-elect 1989-90, pres. 1990-91, publs. com. 1990-91, conf. program planning 1990-91), Nat. Assn. State Univs. and Land Grant Colls. (commn. info. tech. 1992-94), Internat. Fedn. Libr. Assns. and Instns. (sec. ofcl. pubs. sect., gen. info. com. 1985 conf., moderator Latin Am. seminar on ofcl. pubs. 1991, univ. and other rsch. librs. sect. standing com. 1999—), Spl. Librs. Assn. (program com. 1976-77, 80-82, publicity com. 1977-79, chair 1978-79, chair spl. projects com. 1981-82, [illegible] internat. affairs sect. 1984-86), Assn. Libr. Info. Sci. Edn. (chair local arrangements conf. planning com. 1988, 92), Ill. Libr. Assn. (chair election com. 1976-77, exec. bd. 1978-79, 80-84, bd. govt. documents round table 1976-79, chair 1978-79, long range planning com. 1980-84), Tex. Libr. Assn. (pubs. com. 1985-87, legis. com. 1986-87, judge best of exhibits award 1987, task force Amigos Fellowship 1990, del. conf. on librs. and info. svcs., 1991), Va. Libr. Assn. (ad hoc. com. distance learning 1992), Va. State Libr. and Archives (Va. libr. and info. svcs. task force 1991-93, steering com. Arbuthnot lecture 1992-93, coop. continuing edn. adv. com. 1992-94), VIVA (steering com. 1994-98), Chgo. Libr. Club (2d v.p. 1983-84), Richmond Acad. Libr. Consortium (v.p. 1991-92, pres. 1992-93), Beta Phi Mu, Phi Kappa Phi, Phi Alpha Theta, Kappa Delta Pi. E-mail: bjford@uiuc.edu.

FORD, BETTY ANN (ELIZABETH ANN FORD), former First Lady of the United States, health facility executive; b. Chicago, Apr. 8, 1918; d. William Stephenson and Hortence (Neahr) Bloomer; m. Gerald R. Ford (38th Pres. U.S.), Oct. 15, 1948; children: Michael Gerald, John Gardner, Steven Meigs, Susan Elizabeth. Studied, Bennington Sch. of Dance, 1936, 37; studied with Martha Graham, Graham Sch. of Dance, N.Y.C., 1937; LL.D. (hon.), U. Mich., 1976. Dancer Martha Graham Concert Group, N.Y.C., 1939-41; fashion dir. Herpolscheimer's Dept. Store, Grand Rapids, Mich., 1943-48; dance instr. Grand Rapids, 1932-48; First Lady of the United States, 1974—77. Co-founder Susan G. Komen Foundation, 1982; chmn., co-founder The Betty Ford Ctr., Rancho Mirage, Calif., 1982—. Author: autobiography The Times of My Life, 1978, Betty: A Glad Awakening, 1987. Bd. dirs. Nat. Arthritis Found. (hon.); trustee Martha Graham Dance Ctr.; Eisenhower Med. Ctr., Rancho Mirage; hon. chmn. Palm Springs Desert Mus.; nat. trustee Nat. Symphony Orch.; bd. dirs. The Lambs, Libertyville, Ill. Recipient Presidential Medal of Freedom, 1991, Congressional Gold Medal, 1999, Woodrow Wilson Pub. Svc. award, 2003. Republican. Episcopalian. Home: PO Box 1560 Rancho Mirage CA 92270 Office: Betty Ford Center 39000 Bob Hope Dr Rancho Mirage CA 92270*

FORD, CECILIA S. federal agency administrator; Grad., U. Va. Atty. Bus. and Adminstrv. Law Divsn. Health and Human Svcs. Office Gen. Counsel; air deartmental. appeals bd. U.S. Dept. Health and Human Svcs., Washington, 1999—, also bd. dirs. Office: US Dept Health and Human Svcs Departmental Appeals Bd 200 Independence Ave SW Rm 637-D Washington DC 20201

FORD, EILEEN OTTE (MRS. GERARD W. FORD), modeling agency executive; b. N.Y.C., Mar. 25, 1922; d. Nathaniel and Loretta Marie (Laine) Otte; m. Gerard William Ford, Nov. 20, 1944; children: Margaret (Mrs. Robert Craft), Gerard William, M. Katie (Mrs. Andre Balazs), A. Lacey (Mrs. John Williams). BS, Barnard Coll., 1943. Stylist Elliot Clarke Studio, N.Y.C., 1943-44, William Becker Studio, 1945; copywriter Arnold Constable, N.Y.C., 1945-46; reporter Tobe Coburn, 1946; co-founder Ford Model Agy., N.Y.C., 1946—, now chmn. bd. Author: Eileen Ford's Model Beauty, Secrets of the Model's World, A More Beautiful You in 21 Days, Beauty Now and Forever, 1977. Bd. dirs. London Philharmonic, 1948— . Recipient Harpers Bazaar award for promotion internat. understanding., Woman of Yr. in Advt. award, 1983 Office: Ford Modeling Agy 142 Greene St New York NY 10012-3236

FORD, ELIZABETH ANN, administrator, children's advocate; b. Chambersburg, Pa., Apr. 28, 1946; d. James Wilson and Viola Elizabeth (Ewell) F. BS in Elem. Edn., U. Millersville, 1977; postgrad., North Tex. State U., 1983-85, The Union Inst., 1997—. Tchr. elem. sch. Lancaster (Pa.) Pub. Schs., 1978-80; dir. child care ctr. Head Start, Dallas, 1981-84; early childhood specialist II The Child Care Group, Dallas, 1984-87; program dir. Corp. Fun Tex., Austin, 1987-89; dir. spl. projects NAEYC, Washington, 1990—. Co-founder, cons. Chance and Ford Assocs., Austin, 1988-89; early childhood trainer Children's Resources Internat., Washington, 1984—; mem. adv. bd. Edn. Resource Info. Ctr., Champaign, Ill., 1993—; bd. dirs. Edward Mazique Parent Child Ctr., Washington, chair gala com., 1997. Contbr. articles to profl. jours. Chaor pub. rels. The Peoples Cmty. Bapt. Ch., Silver Spring, Md., 1997. Mem. Nat. Women Achievement (charter), Alpha Kappa Alpha. Democrat. Avocations: music, aerobics, reading, travel. Home: 350 Market St W Apt 346 Gaithersburg MD 20878-6404 Office: NAEYC 1509 16th St NW Washington DC 20036-1426

FORD, IRENE ELAINE, pastor; b. West Union, W.Va., Oct. 6, 1927; d. Clurel Cecil Powell and Lillian Violet Gaskins; m. Claudius Arnold Ford, Jan. 24, 1946 (dec. Oct. 20, 1997); children: Richard Freeman, Michael Leroy. Student, Northern C.C., Weirton, W.Va., W.Va. Wesleyan Coll., 1984—87, Duke Divinity, 1984—89. Ordained deacon United Meth. Ch., 1992. Pastor Bristol Charge United Meth. Ch., Bristol, W.Va., 1983—89, pastpr Christ-Owings Charge Shinnston, W.Va., 1989—94, assoc. mem., 1992, pastor Graysville-Washington Lands, 1994—96, pastor Nessly Chapel New Cumberland, W.Va., 1997—. Parish coord. United Meth. Ch., Bristol, W.Va., 1986—89, Shinnston, W.Va., 1989—94; pres., v.p. WHG dist. United Meth. Women, 1980. Pres. W.Va. Congress Parent Tchr. Orgn., 1975—77; sch. bd. mem. Hancock County, 1979—84. Mem.: W.Va. Ann. Conf. (assoc.; deacon). United Methodist. Avocation: family activities. Home: 122 Clearview Ave New Cumberland WV 26047

FORD, JEAN ELIZABETH, former English language educator; b. Branson, Mo., Oct. 5, 1923; d. Mitchell Melton and Annie Estella (Wyer) F.; m. J.C. Wingo, 1942 (div. 1946; m. E. Syd Vineyard, 1952 (div. 1956); m. Vincent Michel Wessling, Feb. 14, 1983 (div. Dec. 1989). AA in English, L.A. City Coll., 1957; BA in English, Calif. State U., 1959; MA in Higher Edn., U. Mo., 1965; postgrad., UCLA, 1959-60, U. Wis., 1966, U. Mo. Law Sch., 1968-69. Cert. English tchr., real estate broker, Mo. Dance instr. Arthur Murray Studios, L.A., 1948-51; office mgr. Western Globe Products, L.A., 1951-55; pvt. dance tchr., various office jobs L.A., 1955-59; social dir. S.S. Matsonia, 1959; social worker L.A. County, 1959-61; 7th grade instr. Carmenita Sch. Dist., Norwalk, Calif., 1961-62; English instr. Leadwood (Mo.) High Sch., 1962-63; dance instr. U. Mo., 1963-66, SW Mo. State U., 1966-68, NW Mo. State U., 1970-76, Johnson County Community Coll., 1976-77; tax examiner IRS, Kansas City, Mo., 1978-80; tax acct. Baird, Kurtz & Dobson, Kansas City, Mo., 1981; dance tchr. Singles Program Village, Presbyn. Ch., Kans., 1981-96. Substitute tchr. various sch. dists., 1976-85; dance chmn. Mo. Assn. Health, Phys. Edn. and Recreation, 1965-66, 68-69, dance chmn. ctrl. dist. AAHPER, 1972-73; vis. author Young Author's Conf., Ctrl. Mo. State U., 1987, 88, 89; speaker Am. Reading Assn., Grandview, Mo., 1990; real estate sales agt., Kansas City, 1980-84; real estate sales broker, Mo., 1990—, Kans., 1990-2000; pvt. practice tax acct., dance tchr., 1984-2002. Author, pub.: Fish Tails and Scales, 1982, 2d edit., 2000; spkr. at librs. Mem. Am. Contract Bridge League, Kansas City Ski Club. Democrat. Presbyterian. Avocations: tennis, swimming, skiing, sailing, bridge. Home and Office: 142 Grandview Dr Bldg 4 #7 Branson MO 65616

FORD, JENNIFER, art educator; d. George Christopher Ford and Carolyn Caplenor. MA in Curriculum and Instrn., Tenn. Technol. U., 1999; BFA in Visual Arts, Mid. Tenn. State U., 1994. Cert. Art Educator Tenn., 1994, Tchr. Grades 1-8 Tenn., 1999, Art Educator Ky., 1994. Art educator Smith County Schools, Carthage, Tenn., 1999—, Dept. of Def. Dep. Schs., Ft. Campbell, Ky., 1995—98. Mem.: Nat. Art Edn. Assn., Order of Ea. Star, Phi Kappa Phi. Methodist. Personal E-mail: alvalee@twlakes.net.

FORD, JO ANNE, artist, educator; b. Mill Valley, Calif., May 17, 1958; d. Robert Emmet and Eunice Peay (McDowell) F.; m. Blaise Smith, May 17, 1989; 1 child, Emmet Smith. AA in Dramatic Arts, AA in Humanities, Coll. of Marin, 1980; BFA, San Francisco Art Inst., 1987; MFA, U. Calif., Berkeley, 2002. Arts educator Lycee Francais, San Francisco, 1993-95, Bay Area Discovery Mus., Sausalito, Calif., 1994-97; Youth in Arts '94, 1994-96. Lectr. facilitator San Francisco Artist's Com., 1994-95; mem. Adaline Kent Award com. San Francisco Artist Com., 1995. Recipient award of Honor Matrix Gallery, 1993, award of Excellence, Calif. State Fair, 1994, award of Merit, Calif. State Fair, 1995, J. Ruth Kelsey Award 2002. Avocations: environmental activism, hiking, reading.

FORD, KARRIN ELIZABETH, music educator, musician; b. Waco, Tex., July 2, 1951; d. Joe Brown Ford and Lillian Pauline Phelps. B in Music Edn. magna cum laude, Baylor U., 1974; MusM, U. Kans., 1978; D in Musical Arts, Cin. Conservatory Music, 1984. With Burrus Fine Arts Acad., Houston Ind. Sch. Dist., 1975—76; asst. prof. music U. of the South, Sewanee, Tenn., 1985—86; assoc. prof. music, univ. organist Belmont U., Nashville, 1986—99. Faculty Tenn. Arts Acad., Nashville, 1987—94; recitalist annual meeting Music Tchrs. Nat. Assn., Mpls., 2000; lectr. in field. Contbr. articles to profl. jours. Mem.: Coll. Music Soc., Internat. Allliance Women in Music, Am. Guild Organists (assoc.; dean Nashville chpt. 1990—91), Pi Kappa Lambda, Mu Phi Epsilon. Achievements include research in historical keyboard music by women composers. Avocations: playing piano, playing organ, gardening, running. Home: 56 Dog Ln Storrs Mansfield CT 06268-2220

FORD, KAY LOUISE, innovation consulting executive; b. Pontiac, Mich., Aug. 2, 1944; d. Norman Avery and Elsa Katherine (Wahlsten) F.; m. Billy Wayne Reed, Aug. 20, 1965 (div. Jan. 1979); children: Matthew Wayne Reed, Bradley Ford Reed. AB, U. Mich., 1965; MA, SUNY, Brockport, 1983. Speech therapist Cmty. Treatment Ctr., Bath, Maine, 1966-68; continuing edn. coord. SUNY, Brockport, 1974-78, grad. asst., 1978-79; contract tng. dir. Monroe C.C., Rochester, N.Y., 1979-86; exec. dir. Livingston Washtenaw Pvt. Industry Coun., Ann Arbor, Mich., 1986-91; dir. devel. McKinley Found., Ann Arbor, 1991-92; v.p. community rels. Regional Coun. Aging, Inc., Rochester, 1992-93; v.p. Drake Beam Morin, Inc., Rochester, 1993-96; cons. KLF Personal PR Assocs., 1993—; sector v.p. Idea Connection Sys., Inc., Rochester, 1996-2000; sr. v.p. Manchester, Inc., Phila., 1999—2004; v.p. Right Mgmt. Cons., 2004—. Contract trainer Cornell U., Rochester, 1983-86, Learning Internat., Buffalo, 1984-87, Jannotta, Bray and Assocs., Chgo., 1992; field instr. U. Mich., 1988-92; adj. instr. SUNY, Brockport, 1993-98. Co-chmn. Internat. Spl. Olympics Ceremonies Com., Brockport, 1979-80, Washtenaw United Way Comm., Ann Arbor, 1987-91, Mich. Theatre Fund Raising, Ann Arbor, 1987-90; bd. dirs. Jazz for Life--On Stage for Kids, Ann Arbor, 1987-90, Peace Neighborhood Ctr., 1991-92; mem. bus. and labor leaders adv. com. Washtenaw C.C.; fund drive and career svcs. coms. Rochester YWCA, 1996-99.. Mem. ASTD, Soc. Human Resource Mgmt., Finger Lakes SHRM (mem. strategic adv. bd.), Finger Lakes ASTD, Nat. Soc. Fund Raising Execs., Planned Giving Coun. Upstate N.Y., Ann Arbor Pers. Assn., Univ. Club Rochester, Rochester Women's Network, Union League of Phila., Forum of Exec. Women-Del. Avocation: collecting antiques. E-mail: kay.ford@right.com.

FORD, LORETTA C. retired dean, educator, consultant, nurse; b. N.Y.C., Dec. 28, 1920; d. Joseph F. and Nellie A. (Williams) Pfingstel; m. William J. Ford, May 2, 1947; 1 child, Valerie. BSN, U. Colo., Boulder, 1949, MS, 1951, EdD, 1961; DSc (hon.), Ohio State Med. Coll., 1997; DSc (hon.), Simmons Coll., 1997, U. Colo., 1997; LLD (hon.), U. Md., 1990; DSc (hon.), U. Rochester, 2000; LHD (hon.), Binghamton U., 2001. RN N.J. Staff nurse New Brunswick Vis. Nurse Svc., 1941—42; supr., dir. Boulder County (Colo.) Health Dept., 1947—58; from asst. prof. to prof. U. Colo. Sch. Nursing, 1960—72; dean Sch. Nursing, DON, prof. U. Rochester, NY, 1972—86, acting dean Grad. Sch. Edn. and Human Devel., 1988—89; vis. prof. U. Fla., 1968, U. Wash., Seattle, 1974, St. Lukes Coll. Nursing, Tokyo, 1987. Mem. educators adv. panel GAO; dir. Security Trust Co., Rochester, Rochester Telephone Co.; internat. cons. in field. Contbr. chapters to books, articles to profl. jours. Mem. adv. com. Commonwealth Fund Exec. Nurse Fellowship PRogram; bd. dirs. Threshold Alt. Youth Svcs., Easter Seal Soc., ARC, Monroe Cmty. Hosp. With Nurse Corps USAF, 1942—46. Named Colo. Nurse of Yr., Colo. Nurses Assn., Alumni of Century, U. Colo. Sch. Nursing Alumni Assn., 1998; recipient N.Y. State Gov.'s award for women in sci., medicine and nursing, Modern Healthcare Hall of Fame award, Modern Health Care Jour., 1994, Lillian D. Wald Spirit of Nursing award, N.Y. Vis. Nurse Svc., 1994, Lifetime Achievement award, Nat. Conf. Nurse Practitioners, 1999, Trailblazer award, Am. Coll. Nurse Practitioners, 2003, Elizabeth Blackwell award, Hobart and William Smith Colls., 2003. Fellow: Nat. League Nursing (Linda Richards award), Am. Acad. Nursing (Living Legend award 1999); mem.: NAS Inst. Medicine (Gustav O. Leinhard award 1990), ANA, APHA (Ruth B. Freeman award), Am. Coll. Nurse Practitioners (Crystal Trailblazers award 2003), Am. Coll. Health Assn. (Boynton award), Sigma Theta Tau, Alpha Omega Alpha (hon.). E-mail: lorettaford@cfl.rr.com.

FORD, LUCILLE GARBER, economist, educator; b. Ashland, Ohio, Dec. 31, 1921; d. Ora Myers and Edna Lucille (Armstrong) Garber; m. Laurence Wesley Ford, Sept. 1, 1946; children: Karen Elizabeth, JoAnn Christine. AA, Stephens Coll., 1942; BS in Commerce, Northwestern U., 1944, MBA, 1945; PhD in Econs., Case Western Res. U., 1967; PhD (hon.), Tarkio Coll., 1991, Ashland U., 1995. Cert. fin. planner. Instr. Allegheny Coll., Meadville, Pa., 1945-46, U. Ala., Tuscaloosa, 1946-47; personnel dir., asst. sec. A.L. Garber Co., Ashland, Ohio, 1947-67; prof. econs. Ashland U., 1967-95, chmn. dept. econs., 1970-75; dir. Gill Ctr. for Econ. Edn. Ashland Coll., 1975-86, v.p., dean Sch. Bus., Adminstrn. and Econs., 1980-86, v.p. acad. affairs, 1986-90, provost, 1992-95; exec. asst. to pres., 1993-95; pres. Ashland Comm. Found., 1995—. Bd. dirs. Peco II, Inc., Western Res. Econ. Devel. Coun., Morgan Freeport Corp., Ohio Coun. Econ. Edn.; lectr. in field; mem. govs. adv. com. on econ. devel. Author: University Economics-Guide for Education Majors, 1979, Economics: Learning and Instruction, 1981, 91; contbr. articles to profl. jours. Mem. Ohio Gov.'s Commn. on Ednl. Choice, 1992; candidate for lt. gov. of Ohio, 1978; trustee Stephens Coll., 1977-80, Ashland U., 1995—, North Cen. State Coll., 1998—; elder Presbyn. Ch.; bd. dirs. Presbyn. Found., 1982-88; chair, trustee Synod-Presbyn. Ch., 1994-2000; active ARC. Named to Ohio Women's Hall of Fame, 2001; recipient Outstanding Alumnus award, Stephens Coll., 1977, Outstanding Profl. award, Ashland U., 1971, 1975, Roman F. Warmke award, 1981, Women of Achievement award, 1998. Mem. Am. Econs. Assn., Nat. Indsl. Research Soc., Am. Arbitration Assn. (profl. arbitrator), Assn. Pvt. Enterprise Edn. (pres. 1983-84), North Ctrl. Assn. Colls. & Schs. (commr.), Omicron Delta Epsilon, Alpha Delta Kappa. Republican. Office: Ashland Co Comm Found 300 College Ave Ashland OH 44805-3803

FORD, MARYESTELLE BEVERLY, piano educator, music researcher; b. St. Paul, Jan. 2, 1908; d. Harvey Louis Leander and Roberta Beverly (Finley) Glick; m. Ira Wilbur Ford, Mar. 23, 1928; 1 child, Mary Lou Ford Falkard. Student, L.A. Conservatory Music, 1957-58, U. So. Calif., 1961-63, UCLA, 1964, El Camino Jr. Coll., Redondo Beach, Calif., 1965-66, Calif. State U., Long Beach, 1966. Pvt. tchr. piano Alderman Studios, Fresno, Calif., 1926-28, El Segundo, Calif., 1928—. Adjudicator South Bay, El Segundo, 1966-71, El Camino Jr. Coll., 1971—. Mem., speech coord., liaison Am. Field Svc., El Segundo, 1950-60. Recipient hon. degrees in music child edn. specialist and pedagogy, Music. Tchrs. Assn. Calif. Plan. Mem. Music Tchrs. Nat. Assn., Piano Guild Internat., Music Tchrs. Assn. Calif. (charter, pres. 1956-58), South Bay Music Tchrs. Assn. (founding, cert. tchr., pres. 1956-58), Order Ea. Star, Bridge Club. Avocations: accompanying on piano for various organizations, gardening, reading, travel, collecting hummels. Home: PO Box 17010 Anaheim CA 92817-7010

FORD, MAUREEN MORRISSEY, civic worker; b. St. Joseph, Mo., July 1, 1936; d. Albert Joseph and Rosemary Kathryne (FitzSimons) Morrissey; m. James Henry Lee, Feb. 12, 1954; children: Kathryne Elizabeth, Maryellen, James Henry Lee III(dec.), William Charles, Maureen Lee. Student, U. N.Mex., 1953-54, U. Bridgeport, Conn., 1966-68; BS, Fairfield U., 1986, postgrad. in applied ethics, 1986—. Charity and sch. vol., 1959—; fundraiser for cmty. causes, mus., agys., 1964—; active presdl. campaign Barry Goldwater, 1963-64; congl. campaign Senator Lowell Weiker, 1968; pre-sch. tchr. Earth Place, 1966-68, trustee, v.p. bd. dir., 1968-75; assoc. program in applied ethics Fairfield U., 1986—. Author: (with Lisa H. Newton) Taking Sides: Controversial Issues in Business Ethics, 1990, 8th edit., 2003. V.p. Women's League, 1966-70; mem. exec. com. Rep. Women's Club, Westport, 1967-68; leader, trainer Troops on Fgn. Soil br. Girl Scouts US, Caracas, Venezuela, 1971-72; founding trustee, treas. Kara Mus., Norwalk, Conn.; mem. adv. coun. Fairfield County (Conn.) for spl. edn. Staples H.S.; bd. dirs. CLASP; mem. exec. com. Group Home Search; pres. Ind. Assocs. Cons. Firm, 1991—; cons., facilitator life planning workshops Merideth Assocs., Westport; v.p., bd. dirs. Isaiah 61:1, Inc., 1989—; active grants com. Bridgeport Pub. Edn. Fund and Devel. Commn., 1984—; mem. 1st selectmen's com. on recycling, 1974-75; bd. dirs. PTA, 1976-79; mem. YWCA of Bridgeport Com. of 100 and Task Force; v.p. bd. dirs. YWCA, 1980-87, pres., 1984-85; v.p. Conf. Women's Orgns., Bridgeport; founding mem. Concerned Women Colleagues of Bridgeport; pres. Jr. League Ea. Fairfield County, Inc., 1977-78; v.p., sec. J.H.L.F. Inc., Westport; mem. grants com. Conn. Cares Hartford Fund, 1995-97. Mem. Assn. Jr. League Am., Westport Tennis Assn. Roman Catholic. Home: 204 Stillson Rd Fairfield CT 06825

FORD, MAUREEN R. insurance company executive; b. 1956; BS in Bus. and Econs., U. Pitts.; MS in Internat. Bus., U. S. Carolina. Sr. v.p. Mass. Life Ins. Co., Boston, 1988—89; vice chmn. and CEO John Hancock Funds, LLC, Boston, 1999—2001; chmn., CEO Berkeley Fin Svcs. Group, LLC, Boston, 2001—; exec. v.p. John Hancock Fin. Svcs., Inc., John Hancock Life Ins. Co., Boston, 2001—; also bd. dirs. John Hancock Subsidiaries, Boston, 2001—. Office: John Hancock Fin Svcs John Hancock Pl Boston MA 02117

FORD, NANCY LOUISE, composer, scriptwriter; b. Kalamazoo, Oct. 1, 1935; d. Henry Ford III and Mildred Wotring; m. Robert D. Currie, June 7, 1957 (div. 1962); m. Keith W. Charles, May 23, 1964. BA, DePauw U., 1957; D of Arts (hon.), Eastern Mich. U., 1986; D of Fine Arts (hon.), DePauw U., 2002. Composer (with Gretchen Cryer): (off-Broadway musicals) Now is the Time for All Good Men, 1967, The Last Sweet Days of Isaac, 1970, I'm Getting My Act Together and Taking It On the Road, 1978, The American Girls Revue, 1998, Circle of Friends, 2001; composer: (Broadway musical) Shelter, 1972; scriptwriter: TV daytime serials Love of Life, 1971—74, Ryan's Hope, 1975; scriptwriter (TV daytime series) Ryan's Hope, 1983—84; scriptwriter: TV daytime serials Search for Tomorrow, 1981—82, Guiding Light, 1977—78, As the World Turns, 1978—80, 1987—95; performer: stage and cabaret. Trustee DePauw U., 1988-97. Recipient Emmy awards, 1983, 84. Mem.: AFTRA, League Profl. Theatre Women N.Y. (bd. dirs), Am. Fedn. Musicians, Actors Equity, Writers Guild Am., Dramatists Guild (mem. coun.).

FORD, NATALIE RUTH, education educator; b. Doylestown, Pa., Aug. 31, 1975; BA in lit. and creative writing (hons.), Bard Coll., Annandale, N.Y., 1997; MA in Renaissance Lit. (hons.), U. York (Eng.), 2002. Reading clinician, vol. St. Labre Indian Sch, Ashland, Mont., 1998—99; tchr., tutor, vol. Kilinik HS, Nunavut, Canada, 1999—2000; libr. asst. Ctrl. Bucks HS West, Doylestown, Pa., 2000; English lang. prof. Barcelona, 2002—03. Author: (poem) Native Ground, 2002, Grace, 2003. John Bard scholar in lang. and lit., Bard Coll., 1995—96, Excellence and Equal Cost scholar, 1993—97. Avocations: foreign language study, chess, yoga, running, travel, painting.

FORD, SALLY J. physical education educator; b. Vincennes, Ind., July 2, 1950; d. Marion C. and Peggy A. (Clark) Ford; 1 child from previous marriage, Chanda D. BA, McKendree Coll., 1973; MS, Eastern Ill. U., 1980; PhD, So. Ill. U., 2000. Tchr., coach Effingham (Ill.) HS, 1974-80; head coach Bradley U., Peoria, Ill., 1980-83; exercise physiologist Curtiss Ave. Clinic, Sarasota, Fla., 1985-87; conditioning coord. Kansas City Royals, 1987-88; prof. Pima CC, Tucson, 1989—2001, Tusculum Coll., Greeneville, Tenn., 2001—. With U.S. Men's Sprint Com., 1982—86, Competitive Edge, Calif., 1993—95. Named to Sports Hall of Fame, McKendree Coll., 1991. Mem.: Clinics Speed Devel., Athletic Congress, Nat. Strength and Conditioning Assn., N.Am. Soc. Sport Mgmt., Am. Alliance Health, Physical Edn., Recreation and Dance. Avocations: running, weightlifting. Office: Tusculum Coll Erwin Hwy Greeneville TN 37743

FORDEN, DIANE CLAIRE, magazine editor; b. N.Y.C., Apr. 6, 1951; d. Joseph Anthony and Helen (Nash) F. BA in English Edn. summa cum laude, Montclair (N.J.) State U., 1973. Fashion editor Seventeen Mag., N.Y.C., 1975-81; fashion and beauty dir. YM Mag., N.Y.C., 1981-85; fashion dir. Avon Fashions, N.Y.C., 1985-87, Prima Mag., N.Y.C., 1987-88; from fashion and beauty editor to editor in chief and v.p. Bridal Guide Mag., N.Y.C., 1989—. Author: How to Have an Elegant Wedding-Without Going Broke. Mem. Am. Soc. Mag. Editors, Fashion Group Internat., N.Y. Women in Comms. Avocations: piano, biking, skiing, photography. Home: 10 River Rd Apt F Nutley NJ 07110-3459 Office: Bridal Guide Mag 3 E 54th St New York NY 10022-3108

FORDICE, PATRICIA OWENS, civic leader, former state first lady; b. Jackson, Miss., Nov. 27, 1934; d. Lloyd Leon and Veo (McLelland) Owens; m. Daniel Kirkwood Fordice, Aug. 13, 1955 (div. Feb. 2000); children: Angela Leigh, Daniel Kirkwood III, Hunter Lloyd, James Owens. Student, Christian Coll., Columbia, Mo., 1952-53, Memphis State U., 1953-54. First lady State of Miss., Jackson, 1992-2000. Host radio talk show. Co-host TV show Woman to Woman. Responsible for art exhibit Palaces of St. Petersburg Russian Imperial Style, Jackson, 1996, Splendors of Versailles exhbn., Jackson, 1998, Majesty of Spain, 2001; creator Spendors of Miss. Project, Bucks for Books; host, hon. chmn. Internat. Ballet Competition, 1998, also mem. bd.; founder Miss. Gov.'s Initiative for Vol. Excellence Awards; creator SAFETY (Securing Brighter Future for Today's Youth); creator women's health initiative Heart of Miss. Women; hon. chmn., spokesperson for Friends of Children's Hosp.; spokesman Miss. Div. Tourism; hon. chmn. Spl. Olympics, Very Spl. Arts, Miss. Family for Kids; organizer fight against breast cancer Miss. Florist Assn., 1995, Miss. chpt. Am. Cancer Soc., also hosps. and clinics; founder, Power of One, Miss. Woman's Conf., from 1996; co-chmn. abstinence program Miss. Dept. Human Services; hon. pres. Gulf Pines coun. Girl Scouts U.S.A., 1994; past pres. Ofcl. Miss.'s Women's Club; hon. chmn., mem. founding bd. Miss. Commn. Volunteerism, 1993—; active Miss. Blood Svcs.; bd. dirs. Hospice Care Found., Vicksburg, Miss.; active Salvation Army; vol. Toys for Tots; participant Gateway Rescue Mission, 1998, Habitat for Humanity; keyperson key arts program Miss. Arts Commn.; spkr. to numerous chambers of commerce orgns., Rotary and Lions clubs, other civic and charitable groups; vol. Rankin County Human Resource Ctr.; promoter Good Neighbor Day; lobbyist for Medicare coverage of arthritis drugs; hon. chmn. emeritus of bd. Commn. for Internat. Cultural Exch.; bd. dirs. Miss. Symphony; Internat. Ballet Competition; amb. Ageless Heroes awards program Blue Cross & Blue Shield Miss.; spokesperson Arthritis Found; also others. Decorated knight Sovereign Order of Orthodox Knights Hospitaller of St. John of Jerusalem; named Miss.'s Outstanding Philanthropist, 1996; recipient Communicator award Soil and Water Conservation Soc., 1997, Need Knows No Svc. award Salvation Army, 1997, award as outstanding leader and vol. Miss. Blood Svcs., 1998, medal of honor DAR, 1999, medal of excellence Miss. U. for Women, 1999, Steward of Arts and Edn. award Phi Theta Kappa, 1999, Keep Ms Beautiful Louise Godwin award for excellence, 1999; inducted into Miss. Family for Kids' Hall of Fame, 1997. Mem. Nature Conservancy (life), Girl Scouts U.S.A. (life), United Meth. Women (life), Garden Club Soc. Miss. (life), Vicksburg Jr. Aux. (life, pres. 1970). Home: 207 Winter Teal Ct Madison MS 39110-9652

FORD-ROEGNER, PATRICIA A. health services professional; b. Phila., May 25, 1947; AD, Gwynedd Mercy Coll., 1967; BA, West Chester State U., 1969; MSW, U. Pa., 1973. Pres. pub. affairs PFR, Washington, 1992-94; regional dir. Dept. Health and Human Svcs., Atlanta, 1994—. Vice-chair White House Task Force Health Care Reform, 1993. Office: Dept Health & Human Servs 61 Forsyth St SW Ste 5b95 Atlanta GA 30303-8931 E-mail: pfordroegner@osophs.dhhs.gov.

FORE, HENRIETTA HOLSMAN, federal agency administrator; m. Richard L. Fore. AB, Wellesley Coll., 1970; MA, U. No. Colo., 1975. Pres. Stockton Wire Products, Burbank, Calif., 1977-89; asst. adminstr. for pvt. enterprise AID, Washington, 1990-91, asst. adminstr. for Asia, 1991-93; Dir U.S. Mint Dept Treasury, Washington, 2001—. Mem. Com. of 200. Mem. Young Pres. Orgn. Office: U S Mint Headquarters 801 9th Street NW Washington DC 20220

FOREHAND, JENNIE MEADOR, state legislator; b. Nashville; d. James T. and Estelle Meador; m. William E. Forehand, Jr.; children: Virginia, John. BS in Indsl. Rels., U. N.C., Chapel Hill. Reporter Charlotte (N.C.) News, 1954-56; probation counselor Juvenile Ct., Charlotte, 1958; tchr. Anne Arundel County, Md., 1958-60; statis. analyst NIH, Bethesda, Md., 1961-62; interior designer, owner Forehand Antiques and Interiors, Rockville, Md., 1971—; mem. Md. Ho. of Dels., Annapolis, 1978-94, Md. Senate, Annapolis, 1995—. Mem. appropriations com., joint capital budget com., health and environ. subcom., chair Montgomery County delegation transp. com., co-chair com. on mgmt. of pub. funds; mem. Senate jud. proces. com., exec. nominations Com., vice-chmn. Montgomery County Senate delegation; mem. children, youth and families com. Small Mus. Com., Regulatory Rev. Com.; co-chair Fed. Relations com., co-chair MD.Dc.VA Regional Transp. Commn., NIH Bio-Safety Com.; chair econ. devel., transp. and cultural affairs com. So. Legis. Conf., 1994—; mem. So. Tech. Coun.; chair Task Force on Genetic Techs. and Pub. Policy, Nat. Conf. State Legislatures. Mem. planning bd. Montgomery County Health Sys.; consumer rep. Rockville Econ. Devel. Coun., Md. Cmty. Mental Health Adv. Bd.; pres. local civic assn., Girl Scout Adv. Coun., bd. dirs. Montgomery County Hist. Soc., Md. Coll. Art and Design, Rockville Arts Place, Asbuty Meth. Homes; mem. Peerless Rockville Hist. Preservation, Ltd. Recipient Bus. Leadership award Suburban Md. Tech. Coun.; named among Md.'s Top 100 Women; named Outstanding Legislator Montgomery County Med. Soc., and Md. State's Attys. Assn. Mem. AAUW, Women's Caucus of Md. Gen. Assembly (pres.), Women's Polit. Caucus, Nat. Conf. State Legislatures (pres. Women's Network). Office: James Senate Ofc Bldg 110 College Ave Annapolis MD 21401-8012

FORELLE, HELEN (GRACE JANET LEIH), publishing executive, writer, poet; b. Canton, S.D., Jan. 27, 1936; d. Geurt and Ruth Victoria (Hall) Leih; m. John Maxwell Jeffords, Dec. 2, 1955 (div. 1968); children: Ruthanne Shepherd, John Maxwell Jeffords, Pamela Leih Meder. BA, Memphis State U., 1967, postgrad., 1967-69, U. Wuerzburg, Munich, 1970, Technische Hochschule, 1971. Computer programmer, analyst various cos., San Francisco, 1972-77; instr. computer sci. Augustana Coll., Sioux Falls, S.D., 1978-79; project dir. S.D. State Poetry Soc., Sioux Falls, 1984-87; temp. jobs various agencies, Sioux Falls, 1978-88; enumerator U.S. Census Bureau, Sioux Falls, 1989; owner Tesseract Pub., Fairview, S.D., 1989—. Lectr. in field. Author: (pseudonym Mario Edlosi) (trilogy) Which Way the Wind Blows, 1978, Shouting to the Wind, 1996, The Windmill, 1996, (children's story) The Adventures of Mortimer Troll, 1981, If Men Got Pregnant, Abortion Would Be A Sacrament, 1982, (pamphlets) Conversations in a Clinic, 1980, Publication Indexing, a Writers' Guide to Inventory, 1989, (poems) Pearls Among the Swine, 1990, A Classical Garden, 1996, Under the Gun, 1997, (musical comedy) The Tea-Totalers, 1982; editor: South Dakota Authors' Catalog, 1982, 83, 85, 87, The Wash Rag Newsletter; mng. editor, project dir. for S.D. State Poetry Soc.-A Sixty Year Comprehensive Index of Pasque Petals, 1926-1986), 1987; contbr. poetry to popular mags. and newsletters, and cartoons to Broomstick mag. Dir. Women Against Sexual Harassment, Fairview, S.D., 1992-98; recorder Valley of Many Winds S.D. State Libr. Talking Books; judge contests Nat. Fedn. State Socs., 1985, 88. With USN, 1954-56. Recipient Poet of the Year S.D. State Poetry Soc., Sioux Falls,, 1982, 2d place Denver Am. Pen Women contest, 1978, S.D. State Poetry Soc., 1980, best of show S.D. State Fair, 1980, 84, Hon. Mention award Nat. Assn. State Poetry Soc., 1980, 81, also numerous poetry awards. Mem. AAUW, WAVES, Nat. Assn. Atomic Vets. (area commdr.), S.D. State Poetry Soc. (pres. 1985-86), Bardic Round Table (treas. 1988, pres. 1989-91). Avocations: gardening, occasional travel, sewing, crafts. Office: Tesseract Pubs PO Box 164 Canton SD 57013-0164

FOREMAN, CAROL LEE TUCKER, consumer advocate; b. Little Rock, May 3, 1938; d. James Guy and Willie Maude (White) Tucker; m. Jay Howell Foreman, June 13, 1964; children: Guy Tucker, Rachel Marian. AA, William Woods Coll., 1958; AB, Washington U., 1960; postgrad., Am. U.; LLD (hon.), William Woods Coll., 1976. Rsch. asst. Com. Govt. Ops. U.S. Sen., 1961; assoc. Fed. Counsel Assocs., 1961-63; instr. Am. govt. William Woods Coll., Fulton, Mo., 1963-64; exec. asst. to Rep. James Roosevelt, 1964; dir. rsch. & publs. Dem. Nat. Com., 1965-66; Congl. liaison aide HUD, 1967-69; chief info. liaison Ctr. Family Planning Program Devel. Planned Parenthood-World Population, 1969-71; dir. policy coordination Commn. on Population and Am. Future, 1971-72; exec. dir. Citizens Com. on Population and Am. Future, 1972-73, Paul Douglas Consumer Rsch. Ctr., 1973-77, Consumer Fedn. Am., 1973-77; asst. sec. food and consumer svcs. Dept. Agriculture, Washington, 1977-81; dir. U.S. Commodity Credit Corp., 1977-81, U.S. Consumer Coop. Bank, 1977-81; pres. Foreman & Co., 1981-86, Foreman Heidepriem & Mager, 1986—99. Mem. Pres.'s Commn. on White House Fellows, 1996—2001; mem. Nat. Adv. Com. Meat and Poultry Inspection, 1997—2002; adv. com. Joint Inst. Food Safety and Applied Nutrition; mem. adv. com. on agrl. biotech. USDA, 2000—. Editor: Regulating for the Future, 1991. Exec. dir. Ctr. Women Policy Studies, 1983-84, mem. Interdeptl. Task Force on Women, 1973-74; bd. dirs. Consumer's Union, 1982-83, chmn., 1993—; bd. dirs. Food Rsch. & Action Ctr., 1983, Christianity and Crisis, 1990-92; vice chmn. Ctr. Nat. Policy, 1982-84, bd. dirs., 1981-99; trustee Washington U., St. Louis, 1987-95; bd. dirs. Bread for the World, 2000—. Recipient disting. alumni award Washington U., 1979, 2000. Mem. Women's Equity Action League (past pres. local chpt.), Nat. Policy Assn. (dir. 1985-97), Phi Beta Phi. Presbyterian. Home: 5408 Trent St Chevy Chase MD 20815-5514 Office: Consumer Fedn Am 1424 16th St NW Ste 604 Washington DC 20036-2239 E-mail: tuckfore@aol.com.

FOREMAN, JUDY, journalist; b. Ft. Bragg, N.C., 1944; BA in Anthropology/Sociology, Wellesley Coll., 1966; MEd, Harvard U., 1970. City Hall reporter Lowell (Mass.) Sun, 1970-73; gen. assignment reporter Times, London, 1982-83; stringer Boston Globe, 1976-78, sci. and medicine reporter, 1983-95, columnist Health Sense, 1995—. Office: Boston Globe PO Box 2378 Boston MA 02107-2378 also: Boston Globe 135 Morrissey Blvd Boston MA 02125-3310

FOREST, EVA BROWN, nursing administrator, songwriter; b. Ontario, Va., July 7, 1941; d. William Butler and Ruth Pauline (Simpson) Brown; m. Willie J. Forest Jr., Sept. 16, 1961; children: Gerald, Darryl, Angela. AA, Bismarck (N.D.) State Coll., 1981; BSN, U. Mary, Bismarck, 1984. RN, Colo. Charge nurse St. Alexius Med. Ctr., Bismarck, 1984—85, Cedars Health Care Ctr., Lakewood, Colo., 1989—90; staff devel. coord. Park Avenue Bapt. Home, Denver, 1990—91; supr., charge nurse Cedars Health Care Ctr., Lakewood, Colo., 1991—; charge nurse Villa Manor Health Ctr., Lakewood, Colo., 1991—93, Stovall Care Ctr., Denver, 1995—96, supr., 1997—98, supr., charge nurse, 1999—2003. Nursing supr. Rose Terrace Care Ctr., Commerce City, Colo., 2003—. Songwriter, prodr., 1999; recorded (CD) God Has Begun a Good Work in Me, 1999. Vol. for cultural exch. lang., culture and fashions YWCA, Kano, Nigeria; vocalist gospel music workshop, N.D.; pianist adult and children's choir, N.D.; mem. MADD, Habitat for Humanity Internat., HALT, Vols. of Am. Mem. Nat. Multiple Sclerosis Soc., DAV Commdrs. Club, Vols. of Am. Office Phone: 303-716-9346. E-mail: Webmaster@Forest.edu.com.

FORESTER, JEAN MARTHA BROUILLETTE, innkeeper, retired librarian, educator; b. Port Barre, La., Sept. 7, 1934; d. Joseph Walter and Thelma (Brown) Brouillette; m. James Lawrence Forester, June 2, 1957; children: Jean Martha, James Lawrence. BS La. State U., 1955; MA, George Peabody Coll. Tchrs., 1956. Libr. Howell Elem. Sch., Springhill, La., 1956—58; asst. post libr. Fort Chaffee, Ark., 1958; command libr. Orleans Area Command, U.S. Army, Orleans, France, 1958—59; acquisitions libr. Northwestern State U., Natchitoches, La., 1960; serials libr. La. State U., New Orleans, 1960—66, mem. faculty Eunice, 1966—85, asst. libr., 1972—85, assoc. libr., 1985—87, acting libr., 1987—88, dir. libr., 1988—89, libr. emeritus, 1989—, asst. prof., 1972—85, faculty senator, 1978—80, 1985—86, 1987—89; innkeeper Crown'n'Anchor Inn, Saco, Maine, 1989—. Co-author: Robertsons's Bill of Fare; contbr. articles to profl. jours. Active Eunice Assn. Retarded Children. Fellow Carnegie, 1955—56. Mem.: UDC, La. Libr. Assn. (sect. sec. 1971—72, coord. serials interest group 1984—85), Delta Kappa Gamma (chpt. parliamentarian 1972—74, rec. sec. 1984—86), Order Ea. Star, Phi Mu, Phi Gamma Mu, Alpha Beta Alpha. Democrat. Baptist.

FORINASH, CAROLYN COSNER, medical/surgical nurse; b. Clarksburg, W.Va., June 6, 1960; d. Franklin Dee and Carolyn Marlene Cosner; m. Michael Ray Forinash, Aug. 15, 1981; children: Marlana Kay, Machelle Rae. BA in Arts and Sci., Alderson-Broaddus Coll., 1982, BSN, 1983; MSN, W.Va. U., 1997. Cert. nurse of oper. rm. Staff nurse urology/med. surgery United Hosp. Ctr., Clarksburg, 1983—86, staff nurse obste./labor delivery, 1986—89, staff nurse oper. rm., 1986—89, team leader oper. rm., 1990—94, educator, 1994—98, educator home health/hospice, 1998—2000, nurse mgr. hospice, 2000—. Mem.: Sigma Theta Tau. Avocations: reading, travel, golf. Home: 21 Catalpa Heights Stonewood WV 26301 Office: United Hosp Ctr People's Hospice PO Box 1680 Clarksburg WV 26301

FORKAN, PATRICIA ANN, foundation executive; b. N.Y.C., June 13, 1944; d. Robert James and Elaine May F. BA in Polit. Sci., Pa. State U., 1966; postgrad., Am. U., 1968-69. Manpower analyst Dept. Labor, Washington, 1967-69; nat. coord. Fund for Animals, N.Y.C., 1970-76; v.p. program and comms. Humane Soc. of U.S., Washington, 1976-86, sr. v.p., 1987-91, exec. v.p., 1992—. Weekly web-active commentator Soap Box, 1999—2004; bd. dirs. Solar Elec. Light Fund, 1990-2000; mem. U.S. del. Internat. Whaling Commn., 1978, 93, 94 Re-negotiation of Conv. for Regulation of Whaling, 1978, U.S. del. North Pacific Fur Seal Commn., 1985; mem. U.S. Public Adv. Com. to Law of the Sea, 1978-83; bd. dirs. Coun. for Ocean Law; advisor, contbr. weekly TV show Living with Animals, 1985-91; advisor Animal Polit. Action Com.; sr. v.p. Humane Soc. Internat., 1991-; coun. woman Friendship Heights (Md.) Village, 1993-2001; pres. Nat. Assn. Humane and Environ. Edn., 1994—; pres. World-wide Network (Women in Devel. and Environ.), 1998; presdl. appointed mem. trade and environment policy adv. com. U.S. Trade Rep., 2000—. Contbr. articles to environ. and animal welfare publs.; co-host weekly radio show, 1986-87.. Office: Humane Soc of US 2100 L St NW Washington DC 20037-1596

FORKNER, GERALDINE G. art educator, artist; b. Charleston, S.C., July 15, 1945; d. Frank V. (Stepfather) and Bess Good Hazelwood; m. John P. Forkner, May 14, 1967; children: Sam, Rebecca, Julie, Paul. BS, U. Tenn., 1967. Cert. crochet instr. 1998. Pre-sch. tchr. Out-of-Doors Sch., Atlanta, 1980—84; tchr. art 1st Presbyn. Pre-sch., Atlanta, 1985—89; paraprofl. City Schs. Decatur, Ga., 1990—92; co-dir. day camp Venetian Pools Cmty. Assn., Atlanta, 1990—2000; tchr. art Torah Day Sch. Atlanta, 1992—97, Fernbank Elem. Sch., Atlanta, 1994—2000; owner Weaving Arts Studio, Sweetwater, Tenn., 2000—; day camp instr. Children's Mus. Oak Ridge, Tenn., 2001—03. Vol. Atlanta His. Ctr., 1992—2000, Fernbank Mus. of nat. His., 1992—2000, Chattanooga Aquarium, 2001—. Recipient 1st pl. award, Athens Coun. for Arts, 2001, award, Handweavers Guild of Am., 1999, First pl. award for felting, Georgia Nat. Fair, 2000; grantee, Lee Stelzer Heritage Mus., 1999, Nat. Endowment of Arts, 2002—03. Mem.: Nat. Art Educators Assn., So. Highland Craft Guild, Peachtree Handspinners Guild, Chattahoochee Handweavers Guild (sec., historian 1999—2002), Dekalb Investment Club (co-pres. 1998—2000). Home: 566 Randolph Fridley Rd Sweetwater TN 37874

FORMAN, ANN LEE, music educator; b. Waterloo, Iowa, Oct. 26, 1955; d. Merwin Richard and Betty Jane Dieckmann; m. Marc Forman, July 31, 1995; 1 child, Suzanne. BA, St. Olaf Coll., Northfield, Minn., 1977; M in Music Edn., DePaul U., 1996. Tchr. orch. Cedar Falls (Iowa) Cmty. Schs., 1978—84, River Trails Sch. Dist., Mt. Prospect, Ill., 1984—. Dir. orch. DePaul Youth Orch., Chgo., 1995—. Trustee River Trails Edn. Found., Mt. Prospect, 1997—; bd. dirs. River Trails Music Boosters Assn., Mt. Prospect, 1984—. Recipient Caring to Challenge award, Ill. Math. Sci. Acad., 2001. Mem.: Music Educators Nat. Conf., Am. String Tchrs. Assn. (Ill. chpt. Pub. Sch. Tchr. of Yr. 1999). Avocations: reading, gardening, movies. Home: 1122 Hohlfelder Rd Glencoe IL 60022 Office: River Trails Mid Sch 1000 N Wolf Rd Mount Prospect IL 60056

FORMAN, BETH ROSALYNE, specialty food trade executive; b. N.Y.C., Oct. 15, 1949; d. Philip and Dorothy Lea (Vilensky) F. BA in English with honors, NYU, 1971; MA with honors, Columbia U., 1972; MBA in Fin., Rutgers U., 1980. Asst. to contr. Colin Hochstin Co., N.Y.C., 1971-78; instr. Columbia U., N.Y.C., 1974-76; adj. faculty Bergen Community Coll., Paramus, N.J., 1985-87; communications cons. B.R. Forman & Co., Paramus, 1981-87; proposal mgr. Ogden Svcs.Corp., N.Y.C., 1988-89; dir. tech. svcs. Ogden Entertainment Svcs., Rosemont, Ill., 1990-92, dir. mktg. comms. N.Y.C., 1993-96; dir. mktg. Euro-Am. Brands, LLC, Paramus, N.J., 1999—. Bd. dirs. new leadership div. United Jewish Community Bergen County, River Edge, N.J., 1981-87, chmn. fundraiser, 1983, chmn. edn. com., 1983-86, treas., 1984-86; mem. steering com. Viewpoints div. Am. Jewish Com., 1991-93. Pres.'s fellow Columbia U., 1973; recipient Masters award Ogden Svcs. Corp., 1994. Mem. NAFE, Women in Comm. (v.p. spl. programs 1992-93 Chgo. chpt., mem. career devel. com. 1994-95, mem. pub. rels. com. and Matrix awards fundraising com. 1995-96), Columbia U. Club of N.Y., Mensa. Democrat. Avocation: acting. Home: 421 Yuhas Dr Paramus NJ 07652-4125 Office: Euro-Am Brands LLC 15 Prospect St Paramus NJ 07652-2712

FORMAN, DANNA, financial analyst; b. Pell City, Ala., Jan. 20, 1970; d. Ollis and Willene Forman. BA Psychology, DePaul U., Chgo., Ill., 2000—. Supr. billing verification U.S. Cellular, Chgo., 1996—. Mentor PACE Program, Chgo., 2003—03.

FORMAN, LORI ANN, federal agency administrator; b. Sioux Falls, S.D., Dec. 4, 1958; d. Richard William and Duaine Berenice (Erickson) F. BA, Augustana Coll., 1979; M in Pub. Policy, Harvard U., 1981. Cons. OILDECO, Sandvika, Norway, 1980; sr. polit. analyst Decision Making Info., Washington, 1981-83; spl. asst. U.S. Agy. Internat. Devel., Washington, 1985-87, sr. advisor, 1987-89, program officer, 1989-90; exec. v.p. Pacific Mgmt. Resources Inc., Honolulu, 1990; dir. Japan program Nature Conservancy, Arlington, Va., 1990—2001; asst. adminr. bur. for asia and near east USAID, Washington, 2001—. Lectr. in field. Reviewer; (book) Japan's Foreign Aid, 1990; contbg. reviewer (book) Yen for Development, 1990. Vol. Presdls. Youth for Ford, Kansas City, Mo., 1976, Saiki for Senate, Honolulu, 1992; vice chmn. Community Devel. Citizens Adv. Com., Sioux Falls, S.D., 1978-79; mem. internal audit com. Georgetown Luth. Ch., Washington, 1995. Harry S. Truman scholar Truman Found., 1979; ITT Internat. fellow Inst. Internat. Edn., 1980; named one of Ten Outstanding Young People Osaka Jr. C. of C., 1992. Mem. Soc. Internat. Devel., Japan-Am. Soc., Washington Area Bicycle Assn., Asia Soc., Sushi Club. Avocations: reading, cycling, scuba diving, sewing, travel. Office: USAID Bur for Asia and Near East RRB 1300 Pennsylvania Ave Nw Washington DC 20523-4900

FORMAN, SANDRA H. theater educator; b. Charlotte, N.C., July 9, 1944; d. Willis Edward Hopper and Mary Harriet Blackwell; m. Richard Charles Forman, Apr. 16, 1967; children: Rhyan Danette, Anna Regan, Daniel Edward. BA, U. N.C. Greensboro, 1966, MFA, 1971. Instr. Guilford Coll., Greensboro, NC, 1969—72; lectr., asst. prof., assoc. prof. U. N.C. Greensboro, 1977—89; prof. Theatre No. Ky. U., Highland Heights, 1990—. Dir. Va. Shakespeare Festival, Williamsburg, 2002. Author: Your Voice and Articulation, 1984, Public Speaking: Today and Tomorrow, 1989, Only Mystery: Lorca's Poetry etc., 1992; actor: Fox Rock Theatre Co., 2000, N.C. Shakespeare, 1988. Dist. pres.-Mid Atlantic Nat. Coun. Jewish Women, 1982—84. Mem.: Southeastern Theatre Conf., Internat. Hemingway Soc. (chair by-laws com.). Office: No Ky Univ Theatre Dept Nunn Dr Highland Heights KY 41099

FORMENTI, SILVIA C. radiation oncologist; b. Italy; MD, Universita degli Studi di Milano, 1980. Cert. Radiation Oncology 1991. Intern San Carlo Borromeo Hosp., Milan, 1980—83; fellow, hematology, oncology USC Med. Sch., Los Angeles, 1984—85; resident, radiation oncology Nat. Cancer Inst., Milan, 1984—88; resident, radiation oncology USC Sch. Medicine, Los Angeles, 1985—90; assoc. prof. radiation oncology and medicine USC, Keck Sch. Medicine, 1990—2000; assoc. dir. clin. rsch., leader of breast cancer rsch. program NYU Cancer Inst., 2000—; Sandra and Edward H. Meyer chmn. NYU Sch. Medicine, Radiation Oncology Dept., 2000—. Office: NYU Med Ctr Dept Radiation Oncology 566 First Ave New York NY 10016-6402

FORMICA, PALMA ELIZABETH, physician; b. Windber, Pa., June 14, 1928; d. Salvatore M. and Angela (Arrera) F.; m. John Rihacek, 1955 (dec. May 1977); children: Gregory, John, Alycia. BS, U. Pitts., 1948; MD, U. Rome, 1953. Intern Queens Hosp. Ctr., Jamaica, N.Y., 1954, resident in internal medicine, 1955-56; family practitioner pvt. practice, Old Bridge, N.J., 1959—; sch. physician Old Bridge Twp. Bd. Edn., 1959—; chmn. dept. family practice St. Peter's Univ. Hosp., New Brunswick, N.J., 1979—; co-founder, assoc. dir. Robert Wood Johnson Med. Sch., Dept. Family Medicine, New Brunswick, NJ, 1979—. Lay trustee St. Thomas the Apostle Ch., Old Bridge. Fellow Med. Soc. N.J., Am. Acad. Family Physicians; mem. AMA (bd. trustees 1990-99), Am. Acad. Family Practice, Am. Coll. Physician Execs., Am. Diebetic Assn., Acad. Medicine N.J. (pres., bd. dirs., exec. com., awards com.), N.J. Assn. Sch. Physicians, N.J. Acad. Family Practice, Middlesex County Med. Soc. (found. bd. trustees), Soc. Tchrs. Family Medicine, Orgn. State Med. Soc. Pres. Office: Saint Peter's Univ Hosp 254 Easton Ave New Brunswick NJ 08901-1766

FORNERIS, JEANNE M. lawyer; b. Duluth, Minn., May 23, 1953; d. John Domenic and Elva Lorraine (McDonald) F.; m. Michael Scott Margulies, Feb. 6, 1982. AB, Macalester Coll., 1975; JD, U. Minn., 1978. Bar: Minn. 1978. Assoc. Halverson, Watters, Bye, Downs & Maki, Ltd., Duluth, 1978-81, Briggs & Morgan, P.A., Mpls., St. Paul, 1981-83; ptnr. Hart & Bruner, P.A., Mpls., 1983-86; assoc. gen. counsel M.A. Mortenson Co., Mpls., 1986-90, v.p., gen. counsel, 1990-96; with Gen. Counsel, Ltd., Mpls., 1997-98; v.p., sr. counsel Medtronic, Inc., Mpls., 1999—. Instr. women's studies dept. U. Minn., Mpls., 1977-79. Author profl. edn. seminars; contbr. articles to profl. jours. Bd. dirs. Good Will Indusries Vocat. Enterprises, Inc., 1979-81; chmn. bd. trustees Duluth Bar Libr., 1981; mem. United Way Family and Individual Svcs. Task Force, Duluth, 1981. Nat. Merit Assn. scholar, 1971. Fellow Am. Coll. Constrn. Lawyers (bd. dirs.); mem. AMA, Am. Arbitration Assn. (mem. large complex case panel), Minn. State Bar Assn., Minn. Women Lawyers (bd. dirs.), U.S. Dist. Ct. Hist. Soc. (pres.). Democrat. Roman Catholic. Office: Medtronic Inc 7000 Central Ave NE Minneapolis MN 55432-3576 Office Phone: 736-514-3329.

FORNEY, VIRGINIA SUE, educational counselor; b. Little Rock, Sept. 15, 1925; d. Robert Millard and Susan Amanda (Ward) Tate; m. J.D. Mullen, Jr., Oct. 13, 1945 (div. 1966); children: Michael Dunn, Patricia Sue; m. Bill E. Forney, Apr. 29, 1967. Student, Tex. State Coll. for Women, 1943-46; BFA, U. Okla., 1948; postgrad., Benedictine Heights Coll., Tulsa, 1957-58; M.Teaching Arts, Tulsa U., 1969; postgrad., Okla. State U., intermittently, 1969—. Cert. secondary tchr., sch. counselor, vis. sch. counselor, Okla. With Sta. WNAD U. Okla., 1947-49; tchr. lang. arts Tulsa Bd. Edn., 1959-73; women's counselor Tulsa YWCA, 1980; vis. sch. counselor Tulsa County Supt. of Schs. Office, 1980-86, dir. spl. project, 1986-91; owner, dir. Svc. to Families in Bus. and Industry, 1991—. Coord. City Devel. Block grant for Tulsa Helpline Enhanced Access Program, 1999-2000. Mem. budget com. United Way Greater Tulsa, 1980-86; mem. Tulsa County adv. coun. Okla. State U., 1983-85; chairperson Tulsa Coalition for Parenting Edn., 1983-84; chairperson problems of youth study Tulsa Met. C. of C., 1984-85; mem. gen. bd. March of Dimes Greater Tulsa, 1985; pres. evening alliance All Souls Unitarian Ch., 1993-94. Mem. Am. Assn. for Counseling and Devel., Internat. Assn. Pupil Personnel Workers (state bd. dirs. 1982-86), Okla. Assn. Family Resource Programs (regional v.p. 1982-86, state pres. 1986-87), Program Internat. Ednl. Exchange (community coord. for Tulsa 1986-90), LWV Okla. (chairperson juvenile justice study 1976-77), LWV Met. Tulsa (mem. exec. bd. 1993-95), Tulsa Parents as Tchrs. Inc. (founding pres. 1991-92, exec. bd. 1992-96). Democrat. Unitarian Universalist. Avocation: piano.

FORNI, PATRICIA ROSE, dean; b. St. Louis, Feb. 14, 1932; d. Harold and Glenda M. (Keay) Brown. BSN, Washington U., St. Louis, 1955, MS (USPHS trainee), 1957; PhD (USPHS fellow), St. Louis U., 1965; postgrad. (USPHS scholar), U. Minn., summers 1968, 70. Staff nurse McMillan EENT Hosp., St. Louis, summer 1955, Renard Psychiat. Hosp., St. Louis, part-time 1955-57; rsch. asst. Washington U. Sch. Nursing, St. Louis, 1957-59, rsch. assoc., 1959-61, asst. prof., 1964-66, assoc. dean in charge grad. edn., assoc. prof. gen. nursing sci., 1966-68; assoc. prof. pub. health nursing Wayne State U., Detroit, 1968-69; asst. dir. for manpower and edn. Ill. Regional Med. Program, Chgo., 1969-71; project dir. Midwest Continuing Profl. Edn. for Nurses, St. Louis U., 1971-75; dean, prof. nursing So. Ill. U., Edwardsville, 1975-88; dean Coll. Nursing U. Okla., Oklahoma City, 1988—2004, prof. Coll. Nursing, 1988—. Grant proposal reviewer Divsn. Nursing, USPHS, 1972-79, 88, 91, NSF, 1978, U.S. Dept. Edn., 1980; mem. Ill. Implementation Commn. on Nursing, 1975-77, Okla. State Health Plan Adv. Com., 1994—. Mem. peer rev. panel Nursing Outlook, 1987-91; mem. editl. bd. Health Care for Women Internat., 1984—, Jour. Profl. Nursing, 1988-90. Chairwoman articulation of nursing programs task force Okla. State Regents for Higher Edn., 1990-91; bd. dirs. Greater St. Louis Health Sys. Agy., 1976-81, Adult Edn. Coun. Greater St. Louis, 1973-76, Edwardsville unit Am. Cancer Soc., 1981-88. Fellow WHO, Sweden, Finland, 1985. Mem. Nat. League for Nursing (accreditation site visitor 1979—, nominating com. Coun. Baccalaureate and Higher Degree Programs 1979-82, pub. policy and legis. com. 1991-95, bd. dirs. 1991-93, treas. 1991-93, mem. fin. com. 1991-95), Nat. League for Health Care (trustee 1991-93), Nat. League for Nursing Accrediting Commn. (peer review panel, baccalaureate and higher degree programs 1997-2000, commr. 2000-, chmn. 2001-), Am. Nurses Assn. (chmn. continuing edn. publs. com. 1975-76), Mo. Nurses Assn. (chmn. edn. com. 1973-77), Greater St. Louis Soc. Health Manpower Edn. and Tng. (chmn. legis. com. 1974-75), Midwest Alliance in Nursing (1st governing bd. 1979-80, 93-96, chmn. nominations com. 1980, 81, mem. fin. com. 1993-94, chair fin. com. 1994-96, treas. 1994-96, pres. 1998-2000), Am. Assn. Colls. Nursing (program com. 1978-82, mem.-at-large, bd. dirs. 1990-92, chair rsch. com. 1990-92), Ill. Coun. Deans/Dirs. Baccalaureate and Higher Degree Programs in Nursing (chmn. 1979-81), Am. Acad. Nursing (treas., chairwoman fin. com., mem. gov. coun. 1989-93, editor Newsletter 1982-87), Ill. Nurses Assn. (commn. on adminstrn. 1983-87, commn. on edn. 1987-89), Okla. Nurses Found. (pres. bd. trustees 1990-93), Sigma Theta Tau Internat. (charter mem. Epsilon Eta chpt. 1980). Office: U Okla Coll Nursing PO Box 26901 Oklahoma City OK 73190-0001

FORREST, IRIS, publisher; b. N.Y.C., Dec. 4, 1925; d. Elliot Albert and Sade (Roth) Daitz; children: Richard Lee, Douglas Edward. BA, Finch Coll., 1944. Editor/publisher: Computer Tales of Fact and Fantasy, 1993, Computer Legends, Lies and Lore, 1994. Mem. Actors Equity Assn., Publishers Mktg. Assn., Fla. Publishers Assn. Avocations: dance, tennis. Office: Ageless Press PO Box 5915 Sarasota FL 34277-5915 Office Phone: 941-952-0576.

FORREST, KATHERINE VIRGINIA, writer; b. Windsor, Ont., Can., Apr. 20, 1939; d. Leland Wilson and Mary Elizabeth (Gilhuly) McKinlay. Student, Wayne State U., UCLA. With GM Corp., Detroit, Mich., 1957-62, Technicolor, Inc., L.A., 1962-72; adminstr., mgr. Reynolds Metals Co., L.A., 1972-78; sr. editor The Naiad Press, Tallahassee, Fla., 1983-95. Author: Curious Wine, 1983, Daughters of a Coral Dawn, 1984, Amateur City, 1984, An Emergence of Green, 1986, Murder at the Nightwood Bar, 1987, Dreams and Swords, 1987, The Beverly Malibu, 1989, Murder by Tradition, 1991, Flashpoint, 1994, Liberty Square, 1996, Apparition Alley, 1997, Sleeping Bones, 1999, Daughters of an Amber Noon, 2003, Hancock Park, 2004; editor numerous books. Mem. PEN Internat.

FORREST, LINDA SUE, music educator; b. Oklahoma City, June 4, 1947; d. Paul Francis and Vivian Bell Winchester; m. Robert Claude Forrest, Jr.; children: Robin Lynn, Jon Ryan. BA in Music Edn., Oklahoma City U., 1969; MA in Music Edn. (Kodaly), U. Okla., 1992. Orff cert. levels I, II and III 1989, Kodaly cert. 1993, registered nat. music educator MENC, 1997. Vocal music tchr. New World Sch., Oklahoma City, 1968—72; substitute vocal music tchr. Oklahoma City, 1979—80; vocal music tchr. Trinity Episc. Sch., Oklahoma City, 1980—81, Apollo Elem. Sch., Oklahoma City, 1981—83, Harvest Hills Elem. Sch., Oklahoma City, 1983—. Ch. organist First Luth. Northwest Bapt. Ch., Oklahoma City, 1966, N.W. Bapt. Ch., 1969—76, Putnam City Bapt. Ch., Cherokee Hills Bapt. Ch., 1977—89, Cherokee Hills Bapt. Ch., 1990—2000; asst. dir., accompanist Putnam City Honor Chorus, Oklahoma City, 1994—; ch. organist Crossings Cmty. Ch., Oklahoma City, 2001—; accompanist Putnam City Honor Chorus, Oklahoma City, 1994—2002. Composer (music books): Orffestration Series Vol. 1-15, 1987—2003; arranger (music book) It's a Small World, 1999, (music book) Deck the Hall with Holiday Sounds, 2001. Mem.: Okla. Music Educators Assn., Okla. Orff Soc. (pres. 1989—91), Nat. Orff Soc., Gamma Phi Beta. Republican. Bapt. Avocations: tennis, sewing, crafts, quilting. Office: Harvest Hills Elem Sch 8201 NW 104 Oklahoma City OK 73162 E-mail: lfnotes@sbcglobal.net.

FORRESTER, PATRICIA TOBACCO, artist; b. Northampton, Mass., 1940; Student, Yale Summer Sch. Music and Art, 1961; BA, Smith Coll., 1962; BFA, Yale U., 1963, MFA, 1965. Resident Yaddo Found., 1979, 81, The MacDowell Colony Residency, 1980, Hand Hollow Found., 1981, San Francisco Mus. Art, 1967. One woman shows include Trutton Gallery, San Francisco, 1968, Capper's Gallery, San Francisco, 1970, William Sawyer Gallery, San Francisco, 1974, 81, 83, Smith Coll. Fine Arts Bldg., Northampton, 1975, M. H. de Young Meml. Mus., San Francisco, 1977, Kornblee Gallery, N.Y.C., 1978, 79, 81, 82, 83, Fendrick Gallery, Washington, 1978, 79, 81, 88, 90, Sebastian Moore Gallery, Denver, 1981, Contemporary Art Ctr., Honolulu, 1984, Frick Gallery, U. Pitts., 1984, 87, U. Conn., 1984, New Orleans Acad. Fine Arts, 1984, 91, Mattingly-Baker Gallery, Dallas, 1985, Fischbach Gallery, N.Y.C., 1987, 89, 90, 92, Reynolds/Minor Gallery, Richmond, Va., 1987, Braunstein/Quay Gallery, San Francisco, 1987, 89, 91, 94, 98, 2001, Gail Severn Gallery, Sun Valley, Idaho, 1988, Sierra Nevada Mus., Reno, 1988, N.Y. Stock Exch. Bldg., N.Y.C., 1989, Luria Gallery, Bay Harbor Island, Fla., 1990, Kalamazoo Inst. Arts, 1991, Stephen Scott Gallery, Balt., 1992, 97, Addison/Ripley Gallery, Washington, 1993, 96, 99, Gerald Peters Gallery, Santa Fe, 1994; exhibited in group shows Mattingly-Baker Gallery, Dallas, 1982, Springfield (Mo.) Art Mus., 1983, Pa. Acad. Fine Arts, Phila., 1983, Art Inst. Chgo., 1983, Corcoran Gallery, Washington, 1984, Bklyn. Mus., N.Y.C., 1985, William Sawyer Gallery, San Francisco, 1985, 88, Coll. of Mainland, Texas City, Tex., 1985, William's Coll. Art Ctr., Williamstown, Mass., 1985-86, Akron (Ohio) Art Mus., 1985-86, Madison (Wis.) Art Ctr., 1985-86, San Francisco Mus. Art, 1985-86, DeCordova and Dana Mus. Art, Lincoln, Mass., 1985-86, Archer M. Huntington Art Gallery U. Evanston, Ill., 1985-86, William's Coll. Art Ctr., Williamstown, Mass., 1985-86, Akron (Ohio) Art Mus., 1985-86, Madison (Wis.) Art Ctr., 1985-86, Metro. Mus., Miami, 1986, Springfield (Mo.) Art Mus., 1986, Art Mus. Santa Cruz County, 1987, The Sierra Nevada Mus. Art, Reno, Nev., 1988, William Sawyer Gallery, San Francisco, 1988, Kohler Arts Ctr., Sheboygan, Wis., 1988, Grand Ctrl. Art Galleries, N.Y.C., 1989, Fendrick Gallery, Washington, 1989, Gallery K., Washington, 1989, The Palmer Mus. Art, Pa., 1990, Steven Scott Gallery, Balt., 1990, Am. Acad. and Inst. Arts and Letters, N.Y.C., 1991, The Gallery at Bristol-Myers Squibb, Princeton, N.J., 1991, The Noves Mus., N.J., 1991, Ctr. Contemporary Arts, Miami, 1991, Nat. Mus. Women in the Arts, 1991-92, 2000, The Miyagi Mus. Art, Sendai, Japan, 1991-92, Sogo Mus. Art, Yokohama, Japan, 1991-92, Tokushima (Japan) Mod. Art Mus., 1991-92, Mus. Modern Art, Shiga, Japan, 1991-92, Kochi (Japan) Prefectural Mus. Folk Art, 1991-92; Kavesh Gallery, Ketchum, Idaho, 1993, Nat. Acad. Design, N.Y.C., 1993, Sewall Art Gallery Rice U., Houston, 1993, Gerald Peters Gallery, Santa Fe, N. Mex., 1993, Philbrook Mus., Davenport Mus., 2000, Meridian Internat. Ctr., Traveling to Vietnam, China, Singapore, Indonesia, 2000; represented in numerous pub. and pvt. permanent collections including The Achenbach Found., Art Inst. Chgo., Hawaii Arts Ctr., Indpls. Mus. Art., Meml. Art Gallery, Oakland Mus., N.Y. Pub. Lib., San Antonio Mus. Art, San Francisco Art Commn., Springfield Mus., The British Mus., The Brooklyn Mus., University Art Mus., Corcoran Gallery, Nat. Mus. Am. Art, Nat. Mus. for Women in the Arts; others. Guggenheim fellow in printmaking, 1967. Mem. Nat. Acad. Design, Phi Beta Kappa. Address: Addison Ripley Fine Art 1670 Wisconsin Ave NW Washington DC 20007

FORRINGER, DEBORAH LEE, music educator; b. Camp Le June Marine Corp Base, N.C., Oct. 7, 1952; d. Alfred Eugene and Phyllis Ilene (Wilson) Goldinger; m. Kenneth Robert Forringer, June 8, 1974; children: Teresa Elaine, Letitia Marie. BS in Music Edn., Mansfield (Pa.) U., 1973; MA, Ind. U., 1979. Music tchr. Armstrong Sch. Dist., Ford City, Pa., 1974—. Author: (article) Pa. Music Educators Jour., 2003. Band mem. Armstrong County Cmty. Concert, 1984—. Grantee, Pa. Ho. Reps., 2000, 2003, Shopa-Ames Dept. Store, 2002, 2004. Mem.: Armstrong Edn. Assn.,

NEA, Music Educators Nat. Conf., Pa. Music Educators Assn. (pres. dist. 3 1986—88, v.p. dist. 3 1984—86, curriculum instrn. dist. 3 1994—, Citation of Excellence 1996). Baptist. Achievements include Accepted to team 12 tchrs. to tch. during summer in China. Avocations: reading, sewing, travel. Home: RR 4 Box 324 Kittanning PA 16201 Office: Shannock Valley Elem Sch Main St Rural Valley PA 16249

FORSHEE, GLADYS MARIE, writer, insurance agent; b. Loveland, Colo., July 1, 1942; d. Henry William Hansen and Bird Marie Smith; m. Larry Bill Forshee, Aug. 27, 1960 (widowed Dec. 1992). Cert. ins. agt. Customer svc. rep., acct. mgr. various ins. agys., Denver, 1970—2000; owner Superior Janitorial Svc., Colo., 1975—2000, A Appletree Pub., Superior, 1991—. Author, pub.: (history book) Where Memories Linger, 1994, (cookbook) A Superior Centennial, Culinary Fest Cookbook, 1996, also 11 researched, published and continous updated family histories. Asst. organizer Superior Hist. Soc., 1998; town clk., recorder Town of Superior, 1970—73; cmty. svc. dir. Colo. State Grange, Aurora, 1992—99, Boulder county dep., 1999—2001; rsch. asst. Nat. Archives, Lakewood, Colo.; asst. organizer Superior (Colo.) Vol. Fire Dept., 1972—81; mem., vol. Adams County Hist. Soc., Henderson, Colo., 1991—2004; mem., vol. citizens adv. com. Boulder County Recycling and Composting Authority, 2000—01; chmn. Boulder County Hist. Preservation, 2003—04; mem. Boulder County Resource Conservation Adv. Bd., 2002—04, chair, 2003—04; mem. Adams County Centennial Roundtable, 2002; mem. various state hist. and geneal. socs.; citizen adv. Town of Superior, Colo., 2003—04; event coord. Christian Clown Posse, 2003. Mem.: Green Valley Grange. Avocations: gardening, crocheting, camping, reading, playing the stock market. Home: 404 S 3d Ave Superior CO 80027

FORSTROM, JUNE ROCHELLE, professional society administrator; b. Douglas County, Minn., June 24, 1932; d. George Dewey and Borghild Otillia (Sahl) Nelson; m. Keith William Forstrom, June 23, 1951; children: Mark William, Dawn Rochelle. Grad. high sch., St. Paul. Adminstr. rsch. grants, coord. comm. Geol. Soc. Am., Boulder, Colo., 1973—. Recipient Disting. Service award, Geological Soc. of Am., 1998. Republican. Lutheran. Avocations: reading, music, running, creative stitchery, travel. Home: 7705 Baseline Rd Boulder CO 80303-4707 Office: Geol Soc Am 3300 Penrose Pl Boulder CO 80301-1806

FORSYTH, BEVERLY K. language educator, writer; b. Memphis, June 05; d. Marian Davidson Roy and Oakley Eugene Stover, Johnny Roy. AA in Mass Comm., Odessa (Tex.) Coll.; BA in Mass Comm., U. Tex., Odessa, MA in English, 1995; PhD in English, Union Inst., Cin., 2001. Author: (travel guide book) The Texas Monthly Guidebook to Texas. 3rd edition, 1993; co-author: (anthology) American Women Writers, 1900-1945, A Bio-Bibliographical Critical, 2000; author: (short stories) La Gringa Is My Name, 1999, Pontotoc Witch, 2000, One Last Secret, 2003, Amazon Heart, 2003, The Knock, 2002, Shadow's Edge, 2003; contbr. articles to profl. jours. Grantee Grace Mitchell/Learner Coun. Rsch. Travel, Union Inst., 2000; scholar, 2000, Agnes Rettig, 2000. Mem.: W. Tex. Writers, Tex. Assn. Creative Writing Tchrs., Tex. Coun. Tchrs. English (Pres.'s Classroom Rsch/Travel Study grantee 2001), Tex. C.C. Tchrs. Assn., Conf. Coll. Tchrs. English (exec. bd. councilors 2002—), S. Ctrl. MLA, Tex. Popular Culture Assn., S.W. Popular Culture Assn., Am. Culture Assn., Sigma Kappa Delta, Sigma Tau Delta (life). Office: Odessa Coll 201 W University Odessa TX 79761 Office Phone: 432-335-6661. Business E-Mail: bforsyth@odessa.edu.

FORSYTH, ILENE HAERING, art historian; b. Detroit, Aug. 21, 1928; d. Austin Frederick and Eleanor Marie (Middleton) H.; m. George H. Forsyth, Jr., June 4, 1960. AB, U. Mich., 1950; AM (univ. fellow), Columbia U., 1955, PhD (Fulbright, AAUW, Fels Found. fellow), 1960. Lectr. Barnard Coll., 1955-58; instr. Columbia U., 1959-61; mem. faculty U. Mich., Ann Arbor, 1961—, prof. history of art, 1974-97, prof. emerita, 1998—, Arthur F. Thurnau prof., 1984—; vis. prof. Harvard U., 1980; Mellon vis. prof. U. Pitts., 1981; vis. prof. U. Calif., Berkeley, 1996. Mem. Nat. Com. History Art, 1975-97; bd. dirs. Internat. Ctr. Medieval Art, 1970-95, v.p., 1981-85; mem. supervisory com. Woodrow Wilson Found., 1985-88; Rome prize juror Am. Acad. in Rome, 1986-88; bd. advisors Ctr. Advanced Study in the Visual Arts, Nat. Gallery Art, 1985-88; mem. vis. com. medieval dept. Met. Mus. Art, N.Y.C., 1990-95; Samuel H. Kress prof. Ctr. Advanced Study in the Visual Arts, Nat. Gallery Art, 1998-99, bd. advisors, 1999-2000. Author: The Throne of Wisdom, 1972 (Charles Rufus Morey Book award 1974), The Uses of Art: Medieval Metaphor in The Michigan Law Quadrangle, 1993 (Annie award for non-fiction 1994); co-editor: Current Studies on Cluny, 1988; contbr. articles to profl. jours. Rackham research grantee and fellow, 1965-66, 75-76; grantee Am. Council Learned Socs., 1972-73; mem. Inst. Advanced Study Princeton, 1977 Mem. Coll. Art Assn. (dir. 1980-84), Archaeol. Inst. Am., Medieval Acad. Am. (bd. advs. 1985-86, editorial bd. 1986-90), Medieval Club N.Y., Soc. francaise d'archéologie, Soc. Archtl. Historians, Acad. Arts, Scis. et Belles Lettres Dijon (France), Centre de recherches et d'études préromanes et romanes. Home: 5 Geddes Hts Ann Arbor MI 48104-1724 Office: U Mich Dept Art History Ann Arbor MI 48109

FORTE, MARY L. consumer products company executive; With Federated Dept. Stores, The May Dept. Stores Co., Inc., Macy's; v.p. Housewares Divsn. Rich's Dept. Store, 1989—91; sr. v.p. Bon Marchi Home Divsn. The Federated Dept. Store, 1991—94; sr. v.p. QVC Home Shopping Network, 1994; from pres. Gordon's to pres., CEO Zale Corp., Irving, Tex., 1994—2002, pres., 2002—, CEO, 2002—. Office: Zale Corp 901 W Walnut Hill Ln Irving TX 75038-1003

FORTENBERRY, DELORES B. dean; b. McComb, MS, Jan. 31, 1933; d. Isaac and Maude Elma (Carmel) Brown; m. John Prowell, Jan. 22, 1956 (div. 1960); children: Dennis A. Prowell, Stevie G. Prowell; m. Fred D. Fortenberry, Dec. 3, 1971. BS, Jackson State U., 1963; MA, Ball State U., 1974, EdD, 1988. Sci. & math. tchr. McComb (Ms.) Pub. Schs., 1962-65; sci. tchr. Chgo. Pub. Schs., 1965-68; sci., art tchr. E. Chgo. Pub. Sch., Ind., 1968-80; sci. tchr. Ball State U. Lab Sch., Muncie, IL, 1980-81; sci., math. tchr., gen. edn. E. Chgo. Pub. Sch., Ind., 1981-89, dean, 1989—. Pres. Dist. Sci. Fair com., McComb, Miss., 1964-65; nat. chairperson Pike County Agrl. H.S. Alumni, Chgo., 1991-2000, Pike County Agrl. H.S. scholarship fund; chmn. sci. com. Nat. Alliance Black Sch. Educators, Washington, Chgo. Alliance Black Sch. Educators, 1984-86. Fellow NSF, 1963-64, Ball State U., 1980-81; sabbatical leave E. Chgo. Pub. Sch., 1980-81. Mem. AAUW, Nat. Alliance Black Sch. Educators, Chgo. Alliance Black Sch. Educators (certificate 1986), Afro-Am. History Club (chairperson 1999-2000), Pike County Agrl. H.S. Alumni (nat. chairperson 1991-2000, recipient plaques 1992-94, 96-98), Am. Fedn. Tchrs., Nat. Sci. Tchrs. Assn., Hoosier Assn. Sci. Tchrs., Assn. Supervision and Curriculum Devel., Kappa Delta Pi, Gamma Phi Delta (basilieus, 1968-73), Phi Delta Kappa. Avocations: reading, travel, collecting recipes, collecting black history materials, sports. Home: 831 E 192nd St Glenwood IL 60425-2005 Office: Ctrl High Sch 1100 W Columbus Dr East Chicago IN 46312-2582

FORTENBERRY, VANESSA LEA, media specialist, voice educator; b. Atlanta, Dec. 26, 1954; d. Spear and Zelma Ruth Rucker; children: Thomas Roderick Howard, Teresa Deja'tori Henderson. BA in Music Edn., Clark Coll., 1977; MEd in Media, State U. West Ga., 2002. Cert. media specialist Profl. Stds. Commn. Ga., 2003, Music Profl. Stds. Commn. Ga., 2002. Customer svc. City of Atlanta, 1980—94; music specialist Dekalb County Sch. Sys., Decatur, Ga., 1994—2003, libr. media specialist, 2003—. Voice instr. Century Music, Decatur, 1996—; summer camp instr. Music in Motion, Decatur, 2000—01; choral dir. Uzee Philharm. Youth Symphony, Stone Mountain, Ga., 2003—03. Grantee, Jr. League Dekalb County, 2003; Wilma Sowell Cravey Libr. Media Specialist scholar, The Dekalb County Sch. Sys. Dept. Ednl. Media, 2002. Mem.: ALA (assoc.), PA Ga. Educators (assoc.), Nat. Assn. for Music Edn. (assoc.), Phi Kappa Phi (assoc.).

FORTIN, JUDY, cable news anchor; BA in Govt. and French, Bowdoin Coll. Gen. assignment reporter various stas.; nat. corr. CNN Newsource, Atlanta, 1990; anchor CNN Airport Network, Atlanta; weekend anchor CNN Headline News, Atlanta. Recipient AP awards. Office: c/o CNN 1 CNN Ctr NW Atlanta GA 30303-2762

FORTNER, NELL, professional athletics coach; b. Jackson, Miss. BS, U. Tex., 1982; MS, Stephen F. Austin U., 1987. Asst. coach women's basketball Stephen F. Austin U., Nacogdoches, Tex., 1986—90, Louisiana Tech U., 1991—95, USA Nat. Team, 1995—96; head coach women's basketball Purdue U., West Lafayette, Ind., 1996—97; head coach women's basketball, gen. mgr. Ind. Fever Women's Nat. Basketball Assn., Indpls., 1999—. Head coach women's basketball USA Basketball, 1997—2000, FIBA World Championship, 1998, R.William Jones Cup Tournament, Taiwan, 1998. Named Coach of Yr., Big Ten Conf., 1997, Nat. Coach of Yr., Basketball Times, 1997; recipient Gold medal, Olympic Games, 2000, FIBA World Championships, 1998, Olympic Games, 1996. Office: Indiana Fever 125 S Pennsylvania St Indianapolis IN 46204*

FORYST, CAROLE, computer electronics executive; b. Chgo., Apr. 08; d. James M. and Marie V. Foryst; m. Anthony H. Cordesman, Feb. 14, 1976; children: Justin G., Alexander Scott. Student, Rosary Coll., 1958-61, Cite Universite de Grenoble, France, 1961, Hunter Coll., 1964-67, Roosevelt U., 1970-71. Fin. reporter Chgo. Sun-Times, 1969-72, L.A. Times, 1972; staff asst. to sec. U.S. Dept. Treasury, Washington, 1973-76; dep. dir. pub. affairs U.S. Dept. Interior, Washington, 1976; asst. v.p. Assn. Am. R.R.'s, Washington, 1977-78; v.p. AMTRAK, Washington, 1979-81; assoc. adminstr. budget and policy Urban Mass Transp. Adminstrn., Washington, 1981-84; comml. real estate broker Barnes, Morris & Pardoe, Washington, 1984-88, Larry Hogan & Assocs., Inc., Landover, Md., 1988-93; mortgage broker Mortgage Investment Corp., Vienna, Va., 1993-94, Windsor Mortgage Co, McLean, Va., 1994-95; v.p. ops. Floating Images Inc., Westbury, N.Y., 1997-98, DynaFirm, Inc., Los Alamos, N.Mex., 1998-99, CEO, 1999-2000. Mem. fin. svc. com. Treas. Dept., Fed. Credit Union, 1991-93, Pub. Internat. Bus. Insights, 1991-93, Hotels and Comm. Real Estate Co., 1993-. Republican. Home: PO Box 1114 Corrales NM 87048-1114 Office: PO Box 1114 Corrales NM 87048-1114

FOSCARINIS, MARIA, lawyer; b. N.Y.C., Aug. 8, 1956; d. Nicolas and Rosa F. BA, Barnard Coll., 1977; MA, Columbia U., 1978, JD, 1981. Bar: N.Y. 1982, U.S. Dist. Ct. (so. and ea. dists.) N.Y. 1983, D.C. 1986, U.S. Dist. Ct. D.C., U.S. Ct. Appeals (D.C. cir.). Law clk. to judge U.S. Ct. Appeals (2d cir.), N.Y.C., 1981-82; assoc. Sullivan & Cromwell, N.Y.C., 1982-85; counsel Nat. Coalition for Homeless, Washington, 1985-89; founder and dir. Nat. Law Ctr. on Homelessness and Poverty, Washington, 1989—. Notes editor Columbia U. Law Rev., 1980-81. Harlan Fiske Stone scholar, 1978-79; John Dewey fellow. Mem. ABA (commr. homelessness and poverty, 1989-95). Office: Nat Law Ctr Homelessness and Poverty 1411 K St NW Ste 1400 Washington DC 20005-3404 Home: 1752 Swann St NW Washington DC 20009-5535

FOSDICK, CORA PRIFOLD (CORA PRIFOLD BEEBE), management consultant; b. San Francisco, Nov. 9, 1937; d. George and Beatrice (Ebni) Prifold; m. Ronald Beebe, Jan., 1959 (div.); m. Donald James Fosdick, Oct. 12, 1997. Student, Hollins Coll., Va., 1955-57, Am. U., 1957-58; BA, U. Mich., 1959, MA, 1961; LHD (hon.), Southeastern U., 1993. Adminstrv. asst. Am. Polit. Sci. Assn., 1962-64; research assoc. Inst. Comparative Studies of Polit. Systems, Washington, 1963-65; program planning and evaluation specialist U.S. Office Edn., Washington, 1965-68, planning coordinator, 1968-73, dir. planning and budget div., 1973-80; prin. dep. asst. sec. for elem. and sec. edn. Dept. Edn., Washington, 1980-81; asst. sec. adminstrn. U.S. Treasury Dept., Washington, 1981-84; dir. office of policy, budget and program mgmt. OSWER, EPA, Washington, 1984-86; dir. office of planning, budget and evaluation Dept. Commerce, Washington, 1986-87; commerce & justice br. chief Office of Mgmt. and Budget, 1987-94, advisor to assoc. dir. gen. govt. and fin., 1994; exec. dir. adminstrn., chief fin. officer Office of Thrift Supervision, Washington, 1994-99; v.p. Jefferson Consulting Group, Washington, 1999—2002; ind. cons. Washington, 2002—. Mem. women's com. Washington Performing Arts Soc., 1983—; mem. Coun. for Excellence in Govt. Recipient HEW Superior Svc. award, Presdl. Rank award, 1989; Inst. World Affairs fellow, 1956, Am. Edn. Abroad former fellow, 1960. Fellow: Nat. Acad. Pub. Adminstrn. (vice chair 2002—03, bd. dirs., chair audit com.); mem.: Assn. Assn. Execs., Nat. Press Club, Exec. Women in Govt. Program and Budget Analysis. Home: 1415 N Pegram St Alexandria VA 22304-1933 E-mail: corabeebe@aol.com.

FOSGATE HEGGLI, JULIE DENISE, producer; b. El Paso, Tex., Feb. 17, 1954; d. Orville Edward and Patricia (Ward) Fosgate; m. Bjarne Heggli, June 20, 1980; children: Elise Mai, Kristin April. BA in Broadcasting, U. So. Calif., 1976, MA in Journalism, 1978. On-board editor Royal Viking Line, San Francisco, 1978-80; editor Stentor, Trondheim, Norway, 1981; staff Grunion Gazette, Long Beach, Calif., 1981; news editor Nine Network Australia, Los Angeles, 1981-82; editor South Coast Metro News, Costa Mesa, Calif., 1981-82; v.p. The Newport Group, Newport Beach, Calif., 1982-85; exec. editor Orange County This Month, Newport Beach, 1985; exec. dir. mktg. Gen. Group Cos., Harbor City, Calif., 1985-87; sr. v.p. mktg. Automax Corp., L.A., 1987-88, Gen. Group Internat., Harbor City, Calif., 1988-90; assoc. producer Zoo Life TV Spls., L.A., 1991, NBC News, Burbank, Calif., 1992-94; v.p. mktg. Western Nat., Scottsdale, Ariz., 1994-99; sr. v.p. mktg. CNA Nat. (formerly Western Nat.), Scottsdale, 2000—. Mem. Phi Beta Kappa. Avocations: collecting, reading, art. Home: 9640 E Davenport Dr Scottsdale AZ 85260-1426 Office: CNA Nat 4150 N Drinkwater Blvd Scottsdale AZ 85251-3611

FOSHER, MARY JANE, humanities educator; b. Shakopee, Minn., Dec. 19, 1946; d. William Harold and Mary Agnes (MacEachern) Block; children: Cassandra, Jonathan. BA, Notre Dame Coll., 1969; MS, U. N.H., 1987. English tchr. Raymond (N.H.) High Sch., 1980—2003; dir. English curriculum Raymond Sch. Dist., 1987—. Bd. dirs. A Safe Place, Portsmouth, N.H., 1993-96. Mem. Nat. Coun. Tchrs. English, NOW (sec. Seacoast chpt. 1994—), N.H. Assn. Tchrs. English (bd. dirs. 1995—), N.H. Coun. Tchrs. English. Democrat. Avocations: kayaking, cross country skiing, reading. Office: Iber Holmes Cove MS School St Raymond NH 03077

FOSSLAND, JOEANN JONES, professional speaker, personal coach; b. Balt., Mar. 21, 1948; d. Milton Francis and Clementine (Bowen) Jones; m. Richard E. Yellott III, 1966 (div. 1970); children: Richard E. IV, Dawn Joeann; m. Robert Gerard Fossland Jr., Nov. 25, 1982. Student, Johns Hopkins U., 1966-67; cert., Hogan's Sch. Real Estate, 1982. Cert. values coach, behaviors coach, 1998, GRI; master cert. coach. Owner Kobble Shop, Indiatlantic, Fla., 1968-70, Downstairs, Atlanta, 1971; seamstress Aspen (Colo.) Leather, 1972-75; owner Backporch Feather & Leather, Aspen and Tucson, 1975-81; area mgr. Welcome Wagon, Tucson, 1982; realtor assoc. Tucson Realty & Trust, 1983-85; mgr. Home Illustrated mag., Tucson, 1985-87; asst. pub., gen. mgr. Phoenix, Scottsdale, Albuquerque, Tricities Tucson Homes Illustrated, 1990-93; pres. Advantage Solutions Group, Cortaro, Ariz., 1993—. Power leader Darryl Davis Seminars Power Program, 1995—; personal and profl. coach.; instr. Women's Coun Realtors, 1999—. Designer leather goods (Tucson Mus. Art award 1978, Crested Butte Art Fair Best of Show award 1980); author: Personal and Professional Coaching: Coach University, Certified Training Program, 1996. Voter registrar Recorder's Office City of Tucson, 1985-91; bd. dirs. Hearth Found., Tucson, 1987-96, pres., 1994; bd. dirs. Ariz. Integrated Residential & Ednl. Svcs., Inc., 1989-95, pres. 1994-95). Mem. NAFE, Internat. Fedn. Coaches (master cert. coach), Women's Coun. Realtors (leadership tng. grad. designation, pres. Tucson chpt. 1995, Ariz. state gov. 1997-98, v.p. Region IV, 2000, Tucson Affiliate of Yr. award 1991, Ariz. State Mem. of Yr. 1999), Tucson Assn. Realtors (Affiliate of Yr. award 1988). Democrat. Presbyterian. Avocations: tennis, gardening, reading, travel, public speaking. Office: Advantage Solutions Group PO Box 133 Cortaro AZ 85652-0133 E-mail: joeann@joeann.com.

FOSSUM, RUTH N. musician; b. Maxbass, N.D., Oct. 25, 1922; d. Minnick Fossum and Gussty Jeannette Lewison. BS, Minot State U., 1947; postgrad. in advanced music study, U. Minn. Pvt. musician, ch. organist and choir dir., Fargo, ND, 1951—. Mem.: Music Tchrs. Nat. Assn., Nat. Fedn. Music Clubs (officer), Am. Guild Organists, Sigma Alpha Iota. Avocations: sewing, stamping, gardening, exercise. Home: 1206 2nd Ave S Fargo ND 58103

FOSTER, BONNIE GAYLE, operating room nurse, real estate agent; b. Valentine, Nebr., Dec. 3, 1940; d. Isaac Robert and Helen Anita (Tucker) Bingham; m. Floyd E. Foster, July 4, 1973; m. Daniel A. Plummer, Aug. 8, 1963 (div. Oct. 1971). AA, RN, Oakland City Coll., 1963; BA in Sociology, U. Mo., Kansas City, 1975, M in Edl. Adminstrn., 1978. RN Calif., Kans., Mo., cert. plastic surg. nursing. RN staff O.R. Herrick Hosp., Berkeley, Calif., 1963—64, Kaiser Hosp., Oakland, 1963—64; RN staff oper. room U. Kans. Med. Ctr., Kansas City, 1964—65; RN oper. room Rsch. Med. Ctr., Kansas City, Mo., 1965—78; RN, oper. room supr. Broadway Surg. Ctr., Kansas City, Mo., 1979—86; RN oper. room Menorah Med. Ctr., Kansas City, Mo., 1986—94, Sierra Surgi-Ctr., Walnut Creek, Calif., 1994—; realtor assoc. Pacific Real Estate Svcs., Pleasanton, Calif., 2003—. In svc. instr. Rsch. Hosp. and Med. Ctr., Kansas City, Mo., 1966—72, instr. CPR, 1976—88. Bus. assoc. Network Mktg.; chairperson fund raising program St. Paul's Episcopal Ch., Lee's Summit, Mo., 1976—94, chairperson bldg. expansion program, 1976—94, vestry mem., 1976—94; active St. Clare's Episcopal Ch., Pleasanton, 1994—. Mem.: Assn. Oper. Rm. Nurses (past pres. Greater Kansas City chpt., sec., chairperson Career Fair, co-chairperson Oper. Rm. Nurse of the Yr., panel moderator two-day inst., mem. several coms.). Republican. Episcopalian. Avocations: bicycling, hiking, golf, bridge, gardening. Home: 7567 Maywood Dr Pleasanton CA 94588 Office: Sierra Surgi-Ctr Clin Coor Plastic ENT Maxillary Facial 1601 Ygnacio Valley Rd Walnut Creek CA 94598 Address: Pacific Real Estate Svc 6150 Stoneridge Mall Rd Ste 105 Pleasanton CA 94588

FOSTER, COLLEEN, library director; BA in English Lit., Coll. Notre Dame, Belmont, Calif., 1967; MLS, U. Denver, 1968. Br. reference libr. San Francisco Pub. Libr., 1968-69; reference libr. Stockton-San Joaquin County Pub. Libr., Calif., 1969-77, audiovisual libr., 1977-78, br. supr., 1978-81, libr. divsn. mgr. for adult svcs., 1990-92, dep. dir. libr. svcs., 1992-94, dir. libr. svcs., 1994—. Five gallon blood donor, Delta Blood Bank; mem. League of Women Voters of San Joaquin County, 1981—, sec., 1983-84, mem. speakers bureau, pros and cons presenter, 1985—, voter editor (newsletter), 1984-88, voter distbn. coord., 1991-97, participant candidates' forum, 1984-92, bd. dirs., 1983-84, 88-90, mem. League Study Com.; mem. Leadership Stockton, Class of 1995; reading tutor vol. Marshall Middle Sch. HOSTS (Help One Student to Succeed), 1996—. Mem. ALA, ACLU, NOW, MADD, Calif. Libr. Assn. (coun. mem. 1984-91, chair Coun. Rules Com. 1986, 88-89, bd. dirs. Calif. Soc. Librs. 1987-89, chair Bylaws Reorganization Com. 1990, mem. future of the profession task force, 1995, sec., treas. Calif. County Librs. Assn. 1995, mem. assembly 1995-98, mem. Conf. Planning Com. 1996, Fin. Com. 1996-98, Exec. Com. 1997-98, Mgmt. Svcs. Divsn. Excellence in Libr. Mgmt. award 1997), Habitat for Humanity, So. Poverty Law Ctr., Amnesty Internat., Greenpeace, Nature Conservancy, World Wildlife Found., Sierra Club, Rotary (Stockton chpt., vol. Asparague Festival 1994—, Rotary Read-in 1994—, Su Salud Health Fair 1995). Office: Stockton-San Joaquin County Pub Libr 605 N El Dorado St Stockton CA 95202-1907 Fax: 209-937-8683.

FOSTER, CRYSTAL ANN, elementary school educator; b. Hammond, La., May 5, 1975; d. Jerod and Katherine Ann Foster; children: Daven Lucas Lavigne, Kyle Alexander. BA, Southea. U., Hammond, La., 1998. Cert. tchr. type B La. 2nd grade tchr. Ascension Parish, Donaldsonville, La., 1999—. Grantee, Ascension Fund, 2000—01. Home: 18200 Hwy 16 Port Vincent LA 70726 Personal E-mail: fosterc@teacher.com.

FOSTER, FAITH WILHELMINA, school counselor, educational consultant; d. William and Estelle (Taylor) Smith; m. Esau Foster Sr., Aug. 21, 1971 (div. 1988); children: Esau II, Shani Lynn. BS, Ctrl. State U., 1965; MEd, Kent State U., 1970. Lic. profl. counselor; cert. tchr., prin. Tchr. Cleve. Pub. Schs., 1965-69, 70-71; counselor University City (Mo.) Pub. Schs., 1972-75; probation officer criminal courts Allegheny County, Pitts., 1977-80; counselor Cleveland Heights/University Heights Bd. Edn., 1983—; career edn. counselor Upward Bound, 1983-96. Author: Career Education in Middle School Education, 1974. Mem. citizens adv. coun. City of Cleveland Heights, 1991-96; chairperson civil rights AFT, Cleveland Heights/University Heights, 1993—; chairperson Sch. Am., 1992-97, Delta Acad., 1997—. Mem. ASCD, Phi Delta Kappa. Avocations: reading, sewing. Home: 1080 Rushleigh Rd Cleveland OH 44121-1444

FOSTER, JAN S. special education educator; b. Eldorado, Ill., Nov. 15, 1950; d. James H. and Rosemary S. (Triplett) Richey; m. Alan Joe Foster, Dec. 15, 1972; children: Michelle Daye, James Joseph. AS, Southeastern Ill. Coll., Harrisburg, 1972; BS in Spl. Edn., Ea. Ill. U., 1998. Bookkeeper Money Stretcher Newspaper, Galatia, Ill., 1980—88; tchrs. aide Galatia Cmty. Dist. 1, 1988—98, after sch. tutoring, 1999—; spl. edn. tchr. Joppa (Ill.) Sch. Dist., 1998—99, Galatia Cmty. Dist. 1, 1999—. Vol. Spl. Olympics, Galatia, 1996—97; Sunday sch. tchr. Galatia Ch., 1990—96. Mem.: Galatia Edn. Assn. (activity chmn. 2000—), Young Reps., Illinois 4-H Club, Lions. Republican. Baptist. Avocations: cooking, shopping, gardening, antiques. Home: 500 E Church St Galatia IL 62935 Office: Galatia Jr High Sch R # 1 Galatia IL 62935

FOSTER, JODIE (ALICIA CHRISTIAN FOSTER), actress, film director, film producer; b. L.A., Nov. 19, 1962; d. Lucius and Evelyn (Almond) F.; children: Charles, Kit BA in Lit. cum laude, Yale U., 1985. Acting debut in TV show Mayberry, R.F.D, 1969; numerous other TV appearances including My Three Sons, The Courtship of Eddie's Father, Gunsmoke, Bonanza, Paper Moon, 1974-75; TV spl. The Secret Life of T.K. Dearing, 1975; TV movies include Rookie of the Year, Smile, Jenny, You're Dead; motion picture appearances include Napoleon and Samantha, 1972, One Little Indian, 1973, Tom Sawyer, 1973, Alice Doesn't Live Here Anymore, 1974, Taxi Driver, 1976 (Acad. award nominee for Best Supporting Actress), Echoes of a Summer, 1976, Bugsy Malone, 1976, Freaky Friday, 1976, Moi, Fleur Bleue, 1977, Casotto, 1977, The Little Girl Who Lives Down the Lane, 1977, Candleshoe, 1977, Foxes, 1980, Carny, 1980, O'Hara's Wife, 1982, Hotel New Hampshire, 1984, The Blood of Others, 1984, Five Corners, 1987, Siesta, 1987, Stealing Home, 1988, The Accused, 1988 (Acad. award for Best Actress, 1989), Backtrack, 1989, The Silence of the Lambs, 1991 (Golden Globe award for Best Actress in Drama, 1992, Acad. award for Best Actress, 1992, BAFTA award for best actress, 1992), Shadows and Fog, 1992, Sommersby, 1993, Maverick, 1994, Contact, 1997, Anna and The King, 1999, Panic Room, 2002; dir., actress: Little Man Tate, 1991; prodr., actress: Mesmerized, 1986, Nell, 1994 (Acad. award nominee for Best Actress 1995), The Dangerous Lives of Altar Boys, 2002; dir., prodr. Home For the Holidays, 1995; exec. prodr. (Showtime) Babydance, 1998, Waking the Dead, 2000. Recipient Golden Globe award, 1989. Office: EGG Pictures Production Co Jerry Lewis Annex 5555 Melrose Ave Los Angeles CA 90038-3112

FOSTER, JOY VIA, retired library media specialist; b. Besoco, W.Va., Aug. 11, 1935; d. George Edward and Burgia Stafford (Earls) Via; m. Paul Harris Foster, Jr., Dec. 8, 1956 (dec. Dec. 20, 1962); children: Elizabeth Lee, Michael Paul. BS, Radford Coll., 1971; MS, Radford U., 1979. Cert. pub. sch. libr., Va. Clk. Va. Tech. and State U., Blacksburg, 1955-57, Christiansburg (Va.) Primary Sch., 1971-73, [illegible]; Auburn Mid. and High Sch., Riner, Va., 1985-00; ret., 2000. Meml. chmn. Am. Cancer Soc., Christiansburg, 1965—66; block worker, 1985—91; area chmn. Am. Heart Fund, Christiansburg, 1990—93; pres. Montgomery County Ret. Tchrs. Assn., 2002—04; trustee Montgomery-Floyd Regional Libr. Bd, 2003—. Mem.: Va. Ednl. Assn., Va. Ednl. Media Assn. (Meritorious Svc. award 1999). Presbyterian. Avocations: reading, bowling, flea marketing, antique collecting.

FOSTER, KIM, art dealer, gallery owner; b. Washington, Nov. 22, 1956; d. James R. and Clair Lynn (Block) Foster; m. Antonio Petracca, Oct. 30, 1994. BA, Sarah Lawrence Coll.; MA, Johns Hopkins U. Lic. stockbroker, N.Y. Asst. treas. Bankers Trust Co., N.Y.C., 1980-83; asst. v.p. Marine Midland, N.Y.C., 1984-85; commodities credit mgr. Shearson Lehman, N.Y.C., 1985-86; v.p. Bayerische Vereinsbank, N.Y.C., 1988-94; pres. Kim Foster Gallery, N.Y.C., 1993—. Bd. dirs. Foster Holdings, Inc., Pitts. Speech writer Gov. James R. Thompson, Chgo., 1975. Mem. Mus. Modern Art., Whitney Mus. Am. Art. Republican. Jewish. Avocations: swimming, travel. Office: Kim Foster Gallery 529 W 20th St New York NY 10011-2800 Office Phone: 212-229-0044. E-mail: kimfoster1@hotmail.com.

FOSTER, LINDA TIMBERLAKE, state legislator; b. Portland, Maine, Feb. 8, 1943; m. Bernard Scott; 3 children. BS, U. Maine, 1965. Rep. Hillsborough Dist. 10 N.H. State Ho. of Reps., 1992—; policy leader Dem. Party, NH. Bd. dirs. Family Strength. Mem. N.H. Assn. Residential Care Homes (adv. bd.), So. N.H. Svcs. (exec. bd.), Phi Kappa Phi. Office: NH Ho of Reps Com on Fin State Capitol Concord NH 03301

FOSTER, LUCILLE CASTER, school system administrator, retired; b. Vallejo, Calif., Sept. 28, 1921; d. Lewis Caster and Mabel Estelle (Witt) Beidleman; m. Donald Foster, Nov. 21, 1942 (deceased). AB in History, U. Calif., Berkeley, 1943; MA in Elem. Edn., San Francisco State U., 1953; EdD, Stanford U., 1959. Cert. sch. adminstr., Calif. Elem. tchr. Alameda (Calif.) Unified Sch. Dist., 1948-55; curriculum cons. Laguna Salada Elem. Sch. Dist., Pacifica, Calif., 1955-60, asst. supt., 1960-81; ret., 1981. Fir br. Children's Med. Ctr. No. Calif. Co-author (handbooks) Selling Ventures, 2000, Grant Writing 4th edit., 2002, Fundraising, 2d edit., 2002, Resource Development, 2002; contbr. articles to Calif. Jour. Elem. Edn., 1957, 61. Mem. AAUW (Santa Rosa br.), Can. Fedn. Univ. Women (hon. life), Internat. Fedn. U. Women, Calif. Sch. Adminstrs. Assn. (life), Calif. Tchrs. Assn. (life), Calif. Sch. Personnel Commrs. Assn. (life), Nat. Assistance League, Assistance League Sonoma County (hon. life), Pi Lambda Theta, Delta Zeta. Avocations: community volunteer, bridge, travel. Home: 245 Mockingbird Cir Santa Rosa CA 95409-6245 Fax: 707-538-2584.

FOSTER, M. JOAN, lawyer; b. Cin. d. William and Marguerite (DeHaven) Moeller; children: Peter Graf, James DeHaven. BA, Duke U., 1961; JD cum laude, Seton Hall U., 1976. Bar: N.J. 1976, U.S. Dist. Ct. N.J. 1976, U.S. Ct. Appeals (3d cir.) 1980, U.S. Dist. Ct (no. dist.) Calif. 1982. Assoc. Lowenstein, Sandler, Kohl, Fisher & Boylan, Roseland, N.J., 1976-79, Grotta, Glassman & Hoffman, PA, Roseland, 1980-85, prin., 1986—. Adj. prof. Seton Hall Law Sch., Newark, 1978-80. Trustee N.J. Symphony Orch., Newark, 1989—, vice chair, 1997—. Mem. ABA (labor and employment law sect. 1980—, internat. law sect. 1988—), N.J. State Bar Assn. (exec. com. labor and employment sect. 1982—, editor-in-chief 1984-88, sec. 1991-92, vice chair 1992-93, chair 1993-94, health and hosp. law sect. 1988—), N.J. Pub. Employer Labor Rels. Assn. (trustee 1993—), N.J. Network of Bus. and Profl. Women (trustee 1980—, pres. bd. trustees 1991-93), U.S. Dist. Ct. Hist. Soc. (trustee, exec. com. N.J. dist. 1989-92). Office: Grotta Glassman & Hoffman PA 75 Livingston Ave Ste 13 Roseland NJ 07068-3701

FOSTER, MARY CHRISTINE, film producer; b. L.A., Mar. 19, 1943; d. Ernest Albert and Mary Ada (Quilici) Foster; m. Paul Hunter, July 24, 1982. BA, Immaculate Heart Coll., L.A., 1967; M in TV News Documentary, UCLA, 1968. Dir. R & D Metromedia Producers Corp., L.A., 1968-71; dir. devel. and prodn. svcs. Wolper Prodns., L.A., 1971-76; mgr. film programs NBC-TV, Burbank, Calif., 1976-77; v.p. movies and mini series Columbia Pictures TV, Burbank, 1977-81, v.p. series programs, 1981; v.p. program devel. Group W. Prodns., L.A., 1981-87; agt. The Agency, L.A., 1988-90, Shapiro-Lichtman Agy., L.A., 1990-99; ind. prodr., 1999—. Lectr. in field. Creator (TV series) Sullivan, 1985, Auntie Mom, 1986; author: Immaculate Heart H.S., L.A., 2002—, 100 Year Anniversary Book, 2003. Trustee Immaculate Heart H.S., L.A., 1980—; mem. exec. com. Humanitas Awards Human Family Inst., 1985—; mem. cmty. devel. com. Immaculate Heart Cmty., 2001—; mem. exec. com. L.A. Roman Cath. Archdiocesan Comm. Commn., L.A., 1986—90; bd. dirs., treas. Catholics in Media, 1992—; mem. vol. com., writer tour script, book, newsletter and website Cathedral of Our Lady of Angels, 2002—; chmn. pastorial coun. St. Francis of Assisi, 2003—, chmn. stewardship com. and renovation com. Mem.: NATAS, Women in Film (bd. dirs. 1974—78). Democrat. E-mail: fosterc@aol.com.

FOSTER, ROSEMARY ALICE, lawyer, artist; b. Independence, Iowa, Oct. 2, 1944; d. James Charles Mooney and Hilda Marie Engelkes; m. Monty Foster, July 20, 1979 (dec. Jan. 17, 2000); 1 child, Daisy Ward. BA, Drake U., 1964; JD, George Washington U., 1967; MA in Psychology, U. Utah, 1973. Bar: D.C. 1968. Supr. neighborhood probation unit Second Dist. Juvenile Ct., Salt Lake City, 1968—73; legal cons. State of Idaho, Boise, Idaho, 1973—74; atty. Nat. Ctr. Law Handicapped, South Bend, Ind., 1974—75; adminstrv. law judge Wash. Office Adminstrv. Hearings, Olympia, Wash., 1976—2001; with STEPS Program Cmty. Mental Health, Homer, Alaska, 2001—02; hearing officer Workers Compensation Dept. Labor, Anchorage, 2002—. Exhibitions include Artist's Gallery, Olympia, Wash., 1995—97, Cuyamungue Stone Co., Homer, Alaska, 2003, Mystic Enterprises, 2003. Vol. Youth Ct., Olympia, 1998—2001; mem. Alaska Women's Polit. Caucus, Anchorage, 2003; bd. dir. South Peninsula Women's Svcs., Homer, Alaska, 2000—02. Recipient Svc. award, State of Wash., 2001. Mem.: LWV. Democrat. Roman Catholic. Office: 2440 E Tudor Rd Anchorage AK 99507

FOSTER, SALLY, interior designer; b. New Orleans, Nov. 6, 1927; d. Charles Shearer and Bessie Long Foster; m. Harold Barnett McSween, Dec. 21, 1948 (div. Mar. 1979); children: John Charles McSween, Robert Douglas McSween, Elizabeth McSween, Sally McSween Ward. BA, Tulane U., 1948. Interior designer, owner Sally Foster Designs, Alexandria, La., 1979—. Bd. dirs., past pres. Alexandria Mus. Art, 1988—92, 1999—, Kent Plantation House, Alexandria, 1964—67, 1998—; founding mem. bd. dirs. Rapides Symphony Orch., Alexandria, 1973. Mem.: Alexandria Jr. League (pres. 1963—64), Nat. Soc. Colonial Dames Am., Alexandria Golf and Country Club, Alexandria Rotary Club, Chi Omega. Republican. Episcopalian. Avocations: antiques, travel, food, reading. Office: Sally Foster Designs 1307 Windsor Pl Alexandria LA 71303-2751

FOSTER, SCARLETT LEE, investor relations executive; b. Charleston, W.Va., Dec. 14, 1956; d. William Christoph Foster, Jr. and Anne (Howes) Conway. B in Comm., Bethany Coll., 1979; MBA, Washington, 2000. Dir. pub. rels. Allergy Rehab. Found., Charleston, 1979-80; dir. pubs. Contractors Assn. W.Va., Charleston, 1980-82; comm. rep. Monsanto Co., Nitro, W.Va., 1982-84, 1984-87, mgr. environ. and community rels. St. Louis, 1987-89, mgr. pub. rels., 1989-91, mgr. fin. pub. rels., 1991-93, dir. pub. rels., 1993-94, dir. pub. affairs, 1994-2001, dir. investor rels., 2001—. Trustee Bethany (W.Va.) Coll., 1994—. Named Outstanding Alumni of Achievement Bethany Coll., 1990. Mem. Nat. Investor Rels. Inst. Episcopalian. Avocations: biking, reading, cooking, gardening. Office: Monsanto Co A2SP 800 N Lindbergh Blvd # A2sp Saint Louis MO 63167-0001 E-mail: scarlett.l.foster@monsanto.com.

FOSTER, SUTTON, actress; b. Statesboro, Ga., Mar. 18, 1975; Postgrad., Carnegie Mellon U., Hunter Coll., N.Y.C. Actor: (Broadway musical) Grease, Annie, Scarlet Pimpernel, Les Misérables, Thoroughly Modern Millie (winner Tony award for Best Performance by a Leading Actress in a Musical, 2002). Office: Marquis Theatre 211 W 45th St New York NY 10036

FOSTER, TEREE E. law educator, dean; BA in English Lit., U. Ill., Chgo., 1968; JD, Loyola U., Chgo., 1976. Bar: Ill. 1976, U.S. Dist. Ct. (no. dist.) Ill. 1976, U.S. Dist. Ct. (we. dist.) Okla. 1976, U.S. Ct. Appeals 7th and 10th cirs.) 1983, Okla. 1984. Admissions officer U. Ill., Chgo., 1968-69; co-dir. Dept. Def., Hanau, Germany, 1969-72; intern Office of State Appellate Defender, Springfield, Ill., 1974; law clk. Philip H. Corboy and Assocs., Chgo., 1974-76; instr., teaching asst. Loyola U., Chgo., 1975-77; jud. law clk. U.S Ct. Appeals, Chgo., 1976-77; of counsel Hastie & Kirschner, Oklahoma City, 1984-90; from asst. prof. to assoc. prof. U. Okla., Norman, 1980-83, prof., 1983-93, assoc. dean, 1990-92; dean, prof. law U. W.Va., Morgantown, 1993-97, mem. bd. advisors, 1994-96, facilitator social justic common ground forum, 1994-97; dean, prof. law DePaul U., Chgo., 1997—. Vis. prof. U. Denver, 1992-93, U. Fla., 1988-89, Ohio State U., 1987-88; mem. Chgo. com. Chgo. Coun. on Fgn. Rels., 1997—; mem. Chgo. Lawyers Com. for Civil Rights under Law, 1997—. Contbr. articles to profl. jours. Host Perspectives, 1986-87, The Law in Your Life, 1995-97, Legal Lines, 1996-97; co-host Encounter, 1983-85; gov. bd. W.Va. Rape and Domestic Violence Info. Ctr., 1993-97, W.Va. Women's Alliance, 1993-97, Okla. Com. Prevention Child Abuse, 1990-93; instr. Rite Christian Initiation Adults St. Thomas More U., 1983-87; exec. com. Southwest Ctr. Human Rels. Studies, 1983-86, directorship search com., 1984-85; task force Quality of Okla. Life, 1983-84; mem. Chgo. com. Chgo. Coun. on Fgn. Rels., 1997—; mem. Chgo. Com. for Civil Rights Under Law, 1997—. Mem. ABA, Ill. Bar Assn., Soc. Am. Law Tchrs., Assn. Am. Law Schs., Am. Judicature Soc. Home: 851 W Roscoe St Chicago IL 60657-2303 Office: DePaul U Office of Dean College of Law 25 E Jackson Blvd Chicago IL 60604-2289

FOSTER, WILLETTA JEAN, music educator; b. Paris, Tex., Feb. 18, 1939; d. Eugene Curtis and Lyda Willetta (Murphy) Lawhorn; m. Paul Kenneth Foster, Mar. 4, 1961 (dec. Nov. 1986); 1 child, Paulette LaRee Foster Galbraith. AA, Tyler Jr. Coll., 1959; BS, Tex. Women's U., 1961, postgrad., 1961-63. Tchr. music pvt. practice, Ft. Worth, Houston, Tyler, Tex., 1959—; dir. music West U. Meth. Ch., Houston, 1965-67; devel. specialist, tchr. music Palmer Sch., Houston, 1983-88; tchr. music Duchesne Acad., Houston, 1984-91, U. St. Thomas Sch. Little Children, Houston, 1989-90; co-owner, devel. specialist, program dir. Acad. Skills Svcs. Learning Ctr., Houston, 1983-88; instr. U. Tex., Tyler, 1993-95; developer, dir. Acad. Skills & Knowledge, Tyler, 1996-98; devel./cognitive cons. Bay Waveland Sch. Dist., Bay St. Louis, Miss., 1998—. Cons. and spkr. in field. Author, composer: (albums) These Are Me, I Can Be Any of These, Listen It's the Singing Me, Watch It's the Dancing Me, Bravo It's the Creative Me, I Can Go Left, Right, All About, My World and Me, Shh-It's the Listening Me; author: (video) I Can Run I Can Read. Big sister Convent of the Good Shepherd, Houston, 1965-66; vol. Rep. County Hdqrs., Houston, 1964. Recipient Book Golden Deeds, Exch. Club Houston, 1986. Mem. Nat. Music Tchrs. Assn., Am. Contract Bridge League, Tex. Music Tchrs. Assn., Tyler Music Tchrs. Assn. (treas. 1993-96). Presbyterian. Avocations: needlework, bridge, gardening, reading. Home: 126 Engman Ave Bay Saint Louis MS 39520-2116 Office: Bay-Waveland Sch Dist Bay Saint Louis MS 39520

FOSTER-WELLS, KAREN MARGARET, artist; b. Pasadena, Calif., Oct. 26, 1942; d. Ray Russell Foster and Margaret Victoria Ray; m. David Roycroft Rory Wells, Sept. 17, 1988; children; John McCarthy, Sabisha Friedberg. AA, Orange Coast Coll., Costa Mesa, Calif., 1962; student, U. Calif., Irvine, 1967-68, Laguna Beach Sch. Art/Design, Calif., 1965-67. Illustrator, 1963—. One-woman shows include Santa Barbara (Calif.) of Natural History, 1979, Morro Bay (Calif.) Mus. of Natural History, 1988, Great Western Bank, San Luis Obispo, Calif., 1989, Cayucos (Calif.) Art Assn., 1993, Chelsea Bookshop, Paso Robles, Calif., 1993, Paso Robles Art Assn. Gallery, 1993, Wild Horse Found., Santa Barbara, Summerwood Winery, 2002; group exhbns. include Waterside Gallery, Morro Bay, Calif., 1997, 98, Johnson Gallery and Framing Studio, San Luis Obispo, 1999, 2000, Coll. of Creative Studies, Santa Barbara, 2000, Santa Barbara Mus. Natural History, 2000, Carnegie Western Art Gallery, Paso robles, 2000-2001, San Luis Obispo Art Ctr., 2001, Cayucos Art Assn., 2001, Biennale Internazionale Dell'arte Contemporanea, Florence, Italy, 2003, Mid-State Fair (Artist Achievement award 2003), Quick Draw Cowboy Festival, Santa Clarita, 2003, 2004, Cattlemen's Western Art Show, Paso Robles, 2004, (with pianist Hilary Anderson) Painting Concert, 2004; artist (cover) The Path of Return, 2001, Monterey Mus. Art, 2002. Recipient Bronze medal Art of Calif. Discovery awards, 1993, 1st Pl. Calif. Mid-State Fair Art Show, 1994, 98, 1st Pl. and Coord. award Calif. Mid-State Fair Art Show, 2000, Best of Show Paso Robles Art Assn., 2000, Color of Autumn award Paso Robles Art Assn., 2004. Mem. The Oak Group, Calif. Art Club, San Luis Outdoor Painters Enterprise (co-founder), Am. Soc. Portrait Artists, Women Artists of the West. Avocations: horses, natural history. Office: Karen Foster Artist dot com PO Box 1114 Templeton CA 93465 Office Phone: 805-239-8413. E-mail: horseart@tcsn.net.

FOTI, MARGARET, medical association administrator, editor, consultant; b. Phila., Dec. 15, 1944; d. Samuel A. and Margaret M. (DiBiase) F. BA, Temple U., 1975, MA in Comm., 1985, PhD in Comm., 1995; MD (hon.), U. Rome, 2003. Tech. editor U. Pa., Phila., 1962-64, asst. to bus adminstr., 1964-65; sr. editorial asst. Cancer Rsch. Jour., Phila., 1965-69, mng. editor, 1969—; CEO, Am. Assn. Cancer Rsch., Phila., 1982—. Adminstrn., pub. edn., devel., editorl. and pub. cons., lectr. in field. Contbr. articles to profl. jours. Pres. Nat. Coalition for Cancer Rsch., 1994-96. Recipient cert. of appreciation Am. Assn. Cancer Rsch., 1975, 85, 90, 99, Woman of Distinction award, 1999, Cino del Duca award, 2000, Ville de Paris award, 2000, award City of Trento, Italy, 2002, Solemn Encomium recognition U. Palermo, Italy, 2003. Mem.: AAAS, European Assn. Cancer Rsch., Coun. Engrs. and Sci. Soc. Execs., Coun. Biology Editors (pres. 1980—81), Soc. for Scholarly Publs. (pres. 1996—97), Internat. Fedn. Sci. Editors, European Assn. Sci. Editors, European Assn. Cancer Rsch. (disting.), Am. Assn. Cancer Rsch., Am. Soc. Assn. Execs., Japanese Cancer Assn. (hon.). Democrat. Roman Catholic. Home: 220 Locust St Apt 24A Philadelphia PA 19106-3932 Office: Am Assn Cancer Rsch 615 Chestnut St 17th Fl Philadelphia PA 19106-4404 E-mail: foti@aacr.org.

FOTOPOULOS, DANIELLE, former soccer player; b. Camp Hill, Pa., Mar. 24, 1976; Student, U. Fla. Mem. U.S. Nat. Women's Soccer Team, 1996—. Recipient Southeastern Conf. Player of Yr. award, 1996. Achievements include appeared twice in Faces in the Crowd, Sports Illustrated. Office: US Soccer Fedn 1801-1811 S Prairie Ave Chicago IL 60616

FOTOVICH, SISTER URSULA ANN, nun, religious organization administrator; d. Stephen Vida and Helen Barbara Fotovich. AA, Kansas City (Kans.) C.C., 1972; BS in Edn., Emporia State U., 1974; MS in Ednl. Adminstrn., U. Dayton, 1986. Cert. tchr. Kans. Nun Sisters St. Joseph, Wichita, 1974—, congl. sec., 1993—96; level 1 tchr. spl. edn. Holy Family Ctr., Wichita, Kans., 1974—75; elem. tchr. Parsons (Kans.) Cath. Sch., 1977—81, Holy Name Sch., Coffeyville, Kans., 1981—84; elem. prin. Holy Savior Cath. Sch., Wichita, 1984—90, St. Mary Cath. Sch., Newton, Kans., 1990—92; elem. tchr. St. Anne Cath. Sch., Wichita, 1996—98, St. Cecilia Cath. Sch., Haysville, Kans., 1998—99; diocesan dir. missions Cath. Diocese Wichita, 2000—. Mem.: U.S. Cath. Mission Assn. Avocations: play [illegible], quilting, embroidery, crafts. Office: Cath Diocese Wichita 424 N Broadway Wichita KS 67202-2377

FOUBERG, GLENNA M. career planning administrator; b. Ashley, N.D., Sept. 1, 1942; m. Rod Fouberg; children: Robert, Dan. Student, N.D. State U., 1960—61; BS in Secondary Edn., No. State U., 1963, psychol. examiner's endorsement, 1980, Doctorate (hon.), 2002; MEd in Guidance and Counseling, S.D. State U., 1968; postgrad., 1971—. English tchr., drama dir., Sisseton, SD, 1963—64; English tchr., 1965—67, Eielson AFB, Fairbanks, Alaska, 1964—65; English tchr., guidance counselor Bristol, SD, 1967—69, Webster, SD, 1968—71; tchr. Holgate Jr. H.S., Aberdeen, SD, 1973—90; coord., tchr. Alt. Learning Ctr. Ctrl. H.S., SD, 1990—2002; chief examiner GED testing Aberdeen Career Planning Ctr., 2002—. Mem. S.D. State Bd. Edn., 1998—, pres., 2002—; mem. editl. com. Ctr. Applied Rsch.; mem. nominating com. Nat. State Tchrs. Yr.; adj. prof. English No. State U.; presenter in field. Co-chair Aberdeen Arts Festival; bd. mem., membership drive chmn., pres. Cmty. Concert Assn.; mem. health adv. com. Northeastern Mental Health Ctr. and Brown County; block worker Am. Cancer Soc., Heart Fund, March of Dimes, Easter Seals; active Alexander Mitchell Libr. Found. Bd.; co-chair Rails Club United Way; bd. dirs., office coord. Aberdeen Swim Club; fund raising com. Act II Cmty. Theater, S.D. Humanities Fund; co-chair Jr. Achievement, 2001—03. Recipient Sertoma Svc. to Mankind award, F.O.E. Eagles Edn. award, Golden Deed award, Exch. Club, George award, Aberdeen Area C. of C., award, Optimist Club, Spl. Contbns. award, S.D. Assn. Guidance Counselors, 2001, Outstanding Grad. award, S.D. State U. Guidance and Human Resources Dept., 2002. Mem.: NEA, State Profl. Practices Commn. (charter), Local Reading Coun., N.E. S.D. Reading Coun., Aberdeen Edn. Assn. (mem. comm. com.), S.D. Edn. Assn., Nat. Coun. Tchrs. English, Kappa Delta Pi, Phi Delta Kappa (v.p. membership, pres.), Delta Kappa Gamma (mem. rsch. com.). Office: Aberdeen Career Planning Ctr 420 S Roosevelt Aberdeen SD 57402-4730 also: 203 Third Ave SE Aberdeen SD 57401

FOUCHA, LAURA THERESA, computer graphics designer, film maker, writer; b. New Orleans, Mar. 24, 1947; d. Frederick Lake and Lucille Mary (Normand) F. BA, U. New Orleans, 1973. Reg. radiologic technologist. Radiologic technologist Uptown Physicians Group, New Orleans, 1969-73; dept. mgr. D.H. Holmes, New Orleans, 1969-73; asst. mgr. Gen. Cinema Theatres, New Orleans, 1973-75; computer graphics designer New Orleans, 1975—; videographer Lens To Creation, New Orleans, 1993—. Camerawoman New Orleans Women in Video, 1982-89. Film maker: Gunchase to Nowhere, 1970 (1st prize 1970); author: (book) Tribunal of Anarchy, 1995. Vol. City of New Orleans, 1962-64; campaign worker Candidates Campaigns, 1964-74; activist NOW, New Orleans, 1979—. Recipient Certificate of Recognition award City of New Orleans, 1962, Key to the City, 1965, Cert. of Appreciation Vet's. Adminstrn., 1963, Best Actress award New Orleans Cmty. Theater, 1979. Mem. NOW (New Orleans chpt. pres. 1986-88), Agenda For Children, Timberwolf Preservation Soc., Soc. for Creative Anachronism, Ravenswood Archery Assn. (pres. 1995—). Avocations: archery, reading, movies, dance, video editing. Home: PO Box 113247 Metairie LA 70011-3247

FOUCHT, JOAN LUCILLE, retired elementary school educator, retired counseling administrator; b. Glenford, Ohio, Feb. 26, 1931; d. Byron Ralph and Elsie Pauline (Tavenner) Foucht. BS in Elem. Edn., Ohio State U., 1953, MA in Guidance, 1967. Elem. sch. tchr. Southwood Elem. Sch., Columbus, Ohio, 1953—55, Suffern (N.Y.) Pub. Sch., 1955—56, N.E. Elem. Sch., Upper Montclair, NJ, 1956—60, Hubbard Elem. Sch., Columbus, 1960—67, Medary Elem. Sch., Columbus, 1986—93; counselor Medina Jr. H.S., Columbus, 1967—70; elem. sch. counselor various schs., Columbus, 1970—86; ret., 1993; sub. tchr., 1996—. Elected delegate Ohio Edn. Assn. and Nat. Edn. Assn. Conv., 1966—77; treas. Columbus Assn. of Classroom tchr., 1964—66, pres. elect, 1966—67, pres., 1967—69; human rels. chairperson, coorndinated tchr. edn. study with Ohio State Univ., Sch. desegregation. Columbus Edn. Assn., 1973—77. Contbr. articles Career Education Interest Groups Ohio Sch. Coun., 1968. Counselor, advisor 4H Club, Columbus, 1971—73; pres. Women's Assn. Columbus Symphony Orch., 1991—92, Women's Assn. Symphony Columbus Orch., 2000—01; program chairperson bus. and prof. unit Women's Assn. Columbus Symphony Orch., 1990—2000, 2002—03; choir mem. Overbrook Presbyn. Ch., Columbus, 1945—. Recipient Rsena B. Willis Award, Nat. Edn. Assn. Convention, 1975, Coun. Award of the Yr. for Creative Multicultral Programs, Ohio Sch., 1982. Mem.: AAUW (choral group 1988—2002, membership treas. 1996—2001, co chairperson 2002—04), Clintonville Women's Club (chairperson bridge groups 1988—2001), Alpha Delta Kappa (chpt. pres. 1986—88). Democrat. Presbyterian. Avocations: gardening, music, travel, theater, reading. Home: 225 Webster Pk Columbus OH 43214

FOUDY, JULIA MAURINE, professional soccer player; b. San Diego, Jan. 23, 1971; m. Ian Sawyers, July 1995. BSW in Biology, Stanford U., 1993. Mem. U.S. Women's Nat. Soccer Team, 1988—; profl. soccer player San Diego Spirit, 2001—03. Color commentator Men's World Cup, ESPN, 1998. Mem. Tyresco Football Club, Sweden, 1994; pres. Women's Sports Found. Named World Cup Champion, 1991, 1999; recipient Gold medal, Centennial Olympic Games, 1996, FIFA Fair Play award, 1997, Silver medal, Sydney Olympic Games, 2000. Achievements include appeared on cover Women's Soccer World mag., 1997; mem. championship team World Championships, Sweden, 1995; CONCACAF, Montreal, 1994. Office: c/o US Soccer Fedn 1801 S Prairie Ave # 1811 Chicago IL 60616-1319

FOULADVAND, HENGAMEH, artist; b. Tehran, Iran; naturalized U.S. citizen, 1974; d. Mansour and Mahin F.; m. Masoud B. Mansouri, Feb. 20, 1981; 1 child, Tia. BA, San Jose State U., 1976; M, Calif. State U., 1979. Exec. dir. Iranian Modern Arts, 1998—. Art cons. T.H.E. Graphics & Design, 1990-96; graphic & prodn. cons. Metro Lables, 1994-96. Exhibited in solo and group shows including Columbia U., N.Y.C., 1989, L.I. U., 1989, 91, Strathmore Arts Ctr., Md., 1991, Port Washington Pub. Libr., 1991, Huntington Arts Coun., Hecksher Mus., 1993, 95, McArthur Airport Terminal Bldg., L.I., 1996-97, Columbia U., Hamilton Bldg., N.Y.C., 1997, Lindberg Gallery, N.Y.C., 1999, GORA Gallery, Montreal, 1999, La Maison Francaise, Columbia, 2000; represented in permanent collections Ency. Iranica Found., N.Y., Line & Tone Typographics, N.Y., numerous pvt. collections; mem. editl. bd.: Tavoos Art Quarterly, 1999-. Mem. N.Y. State Coun. Arts, N.Y. Found. Arts, Huntington Art League and Coun. Long Island. Home: 34 Lisa Dr Dix Hills NY 11746 E-mail: hengamehf@earthlink.net.

FOULKE, JUDITH DIANE, health physicist; b. Bucyrus, Ohio, Nov. 22, 1945; d. Lawrence Kern Foulke and Alberta Amelia (Foulke) Houpt; m. Mark Allen Elrod, July 17, 1981. BA, St. Mary of the Springs, 1967; MS, U. Mich., 1969; PhD, Purdue U., 1973. Health physicist NASA Goddard Space Flight Ctr., Greenbelt, Md., 1969-71, U.S. Atomic Energy Commn., Washington, 1973-77; radiobiologist U.S. Nuc. Regulatory Commn., Washington, 1977-87; health physicist U.S. Dept. Energy, Washington, 1987—. Mem. Spires Brass Band, Frederick, Md. Mem. AAAS, Am. Nuc. Soc., Health Physics Soc. Democrat. Roman Catholic. Home: 10 Sunnyview Ct Germantown MD 20876-4025

FOULSTON, NOLA TEDESCO, lawyer; b. Mt. Vernon, N.Y., Dec. 14, 1940; d. Dominick J. and Theresa M. (Pellino) Tedesco; m. Steven L. Foulston, Jan. 2, 1983; 1 child, Andrew. BA, Ft. Hays State U., 1972; postgrad., U. Kans., 1972-73; JD, Washburn U., 1976. Bar: Kans. 1977,

U.S. Dist. Ct. Kans., U.S. Ct. Appeals (10th cir.). Asst. dist. atty. 18th Jud. Dist., Dist. Atty.'s Office, Wichita, Kans., 1977-81; assoc. Foulston, Siefkin, Powers & Eberhardt, Wichita, 1981-86; ptnr. Foulston & Foulston, Wichita, 1986-89; dist. atty. Office of Dist. Atty. Eigthteenth Jud. Dist. Sedgwick County Courthouse, Wichita, 1989—. Bd. dirs., legal counsel YWCA, Wichita, 1978-83, pres. 1980-81; active YWCA's Women's Crisis Ctr., Wichtia Area Sexual Assault Ctr.; bd. dirs. Exploited and Missing Children's Unit, Project Freedom, Community Corrections, County-Wide Substance Abuse Task Force, State of Kans. Law Enforcement Coordinating Com., Community Rels. Task Force, Inter-Agy. Truancy Adv. Com., Women's Rsch. Inst., Crime Stoppers of Wichita Adv. Bd.; apptd. by Gov. Hayden of Kans. to the Weigand Commn. on State Expenditures. Named one of Outstanding Young Women of Am., Outstanding Young Wichitan, Wichita Jaycees, 1990; recipient Alumni Achievement award Ft. Hays State U., 1992, Law Enforcement Commendation medal SAR, 1992. Mem. ABA, Kans. Bar Assn., Wichita Bar Assn. (Outstanding Atty. of Achievement 1992), Nat. County and Dist. Attys. Assn., Kansas County and Dist. Attys. Assn., Golden Key (hon.). Democrat. Roman Catholic. Office: 535 N Main Wichita KS 67203-3702

FOUNTAIN, CLARA GARRETT, archivist, librarian; b. Danville, Va., May 22, 1941; d. Albert Earle and Evelyn Hull (Steele) Garrett; 1 child, Marc. AA, Averett Coll., Danville, Va., 1962; BA, U. N.C., 1964, MLS, 1985. Libr. Danville/Pittsylvania County Schs., Danville, Va., 1966—84; archivist Dan River, Inc., Danville, 1981—85; ref. libr. Ferrum Coll., Va., 1986—88; ref. libr., archivist Averett Coll., Danville, 1989—2001, Averett U., Danville, 2001—. Author: (children's book) The Wreck of the Old 97, 1976, (history book) Danville: A Pictorial History, 1979, Danville, Va.: Postcard History, 2000. Mem.: Danville Hist. Soc., Va. Libr. Assn., Danville Mus. Fine Arts and History. Office: Averett University Blount Library 344 W Main St Danville VA 24541

FOUNTAIN, KAREN SCHUELER, physician; b. Aberdeen, S.D., Oct. 14, 1947; BA, No. State Coll., Aberdeen, S.D., 1968; MD, U. Md., Balt., 1972. Diplomate Nat. Bd. Med. Examiners, Am. Bd. Radiology in Therapeutic Radiology. Intern Md. Gen. Hosp., Balt., 1972-73, resident in radiation oncology, 1973-74; fellow in radiation oncology Mayo Clinic, Rochester, Minn., 1974-76, cons. in oncology, 1976-81; clin. asst. prof. Columbia U., N.Y.C., 1981-83, residency program dir. dept. radiation oncology, 1981-93, clin. assoc. prof., 1983—2001. Mem. med. bd. Presbyn. Hosp., N.Y.C., 1983-86; faculty coun. mem. Columbia U., 1982-89; del. N.Y. State Radiological Soc., N.Y.C., 1987—. Fellow Am. Coll. Radiology (councilor 1999—), N.Y. Acad. Medicine; mem. Am. Soc. Therapeutic Radiology and Oncology, Radiol. Soc. N.Am., Am. Radium Soc., Am. Soc. Clin. Oncology, Am. Assn. for Women Radiologists (bd. dirs. 1995-96), N.Y. Roentgen Soc. (sect. chmn. 1989-90), N.Y. State Radiol. Soc. (bd. dirs. 1996-2002). Office: Long Island Radiation Therapy 1129 Northern Blvd Manhasset NY 11030

FOUNTAIN, LINDA KATHLEEN, health science association executive; b. Fowler, Kans., Apr. 30, 1954; d. Ralph Edward and Ruth Evelyn (Cornelson) Young; m. Andre Fountain. BS in Nursing, Cen. State U., Edmond, Okla., 1976. RN, Okla. Staff nurse med./surg. and coronary care unit Presbyn. Hosp., Oklahoma City, 1976-79; mgr. nursing Hillcrest Osteo. Hosp., Oklahoma City, 1979-80; staff nurse, mgr. Oklahoma U. Teaching Hosp., Oklahoma City, 1981-82; pres. New Life Programs, Oklahoma City, 1981-88, Nursing Entrepreneurs, Ltd., Oklahoma City, 1988—; mgr. Internat. Health Supply, Oklahoma City, 1988—. Coord. lactation cons. program State of Okla., 1981-98, new life car seat rental program at various hosps., 1983-92, also speaker Success Co., Oklahoma City, 1984—; owner Rainbows Overhead Graphic Media, Oklahoma City, 1984-91; speaker in field. Founder Praxis Coll., Oklahoma City, 1988. Named Mentor of Yr., Okla. Metroplex Childbirth Network, Oklahoma City, 1984; honored for vol. work with families and rescue after Oklahoma City bombing, U.S. Dept. Justice, 1995. Mem. Am. Nurses Assn., Internat. Lactation Cons. Assn., Internat. Platform Assn., Bodyworkers and Wellness Therapies Assn. Avocations: gemology, travel. Office Phone: 405-858-7722.

FOUNTILA, SALLIE MARIE, educational specialist; b. Lake Charles, La., Feb. 28, 1934; d. Fred and Lillian Leola (Neal) Fountila; children: Preston Comings Williams, Kelly Jones Williams, Walter F. Williams, Ida Williams. BA, So. U., Baton Rouge, La., 1955; MEd, McNeese State U., Lake Charles, 1962; postgrad., UCLA, 1990-93. Nat. cert. counselor, nat. cert. career counselor. Tchr. social studies Calcasieu Parish Sch., Lake Charles, 1955-62; instr. history So. U., 1963-68; tchr. social studies Centennial H.S., L.A., 1969-74; career counselor Los Angeles County Office of Edn., L.A., 1974-86, cons., 1986-98. Mem. choir Messiah Bapt. Ch., v.p., 1978, mem. bd. Christian edn., 1969. Mem. AAUW (pres. 1990-92), Calif. Assn. Multicultural Counselors (pres. 1985-87), Alpha Kappa Alpha. Democrat. Home: 2702 S Harcourt Ave Los Angeles CA 90016-2829

FOUQUET, ANNE (JUDY FUQUA), musician, music educator; b. Wurtland, Ky., Oct. 2, 1938; d. John Paul and Garnet May (Gibson) Hillman; m. Warren Russell Fuqua, Dec. 21, 1961 (div. Dec., 1992); children: Bryan David, Faith Fuqua-Purvis, Paul Carroll. BMus., Am. Conservatory, Chgo., 1962; MMus., No. Ill. U., 1967; MFA, U. Iowa, 1971, D in Musical Arts, 1997. Organist various churches and denominations, Ill., 1960—; profl. accompanist Wis., Ill., 1970—; piano instr. Beloit (Wis.) Coll., 1972—; instr. Rockford (Ill.) Coll. Acad., 1991—; ind. instr. Keyboard Studio, Rockford, Ill., 1971—; clarinet player Rockford (Ill.) Park Band, 1995—. Composer: (song cycle soprano) Spinner of the Seasons, 1987, (suite for flute and hapsichord) Issar Suite, 1992; author: (play) Miracle of Love, 1982; (novel) If It Hadn't Been for Joel, 1980; (memoirs) Daddy Was a Farmer, Mother Was a City Girl, 1999; concert artist duo-piano with Robin Wooten, 1999, 2001; solo harpsichord recitals, 2001, 02. Mentor Helping One Student To Succeed, Structured Reading, Kishwaukee Sch., Rockford, Ill., 1997-98, adult lit. tutor READ Chatanooga, 1999—; interim organist, choirmaster Trinity Luth. Ch., 2000, Northminster Presbyn. Ch., Chattanooga, summer 2001; organist St Thaddeus Episcopal Ch., 2003—; Suzuki piano instr. Tenn. Valley area, 1998—; active concert artist, harpsichord, and piano. Nominee Best Classical Pianist Rockford Area Music Industry, 1996. Mem. Am. Guild of Organists, Music Tchrs. Nat. Assn., Ill. Music Tchrs. Assn. (adjudicator 1994-97), Kishwaukee Valley Concert Band, Szuki Assn. of the Americas, Midwest Hist. Keyboard Soc., Mendelsson Club (founder composer showcase concerts Rockford 1991-97, bd. dirs. 1993-97), Am. Fedn. of Musicians, Tenn. Music Tchrs. Assn. (adjudicator 1999-2000), Sierra Club. Avocations: hiking, langs. (German, French, Hebrew), cooking, gardening, astronomy. Office: Cadek Conservatory Music U Tenn Chattanooga 724 Oak St Chattanooga TN 37403-2406

FOUQUET, KRISTIN K. writer, photographer; b. New Orleans, Sept. 18, 1970; m. Errol David Fouquet, Dec. 13, 1996. AS in Funeral Svcs. Edn., Delgado C.C., New Orleans, 1991; BA in Philosophy, U. of New Orleans, 1995. Photographs in textbook, Two People in a Restaurant; author: (plays) Can She Cook? (Hon. Mention, 2002), (short story) Devotion; photographs, Chicken Ciarmello. Personal E-mail: kfouquet@cox.net.

FOURNET, LISA CLARK, music educator; d. William Spiva and Patsy Dunigan Clark; m. Dickens Quin Fournet, May 13, 2000. MusB, U. Miss., 1983; MusM Edn., Miss. State U., 1986. Choral music tchr. Ridgeland H.S., Miss., 2002—, Holmes C.C., Goodman, Miss., 2001—02; music tchr. Neshoba Ctrl. H.S., Philadelphia, Miss., 1995—2000; pvt. piano studio Louisville, Miss., 1986—95; organist/youth choir dir. First Presbyn. Ch., Louisville, 1987—95. Musician teacher. Life mem. Louisville Jr. Aux., Louisville, 1987—2003; regional dir. Miss. Jr. Miss Assn., Meridian, Miss., 1993—95; mem. Lydian Music Club, Philadelphia, Miss., 1995—2000. Recipient Miss Miss. Farm Bur., Miss. Farm Bur. Fedn., 1981. Mem.: Miss. Profl. Educators, Music Educators Nat. Conf., Am. Choral Directors Assn. Avocations: Nascar fan, travel, judging pageants.

FOUST, DONNA ELAINE MARSHALL, women's health nurse; b. Sacramento, May 11, 1959; d. Donald H. and Diana Janet (O'Day) Marshall; m. Jennings Franklin Foust, Mar. 29, 1980; children: Andrew Donald, Sheri Diane. LPN, Harriman Vocat. Sch., 1979; ADN, Walter State C.C., 1983. RN, Tenn.; cert. RN first asst., CNOR. Staff nurse labor and delivery Meth. Med. Ctr., Oak Ridge, Tenn., 1979-83, staff nurse oper. rm., 1983-90; 1st asst. ob/gyn office Women's Health Assocs., Oak Ridge, 1988—. Mem. Assn. Oper. Rm. Nurse, RN First Asst. Specialty Assembly. Democrat. Avocations: computers, photography, reading, cross stitch. Home: 2512 Clinton Hwy Powell TN 37849-7613 Office: Westmall Med Park 200 New York Ave Ste 150 Oak Ridge TN 37830-5227 also: 9330 Park West Blvd Ste 300 Knoxville TN 37923-4311 E-mail: whapc@icx.net.

FOUST, JEAN LOUISE, physical therapist; b. Pitts., June 20, 1932; d. Clyde Aiken Fellows and Wilma Anne Deirker; children: Reik Alan, Robert Clyde, Linda Lee. Grad., D.T. Watson Sch. Physiatrics, 1954; BS, U. Pitts., 1955. Lic. physical therapist Pa. Physical therapist Easter Seals, Pitts., 1954—58, Bethlehem, 1968—80; phys. therapist Bethlehem Area Sch. Dist., 1980—93; physical therapist United Cerebral Palsy, 1993—2000. Phys. therapist as needed two local nursing homes, Bethlehem/Allentown area2003. Vol. Musikfest, Chriskindlmant. Republican. Presbyterian. Avocation: swimming.

FOUSTE, DONNA H. association executive; b. N.Y.C., Feb. 26, 1944; d. Donald Lynn and Edna (Parker) Ham; m. James Edward Fouste, Nov. 2, 1980. AA in Mgmt. and Supervision, Coastline Community Coll., Fountain Valley, Calif., 1980; BS in Organizational Behavior, U. San Francisco, 1985, MS in Orgnl. Devel., 1988. Officer mgr., bus. mgr. Fulwider, Patton, Rieber, Lee & Utecht, L.A., 1971-79, 89-91; patent adminstrn. specialist Discovision Assocs., Costa Mesa, Calif., 1979-82; law office mgr. City of Anaheim, Calif., 1982-89; exec. dir. Orange County Bar Assn., Santa Ana, Calif., 1992—. Instr. Rancho Santiago Coll., Santa Ana, with legal asst. program, 1987—; instr. U. Calif., Irvine, 1997; mem. adv. bd. Pub. Svc. Inst., Santa Ana, 1986-88. Patron Friends of South Coast Repertory, Costa Mesa, Calif., 1985; mem. applause chpt. Performing Arts Ctr., Costa Mesa, 1986-87. Recipient Silver medal in Chess Corp. Challenge, 1988, Tribute to Women award YWCA, 1997, Spirit of Volunteerism award Vol. Ctr. of Greater Orange County, 1996. Mem. Assn. Legal Adminstrs., Nat. Assn. Bar Execs. (membership chair 1999), State Bar Calif. (minimum continuing legal edn. com.), Am. Soc. Assn. Execs., So. Calif. Soc. Assn. Execs., Execs. of Calif. Law Assns. Avocations: gourmet cooking, skiing, gardening. Office: Orange County Bar Assn PO Box 17777 Irvine CA 92623-7777

FOUTCH, KARAN, marketing professional; b. Missouri Valley, Iowa, July 7, 1969; d. Mary Jane Foutch. BBA, Iowa State U., Ames, Iowa, 1991. Info. referral coord. U.S. Army Heidelberg Youth Svcs., Heidelberg, Germany, 1993—96; mktg. specialist 26th Area Support Group Mktg. Divsn., Heidelberg, Germany, 1996—98; mktg. rsch. analyst 26th Area Support Group Mktg. Divsn. - U.S. Army, Heidelberg, Germany, 1998—2000; mktg. rsch. specialist U.S. Army Cmty. & Family Support Ctr., Alexandria, 2000—. Mem.: Am. Mktg. Assn. Avocations: swimming, softball. Office: US Army Cmty & Family Support Ctr 4700 King St Alexandria VA 22302

FOUTS, ELIZABETH BROWNE, psychologist, metals company executive; b. New Orleans, July 5, 1927; d. Donovan Clarence and Mathilde Elizabeth (Hanna) B.; m. James Fremont Fouts, June 19, 1948; children: Elizabeth, Donovan, Alan, James. BA, Tulane U., 1948; MS, N.E. La. U., 1973, postgrad., 1984. Cert. sch. psychologist, La.; cert. reality therapist, La. Instr. spl. edn., psychol. cons. N.E. La. U., Monroe, 1971-73; sch. psychologist Ouachita Parish Schs., Monroe, 1973-87; sec.-treas. Fremont Corp., Monroe, 1967—, Auric Metals Corp., Salt Lake City, 1975-99. Dir. La Fonda Hotel, Santa Fe, N.Mex., 1993—; pres. Sunbelt Reality Therapist, 1989-90. Exec. bd. Episc. Diocese Western La., 1986-87, 99-2002, commn. ministry, 1987-94; res. family resource ctr. N.E. La. U., 1993-94; bd. dirs. Assn. for Retarded Citizens, Monroe, 1982-88, treas., 1984, pres., 1987. Named Outstanding Sch. Psychologist, State of La., 1987. Mem. Nat. Assn. Sch. Psychologists, La. Sch. Psychologists Assn. (pres. 1978-79, Outstanding Woman Sch. Psychologist 1984, newsletter editor 1988-93). Avocations: walking, swimming. Home: PO Box 7070 Monroe LA 71211-7070 Office: 4002 Bon Aire Dr Monroe LA 71203-3015

FOUTZ, CLAUDIA, state agency administrator; BS in Econs., U. Calif., Davis. Audit divsn. chief Calif. State Employment Devel. Dept.; chief dep. dir. Calif. Dept. Consumer Affairs; exec. officer Calif. State Bd. Pharmacy; exec. dir. Calif. Optometric Assn., Ariz. Bd. Med. Examiners, Phoenix. Pres.-elect Nat. Coun. Licensure, Enforcement and Regulation. Mem. Calif. Soc. Assn. Execs. (mem. strategic planning com.). Office: Ariz Bd Med Examiners 1651 E Morten Ave Ste 210 Phoenix AZ 85020-4613

FOWLER, ANDREA, teachers academy administrator; Dir. Delta Tchrs. Acad., Atlanta; dir. Delta Tchrs. Acad., sr. program exec. Nat Faculty, Atlanta, v.p. programs, to 1998; cons. for edn. and non-profits Atlanta, 1998—. Office: Nat Faculty 83 Dartmouth Ave Avondale Estates GA 30002-1412

FOWLER, BARBARA HUGHES, classics educator; b. Lake Forest, Ill., Aug. 23, 1926; d. Fay Orville and Clara (Reber) Hughes; m. Alexander Murray Fowler, July 14, 1956; children: Jane Alexandra, Emily Hughes. BA, U. Wis., 1949; MA, Bryn Mawr Coll., 1950, PhD, 1955. Instr. classics Middlebury (Vt.) Coll., 1954-56; asst. prof. Latin Edgewood Coll., Madison, Wis., 1961-63; mem. faculty U. Wis., Madison, 1963—, prof. classics, 1976—, John Bascom prof., 1980—, prof. emeritus, 1991—. Author: The Hellenistic Aesthetic, 1989, The Seeds Inside a Green Pepper, 1989, Hellenistic Poetry, 1990, Archaic Greek Poetry, 1992, Love Lyrics of Ancient Egypt, 1994, Songs of a Friend, 1996, Vergil's Eclogues, 1997; also articles. Fulbright scholar Greece, 1951-52; Fanny Bullock Workman travelling fellow, 1951-52 Mem. Am. Philol. Assn., Archaeol. Inst. Am. Office: U Wis 910 Van Hise Hall Madison WI 53706 Home: 2210 E Newton Ave Shorewood WI 53211-2614

FOWLER, BETH, actress; b. Jersey City, Nov. 1, 1940; Actor: (Broadway plays) Gantry, 1970, A Little Night Music, 1974, 1600 Pennsylvania Avenue, 1976, Peter Pan, 1979—81, Baby, 1984, Take Me Along, 1985, Teddy & Alice, 1987—88, Sweeney Todd, 1989—90 (Tony nominee best actress musical, 1990), Beauty and the Beast, 1994 (LA Ovation award), Bells Are Ringing, 2001, The Boy From Oz, 2003 (Tony nominee best featured actress musical, 2004). Office: Imperial Theatre 249 W 45th St New York NY 10036*

FOWLER, JENNEFER RAE, sculptor; b. Bay City, Tex., Feb. 14, 1973; d. Bobby Owens and Ygerne Roxanne Michalec Hubbell; 1 child, Lexis DeVoe Beauford. Student, Richland Jr. Coll., 1991, 92; BFA with honors, U. Ctrl. Ark., 1998; MFA, U. Ark. Little Rock, 2001. Intern, apprentice Richard Hunt Studios, Chgo., 1997; tech. asst. Chgo. Fine Art Foundry, 1997, Hunt Studios, Chgo., 1997; sculptor disability svcs. U. Ctrl. Ark., Conway, 1998; tchr. Assn. Retarded Citizens, Little Rock, 1999, U. Ala.-Little Rock Share Am. Cmty. Outreach Program, 2001—; tchr. sculpture Gallery B, 2002. Mem. com. Kramer Artist Coop., Little Rock, 1997; v.p. Kramer Sch. Artist Coop. Moon Meditation, 1997, exhibited in group shows at U. Ctrl. Ark., Conway, 1997, 1998, Woman's City Club, 1999, Ctrs. Youth and Family, 1999, Art Found., Hot Springs, 1999, 2000, Youth Home Inc. Eggshibition, 2002. Scholar U. Ctrl. Ark., 1998. Mem. Art History Assn. (v.p. 1997). Democrat. Avocations: painting with oil, watercolors, acrylic, camping, canoeing, swimming, figure drawing. Home: 5900 N Country Club Blvd Little Rock AR 72207-4349

FOWLER, JOANNA S. chemist; b. Aug. 9, 1942; BA, U. South Fla., 1964; PhD in Chemistry, U. Colo., 1968. Rsch. assoc. U. East Anglia, Eng., 1968-69; rsch. assoc. in organic chemistry Brookhaven Nat. Lab., Upton, N.Y., 1969-71, chemist, 1971—. Mem. Soc. Nuclear Medicine, Am. Chem. Soc. (co-recipient Gustavus John Esselen Award for Chemistry in the Pub. Interest, northeastern sect., 1988, Francis P. Garvin & John M. Olin Medal, 1998). Office: Brookhaven Nat Lab Chem Dept Bldg 555A Upton NY 11973

FOWLER, KATHLEEN BROWN, parochial school educator, department chairman; b. Leavenworth, Kans., Feb. 15, 1954; d. Elwood Hansel Brown and Doris Irene Risinger Brown; m. John Dowdy Fowler; children: Matthew Connor, Jessica Kristine. MPA in Performing Arts, Okla. City U., Oklahoma City, 1986. Tchr. H.M. King H.S., Kingsville, Tex., 1990—93; tchr., dept. chair Incarnate Word Acad., Corpus Christi, Tex., 1994—. Singer Corpus Christi Chorale, Corpus Christi, 1991—2000. Recipient "Sammy" - Acting Award, Harbor Playhouse, 1994, Tchr. of Yr., Tex. State Fine Arts, 2002. Mem.: Delta Kappa Gamma (Treas. 2000—02). Methodist. Home: 4321 Saint George Dr Corpus Christi TX 78413 Office: Incarnate Word Academy 2910 S Alameda Corpus Christi TX 78413

FOWLER, LINDA MCKEEVER, health facility administrator, educator; b. Greensburg, Pa., Aug. 7, 1948; d. Clay and Florence Elizabeth (Smith) McKeever; m. Timothy L. Fowler, Sept. 13, 1969 (div. July 1985). Nursing diploma, Presbyn. U. Hosp., Pitts., 1969; BSN, U. Pitts., 1976, M in Nursing Adminstrn., 1980; D in Pub. Adminstrn., Nova U., 1985. Supr., head nurse Presbyn. Univ. Hosp., Pitts., 1969-76; mem. faculty Western Pa. Hosp. Sch. Nursing, Pitts., 1976-79; acute care coord. Mercy Hosp., Miami, 1980-81; asst. adminstr. nursing North Shore Med. Ctr., Miami, 1981-84, v.p. patient care, 1984-88, Golden Glades Regional Med. Ctr., Miami, 1988-89, Humana Hosp.-South Broward, Hollywood, Fla., 1989-91, assoc. exec. dir. nursing; v.p., chief nursing officer Columbia Regional Med. Ctr., Bayonet Point, 1991-96; COO, chief nursing officer Greenbrier Valley Med. Ctr., 1996-97; quality mgmt. coord. Greenbrier Valley Hospice, 1997-98; pvt. practice healthcare cons., 1998-99; chief nursing officer Marlboro Park Hosp., 1999—2002; pvt. practice healthcare cons., 2002—; chief clin. officer Intermedical Hosp. of S.C., 2003—. Mem. adj. faculty Barry U., Miami, 1984-97, Broward C.C., Ft. Lauderdale, 1984-85, Nova U., 1986-87; cons. Strategic Health Devel. Inc., Miami Shores, Fla., 1986-90, So. Coll., Cleveland, Tenn., 1995-96. Dept. HEW trainee, 1976, 79-80; bd. dirs. Pasco County Am. Cancer Soc., 1992-95. Mem. Am. Orgn. Nurse Execs. (legis. com. 1988-90), Fla. Orgn. Nurse Execs. (bd. dirs. 1986-88), S.C. Orgn. Nurse Execs., South Fla. Nurse Adminstrs. Assn. (sec. 1983-84, bd. dirs. 1984-86), U. Pitts. Alumni Assn., Presbyn. U. Alumni Assn., Portuguese Water Dog Club Am. (bd. dirs. 1988-89), Ft. Lauderdale Dog Club (bd. dirs. 1981-82, 83-85, v.p. 1982-83), Am. Kennel Club (dog judge), Moore County Kennel Club, Sigma Theta Tau. Lutheran. Office: Taylor at Marion Sts Columbia SC 29220

FOWLER, MARTI, fine arts consultant; b. St. Louis, Mar. 25, 1952; d. Chester Felix and Emily (Kohout) Czarcinski; m. Robert Lee Fowler, Mar. 26, 1988. BA, So. Ill. U., 1973, MA, 1981. Cert. tchr. English, speech and theatre, Mo. Tchr. asst. Hazelwood Sch. Dist., St. Louis, 1974-76; instr. Jefferson Coll., 1991-92, St. Louis C.C. at Meramec, St. Louis, 1990-98; tchr. Hazelwood East H.S., St. Louis, 1976-97; dept. chair fine arts Hazelwood East H.S. and Kirby Jr. H.S., 1997-99; cons. fine arts Hazelwood Sch. Dist., 1999—2003; owner, prodr. Interactive Ednl. Video LLC, 2003—. Co-playwright/lyricist: (musical theatre) Difficult Choices, 1988; dir. and choreographer numerous prodns., 1973—; co-producer: Practical Technical Theatre-Interactive Educational DVD Series, 2003-. Recipient Adminstr. of Yr. award, Mo. Thespians Ednl. Theatre Assn., 2001—02. Mem. Am. Alliance for Theatre in Edn. (Mo. state chmn. 1993-97, Dina Reese Evans award 1998), Theatre Edn. Assn. (Mo. State chmn. 1993-97, coord. Mo. State Thespian Conf. 1996, 99, Dina Rees Evans award for theatre in our schs. advocacy), Mo. State Thespian Bd. Dirs., Speech Theatre Assn. of Mo., Internat. Thespian Soc., Zeta Phi Eta (pres. 1972-73). Avocations: attending theatre, reading. Home: 15685 Silver Lake Ct Chesterfield MO 63017-5128 E-mail: marti@interactiveeducationalvideo.com.

FOWLER, SANDRA LYNN, poet; b. W. Columbia, W.Va., Feb. 4, 1937; d. Okey Donly and Ramona Jean Fowler. Author: In the Shape of Sun, 1972—73, The Colors Cry in Rain, 1983, Ever Sunset, 1992; assoc. editor: poetry jour. Ocarina, 1978—89. Hon. mem. steering com. Clinton-Gore Campaign, Washington, 1991, 1995, Gore-Lieberman Campaign, Washington, 1999. Democrat. Avocations: reading, music, collecting classical movies. Home: Rte 1 Box 50 West Columbia WV 25287

FOWLER, SUSAN MICHELE, real estate broker, entrepreneur; b. East Liverpool, Ohio, Jan. 6, 1952; d. George Robert and Mary Helen (Gilliland) F.; m. Paul Joseph Cusumano, Nov. 5, 1988. BA, West Liberty Coll., 1973; MEd, Kent State U., 1995. Lic. real estate broker, Ohio. Sales rep. Tropic-Cal, L.A., 1974-76; project mgr. R&B Enterprises, L.A., 1977-80; regional leasing mgr. First Union Mgmt., Inc., Cleve., 1981-82; comml. real estate broker Adler, Galvin, Rogers, Inc., Cleve., 1983-86, Coldwell Banker Comml. Real Estate, Cleve., 1986-90; pres. Comml. Real Estate Co., Cleve., 1990—; owner Susan M. Fowler Comml. Real Estate Co., Chagrin Falls, Ohio, 1990—, Empower Yourself Seminars, Chagrin Falls, 1992—; v.p., dir. offices First Union Real Estate Investment Trust, Cleve., Susan M. Fowler Comm. Real Estate Svcs., Inc., Chgo., 2000—, Susan M. Fowler Comml. Real Estate Svcs., Inc., Hoffman Estate, Ill., 2000—. Pres. Christopher Real Estate Investment, Cleve., 1989—, Christopher Mgmt. Co., Cleve., 1989—; founder, speaker Empower Yourself Seminars, 1992. Trustee, pres. West Side Community Mental Health Ctr., Cleve., 1985—; trustee, v.p. Child Conservation Coun., Cleve., 1988—; trustee Big Bros. and Big Sisters Greater Cleve., 1989, Visions for Youth, 1991; mem. Cleve. Mus. Art, Geauga County Humane Soc., Fairmount Arts Centre. Mem. Comml. Real Estate Women, Cleve. Area Bd. Realtors (speakers bur.), Nat. Assn. Realtors, Ohio Assn. Realtors, Cleve. Mus. Art, Pine Lake Trout Club. Home: 1014 Oakland Dr Barrington IL 60010-6307

FOWLER, TERRI (MARIE THERESE FOWLER), artist; b. Decatur, Ga., Sept. 26, 1949; d. John Francis and Marjorie Herndon; m. John Charles Fowler, July 29, 1972; children: Courtney Marie, Douglas Edwin. Studied with Carolyn Wyeth, Wyeth Sch. Art, 1972. Speaker to arts groups, schools. One-man shows include Hampden Sydney Coll., 1973, Longwood, Coll., 1976, C&S Bank, Camden, S.C., 1979, Benfield Gallery, 1985-99; exhibited in cen. chpt. Va. Mus., 1973 (recipient award 1973), Colonial Williamsburg, 1974-77, Md. St. House, Md. St. Senate, 1983-85; works selected by Am. Heart Assn. for Holiday Card Series, 1986-87, commnd. Prince Edward County Bicentennial Com., 1976; represented in many nat. and internat. pvt. collections. Active Girl Scouts Am. ctrl. Md.; sec. citizens adv. com. Annapolis Mid. Sch. Mem. Balt. Watercolor Soc., Md. Fedn. Art. Annapolis Watercolor Club., San Diego Watercolor Soc., U.S. Naval Acad. Womens Club and Garden Club. Avocations: reading, flower arranging, gardening. Home: 123 Groh Ln Annapolis MD 21403-4008

FOWLER, TILLIE KIDD, lawyer; b. Milledgeville, Ga., Dec. 23, 1942; d. Culver and Katherine Kidd; m. L. Buck Fowler, 1968; children: Tillie, Elizabeth. BA in Polit. Sci., Emory U., 1964, JD, 1967. Legis. asst. Rep.

Robert G. Stephens, 1967—70; counsel White House Office of Consumer Affairs, 1970—71; mem. 103d-106th Congresses from 4th Fla. dist., 1993—2001, mem. armed svcs. com., transp. and infrastructure com.; majority dep. whip; chmn. transp. subcom. on oversight, investigation & mgmt.; atty. Holland & Knight, Washington, 2001—; chmn. Def. Policy Bd. U.S. Dept. Def., Washington 2003—. Yua Chm Hu Nen Civil Prac Jr. League, Jacksonville, Fla., 1982—83; chmn. Fla. Humanities Coun., 1989—91; pres. Jacksonville City Coun., 1989—90, mem. 1985—91; mem. bd. visitors U.S. Naval Acad., 1995—; chmn. ho. page bd., 1996—; mem. Chief of Naval Ops. Executive Bd., 2003—. Republican. Office: Holland & Knight 2099 Pennsylvania Ave NW Ste 100 Washington DC 20006*

FOWLER, VIVIAN DELORES, insurance company executive; b. Knoxville, Tenn., Sept. 26, 1946; d. Rance James Pierce and Margaret Willadene (Crowe) Compton; m. James Hubert Fowler, May 12, 1979. Student, U. Tenn., Knoxville. CPCU. Clk. The Travelers Ins. Co., Knoxville, 1967-84, adminstv. staff, 1984, comml. mktg. asst., 1984-86, comml. account analyst Nashville, 1986-89, sr. account analyst, 1989-90, account mgr., 1990-93, regional asst. mgr. small bus. unit coml. lines Atlanta, 1993—; regional underwriting mgr. select accounts mktg. Travelers/Aetna Ins. Co. (name changed to St. Paul Travelers), Atlanta, 1996. Lay witness speaker, United Meth. Ch., Knoxville 1979-82; charter mem. St. Thomas Hosp. Found. Soc., 1990; mem. Arthritis Found., 1991. Mem. NAFE, Soc. CPCU, Soc. Cert. Ins. Counselors (cert. 1987), Nat. Assn. of Ins. Women (cert. Profl. Ins. Woman 1975), Internat. Platform Assn., Ins. Professionals of Atlanta, 1998. Republican. United Methodist. Home: 604 Ashley Forest Dr Alpharetta GA 30022-6133 Office: Travelers Property and Casulty Co 4400 Northpoint Pkwy Alpharetta GA 30022-2429 E-mail: vfowler@travelers.com.

FOWLKES, JANET STUDARD, secondary school educator; d. Paul Elton and Anna Frances Studard; m. John Michael Fowlkes, Feb. 28, 1986; 1 child, Rachel Anne. Assocs. degree, Dyersburg State C.C., Tenn., 1977; BS in Home Econ. Edn., U. Tenn., Martin, 1980. Banking First Citizens Nat. Bank, Dyersburg, 1981—82; mfg. sales rep. Brown and Williamson, Louisville, 1982—91; salesperson Beauty Connection, Paducah, Ky., 1991—92; educator Dyer County H.S., Newbern, Tenn., 1992—. Mem. Delta Kappa Gamma (co-chair mem. 2001—02). Baptist. Avocations: painting, piano, rancher.

FOWLKES, NANCY LANETTA PINKARD, social worker; d. Amos Malone and Nettie (Barnett) Pinkard; m. Vester Guy Fowlkes, June 4, 1955 (dec. 1965); 1 child, Wendy Denise. BA, Bennett Coll., 1946; MA, Syracuse U., 1952; MSW, Smith Coll., 1963; MPA, Pace U., 1982. Dir. publicity Bennett Coll., Greensboro, N.C., 1946-47, 49-50; asst. editor Va. Edn. Bull. ofcl. organ Va. State Tchrs. Assn., Richmond, 1950-52; asst. office mgr. Cmty. Svc. Soc., N.Y.C., 1952-55; social caseworker, asst. supr. Dept. Social Svcs. Westchester County, White Plains, N.Y., 1959-67, supr. adoption svcs., 1967-77, supr. adoption and foster care, 1977-89. Mem. adv. bd. White Plains Adult Edn. White First v.p. Eastview Jr. H.S., 1970-71; area chmn. White Plains Cmty. Chest, 1964; sec. Mt. Vernon Concert Group, 1952-54; fund raising co-chmn. Urban League Guild of Westchester, 1967; pres. White Plains Interfaith Coun., 1972-74; pres. northeastern jurisdiction United Meth. Ch., 1988-92; chmn. adminstrv. bd. Meth. Ch., 1970-72, 82-83, vice chmn., 1978-80, vice chmn. trustees, 1973-77, treas., 1978-83; lay spkr., v.p. Met. dist. United Meth. Women, 1977-79, exec. bd. N.Y. conf.; N.Y. conf. rep. Upper Atlantic Regional Sch., 1981-83, mem. nominating com., 1982-83, trustee N.Y. conf., 1982-88, pres. N.Y. conf., 1983-87; bd. dirs. Global Ministries United Meth. Ch., 1988-96, women's divsn., 1988-96, v.p. chair sect. finance women's divsn., 1992-96, supt., 1997—, chair program divsn. N.Y. conf., 1989-93; v.p. superintendency commn. Met. North Dist., 1997—; chair Episcopal residence N.Y. Conf. Episcopacy Com., 1997—; mem. N.Y. Conf. Bd. Ordained Ministry, 2000—; chmn. Dist. Coun. on Ministry, 2002-; bd. dirs. Family Svc. Westchester, Bethel Meth. Home, Ossining, N.Y., White Plains YWCA, 1985-93, Scarritt Bennett Ctr., Nashville, 1990-2000, Gum Moon Women's Residence, San Francisco, 1992-96, White Plains-Greenburg NAACP, 1993-98. Mem. NASW, Acad. Cert. Social Workers, Jack and Jill of Am. Inc. (chpt. pres. 1954-56, regional sec.-treas. 1967-71), Nat. Bus. and Profl. Women's Club (chpt. sec. 1954-56), Internat. Platform Assn., Theta Sigma Phi (sec.-treas.), Zeta Nu Omega, Alpha Kappa Alpha (pres. 1960-64, treas. 1975-78), Regency Bridge Club (pres. 1963-65). Home: 107 Valley Rd White Plains NY 10604-2316

FOX, BETTY, financial services executive; b. Chgo., July 30, 1935; d. Abraham and Lucille (Manesewitz) Axelrod; children: Deborah Kravitz, Esther Fox, Adam Fox. Student, U. Ill., Chgo., 1953; CLU, The Am. Coll., 1989, ChFC, 1990. Art tchr. Suburban Fine Arts Ctr., Highland Park, Ill., 1963-75; commodities broker Rosenthal et al, Chgo., 1975-78; registered rep. AXA Advisors, LLC, Northbrook, Ill., 1978—. Painter represented in nat. collection (blue ribbon award 1971). Bd. dirs., past pres., art tchr./painter Suburban Fine Arts Ctr., Highland Park, Ill., 1962—; vol Jewish Vocat. Svc., Chgo.; active Alliance for Mental Illness. Recipient Purchase prize Kemper Ins. Co., Nat. Wine Art Competition. Mem. Nat. Assn. Life Underwriters, Million Dollar Round Table, Chgo. Women Ins. Assn. (treas. 1989), Nat. Assn. Women Life Underwriters, Lake County Life Underwriters, 500 Club (pres. 1990, agy. CLU advisor 1989-92, chmn. Agts. Forum 1992-94), Axa Group. Office: 601 Skokie Blvd Ste L2 Northbrook IL 60062

FOX, DAWNE MARIE, safety scientist; b. West Lafayette, Ind., Aug. 3, 1948; d. Gerhard P. and Betty M. (Norris) F.; m. Gerald C. Newmeyer, Oct. 4, 1969 (div. 1981); children: Mimie, Jerry. Grad. magna cum laude, Lord Fairfax, Middletown, Va., 1979; grad., Casper (Wyo.) Coll., 1985; cert. in indsl. safety and health, Ga. Inst. Tech., 1998, cert. in hazardous material mgmt., cert. in environ. mgmt., cert. in constrn. safety and health, Ga. Inst. Tech., 1999. Cert. environ. trainer Nat. Environ. Tng. Assn.; EPA cert. instr. in asbestos abatement, supr., insp. and mgmt. planner, project designer tng. courses; approved instr. occupl. safety and health adminstrn., U.S. Dept. Labor, Nat. Tng. Inst.; cert. in indsl. safety and health; registered environ. mgr. Nat. Registry Environ. Profls.; cert. hazardous materials mgr. Inst. Hazardous Material Mgrs. Regional safety coord. Milchem Inc., Casper, 1979-83; safety dir. Energy Insulation Inc., Casper, 1983-85; safety mgr. Western States Constrn., Loveland, Colo., 1985-86; safety officer Govt. of D.C., 1987-89; dir. safety, health svcs. Denver and Rio Grande R.R., Denver, 1989-90; safety mgr. Browning-Ferris Inc., Hyattsville, 1990-91; sr. safety scientist Gen. Physics Corp., Columbia, Md., 1991—. Cons., Casper, 1983-85. Instr. ARC, Casper, 1981-85, Am. Heart Assn., Casper, 1982-85; spl. aide to Spl. Olympics, Casper, 1983-85. Mem. Nat. Safety Coun., Am. Soc. Safety Engrs. (v.p. 1982-83, pres. 1983-84, Safety Profl. award 1982), Assn. Am. Railroads Safety Coun. (past del.). Republican. Roman Catholic. Avocations: skiing, bowling. Home: 8706 Mission Rd Jessup MD 20794

FOX, DEBRA L. educational association administrator, business owner; m. Jules Rosen; children: Adam, Josh, Daniel, Rebecca. Gen. assignment reporter WTAE-TV, 1976—86; founder, owner, CEO Fox Learning Systems Inc. (formerly Fox FarSight Prodn.), 1997—. Named One of Pa. Best 50 Women in Bus., 2004. Office: Fox Learning Systems Inc 401 Washington Ave Bridgeville PA 15017*

FOX, DONNA BRINK, music educator; b. Pipestone, Minn., June 7, 1950; d. Carroll Marion and Nellie (De Groot) Brink; m. George Bernard Fox, Aug. 30, 1975; 1 child, Elizabeth Ann. BA, Calvin Coll., 1972; MMus, Ohio U., 1975; PhD, Ohio State U., 1982; postgrad. Mgmt. Devel. Program, Harvard U., 1996. Music tchr. Calvin Christian Schs., Grand Rapids, Mich., 1972-74; vis. instr. Ohio U., Athens, 1975-76; asst. prof. Ill. State U.,

Normal, 1980-84; from asst. prof. to prof. Eastman Sch. Music, Rochester, NY, 1984—98, Eisenhart Prof. Music Edn., 1998—, chair music edn. dept., 1992—2001, dir. summer session, 1998—2000. Bd. dirs. Aesthetic Edn. Inst., Rochester, NY, 1994—2000; cons. in field. Grantee Young Audiences of Rochester, 1994, 95; recipient Eisenhart award for Disting Tchg. Wntmnr Vnh ot Minni 1006; O ommanding Alumni award Ohio U., 1994. Mem. ASCD, Am. Edn. Rsch. Assn., Nat. Assn. Music Young Children, Music Educators Nat. Conf. (early childhood spl. rsch. interest group 1986-90, grantee, 2002), Am. Orff-Schulwerk Assn. (rsch. adv. review panelist 1992-96), N.Y. State Sch. Music Assn. (chair early childhood group 1991-95). Office: Eastman Sch Music 26 Gibbs St Rochester NY 14604-2599 Home: 8 Cambridge Cir Victor NY 14564 Office Phone: 585-274-1544.

FOX, ELAINE SAPHIER, lawyer; b. Chgo., Nov. 18, 1934; d. Nathan Abraham and Rhoda M. (Schneidman) Saphier; m. Alan A. Fox, Apr. 25, 1954; children: Susan Fox Lorge, Wendy Fox Schneider, Mimi. BS, Northwestern U., 1955; JD, Ill. Inst. Tech., 1975. Bar: Ill., 1975, U.S. Dist. Ct. (no. dist.) Ill., 1975, U.S. Ct. Appeals (7th cir.) 1975, U.S. Ct. Appeals (fed. cir.) 1985. Trial atty. NLRB, Chgo., 1975-80; assoc. Hinsh & Schwartzman, Chgo., 1980-81, Gottlieb & Schwartz, Chgo., 1981-84, ptnr., 1984-90, D'Ancona & Pflaum, Chgo., 1990—. Co-editor in chief How to Take a Case to the NLRB, 7th edit.; contbr. articles to profl. jours. and mags. Bd. dirs., exec. com. Am. Cancer Soc., Chgo., 1993—; mem. nat. and local governing coun. Am. Jewish Congress, Chgo., 1991—; bd. dirs. Jewish Vocat. Svc. Mem. ABA (subcom. NLRB practice and procedures, employ-ment and labor law, labor and employment law com., Women Rainmakers, midwest regional mgmt. chair NLRB practice and procedure com.), Women's Bar Assn., Chgo. Bar Assn. (labor and employment rels. vice chmn. 1989-90, chmn. 1990-91, co-chmn. Alliance for Women 1994-95, co-chair bd. mgrs. 1996-98), Decalogue Assn. Avocations: swim-ming, walking, reading, theater, art. Office: Dancona and Pflaum 11 E Wacker Dr Ste 2800 Chicago IL 60601-2101 E-mail: efox@dancona.com.

FOX, ELEANOR MAE COHEN, lawyer, educator, writer; b. Trenton, N.J., Jan. 18, 1936; d. Herman and Elizabeth (Stein) Cohen; children: Douglas Anthony, Margot Alison, Randall Matthew. BA, Vassar Coll., 1956; LLB, NYU, 1961. Bar: N.Y. 1961, U.S. Dist. Ct. N.Y. 1964, U.S. Supreme Ct. 1965. Ptnr. Simpson Thacher & Bartlett, 1970—76, of counsel, 1976—; prof. Law Sch. NYU, 1976—, Walter J. Derenberg prof. trade regulation, 1999—. Lectr. on antitrust and interntat. competition policy, globalization markets; mem. Pres. Carter's Nat. Commn. Rev. Antitrust Laws and Procedures, 1978-79; mem. adv. bd. Bur. Nat. Affairs Antitrust and Trade Regulation Reporter, 1977—; trustee NYU Law Ctr. Found.; 1974-92; trustee Lawyers' Com. Civil Rights Under Law, 1988—; mem. Coun. Fgn. Rels., 1993—; mem. Pres. Clinton's internat. competition policy adv. com. to advise the U.S. Atty. Gen., 1997-2000. Author: (with Byron E. Fox) Corporate Acquisitions and Mergers, Vol. 1, 1968, Vol. 2, 1970, Vol. 3, 1973, Vol. 4, 1981, rev. edit., 2003; (novel) W.L., Esquire, 1977, (with Lawrence A. Sullivan and Rudolph Peritz) Cases and Materials, 2004, U.S. Antitrust in Global Context, 2004, (with G. Bermann, R. Goebel, W. Davey) European Union Law, Cases and Materials, 2002, The Compe-tition Law of the European Union--Cases and Materials, 2002; (with J. Fingleton, D. Neven, P. Seabright) Competition Policy and the Transfor-mation of Central Europe, 1996; mem. bd. editors N.Y. Law Jour., 1976-99, Antitrust Bull., 1986—; mem. adv. bd. Rev. Indsl. Orgn., 1990-2001, EEC Merger Control Reporter, 1992—, Gaceta Juridica la CE y de la Competencia, 1992-2001, World Competition: Law and Economics Re-view, 1999—, Inst. for Consumer Antitrust Studies, 2002--. Fellow Am. Bar Found., N.Y. Bar Found.; mem. ABA (chmn. merger com. antitrust sect. 1974-77, chmn. publs. com. 1977-78, chmn. Sherman Act com. 1978-79, mem. council antitrust sect. 1979-83, 90-94, vice chmn. antitrust sect. 1992-94, chair NAFTA Task Force, 1993-99), N.Y. State Bar Assn. (chmn. antitrust sect. 1978-79, mem. exec. com. antitrust sect. 1979-83), Fed. Bar Council (trustee 1974-76, v.p. 1976-78), Assn. of Bar of City of N.Y. (v.p. 1989-90, exec. com. 1977-81, chmn. trade regulation com. 1973-76, lawyer advt. com. 1976-77, chmn. com. on U.S. in a global economy, 1991-94), Am. Law Inst., Assn. Am. Law Schs. (chmn. sect. antitrust and econ. regulation 1981-83), NYU Law Alumni Assn. (bd. dirs. 1974-79, 87-91), Am. Fgn. Law Assn. (v.p. 1979-82, 98-2001).

FOX, GLORIA L. state representative, state legislator; b. Boston, Mass., Mar. 18, 1942; Cmty. fellows program, M.I.T., 1974. Legis., Mass., 1985—. Mem. Million Man March, Mobilization Polit. Action Com., Salvation Army Day Care Ctr., Urban League Guild Eastern Mass., Mass. Halfway House Assn.; mem. task force Pregnant and Parenting Addicted Women and their Children, Women in Poverty. Mem. NAACP, Nat. Caucus Black State Legislators, MIT Cmty. Fellows Program Alumnae Assn., Phi Theta Kappa, Mass. Caucus Women Legislators. Democrat. Office: State Ho Rm 167 Boston MA 02133

FOX, GRETCHEN HOVEMEYER, freelance editor, genealogical con-sultant; b. Erie, Pa., Jan. 2, 1940; d. Ernst Henry and Marjory Etta (Hollister) Hovemeyer; m. Kenneth Roland Fox, Apr. 23, 1989. AB, Radcliffe Coll., 1961. Manuscript sec. Internat. Tax Program Harvard U. Law Sch., Cambridge, Mass., 1961-63, copy editor, 1963-65, editorial asst., 1965-66, publs. assts., 1966-76, editorial and pub. dir., 1976-89; freelance editor, cons. pub. and genealogy Cambridge, 1989—; database/rsch. asst. innovations program John F. Kennedy Sch. of Govt., Harvard U., Cam-bridge, Mass., 1991-93, staff asst. innovations program, 1993—2002; int., 2002—. Mem. New Eng. Hist. Geneal. Soc., Orange County Geneal. Soc. (pub. cons. 1983-91) Sullivan County (N.Y.) Hist. Soc., DAR (chpt. registrar, chpt. historian 1978-83).

FOX, INGRID, curator; b. Shoemaker, Calif., June 14, 1945; d. Mel V. and Margaret (Hubert) Allex; m. Frederick B. Fox Jr., Sept. 1, 1973; children: Vanessa Verena, Frederick Bain. AD in Design, Parsons Sch. Design, N.Y.C., 1968; BFA, The New Sch., N.Y.C., 1977. Graphic designer Pfizer, Inc., N.Y.C., 1988-1992, curator, 1992—. Designer Montgomery Winecoff & Assocs., N.Y.C., 1969—75. Mem.: Art Table, Nat. Art Exhbns. by the Mentally Ill (bd. mem.), Internat. Assn. Profl. Art Advisors (treas./bd. mem.). Episcopalian. Avocations: crafts, designing. Home: 22 Pomander Walk Ridgewood NJ 07450-3711 Office: Pfizer Inc 235 E 42nd St New York NY 10017-5755

FOX, JANIE, environmental engineer; b. Oliver Springs, Tenn., Dec. 22, 1955; d. Douglas P. and Ina H. Scarbrough; children: Lorie, Joseph, Stephanie Grant, Sarah. Student, Roane State C.C., Harriman, Tenn., 1978—79. Cert. environ. technician, 1993. Sr. constrn. asst. Stone & Webster Constrn. Corp., Spring City, Tenn., 1997; tech. support technician Lockheed Martin Energy Systems, Oak Ridge, Tenn., 1998; subject matter expert/records mgr. Mfg. Scis. Corp., Oak Ridge, Tenn., 1998—99; records mgr. British Nuc. Fuels Ltd., Oak Ridge, Tenn.; engring. supr., document control Morrison Knudsen Corp., Oak Ridge, Tenn., 1990—94; asst. project mgr., records mgr. Foster Wheeler Environ. Corp., Oak Ridge, Tenn., 1999—; tech. writer Knight-Jacobs, Oak Ridge, 2001—03; engring. tech. Mesa Assocs., Oak Ridge, 2002—03, REMOTEC, Inc., 2003. Cons. CDI Tech. Svcs., Oak Ridge, 1998—. Author: A Hard Night's Day, 2002, Raised Right, 2003. Mem.: Assn. Records Mgrs. and Adminstrs., Women's Profl. Billiard's Assn. Avocations: writing, billiards. Home: 304 Florida Ave Oak Ridge TN 37830

FOX, JEANNE MARIE, lawyer; b. Phila., May 30, 1952; d. Samuel Cooper and Palmira Caroline (Ungerbuehler) F.; m. Stephan DeMicco, Sept. 29, 1979. BA, Douglass Coll., Rutgers U., New Brunswick, 1975; JD, Rutgers Sch. of Law, Camden, 1979; completed Program for State and Local Govt. Execs., Harvard U., 1990. Letter carrier U.S. Post Office,

Wildwood, 1971, Delran, 1973, Willingboro, 1976; intern U.S. Dept. of Environ. Protection, Edison, Phila., 1974, 77; law clerk Bd. of Pub. Utilities, Newark, N.J., 1978, N.J. Supr. Court, Camden, N.J., 1978, 79; policy dir. N.J. Democrat. State Com., Trenton, N.J., 1979-80; atty. N.J. Offices of tho Pub Advooto, 1980 81; ramintory attnon ALL UL J.J. Utilities, Newark, 1981-85, dep. dir., 1985-87; dir. N.J. Bd. of Pub. Utilities, Newark, 1987-90, sr. advisor for policy and mgmt., 1990-91; chief of staff N.J. Dept. of Environ. Protection and Energy, Trenton, 1991-92; dep. commr. N.J. Dept. Environ. Protection and Energy, Trenton, 1992-93, commr., 1993-94, commr. Delaware River Basin Commn., 1991-94; re-gional adminstr. Region II, EPA, N.Y.C., 1994-2001. Vis. lectr. in pub. and internat. affairs Woodrow Wilson Sch., Princeton U., 2001; vis. disting. lectr. Bloustein Sch. Planning & Pub. Policy Rutgers U., 2001; pres. N.J. Bd. Pub. Utilities, Newark 2002—. Mem. Commn. on Status of Women, Middlesex, 1985—94, chmn., 1985—89; bd. dirs. Douglass Coll. Assoc. Alumnae, 1986—2001; trustee Rutgers U., 1989—2001; mem. N.J. Commn. on Sex Discrimination in Statutes, 1989—94; bd. dirs. Del.-Raritan coun. Girl Scouts USA, co-chair devel. com., 2001—; del. Dem. Nat. Conf., 1992; pres. Middlesex County Women's Polit. Caucus, 1984—86; v.p. Nat. Women's Polit. Caucus, 1991—94, mem. steering and adminstrn. coms., 1989—94; chmn. Dem. Task Force Women's Polit. Caucus, NJ, 1991—94; co-chair edn. and tng. com. Women's Polit. Caucus of N.J., 2001—; pres. Women's Polit. Caucus N.J., 1988—91, bd. dirs., 2001—. Named Outstanding Young Woman N.J., N.J. Woman of Achieve-ment, N.J. Women's Clubs and Douglass Coll., 1986, Jerseyan of Week, Star Ledger, 1986, Bus. and Profl. Woman of Yr., Bus. and Profl. Women, 1993, Environmentalist of the Yr., N.J. Environ. Lobby, 2001; recipient Alumni Meritorious Svc. award Rutgers U. Alumni Fedn., 1991, award Douglass Soc., 1994, Waterfront Visionary award N.Y. League Conserva-tion Voters, 2000, Corwin award Douglass Coll., 2002; honored in Rutger U.'s Hall of Disting. Alumni, 1997. Mem. Nat. Women's Polit. Caucus (U.N. chpt. 2000) Barbara Boggs Sigmund award 2000), N.J. State Bar Assn., Rutgers Sch. of Law Alumni Assn., Rutgers Club. Democrat. Home: 227 New York Ave New Brunswick NJ 08901-1715 Office: NJ Bd Pub Utilities Two Gateway Ctr Newark NJ 07102

FOX, KELLY DIANE, financial advisor; b. Brockton, Mass., Sept. 9, 1959; d. James H. and Betty Jane (Calloway) F.; m. Alan David Goldberg, July 6, 1985; 1 child, Andrew Jason. BA, Allegheny Coll., 1980; postgrad. in Bus. Adminstrn., Suffolk U., 1983—84; student, Temple U., London, 1978, Syracuse U., 1979. Cert. fin. planner practitioner. Asst. mgr. Casual Male, Braintree, Mass., 1980, Hit or Miss, Braintree, 1981-82; merchan-diser Foxmoor, West Bridgewater, Mass., 1982; distbr. Hill's Dept. Stores, Canton, Mass., 1982-85; asst. buyer BJ's Wholesale Club, Natick, Mass., 1985-92; advanced advisor team, personal fin. advisor Am. Express Fin. Advisors, 1993—. Am. Express Fin. Advisors Boston steering com., diversity chair 1995-96; mem. spkrs. bur. Women's Union, 1997-2001; contbr. ADVICE + program State Atty. Gen.'s Office for Elder Affairs; guest lectr. MBA in a Day program Wheaton Coll.; mem. Mass. Dept. Edn. Gifted and Talented Adv. Coun.; founder Women's Resource Room, 1995-97; bd. dirs. New Hope, Inc., 1996-98; co-founder The Women's Connection, 2001—; founding bd. dirs., treas. Women at Work Mus., 2003. Contbr. columns in newspapers The Sun Chronicle Newspaper, 2002-04. Treas., bd. dirs. Attleboro Area Couc. Children, 1993—; bd. dirs. Attleboro Area Parents Anonymous, 1996, 1996—98; cheerleading coach Avon High Sch., Mass., 1982—83; co-chair enrichment program Falls Elem. Sch., 1994—95, 1997—98; mem. John Woodcock Sch. Coun., 1993—94; vol. Foxborough Regional Charter Sch. SABIS. Recipient Woman of Achieve-ment award, Attleboro Area Bus. and Profl. Women, 2003, Athena award, 2004. Methodist. Avocations: theater, travel, bell choir, art galleries. Office Phone: 508-695-2336. Business E-Mail: Kelly.D.Fox@AEXP.com.

FOX, LESLIE B. real estate company executive; b. Denver. Exec. mgmt. positions NHP, Inc.; sr. mgmt. positions Asset, Investors Corp., Comml. Assets, Inc., 1993—96, pres., 1996—97; exec. v.p., COO, exec. v.p., investment mgmt. Lexford Residential Trust, 1997—99; pres., Lexford divsn. Equity Residential, Chgo., 1999—2001, exec. v.p., 0999—, chief info. officer, 2001—. Office: Equity Residential 2 N Riverside Plaza Chicago IL 60606

FOX, MARGERY Q. anthropology educator; b. N.Y.C., Mar. 30, 1928; d. Otto Henry Court Quitzau and Marguerite Elisabeth Ernst; m. Frederick B. Fox, Nov. 25, 1954 (dec. Sept. 1991); children: Peter Q., Hugh Charles. BA, Smith Coll., 1949; MA, NYU, 1967, PhD, 1973. Asst. designer Max Liebman Prodns. (NBC-TV), N.Y.C., 1951-56, various Broadway prodns., N.Y.C., 1953-60; prof. anthropology/sociology Fairleigh Dickinson U., Teaneck, N.J., 1967-87. Adj. prof. Hawaii Pacific U., Honolulu, 1973-74; founder women's studies program Fairleigh Dickinson U., Teaneck, 1977; lectr. R.S.V.P., Paramus/Teaneck, 1992—; project dir. NEH Grant, 1983. Author: (with others) Women as Healers, 1989; author: book and lyrics Queen, 2003; contbr. articles to profl. jours. Co-dir. Women's Outreach Ctr., Teaneck, 1978-80. Pre-doctoral Rsch. grantee NSF, 1971; Rsch. grantee Fairleigh Dickinson U., 1976, 87. Avocations: walking, hiking, bridge, theatre-going. Home: 200 Winston Dr Apt 804 Cliffside Park NJ 07010-3214

FOX, MARIANN PALOMBO, supervisor, music educator; b. Aliquippa, Pa., Dec. 1, 1968; d. Natalino J. and Elvira Palombo; m. Todd A. Fox, June 14, 2003. BA, Seton Hill Coll., 1991; M in Music Edn., Youngstown State U., 1996. Cert. music tchr. Pa., supr. curriculum/instrn. Pa. Secondary music tchr., choral dir. Aliquippa (Pa.) Sch. Dist., 1992—97; mid. sch. music tchr., choral dir. Quaker Valley Sch. Dist., Sewickley, Pa., 1997—2000; fine arts supr., sr. high choral dir. Mt. Lebanon (Pa.) Sch. Dist., 2000—. Mem.: ASCD, Pa. Sch. Bds. Assn., Am. Choral Dirs. Assn., Music Educators Nat. Assns., Arts Edn. Collaborative (mem. steering coun. mem., chairperson advocacy and awareness 2001), Seton Hill U. Alumnae (bd. dirs. 2002). Office: Mt Lebanon Sch Dist 7 Horsman Dr Pittsburgh PA 15228 E-mail: mfox@mtlsd.net.

FOX, MARY ANN WILLIAMS, librarian; b. Savannah, Ga., Jan. 16, 1939; d. Alton F. and Arthur (Colquitt) Williams; m. William Francis Fox, Dec. 26, 1960 (div. 1984); children: Katherine Frances, William Francis Jr. BA, U. Ga., 1960; MLS, Rutgers U., 1984. Libr. Metuchen (N.J.) Pub. Libr., 1983-85, Mable Smith Douglas Libr. Rutgers U., New Brunswick, N.J., 1984, Firestone Libr. Princeton (N.J.) U., 1985, The Hun Sch. of Princeton, 1985—. Bd. dirs. Ctrl. Jersey Regional Libr. Coop., 1997—, Region 5 Libr. Coop., N.J., 1985-92. Trustee East Brunswick (N.J.) Pub. Libr., 1979-92; bd. dirs. Ctrl. Jersey YWCA, New Brunswick, 1985-88, Ctrl. Atlantic Conf. United Ch. of Christ, 1985-88. Mem. ALA, N.J. Libr. Assn., N.J. Ind. Sch. Assn. (chair libr. sect. 1988—), Edn. Media Assn. N.J. (bd. dirs. 1987-92), Librs. of Middlesex (pres.). Democrat. Mem. United Ch. of Christ. Home: 10 Redcoat Dr East Brunswick NJ 08816-2759 Office: Hun Sch Princeton 176 Edgerstone Rd Princeton NJ 08540 E-mail: mafox@hun.k12.nj.us.

FOX, MARYE ANNE, university chancellor, chemistry educator; b. Canton, Ohio, Dec. 9, 1947; m. James K. Whitesell, 1990; stepchildren: Christopher Whitesell, Robert Whitesell; children: Robert, Michael, Mat-thew. BS, Notre Dame Coll. of Ohio, 1969; MS, Cleve. State U., 1970; PhD, Dartmouth Coll., 1974; postgrad., U. Md., 1974-76; DSc (hon.), Notre Dame Coll., 1994, Cleve. State U., 1998; JD (hon.), Sandhills Cmty. Coll., 2000; degree (hon.), Universite Pierre et Marie Curie, 2001; LHD (hon.), Texas A&M, 2002; degree (hon.), Universidad Nacional de Educacion a Distancia, Madrid, 2003. Prof. chemistry U. Tex., Austin, 1976-91, Row-land Pettit Centennial prof., 1986-92, M. June and J. Virgil Waggoner regents chair chemistry, 1992-98, v.p. rsch., 1994-98; chancellor N.C. State U., Raleigh, 1998—; chancellor-elect U. Calif. San Diego, 2004. Mem. Nat. Sci. Bd., 1991-96, vice-chair, 1994-96; bd. dirs. Kenan Inst. Engring.,

Tech., and Sci., 1998—, Microelectric Ctr., NC, 1998—, mem. sci. adv. bd. Robert A. Welch Found., 1998—, David and Lucile Packard Found., 1998—; mem. Coun. on Competitiveness, 1999—; bd. trustees Nat. Inst. Statistical Sciences, 2000—; bd. dirs. Nat. Inst. Environment, 2001—, Boston Sci. Inc., 2001—, mem. President's Adv. Coun. of Advisors on Sci. and Tech., 2001—; bd. dirs. NC Bd. Sci. and Tech., 2002—, PPD Inc., 2002—, Red Hat Inc., 2002, Nat. Assn. State Universities and Land Grant Coll., 2003— Assoc. editor Jour. Am. Chem. Soc., 1986-94; mem. adv. bd. Jour. Organic Chemistry, Chem. Engring. News, Chem. Rev. Bd. trustees U. Notre Dame, 2002—; bd. dirs. N.C. Citizens for Bus. and Industry, 2003—. Recipient Agnes Faye Morgan Rsch. award Iota Sigma Pi, 1984, Arthur C. Cope scholar award Am. Chem. Soc., 1988; Garvan medal Am. Chem. Soc., 1988, Havinga medal Leiden U., 1991, Monie A. Ferst award, 1996; named to Hall of Excellence, Ohio Found. Ind. Colls., 1987, The Best of the New Generation, Esquire Mag., 1984; Alfred P. Sloan Rsch. fellow, 1980-82, Camille and Henry Dreyfus tchr. scholar, 1981-85. Fellow AAAS, Assn. Women in Sci.; mem. NAS (co-chair, Govt.-Univ.-Industry Rsch. Roundtable, 1999-), Am. Acad. Arts and Sci., Am. Philos. Soc., Sigma Xi (pres. 2001-02). Office: NC State U Chancellor's Office PO Box 7001 Raleigh NC 27695-0001*

FOX, MURIEL, retired public relations executive; b. Newark, Feb. 3, 1928; d. M. Morris and Anne L. (Rubenstein) F.; m. Shepard G. Aronson, July 1, 1955; children: Eric R., Lisa S. Student, Rollins Coll., 1944-46; BA summa cum laude, Barnard Coll., 1948. Art critic, bridal editor Miami (Fla.) News, 1946; reporter U.P.I., 1946-48; polit. speechwriter, publicist, 1949-50; from TV-radio writer to exec. v.p. Carl Byoir & Assos., N.Y.C., 1950-85; pres. subs. MediaCom Comm. Tng., 1975-85, By/Media Inc., 1981-85; sr. cons. Hill & Knowlton, Inc., 1986-90. Dir. Harleysville Ins. Co., Rorer Group Inc.; Co-chmn. Vice Presdl. Task Force on Women, 1968; mem. steering com. Women's Forum, 1974-79, pres., 1976-78; mem. Women's Econ. Adv. Com., N.Y.C., 1974-78; mem. nat. adv. com. Nat. Women's Polit. Caucus; nat. adv. bd. Women Today, Ethnic Woman Bd. dirs. N.Y. Diabetes Assn., 1956-66, Holy Land Conservation Fund, United Way of Tri-State, Internat. Rescue Com., 1977-84; v.p. Rockland Ctr. for the Arts, 1985—; pres. Hickory Hill Coop., Inc., 1995-99; chair bd. dirs. Vet. Feminists of Am., 1997—. Named one of 100 Top Corp. Women Bus. Week mag., 1976; recipient Matrix award Women in Communications, 1977, Bus. Leader of Year award ADA, 1979; Disting. Alumna award Barnard Coll., 1985, Eleanor Roosevelt Leadership award, 1985 Mem.: NOW (v.p. 1967—70, chmn. bd. 1971—73, chair nat. adv. com. 1973—74, bd. dirs. legal def. and edn. fund 1974—, v.p. fund 1977—78, pres. 1978—81, chair bd. 1981—92, hon. chair bd. 1993—, founder, Muriel Fox Comm. Leadership award 1991, Our Hero award 1995, Caroline Lexow Babcock award 1997), Am. Arbitration Assn. (bd. dirs. 1983—87), Am. Women in Radio and TV (bd. dirs. 1950—51, chair nat. publicity com. 1955—57, chair nat. pub. rels. com. 1957—59, Achievement award 1983), Vet. Feminists of Am. (chair bd. dirs. 2000—). Home and Office: 66 Hickory Hill Rd Tappan NY 10983-1804 E-mail: mfox66@optonline.net.

FOX, PAULA (MRS. MARTIN GREENBERG), writer; b. N.Y.C., Apr. 22, 1923; d. Paul Hervey and Elsie (de Sola) F.; m. Richard Sigerson (div. 1954); children: Adam, Linda, Gabriel; m. Martin Greenberg, June 9, 1962. Student, Columbia U. Condr. writing Seminars U. Pa. Author: 22 children's books and 6 novels, including How Many Miles to Babylon, 1966, Portrait of Ivan, 1968, Blowfish Live in the Sea, 1970; (novels) Poor George, 1967, Desperate Characters, 1970, The Western Coast, 1972, The Slave Dancer, 1974 (John Newbery medal), The Widow's Children, 1976, The Little Swineherd and Other Tales, 1978, A Place Apart, 1983 (Am. Book award), A Servant's Tale, 1984, One-Eyed Cat, 1985 (Newbery honor book 1985), Maurice's Room, 1985, The Moonlight Man, 1986, The Stone-Faced Boy, 1987, The Village by the Sea, 1988, Lily and the Lost Boy, 1989, The God of Nightmares, 1990, Monkey Island, 1991, Amzat and His Brothers, 1993, Western Wind, 1993, The Eagle Kite, 1995, Radiance Descending, 1997, Borrowed Finery: A Memoir, 2000 (PEN/Martha Albrand award). Recipient Arts and Letters award Nat. Inst. Arts and Letters, 1972, Hans Christian Andersen medal, 1978, fiction citation Brandeis U., 1984, Empire State award for children's lit., 1994; Guggenheim fellow, 1972. Mem. Authors League, Am. Acad. Arts and Letters (recipient medal and cash award). Office: care Robert Lescher 47 E 19th St New York NY 10003-1323

FOX, RENÉE CLAIRE, sociology educator; b. N.Y.C., Feb. 15, 1928; d. Paul Fred and Henrietta (Gold) F. AB summa cum laude, Smith Coll., 1949, LHD, 1975; PhD, Harvard U., 1954; MA (hon.), U. Pa., 1971, U. Oxford, 1996; ScD (hon.), Med. Coll. Pa., 1974, St. Joseph's Coll., Phila., 1978; D (hon.), Katholieke U., Leuven, 1978; LHD (hon.), La Salle U., Phila., 1988; DSc (hon.), Hahnemann U., 1991, U. Nottingham, Eng., 2002. Rsch. asst. Bur. Applied Social Rsch., Columbia U., 1953-55, rsch. assoc., 1955-58; lectr. dept. sociology Barnard Coll., 1955-58, asst. prof., 1958-64, assoc. prof., 1964-66; lectr. sociology Harvard U., 1967-69; rsch. fellow Ctr. Internat. Affairs, 1967-68, rsch. assoc. program tech. and soc., 1968-71; prof. sociology, psychiatry and medicine U. Pa., Phila., 1969-98, Annenberg prof. social scis., 1978-98, chmn. dept. sociology, 1972-78, Annenberg prof. social scis. emerita, 1998—. Rsch. assoc. Refugee Studies Centre, Queen Elizabeth House, U. Oxford, 1998—; sci. advisor Centre de Recherches Sociologiques, Kinshasa, Zaïre, 1963-67; vis. prof. sociology U. Officielle du Congo, Lubumbashi, 1965; vis. prof. Sir George Williams U., Montreal, summer 1968; Phi Beta Kappa vis. scholar, 1973-75; dir. humanities seminar med. practitioners NEH, 1975-76; maitre de cours U. Liège, Belgium, 1976-77; vis. prof. Katholieke U., Leuven, Belgium, 1976-77; Wm. Allen Neilson prof. Smith Coll., Mass., 1980; dir. d'Études Associè, Ecole des Hautes Etudes en Sciences Sociales, Paris, summer 1989; George Eastman vis. prof. Oxford U., 1996-97; vis. scholar Tokyo Med. and Dental U., 2001; mem. bd. clin. scholars program Robert Wood Johnson Found., 1974-80; mem. Pres.'s Commn. on Study of Ethical Problems in Medicine, Biomed. and Behavioral Rsch., 1979-81; dir. human qualities of medicine program James Picker Found., 1980-83; Fae Golden Kass lectr. Harvard U. Sch. Medicine and Radcliffe Coll., 1983, Kate Hurd Mead lectr. Med. Coll. Pa./Coll. Physicians Phila., 1990, Lori Ann Roscetti Meml. lectr. Rush-Presbyn.-St. Luke's Med. Ctr., Chgo., 1990; vis. scholar Women's Ctr., U. Mo., Kansas City, 1990, vis. scholar Case Western Res. Sch. of Med., 1992; opening address 13th Internat. Conf. on Social Scis. and Medicine, Hungary, 1994, vis. prof. U. Calif., San Francisco Sch. of Medicine, 1994; lectr. founds. of medicine Faculty of Medicine McGill U., Montreal, 1995; Supernumerary fellow Balliol Coll. Oxford U., 1996-97; WHR Rivers disting. lectr. dept. social medicine Harvard Med. Sch., 1998; assembly series lectr. Washington U., St. Louis, 1998; William J. Rashkind Meml. lectr, Am. Heart Assn., 1998, Salinger-Forlang lectr. U. Tex. Health Scis. Ctr. at San Antonio, 1999, Frances H. Schlitz lectr. U. Kans., Wichita, 2002; affiliated faculty Solomon Asch Ctr. for Study of Ethnopolit. Conflict, U. Pa., 2001—; sr. fellow Ctr. Bioethics, U. Pa., 1999-; Stambaugh lectr. U. Louisville Sch. Medicine, 2004. Author: Experiment Perilous, 1959, (with Willy DeCraemer) The Emerging Physician, 1968, (with Judith P. Swazey) The Courage to Fall, 1974, rev. edit. 1978, 2002, Essays in Medical Sociology, 1979, 2d edit., 1988, L'Incertitude Medicale, 1988, The Sociology of Medicine: A Participant Observer's View, 1989, (with Judith P. Swazey) Spare Parts: Organ Replacement in American Society, 1992, In the Belgian Château: The Spirit and Culture of European Society in an Age of Change, 1994, French language edit., 1997, Organ Transplantation: Meanings and Realities (edited with Stuart Youngner and Laurence O'Connell), 1996, (in Japanese) Looking Intimately at Bioethics: Fifty Years as a Medical Sociologist, 2003; assoc. editor: Am. Sociol. Rev, 1963-66, Social Sci. and Medicine; mem. editl. com.: Ann. Rev. Sociology, 1975-79; assoc. editor Jour. Health and Social Behavior, 1985-87, Perspectives in Biology and Medicine, 1996—; mem. editl. adv. bd. Tech. in Soc., Sci., 1982-83; mem. editl. bd. Bibliography of Bioethics, 1979—, Culture, Medicine and Psychiatry, 1980-86, Jour. of AMA, 1981-94, Am. Scholar, 1994-99, Current Revs. in Publs., 1994—, Am. Jour. Bioethics, 1999—; vice chair adv. bd. Am. Jour. Ethics and Medicine; contbr. articles to profl. jours.; A Festschrift published in his honor: Society and Medicine: Essays in Honor of Renée Fox, 2003. Bd. dirs. Medicine in Pub. Interest, 1979-94; mem. tech. bd. Milbank Meml. Fund, 1979-85; mem. overseers com. to visit univ. health svcs. Harvard Coll., 1979-86; trustee Russell Sage Found., 1981-87; vice chmn. bd. dirs. Acadia Inst., 1990-97; mem. adv. com. Sch. Nursing LaSalle U., 1998—; mem. external bd. Ctr. for Bioethics, Columbia U., mem. advancement com. King Baudouin Found. U.S. Inc., 1998—, mem., sec. bd. dirs. Acadia Inst., 2002—; mem. info. sci. adv. coun. Innovia Found., Netherlands, 2002—; mem. external bd. Ctr. for Bioethics, Columbia U., 2002—; mem. Internat. and Sci. Adv. Coun., 2002—. Recipient E. Harris Harbison Gifted Tchg. award Danforth Found., 1970, Radcliffe Grad. Soc. medal, 1977, Lindback Found. award for tchg. U. Pa., 1989, Centennial medal Grad. Sch. Arts and Scis. Harvard U., 1993, Chevalier de l'Ordre de Leopold II (Belgium), 1995; Wilson Ctr., Smithsonian Instn. fellow, 1987-88, Guggenheim fellow, 1962, Sr. fellow Ctr. Bioethics U. Pa., 1999—, Emeritus fellow Andrew W. Mellon Found., 2004-; Fulbright Short-Term Sr. scholar to Australia, 1994; 1st W.H.R. Rivers Disting. lectr. Harvard Med. Sch., 1998. Fellow African Studies Assn., AAAS (dir. 1977-80, chmn. sect. K 1986-87), Am. Sociol. Assn. (coun. 1970-73, 79-81, v.p. 1980-81), Am. Acad. Arts and Scis. (co-chair Class III section I membership com., 1994-96), Inst. Medicine of NAS (coun. 1979-82), Inst. Soc., Ethics and Life Scis. (founder, gov.); mem. AAUP, AAUW, Assn. Am. Med. Colls., Social Sci. Rsch. Coun. (v.p., dir.), Ea. Sociol. Soc. (pres. 1976-77, Merit award 1993), N.Y. Acad. Scis., Soc. Sci. Study Religion, Inst. Intercultural Studies, 1969-93, (asst. sec. 1969-78, sec. 1978-81, 89-92, v.p. 1987-89), Am. Bd. Med. Specialists, Coll. of Physicians of Phila. (coun. 1993-98), Phi Beta Kappa (senate 1982-87, Ralph Waldo Emerson book award com. 1998-2001). Home: The Wellington 135 S 19th St #1104 Philadelphia PA 19103-4912 E-mail: rcfox@ssc.upenn.edu.

FOX, SALLY G. state legislator, lawyer; b. Omaha, Jan. 30, 1951; m. Michael Sirotkin; 2 children. BA, U. Wis., 1972; JD, SUNY, 1975. Pvt. practice law; mem. Vt. Ho. of Reps., Montpelier, 1987—. Majority whip, 1995—, mem. jud. rules and jud. retention coms.; justice of peace. Mem. Criminal Justice Cabinet, Supreme Ct. Jud. Edn. Com., Gender Bias Implementation Task Force, Essex and Chittenden County Dem. Com.l active Vt. Children's Forum, Ct. Child Safety Coalition; bd. dirs. United Cerebral Palsy Vt. Mem. Vt. Bar Assn. Home: 21 Weed Rd Essex Junction VT 05452-2723 Office: Vt Ho of Reps 115 State St Montpelier VT 05633-0001

FOX, SARAH, lawyer; b. Buffalo, Dec. 12, 1951; d. Austin McCracken and Jean McLean (Coatsworth) F. BA, Yale U., 1973; JD, Harvard U., 1982. Bar: N.Y. 1982, D.C. 1983. Reporter Buffalo Courier-Express, 1973-79; staff counsel Internat. Union of Bricklayers & Allied Craftsmen, Washington, 1982-90; chief labor counsel Senate Labor and Human Resources Com., Washington, 1990-94, minority chief labor counsel, 1995-96; bd. mem. NLRB, Washington, 1996—. Office: NLRB 1099 14th St NW Ste 11300 Washington DC 20005-3419

FOX, STACY, automotive executive; B, JD, U. Mich. Former assoc. Mintz, Levin, Cohn, Ferris, Glovskky & Popeo, P.C., Boston; former gen. counsel Unisys Fin. Corp.; group counsel automotive systems group and plastics tech. group Johnson Controls, Inc., 1989—93, group v.p., gen counsel automotive systems group, 1993—2000; sr. v.p. corp. transactions and legal affairs Visteon Corp., Dearborn, Mich., 2000—. Named one of 100 Leading Women in Automotive Industry, Automotive News, 2000. Office: Visteon Corp 1700 Rotunda Dr Dearborn MI 48120

FOX, VIVICA, actress; Movies include Independence Day, 1996, Set It Off, 1996, Booty Call, 1997, Soul Food, 1997, Idle Hands, 1999, Teaching Mrs. Tingle, 1999, Little Secrets, 2001, Juwanna Mann, 2002, Boat Trip, 2002, Kill Bill: Vol. 1, 2003, Ride or Die, 2003, Motives, 2004, Ella Enchanted, 2004, Kill Bill: Vol. 2, 2004; (TV) Solomon, 1997, A Saintly Switch, 1999, City of Angels, 2000. Office: William Morris Agy 151 S El Camino Dr Beverly Hills CA 90212-2775

FOX-CLARKSON, ANNE C. computer company executive; 1 child. BS in Edn., Bucknell U., 1967; MS in Reading, Syracuse U., 1973, PhD in Tchr. Edn., 1975. Cert. elem. tchr., adminstr., Idaho. Postdoctroal work in edn. adminstrn. U. Idaho; elem. sch. tchr.; prin., supt. pub. schs., 1978-84; assoc. prof. ednl. adminstrn. Gonzaga U., 1987-94; supt. pub. instrn. State of Idaho, 1995-98; v.p. ednl. markets Shop2gether.com, 2000; pres. Human Resources Dynamics, Inc., Boise, 2001—. Mem. State Bd. Edn., State Land Bd., State Libr. Bd., State Endowment Fund, State Investment Bd.; pres., co-founder Children's Village Homes for Abused Children; grant writer, mgmt. cons.; spkr. in field. Former pres. Idaho State Elem. Prin. Assn., Wash. State Univ. Profl. Adminstr. Assn.

FOX-GENOVESE, ELIZABETH ANN TERESA, humanities educator, educator; b. Boston, May 28, 1941; d. Edward Whiting and Elizabeth Mary (Simon) Fox; m. Eugene Dominick Genovese, 1969. BA, Bryn Mawr Coll., 1963; MA, Harvard U., 1966, PhD, 1974; LittD (hon.), Millsaps Coll., 1992. Teaching fellow Harvard U., Cambridge, Mass., 1965-66, 1967-69; asst. prof. U. Rochester, N.Y., 1973-76, assoc. prof., 1976-80; prof. SUNY, Binghamton, 1980-86, Emory U., Atlanta, 1986—, Eleonore Raoul prof. of humanities, 1988—. Adj. prof. Auburn (Ala.) U., 1987; Eudora Welty prof. Millsaps Coll., 1990, Mem. Nat. Coun. Humanities, 2003-. Author: Origins of Physiocracy, 1976, (with others) Fruits of Merchant Capital, 1983, Within the Plantation Household, 1988, Feminism Without Illusions, 1991, Feminism Is Not the Story of My Life: How the Elite Women's Movement Has Lost Touch with the Real Concerns of Women, 1996, Women and the Future of the Family 2000; co-editor: Reconstructing History: The Emergence of a New Historical Society, 1999; mem. editl. adv. bd. First Things; mem. editl. bd. Books and Culture; editor Jour. Hist. Soc., 1999—; contbr. numerous articles to profl. jours. Mem. acad. adv. bd. Inst. for Am. Values, 1994—; adv. bd. Campaign for the Am. Family, 1995—, Ind. Women's Forum, 1993—. Recipient Nat. Humanities Medal, 2003. Mem. LWV, MLA, Soc. Am. Historians, The Hist. Soc. (mem. exec. com.), So. Hist. Assn. (life), So. Assn. for Women Historians (life), Am. Comparative Lit. Assn. (adv. bd. 1991-95), Orgn. Am. Historians (life, proglram com. 1991), Am. Studies Assn. (program com. 1987), Soc. for Study So. Lit. (exec. coun. 1990-93), South Atlantic MLA (chair women's studies network 1989-90), Social Sci. Hist. Assn. (exec. coun. 1986-88), Am. Hist. Assn., Am. Polit. Sci. Assn., Assn. of Lit. Scholars and Critics, Am. Acad. Liberal Edn. (bd. dirs.), Nat. Coun. on Hist. Standards (steering commn.), Hist. Soc. (mem. exec. com.), Atlanta Hist. Assn. (acad. adv. com.), Am. Antiquarian Soc., Nat. Alumni Forum (adv. bd.), Cosmos Club, Harvard Club of Boston. Roman Catholic. Avocations: family, films, fashion, reading, major league baseball. Home: 1487 Sheridan Walk NE Atlanta GA 30324-3253 Office: Emory U Dept History Atlanta GA 30322-0001*

FOXLEY, CECELIA HARRISON, commissioner; BA in English, Utah State U., 1964; MA in English, U. Utah, 1965, PhD in Ednl. Psychology, 1968. English tchr. Olympus H.S., Salt Lake City, 1965-66; asst. prof. edn., assoc. dir. student activities U. Minn., Mpls., 1968-71; from asst. prof. to assoc. prof., asst. dean Coll. Edn. U. Iowa, Iowa City, 1971-81; prof. psychology Utah State U., Logan, 1981-85, from asst. v.p. student svcs. to assoc. v.p. for student svcs. and acad. affairs, 1981-85; assoc. commr. for acad. affairs Utah State Bd. Regents, Salt Lake City, 1985-93, commr., 1993—. Utah rep. Am. Coun. on Edn. Office Women in Higher Edn., 1982-92; mem. nat. adv. coun. on nurse tng. U.S. Dept. Health and Human Svcs., 1987-91; mem. nat. adv. bd. S.W. Regional Ctr. for Drug Free Schs., 1988-93; mem. edn. bd. Utah Alliance for Edn. and Humanities, 1989-93; mem. prevention subcom. Utah Substance Abuse Coordinating Coun., 1991-93; mem. exec. bd. U.S. West Comm., 1995—; mem. adv. bd. Salt Lake Buzz, 1995—; active Consortium for Women in Higher Edn. Bd., 1981-85, Utah State Libr. Bd., 1990-93, Compact for Faculty Diversity, 1994—; presenter in field; cons. in field. Author: Recruiting Women and Minority Faculty, 1972, Locating, Recruiting, and Employing Women, 1976, Non-Sexist Counseling: Helping Women and Men Redefine Their Roles, 1979; co-author: The Human Relations Experience, 1982; editor: Applying Management Techniques, 1980; co-editor: Multicultural Nonsexist Education, 1979; author chpts. to books; contbr. articles to profl. jours. Grantee Utah State Dept. Social Svcs., 1984-85, 85-86; recipient Pres. Leadership award Assn. Utah Women Edn. Adminstrs., 1990, Disting. Alumni award Utah State U., 1991. Mem. APA, Am. Assn. Counseling and Devel., Am. Coll. Pers. Assn., Nat. Forum Sys. Chief Acad. Officers, State Higher Edn. Exec. Officers (mem. exec. com. 1994—), Western Interstate Cooperative Higher Edn. (mem. exec. com. 1994—). Office: Utah State Bd Regents 355 W North Temple Salt Lake City UT 84180-1114

FOXWELL, ELIZABETH MARIE, editor; b. Somerville, N.J., Aug. 30, 1963; d. James Adolph and Rita Ann (Drohan) F. BS in Journalism, U. Md., 1985; MA in Liberal Studies with distinction, Georgetown U., 1990. Coord. publs. internat. student exch. program Georgetown U., Washington, 1987-91; editor Am. Assn. Colls. for Tchr. Edn., Washington, 1992-97, dir. publs. and mktg., 1994-97; publs. mgr. Soc. for Am. Archaeology, 1998-2000; pubs. dir. section internat. law and practice Am. Bar Assn., 2000—02; mng. editor Heldref Pubs., 2001—. Bd. dirs. Malice Domestic, Bethesda, Md., publicity liaison, 1988-94, vice-chair, 1993-95, chair, 1995-97; bd. dirs. Mystery Writers of Am., 2003—; presenter Vera Brittain Centenary Conf., 1993, Popular Culture Assn. Conf., 1995-96. Editor: The Usual Suspects, 1992—95, The 3rd Degree, 2003—04; contbg. editor: MysteryScene, 2000—; co-editor: (anthologies) Malice Domestic 5, 1996, Malice Domestic 6, 1997; editor: Malice Domestic 7, 1998, Malice Domestic 8, 1999, Malice Domestic 9, 2000, Malice Domestic 10, 2001; co-editor: Murder, They Wrote I, 1997, Murder, They Wrote II, 1998, More Murder, They Wrote, 1999; editor (in-chief): The Armchair Detective, 1997—98; contbr. (short stories) Crime Through Time II, 1998, Cat Crimes Through Time, 1999, Crime Through Time III, Crafty Cat Crimes, 2000, Blood on Their Hands, 2003; contbr. articles to profl. jours.; mng. editor CLUES: A Jour. of Detection, 2004 ; author: Chesapeake Crimes, 2004. Recipient 2d prize in play contest N.J. Ctr. for the Performing Arts, 1981, honorable mention in writing contest Interlochen Arts Acad., 1981, 1st prize Cape Fear (N.C.) Crime Festival Short Story Contest, 2003. Mem.: Sisters in Crime, Mystery Writers Am. Address: PO Box 6267 Arlington VA 22206

FOXWORTH, JO, advertising agency executive; b. Tylertown, Miss. Grad. in Journalism, U. Mo. Exec. McCann-Erickson, Interpub. Group of Cos.; owner Jo Foxworth Inc., N.Y.C., 1968—; co-owner Foxworth-Gold, Inc. Author: Boss Lady, 1979, Wising Up, 1981, Boss Lady's Arrival and Survival Plan, 1986, The Bordello Cookbook, 1997, Murder Under Wraps, 2002. Named to AAF Hall of Fame, 1997. Office: 740 Broadway New York NY 10003-9518

FOXWORTH, JOHNNIE HUNTER, retired state agency administrator; b. Anderson, S.C., Feb. 13, 1921; d. John Ira and Bessie (Hatton) Hunter; m. Marvin Ardell, Sept. 21, 1941. Attended colls., univs., Atlanta, Bridgeport, Conn. Cashier examiner, office supr. Motor Vehicle Dept., State Conn., Bridgeport, 1957—72; br. office mgr. various locations in state, 1972—77; br. office dist. supr. Wethersfield, Conn., 1977—81; asst. dir., 1981—85; cons., tng. instr., 1985—88; ret. Writer: manual in field. Mem. Commrs. Affirmative Action Com., 1987. Recipient Profl. Achievement award, Bridgeport chpt. Nata. Bus. and Profl. Women, 1972, (2) Disting. Managerial Svc. award, State of Conn., Wethersfield, 1982, Woman of Yr. award, Nat. Coun. Negro Woman, Bridgeport, 1972. Mem.: The Links, Inc. (Waterbury) (pres. 1980—85), Les Treize (Bridgeport) (pres. 1966—68). Home: 496A Heritage Village Southbury CT 06488-1525

FOXX, VIRGINIA ANN, state legislator, small business owner; b. N.Y.C., June 29, 1943; m. Thomas A. Foxx. AB, U. N.C., Chapel Hill, 1968, MA in CT, 1972; EdD, U. N.C., Greensboro, 85. Pres., cons. Md. C.C.; owner, operator plant nursery, Banner Elk, N.C.; mem. N.C. Senate, Raleigh, 1995—. Ranking minority mem. appropriations on gen. govt. com.. mem. appropirations and base budget com., children and human resources com., commerce com., edn. and higher edn. com., fin. com., info. tech. com. Mem. Watauga County Bd. Edn., 1976-88. Mem. Nat. Assn. Women Legislators, Am. Legis. Exch. Conf., NCCBI, N.C. Ctr. for Pub. Policy Rsch., N.C. Women's Forum. Republican. Office: NC Senate 1120 Legis Bldg 16 W Jones St Raleigh NC 27601-1030 also: 11468 Hwy 105 Banner Elk NC 28604

FOY, PATRICIA SOLESBEE, music educator; b. Greenville, S.C., Apr. 28, 1955; d. Luke Julian and Betty (Sprouse) Solesbee; m. David Strickland Foy; children: Robert Strickland, David Christopher. MusB, Converse Coll., 1977; M of Music Edn., U. S.C., 1980, PhD, 1988. Pvt. practice, SC, 1976—84; music tchr. Sch. Dist. Greenville (S.C.) County, 1978—79; choral music tchr. St. John's H.S., Darlington, SC, 1980—84; music tchr. Darlington (S.C.) County Schs., 1985—86, Fair Oaks Elem. Sch., Marietta, Ga., 1986—90; assoc. prof. music edn. Converse Coll., Spartanburg, SC, 1990—. Steering com. Arts in Basic Curriculum Project, Rock Hill, SC, 1994—; chair performance-based stds. com. for music tchr. edn. S.C. Dept. Edn., Columbia, 2001—02, coord. com. for the revision of the S.C. visual and performing arts stds., 2001—03; choral adjudicator Music in the Parks/Festivals of Music, Douglassville, Pa., 1992—. Music dir. Sharon United Meth. Ch., Greer, SC, 1997—; bd. dirs. Cmty. Concert Assn., Hartsville, SC, 1980—84. Grantee Music Technology grant, S.C. Dept. Edn., 2001, Arts in Basic Curriculum grant, S.C. Arts Commn., 2001—04. Mem.: S.C. Music Educators Assn. (chair tchr. edn. 1997—2001, pres.-elect 2001—03, pres. 2003—), Soc. for Music Tchr. Edn., Nat. Assn. for Music Edn., Pi Kappa Lambda. Methodist. Office: Converse Coll 580 E Main St Spartanburg SC 29302 Business E-Mail: patti.foy@converse.edu.

FRADY, RITA R. music educator, information technology manager; d. Laurence Herbert and Evelyn T. Rice; m. Lamar K. Frady, Aug. 29, 1981; children: Leigha A., Keith B. MusB in Piano Performance, West Ga. Coll., 1980. Tchr. Cert. T-4 Ga., 1991. Music tchr. K-6 Cherokee County Bd. of Edn., Canton, Ga., 1991—. Intech redelivery Cherokee County Bd. of Edn., Canton, Ga., 2003—. Pres., v.p. Cherokee Basketball Boosters, Canton, Ga., 2000—02. Mem.: Music Educators Nat. Conf. Avocations: Tae Kwon Do, reading, travel. Office: Canton Elementary Sch 712 Marietta Hwy Canton GA 30114 Home: PO Box 4925 Canton GA 30114-0246

FRAHM, KAREN FOLEY, epidemiologist; b. Detroit, Oct. 9, 1959; d. Louis Vincent and Barbara Jean Foley; m. Jeffry Roger Frahm, June 3, 1989; children: Amy Marie, Patrick Louis. BS, Mich. State U., 1981; MPH, U. Mich., 1985. Cert. infection control Bd. Infection Control and Epidemiology Inc. Rsch. asst. Wayne State U., Detroit, 1981—84; staff specialist in infection control U. Mich. Hosps., Ann Arbor, 1985—87; epidemiologist St. Mary Hosp., Livonia, Mich., 1987—89; infection control practitioner VA Med. Ctr., Lebanon, Pa., 1989—93, quality mgmt. coord. Saginaw, Mich., 1993—96; infection control practitioner Bay Reginal Med. Ctr., Mich., 1996—. Spkr. various cancer support groups. Contbr. articles to profl. jours. Scholar, U. Mich. Sch. Pub. Health, 1994—95. Mem.: Assn. Am. Univ. Women, Assn. Profls. Infection Control, Mich. Soc. Infection Control (treas. 2000). Home: 10660 King Rd Frankenmuth MI 48734-9749 Office: Bay Med Ctr 1900 Columbus Ave Bay City MI 48708

FRAHM, SHEILA, association executive, former government official, academic administrator; b. Colby, Kans., Mar. 22, 1945; m. Kenneth Frahm; children: Amy, Pam, Chrissie. BS, Ft. Hays State U., 1967. Mem. bd. edn. State of Kans., 1985-88; mem. Kans. Senate, Topeka, 1988-94, senate majority leader, 1993-94; lt. gov. State of Kans., 1995-96; mem. from Kans., U.S. Senate, Washington, 1996, exec. dir. Kans. Assn. C.C. Trustees, Topeka, 1996—. Mem. AAUW (Outstanding Br. Mem. 1985), Thomas County Day Care Assn., Shakespeare Fedn. Women's Clubs, Farm Bur., Kans. Corn Growers, Kans. Livestock Assn., Rotary (Paul Harris fellow 1988). Republican. Home: 410 N Grant Colby KS 67701-2036 Office: 700 SW Jackson St Ste 401 Topeka KS 66603-3757 E-mail: sfrahm@colbyweb.com.

FRALIX-GOLD, CAROLYN, nursing educator, consultant, medical/surgical nurse; b. Pulaski, Tenn., Oct. 12, 1951; d. Gardner and Louetta (Miller) Fralix; children: Sean Adams, Amber Holcomb-Keene; m. Ronald David Gold, Jan. 1, 2000. ADN, San Antonio Coll., 1982; BSN, U. Tex. Health Sci. Ctr., San Antonio, 1988; MSN, U. Tex., San Antonio, 1995. RN; cert. EMT, BLS, CPR instr. Tchr., rsch. assoc. U. Tex. Health Sci. Ctr., San Antonio; neonatal ICU Santa Rosa Hosp., San Antonio, 1982; staff devel. coord. St. Rose and Villa Rosa Hosp., San Antonio; cons. for ednl. resources, med. surg. staff nurse Santa Rosa Health Care Corp., San Antonio, 1984-88; med.-surg. pool nurse Meth. Hosp., San Antonio, 1994-95; vocat. nursing instr. St. Philip's Coll., San Antonio, 1991-95; nursing instr. UTHSCSA, 1995-98; assoc. prof. Dept. Nursing San Antonio Coll., 1998-99; rsch. nurse coord. U. Tex. Health Sci. Ctr., San Antonio, 1999; intake coord. SNU Methodist Hosp., 1999—. Adj. faculty dept. nursing U. Tex. Health Sci. Ctr., San Antonio, 2002, S.W. Tex. Meth. Women's Ctr., 2002—; founder, owner Hearts Alive Inc., 2003—; cons. in field. Recipient various scholarships. Mem. ANA, Holistic Nurses Assn., Am. Urol. Assn. Allied, Tex. Nurses Assn., U. Tex. Nursing Alumni Assn. (past treas.), Tex. Jr. Coll. Tchrs. Assn., Rotary, Sigma Theta Tau.

FRAME, NANCY DAVIS, lawyer; b. Brookings, S.D., Dec. 13, 1944; m. J. Davidson Frame, Mar. 28, 1970 (div. Oct. 1994); 1 child, Katherine Adele; m. Kelly C. Kammerer, Oct. 2, 1999. BS, S.D. State U., 1966; MA, Georgetown U., 1968, JD, 1976. Bar: D.C. 1976. Atty., advisor AID, Washington, 1976-81, asst. gen. counsel, 1981-86; dep. dir. Trade and Devel. Agy., Washington, 1986-99. Bd. dirs. Daktronics, Inc. Recipient Superior Honor award AID, 1984, Presdl. Meritorious Rank award, 1993, Disting. Alumnus award S.D. State U., 1998, Presdl. Disting. Rank award, 1998; Fulbright fellow, 1966, NDEA fellow, 1967. Address: Chemin de la Bernarde Route de Lorgues 83300 Draguignan France E-mail: ndframe@hotmail.com.

FRAN, GRANDMA See BROWN, FRANCES LOUISE

FRANANO, SUSAN MARGARET KETTEMAN, arts consultant and adminstrator, musician; b. Kansas City, Mo., Sept. 30, 1946; d. Charley Gilbert and Mary Elizabeth (Bredehoeft) Ketteman; m. Frank Salvatore Franano, Dec. 20, 1969; 1 child, Domenico Frank. AA, Stephens Coll., Columbia, Mo., 1966, BFA, 1967; postgrad., U. Mo., Kansas City, 1967-68, So. Ill. U., Edwardsville, 1968-69. Mgr. Lyric Opera Group, Kansas City, 1976-82; tour coordinator Lyric Opera Kansas City, 1978-85; dir. outreach Kansas City Symphony, 1982-84, asst. mgr., 1984-85, ops. mgr., 1985-86, gen. mgr., 1986-95; exec. dir. Columbus (Ohio) Symphony Orch., 1995-97, Ohio Citizens for Arts, Columbus, 1998—. Guest lectr. Ohio State U., 1999. Regional liaison Mo. Citizens for Arts, Kansas City, 1984-86; regional rep. Am. Guild Mus. Artists, Kansas City, 1977-81; regional ammenities task force mem. Mid-Am. Regional Coun., 1989-95; panelist Nat. Endowment for Arts, 1991-2000, site visitor, 1998—; chmn. group 2 orchs. Am. Symphony Orch. League, 1992-94; site visitor Fla. Dept. Cultural Affairs, 1998—; mem. bd. Statewide Arts Advocacy League Am., Ohio Alliance for Art Edn. Mem. Mo. Citizens for Arts, Ohio Citizens for the Arts, Actors Equity, New Albany Arts Coun., Columbus Mus. Art. Democrat. Roman Catholic. Avocations: tennis, cooking, travel. Office: Ohio Citizens for the Arts 77 S High St Columbus OH 43215-6108

FRANCE, DOROTHY DANIEL, minister; b. Danieltown, Va, Nov. 23, 1926; d. Arthur R. and Susan G. (Waller) Daniel; m. Carl G. France, Aug. 6, 1946 (dec. Nov. 1997); 1 child, Dorothy Gail France Frankle. BA, Bethany Coll., 1950; post grad., William and Mary Coll., 1964, Va. Commonwealth U., 1966. Dir. Army Dir. Svc., Camp Pickett, Va., 1944-46; tchr. Nottoway County Pub. Sch., Crewe, Va., 1950-55, Henrico Pub. Sch., Richmond, Va., 1961-63, Petersburg Pub. Sch., Va., 1964-68; dir. Cmty. Devel., New River Cmty Action, Radford, Va., 1969-73; min. Petunia Christian Ch., Wytheville, Va., 1969-72, Galilee Christian Ch., Wytheville, 1973-75; assoc. dir. CROP/Ch. World Svc., Va., NC, 1975-76; dir. CROP/Ch. World Svc. for Va., Richmond, 1977-80; dir. resource devel. Va. Inst. of Pastoral Care, Richmond, 1980-81; min. Prospect Christian Ch., Dinwiddie, Va., 1982-87; dir. Refugee Resettlement CWS/EMM, Va. Coun. of Ch., Richmond, 1981-91. Cons. on Am. corp. involvement in South Africa Christian Ch., Indpls., 1971. Author: Special Days of the Church Year, 1969, Newness of Life, 1970, Partners in Prayer, 1986, Welcome to the United States An Orientation Guide for Refuges, 1988, Blessed Assurance, 1999, (with Jason and David Frankle) You Might Be a Football Fan If....Simplified Game Notes for Would Be Fans, 2000; (with Jason and David Frankle) You Might Be a Basketball Fan If... Simplified Game Notes for Would Be Fans, 2003; author/editor: At Christ's Table, 1997; author: (with others) Go Quickly and Tell, 1973; editl. com. Toward Better Grouping in Reading, 1968. Recipient Valiant Woman award Ch. Women United. Mem. AAUW, Va. Coalition on Nutrition, Delta Kappa Gamma (chair personal growth and devel. com. 1968). Avocations: writing, travel. Home and Office: DDF Enterprises 2968 Silver Maple Dr Fairlawn OH 44333-3295 E-mail: ddfenprise@aol.com.

FRANCESCONI, LOUISE L. electronics executive; b. Calif., Mar. 1953; BA, Scripps Coll., 1975; MBA, UCLA, 1978. With Hughes Missile Systems Co., 1976—98, pres., 1996—98; sr. v.p., dep. gen. mgr. def. systems Raytheon Co., Tucson, 1998—99, v.p., gen. mgr. missile systems, 1999—2002, v.p., pres. missile systems, 2002—. Mem. Ariz. Gov.'s Coun. on Innovation and Tech., 2003—; nat. bd. advisors Eller Coll. Bus. and Pub. Adminstrn., U. Ariz.; bd. trustees Tucson Med. Ctr. Healthcare, Tucson Airport Authority. Office: Raytheon Co 9000 S Rita Rd Tucson AZ 85744*

FRANCHINI, ROXANNE, bank executive; b. N.Y.C., Mar. 20, 1951; d. Tullio and Jean (Brady) Franchini. Student, Emerson Coll., Ricker Coll., New Sch. Social Rsch. With Princess Marcella Borghese divsn. Revlon, N.Y.C., 1972-73, TWA Airlines, 1973-74; asst. to pres. N.Y. Shipping Assn., N.Y.C., 1974-79; benefits mgr. Kidde, Inc., N.Y.C., 1979-83; 2d v.p. pension trust fin. svcs. Chase Manhattan Bank, N.A., N.Y.C., 1983-85, v.p. mgr. global securities, 1985-89; v.p., sales dir. global custody worldwide securities svcs. Citibank, N.Y.C., 1989-91; v.p. Mellon Bank, Pitts., 1991—2001; 1st v.p. Mellon Fin. Corp., Pitts., 2002—. Chair fin. local fund raising campaigns. Mem.: So. Assn. Coll. and Univ. Bus. Offices, Ea. Assn. Coll. and Univ. Bus. Offices, Nat. Assn. Coll. and Univ. Bus. Offices. Home: 1415 Ocean Shore Blvd Ormond Beach FL 32176-3673

FRANCIS, ELIZABETH ROMINE, secondary school educator, theater director; b. Clarksburg, WVa., Sept. 10, 1920; d. John Ransel and Virginia Snider Romine; m. Jack Stanley Francis, Feb. 13, 1943; children: Michael Stanley, John Maurice. BM, WVa. U., 1942, MM, 1963, JD; grad. drama, Ohio U., 1980. Tchr. Elem. Sch., Clarksburg, W.Va., 1942—43, Jr. H.S., Clarksburg, W.Va., 1943—44, Sr. H.S., Clarksburg, W.Va., 1943—45, New Martinville, W.Va., 1960—93; tchr. adult edn. WVa. U. Ext., New Martinville, 1960—70; Fred Waring workshop staff mem. Waring Enterprises, Delaware Water Gap, 1988—90; dir. theater activities Park & Recreation, New Martinsville, W.Va., 1993—2001. Chmn. theater divsn. Parks and Recreation, New Martinsville, W.Va., 1993—2001. Prodr., dir. : (musical theater) Cmty. Theater, 1993—2001. Recipient Acad. Excellence award, State of WVa., 1985. Republican. Methodist. Avocations: golf, bridge. Office: New Martinsville Parks and Recreation 191 Main St New Martinsville WV 26155 Personal E-mail: eliza@ovis.net.

FRANCIS, JUANITA ROSE, environmental engineer, chemist; b. Ganado, Ariz., June 11, 1958; d. James and Anita (Sleuth) F.; 1 child: Dominic James Edward Francis-Segay. BS in Biology, Chem., No. Ariz. U., 1981. Registered environ. mgr. Chemist Navajo Tribal Utility Authority, Ft. Defiance, Ariz., 1982-84, chemist II, 1989-93, environ. engr., 1993—; tchr. chem., physics Many Farms (Ariz.) H.S., 1985-86; student intern NIH, Bethesda, Md., 1988; med. technologist Tsile (Ariz.) Health Ctr., 1988, Chinle (Ariz.) Comprehensive Health Care Facility, 1988-89. Contbr. articles to profl. jours. Mem. Am. Chem. Soc.

FRANCIS, KAREN, painter, television producer; b. Memphis, Apr. 27, 1950; BA in Comm. Arts, Rhodes Coll., 1971; MA, U. Mo., 1973. Cert. tchr., Tenn. Secondary sch. tchr. Memphis City Schs., 1971-72; speech tchr. U. Ga., Athens, 1973-75; dir. computer systems installations Planning Rsch. Corp., McLean, Va., 1976-78; dir. account mgmt. TDX Systems, Cable & Wireless, Vienna, Va., 1978-80; cons. telecommunications MCI, Washington, 1985-87; producer Fairfax Cable Access, Merrifield, Va., 1991-96. Owner Art Promotions, McLean, 1989—. Exhibited paintings in numerous group and one-woman shows and in cyberspace including Mus. Contemporary Art, Washington, 1996, Arts Coun. Fairfax County, Va., 1999, many others; paintings numerous pvt. collections; author screenplay Sisters, 2003. Active Family AIDS Housing Found., 1992, Hospice No. Va., 1991, 92, Friends of Vietnam Vets. Meml., 1992; founding bd. mem. Jobs for Homeless People, 1988-90; founder Non-Violence Award Program, 1998. Avocations: tennis, bridge, poetry, piano. Office: Art Promotions PO Box 3104 Mc Lean VA 22103-3104 Office Phone: 703-893-7482. E-mail: karen@artpro.com., karenartpro@aol.com.

FRANCIS, LYNNE ANN, elementary school educator, music educator; b. Parkersburg, W.Va., May 18, 1961; d. Gale Meyer and Mabel Eileen Hains; m. Randal Craig Francis, June 17, 1989; 1 child, Brent. MusB, SUNY, Fredonia, 1982, MusM, 1984. Summer employee E.I. DuPont, Washington, W.Va., 1980—82; music specialist elem. sch. Marietta City Schs., Ohio, 1984—. Mem.: NEA, Ohio Music Edn. Assn., Music Educator's Nat. Conf., Ohio Edn. Assn., Sigma Alpha Iota. Avocations: crocheting, music, counted cross stitch, photography. Home: 165 Edendale Ln Parkersburg WV 26101 Office: Marietta City Schs 701 3d St Marietta OH 45750

FRANCIS, SHARI, federal agency administrator; BA in edn., Southeast Mo. State U., 1970; MA in edn., U. Mo., St. Louis, 1976. V.p., state relations Nat. Coun. Accreditation Tchr. Edn., Wash., 1992—; sr. policy analyst Nat. Edn. Assn., Wash., DC, 1981—92; staff US Dept. Edn., Elem. Secondary Edn., Wash., 1980; reading spec., tchr., 1970—79. Mem.: Nat. Bd. Profl. Tchg. Standards. Office: Nat Coun Accreditation Tchr Edn 2010 Mass Ave NW Ste 500 Washington DC 20036 E-mail: shari@ncate.org.

FRANCISCO, DEBORAH ANTOSH, educational administrative professional; b. Wilkes-Barre, Pa, Mar. 8, 1952; d. Albert and Marie Iris (Stuka) Antosh; m. John Thomas McCauley, Sept. 11, 1970 (div. Sept. 1983); 1 child, John-Austen; m. John Patrick Francisco, July 28, 1988; 1 child, Theresa. BA, Cedar Crest Coll., Allentown, Pa., 1984; EdM in Ednl. Adminstrn., Rutgers U., 2003. Cert. elem. tchr., Pa.; cert. elem. and nursery sch. tchr., N.J. Elem. tchr. Allentown Sch. Dist., 1984-88; tchr. basic skills Perth Amboy Sch. Dist., NJ, 1988-89, elem. tchr., 1989—90; tchr. St. Matthias, Somerset, NJ, 1993—96; order processor divsn. housing and confs. Rutgers U., 1997—99, asst. mgr. adminstrn. Coll. Ave. campus, 1999—. Democrat. Roman Catholic. Home: 14 Canadian Woods Rd Marlboro NJ 07746-1672

FRANCISCO, JODIE E. realtor, marketing professional, consultant; b. Chicago, Ill., Aug. 18, 1957; d. James Lee LeVitus and Joan Lee (Davis) Kreiter; m. Stephen F. Francisco, June 25, 1995. BS in Advt., U. Ill., Champaign, 1978. Cons. Jelco, Encino, Calif., 2000—; realtor Prudential Calif. Realty/John Aaroe, Encino, Calif., 2001—. Office: Prudential California Realty/John Aaroe 16810 Ventura Blvd Encino CA 91436

FRANCKE, GLORIA NIEMEYER, pharmacist, editor, publisher; b. Dillsboro, Ind., Apr. 28, 1922; d. Albert B. and Fannie K. (Libbert) Niemeyer; m. Donald Eugene Francke, Apr. 15, 1956. BS in Pharmacy, Purdue U., 1942; PharmD (hon.), 1988—; PharmD, U. Cin., 1971; postgrad., U. Mich., 1945. Pharmacist Dillsboro Drug Store, 1943-44; instr. Sch. Pharmacy Purdue U., Lafayette, Ind., 1943; asst. to chief pharmacist U. Mich. Hosp., Ann Arbor, 1944-46; assoc. editor Am. Jour. Hosp. Pharmacy, Washington, 1944-64; asst. dir. divsn. hosp. pharmacy Am. Pharm. Assn., Washington, 1946-56; exec. sec. Am. Soc. Hosp. Pharmacists, Ann Arbor, 1949-60, acting dir. dept. comm. Washington, 1963-64; drug lit. specialist Nat. Libr. Medicine, Bethesda, Md., 1965-67; clin. pharmacy tchg. coord. VA Hosp., Cin., 1967-71; asst. clin. prof. clin. pharmacy Coll. Pharmacy U. Cin., 1967-71; chief program evaluation br. Alcohol & Drug Dependence Svc. VA Ctrl. Office, Washington, 1971-75; dir. Pharmacy Intelligence Ctr. Am. Pharm. Assn., Washington, 1975-85. Mem. Roche Hosp. Pharmacy Adv. Bd., 1971-74; judge for ann. Lunsford Richardson Pharmacy awards, 1963, 64; mem. com. stds. for drug abuse treatment and rehab. programs Joint Commn. Accreditation of Hosps., 1974-75. Author: (with D.E. Francke, C.J. Latiolais and N.F.H. Ho) Mirror to Hospital Pharmacy, 1964; contbr. articles to profl. jours. Bd. dirs., mem. found., co-chair women's bd. Ingleside Presbyn. Retirement Cmty., Washington., 1999-2003. Recipient Harvey A.K. Whitney award Mich. Soc. Hosp. Pharmacists, 1953, Disting. Alumnus award Purdue U. Sch. Pharmacy, 1985, Remington Honor medal, 1987, Career Achievement award Profl. Frat. Assn., 1991, Fedn. Internat. Pharm. Lifetime Achievement in the Practice of Pharmacy award, 1996; also various commendations. Mem. Internat. Pharm. Fedn., Am. Inst. History of Pharmacy (exec. sec. 1968-78), Tex. Soc. Hosp. Pharmacists (hon.), Am. Pharm. Assn. (hon. chmn. 1986, Gloria Niemeyer Francke Leadership Mentor award named in her honor 1995), Am. Soc. Hosp. Pharmacists (Donald E. Francke medal 1995), Kappa Epsilon, Rho Chi. Presbyterian. Home and Office: Apt 441 B 4000 Cathedral Ave NW Washington DC 20016-5289 E-mail: glor238@aol.com.

FRANCKE, LINDA BIRD, journalist; b. NYC, Mar. 14, 1939; d. Samuel Curtis and Janet (King) Bird; m. G.D. Mackenzie, Jan. 12, 1961; 1 son, Andrew Mackenzie; m. Albert Francke III, Oct. 7, 1967; 2 daughters: Caitlin, Tapp. Student, Bradford Jr. Coll., 1958, New Sch. for Social Rsch., 1963—65. Copywriter Young & Rubicam, Inc., N.Y.C., 1960-63, Ogilvy & Mather, Inc., N.Y.C., 1965-67; contbg. editor N.Y. Mag., N.Y.C., 1968-72, 80—; gen. editor Newsweek Mag., N.Y.C., 1972-77; columnist N.Y. Times, 1977—; TV news commentator Spl. Edit., 1978-79. Dir. New Directions; juror Am. Book Awards, 1981; Co-chmn. Writer's Resource Center, Southampton, N.Y. Contbr. (works to anthologies including) The N.Y. Spy, 1967, The Power Game, 1970, Running Against the Machine, 1969, Women: A Book for Men, 1979, Hers: Through Women's Eyes, 1985, America Firsthand, Vol. II: From Reconstruction to the Present, 1994; author: The Ambivalence of Abortion, 1978, Growing Up Divorced, 1983, Ground Zero: The Gender Wars in the Military, 1997; collaborator: First Lady from Plains, 1984, Ferraro: My Story, 1985, A Woman of Egypt, 1987, Daughter of Destiny, 1989, Signature Life, 1998, Life So Far, 2000, On Faith, 2002. Mem. Women's Commn. for Refugee Women and Children, Internat. Rescue Com. Inc.; chmn. East End Choice; candidate N.Y. State Assembly, 2d Dist., 1990; del. to Dem. Nat. Conv., 1992; bd. dirs. Bridgehampton Child Care & Recreational Ctr., Inc., The Retreat. Recipient award Cannes Film Festival, 1969, Nat. Clarion award, 1994; finalist Helen Bernstein Book award Excellence in Journalism, 1998. Mem. Authors Guild, Women's Media Group N.Y.C., Eastville Hist. Soc., Women Mil. Aviators, Inc.

FRANCKE, REND RAHIM, ambassador; b. Baghdad, Iraq, 1949; arrived in U.S., 1981, naturalized, 1987; d. Mahdi Rahim; m. Frederic B. Francke. MA in English, U. Cambridge; MA in French Lit., Sorbonne. Co-founder The Iraqi Found., Washington, 1991—2003, dir., 1991—2003; amb. Iraq Washington, 2003—. Co-author: The Arab Shi'a: Forgotten Muslims, 2000. Office: Bahraini Embassy Iraqi Interests Sect 3502 International Drive NW Washington DC 20008 also: The Iraq Foundation 1012 14th St NW Ste 1110 Washington DC 20005 Home: 7017 Hector Rd Mc Lean VA 22101-2112*

FRANCKE, UTA, medical geneticist, genetics researcher, educator; b. Wiesbaden, Germany, Sept. 9, 1942; arrived in U.S., 1969; d. Kurt and Gertrud Muller; m. Bertold Richard Francke, May 27, 1967 (div. 1982); m. Heinz Furthmayr, July 27, 1986. MD, U. Munich, Fed. Republic Germany, 1967; MS, Yale U., 1985. Diplomate Am. Bd. Pediatrics, Am. Bd. Med. Genetics (bd. dirs. 1981-84). Asst. prof. U. Calif., San Diego, 1973—78; assoc. prof. Yale U., New Haven, 1978—85, prof., 1985—88; prof. genetics Stanford (Calif.) U., 1989—. Investigator Howard Hughes Med. Inst., Stanford, 1989—2000, mem. sci. rev. bd., Bethesda, Md., 1986—88; mem. mammalian genetics study sect. NIH, Bethesda, 1990—94. Profl. advisor March of Dimes Birth Defects Found., White Plains, NY, 1990, Marfan Assn., Port Washington, NY, 1991. Mem.: Am. Soc. Human Genetics (pres. 1999, bd. dirs. Rockville, Md. chpt. 1981—84), Soc. for Inherited Metabolic Disorders, Soc. for Pediatric Rsch., Human Genome Orgn., Inst. Medicine of NAS (assoc.). Avocation: piloting. Office: Stanford U Med Sch Beckman Ctr Stanford CA 94305-5323 E-mail: francke@cmgm.stanford.edu.

FRANCO, ANNEMARIE WOLETZ, editor; b. Somerville, N.J., Sept. 18, 1933; d. Frederick Franz and Bertha (Laugginger) Woletz; m. Frederick Nicholas Franco, June 11, 1977 (dec. Feb. 1998). Student, Wood Coll. of Bus. Editorial asst. Internat. Musician, then assoc. editor, 1965-88, ret., 1988. Republican. Presbyterian. Avocations: writing, music, cooking, travel. Home: 166 Wellstone Dr Palm Coast FL 32164-4111

FRANCO, BARBARA ALICE, museum director; b. N.Y.C., Mar. 16, 1945; d. Alexander and Sarah E. (Johnson) F.; m. John A. Mayer, Apr. 8, 1973; children: Lee, Samantha. BA, Bryn Mawr Coll., 1965; MA, SUNY, Cooperstown, 1966. Curator of decorative arts Munson-Williams-Proctor Inst., Utica, N.Y., 1966-73; curator of collections Mus. of Our Nat. Heritage, Lexington, Mass., 1974-85, asst. dir., 1985-89; asst. dir. for museums Minn. Hist. Soc., St. Paul, 1990-95; exec. dir. The Hist. Soc. Washington, 1995—2003, Penn. Historical and Museum Com., Phila., 2003—. Author exhbn. catalogs; editor: Folk Roots, New Roots, 1988, Ideas and Images, 1992. Mem. Minn. Assn. Museums (chmn. 1992-93). Mem. Bryn Mawr Club (pres. 1982-84). Office: Penn Historical and Museum Com 300 N St Harrisburg PA 17120*

FRANCO, ELAINE ADELE, librarian; b. N.Y.C., Jan. 24, 1948; d. Alexander and Sarah Eleanor (Johnson) Franco; m. James Paul Webster, Dec. 29, 1982 (dec. Sept. 1993). BA magna cum laude, Hope Coll., Holland, Mich., 1969; MLS, U. Mich., 1975, MA, 1976. Cataloger U. Nebr.-Lincoln Librs., 1977-81, prin. cataloger, 1981-90, Shields Libr., U. Calif., Davis, 1990—. Bibliographer: MLA International Bibliography, 1979—, First Printings of American Authors, 1977-79; editor conf. procs. Recipient Disting. Svc award Nebr. Libr. Assn. Coll. and Univ. Sect. 1984. Mem. MLA, ALA (councilor-at-large 1987-91), Calif. Libr. Assn. (pres. access, collections and tech. svcs. sect. 1998-99), Calif. Acad. and Rsch. Librs., Beta Phi Mu. Office: U Calif Shields Libr 100 NW Quad Davis CA 95616-5292 E-mail: eafranco@ucdavis.edu.

FRANCOEUR, SHEILA T. state representative; b. Lowell, Mass., Feb. 18, 1938; m. Ronald Francoeur; two children. BA, Fla. State U., 1971. Banker, ret. 1993; ret., 1993; mem. dist. 85 N.H. Ho. of Reps., 1996—. Mem., chmn. econ. devel. com., City of Hampton; mem. vice-chmn. policy bldg. study com.; mem. mcpl. budget com. Bd. dirs. Leadership Seacoast. Mem. Rotary (v.p., bd. dirs.), AAUW (treas., bd. dirs.). Roman Catholic. Home: 88 Kings Hwy Hampton NH 03842-4317 Office: NH State Legis State House Concord NH 03301 E-mail: sheila.francouer@leg.state.nh.us.

FRANCOMANO, CLAIR ANN, geneticist; BA, Yale U., 1976; MD, Johns Hopkins U. Sch. Medicine, 1980. Resident internal medicine Johns Hopkins U. Sch. of Medicine, Balt., 1980-82, fellow pediat. and med. genetics, 1982-84, asst. prof., 1985-92, assoc. prof., 1992—; clin. dir. Nat. Human Genome Rsch. Inst. Clin. dir. Nat. Human Genome Rsch. Inst., Bethesda, Md., 1996—, chief med. genetics br., 1994-99; assoc. prof. dept. health policy and mgmt. Johns Hopkins U. Sch. of Hygiene and Pub. Health, Balt., 1996—. Office: Nat Human Genome Rsch Inst 10 Center Dr Msc 1852 Bldg 10 Bethesda MD 20892-1852 Fax: 301 496-7157. E-mail: clairf@nhgri.nih.gov.

FRANEY, BILLIE NOLAN, political activist; b. Eveleth, Minn., Sept. 17, 1930; d. Mark and Ann Murray Nolan; m. Neil Joseph Franey; children: Kathleen, Timothy, Nora, Colin, Patrick. Student, Carleton Coll., 1948-49, U. Minn., 1949-50; BA, Coll. St. Scholastica, 1952. Social worker Cath. Welfare, Mpls., 1952-53. Contbr. articles to profl. jours. Chair Indian Affairs, Minn. Mrs. Jaycees, 1962; mem. Charter Commn., White Bear Lake, Minn., 1962-65; pres. White Bear Lake LWV, 1965-67; lobbyist Common Cause of Minn., 1979, Minn. LWV, 1980, AAUW, 1987-89; mem. met. futures task force Met. Coun., 1988-89; co-chair Women Come to The Capitol, Minn. Women's Consortium. Named Outstanding Young Women of Am., 1966; revipient Sister Ann Edward Scholar award The Coll. of St. Scholostica, 1992. Mem. AAUW (pres. 1992-94, St. Paul program v.p. 1990-92, legis. pub. policy chair 1987-89, Minn. chpt. legis. pub. policy v.p. 1987-89, scholarship named for as a gift from St. Paul AAUW 1989, Women as Agts. of Change award 1991, chair St. Paul scholarship trust 2001—), Coun. Met. Area LWV (chair 1981-83, program and study chair 1979-81, bd. mem. 1978-79). Avocations: reading, biking, cross-country skiing, gardening. Home: 1323 Hedman Way Saint Paul MN 55110-3360

FRANEY, CATHERINE T. elementary school educator; b. Ashland, Pa., Nov. 6, 1943; d. George William and Elizabeth (McDonald) Dougherty; m. William George Franey, Nov. 18, 1966; children: William Sean, Molly Elizabeth Suplee, Ryan Patrick, Sarah Jeanne, Emily Therese. BS, U. Md., 1965; postgrad., Trinity Coll., Washington, 1992-96. Elem. sch. tchr., Prince Georges County, Md., 1965-71; life skills tchr. Severn Sch., Severna Park, Md., 1992—. Mem. Ward One Residents Assn., Annapolis, Md., 1995—. Mem. AAUW, ACA, Md. Assn. Counseling and Devel., Delta Gamma Sorority (Beta Sigma chpt. pres. 1964-65).

FRANK, AGNES T. medical librarian; b. Budapest, Hungary; d. Julius Furedi and Maria Szlovak; m. Neil Frank (div. 1971). MLS, Columbia U., 1964. Dir. med. library French & Polyclinic Med. Sch. and Health Ctr., N.Y.C., 1970-74, St. Vincent's Hosp. and Med. Ctr., N.Y.C., 1974—2002. Mem. Med. Libr. Assn. (cert.), Acad. Health Info. Practitioners (sr.). Avocations: travel, yoga, photography. Home: 372 Central Park W Apt 16A New York NY 10025-8211

FRANK, AMÉLIE LORRAINE, marketing professional; b. L.A., Feb. 5, 1960; d. Lawrence Bruce and Phébé Exilda (Brodeur) Frank. BA in English, Creative Writing, U. Calif., Irvine, 1981. Letters editor Petersen Pub., West Hollywood, Calif., 1983-85; owner, writer Mysterious Affairs, Hollywood, 1984-88; script svcs. supr. Universal City (Calif.) Studios, 1985-86; mkt. rschr. Universal Pictures Mktg., Universal City, 1986-94; owner, pub. Sacred Beverage Press, Venice, Calif., 1994—; rsch. coord. Buena Vista Pictures Mktg., Burbank, Calif., 1994—; creative exec. feature film Bring Him Home, 2000. Host poetry readings Hot House Cafe, North Hollywood, 1996—99, Exile Books & Music, 1999—2000; co-dir. Valley Contemporary Poets, 1999—2002; host Killer Poetry, 2000—01; co-webmaster Billybobapalooza Ofcl. Billy Bob Thornton website; creative exec. "Bring Him Home" feature film. Author: (poems) A Resilient Heart and Other Visceral Comforts, 1992, Flame and Loss of Breath, 1996, Doing Time on Planet Billy Bob, 2000; co-author: Drink Me, 1997, Bird Interpretations, 1998; editor: (book) God the Motion Picture, 1994; co-editor: Blue Satellite Jour., 1994—2000; performer spoken word (albums) The Essential Girl, 2001, Retro Hell music reviewer Ind. Revs. Site; CD, Michael Shipp Xcursion "The Adventures of Roosterboy". Facilitator buddy program AIDS Project, L.A., Hollywood, 1988—92; trustee Beyond Baroque, 1999—, artist, cmty. advisor coun., 1998—99; mem. med. staff Disney Disaster Preparedness, Burbank, 1994—. Named L.A. Newer Poet, Beyond Baroque in conjunction with L.A. Poetry Festival, 1999; recipient award for favorite new poetry book, Readership, NEXT Mag., 1996, Spirit of Venice award, 2000. Mem.: NOW, Poetry Soc. Am., Office Profl. Employees Internat. Union (newsletter editor 1991—94), PETA. Green Party. Avocations: reading, choral music, travel, films, working with animals. Office: The Sacred Beverage Press PO Box 10312 Burbank CA 91510-0312 E-mail: poetamelie@aol.com.

FRANK, DEE, artist, educator; b. Greeley, Colo., July 5, 1931; d. Frank Albert Borton and Carolyn Frances Hayden; m. Leslie Arthur Frank, 1959 (div. 1978); children: Edward, David, Barbara. BFA, Idaho State U., 1953. Asst. med. illustrator Oreg. Health Scis. U., Portland, 1953-57, ophthalmic artist and technician, 1960-82; recreation leader U.S. Army, LaRochelle, France, 1957-59; pvt. practice graphic artist Portland, 1982-92; pvt. practice artist, instr., tour leader, 1992—. Elderhostel watercolor instr., 1992—; participant juried shows Watercolor Soc. Oreg., 1977—, N.W. Watercolor Soc., 1979, 82, 88, 89, 92, 96, Rocky Mountain Nat. Watermedia Exposition, 1987, 88, 97. One-person shows include The Main Gallery, Boise, 1990, The Dalles Art Ctr., 1987, Idaho State U., Transition Gallery, 1981, Galos Gallery, Boise, 1995, Artreach Gallery, Portland, 1998, Salem (Oreg.) Art Assn. Bush Barn Gallery, 2000, among others. Active Stanford Parents Club, Portland, 1980-83; vol. Ecumenical workcamp, P.R., 1951. Recipient numerous awards. Mem. Watercolor Soc. Oreg. (bd. mem. 1978-97, newsletter editor 1980-97, pres. 1995-96, Outstanding Svc. award 1992), N.W. Watercolor Soc., The Critique Group, Le Déjuener Français. Avocations: reading, walking, crossword puzzles. Home and Office: Aquarelle Tours PO Box 10 Gladstone OR 97027-0010

FRANK, SISTER ELAINE LOU, sister; b. LaCrosse, Wis., Apr. 16, 1946; d. Jerome H. and Florence A. Frank. BA in Social Welfare, Barry U., 1972, MA in Religious Studies, 1975. Cert. chaplain. Primary tchr. Cath. Sch. Sys., Marathon and Port Charlotte, Fla., 1967—69; asst. to the adminstr. St. Elizabeth Gardens, Pompano Beach, Fla., 1969—73; adminstr. Villa Madonna, Miami, Fla., 1973—75; parish and retreat ministry Sisters of St. Francis, Rochester, Minn., 1975—80; adminstrn. and retreat ministry Tau Ctr., Winona, Minn., 1980—88; hosp./hospice chaplain Mercy Health Center-North Iowa, Mason City, Iowa, 1990—98; retreat ctr. ministry Holy Spirit Retreat Ctr., Janesville, Minn., 1998—. Instl. rev. bd. Mercy Health Ctr.-North Iowa, Mason City, Iowa, 1993—98; coun. area reps. Retreats Internat., Notre Dame, Ind., 2002—. Mem. cmty. policing adv. bd. Police Dept., Mason City, Iowa, 1996—98; hospice vol. Immanuel St. Joseph-Mayo Health Sys., Mankato and Waseca, Minn., 1998—2003; sec. Home Delivered Meals Program, Janesville, Minn., 2001—03; exec. com. Lake Elysian Watershed Assn., Janesville and Elysian, Minn., 2002—03. Mem.: Spiritual Directors Internat., Nat. Assn. of Cath. Chaplains (nat. leadership coun. 1996—98). Dfl. Roman Catholic. Avocations: quilting, bridge, crossword puzzles, reading, sewing. Home and Office: Holy Spirit Retreat Ctr 3864 420th Ave Janesville MN 56048-1102

FRANK, ELIZABETH, literature educator, writer; b. L.A., Sept. 14, 1945; d. Melvin G. and Anne R. Frank; 1 child, Anne Louise Buchwald. Student, Bennington Coll.; BA, MA, PhD, U. Calif., Berkeley. Prof. modern langs. and lit. Bard Coll., Annandale-on-Hudson, NY, 1982—, faculty Ctr. for Cultural Studies, Joseph E. Harry prof. modern langs. and lit. Author: Jackson Pollock, 1983, Louise Bogan: A Portrait, 1985 (Pulitzer prize for biography, 86), Esteban Vicente, 1995; contbr. articles to profl. jours. Fellow, Ford Found., 1967—72, Temple U., 1977, The Newbery Libr., 1977, Am. Coun. Learned Socs., 1977, NEH. Office: Joy Harris Lit Agy 156 5th Ave Ste 617 New York NY 10010-7002 also: Bard Coll Dept Lang & Lit Annandale On Hudson NY 12504

FRANK, ELIZABETH AHLS (BETSY FRANK), art educator; b. Cin., Sept. 27, 1942; d. Edward Henry and Constance Patricia (Barnett) Ahls; m. James Russell Frank, Aug. 10, 1963; children: Richard Scott, Robert Edward. Student, Hiram (Ohio) Coll., 1960-63; BA, U. Denver, 1964; MA, U. South Fla., 1988. Cert. profl. educator. Remedial reading tchr. Willoughby-Eastlake (Ohio) Schs., 1971-72; elem. tchr., grade level chmn. Lee County Pub. Schs., Ft. Myers, Fla., 1972-79, tchr. art, 1979—2002. Mem. arts coun. Lee County Pub. Schs., mem. long range and model schs. planning coms., 1997—98. Contbg. author Davis Art Edn. Publs., Worcester, Mass. Vol. Mann Performing Arts Hall, Fort Myers, 1986-98, Harborside Convention Ctr., 1991-95; sec. Colonial Acres Homeowners Assn., North Fort Myers, Fla., 1994-99. Named Golden Apple Tchr. of Distinction, Lee County Schs. Found., 1991—2002, Lee County Art Educator of Yr., 2001—02; recipient, Seminar Fla. Humanites Coun., 2000. Mem.: NEA, Edison African Violet Soc. (1st v.p. 1997—2000), Tchrs. Assn. Lee County (rep. bd. 1972—99, mem. exec. bd. 1990—91, M.M. Bethune Humanities award 1992), Fla. Edn. Assn., Lee Art Edn. Assn. (pres. 1991—92, founder, Art Educator of Yr. 1991—92), Calusa Nature Ctr., Southwest Fla. Rose Soc., Fla. Art Edn. Assn. (workshop presenter), Nat. Art Edn. Assn., Citrus County Audubon Soc. (sec. 2004—), Audubon of S.W. Fla.. (recording sec. 2002—03, Educator of Yr. 1998), Crystal River Women's Club, Delta Kappa Gamma (v.p. 1986—88, pres. 1988—90, sec. 1996—98, state chmn. arts and crafts com. 1997—99, sec. 2001—03, state mem. world fellowship com., Fla. scholar 1988), Phi Delta Kappa, Phi Kappa Phi. Democrat. Avocations: gardening, camping, boating, arts and crafts, birdwatching. Home: 4583 S Sawgrass Cir Homosassa FL 34448 E-mail: jrfrank@mindspring.com.

FRANK, ELLEN, medical educator, psychiatrist, psychologist, researcher; Grad., Vassar Coll., 1966; M in Eng., Carnegie Mellon U., 1967; PhD in Psychol., U. Pitts., 1979. Prof. psychiatry, psychology U. Pitts., 1979—. Mem. task force on DSM-IV Am. Psychiat. Assn.; chair psychopharmacologic drugs avd. panel FDA; mem. MacArthur Found. Rsch. Network on Psychopathology and Devel.; chair task force on continuing edn. Am. Coll. Neuropsychopharmacology. Grantee Nat. Inst. Mental Health. Fellow: Am. Psychiatric Assn. (hon.); mem.: Inst. Medicine. Office: Bellefield Twrs 8th Fl Pittsburgh PA 15213

FRANK, ERICA, preventive medicine physician; b. Trenton, N.J., June 17, 1962; m. Randall White, 1990; 1 child, Ridge. MD, Mercer U., 1988. Intern Cleve. Clin., 1988-89; resident in preventive medicine Yale U., New Haven, 1989-90; rsch. fellow Stanford U., 1990—93; asst./assoc. prof. Sch. Medicine Emory U., Atlanta, 1993—. Co-editor-in-chief: Preventive Medicine, 1994—99. Recipient Clinician-Scientist award Am. Heart Assn., 1995-96. Office: Emory U 69 Butler St SE Atlanta GA 30303-3033

FRANK, JEAN MARIE, educational administrator, researcher; b. Sheboygan, Wis., July 22, 1954; d. Donald J. and Patricia Gudinas; children: Eric, Andrew, Jennifer. BS in Tech. and Mgmt., U. Md., 1988; MS in Bus., Johns Hopkins U., 1995. Rsch. asst. Howard C.C., Columbia, Md., 1988-92, rsch. analyst, 1992-99, policy specialist, 1996-98, sr. rsch. analyst, 1999—; bd. examiners Program for Ednl. Excellence, 1999—; examiner U.S. Senate Productivity and Md. State Quality Award, 2001. Spl. rsch. projects for Howard County Office Human Rights, Columbia, 1990, Columbia Forum, 1991. Mem. exec. bd. Bryant Woods PTA, Columbia, 1984-86. U. Md. merit scholar, 1985-86, Chancellor's scholar, 1986-87, Kelly Found. scholar, 1987-88. Mem. Am. Coun. on Edn. (instnl. rep. 1994—), Nat. Coun. Rsch. and Planning, Md. Assn. Instnl. Rsch. (exec. com., C.C. segmental rep. 1997-98), Md. Assn. for Higher Edn. (instnl. rep. 1998-99), Md. C.C. Rsch. Group (pres.-elect 1998-99, pres. 1999-2000), Phi Kappa Phi, Alpha Sigma Lambda.

FRANK, JOANN, photographer; b. Phila., Apr. 11, 1947; d. Herbert and Irene Frank. BFA, Moore Coll. Art, Phila., 1968. Photographer (book) 3 Dozen, 1977; one-woman shows include The Halsted 831 Gallery, Birmingham, Mich., 1974, Enjay Gallery of Photography, Boston, 1975, The Witkin Gallery, N.Y.C., 1979, Drew U., Madison, N.J., 1990, exhibited in group shows at U. Kans. Mus. Art, Lawrence, 1974, San Francisco Mus. Modern Art, 1975, Addison Gallery of Am. Art, Andover, Mass., 1975, Balt. Mus. Art, 1977, L.A. Inst. Contemporary Art, 1978, exhibited in group shows, Phila., 1983, exhibited in group shows, IBM Gallery, 1984, Print Club of Phila., 1986, Zabriskie Gallery, N.Y.C., 1989, Drew U., Madison, 1993, Witkin Gallery, 1995, numerous others, Represented in permanent collections Met. Mus. Art, N.Y.C., Bibliotheque Nationale, Paris, San Francisco Mus. Modern Art, Sheldon Meml. Art Gallery, U. Nebr., Lincoln, Australian Nat. Gallery, Canberra, Inst. Photography, Tokyo, New Orleans Mus. Art, U. Kans. Mus. Art, Centro Cultural/Arte Contemporaneo, Mexico City, Estado da Cultura, Lisbon, Portugal, numerous others; photography in numerous pubs.

FRANK, LILLIAN GORMAN, human resources executive, psychologist, management consultant; b. N.Y.C., July 4, 1953; d. Helmuth H. and Ida (Malitsch) Degen; m. Stephen E. Frank, Feb. 10, 2001. BA in Psychology, Lehman Coll., CUNY, 1975; MA in Indsl. Psychology, Case Western Res. U., 1978, PhD in indsl. Psychology, 1979, MBA in Corp. Fin., U. So. Calif., 1986. Econ. benefits asst. Girl Scouts U.S.A., N.Y.C., 1971—75; psychologist Pers. Rsch. Svcs., Cleve., 1975—79; cons. psychologist Pers. Rsch. & Devel. Corp., Cleve., 1977—78; mgr. pers. rsch. 1st Interstate Bank, L.A., 1979—82, v.p., mgr. human resource planning and devel., 1982—85; v.p., mgr. human resource planning and exec. devel. 1st Interstate Bancorp, L.A., 1985—86; exec. v.p., human resources dir. First Interstate Bank of Calif., 1986—90; exec. v.p. human resources First Interstate Bancorp, 1990—96; sr. v.p. human resources Edison Internat., Rosemead, Calif., 1996—2000; prin. Frank Insights, L.A., 2000—. Trustee Autry Mus. Western Heritage, 2001—; bd. dirs. INROADS/So. Calif., 1986—, YMCA of Met. L.A., 2002—. Mem. APA, Soc. for Psychologists in Mgmt. (bd. dirs. 1993-97), Orgn. for Women Execs., Soc. for Human Resources Mgmt. Home and Office: 207 N Glenroy Ave Los Angeles CA 90049-2417 E-mail: lillian@frankinsights.com.

FRANK, LINDA ROSE, nursing educator, clinical specialist, educator; b. Oil City, Pa., May 8, 1951; d. Dominick and rose Frank; m. Mark Hertweck, June 17, 1976. BSN, Pa. State U., 1982; MSN, U. Pitts., 1983, PhD, 1990. Dir. regional clin. svcs. dept. psychiatry Sch. Medicine U. Pitts., 1983—87, dir., 1988—, asst. prof. Grad. Sch. Pub. Health, 1990—. Treas. HIV Nursing Cert. Bd., Washington, 1995—. Bd. dirs. Pitts. AIDS Task Force, 1992—, AIDS Action Coun., Washington, 1996—. Mem. APHA (chmn. health com.), Am. Nurses Assn. (cert. clin. specialist), Assn. Nurses in AIDS Care (cert.), Sigma Theta Tau. Home: 3490 Beechwood Blvd Pittsburgh PA 15217-2943 Office: U Pitts Grad Sch Pub Health 130 De Soto St Pittsburgh PA 15261-0001

FRANK, MARY LOU, retired elementary school educator; b. Cleve., May 18, 1915; d. William Henry and Martha Ann (Brown) Parsons; m. Russell Edward Frank, May 18, 1935; children: Richard Edward, James Russell. BS in Edn., Cleve. State U., 1960; MS in Edn., U. Akron, Ohio, 1967, Miami U., Oxford, Ohio, 1934-35; student, Baldwin-Wallace Coll., 1933-34. Cert. tchr., Ohio. Substitute tchr. Cleve. Pub. Schs., 1963; tchr. elem. Brecksville (Ohio) City Sch. Dist., 1953-71, Lee County Bd. of Edn., Ft. Myers, Fla., 1971-74, ret., 1974. Mem. ambassadors to China from Fla., Children's Palaces Homes Hosps., 1980. Martha Holden Jennings Found. scholar, 1963-64, grantee, 1965. Mem. U.S. Power Squadron Aux. (pilot), Collier Reading Coun., Delta Kappa Gamma. Avocations: boating, travel, oil painting. Home: 61 Impala Ct # 23 Fort Myers FL 33912-6338

FRANK, MARY LOU BRYANT, psychologist, educator; b. Denver, Nov. 27, 1952; d. W. D. and Blanche (Dean) Bryant; m. Kenneth Kerry Frank, Sept. 9, 1973; children: Kari Lou, Kendra Leah. BA, Colo. State U., 1974, MEd, 1983, MS, 1986, PhD, 1989. Tchr. Cherry Creek Schs., Littleton, Colo., 1974—80; grad. dir. career devel. Colo. State U., Ft. Collins, 1980—86; intern U. Del., Newark, 1987—88; psychologist Ariz. State U., Tempe, 1988—93; assoc., lead prof. psychology Clinch Valley Coll. U. Va., Wise, 1992—96, asst. acad. dean, 1993—95; head psychology dept., prof. North Ga. Coll. and State U., Dahlonega, 1996—2001; dean undergrad. and univ. studies, prof. psychology Kennesaw State U., 2001—. Chmn. bd. regents adv. com. Psychology, 2000—01; instr. Colo. State U., Ft. Collins, 1981—82, counselor, 1984—85, Ft. Collins, 1986—87; psychologist Ariz. State U., Tempe, 1989—92; assoc. prof. psychology Clinch Valley Coll. U. Va., 1992—96; spkr. in field. Author: (program manual) Career Development, 1986; contbr. book chpts. on eating disorders and existential psychotherapy, 1996, 1998, 1999, 2002; reviewer: Buros Mental Measurements Yearbook. Bd. dirs. Ct. Apptd. Spl. Advocates, 2000—, Enotah Legis. Dist., Helping Teens Succeed, 2003—; Youth Adv. Coun. Lumpkin County, 2000—02. Mem.: AACSU, AAUP, AAHE, ACES, APA, AACD, Am. Counseling Assn., Ga. ACE Network (mem. exec. com. 2001—), Ga. Assn. Women Higher Edn. (pres. 2001—), Southeastern Psychol. Assn. (chair undergrad. rsch. 1996—2000), Odeka, Phi Beta Kappa, Psi Chi (Ga. Woman of the Yr. com. 1999—2003, vice chair 2003—, documentary project), Pi Kappa Delta, Phi Kappa Phi (Internat. Womans Day program com. 2003, planning com. so. women in pub. svc. conf. 2003—, pres. 2003—, Promotion of Excellence grantee 2002—03). Avocations: music, hiking, reading. Office: Kennesaw State U Off Dean Undergrad & Univ Studies 1000 Chastain Rd - Kennesaw Hall 4443 Kennesaw GA 30144-5591 Office Phone: 770-499-3550. E-mail: mlfrank@kennesaw.edu.

FRANK, NANCY KATHLEEN, minister; b. Flint, Mich., Sept. 28, 1949; d. Larry Brosuis and Lucille Elsie (Knickerbocker) McMahon; m. Daniel Lee Frank, May 27, 1972; children: Lucille Elizabeth Thompson, Kurt Daniel, Jennifer Kathleen Walker. BFA, Ea. Mich. U., 1988; MDiv, Asbury Theol. Sem., 1991. Ordained deacon United Meth. Ch., 1991, ordained elder United Meth. Ch., 1993. Pastor Norway Grace and Faithorn United Meth. Chs., Mich., 1991—94; assoc. pastor Fenton United Meth. Ch., Mich., 1994—96; pastor Swan Valley United Meth. Ch., Saginaw, Mich., 1996—2000, Good Shepherd United Meth. Ch., Dearborn, Mich., 2000—. Ch. redevelopment team mem. Detroit Ann. Conf. United Meth. Ch., Flint, 1997—2001, mem. vison writing team Detroit Ann. Conf., 1997—99; pastor in cmty. practices and pastoral excellence Lilly Endowment - Ch. of the Apostles, Lexington, Ky., 2003—. Watercolor painting, Mission Point. Recipient Ga. Harkness Scholarship award, Bd. of Higher Edn. and Ministry of United Meth. Ch., 1999; Sem. scholar, Detroit Ann. Conf. of United Meth. Ch., 1988—91, Dexter United Meth. Ch., 1988—91, Lilly Endowment grantee for pastoral excellence, Lilly Found., 2003—. Mem.: Detroit Ann. Conf. United Meth. Ch. (pastor 1993—). Avocations: music, singing, travel, reading. Office: Good Shepherd United Methodist Church 1570 Mason Dearborn MI 48124-2813 E-mail: gshepherdumc@peoplepc.com.

FRANK, PAULA FELDMAN, business executive; b. Tulsa; d. Maurice M. and Sarah (Bergman) Feldman; m. Gordon D. Frank, Dec. 15, 1955; children: Cynthia Jan, Margaret Jill. B.S., Northwestern U., 1954. Directed, wrote and appeared in TV films for Nat. Safety Coun., Chgo., 1954-55; appeared in TV commls., 1955-56; asst. prodn. mgr. Kling Films, Chgo., 1956; pres. Gaston Ave. Optical Inc., ret. 1990; Dallas. Social chmn. Baylor Hosp. Vol. Corp., Dallas, 1962—; asst. dir. Des Plaines (Ill.) Theater Guild, 1956-57, Pearl Chappell Playhouse, Dallas, 1962-63, Dallas Theater Center, 1964. Mem. Hockaday Alumni Assn., Tau Gamma Epsilon, Phi Beta, Sigma Delta Tau. Home: 7123 Currin Dr Dallas TX 75230-3645

FRANK, ROBERTA, English language educator; b. N.Y.C., Nov. 9, 1941; d. Norman Berton and Doris (Birnbaum) F.; m. Walter André Goffart, Dec. 31, 1977. BA, NYU, 1962; MA, Harvard U., 1964, PhD, 1968. Asst. prof. U. Toronto, 1968-73, assoc. prof., 1973-78, prof. English, 1978-2000, Univ. prof., 1995-2000, dir. grad studies dept. English, 1980-85, dir. Ctr. for Medieval Studies, 1994-99; Douglas Tracy Smith prof. English Yale U., 2000—. Mem. bus. bd. U. Toronto Press. Author: Old Norse Court Poetry, 1978, also articles; co-editor: Computers and Old English Concordances, 1970, A Plan for the Dictionary of Old English, 1973; gen. editor: Toronto Old English Series, 1976-2003; publs. of Dictionary of Old English, 1984-2003. Recipient Guggenheim award, 1985, Bowdoin prize in humanities Harvard U., 1968. Fellow Medieval Acad. Am. (councillor 1981-84, Elliott prize 1972), Royal Soc. Can.; mem. MLA (mem. Old English exec. com. 1974-78, 95-99), Internat. Soc. Anglo-Saxonists (pres. 1985-87). Home: 171 Lowther Ave Toronto ON Canada M5R 1E6 Office: Yale U Dept English New Haven CT 06520-8302 E-mail: rfrank@chass.utoronto.ca., roberta.frank@yale.edu.

FRANKE-BARRINGER, MICHELE ANNETTE, elementary school educator; b. Kenmore, N.Y., Dec. 10, 1975; d. David Lewis and Gretchen Ardene Franke; m. Thomas Anthony Barringer, July 26, 2003. BA, SUNY, Geneseo, 1998; MEd, U. Mich., 2003. Cert. tchr. Grade tchr. 4th and 5th grade Summit Acad., Huron Twp., Mich., 1998—99, tchr. 2d and 3d grade, 1999—2000; tchr. 1st grade Cranbrook Ednl. Comty., Bloomfield Hills, Mich., 2000—. Co-chair All-Sch. Faculty Coun., Bloomfield Hills, 2002—. Named Tchr. of Week, Detroit Free Press, 2001, 2002, 2003; recipient Harris award, Cranbrook Ednl. Comty., 2003. Mem.: CEC, Coun. for Children with Behavioral Disorders. Avocations: gardening, reading, baking.

FRANKEL, ALICE KROSS, physician, director; b. N.Y.C., Feb. 3, 1929, d. Isidor and Anna (Moscowitz) Kross; m. Julian B. Schorr, May 14, 1951 (div. 1963); children: David, Ellen; m. Marvin E. Frankel, Aug. 22, 1965; 1 stepchild, Eleanor Frankel Perlman; 1 child, Mara. BA, Oberlin (Ohio) Coll., 1949; MD, Columbia U., 1953. Pvt. practice, N.Y.C., 1956-66, 85—, Larchmont, N.Y., 1966-85; assoc. clin. prof. psychiatry Med. Coll. Cornell U., N.Y.C., 1970-90; dir. Child Devel. Ctr. Jewish Bd. Family & Children's Svcs., N.Y.C., 1984—; supervising and tng. psychoanalyst Psychoanalytic Ctr. Tng. & Rsch. Columbia U., N.Y.C., 1984—. Mem. Am. Psychiat. Assn., Am. Psychoanalytic Assn., Am. Acad. Child and Adolescent Psychiatry, Assn. for Child and Adolescent Analysis, N.Y. County Med. Soc., N.Y. State Med. Soc. Democrat. Jewish. Office: Jewish Bd Family Childrens Svcs Child Devel Ctr 120 W 57th St New York NY 10019-3320 Home: 110 Riverside Dr Apt 15B New York NY 10024-3734

FRANKEL, FRANCINE RUTH, political science educator; b. N.Y.C., Aug. 31, 1935; d. William and Dora (Tuchschneider) Goldberg; m. Douglas Vernon Verney, Nov. 28, 1975; stepchildren: Andrew, Jonathan. BA, CCNY, 1956; MA, Johns Hopkins U., 1958; PhD, U. Chgo., 1965. Asst. prof. U. Pa., Phila., 1965-70, assoc. prof., 1970-79, prof., 1979—, prof. South Asian studies, 1978—, chmn. grad. program polit. sci., 1980-83, founding dir. Ctr. Advanced Study of India, 1992—. Vis. fellow Ctr. of Internat. Studies, Princeton (N.J.) U., 1969-73; resident scholar Bellagio Study and Conf. Ctr., 1975; vis. mem. Inst. Advanced Study, 1976; mem.-at-large Commn. Internat. Rels., Nat. Acad. Scis., 1973-79; mem. del. South Asian specialists to China, 1986; founding mem., mem. governing coun. U. Pa. Inst. for Advanced Study of India, New Delhi, 1995—. Author: India's Political Economy, 1947-77, The Gradual Revolution, 1978, Chinese edit., 1990, India's Green Revolution, 1971; editor, contbr. Dominance and State Power in Modern India, Decline of a Social Order, 2 vols., 1989-90, Bridging the Non-Proliferation Gap: India and the United States, 1995, Transforming India, Social and Political Dynamics of Democracy, 2000; contbr. articles on India's polit. economy to profl. jours. Grantee Am. Inst. Indian Studies, 1979-80, Smithsonian Instn., 1983-86, Social Sci. Rsch. Coun., 1989-91; Woodrow Wilson fellow, 1997-98. Mem. Am. Polit. Sci. Assn., Assn. Asian Studies, Coun. Fgn. Rels. Home: 104 Pine St Philadelphia PA 19106-4312 Office: Ctr Advanced Study of India 3833 Chestnut St Philadelphia PA 19104 E-mail: ffrankel@sas.upenn.edu.

FRANKEL, JENNIE LOUISE, writer, composer, playwright; b. Chgo., Aug. 7, 1949; Student, Roosevelt U., 1968, U. Hawaii, 1969-71, Golden West Law Sch., 1976. Fashion model, singer/actor in TV commls., 1967—81, 1979—81; performer Comedy Store and the Improvisation, L.A., 1977—79. Co-author: You'll Never Make Love in this Town Again, 1996 (N.Y. Times Bestseller), Unfinished Lives, 1996, Tales From the Casting Couch, 1996; author; (Detective Sabrina Fortune crime novels) Sex with the Proper Killer, 2003, Natural Blonde Killer, 2003; editor-in-chief Page Turner Pub.; composer network TV theme songs, 1998-99, Youth at the Greek, 1999, Heartwalk L.A. Theme; columnist. Active USO Vietnam Tour, 1968; bd. govs. Hollywood Scriptwriting Inst.; judge Cable Ace Awards, 1987—96. Mem. Acad. TV Arts & Scis. (blue ribbon panel judge), L.A. Women in Music (bd. dirs. 1991-92), Circumnavigators Club. Avocation: comedy. Office: PO Box 346 Sedona AZ 86339-0346

FRANKEL, LOIS J. state legislator; b. N.Y.C., May 16, 1948; BA magna cum laude, Boston U., 1970; JD, Georgetown U., 1973. Rep. dist. 85 Fla. House, Tallahassee, 1986—. Recipient Allen Morris Most Promising Freshman award, 1988, Up and Comers Govt. award S. Fla. Bus. Jour.-Price Waterhouse, 1988, Nelson Poynter Civil Liberties award, 1988, Fla. Brotherhood award, 1989, Weizmann Inst. Sci. award, 1989, Brotherhood award Assn. Retarded Citizens/Fla., 1989, Ann. Legis. award Fla. Children's Forum, 1990, First Legis. award Fla. Student Nursing Assn., 1990, Outstanding Legislator award Fla. Fedn. Bus. and Profl. Women, 1990, Commr.'s award for Prevention of Child Abuse and Neglect U.S. Dept. Health and Human Svcs., 1991, award Am. Heart Assn., 1992, Polit. Courage award Am. Lung Assn., 1992; named Freshman Friend Edn. FTP-NEA, 1987, Citizen of Yr. NASW, 1989, Child Adv. of Yr., 1989, Children's Home Soc., 1989, Child Care Connection, 1990. Mem. NOW, LWV, Fla. Bar Assn., Acad. Fla. Trial Lawyers (Freshman award 1987, Outstanding Legislator award 1990), Fla. Assn. Women Lawyers (past pres. Palm Beach County chpt.), Palm Beach County Bar Assn., Jewish Fedn. Palm Beach County, Exec. Women Palm Beaches (Leadership award 1991), Econ. Devel. Coun. Palm Beach County, Gold Coast Bus. and Profl. Women, Am. Cancer Soc. (bd. dirs. Palm Beach County, Rookie of Yr. award 1994), Jewish Family and Children's Svcs. (dir. Palm Beach

County), Domestic Assault Shelter (founder). Democrat. Avocations: sports, music. Office: 402 S Monroe St Tallahassee FL 32399-6526 Also: Ste 290 1645 Palm Beach Lakes Blvd West Palm Beach FL 33401-2216 E-mail: frankel.lois.web@leg.state.fl.us.

FRANKEL, TERRIE MAXINE, writer, composer, playwright, publisher, producer; b. Chgo., Aug. 7, 1949; d. David and Jewell Frankel. Student, Roosevelt U., 1968, U. Hawaii, 1971, U. Hong Kong, 1979-80. Entertainer USO, Viet Nam, 1968; performer Comedy Store, Improvisation, others, 1969-79; pres. Page Turner Pub., Scottsdale, Ariz. Fashion model, 1967—81. Co-author: You'll Never Make Love in this Town Again, 1996 (N.Y. Times Best Seller List), Unfinished Lives, 1996, (Det. Sabrina Fortune crime novels) Sex With the Proper Killer, 2003, Natural Blonde Killer, 2003; author, editor: Tales from the Casting Couch, 1996, theme song Youth at the Greek, 1998-99,Heartwlk L.A. Theme, 1999; columnist Fabulous Boomer Babes, 1999, sr. editor: The Industry Mag., 2000; model tv commercials, 1971-81. Judge, comedy Cable Ace Award, 1988—96. Mem. Producers Guild of Am. (bd. dirs., sr. editor POV mag. 1990-2001), Hollywood Script Writing Inst. (bd. govs.), Authors Guild, Circumnavigators Club. Avocation: speaking Cantonese and Mandarin Chinese. Home: PO Box 346 Sedona AZ 86339-0346

FRANKENTHALER, HELEN, artist; b. N.Y.C., Dec. 12, 1928; d. Alfred and Martha (Lowenstein) F.; m. Robert Motherwell, Apr. 5, 1958 (div.); m. Stephen DuBrul, June 1994. BA, Bennington Coll., 1949; LHD (hon.), Skidmore Coll., 1969, Hofstra U., 1991; DFA (hon.), Smith Coll., 1973, Moore Coll. Art, 1974, Bard Coll., 1976, NYU, 1979; DFA, Phila. Coll. Art, 1980, Williams Coll., 1980; DFA (hon.), Marymount Manhattan Coll., 1989, Adelphi U., 1989, Washington U., St. Louis, 1989; DArt, Radcliffe Coll., 1978, Amherst Coll., 1979; DArt (hon.), Harvard U., 1980; DFA (hon.), Yale U., 1981, Brandeis U., 1982, U. Hartford, 1983, Syracuse U., 1985, Dartmouth Coll., 1994, Parsons Sch. Design, 1996, U. Pa., 1996, R.I. Sch. Design, 1996, Tufts U., 1998. Tchr., lectr. Yale U., 1966, 67, 70, Hunter Coll., 1970, Princeton U., 1971, Cooper Union, N.Y.C., 1972, Washington U. Sch. Fine Arts, 1972, Skidmore Coll., 1973, Swathmore Coll., 1974, Drew U., 1975, Harvard, 1976, Radcliffe Coll., 1976, Bard Coll., 1977, Detroit Inst. Arts, 1977, NYU, U. Pa., Sch. Visual Arts, Goucher Coll., Wash. U., Yale Grad. Sch., U. Ariz., 1978, Graphic Arts Council N.Y., 1979, Harvard U., 1980, Phila. Coll., 1980, Williams Coll., 1980, Yale U., 1981, Brandeis U., 1982, U. of Hartford, 1983, Syracuse U., 1985, Sante Fe Inst. Fine Arts, 1986, 90, 91; U.S. rep. Venice Biennale, 1966, lectr. in field. One-woman shows include, Tibor de Nagy Gallery, N.Y.C., 1951-58, Andre Emmerich Gallery, N.Y.C., 1959-73, 75, 77, 78, 79, 81, 82, 83, 84, 86, 87, 89, 90, 91, 92, 93, Jewish Mus., N.Y., 1960, Everett Ellin Gallery, Los Angeles, 1961, Galerie Lawrence, Paris, 1961, 63, Bennington Coll., 1962, 78, Galleria dell'Ariete, Milan, 1962, Kasmin Gallery, London, 1964, David Mirvish Gallery, Toronto, 1965, 71, 73, 75, Gertrude Kasle Gallery, Detroit, 1967, Nicholas Wilder Gallery, Los Angeles, 1967, Andre Emmerich Gallery, Zurich, 1974, 80, Swarthmore (Pa.) Coll., 1974, Solomon R. Guggenheim Mus., N.Y.C., 1975, Corcoran Gallery Art, Washington, 1975, Seattle Art Mus., 1975, Mus. Fine Arts, Houston, 1975, 85, 86, Ace Gallery, Vancouver, B.C., Can., 1975, Rosa Esman Gallery, N.Y.C., 1975, 83, 89, 3d Internat. Contemporary Art Fair, Paris, 1976, 81, retrospective Whitney Mus. Am. Art, 1969, Whitechapel Gallery, London, Eng., 1969, Kongress-Halle, Berlin, Kunstverein, Hannover, 1969, Heath Gallery, Atlanta, 1971, Galerie Godard Lefort, Montreal, 1971, Fendrick Gallery, Washington, 1972, 79, John Berggruen Gallery, San Francisco, 1972, 79, 82, Portland (Oreg.) Art Mus., 1972, Waddington Galleries II, London, 1973, 74, Janie C. Lee Gallery, Dallas, 1973, Houston, 1975, 76, 78, 80, 82, Met. Mus. Art, N.Y.C., 1973, Gallery Diane Gilson, Seattle, 1976, Greenberg Gallery, St. Louis, 1977, Galerie Wentzel, Hamburg, Germany, 1977, Jacksonville (Fla.) Art Mus., 1977-78, Knoedler Gallery, London, 1978, 81, 83, USIA exhbn., 1978-79, Atkins Mus. Fine Art, William Rockhill Nelson Gallery Art, Kansas City, Mo., 1978, 80, Saginaw Art Mus., Mich., 1980, Gimpel and Hanover and Andre Emerich Galleries, Zurich, 1980, Gallery Ulysses, Vienna, 1980, Knoedler Gallery, London, 1981, 83, Buschlen/Mowalt Fine Arts, Vancouver, 1989, Mus. Modern Art, N.Y.C., 1989, Douglas Drake Gallery, N.Y.C., 1989, Mizografia Gallery, L.A., 1989, Gerald Peters Gallery, Santa Fe, 1990, Kukje Gallery, Seoul, Korea, 1991, Assn. Am. Artists, N.Y.C., 1992, Knoedler & Co., N.Y.C., 1992, 94, 95, 96, 97, Nat. Gallery Art, Washington, 1993, San Diego Mus. Art, 1993, Mus. Fine Arts, Boston, 1994, Contemporary Arts Ctr., Cin., 1994, Meredith Long and Co., Houston, 1994, 95, 96, 97, Dennos Mus. Ctr. Northwestern Mich. Coll., Travers City, 1995, Tyler Graphics Ltd., Mt. Kisco, N.Y., 1995, Bobbie Greenfield Gallery, Santa Monica, Calif., 1995, Meyerovich Gallery, San Francisco, 1995, Greg Kucera Gallery, Seattle, 1995, Gallery One, Toronto, Canada, 1995, 97, Ace Contemporary Exhbns., L.A., 1996, Tasenda Gallery, L.A., 1997, Remba Gallery, West Hollywood, Calif., 1997, Thomas Segal Gallery, Balt., 1997, numerous others; exhibited in group shows including, Whitney Mus., 1958, 71, 75-79, 82, 89, Carnegie Internat., Pitts., 1955, 58, 61, 64, Columbus Gallery Fine Arts, 1960, Guggenheim Mus., 1961, 76, 80, 82, Seattle World's Fair, 1962, Art Inst. Chgo., 1963, 69, 72, 76, 77, 82, 83, San Francisco Mus. Art, 1963, 68, Krannert Mus., U. Ill., 1959, 63, 65, 67, 80, Washington Gallery Modern Art, 1963, Pa. Acad. Fine Arts, 1963, 68, 76, N.Y. World's Fair, 1964, Am. Fedn. Arts Circulating Exhbn., 1964, U. Austin Art Mus., 1964, Rose Art Mus. Circulating Exhbn., 1964, Detroit Inst. Arts, 1965, 67, 73, 77, U. Mich. Mus. Art, 1965, Md. Inst., 1966, Norfolk Mus. Arts and Scis., 1966, Venice Biennale, 1966, Smithsonian Instn., 1966, Expo '67, Montreal, 1967, Washington Gallery Modern Art, 1967, Ga. Mus. Art, Athens, 1967, U. Okla. Mus. Art, Norman, 1968, Philbrook Art Center, Tulsa, 1968, Cin. Mus., 1968, U. Calif. at San Diego, 1968, Mus. Modern Art, N.Y.C., 1969, 75, 76, 80, 82, Met. Mus., N.Y.C., 1969-70, 76, 79, 81, Va. Mus., Richmond, 1970, 74, 87, Balt. Mus. Art, 1970, 76, 89, Boston U., 1970, Boston Mus. Fine Arts, 1972, 82, 90, Des Moines Art Center, 1973, Mus. Fine Arts, Houston, 1974, 82, Smith Coll. Mus. Art, Northampton, Mass., 1974, El Instituto de Cultura Puertorriquena, San Juan, 1974, Basil (Switzerland) Art Fair, 1974, 76, Finch Coll. Mus. Art, N.Y.C., 1974, S.I. Mus., 1975, Denver Art Mus., 1975, Visual Arts Mus., N.Y.C., 1975, 76, Mus. Modern Art, Belgrade Yugoslavia, 1976, Chrysler Mus., Norfolk, Va., 1976, Everson Mus., Syaracuse, N.Y., Galleria d'Arts Moderna, Rome, 1976, Grey Art Gallery, N.Y.C., 1976-78, 81, Bklyn Mus., 1976-77, 82, Edmonton Art Gallery, Alta., Can., 1977, 78, Albright-Knox Mus., Buffalo, 1978, Fogg Art Mus., Harvard U., 1978, 83, Art Gallery Ont., 1979, Hirshorn Mus. and Sculpture Garden, Washington, 1980, Phoenix Art Mus., 1980, Nat. Gallery Art, Washington, 1981, Tate Gallery, London, 1981, Walker Art Ctr., Mpls., 1981, Milw. Art Mus., 1982, Mus. Fine Arts, Boston, 1982, Whitney Mus. Am. Art, N.Y., 1982, St. Louis Art Mus., 1982, High Mus. Art, Atlanta, 1989, Nelson-Atkins Mus. Art, Kansas City, Nat. Gallery Can., 1990, Williams Coll. Mus. Art, Williamstown, Mass., 1991, Aldrich Mus. Contemporary Art, Ridgefield, Conn., 1992, Mus. Modern Art, Mexico City, 1992, Yokohama Mus. Art, Japan, 1992, Marugame Inokuma-Genichiro Mus. Contemp. Art, 1992, Mus. Modern Art, Wakayama, 1992, Tokushima Modern Art Mus., Japan, 1992, Hokkaido Obihiro Mus. Art, 1993, Whitney Mus. Am. Art, Stamford, Conn., 1993, Gallery One, Toronto, Can., 1994; represented in permanent collections, Bklyn. Mus., Met. Mus. Art N.Y.,, Solomon R. Guggenheim Mus., NYU, Mus. Modern Art, Albright-Knox Art Gallery, Buffalo, Whitney Mus., N.Y.C., U. Mich., High Mus., Atlanta, Milw. Art Inst., Wadsworth Atheneum, Hartford, Newark Mus., Yale U. Art Gallery, U. Nebr. Art Gallery, Carnegie Inst., Pitts., Detroit Inst. Art, Balt. Mus. Art, Univ. Mus., Berkeley, Calif., Bennington (Vt.) Coll., Art Inst. Chgo., Cin. Art Mus., Cleve. Mus. Art, Columbus Gallery Fine Arts, Honolulu Acad. Arts, Contemporary Arts Assn., Houston, Pasadena Art Mus., William Rockhill Nelson Gallery Art, Kans. City, Kans., Kans. City Art Inst., Atkins Mus. Fine Arts, Kans. City, Kans., City Art Mus., St. Louis, Mus. Art, R.I. Sch. Design, Providence, San Francisco Mus. Art, Everson Mus., Syracuse, N.Y., Smithsonian Instn., Walker Art Inst., Mpls., Washington Gallery Modern Art, Wichita Art Mus., Brown Gallery Art, Nat. Gallery Victoria, Melbourne, Australia, Australian Nat. Gallery, Canberra, Victoria and Albert Mus., London, Eng., Tokyo Mus., Ulster Mus., Belfast, No. Ireland, Elvehjem Art Center, U. Wis., Israel Mus.-Instituto Nacional de Bellas Artes, Phila. Mus. [illegible] Mus., Corcoran Gallery Art, Boston Mus. Fine Arts, Springfield (Mass.) Mus. Fine Arts, Witte Mus., San Antonio, Abbott Hall Art Gallery, Kendal, Eng., Mus. Contemporary Art, Nagaoka, Japan, Guggenheim Mus., N.Y.C., 1984, others; was subject of film Frankenthaler: Toward a New Climate, 1978. Trustee Bennington Coll., 1967— . Fellow Calhoun Coll., Yale U., 1968— ; recipient 1st prize for painting Paris Biennale, 1959, Gold medal Pa. Acad. Fine Arts, 1968, Great Ladies award Fordham U., Thomas Moore Coll., 1969, Spirit of Achievement award Albert Einstein Coll. Medicine, 1970, Gold medal Commune of Catania, III Biennale della Grafica d'Arte, Florence, Italy, 1972, Garrett award 70th Am. Exhbn., Art Inst. Chgo., 1972, Creative Arts award Nat. Women's div. Am. Jewish Congress, 1974, Art and Humanities award Yale Women's Forum, 1976, Extraordinary Woman of Achievement award NCCJ, 1978, Alumni award Bennington Coll., 1979, N.Y.C. Mayor's award, 1986, Lifetime Achievement award Coll. Art Assn., 1994, Lotos medal of merit, 1994, Artist of Yr. award, 1995, Jerusalem prize, 1999, Lifetime Achievement award, 1999. Mem. NEA, Am. Acad. (vice-chancelor 1991), Am. Acad. Arts and Scis., Nat. Coun. Arts, Nat. Inst. Arts and Letters. Office: M Knoedler & Co Inc 19 E 70th St New York NY 10021-4907

FRANKL, RAZELLE, management educator; BA in English, Temple U., 1955; MA in Polit. Sci., Bryn Mawr Coll., 1966; MBA in Organizational Devel., Drexel U., 1973; PhD, Bryn Mawr Coll., 1984. Chair codes and ordinance com. Exec Com. Neighborhood Improvement Program, Lower Merion Twp., 1967-68; pres. LWV Lower Merion Twp., 1967-68; v.p. for organizational affairs LWV, Springfield, Mass., 1968-70; chair environ. quality com. LWV Radnor Twp., 1970-71; instr. applied behavioral sci. Drexel U. Sch. Bus., 1972-73; planner office of mental health/mental retardation Dept. Pub. Health, City of Phila., 1971-73, planner office of health planning, 1971-73; coord. for health programs Phila. '76 Inc. (Official Bicentennial Corp.), 1972-74; adj. faculty dept. mgmt. adminstrv. studies divsn. Coll. Bus. Rowan U. (formerly Glassboro State Coll., Rowan Coll.), 1974-77, 81-82; asst. prof. Glassboro (N.J.) State Coll., 1982-88, assoc. prof. dept. mgmt., 1988-95, prof., 1995—2002, prof. emerita, 2002—. Author: Televangelism: The Marketing of Popular Religion, 1987, Popular Religion and the Imperatives of Television: A Study of the Electric Church, 1984; author: (with others) Religious Television: Controversies and Conclusions, 1990, Teleministries as Family Businesses, 1990, New Christian Politics, 1984, Culture Media and Religious Right, 1997, The Encyclopedia of Religion and Society, 1997; contbr. (book chpt.) Transformation of Televangelism: Repackaging of Christian Family Values, 1997, articles to profl. jours. Dir. nat. bd. Allegheny U. Health Scis., chair spring program; chair, bd. dirs. Anti-Violence Partnership of Phila.; founder, chair Friends of Rowan U. Libr., 1995—. Rsch. grantee Rowan Coll. N.J. (formerly Glassboro State Coll.), 1986-87, 90, 91, 93-94, 94-95, All-Coll. Rsch. grantee, 1987-88. Mem. Am. Acad. Mgmt. (chair membership com. div. mgmt. edn. and devel., chair media rels. com., div. women in mgmt.), Soc. for Human Resource Mgmt., Am. Sociol. Assn., Ea. Sociol. Soc., Assn. for Sociology Religion, Religious Rsch. Assn., Soc. for Sci. Study Religion (chair womens caucus), Internat. Sociol. Assn. Home: 536 Moreno Rd Wynnewood PA 19096-1121 E-mail: frankl@rowan.edu.

FRANKLIN, ARETHA, singer; b. Memphis, 1942; d. Clarence L. and Barbara (Siggers) Franklin; m. Ted White (div.); m. Glynn Turman, Apr. 11, 1978. First record at age 12, rec. artist with Columbia Records, N.Y.C., 1961, then with Atlantic records, now with Arista Records; singer: (albums) Aretha, 1961, Electrifying, Tender Moving and Swinging, 1962, Laughing on the Outside, 1963, Unforgettable, Songs of Faith, Running Out of Fools, 1964, Yeah, 1965, Soul Sister, 1966, Queen of Soul, Take It Like You Give It, Lee Cross, Greatest Hits, I Never Loved a Man, Once in a Lifetime, Aretha Arrives, 1967, Lady Soul, Greatest Hits, Vol. 2, Best of Aretha Franklin, Live at Paris Olympia, Aretha Now, 1968, Soul 69, Today I Sing the Blues, Soft and Beautiful, Aretha Gold's, Satisfaction, I Say a Little Prayer, 1969, This Girl's in Love with You, Spirit in the Dark, Don't Play that Song, 1970, Live at the Fillmore West, Young Gifted and Black, Aretha's Greatest Hits, 1971, Amazing Grace, 1972, Hey Hey Now, Firest 12 Sides, 1973, Let Me Into Your Life, 1974, With Every Thing I Feel in Me, You, 1975, Sparkle, Ten Years of Gold, 1976, Sweet Passion, 1977, Almighty Fire, Star Collection, 1978, La Diva, 1979, Aretha, 1980, Who's Zoomin' Who, 1985, One Lord, One Faith, One Baptism, 1987, Aretha Sings the Blues, 1965, 85, Lady Soul, 1988, Through the Storm, 1989, What You See is What You Sweat, 1991, Jazz to Soul, 1992, Aretha After Hours, Chain of Fools, 1993, Unforgettable: A Tribute to Dinah Washington, 1995, Love Songs, 1997, The Delta Meets Detroit, A Rose Is Still A Rose, 1998, Amazing Grace, 1999; actress Blues Brothers, 1980, (films) Shindig! Presents Soul, Shindig! Presents Groovy Gals, 1991, History of Rock 'N' Roll, 1995, Blues Brothers 2000, 1998, (TV films) Bob Hope on Campus, 1975, Aretha Franklin: The Queen of Soul, 1988, (TV miniseries) Motown 40: The Music Is Forever, 1998; performer (Showtime prodn.): Aretha, 1986; performer: (concert tours) in U.S. and Europe. Named Top Female Vocalist, 1967, Number One Female Singer 16th Internat., Jazz Critics Poll, 1968; named to Hollywood Walk of Fame, 1979, Rock and Roll Hall of Fame, 1987; recipient Grammy award for best female rhythm and blues vocal, 1967—74, 1981, 1985, 1987, for best rhythm and blues rec., 1988, for best soul gospel performance, 1972, for best rhythm and blues duo vocal (with George Michael), 1987, Am. Music award, 1984, Kennedy Center Honor, 1994, 1994. Office: care Arista Records c/o Gwen Quinn 6 W 57th St New York NY 10019-3901

FRANKLIN, BARBARA HACKMAN, business executive, former government official; b. Lancaster, Pa., Mar. 19, 1940; d. Arthur A. and Mayme M. (Haller) Hackman; m. Wallace Barnes, 1986. BA with distinction, Pa. State U., 1962; MBA, Harvard U., 1964. Mgr. environ. analysis Singer Co., N.Y.C., 1964—68; asst. v.p. Citibank, N.Y.C., 1969-71; White House staff asst. to the Pres. for recruiting women to govt. Washington, 1971-73; vice chmn. U.S. Consumer Product Safety Commn., Washington, 1973-79; sr. fellow, dir. govt. and bus. program Wharton Sch. U. Pa., Phila., 1980—88; pres., CEO Franklin Assocs., Washington, 1984-92; U.S. sec. commerce Dept. Commerce, Washington, 1992-93; pres., CEO Barbara Franklin Enterprises, Washington, 1995—; commentator Nightly Bus. Report, 1997—. Mem. Pres.'s Adv. Com. for Trade Policy and Negotiations, 1982—86, 1991—92, chair task force on tax reform, 1985—86, mem. NAFTA task force, 1991—92; alt. Rep. and public del. 44th session UN General Assembly, 1989—90; mem. U.S. Comptroller Gen.'s con. panel, 1984—92, 1994—98. Bd. dir. Aetna, Inc., 1979—92, 1993—, chair audit com., 1989—92, 1993—; bd. dir. Dow Chem. Co, 1980—92, 1993—, chair audit com., 1985—92, 1993—2004; bd. dir. MedImmune, Inc., 1995—, Milacron Inc., 1996—, GenVec, Inc., 2002—; trustee Pa. State U., 1976—82; bd. regents U. Hartford, 1986—88; bd. dir. Harvard Bus. Sch., 1988—; co-chmn. Nat. Fin. Com. for George Bush for Pres., 1987—88, Nat. Fin. Com. for George W. Bush for Pres., 1999—2000. Named one of 50 Most Influential Corp. Dirs., Am. Mgmt. Assn., 1990, Outstanding Dir., Board Alert; recipient Disting. Alumni award, Pa. State U., 1972, John J. McCloy award for audit excellence, 1992, Dir. Yr., NACD, 2000. Mem.: Nat. Symphony Orch. (bd. dirs.), Heritage Found. (chair Asian studies adv. coun.), U.S. China Bus. Coun. (vice-chair), Nat. Com. U.S.-China Rels., Coun. Fgn. Rels., Nat. Assn. Corp. Dir. (bd. dirs., Blue Ribbon Commn., CEO evaluation 1994, Blue Ribbon Commn., audit effectiveness 1999, co-chair Blue Ribbon Commn., exec. compensation 2003), Internat. Women's Forum (founding mem.), Bretton Woods com., Union League Club N.Y. Avocations: exercise, hiking, reading, painting. Office: 2600 Virginia Ave NW Ste 506 Washington DC 20037-1905

FRANKLIN, BONNIE GAIL, actress; b. Santa Monica, Calif., Jan. 6, 1944; d. Samuel Benjamin and Claire (Hersch) F. BA, UCLA, 1966. Mem. regional theatres in, N.Y., Mass., Ohio, Maine, N.H., Conn., Pa., 1972-99. Stage appearances include Your Own [illegible], N.Y.C., 1968, Dames At Sea, 1969, Applause, N.Y.C., 1970-72 (Aegis Theatre Club award 1970, Theatre Club award 1970, Outer Critics Circle award 1960-70, Tony nomination), Happy Birthday and Other Humiliations, N.Y., 1987, Frankie & Johnny in the Clair de Lune, 1988, Grace & Glorie, 1996; tv appearances include One Day At A Time, 1975-84. Mem. AFTRA, SAG, Actors Equity Assn., Dirs. Guild Am. Democrat. Jewish. Address: 15745 Royal Oak Rd Encino CA 91436-3907

FRANKLIN, BONNIE SELINSKY, retired federal agency administrator; b. Oakland, Calif., Mar. 17, 1944; d. Harold Joseph and Madge (Warden) Selinsky; m. Alfred Carl Franklin, Jan. 24, 1981; 1 child, Amy Beth. AB in Am. Studies, George Washington U., 1966, MBA in Acctg., 1977. Tax auditor IRS, Baileys Crossroads, Va., 1966-71, from program analyst to tax law specialist Washington, 1971-77, from program analyst appeals to chief procedures sect., 1979-82, tech. asst. to nat. chief appeals, 1985-2000, program mgr., 2000—01, regional analyst conf. Atlanta, 1977-79. Chair Arlingtonians for a Better County, Arlington, Va., 1994-97, archivist, 1999-2000; active Friends of the Libr., Arlington, 1996—. Recipient Albert Gallatin Devoted Svc. award, U.S. Treasury Dept. Mem. LWV (treas. Arlington Va. chpt. 1998-2001, pres. 2001—), AAUW. Democrat. Lutheran. Avocations: reading, travel.

FRANKLIN, CAROL D. electronics company executive; With Grant Thornton, Ltd., Video Display Corp., contr., CFO, treas. Office: Video Display Corp 1868 Tucker Indsl Dr Tucker GA 30084

FRANKLIN, DOROTHY ANN, guidance counselor; b. West Point, Ky., June 30, 1938; d. Raymond and Laura B. (Robards) Williams; m. Herbert Franklin, Mar. 31, 1962; children: Marcus, Lori. BS, Ky. State U., 1960; MEd, U. Louisville, 1969; postgrad., Ind. U., 1973-74, U. Dayton. Cert. in guidance supervision. Tchr. Cardinal Cmty. High Sch., Eldon, Iowa, 1960-61; tchr., counselor Louisville/Jefferson County Schs., Louisville, 1961-72; counselor Monroe County Schs., Bloomington, Ind., 1972-74, Alachua County Schs., Gainesville, Fla., 1974-80, Franklin County Schs., Frankfort, Ky., 1980-84, Sidney (Ohio) City Schs., 1984—. Bd. trustees United Way, Sidney, 1993-96, Riverview Behavior Health Care Ctr., Sidney, 1993-96; mem. steering com., mem.-at-large City of Sidney Comprehensive Plan, 1996-97; mem. adv. bd. Bank One, Sidney, 1994-97; mem. adv. coun. Planned Parenthood, Sidney, 1993-98. Mem. AAUW, NEA, Am. Assn. Counseling Devel., Ohio Edn. Assn., Ohio Sch. Counselors Assn., Sidney Edn. Assn., Tri-County Br. NAACP, Kappa Delta Pi, Alpha Kappa Alpha. Democrat. Baptist. Avocations: real estate, reading, travel. Home: 954 Lakepointe Ct Union KY 41091-9558

FRANKLIN, EVE, state legislator; b. N.Y., Aug. 14, 1954; m. Les Nilson. BSN, Earlham Coll.; MSN, Herbert H. Lehman Coll. Formerly nurse-educator; mem. Mont. Senate, Dist. 21, Helena, 1991—; minority whip Mont. Senate, 1997-98, mem. joint appropriation subcom. on gen. govt. and transp., mem. fish and game com., mem. fin. and claims com., mem. pub. health, welfare and safety com. Democrat. Home: 2707 Dawn Dr Great Falls MT 59404-3633

FRANKLIN, HEIDI ANN, music educator; b. Tracy, Calif., Aug. 25, 1955; d. Edmond Nicholas and Ella Drue Heinbockel; m. Ronald Keith Franklin, Mar. 6, 1982; children: Brandon, Ryan. BMus, Univ. of the Pacific, 1977; MMus, U. of the Pacific, 1980. String instrument specialist Fresno (Calif.) Sch. Dist., 1986—91; dir. of orchestras Buchanan Edn. Ctr., Clovis, Calif., 1991—; condr. jr. symphony Youth Orchestras of Fresno, 1994—99. Adj. prof. Calif. State U., Fresno, 1998—2000; bd. dirs. Fresno Philharmonic, 1990—92. Mem.: Fresno-Madera Counties Music Educators Assn. (orchestra rep. 1998—2000, Outstanding Mid. Sch. Orchestra Dir. 1994), Am. String Tchrs. Assn., Calif. Music Educators Assn. (Outstanding Orchestra Educator 2000). Home: 10202 E Sierra Ave Clovis CA 93611 Office: Buchanan High Sch 1560 N Minnewawa Clovis CA 93611

FRANKLIN, JEANNE F. lawyer; b. N.Y.C., July 22, 1946; BA cum laude, Vassar Coll., 1968; JD, U. Va., 1971. Bar: Mich. 1971, U.S. Dist. Ct. Mich. (ea. dist.) 1975, U.S. Ct. Appeals (10th cir.) 1975, N.Mex. 1977, D.C. 1977, Va. 1981, U.S. Dist. Ct. Va. (ea. dist.) 1984. Sole practice, Alexandria, Va. Fellow: Am. Bar Found.; mem.: D.C. Bar (mem. health law sect.), Va. State Bar (mem. health law sect.), Am. Health Lawyers Assn., Alexandria Bar Assn., Va. Bar Assn. (mem. exec. com. 1997—, pres. 2000—01), ABA. Office: 604 Cameron St Alexandria VA 22314

FRANKLIN, LYNNE, business communications consultant, writer; b. St. Paul, Minn., Aug. 24, 1957; d. Lyle John Franklin and Lois Ann (Cain) Kindseth; stepdau. Thomas John Kindseth; m. Lawrence Anton Pecorella, Sept. 2, 1989; 1 stepchild, Lauren. BA in Psychology and English, Coll. St. Catherine, 1979; MA, Hamline U., 1989. Residential treatment counselor St. Joseph's Home, Mpls., 1979-80; staff writer Comml. West Mag., Mpls., 1980-81; acct. exec. Edwin Neuger & Assocs., Mpls., 1981-83, Hill and Knowlton, Mpls., 1983-84; mgr. pub. rels. Gelco Corp., Eden Prarie, Minn., 1984-86; dir. financial rels. Dunstan & Assocs., Mpls., 1986; cons. MC Assocs., Chgo., 1986-87; v.p. Fin. Rels. Bd., Chgo., 1987—; prin. Wordsmith, Glenview, Ill., 1993—. Trustee Lawrence Hall Youth Svcs.; pres. Skokie Valley chpt., Bus. Networking Internat., 2003; judge achievement awards Internat. Assn. of Bus. Communicators, Mpls., 1986, presenter fin. rels., 1990; judge achievement awards Publicity Club of Chgo., 1992-94; presenter ann. report seminar Nat. Investor Rels. Inst., Chgo., 1992, presenter investor rels. survey, 2003. Author: (novel) Second Sight, 1989. Tchr. Great Books Program, St. Paul, 1976-79, Minn. Literacy Coun., 1985-87. Recipient Ann. Report Excellence award, Fin. World Mag., 1991—98, award, MerComm-ARC Competition, 1992—2003, Nat. Assn. Investors Corp., 1994—2003, Equities Mag., 1999—2002. Office: Wordsmith 2019 Glenview Rd Glenview IL 60025-2849

FRANKLIN, MARGERY BODANSKY, psychology educator, researcher; b. N.Y.C., Mar. 18, 1933; d. Oscar and Barbara (Biber) Bodansky; m. Raymond S. Franklin, Aug. 22, 1962; children— Kenneth, David AB, Swarthmore Coll., 1954; MA, Clark U., 1956, PhD, 1961. Instr. psychology Vassar Coll., Poughkeepsie, N.Y., 1960-62, asst. prof., 1962-64; research assoc. Bank St. Coll. Edn., N.Y.C., 1967-72; prof. Sarah Lawrence Coll., Bronxville, NY, 1965—2002. Dir. Child Devel. Inst. Sarah Lawrence Coll., 2003—. Co-editor: Developmental Processes: Heinz Werner's Selected Writings, 1978, Symbolic Functioning in Childhood, 1979, Child Language: A Reader, 1988, Development and the Arts: Critical Perspectives, 1994; contbr. articles to profl. jours., chpts. to books. Fellow Am. Psychol. Assn. (pres. psychology and arts divsn. 1990-91); mem. Soc. for Rsch. in Child Devel. Avocation: photography.

FRANKLIN, PHYLLIS, retired professional society administrator; b. N.Y.C., Apr. 21, 1932; d. Matthew Pine and Helen Lutsky; m. Irwin Franklin, Apr. 21, 1958 (div. 1971); children: James, Jody. AB, Vassar Coll., 1954; MA, U. Miami, 1965, PhD, 1969; LHD (hon.), George Washington U., 1986. From asst. to assoc. prof. U. Miami, Coral Gables, 1969-80; spl. asst. to dean Coll. Arts & Scis. Duke U., Durham, N.C., 1980-81; dir. English programs MLA, N.Y.C., 1981-85, exec. dir., 1985—2001, ret., 2001. Adj. prof. English programs NYU, 1987-88. Editor ADE Bull., 1981-85. Fellowship, Danforth Found., 1966-68, Am. Council on Edn., 1980-81; stipend NEH, 1971. Mem. USSR Acad. Scis., Am. Coun. Learned

Socs. (bd. dirs. 1987-89, commn. on humanities and social scis. 1987-88, chair conf. secs. 1987-90), Nat. Humanities Alliance (bd. dirs. 1986-88, v.p. 1990-91, pres. 1991-96), Nat. Fedn. Abstracting and Info. Svcs. (bd. dirs. 1994-96). Democrat. Jewish.

FRANKLIN, ROSA G. state legislator, retired nurse; m. James Franklin; 3 children. RN, Good Samaritan Waverly Hosp., Columbia, S.C., 1948; BA in Biology and English, U. Puget Sound, 1968; MA in Social Scis. and Human Rels., Pacific Luth. U., 1974; postgrad., U. Wash., 1974. Ret. nurse; mem. Wash. Senate, Dist. 29, Olympia, 1993—; Dem. whip Wash. Senate, Olympia, 1997, majority whip, 1999-01, pres. pro tem, 2001. Mem. commerce and trade com. Wash. State Senate, mem. health and long term care com., mem. rules com., asst. Dem. fl. leader. Mem. Tacoma Urban League, Safe Streets, South End Neighborhood for Family Safety, Hunger Walk '93; mem. adv. com. Cancer Screening Program for Targeted Populations; bd. dirs. Cascade Blood Bank; bd. advisors Health Edn. Coun, New Phoebe House; adv. bd. Bates Tech. Coll. Named Outstanding Vol. Stafford Study Club, Hon. Citizen award Citizen of Tacoma, Dem. Woman of Yr. Wash. State Fedn. Dem. Women; recipient Thurgood Marshall award African Am. Port of Tacoma, Lifetime Achievement award Wash. Dem. Party, 2000, award Women's Polit. Caucus, 2001, Black Veterans Service award, 2004; named to Wash. State Nurses Assn. Hall of Fame, 2002. Mem. LWV, NAACP, Wash. Assn. C.C. Women's Programs, Pierce County Nurses Assn, Alpha Kappa Alpha. Democrat. Office: PO Box 40429 Olympia WA 98504 Office Phone: 360-786-7656. E-mail: franklin_ro@leg.wa.gov.

FRANKLIN, SHIRLEY CLARKE, mayor; b. Phila., May 10, 1945; d. Eugene Haywood Clarke and Ruth (Lyons) White; m. David McCoy Franklin, Feb. 5, 1972 (div. 1986); children: Kai Ayanna, Cabral Holsey, Kali Jamilla. BA, Howard U., 1968, LLD (hon.), 2002; MA, U. Pa., 1969. Contract compliance officer U.S. Dept. Labor, Washington, 1966-68; instr. social scis. Talledega (Ala.) Coll., 1969-71; from dir. to commr. Dept. Cultural Affairs, Atlanta, 1978-82; chief adminstrv. officer City of Atlanta, 1982-90, exec. officer for ops., 1990—2001; pvt. practice, 1997—; mayor, 2002—. Trustee Atlanta Symphony Orch., 1977-81, Atlanta Found., 1980—; mem. Ga. Council for the Arts, Atlanta, 1979-82, adv. bd. Ga. Women's Polit. Caucus, Atlanta, 1982-84; chmn. expansion arts panel Nat. Endowment for the Arts, Washington, 1980-82; bd. dirs. Nat. Urban Coalition, Washington, 1980-83; dep. campaign mgr. Young for Atlanta, 1981-82; sr. v.p. external rels. Atlanta Com. Olympic Games, 1991-97; majority ptnr. Urban Environ. Solutions, LLC, 1998-. Recipient Disting. Alumni award Nat. Assn. for Equal Opportunity Higher Edn., 1983, Leadership award Atlanta chpt. NAACP, 1987; named to Acad. Women Achievers YWCA Greater Atlanta, 1986. Mem. Nat. Forum Black Pub. Adminstrs. Clubs: Chautauqua Circle. Democrat. Avocations: gardening, traveling, politics, fine arts. Office: City Hall 55 Trinity Ave SW Atlanta GA 30303-3520*

FRANKLIN, SHIRLEY MARIE, marketing consultant; b. Kansas City, Mo., Apr. 13, 1930, d. Eric E. and Marie M. (Kilpatrick) Snodgrass; div. 1967; 1 child, Scot Wesley. BA, State U. Iowa, 1952; MS, Simmons Coll., 1954; MA, Kans. U., 1974. Cert. tchr., Kans., Mass., N.J., Ariz., Calif. Tchr., adminstr. various schs., 1952 76; gifted student program designer Leavenworth County (Kans.) Pub. Schs., 1976-77; sales cons., mgr. Sealight Co., Inc., Kansas City, Mo., 1978-82; dir. chain sales Haagen Dazs Ice Cream Co., Teaneck, N.J., 1982-87, program dir. east apart mgmt. Ice Cream Industry, 1986-88; prin. Shirley Franklin Consulting, Basehor, Kans., 1987—; U.S. brands dir. Mövenpick Co., Zurich, Switzerland, 1990—; mktg. cons. Franklin & Assocs., 1994—. Speaker at dairy industry meetings, seminars. Contbr. articles to profl. jours. and mags. Nat. com. steering com. U.S. Congress Arts Caucus, Washington, 1988—89; foster parent World Vision, Pasadena, Calif., 1986—99; vol. ct. appointed spl. advocate for children in trouble Kans., 1994; steering com. Fred Harvey Mus., 2000—, grant writer, Fred Harvey home restoration, 2000—03; apptd. City Planning Commn., 1996—99; ESL com. Leavenworth City Schs. Recipient Excellence in Sales Promotions award Dairy and Food Industries Supply Assn. Mem. Internat. Ice Cream Assn. (mktg. coun. 1979—), Internat. Platform Spkrs. Assn., Alpha Delta Kappa, Delta Delta Delta. Republican. Episcopalian. Avocations: writing, walking, reading, travel, bridge. Home and Office: 910 Columbia Ave Leavenworth KS 66048-3133

FRANKLIN, VERONICA RENA, psychotherapist; b. Memphis, Nov. 1, 1959; d. Orenzia Self and Katherine Reed-Franklin; life ptnr.. BA, Oral Roberts U., 1983; MEd, U. Minn., Mpls., 1993; postgrad. in sport psychology, U. N.Mex., 1996—97; MA in Counseling, Argosy U., Chgo., 2002. Lectr. kinesiology Tex. A&M U., College Station, 1993; head women's basketball coach Montgomery Coll., Rockville, Md., 1994; dir. sport club U. Minn., Mpls., 1995; tchr. aide Beacon and North Shore Alternative Sch., Chgo., 1999—2000; therapist Thresholds Psychology Rehab. Ctr., Chgo., 2000—. Contbr. articles to profl. publs. Active vol. democratic elections, gay rights. Recipient Fullbright award, 1989—90. Mem.: AAPHERD, NIRSA, Coll. Coaches Assn. Democrat. Home: 3660 N Lake Shore Dr Chicago IL 60613 Office: Thresholds Psychiat Rehab Ctr Mothers Project 1110 W Belmont Chicago IL 60657 E-mail: vfranklin@thresholds.org.

FRANKS, BEVERLY MATTHEWS, psychotherapist, consultant; b. Denver, Mar. 13, 1936; d. William Harry and Helen Catherine Nissen; m. Dean Nolie Matthews, Dec. 12, 1954 (div. July 1974); m. Kenneth W. Franks Jr., May 14, 1988. BS, Colo. State U., 1977, MS, 1981; PhD, U. Wyo., 1988. Diplomate Am. Bd. Psychotherapy; cert. sch. psychologist, nat. bd. cert. sch. psychologist, counselor, lic. profl. counselor Wyo., sch. psychologist Wyo., psychol. technician Wyo. Instr. dept. psychology Colo. State U., Ft. Collins, 1979—80; staff psychologist Poudre R-1 Sch. Dist., Ft. Collins, 1980—83, Natrona County Sch. Dist., Casper, Wyo., 1983—85; counselor Univ. Lab Sch., Laramie, Wyo., 1985—86; clin. therapist Ctrl. Wyo. Counseling Ctr., Casper, 1986—88; staff psychologist Lake Wash. Sch. Dist. # 414, Kirkland, Wash., 1988—89, Fed. Way (Wash.) Pub. Schs., 1989—92, head psychologist, 1992—94; spl. edn. legal cons. B&K Tech., Seattle, 1994—95; psychotherapist Red Buttes Counseling, Laramie, 1996—. Cons. Fed. Way Pub. Schs., 1995, Albany County Pub. Schs., 2002. Mental health therapist Downtown Clinic, Laramie, 1999—2002. Recipient Mature Woman's award, AAUW, 1975—76, Sr. Woman's award, 1976—77; Charles S. Hill Meml. scholar, Colo. State U., 1976—77. Mem.: Laramie Area Mental Health Profls. (treas. 2000—), Nat. Assn. Sch. Psychologists, Am. Psychotherapy Assn., Omicron Nu, Psi Chi, Phi Kappa Phi. Avocation: quilting. Office: Red Buttes Counseling 36 Arrowhead Dr--The Buttes Laramie WY 82070-6824

FRANKS, CANDACE ANN, bank executive; b. Memphis, Nov. 18, 1952; d. James William and Barbara Elizabeth Webb; m. Roger Allen Franks, July 23, 1977; 1 child, Ava Elizabeth. BA, Ark. State U., 1974, MA, 1976; JD, U. Ark., 1979. Bar: Ark. 1979. Gen. counsel Ark. State Bank Dept., Little Rock, 1980-95, dep. bank commr., 1995—. Mem. Gov.'s Task Force to Revise Banking Code, Legis. Task Force to Study NAFTA, 1995, Gov.'s Task Force on Interstate Banking, 1997—; mem. legis. com. Conf. State Bank Suprs., Washington, 1997—. Named one of Top 10 Women in Ark., Ark. Bus. Mag., 1996, 97, 98. Mem. Ark. Bar Assn., Pulaski County Bar Assn., Conf. State Bank Suprs. Office: Ark State Bank Dept Sedgwick Ctr 400 Hardin Rd Ste 100 Little Rock AR 72211-2613 E-mail: cfranks@banking.state.ar.us.

FRANKS, LUCINDA LAURA, journalist; b. Chgo., July 16, 1946; d. Thomas Edward and Lorraine Lois (Leavitt) F.; m. Robert M. Morgenthau, Nov. 1977; children: Joshua Franks Morgenthau, Amy Elinor Morgenthau. BA, Vassar Coll., 1968. Journalist specializing youth affairs, civil strife in No. Ireland UPI, London, 1968-73, N.Y. Times, N.Y.C., 1974-77; freelance writer N.Y. Times Mag., N.Y. Times Book Rev., Talk Mag., The Atlantic, The New Yorker, N.Y. mag., The Nation. Vis. prof. Vassar Coll., 1977-82; Ferris prof. journalism Princeton U., 1983 Author: Waiting Out A War: The Exile of Private John Picciano, 1974, Wild Apples, 1991. Recipient Pulitizer prize for nat. reporting, 1971, N.Y. Newspaper Writers Assn. award, 1971, Nat. Headliners award Soc. Silurians journalism award, 1976, EDI award for print journalism Easter Seals, 1999. Mem. Am. PEN Club (membership bd.), Author's League, Coun. on Fgn. Rels., Writers Rm. Inc. (past pres.). Address: 64 E 86th St New York NY 10028-1016

FRANKS, SUZAN L. R. state legislator; b. Everett, Mass., Sept. 18, 1949; d. Francis and Elsie Robinson; m. Richard A. Franks, Nov. 17, 1950; children: Robinson, Jamisen, Justin.. State rep. N.H. Ho. of Reps., Concord, 1992—; alderman at large City of Nashua, 1998—. Mem. bd. edn. City of Nashua, 1985-86, 89-92. Recipient Master of Boardsmanship award N.H. Sch. Bds. Assn., 1991. Republican. Office: Bd Aldermen 229 Main St Nashua NH 03060-9221

FRANKSON-KENDRICK, SARAH JANE, publisher; b. Bradford, Pa., Sept. 24, 1949; d. Sophronus Ahimus and Elizabeth Jane (Sears) McCutcheon; m. James Michael Kendrick, Jr., May 22, 1982. Customer svc. rep. Laros Printing/Osceola Graphics, Bethlehem, Pa., 1972-73; assoc. editor Babcox Publs., Akron, Ohio, 1973-74, Bill Comms., Akron, Ohio, 1974-75, sr. editor, 1975-77, editor-in-chief, 1977-81; assoc. pub. Chilton Co./ABC Pub., Chgo., 1981-83, pub., 1983-89, group pub. Radnor, Pa., 1989-93; group v.p. Cahners Bus. Info. (formerly Chilton Co.), Radnor, Pa., 1993-98; divsn. v.p. Primedia Intertec, Chgo., 1999—2001. Exec. MBA prof. Northwood U., mem. adv. coun. Mem. oper. com. Primedia Intertec. Recipient Automotive Replacement Edn. award Northwood Inst., 1983, award for young leadership and excellence Automotive Hall of Fame, 1984; bd. dirs. Automotive Hall of Fame. Mem. Automotive Found. for Aftermarket (trustee), Automotive Parts and Accessories Assn. (bd. dirs., exec. com., sec., treas., strategic planning com., edn. com., Disting Svc. award 1993), Automotive Svc. Industry Assn. (bd. dirs. automotive divsn. com.), Automotive Svc. Assn. Mgmt. Inst. (trustee, exec. com.), Palm Beach (Fla.) Polo and Country Club, Winged Foot Golf Club (Mamaroneck, N.Y.). Republican.

FRANK-STROMBORG, MARILYN LAURA, nursing educator; b. Chgo., Jan. 20, 1942; d. Irving and Roseann (Krcek) Frank; m. Paul Stromborg, 1966; children: Nels, Danny. BS, No. Ill. U., 1964, MS, cert. in nursing, No. Ill. U., 1966, EdD, 1974, JD, 1994. RN. Mem. faculty Sch. Nursing U. Ill., Chgo., 1970-71, No. Ill. U., DeKalb, 1976—; acting chair, 1995-96. Part-time mem. nursing faculty U. Loyola U., Chgo., 1974-76, Rush U., Chgo., 1974-76. Author: Primary Care Assessment and Management Skills for Nurses, 1979; editor Instruments for clinical Nursing Research, 1989 (AJN award 1989), Cancer Prevention and Early Detection in Minorities: Culturial Implications, 1993. Founder, vol. trainer De Kalb County Hospice, 1977—; v.p. Am. Cancer Soc., 1977. Capt. USAF, 1966-70. Named Researcher of Yr., Pace U., 1990; grantee Nat. Cancer Inst., NIH, 1984—; Ctr. for Nursing Rsch., 1985-90, Div. Nursing, 1990—. Fellow Am. Acad. Nursing; mem. Midwest Nursing Rsch. Soc. (treas. 1989-91), Oncology Nursing Soc. (chair rsch. com. 1985-87, sec. 1987-89, excellence in cancer nursing edn. award 1991). Avocations: gardening, skiing. Home: 215 Dunkery Dr Sycamore IL 60178-1017 Office: No Ill U Dept Nursing Dekalb IL 60115

FRANSE, KAREN BALCH, editor, small business owner; b. Menomonee Falls, Wis., Sept. 14, 1964; d. William Perry and Kitty (Parker) B.; m. Ulrich Bonn (div. Jan. 1990); m. John E. Franse, July 6, 1996. BA in Comms., Broadcast Journalism, Pepperdine U., Malibu, Calif., 1985; MA in Counseling Psychology, Nat. U., Irvine, Calif., 1995. Cert. mediator. Mktg. coord. Schmidt-Cannon, Inc., City of Industry, Calif., 1986-88; copywriter The Practice Builder Advtg. Agy., Irvine, Calif., 1988; proprietor The Write Stuff, El Toro, Calif., 1989-91; mng. editor Macartist Mag., Santa Ana, Calif., 1989-91; asst. publs. editor Ingram Micro Inc., Santa Ana, Calif., 1988-91; sr. editor CMP Publs. Inc., Irvine, Calif., 1991—2002; psychotherapist trainee College Hosp., Costa Mesa, Calif., 1994-95; owner Franse & Assocs., 2002—. Past mem. bd. dirs., mem.-at-large, v.p. Cedar Glen Homeowners Assn. Mem. Psi Chi Honor Soc. Office Phone: 803-289-7048. E-mail: kfranse@comperium.net.

FRANTZVE, JERRI LYN, psychologist, educator, consultant; b. Huntington Beach, Calif., Sept. 9, 1942; d. Rolland and Marjorie Weiland. Student, Purdue U., 1964-68; BA in Psychology and History, Marian Coll., 1969; MS in Organizational Psychology, George Williams Coll., 1976; PhD in Indsl. and Organizational Psychology, U. Ga., 1979. Sr. mktg. rsch. analyst Quaker Oats Co., Barrington, Ill., 1971-75; asst. prof. sch. of mgmt. SUNY, Binghamton, 1979-83; dir. employee rels. Conoco/DuPont, Ponca City, 1983-88; cons. psychologist Mass., 1988-89; assoc. prof. psychology Radford (Va.) U., 1989-94; mgmt. cons. J.L. Frantzve & Assocs., Bklyn., 1994—; divsn. head human svcs. Coll. New Rochelle, 1991 99, affiliate prof. Milano Grad. Sch. of Mgmt. New Sch. U., N.Y.C., 1999—. Instrn. cons. USAF, Rome, N.Y., 1979-83; dir. Israel Overseas Rsch. Program, Ginozar, Israel, 1982, Japanese Overseas Rsch. Program, Tokyo, 1983; coord. rsch. Ctr. for Gender Studies, Radford U., 1989-94; adj. prof. dept. psychology Bklyn. Coll., 2000—. Author: Behaving in Organizations: Tales from the Trenches, 1983, Guide to Behavior in Organizations, 1983; contbr. articles to profl. jours. Bd. dirs. Broome County Alcoholism Clinic, Binghamton, N.Y., 1980-83, bd. dirs. Broome County Mental Health Clinic, Binghamton, 1981-83; del. Dem. Caucus, Okla., 1985. Mem. APA (com. on women in psychology 1986-88), AAUW, Acad. Mgmt., Internat. Pers. Mgmt. Assn., Assn. for Women in Psychology. Avocations: ceramics, jazz, murder mysteries. Home and Office: 1804 Glenwood Rd Brooklyn NY 11230-1816 E-mail: drj4647@aol.com.

FRANZ, ELIZABETH, actress; b. Akron, Ohio, June 18, 1941; Actress with Broadway credits in: Death of a Salesman, The Cripple of Inishmaan, Brighton Beach Memoirs (Tony and Drama Desk nominations), Broadway Bound, Uncle Vanya, Getting Married, The Cemetery Club, The Octette Bridge Club, The Cherry Orchard, Mornings at Seven, 2002; off-Broadway credits include: Sister Mary Ignatius (Obie award, Drama Desk nomination), Minutes from the Blue Route, The Comedy of Errors; regional credits include: Eleanor of Aquataine in The Lion in Winter (Cleve.), Amanda in The Glass Menagerie, Dividing the Estate (Great Lakes), A View From the Bridge, Woman in Mind (Berkshire Theatre Festival), Dolly in The Matchmaker, Agnes of God, Hamlet, Buried Child, The Wicked Witch in The Wizard of Oz, Miss Haversham in Great Expectations; appeared in numerous TV series and movies including: Roseanne, Sister, A Town's Revenge (Emmy nomination), Notes for My Daughter, Nothing Personal, Shameful Secrets, Face of a Stranger, Dottie, The Rise and Rise of Daniel Rocket, Love and Other Sorrows, A Girl Thing, Death of a Salesman (Emmy nomination, 2000), Gilmore Girls, 2001, Judging Amy, 2001; film credits include: Sabrina, 1995, The Substance of Fire, 1996, The Pallbearer, 1996, Thinner, 1996, Twisted, 1997, Jacknife, 1989, Secret of My Success, 1987, School Ties, 1992 Winner 1999 Tony award for featured actress in Death of a Salesman, also Drama Desk award, Outer Critics Circle award. Office: c/o Michael Slessinger Assocs 8730 W Sunset Blvd Ste 220 Los Angeles CA 90069-2275

FRANZ, HOLLY JO, lawyer, partner; b. Mpls., July 2, 1957; d. Gerald A. and Delores E. (Dahle) F. BS, Mont. State U., 1983; JD, U. Mont., 1986. Bar: Mont., 1986, U.S. Dist. Ct., 1986. Ptnr. Gough, Shanahan, Johnson and Waterman, Helena, Mont., 1986—. Pres. Mont. Water Resources Assn., Helena, 1999-2001.. Author: Montana Law Journal, 1986; contbr. articles to profl. jours. Legis. Com. Women's Law Caucus, Missoula, Mont., pres. or bd. mem. The State Bar of Mont. (Women's Law Sect.), 1986—, treas. Mont. Women's Lobby, Helena, 1990-95. Recipient Award of Merit Mont. Legal Svcs., 1984, Belle Winestine award Mont. Women's Lobby, 1993. Mem. ABA, First Jud. Bar Assn. (pres. 1998—). Avocations: gardening, snow skiing, hiking, wildlife viewing, camping. Office: Gough Shanahan Johnson & Waterman 33 S Last Chance Gulch St Helena MT 59601-4132

FRANZEN, JANICE MARGUERITE GOSNELL, magazine editor; b. LaCrosse, Wis. d. Wray Towson and Anna Heldena (Renstrom) Gosnell; m. Ralph Oscar Franzen, Feb. 15, 1964. BS cum laude, Wis. State U., LaCrosse; MRE, No. Bapt. Theol. Sem. Dir. Christian Writers Inst., 1950—63, dir. studies, 1964-86; fiction editor Christian Life Mag., Wheaton, Ill., 1950-63, woman's editor, 1964-72, exec. editor, 1972-86; mem. editorial bd. Creation House, Wheaton, 1972-86. Speaker writers confs. Author: Christian Writers Handbook, 1960, 61, The Adventure of Interviewing, 1989; editor: Christian Author, 1949-54, Christian Writer and Editor, 1955-63; compiler, contbr.: The Successful Writers and Editors Guidebook, 1977; contbr. articles to various mags. Sec., bd. dirs. Christian Life Missions, Lake Mary, Fla., 1971-95; bd. dirs. Ralph O. Franzen Charitable Found., 1990—, Wesley Luehring Found., 2000—. Home: 140 Windsor Park Dr Apt E201 Carol Stream IL 60188-5314

FRANZETTI, LILLIAN ANGELINA, former automobile dealership owner; b. N.Y.C., Nov. 24, 1925; d. Anthony and Jenny (De Santis) Spilotro; m. Louis Mario Franzetti, Apr. 27, 1946 (dec. Oct. 1986); 1 child, Paul. Clk. typist U.S. Guarantee Ins. Co., N.Y.C., 1943-44, payroll asst. mgr., 1944-46; clk. typist N.J. Div. of Motor Vehicles, Westwood, 1950-54; office mgr. Lakeview Motors, Inc., Woodcliff Lake, N.J., 1954-58, mgr., owner Westwood, 1958-93. Sec. Tri-State Jeep, Eagle Adv. Assn., Tappan, N.Y., 1978-93. Recipient Bus. Mgmt. award, Am. Motors Corp., 1978. Republican. Roman Catholic.

FRASER, ARVONNE SKELTON, former United Nations ambassador; b. Lamberton, Minn., Sept. 1, 1925; d. Orland D. and Phyllis (Du Frene) Skelton; m. Donald M. Fraser, June 30, 1950; children: Thomas Skelton, Mary MacKay, John Du Frene, Lois MacKay (dec.), Anne Tallman (dec.), Jean Skelton Fraser. BA, U. Minn., 1948; LLD (hon.), Macalester Coll., 1979. Staff asst. Office Congressman Donald M. Fraser, 1963-70, adminstrv. asst., campaign mgr., 1970-76; regional coord. Carter-Mondale Com., 1976; counsellor office presdl. pers. The White House, 1977; coord. office women in devel. U.S. Agy. Internat. Devel., Washington, 1977-81; dir. Minn. and Chgo. coms. peace petition dr. Albert Einstein Peace Prize Found., Chgo., 1981-82; co-dir. ctr. on women and pub. policy Hubert H. Humphrey Inst. Pub. Affairs, U. Minn., Mpls., 1982-94; head U.S. del. Commn. On The Status of Women, UN, 1993-94, U.S. rep., amb., 1994; co-founder, dir. Internat. Women's Rights Action Watch, 1985-93. Bd. dirs. Minn. DFL Edn. Found., Internat. Women's Yr. Conf., Mexico City, 1975, UN Commn. on Status of Women, 1974, 78, Internat. Bur. Edn. Conf., Geneva, 1977; cons. Kenya Women's Leadership Conf., 1984; organizer, chairperson Orgn. Econ. Coop. and Develp./Devel. Assistance com./Women in Devel. experts group for aid-donor nations, 1978-80; dir. Ford. Found. Women's Equity Action League Fund Intern Project and World Plan Project, treas. 1974-77, bd. dirs. 1970-77, 81-83, nat. pres. 1972-74, past legis. chairperson Washington office. Author: U.N. Decade for Women: Documents and Dialogue, 1987; (with others) Women in Washington: Advocates for Public Policy, 1983, Women, Politics and the United Nations, 1995. Trustee Macalester Coll., St. Paul, 1982-84, candidate Lt. Gov. Minn., 1986; pres. Friends of Minneapolis Pub. Libr. Recipient Disting. Svc. award Women's Equity Action League, 1977, Superior Honor award U.S. Agy. Internat. Devel., 1981, Elizabeth Boyer award Women's Equity League, 1984, Leader of Leaders Outstanding Achievement award Mpls. YWCA, 1979, Resourceful Woman award Tides Found., 1992; sr. fellow Humphrey Inst. Pub. Affairs U. Minn., 1981-94, emeritus 1995; Prominent Women in Internat. Law award Am. Soc. of Internat. Law, 1995, Mpls. Internat. Citizen award, 1995. Mem. Minn. Bd. Law Examiners. Home and Office: 821 7th St SE Minneapolis MN 55414-1331

FRASER, CATHERINE ANNE, Canadian chief justice; b. Campbellton, N.B., Can., Aug. 4, 1947; d. Antoine Albert and Anne (Slevinski) Elias; m. Richard C. Fraser, Aug. 17, 1968; children: Andrea, Jonathan. BA, U. Alta., Can., 1969, LLB, 1970; ML, U. London, 1972. Assoc., ptnr. Lucas, Bishop & Fraser, Edmonton, Alta., 1972-89; justice Ct. Queen's Bench Alta., Edmonton, 1989-91, Ct. Appeal Alta., Edmonton, 1991-92, chief justice Alta. and NW Ter., 1992—, chief justice Nunavut, 1999—. Dir. Can. Inst. Adminstrn. Justice, 1991-95. Recipient Tribute to Women award YWCA, 1987. Mem. Can. Bar Assn. Office: Ct Appeal Alta Law Courts Bldg Edmonton AB Canada T5J OR2

FRASER, CLAIRE M. research scientist, science administrator; BS in Biology, Rensselaer Poly. Inst., 1977, DSc (hon.), 2002; PhD in Pharmacology, SUNY, Buffalo, 1981; Doctorate (hon.), U. Bergen, Norway, 2000. Tchg. asst. dept. pharmacology and therapeutics SUNY, Buffalo, 1977—81, rsch. assoc. dept. pharmacology and therapeutics, 1981—82, rsch. instr. dept. biochemistry, 1982—83; cancer rsch. scientist III dept. molecular immunology Roswell Park Meml. Inst., Buffalo, 1983—84, cancer rsch. scientist IV dept. molecular immunology, 1984—85; sr. staff fellow Lab. Neurophysiology NINCDS, NIH, Bethesda, Md., 1985—87; sr. staff fellow, chief unit of receptor regulation, receptor biochemistry and molecular biology Lab. Molecular and Cellular Neurobiology, NINDS, NIH, Bethesda, Md., 1987—89; chief sect. on molecular neurobiology Lab. Physiologic and Pharmacologic Studies Nat. Inst. on Alcohol Abuse and Alcoholism, ADAMHA, Rockville, Md., 1989—92; v.p. for rsch., dir. dept. microbial genomics Inst. for Genomic Rsch., Rockville, 1992—98, pres., dir., investigator, 1998—. Mem. com. on countering bioterrorism and domestic animal genomics NRC; mem. rev. com. NSF, Dept. Energy-NIH; lectr. Waksman Found. for Microbiology Lectures Program, 2000, 01; prof. pharmacology George Washington U., 2000, prof. microbiology and tropical medicine, 01. Mem. editl. bd.: Jour. Biol. Chemistry, reviewer sci. jours.: ; contbr. articles to profl. jours. Named to, Md. Top 100 Women, 1997, 2000; recipient Computerworld Smithsonian award for innovation and info. tech., 1998, award, Inst. for Math. and Advanced Supercomputing, 1999, Burroughs Wellcome Fund Visiting Scientist Professorship award, 1999, Fellows award, Rensselaer Alumni Assn., 2002. Office: Inst for Genomic Rsch 9712 Medical Center Dr Rockville MD 20850

FRASER, KAREN, state legislator; m. Tim Malone; 1 child, Hiromi. BA in Sociology, U. Wash., 1966, MPA, 1969. Thurston County commr., 1981-88; mayor City of Lacey, 1976-80, mem. coun., 1973-80; mem. Wash. Senate, Dist. 22, Olympia, 1988—; chair environ. quality and water resources com.; mem. energy, tech., and telecoms. com.; mem. ways and means com.; mem. joint com. on pension policy Wash. Senate, Olympia, 1995—, exec. com. Asia and Pacific parliamentarians conf., 1994-97, co-chair legis. internat. caucus, 1994—, mem. capitol campus design adv. com., 1995—, senate ecology and parks com. chair, 1993-96; chair com. on natural resources, environ. and water. Bd. dirs. Wash. Wildlife and Recreation Coalition; mem. com. Olympic Trials Legacy, 1998—; chair Nisqually River Coun.; founding bd. dirs. Nisqually River Basic Land Trust; trustee State Capital Hist. Assn.; host com. Women's Olympic Marathon Trials Assn., chair chair, 1984; past v.p., treas. Tumwater area coun. Boy Scouts Am. Recipient Legislator of Yr. award Wash. Fedn. State Employees, 1993, Silver Beaver award Boys Scouts Am., Toll Fellow Coun. State Govts., 1993, Legislator of Yr. Wash. Health Care Assn., 1996, Puget Sound Hero, People for Puget Sound, 1995, Woman of Distinction award Pacific Peaks Girl Scouts USA Coun., 1995, Cert. Appreciation Jud. Staff Bd. Indsl. Ins. Appeals, Wash. Fedn. State Employees, 1998, Disting. Leadership Recognition award Assn. Wash. Housing Authorities, 1998,

Program Leadership award Nisqually River Mgmt. Program, 1998, Legis. Citation of Merit award Wash. Recreation and Parks Assn., 1998. Mem. Wash. State Assn. Counties (pres. 1987-98). Democrat. Avocations: outdoor recreation, sailing, hiking, marathon running. Office: 417 John Cherberg Bldg Olympia WA 98504-0001

FRASER, KATHLEEN JOY, poet, creative writing educator; b. Tulsa, Mar. 22, 1935; d. James Ian and Marjorie Joy (Axtell) F.; m. Jack Marshall, July 10, 1960 (div. 1970); 1 child, David Ian; m. Arthur Kalmer Bierman, June 30, 1984 BA in English Lit., Occidental Coll., 1958; doctoral equivalency, San Francisco State U., 1976. Vis. prof. writing, lectr. in poetry The Writer's Workshop, U. Iowa, Iowa City, 1969-71; writer in residence Reed Coll., Portland, Oreg., 1971-72; dir. Poetry Center San Francisco State U., 1972-75, prof. creative writing, 1972-92. Founder-dir. Am. Poetry Archives, San Francisco, 1973-75; founder-editor How(ever), Jour. for poets/scholars interested in modernism and women's innovative writing, 1983-91. Author: (children's book) Stilts, Somersaults and Headstands, 1967; (poetry) What I Want (New and Selected Poems), 1974, New Shoes, 1978, Something (even human voices in the foreground) A Lake, 1984, Notes Preceding Trust, 1988, When New Time Folds Up, 1993, Il Cuore: The Heart, Selected Poems 1970-95, 1997. Recipient Frank O'Hara Poetry prize, 1964; Nat. Endowment for Arts fellow, 1978, Guggenheim fellow, 1981.

FRASER, MARGOT, consumer products company executive; b. Bremen, Germany; Pres., founder Birkenstock Footprint Sandals, Inc., 1972—. Inductee Footwear News Hall of Fame. Office: Birkenstock Footprint Sandals 8171 Redwood Blvd Novato CA 94945-1403

FRASER, MARILYN ANNE, state legislator; b. Concord, N.H., Apr. 24, 1936; d. Louis Nicholas and Clarissa Blanchard N.; m. Maurice Henri Dupuis, 1990; 1 child, John E. Jr. BEd, MEd, U. N.H. Tchr., Concord, 1991-95; co-chmn. Concord Area Transp., 1992—, cons., 1993—, chmn. airport adv. com., 1993—; mem. Concord City Coun., 1991-95, N.H. Ho. of Reps., 1994—. Chmn. state and city rels. N.H. Ho. of Reps., 1995—. Democrat. Address: 84 Branch Tpke #54 Concord NH 03301-5715

FRASER, MARY EDNA, artist, educator; b. Fayetteville, NC, Mar. 20, 1952; d. Claude Ivey and Mary Beasley Burkhead; m. James West Fraser, 1978 (div. 1989); children: Sarah, Rebecca; m. John B. Sperry, Aug. 22, 1993. BS with honors, East Carolina U., 1974. Judge Oreg. Arts Commn. Fellowship Panel, 1993; artist NASA, 1995, Am. Emb., Bangkok, 1996. Book, What The Water Gives Me, 2002; illustrator: A Celebration of the World's Barrier Islands, 2003; one-woman shows include Smithsonian Nat. Air and Space Mus., 1994—95. Contbr., lectr. S.C. Coastal Conservation League, Charleston, 1985—; founding mem. Nat. Mus. Women in the Arts, Washington, Bella A Capella, 2003. Profl. Discipline Individual grant, S.C. Arts Commn., 1988, Project grant, 1992, Individual Fellowship grant, 1998. Mem.: Surface Design Assn. Democrat. Presbyterian. Avocations: music, swimming, singing, yoga. Home: 1723 Oak Point Rd Charleston SC 29412 Studio: PO Box 12250 Charleston SC 29422

FRASER, PAMELA, artist; b. Smyrna, Tenn., 1965; BFA, Sch. Visual Arts, N.Y.C., 1988; MFA, UCLA, 1992. Prof. U. Tenn., Northwestern U.; asst. prof. art dept. Ohio State U., Columbus, 2001—. One-woman shows include Casey Kaplan, N.Y.C., 1998, 2000, exhibited in group shows at Lotus Motel, Inglewood, Calif., 1995, White Columns, N.Y.C., 1996, Exit Art, 1999, Elga Wimmer Gallery, 1999, Pudewil, Berlin, 2000, Wurtembergischer, Stuttgart, 2000, Dundee Ctr. of Contemporary Art, Scotland, 2000, others. Recipient Louis Comfort Tiffany award, 1997; Skowheghan Sch. Painting and Sculpture fellow, 1988. Office: Ohio State Univ Dept Art 146 Hopkins Hall 128 N Oval Mall Columbus OH 43210 Fax: 212-645-7335..*

FRASER, SHEILA, government agency administrator; b. Dundee, Que., Can., Sept. 16, 1950; m. Henri Gagnon; 3 children. BS, McGill U., 1972. Chartered acct., 1974, cert. FCA, 1994. Acct. Ernst & Young, prtnr.; deputy auditor gen., audit opers. Office of Auditor Gen. Canada, Que., Canada, 1999—2001, auditor gen., 2001—. Chair Working Group Environ. Auditing, Sub-Com. Independence Supreme Audit Insts., Internat. Orgn. Supreme Audit Insts.; mem. exec. bd. and bd. govs. Canadian Comprehensive Audit Found. Recipient Prix Emérite, 1993, Gov. Gen.'s medal. Fellow: Inst. Chartered Accts. Ont.; mem.: Canadian Inst. Chartered Accts. (mem. Public Sector Acctng. Bd.). Office: Office of the Auditor Gen of Canada 240 Sparks St Ottawa ON Canada K1A 0G6*

FRATES, MEX (MRS. CLIFFORD LEROY FRATES), civic worker; b. Moweaqua, Ill., Jan. 15, 1908; d. William James and Gertrude (Gunderson) Rodman; m. Clifford L. Frates, Nov. 15, 1935; children: Rodman A., Kent F. Student, Pine Manor Jr. Coll., 1924; BA, U. Okla., 1929. Mem. bd. ARC, Oklahoma City; dir. Community Fund Bd.; trustee Jane Brooks Sch. Deaf, Okla. Art Center, Okla. Coll. for Women; chmn. adv. bd. Mercy Hosp., also trustee; bd. dirs. Okla. State Library, Library for Blind, dir. Jr. Leagues of Am.; mem. bd. Okla. Heritage Assn., Allied Arts of Oklahoma City, Oklahoma City Symphony, YWCA, Blood Inst., Better Bus. Bur.; mem. Children's Rehab. and Edn. Bd.; drive chmn. Central Vol. Bur.; chmn. women's div. United Fund; chmn. Art Center drive; chmn. Oklahoma City Savs. Bond Com.; chmn. Episcopal Women's Conf. Okla.; div. chmn. for Christian social relations; mem. Episcopal Bishop and Council; mem. vestry All Souls Ch. chmn. Re-act campaign for Oklahoma City Vol. Action Center, 1971. Recipient award NCCJ, Humanitarian award Oklahoma City Pub. Sch. Found., 1986, By-Liners award Women in Comm., 1979, Okla. Gov.'s Arts award, 1985, Mary Baker Rumsey award Jr. League Redlands, award for volunteerism Girl Scouts U.S., Richard Clements award United Appeal, Pathfinder award Oklahoma County Hist. Soc., Dean's award Coll. Medicine for Cmty. Svc.; named to Okla. Hall of Fame, 1969. Home: 2607 Warwick Dr Oklahoma City OK 73116-4208

FRATKIN, LESLIE, photographer; b. Schenectady, N.Y., 1960; BA in Comm., SUNY, Albany, 1983. Curator, coord., mgr. touring internat. photography exhbn., film series, web site and book project Sarajevo Self-Portrait: The View From Inside, 1995—. Exhibitions include Barney's, N.Y.C., 1995, Foster Goldstrom Gallery, 1995, Children in Crisis Benefit, Germany, 1997, Riverside Studios, London, 1998, Florence, Italy, 1999; contbg. photographer various publs., 1983—. The Trust for Mutual Understanding grantee, 1997, Individual Project fellow and grantee, Soros Found./Open Soc. Inst., 1997. E-mail: leslief@interport.net.

FRAUENHOFFER, ROSE MARIE, visual artist, cosmetologist; b. Evanston, Ill., July 24, 1926; d. Edward John and Rose Louise (Pantle) Kossow; m. Harold Voight Frauenhoffer, Oct. 14, 1950. Lic. cosmetologist, Ill. Mgr., buyer Del-Mar, Evanston, 1948-52; asst. mgr., buyer House of Harold Salon, Evanston, 1952-2000; mgr. buyer House of Harold Gifts, Evanston, 1952—; mgr. House of Harold Gallery, Evanston, 1952-2000; asst. mgr., designer House of Harold Engraving, Evanston, 1952-2000; artist, designer House of Harold Studio, Evanston, 1999-2000; artist, dir. Peinture de la Monde Studio, Gallery divsn. House of Harold, Evanston, 2000—. Exhibited works in solo shows at Aurelia Gallery, Evanston, Garland Bldg. Gallery, Chgo., Bank of Lincolnwood, Levy Ctr. La-Petite Gallery, Loft Gallery, Skokie, Ill.; group shows at Loft Gallery, John G. Blank Ctr. for Arts, Michigan City, Ind., Margaret Harwell Art Mus., Poplar Bluffs, Mo., Wilmette (Ill.) Pub. Libr., others; exhibited in nat. and internat. art shows. Alumnus, vol. Evanston Citizens Police Acad., 1997—; co-chair Skokie Centennial Art and Craft Fair, 1988. Recipient awards for art. Mem. Skokie Art Guild (v.p. 1980-81, pres. 1981-82), Midwest Watercolor Soc., Nat. Mus. Women in the Arts, Ill. Arts Coun., Evanston Arts Coun. Avocations: gardening, photography, sewing.

FRAVEL, POLLY B. music educator; b. Harrisonburg, Va., Nov. 9, 1953; d. Charles Edward and Eula Rhodes Burkholder; m. Donald O. Fravel, June 13, 1981. BA, Goshen Coll., 1976. Cert. music edn. grades K-12. Elem. music tchr. Page County (Va.) Schs., 1976—79, Harrisonburg (Va.) City Schs., 1979—. Mem.: NEA, Harrisonburg Edn. Assn. (pres. 1998—), Va. Music Educators Assn. (dist. rep. 2003), Va. Edn. Assn. Methodist. Avocation: travel. Home: 749 Northfield Ct Harrisonburg VA 22802

FRAWLEY, SISTER CLAIRE, religious studies educator; b. Elmira, N.Y., Nov. 7, 1929; d. James Edward and Alice (Keating) Frawley. BS, Nazareth Coll., 1957, BA, 1966; postgrad., Siena Coll., 1967, U. Dayton, 1967-68, Cath. U., 1969-73; MRE, Divine Word, 1972. Sch. administr., tchr. Parish Schs., Rochester, Ithaca, Elmira, N.Y., 1950-80. Founder, exec. dir. St. Claires Homes, Escondido Calif., homes for homeless women and children, youth minister, Escondido, established and administered program for youth and young adults. Recipient Women Helping Women award Soroptimists, Womens Internat. Living Legacy award; scholar Nat. U. Mem. NAFE, Assn. of Christian Therapists, Calif. Mental Health Assn., Womens Internat., Coalition of Human Svc. Agencies, Child Abuse Coalition, Inland Dirs. Coalition. Home: # 321 243 S Escondido Blvd # 321 Escondido CA 92025-4116

FRAWLEY BAGLEY, ELIZABETH, government advisor, ambassador; b. Elmira, N.Y., July 13, 1952; m. Smith Bagley; 2 children. BA in French and Spanish cum laude, Regis Coll., 1974; JD in Internat. Law, Georgetown U., 1987. Staff Office Congl. Rels. Dept. State, spl. asst. to Amb. Sol Linowitz, congl. liaison Conf. on Security and Cooperation in Europe, amb. to Portugal, 1993-97, former amb. to Portugal, 1997—. Adj. prof. law Georgetown U. Washington. Home: 1539 29th St NW Washington DC 20007-3061

FRAYSER, MARY STOKES, human services administrator, consultant; b. Keysville, Va., Oct. 14, 1929; d. Goodrich Henry and Elizabeth (Holloway) Stokes; m. James Samuel Frayser, Aug. 24, 1954 (dec. Mar. 1964). BA in Sociology, Va. Union U., 1951; MA in Social Work, Howard U., Washington, 1968, D of Social Work, 1988. Cert. social worker; lic. ind. clin. social worker. Tchr. Lunenburg County Bd. Edn., Victoria, Va., 1951-55; caseworker Dept. Social Svcs., Richmond, Va., 1957-64; social svcs. rep. child welfare divsn. Dept. Pub. Welfare, Washington, 1965-70; social worker supr. Dept. Human Svcs., Family Svcs., Washington, 1970-79, chief, contract residential care, 1979-82, chief continuing svcs., 1982-84, program analyst, 1984-90; dir. tng. & staff devel. Commn. on Social Svcs., Washington, 1990-93; cons. Keysville, Va., 1993—. Cons. D.C. Child Welfare Corsortium, 1979-82; participant task force on standards, regulations for home care agencies, Washington, 1984-85; proposal reviewer U.S. Dept. Human Svcs., Washington, 1984-89; chair guardianship com. Nat. Assn. Adult Protective Svcs. Adminstrs., San Antonio, 1990-91. Author papers, presenter in field. Vol. coord. commn. wards 5 & 7, Washington, 1976-81; cmty. rels. vol. Piedmont Geriat. Hosp., Burkeville, Va., 1995—; bd. dirs., grant writer Cmtys. in Sch., Lunenburg County, Va., 1996-97. Child welfare tng./ednl. leave scholar D.C. Dept. Pub. Welfare, 1966; Kennedy Inst. Ethics fellow Joseph P. Kennedy Jr. Found., Washington, 1989. Mem. NASW, (nominations, leadership identification com. D.C. metro chpt. 1993-95), Nat. Coun. on Aging, The Hastings Ctr. (assoc.), Rotary (Lunenburg County chpt.). Democrat. Avocations: traveling, antiques & collectibles, reading, photography, home decorating. Home and Office: 1358 Tuckers Rd Keysville VA 23947-3303

FRAZEL-LASSETER, CHERYL, newscaster; b. Balt., Oct. 13, 1969; BS summa cum laude, Towson U., 1992. Reporter WMDT-TV, Salisbury, Md., WLEX-TV, Lexington, Ky.; anchor WLBT, Jackson, Miss., 2000—. Office: WLBT 715 S Jefferson St Jackson MS 39201

FRAZER, JENDAYI, political science educator; BA political sci., MA internat. policy/internat. devel., PhD political sci., Stanford U. Dir. african affairs Nat. Security Coun.; fellow Coun. Foreign Relations Internat. Affairs, 1998-99; asst. prof. pub. policy Kennedy Sch. Govt. Harvard U. Vis. fellow Ctr. Internat. Security and Arms Control, Stanford U.; rsch. assoc. Inst. Devel. Studies, U. Nairobi, Kenya. Mem. Women in Internat. Soc. (exec. bd. 1998—). Office: The Kennedy Sch 79 John F Kennedy St Cambridge MA 02138-5801

FRAZER, SUSAN HUME, independent scholar and consultant; b. Hinton, W.Va., Jan. 3, 1949; d. Dennis Ray and Wanda Marrs Hume; m. John Walker Frazer Jr., Oct. 6, 1989; children: Andrew Reno Collier II., Amy Marie Wilson Collier. BA Psychology, Chapman U., 1972; MS Interior Environments, U. Wis., 1992; PhD Art History, Va. Commonwealth U., 2001. V.p., dir. mktg. Signature Cmtys., Alexandria, Va., 1984—88; v.p. mktg. Miller and Smith, McLean, 1988—90; ind. scholar/cons. Am. Architecture and Decorative Arts, Richmond, 1998—. Contbr. articles to profl. jours. Mem.: Soc. Archtl. Historians, Sigma Sigma Sigma (past pres.), Kappa Omicron Nu (hon.), Delta Omicron (hon.). Presbyterian. Avocations: piano, tatter, baking, antiques. Home and Office: 2023 Hanover Ave Richmond VA 23220 E-mail: hume-frazer@erols.com.

FRAZIER, AMY, professional tennis player; b. St. Louis, Mo., Sept. 19, 1972; Prof. tennis player USTA, 1990—. Mem. 1995 U.S. Fed. Cup Team. Named World Team Tennis MVP, 1995. Achievements include winner 7 Career Singles Titles and 4 WTA Career Doubles Titles, WTA Tour. Avocations: ceramics, painting, bicycling. Office: USTA 70 W Red Oak Ln White Plains NY 10604-3602

FRAZIER, CYNTHIA ELLEN, journalist, writer; b. Lakewood, Ohio, June 15, 1952; d. Louis Wickham and Evelyn Mae Frazier; life ptnr. Sharon Marie Gretsch. BA, Bennington Coll., Bennington, Vt., 1975, Calif. State U., Northridge, 1983. Mng. editor Brentwood Media Group, Brentwood, Calif., 1994—96; news editor The Argonaut Newspaper, Marina del Rey, Calif., 1996—. Author: (novels) Desert Snow, (screenplay) Cyber Virus. Mem.: Greater L.A. Press Club. E-mail: cindyfrazier@argienews.com.

FRAZIER, DOUGLAS ALMEDA MCREE, volunteer, former energy facility analyst; b. Soddy, Tenn., Feb. 6, 1923; d. Clarence Douglas and Nannie (Eldridge) McRee; m. Earl Lee Frazier, Aug. 25, 1963. BA, U. Chattanooga, 1944, B of Music, 1949, MEd, 1958. Various positions TVA, Chattanooga, power supply analyst, 1945-87. Vol. for TVA retirees, Chattanooga Visitors Ctr., Chattanooga Health Coun.; mem. Adult Edn. Coun., Chattanooga Employees Recreation Assn., Sr. Neighbors Orch., Chattanooga, 1990—, v.p. Ret. Sr. Vol. Program; organist, pianist Soddy United Meth. Ch.; past sec. Soddy-Daisy H.S. Alumni Assn.; life mem. First Presbyn. Ch.resbyn. Ch. Grand Organist, O.E.S., Tennessee, 1999—; Listed in 1st Families Tenn., 1996. Mem. AAUW (life; past pres., Names Gift award 1965), AARP (past pres., Cmty. Citizen award), DAR, East Tenn. Hist. Soc., Chattanooga Engrs. Club (past. sec., v.p., pres., People-to-People award 1989), U. Chattanooga Alumni Coun., Soddy C. of C., Soddy Lioness Club, Order of Eastern Star (past matron, grand rep. 1965-67, grand rep. Tenn. 1996, 97, grand organist 1999), Soddy High Alumni Assn. (past sec., past pres.), Pilot Club of Chattanooga. Life-long mem. of the First Presbyterian Church of Soddy, Tennessee. Home: 11313 Hixson Pike Soddy Daisy TN 37379-6371 Address: PO Box 223 Soddy Daisy TN 37384-0223

FRAZIER, LINDA JOYCE, county official; b. Dickson, Tenn., May 12, 1955; d. James Franklin and Helen Louise (Pellam) Hayes; m. Henry Garland Frazier, July 17, 1976; 1 child, Henry Garland, Jr. Sec., food processor Dickson (Tenn.) Frozen Food Lockers, 1970-76; sec. B.G. Howell Contractors, White Bluff, Tenn., 1976-78; [illegible] Dickson, 1990-94, dep. recorder, 1978-94, asst. tax collector, 1978-94; trustee County of Dickson, Charlotte, Tenn., 1994—2002, county mayor, 2002—. Sec./bookkeeper Dickson County Emergency Comms. Bd., Dickson, 1988-2001; chair bd. trustees Dickson County Pub. Libr., 1986-98. Trustee on regional bd. dirs. Warioto Regional Libr., Clarksville, Tenn., 1995—; pres. Leadership Dickson County Alumni Assn., 1996-97; vol. Dickson County Cancer Soc.; trustee Dickson County Pub. Libr., 1986-98; bd. dirs. United Way Dickson County, 1998. Mem. County Assn. Mayors, Dickson County C. of C., Dickson County Hist. Soc., Leadership Dickson County Alumni Assn. Avocations: reading, crocheting, gardening. Office: County of Dickson PO Box 267 Charlotte TN 37036-0267

FRAZIER, MARY ANN, artist; b. Tulsa, Okla., Sept. 11, 1937; d. Dolphus Leonard and Elouise (Reedy) Cagle; m. Robert E. Frazier, May 14, 1954 (div. Mar. 1971); children: Robert E. Frazier, Jr. (dec.), Robbyne Elisa. Student, Tulsa C.C., 1990-92; studied with numerous artists, including, David Leffel, Ben Konis, Doug Dawson, William Herring, Mary Russell, Del Gish, others. Oil portrait David Moss, David L. Moss Correctional Ctr., Tulsa; permanent collections of portrait and other paintings in pub. and pvt. collections throughout the U.S. Home: 3338 E 27th Pl Tulsa OK 74114-5910

FREAD, PHYLLIS JEAN, counselor, educator; b. Pahala, Hawaii, May 21, 1927; d. Logan Allen and Joyce (Barnes) Pruitt; m. John W. Fread (dec.); children: James R., John A. BA, Cornell Coll., 1948; MEd, U. Oreg., 1956. Cert. tchr., counselor, Oreg. Tchr. Seattle Pub. Schs., 1948-50, West Valley H.S., Millwood, Wash., 1950-52, Roseburg (Oreg.) Dist. 4, 1954-65, dean students, 1965-80; French instr. Umpqua C.C., Roseburg, Oreg., 1984-93; diagnostic counselor AFS, Portland, Oreg., 1988—, hosting dir., 1990—. Named Vol. of Month, Roseburg C. of C. Mem. AAUW (treas. 1958-63), Zonta Club of Roseburg (pres. 1976-78, 83-84, gov. dist. 8 1996-98). Republican. Methodist. Avocations: music, travel, reading. Home: 879 NW Meadowood Cir Mcminnville OR 97128-9530

FREAR, LORRIE, graphic designer, educator; b. Rochester, N.Y., July 23, 1955; d. Charles Richard and Muriel Jean F; m. John Paul Dodd, Feb. 29, 1992. BFA, Rochester Inst. Tech., 1978, MFA, 1981. Graphic designer Gannett (newspapers), Rochester, N.Y., 1981-82, Robert Meyer Design, Rochester, N.Y., 1981-82, Gregory Fossella Assocs., Boston, 1982-84, McKesson Corp., San Francisco, 1984-88, Landor Assocs., 1985, Great Ideas Advtsg., Buffalo, 1988-99, Lorrie Frear Design, Canandaigua, N.Y., 1990—; lectr. graphic design Rochester Inst. Tech., 1990—. Art dir. Nat. Ctr. Missing & Exploited Children, Rochester, 1998; water safety instr., 1973-93; IDEA cert. fitness instr., 1987-93. Mem. Lake County Garden Club (art dir. 1999—), Genesee Valley Calligraphy Guild, Phi Kappa Phi. Independent. Baptist. Avocations: calligraphy, fitness, movies, gardening, piano. Home: 5434 Lower Egypt Rd Canandaigua NY 14424-8850 Office: RIT Sch Design Coll Imaging Arts & Scis 73 Memorial Dr Rochester NY 14623 E-mail: lxfcad@rit.edu.

FREASIER, AILEEN W. special education educator; b. Edcouch, Tex., Nov. 12, 1924; d. James Ross and Ethel Inez (Riley) Wade; m. Ben F. Freasier, Mar. 9, 1944 (dec.); children: Ben. C., Doretha J. Christoph, Barbara F. McNally Protzman, Raymond E. (dec.), John F. BS HE, Tex. A and I Coll., 1944; MEd, La. Tech. U., 1966; postgrad. 90 hours, La. Tech. U. Tchr. Margaret Roane Day Care Ctr., Ruston, La., 1965-71; tchr. spl. edn. Lincoln Parish Schs., Ruston, 1971-81; individualized edn. program facilitator La. Tng. Inst. Monroe Spl. Sch. Dist. # 1, 1981-89; ednl. diagnostician LTI Monroe (La.) SSD # 1, 1985-95. R.S.V.P. vol. tutor, Lincoln Parish Detention Ctr., 1995—; citizen amb. People Conf. on Edn., Beijing, 1992, South Africa, 1995; presenter in field. Mem. editl. bd.: Jour. Correctional Edn., 1983—95, editor learning tech. sect.:, 1991—95; contbr. articles to ednl. publs. and profl. jours.; author: 5 comml. handwriting duplicating books. Treas. Ruston Mayor's Commn. on Women, 1996—. Named Spl. Sch. Dist. #1 Tchr. of Yr., 1988; recipient J.E. Wallace Wallin Educator of Handicapped award La. Fedn. CEC, 1994, Meritorious Svc. award La. Dept. Pub. Safety and Corrections, 1995, Pres.'s award La. CEC-Tech. and Media, 1997. Mem. AAUW (pres. North La. br. 1995—, state co-chair diversity task force 1993-94, state chmn. diversity com. 1994-2002, state treas. 2001-03, La. Named Gift honoree AAUW Edn. Found. 1994), CEC-Tech. and Media (treas. La. divsn. 1993-96, 2001—, Pres.'s award 1997), Internat. Correctional Edn. Assn. (spl. edn. spl. interest group, newsletter editor 1991-94, chmn. 1994-96, editl. bd. CEA Yearbook of Correctional Edn. 1998—), Nat. Soc. DAR (Long Leaf Pine chpt., regent 1997-99, constitution week chmn. 2000—), Veteran's Patients Com. (chmn., 2000-), Lincoln Parish Ret. Tchrs. Assn. (yearbook editor 1996—, pres. 1998-2000), Phi Delta Kappa (past pres. chpt. 1994-96, newsletter editor 1989-93, 97-98, treas. 2002—), Kappa Kappa Iota (state pres. 1991-92, nat. scholarship com. 1995-97, nat. tech. com. 1997-99, chmn. nat. tech. com. 1999-2000, nat. profl. devel. com. 2001-03, Nat. Scholarship Com., 2003-04, chmn. Eta State Scholarship Com., 2002-03, chmn. bylaws com. 2003—, Eta State Loretta Doerr award 1995, Epsilon conclave pres. 1985-87, 99-2000, v.p. 2003). Home: PO Box 1595 Ruston LA 71273-1595 E-mail: aileenwf@bayou.com.

FRÉCHETTE, LOUISE, international organization official; b. Montreal, Can., July 16, 1946; BA, Coll. Basile Moreau, 1966; licence es lettres degree in history, U. Montreal, 1970; postgrad. diploma in econ. studies, Coll. Europe, Bruges, Belgium, 1978; Doctorate (hon.), St. Mary's U., Halifax, 1993, Kyung Hee U., Seoul, U. Ottawa, U. Toronto, Laval U., Quebec. Mem. General Assembly, Canada, 1972; second sec. Canadian Embassy, Athens, 1972—75; with European Affairs Div., Dept. of External Affairs, Canada, 1975—77; first sec. Canadian Mission to the UN, Geneva, 1978—82; deputy dir. Trade Policy Div., Dept. of External Affairs, 1982—83; dir. European Summit Div., 1983—85; Can. amb. to Argentina, Uruguay, Paraguay, 1985—88; asst. dep. min. for L.Am. and Caribbean Dept. External Affairs and internat. trade, 1988—91; asst. dep. min. for econ. policy and trade competitiveness Ministry of Fgn. Affairs, 1991-92; permanent rep. of Canada UN, 1992-94; assoc. dep. min. Can. Dept. Fin., 1994-95; dep. minister def. Govt. of Can., 1995-98; dep. sec. gen. UN, 1998—. Named Office of the Order of Can., 1998.*

FREDA, LISA M. psychologist; d. Alexander Joseph and Eleanor Rainone Freda; m. David R Hruska, May 25, 2003. PsyD in Psychology, U. Hartford, Conn., 1999. Lic. psychologist RI, N.Y. Psychology intern Maimonides Med. Ctr., Bklyn., 1997—98; psychologist Pesach Tikvah Day Treatment Program, Bklyn., 1998—2000; pediat. psychologist Maimonides Med. Ctr., Bklyn., 2000—01; psychologist Maimonides Devel. Ctr., Bklyn., 1999—2001, Bradley Hosp., East Providence, RI, 2002—. Pvt. practice psychology, Bklyn., 2001—02. Author: (monograph chapter) National Inst. on Alcohol Abuse and Alcoholism Project MATCH Monograph Series. Scholar Champlin scholar, Champlin Found., 1986—91. Mem.: APA, Sigma Xi. Office: Bradley Sch Bradley Hosp 1011 Veterans Memorial Pkwy East Providence RI 02915 Office Phone: 401-432-1503.

FREDEN, SHARON ELSIE CHRISTMAN, state education official; b. Watertown, S.D., Jan. 11, 1941; d. Harlon Arthur and Mildred Lillian (Jensen) Christman; m. Noble Everett Freden, July 3, 1973; 1 child, Anne Victoria. BS, No. State Coll., Aberdeen, S.D., 1962; MA, U. Iowa, 1966; EdD, U. Colo., 1973. Tchr. Manitowoc (Wis.) Pub. Schs., 1962-64, Boulder Valley Pub. Schs., Colo., 1966-70, K-12 lang. arts cons., 1970-72; cons. Colo. Dept. Edn., Denver, 1973-76, 77-80; ITV insvc. coord. Sta. KCPT-

TV, Kansas City, Mo., 1980-81; dir. Kans. Dept. Edn., Topeka, 1981-84, asst. commr., team leader, 1984—2001, 2001—. Editor: Basic Skills: Promising Practices in Colorado, 1979, (with others) Pupil Progress in Colorado, 1978; contbr. chpts. to books. Chmn. precinct com. Broomfield (Colo) Dem. Com., 1978. Recipient leadership award YWCA, 1990; Hildegard Sweet Meml. scholar, 1972. Mem. ASCD, Kans. ASCD, United Sch. Adminstrs., Phi Delta Kappa. Office: Kans Dept Edn 120 E 10th Topeka KS 66612 also: 6021 SW 29th St #A Topeka KS 66614-4269

FREDENBURGH, LISA MARIE, music educator; b. Flint, Mich., Jan. 28, 1964; d. Carol A. and Jack E. Fredenburgh. BA, Luther Coll., Decorah, Iowa, 1986; MusM in Conducting, Vocal Performance, D of Musical Arts, U. Ariz., 1996. Choral dir., music instr. Satanta (Kans.) Pub. Schs., 1986—88; choral dir. Scott City (Kans.) H.S., 1988—90; music dir. Tucson (Ariz.) Masterworks Chorale, 1992—95; instr. voice Ga. So. U., Statesboro, 1995—96; dir. choral activities Meredith Coll., Raleigh, NC, 1996—. Choral dir. N.C. Gov.'s Sch. East, Raleigh, 2000—01. Mem.: Soc. Ethnomusicology, Music Educators Nat. Conf. (co-presenter interest session So. divsn.), Am. Choral Dirs. Assn. (nat. chair women's choirs 2001—, presenter, panel participant 2001). Office: Meredith Coll 3800 Hillsborough St Raleigh NC 27607

FREDERICK, AMY L. science administrator; b. Flint, Mich., Oct. 13, 1972; BA, Cumberland U., Lebanon, Tenn., 1994; MA, Howard U., 1996, PhD, 2000. Tech. commercialization fellow NASA, Greenbelt, Md., 1995—99; program adminstr. Global Sci. and Tech., Inc., Greenbelt, 1999—2000; sr. staff Sci. Applications Internat. Corp., Vienna, Va., 2000—. Presenter in field. Author: The Election of Women and African-American to Congress; contbr. articles to profl. jours. Recipient NASA Goddard Space Flight Ctr. Group award, NASA, 1996; Hawthorne Dissertation fellow, Howard U., 1999, Cumberland U. scholar, 1992—94. Mem.: Phi Sigma Alpha. Office: Science Applicatios Internat Corp 8401 Corporate Dr Landover MD

FREDERICK, ELIZABETH ELEANOR TATUM, watercolor artist, retired educator; b. Clovis, N.Mex., Dec. 22, 1915; d. John Hardy Tatum and Bessie Elizabeth Weathers Tatum; m. George Achias Frederick, June 7, 1937 (dec. Apr. 1991); children: Ronald W., George Douglas, Barbara Elizabeth Frederick Ewing, John Lawrence. BS in Edn., U. N.Mex., 1937, MS, 1943; postgrad., Highland U., Las Vegas, N.Mex., 1944, Ea. N.Mex. U., 1944, 45. Tchr. Ctrl. H.S., Kirtland, N.Mex., 1936-37, Bellview (N.Mex.) H.S., 1940-42, Hot Springs (N.Mex.) Jr. H.S., 1943-45, 1951-53, Hot Springs (N.Mex.) H.S., 1954; ret., 1967. Exhibitions include Sierra Art Soc., N.Mex., Willamette Oaks Retirement Ctr., Eugene, Oreg., 1995, El Paso Mus. Art, N.Mex. Art League, N.Mex. Watercolor Soc., Albuquerque, Represented in permanent collections. Mem. Nat. League Am. Pen Women (pres. Rio Grande br. 1975-76), Sierra Art Soc. (pres. 1974-75, funding and program chmn. 1975-89), N.Mex. Watercolor Soc., Black Range Artists (sec.-treas. 1978-79). Republican. Avocations: sweepstakes, worldwide travel.

FREDERICK, LEAH RUTH, education educator; b. Sandersville, Ga., Sept. 28, 1944; d. Stanley LaMar Sr. and Kate Burns (Bryan) Frederick. BS, Bryan Coll., Dayton, Tenn., 1966; MEd, Fla. Atlantic U., 1968; EdD, U. Ga., 1996. Cert. profl. tchr. Dept. Edn., Fla., 1966, edn. specialist Fla. Atlantic U., 1980. Tchr. Lantana (Fla.) Jr. High, 1966—71; spl. edn. tchr. Meadow Pk. Elem., West Palm Beach, Fla., 1971—72; admintrn., tchr. Alliance Acad., Quito, Ecuador, 1972—90; prof. Simpson Coll., Redding, Calif., 1988—90; assoc. prof. Toccoa Falls (Ga.) Coll., 1990—. Conf. spkr. Assn. Christian Schs., Inc., Quito, Ecuador, 1993, Quito, 97, Manilla, Philippines, 96, Santa Cruz, Bolivia, 2000. Author: (book) Instructional Reading Level Inventory, 1996, (jour. articles) Assn. Christian Schs., Inf., 1997—2003; co-author: Assn. Childhood Edn. Internat., 1995. Presenter Evangelism Explosion, Toccoa, Ga., 1998—; pres. Local Impact Com., Toccoa, Ga., 2002—. Grantee Faculty Devel. Grant, U. Ga., 1993—94. Mem.: Tocca Stephens County Lit. Coun. (sec. 1998—). Independent. Mem. Missionary Alliance. Avocations: travel, furniture restoration, walking. Office: Toccoa Falls Coll PO Box 800296 Toccoa Falls GA 30598

FREDERICK, PAULA F. health facility administrator; b. Portland, Oreg., Apr. 14, 1954; d. Robert Paul and Gertrude Agnes (Krein) F.; m. Stephen Wilson DeBruhl, Aug. 25, 1978 (div. 1992); children: Brandon Frederick DeBruhl, Colin Frederick DeBruhl. BA with honors, Portland State U., 1976, MS, MEd with honors, 1977. Cert. in mental health psycho-therapy Wash.; nat. cert. in addictions specialty (psycho-therapy). Rschr. F.U.D., Fairbanks, Alaska, 1977-80; tchr. Women's Ctr., Knoxville, Tenn., 1980-82; sr. psychotherapist Child and Family Svcs., Family Crisis Ctr., Knoxville, 1980-82; asst. adminstr. Comprehensive Care Corp. Care Unit Hosp., Kirkland, Wash., 1983-88; adminstr. Rader Inst., Auburn, Wash., 1988-93, Seattle, 1993—; program adminstr. Friends of Youth, 2002—. Rsch. asst. Portland (Oreg.) State U., 1976-77; cons. Vancouver (Wash.) Women's Ctr., 1978-80, Knoxville Women's Ctr., 1980-82; sec., treas., bd. dirs. Tenn. Victims of Abuse & Violence Coalition, Knoxville, 1981-82, instr. Bellevue C.C., 1998—. Author, co-author publs. in field. Mem. ACA, State of Wash. Mental Health Counselors Assn. Avocations: hiking, walking, oil painting, reading, dance. Office: Friends of Youth 464 12th Ave Issaquah WA 98027

FREDERICK, ROSEANN, retired medical/surgical nurse; b. Easton, Pa., Dec. 6, 1924; d. Oranjio Pennise and Angeline Guarrera; m. Walter S. Frederick, Feb. 7, 1953 (div. June 2001); children: Stephen, Ann, Jane, Jim, David. Nursing diploma, Sacred Heart Hosp., 1946; student, U. Pa., 1953. Emergency rm. nurse Bklyn. Hosp., 1946—48; pub. health nurse Easton, 1949—53; nurse registry Peninsula Hosp., Burlingame, Calif., 1954—55; staff nurse, head nurse Mills Hosp., San Mateo, Calif., 1956—58, Sequoia Hosp., Redwood City, Calif., 1959—61, Stanford Hosp., Palo Alto, Calif., 1966—. Nurses registry U. Calif. Brain Imaging Ctr., Irvine, 1999—. Mem.: Franciscan Order, Mercy Assn., Italian Cath. Fedn. Avocations: watercolors, computers. Home: 26581 Naccome Dr Mission Viejo CA 92691

FREDERICK, SHELLEY CANNON, artist; b. Longview, Tex., Mar. 2, 1957; d. Robert Jackson and Dorothy Davis Cannon; m. Mark Frederick, Nov. 12, 1982; m. Steven Mark Hilton, Aug. 31, 1975 (div. Nov. 20, 1977); 1 child, Thomas Jack Hilton. AA in Drafting, Kilgore Coll., Tex., 1981; student, U. of Indpls., 2002—. Drafter Design Specialist, Tyler, Tex., Sun Prodn. Co., Longview, Tex., 1982; contract drafter Applied Tech. Svcs., New Orleans, 1983—85; designer Bob Evans Farms, Columbus, 1986; irrigation designer Buckeye Landscape, Columbus, 1988—89; art tchr. John Waldron Art Ctr., Bloomington, Ind., 1992—2001, Columbus Art League, Columbus, Ind., 2001—02. Exhibitions include Selection of Watercolor, Trojan Horse (Monroe County Bank Purchase Award, 2000), Hot, Hotter, Hottest (Outstanding Watercolor, 1999), Patriot (Grand Champion and 1st Pl. Watercolor, 1999), Florida Dreaming, Art Mus. of Sport (Purchase Award, 1998), First Lady of America, Allentown Art Festival (Outstanding Work Purchase Award, 1991), Church at Borchers, So. Ind. Art Ctr. (First Pl., 2000), Hot, Hotter, Hottest, Southside Art League (First Pl. Watercolor, 1999). Mem. Bible Study Fellowship, Columbus, Ind., 1991—2001; bd. dirs. Ind. Artist Club, Indianapolis, Ind., 2003—; mem. DAR, Columbus, Ind., 1997, Brown County Humane Soc., Nashville, Ind., 1991—93; bd. dirs. Brown County C. of C., Nashville, Ind., 1999—2000, Brown County Studio and Garden Tour, Nashville, 1999—2002, Ind. Heritage Artists, Nashville, 2002—. Recipient Merit award, Ind. State Fair, 2002. Mem.: Watercolor Soc. of Ind. (signature mem.), Brown County Artists (assoc.; v.p. 1999—2000). Conservative-R. Christian. Avocations: gardening, computing. Home: 8463 Garrity Rd Freetown IN 47235 Office: Heartworks 8463 Garrity Rd Freetown IN 47235 Personal E-mail: shell_art@iquest.net. E-mail: shell_art@iquest.net.

FREDERICK, SUSAN ANN (PENTZ), music educator; b. Canandaigua, N.Y., Mar. 13, 1963; d. George V. and Majel A. Pentz; m. Dennis A. Frederick, June 8, 1985; children: Zachary, Aaron, Jonathan. BME, Houghton (N.Y.) Coll., 1985; MusM in Edn., Ithaca (N.Y.) Coll., 1991. Cert. tchr. music edn. Tchr. vocal music East Ridge Jr. HS, East Irondequoit, NY, 1985—86, East Ridge HS, East Irondequoit, 1985—86, Rochester City Sch. Dist., 1986—88, Boynton Mid. Sch., Ithaca, 1988—93, Trumansburg Ctrl. Sch., 1993—. Accompanist at weddings. Pianist and organist Lodi (N.Y.) Presbyn. Ch., 1998—, Sunday sch. tchr., 1994—, clk. of session, 1988—91. Mem.: NEA, N.Y. State Music Assn., Music Educators Nat. Chpt. Republican. Avocations: crocheting, knitting, sewing, gardening. Home: 6056 Seneca Rd Trumansburg NY 14886 Personal E-mail: sfrederick@zoom-DSL.com. Business E-Mail: sfrederick@tburg.k12.ny.us.

FREDERICK, VIRGINIA FIESTER, state legislator; b. Rock Island, Ill., Dec. 24, 1916; d. John Henry and Myrtle (Montgomery) Heise; m. C. Donnan Fiester (dec. 1975); children: Sheryl Fiester Ross, Alan R., James D.; m. Kenneth Jacob Frederick, 1978. BA, U. Iowa, 1938; postgrad., Lake Forest Coll., 1942-43, LLD, 1994, MLS, 1999. Freelance fashion designer, Lake Forest, Ill., 1952-78; pres. Mid Am. China Exch., Kenilworth, Ill., 1978-81; mem. Ill. Ho. of Reps., Springfield, 1979-95, asst. minority leader, 1990-95. Alderman first ward, Lake Forest, 1974-78; del. World Food Conf., Rome, 1974; subcom. pensions and employment Ill. Commn. on Status of Women, 1976-79; co-chair Conf. Women Legislators, 1982-85; bd. dirs. Lake Forest Coll., 1995-98, Lake Forest Symphony Guild, 1998—; city supr. City of Lake Forest, 1995-98. Named Chgo. Area Women of Achievement, Internat. Orgn. Women Execs., 1978; recipient Lottie Holman O'Neal award, 1980, Jane Addams award, 1982, Outstanding Legislator award Ill. Hosp. Assn., 1986, VFW Svc. award, 1988, Joyce Fitzgerald Meml. award, 1988, Susan B. Anthony Legislator of Yr. award, 1989, Delta Kappa Gamma award, 1991, Outstanding Legislator award, 1995, Svcs. for Srs. award, Ill. Dept. Aging, 1991, Ethics in Politics award, Rep. Womens's Club, 1992, Woman of Achievement award YWCA North Eastern Ill., 1994, Ill. Women in Govt. award, 1994, Lifetime Achievement award Equip for Equality, 1999. Mem. LWV (local pres. 1958-60, state dir. 1969-75, nat. com. 1975-76), AAUW (local pres. 1968-70, state pres. 1975-77, state dir. 1963-69, nat. com. 1967-69, Legislator of Yr. 1993), UN Assn. (bd. dirs.), Chgo. Assn. Commerce and Industry (bd. dirs.). Home: 1290 N Western Ave Lake Forest IL 60045-1258 E-mail: k16v13@aol.com.

FREDERICKS, DOLORES ELIZABETH, music educator; b. Johnson City, Tenn., Aug. 16, 1952; d. William Alexander and Virginia Rauhof Powers; m. George Washington Fredericks, Nov. 28. MusB in music edn., East Tenn. State U., 1970—74, MusM in music edn., 1996—98. Cert. Tennessee Career Ladder Tchr. - Level II Tenn. State Bd. of Edn., 1990. Music tchr. Kimball Music Co., Johnson City, Tenn., 1971—77; music dir./liturgist/choir dir. St. Mary's Cath. Ch., Johnson City, Tenn. Mem.: Music Educators Nat. Conf. (licentiate), Delta Kappa Gamma (licentiate). Roman Catholic. Avocation: travel. Home: 602 Sharon Drive Johnson City TN 37604 Office: South Side Sch 1011 Southwest Ave Johnson City TN 37604 Personal E-mail: dfmusic@yahoo.com. E-mail: fredericksd@jcs.k12.tn.us.

FREDERICKS, FRANCES M. state legislator, nurse; b. New Orleans, Sept. 23, 1935; widowed. Student, St. Mary's Sch. Nursing, Miss. Gulf Coast Jr. Coll. Mem. Miss. Ho. of Reps., 1991—; vice chmn. local and pvt. com.; mem. judiciary B, penitentiary, pub. health coms.; mem. ways and means com. Mem. bi-racial adv. com. Harrison County Schs. Mem. NAACP, Nat. Coun. Negro Women, A.F.G.E. Local 2238, North Gulfport Civic Club. Democrat. Baptist. Home: PO Box 10186 Gulfport MS 39505-0186 Office: State Capitol Bldg PO Box 1018 Rm 102C Jackson MS 39215

FREDERICKS, SHARON KAY, nurse's aide; b. Grand Rapids, Mich., July 12, 1942; d. Leroy and Edith Luella (Crawford) Fredericks. Cert. in Interior Decorating, LaSalle U., 1975; AAS, Community Svc. Asst., Kalamazoo Valley Coll., 1982; assoc. paralegal studies, Internat. Corr. Schs., Scranton, Pa., 1993; AAS in Bus. Mgmt., Davenport Coll., 1994, BBA in Bus. Adminstrn., 1997. Cashier Goodwill Industries, Battle Creek, Mich., 1963; dishwasher Woolworths, Kalamazoo, 1963; nurses aide Mary L. Bocher, Kalamazoo, 1964-69, Sisters St. Joseph, Nazareth, Mich., 1976-98; kitchen aide Saga Foods, Kalamazoo Valley C.C., 1981-82, Saga Foods, Nazareth Coll., 1983-84; ind. sales rep. Avon, 2000—01. Vol. Portage Ctrl. Jr. and Sr. HS, 1961—62, Bronson Meth. Hosp., Kalamazoo, 1961—62, nurse aide bloodmobiles, 1970—75; nurse aide ARC, 1964—69, Brogess Med. Ctr., 1977, CASA Kalamazoo Juvenile Ct., 1980—86; participant neighborhood watch Vine Neighborhood, Kalamazoo, 1985—88; vol., adminstrv. aide Kalamazoo, 1991—; vol. monitor Kalamazoo Women's Festival, 1991, 1992; mem. grounds com. New Horizon Village, Kalamazoo, 1998, mem. neighborhood watch com., 1999, chair pet com.; active Mich. Campaign for Quality Care, 2002—; foster grandparent sr. svc. elem. sch., 2004—; sec.-treas. Order St. Francis Secular, 1976—79, pres. dir. pres. pub. rels. and bulls., 1979—81; vol. Cath. Family Svcs., 1991—. Named Vol. of the Month, Kalamazoo Regional Psychiat. Hosp., 1976, Vol. of the Week, Cath. Family Svcs., 1993, 1995; recipient John Edgar Hoover Gold medal, 1991; Thomas F. Reed Jr. scholar, Davenport Coll., 1993. Mem.: AARP (Mich. amb. vol. 2002—03, v.p., pub. rels. vol. A.A. chpt. 1020 Kalamazoo br. 2003—), Davenport U. Alumni Assn. Roman Catholic. Avocations: photography, textile painting, helping people, reading, learning wildlife, environmental policies, pet policies, governmental policies. Home: 2310 Inverness Ln Apt 204 Kalamazoo MI 49048-1459

FREDERIKSEN, MARILYNN C. physician; b. Chgo., Sept. 12, 1949; d. Paul H. and Susanne (Ostergren) Conners; m. James W. Frederiksen, July 11, 1971; children: John K., Paul S., Britt L. BA, Cornell Coll., 1970; MD, Boston U., 1974; grad. Exec. Leadership in Acad. Medicine, Allegheny U. Health Scis., 1998. Diplomate Am. Bd. Ob-Gyn., Am. Bd. Maternal-Fetal Medicine, Am. Bd. Clin. Pharmacology. Pediat. intern U. Md. Hosp., 1974-75, resident in pediat., 1975-76; resident in ob-gyn. Boston Hosp. for women, 1976-79; fellow in maternal fetal medicine Northwestern U., 1979-81, fellow clin. pharmacology, 1981-83, instr. ob-gyn., 1981-83, asst. prof. ob-gyn., assoc. clin. pharmacology, 1983-91, assoc. prof. ob-gyn., 1991—, sect. chief gen. ob-gyn., 1993—2001. Mem. gen. faculty com. Northwestern U., Chgo., 1994—97, mem. ob-gyn. adv. panel, 1985—2000, chair ob-gyn. adv. panel, 2000—; mem. U.S. Pharm. Com. Revision, Rockville, Md., 1986—; del. U.S. Pharm. conv. Northwestern U. Med. Sch., 1990, 95, 2000; mem. gen. clinic rsch. ctr. com. NIH, 1989—93, chairperson, 1992—93; mem. Task Force Writing Group on Asthma in Pregnancy, Nat. Heart, Lung and Blood Inst., 1991—92; examiner Am. Bd. Ob-Gyn., 1997—; mem. Task Force Working Group, Nat. Bd. Med. Examiners, 1997—98, mem. acute care com., 1999—2001. Mem. editorial bd. Clin. Pharmacology & Therapeutics, 1993; contbr. numerous articles to profl. jours. Bd. dirs. Cornell Coll. Alumni Assn., Mt. Vernon, Iowa, 1986—90, PRCH, 1997—, Planned Parenthood of Chgo. Area, 1999—, Northwestern Med. Faculty Found., 1995—98. Recipient Pharm. Mfrs. Assn. Found. Faculty Devel. award, 1984-86, Civil Liberties award ACLU, 1991. Fellow Am. Coll. Ob-Gyn.; mem. Soc. Maternal Fetal Medicine, Ctrl. Assn. Obstetricians and Gynecologists (bd. dirs. 1997-99), Am. Soc. Clin. Pharmacology and Therapeutics (bd. dirs. 1994-97), Chgo. Gynecologic Soc. (treas. 1994-97), Phi Beta Kappa. Episcopalian. Avocations: gardening, needlework. Office: Northwestern Perinatal Assocs Stte 1230 680 N Lake Shore Dr Chicago IL 60611 E-mail: mcf810@northwestern.edu.

FREDIANI, DIANE MARIE, graphics designer, interior designer, executive secretary; b. Bklyn., June 20, 1963; d. Albert Michael and Mary (Piantino) F. BFA in Graphic Design, Centenary Coll., 1985, teaching cert., 1991. Cert. graphic designer. Cashier, dept. supr. Reynolds, Hackettstown, N.J., 1982-85, window displays and promotions staff, 1985-86; clerical asst. AT&T, Basking Ridge, N.J., 1986-87, typesetter, bd. artist Parsippany, N.J., 1988-89, project mgr. interior design Basking Ridge, 1989-99, supplier diversity specialist supplier mgmt. divsn., 1999—. Graphic designer St. Mary's Sch., Hackettstown, 1985—; nominee for White House Fellowship Com., 1994. Mem. Centenary Alumni Assn. (forensic judge oral speaking competitions 1993—), N.J. Supplier Diversity Devel. Coun., N.Y./N.J. Minority Purchasing Coun. (sec. 1999—). Roman Catholic. Avocations: photography, painting, reading, going to sporting events. Home: 203 Hudson Ct Hackettstown NJ 07840-1690 Office: AT&T 295 N Maple Ave Basking Ridge NJ 07920-1025

FREDRICK, SUSAN WALKER, tax company manager; b. Painesville, Ohio, Nov. 17, 1948; d. Floyd Clayton and Margaret (Merkel) Walker; m. Stephan Douglas Fredrick, Oct. 20, 1973. BS, Mt. Union Coll., Alliance, Ohio, 1970; MS, U. Conn., 1973. Rsch. asst. Boyce Thompson Inst., Yonkers, NY, 1971-74; dir. quality control Lawley, Matusky, Skelly, Tappan, NY, 1974-75; field supr. Ecological Analysts, Middletown, NY, 1975-76; scientist Pandullo Quirk Assocs., Wayne, NJ, 1976-78; editor Biosis. Info. Service, Phila., 1978-80; tax preparer H&R Block, Inc., Malvern, Pa., 1978-80, dist. mgr. King of Prussia and West Chester, Pa., 1980—2002, franchise dist. mgr. Easton, Md., 2002—. Guest lectr. Temple U., 1981-86. Mem. Nat. Assn. Enrolled Agts., Pa. Soc. Enrolled Agts., Nat. Assn. Underwater Instrs. (active instr.), Keystone Divers Club (West Chester, Pa.). Avocations: scuba diving, hiking, swimming. Office: 8719 Brooks Ln Unit 1 Easton MD

FREDRICKSON, KAREN LORAINE, librarian; b. Kansas City, Mo., Sept. 27, 1952; d. Kenneth Eugene Kruse and Loraine Lulu (Neugebauer) Morse; m. Timothy Dean Cox, Sept. 1, 1973 (dec. Sept. 1984); m. David Dean Fredrickson, June 10, 1989; children: Jennifer, Rachel. BS, Cen. Mo. State U., 1974, MS, 1979. Cert. tchr. Kans., Mo. Tchr./libr. Lone Jack (Mo.) Schs., 1974-76; tchr. Clarksville-Montgomery County Schs., Tenn., 1977, tchr./libr. St John's Luth. Sch., Indpls., 1978-82; libr. media specialist Lawrence (Kans.) Public Schs., 1985—. Mem. Lawrence In-Svc. Coun., 1986-88. Recipient Kans. Ednl. Excellence Program award Southwestern Bell, Lawrence, 1991. Mem. ALA, Am. Assn. Sch. Libr., Kans. Assn. Sch. Libr. Luth. Avocations: sewing, crocheting. Office: Langston Hughes Sch 1101 George Williams Way Lawrence KS 66049 E-mail: klfredri@usd497.org.

FREDRICKSON, MARILYN H. secondary school educator, art educator, artist; d. Herbert H. and Hazel I. Fredrickson. BA, Waldorf Jr. Coll., Forest City, Iowa, 1961; BS, Luther Coll., 1963; MS, Winona State U., 1972. Visual arts educator Kasson (Minn.)-Mantorville H.S., 1963—, art dept. head, 1963—. Mentor to new educators Kasson Mantorville Schs., 1972—, mem. H.S. curriculum com., 2000—, visual arts scholarship fund head art dept., 2000—. Supt. art dept. Goodhue County Fair Assn., Zumbrota, 1973—; visual arts tchr. Cmty. Edn., Rochester, Kasson and Zumbrota, 1980—. Named Tchr. of Yr., K-Mantorville Edn. Minn., 1999. Mem.: Minn. Edn. Assn. (Tchr. of Excellence award 1999), Minn. Art Educators (Minn. State Art Educator of Yr. 2002), Nat. Art Educators. Lutheran. Avocations: painting, calligraphy, pottery, quilting, gardening. Home: 42970 County 4 Blvd Zumbrota MN 55992

FREDRIK, BURRY, theatrical producer, director; b. NYC, Aug. 9, 1925; d. Fredric Kreuger and Erna Anna (Burry) Gerber; m. Gerard E. Mounier, Dec. 27, 1945 (div. 1949). Grad., Sarah Lawrence Coll., 1947. Ind. theatrical dir., producer, U.S. and abroad, 1955—; lit. mgr., dir. Boston Post Road Stage Co., 1988-92; artistic dir. Fairfield County Stage Co. (formerly Boston Post Road Stage), 1992-93. Prodr.: (Broadway plays) Too Good to be True, 1964—65 (nominated Tony award, 1965), Travesties, 1976 (Tony award, 1976), An Almost Perfect Person, 1977, The Night of the Tribades, 1978, To Grandmother's House We Go, 1981, The Royal Family, 1975—76 (Drama Desk award, 1976), (off-Broadway plays) Thieves Carnival, 1955 (Spl. Tony award, 1955), Exiles, 1956 (OBIE award, 1956), Buried Child (Pulitzer prize, 1980); dir.: (nat. tours) Misalliance, 1953, Milk and Honey, 1963, Dark at the Top of the Stairs, 1958, Dear Love, 1971, To Grandmother's House We Go, 1982, (off-Broadway prodns.) The Decameron, 1961, Catholic School Girls, 1981, (Broadway prodn.) Wild and Wonderful, 1972; prodr.: (off-Broadway) Pretzels, 1974; dir.: (plays, Sad Hotel) White Barn Theatre, 2001—; (plays, Swansong), 2002—. Chmn. Weston Commn. Arts, 1997—2000; mem. fin. commn., trustee Long Wharf Theatre, New Haven, 1998—. Recipient Disting. Adv. Arts award, State of Conn. Commn. Arts, 2001. Home and Office: 51 Hillside Rd N Weston CT 06883-1513 Home Fax: 203-222-9478.

FREE, ANN COTTRELL, writer; b. June 4, 1916; d. Emmett Drewry and Emily (Blake) Cottrell; m. James Stillman Free, Feb. 24, 1950; 1 child, Elissa. Grad., Collegiate Sch. for Girls, Richmond, 1934; student Richmond divsn., Coll. William and Mary (now Va. Commonwealth U.), 1934-36; AB, Barnard Coll. Columbia U., 1938. Reporter Richmond Times Dispatch, 1938-40; Washington corr. Newsweek, 1940-41, Chgo. Sun, 1941-43, N.Y. Herald Tribune, 1943-46; pub. info. dir., China corr. UN Relief-Rehab. Adminstrn., China Mission, Shanghai, 1946-47; corr. Mid. and Near East and Europe, 1947-48; writer-photographer Marshall Plan, Washington/Western Europe, 1949-50; Washington corr. N.Am. Newspaper Alliance, 1955—85; former Washington editor EnviroSouth Quar., 1977-82; freelance writer. Pres. Flying Fox Press. Author: (book) Forever the Wild Mare, 1963, Animals, Nature and Albert Schweitzer, 1982, No Room, Save in the Heart, 1987, Since Silent Spring: Our Debt to Albert Schweitzer and Rachel Carson, 1992; contbr. oral history Animal Advocacy, Columbia U., oral history Telling Their Story is All I Can Do, 2001. Hon. founding mem. Friends of the Rachel Carson nat. Wildlife Refuge; chmn. Mrs. Roosevelt's Press Conf. Assn., 1943; cons. expert Rachel Carson Coun.; v.p. Vieques (P.R.) Humane Soc.; past coord. Albert Schweitzer Summer Fellows Program; past bd. dirs. Albert Schweitzer Fellowship; pres. Albert Schweitzer Coun. Animals and Environment; trustee Albert Schweitzer Animal Welfare Fund. Named to Va. Comms. Hall of Fame, 1996; recipient Dodd Mead-Boy's Life Writing award, 1963, Albert Schweitzer medal, Animal Welfare Inst., 1963, Jr. Book award cert., Boys Club Am., 1964, Humanitarian of the Yr. award, Washington Animal Rescue League, 1971, Montgomery County Humane Soc., 1971, Washington Humane Soc., 1983, News Writing award, Dog Writers Assn., 1975, 1978, Rachel Carson Legacy award, 1987, Disting. Alumni award, Collegiate Schs., 1992, Cert. Appreciation for role in establishing Rachel Carson Nat. Wildlife Refuge, Dept. Interior Fish and Wildlife Svc., 1995, Lifetime Svc. award, Washington Animal Rescue League, 1997. Mem.: Am. News Women's Club, Nat. Press Club, Soc. Woman Geographers. Home: 4700 Jamestown Rd Bethesda MD 20816-2923 also: 56 Bell's Ln Lantz Mill Edinburg VA 22824 E-mail: anncottrellfree@aol.com.

FREE, HELEN MURRAY, chemist, consultant; b. Pitts., Feb. 20, 1923; d. James Summerville and Daisy (Piper) Murray; m. Alfred H. Free, Oct. 18, 1947; children: Eric, Penny, Kurt, Jake, Bonnie, Nina. BA in Chemistry, Coll. of Wooster, Ohio, 1944, DSc (hon.), 1992; MA in Clin. Lab. Mgmt., Ctrl. Mich. U., 1978, DSc (hon.), 1993. Cert. clin. chemist Nat. Registry Cert. Chemists. Chemist Miles Labs., Elkhart, Ind., 1944—78, dir. mktg. svcs. rsch. products divsn., 1978-82; chemist, mgr., cons. diagnostics divsn. Bayer HealthCare, Elkhart, 1982—. Mem. adj. faculty Ind. U., South Bend, 1975—96. Author (with others): (books) Urodynamics and Urinalysis in Clinical Laboratory Practice, 1972, 1976; contbr. articles to encys. and profl. jours. Bd. dirs. Nat. Inventors Hall of Fame Found.; women's chmn. Centennial of Elkhart, 1958; mem. adv. bd. Intellectual Property Sch. Law, Akron U.; indsl. adv. bd. chemistry/chem. engring. Tri-State U., Angola, Ind. Named Woman of Yr., YWCA, 1993, Kilby Found. laureate, 1996;

named to Hall of Excellence, Ohio Found. Ind. Colls., 1992, Nat. Inventors Hall of Fame, 2000, Engring. and Sci. Hall of Fame, 1996; recipient Disting. Alumni award, Coll. of Wooster, 1980, award, Medi Econ. Press, 1986, Nat. Leadership award, Lab. Pub. Svc., 1994. Fellow: AAAS, Royal Soc. Chemistry, Am. Inst. Chemists (co-recipient Chgo. award 1967); mem.: Nat. Com. Clin. Lab. Stds. [illegible] Clin. Lab. Sci. (chmn. assembly, Achievement award 1976), Soc. Chem. Industry (hon.), Assn. Clin. Scientists (diploma of honor 1992), Am. Assn. Clin. Chemistry (coun., bd. dirs., nat. membership com., nominating com. and pub. rels. com., coord. profl. affairs, pres.), Am. Chem. Soc. (pres. 1993, bd. dirs., chmn. Chemistry Week task force, bd. com. pub. affairs and pub. rels., chmn. women chemists com., internat. activities com., grants and awards com., prof. and mem. rels. com., nominating com., coun. policy pub. affairs and budget, councilor, chair Progress project, Garvan medal 1980, Svc. award local chpt. 1981, co-recipient Mosher award 1983, 1st recipient Helen M. Free Pub. Outreach award 1995, Helen M. Free award named in her honor 1995), Altrusa (pres. 1982—83, bd. dirs.), Sigma Delta Epsilon (hon.), Iota Sigma Pi (hon.). Presbyterian. Achievements include patents in field. Home: 3752 E Jackson Blvd Elkhart IN 46516-5205 Office: Bayer HealthCare Diagnostics Divsn 1884 Miles Ave Elkhart IN 46514-2291 E-mail: Hmfree23@aol.com., helen.free.b@bayer.com.

FREE, MARY MOORE, biological and medical anthropologist; b. Paris, Tex., Mar. 6, 1933; d. Dudley Crawford and Margie Lou (Moore) Hubbard; m. Dwight Allen Free Jr., June 26, 1954 (dec.); children: Hardy (dec.), Dudley (dec.), Margery, Caroline. Student, Ward-Belmont Coll., 1951; BS, So. Meth. U., 1954, MLA, 1981, MA, 1987, PhD, 1989. Instr. So. Meth. U., Dallas, 1982-89, prof. continuing edn., 1989-90; prof. So. Meth. U., Dedman Coll., Dallas, 1990—; adj. asst. prof. dept. anthropology So. Meth. U., Dallas, 1990—. Prof. Richland C.C., Dallas, 1986; house anthropologist Baylor U. Med. Ctr., mem. adv. bd. Inst. for Study of Earth and Man, 1995, preceptor clin. edn. affiliation, 1990—, chair Class 1954 sustentation drive, organ/tissue transplantation task force, 1997; cardiothoracic transplantation team Baylor U. Med. Ctr., S.W. transplantation team Baylor U. Med. Ctr./U. Tex. Southwestern Med. Sch., 1990— (cardiothoracic transplantation award for excellence in svc., 1998); adv. bd. geriatrics Vis. Nurse Assn., Dallas, 1984-91; presenter in field anthropology, medicine, women's issues; bd. Dedman Coll. SMU Excellence in Sci. Lecture Series, Dallas Soc. SMU, Collegium de Vinci, SMU; contbr. AMA/JAMA protocol on authorship; spokesperson, adv. bd. Lisa Landry Childress Found. for Organ Donation Awareness. Author: The Private World of the Hermitage: Lifestyles of the Rich and Old in an Elite Retirement Home, 1995; contbr. numerous chpts. in sci. books, ednl. TV, and articles to Anthropology Newsletter, Am. Anthropologist, Am. Jour. Cardiology, Cahiers de Sociologie Economique et Culturelle-Ethnopsycholie, Jour. Heart Failure, Jour. Internat. Soc. Dermatology, Jour. Leadership Ctr., Baylor Health Care System, Jour. Lisa Landry Childrens Found., ; mem. editl. bd. Baylor U. Med. Ctr. Procs.; editor/contbr. Jour. Kimberly H. Courtwright and Joseph W. Summers Inst. of Metabolic Disease, BUMC, 1998; contbr. numerous articles to profl. jours. Bd. dirs. New Hearts and Lungs, Baylor Med. Ctr., 1994—, Lisa Landry Childress Found. for Organ Donor Awareness, Victims Outreach, 1997—, Isis Soc. and internat. issues com. Baylor U. Med. Ctr.; active various svc. and social orgns. Named one of Notable Women of Tex., 1984; recipient Outstanding Svc. Cardiothoracic Transplantation award Baylor U. Med. Ctr., 1998; provide Dr. Mary Moore Free Endowment for grad. study fieldwork in anthropology So. Meth. U. Fellow Am. Anthrop. Assn., Inst. for Study of Earth and Man; mem. AAAS, Internat. Soc. Heart Failure (sci. adv. bd.), Internat. Acad. Cardiology Inc. (internat. sci. adv. bd.), Internat. Congress Heart Disease (internat. sci. adv. bd.), Internat. Soc. Heart Disease (sci. adv. bd.), Soc. Heart Edn. (sci. adv. bd.), Dallas Women's Club, Dallas Petroleum Club, Brook Hollow Golf Club, Pi Beta Phi. Methodist. Achievements include development of position of house anthropologist in non-academic medical center, community medicine program; cross-cultural research on old age, women and cardiology. Home: 4356 Edmondson Ave Dallas TX 75205-2602 Office: Baylor U Med Ctr 3500 Gaston Ave Dallas TX 75246-2096

FREEBORN, JOANN LEE, state legislator, farmer, former educator; m. Warren S. Freeborn Jr. BS, Kans. State U., 1966. Mem. from Dist. 107, Kans. State Ho. of Reps., 1992—, chmn. environ. com., mem. agr. com., mem. fed. and state affairs com. Home: 1904 N 240th Rd Concordia KS 66901

FREECE, DEBBIE ANN, trade association executive; b. Dayton, Ohio; d. Lloyd M. and Dorothy E. (Deblin) Cannon; m. Eric W. Freece; children: Ian C., Katelyn A. BSN, Ohio State U., 1974, MS, 1979. Cert. gerontol. nurse ANCC. DON Arlington Ct. Nursing Home, Columbus, Ohio, 1974-78; project dir. Ohio Dept. Health, Columbus, 1979-82; pvt. practice geriatric nurse cons. Columbus, 1983-91; exec. dir. Mid-Ohio Dist. Nurses Assn., Columbus, 1991—. Cons. Ohio Tchg. Network, Columbus, 1987-90, Ohio Health Care Bd., Columbus, 1993-95, Legis. Study Com., Columbus, 1993-95; mem. citizen adv. bd. Columbus Developmental Ctr., 1993-96; bd. trustees Franklin County Resdl. Svcs., 1996—. Pres. Evangelical Luth. Ch. Women Ascension Luth. Ch., Columbus, 1985-88, pres. presch. bd., 1990-93; sec. Whetstone HS PTA, 2002—. Mem. Ohio Nurses Assn. (del. 1995—, Dorothy A. Cornelius Leadership fellow 1995), Alpha Tau Delta Epsilon Pi (sec. 1990-95 1998—), Sigma Theta Tau. Republican. Office: Mid-Ohio Dist Nurses Assn 1460 W Lane Ave Columbus OH 43221-3949

FREED, RITA EVELYN, curator, Egyptologist, educator; b. Newark, June 29, 1952; d. Samuel David and Gertrude (Housman) F. BA in Classical and Nr. Ea. Archaeology, Bibl. Studies, Wellesley Coll.; cert. in museology, MA, PhD, NYU. Exhbn. asst. Egypt's minor arts Mus. Fine Arts, Boston, 1978-82, joint head dept. art of ancient world Ancient Egyptian, Nubian and Near Ea. Art Norma-Jean Calderwood Curator, 1989—; curator Egyptian exhbn. univ. gallery U. Memphis, 1983, curator Egyptian antiquities, founding dir., 1984-89, assoc. prof. dept. art, 1983-89; adj. prof. Wellesley Coll., 1991—. Part-time rsch. asst. dept. Egyptian and classical art Bklyn. Mus., 1976-78; rschr. Egyptian dept. Met. Mus. Art, 1977-78, lectr. dept. pub. edn., 1978; lectr. art Adelphi U., 1978-79; mem. archaeol. survey team Idalion Excavations, Dhali, Cyprus, 1973; site supr. excavation of Philistine temple, Tel Qasile, Tel Aviv, 1973; field archaeologist expdn. photographer Mendes Excavations, Ea. Delta, Egypt, 1977; small finds registrar Memphis Excavations, Mitrahineh, Egypt, 1988; epigrapher Giza Mastabas Project, Egypt, 1989; co-project dir. Boston-Penn Expdn., Bersheh, Egypt, 1990, Saqqara, Egypt, 1992—. Contbr. articles and revs. to profl. jours. and books; author exhbn. catalogues. U.S. trustee Schiff-Giorgini Found.; mem. Amarna Rsch. Found. Ford Found. fellow, Slater Fgn. Study fellow; Trustee fellow and Durant scholar of Wellesley Coll.; NSF rsch. grantee. Mem. Am. Rsch. Ctr. in Egypt (bd. govs.), Soc. for Study Egyptian Antiquities, Egypt Exploration Soc., Egyptological Seminar, Internat. Assn. Egyptologists (N.Am. rep.), Internat. Coun. Mus. (Am. rep.), Am. Assn. Mus., Com. Internat. Egyptology (former chmn.), Phi Beta Kappa. Office: Mus Fine Arts 465 Huntington Ave Boston MA 02115-5597

FREEDLENDER, SUSAN See HOMESTEAD, SUSAN E.

FREEDMAN, HELEN E. justice; b. N.Y.C., Dec. 15, 1942; d. David Simeon and Frances (Fisher) Edelstein; m. Henry A. Freedman, June 7, 1964; children: Katherine Eleanor, Elizabeth Sarah. BA, Smith Coll., 1963; JD, NYU, 1967. Bar: N.Y. 1970, U.S. Dist. Ct. (so. and ea. dists.), U.S. Supreme Ct. 1979. Staff atty. office of gen. counsel Am. Arbitration Assn., N.Y.C., 1967-69; assoc. Hubbel, Cohen & Stiefel, N.Y.C., 1970-71, Shaw, Bernstein, Scheuer, Boyden & Sarnoff, N.Y.C., 1971-74; law sec. Civil Ct., N.Y.C., 1974-76; sr. atty. housing litigation bur. N.Y.C. Dept. Housing Preservation and Devel., 1976; supervising atty. Dist. Coun. 37 Legal Svcs. Plan, N.Y.C., 1976-78; judge Civil Ct., N.Y.C., 1979-88; acting justice Supreme Ct., N.Y.C., 1984-88, justice, 1989-95; apptd. to appellate term 1st dept. NY Supreme Ct., N.Y.C., 1995-99, apptd. to comml. divsn., 2000—, pres. judge mass tort litigation panel, 2002—. Co-chair State Judges Mass Tort Litigation Com.; mem. pattern jury instrns. com., Supreme Ct. Justices; adj. prof. N.Y. Law Sch., 1999, 2000, 02; [illegible] Objections, 1999, rev. edits., 2000, 01, 02; contbr. articles to profl. jours. Recipent Disting. Alumna award Smith Coll., 2000. Fellow Am. Bar Found., N.Y. State Bar Found.; mem. ABA (chair small claims ct. com. 1986-89, bioethics com. nat. conf. spl. ct. judges, N.Y. State Ct. del. to ann. meetings, nat. conf. spl. ct. judges, 1987, 88, Spl. Cts. Conf. award 1987, 88, 93, Jud. Excellence award 1998), Nat. Assn. Women Judges, N.Y. State Bar Assn. (del.), N.Y. Fed. State Jud. Coun., N.Y. Women's Bar Assn., N.Y. State Assn. Women Judges (pres. 1995-97), Assn. of Bar of City of N.Y. (mem. various coms., chair com. med. malpractice, v.p. 1994-95), Judges and Lawyers Breast Cancer Alert (pres.). Home: 150 W 96th St New York NY 10025-6469 Office: NY Supreme Ct 60 Centre New York NY 10007-1488

FREEDMAN, JUDITH GREENBERG, state legislator, importer; b. Bridgeport, Conn., Mar. 11, 1939; d. Samuel Howard and Dorothy (Hoffman) G.; m. Samuel Sumner, Dec. 24, 1964; 1 child, Martha Ann. Student, Boston U., 1957-58, U. Mich., 1958-59; BS, So. Conn. State U., 1961, MS, 1972. Tchr. Hollywood (Fla.) Pub. Schs., 1961-62, White Plains (N.Y.) Pub. Schs., 1962-64, Wilton (Conn.) Pub. Schs., 1964-66, Weston (Conn.) Pub. Schs., 1966-72, tutor, 1977-80, tchr., 1982-84; owner Judith's Fancy, Westport, Conn., 1984—; mem. Dist. 26 Conn. Senate, Hartford, 1987—. Ranking mem. human svcs. com., 1987—88; ins. com., 1987—94; ranking mem. appropriations com., 1989—94; chmn. program rev. and investigation, 1992—94; chmn. commn. on innovation and productivity, 1994—; dep. pres. pro tem Conn. Senate, 1995—97, 1995—, ranking mem. edn. com., 1997—2000, chair edn. com., 1998—2000, asst. minority leader, 1998—, co-chair edn. sub. com. appropriations, 1998—, mem. legis. mgmt. com., 1998—, mem. appropriation com., 1998—, ranking mem. higher edn. com., 2002—; mem. exec. com. ea. region Coun. State Govts.; chair program rev. and investigation, 2000—; dep. minority leader, 2000; edn. commn. of the states Conn. steering com., 2000. Pres., v.p. 4th Congl. Rep. Women's Assn., 1976-80; pres. Rep. Women of Westport, 1976-79; mem. Bd. Edn., Westport, 1983-87, 89—; treas. Conn. Order Women Legislators. Mem. Order of Women Legislators (treas.). Jewish. Avocations: reading, art, golf. Home: 17 Crawford Rd Westport CT 06880-1823 Office Phone: 860-240-8826.

FREEDMAN, MARYANN SACCOMANDO, lawyer; b. Buffalo, N.Y., Sept. 12, 1934; d. James Vincent Saccomando and Rosaria Rizzo; m. Robert P. Freedman, Apr. 9, 1961; children: Brenda M., Donald V. JD, U. Buffalo, 1958. Bar: N.Y., 1959; U.S. Dist. Ct. (we. dist.) N.Y., 1959; U.S. Bankruptcy Ct., 1959. U.S. Supreme Ct., 1963. Law clk. Saperston, McNaughton & Saperston, 1957-59, assoc., 1959-61; ptnr. Freedman & Freedman, 1961-75, 93-95; confidential legal rsch. asst. Buffalo City Ct., 1972-75; asst. atty. gen. N.Y. State Dept. of Law, 1975-77; law clk., matrimonial referee, hearing referee N.Y. State Supreme Ct., 1977-90, 80-90; spl. counsel Lavin & Kleiman, 1991-95; of counsel Cohen & Lombardo, P.C., 1995—. Hearing referee Jud. Conduct Commn., 1998—; founder and panel mem. Alliance for Dispute Resolution, 1997—; arbitrator, mediator U.S. Arbitration and Mediation of Upstate N.Y., 1992-94, arbitrator Am. Arbitration Assn., 1985—; lectr. Buffalo & Erie Co. Police Acad., 1975-86, Erie Co. Emergency Med. Tech. Tng. Program, 1975-83; asst. prof. paralegal studies Erie C.C., 1975-76; guest lectr. SUNY Coll., Buffalo, others. Contbr. articles to profl. jours. and publs. Mem. numerous civic orgns. including steering com. Women's Pavilion Pan Am 2001, 1999—, Italian-Am. Women of We. N.Y., 1994—, Temple Beth Zion Sisterhood, Buffalo Geol. Soc., others. Named Western N.Y. Women's Hall of Fame, 2001; recipient Outstanding Italian Am. Woman award, Ann. of Italian Am. Women, Western N.Y., 1989, Woman of Yr. award, Buffalo Philharmonic Orchestra, 1993. Mem.: ABA (ho. of dels. 1986—2002), Legal Svcs. for the Elderly (dir. 1978—85, others), Legal Aid Bur. (bd. dirs. 1980—81), Vol. Lawyers Project (adv. coun. 1982—86), Assn. Women Lawyers, Mid-Atlantic Conf. of State Bar Pres., N.Y. State Bar Jour. (bd. editors 1983—97), Pre-Trial Svcs., Inc. (pres. 1981), Erie County Aid to Indigent Prisoners Soc., Inc. (pres. 1981—82), Erie County Bar Found. (treas. 1962—63, bd. dirs. 1974—77, others), Erie County Bar Assn. (v.p. 1980—81, pres. 1981—82, others), N.Y. State Bar Found. (bd. dirs. 1982—, v.p. 1994—97, pres. 1997—2000, others), N.Y. State Bar Assn. (exec. com. 1982—89, sec. 1984—86, pres.-elect/chair ho. of dels. 1986—87, pres. 1987—88, Ruth G. Schapiro award 1994, others). Avocations: rocks, music, gardening, reading. Office: Cohen & Lombardo PC 343 Elmwood Ave Buffalo NY 14222-2203

FREEDMAN, SANDRA WARSHAW, former mayor; b. Newark, Sept. 21, 1943; m. Michael J. Freedman; 3 children. BA in Govt., U. Miami, 1965. Mem. Tampa (Fla.) City Coun., 1974—, chmn., 1983-86; mayor City of Tampa, 1986-95. Author: Specialties of the House (Recipes for People on the Go!), 2002. Bd. dirs. Jewish Cmty. Ctr., Boys and Girls Clubs Greater Tampa, Hillsborough Coalition for Health, Tampa Cmty. Concert Assn., Hillsborough Edn. Found., Judeo Christian Clinic, NCCJ, Human Rights Task Force; mem. sports adv. bd. Hillsborough Community Coll., 1975-76; sec. Downtown Devel. Authority, 1977-78; bd. dirs., v.p. Fla. Gulf Coast Symphony, 1979-80; vice chmn. Met. Planning Orgn., 1981-82; corp. mem. Neighborhood Housing Service; bd. fellows U. Tampa; mem. steering com. Hillsborough County Council of Govt.'s Constituency for Children; mem. exec. bd. Tampa/Hillsborough Young Adult Forum; chmn. bd. trustees Berkeley Prep. Sch.; trustee Tampa Bay Performing Arts Ctr., Inc., Tampa Mus.; mem. ethics com. Meml. Hosp.; mem. Tampa Preservation, Inc., Tampa/Hillsborough County Youth Council, Davis Islands Civic Assn., Tampa Hist. Soc., Met. Ministries Adv. Bd., Rodeph Sholom Synagogue, Sword of Hope Guild of Am. Cancer Soc., Friends of Arts. Recipient Spessar L. Holland Meml. award Tampa Bay Com. for Good Govt., 1975-76, Human Rights award City of Tampa, 1980, award Soroptimist Internat. Tampa, 1981, Status of Women award Zonta of Tampa II, 1986, Woman of Achievement award Bus. & Profl. Women, Jewish Nat. Fund Tree of Life award, Disting. Citizen award U. South Fla., 1995, Nat. Conf. of Christian and Jews Humanitarian award, 1995; named to Fla. Home Builders Hall of Fame. Mem. Hillsborough County Bar Aux., Greater Tampa C. of C., C. of C. Com. of 100 (exec. com.), Fla. League of Cities (bd. dirs.), Tampa Urban League, Nat. Council Jewish Women, U. Miami Alumni Assn., Athena Soc., Hadassah. Office: 3435 Bayshore Blvd Apt 700 Tampa FL 33629-8827

FREEDMAN, WENDY LAUREL, astronomer, educator; b. Toronto, Ont., Can., July 17, 1957; arrived in U.S., 1984; d. Harvey Bernard and Sonya Lynn Freedman; m. Barry F. Madore, June 23, 1985. BSc, U. Toronto, 1979, PhD in astronomy and astrophysics, 1984. Fellow Carnegie Observatories, Pasadena, Calif., 1984-87, faculty, 1987—, 2003—, Crawford H. Greenewalt chair dir., 2003—. Bd. dirs. Assn. Univs. for Rsch. in Astronomy, Inc., Washington; co-chair com. on astronomy and astrophysics NRC, 2002—. Fellow AAAS; mem. Nat. Acad. Scis., Am. Astron. Soc. Office: Carnegie Observatories 813 Santa Barbara St Pasadena CA 91101-1292*

FREEMAN, ANNE FRANCES, artist, freelance/self-employed illustrator; b. Milw., Sept. 13, 1936; d. Edward Joseph and Agatha Gertrude (Mihm) Huether; m. John Henry Freeman, June 27, 1964; children: John Edward, Robert William. BA, Elmira Coll., 1964. Rsch. assoc. The Corning (N.Y.) Mus. Glass, 1957-59, coord. ednl. svcs., 1959-61, curator edn., 1962-63; freelance graphic artist, writer Corning Glass Works, 1963-64; asst. to dir. communications & employee rels. Crouse Hinds Corp., Syracuse, N.Y., 1964-65; freelance artist Southborough, Mass., 1977—. Tchr., jr. curator The Corning Mus. Glass, 1961-63, editor jr. curator's newsletter, 1961-63. Author: Glass and Man, 1962. Chair Southborough Sch. Bd., 1976-77, Algonquin Regional High Sch. Com. Bd., Northborough, Mass., 1978-79; treas. Southborough Cultural Arts Coun., 1983-85, chmn., 1986. Mem. [illegible] Doll Artists, Friends of Southborough Arts Ctr., Cape Cod Art Assn., Chatham Art Ctr., ARTS Worcester. Roman Catholic. Avocations: designing clothes, writing, dollmaking and costume design.

FREEMAN, BABA FOSTER, editor; d. Festus Finley and Beatrice Michelson Foster; m. Monroe E. Freeman Jr, 1959; children: Emily Freeman Jones, Roger, Andrew. BA in Polit. Economy, Bennington Coll., 1948. Mem. editl. staff The Blue Ridge Herald, Purcellville, Va., 1949—50; clk. Office Sci. Pers. Nat. Acad. Sci., Washington, 1950—52; head info. svcs. sect., Ops. Evaluation Group Office of Chief of Naval Ops., Washington, 1952—59. Rsch. dir. New Town Publs., Reston, Va., 1980—96. Dir., bull. editor LWV of Fairfax Area, 1967—71, v.p., 1999—; vol. Fairfax County Pub. Libr., 1976—; dir. governing bd. Reston Cmty. Ctr., 1976—80; commr., coach Reston Soccer Assn., 1978—82; bd. dirs. Reston Interfaith Housing Inc., 1980—93; Centreville (Va.) dist. rep. Adv. Social Svcs. Bd., Fairfax County, 1986—95; Hunter Mill dist. rep. Human Svcs. Coun., Fairfax County, 1997—; del. conv. LWV of the U.S., Washington, 2000; del. ann. coun. Diocese of Va., 1986—92. Office: LWV - Fairfax Area 4026 Hummer Rd Ste 214 Annandale VA 22003 E-mail: lwvfa@ecoisp.com.

FREEMAN, CAROL LYN, business administrator; b. Loraine, Tex., May 3, 1949; d. James R. and Flora Lee (Tibbs) Turnbow; m. Donald Lee Freeman, July 2, 1987; children: Tracy Lyn, Warton Irvin, Rian, Makai Jenkins, Merritt Freeman. Student, Western Tex. Coll., Snyder. Pres. DC Sports, Roscoe, Tex.; purchasig agt. Bearings Inc., Sweetwater, Tex., Abilene, Tex.; in ops. Abilene Bearing Co.; br. mgr. Bearings Inc., Abilene, Tex.; computer programmer Freeman & Sons. Trucking, Roscoe, Tex. Co-owner DC Sports, Roscoe. Mem. NAFE. Address: 5249 Meadowick Ln Abilene TX 79606-4335

FREEMAN, CAROLYN RUTH, radiation oncologist; b. Kettering, Eng., Jan. 2, 1950; emigrated to Can., 1974, naturalized, 78; d. Ivor Thomas and Winifred Mary (Scotney) F.; m. J.C. Negrete, July 25, 1981. Student, King's Coll. London U., 1967-69; MB, BS, Westminster Med. Sch. London U., 1972. Prof., chmn. dept. radiation oncology, faculty medicine McGill U., Montreal, 1979—; radiation oncologist-in-chief McGill U. Hosps., Montreal, 1979—. Contbr. articles to med. publs. Fellow Royal Coll. Physicians (Can.); mem. Can. Assn. Radiol. Oncologists (pres. 1991-93), Am. Soc. Therapeutic Radiology and Oncology. Home: 4270 deMaisonneuve W Montréal QC Canada H3Z 1K6 Office: 1650 Cedar Ave Montréal QC Canada H3G 1A4 E-mail: carolyn.freeman@muhc.mcgill.ca.

FREEMAN, CORINNE, financial services, former mayor; b. N.Y.C., Nov. 9, 1926; d. Bernard J. Hirschfeld and Sidonie (Daxe) Lichtenstein; m. Michael S. Freeman, Mar. 14, 1948; children: Michael L., Stephan J., Adelphi Coll. Sch. Nursing, 1944-47. RN, N.Y., Mass. Nurse numerous hosps. in N.Y. and Mass., 1948-64; mayor, 1977-85; mem. Pinellas County Sch. Bd., St. Petersburg, Fla., 1989-98, chmn., 1996-98; bd. trustees Palms of Pasadena Hosp., St. Petersburg, 1998—. Fin. advisor Prudential Securities; bd. dirs. Creativity in Child Care. Chmn. Social Svc. Allocations Com., St. Petersburg, 1972-76, City Budget Rev. Com., 1973-76, Youth Svc. System, Pinellas County, 1975-76, West Coast Regional Water Supply Authority; past mem. community redevel. com. U.S. Conf. of Mayors; past pres. Fla. League Cities; past mem. Pinellas County Mayors Coun.; past mem. Nat. League of Cities Revenue and Fin. Task Force; pres. LWV, St. Petersburg, 1970-72, 75-76; trustee Fire Pension Bd., St. Petersburg, 1989-92, Bayfront Med. Ctr.; dir. Palms of Pasadena Hosp., 1999-2003; adv. com. Jr. League St. Petersburg, 1990-92. Recipient Disting. Alumni award Adelphi U. Mem. Fla. Nursing Assn. Mem.: Treasure Island Yacht and Tennis Club (bd. dirs. 2004). Republican. Home: 2101 Pelham Rd N Saint Petersburg FL 33710-3659 Office: 5858 Central Ave Saint Petersburg FL 33707-1728 E-mail: corinne_freeman@prusec.com.

FREEMAN, DONNA COOK, small business owner; b. Waldron, Ark., Apr. 18, 1937; d. Oliver Raymond and Lura Edna (Doyel) Cook; m. Clarence Lee Freeman, Jan. 21, 1954; children: Scott, Kevin, Steven, Melissa, Melinda. Staff dept. aquaculture U. Calif. Bodega Marine Lab., 1976—77; real estate assoc., 1978—82; co-owner fishing vessel Noyo Belle, 1981—84; ptnr. Freeman's Union 76 Svc., Bodega Bay, 1983—93; owner, designer Compass Rose Gardens, 1986—. Vice chmn. Shoreline Trust Ednl. Program Svcs., 1981—85; founding chmn. Bodega Bay Fisherman's Festival, 1973—74, 1983; chmn. Spud Point Adv. Bd., 1985—; grand juror Sonoma County, Calif., 1983—84; hon. dir. Sonoma County Fair, 1995—; dir. Bodega Bay Fire Protection Dist., 1987—; alt. mem. Dem. Ctrl. Com., 1982; mgr. polit. campaign, 1984; bd. dirs. Bodega Bay Area Rescue, 1973—74; mem. local bd. SSS, 1982—; bd. dirs. Sonoma County Fair, 1985—95, Coastal Fisheries Found., 1986—; mem. regional adv. bd. Sonoma County Libr. Commn., 2002—. Mem.: Bodega Bay Cmty. Assn., Bodega Bay C. of C. (pres. 1979—81, bd. dirs. 1982—86), Bodega Bay Fisherman's Aux., Bodega Bay Grange. Home: 1409 Hwy 1 N Bodega Bay CA 94923-9716 E-mail: donna@compassrosegardens.com.

FREEMAN, ELAINE LAVALLE, sculptor; b. Boston, May 22, 1929; d. John and Ellen (Tufts) Lavalle; m. Felix Joachim Freeman, Jr., June 16, 1951 (div. 1974); children: John Lavalle, William Baker, Ellen Candler. Student, NAD, 1973, Art Students League, N.Y.C., 1947-49, 70-73; BA, Fordham U., 1986. Profl. sculptor, N.Y.C. and Southampton, N.Y., 1973—; instr. Sculpture Ctr. Sch., N.Y.C., 1977-81; vol. gallery asst. Sculpture Ctr., N.Y.C., 1979-2000. Exec. com., sec., bd. trustees Sculpture Ctr., N.Y.C., 1985-2000. One-woman shows include Wheeler Gallery, Providence, 1979, Sculpture Ctr., N.Y.C., 1977, Southampton Gallery, N.Y.C., 1975; exhibited in group shows at Nat. Acad., Audubon Artists, Allied Artists, Parrish Mus., Nat. Arts Club, Am. Standard Corp. Gallery, Sculpture Ctr. Gallery, Huntington Twp. Art League, East Edn Arts Coun., others, 1973—; permanent collection include Martha Graham Sch. Contemporary Dance, Health Mgmt. Resources, N.Y., Southampton Hosp. Bd. dirs. Southampton Fresh Air Home for Crippled Children, 1980-86, sec., 1981-83, treas. 1980. Recipient Judges award Parrish Art Mus., Southampton, 1974, Am. Carving Sch. award Allied Artists, N.Y.C., 1977. Mem. Catharine Lorillard Wolfe Art Club (bd. dirs. 1997—, v.p. sculpture 1998-2001, 1st v.p. 2001—, 1st prize sculpture 1994, Anna Hyatt Huntington award 1983), Southampton Bathing Corp., Colony Club, Meadow Club. Democrat. Episcopalian. Avocations: travel, tennis, watercolor painting. Home: 132 Post Ln Southampton NY 11968-4919

FREEMAN, J. P. LADYHAWK, vicar, underwater exploration, security and transportation executive, educator, fashion model, legislative advocate; b. Berkley, Calif., Feb. 21, 1951; d. Gilbert Richard Freeman (dec.) and P.M. (Ann) Raistrick; children: Jennifer Patricia (dec.), Schne F. (dec.). BA in English, Davis & Elkins Coll., W.Va., 1973; grad., USAF Air Weapons Controller Sch., Tyndall AFB, Fla., 1973, USAF Air Command and Staff Coll., 1982, U.S. Marine Corps Command and Staff Coll., 1982, Dept. Def. Computer Inst., 1984; M in Aviation M in Aviation Mgmt., postgrad., Embry-Riddle Aeronautical U., Daytona Beach, Fla., 1986; grad., USAF Air War Coll., Montgomery, Ala., 1988. Cert. EMT; ordained vicar Universal Ch., 2002. Mem. 56th spl. ops. rescue for Southeast Asia NKP Royal Thai Air Force Base, 1974, 75; chief wing radar standardization/evaluation RAF Alconbury, England, 1980-83; commdr. joint U.S. forces Operation Raleigh, 1986; support chief of staff Hdqs. NORAD, Colorado Springs, Colo., 1987-89; dep. base commdr. NATO Hdqs. Allied Forces No. Europe, Norway, 1989-91; chief airport mgmt. divsn. Whiteman AFB, Knob Noster, Mo., 1991-93; dir. spl. projects USAF Acad. Regional Hosp., Colorado Springs, 1993-94; systems performance specialist Colo. Sport & Spine Rehab., Colorado Springs, 1994-95; dir. FLEET Internat. Explorations and Svcs. Co., Colorado Springs, 1995-97; fashion model, 1996—2001; vicar, 2002—. Spl. adv. for anti and counter terrorist security design for 1994 Internat. Olympic Games, Oslo, Norway, 1989-91; designer Automated Provider Credentialing System USAF Acad. Regional Hosp., USAF Acad., Colo., 1993-94; spl. adv. comms. NATO German High Commd., 1977-80; paralyzed Vet. of Am., sr. legist. advocate. U.S. Congress for Colo., Mont. Ut. and Wyo., 2002-; experience in 37 countries. Poet, poems included in numerous anthologies. Mem. bd. dirs. Johnson County (Mo.) United Way, 1991-93; surgery life support specialist ARC, USAF Acad. Regional Hosp., 1993-95; mem. nat. scholarship com. Red River Valley Fighter Pilots Assn., 1993—; hosp. vol., med. technician, provider credentialing system designer, oral surgery life support system specialist. Recipient 53 awards and decorations including Defense Meritorious svc. medal with 1 oak leaf cluster, Meritorious Svc. medal with 2 oak leaf clusters, Joint Svc. Commendation medal with 1 oak leaf cluster, air force commendation medal, Armed Forces Expeditionary medal with 2 bronze stars, 2 Humanitarian Svc. medals, 2 Kuwait Liberation medals, 2 Southwest Asia medals; named Adminstrsn. Officer of Yr. USAF, 1986; named one of the six top Support Officers USAF, 1986-87; 1st woman named dir. Fleet Internat. Mem. VFW, DAV, Am. Legion, Air Force Assn., Soc. of Profl. Journalists, Assn. of Old Crows, Lambda Lambda Lambda, Alpha Phi Omega, Iota Beta Sigma. Mem. United Anglican Ch. Avocations: writing, skiing, horseback riding, oil painting, music. Home: 4861 Chaparral Rd Colorado Springs CO 80917-1413 Office: FLEET Internat Explorations & Svcs Co PO Box 14192 Colorado Springs CO 80914-0192

FREEMAN, LESLIE JEAN, neuropsychologist, researcher; b. San Diego, Feb. 17, 1965; d. Richard Joseph and Jean Doris (Weber) Currier; m. Drue Scott Freeman, Sept. 6, 1986. BA, U. Calif., Irvine, 1989; MA in Clin. Psychology, Antioch U., L.A., 1992; postgrad., Calif. Sch. Profl. Psychology, Fresno, 1993-98. Marriage, family and child counselor intern So. Calif. Counseling Ctr., L.A., 1990-93; marriage, family, child counselor intern/psychology intern Bakersfield (Calif.) Med. Hosp., 1993-94; intern, resident in neuropsychology pvt. practice and Drs. Hosp., Modesto, Calif., 1994-97; resident in neuropsychology VA Med. Ctr., Cleve., 1997-98; resident, fellow in neuropsychology U. Rochester (N.Y.) Med. Ctr., 1998—. Guest lectr. in field. Contbr. articles to profl. jours. Mem. APA, Nat. Acad. Neuropsychology, Internat. Neuropsychol. Soc., Am. Neuropsychiat. Assn., Calif. Assn. Marriage and Family Therapy, Calif. Assn. Psychology Providers. Avocations: collecting first edition mystery novels, collecting original animation art and disneyana, cooking, skiing, photography. Home: PO Box 765 Kent OH 44240-0015 Office: U Rochester Rochester NY 14642-0001

FREEMAN, MARY BETH, state representative; b. Chesterfield, SC, July 22, 1938; d. Leon Barton and Maggie Lee (Streater) Robeson; m. Preston R. Freeman, Nov. 11, 1956; children: Elizabeth F. Roumillat, Preston R. Jr. Ret. pers. mgr.; mem. SC Ho. of Reps., 2001—. Adv. bd. Cheraw Sch. Dist.; mem. Cheraw Town Coun.., 1984—92. Mem.: United Meth. Women, Rotary. Democrat. Office: State Capitol 304 A Blatt Bldg Columbia SC 29211

FREEMAN, MARY LOUISE, state legislator; b. Willmar, Minn., Oct. 21, 1941; d. James Martin and Luella Anna (Backlund) Hawkinson; children: Mark D., Sara L., Cary D., Maret S. BA, Gustavus Adolphus Coll., 1963. Substitute tchr. Arrowhead Edn. Assn., Storm Lake, Iowa, 1982-93; tchr., cons. Midwest Power, Des Moines, 1991-94; mem. Iowa Senate from 5th dist., Des Moines, 1994—. Mem. Iowa State Bd. Health, 1988-94; mem. early childhood intervention com., 1994—, mem. disaster prevention svcs. com., 1994—. Del. alt. Rep. Nat. Conv., Kansas City, 1976; active Midwest-Can. Relations Co., 1994—. Mem. Am. Legis. Exch. Coun., Nat. Coun. State Govts., Buena Vista County Farm Bur., Storm Lake C. of C., Delta Kappa Gamma. Lutheran. Home: 203 Lake St Alta IA 51002-1228 Office: Iowa State Senate State Capitol Des Moines IA 50319-0001

FREEMAN, MYRNA FAYE, county schools official; b. Danville, Ill., Oct. 30, 1939; d. Thomas Gene and Dorothy Olive (Chodera) F.; m. Lonnie Lee Choate, Aug. 16, 1959 (div. 1987); children: Leslie Rene, Gregory Lonn. BA in Pub. Adminstrn., San Diego State U., 1977, MA in Edn. Adminstrn., 1987. Employee benefits mgr. City of San Diego, 1974-84; dir. San Diego County Office Edn., San Diego, 1984—. Instr. Sch. Bus. Mgrs. Acad., Assn. Calif. Sch. Adminstrs., 1985—, Ins. Edn. Assn., Cert. Employee Benefits Specialist courses, 1991—. Author: Adm. Impact of Implement Leg. 1987; Author: Article Risk Mgmt.-Emp. Benefits 1985, Risk Mgmt.-Workers' Comp. 1986, Risk Mgmt.-Loss Control 1986. Mem. Kaiser Consumer Coun., 1977-84, pres., 1979-80; bd. dirs. S.D. County Affirmative Action Adv. Bd., 1985; mem. adv. com. Vista Health Plan Pub. Policy, 1994—; adv. coun. Kaiser On-the-Job, 1994—. Recipient Appreciation award COMBO-Cultural Arts of San Diego 1977. Mem. Risk Ins. Mgmt. Soc. (pres. San Diego chpt. 1988), Calif. Assn. Sch. Bus. Ofcls. (chmn. risk mgmt. R&D comm. 1987-88), San Diego Group Ins. Claims Coun. (pres. 1987), S.D. Employers Health Cost Coalition (vice-chmn. 1987), Calif. Women in Govt. (bd. dirs. 1983-84), Calif. Assn. of Joint Powers Authority, Pub. Agys. Risk Mgmt. Assn., Pub. Risk Ins. Mgmt. Assn., Internat. Found. Employee Benefits Plans, San Diego Workers' Compensation Forum, Sigma Kappa, Phi Kappa Phi, Internat. Platform Assn Republican. Methodist. Home: 1545 Northrim Ct # 272 San Diego CA 92111-7341 Office: San Diego County Office Edn 6401 Linda Vista Rd Rm 505 San Diego CA 92111-7319 Office Phone: 858-292-3773. E-mail: ffreeman@sdcoe.k12.ca.us.

FREEMAN, PATRICIA ELIZABETH, library and education specialist; b. El Dorado, Ark., Nov. 30, 1924; d. Herbert A. and M. Elizabeth (Pryor) Harper; m. Jack Freeman, June 15, 1949; 3 children. BA, Centenary Coll., 1943; postgrad., Fine Arts Ctr., 1942-46, Art Students League, 1944-45; BSLS, La. State U., 1946; postgrad., Calif. State U., 1959-61, U. N.Mex., 1964-74; EdS, Peabody Coll., Vanderbilt U., 1975. Libr. U. Calif., Berkeley, 1946-47; libr. Albuquerque Pub. Schs., 1964-67, ind. sch. libr. media ctr. cons., 1967—. Painter lithographer; one-person show La. State Exhibit Bldg., 1948; author: Pathfinder: An Operational Guide for the School Librarian, 1975, Southeast Heights Neighborhoods of Albuquerque, 1993; compiler, editor: Elizabeth Pryor Harper's Twenty-One Southern Families, 1985; editor: SEHNA Gazette, 1988-93, N.Mex. AAUW, 1999—. Mem. task force Goals for Dallas-Environ., 1977-82; pres. Friends of Sch. Librs., Dallas, 1979-83; v.p., editor Southeast Heights Neighborhood Assn., 1988-93. With USAF, 1948-49. Honoree AAUW Ednl. Found., 1979, 96; vol. award for outstanding service Dallas Ind. Sch. Dist., 1978; AAUW Pub. Service grantee 1980. Mem. ALA, AAUW (dir. Dallas 1976-82, Albuquerque 1983-85, 2003--, N.Mex. 1999—), LWV (sec. Dallas 1982-83, editor Albuquerque 1984-88, editor N.Mex. 2004—), Nat. Trust Historic Preservation, Friends for the Pub. Libr., Colorado Springs Fine Arts Ctr., N.Mex. Symphony Guild, Alpha Xi Delta. Home: 612 Ridgecrest Dr SE Albuquerque NM 87108-3365

FREEMAN, PEGGY RENEA, accountant; b. Gadsden, Ala., Oct. 8, 1966; d. Russell Leon and LaVada Inez (Weaver) Lemons; m. Robert Stanley Freeman, Mar. 15, 1986; children: Teri Inez, Robert Kyle. AS, Gadsden State C.C., 1986; BS, Jacksonville (Ala.) State U., 1993. Office clk. R.L. Polk & Co., Gadsden, 1984-85; sec. Shamrock Rentals, Gadsden, 1986; bookkeeper Ala. Contrs. Equipment, Gadsden, 1986-87, City of Hokes Bluff, Ala., 1988; tutor Gadsden State C.C., 1991-92; editor H & R Block, Gadsden, 1991-93; tax preparer Student Acctg. Assn., Jacksonville, 1992-93, Ret. Sr. Volunteer, Gadsden, 1994, Steed Acctg. Svcs., Attalla, Ala., 1995-96; acct. Delphi Packard Electric Systems, Gadsden, Ala., 1995-96, Kirkland & Co., Gadsden, 1997—99, Steven Vaughn Constrn. Co., 1999—2002; office mgr. Pettus Materials, Inc., 2000—. Fin. sec. Meadowbrook Bapt. Ch., 2003. Avocations: children's sports, horseback riding, softball. Home: 5032 Louise St Gadsden AL 35903-4728

FREEMAN, SHAREE M. federal agency administrator; b. N.Y. BA, St. Lawrence U.; JD, Georgetown U. Law clk. Norma Holloway Johnson U.S. Dist. Ct. D.C., Washington; asst. dist. atty. Phila., 1982—84; with Solicitor's Office U.S. Dept. Interior, 1984—97, acting asst. solicitor Gen. Indian Legal Activities, atty. advisor; counsel U.S. Ho. of Reps. Internat. Rels. Com., 1997—2001; dir. cmty. oriented policing svcs. U.S. Dept. Justice, Washington, 2001—. Office: US Dept Justice Cmty Oriented Policing Svcs 1100 Vermont Ave NW Washington DC 20005-3505

FREEMAN, SUSAN TAX, anthropologist, educator, culinary historian; b. Chgo., May 24, 1938; d. Sol and Gertrude Tax.; m. Leslie G. Freeman, Jr., Mar. 20, 1964; 1 dau., Sarah Elisabeth. BA, U. Chgo., 1958; MA, Harvard U., 1959, PhD, 1965. Asst. prof. anthropology U. Ill., Chgo., 1965-70, assoc. prof., 1970-78, prof., 1978—, prof. emerita, 1999—, chmn., 1979-82. Rsch. assoc. dept. sociology and anthropology Mont. State U., Bozeman, 1992—; panelist NEH, Council for Internat. Exchange of Scholars; mem. anthropology screening com. Fulbright-Hays Research Awards, 1975-78; mem. ad hoc com. on research in Spain Spain-U.S.A. Friendship Agreement, various yrs., 1977-84; field researcher Mex., 1959, Spain, 1962—, Japan, 1983; instr. Radcliffe Coll. Seminars on Food in History and Culture, 1998. Author: Neighbors: The Social Contract in a Castilian Hamlet, 1970, The Pasiegos-Spaniards in No Man's Land, 1979; assoc. editor: Am. Anthropologist, 1971-73, Am. Ethnologist, 1974-76; editl. bd. Gastronomica, 2000—. Fellow Inst. for the Humanities, U. Ill. Chgo., 1987-88; Wenner-Gren Found. for Anthrop. Research grantee, 1966, 83; NIMH grantee, 1967, 68-71; NEH fellowships, 1978-79, 89-90. Fellow Am. Anthrop. Assn. (nominating com. 1981-82, Centennial Adv. Commn. 1999-2002), Royal Anthrop. Inst. Gt. Britain and Ireland; mem. Soc. for Anthropology of Europe (exec. com. 1987-88), Soc. Spanish and Portuguese Hist. Studies (exec. com. 1990-92), Coun. European Studies (steering com. 1980-83), Internat. Inst. Spain (corporator, bd. dirs. 1982-87, 2000-2003), Centro Estudios Sorianos (hon.), Assn. Anthropologia Castilla y Leon (hon.). Home: PO Box 369 Whitehall MT 59759 Office: U Ill Dept Anthro M/C 027 1007 W Harrison St Chicago IL 60607-7135 Office Phone: 312-413-3570.

FREEMAN-WILSON, KAREN, former attorney general, prosecutor, educational association administrator; m. Carmen Wilson; 1 child, Jordan ; 3 stepchildren. BA cum laude, Harvard Coll., 1982, JD, 1985. Pub. defender Lake County; ptnr. Freeman-Wilson and Lewis; dir. Ind. Office Drug Control Policy; atty. gen., chief legal officer State of Ind., judge drug ct.; pub. defender, exec. dir. Ind. Civil Rights Commn.; dep. prosecutor Lake County, 1985—88; exec. dir. Ind. Civil Rights commn., 1989—92; judge Gary City Ct., 1994—2000; atty. gen. State Ind., Indpls., 2000—01; exec. dir. Nat. Drug Ct. Inst., 2002—; CEO Nat. Assn. Drug Ct. Profls., 2002—. Instr. Valparaiso U. Law Sch., Ind. U. Sch. Law; bd. dirs. Conf. for Legal Edn. and Opportunity, Ind. Supreme Ct. Trainer rape awareness Gary Commn. for Women; active Harbor House; bd. dirs. Rainbow Shelter. Democrat. Address: 4900 Seminary Rd Ste 320 Alexandria VA 22311 Business E-Mail: kfwilson@nadcp.org.

FREEMOND WOODS, RENÉE, secondary school educator; d. Joseph Wolf and Mamie Sarah Freemond; m. Paul William Woods, May 12, 1990 (div. Sept. 27, 2001). BA, Northeastern U., 1974, MEd, 1983, postgrad., 1991. Cert. tchr. Ill. Tchr. elem. sch., Evanston, Ill., 1975—78; tchr. mid. sch. River Forest, Ill., 1980—82; tchr. jr. h.s. Buffalo Grove, Ill., 1983—. Tutor pvt. lesson; mentor Dist. 65, Dist. 102, Ill., 1998. Exec. bd. dirs. Dist. #102 Union, Buffalo Grove, 1998—; founding mem. U.S. Holocaust Mus., Washington, 1993—; mem. Simon Weisenthal Ctr., Washington, 1995—. Mem.: PTA, NEA, Amnesty Internat., Ill. Edn. Assn. Avocations: travel, movies, reading, home improvement, charity work. Office: Aptakisic-Tripp Dist # 102 1231 Weiland Buffalo Grove IL 60089 Office Phone: 847-353-5500.

FREEMONT, ANDRIA SHAMONA, laboratory administrator; b. Monroe, La., Mar. 10, 1971; d. Billy Joe Freemont and Barbara Jean Tillman. BS in Chemistry, Jackson State U., 1993. Lic. analyst, State of Ga. Rsch. scientist Upjohn Pharm. Co., Kalamazoo, Mich., 1993-94; chemistry tchr. Carroll H.S., Monroe, 1994-95; extraction chemist Analytical Svcs., Inc., Atlanta, Ga., 1997; sr. forensic toxicologist Ga. Bur. Investigation, Decatur, 1997-2000; adminstr. Biolab Inc., Decatur, 2001—. Lectr. Ga. Prosecution Attys. Coun., Atlanta, 1998-2000; with Howard Hughes Rsch. program, Jackson, Miss., 1989-93. Mem. Am. Chem. Soc., Alpha Kappa Alpha Sorority, Inc., Beta Kappa Chi Honor Soc., 1991. Democrat. Roman Catholic. Avocation: reading mystery novels. Office: 121 New St Decatur GA 30030 Home: 7307 Jefferson Sq Ct Decatur GA 30030-1791 E-mail: afreemont@usa.net.

FREESE, KATHERINE, physicist, researcher; b. Freiburg, Germany, Feb. 8, 1957; came to U.S., 1957; d. Ernst and Elisabeth Gertrude Maria (Bautz) F.; 1 child, Douglas Quincy Adams. BA, Princeton U., 1977; MA, Columbia U., 1981; PhD, U. Chgo., 1984. Postdoctoral fellow Harvard/Smithsonian Ctr. for Astrophysics, Cambridge, Mass., 1984-85, Inst. for Theoretical Physics, Santa Barbara, Calif., 1985-87, U. Calif., Berkeley, 1987-88; asst. prof. physics MIT, Cambridge, 1988-91; prof. physics U. Mich., Ann Arbor, 1991—. Gen. mem. Aspen Ctr. for Physics, 1991—; bd. dirs. Inst. for Theoretical Physics. Contbr. articles to profl. jours. William Rainey Harper fellow U. Chgo, 1982; Sloan Found. fellow, 1989; Presdl. Young Investigator NSF, 1990, rsch. grantee, 1991, 94; Presdl. fellow U. Calif., 1987. Mem. Am. Phys. Soc., Assn. for Women in Sci. Democrat. Avocations: water polo, swimming, skiing, tennis. Office: U Mich Dept Physics Ann Arbor MI 48109

FREESE, LAURA ANN, social worker, consultant; b. Bloomington, Ind., Oct. 6, 1960; d. Donald Gordon and Georgie Ann Freese; 1 child, Hannah Meryl. BS, Bridgewater State Coll., 1991; MSW, U. So. Ind., 1997; postgrad., U. Louisville, 2003. LCSW Ky., Ind. Program dir. Vinfen Corp., Cambridge, Mass., 1992—95; adminstrv. dir. Spencer County Hospice, Rockport, Ind., 1996—97; therapist So. Hills Counseling Ctr., Jasper, 1997; behavior specialist RiverValley Behavioral Health, Owensboro, Ky., 1997—98, therapeutic foster care program mgr., 1998—2000; in-home therapist Christian Ch. Homes Ky., Henderson, 2000—01; ednl. cons. Ea. Ky. U., Owensboro, 2001—. Item writer Assn. Social Work Boards, Culpeper, Va., 1999—2001, exam. com. mem., 2001—; com. mem. RiverValley Behavioral Health Human Rights Com., Owensboro, 2000—01. Contbr. articles to profl. jours. Vol. Ct. Apptd. Spl. Advocates, Owensboro, 1999—2002; bd. mem., sec. St. Bernard Sch. Bd., Rockport, Ind., 2002. Recipient Star award, The Vol. Ctr., 2000. Mem.: NASW. Office: Cabinet for Health and Family Svcs 311 W 2nd St Owensboro KY 42301 E-mail: laura.freese@mail.state.ky.us.

FREESE, MELANIE LOUISE, librarian, educator, assistant dean; b. Mineola, NY, May 12, 1945; d. Walter Christian and Agnes Elizabeth (Jensen) F. BS in Elem. Edn., Hofstra U., 1967, MA in Elem. Edn., 1969; MLS, L.I. U., 1977. Cert. tchr., N.Y. Bibliographic searcher acquisitions dept. Adelphi U. Swirbul Libr., Garden City, N.Y., 1973-79, res. desk libr., 1979-83; catalog libr., assoc. prof. Hofstra U. Axinn Libr., Hempstead, N.Y., 1984—, asst. dean, chair libr. tech. svcs., 1998—2000, sr. cataloger, 2000—. Ch. librarian St. Peters Evang. Luth. Ch., Baldwin, N.Y., 1977—. Founder libr. Salvation Army Wayside Home and Sch. for Girls, Valley Stream, N.Y., 1993. Mem. ALA, Nassau County Libr. Assn. (corr. sec. acad. and spl. librs. divsn. 1986-88, v.p., pres.-elect 1989-90, pres. 1991), Bus. and Profl. Women's Club (pres. Nassau County chpt. 1990-92, 95-97, Woman of Yr. 1994). Republican. Avocations: needlework, knitting, crocheting. Office: Hofstra U Axinn Library 1000 Fulton Ave Hempstead NY 11550-1030 Office Phone: 516-463-6423.

FREESEMANN, LEANNE CLAIR (LUIKART), music educator; b. Sioux City, Iowa, July 19; d. Edwin Hastings and Nancy Clair Conway Luikart; m. Grant Lee Luikart, June 3, 1989; children: Jenava Ann, Josiah Daniel. BA, Oral Roberts U., Tulsa, Okla., 1990. Cert. elem. and secondary music tchr. Okla., 1990. Secondary vocal music dir. Victory Christian Sch., Tulsa, Okla., 1990—. Min., music dir. Prophetic Sound Ministries, Broken Arrow, Okla. Traveling min., chapel supr., music dir. Prophetic Sound Ministries, Broken Arrow Ok, Okla. Named Tchr. of Yr., 1998, 2000. Mem.: Okla. Music Educators Assn. (assoc.). Achievements include first to Training young musicians for the Ministry. Avocations: study of the Jewish roots of Christianity, fishing, antiques, history, reading. Home: 1617 W Delmar St Broken Arrow OK 74012 Office: Victory Christian Sch 7700 S Lewis Tulsa OK 74136

FREIBERGER, KATHERINE GUION, composer, retired piano educator; b. Mineral Wells, Tex., May 2, 1927; d. Waldo Burton and Kate Francis (Guion) Lasater; m. John Jacob Freiberger, July 22, 1950. AA, HocKaday Jr. Coll., Dallas, 1946; BA, U. Tex., 1949; MusB, So. Meth. U., 1966. Tchr. Dallas Ind. Schs., 1949-50; pvt. practice piano tchr. Dallas, 1961-85. Composer piano solos and duets, chamber, choral and incidental music. Mem. Dallas Civic Chorus, 1962-69, 72-76, chorus Dallas Civic Opera, 1959; alto soloist Preston Hollow Presbyn. Ch., Dallas, 1956-63; alto soloist, dir. youth choir Churchill Way Presbyn. Ch., Dallas, 1963-70; sole trustee David W. Guion Edn. and Religious Trusts I and II, Dallas, 1978-91; bd. dirs. Dallas Music Tchrs. Assn., 1979-91, Voices of Change, Dallas, 1980s, Dallas Civic Music, 1970s-80s, Durango/Purgatory Music in the Mts., Colo., 1990—, The Dallas Opera, 1989-97;artist in residence com. Ft. Lewis Coll., Durango, Co., 1998—.) Recipient, Elizabeth Mathias Award, Prof. Achievement, 2001. Mem. Musical Arts Club, Mu Phi Epsilon Alumni (First prize for composition 1989, Elizabeth Mathias award 2001). Home: 3825 Hawthorne Ave Dallas TX 75219-2212

FREIBERT, LUCY MARIE, humanities educator; b. Louisville, Oct. 19, 1922; d. Joseph Anthony and Amelia Josephine (Stich) F. BA in English, Nazareth Coll., 1957; MA in English, St. Louis U., 1962; PhD in English, U. Wis., 1970. Joined Sisters of Charity of Nazareth. Elem. tchr. St. Cecilia Sch., Louisville, 1947-51, Holy Name Sch., Louisville, 1951-57; secondary tchr. Presentation Acad., Louisville, 1957-60; prof. English Spalding Coll., Louisville, 1960-71, U. Louisville, 1971-93, prof. emerita of English, 1993—. Co-editor: Hidden Hands, An Anthology of American Women Writers, 1790-1870, 1985; contbr. articles to profl. jours. Named Woman of Distinction, Ctr. for Women and Families, 1993. Mem. MLA (life), NOW, Nat. Women's Studies Assn., Melville soc. Roman Catholic. Home: 1507 Hepburn Ave # 2 Louisville KY 40204-1617 Office: U Louisville Dept English Louisville KY 40292-0001

FREID, STEPHANIE LYNNE, writer, educator; d. Alan Isadore and Patricia Ruth Freid; m. Tonny Bruun Madsen, Sept. 6, 2001; 1 child, Raphael Max Bruun Madsen. BA, U. Cin., 1986, Tel Aviv U., 1984. Translator, stringer N.Y. Times, Jerusalem, 1988—90; prodr. NBC News, Tel Aviv, 1988; prodr., corr. Reuters Jerusalem, 1996—2001, chief client liaison, 1994—96, prodr., corr. Reuters San Francisco, 1997—2001; freelance writer San Francisco, 1996—. Career spkr. San Francisco Pub. Schs., 2001—. Co-author: (chpt. to book) I Really Should Have Stayed Home. Vol. Little Bros., San Francisco, 2002—03, Friends of the Elderly, San Francisco, 2002—03; literacy vol. San Francisco Sch. Vols., 2000—01. Scholar, Cin. Israel-Am. Orgn., 1982. Mem.: Media Bistro (assoc.). Personal E-mail: stefanella@sbcglobal.net.

FREIDEL, JUDY ANN, artist; b. Madison, Wis., June 11, 1955; d. Robert Leo and Agnes Theresa (Langer) F. BA in Art, U. Ctrl. Ark., 1977. Owner, artist Red Hen Studio, Hot Springs, Ark., 1991—. Freelance comml. artist and illustrator, 1977—; represented by Anderson Gallery. Artwork included in American Artist of the Bookplate, 1993, Best of Colored Pencil II, 1994, Creative Colored Pencil, 1995; represented in pvt. collection St. Joseph Regional Health Ctr. Mem. Colored Pencil Soc. Am. Roman Catholic. Avocations: competitive running, needlework, gardening.

FREIDHEIM, LADONNA, dance company director; b. Chgo., Nov. 15, 1967; d. J. Thomas and Janet Rae (Garr) F. BS, U. Ill., 1991. Corp. asst. dir. Advanced Quality Custom Graphics, Champaign, Ill., 1990-91; adminstrv. coord. Classical Symphony Orch., Chgo., 1991-92; adminstrv. asst. Chgo. Sinfonietta, 1992-93; bus. mgr. Organic Theater, Chgo., 1993-94, mng. dir., 1994-96, Hedwig Dances, Chgo., 1997—. Lighting designer, 1992-95; founding mem. Lucid Theatre Co. Bd. dirs. Ministry to the Disadvantaged, Champaign; vol. phys. assistance Rehab. Inst., Chgo., 1993-96; vol. dance instr. Pace Program, Evanston, 1993; vol. Children's Meml. Hosp., Chgo., 1996-99. Roman Catholic. Avocations: lighting design, exercise, cycling. Office: Hedwig Dances Chgo Cultural Ctr 78 E Washington Chicago IL 60606

FREIDHEIM, LYNN, not-for-profit fundraiser; Degree, Sch. Fgn. Svc., Georgetown U., Thunderbird Internat. Mgmt. Sch. Mktg. positions with Pillsbury, Mpls., Novartis, NJ; dir. corp. partnerships and alliances US Fund for UNICEF, NYC. Mem.: NY Women in Comm. Office: US Fund for UNICEF 333 E 38th St New York NY 10016 Business E-Mail: lfreidheim@unicefusa.org.*

FREILICH, JOAN SHERMAN, utilities executive; b. Albany, N.Y., Nov. 3, 1941; d. Julius and Bess (Bergner) Sherman; m. Sanford J. Freilich, Jan. 24, 1965. AB in French magna cum laude, Barnard Coll., 1963; MA in French, Columbia U., 1964, PhD in French, 1971, MBA in Fin., 1980. Instr. CCNY, Columbia U., N.Y.C., 1965-75; tchr. Walden Sch., N.Y.C., 1970-74; asst. to dean Coll. of New Rochelle, N.Y., 1974-75, dir. admissions, 1975-78; sr. acct. Consol. Edison Co. N.Y., N.Y.C., 1978-81, mgr. acctg. rsch., 1981-82, contr. power generation, 1982-86, gen. mgr. power generation, 1986-89, exec. asst. to pres., 1989, asst. v.p. corp. planning, 1989-90, v.p. corp. planning, 1990-92, v.p., contr., chief acctg. officer, 1992-96, sr. v.p., CFO, 1996-98, exec. v.p., CFO, 1998—; also bd. dirs. Consol. Edison, Inc. and Consol. Edison of N.Y., Inc., N.Y.C. Author: Paul Claudel's "Le Soulier de satin": A Stylistic, Structuralist and Psychoanalytic Interpretation, 1973; assoc. editor Claudel Studies, 1973-78; contbr. articles to profl. jours. Trustee Citizens Budget Commn.; bd. trustees Coll. New Rochelle; mem. president's coun. The Cooper Union. Publ. grantee Humanities Rsch. Coun. Can., 1972; Pres.'s fellow Columbia U., 1964, Henry Todd fellow, 1967; recipient scholarship N.Y. State Bd. Regents, 1959, Nat. Merit Found., 1959, Columbia U., 1965; Civic Spirit Award, Women's City Club of N.Y., 1999. Mem.: N.Y. State Women in Comms. and Energy (steering com.), YWCA Acad. of Women Achievers, Phi Beta Kappa, Beta Gamma Sigma. Office: Consolidated Edison Co NY 4 Irving Pl New York NY 10003-3598*

FREILICHER, JANE, artist; b. N.Y.C., Nov. 29, 1924; d. Martin and Bertha (Niederhoffer); m. Joseph Hazan, Feb. 17, 1957; 1 dau., Elizabeth. AB, Bklyn. Coll., 1947; postgrad., Hans Hoffman Sch. Fine Arts, 1947; MA, Columbia U., 1948. Vis. lectr., critic art schs., colls. One-woman shows include Tibor de Nagy, 1952-68, 98, 2000, 02, 04, John Bernard Myers Gallery, 1971, Fischbach Gallery, 1975, 77, 79-80, 83, 85, 88, 90, 92, 95, Utah Mus. Fine Arts, 1979, Lafayette Coll., 1981, Kansas City Art Inst., 1983, David Heath Gallery, Atlanta, 1990, Reynolds Gallery, Richmond, Va., 1993, Nat. Acad., 2002; group exhbns. include Met. Mus. Art, 1979-80,

Denver Art Mus., 1979, Pa. Acad., 1981, Am. Acad. and Inst. of Arts and Letters, 1981, 84-85, Bklyn. Mus. 1984, Yale U., 1986, Tibor de Nagy Gallery, 1992, Whitney Mus., 1955, 72, 95, Whitney Mus., Stamford, Conn., 1999, Artists Eye NAD, 2002, Women of Acad. NAD, 2003; curator Nat. Acad., 2002; represented in permanent collections Met. Mus. Art, [illegible] Bklyn. Mus., [illegible] Rose Art Mus., Whitney Mus., Cleve. Mus. Art, San Francisco Mus. Art, others; travelling retrospective in Currier Gallery Art, Parrish Mus., Contemporary Arts Mus., McNay Mus., 1986-87; illustrator Turandot and Other Poems, 1953, Paris Review, 1965, Descriptions of a Masque, 1998. Recipient Eloise Spaeth award Guild Hall Mus., East Hampton, N.Y., 1991, Lifetime Achievement award Guild Hall Mus., 1996; AAUW fellow, 1974; Nat. Endowment Arts grantee, 1976; Benjamin West Clinedinst Meml. medal Artists' Fellowship, 1997. Mem. NAD (academician) (Saltus Gold medal 1987, Benjamin Altman landscape prize 1995, Edwin Palmer prize 2003), Am. Acad. Arts and Letters.

FREIMAN, LELA KAY, retired secondary school educator; b. Canton, Miss., Oct. 2, 1939; d. Lyle K. and Mae Susan (Billman) Linch; m. James F. Freiman, Sept. 5, 1965 (div. Feb. 1975); 1 child, Jennifer Leigh. Student, Northwestern State Coll., Natchitoches, La., 1957-59; BA, U. Iowa, 1962; MEd, U. Ariz., 1977. Tchr. speech, English and drama Sturgeon Bay (Wis.) H.S., 1962-65; spl. edn. tchr. Naylor Jr. H.S., Tucson, 1975-83; tchr. drama Sahuaro H.S., Tucson, 1983-97. Summer camp dir. Sahuaro coun. Girl Scouts U.S.A., Tucson, 1977-87; mem. adv. coun. drama dept. U. Ariz., Tucson; participant Nat. faculty for Humanities, Santa Fe, Tucson, 1988-89; bd. dirs. Live Theatre Workshop, 2001-; sec. Ariz. Alliance Arts Ed., 2001-03. Former leader, trainer, camp dir. Girl Scouts U.S.A., Sturgeon Bay, Wis. Rapids, Waukesha, Wis., Ariz., rep. Nat. Leadership Conf., Washington, 1983, bd. dirs. Sahuaro coun., 1992-95; first aid com., instr. AFA, CPR ARC, Tucson; instr. CPR Am. Heart Assn.; Sunday sch. tchr., supt., mem. coun. Luth. Chs., Wis. Rapids, Waukesha, now Tucson; v.p. bd. dirs. S.W. Actors Studio, Tucson, 1987-92; adult mem. Ariz. State Thespian Bd., 1992-97; h.s. page editor Tucson Theatre Scene; sec. Live Theatre workshop Bd., 2002—. Recipient Thanks Badge, Sahuaro coun. Girl Scouts U.S.A., 1976, 88, Cross and Crown award Luth. Scouters So. Ariz., 1983, Mainstream Tchr. of Yr. award Assn. for Retarded Citizens So. Ariz., 1989. Mem. NEA (ret.), Am. Alliance for Theatre and Edn., Ariz. Theatre Alliance (state sec. 1989-90, state treas. 1990-91, state bd. 1998, 2000-03, exec. dir. 1998-2000, com. to draft curriculum guidelines for Ariz. Ho. of Reps., Theatre Educator of Yr. 1994-95), Ariz. Edn. Assn. (ret.), Ariz. Prodn. Assn. (sec. so. Ariz. chpt. 1997-99), Cougar Found. (bd. dirs. 1997-2002), Pima County Ret. Tchrs. Assn., Sahuaro Speculators. Avocations: camping, travel, reading. Home: 7517 E Beach Dr Tucson AZ 85715-3649 E-mail: lelar@mindspring.com.

FREITAG, ANNA CAROL, endocrinologist, internist; b. Norwalk, Conn., Dec. 26, 1964; d. Arthur Richard and Sofia Boccanfuso Freitag. BA, Smith Coll., 1986; MD, U. Conn., 1994. Diplomate in internal medicine, endocrinology, diabetes and metabolism Am. Bd. Internal Medicine. Assoc. in rsch. Yale Sch. of Medicine, New Haven, Conn., 1986-90, U. Calif. San Diego Sch. of Medicine, 1990; resident in internal medicine N.Y. Hosp.-Cornell Med. Ctr., N.Y.C., 1995-97; fellowship in endocrinology and metabolism Albert Einstein Coll. of Medicine/Montefiore Med. Ctr., Bronx, 1997-99; endocrinologist, internist The Norwalk (Conn.) Med. Group, P.C., 1999—. Instr. endocrinology Albert Einstein Coll. of Medicine, 1998-99; attending physician in medicine and endocrinology Montefiore Med. Ctr., Bronx, 1997-99; instr. phys. diagnosis Cornell U. Med. Coll., N.Y.C., 1997, instr. medicine, G.I. physician asst. program, 1997. Editor-in-chief (newsletter) The Forum, 1997-98; contbr. articles to profl. jours. Fellow ACP; mem. AMA (resident del. 1995-99, reference com. mem. 1997, Physician's Recognition award 1999), Am. Med. Women's Assn. (bylaws com. 1997-99), Women's Med. Soc. of Fairfield County (bd. dirs. 2000--), N.Am. Menopause Soc., Am. Diabetes Assn. (governing coun. Fairfield County), Am. Thyroid Assn., The Endocrine Soc. Republican. Roman Catholic. Avocations: tennis, skiing, scuba, photography, writing. Home: 5 Butternut Ln Norwalk CT 06851-1009 Office: Norwalk Med Group PC 40 Cross St Fl 4 Norwalk CT 06851-4647

FREITAG, CAROL WILMA, state official, political scientist; d. Lowell William and Lois Marie (Robertson) Petersen; m. Henry Wesley Freitag, 1961 (dec. Nov. 1985); children: Bonita, Henry. Diploma in Dental Hygiene, Northwestern U., 1959; BA, Purdue U., Hammond, Ind., 1988. Registered dental hygienist, Ill. Pvt. practice dental hygiene Henry W. Freitag, D.D.S., Homewood, Ill., 1959-85; mem. group practice Chgo., 1970; faculty, interim dir. dental hygiene Prairie State Coll., Chgo. Heights, Ill., 1971-72; pvt. practice James J. Kreuz, D.D.S., Homewood, 1985-90. Contbr. articles to profl. jour. Chair US Constn. Bicentennial Commn., Village of Matteson, Ill., 1986-89; pres. Matteson Hist. Soc., 1987-89; panel spkr. South Suburban Heritage Assn., Homewood, 1990. Calumet rep. Bicentennial Com. Purdue U., 1988; vis. com. Northwestern Dental Sch., 1997-98; mem. centennial celebration com. Bloom Twp. HS, 2000; mem. Hist. Columbia Found. 2003—. Recipient Key to City, Village of Matteson, 1990, Svc. award Northwestern U., 1980, Good Neighbor award Village of Matteson, 1989, Outstanding Alumni 1950's Decade award Bloom Twp. H.S., 2000. Mem. Am. Dental Hygienists' Assn. (chair Am. Session Program 1975), Ill. Dental Hygienists Assn. (pres. 1968-69, bd. dirs., Merit award 1979), G.V. Black Soc. (leader, pres. 1997-2001), Evelyn E. Maas Soc. (pres. 1989-90, bd. dirs., Merit award 1993), Northwestern Dental Sch. Alumni Assn. (bd. dirs. 1969-2001, pres. 1977-78, v.p. 1976-77, 90-93), Acad. Polit. Sci., Sigma Phi Alpha, Alpha Chi. Avocation: travel. Home: 117 Oak Trace Ct Chapin SC 29036

FREMGEN, DARLENE, manufacturing specialist; b. Schenectady, N.Y., July 19, 1958; d. Jacob Scott and Diane Stepler Miner. Cert. in clerical office procedures, Shippensburg U., 1987; student, U. Mass., 1996, Hagerstown C.C., 1997—99. Cook Denny's Restaurant, Chambersburg, Pa., 1985; assembler, casepacker Pet Ritz/Van De Kamp, Chambersburg, 1985—87; constrn. site sec. Guilford Assocs., Chambersburg, 1987—89; radiator/valve assembler Grove Worldwide, Shady Grove, Pa., 1989—. Critic poetry, 1999—. Author: (poems) High Hopes, 1998, Cancel The Normal, 1996, Memorial Day Tribute (Editor's Choice award, 1994, Outstanding poets award, 1994), Cats Eyes Through Windowsills, 2003. Recipient Ogden Nash award, Triangle Pub., 1973. Mem.: Pa. Poetry Soc., Nat. Mus. Women in Arts, Internat. Soc. Poets, James Madison Bldg.-Libr. Congress (assoc.). Avocations: genealogy, poetry. Home: PO Box 256 Greencastle PA 17225

FRENCH, BARBARA C. state representative; b. Norwood, Mass., July 1, 1926; divorced; children: Michael, Susan. BS, U. N.H., 1948, Sch. Nursing, N.Y. Hosp., 1950; MEd, Mt. St. Mary, 1967. Clin. instr. N.H. State Hosp., 1953-55; child welfare social worker N.H. Dept. Welfare, 1960-63; sch. nurse Union Sch. Dist., Concord, 1963-90; drug edn. cons. N.H. Detp. Edn., 1974-75; mem. dist. 3 N.H. Ho. of Reps., Concord, 1992-94, 96—. Author: After the Crash, Jour. of Christian Nursing, 1986. Mem. Henniker Recycling Com., N.H. Coalition Against Gambling Expansion, Henniker Peace Group, Ptnrs. of the Ams., N.H. Women's Lobby Tax Equity Task Force. Mem. Nat. Sch. Nurses Assn. (bd. dirs. 1972-78, sec./treas. 1978-79, N.H. Sch. Nurse of Yr. 1990), NEA, N.H. Ret. Educators Assn. (pres.), AARP. Congregationalist. Home: 17 Fairview Ave Henniker NH 03242-3310

FRENCH, CANDACE LEE, elementary school educator, music educator; b. Springfield, Mo., Aug. 17, 1956; d. Ronald Lee and Fern Elizabeth Affolter; m. Everett Earl French, Dec. 20, 1980; children: Gregory, Geoffrey. BS in Edn., So. Mo. State U., 1979, MEd in Music Edn., 1987. Tchr. piano, voice pvt. practice, Springfield, Mo., 1978—2003, Willard, 1978—2003; choral dir. Willard Jr. High Sch., 1979—; choir dir. Ctrl. Christian Ch., Springfield, 1995—. Mem.: Music Edicators Nat. Conf., Mo. State Tchrs. Assn.

FRENCH, CATHERINE E. WOLFGRAM, engineering educator, researcher; b. Dec. 17, 1957; BS in Civil Engring., U. Minn., 1979; MS in Civil Engring., U. Ill., 1980, PhD in Civil Engring., 1984. Rsch. and tchg. asst. dept. civil engring. U. Ill., Urbana-Champaign, 1979-83; asst. prof. dept. civil engring. U. Minn., Mpls., 1984-90, assoc. prof. dept. civil engring., 1990-97, prof., assoc. head dept. civil engring., 1997-2000. Mem. external adv. com. FEMA external adv. com. Earthquake Engring. Simulation Facility U. Nev., Reno, 1994-97. Erskine fellow U. Canterbury, New Zealand, 1995, Fulbright Travel fellow New Zealand, 1995; recipient Presdl. Young Investigator award NSF, 1985, R.J. Boase award for contbns. to prestressed concrete rsch. Reinforced Concrete Rsch. Coun., Young Civil Engrs. Achievement award U. Ill. Civil Engring. Alumni Assn., 1987, Minn. Young Civil Engr. of Yr. Minn. Soc. Profl. Engrs., 1989, Faculty Award for Women, 1991-96, Bonestroo, Rosene, Anderlik and Assoc. Undergrad. Faculty award, 1994. Fellow Am. Concrete Inst. (com. 318 std. bldg. code 1996—, bd. dirs. Iowa-Minn. chpt. 1987-91, pres. 1991, Outstanding Chpt. award 1991, Kennedy award 2004, bd. dirs. 1996-91); mem. ASCE (award for Outstanding Svc. as Faculty Adv. to student chpt. 1986-90, 1986, Edmund Friedman Young Engr. award for Profl. Achievement 1989, U. Minn. Gordon L. Starr award Outstanding Faculty Contbn. to student chpt. 1990, Raymond C. Reese Rsch. prize 1990, mem. structures com. Minn. 1986-90, pres. Minn. chpt. 1996-97), Earthquake Engring. Rsch. Inst. (Travel grant 1988, 2000), Precast/Prestressed Concrete Inst. (seismic com.), Transportation Rsch. Bd. (concrete bridges com.), Minn. Surveyors and Engrs. Soc. Achievements include research in behavior of reinforced concrete and prestressed concrete structures subjected to lateral loads, bond strength and durability of reinforcement in concrete, investigation of causes and methods to eliminate cracking in the fabrication of prestressed bridge girders, application of high strength concrete to prestressed systems, investigation of mechanical properties of high strength concrete and structural behavior of prestressed bridge girders fabricated with high strength concrete, development of testing method "effective force testing" for real-time earthquake simulation. Office: U Minn Dept Civil Engring 122 Civil Engring Bldg 500 Pillsbury Dr SE Minneapolis MN 55455-0233 Business E-Mail: cfrench@umn.edu.

FRENCH, DORRIS TOWERS BRYAN, volunteer; b. Kissimmee, Fla., May 15, 1926; m. Lawrence Cornwell French, Sept. 7, 1947; children: Layne Bryan, Leyland Bradley. Student, Art Inst., Costa Rica, 1940-42; BFA, Tulane U., 1946; student, U. Mex., 1943-44. Fabric designer Wembley Co., 1945-46; designer silver and jewelry New Orleans, 1945-47; head art dept. pvt. sch., 1947. Columnist From the Mayor's Desk; editor pub. Paw Prints, 1981-93. Founder, v.p. Peoples Animal Welfare Soc., 1977-96; past art dir., coord. internat. gladiola show Garden Club, Binghamton. Mem. AAUW, Zeta Tau Alpha. Avocations: animal welfare, writing, art. Home: 3510 Aransas St Corpus Christi TX 78411-1302

FRENCH, ELIZABETH IRENE, biology educator, violinist; b. Knoxville, Tenn., Sept. 20, 1938; d. Junius Butler and Irene Rankin (Johnston) F. MusB, U. Tenn., 1959, MS, 1962; PhD, U. Miss., 1973. Tchr. music Kingsport (Tenn.) Symphony Assn., 1962-64, Birmingham (Ala.) Schs., 1964-66; NASA trainee in biology U. Miss., Oxford, 1969-73; asst. prof. Mobile (Ala.) Coll. (name now U. Mobile), 1973-83, assoc. prof., 1983-94, prof., 1994—. Orch. contractor Am. Fedn. Musicians, 1983—; 1st violin Kingsport Symphony Orch., 1962-64, Birmingham Symphony Orch., 1964-66, Knoxville Symphony Orch., 1955-62, 66-68, Memphis Symphony Orch., 1970-73, Fairhope (Ala.) Concert Series, 1998, Mobile Symphony Orch., 1974—, Pensacola Symphony Orch., Gulf Coast Symphony Orch. Violin recitalist Ala. Artists Series, 1978-81, Fairhope (Ala.) Concert Series, 1998. Mem. project Choctaw Nat. Wildlife Refuge, 1997-98. Named Career Woman of Yr., Gayfer's, Inc., 1985. Mem. Assn. Southeastern Biologists, Human Anatomy and Physiology Soc. (nat. com. to construct standardized test on anatomy and physiology), Wilderness Soc., Ala. Acad. Scis. (presenter 1996), Ala. Ornithol. Soc., Mobile Bay Audubon Soc. (bd. dirs. 1997—), Am. Fedn. Musicians, Ala. Fedn. Music Clubs (chmn. composition contest 1986-90, historian 1991-94), Schumann Music Club (pres. 1977-79, 85-87, 94-97, 2000-03). Republican. Roman Catholic. Avocations: camping, photography, birdwatching. Home: 36 Ridgeview Dr Chickasaw AL 36611-1317 Office: U Mobile PO Box 13220 Mobile AL 36663-0220

FRENCH, HILARY F. foundation administrator; V.p. rsch. Worldwatch Inst., Washington. Contbr. articles to profl. jours. Office: Worldwatch Inst Ste 800 1776 Massachusetts Ave NW Washington DC 20036-1995 E-mail: hfrench@worldwatch.org.

FRENCH, LEURA PARKER, secondary educator; b. Owensville, Ind., June 4, 1926; d. Arthur William and Mildred Ruth Parker; m. Alvin L. French, July 14, 1947 (dec. Sept. 1996); children: Bruce A., Dwight L. BA cum laude, God's Bible Sch. and Coll., 1950; BS in Edn., Wesleyan U., Marion, Ind., 1952; MS in Edn., Butler U., 1961; postgrad., U. Calif., Davis, 1970—73. Tchr. Moorhead Jr. H.S., Indpls., 1957-58, Washington H.S., Indpls., 1962-63, Bella Vista H.S., Fair Oaks, Calif., 1963-65, Casa Roble H.S., Orangevale, Calif., 1967-84, Valley Oak H.S., Oakdale, Calif., 1987—. Study tours for WWII in Europe, China, Hong Kong, Bangkok, Singapore. Co-author booklet: Goals and Objectives for the San Juan Unified School District's Reading Program, 1972. Active Free Meth. Ch., Indpls., 1953-62, Orangevale, 1963-85, 89-96, Oakdale, 1985-89. Fellow Calif. Tchrs. Assn. Republican. Avocations: reading, research, writing, travel. Home: 1100 Roseville Pkwy #317 Roseville CA 95678-5351

FRENCH, MARILYN, writer, critic; b. N.Y.C., Nov. 21, 1929; d. E. Charles and Isabel (Hazz) Edwards; m. Robert M. French, Jr., June 4, 1950 (div. 1967); children: Jamie, Robert. BA, Hofstra Coll., 1951, MA, 1964; PhD, Harvard U., 1972. Secretarial, clerical worker, 1946-53; lectr. Hofstra Coll., 1964-68; asst. prof. Holy Cross Coll., Worcester, Mass., 1972-76; Mellon fellow Harvard U., 1976-77; writer, lectr., 1967—. Author: (criticism) The Book as World: James Joyce's Ulysses, 1976, Shakespeare's Division of Experience, 1981, (novels) The Women's Room, 1977, The Bleeding Heart, 1980, Her Mother's Daughter, 1987, Our Father: A Novel, 1994, My Summer with George, 1996, (nonfiction) Beyond Power: On Women, Men and Morals, 1986, The War Against Women, 1992, A Season in Hell, 1998, From Eve To Dawn: A History of Women, Vol. I-III, 2002—03, introductions to Edith Wharton's Summer and The House of Mirth, 1981. Mem. Virginia Woolf Soc., Phi Beta Kappa.

FRENCH, PATSY J. property manager, state representative; b. Randolph, Vt., Aug. 22, 1949; m. Patrick French; 2 children. BS in Edn., U. Vt., 1972. Owner, mgr. rental property; rep. Vt. State Ho. Reps., 2003—. Democrat. Home: 886 Harlow Hill Randolph VT 05060

FRENCH, SARA LILLIAN, humanities educator, writer; d. Robert Lewis and Esther Griswold French. Deuxieme Degre, U. Stendahl, Grenoble, France, 1989; A.B., Wells Coll., Aurora NY, 1990; M.A., SUNY, Binghamton, 1993, PhD, 2000. Vis. asst. prof. Wells Coll., Aurora, NY, 2000—. Contbr. articles to scholarly book, Widowhood and Visual Culture in Early Modern Europe. Sec. Griswold Family Assn. of Am., Inc., Wethersfield, Conn., 1999—2003; sr. v.p. Onondaga Soc., Children of the Am. Revolution, Syracuse, NY. Recipient Hon. State Pres., N.Y. State Soc., Children Am. Revolution, 1987. Mem.: DAR (Henrick Hudson chpt.), DAR (Comfort Tyler chpt.) (assoc.), Nat. Soc. Daughters of Founders and Patriots of Am., Continental Soc., Daughters of Indian Wars, Descendants of the Knights of the Garter and Friends of St. George's Chapel, Windsor (life), Nat. Soc. Americans of Royal Descent (life). Office: Wells College Aurora NY 13026 E-mail: sfrench@wells.edu.

FRENCH, STEPHANIE TAYLOR, corporate philanthropist; b. Newark; d. William Taylor and Connie V. French; m. Amory Houghton III, Sept. 8, 1979 (div.); children: Christina French Houghton, Amory Taylor Houghton. BA, Wellesley Coll., 1972; MBA, Harvard U., 1978. Freelance on-air performer, prodr. San Francisco and Oakland radio and cable TV stas., 1973-76; dir. European Gallery, San Francisco, 1974-75; acct. exec. Young & Rubican, N.Y.C., 1978-79; acct. supr. Rives Smith Baldwin & Carlberg, Houston, 1980-81; mgr. cultural affairs and spl. programs Philip Morris Cos. Inc., N.Y.C., 1981-86, dir. cultural and contbns. programs, 1986-90, v.p. corp. contbn. and cultural programs bds., 1990—2001; ind. art. cons., 2001—. Bd. dirs. Joffrey Ballet of Chgo., Contemporary Art, Dance Com. Juilliard Sch., Am. Craft Mus., Parsons Dance Co., Nat. AIDS Fund, The Thomas S. Kenan Inst. for the Arts, Harkness Ctr. for Dance Injuries, Bus. Com. of the Met. Mus. Art, Arts and Edn. Adv. Coun. for Harvard Grad. Sch. Edn., New Mus. Contemporary Art, Ballet Tech, Career Transitions for Dances; bd. adv. com. Bill T. Jones/Arnie Zane Co.; mem. dance com. Juillard Sch.; apptd. mem. Gov. of N.Y. to Empire State Arts Commn., Mayor of N.Y.C. to the N.Y.C. Econ. Devel. Corp. Mem. Harvard Bus. Sch. Network of Women Alums, Wellesley Club.*

FRESCH, MARIE BETH, court reporting company executive; b. Norwalk, Ohio, Jan. 16, 1957; d. Ralph Roy and Vonda Mae (Brunkhorst) Spiegel; m. James R. Fresch, Aug. 5, 1978; 1 child, Alexandra Jane. AS in Bus., Tiffin U., 1977; cert. in ct. reporting, Acad. Ct. Reporting, 1979. Registered profl. reporter, Ohio. Ofcl. reporter Seneca County Common Pleas Ct., Tiffin, Ohio, 1979-80; owner, operator Marie B. Fresch & Assocs., Norwalk, 1980—. Coach indoor and outdoor Soccer teams, 1994-99, summer softball teams, 1994—, girls volleyball coach, 1999-2002; leader Girl Scouts Am., 1995-2002, sch. organizer, team leader, 1997-2002, parade organizer, 1998-2002. Recipient Cert. of Merit, Nat. Ct. Reporters Assn., 1990; named Outstanding Leader, Girl Scout Coun., 1998, Outstanding Vol., 2000. Mem. Nat. Ct. Reporters Assn., Ohio Ct. Reporters Assn. (student promotions and pub. rels. coms. 1986-90, dist. rep. 1994-95, fundraising com. 1993-96), NOW (sec. Port Clinton chpt. 1984-86, treas. 1986-87, 91), Am. Legion Aux., Kappa Delta Kappa. Lodges: Order of Eastern Star (esther 1979-81). Democrat. Methodist. Avocations: swimming, biking, gardening, hiking. Home and Office: 47 Warren Dr Norwalk OH 44857-2447 Office Phone: 419-668-7394. E-mail: MBF1@AccNORWALK.com.

FRESH, LINDA LOU, government official; b. Ashland, Pa., June 29, 1957; d. Harold Foster and Norma Jean (Thomas) Geist; m. Bruce Alan Fresh, June 18, 1977; 1 child, Niccole Patricia. AA in Bus. Mgmt., U. Md., Okinawa, Japan, 1981; BS in Psychology, U. Md., Heidelberg, Germany, 1987; EdM in Counseling, Boston U., Heidelberg, 1994. Clinic liaison specialist U.S. Army, Augsburg, Germany, 1985, fin. counselor New Cumberland, Pa., 1989-92, Hanau, Germany, 1992-94; family support program specialist U.S. Army Res., Ft. Belvoir, Va., 1994-95; family life specialist USAF, Washington, 1995-96; family advocacy prevention and edn. specialist USN, Washington, 1996-99; EEO mgr., fed. women's program mgr., mgr. Upward Mobility program, EAP counselor FBI, Washington, 1999—, sexual harassment coord., 2000—. Mem. interagy. com. Fed. Women's Program, Washington, 1999; spl. asst. Fed. Women's Program to Federally Employed Women's Nat. Pres. and Bd. Mem. Mus. for Women in Arts, Women's Meml. With U.S. Army, 1975-78. Mem. AAUW, Women in Mil. Svc. for Am., Women's Army Corps Vets. Assn., Federally Employed Women (exec. v.p. N.W. D.C. chpt.), Women in Fed. Law Enforcement Inc., Toastmasters. Avocations: travel, movies, writing, reading, teaching. Home: 12993 Queen Chapel Rd Woodbridge VA 22193 Office: FBI 935 Pennsylvania Ave NW Washington DC 20535-0001

FRESHWATER, SHAWNA MARIE, neuropsychologist, clinical psychologist, cognitive neuroscientist; b. Roseau, Minn., Aug. 10, 1964; d. Robert D. and Andrea K. Porter; children: Michaël, David. BA (magna cum laude), U. Miami, 1995; MS in Clin. Psychology, Nova Southeastern U., Ft. Lauderdale, 1996, PhD, 2000, postdoc., 2002. Lic. Psychology Fla., 2001. Behavioral medicine/health psychology trainee Behavioral Medicine Clin. Rsch. Ctr., U. Miami, 1993—95; psychology intern Cmty. Mental Health Ctr., Nova Southeastern U., Ft. Lauderdale, 1995—96, psychology intern child and adolescent traumatic stress program, 1995—96, psychology intern program for seriously emotionally disturbed, 1995—96; intern Brain Injurty Rehab. Program, Ft. Lauderdale, 1996—97, Bnef Psychotherapy Program, Ft. Lauderdale, 1997—98, V.A. Hosp., Miami, 1997—99, resident East Orange, NJ, 2000, Cornell Med. Ctr., N.Y.C., 2000, N.Y. Presbyn. Hosp., N.Y.C., 2000; postdoc. fellow, faculty rschr. dept. Neurology U. Fla., Gainesville, 2000—02; dir., pres. Neuropsychological Inst., P.A., Miami, 2002—. Author: (jour. article) Nineteenth Ann. Procs. of Soc. for Behavioral Medicine, 1998, The Clin. Neuropsychologist, 1998, Archives of Clin. Neuropsychology, 1999—2000, Jour. of Clin. Geropsychology, 2001. Mem.: Fla. Soc. Neurology, Internat. Neuropsychological Soc., Nat. Acad. Neuropschology, APA, Phi Theta Kappa, Phi Kappa Phi, Phi Beta Kappa. Office: Neuropsychological Inst PA 2999 NE 191st St Ste 240 Aventuia FL 33180

FRETZ, DEBORAH MCDERMOTT, oil industry executive; m. Philip Fretz; two children. BS in Biology and Chemistry, Butler U., 1970; MBA, Temple U., 1977. Virologist Merck, Sharp & Dohme; fin. analyst Sun Co., Inc., 1977—, mgr. fin. analysis group, 1985-88, dir. wholesale fuels mktg., 1988-89, gen. mgr. fuels, 1989; pres. Sun Pipe Line Co. and Marine Terminals Sunoco, Inc., 1991—; sr. v.p. logistics Sunoco, Inc., 1994—2000; sr. v.p. lubricants Sunoco, Inc., 1997—2000, sr. v.p. MidContinent Refining, Mktg. and Logistics, 2000; pres., COO Sunoco Logistics Ptnrs., LP, 2001. Dir. GATX Corp., Cooper Tire and Rubber Co. Office: Sunoco Logistics Ptnrs LP Ten Penn Ctr 1801 Market St Ste Sl Philadelphia PA 19103-1699*

FREUND, CYNTHIA M. dean; BSN, Marquette U., 1963; MSN, U. N.C., 1973, FNP, 1974; PhD in Bus. and Health Adminstrn., U. Ala., 1981. Staff nurse McHenry (Ill.) Hosp., 1963, 64-65, VA Hosp., Wood, Wis., 1963-64; instr. Milw. County Instns., Wauwatosa, Wis., 1965-68, supr. Milw. County Rehab. and Chronic Disease Hosp., 1968-70; instr. Sch. Nursing U. Wis., Milw., 1972-73; dir. FNP program Area L Health Edn. Ctr., Tarboro, N.C., 1973-74; asst. prof., assoc. dir. FNP program U. N.C., Chapel Hill, 1974-78, assoc. prof., chair social and adminstrv. sys. dept., 1984-92, dean, prof. nursing, 1992-99, prof. nursing, dean emeritus, 1999—; asst. prof. U. Pa., Phila., 1981-84, sr. rsch. assoc. Leonard Davis Inst. Health Econs., 1981-84, dir. MSN nursing adminstrn. program, PhD in nursing/MBA joint degree, 1981-84. Mem. Gov. Advocacy Com. for Children and Youth State of Wis., 1973; bd. dirs. N.C. Ctr. for Child and Family Health, 1996, N.C. Inst. Medicine, 1996—; mem. N.C. Med. Data Base Commn., N.C. Gen. Assembly, 1985-89; mem. nursing adv. panel P.E.W. Health Professions Commn., 1991-92; mem. nat. adv. com. for project future requirements for nurse practitioners and nurse midwives Dept. Health and Human Svcs., 1993-94, mem. joint adv. com. to project future requirements for primary care physicians, and others, Bur. Health Professions, 1994-95; cons., presenter in field. Author: (with D. del Bueno) Power and Politics in Nursing Administration, 1986 (Am. Jour Nursing Book of Yr. 1986), Nursing: A Kaleidoscopic View, 1991 (Am. Jour. Nursing Book of Yr. 1991); author chpts. to books; mem. editl. bd. Nursing Econs., 1982-84, manuscript reviewer, 1982—; manuscript reviewer Jour. Profl. Nursing, 1984—, Health Svc. Rsch., 1984—, Planning for Higher Edn., 1986; contbr. articles to profl. jours. Bd. dirs. N.C. Ctr. Child and Family Health, 1996, N.C. Inst. Medicine, 1996—. Pub. Health Svc. Doctoral fellow Nat. Ctr. for

Health Svcs. Rsch., 1980-81, Rsch. fellow Nat. Health Care Mgmt. Ctr., 1980-81; recipient Profl. Svc. Alumni award Marquette U., 1992. Fellow Am. Acad. Nursing; mem. ANA (vice-chair coun. FNP and clinicians 1977-78, cert. adult nurse practitioner 1977, Jessie M. Scott award 1990), Nat. League Nursing, Acad. Mgmt., Am. Orgn. Nurse Execs., Am. Hosp. Assn. Office: U NC Sch Nursing Cb 7460 Carrington Hl Chapel Hill NC 27599-0001

FREUND, DEBORAH MIRIAM, transportation engineer; b. Bklyn., Apr. 9, 1957; d. Harry and Bertha (Fried) F.;m. Garey Douglas White, Feb. 22, 1981. BSCE, Washington U., 1979, MSc, 1982. Registered profl. engr., Tex. Grad. rsch. asst. Washington U., St. Louis, 1979-81; transp. planning engr. Mid-Am. Regional Coun., Kansas City, Mo., 1981-83; civil engr. Fed. Hwy. Adminstrn., Washington, 1983-85, rsch. hwy. engr., 1985-90, transp. specialist, 1990-92, sr. transp. specialist, 1992—99; sr. transportation specialist Fed. Motor Carrier Safety Admin., 2000—. Nat. tech. expert for vehicle rsch., 2001—; mem. com. operator and vehicle performance and simulation Transp. Rsch. Bd., Washington, 1993—96, mem. com. on vehicle user characteristics, 1997—2003, mem. com. on frt. econs. and regulation, 2000—, mem. com. on truck and bus safety, 2003—; presenter in field. Recipient award for meritorious achievement, Sec. of Transp., 1996, Forest R. McFarland Award, Soc. of Automotive Engrs., 2003; fellow, Coun. for Excellence in Govt., Washington, 1995—96. Mem. ASCE (sec. hwy. divsn. rsch. com. 1988-90), Soc. Automative Engrs. (co-chair total vehicle com. 1997—), Inst. Transp. Engrs., Sigma Xi (assoc.). Achievements include leadership in research on commercial motor vehicle driver safety; innovation in pavement infrastructure information systems. Office: Fed Motor Carrier Safety Adminstrn 400 7th St SW Washington DC 20590-0001 Office Phone: 202-366-4009. E-mail: dmfreund@go-nci.com.

FREUND, EMMA FRANCES, medical technologist; b. 1922; d. Walter R. and Mabel W. (Loveland) Ervin; m. Frederic Reinert Freund, March 4, 1953; children: Frances, Daphne, Fern, Frederic. BS, Wilson Tchrs. Coll., Washington, 1944; MS in Biology, Cath. U., Washington, 1953; MEd in Adult Edn., Va. Commonwealth U., 1988. Tchr. math and sci. D.C. Sch. Sys., Washington, 1944-45; technician in parasitology lab. U.S. Dept. Agr., Beltsville, Md., 1945-48; histologic technician dept. pathology Georgetown U. Med. Sch., Washington, 1948-49; clin. lab. technician Kent and Queen Anne's County Gen. Hosp., Chestertown, Md., 1949-51; histotechnologist Med. Coll. Va. Hosp., Richmond, Va., 1951—. Cons. profl. meetings and workshops; exam. coun. Nat. Credentialing. Agy. Med. Lab. Pers. Co-author: (mini course) Instrumentation in Cytology and Histology, 1985; editor Histo-Scope Newsletter. Asst. den leader Robert E. Lee coun. Boy Scouts Am., 1967-68, den leader, 1968-70. Mem. AAAS, NAFE, AAUW, APS, Am. Mgmt. Assn., Am. Soc. Clin. Lab. Sci. (rep. to sci. assembly histology sect. 1977-78, chmn. 1983-85, 89 96), Va. Soc. Med. Tech. (Richmond chpt. corr. sec. 1977-78, bd. dirs. 1981-82, pres. 1984-85), Va. Soc. Histotech. (pres. 1994-96), Nat. Credentialing Agy. (clin. lab. specialist in histotech., clin. supr. clin. lab. dir.), N.Y. Acad. Scis., Am. Assn. Clin. Chemistry (assoc.), Am. Soc. Clin. Pathology (assoc.; cert. histology technician), Nat. Geog. Soc., Va. Govtl. Employees Assn., Nat. Soc. Histotech. (by-laws com. 1981—, C.E.U. com. 1981—, program com. regional meeting 1984, 85, 87, 97, 2000, chmn. regional meeting 1987, program chmn. state meeting 1998-99, Conv. scholarship award 1997, Clin. Chemists' Recognition award 1995, 98, 2002), Am. Mus. Natural History, Smithsonian Inst., Am. Mgmt. Assn., Am. Chem. Soc., Am. Soc. Quality, Clin. Lab. Mgmt. Assn., Van Slyke Soc., Soc. Human Resource Mgmt., Nat. Soc. Hist. Preservation, Math. Assn. Am., Sigma Xi, Phi Beta Rho, Kappa Delta Pi, Phi Lambda Theta. Home: 1315 Asbury Rd Richmond VA 23229-5305

FREY, JOANNE ALICE TUPPER, art educator; b. Wakefield, Mass., Jan. 16, 1931; d. Arthur Andrew Tupper, Elva June Goddard, Joanne Alice Tupper; m. John Oscar Frey, June 14, 1953 (dec. Oct. 2000); children: David J., Donald A., Dale R., Alexandria Brennan. Grad. honors, Vesper George Sch. Art, Boston, 1951; student art history, NTL Art Gallery, London, 1979. Tchr. art Wishing Well Cards, Everett, Mass., 1951—54, Sarrin Studio, Wakefield, Mass., 1960—96; tchr. art oil, acrylic, and watercolor Wakefield H.S., Wakefield, 1997—. Antique and current doll authority; lectr. in field. Asst. resident dir. Boit Home for Women, Wakefield, Mass., 1996—; bd. dirs. The Hartshorne House. Mem.: Collie Fancier League of N.E., The Kosmos Club (decorator 1997—). Republican. Congregationalist. Avocations: painting, reading, walking, gardening, art history. Home: 701 Haverhill St Reading MA 01867

FREY, JULIA BLOCH, French language educator, art historian educator; b. Louisville, July 25, 1943; d. Oscar Edgeworth and Jean Goldthwaite (Russell) Bloch; m. Roger G. Frey, Dec. 27, 1968 (div. Mar. 1976); m. Ronald Sukenick, Mar. 9, 1992. BA, Antioch Coll., 1966; MA, U. Tex., 1968; MPhil, Yale U., 1970, PhD, 1977. Instr. Brown U., Providence, 1972-73; chargé de cours U. Paris, 1974-75; lectr. Yale U., New Haven, 1975-76; prof. Inst. Internat. Comparative Law, U. San Diego, Paris, 1979-89, adminstrv. dir., 1989; prof. French, art history U. Colo., Boulder, 1976—2001, prof. emeritus, 2002—, dir. undergrad. studies, 1985-95, assoc. chmn. for grad. studies, 1996-97, 98-99, chmn., 1999. Guest prof. Sarah Lawrence Coll., Bronxville, N.Y., 1983; curator Toulouse-Lautrec Met. Mus. Art Denver Art Mus., 1999, Toulouse-Lautrec, Museo Vittoriano, Rome, 2003-04. Author: Toulouse-Lautrec, a life, 1994, Toulouse-Lautrec l'homme qui aimait les femmes, 1996; editor: Gustave Flaubert's La Lutte du Sacerdoce et de L'Empire (1837), 1981; contbr. articles and monographs to profl. publs., chpts. to books; translator: René. Recipient Conn. Grad. Study award, 1970-73; grantee NDEA, 1967, Brown U. Research and Travel, 1973, Boulder Arts Com., 1979, 80, Ctr. for Applied Humanities, 1985, S.W. Inst. for Research on Women, 1985-86, NEH, 1986; fellow NDEA, 1966-68, Yale U., 1968-72, Gilbert Chinard, Inst. Français de Washington, 1977, Big 12 2000, Humanities Rsch. Ctr., Australian Nat. U., 2000; Pen Ctr. USA West Lit. award for non-fiction, 1995; Finalist Nat. Book Critics Cir. award for Biography, 1994. Mem. MLA, PEN U.S.A., Coll. Art Assn., Yale Club. Unitarian Universalist. Home: 355 8th Ave New York NY 10001 E-mail: julia.frey@aya.yale.edu.

FREY, LUCILLE PAULINE, social studies educator, consultant; b. Huggins, Mo., Aug. 1, 1932; d. Albert Raymond and Gladys Pearl (Maxville) F. BS in Edn., Southwest Mo. State U., 1955; MA in English, Mo. U., 1963; MAT, Alaska Pacific U., 1975; PhD in Women's Studies, Union Grad. Inst., 1985. Tchr. Tex. County Rural Schs., Plato, Mo., 1949-53, Sullivan (Mo.) Pub. Schs., 1953-57, Anchorage Pub. Schs., 1957-70; social studies coord., 1970-75; ednl. cons. The Learning Tree, Alaska, 1975-85. Adj. prof. U. Alaska, 1970-77; owner Women's Bookstore, Anchorage, 1981-84; comml. fisherwoman Net Prophets, Bristol Bay, Alaska, 1980-85; real estate salesperson Dynamic Properties, Anchorage, 1989-94, Century 21 Peterson, Hermitage, Mo., 1995—. Author: (textbook) Eyes Toward Icebergia, 1963; editor: Women of Alaska Workbook, 1974, Alaska Studies Curriculum, 1975, Athabaskan Curriculum, 1980. Founding mem. Alaska Women's Edn. Caucus, Anchorage, 1970; mem. Alaska Women's Polit. Caucus, Anchorage, 1972; organizer various state edn. confs., 1976-83, women's conf., Alaska, 1982. Recipient Gov's. Vol. award, Alaska, 1984; named to Women's Hall of Fame, Alaska, 1991. Mem. NEA (Women's Right award 1979, Renowned Alaskan award, 1986), Profl. Women's Assn. (sec.), Mo. Realtor's Assn., Union Grad. Inst. (mem. doctoral com.), Ozark Bd. Realtors, Lake Area Friendship Club. Progressive. Avocations: gardener, birdwatcher, historian, political activist. Home: RR 1 Box 1965 Urbana MO 65767-9639

FREY, MARGO WALTHER, career counselor, columnist; b. Watertown, Wis., July 1, 1941; d. Lester John and Anabel Marie (Bergin) Walther; m. James Severin Frey, June 29, 1963; children: Michelle Marie Frey Loberg, David James. BA in French, Cardinal Stritch Coll., 1963; MS in Ednl. Psychology, U. Wis., Milw., 1971; EdD in Adult Edn., Nova U., 1985. Nat. bd. cert. career counselor; approved profl. counselor, Wis. Acad. counselor biology dept. Ind. U., Bloomington, 1975-76; dir. career planning and placement Cardinal Stritch Coll., Milw., 1977-89; pres. Career Devel. Svcs., Inc., Milw., 1989—. Weekly columnist Milw. Journ. Sentinel, 1994-95, 98—. Mem. Bloomington (Ind.) women's commn. com. on employment assessment Displaced Homemakers Task Force, 1975. Named to Practitioner's Hall of Fame, Nova U., 1985. Mem. ASTD (bd. dirs. 1992), Wis. Career Planning and Placement Assn. (bd. dirs. 1987), Wis. Assn. Adult and Continuing Edn. (bd. dirs. 1983-85), Milw. Coun. Adult Learning, Human Resource Mgmt. Assn., Tempo (bd. dirs. 1995-97). Avocations: reading, swimming. E-mail: margocds@execpc.com.

FREY, MARY ELIZABETH, artist; b. Yonkers, N.Y., Nov. 25, 1948; d. Harold and Matilda F.; m. William M. Bennett, Jan. 31, 1976; children: Jacob F. and Nicholas F. BA in Fine Arts, Coll. New Rochelle, 1970; postgrad., Pratt Inst., 1970-71; MFA in Photography, Yale U., 1979. Instr. photography Project Art Ctr., Cambridge, Mass., 1975-77, dir. photography, 1976-77; prof. photography Hartford Art Sch., West Hartford, Conn., 1989—. NEA, Washington, 1994; vis. artist Harvard U., Cambridge, 1984, Cooper Union, N.Y.C., 1985, Yale U., New Haven, 1986, NYU, N.Y.C., 1987, Cornell U., Ithaca, N.Y., 1988, Northfield Mt. Hermon, Northfield, Mass., 1989, Mills Coll., Oakland, Calif., 1989, Hampshire Coll., 1992; Harnish vis. artist Smith Coll., Northampton, Mass., 1994-95; guest lectr. Hudson River Mus., Yonkers, N.Y., 1984, Hartford Art Sch., 1988, Smith Coll. Mus. Art, Northampton, 1994. One-woman shows include Panopticon Gallery, Boston, 1974, Hollins College (Va.) Art Gallery, 1977, Project Art Ctr., Cambridge, Mass., 1979, Hudson River Mus., Yonkers, N.Y., 1984, Blue Sky Gallery, Portland, 1985, ZONE Art Ctr., Springfield, Mass., 1988, Ledel Gallery, N.Y.C., 1989, Arno Maris Gallery, Westfield, Mass., 1991, Springfield (Mass.) Mus. of Fine Arts, 1993, Ariz. State U., 1994, Laelia Mitchell Gallery, Boston, 1995, Marlboro (Vt.) Coll., 1998; group shows include Commonwealth Armory, Boston, 1974, Project Art Ctr., Cambridge, 1975, Boston City Hall, 1976, Yale U., New Haven, 1977, Webb & Parsons Gallery, New Bedford, Mass., 1978, Pleasant St. Gallery, Amherst, Mass., 1979, Hampshire Coll., Amherst, 1980, Light Gallery, N.Y.C., 1981, Memphis Acad. Art, 1982, Carpenter Ctr. for Visual Arts, Cambridge, 1984, Blue Sky Gallery, Portland, 1985, Mus. Modern Art, N.Y.C., 1986, Aperture Gallery, N.Y.C., 1986, 87, Real Art Ways, Hartford, Conn., 1988, MS Gallery, Hartford, 1990, Smith Coll. Mus. Art, Northampton, 1992, 100 Pearl St. Gallery, Hartford, 1993, Artspace, New Haven, 1994, ICP-Midtown Eye of the Beholder, 1997, Coll. of N.J., 2002, Smithsonian Instn., 2001, others; represented in permanent collections at Art Inst. Chgo., Mus. Fine Arts, Houston, Smith Coll. Mus. Art, Northampton, Internat. Polaroid Collection, Cambridge, Mus. Modern Art, N.Y.C., Coca-Cola Corp., Atlanta, Bank of Boston, Springfield Tech. C.C., Avon Corp., others. Home: 70 Firglade Ave Springfield MA 01108-2531

FREY, VIOLA, sculptor, educator; b. Lodi, Calif., Aug. 15, 1933; AA, Delta Coll.; BFA, Calif. Coll. Arts and Crafts; MFA, Tulane U. Prof. ceramics Calif. Coll. Arts and Crafts, 1965—; chmn. dept. ceramics Noni Eccles Treadwell Ceramic Arts Ctr. One woman shows at Whitney Mus. Am. Art, 1984, Moore Coll. Art, Phila., 1984; exhibited sculpture in numerous shows including Calif. State U., Fullerton, 1977, San Francisco Mus. Modern Art, 1978, A Century of Ceramics in the U.S. Everson Mus. Art, Syracuse, N.Y., 1979, Renwick Mus., Washington, 1979, Cooper-Hewitt Mus., N.Y., 1979, Crocker Art Mus., Sacramento, Oakland (Calif.) Mus., St. Louis Mus. Art, Huntsville (Ala.) Mus. Art, Seattle Art Mus. Grantee Nat. Endowment Arts, 1978, 86. Office: c/o Rena Bransten Gallery 77 Geary St San Francisco CA 94108-5723

FREYD, JENNIFER JOY, psychology educator; b. Providence, Oct. 16, 1957; d. Peter John and Pamela (Parker) F.; m. John Q. Johnson, June 9, 1984; children: Theodore, Philip, Alexandra. BA in Anthropology magna cum laude, U. Pa., 1979; PhD in Psychology, Stanford U., 1983. Asst. prof. psychology Cornell U., 1983-87, mem. faculty coun. of reps., 1986-87; assoc. prof. psychology U. Oreg., Eugene, 1987-92, prof., 1992—, mem. dean's adv. com., 1990-91, 92-93, mem. exec. com. Ctr. for the Study of Women in Soc., 1991-93, mem. child care com., 1987-89, 90-91. Elected mem. faculty coun. of reps. Cornell U., 1986-87; mem. dean's adv. com. U. Oreg., 1990—, exec. com. Ctr. for Rsch. Study of Women in Soc., 1991-92, Inst. of Cognitive and Decision Scis., 1991-94; mem. instl. rev. bd. U. Oreg., 2002—. Author: Betrayal Trauma: The Logic of Forgetting Childhood Abuse, 1996 (Disting. Publ. award Assn. of Women in Psychology 1997, Pierre Janet award Internat. Soc. for Study Dissociation 1997), Spanish edit., 2003; co-editor: (with A.P. De Prince) Trauma and Cognitive Science: A Meeting of Minds, Science, and Human Experience, 2001; mem. editl. bd. Jour. Exptl. Psychology: Learning, Memory, and Cognition, 1989-91, Gestalt Theory, 1985—, Jour. of Aggression, Maltreatment, and Trauma, 1997—, Jour. of Psychopathology and Behavioral Assessment, 2001-2003, Jour. Trauma Practice, 2003—, Jour. of Trauma and Dissociation, 1999-2003, assoc. editor, 2004 ; guest reviewer Am. Jour. Psychology, Am. Psychologist, others; contbr. articles to profl. jours. Recipient Grad. fellowship NSF, 1979-82, Univ. fellowship Stanford U., 1982-83, Presdl. Young Investigator award NSF, 1985-90, IBM Faculty Devel. award, 1985-87, fellowship Ctr. for Advanced Study in the Behavioral Scis., 1989-90, John Simon Meml. fellowship Guggenheim Found., 1989-90, Rsch. Scientist Devel. award NIMH, 1989-94, Pierre Janet award Internat. Soc. for the Study of Dissociation, 1997; other rsch. funding. Fellow AAAS, APA (liaison divsn. 35 to sci. directorate 1998—), Am. Psychol. Soc.; mem. Psychonomic Soc., Internat. Soc. for the Study of Traumatic Stress, Sigma Xi. Office: U Oreg 1227 Dept Psychology Eugene OR 97403-1227

FREYER, DANA HARTMAN, lawyer; b. Pitts., Apr. 17, 1944; m. Bruce M. Freyer, Dec. 21, 1969. Student, L' Institut De Hautes Etudes Internationales, Geneva, 1963-64; BA, Conn. Coll., 1965; postgrad., Columbia U., 1968, JD, 1971. Bar: N.Y. 1972, Ill. 1974, U.S. Dist. Ct. (no. dist.) Ill. 1974, U.S. Ct. Appeals (7th cir.) 1976, U.S. Supreme Ct. 1977, U.S. Dist. Ct. (so. dist.) N.Y. 1978, U.S. Dist. Ct. (ea. dist.) N.Y. 1981, U.S. Ct. Appeals (2d cir.) 1982. Staff atty. Legal Aid Soc. Westchester County, Mt. Vernon, N.Y., 1971-72; assoc. Friedman & Koven, Chgo., 1973-77, Skadden, Arps, Slate, Meagher & Flom, LLP, N.Y.C., 1977-88; spl. counsel Skadden, Arps, Slate, Meagher & Flom, N.Y.C., 1988-93, ptnr., 1994—. Pres. Westchester Legal Services, Inc., White Plains, N.Y., 1985-87, bd. dirs., 1978-98; U.S. Coun. for Internat. Bus. Arbitration Com.; London Ct. of Internat. Arbitration; adv. bd. World Arbitration and Mediation Report. Mem. ABA, Bar Assn. of City of N.Y., Internat. Bar Assn. Office: Skadden Arps Slate Meagher & Flom LLP 4 Times Sq Fl 48 New York NY 10036-6522

FREYER, VICTORIA C. fashion and interior design executive; b. Asbury Park, N.J. d. Spiros Steven and Hope (Pappas) Pappaylion; m. Cyril Steven Arvanitis, Dec. 26, 1950 (div. 1975); children: Samuel James, Hope Alexandra. BA, Georgian Court Coll., 1950; student, N.Y. Sch. Interior Design, 1971-72. Mgr. Homestead Restaurant, Ocean Grove, N.J., 1946-58; art supr. Lakewood (N.J.) Pub. Schs., 1950-51; interior designer London, 1975-76, F. Korasic Assocs., Oakhurst, N.J., 1977-78; owner, operator Virginia Interiors, McLean, Va., 1974-90; interior designer Anita Perlut Interiors, McLean, 1986; owner, operator Victoria Freyer Interiors, McLean, 1986—; fashion cons. Nordstrom Splty. Store, McLean, 1988-92, fashion seminar coord. Tysons Corner, Va., 1992—. Lectr. Girl Scouts U.S., Rep. Women of Capitol Hill, Washington Hosp. Ctr., Women's Am. ORT, Nat. Assn. Cath. Women, Bethesda Naval Hosp., NIH, others. Pres. Monmouth County Med. Aux., 1964; originator 1st lecture series Monmouth Coll., Long Branch, N.J., 1965; guest moderator Alexandria (Va.) Hosp. Series, 1988; mem. Women's Symphony Com., Washington, 1988—; guest speaker Girl Scouts U.S. Coun. Nation's Capitol, 1988-90, Nuclear Energy Coun., 1989, pers. dept. CIA, 1989-90, Internat. Women's Group Washington, 1989-90. Recipient Recognition awards Girl Scout Coun. Nation's Capitol, 1991, No. Region Beta Pi, 1991, Beta Sigma Pi, 1991. Mem. AAUW (program chmn. 1968, guest speaker many orgns.). Greek Orthodox. Avocations: greek and roman archeology and antiquities, painting, gourmet cooking, traveling. Home and Office: 7630 Provincial Dr Mc Lean VA 22102-7652

FREYERMUTH, VIRGINIA KAREN, art educator; BFA cum laude, Boston U., 1973, MFA, 1975; edn. cert., Suffolk U., 1975; PhD in Interdisciplinary Studies, Art Edn., Union Inst. and U., 2003. Cert. art tchr., Mass. Grad. asst. Boston U., Mass., 1973-75; art tchr. Quincy Pub. Sch., Mass., 1975-76, Plymouth Pub. Sch., Mass., 1976-78, 83-85; painting tchr. Brockton Fuller Mus. Art, Mass., 1978-79; art coord. grades K-12 Duxbury Pub. Sch., Mass., 1985-99; vis. lectr. art edn. U. Mass., Dartmouth, Mass., 1999—. Art reviewer Patriot Ledger, Quincy, 1975-85; dir. Freyermuth Fine Arts Ctr., Plymouth, 1990-94; mem. adv. coun. Mass. Field Ctr. Tchg. & Learning, 1993-96; tchr. in electronic residence MCET, Cambridge, 1993-95; instr. art Massasoit C.C., Brockton, 1991-92; dir. Helen Bumpus Gallery, Inc., Duxbury, 1992-94; forum tchr. Goals 2000 U.S. Dept. of Edn., 1994—, internat. space camp, 1994. Columnist Learning for Life, 1994. Mem. commn. on common core of learning Mass. Dept. Edn., 1993-94; bd. dirs. Mass. Alliance for Arts Edn., 1994-95. Named Mass. Tchr. of Yr., Mass. Dept. Edn., 1994, Nat. Outstanding Visual Art Tchr., Walt Disney and McDonald's, 1995, 1995-96 Profiled in Disney Channel. Mem. Mass. Art Edn. Assn., Nat. Art Edn. Assn., Tchr. Leadership Acad. Mass. (bd. dirs.), Lucretia Crocker Acad. of Tchg. Fellows (bd. dirs.). Office: PO Box 6132 Plymouth MA 02362-6132

FREYMUELLER, CYNTHIA LOUISE, educational consultant; b. Chgo., July 29, 1940; d. Eugene Willard and Dorothy Harriet (Rutstrom) Larson; m. John Craig Freymueller; children: Jeffrey T., Brian J., Sarah S. BA, San Diego State U., 1962; GATE cert., U. Calif., Riverside, 1982. Cert. elem. tchr., K-8, Calif. Tchr. LaMesa Spring Valley Sch. Dist., 1962-64, Ctrl. Sch. Dist., Rancho Cuca, Calif., 1976-81; mentor, tchr. Snowline J.U. Sch. Dist., Phelan, Calif., 1981-95, reading cons., 1995—. Recipient Hon. Svc. award PTA Ctrl. Sch., 1978, Foothill Coun. PTA, 1979. Mem. AAUW (v.p.), Mountain Desert Reading Assn., Calif. Reading Assn., Delta Kappa Gamma (1st v.p.). Avocations: reading, sewing, sports, gardening, traveling. Home: 18524 Kamana Rd Apple Valley CA 92307-1454

FREYTAG, SHARON NELSON, lawyer; b. May 11, 1943; d. John Seldon and Ruth Marie (Herbel) Nelson; children: Kurt David, Hillary Lee. BS with highest distinction, U. Kans., Lawrence, 1965; MA, U. Mich., 1966; JD cum laude, So. Meth. U., 1981. Bar: Tex. 1981, U.S. Dist. Ct. (no. dist.) Tex. 1981, U.S. Ct. Appeals (5th cir.) 1982, U.S. Supreme Ct. 1993, U.S. Dist. Ct. (so. dist.) Tex. 2001, U.S. Ct. Appeals (8th cir.) 2001, U.S. Ct. Appeals (fed. cir.) 2002. Tchr. English, Gaithersburg (Md.) H.S., 1966—70; instr. English, Eastfield Coll., 1974-78; law clk. U.S. Dist. Ct. (no. dist.) Tex., 1981-82, U.S. Ct. Appeals (5th cir.), 1982; ptnr., chmn. appellate practice sect. Haynes and Boone, Dallas, 1983—. Vis. prof. law So. Meth. U., 1985-86. Editor-in-chief Southwestern Law Jour., 1980-81; contbr. articles to profl. jours. Bd. dirs. Ctr. for Brain Health; dir. devel. bd. U. Tex. at Dallas; co-chmn. task force on appellate advocacy Cou. of Appellate Lawyers. Recipient John Marshall Constl. Law award, Baird Cmty. Spirit award, 1995, named Tex. Super Lawyer, 2003; Woodrow Wilson fellow. Mem. ABA (litigation sect., co-chmn. subcom. on appellate rules), Fed. Bar Assn. (co-chmn. appellate practice and adv. sect. 1990-91), Tex. Bar Assn. (appellate coun. 1995-98), State Bar Tex. (bd. dirs., exec. com. 1997-2001), Dallas Bar Assn. (appellate coun., chair, courthouse com.), Coun. of Appellate Lawyers (co-chair task force on appellate advocacy), Higginbotham Inn of Ct. (former barrister), Order of Coif, Phi Beta Kappa. Lutheran. Office: Haynes & Boone 3100 Bank of America Plz Dallas TX 75202 E-mail: freytags@haynesboone.com.

FRIARS, EILEEN M. bank executive; b. Holden, Mass., June 3, 1950; d. Gordon Edward and Marjorie Ella Friars. BA, Simmons Coll., 1972; MBA, Harvard U., 1974. Mgmt. asst. U.S. Govt. Office Mgmt. and Budget, Washington, 1974-76; sr. v.p., dir. fin. svcs. practice The MAC Group, Chgo., 1976-90; sr. exec. v.p. C&S/Sovran, Virginia Beach, Va., 1990-92; pres. card svcs. Nations Bank, Charlotte, N.C., 1992-98; pres. consumer credit card svcs. Bank of Am., Charlotte, 1998-99. Mem. vis. com. Harvard Bus. Sch., 2000-; mem. adv. bd. McColl-Garella, 2003-. Editor: Financial Services Handbook; contbr. articles to profl. jours. Pres. Charlotte Repertory Theatre, 1997—98; bd. dirs. Com. of 200, Chgo., 1997—2003; trustee. Simmons U., Boston, 1997—, chair fin. com. Named Outstanding Bus. Leader, Northwood U., Palm Beach, Fla., 1998. Mem. Harvard Bus. Sch. Club Charlotte. Avocations: theatre, hiking, writing, yoga.

FRIAUF, KATHERINE ELIZABETH, metal company executive; b. Balt., Oct. 13, 1956; d. John Beecher Friauf and Elizabeth Withers (Wilson) Struever. Student, Columbia Coll., Chgo., 1979-81. Cert. sound engr. Owner, operator Midwest Emery Freight System, Chgo., 1978-80; driver BCB Dispatch, Inc., Rochester, N.Y., 1980-88, dispatcher, systems analyst LeRoy, N.Y., 1988-89; corp. controller Rochester Plating Works, Inc., 1988—; owner Rochester Vibratory Inc., 1991—. Dir. Rochester Plating Works, Inc., 1988-91. Mem. NAFE, Rochester Women's Network (patron mem.). Presbyterian. Avocations: classical piano, photography, gardening, gourmet cooking. Office: Rochester Vibratory Inc 4 Cairn St Rochester NY 14611-2416

FRIDAY, KATHERINE ORWOLL, artist; b. Granite Falls, Minn., Dec. 3, 1917; d. Melvin Sylvester and Anna Elizabeth (Hustvedt) Orwoll; m. Erling Bjarne Struxness, May 8, 1943 (div. 1961); children: John Eric, Mimi Ann McNicholas, Mari Struxness; m. George Edward Friday, Apr. 12, 1969 (dec. Jan. 1997). Student, U. Minn., 1935-36, 40-41, Frederick Mizen Sch. of Art, Chgo., 1941. Designer, illustrator Josten's, Owatonna, Minn., 1936-39, 42-43; layout artist Tempo Inc., Chgo., 1941-42, Vogue-wright Studios, Chgo., 1943-44; layout, illustration Allan D Parson Advt. Agy., Chgo., 1945, Ad-Art, Wichita, Kans., 1952-54, 63; indsl. designer Harold W. Darr Assoc., Mpls., 1959-61; layout, illustration Lydiard Assoc., Mpls., 1961—62; owner Skyline Studio, Mpls., 1962—66; layout, illustration Comm. Cons., Wilmington, Del., 1971; freelance illustration, med. illustration dept. pathology U. Chgo., Chgo., 1946-48; freelance illustrator Hutchinson, Kans., 1948—52, 1954—58; art dir. SPF Adv., Intermedia, Mpls., 1966-69, Arne Westerman Adv., Portland, Oreg., 1970-71, Battle Advt., Wyncote, Pa., 1971-72; creative dir., owner A'La Carte Advt./Art, Bellevue, Wash., 1973-77; graphic illustration Courseware, Moffat Field, Mountain View, Calif., 1978, Quantic, Los Altos, Calif., 1979—; ret., 1982; represented by Belinki-Duprey Art Gallery, Portland Art Mus. Rental Gallery. Tchr. watercolor, colored pencil, pastel techniques; curator, judge internat. miniature art exhibit Festival of the Arts, Lake Oswego, Oreg., 2002. Exhibitions include Westminster Gallery, London, 1995, Hobart, Tasmania, 2000. Recipient Best of Show award, Internat. Miniature Art Show, Kirkland, Wash., 1997, hon. mention, 1998, 4th pl., 1999, 3d pl., 2001. Mem.: N.W. Artists' Support Group, Oreg. Soc. Artists, Main St. Art. Soc. (Best of show, 1st pl. and 2d pl. awards 2002, Best of Show, 1st and 2d pl. awards, 3d pl., Merit award, Best of Show, 1st pl. oil, 1st pl. watercolor 2003), Painters Showcase (Grand award 1999, Judges Choice award 2000—02), Oreg. Colored Pencil Soc. (2d pl. N.W. Regional show 2000—02), Watercolor Soc. Oreg. (Achievement award 1998, 2002), Cider Painters of Am. (award of excellence 1992—94, 1st in floral 1993, still life 1995, portrait 1995, award of excellence 1997, portrait 1998, Pres. award 1999, award of excellence 2001, Pres. award 2002, signature mem.), Ga. Miniature Artists Soc. (2d pl. and 3d pl. 1990, 1st pl. 1991, 1994, Merit award 1997), Miniature Art Soc. Fla. (1st pl. 1989—90, 2d pl. 1994—95,

1st pl. 1997—98, 2d pl. 1999, 1st pl. 2002—03), Miniature Artists of Am. (hon. signature), Colored Pencil Soc. Am., N.W. Watercolor Soc. (assoc.), Miniature Painters, Sculptors, Gravers Soc. (assoc. 3d pl. 1990, 1st pl. 1996, 1st of show 1998, 2d and 3d pl. 1999, Grumbacher award, 2d pl. 2001). Avocations: painting, drawing, reading, music.

FRIDAY, LEAH REBECCA, portfolio manager; b. Houston, Nov. 12, 1968; d. Jerry Jefferson and Verena (Shuttlesworth) Bennett; m. Charles Kevin Friday, Aug. 26, 1995. BS, Tex. A&M U., 1991. CFA. Fixed income product specialist Am. Funds Group, L.A., 1992—95; portfolio mgr. King Investment Advisors, Houston, 1995—. Mem.: Houston Soc. Fin. Analysts (edn. com. 1999—2001, edn. chmn. 2001—04, secr. 2002—03, treas. 2003—04), Kappa Alpha Theta. Republican. Avocations: running, biking, tennis, reading, triathlons. Office: King Investment Advisors 1980 Post Oak Blvd #2400 Houston TX 77056

FRIDAY, NANCY, author; b. Pitts., Aug. 27, 1938; d. Walter and Jane (Colbert) F.; m. Norman Pearlstine, 1988 Student, Wellesley Coll. Editor Islands in the Sun, 1961-63. Author: My Secret Garden, 1973; Forbidden Flowers, 1975; My Mother, My Self, 1977, Men in Love: Men's Sexual Fantasies: The Triumph of Love over Rage, 1980; Jealousy, 1985; Women on Top: Women's Sexual Fantasies of Power, Self Exploration and Insatiable Lust, 1991; The Power of Beauty, 1996.

FRIDLEY, SAUNDRA LYNN, private investigator; b. Columbus, Ohio, June 14, 1948; d. Jerry Dean and Esther Eliza (Bluhm) F. BS, Franklin U., 1976; MBA, Golden Gate U., 1980. Accounts receivable supr. Internat. Harvester, Columbus, Ohio, San Leandro, Calif., 1972-80; sr. internal auditor Western Union, San Francisco, 1980; internal auditor II County of Santa Clara, San Jose, Calif., 1980-82; sr. internal auditor Tymshare, Inc., Cupertino, Calif., 1982-84, divsn. contr., 1984; internal audit mgr. VWR Scientific, Brisbane, Calif., 1984-88, audit dir., 1988-89; internal audit mgr. Pacific IBM Employees Fed. Credit Union, San Jose, 1989-90, Westaff, Inc., Walnut Creek, Calif., 1990—2002; lic. pvt. investigator, owner Fridley & Assoc., 2000—. Dir. quality assurance, 1992-98, v.p. audit and investigations, 1998-2002; owner Dress Fore the 9's, Brentwood, Calif., 1994—; pres., founder Bay Area chpt. Cert. Fraud Examiners, 1990. Commr. Brentwood Art Commn., 2003—; mem. Brentwood Bus. Alliance. Mem. NAFE, Calif. Assn. of Lic. Investigators, No. Calif. Fraud Investigators Assn., Friends of the Vineyards, Internal Auditors Speakers Bur., Assn. Cert. Fraud Examiners (founder, pres. Bay area chpt., we. regional gov. 1996-97, Disting. Achievement award 1997, 98), Inst. Internal Auditors (pres., founder Tri-Valley chpt., internat. seminar com., internat conf. com.) Avocations: woodworking, gardening, golfing. Home: 19 Windmill Ct Brentwood CA 94513-2502 Office: Fridley & Assocs 613 1st St # 19 Brentwood CA 94513 also: Dress Fore The 9's 613 1st St Ste 19 Brentwood CA 94513-1322 Office Phone: 800-306-3673. E-mail: saunief@aol.com.

FRIED, ELEANOR REINGOLD, psychologist, educator; b. Quantico, Va., Jan. 4, 1943; d. Morris and Eleanor (Wilson) R.; divorced, 1984; children: Joshua Mark, Noah Seth, Adam Lawrence. BS cum laude, Boston U., 1964; MS in Clin. Sch. Psychology, CUNY, 1971; postgrad. Fordham U., 1971-73; MA in Clin. Psychology, The Fielding Inst., 1980, PhD in Clin. Psychology, 1981. Lic. psychologist, N.J. Psychology intern Roosevelt Hosp., N.Y.C., 1971-73; cons. Inwood House, N.Y.C., 1971-83; staff therapist Univ. Consultation Center Mental Hygiene, Bronx, N.Y., 1974-79, clin. instr., 1976-80; sr. clin. psychologist moderate security unit North Princeton Developmental Ctr., 1983-98; cons. Early Childhood Learning Center, Paramus, N.J., 1978-80, Found. for Religion and Mental Health, Briarcliff Manor, N.Y., 1979-82, Inwood House, N.Y.C., 1981-83, prin. clin. psychologist Ewing Residential Ctr., Trenton, N.J., 1987-88, Ind. Child Study Teams, East Orange, N.J; pvt. practice, Princeton, N.J.; ct. expert in forensic psychology; exec. dir. Ea. Profl. Group. Fellow Am. Bd. Forensic Examiners; mem. APA (assoc.), N.J. Psychol. Assn., Nat. Assn. Treatment Sex Offenders, Kappa Tau Alpha. Office: Ea Profl Group 601 Ewing St Ste C20 Princeton NJ 08540-2758 E-mail: fried@nerc.com .

FRIED, LINDA P. medical educator; b. N.Y.C., 1949; MD, Rush Med. Coll., 1979; MPH, Johns Hopkins U., Balt., 1985; BA in Polit. Sci., Colgate U. Diplomate Am. Bd. Internal Medicine. Intern Rush Presbyn. St. Luke's Med. Ctr., Chgo., 1979—80, resident in internal medicine, 1980—82; fellow in internal medicine Johns Hopkins Med. Inst., Balt., 1982—85, fellow in epidemiology, 1983—85, fellow in geriatrics, 1985—86; legis. dir. Congresswoman Connie Morella, Washington, 1987—98; prof. medicine, epidemiology and health policy Johns Hopkins U., Balt.; staff Johns Hopkins Hosp. Geriatrician and dir. Johns Hopkins Ctr. on Aging and Health; vice chair clin. epidemiology and health svcs. rsch. Johns Hopkins Dept. Medicine, mem. pres.'s coun.; advisor Paul Beeson Faculty Scholars in Aging Rsch., Health and Retirement Survey; staff liaison Congl. Caucus for Women's Issues, 104th Congress. Contbr. articles to prof. jours.; mem. editl. bd. Jour. Gerontology, Am. Jour. of Medicine. Pres. Women's Policy, Inc., 1999—. Recipient Archstone award, APHA, 2000, Marion Spenser Fay award for the 2000 Disting. Woman Physician/Scientist, Herbert R. DeVries Disting. Rsch. award, Coun. on Aging and Adult Devel., 2000; fellow Exec. Leadership in Acad. Medicine Program fellow; scholar Kaiser Found. scholar in gen. internal medicine. Fellow: Am. Heart Assn. (Coun. on Epidemiology and Prevention); mem.: ACP, SGIM, SER, AGS, Inst. of Medicine of NAS. Office: Johns Hopkins Med Inst 2024 E Monument St Ste 2-700 Baltimore MD 21205

FRIEDAN, BETTY, writer, feminist leader; b. Peoria, Ill., Feb. 4, 1921; d. Harry and Miriam (Horwitz) Goldstein; m. Carl Friedan, June 1947 (div. May 1969); children: Daniel, Jonathan, Emily. AB summa cum laude, Smith Coll., 1942, LHD (hon.), 1975, SUNY, Stony Brook, 1985, Cooper Union, 1987; Doctorate (hon.), Columbia U., 1994. Rsch. fellow U. Calif., Berkeley, 1943; lectr. feminism univs., women's groups, bus. and profl. groups in U.S. and Europe; founder NOW, 1st pres., 1966-70, chairwoman adv. com., 1970-72, mem. bd. dirs. legal def. and edn. fund; organizer Nat. Women's Polit. Caucas, 1971, Internat. Feminist Congress, 1973, First Women's Bank, 1973, Econ. Think Tank for Women, 1974; v.p. Nat. Assn. Repeal Abortion Laws, 1970-73. Disting. vis. prof. sch. journalism and studies of women and men in soc., U. So. Calif., 1987; vis. prof. sociology Temple U., 1972, Queens Coll., 1975; vis. lectr. Calhoun Coll., fellow Yale U., 1974; lectr. New Sch. Social Research, N.Y.C., 1971; sr. research assoc. Ctr. Social Scis., Columbia U., N.Y.C., 1979-81; bd. dirs. NOW Legal Defense and Education fund; co-chmn. Nat. Comms. Women's Equality; del. White Ho. Conf. on Family, 1980; del. UN Decade for Women Confs. in Mexico City, Copenhagen, Nairobi; mem. LORAN Commn. Harvard Community Health Plan; vis. scholar U. S. Fla., Sarasota, 1985; Disting. vis. prof. Sch. Journalism and Social Work Sch. U. So. Calif., Cornell U., Ithaca, N.Y., 1998—. Author: The Feminine Mystique, 1963, It Changed My Life: Writings on the Women's Movement, 1976, The Second Stage, 1981, The Fountain of Age, 1993, Beyond Gender: The New Politics of Family and Work, 1998, Life So Far, 2000; mem. editl. bd. Present Tense mag.; contbg. editor McCall's mag., 1971-74; contbr. Atlantic Monthly; contbr. articles to New York Times, Cosmopolitan, Saturday Rev., Family Circle, Good Housekeeping, McCall's, Newsweek, American Behavioral Scientist, Social Policy, and others; papers being collected by Schlesinger Libr. Harvard U. Mem. exec. com. Am. Jewish Congress, co-chair nat. commn. women's equality, 1984-85; mem. nat. bd. Girl Scouts USA, 1976-82; mem. N.Y. County Democratic Com. Recipient Humanist of Yr. award, 1974, Eleanor Roosevelt Leadership award, 1989; Inst. Politics fellow Kennedy Sch. Govt., Harvard U., 1982, rsch. fellow Ctr. Population Studies, Harvard U., 1982-83, Chubb fellow Yale U., 1985, Andrus Ctr. Gerontology fellow U. So. Calif., 1986, guest scholar Woodrow Wilson Ctr. for Internat. Scholars, 1995-96, disting. vis. prof. George Mason U., 1995, Mt. Vernon Coll., 1996; Ford Found. grantee, 1998. Mem. AFTRA, PEN, Author's Guild, Women's Ink, Women's Forum, Mag. Writers, Am. Soc. Journalists and Authors (1st recipient Mort Weisinger award for outstanding mag. journalism 1979, Author of Yr. 1982), Assn. Humanistic Psychology, Am. Sociology Assn., Gerontol. Soc. Am., Cosmos Club, Nat. Press Club, Phi Beta Kappa. Address: 2033 Columbia Rd NW Washington DC 20009-1352

FRIEDEN, JANE HELLER, art educator; b. Norfolk, Va., Aug. 25, 1926; d. Samuel Ries and Saida (Seligman) Heller; m. Joseph Lee Frieden, Dec. 23, 1950 (dec. 1990); children: Nancy Frieden Crowe, Robert M., Andrew M. AA, Coll. of William and Mary, Norfolk, Va., 1945; BA, Coll. of William and Mary, Williamsburg, Va., 1947; MA, Columbia U., 1950. Lic. pvt. pilot. Tchr. art City of Norfolk Pub. Schs., 1947-48, Hudson Day Sch., New Rochelle, N.Y., 1948-49, Mt. Vernon (N.Y.) Pub. Schs., 1949-50, City of Norfolk Pub. Schs., 1950-51; prof. art Coll. William and Mary Extension, Williamsburg, 1957-72, U. Va. Extension, Norfolk, 1972-78, Cmty. Colls. State of Va., Chesapeake and Hampton, 1978-82, St. Leo Coll., Norfolk, 1982-95; advocate Chrysler Mus. Art, 2003—. Travel agt., 1977-89. Author: (dictionary) A is For Art, 1978-82; artist water color paintings and ink drawings at several shows. Asst. Gen. Douglas MacArthur Meml. Archives, Norfolk, 1945—95; vol. Chrysler Mus. Art, Norfolk, 1991—, advocate, 2003—, amb.; vol. Va. Symphony Aux., 1992—98, Norfolk Little Theatre Box Office, 1991—, Meals on Wheels, 1962—66, Make a Wish Found., 1996, ARC, 1953—95, Grey Lady Project, 1956—62, Bloodmobile Project, 1966—80, Va. Zool. Soc., 1996; tchr. drawing Ghent Venture, 1993; reader for the visually handicapped Intouch Network WHRO-Radio, 1991—; archives com. Ohef Sholom Temple; bd. dirs. Norfolk Little Theatre, 1996; vol. career svcs. Coll. William and Mary, 1992—; drawing tchr. Norfolk Sr. Ctr., 1998—99; vol. docent USS Wisconsin BB 64, Hampton Roads Naval Mus., 2001—. Mem. Ninety-Nines (treas. 1978-85), Tidewater Artists Assn. (bd. dirs. 1975-80, 91—, treas. membership com.), Tidewater Orchid Soc., Am. Orchid Soc., Norfolk Soc. Arts, United Daus. Confederacy, Hermitage Soc., Norfolk Ex Libris Soc. Coll. William & Mary (steering com. 1993—), Va. Belles (reunion com. 1993—), Chesapeake Watercolor Soc. Republican. Jewish. Avocations: drawing and water color painting, raising orchids, travel. Home: 221 Oxford St Norfolk VA 23505-4354 E-mail: flymum@earthlink.net.

FRIEDHABER-HARD, SUSAN MARGARET, school media specialist, educator; b. Holyoke, Mass., July 11, 1944; d. John Herbert and Anne Mary (Pruzinsky) Friedhaber; m. Robert Osvath, Feb. 17, 1973 (div. 1990); 1 child, Rebecca Jeanne Osvath. BA, Daemen Coll., 1967; MLS, State Univ. Coll., Geneseo, 1974; postgrad., Christ the King Sem., East Aurora, N.Y., 1999—. Tchr. English and French, DeSales H.S., Columbus, Ohio, 1967-68; housemother St. Vincent's Orphanage, Columbus, 1968; tchr. English and French Mater Dei H.S., New Monmouth, NJ, 1968-69; records libr. Children's Aid Soc., Buffalo, 1970; tchr. English, French and religion, libr. Archbishop Carroll H.S., Buffalo, 1970-74; libr. asst. Arcade (N.Y.) Free Libr., 1975-81; sch. libr. Pioneer H.S., Yorkshire, NY, 1981—, chmn. libr. dept., 1989-94, 2000—, co-chmn. libr. dept., 1998—99. Mem. coun. Cattaraugus-Allegany Sch. Libr. System, 1986-90, chmn. coun., 1989-90; lector, mem. liturgy com. St. Joseph's Ch., Bliss, N.Y., 1987-90. Mem. Citizens' Activist Group to fight zoning change, Arcade, 1982-83; tchr. St. Mary's Ch., East Arcade, N.Y., 1977-84, 97-2002, lectr., 1980-84, 97—; mem. N.Y. State Hist. Assn., 1986-2003, The Eighth Air Force Hist. Soc. Western N.Y., 1994—. Mem. ALA, AAUW, Am. World War II Orphans' Network, N.Y. Libr. Assn., Sch. Libr. Assn. Western N.Y., Arcade Hist. Soc., Enchanted Mountains Sch. Libr. Assn. (treas. 1993-94, v.p. 1994-95, pres. 1995-96), Second Air Divsn. Assn. Roman Catholic. Office: Pioneer High Sch Libr PO Box 639 Yorkshire NY 14173-0639 Home: 146 Skyview Dr Arcade NY 14009-9521 Office Phone: 716-492-9324.

FRIEDLAND, BILLIE LOUISE, former human services administrator; b. Los Alamos, N.Mex., Jan. 6, 1944; d. William Jerald and Harriet Virginia (Short) Van Buskirk; m. David Friedland. BS in Edn., California U. of Pa., 1972, MS in Psychology, 1986; EdD, W.Va. U., 1998. Sales mgr., buyer Friedland's Ladies Ready-To-Wear, Monessen, Pa., 1969-72; tchr. Belle Vernon (Pa.) Area Schs., 1973-74; head social scis. dept. Yeshiva Achei Tmimim, Pitts., 1974-75; caseworker, outreach to children and their families project Fayette County Mental Health and Mental Retardation Clinic, Uniontown, Pa., 1975, ctr. supr. outreach to children and their families project, 1976; case mgr., family support svcs. coord. Diversified Human Svcs. Inc., Monessen, 1978-89, supr. cmty. living arrangements, 1989-92; grad. asst. Affiliated Ctr. for Devel. Disabilities W.Va. U., Morgantown, 1992-93, grad. asst. dept. spl. edn., 1993-98, coord. inclusive schooling project, 1998-99; asst. prof. spl. edn. Ea. Ill. U., Charleston, 1999—2002, Del. State U., 2002—. Founder 1st Infant/Toddler Day Care Project, Fayette County, 1976-78. Mem. NAACP, CEC (sponsor student chpt.), Am. Assn. Mental Retardation, Assn. Supervision & Curriculum Devel., Am. Conf. Rural Spl. Edn. (reviewer RSEQ), W.Va. Fedn. Coun. for Exceptional Children (past pres. divsn. mental retardation/devel/ disabilites), Phi Delta Kappa, Sigma Rho Epsilon. Avocations: cross country skiing, canoeing, backpacking, hiking, bicycling. Office: Del State U EH 233 Edn & Human Performance 1200 N Dupont Hwy Dover DE 19901 Office Phone: 302-587-6744. E-mail: bfriedla@desu.edu.

FRIEDLANDER, PATRICIA ANN, marketing professional, writer; b. Chgo., May 9, 1944; d. James Farrell and Therese Mary (Pfeiler) Crotty; m. Daniel B. Friedlander, July 3, 1971 (div. Apr. 1978); children: Michael Derek, David Colin; m. Lisa Tolva, Sept. 23, 2000. BA, Cardinal Stritch Coll., 1966; MA, U. Wis., Milw., 1968; postgrad., U. Chgo., 1968-69, U. London, 1968—. Instr. U. Wis., Milw., 1966-68, Chgo. State U., 1968-71, Argo Cmty. H.S., Summit, Ill., 1971-73, Park Dist., Park Forest South, Ill., 1973-77; counselor Will County Mental Health Clinic, Park Forest South, 1977-78; sales rep. Prentice-Hall, Inc., Englewood Cliffs, N.J., 1978-84; nat. sales mgr. Dow Jones-Irwin, Homewood, Ill., 1984-87; dir. mktg. Nat. Textbook Co., Lincolnwood, Ill., 1987-88; mgr. mktg. Scott Foresman & Co., Glenview, Ill., 1988-90; corp. advt. dir. Giltspur, Inc., Itasca, Ill., 1990-96; dir. Mktg. Comms. Exhibitgroup/Gitspur, Roselle, Ill., 1996-98; sales exec. Derse Exhibits, Chgo., 1998-99; dir. mktg. Exhibitor Mag. Group, 1999-2000; pres. Word-Up! Comms., 2000—. Dir. Printer's Row Bookfair, Chgo., 1985; cons.; spkr. and author in trade show. Den mother Cub Scouts Am., Park Forest South, 1981-84. Mem. Bus. Mktg. Assn., Health Care Conv. and Exhibitors Assn., Trade Show Exhibitors Assn. Avocations: piano, reading, cycling, swimming. Home and Office: Word-Up! 2320 W Farwell Ave Chicago IL 60645-4735 E-mail: pat@patfriedlander.com.

FRIEDLI, HELEN RUSSELL, lawyer; b. Indpls., July 8, 1956; d. William F. and Helen F. Russell; m. E. Kipp Friedli, May 19; children: Katherine, Laura. BS, Purdue U., 1977; JD, Ind. U., 1980. Bar: Ill. 1980. Ptnr. McDermott, Will & Emery, Chgo., 1980—. Office: McDermott Will & Emery 227 W Monroe St Ste 3100 Chicago IL 60606-5096 E-mail: hfriedli@mwe.com.

FRIEDMAN, ALICE DIANE, internist, gastroenterologist, educator; b. Houston, Aug. 21, 1957; d. Ben and Susanna Rose (Stern) F. BS in Medicine, Tex. A&M U., 1979, MD, 1981; MS in Aerospace Medicine, Wright State U., 1994. Lic. physician, Tex. Resident in internal medicine U. of Va. Affiliated Hosp., Roanoke-Salem, Va., 1981-84; fellow in gastroenterology U. Md. Hosp., Balt., 1984-86; pvt. practice Mahorner Clinic, New Orleans, 1986-87, Lubbock, Tex., 1988-92; resident in aerospace medcine Wright State U., Dayton, Ohio, 1992-94; rsch. asst. Logicon Inc., Dayton, 1993-94; asst. prof. in internal medicine U. Ark. for Med. Scis., Little Rock, 1994—97; pvt. practice Kansas City, Kans., 1997—2001, Brenten Arrow, Okla., 2001, Austin, Tex., 2001—. Instr. U. Md., Balt., 1984-86; clin. asst. prof. Tex. Tech. U., Lubbock, 1989-91; cons. Dayton-Vets. Hosp., 1993-94. Contbr. case reports, abstracts, studies to profl. publs. Bd. dirs. S.W. Lubbock Kiwanis, 1989-92. Rsch. grantee Schering Inc., 1995. Fellow ACP, Am. Coll. Gastroenterology; mem. AMA, Am. Gastroenterol. Assn. Avocations: pilot, tae kwan do, racquetball, astronomy. Office: Austin Diagnostic Clinic 12221 Mapae Expressway North Austin TX 78758

FRIEDMAN, D. DINA, writer, educator; b. Tacoma Park, Md., June 13, 1957; d. Stanley David and Susan Loeserman Friedman; m. Shel Horowitz, Oct. 9, 1983; children: Alana Horowitz Friedman, Rafael Horowitz Friedman. BA in English, Cornell U., 1978; MSW, U. Conn., 1987. Co-dir. Accurate Writing & More, Northampton, Mass., 1987—; instr. Mt. Holyoke Coll., South Hadley, Mass., 1997—2002; instr. sch. mgmt. U. Mass., Amherst, 2000—. Writing workshop leader Amherst Writers and Artists, 1987—99; tchr. pub. speaking U. Mass., 1987—89. Co-founder Save the Mountain, Hadley, Mass., 1999—. Recipient Pallas award, Athena Press, 1988, Reed Smith prize, Amelia Mag., 1989. Mailing: PO Box 1164 Northampton MA 01061

FRIEDMAN, DANIELLE, social worker; b. Bklyn., Dec. 16, 1977; d. Martin and Arlene Dena Friedman. BA, Stern Coll. for Women, N.Y.C., 1998; MSW, Columbia U., N.Y.C., 2000. LCSW N.Y. Grad. asst. Yeshiva U., N.Y.C., 1998—2000; social worker Montefiore Med. Ctr., Bronx, NY, 2000—01, Columbia Presbyn. Med. Ctr., N.Y.C., 2001—. Democrat. Jewish. Avocations: reading, crossword puzzles. Home: 65 W 85th St Apt A New York NY 10024 Office: Columbia Presbyn Med Ctr 622 W 168th St New York NY 10032

FRIEDMAN, FRANCES, public relations executive; b. NYC, Apr. 8, 1928; d. Aaron and Bertha (Itzkowitz) Fallick; m. Clifford Jerome Friedman, June 17, 1950; children— Kenneth Lee, Jeffrey Bennett. BBA, CCNY, 1948. Dir. pub. rels. Melia Internat., Madrid, N.Y.C., 1971-73; sr. v.p. Lobsenz-Stevens, N.Y.C., 1973-75; exec. v.p. Howard Rubenstein Assocs., N.Y.C., 1975-83; pres., prin. Frances Friedman Assocs., N.Y.C., 1983-84; pres., chmn. bd. dirs. GCI Group Inc., N.Y.C., 1984-91, pub. rels. and editl. cons., 1991-93; mng. dir. L.V. Power & Assoc., Inc., 1993-97; pub. rels. cons. N.Y.C., 1997—. Media cons. White Ho. on Women's Issues, 1995; participant in Vital Voices Confs., Hillary Clinton's program for women in emerging democracies, 1996; feature writer Kenttribune.com, 2003—. Mem. editl. staff: Kenttribune.com, 2003. Bd. dirs. United Nations Assn. (NW Ct. chpt.), 2003, Morris-Jumel Mansion, 1999-2001, Contemporary Guidance Svcs, 1999, 2001, City Coll. Fund, N.Y.C., 1970-79; mem. adv. bd. League for Parent Edn., N.Y.C., 1961-65; editor South Shore Democratic Newsletter, North Bellmore, N.Y., 1958-61, press sec. N.Y. State Assembly candidate, 1965, N.Y. State Congl. candidate, 1968; officer Manhasset Dem. Club, N.Y., 1965-69; mem. adv. com. N.Y.C. Coun. candidate, 1985. U. New Haven Bartels fellow, 1993. Mem. Pub. Rels. Soc. Am., Women in Comm. (Matrix award for pub. rels. 1989), The Counselors Acad., Pride and Alarm, City Club N.Y. Democrat. Jewish. Home: 30 Appalachian Rd Kent CT 06757-1009 Personal E-mail: ffried2078@aol.com.

FRIEDMAN, FRANCES WOLF, political fund raiser; b. Ft. Worth, June 14, 1940; d. Tobian Alexander and Ann (Katz) Wolf; m. Christopher I. Newman (div. 1984); children: Peter A., J. Hope; m. Frederick Friedman Sr., Jan. 3, 1986; stepchildren: Danielle F., David J. BA in Polit. Sci., Tulane U., 1961. Motion picture film prodn. office coord. Columbia Pictures Corp. Paramount Pictures, N.Y.C., 1965-72, Metro Goldwyn Mayer, N.Y.C., 1965-72; dir. vols. Congressman Bill Green, N.Y.C., 1984-86, fin. dir., 1988-92; nat. dir. Modrnpac, N.Y.C., 1993-2001. Bd. dirs. Family Connections, 1998—; domestic violence task force chair Adv. Bd. on the Status of Women-Essex County, Newark, 1997-2000; mem., co-founder Essex County Coalition on Domestic Violence Svc. Providers, Newark, 1997—. Mem. pub. rels. Concert Artists Guild, N.Y.C., 1982-84, LWV, Millburn-Short Hills, N.J., 1996—; v.p. Rep. Club, Millburn-Short Hills, 1996—; freeholder-at-large candidate Rep. Party, Essex County, N.J., 1996. Avocation: gardening. Home: 14 Cross Gates Short Hills NJ 07078-2106

FRIEDMAN, JANE, publishing executive; BA in English, NYU, 1967. Joined Random House, 1968, with publicity dept., exec. v.p. Knopf Pub. Group, pub. Vintage Books, founder, pres. Random House Audio, exec. v.p. Random House Inc., mem. exec. com.; pres., CEO HarperCollins, N.Y.C., 1997—. Co-chair pub. divsn., vice chair entertainment, media and comms. divsn. UJA; mem. Am. adv. com. Jerusalem Internat. Book Fair; chmn. bd. dirs., adv. com. Assn. Am. Pubs.; bd. dirs. Poets and Writers; adv. com. Literacy Ptnrs., Yale U. Press. Named Person of Yr., LMP, 1999; named one of 200 Women Legends, Leaders and Trailblazers, Vanity Fair, 1998, N.Y.'s 100 Most Influential Women in Bus., Crain's N.Y. Bus., 1999, Am.'s 100 Most Important Women, Ladies Home Jour., 1999, 101 Most Important People in Entertainment, Entertainment Weekly, 1999—2002; recipient Matrix award, Women Who Change the World, 2001. Office: HarperCollins 10 E 53rd St New York NY 10022-5299*

FRIEDMAN, JOAN M. accounting educator; b. N.Y.C., Nov. 30, 1949; d. Alvin E. and Pesselle Gail (Rothenberg) F.; m. Charles E. Blair III, Sept. 20, 1992. AB magna cum laude, Harvard U., 1971; MA, Courtauld Inst., U. London, 1973; MS with honors, Columbia U., 1974; MAS, U. Ill., 1993. CPA, Ill. Asst. research librarian Beinecke Library, New Haven, Conn., 1974-75; asst. research librarian Yale Ctr. for Brit. Art, New Haven, Conn., 1975-76, curator of rare books, 1976-90; computer cons., teaching asst. dept. accountancy U. Ill., Champaign, 1990-95; vis. asst. prof. acctg. Ill. Wesleyan U., Bloomington, Ill., 1995-99, asst. prof. acctg., 1999—. Cons. Johns Hopkins U., Balt., 1983; tchr. Sch. Library Service Columbia U., 1983-88, Sysop WordPerfect Users Forum on CompuServe, 1987-2000, Sysop, Tapcis Forum on CompuServe, 1988-95. Author: Color Printing in England, 1978; contbr. articles in field Recipient student achievement award Fedn. Schs. Accountancy, 1993; Nat. Merit scholar Harvard U., 1967; Moss Accountancy fellow U. Ill. 1990. Mem. ALA (chmn. rare books and manuscripts sect. 1982-83), Bibliog. Soc. Am. (coun. 1982-86, sec. 1986-88), Am. Printing History Assn., Phi Beta Kappa, Beta Phi Mu. Clubs: Grolier (N.Y.C.); Elizabethan (New Haven). Jewish. Avocations: microcomputers, bicycling. Office: Ill Wesleyan U Divsn Bus & Econs PO Box 2900 Bloomington IL 61702-2900 E-mail: jfriedma@titan.iwu.edu.

FRIEDMAN, KENNI, healthcare company official, councilwoman; BA, UCLA, 1963, MBA, 1964. Councilwoman City of Modesto, Calif., 1991-99, vice mayor, 2000—; mem. bd. Sutter-affiliated Meml. Hosps. Assn., Sacramento, chmn. bd., 1993-95; bd. dirs. Sutter Health Inc., Sacramento. Bd. dirs. Sutter Gould Med. Found., Modesto; active League Calif. Cities, United Way Sanislaus County, Modesto Symphony Assn.; former mem. state bd. dirs. and nat. bd. dirs. LWV; mem. policy bd. San Joaquin Valley Unified Air Pollution Control Dist. Mem. Modesto C. of C. (bd. dirs.). Office: Sutter Health Inc 2200 River Plaza Dr Sacramento CA 95833-4134

FRIEDMAN, LYNN JOSEPH, counselor; b. New Orleans, Jan. 12, 1949; d. Leonard Cerf and Paula Rose (Levy) Joseph; children; Rebecca, Naomi. BS, La. State U., 1970; MEd, U. Tex., 1971; PhD, U. New Orleans, 1995. Tchr. Orleans Parish Schs., New Orleans, 1971-73; rehab. counselor L.A. Div. Rehab. Svcs., Metairie, 1973-87, Intracorp, Metairie, 1987-91, GAB Robins/Med Insights, Metairie, 1991—. Counselor Metro Battered Women, Metairie, 1990-92; edn. dir. Congregation Gates of Prayer, New Orleans, 1971-75; nat. mgr. Crisis Intervention Program. Contbr. articles to profl. jours. Named Counselor of Yr. Goodall Rehab., 1980; recipient Cert. Appreciation Nat. Assn. Ret. Citizens, 1974, Magnolia Sch., 1976. Mem. ACA (La. Grad. Student of Yr. 1991), Nat. Rehab. Assn. (La. Counselor of

Yr. 1979), Chi Sigma Iota (treas. 1990-91, v.p. 1991-92). Democrat. Jewish. Home: 4721 Loveland St Metairie LA 70006-4027 Office: GAB Robins/Med Insights 4721 Loveland St Metairie LA 70006-4027

FRIEDMAN, MARIA ANDRE, public relations executive; b. Jackson, Mich., June 12, 1950; m. Stanley N. Friedman; children: Alexandra, Adam. BA cum laude, U. Md., 1972, MA, 1979; DBA, Nova U., 1993. Writer U.S. Bur. Mines, Washington, 1973-78; head writer Nat. Ctr. Health Svc. Rsch./Healthcare Tech. DHHS, Rockville, Md., 1978-85; chief publs. and info. br. Agy. for Healthcare Policy and Rsch., 1986-89; dir. office pub. affairs Healthcare Fin. Adminstrn., Washington, 1990—, acting assoc. adminstr. for comm., 1992-93, sr. rsch. advisor Balt., 1994-95, dir. disemination staff ORB, 1995-96, sr. advisor for ins. reform, 1997-99, Y2K outreach coord. for medicaid program, 1999—. Mem. Assn. Health Svcs. Rsch., Acad. of Mgmt. Office: Health Care Fin Adminstrn 7500 Security Blvd Baltimore MD 21244-1849 Home: 12535 Heurich Rd Silver Spring MD 20902-1441

FRIEDMAN, MARLA ILENE, director, educator; b. Miami, Fla., Sept. 19, 1972; d. Alice and Joseph Ostrower; m. Marc Richard Friedman, Feb. 27, 1999. BS, Emerson Coll., 1995, MA, 1996; postgrad., Nova Southea. U., 1998—. Regional dir. Bus. Network Internat., Albuquerque, 1992—94; intern, account asst. Ward Rovner Pub. Rels., Boston, 1994—95; mktg. project mgr. Nova Southea. U., Ft. Lauderdale, Fla., 1997—99, mktg. mgr., 1999—2000, adj. faculty mem., 1999—; assoc. dir. internat., online & grad. programs Nova Southea. U. Law Ctr., Ft. Lauderdale, 2000—. Co-facilitator Thyroid Cancer Survivors, Ft. Lauderdale; team capt. Multiple Sclerosis Soc. 150 Bike Ride, Fla. Mem.: Am. Mktg. Assn. (assoc.). Office: Nova Southea U Law Ctr 3305 College Ave Fort Lauderdale FL 33314 E-mail: friemar@nova.edu.

FRIEDMAN, MARLA LEE, marketing professional; b. Chgo., May 26, 1953; d. Martin P. and Charlotte K. (Beilenson) F. BSC in Commerce, DePaul U., Chgo., 1977; MBA wih honors, Roosevelt U., Chgo., 1985. Gen. mgr., adminstr. Chgo. Ctr. for Devel. Learning, Inc., Ill., 1975—77; dist. health claims adminstrn. analyst Washington Nat. Ins. Co., Evanston, Ill., 1977—80; unit coord. computer resource liaison Luth. Gen. Hosp., Pk. Ridge, Ill., 1980—99; pres., owner Dancing By Candlelight, 1995—; media & investor rels. prof.. IPA, Buffalo Grove, Ill., 2000—01; dir. mktg. programs Samples & Surveys, Northbrook, Ill., 2001; acting dir. mktg. & publ. rels. Penworthy Ctrl., Glenview, Ill., 2002; scheduling coord. Nurse Staffers, Rosemont, Ill., 2003—. Mem. associated writing programs George Mason U. Contbr. prose poem Chips Off the Writer's Block, 1992, columnist, 1994; contbr. poem Guided By Voices Anthology, 1998, Best Poets of the 20th Century, 2000, Best Poets of 2000, 2000, Sound of Poetry, 2001; author short stories, children's stories, novels and articles. Recipient Editors Choice award N.Am. Poetry Open Competition, 1998, awards for nonfiction articles. Fellow Life Mgmt. Soc. (cert. fin. scis.); mem. NAFE, Acad. Am. Poets. Avocations: drama, music, creative cookery. Home: PO Box 1292 Morton Grove IL 60053-7292 E-mail: beyondpage2@yahoo.com.

FRIEDMAN, MILDRED, architectural and design educator, curator, consultant; b. L.A., July 25, 1929; d. Nathaniel and Hortense (Weinsveig) Shenberg; m. Martin Friedman; children: Lise, Ceil, Zoe. BA, UCLA, 1951, MA, 1952; DFA (hon.), Mpls. Coll. Art, 1981; DFA, Hamlin U., 1987. Instr. design L.A. City Coll., 1952-54; archtl. designer Cerny Assocs., Mpls., 1957-69; design curator Walker Art Ctr., Mpls., 1970-90; freelance cons. N.Y.C., 1990—. Mem. arch. and design panel Nat. Endowment Arts, 1975—78, mem. policy panel design arts, 1979—82, mem. presdl. design awards jury, 1991; mem. vis. com. Sch. Arch. and Planning MIT, 1985—88; mem. vis. com. Grad. Sch. Design Harvard U., 1994—; bd. dirs. Internat. Design Conf., Aspen, 1989—91, Chgo. Inst. Arch. and Urbanism, 1990—93, Nat. Inst. Archtl. Edn., 1993—; mem. deisgn jury Am. Acad. Rome, 1991; gueest instr. UCLA, 1992; mem. jury to select architect for Whitehall Ferry Terminal, N.Y.C., 1992; vis. instr. Harvard U., 1993; cons. Battery Park City Authority, N.Y.C.; guest curator Bklyn. Mus., 1992—2002; guest curator for Frank Gehry retrospective exhbn. Solomon R. Guggenheim Mus., N.Y.C., 2001; guest curator for Vital Forms exhbn. Bklyn. Mus. Art, 2001—02. Author, editor: Gehry Talks, 1999; editor Design Quar., 1970-91, numerous catalogues. Recipient Outstanding Achievement award YWCA, 1984, Outstanding Svc. award U. Minn., 1991; fellow Intellectual Interchange program Japan Soc., 1982, Chrysler Design award, 2002; grantee Nat. Endowment Arts, 1992-93, Graham Found. for Advanced Studies in Fine Arts, 1997; recipient Graham Found grant for Design Quar. Anthology. Mem. AIA (hon., nat. awards jury 1981, 87, bd. dirs. Minn. chpt. 1984-86, Inst. Honors 1994).

FRIEDMAN, PAMELA RUTH LESSING, financial consultant, writer; b. N.Y.C., Jan. 15, 1950; d. Fred William and Helen D. Lessing; children: Elizabeth Lessing, Paul Lessing. BA, U. Rochester, 1972; MSLS, U. N.C., Chapel Hill, 1974. Dep. libr. Am. Soc. Internat. Law, Washington, 1974-76; with edn. dept. Nat. Air and Space Mus., Smithsonian Inst., Washington, 1976-84; ind. cons. fin. and art Boulder, Colo., 1984—; pub. C.S.B. Co., Boulder, 1989—. Lectr. in fields, 1989—; cons. Denver Art Mus., 1989-91, Asian Art Coordinating Coun., Denver, 1990—; pres. Kylin Resources, Boulder, Colo., 1995—; —race ofcl., U.S. Ski Assn., 1998—; v.p. Linking Human Sys. (LINC), Boulder, 1997—. Author: (reference book) Chinese Snuff Bottles, 1990, The First Week with My New P.C.: A Very Basic Guide for Mature Adults and Everyone Who Wants to Get Connected, 2000, The First Week with My New iMac: A Very Basic Guide for Mature Adults and Everyoneho Wants to Get Connected, 2001, The First Week with My New Digital Organizer: A Very Basic Guide to Palm OS Personal Digital Assistants, 2002, The First Week with My New Digital Camera, 2003; editor: (reference book) Flight Service Directory, 1975. Rep. S.E.V.A.B., Smithsonian Instn., 1979-81, mem. exec. bd. docent coun. Nat. Air and Space Mus., 1977-81; mem. trustee coun. U. Rochester, N.Y., 1992-98, mem. vis. com. coll. of arts and scis. U. Rochester, 1994—; bd. dirs., mem. exec. com. bd., treas. Colo. Music Festival, Boulder, 1983-89; mem. exec. bd. Women's Incentive Fund Colo. U., Boulder, 1988-91; rep. Leadership Boulder, 1986-87; v.p. bd. dirs. Lessing Found., N.Y., 1988—; mem. exec. bd. Interfaith Coun., Boulder, 1987-90; dir. exec. bd. LINC Found., 2002—, Vail Film Festival, 2002—; life mem. RAF Mus., 1977—. Recipient Internat. Gold Test Pin award Swiss Skiing Fedn., St. Moritz, 1975. Mem. Internat. Chinese Snuff Bottle Soc., Army and Navy Club (Washington), Beach Point Club (Mamaroneck, N.Y.), Game Creek Club (Vail, Colo., adv. bd. 2001—). Avocations: private aviation, amateur radio, skiing, sailing, scuba diving, collecting. Home and Office: 503A Kalmia Ave Boulder CO 80304-1733

FRIEDMAN, PENNY, lawyer; b. Cleve., Dec. 24, 1951; d. Harold Emanuel and Ruth (Resnick) F.; children: Rachel, Leah. AB in Econs. with high honors, U. Mich., 1973, JD cum laude, 1977. Bar: Ohio 1977. Atty. Taft, Stettinius & Hollister, Cin., 1977-80; v.p. property devel. Gt. Am. Broadcasting Co. (formerly Taft Broadcasting Co.), Cin., 1980-88; real estate portfolio mgr. Bartlett & Co., Cin., 1988-98; pres. Benefactors, LLC, 1998—. Mem. Cin. Downtown Progress Com., 1991-95, mem. exec. com., 1993-95; v.p. Cin. chpt. Am. Jewish Com., 1992-96, pres. 1996-98, mem. exec. com., 1990—; v.p. Leadership Cin. Alumni Assn., 1987-89; chmn. Family Svc. Cin. Area, 1991-92, pres., 1988-90, v.p., 1985-88, trustee, 1979-93, trustee emeritus, 1993—; vice-chmn. Cin. Devel. Fund, 1989-95; vice chmn. Devel. Corp. Cin., 1990-92, trustee, 1989-92; bd. dirs. Cin. Ctr. for Devel. Disorders, 1979-85, Seven Hills Neighborhood Houses, 1981-86; trustee Cin. Arts Assn., 1992—, mem. exec. com. 1994—; trustee Downtown Cin., Inc., 1998-2004, Cin. Psychoanalytic Inst., 1994-2002, The Wellness Cmty., 1999-2002; vice chair, trustee Knowledgeworks Found., 1999—; trustee Found. Family Svc., 2000— (v.p. 2002—), Greater Cin. Arts and Edn. Ctr., 1999—; trustee Project Grad. Cin., 2003—. Mem. Cin. Bar Assn., Phi Beta Kappa. Office: BeneFactors LLC 312 Walnut St Ste 3560 Cincinnati OH 45202-4026 E-mail: benefactors@fuse.net., psoul@aol.com.

FRIEDMAN, POLLY, public relations executive, marketing professional; b. Orange, N.J., Nov. 9, 1932; d. Sidney and Doris (Simons) Adler; m. Eugene M. Friedman, Jan. 14, 1954; children: Robert A. Friedman, Nancy Friedman Meagher. Student, Beaver Coll., 1951-53, NYU, 1953-54. Dir. pub. rels. Albert Einstein Med. Ctr., Phila., 1975-77, Pa. Coll. Optometry, Phila., 1977-79; mgr. media project devel. Sun Oil Co., Phila., 1979-86; dep. dir. Greater Phila. Econ. Coalition, Phila., 1986-88; exec. dir. The Nat. Constitution Ctr., Phila., 1992-94; pres. Polly Friedman & Assoc., Phila., 1988—; dir. mktg. Grant Thornton, Phila., 1995—. Com. mem. White House Conf. on Small Bus., Pa.; hon. bd. mem. Nat. Archives Week, Phila., 1993; conf. spkr. Nat. Park Svc., Washington, 1993, Nat. Parks and Conservation Assn., 1993, 94, Nat. Newspaper Assn., 1993; mem. adv. com. Ambler Music Festival at Temple U., Phila., 1992-94; mem. pub. rels. coun. Phila. Coalition on Domestic Violence, 1986, 87; cons. Fed. Res. Bank, Phila., 1994—. Recipient Silver Anvil Best Pub. Rels. Event award Pub. Rels. Soc. of Am., 1979, Pepperpot award (Phila. chpt.), 1979, Best Pub. Affairs Radio Series Pa. Assn. Broadcasters, 1993. Avocations: sailing, stone carving. Office: 2001 Market St Philadelphia PA 19103-7044

FRIEDMAN, RACHELLE, music retail executive; b. Israel; m. Joseph Friedman; children: Jason, Daryn. Grad., Poly. Inst. of Brooklyn. Co-founder, co-CEO J & R Music World, N.Y.C., 1971—, J & R Computer World, N.Y.C., 1990—. Adv. bd. Dealerscope mag. Trustee Poly. U. N.Y. (bd. dirs. Y.E.S. Ctr. Promise Fund); bd. dirs. Heritage Trails., Alliance Downtown N.Y.; Grammy Awards host com. Mem. Nat. Assn. Record Merchandisers (mem. bd. dirs., chmn., 1998-99). Avocations: travel, boating, working out, reading. Office: J & R Music World 23 Park Row New York NY 10038-2397*

FRIEDMAN, ROSELYN L. lawyer, mediator; b. Cleve., Dec. 9, 1942; d. Charles and Lillian Edith (Zalzneck) F. BS, U. Pitts., 1964; MA, Case Western Res. U., 1967; JD cum laude, Loyola U., Chgo., 1977. Bar: Ill. 1977, U.S. Dist. Ct. (no. dist.) Ill. 1977. Mem. legal dept. No. Trust Co., Chgo., 1977-79, assoc. Rudnick & Wolfe, Chgo., 1979-84, ptnr. 1984-95, Sachnoff & Weaver, Ltd., Chgo., 1995—, ptnr., chmn. dept. estates and trusts, 2002—. Mem. Loyola U., Chgo. law rev.; mem. profl. adv. com. Chgo. Jewish Fedn., chmn., 1999-2001; mem. profl. adv. com. Chgo. Cmty. Trust, 2001-. Trustee Jewish Women's Found., 1997—2001; mediator Ctr. for Conflict Resolution, 2000—. Fellow Am. Coll. Trust and Estate Counsel; mem. ABA, Am. Jewish Congress (gov. coun. Midwest region 1995-97), Chgo. Bar Assn. (cert. appreciation continuing legal edn. program 1984, chmn. trust law com. 1989-90), Chgo. Estate Planning Coun. (program com. 1992-94, 98-2000, membership com. 1997-98, bd. dirs. 2001-2003), spkr. Ill. Inst. CLE, Chgo. Fin. Exch. (bd. dirs. 1995-97, sec. 1996-97). Office: Sachnoff & Weaver Ltd 30 S Wacker Dr Ste 2900 Chicago IL 60606-7413 E-mail: rfriedman@sachnoff.com.

FRIEDMAN, SOFIA, social sciences educator, nutritionist, educator; b. San Carlos, Uruguay, Oct. 7, 1940; arrived in USA, 1988; d. Israel Iser and Szajndla Lea (Lebensohn) Friedman; m. Salomao Nejman, Dec. 26, 1959 (div. June 10, 1980); children: Helena (Nejman) Bardusco, Regina Nejman, Susana Nejman. BS nutrition, Univ. Rio De Janeiro, Rio de Janeiro, Brazil, 1979; MA social comm., Fed. Univ. of Rio de Janeiro, Rio de Janeiro, Brazil, 1987; MA polit. sci., City Univ. of Rio de Janeiro, New York, NY, 1995; PhD internat. studies, Fairfax Univ., London, Eng., 2000. Cert. Yoga Instr. Vayuananda Yoga Ctr./ Rio de Janeiro, Brazil, 1974, Internat. Sivananda Yoga Vedanta Ctr./Paradise Is., Bahamas, 1983. Asst. prof. Univ. of Rio de Janeiro, Rio de Janeiro, 1980—88; adj. instr. Hudson County Cmty. Coll., Jersey City, NJ, 1995—97, Stevens Inst. of Tech., Hoboken, NJ, 1997, La Guardia Cmty. Coll., NY, NY, 1995—2000. Founder, owner Redefining Life After Fifty ednl. seminars, Hoboken, 1997—. Author: (MA thesis dissertation) Food Scarcity and Abundance: Analysis of a Food Sys. in Natividade, Rio de Janeiro, 1987, The Emergence of a Condition of Food Insecurity in Brazil During the 1964-1985 Military Regime and the Rise of Civil Soc., 1995, (book) Brazil 1960-1990: Structures of Power and Processes of Change, 2003. Democrat. Jewish. Home and Office: 159 14th St Apt 5 Hoboken NJ 07030

FRIEDMAN, SUE TYLER, technical publications executive; b. Nürnberg, Germany, Feb. 28, 1925; came to U.S., 1938; d. William and Ann (Federlein) Tyler (Theilheimer); m. Gerald Manfred Friedman, June 27, 1948; children: Judith Fay Friedman Rosen, Sharon Mira Friedman Azaria, Devora Paula Friedman Zweibach, Eva Jane Friedman Scholle, Wendy Tamar Friedman Spanier. Student, Beth Israel Sch. Nursing, 1941-43. Exec. dir. Ventures and Publs. Gerald M. Friedman, 1964-90; owner Tyler Publs., Watervliet and Troy, N.Y., 1978-86; treas., dir. Northeastern Sci. Found., Inc., Troy, 1979—; treas. Gerry Exploration, Inc., Troy, 1982-88; office mgr. Rensselaer Ctr. Applied Geology, Troy, 1983—. Pres. Pioneer Women/Na'amat, Tulsa, 1961-64, treas., Jerusalem, Israel, 1964, pres., Albany, N.Y., 1968-70; bd. dirs. Temple Beth-El, 1965—, dir. Hebrew Sch., 1965-80; mem. social program com. Internat. Sedimentological. Congress, 1979. Named Hon. Alumna, Dept. Geology, Bklyn. Coll. at CUNY, 1989; Sue Tyler Friedman medal for distinction in history of geology created in her honor Geol. Soc. London, 1988; recipient Disting. Svc. award Temple Beth-El, 1991, Scroll of Honor, State of Israel Bonds, 1981. Mem. Geology Alumni Assn. (hon.). Avocation: world travel. Office: Northeastern Sci Found Inc/Bklyn Coll CUNY Rensselaer Ctr Applied Geology PO Box 746 Troy NY 12181-0746

FRIEDMAN, SUSAN LYNN BELL, economic development professional; b. May 23, 1953; d. Virgil Atwood and Jean Loree (Wiggins) B.; m. Frank H. Friedman, July 31, 1976; 1 child, Alex Charles. BA, Purdue U., 1975; MSc, Ind. State U., 1981. Asst. dir. pub. rels. Vincennes U. Jr. Coll., Ind., 1977-83; dir. Knox County C. of C., Vincennes, 1983-84; asst. to pres. Am. Assn. Cmty. and Jr. Colls., Washington, 1985-87; owner, pres. SBF Promotions, 1987—; mgr., program developer Family Resources, Inc., 1988-89; partnership coord. Beaufort (S.C.) County Sch. Dist., 1989-90; job tng. coord. Heart of Ga. Tech. Inst., 1990-92, v.p. econ. devel., 1992-96; exec. dir. Tex. Assn. Ptnrs. in Edn., 1996-98; dir. regional bus. assistance Thomas Jefferson Partnership for Econ. Devel., 1999—. Mem. Leadership Class, Charlottesville, Va., 2000; pres. Annandale BPW, Vincennes, Ind., BPW Dublin and Capital City; newsletter adv. coord. Focus Women's Ctr.; mem. sch. bd. Albermarle Pub. Schs., Va., 2004—; bd. dirs. I Have A Dream Found., 2001—. Hoosier scholar, 1971, 1972. Mem. NAFE, LWV (v.p. chpt. 1982-84, pres. 2000-2002), ACLU, Nat. Assn. Ptnrs. in Edn., NOW, Rotary (v.p. 2000-01), Albemarle County Rotary. Home: 2544 Brandermill Pl Charlottesville VA 22911-8253 Office: PO Box 1525 Charlottesville VA 22902

FRIEDMANN, ELIZABETH CARROLL, writer, editor; b. Nashville, Tenn., Jan. 3, 1941; BA, U. Tenn., 1962; MA, U. Fla., 1979. Freelance travel writer mags. and newspapers, Jacksonville, Fla., 1979—85; reporter and feature writer Florida Times-Union, Jacksonville, 1965—68; lectr. to adj. asst. prof. of English Jacksonville U., 1979—86; book reviewer Florida Times-Union, Jacksonville, 1975—88; columnist and feature writer Jacksonville Mag., Jacksonville, 1979—88; ind. scholar and rschr., 1988—. Mem. Laura (Riding) Jackson Bd. Literary Mgmt., 1991—; project dir. Kalliope On the Air/Cable TV series, 1980—88; founding editor, project dir. Kalliope: A Jour. of Women's Art, 1978—88; numerous other coms., panels in field. Co-editor: Four Unposted Letters to Catherine, by Laura Riding, 1993; co-editor: (with Alan J. Clark) The Word "Woman" and Other Related Writings, by Laura (Riding) Jackson, 1993; co-editor: (with Alan J. Clark and Robert Nye) First Awakenings, The Early Poems of Laura Riding, 1992. Home: 2355 South Ponte Vedra Blvd Ponte Vedra Beach FL 32082

FRIEDMANN, PATRICIA ANN, writer; b. New Orleans, La., Oct. 29, 1946; d. Werner and Marjorie Sybil (Cahn) F.; m. Robert E. Skinner, Mar. 17, 1979 (div. Nov. 1996); children: Esme Friedmann, Werner Skinner; m. Edward G. Muchmore, Nov. 11, 1999. AB, Smith Coll., 1968; MEd, Temple Univ., 1970; ABD, Univ. Denver, 1975. Fiction workshop facilitator, New Orleans, 1994—99; writer-in-residence Tulane U., 2001; reviewer Publishers Weekly, Brightleaf, Times-Picayune, 1993—99; spkr. in field. Author: Too Smart to Be Rich, 1988, The Exact Image of Mother, 1991, Eleanor Rushing, 1999 (Barnes & Noble Discover Great Writers selection, Borders Original Voices selection), Odds, 2000, Secondhand Smoke, 2002 (Book Sense 76 selection), (play) The Accidental Jew as part of Native Tongues, 1994, Lovely Rita as part of Native Tongues, 2000; contbg. author: The New Great American Writers Cookbook, 2003, Christmas Stories from Louisiana, 2003; author short stories. Mem. Authors Guild. Home: 8330 Sycamore Pl New Orleans LA 70118-2941 E-mail: afreelunch@aol.com.

FRIEDMANN, ROSELI OCAMPO, microbiologist, educator; b. Manila, Nov. 23, 1937; came to U.S., 1968; d. Eliseo Amio and Generosa (Campana) Ocampo; m. Emerich Imre Friedmann ; children: Maria Roseli, Rodolfo. BSc in Botany, U. Philippines, 1958; MSc in Biology, Hebrew U. of Jerusalem, 1966; PhD in Biology, Fla. State U., 1973. Rsch. assoc. Inst. Sci. and Tech., Manila, 1958-67; rsch. asst. Queen's U., Kingston, Ont., Can., 1967-68; tchg. asst. Fla. State U., Tallahassee, 1968-73, rsch. assoc., 1973—75; from asst. prof. dept. biology to assoc. prof. Fla. A&M U., 1975-87, prof., 1987—2000, prof. emeritus, 2000—; prin. investigator NASA Ames Rsch. Ctr., Moffett Field, Calif., 2000—. Contbr. articles to profl. jours. Recipient Resolution of Commendation, State of Fla., Tallahassee, 1978, Antarctic Svc. medal U.S. Congress, NSF, 1981. Mem. Soc. Phycologigue France, Phycological Soc. Am., Planetary Soc., AAAS, U.S. Fedn. Culture Collections, Am. Soc. Microbiology, Assn. Women in Sci., Sigma Xi. Avocations: cooking, classical music, photography, travel, cats. Office: NASA Ames Rsch Ctr Mail Code 245 3 Moffett Field CA 94035-1000 Home: 300 E 59th St Apt 1402 New York NY 10022-2054 E-mail: ifriedmann@mail.arc.nasa.gov.*

FRIEDRICH, MARGRET COHEN, guidance and student assistance counselor; b. Balt., June 4, 1947; d. Joseph Cohen and Judith (Kline) Cohen Roisman; m. Jay Joseph Friedrich, May 16, 1971; children: David Benjamin, Marc Adam, Samantha Lauren. BEd, U. Miami, Fla., 1969, MEd, 1970; PhD, Internat. U., 2003. Cert. alcoholism and addiction counselor, alcoholism and drug counselor. Grad. asst. U. Miami, Coral Gables, Fla., 1969-70; tchr. Balt. Bd. Edn., 1970; guidance counselor Ridgewood Bd. Edn., N.J., 1970—, student asst. coord., 1986—, chmn. student assistance com., 1986—. Alcoholism counselor Bergen County Dept. Health, Paramus, N.J., 1981-82; in-service tchr. Ridgewood Bd. Edn., 1983, supr., coordinator peer counseling program H.S., 1978-93; with Assn. Mental Health and Counseling of No. N.J., 1985-89; pres. BFT, Maggie Assoc.; exec. officer BFPR; cons. N.J. Student Assistance Program, student asst. cons. N.J. Dept. Edn., chmn. student asst. com.; presenter Coll. Bd. Conf., 1992, CEEB Conf., Phila., 1992; working gorup partnership for Cmty. Health Addiction Prevention, Bergen City, 1997. Author tech. papers. Exec. bd. Hadassah, Ridgewood-Glen Rock, N.J., 1971-80; youth leadership com. United Jewish Appeal, Bergen County, 1974-75; sec. Bergen County Youth Com. Substance Abuse, Paramus, 1980-90, conf. coord. com., 1983; treas. Ridgewood Coalition Substance Use and Abuse, 1990-94, Ridgewood Substance Abuse Prevention Commn., 1989-91, participant Pres.'s Drug Free Am.; facilitator Gov.'s N.J. Drug-Free Teleconf.; co-chmn. fundraiser, treas. United Parents/Safe Homes, Ridgewood, 1984; mem. core com. Ridge Against Drugs; lectr./educator Passaic County Juvenile Conf. Com., Paterson, N.J., 1984; mem. steering com. Bergen County Addictions Prevention Working Group-Partnership Cmty. Health. Reisman scholar, 1969; U. Miami teaching asst., 1970, recipient Recognition award, 1968, Disting. Leadership award N.J. Assn. St. Asst. Profls. Mem. N.J. Assn. Alcoholism and Drug Counselors, Nat. Assn. Suicidology, N.J. Edn. Assn., Ridgewood Edn. Assn., Bergen County Edn. Assn., N.J. Task Force on Women and Alcohol, Nat. Assn. Coll. Adminstr. Counselors, N.J. Personnel and Guidance Assn., Women of Accomplishment, Sigma Delta Tau (exec. bd. 1965-69). Democrat. Jewish. Office: Ridgewood High Sch Ridgewood NJ 07451

FRIEND, CYNTHIA M. chemist, educator; b. Hastings, Nebr., Mar. 16, 1955; d. Matthew Charles and Elise Germaine Friend; children: Ayse K., Kurt Y. BS, U. Calif., Davis, 1977; PhD, U. Calif., Berkeley, 1981. Postdoctoral assoc. Stanford (Calif.) U., 1981-82; asst. prof. Harvard U., Cambridge, Mass., 1982-86, assoc. prof., 1986-89, prof., 1989—. Rsch. collaborator Nat. Synchrotron Light Source/Brookhaven Nat. Labs.; Lucy Pickett lectr. Mt. Holyoke Coll., 1991; Cargill lectr. U. South Fla., 1992; Robert Welch lectr., Bernhard vis. fellow Williams Coll., 1992; Procter & Gamble lectr. U. Cin., 1993. Recipient Presdl. Young Investigator award NSF, 1985, Am. Chem. Soc. Garvan medal, 1990, Iota Sigma Pi Agnes Fay Morgan award, 1991. Mem. Am. Phys. Soc., Am. Chem. Soc. (Francis P. Garvan-John M. Olin medal 1990), Am. Vacuum Soc., Phi Beta Kappa (hon., Iota chpt.). Avocations: golf, swimming, weightlifting. Office: Harvard U Dept Chemistry 12 Oxford St Cambridge MA 02138-2902

FRIEND, PATRICIA A. trade association administrator; b. Aug. 28, 1946; Student, Northeastern State Coll. Flight attendant United Airlines, 1966—. Mem. Dept. Transp. Rapid Response Team for Aircraft Security, 2001—. Mem.: Am. Fed. Labor Unions-Congress Indsl. Orgns., Assn. Flight Attendants (head United Coun. 8/ORD Chgo. local 1980—82, internat. pres. 1995—, v.p.). Mailing: 5th Fl 1275 K St NW Washington DC 20005*

FRIES, HELEN SERGEANT HAYNES, civic leader; d. Harwood Syme and Alice (Hobson) Haynes; m. Stuart G. Fries, May 5, 1938. Student, Coll. William and Mary, 1935-38. Mem. nat. nurses aid com. ARC, 1958-59; dir. ARC Aero Club, Eng., 1943-44; supr. ARC Clubmobile, Europe, 1944-46; mem. women's com. Nat. Symphony Orch., Washington, 1959—, chmn. residential and fund dr. for apts., 1959; bd. dirs. Madison Country Rep. Club, 1969-70; mem. nat. coun. Women's Nat. Rep. Club N.Y., 1963—, chmn. hospitality com., 1963-65; bd. dirs. League Rep. Women, 1952-61; patron mem., vol. docent Huntsville Mus. Art, Huntsville Lit. Assn.; vol. docent Weeen House, Twickenham Hist. Preservation Dist. Assn., Inc., Huntsville; mem. The Garden Guild, Huntsville, The Collectors Guild Constn. Hall Village, Huntsville, Hist. Huntsville Found., Huntsville Mus. Art., Corcoran Art Gallery. Recipient cert. of merit 84th Divsn., U.S. Army, 1945. Mem.: DAR, Assn. Preservation Va. Antiquities, Turkish-Am. Assn., English Speaking Union, Greensboro Soc. Preservation, Nat. Trust Hist. Preservation, Va., Nat., Valley Forge (Pa.), Eastern Shore Va., Nat. Soc. Colonial Dames Am., Daus. Am. Colonists, Huntsville-Madison County hist. socs., Friends of Ala. Archives, Nat. Soc. Lit. and Arts, Va. Hist. Soc., Cmty. Ballet Assn. Inc. (life bd. dirs.), Bot. Garden Club, Heritage Club, Redstone Yacht Club, Garden Club, Army-Navy Country Club, Capitol Hill Club, Washington Club, Army-Navy Club. Address: 6200 Oregon Ave NW Apt 480 Washington DC 20015-1549

FRIES, REBECCA KAY, director, special education educator; d. Eugene Charles and Marie Wilhelmenia Combs; m. Richard Warren Fries, Aug. 15, 1970. BA, Concordia Tchrs. Coll., River Forest, Ill.; MA, U. Iowa, Iowa City, Iowa; EdD, U. Ill. - Urbana-Champaign, Champaign, Ill. Dir. of spl. edn. Lincolnway Area Spl. Edn. Coop., New Lenox, Ill., —, Joliet Pub. Elem. Sch. Dist. 86, Joliet, Ill.; coord. of diagnostic services Joliet Pub. Elem. Sch. - Dist. 86, Joliet, Ill., sch. psychologist; elem. sch. counselor Cedar Rapids Pub. Sch., Cedar Rapids, Iowa, sch. psychologist. Mem.: Delta Kapppa Gamma Internat. - Rho Chpt. (chpt. pres. 2000—02).

Independent. Office: Lincolnway Area Spl Edn Coop 20700 S Schoolhouse Rd New Lenox IL 60451 E-mail: rfries@lwhs.will.k12.il.us.

FRIESS, DONNA LEWIS, children's rights advocate; b. L.A., Jan. 16, 1943; d. Raymond W. Lewis, Jr. and Dorothy Gertrude (Borwick) McIntyre; m. Kenneth E. Friess, June 20, 1964; children: Erik, Julina, Daniel. BA in Comm., U. So. Calif., 1964; MA in Comm., Calif. State U., Long Beach, 1966; PhD in Psychology, U.S. Internat. U., San Diego, 1993. Cert. tchr., Calif. Prof. human comm. Cypress (Calif.) Coll., 1966—. Lectr. survivors of abuse, 1990—, mental health profls., 1990—; guest expert (TV) Sally Jessy Raphael, 1993, Leeza Gibbons Talk Show, 1994, Sonja: Live, 1994, Oprah Winfrey Show, 1991, others; presenter, spkr. in field. Author: Relationships, 1995, Just Between Us: A Guidebook for Survivors of Childhood Trauma, 1995, Cry the Darkness, 1993, European edit. 1995, Danish edit., 1999, Korean edit., 1995, Norwegian edit., 1998, Circle of Love: Secrets to Successful Relationships, 1996, 2d edit., 2002, Whispering Waters: The Story of Historic Weesha, 1998, Chronicle of Historic Weesha and the Upper Santa Ana River Valley, 2000; contbr. articles to mags. Del. to round table discussion on victims' issues U.S. Justice Dept., 2002, apptd. consortium for victims affairs, 2003; nat. consortium of victim assistance experts U.S. Dept. Justice, 2003—, adv. bd. Recipient Author's award U. Calif. Friends of Libr., 1996, recognition from U.S. Justice Dept. for outstanding efforts to stop child abuse, 1995, Lee Steelmon award, Recognition cert. for work to prevent child abuse Calif. State Senate, 2000, Orange County (Calif.) Bd. Suprs.' Resolution for Outstanding Efforts for Children, 2000, Outstanding Speech Faculty award Calif. State U., 2001. Mem. Am. Coalition Against Child Abuse (founder), Task Force for ACCA to Educate American Judges on Issues of Sexual Abuse, One Voice, Calif. Psychol. Assn., Western Social Sci. Assn., Child Abuse Listening and Mediating (bd. dirs.), Am. Profl. Soc. on Abuse of Children, Mother Against Sexual Abuse (bd. dirs.), Laura's House for Battered Women (bd. dirs.), Calif. Tchrs. Assn., Faculty Assn. Calif. C.Cs., Speech Communication Assn. of Am., U.S. Internat. U. Alumni Assn. (bd. dirs.). Avocation: painting on porcelain. Office: Cypress College Dept Human Communications Cypress CA 90630 E-mail: donafriess@aol.com.

FRIESS, LYNN, state agency administrator; 4 children. BA, U. Wis. Bd. dirs. Wyo. Bus. Coun.; co-owner Friess Assocs. Adv. Life Enrichment Found.; fundraiser Grand Teton Music Festival & Matchpoint. Office: Wyo Bus Coun 214 W 15th Cheyenne WY 82002

FRIESZ, MARY LEE, freelance/self-employed poet; b. Little Rock, Ark., Apr. 13, 1940; d. E. Lee and Lala Maurine (Bain) Franklin; m. David Wilson Dubbell, Jan. 28, 1961 (div. Aug. 1982); children: Cheryl Blaine Dubbell Knight, Paul Fremont Dubbell; m. Donald Stuart Friesz; July 5, 1985; children: Mark Allan Friesz, Carol Ann Friesz Leslie. BA in Psychology, U. Ark., 1962. Sec. Stanford U., Palo Alto, Calif., 1962-63; tchr. aide Pedregal Sch., Palos Verdes, Calif., 1974-78; corp. sec. Pel-Freez Biols., Inc., Palos Verdes, Calif., 1978-81; asst. mgr. May Co., Rolling Hills Estates, Calif., 1981-82; investment counselor Am. Savs. & Loan, Redondo Beach, Calif., 1982-84; founder, editor Mustard Seed Poetry, Palos Verdes, 1995—. Author books of poetry. Dir; Poetry By The Sea, Serenos de Point Vicente (televised, 1997-99). Mem. membership com. Assistance League San Pedro/South Bay, 1994-95; leader cmty. Bible study core Palm Desert Cmty. Presbyn. Ch., Palm Desert, Calif., 2003—. Recipient Cmty. Svc. award South Bay Panhellenic Coun., 1996. Mem. Palos Verdes Woman's Club (first v.p.), S.W. Manuscripters, So. Calif. Fedn. Zeta Tau Alpha (pres. 1994-95, pres. local chpt. 1990-91, cert. merit Nat. coun. 1994), Surfwriters (treas. 1994-99), Arts Coun. Torrance (sec.), Phi Beta Kappa. Home: 38 Maximo Way Palm Desert CA 92260 Office: Mustard Seed Poetry 38 Maximo Way Palm Desert CA 92260

FRINK, JEANNE RAE RUNDELL, artist; d. Edward L. Johnson and Rachel M. Enhelder; m. Robert D. Frink; stepchildren: David, Caron, Ann, Rob; 1 child, Eric F. Rundell. BA, U. Minn., 1996. Jewelry design Jeanne Rundell Design, St.Paul, Minn., 1988—92; fine arts, painting Studio 342 Fine Art, St.Paul, Minn., 1996—. Mktg. services mgr. Sanborn, Eden Prairie, Minn., 1987—89; art dir. Land O' Lakes, Inc., Arden Hills, Minn., 1975—86; graphic designer Environ. Edn. Consulting Found., Golden Valley, Minn., 1971—75. Graphic designer St.Clements Episcopal Ch., St.Paul, Minn., 1991. Recipient Art award, Wayland Acad., 1967. Mem.: Walker Art Ctr., Nat. Mus. of Women in the Arts, Mpls. Inst. of Arts, Nature Conservancy, Ocean Conservancy, Golden Key.

FRISCH, ROSE EPSTEIN, population sciences researcher; b. N.Y.C., July 7, 1918; m. David H. Frisch; children: Henry J., Ruth Frisch Dealy. BA, Smith Coll., 1939; MA, Columbia U., 1940; PhD, U. Wis., 1943. Assoc. prof. population scis. Harvard U., Cambridge, Mass., 1984-92, assoc. prof. emerita, 1992—. Author: (book) Female Fertility and the Body Fat Connection, 2002; contbr. articles to profl. jours. John Simon Guggenheim Meml. fellow, 1975-76. Fellow Am. Acad. Arts and Scis.; mem. AAAS, Endocrine Soc. Am., Population Soc. Am., Sigma Xi (nat. lectr. 1989-90). Office: Harvard U Ctr Population Studies 9 Bow St Cambridge MA 02138-5103 Office Phone: 617-495-3013.

FRISCIA, ARLINE M. assemblywoman; BA in music, Caldwell Coll.; MA in adminstrn. and supervision, Seton Hall U. Councilwoman at large Woodbridge Twp., 1988—91; assemblywoman N.J. Gen. Assembly, 1996—; assoc. minority leader, 1998—2001; asst. majority whip, 2002—; vice chair Woodbridge Twp. Dem. Party. Bd. mgrs. Roosevelt Hosp. Democrat. Office: 245 Main St Woodbridge NJ 07095 E-mail: AswFriscia@njleg.org.

FRISINA, JENNIFER LYNNE, music educator; b. Schenectady, N.Y., June 29, 1956; d. James Alexander and Anne Myers Steele; m. Vincent Charles Frisina, Jr., June 24, 1978; children: David Vincent, Christopher James, Jessica Lynne. B in Music Edn., Jacksonville U., 1977; M in Music Edn., Fla. State U., 1978. Pvt. cello instr., Charlotte, NC, 1980—; orch. dir. Charlotte-Mecklenburg Schs., 1981—. Cellist Lyric Arts String Quartet, Charlotte, 1980—, Charlotte Civic Orch., 1990—. Choir mem. Advent Luth. Ch., Charlotte. Composer's grantee, Cultural Edn. Collaborative, Randolph Mid. Sch., 2001—02. Mem.: Music Educator's Nat. Conf. (sec. N.C. orch. divsn. 2002—). Avocation: needlecrafts.

FRISTOE, MACALYNE, speech-language pathologist, psychologist, educator, writer; b. Nashville, Mar. 14, 1931; d. George Miller and Brownie Appleton Watkins; m. James Houston Fristoe, June 4, 1953 (div. Nov. 1964); children: James Houston Jr., Andrew McLean; m. John Leiper Freeman, Jr., Jan. 20, 1966 (div. Oct. 1973). BA cum laude, Vanderbilt U., 1953, MS, 1960, PhD, 1972. Lic. speech pathologist, Ind. Health Prof. Bur. Speech clinician East Tenn. Hearing & Speech Ctr., Knoxville, Tenn., 1953—54; speech clinician, speech pathologist Bill Wilkerson Hearing & Speech Ctr., Nashville, 1955—60, asst. dir. speech clinic, 1964—67; instr. speech pathology Sch. Medicine Vanderbilt U., Nashville, 1960, 1964—67, instr. psychology, 1971—72, asst. prof., 1972—74; dir. lang. intervention study project Ctr. Devel. & Learning Disorders Med. Ctr., U. Ala., Birmingham, 1974—76; asst. prof. to assoc. prof. dept. biocomm. U. Ala., Birmingham, 1974—76; dir. speech clinic Purdue U., West Lafayette, Ind., 1976—79, assoc. prof. to prof. dept. audiology & speech scis., 1976—96, dir. grad. programs dept. audiology and speech scis., 1986—90, 1992—96, assoc. dept. head audiology and speech scis., 1993—96, assoc. prof. to prof. dept psychol. scis., 1982—96, prof. emerita, 1996—. Speech clinician Nashville-Davidson County Schs., Nashville, 1955—57; cons. Vanderbilt Hosp., 1957—60, L.B. Wallace Devel. Ctr., Decatur, Ala., 1974—78; rsch. NIH-NIAMDD kidney disease contract Vanderbilt Med. Ctr., 1971—74; mem. adv. bd. Ind. Resource Ctr. for Autism, Ind. U., Bloomington, 1986—94, Steer Speech and Hearing Clinics, Purdue U., 2000—02; reviewer NIH, Bethesda, Md., 1990—96; sci. reviewer Nat. Inst. Neurological and Commn. Disorders and Stroke, NIH, Nat. Inst. Child Health and Human Devel., Nat. Inst. Deafness and Commn. Disorders, Sensory Disorders and Lang. Study sect. NIH, NSF, March of Dimes, Purdue U.; spkr. in field. Assoc. editor Jour. Childhood Comm. Disorders, 1975-78, reviewer, 1978-82; mem. pub. bd. CEC Divsn. Children with Comm. Disorders, 1977-79; editl. cons. Jour. Speech and Hearing Disorders, 1977-79, 1982—, Mental Retardation, 1977-80, Augmentative and Alternative Comm.; cons. editor Am. Jour. Mental Deficiency, 1979-83; reviewer Jour. Applied Rsch. in Mental Retardation; contbr. numerous articles to profl. jours.; co-author, developer: Filmstrip Articulation Test, 1966, Goldman-Fristoe Test of Articulation, 1969, Goldman-Fristoe-Woodcock Test of Auditory Discrimination, 1970, Goldman-Fristoe-Woodcock Auditory Skills Test Battery, 1975, Goldman-Fristoe Test of Articulation 2, 2000; author: Language Intervention Systems for the Retarded, 1975; editor: (book) Four Language Intervention Systems, 1977. Recipient Women in Rsch. award Kennedy Inst. Johns Hopkins U., Balt., 1976; scholar Vanderbilt U., 1952-53; fellow Nat. Def. Edn. Act., 1969; traineeship U. Miami, 1956, Columbia U., 1966, Vanderbilt U., 1969-70, 1970-71. Fellow APA, Am. Speech Lang. Hearing Assn. (cert. clin. competence in speech pathology), Am. Assn. Mental Retardation (v.p. comm. disorders 1985-86, pres. comm. disorders divsn. 1986-87); mem. Nat. Coun. Comm. Disorders (rep.), Phi Beta Kappa, Sigma Xi.

FRITSCH-STEWART, ANTOINETTE M. education educator; b. Chgo., Dec. 30, 1946; d. Edward Paul Fritsch and Pearl M. Konecki-Fritsch; AA, Richard J. Daley U., 1992; student, Chgo. State U., 1997—. From mail clk. to underwriter asst. Kemper Ins., Chgo., 1965—75, underwriter asst., 1975—77; vet. advisor City Colls. Chgo., 1977—. Bd. dir. Commn. Vets. Edn., Washington; mem. Sch. Cons. Commn., St. Louis, 2000—01. Author: Family History Jackson-Riley Family of Poplar Hill, 2002, Self Audit For Certifying Officials, 2003. Bd. dir. Christ Universal Temple, Chgo., 1998—. Recipient Dedicated Svc. award, City of Chgo. Mem.: Assn. Vet. Edn. Certifying Officials (v.p. 2002—, pres. 2000—01, sec. 1999—2000). Avocation: genealogy. Office: Richard J Daley College 7500 S Pulaski Rd Chicago IL 60652

FRITZ, BARBARA JEAN, occupational health nurse; b. Helena, Mont., Sept. 16, 1936; d. Marion Caldwell and Clara K. (Bernard) Heffern; m. Bernard John Fritz Sept. 2, 1961; children: Cathleen, Stephen, Elizabeth. Diploma in nursing, Sacred Heart Sch. Nursing, 1957; BS in Nursing, St. Louis U., 1959; postgrad., Oreg. State U., Portland State U., Oreg. Health Scis. U. Cert. occupl. health nurse. Occupl. health nurse Chloride Western Battery, Portland, Oreg., 1984-85; occupl. health nurse unit mgr. Pub. Health Dept. Fed. Occupl. Health, Portland, 1985-86; occupl. health relief nurse James River Corp., Portland, 1986-88; occupl. health nurse Harder Mech./James River Site, Camas, Wash., 1988; health & safety mgr. Armour Foods, Portland, 1988-90; occupl. health cons. Pacific Rim Occupl. Health & Safety Svcs., Portland, 1990—2004; occupl. health nurse mgr. Toyota Vehicle Processing, Inc., Portland, 1992-95; med. case mgr. Gates McDonald, Beaverton, Oreg., 1995-96; temp. occupl. health mgr. L.S.I. Logic, Gresham, Oreg., 1997. Relief occupl. health cons. Atlas, Copco, Wagner Mining, Portland, 1986-99; instr. in field. Chmn. northeast citizen's adv. Portland Planning Commn., 1988, com. historic landmarks, 1988; mem. Urban Tour Group, Portland; leadership group Mid-County Sewer Project, 1991-92; vol. Portland Ctr. Performing Arts. Recipient Cert. of Appreciation, 25th Anniversary of Urban Tour Group, 1995. Mem. Am. Assn. Occupl. Health Nurses, Oreg. State Assn. Occupl. Health Nurses (registered lobbyist, historian 1992-96, govtl. affairs co-chair 1995-96, chair 1996-97, Nat. Govtl. Affairs award 1996, 98). Democrat. Roman Catholic. Achievements include being instrumental in inclusion of occupational health professionals in Oregon state worksite redesign grant program. Home and Office: 4705 NE Ainsworth St Portland OR 97218-1818 Office Phone: 503-288-1027. E-mail: prohealthme@msn.com.

FRITZ, JEAN GUTTERY, writer; b. Hankow, People's Republic China, Nov. 16, 1915; d. Arthur Minton and Myrtle (Chaney) Guttery; m. Michael Fritz, Nov. 1, 1941; children: David, Andrea. BA, Wheaton Coll., Norton, Mass., 1937, LittD (hon.), 1987, Washington and Jefferson Coll., 1982. Rsch. asst. Dobbs Ferry (N.Y.) Libr., 1937—41, children's libr., 1955—57; founder, instr. Jean Fritz Writers' Workshops, Katonah, NY, 1962—70; tchr. Bd. Co-operative Ednl. Svc., Westchester County, NY, 1971—73; faculty mem. Appalachian State U., Boone, NC, 1980—82. Author: Fish Head, 1954, The Late Spring, 1957, The Animals of Doctor Schweitzer, 1958, The Cabin Faced West, 1958, How to Read a Rabbit, 1958, Brady, 1960, I, Adam, 1963, Magic to Burn, 1964, Early Thunder, 1967, George Washington's Breakfast, 1969, Cast for a Revolution, 1972, And Then What Happened, Paul Revere?, 1973, Why Don't You Get a Horse, Sam Adams?, 1974, Where Was Patrick Henry on the 29th of May?, 1975, Who's that Stepping on Plymouth Rock?, 1975, Will You Sign Here, John Hancock?, 1976, The Secret Diary of Jeb and Abigail, 1976, What's the Big Idea, Ben Franklin?, 1976, Can't You Make Them Behave, King George?, 1977, Brendon the Navigator, 1979, Stonewall, 1979, Where Do You Think You're Going, Christopher Columbus?, 1980, The Man Who Loved Books, 1981, Traitor: The Case of Benedict Arnold, 1981, The Good Giants and the Bad Pukwudgies, 1981, Homesick: My Own Story, 1982 (Am. Book award 1983, Child Study Book award 1983, Honor Book, Newberry Medal Book 1983), China Homecoming, 1985, The Double Life of Pocahontas, 1983 (Boston Globe/Horn Book award 1984), Make Way for Sam Houston, 1986 (Western Writers award 1987), Shh! We're Writing the Constitution, 1987, China's Long March, 1988, The Great Little Madison, 1989, Bully for You, Teddy Roosevelt!, 1991, Around the World in 100 Years, 1994, Harriet Beecher Stowe and the Beecher Preachers, 1994, You Want Women to Vote, Lizzie Stanton?, 1995, Why Not, Lafayette?, 1999, Leonardo's Horse, 2001. Recipient Christopher award Cath. Library Assn., 1982, Regina Medal Cath. Library Assn., 1985, Laura Ingalls Wilder award ALA, 1986, Nat. Humanities medal, 2003. Home: 50 Bellewood Ave Dobbs Ferry NY 10522-2302 Office: Gina MacCoby Literary Agy Ste 1010 1123 Broadway New York NY 10010*

FRITZ, MARY ANN, elementary school educator; b. Huron, S.D., July 23, 1951; d. Marvin Frederick and Gertrude Irene White; m. Harry M. Fritz, May 24, 1975; children: Jennifer, John. BA, S.D. State U., 1973; MA, Ball State U., Muncie, Ind., 1978. Cert. Orff Inst., Salzburg, Austria, 1974, Orff Schulwerk Levels I to II. Elem. music tchr. Rapid City (S.D.) Pub. Schs., 1974—77, 1978—80, Shrine of St. Anne, Arvada, Colo., 1980—81, Laramie County Sch. Dist. #1, Cheyenne, Wyo., 1981—. Exec. dir. Cheyenne All-City Children's Chorus, 1982—; handbell quartet ringer Quarter Notes, First United Meth. Ch., Cheyenne, 1998—; condr. workshops in field. Past faculty rep. Buffalo Ridge PTO; dir. Celebration Singers First United Meth. Ch., past dir., ringer Celestial Bells, past bd. trustees. Recipient Tchr. of the Mo. award, Cheyenne Rotary Club, 1993; scholar Fulbright scholar, 1973. Mem.: Am. Guild of English Handbell Ringers, Choristers Guild, Am. Choral Dirs. Assn. (Wyo. R&S children's choir chmn.), Orgn. of Am. Kodaly Educators, Am. Orff Schulwerk Assn. (treas. 1988—, fundraising com. 1988—, membership com. 1986—, pres. 1984—86), Music Educators Nat. Conf., Wyo. Music Educators Assn. (Music in our Schs. Mo. chmn. 1996—2000, sec. 1987—89, elem. v.p. 1985—87, S.E. Dist. Music Tchr. of the Yr. 2001), Phi Kappa Phi, Delta Kappa Gamma. Republican. Methodist. Avocation: musical activities. Home: 5725 Blue Bluff Cheyenne WY 82009 Office: Laramie County Sch Dist #1 Buffalo Ridge Elem Sch 5331 Pineridge Ave Cheyenne WY 82009

FRITZ, MARY G. state legislator; b. Cambridge, Mass., May 8, 1938; d. Patrick John and Kathleen Sherry; m. William W. Fritz, Aug. 24, 1963; children: William Jr., Kathleen, Michael, Heather, Matthew, David. BA, Emmanuel Coll., Boston, 1959. Cert. tchr., Conn. Tchr. Wallingford (Conn.) Bd. Edn., 1979-83; dir., owner nursery sch., Yalesville, Conn., 1969-78; mgr. furniture store, 1977-81; legislator 90th dist. State of Conn., 1983-84, 87—. Bd. govs. Mid-State Med. Ctr., 1998—; mem. adv. coun. August Daily Intervention Ctr., Cheshire, 1985—. Mem. Heritage Quilters, Cheshire Grange. Democrat. Roman Catholic. Home: 43 Grove St Wallingford CT 06492-1606

FROBOM, LEANN LARSON, lawyer; b. Ramona, S.D., May 31, 1953; d. Floyd Burdette and Janice Anne (Quist) L.; m. Richard Curtis Finke, May 19, 1973 (div. Jan. 1978); 1 child, Timothy; m. Dwayne Jeffery LaFave, May 31, 1981 (div. 1992); children: Jeffrey, Allison; m. Jerome B. Frobom, Aug. 21, 1999. BS, U. S.D., 1974, JD with honors, 1977. Bar: S.D. 1977, U.S. Dist. Ct. S.D. 1977, U.S. Ct. Appeals (8th cir.) 1977, N.D. 1978, U.S. Dist. Ct. N.D. 1978, Iowa 1998, Nebr. 2001. Asst. atty. gen. State of S.D., Pierre, 1977-78, 79-81; assoc. Bjella, Neff, Rathert & Wahl, Williston, ND, 1978-79, Tobin Law Offices, P.C., Winner, SD, 1981-83; assoc. dean, asst. prof. U. S.D. Sch. Law, Vermillion, 1983-86, dir. continuing legal edn., 1983-89, assoc. prof. law, 1986-89; ptnr. Aho & LaFave, Brookings, SD, 1990-91; pvt. practice Brookings, 1991-92; asst. U.S. atty. U.S. Dist. S.D., 1992-97; gen. counsel S.D. Auto Group, Inc., Sioux Falls, 1997-98; atty. Hughes Law Offices, Sioux Falls, 1998-99, Cline Williams Wright Johnson & Oldfather, Lincoln, Nebr., 1999—2003, Nebr. Legal Svcs., 2003—; seasonal tax preparer H&R Block Co., 1999—. Mem. S.D. Bd. Pardons and Paroles, 1987-90, chmn., 1989-90; comml. arbitrator Am. Arbitration Assn., 1985-92; prof. Kilian C.C. Contbr. articles to profl. jours. Mem. planning coun. Nat. Identification Program for Advancement Women in Higher Edn. Adminstrn., Am. Coun. on Edn., S.D., 1984-90; bd. dirs. Mo. Shores Women's Resource Ctr., Pierre, 1980, W.H. Over Mus., Vermillion, 1986-87, S.D. Vol. Lawyers for Arts, 1987-92, Brookings Interagy. Coun., 1990-91, Brookings Women's Ctr., 1990-94; sec. Mediation Ctr., Inc. Named S.D. Woman Atty. of Yr. Women in Law U. S.D., 1985. Mem. Epsilon Sigma Alpha (S.D. coun. sect. 1985-86). Episcopalian. Avocation: reading. Home: 4911 High St Lincoln NE 68506-3970 Office: 941 'O' St Ste 825 Lincoln NE 68508 Office Phone: 402-435-2161.

FROEBER, SARAH MARJORIE, actress, playwright, educator; b. Hollis, Okla., Dec. 15, 1946; d. Robert Jones and Marjorie Husband F.; m. John Peter Nussbaumer (div.); 1 child, Eric Robert Nussbaumer; m. Jeffrey Charles Lambdin, June 27, 1987. BA, Duke U., 1968; MA, Columbia U., 1969. Psychometrist Child Devel. Rsch. Project, N.Y.C., 1969-71; evaluator street acad. program N.Y. Urban League, N.Y.C., 1971-72; rsch. asst. Program Rsch. Media Assocs., N.Y.C., 1972-73, City Coll. N.Y., N.Y.C., 1973-74; instr. and dir. day care ctr. Vance-Granville C.C., Henderson, N.C., 1977-81; dir. day care ctr. Frank Porter Graham Child Devel. Ctr., Chapel Hill, N.C., 1981-84. Artistic dir., playwright Jelly Ednl. Theater, Carrboro, N.C., 1996-2000; playwright, dir. Scroggs Elem. Sch., Chapel Hill, N.C., 2000, McDougle Elem. Sch., Chapel Hill, 2000; instr. drama program Duke U., Durham, N.C., 1995—; bd. dirs. drama program Duke U., Durham; bd. dirs. Americal Corp., Henderson. Actor regional stage cos., film, radio, and audiotape, 1985—; author (play for children) Samuel and the Wishards, 1996, Melvin the Pelican, 1997, The Prince Who Was Afraid of Peanut Butter, 1997, The Great Nut Hunt, 1998, Wheelchair Dancer, 1999, Spiders on Strike, 2000, Getting Help, 2000, Dolphins and Grolphins and the Keys to Success, 2000, Lovely, Lovely, Lily Pad, 2000. Mem. SAG, Actors Equity Assn. Avocations: yoga, dance, cross country skiing, singing. Home: 3211 Gait Way Chapel Hill NC 27516-7607 E-mail: froeber@mindspring.com.

FROELICH, BEVERLY LORRAINE, foundation director; b. Vancouver, B.C., Can., Oct. 23, 1948; came to U.S., 1968; d. Kenneth Martin and Ethel Pulham; m. Eugene Leonard Froelich, Dec. 26, 1971; children: Craig, Grant. Cert. in fundraising, U. So. Calif., 1986; profl. designation in pub. rels., UCLA, 1987. Cert. fund raising exec. Contract analyst Universal Studios, Calif., 1968-71; exec. dir. Olive View, UCLA Med. Ctr. Found., Sylmar, Calif., 1987—. Pres. Beverly Froelich Pub. Rels., Sherman Oaks, Calif., 1988-90; prin. Tracy Susman & Co., Sherman Oaks, 1986-88. Co-author: (program) Overcoming Chronic Arthritis Pain, 1989; contbg. writer hosp. earthquake preparedness guidelines Hosp. Coun. So. Calif., 1991. Founder San Fernando Valley br. Arthritis Found., Encino, 1983, pres., 1983-87, mktg. com.; bd. dirs. health care com. Valley Industry and Commerce Assn. Recipient Nat. Vol. Svc. award Arthritis Found., 1986, Jane Wyman Humanitarian award Arthritis Found., 1991, Disting. Svc. award Arthritis Found., 1990, Marilyn Magaram award for Cmty. Svc., 1997. Mem.: Assn. Fundraising Profls. (pres. San Fernando Valley chpt., Fundraising Profl. of Yr. 2000, Fundraising Profl. of Yr.), Valley Industry and Commerce Assn., UCLA Alumni Assn. Avocations: hockey, music. Office: Olive View Med Ctr Found Cottage J2 14445 Olive View Dr Sylmar CA 91342-1437

FROETSCHER, JANET, social services administrator; m. Roy Froetscher; 2 children. Bachelor's Degree, U. Va., 1981; M in Mgmt., Northwestern U., 1983. Leveraged buyout specialist First Chgo. Corp.; v.p. corp. fin. Bankers Trust Co., N.Y.C.; founding mng. ptnr. Exec. Options; exec. dir. Fin. Rsch. and Adv. Com. Civic Com. of the Comml. Club Chgo., 1992—99; sr. v.p. seminars Aspen Inst., 1999—2000, exec. v.p., 2000—01, COO, 2001—02; pres., CEO United Way Chgo., 2003, United Way Met. Chgo., 2003—. Named mem. Coun. of 100, Northwestern U., mem., The Chgo. Network; named one of Chgo. Most Influential Women, Crain's Chgo. Bus., 1996, 40 under 40, 1997; Henry Crown fellow, Aspen Inst., 1998. Office: United Way Met Chgo 560 W Lake Chicago IL 60661*

FROIMOVITZ, FELICIA STACEY, psychologist; d. Howard B. Froimovitz and Susan G. Turk. BA, SUNY, 1996; MEd, Columbia U., 1999. Sch. psychologist Belleville (N.J.) Pub. Schs., 1999—2002, Pompton Lakes (N.J.) PUb. Schs., 2002—. Mem.: Nat. Assn. Sch. Psychologists, Am. Psychol. Assn.

FROLICK, PATRICIA MARY, retired elementary school educator; b. Portland, Oreg., May 17, 1923; d. Fred Anthony and Clara Cecelia (Riverman) F. BS in Edn., Marylhurst Coll., 1960; MS in Edn., Portland State U., 1970; student, U. Oreg., 1975; MA in Theology, St. Mary's Coll., Moraga, Calif., 1977. Joined Roman Cath. Order Sisters of Holy Names of Jesus and Mary, 1943. Left order in 1974. Elem. sch. tchr. Catholic Sch. System, Oreg., 1943-69; tchr., libr. Hood River Pub. Schs., 1970-74, Bend-La Pine (Oreg.) Pub. Schs., 1981-93; ret., 1993. Part-time tchr.'s asst., Portland, 1993—2000. Mem. NEA, Oreg. Edn. Assn., Met. Mus. Art (assoc.), Nat. Mus. Women in Arts (charter). Democrat. Roman Catholic. Avocation: watercolor and oil painting. Home: 3465 SE 153rd Ave Portland OR 97236-2265

FROMAN, SANDRA SUE, lawyer; b. San Francisco, June 15, 1949; d. Jay and Beatrice Froman. AB with honors, Stanford U., 1971; JD, Harvard U., 1974. Bar: Calif. 1974, U.S. Dist. Ct. (cen. dist.) Calif. 1974, U.S. Dist. Ct. (so. dist.) Calif. 1976, U.S. Dist. Ct. (no. dist.) Calif., U.S. Ct. Claims 1979, U.S. Tax Ct. 1984, Ariz. 1985, U.S. Dist. Ct. Ariz. 1985, U.S. Ct. Appeals (9th cir.) 1986, U.S. Supreme Ct. 1986. Assoc. Loeb & Loeb, L.A., 1974-80, ptnr., 1981-84; assoc. Bilby & Schoenhair, P.C., Tucson, 1985, shareholder, 1986-89; ptnr. Snell & Wilmer, Tucson, 1989-99. Vis. asst. prof. law U. Santa Clara, Calif., 1983-85; mem. Pima County Commn. on Trial Ct. Appointments, 1996-98. Trustee NRA Civil Rights Def. Fund, 1992-98, NRA Found., pres. 1997-2000; bd. dirs., 1st v.p. NRA, 1992—. Mem. Ariz. Bar Found. (pres. 1996—), Nat. 4-H Shooting Sports Found. (pres. 2002—), Wildlife for Tomorrow Found. (pres. 1999—). Office: Ste 140 200 W Magee Rd Tucson AZ 85704-6492

FROMAN, VERONICA ZASADNI, career officer; BA in Polit. Sci., Seton Hill Coll.; grad., Armed Forces Staff Coll. Commd. U.S. Navy, 1970; advanced through grades to rear admiral, 1995; Naval Air Sta., Milton, Fla., 1970-72; Navy Recruiting Area Four, Columbus, Ohio, 1972-79; exec. officer Personnel Support Activity, Pearl Harbor, Hawaii, 1979-81; with Manpower Planner Joint Staff, 1983-86; commanding officer Personnel Support Activity, Pearl Harbor, 1986-90; Naval Edn. Tng. Support Ctr. Pacific, San Diego, 1981-83; exec. officer Naval Sta., Norfolk, Va., 1986-90; head edn. tng. staff placement Bur. Naval Personnel, Washington, 1990, also head gen. unrestricted line assignment br., 1990-93; commanding officer Naval Sta., Charleston, S.C., 1993-95; dir. manpower personnel Joint Staff, 1995-97; commander Naval Base, San Diego, 1997-2000; dir. FIMD USN, Arlington, Va., 2000—. Decorated Def. Disting. Svc. medal, Legion of Merit; named San Diego Press Club Headliner, 1998, San Diego Soroptomists' Woman of Accomplishment, 1998, Adv. of Yr., Nat. Assn. Women Bus. Owners, 1998. Office: Naval Sea Systems Command SE#1100 1333 Issac Hull Ave Washington DC 20376-1100

FROMBERG, JEAN STERN, school system administrator; b. Roanoke, Va., Jan. 4, 1943; d. Ernest George and Marianne (Stamm) Stern; m. Aug. 26, 1968 (div. 1989); children: Nathan, Eric, Craig, Brian, Laura; m. Zachary Fromberg, Nov. 14, 1999. BA, Coll. William and Mary, 1965; MA, Wichita State U., 1986, specialist degree, 1989. Cert. permanent tchr. German, N.Y.; cert. supt., bldg. adminstr., Kans., Colo., N.Y., Va., N.H., Ohio, Ariz., Pa., Ky. Rural community devel. vol. Peace Corps, Turkey, 1965-67; tchr. German, Spanish and English Kenmore (N.Y.)-Tonawanda Sch. Dist., 1967-70; tchr. German Grand Island (N.Y.) Sch. Dist., 1978-82, coord. adult edn., prin., 1982; grad. rsch. asst. Wichita (Kans.) State U., 1984-86, instr. German, 1985; asst. prin. Unified Sch. Dist. 259, Wichita, 1986-88; supt., high sch. prin. Unified Sch. Dist. 314, Brewster, Kans., 1988-91; supt. Unified Sch. Dist. 271, Stockton, Kans., 1991-93; dir. edn. Computer Learning Ctr., Alexandria, Va., 1993; sr. dir. distbr. Nat. Safety Assocs., Lorton, Va., 1993-96; dir. KinderCare Learning Ctr., Alexandria, 1994; dir. edn. Gesher Jewish Day Sch. of No. Va., Fairfax, 1994; dir. Kinder Care Learning Ctr., Vienna, Va., 1994-95, Children's World Learning Ctr., Lake Ridge, Va., 1995-98; dir. adminstrn. Sanz Sch., Inc., Washington, 1998—. Mem. sch. community adv. coms., N.Y., Kans., 1975-86; chmn. Com. To Revise Fgn. Lang. Curriculum, Grand Island, 1981-83; judge Kans. Fgn. Lang. Competition, 1987. Contbr. numerous articles on ednl. leadership to profl. jours. Pres. Grand Island Food Coop., 1978-83, Waterford Food Coop., Wichita, 1983-88. Mem. ASCD, Am. Assn. Sch. Adminstrs., Nat. Assn Secondary and Elem. Sch. Prins., Am. Assn. Tchrs. German, Kans. Assn. Sch. Adminstrs., Kans. Unified Sch. Adminstrs., AAUW (active local, regional and state levels 1973—), Phi Kappa Phi, Phi Delta Kappa, Nat. Supts. Acad., Ankadaşlar-Returned Peace Corps Vols. of Turkey (bd. dirs. 1993-99, pres. 1996-98, area coord. 1993-2002). Avocations: gourmet cooking and baking, reading, gardening, swimming, sewing. Home: 8513 Farrell Dr Chevy Chase MD 20815-3849 Office: Sanz Sch Inc 8455 Colesville Rd Silver Spring MD 20910 Office Phone: 301-608-3685. E-mail: zjfromberg@earthlink.net.

FRONTIERE, GEORGIA, professional football team executive; b. St. Louis; m. Carroll Rosenblum, July 7, 1966 (dec.); children: Dale Carroll, Lucia; m. Dominic Frontiere. Pres., owner L.A. Rams, NFL, 1979—; now mng. ptnr. St. Louis Rams. Bd. dirs. L.A. Boys and Girls Club, L.A. Orphanage Guild, L.A. Blind Youth Found. Named Headliner of Yr. L.A. Press Club, 1981. Office: St Louis Rams 1 Rams Way Earth City MO 63045-1525 also: Transworld Dome 701 Convention Plz Saint Louis MO 63101

FROST, ELIZABETH ANN MCARTHUR, physician; b. Glasgow, Scotland, Oct. 29, 1938; came to U.S., 1963; d. Robert Thomas and Annie M. (Ross) F.; m. Wallace Capobianco, Sept. 4, 1965 (dec. May 1988); children: Garrett, Ross, Christopher, Neil. MBChB, U. Glasgow, 1961. Diplomate Am. Bd. Anesthesiology, Royal Coll. Ob-Gyn., London. Intern in surgery Royal Infirmary, Glasgow, 1961-62; intern in medicine Victoria Infirmary, Glasgow, 1962; intern in obstetrics Royal Maternity Hosp., Glasgow, 1962-63; resident in internal medicine Englewood (N.J.) Hosp., 1963-64; resident in anesthesiology N.Y. Hosp., N.Y.C., 1964-66; instr. in anesthesiology Albert Einstein Coll. Medicine, Bronx, N.Y., 1966-68, asst. prof. to assoc. prof., 1968-81, prof. anesthesiology, 1981-91, mem. dept. history of medicine, 1973-91; prof. dept. anesthesiology N.Y. Med. Coll., Valhalla, N.Y., 1992-99; clin. prof. dept. anesthesiology Mt. Sinai Med. Ctr., N.Y.C., 2000—; attending anesthesiology VA Bronx, 2000—. Book reviewer New Eng. Jour. of Medicine, 1983—; editor Preanesthetic Assessment, Anesthesiology News, 1984—, Gen. Surgery News, 1991; author/contbr. books; contbr. articles to profl. jours. Mem. N.Y. State Soc. Anesthesiologists, Am. Soc. of Anesthesiologists, Assn. of Univ. Anesthesiologists, Soc. of Neurosurg. Anesthesia and Neurologic Supportive Care, Am. Assn. of Neurol. Surgeons, Anesthesia History Assn. Home: 2 Pondview West Purchase NY 10577 E-mail: ElzFrost@aol.com.

FROST, ELLEN ELIZABETH, psychologist; b. N.Y.C. d. John Joseph and Josephine Mary (Cornell) F.; m. Jerry Melnick, Jan. 8, 1982; children: Mariel Frost, Matt James. BA magna cum laude, St. John's U., 1969; MA, Fordham U., 1971, PhD, 1982; candidate NYU Postdoctoral Program for Psychotherapy and Psychoanalysis, 1982-84. Cert. Eye Movement Desensitization Reprocessing tng., 2000. Clin. psychology intern Columbia-Presbyn. Psychiat. Inst., N.Y.C., 1972-73; asst. team leader staff psychologist Bensonhurst inpatient unit South Beach Psychiat. Ctr., Bklyn., 1973-75, sr. psychologist, Bensonhurst outpatient dept., 1975-81, assoc. psychologist, supr., 1982-89; dir. Phobia Svc., 1982-89; pvt. practice, 1983—; clin. supr. New Hope Guild, Bklyn., 1983—2000. Faculty L.I. Inst. Mental Health, 1990-97, supr., 1993-97. N.Y. State regents fellow, 1969-72; USPHS fellow, 1969-72. Mem. Am. Psychol. Assn., EMDR Internat. Assoc., Sigma Xi. Office: 200 E 33rd St Apt 25J New York NY 10016-4831 E-mail: efrostphd@aol.com.

FROST, ELLEN LOUISE, political economist; b. Boston, Apr. 26, 1945; d. Horace Wier and Mildred (Kip) F.; m. William F. Pedersen, Jr., Feb. 2, 1974; 1 son by previous marriage, Jai Kumar Ojha; children: Mark Francis Pedersen, Claire Ellen Pedersen. BA magna cum laude, Radcliffe Coll., 1966; MA, Fletcher Sch. Law and Diplomacy, 1967; PhD, Harvard U., 1972. Teaching fellow, instr. Harvard U., Wellesley Coll., 1969-71; legis. asst. Office of Senator Alan Cranston, Washington, 1972-74; fgn. affairs officer Dept. Treasury, Washington, 1974-77; dep. dir. Office of Internat. Trade Policy and Negotiations, 1977; dep. asst. sec. of def. for internat. econ. and tech. affairs Dept. Def., Washington, 1977-81; dir. govt. programs Westinghouse Electric Corp., Washington, 1981-88; corp. dir., internat. affairs United Techs. Corp., Washington, 1988-91; sr. fellow Inst. for Internat. Econs., Washington, 1992-93, 95-98, vis. fellow; counselor to U.S. Trade Rep., Washington, 1993-95. Author: For Richer, For Poorer: The New U.S.-Japan Relationship, 1987, Transatlantic Trade: A Strategic Agenda, 1997; co-editor: The Global Century, 2001. Trustee Aspen Inst. Berlin, 1990-92. NSF trainee, 1967-69 Mem. Internat. Inst. Strategic Studies, Coun. Fgn. Rels., Phi Beta Kappa.

FROST, LINDA GAIL, clergyman, hospital chaplain; b. Louisville, Feb. 26, 1950; d. Halqua Mildon and Christena (Crisp) F. BA, Georgetown (Ky.) Coll., 1972; MDiv, So. Bapt. Sem., Louisville, 1978, DMin, 1982. Ordained to ministry Bapt. Ch., 1978; bd. cert. chaplain. Social worker Dept. Pub. Welfare, Corpus Christi, 1972-76; assoc. to pastor Walnut St. Bapt. Ch., Louisville, 1979-89; chaplain, clin. supr. Koala Hosp., Columbus, Ind., 1989-92; dir. chaplain svcs. Caritas Med. Ctr., Louisville, 1993—. Advisor pastoral svcs. Hospice of S.E. Ind., Jeffersonville, 1993-98. Author: A Legacy in Missions and Ministry, 1993; contbg. author: Women at the Well, 2003. Bd. dirs., pres. Neighborhood Devel. Corp., Louisville, 1979-89; mem., sec. Old Louisville Neighborhood Coun., 1979-87; active ARC Disaster Svcs., 1999—. Mem.: Ky. Chaplain Assn. (pres. 1999—).

FROST-KNAPPMAN, ELIZABETH (LINDA ELIZABETH FROST-KNAPPMAN), publishing executive, editor, writer; b. Washington, Oct. 1, 1943; d. Edward Laurie and Lorena (Ameter) Frost; m. Edward William Knappman, Nov. 6, 1965; 1 child, Anna Knappman. BA, George Washington U., 1965; postgrad., U. Wis., 1966, NYU, 1966. Editor Natural History Press, N.Y.C., 1967-69, William Collins and Sons, London, 1970-71; sr. editor Doubleday and Co., N.Y.C., 1972-80, William Morrow and Co., Inc., N.Y.C., 1980-82; founder, pres. New Eng. Pub. Assocs. Inc., Chester, Conn., 1982—. Lectr. New Eng. colls. and univs. Author: The World Almanac of Presidential Quotations, 1993, The ABC-CLIO Companion to Women's Progress in America, 1994 (Outstanding Acad. Book-Reference of Yr. award ALA), The Quotable Lawyer, 1986, 1998, Women Suffrage in America: An Eyewitness History, 1992, Courtroom Dramas, 3 vols., 1997; gen. editor: (CD-ROM) American Journey: Women in America, 1994, Women's Rights on Trial, 1998. Mem. Assn. Authors Reps., Authors Guild, Am. Soc. Journalists and Authors. Avocations: knitting, tennis, travel, reading, piano. Office: New Eng Pub Assocs Inc PO Box 5 Chester CT 06412-0005 E-mail: nepa@nepa.com.*

FROT-COUTAZ, CECILE, television producer; b. Chambery, France, Apr. 18, 1966; m. M. Eliot Charles, Dec. 29, 2001; 1 child, Amelie. BA in Bus., U. Paris, 1988; MBA, INSEAD, 1994. Assoc. Mercer Mgmt. Consulting, London, 1988—93; exec. corp. strategy Pearson Group, London, 1994—98; dep. chief exec. officer So. Europe, mng. dir. France Pearson TV, Paris, 1998—2000, head digital media, 2000—01; exec. v.p. comml. and ops. FremantleMedia N.Am., LA, 2001—02, COO prodn. Santa Monica, Calif., 2002—, exec. prodr. Am. Idol, 2002—. Office: Fremantle Media Productions North America Inc 2700 Colorado Ave Ste 450 Santa Monica CA 90404*

FRUEHLING, ROSEMARY THERESE, publishing executive, author; b. Gilbert, Minn., Jan. 23, 1933; d. Tony and Mary (Scalise) Leoni; 1 child, Shirley Adzick. BS, U. Minn., 1954, MA, 1968, PhD, 1980. Cert. vocat. tech. inst. dir.; cert. in bus. edn. Mgr. instructional svcs. State Bd. Voc-Tech. Edn., St. Paul; dir. Minn. Software Office State of Minn., St. Paul; mgr. office tech. Gregg, McGraw Hill, Mpls.; pres. EMC/Paradigm Pub. Inc. (Coll. Divsn.), St. Paul, Minn. Nat. cons. editor SRA. Author: (textbooks) Communicating for Results: Write to The Point, Office Systems: People, Procedures and Technology, Business Communications: A Case Method Approach, Business Writing: Integrating Process and Purpose, Psychology: Realizing Human Potential, Working at Human Relations, Your Attitude Counts, Communicating for Results, Working in Teams. Mem. Am. Vocat. Assn., Minn. Vocat. Assn., Nat. Bus. Edn. Assn., Delta Pi Epsilon. Office: EMC Corp 875 Montreal Way Saint Paul MN 55102-4245

FRUEHWALD, KRISTIN G. lawyer; b. Sidney, Nebr., May 15, 1946; d. Chris U. and Mary E. (Boles) Bitner; m. Michael R. Fruehwald, Feb. 23, 1980; children: Laurel Elizabeth, Amy Marie. BS with highest distinction in History, U. Nebr., 1968; JD summa cum laude, Ind. U., 1975. Bar: Ind. 1975, U.S. Dist. Ct. (so. dist.) Ind. 1975. Assoc. Barnes & Thornburg, Indpls., 1975-81, ptnr., 1982—. Spkr. in field. Contbr. articles to profl. jours. Trustee The Orchard Sch., 1993—, chmn., 1997—98; bd. dirs. Indpls. Parks Found., 1995—2000, Arts Ind., 1994—98, Ind. Continuing Legal Edn. Forum, 1993—2001, pres., 2000—01; bd. dirs. Indpls. Bar Found., 1992—, chmn., 1997—99; bd. dirs. James Whitcomb Riley Meml. Assn., 1995—, treas., 2000—; bd. dirs. Planned Giving Group Ind., Fedn. Cmty. Defenders, Inc., 1993—99, pres., 1999—2001; bd. dirs . Ind. affiliate Am. Heart Assn., 1977—81, vice chmn. Marion County chpt., 1981; bd. dirs. through pres. Indpls. Bar Found., 1994—2001. Fellow: ABA (chmn. distributable net income subcom 1985—91, sect. taxation, mem. real property, probate and trust sect.), Ind. State Bar Assn. (chmn. probate, trust and real property sects. 1987—88, mem. ho. of dels. 1987—, bd. mgrs. 1989—90, treas. 1996—97, chair ho. of dels. 1998—99, pres. 2001—02, mem. sect. taxation), Ind. Bar Found. (bd. dirs. 2003—), Am. Coll. Trust and Estate Counsel (chmn. Ind. state laws com. 1992—95); mem.: Ind. Code Study Commn., Internat. Assn. Fin. Planners, Indpls. Estate Planning Coun., Indpls. Bar Assn. (chmn. estate planning and adminstrn. sect. 1982—83, chmn. long range fin. planning com. 1988—89, pres. 1993). Office: Barnes & Thornburg 11 S Meridian St Indianapolis IN 46204-3535 E-mail: kris.fruewald@btlaw.com.

FRUEN, LOIS, secondary school educator; Chemistry tchr. Breck Sch., Mpls. Recipient James Bryant Conant award High Sch. Chemistry Teaching, 1992. Office: The Breck Sch 123 Ottawa Ave North Minneapolis MN 55422

FRUIHT, DOLORES GIUSTINA, artist, educator, poet; b. Portland, Oreg., Mar. 9, 1923; d. Erminio and Irene (Onorato) Giustina; m. Thos. Herman Fruiht, Dec. 20, 1947 (div. 1976); children: Justina, Bryce, Bradford, Erica, Renee. BS, RN, U. Portland, 1944; attended, U. San Francisco, 1971. Nurse, Nurse Corps U.S. Army, 1944-46; intravenous nurse St. Vincent's Hosp., Portland, 1946; staff nurse Dr. Shepard, Eugene, Oreg., 1947-49; surg. nurse Sacred Heart Hosp., Eugene, Oreg., 1949-52; tchr. Ursulina High Sch., Santa Rosa, Calif., 1976-78; artist Angela Ctr. for Adult Edn., Santa Rosa, Calif., 1978-88. Juror Bodega Bay Fisherman's Festival, Calif., 1992, Sebastopol Ctr. for the Arts, 1995. One woman shows include: "Expressions in Art", Abstract Photography, Paintings, and Images in Clay, Sonoma County Mus., Santa Rosa, 1992, Pottery Exhibit, Angela Ctr., 1980, Sonoma, 1976; exhibited in group shows at: Oreg. State U., 1999, Cultural Arts Coun. Sonoma County, 1998, Sebastopol Libr., 1992, Bodega Bay Allied Arts, 1991, 93-96, Nor Cal. State Art Exhibit, Nat. League of Am. Pen Women, Souverain Winery, 1985, "Tibetan Faces", Photography, Calif. Mus. of Art, Santa Rosa, 1985, Photography Exhibit, Angela Ctr., 1982, "The Healing Celebration of Art", Photography, San Francisco Civic Auditorium, 1981, Photography Show, Angela Ctr., 1980, Pottery Exhibit, 1975; contbr. articles to numerous profl. jours.; disting. lectr. Diplomat City of Sonoma, Russia, 1988. 1st Lt. U.S. Army Nurse Corps, 1944-46. Decorated Bronze Star for Luzon Campaign U.S. Army. Mem. Nat. League of Am. Pen Women (Biennial Selection award, 1986, Excellence award, 1985). Roman Catholic. Avocations: hiking, golfing, reading. Office: 1519 Parsons Dr Santa Rosa CA 95404 Home: PO Box 823 Bodega Bay CA 94923

FRUSTI, DOREEN KAYE, nursing administrator; BSN summa cum laude, Augustana Coll., 1970; MS in Ednl. Psychology and Counseling, Winona State U., 1979, postgrad., 1988—. RN, Minn. Developer, implementor group therapy program acute psychiat. unit McKennan Hosp., Sioux Falls, S.D., 1970; asst. head nurse gen. surgery Rochester (Minn.) Meth. Hosp., 1970-73, head nurse nephrology and renal transplant, 1973-78, instr. electrocardiology, 1975, asst. DON, 1978-83, mem. facility and program devel. chem. dependence svcs., 1981-83, mem. adminstrv. com., 1983-85, mem. lab. medicine study, 1978, mem. weekend phys. medicine feasibility study, 1978-79, mem. liason com., 1978-80, mem. hospice feasibility study, 1978-82, clin. DIN, 1978-91, mem. mgmt. coun., 1987—, mem. clean air task force com., 1986-87, mem. tornado and disaster coms., 1986-88, mem. nursing info. system steering com., 1987-91, joint head nurse planning com., 1988-91, chair dept. nursing, 1991—; grad. intern supr. Winona (Minn.) State U., 1983-88; co-instr. chem. dependence course Rochester Community Coll., 1985; cons. Meth. Hosp. Indpls., 1989. Adj. asst. prof. St. Mary's Coll., Winona, 1986—; mem. cons. com. on alcoholism and drug dependence unit Mayo Clinic, 1980-91, adminstrv. mgmt. com., 1983-88, adolescent chem. dependence unit, 1984-88, mgmt. forum, 1988—, coordinating com., 1988-90, smoking cessation program com. Mayo Med. Ctr., 1985-89, smoke free implementation task force, 1987; cons. Genesee Hosp., Rochester, N.Y., 1989. Mem. hypertension screening program Bethel Luth. Ch., 1976, stewardship com., 1976-78, usher, 1985—, group discussion facilitator, 1985-90, chair, 1986-89, chair pers. and exec. coms., 1987-89, capt., 1988—, lead usher, 1991—; del. dist. conv. Am. Luth. Ch., 1987; del. synodical conv. Evang. Luth. Ch. Am., 1988; chair Outpatient Observation Task Force, 1990-91, steering com. Nursing Ops. Assessment, 1990-91, Incident Report Task Force, 1990-91, Allied Health, 1992—; mem. Bread of the World, 1989—; mem. ops. bd. dirs. Probation Offenders Rehab. and Tng., 1987-90, chair pers. com., 1988-90; supr. Roundtable, 1992—. Mem. Dist. F Orgn. Nurse Execs., Am. Orgn. Nurse Execs., Minn. Orgn. Nurse Execs., Minn. Nurses Assn. (del. 1971, 77, 81, 83, program com. 6th dist. 1973-75, chairperson, 1975-77, adv. bd. com., pres. 1977-79, long range planning com. 1978-79, entry level task force 1981, nursing svc. adminstrn. exec. and legis. coms. 1981-82, nominating com. 1981-83), Sigma Theta Tau (Kappa Mu chpt.). Home: 2100 Valkyrie Dr NW Apt 108 Rochester MN 55901-2451 Office: Rochester Meth Hosp 200 1st St SW Rochester MN 55905-0001

FRUTH, BERYL ROSE, physician; b. Carey, Ohio, Mar. 27, 1952; d. Oscar W. and Alice (Arnett) Fruth. BA in Chemistry magna cum laude, Asbury Coll., 1973; MD, Ohio State U., 1977. Diplomate Am. Acad. Family Practice. Intern Grant Hosp., Columbus, Ohio, 1977-78, resident, 1978-79, chief resident, 1979-80; pvt. practice Columbus, 1980-93; family physician Columbus Community Physicians, Inc., Grove City, Ohio, 1993—98; med. dir. Meml. Physicians Inc. Urgent Care, Marysville, Ohio, 1998—2000, Vets. Med. Ctr., Chillicothe, Ohio, 2000-01, primary care team physician, 2000—03; dir. women's health Oakland Pk. Outpatient Clinic, Ft. Lauderdale, Fla., 2003—. Asst. dir. family practice residency Grant Hosp., 1980-81; med. dir. Columbus Dispatch, 1983-93, St. Anthony Breast Evaluation Ctr., 1986—, Physicians House Call, Columbus, 1998—; lectr. Columbus Cancer Clinic, 1984; mentor family practice dept. Ohio State U., physician preceptor Sch. Medicine. Contbr. Ohio State U. Med. Sch. Learning Module in Alcoholism, 1983-84. Named Alumna of Yr. Vanlue Sch., Ohio. Fellow Am. Acad. Family Physicians; mem. AMA, Am. Med. Women's Assn., Acad. Family Practice. Address: Oakland Pk Outpatient Clinic 5599 N Dixie Hwy Fort Lauderdale FL 33334 Home: 1900 S Ocean Blvd Apt 10N Pompano Beach FL 33062-8022

FRY, ANNE EVANS, zoology educator; b. Phila., Sept. 11, 1939; d. Kenneth Evans and Nora Irene (Smith) F. AB, Mount Holyoke Coll., 1961; MS, U. Iowa, 1963; PhD, U. Mass., 1969. Instr. Carleton Coll., Northfield, Minn., 1963-65; asst. prof. Ohio Wesleyan U., Delaware, 1969-74, assoc. prof., 1974-80, prof., 1980—, Helen Whitelaw Jackson univ. prof., 1999—. Contbr. articles to profl. jours. Recipient Welch Teaching award Ohio Wesleyan U., 1976. Mem. AAAS, Am. Inst. Biol. Scis., Soc. for Integrative and Comparative Biology, Ohio Acad. Sci., Soc. Devel. Biology, Sigma Xi. Office: Ohio Wesleyan U Delaware OH 43015 E-mail: AEFry@owu.edu.

FRY, CATHERINE HOWARD, publishing executive; b. Vicksburg, Miss., Jan. 6, 1952; d. Z.B. and Letty (Lassiter) F. BS, La. State U., 1974, MA, 1977. Dir. Baton Rouge Eye Bank, 1977-79; promotion mgr. La. State U. Press, Baton Rouge, 1979-83, mktg. mgr., 1983-89, asst. dir., mktg. mgr., 1989-94, assoc. dir., mktg. dir., 1994-95; dir. U. S.C. Press, Columbia, 1995—. Adj. prof. Manship Sch. Mass. Comm. La. State U., 1994; faculty mem. Acad. Scholarly Pub., Charleston, 1996, New Orleans Writers Conf., 1990; spkr. in field. Mem. Assn. Am. Univ. Presses (chair mktg. workshop 1987, mem. mktg. com. 1985-94, chair mktg. com. 1986-87, nominating com. 1992-93, chair equal opportunity com. 1993 95), Pubs. Assn. South (bd. dirs. 1984-87), S.C. Book Festival (bd. dir. 1997—), Jr. League Columbia (sustaining), Mortar Bd. Alumni Assn., Omicron Delta Kappa, Chi Omega. Democrat. Episcopalian. Office: U SC Press 937 Assembly St Fl 8 Columbia SC 29208-0001 E-mail: cfry@sc.edu.

FRY, HEDY, member of parliament; 3 children. MD, Royal Coll. Surgeons, Dublin, Ireland, 1968. Pvt. practice; mem., sec. of state (multiculturalism) (status of women) Can. Parliament/Vancouver Ctr., Ottawa, 1996—2002; chair B.C. Caucus, 2002—; mem. spl. com. on non-med. use of drugs, mem. standing com. on health, standing com. on justice and human rights Can. Parliament, Ottawa, Canada, 2002. Dr. Hirsh Rosenfeld Disting. Lectr. in family medicine McGill U., 1994; featured on Doctor-Doctor, CBC TV series, 1985-89. Mem. editl. bd. Med. Post. Mem. com. Royal Commn. on Reproductive Technologies.dn. Learning for Living Adv. Bd.; mem. Mayor's Spl. Com. on Urban Natives; bd. dirs. St. George's sch., 1989-91; adv. bd. B.C. Physicians Against Nuclear War; co-chair Liberal Party Health and Social Issues sect., Aylmer Conf., 1992, mem. Leader's Nat. Task Force on Women, 1992-93; parliamentary sec. Min. of Health, 1993-96, mem. task force on reform of social security sys., 1994, standing com. on health, 1994, subcom. on AIDS, mem. caucus com. on social policy. Recipient Cmty. Svc. award Commonwealth Caribbean Club, 1991, Black Achievement award, 1994, Congress of Black Women award, 1994. Mem. B.C. Fedn. Med. Women (pres. 1977), Vancouver Women's Network, Vancouver Med. Assn. (pres. 1988-89), B.C. Med. Assn. (pres. 1990-91, chief negotiator 1991-93), Can. Med. Assn. (chair obstetrics task force 1986-87, chair multiculturalism com. 1992-93), Coun. of Healthcare and Promotion (B.C. rep. 1984-92). Avocations: travel, gardening, reading.*

FRY, JUDY ARLINE, hypnotherapist; b. Great Falls, Mont., July 25, 1938; d. Ernest Leroy and Leota M. (Lyon) Workman; m. Kenneth J. Fry, Nov. 11, 1956 (div. 1974); children; Kenneth J., Kathy K. Student, Calif. State U., Northridge, 1978. Cert. clin. hypnotherapist. Co-owner, dir. Artistic Designs in Iron, Huntington Beach, Calif., 1969-73; ops. mgr., sales coord., purchasing agt. Komfort Industries Inc., Santa Ana, Calif., 1974-75; corp. adminstr. OEM accounts Greer Hydraulics, Inc., City of Commerce, Calif., 1975-81; office svc. supr. Pacific Pumps/Dresser Industries, Inc., Huntington Park, Calif., 1981-83, aftermarket order entry mgr., 1983-84; ops. dir., dir. pub. rels. Calif. Assn. Real Estate Investors, Laguna Niguel, 1986-87; founder, co-owner Advance Resource Ctr., Garden Grove, Calif., 1987-94, North Las Vegas, 1994—. Author two books. Mem. Nat. Mgmt. Assn., United Hypnotherapists Calif., Internat. Assn. Clin. Hypnotherapists (past pres. Orange County chpt.). Home: 4475 Aerial Way # 231 Eugene OR 97402-8733 Office: Advance Resource Ctr 4404 Fenton Ln North Las Vegas NV 89032-0141

FRY, MAUREEN SHEA, director, educator; d. James Matthias Shea, Jr. and Leona Catherine Gore; m. Philip Francis Fry, Aug. 22, 1964; children: Philip Michael, Brian James. BA in English, Coll. Notre Dame Md., 1964; MA in English Lit., U. Dayton, 1972. Adj. instr., instr. Wright State U., Dayton, 1973—80; adj. instr. Edison State C.C., Piqua, Ohio, 1979—80, Urbana (Ohio) U., 1982—83; vis. asst. prof., adj. instr. Wittenberg U., Springfield, Ohio, 1979—88, asst. dir. writing ctr., 1979—88, dir. writing ctr., 1988—. Grad. tchg. asst. U. Dayton, Ohio, 1970—72. Mem. Ohio Environ. Coun., Columbus, Ohio, 2000—; aide, asst. Kara Anastasio for Congress, Yellow Springs, Ohio, 2002. Mem.: AAUW (treas.), Nat. Writing Ctrs. Assn., Coun. Writing Program Adminstrs., Sierra Club. Democrat. Avocations: poetry, gardening, furniture refinishing, swimming. Office: Wittenberg U Box 720 Springfield OH 45501

FRY, THERESA EILEEN, therapeutic foster care aide; b. Bellefonte, Pa., July 20, 1968; d. James Allen Boob, Eileen Betty Boob; m. Shawn William Fry; children: Teri Shaffer, Melinda Shaffer. Student in social work, Lock Haven U., 1999—2003. Cert. nurse asst., 1991. Resident asst. Alterra, State College, Pa., 1998—99; technician mental health Meadows Psychiat. Ctr., Centre Hall, Pa., 2000—01; sec. Social Work Club, Lock Haven, 2000—; therapeutic foster care aide Hope For Kids, Inc., 2002—. Counselor Risk Reduction Test The Aids Project, State College, 2000—. Mem.: NASW (Pa. chpt., com. on nominations and leadership identification). Democrat.

Methodist. Avocations: camping, hunting, fishing, travel. Home: 102 Front St Centre Hall PA 16828 Personal E-mail: theresa16828@yahoo.com.

FRYE, DELLA MAE, portrait artist; b. Roanoke, Va., Feb. 16, 1926; d. Henry Vetchel and Helen Lavinia Theradosia (Eardley) Pearcy; m. James [illegible] Frye, [illegible]; children: [illegible] Frye, James Marvin, David Scott. Student, Hope Coll., 1968, Grand Valley State Coll., 1969-71. Asst. med. records librarian Bapt. Hosp., Little Rock, 1944; receptionist, sec. Stephens Coll., Columbia, Mo., 1945-46; art tchr. Jenison (Mich.) Christian Sch., 1965-67, pvt. classes, 1964-74; realtor, 1978-80; with Diversified Fin., 1979-82; portrait artist, 1967—. Cons. World Traders, Grand Rapids, Mich., 1986—. Author various poems; exhbns. include Salon Des Nations (cert. honor), 1984, Ann Arbor (Mich.) Art Guild, Kalamazoo Artists, Internat. Art Gallery, Hawaii, La Mandragore Gallery Internationale D'Art Contemporain, songwriter: (album) I Love America, 2000-2002 Pres. mother's club Jenison Christian Sch., 1965-66; treas. Band Boosters, Jenison, 1966. Recipient awards for nat. contests in portrait painting. Republican. Baptist. Avocations: songwriting, swimming. Home: 7677 Steele Ave Jenison MI 49428 also: 8901 SE 120th Pl Belleview FL 34420 Mailing: PO Box 2484 Grand Rapids MI 49501-2484

FRYE, HELEN JACKSON, federal judge; b. Klamath Falls, Oreg., Dec. 10, 1930; d. Earl and Elizabeth (Kirkpatrick) Jackson; m. William Frye, Sept. 7, 1952; children: Eric, Karen, Heidi; 1 adopted child, Hedy; m. Perry Holloman, July 10, 1980 (dec. Sept. 1991). BA in English with honors, U. Oreg., 1953, MA, 1960, JD, 1966. Bar: Oreg. 1966. Public sch. tchr., Oreg., 1956-63; with Riddlesberger, Pederson, Brownhill & Young, 1966-67, Husband & Johnson, Eugene, 1968-71; trial judge State of Oreg., 1971-80; U.S. dist judge Dist. Oreg. Portland, 1980-95; sr. judge U.S. Dist. Ct., Portland, 1995—. Mem. Phi Beta Kappa. Office: 1107 US Courthouse 1000 SW 3rd Ave Portland OR 97204-2930

FRYE, LATOYA AISHA HORTENSE, banking administrator; d. Lester Alton and Pansy Moraine (Williams) Frye. AS in Bus. Adminstrn., Piedmont Va. C.C., Charlottesville, Va., 1999; BS in Mktg., Va. Commonwealth U., 2000. Resident asst. Va. Commonwealth U., Richmond, 1998—2000; intern personal banker Bank of Am., Richmond, 1999; intern computer instr. Collis-Warner Found., Alexandria, 2000; mgmt. assoc. Wachovia Bank, Charlottesville, 2001—03, br. mgr., 2003—. Vol. Salvation Army, Charlottesville, Va., 2002—. Mem.: Am. Mktg. Assn., Inroads/Richmond Inc. (Outstanding Acad. Achievement award 1999—2000), Golden Key, Phi Kappa Phi. Avocations: aerobics, rollerblading, tennis. Office: Wachovia Bank 123 E Main St Charlottesville VA 22902

FRYE, LINDA BETH (LINDA BETH HISLE), elementary, secondary education educator; b. Apr. 15, 1947; d. Roland Earl Jr. Hisle and Paralee M. Jones; m. Dennis Franklin Frye; children: Byron Franklin, Cody Earl, Matthew Cole. BA in Art and Elem. Edn., E. Ctrl. State U., Ada, 1970; M.Ed. in Elem. Edn., E. Tex. State U., Commerce, 1975. Tchr. Sherman (Tex.) Ind. Sch. Dist., 1969—2002. Specialist in lang., learning disabilities in spl. edn. Recipient Tex. Instrument Invention Conv. award, Tchr. award, Tex. Instrument Invention Convention; grantee Ada City Sch. Foundation, Ada City Sch. Foun. Mem.: Church of Christ. Home: 8380 CR 3510 Ada OK 74820-9619 Office: P O Box 2015 Ada OK 74821-1701

FRYMAN, ALISON LEIGH, bank executive; b. Atlanta, Feb. 25, 1965; d. Darrell Clifford and Barbara Sue Kamrath; m. Paul Michael Fryman, Apr. 28, 1985; 1 child, Paul Blake. Grad. H.S., Richardson, Tex. Lic. gen. lines ins. Tex., 2002; Series 6 And 63 Tex., 2002. Br. mgr. Bank United, Mckinney, Tex., 1986—2001, Chase Bank, Mckinney, Tex., 2001—03, Regions Bank, Dallas, 2003—. Mem. acquisition team Bank United, Mckinney, 1997—98. Mem.: C. of C. (assoc.). Home: 519 County Rd 698 Farmersville TX 75442 Office: Regions Bank 1337 W McDermott Allen TX 75013 Office Phone: 214-509-9399. Office Fax: 214-509-9431.

FRYXELL, GRETA ALBRECHT, marine botany educator, oceanographer; b. Princeton, Ill., Nov. 21, 1926; d. Arthur Joseph and Esther (Andreen) Albrecht; m. Paul A. Fryxell, Aug. 23, 1947; children: Karl Joseph, Joan Esther, Glen Edward. BA, Augustana Coll., 1948; MEd, Tex. A&M U., 1969, PhD, 1975. Tchr. math and sci. jr. high schs., Iowa, 1948-52; research asst. Tex. A&M U., College Station, 1968-71, research scientist, 1971-80, asst. prof. oceanography, 1980-83, assoc. prof., 1983-86, prof., 1986-94, prof. emeritus, 1994—; adj. prof. botany U. Tex., Austin, 1993—. Vis. scientist U. Oslo, 1971; chmn. adv. commn. Provasoli-Guillard Ctr. for Culture Marine Phytoplankton, Bigelow Lab, Maine, 1985-87; hon. curator N.Y. Bot. Garden, 1992—; courtesy prof. U. Oreg., 1994—; sr. rsch. scientist U. Tex. Marine Sci. Inst., 1996—. Editor: Survival Strategies of the Algae, 1983; contbr. articles to profl. jours. Recipient Outstanding Woman award Brazos County, College Station, 1979, Outstanding Achievement award Augustana Coll., Rock Island, Ill., 1980; Faculty Disting. Achievement award in rsch. Tex. A&M U., 1991, Geoscis. and Earth Resources Adv. Coun. medal, 1993; grantee NSF. Fellow: AAAS; mem.: ACLU, Oceanographic Soc., Tex. Assn. Coll. Tchrs., Internat. Diatom Soc. (coun. 1986—92), Am. Soc. Plant Taxonomists, Internat. Phycol. Soc., Brit. Phycol. Soc., Phycol. Soc. Am. (editl. bd. 1976—79, 1982—85, chair Prescott award com. 1991, award of Excellence in Phycology 1996). Democrat. Unitarian-Universalist. Office: U Tex Sch Biol Scis Sect Integrative Biology Austin TX 78712

FRYZ, LINDA ANN, real estate broker; b. Pitts., Dec. 16, 1960; d. George Frederick and Ethel Ann Wolber; m. Joseph Michael Fryz, May 2, 1992. Cert. real property adminstr./broker 1987, property mgr. 1991. Type-setter Electro-Comp, Pitts., 1978—80; property mgr. Grubb and Ellis, Pitts., 1980—92; v.p., asst. mgr. J.S. Karlton Co., Pitts., 1992—99, Independence Mgmt. Co., Pitts., 1999—. Bd. dirs., treas. Office Bldg. Assn. of Pitts., 1996—2002, Mgrs., Owners and Contractors Assn., Pitts., 2002—03. Vol. Bethlehem Haven, Pitts., 1997—2003, Radio Info. Svcs., Pitts., 1999—2003. Mem.: Bldg. Owners and Mgrs. Assn., Inst. Real Estate Mgmt., Duquesne Club. Avocations: swimming, travel, cross stitch, reading, physical fitness. Home: 1622 Blackburn Heights Dr Sewickley PA 15143 Office: Independence Mgmt Co Inc 650 Smithfield Pittsburgh PA 15222 E-mail: lfryz@centrecitytower.com.

FU, KAREN KING-WAH, radiation oncologist; b. Shanghai, Oct. 15, 1940; came to U.S., 1959, naturalized, 1975; d. Ping Sen and Lein Sun (Ho) F. Student, Ind. U., 1959-61; AB, Barnard Coll., Columbia U., 1963, MD, 1967. Cert. radiation oncologist. Intern Montreal Gen. Hosp., Que., Can., 1967-68; resident Princess Margaret Hosp., Toronto, Ont., Can., 1968-69, Stanford U. Hosp., Calif., 1969-71; instr. U. Utah, 1971-72; clin. instr. U. Calif., San Francisco, 1972-73, asst. prof., 1973-76, assoc. prof., 1976-82, prof., 1982—2000, prof. emeritus, 2000—, vice chmn., 1994-95, rsch. assoc. Cancer Research Inst., 1973-96. Contbr. articles to profl. jours. Mem. San Francisco Opera Guild, San Francisco Symphony Assn., San Francisco Ballet, Calif. Acad. Sci., De Young Mus. Grantee Am. Cancer Soc., 1982, 86, NIH, 1982, 87. Fellow Am. Coll. Radiology; mem. Am. Soc. Therapeutic Radiologists, Am. Med. Women's Assn., Calif. Radiation Therapy Assn., Calif. Radiol. Soc., No. Calif. Acad. Clin. Oncology, Radiation Research Soc., Am. Soc. Clin. Oncologists, Assn. Women in Sci. Office: U Calif San Francisco Dept Radiation Oncology PO Box 226 San Francisco CA 94143-0226

FUCHS, ANNE SUTHERLAND, magazine publisher; b. Volta Redonda, Brazil, Apr. 19, 1947; d. Paul Warner and Evelyn Coffman; m. James E. Fuchs, Feb. 6, 1982 Student, U. Paris at Sorbonne, 1967-68, Western Coll. for Women, 1966-67; BA, NYU, 1969. Registered architect. V.p., pub. Woman's Day Spl. Interest Mags.-CBS Mags., N.Y.C., 1980-82, Cuisine Mag., CBS Mags., N.Y.C., 1982-84; v.p., pub. Woman's Day mag. DCI Comm., Inc., N.Y.C., 1985-88; sr. v.p., pub. ELLE mag., N.Y.C., 1988-90, Vogue, N.Y.C., 1991—94; group pub. dir., sr. v.p. Harper's Bazaar/Hearst Mag., N.Y.C., 1994—2001; global CEO, chmn., mgmt. bd. Phillips, dePUry & Luxembourg, 2001—02; exec. v.p. LVMH Group, 2002; cons., 2003[illegible] Chmn. mag. and print com. U.S. Info. Agy., 1989—. Author: (other) The Modular Pattern, 1945, British Prefabricated School Construction, 1962; other, Sch. Constrn. Systems Devel., 1964; contbr. numerous articles to profl.jours; other, De Laveaga Elem. Sch., Santa Cruz, Calif., 1966, Silvercreek High Sch., San Jose, Calif., 1969, Canady Hall Harvard U., 1974, Aaron Davis Hall, CCNY, 1978. Chmn. women's bd. Madison Sq. Boys and Girls Club, N.Y.C.; mem. Com. 200, USIA; bd. dirs. N.Y.C. Partnership, N.Y.C. Partnership Found. Recipient Innovation in Bldg. award, Am. Builder, 1965, Services to Building Industry award, Engring. News Record, 1966, Gov.'s Design award, State of Calif., 1966, Quarter Century award, Bldg. Rsch. Adv. Coun., 1977, named Constrn. Man of Yr., Engring. News Record, 1968; fellow Fulbright fellow, England, 1955—56. Mem. Fin. Women's Assn. N.Y., N.Y. Jr. League, Advt. Women of N.Y., Women in Communications, Women's Forum, Com. of 200, Fin. Women's Assn. N.Y. Clubs: Economic (N.Y.C.). E-mail: afuchs@hearst.com.

FUCHS, BETH ANN, research engineer; b. Moberly, Mo., July 22, 1963; d. Larry Dale and Marilyn Sue (Summers) Williams; m. Fred Albano Fuchs Jr., Sept. 30, 1989. AA, Cottey Coll., 1983; BS in Engring., U. N.Mex., 1987. Bookkeeper, chemistry technician U. N.Mex., Albuquerque, 1984-88; rsch. engr. Sandia Nat. Labs., Albuquerque, 1988-97; rsch. engr., cleanroom mgr. Ctr. for High Tech. Materials, U. N.Mex., 1997—. Contbr. articles to profl. jours. Republican. Avocations: cooking, counted cross stitch, bowling. Home: 336 Espejo St NE Albuquerque NM 87123-1111 Office: U NMex Ctr for High Tech Materials 1313 Goddard St SE Albuquerque NM 87106-4343

FUCHS, ELAINE V. molecular biologist, educator; b. Hinsdale, Ill., May 5, 1950; d. Louis H. and Viola L. (Lueck) F.; m. David T. Hansen, Sept. 10, 1988. BS in Chemistry with honors, U. Ill., Urbana, 1972; PhD in Biochemistry, Princeton U., 1977. Postdoctoral fellow dept. biology MIT, 1977-80; asst. prof. U. Chgo., 1980-85, assoc. prof., 1985-88, prof. dept. molecular genetics and cell biology, 1989—, Amgen prof. basic scis., 1993—, investigator, Howard Hughes Med. Inst., 1988—. Assoc. editor Jour. Cell Biology, 1993—; contr. numerous articles to profl. jours. Recipient R.R. Benesely award Am. Assn. Anatomists, 1988, Searle Scholar award Chgo. Cmty. Trust, 1981-84, Presdl. Young Investigator award NSF, 1984-89, NIH Merit award, 1993, 98, Wm. Montagna award Soc. Investigative Dermatology, 1995, Keith Porter Lecture award Am. Soc. Cell Biology, 1996, Sr. Woman Achievement award, 1997; named Harvey Lectr., 1999. Fellow Am. Acad. Arts and Scis., Am. Assn. Microbiology; mem. NAS (elected mem.), Inst. Medicine of NAS, Phi Beta Kappa. Office: U Chgo Howard Hughes Med Inst Dept Molecular Genetics 5841 S Maryland Ave Rm 314N Chicago IL 60637-1463

FUCHS, LILLIAN, classical musician, educator, composer; d. Philip and Kate (Weiss) F.; m. Stein Ludwig; children: Barbara Stein Mallow, Carol Stein Amado (twins). Grad. in Violinwith highest honors, Juilliard Sch. Music. Mem. Perole String Quartet; tchr. viola and chamber music Juilliard Sch. Music; composer viola and violin solos. Instr. Aspen Music Sch. Festival; recorded Mozart duos for violin, viola and symphony concertante with Joseph Fuchs. Composer, published studies, sonatas for viola solo; arranger violin and viola concerts. Recipient Artist Tchr. award, 1979, award Am. Viola Soc., 1981, award Music Edn. Assn. of N.J., 1960, Morris Loed prize, Isaac Newton Seligman prize; one of 1st viola artists to perform and record 6 cello suites by J.S. Bach on the viola. Home: 186 Pinehurst Ave New York NY 10033-1729 Office: The Juilliard Sch Lincoln Ctr New York NY 10023

FUCHS, NORA KAY, business manager; b. Aza Kuwar, Okinawa, Aug. 15, 1962; d. Samuel L. and Darlene L. (Simpson) Carrier; m. Robin Lynn Fuchs, Sept. 28, 1985 (div. Nov. 1996). Student, Lincoln Land C.C., 1983, Springfield Coll., 1984. Teller supr. Capital Bank, Springfield, Ill., 1982-87; owner Bearfootin' Tanning, Springfield, 1986-90; treas., mgr. Carriers Plus, Springfield, 1996—. Mem. NAFE, Assn. Mail and Parcel Carriers. Avocation: collecting teddy bears and precious moments. Office: The Mail Rm 1136 W Jefferson St Springfield IL 62702-4867

FUDA, SIRI NARAYAN K.K. (ELAINE T. BARBER), director; b. Albany, N.Y., June 13, 1941; d. Adam Henry and Anna Mae Farrell Barber; m. Michael G. Fuda, Nov. 23, 1962; children: Meredith-Anne Costello, Melanie Elsie Henderson, Michelle Germanne Fuda. BA in English with honors, SUNY, Albany, 1963, MA in English Lang. and Lit., 1965; postgrad., SUNY, Buffalo, 1967; MS in Exceptional Edn., Buffalo State Coll., 1982. Tchr. Albany Pub. Sch. Sys., 1964-67, curriculum developer, 1966-67; tchr. Buffalo Pub. Schs., 1981-99; dir. Ctr. for Healthy, Happy, Holistic Living, Buffalo, 1987—. Adj. prof. Buffalo State Coll., 1993—; edn. cons. just buffalo lit. ctr., 1990-99; yoga tchr. Women's Wellness Ctr. Western N.Y., 1999—, others; cons. SUNY, Buffalo, 1999; coord. Buffalo State Coll./Buffalo Pub. Schs. coop. program, 1993-99; writer-in-residence Khalsa Women's Tng. Camp, Espinola, N.Mex., 1993-94, just buffalo lit. ctr., 1994; developer, instr. Creative Writing Workshops, Buffalo, Santa Fe; reader Erie and Niagara County Writers Assn.; presenter workshops on yoga for personal stress reduction, expectant mothers and infants, and as metatherapy for emotionally disturbed students. Contbg. editor to lit. anthology Life Junkies: On Our Own, 1990; author: (poetry collections) Unconditional Love: The Sapphire Poems, 1992, Dancing with the Guru, 1994.; contbr. articles to profl. jours., poetry to Buffalo News, others. Founding mem. Lexington Real Foods Co-op, Buffalo, 1971; bd. dirs. Elmwood Ave. Bus. Assn., Buffalo, 1980-83; founder Children's Rm. Co-op Day Care Ctr., Buffalo, 1972-73. Recipient Labor in Lt. award AFL-CIO, Buffalo, 1995; grantee Arts Coun., Buffalo and Erie County, 1990. Mem. Buffalo Tchrs. Fedn. (coun. of dels. 1984-91), just buffalo lit. ctr., Internat. Kundalini Yoga Tchrs. Assn. Democrat. Sikh. Avocation: gardening. Home: 460 Ashland Ave Buffalo NY 14222-1502 Office: Ctr for Healthy Happy Holistic Living 460 Ashland Ave Buffalo NY 14222-1502 E-mail: SiriNarayan@aol.com.

FUDGE, ANN MARIE, advertising executive; b. Washington, Apr. 23, 1951; d. Malcolm R. and Bettye (Lewis) Brown; m. Richard E. Fudge, Feb. 27, 1971; children: Richard Jr., Kevin. BA, Simmons Coll., 1973; MBA, Harvard U., 1977; DHL (hon.), Adelphi U., 1995, Howard U., 1998, Simmons Coll., 1998, Marymount Coll., 1999. Manpower specialist GE, Bridgeport, Conn., 1973-75; mktg. asst. Gen. Mills, Mpls., 1977-78, asst. product mgr., 1978-80, product mgr., 1980-83, mktg. dir., 1983-86; assoc. dir., strategic planning Gen. Foods, White Plains, N.Y., 1986-87, mktg. dir., 1987-89, v.p. mktg. and devel., 1989-91, exec. v.p., gen. mgr., 1991-94; exec. v.p. Kraft Foods, 1994-97; pres. Maxwell House Coffee Co., White Plains, N.Y., 1994-97, Maxwell House Coffee and Post Cereal, Tarrytown, NY, 1997—2001; chmn., CEO Young & Rubicam, Inc., 2003—, Y&R Advt. Bd. dirs. GE, Marriott Internat.; trustee Am. Grad. Sch. Internat. Mgmt., Brookings Instn. Bd. dirs. Women's Econ. Devel. Corp., St. Paul, 1984-86; chair allocations panel United Way, Mpls., 1983-86; vol. Big Sisters/Big Bros., Fairfield County, Conn., 1988-90; bd. govs. Boys and Girls Clubs Am. Recipient Leadership award YWCA, Mpls., 1980, Black Achievers award Harlem YMCA, 1988, Candace award Nat. Coalition of 100 Black Women, 1991-92, Corp. Women's Network award, 1994, She Knows Where She's Going award Girls, Inc., 1994, Alumni Achievement award Harvard Bus. Sch., 1998; named Woman of Yr., Glamour Mag., 1995, Ad Woman of Yr., Advt. Women of N.Y., 1995, Sara Lee Frontrunner award, 1999, one of 50 Most Powerful Women in Am. Bus., Fortune mag. Mem. Exec. Leadership Coun. (pres. 1994-96, Achievement award 2000), Com. of 200, NY Women's Forum, Coun. on Fgn. Rels. Office: Y&R Advt 285 Madison Ave New York NY 10017-6486

FUENTES, DENISE IRIS, [illegible] administrator, sales representative; b. Skokie, Ill., May 12, 1970; d. Hugo and Gladys Fuentes. BS, Cumberland Coll., 1994. Cert. troubleshooting tech. support 3d level Dept. Children and Families, Fla., 1996. Telecom. specialist iii Dept. Children and Families, Ft. Lauderdale, Fla., 1994—97; client services coord./sales rep. VizuAll, Inc., Hollywood, Fla., 1997—. Asst. Sunday sch. tchr. U. Bapt. Ch., Coral Gables, Fla., 2000—01. Independent. Avocations: travel, swimming, working out. Office: VizuAll Inc 2719 Hollywood Blvd Hollywood FL 33020 Personal E-mail: denise0512@juno.com.

FUENTES, SONIA PRESSMAN, lawyer; b. Berlin, May 30, 1928; came to U.S., 1934; d. Zysia and Hinda (Dombek) Pressman; m. Roberto Fuentes, Oct. 24, 1970 (div. Mar. 1980); 1 child, Zia Monina. BA, Cornell U., 1950; LLB sum cum laude, U. Miami, 1957. Bar: Fla. 1957, D.C. 1959, U.S. Supreme Ct. 1961. Claims atty. Office Alien Property U.S. Dept. Justice, Washington, 1957-59; legal asst. to chmn. NLRB, Washington, 1959-65; chief legis. counsel div. EEOC, Washington, 1965-73; sr. atty. GTE Svc. Corp., Stamford, Conn., 1973-81; dir. compliance mgmt. TRW, Inc., Cleve., 1981-84; atty. HUD, Washington, 1985-93, ret., 1993. Cons. Women's Bur., Dept. Labour, Ont., Can.; witness select com. Ho. of Lords, Eng.; Am. specialist USIA, Europe, S.E. Asia, Japan; legis. fellow HUD, 1988; subcom. on labor U.S. Senate, spl. asst. to Congresswoman Nancy Pelosi. Contbr. articles on employment discrimination to profl. jours. Mem. NOW (founder), Women's Equity Action League (founder), Federally Employed Women (founder), Women in Mgmt. (founder), Vet. Feminists Am. (charter), Nat. Woman's Party (bd. dirs.), Phi Beta Kappa. Democrat. Jewish.

FUENTEZ, TANIA MICHELE, journalist; b. N.Y.C., Nov. 21, 1966; d. C. Pedro Alvarez Carr and E. Kay (Samuels) Queally. BA in Comm. and Rhetorical Studies, Marquette U., 1991; MA in Mass Media Comm., U. Akron, 1996. Asst. rschr. V.I. Legislature, St. Thomas, 1991; reporter V.I. Daily News, St. Thomas, 1993-95; instr. news writing U. Akron, Ohio, 1995-96; copy editor Observer Times, Fayetteville, N.C., 1997, Beacon Jour., Akron, 1997-2000; newswoman, writer AP, Atlanta, 2000—02, nat. desk editor NYC, 2002—. Adv. bd. diversity com. V.I. Daily News, 1993-95. Contbr. articles to profl. jours. Bd. dirs. U.S. V.I. League of Women Voters, 1994-95; mem. Am. Cancer Soc., 1993-95, mem. St. Thomas Arts Coun., 1992-95. Recipient Cmty. Svc. award Pan African Support Group, 1995; scholar John S. Knight Meml. Fund, 1996, U. Akron, 1995-96. Mem. ESL (asst., participant 1989), Soc. Profl. Journalists, Nat. Assn. Hispanic Journalists, Nat. Assn. Black Journalists, Newspaper Guild (local 1), N.E. Ohio Assn. Black Journalists, Am. Copy Editors Soc., Comm. Workers Am.-AFL-CIO, Atlanta Press Club. Roman Catholic. Avocations: writing, traveling, chinese martial arts, photography, hiking. Office: 50 Rockefeller Ctr New York NY 10020

FUERSTNER, FIONA MARGARET ANNE, ballet company executive, ballet educator; b. Rio de Janeiro, Apr. 24, 1936; d. Paul G. and Agnes Ethel (Stothard) F.; m. Dane LaFontsee, June 7, 1969 (div. 1992); 1 child, Liana Marie. Studied with San Francisco Ballet, Royal Ballet (London), Ballet Rambert (London) Ballet Theatre Sch. (N.Y.C.), Sch. Am. Ballet (N.Y.C.). With corps de ballet San Francisco Ballet, 1952-55, soloist, 1955-58, prin. dancer, 1958-62; toured with Walter Terry's Am. Dances, 1962-63; prin. dancer Les Grands Ballets Can., Montreal, 1963-64, Am. Choreographer's Co. of N.Y., 1964, Pa. Ballet, 1965-68, 1968-74, ballet mistress, instr. co. class, apprentice class, 1974-77, ballet mistress, instr. co. class, 1977—86; ballet mistress Nashville Ballet, 1986-87, ballet mistress, asst. to artistic dir., 1987-91; ballet mistress Milw. Ballet, 1990-95, asst. to artistic dir. ballet mistress, 1995—2003. Guest dancer Ballet Concerto, Miami, 1967, 68, Erie Civic Ballet, 1969; guest instr. Marsha Woody Dance Acad., Beaumont, Tex., 1974, U. Louisville, 1977-78, co. class San Francisco Ballet, 1985, Tenn. Assn. Dance Nashville Conf., 1988, So. Regional Workshop Chgo., Nat. Assn. Dance Masters in Nashville, 1989, BalletMet, 1991, Memphis Classical Ballet, 1992, 97, 99, Nashville Ballet, 1992; guest ballet mistress BalletMet, 1993; faculty tchr. Sch. of Pa. Ballet, 1977-78, 78-86; organized concert group, ballet mistress, dancer Pa. Ballet, 1971; mem. dance panel Nat. Found. Advancement in the Arts, 1995-98; master tchr. South Eastern Regional Ballet Assn. Festival, 1998, Nat. Found. for Advancement in the Arts, 1999, 2001; guest tchr. Ind. U. Ballet Dept., 2000, Western Mich. U., 2002; vis. asst. prof. dance Wright State U., 2004, Dance-Spring Quarter, 2004; dance panelist Midwest Regional, Nat. Found. for Advancement in the Arts, 2001, 02. Staged Allegro Brillante, Sch. Pa. Ballet Student Showcase, 1986, Nashville Ballet, 1988, Madrigalesco, Pacific NW Ballet, 1981, (parts) Nutcracker, Nashville Ballet, 1989, Carmina Burana (Butler), Milw. Ballet, 1989, Scotch Symphony, Pa. Ballet, 1993, Carmina Burana, Alberta Ballet, 1993, Concerto Barocco, Ballet Omaha, 1994, Ballet Met, 1995, Serenade, Milw. Ballet Sch., 1994, 95, 96, Serenade, Milw. Ballet, 1998-99, Serenade, Western Mich. U., 1999-2000, Concerto Barocco, The Four Temperaments for Milw. Ballet, 1999-2000, Allegro Brillante for Milw. Ballet, 2000-01, (excerpts) Who Cares?, Western Mich. U., 2003, Serenade, Wright State U., 2004. Office Phone: 414-254-4086. E-mail: fionafio@earthlink.net.

FUES, MARIANNE COLE, multi-media specialist; b. Sedalia, Mo., Aug. 29, 1945; d. Leslie Carl and Columbia Jane Cole; m. Donald Frederick Fues, Oct. 21, 1967; children: Jennifer Nicole, Michael Frederick. BS in Home Econ., U. Mo., 1967, MLS, 1994. Home econ. tchr. Columbia (Mo.) Pub. Schs., 1985—87, libr. media specialist, 1989—91; libr. asst. Columbia Coll., 1988—89; libr. media specialist Boone County R-IV Schs., Hallsville, Mo., 1991—2000, Jefferson City (Mo.) Pub. Schs., 2000—. Advt. mgr. Media Horizons, 1994—99; bd. dirs. COIN, Columbia, 1997—2000; governing bd. MOREnet Consortium, Columbia, 1996—2000. Mem.: MLA, AASL, AAUW, ALA, Hallsville Cmty. Tchrs. Assn. (pres. 1996—97), Mo. State Tchrs. Assn., Mo. Assn. Sch. Librs. (treas. 1998—99, 2d v.p. 1999—2000, 1st v.p. 2000—01, pres. 2001—02). Avocations: reading, travel. Home: 1 East Burnam Rd Columbia MO 65203 Office: Jefferson City HS 609 Union St Jefferson City MO 65101

FUFUKA, NATIKA NJERI YAA, retail executive; b. Cleve., Feb. 21, 1952; d. Russell and Mindoro Reed. AA, AAB, Cuyahoga Community Coll., Cleve., 1973; BA, Mich. State U., 1975; postgrad., Cleve. State U. Asst. pers. dir. May Co., Cleve., 1975-78; merchandiser J.C. Penney, Cleve., 1978-80; sports mgr. Joseph Hornes, Cleve., 1980-81; fashion buyer Higbee, Cleve., 1981-86; exec. v.p. Mindoro & Assocs., 1982—; merchandise exec. Fashion Bug, Euclid, Ohio, 1986-92; pres., CEO Mindy's Return to Fashion, Cleve., 1993—. Vice chair Joint Com. on Medicaid Provider Impact for State of Ohio, 1992; mem. Mayor's Census Task Force, Cuyahoga County Women Bus. Enterprise Adv. Coun., Cleve. Female Bus. Enterprise Adv. Coun., Greater Cleve. Growth Assn. (pub. affairs com.), Displaced/Single Parent Homemakers Adv. Coun., Cuyahoga Cmty. Coun., Cuyahoga Hills Boys Adv. Coun., Black Aspiration Week Celebrationcom. Cleve. State U., 1990, cmty. rels. coun. Cleve. Job Corp., 1996, African Am. com. Cleve. Found., 1996, nat. nomination com. Outstanding Young Woman of Am., 1998, Outstanding Young Man of Am., 1998; chair Centralized Resource Referral Svc. Panel United Way, 1993, mem. Gen. Assembly, 1993—, United Way Appeal Com., 1996, leadership devel. program; active Citizen League, Cleve. Mus. Art, Playhouse Square Found., Women in Apptd. Office Project, Planned Parenthood Greater Cleve., WCPN Radio.; bd. dirs. Ohio Youth Adv. Coun., Women Cmty. Found., 1993—, Career Beginning Program Bd., 1993—, Nat. Ctr. Non-Profit; mem. Nat. Coun. Christians and Jews, 1996. Ford Found. scholar, 1975; recipient Jesse Jackson Voter Registration award, 1984, Leadership award United Way, 1991, Cert. Appreciation award, 1998, 2001, Vol. Leadership recognition City of Cleve., 1991, Cmty. Rels. Coun. Svc. award Cleve. Job Corps., 1998. Mem. NAFE, Nat. Nominating Bd. Outstanding Ams., Assn. MBA Execs., Black Profl. Assn., Nat. Assn. Negro Bus./Profl. Women, Am. Profl. Exec. Women, Am. Women Bus. Assn., Nat. Assn. Black Female Entrepreneurs, Severance Merchant Mall Orgn., Op. Big Vote, Nat. Coun. Negro Women, Nat. Polit. Congress Black Women (nat. founder mem., founder mem. Ohio state chpt.), Nat. Hook-Up, 100 Black Women Coalition, Black Congl. Caucus Braintrust, Small Minority Bus. Braintrust, Corp. Braintrust, Nat. Non-Profit Bds., Black Women Agenda, Black Women Roundtable, Black Focus (pres. bd. trustees), 21st Congl. Dist. Caucus (exec. bd. mem., chair bus. women com., certs. of appreciation for outstanding svc. 1985, 86), Urban League Greater Cleve., Op. Push of Greater Cleve. (bd. dirs.), Project Vote (asst. dir., Voter Registration award 1984), Midwest Vote Project, Women Vote Project, WomenSpace, United Black Fund, Greater East Cleve. Dem. Club, Minority Women Polit. Action Com., LWV, Cuyahoga Women Polit. Caucus, Ohio Pub. Interest Campaign, Ohio Rainbow Coalition, Ohio Dem. Women Com., Network Together, Black Elected Dem. Ofcls. Ohio, Cleve. City Club, 16th Dist. Club, Project M.O.V.E, Kinsman Youth Devel. Program and Scholarship Cmty. Liasion. Democrat. Pentecostal. Avocations: collecting african art, golf. Office: One Chagrin Highlands 2000 Auburn Drive Ste 200 Beachwood OH 44122

FUGELBERG, NANCY JEAN, retired music educator; b. Tarentum, Pa., Mar. 6, 1947; d. Stanley and Mary (Struhar) Homer; m. Darrell Marvin Fugelberg, Aug. 27, 1977. B in Music Edn., Mt. Union Coll., 1969; postgrad., Kent State U., 1973-76; EdM in Curriculum and Instrn., Ashland U., 1989. Cert. master piano classes and music lt. Mozarteum, Salzburg, Austria. Music tchr. Alliance (Ohio) Sch. Dist., 1969-70, Minerva (Ohio) Sch. Dist., 1970-99, ret., 1999—. Pianist musicals Carnation Players, Alliance, 1969—72. Asst. organist, accompanist various chs.; organist 1st Imannuel United Ch. of Christ, Alliance, 1969—85. Named to Outstanding Young Women Am., 1981. Mem.: NEA, Ohio Edn. Assn., Minerva Tchrs. Assn., Alliance Area Ret. Tchrs. Assn., S.C. Ret. Tchrs. Assn., Ohio Ret. Tchrs. Assn., Mu Phi Epsilon (chpt. v.p. 1980—82, pres. 1982—84, historian and music therapy chmn. 1984—, Alumni Svc. award 1983, 1984). Republican. Avocations: plants, travel, keyboards, gives various musical programs. Address: 345 S Rockhill Ave Alliance OH 44601-2257

FUGGI, GRETCHEN MILLER, education educator; b. Westerly, R.I., Aug. 26, 1938; d. John Louis and Harriet (Scheid) M.; m. William Joseph Fuggi, Aug. 15, 1960; children: Gretchen, Juliann, John, Kristen. BS, So. Conn. State U., 1960, MS, 1969, 6th yr. diploma, 1991, 6th yr. Ednl. Leadership diploma, 1994. Reading cons. Washington Magnet Sch., West Haven, Conn., 1974—; adj. prof. So. Conn. State U., New Haven, 1988—. Pres. Cath. Charity League of Greater New Haven, 1989-90; bd. dirs. New Haven Symphony Aux., 1992—. Named Tchr. of Yr., West Haven Fedn. Tchrs., 1998-99. Mem. AAUP, Internat. Reading Assn., Conn. Reading Assn., Stonington Hist. Soc. of Conn., Delta Kappa Gamma Soc. Internat., Grad. Club New Haven. Roman Catholic. Home: 19 Westview Rd North Haven CT 06473-2013 E-mail: Fuggi@Juno.com.

FUHRMAN, SUSAN H, education educator; BA in history with highest honors, Northwestern U., 1965, MA in history, 1966; PhD in polit. sci. and edn., Columbia U., 1977. Prof. of edn. policy Eagleton Inst. of Polit. at Rutgers U., 1989—95; prof., dept. of pub. policy Rutgers Edward J. Bloustein Sch. of Planning and Pub. Policy, 1994—95; dean grad sch. edn. U. Penn, 1995—. Bd. mem. Carnegie Found. for the Advancement of Tchg.; founder and chmn. Consortium for Policy Rsch. in Edn. (CPRE), 1985—; mem. of coun. Corp. and Sch. Partnerships of the Coca-Cola Found.; former co-chair Nat. Adv. Panel for the Third Internat. Math and Sci. Study. Editor: From the Capitol to the Classroom: Standards-Based Reform in the States, One Hundredth Yearbook of the National Society for the Study of Education, 2001, Designing Coherent Education Policy: Improving the System, 1993; co-editor (with Jennifer O'Day): Rewards and Reform: Creating Educational Incentives that Work, 1996; co-editor: (with Melissa Carr) Making Money Matter: Equity and Adequacy in Education Finance, 1999. Achievements include research in state education reform, state local relationships, state differential treatment of districts, federalism in education, incentives and systemic reform, legislatures and education policy. Office: The Graduate Sch Penn State U 114 Kern Bldg University Park PA 16802

FUJII, SHARON M. federal agency administrator; BA, U. Washington, 1966, M in Social Work, 1969; PhD, Brandeis U., 1975. Sr. v.p. Gerontological Planning Assn., 1975-77; prin. investigator Pacific-Asian Elderly Rsch. Project, 1977-79; program analyst Office of Refugee Resettlement, 1978-79, regional dir., 1979-80; regional dir., adminstrn. for children and families Dept. Health and Human Svcs., 1980-86; regional adminstr., adminstrn. for children and families, 1986—. Mem. Pres. Fed. Coun. on Aging, 1975-78. Health, Edn. and Welfare fellow, 1978-79. Office: Dept Health & Human Svcs 50 United Nations Plz Rm 450 San Francisco CA 94102-4912

FUJIOKA, JO ANN OTA, educational administrator, consultant; b. Bellflower, Calif., Apr. 30, 1939; d. Richard Masayoshi and Lillian Chiyono (Ihara) Ota; m. Arthur Fujioka, Feb. 19, 1961; 1 child, Dana Kay. BSN, U. Colo., 1961, MSN, 1970; PhD, Colo. State U., 1987. RN; cert. adminstr., supt., spl. edn. dir., sch. nurse, vocat. edn. adminstr., instr. Nurse pub. health, psychiat. Denver Gen. Hosp., Denver Vis. Nurse Svc., 1961-71; sch. nurse Jefferson County Sch. Dist., Golden, Colo., 1971-76, mgr. program, supr. sch. health program, 1976-79, mgr. spl. edn. and related svcs., adminstr. elem. bldg., 1979-95; cons. Fujioka Cons., Denver, 1995—. Cons. Ctrl. Kans. Bd. Coop. Ednl. Svcs., Salina, 1992, Denver Children's Home, 1996, Colo. Assn. of Family and Children's Agencies, 1997, Colo. Mediation Project, 1998. Contbr. articles to profl. jours. Vice chmn. bd. dirs. Creative Exch., 1997—99, chmn. bd. dirs., 1999—2001, mem. adv. bd., 2002—; mem. edn. adv. com. PBS, 2001—; mem. Cross Cultural Dialogue, 2001—; hon. bd. dirs. Colo. Women's Hall of Fame, 2002—. Mem.: AAUW, NOW, Jefferson County Adminstrs. Assn., Colo. Sch. Health Coun. (pres. 1978—80), U. Colo. Health Scis. Ctr. Srs. Assn. (chpt. pres. 1992—94, Internat. Dist. IV project grant dir. 1993, fall conf. chair 1993—, bd. dirs., sec. 1997—, Internat. Dist. IV project grant dir. 1999, internat. coord. for ethical leadership project 2000—, bd. dirs. 2000—, sec. 2000—03, v.p. internat. bd. dirs. 2001—), Am. Assn. Sch. Execs., Alliance Profl. Cons. (exec. bd.), Colo. Women's Hall of Fame (hon. bd. dirs. 2002—), Public Broadcasting System (edn. adv. bd. 2001—), Japanese Am. Nat. Mus., Cross Cultural Dialogue, Phi Delta Kappa (internat. del. 1993, area coord. 1996—2001, internat. v.p. bd. dirs. 2001—, internat. pres. elect 2003—, Douglas County Chpt. award 1999, Denver U. Chpt. Svc. award 1999, Jefferson County Chpt. Svc. award 2001). Democrat. Buddhist. Avocations: crossword puzzles, jigsaw puzzles, crocheting, tai chi, reading. Home and Office: 540 S Forest St #K Denver CO 80246-8164

FUJITSUBO, LANI CHARLENE, psychology educator; b. L.A., June 21, 1954; d. WIlliam Sadao and Sylvia Toshiko Fujitsubo. BA, SCC, Costa Mesa, Calif., 1980; MA, U.S. Internat. Univ., San Diego, 1988, PhD, 1991. Lic. psychologist, Oreg., Alaska. Psychology intern Children's Hosp., Orange, Calif., 1990-91; prof., psychologist U. Alaska, Fairbanks, 1991-93; prof. So. Oreg. Univ., Ashland, 1993—, dir. testing, 1994—. Pvt. practice, Ashland, 1993—; cons., 1991—. Bd. dirs. Girl Scout Coun., Winema, Oreg. Mem. Am. Psychol. Assn., Western Psychol. Assn., Oreg. Psychol. Assn., Assn. Women in Psychology. Democrat. Avocations: stained glass, piano, hiking, travel. Office: So Oreg U 1250 Siskiyou Blvd Ashland OR 97520-5010

FUKUNAGA, CAROL A. state legislator, lawyer; b. Dec. 12, 1947; BA, JD, U. Hawaii. Pvt. practice, Honolulu; mem. Hawaii Ho. of Reps., Honolulu, 1978-82, 86-92, Hawaii Senate, Dist. 12, Honolulu, 1992—; co-chair ways and means com., mem. health and human svcs. Hawaii Senate, Honolulu, mem. labor and environment com. Exec. officer Office of the Lt. Gov., Honolulu, 1982-86; hearings officer Hawaii Pub. Employees Rels. Bd.; mem. coord. com. Hawaii Dem. Action, 1985; platform co-chair State Dem. Conv., 1984; bd. dirs. Hawaiian Air; mem. Japanese Am. Citizens League, Sex Abuse Treatment Ctr. Mem. Hawaii Women Lawyers. Democrat. Office: State Capitol 415 S Beretania St Rm 210 Honolulu HI 96813-2407

FUKUSHIMA, BARBARA NAOMI, financial advisor; b. Honolulu, Apr. 5, 1948; d. Harry Kazuo and Misayo (Kawasaki) Murakoshi; m. Dennis Hiroshi (div. 2001); 1 child, Dennis Hiroshi Jr. BA with high honors, U. Hawaii, 1970; postgrad., Oreg. State U., 1971, 73, U. Oreg., 1972. Intern Coopers & Lybrand, Honolulu, 1974; auditor Haskins & Sells, Kahului, Hawaii, 1974-77; pres. Book Doors, Inc., Pukalani, Hawaii, 1977-97, Barbara N. Fukushima CPA, Inc., Wailuku, Hawaii, 1979-86, sec. treas. Target Pest Control, Inc., 1979-96; internal auditor, acct. Maui Land & Pineapple Co., Inc., Kahului, Hawaii, 1977-80; auditor Hyatt Regency, Maui, Hawaii, 1980-81; ptnr. D & B Internat., Pukalani, Hawaii, 1980-91; instr. Maui C.C., 1982-85; fin. advisor Merrill Lynch, Pierce, Fenner & Smith, Inc., 1986—. Recipient Phi Beta Kappa Book award, 1969. Mem.: AICPA, Hawaii Soc. CPAs, C. of C. of Hawaii, Phi Beta Kappa. Christian. Home: 1088 Bishop St Apt 1117 Honolulu HI 96813-3134 Office: 1001 Bishop St PH Honolulu HI 96813-3429 E-mail: barbnf@yahoo.com.

FULBRIGHT, HARRIET MAYOR, educational association administrator; b. N.Y.C., Dec. 13, 1933; d. Brantz and Evelyn (Griswold) M.; m. William Watts, Aug. 4, 1954 (div. 1975); children: Evelyn G. Ward, Shelby Funk, Heidi H. Mayor; m. J. William Fulbright, Mar. 10, 1990. BA, Radcliffe Coll., Cambridge, Mass., 1955; MFA, George Washington U., 1975; LLD (hon.), U. Scranton, 1986; LHD (hon.), L.I. U., Bank St. Coll., U. Devel. Studies, Tamale, Ghana. Chair art dept. Maret Sch., Washington, 1975-80; asst. dir. Congl. Arts Caucus, Washington, 1980-82, Alliance of Ind. Coll. Art, Washington, 1982-84; exec. sec. Internat. Congress Art History, Washington, 1984-87; exec. dir. Fulbright Assn., Washington, 1987-91, pres. The Ctr. for Arts in the Basic Curriculum, Washington, 1991-96; exec. dir. Pres.'s Com. on the Arts and the Humanities, 1997-2000. Vice chair Reves Internat. Ctr., 1994-97, chmn. 1997-; mem. J.W. Fulbright Fgn. Scholarship Bd., 1992-98, Acad. for Ednl. Devel., 1995—; pres. Fulbright Internat. Ctr., 1996—; chmn. UNESCO leadership coun. U. Bahcesehir, Istanbul, Turkey, 2002-; unofficial amb. Fulbright Program's 50th Ann. Author: How To Get Your Own Pre-School Play Group; editor: Fulbrighters Newsletter. Pres. Maret Sch. Bd., 1975; exec. dir. Pres.'s Com. for Arts and Humanities, 1997—2000; mem. U.S. Cuba Policy Project, Ctr. for Nat. Policy, 2001—. Honoree, Young Audiences, 1994; recipient El Order de Manuel Amador Querrero (Panama's highest civilian award), 1997, Arts in Edn. award Fillmore Arts Ctr., 2001, Medal Cross of the Order of Merit, Hungary, 2002, Hubert H. Humphrey Humanitarian award Assn. Tchrs. of Social Studies, 2003. Mem. Nat. Coun. Stds. in the Arts. Office Phone: 703-351-5717. E-mail: hmful@aol.com.

FULKERSON, JULIE MARIA, illustrator; d. James Thomas and Mary Frances Fulkerson; m. Jeffrey Alan Dillon. BS in Wildlife, Purdue U., 1988; MS in Wildlife Biology, La. State U., 1990, AD in Graphic Design, Mt Hood C.C., 2001. Wildlife biologist U.S. Fish and Wildlife Svc., 1993—2001; owner Wildland Graphics, Canby, Oreg., 2001—. Mem.: Self-Employed Creative Profls.

FULKERSON, SUE ELLEN, poet; b. Zanesville, Ohio, Dec. 14, 1943; d. Arthur Amos and Helen Marie Bryan; m. Larry Dean Fulkerson, Apr. 5, 1968; children: Rebecca, Matthew. BA in Social Work, Valparaiso U., Ind., 1966. Probation officer Muskingum County Juvenile Ct., Zanesville, Ohio, 1966—67; caseworker Muskingum County Welfare Dept., Zanesville, 1967—68; social worker Franklin County Children Svcs., Columbus, Ohio, 1968—70; income maint. worker Muskingum County Welfare Dept., Zanesville, 1977—80; foster care coord. Muskingum County Children Svcs., Zanesville, 1980—81; social worker ODC Nursing Home, Zanesville, 1987—88; ret., 1988. Author: (book of poetry) Poems for Life's Seasons, 1999; contbr. poems to profl. pubs. Vol. Assisted Living Cmty., Zanesville; mem. Rep. Nat. Com., 2000—03, Trinity Luth. Ch. Recipient Editors Choice award for poem Autumn, Nat. Libr. Poetry, 1993, Editor's Choice award for poem Summer's Farewell, 1997, Editor's Choice award for outstanding achievement in poetry for poem The Autumn Leaves, 2002, Poetry Cert. of Recognition, Famous Poet Soc., 2001, Editor's Choice award outstanding achievement in poetry for poem One Summer Day, Internat. Libr. Poetry, 2003. Mem.: Acad. Am. Poets, Gideons Internat. (sec. 1985—99). Avocations: reading, making bookmarks, photography. Home: 3275 Buena Vista Cir Zanesville OH 43701 E-mail: verse_maker@msn.com.

FULLARD, HENRIETTA, minister; d. Henry Graham and Janie Lillie Scott; children: Adrienne Yolanda Small, John Harold. BS, S.C. State U., Orangeburg, 1964; MA, Columbia U., 1972; MDiv, New Brunswick (N.J.) Theol. Sem., 1992; EdD (hon.), Faith Coll., Mobile, Ala., 1993—94, DD (hon.), 1994—94. Cert. sch. adminstrn. St. John's U., 1982. Endocrinology rschr. Interfaith Hosp. (formerly Bklyn Jewish Hosp.), Bklyn., 1964—65; tchr. Andrew Jackson HS, Cambria Heights, NY, 1965—90, asst. prin. sci. Cambria Heights, NY, 1990—94; prin. Math., Sci. Rsch. And Tech. Magnet HS, Cambria Heights, NY, 1994—99; pastor Bethel AME Ch., Arverne, NY, 1995—. CEO Bethel Arverne Cmty. Devel. Corp., Arverne, NY, 1999—; founder, job-trainer, developer Bethel Home Health Aide Program. Advisor Arverne (N.Y.) Civic Assn., 2000—03; mem. Cmty. Planning Bd. 14, Arverne, NY, 1998—2003; v.p. Rockaway/inwood Ministerial Coalition, Far Rockaway, NY, 1999—2003; mem. AME Ch. Ministerial Alliance, N.Y.C., NY, 1995—2003, Habitat For Humanity, Jamaica, NY, 2000—03; pres. S.E. Queens Clergy For Cmty. Empowerment, Inc., Jamaica, NY, 1999—2003; sec. adv. bd. York Coll., Jamaica, NY, 1998—2003; adv. bd. St. John's Episcopal Hosp., Far Rockaway, NY, 1999—2003. Recipient Congl. Record Award Of The 107Th Session, U.S. Ho. of Reps., 2002, Women Of The Millennium award, Nat. Coun. Of Negro Women, 2000, citation, N.Y. State Assembly, 1998, Nassau County, N.Y., 2000, Svc. To Women award, Ladies Of Distinction, Inc., 2002. Democrat. Avocation: travel. Office: Bethel AME Church 215 Beach 77th St Arverne NY 11411 Personal E-mail: hefullard@aol.com.

FULLENWIDER, NANCY VRANA, composer, dancer, musician, educator; b. Sheridan, Wyo., May 9, 1940; d. Jacob Allen and Edith Martha (Tripp) Fullenwider; m. Linsfred Leroy Vrana, Apr. 26, 1980. BA summa cum laude, U. Denver, 1962, MA, 1971, postgrad., 1974. Prin. dancer, instr. Colo. Ballet and Colo. Ballet Ctr., Denver, 1958-80; owner, instr. Idaho Springs (Colo.) Sch. Ballet, 1962-67, Sch. Ballet, Parker, Colo., 1974-79. Curriculum developer Career Edn. Ctr., Denver Pub. Schs., 1973; grad. asst. U. Denver, 1974; guest artist, choreographer, composer Young Audiences, Denver, 1975-80; instr. ballet Ballet Arts Ctr., Denver, 1992-98, Colo. Dance Ctr., Littleton, 1992—; music dir., accompanist for Western Chamber Ballet, Denver, 1994-98, Colo. Ballet, 1999, Arvada Ctr., 1998, Ballet Arts, 1998, Internat. Sch. Ballet, 2000. Composer (CD's) To the Pointe, 1997, Brava!, 1999, Curtain Call, 2000, Inner Dance, 2002; commissioned ballet works performed at Auditorium Theatre, Denver, 2000, Arvada Ctr. for Performing Arts, Colo., 1991, Aurora (Colo.) Fox Arts Ctr., 1989-92, Buell Theatre, Colo., 1993, Cleo Parker Robinson Dance Theatre, Colo., 1992, 2003, 04, Colo. Springs Fine Arts Ctr., 1991, Houston Fine Arts Ctr., Colo., 1971, San Luis Arts Festival, Colo., 1990, Bonfils Theatre, Colo., 1971, Denver Civic Theatre, 2000, Auditorium Theatre, Denver, 2000, 01, (TV series) Providence, 2000, (piano) DCPA, Denver, Colo., 2004. Grantee Douglas County Schs., Colo., 1998. Mem. Phi Beta Kappa, Alpha Lambda Delta. Avocations: hiking, fly fishing, theatre, concerts.

FULLER, ANNE ELIZABETH HAVENS, English language and literature educator, consultant; b. Pomona, Calif., Jan. 20, 1932; d. Paul Swain and Lorraine Elizabeth (Hamilton) Havens; m. Martin Emil Fuller, II, June 17, 1961; children: Katharine Hamilton, Peter David Takashi. AB, Mount Holyoke Coll., 1953; BA (Fulbright scholar), Somerville Coll., Oxford U., 1955, MA, 1959; PhD (Univ. fellow), Yale U., 1958. Instr. English, Mount Holyoke Coll., 1957-59; instr. Pomona Coll., 1959-61; asst. prof. U. Fla., Gainesville, 1961-63; lectr. U. Denver, 1964-68, 71-73; assoc. prof., chmn. center for lang. and lit. Prescott (Ariz.) Coll., 1968-70; tchr. Colo. Rocky Mountain Sch., 1970-71; dean of faculty Scripps Coll., Claremont, Calif., 1973-80, prof. English, 1973-80; spl. asst. to pres., sec. to corp. Claremont U. Center, 1981-83; v.p. for acad. affairs Austin Coll., Sherman, Tex., 1982-84, faculty mem., 1984-96. Mem. SW dist. Rhodes Scholar Selection Com., 1975-83 Bd. dirs. Am. Council on Edn., 1979-81. Mem. Assn. Am. Colls. (dir. 1977-81, chmn. 1980-81), Am. Conf. Acad. Deans (dir. 1976-79), Commn. on Women in Higher Edn., Am. Assn. Higher Edn., Modern Lang. Assn. Am. Democrat. Episcopalian. Home: 11304 Pinos Altos Ave NE Albuquerque NM 87111-5701 E-mail: ahnefu@nmia.com.

FULLER, BETTY STAMPS, music educator; b. Prentiss, Miss., Feb. 19, 1938; d. Henry Buford and Genevieve (Bozeman) Stamps; m. Allan Riggs Fuller, Dec. 19, 1957 (dec. May 1987); children: Melodie, Valerie. Attended, Miss. Coll., 1958; BA, McNeese State U., 1983; post grad., Loyola U., 1985. Music tchr. Episcopal Day Sch., 1975—84, Our Lady's Sch., 1985—. Mentor tchr. Alliance for Cath. Edn., Notre Dame U., Notre Dame, Ind., 2000—01. Coord. youth orch. Miss. Coll., Clinton, Miss., 1967—72; bd. mem. Lake Charles (La.) Symphony Orch., 1975—77. Named Citizen of the Day, KLOU Radio Station, Lake Charles, 1975; Fine Arts grant, La. Divsn. of Arts, 1994—95, Arts and Humanities Coun. SW La., 1996. Mem.: Nat. Cath. Edn. Assn. Episcopal. Avocations: production of musical plays, visual arts, historical preservation, environmental activities. Home: 2715 Roxton St Sulphur LA 70663

FULLER, BONNIE, editor; Editor-in-chief YM, 1989—94; founding editor Marie Claire, 1994—96; dep. editor Cosmopolitan, 1996—97; editor-in-chief Cosmopolitan Hearst Mags., N.Y.C., 1997—98; editor-in-chief Glamour, Conde Nast, 1998—2001; editor US Weekly, 2002—03; exec. v.p. Am. Media Inc., Boca Raton, Fla., 2003—, chief editl. dir., 2003—. Office: Star Magazine American Media Inc 5401 NW Broken Sound Blvd Boca Raton FL 33487

FULLER, CASSANDRA MILLER, applications specialist; b. Norwalk, Conn., Dec. 10, 1965; d. George Louis and Bernice (Simmons) Miller; m. David Norman Fuller, Dec. 24, 1988; 1 child, Jessica Ashley. BS, S.C. State Coll., 1987; MBA, U. Bridgeport, 1995. Interior decorator's apprentice Marty Rae Interiors, Orangeburg, S.C., 1984-85; asst. mgr. Dairy Queen, Orangeburg, S.C., 1986-87; day mgr. The Bedford, Stamford, Conn., 1987-88; dept. mgr. Burlington Coat Factory Warehouse, Danbury, Conn.; asst. mgr. Kidstuff, Inc., Orange, Conn., 1989-92; Postage By Phone customer assistance specialist Pitney Bowes, Stamford, Conn., 1992-95, programmer analyst, 1996-98; applications specialist GE Capital Vendor Fin. Svcs., Danbury, Conn., 1998—. Cons. Orangeburg Metro Transit 1987. Mem. Nat. Assn. Negro Bus. and Profl. Women's Clubs Inc., Nat. Black MBA Assn., NAFE, African Am. Forum, Kappa Omicron Phi. Democrat. Baptist. Office: GE Capital Corp Vendor Fin Svcs 10 Riverview Dr Danbury CT 06810-6268

FULLER, JEAN, school system administrator; AA, Bakersfield Cmty. Coll.; BA, Calif. State U., Fresno, 1972; MPA, Calif. State U., LA, 1982; PhD in Ednl. Policy and Orgnl. Studies, U. Calif., Santa Barbara, 1989. Cert. tchr. comm., English, Soc. Sci. Calif. State U., 1972. Elem. and secondary tchr., 1972—80; elem. and mid. sch. prin. Westside Union Sch. Dist, Calif., 1980—83, cons. 803 computer, 1987; elem. prin. and dir. of tech. svcs. Keppel Union Sch. Dist, 1983—88, dir. state and fed. projects, spl. edn. and pers., 1988, asst. supt., 1988—90, supt., 1990—99, Bakersfield City Sch. Dist, 1999—. Attendee U. So. Calif. Supt. Symposium, LA, 1991, Harvard Grad. Sch. of Edn. Supt. Seminars, Cambridge, Mass., 1998, Cambridge, 99; mem. Kern County Supt.'s Adv. Bd., 1999—. Mem. Jim Burke Ednl. Found., Vision 2020 Ednl. Com.; Mayor's Youth Devel. Coun.; mem. Kern County Network Children Bd.; bd. dir. Boys and Girls Club, 2002—, mem. mktg. com., 2002—. Recipient Calif. Supt. of Yr., Am. Assn. of Sch. Adminstrs., 1995, Nat. Leadership Learning award, 1998. Mem.: Am. Assn. of Sch. Adminstrs. Office: Bakersfield City Sch Dist 1300 Baker St Bakersfield CA 93305*

FULLER, KAREN BETH, marriage and family therapist; b. Brownwood, Tex., Aug. 19, 1949; d. Alfred Earl and Iva LaVerne (Neal) Ross; m. Philip Storey Fuller, Dec. 28, 1968; children: Philip Paul, Lara Kristen. BS in Psychology, S.W. Tex. State U., 1974; MA in Psychology, Goddard Coll., 1987. Lic. profl. counselor, Tex.; lic. marriage and family therapist, Tex. Marriage and family therapist Behavioral Medicine Assocs., Wichita Falls, Tex., 1986-91; nat. seminar coord. LifeCare Counseling, Ft. Worth, 1991-93; v.p., COO Focus Counseling Assocs., Ft. Worth, 1993—. Seminar leader Focus Counseling Assocs., Ft. Worth, 1991—. Co-author: Who Am I? Christ-Centered 12 Step Program, 1993. Mem. sch. bd. Lake Country Christian Sch., Ft. Worth, 1997. Mem. Am. Assn. Marriage and Family Therapy (clin. mem.). Republican. Baptist. Home: 7425 Lochwood Ct Fort Worth TX 76179-3135 Office: 7425 Lochwood Ct Fort Worth TX 76179-3135

FULLER, KATHRYN SCOTT, environmental association executive, lawyer; b. N.Y.C., July 8, 1946; d. Delbert Orison and Carol Scott (Gilbert) F.; m. Stephen Paul Doyle, May 29, 1977; children: Sarah Elizabeth Taylor, Michael Stephen Doyle, Matthew Scott Doyle. BA English, Am. Lit., Brown U., 1968, LHD (hon.), 1992; JD with honors, U. Tex., 1976; postgrad., U. Md., 1980-82; DSci. (hon.), Wheaton Coll., 1990; LLD (hon.), Knox Coll., 1992. Bar: Tex. 1977, D.C. 1979. Rsch. asst. Yale U., New Haven, Conn., 1968-69, Am. Chem. Soc., 1970-71, Harvard U. Mus. Comparative Zoology, Cambridge, Mass., 1971-73; law clerk Dewey, Ballantine, Bushby, Palmer & Wood and Vinson & Elkins, N.Y.C., Houston, 1974-76, U.S. Dist. Ct. (so. dist.), Tex., 1976-77; atty., advisor Office Legal Counsel Dept. Justice, Washington, 1977-79, atty. Wildlife and Marine Resources sect., 1979-80, chief Wildlife and Marine Resources sect., 1981-82; exec. v.p., dir. Traffic USA, pub. policy, gen. counsel World Wildlife Fund, Washington, 1982-89, pres., CEO, 1989—. Contbr. articles to profl. jours.; bd. dirs. Alcoa Inc., 2002—, Student Conservation Assn., Fondo Mexicano para la Conservacion de la Naturaleza; mem. World Bank Adv. Com. on Sustainable Devel. Bd. trustees Ford Found., Brown U. Recipient William Rogers Outstanding Grad. award Brown U., 1990, UN Environment Programme Global 500 award, 1990; Named outstanding woman law student Tex. scholar, 1975. Mem. State Tex. Bar, D.C. Bar, Coun. Fgn. Rels., Zonta Internat. (hon.). Avocations: squash, trekking, scuba diving, gardening, fishing. Office: World Wildlife Fund 1250 24th St NW Fl 6 Washington DC 20037-1193*

FULLER, MARTHA M. poet; Author: Tattle Tales, 1997, Days Gone By, 1997 (Editor's Choice award Nat. Libr. Congress), Sounds of Poetry, 1998, After Thoughts, 2002, among others. Recipient numerous awards. Mem. Poetry Hall of Fame, Internat. Soc. Poets. Home: 34 Worthington Dr Apt 202 Westbrook CT 06498-1994 E-mail: quidfit@snet.net.

FULLER, S(HERI) MARCE, energy executive; BSEE, U. Ala.; MS in Power System Engring., Union Coll. Student engr. Ala. Power (subs. The So. Co.), 1980-83; engr. power system engring. dept. GE, 1983-85; electric system planning engr. Ala. Power (subs. The So. Co.), 1985-87; sr. fin. analyst corp. finance So. Co. Svcs., 1987-89, prin. strategic planning, asst. [illegible] 1990-91; [illegible] So. Electric (subs. The So. Co.), 1991; v.p. domestic bus. devel. So. Electric, 1994-96, sr. v.p. domestic ops., 1996; pres., CEO Mirant Corp., Atlanta, 1999—. Bd. dirs. Curtiss-Wright Corp., Earthlink; chairperson electricity adv. bd. U.S. Dept. Energy; mem. bd. councilors The Carter Ctr.; mem. Pres. Internat. Bd. Advisors, Philippines. Trustee Atlanta Internat. Sch. Office: Mirant 1155 Perimeter Ctr W Atlanta GA 36338*

FULLER-MCCHESNEY, MARY ELLEN, sculptor, writer, publisher; b. Wichita, Kans., Oct. 20, 1922; d. Edward Emory and Karen Mabel (Rasmussen) Fuller; m. Robert Pearson, Dec. 17, 1949. AA, U. Calif., Berkeley, 1943. Staff writer Currant; rschr. Archives of Am. Art; publisher Sonoma Mt. Publishing Co. Author: (art book) A Period of Exploration, 1973, Robert McChesney: An American Painter, 1996, 3 mystery novels, short stories, poems, articles; exhibitions include Syracuse (N.Y.) Mus., San Francisco Mus., Oakland (Calif.) Mus., Calif. State U., Sonoma, Santa Rosa Civic Ctr., U. Calif., Davis, San Jose (Calif.) State U., U. Calif. Ctr. U. Oaxaca, San Francisco art festivals, galleries, prin. works include Dos Leones, San Francisco Gen. Hosp., 1974, Children's Sculpture Park, Salinas Cmty. Ctr., 1976, Falcon, Andrew Hill High Sch., San Jose, Calif., 1977, Yuba Totem,Yuba Lion, Dept. Motor Vehicles Bldg., Calif., 1983, Playground, Portsmouth Square, San Francisco, 1982, Olympic Lions, Squaw Valley, Calif., 1983, Stratford Meml. Lion and Bear, Petaluma (Calif.) Libr., 1983, Anshen-Mays Birdbath, Sausalito, Calif., 1984, West Side Pump Sta., San Francisco, 1979, 4 garden sculptures, L.A. State Office Bldg., 1987, Walnut Creek Totem, 1992, Seach Park, Santa Cruz, Calif., 1993, Utah Arts coun. Bear v Rams, Salt Lake City, 1999, sculptures, Becky Temko Park, Berkeley, Calif., 2000, Rainbow Ridge Park, Reno, Nev., 2001, Gala Chamberlain Fountain, Santa Rosa, Calif., 2002, Garden Lion, Sonoma State U., Rohnert Park, Calif., 2002, Lady of the Beasts sculpture, Animal Shelter, Petaluma, Calif., 2003. Ford Found. fellow, 1965-66; Nat. Endowment Arts grantee, 1975. Home: 2955 Sonoma Mt Rd Petaluma CA 94954

FULLERTON, DAVINA, art historian, consultant, researcher; b. London, July 29, 1931; came to U.S., 1957; d. David George and Elsa Victoria Mandler; m. Kenneth James Fullerton, Aug. 16, 1952; children: Victoria, Honor. BS, London U., 1952, Boston U., 1972, MEd, 1974; Mus. Studies Cert., Tufts U., 1992. Jr. physiotherapist St. Mary's Hosp., London, 1953-54, sr. physiotherapist, 1954-57; physiotherapist Framingham (Mass.) Union Hosp., 1958-72; homecare physiotherapist Easter Seals, Boston, 1973-83; cons. physiotherapist Sudbury (Mass.) Pines, 1983-86; coord. pub. edn. Harvard U. Art Museums, Cambridge, Mass., 1990-98; lectr., art historian Humanities Internat., Boston, 1998—. Actor, appearing in numerous plays, 1959-90; voice-over for commls., 1970s—. Eucharistic lay min. St. Elizabeth's Ch., Sudbury, 1980-92, also thrift shop mgr.; lay reader Ch. of Messia, Woods Hole, Mass., 1992—. Mem. Doric Dames Inc. (bd. dirs. 1986—, exec. v.p. 1986-88). Episcopalian. Avocations: reading, gardening, swimming, exercise. Home: 44 Carey Ln Falmouth MA 02540-1604

FULLERTON, FAYE ELLEN, academic administrator; b. Red Bud, Ill., July 7, 1957; d. Albert Warren and Cleota Marie Sinn Fullerton. BS, So. Ill. U., Carbondale, 1978, MSEd, 1983; EdD, U. Mo., St. Louis, 1998. Cert. Counselor Nat. Bd. of Cert. Counselors, 1998. English/journalism tchr. Sparta H.S., Sparta, Ill., 1978—83; guidance counselor Calhoun H.S., Hardin, Ill., 1983—87; supr. of assessment and instl. rsch. St. Louis Cmty. Coll.-Florissant Valley, St. Louis, 1987—92; dir. of counseling East Ctrl. Coll., Union, Mo., 1992—98; v.p., student svcs. Lincoln Land C.C., Springfield, Ill., 1998—. Pres. Ill. C.C. Chief Student Svcs. Officers, Springfield, Ill., 2002—. Mem. Women in Mgmt., Springfield, Ill., 2002; elder, mem. of session John Knox Presbyn. Ch., Florissant, Mo., 1996—98; mem., bd. of deacons First Presbyn. Ch., Springfield, Ill., 2003. Mem.: Mo. C.C. Assn. (pres. of profl. sect. 1996—97), Nat. Coun. of Student Devel., Nat. Assn. of Student Pers. Adminstr. Presbyterian. Avocations: travel, photography. Office: Lincoln Land C C 5250 Shepherd Rd PO Box 19256 Springfield IL 62794-9256 E-mail: faye.fullerton@llcc.edu.

FULLERTON, GAIL JACKSON, retired academic administrator; m. Stanley James Fullerton, Mar. 27, 1967; children by previous marriage—Gregory Snell Putney, Cynde Putney Mitchell. BA, U. Nebr., 1949, MA, 1950; PhD, U. Oreg., 1954. Lectr. sociology Drake U., Des Moines, 1955-57; asst. prof. sociology Fla. State U., Tallahassee, 1957-60, San Jose (Calif.) State U., 1963-67, assoc. prof., 1968-71, prof., 1972-91, dean grad. studies and rsch., 1972-76, exec. v.p. univ., 1976-78, pres., 1978-91; ret., 1991. Bd. dirs. Assoc. Western Univs., Inc., 1980-91; mem. sr. accrediting commn. Western Assn. Schs. and Colls., 1982-88, chmn., 1985-86; mem. Pres.'s Commn. NCAA, 1986-91; bd. dirs. Am. Coll. Assn., 1991. Author: Survival in Marriage, 2d edit, 1977, (with Snell Putney) Normal Neurosis: The Adjusted American, 2d edit, 1966. Carnegie fellow, 1950-51, 52-53; Doherty Found. fellow, 1951-52. Mem. Phi Beta Kappa, Chi Omega.

FULLERTON, JEAN LEAH, retired language educator, researcher, census researcher; b. Johnstown, Pa., Aug. 5, 1929; d. Elmer Michael Daily and Mary Elizabeth Daily (Schultz); m. Bernell Houston Fullerton, Nov. 8, 1952; children: Kenneth Leon, Brian Hugh, Michele Marie Kelley, Madeline Elizabeth McMahon. BA, Seton Hill Coll., Greensburg, Pa., 1951; MS, Towson U., Md., 1980. Cert. tchr. English Md., 1969, Md., 1994. Tchr. English Balt. County Sch. Sys., Towson, Md., 1967—89; interviewer/rschr. Census Bur. US Dept. Commerce, Phila., 1990—. Author poetry. Vol. Rep. Party, Towson, 1960—82. Roman Catholic. Avocation: genealogy. Home: 185 Sandyhook Road Ocean Pines MD 21811 Personal E-mail: fullerton@mchsl.com.

FULLERTON, STEPHANIE MALIA, research scientist; b. Hilo, Hawaii, July 6, 1967; BA, Occidental Coll., 1989; postgrad. diploma, U. Oxford, Eng., 1990, DPhil, 1995. Lectr. U. Durham, Durham, England, 1995—98; rsch. assoc. Pa. State U., U. Park, Pa., 1998—. Contbr. articles to profl. jours. Scholar Rhodes scholar, Rhodes Trust, Oxford, Eng., 1989—92. Mem.: UK Genetical Soc. (univ. rep. 1996—98), Soc. Molecular Biology & Evolution, Am. Assn. Phys. Anthropology, Am. Human Genetics Soc. Democrat. Avocations: bicycling, reading, choral singing. Office: Pa State U Dept Anthropology 409 Carpenter Bldg University Park PA 16802

FULLING, SHARON S. college nursing program director; RN, St. Mary's Hosp. Sch. Nursing, Evansville, Ind., 1959; BSN, U. Evansville, 1978, MSN, 1981. Asst. dean, Dir. Nursing Mississippi County C.C., Blytheville, Ark., 1981—, mem. profl. standards com. Chmn. by-laws com. Ark. Nursing Rsch. Consortium, Coun. of Nurse Adminstrs. of Nursing Edn. in Ark.; mem., past recorder for Coun. of Deans and Dirs. for RN Edn. of Ark. State Bd. Nursing, past chmn. ADN coun.; presenter health care career symposiums. Mem. adv. bd. Mississippi County Dept. Pub. Health. Mem. ANA, Ark. Nursing Assn., Ark. League for Nursing Assn., Ark. State Nursing Assn., Ark. Nurses Assn., Ark. Orgn. for Advancement of Assoc. Degree Nursing, Sigma Theta Tau. Office: Miss County CC PO Box 1109 Blytheville AR 72316-1109

FULMORE, MARYANN, state agency administrator; b. Mar. 19, 1952; d. William Stewart and Etta Grace Anderson; m. Clifton Fulmore, Mar. 29, 1980. BA, N.C. Ctrl. U., Durham, 1974; MA, Kean U., Union, N.J., 1985. Cert. counselor dept. labor, N.J. Sr. vocat. counselor divsn. employment and tng. State of N.J., Plainfield; discretionary grants coord. Union County Dept. Human Svcs./Divsn. Employment and Tng., Elizabeth, N.J., 1992-98, dir. ops., 1998—. Editor-in-chief newsletter Shiloh Bapt. Sentinel, 1993-99. Recipient Women of Excellence award Union County Commn. on Status of Women, 1998, Freeholder Resolution award Bd. Chosen Freeholders, Union County, 1998. Mem. Nat. Assn. [illegible] Plainfield Brunswick br., Svc. award 1994-98), Garden State Employment and Tng. Assn., Shiloh Bapt. Ch. Women's Fellowship. Office: County Adminstrn Bldg Human Svcs Dept Elizabethtown Plz Elizabeth NJ 07207

FULTON, ADDIE RUTH, minister, social worker; b. Kingstree, South Carolina, U.S.A., Sept. 15, 1953; d. James and Dillie Mae (Snow) Fulton. M.A. Elem. Ed., SC. St. Coll., Orangeburg, SC., 1984—86. Pastor/co-pastor Bethlehem Ch. of Christ, 1978—; coun./intake coord. Action/Vista, Phila., 1988—90; home-based MH/MR tchr. NW. MH/MR CDC Ctr., Phila., 1987—88. Resident dir., asst. dir. edn. Legare Hall & Morris Coll., Sumter, SC, 1977—84. Mem.: Santee Round-Up Program. Home: POB 1054 Kingstree SC 29556

FULTON, CARLA RAE, human resources manager; b. Clarion, Iowa, July 18, 1953; d. Don C. and Marietta (Walker) Greenfield; m. Kenneth W. Townsley, May 24, 1975 (div. 1987); m. James P. Fulton, July 17, 1994. BA, U. North Tex., 1975, MBA, 1982. Human resources specialist Mobil Oil Corp., Dallas, 1976-82; human resources mgr. S & A Restaurant Corp., Dallas, 1982-85; sr. compensation analyst Frito-Lay, Dallas, 1985-86; asst. dir. human resources Fed. Home Loan Bank, Dallas, 1986-89; sr. mgr. human resources DSC Communications Corp., Plano, Tex., 1989-92, Pier I Imports, Fort Worth, 1993-96; dir. human resources Nations Credit, Dallas, 1996—97; v.p. human resources Summit Global Ptnrs., Dallas, 1997—. Mem. adv. coun. Seay Behavioral Ctr. Mem. Soc. Human Resource Profls., Dallas Human Resource Mgmt. (v.p. 1986-90), Nat. Human Resource Systems Profls. (sec. 1986), Dallas Human Resource Systems Profls. (founding mem., pres. 1985-86). Republican. Methodist. Avocations: gardening, antiques. Home: 7111 Mimosa Ln Dallas TX 75230-5441

FULTON, CHERYL L. customer service administrator; b. Chgo., Feb. 21, 1947; d. Theodore E. and Elsie A. Whiffen; m. Richard L. Gniadek, Nov. 15, 1969 (dec. Feb. 1979); m. Richard J. Fulton, Sept. 2, 1995. BSBA, Ill. State U., 1969. Prodn. sec. Universal Tng. Systems, Lincolnwood, Ill., 1969-71; exec. sec. Alliance Am. Insurers, Chgo., 1971-78; temp. sec. Kelly Svcs., Grand Rapids, Mich., 1978-79; sec. Honeywell, Internat., Grand Rapids, Mich., 1979—80, sales corr., 1980—81, adminstr. customer quality Ft. Washington, Pa., 1981—84, rep. customer svc. Valley Forge, Pa., 1984—88, fin. acct. Ft. Washington, 1987—91, br. support supr. Valley Forge, 1991—92, supr. Regional Customer Svc. Ctr. Ft. Washington, 1992—95, field svcs. mgr., 1995—. Mem. NAFE, Am. Bus. Women's Assn. (New Directions Charter chpt., pres. 1986, Woman of Yr. 1985), Instrument Soc. Am. (treas., edn. com. Phila. sect., sec., treas., 3d v.p., 2d v.p., 1st v.p., pres. 1994-95). Democrat. Roman Catholic. Avocations: needlework, skiing, reading. Home: 857 Thoreau Ct Warminster PA 18974-2057 Office: Honeywell Internat 1100 Virginia Dr Fort Washington PA 19034-3264

FULTON, JO ANN, lawyer; b. 1951; BA in History, U. Wyo., JD, 1989. Atty. Fulton Law Office, Laramie, Wyo., 1992—. Mem. Wyo. State Bd. Edn., 2000—, chmn., 2003—. Office: Fulton Law Office PC PO Box 1267 1002 S 3rd St Laramie WY 82073-1267 Address: Wyo Dept Edn Hathaway Bldg 2nd Fl 2300 Capitol Ave Cheyenne WY 82002-0050

FUNDERBURG, JAN, telecommunications industry executive; Numerous positions including operator svcs., human resources, network ops., sales, mktg. Bellsouth Corp., v.p. customer svcs., 1997—2002, pres. interconnection svcs., 2002—. Active Am. Cancer Soc., Woodruff Arts, Jr. Acheivement, United Way; bd. dirs. ARC Disaster Svcs. Divsn. Recipient Outstanding Woman Achievement award, YWCA, 1997, Person Yr. award, Ga. Interconnection Assn., 1988. Office: Bellsouth Corp 1155 Peachtree St NE Atlanta GA 30309-3610

FUNG, AMY SHU-FONG, accountant; b. Hong Kong, Sept. 23, 1949; came to U.S., 1970; d. Wing-Chee and Fung-Siu (Tsang) Leung; m. Gee-You Fung, Mar. 17, 1970; children: Alice, Deborah. BS in Acctg., CUNY, 1982. Acct. Cath. Charities Diocese of Bklyn. Inc., N.Y.C., 1982-83; sr. acct. Beth Israel Med. Ctr., N.Y.C., 1983-85, St. John Episcopal Home for Aged and Blind, N.Y.C., 1986-87, Internat. Ctr. for Disabled, N.Y.C., 1988-91, United Jewish Appeal-Fedn. Jewish Philanthropies N.Y., N.Y.C., 1992-94. Avocations: music, cooking, theater, travel. Home: 359 Colon Ave Staten Island NY 10308-1415

FUNG, FLORA LIK-YUEN, statistician, consultant; b. Hong Kong, China, Jan. 10, 1950; came to U.S., 1969; d. Kon-Hung and Yuen-Chan (Tung) Tsang; children: Christopher Mon-Chee, Stepanie Mon-Taine. BS in Math., Iowa State U., 1972; MA in Biostats., U. Calif., Berkeley, 1974, MPH in Epidemiology, 1979. Tchg. asst. U. Calif., Berkeley, 1972-74; rsch. assoc. Univ. Calif., Berkeley, 1976-79, Lawrence Berkeley Lab., Berkeley, 1979; programmer analyst Eastman Kodak, Rochester, N.Y., 1980-85; analyst, programmer U. So. Calif., L.A., 1986-90, So. Calif. Edison Co., Rosemead, Calif., 1990-93; analyst U. So. Calif., L.A., 1994-95; analyst, programmer Prudential Ins. Co., Woodland Hills, Calif., 1995-97; actuarial systems analyst Blue Cross of Calif., Woodland Hills, 1997—. Cons. Infotech. Co., Culver City, Calif., 1994, U. So. Calif. Med. Sch., 1994-95. Mem. Am. Stats. Assn., Toastmaster Club (v.p. local chpt. 1991-93), Pi Mu Epsilon (Hon. Math. award 1972). Avocations: piano, theatre, musicals, reading, classical music. Home: 17302 Avenida Herradura Pacific Palisades CA 90272 Office: Blue Cross of Calif Oxnard St Woodland Hills CA 91367

FUNG, ROSALINE LEE, language educator; b. China, May 14, 1944; came to U.S., 1963; d. Frank Kwok-Wai and Teresa Wai-Hing (Cheung) Lee; m. Stephen Ying-Chung Fung, Aug. 23, 1968. BA, Briar Cliff Coll., 1966; MA, Idaho State U., 1968. Instr. Highland C.C., Freeport, Ill., 1968-69, Merced (Calif.) Coll., 1969-70; tchr. Linden (Calif.) High Sch., 1970-84; prof. San Joaquin Delta Coll., Stockton, Calif., 1984—. Cons. in field. Author: (textbooks) ESL Writing Manual, 1992, Patterns for Success, 4 vols., 1997, Basic Composition, 1997, Writing Essays, 1998, Writing Paragraphs, 1999. Coord. cultural exch. San Joaquin Delta Coll., 1995, 96, 98. Mem. NEA, Calif. Tchrs. Assn. Avocations: reading, writing, concerts, theater, surfing the net. Office: San Joaquin Delta Coll 5151 Pacific Ave Stockton CA 95207-6304 Office Phone: 209-954-5252. E-mail: rfung@deltacollege.edu.

FUNG-CHEN-PEN, EMMA TALAUNA SOLAITA, librarian, program director; b. Pago Pago, Am. Samoa, Sept. 4, 1951; d. Talauna and Ema (Tauoa) S.; m. Su'a oelu T. Fung-Chen-Pen, Nov 1, 1971; children: John Kevin, Juliet Ruth, Jacqueline Josie, Jennifer Lorna, Jonathan Emosi. AA Gen. Edn., Am. Samoa C. C., 1973, AS Libr. Studies, 1974; BA, Brigham Young U., Honolulu, 1977; MS in Librarianship, U. Hawaii, 1979. Libr. clerk Libr. Svcs., Pago Pago, 1971-74, libr. technician, 1974-76, libr. II, 1976-79, program dir., 1980—. Sec. Seventh Day Adventist Leone (Am. Samoa) Ch., 1990-94; dir. Seventh Day Adventist Leone Pathfinder, 1993—; pres. Parent-Tchr. Assn.-Sch., 2000-; active SDA Sch. Bd., 1991-98, mem. exec. bd. Samoa Mission, 1999-; mem. libr. bd. Feleti Barstow Pub., 2000-; mem. Samoa bd. dirs., coun. Read to Me, 1998-; mem. TV ministry bd. Leone SDA Ch., 1999-. Avocations: volleyball, reading, walking. Home: PO Box 1952 Pago Pago AS 96799-1952 Office: Am Samoa-Office of Lib Svcs PO Box 1329 Pago Pago AS 96799-1329

FUNK, CARLA JEAN, library association executive; b. Wheeling, W.Va., Sept. 21, 1946; d. David H. and Jean (Duffy) Belt. BA in Psychology, Northwestern U., 1968; MLS, Ind. U., 1973; MBA, U. Chgo., 1985. Libr. adult svcs. Northbrook (Ill.) Pub. Libr., 1973-77; dir. Warren-Newport Pub. Libr. Dist., Gurnee, Ill., 1977-80; cons. Suburban Libr. Sys., Burr Ridge, Ill., 1980-83; dir. automation and tech. svcs., med. student svcs. AMA, Chgo., 1983-92; exec. dir. Med. Libr. Assn., Chgo., 1992—. Adj. faculty Dominican U., 1980—. Contbr. articles to profl. jours. Mem. Internat. Fedn. Libr. Assns. and Insts. (treas., mgmt. libr. assn. sec.), Am. Soc. Assn. Execs. (cert. assn. exec.), Assn. Forum of Chicagoland, Beta Phi Mu, Delta Zeta. Home: 345 W Fullerton Pkwy #2707 Chicgao IL 60614 Office: 65 E Wacker Pl Ste 1900 Chicago IL 60601-7246 E-mail: funk@mlahq.org.

FUNK, VICKI JANE, librarian; b. Frankfurt am Main, Hesse, Federal Republic of Germany, Apr. 7, 1951; d. George N. and Maymie Lou Funk; m. David Robert Koble, July 11, 1986. BS, Ind. State U., 1971; MLS, Okla. U., 1975; cert. in comparative libraries, Oxford U., Eng., Summer 1978; cert. in Scottish lit., St. Andrews U., Scotland, Summer 1985. Elem. open concept team tchr. Plainfield (Ind.) Pub. Schs., 1971-72; media specialist, tchr. elem. schs. Enid (Okla.) Pub. Schs., 1972-73, librarian, 1973-74; libr. media specialist Bartlesville (Okla.) Sr. H.S., 1975-96. Chmn. library evaluation teams North Cen. Assn., Okla., 1982-86; pres. V.I.E.W. adv. bd. Okla. State Dept. Vocat. Edn., 1980-81; tchr. pub. library continuing adult edn. program, Bartlesville 1986. Storyteller Ednl. TV Bartlesville Cable, 1975-77, Oral Children's Program Pub. Library, 1985-86; book reviewer Okla. State Dept. Libraries "Gushers and Dusters", 1986-87; mem. book rev. selection com. Bartlesville Pub. Library. V.P. Friends of the Pub. Library, Bartlesville, 1986. Recipient Outstanding Svc. award Okla. Dept. Vocat. Edn., 1981; Emiline Libr. scholar Ind. State U., 1970; Innovative Edn. grantee Bartlesville Pub. Edn. Found., 1990, 91. Mem. NEA, AAUW (edn. officer 1980-81), Okla. Edn. Assn., Bartlesville Edn. Assn., Bartlesville Art Assn., Okla. Libr. Assn., Kappa Kappa Iota (v.p. 1990-91, secd. 1996-98). Democrat. Presbyterian. Avocations: bridge, traveling, skiing, acting, oil painting.

FUNKHOUSER, CATHERINE G. music educator; b. Sistersville, W.Va., Jan. 18, 1957; d. Harold Cales and Eleanor Mitchell Givens; m. Greg Wendell Funkhouser, July 25, 1981; children: Erik Wendell, Megan Marie. B of Applied Music, B of Music Edn., W.Va. U., 1978. Dir. music and youth 1st United Ch. Christ, Canton, Ohio, 1979—81; dir. music Clayton (Ga.) Bapt. Ch., 1984—86; voice and piano tchr. Rabun Gap (Ga.) Nacoochee Sch., 1988—91, 1993—95; paraprofl. Clayton Elem., 1996—2000, music tchr., 2000—. Named Rabun County Tchr. of Yr., Rabun County Bd. Edn., 2004. Mem.: Ga. Music Educator Assn., Music Educators Nat. Conf., Am. Orff Schulwerk Assn. Avocations: reading, sewing. Office: Clayton Elem 837 US Hwy 76 W Clayton GA 30525

FUNKHOUSER, ERICA, writer, writing educator; b. Cambridge, Mass., Sept. 17, 1949; d. Elmer Newton and Gladys McFeeley Funkhouser; children: Justin, Sophie. BA, Vassar Coll., 1971; MA, Stanford U., 1973. Part-time lectr. dept. writing and humanistic studies MIT, Cambridge, Mass., 1998—. Author: Sure Shot and Other Poems, 1992, The Actual World, 1997, Pursuit, 2002. Fellow, McDowell Found., 1994. Mem.: Acad. Am. Poets, Poetry Soc. Am., PEN New Eng. Office: MIT Dept Writing and Humanistic Studies Rm 14E 303 Cambridge MA 02139-4307

FUQUA, JUDY See FOUQUET, ANNE

FURCRON, CHARNE DELISE, dancer; b. Atlanta, Sept. 10, 1963; d. James Louis and Parrie Lee (Carter) Furcron. BFA, Tex. Christian U., 1985; MA, Goucher Coll., 1989, Ga. Sch. Profl. Psychology, Atlanta, 1989. Lic. profl. counselor Ga., 2001, registered dance therapist Am. Dance Therapy Assn., 1989. Expressive arts therapist West Paces Ferry Hosp., Atlanta, 1988—89; activity therapist/rehab. Skyland Trail, Atlanta, 1989—92; dance therapist Fulton County, Atlanta, 1992—97, Northside Hosp., Atlanta, 1989—2000; jr. co. and Stepping Stones dir. Moving in the Spirit, Atlanta, 2000—. Choreographer DeKalb County Bd. Edn., Decatur, Ga., 2001—; choreographer, co. mem. Moving in the Spirit, Atlanta, 1993—; collaborating artist Beacon Dance, Decatur, 1991—99, adv. bd., 1992; choreographer, co. mem. Dance for Everyone, Atlanta, 1991—95; artist in residence City of Atlanta Bur. Cultural Affairs, 1997, Westchester Sch. Arts Residency, 2000, Dancing Together Residency, 2000, Spl. Audience, Inc., 1994. Recipient Panelist, Gov.'s Honors Program of Ga., 2001; grantee City of Atlanta Bur. Cultural Affairs, 1995—97. Mem.: Sacred Dance Guild, Dance Educators of Ga., Nat. Bd. Cert. Counselors, Am. Dance Therapy Assn. (treas. Atlanta chpt. 1996—2001, pres. 1994—96), Alternate Roots, Atlanta, Alpha Kappa Alpha (Lambda Epsilon Omega chpt.). Roman Catholic. Avocations: gardening, theater, refinishing antiques, cultural arts events, water sports. Office: Moving in the Spirit 750 Glenwood Ave Atlanta GA 30316 E-mail: chafur@yahoo.com.

FUREY, ANNEMARIE PATRICIA, apparel designer; b. Kingston, N.Y., Oct. 11, 1966; d. Peter Joseph II and Anne Barbara (Cioffi) F.; m. Todd Douglas Sheinfeld, Sept. 10, 1994 (div. Sept. 2003); children: Parker Hale, Jascha Anne. BFA, RISD, 1988. Product mgr. Mast Industries, Andover, Mass., 1988-91; head sweater designer Boston Traders, Lynn, Mass., 1991-92; product mgr. Burton Snowboards, Burlington, Vt., 1992-95; v.p. R&D Turtle Fur, Morrisville, Vt., 1995—2001; creative CEO Turtle Fur and Nordic Gear Cos., 2001—. Spkr. in field. Vol. Mad River Valley Winter Carnival, Waitsfield, Vt., 1992—. Avocations: disc jockey, snowboarding, sea kayaking, hiking, tng. labrador retriever. Home: PO Box 534 Waitsfield VT 05673-0534 Office: Turtle Fur Co 1 Lamolle Industrial Pkwy Morrisville VT 05661

FURLOW, BRENDA J. religious studies educator, consultant; d. L. T. and Thelma M. Thomas; m. Rocket P. Furlow, Dec. 5, 1971; children: Jacquetta A. Furlow-Ellis, La'Chaundra A. BS, Athens State U., 1997; MDiv, Samford U., 2003. Contract specialists Dept. Army, Anniston, Ala., 1982—93, contract adminstr. Heidelberg, Germany, 1993—96; contracting officer U.S. Corps Engrs., Huntsville, Ala., 1997—2001; dir. Christian edn. St. Luke Missionary Bapt. Ch., Huntsville, 2002—. Marriage and family counselor B.F. Ministries, Huntsville, 2000—. Counselor Downtown Rescue Mission, Huntsville, 2003; com. pres. Prog. Nat. Bapt. Conv., Washington, 2001; com. mem. Greater Huntsville Interdenominational Ministerial Fellowship, Huntsville, 1998; vice moderator Flint River Missionary Bapt. Assn., Huntsville, 2000. Home: 9020 Craigmont Rd SW Huntsville AL 35802 Office: St Luke Missionary Baptist Church 1800 Sparkman Dr Huntsville AL 35810 Personal E-mail: preacherwo@knology.net.

FURMAN, LAURA, writer, educator; b. Bklyn., N.Y., Nov. 19, 1945; d. Sylvan S. and Minnie Airov Furman; m. Joel Warren Barna; 1 child, Solomon Barna. BA, Bennington Coll., 1968. Prof. engring. U. of Tex., Austin, Tex., 1988—. Series editor O'Henry Prize Story Awards, N.Y.C., 2003—. Author: (short stories) The Glass House, 1981 (Jesse Jones award Tex. Inst. of Letters, 1981), (novel) The Shadow Line, 1982, (short stories) Watch Time Fly, 1983, (novel) Tuxedo Park, 1987, (memoir) Ordinary Paradise, 1998, (short stories) Drinking with the Cook, 2001. Mem. Corp. Yaddo, Saratoga Springs, NY, 1987. Recipient CAPS award in Fiction, N.Y. State Coun. on the Arts, 1976, Ritchie-McGinnis award for Best Fiction, S.W. Rev., 2000, prize, Smart Family Found. & Yale Rev., 2001; fellow Dobie-Paisano fellowship, U. of Tex. at Austin & Tex. Inst. of Letters, 1981, John S. Guggenheim Found., 1982. Mem.: Authors Guild. Jewish. Office: U Tex at Austin English Dept B5000 One University Ave Austin TX 78712-1164 E-mail: ljfurman@mail.utexas.edu.

FURMAN, SUE, owner public relations agency; b. Phila., Aug. 3, 1945; d. Seymour and Ruth (Pripstein) Costilo; m. Richard A. Furman, Aug. 20, 1966; children: Michael Brett (dec.), Deborah Elizabeth. BA in comm., Temple U., Phila., 1982. Prodn. asst., prodr., dir. Sta. WPHL-TV 17, Phila.,

1981-84; spl. events coord. Sta. KYW-TV 3, Phila., 1984-88; dir. mktg. Oxford Valley Mall, Langhorne, Penn., 1989-90; v.p. The Hayes Group, Dresher, Penn., 1992-95; pres. Furman Comm., Blue Bell, Penn., 1995—. Cons. Internat. Franchise Assn., Washington, 1995. Mem. Greater Phila. C. of C. (bd. dirs.). Home: 105 Muirfield Dr Blue Bell PA 19422-1294 Office: Furman Comm 1166 Dekalb Pike Blue Bell PA 19422

FURNESS, JANET ELISABETH, social work educator; b. Newark, Nov. 25, 1948; d. Charles Yardley and Margaret Sutherland F.; children: Philip Andrew Spressart, Jessie Marie Spressart. BS, Phila. Biblical U., 1970; MSW, Rutgers U., 1972; postgrad., U. Rochester, 1997—. Dir. child welfare Goodwill Home and Rescue Mission, Newark, 1972-82; dir. child placement svcs. Christian Homes for Children, Hackensack, N.J., 1982-86; dir. statewide vol. programs Mental Health Assn. N.J., Montclair, 1987-94, dir. children's mental health legis. advocacy, 1987-94; assoc. dean, asst. prof. Carver Sch. Ch. Social Work, So. Bapt. Theol. Sem., Louisville, 1994-95; acting dean Carver Sch. Ch. Social Work So. Bapt. Theol. Sem., Louisville, 1995-96; assoc. prof. social work Roberts Wesleyan Coll., Rochester, N.Y., 1996—. Chair parents and profls. in partnership statewide conf. Mental Health Assn. N.J., New Brunswick, 1990; chair legal issues task force Children's Svc. Coordinating Coun., N.J. Dept. Human Svcs., Trenton, 1990-94; cons. to pub. schs. regarding edn. reform Ky. Edn. Reform Act, Louisville, 1994-95; founding mem., leadership team mem. Christians Supporting Cmty. Orgn., Denver, 1997. Contbr. chapters to books. Mem., adv. Rochester Area Children's Collaborative, 1996—. Mem. NASW (cert.), Acad. Cert. Social Workers, N.Am. Assn. Christians in Social Work (sec./treas. 1987-89, pres. 1995-97, co-chair ann. conv. 2002), Coun. on Social Work Edn. Evangelical Covenant. Avocations: soprano vocalist, organist, pianist. Office: Roberts Wesleyan Coll 2301 Westside Dr Rochester NY 14624-1933 E-mail: furnessj@roberts.edu.

FURNEY, LINDA JEANNE, state legislator; b. Toledo, Sept. 11, 1947; d. Robert Ross and Jeanne Scott (Hogan) F. BS in Edn., Bowling Green State U., 1969; postgrad., U. Toledo. Tchr. Washington Local Schs., Toledo, 1969-72, Escola Americano do Rio de Janiero, 1972-74, Springfield Schs., Holland, Ohio, 1977-83; council mem. City of Toledo, 1983-86; mem. Ohio Senate from 11th dist., Columbus, 1987—. Mem. edn. com., rules com., reference and oversight com., fin. com., econ. devel. com. hwys. and transp. com., state and local govt. and vet. affairs com., asst. minority leader Ohio State Senate, Columbus, 1997-99. Dem. precinct committeewoman Toledo, 1980-90; mem. Toledo Bd. Edn., 1982-83. Recipient Citizen award Ohio Assn. Edn. Young Children, Stanley K. Levinson award Planned Parenthood Northwest Ohio, Educator of Yr. award Phi Delta Kappa, Milestone award Toledo YMCA, Pres. award Ohio Rehab. Assn.; named Person of Yr., Ohio Vocational Assn. Mem. NOW, AAUW, NAACP, ACLU (Found. award), Toledo Mus. Art, Toledo Zoo, Manhattan Dance Co. Home: 2626 Latonia Blvd Toledo OH 43606-3620 Office: Ohio Senate Senate Bldg Rm 051 Columbus OH 43215

FURNISS, WENDY HAGSTROM, public health services administrator; b. Hartford, Conn., Mar. 30, 1949; BSN summa cum laude, Duke U., 1971; MS in Nursing Adminstrn., U. Conn., 1989. Instr. nursing St. Francis Hosp. and Med. Ctr., Hartford, 1976-77; case mgr. Conn. Cmty. Care, Inc., Hartford and Bristol, 1980-90, adminstrv. supr., 1983-90; supervising nurse cons. Dept. Pub. Health, State of Conn., Hartford, 1990-95, pub. health svcs. mgr., 1995—. Lectr. in field. Mem. Am. Nurses Assn. in Gerontologic Nursing (cert.), Sigma Theta Tau, Phi Kappa Phi. Office: Conn Bd of Examiners for Nursing Divsn of Health Systems 410 Capitol Ave # 12 Hartford CT 06106-1367

FURSE, ELIZABETH, former congresswoman, small business owner; b. Nairobi, Kenya, 1936; came to U.S., 1958, naturalized, 1972; children: Amanda Briggs, John Briggs; m. John Platt. BA, Evergreen State Coll., 1974; postgrad., U. Wash., Northwestern U., Lewis and Clark Coll. Dir. Western Wash. Indian program Am. Friends Svc. Com, 1975-77; coord. Restoration program for Native Am. Tribes Oreg. Legal Svc., 1980-86; co-owner Helvetia Vineyards, Hillsboro, Oreg.; mem. 103rd-105th Congresses from 1st Oreg. dist., 1993-98, mem. commerce com. Exec. dir. Inst. for Tribal Govt., Portland State U. Co-founder Oreg. Peace Inst., 1985. Address: 22485 NW Yungen Rd Hillsboro OR 97124-8146 also: Inst Tribal Govt PO Box 751 Portland OR 97207

FURST, GRETA LENETSKA, entertainer, writer, travel agent; b. N.Y.C., May 15, 1932; d. Harry and Heloise (Altschul) Lenetska; m. Lionel A. Furst, June 15, 1967; children: Valeri Furst Wauschek, Larry M. Student, UCLA, 1951-54. Sales clk. Saks Fifth Ave., N.Y.C., 1950-51, credit and control clk. Beverly Hills, Calif., 1951-53; asst. chief insp. Hoover Electric, West Los Angeles, Calif., 1953-54; office mgr. Craig & Randall Constrn., L.A., 1954-59; restaurant owner The Coffee Palace, L.A., 1958-61; internat. performer, singer in worldwide tours USO, L.A., 1960-63; performer, singer, actor self employed, 1963—; profl vol. L.A. Free Clinic, others, 1970—. Prodr., dir. Beverly Hills Follies, Beverly Hills C. of C., 1992; regular performer Srs. Entertaining Srs., 1997—. Composer songs; painter portraits; one-woman show Here I Go Again, 1999. Bd. dirs., pres. Friends of the L.A. Free Clinic, 1972—; trustee L.A. West Mosquito Abatement Dist., 1978-83; mem. Bverly Hills Traffic and Parking Commn., 1992-2000, chair, 1995; mem. adv. com. Access Svcs., 1997—. Recipient Agy. Leadership award United Way Greater L.A., 1995, Frances Helfman award L.A. Free Clinic, 1998, resolution Calif. State Assembly, 1998, others. Mem. NATAS, SAG, AFTRA, AGVS, Srs. Entertaining Srs., Bronx H.S. of Sci. West Coast Alumni. Democrat. Jewish. Avocations: portraiture, travel, reading, community service.

FURST-BOWE, JULIE, academic administrator; BA in Journalism, U. Wis., Eau Claire, 1985; MS in Media Tech., U. Wis.-Stout, 1986; cert. in tng. and human resource devel., U. MInn., 1995. Media dir. libr. and media svcs. U. Wis., Waukesha, 1986—87, media specialist Media Devel. Ctr. Eau Claire, 1987—90; mem. faculty U. Wis.-Stout, Menomonie, 1990—94, assoc. prof., 1999, prof., 1999—, dir. grad. program, 1995—97, chmn. dept. comms., 1996—98, assoc. vice chancellor divsn. acad. and student affairs, 1998—, acting dir. Office Continuing Edn., 1998—99. Presenter in field. Contbr. articles to mags. and profl. publs., chpts. to books. Vol. Bolton Refuge House, 1988—98, Challenges and Chouces Career Workship for Young Women, 1988—98, Eau Claire Devel. and Tng. Ctr., 1997; mem. steering com. Eau Claire Women's Network, 1992, 1996; mem. Leadership Chipewa Valley, 1995, Inst. for Learning in Retirement, 1998—99; co-chmn. Menomonie Plan Com., 1997—99. Grantee, U. Wis.-Stout, 1994—97, U. Wis. Sys., 1997—2000. Mem.: AAUW, Wis. Vocat. Assn., Wis. Women in Higher Edn. Leadership., Wis. Edn. Media Assn. (bd. dirs. 1993—96, chmn. pub. rels. com. 1993—96, editor Wis. Ideas in Media jour. 1992—96), Profl. and Orgnl. Devel. Network, Profl. and Orgnl. Devel. Network (reviewer To Improve the Academy 1998—), North Ctrl. Assn. Summer Schs., Midwest Assn. Grad. Schs., Assn. Ednl. Comms. and Tech. (del. nat. leadership conf. 1994, Ednl. Found. Mentor scholar 1993), Acad. Human Resource Devel. (proposal reviewer, session facilitator 1997—2000, reviewer Internat. Jour. Tng. and Devel. 1998—), Am. Assn. Adult and Continuing Edn., ASTD (HRD prof.'s forum editor 1997, bd. dirs. N.W. Wis. chpt. 1994—97). Office: U Wis-Stout 303 Adminstrn Bldg 712 S Broadway Menomonie WI 54751-0790

FURSTMAN, SHIRLEY ELISE DADDOW, advertising executive; b. Butler, N.J., Jan. 26, 1930; d. Richard and Eva M. (Kitchell) Daddow; grad. high sch.; m. Russell A. Bailey, Oct. 1, 1950 (div. Oct. 1967); m. William B. Furstman, Dec. 24, 1977. Asst. corporate sec. Hydrospace Tech., West Caldwell, N.J., 1960-62; sec. to pres. R.J. Dick Co., Totowa, N.J., 1962-63, Microlab, Livingston, N.J., 1963; asst. corporate sec. Astrosystems Internat., West Caldwell, N.J., 1963-65; corporate sec. Internat. Controls Corp., Fairfield, N.J., 1965-73; sec. to pres. Global Financial Co., Nassau, Bahamas, 1974-75; office mgr. Internat. Barter, Nassau, 1975-76; sec. to pres., corp. sec. Haas Chem. Co., Taylor, Pa., 1976-77; asst. to pres., pub. Am. Home mag., N.Y.C., 1977-78; v.p., office mgr. Gilbert, Whitney & Johns, Inc., Whippany, N.J., 1979-95; ret., 1996. Home: 4 Oceans West Blvd Apt 606D Daytona Beach FL 32118-5977

FURTADO, BEVERLY ANN, financial aid administrator; b. Bellville, Ill., Feb. 2, 1951; d. George C. and Bertha D. Carroll; m. James R. Furtado, July 18, 1970; children: Jeffrey, Cynthia. AS in Criminal Justice, Fisher Coll., Boston, 1994; BA in Liberal Studies, Western New Eng. Coll., 1998. Fin. aid counselor Fisher Coll., Boston, 1999; career cons. Job Tng. and Edn. Corp., Hyannis, Mass., 1998—2000; fin. aid assoc. Labouré Coll., Boston, 2000—01; fin. aid specialist Quincy Coll., Mass., 2001—; assoc. fin. aid dir. Quincy, Mass. Avocations: reading, quilting, sewing. Home: 781 Cotuit Rd Mashpee MA 02649 Office: Quincy Coll 34 Coddington St Quincy MA 02169

FURTADO, NELLY KIM, vocalist; b. Victoria, B.C., Can., Dec. 2, 1978; Singer: (albums) Whoa Nelly!, 2000 (Grammy award for Best Female Pop Performance, 2002), Folklore, 2003. Named one of Fun and Fearless Females, Cosmopolitan Mag., 2002. Office: Dreamworks SKG 1000 Flower St Glendale CA 91201*

FURTADO-LAVOIE, JULIA, management consultant, accountant; b. Fall River, Mass., July 22, 1964; d. Manuel Lawrence and Mary Gloria (Mello) Furtado; m. Michael Cavoie. Student, U. Mass., Dartmouth, 1987, Emerson Coll., Boston, 1987-89. Dist. sales mgr. InterPay Inc., Mansfield, Mass., 1996—2003; sales payroll cons. Paychex, Inc., Providence, 2003—. Cons. Start Me Up, Dartmouth, 1993—. Recipient Freedom Torch award ABC6 and Providence Jour., 1996. Mem. C. of C. (amb.). Avocations: reading, cats, theatre, opera. Home: 6 Ashley St South Dartmouth MA 02748-2808 Office: 501 Wampanoag Tr East Providence RI 02915

FURTH, KAREN J. artist; BA in Am. History, U. Pa., 1983; MA in Photography, NYU, 1988. Biomed. photographer Rockefeller U., 1988—89; photographer Smithsonian Instn., 1989—94; tchr. Trinity Sch., 1990; freelance photographer, 1994—; tchr., cons. Ctr. Urban Cmty. Svcs. The Times Sq., 1994—; tchr. Internat. Ctr. Photography at The Point, N.Y.C., 1998—. One-woman shows include Washington Sq. East Galleries, N.Y.C., 1988, 494 Gallery, 1991, 1992, 1994, Pulse Art Gallery, 1997, exhibited in group shows at Oswego Civic Art Ctr., 1988, 494 Gallery, 1991, 1992, Synchronicity Space, 1995, Pulse Art Gallery, 1996, Golin/Harris, 1998, others, curatorial projects include, The Times Sq. Photography Project, Met. Transp. Authority, 1999; presenter in field; contbr. articles to profl. jours.; Represented in permanent collections J.P. Morgan, Mt. Sinai Hosp., others. Recipient Gilbert Graphic Paper award, 1993; fellow Open Soc. Inst. Individual Project fellow, Soros Found., 1997; scholar Faculty scholar, U. Pa., 1979—83; Internat. Outreach grante, 1993—94.

FURTH, YVONNE, advertising executive; BS in Mktg., postgrad., Georgetown U., DePaul U. Asst. account exec. Draft Worldwide, 1981—88, gen. mgr., 1988—92, pres. of Chicago office, 1992—96, pres. & COO US operations, 1996—2001, pres., COO, 2002—. Mem.: Chgo. Assn. Direct Mktg. Direct Mktg. Assn. Office: Draft Chicago 633 N St Clair St Chicago IL 60611

FURUI, SACHIKO, language educator, consultant, artist; b. Osaka, Japan, Nov. 18, 1948; d. Kazuo and Setsuko Furui. Student, Chuo U., Tokyo, 1968—72; diploma, Osaka Lang. Sch., 1984; AS, Bunker Hill Coll., Mass., 1988. Lang. cons. Chinese Women's Club, Woburn, Mass., 1986, Japan Soc. Boston, 2000—, English League, Cambridge, Mass., 2001—; lang. tchr. Arlington (Mass)-Nagaoka Sister City Com., 1987, Lynnfield (Mass.) Elem. Sch., 1988, Endicott Coll., Beverly, Mass., 1992—93, Berlitze Lang. Ctr., Wellesley, Mass., 1993—, Salem (Mass.) State Coll., 1993—2002. Cover designer (book) After the Fact, 1994; editor: Japanese mag., 1997—. Mem. adv. com. Children's Ctr. Woburn, 1991—93, bd. dirs., 1991—92. Recipient nat. juried show, Mountain Art Show, 2000, St. Cloud Art Coun., 1999; grantee, Melrose Art, 1987. Mem.: Nat. Women for Art, Winchester Art Network, Cambridge Art Assn. Avocations: Koto player, history, travel, yoga. Home and Studio: 14 George Rd Winchester MA 01890

FUSCO, AURILLA MARIE, director; d. Delmar A. and Catherine F. (Bryan) Thibodeau; m. John A. Fusco (div.); 1 child, Craig L. Jr. BS in Paralegal/Govt. Bus., U. Md., 1986; MPA, Troy State U., 1990; postgrad., Concord Sch. Law. Staff asst. to Sen. George J. Mitchell U.S. Senate, Washington, 1981—85, staff asst. to Sen. Albert Gore, Jr. Nashville, 1985—86, staff asst, office mgr. subcom. on children, families, drugs and alcoholism, 1987; program analyst, adminstrv. officer Dept. of the Army, Germany, 1987—91; dir. child care River Valley Child Devel., Huntington, W.Va., 1992—97; exec. dir. Child Advocates of Blair County, Altoona, Pa., 1998—2001; regional mr. capital gifts Bucknell U., Lewisburg, Pa., 2001—04; dir. devel. Main Campus Librs. Georgetown U., Washington, 2004—. Presenter Nat. Assn. for Edn. of Young Children; cons. W.Va. Welfare Reform Coalition, 1996—98; exec. dir. nonprofit R&D Gamday, LLC, Altoona, Pa., 2000—. Co-chair Children's Issues Advocates, W.Va., 1997—98; pres. Jr. League, Huntington, 1997—98; sustainer adviser Jr. League Williamsport, 2003—04; bd. dirs. AIDS Resource Alliance, Williamsport, Pa., 2002—. Mem.: Sunrise Rotary.

FUSILLO, ALICE ELBERT, retired sociologist, sculptor; b. Balt., Dec. 13, 1922; d. Francis Wilson and Alice Margaret (Jones) Zeigler; m. Matthew Henry Fusillo, Sept. 13, 1947 (dec. Aug. 3, 1980); children: Lawrence Joseph, Lisa Ann, Jessica Jean, Susan Frances. BS, U. Md., 1948, MA, 1966. Pub. health analyst NIH, Bethesda, Md., 1968—74; statistician Bur. Census, SESA, Suitland, Md., 1974; consumer sci. specialist FDA, Washington, 1974—79; statistician Dept. Health and Human Svcs., Washington, 1979—88; sculptor Washington, 1988—. Contbr. articles to profl. jours.; exhibitions include Carego Foxley Leach Gallery, Washington, D.C., 1991, Whitehall Gallery, Corcoran, Washington, 1990, Washington Square Sculpture Show, 2003. Recipient Mary Lay Sculpture award, Corcoran Sch. Art, 1986, Visual Art award, Capitol Hill Art League, 2002. Mem.: AAUW, Goodwill Industries, Washington Sculptors Soc., Internat. Sculpture Ctr., The Art League (Best in Show 1988), Sierra Club. Achievements include patents for Dying Swan sculpture. Avocations: landscape and portrait painting, ballroom dancing. Home: Apt N604 560 N St SW Washington DC 20024-4617

FUSILLO, NANCY MARIE, medical/surgical, oncological, pediatric, community health and family nurse practitioner; b. Washington, Sept. 15, 1948; d. Leonard and Yolanda Rita (Tolatta) F. AA, Montgomery Jr. Coll., Takoma Park, Md., 1969; BA, U. Md., 1971; ADN, Daytona Beach C.C., 1986; BSN, U. South Fla., 1988; MS, Nat. Louis U., Tampa, Fla., 1992; MSN in Family Nurse Practitioner Program, U. Tampa, 2002. RN; cert. chemotherapy nurse 1991, med.-surg. nurse 1993, intravenous nurse 1993, oncology nurse, 1993,; diabetic educator, 1994, family nurse practitioner, 2003. Med.-surg. staff nurse Palms of Pasadena Hosp., St. Petersburg, Fla., 1986-87; home health nurse Paragon Nursing Fla., Inc., Clearwater, 1987-94; staff and home health nurse Upjohn Olsten Gentiva Intel Staff Healthcare Svcs., Clearwater, Fla., 1987—; intravenous nurse clinician New Eng. Critical Care, Tampa, 1989-91; oncology and med.-surg. nurse Suncoast Hosp., Largo, Fla., 1991-92; neonatal and pediat. clinician Pediat. Health Choice, Tampa, 1993-97; nurse clin. pediat., neonatal Pediat. Svcs. Am., St. Petersburg, Fla., 1994-96; nurse Hospice of Fla. Suncoast, 1990—; chemotherapy infusion nurse Fla. Cmty. Cancer Ctrs. Am., 2000—; staff nurse med. oncology unit St. Anthony's Hosp., 2001—02. Pub. educator nurse Am. Cancer Soc., 1987—; item reviewer Nat. Coun. State Bds. Nursing, 1999; breast and cervical cancer sub-com., chair tell-a-friend mammogram project Am. Cancer Soc., 2001—; cmty. educator ARNP St. Petersburg Gen. Hosp., Fla., 2003. Manuscript reviewer: Jour. Hospice and Palliative Nursing, 2002—. Vol. nurse cmty. outreach program St. Anthony's Hosp., 1990—, distributor newspaper Voice of the Diabetic, Sojourn Bears for Cancer Patients, 2000—. Recipient Masters scholar, Oncology Nursing Soc. Found., 2002. Mem. Oncology Nurses Soc., Infusion Nurses Soc. (editl. rev. bd. 1995), Am. Cancer Soc.

FUTCH, DOROTHY HELEN, librarian, paralegal; b. Alachua, Fla., Aug. 17, 1931; d. David Malcolm and Burdine (Slaughter) Futch. BA, Fla. State U., 1951; MS, Simmons Coll., 1960; cert. paralegal, City Coll. San Francisco, 1980. Cataloger Oakland (Calif.) Pub. Libr., 1961—76; file supr. Orrick, Herrington & Sutcliffe, San Francisco, 1977—80; probate paralegal R.E. Neuman Probate Referee, San Francisco, 1982—89; database mgr. Natkin, Weisbach, Higginbothan, San Francisco, 1990—93; adminstr. Cool Shades Internat., San Francisco, 1995—. Editor: (newsletter) Oak Leaves, 1969—76; translator: Astucia, 1995—2000. Pres. Oakland Pub. Libr. Staff Assn., 1973; active Rep. Nat. Com., 2003—. Lewis State Tchrs. scholar, State of Fla., Tallahassee, 1948—51. Mem.: Luis Inclan Soc. (pres. 2003—), Gamma Phi Beta. Republican. Baptist. Home: Apt 212 631 O'Farrell San Francisco CA 94109

FUTTER, ELLEN VICTORIA, museum administrator; b. N.Y.C., Sept. 21, 1949; d. Victor and Joan Babette (Feinberg) F.; children— Anne Victoria, Elizabeth Jane. Student, U. Wis., 1967-69; AB magna cum laude, Barnard Coll., 1971; JD, Columbia U., 1974, LLD (hon.), 1984, Hamilton Coll., 1985, N.Y. Law Sch.; DHL (hon.), Amherst Coll., Hofstra U., 1994, CCNY, 1996, L.I. City Coll., 1995, Yale U., 2000; DL, Columbia U. Bar: N.Y. 1975. Assoc. Milbank, Tweed, Hadley & McCloy, N.Y.C., 1974-80; acting pres. Barnard Coll., N.Y.C., 1980-81, pres., 1981-93, Am. Mus. Natural History, N.Y.C, 1993—. Bd. dirs. Bristol Myers Squibb, Am. Internat. Group, JP Morgan Chase, Consol. Edison of N.Y., Overseer Meml. Sloan Kettering Cancer Ctr., N.Y.; trustee Am. Mus. Natural History. Recipient L. Sachar award Brandeis U., Elizabeth Cutter Morrow, Distinction medal Barnard Coll., Excellence medal Columbia U., Gold medal award Nat. Inst. Social Scis., Legacy Conservation award Theodore Roosevelt Sanctuary, Visionary award New Vision in Pub. Sch. Mem. ABA, Am. Acad. Arts and Scis., N.Y. State Bar Assn., Assn. Bar City N.Y., Nat. Inst. Social Scis., Coun. Fgn. Rels., Cosmopolitan Club, Century Club, Phi Beta Kappa. Office: Am Mus Natural History Central Park West at 79th New York NY 10024*

FYDA-MAR, MARY CATHERINE, systems engineer, director; b. Oil City, Pa., Aug. 4, 1952; d. John Joseph and Lela Marie (Thompson) Fyda; m. Thomas Webb Mar, June 17, 1978; 1 child, Christina Ann. BS, Mich. State U., 1973, MA, 1975. Exec. dir. H.E.R.E. Rape Crisis Clinic, Placentia, Calif., 1977-78; lectr. Calif. State U., Fullerton, 1978; software engr., project engr. Rockwell Internat., Anaheim, Calif., 1978-91, systems engr., 1996; computer tchr. Fairmont Pvt. Sch., Anaheim Hills, Calif., 1992-94; sr. engring. specialist The Boeing Co., Anaheim, Calif., 1996—2001, dir. engring. resources, 2001—. NSF fellow, 1974; Nat. Merit scholar, 1970. Mem. IEEE, Project Mgmt. Inst., Nat. Mgmt. Assn., Phi Kappa Phi, Phi Beta Kappa. Democrat. Episc. Office: The Boeing Co 3370 E Miraloma Ave Anaheim CA 92806-1911 E-mail: mary.c.fyda-mar@boeing.com.

FYFE, DORIS MAE, elementary school educator; b. Shelby, Nebr., Sept. 5, 1930; d. Harold William Fyfe and Mae Emma Schmid. Assoc. in Elem. Edn., Scottsbluff Jr. Coll., Nebr., 1957; BS in Elem. Edn., Peru State Tchrs. Coll., Nebr., 1963; M in Urban Edn., U. Nebr., Omaha, 1980. Cert. K-12 tchr. Nebr. Tchr. K-8, Polk County Schs., Shelby, 1947—50, Banner County Schs., Harrisburg, Nebr., 1950—53; tchr. 2d grade Albin Consol. Schs., Albin, Wyo., 1953—57; prin., tchr. K-2, Union Pub. Schs., Nebr., 1957—61; tchr. 2d grade Nebraska City Pub. Schs., Nebr., 1961—63; intermediate tchr. Omaha Pub. Schs., 1963—90, substitute tchr., 1990—; adj. faculty Grace U., Omaha, 1984—. 4-H leader Agr. Coll. Ext. Svc. Polk County, 1947—50; vol. tutor Uta Halee Girls' Village, Omaha, 1995—; active Harvey Oaks Bapt. Ch., 1962—; dir. Midway Bible Camp, Thompson, Canada, 1970—90. Mem.: Omaha Area Ret. Tchrs. Assn., Olympian Club. Republican. Avocations: stamp collecting/philately, doll collecting, pencil collecting. Home: 6222 Ponderosa Dr Omaha NE 68137-4231

GABALDON, DIANA, writer; b. 1950; d. Jacqueline (Sykes) Gabaldon; m. Doug Watkins; children: Laura Juliet, Samuel Gordon, Jennifer Rose. MS in Marine Biology, PhD in Ecology. Asst. prof. rsch. environ. studies; freelance writer. Author: Outlander, 1991 (Best First Novel award B. Dalton bookstores 1991, Best Book Yr. award Romance Writer's Am. 1991), Dragonfly in Amber, 1992, Voyager, 1994, Drums of Autumn, 1997, Fathers and Daughters: A Celebration in Memoirs, Stories, and Photographs, 1999, The Outlandish Companion, 1999; software reviewer Byte mag.; contbr. articles to profl. jours.; author comic strips Disney. Office: Bantam Doubleday/Del 1540 Broadway Ste 9E New York NY 10036-4040

GABARRA, CARIN LESLIE, professional soccer player, professional soccer coach; b. East Orange, N.J., Jan. 9, 1965; m. Jim Gabarra. Degree in bus. mgmt., U. Calif., Santa Barbara, 1987. Mem. U.S. Nat. Women's Soccer Team, 1987—96; head coach, women's soccer Westmont Coll., 1987—88; asst. coach, women's Soccer Harvard U., Boston, 1988—93; head coach, women's soccer Navy, 1993—. Mem. U.S. Olympic World Festival team, 1986—89; mem. women's soccer U.S. Naval Acad., 1993. Named U.S. Soccer's Female Athlete of Yr., 1987, 1992; named to, U. Calif.-Santa Barbara Athletic Hall of Fame; recipient Golden Ball, FIFA Women's World Championship, China, 1991, gold medal, Atlanta Summer Olympic Games, 1996. Achievements include ranked as 3d-leading goal scorer in U.S. women's history; mem. CONCACAF Championship team, 1993, 94. Office: c/o US Soccer Fedn 1801 S Prairie Ave # 1811 Chicago IL 60616-1319

GABEL, CONNIE, chemist, educator; b. Green Bank, W.Va. d. William Ashby and Marie Lowry; m. Richard Gabel; children: Greg, Keith, Debbie. BS in Chemistry magna cum laude, James Madison U.; MA in Ednl. Adminstrn. summa cum laude, U. Colo., 1984, PhD in Ednl. Leadership and Innovation, 2001. Tchg. asst. U. Wis., Madison, 1969-70, specialist endocrinology, 1970-71; tchr. Dept. Def. Schs., Tokyo, 1972-74, Poudre R-1 Schs., Ft. Collins, Colo., 1975-78, Boulder (Colo.) Valley Schs., 1985-87, 96-98, intern asst. prin., 1984-85; intern supt. Jefferson County Schs., Golden, Colo., 1992; tchr. Mapleton Pub. Schs., Thornton, Colo., 1992-95; internat. studies Egyptian program Regis U., Denver, 1994; instr. chemistry Colo. Sch. Mines, 1995-98; dean students Horizon HS, Thornton, Colo., 1995-96; project 2061 coord. dept. chemistry/edn. U. Colo., Denver, 1998-2000; instr. St. Mary's Acad., Englewood, Colo., 2000—03, Met. State Coll. Tchr. Edn. and Chemistry, Denver, 2004—. Cons. sch. fin. Colo. Dept. Edn., Denver, 1984; rschr. AMC Cancer Rsch. Ctr., Denver, 1993, Colo. U. Med. Ctr., Denver, 1994; display tech. Boulder-Chemistry Rsch., 1995. Charter mem., pres. Friends Louisville (Colo.) Libr., 1985—; charter mem. Nat. Women's History Mus.; charter mem., pres., v.p. Coal Creek Rep. Women, Louisville, 1987—; sec., mem. Boulder County Reps., 1988—98, precinct chair; mem. Nat. Rep. Women, Washington, 1987—; sec. Dist. 17 Colo. Senate, Dist. 13 Colo. Ho., 1993—2002; mem. Colo. Fedn. Rep. Women, 1987—, Colo. Rep. Ctrl. Com. Mem.: AAUW, AAAS, ASCD, NY Acad. Sci., Math., Engring. and Sci. Achievement (dir., advisor 1992—97, mem. state level adv. bd. 1992—96), Colo. Chemistry Tchrs.

Assn., Colo.-Wyo. Acad. Sci., Colo. Assn. Sci. Tchrs., Nat. Soc. Study Edn., Nat. Assn. Rsch. Sci. Tchg., Am. Chem. Soc., Nat. Assn. Sci. Tchrs., Am. Ednl. Rsch. Assn., Phi Delta Kappa. Avocations: reading, hiking, gardening. Business E-Mail: cgabel@mscd.edu.

GABEL, KATHERINE, retired academic [illegible] Rochester, N.Y., Apr. 9, 1938; d. M. Wren and Esther (Conger) G.; m. Seth Devore Strickland, June 24, 1961 (div. 1965). AB, Smith Coll., Northampton, Mass., 1959; MSW, Simmons Coll., 1961; PhD, Syracuse U., 1967; JD, Union U., 1970; bus. program, Stanford U., 1984. Psychol. social worker Cen. Island Mental Health Ctr., Uniondale, N.Y., 1961-62; psychol. social worker, supt. Ga. State Tng. Sch. for Girls, Atlanta, 1962-64; cons. N.Y. State Crime Control Coun., Albany, 1968-70; faculty Ariz. State U., Tempe, 1972-76; supt. Ariz. Dept. of Corrections, Phoenix, 1970-76; dean, prof. Smith Coll., 1976-85; pres. Pacific Oaks Coll. and Children's Sch., Pasadena, Calif., 1985-98; western region v.p. Casey Family Program, Pasadena, 1998—2001; cons. svcs., 2001—. Advisor, del. UN, Geneva, 1977; mem. So. Calif. Youth Authority, 1986-91. Editor: Master Teacher and Supervisor in Clinical Social Work, 1982; author report Legal Issues of Female Inmates, 1981, model for rsch. Diversion program Female Inmates, 1984, Children of Incarcerated Parents, 1995. Vice chair United Way, Northampton, 1982-83; chair Mayor's Task Force, Northampton, 1981. Mem. Nat. Assn. Social Work, Acad. Cert. Social Workers, Nat. Assn. Edn. Young Children, Western Assn. Schs. and Colls., Pasadena C. of C., Athenaeum, Pasadena Rotary Club. Democrat. Presbyterian. Avocations: collecting, S.W. Indian art, aviary. E-mail: gabelk@prodigy.net.

GABELER, JO, artist; b. Baton Rouge, Feb. 14, 1931; d. Gustav Adolph Jr. and Ruth Hart Stein; m. Charles Pierce Gabeler Jr., Feb. 17, 1951 (div. Feb. 1973); children: Ann Speed, Charles Pierce III, T. Dolph, Caroline Hart. BA, Stephens Coll., 1950; studied with Edward Betts, Judi Betts, Al Brouillete, Jeanne Dobie, Ray Ellis, Dong Kingman, Fred Messersmith, Tony Van Hasselt, Millard Wells, Charles Reid. Illustrator: (with others) The Golf Courses at the Landings on Skidaway Island, 1993, The Galley Collection, 1998. One-woman shows include Elliott Mus., Stuart, Fla., 1986, Scarborough House, Savannah, 1988, John Tucker Fine Arts, 2000; exhibited in two-person show Al Stine Gallery, Anderson, S.C., 2002; exhibited in group shows at Fla. Watercolor Soc., Mus. Arts and Scis., Daytona, Fla., 1978, Brevard Art Ctr. and Mus., Melbourne, 1981, State Capitol, Tallahassee, 1982, Boca Raton Mus. Art, 1984, 86, Houston Pub. Libr., 1981, Galveston (Tex.) Art League, 1983; represented in permanent collections The Moody Found., Elliott Mus., The Rosenberg Libr., Transco Energy Co. Houston, Allied Bank of Seabrook, Tex. Now Hang with the Dolphin and the Mermaid, Thunderbolt, Georgia, Gallery 209, Savannah, 2004. Mem. Fla. Watercolor Soc. (Pres.'s award 1981, 82, Purchase award 1986, signature life mem.), Salmagundi Club, Galveston Art League (pres. 1981-82, Purchase award 1982), Profl. Artist Guild, Landings Art Assn. (pres. 1990). Home: 11 Mainsail Xing Savannah GA 31411-2723 Office: Gallery 209 209 River St Savannah GA 31401 Home Fax: 912-598-9817.

GABLE, KAREN ELAINE, health science educator; b. Des Moines, Nov. 12, 1939; d. John E. and Mabel I. (Davis) Clay; m. Robert W. Gable, Jr., Feb. 4, 1961; children: Susan Kay, Barbara Lynne, R. J. Kent. AS, 1969; BS in Edn., Ind. U., Indpls., 1976, MS in Edn., 1979, EdD, 1985. Registered dental hygienist Ind. U., cert. dental asst. Ind. U. From clin. instr. dental hygiene program Sch. Dentistry to assoc. prof. Ind. U., Indpls., 1976—94, assoc. prof. Sch. Health and Rehab. Scis., 1994—, program dir., 1994—2003, chair dept. health sci., 2002—. Contbr. articles to profl. jours. Recipient Disting. Dental Hygiene Alumna award, Ind. U. Sch. Dentistry. Mem.: ACTE/Health Occupations Edn. (mem. policy bd. 2002—), Ind. Career and Tech. Edn. Assn. (Outstanding Svc. awards), Ind. Dental Hygienists Assn. (sec.), Ind. Health Careers Assn. (pres.-elect, pres.), Health Occupations, Supvs. and Tchr. Educators Coun. (treas., pres.), Sigma Phi Alpha. Office Phone: 317-278-1353.

GABLES, SHON, newscaster; 1 child. BA in econs., U. Okla., 1992. News dir., host KVSP Radio, Oklahoma City; assoc. prodr. KWTV; morning news anchor, gen. assignment reporter WDIV-TV, Detroit; co-anchor CBS 2 News This Morning, NY, 2003—. Mem. bd. Youth-At-Risk, NY; mentor VIP Mentoring. Reservist U.S. Army. Recipient NYC Excellence in Media award, 2003, Lee Evans Outstanding Journalist award, 2003. Office: WCBS-TV 524 W 57 St New York NY 10019*

GABLIK, SUZI, art educator, writer; b. N.Y.C., Sept. 26, 1934; d. Anthony Julius and Geraldine (Schwartz) G. BA, Hunter Coll., 1955. Vis. prof. art Sydney Coll. Arts, 1980, U. of the South, Sewanee, Tenn., 1982, 84, U. Calif., Santa Barbara, 1985, 86, 88, Va. Commonwealth U., Richmond, 1987, Va. Tech., Blacksburg, 1990, U. Colo., Boulder, 1990. Endowed lectr. U. Victoria, B.C., 1983, Colo. Coll., 1983, U. Santa Barbara, 1985, Va. Tech., 1989. Author: Magritte, 1979, Has Modernism Failed?, 1984, The Reenchantment of Art, 1991, Conversations Before the End of Time, 1995, Living the Magical Life, 2002. Recipient Lifetime Achievement award, Women's Caucus for Art, 2003. Home: 3271 Deer Run Rd Blacksburg VA 24060-9075 E-mail: suzi@swva.net.

GABOR, ZSA ZSA (SARI GABOR), actress, cosmetics executive; b. Budapest, Hungary, Feb. 6, 1917; m. Conrad Hilton (div.); 1 child, Francesca Hilton; m. George Sanders (div.); m. Prince Frederick von Anholt, 1986. Ed. in., Budapest and Lausanne, Switzerland. Chmn. bd. Zsa Zsa Ltd. Stage debut, Europe; appeared in motion pictures Lovely to Look At, We're Not Married, The Story of Three Loves, Lili, Moulin Rouge, Three Ring Circus, Death of a Scoundrel, Girl in the Kremlin, For the First Time, Boys Night Out, 1962, Picture Mommy Dead, 1966, Jack of Diamonds, 1967, Won Ton Ton, The Dog Who Saved Hollywood, 1976, Hollywood, Here I Come, 1980, A Nightmare on Elm Street 3: Dream Warriors, 1987, Happily Ever After (voice), 1990, Naked Gun 2 1/2: The Smell of Fear, 1991, The Naked Truth, 1992, Est & Ouest: Les Paradis Perdus, 1993, The Beverly Hillbillies, 1993, A Very Brady Sequel, 1996; star stage prodn. Arsenic and Old Lace, 1975; author: Zsa Zsa's Complete Guide to Men, 1969, How to Get a Man, How to Keep a Man, How to Get Rid of a Man, 1971, one lifetime is not enough, 1991; exercise video: It's Simple, Darling, 1993.

GABOW, PATRICIA ANNE, internist; b. Starke, Fla., Jan. 8, 1944; m. Harold N. Gabow, June 21, 1971; children: Tenaya Louise, Aaron Patrick. BA in Biology, Seton Hill Coll., 1965; MD, U. Pa. Sch. Medicine, 1969. Diplomate Am. Bd. Internal Medicine, Am. Bd. Nephrology, Nat. Bd. Med. Examiners; lic. Colo. Internship in medicine Hosp. of U. of Pa., 1969-70; residency in internal medicine Harbor Gen. Hosp., 1970-71; renal fellowship San Francisco Gen. Hosp. and Hosp. of U. Pa., 1971-72, 72-73; instr. medicine divsn. renal diseases, asst. prof. U. Colo. Health Scis. Ctr., 1973-74, 74-79, assoc. prof. medicine divsn. renal diseases, prof., 1979-87; chief renal disease, clin. dir. dept. medicine Denver Gen. Hosp., 1973-81, 76-81, dir. med. svcs., 1981-91; CEO, med. dir. Denver Health and Hosps., 1992—. Intensive care com. Denver Gen. Hosp., 1976-81, med. records com., 1979-80, ind. rev. com., 1978-81, continuing med. edn. com., 1981-83, animal care com., 1979-83; student adv. com. U. Colo. Health Scis. Ctr., 1982-87, faculty senate, 1985, 86, internship adv. com., 1977-92; exec. com. Denver Gen. Hosp., 1981—, chmn. health resources com., 1988-90, chmn. pathology search com., 1989, chmn. faculty practice plan steering com., 1990-92. Mem. editorial bd. EMERGINDEX, 1983-93, Am. Jour. of Kidney Disease, 1984-96, Western Jour. of Medicine, 1987-98, Annals of Internal Medicine, 1988-91, Jour. of the Am. Soc. of Nephrology, 1990-97; contbr. numerous articles, revs. and editorials to profl. publs., chpts. to books. Mem. Mayor's Safe City Task Force, 1993; mem. sci. adv. bd. Polycystic Kidney Rsch. Found., 1984-96, chmn., 1991; mem. sci. adv. bd. Nat. Kidney Found., 1991-94; mem. Nat. Pub. Health and Hosps. Inst. Bd., 1993-2001, 03—. Recipient Sullivan award for Highest Acad. Average in Graduating Class, Seton Hill Coll., 1965, Pa. State Senatorial scholarship, 1961-65, Kaiser Permanente award for Excellence in Tchg., 1976, Ann. award to Outstanding Woman Physician, 1982, Kaiser Permanente Nominee for Excellence in Tchg. award, 1983, Seton Hill Coll. [illegible] Alumna Leadership award, 1990, Florence Rena Sabin award U. Colo., 2000, Nathan Davis award AMA, 2000, Good Housekeeping Women in Govt. award, 2002; named one of The Best Doctors in Am., 1994-95, 2002; grantee Bonfils Found., 1985-86, NIH, 1985-90, 91-96, 96-2000, W.K. Kellogg Found., 1997—, AHRQ, 2000-03; named to Colo. Women's Hall of Fame, 2004. Mem. Denver Med. Soc., Colo. Med. Soc., Am. Fedn. Clin. Rsch., Am. Physiol. Soc., Polycystic Kidney Disease Rsch. Found. (sci. advisor 1984-96), Western Assn. Physicians, Nat. Kidney Found. (sci. adv. bd. 1987-91), Women's Forum of Colo., Inc., Assn. Am. Physicians. Roman Catholic. Office: Denver Health 660 Bannock St Denver CO 80204-4506

GABRIEL, JUDITH A. bodywork therapist, educator, writer; b. Reading, Pa., July 14, 1949; d. Daniel Jacob and Alma Geraldine (Wengel) Tobias; m. Cleon Jay Hertzog, Oct. 5, 1974 (div. 1987). BS, Kutztown U., 1971, MEd, 1977; cert. massage therapist, Pa. Sch. Muscle Therapy, Phila., 1989; further tng., U.S. and Sweden. Cert. tchr. Pa., bodywork therapist. Tchr. Hamburg (Pa.) Area Sch. Dist., 1971-96; bodywork therapist, owner, operator Judith Gabriel Integrational Bodywork, Reading, Pa., 1989—; Rebirther (breathwork counseling) Reading, Pa., 1988—. Presenter WIOV Radio, 1997; asst. Patrick Collard's Internat. Apprenticeship, 1997, 98, 99; prodr. concert A Tribute to John Denver: The Man and His Music, Kempton, Pa., 2000; prodr. A Tribute to John Denver: The Man and His Music concert, Kempton, Pa., 2001; organizer Hibernia County Park, Pa., 2002; pres., CEO, The John Denver Meml. Found., Inc.; presenter Tuly's Conf. for Women, Reading, Pa., 2003; prodr., pres./CEO John Denver Meml. Found., Inc.; prodr. concert A Tribute to John Denver: The Man and His Music, Hibernia County Park, Pa., 2002; presenter Tulip Conf. for Women, Reading, Pa., 2003. Choir singer various chs., Reading; stress mgmt. demonstrator Berks Advocates Against Violence, Reading, 1997. Recipient Corp. Achiever award, Multiple Sclerosis Found., 2002. Mem.: Berks C. of C., Assoc. Bodyworkers and Massage Profls. (cert. massage therapist, cert. bodywork therapist). Avocations: reading, walking, singing, meditation, travel.

GADBERRY, VICKI LYNN HIMES, librarian; b. Frederick, Md., Jan. 3, 1950; d. Guilford Swisher and Eloise Alberta (Twentey) Himes; m. Eric Brett Gadberry, Aug. 15, 1971. BS, U. Md., 1971; MLS, U. S.C., 1974; postgrad., Penland Sch. Crafts, 1989, 96, Sul Ross State U., 1997-98. Cert. media coord. N.C. Dept. Pub. Instrn. Media coord. N.C. Pub. Schs., Fayetteville, 1976-78, Hendersonville, 1980-85, Asheville, 1985-88; pub. svcs. coord. Mars Hill (N.C.) Coll., 1990-92, reference svcs. libr., 1992-97; asst. exec. dir., adminstrn. Fort Davis (Tex.) C. of C., 1998—; owner Off The Wall Photos & Art, 2001—. On-site dir. Children's Art in the Mountains Program, Marshall, N.C., summer 1992, tchr. fiber art, summer 1990; artist-in-residence Mountain Arts Program, Waynesville, N.C., 1990. Project designer book: Molas!, 1998; contbr. articles, revs., index to profl. publs. Mem. planning com. Beacon Handloom Weaving Show, Asheville, N.C., 1988, 90-92, chair, 1989; bd. dirs. Children's Art in the Mountains Program, Marshall, N.C., 1991-93. Mem. Handweaver's Guild Am. (orgnl. C.O.E. Weaving com. co-chair 1992-94). Avocations: weaving, photography. Home: PO Box 393 Fort Davis TX 79734-0393 E-mail: gadberry@overland.net.

GADDIS ROSE, MARILYN, literature educator, translator; b. Fayette, Mo., Apr. 2, 1930; d. Merrill Elmer and Florence Georgia (Lyon) Gaddis; m. James Leo Rose, Dec. 23, 1956 (div. 1966); m. Stephen David Ross, Nov. 16, 1968; 1 child, David Gaddis Ross. BA, Central Meth. Coll., 1952; MA, U. S.C., Columbia, 1954-55; PhD, U. Mo., 1958; LHD, Ctrl. Meth. Coll., 1987. Instr. Stephens Coll., Columbia, Mo., 1958-68; assoc. prof. Ind. U., Bloomington, 1968; prof. comparative lit. SUNY, Binghamton, 1968—, disting. svc. prof., 1991—, dir. translation program, 1973—2002. Translator: (book) Axel, 1970, 1986, Eve of the Future Eden, 1981, Lui: A View of Him, 1986, Adrienne Mesurat, 1991, Volupté, The Sensual Man, 1995, Translation Horizon, 1996, Translation and Literary Criticism, 1998, Beyond the Western Tradition, 2000; editor, contbr.: book Translation Spectrum, 1981; editor: Translation Perspectives; contbr. articles to profl. jours. Fulbright fellow, U. Lyon, France, 1953—54, Humanities Rsch. Centre Sr. fellow, Australian Nat. U., 1977. Mem.: MLA (del. assembly 1974—78, pres. N.E. sect. 1975—76, del. assembly 1984—87, exec. coun. 2004—), Am. Translators Assn. (bd. dirs. 1986—88, mng. editor series 1986—96, endowed lectr. 1998—, Spl. Svc. award 1983, 1995, Alexander Gode award 1988), Am. Lit. Translators (sec.-treas. 1981—83), PEN N.Y. Home: 5 Riverside Dr Apt 204 Binghamton NY 13905-4644 E-mail: mgrose@binghamton.edu.

GADIESH, ORIT, management consulting executive; b. Haifa, Israel, Jan. 31; BA in psychology, Hebrew U., Israel, 1973; MBA, Harvard Bus. Sch., 1977. With Israeli Army; asst. prof. Hebrew U., Israel; with Bain & Co., Boston, 1977—, head Boston office, 1991—93, chmn., 1993—. Mem.: Coun. Fgn. Rels. Office: Bain & Co Two Copley Pl Boston MA 02116

GAETANO, JOY M. human resources executive; BA, Youngstown State U.; MS, Case Western Reserve U.; MBA coursework, Rider Coll. West region human resource mgr. U.S. Filter Corp., 1995—96, dir. human resources, v.p. human resources, sr. v.p. corp. human resources, 1999—. Office: US Filter Corp 181 Thornhill Rd Warrendale PA 15086

GAFFIN, JOAN VALERIE, secondary school educator; b. N.Y.C., Nov. 25, 1947; d. William John and Louise Eleanor (Liebig) Philibert; m. Ira Martin Gaffin, May 7, 1981. BS in Bus. Edn., Rider U., 1971; MA in Student Personnel Svcs., Montclair State U., 1978. Cert. coop. bus. edn. coord., bus. edn. adminstr. and coord. Bus. edn. instr., coord. Econ. Manpower Corp., N.Y.C., 1971-72; bus. edn. coord., educator Northern Valley Regional H.S., Old Tappan, N.J., 1972—; gymnastics instr. Twp. of Teaneck, NJ, 1985—2000. Adj. grad. prof. Montclair State U., Upper Montclair, NJ, 1994—. Recipient Outstanding Tchr. of the Yr. award, N.J. Gov., 1986. Mem.: NEA, Nothern Valley Edn. Assn. (sec. 1978—80, 1985—86, 1991—92, Tchr. Recognition award 1990—91), N.E. Bergen Ind. Assn. (treas., bd. dirs. 1978—), N.J. Coop. Bus. Edn. Coords. Assn. (Bergen sector sec., pres., Coord. of the Yr. 1993), Eastern Bus. Edn. Assn. (Educator of the Yr. 1993), N.J. Edn. Assn., N.J. Bus. Edn. Assn. (mem. legis. com. 1990—92, bd. dirs. 1991—95, chmn. critical issues task force 1991—95, N.J. Bus. Tchr. of the Yr. 1993), Nat. Bus. Edn. Assn. Avocations: traveling, reading, cooking, exercising, antiquing. Home: 852 W Crescent Ave Allendale NJ 07401-2129 Office: Northern Valley Regional HS 140 Central Ave Old Tappan NJ 07677 Office Phone: 201-784-1600 4450. Business E-Mail: gaffin@nvnet.org.

GAFFNEY, ELIZABETH MALLORY, editor, writer, literature educator, translator; b. N.Y.C., N.Y., Dec. 22, 1966; d. Richard Waring and Ann Walker Gaffney; m. Alexis David Boro, July 15, 1995. BA, Vassar Coll., 1988; MFA, Bklyn. Coll., 1997. Mem. editl. staff The Paris Rev., N.Y.C., 1988—93, mng. editor, 1993—95, editor-at-large, 1995—, also trustee. Writing tchr. NYU, N.Y.C., 1997—. Translator: The Arbogast Case, 2003, The Pollen Room, 1998, Invisible Woman, 2000, author short stories. Resident/fellow, MacDowell Colony, Peterborough, N.H., 1996, 1997, Blue Mountain (N.Y.) Ctr., 1999, Yaddo, Saratoga Springs, N.Y., 2000, 2001. Mem.: Phi Beta Kappa. Democrat. Avocations: hiking, kayaking, bicycling, camping. Office: The Paris Rev 541 E 72 St New York NY 10021

GAGAN, JAMIE LISA, emergency physician, artist; b. Portland, Maine, July 21, 1954; d. James Ephraim Gagan and Gertrude Durgin; m. Alan S. Rogers, June 12, 1993; 1 child, Emma Francesca Gagan Rogers. BS in Biochemistry, U. Vt., 1976, MD, 1982. Bd. cert. emergency medicine Am. Bd. Med. [illegible] physician St. Vincent Hosp., Santa Fe, 1987—, med. dir. sexual assault nurse examiner program, 1997—. Assoc. prof. family and cmty. medicine U. N.Mex., Albuquerque, 1988—; staff physician Santa Fe AIDS Wellness Program, 1988—94; med. dir. Santa Fe County EMS, 1990—96; mem. mentoring program dept. emergency medicine St. Vincent Hosp., Santa Fe, 1999—. Recipient 2nd pl. mixed media award, Steamboat Springs (Colo.) Arts Coun., 2000; scholar, Joseph Collins Found., 1979—82. Fellow: Am. Coll. Emergency Physicians; mem.: Physicians for Human Rights, N.Mex. Coll. Emergency Physicians (signature mem.), N.Mex. Watercolor Soc. (Artisan's award 1999). Avocations: cooking, skiing, travel, art. Home: PO Box 803 Tesuque NM 87574 Office: St Vincent Hosp 455 St Michaels Dr Santa Fe NM 87505

GAGE, BEAU, artist; b. Rye, N.Y., Dec. 3, 1945; d. John Alden and Frances (Johnston) G.; m. Glenn A. Ousterhout, May 24,1980. BA, St. John's Coll., Santa Fe and Annapolis, Md., 1971; student, Internat. Ctr. Photography, N.Y.C., 1981-82, 82-83, Art Students League N.Y., 1983-87, The Sculpture Ctr. Sch., N.Y.C., 1985-87, Nat. Acad. Design, 1988-89. Staff asst. to the pres. The White House, Washington, 1972-73; key accounts mgr. Sterling Drug, Inc., Montvale, N.J., 1975-79. Works exhibited at Internat. Ctr. Photography, 1981-83, Art Students League, 1984-87, The Sculpture Ctr., 1985-87, Westbeth Gallery, N.Y.C., 1984, 86, Sotheby's Auction House, 1990, others; permanent pub. sculpture Jacksonville (Fla.) Jaguars, Inc.; permanent exhbn. Jacksonville Mus. Sci. & History. Supporter, guild mem. Martha Graham Dance Co., N.Y.C., 1989—; canopy assoc. Rainforest Alliance, 2000—; mem. adv. bd. Buglisi/Foreman Dance Co., N.Y.C., 2001—; leader Perlman Music Program, N.Y.C., 2001—. Fellow Mus. Modern Art; mem. Met. Mus. Art, Internat. Ctr. Photography, Orgn. Ind. Artists, The Nature Conservancy, Mass. Soc. Mayflower Descendants, Poets House (N.Y.C.). Avocations: astronomy, sailing, yoga. Home: 320 E 46th St Apt 34E New York NY 10017-3039 E-mail: beau7gage@aol.com.

GAGE, MIRIAM BETTS, retired nutritionist; b. Nelsonville, Ohio, Jan. 9, 1928; d. Charles Donald and Lillian Mary (Linscott) B.; m. Robert Averill Gowdy, Oct. 12, 1950 (div. 1977); children: Carol Jo, Robert Jr., Bruce; m. George Joel Gage, Aug. 16, 1997. BA in Home Econs., Ohio Wesleyan U., 1949; postgrad., Duke U., 1949-50, Calif. State U., L.A., 1975-76. Registered dietitian. Pvt. practice dietitian, L.A., 1977-91; cons. Nat.-in-Home Health, Van Nuys, Calif., 1984-87; clin. dietitian Lake Mead Hosp., 1991-94; pvt. practice Las Vegas, Nev., 1994-97; contract dietitian Pulse Health Svcs., Las Vegas, 1995-97; ret., 1997. Mem. Am. Diabetes Assn. (con. San Fernando Valley unit 1976-80, bd. dirs. N.W. chpt. 1977-82), Nev. Dietetic Assn. (nominating com. 1995-97), So. Nev. Dietetic Assn. (mem. chmn. 1991-92, pres. 1993-94), Cons. Nutritionists (chmn.-elect So. Calif. chpt. 1979-81), Calif. Dietetic Assn. (chmn. diabetes care practice 1979-81), Am. Heart Assn. (governing bd. N.W. chpt. 1988-89). Republican. Methodist. Home: 10813 Brinkwood Ave Las Vegas NV 89134-5248 Business E-Mail: miriamgage@acninc.net.

GAGEN, GINA, psychotherapist; d. John David and Barbara Jeanne Gagen. BA in Psychology, BA in Sociology, Ea. Ill. U., 1984; MA in Psychology, Our Lady of the Lake U., 1999; MA in Health Care Adminstrn., Tex. Woman's U. Asistant gen. mgr. Hearthstone Assisted Living, Houston, 1998—2000; caseworker ii Tex. Dept. of Protective and Regulatory Svcs., Houston, 2000; counselor Mitchell Group Homes, Peterborough, Canada, 2001; intake counselor United Behavioral Health, Houston, 2002—. Vol. Houston (Tex.) Area Women's Ctr. Mem.: APA (assoc.), Am. Assn. of Marriage and Family Therapists (assoc.), Tex. Assn. of Marriage and Family Therapists (assoc.), Psi Chi (life). Methodist. Avocations: travel, scuba diving, swimming.

GAGNE, MARY, academic administrator; Dir. Tex. Acad. Leadership in the Humanities Lamar U., Beaumont, 1998—. Recipient Blue Ribbon awards U.S. Dept. Edn., 1986-87, 90-91, Exec. Educator Best Prin. award, Nat. Tchg. award NCEA, Coca Cola Educator of Distinction award. 2000. Address: PO Box 10062 Beaumont TX 77710-0062 E-mail: gagneml@hal.lamar.edu.

GAGNE, NANCY LYNN, music educator, musician; b. Everett, Mass., Nov. 6, 1962; d. William Donald and Carolyn Mildred Wilderman; m. James Michael Gagne, Dec. 31, 1988. MusB, Crane Sch. of Music, 1980—84; MusM, Hartt Sch. of Music, 1987—89. Cert. Music K-12 State of NY, 1984. Instrumental music tchr. New Lebanon Ctrl. Schools, NY, 1984—87; tchr. of woodwind techniques Hartt Sch. of Music, Hartford, Conn., 1987—89; instrumental music tchr. Webutuck Ctrl. Schools, Amenia, NY, 1989—. Pre-k spl. ed music cons. Region One Sch. Dist., Falls Village, Conn., 1989; dir. summer day camp Town of Nassau, NY, 1985—87; v.p. Dutchess County Music Educators Assn., Poughkeepsie, NY, 1994—96, pres., 1996—98; bassoonist Pandean Wind Quintet, Hudson, NY, 1994—, Barocco Wind Trio, Red Hook, NY, 1996—. Musician: Chatham Theater Co., Stissing Theater Guild, Webutuck Drama Soc.; conductor (plays) Once Upon A Mattress; dir.: (plays) Little Shop of Horrors; guest conductor (concert) Columbia County All-County Festival. Mem. adminstrv. coun. Hillsdale United Meth. Ch., NY, 1994—98; mem. pastor-parish rels. com. United Meth. Ch., Hillsdale, NY, 1994—98, communion steward Craryville, NY, 1999; mem. Rockland County Girl Scouts, New City, NY, 1978—80. Recipient Crane Departmental scholar, Crane Sch. of Music, 1984, Excellence in Tchg. Music, 1984; Full Tchg. assistantship, Hartt Sch. of Music, 1987—89. Mem.: Music Educators Nat. Conf., NY State Sch. Music Assn., Dutchess County Music Educators Assn. (pres. 1996—98), Pi Kappa Lambda. Protestant. Avocation: golf. Home: PO Box 655 Copake NY 12516 Office: Webutuck Central Schools Haight Rd Amenia NY 12501

GAGNON, LAURA CHRISTINE, financial analyst; b. Lakefield, Minn., Aug. 17, 1961; d. Arlo Theodore Jochims and Margaret Mary Klingsporn; m. Joseph Widlund Gagnon, May 5, 1990; children: Maria, Joseph, John, Samuel. BS, Winona State U.; MBA, Vanderbilt U., 1986. Analyst, portfolio mgr. St. Paul Cos., Inc., 1986—95, asst. v.p., v.p. corp. planning, 1995—99, v.p. investor rels., 1999—. Mem.: Nat. Investor Rels. Inst., Twin Cities Soc. Security Analysts, Assn. Investment Mgmt. Rsch., Assn. Ins. and Fin. Analysts. Republican. Roman Catholic. Avocations: teaching religious education, golf, fishing. Office: St Paul Cos Inc 385 Washington St Saint Paul MN 55102 E-mail: laura.gagnon@stpaul.com.

GAHALA, ESTELLA MARIE, writer, consultant; b. Alva, Okla., Mar. 28, 1929; d. Ivan Grant Crouse and Margaret Estella Beck; m. Dale Lowell Lange, Apr. 17, 1998; m. John W. Gahala, Nov. 27, 1964 (dec. Aug. 1, 1989). BA magna cum laude, Wichita (Kans.) State U., 1953; MA, Middlebury (Vt.) Coll., 1963; PhD, Northwestern U., 1980. Tchr. Highland Pk. HS, Topeka, 1953—57, Amarillo (Tex.) HS, 1957—60, Glenbrook North HS, Northbrook, Ill., 1960—64; dept. chmn. Evanston (Ill.) Township HS, 1964—73; dir. curriculum Lyons Township HS, LaGrange, Ill., 1973—84; author, cons. Scott Foresman Pub., Glenview, Ill., 1984—94, McDougal Littell Pub., Boston, 1994—. Pres. Gahala Assocs., Pk. Ridge, Ill., 1980—96. Author: Son et Sens, 1984, Dis-moi, 1993, En Español, 2000; contbr. articles to profl. jours. Chpt. pres. Am. Assn. Tchrs. French, 1970—72, mem. exec. coun., 1976—81; vol. Albuquerque (N.Mex.) Mus. Art, 1987—2003, Presbyn. Hospice Care, Albuquerque, 1991—2003. Named Chevalier Palmes Académiques, French Ministry Edn., 1975. Mem.: Am. Coun. Fgn. Langs. Democrat. Avocations: art, genealogy, working with homeless and abused women. Home and Office: 2315 Madre Drive NE Albuquerque NM 87112

GAIA, JENNIFER T. customer support specialist; b. Memphis, Tenn., June 30, 1977; d. Gerald W. and Glenda T. Tatum; m. Richard A. Gaia. Attended, Christian Bros. U., 1995—96; BA, U. Memphis, 2001. Customer svc. supr. Terminix Internat. Co., L.P., Memphis, 1995—98; ops. planning analyst Stream Internat., Memphis, 1998—99; call ctr. shift mgr. PlanetRx-.com Inc., Memphis, 1999—2001; customer care team mgr. TeleCorp PCS, Memphis, 2001—01; workforce mgr. Scholastic, Inc., Jefferson City, Mo., 2001—03; customer support spec. Schering-Plough, Inc., Memphis, 2003—. Scholar Presdl. Scholarship, Christian Bros. U., 1995. Mem.: NAFE, Soc. Workforce Planning Profls.

GAILEY, JOAN DALE, retired finance educator; b. Beaver Falls, Pa., May 10, 1940; d. Irvin D. and Elizabeth Jane (Hollander) Anderson; m. Ronald L. Gailey, Aug. 15, 1957; 1 child, Ronald. BSBA, Geneva Coll., 1975; MBA, Youngstown State U., 1980; PhD, U. Pitts., 1987. Libr. tech. Community Coll. Beaver County, Monaca, Pa., 1969-74; customer liaison, floor supr. LTV Steel, Aliquippa, Pa., 1975-79; instr. Youngstown (Ohio) State U., 1980-83; asst. prof. bus. mgmt. Kent State U., East Liverpool, Ohio, 1984-91, assoc. prof. bus. mgmt., 1992—, prof. bus. mgmt., 1998—, prof. Trumbull campus Warren, Ohio, 2001—02, prof. East Liverpool campus, 2003, prof. emeritus, 2003. Cons. in bus. mgmt., 1988—; dir. Kent State East Liverpool Bus. Resource Ctr. Abstract editor Interface, 1994, 95, 96, 97, proceedings editor, 1998; co-editor: Humanities and Technology Rev., 1999—; contbr. articles to profl. jours. Mem. Rochester (Pa.) Area Planning Commn., 1989, Rochester Area Mktg. Com., 1990; tutor Adult Lit. Coun., Monaca, 1984-91; mem. adv. bd. Ret. Sr. Vol. Program, Lisbon, Ohio, 1990, vice chair, 1993-2000, facilitator Columbiana County Mini-Loan Fund, 1994-96. Recipient Kent State Teaching Devel. award, 1990, Kent State Profl. Devel. award, 1992; tchg. coun. grantee Kent State U., 1997-98, Summer award Univ. Tchg. Coun., 1999. Mem. Am. Ednl. Rsch. Assn. (editor newsletter 1993-94, program chair 1992), Nat. Assn. Indsl. Tech., Midwest MLA, Ohio Bus. Tchrs. Assn., Humanities and Tech. Assn. (exec. bd. dirs. 1997—), Assn. for Bus. Comm., Alpha Mu (Outstanding Mktg. Tchr. 1983). Office: Kent State U East Liverpool OH E-mail: jgailey@kent.edu.

GAILLARD, MARY KATHARINE, physics educator; b. New Brunswick, N.J., Apr. 1, 1939; d. Philip Lee and Marion Catharine (Wiedemayer) Ralph; children: Alain, Dominique, Bruno. BA, Hollins (Va.) Coll., 1960; MA, Columbia U., 1961; Dr du Troiseme Cycle, U. Paris, Orsay, France, 1964, Dr-es-Sciences d'Etat, 1968. With Ctr. Nat. Rsch. Sci., Orsay and Annecy-le-Vieux, France, 1964-84, head rsch. Orsay, 1973-80, Annecy-le-Vieux, 1979-80, dir. rsch., 1980-84; prof. physics, sr. faculty staff Lawrence Berkeley lab. U. Calif., Berkeley, 1981—. Morris Loeb lectr. Harvard U., Cambridge, Mass., 1980; Chancellor's Disting. lectr., U. Calif., Berkeley, 1981; Warner-Lambert lectr. U. Mich., Ann Arbor, 1984; vis. scientist Fermi Nat. Accelerator Lab., Batavia, Ill., 1973 74, Inst. for Advanced Studies, Santa Barbara, Calif., 1984, U. Calif., Santa Barbara, 1985; group leader L.A.P.P., Theory Group, France, 1979-81, Theory Physics div. LBL, Berkeley, 1985-87; sci. dir. Les Houches (France) Summer Sch., 1981; cons., mem. adv. panels U.S. Dept. Energy, Washington; cons. Nat. Sci. Bd., 1996-97, 2002, bd. dirs., 1997-2002. Co-editor: Weak Interactions, 1977, Gauge Theories in High Energy Physics, 1983; contr. articles to profl. jours. Recipient Thibaux prize U. Lyons (France) Acad. Art and Sci., 1977, E.O. Lawrence award, 1988, J.J. Sakurai prize for theoretical particle physics, APS, 1993; Guggenheim fellow, 1989-90. Fellow Am. Acad. Arts and Scis., Am. Phys. Soc. (mem. various coms., chair com. on women, J.J. Sakurai prize 1993); mem. AAAS, NAS, Am. Philos. Soc. Office: U Calif Dept Physics Berkeley CA 94720-0001

GAINES, BARBARA, theater director; Degree, Northwestern U., 1969. Founding artistic dir. Chgo. (Ill.) Shakespeare Theatre, 1997—. Artistic dir. Globe Theatre, London; bd. trustees Northwestern U.; panel me. NEA. Mem. editl. bd.: Chgo. (Ill.) Reporter. Recipient Jeff award. Office: Chicago Shakespeare Theatre 800 E Grand Ave Chicago IL 60611*

GAINES, BRENDA, financial services company executive; Formerly with U.S. Dept. Housing & Urban Develop., Chgo.; former head Chgo. Housing Authority; past dep. chief staff Office of Mayor, Harold Washington, Chgo.; advanced through co. in govt. and cmty. rels. to sr. v.p. residential lending Citibank, Chgo., 1988—92; sr. v.p. Diners Club N.Am. (subsidiary of Citigroup), Chgo., 1992—99; pres. Diners Club N.Am., Chgo., 1999—. Mem. Diners Club Internat. Global bd. Office: Citicorp Diners Club NAm 8430 Bryn Mawr Ave Chicago IL 60631 E-mail: brenda.gaines@citicorp.com.

GAINES, KENDRA HOLLY, English language educator, editorial and writing consultant; b. Chgo., Dec. 6, 1946; d. Reuben B. and Frances P. Gaines; m. Kenneth C. Wolfgang, Feb. 18, 1989. BA with distinction, Mt. Holyoke Coll., 1968; MA with honor, Claremont Grad. Sch., 1971; MA, Northwestern U., 1974, PhD, 1982. Cert. life secondary and community coll. tchr., Calif., Ariz. Tchr. English, Claremont (Calif.) Collegiate Sch., 1969-72; teaching asst. Northwestern U., Evanston, Ill., 1975-78; instr. English, U. Mich., Ann Arbor, 1978-79; assoc. editor Scott, Foresman Co., Glenview, 1983-85; instr. English, sr. career tutor U. Ariz., Tucson, 1985—2002, mgr. Grad. Writing Resource website, 2002—; instr., faculty advisor Pima Cmty. Coll., Davis-Monthan AFB, Ariz., 1987—2002. Head Grad. Writing Inst., U. Ariz., 1996—2002; editl. cons., freelance writer, 1969—; lectr. Suzhou U., Nanjing Normal U., China, 1999; mem. adv. bd. translation studies Pima C.C.; writing cons. U. Ariz. Coll. Law; trainer S.W. Gas Corp.; writing cons. to Arizona Daily Star newspaper, Tucson, 2002—. Contbr. articles to various publs.; writer radio scripts Holiday World of Travel, 1969—2000. Elected to The Imperial Russian Order of St. John of Jerusalem Ecumenical Found. (Knights of Malta), N.Y.; grantee State of Calif., 1970; Mills fellow, 1971; fellow Northwestern U., 1973-76. Mem. MLA, Nat. Coun. Tchrs. English, AAUW. Avocations: travel, photography, music, creative writing, aerobics. Home: 925 N Jerrie Ave Tucson AZ 85711-1153 Office: U Ariz Grad Coll Tucson AZ 85719 E-mail: kgaines@email.arizona.edu.

GAINES, LA DONNA ADRIAN See SUMMER, DONNA

GAINES-MASAK, ANNE FARLEY, artist, art educator; b. Grand Rapids, Mich., May 19, 1954; d. Ralph Clay and Nancy Bogue (Farley) G.; m. David Michael Masak, Nov. 26, 1999; stepchildren: Chad, Ryan. BA magna cum laude, Principia Coll., 1976; MA, MFA, Bowling Green State U., 1980. Instr. in color theory and fashion drawing Internat. Acad. Design and Tech., Chgo., 1987-92, 2000—; commd. muralist Sara Lee Bakery Headqtrs., Chgo., 1992-93; artist in residence Chgo. Jr. Sch., Elgin, Ill., 1993-94, art tchr. grades 1-8, 1994-95; vis. asst. prof. art Ripon (Wis.) Coll., 1995-97; adj. prof. of art and humanities Moraine Valley C.C., Palos Hills, Ill., 1997-99. Vis. scholar Principia Coll., Elsah, Ill., 1989; owner, artist Pilsen Screens, Chgo., 1990—; mem. adv. bd. Collegiate Press, 1998—; instr. at art workshops, Chgo., Mich., Fla. Illustrator: (book) From Greek to Graffiti, English Words that Survive and Thrive, 1981, (cover design) A Walking Tour of Wicker Park by Elaine Coorens, 2003; artist solo exhbns. include Lighthouse Gallery, Tequesta, Fla., 1983, South Haven (Mich.) Ctr. for Fine Arts, 1990, Wilderness at A.R.C. Gallery, Chgo., 1995, Strange Yards and Other Eulogies, Harper Coll., Palatine, Ill., Outer Depictions/Inward Questions, De Caprio Gallery, Moraine Valley C.C., Palos Hills, Ill., 1997, A.R.C. Galllery, Chgo., 2000, (book cover) Wicker Park: A Walking Tour Guide, 2003; selected group exhbns.: Stockton State Coll., Pomona, N.J., 1985, Ill. State Mus., Springfield, 1985, Ukranian Inst. Art, Chgo., 1988, Alice and Arthur Baer Juried Competition, Beverly Art Ctr., Chgo., 1989, Quincy (Ill.) Art Ctr., 1989, Watercolor Alternatives -4 Chgo. artists- South Bend Art Ctr., Women's Art League Gallery, 1990, Botanics Gallery 10, Rockford, Ill. (1st place), 1991, Sacred Arts, Billy Graham Ctr. Mus., Wheaton (Ill.) Coll., 1992, Chgo. Botanic Gardens, Glencoe, Ill., 1992, Barrington (Ill.) Area Arts Coun. Gallery, 1993, Coll. Lake County, Grays Lake, Ill., 1993, Caestecker Gallery, Ripon (Wis.) Coll., 1995, P.E.A.C.E. Gallery, Chgo., 1996, Mus. Sci. and Industry, Chgo., 1996, Jacqueline Ross Gallery, Chgo., 1998; works in pub. collections: Thirteenth Floor Gallery, Chgo., 2000, Am. Nat. Bank, Chgo., Borg Warner, Chgo., Bowling Green (Ohio) State U., Ernst & Young, Chgo., G.A.T.X. Corp., Chgo., Harper Elem. Sch., Wilmette, Ill., Nat. Soc. Am. Colls. and Univs., Washington, D.C., Rockford Art Mus., Sara Lee Bakery, Chgo.; major commns. include 21 x 8 mural, Conf. Rm., Bowling Green (Ohio) State U., 1979, 4 20 x 12 painted solar fabric murals, Sara Lee Bakery, Chgo., 1992-93, mixed media installation and watercolors, office suite, Fox Valley Neurosurgery, McHenry Ill., 1995, 4 mixed-media panels Valley Hosp., Ridgewood, N.J., 1999, 5 x 8 painting mix media, 17th Church Christ, Chgo., 2001, 6 x 9 folding screen, Lockhart Nature Ctr., Lake Forest, Ill., 2001; chief designer, coord. set design PM&L Theater, Antioch, Ill. Lectr. com. chmn. 17th Ch. of Christ, Scientist, Chgo., 1996-98. Named Accomplished Grad. Honoree in Fine Arts, Bowling Green (Ohio) State U., 1992; grantee: Ill. Arts Coun., Chgo., 1986, Ripon (Wis.) Coll., 1995, 96. Mem. Nat. Assn. Women Bus. Owners, Coll. Art Assn., Women's Caucus for Arts, Chgo. Artists Coalition, A.R.C. Gallery (grant chmn., chair self-portrait show 1984-86), Pilsen Artists (chair open house 1981, 90, fund raising 1991-95). Avocations: playing classical piano, choral singing, gourmet cooking, renovating victorian houses. Home: 713 W 19th St Chicago IL 60616-1023 Office: Pilsen Screens 1839 S Halsted St Chicago IL 60608-3455 E-mail: gainesart@aol.com.

GAISSER, JULIA HAIG, classics educator; b. Cripple Creek, Colo., Jan. 12, 1941; d. Henry Wolseley and Gertrude Alice (Lent) Haig; m. Thomas Korff Gaisser, Dec. 29, 1964; 1 child, Thomas Wolseley. AB, Brown U., 1962; MA, Harvard U., 1966; PhD, U. Edinburgh, Scotland, 1966. Asst. prof. Newton (Mass.) Coll., 1966-69, Swarthmore (Pa.) Coll., 1970-72, Bklyn. Coll., 1973-75, assoc. prof. dept. Latin Bryn Mawr (Pa.) Coll., 1975-84, prof., 1984—. Martin Classical lectr. Oberlin Coll., 2000. Author: Catullus and his Renaissance Readers, 1993, Pierio Valeriano On the Ill Fortune of Learned Men, 1999, Catullus in English, 2001; editor Bryn Mawr Latin Commentaries, 1983—. Mem. Mid-East sel. com. Marshall Scholarships, Washington, 1975-89, chmn., 1984-89; mem. mng. com. Intercollegiate Ctr. for Classical Studies in Rome, Stanford, Calif., 1984-92, chmn., 1988-92. Decorated MBE; named Marshall scholar, U. Edinburgh, 1962—64, Phi Beta Kappa Vis. scholar, 1996—97, ACLS Travel grantee, 1985, fellow, ACLS, 1989—90, NEH sr. fellow, 1985—86, 1993—94, 1999; recipient NEH summer stipend, 1977, rsch. grantee, Am. Philos. Soc., 1980, 1993. Mem. Am. Philol. Assn. (dir. 1985-88, pres. 2000), Renaissance Soc. Am., Internat. Neo Latin Soc. Office: Bryn Mawr Coll Dept Latin Bryn Mawr PA 19010

GAJIC, RANKA PEJOVIC, secondary school educator; b. Mostar, Bosnia-Herzegovina, Apr. 30, 1928; came to U.S., 1953; d. Radovan Ilija and Darinka Ducic Pejovic; m. Sreten Gajic, Sept. 26, 1954 (dec. Apr. 1991). Student, Belgrade (Yugoslavia) U., 1947-52; B Art Edn., Northeastern Ill. U., 1973; M Slavic Langs. and Lit., U. Ill., Chgo., 1979, ABD, 1990; MLS, Chgo. State U., 1987; PhD in Edn., Century U., 1995. Acct. Field Enterprises Ednl. Corp., Chgo., 1955-59; ins. policy writer Alexander & Co. Ins., Chgo., 1959-64; fgn. ind. travel agt. Am. Express, Chgo., 1964-69; tchr. Chgo. Pub. Schs., 1974-84, 85—; tchg. asst. U. Ill., Chgo., 1984-85. Exhibited paintings in group shows at Northeastern Ill. U., Chgo., 1976 (3d prize) Mus. Sci. and Industry, Chgo., 1976 (Hon. Mention), North River Gallery, Chgo., 1977, 79 (2d prize 1977, Hon. Mention 1979). Chgo. State U. scholar, 1986; recipient Nat. Collegiate award U.S. Achievement Acad., 1987, Am. Medal of Honor ABI, 2000, Lifetime Achievement award IBC, Cambridge, Eng., 2002, Women of Yr. award ABI, 2002. Mem. Am. Assn. for Advancement of Slavic Studies, U. Ill. Alumni Assn. (life), Mus. Contemporary Art (comm. chair North Side Affiliates chpt. 1999—), Golden Key Nat. Honor Soc. Avocations: art, literature, languages, travel. Home: 5901 N Sheridan Rd Apt 12J Chicago IL 60660-3638

GAJL-PECZALSKA, KAZIMIERA J. retired surgical pathologist, pathology educator; b. Warsaw, Nov. 15, 1925; came to U.S., 1970; d. Kazimierz Emil and Anna Janina (Gervais) Gajl; widowed; children: Kazimierz Peczalski, Andrew Peczalski. Student, Jagiellonian Univ., Cracov, Poland, 1945-47; MD, Warsaw U., Poland, 1951, PhD in Immunopathology, 1964. Diplomate Polish Bd. Pediatrics, Polish Bd. Anatomic Pathology, Am. Bd. Pathology. Attending pediatrician Children's Hosp. for Infectious Diseases, Warsaw, Poland, 1953-58, head, pathology lab., 1958-65; adj. prof. Postgrad. Med. Sch., Warsaw, Poland, 1965-70; fellow U. Minn., Mpls., 1970-72, asst. prof. dept. pathology, 1972-75, assoc. prof. dept. pathology, 1975-79, prof. dept. pathology, 1979-00, dir. immunophenotyping and flow lab., 1974-00, dir. cytology dept. pathology, 1976-95; ret., 2000. Author chpts. to book; contbr. of numerous papers to profl. jours. Fellow WHO, Paris, 1959, London, 1962, Paris, 1967, U.S. Pub. Health Svcs. fellow, 1968-69; recipient Scientific Com. award Polish Ministry of Health and Social Welfare, 1964. Mem. Am. Soc. Experimental Pathology, Am. Soc. Cytology, Internat. Acad. Pathology, British Soc. Pediatric Pathology, Polish Soc. Pathology, Polish Soc. Pediatricians. Roman Catholic. Avocations: music, skiing. Office: U Minn Dept Pathology U Health Ctr PO Box 609 Minneapolis MN 55455

GALA, CANDELAS S. literature educator, language educator; b. Santander, Cantabria, Spain, Nov. 13, 1948; arrived in U.S., 1972; d. José Sánchez and Isabel Gala; children: Isabel Gala Newton, Ryan Antonia Newton. BA in Modern Philology, U. Salamanca, Spain, 1972; MA, U. Pitts., 1978, PhD, 1980. Lectr. St. Ursula's Grammar Sch., London, 1972—73, Carlow Coll., Pitts., 1973—74; tchg. asst., tchg. fellow U. Pitts., 1975—78; instr. Wake Forest U., Winston-Salem, NC, 1978—81, asst. prof., 1981—85, assoc. prof., 1985—91, full prof., 1991—, chmn. romance langs., 1996—, Wake Forest prof., 2000—. Author: Lorca: Book of Poems or the Adventures of a Quest, 1986, Lorca: Writing in a Trance Book of Poems and Diván at the Tamarit, 1992, Understanding Federico García Lorca, 1995, Collection of Critical Essays on Spanish and Latino Women Writers in the U.S., 1996; editor: Ensayos Críticos; contbr. articles to profl. jours. Mem.: MLA, Asociación Internat. de Hispanistas, Asociación de Licenciados y doctores españoles, South Atlantic MLA. Office: Wake Forest Univ Dept Romance Langs 7566 Reynolda Sta Winston Salem NC 27109

GALANDIUK, SUSAN, colon and rectal surgeon, educator; b. N.Y.C., Mar. 6, 1957; d. Joseph and Dora (Neu) G.; m. Hiram C. Polk Jr., Dec. 22, 1991. BS cum laude, SUNY, Albany, 1976; MD summa cum laude, Julius Maximilians U., Wuerzburg, Germany, 1982. Diplomate Am. Bd. Surgery, Am. Bd. Colon and Rectal Surgery. Surg. intern Chirurgische Univ. Klinik, Julius Maximilians U., Wuerzburg, Germany, 1982-83, Cleve. Clinic Found., 1983-84, surg. resident, 1984-88; Price fellow in surg. rsch., dept. surgery U. Louisville, 1988-89, colon and rectal surgery fellow dept. surgery, 1989-90, instr. dept. surgery, 1990-91, asst. prof. dept. surgery, 1991-96, assoc. prof., 1996-2001, program dir. sect. colon and rectal surgery, 1999—, prof., 2001—; dir. Price Inst. Surg. Rsch., 2001—. Presenter in field. Editl. bd. Digestive Surgery, Mayor Clin. Procs., Diseases Colon Rectum, Archives of Surgery; contbr. chpts. to books, articles to profl. jours. Chmn. fund raising com. ARC, Louisville, 1993, 1995—97, bd. dirs., 1997—2000, chmn. bd., 2001—03; bd. mem. Fund for the Arts, 1996—2003; chair med. adv. com. Ky. chpt. Crohn's and Colitis Found. Am., Louisville, 1993—97, 1999—2003. William E. Lower Fellow Thesis prize Cleve. Clinic Found., 1986. Fellow ACS, AAUP, Am. Soc. Colon and Rectal Surgeons (mem. chair young rschrs. com. 1996—, mem. program com. 1994-96, trustee rsch. found., 2001—, membership com., 2000—); mem. AMA, Am. Med. Women's Assn., Am. Soc. Microbiology, Assn. Acad. Surgery, Assn. Women Surgeons, Collegium Internat. Chirurgiae Digestivae, Jefferson County Med. Soc., Ky. Med. Assn. (mem. cancer com.), Louisville Surg. Soc., Hiram C. Polk Jr. Surg. Soc., Ohio Valley Soc. Colon and Rectal Surgeons, Priestly Soc., Soc. Surgery of Alimentary Tract, Soc. Am. Gastrointestinal Endoscopic Surgeons, Soc. Surg. Oncology (mem. corp. rels. and issues, govt. affairs coms.), Southea. Surg. Congress (councillor 1997-99), Surg. Infection Soc., Soc. Univ. Surgeons, Am. Soc. Gastrointestinal Endoscopists, Ctrl. Surg. Assn., Western Surg. Assn., Am. Gastroent. Assn., So. Surg. Assn., Am. Gastroenterol. Assn., Am. Soc. Human Genetics, Am. Soc. Clin. Oncology, Assn. Program Dirs. in Colon & Rectal Surgery, Soc. Pelvic Surgeons, Assn. Program Dirs. in Colon and Rectal Surgery, Surg. Biol. Club I. Greek Catholic. Office: U Louisville Dept Surgery 550 S Jackson St Louisville KY 40202-1622 Office Phone: 502-852-4568. E-mail: S0gala01@gwise.louisville.edu.

GALANTE, ANN MURIEL, municipal official; b. N.Y.C., May 20, 1929; d. Johnson D. and Anna Francis (Donavan) Boyd; m. James Vincent Galante, June 25, 1949; children: Patricia, Ann, James, Margaret, Joseph. BS in Pub. Adminstrn., SUNY, Old Westbury, 1986; MA in Liberal Studies, Empire State Coll., SUNY L.I. Ctr., 2000. Trustee Village of Mineola, N.Y., 1982-85, mayor, 1985-91; receiver of taxes Town of North Hempstead, Manhasset, N.Y., 1992—. Mem. N.Y. State Gov.'s Task Force on State Mandates, N.Y.C., 1989-90, N.Y. State Gov.'s Task Force on Sexual Harassment, N.Y.C., 1993-94. Active numerous cmty., ednl., religious, sr. citizen, youth and women's orgns.; past pres. Mineola Welcome Wagon (now Friends and Neighbors); former mem. bd. dirs. Am. Heart Assn.; mem. citizenship com. Nassau County 4-H Clubs, Plainview, N.Y., 1983-87; com. mem. Nassau County Dem. Com., Carle Place, N.Y., 1991—; del. 19th Dist. Jud. Conv., Hauppauge, N.Y., 1992—; Presdl. elector N.Y. State Electoral Coll., Albany, 1996; mem.-at large bd. dirs. Shelter Rock dist. Boy Scouts Am., 1996-97; co-founder Mineola Homebound Svc.; eucharistic min. Corpus Christi Ch., Mineola, 1981—, also past chmn. justice and peace com., renew 2000 com., 100th anniversary com.; trustee Mineola Hist. Soc., 1990—; active Mineola Mustang Run Com., Mineola Bicentennial of Constn. Com.; charter mem. Circle of Friends Soc., Girl Scouts U.S.A., Nassau County; co-founder Mineola Friends of A. Holly Patterson Nursing Home, Mineola Homebound Svc.; mem. master plan and planning com. Village of Mineola, Pres.'s Coun. L.I. Womens Agenda; mem. steering com. L.I. Railroad Mineola Downtown Revitalization Study; co-chair N.H. com. against domestic violence; del. Dem. Nat. Conv., 2000. Named hon. fire chief Mineola Fire Dept., 1985, Outstanding Friend, Corpus Christi Sch., 1996, Disting. Grad., Empire State Coll., 1996, Woman of Yr., Mineola Welcome Wagon; recipient numerous awards for cmty. svc., including Mother of Yr. award Southeastern Dist. Elks Club, Humanitarian award Nassau County Dem. Com. Mem. Tax Receivers and Collectors Assn., N.Y. State Assn. Towns, Soroptimists Internat. of Nassau County (past pres., Woman of Distinction award 1995), Am. Assn. Ret. Persons, Rotary. Roman Catholic. Avocations: travel, theatre, women's history research, walking, swimming. Office: Town of North Hempstead PO Box 3000 Manhasset NY 11030-3000 E-mail: galantea@northhempstead.com.

GALANTE, JANE HOHFELD, pianist, music historian; b. San Francisco, Feb. 14, 1924; d. Edward and Lillian (Devendorf) Hohfeld; m. Clement Galante, Dec. 26, 1956; children: Edward Elio, John Clement. AB, Vassar Coll., 1944; MA, U. Calif., Berkeley, 1949. Instr. U. Calif., Berkeley, 1948—51, Mills Coll., Oakland, Calif., 1951—54. Founder, dir. Composers' Forum of San Francisco, 1946-56. Music editor Berkeley, A Jour. Modern Culture, 1944-52; concert pianist German tours for USIS, 1952-54; Young Audience Concerts, San Francisco, 1963-70; mem. Lyra Chamber Music Ensemble, 1980-90; transl.: Darius Milhaud (Paul Collaer) including revised and edited catalog Milhaud's Compositions, 1988, Darius Milhaud: Interviews with Claude Rostand, 2002. Trustee Morrison Chamber Music Ctr., San Francisco State U., 1956—; hon. trustee San Francisco Conservatory Music, 1970-99; co-founder San Francisco Friends of Chamber Music, 1999. Decorated chevalier de l'ordre des arts et des lettres; recipient Disting. Svc. award Chamber Music Am., 1992, Pres.'s medal San Francisco State U., 1998. Mem. Am. Fedn. Musicians.

GALANTER, RUTH, city official; Grad., U. Mich.; MA, Yale U. Chair South Coast Regional Coastal Commn.; city coun. 6th dist. L.A., 1987—. Mem. Am. Pub. Health Assn. Office: City Hall 200 N Main St Rm 515 Los Angeles CA 90012-4103

GALBRAITH, NANETTE ELAINE GERKS, forensic and management sciences company executive; b. Chgo., June 15, 1928; d. Harold William and Maybelle Ellen (Little) Gerks; m. Oliver Galbraith III, Dec. 18, 1948; children: Craig Scott, Diane Frances. BS with high honors with distinction, San Diego State U., 1978. Diplomate Am. Bd. Forensic Document Examiners. Examiner of questioned documents San Diego County Sheriff's Dept. Crime Lab., San Diego, 1975-80; sole prop. Nanette G. Galbraith, Examiner of Questioned Documents, San Diego, 1980-82; pres., examiner of questioned documents Galbraith Forensic & Mgmt. Scis., Ltd., San Diego, 1982-97; cons., 1997—. Keynote spkr. Internat. Assn Forensic Scis., Adelaide, South Australia, 1990. Contbr. articles to profl. jours. including Jour. Forensic Scis., Forensic Sci. Internat., Internat. Jour. Forensic Document Examiners. Fellow: Am. Acad. Forensic Scis. (del. to Peoples Rep. of China 1986, USSR 1988, questioned documents sect.); mem.: Southwestern Assn. Forensic Document Examiners (charter), Am. Soc. Questioned Document Examiners (life; jour. editl. bd. 2000—), 1909 Univ. Club San Diego, Southwestern Yacht Club (life), Phi Kappa Phi. Republican. Episcopalian. E-mail: nggalbrait@aol.com.

GALBRAITH, RUTH LEGG, retired university dean, home economist; b. Lecompte, La., Nov. 5, 1923; d. Byron S. and Dora Ruth (Lindley) Legg; m. Harry W. Galbraith, June 16, 1950; 1 son, Allan Legg. BS, Purdue U., 1945, PhD, 1950. Chemist E.I. duPont de Nemours, Waynesboro, Va., 1945-46; textile chemist Gen. Electric Co., Bridgeport, Conn., 1946-47; teaching asst. Purdue U., 1947-48, research fellow, 1948-50; prof. textiles and clothing U. Tenn., Knoxville, 1950-55; asso. prof. U. Ill., Urbana, 1956-64, prof., 1964-70, chmn. textiles and clothing div., 1962-70; prof., head consumer affairs dept. Auburn (Ala.) U., 1970-73; dean Sch. Home Econs., head home econs. research, 1973-85. Mem. task force on quality of living Dept. Agr., 1967 68; mem. nat. adv. com. Flammable Fabrics Act, 1971-73; mem. U.S. Dept. Agr. Com. of Nine, 1981-83, chmn., 1983 Mem. editorial bd.: Research Jour. Home Econs., 1973-77, chmn. policy bd., 1978-80; contbr. articles to profl. jours. Recipient Disting. Alumni award Purdue U., 1970 Fellow Am. Inst. Chemists; mem. Am. Home Econs. Assn. (chmn. agy. mem. unit 1975-76, chmn. research sect. 1978-80, Outstanding Home Economist award 1984), Ala. Home Econs. Assn. (pres. 1983-84), Am. Assn. Textile Chemists and Colorists, Am. Chem. Soc., ASTM (3d v.p. com. D-13 textiles 1975-79), Assn. Adminstrs. Home Econs., Nat. Council Adminstrs. Home Econs., AAUW, Sigma Xi, Omicron Nu, Phi Kappa Phi, Delta Kappa Gamma. Home: 368 Singleton St Auburn AL 36830-6317

GALBREATH, MARGARET ANNE, market research analyst; d. Mark and Lorinda Galbreath. BSBA, Babson Coll., 2000. Sr. ops. asst. Staples.com, Framingham, Mass., 2000; market rsch. analyst U. Tex. Sys. - UTTC, Austin, Tex., 2001—. Com. chair Tex. Distance Learning Assn., Austin, 2002—03. Mem.: Tex. Distance Learning Assn. (assoc.), Internat. Assn. Bus. Communicators (assoc.), Am. Mktg. Assn. (assoc.). Avocations: running, painting, cooking, entertaining. Office: U Tex Sys - UTTC 210 W 6th St Ste 2100 Austin TX 78701 Personal E-mail: mgalbreath@utsystem.edu.

GALCZYNSKI, VALERIE ERTTER, music educator, soprano; b. Spangler, Pa., Jan. 2, 1961; d. James Robert and Barbara Vallery Ertter; m. Barry Anthony Galczynski, June 16, 1984; 1 child, Nicholas James. BS in Music

Edn., Pa. State U., University Park, 1982; MEd, St. Frances U., Loretto, Pa., 1991; Prin. Certification, Calif. U. of Pa., 2003—. Cert. music specialist K-12, instructional I and II Pa., 1982. Gen. music educator Ctrl. Cambria Elem. Sch., Ebensburg, Pa., 1982—83; choral music dir. Cambria Heights H.S., Patton, Pa., 1983—; adj. prof. music Mt. Aloysius Coll., Cresson, Pa., 1999—2000, St. Frances U., Loretto, Pa., 1999—2001; music supr. Cambria Heights Sch. Dist., Patton, Pa., 2002—. Soprano vocalist and soloist Johnstown Symphony Singers and Chorus, Pa., 1982—88, Blair Concert Chorale, Altoona, Pa., 1989—97; nat. honor soc. advisor Cambria Heights H.S., Patton, Pa., 1994—; soprano vocalist Mendelssohn Choir of Pitts., Pa., 1998—; vacation Bible sch. music instr. St. Benedict Cath. Ch., Carrolltown, Pa., 1999—2000; soprano vocalist Robert Page Festival Singers, Pittsburgh, Pa., 2000—. Prodr.(choreographer, composer and director): Cambria Heights First Ann. Madrigal Dinner, 2002; singer (actor): (cmty. theater) The Sound of Music, West Side Story, The Mikado, H.M.S. Pinafore; singer: St. Frances Univ. Alumni Dinner, Faculty Recognition Awards Dinner, Stoakes Mass of Remembrance, (civic award dinnners) Patton Chamber of Commerce; dir.(choreographer, producer, editor): (H.S. mus. prodns.). Vocalist for Gov. Tom Ridge, Blair Concert Chorale, Altoona, Pa., 1996. Recipient Disney Am. Tchr. Award nominee, Walt Disney Co., 1999. Mem.: NEA (licentiate), Pa. Music Educators Assn., Am. Choral Dirs. Assn., Cambria Heights Edn. Assn. (licentiate), Music Educators Nat. Conf. (licentiate), Pa. State U. Alumni Assn. (life), Mu Phi Epsilon Musical Honor Frat. (life). Roman Catholic. Avocations: singing, reading, travel, especially to Walt Disney World, being a soccer mom. Home: 119 Joy's Dr Carrolltown PA 15722 Office: Cambria Heights HS 426 Glendale Lake Rd Patton PA 16668 Business E-Mail: vgalczynski@chsd.k12.pa.us.

GALE, MARTHA JAYNE, lawyer; b. Ft. Wayne, Ind., Aug. 20, 1945; d. Francis LaMoyne and Maxine Ann (Taylor) G. BS, Cornell U., 1967; JD, Temple U., 1975; diploma, Phila. Sch. Psychoanalysis, 1996. Probation officer N.Y. City Cts., Bronx, 1967-70; law clk. Hon. Matthew Bullock, Phila., 1975-78; asst. atty. gen. Pa. Dept. Justice, Phila., 1978-81; chief asst. city solicitor City of Phila. Law Dept., 1981-86; adminstr. Legal Rsch., Inc., Phila., 1986-92; assoc. Law Offices Barry Ginsberg, Phila., 1992—. Mem. Pa. Trial Lawyers Assn., Phila. Bar Assn., Phila. Trial Lawyers Assn. Avocation: acting. Home: 1420 Locust St Apt 14F Philadelphia PA 19102-4209 Office Phone: 215-569-8700. Personal E-mail: marthag820@aol.com.

GALE, REBECCA J. artist; b. Dec. 24, 1963; m. Anthony B. Gale, Dec. 18, 1982; children: Anthony B. II, Cassandra M., Kimberly E. Pres. Edmond Art Assn., Edmond, Okla., 1997—98; therapeutic art facilitator The Delores Project (homeless womens shelter), Denver, 2000—. Featured artist (magazine article) The Artists Sketchbook Mag., featured illustrator (magazine) Kite Tales Mag., featured artist (newspaper) The Elbert County News; exhibitions include Pastel Society of West Coast, Boulder Art Assn., Englewood Arts Nat. Juried Art Show, Pastel Painters Maine, No. Colo. Artists Assn. Mem. com. fundraising efforts The Delores Project, Denver, 2000—03; mem. com. empty bowl Douglas County Women's Crisis Ctr., Castle Rock, 2003—04. Mem.: Pastel Soc. Colo. (assoc.), Soc. Children's Book Writers and Illustrators (assoc.), Parker Artists Guild. Conservative. Baptist. Avocations: running, hiking, reading, travel, volleyball. Home: 35696 Darting Bird Ride Elizabeth CO 80107 Personal E-mail: rebeccagaleart@aol.com.

GALE, TRISTAN, Olympic athlete; b. Ruidoso, N.Mex., Aug. 10, 1980; Student, Salt Lake C.C. Mem. U.S. skeleton team Winter Olympic Team, Lake Placid, NY. Named Am.'s Cup champion, 2001, Am.'s Cup champion, 1st pl., Lake Placid, 2001, Calgary, 2001; recipient Gold medal, 2002 Winter Olympics, 1st pl., U.S. Olympic Team Trials, 2002, 1st, 2d, 3d pl. 1st 3 races, Nat. Team Trials, 2001. Office: US Bobsled and Skeleton Fed PO Box 828 421 Military Rd Lake Placid NY 12946-0828

GALEF, SANDRA RISK, state legislator, teacher; b. LaCrosse, Wis., May 7, 1940; d. William P. and Christine Risk; m. Steven Allen Galef, Mar. 30, 1963 (dec.); children: Gregory Todd, Gwendolyn. BS, Purdue U., 1962; MS in Edn., U. Va., 1965. Tchr. Albemarle Schs., Charlottesville, Va., 1962-65, Scarsdale (N.Y.) Schs., 1965-67; mem. Westchester County Bd. Legislators, 1980-93, minority leader, 1984-93; mem. N.Y. State Assembly, Dist. 90, 1993—, chair com. on librs. and ednl. tech. Bd. dirs. Westchester County Children's Hosp. Found., 1998—, Bethel Nursing Home, 1999—2003; bd. dirs. United Way No. Westchester, 1973—, pres., 1979-80, v.p., 1975-79; trustee Ossining (N.Y.) Pub. Libr., 1975-80, Briarcliff (N.Y.) Nursery Sch., 1974-76; pres. chpt. LWV, 1973-75; chair Ossining Youth Employment Svc., 1977-80; bd. dirs Day Care Coun. Westchester, 1976-79; pub. affairs chair Jr. League Westchester-on-Hudson, Tarrytown, 1978-80, mem. tng. com., 1980-85; mem. adv. bd. Children's Village, Dobbs Ferry, N.Y., 1984—, Interfaith Coun. for Action, Ossining, 1983—; mem. Ossining Upward Bound Substance Abuse Coun., 1984—, Ossining Restoration Com., 1975-77; mem. nominating com. White Plains chpt. ARC, 1985-86; bd. dirs. Phelps Meml. Hosp. Ctr., Vis. Nurse Svcs. Westchester. Recipient Harold J. Marshall award United Way No. Westchester, 1981. Mem. N.Y. Assn. Counties (v.p. 1984-85, pres. 1985, mem. steering com. 1989-92, Legislator of Yr. 1993), Westchester Mcpl. Planning Fedn. (bd. dirs. 1982—), Westchester 2000 (mem. task force 1985), Ossining C. of C. Avocations: gardening, sewing, crafts, decorating. Office: 2 Church St Ossining NY 10562-4802

GALEN, ELAINE, painter; b. Bklyn., July 12, 1928; BA, U. Pa., 1951; MA, NYU, 1963. Instr. NYU, 1970-73, Prairie State Coll., Ill., 1974-79, Lake Forest (Ill.) Coll., 1979-80; assoc. prof. SUNY, Purchase, 1981—. Instr. Manhattanville Coll., Purchase, 1981-89, Columbia U., N.Y.C., 1984-89; vis. artist Ben Gurion U., Israel, 1997-98. Exhibited in group shows at Whitney Mus. Am. Art, NYC, 1961, Bklyn. Mus. Internat., 1963, 78, Pa. Acad. Fine Arts, Peale House., 1972, State Mus. Ill., 1974, Art Inst. Chgo., 1978, Jewish Mus., 1988, Soho 20, NYC, 1988, 90, 92, 94, Neuberger Mus., Purchase, NY, 1992-94, Tampa Mus. Art, 1994, Gallery 1756, Chgo., 1996, 99, Concordia (NY) Gallery, 2002, Monique Goldstrom Gallery, 2002-03, Studio Gallery, NY, 2004, NY Pub. Libr., 2003-04, others; collections include U.S. Info. Agy., Cyprus, Israel Mus., Jerusalem, NY Pub. Libr., U. Arts Libr., Phila., Nat. Liberty Mus., Phila., Pa., Neuberger Mus., NYC, James A. Michener Mus., Doylestown, Pa., Miss. Mus., Jackson, others. Florsheim grant, 1991.

GALESI, DEBORAH LEE, fine artist; b. Paterson, N.J., Oct. 08; d. John Michael Galesi and Ethel Marchitti; m. Samuel Corbinelli, Oct. 3, 1997. BFA, U. Colo.; pvt. student, Raymond Whyte and, Gene Scarpentoni/Art Students League, N.Y., Ben Long, Florence; Master Program, Villa Schifanoia/Inst. of, Florence. One-woman shows include: Lo Sprone, Florence, Italy, 1983, Spinetti Gallery, Florence, 1985, Benvenuti Gallery, Venice, 1986, Salaria Gallery, Spoleto, 1987, Lo Spirale, Prato, Italy, 1988, Traghetto Gallery, Venice, 1987; works exhibited at: U. Colo., Boulder, 1980, N.Y. Gallery, N.Y.C., 1981, N.J. Gallery, 1981, U. Avignon, France, 1981, Sieve Art Expo, Pontassieve, Italy, 1984, Cenacolo Gallery, Florence, 1985, Modigliani Gallery, Milan, 1990, Art Expo, Verona, 1990, Palazzo Congressi, Salsomaggiore, 1995, Palazzo, Florence, 1996, Montserrat Gallery N.Y., 1997. Vol. Natural Resource Def. Coun., Washington, Pacific Whale Found., Hawaii, Ctr. for Marine Conservation, Washington, WWF, Greenpeace. Winner competition Nat. Art Ctr., N.Y., 1978, others; recipient Stewardess of Ctr. of Light and Harmony award, Sierra Club. Mem. Ptnrs. of Destiny. Avocations: scuba diving, music, rollerblading, chinese painting, piano. Office: PMB 523 PO Box 959 Kihei HI 96753-0959

GALINSKY, DEBORAH JEAN, county official; b. Oakland, Calif., Jan. 22, 1951; d. Jerome James and Barbara Ann (Ball) G.; m. William H. Furr III, Sept. 27, 1997; 1 child by previous marriage, Lauren Rachel Lipscomb. BSW, Bowie State U., 1978. Cert. housing counselor. Substitute tchr. Anne Arundel County Schs., Ft. Meade, Md., 1972-74; addictions counselor Dept. of Health, Ellicott City, Md., 1977-78; coord. dept. Citizens Svcs., housing program specialist Housing and Cmty. Devel., Ellicott City, 1979; coord. youth teen devel. County of Howard, Ellicott City, 1978—; tchr. Rapides Parish Sch. Bd., Pineville, La., 1996—, arts and crafts youth tchr., 1997. Rep. Inter-Agy. Com., Ellicott City, 1990-93; computer instr. Aerie; tchr. Cabrini Sch., Alexandria, La. Author homeownership programs. Vol. Bethany United Meth. Ch., Ellicott City, 1987; tchr. Woodland Presbyn. Ch., Pineville. Fellow Nat. Assn. Housing and Revel. Ofcls.; mem. Nat. Fedn. Housing Counselors, Assn. Cmty. Svcs. (counselors rep.). Democrat. Avocations: dance choreographing, creative art crafts, water aerobics, bicycling, camping. Office: County of Howard Housing & Comm Devel Dept 3450 Court House Dr Ellicott City MD 21043-4330 Home: PO Box 148 Westbrook ME 04098-0148

GALITELLO-WOLFE, JANE MARYANN, artist, writer; b. Torrington, Conn., Aug. 27, 1942; d. Morris D. and Rose A. (Abate) Galitello; children: Henry Berg III, Jason Sterling, Marissa Tracy. Student, Ward Sch. Elec., 1961, Porter-Chester Coll., 1982. Nurse aide, Palm Bay, Fla., 1989; decorator, designer Waterbury, Conn.; electronic engr. Torrington, Conn.; sales rep. Thomaston, Conn.; dance tchr. San Jose, Calif.; freelance artist, writer Torrington. Host radio show C.C. Fla., Ct. Teen St. Ministry. Author: Your Gift of Life, 1991 (award 1993), 2d edit., 2002, Snow Bird Melt, 1991, Tody, Heart Desire, Jumping for Jesus, World Wide Irrigation System, 2002; published 3 songs including Let Jesus Take Your Hand - Set You Free, You Answer All My Prayers, Unity Song; inventor hurricane, tornado and fire shelters. Faith healer; active Govt. for Abuse Through Nation and Unity of Nation; advocate for the homeless; active United We Stand in Love; min. Your Gift of Life, WBCC-CoCo Radio. Home: PO Box 61851 Palm Bay FL 32906-1851

GALIZZI, MONICA, economics educator; b. Piacenza, Italy, Nov. 12, 1961; arrived in U.S., 1987; d. Giovanni and Giuliana (Vecchiotti) G.; m. Enrico Cagliero, June 25, 1994; children: Diana Anna, Erica B. BS, U. Cattolica, Milan, Italy, 1986; M in Polit. Economy, Boston U., 1990, PhD in Econs., 1994; D in Polit. Economy, U. Milan, Italy, 1990. Rsch. asst. dept. econs. Cath. U., Milan, Italy, 1986-87; instr. micro- and macroeconomics, dept. econs. Boston U., 1989-92; postdoctorate rsch. fellow in econs. of labor markets U. Limburg, Maastricht, The Netherlands, 1993-94; economist Workers Compensation Rsch. Inst., Cambridge, Mass., 1994-98; adminstrv. dir. program on children Nat. Bur. Econ. Rsch., Cambridge, 1998-99; asst. prof. dept. econs. U. Mass., Lowell, 1999—. Co-author (with L. Boden): What Are the Most Important Factors Shaping Return to Work? Evidence from Wisconsin, 1996; co-author: (with Boden and T. Liu) The Workers' Story: Results from a Survey of Workers injured in Wisconsin, 1998; co-author: (with G. Gotz and T. Lin) Predictors of Multiple Workers' Compensation Claims in Wisconsin, 2000; contbr. articles to profl. jours. Mem.: Workers' Compensation Rsch. Group, European Econ. Assn., Am. Econ. Assn. Home: 76 Paul Revere Rd Lexington MA 02421-6638 Office: U Mass Lowell Dept Econs 1 University Ave Lowell MA 01854-2881 E-mail: monica_galizzi@uml.edu.

GALL, BETTY BLUEBAUM, office services company executive; b. Williamson, W.Va., June 11, 1944; d. Thomas Jefferson Bluebaum and Ollie Mae (Moore) Bluebaum Walker; Charles B. Walker (stepfather); 1 child, Thomas Ethan. Ptnr., dir. Chicagoland Register, dating svc., Chgo., 1974-84; cooking instr. Elizabeth Benson Internat. Cooking Lessons, 1978-84; owner Ethnic Party People Catering, 1981-92, Phone-A-Friend Dating Svc., Chgo., 1984-90, Betty Gall Office Svcs., Chgo., 1984—; office mgr. Myers & Assocs., 1998—2000. Contbr. poetry to Nat. Libr. Poetry, 1997, 98. Mem. comm. dept. Little City Found., 1989-91. Home: 6314 N Troy St Chicago IL 60659-1414 E-mail: bettygall44@hotmail.com.

GALL, LENORE ROSALIE, educational administrator; b. Bklyn., Aug. 9, 1943; d. George W. Gall and Olive Rosalie (Weekes) Gall Bryant. AAS, NYU, 1970, cert. tng. and devel., 1975, BS in Mgmt., 1973, MA in Counselor Edn., 1977; EdM, EdD, Columbia U., 1988. Various positions Ford Found., N.Y.C., 1967-75; dep. dir. career devel. Grad. Sch. Bus., NYU, N.Y.C., 1976-79; dir. career devel. Pace Lubin Sch. Bus., N.Y.C., 1979-82, Sch. Mgmt., Yale U., New Haven, 1982-85; asst. to assoc. provost Bklyn. Coll., 1985-88, asst. to provost, 1988-91; asst. to v.p. acad. affairs Fashion Inst. Tech., 1991-94; asst. provost curriculum and instrn. N.Y.C. Tech. Coll., 1994-2000, dean students and acad. svcs., 2000—. Adj. asst. prof. LaGuardia C.C., L.I. City, N.Y., 1981-90, Sch. Continuing Edn. NYU, 1983-84; dir., sec. devel. workshop Coll. Placement Svcs., Bethlehem, Pa., 1978-81. Bd. dirs. Langston Hughes Cmty. Libr., Corona, N.Y., 1975-83, 86-92, chair, 1975-79, 82-83, 89-92, 2d v.p., 1986, 1st v.p., 1987-88, chair awards com. Dollars for Scholars, Corona, 1976-99, pres., 1999-2003; active audience devel. task force Dance Theatre of Harlem, 1992-98, hon. co-chmn., 1994-95; active alumni coun. Tchrs. Coll., Columbia U., 2000—; bd. trustees Renaissance Charter Sch., 2002, Queens (N.Y.) Borough Pub. Libr., 2003. Recipient Concerned Women of Bklyn., Inc., 1994, Edn. award Stuyvesant Heights Lions Club, Bklyn., N.Y., 1997, Edn. award Girls HS Alumni Assn., Bklyn., N.Y., 2003, Edn. award Key Women Am., Concourse Village Beach, 2003; grantee Jewish Fedn. for the Edn. of Women, 1986-87. Mem. AAUW, Assn. Black Women in Higher Edn. (exec. bd., membership chair, pres.-elect 1988, pres. 1989-93), Am. Assn. Univ. Adminstrs., Nat. Assn. Univ. Women (chaplain 1987-88, 2d v.p. 1988, 1st v.p. 1988-92, dir. N.E. sect. 1993-96, nat. 2d v.p. 1996-98, nat. first v.p. 2000-2002, nat. pres. 2002), Tchr.'s Coll./Columbia U. Alumni Coun. (chmn. nominating com. 2001-), Nat. Assn. Women in Edn., Black Faculty and Staff Assn. Bklyn. Coll. (1st vice-chair 1986-87, chair 1987-88), New Haven C. of C. (chmn. women bus. and industry conf. 1984), Nat. Coun. Negro Women Inc. (life, 1st v.p. North Queens sect. 1986-89, pres. 1989-93), Nat. Assn. Negro Bus. & Profl. Women's Club (Sojourner Truth award 1991), Phi Delta Kappa, Kappa Delta Pi, Pi Lambda Theta, Delta Sigma Theta (chmn. nominating com. Queens Alumni chpt. 2001-03, chmn. tri-com.-arts and letters, project ch., May Week 1999-2002). Mem. A.M.E. Ch. Office: NYC Coll Tech 300 Jay St Jackson Heights NY 11201-1909

GALL, MARY SHEILA, federal agency administrator; 2 children. BA, Rosary Hill Coll., 1971; MS in Edn., Old Dominion U., 1998. Staff mem. various mems. of Senate and Ho. of Reps., 1971-79; sr. legis. analyst study com. Ho. of Reps., 1980-81; dep. domestic policy adviser Office of V.P. of U.S., 1981-86; counselor to dir. U.S. Office Pers. Mgmt., 1986-89; asst. sec. human devel. svcs. HHS, Washington, 1989-91; commr. U.S. Consumer Product Safety Commn., Washington, 1991—. Chair Pres.'s Task Force on Adoption, 1987-89. Dir. rsch. George Bush for Pres. campaign, 1979-80; mem. Reagan-Bush Presdl. campaign and transition team, 1980-81; tchr. Sunday sch. Republican. Office: US Consumer Product Safety C Washington DC 20207-0001

GALL, PAMELA JANE, art educator; b. York, Pa., Apr. 14, 1952; m. Russ Julius Gall, July 9, 1988. BS in art edn., Pa. State U., 1970—74, MEd in art edn., 1984. Mid. level art specialist Littlestown Area Sch. Dist., Littlestown, Pa., 1974—. Region 7 rep. Pa. Art Edn. Assn., Pa., 1987—90, mid. level divsn. dir., Pa., 1991—94, state conf. chair, Pa., 1993, sec., Pa., 1994—99, Pa., 2001—; ea. region mid. level divsn. dir. elect Nat. Art Edn. Assn., Reston, Va., 2003—; sponsor of chpt. 23 Nat. Jr. Art Honor Soc., L:ittlestown, Pa., 1991—; fine arts coord. Littlestown Area Sch. Dist., Littlestown, Pa. Tchr. St Paul's Luth. Ch. Vacation Bible Sch., Hanover, Pa., 1996—2003. Recipient Pa. Outstanding Nat. Jr. Art Honor Soc. Sponsor, Pa. Art Edn. Assn., 2002, Nat. Outstanding Nat. Jr. Art Honor Soc. Sponsor, Nat. Art Edn. Assn., 2003. Mem.: Adams County Art Teachers Assn., Nat. Art Edn. Assn. (ea. region mid. level dir. elect 2003, Nat. Outstanding Nat. Jr. Art Honor Soc. Sponsor 2003), Pa. Art Edn. Assn. (sec. 2001—03), Delta Kappa Gamma Edn. Soc. (US forum chair 2001—02, 2003 Album of Distinction 2003). Office: Littlestown Area School District 75 Maple Ave Littlestown PA 17331 Office Phone: 717-359-4146. E-mail: galln@lasd.k12.pa.us

GALL, SIMONE ELLEN, music educator; b. Elyria, Ohio, Sept. 7, 1950; d. Rudy and Dorothy Maravich; m. Steven Joseph Gall, June 30, 1974; children: Julie Jeannine, Melanie Nicole. B of Music Edn., Bowling Green State U., 1972. Vocal music tchr. K-6 Elyria City Schs., 1972—78; vocal music tchr. K-8 Amherst (Ohio) Exempted Village Schs., 1985—; dir. Amherst Comty. Chorus, 1996—. Dir. St. George Serbian Orthodox Ch. Choir, Lorain, Ohio, 1980—2000; dir. music Sandstone Summer Theater, Amherst, 1995—97. Named Lorain Internat. Queen, Lorain Internat. Festival, 1968. Mem.: Music Educators Nat. Conf., Ohio Edn. Assn. Democrat. Avocations: performing at retirement centers and nursing homes, singing and playing for weddings, organizing class reunions. Home: 764 Terra Ln Amherst OH 44001 Office: Amherst Jr H S 548 Milan Ave Amherst OH 44001 E-mail: simonegall51@aol.com.

GALLAGHER, ANNE PORTER, communications executive; b. Coral Gables, Fla., Mar. 16, 1950; d. William Moring and Anne (Jewett) Porter; m. Matthew Philip Gallagher, Jr., July 31, 1976 (div. July 1998); children: Jacqueline Anne, Kevin Sharkey. BA in Edn., Stetson U., 1972. Tchr. elem. schs., Atlanta, 1972-74; sales rep. Xerox Corp., Atlanta, 1974-76, Rosslyn, Va., 1976-81, No. Telecom Inc., Vienna, Va., 1981-84, account exec., 1984-85, sales dir., 1985-91, mktg. dir., 1995-96; v.p. Fed. Pub. Sector Timeplex Fed. Sys., Inc., Fairfax, Va., 1995-96; bus. devel. dir. Informix Software, Vienna, 1996-97; sr. v.p. Tricor Industries Inc., Alexandria, Va., 1997-98; sr. v.p. fed. sys. Metromedia Fiber Network, McLean, Va., 1999—2002; sr. v.p. bus. devel. Source1 Techs., Arlington, Va., 2002—. Mem. Info. Tech. Assn. Am., Pi Beta Phi. Episcopalian. Avocations: running, working out. Home: 4643 Kirkland Pl Alexandria VA 22311-4949 Office: Source 1 Techs 2111 Wilson Blvd Ste 700 Arlington VA 22201 Office Phone: 703-626-9466. E-mail: AGallagher@aol.com.

GALLAGHER, CYNTHIA, artist, educator; b. N.Y. BFA in Painting, Phila. U. of Arts, 1972; MFA in Painting, Queens Coll., 1974. Instr. N.Y. Inst. Tech., N.Y.C., 1974-88; adj. prof. CUNY, Queens Coll., N.Y.C., 1974—90; instr. foundations dept. Parsons Sch. Design, 1994—2001. Critic Brown U., 1994, R.I. Sch. Design, 1994, Cooper Union for Advancement of Sci. and Art, 1994; selection com. vis. artists Fashion Inst. Tech., 1992-93; graphics cons. N.Y. State Found. Arts, 1978; vis. critic NYU, N.Y.C., N.Y., 1974-75; adj. asst. prof. Phila. (Pa.) Coll. Art, 1976—, Fashion Inst. Tech., N.Y.C., N.Y., 1976—; instr. summer sch. music and art Yale U., Norfolk, Conn., 1980—. One-woman shows include 55 Mercer St., N.Y.C., 1976, 1978, Grace Borgenicht Gallery, 1981, Luise Ross Gallery, 1988, Edward Thorden Gallery, Gothenborg, Sweden, 1989, Charles More Gallery, Phila., 1990, 1991, Mary Ryan Gallery, N.Y.C., 1992, Espace Crois, Barangnon, Toulouse, France, 1993, Johnson & Johnson, New Brunswick, N.J., 1998, exhibited in group shows at Weatherspoon Mus., Greensboro, N.Y.C., 1982, Castelli Graphics, N.Y.C., 1983, Bess Culter Gallery, 1984, Parrish Art Mus., Southampton, L.I., N.Y., 1991, Tiffany's, N.Y.C., 1993, Inst. for Art and Urban Resources, Inc., L.I. City, N.Y., 1982, Nat. Mus. Women in the Arts, Washington, 1996, Montclair (NJ) Mus. Art, 1997, Represented in permanent collections Met. Mus. Art, N.Y.C., Best Inc., Citibank, 1st Nat. Bank Chgo., Home Ins. Co., Owens Corning Corp., Salomon Bros., Shearson-Lehman Am. Express, N.Y.C., San Francisco, Skadden, Arts, Slate, Meagher and Flom, Johnson, Nat. Mus. of Women in the Arts, Whitney Mus. Am. Art, Met. Mus. Art, Nat. Women's Mus., Washington, D.C.; contbr. articles to profl. jours. Mem. adv. bd., bd. dirs. YWCA Elsa Mott Ives Gallery, 1992, curator, 1993. Grantee, Creative Artists Pub. Svc. Program, 1981—82, Nat. Endowment for Arts, 1983—84, 1989—90, N.Y. Found. for Arts, 1989—90.

GALLAGHER, ELIZABETH WORRELL, fund raising consultant; b. Phila., June 9, 1936; d. Granville II and Marguerite (Boyle) Worrell; m. William J. Gallagher, Mar. 21, 1981; children: Liza Powell, Lynne Samson, Sara Noon, Lawrence Coughlin. BA, Sweet Briar Coll., 1958. Assoc. Marsteller, McCade, Inc., Washington, 1971-74; dir. devel. Nat. Cathedral Sch., Washington, 1974-88; assoc. Russell Reynolds, Inc., Washington, 1988-90; exec. dir. devel. Georgetown U., Washington, 1990-94; sr. cons. Marts & Lundy, Inc., Lyndhurst, N.J., 1994—. Office: Marts & Lundy Inc 1280 Wall St W Lyndhurst NJ 07071-3517

GALLAGHER, ELLEN, artist; b. Providence, 1965; Student, Sch. Mus. Fine Art, Boston, 1992, Skowhegan Sch. Art, 1993. One-woman shows include Akin Gallery, Boston, 1992, Mario Diacono Gallery, 1994, Mary Boone Gallery, N.Y., 1996, Anthony d'Offay Gallery, London, 1996, Gagosian Gallery, 1998, Ikon Gallery, Birmingham, 1998, Galerie Max Hetzler, Berlin, 1999, exhibited in group shows at Brandeis U., Waltham, 1993, Mus. Fine Arts, Boston, 1993, Inst. Contemporary Art, 1994, 1996, Mus. Fine Arts, 1995, Whitney Mus. Am. Art, N.Y., 1995, Whitechapel Art Gallery, London, 1996, Mario Diacono Gallery, Boston, 1997, De Beyerd Ctr. Contemporary Art, Breda, The Netherlands, 1998, others, Represented in permanent collections Mus. Modern Art, N.Y., Whitney Mus. Am. Art, Met Mus. Art, Guggenheim Mus., Mus. Fine Art, Boston, Mus. Contemporary Art, L.A., Denver Mus. Art, Moderna Museet, Stockholm; featured in numerous articles and revs. Ann. Gund fellow, 1993, Provincetown Fine Arts Work Ctr. fellow, 1995, Joan Mitchell fellow, 1997. Office: care Mario Diacono Gallery 207 South St Boston MA 02111-2723

GALLAGHER, KATHRYN KASICH, elementary school educator; b. Litchfield, Ill., Dec. 30, 1951; d. William and Joan Teresa (Jatcko) Kasich; m. Larry Eugene Gallagher, Oct. 25, 1980; children: Vanita Eleanor, Michael Edward. BA in French, So. Ill. U., Edwardsville, 1974, MS in Elem. Edn., 1978, BA in Music, 1988. Ind. piano/voice tchr., Edwardsville, 1971—; instructional aide Edwardsville Jr. H.S., 1978-79, Montessori Sch., Edwardsville, 1979-80; organist St. Boniface Ch., Edwardsville, 1988-91; singer/soprano St. Louis Chamber Chorus, 1989-94; music dir. Sts. John & James, Ferguson, Mo., 1991-95; tchr. Our Lady of Fatima, Florissant, Mo., 1994-97, St. Ambrose Sch., Godfrey, Ill., 1997—. Music dir. Cath. Campus Ministries, Edwardsville, 1998—. Mem. pastoral coun. St. Boniface Ch., Edwardsville, 1988-93; mem. friends of Music, So. Ill. U.-Edwardsville, 1997—, friends of Watershed Nature Ctr., Edwardsville, 1996—; cantor St. Boniface/St. Mary's, 1986-94. Mem. Nat. Guild of Piano Tchrs., Nat. Music tchrs. Assn., Ill. State Music Tchrs. Assn., Choristers Guild. Democrat. Roman Catholic. Avocations: swimming, knitting, cooking. Office: St Ambrose Catholic Sch 820 Homer Adams Pkwy Godfrey IL 62035

GALLAGHER, LINDY ALLYN, banker, financial consultant; b. Kalamazoo, Sept. 27, 1954; d. Karl P. Joslow and Audrey S. Phillips; m. Thomas J. Gallagher, Nov. 29, 1975; children: James Allyn Buckley, Phillip Graham, Charles Bedloe. BS, U. Pa., 1975; MBA, Columbia U., 1982. Mem. faculty, rschr. U. Pa., Phila., 1976-80; corp. banking officer Bank of Montreal, N.Y.C., 1982-84; v.p. Citibank NA, N.Y.C., 1984-89; v.p., mgr. Chase Manhattan Bank, N.Y.C., 1989-90; pres. The Allyn Co., New Canaan, Conn., 1990-99; prin. State Street Global Advs., 1999; pvt. fin. cons., 2000—. Treas., dir. 957 Lexington Corp., 1981-87. Editor Columbia Jour. World Bus., 1980-82. Mem. Women's Nat. Rep. Club, 1986—; commr. Town of New Canaan, 1991-99; treas., sec. Young Women's League New Canaan, Inc., 1992-94; bd. dirs. Charlotte Latin Sch., 2000—. Mem. Stanwich Club, The Penn Club (N.Y.C.), The Breakers Club. Republican. Episcopalian.

GALLAGHER, M. CATHERINE, English literature educator; b. Denver, Feb. 16, 1945; d. John Martin and Mary Catherine Sullivan; m. Martin Evan Jay, July 6, 1974; children: Margaret Shana, Rebecca Erin. BA, U. Calif., Berkeley, 1972, MA, 1974, PhD, 1979. Asst. prof. U. Denver, 1979-80, U. Calif., Berkeley, 1980-84, assoc. prof., 1984-90, prof., 1990—. Author: The Industrial Reformation of English Fiction, 1985, Nobody's Story, 1994; co-author: The Making of the Modern Body, 1987, Practicing New Historicism, 2000; editor Representation, 1983—. Guggenheim fellow Guggenheim Found., 1989; fellow NEH, 1990, ACLS, 1990, Mem. MLA (del. assembly mem. 1985-86, exec. com. lit. criticism divsn. 1991-94), Am. Acad. Arts and Scis., Acad. Lit. Studies, Brit. Studies Assn., The Dickens Soc. Office: U Calif Dept English Berkeley CA 94720-0001

GALLAGHER, PATRICIA E. government agency administrator; BA in Pub. Adminstrn. and Urban Studies, Elmhurst Coll., Ill.; MA in Pub. Policy Analysis, Northwestern U. Prin. P. Gallagher & Assocs., Chgo.; mgr. Chgo. River Devel. Plan; asst. commr. open space planning City of Chgo. Dept. Planning, dep. commr. strategic planning, 1999—2001; exec. dir. Nat. Capital Planning Commn., Washington, 2001—. Contbr. articles to profl. jours. Loeb fellow, Harvard U., 1999—2000. Office: Nat Capital Planning Commn 401 9th St NW Washington DC 20576 Office Phone: 202-482-7200.

GALLAGHER, PAULA, minister, musician; d. Paul John Gallgher and Margaret Jewel Denton. MusB, Marywood Coll., Scranton, Pa., 1969, MRE, 1985; MusMEd, Hartt Coll., U. Conn., Hartford, 1980; student, Gonzaga U. N.W. Bibl. Inst., Spokane, Wash., 1988—90, Santa Fe Spirituality Inst., 1985—2003. Cert. catechist and master catechist N.Mex.; tchr. Pa. Music edn. dir. Our Lady Queen of Martyrs, Forest Hills, NY, 1969—73; music edn., art dir. Our Lady of Mercy, Forest Hills, NY, 1970—73; music dir. St. Mary of the Mt. H.S., Pitts., 1973—74; music edn., art dir. St. Rosalia, Pitts., 1974—77; music chair Seton Cath. H.S., Pittston, Pa., 1977—82; core mem. House of Prayer Our Lady of the Lake, Verona, NJ, 1982—84; core mem. Avila Ctr., Kelowna, Canada, 1984—92; liturgy dir. St John the Baptist, Santa Fe, 1992—95; liturgy, RCIA dir. Santa Maria de la Paz, Santa Fe, 1995—2003. Student tchr supr. Marywood Coll., Pittston, Pa., 1978—79; Diocesan liturgy commn. sec. Diocese of Scranton, Pa., 1977—82; Diocesan Sister's coun. sec. Diocese of Newark, 1982—84; liturgy chair St Pius, Immaculate Conception, Kelowna, BC, Canada, 1985—92; diocesan liturgy commn. Diocese of Nelson, BC, Canada, 1986—92; deanery chair-person Kelowna, BC, Canada, 1989—92; diocesan pastoral Coun. Diocese of Nelson, BC, Canada, 1988—91, co-chair for diocesan synod, BC, Canada, 1989; mus. dir. Diocesan Celebrations of Faith, Kelowna, BC, Canada, 1986—90; worship presenter Archdiocese of Santa Fe, Albuquerque, 1993—94; music dir. Archdiocesan Priest's Retreat, Santa Fe, 1996—2000, Archdiocesan Ordination Mass, Santa Fe, 2001; retreat dir. IHM Christian Life Cmty.; presenter in field. Active So Other Might Eat, Washington, 1980; vol. Hospice, 1993, Red Cross, 2000; jurist Santa Fe Courts, 1999. Mem.: Nat. Forum on the Catechumenate, Nat. Assn. of Pastoral Musicians. Avocations: photography, writing, graphic arts. Office: Santa Maria de la Paz Cath Cmty 11 Coll Ave Santa Fe NM 87508-9225 Business E-Mail: liturgy@smdlp.org.

GALLAGHER, PAULA MARIE, real estate appraiser; b. Omaha, Nov. 10, 1959; d. Kenneth Leroy and Phyllis Virginia (Stopak) G. Diploma, Nebr. Coll. Bus., 1979; student, Met. Tech. C.C., Omaha, 1979—81, U. Nebr., 1981—85, Coll. St. Mary, 1986—90; BS, Bellevue U., 1993. Lic. real estate appraiser and broker, Nebr. Legal sec. McCormick Cooney Mooney & Hillman P.C., Omaha, 1979; word processor Firstier Bank, Omaha, 1979-83, staff asst., 1983-84; sec. Morrissey Appraisal Svcs., Omaha, 1984; appraiser trainee Morrissay Appraisal Svcs., Omaha, 1985-88, real estate appraiser, 1988—. Residential mem. Am. Inst. Real Estate Appraisers. Mem.: Am. Bus. Women's Assn. (rec. sec. 1984—85, treas. 1988—89, Woman of Yr. award 1989), Appraisal Inst. (sr. residential appraiser), Omaha Women's C. of C. (mem. edn. com. 1990—92, mem. fin. com. 1991—2003, dir. cmty. recognition 1992, dir. edn. 1993, chmn. fin. style show 1995, pres.-elect 1996, pres. 1997, immediate past pres. 1998). Roman Catholic. Avocations: needlepoint, counted cross stitch, sewing, reading. Home: 16617 Monroe St Omaha NE 68135-2906 Office: Morrissey Appraisal Svcs 13825 P St Omaha NE 68137-2701

GALLAGHER, SANDRA ANN, music educator; b. New Prague, Minnesota, USA, Aug. 20, 1948; d. Walerine Raymond and Georgia Ann Solheid; m. David Michael Gallagher, July 14, 1979; 1 child, Katherine Elizabeth. BSCI, U. Minn., Mpls., Minn., 1970. Music educator Shakopee Pub. Sch., Shakopee, Minn., 1970—79, Ohumwa Pub. Sch, Ohumwa, Iowa, 1979—80, Shakopee Pub. Sch., Shakopee, Minn., 1980—81, New Prague Pub. Sch., New Prague, Minn., 1986—. Ch. musician St. Wenceslaus, New Prague, Minn., 1982—86. Mem. arts coun. New Prague Arts Coun., New Prague, Minn., 1999—; dir. Cmty. Band, New Prague, Minn., 1993—. Recipient Music Educator of the Yr., MENC-MMEA (Minn. Music Educators Assoc.), 1997. Mem.: Women Band Dir. Internat., Music Educators Nat. Conf., Minn. Music Educators Assoc. Avocations: reading, theater. Home: 318 Pershing Ave N New Prague MN 56071 Office: New Prague High School 221 12th St NE New Prague MN 56071

GALLAGHER-DALTON, TONYA MARIE, family support specialist; b. Great Falls, Mont., Aug. 2, 1971; d. Ronald A. and Sherry E. (Morris) G. BA in Psychology, BA in Comm. Studies, U. Mont., 1994, M in Interdisciplinary Studies, 1999. Cert. family support specialist II, Mont. Project asst./resource coord VVCAP, Missoula, Mont., 1993-96; grad. asst. dept. psychology U. Mont., Missoula, 1996-97; family support specialist Western Mont. Comprehensive Devel. Ctr., Missoula, 1997—. Mem. coun. Youth in Crisis Coalition, 1995—; bd. dirs. MCAT, 1999. Vol. coord. AmeriCorps, Missoula, 1996-2000; crisis vol. YWCA Domestic Violence Assistance Program, 1992-95. Recipient Children And Youth scholarship award Am. Legion, 1993, Heisey award Mont. Cascade Coun., 1992; Mountain West Regional scholar Golden Key Nat. Honor Soc., 1994-95; Early Intervention scholar, 1994-97. Mem. AAUW, Grad. Student Assn., Psi Chi, Alpha Phi (treas. 1989). Lutheran. Avocations: stamp collecting, coin collecting, poetry, skiing, hiking. Home: PO Box 2166 Kalispell MT 59903 Office: Western Mont Comprehensive Devel Ctr 945 4th Ave E Kalispell MT 59901

GALLARDO, HENRIETTA CASTELLANOS, writer; b. San Antonio, July 16, 1934; d. Francisco Garcia and Elisa Duarte (Moreno) Castellanos; m. Albert Joseph Gallardo, Aug. 19, 1965; children: Frank Cantu, Roger Cantu (dec.), Gloria Michelle. Cert., Draughn's Bus. Coll., San Antonio, 1952. Sec. Kelly Air Force Base, San Antonio, 1952-53; exec. sec. U. Tex., Dallas, 1974-82; interior decorator Plano, Tex., 1983-85; writer. Author: Tangled Web of Destiny, 1992, Marsh & Co., 1993, Everyday Heroes, 2002. Democrat. Roman Catholic. Avocations: photography, travel, reading, charity work. Home: 2212 Parkhaven Dr Plano TX 75075-2013

GALLARDO, SANDRA SILVANA, producer; b. Bronx, Jan. 13, 1947; d. Edward Francis and Grace (Mallory) G.; m. Gerald O'Connor, Jan. 21, 1968 (div. 1978); m. Billy Burrows, Sept. 21, 1985. Student, HB Studio, N.Y.C., 1964-72, CCNY, 1964-66. CEO Gallardo Studios, North Hollywood, Calif., 1980—; pres. Camellia Prodns., Studio City, Calif., 1987—. Guest spkr. IRS, Hollywood, Calif., 1990. Prodr., dir., writer The Acting Class, 1988; author: The Winning, 1998, Acting for Success, 1999 (Academic World Star); motion pictures include (co-star) Solar Crisis, The Windwalker, Death Wish II, (star) Out of the Dark, (star) The Tin Angel; movies of the week spls. and pilots include (star) Prison Stories: Women on the Inside, Calendar Girl Murders, (PBS spl., star) The People vs. Inez Garcia, (recurring) Days of Our Lives; co-author (with Billy Drago): The Anger; episodic TV include (recurring) NYPD Blue, Lou Grant, (co-star) E R, (guest star) Babylon 5, (guest star) Providence, (guest star) Strong Medicine, Golden Girls, (guest star) Ressurection Blvd., (guest star) Kingpin; starred on stage in American Mosaic. Recipient Bronze Star halo So. Calif. Motion Picture Coun., 1985, Golden Eagle award Nosotros, 1989. Mem. SAG (guest spkr. 1988-96), Am. Fedn. TV Arts Scis., Am. TV Arts & Scis., Equity. Avocations: writing, paddle tennis, hiking, museums. Studio: Studio 1500 11440 N Chandler North Hollywood CA 91601 Office: Camellia Prodns # 1500 11440 N Chandler Blvd North Hollywood CA 91601 Office Phone: 818-752-2588. E-mail: SGalla2222@aol.com.

GALLARELLO, JOSEPHINE, performing arts educator, director; b. N.Y.C., June 2, 1942; d. Amedeo and Angelina Ammirata; m. John R. Gallarello, Aug. 1, 1965; children: Victoria Angela, Josephine M., John Amedeo. BS in music edn., NYU, 1964; MS in music edn., Queens Coll., 1966; profl. dip., Long Island U., 1994. Music tchr. So. Huntington Schs., Huntington Station, NY, 1964—68; soprano singer self employed, Long Island, NY, 1976—80; choral tchr. Sachem Schs., Holtsville, NY, 1980—86; choral dir. Kings Park (NY) Schs., 1986—96; dir. fine and performing arts Hauppauge (NY) Schs., 1996—. Past pres. NY Sch. Coun. of Admin. of Music Edn., Suffolk County, 1996—, Suffolk County Music Edn. Assoc., 1964—; fellow mem. PTA, So. Huntington, 1964—69, Kings Park, 1975—85, Hauppauge, 1996—. Mem.: NY State Coun. Admin. of Music Edn., Elem. Secondary PTA So. Huntington NY (life). Republican. Roman Catholic.

GALLEGOS, MARY, state representative; Attended, Portland State U. State rep., dist. 29 Oreg. House Rep., Salem, 2002—. Republican. Office: 900 Court St NE H-288 Salem OR 97301

GALLEHUE, DAWN E. voice educator; b. Springfield, Ohio, May 7, 1978; d. John Michael and Lois Carolyn Gallehue. MusB in music edn., Bowling Green State U., 2001. Music tchr. Talawanda HS, Oxford, Ohio, 2001—. Scheduling com. Talawanda HS, 2002—03, music curriculum supr., 2002—03. Musician (arranger): (choral works) All My Trials, 1999 (Best Non Published Work, 2000). Dir., musician Oxford Cmty. Band, 2001—04; actor, singer Oxact, Miami U., Oxford, 2003. Recipient Oxford Cmty. Found. grant, 2003. Mem.: Talawanda Edn. Assoc., Am. Choral Dirs. Assoc., Ohio Music Educators Assoc. Home: 301 Brookview Ct Apt 4 Oxford OH 45056-2131 Office: 101 W Chestnut Oxford OH 45056

GALLES, KRISTEN, lawyer; b. Cedar Rapids, Iowa; d. Joseph Galles, Sr. and Madeline Galles. BA summa cum laude, Econs. and Spanish, Creighton U., 1987; JD with hons., Wash. U., 1990. Bar: Calif. 1990, D.C. 1993, Nebr. 1996, Va. 1996, U.S. Dist. Ct., (no. dist.) Calif. 1990, U.S. Dist. Ct. (ea. dist.) Calif. 1991, U.S. Dist. Ct. D.C. 1993, U.S. Dist. Ct. Md. 1994, U.S. Dist. Ct. Nebr. 1995, U.S. Dist. Ct. (we. dist.) Mich. 1998, U.S. Ct. Appeals (9th cir.) 1990, U.S. Ct. Appeals (11th cir.) 1995, U.S. Ct. Appeals (4th cir.) 1999, U.S. Ct. Appeals (10th cir.) 2000, U.S. Ct. Appeals (6th cir.) 2000, U.S. Ct. Appeals (2d cir.) 2002, U.S. Supreme Ct. 2000. Legal fellow U.S. Senate office of J. Robert Kerrey, Washington, 1990; atty. Sheppard, Mullin, Richter & Hampton, San Francisco, 1990—93, Powell, Goldstein, Frazer & Murphy, Washington, DC, 1993—96, Equity Legal, Alexandria, Va., 1996—. Adj. prof. Nat. Sch. of Law George Wash. U., Washington, 1996—99. Vol. domestic violence clinic Women Inc., San Francisco, 1991—93; vol. Legal Svcs.Program Bar Assn. San Francisco, 1990—93; vol. Whitman Walker Clinic, Washington, 1994—2000; vol. voting rights project Lawyers Com. for Civil Rights, Washington, 2002; Dem. legal com. voting rights project Mark Warner gubanatorial campaign, Alexandria, 2001; bd. dir. YWCA, San Francisco, 1992—93. Scholar, Wash. U., 1987—90, Creighton U. Mem.: AAUW, ABA Individual Rights and Responsibilities Sect. (vice chmn. state constl. rights com. 1997—99, vice-chair com. on the rights of women 1998—2002, labor & employment sect., co-chair com. on the rights of women 2002—, Com. of the Yr. award 2002), State Bar Calif. (Wiley Manuel Pro Bono award 1992), Women's Sports Found. (consulting atty.), Bar Assn. of San Francisco (named Vol. Atty. of the Month 1992, named Vol. Attys. of Yr. 1991, 1992), GAYLAW (bd. dirs. 1998—2001, membership coord. 1998—), Met. Wash. Employment Lawyers' Assn., Nat. Ctr. for Lesbian Rights (consulting atty.), San Francisco Women Lawyers Alliance (sexual harassment guidelines com. (1991-1992) 1991—99), Nat. Lesbian & Gay Lawyers Assn. Achievements include several significant legal civil rights and Title IX athletics victories. Avocations: sports, civil rights advocacy, travel, history & current events. Home: 10 Rosecrest Avenue Alexandria VA 22301

GALLETTI, MARIE ANN, English language and linguistics educator; b. N.Y.C., Nov. 25, 1944; d. Fidel G. and Marie Theresa (Chaumard) G.; m. Wayne Lee Mitchell. BA cum laude, Queens Coll. CUNY, 1965; MA, Hunter Coll. CUNY, 1971; M in Counseling, Ariz. State U., 1981. Prof. English Glendale (Ariz.) Cmty. Coll. Maricopa Cmty. Coll. Dist., 1975—. Co-editor: (anthologies) Native American Substance Abuse, 1982, American Indian Families: Developmental Strategies, 1982. Mem. Nature Conservancy, 1984—, World Wildlife Fund, 1984—, Humane Soc. of U.S., 1984—, Ellis Island Found., 1986—; founding mem. 390th Meml. Mus. Found., Tuscon, 1994. Recipient Regents' scholarship N.Y. State Bd. Regents, 1961. Mem. AAUP, Phi Beta Kappa (founding v.p. Phoenix met. area chpt. 1981-83), Phi Delta Kappa. Office: Glendale Cmty Coll 6000 W Olive Ave Glendale AZ 85302-3006

GALLIAN, VIRGINIA ANNE, music educator; b. St. Louis, Dec. 29, 1933; d. Martin Charles and Flora Olinda (Rocklage) Schake; children: John Charles (dec.), Paige Renee. BS, U. Mo., 1955, MS, 1966; student, U. San Jose, Calif., 1961, U. North Tex., Denton, 1971. Tchr. Hazelwood (Mo.) Pub. Schs., 1955, Ft. Dix Post Sch., Trenton, N.J., 1956, Ft. Bragg Post Sch., Fayetteville, N.C., 1956-58, Fergusen-Florrisant (Mo.) Pub. Schs., 1958-59; music supr. Jefferson City (Mo.) Pub. Schs., 1959-60; tchr. Union Sch. Dist., San Jose, 1960-63, 67, 68, Bridgeport (Calif.) Pub. Schs., 1963-65, Columbia (Mo.) Pub. Schs., 1965-67; music tchr. Denton Ind. Sch. Dist., 1970-95; adj. Tex. Woman's U., 1996—2000. Instr. U. North Tex., 1995. Trustee Denton Ind. Sch. Dist., 1999—; mem. Greater Denton (Tex.) Arts Coun., 1995—, Denton Cmty. Bd., 1982—. Mem. AAUW, Tex. State Tchrs. Assn. (lobbyist 1985—, bd. dirs. 1988-93), Denton Edn. Assn. (chmn. 1985-95), Denton C. of C., Kiwanis (bd. dirs. 2003—), Sigma Alpha Iota (chaplain 1972-74), Phi Delta Kappa, Pi Lambda Theta. Republican. Methodist. Avocations: reading, gardening, sewing, travel, piano and flute.

GALLIEN, SANDRA JEAN, social worker; b. Winchester, Mass., May 13, 1956; d. William Joseph and Shirley Ann (Ewing) Treacy. BA in Early Childhood Edn., U. Mass., 1979; Cert. Advance Study in Adminstrn., Mgmt., Harvard U., 1987; MBA in Mgmt., U. Conn., 1997; MSW, U. Conn., W. Hartford, 1998. Counselor Greater Newburyport Edn. Collaborative, Danvers, Mass., 1991-93; rsch. asst. Inst. African Am. Studies U. Conn., Storrs, 1995-98, rsch. asst. Inst. Advancement Polit. Social Work Practice W. Hartford, 1996-98; intern Conn. Women's Edn. and Legal Fund, Hartford, 1996-97, United Way, Rocky Hill, Conn., 1997—. Contbr. papers to Credit Rsch. Found., 1989. Town precinct coord. congl. campaign, Reading, Mass., 1974; mem. Coventry Dem. Town Com., 1997-99, Unitarian Universalist Soc., East Manchester, Conn., 1999—. Mem. NASW, U. Mass. Alumni Assn., U. Conn. Grad. Bus. Assn. (founder), Emily's List. Avocations: leather and wreath crafting, softball, basketball, writing. Home: 16 Vernon Ave Unit 50 Vernon Rockville CT 06066-6701 E-mail: Sandy.Gallien@ctunitedway.org.

GALLIMORE, MARGARET MARTIN, poet; b. Winston Salem, Mar. 20, 1947; d. Holland Henry and Dallas Cornell (Robbins) Martin; m. Elmer Harold Holden Jr., Feb. 14, 1965; children: Andrew Harold, Amy Darlene, John Alan; m. Timothy Milton Gallimore, May 9, 1986. Student, High Point (N.C.) Coll., 1988. With AT&T Network Sys., Winston-Salem, 1965-69, 73-75, prodn. operator, 1979-89; real estate salesperson Lambe-Young Real Estate Co., Kernersville, NC, 1975-79; leasing cons. Vinyard Gardens Apt./S.E. Atlantic Properties, Winston-Salem, 1994-95; comm. assoc. AT&T Phone Ctr., Winston-Salem, 1995-96; real estate salesperson Triad Piedmont Properties, Kernersville, 1996; real estate broker Winston-Salem, 1996—; asst. cmty. mgr. Lindsey Manor Apts./Steven D. Bell & Co., Kernersville, 1997; kitchen asst. child nutrition dept. Winston-Salem/Forsyth County Schs., 2001—. Author poetry. Recipient Editors Choice awards (2) Nat. Libr. of Poetry, 1995, 97; named to Internat. Poetry Hall of Fame, Nat. Libr. Poetry, 1996. Mem. Internat. Soc. Poets (Disting. mem.).

GALLINGER, LORRAINE D. prosecutor; b. Sept. 2, 1948; BS, U. Wyo., 1970; JD, Cath. U. Am., 1975. Bar: D.C., Mont. 1st asst. U.S. atty. Dept. Justice, Billings, Mont., 1976-85, 91, sr. litigation counsel, chief civil divsn., 1985-91, acting U.S. atty., 1991-93; first asst. U.S. Attys. Office, Billings, Mont., 1993—. Instr. Atty. Gen. Advocacy Inst. Recipient Dir.'s Superior Performance award AUSA, 1988. Office: US Attys Office PO Box 1478 Billings MT 59103-1478

GALLO, HANNA M. state legislator; b. Colorado Springs, Colo., Nov. 21, 1956; m. Russelle Gallo; children: Julie, Laura. BS in Communicative Disorders, U. R.I., 1995, MS in Speech Lang., 1997. CCRI. Speech lang. pathologist South Kingstown (R.I.) Sch. Dept.; mem. R.I. Senate, Dist. 12, Providence, 1998—. Mem. corps. com. R.I. State Senate, legis. com. Democrat. Office: RI State Senate State House Providence RI 02903 E-mail: sen-gallo@rilin.state.ri.us.

GALLO, JOAN ROSENBERG, lawyer; b. Newark, Apr. 28, 1940; BA in Psychology, Boston U.; postgrad. studies in Counseling, We. Md. Coll.; postgrad studies in Clin. Psychology, We. Grad. Sch. Psychology; JD magna cum laude, U. Santa Clara, 1975. Bar: Calif. 1975. Assoc. with Cynthia Mertens U, Santa Clara, Calif., 1975-76; sr. law clk. U.S. Dist. Ct., Calif., 1976-78; assoc. Decker and Collins, San Jose, Calif., 1978-79; from dep. city atty. to city atty. City of San Jose, 1979-2000; ptnr. Terra Law LLP, San Jose, 2000—. Mem. Psi Chi. Office: Terra Law LLP 60 S Market St Ste 200 San Jose CA 95113-2333 E-mail: jgallo@terra-law.com.

GALLOP, JANE (JANE ANNE GALLOP), women's studies educator, writer; b. Duluth, Minn., May 4, 1952; d. Melvin Gordon and Eudice Zelda (Titch) G.; children: Max Blau Gallop, Ruby Gallop Blau. BA, Cornell U., 1972, PhD, 1976. Lectr. French Gettysburg (Pa.) Coll., 1976; asst. prof. Miami U., Oxford, Ohio, 1977-81, assoc. prof., 1981-85; prof. women's studies Rice U., Houston, 1985-87, Autrey prof., 1987-90; prof. English U. Wis., Milw., 1990-92, Disting. prof., 1992—. NEH vis. prof. Emory U., Atlanta, 1984-85; Hill vis. prof. U. Minn., Mpls., 1987; dir. seminar for coll. tchrs. NEH, Milw., 1985, 88; instr. Sch. of Criticism and Theory, Dartmouth Coll., 1991. Author: Intersections, 1981, The Daughter's Seduction, 1982, Reading Lacan, 1985, Thinking Through the Body, 1988, Around 1981, 1992, Feminist Accused of Sexual Harassment, 1997,Anecdotal Theory, 2002, Living with His Camera, 2003; editor: Pedagogy, 1995. Guggenheim fellow, 1983-84. Mem. MLA. Office: U Wis PO Box 413 Milwaukee WI 53201-0413 Office Phone: 414-229-6402. E-mail: jg@uwm.edu.

GALLOWAY, CATHERINE BLACK, publishing executive; b. Birmingham, Ala., Oct. 24, 1954; d. Robert Lee and Catherine Hicks Black; m. Michael Galloway, Aug. 25, 1984. Editl. prodn. coord. So. Med. Jour., Birmingham, Ala., 1975—2002, mng. editor, 2002—. Sec., treas. Vocat. Resources, Inc., Birmingham, 1997—. Mem.: Am. Med. Writers Assn. (cert. core curriculum program 1983). Office: Southern Medical Journal 35 Lakeshore Drive Birmingham AL 35209 Office Phone: 205-945-1840 143. E-mail: cgalloway@sma.org.

GALLOWAY, EILENE MARIE, space and astronautics consultant; b. Kansas City, Mo., May 4, 1906; d. Joseph Locke and Lottie Rose (Harris) Slack; m. George Barnes Galloway, Dec. 23, 1924; children: David Barnes, Jonathan Fuller. Student, Washington U., St. Louis, 1923-25; AB, Swarthmore Coll., 1928; postgrad., Am. U., 1937-38, 43; LLD (hon.), Lake Forest Coll., 1990, Swarthmore Coll., 1992. Tchr. polit. sci. Swarthmore Coll., 1928-30; editor Student Svc., Washington, 1931; staff mem. edn. div. Fed. Emergency Relief Adminstrn., 1934-35; asst. chief info. sect. div. spl. info Library of Congress, 1941-43; editor abstracts Legis. Reference Svc., 1943-51, nat. def. analyst, 1951-57, specialist in nat. def., 1957-66; sr. specialist internat. rels. (nat. security) Congl. Rsch. Svc., 1966-75, cons. internat. space activities, 1975—. Staff mem. Senate Fgn. Rels. Com., 1947; profl. staff mem. U.S. group Interparliamentary Union, 1958-66; cons. Senate Armed Svcs. Com., 1953-74, Ford Found., 1958; spl. cons. Spl. Senate Com. on Space and Astronautics, 1958; spl. cons. to Senate Com. on Aero. and Space Sci., 1958-77; cons. to Senate Com. on Commerce, Sci. and Transp., 1977-82; chmn. com. edn. and recreation Washington, 1937-38; forum leader, 1976-79; guest Soviet Acad. Sci., 1982, adult edn. U.S. Office Edn., 1938; mem. Internat. Inst. Space Law of Internat. Astronautical Fedn., 1958—, U.S. bd. dirs., v.p., 1967-79, hon. dir., 1979—, Fedn. ofcl. observer at sessions UN Com. on Peaceful Uses Outer Space and legal sub-com., 1970-94, com. for rels. with internat. orgns., 1979—; space law and sociology com. Am. Rocket Soc., 1959-62; adv. panel Office Gen. Counsel, NASA, 1971; adviser outer space del. U.S. Mission to UN Working Group on Direct Broadcast Satellites, 1973-75; observer UN Conf. Exploration and Peaceful Uses of Outer Space, Vienna, 1982; lectr. NAS, 1972, U.S. CSC, Exec. Seminar Ctr., Oak Ridge, 1973-78; ednl. counselor Purdue U., 1974; lectr. Inst. Air and Space Law McGill U., 1975, Inter Am. Def. Coll., 1977-78, U. Akron, 1984, 91; mem. panel on solar power for satellites and U.S. space policy Office Tech. Assessment, 1979-80, 82-86, cons., 1982; cons. COMSAT, 1983, FCC Commn. on U.S. Telecomm. Policy, 1983-87; spkr. internat. space law UN, N.Y.C., 1995; mem. NASA Nat. Adv. Com. on Internat. Space Sta., 1996-99, NASA Spaceflight Adv. com., 2000-03, UN seminar Space Futures and Human Security, Alpbach, Austria, 1997, chmn. Session in Internat. Astronautical Fed. Congress Concepts of Space Law, 1997; active European Space Agy. Internat. Lunar Workshop, 1994, 97; chair UN Workshop UNISPACE III Space Treaties: Strengths and Needs, Vienna, Austria, 1999. Author: Atomic Power: Issues Before Congress, 1946; author: (with Bernard Brodie) The Atomic Bomb and the Armed Services, 1947; author: History of United States Military Policy on Reserve Forces, 1775-1957, 1957, The Community of Law and Science, 1958, United Nations Ad hoc Committee on Peaceful Uses of Outer Space, 1959. Pres. Theodore Von Karman Meml. Found., 1973-84; mem. alumni council Swarthmore Coll., 1976-79; mem. organizing com., author symposium on Conditions Essential For Maintaining Outer Space for Peaceful Uses, Peace Palace, Netherlands, 1984; bd. advisers Student for Exploration and Devel. of Space, 1984—. Rockefeller Found. scholar-in-residence, Bellagio, Italy, 1976; elected to Coun. of Advanced Internat. Studies, Argentina, 1985, Uruguyan Centro de Investigacion y Difusion Aeronautica-Expacial, 1985; recipient Andrew G. Haley gold medal Internat. Inst. Space Law, 1968, Disting. Svc. award Libr. Congress, 1975, NASA Gold Medal for Pub. Svc., 1984, USAF Space Command plaque, 1984, Internat. Acad. Astronautics' Theodore Von. Karman award, 1986, Women in Aerospace Lifetime Achievment award Internat. Inst. Space Law, 1989, Leadership award NASA Johnson Space Ctr., 1997, Cologne U. Inst. Air and Space Law and German Aerospace Ctr. award, 2003; Wilton Park fellow, Eng., 1968, NASA award for contbns. to internat. space sta., 1999; Eilene M. Galloway award established by Internat. Acad. Space Law, 2000. Fellow: AIAA (tech. com. on legal aspects of aeros. and astronautics 1980—84, internat. activities com. 1985—, European space agy. internat. lunar workshop 1994, Pub. Svc. award and medal 2003, Pub. Policy award 2002), Internat. Acad. Astronautics (trustee emeritus, Social Scis. award 1999, Moot Ct. award 2002), Am. Astronautical Soc. (John F. Kennedy

Astronautics award 1999); mem.: Nat. Aeronautic Assn. (Katharine Wright award 2003, 2003), Internat. Law Assn., Am. Soc. Internat. Law, LWV (chmn. study groups housing, welfare in D.C. 1937—38, mem. tech. com. on law and sociology task force on legal aspects 1979—), World Peace Through Law Ctr., Lamar Soc. Internat. Law, Kappa Alpha Theta, Delta Sigma Rho, Phi Beta K[illegible] Home and Office: 4012 29th Pl NW Washington DC 20008-2105

GALLOWAY, JANICE, writer, editor; b. Kilwinning, Scotland, Dec. 2, 1956; d. James and Janet (McBride) G.; 1 child, James Alexander Galloway McNaught. MA, Glasgow U., 1978. Tchr. Strathclyde Regional Coun., Ayrshire, Scotland, 1980-90. Music critic. Editor (with Hamish Whyte): New Writing Scotland, 1990, 1991, 1992; author: The Trick is to Keep Breathing, 1990, Foreign Parts, 1994, Where You Find It, 1996, Clara, 2002 (Saltire book of yr., 2002), Boy Book See, 2002; author: (with sculptor Anne Bevan) +Rosengarten, 2004; librettist (with sculptor Anne Bevan): Pipelines, librettist (with composer Sally Beamish): Operas Monster. Recipient Mind/Allan Lane prize, 1990, Cosmopolitan/Perrier award, 1991, E.M. Forster award in lit. Am. Acad. Arts and Letters, 1994, McVitie's prize for Scottish Writer of the Yr., 1994, Saltire prize, 2002; Times Literary Supplement Rsch. fellow Brit. Libr., 1999. Office: care Jonathan Cape 20 Vauxhall Bridge Rd London SW1 6RB England also: care Derek Johns AP Watt Agy 20 John St London WCIN 2DR England E-mail: djohns@apwatt.co.uk.

GALLOWAY, JUDY A. deputy commissioner; BS in Bus. Adminstrn., Ga. State U.; postgrad., U. Colo., Denver. Program specialist Atlanta Regional Office, Dept. Health and Human Svcs.; deputy regional commr., ACF-Region VIII office Adminstrn. Children and Families, U.S. Dept. Health and Human Svcs., 1998—2000, deputy regional commr., Office of Early Childhood Programs, 2000—. Office: Denver Fed Office 1961 Stout St Denver CO 80294-3538

GALLOWAY, LILLIAN CARROLL, modeling agency executive, consultant; b. Hazard, Ky., Sept. 23, 1934; d. William Zion and Clemma (Lewis) Carroll; m. Thomas Roddy Galloway, Dec. 2l, 1957; children: David Junkin, Scott Thomas, Donald Lewis. Student, Cumberland Coll., l955, Ea. U., Richmond, Ky., l956, U. Cin., l958, John Robert Powers Sch., Cin., 1958. Tchr. Vandalia (Ohio) Elem. Sch., l954-56, Kenwood Elem. Sch., Louisville, l956-57, Cin. Pub. Schs., l957-64; founder, pres. Fairfax Model Agy., Washington, l964-67, Cin. Model Agy. Internat., 1967—, Lillian Galloway Modeling Acad., Cin., l97l—, Children Model Agy. Internat., Cin., 1985—, Lillian Galloway Fashion Show Prodn. Co., 1998—. Cons., co-owner John Robert Powers Modeling Sch., Cin., 1957-64; pres. Student Model Bds., Cin., 1984—; dir. Career Day, Cin., 1967—. Mem. Cin. Better Bus. Bur., 1967—; trustee Knox Presbyn. Ch., Cin. Named Cin.'s Outstanding Bus. Woman, Sta. WCPO-TV, l985, Outstanding Alumni, Cumberland Coll., 1988. Mem. DAR, Modeling Assn. Am. (chmn. convs. 1975-77), Am. Modeling Assn. Internat. (pres. 1976-77), Cin. Advertisers Club (membership and program coms., Outstanding Bus. Woman award 1985), Exec. Women Internat. (program com., chmn. bd. dirs. 1986, Woman of Achievement award 1986), Cin. C. of C., Cumberland Coll. Alumni Assn. (pres. 1982), English Speaking Union, Order Ky. Cols., Cin. Woman's Club (bd. dirs. 1992—, lecture/entertainment chmn. 1992-95), Town Club (bd. dirs. 1988—), Order Ea. Star (organist 1953—). Republican. Avocations: art, french antiques, gardening, music, travel. Home: 6027 Stirrup Rd Cincinnati OH 45244-3917 Office: 6047 Montgomery Rd Cincinnati OH 45213-1611

GALLOWAY, PATRICIA DENESE, civil engineer; b. Lexington, Ky., June 14, 1957; d. Howard John and Maudine Lou (Jones) Frisby; m. Kris Richard Nielsen, Mar. 16, 1987. BS in Civil Engring., Purdue U., 1978; MBA, N.Y. Inst. Tech., 1984; candidate, Kochi U., Japan, 2003—. Registered profl. engr. Ky., N.Y., N.J., Ariz., Wis., Wyo., Fla., Wash., Colo., Pa., Man., Can., Australia. Project engr., inspector CH2M Hill, Milw., 1978-79, master program scheduler, 1979-81; sr. cons. Nielsen-Wurster Group, N.Y.C., 1981-83, sr. engr., 1983-84, v.p., 1984-85, prin., exec. v.p., 1985-99, pres., 1999-2000, CEO, pres., 2001—04, CEO, 2004—. Pres. subs. cor., 1988-90; also bd. dirs.; lectr. Columbia U., U. Wis.-Madison; vis. prof. Kochi U.; presenter to numerous orgns; ptnr. Unionville Vineyards, Ringoes, N.J.; pres. Unionville Aviation; gen. ptnr. Unionville Ranch, L.L.C., Wash.; chief exec. Nielson-Wurster Asia Pacific, Melbourne, Australia, 2001—; bd. dir. Civil Engring. Rsch. Found.; adv. bd. Civil Engring. Rsch. Found., 2000—, exec. com., 2001—. Contbr. articles to profl. jours. Named one of Top 10 Women in Constrn., Engring. New Record, 1986, one of Top 10 Women, Glamour Mag., 1987, 88, White House fellow regional finalist, 1990, Ky. Col., Gov. Patten, Sts. of Ky., 2002; named to Lafayette H.S. Hall of Fame, 2001; recipient Nat. Leadership Coun. Capital award, 1990, Engr. of Yr. award Mercer County Profl. Engrs., 1990, Nat. Leadership award Profl. Women in Constrn., 1995, Fed. Infrature Design award Whitehouse Commn., 1999, Upward Mobility award Soc. Women Engrs., 2003, Tribute to Women in Industry award, YWCA, 2004; named Disting. Engring. Alumnus, Purdue U., 1992, Celebration of Women, NAE, 2000. Fellow ASCE (instr. constrn. claims course, bd. chair task com. on women in civil engring. 1998—2000, internat. dir., bd. dirs. 1992-95, chmn. membership com. 2001—, pres.-elect 2003—, pres., bd. dirs. 2004 (1st woman); mem. NSF (dir. engring. 2004-), YWCA (Tribute to Women award), Am. Assn. Engring Socs., Nat. Soc. Professional Engrs., Am. Arbitration Assn., Professional Women in Construction, The Acad. Experts, UK, The Inst. Engrs., Australian Fellow, Soc. Women Engrs. (pres. Wis. chpt. 1980, pres. N.Y. chpt. 1982, Disting. New Engr. 1980, Mobility award 2003-), Project Mgmt. Inst. (dir. pub. bd.), Am. Assn. Cost Engrs., Am. Nuclear Soc., Garden State Wine Growers Assn. (pres. 1990-92), Somerset County C. of C. (most outstanding woman in bus. and industry 1987), Purdue Engring. Alumni Assn. (bd. dirs., 1975-2001), Toastmasters, Sigma Kappa (fin. com. 1993-97), Tau Beta Pi. Republican. Methodist. Avocations: scuba diving, cross-country skiing, hiking, horseback riding, wine making. Office: Nielsen-Wurster Group 345 Wall St Princeton NJ 08540-1518 Fax: 1-609-497-3412. Office Phone: 509-857-2235. E-mail: patnwg@aol.com.

GALLOWAY, SHARON LYNNE, special education educator; b. Pensacola, Fla., Jan. 2, 1951; d. Richard Earl and Beatrice Kathlyn (Stone) G. AA, Pensacola Jr. Coll., 1995; BA, U. West Fla., 1998, MEd, 2000. Professionaly Recognized Spl. Educator. Travel counselor, trainer Gulf Breeze (Fla.) Travel, 1985-95; sign lang. interpreter Pensacola Jr. Coll., 1995-97; tchg. intern Sherwood Elem., Pensacola, 1997-98; tchr. Sherwood Elementary, Pensacola, FL, 1998—. Coord. deaf ministries Gulf Breeze United Meth. Ch., 1995-2000, interpreter, 1995—, youth counselor anchor program, 1996-98; vol. Habitat for Humanity, Gulf Breeze, Pensacola, 1994-96, Gulf Coast Sports Ability Games, 1996, Special Olympics, 1999-02; interpreter Ala.-West Fla. Annual Conf. United Meth. Ch., Montgomery, Ala., 1996—; server, cleanup com. Loaves and Fishes, Pensacola, 1996-97; reading camp tchr. U. West Fla., Pensacola, 1997, 99. Mem. NEA, Internat. Reading Assn., Student Coun. Exceptional Children (mem. chair 1996-98) Golden Key Internat. Honor Soc. (chpt. webmaster 1998-2002, chpt. treas. 1998), Coun. for Exceptional Children, Coun. for Children with Behavioral Disorders, Coun. for Children with Learning Disabilities, Alpha Sigma Lambda, Phi Delta Kappa (bd. dirs., chpt. webmaster, 2001—). Avocations: gardening, carpentry, interior design, webpage design. Home: 3367 Crestview Ln Gulf Breeze FL 32563 Office: Sherwood Elem Sch 501 Cherokee Trl Pensacola FL 32506-3519

GALLUP, JANET LOUISE, management consultant; b. Rochester, N.Y., Aug. 11, 1951; d. John Joseph and Mildred Monica (O'Keefe) VerHulst; 1 son, Jason Hicks. BA, Hofstra U., 1973; MA, Calif. State U., 1979. Asst. trader E.F. Hutton, N.Y.C., 1975; instr. Calif. State U., Long Beach, 1978-79, grad. asst., 1979; fin. analyst Rockwell Internat., Seal Beach, Calif., 1979-85, coord. mgmt. and exec. devel. and succession planning, 1985-91; mgr. orgn. and employee devel. activities Hughes Aircraft, 1991-95; mgr. tng. ops. Smart & Final Co., L.A., 1995-98; mgr. human resources devel. [illegible] J. Gallup Cons., 2002—. Vol. Working Wardrobes of Orange County, Sr. Meals. Democrat. Personal E-mail: jlgallup@mindspring.com.

GALLUP, PATRICIA, computer company executive; Grad., U. Conn., 1979. Chair PC Connection, Inc., Milford, Mass., 1982—, CEO, 2002—, pres., 2003—. Named Entrepreneur of Yr., Ernst & Young, 1998, 2003, N.H. High Tech. Coun., 2003; named one of Top 50 Women Bus. Owners in U.S., Working Woman, 2000—03. Office: PC Connection Inc Rt 101A 730 Milford Rd Merrimack NH 03054-4631

GALLUP, PATRICIA SUE, architect; b. Tampa, Fla., June 29, 1957; d. Theodore Maxwell and Virginia Lou Raley; m. Timothy Michael Gallup; children: Jennifer, Nathan. BArch, U. Okla., 1988. Specifier Dewberry Design Group Inc., Tulsa, Okla., 1999—. Mem.: Constrn. Specifications Inst.

GALLUP RICCI, JANICE ELIZABETH, music educator; b. Glens Falls, N.Y., Mar. 13, 1959; d. Franklin Delano Gallup and Betty Irene Bettles; m. Richard James Ricci Jr., Aug. 20, 1991 (dec. Sept. 1995); 1 child, Nicholas Basil. BA Music Edn., St. Leo U., 1981; MS Edn., SUNY, Plattsburgh, 1992. Tchr. Pasco County Sch. System, San Antonio & Dade County, Fla., 1981—87, Minerva Ctrl. Sch., Olmsteadville, NY, 1987—, concert coord., 1998—. Bd. dirs. Cornell Coop. Ext., Warren County, NY, 1998—2002. Recipient State and Nat. awards in music, DAR, 1998, 2000, 2001. Mem.: Minerva Tchrs. Orgn., Music Educators Nat. Conf., Gamma Alpha. Republican. Episcopalian. Avocations: motorcycling, bicycling, songwriting, travel. Home: PO Box 461 Warrensburg NY 12885

GALUS, CLARA P. philosopher, educator; b. June 12, 1935; BS in Edn., Bennett Coll., Rio de Janeiro, 1956; MS in Edn., Russell Sage Coll., 1975; PhD in Counseling, Progressive U., Sacramento, Calif., 1998. Prin. ARI Elem. Sch., Rio de Janeiro, 1957—61; adj. prof. Hispanic studies SUNY, Albany, 1969—72; adj. prof. Schenectady (N.Y.) C.C., 1983—86; adult edn. educator N.Y. State Correctional Facility, Ossining, 1986—88; ednl. cons. Ctr. for Human Devel., Albany, NY, 1989; spanish tchr. House Internat. Sch., Schenectady, 1989—90, prof. Chinese Paint and History, 2001—. Justice of the peace Albany (N.Y.) Ct. House, 2001—. Mem.: ASCD, AAUP, Albany Bar Assn., Tng. and Devel. Soc., Am. Counseling Assn. Address: PO Box 5874 Albany NY 12205

GALVAN, ALICIA ZAVALA, pharmacist; b. Saginaw, Mich., May 4, 1949; m. Oscar A. Galvan; children: Alicia Galvan Davis, Oscar Jr., Teresa G. AS, San Antonio C.C., 1970; BS in Pharmacy, U. Tex., 1973. Registered pharmacist, Tex. Staff pharmacist Galvan Pharmacy, San Antonio, 1973-94, pharmacist in charge, 1994—; pres. Galvart Press, San Antonio, 1993—. Pharmacy cons. Galvan Pharmacy, 1973—. Contbr. works to mags. Recipient 1st Angel award Alamo Writers Unltd. Mem. Am. Pharm. Assn., Nat. Notary Assn., Tex. Pharm. Assn., Bexar County Pharm. Assn., San Antonion Poets Assn. (poet laureate). Avocation: painting. Office: Galvan Pharmacy PO Box 15764 San Antonio TX 78212-8964 E-mail: SorSevilla@aol.com.

GALVIN, KATHLEEN MALONE, communications educator; b. N.Y.C., Feb. 9, 1943; d. James Robert and Helen M. (Sullivan) G.; m. Charles A. Wilkinson, June 19,1973; children: Matthew, Katherine, Kara. BS, Fordham U., 1964; MA, Northwestern U., 1965, 80, PhD, 1968. Tchr. Evanston (Ill.) Township High Sch., 1967-72; asst. prof. Northwestern U., Evanston, 1968-73, assoc. prof., 1973-78, prof., 1978—, assoc. dean, 1988-2001. Presenter workshops in field. Author: Listening by Doing, 1986; sr. author: Family Communication, 6th edit., 2004; co-author: Person to Person, 5th edit., 1996, Basics of Speech, 3d edit., 1998; co-editor: Making Connections, 3d edit., 2002, Communication Works!, 2000; contbr. articles to profl. jours.; developer, instr. 26-video series on Family Communication (PBS Adult Satellite Sys.). Office: Northwestern U Comm Studies Dept 2240 N Campus Dr Evanston IL 60208-3545 Office Phone: 847-251-6183.

GALVIS Y ASSMUS, PATRICIA, computer animator, educator, filmmaker; b. Cucuta, Colombia, July 20; d. Lucio Enrique Galvis and Gloria Assmus; 1 child, Ria Jocet Bailey-Galvis. BA Studio Art, Calif. State Univ., 1987; MFA, Calif. Inst. Arts, 1991. Assoc. prof. U. Mass., Amherst, 1991—. Dir. Ctr. Rsch. in Art and Tech., 1996—. Prodr., dir. : (films) Stages, 1999; producer, dir. (films) EOS, 2003; dir.: (films) Sal Vijua (Director's Award, 1994); editor: ACM SIGGRAPH Computer Graphics Quar. Fellow Lilly Tchg., Ctr. Tchg.; grantee Prodn., Interactive Entertainment Techs.

GAMBLE, DESIRATA, artist, poet; b. Wilkesboro, NC; d. Robert Lee and Mary Etta Gamble; m. David Bullins, Feb. 14; 1 child, Zoe Bullins. AA with honors, Surry C.C., Dobson, N.C., 1983; BA in Psychology, U. N.C., Wilmington, 1985, BA in Studio Arts, 2001; postgrad., U. Ga., 1985—87, PhD candidate social psychology. Proofreader Joan S. Northrop, Wilmington, 1984—85; artist U. N.C., Wilmington, NC, 1996—2002; artist transp. MerleFest, Wilkesboro, NC, 1994—2001; asst. to Merle Fest artist transp. coord. David C. Bullins, 2002—04. One-woman shows include The Morning Dew, Winston-Salem, N.C., 1997—98, Claude Howell Gallery, Wilmington, 1998, The Deluxe, Wilmington, N.C., 1998—99, The Beanstalk, Boone, NC, 1999—2001, Daughtry's Old Books, Wilmington, NC, 2003, William Vance Nichols/Wilkes Art Gallery, 2003; artist, poet: Sights of the Wind, Her White Hair Peeps and We Heard the Music for Miles, 1985 (Book award for poetry U. N.C. Wilmington); Represented in permanent collections Daniel Hall, Wilkes C.C., Wilkesboro, NC; author: numerous poems. Mem.: AAUW, Acad. Am. Poets, Southeastern Ctr. for Contemporary Art, Ala. State Poetry Soc. Personal E-mail: gambled1@excite.com.

GAMBLE, JACQUELYN VALDENA, secondary school educator; d. Jerome Matthew and Mildred Francis Gamble. BA, MEd, S.C. State U., 1975. Tchr. Orangeburg (S.C.) Consol. # 5, 1979—. Grade level chairperson Whittaker Elem. Sch., Orangeburg, 1982—96. Advisor Just Say No Club, Orangeburg, 1980—2003; vol. Dem. Party, Orangeburg. Mem.: NAACP (life), Am. Bus. Women of Am. (assoc.), S.C. Edn. Assn. (life; S.C. edn. bldg. rep. 1996—), Habitat for Humanity (assoc.), Delta Sigma Theta (life). Democrat. Methodist. Avocations: travel, reading mysteries, cooking, swimming, jogging. Home: 3298 Hunter Dr Orangeburg SC 29118

GAMBLIN, CYNTHIA MACDONALD, mathematics educator, lobbyist; b. Chgo., Sept. 12, 1946; d. Robert Eugene and Janice (Billings) MacD.; m. James Bradford Gamblin, Sept. 6, 1969 (div. June 1980). BS, Washington U., St. Louis, 1969, MA in Teaching, 1971. Cert. tchr., Fla., Mo.; lic. basic ground instr. FAA. Tchr. maths. Mary Inst., St. Louis, 1969-70; exec. sec. Coalition for the Environment, St. Louis, 1971-72; office mgr. Around the World Food Corp., St. Louis, 1972-73; tchr. maths. Dunedin (Fla.) High Sch., 1973—. Mem. pub. policy com. Juvenile Welfare Bd., St. Petersburg, Fla., 1979-98, co-chmn. legis. subcom., 1989-90; advisor DHS Sailing Club, 2002—. Mem. Pinellas Classroom Tchrs. Assn. (lobbyist St. Petersburg chpt. 1979-92), Ctr. for Fla.'s Children, Jr. League of Clearwater, Phi Delta Kappa. Republican. Avocations: pilot, sailing, reading. Home: 1441 Fairway Dr Dunedin FL 34698-2270

GAMBREL, KIMBERLY, lawyer; b. Cincinnati, Ohio, Dec. 13, 1960; d. Arvil Lee and Helen Gambrel. BA, Miami U., 1979—83, MA, 1984; JD, U. of Cin. Coll. of Law, 1985—88. Bar: Ohio 1988. Law clk. Hamilton County Ct. of Common Pleas, Cin., 1989—90; assoc. Killworth, Gottman, Hagan & Schaeff, L.L.P., Dayton, Ohio, 1990—94, ptnr., 1994—. Urban Morgan Inst. for Human Rights fellowship, Urban Morgan Inst. for Human Rights, 1985—88. Mem.: ABA, Dayton Women's Bar Assn., Dayton Intellectual Property Law Assn. (second v.p. 2003), Ohio Women's Bar Assn., [illegible] Intellectual Property Law Assn. Office: Killworth Gottman Hagan & Schaeff 1 Dayton Ctr 1 S Main St Ste 500 Dayton OH 45402-2023 E-mail: gambrelk@kghs.com.

GAMBRELL, LUCK FLANDERS, corporate executive; b. Jan. 17, 1930; d. William Henry and Mattie Moring (Mitchell) Flanders; m. David Henry Gambrell, Oct. 16, 1953; children: Luck G. Davidson, David Henry, Alice Kathleen, Mary G. Rolinson. Grad., St. Mary's Coll., 1948; AB, Duke U., 1950; diplome d'etudes françaises, L'Institut de Touraine, Tours, France, 1951. Chmn. bd. LFG Co., 1960—. Mem. State Bd. Pub. Safety, 1981—90, Chpt. Nat. Cathedral, Washington, 1981—85, World Svc. Coun. YWCA, 1965—; chmn. bd. dirs. Student Aid Found., Atlanta, 1992—99; mem. Bd. Councilors The Carter Ctr., Emory U.; mem. bd. advisors Emory U., 2001—; coun. mem. Presbytery Greater Atlanta, 1988; elder First Presbyn. Ch., Atlanta; bd. dirs. Atlanta Symphony Orch., 1982—85. Recipient East Ga. Coll. Student Ctr. named in her honor, Swainsboro, Ga., 2002. Mem.: Atlanta Jr. League, Alpha Delta Pi.

GAMBRELL, SARAH BELK, retail executive; b. Charlotte, NC, Apr. 12, 1918; d. William Henry and Mary (Irwin) Belk; m. Charles Glenn Gambrell (dec.); 1 child, Sarah Belk Gambrell Knight. BA, Sweet Briar Coll., 1939; D in Humanities (hon.), Erskine Coll., 1970, U. N.C., Asheville, 1986, Furman U., 1997, Johnson C. Smith U., 2003. Dir. Belk Inc., 1947—. Bd. consulators Erskine Coll. and Sem.; trustee Warren Wilson Coll., Swannanoa, NC, Charlotte Mus. of History; nat. bd. asset mgmt. and devel. com. YWCA; hon. trustee Cancer Rsch. Inst.; hon. trustee emeritus Princeton (N.J.) Theol. Sem.; bd. dirs. Parkinson's Disease Found., N.Y.C., N.C. Cmty. Found., Raleigh, Charlotte Philharmonic Orch., N.C. Transp. Mus., Spencer, NC; hon. bd. dirs. YWCA, N.Y.C.; bd. dirs. YWCA of Ctrl. Carolinas. Mem. Fashion Group, Inc. (N.Y.C.), Jr. League Charlotte, Nat. Soc. Colonial Dames, DAR. Home: 300 Cherokee Rd Charlotte NC 28207-1908 Office: Belk Inc 2801 W Tyvola Rd Charlotte NC 28217-4500

GAMIERE, CONSTANCE ANNE, education educator, counselor; b. Cleve., Nov. 26, 1942; d. Charles Lincoln and Mary Carmella (Zappola) G.; m. Conlon Stephan Keator, Sept. 11, 1974. BS in Edn., Miami U., 1965, MEd, 1969, Pupil Pers. Degree, 1971. Cert. c.c. instr., Calif. Coll. instr., counselor Monterey (Calif.) Peninsula Coll., 1974—, co-chair creative arts divsn., 1997—; tchr. Rushville Consold. Sch., Ind., 1973-74; grad. asst./instr. Miami U., Oxford, Ohio, 1968-71; tchr. Lakewood (Ohio) Schs., 1966-68, Cleveland Heights (Ohio) Schs., 1965-66. Costume designer Mac N Ava Film Prodn., Monterey, 1984-90, make-up designer, 1984-90, Chapparrel Prodns., Monterey, 1988, costume asst., John Pytka Prodns., Hollywood, Calif., 1988. Designer theatre costumes All Main Stage Prodns., 1974-97 (ann. Bay Area Region Best awards). Costume designer for Larkin House, Calif. Parks Dept., Monterey, 1987, Squid Festival, Monterey Chamber, 1985. Mem. Calif. Tchrs. Assn., Faculty Assn. of Calif. C.C., NEA, Costume Soc. Am., Bay Area Costumer's Guild. Avocations: gardening, travel, art collecting, play flute, piano. Home: 949 14th St Pacific Grove CA 93950-4901 Office: Monterey Peninsula Coll 980 Fremont St Monterey CA 93940-4799

GAMMILL, KATHRYN DENISE, elementary school educator; b. Clarksdale, Miss., Mar. 1, 1971; d. Lillie C. and Bobby G. Gammill. BS, Delta State U., 1994, MEd, 1998. Tchr. West Bolivar Elem. Sch., Rosedale, Miss., 1994—. Mem., supporter Young Rep., Washington, 2000—03; Sunday sch. dir. for children's dept., Sunday sch. tchr., libr. com. Calvary Bapt. Ch., Cleveland, Miss., 1998—2003. R-Consevative. Baptist. Achievements include Nominated for Disney's Teacher of the Year by a former student. Personal E-mail: katy121997@yahoo.com.

GAMPEL, ELAINE SUSAN, investment company executive, consultant; b. New Haven, Apr. 12, 1950; d. Stanley Irwin and Marion (Levine) G.; m. Alan Joseph Tedeschi, Sept. 9, 1984; children: Zachary Joseph Gampel Tedeschi, Matthew Samuel Gampel Tedeschi. BS in Spl. Edn., Boston U., 1972; MS in Counseling, So. Conn. State U., New Haven, 1975; cert. investment mgmt. analyst, Wharton Sch. Bus., 1990. Spl. edn. tchr. Ansonia (Conn.) Pub. Schs., 1972-77; v.p., investment mgmt. cons. Paine Webber Inc., Denver, 1977-89; v.p. investments Dean Witter Reynolds, Denver, 1989-93, 1st v.p. investments, sr. cons., 1993-2000, sr. v.p. investments, sr. cons., 2000—, wealth advisor, 2002—. Bd. dirs. United Cerebral Palsy of Denver, 1984-93; outside editorial bd. Denver Post, 1991-94; chair investment com. Women's Found. Colo., Denver, 1995-97, treas. 1998, 99, chair bd. trustees, 2002; elected mem. Women's Forum of Colo., 2002; cmty. bd. Denver Nuggets, 1992-95. Recipient Women Leaders of Excellence award, Colo. Women's Leadership Coalition, 2003. Mem. Investment Mgmt. Cons. Assn. (membership com., cert. com. 1990—), Denver Soc. Security Analysts. Avocations: tennis, running, biking. Office: Morgan Stanley 370 17th St Ste 5100 Denver CO 80202-5651

GAND, GAYLE, chef; m. Rick Tramonto. Ry chef, owner Tru, Chgo., 1999—; chef Jam's, N.Y.C., 1985, Gotham Bar & Grill, N.Y.C., Strathallen Hotel, Rochester, NY, Carlos', Highland Park, Ill.; pastry chef The Pump Room, Chgo.; chef Cafe 21, Chgo., Bice, Chgo., Bella Luna, Chgo., Stapleford Park, London, Charlie Trotter's, Chgo.; chef, owner Trio, Chgo., 1993, Brasserie T, Chgo., 1995, Vanilla Bean Bakery, Chgo., 1996—98. Appeared on TV programs : Baker's Dozen, Chef du Jour, Ready, Set, Cook!, Cooking With Julia. Named one of Top Ten Best New Chefs, Food & Wine, 1994; recipient award, James Beard Found., 2001. Office: 676 N St Clair Chicago IL 60611

GANDY, KIM ALLISON, feminist organization executive, lawyer; b. Bossier City, La., Jan. 25, 1954; d. Alfred K. and Roma Rae (Young) Gandy; m. Christopher Lornell; children: Elizabeth Cady, Katherine Eleanor. GBS, La. Tech. U., 1973; JD, Loyola U., 1978. Bar: La. 1978, U.S. Dist. Ct. (ea. and we. dists.) La. 1980, U.S. Supreme Ct. 1981, U.S. Ct. Appeals (5th cir.) 1982. Mgr. South Ctrl. Bell Tel. Co., New Orleans, 1973—77; asst. dist. atty. Orleans Parish, New Orleans, 1978—79; sole practice New Orleans, 1979—. Guest lectr. in field. Treas. ERA United Coalition La., 1977—78; chmn. New Orleans del. La. Dem. Conv., 1980, 1982; vice chmn. New Orleans del., 1984; dir. Women's Lobby Network, 1980—85; founder Greater New Orleans Assn. Dem. Women, 1984. Named New Orleans Outstanding Young Career Woman, New Orleans Bus. and Profl. Women, 1980; named one of New Orleans 100 Women in Forefront, 1986; recipient Law Alumni award, Loyola U., 1976, Milton Sheen award, 1978. Mem.: ABA, Assn. Women Attys., La. Trial Lawyers Assn., La. Bar Assn., NOW (nat. sec. 1987—91, exec. v.p. 1991—2001, pres. 2001—, Mid-South reg. dir. 1983—87, Woman of Yr.). Office: NOW 733 15th St 2nd Fl Washington DC 20005*

GANLEY, BETTY, artist; b. Rahway, N.J., Sept. 18, 1942; d. Walter George and Margaret Charlotte Kenney; m. John Charles Ganley, Feb. 6, 1965 (dec.); children: Scott Michael, Kyle Andrew, David Sean. Diploma in Nursing, Muhlenberg Sch. Nursing, Plainfield, N.J., 1965. RN Va., Md., N.J. Part-time nurse Holy Cross Hosp., Silver Spring, Md., 1979—2003. Artist-contbr., Fresh Flowers, The Best of Flower Painting, 1996, Splash 5 - The Glory of Color, 1998, The Artistic Touch 3, 1999, Splash 5, 2000, Splash 7, The Quality of Light, 2001, Splash 7, A Celebration of Light, one-woman shows include NIH, 1995, Glenview Mansion, Rockville, Md., 1997, The Manor House, Green Spring Gardens Pk., Alexandria, Va., 2002, exhibited in group shows at Quiet Waters Gallery, Annapolis, Md., 1996, Black Rock Art Ctr., Germantown, Md., 2003; cover artist, contbr. article

Elan mag., 2000. Named One of Nieman Marcus' Top 10 Artists of 2000; named one of Top 100, Arts for the Parks, 2001; recipient numerous awards for artwork, 1994—, Best of Show for watercolor, Rockville Art League, 2001, McLean Art Club, Emerson Ramp Gallery Show, 2001, Potomac Valley Watercolor Soc., Bohrer Park Show, 2001, Best of Show, Vienna Art Soc., 1999, Best of Show and 1st Place for watercolor, Rockville Art League ann. spring show, 1997, Spl. award for watercolor, Va. Watercolor Soc. ann. Art Show, 2000, Top 10, Still Life Comp., Australian Artist Mag., 2004, numerous others. Mem.: Washington Watercolor Soc., Balt. Watercolor Soc., Va. Watercolor Soc., Potomac Valley Watercolor Soc., Internat. Soc. of Marine Painters, Reston Art League, Vienna Art Soc., So. Watercolor Soc., Rockville Art League. Home: 713 Forest Park Rd Great Falls VA 22066

GANN, PAMELA BROOKS, academic administrator; b. 1948; BA, U. N.C., 1970; JD, Duke U., 1973. Bar: Ga. 1973, N.C. 1974. Assoc. King & Spalding, Atlanta, 1973; 1975assoc. Robinson, Bradshaw & Hinson, P.A., Charlotte, 1974; asst. prof. Duke U. Sch. Law, Durham, 1975—78, assoc. prof., 1978—80, prof., 1980—99, dean, 1988—99; pres. Claremont McKenna Coll., Claremont, Calif., 1999—. Vis. asst. prof. U. Mich. Law Sch., 1977; vis. assoc. prof. U. Va., 1980 Author: (with D. Kahn) Corporate Taxation and Taxation of Partnerships and Partners, 1979, 83, 89; article editor Duke Law Jour. Mem. Am. Law Inst., Coun. Fgn. Rels., Order of Coif, Phi Beta Kappa Office: Claremont McKenna Coll Office Pres 500 E 9th St Claremont CA 91711-5903

GANNAWAY, CAROLYN MARIE, elementary school educator; b. Kenosha, Wis., Sept. 30, 1949; d. Nicholas and Rose Lucy (Manna) Bordo; m. Paul Joseph Gannaway, May 2, 1970; children: Steven, Michael, Jason, Gregory. BA in English, U. Wis.-Parkside, Kenosha, 1971; MA in Classroom Guidance and Counseling, Carthage Coll., 1989. Cert. tchr., Wis. Tchr., team leader Racine (Wis.) Unified Sch. Dist., 1972—. Named Tchr. of Yr., Wis. PTA, 1995. Avocations: reading, needlepoint, crafts, computers. Office: Gilmore Mid Sch 2330 Northwestern Ave Racine WI 53404-2521 Office Phone: 262-619-4260.

GANNON, SISTER ANN IDA, retired philosophy educator, former college administrator; b. Chgo., 1915; d. George and Hanna (Murphy) G. AB, Clarke Coll., 1941; A.M., Loyola U., Chgo., 1948, LL.D., 1970; PhD, St. Louis U., 1952; Litt.D., DePaul U., 1972; L.H.D., Lincoln Coll., 1965, Columbia Coll., 1969, Luther Coll., 1969; LHD, Augustana Coll., 1969; L.H.D., Marycrest Coll., 1972, Ursuline Coll., 1972, Spertus Coll. Judaica, 1974, Holy Cross Coll., 1974, Rosary Coll., 1975, St. Ambrose Coll., 1975, St. Leo Coll., 1976, Mt. St. Joseph Coll., 1976, Stritch Coll., 1976; LHD, Stonehill Coll., 1976, Elmhurst Coll., 1977, Manchester Coll., 1977, Marymount Coll., 1977; L.H.D., Governor's State U., 1979; LHD, Seattle U., 1981, St. Michael's Coll., 1984, Nazareth Coll., 1985, Holy Family Coll., 1986, Keller Grad. Sch. Mgmt., Our Lady of Holy Cross Coll., New Orleans, 1988. Mem. Sisters of Charity, B.V.M.; tchr. English St. Mary's High Sch., Chgo., 1941 47; residence, study abroad, 1951; chmn. philosophy dept. Mundelein Coll., 1951-57, pres., trustee, 1957—75, prof. philosophy, 1975-85, emeritus faculty, 1987—, archivist, 1986—. Contbr. articles philos. jours. Mem. adv. bd. Sec. Navy, 1975—80, Chgo. Police Bd., 1979—89; bd. dirs. Am. Coun. on Edn., 1971—75, chmn., 1974—75; nat. bd. dirs. Girl Scouts USA, 1966—74, nat. adv., 1976—85; trustee St. Louis U., 1974—87, Ursuline Coll., 1978—92, Cath. Theol. Union, 1983—89, DeVry, Inc., 1987—98, Duquesne U., 1989—91, Montay Coll., 1993—95, Mundelein Coll., 1957—75; bd. dirs. Newberry Libr., 1976—, WTTW Pub. TV, 1976—, Parkside Human Svcs. Corp., 1983—89. Recipient Laetare medal, 1975, LaSallian award, 1975, Aquinas award, 1976, Chgo. Assn. Commerce and Industry award, 1976, Hesburgh award, 1982, Woman of Distinction award Nat. Conf. Women Student Leaders, 1985, Outstanding Svc. award Coun. Ind. Colls., 1989, Woman of History award for edn. AAUW, 1989; named One of 100 Oustanding Chgo. Women, Culture in Action, 1994, Alpha Sigma Nu, 1996. Mem. Am. Cath. Philos. Assn. (exec. coun. 1953-56), Assn. Am. Colls. (bd. dirs. 1965-70, chmn. 1969-70), Religious Edn. Assn. Am. (pres. 1973, chmn. bd. 1975-78), North Cen. Assn. (commn. on colls. and univs. 1971-78, chmn. exec. bd. 1975-77, bd. dirs.), Assn. Governing Bds. Colls. and Univs. (bd. dirs. 1979-88, hon. bd. dirs. 1989-92). Home: Wright Hall 6364 N Sheridan Rd Chicago IL 60660-1726 Office: Loyola U Office Archives Sullivan Ctr 6525 N Sheridan Rd Chicago IL 60626-5344 E-mail: aganno2@luc.edu.

GANNON, PATRICIA J. academic administrator; b. Methuen, Mass., June 1965; d. Richard Edward and Barbara Lee Gannon. BA, Coll. Holy Cross, 1987; MPA, Suffolk U., 1997. Mng. dir. adminstrn., dir. non-profit fin. Mass. Indsl. Fin. Agy., Boston, 1989-95, exec. dir., 1995; sr. mng. dir. fin. programs Mass. Devel. Fin. Agy., Boston, 1996-99; v.p. fiscal affairs, CFO Merrimack Coll., North Andover, Mass., 1999—. Mem. Pi Alpha Alpha. Avocations: decorative furniture painting, gardening, travel. Office: Merrimack Coll Office of Fiscal Affairs 315 Turnpike St North Andover MA 01845-5806

GANT, LESYLE K. systems engineer; b. Shreveport, Jan. 28, 1969; d. Wilson and Loyace Perkins Gant. BS in elec. engr., So. U., A&M Coll., 1991; MS in elec. engr., Ga. Inst. of Tech., 1993. Sci. staff mem. Nortel Networks, Richardson, Tex., 1994—98, sr. verification engr., 1998—2001, Elastic Networks, Paradyne Network, Alpharetta, Ga., 2001—02; sys. test engr. Volt svcs. Group, Proxim Corp., Duluth, Ga., 2002—. Mem.: Soc. Women engrs. Democrat. Bapt.

GANTT, ELISABETH, plant biology educator, researcher; b. Gakovo, Yugoslavia, Nov. 26, 1934; m. R. Raymond, 1958; 1 child. BA, Blackburn Coll., 1958; MSc, Northwestern U., 1960; PhD in Biology, 1963. NIH rsch. assoc. microbiology Dartmouth Coll. Med. Sch., 1963-66, Smithsonian Inst. Radiation Biology Lab., 1966-88; prof. plant biology U. Md., 1988—; co-dir. MOCB. Mem. bd. fellows and assocs. Nat. Rsch. Coun., 1973-76. Recipient Darbaker prize Botany Soc., 1981, G.M. Smith medal NAS, 1994. Fellow AAAS, Am. Inst. Biological Sci., Am. Soc. Photobiology, Am. Soc. Plant Physiologists (v.p. 1988, pres. 1989), Phycol. Soc. Am. (v.p. 1977, pres. 1978), Japan Soc. Plant Physiologists, Nat. Acad. Sci. Achievements include research in structure of photosynthetic apparatus; characterization of carotenoids and photosynthetic membrane structure. Office: U Md Dept Cell Biol and Molecular Genetics College Park MD 20742-0001

GANTZ, NANCY ROLLINS, hospital administrator, nursing administrator, consultant; b. Buffalo Center, Iowa, Mar. 7, 1949; d. Troy Gaylord and Mary (Emerson) Rollins. Diploma in nursing, Good Samaritan Hosp. and Med. Ctr., Portland, Oreg., 1973; BSBA, City U., 1986; MBA, Kennedy-Western U., 1987, PhD, 1991; postgrad. Exec. Program, Wharton Bus. Sch., 1007. Nurse ICU Good Samaritan Hosp., 1973-75; charge nurse Crestview Convalescent Hosp., Portland, 1975; dir. nursing svcs. Roderick Enterprises, Inc., Portland, 1976-78, Holgate Ctr., Portland, 1978-80, nursing cons. in field of adminstrn., 1980-84, coord. CCU; mgr. ICU/CCU Tuality Cmty. Hosp., Hillsboro, Oreg., 1984-86; head nurse ICU, cardiac surgery unit, coronary care unit Good Samaritan Hosp. & Med. Ctr., Portland, 1986-88, mgr. critical care units, 1988-92, asst. v.p. patient care svcs., 1992-93; dir. heart ctr. Deaconess Med. Ctr., Spokane, Wash., 1992-93; asst. exec. dir. Children's Cancer Ctr. King Faisal Specialist Hosp. and Rsch. Ctr., Riyadh, Saudi Arabia, 1994-96; asst. adminstr., chief nurse exec. King Fahad Nat. Children's Cancer and Rsch. Ctr., Riyadh, 1996-99; dir. pediatric intensive svcs./solid organ transplantation St. Louis Children's Hosp., 2000—02; pres. Emerson Rollins Internat. Cons. Assocs., 2002—; v.p. patient care svcs. Wishard Health Svcs., Indpls., 2002—03. Mem. spkrs. bur. Nurses of Am.; mem. task force Oreg. State Health Divsn. Rules and Regulations Revisions for Long Term Health Facilities and Hosp., 1978-79; numerous internat. and nat. speaking presentations; mem. Cons. Consortium, Inc., 1997-2003; developer Cultural Appreciation through Profl. Practice and Synergy. Contbr. chpts. to books and articles to profl. jours. Recipient Wharton Fellow, U Pa. Wharton Bus. Sch., 1997. Mem.: AONE Coun. Nurse Mgrs. (bd. dirs. region 9 1991—92), AONE, ANA (cert.), AACN (chpt. cons. region 18 1978—7989, mgmt. SIC region 18 1990—92, pres. elect greater Portland chpt. 1985—86, pres. 1986—87, bd. dirs. 1985—), Geriatric Nurses Assn. Oreg. (founder, charter pres.), Am. Heart Assn., Sigma Theta Tau. Office: Tower One Ste 3000 225 East North St Indianapolis IN 46204 E-mail: rollinsgantzinternational@msn.com.

GANTZ, SUZI GRAHN, special education educator; b. Chgo., May 17, 1954; d. Robert Donald and Barbara Edna (Ascher) Grahn; m. Louis Estes Gantz, July 11, 1976; children: Christopher, Joshua. BS in Edn. of Deaf and Hard of Hearing, U. Ill., 1976. Tchr. A.G. Bell Sch., Chgo., 1976-80, 88—, facilitator Edn. Connection grant, 1999-2001; sales asst. Bob Grahn & Assocs., Chgo., 1982-84; with sales dept. Isis/My Sisters Circus, Chgo., 1984-86; interpreter Glenbrook North High Sch., Northbrook, Ill., 1986-87; interpreter, aide Lake Forest (Ill.) Dist. 67, 1987-88. Mem. Northbrook Citizens for Drug and Alcohol Alliance, 1988—; cubmaster Boy Scouts Am., Northbrook, 1990-93. Mem. Ill. Tchrs. of the Hearing Impaired, A.G. Bell Soc., Coun. on Exceptional Children. Avocations: dance, swimming. Home: 485 Laburnum Dr Northbrook IL 60062-2259 Office: AG Bell Sch 3730 N Oakley Ave Chicago IL 60618-4813 Office Phone: 773-534-5150. Personal E-mail: shopatnord@comcast.net.

GANULIN, JUDY, public relations professional; b. Chgo., May 2, 1937; d. Alvin and Sadie (Reingold) Landis; m. James Ganulin, June 23, 1957; children: Stacy Ganulin Clark, Amy Ganulin Lowenstein. BA in Journalism, U. Calif., Berkeley, 1958. Copywriter-sec. Joe Connor Advt., Berkeley, 1958; exec. sec. Prescolite Mfg. Co., Berkeley, 1958-59; info. officer Office of Consumer Counsel, Sacramento, 1959-61; pub. rels. positions various polit. campaigns, Fresno, Calif., 1966; adminstrv. asst., editor, mktg. Valley Pubs., Fresno, 1971-80; staff asst. to county supr. Bd. Suprs., Fresno, 1980-82; field rep. Assemblyman Bruce Bronzan, Fresno, 1982-84; prin. Judy Ganulin Pub. Rels., Fresno, 1984—. Speaker new bus. workshop SBA/Svc. Corps Ret. Execs., Fresno, 1990—. Active Hadassah, Fresno, 1975—; pres. Temple Beth Israel Sisterhood, Fresno, 1976; panelist campaign workshop Nat. Women's Polit. Caucus, Fresno, 1994, 2001, publicity chmn. ctrl. Calif. chpt., 1999—2000, mem. C. of C. Art and Wine Festival Com., 1999—2000, Juvenile Justice Ctr. Task Force, 2001, Valley Women's Polit. Fund; bd. dirs. Temple Beth Israel, Fresno, 1972—75, Planned Parenthood Ctrl. Calif., Fresno, 1986—91, Empty Bowls, Sr. Companion Program. Mem. Pub. Rels. Soc. Am. (accredited pub. rels. practitioner, pres. Fresno/Ctrl. Valley chpt. 1994), Am. Mktg. Assn. (pres. ctrl. Calif. chpt. 1987-88), Calif. Press Women, Fresno Advt. Fedn., Fresno Comm. Network (v.p., pres. 1991-93), Fresno C. of C. (mem. mktg. com. 1988—), Fresno Comm. Network (formerely Pub. Rels. Roundtable) . Democrat. Avocations: traveling, reading, cooking. Office: Judy Ganulin Pub Rels 1117 W San Jose Ave Fresno CA 93711-3112 E-mail: jganulin@comcast.net.

GAPPA, JUDITH M. university administrator; Student, Wellesley Coll., 1957-60; BA in Music, George Washington U., 1968, MA in Musicology, 1970; EdD in Ednl. Adminstrn., Utah State U., 1973; cert. Inst. for Ednl. Mgmt., Harvard U., 1980. Lectr. George Washington U., Washington, 1968-69; dir. fine arts program The York Sch., Monterey, Calif., 1970; program cons. Western Interstate Commn. for Higher Edn., Boulder, Colo., 1973; coord. affirmative action program Utah State U., Logan, 1973-75, dir. affirmative action/equal opportunity programs, asst. prof., 1975-77, 78-80, project dir., 1979-81; sr. staff assoc. Nat. Ctr. for Higher Edn. Mgmt. Systems, Inc., Boulder, 1977-78; assoc. v.p. for faculty affairs, dean of faculty, prof. San Francisco State U., 1980-91; sr. assoc. Am. Assn. Higher Edn., 1995-97; prof. Purdue U., West Lafayette, Ind., 1991—, v.p. human rels., 1991-98. Served on numerous coms., couns. Utah State U., San Francisco State U.; cons. Assn. Governing Bds., 1994, U. Mich., Duluth, 1992, Calif. State U. Human Resources Mgmt. Office, 1992, Am. U., Washington, 1987, No. Rockies Consortium for Higher Edn. Conf., 1985, So. Utah State Coll., 1982, Nat. Ctr. for Rsch. in Vocat. Edn., 1980-81, Hood Coll., 1982-84, Am. Insts. for Rsch. in Behavioral Scis., 1980-81; condr. workshops on edn. Co-author: The Invisible Faculty, 1993; mem. editl. bd. Rev. of Higher Edn., 1994-97; contbr. numerous articles to profl. jours. Grantee Lilly Endowment, 1995, United Techs. Corp., 1992, TIAA-CREF/Lilly Endowment, 1990, Calif. State U., 1985, San Francisco State U., 1981, HEW, 1979-81, Nat. Inst. Edn., 1977, Utah State U., 1977, Fed. workshop grant, 1976, State of Utah, 1975, 76. Mem. Western Assn. Schs. and Colls. (accreditation team mem. Calif. State U.-L.A. 1990), Am. Assn. for Higher Edn. (sr. assoc. Washington chpt. 1995-97), Assn. for Study of Higher Edn. (nat. adv. bd. ASHE-ERIC Higher Edn. Report Series 1990-91, editl. bd. Rev. of Higher Edn. 1994-97, nominating com. 1986-87, program com. for 1986 nat. conf., membership com. 1982-84, conf. com. 1983, editl. bd. Rev. of Higher Edn. 1994-97), Am. Coun. on Edn. Nat. Identification Program (No. Calif. state coord. 1988-91). Office: Purdue Univ Sch Edn 1446 Liberal Arts Rd West Lafayette IN 47907-1075

GAPSTUR, SUSAN MARY, cancer epidemiologist, educator, researcher; b. Mpls., Nov. 14, 1960; d. Michael and Mary Monica Gapstur. BS, U. Wis., La Crosse, 1983; MPH, U. Minn., 1989, PhD, 1993. Rsch. technician Mayo Clinic and Found., Rochester, Minn., 1984-87; rsch. assoc. U. Ariz., Tucson, 1993-94; asst. prof. dept. preventive medicine Northwestern U., Chgo., 1994—. Grant reviewer NIH, 1996—, Dept. Def., 1998—. Contbr. over 30 articles to med. jours., including Jour. AMA, Am. Jour. Physiology, Am. Jour. Epidemiology, Cancer Epidemiology. Predoctoral fellow U. Minn., 1990-92; rsch. grantee Lynn Sage Breast Cancer Found., 1996, Washington Square Health Found., 1998-00, Nat. Cancer Inst., 1998-02. Mem. Soc. for Epidemiologic Rsch., Am. Assn. Cancer Rsch., Am. Soc. Preventive Oncology (session chmn. 1993, 97). Avocations: hiking, canoeing. Office: Northwestern U Dept Preventive Medicine 680 N Lake Shore Dr 1102 Chicago IL 60611-4402

GARBACZ, PATRICIA FRANCES, school social worker, therapist; b. Hamtramck, Mich., Nov. 26, 1941; d. Stanley and Frances (Harubin) G. BS, Siena Heights Coll., 1969; M. Pastoral Counseling, St. Paul U., Ottawa, Can., 1972; ThM, St. John Provincial Sem., 1983; MSW, Wayne State U., 1989. Cert. social worker Acad. Cert. Social Workers; cert. sch. social worker; lic. marriage and family therapist; cert. addictions counselor level I. Assoc. dir. vocations Archdiocese of Detroit, 1975-77; co-dir. of inst. for women Archdiocese of Lusaka (Zambia), 1977-78; pastoral minister Archdiocese of Detroit, 1979-80, assoc. dir. preformation, 1980-84; tchr., ministry coord. Bishop Borgess High Sch., Redford, Mich., 1984-86; tchr., dept. chair Aquinas High Sch., Southgate, Mich., 1986-88; therapist Community Coun. on Drug Abuse/Livonia (Mich.) Counseling, 1988-89; substance abuse therapist Oxford Inst., St. Clair Shores, Mich., 1989-91; sch. social worker Lakeshore Pub. Schs., St. Clair Shores, 1990—; therapist Macomb Child Guidance, 1989-96. Mem. NASW, Am. Assn. Marriage and Family Therapists, Mich. Assn. Sch. Social Workers. Avocations: reading, walking, piano, dulcimer, spinning and weaving.

GARBE-MORILLO, PATRICIA ANN, preservationist; b. Paterson, N.J., Nov. 27, 1946; d. William Richard Garbe and Margaret Mary Quinn; m. Manuel Enrique Morillo, Sept. 9, 1985; 1 child, Christina Patricia Morillo. BA, U. Miami, Coral Gables, 1969; MA, U. Ariz., 1971; PhM, Columbia U., 1976. Truck driver N.Y. Daily News, N.Y.C., 1974—76; bus. mgr., contbr. Talking Wood environ. mag., Pompton Lakes, NJ, 1979—81; archtl. historian Divsn. Cultural and Hist. Affairs Bergen County Dept. Pks., Hackensack, NJ, 1981—83; archtl. historian Urban Rsch. & Design divsn., Jersey City Dept. Housing, 1983—85; preservation specialist N.Y.C. Landmarks Preservation Commn., 1985—95; preservation officer Bergen County Dept. Pks. divsn. Cultural and Hist. Affairs, Hackensack, NJ, 1996—. Apprentice archaeologist archeol. excavations, Mexico, 1972—73; cons. N.J. State Hist. Preservation Consulting List, 1983—; chmn. Closter (N.J.) Hist. Preservation Commn., 1998—; prin. Preservation Planning & Heritage Devel., Closter, 1996—. Author (annotated bibliography): Kroeber Anthropological Society Papers, 1971; author: Closter and Alpine, 2001; project dir., tombstone restoration and mus. exhibit Closter: This is Your History, 1997 (Bergen County Historic Sites adv. bd. award); editor: Raid! The Tory Raid on Closter, May 9, 1779, 1999. Apptd. mcpl. historian Borough of Closter, 1996—; mem. environ. and hist. com. N.J. State Dem. Com., Rutgers U., 1981—83; mem. Closter Bus. & Industry Adv. Com., 1995—98; design advisor Downtown Renaissance Com., Closter, 1996—98. Recipient Women's Heritage Keeper award, Bergen County and N.J. State Assembly, 1999, Vol. of Yr. award, Bergen County, 1999, Hist. Preservation Leadership award, 2003; fellow Ford Found., 1972. Mem.: Preservation New Jersey, Miami Design Preservation League, Nat. Trust for Historic Preservation, Closter Hist. Soc. (founder, pres. 1996—). Avocations: travel, gardening, Cuban culture and architecture, museums. Home: 68 Taylor Dr Closter NJ 07624

GARBER, BETH CAROL, early childhood educator, music educator; b. Miami Beach, Fla., Oct. 1, 1952; d. Seymour Albert Bender and Marian Jane Ascher; m. Harold Garber, Feb. 19, 1984; 1 child, Mathew Eric. BS in Edn., U. Hartford, 1974; MA in Student Personnel Svcs., Kean Coll. N.J., 1981; MA in Rehab. Counseling, Seton Hall U., South Orange, N.J., 1985. Cert. tchr. handicapped N.J., 1975, student personnel svc. instr. N.J., 1982, rehab. counselor N.J., 1985, elem. tchr. N.J., 1991. Resource rm. tchr. Lafayette Mid. Sch., Elizabeth, NJ, 1975—78, Battin Career Ctr., Elizabeth, NJ, 1978—81; learning resource ctr. tchr. Union County Regional High Schs., Springfield, NJ, 1981—83; rehab. specialist Ctrl. Rehab. Assocs., Freehold, NJ, 1985—87; music specialist tchr. Sundance Sch., North Plainfield, NJ, 1988—90; nursery dir., lead tchr. Bayonne Jewish Cmty. Ctr., NJ, 1990—91; music tchr. TMR program Jointure for Cmty. Adult Edn., Bound Brook, NJ, 1992—95; head tchr., music specialist Wee People, Bound Brook, NJ, 1991—96; music specialist Jewish Edn. Assn., Ctr. for Spl. Edn., Whippany, NJ, 1996—; head tchr., music dir. Mountain Top Presch. and Kindergarten, Warren, NJ, 1996—. Ednl. cons. Teen Parent Program, Elizabeth, NJ, 1978; Judaic programming cons. Mountain Top Presch. and Kindergarten, Warren, NJ, 1996—, mentor, 2000—01. Vol. Somerset County Food B ank, Bound Brook, NJ; mem. Somerset County Mental Health Players, Bridgewater, NJ; coord. Interfaith Hospitality Network, Temple Beth-El, Hillsborough, NJ, 2002—, founding mem. adult choir, mem., past pres. Sisterhood, 1996—98. Named Outstanding Child Care Profl., Somerset Alliance for the Future, 1993; fellowship, Seton Hall U., 1983. Mem.: Nat. Assn. Edn. of Young Children, N.J. Assn. for Edn. of Young Children, Rho Chi Sigma (pres. 1983—84). Avocations: guitar, family and friends, reading, travel, performing in community theater.

GARBER, DOROTHY HELEN, rancher, artist; b. Fredricktown, Mo., Oct. 7, 1917; d. Chester Payton and Bessie Belle (Sykes) Brewington; m. H. Derwood Garber, 1933 (dec.); children: Patricia Kay, Marici Lea; m. Samuel T. Ramey, Sept. 1959 (div. Dec. 1971). Rancher Patty K. Ranch, Hotchkiss, Colo., 1945—. Bookkeeper, owner Garber Clo, Hotchkiss, 1954-56, co-owner, mgr., 1966-80; owner, mgr., buyer Dorothy's, Hotchkiss, 1956-66. Artist, judge, exhibitor, lectr. and demonstrator; retrospective art exhibit Gallery Connections Hotchkiss, Colo., 1997. One-woman shows include Western Colo. Ctr. for Arts, Grand Junction, Hotel Colorado Art Gallery, Glenwood Springs, Colo., Aristracrat, Paonia, Colo., Finishing Touch Gallery, Hotchkiss, Pavilion, Montrose, Colo., etc.; exhibited in group shows at Montrose Pavilion, Mitchell Mus., Trinidad, Colo., Old Pass Gallery, Raton, N.Mex., Doherty Gallery, Delta, Colo., Castano Gallery, Denver, Rocky Mountain Nat. Watercolor Exhibition, Golden, Colo., San Diego Internat. Watercolor Soc. Exhibition, State Fair Fine Arts Gallery, Albuquerque, The Tubac Mus., Tubac, Ariz., Albuquerque Mus. Fine Arts, Western Colo. Ctr. for Arts, Grand Junction, Gallery Connections, Hotchkiss, Colo., 1997, Catherine Lorillard Wolf Art Club, N.Y.C., 1998, others. Mem. Western Fedn. Watercolor (signature mem.), N.Mex. Watercolor Soc., Western Colo. Watercolor Soc. (founder, past pres., adv. bd.), Hotchkiss Fine Arts (past pres., charter mem.), Delta Fine Art. Democrat. Baptist. Home and Office: 697 3950 Dr Hotchkiss CO 81419-9639

GARBER, KATHERINE, special education educator; b. Granite City, Ill., Mar. 13, 1975; d. Anton Fredrick and Carol Jean Garber. AA, Belleville Area Coll., 1995; BS, So. Ill. U., 1998. Tchr. Lots-of-Tots Daycare, Granite City, Ill., 1994—98; sub. tchr. Harris Elem. Sch., Madison, Ill., 1999; alternative edn. tchr. Coord. Youth and Human Svcs., Granite City, Ill., 1999—2002; spl. edn. tchr. Riverview Ctrl. Middle Sch., St. Louis, 2002—. Camp counselor Camp Roxy, Roxana, Ill., 1997; advisor Junior Achievement, Edwardsville, Ill., 1997—98. Class A vol. Special Olympics, Granite City, Ill., 1999—; vol. March of Dimes Walk-a-Thon, Edwardsville, 1995; mem. Madison Jr. Svc., 1996—98. Mem.: NEA, Mo. Edn. Assn., Ill. Edn. Assn., Coun. for Exceptional Children, So. Ill. Univ. Alumni Assn. Avocations: swimming, bicycling, shopping, camping, walking. Home: 2209 Grand Ave Granite City IL 62040

GARBER, NARA THEA, filmmaker; b. N.Y.C., Apr. 6, 1970; d. Donald Graham Garber and Ikuyo Tagawa Garber; m. Benjamin Dale Wolf, Aug. 28, 1999. AB in English, Harvard-Radcliffe, 1991; MFA in Film, Columbia U., 1999. Rschr., writer travel guidebook Let's Go (Italy), Cambridge, Mass., 1991; tchr. Latin, adminstr. St. Anns Sch., Bklyn., 1991—94, coll. counselor, 1994—98; co-pres. Topiary Prodns., Inc., Bklyn., 1998—. Dir., writer : (films) A Quiet Chapter, 1997 (1st pl. award N.Y. Student Film/Video Festival, Best Short Narrative, South Bronx Film Festival); Pas de Deux, 1999 (Silver Bear, Austria's Festival of Nations, Outstanding Narrative Short, CineWomenNY); locations mgr. Baby John Doe, 1996; editor (films, 24), 1999; (films, Fat Chance), 2000; (films) Amour Infinity, 2000 (Best Film, Jamaican Film Festival, Audience Choice award L.A. Black Film Festival); Business Class, 2002; dir. photography, editor (films, Central Nam), 1999; dir. photography (films) A Day in the Park, 2000; The Dead and the Dying, 2001; dir. photography, editor Under Pressure, 2001; Welcome to Purgatory, 2002; (films, Jihad!), 2002—03; dir. photography (films) Mimmo & Paulie, 2003; (documentaries) Power, 2001. Democrat. Home: 22 Vernadah Pl Brooklyn NY 11201 E-mail: naragarber@topiaryproductions.com.

GARCEAU, JO MILLS, writer; b. Portland, Oreg., Nov. 10, 1932; d. M. Pierre Mills and Mary Elizabeth Kies. BA in Polit. Sci., U. of Oreg., 1953; MA in Human Values, San Francisco Theol. Sem., 1982. Exec. sec. The Boeing Co., Seattle, 1959—65; campaign dir. Dan Evans for Gov. Com., Spokane, Wash., 1968; asst. to the gov. Office of the Gov. State of Wash., Olympia, Wash., 1969—72, cabinet dir., 1972—76; campus min. The Evergreen Coll. Campus Ministry, Olympia, 1977—82; asst. min. Ananda Ch., Nevada City, Calif., 1982—89; writer Boring, Oreg., 1990—; customer svc. assoc. PacifiCorp, Portland, 1996—. Chmn. affirmative action com. State of Wash., Olympia, 1973—77, mem. intergovtl. pers. adv. coun., 1975—77. Chmn. budget com. United Way, Olympia, Wash., 1974—78; v.chmn. 47th Legis. Dist. Rep. Party, Renton, Wash., 1960—63; co-chmn. Dan Evans for Gov. Legis. Com., Renton, 1963—64, Treadwell for Congress Com., Spokane, Wash., 1967; chmn. The Evergreen Coll. Campus Ministry, Olympia, 1976—78; dir. parish renewal project St. Michael's Parish, Olympia, 1981—82; bd. dir. Wash. Coun. of Ch., Seattle, 1977—82. Fellow Walden fellow, 1998; grantee, State of Oreg., 1949—51; scholar Hazel P. Schwering scholarship, U. of Oreg., 1952. Mem.: Nat. Assn. Securities Dealers (arbitrator 2003—), Willamette Writers (asst. treas. 2002), Pacific N.W. Writers, Oreg. Astrological Soc. Liberal. Buddhist. Avocations: car camping, astrology, psychology, spirituality.

GARCHIK, LEAH LIEBERMAN, journalist; b. Bklyn., May 2, 1945; d. Arthur Louis and Mildred (Steinberg) Lieberman; m. Jerome Marcus Garchik, Aug. 11, 1968; children— Samuel, Jacob BA, Bklyn. Coll., 1966. Editorial asst. San Francisco Chronicle, 1972-79, writer, editor, 1979-83, editor This World, 1983-84, columnist, 1984—; also author numerous book and movie reviews, features and profiles. Author: San Francisco; the City's Sights and Secrets, 1995; panelist (radio quiz show) Mind Over Matter; contbr. articles to mags. Vice pres. Golden Gate Kindergarten Assn., San Francisco, 1978; pres. Performing Arts Workshop, San Francisco, 1977-79; bd. dirs. Home Away From Homelessness, 1994-99. Recipient 1st prize Nat. Soc. Newspaper Columnists, 1992. Mem. Deutsche Music Verein, Newspaper Guild. Democrat. Jewish. Home: 156 Baker St San Francisco CA 94117-2111 Office: San Francisco Chronicle 901 Mission St San Francisco CA 94103-2905 Office Phone: 415-777-8426. E-mail: lgarchik@sfchronicle.com.

GARCIA, ANGELA G. lawyer; b. Manila, Philippines, 1960; BA cum laude, Mount Holyoke U., 1982; MPhil, U. Cambridge, 1984; JD cum laude, Georgetown U., 1989. Bar: N.Y. 1990, D.C. 1990, U.S. Dist. Ct. (so. and ea. dists.) N.Y. 1994, U.S. Ct. Appeals (2d cir.) 1996. Law clk. Hon. James Belson D.C. Ct. Appeals, 1989—90; atty. Skadden, Arps, Slate, Meagher & Flom LLP, N.Y., 1990—97, ptnr., 1997—. Office: Skadden Arps Slate Meagher & Flom LLP Four Times Sq New York NY 10036*

GARCIA, ASTRID J. newspaper executive; b. Caguas, Puerto Rico, Sept. 6, 1950; m. Robert Gillespie; children: Robert, Richard. BA with distinction, Barnard Coll., 1972; JD, Bklyn. Law Sch., 1980. Bar: N.Y. 1980. Dir., lighting designer various theatres, N.Y.C., 1972-74; equal employment opportunity specialist Gen. Svcs. Adminstrn. Fed. Govt., Region II, N.Y.C., 1974-76; paralegal So. Dist. N.Y. U.S. Atty.'s Office, N.Y.C., 1976-80; atty. Puerto Rican Legal Def. and Edn. Fund, N.Y.C., 1980-81, NLRB, N.Y.C. and Hartford, Conn., 1981-85; mgr. employee rels. dept. human resources The Hartford Courant, 1985-87; asst. dir. human resources The Miami (Fla.) Herald, 1987-90; v.p., dir. employee rels. St. Paul Pioneer Press, 1990-94; sr. v.p. human resources and labor, dir. labor rels. Jour. Comm., Milw., 1994-97; sr. v.p. ops. Milw. Jour. Sentinel, 1997—. Mem. N.Y. Bar Assn. Office: Milw Jour Sentinel PO Box 661 Milwaukee WI 53201-0661

GARCIA, BEATRICE MAUDE, social worker; b. Boston, Jan. 18, 1929; d. George Louis and Beatrice Lawrence (White) Joughin; m. Edward P. Black, June 4, 1950 (dec.); children: Victoria, Edward, Barbara; m. Marvin Victor Aquirre, May 10, 1956 (div.); children: Deborah, Michael; m. Peter Charles Garcia, Aug. 13, 1961. BA in Anthopology with honors and distinction, Sonoma State U., 1971; MA in Anthropology, San Francisco State U., 1979; postgrad., Sonoma State U., 1982—. Coord. Boyle Heights Coalition, L.A., 1953-55; dir. Truman Boyd Housing Assn., Long Beach, Calif., 1961-63; med. records supr. Crestview Hosp., Petaluma, Calif., 1979-81; investigator, ombudsman Sonoma County Ombudsman, Santa Rosa, Calif., 1984—88; dir. sr. svcs. Ctrl. YMCA, San Francisco, 1988-90; dir. case mgmt. East Valley Sr. Ctr., North Hollywood, Calif., 1994-98, regional mgr. Region VII, long term care ombudsman L.A., 2001—. Organizer campaigns Dem. Orgn., Santa Maria, Calif., 1964, Vallejo, Calif., 1968; sec. Red Banks Oaks Assn., 1998—, Dem. Club High Desert, 1999—. Mem. AAUW (sec. Antelope Valley chpt. 1999—), No. Calif. Manx Assn. (adminstrv. 1999—). Democrat. Episcopalian. Avocations: reading, travel, antiques. Home: 4030 Lexington Ct Palmdale CA 93552-4356

GARCIA, BETH BAXTER, sculptor, writer; b. Oakland, Calif., Jan. 4, 1918; d. Howard Edward and Rena (Scott) Baxter; m. John Locke García, 1942 (div. 1974); children: Baxter Juan, Holland Gene. BA in Creative Art, Mills Coll., 1939, MA in Creative Art, 1941. One person shows include Carmel (Calif.) Art Assn., 1978; two person shows include Villa Montalvo, Saratoga, Calif., 1964, New Monterey Ctr., Monterey, Calif., 1967; exhibited in group shows Dallas Mus. Fine Art, 1959, Oakland (Calif.) Mus. Art, 1959, Calif. State Fair, Sacramento, 1965, Monterey County Fair, 1956-65, Ch. of the Wayfarer, Carmel, 1967, Carmel Art Assn., 1956—. Recipient Popular award Ch. of the Wayfarer, 1967, 1st prize ribbons Monterey County Fair Fine Arts, 1956, 57, 58, 63, 64, 65, 1st Ann. Chamber Arts award Portland (Oreg.) Chamber, 1980. Mem. Carmel Art Assn. (bd. dirs. 1958-59, 77-79, 85-86). Avocations: reading, collecting porcelain animals, swimming. Home: 25673 Flanders Dr Carmel CA 93923-8323 Office Phone: 831-624-5615. E-mail: hollandgarcia@sbcglobal.net.

GARCIA, BONNIE, state official; b. N.Y.C. m. Javier Garcia; children: Melissa, Javier. BS in Workforce Edn. and Devel., So. Ill. U. Owner consulting bus.; state assembly mem. Dist. 80 Calif. State Assembly, 2002—. Mem. edn. com.; mem. human svcs. com.; mem. local govt. com.; vice-chair jobs, econ. devel., and economy com.; mem. Coachella Valley Health Partnership, DCA Riverside County Energy Task Force Com., FISH Food Bank, Inland Empire Cmty. Devel. Corp. Republican. Mailing: Rm 4102 PO Box 942849 Sacramento CA 95814 Office: Ste B 68-700 Avenida Lalo Guerrero Cathedral City CA 92234

GARCIA, CHRISTINE, academic administrator, educator, researcher; B Govt., U.Nex., 1961, M Polit. Sci. in Edn., 1964; PhD Polit. Sci., U. Calif., Davis, 1972. Prof. polit. sci. U. N.Mex., 1970—, asst. dir. divsn. govt. rsch., 1970—72, asst., assoc. dean Coll. Arts and Scis., 1975—80, dean coll. Arts and Scis., 1980—86, v.p. acad. affairs, 1987—90, interim provost, v.p. acad. affairs, 1993, 1998—2000, pres., 2002—. Tchr. various u.; rschr. in field. Author (editor): 10 books, 50 monographs; contbr. articles, chapters to books. Office: U NMex 115 Civic Plz Dr Taos NM 87571

GARCIA, EDNA I. state legislator, secondary education educator; b. Humacao, P.R., Feb. 16, 1951; d. Agustin and Benigna Garcia; children: Clemente, Myrna. BA, Internat. Inst. of Ams., Hato Rey, P.R., 1983; postgrad., U. Bridgeport, 1985, Housatonic Coll., Bridgeport, Conn., 1989; MA in Bilingual Edn., Fairfield U., 1995; student paralegal studies, Profl. Career Devel. Inst., Atlanta, 1990—. Notary pub. Coord. social svc., outreach worker Spanish Am. Devel. Agy., Bridgeport, 1973-79; tchr. English, Dept. Pub. Edn., Carolina, P.R., 1979-83; ESL tchr. Bassic High Sch., Bridgeport, Conn., 1985-95; rep. 128th dist. Conn. Ho. Reps., 1992—, chair exec. and legis. nominations com., legis. black and Puerto Rican caucus, vice chair edn. com., mem. judiciary com. Mem. citizens adv. com. on contract compliance Mayor's Office; mem. Dem. Town Com., 1992—; bd. dirs. Kennedy Ctr., Inc., 1994—. Recipient Humanitarian award Conn. Edn. Assn., 1988, Jefferson award Sta. WTNH-TV Channel 8, 1991, Outstanding Achievement award The Hispanic Soc., Inc., 1991. Mem. NAFE, NOW, ASPIRA (founding mem.), ATENO (founding mem.), Nat. Hispanic Caucus of State Legislators, Latinos for Progress, Nat. Assn. Latino Elected Ofcls. Democrat. Address: PO Box 5887 Bridgeport CT 06610-0887

GARCIA, ELISA DOLORES, lawyer; b. Bklyn., Nov. 8, 1957; d. Vincent Garcia, Jr. and Dolores Elizabeth (Canedo) Marmo; m. John Jay Hasluck, Feb. 28, 1987; children: Brooke Elisabeth, John Neville. BA, MS, SUNY, Stony Brook, 1980; JD, St. John's U., 1985. Bar: N.Y. 1986. Cons. Energy Devel. Internat., Pt. Jefferson, N.Y., 1980-83; assoc. Willkie Farr & Gallagher, N.Y.C., 1985-89; sr. counsel GAF Corp./Internat. Specialty Products, Wayne, N.J., 1989-94; regional counsel for L.Am., Philip Morris Internat., Rye Brook, N.Y., 1994-2000; exec. v.p., gen. counsel Domino's Pizza, LLC, Ann Arbor, Mich., 2000—. Mem. Glen Rock (N.J.) Planning Bd., 1992-95, chmn., 1994-95. Mem. ABA, N.Y. State Bar Assn., Mich. Bar Assn., Am. Corp. Counsel Assn. (dir. Mich. chpt.). Roman Catholic. Avocations: gardening, scuba diving. Office: Domino's Pizza LLC PO Box 997 30 Frank Lloyd Wright Dr Ann Arbor MI 48106-0997 E-mail: garciae@dominos.com

GARCIA, FRANCES, accountant; b. Wichita Falls, Tex., July 21, 1941; d. Genaro Garcia and Rosalia Nunez. BBA, Midwestern State U., 1968. Audit mgr. Arthur Andersen and Co., Austin and Dallas, Tex., 1968-77; commr. U.S. Copyright Royalty Tribunal, Washington, 1977-82; auditing ptnr. Quezada Navarro and Co., L.A., 1982-86; dir. of recruiting U.S. Gen. Acctg. Office, Washington, 1986—, dir. internal evaluation, 1994—96; inspector gen. Orgn. of Am. State, 2002—, chmn. bd. external auditors, 2002—. Mem. Am. Assn. Hispanic CPAs (pres. 1987-90), Spanish Edn. Devel. Ctr. (treas. 1992—). Home: 2510 Virginia Ave NW Washington DC 20037-1904

GARCIA, FRIEDA, community foundation executive; BA, New Sch. Social Rsch., 1964; AA (hon.), Roxbury C.C., 1987. Social worker Roxbury (Mass.) Multi-Svc. Ctr., 1966-71; exec. dir. La Alianza Hispana Inc., 1971-73; cmty. fellow MIT, Boston, 1974; spl. asst. to gov. Commonwealth of Mass., Boston, 1974-75; dir. consultation and edn. Solomon Carter Fuller Mental Health Ctr., Boston, 1975-81; pres. United South End Settlements, Boston, 1981—. Bd. dirs. Local Initiatives Support Corp. Chair Boston Found.; bd. dirs. Lincoln Filene Ctr. for Citizenship & Pub. Affairs, Associated Grantmakers of Mass.; trustee Isabella Gardner Mus. Recipient Drum Maj. for Peace award Martin Luther King Jr. Ann. Breakfast, 1981, Abigail Adams award Mass. Women's Polit. Caucus, 1993, Mass. Legis. Black Caucus award, 1995. Mem. The Boston Panel of Agy. Execs., Boston Pvt. Industry Coun. (bd. dirs.), Coun. of Foundations, Women & Founds./Corp. Philanthropy, Hispanics in Philanthropy. Office: United South End Settlements Harriet Tubman House 566 Columbus Ave Boston MA 02118-1181

GARCIA, JENNIFER, music educator; b. Charleston, W.Va., Apr. 22, 1976; d. George A. Brown, Jr. and Anna C. Brown; m. John R. Garcia, II, July 8, 2000. BA cum laude in Music Edn., BA cum laude in Ch. Music, Alderson-Broaddus Coll., 1999. Cert. tchr. W.Va. Dept. of Edn., 1999, Mass. Dept. of Edn., 2002. Music tchr. grades 4-12 Kanawha County Schs., Charleston, W.Va., 1999—2000; music tchr. grades k-8 Methuen (Mass.) Pub. Schs., 2001; music tchr. grades k-4 Chelmsford (Mass.) Pub. Schs., 2001—. Handbell choir dir. Hanscom (Mass.) Chapel, 2002—, children's choir dir., 2000—02. Musician: (performance) Music of the Night, 2003. Pilgramage to UN Odd Fellows Lodge, 1992. Recipient Academic and Citizenship award, Epsilon Tau Eta Sigma, 1999, Meml. award, E. W. Billings, 1999. Mem.: Student Music Educators Nat. Conf. (pres., sec., treas. 1997—99), Music Educators Nat. Conf. Home: 114 Ent Road Hanscom AFB MA 01731 Office: Chelmsford Public Schools 290 Richardson Rd North Chelmsford MA 01863

GARCIA, JULIA THERESA, secondary school educator; b. N.Y.C., Aug. 30, 1923; d. Ignatius Colletti-Riena and Julia Pendeleur; m. Frank Leonard Garcia, May 26, 1949 (dec. Aug. 1995); children: Julia, Frank, Annette. BA, Hunter Coll., 1951; MA, Columbia U., 1956. Cert. tchr. chemistry N.Y., asst. prin. supervision phys. scis. N.Y. Tchr. gen. sci. Alfred E. Smith Jr. H.S. Bd. Edn. N.Y.C., tchr. chemistry Alfred E. Smith H.S., asst. prin. supervision phys. scis. Alfred E. Smith H.S., prin. summer sch. Alfred E. Smith H.S. Bd. examiner sci. and math. Bd. Edn. N.Y.C., 1984—89. Active Diabetic Assn. Recipient award for dedicated svc. to children, N.Y.C. Sci. Chmn.'s Assn., 1989. Mem.: Phi Delta Kappa, N.Y.C. Acad. Sci.

GARCIA, JULIET VILLARREAL, university administrator; m. Oscar E. Garcia; two children. Grad. in Comm. and Linguistics, U. Tex. Pres. U. Tex. at Brownsville, Tex. Southmost Coll. Bd. dirs. Fed. Res. of Dallas/San Antonio br. of Tex. Commerce Bancshares Inc.; past bd. dirs. Am. Coun. Edn., chmn. bd. dirs. 1995. Bd. dirs. Carnegie Found. for Advancement of Teaching, Pub. Welfare Foun.; vice-chair adv. com. on Fin. Aid; appointed mem. White House Initiative on Ednl. Excellence for Hispanic-Ams. Named Woman of Distinction Nat. Conf. of Coll. Women Student Leaders, 1995, one of most influential Hispanics Hispanic Bus. Mag. Office: U Tex & Tex Southmost Coll Office of Pres 80 Fort Brown St Brownsville TX 78520-4956

GARCIA, JUNE MARIE, librarian; b. Bryn Mawr, Pa., Sept. 12, 1947; d. Roland Ernest and Marion Brill (Hummel) Traynor; m. Teodosio Garcia, July 17, 1928; children: Gretchen, Adrian. BA, Douglass Coll., 1969; MLS, Rutgers U., 1970. Reference libr. New Brunswick (N.J.) Pub. Libr., 1970-72, Plainfield (N.J.) Pub. Libr., 1972-75; br. mgr. Phoenix Pub. Libr., 1975-80, extension svcs. adminstr., 1980-93; dir. San Antonio Pub. Libr., 1993-99; CEO, CARL Corp., Denver, 1999-2001; v.p., chief amb. TLC/CARL, Denver, 2001—02; mng. ptnr. Dubberly Garcia Assocs., 2002—, E-Learn Librs., Inc., 2004—. Recipient Productivity Innovator award City of Phoenix, 1981. Mem. ALA (life, coun. 1986-90, 93-2001, pres. Pub. Libr. Assn. 1991-92, new stds. task force 1983-87, goals, guidelines and stds. com. 1986-90, chairperson 1987-90, resource allocation com. 1998-99), Freedom to Read Found. (bd. dirs.), Ariz. State Libr. Assn. (pres. 1984-85, Libr. of Yr. award 1986, Pres.'s award 1990), Beta Phi Mu. Office: 1195 S Harrison St Denver CO 80210 Office Phone: 303-757-7420.

GARCIA, KATHERINE LEE, controller, accountant; b. Portland, Oreg., Nov. 4, 1950; d. Gerald Eugene and Dolores Lois (Erickson) Moe; m. Buddy Jesus Garcia; Nov. 19, 1977; children: Kevin, Brett, Rodd. BS cum laude, U. Nev., 1976. CPA Idaho, Nev.; cert. pub. fin. officer 2001. Retail clk. Raleys, Food King, Reno, 1968-76; sr. acct. Pieretti, Wilson and McNulty, Reno, 1976-78, Deloitte Haskins and Sells, Boise, Idaho, 1979-81, Washoe County, Reno, 1981-83, chief dep. comptr., 1983-94, comptroller, 1994—. Treas., bd. dirs. Friends of 4 (pub. TV), Boise, 1979-81; tutor RAD program, 1995-97; treas. Sierra Miners, 1998-99. Recipient Cert. of Excellence in Fin. Reporting, Govt. Fin. Officer's Assn., 1982—. Mem. AICPA, Nev. Soc. CPAs (chmn. state and local govt. com. 1992-93, 98—), Govt. Fin. Officers Assn. (mem. spl. rev. com. 1989-97, state rep.), Nev. Govt. Fin. Officers Assn. (treas. 1989-91), U. Nev. Reno Found. (trustee, audit com.). Republican. Avocations: jogging, sewing, biking, reading. Home: 655 Joy Lake Rd Reno NV 89511-5766 Office: Washoe County PO Box 11130 Reno NV 89520-0027 E-mail: kgarcia@mail.co.washoe.nv.us.

GARCIA, LAURA CATHERINE, emergency and disaster preparedness consultant; b. Hollywood, Fla., Mar. 11, 1957; d. Thomas Tubens and Felicia (Acebal) Garcia; children: Kristin Kaplan, Natalie, Jonathan, Diana. BSEE, U. Miami, 1979. Utilities exec. Fla. Power and Light Co., Miami, 1980-93, ops. mgr. Dade County, 1991-93; pres. L.G.K. Assocs., Inc., Ft. Lauderdale, Fla., 1993—. Counselor Soc. Abused Children, Kendall, Fla., 1985-86; instr. Jr. Achievement, Miami, 1986-87, Adult Illiteracy Program, 1987; bd. dirs. YWCA, 1988-92, Convenant House, 1995-96; instr. Youth Ministry, 1999-2002, CHARLEE program, 2000—. Early admission scholar U. Miami, 1975; recipient Hurricane Andrew Hero award Dade County Rebuilding Program, 1993. Mem. Leadership Miami Assn., Greater Miami C. of C. Clubs: Hurricane. Republican. Roman Catholic. Avocations: doll collecting, piano, scuba diving. Office: LGK Assocs Inc 6738 NW 110th Way Parkland FL 33076-3828 E-mail: lgkassoc@mindspring.com.

GARCIA, MOTHER MAGDA LETICIA, sister, consultant; b. Guadalajara, Jalisco, Mexico, Aug. 28, 1939; arrived in U.S., 1960, naturalized, 1983; d. Gumersindo L. Garcia and Maria de Jesus Rodriguez de Garcia. BA in acctg., St. Mary's Coll., Los Angeles, 1976. Admitted to Poor Clare Missionary Sisters, 1962; accredited Bd. of Immigration Appeals, Falls Ch., Va., 2000. Sec. Guadalajara divsn. Colgate Palmolive Co., 1955—60; postulant Poor Clare Missionary Sisters, Cuernavaca, Mexico, 1960, novice San Gabriel, Calif., 1960—62, first profession Gardena, 1962—67, 2d profession Santa Ana, 1967, regional superior Garden Grove, 1967—76; gen. superior and foundress Sisters of Our Lady of Guadalupe and St. Joseph, Gallup, N.Mex., 1976—. Foundress Prayer and Svc., 1976, Chapel of Perpetual Adoration, 1984—; cons. Cath. Legal Immigration Network, Inc., 1983—. Mem. Northside Forgotten No Longer, Gallup, 1997, Gallup C. of C., 1997; spiritual dir. Blue Army of Our Lady of Fatima, 1981—; adv. bd. Diocesan Sisters Coun., Gallup, 2000. Recipient 3 excellence and svc. awards, U.S. Immigration and Naturalization Svc., 1988. Achievements include founding three orphanages for children in Guadalajara, Mexico. Avocation: establishing family type orphanages. Office: Casa Reina 215 E Wilson Gallup NM 87301 E-mail: guadalupesrs@cnetco.com.

GARCIA, MARIA LUISA, biochemist, researcher; b. Valladolid, Spain, Oct. 9, 1953; came to U.S., 1979; d. Baldomero and Dolores (Garcia) G.; m. Gregory Kaczorowski, June 21, 1982. PhD, Autonoma U., Madrid, 1979. Sr. rsch. biochemist Merck & Co., Rahway, NJ, 1985—87, rsch. fellow, 1987—91, sr. rsch. fellow, 1991—97, sr. investigator, 1997—2003, disting. sr. investigator, 2003—. Invited speaker, presenter papers in field. Contbr. numerous articles and revs. to profl. jours.; patentee in field. Mem. AAAS, Am. Soc. Biol. Chemists, Biophys. Soc., N.Y. Acad. Sci. Home: 5 Ashbrook Dr Edison NJ 08820-4318 Office: Merck Rsch Labs PO Box 2000 Rahway NJ 07065-0900 E-mail: maria_garcia@merck.com.

GARCIA, MARY HELEN, state representative; b. Las Cruces, N.Mex., July 14, 1937; m. George Garcia; 2 children. BS, N.Mex. State U., 1960, M, 1976. Tchr. Gadsden (N.Mex.) Pub. Schs., 1960—61, Las Cruces Pub. Schs., 1967—92, dir. instr., 1993—99, elem. sch. prin., 1984—93, 1999—; state rep. dist. 34 N.Mex. Ho. of Reps., Santa Fe, 2002—, vice chair, voters and elections com., mem. appropriations and fin. com. Co-chair United Fund Campaign, 1971; chair Methens March of Dimes., N.Mex. and Dist. Dem. Party, 1997—. Mem.: NEA, Internat. Assn. Reading, Dona Ana Arts Coun., Assn. Curriculum and Design, Pan Am. Round Table, La Casa Shelter for Domestic Violence, Las Cruces Jr. Women's Club, Phi Delta Kappa. Democrat. Roman Catholic. Office: State Capitol Room 413B Santa Fe NM 87503

GARCIA, MARY JANE MADRID, state legislator; b. Dona Ana, N. Mex., Dec. 24, 1936; d. Isaac C. and Victoria M. Garcia. AA, San Francisco City Coll., 1956; BS, N.Mex. State U., 1982, BA in Anthropology, 1983, MA in Anthropology, 1985. Interpretor, translator to USAF Capt., Hotel Balboa, Madrid, Spain, 1962-63; exec. sec. to city mgr. City of Las Cruces, N.Mex., 1964-65; adminstrv. asst. RMK-BRJ, Saigon, Socialist Rep. Vietnam, 1966-72; owner Billy the Kid Gift Shop, Mesilla, N.Mex., 1972-81; pres., owner Victoria's Night Club, Las Cruces, 1981—; state senator Dist. 38 N.Mex. With archaeol. excavations N.Mex. State U. Anthropology Dept., summer 1982, spring 1983; bd. dirs., sec-treas. Dona Anna Mutual Domestic Water Assn.; mem. Subarea Council Health Systems Agy., 1979; bd. dirs. Sun Country Savings Bank, Las Cruses, 1985; treas. Toney Anaya for U.S. Senate, 1978; active Toney Anaya for N.Mex. Gov., 1979-82. Mem. N.Mex. Retail Liquor Assn. Democrat. Roman Catholic. Address: Majority Whip 226 Issac Garcia Rd PO Box 22 Dona Ana NM 88032-0022

GARCIA, MELVA YBARRA, counseling administrator, educator; d. Estanislaso B and Ofelia M Ybarra; m. Frank Garcia, Dec. 28, 1974; children: Ruben Jesus, Luis Francisco, Ramon Estanislado. Student, San Francisco State U., 1969—72; B.A. in Sociology, Calif. State U., Hayward, 1974, MS in Counseling, 1983; PhD (hon.), U. Calif.-Berkeley, 1992. Cert. cmty. coll. counselor Calif., 1986, student pers. workers credential Calif., 1986. Dir. Chicano student counseling ctr. Wash. State U., Pullman, 1984—86; Chicano studies advisor U. of Calif., Berkeley, 1987—92; counselor/instr. Chabot Coll., Hayward, Calif., 1992—. Co-author (counseling manual) Counseling Chicanos: The Affects of Racial and Cultural Stereotype, 1985. Mem. Self-Help for the Hard of Hearing, 2001—; sponsor Children's Internat., Kansas City, Mo., 2002—; mem. La Alianza, Hayward, Calif., 1993; mentor Puente Program, Chabot Coll., 1992—; advisor Wash. State U.; ptnr. Spl. Olympics, 1995—; assoc. mem. Nat. Coun. of La Raza, Washington, 2000—. Mem.: Assn. Main United Farm Workers, So. Law Poverty Ctr., Chabot-Las Positas Faculty Assn., Faculty Assn of Calif. Cmty. Colls., Chicano/Latino Edn. Assn. (mem., 1992-present, co-chair 1998—99), NACADA. D-Liberal. Catholic. Avocations: travel, aerobics. Office: Chabot College 25555 Hesperian Blvd Hayward CA 94545 E-mail: mgarcia@chabotcollege.edu.

GARCIA, MINERVA A.F. bacteriologist, research and clinical laboratory scientist; b. Santiago, Dominican Republic, Nov. 1, 1959; arrived in U.S., 1969; d. Seferino Frias and Lydia Hernandez; m. Jose N. Garcia, Aug. 25, 1985; 1 child, James. BS in Biology, St. Francis Coll., 1984; postgrad. Wagner Coll. Bacteriologist, S.I., NY. Poet Anthologies, 1994, Newspapers and Mags. Recipient award, Anaerobic Bacteriology, 1992, Mayor's scholarship, N.Y.C. Honor Citation award. Mem.: AAUW, Alliance for Prudent Use of Antibiotics, Am. Chem. Soc., N.Y. Acad. Scis., Am. Soc. Microbiology. Home: 29 Pontiac St Staten Island NY 10302-2213

GARCIA, NORMA GARZA, county treasurer; b. Donna, Tex., Oct. 5, 1950; d. Zacarias H. and Olivia (Cavazos) Garza; m. George A. García, Dec. 20, 1977 (div. Mar. 1993); children from previous marriage: Martha Ann, Lucas Aaron, Jorge Antonio II. Stenographer, San Antonio C.C., 1968; student, Pan Am. U., 1969-70, Southmost Coll., 1984. Cert. county treas. Tex. Assn. Counties; cert. investment officer Tex. Assn. Counties. Employment interviewer, supr. Tex. Employment Commn., Weslaco, 1969-80; real estate agt. M.F. Red Connor & Assocs., Weslaco, 1984-85; asst. dir. CBM Edn. Ctr., San Benito, Tex., 1985-87; legis. asst. State Rep. Juan Chuy Hinojosa, McAllen, Tex., 1987-88; income tax return preparer, co-owner H&R Block, Rio Grande City, Tex., 1988-95; county treas. Hidalgo County, Edinburg, Tex., 1995—. Child support investigator Tex. Atty. Gen., McAllen, 1993-94. Mayor City of Mercedes, Tex., 1986-93; dir. Amigos del Valle, McAllen, 1989-93; bd. mem. Planned Parenthood Hidalgo County, McAllen, 1990-92; pres., coun. of govts. Lower Rio Grande Valley Devel. Coun., McAllen, 1992-93; pres. Assn. Mayor, Coun. Mems. and Commrs., Austin, Tex., 1993; mem. County Treas.'s Polit. Action Com., Austin, 1995—. Named Outstanding Profl. Woman, Bus. and Profl. Women's Club, McAllen, 1988, Woman of the Yr., Mercedes C. of C., 1988, Outstanding Hispanic Mayor, Assn. Hispanic Mcpl. Ofcls., Austin, 1992. Democrat. Roman Catholic. Avocations: cake decorating, baking, piano, reading. Office: Hidalgo County Courthouse Annex Bldg Edinburg TX 78539

GARCIA, OFELIA, dean; b. Havana, Cuba, Feb. 12, 1941; d. Ramon Garcia-Castro and Nieves (Gomez de Molina) Garcia. Student, Escuela de Bellas Artes, Havana, 1958-60; BA, Manhattanville Coll., 1969; MFA, Tufts U., 1972; postgrad., Duke U., 1973-75; D. Fine Arts (hon.), Atlanta Coll. Art, 1991. Asst. prof., art dept. chair, div. dir. humanities and fine arts Newton (Mass.) Coll., 1969-75; dir. studio art Boston Coll., Chestnut Hill, Mass., 1975-76; exec. dir. The Print Club, Phila., 1978-86; critic Pa. Acad. Fine Arts, Phila., 1982-86; pres. Atlanta Coll. Art, 1986-91, Rosemont (Pa.) Coll., 1991—95; sr. fellow Am. Coun. on Edn., 1995—97; dean, coll. arts and comm., prof. William Paterson U., 1997—. Visual arts panelist State Coun. of the Arts, Pa. and N.J., 1985-86, Ga., 1990-91; mem. vis. com. dept. art and architecture Lehigh (Pa.) U., 1990-96; bd. mgrs. Haverford Coll., 1992—. Artist exhibitions of prints and drawings; curator, juror numerous nat. and internat. or regional art exhibitions. Nat. pres. Women's Caucus for Art, 1984-86; bd. dirs. Am. Coun. on Edn., 1993-96; co-chair Mayor's Commn. for Women, City Phila., 1992-97; Arts Adv. Com. Barnes Found. Bd., 1992-95; trustee Jersey City Mus., 2000—, bd. chair, 2001--; bd. dirs. Caths. for Free Choice, 2000—. Recipient Am. Bookbuilders prize

Boston Mus. Sch., 1969, Park Found. award, 1974; Kent fellow Danforth Found., 1975-80. Fellow Soc. for Values Higher Edn.; mem. Coll. Art Assn. Am. (bd. dirs. 1986-90, bd. coms. 1986-92), Commn. on Women in Higher Edn., Am. Coun. on Edn. (chair 1990-91), So. Assn. Colls. and Schs. (accreditation evaluator 1990-91), ArtTable, Inc. Roman Catholic. Office: William Paterson U 300 Pompton Rd Wayne NJ 07470-2152 Office Phone: 973-732-2232. E-mail: garciao@wpunj.edu.

GARCIA, SARA KRUGER, lawyer; b. San Antonio, Dec. 12, 1975; d. Daniel Yahr and Chaddie Bruckman Kruger; m. Ryan Matthew Garcia. BA cum laude, Bryn Mawr Coll., 1997; JD, U. Tex., 2000. Rsch. atty. Supr. Ct. Calif., San Jose, 2001—. Mediator, Tex., 1999—, Calif., 1999—. Recipient Peggy Guggenheim Internat. Studentship. Mem.: Nat. Order of Barristers. Home: 6600 Walebridge Ln Austin TX 78739-2025

GARCIA, SUSAN BREAUX, multi-media specialist, consultant; m. Gerard Garcia; children: Brandon, Caroline, Benjamin. BS in English Edn. magna cum laude, La. State U., 1973, MLS, 1977. Cert. secondary English, libr. sci. tchr. La. Elem. sch. libr. Iberia Parish Sch. Sys., Jeanerette, La., 1974—82, HS libr., 1982—93, dist. libr., media specialist supr. New Iberia, La., 1993—. Cons. storytelling Iberia Parish Sch. Sys., New Iberia, 1978—; cons. libr. sci. U. Southwestern La., Lafayette, 1995—2002, adj. instr. libr. sci.; storyteller. From pres. to sec. Entre Nous Club, Jeanerette, 1976—2004, chmn. Reading is Fundamental Project, 1979—2004; bd. dirs., sec. Friends of Iberia Parish Libr., New Iberia, La., 1998—2004; lector St. John the Evangelist Ch., Jeanerette, 1980—2004, mem. parish coun., 1999—2001. Named Outstanding Young Educator of La., La. Jaycees, 1980, Outstanding Young Educator, Jeanerette Jaycees, 1980, Outstanding Club Mem., Entre Nous Club, 1987, 1991; recipient Achievement award, Nat. Coun. Tchrs. English, 1970; scholar, La. State U. Alumni Fedn., 1970—73; Nat. Merit scholar, Texaco Merit scholar, Nat. Merit Scholarship Corp., 1970—73. Mem.: ALA, Title I Spl. Interest Coun., La. Reading Assn., Internat. Reading Assn., La. Libr. Assn., La. Assn. of Parish Textbook Administrs. (sec. 1999—2002), Alpha Beta Alpha, Alpha Lambda Delta, Beta Phi Mu, Phi Kappa Phi. Roman Catholic. Avocations: reading, storytelling, travel. Office: Iberia Parish Sch Sys 1204 Lemaire St New Iberia LA 70560 Office Phone: 337-364-7641.

GARCIA Y CARRILLO, MARTHA XOCHITL, pharmacist; b. Austin, Tex., Dec. 7, 1919; d. Alberto Gonzalo and Guadalupe Eva (Carrillo) Garcia; m. Jerjes Jose Rodriguez, Oct. 9, 1943 (dec. 1987); children: Marie Eugenia, Jerjes Alberto, Nicanor Francisco. BS in Pharmacy, U. Tex., 1944. RPh, Tex. Retail pharmacist Ward Drug Store, Austin, Tex., 1952-57, Sommer's Drug Store, San Antonio, 1957-62, Skillern's Drug Store, Dallas, 1962-66; hosp. pharmacist Brackenridge Hosp., Austin, 1968-75; retail pharmacist Thorp Lane Pharmacy, San Marcos, Tex., 1975-77, The Pharmacy, San Marcos, 1975-79, MHMR Pharmacy, Austin, 1975-78, Ace Drug Co., Austin, 1979-82; ret. Contbg. author: The New Handbook of Texas, 1996. Recipient Citation of Achievement Tex. State Bd. Pharmacy, 1996. Mem. Am. Pharm. Assn. (emeritus mem.), Tex. Pharmacy Assn., Capitol Area Pharmacy Assn., Tex. State Hist. Assn., Ex-Students Assn. U. Tex. (life, Golden Anniversary cert. 1994). Republican. Avocations: reading, playing piano, current events, pharmacy medicine. Home: 21107 Ridgeview Rd Lago Vista TX 78645-4617

GARD, BEVERLY J. state legislator; b. N.C., Mar. 8, 1940; m. Donald Gard; children: David, Doug. BS, U. Tenn., Chattanooga; grad. studies, U. Tenn. Biochemist Eli Lilly & Co.; councilwoman City of Greenfield, Ind., 1976-88; mem. Ind. State Senate from 28th dist., 1988—. Mem. Hancock Assn Retarded Citizens, Ind. Assn. Cities and Towns. Republican. Methodist. Office: Ind Senate Dist 28 200 W Washington St Indianapolis IN 46204-2728

GARDE, SUSAN REUTERSHAN, accountant; b. Southampton, N.Y., Sept. 5, 1953; d. Robert Gordon and Ann Patricia (Cronin) Reutershan; m. John Franklin Garde III, May 20, 1989 (div. 2000); children: John Franklin IV, Sean Robert. BS, Skidmore Coll., 1975; MBA, Fla. Inst. Tech., 1983, MS in Mgmt., 1991. Budget analyst Grumman Aerospace Corp., Bethpage, NY, 1975-76, program planner, 1976-79, sr. budget planner Stuart, Fla., 1979-81, program planner, 1981-82; adminstr. rsch. ctr. United Techs., Inc., West Palm Beach, Fla., 1982-86, sr. adminstr., 1986-87, 1988-94; cost acct. Harbor Br. Oceanog. Inst., Inc., Ft. Pierce, Fla., 1994-96, sr. cost acct., 1996—. Mem.: Am. Bus. Women's Assn. (pres. Orchid chpt. 1986—87, pres. Sailfish chpt. 1985, Woman of the Yr. Citrus chpt. 2000), Skidmore Alumni Assn., Skidmore Club S.E. Fla. Republican. Congregationalist. Avocations: reading, coin collecting, needlepoint. Office: Harbor Br Oceanog Inst 5600 US Highway 1 N Fort Pierce FL 34946-7320 Home: 286 14th Ave Vero Beach FL 32962-2718 E-mail: SueGarde@excite.com., garde@hboi.edu.

GARDEBRING, SANDRA S. academic administrator; Grad., Luther Coll., Decorah, Iowa; JD, U. Minn. Dir. Region 5 U.S. EPA; commr. Minn. Pollution Control Agy., Minn. Dept. Human Svcs.; judge Minn. Ct. Appeals; assoc. justice Minn. Supreme Ct., 1991-98; v.p. univ. rels. U. Minn., 1998—. Bd. dirs. Nature Conservancy of Minn., Regions Hosp. Health Connection, Greater Mpls. Conv. and Visitors Assn. Office: U Minn Univ Rels 3 Morrill Hall 100 Church St SE Minneapolis MN 55455-0110

GARDENIER, TURKAN KUMBARACI, statistical company executive, researcher; b. Istanbul, Turkey, Nov. 10, 1941; arrived in U.S., 1958; d. Celal and Aysel (Triandafilidu) K.; m. Harry M. Peyser, Nov. 24, 1966 (div. Aug. 1968); m. John Stark Gardenier, June 18, 1977; children: Pamela Lee, George HalilBonneval, Jason Celal Stark. AB, Vassar Coll., 1961; MA, Columbia U., 1962, PhD, 1966. Ops. rsch. scientist IIT Rsch. Inst., Chgo., 1966-68; asst. prof., chmn. Middle East Tech. U., Ankara, Turkey, 1968-70; vis. scientist Brookhaven Nat. Labs., Upton, L.I., NY, 1970-71; assoc. dir. Pfizer Pharms., N.Y.C., 1971-73; asst. prof. N.Y. State Maritime Coll., Bronx, NY, 1973-78; health scientist U.S. EPA, Washington, 1978-81; assoc. prof. Am. U., Washington, 1982-84; pres. Pragmatica Corp., Vienna, Va., 1982—. Tech. cons. Analytic Services Corp., Arlington, Va., 1982-90; expert U.S. Energy Info. Adminstrn., Washington, 1982-84; statis. expert EEO, 1990—, statis. cons. Engring. Computer Optecnomics, Annapolis, Md., 1977—; cons. C.R. Cushing Co., Marine Engring., N.Y.C., 1974-77. Organizer, pub. Symposium on Data Efficiency Design; preprocessing pub. Garden-ear Math./Stat. Series for Quanititative Literacy. Corp. mem. Am. Friends of Turkey, McLean, Va., 1983-89; com. mem. World Mut. Service Com., N.Y.C., 1982—; bd. dirs., v.p. Friends of Am. BoardSchs. in Turkey, 1986-88, Am. Turkish Assn., Washington, 1988-90, Washington parents rep. Foxcroft Sch., Middleburg, Va., 1981-84. Grantee, NSF, 1980, CENTO, 1969. Mem. Am. Statis. Assn. (audio-visual graphics com. 1979), Ops. Rsch. Soc. Am. (fin. com. 1980), Soc. Computer Simulation (assoc. editor jour. 1980-84), Soc. Risk Analysis (fin. com. 1980), AAAS (symposium organizer 1979-2003). Avocations: swimming, photography, music composition, multi-media training. Office: Pragmatica Corp 246 Maple Ave E Vienna VA 22180 Home: 115 St Andrews Dr NE Vienna VA 22180-3660

GARDINER, PAMELA NAN, performing arts company executive; m. David Edward Miller, 1974 (div. 1988); m. Anton Labuschagne, 1988 (div. 1999). BA, U. Wis.; MA, Columbia U.; JD, Case Western Res. U. Bar: Ohio, Wis., Fla. Trust officer Cleve. Trust Co., 1975-78; asst. dean acad. affairs Coll. Letters and Sci. U. Wis., 1978-84; exec. dir. Madison Festival of the Lakes, 1984-88, Miami (Fla.) City Ballet, 1988—. Bd. dirs. Performing Arts Ctr. Found., Miami Beach Prodn. Industry Coun. Office: Miami City Ballet 2200 Liberty Ave Miami Beach FL 33139-1641*

GARDNER, ANNE LANCASTER, judge; b. Corpus Christi, Tex., Aug. 19, 1942; d. Jack Quinn and DeWitte (Benton) Lancaster; m. Terry Gardner; 1 child, Travis Gregory. BA, U. Tex., 1964, LLB, 1966. Bar: Tex. 1966. Asst. dir. CLE State Bar Tex., 1966-67; law clk. to U.S. Dist. Ct. judge, 1967-71; ptnr. Simon, Peebles, Haskell, Gardner & Betty, Ft. Worth, 1971-85, McLean, Sanders, Price, Head & Ellis, P.C., Ft. Worth, 1985-88, Shannon, Gracey, Ratliff & Miller, Ft. Worth, 1988-2000, chair appeals sect.; justice Ct. of Appeals (2d dist.) Tex., 2000—. Mem. adv. commn. State Bd. Legal Specialization Appellate Civil Law, chair, 1993-94; mem. Tex. Supreme Ct. adv. com., 1993-98; chmn. merit selection Panel for U.S. Magistrate Judges, no. dist. Tex., 1995. Editor legal jours. Fellow Tex. Bar Found. (life); mem. ABA, Tarrant County Bar Assn. (dir., v.p., pres.-elect 1993, pres. 1994), Tex. Assn. Def. Counsel (bd. dirs.).

GARDNER, BONNIE MILNE, theater educator; b. Cleve., Oct. 17, 1954; d. Alexander Robert and Lois Chase Milne; m. Bruce Andrew Gardner, July 9, 1977; children: Jesse Milne, Elizabeth Milne. BA in Theatre, Ohio Wesleyan U., 1977; MA in Theatre, U. Akron, 1980; PhD in Theatre, Kent State U., 1985. Intern Meri Mini Players, N.Y.C., 1975; mng. dir. Theatre on the Square, Brecksville, Ohio, 1976—79; pub. rels. dir. Fairmount Theatre of the Deaf, Cleve., 1980—81; doctoral fellow Kent State U. Sch. of Theatre, 1981—84; dir. Kent State U., Youth Enrichment Program, 1982—83; instr. U. Akron, 1984—85; prof. theatre Ohio Wesleyan U., Delaware, 1985—. Author: The Emergence of the Playwright- Director in American Theatre, 2001, Columbus Dispatch, 1999 (short play contest finalist, 1999); contbr. articles various profl. jours. Adv. bd. mem. Arts Edn. Ohio Dept. of Edn., 1996—2002; mem. program rev. bd. Theatre Edn. Ohio Dept. of Edn., 1998—2000; program bd. mem. Del. County Cultural Arts Ctr., Ohio, 1990—92. Individual Artist grantee, Playwrights Ohio Arts Coun., 1994. Mem.: Ohio Theatre Alliance, Ohio Alliance for Arts Edn., Assocs. for Theatre in Higher Edn., Dramatists Guild. Unitarian Universalist. Office: Ohio Wesleyan U Theatre 45 Rowland Ave Delaware OH 43015

GARDNER, ELIZABETH ANN HUNT, artist, poet, genealogist; b. Chgo., Aug. 8, 1916; d. William Luther and Elizabeth (Miller) Hunt; m. Vernon Everett Gardner, Mar. 25, 1950. Student, Wilson Tchrs. Coll., Washington, 1934-35. Art instr. Studio 6624, Falls Church, Va., 1968—. Vol. arts tchr. Anderson Orthopedic Hosp., Arlington, Va., 1958-66; flower judge, Alexandria, Va., 1965. Author and photographer: Accidental Surprises in Art, Spotlight on Little Mountain Garden Gems, Collection of Poetry on Current Themes Hand Illuminated; photographer numerous color photographs Framed Restoration Worn Thin Keepsake Copy Salvadore's Msytical Art, 2004; exhbn. Smithsonian Inst., Washington; one-woman show at Bowie Art Ctr., 1997; oil paintings, watercolors, brass rubbings included in area exhbns. including Brevard, N.C., 2004; presenter recitation of original compositions including Winter Wonderland, Shut-In, Easter, Easter Haiku, 2004, Mother's Day, Father's Day. Mem. Washington Figure Skating Club, North Star Astronomy Club (Asheville, N.C.), Nat. Audubon Soc., Cornell Lab. Ornithology, Nat. Wildlife Fedn., Shillelaghs the Travel Club. Unitarian Universalist. Avocation: ornithology. Office Phone: 828 693-0429.

GARDNER, GEORGIA ANNE, state legislator; 2 children. Mem. Wash. Senate, Dist. 42, Olympia, 1998—; vice chair transp. com. Wash. Legislature, Olympia, mem. agr. and rural econ. devel. com., mem. commerce, trade, housing and fin. instns. com., vice chair state and local govt. com., mem. legis. transp. com., mem. joint legis. audit and rev. com., mem. joint adminstrv. rules rev. com., mem. Nat. Conf. State Legis. Fed. Budget and Tax. com. Bd. dirs. Bellingham/Whatcom County Conv. and Vis. Bur.; mem. Blaine County Planning Commn.; founding bd. dirs., treas. Computers for Kids; mem. United Meth. Ch.; mem. Blaine City Coun., 1990-97, Whatcom County Charter Rev. Commn., 1995. Recipient Thomas L. George award Blaine Woman of Yr., Westside Record Jour., 1999. Mem. Assn. Wash. Cities, Kiwanis. Democrat. Avocations: water color painting, traveling. Office: 424 John Cherberg Bldg Olympia WA 98504-0001

GARDNER, JANET PAXTON, journalist, film/video producer; b. Dayton, Ohio, Sept. 6, 1940; d. Edward Tytus and Mary Elizabeth (Paxton) G.; m. George Karl Debreczeny, Sept. 10, 1964 (div. Feb. 1970); 1 child, Karl Philip; m. George Edward Bradshaw Morren, Jr., Nov. 6, 1980. BFA in Art and Architecture, Cooper Union, 1965; MFA in Film Prodn., NYU, 1971; postgrad., Columbia U., 1976. Film editor, assoc. prodr. Sta. WRC-TV, NBC, Washington, 1972; asst. film editor NBC News, N.Y.C., 1973-74; newswriter, field prodr. NewsCenter4 NBC, N.Y.C., 1974-75; freelance film editor CBS News, N.Y.C., 1976-79; staff reporter, feature writer The Plain Dealer, Cleve., 1979-81; edn. columnist, editor Glamour mag., N.Y.C., 1981-82; staff writer Asbury Park Press, Neptune, N.J., 1985-86; press officer UN, 1989; owner, mgr. prodr. The Gardner Documentary Group, N.Y.C., 1991—. Mem. adj. faculty journalism Univ. Coll., Rutgers U., Newark, 1988-92, Montclair State Coll., Upper Montclair, N.J., 1992; mem. L.A. Times pub.-prof. exch. program, 1989. Prodr., dir., writer documentary videos The United Nations: It's More Than You Think, 1991, Vietnam: Land of the Ascending Dragon, 1993, Children of the Night & Starting Over, 1994, A World Beneath The War, 1996, Dancing Through Death: The Monkey Magic & Madness of Cambodia, 1999, Precious Cargo: Vietnamese Adoptees Come of Age, 2001, Siberian Dream, 2004; editor CBS News documentary film The Black Robes, 1978; prodr. Preparing To Give Birth, 1977, Choices in Childbirth, 1977, (film) Inside Ladies Home Jour., 1970; contbr. to NY Times, Phila. Inquirer, Boston Globe, Newsday, The Nation, Glamour, Working Women, New Woman, Diversion, Health Week, Indochina Newsletter, NJ Monthly, also others. Co-chair peace and social order com. Religious Soc. of Friends, Princeton, N.J., 1994; participant U.S.-Indochina Reconciliation Project Del. to Vietnam, 1987, to Cambodia, 1990. Nominee Emmy award Outstanding Hist. Programming, NATAS, 1997; recipient spl. citation, Edn. Writers Assn., 1983, 2d place award for news reporting, N.J. Press Women, 1990, 1st place award for newspaper feature writing, 1990, cert. of merit, Media & Methods mag., 1992, Lowell Thomas award for video on Vietnam, Soc. Am. Travel Writers Found., 1993, Bronze Apple award, Nat. Edn. Film and Video Festival, 1993, Golden Eagle award, CINE, 1994, 1999, 2001, Spl. Jury award, 2001, Silver Apple award, Nat. Edn. Film and Video Festival, 1997, Best Feature Reporting TV award, Soc. Profl. Journalists N.Y. chpt. Deadline Club, 1998, 2001, Bronze medallion (nat. award), Sigma Delta Chi, Best Feature Reporting TV award, Soc. Profl. Journalists N.Y. chpt., 2001, award, Chgo. Internat. Film Festival, 2002; fellow Woolrich writing fellow, Columbia U. Sch. Gen. Studies, 1976. Mem. Soc. Profl. Journalists (juror nat. mag. awards 1985, scholastic press awards 1986, chief juror editl. writing awards 1988), Investigative Reporters and Editors, Internat. Documentary Assn., North Jersey Press Club (2d place award for bus. feature writing 1990, 1st place award 1991, 1st place award for best documentary 1992, 2d place award for feature photography 1993), N.Y. Women in Film and TV. Avocation: travel. Home: 180 Riverside Dr Apt 2D New York NY 10024 Office: Ste 2420 330 W 42d St New York NY 10036-6902

GARDNER, KATHLEEN D. gas company executive, lawyer; b. Fayetteville, Ark., July 14, 1947; d. Harold Andrew and Bess (Gunn) Dulan; m. Robert Gardner, June 7, 1969 (dec. Sept. 1974); m. Cecil Alexander, Feb. 4, 1995; 1 child, Christina Ann. BS, U. Ark., 1969, JD, 1978; MA, U. Ala., 1972. Atty., corp. officer SW Energy Co., Fayetteville, 1978-85; asst. gen. counsel, asst. v.p. Reliant Energy Akrla a divsn. of Reliant Energy Resources, Little Rock, 1985-86, gen. counsel, v.p., 1986-2000, sr. v.p., 2000—. Chmn. Regional Tng. Program, Birmingham, Ala., 1972-75. Bd. dirs. the New Sch. Fayetteville, 1978-79, Robert K. Gardner Meml. Fund, Fayetteville; past bd. dirs. Keep Ark. Beautiful Commn., Ballet Ark., Ark. Mus. Sci. and History, Vis. Nurse Corp. Named Outstanding Young woman Fayetteville Jaycettes, Ark. Jaycettes, recipient Woman of Achievement in Energy award, 1990; named to Top 100 Women in Ark., Ark. Bus. Newspaper, 1995, 96, 97, 98, 99, 2000. Mem. ABA, Ark. Bar Assn. (sec. natural resources sect. 1981), Pulaski County Bar Assn., Am. Gas Assn., DAR, Ark. Assn. Def. Counsel, Am. Arbitration Assn. (Ark. adv. coun.), Alpha Delta Pi. Episcopal. Office: Reliant Energy Arkla Reliant Energy Resources Co 401 E Capitol Ave Ste 102 Little Rock AR 72202-2459

GARDNER, KERRY ANN, librarian; b. Honolulu, May 19, 1955; d. Byron Patton and Claire Gardner. BA in Polit. Sci. magna cum laude, Temple U., 1976; MA in L.Am. Studies, U. Ariz., 1983, MLS, 1990. Documents libr. FMC Corp., Chgo., 1977-78; grad. rsch. asst. U. Ariz., Tucson, 1983-86; rsch. cons., 1983-92; libr. asst. I Phoenix Pub. Libr., 1988-89; mgr. faculty resource libr., English 2d lang. U. Ariz. Ctr., 1989—90; project mgr. U. Ariz., 1990-92; mgr. faculty resource libr., English 2d lang. U. Ariz. Ctr., 1991—92; pub. svcs. libr. Bryan Wildenthal Meml. Libr., Sul Ross State U., Alpine, Tex., 1992-95; libr. dir. Am. U., Dubai, United Arab Emirates, 1995-96; literacy libr. Sterling Mcpl. Libr., Baytown, Tex., 1996-98; libr. Valle Verde campus, El Paso C.C., Tex., 1998—, co-head libr., 2001—02. Indexer Hispanic Am. Periodicals Index, 1995; maintain GPO Access Web site, 1998—. Contbr. articles to profl. publs. Tchr. English Literacy Vols. Am., 1991-92, 96-98. Named Libr. of Yr., Border Regional Libr. Assn., 2001; grad. scholar, U. Ariz., 1976—77, 1981—82. Mem.: NEA, ALA, Tex. Faculty Assn., Tex. C.C. Tex. Assn., Assn. Borderlands Scholars, Border Regional Libr. Assn. (chair publicity com. 1999—2002, chair. Libr. of the Yr. com. 2002—03), Assn. Coll. and Rsch. Librs., Tex. Libr. Assn. (legis. com. coll. and univ. librs. divsn. 1993—94), Beta Phi Mu. Avocations: travel, birding. Office: El Paso C C Valle Verde Campus PO Box 20500 El Paso TX 79998-0500

GARDNER, LIZ See WEDDINGTON, ELIZABETH GARDNER

GARDNER, MARY JOSEPHINE, management development consultant; b. Lebanon, Pa., Sept. 10, 1943; d. John Edward and Gertrude Marie (Scanlon) G.; divorced; children: Susan Lupack, Joyce Lupack. BA magna cum laude, Fordham U., 1971; MA, Columbia U., 1983. Tchr. Cardinal Spellman H.S., Bronx, N.Y., 1971-77; asst. tng. specialist Prudential Ins. Co., Newark, 1977-79; mgr. tng. and devel. Am. Express Co., N.Y.C., 1979-82; v.p. Chase Manhattan Bank, N.Y.C., 1982-84; pres. Gardner Enterprises, N.Y.C., 1984—, Marblehead, Mass., 1991—, WorkVision, Marblehead, 1999. Mem. faculty Am. Women's Econ. Devel. Corp., 1985-89, adj. instr. Grad. Sch. Mgmt., New Sch. for Social Rsch., N.Y.C., 1986-89; bd. dirs. Consortium for Breakthroughs in Women's Leadership. Mem. Culver Lake (N.J.) Water Quality Com., 1985-90; vol. Marblehead Eco-Farm, 1995-96; vol. coord. Me and Thee Coffee House, Marblehead, 1995—, Marblehead Arts Festival, 1991—; vol. cons. Boston Mgmt. Consortium, 1996—; vol. Boston Mayor's Leadership Devel. Program; vol. cons. on performance mgmt. to Boston Pub. Schs.; vol. Boston Police Dept.; active Murder Victims Families for Reconciliation; mem., pastoral assoc. Unitarian Universalist Ch. of Marblehead, 1997—. Avocation: gardening. Home: 22 Circle St Marblehead MA 01945-3502 Office: WorkVision 22 School St Marblehead MA 01945-3327 E-mail: mgardner@workvision.com.

GARDNER, SANDI B. biology educator; b. Chicago Heights, Ill., June 24, 1959; d. Robert S. and Lenore M. (D'Arcy) Bushor; m. Daniel E. Gardner, Apr. 16, 1988 (div. 1997); m. Philliip K. Duncan, Feb., 2004; 1 child, C(atherine) J. BS in Phys. Edn./Recreation, U. Ill., Chgo., 1981; MS in Environ. Biology, Govs. State U., University Park, Ill., 1988; postgrad., Ill. Inst. Tech., Chgo., 1993-95, PhD, Walden U., Mpls., 1997. Profl. scout Wau Bon Girl Scout Coun., Fond Du Lac, Wis., 1981-82; pre sch. tchr. Anita M. Stone Ctr., Flossmoor, Ill., 1982-84, Alsip (Ill.) Pre-Sch., 1984-85; tchg. asst. Govs. State U., 1986-89; park ranger Ind. Dunes Nat. Lakeshore, Porter, 1986-92; prof. biology South Suburban Coll., South Holland, Ill., 1990-96. Adj. prof. Ind. U.-N.W., Gary, 1990—92, Govs. State U., 1989—93; mem. spl. populations adv. bd. South Suburban Mental Health, South Holland, 1992—94; staff develop./curriculum specialist Purdue U., 1995—96, adj. faculty, 1996; prof. biology Triton Coll., River Grove, Ill., 1996—, chair sci. dept., 2001—, adv. pre-profl. orgn., 2002, faculty advisor, 2003—, grad. sch. advisor, 2003—; cons. Taylor U., Ft. Wayne, Ind., 1999—2001; grad. sch. adv. Excelsior U., NY, 2003—; workshop presenter, cons. in field. Author: Relationship Between Computer Anxiety and Computer Use, 1996, WebWeaver Environmental Science Online, 2001, Lab Manual Genetics, 2002; co-author: Case Studies for Anatomy and Physiology, 1992, Lab Manual for General Biology, 1994, 1999, 2001, Teachers/Student Guide to Virtual Biology Laboratory CD-ROM, 1997, WebWeaver Study Guide, 1998; editor: McGrawHill Pub., 2003, Pearson Pub., 2003. Leader, vol., trainer Calumet coun. Girl Scouts U.S., Highland, Ind., 1981-84, 93—; vol. Lincoln Park Zoo, 1986-88, Brookfield Zoo, 1996-2000; coach AYSO Soccer, River Forest, Ill., bd. dirs. 1999; adv. Phi Theta Kappa Triton Coll, River Grove, Ill., 1996-2000; vol. mentor West Lake Hosp., 2002; vol. Amb. Walden U., 2002; co-chair accreditation com. NCA, 2003. Recipient Spl. Achievement award Nat. Park Svc., 1988; Hand-On Sci. for Tchrs. award EPA, 1992; grantee R&D Triton, 1998—, On-line Biology, 1999, Plastination, 1999, HECA, 1999-2000, On-Line Tutoring Ctr., 2000-01. Mem. Nat. Sci. Tchrs. Assn., Nat. Assn. Biology Tchrs., Ill. Assn. C.C. Biology Tchrs. (pres. 1999-2001), Phi Delta Kappa (v.p. membership 1999-2003). Home: 115 S Euclid Oak Pk K River Forest IL 60302 Office: Triton Coll 2000 N 5th Ave River Grove IL 60171-1907 E-mail: sbgardner@aol.com.

GARDNER, SHERYL PAIGE, gynecologist; b. Bremerton, Wash., Jan. 24, 1945; d. Edwin Gerald and Dorothy Elizabeth (Herman) G.; m. James Alva Beat, June 20, 1986. BA in Biology, U. Oreg., 1967, MD cum laude, 1971. Diplomate Am. Bd. Ob-Gyn. Intern L.A. County Harbor Gen. Hosp., Torrance, Calif., 1971-72, resident in ob-gyn., 1972-75; physician Group Health Assn., Washington, 1975-87; pvt. practice Mililani, Hawaii, 1987—. Med. staff sec. Wahiawa (Hawaii) Gen. Hosp., 1994-95. Mem. Am. Coll. Ob-Gyn., Am. Soc. Colposcopy and Cervical Pathology, Hawaii Med. Assn., N.Am. Menopause Soc., Sigma Kappa, Alpha Omega Alpha. Democrat. Avocation: supporter numerous environ., peace and social concern groups. Office: 95-1249 Meheula Pkwy Ste B10A Mililani HI 96789-1763

GARDUNIA, SHARON STRAWSBURG, secondary school educator; b. Springfield, Ohio, Sept. 5, 1941; d. Benjamin Lawton and Winifred Edythe Strawsburg; children: Shelley Jo Watters, Vincent Reid Harmon, Shelby Joy Strong. BS in edn., Wittenberg U., 1960—65; MEd, E. Tenn. State U., 1981—82, N.W. Nazarene U., 2000—01. Cert. spl. edn. Ohio State Bd. of Ed., 2002, Idaho, 2001, Ore., 1999. Tchr. - md North High School-Springfield City Schools, Springfield, Ohio, 2002—; inclusion specialist Nampa City Schools, Nampa, Idaho, 2001—02. Presenter - workshops N.W. Nazarene U., Nampa, Idaho, 2000—01. Author: (novel) A Story with an Interesting Twist. Precinct leader, sec., del. Ga. Rep. Party, Conyers, Ga., 1989—92. Rotarian Edn. grant, Rotary Club of Springfield, OH, 2003. Mem.: Coun. of Exceptional Children. R-Consevative. Protestant. Avocations: reading, live theater, travel, dance. Office: North High School 701 E Home Rd Springfield OH Office Phone: 937-342-4100. Personal E-mail: sgardunia@aol.com.

GAREY, PATRICIA MARTIN, artist; b. State College, Miss., Nov. 11, 1932; d. Verey G. Martin and Eva Myrtle Jones; m. Donald L. Garey, Aug. 1, 1953; children: Deborah Anne Garey Furst, Elizabeth Laird Garey Jones. BS in Costume Design, Tex. Women's U., 1953; MFA, Tex. Tech. U., 1973; postgrad. in art history, Two-Dimensional Studio Art, 1970-73. Prodn. mgr. Cox Advt. Agy., Roswell, N.Mex., 1958-63; art instr. Coll. of Southwest, Hobbs, N.Mex., 1967-69, 72-73, prof. art history, art appreciation, 1974-76; studio artist Hobbs, 1976—; prof. art/painting and drawing N.Mex. Jr. Coll., 1997-98. Instr. Cloudcroft Artists Sch., N.Mex., 1991; prof. drawing, painting N.Mex. Jr. Coll.; prof. art hist. Coll. of Southwest, 1999—2001; rep., drawing instr. Villa Maria Ctr. for the Arts, Perugia, Italy, 1996; apptd. N.Mex. Arts Commn., 1999; artist-in-residence N.Mex. Art Commn., Santa Fe, 1975—76. Artist (one-woman shows) Sand Hills Mus., Kermit, Tex., 1968, N.Mex. Jr. Coll., Hobbs, 1969, 1985, Coll. of SW, 1974, 1979, Sangre de Cristo Arts Ctr., Pueblo, 1979, U. Tex. of Permian Basin, Odessa, 1980, N.Mex. Jr. Coll., (represented by) Beverly Gordon Gallery, Dallas, Sylvia Ullman Am. Crafts, Cleve., Design Today, Lubbock, Tex., El-Dor Galleries Old-Town, Albuquerque, Front Room Gallery, Dallas, Tex. Art Gallery, Galeria de la Paloma, Santa Fe, (exhibitions) Roswell Mus. Art, Four Women Artists of Hobbs, N.Mex., 1966, Lubbock Mcpl. Garden and Arts Ctr., 1966, Laguna Gloria Art Mus., 1968—, Southeastern N.Mex. Small Painting Exhibit, 1975 (2d pl., 1966, 2d pl. Graphics, 2d pl. Sculpture, 2d pl. Acrylics, 1st pl. Ceramics, 1st pl. Drawing, 2d pl. Painting), Americas Gallery, Taos, 1974, Blair Gallery, Santa Fe, 1976, Mus. Fine Arts, 1976, Tex. Tech. U. Grad. Show, 1977, Little Rock Art Ctr., Ark., 1978, Hills Gallery, Santa Fe, 1979, Llano Estacado Art Assn., Dallas Mus. Fine Art, 1986, 1987, 1988, 1990, Beaux Arts Ball Art Auction, 1990, Okla. City Mus. Art nat. drawing competition, Little Rock Art Ctr., El Paso Sun Carnival, Tex., Govs. Gallery, State Capitol, Santa Fe, 1997, L.E.A.A., Hobbs, N.Mex., 1999 (Best of Show, 1st pl. watercolor), (permanent collections) Home Scis. Dept., Tex. Tech. U., The Round House/State Capitol, Santa Fe, Villa Maria Ctr. for the Arts, Raimondi Collection, Perugia, Italy, docent Meadows Mus. of Art So. Meth. U., Dallas, 1990, Govs. Invitiational, Govs. Gallery, 1996, 35 Clay Workers of N.Mex., artist (exhibitions) Southeastern N.Mex. Small Painting Exhibit, 1976, 1987, 1988, 1990, (permanent collections) State Capitol, Santa Fe, N.Mex. Jr. Coll. Arts commr. State of N.Mex., 1999—2002, N.Mex. Arts Commn., 1999—2003; artistic bd. S.W. Symphony, Hobbs, 1987—99; Bd. dirs. The Bridge Breast Ctr., Dallas, 1992—93, Llano Estacado Art Assn. Recipient Best of Show award for mixed media Llano Estacado Art Assn. Regional Show, Hobbs, N.Mex., 1996, Best of Show award for ceramics, 1999, 1st pl. award for watercolor, 1999. Mem. Delta Phi Delta, Chi Omega. Democrat. Methodist. Avocations: swimming (mem. Sr. Olympics N.Mex. Nat. Swim Team 1997), southern cooking, piano, classical music, book collecting. Studio: 315 E Alto Dr Hobbs NM 88240-3905 also: Piney Woods Cloudcroft NM 88350

GARFIELD, WINIFRED L. nursing administrator; b. Fredericksted, St. Croix, V.I., July 28, 1941; d. Walter Antonio and Idalia Crystalia (Stephens) L.; m. Victor Conrad Garfield, June 30, 1968; children: Vilma Cecilia, Victor Conrad, Vynette Crystine, Vivicka Celeste. RN, St. Lukes Sch. Nursing, Ponce, P.R., 1962; grad. anesthesiology for nurses, Harlem Hosp. Sch., 1966. RN, CRNA, AANA. Staff nurse Knud Hansen Hosp., St. Thomas, V.I., 1962-64, nurse anesthetist, 1966-70, nurse anesthetist supr., 1970-89, respiratory therapy instr., 1976-77; campus nurse U. of V.I., St. Thomas, V.I., 1979-82; first aid instr., trainer ARC, St. Thomas, V.I., 1973-80; supr. anesthesia and respiratory svc. St. Thomas Hosp., St. Thomas, V.I., 1980-89; exec. dir. V.I. Bd. of Nurse Licensure, St. Thomas, V.I., 1989—. Nurse cons. Educare Sch., Inc., 1970—, asst. dir., 1980—. Recipient Disting. Nurse Cons. award Dept. of Health Office of Commr., 1982, named Nurse of the Year V.I. Licensed Practical Nurse Assn., 1986. Mem. V.I. Nurses Assn. (v.p. 1963-64), Chi Eta Phi (historian, 1963-64), Eta Phi Beta (Alpha Chi chpt). Democrat. Roman Catholic. Avocations: reading, gardening, traveling. Home: 394-140 Anas Retreat Charlotte Amalie VI 00803 Office: VI Bd of Nursing Licensure Veterans Dr Sta Charlotte Amalie VI 00803

GARFIELD-WOODBRIDGE, NANCY, writer; b. N.Y.C. d. Solomon and Betty Silbowitz; m. George Charles Woodbridge, Apr. 20, 1980; children from previous marriage: Maurice Garfield, Joshua Garfield. BA in Lit., Bennington Coll., 1955; MS in Edn., Hofstra U., 1972, postgrad., 1973. Cert. tchr. K-8, English 7-9 N.Y. Editl. asst. Wenner Gren Found. Anthropol. Rsch., N.Y.C., 1952—55; picture editor Forbes Mag., N.Y.C., 1955—56; editor-in-chief The Gifted Child Mag., N.Y.C., 1957—58; v.p. Info. Retrieval Systems, Great Neck, NY, 1958—72; rsch. assoc. to v.p. and editor N.Y. Inst. Tech., Westbury, 1972—73; dir. spl. projects Girl Scouts of USA, N.Y.C., 1973—2000; children's author, 2000—. Spkr. v.p.'s task force on youth employment, Little Rock, 1979, gov.'s conf. on juvenile justice, Baton Rouge; presenter Edn. Commn. for the States, Denver, 1979. Author: The Tuesday Elephant, 1968, The Dancing Monkey, 1970, Juvenile Justice, 1981; contbr. articles to profl. jours. and mags. Vol. Kennedy Kenya Airlift Program, N.Y.C., 1962, Biafran Refugee Campaign, N.Y.-London, 1967; fundraiser Sara's Ctr. Very Spl. Arts Festival, L.I. to Washington. Scholar Breadloaf Writers Conf., Vt., 1967. Mem.: Acad. Am. Poets, The Author's Guild, Milford Fine Arts Coun., Soc. Children's Book Writers and Illustrators. Avocations: travel, reading, opera, painting, photography.

GARFINKEL, JANE E. lawyer; b. N.Y.C., Dec. 2, 1952; d. Albert E. and Rita H. (Halpern) G.; m. Louis F. Solimine, May 20, 1979. BA, Wheaton Coll., 1974; MA, U. Mich., 1975, JD, 1979. Bar: Ohio 1980. Assoc. Smith & Schnacke, Cin., 1980-88, ptnr., 1988-89, Thompson Hine LLP, Cin., 1989—. Office: Thompson Hine LLP 312 Walnut St Ste 1400 Cincinnati OH 45202-4089 E-mail: jane.garfinkel@thompsonhine.com.

GARFINKLE, ELAINE MYRA, writer; b. Canton, Ohio, July 24, 1936; d. Clifford and Dora Adelman Margolis; m. Jack George Garfinkle, Dec. 27, 1959; 1 child, Marcia Lizabeth. Grad. H.S., Canton. Gen. mgr., editor, pub. Stark Jewish News, Inc., Canton, 1970—83; owner, writer, rschr. Canton Writing Svc., 1978—90; pres., treas. Marce Pubs., Inc., Canton, 1979—83; owner, rschr. Leo Rsch. unlimited, Canton, 1979—83; cmty. rels. supr. Goodwill Rehab., Canton, 1984—87; advt. exec. Cmty. Newspapers, Massillon, Ohio, 1987—91. Historian, pub., compiler, author Through the Years, the Informal History of the Canton Area Jewish Community 1870-2003, 63 vols. Program presenter area nursing homes, 1999—2003; historian on local spl. PBS program on history of Canton, Ohio; adv. U.S. Holocaust Meml. Mus.; supporter Goodwill's Amb. of Goodwill; trustee Cleve. Jewish Genealogy Soc.; advocate for spl. edn., sr. adult and consumer product affairs; mem., supporter Stark County Hist. Soc., McKinley Mus.; vol. and program presenter Canton Jewish Cmty. Ctr. Mem.: Friends of Ctr. Jewish History, Ohio Libr., Am. Friends Hebrew U., Leo Baeck Inst., Friends North Canton, YIVO Inst. Jewish Rsch., Am. Jewish Hist. Soc., Canton Jewish Cmty. Fedn. (edn. com. mem., Outstanding Svc. award 1996—2002), Internat. Jewish Women (life; past pres., treas.), Am. Heart Assn. (cmty. rels. com. 1992—96, Outstanding Svc. award 1992—96), Am. Sephardi Fedn., Nat. Geographic Soc., Hadassah (former edn. com. mem., program presenter 2003), Anti-Defamation League, Women's League Conservative Judaism, Shaaray Torah Sisterhood (former social action chmn.). Jewish. Avocations: photography, practical psychology, music, reading, studying Jewish history.

GARG, RAJNI, chemist, researcher; b. Meerut, India, Oct. 4, 1963; arrived in U.S., 1997; d. Jai Prakash Garg and Tara Devi; m. Sunil Kumar, Dec. 8, 1990; children: Paras Kumar, Shubham Kumar. BSc in Chemistry, Meerut U., India, 1982, MSc in Organic Chemistry, 1984, B.Ed., 1986; MPhil, Delhi U., India, 1988; PhD, Birla Inst. Tech. and Sci., Pilani, India, 1996. Lectr. Birla Inst. Tech. and Sci., Pilani, India, 1991—96; post doctoral rsch. assoc. Pomona Coll., Claremont, Calif., 1997—2002; rsch. assoc., prof. Clarkson U., Chemistry Dept., Potsdam, NY, 2002—. Contbr. articles to profl. jours. Recipient S.R. Palit award, Indian Chem. Soc., 1995; scholar, Govt. India, 1978—84. Mem.: Sci. Congress India, Am. Chem. Soc. Hindu. Avocations: reading, cooking, traveling, charity. Office: Clarkson U Chemistry Dept PO Box 5810 Potsdam NY 13699

GARIBALDI, MARIE LOUISE, former state supreme court justice; b. Jersey City, Nov. 26, 1934; d. Louis J. and Marie (Serventi) G. BA, Conn. Coll., 1956; LLB, Columbia U., 1959; LLM in Tax. Law, NYU, 1963. Atty. Office of Regional Counsel, IRS, N.Y.C., 1960-66; assoc. McCarter & English, Newark, 1966-69; ptnr. Riker, Danzig, Scherer, Hyland & Pernutti, Newark, 1969-82; assoc. justice N.J. Supreme Court, Newark, 1982-2000. Contbr. articles to profl. jours. Trustee St. Peter's Coll.; co-chmn. Thomas Kean's campaign for Gov. of N.J., 1981, mem. transition team, 1981; mem. Gov. Byrne's Commn. on Dept. of Commerce, 1981, bd. dirs, Crown Holdings, 2000-. Recipient Disting. Alumni award NYU Law Alumni of N.J., 1982; recipient Disting. Alumni award Columbia U., 1982 Fellow Am. Bar Found.; mem. N.J. Bar Assn. (pres. 1982), Columbia U. Sch. Law Alumni Assn. (bd. dirs.) Roman Catholic.*

GARING, IONE DAVIS, civic worker, club woman; b. Huntsville, Ala., Jan. 8, 1930; d. Drury McNary and Ione (Thompson) Davis; m. John Seymour Garing, Apr. 26, 1952; children: John Davis, Susan Carolyn. BSc in Edn. cum laude, Ohio State U., 1951. Tchr. Columbus (Ohio) Pub. Schs., 1952-54, Upper Arlington Pub. Sch., Columbus, 1957-58; libr. Newton (Mass.) Libr., 1955; interviewer audits and surveys Elmo Roper, Boston, 1956. Mem. adv. com. Sch. Com. on Spl. Edn., Lexington, Mass., 1979-80; mem. adv. bd. Cary Meml. Libr., Lexington, 1989—. Active numerous civic orgns., including mem. Town Meeting, Lexington, 1980-2002; mem. Lexington 2020 Vision Study, 2001; mem. exec. bd. Lexington Dem. Com., 1987-89, mem., 1986—; del. Mass. Dem. Convs., 1986, 88, 90, 92, 94, 96, 98, 2000, 2002; mem. exec. bd. Friends Coun. on Aging, 1986, PTA's, 1965-79; vol. Meals on Wheels, 1985-89; pres. United Meth. Women, Lexington, 1973-75; bd. dirs. Meth. Weekday Sch., 1971-80; co-organizer 1st town-wide hazardous waste collection in U.S., Lexington, 1983; vol. Lexington Hist. Soc., 1978—; co-founder, chmn. Friends of Cary Meml. Libr. Orgn., 1990-97, bd. dirs., 1990—; founding mem., treas., Precint 8 Residents Assn., 1996-03. Mem. LWV (pres. Lexington 1983-85), AAUW (Mass. long range planning com.), DAR (vice regent 1977-80, Mass. chmn. scholarships and loan com. 1980-83), Florence Crittenton League, Outlook Club (pres. 1985-87, chmn. scholarships com. 1990-2002), Lexington Field and Garden Club (2d vice-pres. 2000-2002), North Shore Rock and Mineral Club (Peabody, Mass.), Brookline Bird Club, Minute Man Nat. Pk. Assn., Alpha Chi Omega. Avocations: conservation, gardening, bird watching, genealogy, travel. Home: 157 Cedar St Lexington MA 02421-6507

GARITY, KATHLEEN, medical/surgical nurse, director; d. Mary Murphy; m. Donald Garity; children: Hannah Caitlin, Katherine Mary. BSN, BS in Psychology, Old Dominion U., 1980; MSN, Cath. U. Am., 1987. RN Va. Heart transplant coord. Fairfax Hosp., Falls Church, Va., 1986—88; cons. APACHE Med. Systems, Washington, 1987—89; nurse Fed. Occupl. Health, Washington, 2002—; pres., dir. of care coordination Compassionate Care Associates, Burke, Va., 2002—. Wise fellow, George Wash. Med. Ctr., 1985, nurse traineeship fellow, US Govt., 1986. Mem.: Omicron Delta Kappa (life), Sigma Theta Tau (life). Avocations: travel, snorkeling, scuba diving.

GARLAND, LARETTA MATTHEWS, psychologist, educator, nursing educator; b. Jacksonville, Fla. d. Wilburn L. and Clyde-Marian (Chamberlin) Matthews; m. John B. Garland, Mar. 2, 1946; children: John Barnard, Brien Freeling, Amy-Gwin. Diploma, Fla. State Sch. Nursing, 1942; BSN, Emory U., 1950, MA, 1953; BA in Edn., U. Fla., 1951; cert. cardiovascular nurse specialty, Tex. Med. Ctr., 1965; EdD, U. Ga., 1975; postgrad. in counseling and guidance, Ga. State U., 1969; grad. cert. in gerontology, 1981. Cert. nat. counselor. Office and staff nurse, Lakeland, Fla., 1942, 45; nurse ARC, Buffalo, 1956; asst. prof. nursing Med. Coll. Ga., 1965-67; instr. Emory U., 1952-54, assoc. prof., 1967-71, prof., 1972-86, prof. emeritus, 1987—. Ednl. psychologist, dir. gerontol. nurse practitioner program, 1978-80, asst. to dean, 1983-86. Author: (with Carol Bush) Coping Behavior and Nursing, 1982; contbr. articles to profl. jours. With Nurse Corps, U.S. Army, 1942-45. Decorated 2 Bronze Stars; recipient Outstanding Tchg. award Emory U. Sch. Nursing Grad. Srs., 1977, Appreciation award So. Region Constituent Leagues, Nat. League for Nursing award, 1987, Mabel Korsell award of appreciation Ga. League Nursing, 1987, Spl. Recognition award Ga. Nurses Assn., 1988, 90, Nurse of Yr. award, 1992, Appreciation award Ga. Assn. Nursing Students, 1990, Van de Vrede award Ga. League Nursing, 1993; HEW fellow, 1967-68. Mem. APA, AACD, ANA, Ga. Assn. Nursing Students (hon.), Nat. League Nursing, Bs. and Profl. Women, China Burma India VA Assn. (mem. nat. bd. 1993—), 14th Air Force Asssn. (Flying Tigers), Hump Pilots Assn., Ormond Beach Womens Club, Ormond Beach Hist. Trust, Nat. Assn. Women Vet. (steering com.), Women in Mil. Svc. Meml. Found. (charter), ARC Nurses, Panhellenic Assn., Hist. Trust, Alpha Chi Omega, Sigma Theta Tau, Kappa Delta Pi, Alpha Kappa Delta, Omicron Delta Kappa. Office: Emory U Nell Hodgson Woodruff Sch Atlanta GA 30322-0001

GARLETTS, TWILA UMBEL, advocate; b. Uniontown, Pa., Dec. 17, 1955; d. Wade and Margaret Theresa (Rocheck) U.; m. Gary Paul Garletts; 1 child, Nathan Umbel. BA summa cum laude, U. Pitts., 1987. Sales rep., receptionist Uniontown (Pa.) Newspapers, Inc., 1973-88; sec., ins. coord. Dr. Ronald R. Sepic, D.D.S., Uniontown, 1989-93; keyboarder Tapsco, Inc., Akron, Pa., 1994—99, Archtype, Lancaster, Pa.; Reiki Master energy healing practice, 2003—. Contbr. poetry to anthologies. Active numerous movements involving children rights and healthcare issues; co-founder Treasures of Human Expression Arts Coun.and The Greater Uniontown Chorale. Mem. animal rights orgns. Republican. Presbyterian. Avocations: church committees and choirs, holistic spirituality, alternative healing. Home: 1311 Roosevelt Ave Havertown PA 19083-3016

GARLING, TINA LOUISE, data processing coordinator; b. Granville, Ohio, Sept. 24, 1974; d. Albert Alvin Jr. and Fern Demple (Neece) G. BBA, U. Cin., 1996. Waitress Cin. Faculty Club, 1993-94; customer asst. JC Penney Outlet, Columbus, 1991-96; telephone interviewer B&B Rsch., Grandview, Ohio, 1996; tabulations specialist Saperstein Assocs., Columbus, 1996-98, data processing coord., 1998—. Coll. bd. Procter & Gamble, Cin., 1994-95. Mem. AAUW, Human Soc. of the U.S., World Wildlife Fund, Nat. Audubon Soc. Methodist. Avocations: tennis, volleyball, hiking, roller blading, shopping. Home: 7666 Broadwyn Dr Reynoldsburg OH 43068-2612

GARMAN, RITA B. judge; b. Aurora, Ill., Nov. 19, 1943; m. Gill Garman; children: Sara Ellen, Andrew Gill. BS in econs., U. Ill., 1965; JD with distinction, U. Iowa, 1968. Asst. state atty. Vermilion County, 1969—73; pvt. practice Sebat, Swanson, Banks, Lessen & Garman, 1973; assoc. cir. judge, 1974—86; cir. judge Fifth Jud. Cir., 1986—95, presiding cir. judge, 1987—95; judge Fourth Dist. Appellate Ct., 1996—2001; Supreme Ct. justice Ill. State Supreme Ct., 2001—. Mem.: Ill. Judge's Assn., Vermilion County Bar Assn., Iowa Bar Assn., Ill. State Bar Assn. Office: 3607 N Vermilion Ste 1 Danville IL 61832

GARMAN, TERESA AGNES, state legislator; b. Ft. Dodge, Iowa, Aug. 29, 1937; d. John Clement and Barbara Marie (Korsa) Lennon; m. Merle A. Garman, Aug. 5, 1961; children: Laura Ann Garman Hansen, Rachel Irene Garman Coder, Robert Sylvester, Sarah Teresa Garman Powers. Grad. high sch., Ft. Dodge. With employee relations dept. 3M Co., Ames, Iowa, 1974-86; mem. Iowa Ho. of Reps., Des Moines, 1986—. Asst. majority leader, mem. platform com., del. Rep. Nat. Conv., 1988, del., mem. platform com., 1992, del., 1996; mem. Iowa Rep. Ctrl. Com. Mem. Rep. Farm Policy Coun., Story County Rep. Women, Story County Pork Prodrs., Farm Bur., Story City C. of C., Nev. C. of C. Roman Catholic. Avocations: horseback riding, gardening. Home: 1799 Old Bloomington Rd Ames IA 50010-9469 Office: State Capitol Des Moines IA 50319-0001

GARMANY, CATHARINE DOREMUS, astronomer; b. N.Y.C., Mar. 6, 1946; d. Edwin and Janet (MacMaster) Doremus; children: Richard, Jeffrey. BS, Ind. U., 1966; MS, U. Va., 1968, PhD, 1971. Rsch. assoc. U. Va., Charlottesville, 1971-73; rsch. assoc. Joint Inst. for Lab Astrophys. U. Colo., Boulder, 1977-84, sr. rsch. assoc. Joint Inst. for Lab Astrophys., 1984-2000; dir. Fiske Planetarium, 1991-2000; dir. astronomy Astronomy, Oracle, Ariz., 2000—. Contbr. articles to profl. jours. Recipient Annie J. Cannon award AAUW, AAS, 1976; grantee NASA, NSF. Office: Biosphere 2 Atronomy Bldg 32540 S Biosphere Rd Oracle AZ 85623 E-mail: katy@astro.bio2.edu.

GARMEL, MARION BESS SIMON, retired arts journalist; b. El Paso, Tex., Oct. 15, 1936; d. Marcus and Frieda (Alfman) Simon; m. Raymond Lewis Garmel, Nov. 28, 1965 (dec. Feb. 1986); 1 child, Cynthia Rogers; 1 stepchild, Christine Blum. Student, U. Tex., El Paso, 1954-55; BJ, U. Tex., Austin, 1958. Exec. sec. Nat. Student Assn., Phila., 1958-59, pub. rels. dir., 1960-61; sec. World Assembly Youth, Paris, Brussels, 1959-60; dictationist Wall Street Jour., Washington, 1961; libr., staff writer Nat. Observer, Silver Spring, Md., 1961-70; art critic Indpls. News, 1971-91, editor Free Time sect., 1975-91, critic radio and TV, 1991-95; theater critic Indpls. Star and News, 1995-99; television critic Indpls. News, 1995-99; theater critic Indpls. Star, 1999—2002, ret., 2002. Mem. Nat. Fedn. Press Women (1st Place Critics award 1974), Ind. Soc. Profl. Journalists (1st place criticism 2002), Hadassah Women's Zionist Orgn. Am. (life), Women's Press Club Ind. (1st Place Critics award 1995, 2002). Jewish. Avocation: tennis. Home: 226 E 45th St Indianapolis IN 46205-1712 E-mail: mgarmel@earthlink.net.

GARMIRE, ELSA MEINTS, electrical engineering educator, consultant; b. Buffalo, Nov. 9, 1939; d. Ralph E. and Nelle (Gubser) Meints; m. Gordon P. Garmire, June 11, 1961 (div. 1975); children: Lisa, Marla; m. Robert Heathcote Russell, Feb. 4, 1979. AB in Physics, Harvard U., 1961; PhD in Physics, MIT, 1965. Rsch. scientist NASA Electronics Rsch. Ctr., Cambridge, Mass., 1965-66; rsch. fellow Calif. Inst. Tech., Pasadena, 1966-73; sr. rsch. scientist U. So. Calif. Ctr. for Laser Studies, L.A., 1974-78, prof. elec. engring. and physics, 1981-95, assoc. dir. Ctr. for Laser Studies, 1978-83, dir., 1984-95, William Hogue prof. of engring., 1992-95; dean Thayer Sch. Engring. Dartmouth Coll., Hanover, N.H., 1995-97, prof. engring., 1997—. Vis. fellow Standard Telecommunication Labs., Eng., 1973-74; cons. Aerospace Corp., L.A., 1975-91, sci. adv. bd. Air Force, Washington, 1985-89, TRW, L.A., 1988-89, McDonnell Douglas, St. Louis, 1990-93; mem. com. Nat. Medal Sci., 1996—. Contbr. over 200 sci. papers and articles to profl. publs.; patentee in field. Recipient Soroptimist Achievement award Soroptimist Club L.A., 1970, K.C. Black Award N.E. Electronics Rsch. and Engring. Meeting, 1972, Soc. Women Engrs. Achievement award 1994, U. So. Calif. Rschr. award, 1994; named Mademoiselle Women of Yr. Mademoiselle Mag., 1970. Fellow IEEE (bd. dirs. 1985-89), Optical Soc. Am. (bd. dirs. 1983-86, pres. 1992, 93), Am. Phys. Soc. (bd. dirs. 1994-97), Am. Acad. Arts and Scis., NAE (life), Soc. Women Engrs. (life, Achievement award 1994). Democrat. Avocations: music, gardening. Office: Dartmouth Coll Thayer Sch of Engring Hanover NH 03755-8000

GARNER, CARLENE ANN, fundraising consultant; b. Dec. 17, 1945; d. Carl A. and Ruth E. (Mathison) Timblin; m. Adelbert L. Garner, Feb. 17, 1964; children: Bruce A., Brent A. BA, U. Puget Sound, 1983. Adminstrv. dir. Balletacoma, 1984-87; exec. dir. Tacoma Symphony, 1987-95; prin. New Horizon Cons., Tacoma, 1995-98; co-owner Stewardship Devel., 1998—. Cons. Wash. PAVE, Tacoma, 1983-84. Treas. Coalition for the Devel. of the Arts, 1992-94; pres. Wilson High Sch. PTA, Tacoma, 1983-85; chmn. Tacoma Sch. Vol. Adv. Bd., 1985-87; pres. Emmanuel Luth. Ch., Tacoma, 1984-86, chmn. future steering com., 1987-93; sec.-treas. Tacoma-Narrows Conf., 1987-98; vice chmn. Tacoma Luth. Home, 1996-98; pub. mem. Wash. State Bd. Pharmacy, 1993-98. Mem. N.W. Devel. Officers Assn. (chair Tacoma/Pierce County com. 1994-96), Jr. Women's Club Tacoma (pres. 1975-76, pres. Peninsula dist. 1984-86), Gen. Fedn. Women's Club-Wash. State (treas. 1988-90, 3d v.p. 1990-92, 2d v.p. 1992-94, 1st v.p. 1994-96, pres. 1996-98, Clubwoman of Yr. 1977, Outstanding FREE chmn. Gen. Fedn. 1982), Commencement Bay Woman's Club (pres. 1990-92), Gen. Fedn. of Women's Club (bd. dirs., chair nat. conv. 1995, state pres. 1996-98, chair cmty. improvement program 1998-2000, treas. 2000—02, recording sec. 2002-). Lutheran. E-mail: cagarner@mindspring.com.

GARNER, CINDY ANNE, account executive; b. Fayetteville, N.C., Aug. 2, 1957; d. William Marvin and Virginia Ruth (Wheeler) G. MAT, BA, Rollins Coll., 1979. Collector Creditors Mercantile, Inc., Orlando, Fla., 1980-82; supr. collection Credinrs Mercantile Inc., Orlando, Fla., 1982-83, mgr. collection, 1983-84, regional mktg. dir., 1984-86; mgr. collection AMI Tampa (Fla.) Cen. Bus. Office, 1986-87, dir., 1987-89; pres. Marc Inc., Charlotte, N.C., 1989—. Recipient Charlotte Bus. Jour. Women in Bus. Achievement award, 1997. Mem. Am. Guild Patient Account Mgmt. (publs. com. 1990-91, 2d v.p. Carolina chpt.), Am. Collectors Assn. (edn. coun. 1997—), Nat. Fin. Mgmt. Assn., Nat. Health Collectors Assn., Internat. Fellowship of Cert. Collectors. Avocations: golf, cross country skiing, snowmobiling, photography, bowling. Office: 701 Forest Point Cir Charlotte NC 28273-5609

GARNER, JENNIFER, actress; b. Houston, Apr. 17, 1972; d. Bill and Pat Garner; m. Scott Foley, Oct. 19, 2000. BFA, Dennison U, 1996. Actor: (TV miniseries) Danielle Steele's Zoya, 1995; (TV films) Harvest of Fire, 1996, The Player, 1997; (TV series) Significant Others, 1998, The Time of Your Life, 1999—2000, Alias, 2001— (Golden Globe Award for Best Actress in a Television Series, 2001); (films) Dude, Where's My Car, 2000, Pearl Harbor, 2001, Deconstructing Harry, 1997, Washington Square, 1997, Mr. Magoo, 1997, In Harm's Way, 1997, Rennie's Landing, 2001, Catch Me if You Can, 2002, Daredevil, 2003, 13 Going On 30, 2004.*

GARNER, JO ANN STARKEY, retired elementary and special education educator; b. Ft. Hamilton, N.Y., Dec. 25, 1934; d. Joseph Wheeler and Irene Dorothy (Vogt) Starkey; m. James Gayle Garner, Mar. 2, 1957; children: Mary Vivian Pine, Margaret Susan Gillis, Kathryn Lynn. BA in History, Govt., Law, U. Tex., Austin, 1956; postgrad., Trinity U., 1973. Cert. deaf edn. and elem. tchr., Tex. Kindergarten tchr. Platenstrasse Internat. Sch., Frankfurt, Fed. Republic Germany, 1964-66; tchr. of deaf Sunshine Cottage Sch. for Deaf, San Antonio, 1966-2000; ret., 2000. Speech cons. Trinity U., 1978, cooperating tchr., 1978-87; fiesta coord. Sunshine Cottage. Active San Antonio Fiesta Commn., Poweshiek County Iowa Geneal. Soc.; chmn. book purchasing com. San Antonio Geneal. and Hist. Soc. Mem. Tex. (charter) and Nat. Alexander Graham Bell Assn., Tex. State Geneal. and Hist. Soc., Rep. Nat. Com., German-Texan Heritage Soc., Pioneers of Ind., Olde Mecklenburg Geneal. Soc. N.C., Pioneers of Ill., Ill. Geneal. Soc., Madison County (Ill.) Geneal. Soc., Tex. Pioneers, Alpha Delta Pi. Republican. Mem. Catholic Episcopal Ch. Avocations: writing, painting, history, genealogical research, science. Home: 2027 Edgehill Dr San Antonio TX 78209-2023

GARNER, JOYCE CRAIG, artist; b. Covington, Ky., Dec. 4, 1947; d. William Fayette and Mildred Ollie (Hodge) Craig; m. Gordon Reed Garner, Aug. 19, 1967; children: Angie Reed, Craig Charles, Scott William, Will Michael. BS, U. Ky., 1968. One-woman shows include Ctrl. Bank Gallery, Lexington, 1988, 91, Yvonne Rapp Gallery, Louisville, 1989, 91, 93, 94, Bluegrass Airport Gallery, Lexington, 1991, Headley-Whitney Mus., Lexington, 1992, Malton Gallery, Cin., 1994, Jewish Cmty. Ctr., Louisville, 1995, Hot House Gallery, Indpls., 1996, 98, Carnegie Art Ctr., Covington, Ky., 1997; group exhibits include Three Rivers Arts Festival, Pitts., 1995, Turman Gallery Ind. State U., Terre Haute, 1995, 96, Louisville Visual Art Assn., 1995, 96, Indiana (Pa.) U., 1995, 96, Indpls. Art Ctr., 1995, 96,

Carnegie Art Ctr., Covington, Ky., 1995, 96, Midwest Mus. Am. Art, Elkhart, Ind., 1995, 96, many others; represented in permanent collections Grand Ctrl. Office Bldg., St. Louis, U. Hosp., Cin., St. Luke's Hosp., Newport, Ky., Assn. Met. Sewage Agys., Washington, C.P.I. Corp., St. Louis, KAISER, Atlanta, Ctrl. Bank, Lexington, Balke Properties, St. Louis, Brown & Williamson, Louisville, Riscorp., Sarasota, Fla., Peach Tree Ctr., Internat. Tower, Atlanta, others; art in embassies program U.S. Mission to European Cmtys., Brussels. Resident fellow Hambidge Ctr., 1994. Unitarian-Universalist. Home: 7300 Happy Hollow Rd Prospect KY 40059-9356

GARNER, JUNE BROWN, journalist; b. Detroit, July 19, 1923; d. Simpson and Vela (Wilkerson) Malone; m. Warren C. Garner, June 28, 1961; 1 dau., Sylvia G. Mustonen. Student, Wayne State U., 1941. Columnist, classified advt. mgr. Mich. Chronicle, Detroit, 1945-74; columnist Detroit News, 1974-87, Mich. Chronicle, 1990-92; CFO Warren Garner Realty, Southfield, Mich., 1992-96; reading tchr. North Tazewell (Va.) Elem. Sch., 1996—. Author: June Brown's Guide to Let's Read, 1981, June Brown's Tool Kit, 2000. Founder The Let's Read Summer Sch., 1980—. Recipient Best Column awards Detroit Press Club, 1971, 72, Nat. Newspaper Pubs. Assn., 1968, 69, Sch. Bell award Mich. Edn., Assn., 1989, Am. Promise award, 1999, Tazewell County Pub. Sch. award, 1998. Mem. S.W. Va. Reading Coun. Methodist. Home: 107 Vernon Ave Tazewell VA 24651-1432 E-mail: june_garner@hotmail.com.

GARNER, LANI ALOHA, music educator; b. Norman, Okla., May 4, 1969; d. Sherril Duane and Dolores Leilani Christian; m. William Chester Garner, May 25, 1991; children: Lauren Ashley, Christian Edward. MusB in Edn. with honors, U. Okla., 1992. Cert. Kodaly 1 U. Okla., 1991. Music edn. specialist Norman Pub. Schs., 1992—. Music dir. children's choir grades kindergarten-first McFarlin Meth. Ch., Norman, 1990—91; choir dir. children's choir St. Michael's Episcopal Ch., Norman, 1991—92; children's choir St. John's Episcopal Ch., Norman, 1993—94, children's choir 3 yr. olds - 5th grade, 1999—2001, Christmas pageant dir., 1999—2001; music dir. 4th and 5th grade honor choir Kennedy Elem., Norman, 1992—2000, Monroe Elem., Norman, 2000—01; music dir. Manyawi!, World Music Ensemble, Norman, 2001—. Vol. counselor Birthright Am., Norman, 1988—91; facilitator Bringing Christ Home, Norman, 1997—99. Recipient Rotary Internat. Group Study Exch. Mem. to Norway, Rotary Internat., 2001; grantee, Norman Pub. Schools Found., 1991, 2001, 2002. Mem.: Okla. Educators Assn., Profl. Educators Norman, Music Educators Nat. Conf., Nat. Educators Music Assn., Okla. Music Educators Assn. Democrat. Episcopalian. Avocations: camping, skiing, aerobics, travel. Office: Monroe Elementary School 1601 South McGee Norman OK 73072 E-mail: lgarner@norman.k12.ok.us.

GARNER, SHIRLEY IMOGENE, retired music educator; b. Silverton, Oreg., June 8, 1932; d. Julius Edgar and Amelia Christine (Preszler) Herr; m. Steven Mead Garner, Feb. 24, 1952 (div. Dec. 15, 1987); children: Shelia Christine Garner-Ward, Steven. MusB with honors, Univ. Oreg., Eugene, 1957. Elem. tchr. Springfield USD, Oreg., 1957—58; vocal music tchr. Berkeley USD, Calif., 1958—61, San Jose USD, Calif., 1961—66; lit. tchr. Napa USD, Calif., 1966—67; vocal music tchr. San Jose USD, Calif., 1968—99, ret., 1996, taught part-time, 1996—99. Choir dir. various ch., Oreg., Calif., 1955—83, Pilgrim Haven Ret. Home, Los Altos, Calif., 1969—72, The Fun Time Singers, Campbell, Calif., 2000—02. Edn. adv. com. Restoration of the Statue of Liberty and The Bicentennial of the Constitution, Washington, 1986; vol. Castillero Music Performance. Recipient Hall of Fame award, Youth Focus., Inc., 1993. Mem.: Music Educators Nat. Conf. Presbyn. Achievements include started Castillero Middle Sch. annual music performance at the San Jose Ctr. for performing arts with 2 choirs and profl. performer in 1989; Nov. 2003, will be the 15th annual performace in moring /afternoon and pub. evening performance with about 450 students-5 choirs, 2 bands. orchr. and dance team. Avocations: gardening, flower arranging, reading. Home: 1085 Tasman Dr Space 805 Sunnyvale CA 94089

GARNER, SHIRLEY NELSON, English language educator; b. Waxahachie, Tex., Aug. 8, 1935; d. Cleo and Ruby D. Nelson; m. Frank L. Garner, Nov. 24, 1972; children: Hart Phillip, Celia Ann. AB magna cum laude, U. Tex., 1957; MA, Stanford U., 1966, PhD, 1972. Instr. Stanford (Calif.) U., 1964-65, instr., asst. to dir. fresh composition, 1967-70; asst. prof. U. Minn., Mpls., 1972-76, assoc. prof., 1976-86, assoc. mem. faculty Women's Studies, 1980—, prof., 1986—, chair Women's Studies, 1989-90, dir. Ctr. Advanced Feminist Studies, 1990-94, chair English dept., 1994—2000, assoc. dean grad. sch., 2001—. Editor: (with Personal Narratives Collective) Interpreting Women's Lives: Feminist Theory and Personal Narratives, 1989, (with Madelon Sprengnether) Shakespearean Tragedy and Gender, 1995, Antifeminism in the Academy, 1996, (with VeVe Clark, Ketu Katrak, and Margaret Higonnet) Is Feminism Dead?, 2000; editor, contbg. author: (with Clare Kahane and Madelon Sprengnether) The (M)other Tongue: Essays in Feminist Psychoanalytic Interpretation, 1985; contbg. author: Bad Shakespeare: Revaluations of the Shakespeare Canon, 1988, Seduction and Theory: Readings of Gender, Representation and Rhetoric, 1989, Shakespeare's Personality, 1989, Novel Mothering, 1991, Feminism and Psychoanalysis, Feminism and Philosophy: Essential Readings in Theory, Reinterpretation and Application, 1992, The Intimate Critique: Autobiographical Literary Criticism, 1993; founder, mem. editl. bd. Hurricane Alice, 1983—; mem. editl. bd. Signs, 1992—; contbr. articles, revs. to profl. jours. Scholar Phillips Petroleum Found., 1953-57; Woodrow Wilson fellow, 1959-60, Sorptimists' fellow, 1965-66, 66-67; grantee U. Minn. 1974-76, 81, 87-88, Bush Sabbatical, 1984-85, Office Internat. Edn., 1988, CIA, 1981, 84-90, UROP, 1991-92. Mem. MLA (co-chairperson Marriage and the Family in Shakespeare divsn., Shakespeare sect. 1979, chairperson 1980-82, chair, co-chair various seminars, symposia), Nat. Women's Studies Assn., Midwest Modern Lang. Assn. (sec. Shakespeare sect. 1972, chairperson 1973, nominations com. 1974-77, sec. Women and Lit. sect. 1978-79, chairperson 1980-81, nomination com. Women and Lit. sect. 1981-84), Shakespeare Assn. Office: U Minn English Dept 207 Church St SE Minneapolis MN 55455-0134

GARNETT, KATRINA A. information technology executive; b. Brisbane, Australia, Oct. 17, 1961; BS, SUNY; MBA, Webster U., Geneva, Switzerland. CEO, pres. Cross Worlds Software, Burlingame, Calif., 1996—. Office: Cross Worlds Software 577 Airport Blvd Ste 800 Burlingame CA 94010-2024

GARNETTE, CHERYL PETTY, government agency administrator; BS in Math., MA in Measurement and Stats., U. Md. With Model Secondary Sch. for the Deaf; dir. tech. in edn. programs Office Innovation and Improvement U.S. Dept. Edn., Washington. Comm. dir. Assn. for Ednl. Comm. and Tech. Editor: (Rsch. Notes column) Jour. Ednl. Computing Rsch. Office: US Dept Edn Rm 522G Capitol Pl 555 New Jersey Ave NW Washington DC 20208

GARNISS, JOAN BREWSTER, musician, educator; b. Bangor, Maine, Aug. 10, 1940; d. William Ayer Brewster and Constance Miriam (Witham) Page; adopted d. Woodrow Evans Page; m. Howard Freeman Garniss, Aug. 26, 1962; children: Gretchen, Jonathan. MusB, Boston U., 1962, MusM, 1991. cert. music tchr., Music Tchr. Nat. Assn. Pvt. practice, Dover-Foxcroft, Maine, 1954-58, Hingham, Mass., 1963-65, Waltham, Mass., 1974—. Musician: (albums) En blanc et noir, 2001, Duo Con Anima, 1987—, (accompanist) Wintersauce Chorale, 1984—86, U. Mass., 1988—. Co-founder, pres. Waltham Band Parents, 1979-82, Waltham Music Festival, 1994-97; pres. Friends Waltham Pub. Libr., 1980-83 (bd. dir. 1980-89, 1995—); trustee Waltham Pub. Libr., 1986—, co-chmn. fundraising com., 1995-96; dir. children's choir, All Saints Ch., 1963-66; vol. Boston Pub. Sch., 1969-73; active City Coun. Citizens Com. Transp., Waltham, 1977. Mass. Cultural Affairs Coun. grantee, 1988-89. Mem. UUA/MA N.E. Dist. (human rels. chmn. 1967-70), LWV (v.p. 1979-83, pres. 1983-85, sec. 1997-2003, bd. dir., 2003—, Outstanding Mem. award, 1995), Music Tchrs. Nat. Assn.(rep. East Divsn. Cmty. Outreach, 1995-97,) Ind. Music Tchr. Forum oversight com., 1997-99, Mass. Music Tchrs. Assn. (v.p. 1987-91, pres.-elect 1991-93, pres. 1993-97, immediate past pres. 1997-99), New England Piano Tchr. Assn. (co-chmn. junior recitals com. 1982-88, student master class 1988-90, dir. 1988-90, chair Ensemble Festival, 2000—), Mass. Libr. Trustees Assn., Lexington Music Club, Mu Phi Epsilon, Pi Kappa Lambda. Avocations: needlework, travel, reading, grandchildren.

GAROFALO, JANEANE, actress, comedienne; b. Newton, N.J., Sept. 28, 1964; BA in History and Am. Studies, Providence Coll. Co-anchor Air America, 2004—. TV appearances include The Ben Stiller Show, 1992-93, The Larry Sanders Show, 1992-97, Saturday Night Live, 1994-95, Comedy Product, 1995, emcee, prodr., (movies) Late for Dinner, 1991, Armistead Maupin's Tales of the City, 1993, Reality Bites, 1994, Bye Bye Love, 1995, Cold Blooded, 1995, The Truth about Cats and Dogs, 1996, HBO 1 Hour Special, 1997; appearances include (films) The Cable Guy, 1996, Larger Than Life, 1996, Sweethearts, 1997, Touch, 1997, Romy and Michele's High School Reunion, 1997, Cop Land, 1997, Clay Pidgeons, 1997, The Matchmaker, 1997, Permanent Midnight, 1998, Dog Park, 1998, Half Baked, 1998, Thick as Thieves, 1999, Steal This Movie, 1999, The Minus Man, 1999, Dogma, 1999, Can't Stop Dancing, 1999, 200 Cigarettes, 1999, Mystery Men, 1999, Steal This Movie, 2000, The Independent, 2000, Titan A.E., 2000, The Adventures of Rocky and Bullwinkle, 2000, The Cherry Picker, 2000, Wet Hot American Summer, 2001, The Search for John Gissing, 2001, The Laramie Project, 2002, Martin and Orloff, 2002, Big Trouble, 2002, Manhood, 2003, Wonderland, 2003, Nobody Knows Anything, 2003, Ash Tuesday, 2003, Junebug and Hurricane, 2004; co-author (with Ben Stiller) Feel This Book, 2000. also: UTA Inc 9560 Wilshire Blvd Fl 5 Beverly Hills CA 90212-2401 Office: Ste 700 9460 Wilshire Blvd Beverly Hills CA 90212-2713

GARONZIK, SARA ELLEN, stage producer; b. Phila., Jan. 12, 1951; d. Milton and Bernice (Kohn) G. BA in Spanish cum laude, Temple U., 1972. Producing artistic dir. Phila. Theatre Co., 1982—. Bd. dirs. Arts and Bus. Coun. Greater Phila., Artreach, Phila. Theatre Co., Theatre Alliance Greater Phila. Recipient prize Sigma Delta Pi, 1972, award of Honor, Alumnae Assn. Girls H.S., 1997. Office: Phila Theatre Co 230 S 15th St Philadelphia PA 19102 Business E-Mail: sgaronzik@phillytheatreco.com.

GARRABRANT, DOROTHY OLSON, retired social worker, psychotherapist; b. Eldora, Iowa, May 17, 1940; d. Lowell Graham Olson and Alice Marion Clampitt; m. John Charles Olsa III, Dec. 30, 1966 (div. Oct. 1, 1971), children: John C. Olsa IV, Aaron Curtis Olsa; m. Roger Roy Halleck, July 7, 1973 (div. Aug. 1986); m. Ward Andrew Garrabrant, Sept. 4, 1988. BS in English and Speech, Iowa State U., 1964; MSW, U. Cin., 1993. Lic. ind. social worker Ohio, LCSW Ind., cert. chem. dependency counselor Ohio. English tchr. pub. schs., Iowa and Fla., 1964—66; welfare worker Lee County Dept. Pub. Welfare, Ft. Myers, Fla., 1966—68; children's protective svcs. worker Iowa Dept. Social Svcs., Marshalltown, 1968—81; cert. adoption investigator Marshalltown, 1982—87; children's svcs. worker Hamilton County Dept. Human Svcs., Cin., 1987—94; family therapist Ctrl. Psychol. Clinic/Alcohol and Substance Abuse, Cin., 1994—97; mental health therapist Cin. Counseling, 1997—98, Cath. Social Svcs., Cin., 1999—2002. Mem. group home adv. bd. Youth Group Home, Marshalltown, 1977—80. Exch. dir., amb., v.p., comm. chair Friendship Force, Cin., 1990—2003; singer ch. and cmty. choirs, Marshalltown and Cin., 1981—2003; mentor coll.-level class Edn. for Ministry, Cin., 1999—2003; pub. rels. staff, conv. del. Rep. Party, Marshalltown, 1980—87. Named Outstanding Foster Care Worker, Foster Parents Group, Cin., 1991. Mem.: Alpha Chi Omega. Episcopalian. Avocations: international relations, nature, music, reading, photography.

GARRAHAN-MASTERS, MARY PATRICIA, retired social worker, writer; b. Phila., June 6, 1951; d. Francis Edward and Mary Patricia McElduff Garrahan; m. Thomas Anthony Masters Mastrangelo, June 5, 1995 (div. Feb. 2000). Student, Georgetown U., 1971-72, Facultad Filosofia y Letras, Madrid; BA in Sociology with honors, Villanova (Pa.) U., 1973; M in Social Sci., M in Law and Social Policy, Bryn Mawr (Pa.) Coll., 1983. Geriat. case worker Schuylkill County Area Agy. on Aging, Pottsville, Pa., 1974-79; social svc. dir. Dowden Nursing Home, Newtown Sq., Pa., 1980-84; dir. admissions St. Francis County Ho., Darby, Pa., summer 1981; tchr. Delaware County Coll., Media, Pa., 1984; med. social worker VA Med. Ctr., Lebanon, Pa., 1985-88, Phila., Pa., 88-90. Part-time staff coord. Garrahan Equipment Inc., Havertown, Pa., 1973-92; part-time social worker Delta-T Home Health Agy., Bryn Mawr, 1992-97. Contbr. poetry to Lynx mag. Villanova U. Assoc. mem. Rep. Nat. Com., Washington, 1993-99; Eucharistic minister St. Richard's Roman Cath. Ch., Barnesville, Pa., 1974-79. Mem. Internat. Hypnosis Hall Fame Guild Inc., Nat. Assn. Ret. Fed. Employees, Soc. Friends of Touro Synagogue (assoc. mem.), Alpha Zeta Delta. Home: 2707 Stoneham Dr West Chester PA 19382-6649

GARRARD, PATRICIA RENICK, elementary school educator; b. Miami, Fla., Mar. 9, 1950; d. Ralph Apperson and Elizabeth (Henry) Renick; m. Walter Martin Garrard, Dec. 29, 1972; children: Elizabeth, Danielle. BA, Fla. State U., 1972. Tchr. St. Lawrence Sch., North Miami Beach, Fla., 1972—73, Citrus Grove Jr. H.S., Miami, Fla., 1973—76, Hialeah Jr. H.S., Fla., 1977—79; tchr. lang. arts Pioneer Mid. Sch., Cooper City, Fla., 1979—, chair dept. lang. arts, 1996—. Tchr. cons. South Fla. Writing Project, Ft. Lauderdale, 2001—. Mem.: Nat. Coun. Tchrs. English, Fla. Coun. Tchrs. English, Broward Coun. Tchrs. English, Alpha Chi Omega (province officer 1987—93), Kappa Delta Pi. Roman Catholic. Home: 10427 SW 53 St Fort Lauderdale FL 33328 Office: Pioneer Middle Sch 5350 SW 90th Ave Cooper City FL 33328

GARRELS, ANNE, news correspondent; b. July 2, 1951; m. Vint Lawrence Garrels. Grad., Harvard U., 1972. Various positions ABC News, 1975—85, Moscow bur. chief, Ctrl. Am. corr., 1984—85; State Dept. corr. NBC News, 1985—88; fgn. corr. Nat. Pub. Radio, Washington, 1988—. Recipient Alfred I. duPont-Columbia U. award, 1992, duPont-Columbia award, 1996, Whitman Bassow award, Overseas Press Club, 1999, Alumnae Recognition award, Radcliffe Assn., 2002, Courage award, Internat. Women's Media Found., 2003, George K. Polk award for radio reporting, 2004; Edward R. Murrow fellow, Coun. on Fgn. Rels., 1996. Mem.: Com. to Protect Journalists (bd. mem.). Office: NPR 635 Massachusetts Ave NW Washington DC 20001-3753

GARRELS, SHERRY ANN, lawyer; b. Chgo., Feb. 5, 1956; d. William Henry and Jacqueline Ann G.; m. Timothy Anthony Marion, Aug. 1, 1987 (div. June 1988); 1 child, William Garrels-Marion; 1 child, Georgianna Garrels-Rogers. BA, Barat Coll., 1980; certificate, Trinity Coll., 1989; JD, Western State U., 1990. Bar: Calif. 1992, U.S. Dist. Ct. (ctrl. dist.) Calif. 1992, U.S. Dist. Ct. (no. dist.) Calif. 1993, U.S. Dist. Ct. (so. dist.) Calif. 1996, U.S. Ct. Appeals (9th cir.) 1994, U.S. Tax Ct. 1996. Pvt. practice, Huntington Beach, Calif., 1992—; judge pro tem West Justice Ctr., Westminster, Calif., 1998—. Arbitrator Nat. Panel Consumer Arbitrators, Huntington Beach, 1996, State Panel Consumer Arbitrators, Huntington Beach, 1996, Better Bus. Bureau, 1996—, U.S. C. of C., 1996, Huntington Beach C. of C., 1996. Editor The Dictum, 1989. Active 4th of July Exec. Bd., Huntington Beach, 1996—. Mem. Assn. Trial Lawyers, L.A. Trial Assn., Orange County Bar Assn., St. Bonny Golf Classic (dir. 1991-97), Delta Theta Phi. Republican. Presbyterian. Avocations: swimming, golf, scuba diving. Office: 5942 Edinger Ave Ste 113-702 Huntington Beach CA 92649-1763 also: West Justice Ctr 8141 13th St Westminster CA 92683-4593 Fax: 714-374-0104.

GARRETT, CELIA ERICA, human services administrator, consultant; b. Asheville, N.C., Mar. 31, 1945; d. Willie Thomas and Barbara Anne (Roberts) Garrett. BA, N.C. Ctrl. U., 1967; MSSW, Columbia U., 1978. Caseworker Human Resource Adminstrn., N.Y.C., 1967-74, Adminstrn. for Children's Svcs., N.Y.C., 1974-85, supr. emergency children's svcs., 1985-88, dir. field office emergency children's svcs., 1988—; mental health profl. Trustees of Columbia U. CSS Program, 1979—; cons. Harlem Restoration Project Inc., 1998—. Cons. El Guapo, N.Y.C., 1998—; field instr. Columbia U., 1992—, Hunter Coll., N.Y.C., 1992—; adj. prof. NYU, 1991—. Mem. NASW, Delta Sigma Theta. Democrat. Roman Catholic. Avocations: reading, cooking. Home: 650 Lenox Ave Apt 3J New York NY 10037-1043

GARRETT, DEBRA ANNE, music educator; b. New Albany, Ind., Jan. 9, 1954; d. David Paul and Doris Jean Thomas; m. David B. Garrett, Aug. 26, 1978 (div. Sept. 1989); 1 child, Nathaniel David. BS, Ball State U., 1976, MusM, 1999. Prin. cellist Civic Theater, Grand Rapids, Mich., 1979—80; cellist Fairmont Hotel, New Orleans, 1981; tchr. Shreveport Sch., 1981—82; cellist Shreveport (La.) Symphony, 1981—83; pvt. tchr. Louisville, 1978—; freelance cellist, 1988—; dir. orch. Jefferson County Pub. Schs., Louisville, 1996—; chair dept. Robert Frost Mid. Sch., Louisville, 1997—2002. Judge Overstreet Music Competition, Louisville, 2003. Mem.: Ky. Cello Club, Musicians Union, Am. String Tchrs. Assn., Music Educators Nat. Conf. Avocations: reading, gardening. Home: 786 Captain Frank Rd New Albany IN 47150 Office: Fern Creek Traditional HS 9115 Fern Creek Rd Louisville KY 40291

GARRETT, FLORENCE ROME, poet; b. Bklyn., Sept. 10, 1912; d. George and Blanche Alice (Smith) Rome; m. Elmer Ellsworth Garrett, June 2, 1934 (dec. Oct. 1993); children: Susan Taylor, James Garrett. Profl. accompanist, N.Y., Conn., 1930-61; piano tchr. L.I., N.Y., 1930-55; editor Flume Press, Bridgewater and Hebron, Conn., 1975—. Poetry lectr., L.I., N.Y.; dir. poetry workshops, Conn. Author, editor: Looking for a View, 1997, Light Coming, 1995; author: A Sprig of Lilac, 1990, Japanese Sketches, 1980, Bridgewater Morning, 1986, The Mill and Us, 1978, On the Hill, 1977, More than the Quiet Pond, 1969, Edge of Day, 1954, More than All, 2001. Mem. Roxbury Dem. Town Com., 1972-73, Nat. Dem. Com., Hebron, Conn., 1992-98. Book inclusion in the collection The Ko MUs. of Haiku, Japan; works included in Walt Whitman Collection. Fellow Acad. of Poetry and Lit.; mem. Nat. League of Am. Pen Women (br. pres. L.I. br. 1954-56, poetry chair Conn. Pioneer br. 1959-61). Home and Office: Flume Press 18 River Rd Hebron CT 06248-1430

GARRETT, JILL HOPE, broadcast journalist; b. N.Y.C., Aug. 7, 1954; d. Carlton Ray and Mary Hope (Jackson) G. Grad. high sch., Wilkes-Barre, Pa., 1972. Clk.-stenographer EEOC, Washington, 1973; ministry, 1974-76; sec. prodn. asst. Sta. WBAX Radio, Edwardsville, Pa., 1976-77; photographer, reporter Sta. KJAC-TV, Port Arthur, Tex., 1977-79; news producer Sta. WVIA TV, Pittston, Pa., 1979-80; reporter Sta. WNYT-TV, Albany, N.Y., 1980-83; morning anchor/reporter Sta. WCPO-TV, Cin., 1983-90; healthwatch reporter, prodr. Sta. WNEP-TV, Scranton, Pa., 1990—. Former vol. Clin. Edn. Foundation public television. Home: 438 S River St Wilkes Barre PA 18702-3725 Office: Sta WNEP TV 16 Montage Mountain Rd Scranton PA 18507-1753

GARRETT, LAURIE, science correspondent; b. L.A., Sept. 8, 1951; d. Banning and Lou Ann (Pierose) G. Grad. with honors, U. Calif., 1975, postgrad. With KPFA, Berkeley, Calif., Calif. Dept. Food and Agr.; freelance journalist So. Europe, E. Africa, 1979; freelance reporter, 1980-88; sci. corr. Newsday, N.Y.C., 1988—. Vis. fellow Harvard Sch. Pub. Health, 1992-93. Author: The Coming Plague: Newly Emerging Diseases in a World Out of Balance, 1994; contbr. articles to periodicals including Omni, Washington Post, L.A. Times, Foreign Affairs, others; TV appearances include Dateline, McNeil/Lehrer Newshour, Nightline, others; contbr. reports including Science Story (George Foster Peabody Broadcasting award 1977), Hard Rain: Pests, Pesticides, and People (Edwin Howard Armstrong Broadcast award 1978), The VDT Controversy (Nat. Press Club award Best Consumer Journalism 1982), Why Children Die in Africa (Media Alliance Meritorious Achievement award in Radio 1983, World Hunger Media award First Prize 1987), AIDS in Africa (J.C. Penney/Mo. Journalism Cert. Merit, award of Excellence Nat. Assn. Black Journalists Second Place, 1989), Breast Cancer (Best Beat Reporter Deadline Club N.Y. 1993, First Place N.Y. State AP Writing Contest Press Club L.I., Soc. Silurians 1994), AIDS in India (Bob Considine award Overseas Press Club Am. 1995), Ebola Virus Outbreak in Zaire (Pulitzer prize in Explanatory Journalism, 1996). Office: Newsday 235 Pinelawn Rd Melville NY 11747-4250 also: care Charlotte Sheedy 65 Bleecker St New York NY 10012-2420

GARRETT, MARY JANE, director; b. Houston, Oct. 16, 1961; d. Neitha Mae Freeman. BS in Home Econs., Prairie View A&M U., 1985; child devel. assoc. cert., Houston CC Sys., 2000; postgrad., Tex. So. U., 2003—. Cert. Child Devel. Assn. Owner, operator Ms. Mary's Day Home Care, Houston, 1991—96; dir. Kiddie Coll. Ctr., Houston, 1996—97; tchr. Young Scholar Acad., Houston, 1997—98; ctr. mgr. Village Green Head Start, Houston, 1998—99; asst. ctr. mgr. South Willow Head Start, Houston, 1999—2002, ctr. mgr., 2003; asst. ctr. mgr. Cook Rd. Head Start, Houston, 2003—. Vol. worker Ada Edward Campaign, Houston, 2001; active Christmas Wish Tree Program Salvation Army, Houston, 2001—02; mentor Cmtys. in Sch., Houston, 2002—03. Mem.: Houston Area Assn. for Edn. Young Children, Nat. Black Child Devel. Inst., Nat. Head Start Assn. Democrat. Avocations: bowling, painting, baking, speed walking, party planning. Home: 5500 Martin Luther King Blvd #3 Houston TX 77021

GARRETT, ROBIN SCOTT, public information officer; b. Sparta, NC, Jan. 24, 1965; d. Milton William Scott, Peggie Adams Scott; m. William Earle Garrett; 1 child, Nicolas. BS Mgmt. and Mktg., Univ. SC, 2004. Medical Clerk WJBD VA Medical Center, Columbia, SC, 1986—86; Sec./Steno. WJBD VA Med. Ctr., Columbia, SC, 1986—91, Civilian Pay Technician, 1991—95, Lead Civilian Pay Technician, 1995—97, Fiscal Admin. Sup., 1997—2000. VALUE (VA Leadership Upward Expectations) Graduate Dept of Veterans Affairs, Atlanta, 1999—2000; developed new strategy on budgeting salaries VA Med. Ctr., Columbia, SC, 2000; conducted feasibility study on establishing an adult day care facility WJBD VA Med. Ctr., Columbia, SC, 1999; prepared strategic mgmt. plans Edward Jones Investments, Columbia, SC, 2002, Ashley Fetner Fine Art Photography, Columbia, SC, 2002. Notary Pub. State of SC, Columbia, SC, 1996—2006. Named Fed. Woman of Yr., 1995; recipient CPCU Mem. Scholarship, Lanville Mengedoht, 2003. Mem.: National Society of Collegiate Scholars (life), Golden Key National Honor Society (life), Beta Gamma Sigma (life), Phi Beta Kappa (life). Baptist. Avocation: photography, travel, hiking, reading, music. Home: 101 Fox Run Dr Hopkins SC 29061-9231 Personal E-mail: rgarrett@sc.rr.com.

GARRETT, SANDY LANGLEY, school system administrator; b. Muskogee, Okla., Feb. 8, 1943; 1 child, Charles Langley (Chuck). BS in Elem. Edn., Northeastern U., Tahlequah, Okla., 1968, MS in Counseling, 1980; grad. John F. Kennedy Sch. Govt., Harvard U., 1989. Lic. tchr., adminstr., supt. std., Okla. Tchr. Hilldale Schs., Muskogee, Okla., 1968-80; coord. gifted program Hillsdale Schs., Muskogee, Okla., 1980-82; coord. gifted and talented State Dept. Edn., Oklahoma City, 1982-85, dir. rural edn., 1985-87, exec. dir. ednl. svcs., 1987-88, state supt. pub. instrn., 1991-95;

sec. edn. Gov.'s Office, Oklahoma City, 1988—; state supt. pub. instrn. State Dept. Edn., Oklahoma City, 1991—. Chair State Bd. Edn., Oklahoma City, 1991—, State Vo-Tech. Edn., Oklahoma City, 1991—; bd. dirs. So. Regional Edn. Bd.; regent Okla. Colls., 1991—; mem. Nat. Coll. Bd. Equality Project; chair. Okla. Lit. Initiatives Commn.; mem. So. Regional Ednl. Bd. Co-author: (curriculum guide) Gifted Galaxy; mem. editorial bd. Rural and Small Schs.; contbr. articles to profl. jours. Co-chair Dem. Party, Muskogee, 1978; del. Dem. Nat. Conv., N.Y.C., 1980, 82; mem. Leadership Okla., 1990. Recipient Cecil Yarbrough award, 1989, Claude Dyer Legis. award, 1989. Mem. Muskogee County Ednl. Assn., Delta Kappa Gamma, Phi Delta Kappa, Delta Kappa Gamma. Methodist. Avocations: tennis, swimming, computer programming, travel, politics. Office: State Dept Edn 2500 N Lincoln Blvd Oklahoma City OK 73105-4503

GARRETT, SHARON, health services company executive; B in Econs., MPH, PhD, UCLA. Formerly with Hyatt Med. Enterprises, VA, Am. Heart Assn., Cath. Hosp. Assn., Calif. Dept. Health Svcs.; former dep. dir. UCLA Med. Ctr.; chief info. officer The Walt Disney Co., 1989—2000; exec. v.p. enterprise svcs. PacifiCare Health Systems, Inc., Cypress, Calif., 2000—. Bd. dirs. Ross Stores, Corio. Office: PacifiCare Health Systems Inc 5995 Plaza Dr Cypress CA 90630

GARRETT, SHIRLEY GENE, nuclear medicine technologist; b. Evanston, Ill., Apr. 19, 1944; d. Nathan and Emma Louise (Uecker) G. AA, Oakton C.C., 1977; AS in Nuc. Medicine, Triton Coll., 1980; BA, Northea. Ill. U., 1983; MA, Govs. State U., University Park, Ill., 1985. Cert. nuclear medicine technologist. Nuc. medicine technologist Chgo. Osteo. Hosp., 1980-88, Little Co. of Mary Hosp., Evergreen Park, Ill., 1989; nuclear medicine technologist Lutheran Gen. Hosp., Lincoln Park, Ill., 1989; nuc. medicine technologist Mt. Sinai Hosp., Chgo., 1990-92; technologist nuc. medicine Swedish Covenant Hosp., Chgo., 1992-93; pres. Providence Hosp. of Cook County, Chgo., 1994—. Contbr. articles to profl. jours. Vol. Ravenswood Hosp., Chgo., 1986-2000, Mt. Sinai Hosp., 1990-92, Congl. Health Ministry, Ch. of St. Lukes. Mem. Soc. Nuc. Medicine (mem. bylaws com. technologist sect. Ctrl. chpt. 1982-83, 85-86, 92-2000, mem. continuing edn. com. 1986-87, chmn. nominating com. 1987-88, 92-93, mem. edn. com. 1988-89, pres.-elect 1989-90, mem. bd. govs. 1990-92, 97-2000, pres. 1991-92, chmn. bylaws com. 1992-93, bd. govs. ctrl. chpt. 1997-2000), Assoc. and Tech. Affiliates Chgo. Area (coord. edn. 1981-84, mem. adv. bd. 1983-84, 87-88, 96-97, pres. 1985-87, chmn. nominating com. 1987-89). Lutheran.

GARRETT, SUSAN, state senator; b. Lake Forest, Ill., Feb. 11, 1950; m. Scott Garrett; children: Brett, Liz. BA Polit. Sci., Lake Forest Coll. State Senator US Senate, Dist. #29, Ill., 2003; State Rep. House of Rep., Ill., 1998—2002. Legis. assignment Comm. on Ed.; mem. Health & Human Svc.; vice-chairperson Trans.; mem. HHS-BDD subcommittee; subchairperson Health & Human Svc. Health Care; mem. Health and Human Svc. Subcommittee on Behavioral and Devel.. Disabilities. Mem.: Market Square 2000 (Bd. of Dir.), Susan Garrett Marketing Assoc. (founder). Democrat. Episcopalian. Office: Capitol M118 Capitol Bldg Springfield IL 62706 also: District 425 Sheridan Rd Highwood IL 60040

GARRETT, SUSAN, music educator; d. A. K. and Elsie Herrmann Guthrie; m. Donald Garrett; children: Alan K., Philip T. BS, Tenn. Technol. U., 1972; Kodály Music Edn. Cert., Capital U., 1997. Musican Chattanooga Symphony & Opera, 1975—2000; choral dir. Lake Forest Mid. Sch., Cleveland, 1983—2003. Singer Choral Arts Chattanooga, 1995—; instr. kodály summer certification course U. Tenn., Chattanooga, 2001—02; presenter in field. Co-director (concert for U. Tenn. Chattanooga Music Edn. Assn. Conf.) Trewhitt Junior High Choir. Mem.: East Tenn. Vocal Assn. (area rep. 2002—03), SE Chpt. Kodály Educators (sec.-treas. 2001—, pres. 1997—98). Office: Lake Forest Mid Sch 610 Kile Lake Rd SE Cleveland TN 37323

GARRETT, VIKKI RAE, transportation planner; b. Pensacola, Fla., Jan. 17, 1967; d. Edgar Ray and Patricia Ann (Lodge) G. AA, Pensacola Jr. Coll., 1987; BS, U. West Fla., 1990, MPA, 2001. Transp. planner Fla. Dept. of Transp., Pensacola, 1992-97, Hamilton Smith and Assocs. Inc., Gulf Breeze, Fla., 1997—2000, Escambia County Engring. Dept., 2000—03; prin., owner Garrett Consulting Svcs., Inc., 2003—. Mem.: Inst. Transp. Engrs., Am. Planning Assn. Home: 1411 E Lee St Pensacola FL 32503-5623 Office Phone: 850-438-6469.

GARRIS, ANNETTE D. FAILE, medical, surgical, and rehabilitation nurse; b. Homestead, Fla., July 3, 1963; d. Rex Pyron and Margie Ruth (Jordan) Faile; m. Larry Allen Garris, June 5, 1987; children: Lanette and Tiffany. LPN, Lancaster (S.C.) Vocat. Sch., 1987; ADN, U. S.C., Lancaster, 1990. RN, S.C.; cert. rehab. nurse. Nursing asst. Marion Sims Nursing Ctr., Lancaster; nurse Piedmont Med.Ctr., Rock Hill, S.C., Lancaster County Care Ctr., Lancaster, Rebound Inc., Lancaster, Elliot White Springs Meml. Hosp., Lancaster; RN, asst. dir. nursing Rebound, Inc., Lancaster. Asst. dir., Nursing at Meadow Haven Rehab. & Specialty Care Ctr., Rock Hill, SC, transitional care coord., Rehab. Care, Lancaster, SC, dir. case mgmt., Springs Hosp., Lancaster, SC. Recipient Francine Manion award, 1990. Home: 2468 Golf Course Rd Lancaster SC 29720-8416

GARRISON, ALTHEA, government official; b. Hahira, Ga., Oct. 7, 1940; d. Charles and Lenora Mae (Davis) G. AS, Newbury Jr. Coll., 1978; BS, Suffolk U., 1982; cert. in social studies, Harvard U., 1986; MS, Lesley Coll., 1984. Counselor, supr. Charlotte House Dorchester (Mass.), 1977-77; with EDP dept., sr. assessor Mass. Dept. Revenue, Boston, 1979-81; sr. examiner Office State Compt., Boston, 1982-90; human resource mgr. Office of State Comptr. Commonwealth of Mass., 1991—; state rep. gen. ct. 5th suffolk Rep. Dist., Mass., 1992-95. Bd. dirs. Uphams Corner Health Ctr., Dorchester, 1983—, v.p., 1987—, Disting. Svc. award, 1991. Charter mem. adv. bd. Christian Record Braille, Lincoln, Neb., 1983; alumna coun. Lesley Coll. Grad. Sch., Cambridge, Mass., 1986-88; active Nat. Rep. Congl. Com., 1988—, Rep. Presdl. Task Force, 1989—, Met. Area Planning Coun., 1994; charter founder Ronald Reagan Rep. Ctr., Washington, 1989; nominee City Coun. Dorchester, 1989, State Rep. Rep. Primary, 1990; town com. woman Ward 13, Boston, 1992, commn. vice-chair, treas. city com., 1994-96; exec. com. Met. Area Planning Coun., 1995-98; apptd. Notary Pub., 1994—, Justice of Peace, 1997; mem. Irish Immigration Ctr., 1996-98; coord. Toys for Tots, Office State Comptr., 1997; hon. mem. Profl. Women's Adv. Bd., 1999, Am. Biog. Inst., 1999. Recipient Senator's citation Commonwealth Mass., 1982, Merit medal Rep. Task force, 1989, Appreciation cert. Mass. Rep. Party, Outstanding Vol. award Suffolk U., 1991, Achievement cert. Conf. New Legislators, 1993, Rep. Leadership award, 1993-94, Book award Dearborn Middle Sch., 1994, Legis. Yr. award Gtr. Boston Labor Coun. AFL-CIO, 1994, Excellent Svc. award Holborn, Gannett, Gaston, Otisfield Betterment Assn., 1995, Cmty. Svc. Honor award Winthrop St. Crime Assn., 1996, Benefactor Cert. Mayo Found., 1998, Membership Achievement award WGBH, 1999, Cert. of Appreciation, Uphams Corner Health Ctr., 1999; hon. fellow John F. Kennedy Libr., 1987-90; named one of 100 Women Making History North Shore Women's Coalition, Rep. Presdl. Legion of Merit Honor Roll, 1993; cert. of appreciation USMC Res.; Cmty. Svc. Honor award Winthrop Street Crime Assn., 1996. Mem. Am. Mgmt. Assn., Nat. Assn. Govt. Employees (negotiator, organizer 1979-81), Suffolk U. Gen. Alumni Assn. (bd. dirs. 1986-89), Heritage Found., Nat. Found. Cancer Rsch. (hon., citation 1991), DAV Comdrs., World War II Soc. (charter mem. 2000). Roman Catholic. Avocations: walking, music, reading, research. Home: 18 Jerome St Apt 2 Dorchester MA 02125-2021

GARRISON, ARLENE ALLEN, engineering executive, engineering educator; BA in Liberal Arts, U. Tenn., 1975, PhD in Analytical Chemistry, 1981, BSEE, 1988. Instr. analytical chemistry, grad. rsch. asst. U. Tenn., Knoxville, 1975-81, rsch. assoc., 1981, sr. electonic design engr. dept. chemistry, 1985-89, rsch. asst. prof. dept. chemistry, 1989—, dir. measurement and control engring. ctr. Coll. Engring. U. Tenn., Knoxville; licensing exec. U. Tenn., Knoxville, 1998-99, dir. industry programs and tech. transfer, 1999-2000, asst. v.p., 2000—. Mem. NRC bd. assessment for Nat. Inst. Standards and Tech., Panel for Chem. Sci. and Tech., 1996-2001; mem. chemistry dept. alumni steering com. U. Tenn. Knoxville, 1994—; participant in NATO Advanced Study Inst. on Analytical Applications of Fourier transform infrared to Molecular and Biolog. Systems, Florence, Italy, 1980; organizer insl. spectroscopy symposium Internat. Conf. on Raman Spectroscopy, Hong Kong; co-chair Soc. Photo-Optical Instrumentation Engrs. conf. on optical methods for chem. process control, 1994; sci. bd. Iternat. Forum Process Analytical Chemistry, 1993—; presenter in field. Contbr. over 29 articles to profl. jours. Chair bd. trustees Fountain City United Meth. Ch., 1991-94; sec. Wesley Found. Bd., 1992-93; bd. dirs. Appalachian Sci. Fair, 1993-2003, WATTec, 1994-96, Discovery Ctr., 1995-98; mem. Pub. Bldg. Authority, 1995-2003, chair, 2000-02. Recipient Chancellors Citation for extraordinay cmty. svc., 1993. Mem. Soc. for Applied Spectroscopy (Meggars award 1982), Soc. of Photo Instrumentation Engrs., Coblentz Soc. (bd. mgrs. 1989-92, pres. 1997-98), Am. Chem. Soc. (sec. East Tenn. sect. 1988-90, chair-elect 1991, chair 1992, steering com. divsns. chem. edn. and analytical chemistry, chair Williams Wright award com. 1991, 92). Phi Beta Kappa, Phi Kappa Phi, Alpha Lambda Delta. Office: U Tenn Office Rsch and Info Tech 409 Andy Holt Tower Knoxville TN 37996-0147 Business E-Mail: garrison@tennessee.edu.

GARRISON, BARBARA JANE, chemistry educator; b. Big Rapids, Mich., Mar. 7, 1949; BS, Ariz. State U., 1971; PhD in Chemistry, U. Calif., Berkeley, 1975. Rsch. fellow in chemistry Purdue U., Lafayette, Ind., 1975-77; lectr. U. Calif., Berkeley, 1977-78; from asst. prof. to assoc. prof. Pa. State U., University Park, 1979-86, prof. chemistry, 1986—, head dept. chemistry, 1989-94, Disting. prof. chemistry, 2000—02, Shapiro prof. chemistry, 2002—. Vis. asst. prof. Purdue U., 1978-79; vis. assoc. chemistry Calif. Inst. Tech., 1985-86. Alfred P. Sloan Found. rsch. fellow, 1980. Fellow Am. Phys. Soc., Am. Vacuum Soc.; mem. Am. Chem. Soc. (Francis P. Garvan - John M. Olin medal 1994). Office: Pa State U Dept Chemistry 152 Davey Lab University Park PA 16802-6300

GARRISON, CAROL Z. academic administrator; b. Upper Montclair, N.J. BA, U. N.C., Chapel Hill, 1974; MS in nursing, U. Ala., Birmingham, 1976; PhD, U. N.C., Chapel Hill, 1982. Cert. nurse practitioner, U. Ala. Birmingham, 1978. Asst. prof. nursing U. Ala., Birmingham, 1976—78, U. N.C., 1978—82; faculty U. S.C., 1982—92, prof. and chair epidemiology and biostatistics, 1992—97, assoc. provost, 1994—97, dean grad. sch., 1994—97; provost U. Louisville, 1997—2002, acting pres., 2002; pres. U. Ala., Birmingham, 2002—. Office: AB 7070 1530 3rd Ave S Birmingham AL 35294-0110*

GARRISON, ELIZABETH JANE, artist; b. Elmira, N.Y., Feb. 11, 1952; BFA, Ringling Sch. Art and Design, 1973; postgrad., Mansfield U., 1976-78; MS, Fla. State U., 1980. Exhibits include Mus. Contemporary Art, The Netherlands, Mus. Fine Arts, St. Petersburg, Fla., Renwick Gallery, The Smithsonian Inst., Washington, and others; represented in permanent collections Yale U. Art Gallery, New Haven, Conn., Kunstgewerbe Mus., Berlin, Honolulu Acad. Arts. Nat. Endowment Arts fellows, 1981, 88; Saltonstall Found. grantee, 1996. Home: 317 Elm St Ithaca NY 14850-3018

GARRISON, F. ELAINE, copy editor; b. Trenton, Mo., Jan. 16, 1957; d. Eugene and Arlene (Elliott) G. AA, Trenton Jr. Coll., 1976; B in Mass Comm., Ctrl. Mo. State U., 1978. Features editor Daily Dunkin Democrat, Kennett, Mo., 1981-89; agriculture editor Daily Am. Republic, Poplar Bluff, Mo., 1989-90; news editor News Guardian, Cape Girardeau, Mo., 1990; state editor Mo. Agri-News, Columbia, 1990-91; news editor, copy desk chief, features editor Sedalia (Mo.) Democrat, 1991—98; copy editor Quad City Times, Davenport, Iowa, 1998—99, The Kansas City (Mo.) Star, 1999—. Bd. dirs. Mo. Bootheel Humane Soc., Kennett, 1980-86, pres., 1987. Methodist. Avocations: pets, photography, fine arts. Office: The Kansas City Star 1729 Grand Blvd Kansas City MO 64108

GARRISON, GENEVA, retired administrative assistant; b. Bowling Green, Ky., Feb. 14, 1933; d. Claude Harrison and Helen (Bohannon) Garrison; m. Marion Murphey Dare, Jr., Aug. 1955 (div. Mar. 1972); 1 child, Marcus Glenn. AAS, U. Louisville, 1975, BLS summa cum laude, 1977. Tchr. behavior disorders, learning disabilities, mentally handicapped Jefferson County Schs., Louisville, 1974—77; coord. parent edn. project U. Louisville, 1977—79; exec. sec. to dir. AHES Western Ky. U., Bowling Green, 1980, sec., asst. to dir. devel., 1980—84, exec. sec. to exec. v.p. adminstrv. affairs, 1984—87, sec. to pres., 1987—89; ret., 1989. Part-time crisis counselor LifeSkills Inc., Bowling Green, 1993—96. Author: (poetry) to profl. jours. Recipient Omicron Delta Kappa Outstanding Grad. Sr. award, U. Louisville, 1978. Mem.: AAUW, DAR, Warren County Ret. Tchrs. Assn., Ky. Ret. Tchrs. Assn., Oak Ridge Camera Club, So. Appalachian Nature Photography Club, Internat. Soc. Poets, Phi Kappa Phi (scholar 1978). Avocations: photography, nature walks, book collecting, fashion . Home: 733 Newman Way Bowling Green KY 42104-3810

GARRISON, KATHRYN ANN, retired nutritionist; b. Prentiss, Miss., Dec. 30, 1929; d. Brooks Hilton and Irene Dale Polk; m. Rufus James Garrison, Dec. 30, 1953; children: Rufus James Garrison Jr., Karen D. Garrison Goff, David B. BS in Instnl. Mgmt., U. So. Miss., 1952. Dietetic intern Vanderbilt U. Hosp., Nashville, 1953; staff dietitian Bapt. Hosp., Nashville, 1954, Children's Hosp., Louisville, Ky., 1954; cons. Murfreesboro (Tenn.) Med. Clinic, 1980-89; registered dietitian, 1989-96; ret., 1996. Pres., gen. mgr. Mid. Tenn. Choral Soc., 1983—; gen. mgr. Orpheus Vocal Competition, 1995—. Recipient Cmty. Svc. award, Daily News Jour. and Sun Trust Bank, 1999. Baptist. Avocations: music, travel, antiques, art. Home: 1941 Veranda Pl Murfreesboro TN 37130-3267

GARRISON, LATREASE E. association executive; b. Petersburg, Va., Aug. 8, 1972; d. Larry Boyd and Ruby (Williams) Evans; m. D'Vell Medley Garrison, Mar. 15, 1997; 1 child, Testimony Faith. BS in Chemistry, Howard U., 1995; postgrad., Strayer U., 1998—. Editl. sec. Am. Chem. Soc., Washington, 1992-95, program asst., 1995-96, staff asst., 1996-97, staff assoc., 1997-98, sr. staff assoc., student affiliates program, 1998-99, program mgr., 1999—2001, sr. edn. program mgr., 2001—. Editor Chemistry, 2003—; editor (newsletter) FANmail, 1998—. Active Antioch Bapt. Ch. Mem. Am. Chem. Soc., Alpha Kappa Alpha Sorority, Inc. Avocations: travel abroad, reading, writing poetry, cooking. Home: 5408 Quaint Dr Woodbridge VA 22192-5612 Office: Am Chem Soc 1155 16th St NW Washington DC 20036-4800

GARRISON, SUEANN, psychologist; b. Buenos Aires, July 14, 1972; arrived in U.S., 1978; d. Joel Richard Garrison and Nancy Susana Casella-Garrison; m. Frank Joseph Vazzana, June 23, 2001. BA, U. Miami, 1993; MA, Tex. Tech U., 1997, PhD, 2000. Lic. psychologist Fla. Dir. sexual trauma program Bay Pines VAMC, Fla., 2001—. Republican. Roman Catholic. Avocations: reading, gardening, exercising, home renovation.

GARRISON, WANDA BROWN, environmental consultant; b. Madison County, N.C., Sept. 16, 1936; d. Roy Lee Brown and Zella Arizona (Miller) Brown Hannah; m. Charles Mitchell Garrison, July 9, 1955; children: Roy Lee, Marsha Joan; 1 step-son, Charles Mitchell, Jr. Student air-line hostess, Weaver Airlines, St. Louis, 1954-55; student, Haywood Tech. Coll., Clyde, N.C., 1967-68, IBM, Asheville, N.C., 1977; student data processing, Agy. Record Control, Atlanta, 1978. Operator Day Co., Waynesville, N.C., 1954-57; driver Haywood County Schs., Waynesville, 1970-71; operator Am. Enka, N.C., 1972-75; bookkeeper L.N. Davis Ins. Co., Waynesville, 1975-80; stock preparation Champion Internat., Canton, N.C., 1980-89. Cons. Garrison and Assocs. Environ. Solutions, Pensacola, Fla., 1990—2001. Pres. Fire Dept. Aux., Crabtree, NC, 1973—; sec.-treas. James Chapel Bapt. Ch., Haywood County, NC, 1965—77; pres. Women Mission Union Crabtree Bapt. Ch., Haywood County, 1977—80; v.p. Gideon Aux., Haywood County, 1982—84, pres., 1984—87; state aux. follow-up rep., 1984—87; state zone leader, 1987—88. Recipient Life Saving plaque Lion's Club, Waynesville, 1972. Mem. AFL-CIO. Republican. Home: 513 S 2nd St Pensacola FL 32507-3313

GARRISON-FINDERUP, IVADELLE DALTON, writer, educator; b. San Pedro, Calif., Oct. 4, 1915; d. William Douglas and Olive May (Covington) Dalton; m. Fred Marion Garrison, Aug. 8, 1932 (dec. Nov. 1984); children: Douglas Lee, Vernon Russell, Nancy Jane; m. Elmer Pedersen Finderup, Apr. 8, 1994 (dec. Oct. 1997). BA, Calif. State U., Fresno, 1964; postgrad., U. Oreg., 1965, U. San Francisco, 1968. Cert. secondary tchr., Calif. Tchr. Tranquillity (Calif.) H.S., 1964-78, West Hills Coll., Coalinga, Calif., 1970-74. Lectr. in field. Author: Roots and Branches of Our Garrison Family Tree, 1988, Roots and Branches of Our Dalton Family Tree, 1989, The History of James' Fresno Ranch, 1990, 3d edit., 1993, There is a Peacock on the Roof, 1993; (with Vernon R. Garrison) William Douglas Dalton, a Biography, 1995, Sam (The Cat That Thought He Was a Boy), 1997, Amanda and Her Feathered Friends, 1997, Freddy Goes on a Trailer Outing, 1998, David Learns to Count, 1998, Laura and the Lizard: a fairy tale, 2001. Mem. DAR (sec. 1987-89, regent 1989-91, regent Fresno chpt. 1999-2001, scholarship chmn. 2002, nat. recognition for excellence in cmty. svc. Cert. of Award 1995), Nat. Trust for Hist. Preservation, Frazier Clan N.Am., Fresno City and County Hist. Soc. (life), Fresno Archaeology Soc. (sec. 1994), Children of the Am. Revolution (life patriot, sr. pres. 1991-97), Westerners Internat., Fresno Gem and Mineral Soc., Thora # 11 Dannebrog, Friends of the Libr. (Fresno), Chaffee Zoolog. Gardens of Fresno, Archaeological Inst. Am. (San Joaquin Valley chpt., charter mem.), Fresno County Archaeological Soc, Fresno Met. Mus., Baker Hist. Mus. (life), Fresno Gem and Mineral Soc. Republican. Lutheran. Avocations: quilting, knitting. Office: Garrison Libr 3427 Circle Ct E Fresno CA 93703-2403

GARRISON-JACKSON, ZINA, retired professional tennis player; b. Houston, Nov. 16, 1963; m. Willard Jackson. Mem. U.S. Olympic tennis team, 1988 (Bronze Medal in Singles and Gold Medal in Doubles - with Pam Shriver). Winner tournaments including Wimbledon Jr. Singles, 1981, U.S. Open Jr. Singles, 1981, U.S. Open Doubles Title (with Mary Joe Fernandez), 1993, Can. Doubles, 1986, 87, Birmingham, 1990; finalist Wimbledon, 1990. Office: c/o USTA 70 W Red Oak Ln White Plains NY 10604-3602 also: c/o Advantage International 1751 Pinnacle Dr Ste 1500 Mc Lean VA 22102-3833

GARRISS, PHYLLIS WEYER, music educator, performer; b. Hastings, Nebr., Dec. 25, 1923; d. Frank Elmer and Mabelle Claire (Carey) Weyer; m. William Philip Garriss, Aug. 28, 1954; children: Daniel, Meredith, Margaret. AB, MusB, Hastings Coll., 1945; MusM, U. Rochester, 1948. Instr. DePauw U., Greencastle, Ind., 1948-51; assoc. prof. music Meredith Coll., Raleigh, N.C., 1951-94, assoc. prof. emerita, part-time prof., 1994—. Instr. Cannon Music Camp, Appalachian State U., Boone, N.C., 1973-98; vis. instr. Ball State U., Muncie, summers 1951, 53; dir. Lamar Stringfield Chamber Music Camp, Meredith Coll., 1980—; bd. dirs. Raleigh Symphony Orch., Raleigh Chamber Music Guild; mem. various symphonic groups as violinist, including Roanoke Symphony, Raleigh Civic Symphony, Duke U. Symphony, Tri-City Chamber Orch., Raleigh Symphony Orch., Capital Chamber Music Ensemble. Mem. Raleigh Civic Coun., 1958-60; bd. dirs. Raleigh Comty. Mus. Sch., 1993-97, N.C. Fedn. Music Clubs, 1988-96; mem. PEO. Recipient Medal of Arts, City of Raleigh Arts Commn., 1987. Mem. Am. String Tchrs. Assn. (corr. sec. 1950-54, Disting. Svc. award 1979), Music Tchrs. Nat. Assn., Music Educators Nat. Conf., Local 500 Musicians Assn. (bd. dirs. 1980—), Raleigh Music Club (pres. 1958-60, 93-95), Pi Kappa Lambda, Mu Phi Epsilon. Democrat. Presbyterian. Avocations: cooking, traveling. Home: 3400 Merriman Ave Raleigh NC 27607-7004 Office: Meredith Coll 3800 Hillsborough St Raleigh NC 27607-5237

GARROTT, FRANCES CAROLYN, architectural technician; b. Bowling Green, Ky., Mar. 10, 1932; d. Irby Reid and Carrie Mae (Stahl) Cameron; m. Leslie Othello Garrott, Oct. 12, 1951 (dec. Feb. 1978); adopted children: Carolyn Maria, Karen Roxana children: Dennis Leslie, Alan Reid; m. Raymond William Scerbo, May 31, 1978 (div. Oct. 1990). Student, Fla. State U., 1951, St. Petersburg Jr. Coll., 1962-74; grad., Pinellas Vocat. Tech. Inst., 1975. With Sears, Roebuck and Co., Rapid City, S.D., 1951-52, St. Petersburg, Fla., 1961-62; bookkeeper Ohio Nat. Bank, Columbus, 1953-54, Sunbeam Bakery, Lakeland, Fla., 1955-56; with Christies Toy Sales, Pennsauken, N.J., 1958-60; exec. sec. Gulf Coast Automotive Warehouse, Inc., Tampa, Fla., 1970-73, office mgr., 1975-78; sec., treas., chief pilot, co-owner Tech. Devel. Corp., St. Petersburg, Fla., 1970-78. Freelance archtl. draftsman and designer, archtl. cons., constrn. materials estimator, Lakeland, Fla., 1995—, Seminole, Fla., 1975—95. Fla. judge Vocat. Indsl. Clubs Am. Skills Olympics, 1986. Nat. Assn. Women in Constrn. scholar, 1974. Mem. Nat. Assn. Women in Constrn. (scholar 1974), Alpha Chi Omega. Democrat. Home: 8156 Timberidge Loop W Lakeland FL 33809-2357

GARROU, LINDA, state legislator; b. Atlanta, Jan. 17, 1943; m. John L.W. Garrou. AA, Sullins Coll., 1962; BS in Edn., U. Ga., 1964; MA, U. N.C., 1967. Tchr. social studies Jordan H.S., 1964-66; asst. adminstr. Forsyth County Juvenile Justice Coun., 1972-81; dist. adminstr. AOCL, 1987-94, regional adminstr., 1994—; senator N.C. State Senate, Raleigh, 1998—. Mem. agr./environ./natural resources, appropriations on edn./higher edn., appropriations/base budget, children and human resources, edn./higher edn. coms. N.C. State Senate, vice chair info. tech., mem. select com. on tobacco settlement issues. Mem. Leadership Winston-Salem, Piedmont Triad Leadership, Winston-Salem Jr. Leaguek Big Brother/Big Sister, Gov.'s Advocacy Coun. for Children and Youth, Commn. on Family, N.C. Advocacy Coun. Democrat. Office: NC State Senate 522 Legislative Office Bldg Raleigh NC 27601-2808 E-mail: Lindag@s.ncga.state.nc.us.

GARRY, COLLEEN M. state legislator; B.S., U. of Lowell; J.D., Suffolk U. Sch. of Law. Mem. Mass. Ho. of Reps., Boston, 1995—, house and joint counties commt., commerce and labor cmmt., criminal justice commt. Democrat. Office: State House Rm 473-G Boston MA 02133

GARTH-LEWIS, KIMBERLEY, state official, public policy educator; b. Sacramento, Calif. children: Shavaugn, Veronica. BS, U. San Francisco, 1981; MPA, Golden Gate U., 1986, DPA, 1992. Cert. lifetime credential for pub. adminstrn. and colls. Rschr. in neurology U. Calif.-San Francisco Med. Ctr., 1978—81; ins. investigator Equifax Svc., Calif. and Nev., 1982—85; exec. asst. U.S. Embassy, London, 1985—86, Dept. Def. Dependent Sch., England, 1986—87; cons. Calif. Legislature, Sacramento, 1988—92; lobbyist Calif. Correctional Peace Officers Assn., Sacramento, 1992—95; prof. Calif. State U., 1993—95, U. San Francisco, San Francisco, 1992—; criminal justice specialist Office of Gov. of Calif., 1999—2002; cons. Dept. of Edn., Calif., 2002—. Cons., owner KAGL & Affiliates, Inc., Sacramento, 1995—; chmn. welfare reform Human Svcs. Coord. Coun., Sacramento, 1999; cons. Bur. Justice Correctional, 1999—; bd. dirs. Calif. Criminal

Justice Inst., 2002. Bd. dirs. NAFE, Calif., 1990—92. Recipient Calif. Resolution, Calif. State Legislature, 1990, Outstanding Woman's award, YWCA, 1999. Avocations: reading, running. Home: PO Box 293402 Sacramento CA 95828 Office Phone: 916-689-2797.

GARVENS, ELLEN JO, art educator, educator, artist; b. Omro, Wis., Aug. 15, 1955; d. Leonard Kenneth and Eugenia Mary (Wetter) G.; m. James Patrick Phalen, Oct. 18, 1988; children: Cole Garvens Phalen, Mason Garvens Phalen. BS in Art, U. Wis., 1979; MA, U. N. Mex., 1982, MFA, 1987. Asst. prof. of art Oberlin (Ohio) Coll., 1990-94; assoc. prof. art U. Wash., Seattle, 1994—. Artist: one person shows include: Humboldt State, 2000, Jayne H. Baum Gallery, N.Y.C., 1986, 89, 93, Wooster (Ohio) Mus. of Art, U. R.I., Kingston. Recipient Wis. Women in Arts award Madison, 1978, Fullbright Hays scholarship Internat. Comm. Agy., Washington, 1979-80; grantee, NEA, Washington, 1986, HC Powers grant, Oberlin Coll., 1991, Royalty Rsch. Fund grant, U. Wash., 1996, Artist Trust Washington State fellowship, 2000—. Home: 19518 67th Ave NE Kenmore WA 98028-3447 Office: U Wash Sch of Art PO Box 353440 Seattle WA 98195-3440 E-mail: elgarv@u.washington.edu.

GARVEY, ARLENE P. library media specialist; b. Butte, Mont., Aug. 6, 1946; d. Michael Joseph and Dorothy Louise G. BS in Edn., Ea. Mont. Coll., 1973; MA, Lesley Coll., 1993. Libr. Butte Silver Bow, 1965-71, Whitehall (Mont.) H.s., 1973-75, Sweetgrass County HS., Big Timber, Mont., 1975-78; libr., media specialist Sch. Dist. #1, Butte, 1979—. Mem. Am. Fedn. Tchrs., Mont. Fedn. Tchrs., AAUW. Democrat. Roman Catholic. Avocations: walking, reading, writing, traveling. Home: 1030 W Gold St Butte MT 59701-2216

GARVEY, JANE, public relations executive; BA, Mount Saint Mary Coll.; MA, Mount Holyoke Coll.; fellowship program for pub. leaders, Harvard U. Assoc. commr. Mass. Dept. Pub. Works, Boston, commr., 1988-91; dir. Logan Internat. Airport, Boston, 1991-93; dep. adminstr. Fed. Hwy. Adminstrn. U.S. Dept. Transp., Washington, 1993-97, acting adminstr. Fed. Hwy. Adminstrn., 1997, apptd. 14th adminstr. FAA, 1997—2003; exec. v.p., chmn. APCO Worldwide, 2003—. Lectr., rsch. scientist Ctr. for Transp. and Logistics, MIT, 2003—. Office: APCO 1615 L St NW, Ste 900 Washington DC 20036

GARVEY, JEANNE WOLTER, state legislator, realtor; b. Bridgeport, Conn., Jan. 13, 1939; d. Henry Adolph and Bertha Helen (Morazes) Wolter; m. Henry Hulton Garvey, Jr., Apr. 28, 1962 (dec. June 1998); children: Henry Hulton, III, Kendra Garvey Owen, Colleen Elizabeth; m. William J. Stay, Sept. 11, 1999. Student, Western Conn. State U., Naugatuck C.C. Grad. Real Estate Inst. Rsch. lab. asst. Nestle Co., New Milford, Conn., 1957-63; realtor, appraisor DeVoe Realty Co., New Milford, 1976-93, Settlers and Traders Realtors, New Milford, 1993—; mem.. Conn. Ho. of Reps., Hartford, 1993—. Mem. various coms. New Milford Bd. Realtors, 1976—, Conn. Bd. Realtors, Hartford, 1976—, House Ranking mem. General Assembly's Human Svcs. Com., mem. Transportation, Legis. and Exec. coms., former mem. Appropriations com. Mem., past. dir. New Milford Hist. Soc., 1971—; mem. New Milford Rep. Town Com., 1993—. Recipient advocate of year award TBICO, 1997, Paul Harris Fellow New Milford Rotary Club. Mem. Nat. Order Women Legislators, Nat. Conf. State Legislators (mem. transp. com.), Nat. Assn. Realtors (various coms. 1976—), Conn. Fed. Rep. Women, 6th Congressional Dist, Rep. Women's Club, Am. Legis. Exchange Coun. Roman Catholic. Avocations: gardening, classical music, learning to play piano. Office: Conn Legis Office Bldg Capital Ave Hartford CT 06106

GARVEY, JOANNE MARIE, lawyer; b. Oakland, Calif., Apr. 23, 1935; d. James M. and Marian A. (Dean) G. AB with honors, U. Calif., Berkeley, 1956, MA, 1957, JD, 1961. Bar: Calif. bar 1962. Assoc. firm Cavaletto, Webster, Mullen & McCaughey, Santa Barbara, Calif., 1961-63, Jordan, Keeler & Seligman, San Francisco, 1963-67, ptnr., 1968-88, Heller, Ehrman, White & McAuliffe, 1988—. Bd. dirs. Mexican-Am. Legal Def. and Ednl. Fund; chmn. Law in a Free Soc., Continuing Edn. of Bar; mem. bd. councillors U. So. Calif. Law Center. Recipient Paul Veazy award YMCA, 1973, Internat. Women's Yr. award Queen's Bench, 1975, honors Advs. for Women, 1978, CRLA award, Boalt Hall Citation award, 1998, Judge Lowell Jensen Cmty. Svc. award, 2001, Margaret Brent award, 2003, Latcham State and Local Disting. Svc. award, 2003. Fellow Am. Bar Found.; mem. ABA (gov., state del., chmn. SCLAID, chmn. delivery of legal svcs.), Calif. State Bar (v.p., gov., tax sect., del., Jud Klein award, Joanne Garvey award), San Francisco Bar Assn. (pres., pres. Barristers), Am. Law Inst., Calif. Women Lawyers (founder), Order of Coif, Phi Beta Kappa. Democrat. Roman Catholic. Home: 16 Kensington Ct Kensington CA 94707-1010 Office: 333 Bush St San Francisco CA 94104-2806 Office Phone: 415-772-6729. Business E-Mail: jgarvey@hewm.com.

GARVEY, SHEILA HICKEY, theater educator; b. Erie, Pa., Dec. 23, 1949; d. Robert Francis and Mary Virginia (Sullivan) H.; children: Sean Timothy, Darragh Burgess. BS, Emerson Coll., 1971; MA, Northwestern U., 1973; PhD, NYU, 1984; grad., The Circle in the Square, N.Y.C., 1975. Preceptor NYU, N.Y.C., 1978-80; sabbatical replacement Rutgers U., Camden, N.J., 1980-81; asst. prof. Dickinson Coll., Carlisle, Pa., 1981-88; full prof. So. Conn. State U., New Haven, 1988—. Editor: Jason Robards Remembered, 2002; contbr. articles to profl. jours. Scholar JFK Ctr. Performing Arts, Am. Coll. Theatre Festival, 1993; Rsch. grantee Dickinson Coll., 1987-88, So. Conn. State U., 1988-90, 92, 94, 98, 2003, Faculty Devel. grant, 1988-90, 92, 94, 97; Dana fellow Dickinson Coll., 1987. Mem. New Eng. Theatre Conf. (bd. dirs., coll. divsn. 1992-95, chair coll. and univ. com. 1991-95, life mem. Coll. Fellows), Eugene O'Neill Soc. (pres. 2000-02, v.p. 2001—), Conn. Critics' Cir., Conn. Critics Cir. (bd. dirs.). Roman Catholic. Home: 273 Knob Hill Dr Hamden CT 06518-2737 Office: So Conn State U 501 Crescent St New Haven CT 06515-1330

GARVIN, GERALDINE MCKINLEY, retired psychology educator; b. Boyne City, Mich., Jan. 3, 1922; d. Donald A. and Isabel M. (Phillips) McKinley; m. James Hinkley Garvin; children: James H., Jr., Nancy Garvin Shor. BA with honors, Wellesley Coll., Wellesley, 1943; MEd, U. Del., Newark, 1962. Cert. tchr., Del. Historian war records project U.S. Govt., Washington, 1943-44; adminstr. U.S. Govt. Bermuda Base Command, Bermuda, 1945-46, Del. Preschool Assn., Wilmington, 1949-77; prof. pyschology Widener U., Del., 1966-84. Editor: Delaware Women Remembered, 1977, S Legacy from Delaware Women, 1982. Jr. bd. Med Ctr. of Del., 1965—; mem. Foster Care Rev. Bd., apptd. by Gov. duPont, Del., 1977; bd. dirs. United Way, 1985-89; moderator Women of Westminster, 1990-92; deacon, 1993-98, elder, 1999-2002, Westminster Presbyn. Ch.; pres. Mental Health Assn. Del., 1985-89. Scholar Durant scholarship. Mem. Lincoln Club, Del. World Affairs Coun., English-speaking Union (nat. bd. mem., chair Region III, pres. Del. br., 2000-01, bronze life master), Phi Beta Kappa. Presbyterian. Avocations: duplicate bridge, travel, tennis, gardening. Home: 2302 Delaware Ave Wilmington DE 19806-1216

GARWOOD, JULIE, writer; b. 1946; Author: (novels for young adults) A Girl Named Summer, 1985, (as Emily Chase) What's A Girl to Do, 1985, (historical romance novels) Gentle Warrior, 1985, Rebellious Desire, 1986, Honor's Splendor, 1987, The Lion's Lady, 1988, The Bride, 1989, Guardian Angel, 1990, The Gift, 1990, The Prize, 1991, The Secret, 1992, Castles, 1993, Saving Grace, 1993, Prince Charming, 1994, For the Roses, 1995, The Wedding, 1996, One Pink Rose, One White Rose, One Red Rose, Come the Spring, 1997, The Wedding, 1998, Ransom, 1999, Heartbreaker, 2000, Killjoy, 2002. Office: PO Box 7574 Leawood KS 66207-0574

GARY, JULIA THOMAS, retired minister; b. Henderson, N.C., May 31, 1929; d. Richard Collins and Julia Branch (Thomas) G. BA, Randolph-Macon Woman's Coll., 1951; MA, Mt. Holyoke Coll., 1953; PhD in Chemistry, Emory U., 1958; MDiv cum laude, Candler Sch. Theology, 1986. Ordained to Meth. Ch. as deacon, 1986, as elder 1989. Instr. Mt. Holyoke Coll., South Hadley, Mass., 1953-54, Randolph-Macon Woman's Coll., Lynchburg, Va., 1954-55; from asst. prof. to prof. chemistry Agnes Scott Coll., Decatur, Ga., 1957-84, dean, 1969-84; pastor-in-charge St. Matthew United Meth. Ch., East Point, Ga., 1987-92. Bd. dirs. Global Health Action, Inc., Atlanta, treas., 1991-97, v.p., 1997—; chmn. coord. coun. Decatur Area Emergency Assistance Ministry, 1995-96. Contbr. articles to profl. jours. Recipient Alumnae Achievement award Randolph-Macon Woman's Coll., 1990. Mem.: Sigma Xi, Phi Beta Kappa. Avocations: music, gardening. Home: 117 Bruton St Decatur GA 30030-3767 Personal E-mail: REVJTG@aol.com.

GARY, NANCY ELIZABETH, nephrologist, academic administrator; b. N.Y.C., Mar. 4, 1937; d. Walter Joseph and Charlotte Elizabeth (Sayer) G. BS, Springfield (Mass.) Coll., 1958; MD, Med. Coll. Pa., 1962. Diplomate Am. Bd. Internal Medicine, Am. Bd. Nephrology. Resident Nassau County Med. Ctr., East Meadow, N.Y., 1962-64, St. Vincent's Hosp. and Med. Ctr., N.Y.C., 1964-65, chief renal sect., 1967-74; fellow in nephrology Georgetown U. Med. Ctr., Washington, 1965-67; instr. medicine NYU Sch. Medicine, N.Y.C., 1968-74; asst. prof. U. Medicine and Dentistry of N.J.-Rutgers Med. Sch., Piscataway, 1974-76, assoc. prof., 1976-81, prof., 1981-88, assoc. dean, 1981-87, exec. assoc. dean, 1987-88; dean Albany (N.Y.) Med. Coll., 1988-90; sr. med. adv. to adminstr. health care financing HHS, Washington, 1990-92; clin. prof. medicine George Washington U. Sch. Medicine, 1991—; prof. medicine Uniformed Svcs. U. Health Scis., Bethesda, Md., 1992—, exec. v.p., dean Sch. Medicine, 1992-95; dean emeritus, 1996; clin. prof. Howard U. Coll. Medicine, Washington, 1992—; pres., CEO Ednl. Commn. Fgn. Med. Grads., Phila., 1995—2001. Contbr. chpts. to books, articles to profl. jours. Robert Wood Johnson Health Policy fellow NAS Inst. Medicine, 1987-88; recipient Joseph F. Boyle, M.D. award for Disting. Pub. Svc., Am. Soc. Internal Medicine, 1992. Mem. ACP (Master), AMA, Nat. Kidney Found., Alpha Omega Alpha. Office: Ednl Commn Fgn Med Graduates 3624 Market St Fl 4 Philadelphia PA 19104-2614

GARZA, MELITA MARIE, journalist; b. Madrid, Oct. 19, 1959; came to U.S., 1961; d. Carlos Mario and Linda Rose (Caballero) G. BA, Harvard U., 1983; postgrad., Poynter Inst. Reporter, writer L.A. Times, 1984-85, Milw. Jour., 1986-89, Chgo. Tribune, 1989—. Discussion leader Am. Press Inst., Reston, Va., 1995; spkr., instr. Wilmington (Del.) Writers Workshop, 1995. Bd. dirs. SciTech mus., Aurora, Ill., 1991—; mem. com. on fgn. rels. Chgo. Coun. on Fgn. Rels., 1991—. Named one of top 20 young people in U.S. newspaper industry Newspaper Assn. Am., 1993, one of 100 Women Making a Difference Today's Chgo. Women, 1996; recipient Excellence in Journalism award Ill. Coalition for Immigrant and Refugee Protection, 1995, Cardinal's Comm. award for Profl. Excellence Archdiocese of Chgo., 1996. Mem. Nat. Assn. Hispanic Journalists (v.p. bd. dirs. 1989-94, Pres.' award 1994), Internat. Women's Media Found., Harvard Club of Chgo. (v.p. 1993-94), Radcliffe Club of Chgo. (pres. 1993-94). Roman Catholic. Avocations: tennis, aerobics, cooking, sewing, reading. Office: Chgo Tribune 435 N Michigan Ave Chicago IL 60611-4066

GARZARELLI, ELAINE MARIE, economist; b. Phila., Oct. 13, 1952; d. Ralph J. and Ida M. (Pierantozzi) G.; BS, Drexel U., 1973, MBA, 1977, Ph.D, 1992. With A.G. Becker, N.Y.C., 1973-84, v.p., economist, 1975-84, mgn. dir., 1984; ptnr., portfolio mgr. Lehman Bros. Inc., 1984-94; prin. Garzarelli Internat. Inc., Delray Beach, Fla., 1994—; lectr. in field. Named Businesswoman of Yr. Fortune Mag., 1987, # 1 in Quantitative Analysis, Instl. Investor Annual Contest. Mem. Nat. Assn. Bus. Economists, Women's Fin. Assn., Am. Statis. Assn., Women's Bond Assn. Developer Sector Analysis (econometric model for predicting industry profits and stock price movements, also predicted stock market crash of 1987).

GASCHEL-CLARK, REBECCA MONA, special education educator; b. Hudson, N.Y., Sept. 10, 1972; d. Michael Anthony and Ellen Michele (Wright) Gaschel; m. Eric Clark, Nov. 8, 1997. BS in Spl. Edn., Early Childhood Edn., U. Hartford, 1994, MEd, 1997. Cert. spl. edn. tchr., Conn., pre-kindergarten-12. Spl. edn. educator Regional Sch. Dist. #1, Falls Village, Conn., 1994—. Mem. consultation team Salisbury Ctrl. Sch., Lakeville, Conn., 1996—, Lector Ch. of the Resurrection, Germantown, N.Y., 1989—. Named tchr. of elem. sch. Exemplary Program, Conn. Assn. of Schs., 1996. Mem. Phi Delta Kappa, Alpha Chi, Kappa Delta Pi. Democrat. Roman Catholic. Avocations: water skiing, opera, cooking, camping. Office: Regional Sch Dist # 1 246 Warren Tpke Falls Village CT 06031-1600

GASCOINE-MOLINA, JILL VIOLA, actress, writer; b. London, Apr. 11, 1937; d. Francis Gascoine and Irene Ethel Greenwood; m. William Keith, Mar. 18, 1965 (div. June 1973); children: Sean William, Adam Francis; m. Alfred Molina, Mar. 1, 1985. Student, Theatre Sch., London. Actress theater, TV, films, London. Author: Addicted, 1994, Lilian, 1996, Just Like A Woman, 1997. Named Best Actress on TV, TV Times Mag. Viewers Vote, 1983, 1984. Avocation: designing gardens.

GASH, LAUREN BETH, lawyer, state legislator; b. Summit, N.J., June 11, 1960; d. Ira Arnold and Sondra Regina (Stetin) G.; m. Gregg Allen Garmisa, June 12, 1983; children: Sarah, Benjamin. BA in Psychology, Clark U., 1982; JD, Georgetown U., 1987. Bar: Ill. 1989. Projects dir. U.S. Senator Alan Dixon, Washington, 1981-83; statewide constituency coord., dir. Women for Simon, U.S. Senator Paul Simon, Chgo., 1990; aide State Rep. Grace Mary Stern, Highland Park, Ill.; atty. Prairie State Legal Svcs., Waukegan, Ill.; mem. Ill. State Ho. of Reps., chair judiciary-criminal com. Mem. women's health adv. bd. Highland Park Hosp., southeast adv. bd Coll. Lake County, JUF govt. agencies divsn. campaign cabinet, 1999, chair, Highland Park 2000 com., human needs subcom. Women in Law as 2d Career grantee; recipient Disting. Svc. award Ill. Com. for Honest Govt., 1996, Best Legis. Record Voting award Ind. Voters Ill., 1996; named Legis. of Yr. Alliance for the Mentally Ill, 1997. Mem. Ill. State Bar Assn. (mem. com. cmty. involvement), Formerly Employed Mothers at the Leading Edge (co-founder North Shore chpt.), Chgo. Women in Govt. Rels., Women Employed, Ravinia PTA (bd. dirs., polit. action chair), Com. for Interdist. Cooperation, North Shore Synagogue Beth El (social action com.) LWV (bd. dirs. Highland Park chpt., bd. dirs. Lake County chpt.). Avocations: flute, french, spanish. also: 2052-I Stratton Bldg Springfield IL 62706-0001 Office: 1345 Forest Ave Highland Park IL 60035-3456

GASKEY-SPEAR, NANCY JANE, nurse anesthetist; b. California, Pa. d. Frank and Rose Gaskey; m. Robert L. Spear (dec. Jan. 1998). RN, Mercy Hosp., Pitts., 1960, Nurse Anesthetist, 1963; BS in Nursing Edn., California (Pa.) U., 1970; MEd in Curriculum and Supervision, U. Pitts., 1975, PhD in Edn. Comm. and Tech., 1983. Cert. nurse anesthetist; RN, Pa. Staff nurse Mercy Hosp., Pitts., 1960-61, staff nurse anesthetist, 1963-70; dir. Sch. Nurse Anesthesia Western Pa. Hosp., Pitts., 1970-86; staff nurse anesthetist Western Pa. Anesthesia Assocs. Ltd., Western Pa. Hosp., Pitts., 1987—. On-site visitor Coun. on Accreditation Nurse Anesthesia Ednl. Programs, Schs., 1981-86; ednl. cons. Nursing Expo, Pitts., 1982; mem. Allegheny County Bd. Health, Pitts., 1976-85; instr. workshops, seminars, various orgns. Prodr. slide/cassette: Radial Artery Cannulation, Western Pa. Hosp. Sch. Anesthesia Recruitment, Instrns. for Assembling the Gould Transducer Pressure Monitoring Sys., Brachial Plexus Blocks: Interscalene Technique, Evolution of Inhalation Anesthesia; prodn. coord. videotapes Close-Ups in Anesthesia; contbr. articles to profl. jours.; mem. editl. bd. Current Revs. for Nurse Anesthetists; profl. corr. Antique Collector, Salem, Ohio, Bee Pub. Co., Newtowne, Conn. Recipient Cmty. Citation of Merit Allegheny County Bd. Commrs., 1985. Mem. Am. Assn. Nurse Anestetists (edn. com. 1973-74, rsch. in action recognition award 1985), Pitts. Bibliophiles, Mid-Atlantic Assn. Nurse Anesthetists (sec.-treas. 1970-71, chmn. elect 1971-72, chmn. 1972-73, chmn. program com. 1973-74), Southwestern Pa. Soc. Nurse Anesthetists (pres. 1972-73), Pa. Assn. Nurse Anesthetists (trustee 1972-74, pub. rels. com. 1972-74, safety com. 1974-75, pres.-elect 1975-76, pres. 1976-77, editor Pennsylvania Tidings 1976-77, founder, chmn. spl. com. Assembly Sch. Faculty), Hosp. Coun. Western Pa. (anesthesia circuits project com. 1982-83). Avocations: photography, antiques, art, gardening. Home: 552 N Neville St Pittsburgh PA 15213-2855 Office: Western Pa Hosp Liberty Ave Pittsburgh PA 15224

GASKILL, MARY, state official; b. Clyde, Mo., Dec. 1, 1941; Student, N.E. Mo. R VI, Gard Bus. U. State rep., Iowa, 2003—. Mem. econ. devel. appropriations com.; mem. environ. protection standing com.; mem. local govt. standing com.; mem. state govt. com.; county auditor; commr. elections; control auditor IHCC Elections; mem. County Safety and Wellness Coms.; bd. dirs. IMWCA; mem. Com. on the Future, Law Enforcement Steering Com., Elections LEgis. Com. Mem. City of Ottumwa Strategic Planning, County/City Jail Planning, Conv. and Visitors Bur., Govt. Affairs Com., Foster Care Rev. Bd., Wapello County Dem. Party Cen. Com.; lector, usher, mem. worship and prayer com. St. Mary's Ch. Mem.: LWV, Ottumwa C. of C., AIS Users Orgn. (pres.), 5th Dist. Auditors Assn. (pres.), Iowa State Assn. County Auditors (mem. com. on the future). Office: State Capitol E 12th and Grand Des Moines IA 50319

GASKIN, FELICIA, biochemist, educator; b. Carlisle, Pa., Jan. 17, 1943; d. Joseph A. and Wanda J. (Rakowski) G.; m. Shu Man Fu, Nov. 29, 1969; children: Kai-Ming, Kai-Mei. AB in Chemistry, Dickinson Coll., Carlisle, Pa., 1965; MA in Organic Chemistry, Bryn Mawr Coll., 1967; PhD in Biochemistry, U. Calif., San Francisco, 1969. Postdoctoral fellow Stanford U., Palo Alto, Calif., 1969-71; rsch. assoc. Rockefeller U., N.Y.C., 1971-72, Columbia U., N.Y.C., 1972-74; asst. prof., then assoc. prof. Albert Einstein Coll. Medicine, N.Y.C., 1974-82; prof. Sch. Medicine U. Okla., Oklahoma City, 1982-88, U. Va., Charlottesville, 1988—. Mem. Okla. Med. Rsch. Found., 1982-88. Contbr. articles to profl. jours. Recipient rsch. career devel. award NIH, 1975-80; Nat. Inst. Neurol. Diseases and Stroke spl. fellow, 1972-74. Mem. AAAS, Am. Soc. Biochemistry and Molecular Biology, Am. Soc. for Cell Biology, Soc. Neurosci. Office: U Va Sch Medicine Box 800203 Charlottesville VA 22908-0001

GASKINS, KAREN D. neuroscientist, psychotherapist; b. Ft. George Meade, Md., Mar. 23, 1953; d. Melvin Whittier Gaskins Sr. and Geneva Katherine Hill. ASN, Prince George's C.C., Largo, Md., 1977; BS in Neuropsychology, U. Md., 2000, postgrad. Nurse mgr. Washington Adventist Hosp., Takoma Park, Md.; pers. specialist Pvt. Industry, Garden Grove, Calif., fin. rep. Capitol Heights, Md.; substitute tchr. Prince George's Pub. Schs., Upper Marlboro, Md., 1998-2000, Anne Arundel County Sch. Sys., 2000—. Editor Deliverance; author of poetry. Soloist Riverton (N.J.) Civic Chorus, 1984-89; soprano Mendelsohn Choir, Phila., 1988-89, Nat. Christian Choir, Md., 1995-96; min. rep. Nat. Conf. Christians and Jews, Cherry Hill, N.J., 1989 90; cert. cathetist St. Pius X Cath. Ch., 1994. Mem. Noetic Sci. (neuroscientist). Avocations: classical voice, ballet/pointe, reading, writing, germanic cultures. E-mail: tanne20721@yahoo.com.

GASPAR, ANNA LOUISE, retired elementary school educator, consultant; b. Chgo., May 12, 1935; d. Miklos and Klotild (Weiss) G. BS in Edn., Northwestern U., 1957. Cert. elem. tchr., Calif. Tchr. 6th grade Pacific Palisades Elem. Sch., L.A., 1957-58; tchr. 1st grade Eastman St. Elem. Sch., L.A., 1959, Glassell Park, L.A., 1959-62, Stoner Ave. Elem. Sch., L.A., 1962-67; 2nd-4th grade tchr. Brentwood Elem. Sch., L.A., 1967-78; tchr. 4th and 5th grades Brockton Ave. Elem. Sch., L.A., 1978-90; vol., established Swakopmund Tchrs. Resource Ctr., Peace Corps, Namibia, 1991-93; tchr. English, Atlantic Sr. Primary Sch., Swakopmund, Namibia, 1992; career info. cons. Peace Corps., 1991—; substitute tchr. Hebrew Acad./Pre-Primary, Las Vegas, 1994-2000. Mem. Elderhostel Programs: Alaska, 2000, Victoria BC, 2000, Hungary, 2001, Banff Ctr. Can. 2002, Mpls., 2002, San Francisco, 2002, Phoenix Valley, 2003, Santa Fe, 2003, Taos, N.Mex., 2003, Albuquerque, 2003; mem. Bet Knesset Bamidbar Temple. Mem.: Calif. State Ret. Tchrs. Assn., So. Nev. Peace Corps Assn., Peace Corps, Northwestern U. Alumni Assn. Democrat. Jewish. Avocations: world travel, playing piano, art, collecting costume dolls, folk music. Home: 2700 Hope Forest Dr Las Vegas NV 89134-7322

GASPARRINI-ETHERIDGE, CLAUDIA, publishing company executive, scientist, writer; b. Genova, Italy, Apr. 25, 1941; arrived in US, 1984; d. Corrado and Tina (Pizzuti) G.; m. James K. Etheridge, Oct. 15, 1998. D in Earth Scis., U. Rome, 1965; cert. in English, U. Cambridge, Eng., 1965, Pitman Inst., London, 1965. Sr. tech. U. Toronto, Can., 1966-67, rsch. asst., 1967-70, rsch. assoc., 1970-72; phys. scientist II Geol. Survey Can., Ottawa, 1973; rsch. scientist Nat. Inst. for Metallurgy (now Mintek), Johannesburg, 1974-75; ind. cons. Toronto, 1976; pres., owner Minmet Sci. Limited, Toronto, 1977—, Jacksonville, Fla., 1982-86, Tucson, 1986—2000, The Space Eagle Pub. Co., Inc., Toronto, Tucson, 1986—, 1987—; writer, pub., 1989—. Adviser Chinese chpt. Internat. Precious Metals Inst., 1996—2000; guest lectr. U. Heidelberg, 1990, 91, Inst. Precious Metals, Kunming, China, 1984, U. Padua, U. Florence, 1995; presenter in field. Author: Gold and Other Precious Metals-The Lure and the Trap, 1989, How to Get the Most Out of the Legal System Without Spending a Fortune, 1990, Gold and Other Precious Metals-From Ore to Market, 1993, Murder of the Mind-The Practice of Subtle Discrimination, 1993, Murder of the Mind-The Practice of Subtle Discrimination, rev. 2d edit., 1996, When You Make the Two One, 1994, When You Make the Two One, rev. 2d edit., 1996; author: (as Gloria J. Duv) How to Run a Successful Mail Order Business by Defrauding the Public, 1995; author: Deceit-The Fad of the Nineties, 1997, Gold and Other Precious Metals-Occurrence, Extration, Applications, 2000, From Darkness to Light, 2001, Mechanics-Doctors, Does the Quality of Their Assistance Justify the Fees?, 2002, Subtle Discrimination, 2003, The Enemy Within, 2003; mem. bd. editors: Chinese mag. Gold Sci. and Tech., 1996—2000; contbr. articles to profl. jours. and books. Scientist Sci. by Mail Program, Boston Mus. Sci., 1991-92; mem. rsch. bd. advisors Am. Biog. Inst., Raleigh, N.C., 1990—; hon. mem. Internat. Biog. Ctr. Adv. Coun., Cambridge, Eng., 1992—. Recipient Cert. Appreciation Outstanding Svc. Internat. Precious Metals Inst., 1994; named hon. mem. organizing com. Internat. Conf. on Precious Metals, Kosice, Slovakia, 1995. Avocations: classical music, computers and computer applications, collecting books, crystals, precious and semi-precious stones. Home and Office: 7990 E Snyder Rd Apt 4108 Tucson AZ 85750-9007 Office: Minmet Sci Ltd/ The Space Eagle Pub Co Inc 1210 Sheppard Ave E # 200 North York ON Canada M2K 1E3 also: Via Ugo de Carolis 62 00136 Rome 00136 Italy E-mail: claudiaetherigde@thespaceagle.net.

GASPARRO, MADELINE, banker; b. Jersey City, Oct. 5, 1928; d. Donato and Anna (D'Urso) D'Achille; m. Dominick J. Gasparro, Apr. 30, 1949; children: Dorothy, Joseph, Donato, Frank. Grad. high sch., Jersey City. Cert. St. Aloysius Eucharistic Min. 2003. Salesperson credit dept. and employee sales J.C. Penney, Parlin, N.J.; head teller Amboy Madison Nat. Bank, Old Bridge, N.J., bank mgr., br. mgr., 1983-97; ret., 1997. Chpt. chmn. South Amboy Hosp., mem. fin. com.; eucharist minister St. Bernadette Ch. of Parlin. Mem. NAFE, Nat. Assn. Bank Women (past hostess), Fin. Women Internat. (chmn. membership Raritan Bay group 1990-91, v.p. 1991-92, pres. 1992-93), Altar Rosary Soc. (past pres.). Address: 12 Baltusrol Dr Jackson NJ 08527-3991 E-mail: domgas@aol.com.

GASPER, JO ANN, consulting firm executive; b. Providence, Sept. 25, 1946; d. Joseph Siegleman and Jeanne Van Matre Shoaf; m. Louis Clement Gasper, Sept. 21, 1974; children: Stephen Gregory, Jeanne Marie, Monica Elizabeth, Michelle Bernadette (dec.), Phyllis Anastasia, Clare Genevieve. BA, U. Dallas, 1967, MBA, 1969. Adminstrv. asst. U. Dallas, 1964-68; asst. dir. adminstrn. Britton Convalescent Ct[illegible] 1964-68; pres. Medicare Ctrs., Inc., Dallas, 1968-69; bus. mgr., treas. U. Plano, Tex., 1969-72; ins. agt. John Hancock Ins. Co., Dallas, 1972-73; systems analyst Tex. Instrument, Richardson, 1973-75; pvt. practice acctg., bus. cons. McLean, Va., 1976-81; editor, pub. Congl. News for Women and the Family, McLean, Va., 1978-81, Register Report, McLean, Va., 1980-81; dep. asst. sec. for social services policy HHS, Washington, 1981-85; exec. dir. White House Conf. on Agys., HHS, Washington, 1982-85; dep. asst. sec. for population affairs HHS, Washington, 1985-87; policy advisor to under sec. U.S. Dept. Edn., Washington, 1987-88, cons.; pres. Franklin Pk. Assocs., 1989—; exec. dir. Nat. Assn. for Abstinence Edn., 1989-94; mgr. TSR, 1995-98. Tchr. Grapevine-Colleyville Ind. Sch. Dist., 1998—. Co-chmn. St. John's Refugee Resettlement Commn., Va., 1977; bd. dirs., treas. Coun. Inter-Am. Security, Washington, 1978-80; active Fairfax County Citizens Coalition for Quality Child Care, Va., 1979-80; del. White House Conf. on Families, Va., 1979-80; mem. U.S. adv. Inter-Am. Commn. on Women, OAS, 1982-85; U.S. del. XVI Pan Am. Child Congress, Washington, 1984; mem. nat. family policy adv. bd. Reagan-Bush Campaign, 1980; mem. City of Colleyville Planning and Zoning Comm., 2000-02. Recipient Eagle Forum award, 1979, Wanderer Found. award, 1980, Bronze medal HHS, 1982; named Outstanding Conservative Woman, Conservative Digest, 1980, 81 Mem. Exec. Women in Gov. (treas. 1985, sec. 1986) Roman Catholic.

GASPERINI, ELIZABETH CARMELA (LISA GASPERINI), marketing consultant, graphic designer; b. Newark, Sept. 26, 1961; d. Enrico Caesar and Wanda Claudia (Stanziale) G. BFA, Caldwell (N.J.) Coll., 1983. Advt. specialist J.C. Penney Corp., Wayne, N.J., 1982-83; asst. prodn. mgr. Internat. Postal Mktg. Corp., Montville, N.J., 1983-84; art dir. Healy, Dixcy & Forbes, W. Caldwell, N.J., 1984-86; sr. mktg. specialist Am. Varityper Corp., E. Hanover, N.J., 1986-88; product promotion mgr. Brother Internat. Corp., Somerset, N.J., 1988-90; mktg. specialist Ishida USA Inc., Lincoln Park, N.J., 1990-92; mktg. promotions mgr. Nat. Electronic Info. Corp., Secaucus, N.J., 1992-95; self-employed mktg. cons. Towaco, N.J., 1995-96; mgr. mktg. svcs. AmeriHeath Ins. Co. N.J., Iselin, N.J., 1996-98; mktg. cons. Towaco, N.J., 1998—; mgr. client segment mktg. Merck-Medco Managed Care LLC, 2000—. Telemktg. specialist Sears, Roebuck & Co., Fairfield, N.J., 1984-96; owner, cons. Gasperini Graphics, Towaco, N.J., 1984—; art cons. Italico Pubs., Livingston, N.J., 1982-92. Mem. N.J. Art Assn., N.J. Italian-Am. Assn. (cons. 1982-92). Republican. Roman Catholic. Avocations: photographer, painter, pianist, crafts designer, unique and antique jewelry collector. Home and Office: 10 Willard Ln Towaco NJ 07082-1517

GASPERONI, ELLEN JEAN LIAS, interior designer; b. Rural Valley, Pa.; d. Dale S. and Ruth (Harris) Lias; student Youngstown U., 1952-54, John Carrol U., 1953-54, Westminster Coll., 1951-52; grad. Am. Inst. Banking; m. Emil Gasperoni, May 28, 1955; children: Sam, Emil, Jean Ellen. Mem. Coeurde Coeur Heart Assn., Orlando Opera Guild, Orlando Symphony Guild. Mem. Jr. Bus. Women's Club (dir. 1962-64), Sweetwater Country Club (Longwood, Fla.); Lake Toxaway Golf and Country Club (N.C.). Presbyterian. Home: 1126 Brownshire Ct Longwood FL 32779-2209 also: 92 Cold Mountain Rd Lake Toxaway NC 28747-9630

GASQUE, DIANE PHILLIPS, mortgage manager; b. Madison, Wis., Mar. 31, 1954; d. Codie Odel and Ruth Elaine (Oimoen) Phillips.; m. Wyndham Henry Burriss, Feb. 5, 1977 (div. 1989); m. Allard Harrison Gasque, Nov. 14, 1992; 1 child, Folline Elaine Gasque. BA, Midlands Tech., Columbia, S.C. Cert. Notary S.C. With inventory control Oxford Industries, Columbia, S.C.; processing agent NCR, Columbia, S.C.; comml. loan officer S.C. Nat., Columbia, S.C.; personnel dir. Witten Sales, Columbia, S.C.; funding agt. Resource Bankshares Mortgage Group, 1995—, sr. specialist. Mem.: Order of Confederate Rose. Republican. Presbyterian. Avocations: bowling, coin collecting. Home: 3728 Linbrook Dr Columbia SC 29204-4438 Fax: (803) 741-3595. E-mail: dgasque@sc.rr.com.

GASS, CYNTHIA ANN, music educator; b. Tulsa, Okla., June 27, 1958; d. Bruce Edward and Ruth Ellen Gass. B in Music Edn. in Voice, Okla. State U., 1980; MusM in Performance, U. Southwestern La., 1987. Vocal music dir. Emerson Jr. H.S., Enid, Okla., 1980—85, Lafayette (La.) H.S., 1987—90, Will Rogers H.S., Tulsa, 1990—94, Ponca City (Okla.) H.S., 1996—2003; assoc. vocal music dir. Norman (Okla.) North H.S., 2003—. Named Dir. of Distinction, Okla. Secondary Schs. Activity Assn., 1997, 1998, 2001, 2003. Mem.: NEA, Okla. Choral Dirs. Assn. (N.E. rep. bd. dirs. 2001—03), Music Educators Nat. Conf., Am. Choral Dirs. Assn. Office: Norman North High Sch 1809 Stubbeman Ave Norman OK 73069

GASS, GERTRUDE ZEMON, psychologist, researcher; b. Detroit; d. David Solomon and Mary (Goldman) Zemon; m. H. Harvey Gass, June 19, 1938; children: Susan, Roger. BA, U. Mich., 1937, MSW, 1943, PhD, 1957. Lic. clin. psychologist, Mich. Mem. faculty Merrill-Palmer Inst., Detroit, 1958-69, lectr., 1967; mem. faculty Advanced Behavioral Sci. Ctr., Grosse Pointe, Mich., 1969-72; pvt. practice clin. psychology Birmingham, Mich., 1972—. Adj. prof. psychology U. Detroit, 1969-75; cons. Continuum Ctr. Oakland U., Rochester, Mich., 1961-77, Traveler's Aid, Detroit, 1959-75; pres. Shapero Sch. Nursing, Detroit, 1967-72, cons. 1958-78; psychol. cons. Physician's Ins. Co. of Mich., 1988—, mgmt. Mich. Bell Telephone, 1979-82. Mem. Adv. Com Sch. Needs, 1954-56; trustee Sinai Hosp. Detroit, 1972-99; bd. dirs. Tribute Fund United Cmty. Svcs., 1955-67. Fellow Am. Assn. Marriage-Family, Am. Orthopsychiatric Assn. (v.p. 1975-76), Mich. Psychol. Assn.; mem. Am. Psychol. Assn., Psychologists Task Force (v.p. 1977-84), Mich. Inter-Profl. Assn. (pres. 1976-78), Mich. Assn. Marriage Counselors (1979-80, pres. 1979-80), Mental Health Adv. Svc., Blue Cross and Blue Shield of Mich., Phi Kappa Phi, Pi Lambda Theta. Home and Office: 6155 E Longview Dr East Lansing MI 48823

GASS, ROSARIO, artist; arrived in U.S., 1953; d. Luis and Amelia F. de Pena; m. James M. Gass (dec.); children: Beatrice Amelia, William Harlan, James Paul, Laura Elena. Sec.-treas. Calif. Assn. Ind. Bus. Inc. Exhibitions include in Calif., Represented in permanent collections in Mex., Irvine, Calif., Long Beach, Calif., Albuquerque. Recipient Gov.'s Golden Bear award, Sacramento, 1997. Avocations: travel, art, classical music, crafts.

GASS, WANDA, engineering executive; BSEE, Rice U., 1978; MS in Biomedical Engring., Duke U., 1980. From mem. staff to fellow Tex. Instruments Inc., Dallas, 1980—, fellow. Mentor Infinity Project So. Meth. U. Founder Women of TI Fund; leader Sr. Summit Women in Computing. Named to Women in Tech. Internat. Hall Fame, 2003. Mem.: IEEE, Solid State Circuits Soc. (chmn. 2000—02), Signal Processing Soc. (chmn. 1997—99). Office: Texas Instruments Inc 12500 TI Blvd Dallas TX 75222*

GASTON, MARILYN HUGHES, health facility administrator; b. Cin. children: Amy Marie, Damon Allen. AB in Zoology, Miami U., Oxford, Ohio, 1960; MD, U. Cin., 1964. Diplomate Am. Bd. Pediats. Intern Phila. Gen. Hosp., 1964—65; resident in pediat. Childrens Hosp. Med. Ctr., Cin., 1965—67, asst. dir. out-patient dept., 1967—68, Convalescent Hosp. for Children, Cin., 1968—69; med. dir. Lincoln Heights (Ohio) Health Ctr., 1969—72; dir. Sickle Cell screening clinic Cin. Health Dept., 1972—76; med. expert Nat. Heart, Lung & Blood Inst./NIH, Bethesda, 1976—79; commd. 2d lt. USPHS, 1979—89; dir. divsn. medicine Bur. Health Professions, Rockville, Md., 1989—90; dir., asst. surgeon gen., assoc. adminstr. for bureau Bur. Primary Health Care, Rockville, Md., 1990—2002; chief medical officer National Minority Health Month, 2002—. Instr. pediats. U. Cin. Coll. Medicine, 1967—68, asst. clin. prof. divsn. cmty. pediats., 1968—70, asst. prof. pediats., 1970—76, assoc. prof. pediats., 1976—77; asst. clin. prof. pediats. Cin. Tech. Coll., 1974—76, Howard U. Coll. Medicine, 1978—91, Uniformed Svcs. U. the Health Scis., 1987—; attending pediatrician Children's Hosp. Med. Ctr., 1969—76, attending pediatrician and clinician, 1969—76, dir. med. staff, 1969—76; attending pediatrician Bethesda Hosp., 1974—76; pediatrician Hosp. Albert Schweitzer Deschapelles, Haiti, 1967; presenter, lectr., spkr. in field. Author: AL Bibliography: Comprehensive Sickle Cell Centers, 1977; co-author (with C.L. Calhoun), 1981; author: Management and Therapy of Sickle Cell Disease, 1984, 1988, Prime Time: The African American Woman's Complete Guide to Midlife Health and Wellness, 2003; author: (with others) Newborn Screening for Sickle Cell Disease and Other Hemoglobinopathies, 1989; contbr. articles to profl. jours. Co-chair Nat. Sickle Cell Dirs., 1974; med. advisor Sickle Cell Awareness Group, 1971—77, State Crippled Children's Svcs., 1975—77; bd. trustees Child Health Assn., 1974—77; bd. dirs. U. Cin. Found., 1989—, George Washington U. Life Scis., 1993—, U. Md. Ctr. for Minority Rsch. External Adv. Bd., 1993—, Komen Found. for Breast Cancer, Wellesley Ctr. for Women, Nat. Black Woman's Health Project. Named Woman of the Yr. in Medicine, Harriet Tubman Black Women's Dem., 1976; named one of Outstanding Young Women in Am., 1973, Outstanding Black Women in Cin., 1974; named to Ohio Women's Hall of Fame, 1990; recipient Phyllis Wheatley award, State of Ohio, 1975, Hildrus A. Poindexter award, Pub. Health Svcs., 1990, State of Ohio Gov.'s award, 1987, Disting. Alumnae award, U. Cin., 1989, Pub. Health award, D.C. Health Care for the Homless Project, Inc., Nathan Davis award, AMA. Mem.: APHA, AAAS, Inst. of Medicine/NAS, N.Y. Acad. Scis., Am. Med. Women's Assn., Am. Pediat. Soc., Am. Soc. Hematology, Nat. Med. Assn. (Living Legend award), Nat. Assn. Med. Minority Educators, Am. Acad. Pediats., Alpha Kappa Alpha, Sigma Delta Epsilon. Office: Nat Minority Health Month 1101 Pennsylvania Ave, NW, Ste 820 Washington DC 20004

GATCH, FRANCES ANNE, retired small business owner; d. Owen Thomas King and Mary Allie Foster; m. Ronald Vernon Gatch, Sept. 25, 1976 (div. June 6, 2002); 1 child, Diane Michelle. AA, Daytona Beach (Fla.) Jr. Coll., 1975—79. Bus. co-owner AiReed Filter Products, Daytona Beach, 1972—2000; ret. Author: (genealogy record) The Gatch Family of South Carolina. Mem., pres., state dir. Daytona Beach Jaycee Aux., 1974—82; mem., v.p., sec. Bonner Elem. PTA, Daytona Beach, 1986—92; mem., pres. Halifax River Toastmistress Club, Daytona Beach, 1978—81. Named Woman of the Yr., Daytona Beach Jaycee Aux., 1977, Jayceette of the Yr., Daytona Beach Jaycees, 1979, Outstanding Young Women of Am., 1980; recipient Outstanding Aux. award, Daytona Beach Jaycee Aux., 1979, Today's Woman Essay award, Fla. Jaycee Aux., 1979, Golden Apple award, Bonner Elem. PTA, 1991, Outstanding Young Women of Am., 1980. Mem.: Phi Theta Kappa. Avocations: needlepoint, reading.

GATES, AUDREY CASTINE, city government administrator; b. Napoleonville, La., Dec. 9, 1937; d. Lawrence Curtis and Ethel (Ray) Castine; m. George M. Gates III, Nov. 22, 1959; children: George M. IV, Geoffrey L. BA in Fgn. Langs., Dillard U., 1958. Tchr. Orleans Parish Sch. Bd., New Orleans, 1959-69; asst. dir. consumer affairs City of New Orleans, 1972-85, dir. residential parking, 1985-89; prin. analyst New Orleans City Coun., 1989-94, dir. rsch., 1994—. Fellow Loyola Inst. Politics, Metro. Area Com.; mem. Palm Air Civic Assn. Mem. Govt. Rsch. Assn., Delta Sigma Theta. Office: 1300 Perdido St Rm Le2 New Orleans LA 70112-2125

GATES, LISA, private chef, caterer; b. Washington, July 11, 1955; d. Chester Robert and Peggy Jean (Dalton) Gates; m. Sergio Vivoli, Nov. 3, 1978 (div. Nov. 1984); m. Mitchell Cohen, Sept. 21, 1987 (div. Febr. 1995). AA, Fleming Coll., Florence, Italy, 1974. Dir. The Am. Sch. in Switzerland, Lugano, 1974-80; counter person Bar Gelateria Vivoli, Florence, 1978-80; costumer, choreographer, scene designer English Theatre of Florence, 1978; tchr. Dance Sch. Theatre, Florence, 1978-81; sec., treas. Vivoli Da Firenze, Inc., L.A., 1981-82; event coord. Calif. Catering Co., Beverly Hills, Calif., 1983; chef, sales rep. St. Germain To Go, West Hollywood, Calif., 1984; chef, cons. Posh Affair Catering Co., L.A., 1984-87; owner, chef, party planner Lisa Gates-Vivoli Catering, L.A., 1985—; catering mgr. Maple Drive Restaurant, Beverly Hills, 1990-91; pvt. chef, 1991—2001, 2001—. Mem. Mus. Contemporary Art, L.A., L.A. County Mus. Art, L.A. Music Ctr. Unified Fund. Recipient Outstanding Achievement in Art award Bank of Am., Miraleste, Calif., 1972. Mem. Am. Inst. Wine and Food, Roundtable for Women in Foodsvc., Women Chefs and Restaurateurs. Democrat. Avocations: dance, dining, music. Home and Office: 1227 N Orange Grove Ave West Hollywood CA 90046-5311

GATES, MARTINA MARIE, food products company executive; b. Mpls., Mar. 19, 1957; d. John Thomas and Colette Clara G. BSBA in Mktg. Mgmt. cum laude, U. St. Thomas, 1984, MBA in Mktg., 1987. Tchrs. asst. Mpls. Area Vocat. Tech. Inst., Mpls., 1978-79; sec., regional sales mgr. Internat. Multifoods, Mpls., 1979, sec. bakery mix, mktg. mgr., 1979-80, sec., v.p. sales and new bus. devel., 1980, customer svc. rep. regional accounts, 1980-81, customer svc. rep. nat. accounts, 1981-82, credit coordinator indsl. foods divsn., 1982-85, asst. credit mgr. consumer foods divsn., 1985, advt./sales promotion mgr. indsl. foods divsn., 1985-86, asst. credit mgr. fast food and restaurant divsn., 1986-87, dir. devel. USA and Can. franchise area, 1987-89; dir. franchise devel. FIRSTAFF, Inc., Mpls., 1989-90; dir. adminstrn. Robert Half Internat., Inc., Mpls., 1990-94; dir. client svcs. The NPD Group, Inc., Chgo., 1994—. Vol. seamstress Guthrie Theater Costume Shop, Mpls., 1975—; alumni mem. New Coll. Student Adv. Council St. Thomas, St. Paul, 1984—; vol. Mpls. Aquatennial, 1987. Mem. Streeterville Orgn. of Active Residents, Omicron Delta Epsilon. Avocations: golf, fine arts, needlework, tennis, skiing.

GATES, SUSAN INEZ, magazine publisher; b. San Francisco, Jan. 14, 1956; d. Milo Sedgewick and Anne (Phelger) Gates. BA in English, French magna cum laude(hon.), U. Colo., 1978; MS in Journalism, Columbia U., 1983. With GEO Mag., N.Y.C., 1978—79, New York Mag., N.Y.C., 1981—82, Ladd Assoc., N.Y.C., 1983—85, Mc Namee Cons., N.Y.C., NY, 1986—88; founding pub. BUZZ Mag., L.A., 1989—97; co chmn. Mind Over Media, L.A., 1997—. Contbg. writer San Francisco Chronicle Book Rev., 1983-86. So. Calif. adv. bd. natural resources def.coun., L.A., 1989-96. Mem. Advt. Club of L.A. (bd. dir. 1995-98), Phi Beta Kappa. Personal E-mail: sigates@adelphia.net.

GATEWOOD, TELA LYNNE, lawyer; b. Cedar Rapids, Iowa, Mar. 23; d. Chester Russell and Cecilia Mae (McFarland) Weber. BA with distinction, Cornell Coll., Mt. Vernon, Iowa, 1970; JD with distinction, U. Iowa, 1972. Bar: Iowa 1973, Calif. 1974, U.S. Supreme Ct. 1984. Instr. LaVerne Coll., Pt. Mugu, Calif., 1973; asst. city atty. City of Des Moines, 1973-78; sr. trial atty. and supervisory atty. EEOC, Dallas, Phila., 1978-91, acting regional atty. Dallas Dist., 1987-89, adminstrv. judge Dallas, 1991-94; adminstrv. law judge Social Security Adminstrn., Oklahoma City, 1994—. Bd. dirs. Day Care Inc., Des Moines, 1975-78, sec., 1977, pres., 1978. Mem. ABA (labor law, litigation, govt. svc., judiciary sects.), NAFE, Nat. Assn. Female Judges, Fed. Bar Assn., U.S. Supreme Ct. Bar Assn., Calif. Bar Assn. Office: Social Security Adminstrn Office of Hearings and Appeals 420 W Main St Ste 400 Oklahoma City OK 73102-4435

GATH, JEAN MARIE, architectural firm executive; BS, SUNY, New Paltz; M in City and Regional Planning, Pratt Inst. Prin. Hardy, Holzman, Pfeiffer Assocs. LLP, N.Y.C., 2001—03, ptnr., dir. planning, 2003—. Fellow: Inst. for Urban Design; mem.: Soc. for Coll. and Univ. Planning, Am. Planning Assn. Office: HHPA 10th Fl 902 [illegible] NY 10010

GATI, TOBY T. international advisor; b. Bklyn., July 27, 1946; m. Charles Gati; 2 children; 3 stepchildren. BA, Pa. State U., 1967; MA in Russian Lit., Columbia U., 1970, M in Internat. Affairs, 1972. Rsch. asst, project dir., dep. v.p., v.p., sr. v.p. UN Assn. of the U.S.A., 1972-93; spl. asst. to the pres. for nat. security affairs Nat. Security Coun., sr. dir. for Russia, Ukraine and Eurasian States, 1993; asst. sec. for intelligence and rsch. Dept. State, Washington, 1993-97; sr. internat. advisor Akin Gump Strauss Hauer & Feld LLP, Washington, 1997—. Commentator CNN Headline News and CNN; cons. ABC World Tonight, 1986, Ford Found., 1987-89, BDM Internat., 1989; mem. Coun. on Fgn Rels., Internat. Inst. for Strategic Studies. Home: 5137 Macomb St NW Washington DC 20016-2611 Office: Akin Gump Strauss Hauer & Feld LLP Ste 400 1333 New Hampshire Ave NW Washington DC 20036-1564 E-mail: tgati@akingump.com.

GATIPON, BETTY BECKER, medical educator, consultant; b. New Orleans, Sept. 8, 1931; d. Elmore Paul and Theresa Caroline (Sendker) Becker; m. William B. Gatipon, Nov. 22, 1952 (dec. 1986); children: Suzanne, Ann Gatipon Sved, Lynn Gatipon Pashley. BS magna cum laude, Ursuline Coll., New Orleans, 1952; MEd, La. State U., 1975, PhD, 1983. Tchr. Diocese of Baton Rouge, 1960-74, edn. cons. to sch. bd., 1974-78; dir. Right to Read program Capital Area Consortium/Washington Parish Sch. Bd., Franklington, La., 1978-80; dir. basic skills edn. Capital Area Consortium/Ascension Parish Sch. Bd., Donaldsonville, La., 1980-82; instr. Coll. Edn. La. State U., Baton Rouge, 1982-84; evaluation cons. La. Dept. Edn., Baton Rouge, 1984-85; dir. basic skills edn. Capital Area Basic Skills/East Feliciana Parish Sch. Bd., Clinton, La., 1985-86; program coord. La. Bd. Elem. and Secondary Edn., New Orleans, 1987-89; dir. divsn. of med. edn., dept. family medicine Sch. Medicine La. State U. Med. Ctr., New Orleans, 1989—. Evaluator East Feliciana Parish Schs., 1982-86; presenter math. methods workshops Ascension Parish Schs., 1980-84. Author curriculum materials, conf. papers; contbr. articles to edn. jours. Curatorial asst. La. State Mus., New Orleans, 1987—; soprano St. Louis Cathedral Concert Choir, New Orleans, 1988—; chmn. Symphony Store, New Orleans Symphony, 1990—; lector St. Francis Xavier Ch. Mem. Am. Ednl. Rsch. Assn., Assn. Am. Med. Colls., Midsouth Ednl. Rsch. Assn., La. Ednl. Rsch. Assn., Soc. Tchrs. Family Medicine, New Orleans Film and Video Buffs, Phi Kappa Phi, Phi Delta Kappa. Roman Catholic. Avocations: music, aerobic walking, classic movies. Home: 105 10th St New Orleans LA 70124-1258 Office: LA State U Med Ctr Sch Medicine 1542 Tulane Ave New Orleans LA 70112-2825 Office Phone: 504-568-4570.

GATISON, KAREN ANN, private school educator; b. Bridgeport, Conn., Apr. 1, 1953; d. Harold George and Teresa Mary Russer; children: Jonathan Isaiah, Denise Nicole. AS in Office Tech. and Mgmt., Ctrl. Fla. C.C., Ocala, 1992, AA in Bus. Mgmt., 1994; BA in Bus. Mgmt., St. Leo Coll., 1996. Tchr. Cambridge Acad., Ocala, Fla., 1996—. Bd. dirs. Help Agy. Forest, Silver Springs, Md. Mem.: NAFE, Nat. Bus. Edn. Assn., Nat. Women's History Project, Nat. Coun. Tchrs. Math., Phi Beta Lambda (profl. divsn. 1995—, historian 1993—94, Most Valuable Mem. 1994). Home: 2702 NE 22d Ct Ocala FL 34470-3850 Office: Cambridge Acad 3855 SE Lake Weir Rd Ocala FL 34480-9152 E-mail: karen@cambridgeacademy.com.

GATLIN, NOVELLA ANNA MARIA, collection specialist, business consultant; b. St. Louis, Nov. 23, 1942; d. George Wilbur Thompson and Flossie Lavetta Carter; m. Alton Lee Gatlin, Mar. 3, 1962; children: Kimberly Ann, Michael David. AA in Liberal Arts, Forest Park C.C., St. Louis, 1973; postgrad., LaSalle Extension U., Chgo., 1973-80. Cert. master profl. credit exec. Clk. for various depts. City of University City, Mo., 1971-82, dep. collector fin. dept., 1982-88, collection specialist fin. dept., 1988—. Bus. cons. Jr. Achievement of Miss. Valley, University City, 1991—. Writer Credit Profls. Internat. Connection quar. newsletter, 1995, 96, 98, St. Louis Credit Profls. Internat. quar. newsletter, 1996. With U.S. WAC, 1961-62. Recipient 5 Yr. Svc. award Jr. Achievement Miss. Valley, 1996. Mem. Internat. Credit Assn. Mo. (chmn., writer quar. newsletter 1995-96, 97-98, 2d v.p. 1995-96, 1st v.p. 1996-97, pres. 1997-98), Mo. Credit Assn. (bd. dirs. 1992-94), Credit Profls. Internat. (public rels. com. 1995-96, 96-97, chmn. cert. comm. CERF 1998—, public rels. com. CERF 1997-98, bd. dirs. 1997—, ICA Dist. VII 1997—, St. Louis credit prof. treas. 1990-91, 97-98, v.p. 1991-92, pres. 1992-93, 94-95, 95-96, 96-97, past. pres. 1993-94, 97-98, credit profl. of yr. award 1992-93, credit profl. of yr. award dist. VII 1995-96, Lifetime Achievement award, individual excellence in edn. dist. VII 1996, dist. VII treas. 1994-95, dist. VII 2d v.p. 1995-96, dist. VII 1st v.p. 1996-97, dist. VII pres. 1997-98), Credit Prof. Internat. Bd. Dirs., 1997-98, Internat. Credit Assn. of Greater St. Louis, (edn. comm. 1998, disting. svc. award, 1998). Avocations: music, travel. Office: City of University City 6801 Delmar Blvd University City MO 63130-3104

GATONS, ANNA-MARIE KILMADE, government official; b. Albany, N.Y., Oct. 21, 1946; d. Daniel Joseph Jr. and Tomasina (Fallone) Kilmade; m. Robert A. McCarthy, Sept. 3, 1967 (div. Apr. 1990); children: Daniel Kilmade McCarthy, Kevin Michael McCarthy; m. Paul K. Gatons, July 28, 1991. BA, Coll. of St. Rose, 1970. Staff support positions HUD, Washington, 1976-79, mgmt. analyst, 1979-81, staff budget analyst, 1981-83, chief of the budget and legislation coord. br., 1983-91, dir. exec. secretariat, 1992-95; dir. exec. secretariat for atty. gen. Dept. of Justice, Washington, 1995—2001; corr. mgmt. officer Office of Asst. Atty. Gen. for Adminstrn., Washington, 2001—02; dir., exec. sec. Immigration and Naturalization Svc., Washington, 2002—03; dir., exec. secretariat U.S. Immigration and Customs Enforcement, Dept. Homeland Security, Washington, 2003—. Mem. St. Rose Alumni Assn. Roman Catholic. Avocations: reading, needlework, decorating. Home: 7705 Huntsman Blvd Springfield VA 22153-3912 Office: US Immigration and Customs Enforcement Exec Secrt Rm 7045 Dept of Homeland Sec 425 I St NW Washington DC 20530

GATTING, CARLENE J. lawyer; b. Hartford, Conn., Apr. 12, 1955; d. Charles W. and Jean A. (Murkowicz) G. BS, U. Conn., 1977; JD, Rutgers U., 1983. Counsel Skadden, Arps, Slate, Meagher & Flom, N.Y.C., 1987—. Mem. ABA. Office: Skadden Arps Slate Meagher & Flom 4 Times Sq Fl 24 New York NY 10036-6595

GATTO, CAROLYN MICHELE, editor-in-chief; BA in English, U. Va., 1973. Mng. editor, assoc. editor Garden City (N.Y.) Leader, 1973-76; sr. editor Woman's Day Spl. Interest Publs. Hachette Filipacchi Mags., N.Y.C., 1976-87, mng. editor, 1987-91, editor-in-chief, 1991—, v.p., 1996—. Chair comm. com. Coll. Trustees, U. Va., Charlottesville, 1991—. Trustee Project Row Houses Found., 1998—. Recipient Editl. award Dallas Home Furnishings Mkt., 1987, Writer Hall of Fame award Internat. Home Furnishings Mkt., 1989, FOLIO Editl. Excellence award, 1994, Honor award Nat. Trust Hist. Preservation, 1997. Mem. Internat. Furnishings Design Assn. (v.p. comm. 1992), Am. Soc. Mag. Editors, Women in Comm. Office: Womans Day Spl Interest Publs Editor-in-chief 1633 Broadway Fl 42 New York NY 10019-6708 Fax: 212-489-5621.

GAUCHER, JANE HEYCK, retail executive; b. Houston, Feb. 11, 1936; d. Theodore Richard and Gertrude Paine (Daly) Heyck; m. Donald Holman Gaucher, June 15, 1957 (dec.); children: Susan Heyck Merrill, Beverly Jane. AB cum laude, Brown U., Providence, 1957. Mgr. Bride and Groom Registry Berings, Houston, 1990-99; asst. mgr. Pavillon Christofle, Houston, 1999—2002; mktg. rep. dinnerRings, 2002—. Pres. Antique Study Group, Houston, 1974-75. Bd. dirs. Jr. League Houston, 1963, sustaining bd., 1990-93; mem. Kinkaid Sch. Alumni Bd., Houston, 1995-98, Mus. So. History Bd., 2000-. Avocations: tennis, running, golfing, mah jongg, bridge. Home: 1905B Potomac Dr Houston TX 77057-2921

GAUDET, JEAN ANN, retired librarian, educator; b. Oakland, Calif., Dec. 28, 1949; d. Edwin Joseph and Teresa Maureen (McDonnell) G. BS, Madison Coll., Harrisonburg, Va., 1971; MLS, George Peabody Coll. for Tchrs, Nashville, 1973. Libr., gifted edn. tchr. Prince William County Schs., Manassas, Va., 1971—2003, ret., 2003. Chmn. PSHS Site-Based Mgmt. Com., Dumfries, Va., 1989-92, 98-2001; chmn. Cmty. Choir, Woodbridge, Va., 1983-85; citizen ambassador People to People, Russia and Poland, 1992, China, 1993, 2000, Australia, 1994. Named Prince William Assn. for Edn. of Gifted Tchr. of Yr., 1998. Mem. ALA, Va. Edn. Media Assn., Va. Assn. for Edn. of Gifted, Delta Kappa Gamma (sec. 1994—), Beta Phi Mu, Alpha Beta Alpha. Home: 16820 Francis West Ln Dumfries VA 22026-2110 Personal E-mail: gaudetja@cs.com.

GAUDIANI, CLAIRE LYNN, retired academic administrator; b. Venice, Fla., Nov. 10, 1944; d. Vincent Augustus and Vera (Rossano) Gaudiani; m. David Graham Burnett; children: David Graham, Maria. BA, Conn. Coll., 1966; MA in French and Italian, Ind. U., 1969, PhD in French and Italian, 1975; PhD (hon.), Purdue U., 1989, Whitman Coll., 1989. Asst. prof. Purdue U., W. Lafayette, Ind., 1977—80, Emory U., Atlanta, 1980—81; sr. fellow in romance langs., acting assoc. dir. Joseph H. Lauder Inst. Mgmt. and Internat. Studies U. Pa., Phila., 1981—88; pres. Conn. Coll., New London, 1988—2001; sr. rsch. scholar Yale Law Sch., 2001—. Mem. commn. internat. edn. Am. Coun. Edn.; bd. dirs. So. NEw ENg. Telephone Co.; cons. Dana Found., Exxon Found., Rockefeller Found. Author: The Cabaret Peotry oof Theophile de Viau: Texts and Traditions, 1980, Teaching Writing in the Foreign Language Curriculum, 1981; co-author (with Carol Herron and others): Strategies for Development of Foreign Language and Literature Programs, 1984; contbr. articles to profl. jours.; author: The Greater Good: How Philanthropy Saves American Capitalism, 2003. Chair assessment task force United Way, New London, 1988; hon. chair Summer Music Fund, 1988; trustee Hazen Found.; bd. dirs. Eugene O'Neill Theatre Ctr. Recipient Coll. medal, Conn. Coll., 1987; fellow rsch. fellow, Nat. Humanities Ctr., 1980—81, Am. Coun. Learned Socs., 1976—77. Mem.: MLA (adv. com. fgn. lang. programs 1988—), Conn. World Trade Assn. (bd. dirs.), Am. Assn. Higher Edn. (bd. dirs. 1988—), Phi Beta Kappa. Roman Catholic. Office: Yale Law School P O Box 208215 New Haven CT 06520

GAUFF, LISA, broadcast journalist; b. Seattle; d. Joseph F. and Patricia A. (Lee) G. BA in Comm., U. Wash., 1987; MA in Journalism and Pub. Affairs, Am. U., 1988. Pub. info. asst. King County Coun., Seattle, 1985-86; reporter Sta. KUOW-FM, Seattle, 1985-86; news anchor Sta. KCMU-FM, Seattle, 1986-87; TV field prodr. Group W/Newsfeed Network, Washington, 1988-89; anchor, reporter Capitol TV, Washington, 1989-90, Newschannel 8, Washington, 1991-93; prodr., writer Sta. WJLA-TV, Washington, 1990-91; weekend anchor Sta. WHTM-TV, Harrisburg, Pa., 1993-94; morning anchor Sta. WJW-TV, Cleve., 1994-97; traffic anchor Sta. KNX-AM, L.A., 1998—2001, pub. rels. cons., 2001—. Freelance reporter KCBS-TV, KABC-TV, UPN-TV, Fox TV, Sunworld, Satellite News, Media Gen., NPR Radio, Shadow Broadcasting, 1988-89; ind. video prodr. 1989-91. Host, editor TV documentary Coming to Terms, 1993. Bd. dirs. NE Ohio AAU Baseball Com., 1995-96; moderator Ohio Acad. Decathalon, Cleve., 1995, 96; vol. United Way, Cleve., 1995, 96; honorary chair Women's Ctr. Greater Cleve., 1995; celebrity spokesperson Cleve. Christian Home for Children, 1995. Recipient John Merriman award Writer's Guild Am., 1988, Appreciation cert. United Negro Coll. Fund, 1995, 96; named One of 20 Top Women in Media, Washington D.C. Tchrs. Assn., 1993. Mem. NATAS, AFTRA. Avocations: art history, skiing, quiz shows. Office: Sta KNX-AM 6121 W Sunset Blvd Los Angeles CA 90028-6423

GAUGER, MICHELE ROBERTA, photographer, studio administrator, corporate executive; b. Elkhorn, Wis., Feb. 28, 1949; d. Robert F. and Christiane J. (Guiffaut) Marszalek; m. Richard C. Gauger, May 3, 1969 (div.). Student, U. Wis., Superior, 1967-69, U. Wis., Whitewater, 1978-80, Winona Sch. Profl. Photography, Chgo., 1984-91; MA in Photography, 1994. Wedding photographer Fossum Studio, Elkhorn, 1973-78; owner Photography by Michele, Whitewater, 1978-81; pres., photographer, mgr. Michele Inc. Wis., Whitewater, 1981—, Foxes Reg., 1987. Instr. Whitewater Experience (Sch.), 1997—2004, Yucatan Experience, 2003; spkr., lectr. in field. Contbr. articles to profl. jours.; exhibitions include Chinese Nat. Gallery, Beijing, 1987, 1988 (2d pl. award, 1988), 1989 (Bronze medal, 1989), 1991, 1994, 1995, 1996 (Bill Stockwell Lifetime Achievement award, 1995). Mem. Nat. Arbor Found., Nebr., 1984—. Named to Wis. Ct. Honor, 1991, 1996; recipient 1st pl. Wedding Photography award, Internat. Wedding Photography, 1983, 1984, 1987, 1988, 1989, 1991, 1996, 2s pl. award, 1985, 1996, Grand award, 1988. Mem.: N.Am. Hunters Assn., Winona Sch. Profl. Photography Alumni Assn., Wedding & Portrait Photo Internat. Photographers Assn. (Lifetime Achievement award 2003), Profl. Photographers Am. (Nat. Loan Collectional 1984, Epcot Exhibit 1996), Whitewater C. of C., Turtle Lake Sportsman Club (chmn. bd. dirs. 2001—03). Republican. Roman Catholic. Avocations: world travel, big game hunting, horseback riding, cooking. Home and Office: Michele Inc N7240 Sand Pyramid Rd Whitewater WI 53190-4479

GAUGHAN, PATRICIA ANNE, judge; b. Cleve., Oct. 21, 1953; d. John James and Alma Marie (Friedmann) G.; m. Roger Andrew Andrachik, Apr. 24, 1987; children: Brett Gaughan, Kathryn Gaughan. BA, St. Mary's Coll., 1975; JD, U. Notre Dame, 1978. Bar: Ohio 1978, Ind. 1978. Asst. county pros. Cuyahoga County Pros. Office, Cleve., 1978-83, 84-87; asst. U.S. atty. U.S. Atty.'s Office, Cleve., 1983-84; assoc. Reid, Johnson, Downes, Andrachik & Webster, Cleve., 1984-87; judge Common Pleas Ct. Cuyahoga County, Cleve., 1987-96, exec. com., 1993-96; judge U.S. Dist. Ct. (no. dist.) Ohio, Eastern divsn., 1996—. Adj. prof. trial advocacy Cleve. Marshall Coll. of Law, 1983-87; mem. rules adv. com. Supreme Ct. of Ohio, Columbus, 1991-97; mem. paralegal studies adv. bd. Notre Dame Coll., Cleve., 1991—. Bd. dirs. Nat. Conf. Met. Cts., 1993—, Newburgh House of Hope, Cleve., 1994-96, Conflict Resolution Ctr., Cleve., 1995-98; mem. children's trust fund bd. Cuyahoga County Commrs., Cleve., 1984-92; v.p. Leukemia Soc., Lymphoma Soc. Mem. Ohio State Bar Assn., Ohio Jud. Conf. Assn., Cleve. Bar Assn. (trustee 1994-97), Cuyahoga County Bar Assn., Fed. Judges Assn., Fed. Cir. Bar Assn., Am. Judicature Soc., Common Pleas Ct. Judges Assn., Harold H. Burton Inn of Ct. (master of the bench 1991-96), Kappa Gamma Pi. Office: US Dist Ct 201 Superior Ave E Ste 202 Cleveland OH 44114-1201

GAULT, JEANNIE SUZANNE, elementary school educator; b. Pensacola, Fla., Sept. 20, 1953; d. Arthur Boucher Boyd and Genevieve Grace (Daniel) Alvers; m. Michael Alan Gault, Nov. 20, 1993. BFA, Bowling Green State U., 1975; A in Comml. Art, U. Akron, 1984. Cert. tchr. Ohio. Art tchr. Jefferson Local Schs., Irondale, Ohio, 1975—76, Mapleton Local Schs., Ashland, Ohio, 1976—87, Loudonville (Ohio) Perrysville Schs., 1987—. Mem.: Ohio Art Edn. Assn., Ohio Edn. Assn. Republican. Methodist. Avocations: golf, crocheting, walking, drawing, painting. Home: 1244 Township Rd 1253 Ashland OH 44805 Office: Loudonville Perrysville Schs 210 E Main St Loudonville OH 44842

GAULT, JUDITH, piano teacher; b. Chgo., Jan. 11, 1934; d. Ray and Marguerite Louise Adkins; m. Richard J. Gault, Dec. 18, 1955; children: Laura, Sarah, Thom, David. BM, Western Mich. U., 1956. Cert. Nat. Music Tchrs. Assn. Pvt. piano tchr., 1960—; pianist Buchanan (Mich.) Pub. Schs., 1970—; dir. organist Ministry of Music, Buchanan, 1970—; dir. corp. choir Tyler BlueNotes, Niles, Mich., 1975—; orchestra dir. Brandywine Schs., Niles, 1964-70; choral dir. Area Choir, Buchanan, 1987-97. Actress various musicals and plays, 1970-90; dir. various choirs and cantatas, Buchanan and Niles, Mich., 1968—; Piano recitals and planner of Monster Concerts, South Bend, Ind., 1960—; singer chior tours of Europe and Canegie Hall, N.Y., 1982-99. Chmn. Buchanan Fine Arts Coun., 1980; pres. South Bend Area Piano Tchrs. Assn., 1990—; officer South Bend Symphony Guild, 1980-90; mem. South Bend Art League, Niles League of Women Voters, 1980-90. Mem. Nat. Piano Guild, Nat. Federation Music Clubs. Republican. Presbyterian. Avocations: traveling, tennis, racquet ball. E-mail: JNRGault@aol.com.

GAULT-STOVALL, SHERI ZELDA-LYNN, property manager, consultant; b. Gary, Ind., Nov. 12, 1955; d. James Wylie and Vivian Louise Gault; m. Thurman R. Stovall, Aug. 5, 1995. BA, Doane Coll., Crete, Nebr., 1987; MS, Spertus Inst., Chgo., 1991. Site coord., counselor Chgo. Dept. Pub. Health, Chgo., 1989—93; program coord. Midwest Aids Tng. Edn. Ctr., Univ. Chgo., 1993—96; site dir. Chase House, Chgo., 1996—2000, assoc. dir., 2000—02; property mgr. Steven Jerold Mgmt., Chgo., 2003—. Cons. Midwest Aids Tng. Edn. Ctr., Chgo., 1997—; planning coun. mem. City of Chgo HIV/AIDS Planning Coun., Dept. Pub. Health, Chgo., 2000—03. Contbr. articles to profl. jour. Crisis worker, vol. South Suburban Family Shelter, Homewood, Ill., 1997—. Avocations: walking, reading, paper tole art, miniature golf, drawing.

GAUMOND, LYNN E. elementary school educator; b. Meriden, Conn., July 15, 1953; d. Richard Drake and Jean (Hall) Anderson; m. Gary Williams Gaumond, June 28, 1975; children: Jeffrey Ross, Kara Marie. BS in Edn. magna cum laude, Plymouth (N.H.) State Coll., 1975; MEd summa cum laude, U. Hartford, 1978. Tchr. grade 6 Squadron Line Sch., Simsbury, Conn., 1975-84, tchr. grade 3, 1984-86, tchr. kindergarten, 1986-89; tchr. grade 1 Tootin Hills Sch., West Simsbury, Conn., 1989—2000. Adj. prof. U. Hartford, 2002-; tchr. in residence bur. program and tchr. evaluation Conn. State Dept. Edn., 2000-2001, U. Hartford Magnet Sch., West Hartford, Grades 1, 2001-2003; logical math. essentialist, 2003-; cons. math program Primary Math. Series, Scholastic Book Pub., 1992-93; cons. math. manipulative project LEGO/DACTA, Enfield, Conn., 1990-91; tchr. PIMMS math recovery, 2002-. Contbg. writer/editor math program: Math Place, 1993-94; contbg. writer: CSDE Tchg. Handbook Portfolio. Mem. faculty, portfolio benchmarking, trainer, scorer, leader CSDE elem. edn., 1997-; trainer Ind. State Tchr.'s Portfolio, 2001, 2002; instr. CSDE Numeracy Acad., 1998-2000; com. mem. troop 177 Boy Scouts Am., Canton, Conn., 1992; coun. mem. Girl Scouts U.S., Canton, 1991—, leader troop 828, Canton, 1991—; mem. PTO, Canton Pub. Schs., 1985—; mem. Concerned Citizens for Canton, 1992—; bd. dirs. Canton Youth for Environ. Awareness, 1994—. Recipient Presdl. Award for Excellence in Sci. and Math. Teaching, NSF, 1993, state awardee, 1992, 93; Assoc. Tchrs. of Math. in Conn. grantee, 1993, semifinalist Conn. Tchr. of Yr., 2003, CREC Tchr. of Yr., 2003. Fellow Acad. for Edn. in Math., Sci. and Tech.; mem. NEA, ASCD, Conn. Edn. Assn., Simsbury Edn. Assn., Nat. Coun. Tchrs. Math., Assoc. Tchrs. of Math. in New Eng., Assoc. Tchrs. Math. in Conn., Coun. of Presdl. Awardees in Math., Soc. of Elem. Presdl. Awardees, Coun. for Elem. Sci. Internat., Nat. Sci. Tchrs. Assn. Democrat. Avocation: gardening. Home: 18 High Hill Rd Canton CT 06019-2225 Office: U Hartford Magnet Sch 196 Bloomfield Ave West Hartford CT 06117

GAUS, LYNN SHEBESTA, school administrator; b. Manitowoc, Wis., Dec. 16, 1955; d. Joseph J. Shebesta and Shirley Ann (Pietras) Kent; m. John Michael Gaus, Jr. BS, U. Wis., La Crosse, 1978; MS, Mankato State U., 1986; postgrad., Harvard U., 1992. Admissions counselor Silver Lake Coll., 1980-83; asst. dir. admissions Mankato (Minn.) State U., 1983-88; dir. admissions Lakeland Coll., Sheboygan, Wis., 1988-90; dean of admissions and fin. aid Wayland Acad., Beaver Dam, Wis., 1990-95; econ. devel. profl. N.E. Wis. Tech. Coll., Green Bay, 1995-2000; adminstr., prin. St. Mary's Sch., Luxemburg, Wis., 2000—01, St. Philip the Apostle Sch., Green Bay, 2001—02; dir. Am. Red Cross, Manitowoc, 2002—. Cons. to admissions Northwestern Military/Naval Acad., Lake Geneva, Wis., 1992; adj. instr. N.E. Wis. Tech. Coll., Lakeland Coll.; presenter, workshop presenter in fiel. Editor, designer, publisher (ednl. insts. brochures, viewbooks), 1986-93. Bd. dirs. Big Bros.-Big Sisters, Manitowoc, 1989, Girl Scouts U.S.A., Green Bay, 1996-98. Mem. Green Bay Area C. of C. (advance econ. devel. com., advance retention com.), Civitan (bd. dirs., v.p. Mankaato 1986-88), Rotary (bd. dirs., pres. DePere, Wis.). Avocations: skiing, camping, golf, cooking, gardening. Home: 448 N Good Hope Rd De Pere WI 54115-2405 Office: Am Red Cross 205 N 8th St Manitowoc WI 54220 E-mail: arclynng@lsol.net.

GAUTHIER, AMY, campus administrator; b. New Roads, La. d. Roland and Mary Carter Gauthier. BS in Acct., So. U., Baton Rouge, 1986, MEd in Counselor Edn., 1992. Counselor So. U., Baton Rouge; acct. Jumonville Meml. campus La. Tech. Coll., New Roads, counselor Slidell campus, couselor Jumonville Meml. campus; now campus adminstr. La. Tech. Coll.-Jumonville Meml. Campus, New Roads. Columnist: Pointe Coupee Banner. Founder The Workplace Found. Mem.: La. Assn. Student Fin. Aid Adminstrs. Avocations: dance, writing. Office: La Tech Coll Jumonville Meml Campus PO Box 725 New Roads LA 70760

GAUVEY, SUSAN KATHRYN, judge; b. Van Wert, Ohio, Mar. 1, 1948; d. Richard David and Asta Walburga (Frericks) G.; m. David E. Kern, May 10, 1975; children: Megan E. Gauvey-Kern, Kevin C. Gauvey-Kern, Elizabeth H. Gauvey-Kern. Student, Georgetown U., 1968-69; BA cum laude Polit. Sci., Rosary Coll, River Forest, Ill., 1970; JD, Northwestern U., 1973; postgrad. Mental Hygiene, Johns Hopkins U., 1976-77. Bar: Wash. 1974, Md. 1975. Law clerk to fed. dist. ct. judge We. Dist. Ct., Seattle, Wash., 1973-74; staff atty. Mental Health Law Project Legal Aid Bur., Balt., 1975-77, chief Mental Health Law Project, 1977-79; asst. atty. gen. Dept. Health and Mental Hygiene Office of Atty. Gen., Balt., 1979-81, asst. atty. gen. Civil Divsn., 1981-86, prin. counsel trial litigation, 1984-86; with litigation divsn. Venable, Baetjer and Howard L.L.P., Balt., 1986-96; magistrate judge U.S. Dist. Ct. for Md., Balt., 1996—. Contbr. articles to profl. jours. Chair bd. dirs. Marian House for Women. Mem. Nat. Assn. Women Judges, Wranglers Law Club, Lawyers' Roundtable. Democrat. Office: US Courthouse 101 W Lombard St Baltimore MD 21201-2605

GAVIN, LESLEY CATHERINE, architecture educator, consultant; b. St. Andrews, Scotland, May 6, 1968; d. Anthony John and Charlotte Donaldson Gavin. BArch, Edinburgh Coll. of Art, 1986—91; MSc in Computing & Design, U. E. London, 1991—92; MBA, London Bus. Sch., 2001—03. Archtl. asst. J+F Johnson & Ptnrs., Edinburgh, Scotland, 1990—91; lectr., architecture The Robert Gordon U., Aberdeen, Scotland, 1992—95; built environment The Open U., Milton Keynes, England, 1995—96; arch. Hurley Robertson Assocs., London, 1996—98; lectr., architecture U. Coll. London, 1998—. Dir. 4D Trading Ltd., London, 2001—03. Contbr. articles to profl. jours. Mem.: London VR Group, Internat. Astronautical Fedn. (mem., space, edn. and outreach com. 2000), Royal Inst. of Brit. Archs. Office: Univ Coll London Gower St London WC1E 6BT England

GAVIN, MARY ELLEN, consultant; b. Chgo. d. Francis Edward and Agnes Mary (Rolder) Des Enfants; m. William Francis Gavin; children: Michael James, Terence Francis. MBA, U. Palmers Green, Eng., 1999. Lic. pvt. investigator. Analyst A.C. Nielsen, Chgo.; asst. br. mgr. Borg-Warner Fin. Svc., Chgo.; asst. leasing mgr. Borg-Warner Leasing, Chgo., midwest leasing mgr.; v.p. Gen. Equipment Leasing, Chgo.; leasing mgr. Pitney Bowes Credit Corp., Chgo.; ind. rep. Gen. Elec. Mobile Radio & Tele., Chgo.; pres. Gavin Communications, Annapolis, Md.; owner Gavin & Assocs., Chantilly, Va. Adult edn. tchr. Fairfax County, 1996—, Nova C.C., 2000—. Author: And Still We Celebrate, 2001, We Celebrate the Macabre, 2002, We Celebrate Food for the Soul; editor: Post War Letter Messages From the Heart, 1997. Mem.: The Writers of Chantilly (founder), Nat. Assn. Writers, Women in Mgmt., Wash. Ind. Writers, Internat. Women's Writing Guild, Associated Writing Program George Mason Univ., Nat. Writers Assn. Republican. Roman Catholic. Home and Office: 127 Richland Dr W Mandeville LA 70448-6332 E-mail: maryellengavin@yahoo.com.

GAVIN, MARY JANE, medical and surgical nurse; b. Prairie Du Chien, Wis., Sept. 1, 1941; d. Frank Grant and Mary Elizabeth Wolf; m. Alfred William Gavin, Nov. 9, 1963; children: Catherine Heidi Elizabeth, Carl Alfred Eric. Student, North Cen. Coll., Naperville, Ill., 1959-61; BS, RN, U. Wis., 1964; postgrad., Deepmuscle Tng. Ltd., 1980; postgrad. in deep muscle therapy. RN, Wis. Staff nurse U. Wis. Hosps., Madison; RN home response VA, Milw. Unit chair Badger Girls State, 1991—; mem. Wis. Am. Legion Aux.; mem. task force for handicapped Eastside Wis. Evang. Luth. Ch., Madison, 1993. U. Wis. scholar. Mem. Monona Grove Am. Legion Aux. (pres. Unit 429 1990—). Home: 702 Fairmont Ave Madison WI 53714-1424

GAVIN, PAULA LANCE, investment company executive; b. Nassau, N.Y., July 25, 1945; d. Paul P. and Gisela M. (Saume) Lance; m. John J. Gavin, July 23, 1983; children: Jennifer, Jason. BA, U. Del., 1967. With AT&T, N.J., 1967-90; pres. YMCA of Greater N.Y., N.Y.C., 1990—2004; with Jacobson Ptnrs., N.Y.C., 2004—. Bd. dirs. Childtime Learning Centers, Novi, Mich., 2002—. Bd. dirs. N.Y.C. Partnership and C. of C. Named to U. Del. Wall of Fame, 1998. Office: Jacobson Ptnrs 595 Madison Ave New York NY 10022*

GAVIN, SARA, public relations executive; b. Minn. Degree in History and Polit. Sci., Coll. St. Catherine, St Paul, Minn. Investor rels. programs Doremus & Co.; v.p. Hill and Knowlton/Twin Cities, Dorn Swenson Meyer, 1985-86; exec. v.p. Mona Meyer McGrath, 1986-93; pres. Mona Meyer McGrath & Gavin (Shandwick), Minn., 1993-95; mgr. dir. Shandwick Internat., 1995—. Bd. dirs. Minn. Women's Economic Round Table; trustee Coll. of St. Catherine, Minn. Pub. Radio. Recipient various awards PRSA, IABC. Mem. PRSA, Recognized Phi Beta Kappa. Office: Shandwick Ste 500 8400 Normandale Lake Blvd Minneapolis MN 55437-3889

GAVRILOFF, KATRINA, writer; b. Erie, Pa., Aug. 5, 1978; d. Perry Richard and Susan Loraine Gavriloff. BA in English, Pa. State U., 2000. Asst. support technician Am. Online, Inc., Reston, Va., 2000—01; sr. tech. writer Am. Online, Inc. Systems Ops., Reston, Va., 2001—. Tool com., tool documentation, aided in tng. new writers Am. Online, Inc., Multi-departmental, Reston, Va., 2002—03; spkr. Pa. State U. Mem.: Soc. Tech. Communication. Avocations: travel, reading, theater. Personal E-mail: wutangaler@aol.com.

GAWEL, MAUREEN SALTZER, newspaper executive; b. Winchester, Mass., Mar. 21, 1959; d. William Charles Saltzer and Janet Ann Child; m. O. Lee Brotherton, June 27, 1981 (div. 1984); m. Robert Chester Gawel, Oct. 14, 1995; 1 child, Lauren Roberta. BS in Journalism summa cum laude, Boston U., 1981; postgrad., Northeastern U., Boston, 1984, U. Calif., Riverside, 1994, Stanford U., 1999, Northwestern U., 2001. Freelance corr. Concord (N.H.) Monitor, 1981-82; advt. sales rep. N.H. Times, Concord, 1981-82, circulation mgr. 1982-83; circulation and promotion mgr. Century Publs. Inc., Winchester, Mass., 1983-84, asst. gen. mgr., 1984-85; ad dir., ops. mgr. Provincetown (Mass.) Adv., 1985-86; gen. mgr. Healdsburg (Calif.) Tribune, Lesher Comm., 1986-87, Valley Times, Lesher Comm., Pleasanton, Calif., 1987-90; corp. oper. bd. dirs. Lesher Comm. Inc., Walnut Creek, Calif.; pub., v.p. Victor Valley Daily Press and Barstow Desert Dispatch divsn. Freedom Comm., Victorville, Calif., 1990-96; pub. Ft. Pierce (Fla.) and Port St. Lucie Tribune divsn., Freedom Comm., 1996-2000; pres. Ea. N.C. Comm. divsn. Freedom Comm., 2000—02; pub. Appeal-Dem. Freedom Cmty. Newspapers, 2003—, v.p. Pacific region, 2003—. Bd. dirs. United Way St. Lucie County, 1997-2000, Leadership St. Lucie, 1997-99, Camp Hidden Hammock, Am. Heart Assn., 1997-99, Manatee Observation and Edn. Ctr., St. Lucie County Sch. Readiness Bd., Exch. Club Castle, 1998-2000, St. Lucie County C. of C., 1998-2000, Boys and Girls Club, 1997-2000, Montessori Childrens Sch., 2000-01, Yuba-Sutter United Way, 2003—, Yuba-Sutter C. of C., 2003—, Fremont-Rideout Found., 2003—. Recipient Woman of Achievement award Bus. and Profl. Women, San Orco, 1991, Golden Nike award, 1991, 94, Hall of Fame-Bus. award for State of Calif., 1992, Humanitarian award Desert Comtys., United Way, 1991, Outstanding Exec. Achievement award U. Calif. Riverside, 1994-95; named Citizen of Yr., Boy Scouts Am. Serrano Dist., 1994, St. Lucie County Citizen of Yr., March of Dimes, 1999. Mem. Newspaper Assn. Am., So. Newspaper Pubs. Assn. (com. chair), Rotary. Avocations: skiing, reading, oenology, sailing. Home: 546 Raddison Dr Yuba City CA 95991 Office: Appeal-Democrat 1530 Ellis Lake Dr Marysville CA 95901

GAWRONSKI, ELIZABETH ANN, retired army officer; b. Panama City, Fla., Oct. 11, 1943; d. Myron Harvey Belyeu Sr. and Irene (Sewell) Belyeu Coates; m. Kenneth E. Gawronski Sr., Sept. 16, 1972; 1 child, Kenneth Edward Jr. BS in Edn., Fla. State U., 1965; MA in Edn., U. Ala., 1974, EdS, 1975. Commd. 2d lt. USAR, 1965, advanced through grades to lt. col., 1986; comdr. Women's Army Corps, Aberdeen Proving Ground, Md.; asst. to chief-of-staff U.S. Army Missile Command, Redstone Arsenal, Ala.; officer-in-charge, instr. Women's Army Corps Sch., Ft. McClellan, Ala.; ops. officer 3392d USAR Sch., Huntsville, Ala.; occupl. splty. instr. 1163d USAR Sch., Bronx, NY; pers. mgmt. staff Adjutant Gen. Corps; staff officer LOGEX, Ft. Lee, Va., pers. staff officer Camp Pickett, Va.; postal staff officer Mil. Postal Svc. Agy., Alexandria, Va.; insp. gen. U.S. Army Missile Sch., Redstone Arsenal, sr. staff officer, various positions, 1988-94; comdg. officer 184th IMA Detachment, Redstone Arsenal, 1994-96; ret., 1996. Exhibitions include Signature 2000, Signature 2001, Limelight Series, 2002, Monte Sano Art Show, 2003. Vol. Huntsville City Schs., 1988-96, Boy Scouts Am., Huntsville, 1993-95, Huntsville Art League, 1997. Decorated Meritorious Svc. medal. Mem.: Watercolor Soc. Ala., Internat. Soc. Exptl. Artists, Res. Officers' Assn. (life), Phi Delta Kappa, Kappa Delta Pi. Methodist. Home: 8044 Lauderdale Rd SW Huntsville AL 35802-2916

GAY, FAITH E. lawyer, educator; BA with honors, Duke U., 1982; JD, Northwestern U., 1986. Bar: N.Y. 1987, U.S. Dist. Ct. (so. and ea. dists.) N.Y. 1987, U.S. Ct. Appeals (2d cir.) 1991, Tex. 1997, Ill. 1997, Fla. 1997, U.S. Ct. Appeals (8th cir.) 1999. Supervising atty., dep. chief civil rights divsn. U.S. Atty.'s Office for Ea. Dist. N.Y., N.Y.C., also dep. chief spl. prosecutions unit; ptnr. Sidley & Austin, N.Y.C. Instr. seminar complex criminal litigation Fordham U. Sch. Law, 1992. Angier B. Duke meml. scholar Duke U. Office: Sidley & Austin 875 3d Ave New York NY 10022 Fax: 212-906-2021. E-mail: fgay@sidley.com.

GAY, SARAH ELIZABETH, lawyer; b. Cambridge, Mass., May 24, 1950; d. Frank Smith and Jane (Spencer) Fussner; m. Kirk D. Gay; 1 child, John Russell. BA, Harvard/Radcliffe, 1972; JD, U. Oreg., 1975. Bar: Alaska 1976, U.S. Dist. Ct. Alaska 1976, U.S. Ct. Appeals (9th cir.) 1976, U.S. Supreme Ct. 1980. Assoc. Ely, Guess & Rudd, Anchorage, 1975-77; asst. atty. gen. natural resources sect. State of Alaska, Anchorage, 1977-88, asst. atty. gen. oil spill sect., 1989-91, sect. supr. natural resources sect., 1991-93; corp. counsel Alaska Safari, Inc., Alaska's Valhalla Lodge, Inc., Anchorage, 1993—; pvt. practice Anchorage, 1993—. Workshop leader U. Oreg. Law Sch., Eugene, 1989; chmn. Anchorage Mcpl. Airports Adv. Com., 1990-93; food safety adv. com. dept. Environ. Conservation, State Alaska, 2000—. Mng. bd. editor U. Oreg. Law Rev., Eugene, 1975. Citizens' adv. bd. Land Conservation & Devel. Bd., Salem, Oreg., 1975. Mem. Alaska Bar Assn.

Law Examiners, Phi Delta Phi. Avocations: commercial pilot, sport fish lodge operator. Address: Valhalla Lodge Nondalton AK 99640 Office Phone: 907-248-4235. Business E-Mail: sarah@valhallalodge.com.

GAY, SUSAN MATTHEWS, publishing professional; b. Atlanta, Dec. 14, 1954; d. Brinton Bizzelle, Jr. and Evelyn (Ward) G.; m. Jonathan P. Andrews, Dec. 14, 1991; children: Katherine Rose Andrews, Paul Brinton Andrews. BS, Presbyn. Coll., 1976; MA, Emory U., 1980. Continuing edn. coord. Emory U. Sch. of Medicine, Atlanta, 1976-79; editor Ctrs. for Disease Control, Atlanta, 1979; editor, sr. editor Butterworth Pubs., Inc., Boston, 1979-82; sr. editor to exec. editor Grune & Stratton, Inc., N.Y.C., 1982-85; exec. editor J.B. Lippincott, Inc., Phila., 1986-88; exec. editor to editor-in-chief Mosby, Inc., Phila., 1988-95; v.p., pub. Williams and Wilkins (Waverly, Inc.), Balt. and Phila., 1995-99; pres., CEO InfoBrand Pub. Inc., Phila., 1999—. Spkr. Thomas Jefferson Med. Coll., Phila., 1997, others. Co-author: (book) Clinical Methods Learning System, 1979. Sec. Presbyn. Coll. Alumni Assn., Clinton, S.C., 1980-81; bd. dirs. New Gulph Children's Ctr., Villanova, Pa., 1996-98, Found. for Architecture, Phila., 1989-91. Mem.: Am. Med. Pubs. Assn. (pres. 2000—01), Am. Med. Writers Assn. (bd. dirs., chmn. audiovisual sect. 1978—85). Avocations: hist. architecture, design, gourmet cooking.

GAYDOS, MARY, writer, researcher, actress; b. Marblehead, Ohio, Feb. 13, 1936; d. George Joseph Gaydos and Dorothy Marian Vargosick Saunders. BFA, Ohio U., 1958; MLS, Queens Coll., 1972. Narrator various art programs, cable TV, 1992—. Actress off-broadway, cinema, TV, 1958-70; writer, moderator (radio series) Fgn. Film Industry, 1970-71; prodr. Milliken Fabric's Fashion Show, 1978; book rev. critic MD Med. Newsmag., N.Y.C., 1973-76; stage mgr. Women in the Performing Arts Festival at Lincoln Ctr., 1977; narrator (film) The Art and Architecture of Belgrade and Kosovo (honoree World Lang. Inst., N.Y.C, 2001); narrator dedication of Nikola Tesla Meml. sponsored by Hons. R. Giuliani and G. Pataki, N.Y.C., 2001.; host of Broadway's 47th Ann. Drama Desk awards, 2002, 48th Ann. Drama Desk awards, 2003, 26th Ann. Medieval Festival, Cloisters Mus./Met. Mus. Art, 2003. Fundraiser for non-profit orgns. including Skowhegan Sch. of Art and Design, The Spanish Inst., Legal Aid Soc., Nat. Energy Found., Archdiocese of N.Y.'s Inner-City Scholarship Fund, 1979-87. Named honoree, World Lang. Inst., 2001; recipient Mayor's Merit award, Hon. Ed T. Koch, N.Y.C., 1989. Mem. Actors Equity Assn., Screen Actors Guild, C.G. Jung Found., Am. Teilhard Assn. for the Future of Man, Am. Soc. of Psychical Rsch. Home: 101 W 85th St Apt 6-12 New York NY 10024-4487 E-mail: marygaydos@hotmail.com.

GAYLE, HELENE D. public health physician; b. Buffalo; BS in Psychology cum laude, Columbia U., 1976; MD, U. Pa., 1981; MPH, John Hopkins U., 1981. Diplomate Am. Bd. Pediats. Intern then resident in pediats. Children's Hosp. Nat. Med. Ctr., Washington, 1981-84; epidemic intelligence svc. officer br. epidemiology divsn. nutrition Ctr. Health Promotion and Edn., 1984-86; preventive medicine resident divsn. evaluation and rsch. office internat. health program Ctrs. Disease Control Ga. State Dept. Health, 1986-87; med. epidemiologist pediats. and family studies sect., AIDS program Ctrs. Disease Control, 1987-89, acting spl. asst. minority HIV policy coordination office dep. dir. (HIV), 1988-89, asst. chief sci., 1989-90, chief internat. activity divsn. HIV/AIDS, 1990-92, assoc. dir. Washington, 1994-96; agy. AIDS coord., chief divsn. HIV-AIDS Agy. Intl. Devel., Washington, 1992-94; dir. Nat. Ctr. HIV, Sexually Transmitted Diseases and Tb Prevention Ctrs. Disease Control, Atlanta, 1995—. Lectr. Sch. Medicine Morehouse U., 1987—92; lectr. masters in pub. health program Emory U., Atlanta, 1989, 90, clin. asst. prof. cmty. medicine, 1996—; cons. WHO, others; bd. dir. Africa Am. inst. Global Health Coun., Internat. Ctr. Rsch. in Women; dir. HIV/AIDS and Tb program Bill & Melinda Gates Found., 2001—. Contbr. articles to profl. jours. Adm. USPHS. Merit scholar, 1981; recipient Henrietta and Jacob Lowenburg prize, 1981, Model Excellence award Colgate-Palmolive Co., 1992. Mem. AAS, AMA, APHA, Am. Coll. Epidemiology, Internat. AIDS Soc., Soc. Against AIDS in Africa, Inst. Medicine, Coun. Fgn. Rels. Mailing: PO Box 23350 Seattle WA 98102 E-mail: heleneg@gatesfoundation.org.

GAYLE, KING, editor; m. Bill Bumpus (div.); 2 children. Prodn. asst., Wash. DC, Balt.; co-host with Maury Povich NBC talk show Cover to Cover; news anchor WFSB-TV, Hartford, 1981—; host The Gayle King Show, 1997; editor-at-large O: The Oprah Mag. Actor: (films) A Little Bit of Lipstick, 2000. Office: O: The Oprah Mag 1700 Broadway New York NY 10019 Office Phone: 212-903-5187.*

GAYLE, MONICA, broadcast journalist; b. Wenatchee, WA, Mar. 3, 1960; BA Journalism, Wash. State U., 1982. Anchor, gen. assingment reporter Sta. KNSD-TV, San Diego, 1990-92; co-anchor CBS News Up to the Minute, N.Y.C., 1992-93, CBS Morning News, N.Y.C., 1993—97; anchor Sta. WJBK-TV, Detroit, 1997—. Recipient 2 Emmys and 3 Sigma Delta Chi awards. Office: WJBK FOX 2 Box 2000 Southfield MI 48037-2000

GAYLOR, SUSAN ROLAND, social worker; b. Roanoke, Virginia, May 8, 1957; d. Clyde Garland and Mildred Grant Roland; m. John Randolph Gaylor, II, June 10, 1995; children: John Randolph III, Jessica Ryan. BS, Old Dominion U., Norfolk, Va., 1975—80; MSW, Norfolk State U., Va., 1982—84; MBA, Averett U., Danville, Va., 2001—03. Cert. ACSW Nat. Assn. Social Workers, 1996. Clin. social work Family Services, Atlanta, 1984—85; dir. The Turning Point, Roanoke, Va., 1986—88; clin. social worker Roanoke City DSS, Va., 1988—92; tng. specialist Dept. of Human Svc., Washington, 1992—94; tng. mgr. VI SSTA, Roanoke, Va., 1975—80. Contbr. book Days in the Lives of Social Workers, 1996. Mem. Child Welfare Task Force Radford U., Radford, Va., 2000—; pres., bd. dir. CASA found., Roanoke, Va., 2003; pres. Coun. of PTA, Roanoke, Va., 1998—2000. Office: VISSTA 210 First St Ste 405 Roanoke VA 24011 Personal E-mail: Dobbs95@aol.com.

GAYNOR, ELLEN ROSE, hematologist; b. Chgo., 1948; MD, U. Wis., 1978. Cert. Am. Bd. Internal Medicine, 1982, in Med. Oncology 1985, in Hematology 1986. Intern Loyola U. Med. Ctr., Maywood, Ill., 1978—79, resident, 1979—82, fellow, oncology, 1980—81; fellow, hematology and oncology U. Chgo., 1982—84; assoc. prof. Loyola U., Stritch Sch. Medicine, Maywood, Ill. Office: Loyola Univ Health Sys 2160 S First Ave Maywood IL 60153

GAYNOR, MARGARET CRYOR, program director; b. Oak Park, Ill. children: Andrew Thorp, Mary Leland. Student, Wellesley Coll., U. Ariz.; BA in Am. Studies, George Washington U., 1974; postgrad., Fed. Exec. Inst. Caseworker, spl. asst. U.S. Senate, Washington, 1962-65, 69-70; assoc. dir. for congl. rels. U. S. OEO, Washington, 1970-73; dir. Office of Govt. Rels. Smithsonian Instn., Washington, 1973-92, dir. Office of Policy and Program Devel., 1992-94, asst. dir. Office Planning Mgmt. and Budget, 1995—. Founding mem. Exec. Women in Govt.; vestry Christ Ch., Alexandria; former mem. Alexandria Archaeology Commn. Home: PO Box 20623 Alexandria VA 22320-1623

GAYOSKI, KATHLEEN MARY, counselor, minister; d. Thomas and Katherine Ida Gayoski. RN, Mercy Hosp. Sch. Nursing, Springfield, Mass., 1971; MA in Psychology and Religion, Andover Newton (Mass.) Theol. Sch., 2000; cert. holistic health counselor, Inst. Transformational Studies, Rockport, Mass., 2002; postgrad., Inst. Transformational Studies, 2003, Elfinstone Coll., 2003—. RN Mass., cert. epidemiologist, CDC; ordained min. Universal Life Ch., 1997; cert. Reiki master tchr. Crystal Crossing Holistic Resource Ctr., Tapas accupressure technique Tapas Assn., Mass., Am. Soc. Alternative Therapists C.O.R.E. Counselor Inst. Transformational Studies, batter's treatment counselor EMERGE/Mass., Nat. Crisis Responder, Debriefer and Chaplain Nat. Office of Victims Assistance, traumatic bereavement specialist and death notification specialist MADD, 1979. Psychiat. RN specialist Mass. Dept. Mental Health, Taunton, 1971—72, RN, health prevention specialist, alcohol rehab. counselor South Miami (Fla.) Hosp., 1972—73, state epidemiologist, RN Mass. Dept. Pub. Health, Boston, 1973—97; coord., traumatic bereavement specialist and trainer Project REACH, Ctr. for Health and Human Svcs., Inc, New Bedford, Mass., 1997—2002; ordained min., crisis chaplain Tender Spirit Ministries, Rochester, Mass., 1997—; cert. holistic health counselor, profl. lectr. and educator Eagle Feathers Healing Arts Garden, Wareham, Mass., 2002—. Poet, author, clay artist Eagle Feathers Healing Arts Garden, 2002—; poet, author, artist Tender Spirit Ministries, 1997—; author Mass. Med. Assn., Boston, 1995. Mem. com. Rochester Meml. Sch., 1982—88; commr. Rochester Pk. Dept., 1988—91; chairperson South Ea. Ednl. Collaborative, New Bedford; publicity dir. Emmaus Cmty., East Freetown, Mass., 1985—88; chaplain, counselor World AIDS Day. Named to Wall of Tolerance, 2003; recipient cert. appreciation, Bur. Family and Cmty. Health, Mass. Dept. Pub. Health, 1997, Silent No More cert. appreciation, U.S. Dept. Justice, 1999, Cert. of Achievement, MADD, 1999, cert. recognition for spiritual care for Egyptian Air Crash, ARC, 1999, letter appreciation for svc. response, Can. Consulate, 1999, cert. recognition for svc. to edn., ORPEA for crisis intervention and bereavement counseling, Old Rochester Regional Sch. Dist., 2000, cert. recognition, Sen. Edward M. Kennedy, U.S. Senate, Washington, 2001. Mem.: Nat. Office Victims Assistance Crisis Response Team, Greater New Bedford Trauma Response Team, Am. Soc. Alternative Therapists, Sisters of Mercy of the Ams. (assoc.; poet, author, nat. lectr.), Nat. Grange. Avocations: travel, writing, reading, expressive clay figures, hiking. Office: Eagle Feathers Healing Arts Garden 191 Main St Wareham MA 02571 Office Phone: 508-245-2860. E-mail: efhealingarts@aol.com.

GAYVORONSKY, LUDMILA, artist, educator; b. Kharkov, Ukraine, Dec. 4, 1939; arrived in U.S., 1980; d. Pavel Nikanorovich Nikitin and M. Eva Lazarevna Skibityanskaya; m. Alexander Vitalievich Eremenko, June 9, 1996; 1 child, Gleb. Diploma in Meteorology, Hydrometeorol. Inst., Odessa, Ukraine, 1961; PhD in Geography, World Meteorol. Ctr., Moscow, 1965; BFA, Acad. Fine Art, Moscow, 1968. Engr.-climatologist Climatol. Obs., Samara, Russia, 1961-62; engr.-agrometeorologist World Meteorol. Ctr., Moscow, 1965-66; editor Inst. Tech. Info., Moscow, 1966-68, chief editor, 1969-79; instr. fine art Sts. Cosmas & Damian Human Svcs. Ctr., S.I., NY, 1983-93; prof. fine art Lebanon (N.H.) Coll., 1997—. Artist stage art constrn. for Childrens Week, Lincoln Ctr., N.Y.C., 1990, wall mural for Sinergia, Inc., N.Y.C., 1992-93, wall mural Town of Newport, N.H., 1998, backdrop panel Dicken's Fair, 1997. Recipient Gold medal Festival of Art, Moscow, 1968, Jurors prize distinction Spring Art Competition, Moscow, 1969, medal of honor Ukrainian Inst. Am., N.Y.C., 1988, cert. of appreciation USCG, Governors Island, N.Y., 1989, Jurors prize distinction Sunapee (N.H.) Art Fair, 1999; named acad. knight Acad. Verbano, Italy, 1999. Mem. World Phenomenological Inst. (artist-in-residence 1997—), N.H. Art Assn., Acad. Fine Arts, Acad. Verbano (Italy). Mem. Orthodox Ch. Of Am. Home: 26 Church St Newport NH 03773-1908 E-mail: ludmila.gayvoronsky@verizon.net.

GAZAWAY, BARBARA ANN, music educator, art educator; b. Lebanon, Pa., Jan. 7, 1942; d. Ammon Mark Brubaker and Margaret (Lesher) Dierwechter; m. Hal Prentiss Gazaway; children: Farideh Dunford, Ramin Dunford, Ammon Dunford, Lavada Kahumoku, Rene Dunford. BS in Music Edn., West Chester State U., 1963; cert. in elem. edn., Brigham Young U., 1979. Cert. Multiple Subject Tchg. Credential 1984, type A tchg. cert. 1990. Elem. music tchr. Oxford (Pa.) Sch. Dist., 1963—65; elem. classroom tchr. Lebanon (Pa.) Sch. Dist., 1965—67; elem. music tchr. U.S. Dept. Edn., European Area, Bad Kreuznach, Germany, 1968—70, elem. classroom tchr. Darmstadt, Germany, 1972—74, elem. music tchr. Alconbury, England, 1974—75; instrumental music instr. Lebanon (Pa.) Cath. H.S., 1976—78, h.s. music tchr., 1976—77; music instr. Brigham Young U., Provo, Utah, 1978—79; elem. vocal music tchr. Bennett Valley Union, Santa Rosa, Calif., 1987—89; elem. vocal music instr. Anchorage Sch. Dist., 1990—2000; pvt. practice, 2001—. Owner, dir. Millcreek Nursery Sch., Newmanstown, 1975—76; instr. Homestay Am. Japanese Exch. Program, Santa Rosa, Calif., 1987; show pianist Marquee Theater, Santa Rosa, Calif., 1985—85; governess, Stuttgart, Germany, 1967—68; opermädchen Internat. Student Info. Svc., Mautern, Austria, 1967; singer, waitress The Harbor View, Martha's Vineyard Is., Mass., 1964; singer, baker, pianist The Inn, Mt Gretna, Pa., 1963; active Experiment in Internat. Living Home Stay Program, Switzerland, 1962; gasthaus worker Am. Student Info. Svc., Feldkirch, Austria, 1965; pres. Internat. Reading Assn. Campus Chpt. Singer: Sister Quartet, 1956—64. Family Coun. sec. Anchorage Pioneer Home, 2001—02; sec. Alpine Condominium Assn., Anchorage, 2001—02; chair Beautification Com., Anchorage, 2001—02; co-chair County Rep. Com., Santa Rosa, 1984—84; co-chair mission com. Trinity Christian Reformed Ch., Anchorage, 2001—02, co-facilitator divorce recovery program, 1999—. Mem.: NEA, Internat. Reading Assn. (pres.), Music Educators Nat. Conv. Avocations: travel, hiking, reading, gardening, cooking. Home and Studio: 8620 Boundary Ave Anchorage AK 99504 Personal E-mail: gazaway_barbara@hotmail.com.

GEALT, ADELHEID MARIA, museum director; b. Munich, May 29, 1946; came to U.S., 1950; d. Gustav Konrad and Ella Sophie (Daeschlein) Medicus; m. Barry Allen Gealt, Mar. 15, 1969. BA, Ohio State U., 1968; MA, Ind. U., 1973, PhD, 1979. Registrar Ind. U. Art Mus., Bloomington, 1972-76, curator Western art, 1976—, acting/interim dir., 1987-89, dir., 1989—. Adj. assoc. prof. H.R. Hope Sch. Fine Arts, Ind. U., Bloomington, 1985—89, assoc. scholar, 1986, assoc. prof., 1989—; mem. nat. adv. coun. Valparaiso U. Art Mus.; commr. Indiana Arts Commn., 1997—2001. Author: Looking at Art, 1983, Domenico Tiepolo The Punchinello Drawings, 1986; co-author: Art of the Western World, 1989, Painting of the Golden Age: A Biographical Dictionary of Seventeenth-Century European Painters, 1993, Domeinco Tiepolo: Master Draftsman, 1996, Giandomenico Teipolo, Disegni dal mondo, 1996; contbg. author Critic's Choice, 1999. Grantee Nat. Endowment for Arts, 1982, 83, Am. Philos. Soc., 1985, NEH, 1985, Samuel H. Kress Found., 1999-2000. Mem. Assn. Art Mus. Dirs. Office: Ind U Art Mus 7th St Bloomington IN 47405-3024

GEAR, KATHLEEN O'NEAL, archaeologist, writer; b. Tulare, Calif., Oct. 29, 1954; d. Harold Arthur and Wanda Lillie O'Neal; m. W. Michael Gear, Oct. 1, 1982. BA cum laude, Calif. State U., Bakersfield, 1976; MA summa cum laude, Calif. State U., Chico, 1979. Sr. mus. preparator Mus. Cultural Hist., L.A., 1980; city historian City of Cheyenne, Wyo., 1980-81; state historian U.S. Dept. Interior, Cheyenne, 1981-82, archeologist, 1982-86; buffalo ranch mgr. Red Canyon Ranch, Thermopolis, Wyo., 1992—; author TOR Books, DAW Books, Warner Books, N.Y.C., 1986—; prin. investigator Wind River Arch. Co., Thermopolis, 1990—. Bd. dirs. U. Press Colo., Boulder. Author: (historical) Sand in the Wind, 1990, This Widowed Land, 1993, Thin Moon and Cold Mist, 1995, (sci. fiction) An Abyss of Light, 1990, Treasure of Light, 1990, Redemption of Light, 1991, (booklet) Cheyenne and the Development of Wyoming, 1981; author (with W. Michael Gear): People of the Wolf, 1990, People of the Fire, 1991, People of the Earth, 1992, People of the River, 1992, People of the Sea, 1993, People of the Lakes, 1994, People of the Lightning, 1995, People of the Silence, 1996, People of the Mist, 1997, People of the Masks, 1998, The Visitant, 1999, The Summoning God, 2000, Dark Inheritance, 2001, Bone Walker, 2001, Raising Abel, 2002, People of the Owl, 2002, People of The Raven, 2003; contbr. articles to various mags. Scholar Am. Bible Study, 1975-76, Calif. State scholar Calif. State U., 1972-76. Mem. Nat. Bison Assn., Am. Assn. Physical Anthropologists, Am. Anthro. Assn., Soc. Hist. Archaeology, We. Writers Am., Sci. Fiction Writers of Am. Avocations: hunting, fishing, reading, camping, hiking. Home and Office: PO Box 1329 Thermopolis WY 82443-1329

GEARY, HILARY R. society editor; d. J. Jeffrey Roche and Sidney B. Wood; m. John W. Geary II, Apr. 28, 1973 (dec. 1995); children: Alfred, John; m. Peter Green, 2000 (div. 2002). Student, Finch Coll. Society editor Quest Mag. Mem.: Southampton Rose Soc. Office: QUEST Media 920 Third Ave 6th Fl New York NY 10022 Office Phone: 646-840-3404 ext. 106. Office Fax: 646-840-3408.*

GEARY, MARIE JOSEPHINE, art association administrator; b. Boston, Dec. 1, 1933; d. Vincent and Maryanne (DeAngelo) Bianco; m. John Francis Geary, Oct. 11, 1959; 1 child, John Francis Jr. Grad., Medford H.S., 1951. Registrar grad./postgrad. div. Tufts U. Sch. Dental Medicine, Boston, 1951-60; reporter, arts editor Chelmsford (Mass.) Newsweekly, 1970-82; owner, mgr. Village Sq. Art Gallery, Chelmsford, 1976-80; founder, owner A Way With Words, Chelmsford, 1980—; founder, dir. Eastcoast Quilters Alliance, Westford, Mass., 1988—. Mktg. cons. Westford Regency Inn, 1991; cons. to arts orgns. for seminar planning, curator exhibits, 1999—. Contbr. articles to profl. mags. Pub. rels. dir. New England Quilt Mus., Lowell, 1986-88; founder, pres. Chelmsford Art Soc., 1970-75; founder, bd. dirs. Chelmsford Cultural Coun., 1980-84; founder, dir. pub. rels. Chelmsford Crafters, Inc., 1976-80; publicity dir. Chelmsford Town 4th of July Celebration, 1971-74; founder Women in Bus. Conf., 1994. Mem. Am. Quilting Soc., Chelmsford Quilters (pres. 1985-89, 99-2003), New Eng. Quilters Guild (Compass editor 1985-88), Chelmsford Book Discussion Soc., Quilters Connection (Quiltations editor 1992-93, v.p. 1994-95, pres. 1995-96), Middlesex Women's Network, Women in Bus. (formed 1993, coord. 1st conf. 1994), Enterprising Women. Republican. Roman Catholic. Avocations: art, antiques, reading, economics, marketing trends. Home: 38 Amble Rd Chelmsford MA 01824-1968 Office: Eastcoast Quilters Alliance PO Box 711 Westford MA 01886-0021 E-mail: eqaquilter@aol.com.

GEBBIE, KATHARINE BLODGETT, physicist; b. Cambridge, Mass., July 4, 1932; BA, Bryn Mawr Coll., 1957; BSc, U. London, 1960, PhD, 1965. Rsch. assoc. astrophysics JILA, U. Colo., 1967-68, lectr. physics and astrophysics, 1974-77; physicist Nat. Bur. Standards, 1968-85, supervisory physicist, 1985-89; dir. physics lab. Nat. Inst. Standards and Tech., 1990—. Adj. prof. astrophys., planetary and atmospheric scis. U. Colo., 1977-90. Fellow Am. Phys. Soc.; mem. AAAS, Internat. Com. Weights and Measures, Sigma Xi. Achievements include rsch. in planetary nebulae, stellar atmospheres; physics of solar atmosphere. Office: Nat Inst Standards & Tech 100 Bureau Dr # Ms8400 Gaithersburg MD 20899-0003

GEBBIE, KRISTINE MOORE, health science educator, health official; b. Sioux City, Iowa, June 26, 1943; d. Thomas Carson and Gladys Irene (Stewart) Moore; m. Lester N. Wright; children: Anna, Sharon, Eric. BSN, St. Olaf Coll., 1965; MSN, UCLA, 1968; DPH, U. Mich., 1995. Project dir. USPHS Tng. Grant, St. Louis, 1972—77; coord. nursing St. Louis U., 1974—76, asst. dir. nursing, 1976—78, clin. prof., 1977—78; adminstr. Oreg. Health Div., Portland, 1978—89; sec. Wash. State Dept. Health, Olympia, 1989—93; coord. Nat. AIDS Policy, Washington, 1993—94; assoc. prof. Sch. Nursing Columbia U., 1994—; assoc. prof. Oreg. Health Scis. U. Portland, 1980—90. Chair secretarial panel on evaluation of epidemiologic rsch. activities U.S. Dept. Energy, 1989—90; mem. Presdl. Commn. on Human Imunodeficiency Virus Epidemic, 1987—88. Author (with Deloughery and Neuman): Consultation and Community Orgn., 1971; author: (with Deloughery) Political Dynamics: Impact on Nurses, 1975; author: (with Scheer) Creative Teaching in Clinical Nursing, 1976. Bd. dirs. Lusth. Family Svcs. Oreg. and S.W. Wash., 1979—84, Oreg. Psychoanalytic Found.1, 1983—87. Recipient Disting. Alumna award, St. Olaf Coll., 1979; scholar Disting. scholar, Am. Nurses Found., 1989. Fellow: Am. Acad. Nursing; mem.: Am. Soc. Pub. Adminstrn. (Adminstrn. award II 1983), N.Am. Nursing Diagnosis Assn. (treas. 1983—84), Inst. Medicine, Am. Pub. Health Assn. (exec. bd.), Assn. State and Territorial Health Ofcls. (pres. 1984—85, exec. com. 1980—87, McCormick award 1988). Office: Columbia U Sch Nursing 630 W 168th St New York NY 10032-3702 Office Phone: 212-305-1794. E-mail: KMG24@columbia.edu.

GEBO, SUSAN CLAIRE, consulting nutritionist; b. Bristol, Conn., June 22, 1954; d. Ernest Edward and Lena Clara (Jullian) G.; m. Joseph Louis Vasile, Oct. 10, 1987. BS, Cornell U., 1976; MPH, U. Mich., 1980. Registered dietitian. Pub. health nutritionist Navajo & Apache County Health Dept., Holbook and St. Johns, Ariz., 1976-77; coord., WIC nutritionist Miss. State Bd. Health, Tupelo, 1977-78; asst. state WIC nutrition coord. Conn. Dept. Health Svcs., Hartford, 1978-79; nutritionist Cmty. Health Svcs., Hartford, 1981-84; pvt. practice West Hartford, Conn., 1983—; faculty, nutritionist U. Conn. Family Medicine Residency Program, Hartford, 1985—; nutritionist Wesleyan U., Student Health Svcs., Middletown, Conn., 1988—. Adj. faculty U. Hartford, West Hartford, 1981-88, So. Conn. State U., New Haven, 1985-2002, Albertus Magnus Coll., 1991-2000, St. Joseph Coll., West Hartford, 1992—, Manchester C.C., 1994—; fellow Nat. Nutrition Consortium, Washington, 1980. Author: What's Left to Eat?, 1992; writer (video) The Diet Interview: A Guide for Paraprofessionals, 1980, featured in video Culinary Hearts Kitchen Course, Am. Heart Assn., 1988, panenelist (PBS-TV spl.) Women's Hearts at Risk, 1996, featured nutrition expert (PBS-TV series) 3 episodes America's Walking, 2003. Bd. dirs. Am. Heart Assn., Hartford, chmn. program com. greater Hartford br., 1989-91; mem. com. State Communications, 1991-94, media spokesperson, 1991— (Outstanding program award 1990, Outstanding HeartGuide Spokeswoman 1990, Time, Feeling, and Focus award, 1992). Mem. AAUP, Am. Pub. Health Assn., Am. Dietetic Assn., Conn. Dietetic Assn. (co-chmn. pub. rels. com. 1991-93, mem. media spokesperson com. 1993-98, Registered Dietitian of Yr., 1994, del. 1996-99). Avocations: walking, photography, gardening. Office: 854 Farmington Ave West Hartford CT 06119-1587 Office Phone: 860-232-5415. E-mail: sgebo1@prodigy.net.

GEDDES, BARBARA SHERYL, communications executive, consultant; b. Poughkeepsie, NY, May 27, 1944; d. Samuel Pierson and Dorothy Charlotte (Graham) Brush; m. James Morrow Geddes, Feb. 24, 1968 (div. Dec. 1980); 1 child, Elisabeth. BA, Skidmore Coll., 1968. Project leader Four-Phase Systems, Cupertino, Calif., 1976—77, Fairchild Co., San Jose, Calif., 1979—80; mgr. tech. publs. Mohawk Data Scis., Los Gatos, Calif., 1977—79; project mgr. Advanced Micro Computers, Santa Clara, Calif., 1980—81; mgr. tech. publs. Sytek Inc., Mountain View, Calif., 1981—83; v.p. comms. sys. Strategic Inc., Cupertino, 1983—86; pres., mng. ptnr. Computer and Telecomms. Profl. Svcs., Mountain View, Calif., 1986—89; v.p. corp. mktg., sec. First Pacific Networks, Sunnyvale, Calif., 1988—94; pres. Auration, Inc., Palo Alto, 1994—; v.p. mktg., corp. sec. Tachyon Semiconductor Corp., San Jose, 1999—. Cons. H-P, Varian, Aydin Energy, Chemelex, also others, 1972—; v.p. Conf. Recorders, Santa Clara, 1975—77; advisor Tele-PC, Morgan Hill, Calif., 1983—88. Editor: Mathematics/Science Library, 7 vols., 1971; contbr. numerous articles to profl. jours. Advisor Los Altos Hills Planning Commn., Calif., 1978—79; mem. Santa Clara County Adoptions Adv. Bd., 1971—73, Las Cumbres Archtl. Control Commn., Los Gatos, 1983. Named N.Y. State Regents merit scholar, 1962. Mem.: Women in Comms. (pres. San Jose 1983—84), Bus. and Profl. Advt. Assn., Nat. Soc. for Performance and Instrn., Assn. for Computing Machinery (editor 1970—72). Democrat. Home: 10072 Senate Way Cupertino CA 95014-5710 Personal E-mail: sherry@netmagic.net.

GEDDES, LANELLE EVELYN, nurse, physiologist; b. Houston, Sept. 15, 1935; d. Carl Otto and Evelyn Bertha (Frank) Nerger; m. Leslie Alexander Geddes, Aug. 3, 1962. BSN, U. Houston, 1957, PhD, 1970. Staff nurse Houston Ind. Sch. Dist., 1957-62; instr. to asst. prof. physiology Baylor U. Coll. Medicine, 1972-75; asst. prof. nursing Tex. Women's U., 1972-75; prof., head Purdue U. Sch. Nursing, Lafayette, Ind., 1975-91. Contbr. chpts. to books, articles to med. jours. Recipient tchg. awards. Mem. Am. Nurses Assn., Am. Assn. Critical-Care Nurses, AAAS, N.Y. Acad. Scis., Phi Kappa Phi, Sigma Theta Tau, Iota Sigma Pi. Lutheran. Office: Purdue Univ West Sch Nursing Lafayette IN 47907

GEDEON, LUCINDA HEYEL, museum director; b. Port Chester, N.Y., Oct. 13, 1947; d. Philip H. and Isabel (Oldham) H.; m. Francis A. Sprout, Feb. 8, 1987. BA, Calif. State U., Long Beach, 1978; MA, UCLA, 1981, PhD, 1990. Asst. curator Grunwald Ctr. UCLA, 1978-81, asst. dir. Grunwald Ctr., 1981-83, acting dir. Grunwald Ctr., 1983-85; chief curator Ariz. State U. Art Museum, Tempe, 1985-91; dir. Neuberger Mus. SUNY, Purchase, 1991—. Author: (exhbn. catalogues) Tamarind: Los Angeles to Albuquerque, 1985, Fiber Concepts, 1989 (book) The Art of Leonard Lehrer, 1986; gen. editor: Melvin Edwards Sculpture: A Thirty Year Retrospective, 1993, Shared Beginnings Separate Passages: A Retrospective of the Work of Carol Anthony and Elaine Anthony, 1996, June Wayne; A Retrospective, 1997, Elizabeth Catlett Sculpture: A Fifty-Year Retrospective, 1998, Marisol, 2001, Toshiko Takaezu, 2001, Grace Hartigan, 2001; contbr. articles to profl. jours. Chairperson Tempe Mcpl. Arts Commn., 1989-90; bd. dirs. Balboa Art Conservation Ctr., San Diego, 1986-91, Arttable, N.Y., 1995-98, Westchester Arts Coun., 1998—. Recipient Individual Arts award Westchester Arts Coun., 2002, Chancellor's award Excellence, SUNY, 2002; Edward A. Dickson History of Art fellow UCLA, 1984, Afro-Am. Studies fellow, 1984. Mem. Am. Assn. Mus., Assn. Art Mus. Dirs. Office: Neuberger Mus Art SUNY at Purchase 735 Anderson Hill Rd Purchase NY 10577-1402 E-mail: lucinda.gedeon@purchase.edu.

GEDO, JULIE, secondary school educator; d. Stephen M. and Donna G. Gedo; 1 child, Nicholas M. BS in Math., No. Ky. U. Educator Sch. Dist. Palm Beach County, West Palm Beach, Fla., The Benjamin Sch., West Palm Beach. Mem.: Palm Beach County Tchrs. Math., Fla. Educators Assn., Phi Theta Kappa. Serbian Orthodox. Avocation: pure breed dog rescue.

GEE, GAIL MARIE, retired medical society executive; b. Berkeley, Calif., Dec. 27, 1926; d. Floyd E. and Mildred J. (Brunty) White; m. Melvin M. Gee, Nov. 25, 1947 (dec. Apr. 1993); children: Douglas Melvin, Cathy Diane Gee Bridges. BA, U. Calif., Berkeley, 1948. Cert. med. staff coord., record technician, healthcare quality profl. Mem. staff secretarial and med. staff svcs. Columbia Way and Sierra Hosps., Sonora, Calif., 1955-76; dir. med. records, med. staff coord. Sierra Hosp., Sonora, 1976-80; coord. med. staff svcs. Sonora (Calif.) Cmty. Hosp., 1980-91, coord. quality assurance, 1983-87; ret., 1991. Exec. sec. Tuolumne County Med. Soc., Sonora, 1978-91. Sec. Tuolumne County Farm Bur., Sonora, 1958-65; pres. Women's Soc. Christian Svc., Sonora Meth. Ch., 1960-61; pres. Alpha Iota chpt. Omega Nu, Sonora, 1971-72. Recipient Cert. of Appreciation, No. San Joaquin Area Health Edn. Ctr., 1984. Mem. AAUW (pres. Sonora Br. 1968-70), Nat. Assn. Med. Staff Svcs., Calif. Assn. Med. Staff Svcs., Delta Zeta Alumnae. Avocations: reading, gardening, duplicate bridge. Home: PO Box 395 Sonora CA 95370-0395

GEE, SHARON LYNN, funeral director, educator; b. Berea, Ohio, Jan. 11, 1963; d. Donald Edward Gee and Janet Lee Floyd. Cert. in mortuary sci., Wayne State U., 1986, BS Psychology, 1987. Mortuary sci. lic. Mich., Nat. Bd. Cert. Funeral Dir. Mgr., funeral dir. Pixley Funeral Home, Keego Harbor, Mich., 1996—; lectr. instr. dept. mortuary sci. Wayne State U., Detroit, 1996—2003, asst. prof. embalming, 2003—. Recipient Residential Beautification award, City of Royal Oak, Mich., 1993. Mem.: West Bloomfield C. of C., Tri City Bus. Assn., Mich. Embalmers Soc. (pres. 2000—), Mich. Funeral Dirs. Assn., Nat. Funeral Dirs. Assn. (pursuit of excellence achievement award 1997—), Optimist Internat., Keego Harbor Chpt. (Keego Harbor chpt.), A-Dock Sailing Club. Avocations: sailing, circa 1910 home renovation and restoration. Office: Pixley Funeral Home Godhardt-Tomlinson Chapel 2904 Orchard Lake Rd Keego Harbor MI 48320 Business E-Mail: ad7158@wayne.edu.

GEER, JERRI DIANE, retired career officer, photographer; b. Kilgore, Tex., Oct. 28, 1946; d. James Hallead and Lois Pearl (Bryant) G. BS, U. Southwestern La., 1969; AA, N. Seattle C.C., 1986; BFA, U. Washington, 1989. Phys. edn. tchr. Orleans Parish Schs., New Orleans, 1969-71, L.A. Unified Sch. Dist., 1971-72; ensign USCG, 1973, advanced through grades to lt., 1979, aide to the admiral, 1975-76, legal counselor, 1978-82, human rels./civil rights officer, 1978-82, sr. watch officer, marine safety officer, 1979-82, ret., 1982. Photographer: (for book) Photographer's Forum, Best of College Photography Annual, 1989; exhibited in group shows U. Washington, No Boundaries N.W. Travel Art Exhibit, 1993-94, 95-96 (Juror's Special Recognition 1993), Arts Commn., City of Sea-Tac, Washington, 1995. Decorated Meritorious Unit Commendation with silver letter and gold star; recipient Gold medal, Nat. Vet. Creative Arts Festival, 2002. Mem. Nat. Mus. Women in Arts (charter mem.), Women in Mil. Svc. Meml. (charter mem.), Photographic Coun. Seattle, Seattle Art Mus., Disabled Am. Vets., USCG Officer's Assn. Democrat. Avocations: travel, camping, writing poetry, drawing, art. Home: 15835 26th Ave NE Shoreline WA 98155-6436

GEER, LOIS MARGARET, music educator; b. Bethlehem, Pa., Mar. 16, 1957; d. Francis Levere Sterner and Doris Valeria Sterner-Young; m. Richard Charles Geer, July 21, 1994. MusB, U. Hartford, 1982. Cert. tchg. CT, 2001. Tchr. music Music, Movement and More, Hartford, Conn., 1982—91; tchr. elem. sch. music Old Saybrook Pub. Schs., Conn., 1992—. Dir. assoc. music Plainville Congl. Ch., Conn., 1991—96; dir. youth music Westbrook Congl. Ch., 1997—2003, dir. bell choir, 1997—2003. Singer weddings, funerals, events. Recipient Tchr. Yr., Kathleen E. Goodwin Sch. Faculty, 1993—94. Mem.: Old Saybrook Edn. Assn. (treas. 2002—03), Am. Guild English Handbell Ringers, Am. Orff Schulwerk Assn., Chorsters' Guild (assoc.), Music Educators' Nat. Conf. (assoc.). Avocations: cooking, walking, travel. Office: Kathleen E Goodwin Elem Sch 80 Old Boston Post Rd Old Saybrook CT 06475

GEERTZ, HILDRED STOREY, anthropology educator; b. N.Y.C., Feb. 12, 1927; d. Walter Rendell and Helen (Anderson) Storey; m. Clifford Geertz, 1948 (div. 1979); children: Erika, Benjamin. BA, Antioch Coll., Yellow Springs, Ohio, 1948; PhD, Radcliffe Coll., 1956. Lectr. U. Chgo., 1963-68; assoc. prof. to prof. anthropology Princeton (N.J.) U., 1970-98, ret., 1998. Chmn. dept. anthropology Princeton U., 1972-77, 86, 88-89. Author: The Javanese Family, 1961, (with Clifford Geertz) Kinship in Bali, 1974, Images of Power: Balinese Paintings Made for Gregory Bateson and Margaret Mead, 1994, The Life of a Balinese Temple: Artistry, Imagination, and History in a Peasant Village, 2004 (with Geertz and Lawrence Rosen) Meaning and Order in Moroccan Society, 1979; editor: State and Society in Bali, 1992.

GEESA, SUSAN LOUISE, special education educator; b. Richmond, Ind., Mar. 2, 1952; d. George Emery and Dorothy Louise Sauer; m. Roy O. Geesa, Dec. 29, 1974; children: Rachel Louise, Jeffrey Roy. BS, Taylor U., 1974; MS, Ind. U., 1975. Spl. educator moderately and mildly handicapped Perry Twp. Schs., Southport, Ind., 1974—85; spl. educator multiply handicapped Hancock-South Madison Joint Svcs., Greenfield, Ind., 1990—, mem. spl. educators adv. coun., 1990—, coach Spl. Olympics, 2002—. Mem. com. playground for disabled population, 2001; chmn. disability awareness programs, 1996—; leader Girl Scouts USA, Granger, Ind., 1988—90, New Palestine, Ind., 1990—2001. Named ARC Educator of Yr., ARC of Handcock County, Greenfield, 1997. Mem.: Assn. Retarded Citizens Hancock County, Coun. for Exceptional Children, Ind. State Tchrs. Assn. Avocations: travel, music, theater, volunteer work. Office: Harris Elem Sch 200 W Park Ave Greenfield IN 46140

GEFFNER, DONNA SUE, speech pathology/audiology services professional, audiologist, educator; d. Louis and Sally (Weiner) Geffner. BA magna cum laude, Bklyn. Coll., 1967; MA, NYU, 1968, PhD (NDEA fellow), 1970; postgrad., Advanced Inst. Analytic Psychology, 1973—75; EdD (hon.), Providence Coll., 2003. Asst. prof. Lehman Coll., 1971-76; assoc. prof. dept. speech St. John's U., 1976-81, prof., 1982—. Dir. Speech and Hearing Ctr., 1976—, chmn. dept. speech comm. scis. and theater, 1983—92, developer M.A. program in speech pathology and audiology and doctoral consortia, 2004, dir. grad. program in speech-lang. pathology and audiology, 1992—; pvt. practice, 1980—; cons. to corp. execs.; TV prodr. and hostess NBC, 1977—78, CBS, 1978—79; active N.Y. State Licensure Bd., 1993—97. Issue editor: Jour. Topics Lang. Disorders, 1980; editor: ASHA monograph, 1987; contbr. articles to profl. jours., chapters to books. Recipient Emmy nomination for outstanding instrnl. program, 1978, award, Pres.'s Com. Employment Handicapped, Disting. Achievement award, N.Y.C. Speech-Lang.-Hearing Assn., 1994, Honors, L.I. Speech-Lang.-Hearing Assn., 1998; grantee, CUNY Rsch. Found., 1972, N.Y. State Dept. Edn., 1976—78. Fellow: Am. Speech, Lang. and Hearing Assn. (legis. councillor 1978—87, 1988—90, 1990—94, ednl. standards bd., v.p. acad. affairs 1995—97, pres.-elect 1998, pres. 1999, past pres. 2000); mem.: Am. Guidance Svc. (mem. bd. advisors), Audiology Study Group N.Y., N.Y. State Speech and Hearing Assn. (pres. 1978—80, honors). Office: St John's U Speech and Hearing Ctr 8000 Utopia Pkwy Jamaica NY 11432-1343 E-mail: geffnerd@StJohns.edu.

GEHLERT, SALLY OYLER, dental hygienist, consultant; b. Cin., Feb. 12, 1949; d. Ralph Thomas and Inez R. (Morgan) Oyler; m. Robert Gehlert; 1 child, Chloe. AS, U. Cin., 1971, M in Ednl. Adminstrn., 1976; BS in Allied Health Edn., U. Ky., 1974. Registered dental hygienist, Ohio. Dental hygienist, Cin., 1971—; dental cons. Proctor & Gamble Corp., Cin., 1985-95, John O. Butler Co., Chgo., 1990—, Cin., 1985—. Adv. bd. John O. Butler Co., Chgo.; cons. in field. Edit. adv. Journal of Dental Hygiene, 1993; author ednl. programs for dental profls. Mem. Am. Dental Hygienist Assn., Ohio Dental Hygienist Assn., Cin. Dental Hygienist Assn. Home: 2476 Walnutview Ct Cincinnati OH 45230-2455 Office Phone: 513-235-0569. E-mail: sallygehlert@fuse.net.

GEHM, DENISE CHARLENE, ballerina, arts administrator; b. Miami, Fla., Dec. 14, 1951; d. Charles William and Verna Mae (Wiley) Gehm; m. Gary Edward MacDougal, June 15, 1992. BA cum laude, NYU, 1994; MA, Columbia U., 1998; studied ballet with, George Milenoff, Thomas Armour. Soloist ballerina Harkness Ballet, N.Y.C., 1970-71, Nat. Ballet Washington, 1971-73; prin. ballerina Chgo. Ballet, 1974, Ballet de Caracas, Venezuela, 1975; featured ballerina Joffrey Ballet, N.Y.C., 1976-91. Appeared in Broadway plays : West Side Story, 1979; Phamtom of the Opera, 1988, with Rudolf Nureyev in : Nijinsky's L'Apres-Midi d'Un Faune, 1979; prin. dancer : Homage to Diaghilev, Broadway and State Theatre N.Y., 1979; featured roles include : Joffrey's Nutcracker; Arpino's Suite St.-Saens; Cranko's Taming of the Shrew; Ashton's Midsummer Night's Dream; Robbin's N.Y. Export Opus Jazz. Bd. dirs. Lincoln Ctr. Inst.; dir. Fund for Dance, 1994. Recipient Founders Day award NYU, 1994, Disting. Alumni award NYU Gallatin Sch., 1998; Harkness House for Ballet Arts scholar, 1969. Episcopalian.

GEHRING, KARIN, real estate broker; b. Mannheim, Germany, Aug. 22, 1957; arrived in U.S., 1990; d. Heinz and Hedwig Dierdorf; children: Mark, Frank. Pre-need mgr. Lauderdale Meml. Pk., Ft. Lauderdale, Fla., 1995—96; real estate sales Port Charlotte, Fla., 1996; prin., owner Gehring Realty Inc., Port Charlotte, 2001—. Office: Gehring Realty Inc 2265 Tamiami Tr E Port Charlotte FL 33952

GEHRING, PATTI J. principal; d. Peter Edward Brunner and Sandra Ann Howdyshell; m. Jeffrey A. Gehring, July 20, 1992; children: Kyle, Lacey, Ryan. AA, Charles County C.C., LaPlata, Md.; BA with honors, St. Mary's Coll. Md., 1992; M in Ednl. Adminstrn. with honors, Trinity Coll., Washington, 2002. Cert. tchr. Md. State Dept. Edn. Tchr. St. Mary's Sch., Bryantown, Md., 1993—2002; prin. Little Flower Sch., Great Mills, Md., 2002—. Mem.: ASCD, Nat. Cath. Edn. Assn. Office: Little Flower Sch Point Lookout Rd Great Mills MD 20634

GEHRIS, TAMAR K. biologist; b. Allentown, Pa., June 21, 1978; d. Phanny and Annie May Nhek; m. Kim L. Gehris, Jr., Oct. 12, 2001; 1 child, Braedan Mikael. BS in Biology, Moravian Coll., Bethlehem, Pa., 2001. Lab asst. Health Network Labs., Allentown, Pa., 1998—2000, sr. lab. asst., 2000—01; biologist in histopathology Merck and Co., Inc., West Point, Pa., 2001—. Coord. chem. spill team and safety Pathology Labs., Merck and Co., Inc., West Point, Pa., 2002—. Recipient Mabel Riker scholarship, Pa. State U., 1997—98. Mem.: Tri-Beta Biol. Honor Soc. Democrat. Avocations: book club member, fishing, painting, crafts, hiking. Office: Merck and Co Inc PO Box WP45-242 Sumneytown Pike West Point PA 19486

GEHRKE, KAREN MARIE, retired accountant; b. Gaylord, Minn., Apr. 12, 1940; d. Stanley Henry and Frieda Marie (Hammel) Ostermann; m. Orville Raymond Gehrke, Oct. 21, 1961 (div. Aug. 1994); children: Kimberly, Karla, Kent. Grad. high sch., Gaylord, 1958. Inspector Fingerhut Mfg., Gaylord, 1959-60; rewinder 3M, Hutchinson, Minn., 1960-61, packer, 1971-72; sec. Boehmke Ins. Agy., Gaylord, 1961-63, Law Office of H.A. Knobel, Gaylord, 1964-68; teller First State Fed. Savs. and Loan, Hutchinson, 1969; sec. Wally's Tire Shop, Hutchinson, 1970, Lyle R. Jensen, CPA, Hutchinson, 1974-84; owner Karen M. Gehrke L.P.A., Hutchinson, 1984—2001; ret., 2001. Mem. Nat. Assn. Female Execs., Nat. Soc. Pub. Accts., Minn. Assn. Pub. Accts., Hutchinson Area C. of C.

GEIBEL, SISTER GRACE ANN, college president; b. Sept. 17, 1937; BA in Piano and Music Edn., Carlow Coll., 1961; MA in Music Edn., U. Rochester, 1967, PhD in Music, 1975. Tchr. elem. and high schs., 1959-67; ch. musician, 1972-80; assoc. prof. and co-chmn. music dept. Carlow Coll., Pitts., 1981-82, acting acad. dean, 1982-83, dean, 1983-88, v.p. acad. affairs, 1984-88, pres., 1988—. Mem. pres.'s coun. Pitts. Coun. on Higher Edn., numerous other ednl. orgns. Bd. dirs. Program for Female Offenders, United Way of Allegheny County, Oakland Cath. H.S., Women's Coll. Coalition, Global Links, Pitts. Opera, Pitts. Pub. Theater; mem. adv. bd. Pitts. Symphony Soc. Mem. Pitts. Athletic Assn., Duquesne Club, Zonta Club. Office: Carlow Coll Office of the President 3333 5th Ave Pittsburgh PA 15213-3109*

GEIER, DENISE B. director; d. Edward C. and Margaret F. Brim; m. Steven Geier, Oct. 22, 1972; children: Jeffrey S., Dennis M. BA, Montclair (N.J.) State, 1970; MA, Georgian Ct., 1992; EdD, Rutgers U., 1997. Cert. tchr. N.J., 1970, student personnel svcs. N.J., 1991, prin. N.J., 1993. Prin. Matawan (N.J.) Pub. Schs., 1995—98, East Windsor (N.J.) Pub. Schs., 1998—2000; dir. of curriculum Middletown (N.J.) Twp. Pub. Schs., 2000—. Adj. prof. Monmouth U., West Long Br., NJ, 1999—2000; presenter in field. Contbr. articles to mags. Book reviewer Ctrl. Jersey Libr. Coop., Neptune, NJ, 1996. Grantee, The Nat. Gallery of Art and Dodge Found., 1995, The Principals Ctr. for the Garden State, 1997, Mary Owen Borden Found., 1998, Fulbright Meml. Tchr. Fund, 2000, Tchr. Institute:Art and Tech. grant, Nat. Gallery of Art, 2002. Home: 22 Pheasant Drive Marlboro NJ 07746 Personal E-mail: dbgeier@hotmail.com.

GEIER, SHARON LEE, special education educator; b. Dayton, Ohio, Nov. 21, 1943; d. Robert Stanley Murphy and Mary Frances (Ross) Briggs; m. Arthur M. Geier, Jan 23, 1965; children: Arthur William, Bradford Robert. BA, Wilmington (Ohio) Coll., 1965; cert. spl. edn., Wright State U., 1976; MS in Edn., U. Dayton, 1995. Cert. elem. tchr., Ohio, edn. handicapped. Tchr. 1st grade Fairborn (Ohio) City Schs., 1965-66, Kettering (Ohio) City Schs., 1967-71, Xenia (Ohio) City Schs., 1975-81, tchr. 3rd grade, 1981-82, tchr. learning disabled, 1982—. Tchr. specifically learning disabled Camp Progress Centerville (Ohio) Schs., summers, 1977, 78; coord. MicroSoc. Program, 1995-2000, 2002-04. Founder, pres. Twig 6 Children's Med. Ctr. Aux., Dayton, 1971-73, chmn. Jr. Aux., 1972-74. Recipient Doer award Miami Valley Regional Ctr. and Dayton Area Citizens for Spl. Edn., 1988; Martha Holden Jennings scholar, 1980-81; named Spl. Educator of Yr., Spl. Edn. dept. Ctrl. State U., 1993. Mem. AAUW, ASCD, Coun. Exceptional Children (Outstanding Chpt. Pres. Ohio Fedn. 1989, pres. Greene County chpt. 1987-89, treas. Ohio divsn. learning disabilities 1989-91, pres. 1991-93, treas. Greene County chpt. 1999—), Ohio Fedn. Coun. for Exceptional Children (liaison S.W. region 1989-94, liaison chmn. 1992-93, 93-94, sec. 1994-97, v.p. 1997-98, pres. elect 1998-99, pres. 1999-2000, past pres. 2000-01, Tchr. of Yr., 2003), Green Key Honor Soc. Republican. Avocations: reading, music, painting, plants, aerobics. Home: 1134 Napa Rdg Centerville OH 45458-6017 E-mail: sgeier89@aol.com.

GEIGER, CAROL LYNN, educational therapist; b. Reading, Pa., Aug. 22, 1956; d. Elden Claude and Peggy Joyce Schwartz; m. Robert William Geiger, Aug. 6, 1977; children: David, Rebecca, Nathan, Joanna. BA in English Edn., Messiah Coll., Grantham, Pa., 1978; MA in Counseling, Ashland (Ohio) U., 1984. Missionary Br. in Christ World Missions, Colombia, 1984—98; tchr. Elcamino Acad., Bogota, Columbia, 1987—97; counselor Hermandad en Cristo, Bogota, Columbia, 1986—97; ednl. therapist Philhaven, Mt. Gretna, Pa., 1998—. Bd. dirs., advisor CEPAS, Bogota, 1995—97. Author: Cominando en el Discipulado, 2001. Recipient Alumni Christian Svc. award, Messiah Coll., 1997. Mem.: Coun. for Exceptional Children. Avocations: reading, writing, walking. Home: 529 Fremont St Lancaster PA 17603 Office Phone: 717-845-2482.

GEILING, LOUISE ELIZABETH, elementary school educator, secondary school educator; b. New Milford, N.J., Aug. 25, 1934; d. Samuel and Susan Lagrotteria; m. Jacob V. Geiling, Apr. 17, 1960 (dec. Apr. 1998); children: Janet Darvin, Lois Nagie. BS, Montclair State U., N.J., 1955; MA, Montclair State U., 1959; postgrad., William Paterson Coll., Monmouth Coll. Cert. tchr. K-8, tchr. 9-12 in social studies, geography, guidance counselor. Tchr. 4th grade Roosevelt Sch., River Edge, NJ, 1955—56; tchr. reading specialist, guidance counselor Bergenfield Jr./Sr. H.S., NJ, 1956—60; tchr. learning disabilities, elem. and mem. child study team River Vale Schs., 1971—81, tchr. gifted and talented, 1981—85, elem. tchr., 1985—94; substitute tchr. grades K-8 Waldwick Bd. Edn. and Allendale Bd. Edn., NJ, 1994—2001. Contbr. poetry to profl. pubs. CCD tchr. Assumption Parish, Emerson, NJ, 1962—64; tchr. CCD St. Elizabeth Parish, Wyckoff, NJ; leader Girl Scouts U.S., Park Ridge, NJ, 1971—73. Recipient A+ Tchr. award, Students of River Vale, 1990. Mem.: AAUW (charter, v.p. 1962—64), Jr. Women's Club (v.p. 1965—67). Roman Catholic. Avocations: piano, bridge, writing, sports. Home: 181 Mabie Ct Mahwah NJ 07430

GEISELHART, LORENE ANNETTA, English language educator; b. Rake, Iowa, June 28, 1929; d. Charles Tobias and Altha May (Mills) Knutson; m. James Willis Geiselhart, June 1, 1947 (div. 1971); children: Nancy Joyce, Larry Paul, Richard Ray, Kathleen Ann. Cert., Luther Coll., 1949; BA, U. No. Iowa, 1965, MA, 1989; postgrad., U. Iowa, 1990—. Pub. sch. tchr., Postville, Iowa, 1947-48; adminstrv. asst. to county supt. schs. Decorah, Iowa, 1948-49; pub. sch. tchr. Galesville and Trempealeau, Wis., 1949-51, Iowa Braille and Sight-Saving Sch., Vinton, 1959-70, South Winneshiek Community Sch., Ossian, Iowa, 1970-94; instr. English to univ. students Nanchong Inst. Edn., Sichuan, China, 1995-96. Student tchr. supr. Luth. Coll., Decorah, 1971-94. Sec. Calmar (Iowa) Improvement Assn., 1987-92; active Calmar Luth. Ch. Coun., 1975-80, 89-91, mem. choir, 1975-80, pres. Ch. Circle, 1975-77, 88-92. Mem. AAUW (pres. 1969-70, 96-2000, sec. 1990-92), NEA, Iowa Reading Coun., Iowa State Edn. Assn., NE Iowa Rosemaling Assn. (sec. 1991-94), Delta Kappa Gamma (pres. Beta Eta chpt. 1978-81, state fellowship com. 1982-84, grantee 1988). Democrat. Avocations: rosemaling, golf, bridge, painting, reading.

GEISELMAN, LUCYANN, college president; m. Robert L. Harrington; 1 child, Gabriella. BA in Religion, MA in Theology, Tex. Christian U.; PhD in Edn., U. Chgo. Former v.p. Eisenhower Med. Ctr., Rancho Mirage, Calif.; v.p. for planning and Advancement Calif. Inst. of Arts, 1989-91; pres. Mt. Vernon Coll., Washington, 1991—. Office: Mt Vernon Coll Office of Pres 2100 Foxhall Rd NW Washington DC 20007-1150

GEISER, ELIZABETH ABLE, publishing company executive; b. Phillipsburg, N.J., Apr. 28, 1925; d. George W. and Margaret I. (Ross) G. AB magna cum laude, Hood Coll., 1947. Promotion mgr. coll. dept. Macmillan Co., N.Y.C., 1947-54; promotion mgr. R.R. Bowker, N.Y.C., 1954-60, sales mgr., 1960-67, dir. mktg., 1967-70, v.p., 1970-73, sr. v.p., 1973-75, sr. v.p., pub. book divsn.; adj. prof., dir. U. Denver Pub. Inst., 1976—; sr. v.p. Gale Rsch. Co., 1976-91, cons., 1991—. Cons. Excerpta Medica, Elsevier, 1976-82; lectr. pub. procedures Radcliffe Coll., 1966-75; lectr. schs. libr. sci. U. Wash., U. So. Calif.; panel mem. TV series Living Library, 1970 Editor: The Business of Book Publishing, 1985; contbr. Manual of Bookselling, 1969. Trustee Hood Coll., 1993-99. Inducted into Publishing Hall of Fame, 1988. Mem. Assn. Am. Pubs. (exec. coun. prof. and scholarly pub. divsn. 1989-91, adv. coun. Frankfurt book fair 1971, sch. and libr. promotion and mktg. com. 1972-76, bd. dirs. 1982-85), ALA (pres. exhibits roundtable 1968-70, bd. dirs. exhibits roundtable 1968). Presbyterian. Home: 3329 E Bayaud Ave Denver CO 80209 Office: Pub Inst 335 E 51st St Apt 5E New York NY 10022-6765 Office Phone: 212-752-8652. E-mail: egeiser@worldnet.att.net.

GEISINGER, JANICE ALLAIN, accountant; b. Iroquois County, Ill., June 21, 1927; d. Carl Oliver and Constance Kathryn (Risser) Irps Allain; m. Robert Bond Geisinger, Oct. 17, 1947 (div. 1976); children: Jacque K., Holly D., Terry Joe. AA, Blackburn U., Carlinville, Ill., 1947. Lab. technician Mich. Health Lab., East Lansing, 1947-48; with Southwestern Bell Telephone, Tulsa, 1948-49; bookkeeper Geisinger Ent., Dallas, 1951-69; salesman Earl Page Real Estate, Irving, Tex., 1969-71; food purchaser Town & Country vending, Dallas, 1971-75; bookkeeper/sec. Belco C & I Wiring Inc., Irving, 1976-85; leasing bookkeeper Copiers Etc., Inc., Dallas, 1985-89; bookkeeper Kennedy Elec. Inc., Mesquite, Tex., 1989; ret., 1990. Cons. Ross Mech., Irving, 1989—; bookkeeper Metroplex Dental Group (now Dr. Julian M. Chong), 1990—, Limpede, Inc., 1999—. Crew leader Census Bur., Dallas, 1990. Mem. Am. Contract Bridge Assn. Avocations: flying, gardening, knitting, rug making. Home: 1216 E Grauwyler Rd Irving TX 75061-5031

GEISLER, KAY, transportation executive; b. Indianapolis, May 24, 1951; d. Willis Manson and Virginia Mae (Altopp) Scobee; m. Donald Adam Geisler, June 26, 1971; 1 child, Melinda Kay Geisler. Co-owner/corp. sec. Geisler Trucking, Inc., Lebanon, Ind., 1980—; city council woman Lebanon, Ind., 1996—. Bd. dirs. Boone Co. Solid Waste, Lebanon, Ind., 1994—, Well Head Protection, Lebanon, 1998; mem. Teen Pregnancy Coun., 1998, Ind. Assn. Cities and Towns, Indianapolis, 1996, Boone Co. Republican Women, 1996, Boone Co. Symphony, 1997. Mem. Nat. League of Cities, Zonta Club of Lebanon (pres. 1994-96), Zonta Internat. (area 4 dir.

1996-98; dist. 6 sec. 1998-2000), Smile-A-While Homemakers Ext. Club (pres. 1992-94), Ulen Country Club, Kappa Kappa Kappa (Alpha Beta chpt.). Avocation: golf. Home: 2302 Golfside Dr Lebanon IN 46052-8175

GEISLER, SHERRY LYNN, magistrate; b. Durango, Colo., Aug. 18, 1956; d. George Walter and Evelyn Ruth (MacLean) Geisler; m. Harvey Lee Slade, June 6, 1981 (div. Aug. 11, 1993); 1 child, Sherry (Rachel) Orona. Grad. H.S., Springerville, Ariz., 1974; student, Northland Pioneer Coll., Springerville, Ariz., 1986-90, Res. Police Acad., 1986. Clk. Round Valley Justice Ct., Springerville, 1981-84, chief clk., 1984-88, office mgr., judge pro tem, 1988-93, justice of the peace, 1993—; city magistrate City of Springerville and Eagar, Ariz., 1993—. Mentor judge Ariz. Supreme Ct., 1994—; edn. chair Ariz. Justice Ct. Assn, 1994-96. Mem. Nat. Judges Assn. (dir. State of Ariz.), Am. Judges Assn., Ariz. Cts. Assn., State of Ariz. Justice of the Peace Assn. (pres. 1995-99). Ariz. Magistrates Assn. Democrat. Avocations: crafts, gardening, travel, scuba diving. Home: PO Box 1202 Springerville AZ 85938-1202 Office: Round Valley Justice Ct PO Box 1356 Springerville AZ 85938-1356

GELB, JUDITH ANNE, lawyer; b. NYC, Apr. 5, 1935; d. Joseph and Sarah (Stein) G.; m. Howard S. Vogel, June 30, 1962; 1 child, Michael S. BA, Bklyn. Coll., 1955; JD, Columbia U., 1958. Bar: N.Y. 1959, U.S. Dist. Ct. (so. and ea. dists.) N.Y. 1960, U.S. Ct. Appeals (2d cir.) 1960, U.S. Ct. Mil. Appeals 1962. Asst. to editor N.Y. Law Jour., N.Y.C., 1958-59; confidential asst. to U.S. atty. ea. dist. N.Y., Bklyn., 1959-61; assoc. Whitman & Ransom, N.Y.C., 1961-70, ptnr., 1971-93, Whitman Breed Abbott & Morgan LLP, N.Y.C., 1993-2000, Winston & Strawn LLP, NYC, 2000—. Mem.: ABA (individual rights sect., real property and trust law sect.), Assn. Bar City N.Y., N.Y. State Dist. Attys. Assn., N.Y. State Bar Assn. (trusts and estates com.), Fed. Bar Coun., Columbia Law Sch. Alumni Assn. (bd. dirs.), Princeteon Club. Home: 169 E 69th St New York NY 10021-5163 Office: Winston & Strawn LLP 200 Park Ave New York NY 10166-0005 Business E-Mail: jgelb@winston.com.

GELBER, DANIELLE ARNA, broadcast executive; d. Morris and June Beverly Claman; m. Stephen Carl Gelber, Oct. 24, 1999; 1 stepchild, Joshua Austin 1 child, Alexandra Dylan ; m. Stephen Carl Gelber (div.). BA, U. Calif., 1976—80; MA, Am. U., Washington, DC, 1980—82. Dir. of TV devel. Spelling TV, Inc., Los Angeles, Calif., 1983—92; sr. v.p. drama series programming Fox Broadcasting Co., Los Angeles, Calif., 1992—2000; v.p. original series programming Showtime Networks, Inc., Los Angeles, Calif., 2001—04, sr. v.p. original series programming, 2004—. Mem. Acad. TV Arts And Sciences, Los Angeles, Calif., 1987—; Am. U. nat. adv. bd. Am. U. Sch. Of Comm., Washington, 2002—. Recipient Multichannel News Wonder Woman Of The Year, 2003. Mem.: Acad. of TV Arts And Sciences. Avocations: guitar, photography, travel. Office: Showtime Networks Inc 10880 Wilshire Blvd Los Angeles CA 90024

GELBERG, LILLIAN, family medicine physician, educator; b. L.A., May 14, 1955; married; 3 children. BA, UCLA, 1977; MD, Harvard U., 1981; MSPH, UCLA, 1987. Diplomate Am. Bd. Family Practice. Robert Wood Johnson Found. clin. scholar UCLA/VA, 1984-86; asst. prof. UCLA, 1987-97, assoc. prof., 1997—, George F. Kneller prof. family medicine, 2001—. Contbr. chpts. to books, articles to profl. jours. Vol., com. chair various family clinics, Venice, Calif., 1984—. Recipient CAFP 1st Rsch. Excellence award, 2001; Robert Wood Johnson Found. scholar UCLA, 1984-86, Robert Wood Johnson faculty scholar, 1995-2001. Fellow Am. Acad. Family Physicians; mem. Soc. Gen. Internal Medicine, Assn. Health Svc. Rsch. (Young Investigator award 1995, Article of the Yr. award 1997), Soc. of Tchrs. of Family Medicine, Am. Pub. Health Assn., Inst. Medicine (elected 2003). E-mail: gelberg@ucla.edu.*

GELFAND, JULIA MAUREEN, librarian; b. Cleve., Sept. 26, 1954; d. Lawrence Emerson and Miriam J. Ifland Gelfand; m. David Bruce Lang, Apr. 30, 1995. AB, Goucher Coll., 1975; MS in Libr. Sci., MA, Case Western Res. U., 1977. Reference libr. Penrose Libr. U. Denver, 1977-81; reference libr., bibiliographer U. Calif., Irvine, 1981-86, applied sci. and engring. libr., 1986—. Adj. faculty Sch. Info. Resources and Libr. Sci., U. Ariz., Tucson, 1998— Editor: (jour.) Grey Lit., 2000; co-editor: (jour.) Libr. Hi-Tech. News, 2001—. Bd. dirs. Orange County chpt. Am. Jewish Com., 1999—. Recipient U.S./UK Fulbright award Fulbright Commn., 1992-93, Literati award for excellence in Grey Lit., MCB Univ. Press, 1999, Literati award for leading elders MCB U. Press, 2003. Mem. ALA, AAAS, Am. Soc. Engring. Edn., Soc. Scholarly Pub., Internat. Fedn. Lib. Assns. (chmn. sci. tech. sect., 2001—). Democrat. Jewish. Office: U Calif Sci Libr Irvine CA 92623-9556 E-mail: jgelfand@uci.edu.

GELLAR, SARAH MICHELLE, actress; b. Apr. 14, 1977; d. Arthur and Roselen Gellar; m. Freddy Prinze Jr., 2002. Appearances include (TV movie) Invasion of Privacy, 1983, (TV series) All My Children (Daytime Emmy award for outstanding younger leading actress in a daytime drama series 1995) 1993-96, Buffy The Vampire Slayer, 1997-2003, (films) I Know What You Did Last Summer, 1997 (Blockbuster Entertainment award for favorite best supporting actress-horror, MTV Movie award for best breakthrough performance), Scream 2, 1997, Beverly Hills Family Robinson, 1997, Cruel Intentions, 1999, Simply Irresistable, 1999, Scooby Doo, 2002, Harvard Man, 2002, Scooby-Doo 2: Monsters Unleashed, 2004, numerous others, also TV comms. Avocations: Tae Kwon Do, kickboxing, gymnastics. Office: ICM 8942 Wilshire Blvd Beverly Hills CA 90211-1934

GELLER, BUNNY ZELDA, poet, author, publisher, sculptor, artist, photographer; b. N.Y.C., May 21, 1926; d. Herman and Shirley (Shoenfeld) Juster; m. Lester Roy Geller; children: Judy Lynn, Robert Douglas, Sheryl Sue, Wayne Mitchell. Student, UCLA, 1944-46, Fla. Internat. U., 1989-97. Invited artist Pegasus Internat. Corp., N.J., 1981-85, Internat. Art Expo., N.Y., 1982-83; invited guest artist Broward County Main Lib., Ft. Lauderdale, Fla., 1988; pres. BZG Enterprises. Author: Bunny Geller Original Poetry, 1995, Destiny, 1995, Choices (poetry), 1996, The Monkey and the Parakeet (A Poetic Tale for Children), 1997, Kaleidoscope (poetry), 1997, Impressions (poetry), 1999, Bunny Geller Original Sculpture, 1985; one woman sculpture shows include Bowery Savings Bank, N.Y.C., 1978, Lynn Kottler Galleries, N.Y.C, 1978, Hollywood (Fla.) Art Mus., 1978-79, Broward County Main Libr., Fla., Hallandale Cultural Ctr., 1996; group exhbns. include All Broward Exhibit 78, Ft. Lauderdale, Fla., 1978, Old Westbury Hebrew Congregation, Westbury, N.Y., 1978, De Ligny Galleries, Ft. Lauderdale, Fla., 1979, 1983-84, Internat. Treas. Fine Art, Plainview, N.Y., 1978, 79, 80, 81, Artists Equity Assn. Hollywood (Fla.) Art Mus., 1979, Limited Edition Galleries, Bal Harbour, Fla., 1979, Temple Beth-El, Boca Raton, Fla., 1979, Expo 79, Pompano, Fla., 1979, Hilda Rindom Galleries, Hallendale, Fla, 1980, Jockey Club Art Gallery, Miami, 1980, 81, 83, 84, Gallery SO-HO 7, Ltd., Great Neck, N.Y., 1979-80, Exhibition of Fine Art Nassau Mus. of Fine Art Assn., 1985, Gallery at Turnberry, Turnberry Isle, Fla., 1980-81, Galleria Martin, Palm Beach, Fla., 1981, Contextual Fine Arts, Ft. Lauderdale, Fla., 1980-81, Art and Culture Ctr. of Hollywood (Fla.), 1981, Miami Convention Ctr., 1981, Anita Gordon Gallery, Inc., North Miami Beach, 1981, Collier Art Internat., Ltd., Westbury, N.Y., 1981, Tavistock Country Club, Haddonfield, N.J., 1982, Internat. Art Expo, N.Y.C., 1982, 83, Ohio All Arabian Show and Buckeye Sweepstakes, Columbus, 1982, West Elec. Co., Hopewell, N.J., 1982, Devon (Pa.) Arabian Horse Show, 1982, Bondstreet Art Gallery, Pitts., 1982, Blumka II Gallery, N.Y.C., 1982, Korby Gallery, Cedar Grove, N.J., 1982, Washington Internat. Horse Show, Gaithersburg, Md., 1982, Pegasus Internat. Corp., Pennington, N.J., 1981, 82, 83, 84, 85, Patricia Judith Art Gallery, Boca Raton, Fla., 1983-84, Panache Gallery, Ft. Lauderdale, Fla., 1983, The Nelson Rockefeller Collection, Inc., N.Y.C., 1983, Shorr Goodwin Gallery, N.Y.C., 1983, Carrier Found. Auxiliary, Belle Meade, N.J., 1983, First Annual Internat. Wildlife Exposition, Atlantic City, N.J., 1983, Amann Gallery, Inc., Palm Beach, Fla., 1984-85, Robert's One-of-a-Kind, Bal Harbour, Fla., 1984, Hallandale (Fla.) Pub. Lib., 1984-85, Galleria Camhi, Bar Harbor Is., Fla., 1984-85, Tatem Galleries, Ft. Lauderdale, Fla., 1984-85, Westbury (N.Y.) Meml. Lib., 1984, Trenton Country Club, 1984, Designers' Showcase 1985 Cacholmara, Glen Cove, N.Y., 1985, UN Conf., Nairobi, 1985, Hallandale Cultural Ctr., Fla., 1998; sculptures on permanent exhibits; featured in (book) Artists/USA, 1979-80, The Am. Album, Nat. Mus. Women Arts permanent collection, Washington, 1985, Art Expo N.Y. catalogue, 1982, 83, 92, Limited Collectors Edition, 1982, Town and Country mag., 1982, Gold Coast Life mag., 1983, Art in America mag., 1983-84, Sunstorm Arts Mag., 1984; represented in permanent collection Kushi Found.; Wrote words, music to song One World, 1989. Pres. Sisterhood Westbury Hebrew Congregation, Westbury, N.Y., 1967-69; judge Fine Art and Craft Show, Ft. Lauderdale, Fla., 1979-81; art adv. coun. Westbury Meml. Libr., 1990-94. Recipient 1st prize Carrier Found. Aux. 2d Ann. Arts Festival, 1983; named to Internat. Poetry Hall Fame, 1996, Merit award, Hallandale Beach, Fla., 2004; inducted into Internat. Libr. Photography, 2002. Mem. Nat. Mus. Women in the Arts (assoc.), Nat. Libr. Poetry (Editor's Choice award 1995, published in Best Poems of the 90s 1996), Internat. Soc. Poets (disting. mem. 1995, Poet of Merit 1995, semi-finalist symposium 1995, inducted into Internat. Poetry Hall of Fame 1996), Nat. Trust for Historic Preservation. Avocations: tennis, all sports, cultural events, national events, art shows. Home: 400 Diplomat Pkwy Apt 711 Hallandale FL 33009

GELLER, DEBRA F. academic administrator, educator; BA cum laude, U. So. Fla., 1986; MBA, Calif. Coast U., 1998; EdD, UCLA, 2004. Cert. salary adminstrn. ACA/World at Work, 1999. Asst. to dir. nursing systems UCLA Med. Ctr., 1992—94; bus. officer campus human resources UCLA, 1994—99, chief adminstrv. officer student and campus life. Instr. L.A. City Coll. Chair, nominating com. Univ. Credit Union, 2001—02. Recipient Witness Program Wall of Fame, UCLA Sch. of Law. Mem.: Soc. Human Resource Mgmt., ACA/World at Work. Office: UCLA Box 951626 Los Angeles CA 90095-1626 E-mail: dgeller@saonet.ucla.edu.

GELLER, ESTHER (BAILEY GELLER), artist; b. Boston, Oct. 26, 1921; d. Harry and Fannie (Geller) G.; m. Harold Shapero, Sept. 21, 1945; 1 child, Hannah. Diploma, Sch. Boston Mus. Fine Arts, 1943. Tchr. Boston Mus. Sch., 1943, Boris Mirski Sch., 1945-49. Art cons. Leonard Morse Hosp., Natick, Mass. One-woman shows at Boris Mirski Art Gallery, Boston, 1945-46, 49, 52, 61, Addison Gallery Am. Art, Children's Art Centre, Andover, Mass., 1953-55, Mayo Gallery, Provincetown, Mass., 1958, Marion (Mass.) Art Centre, 1966, St. Mark's Sch., Southboro, Mass., 1969, Decenter Gallery, Copenhagen, 1969, Regis Coll., Weston, Mass., 1970, Am. Acad. Gallery, Rome, 1971, Newton (Mass.) Libr., 1973, Newton Art Centre, 1978, Artworks of Wayne, Providence, 1979, Stonehill Coll., Easton, Mass., 1986; 2-person show at The Ctr. for Arts in Natick, 2001; exhibited in group shows at San Francisco Mus., Va. Mus. Art, Chgo. Art Inst., Worcester Art Mus., U. Ill., Smith Coll., Inst. Contemporary Art, DeCordova Mus., USIA traveling show, USIS circulating exhbn., Far East, Boston Mus., Regis Coll., 1984, Danforth Mus. Art, 1995, Boston Ctr. for Arts, 1997, Firehouse Artists Show, Natiek, 1998, Univ. Place, Cambridge, 1999, Mass. State House, Boston, 2000, Boston U. Art Gallery, 2002, Visionary Decade Thorne-Sagendorph Art Gallery, Keene, N.H., 2003. Cabot fellow, 1949; Studios Am. Acad. fellow, 1949-50, 70-71, 75; MacDowell Colony-Yaddo fellow, 1945, 67, 69 Mem. Boston Visual Arts Union, Arts Wayland Assn. Home: 9 Russell Cir Natick MA 01760-1223 Studio: 5 Summer St Natick MA 01760-4511

GELLER, ETHELL A. consulting clinical psychologist; b. Linz, Austria, Sept. 26, 1946; came to U.S., 1948; d. Abraham and Orinka (Brown) Avram; m. Ronald D. Geller, June 2, 1968. BA summa cum laude, Hunter Coll., 1970, MA, 1972; PhD, CUNY, 1977. Diplomate in Profl. Psychology Internat. Acad. Behavioral Medicine, Counseling and Psychotherapy. Prof. psychology Hunter Coll., N.Y.C., 1977-79; staff psychologist Albert Ellis Inst. for Psychotherapy, N.Y.C., 1979-89; pvt. practice clin. psychology, N.Y.C., 1980—. Rschr. in field. Contbr. articles to profl. jours. Mem. APA, N.Y. Acad. Scis., Am. Assn. Behavior Therapy, Soc. for Behavioral Medicine, Inst. for Rational Emotive Psychotherapy, Phi Beta Kappa. Avocations: cooking, martial arts, travel, languages, music. Office: 952 5th Ave New York NY 10021-1740

GELLER, JANICE GRACE, nurse; b. Auburn, Ga., Feb. 25, 1938; d. Erby Ralph and Jewell Grace (Maughon) Clack; m. Joseph Jerome Geller, Dec. 23, 1973; 1 child, Elizabeth Joanne. Student, LaGrange Coll., 1955-57; BS in Nursing, Emory U., 1960; MS, Rutgers U., 1962. Nat. cert. group psychotherapist; cert. clin. nurse specialist. Psychiat. staff nurse dept. psychiatry Emory U., Atlanta, 1960; nurse educator Ill. State Psychiat. Inst., Chgo., 1961; clin. specialist in mental retardation nursing Northville, Mich., 1962; faculty Coll. Nursing Rutgers U., Newark, 1962-63, faculty Advanced Program in Psychiat. Nursing, 1964-66; faculty Coll. Nursing U. Mich., Ann Arbor, 1963-64; faculty, Teheran (Iran) Coll. for Women, 1967-69; clin. specialist psychiat. nursing Roosevelt Hosp., N.Y.C., 1969-70; faculty, guest lectr. Columbia U., N.Y.C., 1969-70; supr. Dept. Psychiat. Nursing Mt. Sinai Hosp., N.Y.C., 1970-72; pvt. practice psychotherapy N.Y.C., 1972-77, Ridgewood, N.J., 1977-96. Faculty, curriculum coord. in psychiat. nursing William Alanson White Inst. Psychiatry, Psychoanalysis and Psychology, N.Y.C., 1974-84; mem. U.S. del. of Community and Mental Health Nurses to People's Republic of China, 1983. Contbr. articles to profl. jours.; editorial bd. Perspectives in Psychiat. Care, 1971-74, 78-84; author: (with Anita Marie Werner) Instruments for Study of Nurse-Patient Interaction, 1964. Mem. Bergen County Rep. Com., 1989. Recipient 10th Anniversary award Outstanding Clin. Specialist in psychiat.-mental health nursing in N.J., Soc. Cert. Clin. Specialists, 1982; Fed. Govt. grantee as career tchr. in psychiat. nursing, Rutgers U., 1962-63; cert. psychiat. nurse and clin. specialist, N.J., N.Y. Mem. AAAS, ANA (various certs.), N.C. Nurses Assn., Soc. Cert. Clin. Specialists in Psychiat. Nursing (chmn.), Coun. Specialists in Psychiat./Mental Health Nursing, Am. Group Psychotherapy Assn. (cert. group psychotherapist), Am. Assn. Mental Deficiency, World Fedn. Mental Health, Sigma Theta Tau. Address: 307 Chatterson Dr Raleigh NC 27615-3137 Fax: (919) 518-0495.

GELLMAN, GLORIA GAE SEEBURGER SCHICK, marketing professional; b. La Grange, Ill., Oct. 5, 1947; d. Robert Fred and Gloria Virginia (McQuiston) Seeburger; m. Peter Slate Schick, Sept. 25, 1978 (dec. 1980); 2 children; m. Irwin Frederick Gellman, Sept. 9, 1989; 3 children. BA magna cum laude, Purdue U., 1969; student, Lee Strasberg Actors Studio; postgrad., UCLA, U. Calif.-Irvine. Mem. mktg. staff Seemac, Inc. (formerly R.F. Seeburger Co.); v.p. V.I.P. Properties, Inc., Newport Beach, Calif.; pres. Glamglo Prodns. Host radio show Orange County Art Bytes, Sneak Previews from the Orange County Performing Arts Ctr.; prodr. corp. videos; co-prodr. PBS TV series Bus. Beyond Borders. Profl. actress, singer, artist, writer; TV and radio talk show hostess, Indpls.; performer radio and TV comms.; feature writer arts and entertainment column H mag., The Grand Tour mag.; co-prodr. Fullerton: Then and Now (PBS); exec. prodr. (video) Paris Air Show, 2003, Tibet: Beyond Mystique (PBS). Mem. Orange County Philharm. Soc., bd. dirs. women's com.; mem. Orange County Master Chorale, Orange County Performing Arts Ctr., v.p., treas. Crescendo chpt. OCPAC Ctr. Stars, 1st v.p. membership; bd. dirs. Newport Harbor (Calif.) Art Mus., v.p. membership, mem. acquisition coun.; bd. dirs., mem. founders soc. Opera Pacific, mem. exec. com. bd. dirs.; patron Big Bros./Big Sisters Starlight Found.; mem. Visionaries Newport Harbor Mus., Designing Women of Art Inst. Soc. Calif.; past pres. Opera Pacific Guild Alliance; past pres. Spyglass Hill Philharm. Com.; v.p. Pacific Symphony Orch. League, chair endowment sect., spl. events chair; bd. dirs. Pacific Symphony Orch., v.p. cmty. affairs, vice chair vol. devel.; mem. UCI Found. of U. Calif. Irvine Bd., mem. devel. com., honors com., pub. affairs and advocacy com.; mem. social scis. dean's adv. coun. U. Calif., Irvine; chmn. adv. coun. Cold War Studies Ctr., Chapman U.; chmn. numerous small and large fundraisers; mem. com. Red Cross; mem. Fashionables of Chapman U.; bd. dirs. Sta. KOCE PBS TV; founder UCI Humanities Assocs.; bd. dirs., exec. com., nominating com., 25th annivarsary com., devel. com., vice chmn. vol. devel. Pacific Symphony; pres. Symphony of 100. Recipient Lauds and Laurels award U. Calif., Irvine, 1994, Gellman Courtyard Sculpture honoring contbn. to Sch. of Humanities, U. Calif., Irvine, Most Outstanding Vol. award Pacific Symphony, 2002, Most Outstanding Vol. award Pacific Symphony Orch. League, 2002; nominated Emmy award 2004. Mem. AAUW, AFTRA, SAG, Internat. Platform Assn., Actors Equity, U. Calif.-Irvine Chancellor's Club, U. Calif.-Irvine Humanities Assocs. (founder, pres., bd. dirs.), Mensa, Orange County Mental Health Assn., Seneca Network, Balboa Bay Club, U. Club, Club 39, Islanders, Covergirls, Pacific Symphony Supper Club (founder), Pacific Symphony "Symphony 100" (pres., founder), Alpha Lambda Delta, Delta Rho Kappa. Republican. Home: PO Box 1993 Newport Beach CA 92659-0993

GELOSO-BARONE, ROSALIA A. lawyer; b. Rye, N.Y., Apr. 21, 1962; d. Vincent M. and Patricia (Checca) G. BA in Journalism with honors, Boston Coll., 1984; JD cum laude, Pace U., 1988. Bar: N.Y. 1988, Conn. 1988, U.S. Dist. Ct. (so. and ea. dists.) N.Y. 1988. Project asst. Fin. Acctg. Standards Bd., Stamford, Conn., 1984-85; legal asst. Merrill Lynch Realty, Inc., Stamford, 1985-86, U.S. Attorney's Office, N.Y.C., 1987-88; legal asst./staff atty. Westchester County Attorney's Office, White Plains, N.Y., 1988-92; sr. staff atty. U.S. Dist. Ct. (so. dist.) N.Y., 1995-98; law lectr. bus. dept and legal assistant program Norwalk (Conn.) C.C., 1998—. Adj. prof. bus. law Norwalk C.C., Berkeley Coll., Katherine Gibbs Sch., U. Conn., 1992-95. Alumni admissions counselor Boston Coll., Fairfield County, Conn., 1984—. Recipient Merit Scholarship Pace Law Sch., 1986-88. Mem. ABA, N.Y. State Bar Assn., Conn. Bar Assn.

GELTZER, SHEILA SIMON, public relations executive; b. N.Y.C. d. Sidney E. and Bertie (Rome) Simon; m. Howard E. Geltzer, Sept. 10, 1967; children: Jeremy Niles, Gabriel Lewis. BA, Queens Coll., 1961. With Philip Lesly Co., N.Y.C., 1962-63, Benjamin Co., N.Y.C., 1963-68; ptnr. Simon and Geltzer, Inc., N.Y.C., 1968-74, Ries and Geltzer, N.Y.C., 1974-79; pres. Geltzer and Co., Inc., N.Y.C., 1979—2000; mng. dir., exec. prin. Publicis Dialog, N.Y.C., 2000—. Mem. Pub. Relations Soc. Am. (counselors acad.), Women in Communications, Women in Pub. Relations, Nat. Council of Women. E-mail: sgeltzer@geltzerco.com.

GELZER, LOIS AUGE, foundation administrator; b. Chicago, Oct. 9, 1942; d. William and Fern Bernice (Schwinkendorff) Auge; m. Lawrence Arthur Gelzer, Jr. (dec. Feb. 26, 1999); 1 child, Henry Lawrence. BA, No. Ill. U., 1964; MS in Edn., Shores Acad. Collegia, Miami Shores, Fla., 1982, M in Computer Sci., 1986. Cert. tchr. Ill., Mass., instr. USCG Aux., 1975. Tchr. Mc Henry Pub. Schs., Ill., 1964—65, No. Chicago Cmty. HS, 1965—69, Shores Acad., Miami Shores, Fla., 1980—82; tutor Gelzer Tutoring Svc., Oak Bluffs, Mass., 1983—94; tchr. Office for Job Partnerships, Edgartown, 1986—88, Fisher Jr. Coll., Hyannis, 1987; developer foundation not yet finalized, Oak Bluffs, 1995—2000, Cape Elizabeth, Maine, 2000—. Instr. USCG Aux., Martha's Vineyard, Mass., 1975—78. Contbr. to mags. and books. Communicator USCG Aux. Flotilla 1-1105, Martha's Vineyard, 1974—79; mgr. The Four PMers Net, 1992—95, Secretary-Treasurer, 1988—97; vol. 3 non-partisan polit. campaigns for selectman, Oak Bluffs, 1974—76; vol. tchrs.' aide Oak Bluffs Sch., 1977; Sunday sch. tchr. Trinity Unitd Meth. Ch., Oak Bluffs, 1977—79. Recipient award for five assists in one night, USCG, 1974. Mem.: AAUW, NAFE, No. Ill. U. Alumni Assn. (life). Meth. Avocations: stamp collecting/philately, genealogy, music, cooking, amateur radio. Home: 58 Hunter Pl Cape Elizabeth ME 04107

GEMMELL-AKALIS, BONNI JEAN, psychotherapist; b. Lansing, Mich., Mar. 11, 1950; d. James Stewart Gemmell and Alpha Alice (Hackenberg) Vanden Bosch; m. Gary Alfred Eddy, Jan. 1, 2001; 1 stepchild, Patrick Eddy ; children: Scott Aaron, Ty Alexander, Zachary Alan. BS, Ctrl. Mich. U., 1972, MA, 1974. Ltd. lic. psychologist, Mich.; cert. social worker, Mich. Clin. psychologist, sr. mental health therapist Lincoln Ctr. for Emotionally Disturbed Children & Youth, Lansing, 1974-77; outpatient psychologist Grand Rapids (Mich.) Child Guidance Clinic, 1978-81; pvt. practice Grand Rapids Psychiat. Svcs., 1981-88, 96—, Associated Therapists, Inc., Grand Rapids, 1988-96, pres., 1989-90. Grad. fellow Ctrl. Mich. U., 1972-73. Mem. Mich. Psychoanalytic Coun., Mich. Women Psychologists, Mich. Assn. Profl. Psychologists, Am. Group Psychotherapy Assn. (founder nat. registry 1996), Grand Rapids Area Psychology Assn., Psi Chi. Home: 632 Duxbury Ct SE Grand Rapids MI 49546-9605 Office: 1025 Spaulding Ave SE Ste B Grand Rapids MI 49546-3703 Office Phone: 616-285-9141.

GENARDO, KIM, newscaster; 1 child, Karen Elissa. Grad., Northwestern U. Weekend anchor WGHP, Greensboro, NC; weekend anchor, reporter Evansville, Ind., Clarksburg, W.Va.; anchor NBC 17, Raleigh, NC. With Am. Bus. Women's Assn., Am. Soc., DARE. Avocations: crafts, music. Office: NBC 17 Studios 1205 Front St Raleigh NC 27609

GENDLER, ELLEN, dermatologist; b. Bklyn., Feb. 15, 1956; MD, Columbia U., 1981. Diplomate Am. Bd. Dermatology. Resident in dermatology NYU Med. Ctr., N.Y.C., 1982—85; pvt. practice dermatology N.Y.C., 1985—. Clin. assoc. prof. dept. dermatology NYU Sch. Medicine, N.Y.C., 1990—. Office: 1035 Fifth Ave New York NY 10028

GENDREAU, BERNICE MARIE, retired women's health nurse; b. Danforth, Maine, Oct. 11, 1934; d. Henry Augustus Harding and Leah Orale (Gould) Crossman; m. Scott Andrew Dunn, Oct. 19, 1957 (dec. June 1986); children: Audrey M. Clune, E. Lee Dunn Shirland, Janet L. Dunn Doucette, John E. II; m. Leo Maurice Gendreau, Jan. 25, 1997; stepchildren: Kathy Gallimore, Leo Gendreau II, Gail Googins, Roland Gendreau. Diploma in nursing, Ea. Maine Med. Ctr., Bangor, 1975. RN, Maine. Psychiat. aide to LPN, RN State of Maine, Bangor, 1953-76; aide, charge aide, charge LPN, med. nurse to supr. ob/gyn Ea. Maine Med. Ctr., 1976-95, ret., 1995. Vol. March of Dimes; organist, pianist, choir dir., Sunday Sch. tchr., Faith Bible Ch., Olarnon, Maine, 1957-82. Democrat. Baptist. Avocations: needlework, reading, continuing education.

GENDRON, MICHÈLE MARGUERITE MADELEINE, librarian; b. Paris, Mar. 15, 1947; came to U.S., 1950; d. Gerard Joachim and Denise Marie Louise (Le Morvan) G. BA, Orlinda Pierce Coll. for Women, Athens, Greece, 1969; MS, U. Ill., 1971. Libr. Free Libr. Phila., 1971-75, head, Kingsessing Br., 1975-76, head, Ramonita G. de Rodriguez Br., 1976-91, curator spl. collections ctrl. children's dept., 1991-92, head, lit. dept., 1992—. Cons. devel. Hist. Children's Lit. Collection Montgomery County-Norristown (Pa.) Pub. Libr., 1993-94; organizing mem. Pa. Libr. Assn.'s 1st Conf. Svcs. to Youth, Harrisburg, Pa., 1987-89, Women's Network's 1st Conf. on P.R. Woman in Phila., 1981. Author: (bibliographies) Booklist, 1983; contbr. bibliographies Destination World, 1979, Stories to Share, 1985. Trustee Legal Svcs. Fund Dist. Coun. 47 of Am. Fedn. State, County and Mcpl. Employees, 1985-95, mem. exec. bd. Local 2186, 1996—. Recipient Charles Scribner award Scribner Pub., 1976, Nat. Security Forum, Air War Coll., 1985. Mem. ALA (Assn. Libr. Svcs. Children, Mildred Batchelder award selection com. 1979-81, 85-87, internat. rels. com. 1981-85, chair 1984-85, libr. instrn. round table 1991-93), Pub. Libr. Assn. (mktg. to pub. librs. 1991—, svcs. to multicultural populations 1991, sec. exec. com. mktg. pub. libr. svcs. sect. 1995-96), Alliance Francaise de Phila., Franklin Inn Club, Beta Phi Mu. Roman Catholic. Office: Free Libr of Phila Lit Dept 1901 Vine St Philadelphia PA 19103-1116

GENDRON, SUSAN ANN, commissioner, educator; b. Tewksbury, Mass. m. Mark Gendron; children: Stacey, Matthew. BS in Elem. and Secondary Edn., MS in Ednl. Adminstrn., U. So. Maine, Gorham. From tchr. to supt. Scarborough Pub. Schs., Maine; supt. Windham Sch. Dist., 1997—2003; commr. of edn. State of Maine, Augusta, 2003—. Mem.: Maine Sch. Supts Assn. (Disting. Educator award 2001, Supt. of Yr. award 2002). Office: Commr of Edn State House Sta #23 Augusta ME 04333 E-mail: susan.gendron@maine.gov.

GENESI, SUSAN PETROVICH, school system administrator; b. Philipsburg, Pa., Mar. 24, 1957; d. Richard and Margaret (Ohs) Petrovich; 1 child, Lindsay Margaret. BS in Elem. Edn., Pa. State U., 1981, cert. ednl. adminstrn., 1998, MA in Edn. Adminstrn., 1999; PA Superintend Ency Letter of Eligibility, 2002. Cert. elem. tchr., Pa.; cert. kindergarten tchr., Pa.; cert. instrnl. tech. specialist; cert. grant specialist. Adminstr. Philipsburg-Osceola Area Sch. Dist., Pa., 1981—, prin., 1998. Commr. Pa. Profl. Stds. and Practices Commn., Harrisburg, Pa., 1995—; mem. content validation panel for early adolescence English Nat. Bd. for Profl. Tchg. Stds., Atlanta, 1997; workshop presenter on topics of coop. learning; presenter Keystone State Reading Assn., Hershey, Pa., 1995, 96; coop. tchr. Pa. State U., State College, 1994—; mem. various coms. throughout the sch. dist. Contbr. articles to profl. jours. Mem. Philipsburg Bicentennial Com., 1996-97; organizer Philipsburg Elem. Philipsburg Days, 1994. Mem. ASCD, NEA, Pa. State Edn. Assn., Philipsburg-Oceola Area Edn. Assn. (com. 1981—), Phi Delta Kappa. Republican. Presbyterian. Avocations: traveling and shopping with daughter, computer technology, exploring new trends in education and technology, relaxing at the beach. Office: North Lincoln Elem Sch/ Wallaceton Boggs Elem Sch 200 Short St Philipsburg PA 16866-2640 E-mail: sxg23@psu.edu.

GENÉT, BARBARA ANN, accountant, travel counselor; b. N.Y.C., Oct. 14, 1935; d. Arthur Samuel and Louise Margaret (Scheider) G. Profl. cert. in acctg., U. Calif., La Jolla, 1995, student, 1996—; BS of Acctg., U. Phoenix, 2001; MBA, Keller Grad. Sch. Mgmt., 2003. Asst. to chmn. bd., asst. v.p. pub. rels. Brink's Inc., Chgo., 1976-78; co-owner, pres. Ask Mr. Foster, Chgo., 1982-90; with Profl. Cmty. Mgmt., Laguna Hills, Calif., 1990-92; travel counselor E.J. Brown & Assocs., San Diego, 1992-94; tchr.'s asst. U. Calif-San Diego, La Jolla, 1996—. Rep. Becker CPA-CMA Rev., San Diego, 1995— Becker scholar, 1995, scholar Marks CPA Rev., 1996. Mem. Am. Soc. Woman Accts., Inst. Mgmt. Accts., Inst. Cert. Travel Agts., Order Ea. Star, Ladies of Shrine N.Am., Zonta Internat. of La Jolla (treas. 1998-2000). E-mail: barbaragenet@cox.net.

GENETT-SCHRADER, ANN G. public relations executive; b. Glendale, Calif., Apr. 22, 1945; d. James Charles Genett, Gladys Miller Genett; m. John Charles Schrader. BA cum laude, U. Houston, 1967. Tchr. English, journalism Coll. of Bahamas, Nassau, The Bahamas, 1976—79; publs. editor Am. Airlines, Inc., Ft. Worth, 1979—90; corr. supr. Mary Kay Cosmetics, Dallas, 1997—2000; mgr. mktg. commn. Carter BloodCare, Bedford, 2000—02; media rels. mgr. Carter & Burgess, Inc., Ft. Worth, 2002— Comm. cons., Bedford, 1994—97. Author: Careers: Women in Aviation, 1975. HEB leadership class of 2001 Hurst/Euless/Bedford C. of C., Bedford, 2001—01; mem. Bedford Beautification Commn., 2001; tutor, mentor Adopt-a-School, 2001. Named Best Airline Newspaper, Airline Editors Forum of the Air Transport Assn, 1981, 1982. Mem.: Soc. Profl. Journalists, Pub. Rels. Soc. Am. (treas. 2003). Avocations: marathons, gardening, travel, photography. Office: Carter & Burgess Inc 777 Main St Fort Worth TX 76012 Business E-Mail: Genett-SchraderAG@c-b.com.

GENGOR, VIRGINIA ANDERSON, financial planning executive, educator; b. Lyons, N.Y., May 2, 1927; d. Axel Jennings and Marie Margaret (Mack) Anderson; m. Peter Gengor, Mar. 2, 1952 (dec.); children: Peter Randall, Daniel Neal, Susan Leigh. AB, Wheaton Coll., 1949; MA, U. No. Colo., 1975, MA, 1977. Cert. fin. planner Coll. Fin. Planning. Chief hosp. intake svc. County of San Diego, 1966-77; chief Kearny Mesa Dist. Office, 1977-79, Dept. Children of Ct., 1979-81, chief child protection svcs., 1981-82; registered rep. Am. Pacific Securities, San Diego, 1982-85; registered tax preparer State of Calif., 1982—; registered rep. (prin.) Sentra Securities, 1985—; assoc. Pollock & Assocs., San Diego, 1985—86; pres. Gengor Fin. Advisors, 1986—. Cons. instr. Nat. Ctr. for Fin. Edn., San Diego, 1986-88; instr. San Diego Community Coll., 1985-88. Mem. allocations panel United Way, San Diego, 1976-79; children's cir. Child Abuse Prevention Found., 1989—; chmn. com. Child Abuse Coord. Coun., San Diego, 1979-83; pres. Friends of Casa de la Esperanza, San Diego, 1980-85, bd. dirs., 1980—; 1st v.p. The Big Sis. League, San Diego, 1985-86, pres., 1987-89. Mem. NAFE, AAUW (bd. dirs.), Fin. Planning Assn., Inland Soc. Tax Cons., Nat. Assn. Securities Dealers (registered prin.), Nat. Ctr. Fin. Edn., Am. Bus. Women's Assn., Navy League, Freedoms Found. of Valley Forge, Internat. Platform Assn. Presbyterian. Avocations: community service, travel, reading. Home: 6462 Spear St San Diego CA 92120-2929 Office: Gengor Fin Advisors 4950 Waring Rd Ste 7 San Diego CA 92120-2700 E-mail: vgengor@cox.net.

GENIA, VICKY, psychologist; b. N.Y.C., June 6, 1950; d. Vincent and Victoria (Bondzio) Auletta; m. Howard D. Genia Jr., Feb. 26, 1971 (div. Nov. 1984); 1 child, Howard D. III; m. Billy G. Witt, Jan. 11, 1985. BA in Math., Buffalo State Coll., 1971; MA in Psychology, U. No. Colo., 1981, D of Counseling Psychology, 1989. Lic. psychologist Md., Washington. Psychologist Ctr. Psychol. and Learning Svcs. Am. U., Washington, 1990—. Adj. prof. dept. psychology Am. U., 1995-96. Author: Counseling and Psychotherapy of Religious Clients, 1995; contbr. articles to profl. jours. With U.S. Army, 1974-76. Mem. Am. Psychol. Assn., Soc. Scientific Study Religion, Religious Rsch. Assn. Home: 1945 1/2 Calvert St NW Washington DC 20009-1501 Office: Am U 4400 Massachusetts Ave NW Washington DC 20016-8003

GENIS, ALICE SINGER, psychologist; b. Vilnius, Lithuania, June 8, 1926; d. Nahum Signer and Miriam Singer (Smith) Galerkin; widowed; children: naomi Genis-Mazin, Robert Genis. Esq., Ludwig Maximillian U., Munich, 1950; BA, Pace U., 1974; MA, Mercy Coll., Dobbs Ferry, N.Y., 1978, Coll. of New Rochelle, 1983. Cert. sch. psychologist. Lab. tech. Queens Gen. Hosp., N.Y.C., 1952-55; with Daycare Ctr. Presbyn. Ch., Peekskill, N.Y., 1972-73; psychologist Mental Health Clinic, Peekskill, 1978-80; asst. sch. psychology Pines Bridge Sch., Yorktown, N.Y., 1980-82; biofeedback therapist Med. Cmty. Ctr., Cortland, N.Y., 1985-94; sch. psychologist BOCES, Yorktown, N.Y., 1983-85. Presenter in field. Contbr. articles to profl. jours. Vol. Hosp. Aux., Peekskill, 1962-98; com. Heart Fund Ball, Westchester, 1970s, 80s; pres. Norchester Hadassam, Peekskill, 1983-85, 88-91; mem. The Field Libr., Peekskill. Named Woman of Merit, Westchester Hadassh, White Plaines, N.Y., 1996; recipient New Life award Israel Bonds, Peekskill, 1979, Presl. awards Norchester Hadassah, 1985, 91. Mem. Nat. Assn. Sch. Psychologists, Biofeedback and Psychophysiology Performing Ctr. for the Arts. Avocations: music, piano, swimming, gardening, travel. Home: 1 Birchwood Ln Cortlandt Manor NY 10567-6709

GENN, NANCY, artist; b. San Francisco; d. Morley P. and Ruth W. Thompson; m. Vernon Chathburton Genn; children: Cynthia, Sarah, Peter. Student, San Francisco Art Inst., U. Calif., Berkeley. Lectr. on art and papermaking Am. Ctrs. in Osaka, Japan, Nagoya, Japan, Kyoto, Japan, 1979-80; guest lectr. various univs. and art mus. in U.S., 1975—; vis. artist Am. Acad. in Rome, 1989, 94, 2001. One woman shows of sculpture, paintings include, De Young Mus., San Francisco, 1955, 63, Gumps Gallery, San Francisco, 1955, 57, 59, San Francisco Mus. Art, 1961, U. Calif., Santa Cruz, 1966-68, Richmond (Calif.) Art Center, 1970, Oakland (Calif.) Mus., 1971, Linda/Farris Gallery, Seattle, 1974, 76, 78, 81, Los Angeles Inst. Contemporary Art, 1976, Susan Caldwell Gallery, N.Y.C., 1976, 77, 79, 81, Nina Freudenheim Gallery, Buffalo, 1977, 81, Annely Juda Fine Art, London, 1978, Inoue Gallery, Tokyo, 1980, Toni Birckhead Gallery, Cin., 1982, Kala Inst. Gallery, Berkeley, Calif., 1983, Ivory/Kimpton Gallery, San Francisco, 1984, 86, Eve Mannes Gallery, Atlanta, 1985, Richard Iri Gallery, L.A., 1990, Harcourts Modern and Contemporary Art, San Francisco, 1991, 93, 96, Am. Assn. Advancement of Sci., Washington, 1994, Anne Reed Gallery, Ketchum, Id., 1995, Michael Petronko Gallery, N.Y., 1997, Mills Coll. Art Mus., Oakland, Calif., 1999, Takada Gallery, San Francisco, 1999, 2000, 2003, Ulivi Gallery, Prato, Italy, 2002, Fresno Art Mus., Calif., 2003, Bolinas Mus., Calif., 2003; group exhbns. include San Francisco Mus. Art, 1971, Aldrich Mus., Ridgefield, Conn., 1972-73, Santa Barbara (Calif.) Mus., 1974, 75, Oakland (Calif.) Mus. Art, 1975, Susan Caldwell, Inc., N.Y.C., 1974, 75, Mus. Modern Art, N.Y.C., 1976, traveling exhbn. Arts Coun. Gt. Britain, 1983-84, Inst. Contemporary Arts, Boston, 1977, J.J.Brookings Gallery, San Francisco, 1997, Portland (Oreg.) Art Mus., 1997—, Takada Gallery, San Francisco, 1999, 2000; represented in permanent collections Mus. Modern Art, N.Y.C., Albright-Knox Art Gallery, Buffalo, Libr. of Congress, Washington, Nat. Mus. for Am. Art, Washington, L.A. County Mus. Art, Art Mus. U. Calif., Berkeley, McCrory Corp., N.Y.C., Mus. Art, Auckland, N.Z., Aldrich Mus., Ridgefield, Conn., (collection) Bklyn. Mus., (collection) U. Tex., El Paso, Internat. Ctr. Aesthetic Rsch., Torino, Italy, Cin. Art Mus., San Francisco Mus. Modern Art, Oakland Art Mus., L.A. County Mus., City of San Francisco Hall of Justice, Harris Bank, Chgo., Chase Manhattan Bank, N.Y.C., Modern Art Gallery of Ascoli Piceno, Italy, Mills Coll. Art Mus., Oakland, Calif., Mills Coll. of Art, Oakland, Calif., Leighton Gallery, Blue Hill, Maine, various mfg. cos., also numerous pvt. collections; commd. works include, Bronze lectern and 5 bronze sculptures for chancel table, 1st Unitarian Ch., Berkeley, Calif., 1961, 64, bronze fountain, Cowell Coll., U. Calif., Santa Cruz, bronze menorah, Temple Beth Am, Los Altos Hills, Calif., 1981, 17, murals and 2 bronze fountain sculptures, Sterling Vineyards, Calistoga, Calif., 1972, 73, fountain sculpture, Expo 1974, Spokane, Wash; vis. artist Am. Acad., Rome, 1989. U.S./Japan Creative Arts fellow, 1978-79; recipient Ellen Branston award, 1952; Phelan award De Young Mus., 1963; honor award HUD, 1968 Home: 1515 La Loma Ave Berkeley CA 94708-2033

GENOVA, DIANE MELISANO, lawyer; b. Aug. 8, 1948; d. Joseph Louis and Ines (Fiumana) Melisano; m. Joseph Steven Genova, Jan. 15, 1983; children: Anthony Robert, Matthew Edward. AB, Barnard Coll., 1970; postgrad., Harvard U., 1970-71; JD, Columbia U., 1975. Assoc. Milbank, Tweed, Hadley & McCloy, N.Y.C., 1975 80; v.p., asst. resident counsel Morgan Guaranty Trust Co. N.Y., N.Y.C., 1981-90, mng. dir., assoc. gen. counsel, 1990-2000, J.P. Morgan Chase & Co., N.Y.C., 2001—03; co-gen. counsel Investment Bank, 2003—. Harlan Fiske Stone scholar, 1972-75. Mem. Assn. of Bar of City of N.Y., N.Y. State Bar Assn., Internat. Swaps and Derivatives Assn. (bd. dirs. 1999). Roman Catholic. Office: J P Morgan Chase & Co 270 Park Ave New York NY 10022 E-mail: genova_diane@jpmorgan.com.

GENSHAFT, JUDY LYNN, psychologist, educator; b. Canton, Ohio, Jan. 7, 1948; d. Arthur I. and Leona (Caghan) G. BA, U. Wis., 1969; MA, Kent State U., 1973, PhD, 1975. Lic. psychologist, Ohio; sch. psychologist Canton (Ohio) City Schs., 1972-75; asst. prof. Ohio State U., 1976-81, assoc. prof., asst. chmn., 1981-85, prof., 1985—92, asst. chair, 1985-86, chair, 1987—92, presdl. intern, acting assoc. provost, 1986-87; dean Sch. Edn. SUNY, Albany, 1992-95, interim v.p. for acad. affairs, 1995-97, provost, v.p. acad. affairs, 1997-2000; pres. U. So. Fla., Tampa, 2000—. Psychiat. social worker Canton Mental Health Clinic, 1970-72; vis. prof. U. British Columbia, Vancouver, Can., 1976-81. Contbr. numerous articles and book chpts. to profl. publ. Mem. Ballet Met., Columbus, 1986; cons. League Against Child Abuse, Columbus, 1978—, Bur. Vocat. Edn., Columbus, 1980—; mem. adv. bd. Support for Talented Students, Columbus, 1985—; bd dirs. H. Lee Moffitt Cancer Ctr. and Rsch. Inst., Fla. High-Tech Corridor, Greater Tampa Bay C. of C., Tampa Bay Partnership, Coun. of 100 (chair-designate). Nat. Rsch. grantee, 1984-85; recipient Kathryn Schoen Endowment award, 1986, Huelsman award, 1988, Hon. award Ohio Dept. Edn., 1984, Disting. Affirmative Action award, 1991, Leadership award Nat. Sch. Devel. Coun., Shirley A. Ryals award, Prevent Blindness, 2003. Mem. Am. Psychol. Assn., Nat. Assn. Sch. Psychologist, (sec. 1983-85, Presl. award 1982, 85, 87), Am. Assn. Counseling and Devel., Internat. Assn. Sch. Psychologists, Ohio Sch. Psychologist Assn. (ethics chmn. 1985-86), Sigma Xi. Avocations: sports, reading. Office: U So Fla Pres Office 4202 E Fowler Ave Tampa FL 33620-8000*

GENTILCORE, EILEEN MARIE BELSITO, elementary school principal; b. Glen Cove, N.Y. d. Samuel Francis and Nellie Theresa (McKenna) Belsito; m. James Matthew Gentilcore, Aug. 4, 1951; children: Kevin, John, Scott. BS in Edn., SUNY, Potsdam; MS in Edn., Hofstra U., 1968, profl. diploma, 1976, EdD, 1979. Tchr., first grade Sea Cliff, N.Y., 1951-52; founder, pre-K Germany Officers Sch., Munich, 1952-53; tchr., first grade Peekskill (N.Y.) Schs., 1953-54; tchr., second grade Syosset, N.Y., 1954-55, reading cons., 1970-84, head tchr., 1974-84, prin., 1985-96; ret., 1996. Bicentennial adv. bd. Syosset Community, 1976; adv. bd. mem. Telicare, Uniondale, N.Y., 1978-80; cons. in field. Author: Developmental Learning, 1979. Organizer med. team to Honduras, 1998; mem. Nassau County Graffiti Task Force, 1994—. N.Y. State PTA fellow, 1971, 72, 73, Hofstra fellow, 1971; recipient Jenkins award N.Y. State PTA, 1968, Hon. Life, 1976, Pius X award Rockville Ctr. Diocese, 1985, Disting. Svc. award, N.Y. State PTA Dist., 1996, Teddy Roosevelt Achievement award, 1999, Award for outstanding svc. Rotary Internat., 1999, Abe Gordon Rotary Internat. V.P. Outstanding Svc. award, 2000, R.I. Internat. Achievment award, 2000. Citation for meritorious svc., R.I. Internat. Found., 2002, Rotary Internat. Svc. Above Self award, 2003, Zone 32 Disting. Past Dist. Gov. award, Barcelona, Spain, 2002; named Woman of Distinction, N.Y. State Senate, 1998, Woman of Distinction, Syosset-Woodbury Rep. Club and Senator Carl Marcellino, 1999; grantee Karla Project, 1998; honoree Gift of Life Inc., 1999, Internat. Task Force for Children at Risk, Rotary Internat. Literary Task Force Coord. Zone 32, 2003-04, Queens Coun. Boy Scouts Am., 2003. Mem.: Syosset Prins. (pres. 1992), Rotary (pres. Syosset-Woodbury 1993—95, gov. aide 1995, Gift of Life pres. 1996—97, vocat. dir. dist. 7250 1996—97, med. mission to Honduras 1997, 1st woman dist. gov. dist. 7250 1998—99, Children at Risk Task Force 2000—, conf. chair Zone 32 2000—, coord. RI literacy task force zone 32 2003—, chair RI centennial com. dist 7250 2003—, med. mission to Russia 1995 dist. 7250, coord. Internat. Children at Risk task force, v.p., coord. Internat. Avoidable Blindness task force 2002—, launched Operation Mitch, Honduras, N.Y. State Senate Woman of Distinction 1998, Internat. Achievement award 1999, Meritorious Svc. citation 2002, Disting. Past Dist. Coord. citation 2002, Internat. Global award 2002, Paul Harris fellow, Svc. Above Self award 2003), Kappa Delta Pi, Alpha Sigma Omicron. Roman Catholic. Avocations: swimming, writing, reading, gardening. Fax: 516-921-0206.

GENTILE, CAROLINE D. adult education educator; b. Presque Isle, Maine, Jan. 24, 1924; d. Gerado and Donata G. BS, Boston U., 1946; MA, NYU, 1952; postgrad., U. Wis., Columbia; LHD, U. Maine, Presque Isle, 1996. Instr. Aroostook State Normal Sch., Presque Isle, Maine, 1946-52; asst. prof. Aroostook State Tchrs. Coll., Presque Isle, 1952-58, assoc. prof., 1958-69, Aroostook State Coll. of the U. Maine, Presque Isle, 1969-71, U. Maine, Presque Isle, 1971—. Cons., editor: History of the Presque Isle Recreation Program. Organizer, founder Presque Isle Ice Skating Program; dir. ARC; mem. Presque Isle Parks and Recreation Bd.; bd. dirs. Opportunity Tng. Sch., chair bd. Mem. AAUP, AAUW, Maine Bus. and Profl. Women (pres. 1990-91), Delta Kappa Gamma (pres. 1986-88). Avocations: dance, sports, gardening, reading. Home: 13 Dudley St Presque Isle ME 04769-2423 Office: U Maine 181 Main St Presque Isle ME 04769-2844

GENTILE, GLENNA LEE, psychologist, educator; b. Chippewa Falls, Wis., July 20, 1945; d. Henry J. Carmical and Donna Mae Henneman Carmical; m. Richard John Gentile, Feb. 5, 1972; children: Joseph, Todd, Jennifer. BS in Applied Psychology cum laude, Bemedji State U., 1990; MA in Human Devel., St. Mary's U., Winona, Minn., 1994; postgrad., U. Wis., Superior, 1994—96. Lic. marriage and family therapist. Therapist Range Mental Health, Hibbing, Minn., 1982—2000, Range Regional Health Svc., Hibbing, 2000—. Adj. instr. Arrowhead U., Bemedji, Minn., 1998—2000; instr. psychology Hibbing C.C., 2002—. Exchange student host parent, 1995—96; elder 1st Presbyn. Ch., 1988—91, trustee, 2003—. Mem.: Minn. Assn. Marriage Family Therapy (approved supr. 1998—), Am. Assn. Marriage Family Therapy, Take Stock (v.p. 1998—). Avocations: quilting, travel, genealogy. Home: 2016 9th Ave E Hibbing MN 55746

GENTILE, LIZ, state representative; b. Detroit, Jan. 2, 1958; m. Zachary Gentile; children: Christie, Patrick. Acct. mgr. KGWC-TV, Casper, Wis., 1999—2000, KTWO-TV, Casper, 2000—; state rep. dist. 36 Wyo. Ho. of Reps., Cheyenne, 2002—. Candidate Wyo. Ho. of Reps., 2000. Democrat. Office: State Capitol Cheyenne WY 82002

GENTILE, MARY O'CONNOR, principal; b. Worcester, Mass. d. John D. and Evelyn A. O'Connor; m. Francis V. Gentile, July 8, 1972; children: Richard, Mary, Christopher, Evelyn. BA, Chestnut Hill Coll., 1966; MA, Boston Coll., 1968; MEd in Reading, Northeastern Coll., 1972; MEd, Villanova U., 1977; EdD, Widener U., 2002. Cert. educator, Pa., Mass. Reading specialist Dedham (Mass.) Sch. Dist., 1967-70, Franklin (Mass.) Sch. Dist., 1970-72; supr. curriculum and instrn. Bensalem (Pa.) Sch. Dist., 1972—99, prin., 1999—. Mem. AAUW (bd. mem. 1973-79), Order Sons of Italy in Am. (Montemuro Lodge); mem. Internat. Reading Assn. (bd. mem. Bucks County coun. 1991—), Bucks County Fed. Program Coords. (chair 1992-99). Office: Bensalem Sch Dist 3000 Donallen Dr Bensalem PA 19020-1829

GENTRY, ALBERTA ELIZABETH, elementary school educator; b. Richter, Kans., Feb. 10, 1925; d. John Charles and Dessie Lorena (Duvall) Briles; m. Kenneth Neil Gentry, June 1, 1947; children: Michal Neil, Alan Dale, Elisa Ann. BE, Emporia (Kans.) Tchrs. Coll., 1975. Cert. tchr., Kans. Tchr. Chippewa Rural Sch., Ottawa, Kans., 1943-44; prin., tchr. Pomona (Kans.) Grade Sch., 1944-47, tchr., 1960 61, Silverlake Rural Sch., Pomona, 1947-48, Hawkins Rural Sch., Ottawa, 1948-49, Davy Rural Sch., Ottawa, 1950-53, Eugene Field Sch., Ottawa, 1953-54, Centropolis Grade Sch., Ottawa, 1964, Appanoose Elem. Sch., Pomona, 1964-90, ret., 1990. Trainer student tchr., 1985-86. Author: Proven Ideas for Classroom Teachers, 1988. Project leader, supporter 4-H, Franklin County, Kans., 1963-67; den mother Boy Scouts Am., Ottawa, 1955-66; dir. Bible sch., tchr. Trinity Meth. Ch., Ottawa, 1955-70, supt., 1955-66, mem. choir, 1947—. Named to Kans. Tchrs. Hall of Fame, 1991. Mem. NEA, Kans. Tchrs. Assn., Kans. Edn. Assn., Alpha Delta Kappa (sec. 1988-90). Republican. Methodist. Avocations: bird watching, arts and crafts, family genealogy, flower gardening, music. Home: PO Box 2 Pomona KS 66076-0002

GENTRY, MARGARET BURTON, retired elementary school teacher; b. Iva, SC, Oct. 19, 1939; d. Emory Goss and Olivia (Copeland) Burton; m. Aubrey Lee Gentry, July 5, 1981 (dec. Apr. 1991). AA, Anderson (S.C.) Coll., 1962; BS, East Tenn. U., 1964; Cert. Grad. Study, U. Ga., 1969-72; postgrad., Clemson U., 1969-72. Cert. tchr., Ga.; cert. poll mgr., 2002. Salesperson Browns Five and Ten Store, Iva, 1958-61; adminstrv. asst. SC Hwy. Dept., Anderson, 1962; spl. asst. to prof. govt. and history East Tenn. State U., Johnson City, 1962-64; tchr. grade 4 DeKalb County, Decatur, Ga., 1964-71; adminstrv. asst. Poinsettia Heat and Treat Co., Anderson, 1965; tchr. grade 4 Elbert County, Elberton, Ga., 1971-99; ret., 1999. Researcher for pictorial history of Iva Reviva Civic and Cmty. Devel., 1998-99; pres. Willing Workers Class, Iva, 1998—; del. Saluda Bapt. Assn., Iva, 1999—; cert. nat. poll mgr. for presdl. and local elections, 2000-. Work scholar Anderson Coll., 1960-62; named. Girls Aux. Queen Union Bapt. Ch., Iva, 1955. Mem. NEA, Ga. Assn. Edn. (rep. plant facility 1979-80, Gift/Letter of Appreciation 1999, cert. poll mgr. 2002), Ga. Retired Tchr., SC Retired Tchr., Elbert County Assn. Edn., Anderson County Ret. Educators Assn., Tartan Cross Soc. Republican. Baptist. Avocations: travel, sewing, genealogy, music, gardening. Home: 311 W Jackson St PO Box 474 Iva SC 29655-0474

GEO-KARIS, ADELINE JAY, state legislator; b. Tegeas, Greece, Mar. 29, 1918; Student, Northwestern U.; LLB, DePaul U. Bar: Ill. Founder Adeline J. Geo-Karis and Assocs., Zion, Ill.; former mcpl., legis. atty. Mundelein, Ill., Vernon Hills, Ill., Libertyville Twp., Ill., Twp. Long Grove (Ill.) Sch. Dist. Justice of peace; former asst. state's atty.; mem. Ill. Ho. of Reps., 1973-79; mem. Ill. Senate, 1979—, asst. majority leader, 1992—; former mayor City of Zion, Ill. Served to lt. comdr. USNR. Res. ret. Recipient Americanism medal DAR; named Woman of Yr. Daughters of Penelope, Outstanding Legislator Ill. Fedn. Ind. Colls. and Univs., 1975-78, Legis. award Ill. Assn. Park Dists., 1976; Sponsor Guilty but Mentally Ill law. Greek Orthodox. Office: Ill State Senate State Capitol Springfield IL 62706-0001

GEOPFERT, KELLI RENEE, rehabilitation services professional; b. Oklahoma City, Okla., May 6, 1961; d. Donald H. Henry and Gwendolyn Jenoah Swafford; 1 child, Noah Riley. AA, Rose State, 1981; BS, U. Ctrl. Okla., 1984, MS, 1985. Tchr. Ranchwood Sch., Moore, Okla., 1987—89; jewelry designer Embellishments, Newcastle, Okla., 1989—94; unit coord. Hillcrest Health Ctr., Oklahoma City, 1994—2002; unit coord., case mgr. Pinnacle Rehab. Physician's Hosp., Oklahoma City, 2002—. Author (poetry): Mind in Motion, 1987, Authors Unknown, 1987. Mem.: Am. Cancer Soc., Am. Wildlife Fedn., Alpha Chi. Democrat. Avocations: reading, music, writing. Office: Physicians Hosp Pinnacle Rehab 3100 SW 89th Oklahoma City OK 73159*

GEORGE, CATHY L. music educator; d. Ruth Paup George and Lynn George; 1 child, Winter Raine Willoughby. BA, Calif. State U., Fresno, 1987; MA, So. Oreg. U., Ashland, 2002. Cert. music tchr. Calif., 1987. Dir. of bands Denair (Calif.) Unified Sch. Dist., 1992—; adj. instr. Merced (Calif.) Coll., 1997—2003. Freelance percussionist. Bd. mem. Modesto Youth Symphony, Modesto, Calif., 2003; music educator Modesto Youth Orch., Modesto, Calif. Recipient subject of article, Sch. Band and Orch. Mag., 2003. Mem.: Stanislaus County Music Educators Assn. (pres. 2002—), Calif. Band Directors Assn. (assoc.). Democrat. Office: Denair Unified Sch Dist 3460 Lester Rd Denair CA 95316

GEORGE, CHRISTINE, mental health services professional, supervisor, writer; d. Raymond Asfar and MaryAnn Asfar-Unis; m. Steve W. George. BA, U. Pitts., Johnstown, 1991—96. LPN, Pa., 1989. Adj. instr. Cambria County CC, Johnstown, Pa., 1997—98; pub. rels. dir. So. Alleghanies Mus. of Art, Loretto, Pa., 1999; caseworker Cambria County Mental Health Unit, Johnstown, Pa., 2000—03, caseworker supr., 2003—; waiver unit Cambria County Area Agy. on Aging, Johnstown, Pa. Contbr. non fiction short story Babajim (cash, 1996); author (humanities scholar): (short story) Goin' to California (cash, 1996). Tchr.; past supt. Recipient Humanites Prose Writing award, U. of Pitts. - Johnstown, 1996; grantee Grad. Assistantship, Ind. U. of Pa, 1997, Humanities Divsn. scholar, U. of Pitts. - Johnstown, 1996. Avocations: soccer, nutrition, reading, travel, education. Office: Cambria County Area Agency on Aging 110 Franklin St Ste 400 Johnstown PA 15901

GEORGE, GAY, lawyer; b. Hollywood, Calif., Mar. 3, 1955; d. Wallace Erby and Audrey Eva Elizabeth George; m. David Scott Bohle, Oct. 26, 1979. BS, Calif. Poly. U., 1977; MBA, U. Wyo., 1993, JD, 2001. Bar: Wyo. 2001. Peace Corps vol. U.S. Govt., Apia, Western Samoa, 1979—80; quality assurance mgr. Arnott's Biscuits, Auckland, New Zealand, 1981—88; R&D mgr. ETA Foods Ltd., Auckland, 1988—90; tech. writer G&G Enterprises, Laramie, Wyo., 1991—98; law clk. to Hon. Barton R. Voigt Wyo. Supreme Ct., Cheyenne, 2001—03; corp. counsel Blue Cross Blue Shield Wyo., Cheyenne, 2003—. Contbr. chapters to books. Avocations: reading, films, theater, camping, backpacking.

GEORGE, JEAN CRAIGHEAD, author, illustrator; b. Washington, July 2, 1919; d. Frank Cooper and Carolyn (Johnson) Craighead; m. John L. George, Jan. 28, 1944 (div. Jan. 1964); children: Twig George Pittenger, John Craighead, Thomas Lothar. BA, Pa. State U., 1941. Reporter Washington Post, 1943-44; artist Pageant mag., 1945; reporter United Features, 1945-46; roving editor Reader's Digest, 1966-80; continuing edn. tchr. Chappaqua, N.Y., 1960-68. Author, illustrator: My Side of the Mountain, 1959, Summer of the Falcon, 1962, Gull Number 737, 1964, The Thirteen Moons, 1967-69, Coyote in Manhattan, 1968, River Rats, Inc., 1968, Who Really Killed Cock Robin, 1972, Julie of the Wolves, 1972, American Walk Book, 1978, Cry of the Crow, 1980, Journey Inward, 1982, The Talking Earth, 1983, One Day in the Alpine Tundra, 1984, How to Talk to Your Animals, 1985, One Day in the Prairie, 1986, Water Sky, 1987, (mus.) One Day in the Woods, 1988, The Shark Beneath the Reef, 1989, On the Far Side of the Mountain, 1990, One Day in the Tropical Rain Forest, 1990, The Missing 'Gator of Gumbo Limbo, 1992, The Fire Bug Connection, 1993, The First Thanksgiving, 1993, Dear Rebecca, Winter Is Here, 1993, Animals Who Have Won Our Hearts, 1994, Julie, 1994, To Climb a Waterfall, 1995, Acorn Pancakes & Dandelion Salad, 1995, There's an Owl in the Shower, 1995, Everglades, 1995, The Case of the Missing Cutthroat Trout, 1996, The Tarantula in My Purse, 1996, Look to the North, A Wolf Pup Diary, 1997, Julie's Wolf Pack, 1997, Arctic Son, 1997, Rhino Romp, 1998, Giraffe Trouble, 1998, Dear Katie, the Volcano Is a Girl, 1998, Survival Filmstrips, 1984, (film) My Side of the Mountain, 1965, Nature Filmstrips, 1978-80, One Day in the Woods Musical for Children (music by Chris Kubie), 1997, Elephant Walk, 1998, Gorilla Gang, 1999, Morning, Noon and Night, 1999, Frightful's Mountain, 1999, Snow Bear, 1999, How to Talk to Your Dog, 2000, How to Talk to Your Cat, 2000, Nutik, the Wolf Pup, 2001, Nutik & Amaoq Play Ball, 2001, Tree Castle Island, 2002, Cliff Hanger, 2002, Frightful's Daughter, 2002, Fire Storm, 2003, Charlie's Raven, 2004, Snowboard Twist, 2004, (play) Julie of the Wolves, 2004. Recipient Aurianne award, 1957, Newbery Honor Book award, 1961, medal, 1973, Hans Christian Andersen Honor List award, 1964, Pa. State Woman of Yr. award, 1968, World Book award, 1971, Kerlan award, 1982, U. So. Miss. award, 1986, Washington Irving award, 1991, 92, Knickerbocker award, 1991, Washington Post Children's Book Guild award, 1998, Empire State award, 1998, runner-up Lamplighter award, 2002, Regina medal Cath. Libr. Assn., Literary Lights award for children's lifetime work Boston Pub. Libr., 2003, Ludington award Am. Paperback Assn., 2004. Address: 20 William St Chappaqua NY 10514-3114

GEORGE, JOYCE JACKSON, lawyer, judge emeritus; b. Akron, Ohio, May 4, 1936; d. Ray and Verna (Popadich) Jackson; children: Michael Eliot, Michelle René. BA, U. Akron, 1962, JD, 1966; postgrad., Nat. Jud. Coll., Reno, 1976, NYU, 1983; LLM, U. Va., 1986. Bar: Ohio 1966, U.S. Dist. Ct. (no. dist.) Ohio 1966, U.S. Ct. Appeals (6th cir.) 1968, U.S. Supreme Ct. 1968. Tchr. Akron Bd. Edn., 1962-66; asst. dir. law City of Akron, 1966-69, pub. utilities advisor, 1969-70, asst. dir. law, 1970-73; pvt. practice Akron, 1973-76; referee Akron Mcpl. Ct., 1975, judge, 1976-83, 9th dist. Ct. Appeals, Akron, 1983-89, Peninsula, Ohio, 1989; U.S. atty. No. Dist., Ohio, 1989-93; v.p. adminstrn. Telxon Corp., Akron, 1993-96; pres. Ind. Bus. Info. Svcs., Inc., Akron, 1996—. Tchr., lectr. Ohio Jud. Coll., Nat. Jud. Coll.; cons. in field. Author: Judicial Opinion Writing Handbook, 1981, 3d edit., 1993, 4th edit., 1998, Referee's Report Writing Handbook, 1992; contbr. articles to profl. publs. Recipient Outstanding Woman of Yr. award Akron Bus. and Profl. Women's Club, 1982; Alumni Honor award U. Akron, 1983, Alumni award U. Akron Sch. Law, 1991; Dept. Treasury award, 1992; named Woman of Yr. in politics and govt. Summit County, Ohio, 1983. Mem.: ABA, Akron Bar Assn., Ohio Bar Assn. Fax: 330-668-2910.

GEORGE, JULIANNE MARY, music educator, conductor; b. Martinez, Calif., July 16, 1964; d. Robert Joseph and Marjorie C. George. BA, U. of the Pacific, Stockton, Calif., 1987. Tchr. instrumental music Sequoia Mid. Sch., Pleasant Hill, Calif., 1993—, chair dept., 2001. Mem.: NEA, Calif. Tchrs. Assn., Music Educators Nat. Conf., Am. String Tchrs. Assn., Nat. Assn. String Educators, Interant. Assn. Jazz Educators, Calif. Music Educators Assn. Avocations: tennis, birdwatching. Home: 1025 Merrithew Drive Martinez CA 94553 Office: Sequoia Middle School 265 Boyd Road Pleasant Hill CA 94523 Office Phone: 925-934-8174. Office Fax: (925) 946-9063.

GEORGE, JULIE BERNY, physician, epidemiologist; b. Nigeria, Feb. 12, 1953; arrived in U.S., 1976; d. George Akabogu and Marie-Therese Nzeribe; m. Joshua George, Feb. 14, 1976 (div. Dec. 1978); 1 child, Michael Ifeanyi ; m. Richard R. Land, Aug. 12, 1998. MD, Med. Coll. Va., 1984; MPH, UCLA, 1987; MOH, Harvard Sch. Pub. Health, 1994. Diplomate Am. Bd. Family Practice, Am. Bd. Preventive Medicine. Med. practitioner Advantage Care/Prairie Med. Group, L.A., 1988-90; med. epidemiologist Ctrs. for Disease Control, Atlanta, 1990-92; HIV/AIDS surveillance WHO, Brazzaville, Congo, 1992-93; sr. physician Exxon Chem. Co., Houston, 1996—2001; sr. assoc. cons. Mayo Clinic, Rochester, Minn., 2001—03; asst. prof. preventive med. Mayo Med. Sch., Rochester, Minn., 2003—; public health officer Kern County Dept. Public Health Preparedness, 2004—. Lt. comdr. USPHS, 1990—92. Fellow: Am. Bd. Preventive Med., Am. Acad. Family Practice. Roman Catholic. Avocations: classical music, jazz, theater, foreign travel, reading. E-mail: juliebag@hotmail.com.

GEORGE, KATIE, lawyer; b. Chillicothe, Ohio, Sept. 4, 1953; d. Harry Paul and Tina Lillian George; m. Nov. 25, 1972 (div. Nov. 1983); 1 child, Alison; m. Timothy John Nusser, June 30, 1985. BBA, U. Toledo, 1983, JD, 1986, MBA, 1989. Bar: Ohio 1987, U.S. Dist. Ct. (no. dist.) Ohio 1993, Fla. 1994. Law clk. Allotta, Singer & Farley, Co., LPA, Toledo, 1985-86; mgmt. specialist Dept. Pub. Utilities City of Toledo, 1987-91, acting commr. Dept. Health, 1992-93, acting mgr. Dept. Pub. Safety, 1991-94; pvt. practice Toledo, 1987-96, Pensacola, Fla., 1996—; asst. dist. legal counsel State of Fla., 1996-97, chief legal counsel, 1997—. Part-time instr. U. Toledo, 1987-88, U. West Fla., 1997. Bd. dirs. Toledo BlockWatch, 1993, Ohio Pub. Employers Labor Rels. Assn., 1991-92; mem. Missing and Exploited Children Comprehensive Action Program, 1997-99. Mem. Fla. Bar Assn., Escambia Santa Rosa Bar Assn. Avocations: gardening, photography, scuba diving. Office: 160 Governmental Ctr Ste 601 Pensacola FL 32502-5734

GEORGE, KRISTI KAY, music educator; b. Kearney, Nebr., Feb. 22, 1955; d. Amos George and Genevieve Eloise (Bosle) Wietjes; m. Richard Dean George, June 30, 1984; children: Britta Rose, Tyler Christian. BA in Music Edn., Kearney State Coll., 1977, MA in Music Edn., 1982. Tchr. music Minatare Pub. Sch., Nebr., 1977—78, Bladen Pub. Sch., 1978—79, Elwood Pub. Sch., 1979—81, Poudre Sch. Dist., Ft. Collins, Colo., 1982—90, Loomis Pub. Sch., Nebr., 1990—96, Southeast Nebr. Consolidated Sch., Stella, 1996—98, Coulee-Hartliner Sch. Dist., Couler Cuty, Wash., 1998—2003. Dir. choir, bell choir, childrens choir Trinity Luth. Ch., Lexington, Nebr., 1990—99, dir. choir Auburn, 1996—98. Mem.: NEA, Coulee-Hartline Edn. Assn. (sec. 1997—98). Avocations: boating, hiking. Home: 419 N 3d Coulee City WA 99115

GEORGE, LINDA SHUMAKER, freelance/self-employed writer; b. Lenoir, N.C., Sept. 24, 1949; d. Thomas Craig and Mary Poole Shumaker; m. Richard George, Feb. 14, 1986; 1 child, Alexander Thomas Oscar. BA, NYU, 1971; MA, Harvard U., 1975, PhD, 1980. V.p. internat. divsn. Mfrs. Hanover Trust Co., N.Y.C., 1981-87; adj. asst. prof. dept. history Drew U., Madison, N.J., 1989-91; vis. scholar Hagop Kevorkian Ctr. for Near Ea. Studies NYU, 1992-93; lectr. in Mid. Ea. langs. and civilizations Columbia U., N.Y.C., 1992-94; freelance writer, 1992—. Author: The Golden Age of Islam, 1998, Letters from the Homefront: World War I, 2001, Around the World in 800, 2002; editor: Far Brook Bull., 1995—2001. Charles McConn scholar NYU, 1967-68; fellow Ctr. for Arabic Study Abroad, Cairo, 1973-74; Radcliffe grantee for grad. women Harvard U., 1980, summer seminar for coll. tchrs. grantee NEH, 1991. Mem. The Authors Guild, Am. Rsch. Ctr. in Egypt (fellow 1977-78), Mid. East Studies Assn., Soc. Children's Book Writers and Illustrators. Avocations: opera, ice hockey.

GEORGE, MARGARET Y. retired educator; b. Pitts., Oct. 14, 1926; d. Alfred Clyde and Elizabeth Beatty Young; m. Robert Shortreed, Nov. 1947; children: Rebecca, Laurie, Andrea; m. Charles Hilles George, Jan. 20, 1960; 1 child, Jessica. BS, U. Pitts., 1957, MA, 1959, PhD, 1964. Author: The Warped Vision, 1966, A Study of Mary Wollstone Craft, 1970, Women in Early Capitals of England, 1988. Grantee, Woodrow Wilson Found., 1956—61, Carnegie Mellon Found., 1961—62. Home: 25 The Strand New Castle DE 19720

GEORGE, MILDRED M. retired sentencing advocate; b. Erie, Pa., Apr. 6, 1925; d. John Alexander and Hannah Clare (Mowrey) McKinnon; m. Edward Michael George, Apr. 24, 1949 (dec. Feb. 1993); children: Edward M. Jr., David, Sarah, John (dec.), Hannah. AS, Palm Beach Jr. Coll., 1974; BA, Fla. Atlantic U., 1985. Cert. in mental health tech. Aide Fla. Parole Commn., Delray Beach, 1974-76, Dept. Offender Rehab., Delray Beach, 1976-78; probation supr. Dept. Corrections, Delray Beach, 1978-85; program dir. divsn. comprehensive alternatives Office of Pub. Defender, West Palm Beach, Fla., 1985—2001, ret., 2001. Cons. Sentencing project, Washington, 1993; advisor Legal Case Mgmt. project, Tallahassee, 1994-97; pres., bd. dirs. PRIDE, Inc., West Palm Beach, 1995—. Bd. dirs. Urban League, West Palm Beach, 1985-95 (Appreciation award, 1990, Svc. award, 1996), Wayside House; pres. bd. dirs. Emergency Med. Assistance; active Am. Civil Liberties Union, 1986— (Freedom award, 1995), Freedom of Choice, Inc., Palm Beach County, 1990-98, Fla. Women's Consortium, 1990—; mem. polit. action com. Planned Parenthood, South Palm Beach County, Fla.; v.p. NOW. With USN, 1945—47. Recipient Davis Productivity award Fla. TaxWatch, 1991, Svc. to Indigents award PRIDE, 1992, Women in Leadership award Public Svc. Sector Exec. Women of the Palm Beaches, 1993, Appreciation award Comprehensive Alcohol Rehab. program, 1994, Pioneer award, 1995, Butterfly award Wayside House, 1994, Cert. of Appreciation The Sentencing Project, 1996, Women of Distinction award Soroptimist Internat., 1997, Urban Beacon of Light award, 1997. Mem. NOW (Susan B. Anthony award, 1996), Mental Health Assn., Nat. Assn. Sentencing Advocates (bd. dirs.), Human Svcs. Coalition of Palm Beach County, Partnership for Drug Free Cmty. (chair), Palm Beach Assn. Criminal Defense Lawyers (certificate of Recognition, 1996), Fortune Soc.(life), Nat. Legal Aid and Defender Assn. Home: 86 Macfarlane Dr Delray Beach FL 33483-6959 E-mail: mimgeorge86@cs.com.

GEORGE, SARAH B. museum director; Dir. Utah Mus. of Natural History, Salt Lake City. Office: Utah Mus Natural History U Utah 1390 E Pres Cir Salt Lake City UT 84112

GEORGES, MARA STACY, lawyer; b. Sept. 2, 1963; JD, Loyola U., 1988; BA, U. Notre Dame, 1985. Ptnr. Rock, Fusco, Reynolds, Crowe & Garvey, 1995-97; 1st asst. corporation counsel City of Chgo., 1997-99, corporation cousel, 1999—.

GEORGOPOULOS, MARIA, architect, artist, inventor; b. Moussata, Cefalonia, Greece, Apr. 2, 1949; came to U.S., 1973; d. Vassilios and Joulia Georgopoulos; 1 child, Demetrios. BArch, Nat. Poly. Sch. Greece, Athens, 1972; MS, Columbia U., 1976. Registered architect, N.Y., Greece. Project mgr. Architects Design Group, N.Y.C., 1976—79, Griswold, Heckel & Kelly, N.Y.C., 1979—80; project dir. Lehman Bros., Kuhn Loeb Inc., N.Y.C., 1980—85; v.p. L.F. Rothschild Inc., N.Y.C., 1985—89; corp. art collection archivist, dir. facilities mgmt. The Dreyfus Corp., N.Y.C., 1989—. Mem. AIA, Greek Inst. Architects, Douglaston (N.Y.) Club. Home: 14 Melrose Ln Douglaston NY 11363-1221 Office: The Dreyfus Corp 200 Park Ave New York NY 10166-0099

GEORGULAS, SUSAN BETH, sales and marketing executive; b. Balt., Oct. 13, 1960; d. Peter Paul Georgulas and Nancy Margaret Law. BA in English, U. Md., 1982. Various positions including sales rep., field mktg. mgr. E & J Gallo Winery, Balt., 1984-87; from region mgt. to nat. accounts mgr. Heublein Inc./IDV, Seattle, 1987-97; dir. sales and mktg. Skyway Luggage Co., Seattle, 1997—. Mem. Seattle Jr. League. Republican. Roman Catholic. Avocations: skiing, gardening, hiking, travel. Office: Skyway Luggage Co 10 Wall St Seattle WA 98121-1320

GEPFORD, BARBARA BEEBE, retired nutrition educator; b. Buffalo, N.Y., Sept. 2, 1930; d. Kenneth Hildreth and Martha Bell (Griswold) Beebe; m. William George Gepford, Dec. 28, 1952; children: David, Scott, Joanna, Andrea. BS in Home Econs. Edn., Iowa State U., 1952. Nutrition instr. Sidon Girl's Sch., Lebanon, 1953-56; instr. textiles and clothing Beirut Univ. Coll., Lebanon, 1955-56, 62-63; nutrition cons. Hong Kong Coun. of Social Svcs., 1967-71; commd. fraternal worker Presbyn. U.S.A., Lebanon, Hong Kong, 1953-71; mgr. Lila's Fabric Store, Cambridge, Ohio, 1973-74. Overseas missionary advisor to Assembly Coun. of Presbyn. Ch., U.S.A., 1971-72. Elder Presbyn. Ch., New Concord, Ohio, 1974-79, mem. com. on Ministry, Detroit, 1987-94; pres. Presbyn. Women of Littlefield Ch., 1987-89; vice-moderator Presbyn. Women of Presbytery of Detroit, 1985-87, moderator, 1997-99; synod of covenant women's rep. Churchwide Coordinating Team of Presbyn. Women, 1999-2002; chair Presbyn. Women Triann. Global Exch. to Africa, 2002-03; advisor YWCA Head Start Program, Dearborn, Mich., 1988-91; bd. dirs. YWCA, 1985-96, pres., 1993-95. Named Ohio Mother of the Yr., Am. Mothers Com., New Concord, 1978. Mem., AAUW (bd. dirs. 87-89, internat. rels. area rep.). Democrat. Avocations: reading, gardening, sewing, knitting. Home: 9421 Westwind Dr Livonia MI 48150-4530 E-mail: barbbgepford@msn.com., wiamfrd@msn.com.

GERACE, DEBORAH COBB, music educator; b. Covington, Ky., Feb. 7, 1948; d. Willis B. and Florence Christophel Cobb; m. Michael E. Gerace, Aug. 1, 1970. B.Mus.Edn., Ea. Ky. U., 1970. Cert. tchr. Ga. Music tchr. Decatur County Schs., Greensburg, Ind., 1970—72, Brookville City Schs., Ind., 1973—74; mgr. Malibu Apts., College Park, Ga., 1976—78; choral dir. Fulton County Schs., College Park, 1978—83; and chorus tchr. Archdiocese of Atlanta, 1984—97; tchr. music, handbells, band The Walker Sch., Marietta, Ga., 1997—. Musical dir. Southside Theatre Guild, Fairburn, Ga., 1977—78; audio describer Very Spl. Arts, Atlanta, 1995—; singer, booking agt. Vintage Vocals, Kennesaw, Ga., 1990—. Musical work/album, Southern, Sacred and Celtic, 1997, musical work, For the Guys, 2001, The Prayer Whisperer, 2000. Vol. Employer Support for Guard and Res., Atlanta, 1996—; vol., cultural olympiad Centennial Olympics, Atlanta, 1996. Recipient Appreciation award, The Mighty 8th Air Force, 1998, Employer Support for Guard and Res., 1994, Make a Difference Day award, Points of Light Found., 1998, Golden Rule award, J.C. Penney/United Way, 1995, Svc. award, USO, 1994, Appreciation award, 50th Ann. V-E Ceremony, 1995; grantee Summer sabbatical grantee, The Walker Sch., 2000. Mem.: Music Educators Nat. Conf., Am. Guild of English Handbell Ringers, Ga. Music Educators Assn. Republican. Episcopalian. Avocations: singing, kayaking, piano, guitar, dogs. Office: The Walker Sch 700 Cobb Pkwy N Marietta GA E-mail: mgturnip@mindspring.com.

GERACI, MARIA CATHERINE, mental health nurse practitioner, educator; b. New Orleans, Jan. 31, 1972; d. Dominick Giovanna Geraci and Jananne Catherine Muller; 1 child, Micah Isabella. BSN, La. State U., 1997; MS in Nursing, U. South Ala., 2003. RN 1997. Nurse Denver Health Med. Ctr., 1997—; nursing supr. Milestone Staffing, 2003—. Grantee, USDHHS. Washington, 2002—03. Mem.: Alpha Theta Chi, Sigma Theta Ta, Zeta Tau Alpha (alumnae rels. bd. 1991—). Home: 5159 Dover St Arvada CO 80002 Office: Denver Health Med Ctr 777 Bannock St Denver CO 80204

GERALD, CAROLYN AILEEN T. emergency physician; b. Hattiesburg, Miss., 1943; MD, U. Miss., 1980. Diplomate Am. Bd. Emergency Medicine. Intern USPHS, New Orleans, 1980-81; mem. staff Wesley Med. Ctr., Hattiesburg, Miss., Marion County Hosp., Columbia, Miss., Forrest Gen. Hosp., Hattiesburg, Miss., Gulf Coast Med. Ctr., Biloxi, Miss., Hancock Med. Ctr., Bay St. Louis; ind. contractor emergency medicine. Adj. faculty Ctr. for Cmty. Health, student health svc. physician U. So. Miss.; ind. contractor emergency medicine. Contbr. articles to profl. publs. Mem. AMA, Am. Bd. Quality Assurance and Utilization Rev. Physicians, Am. Coll. Emergency Physicians, Miss. State Med. Assn. Address: 410 Brooklyn to Janice Rd Brooklyn MS 39425

GERALD, EMMA JANE, minister; b. Mullins, S.C., Sept. 9, 1951; d. Willie Monroe and Sarah Leola Gerald; m. Winfred C. Ross, Sept. 30, 1972 (div. 1978); children: Nicole A. Ross, Douglas B. Ross; m. Jessie Bridges, 1978 (dec. 1979). AS, Highland Park Coll., 1974; BA, Spring Arbor U., 1998; MS, Ctrl. Mich. U., 2003. Ordained min. Greater Ebenezer Bapt. Ch., 1980. Pastor Pillar of Faith, Detroit, Pillar of Faith Prophetic and Deliverance Ministries, Kennesaw, Ga. Owner Skin Care, Kennesaw. Author: (book) Interviewing for Professionals, 1997; rschr.: book National Baptist Training Manual. Min. Divine Word Comty. Ch., 2001. Avocations: reading, driving.

GERALDEZ, MARIA-TERESA DE JESUS, investment advisor, small business owner; b. Binalbagan, Philippines, Sept. 23, 1955; arrived in U.S., 1981; d. Horacio Calixto and Nenna Austria De Jesus; m. Roberto Z. Geraldez, Feb. 23, 1980; children: Marc Christian Jose, Kimberly Ann, Courteney Louise. BS in Commerce, St. Scholastica's Coll., 1976, St. Josephs Coll., 1977. Lic. realtor Calif., 1987, registered broker NASD, 1993, lic. life ins. sales 1983. Prin., owner Tess Robert & Assocs., LA, 1987—; fin. advisor Prudential Securities Inc., Pasadena, Calif., 1998—2003, TS Geraldez, A Fin. Cons. Practice, LA, 2003—. Mem. fin. com. Notre Dame Acad., Culver City, Calif., 2001—. Mem.: Fin. Planning Assn., Exec. Womens Golf Assn., Rotary. Roman Cath. Avocations: golf, tennis, gardening, movies, reading. Office: TS Geraldez A Fin Cons Practice 445 S Figuerda St 2610 Los Angeles CA 90071

GERARD, SUSAN, state senator; Bachelors degree, Drake U., 1972; MBA, Ariz. State U., 1977. Rep. rep. dist. 18 Ariz. Ho. of Reps.; Rep. senator dist. 18 Ariz. State Senate, 2000—; retail mgr., merchandising assoc., 1978. Mem. banking and ins. and govt. coms. Ariz. State Senate, chmn. health com.; mem. Fleming Fellows Bd., Nat. Conf. State Legislators Nat. Forum for State Health Policy Leadership, Ariz. Acad. Town Hall. Mem. AIDS Task Force, Phoenix, Marcus House Bd. Recipient Outstanding Leadership award Ariz. Assn. Managed Care Plans, Freedom of Info. award Ariz. Newspaper Assn., Nat. Child Advocate of Yr. award, 2002. Office: Ariz State Senate State Capitol Rm 303 1700 W Washington Phoenix AZ 85007-2890 E-mail: sgerard@azleg.state.az.us.

GERARD-SHARP, MONICA FLEUR, communications executive; b. London, Oct. 4, 1951; came to U.S., 1975; d. John Hugh Gerard-Sharp and Doreen May (Kearney) Dewhurst; m. Ali Edward Wambold, Nov. 21, 1981; children: Marina, Daniela, Dominica. BA in Philosophy and Lit. with honors, U. Warwick, Eng., 1973; MBA in Fin., Mktg. and Internat. Bus., Columbia U., 1980. Editor Inst. Chem. Engrs., London, 1973-74; sub-editor TV Times, London, 1974-75; press officer, editor UN, N.Y.C., 1975-78; bus. mgr. Time-Life Video, N.Y.C., 1980-81; mgr. fin. analysis Time-Life Films, N.Y.C., 1981; v.p. T.V.I.S., N.Y.C., 1982-83; dir. strategy and devel. HBO, ATC, N.Y.C., 1984-85; asst. treas., officer Time Inc., N.Y.C., 1985—87; pub. Travel Today and other mags. Fairchild Pubs. subs. Capital Cities/ABC, N.Y.C., 1987-88; dir. video programming Fairchild Pubs., Capital Cities/ABC, N.Y.C., 1988-89; pub. Entrée and Home Fashions Mags., N.Y.C., 1988-90; pres. Monali Inc., N.Y.C., 1991—. Cons. UN Bus. Council, N.Y.C., 1979; bd. rep. U.S.A. Network, N.Y.C., 1983-85. Editor: Everyone's United Nations, 1977; contbg. editor Asia Pacific Forum, 1976-77; contbr. articles to profl. jours. and mags., 1973-78. Treas. Help the Aged, Eng.; nat. devel. bd. Chances for Children, 1995-, pres. 2001-; adv. bd. Am. Mus. Natural History, 1998—; pres. bd. Am. Friends of Royal Ct. Theatre, 1998-2000. Bronfman fellow, 1979-80. Mem. Nat. Acad. Cable Programming, Am. Film Inst., Beta Gamma Sigma. Roman Catholic. Avocations: antiques, photography, wildlife. Home: Deer Park 128 Sunset Hill Rd Pleasant Valley NY 12569 Office: Monali Inc 26 E 80th St New York NY 10021-0110

GERBERDING, JULIE LOUISE, federal agency administrator; b. SD; married. BA in chemistry and biology, MD, Case Western Reserve U., Cleve.; MPH, U. Calif., Berkeley, 1990. Intern and resident in internal medicine U. Calif., San Francisco, fellow in clin. pharmacology and infectious diseases; assoc. clin. prof. medicine Emory U.; assoc. prof. medicine, epidemiology and biostatistics U. Calif., San Francisco; founder, dir., Epidemiology Prevention and Interventions Ctr. San Francisco Gen. Hosp., 1987—98; dir., divsn. healthcare quality promotion CDC, 1998—2001, acting deputy dir. sci., 2001—02, dir., 2002—. Dir., Prevention Epicenter U. Calif., San Francisco; mem., bd. scientific counselors CDC, mem., HIV adv. com., mem., scientific program com.; mem. Nat. Conf. Human Retroviruses; cons. NIH, AMA, Occupational Safety and Health Adminstrn., Nat. AIDS Commn., U.S. Congress, and WHO. Edtl. bd. Annals of Internal Medicine, assoc. editor Am. Jour. Medicine, contbr. to profl. publs. and textbooks. Fellow: Infectious Diseases Soc. Am. (chair and co-chair com. profl. devel. and diversity, mem. nominations com., co-chair. annual program com.); mem.: Soc. for Healthcare Epidemiology Am. (mem. AIDS/Tuberculosis com., bd. acad. counselor), Am. Soc. Clin. Investigation, Alpha Omega Alpha, Phi Beta Kappa. Achievements include first female director for the CDC. Office: CDC 1600 Clifton Rd NE 214 Atlanta GA 30333

GERBERG, JUDITH LEVINE, human resource company executive; b. NYC, Mar. 21, 1940; d. Murray Joseph and Pearl (Berens) Levine; 1 child, Lilia Anya Berens. BS in Comparative Lit., Columbia U., 1963, postgrad. in organizational devel., 1989; MA in Psychology and Art, NYU. Registered art therapist; cert. clin. mental health counselor; nat. cert. counselor, career mgmt. profl. Program dir. Women's Selling Game, N.Y.C., 1979-84; mem. faculty Parsons Sch. Design, N.Y.C., 1979-85; pres. Gerberg & Co., N.Y.C., 1984—. Orgnl. devel. mgmt., leadership devel., valuing diversity, team bldg., comm. skills, stress mgmt.; founder Powerhouse, 1st outplacement for creative profls.; mem. N.Y. steering com. Women's Study in Religion Program Harvard Div. Sch.; pres. Career Counselors Consortium, 2000-. Co-author: The New York Women's Directory, 1973; contbr. articles and book revs. to various publ. Chmn. pub. rels. Profl. Women's Caucus, 1972; facilitator NYC Contr.'s Women's Econ. Task Force, 1994-95; mem. Harvard Divinity Sch.: Women in Religion Leadership Conf. NY State scholar. Mem.: Career Counselors Consortium (pres. 2000—03), Internat. Assn. Career Mgmt. Profl. (co-chair future focus com.), Women's Venture Fund, Fin. Women's Assn. (bd. dirs. 2003), The Forum at Stephen Wise (co-chmn. 1986—87), N.Y. Art Therapy Assn., Am. Art Therapy Assn. (life; bd. dirs. 1980—84). Office: 250 W 57th St Ste 2315 New York NY 10107-2315 Office Phone: 212-315-2322. Office Fax: 212-315-2324. E-mail: judith@gerberg.com.

GERBERICH, SUSAN GOODWIN, epidemiologist, educator, medical researcher; b. Cortland, N.Y. d. Arthur George and Elizabeth Pratt Goodwin; m. William Warren Gerberich; children: Bradley Kent, Brian Keith, Beth Clarice. BS summa cum laude, U. Minn., 1975, MS, 1978, PhD, 1980. Prof. U. Minn., Mpls., 1983—; dir. Regional Injury Prevention Rsch. Ctr., Mpls., 1987—, Ctr. for Violence Prevention and Control, Mpls., 1994—. Pres. Gerberich, Inc., Shorewood, Minn., 1985—; cons. Injury Prevention/Epidemiology, 1985—; cons. Nat. Inst. for Occupl. Safety and Health and Ctrs. for Disease Control. Contbr. articles to profl. jours. Trauma adv. com. Minn. Dept. of Health, Mpls., 1999—, mem. Brain and Spinal Cord adv. com., 1993—. Named to Blue Ribbon Panel Nat. Inst. for Occupl. Safety and Health, Washington, 1990-93, 96, Ctr. for Disease Control, Atlanta, 1986-91. Mem. APHA (gov. coun. 1994-96,98-2003), Injury Control and Emergency Health Svcs., Soc. for Epidemiol. Rsch. Avocations: tennis, golf, sailing, rollerblading. Office: EOH/SPH/U Minn/MMC 807 420 Delaware St SE Rm 1156 Minneapolis MN 55455-0374 E-mail: gerbe001@umn.edu.

GERBI, SUSAN ALEXANDRA, biology educator; b. N.Y.C., 1944; d. Claudio and Jeannette Lena (Klein) Gerbi; m. James Terrell McIlwain, Apr. 10, 1976. BA, Barnard Coll., 1965; MPhil, Yale U., 1968, PhD, 1970. NATO and Jane Coffin Childs Fund fellow Max-Planck Institut fur Biologie, Tubingen, Fed. Republic Germany, 1970-72; asst. prof. biology Brown U., Providence, 1972-77, assoc. prof., 1977-82, prof., 1982—. Dir. grad. tng. program in molecular and cell biology, 1982-87, asst. dir. grad. program in molecular biology, cell biology and biochemistry, 1987-89, vice-chair sect. molecular, cellular and devel. biology, 1990-94, chair dept. molecular biology, cell biology and biochemistry, 1994—; vis. assoc. prof. Duke U., Durham, N.C., 1981-82; mem. genetics research grants rev. panel NSF, 1979-80; mem. genetic basis of disease com. NIH, 1980-84. Contbr. articles to profl. jours. Dist. commr. Palmer River Pony Club, 1973-75. N.Y. State Regents scholar, 1965; NIH fellow, 1966-70; NIH research grantee, 1974—, research career devel. award, 1975-80; recipient Gov.'s award for sci. achievement State of R.I., 1993. Mem. Fedn. Am. Socs. Exptl. Biology (pub. policy com. 1994-97, chair consensus conf. on grad. edn. 1996), Assn. Am. Med. Colls. (pub. policy com. 1994-98, chair grad. rsch. edn. and tng. group 1999), Am. Soc. for Cell Biology (program chair 1986, council mem. 1988-90, pub. policy com. 1991-97, pres. 1993), Soc. for Devel. Biology, Genetics Soc., RNA Soc., Sigma Xi (nat. lectr.). Office: Brown Univ Biomedical Divsn Providence RI 02912-0001

GERBINO, ROBINANN LOUISE, real estate agent, pharmaceutical executive; b. Bklyn., Oct. 6, 1954; d. Angelo M. and Louise Alice Fierro. AAS in Med. Tech., SUNY, Farmingdale; BA in Social Sci., Adelphi U., 1982, MBA, 1990; postgrad., L.I.U. Quality auditor Altana Inc., Melville, NY, 1992—94; quality assurance mgr. Tishcon, Westbury, NY, 1994—95, Citation Inc., Farmingdale, 1995—96; quality control mgr. Per Pak/Orlandi, West Babylon, NY, 1997; regulatory affairs mgr. Time-Cap Labs., Inc., Farmingdale, 1998—2003; quality compliance contr. Endo Pharms., Garden City, NY, 2003—. Real estate assoc. Mem.: Bus. and Profl. Women's Club. Home: 75 W 22d St Deer Park NY 11729 Business E-Mail: lgerbino@suffolk.libr.ny.us.

GERDNER, LINDA ANN, nursing researcher, educator; b. Burlington, Iowa, Sept. 17, 1955; d. Richard Paul and Edna Marie Gerdner. AA, Southeastern C.C., 1975, ADN, 1977; BSN, Iowa Wesleyan Coll., 1980; MA, U. Iowa, 1992, PhD, 1998. RN, Iowa, Ark., Minn. Staff devel. coord. Elm View Care Ctr., Burlington, Iowa, 1985—88, DON, 1988—89; tchg./rsch. asst. U. Iowa Coll. Nursing, Iowa City, 1989-92; nursing faculty Grand View Coll., Des Moines, 1992-93; project dir. Nat. Caregiver Tng. Project, U. Iowa Coll. Nursing, 1992-97, predoctoral fellow, 1996-98; postdoctoral fellow/faculty dept. psychiatry U. Ark. Med. Scis., VA Med. Ctr., Little Rock, 1998—2000; asst. prof. U. Minnesota Sch. Nursing, 2001—. Presenter in field; cons. Alverno Health Facility, Clinton, Iowa, 1997—. Mem. referee panel Clin. Nursing Rsch., 1997—, Western Jour. Nursing Rsch., 1998—, Jour. Gerontol. Nursing, 1999—, Internat. Jour. Geriatric Psychiatry, 2000—, Internat. Psychogeriatrics, 2002—, Alzheimer's Disease and Related Disorders, 2002—, Nursing Research, 2003—; contbr. chapters to books, articles to profl. jours. Recipient AARP Andrus Found. grad. fellowship in gerontology Assn. Gerontology in Higher Edn., 1996-97, Rsch. award Am. Soc. Aging, 1999. Mem.: ANA, Coun. Nursing and Anthropology, Am. Assn. Geriatric Psychiatry, Midwest Nursing Rsch. Soc. (Outstanding Poster award 1993), Mid-Am. Contress on Aging (Best Grad. Paper award 1994), Am. Geriatric Soc., Internat. Psychogeriatric Assn. (task force on behavioral and psychol. symptoms of dementia 1999—, scientific advisory com. 2001, IPA/Bayer Rsch. award 1999), Sigma Theta Tau (Best of Image award 1997). Avocations: reading, traveling, walking, music, photography. Home: 1160 Cushing Cir Apt 318 Saint Paul MN 55108 Office: Weaver-Densford Hall 308 Harvard St SE Minneapolis MN 55455-0353 E-mail: gerdn001@umn.edu.

GEREAU, MARY CONDON, political corporate executive; b. Winterset, Iowa, Oct. 10, 1916; d. David Joseph and Sarah Rose (Stack) Condon; m. Gerald Robert Gereau, Jan. 14, 1961. Student, Mt. Mercy Jr. Coll., 1935-37; BA, U. Iowa, 1939, MA, 1941. Program dir. ARC, India, 1943-45; dean of students Eastern Mont. Coll., 1946-48; supt. pub. instrn. State of Mont., 1948-56; sr. legis. cons. NEA, 1967-73; dir. legis. Nat. Treasury Employees Union, 1973-76; legis. asst. to Senator Melcher Mont., 1976-86; pres. Woman's Party Corp., 1991—. Co-chmn. Truman Commerative Com., 1994—. Contbr. articles on state govt. and edn. to profl. jours. Nat. chmn. Equal Rights Ratification Coun.; pres. Coun. Chief State Sch. Officers, 1956; exec. bd. Rural Edn. Assn., 1953—56; mem. campaign staff Kennedy, Johnson, Humphrey, Jackson; v.p. Nat. Women's Party, 1984—91; mem. Westmoreland Dem. com.; bd. dir. Coun. Chief State Sch. Officers, 1953—56. Named Conservationist of Yr. Mont. Conservation Coun., 1952, Roll Call Cong. Staffer of Yr., 1985; recipient Disting. Svc. State Sch. Officers, 1956, medal of honor Vet. Feminists of Am., 2000. Mem. U.S. Congress Burro Club (pres. 1983-84), Mont. State Soc. of Wash. E-mail: grg1@3n.net.

GEREIGHTY, ANDREA SAUNDERS, polling company executive, poet; b. New Orleans, July 20, 1938; d. Andrew Jackson and Jeanne Teresa (Martin) Saunders; m. Dennis Anthony Gereighty Jr., May 19, 1959 (wid.); children: Deni Ann, David Dennis, Peggy T. Cert., Exeter Coll., Oxford, Eng., 1972; BA, U. New Orleans, 1974, MA in English with distinction, 1978. Cotton analyst Anderson-Clayton, Metairie, La., 1956; records retrieval profl. Shell Oil Co., New Orleans, 1956-60; census coord. St. Vincent De Paul Ch., New Orleans, 1960-65; bldg. funds dir. St. Francis Xavier Ch., Metairie, 1965-70; tchr. spl. edn. Deckbar Elem. Sch., Jefferson, La., 1966-70; tchr. English Chalmette (La.) H.S., 1971-73; assoc. prof. English dept. U. New Orleans, 1973-75; tchr. secondary edn. Berlin-Am. H.S., 1980-81; owner, founder, CEO New Orleans Field Svcs. Assocs., 1974—. Guest speaker Delgado Coll., New Orleans, 1989; guest presenter Rabouin Vo-Tech., New Orleans, 1980; lectr., guest presenter poetry at New Sarpy Sch., 1994-95; guest presenter St. Mark's Episcopal Ch., Latter Libr., N.O. Pub. Libr., others. Author: (public opinion polls book) Asking Q's, 1980; (poetry) Illusions and Other Realities, 1974, Restless for Cool Weather, 1990, Season of the Crane, 1994; publ., editor Desire Street, 1997—; author numerous poems. Recipient Coda award Poets and Writers, 1983, Poetry award of honor Nat. League Am. Pen Women, 1973, Deep South Writers, 1984, 88, 90, 92, 94, 95, 96, 97, 98, 99, 2d place award Nuyarikin Poet's Cafe, N.Y.C., Ellipsis Poetry prize, 1983, 85, 87, 90, other poetry awards. Mem. Am. Mktg. Assn., Mktg. Rsch. Assn., Nat. Geneal. Soc., Jefferson Geneal. Soc., Geneaol. Soc. of New Orleans, New Orleans Poetry Forum (dir. 1990—), New Orleans Track Club. Democrat. Roman Catholic. Avocations: writing poetry, jogging, genealogy, dogs, camping. Office: New Orleans Field Svcs 257 Bonnabel Blvd Rear Office Metairie LA 70005-3738

GERGECEFF-COOPER, LORRAINE, artist, consultant; b. Ill. d. Harry Robert and Grace Johnson; m. George William Gergeceff (dec. 1984); m. John Cooper, Jr., May 30, 1992 (dec. 2002); children: Jill Gergeceff Lohnes, Jon Rice Gergeceff. Cert., Internat. Sommerakad., Salzburg, Austria, 1962, Sch. Landscape Painting, Dordogne, France, 1973; BS, So. Ill. U., 1953; MFA, U. Guanajuato, San Miguel Allende, Mex., 1970. Tchr., gallery dir. Ursuline Acad., Oakland, Mo., 1962-70; instr. McKendree Coll., Lebanon, Mo.; artist Forum Creative Dynamics, St. Louis, 1995, Unique Paintings, Webster Groves, Mo., 1997-98; owner LorPaint Gallery, Webster Groves, 1998—. Cons. JDR 3 Through Awareness Classroom Environment; founder, dir. Ursuline Art Gallery, Oakland, Mo. Author: Careers in Art, Self Designed Fabrics; one woman shows at Kinsella Gallery, Long Art Gallery, Ursuline Art Gallery, Notre Dame Coll., University City Libr., St. Louis U.; group shows include St. Louis Art Mus., Art Mus. St. Louis, Bellas Artes, Cuernavaca, Mex., Mus. Arts and Scis., Mo. Hist. Soc., Spete Kukla Gallery, Samos, Greece, Internat. Acad. Fine Arts, Salzburg, Austria, Highland Gallery, Atlanta, St. Louis Artists' Guild, 2002, Galeria Osman, Mex., Creative Art Gallery, St. Louis, 2001, 02, Centro Cultural El Nigromante, San Miguel de Allende, Mex., Art Expo '96, Webster Groves, Mo., Nat. Mus. Women in the Arts, Mo. Water Colo Assn., St. Peter's Cultural Art Ctr., 2001, 2002, 2003, Oil and Acrylic Nat. Exhbn., 2001, Collector's Choice, St. Louis, 2002, 2003, CJ Mggs Art Gallery, 2002, Oil and Acrylic Nat. Exhibit, 2002. Backer Repertory Theater, Webster Groves, Mo., 1996—. Best of Show Kinsella Gallery, Long Art Gallery, Ursuline Art Gallery; recipient prize St. Louis Artists' Guild, 1969, 71, 75; named Outstanding Secondary Educator, 1971. Mem. St. Louis Art Mus., Chgo. Art Inst., Guild of Opera Theater, Art St. Louis, St. Lousi Artists' Guild (spl. events, prize 1969, 71, 75), St. Louis Watercolor Soc. (signature), Soc. Multi Media Layerists. Avocations: travel, sailing, reading. Address: LorPaint Gallery 16 N Gore Ave Ste 201 Webster Groves MO 63119-2315 E-mail: lorpaint@aol.com.

GERHARDT, CAROL ASHBY, visual artist; b. Wabash, Ind., Aug. 10, 1946; d. Dale Martin Ashby and Helen Irene Harper; 4 children from previous marriage. BS, U. Houston, 1986, postgrad., 1994—96. Exec. dir. Penguin Photography Studio, Houston, 1986—87, photographer, 1987—90; photojournalism faculty North Harris County Coll., Houston, 1990—92; art faculty Houston Ind. Sch. Dist., 1992—2003. Exhibitions include UN/UNIFEM, Marias do Mundo, Brazil, 2001, Diverse Works Art Space, Houston, 1996.

GERHART, GLENNA LEE, pharmacist; b. Houston, June 11, 1954; d. Henry Edwin and Gloria Mae (Mrnustik) G. BS in Pharmacy, U. Houston, 1977. Registered pharmacist, Tex. Staff pharmacist Meml. City Med. Ctr., Houston, 1977—84; asst. dir. pharmacy Meml. Hosp.-Meml. City Med. Ctr., Houston, 1984-98; pharmacy supr. Meml. Hermann-Meml. City Hosp. Pharmacy, Houston, 1998—; investigational drug pharmacist Meml. City Med. Ctr., Houston, 2000—; staff pharmacist Christus St. Catherine Health and Wellness Ctr., 2000—02. Active Humane Soc. U.S. Mem.: Pharm. and Therapeutics Soc., Houston-Galveston Area Soc. Hosp. Pharmacists, Tex. Soc. Health-Sys. Pharmacists, Tex. Pharm. Assn., Am. Soc. Hosp. Pharmacists, Am. Pharm. Assn., Nat. Birman Fanciers, Houston SPCA, U. Houston Alumni Orgn. (life), Humane Soc. U.S., Plumeria Soc. Am., Greentrails Ladies Club, Nat. Cougar Club, Houston Cat Club, Slavonic Benevolent Order of Tex. SPJST Lodge #88, Kappa Epsilon. Republican. Methodist. Avocations: reading, gardening, running, raising cats. Home: 25527 Winston Hollow Katy TX 77494 Office: Memorial Hermann-Memorial City Hosp 921 Gessner Houston TX 77024-2312 E-mail: glenna_gerhart@mhhs.org., glennacat@aol.com.

GERHART, LORRAINE PFEIFFER, reading specialist, educator; b. Porterfield, Wis., Mar. 13, 1939; d. Frank William and Michalena Mary (Kroll) Pfeiffer; m. Adolph Dietrich Gerhart, June 20, 1964; 1 child, Monika. BS, U. Wis., Oshkosh, 1961; cert. reading specialist, Carroll Coll., 1966; MA in Reading, Cardinal Stritch Coll., 1975. Classroom tchr. Elmbrook Schs., Brookfield, Wis., 1961-67, reading specialist, 1967—, team leader and specialist, 1988—95; lectr., workshop coord. Cardinal Stritch Coll., 1975—95. Acad. staff U. Wis., Oshkosh, Madison. Co-author: Study Skills, 1977; cons. author for manuals with filmstrip set, 1979; cons. for reading strategies Scott Foresman Soc. St. text, 1988, 90; contbr. Middle School Content Reading, Middle School Thematic Series. Mem. fin. com. Village of Lac La Belle, 1983-84. Recipient Celebrate Literacy award Waukesha Reading Coun., 1986, 96. Mem. ASCD, Internat. Reading Assn. (mem. adv. bd. Jour. of Reading 1989-90, book reviewer Signal, 1975—90), N.E. Reading Coun., Wis. State Reading Assn. (pres. 1990-91, Friend of Literacy award 2000), Mllw. Area Reading Coun., Nat. Coun. Tchrs. English., Delta Kappa Gamma. Republican. Roman Catholic. Avocations: reading, gardening, hiking, taking rubbings, making books. Home: 901 Fj St Crivitz WI 54114-1544 Office: 901 FJ St Crivitz WI 54114-1549

GERING, SANDRA EILEEN, art dealer, curator; b. Washington, Oct. 5, 1942; d. Jack and Marian (Brill) Marks; m. Norman Charles Gering, May 30, 1964 (div. Nov. 1987); children: Brett Michael, Craig Stephen. AS, U. Bridgeport, 1962. Owner, pres. Sandra Gering Gallery, N.Y.C., 1985—. Adv. bd. Genart, N.Y.C., 1993—; founder, pres. Friends of E.1027, 1999—. Pub. (catalogues) Anastasi, Bradshaw, Cage, Marioni, Rauschenberg, Tobey, 1990, William Anastasi, 1991, Dove Bradshaw: Works, 1969-93, 1993. Mem. Art Table. Avocations: yoga, tennis, zen buddhism, travel. Home: 14 W 11th St New York NY 10011-8629

GERLACH, JEANNE ELAINE, English language educator; b. Charleston, W.Va., Oct. 20, 1946; d. Lafayette and Edith Lorraine (Robinson) Marcum; m. Roger Thomas Gerlach Sr., Dec. 30, 1966; children: Roger Thomas Jr., Kristen Elaine. BS, W.Va. State Coll., Institute, 1974; MA, W.Va. State Coll., 1979; EdD, W.Va. U., 1985, U. North Tex., 1992. Lang. arts tchr. Ohio County Schs., Wheeling, W.Va., 1974-79; English instr. West Liberty (W.Va.) State Coll., 1979-82; continuing edn. instr. Seattle Pacific U., 1982-85; asst. prof. English W.Va. U., Morgantown, 1985-86, Tarrant County Jr. Coll., Ft. Worth, 1986-88; dir. Communications Unlimited, Dallas, Pitts., 1986—; assoc. prof. English edn. W.Va. U., Morgantown, 1989-97, spl. asst. to the provost, 1994-97, dir. ctr. women's studies, 1993-94; dean coll. edn. U. Tex., Arlington, 1997—, assoc. v.p. K-16 initiatives, 2003—. Cons. to bus. and corps., 1986—; co-dir. advanced writing project W.Va. U., Morgantown, 1989, lang. arts camps, 1988, 89, 90, young writers inst. Editor: English Internat.; contbr. articles to profl. jours. Mem. LWV, W.Va., DAR, Young Republicans, W.Va. Faculty Devel. grantee W.Va. U., 1989; recipient 1st. place Creative Writing award W.Va. Women's Clubs, 1976. Mem. AAUW, AAUP, Nat. Coun. Tchrs. English (chair women's com. 1986—, chair nominating com. 1988-89, Outstanding Tchr. in Coll. of Human Resources and Edn. award W.Va. U. 1992, Rewey Belle Inglis award 1992), Am. Ednl. Rsch. Assn., W.Va. U. Alumni Assn. (sec. 1990, pres.), Nat. Women's Studies Assn., Nat. Soc. Daus. Am. Revolution. Republican. Methodist. Avocations: tennis, golf, writing poetry, photography, doll collecting. Office Phone: 817-272-7185.

GERMAIN, CLAIRE MADELEINE, law librarian, educator, lawyer; b. Chaumont, France, Sept. 22, 1951; d. Pierre and Jeanne (Despujols) G.; m. Stuart M. Basefsky, Aug. 16, 1976; 1 child, Nicolas. Licence-es. lettres, U. Paris, 1971, LLB, 1974; M in Comparative Law, La. State U., 1975; M in Law Librarianship, U. Denver, 1977. Reference librarian Duke U. Law Library, Durham, N.C., 1977-80, head reference librarian, 1982-84, asst. librarian, sr. lectr. comparative law, 1984-89, assoc. dir., sr. lectr. comparative law, 1989-93; Edward Cornell law libr., prof. law Cornell U., Ithaca, N.Y., 1993—. Research fellow Max Planck Inst., Hamburg, Federal Republic of Germany, 1980. Author: Germain's Transnational Law Research: A Guide to Attorneys, 1991, (with Szladits) Guide to Foreign Legal Materials, French, 2d edit., 1985; contbr. and editor articles to profl. jours. Mem. Am. Assn. Law Librs. (chair fgn. law sect. 1985-86, v.p., pres.-elect 2004-, chair-elect sect. librs. 2003-), ABA, Am. Assn. Law Schs. (chair libr. and tech. com.). Roman Catholic. Office: Cornell Law Libr Myron Taylor Hall Ithaca NY 14853 E-mail: cmg13@cornell.edu.

GERMAN, JUNE RESNICK, lawyer; b. N.Y.C., Feb. 24, 1946; d. Irving and Stella (Weintraub) Resnick; m. Harold Jacob German, May 31, 1974; children: Beth Melissa, Heather Alice, Bret. BA, U. Pa., 1965; JD, NYU, 1968. Bar: N.Y. 1968, U.S. Dist. Ct. (ea. and so. dists.) N.Y. 1974, U.S. Ct. Appeals (2d cir.) 1973, U.S. Supreme Ct. 1973. Atty., sr. atty., supervising atty. Mental Health Info. Svc., N.Y.C., 1968-77; atty., advisor Course in Human Behavior Mems. of N.Y. State Judiciary, Nassau and Suffolk County, 1980; pvt. practice Huntington, N.Y., 1985—. Contbg. author: Bioethics and Human Rights, 1978, Mental Illness, Due Process and the Acquitted Defendant, 1979; contbr. chpts. to books, articles to profl. jours. Chmn. Citizen's Ad Hoc Com. Constrn. of the Dix Hills Water Adminstrn. Bldg., Huntington, N.Y., 1985-90; mem. Citizens Adv. Com. for Dix Hills Water Dist., Huntington, 1992—; dir. House Beautiful Assn. at Dix Hills, 1986—, Citizens for a Livable Environment and Recycling, Huntington, 1989-93; active Suffolk County (N.Y.) Dem. Com., 1986—, Deer Park Avenue Task Force, Town of Huntington, 1997-98, Dix Hills Revitalization Com., 1999-2000. Mem. Suffolk County Bar Assn. Jewish. Avocations: tennis, hiking, travel. Office: 150 Main St Huntington NY 11743-6908 Office Phone: 631-271-8711. E-mail: junegerman@hotmail.com.

GERMAN, LYNNE CUMMINGS, music educator; b. Columbus, Ohio, Feb. 25, 1958; d. W. Dean and Naomi Faye (Cook) Cummings; m. Kenneth W. German, July 31, 1982; children: Madelaine Anne, Eliza Lynne, Brooke Nicole, Iris Noel. BS in Music Edn., Bob Jones U., 1980, MA in Piano, 1982. Dir. Southside Christian Sch. Flute Choir, Greenville, S.C., 1981-82; founder, owner, tchr. German Piano Studio, Mt. Crawford, Va., 1983—; tchr. James Madison U., Harrisonburg, Va., 1989-94; dir. Harrisonburg Flute Choir, 1994-95, Grace Covenant Ch. Vocal Choir and Brass Choir, Harrisonburg, 1995—. Spkr. in field. Contbr. articles to profl. jours. Mem. Nat. Guild Piano Tchrs., Musi. Tchrs. Nat. Assn., Va. Music Tchrs. Assn. (western Va. chpt. music theory chmn. 1995—), Harrisonburg Piano Tchrs. Forum. Avocations: composing, arranging music, writing, hiking, bicycling. Home and Office: 5006 Cross Keys Rd Mount Crawford VA 22841-2535

GERRARD, RUTH ANN, retired English educator; BA, Coll. of Wooster, 1962, MA in Tchg., 1967; postgrad., Youngstown (Ohio) State U., 1975-79, Kent (Ohio) State U. Cert. tchr., supr. English instr. Orrville (Ohio) City Schs., 1962-64, Boardman Local Schs., Youngstown, Ohio, 1964-66, Wooster (Ohio) City Schs., 1967-69, Youngstown State U., 1969-71; gifted coord. Austintown Local Schs., Youngstown, 1977-96, English instr., 1971-96. Curriculum coms. Austintown Schs., workshop leader state and nat. orgns. Contbr. to publs. Spkr. various orgns.; elder Presbyn. Ch., 1985-90, 93—. Martha Holden Jennings scholar Jennings Found., 1987-88; recipient Tchr. of Yr. PTA. Mem. AAUW, Phi Delta Kappa, Delta Kappa Gamma 1968— (chapt. pres. 1990-98), docent Butler Inst. Am. Art. Avocations: painting, sketching, reading, gardening.

GERRATANA, THERESA B. state legislator; b. New Britain, Conn., Oct. 7, 1949; d. Steven Jr. and Mary Ann (Luppino) Bielinski; m. Frank J. Gerratana, 1977; children: Frank L., Gregory J. BS, Ctrl. Conn. State U., 1975. Justice of peace, New Britain, 1985-93; mem. ethics commn. City of New Britain, 1990-93; mem. Dist. 23 Conn. Ho. of Reps., 1993—. Pres. Jr. League of Greater New Britain, 1990-92. Mem. LWV (pres. 1986-88). Address: 674 Lincoln St New Britain CT 06052-1833 Office: Conn Ho of Reps State Capitol Hartford CT 06106

GERRIETTS, VIVIAN JANE, music educator; b. Pekin, Ill., Jan. 18, 1952; d. Carl Henry Deppert and Elsie Mae Uhlman; m. George Steven Gerrietts, Dec. 27, 1975; children: Isaac Matthew, Lee Quentin. BS, U. Ill., 1974. Music tchr. Thomasboro (Ill.) Elem., 1974—78; tchr. Green Valley (Ill.) Grade, 1980—81; cmty. worker 4H Tazewell County Coop. Ext. Svc., Pekin, Ill., 1989—92; music tchr. Delavan (Ill.) CUSD #703, 1992—. Choir dir. St. Paul United Ch. of Christ, Pekin, 1978—, mem. pipe organ select com., 1981; mem. Prairie Wind Ensemble, Pekin Mcpl. Band. 4H leader, fair supt., Green Valley and Tazewell County, 1978—2003; village trustee Green Valley, Ill., 2003. Recipient Outstanding Achievement Arts award, YWCA, 2000. Mem.: Musicians Local 301, Ill. Music Educators Assn., Music Educators Nat. Conf. Avocations: world drumming, gardening, lighthouses, genealogy, photography. Home: 106 Linden Green Valley IL 61534 Office Phone: 309-244-8283.

GERRITSEN, MARY ELLEN, vascular and cell biologist; b. Calgary, Alta., Can., Sept. 20, 1953; came to U.S., 1978; d. Thomas Clayton and Alice Irene (Minton) Cooper; m. Paul William Gerritsen, May 24, 1975 (div. 1977); m. Thomas Patrick Parks, Oct. 11, 1980; children: Kristen, Madelene. BSc summa cum laude, U. Calgary, 1975, PhD, 1978. Postdoctoral fellow U. Calif., San Diego, 1978-80; asst. prof. N.Y. Med. Coll., Valhalla, 1981-86, assoc. prof., 1986-90; sr. staff scientist Pharm. divsn. Bayer Corp., West Haven, Conn., 1990-93, head inflammation exploratory rsch., 1990-96, prin. staff scientist, 1993-97; vis. scientist Harvard U., 1996, assoc. dir. Cardiovascular Rsch., 2000—. Cons. Insite Vision, Alameda, Calif., 1987-89, Boehringer Ingelheim Pharms., Ridgefield, Conn., 1985-88; adj. assoc. prof. N.Y. Med. Coll., 1990-99. Mem. editorial bd. Microvascular Rsch., 1988-96, Am. Jour. Physiology, 1993—, Am. Jour. Cardiovascular Pathology, 1996—, Circulation Rsch., 1997-99, Endothelium, 1999—; editor-in-chief Microcirculation, 1993-98; cons. editor, 1998—; editor N.Am. Vascular Biology Orgn. Newsletter; contbr. articles to profl. jours. I. W. Killam Found. fellow, 1976, Med. Rsch. Coun. Can. fellow, 1978. Mem. Am. Soc. for Pharmacology and Exptl. Therapeutics, Am. Physiol. Soc., Assn. Rsch. on Vision and Ophthalmology, Am. Soc. Investigational Pathology, Soc. Leukocyte Biology, Am. Soc. Cell Biology, Microcirculatory Soc. (mem. coun. 1989-92, chairperson publs. com. 1991-93, Mary Weideman award 1985, Young Investigator award 1984), N.Am. Vascular Biology Orgn. (mem. steering com. 1993, mem. coun. 1994-97, editor-in-chief newsletter 1994-97, sec.-treas. 1997-99, pres.-elect 1999). Avocations: running, step aerobics, horticulture. Office: Genentech Inc MS 42 1 Dna Way South San Francisco CA 94080-4990

GERRY, DEBRA PRUE, psychotherapist, recording artist, writer; b. Oct. 9, 1951; d. C.O. and Sarah E. Rawl; m. Norman Bernard Gerry, Apr. 10, 1981 (div. 1998); 1 child, Gisele Psyche Victoria. BS, Ga. So. U., 1972; MEd, Armstrong State U., 1974; PhD, U. Ga., 1989. Cert. Ariz. Bd. Behavioral Health Examiners. Spl. edn. tchr. Chatham County Bd. Edn., Savannah, Ga., 1972-74; edn. and learning disabilities resource educator Duval County Bd. Edn., Jacksonville, Fla., 1974-77; ednl. resource counselor spl. programs adminstr. Broward County Bd. Edn., Ft. Lauderdale, Fla., 1977-81; pvt. practice Scottsdale, Ariz., 1990—. Contbr. author coll. textbooks; contbr. articles to profl. jours.; prodr. musical album Welcome to this World. Vol., fundraiser, psychol. cons., group leader Valley AIDS Orgns., Phoenix, 1990-96; fundraiser Hosp. Health Edn. Programs, Scottsdale, 1992-93; mem. com. for women's issues Plz. Club, Phoenix, 1992-93; pres. Laissez Les Bon Temps Rouler, Wrigley Club, Phoenix, 1993-96; mem. bd. Sojourner' Ctr., 1996, exec. bd., 1997-98, v.p., 1999; exec. bd. Breast Found., Inc., Phoenix, 1997-98; appointee Ariz. Supreme Ct., Foster

Care Rev. Bd., Phoenix, 1996-2001. Recipient Rudy award Shanti Orgn., 1991. Mem. APA, NOW, ACA, Internat. Soc. Poets (disting., Poet of Merit award 1996), Nat. Assn. Women Bus. Owners, Assn. for Multicultural Coun., Assn. for Specialists in Group Work, Mensa, Phi Delta Kappa, Kappa Delta Epsilon, Sigma Omega Phi, Kappa Delta Pi. Avocations: ballroom dancing, playing musical instruments, singing, travel, [illegible] E-mail: dgerryphd@aol.com.

GERSHANSKY, LIBBY MEG, secondary school educator; d. Sarah Felker and Samuel Tatt; m. Ira S. Gershansky, Jan. 26, 1974; 1 child, Sarah Jessica. MA, Adelphi U., 1992; cert in ednl. leadership, CUNY, 2000. Cert. tchr. English to spkrs. other langs. N.Y., tchr. Spanish N.Y., sch. adminstr. and supr. N.Y. Grad. fellow Bklyn Coll., CUNY, 1975—80, asst. to higher edn. officer, 1980—89; tchr. Spanish and ESL Lafayette HS, Bklyn., 1989—99, coord. ESL and title VII bilingual scholars acad., 1993—99; staff developer New Dorp HS United Fedn. Tchrs./Tchr. Ctr., S.I., NY, 1999—. Sch. bd. chair Temple Israel Reform Congregation, S.I., 1986—2003. Recipient Cmty. Svc. award, Coun. Jewish Orgns., 1996, United Jewish Appeal/Fedn., 2003, citation for Cmty. Svc., N.Y.C. Coun., 1996; grantee, United Fedn. Tchrs., 1996. Mem.: ASCD, Internat. Reading Assn., Nat. Staff Devel. Coun., Tchrs. English to Spkrs. Other Langs. Personal E-mail: eng2ndlang@aol.com. Business E-Mail: lgershansky@ufttc.org.

GERSHON, NINA, federal judge; b. Chgo., Oct. 16, 1940; d. David and Marie Gershon; m. Bernard J. Fried, May 15, 1983. BA, Cornell U., 1962; LLB, Yale U., 1965; postgrad., London Sch. Econs., 1965-66. Former magistrate judge U.S. Dist. Ct. (so. dist.) N.Y., N.Y.C.; U.S. dist. judge Eastern Dist. N.Y., Bklyn., 1996—. Fulbright scholar. Office: US Courthouse 225 Cadman Plz E Brooklyn NY 11201-1818

GERSKE, JANET FAY, lawyer; b. Nov. 14, 1950; d. Bernard G. Gerske and L. Fay (Knight) Capron. BS, Northwestern U., 1971; JD, U. Mich., 1978. Bar: Ill. 1978, U.S. Dist. Ct. (no. dist.) Ill. 1978. Pvt. practice, Chgo., 1978—80, 1984—2002; assoc. Jerome H. Torshen Ltd., Chgo., 1980—84. Chpt. chair Ind. Voters Ill./Ind. Precinct Orgn., Chgo., 1982—83; co-chmn. Ill. Women's Agenda Com., 1985—88, fin. officer, 1987—88; dir. Chgo. Abused Women Coalition, 1986—90, sec., treas., 1988—90; co-chair legal status of women com. Young Lawyers sect. Chgo. Bar Assn., 1984—85; co-chair rights of women com. Ill. Women's Bar Assn., 1985—86, dir., 1988—90. Democrat. Home: 850 W Oakdale Ave Chicago IL 60657-5122

GERSONI-EDELMAN, DIANE CLAIRE, author, editor; b. Apr. 16, 1947; d. James Arthur and Edna Bernice (Krinski) Gersoni; m. James Neil Edelman, Oct. 5, 1975; children: Michael Lawrence, Sara Anne. Asst. editor, then assoc. editor Sch. Libr. Jour. Book Rev., 1968—72; freelance writer, 1972—74, 1977—; writer, editor Scholastic Mags., Inc., N.Y.C., 1974—77. Cons., spkr. in field. Author: Sexism and Youth, 1974, Work-Wise: Learning About the World of Work from Books, 1980; contbr. articles and book revs. to anthologies, newspapers and mags.

GERSTENBERGER, DONNA LORINE, humanities educator; b. Wichita Falls, Tex., Dec. 26, 1929; d. Donald Fayette and Mabel G. AB, Whitman Coll., 1951; MA, U. Okla., 1952, PhD, 1958. Asst. prof. English U. Colo., Boulder, 1958-60; prof. U. Wash., 1960-96, prof. emeritus, 1996—, chmn. undergrad. studies, 1971-74, assoc. dean Coll. Arts and Scis., dir. Coll. Honors and Office Undergrad. Studies, 1974-76, chmn. dept. English, 1976-83, vice chmn. faculty senate, 1984-85, chmn. faculty senate, 1985-86. Cons. in field; bd. dirs. Am. Lit. Classics; mem. grants-in-aid com. Am. Coun. Learned Socs.; chmn. region VII, Mellon Fellowships in Humanities, 1982-92; mem. adv. com. Grad. Record Exams, 1990-93, Coun. Internat. Exch. of Scholars, 1992-95. Author: J.M. Synge, 1964, 2d edition, 1988, The American Novel: A Checklist of Twentieth Century Criticism, vols. I and II, 1970, Directory of Periodicals, 1974, The Complex Configuration: Modern Verse Drama, 1973, Iris Murdoch, 1974, Richard Hugo, 1983; editor: Microcosm, 1969, Swallow Series in Bibliography, 1974—; assoc. editor: Abstracts of English Studies, 1958-68; founder, editor jour. Seattle Rev., 1983-96. Bd. dirs. N.W. Chamber Orch., Seattle, 1975-78, Wash. Friends Humanities, 1991—; trustee Wash. Commn. Humanities, 1985-91, pres., 1988-90; mem. vis. com. Lehigh U., 1987-92; pres. Am. Commn. for Irish Studies/West, 1989-91. Grantee Am. Council Learned Socs., 1962, 88, Am. Philos. Soc., 1963 Mem. MLA, Am. Com. Irish Studies. Office: U Wash Box 354330 Dept English Seattle WA 98195-4330

GERSTENBERGER, VALERIE, media coordinator; b. Amherst, Ohio, Sept. 7, 1913; d. Frank Abraham Eppley and Ethel Elizabeth Dute; m. William Jacob Jenkins, Aug. 13, 1944 (div. May 1964); m. Henry Louis Gerstenberger, Nov. 8, 1984 (dec. Aug. 2001). BA, Baldwin-Wallace Coll., 1936; MA, Kent State U., 1963; postgrad., U. Iowa, 1938—39. Asst. drama dir. Baldwin-Wallace Coll., Berea, Ohio, 1936—38; English/speech tchr. St. Elmo (Ill.) H.S., 1940—42, Clearview H.S., Lorain, Ohio, 1942—57; speech tchr. Kent State U., Elyria, Ohio, 1963—66, Cleve. State U., Lakewood, Ohio, 1966—70; media coord. Amherst (Ohio) Pub. Schs., 1957—80; drama dir. Amherst (Ohio) Pub. H.S., 1957—60, 1975—78. Mem./pres. Amherst Pub. Libr. Bd., 1963—92; cons. for libr. expansion Am. Pub. Libr., 1972—73; costume designer various orgns. Various civic positions and contbns. including founding of Community Theater, local edn. programs and cataloging documents for Amherst Hist. Soc.; founder Amherst Heritage House Mus., 2002. Named to Gallery of Success, Amherst (Ohio) HS, 1987, Ohio Cmty. Theatre Assn. Hall of Fame, 2003; recipient Merit award, Baldwin Wallace Coll., 1986; Paul Harris fellow, Rotary Internat., 1983. Mem.: Amherst Hist. Soc., Phi Mu. Republican. Congregationalist. Home: 439 Shupe Ave Amherst OH 44001

GERSTING, JUDITH LEE, computer scientist, educator, computer scientist, researcher; b. Springfield, Vt., Aug. 20, 1940; d. Harold H. and Dorothy V. (Kinney) MacKenzie; m. John M. Gersting, Jr., Aug. 17, 1962; children: Adam, Jason. BS, Stetson U., 1962; MA, Ariz. State U., 1964, PhD, 1969. Assoc. prof. computer sci. U. Ctrl. Fla., Orlando, 1980-81; asst. prof. Ind. U., Purdue U., Indpls., 1970-73, assoc. prof., 1974-79, prof., 1981-93, U. Hawaii, Hilo, 1994—. Staff scientist Indpls. Ctr. Advanced Rsch., 1982—84. Author: (book) Mathematical Structures for Computer Science, 2003; contbr. articles to sci. jours. Mem.: Assn. Computing Machinery. Avocations: youth soccer, reading. Office: U Hawaii 200 W Kawili St Hilo HI 96720-4075 E-mail: gersting@hawaii.edu.

GERSTNER, MARY JANE, nurse; b. Rochester, N.Y., June 27, 1953; d. Thomas J. and Jane E. Gerstner. Diploma, St. Joseph's Hosp. Health Ctr. Sch. Nursing, 1974; BSN, Nazareth Coll., 1982. Cert. RN N.Y. Staff nurse oper. rm. U. Rochester Med. Ctr./Strong Meml. Hosp., 1974-79, staff nurse ob.-gyn. unit, 1981-83, 84-86; staff nurse oper. rm. St. Mary's Hosp., Rochester, 1983-84, Genesee Hosp., Rochester, 1985-95; nurse 1st asst. Genesee Valley Plastic Surgery, Canandaigua, N.Y., 1995; staff nurse oper. rm. U. of Rochester (N.Y.) Med. Ctr., 1996-00, nurse 1st asst., 2000—. Mem.: ARC, Genesee Valley Nurses Assn., Assn. Peri-Operative RNs, Sigma Theta Tau.

GERTNER, NANCY, federal judge, educator; b. May 22, 1946; d. Morris and Sadie Gertner; m. John C. Reinstein, Apr. 27, 1985; 3 children. BA cum laude with honors, Columbia U., 1967; MA, JD, Yale U., 1971; degree (hon.), New England Sch. Law, 1979, Suffolk U., 1997. Bar: Mass., U.S. Dist. Ct., U.S. Ct. Appeals (1st and 3rd cirs.), U.S. Supreme Ct, 1972. Law clerk to Hon. Luther M. Swygert U.S. Ct. Appeals (7th cir.), Chgo., 1971-72; ptnr. Silverglate, Gertner, Fine & Good, 1973-90, Dwyer, Collora & Gertner, 1990-94; judge U.S. Dist. Ct. Mass., Boston, 1994—. Instr. Sch. Law Boston U., 1972-86, 87-90, 94-95; vis. prof. Law Sch. Harvard U., 1985-86, Yale Law Sch., 1997—; instr. Boston Coll. Law Sch., 1995-98; mem. civic justice adv. com. to U.S. Dist. Ct., 1991; mem. adv. com. U.S. Ct. Appeals (1st cir.), 1991-92. Co-author: The Law of Juries; contbr. articles to legal jours. Bd. dirs. Women's Rights Com. Recipient Mass. Choice award, 1987, Black Educator's Alliance award [illegible] 1988, New England Hudassah award, 1992, Abigail Adams award Mass. Women's Polit. Caucus Edn. Fund., 1994; voted Best Fed. Judge in Mass., 1999. Mem. ATLA (basic trial advocacy course com., vice chair 1985-86), Mass. Acad. Trial Lawyers, Mass. Civil Liberties Union (bd. dirs., Abraham T. Alper award for Excellence in Civil Liberties, 1980), Boston Bar Assn. (lawyers com. for civil rights under law, steering com. 1979—, Hon. William Brennan award 2000), Women Judges Hon. Assn. Office: US Dist Ct 1 Courthouse Way Boston MA 02210-3002 Fax: 617-204-5821.

GERTRUDE, KATY See **WILHELM, KATE**

GERTSENZON, GALINA, music educator; b. Paitygorsk, Russia, Apr. 3, 1946; arrived in U.S., 1981; d. Yefim Olshansky and Hana Berman; m. Igor Gertsenzon, Nov. 8, 1968; 1 child, Elena Gertsenzon Orujev. MusB, Baku Coll. Music, 1964; MusM, Gorky Conservatory, 1970. Prof. music Baku Coll. Music, Azerbaijan, 1970—81; with faculty music Smith Coll., Northampton, Mass., 1985—86; staff pianist U. Mass., Amherst, 1981—82; with music faculty Westfield State Coll., 1983—, Elms Coll., Chicopee, 1982—. Vol. Immingrant Resettlement Program, Springfield, Mass., 1981—. Democrat. Jewish. Avocations: travel, reading.

GERTZ, SUZANNE C. artist; b. Chgo., Sept. 8, 1938; d. Henry A. Feldman and Helen Flanzer; m. Theodore G. Gertz, June 19, 1960; children: Craig M., Candace C., Scott W. Student, Art Inst. Chgo., 1960; BFA, Barat Coll., 1982. Exhibited in group shows at Art Inst. Chgo., San Jacinto Coll., Houston, 2001, New Horizons in Art, Chgo., Lake Forest Art Show, exhibitions include San Bernandino County Mus., Firehouse Gallery, N.Y., Evanston and Vicinity 12th Bienniel Exhbn., The Cmty. Gallery Art Coll. Lake County, Dittmar Gallery, Northwestern U., David Adler Cultural Ctr., Cindy Bordeau Gallery, others. Mem.: Cliff Dwellers Club. Democrat. Jewish. Home: 950 Benson Lane Libertyville IL 60048

GERVAIS, AVIS L. state representative, consumer products company executive; b. Enosburgh, Vt., Sept. 5, 1933; m. Normand G. Gervais; 4 children. Grad., Enosburg Falls H.S. Ret. store owner; hospice LNA; state rep. State of Vt., 1997—. Trustee Enosburg Village; mem. Enosburg Village Planning Commn., Enosburg Econ. Develop. Bd. Mem.: Enosburg Hist. Soc., Modern Dozen Club. Democrat. Roman Catholic. Office: 143 Missisquoi St Enosburg Falls VT 05450

GERVAIS, SISTER GENEROSE, hospital consultant; b. Currie, Minn., Sept. 18, 1919; d. Philip Frederick and Elizabeth Eleanor (Sandgathe) G. BS, Stout State U., Menomonie, Wis., 1945; M. Hosp. Adminstrn., U. Minn., 1954. Joined Sisters of St. Francis, Roman Catholic Ch., 1938; adminstrv. dietitian St. Marys Hosp., Rochester, Minn., 1948-50, adminstrv. asst., 1951-52, asst. adminstr., 1954-63, assoc. adminstr., 1963-71, hosp. adminstr., 1971-81, exec. dir., 1981-85, bd. trustees, 1968-86; hosp. cons., 1985-90. Cons. dietitian Mercy Hosp., Portsmouth, Ohio, 1950-51; bd. dirs. 1st Nat. Bank, Rochester, 1974-78, Fed. Res. Bank Mpls., 1978-86, St. Francis Med. Ctr., LaCrosse, Wis., 1979-87, S.E. Minn. Health Systems Agy., 1978-83, S.E. Minn. Health Coun., 1983-87, Unity Home Health Svcs., Inc., LaCrosse, 1994-95; v.p., sec. Family Health Ctr. LaCrosse, Inc., 1985-91, pres., 1991-93; mem. residency adv. bd. St. Francis-Mayo Family Practice, 1993-95; mem. v.p., bd. dirs. Caledonia Health Care Ctr., 1986-90; bd. dirs. Franciscan Health System, LaCrosse, 1987-94, mem., treas., bd. dirs. Franciscan Cmty. Programs 1985-94. Bd. dirs. United Way of Olmstead County, 1968-73, Sr. Citizens Svcs. Inc., Rochester, Minn., 1988-94, Diocese of Winona Found., 1991-2000; bd. dirs. Madonna Towers, Rochester, 1987—, chair, 1991-97, 2003—; bd. dirs. Olmstead County Hist. Soc., 1994-97, chair, 2003—; bd. dirs. Regina Med. Ctr., Hastings, Minn., 1996-02, Madonna Meadows, 2002—; pres. Poverello Found., Rochester, 1983—; bd. adv. Winona State U. Rochester Ctr., 1985-93; mem. fin. coun. Diocese of Winona, 1986-91; mem. Franciscan Skemp Healthcare Cmty. Bd., LaCrosse, 1995—. Decorated Lady of Equestrian Order of Holy Sepulchre, 1989; recipient Alumni Disting. Service award U. Wis.-Stout, 1978, Teresa of Avila award Coll. of St. Teresa, 1980, Outstanding Achievement award Rochester chpt. U. Minn. Alumni Assn., 1981, Women of Achievement in Area of Bus. award YWCA, 1985, Pro Ecclesiae et Pontifice medal, 1985, Service to Mankind award Sertoma 700 Club, 1987, Mayor's Medal of Honor City of Rochester, 1990, The Athena award, 1994, Outstanding Alumni award Coll. Human Devel., U. Wis.-Stout, 2001; named Boss of Yr., Rochester Jaycees, 1980, named in her honor Sister Generose Gervais Bldg. St. Marys Hosp., 1991; Paul Harris fellow Nat. Rotary Club, 1998. Mem. Cath. Health Assn. U.S. (trustee 1979, vice chair 1981-82, chair 1982-83, speaker membership assembly 1983-84), Am. Coll. Hosp. Adminstrs., Am. Hosp. Assn., Minn. Hosp. Assn., Minn. Conf. Cath. Health Facilities (past dir.), Rochester Area C. of C. Republican. Address: 1216 2nd St SW Rochester MN 55902-1906

GERWIN, LESLIE ELLEN, lawyer, public affairs and community relations executive; b. L.A., May 18, 1950; d. Nathan and Beverly Adele (Wilson) G.; m. Bruce Robert Leslie, July 3, 1978; 1 child, Jonathan Gerwin Leslie. BA, Prescott Coll., 1972; JD, Antioch Sch. Law, 1975; MPH, Tulane U., 1988. Bar: D.C. 1975, N.Y. 1981, U.S. Dist. Ct. D.C. 1977, U.S. Dist. Ct. (so. dist.) N.Y. 1980. Staff asst. U.S. Congress, Washington, 1970-72; cons. Congl. Subcom., Washington, 1972-73; instr. U. Miami Law Sch., Coral Gables, Fla., 1975-76; assoc. prof. law Yeshiva U., N.Y.C., 1976-86; vis. assoc. prof. law Tulane Law Sch., New Orleans, 1983-84; pub. policy cons. New Orleans, 1987—; pres. Ariadne Cons., New Orleans, 1994—; dir. devel. and community rels. Planned Parenthood La., Inc., New Orleans, 1989-90; legal advisor La. Coalition for Reproductive Freedom, 1990-92; exec. v.p. Met. Area Com., New Orleans, 1992-94; exec. dir. Met. Area Com. Edn. Fund, New Orleans, 1992-94. Bd. dirs. Inst. for Phys. Fitness Rsch., N.Y.C., 1982-86, Challenge/Discovery, Crested Butte, Colo., 1977-80; cons. FDA, Washington, 1977-78, U. Judaism, L.A., 1974-75; mem. Met. Area Com. Leadership Forum, New Orleans, 1988; adj. asst. prof. La. State U. Sch. Medicine, 1996—, La. State U. Med. Sch., Dept. of Public Health and Preventive Medicine. Contbr. articles to profl. jours. Mem. Ind. Dem. Jud. Screening Panel, N.Y.C., 1980; bd. dirs. New Orleans Food Bank for Emergencies, 1987-89; profl. adv. com. MAZON-A Jewish Response to Hunger, L.A., 1986-89; bd. dirs. Second Harvesters Food Bank Greater New Orleans, 1989-94, La. State LWV, 1990-91, Anti-Defamation League, New Orleans, 1989-95, Jewish Endowment Found., 1987-93; trustee Jewish Fedn. Greater New Orleans, 1989-95, 97-99, mem. exec. com., 1997-99; trustee Emergency Food and Shelter Program, S.E. La., 1988—; v.p. Tulane U. B'nai B'rith Hillel Found., 1987-90; steering com. Citizens for Pers. Freedom, 1989-91; steering com. Metro 2000, 1989-90; sec. New Orleans sect. Nat. Coun. Jewish Women, 1990-91, state pub. affairs chmn., 1992-96; bd. Contemporary Arts Ctr., 1993-97; chair, bd. advocates Planned Parenthood La., 1995—; v.p. Edn. Tikvat Shalom Conservative Congregation, 1995-97, chair New Orleans Israel Bonds, 1996-98; mem. Cmty. Rels. Com., 1986-99, vice chair, 1995-97, chair 1997-99; adminstr. Area Tng. Ctr., USTA, New Orleans, 1996-2001; v.p. ritual Shir Chadosh Conservative Congregation, 2002—. Fellow Inst. of Politics, 1990-91; scholar Xerox Found., 1972-75; Decorated Order of Barristers; named One of Ten Outstanding Young Women of Am., 1987; recipient Herbert J. Garon Young Leadership award Jewish Fedn. Greater New Orleans, 1990; named YWCA Role Model, 1992. Mem. ABA, N.Y. Bar Assn., N.Y. Acad. Scis., Am. Pub. Health Assn., D.C. Bar Assn., Nat. Moot Ct. Honor Soc., Pub. Health Honor Soc., Calif. State Dem. Club (Key Svc. award 1988), Delta Omega.

GESALMAN, CAROL, minister; b. Greensburg, Pa., Nov. 10, 1946; d. Kasper Frederick and Lois Fern (Carroll) Gesalman; m. Ian Nicholas Polster, Mar. 19, 1995; m. Samuel Francis Rizzo, July 25, 1970 (div.); children: Jonathan Allen Rizzo, Kevin Michael Rizzo. BSc, Bloomsburg (Pa.) State U., [illegible] Theol. Sem., 1988. Tchr. spl. edn. Pitts. (Pa.) Pub. Schs., 1969—72; pastor Christ Evang. Luth. Ch., Baden, Pa., 1988—95; chaplain Oesterlen Svcs. for Youth, Springfield, Ohio, 1995—2000; pastor Fifth Evang. Luth. Ch., Springfield, 1995—. Mem. anniversary com. City of Springfield, 2001—02; bd. dirs. Oesterlen, 2004—, Springfield (Ohio) Civic Theatre, 2001—; mem. Evangelical Lutheran Ch. Am. Mem.: Evang. Luth. Ch. Assn. (mem. worship com. 1997—, pres. Mad River conf. 1998—2000). Avocation: theater. Office: Fifth Evang Luth Ch 1331 E High St Springfield OH 45505-1125

GESKE, JANINE PATRICIA, law educator, former state supreme court justice; b. Port Washington, Wis., May 12, 1949; d. Richard Braem and Georgette (Paulissen) Geske; m. Michael Julian Hogan, Jan. 2, 1982; children: Mia Geske Berman, Sarah Geske Hogan, Kevin Geske Hogan. Student, U. Grenoble, U. Rennes; BA, MA in Tchg., Beloit Coll., 1971; JD, Marquette U., 1975, LLD, 1998, LLD (hon.), 1994; DHL (hon.), Mt. Mary Coll., 1999. Bar: Wis. 1975, U.S. Dist. Ct. (ea. & we. dists.) Wis. 1975, U.S. Supreme Ct. 1978. Tchr. elem. sch., Lake Zurich, Ill., 1970-72; staff atty., chief staff atty. Legal Aid Soc., Milw., 1975-78; asst. prof. law, clin. dir. Law Sch. Marquette U., Milw., 1978-81; hearing examiner Milw. County CETA, Milw., 1980-81; judge Milw. County Circuit Ct., Milw., 1981-93; justice Supreme Ct. Wis., 1993-98; disting. prof. law Marquette U. Law Sch., Milw., 1998—, interim Miles County exec., 2002, interim dean Sch. Law, 2002—03. Dean Wis. Jud. Coll.; mem. faculty Nat. Jud. Coll.; instr. various jud. tng. programs, continuing legal edn. Fellow ABA, mem. Am. Law Inst., Am. Arbitration Assn., Soc. Profls. in Dispute Resolution, Wis. Bar Assn., Wis. Assn. Mediators, Milw. Bar Assn., Nat. Women Judges Assn., 7th Cir. Bar Assn., Alpha Sigma Nu. Roman Catholic. Office: Marquette U Law Sch PO Box 1881 Milwaukee WI 53201-1881

GEST, KATHRYN WATERS, public affairs professional; b. Boston, Mar. 20, 1947; d. Mendal and Anna Waters; m. Theodore O. Gest, May 28, 1972; 1 child, David Mendal. BS, Northwestern U., 1969; MS, Columbia U., 1970. Reporter The Patriot-Ledger, Quincy, Mass., 1968; writer Europe desk Voice of Am., Washington, 1969; reporter St. Louis Globe-Democrat, 1970-77, Congl. Quar., Washington, 1977-78, news editor, 1978-80, asst. mng. editor, 1980-83, mng. editor, 1983-87; St. Louis corr. Time Mag., 1975-77, The Christian Sci. Monitor, 1976-77; press sec. to Sen. William S. Cohen, Washington, 1987-96; chmn., U.S. del. Internat. Labor Orgn. Tripartite Meeting on Conditions of Employment and Work of Journalists, Geneva, 1990; exec. v.p., dir. internat. issues Powell Tate, 1996—. Election observer Nat. Dem. Inst., Albania, 1996, Azerbaijan, 2003. Recipient award for investigative reporting Inland Daily Press Assn., 1975 Bd. dirs. Nat. Press Found. Soc. Profl. Journalists, Women's Fgn. Policy Group, Internat. Women's Media Fund, Nat. Press Club. Office: Powell Tate 700 13th St NW Ste 1000 Washington DC 20005-6618 E-mail: kgest@webershandwick.com.

GETCHELL, SYLVIA FITTS, librarian; b. Dover, N.H., July 3, 1925; d. Perley Irving and Marguerite Elizabeth (Marden) F.; m. L. Forbes Getchell, July 17, 1948; children: Ann Marden, Faith Perley, Edward Fitts, William Forbes. BA in History magna cum laude, U. N.H., 1947; BS in Libr. Sci., Simmons Coll., 1948. Profl. cataloger Libr. Columbia U., N.Y.C., 1948-51, U. N.H., Durham, 1951-52; sch. libr. Newmarket (N.H.) Pub. Schs., 1970-85; curator Stone Sch. Mus., Newmarket, 1966—. Author: Marden Family Genealogy, 1974, Tide Turns on the Lamprey: History of Newmarket, N.H., 1984, Fitts Families: A Genealogy, 1989; co-editor: Piscataqua Pioneers, Selected Biographies of Early Settlers in Northern New England, 2000. Libr. Am. Independence Mus., Exeter, N.H., 1990—, bd. govs., 1992-99; bd. dirs. Newmarket Hist. Soc., 1966—, past pres.; curator Stone Sch. Mus., 1966—; bd.dirs. Piscataqua Pioneers, Portsmouth, N.H., 1969—, past pres.; 18th century re-enactor 1st Newmarket Colonial Militia, 1973—; former chair ann. fund drive local chpt. ARC; past collector, Sun. sch. tchr. Newmarket Cmty. Ch.; former treas. Aux. of N.H. Dental Soc.; mem. N.H. Hist. Soc. Mem. DAR (mem. and past sec. N.H. attic commn. 1994-2000, N.H. state historian 2000—), New Eng. Hist. Geneal. Soc., Newmarket Women's Club (past treas.), Huguenot Soc. N.H., Soc. Daus. Colonial Wars. Republican. Avocations: genealogy, oil painting, needlework, travel. Home: 51 N Main St Newmarket NH 03857-1216

GETER, JENNIFER L. psychologist; b. Washington, Mar. 12, 1970; d. Robert James and Delores Marie Geter. PsyD, Nova Southeastern U., 1997. Lic. clin. psychologist Bd. Examiners in Psychology/Tenn., 2002. Lead children and youth therapist, case mgr. Midtown Mental Health Ctr., Memphis, 1998—2003; clin. psychologist NIA Therapy Svcs., Memphis, 1999—; sch. psychologist Memphis City Schs., 2003—. Singer: (church choir) Greater Cmty. Temple Voices, (gospel choir) Marc Cooper and Friends and Miami Mass Choir. Pres. Greater Cmty. Temple Voices, Memphis, 2002—03. Post Doctoral fellow, U. Tenn., 1997—98. Mem.: APA (assoc.). Mem. Church Of God In Christ. Avocations: music, basketball, swimming, travel. Office: NIA Therapy Services Ste 935 1331 Union Ave Memphis TN 38115

GETSKE, KATHRINE, psychiatric social worker; b. Memphis, Jan. 19, 1937; d. Noble Owen and Annie Lou (Robertson) Fowler; m. Raymond Nicholas Getske, Nov. 27, 1965; children: Philip David, Raymond Nicholas Jr., Barbara Lynn, Virginia Kathrine. BS cum laude, Memphis State U., 1960; MA, Presbyn. Sch. Christian Edn., Richmond, Va., 1962; MSW, U. Tenn., 1989. Lic. cert. social worker, Tenn.; cert. dir. Christian edn. Dir. Christian edn. 1st Presbyn. Ch., Auburn, Ala., 1962-64; social worker ARC, Memphis, 1964-65, Dept. Human Svcs., Memphis, 1985-86; vol. coord. Johnson Aux. to the Regional Med. Ctr., Memphis, 1986-87; psychiat. social worker Memphis Mental Health Inst., 1990-91; med. and psychiat. social worker St. Joseph Hosp., Memphis, 1991-94; therapist Delta Med. Ctr., Memphis, 1999—, Magnolia Counseling Assocs., Batesville, Miss., 2000—; cons. Tri Lakes Med. Ctr., Batesville; psychiat. therapist Alliance Healthcare Sys., Holly Springs, Miss. Pres. Johnson Aux. to Regional Med. Ctr., Memphis, 1985-86; mem. Dixon Gallery, Brooks Mus. League; elder Balmoral Presbyn. Ch.; del. to Cuba, People to People Amb. Program, 2001. Mem. AAUW (pres. Memphis chpt. 1976-78, legis. chair 1990-91, named grant honoree 1985), Acad. Cert. Social Workers, Whitehaven Garden Club, Kennedy Book Club, Beethoven Club, Roseleigh Garden Club (sec.). Republican. Avocations: travel, bridge, reading. Home: 7607 Shady Rose Cv Memphis TN 38119-9109

GETZ, BETTINA, lawyer; b. Davenport, Iowa; BA with honors, Mich. State U., 1976; JD with honors, DePaul U., 1982. Judicial law clk. Ill. Appellate Ct., Chgo., 1982-84; assoc. atty. Isham Lincoln & Beale, Chgo., 1984-87, Mayer Brown & Platt, Chgo., 1987-90, ptnr., atty., 1990—. Mem. Chgo. Inn of Ct. Office: Mayer Brown & Platt 190 S La Salle St Ste 3100 Chicago IL 60603-3441

GETZ, MELISSA B. secondary school educator; b. Balt., May 26, 1969; d. Stanley (adoptive father) and Kathy Getz. BS, Va. Poly. Inst. and State U., 1991; MS, U. Calif., Davis, 1994; tchg. cert., Calif. State U., Sacramento, 1995. Tchr. Berkeley (Calif.) H.S., 1995-96; sci. tchr. Tennyson H.S., Hayward, Calif., 1996—. Cluster leader, East Bay (Calif.) Biotech. Edn. Partnership, 1999-2002; girls tennis coach, Tennyson H.S., 1997-99, Sci. Explorations Club advisor, 2000-01. Bd. dirs. Bridgewater Homeowners Assn., Albany, Calif., 1999—. Mem. ASCD, Nat. Assn. Biology Tchrs. (life), Assn. Women in Sci. (Sacramento Valley and East Bay chpts.), Nat. Sci. Tchrs. Assn., Calif. Sci. Tchrs. Assn., Phi Beta Kappa. Home: 545 Pierce St # 1208 Albany CA 94706 Office: Tennyson H S 27035 Whitman St Hayward CA 94544 E-mail: ntropi@aol.com.

GETZENDANNER, SUSAN, lawyer, former federal judge; b. Chgo., July 24, 1939; d. William B. and Carole S. (Muehling) O'Meara; children—Alexandra, Paul. BBA, JD, Loyola U., 1966. Bar: Ill. bar 1966. Law clk. U.S. Dist. Ct., Chgo., 1966-68; assoc. Mayer, Brown & Platt, Chgo., 1968-74, ptnr., 1974-80; judge U.S. Dist. Ct., Chgo., 1980-87; ptnr. Skadden, Arps, Slate, Meagher & Flom, Chgo., 1987—. Recipient medal of excellence Loyola U. Law Alumni Assn., 1981 Mem. ABA, Chgo. Council Lawyers. Office: Skadden Arps Slate Meagher Flom 333 W Wacker Dr # 2100 Chicago IL 60606-1220

GEWIRTZ, MINDY L. organizational and human relations consultant; b. N.Y.C., Mar. 19, 1951; d. Martin and Miriam (Altman) Lebovicz; m. Gershon C. Gewirtz, Sept. 7, 1971; children: Yussy, Henoch, Sora Leah, Adina, Doniel. MPS, N.Y. Inst. Tech., 1977; MSW, SUNY, Albany, 1981; PhD in Orgnl. Sociology, Boston U., 1995. Lic. ind. clin. social worker; diplomate Am. Bd. Clin. Social Workers. Project coord. Ringel Inst. Gerontology SUNY-Albany, 1980-82; coord. sr. adult dept. Jewish Family Svcs., Albany, 1983-84; dir. eldercare connection long distance caregiving svc. Jewish Family and Children's Svc., Boston, 1984-93; prin. GLS, Inc., Boston, 1988—; postgrad. fellow orgnl. devel. & human resources cons. Boston Inst. Psychotherapy, 1990. Adj. asst. prof. Boston U. Sch. Social Work; cons. Ibis Cons. Group, Cambridge, 1990—; orgn. and mgmt. cons. Boston Digital Equipment Corp., Boston, 1988-92; orgnl. cons. Malden Mills, Lawrence, Mass., 1992-99; presdl. adviser Am. Type Cutter Collection, 2002. Co-author: Sustaining Top Leadership: Promise and Pitfalls in Collaborative Work Systems, 2002; assoc. author: Human Dilemmas in Work Organizations, 1994; contbr. articles to profl. jours. and publs. Mem. Boston Work and Family Forum, New England Human Resources Assn., Greater Boston Orgnl. Devel. Network. Recipient Max Siporin Social Work fellow. Mem. NASW, ACSW (bd. cert. diplomate), Am. Assn. Bus. Women (career advancement fellow), Phi Beta Kappa. Home: 23 Browne St Brookline MA 02446-3804

GEWIRTZ-FRIEDMAN, GERRY, editor; b. N.Y.C., Dec. 22, 1920; d. Max and Minnie (Weiss) G.; m. Eugene W. Friedman, Nov. 11, 1945; children: John Henry, Robert James. BA, Vassar Coll., 1941. Editor Package Store Mgmt., 1942-44, Jewelry Mag., 1945-53; freelance editor promotion dept. McCall's Mag., Esquire, 1953-56; free-lance fashion and gifts editor Jewelers Circular Keystone, N.Y.C., 1955-71; editor, pub. The Fashionables, 1971-74, The Forecast, 1974—, Nat. Jeweler, Ann. Fashion Guide, 1976-80; editor, assoc. pub. Exec. Jeweler, 1980-83; editor The Fashion Source (formerly Internat. Fashion Index), N.Y.C., 1984—; freelance editor and mktg. specialist, 1995—. Ptnr. Gary Gewirtz-Editl. and Mktg.; free-lance editl. wrtier, 1995—. Corr. Internat. Mktg. News. Mem exec. com. Inner City Council of Cardinal Cooke, N.Y.; chairperson women's task force United Jewish Appeal Fedn.; former bd. govs. Israel Bonds; former trustee Israel Cancer Research Fund, Central Synagogue, bd. dirs. Double Image Theater; former pres. women's aux. Brandeis U. Honored guest Am. Jewish Com., 1978; Israel Cancer Research Fund, 1978-81; recipient Disting. Community Service award Brandeis U., 1987; named to Jewelry Hall Fame, 1988. Mem. N.Y. Fashion Group, Nat. Home Fashions League (former pres.), Women's Jewelry Assn. (pres. 1983-87, named editor who has contbd. most to jewelry industry 1984, free lance editor). Home: 45 Sutton Pl S New York NY 10022-2444

GEWURZ, ANITA TARTELL, medical association administrator; b. Buffalo, July 30, 1946; MD, Albany Med. Coll., 1970. Resident in pediat. U. Ill., Chgo., 1971—73; resident in allergy and immunology Rush-Presbyn.-St. Luke's Hosp., Chgo., 1974—76; fellow allergy and immunology Max Samter Inst., Grant Hosp., Chgo., 1976—77, Northwestern U. Med. Coll., Chgo., 1983—85; assoc. prof. immunology/microbiology, pediat. and internal med. Rush U. Med. Coll., Chgo., 1993—2003, prof. immunology/microbiology, pediat. and internal med., 2003—; physician Rush U. Med. Ctr., Chgo., 1974—. Chair, Tng. Program Dirs. Com. Am. Assn. of Allergy, Asthma & Immunology, 2003—04; chair Am. Bd. Allergy and Immunology, 2004—. Office: Rush Univ Med Ctr 1725 W Harrison St Ste 117 Chicago IL 60612*

GEYER, GEORGIE ANNE, syndicated columnist, educator, author, biographer, TV commentator; b. Chgo., Apr. 2, 1935; d. Robert George and Georgie Hazel (Gervens) G. BS, Northwestern U., 1956, LHD (hon.), 1993; postgrad., U. Vienna, Austria, 1956-57; LittD (hon.), Lake Forest Coll., 1980, Coll. Mt. St. Joseph, 1986, Notre Dame, 1986, Wilson Coll., 1987, Linfield Coll., 1987, St. Mary-of-the-Woods Coll., 1989, U. Indpls., 1991, Colby-Sawyer Coll., 1992, Franklin Coll., 1992, Cabrini Coll., 1994; LHD (hon.), Northwestern U., 1984, U. S.C., 1991, Rockhurst (Jesuit) Coll., Kansas City, 1992, Spring Hill Coll., 1993, Lebanon Valley Coll., 1994, Hofstra U., 1995, Loyola U., Chgo., 1996, Westminster Coll., 1996, Govs. State U., 1997, Notre Dame Coll., 1999, Knox Coll., 1999. Reporter Southtown Economist, Chgo., 1958; soc. reporter Chgo. Daily News, 1959-60, gen. assignment reporter, 1960-64, corr. Lat. Am., Ctrl. Am., Soviet Union, Middle East, Europe, 1964-75, roving fgn. corr. and columnist, 1967-75; syndicated columnist Los Angeles Times Syndicate, 1975-80, Universal Press Syndicate, 1981—; Lyle M. Spencer prof. journalism Syracuse U., 1977. Regular news commentator PBS' Washington Week in Review; questioner on Presdl. debate, Oct., 1984; steering com. Aspen Inst. Latin Am. Governance Project, 1981-82; commentator on the BBC; regular panelist Voice of America; sent by Internat. Communication Agy. on 3 worldwide speaking tours on Am. journalism: Nigeria, Zambia, Tanzania and Somalia, 1979, Philippines and Indonesia, 1981, Iceland, Norway, Belgium and Portugal, 1982; rep. Fulbright scholar program 40th anniversary, New Zealand, 1987; commencement speaker various colls., univs. including U. S.Carolina, Rockhurst Coll., St. Mary's Notre Dame; sr. fellow Annenburg Washington, 1992-93; columnist on fgn. policy, internat. affairs The Chgo. Tribune, The Wash. Times, Universal de Caracas, The Dallas Morning News, Diario las Americas, The Denver Post, others; speaker, lectr. in field. Author: The New Latins, 1970, The New 100 Years War, 1972, The Young Russians, 1976; (autobiography) Buying the Night Flight, (Weintal prize citation Sch. Fgn. Svc. Georgetown U. 1984, Chgo. Found. for Lit. award 1984), 1983, reissued, 1996, Guerilla Prince, The Untold Story of Fidel Castro, 1991, Waiting for Winter to End, An Extraordinary Journey Through Soviet Central Asia, 1994, Americans No More: The Death of Citizenship, 1996, Tunisia: A Journey Through the Country that Works, 2003; subjects of interviews include Prince Sihanouk of Cambodia, Yassar Arafat, Anwar Sadat, King Hussein of Jordan, Pres. Khaddafy of Libya, the Ayatollah Khomeini, Sultan Qaboos of Oman, Pres. Juan Peron of Argentina, Pres. Siad Barre of Somalia, Prime Minister Mauno Koivisto of Finland, Anastasio Somoza, Jerzy Urban, Janusz Onyszkiewicz, Prime Minister Edward Seaga of Jamaica, Pres. Ronald Reagan, Pres. George Bush, others; discovered and had first interview with second most-wanted Nazi, Walter Rauff in Tierra del Fuego, Chile, 1966; found Dominican pres. Juan Bosch in hiding in P.R. during Dominican revolution, 1965; held by Palestinians as Israeli spy, 1973; imprisoned in Angola for writing about revolutionary government, 1976; contbr. chpts. to books, articles numerous pubs. Active Orgn. for S.W. Community Chgo., 1960-64; trustee Am. U., Washington, 1981-86; Coun. Fgn. Rels. Recipient 1st prize Am. Newspaper Guild, 1962; 2d prize Ill. Press Editors Assn., 1962; award for best writing on Latin Am. Overseas Press Club, 1967; Merit award Northwestern U., 1968; Nat. Headliner award Theta Sigma Phi, 1968; Maria Moors Cabot award Columbia U., 1970; Hannah Solomon award Nat. Council Jewish Women, 1973; Ill. Spl. Events Commn. Woman's award, 1975; Northwestern U. Alumni award, 1991; Fulbright scholar U. Vienna, 1956-57; Woodrow Wilson fellow Rollins Coll., Winter Park, Fla., 1982; Presdl. Citation award Am. Univ., 1985; Disting. fellow Mortar Bd. Nat. Sr. Honor Soc., Am. U., 1982, Stewart Alaap award Assn. Former Intelligence Officers, 2000, Lifetime Achievement award Soc. Profl. Journalists, 2003; Sr. fellow Annenberg Washington Program, Washington, 1982-83; fellow Soc. Profl. Journalists, 1992; named Outstanding Illinoisian, Ill. State Assn., 2001; named to Hall of Fame of Soc. of Profl. Journalists, 2001. Mem.: Chgo. Coun. Fgn. Rels. (bd. dirs.), Washington Inst., Women's Inst. for Freedom of Press, Internat. Soc. Polit. Psychology, Internat. Inst. Strategic Studies, Inst. Internat. Edn. (bd. dirs.), Women in Comm., Soc. Profl. Journalists, Cosmos Club (1st women mem.), Gridiron Club. Home and Office: The Plaza 800 25th St NW Washington DC 20037-2207 Home Fax: 202-333-3198; Office Fax: 816-932-6658.

GEYER, KAREN LEA, writer; b. Pampa, Tex., June 6, 1952; d. W.D. "Dub" and Mardell (Mask) McKendree; m. David Wesley Geyer, Aug. 11, 1972; children: Nathan David, Neil John William, Kendra Lea. Student, West Tex. State U., 1970-71, Ctrl. Area Tech., Drumright, Okla., 1987. With Drumright News Jour., 1985—86; reporter Drumright Gusher, 1987—88; reporter, Lifestyles editor Cushing (Okla.) Daily Citizen, 1992—98; mng. editor Drumright Gusher, 1999, Cushing Daily Citizen, 2000—01. Editor: (mag.) Young at Heart, Sloat Webster, A Champion Roper, 2003. Recipient 1st Pl. award for feature writing Okla. Newspaper Found. Mem. Okla. Press Assn. (participant news clinics), Okla. Writers Fed., Inc., Cimarron Valley Writers (pres.), Cushing C. of C. (mem. environ. com. 1996—). Republican. Baptist. Avocations: writing, photography. Home: 8439 S 465th West Ave Drumright OK 74030 Office: Drumright Gusher 127 E Broadway St Drumright OK 74030-3801 E-mail: dgeyer7414@aol.com.

GEYER, KATHY VAN NESS, retailer; b. Ft. Lee, Va., July 9, 1954; d. Joseph Clinton and Barbara Lee (Musser) Van N.; m. David Paul Geyer, Mar. 16, 1990 (div. 2002). BS, Purdue U., 1977. Sales mgr. Macy's, Atlanta, 1977 78, asst. buyer, 1978-79, buyer, 1979-80, group mgr., 1980-81, mdse. mgr., 1981-83, store mgr., 1983-84; dist. mgr. Eddie Bauer Inc., Seattle, 1984-85; asst. store mgr. Rich's Dept. Stores, Atlanta, 1985-88; store mgr. Upton's Dept. Stores, Atlanta, 1988-92; instr., dept. chair fashion merchandising div. Bauder Coll., Atlanta, 1992-94; owner, pres. Rings Around the Moon Llamas, Chelsea, Okla., 1994—; realtor Century 21 Group 1, Claremore, Okla., 1995—2003, OklaHomes Realty, Inc., Claremore, 2003—. Avocations: swimming, showing llamas, reading, travel. Home: 10071 S 4220 Rd Chelsea OK 74016-2140 Office Phone: 918-343-3158.

GEYSER, LYNNE M. lawyer, writer; b. Queens, N.Y., Mar. 28, 1938; d. Henry and Shirley Dannenberg; m. Lewis P. Geyser, 1956 (div. 1974); 1 child, Russell B. Geyser. BA, Queens Coll., 1960; JD, UCLA, 1968. Bar: Calif. 1969. Atty. Zagon, Schiff, Hirsch & Levine, Beverly Hills, Calif., 1969-70; atty., registered legis. advocate Beverly Hills, Malibu, Calif., 1973-75; atty. Freshman, Marantz, Comsky & Deutsch, Beverly Hills, Malibu, Calif., 1971-74; prof. law Glendale (Calif.) U. Law, 1974-76, U. Iowa Sch. Law, Iowa City, 1976-77, Pepperdine U., Malibu, 1977-78; pvt. practice Newport Beach, Calif., 1978-81, San Clemente, 1978—. Part-time prof. law Western State Law Sch., Fullerton, Calif., 1978, cons. atty. The Irvine Co., Newport Beach, 1981-86, Std. Mgmt. Co., L.A., 1987-88; instr. Saddleback Coll., Mission Viejo, Calif., early 1990's; lectr., instr. Calif. Assn. Realtors Grad. Realty Inst., 1972-78, U. So. Calif. brokers tng. courses, L.A., 1978-80, UCLA real estate and corp. courses for paralegals, 1973-76; creator and lectr. course on disclosure for licensees, L.A., San Diego and Orange Counties, Calif., 1978-81, faculty advisor, for alumni Glendale U. Coll. Law, 1975-76. Chief articles editor UCLA Law Rev., 1967; adv. bd. The Rsch. Jour., 1976; contbr. poetry and short stories to jours. Mem. exec. bd. L.A. County Art Mus. Contemporary Art Coun., L.A., 1971-73; bd. trustees Westwood (L.A.) Art Assn., 1974; bd. govs. La Costa Beach Homeowners Assn., Malibu, 1975; pres. Dana Point (Calif.) Coastal Arts Coun., 1989-90; teaching participant Jr. Achievement, Newport Beach, 1985. Recipient 6 Am. Jurisprudence awards, 1966-68, 2 West Hornbook awards, 1967; nom. Douglas Law Clk. UCLA Law Sch., 1967. Fellow The Legal Inst.; mem. AALS (chair-elect environ. law sect. 1977), San Clemente Sunrise Rotary, Order of Coif. Avocations: world travel, fine arts, writing, computers, performing arts, graphics. Office: PO Box 4715 San Clemente CA 92674-4715

GFELLER, DONNA KVINGE, clinical psychologist; b. Chgo., Jan. 15, 1959; d. Milton Melvin and Doris Ann (Chapman) Kvinge; m. Jeffrey Donald Gfeller, Aug. 2, 1986. BS in Biol. Scis., Ill. State U., 1980, MS in Clin. Psychology, 1984; PhD in Clin. Psychology, Ohio U., 1987. Lic. psychologist. Staff psychologist Cardinal Glennon Children's Hosp., St. Louis, 1986-87, sr. psychologist, 1988-89, dir. dept. psychology, 1990—. Mem. APA (divsn. clin. psychology, clin. child psychology), Soc. Pediatric Psychology, World Wildlife Fund. Avocations: travel, horseback riding. Office: Cardinal Glennon Children's Hosp 1465 S Grand Blvd Saint Louis MO 63104-1003

GHARIB, SUSIE, television newscaster; b. N.Y.C., Nov. 27, 1950; d. Ali and Homa (Razzaghmanesh) G.; m. Foreydoun Nazem, Jan. 20, 1973; children: Alexander, Taraneh. BA magna cum laude, Case Western Res. U., 1972; M in Internat. Affairs, Columbia U., 1974. Reporter Cleve. Plain Dealer, 1972-73; assoc. editor Fortune Mag., N.Y.C., 1974-83; anchor, reporter Bus. Times/ESPN, N.Y.C., 1983-85; bus. reporter ABC News, N.Y.C., 1986-87; anchor Fin. News Network, N.Y.C., 1989-90, CNBC Network, Ft. Lee, N.J., 1993-98, Nightly Bus. Report, N.Y.C., 1998—. Moderator/host Xerox Corp., Stanford, Conn., 1989-95, KPMG Peat Marwick, N.Y.C., 1992-95; cons. Adam Smith's Money World/PBS, N.Y.C., 1987. Bd. dirs. First Fortis, Inc., 1991-2000, Ice Theatre of N.Y., 1988-90. Mem. Fgn. Policy Assn., N.Y. Fin. Writers Assn., Overseas Press Club, Econ. Club N.Y. (trustee 2003—), Phi Beta Kappa, Sigma Delta Chi. Democrat. Avocations: figure skating, tennis, classical piano. Home: 44 E 73rd St New York NY 10021-4173

GHELF, JENNIFER LYNNE, music educator; b. La Crosse, Wis., Aug. 5, 1973; d. Ralph Earl and Linda Sue Ghelf. BA, Luther Coll., Decorah, Iowa, 1995. Lic. Music Educators Iowa, 1996. H.S. vocal music tchr. Winterset H.S., Iowa, 1996—2002; elem. vocal music tchr. Waukee Elem. Sch., Iowa, 2002—. Asst. dir. of music ministry 1st United Presbyn. Ch., Winterset, Iowa, 2002; choir dir. 1st Christian Ch., Winterset, Iowa, 1996—97. Mem.: Iowa Choral Dir. Assn., Music Educators Nat. Conf. Democrat-Npl. Personal E-mail: jghelf@mchsi.com. E-mail: jghelf@waukee.k12.ia.us.

GHIGLIERI, CATHERINE A. auto loan company executive; b. Toluca, Ill. m. Mark Holland; 1 child, Michael. BBA in Fin., U. Notre Dame; JD, Ga. State U. With Office of the Comptr. of the Currency; apptd. Tex. Banking commr., 1992-99; pres., CEO rateGenius, Inc., Houston, 1999—. Exec. dir. Fin. Commn.; dir. Access to Fin. Svcs.; chmn. Prepaid Funeral Guaranty Fund Adv. Coun. Grad. Class XV-State Tex. Gov.'s Exec. Devel. Program. Mem. State Bar Ga., D.C. Bar, Conf. State Bank Suprs. (sec.-treas., bd. dirs.). Office: rateGenius Inc 1021 Main St Ste 1150 Houston TX 77002

GIACCHI, JUDITH ADAIR, elementary school educator; b. Rochester, N.Y., Dec. 8, 1947; d. William Robert Peters and L. Virginia (Coulter) Peters Sweet; m. Alphonse Robert Giacchi, Aug. 8, 1970; children: Christina Marie, Anthony Robert. BS, SUNY, Buffalo, 1969. Permanent cert. tchr., N.Y. Data processing control clk. Neisner Bros., Inc., Rochester, 1969-70; tchr. Syracuse (N.Y.) City Sch. Dist., 1970—. Tchr. insvcs. and workshops Syracuse sch. dists., 1972—; master tchr. Syracuse U., 1983—; chmn. bldg. level team, 1988—98; collaborative Field Team Rep., mem., 1988—; trainer, ednl. rsch. and dissemination thinking math I, II and III, 2001—; rep. N.Y. State Tchrs. Retirement Sys. convs. and N.Y. State United Tchrs. convs., 1987—89. Contbr. articles to profl. publs. Corr. sec., rec. sec., legis. chmn. Nate Perry Sch. PTA, Liverpool, N.Y., 1983-95; troop aide Girl Scouts U.S.A., Liverpool, 1982-86; rep., mem. strategy com. Syracuse Labor Coun., 1995-97; mem. Union Cities Planning Com., 1997. Recipient award N.Y. State Legislature, 1994, various minigrants. Mem. N.Y. State United Tchrs. Fedn. (rep. convs. 1990-92), Ctrl. N.Y. Romance Writers Group, Onondaga County Tchrs. Assn. (award 1989), Syracuse Tchrs. Assn. (various coms., chief bldg. rep. 1984—). Avocations: reading, writing, needlecrafts, music, computers. Office: Porter Magnet Sch Tech and Career Exploration 512 Emerson Ave Syracuse NY 13204

GIADONE, SUSAN, livestock office manager; b. Pueblo, Colo., Mar. 5, 1956; d. Eugene Joseph and Mary Josephine (Burnham) Ceasar; m. James Lenn, Sept. 13, 1975; children: James Lenn Jr., Eugena Anthonette. Clerk Clark Western Store, Pueblo, Colo., 1974-76; sec. Caprock Feedlots, Leoti, Ks., 1978-98; accounting office Loaf and Jug Stores, Pueblo, 1990-92; accts. payable Vidmar Motor, Pueblo, 1995-97; co-mgr. Gene Cesar Dairy, Pueblo, 1996—; office mgr. Fowler Livestock Exchange, Colo., 1997—. Mem. Pueblo County Stockman's Assn., sec.; mem. Fowler C. of C.; adv. Pueblo County FFA; pres. Pueblo County FFA Alumni, 1992—93; organizer Mo. Day Com., Ranch Rodeo, Fowler, 1999; cmty. rep. White Rock Cmty., 1988—. Mem.: Colo. Cattlemen's Assn. (conv. com., pub. rels. com.), U.S. Team Roping Corp., Fowler Roping Club (sec., treas.). Avocations: nature, music, family, cooking. Home: 67643 Hwy 10 Fowler CO 81039-9613

GIALLOMBARDO, LESLIE, publishing executive; Adv. dir. The Desert Sun, Palm Springs, Calif., The Idaho Statesman, Boise; v.p. adv. The Tennessean, 1995, sr. v.p. mktg., 1999, pres., pub., 2002—. Mgmt. positions Reno (NE) Gazette-Jour., Statesman Jour., Salem, Oreg. Named seven time winner Pres.'s Ring. Office: 1100 Broadway Nashville TN 37203 E-mail: lgiallom@tennessean.com.

GIAMANCO, SCHERRIE V, bank executive; d. Joseph John Viola and Lucille Elizabeth Engelman; children: Maria Luchele Phifer, Evana Joelle Phifer, Paul John, Joseph Paul. BS in mktg., So. Ill. U., 1981—84, MS in speech commn., 1984—86. Outside dir. First Nat. Bank of Nokomis, Ill., 1977—; price support program chief USDA Farm Svc. Agy., Springfield, Ill., 1994—. Adminstrv. aide US Senator Paul Simon, Springfield, Ill., 1991—94, dir. of sales Ramada Hotel Mt. Vernon, Ill., 1988—90. Downstate fin. dir. Simon for Senate, Chgo., 1990; congl. field dir. Ill. Dem. Party, 1988. Mem.: Ill. Agri-Women, Am. Assn. of Univ. Women, Ill. Dem. Women. Home: 3312 Ashley Lane Springfield IL 62707 E-mail: scherrie.giamanco@il.usda.gov.

GIANLORENZI, NONA ELENA, painter, art dealer, educator; b. Virginia, Minn., July 20, 1939; d. Teto Nicholas and Lena Dora (Zini) Gianlorenzi; m. George Michael Devlin, July 20, 1966 (dec. Feb. 1990); children: Gian Loren Kjellesvig Waering, Helena Nicole Devlin Seidel. BA, Bklyn. Coll./CUNY. Painter self employed, N.Y.C., 1960—; asst. dir. Am. Art Gallery, N.Y.C., 1961-67; owner, dir. Asage Art Gallery, N.Y.C., 1977-88; pvt. art dealer Art Space Inc., Bklyn., 1989—. Tchr. art and aesthetics St. Francis Sch. Deaf, Bklyn., 1968-71, Mt. Carmel, Queens, N.Y., 1968-71, Charles Borromeo Sch., Bklyn., 1968-71. Ford fellow, 1992-94, Loy fellow, 1992-94; Art Studio scholar, 1961. Address: 415 Rugby Rd Brooklyn NY 11226-5611

GIANOTTI-FALCIGNO, CONSTANCE ELIZABETH, special education educator; b. New Haven, Sept. 9, 1950; d. Louis Frank and Rowena Lillian (Miller) Gianotti; m. Thomas Bernard Falcigno Jr., May 12, 1990; 1 child, Elizabeth M. Falcigno. BS, So. Conn. State U., 1972; MA, U. Conn., 1982. Tchr. spl. edn. Killingly (Conn.) Bd. Edn., 1972-79, Area Coop. Edn. Svcs., Willimantic, Conn., 1979-83, Madison Bd. Edn., 1983—. Coach cheerleaders Killingly High Sch., 1973-79, mid. sch. cheerleaders, 1986-91, Madison, Spl. Olympics, Willimantic, 1980-84; dramatic Killingly Edn. Assn. Scholarship Fund, 1977-79; active Respit Care, Bolton and Madison, 1979-87; sponsor Hands Alive sign lang. program, Madison, 1990-96; del. citizen amb. program to China People to Peolpe Internat., 1994. Fellow Coun. for Exceptional Children; mem. ASCD, Shoreline Assn. of Retarded Citizens and the Handicapped (bd. dirs. Seneca chpt. 1993-95). Democrat. Methodist. Avocations: walking, sailing, dance. Office: Daniel Hand High Sch Green Hill Rd Madison CT 06443

GIARDI, DIANE M. ceramics educator, sculptor; b. West Hartford, Conn., June 11, 1957; Student, Florence, 1978; BS in Art Edn., U. Vt., 1979; cert. in graphic design, Mass. Coll. Art, 1985; MFA in Ceramics, Syracuse U., 1994. Milieu counselor Kennedy Meml. Hosp. Children, Brighton, Mass., 1979-81, activities coord., 1981-83; art tchr. Creative Ednl. Assocs., Boston, 1981-83; graphic artist, supr. Extraversion, Waltham, Mass., 1983-84; art dir. Info. Gatekeepers, Inc., Boston, 1984-86; art tchr. New Eng. Home for Little Wanderers, Boston, 1986-87; creative dir. Wilde Advtsg. Assocs., Inc., Portland, Me., 1987-89; freelance designer Giardi Designs, Cape Porpoise, Me., 1987-90; ceramics instr. Syracuse (N.Y.) U., 1992, 93, 94; ceramics instr., administr. Heartwood Sch. Art, 1994—96; ceramics prof. U. So. Maine, 1996-97; mem. faculty art Waynflete Sch., Portland, Maine, 1997—2000; mem. arts faculty Ross Sch., East Hampton, NY, 2000—. Ceramics instr. DeCordova Mus. Sch., 1997—2001. One-woman shows include Phoebes Gallery, Syracuse, N.Y., 1994, Eureka Craft Gallery, 1994, Ogunquit Art Assn. Gallery, 1996, Ross Gallery, East Hampton, N.Y., 2003; exhibited in group shows at Danforth St. Gallery, Portland, 1989-90, White Cube Gallery Syracuse U., 1991, Mission Landing Gallery, Syracuse, 1992, Lowe Gallery, Syracuse, 1992, U. La., 1993, U. Tenn., 1993, 12 Rms. 4 Gallery, Syracuse, 1993, Octagon Ctr. for the Arts, Ames, Iowa, 1993, The Upper Gallery, 1993, The Everson Mus. Art, 1993, HUB Galleries and Pa. State U., University Park, 1993, Ea. Wash. U. Gallery Art, Cheney, 1993, West Chester, Pa., 1993, Galleria Mesa, 1994, Lafayette (La.) Art Gallery, 1994, The Newark Mus., 1994, Carnegie Mus. Art, Pitts., 1994, The Potters Gallery, West Chester, Pa., 1994, Hoyt Gallery, New Castle, Pa., 1995, Maine Coast Gallery, Rockport, Maine, 1996, The Ogunquit Art Assn. Gallery, 1996, Kans. State U. Gallery, Manhattan, Kans., 1999, Sandzen Gallery, Lindsburg, Kans., 2000, Denton (Tex.) Arts Ctr., 2003, South Cobb Arts Ctr., Mableton, Ga., 2003, Gallery 510, Decatur, Ill., 2003. Bd. dirs. Danforth St. Gallery, Portland, 1988-90, Grief Support Ctr., 1996-97; active Hospice York, Maine; creator, developer Arts in Hospice, York; developer Grief Support Ctr. for Children and Families, York, Maine; vol. Hospice, 1990—. Grantee Me. Coun. Arts, 1989-90. Mem. Nat. Art Edn. Ass., Am. Craft Coun., Coll. Art Assn., Nat. Coun. Edn. for the Ceramic Arts, Ogunquit Art Assn. (bd. dirs. 1996-97), East End Poets Assn. Home: 170 Laurel Ave Southold NY 11971-5218

GIBB, ROBERTA LOUISE, lawyer, artist; b. Cambridge, Mass., Nov. 2, 1942; d. Thomas Robinson Pieri and Jean Knox Gibb. BS, U. Calif., La Jolla, 1969; JD, New Eng. Sch. Law, 1982; student in Epislemology and Colorusium, MIT, 1972—85. Bar: Mass. 1978. Legal aide Mass. State Legis., 1973; practice law Mass., 1980—. Author: To Boston With Love, 1980, The Art of Inflation, 1981, The Art of Economics, 1982; co-prodr.: (documentary film) Lovins on the Soft Path; contbr. articles to profl. jours.; Exhibited in group shows at Geraci Galleries, Rockport, Mass., 1996—, Rockport Art Assn. Gallery, 1996—, Represented in permanent collections, Nat. Art Mus. Art, Indpls.; prodr.: (TV documentary) Where the Spirit Leads, 1980—, 2000; executor 5 murals, sculptor Albert Einstein, Pres. Carter, Pres. Johnson, Pres. Reagan, Mother Theresa, Eleanor Roosevelt, The Marathon, Fire Dancers, Birth, Olympia, The Family, The Left Handed Squash Player, Basketball, Germain Gliddin, numerous others. Bd. dir. Essex County Environ. and Conservation, Rockport, Mass., 1980-85. Women winner Boston Marathon, 1966, 67, 68, 1st woman to run Boston Marathon, 1966; inducted into Road Runners of Am. Hall of Fame, 1982

Mem.: Inst. Study of Natural Sys. (founder, pres. 1976—), Rockport Art Assn., Nat. Sculpture Soc., Mass. Bar, Boston Athletic Assn., Coll. Club, Club Rome (sec. bd. dirs. 1999—). E-mail: bobbigibb@aol.com.

GIBBONS, CELIA VICTORIA TOWNSEND (MRS. JOHN SHELDON), editor, publisher; b. Fargo, N.D. d. Harry Alton and Helen (Hoog) Townsend; m. John Sheldon Gibbons, May 1, 1935; children: Mary Vee, John Townsend. Student, U. Minn., 1930-33. Advt. mgr. Hotel Nicollet, Mpls., 1933-37; contbg. editor children's mags., 1935—; ptnr. Youth assocs. Co., Mpls., 1942-65; pub. art dir. Mines and Escholier mags., 1954-65; founder Bull. Bd. Pictures, Inc., Mpls., 1954, pres., 1954—. Founder Periodical Litho Art Co., Mpls., 1962, pres., 1962-65; artist Cath. Boy mag., 1938; artist, designer book Palaces That Went To Sea, 1990; chief photographer Cath. Miss mag., 1955; cons., contbg. editor Nereus Pub. Co., 1998-. Mem. Women's aux. Mpls. Symphony Orch.; mem. Ft. Lauderdale (Fla.) Art Mus.; Rep. chairwoman Golden Valley, Minn., 1950; alt. del. Hennepin County Rep. Conv., 1962. Mem. Mpls. Inst. Arts, Internat. Inst., St. Paul Arts and Sci., Art Guild Boca Raton, Woman's Club, Minikahda Club, Deerfield Beach Women's Club. Home: 1416 Alpine Pass Tyrol Hills Minneapolis MN 55416 Office: 1057 Hillsboro Mile Hillsboro Beach FL 33062

GIBBONS, JULIA SMITH, federal judge; d. John Floyd and Julia Jackson (Abernathy) Smith; m. William Lockhart Gibbons, Aug. 11, 1973; children: Rebecca Carey, William Lockhart Jr. BA, Vanderbilt U., 1972; JD, U. Va., 1975. Bar: Tenn. 1975. Law clk. to judge U.S. Ct. Appeals, 1975-76; assoc. Farris, Hancock, Gilman, Branan, Lanier & Hellen, Memphis, 1976-79; legal advisor Gov. Lamar Alexander, Nashville, 1979-81; judge 15th Jud. Cir., Memphis, 1981-83, U.S. Dist. Ct. (we. dist.) Tenn., Memphis, 1983—2002, chief judge, 1994-2000; judge U.S. Ct. Appeals (6th cir.), Memphis, 2002—. Fellow: Memphis and Shelby County Bar Found., Tenn. Bar Found., Am. Bar Found.; mem.: Memphis Bar Assn., Phi Beta Kappa, Order of Coif. Presbyterian. Office: US Ct Appeals 970 Federal Bldg 167 N Main St Memphis TN 38103-1816

GIBBONS, KAYE, writer; b. Nash County, N.C., 1960; Student, U. N.C., Chapel Hill. Author: Ellen Foster (Sue Kaufman award for 1st fiction, Acad. Arts and Letters), A Virtuous Woman, 1989, A Cure for Dreams, 1991 (PEN Revson award, 1990, Heartland prize for fiction, Chgo. Tribune, N.C. Sir Walter Raleigh award), Charms for the Easy Life, 1993, Sights Unseen, On the Occasion of My Last Afternoon, 1998; actor:. Recipient Chevalier de l'Ordre des Arts et des Lettres, Govt. France, 1996. Office: c/o GP Putnam & Sons Publicity 375 Hudson St New York NY 10014

GIBBONS, LEEZA, television talk show host, entertainment reporter; b. Hartsville, SC, Mar. 26, 1957; m. John Hicks, 1980 (div. 1982); m. Chris Quinten, 1988 (div. 1990); 1 child, Lexi ; m. Stephen Meadows, 1991; children: Troy, Nathan. Student, U. S.C. CEO Leeza Gibbons Enterprises; co-host Entertainment Tonight, Hollywood, Calif., 1984—, John and Leeza, Hollywood, 1993; host, exec. prodr. Leeza, 1993—; host/exec. prodr. syndicated radio programs Entertainment Tonight on Radio with Leeza Gibbons, The Entertainment Report, The Top 25 Countdown with Leeza Gibbons, The Leeza Gibbons' Superstar Music Spl. Host Miss Universe Pageant, The Hollywood Christmas Parade; host, co-prodr. (series) Growing Up Together; film appearances include Robocop, 1987, Robocop 2, 1990, Soapdish, 1991, The Player, 1992, Last Action Hero, 1993. Office: Paramount TV 5555 Melrose Ave Los Angeles CA 90038-3112*

GIBBONS, MARY PEYSER, civic volunteer; b. N.Y.C., Dec. 15, 1936; d. Frederick Maurice and Catherine Mary (McKelvey) Peyser; m. John Martin Gibbons, Dec. 26, 1955; children: Catherine Way, Mary Sloan, John, Fredericka Kerr, Myles. Trustee Wadsworth Atheneum, 1978-99, hon. trustee, 2000; trustee Hartford Art Sch., 1985-95; regent U. Hartford, 1988-95—; bd. dirs. Hartford Ballet, 1981-95, Conn. Valley Girl Scouts, 1994-95, U.S. Found. World Fedn., Friends of Museums, 1990—; vol. Com. Art Mus., U.S. and Can., 1982-91; pres. Am. Assn. Mus. Vols., 1983-91, adv. bd. mem., 1991—; corporator St. Francis Hosp., 1990—, Hartford Ballet, 1995-97, Conn. Inst. for the Blind; mem. alumnae bd. divs. Convent of the Sacred Heart, 91th St., N.Y.C. Mem. Hartford Golf Club, Town and County Club. Office: Sefton & Sheil Ltd 1130 Prospect Ave Hartford CT 06105-1124

GIBBONS, PAMELA R. professional athletic trainer; b. Orange, Calif., May 16, 1965; d. Donna L. and Greg S. Crandall(Stepfather), Richard P. Gibbons; 1 child, Savana R. AS in Sports Med./Athletic Tng., Rancho Santiago C.C., 1985; BS in Phys. Edn. and Athletic Tng., Calif. State U., 1989; MA in Ednl. Leadership and Adminstrn., Chapman U., 2001. Cert. athletic trainer 1989, cardiopulmonary resuscitation instr. ARC, 1985, lifeguard tng. instr. ARC, 1996, adv. first aid, basic first aid, basic lifesaving ARC, 1998, first aid for pub. safety personnel instr. ARC, 1998. Head athletic trainer Los Alamitos (Calif.) H.S., 1988—91; personal trainer, fitness instr. Los Caballeros Sports Village, 1990—91; legal asst., investigator Juvenile Law Ctr., Santa Ana, Calif., 1991—94; asst. athletic trainer Chapman U., Orange, 1991—98, head women's swimming coach, 1993—96, head athletic trainer, 1998—. Instr./instr.'s aid Rancho Santiago C.C., 1984—90; substitute tchr. Los Alamitos H.S., 1988—91; part time faculty Chapman U., 1994—; lifeguard tng. instr. City of Orange, 1996—2000; approved clin. instr. Chapman U., 2003—. Mem. ARC. Mem.: Far West Athletic Trainers' Assn., Coll. Athletic Trainers Soc., Nat. Athletic Trainers' Assn. Office: Chapman U One University Dr Orange CA 92866 E-mail: gibbons@chapman.edu.

GIBBONS TANKARD, MELLISA W. education educator; b. Paget, Bermuda, Aug. 4, 1965; d. Carolyn A. Hart Gibbons and Melvin W. Gibbons; m. Radell Recardo Tankard, July 1, 1993; children: Ra'ees Jibri Tankard, Raushon K. S. Tankard. BA, Mt. Allison U., 1984—87; MEd, Howard U., 1987—89, PhD, 1995—2003. Project dir. Jubilee Enterprise of Greater Wash., Washington, 2000—01; adj. prof. Prince George's C.C., Largo, Md., 2001—01, Howard U., Washington, 2002—03. Author: (book) Identifying and Counseling Gifted Black Students. Prin. adv. bd. East Silver Spring Elem. Sch., Md.; bd. mem. Howard U. Early Learning Programs, Washington; gifted and talented liaison East Silver Spring Elem. Sch., Md. Mem.: APA. Islam. Avocations: writing, travel. Home: 1220 East West Hwy #116 Silver Spring MD 20910 Office: Howard University - Child Development 525 Bryant St NW Washington DC 20059 Personal E-mail: mwtankard@gov.bm.

GIBBS, JOHNIE ELIZABETH, information technology manager, educator, consultant; d. John J. and Ruth P. Gibbs. BS in Human Environ. Scis., cum laude, U. Ala., Tuscaloosa, 1984, MS in Consumer Scis., 1985, PhD in Instrnl. Leadership and Instrnl. Tech., 2003. Cert. online tchg. UCLA, 2001. Rsch. asst./assoc. Ctr. for Bus. and Econ. Rsch., U. Ala., Tuscaloosa, Ala., 1986—89; sr. rsch. assoc./computer lab asst. dir. Coll. of Human Environ. Scis., U. Ala., Tuscaloosa, Ala., 1989—94, computer coord., 1994—2001; instr. Dept. of Consumer Scis., U. Ala., 1989—2001; online course developer and online instr. Dept. of Distance Edn., U. Ala., 1999—2003; online program mgr. and cons. Tuscaloosa City Schs.; owner Gibbs Learning Techs., LLC, Northport, Ala., 2004. Editor (project coordinator): (book) Nothing but the Best: A Collection of Recipes from The University of Alabama Family; editor: (magazine/newsletter) Ala. Bus.; senior editor (book) Economic Abstract of Alabama 1989-90, Economic Abstract of Alabama 1987. Vol. webmaster Town of Brilliant, Ala. Mem.: Assn. for the Advancement of Computing in Edn., Internat. Soc. for Tech. in Edn., Am. Assn. for Family and Consumer Scis. (Ala. state sec. 1992—94, past state exec. com., state exec. bd. 1988—94, Ala. New Achiever's award 1993, cert. in family and consumer scis.), Kappa Delta Epsilon, Kappa Delta Pi, Gamma Beta Phi, Golden Key, Phi Upsilon Omicron. Church Of Christ. Personal E-mail: bgibbs@simplecom.net.

GIBBS, JORDAN SMITH, music educator, artist; b. Kinston, N.C., Sept. 11, 1936; d. Ernest Simpson Smith and Nell Brown (Johnson) Griffin; m. Gerald Goodwin Gibbs Jr., July 7, 1956; children: Anne, Stephen. Student, Duke U., 1954-56, George Washington U., 1974-77; Cert. in Piano, Conservatoire Royal de Musique, Mons, Belgium, 1980; BA in Music, Old Dominion U., 1984. Pvt. piano tchr., Cornwall-on-Hudson, N.Y., 1960-61; ch. organist TUSLOG Interdenominational Chapel, Ankara, Turkey, 1962-63; pvt. piano tchr. Mons, Belgium, 1978-79; piano tchr. Friends Sch., Virginia Beach, Va., 1984-86; pvt. piano tchr. Virginia Beach, from 1993; & Duke U. Libr. Assocs., 1989-92. Sec. bd. ARC, West Point, N.Y., 1959-60, hosp. vol., Ft. Sill, Okla., 1961, Ft. hood, Tex., 1969-70, Carlisle, Pa., 1970-71, vol. controller office, Norfolk, Va., 1987-88; asst. leader Girl Scout Mt. Vernon Scout Dist., Alexandria, Va., 1972-73; vol. Meals on Wheels Mt. Vernon Presbyn. Ch., Alexandria, 1972-73, Art League of Alexandria, 1972-73; vol. radiology clinic Internat. Red Cross, Mons, Belgium, 1978-80; sec.-treas. Shape Cycling Club, 1978-79; active docent Chrysler Mus., Norfolk, Va., 1992-99, bd. dirs. glass assocs., 1997-99; mem. worship com., fellowship com., flower guild First Presbyn. Ch., Virginia Beach, Va.; mem. Colonial Williamsburg (Va.) Found. Assocs., Libr. Assocs. Flower Guild, 1997-99; publicity chmn. SHAPE Art Assn., Mons, Belgium, 1978-79, Popular Choice Art Exhibit, SHAPE Hdqs., 1979; piano soloist Rachmaninoff Anniversary Celebration, Georgetown, Washington, 1974. Recipient Radiology Svc. award Red Cross, 1978-80. Mem. Met. Mus. Art, Va. Mus. FineArts, Phillips Collection, The Walters Art Gallery, Ctr. Contemporary Art, Muscarelle Mus. Art, Va. Hist. Soc., Nat. Trust, Nat. Mus. Women in the Arts, Am. Liszt Soc., Inc., Hermitage Found. Aux., Norfolk Soc. of Arts, Linkhorn Park Garden Club (editor yearbook 1992-94, sec. 1994-96, 1st v.p. 1996-98, rec. sec. 1998—, Ann. Flower Arrangements award 1999), Southwood Garden Club (rec. sec. 1971-72, 1st v.p. 1972-73), SACLANT Officers Wives Club (bd. dirs. 1982), Zeta Tau Alpha Alumnae (v.p. 1984-86, Sigma Alpha Iota (bd. dirs. 1980-84, Sword of Honor 1982, Grad. SAI Scholastic award 1984, SAI alumnae treas. 1990-99, treas. 1990-98, Stephen ministry program 1999—). Avocations: golf, tennis, skiing, needlepoint. Home: Virginia Beach, Va. Died Dec. 2002.

GIBBS, JUNE NESBITT, state legislator; b. Newton, Mass., June 13, 1922; d. Samuel Frederick and Lulu (Glazier) Nesbitt; m. Donald T. Gibbs, Dec. 8, 1945 (dec. 2001); 1 child, Elizabeth. BA in Math., Wellesley Coll., 1943; MA in Math., Boston U., 1947; postgrad. computer sci., U. R.I., 1981-84. Mem. from R.I. Rep. Nat. Com., 1969-80, sec., 1977-80; mem. R.I. Senate, Dist. 48, Providence, 1985—2003, R.I. Senate, Dist 12, 2003—. Mem. def. adv. com. Women in Svcs., 1970-72, vice chmn., 1972 Mem. Middletown Town Coun., 1974-80, 82-84, pres., 1978-80. Lt. (j.g.) USNR, 1943-46. Avocation: windsurfing. Home: 163 Riverview Ave Middletown RI 02842-5324 Office: Senate Minority Office State House Providence RI 02903

GIBBS, LINDA DIANA, music educator; d. William M. and Mary L. Gibbs. BA in Music, Tougaloo (Miss.) Coll., 1989; MEd in Sch. Adminstrn. and Supervision, Miss. Coll., 1998. Cert. tchr. Miss., 1994, administrator Miss., 1999. Archival sec. Zenobia Coleman Libr. Tougaloo (Miss.) Coll., 1989—90; data control clk. Am. HealthTech, Jackson, Miss., 1991—93; choral music tchr. Jackson (Miss.) Pub. Sch. Dist., 1993—94, gen. music tchr., 1994—. Mem. Miss. Fine Arts Revision Team, Jackson, 2001—03. Scholarship and challenge bowl chmn. Alpha Kappa Alpha Sorority, Inc., Jackson, Miss., 2000—03. Mem.: Miss. Music Educators Assn. (assoc.; pres. elem. divsn. 2000—02, past pres. 2003—), Music Educators Nat. Conf. (assoc.), Alpha Kappa Alpha (assoc.; spelling bee chmn. 1998—, scholarship chmn. 2000—03, chmn. challenge bowl 2000—03). Baptist. Avocations: piano, singing, cooking, organ, reading.

GIBBS, MARY L. writer, writers' services provider; b. Farmington Hills, Mich., May 2, 1973; d. Morris Whitehead and Elizabeth Sotnik, Thomas Sotnik (Stepfather); m. Gregory W. Gibbs; children: Johnathon, Bethany. Adminstrv. asst. Mobile Edn., Redford, Mich., 1994—96; receptionist Document Svcs., Livonia, Mich., 1996. Tchr.'s asst. The Learning Tree, Livonia, 1996—97; owner Gibbs Ink, Redford, 2001—. Author: (book) Secrets of the Maiden, 2000, Sensible Savings: Money Savers and Makers on the Web, 2002; actor: (Olympic fencing demonstrations) Michigan Renaissance Festival, 2000; editor: (newsletter) The Notebook and Pen, 2001. Founder Writer's Support Network, Redford, 2001—02; color guard coach Redford Union H.S., 2002—. Recipient 1st Pl. award, Writer's Arena monthly contest, 2000. Mem.: Writer's Arena Writing Group (owner 2001—02), Internat. Thespian Soc., Knights of Iron Stage Combat Team, Schoolcraft Coll. Fencing Club (pres. 2000—01, Ladies' Club Champion 1999). Avocations: reading, writing, swing dancing, theater, fencing. Office: Writer's Support Network/Gibbs Ink PO Box 40653 Detroit MI 48239 Business E-Mail: MarytheAuthor@aol.com.

GIBBS, NANCY PATRICIA, lawyer; b. Vancouver, B.C., Can., Dec. 22, 1946; d. Richard Brandreth and Ann Dorothy (Marriott) G.; m. Frank Weber Hughes, Aug. 28, 1971 (div.); 1 dau., Adrianne Elizabeth Hughes. BA in Chemistry, U. Wash., 1968, JD, 1971. Bar: Wash. 1971, U.S. Dist. Ct. (we. dist.) Wash. 1971, U.S. Ct. Appeals (9th cir.) 1972, U.S. Supreme Ct. 1980. Assoc. Davis, Wright, Todd, Riese & Jones, Seattle, 1971-76, ptnr., 1977—. commr. on salaries of state elected officials Washington State Commn., 1987—. Trustee, Seattle Aquarium Soc., 1982-83, 2d v.p., 1983-84; trustee Northwest Chamber Orchestra, 1985-88, mem. exec. com. 1986-87, treas. 1987-88; mem. adv. bd. Sr. Rights Assistance Project, 1978-80, Evergreen Legal Services Corp., 1980-81. Named Newsmaker of Future, Seattle C. of C./Time Mag., 1978; Cathedral fellow Cathedral Assocs., 1983-84. Mem. Seattle-King County Bar Assn. (treas. 1977-79, trustee 1979-82, 2d v.p. 1983-84, 1st v.p. 1984-85, pres. 1985-86), Seattle King County Bar Found. (trustee 1979-82, pres. 1981-82), U. Wash. Law Sch. Alumni Assn. (trustee 1978-82, treas. 1982-83, v.p. 1983-84, pres. 1984-85), Assn. Immigration and Nationality Lawyers, Fed. Bar Assn., ABA (mem. Nat. Met. Bar Leaders Caucus 1985—, mem. exec. com. 1986—), Wash. Bar Assn. (chmn. law related edn. com. 1980-82, disciplinary proceeding hearing officer, 1981—), Phi Alpha Delta. Episcopalian. Club: Wash. Athletic (Seattle); Sand Point Country. Bd. dirs. The Public Defender, 1987—; contbr. articles to profl. jours. Office: Century Sq Century Sq Ste 2600 Seattle WA 98101

GIBBS, PATRICIA HELLMAN, physician; b. Boston, Oct. 22, 1958; d. Frederick Warren and Patricia Christina (Sander) H.; m. Richard D. Gibbs, Dec. 22, 1984; children: Ruth, Samuel, Matthew, Kate, Frank. BA summa cum laude, Williams Coll., 1982; MD, Yale U., 1987. Diplomate Am. Bd. Family Practice. Intern, resident in family practice U. Wash., Seattle, 1987-90; ptnr. Tricia Gibbs, MD and Richard Gibbs, MD, San Francisco, 1990-95; co-founder, med. dir. San Francisco Free Clinic, 1993—. Supervising physician San Francisco Ballet, 1990-95. Co-author: Medical and Orthopedic Issues of Active and Athletic Women-Skiing, 1993, Spine Care-Dance, 1993. Founder Sugar Bowl Acad., 1999. Women's scholar Williams Coll., 1982, Class of '25 Athlete scholar, 1982; named Family Physician of Yr., Calif. Acad. Family Physicians, 1998. Mem. AMA, Am. Acad. Family Physicians, Phi Beta Kappa, Sigma Xi. Avocations: distance running, ski racing, computers. Office: San Francisco Free Clinic 4900 California St San Francisco CA 94118-1115 E-mail: pgibbs@sttc.org.

GIBBS, PATRICIA LEIGH, social sciences educator, researcher; b. Vancouver, B.C., Canada, Dec. 4, 1961; d. Claude Leslie and Margaret Helen Rencher; m. Robert Owen Stayte, June 20, 1997; children: Angus A. Gibbs Stayte, Lachlan A. Gibbs Stayte, Emma Q. Gibbs Stayte. EdB, U. B.C., Can., 1981; MA in Leisure Studies, U. Alta., Can., 1989; MA in Sociology, U. Hawaii, 1995, PhD in Sociology, 1999. Instr. Coll. Rockies, Cranbrook, Canada, 1984—91; faculty human svcs. dept. Malaspina U. Coll., Nanaimo, Canada, 1991—94; lectr. U. Hawaii, Honolulu, 1994—99; assoc. prof. sociology Foothill Coll., Los Altos Hills, Calif., 1999—. Freelance writer. Contbr. chapters to books Cultural Construction and Social Welfare in Hawai'i: Assessing the Role of Alternative Media with Regard to Native Hawaiian Issues., articles to profl. jours. Story evaluator Project Censored: A Media Democracy Orgn., Sonoma State University, Calif., 1997—2003. Recipient Appreciation award, Foothill Alpha Gamma Sigma Hon. Soc., 2003; grantee, Malaspina U. Coll., 1992; scholar, Hawaii Cmty. Found., 1998; vis. scholar Asia Pacific scholar, U. Hawaii, 1994—96; Hawaii Vet.'s Meml. scholar, Hawaii Cmty. Found., 1998. Office: Foothill Coll 12345 El Monte Rd Los Altos Hills CA 94022

GIBBS, SARAH PREBLE, biologist, educator; b. Boston, May 25, 1930; d. Winthrop Harold and Edith Dorothea (Hill) Bowker; m. Robert H. Gibbs, June 9, 1951 (div. 1962); 1 dau., Elizabeth Dorothea; m. Ronald J. Poole, Feb. 2, 1963 (div. 1980); 1 son, Christopher Harold. AB, Cornell U., 1952, MS, 1954; PhD, Harvard U., 1962. Research assoc. Inst. Animal Genetics Edinburgh U., 1963-65; asst. prof. botany McGill U., Montreal, Que., Can., 1966-69, assoc. prof. biology, 1969-74, prof., 1974-98, Macdonald prof. bot., 1998, Macdonald emeritus prof., 1999—. Recipient Darbaker prize, Bot. Soc. Am., 1975, Gilbert Morgan Smith medal, NAS, 2003; fellow, NSF, 1958—61, NIH, 1961—63. Fellow: AAAS, Royal Soc. Can.; mem.: Can. Assn. Univ. Tchrs., Phycol. Soc. Am. (award of excellence 1999), Am. Soc. Cell Biology, Can. Soc. Cellular and Molecular Biology (pres. 1972—73), Phi Kappa Phi, Sigma Xi, Phi Beta Kappa. Home: 70 Henley Ave Montreal QC Canada H3P 1V3 Office: McGill U Dept Biology 1205 Avenue Docteur Penfield Montreal QC Canada H3A 1B1

GIBBY, MABEL ENID KUNCE, psychologist; b. St. Louis, Mar. 30, 1926; d. Ralph Waldo and Mabel Enid (Warren) Kunce; student Washington U., St. Louis, 1943-44, postgrad., 1955-56; B.A., Park Coll., 1945; M.A., McCormick Theol. Sem., 1947; postgrad. Columbia U., 1948, U. Kansas City, 1949, George Washington U., 1953; M.Ed., U. Mo., 1951, Ed.D., 1952; m. John Francis Gibby, Aug. 27, 1948; children— Janet Marie (Mrs. Kim Williams), Harold Steven, Helen Elizabeth, Diane Louise (Mrs. Roderick Rohrich), John Andrew, Keith Sherridan, Daniel Jay. Dir. religious edn. Westport Presbyn. Ch. Kansas City, Mo., 1947-49; tchr. elementary schs., Kansas City, 1949-50; high sch. counselor Arlington (Va.) Pub. Schs., 1952-54; counselor adult counseling services Washington U., 1955-56; counseling psychologist Coral Gables (Fla.) VA Hosp., 1956—; counseling psychologist Miami (Fla.) VA Hosp., 1956—, chief counseling psychology sect., 1982-86; sr. psychologist Office Disability Determination Fla. Hdqrs., 1987-94. Sec. bd. dirs. Fla. Vocat. Rehab. Found. Recipient Meritorious Service citation Fla. C. of C., 1965, President's Com. on Employment of Handicapped, 1965; commendation for meritorious service Com. on Employment of Physically Handicapped Dade County, 1965, named Outstanding Rehab. Profl., 1966, 81; named Profl. Fed. Employee of Year, Greater Miami Fed. Exec. Council, 1966; Outstanding Fed. Service award Greater Miami Fed. Exec. Council, 1966; Fed. Woman's award U.S. Civil Service Commn., 1968, Community Headliner award Theta Sigma Phi, 1968, Outstanding Alumni award Park Coll., 1968, Freedom award The Chosen Few, Korean War Vets. Assn., 1986; certificate of appreciation Bur. Customs, U.S. Treasury Dept., 1969, Fla. Dept. Health and Rehab. Services, 1970. Mem. Am., Dade County (past sec.) psychol. assns., Nat., Fla. (past dir. Dade County chpt.) rehab. assns., Nat. Rehab. Counseling Assn. (past sec.). Patentee in field. Home: 7107 Aberdeen Ave Dallas TX 75230-5406

GIBBY-SMITH, BARBARA, psychologist, nurse; b. Woodburn, Oreg., Dec. 13, 1938; d. Chester Clifton and Marvel Elizabeth (Hill) Gibby; m. Roy Milton Smith, June 2, 1957 (div. June 1990); children: Thomas Clifton, Jeffery Shawn, Mark Anderson. ADN, Chemeketa C.C., Salem, Oreg., 1972; BS, SUNY, Albany, 1980; MS, Western Oreg. State Coll., 1982; D of Psychology, Pacific U., Forest Grove, Oreg., 1993. Diplomate Am. Bd. Profl. Disability Cons., Am. Bd. Specialist, Am. Bd. Forensics Medicine; cert. addiction examiner. Adminstr. Birch St. Manor, Dallas, Oreg., 1973-81; disability determination specialist State of Oreg. Workers' Compensation Dept., Salem, 1983-85; counselor Women's Crisis Ctr., Salem, 1986-88; rehab. counselor Employer Rehab. Svcs., Portland, Oreg., 1985-87; therapist, counselor Pacific U., Hillsboro, Oreg., 1988-89, Forest Grove, 1989-91; intern in psychology Portland State U., 1991-92, Kaiser-Permanente, Salem, 1991-92; resident in psychology Tillamook (Oreg.) Counseling Ctr., 1993-95; hosp. privileges psychology and medicine Quality Healthcare, 1996—; pvt. practice clin. psychology Forest Grove, Oreg., 1993—. Group therapy counselor Women's Crisis Ctr., Dallas, 1982-83; eating disorders group therapy facilitator, Salem, 1986-88; nat. register Doctoral Addiction Examiner. Active Women's Coalition Orgn., Salem, 1988—. Mem. APA, Am. Coll. Forensic Examiners (diplomate), Nat. Bd. Addiction Examiners (diplomate), Oreg. Psychol. Assn., Prescribing Psychologist Assn. (diplomate), Am. Mental Health Alliance (Oreg.). Democrat. Avocations: golf, bicycling, traveling, geneology, walking. Office: Mountain View Counseling Ctr 1911 Mountain View Ln Ste 500 Forest Grove OR 97116-2248

GIBERT, CHARLENE WEST, gifted education educator; b. Ft. Worth; m. Wayne Gibert, 1975; 1 child, Christine. MusB, Tex. Tech U., 1964; MEd, U. Houston, 1978, EdD, 1991. Cert. tchr., profl. counselor, Tex. Elem. tchr. music Lubbock (Tex.) Ind. Sch. Dist., 1965-68; jr. high sch. tchr. lang. arts Clear Creek Ind. Sch. Dist., Houston, 1968-79, tchr. gifted and talented edn. Spring Br. Ind. Sch. Dist., 1981—. Cons. gifted and talented field. Editor, contbr: Biographical Dictionary of Gifted Education, 1988; also articles. Mem. First Presbyn. Ch., Houston. Mem. Nat. Assn. for Gifted Children, Tex. Assn. for Gifted and Talented, T Avocations: music, travel. Home: 1926 Abby Aldrich Ln Katy TX 77449-2817

GIBLETT, ELOISE ROSALIE, hematologist, educator; b. Tacoma, Wash., Jan. 17, 1921; d. William Richard and Rose (Godfrey) Giblett. BS, U. Wash., 1942, MS, 1947, MD with honors, 1951. Mem. faculty U. Wash. Sch. Medicine, 1957—, research prof., 1967—87, emeritus research prof., 1987—. Assoc. dir., head immunogenetics Puget Sound Blood Ctr., 1957—79, exec. dir., 1979—87, emeritus exec. dir., 1987—; former mem. several rsch. coms. NIH. Author: Genetic Markers in Human Blood, 1969; mem. editl. bd. numerous jours. including: Blood, Am. Jour. Human Genetics, Transfusion, Vox Sanguinis; contbr. over 200 articles to profl. jours. Recipient fellowships, grants Emily Cooley, Karl Landsteiner, Philip Levine and Alexander Wiener immunohematology awards, disting. alumna award, U. Wash. Sch. Medicine, 1987. Fellow: AAAS; mem.: NAS, Assn. Am. Physicians, Western Assn. Physicians, Am. Fedn. Clin. Rsch., Internat. Soc. Hematologists, Brit. Soc. Immunology, Am. Assn. Immunologists, Am. Soc. Hematology, Am. Soc. Human Genetics (pres. 1973), Alpha Omega Alpha, Sigma Xi. Home: 6533 53rd Ave NE Seattle WA 98115-7748 Office: Puget Sound Blood Ctr 921 Terry Ave Seattle WA 98104-1256

GIBLIN, NAN J. psychologist, educator; b. Kankakee, Ill., Sept. 18, 1946; d. Kenneth Theodore Johnson and Rose Marie Pocock; m. Walter Patrick Giblin, Oct. 5, 1968; 1 child, Daniel. BS in English Lit., Loyola U. Chgo., 1968, PhD of Ednl. Counseling, 1984; MA in Ednl. Counseling, Northeastern Ill. U. Chgo., 1978. Registered psychologist Ill. Tchr. Sacred Heart Acad., Chgo., 1968—70; asst. prof. Northeastern Ill. U., Chgo., 1985—90; pvt. practice psychology Park Ridge, Ill., 1986—95; assoc. prof., prof. Northeastern Ill. U., Chgo., 1990—. Chair counseling edn. Northeastern Ill. U., Chgo., 1987—92, assoc. dean Coll. Edn., 1992—98, dean Coll. Edn., 1998—; mem. Ill. State Cert. Bd., Springfield, 2001—. Co-author: Finding Help: A Resource Guide to Personal Concerns, Individual Counseling:

Skills and Techniques; co-editor: Family Counseling in School Settings. Mem.: ACA, Am. Assn. Coll. Tchr. Educators. Office: Northeastern Ill Univ 5500 N Saint Louis Chicago IL 60025*

GIBSON, ELISABETH JANE, retired principal; b. Salina, Kans., Apr. 28, 1937; d. Cloyce Wesley and Margaret Mae (Yost) Kasson; m. William Douglas Miles, Jr., Aug. 20, 1959 (div.); m. Harry Benton Gibson Jr., July 1, 1970. AB, Colo. State Coll., 1954-57; MA, San Francisco State Coll., 1967-68; EdD, U. No. Colo., 1978; postgrad., U. Denver, 1982. Cert. tchr., prin., Colo. Tchr. elem. schs., Santa Paula, Calif., 1957—58, Salina, Kans., 1958—63, Goose Bay, 1963—64, Jefferson County, Colo., 1965—66, Topeka, 1966—67; diagnostic tchr. Ctrl. Kans. Diagnostic Remedial Edn. Ctr., Salina, 1968—70; instr. Loretta Heights Coll., Denver, 1970—72; co-owner Ednl. Cons. Enterprises, Inc., Greeley, Colo., 1974—77; resource coord. region VIII Resource Access Project Head Star Mile High Consortium, Denver, 1976—77; exec. dir. Colo. Fedn. Coun. Exceptional Children, Denver, 1976—77; asst. prof. Met. State Coll., Denver, 1979; dir. spl. edn. N.E. Colo. Bd. Coop. Edn. Svcs., Haxtun, Colo., 1979—82; prin. elem. jr. h.s. Elizabeth, Colo., 1982—84; prin., spl. projects coord. Summit County Schs., Frisco, Colo., 1985—92; prin. Frisco Elem. Sch., 1985—91; ret., 2002. Cons. Mont. Dept. Edn., 1978-79, Love Pub. Co., 1976-78, Colo. Dept. Inst., 1974-75, Colo. Dept. Edn., 1984-85, mem. proposal reading com., 1987—; pres. Found. Exceptional Children, 1980-81; pres. bd. dirs. N.E. Colo. Svcs. Handicapped, 1981-82; bd. dirs. Dept. Ednl. Specialists, Colo. Assn. Sch. Execs., 1982-84; mem. Colo. Title IV Adv. Coun., 1980-82; mem. Mellon Found. grant steering com. Dolo. Dept. Edn., 1984-85; mem. Colo. Dept. Edn. Data Acquisition Reporting and Utilization Com., 1983, Denver City County Commn. for Disabled, 1978-81; chmn. regional edn. com. 1970 White House Conf. Children and Youth; bd. dirs. Advs. for Victims of Assault, 1986-91; mem. adv. bd. Alpine Counseling Ctr., 1986-92; mem. placement alternatives commn. Dept. Social Svcs., 1986—; mem. adv. com. Colo. North Ctrl. Assn., 1988-91; sec. Child Care Resource and Referral Agy., 1992—; mem. Child Care Task Force Summit County, 1989-92; mem. tchr. cert. task force Colo. State Bd. Edn., 1990-91; chmn. Summit County Interagy. Coord. Coun., 1989-93. Co-author: (with H. Padzensky) Goal Guide: A minicourse in writing goals and behavioral objectives for special education, 1975, Assaying Student Behavior: A minicourse in student assessment techniques, 1974; contbr. articles to profl. jours. Recipient Vol. award Colo. Child Care Assn., 1992, Ann. Svc. award Colo. Fedn. Coun. Exceptional Children, 1981; San Francisco State Coll. fellow, 1967-68; named Vol. of Season, Hospice of Metro Denver, 2003. Mem. ASCD, Nat. Assn. Elem. Sch. Prins., Colo. Assn. Retarded Citizens, North Ctrl. Assn. (state adv. com. 1988-91), Order Ea. Star, Kappa Delta Pi, Pi Lambda Theta, Phi Delta Kappa. Republican. Methodist. Home: 4505 S Yosemite St Unit 114 Denver CO 80237-2520 E-mail: ejgibson@netzero.net.

GIBSON, FLORENCE ANDERSON, talking book company executive, narrator; b. San Francisco, Feb. 7, 1924; m. V.H. Carlos Gibson, Aug. 30, 1947; children: Nancy Derwent, Christopher Carlos, Katherine Wayne Bolland, Diana Corona. Student, Finch Jr. Coll., N.Y.C., 1941-42; BA in Dramatic Lit., U. Calif., Berkeley, 1944; student, Neighborhood Playhouse, N.Y.C., 1944-45. Radio actress, San Francisco, 1944, 46, 47; chmn. Washington com. Am. Field Svc., 1958-60, 62-65, founder, chmn. Peruvian Com., 1960-62; treas., distbn. mgr. Living Garden and Concern 1975 calendars, 1971-75; sec. exec. com Fgn. Student Svc. Coun., 1970-76; narrator Talking Books Libr. of Congress div. for Blind and Physically Handicapped, 1975-96; narrator Recorded Books, Inc., 1979; founder, pres. Audio Book Contractors, Inc., 1982—. Narrator numberous unabridged books on cassette for 4 companies. Actress, appearing in Blithe Spirit, 1945, Ah, Wilderness, 1946, Traffic Ct. TV series, others, recorded more than 1000 books on cassettes. Bd. dirs. Fgn. Student Svc. Coun., Concern, Inc., Rec. for the Blind, Children's Theater of Washington; vol. in occupational therapy Children's Hosp., Washington, 1949-50; vol. lobbyist student exch. program Am. Field Svc. Recipient 3 Parents' Choice awards, 1983, 84, 86, Audiophile Earphone award, 1999; named Best Female Narrator, Book World, 1989; selected as A Notable Children's Recording, ALA, 1983, 87, 88, 89. Home: 4626 Garfield St NW Washington DC 20007-1025 Office: Audio Book Contractors Inc PO Box 40115 Washington DC 20016-0115 E-mail: flogibsonabc@aol.com.

GIBSON, FRANCES ERNST, music educator; b. San Antonio, Dec. 7, 1925; d. Joseph Omer Ernst and Olga Catherine Ochs; m. Edwin Wray Gibson, Sr. MusB summa cum laude, Our Lady of the Lake U., 1947; MusM, U. Tex., 1970. Faculty piano dept. Our Lady of the Lake U., San Antonio, 1947—51; pvt. music tchr. Fredericksburg, Tex., 1951—. Piano accompanist Point Theater, Ingram, Tex., 1958; ch. organist St. Mary's Cath. Ch., Fredericksburg, 1965-70; participant Internat. Piano Workshops, 1979-91. Co-author: Music Lovers' Cookbook, 1992; performer Tex. Sch. of the Air, Austin, 1947, 125th Ann. Celebration, Fredericksburg, 1972. Free concert arranger Fredericksburg Music Club, Inc., 1987—; chmn. Concert Series, 1987 . Recipient Outstanding Alumni award Our Lady of the Lake U., San Antonio, 1997. Mem. Nat. Guild Piano Tchrs. (local chmn. 1952-93, adjudicator 1975-92), Music Tchrs. Nat. Assn., Fredericksburg Music Club, Inc. (bd. mem., program chair, pres. 1989-93), Frank van der Stucken Internat. Music Festival (bd. mem., program chmn. 1991-94, performer 1991, artistic dir.), Sigma Alpha Iota (Sword of Honor 1943), Sigma Alpha Iota Alumnae (pres. 1950-51), Alpha Chi, Delta Kappa Gamma Catholic Daughters. Roman Catholic. Avocations: reading, traveling, gourmet cooking. Home: 809 W Travis St Fredericksburg TX 78624-2524

GIBSON, GLENDA GALE, special education educator, secondary school educator; b. Tulsa, Okla., May 9, 1968; d. Bennie D. Robertson and Mary Sue Johnston; 1 child, Jake T. BA in Social Studies and Art Edn., Okla. Panhandle State U., 1995; MSc in Spl. Edn., Ft. Hays State U., 2003. Cert. tchr. Okla. State Dept. Edn., 1995, Kans. State Dept. Edn., 1996. Braille transcriptionist, reading speicialist Scott City (Kans.) Mid. Sch., 1995—96; secondary spl. edn. tchr. Scott (Kans.) Cmty. HS, 1999—2000; K-12 gifted facilitator Scott (Kans.) Cmty. Schs., 2000—02; secondary spl. edn. tchr. Garden City (Kans.) HS, 2002—. Mem. core com. Scott City (Kans.) Mid. Sch. Improvment Team, 2000—02; presenter So. Regional Edn. Bd. Staff Devel. Conf., Nashville, 2003; presenter ann. conf. FHSU Katesol, 2004, Kans. State Dept. Edn., 2004. Coach, mentor, judge Kans. History Day, Topeka, 2000—03. Recipient Outstanding Social Studies Degree Grad. award, Okla. Panhandle State U., 1994-1995. Mem.: NEA, Kans. Edn. Assn., Coun. for Exceptional Children, Omicron Delta Kappa. Democrat. Avocations: swimming, hiking, writing, sculpting, painting.

GIBSON, JANNETTE POE, educational consultant; b. Lubbock, Tex., Oct. 29, 1948; d. Hugh Miller and Norma Grace (Harrison) Poe; m. William Carroll Gibson, June 30, 1967; children: Darin L., Arminda L. Gibson Peery, Victoria L. Gibson Dixon. BS, East Tex. State U., 1971, MEd, 1981; postgrad., Tex. A&M U., Commerce, 1992—. Tchr. Como (Tex.)-Pickton Ind. Sch. Dist., 1971-77; tchr., cons. Diocese of Dallas, Diocese of Tyler, Tex., 1982-87; tchr., supr. Hyder Migrant Ctr., Dateland, Ariz., 1987-88; tchr., adult ESL edn. dir. Ariz. Western U., Hyder Campus, 1988-89; tchr. Sulphur Springs (Tex.) Ind. Sch. Dist., 1989-98; cons., presenter Multicultural/Migrant Edn., 1987—; edn. diagnostician Sulphur Springs ISD Spl. Edn. Dept., 1998—. Cons. ESL edn. and early childhood edn. and child devel. U.S. Dept. Edn., 1988-89; profl. adv. com. Sulphur Springs Ind. Sch. Dist., 1990, 92, 96; doctoral adv. bd. East Tex. State U., 1993-96; regional adv. com. migrant edn. Region V111 Svc., 1994-97, advisor Tex. Edn. Agy. assessments of ESL/LEP children, 1997-98; cons. for devel. of culture and lang. bias-free assessments to sch. dists. in Tex.; presenter in fields of migrant edn. and ESL; private cons. assessment in sch. dists., Tex. Mem. AAUW, NEA, Tex. State Tchrs. Assn., TAMU Doctoral Students Assn., TESOL, Classroom Tchrs. Assn. Tex., Tex. Ednl. Diagnosticians Assn., N.E. Tex. Assn. Ednl. Diagnosticians, Mensa, Alpha Chi, Phi Beta Kappa, Kappa Delta Pi. Democrat. Methodist. Avocations: reading, gardening. Home: 1707 Houston St Sulphur Springs TX 75482-2319 Office: 411 College St Sulphur Springs TX 75482-2809

GIBSON, JENNIFER WILLIAMS, music educator; b. Laurinburg, N.C., Jan. 19, 1977; d. Robert Edward and Betty Sue Dupree Williams; m. Andrew Lanier Gibson, Apr. 19, 1964. Bachelor of Music in Edn. and Flute Performance, Meredith Coll., 1995; cert., Selmer U., 1999. Cert. tchr. N.C. Swag Bands Am., Inc., Shaumburg, Ill., 1996—98; clinician George N. Parks Drum Maj. Acad., Amherst, Mass., 1998—2001; dir. Exploris Charter Sch. Orch., Raleigh, NC, 1998—99, Hayesville Mid./H.S. Bands, NC, 1999—. Mem. Clay County Hist. and Arts Coun., Hayesville, NC, 2003—; performer Mountain Heritage Chorus/Orch., Young Harris, Ga., 2003. Grassroots grantee, Clay County Arts Coun., 1999—2002. Mem.: We. Dist. Bandmasters, Music Educators Nat. Conf. (auditions chair 2001—), Sigma Alpha Iota. Republican. Baptist. Avocations: chamber music and ensembles, reading, quilting. Home: 2231 Hwy 64 E Hayesville NC 28904 Office: Hayesville HS 205 Yellow Jacket Dr Hayesville NC 28904

GIBSON, JUDITH W. clinical therapist; b. Syracuse, N.Y., Apr. 27, 1942; d. Nathan Whitney and Helen-Alycia (Fancher) Watson; m. Robert Glenn Gibson, Aug. 1964 (dec. Oct. 1966); 1 child, Heidi. BA in English, Syracuse U., 1978, MA in Religion, 1985, MSW, 1987. LCSW Acad. Cert. Social Workers. Bookkeeper Stickley Furniture, Fayetteville, N.Y., 1965-67; adminstrv. asst. Agway Inc., Dewitt, N.Y., 1967-82; asst. dir. housing Syracuse U., 1983-87; dir. preventive svcs. The Salvation Army, Syracuse, 1990—2002; clinician Psychol. Health Care PLLC, Syracuse, 2002—. Mem. NASW, Sexual Abuse Study Team. Roman Catholic. Avocations: reading, arts, travel. Home: 9 Carriage House E # A Manlius NY 13104-2355 Office Phone: 315-422-0300.

GIBSON, KATHLEEN RITA, anatomy and anthropology educator; b. Phila., Oct. 9, 1942; d. Keath Pope and Rita Irene (Shewell) G. BA, U. Mich., 1963; MA, U. Calif., Berkeley, 1969, PhD, 1970. Teaching assoc. U. Calif., Berkeley, 1965-69; lectr., adj. assoc. prof., then adj. prof. Rice U., Houston, 1973-2000; asst. prof. U. Tex. Health Sci. Ctr., Houston, 1970-73, assoc. prof., 1973-80, prof., 1980—, chair dept. basic sci., 1998—2002. Mem. com. on parenting behavior Social Sci. Rsch. Coun., N.Y.C., 1980-89; mem. fellowship rev. panel NSF, 1992-95; vis. fellow Cambridge U., 1993; vis. scholar Oxford U., 1996. Editor: (with M. Thames and K. Molokon) Genealogy and Demography of the West Main Cree, 1989, (with S. Parker) Language and Intelligence in Monkeys and Apes, 1990, 94, (with A. Petersen) Brain Maturation and Cognitive Development, 1991, (with Tim Ingold) Tools, Language and Intelligence in Human Evolution, 1993, 94, 98, (with Paul Mellars) Modelling the Early Human Mind, 1996, (with Hilary Box) Social Learning in Mammals: Comparative and Ecological Perspectives, 1999 (with Dean Falk) Evolutionary Anatomy of the Primate Neocartin, 2001; contbg. editor Anthropology Newsletter, 1990-93; contbr. articles, commentaries and abstracts in profl. jours. Conf. grantee Wenner Gren Found., 1990, Sloan Found., 1985, travel grantee NSF, 1984, 86, Brit. Soc. Devel. Biology, 1982. Fellow Am. Assn. Phys. Anthropologists, Am. Assn. Anthropologists; mem. AAAS, Am. Assn. Anatomists, Internat. Primatol. Assn., Am. Assn. Dental Schs. (chmn. sect. anatomical scis. 1990), Am. Anthropol. Assn. (chmn.-elect biolog. anthropology sect. 1994-96, chair 1997-98, co-chmn. com. on ethics, 1994-95, chair 1996, chair com. scientific comm. 1997, mem. exec. bd. 1997, 99—2002, chmn. assn. oper. com. 2000—02, mem. nominations com., 2002—), Lang. Origins Soc., Am. Assn. Primatologists (publs. com. 1987-89). Office: Dept Basic Scis U Tex Houston Houston TX 77225

GIBSON, KAY LYNN, education educator; b. Wichita, Kans., Oct. 12, 1948; d. Donald Wayne and Joan Claudine Henrichs; m. Ian Wesley Gibson, July 21, 1973; children: Ashley Sarah Elisabeth, Ethan James. BA in Edn., Wichita State U., 1970, MEd in Ednl. Adminstrn. and Supervision, 1983; PhD, U. of New Eng., Armidale, New South Wales, Australia, 1998. Tchr. Wichita Pub. Schs., Wichita, 1970—71, NSW Dept. of Edn., Sydney, Australia, 1971—73, Kinma Sch., Terrey Hills, Australia, 1973—75, prin., 1976—78; tchr. Cir. Sch. Dist., Towanda, Kans., 1979—80; gifted resource rm. tchr. Wichita Pub. Sch. Dist., 1980—85; elem. sch. tchr. Derby Pub. Sch. Dist., Kans., 1986—89; lectr. A U. of So. Qld., Toowoomba, Australia, 1989—91, lectr. B, 1991—98; asst. prof. Wichita State U., 1998—2004, assoc. prof., 2004—. Editl. adv. bd. TalentEd, Armidale, New South Wales, Australia; conf. convenor Phi Delta Kappa Local Chpt., Wichita, Kans., 2000—01; program reviewer Kans. State Dept. of Edn., Topeka, 1999—; folio reviewer Coun. for Exceptional Children, Arlington, Va. Contbr. articles to profl. jours., chpts. to books. Recipient Outstanding Svc. award, Coll. of Edn. at Wichita State U., 2002, Educator Appreciation award, Wichita State U. Mortar Bd., 2000. Mem.: Kans. Assn. for Gifted, Talented, and Creative (2d v.p. 2002—03, 1st v.p. 2003—04), Phi Delta Kappa (pres. 1999—2001), World Coun. for Gifted and Talented Children, Coun. for Exceptional Children, Nat. Assn. for Gifted Children, Assn. for the Advancement of Computing in Edn., ASCD (assoc.). Democrat-Npl. Achievements include research in Study of the conceptions of giftedness held by urban Australian aborigines. Avocations: travel, reading, gardening, playing piano. Office: Wichita State Univ 1845 Fairmount Wichita KS 67260-0028 Office Phone: 316-978-5569. E-mail: kay.gibson@wichita.edu.

GIBSON, LISETTE L. elementary school educator, music educator; b. St. Louis, Dec. 14, 1945; d. Erwin L. and Anna Marie Lueker; children: Robert, Todd. BA, Concordia, River Forest, Ill., 1967; MA, U. Mich., 1989. Tchr. classroom, music educator St. Paul Lutheran Ch. and Sch., Bay City, Mich.

GIBSON, LUANNE EILEEN, visual artist, educator; m. William Patrick Gibson, May 1, 1982; 1 child, Shayna Nicole. Student, U. Toledo, 1977-1979; BA, Mont. State U., 1993. Ind. visual artist, Bozeman, Mont., 1993—; prin., owner Artifacts Gallery, Bozeman, Mont., 2000—. Art instr. Inst. Lifetime Learning, 1996. Artist (neck piece) The World Diploma of Design & Crafts, 1994. Vol. art tchr. elem. sch., Bozeman, 1994-98; tchr. after sch. program for gifted and talented edn., 1997-98. Mem. Nat. Mus. Women in the Arts, Soc. N.Am. Goldsmiths, Phi Kappa Phi. Avocations: hiking, camping, traveling, cooking, antique collecting. Office: Artifacts Gallery 308 E Main St Bozeman MT 59715 Office Phone: 406-586-3755.

GIBSON, PATRICE VANDEGRIFT, anthropologist, educator; d. Roger Dale and Florence Macrae Vandegrift; m. Chris Gibson, Dec. 31, 1977; children: Jedediah, Lucas. BA, UCLA, 1971, MA, 1973, PhD, 1981. Cert. C.C. tchr. Prof. of anthropology Am. River Coll., Sacramento, 1990—; co-coordinator chimpanzoo program Jane Goodall Inst., Tucson, 1986—. Coord. learning communities for student success Am. River Coll., Sacramento, 1999—2003, co-dir. ctr. for tchg. and learning, 1996—99, 2003—04. Mem.: Soc. for Anthropology in Cmty. Colleges, Am. Anthrop. Assn. Avocations: travel, cooking. Office: American River Coll 4700 College Oak Dr Sacramento CA 95841 E-mail: gibsonp@arc.losrios.edu.

GIBSON-BREHON, DAWN D. performing company executive, consultant; d. Raymond Edward Gibson and Hilda Christine Holness; m. John V. Brehon, Jr., Aug. 16, 1994; children: Michael Andrew Brehon, Matthew Christopher Brehon. MusB, U. Hartford, 1987; MA, U. Wis., Madison, 1991. Co. mgr. Lincoln Ctr. Festival, N.Y.C., 1987—87; theater mgr. Palm Beach C.C., Lake Worth, Fla., 1987—2001; dir. presenting program and world theater Calif. State U. Monterey Bay, Seaside, 2001—. Cons. dance advance program Pew Charitable Trusts, 2000—03; bd. dirs. Assn. Performing Arts Presenters, Washington, 2000—, Chamber Music Am., N.Y.C., 2001—03. Mem. Marina (Calif.) Bus. Assn., 2001—03. Named Businesswoman of the Yr., Marina Bus. Assn., 2003; recipient African-American Achievers, Arts Category award, J.M. Family Enterprises, 2000. Office: California State Univ Monterey Bay World Theater 100 Campus Center #28 Seaside CA 93955-8001 E-mail: dawn_gibson-brehon@csumb.edu.

GIDDINGS, HELEN, personnel management executive; b. Dallas, Apr. 21, 1942; d. Arthur and Catherine (Warren) Ferguson; m. Donald Giddings; children: Lizette, Lisa, Stanley. BA in Bus., U. Tex., 1968. Tng. dir. Sears, Roebuck, Dallas, 1975-77; personnel mgr. Sears, Roebuck & Co., Dallas, 1977-81, dir. community affairs for 11 states, 1979-81; pres. Select Personnel, Dallas, 1981-86; exec. dir. Leadership Dallas, 1985-86; state rep. dist. 109 State of Tex., 1982-86. Trustee Dallas Alliance, 1981—, exec. dir., 1987. Gov. Dallas Symphony, 1980—; elected mem. Dallas Assembly, 1981—; mem. Dist. 6 State Bar Grievance Com.; bd. dirs. Dallas Theatre Ctr., 1984—; exec. dir. Leadership Dallas, 1984, state rep., 1992. Recipient Woman of Yr. award Committee of 100, Dallas, 1980, Achieving Against the Odds award East Oak Cliff-Dallas Ind. Sch. Dist., 1981. Mem. Dallas Black C. of C. (pres. 1981-82), Dallas Hist. Soc. (sec. 1983—, vice-chair), Zeta Phi Beta (Woman of Yr. award 1984), Alpha Phi Alpha (Community Service award 1987). Methodist. Avocations: public speaking, the arts.

GIDWITZ, TERI LYNNE, marketing professional; b. Chgo., Apr. 23, 1961; d. Ralph Wolff and Jane Audrey Gidwitz. BA, U. Mich., 1983; M in Mgmt., Northwestern U., 1985. Asst. account exec. DDB Needham, Chgo., 1985-86; account exec. Sampling Corp. Am., Glenview, Ill., 1987, Feldman Assocs., Chgo., 1987-88; promotion asst. Helene Curtis Industries, Chgo., 1988-90; dir. mktg. Sta. WXRT-FM, Chgo., 1990-97, Sta. WSCR-AM, Chgo., 1991-95, Tunes.com, Chgo., 1997-2000, Household Credit Svcs., 2000—. Advisor Chgo. Beach LLC, 1995-98; dir. Ind. Label Festival, Chgo., 1995-97. Mem. Chgo. Interactive Mktg. Assn. Avocations: music, travel. Home: 1542 W School St Apt E Chicago IL 60657-2191 Office: Household Credit Svcs 200 W Adams St Chicago IL 60606-5208

GIEBEL, MIRIAM CATHERINE, librarian, genealogist; b. Williamsburg, Iowa, Oct. 10, 1934; d. John Timothy and Helen Gertrude (Wright) Donahoe; m. William Herbert Giebel, Sept. 30, 1967; 1 child, Sara Ann Giebel Ward. BS, Marquette U., Milw., 1956, MS in Library Science, Rosary Coll., River Forest, Ill., 1960; cert. in paralegal, Roosevelt U., Chgo., 1992; cert. in family history rsch., Brigham Young U., 1992. Asst. acquisitions dept. Marquette U. Libr., Milw., 1956-58; tech. svcs. libr. Chicago Heights (Ill.) Pub. Libr., 1959-63, ext., reference libr., 1974-99, vol. coord./webmaster, 1999-2000, webmaster, 2000—01, geneal. rschr., 2002—; libr. Little Co. Mary Nursing, Evergreen Park, Ill., 1963-64; asst. libr. hdqrs. ALA, Chgo., 1964-67. Mem.: DAR (chpt. registrar 1994—2001), Fedn. Bus. Profl. Women (state libr. chair 1994—96), Daus. Union Vets. 1861-1865, Daus. Colonial Wars, Dames Ct. Honor, Ill. Cameo Soc. of DAR (state v.p. 1996—99, state pres. 1999—2001), U.S. Daus. of 1812 (chpt. pres. 1991—97, Ill. state registrar 1994—97, Ill. state pres. 1997—99, nat. chair lineage and geneal. records 1997—2000, hon. state pres. life, chpt. registrar 1997—), Soc. Ind. Pioneers (life). Roman Catholic. Avocations: reading, personal genealogical research, Web surfing. Personal E-mail: mirgiebel@aol.com.

GIEGEL, KATHLEEN A. elementary school educator; b. Pitts., Aug. 27, 1957; d. Howard C. and Rita M. Geubtner; m. Michael J. Giegel, Oct. 27, 1978; children: Sarah, Tim. BS in Spl. Edn. summa cum laude, BS in Elem. Edn. summa cum laude, Slippery Rock U., 2003. Presch. instr. YMCA, Pitts.; pharmacy technician U. Pitts. Med. Ctr.; elem. instr. Pine Richard Sch. Dist., Gibsonia, Pa. Mem. Adv. Bd. Autism & Related Disorders, Pitts., 2003. Mem.: Pa. Coun. Tchrs. Math., Nat. Tchrs. Edn. Assn., Coun. Exceptional Children, Phi Theta Kappa, Lambda Epsilon Delta, Sigma Pi Epsilon Delta. Republican. Avocations: music, bicycling, hiking, camping, cross-country skiing.

GIELOW, KATHLEEN LOUISE, career planning administrator, consultant, special education educator; b. Buffalo, July 8, 1951; d. James Elbert and Billie Elaine Robinson; m. Arthur William Gielow, Sept. 1, 1973; 1 child, James Arthur. BS in Edn., SUCNY, Buffalo, 1973, MS in Edn., 1979. Spl. edn. tchr. Buffalo Pub. Schools, 1974—98, career devel. coord., 1998—; ednl. founds. faculty SUCNY, Buffalo, 2001—, prin. investigator, 2002; entrepreneurship coord. Buffalo Employment and Tng. Ctr., 2002—. Profl. devel. provider various ednl. and cmty. orgns., NY, 1997—; profl. conf. workshop presenter, NY, 1998—; conf. workshop presenter Coun. of Gt. City Schs., San Francisco, 1999; careerzone trainer N.Y. State Dept. of Labor, 2000—; cons. Syracuse U., NY, 2001—; career plan trainer N.Y. State Edn. Dept., 2001—; edn. adv. bd. mem. N.Y. State Electric and Gas, Lancaster, 2001—. Editor: (career development best practices collec) Best Practices in Career Development; contbr. nysbest practices in career development Career Development in the Automotive Industry. Vol. Aids Cmty. Svcs., Aids Family Svcs., Buffalo, 1998—2003; eucharistic min. St. Joseph U. Cath. Ch., Buffalo, 2002—03. Recipient Career and Tech. Educator Award, Buffalo Career and Tech. Educators Guild, 2002, Vol. of the Yr., AIDS Cmty. Services, 2003, Partnership Svc. Award, Sch. to Work Family Resource Ctr., 1998; grantee School-To-Work (for Buffalo Pub. Schools), NY State Edn. Dept., 1997-1999, Urban/Rural Opportunity Grant (for BPS), US Dept. of Labor, 1998-2003, Youth Entrepreneurship Matching Grant, Kidsway, Inc., 2000, Workforce Devel. Entrepreneurship Grant, Workforce Investment Bd. of Erie County, 2002, Tech Prep Planning Grant (for BPS), NY State Edn. Dept., 2002-2003. Mem.: Assn. for Career and Tech. Educators Adminstrs. (licentiate), Nat. Educators Assn. (licentiate), Buffalo Tchrs. Fedn. (licentiate). Roman Catholic. Avocations: scrapbooking, travel, reading, musical theater. Home: 300 Hamilton Blvd Kenmore NY 14217-1811 Office: Buffalo Pub Schs 70 W Chippewa Ste 603 Buffalo NY 14202 Personal E-mail: klg7851@aol.com. E-mail: kgielow@buffalo.k12.ny.us.

GIER, KARAN HANCOCK, psychologist; b. Sedalia, Mo., Dec. 7, 1947; d. Ioda Clyde and Lorna (Campbell) Hancock; m. Thomas Robert Gier, Sept. 28, 1968. BA in Edn., U. Mo., Kansas City, 1971; MA in Edn., Webster U., 1974; MA in Counseling Psychology, Western Colo. U., 1981; MEd in Guidance and Counseling, U. Alaska, 1981; PhD in Edn., Pacific Western U., 1989. Nat. cert. counselor. Instr. grades 5-8 Kansas City-St. Joseph Archdiocese, 1969-73; ednl. cons. Pan-Ednl. Inst., Kansas City, 1973-75; instr., counselor Bethel (Alaska) Regional HS, 1975-80; ednl. program coord. Western Regional Resource Ctr., Anchorage, 1980-81; counselor U. Alaska, Anchorage, 1982-83; coll. prep. instr. Alaska Native Found., Anchorage, 1982; counselor USAF, Anchorage, 1985-86; prof. U. Alaska, Anchorage, 1982—; dir. Omni Counseling Svcs., Anchorage, 1984—; prof. Chapman Coll., Anchorage, 1988—93. Workshop facilitator over 100 workshops. Co-author: (book) Coping with College, 1984, Helping Others Learn, 1985, The Tutor Training Handbook, 1996; editor, co-author: book A Student's Guide, 1983, contbg. author: developmental Yup'ik lang. program, 1981; contbr. articles to profl. jours. Mem. Ctr. Environ. Edn., Beta Sigma Phi, Bethel, Alaska, 1976—81. Recipient 3d pl. color photo award, Yukon-Kuskokwim State Fair, 1978, Notable Achievement award, USAF, 1986, Meritorious Svc. award, Anchorage C.C., 1984—88. Mem.: AACD, Nat. Rehab. Counselors, Nat. Rehab. Assn., Alaska Career Devel. Assn., Alaska Assn. Counseling and Devel. (pres.-elect 1989—90), Coll. Reading and Learning Assn. (editor newsletter peer tutor spl. interest group 1988—95, bd. dirs. Alaska state, coord, internat. tutor program, Robert Griffin Long and Outstanding Svc. award, Cert. of Appreciation 1986—93, Spl. Recognition award 1994—95), Wolf Song Alaska, Human Soc. U.S. Wolf Haven Am. Avocations: travel, wolf preservation, photography, music, acting. Home and Office: 8102 Harvest Cir Anchorage AK 99502-4682

GIESE, JUDITH MARIE, minister; d. Carl Christian Giese and Theresa Marie Loew. BA in Elem. Edn., North Ctrl. Coll., 1975; MDiv, Garrett-Evang. Theol. Sem., 1989. Ordained elder No. Ill. Conf. United Meth. Ch. Student asst. pastor First United Meth. Ch., Brookfield, Ill., 1984—87, Faith United Meth. Ch., Lombard, Ill., 1987—88, Westmont (Ill.) United Meth. Ch., 1988—89, pastor Clearing United Meth. Ch., Chgo., 1989—91, Clearing & Asburn United Meth. Chs., Chgo., 1991—95, Plano (Ill.) United Meth. Ch., 1995—2001, Malta (Ill.) and N.W. Malta United Meth. Chs., 2001—. Mem. chaplains com. North Ctrl. Coll., Naperville, 1998—; bd. mem. United Campus Ministries No. Ill. U., DeKalb, 2002—. Avocations: horse owner and rider, antiques, golf, gardening.

GIESSER, BARBARA SUSAN, neurologist, educator; b. Bronx, N.Y., Jan. 21, 1953; d. David and Evelyn (Cohen) G.; m. Philip D. Kanof, June 17, 1979; children: David, Marisa. BS, U. Miami, 1972; MS, U. Tex., Houston, 1974; MD, U. Tex., San Antonio, 1978. Diplomate Am. Bd. Psychiatry and Neurology. Intern Montefiore Hosp., Bronx, 1978-79; resident Bronx Mcpl. Hosp. Ctr. (Albert Einstein Coll. Medicine), 1979-82; asst. prof. neurology Albert Einstein Coll. Medicine, Bronx, 1983-91; med. dir. Gimbel MS Comprehensive Care Ctr., Teaneck, N.J., 1985-90, Rehab. Inst. of Tucson, 1991-95; assoc. prof. clin. neurology Ariz. Health Scis. Ctr., Tucson, 1993—2002; assoc. clin. prof. neurology UCLA, 2002—. Author: Neurology Specialty Board Review, 3d edit., 1986, 4th edit., 1996; contbr. articles to profl. publs. Dean's Tchr. scholar Ariz. Health Scis. Ctr., 1995. Fellow Am. Acad. Neurology (undergrad. edn. subcom. 1999—, Tchr. Recongnition award 2002); mem. Nat. Multiple Sclerosis Soc. (rsch. grant 1989, 97, 2003, mem. profl. adv. com. Desert S.W. chpt. 1994-2000, bd. dirs. 1994-2000, counselor Am. Acad. Neurology sect. on Multiple Sclerosis 1997-99, nat. chair client edn. com. 1999-2003, mem. med. adv. bd. 1999-2003). Office: UCLA Sch Medicine Neurology Reed Neurologic Rsch Ctr 710 Westwood Plz Los Angeles CA 90095

GIEVERS, KAREN A. lawyer; b. Culver City, Calif., Apr. 27, 1949; d. Ernest Conrad and Josephine Theresa (Passolt) Prevost; m. Joseph R. Gievers, Nov. 16, 1968 (dec. Feb. 1987); children: Daniel Steven, Donna Ann; m. Frank J. Bach, Nov. 23, 1997. AA, Miami Dade C.C., 1974; BA, Fla. Internat. U., 1975; JD cum laude, U. Miami, 1978. Bar: Fla. 1978, U.S. Dist. Ct. (so. dist.) Fla. 1978, U.S. Dist. Ct. (mid. and no. dist.) Fla. 1979, U.S. Ct. Appeals (5th cir.) 1979, U.S. Ct. Appeals (11th cir.) 1981, U.S. Ct. Claims 1980, U.S. Supreme Ct. 1982; cert. civil trial atty Fla. Bd. Legal Specialties, 1985, Nat. Bd. Trial Advocacy, 1992. Assoc. Sams, Anderson, Gerstein & Ward, P.A., Miami, 1978, Anderson, Moss, Russo & Gievers, P.A., Miami, 1979-83; ptnr., 1983—87; pvt. practice Karen A. Gievers, P.A., 1987—. Bd. editors: So. Dist. Digest, 1981-85. Lectr. FACT, Miami, 1984; pres. Operation SafeDrive, 1987—; mem. MADD, 1986; bd. trustees We Will Rebuild, 1992-93; candidate treas., ins. commr. State of Fla., 1994, candidate sec. state, 1998. Mem. Fla. Bar Assn. (mem. trial lawyers exec. coun. 1985-88, editor trial lawyers sect. 1984, vice-chmn. evidence com. 1985-88, chmn. 1988-89), Am. Bd. Trial Advocates (pres. elect Fla. 2002), Acad. Fla. Trial Lawyers (chmn. pub. com. 1984-86, bd. dirs. 1985-87, treas. 1988-89, sec. 1987-88, pres. elect 1989-90, pres. 1990-91, recipient Pres.'s award 1986, 90), Assn. Trial Lawyers Am., Dade County Bar Assn. (bd. dirs. 1981-84, 85-87, treas. 1987-88, sec. 1988-89, 2nd v.p. 1989-90, 1st v.p. 1990-91, pres.-elect 1991-92, pres. 1992-93), Dade County Trial Lawyers Assn. (sec. 1984, treas. 1985, pres. 1987), Fed. Bar Assn., Fla. Assn. Women Lawyers, Children's Advocacy Found. (pres., dir. 2000), Zool. Soc. Fla., Fla. Consumer Fedn. (bd. dirs. 1985-87), Lions Internat., Gray Panthers, Banker's, Gov.'s. Democrat. Office: 524 E College Ave Tallahassee FL 32301-2529

GIFFIN, MARGARET ETHEL (PEGGY GIFFIN), management consultant; b. Cleve., Aug. 27, 1949; d. Arch Kenneth and Jeanne (Eggleton) G.; m. Robert Alan Wyman, Aug. 20, 1988; 1 child, Samantha Jean. BA in Psychology, U. Pacific, Stockton, Calif., 1971; MA in Psychology, Calif. State U., Long Beach, 1973; PhD in Quantitative Psychology, U. So. Calif., 1984. Psychometrician Auto Club So. Calif., L.A., 1973-74; cons. Psychol. Svcs., Inc., Glendale, Calif., 1975-76, mgr., 1977-78, dir., 1979-94; rschr. Social Sci. Rsch. Inst., U. So. Calif., L.A., 1981; dir. Giffin Consulting Svcs., L.A., 1994—. Instr. Calif. State U., Long Beach, 1989-90; mem. tech. adv. com. on testing Calif. Fair Employment and Housing Commn., 1974-80, mem. steering com., 1978-80. Mem. APA, Soc. Indsl. Organizational Psychology, Pers. Testing Coun. So. Calif. (pres. 1980, exec. dir. 1982, 88, bd. dirs. 1980-92). Home and Office: 260 S Highland Ave Los Angeles CA 90036-3027 E-mail: peggygiffin@cs.com.

GIFFIN, MARJIE G. writer; b. Columbia City, Ind., Nov. 22, 1951; d. Robert Edwards and Harriett (Brown) Gates; m. Kenneth Neal Giffin, May 17, 1975; children: Christopher, Matthew, Elisabeth Anne. AB in Lit. magna cum laude, Ind. U., 1974; MA in Lit., Butler U., 1982. Cert. tchr., Ind., 1974, gifted and talented edn., 2000. Advt. writer Curtis Pub. Co., Indpls., 1974-75; pub. rels. dir. Dept. Parks and Recreation, Indpls., 1975-76; comms. dir. Acad. Pub. Svc., Indpls., 1976-78; editor Wayne Twp. Sch. Dist., Indpls., 1983-88; assoc. faculty Ind. U./Purdue U., Indpls., 1992-94; freelance writer Indpls., 1978—; rschr./ writer W.B. Brown historical Project, 2001. Mem. grad. sch. arts/scis. alumni bd. Ind. U., 1976-78; bd. dirs. Indpls. Pub. Libr., 1985-86; adv. bd. Ind. U. arts/scis. newsletter, 1977-78. Author: Water Runs Downhill, 1981, If Tables Could Talk, 1988, A Walk Through Time, 1989. Indpls. Zoo, Indpls. Children's Mus.; bd. dirs. Marion County Welfare Bd., 1981-82, Sycamore Sch. Assn., 1998-2001. Honoree Girls, Inc., Indpls. Forum Series, 1991. Honoree Ind. Authors Day, 1990. Mem. Ind. Hist. Soc., Hist. Landmarks found., Acad. Am. Poets, Kappa Alpha Theta. Republican. Roman Catholic. Avocations: water sports, poetry, reading, history, writing. E-mail: mggiffin@aol.com.

GIFFIN, SANDRA LEE, nursing administrator; b. Tacoma, July 16, 1957; d. Clayton Eugene and Carol Lee (Fisher) Peterson; m. Herbert Kent Giffin, May 6, 1989. Diploma, Tacoma Gen. Hosp. Sch. Nursing, 1978; BSN magna cum laude, Pacific Luth. U., 1980; MS, Oreg. Health Scis. U., 1994. Cert. in nursing adminstrn. Staff nurse Mary Bridge Children's Hosp., 1978-81, evening nurse supr., infection control nurse, 1981-83, asst. med./surg. nurse mgr., 1983-84, med./surg. nurse mgr., 1984-89; dept. dir. Oreg. Poison Ctr. Oreg. Health Scis. U., Portland, 1989—, instr., Sch. Nursing, 1994—, dept. dir. nurse cons. program, 1995-2000, interim dir. physician cons. program, 2000. Presenter in field. Author/presenter abstracts in field. Sec. Rocky Butte Neighborhood Assn., 1996; sec. bd. dirs. Make A Wish Found. Oreg., 1989-96; mem. adv. bd. Oreg. Safe Kids Coalition; active Oreg. Interagy. Hazardous Comm. Coun., Oreg. Sch. Health Edn. Coalition. Grantee Agy. for Toxic Substances and Disease Registry/Am. Assn. Poison Control Ctrs., 1992, Oreg. State Health Divsn., 1993-94. Mem. Am. Acad. Ambulatory Care Nursing, Am. Assn. Poison Control Ctrs., N.W. Orgn. Nursing Execs. (apptd. mem. commn. on health care policy 2000). Avocations: skiing, reading, bicycling, travel, cooking. Office: Oreg Poison Ctr 3181 SW Sam Jackson Park Rd Portland OR 97201-3011

GIFFORD, FEREUZA, retired military officer; b. Keene, NH, May 24, 1917; d. John Amos and Leafie Mitchell Gifford; m. John Joseph Pydynkowski Jr., June 1936 (div. June 1941); 1 child, Patricia Mitchell Pydynkowski. Grad., Nat. Maritime Union, 1974; AS in Geology, City Coll. of San Francisco, 1981; AB, Maritime Acad., Piney Point, Md., 1992. Turbo-supercharger tester GE Lynn (Mass.) Riverworks, 1942—43; civilian recruit USN, Boston, Vallejo, Calif., 1943—45; stewardess for convoy SS Fermina, 1947, M.T. Ottawa, San Francisco, 1956, SS United States, N.Y.C., 1960—73, SS Santa Rosa, 1974; mil. petty officer; ret. Author: (poetry) The Falling Rain, 2000 (Editor's Choice award Internat. Libr. of Poetry). Mem.: VFW, Air Force Assn. Achievements include invention of safety handles, Gifford's Lizards, rescuing disabled submarines. Home: 330 Clementina St Apt 621 San Francisco CA 94103-4126

GIFFORD, HEIDI, writer, editor; b. New Haven, Jan. 20, 1961; d. Prosser and Dee Dee (O'Sullivan) Gifford; m. George Melas, July 15, 1995; children: Luke, Lily. BA in English Lit., Yale U., 1983; MPA in Internat. Econs., Columbia U., 1991. Editl. asst. Yale U. Press, New Haven, 1985; asst. to the dir. Gov.'s Office of Fed. Rels., Boston, 1987-89; asst. dir. internat. trade and econs. Coun. on Fgn. Rels., N.Y.C., 1991-94; elections analyst Nightly News with Tom Brokaw/NBC News, N.Y.C., 1995-96; writer and editor Comms. Devel., N.Y.C., 1997—. Assoc. USIA Fgn. Press Ctr., N.Y.C., 1990-91. Mem. Inst. of World Affairs. Episcopalian. Avocations: crew, marathon running. E-mail: heidigiff@earthlink.net.

GIFFORD, MARILYN JOYCE, emergency physician, consultant; b. Denver, Aug. 3, 1943; m. Leslie Arthur and Dorothy Marianne (Stevens) G.; m. Robert Bruce Caplan (div.); children: Eric Louis Caplan, Brian Matthew Caplan; m. Daniel Patrick McKenna, July 17, 1992. AA, Stephens Coll., Columbia, Mo., 1963; BS, Mich. State U., 1965; MD, Mt. Sinai Sch. Medicine, N.Y.C., 1971. Diplomate Am. Bd. Emergency Medicine. Emergency physician Longmont (Colo.) United Hosp., 1974-80, Boulder (Colo.) Cmty. Hosp., 1976-78; dir. emergency svcs. Meml. Hosp., Colorado Springs, Colo., 1980—. Physician advisor Colorado Springs Fire Dept., 1980—; bd. dirs. Nat. Registry Emergency Med. Technicians, Columbus, Ohio, 1983—. Co-author: Protocols for Prehospital Emergency Medical Care, 1984, Prehospital Emergency Care, 1996. Advisor E-911 Authority Bd., Colorado Springs, 1996—. Lt. USNR, 1971-72. Recipient Kim Langstaff Meml. award for excellence Region IV EMs Coun., 1986, Val. Wolhauer award for physician excellence Emergency Med. Technician Assn. Colo., 1982, Pres.'s Leadership award Nat. Assn. Emergency Med. Technicians, 1983, ACEP contbn. in EMS, 2001. Fellow Am. Coll. Emergency Physicians (chair EMS com. 1979-81, Colo. coun. 1978-85); mem. El Paso County Med. Soc. (pres. 1993-94). Avocation: skiing. Office: Meml Hosp 1400 E Boulder St Colorado Springs CO 80909-5599 E-mail: giffordmd@aol.com.

GIFFORD, MARJORIE FITTING, mathematician, educator, consultant; m. Frederick N. Fitting, Feb. 25, 1972 (dec. 1985); m. Forrest W. Gifford, May 28, 1988 (div. 1992). BS in Math., Mich. State U., 1111, PhD in Math. Edn., 1968; AM in Math., U. Mich., 1966; postgrad., U. Nev., Las Vegas, 1994-97. Cert. tchr., Mich., Calif. Tchr. math. in secondary schs., Mich., 1954-61; instr. Lawrence Inst. Tech., Southfield, Mich., 1961-68; grad. asst. Mich. State U., East Lansing, 1966-68; prof. emeritus math. and computer sci. San Jose State U., Calif., 1968-92; instr. math. U. Nev., Las Vegas, 1993-94. V.p. fin. Metra Instruments, San Jose, 1972—82; pres. Metier, San Jose, 1982—98; cons. San Jose Unified Sch., 1969—71. Author: (software) Math Test Generation, 1983; co-author: (book series) Computer Literacy Series, 1983-85, (book) Introduction to Geometry, 1996. Recipient Dean's award for tchg. excellence San Jose State U., 1982; J.C. Plant scholar Mich. State U., 1954; NSF fellow, 1965-66; Fulbright sr. lectr./rsch. grantee, Portugal, 1985-86. Mem. Am. Math. Soc., Calif. Math. Coun., Rotary, Zeta Tau Alpha. Democrat. Roman Catholic. Avocations: gardening, rafting, bridge, photography, painting.

GIFFORD, NANCY (MUMTAZ), artist, poet; b. Youngstown, Ohio, Feb. 24, 1948; d. John S. Baytos and Helen E. Yochman; m. Michael B. Gifford, Feb. 24, 1995; children: Harriet, Ben, Emma, Kristopher. Degree, Kent (Ohio) State U., 1970; student, Fashion Inst. of Am., 1970—71, The Film Sch., Half Moon Bay, Calif., 1975—76. One-woman shows include Argon Gallery, Venice, Calif., 1984, Merging One Gallery, Santa Monica, Calif., 1986, 1987, Carminel Gallery, N.Y.C., 1988, Schreiber/Cutler Gallery, 1988, L.A. County Mus. of Art, 1991, exhibited in group shows at Craft & Folk Art Mus., L.A., 1984, Bowers Mus., 1987, Carnegie Art Mus., 1987 (1st pl. award), Riverside (Calif.) Art Mus., 1988, Mus. of the Hudson Highlands, N.Y., 1989, Mus. of N.Mex., Santa Fe, 1990, Corcoran Gallery, 1990, Naples (Fla.) Art Mus., 2001, HW Gallery, Naples, Fla., 2002; author: (haiku poetry and drawings) The War Room, 2001, Modern Haiku, 2003. Patron, bd. dirs. Naples Art Assn., 1999—; patron Naples Art Mus., 1997—, Haiku Soc. of Am., 2002, Mus. of Contemporary Art, Miami, 2003. Recipient award of excellence, Scarsdale (N.Y.) Art Soc., 1987, Juror's award, Fine Arts of Burbank, Calif., 1987, award of excellence, Gallery 54, N.Y.C., 1988, award of merit, von Liebig Art Ctr., 2003. Avocations: swimming, hiking, yoga. Home: 568 9th St S Ste 354 Naples FL 34102 E-mail: nangifford@home.com.

GIGLI, IRMA, dermatologist, educator, academic administrator; b. Cordoba, Argentina, Dec. 22, 1931; d. Irineo and Esperanza Francisca (Pons de Gigli) Gigli; m. Hans J. Muller-Eberhard, June 29, 1985. BA, Liceo Nacional Manuel Belgrano, Cordoba, 1950; MD, Universidad Nacional de Cordoba, 1957. Intern Cook County Hosp., Chgo., 1957—58, resident in dermatology, 1958—60; fellow in dermatology NYU, 1960—61; mem. faculty Harvard Med. Sch., 1967—75, asso. prof. dermatology, 1972—75; chief dermatology service Peter Bent Brigham Hosp., Robert B. Brigham Hosp., 1971—75; prof. dermatology and exptl. medicine N.Y. U. Med. Center, N.Y.C., 1976—82, mem. Irvington Houst Inst., mem. faculty N.Y. Grad. Sch. Med. Scis., dir. Asthma and Allergic Disease Center for Immunodermatology Studies, 1980—91; prof. medicine, chief div. dermatology U. Calif.-San Diego, 1983—95; prof. medicine and dermatology, vice chair medicine for sci. U. Tex. Health Sci. Ctr., Houston, 1995—; assoc. dir. Inst. Molecular Medicine for Prevention Human Diseases U. Tex., Houston, 1998—2003, dep. dir., 2003—, Walter and Mary Mischer prof. molecular medicine, 1998—; dir. Rsch. Ctr. Immunology and Autoimmune Diseases, 1995—. Mem. Nat. Inst. of Allergy and Infectious Diseases Coun., 1978—79, bd. sci. counselors, 1997—; chmn. study sect. Allergy and Immunology Inst., NIH, 1978—83; mem. Guggenheim Found. Western Hemisphere and Phillippines Com. of Selection; adv. bd. NIH Fogarty Internat. Ctr., 1984—97. Recipient Rsch. award, Am. Cancer Soc., 1970—72, NIH, 1972—76; grantee, Guggenheim Found., 1974—75. Mem.: Am. Acad. Arts and Scis., Henry Kunkel Soc. (councilor 1999—), PEW Latin Am. Fellows Program in Biomed. Scis. (nat. adv. com. 1998—), Inst. Medicine/NAS, Am. Dermatol. Assn., Assn. Am. Physicians, Am. Acad. Allergy, Am. Acad. Dermatology, Am. Assn. Immunologists, Am. Soc. Clin. Investigation, Soc. Investigative Dermatology (hon.; pres. 1990—91, Stephen Rothman Meml. award 1996). Office: U Tex Health Sci Ctr Inst Molecular Medicine 2121 W Holcombe Blvd Houston TX 77030-3303

GIGNAC, JUDITH ANN, utilities executive; b. Detroit, Mich., Mar. 21, 1939; d. Durward Arthur and Gertrude Marian Du Pont; m. Oliver Otto Leininger, July 7, 1990; m. Paul Ross Gignac, Sept. 12, 1964 (div. Apr. 13, 1985); children: Beth Andrea Gignac-Hooper, Christopher Ross. Assoc., Broward Bus. Coll., 1957—58; student, U. of Colo., 1967—69, Cochise Coll., 1975—76, U. of Ariz. - South, 2002. Data processor Kettelle, Colo. Springs, Colo., 1968—69; computer programmer RCA - Ballistic Missile Early Warning Sys., Colo. Springs, 1969—70; elected county supr. Cochise County Bd. of Supervisors, Bisbee, Ariz., 1977—88; vice pres., gen. mgr. Bella Vista Water/Ranches, Sierra Vista, Ariz. Ptnr. Darby, Gignac & Associates, Inc, Sierra Vista, Ariz., 1982—88; mem. Ariz. Assn. of Counties, County Supervisors Assn., Phoenix; dir., sec. Orgn. of U.S. Border Cities & Counties, Ariz.; dir. Governing Bd. of Health Systems Agy. of SE Ariz.; chair San Pedro Water Resources Assn., Sierra Vista, Ariz.; mem. Governor's Workforce Devel. Policy Coun., Phoenix, State Task Force on Wastewater Treatment Facilities Constrn. Grants, Washington, D.C.; dir. Cochise County Water Mgmt. Coun., Bisbee, Ariz.; mem./chair Bur. of Land Mgmt. Pub. Lands Adv. Coun., Safford, Ariz.; dir. Water Utilities Assn. of Ariz., Phoenix, 1989—93, Ariz. Utilities Investor's Assn., 1995—; commr. Upper San Pedro Partnership Adv. Commn., Sierra Vista, Ariz., 2001—; mem./past pres. Ariz. Bd. of Regents, 1994—2002; dir. State C.C. Bd., Phoenix, 1994—2003, United Bank Bd., Phoenix, Bank of Cochise, Sierra Vista, Ariz.; dir./sec. Huachuca Fed. Credit Union, Sierra Vista, Ariz. Dir. Wells Fargo Bank Adv. Bd., Sierra Vista, Ariz., 1999; mem./chair Cochise Coll. Presdl. Adv. Com., Sierra Vista, Ariz.; mem./dir. Sierra Vista C. of C., Ariz.; mem., chair Sierra Vista Bd. of Adjustment, Ariz.; co-chair platform subcommittee 1980 Rep. Nat. Conv., Detroit; keynote spkr. Ariz. Rep. Women; mem./chair Sierra Vista Charter Bd. of Freeholders, Ariz.; chmn. Cochise County Rep. Com., Bisbee, Ariz.; founder/mem./pres. Thunder Mountain Rep. Women, Sierra Vista; treas. Rep. State Party, Phoenix; dir./chmn. Ariz. Town Hall, Phoenix, 1978; dir. U. Found. Sierra Vista, Inc., Ariz. Recipient Woman of the Yr., Bus. & Profl. Women, 1974—75, Disting. Svc. award, U. of Ariz., Coll. of Edn., 2002, Lady of the Yr., Beta Sigma Phi, 1977, Leadership & Comm. award, Toastmasters Internat., 1982, Medal of Honor, DAR, 1988, Woman of the Yr., Cochise County Rep. Com., 1988, Citizen of the Yr., Sierra Vista C. of C., 1994, DeConcini award, Ft. Huachuca 50, 1995, Vision award, Commn. on the Status of Women, 2000, Outstanding Achievement award, U. of Ariz., Coll. of Edn., 2002. Mem.: U. Med. Ctr. (dir. 1995), Upper San Pedro Partnership Adv. Commn. (commr. 2001), Ariz. Town Hall (chmn. of the bd. 2001—03). Avocations: reading, writing, gardening. Home: 1425 Via Viento Sierra Vista AZ 85635 Office: Bella Vista Water Co/Bella Vista Ranches 4055 Campus Dr Sierra Vista AZ 85635 E-mail: jgignac@mindspring.com.

GIKAS, CAROL SOMMERFELDT, museum director; b. St. Louis, Oct. 9, 1950; m. Ken Gikas. Student, U. Mo., 1968-70; BA in Studio Art, U. Ark., Little Rock, 1973; MA, U. Tex., 1977; postgrad., U. Calif., summer 1981. Asst. mus. registrar Art. Arts Ctr., Little Rock, 1972-74; assoc. curator Leeds Gallery, U. Tex., ustin, 1977-80; exec. dir. La. Arts and Sci. Ctr., Baton Rouge, 1980—. Mem. grants adv. panel So. Arts Fedn., 1981, Arts and Humanities Coun. Greater Baton Rouge, 1982, 83, divsn. arts La. Arts Council, 1981, 85; mem. adv. bd. U.S.S. Kidd/La. Naval Mus., Baton Rouge, 1981, 84, La. Dept. Edn., 1981; state rep. to couun. S.E. Mus. Conf., 1984, 85. Sec. Gov.'s Commn. for Anniversary La. Capitol, 1981, 82; trustee ARC, 1986—; mem. Mayor's Commn. for Bicentennial U.S. Constn. Mem. Am. Assn. Mus., Art Mus. Assn. (regional rep. 1983—), Baton Rouge C. of C. (active Goals Conf. 1984, 85, Leadership Greater Baton Rouge 1985, 86). Office: La Arts and Science Ctr Inc PO Box 3373 Baton Rouge LA 70821-3373

GIL, LIBIA SOCORRO, school system administrator; Tchr. L.A. Unified Sch. Dist., 1970; elem. sch. prin. ABC Sch. Dist.; area adminstr., asst. supt. for curricula and instrn. Seattle Pub. Schs.; supt. Chula Vista (Calif.) Elem. Sch. Dist., 1993—2001; chief acad. officer New Am. Schs., 2002—. Author: Principal Peer Evaluation, Promoting Change From Within; co-author: Eight at the Top. Recipient McGraw prize in edn., 2002. Office: New Am Schs Ste 220 675 N Washington St Alexandria VA 22314

GILBERT, ANITA RAE, psychologist, educator; d. Marie Olivia Love; children: Ray Bernard, Lorin D'Andrew. PhD, Wright Inst., Berkeley, Calif., 1981. Lic. clin. psychologist Calif., 2001. Psychology instr. San Francisco City Coll., 1976—78; psychologist Bayview Mental Health Svc., San Francisco, 1980—82; lectr. U. of Calif., San Francisco, 1982—86; neuropsychologist San Francisco Gen. Hosp., 1982—84; forensic psychologist Calif. Dept. of Correction, San Francisco, 1985—; lectr. Calif. State U., Hayward, 1993—96, San Francisco State U., 2003—; clin. program dir. Westside Cmty. Mental Health, San Francisco, 1987—88; psychol. testing program dir. Calif. Med. Facility-Vacaville, Calif., 1984—86. Cons. psychologist Calif. Dept of Mental Health, San Francisco, 1987—88; cons. Asian Am. Residential Treatment Ctr., San Francisco. Mentor Cath. Charities, San Francisco, 1995—98. Fellow Doctoral fellow, APA, 1978—80. Mem.: Soc. for Personality Assessment, APA (assoc.). Achievements include research in depression, women's studies, issues in neuropsychology. Avocations: yoga, travel, exercise program, painting, dance. Personal E-mail: dragilbert@aol.com.

GILBERT, ANTONIA AMELIA, elementary school educator, consultant; b. Birmingham, Aug. 7, 1971; d. William Earl Bryant and Jeanette Ann McMillon. BS in Elem. Edn. (cum laude), U. Ala., 1993, M in Elem. Edn., 1995. Nat. bd. cert. 2000, adminstrv. cert. 2001. Recreation leader, reading tchr. Camp Fire Boys & Girls, Birmingham, Ala., 1991—96; title 1 tchr. Birmingham Pub. Schs., 1994—95, third grade tchr., 1995—. Nat. bd. cert. cons. Birmingham Pub. Schs., 2001—; reading initiative trainer State of Ala. In-svc. Ctr., 2001—; bldg. based team Ctrl. Pk. Elem., Birmingham, 2002—. Adv. com. Martin Luther King Recreation Ctr., Birmingham, 2000—; Sunday sch. tchr. Latter Day Harvest Ch., Birmingham, 2000—. Mem.: Univ. Ala. Alumni Soc., Nat. Coun. Tchrs. of English. Avocation: church choir. Home: 1230 LongbrookDr Bessemer AL 35020 Office: Ctrl Pk Elem Sch 4915 Ave Q Birmingham AL 35208 E-mail: antonia_gilbert@juno.com.

GILBERT, DEBBIE ROSE, entrepreneur; b. Indpls., Jan. 18, 1961; d. James Taylor and Rosemary (Robinson) G. BA, Ind. U., 1984; diploma in computer literacy, St. Augustine Coll., Chgo., 1995. Student typing asst. Shortridge H.S./Indpls. Pub. Schs./Bd. Schs. Commrs., Indpls., 1978-79; substitute tchr. Indpls. Pub. Schs./Bd. Sch. Commrs., 1985-89, Washington Twp. Schs., Indpls., 1992; CHA housewatcher, clothes distbr. The Inner Voice, Inc., Chgo., 1994-95; vol. Lakefront Single Room Occupancy Employment Program, Chgo., 1997—. Dep. registrar O.N.E./Bd. Election Commrs., Chgo., 1996—; mem. People for the Am. Way, Chgo., 1995-96; mem. Access Living, Chgo., 1996—, mem. Southern Poverty Law Ctr., Tchg. Tolerance, Militia Task Force, Klanwatch Org., Montgomery, 1998—. Mem. ACLU, NOW, AAUW, NAACP, The Natl. Mus. of Women in the Arts Org., OWL (The Older Women's League), The Voice of Midlife & Older Women, Wash. D.C., Mental Health Consumer Edn. Consortium, Inc. Democrat. Baptist. Avocations: modeling, singing, race walking, Bingo, reading. Home: 5012 N Winthrop Ave Apt 224 Chicago IL 60640-3124 Office: 4753 N Broadway Ste 632/808 Chicago IL 60640-4986

GILBERT, ELLEN EFFMAN, music educator; b. New London, Conn., May 21, 1969; d. David Garth and Elaine Avery Effman; m. Steven Dale Gilbert, Dec. 25, 1995; 1 child, Eliza Avery. BS in Music Edn., U. Conn., 1991, MMus, 1995; postgrad. in Music Edn., HARTT Sch. of Music, Hartford, Conn., 2001—. Music educator, bilingual Bridgeport (Conn.) Pub. Schs., 1992—93; choral condr. Hartford (Conn.) Camerata Conservatory, 1996—98; music educator Hartford Pub. Schools, 1996—98; choral condr. U. Conn. Treblemakers Cmty. Music Sch. of the Arts, Mansfield, Conn., 2003—; choir dir. Old Mystic (Conn.) Bapt. Ch., 2000—; music educator Mystic (Conn.) Mid. Sch., 1998—. Choral chairperson Ea. Region Music Festival, Waterford, Conn., 2002—; clinician/adjudicator R.I. Music Educators Conf., 2001—04; panel discussion rep. Providence Coll., Providence, 2000—00; presenter/condr. Gt. East Adjudication Festivals, Agawam, Mass., 1998—; presenter Conn. Music Educator's Conf., 2001, 03, 04, All State Elem. Gen. Mus. Conf., 2003, Frankin Pierce Coll., 2003. Singer: Prov. Performing Arts Ctr.; contbr. articles to profl. jours. Member-at-large Stonington (Conn.) Players Thespian Assn., 2003; bd. of Christian edn. Old Mystic Bapt. Ch.; sec. Kodaly Educators of So. New Eng., Hartford, Conn. Grantee Celebration of Excellence, State of Conn., 2000, World Music Drumming in the Classroom, Stonington Edn. Fund, 2002, Recorder Consort, 2000, 100 Best Cmtys. Music Edn., 2002; scholar Young Artist Competition, Nat. Assn. of Teachers of Singing, 1990. Mem.: Am. Choral Directors Assn. (assoc.; presenter Mid. Sch. Festival, West Hartford, Conn. 1999—2003), Kodaly Educators of So. New Eng. (assoc.; sec. 1994—99), Orgn. Am. Kodaly Educators (assoc.), Conn. Music Educators Conf. (assoc.; presenter, Hartford 2001, choral chairperson 2002—03, presenter 2003—), Music Educators Nat. Conf. (assoc.). Democrat. American Baptist. Office: Mystic Mid Sch 204 Mistuxet Ave Mystic CT 06355 Office Phone: 860-536-9613. E-mail: egilbert@stoningtonschools.org.

GILBERT, HELEN DELONG, psychologist, psychoanalyst; b. Lafayette, Ind., Jan. 9, 1939; d. George E. and Ruth A. (Wagoner) DeLong; m. Paul L. Gilbert; children: Amy L., J. Mark; m. James R. Amundsen. BA, DePauw U., 1960; MA, Ind. U., 1973; PhD, The Fielding Inst., Santa Barbara, Calif., 1989. Lic. psychologist, Minn. Tchr. English Greencastle (Ind.) H.S., 1960-62, Pioneer H.S., Ann Arbor, Mich., 1968-70; instr. English DePauw U., Greencastle, 1962-63; instr. folklore Coll. St. Benedict, St. Joseph, Minn., 1973-76; instr. human rels. St. Cloud (Minn.) State U., 1976-80; assoc. dir. admissions Coll. St. Catherine, St. Paul, 1980-82; psychotherapist Office of Wilmer Larson, M.D., Edina, Minn., 1982-84, Oak Grove Psychotherapy Assocs., Mpls., 1984-89; psychologist, psychoanalyst in pvt. practice, St. Paul, 1989-97, Mpls., 1997—. Founder, co-dir. Minn. Inst. for Contemporary Psychoanalytic Studies, Mpls., 1994—. Contbr. chpt. to book. Danforth fellow, 1972. Mem. APA, Minn. Women Psychologists (Dissertation award 1987), Soc. for Psychoanalytic Studies, Mortar Board, Phi Beta Kappa, Kappa Kappa Gamma. Democrat. Avocations: reading, painting, canoe trips, travel abroad. Office: 527 Marquette Ave Ste 1900 Minneapolis MN 55402-1329

GILBERT, JOAN STULMAN, retired public relations executive; b. NYC, May 10, 1934; m. Phil E. Gilbert Jr., Oct. 6, 1968; children: Linda Cooper, Dana McGrk, Patricia Novajosky. Student, Conn. Coll. Women, 1951-53. Br. coord. Vol. Svc. Bur., Westchester, NY, 1970-72; pub. rels. dir. Westchester Lighthouse, 1972-76; exec. dir. Westchester Heart Assn., 1976-77; mgr. cmty. rels. Texaco Inc., White Plains, NY, 1977-97. Vice chmn. ARC; chmn. The Street Theater, 1995—97; bd. dirs. Am. Heart Assn., Westchester Philharm., Jazz Forum Arts; former bd. dirs. Choate Rosemary Hall, United Way of Westchester; former bd. dirs., former trustee Westchester Coun. for the Arts; trustee, former bd. dirs. Teatown Lake Reservation. Recipient award, Youth Theater Interactions, Westchester Hispanic Coalition, Women in Comms., Am. Heart Assn., Am. Diabeters Assn., Westchester Putnam Affirmative Action Program, Arthritis Found., ARC, Urban League Westchester. Mem.: Sales and Mktg. Exec. Westchester (former dir.), Women in Comm. (award), Advt. Club (dir.), Pub. Rels. Soc. Am. (chpt. pres. 1977), Westchester County Assn. Home: The Croft 1595 Spring Valley Rd Ossining NY 10562-1634 E-mail: gilbertjs@aol.com.

GILBERT, LINDA ARMS, education educator, educational administrator; BS in Elem. Edn., Middle Tenn. State U., 1972, MA in Tchg., 1979, EdS in Adminstrn. and Supervision, 1991; EdD in Curriculum and Instrn., Tenn. State U., 1997. 8th grade tchr. Ctrl. Middle Sch., 1972-73; 5th-6th grade band tchr. Mitchell-Neilson Elem. Sch., 1987-90, 5th-6th grade band tchr., K-2 music tchr. Reeves-Rogers Elem. Sch., 1988-90; 5th-6th grade band tchr., K-6 music tchr., chorus tchr. Black Fox Elem. Sch., 1990-98; assoc. dir. instrn., staff devel. Murfreesboro City Schs., 1998—; asst. prof. Mid. Tenn. State U., 2000—. Pvt. music tchr., 1970—; presenter in field; guest conductor mass flute choirs Tenn. Flute Festivals; music adjudicator; adj. prof. Cumberland U., 2001—. Guest columnist for edn. Daily News Jour. Organist Bethel United Meth. Ch., various coms.; active Rutherford 2000, 1991-95; vol. VA Med. Ctr., guest spkr. civic orgns.; mem. Band of Blue Exec. Bd. Middle Tenn. State U.; chairperson edn. com. Am. Cmty. Summit of Rutherford County; bd. dirs. Arts and Humanities Coun.; mem. exec. bd. Murfreesboro Youth Orch., C. of C. Bus. Edn. Partnership. Named Tenn. State Tchr. of Yr., 1998, Radio Educator of Week, Sta. WGNS, Outstanding Tchr. Tenn. Gov.'s Sch. of the Arts, 1995; recipient Apple award WSMV TV's Tchr., 1998, Disting. Classroom Tchr. award, 1992, Spl. Recognition award Tenn. Environ. Edn. Assn.; inducted Band of Blue Hall of Fame, 1998. Mem. ASCD, Nat. Flute Assn., Middle Tenn. Flute Soc., Am. Orff-Schulwork Assn., Tenn. Educators Assn., Music Educators Nat. Conf., Tenn. Elem. Music Educators Assn., Tennesseans for the Arts, Tenn. Bandmasters Assn., Middle Tenn. Sch. Band and Orch. Assn., Middle Tenn. Vocal Assn. (accompanist mass choir 1992), Tenn. Edn. Assn. (human rels com. 1994-96, summer leadership sch. 1994-96, del. to rep. assembly 1992-96), Middle Tenn. Edn. Assn. (pres.), Murfreesboro Edn. Assn. (grievance com. chairperson, exec. bd., profl. adv. com. 1994-96, pres. 1994-96, pres.-elect, other coms.), Phi Kappa Phi, Kappa Delta Pi, Phi Delta Kappa, Delta Omicron, Delta Kappa Gamma. Office: Murfreesboro City Schs 2552 S Church St Murfreesboro TN 37127-6342 E-mail: lgilbert@cityschools.net.

GILBERT, MARGARET BARBOUR, literature educator, poet; d. Robert Bennett Gilbert and Margaret Alice Barbour. BA in German Lang. and Lit. magna cum laude, Hunter Coll., 1980; MA in Creative Writing, CCNY, 1994. English faculty Bergen C.C., 1999—2000, Manhattan Coll., 2000, SUNY/Nassau C.C., 2001; lectr. English, Rutgers U., Newark, 2001—. Author poetry. Recipient grand prize, N.Am. Open Poetry Competition, 1998. Mem.: AAUP, Internat. Soc. Poets (life). Avocations: swimming, reading. Office: Rutgers U Dept English Hill Hall 616 University Heights Newark NJ 07102 E-mail: magilber@andromeda.rutgers.edu.

GILBERT, MARGARET P. university educator, researcher; b. England; d. Peter and Miriam Gilbert. DPhil, Oxford U. Prof. philosophy U. Conn., Storrs, 1983—. Vis. prof. Princeton (N.J.) U., King's Coll., London; vis. fellow Wolfson Coll., Oxford; vis. mem., Herodotus fellow Inst. for Advanced Study, Princeton; rsch. fellow St. Hilda's Coll., Oxford, St. Anne's Coll., Oxford, England. Author: On Social Facts, 1989, Living Together: Rationality, Sociality, and Obligation, 1996, Sociality and Responsibility: New Essays in Plural Subject Theory, 2000, Marcher Ensemble: Essais sur les Fondements des Phenomenes Collectifs, 2003. Rsch. fellow, Am. Coun. Learned Socs., 1989—90, NEH fellow, 2003—. Office: U Conn U-2054 Storrs Mansfield CT 06269-2054

GILBERT, MELISSA, actress; b. Los Angeles, May 8, 1964; d. Paul and Barbara (Crane) G.; m. Bo Brinkman (div.); 1 son, Dakota; m. Bruce Boxleitner, Jan. 1, 1995; stepchildren: Lee, Sam. Student, U. So. Calif. Actress: (TV movies) Little House on the Prairie, 1974, Christmas Miracle in Caulfield, U.S.A., 1977, The Miracle Worker, 1979, The Diary of Anne Frank, 1980, Splendor in the Grass, 1981, Little House: Look Back to Yesterday, 1983, Choices of the Heart, 1983, Little House: Bless All the Dear Children, 1984, Family Secrets, 1984, Little House: The Last Farewell, 1984, Choices, 1986, Penalty Phase, 1986, Family Secrets, Killer Instincts, Without Her Consent, Forbidden Nights, 1990, Blood Vows: The Story of a Mafia Wife, Joshua's Heart, 1990, Donor, The Lookalike, 1990, Conspiracy of Silence: The Shari Karney Story, 1992, With Hostile Intent, 1993, Shattered Trust, 1993, House of Secrets, 1993, Dying to Remember, 1993, Cries From the Heart, 1994, Against Her Will: The Carrie Buck Story, 1994, The Babymaker: The Dr. Cecil Jacobson Story, 1994, Danielle Steel's 'Zoya', 1995, Christmas in My Hometown, 1996, Seduction in a Small Town, 1996, Childhood Sweetheart, 1997, Her Own Rules, 1998, Murder at 75 Birch, 1999, Switched at Birth, 1999, A Vision of Murder: The Story of Donielle, 2000, Sanctuary, 2001, Then Came Jones, 2003; (TV series) Little House on the Prairie, 1974-82, Little House: A New Beginning, 1983, Stand By Your Man, 1992, Sweet Justice, 1994-95 (TV spls.) Battle of the Network Stars, 1978, 79, 81, 82, Celebrity Challenge of the Sexes, 1980, Circus Lions, Tigers and Melissa, Too, 1977, Dean Martin Celebrity Roast, 1984, (stage prodns.) Night of 100 Stars, 1982, The Glass Menagerie, 1985, A Shayna Maidel, 1987 (Outer Critics Circle Award), (feature films) Nutcracker Fantasy, 1979, Sylvester, 1985, Ice House, 1989. Mem.: SAG (pres. 2001—).

GILBERT, PAMELA, strategic services company executive; b. New Brunswick, NJ, Oct. 3, 1958; m. Charles R.E. Lewis, 1995; one child; one stepchild. BA, Tufts U., Medford, MA, 1980; JD, NYU, 1984. NY and DC bar assocs. Dir. consumer program U.S. Pub. Interest Rsch. Group, Washington; dir. Pub. Citizens Congress Watch, Washington; legis. counsel Malkin & Ross, Washington; exec. dir. Consumer Product Safety Commn., Bethesda, Md., 1996-2001; COO, M&R Strategic Svcs., Washington, 2001—. Office: M&R Strategic Svcs 2120 L St NW Ste 400 Washington DC 20037 E-mail: pgilbert@mrss.com.

GILBERT, SUZANNE HARRIS, advertising executive; b. Chgo, Mar. 8, 1948; d. Lawrence W. and Dorothea (Wilde) Harris: children: Kerry, Elizabeth, Gregory. BS, Marquette U.; MBA, U. Chgo., 1985. Fin. analyst Leo Burnett Co., Chgo.; sr. v.p., fin. administrn., sec.-treas. Clinton E. Frank Inc., Chgo., 1975-85; with Campbell-Ewald Co., Detroit, 1985—, grp. sr. v.p. Warren, Mich., exec. v.p., chief fin. and administrv. officer, 1990—. Bd. dirs.; bd. dirs., mem. fiscal control and investment audit coms. AAAA Ins. Co. Ltd. Bd. dirs. Detroit Workforce Devel.; mem. bd. advs. U. Detroit Mercy Coll. of Bus. Recipient Profl. Achievement award Marquette U., 2000. Mem. Am. Assn. Advt. Agys. (fiscal control com.), Econ. Club Detroit, Fin. Execs. Inst. (bd. dirs. Detroit chpt., pres.). Office: Campbell-Ewald 30400 Van Dyke Ave Warren MI 48093-2368

GILBERT-BARNESS, ENID F. pathologist, pathology and pediatrics educator; b. Sydney, Australia, May 31, 1927; arrived in U.S., 1952, naturalized, 1975; d. Christian Henry and Mabel (Milne) Fischer; m. James Bryson Gilbert, Aug. 12, 1954; children: Mary M., Elizabeth A., James C. (dec.), Jennifer E., Rebecca D.; m. Lewis Barness, July 5, 1987. MBBS, U. Sydney, 1950, MD, 1983; DSc (hon.), U. Wis., 1999; MD (hon.), U. Sydney, 1999. Diplomate Am. Bd. Pediat., Am. Bd. Clin. Pathology, Am. Bd. Anatomical Pathology, Am. Bd. Pediat. Pathology. Resident Children's Hosp., Boston, Phila., Washington, Brackenridge Hosp., Austin, Tex.; from asst. prof. to assoc. prof. U. W.Va., 1963-70; from assoc. prof. pathology and pediats. to prof. U. Wis., Madison, 1970-93, Disting. Med. Alumni prof., 1986-93, dir. pediat. pathology, 1970-93, prof. emeritus pathology and pediat., 1993—, Disting. Med. Alumni prof. emeritus, 1993—; prof. pathology, pediats. and ob-gyn. U. So. Fla., 1993—. Author: Introduction to Pathology, 1978, Genetic Aspects Developmental Pathology, 1987, Potters Pathology of the Fetus and Infant, 1997, Atlas Infant and Fetal Pathology, 1998, Metabolic Diseases, 2000, Atlas Embryo Fetal Pathology, 2004, Clinical Use of Pediatric Diagnostic Tests, 2003, Pediatric Autopsy Pathology, 2004; also numerous chpts., articles. Decorated Order of Australia, recipient Disting. Pathologist award, Royal Coll. Pathologists (Australia), 2001; NIH grantee, 1972—92. Mem. Am. Soc. Clin. Pathology, Soc. Pediat. Pathology (pres. 1986-87), Internat. Acad. Pathology, Internat. Pediat. Pathology Assn. (pres. 1990-92), Teratology Soc., Cardiovasc. Soc. S.Am. (hon.), Am. Pediat. Soc., Am. Acad. Pediat., U.S. Can. Acad. Pathology, Arthur Purdy Stout Soc. Surg. Pathology, N.Y. Acad. Sci., Alpha Omega Alpha. Home: 3301 Bayshore Blvd #403 Tampa FL 33629 Office: Tampa Gen Hosp Dept Pathology Tampa FL 33601 Office Phone: 813-844-7565. E-mail: egilbert@tgh.org.

GILBERT-STRAWBRIDGE, ANNE WIELAND, journalist; b. Chgo. d. David and Joy (Arnold) Wiel; m. George Gale Gilbert III (dec.); children: Douglas, Christopher; m. James Murry Strawbridge. BS, Northwestern U. Columnist Chgo. Daily News, 1971-78, United Features Syndicate, 1978-81; reporter NBC-TV Sunday in, Chgo., 1973; guest expert NBC-TV, N.Y.C. Today, 1974—. Mem. Newspapers Features Council. Prodr.: WSNS-TV spl. Collectors World, 1971; performer TV programs, KETC-TV, St. Louis, Donahue, 1975, 77; owner syndicated radio spot The Antique Detective; author: Antique Hunters Guide: For Freaks and Fanciers, 1974, Collecting the New Antiques, 1975, How to Be an Antiques Detective, 1978, Investing in the Antiques Market, 1980, Collectors Guide to American Illustrator Art, 1991, Design and Memorabilia 40s-50s, 1995, Design and Memorabilia 70s-80s, 1996, Collecting of Quilts (syndicated news column) Antique Detective, 1983-2004. Mem. Soc. Illustrators (assoc.), Alpha Gamma Delta. Presbyterian. Address: 854 Pruitt Cove Rd Laurel Springs NC 28644-8349 E-mail: antique1@skybest.com.

GILBREATH, SARAH BURKHART GELBACH, health facility administrator; b. Hagerstown, Md., Feb. 21, 1913; d. George and Carolyne Backer (Knode) Gelbach; m. Ylan Kailo Kealoha, Aug. 21, 1936 (dec. Nov. 9, 1944); 1 child, Ylan K. Kealoha ; m. Junious Dewey Gilbreath, Apr. 13, 1946. BS in Edn., NYU, 1942. RN N.Y., lifetime Red Cross nurse. Newspaper reporter The Herald Mail Publ. Co., Hagerstown, 1929-31; supr., instr. N.Y.C. Dept. Hosps., Seaview, S.I., N.Y., 1934-36, dept. supr. Kings County, Bklyn., 1936-39, supr., edn. dir. Goldwater Rsch. Hosp. Welfare Island, N.Y., 1939-41; asst. dir. nurses Goldwater Rsch. Hosp., Welfare Island, N.Y., 1941-46; supr. Kendall (Fla.) Hosp. Dade County Hosp. Systems, 1948-64; supr. Morris County Nursing Home, Morris Plains, N.J., 1964-74. Author (under pen name S. Burkhart Gilbreath): (book) Prayers of the Amwell Valley, 1987, Henry Stafford Little, Lawyer, 1993, Professor Benjamin B. Warfield, Princeton Clergy, 1996, Prayerful Praise-Sing Again in the Garden, 1999. Nurse Army Res. Hosp. Unit, N.Y. Harbor, Governor's Island, NY, 1939—45. Republican. Presbyterian. Home: PO Box 6010 Chambersburg PA 17201-6610

GILCHREST, BARBARA ANN, dermatologist; b. Port Chester, N.Y., 1945; MD, Harvard U., 1971. Diplomate Am. Bd. Dermatology, Am. Bd. Internal Medicine. Intern Boston City Hosp., 1971-72, resident internal medicine, 1972-73, resident dermatology, 1973-76; fellow photobiology Harvard U., Boston, 1974-75; chief dermatology U. Hosp., Boston, Boston City Hosp. (now Boston Med. Ctr.); prof., chmn. dermatology Boston U. Sch. Medicine, 1985—. Mem. AAAS, Am. Acad. Dermatology, Assn. Am. Physicians, Am. Soc. for Clin. Investigation, Inst. Medicine, Soc. for Investigative Dermatology. Office: Boston U Sch Medicine Dermatology 609 Albany St # J507 Boston MA 02118-2515

GILCHRIST, ANN ROUNDEY, hospice nurse; b. Utica, N.Y., Dec. 21, 1948; d. William Gilchrist and Adele (Cobb) Roundey; married; children: Kristie Ann Hughes, Megean Elizabeth Hughes Holden. Student, Cazenovia Coll., 1967-68; LPN, Utica Sch. Practical Nursing, 1972; postgrad., Mohawk Valley C.C., 1972-75; ADN, SUNY, Morrisville, 1976. RN, Nev.; CNOR. Obstetrics and med., surg. staff nurse St. Elizabeth Hosp., Utica, 1972-76; asst. charge nurse CCU and ICU Mohawk Valley Gen. Hosp., Ilion, N.Y., 1976-78; staff nurse operating room Tucson Med. Ctr., 1978-80, El Dorado Hosp., Tucson, 1978-80; staff nurse oper. room and post anesthesia care unit Tucson Gen. Hosp., 1980-85; charge nurse oper. room Desert Springs Hosp., Las Vegas, Nev., 1985-87, staff nurse GI Lab., 1988-90; charge nurse GI Lab, staff nurse operating room Lake Mead Hosp., Las Vegas, 1991-93; supr. operating room Red Rock Surg. Ctr., Las Vegas, 1993-95; staff nurse Endoscopy Lab., Sunrise Flamingo Surg. Ctr., Las Vegas, 1995-97; RN case mgr. Home Side, at Odyssey Hospice, Las Vegas, 1998—. Mem.: Assn. Hospice and Palliative Care Nurses, So. Nev. Land Cruisers. Avocations: professional doll artist, learther artist, ceramicist, equestrian. Home: 4552 Scott Ave Las Vegas NV 89102-8107 Office: 4011 Mcleod Dr Las Vegas NV 89121-4305 E-mail: annzart@msn.com.

GILCHRIST, ELLEN LOUISE, writer; b. Vicksburg, Miss., Feb. 20, 1935; d. William Garth and Aurora (Alford) G.; children: Marshall Peteet Walker, Jr., Garth Gilchrist Walker, Pierre Gautier Walker. BA in Philosophy, Millsaps Coll., 1967; postgrad., U. Ark., 1976; LittD (hon.), Millsaps Coll., 1987; LHD (hon.), U. So. Ill., 1988, U. Ark., 2000. Freelance writer, journalist. Commentator, morning edit. of news Nat. Pub. Radio, Washington, 1984, 85 Author: The Land Surveyor's Daughter, 1979, In The Land of Dreamy Dreams, 1981, The Annunciation (Book of Month Club alternate in U.S. and Sweden), 1983, Victory Over Japan (Am. Book award 1984), 1984, Drunk With Love, 1986, Falling Through Space, 1987, The Anna Papers, 1988, Light Can Be Both Wave and Particle, 1989, I Cannot Get You Close Enough, 1990 (Miss. Inst. Arts and Letters award 1990, fiction award Miss. Libr. Assn. 1990), Net of Jewels, 1992, Starcarbon, 1994, Anabasis, A Journey to the Interior, 1994, The Age of Miracles, 1995, Rhoda, A Life in Stories, 1995, The Courts of Love, 1996, Sarah Conley, 1997, Flights of Angels, 1998, The CABAL and Other Stories, 1999, Collected Stories, 2000, I, Rhoda Manning, Go Hunting with My Daddy, 2002; (poems) Riding Out the Tropical Depression; contbr. short stories poems to literary publs. Recipient Poetry award U. Ark., 1976, Craft in Poetry award N.Y. Quar., 1978, Fiction award The Prairie Schooner, 1981, Poetry award Miss. Arts Festival, 1968, Saxifrage award, 1983, Fiction award Miss. Acad. Arts and Sci., 1982, 85, Am. Book award Victory Over Japan, 1984, J. William Fulbright prize U. Ark., 1985, Lit. award Miss. Inst. Arts and Letters, 1985, 90, 91; 2 Pushcart prizes, O. Henry Short Story award, 1995; named Woman of Yr. Chi Omega, 2001; grantee NEA, 1979. Mem. Author's Guild.

GILE, MARY STUART, state legislator, educational executive; b. Montreal, Que., Can., Mar. 24, 1936; d. William Gillies and Hazel Irene (Stuart) Sinclair; m. Robert Hall Gile, Mar. 29, 1974; children: D. Christopher, Julia Mary, Robertson Sinclair. BS, McGill U., 1957; EdM, U. NH, 1971; EdD, Vanderbilt U., 1982. Specialist phys. edn. Protestant Sch. Bd. Greater Montreal, 1957-64; kindergarten tchr. White Mountains Sch. Bd., Littleton, NH, 1965-67; dir. Open Door Kindergarten, Salem, NH, 1967-69; coord. State Follow Through, NH, 1969-80, Right to Read, NH, 1973-74; coord. US Sec.'s Initiative in Excellence; Chpt. 1 Edn. Consol. and Improvement Act, 1983-84; sr. cons. edn. State Dept. Edn., Concord, NH, 1969-85; v.p. edn. and devel. Acad. Applied Sci., Concord, NH, 1985-90; prof., dept. head early childhood edn. NH Tech. Inst., Concord, NH, 1990-98. State dept. staff assoc. to U. NH, Durham, 1970—74; mem. Gov.'s Task Force on Sexual Harassment, Concord, NH, 1981—83; chair Trust Fund for Prevention of Child Abuse and Neglect, NH, 1988—92; mem. state child abuse neglect prevention leadership team; mem. State Child Care Adv. Coun., NH, 1994—99; pres. faculty Tech. Inst. and C.C., NH, 1995—97; chmn. State Child Care Adv. Coun., NH, 1997—2001. Pres. Concord Parents and Children, 1977—82; chmn. Citizens Adv. Bd. to Cmty. Devel., 1978—82; bd. gov. Merrimack County United Way, 1983—88; pres. Assn. for Mental Health, NH, 1984—86; Founder Legis. Caucus for Young Children, NH, 1997—; elected to NH legis. Merrimack Dist. 38, 1996—; apptd. to exec. dept. and adminstrn., 1997—98; apptd. to children and family law, bd. dirs., 1999—; U. NH Alumni Assn., 1999. Recipient cert. outstanding achievement NH State Bd. Edn., 1985, NH Dept. Children, Youth and Families award for exemplary leadership and svc., 1999, Providian Child Care leader award, 1999, Honoree DCYF Mary Stuart Gile Award presented to group committed to devel. leadership in early childhood. Mem. NH Assn. for Edn. Young Children (Svc. for Young Children award 1998), Phi Delta Kappa. Congregationalist. Avocations: skiing, music, theater, hiking.

GILES, KATHARINE EMILY (J. K. PIPER), administrative assistant, writer; b. Jackson Hole, Wyo., Jan. 9, 1938; d. William Lamar and Grace Hawley (Domrose) G.; children: Piper Lee Shanks, John Richard Hamlin. Diamond cert., Gemological Inst. Am., 1971. Adminstrv. asst. Matthiesen Equipment Co., San Antonio, 1993-96; driver USA Truck, Van Buren, Ark., 1996—. Top Gun, USA Truck, 148,900 accident free miles, 1997; 147,100, 1998. Author: The Marvelous Bean, 1989, The Lost Trident, 1991, The Missing Crystal, 1992, Jewel of Avalon, 1992, The Lost Kingdom, 1991, The Desert Sun, 1992, The Fire Sled, 1991, Knights of Glass, 1992, Black Pagoda, 1992, Memories from the Kitchen of Grace & Rich Williams, 1992, My Recipe Box, 2000. Home: 6700 Jefferson Paige Rd Lot 265 Shreveport LA 71119-4905

GILES, PHYLLIS LENORE WILLIAMS, retired elementary school educator; b. Fowler, Colo., Oct. 11, 1912; d. Odin Neil and Lillian Valeria (Deutschman) Williams; m. Albert E. Giles, 1943 (dec.); children: Richard Brian, Tyler William BA, U. No. Colo., 1939; MA, Northwestern U., 1964. Elem. sch. tchr., Delearbon, Colo., 1933-34; elem. sch. tchr. La Veta, Colo., 1934-35, Colorado Springs, Colo., 1935-40; exch. tchr Shaker Heights Sch. Dist., 1939-40; tchr. jr. high sch. Colorado Springs, 1939-40; elem. sch. tchr. Montgomery, Ala., 1943, Denver, 1947-48; tchr. Pocatello (Idaho) Jr. High, 1950-51; elem. sch. tchr. Salt Lake City, 1951-53, Park Ridge, Ill., 1953-78. Mem. Cleve. Symphony Chorus, 1939-40, Utah Symphony Chorus, 1951-53; part-time instr. edn. music. Planner weekly classical music programs USO, Colorado Springs, 1941-42; mem. many ch. choirs. Mem. AAUW (chmn. daytime bridge 1988-90, internat. rels. N.W. Suburban br. 1988, 89, 2d v.p. N.W. program, chair 1991-93, networking com., program chmn. 1991-93, AAUW Edn. Found. Scholarship named in honor 1993, 50-Yr. Membership honor 1996), PEO (organized new chpt. in Des Plaines 1939, 1st pres., charter mem. chpt. Denver 1947, selected charter mem. 1986—, chaplain N.W. Suburban Roundtable 1987-88, 2d v.p. 1990-91, mem. planning com., N.W. Roundtable activities, honored 66 yr. mem. 1999, pres. 1999-2001). Congregationalist. Avocations: opera, book review clubs, bridge, reading, foreign affairs. Home: 928 E Grant Dr Des Plaines IL 60016-6209 E-mail: PhyllisGiles@aol.com.

GILFILEN, TERI, artist; b. Columbia, S.C., Aug. 25, 1953; d. William Lee and Hilma Rehard Thomas; m. Dennis Jordan Gilfilen, June 30, 1973; children: Andrea Lee Hanson, Michael Jordan Gilfilen. Student, Ohio State U., 1971-73. Artist-in-sch. Dublin Mid. Sch., Ohio, 1988; mem. selection com. Dublin C. of C., 1987-88; presenter workshops in field. Artist: (book) Best of Watercolor, 1995; contbr. art to profl. jours. (Top 200 award 1994); one-woman shows include Zanesville Art Mus., Ohio, 1992, Middletown Arts Ctr., Ohio, 1994, The Ohio State U., Columbus, 1998. Mem. adv. bd. Dublin Cmty. Ctr., 1988. Mem. Nat. Acrylic Painters Assn. (Gold award 1999, CK award 1999), Salmagundi Nat. Assn. (Kanisky award 1995), Ohio Watercolor Soc. (trustee 1990, 94), Am. Artists Profl. League, Ky. Watercolor Soc. Avocations: fly fishing, archaeology, kayaking. Home: 1203 Sandoway Ln Delray Beach FL 33483-7133

GILFOYLE, NATHALIE FLOYD PRESTON, lawyer; b. Lynchburg, Va., May 4, 1949; d. Robert Edmund and Dorothea Henry (Ward) Gilfoyle; m. Christopher Y.W. Ma, Sept. 9, 1978; children: Olivia Otey. Rohan James. BA, Hollins Coll., 1971; JD, U. Va., 1974. Bar: Mass. 1974, D.C. 1977. Staff counsel Rate Setting Commn., Boston, 1974-76; ptnr. Peabody, Lambert & Meyers, Washington, 1976-84, McDermott, Will and Emery, 1984-96; gen. counsel Am. Psychol. Assn., 1996—. Bd. dirs. ACLU Nat. Capital Area, Washington, 1980-83, St. Columbia's Nursery Sch., 1992-99, D.C. Bar Atty. Client Arbitration bd., chmn., 1994-95. Mem.: ABA, Mass. Bar Assn., Women's Bar Assn., DC Bar Assn. (legal ethics com. 1999—2001, gen. counsel 2002—). Episcopalian. Office: APA 750 1st St NE Washington DC 20002-4241 E-mail: ngilfoyle@apa.org.

GILHAM, JOANNE, state representative; b. Columbia, SC, June 14, 1939; d. Hubert Felder and Evelyn Withers Goldson; m. Louis Benjamin, Jr., Mar. 21, 1958; children: Sherry, Leslye, Joanie, Lynne, Trey. Student, U. SC, Luther Rice Seminary. Tchr. Ridgeland Kindergarten, 1968—72, Calvary Christian Acad., 1974—79; guidance counselor Hilton Head Christian Acad., 1985—89; mem. SC Ho. of Reps., 1999—. Bd. dirs. Forest Beach Assn., 1987—89; adv. bd. SCETV-WJWJ, 1996—97; chmn. credentials com. Beaufort County Rep. Party, 1996—; lay counselor Grace Cmty. Ch., 1989—96; bd. dirs. Beaufort County Commn. Sch., 1996—99. Republican. Office: State Capitol 326 C Blatt Bldg Columbia SC 29211

GILKES, CHERYL LOUISE TOWNSEND, sociologist, educator, minister; b. Boston, Nov. 2, 1947; d. Murray Luke Jr. and Evelyn Annette (Reid) Townsend. BA, MA, PhD, Northeastern U.; postgrad., Boston U., 1988. Lectr. Univ. Coll. Northeastern U., Boston, 1973-78; instr. sociology Boston State Coll., 1974-78, U. Mass., 1976; asst. prof. sociology Boston U., 1978-87; MacArthur assoc. prof. African-Am. studies and sociology

Colby Coll., Waterville, Maine, 1989-2000, MacArthur asst. prof., 1987-89, MacArthur prof. African Am. studies and sociology, 2000—. Vis. lectr. Tufts U., 1974; rsch. assoc., vis. lectr. sociology of religion Harvard U. Div. Sch., 1981-82, vis. lectr. African-Am. religious studies, 1992-93; vis. lectr. Afro-Am. studies Simmons Coll., Chgo. Theol. Sem., 1989, Iliff Sch. Theology, 1989, Temple U., 1989; faculty fellow Bunting Inst. Radcliff Coll., 1982-84; vis. scholar Episcopal Div. Sch., 1992-93; fellow W.E.B. DuBois Inst. for Afro-Am. Rsch., Harvard U., Inst. Advanced Study Religion, Yale U., 1999-2000; host gospel music radio sta. WMHB Waterville, 2002—. Author: If It Wasn't for the Women...: Black Women's Experience and Womanist Culture in Church and Community, 2000; gospel music radio show host Sta. WMHB, Waterville, 2002—; contbr. articles and revs. to profl. jours., chpts. to books. Sec. Cambridge Civic Unity Com., 1978-87; mem. adv. com. Schlessinger Libr., Radcliffe Coll., 1984-86; pres. Cambridge Black Cultural and Hist. Assn., 1978-87; parliamentarian, asst. dean congress Christian Edn. United Bapt. Conv., Mass., R.I. and N.H., 1986—; assoc. min. Union Bapt. Ch., Cambridge, Mass., 1982-97, asst. pastor, 1998—; mem. NAACP. Nat. Fellowships fund dissertation fellow, 1977-78, Socialization Tng. fellow Northeastern U., 1970-73. Fellow: Inst. Advanced Study Religion; mem.: NAACP, Urban League Ea. Mass., Assn. for Sociology of Religion, Soc. Study Black Religion, Soc. Sci. Study of Religion (exec. coun. 1995—97), Sociologists Women in Soc. (lectr. 2002—), Assn. Black Sociologists, Soc. Study of Sybolic Interaction, Am. Acad. Religion, Assn. Humanist Sociology, Soc. Study of Social Problems (v.p. 1990—91), Mass. Sociol. Assn., Ea. Sociol. Soc. (v.p. 1995—96), Am. Sociol. Assn. (Spivak dissertation fellow 1977—78, mem. coun. 1995—98), Delta Sigma Theta, Phi Kappa Phi. Office: Colby Coll Dept Sociology Waterville ME 04901

GILL, DIANE LOUISE, psychology educator, university official; b. Watertown, N.Y., Nov. 7, 1948; d. George R. and Betty J. (Reynolds) G. BS in Edn., SUNY, Cortland, N.Y., 1970; MS, U. Ill., 1974, PhD, 1976. Tchr. Greece Athena High Sch., Rochester, N.Y., 1970-72; asst. prof. U. Waterloo, Ont., Can., 1976-78, U. Iowa, Iowa City, 1979-81, assoc. prof., 1981-86; assoc. prof. sport & exercise psychology U. N.C., Greensboro, 1987-89, prof. Greenboro, 1989—, assoc. dean Greensboro, 1992-97, head dept. exercise and sport sci., 1997-2000, dir. Ctr. for Women's Health and Wellness, 2002—. Author: Psychological Dynamics of Sport and Exercise, 1986, 2000; editor Jour. of Sport and Exercise Psychology, 1985-90; contbr. articles to profl. jours. Fellow AAHPERD (rsch. consortium pres. 1987-89), APA (pres. divsn. 47 exercise and sport 1999-2001), Am. Psychol. Soc., Assn. for Advancement of Applied Sport Psychology, Am. Acad. Kinesiology and Phys. Edn.; mem. N.Am. Soc. for Psychology of Sport and Phys. Activity (pres. 1988-91). Democrat. Office: U NC Dept Exercise and Sport Sci Greensboro NC 27402-6170 E-mail: diane_gill@uncg.edu.

GILL, E. ANN, lawyer; b. Elyria, Ohio, Aug. 31, 1951; d. Richard Henry and Laura (Beeler) G.; m. Robert William Hempel, Aug. 4, 1973; children: Richard, Peter, Mary. AB, Barnard Coll., 1972; JD, Columbia U., 1976. Bar: N.Y. 1977, U.S. Supreme Ct. 1982. Assoc. Mudge, Rose, Guthrie & Alexander, N.Y.C., 1976-77, Dewey Ballantine L.L.P., N.Y.C., 1977-84, ptnr., 1985—2004, Thelen Reid & Priest, N.Y.C., 2004—. Mem. ABA, Nat. Assn. Bond Lawyers. Home: 255 W 90th St New York NY 10024-1109 Office: Thelen Reid & Priest 875 Third Ave New York NY 10022 E-mail: agill@thelenreid.com.

GILL, EVALYN PIERPOINT, editor, writer, publisher; b. Boulder, Colo. d. Walter Lawrence and Lou Octavia Pierpoint; m. John Glanville Gill; children: Susan Pierpoint, Mary Louise Glanville. Student, Lindenwood Coll.; BA, U. Colo.; postgrad., U. Nebr., U. Alaska; MA, Ctrl. Mich. U., 1968. Lectr. humanities Saginaw Valley State Coll., University Ctr., Mich., 1968-72; mem. English faculty U. N.C., Greensboro, 1973-74; editor Internat. Poetry Rev., Greensboro, 1975-92; pres. TransVerse Press, Greensboro, 1981—. Author: Poetry by French Women, 1930-1980, 1980, Dialogue, 1985, Southeast of Here: Northwest of Now, 1986, Entrances, 1996; editor: O. Henry Festival Stories, 1985, 87, Women of the Piedmont Triad: Poetry and Prose, 1989, Edge of Our World, 1990, A Turn in Time: Piedmont Writers at the Millennium, 1999. Bd. dirs. Eastern Music Festival, Greensboro, 1981-85, Greensboro Symphony, 1982-86, Greensboro Opera Co., 1982—, Weatherspoon Art Mus., 1980-; chmn. O Henry Festival, 1985, 95. Recipient numerous poetry prizes, Fortner award St. Andrews Coll., 1995, Altrusa Internat. Cmty. Arts award, Greensboro, 1998. Mem. MLA, Amn. Lit. Translators Assn., N.C. Poetry Soc., Phi Beta Kappa. Home: 2900 Turner Grove Dr N Greensboro NC 27455-1977

GILL, GAIL STOORZA, corporate professional; b. Yoakum, Tex., Aug. 28, 1943; d. Roy Otto and Ruby Pauline (Ray) Blankenship; m. Larry Stoorza, Apr. 27, 1963 (div. 1968); m. Ian M. Gill, Apr. 24, 1981; 1 child, Alexandra Leigh. Student, N. Tex. State U., 1961-63, U. Tex., Arlington, 1963. Stewardess Cen. Airlines, Ft. Worth, 1963; advt. and acctg. exec. Phillips-Ramsey Advt., San Diego, 1963-68; dir. advt. Rancho Bernardo, San Diego, 1968-72; dir. corp. communications Avco Community Developers, San Diego, 1972-74; pres. Gail Stoorza Co., San Diego, 1974—, Stoorza, Ziegaus & Metzger, San Diego, 1974—2002; CEO Stoorza, Ziegaus, Metzger, Inc. (now Stoorza Communications, Co.), 1993—2002; chmn. Stoorza/Smith, San Diego, 1984-85, Stoorza Internat., San Diego, 1984-85; CEO ADC Stoorza, San Diego, 1987—2001, Franklin Stoorza, San Diego, 1993—2001; chmn., CEO The Right Question, LLC. Columnist The San Diego Daily Transcript; bd. dirs. Security Bus. Bank, San Diego. Trustee San Diego Art Found.; bd. dirs. San Diego Found. for Performing Arts, San Diego Opera, Sunbelt Nursery Groups, Dallas; vice chmn. San Diego Convention Ctr. Corp.; mem. bd. San Diego Econ. Devel. Corp., Ind. Colleges of So. Calif. Named Small Bus. Person of Yr. Select Com. on Small Bus., 1984, one of San Diego's Ten Outstanding Young Citizens San Diego Jaycees, 1979; recipient Woman of Achievement award Women in Communications Inc., 1985, Human Unity award, Nat. Conf. Christians and Jews. Mem. Pubs. Soc. Am., Nat. Assn. Home Builders (residential mktg. com.), COMBO, Greater San Diego C. of C (chmn.), Young President's Assn., Arthur Page Soc; Clubs: Chancellors Assn. U. Calif. (San Diego), Pub. Relations, San Diego Press. Methodist.

GILL, LIBBY, television executive; BA in Theater magna cum laude, Calif. State U., Long Beach. Mgr., publicist Embassy Comm. and Columbia Pictures TV, Calif., 1986-89; dir. primetime publicity Columbia Pictures TV/TriStar TV, Calif., 1989-92; v.p. publicity and promotion Sony Pictures Entertainment TV Group, Calif., 1992-94; v.p. pub. rels. west coast Turner Entertainment Group, Calif., 1994-96; sr. v.p. media rels. Universal TV Group, Universal City, Calif., 1996—. Pub. rels. cons. for non-profit orgns., including Deaf Arts Coun. Mem. TV Publicity Execs. Com. (former chmn.). Office: MCA TV 100 Universal City Plz Universal City CA 91608-1002

GILL, MARGARET GASKINS, lawyer; b. St. Louis, Mar. 2, 1940; d. Richard Williams and Margaret (Cambage) Gaskins; m. Stephen Paschall Gill, Dec. 21, 1961; children: Elizabeth, Richard. BA, Wellesley Coll., 1962; JD, U. Calif., Berkeley, 1965. Bar: Calif. 1966. Assoc. Pillsbury, Madison & Sutro, San Francisco, 1966-72, ptnr., 1973-94, mem. mgmt. com., 1973-94, head corp. securities group, mem. assoc., rev. com., 1981-91, chair assoc., rev. com., 1988-91; sr. v.p. legal, external affairs & sec. AirTouch Communications, San Francisco, 1994—. Referee Calif. State Bar Ct., 1979-82; bd. dirs. Consolidated Freightways. Mem. steering com. Trinity Episcopal Ch., Menlo Park, Calif., 1980-82, com. to revise constitution, Diocese Calif., 1981-82; trustee St. Luke's Hosp. Found., San Francisco, 1983-93; mem. adv. coun. Ch. div. Sch. of the Pacific, 1986; bd. dirs. Episcopal Diocese Calif., 1989—; trustee San Francisco Ballet, 1991—; bd. dirs., gen. counsel United Way Bay Area, San Francisco, 1993-94. Fellow Am. Bar Found.; mem. ABA (spl. com. on internat. practice 1979-82, spl. com. negotiated acquisition 1988-90), Calif. Bar Assn. (corp. com. 1982-85, chairperson 1985, exec. com. 1985-88, vice chairperson 1987-88, chair nominating com. bus. law sect. 1988), San Francisco Bar Assn. Republican. Episcopalian. Office: AirTouch Communications One Calif St San Francisco CA 94111

GILL, NIA H. state legislator; BA, Upsala Coll., JD, Rutgers Law Sch. Law clk. McTeer, Walls & Bailey, Greenville, Miss., 1973; legis. aide Sen. Wynona Lipman, N.J., 1973-74; trial atty. N.J. Pub. Defenders Office, Essex & Passaic Counties, N.J., 1976-82; lawyer del. 3d Jud. Conf., 1987—; state legislator N.J. Ho. of Reps. Assembly N.J. State Dist. 27, 1994—, jud. law & pub. safety com. N.J. State Assembly, sr. citizen & social svc. coms., task force on juvenile crime, criminal justice subcom., Dem. task force on crime & corrections; ptnr. Gill & Cohen, P.C., Montclair. Trustee Montclair Pub. Libr., 1978-83, Cmty. Nursing Svc., Montclair, 1986-87; bd. adjustment Montclair Twp., 1985—; bd. dirs. Playwrights Theater N.J., 1993-94, Luna Theater, Montclair. Recipient legal profession award Nat. Coun. Negro Bus. Women, 1985, citizen award Montclair br. NAACP, 1988. Mem. ABA, Assn. Criminal Def. Lawyers N.J. (trustee 1986-89), N.J. State Bar Assn., Garden State Bar Assn., Essex County Bar Assn., Nat. Conf. Black Lawyers, Black Women Lawyers N.J., Assn. Trial Lawyers Am., Isis Literary Guild (pres.). Democrat. Office: NJ Senate Dist 34 425 Bloomfield Ave Ste 2 Montclair NJ 07042-3538

GILL, REBECCA LALOSH, aerospace engineer; b. Brownsboro, Tex., Sept. 17, 1944; d. Milton and Dona Mildred (Magee) LaLosh; m. Peter Mohammed Sharma, Sept. 1, 1965 (div.); m. James Frederick Gill, Mar. 9, 1985; children: Erin, Melissa, Ben. BS in Physics, U. Mich., 1965; MBA, Calif. State U., Northridge, 1980. Tchr., Derby, Kans., 1966; weight analyst Beech Aircraft, Wichita, Kans., 1966; weight engr. Ewing Tech. Design, assigned Boeing-Vertol, Phila., 1966-67, Bell Aerosystems, Buffalo, 1967; design specialist Lockheed-Calif. Co., Burbank, 1968-79; sr. staff engr. Hughes Aircraft Missile Sys., Canoga Park, Calif., 1979-82, project mgr. AMRAAM spl. test and tng. equipment, 1982-85, project mgr. GBU-15 guidance sect., Navy IR Maverick Missile Tucson, 1985-89, project mgr. Navy IR Maverick Missile, Slam Seeker Prodn., 1989-92, TOSH and TOW Internat. program mgr., 1992—. Sec. Nat. Cinema Corp. Com. chmn. Orgn. for Rehab. through Tng., 1971-75; spkr. ednl. and civic groups. Pres. Briarcliffe East Homeowners Assn.; coord. support group Am. Diabetes Assn., chmn. com. fundraising coun. mem. Tucson chpt., walk team capt., 1997, 98, 99; active NOW; block leader Neighborhood Watch. Recipient Lockheed award of achievement, 1977. Mem. NAFE, Soc. Allied Weight Engrs. (dir., sr. v.p., chmn. pub. rels. com.), Aerospace Elec. Soc. (dir.), Tucson Zool. Soc. (bd. dirs.), Hughes Mgmt. Club (bd. dirs., chmn. spl. events, chmn. programs, parliamentarian, 1st v.p., pres.), Women in Def. (sec., Ariz. chpt.), Las Alturas Homeowners Assn. (v.p., pres.), Raytheon Mgmt. Club (chmn. elections com.), Tucson Racquet Club. Republican. Office: Raytheon Missile Sys Bldg 801 MS G25A Tucson AZ 85734

GILLAN, KAYLA J. lawyer; JD, U. Calif., Davis, 1984. Gen. counsel Calif. Pub. Employees Ret. Sys., Sacramento, 1996—. Named one of Top 50 Women Lawyers Nat. Law Jour., 1998. Office: Calif Pub Employees Ret Sys Lincoln Plz 400 P St Sacramento CA 95814-5345

GILLARD, BERYL L. mortgage company executive; d. James Howard and Doris Markland Gillard; life ptnr. Laura Ann Essick, July 23, 1997. BS in Agrl. Bus. Mgmt., U. Del., 1987. Foreclosure/REO sect. head USDA/Centralized Servicing Ctr., St. Louis, 2000—; co-owner, treas. Life Strategies, Inc., Clayton, Mo., 2001—. Bd. dirs., developer website Gateway Alliance, St. Louis, 1998—2001.

GILLEO, SANDRA V. elementary school educator; b. Somerville, N.J., May 8, 1944; d. Sam B. and Frances (Green) Hammer; m. Robert James Gilleo (div. Dec. 1981); children: Robert T.I., Felise V. BA, Trenton (N.J.) State Coll., 1967; MA, Newark State Coll., 1971. Cert. tchr., N.J., Pa. Tchr. elem. Franklin Twp. Sch. Dist., Quakertown, N.J., 1966-67, Bricktown (N.J.) Twp. Sch. Dist., 1967-69; reading specialist Lawrence Twp. Sch. Dist., Lawrenceville, N.J., 1969-72; elem. tchr. New Hope-Solebury (Pa.) Sch. Dist., 1972—. Libr. Village Libr. of Wrightstown, Pa., 1972—; vol. John B. Anderson presdl. campaing, Bucks County, Pa., 1980; mem. Second Monday adv. com. for women, Doylestown, Pa., 1982-894; tchr. Temple Judea of Bucks County, 1991; active James Michener Art Mus., Churchville Nature Ctr. With USNR, 1965-71. Mem. Franklin Twp. Edn. Assn., Brick Edn. Assn., Lawrenceville Edn. Assn., New Hope-Solebury Edn. Assn., Churchville Nature Ctr., Michener Art Mus. Jewish. Avocations: volunteering, tennis, hiking, tap and country western dance. Home: 2650 Windy Bush Rd Newtown PA 18940-3601 Office: New Hope-Solebury Elem Sch N Sugan Rd Solebury PA 18963-9998

GILLESPIE, EVELYN HOPE See NEELY, EVELYN

GILLESPIE, HELEN DAVYS, marketing/industry consultant, analyst, writer; b. San Jose, Calif., Nov. 23, 1954; d. Robert Bruce and Helen Davys (Street) G.; m. Nigel George Haden, May 1, 1982 (div. June 1986). BA in English with honors, Calif. State U., Chico, 1976; postgrad. in English, U. Sheffield, Eng., 1976-77, Calif. State U., Chico, 1977-78. Cert. bus. communicator. Bus. analyst Dun & Bradstreet, San Jose, 1978-80; personal asst. Times Computer Svcs., London, 1980; adminstr. Exec. Aviation, Palo Alto, Calif., 1981; sr. writer/editor Tymnet/McDonnell Douglas, San Jose, 1982-86; mgr. sales support Pactel Spectrum Svcs., Walnut Creek, Calif., 1987; mgr. product communications Varian Assocs., Inc., Sunnyvale, Calif., 1987-90; mgr. mktg. communications Allergan Humphrey, San Leandro, Calif., 1990-91; owner Write Away Comm., San Jose, Calif., 1987—, Isographics Internat., 1994—; mgr. bus. comms. Lockheed Martin Advanced Tech. Ctr., Palo Alto, Calif., 1998-2000; v.p. SciBrain, 2003. Editor, pub. LIMS/Letter, 1994—, LIMSource web site, 1996—. Bd. dirs. and exhibits com. chair Cultural Arts Coun. Sonoma County, 2002. Recipient LIMS award LIMS Inst., 1999. Mem. Bus. Mktg. Assn., Airline Owners and Pilots Assn., Art Inst. Chgo., Mus. Soc. San Francisco, Commonwealth Club, Am. Soc. Quality Control, Sonoma Mus. Visual Arts. Avocations: swimming, windsurfing, english riding/dressage, flying, bicycling, snow and water skiing.

GILLESPIE, MARCIA LOU, tax specialist, accountant, musician; b. Grand Rapids, Mich., Nov. 26, 1942; d. Peter James and Bernice Lucille (DeReus) Muyskens; m. Norman Wayne Edwards, Aug. 15, 1964 (div. Apr. 1977); 1 child, Cary Ann Edwards; m. Eugene Scott Gillespie, Jan. 31, 1988. BA cum laude, U. Pitts., 1973. Enrolled agt. IRS. Acct. San Jose (Calif.) Symphony, 1977-78; agt. Prudential Ins., San Jose, 1978-81; acct. MicroFocus, Palo Alto, Calif., 1981-83; pianist, accompanist Opera Soc., Jr. Colls., San Jose and Napa, Calif., 1976—; contr. Gaston Snow, Palo Alto, 1983; acct. Accountemps, San Francisco, 1983-85, Bernheim Co., San Francisco, 1985-93; acct., tax preparer M.L. Gillespie Tax Svc., Emeryville, Napa, Calif., 1993—. Mem. Better Bus Bur., Oakland, Calif., 1996-97. Sgt., mem. Army Band, U.S. N.G., 1977-2000. Mem. Nat. Assn. Enrolled Agts. Democrat. Avocations: tennis, bowling, home decorating. Office: 1834 1st St # 5 Napa CA 94559-2353 Personal E-mail: marciaea@sbcglobal.net.

GILLESPIE, MARILYN, museum administrator; Dir. Las Vegas Natural History Mus., 1991—. Pres. Bd. Mus. and Attractions, Nev., sec. 1997—. Vol. promoting environ. concerns, homelessness issues, spl. edn. Mem. Am. Assn. Mus., Nev. Mus. Assn., Allied Arts Coun., S.W. Marine Educators Assn., Kiwanis Club (bd. dirs. Las Vegas Territory, program dir. Uptown). Office: Las Vegas Natural History Mus 900 Las Vegas Blvd N Las Vegas NV 89101-1112

GILLESPIE, NORMA, educational advisor; b. Mt. Pleasant, Tex., Oct. 6, 1946; d. Geraldean Margarete and A.W. Fry; m. Lewis James Gillespie; children: Scarlette McCoy, Cassandra Humble, Clay. MA, U.Ctrl.Okla., Edmond, 1993. Instr. Eng. Lit. Seminole (Okla.) State Coll., 1989—2002, ednl. talent search advisor, 2002—. Sponsor Sigma Kappa Delta, Seminole State Coll., 1997—, lit. and drama readings at local canyon. Editor: (publ. of Seminole State Eng. Honor Students) Active Voices; contbr. articles newspaper Wewoka Times, 2000 (AP Card, 2001, 02, 03). Pres. Seminole (Okla.) Arts Coun., 1995—97. Named Tchr. of Yr., Seminole State Coll. students, 1996. Mem.: Wewoka Writers Club, Sigma Kappa Delta (nat. bd. dirs. 2000—), Associated Press (assoc.). Avocation: travel. Office: Seminole State College 2701 Boren Blvd Seminole OK 74868

GILLESPIE, PENNY HANNIG, business owner; b. Schenectady, N.Y., June 4, 1954; d. William Armand and Freda (Penney) H.; m. Kenneth Scofield Keyes, Jr., Sept. 2, 1984 (div. Aug. 1992). Student, U. Ariz., 1972-74. Cert. EMT, Ariz., N.Y.; completion in skills tng. for profls. in Hakomi psychotherapy, Oreg. Co-founder Ken Keyes Coll., Coos Bay, Ore., 1982-91; pvt. practice counseling Eugene, Ore., 1991-95; founder, pres. The Wellness Network, Eugene, Oreg., 1994—. Co-author: Gathering Power Through Insight and Love, 1986, Handbook to Higher Consciousness: The Workbook, 1989; editor: How to Enjoy Your Life in Spite of It All, 1980, The Hundredth Monkey, 1982, Your Heart's Desire, 1983, Your Life Is a Gift, 1987, Discovering the Secrets of Happiness, 1988, Planet-Hood, 1988, The Power of Unconditional Love, 1990. Bd. dirs. Living Love Ch., 1980-91, sec., v.p.; founding bd. dirs., sec., sec.-treas., v.p. The Vision Foundation, Inc., 1982-91; founding bd. dirs., sec., sec.-treas. Cornucopia, The Living Love Ch. of Ky., 1982-91; vol. Victim Advocate Lane County Dist. Attys. Victim/Witness Svcs. Program, Oreg., 1993. Recipient peace award Coalition for Justice and Peace, Ariz. State U. and the Inst. Peace Edn., 1989; award as site mgr. for Anne Frank exhibit Jewish Fedn. Lane County, Ore., 1993. Avocations: piano, bicycling. Home: PO Box 41532 Eugene OR 97404-0369

GILLET, PAMELA KIPPING, special education educator; EdB in Elem. Edn., Chgo. Tchrs. Coll., 1963; MA in Mental Retardation, Northeastern Ill. U., 1966; PhD in Gen. Spl. Edn./Adminstrn., Walden U., 1976. Cert. elem. edn., early childhood edn., learning disabled, mental retardation, behavior disorders, supt., supr. and dir. spl. edn. 4th grade tchr. Dist. # 83 Mannheim, Franklin Park, Ill., 1963—64; h.s. spl. edn. tchr. Dist. # 207 Maine Twp., Park Ridge, Ill., 1964—67, prevocational coord., 1967—69, dept. chmn. spl. edn. dept., 1969—70; dir. EPDA tchr. tng. program Chgo. Consortium Colls. and Univs., Northewst Ednl. Coop., Palatine, Ill., 1970—71; prin. West Suburban Spl. Edn. Ctr., Cicero, Ill., 1971—73; supr. West Suburban Assn. Spl. Edn., Cicero, 1973—75; asst. dir. Northwest Suburban Spl. Edn. Orgn., Palatine, 1975—78, supt. Mt. Prospect, Ill., 1978—96; spl. edn. cons., 1996—. Adj. instr. Northeastern Ill. U., Chgo. State U., Corcordia Coll., Barat Coll., Nat. Coll. Edn., Roosevelt U.; mem. task forces ISBE, 1975—2007, cons. career edn. project, 1977—78, spl. edn. demandate study group, 1983—85; cons. Ednl. Testing Svc.; tchr. edn. coun. Northeastern Ill. U., 1981—97, dean's grant program, 1982—97; workshop leader, 1974—; lectr., cons. in field. Author: Auditory Processes, 1974, rev., 1992, Career Education for Children, 1978, Of Work and Worth: Career Education Programming for Exceptional Children and Youths, 1981; contbr. articles to profl. jours., chapters to books. Bd. dirs. Found. Exceptional Children, 1996—, pres., 1999—2004. Recipient Cmty. Svc. award, Am. Legion, 1976, 1980, Alumnus of Yr. award, Northeastern Ill. U., 1984, Learning Disabilities of Am. Contributors award, Coun. Understanding Learning Disabilities, 1992, Those Who Excel award of excellence, Ill. State Bd. of Edn., 1994, Outstanding Svc. award, Divsn. Mental Retardation and Devel. Disabilities, 1994, Sleznick award, Coun. of Admin. of Spl. Edn., 1996, Outstanding Contbr. award, Coun. Exceptional Children, 1996, Burton Blatt award, Divsn. on Metal Retardation and Devel. Disabilities, 1997, Spl. Edn. Leadership award, Ill. Adminstrs. of Spl. Edn., 1995, Outstanding Spl. Edn. Adminstr. of Yr. award, 1997. Mem.: Found. for Exceptional Children (pres. 2000—04), Ill. Adminstrs. Spl. Edn. (pres. 1994—95), Coun. Exceptional Children (pres. Ill. chpt. 1975—77, bd. govs. 1977—80, pres. mental retardation divsn. 1983—85, bd. govs. 1986, exec. com. 1989—92, v.p. internat. 1992—93, pres.-elect 1993—94, pres. 1994—95, bd. govs. 1996—2000, bd. dirs. 2000—04, Meritorious Svc. award Ill. 1983), Am. Assn. Sch. Adminstrs. Home and Office: 413 Courtley Oaks Blvd Winter Garden FL 34787

GILLETT, MARY CAPERTON, military historian; b. Richmond, Va., Apr. 28, 1929; d. Lewis Hopkins and Mary Caperton (Horsley) Renshaw; m. Richard Clark Gillett, June 7, 1949; children: Richard Clark Jr., Glenn Douglas, Mary Caperton, Priscilla Elizabeth, Blakeney Diana. Student, Wellesley Coll., 1946-49; BA, Am. U., 1966, MA, 1971, PhD, 1978. Historian U.S. Navy Dept., Washington, 1966-69, U.S. Dept. Army, Washington, 1972-96. Author: The Army Medical Department, 1775-1818, 1981, The Army Medical Department, 1818-1865, 1988, The Army Medical Department, 1865-1917, 1995; contbr. articles to profl. jours. Mem. Am. Assn. for History of Medicine, Nat. Wildlife Fedn., We. Hist. Assn., The Nature Conservancy, The Wilderness Soc., The Sierra Club, Nat. Audubon Soc., Audubon Naturalist Soc. Avocations: backpacking, gardening. E-mail: mcgillett@mindspring.com.

GILLETTE, ETHEL MORROW, columnist; b. Oelwein, Iowa, Nov. 27, 1921; d. Charles Henry and Myrne Sarah (Law) Morrow; student Coe Coll., 1939-41; BA, Upper Iowa U., 1959; MA, Western State Coll., 1969; m. Roman A. Gillette, May 6, 1944 (dec. 1992); children: Melody Ann, Richard Allan, William Robert (dec. 1993). Stenographer, Penick & Ford, Cedar Rapids, Iowa, 1941-43, FBI, Washington, 1943-44; tchr. Fayette (Iowa) H.S., 1959-60, Jordan Jr. H.S., Mpls., 1960-64, Montrose (Colo.) H.S., 1964-68; family living, religion editor The News-Record, Gillette, Wyo., 1977-79, columnist Distaff Side, 1979-84. Mem. Western Writers Am., WestWind Writers/NWC (founder, pres. 1992-96), Nat. Writers Club. Contbr. articles to popular mags. Home: 8953 6085 Rd Montrose CO 81401-7217

GILLETTE, FRANKIE JACOBS, retired savings and loan executive, social worker, government administrator; b. Norfolk, Va., Apr. 1, 1925; d. Frank Walter and Natalie (Taylor) Jacobs; m. Maxwell Claude Gillette, June 19, 1976. BS, Hampton U., 1946; MSW, Howard U., 1948. Lic. clin. social worker; cert. jr. coll. tchr., life. Youth dir. YWCA, Passaic, N.J., 1948-50; dir. program Ada S. McKinley Community Ctr., Chgo., 1950-53; program dir. Sophie Wright Settlement, Detroit, 1953-64; dir. Concerted Services Project, Pittsburg, Calif., 1964-66, Job Corps Staff Devel., U. Calif., Berkeley, 1966-69; spl. program coordinator U.S. Community Services Adminstrn., San Francisco, 1969-83; pres. G & G Enterprises, San Francisco, 1985—. Chmn. bd. dirs. Time Savs. and Loan Assn., San Francisco, 1986-87. Commr. San Francisco Human Rights Commn., 1988-93; bd. dirs. Urban Econ. Devel. Corp., 1980-93, San Francisco Conv. and Visitors Bur.; trustee Fine Arts Mus. of San Francisco, 1993—; chmn. San Francisco-Abidjan Sister City Com., 1990—. Mem. Nat. Assn. Negro Bus. and Profl. Women's Clubs (pres. 1983-87), The Links, Inc., Delta Sigma Theta, Inc. Office: G & G Enterprises 85 Cleary Ct Apt 4 San Francisco CA 94109-6518

GILLETTE, MURIEL DELPHINE, nurse; b. Pasadena, Calif., Nov. 10, 1945; d. Edwin and Jean Helen (Fremont) Gillette; m. Larry Houston Potter, Dec. 31, 1971 (dec. 1979); children: Melissa Darlene Genevieve Potter Stephens, Bryan Scott; m. Robert George Baumann Jr., Aug. 18, 1980; 1 child, Robert George III. Student, Western Coll. for Women, Oxford, Ohio, 1963-65; BSN, UCLA, 1968; M of Nursing, Oreg. Health Scis. U., 1991. Sch. nurse, health tchr. Hawthorne (Calif.) Intermediate Sch., 1969-70; nurse St. John's Hosp., Santa Monica, Calif., 1969-71; camp nurse L.A.

Girl Scout Coun., 1969-71; nurse UCLA Med. Ctr., 1967-70; ICU/CCU/pediatrics nurse Mercy Med. Ctr., Roseburg, Oreg., 1971-79; nurse Umpqua Valley Community Hosp., Myrtle Creek, Oreg., 1981-91; camp nurse, health coord. Western Rivers Girl Scout Coun., Roseburg, 1984-90; health edn. dir. City of Myrtle Creek, 1986-91; nurse practitioner Umpgua Nat. Forest, Roseburg and Glide, Oreg., 1991-93; camp nurse, health coord. Oreg. Trail Boy Scout Coun., Roseburg, 1981-91, Western Rivers Girl Scout Coun., Roseburg, 1984-90; cmty. health cons. Roseburg, 1984-98; home health nurse, 1995-98; pub. health nurse State of Alaska, Anchorage, 1998—. Musician quartet, orch., soloist; artist in oils; poet. Bd. dirs. River 'N Dell Day Care Ctr., Myrtle Creek, 1983-85; trustee Augusta Bixler Farms, Inc., Stockton, Calif., 1976—; mem. Douglas County Cancer Screening Com.; vol. ARC, 1982-91. Capt. USAF, 1970-89. Umpqua Valley Hosp. Aux. scholar, 1989; L.A. Watercolor Soc. traveling art collection award, 1963. Mem. UCLA Alumni Assn., Umpqua Valley Hosp. Aux., Oreg. Health Sci. U. Alumni Assn., OES, Delta Zeta. Republican. Presbyterian. Avocations: painting, tennis, music, skiing, raising arabian horses. Home: PO Box 240041 Anchorage AK 99524-0041

GILLICE, SONDRA JUPIN (MRS. GARDNER RUSSELL BROWN), sales and marketing executive; b. Urbana, Ill. d. Earl Cranston and Laura Lorraine (Rose) Jupin; m. Gardner Russell Brown, Jan. 12, 1980; 1 child, Thomas Alan Gillice. BS, Lindenwood Coll., 1968; MBA, Loyola Coll., 1983. Pers. officer N.Y. Citibank, 1968-70, 1st Nat. Bank Chgo., 1970-72; mgr. human resources Potomac Electric Power Co., Washington, 1973-81; dir. pers. U.S. Synthetic Fuels Corp., Washington, 1981-86; v.p. human resources Guest Svcs., Inc., 1987-90, v.p. sales and mktg., 1990-93; sr. v.p. govt. rels. Drake Beam Morin, Inc., 1994-98; pres. RusSon, Inc., 1998—. Bd. govs. Nat. Coal Coun., exec. com. Bd. dirs. Nat. Womens Econ. Alliance, Life With Cancer; chmn. Career & Life Learning Sys., Inc. Mem. AAUW (pres. Falls Church br.), Edison Electric Inst. (chair tng. and mgmt. devel. com.), Soc. for Human Resource Mgmt., Greater Met. Washington Bd. Trade, Soroptimists (pres. Washington chpt. 1979-80), DAR, Army Navy Country Club, Army Navy Club, Soc. Magna Charta Dames, Edgartown Yacht Club, Georgetown Club.

GILLICK, BETSY BRINKLEY, pharmaceutical executive; b. Richmond, Va., May 11, 1959; d. Martha Lou (Caplinger) B. BBA, James Madison U., 1981, MBA, 1983. Procurement analyst Calculon Corp., Germantown, Md., 1983-85; agt. purchasing, subcontracts ORI/Calculon Corp., Rockville, Md., 1986-87, adminstr. contracts, 1987-89; sr. contracts adminstr. ARC Profl. Svcs. Group subs. ORI/Calculon Corp, Rockville, 1989-90, sr. fin. analyst, 1990-93; sr. fin. and contracts analyst Otsuka Am. Pharm. Inc., Rockville, 1993-94, fin. and contracts mgr., 1994-96, R & D bus. mgr., 1996-97, prof. edn. and sci. comm. mgr., 1997—2000, prof. edn. and sci. comm. sr. mgr., 2000—03, assoc. dir. med. affairs, clin. ops., 2003—. Mem. Nat. Contract Mgmt. Assn. Democrat. Presbyterian. Avocations: volleyball, traveling, gardening. Home: 18420 Cape Jasmine Way Gaithersburg MD 20879-4644 Office: Otsuka Am Pharm Inc 2440 Research Blvd Rockville MD 20850-3238

GILLIES, ESTHER HERROON, social worker, educator; b. Toledo, Ohio, Sept. 22, 1941; d. Edwin Anthony and Mary Jane Herroon; m. Bruce North Gillies, Aug. 22, 1969; 1 foster child, Richard Michael Mason. BA, Mary Manse Coll., 1963; MSW, U. So. Calif., 1978. LCSW Calif. Supr. child sex abuse program Los Angeles County DPSS, 1980—85; dir. CSA crisis ctr. Harbor-UCLA Med. Ctr., Torrance, Calif., 1987—88; dir. So. Calif. tng. ctr. Children's Inst. Internat., L.A., 1985—90; exec. dir. Children's Ctr. of Antelope Valley, Lancaster, Calif., 1991—2000; bur. chief L.A. County Divsn. Children and Family Svcs. (Child Protective Svcs.), 2000—01; clin. assoc. prof. U. So. Calif. Sch. Social Work, L.A., 2002—. Cons., trainer, 1982—2002; advisor Calif. State Commn. on Sex Exploitation of Children, Sacramento, 1983—86; mem. Calif. Children's Justice Act Task Force, Sacramento, 1993—94; advisor Calif. VOC Peer Rev. Bd. Control, Sacramento, 1993—2000; team mem., author, Calif., 2001. Contbr. chapters to books. Convenor, chair Children's Planning Coun.-SPAI, Antelope Valley, 1996—2000; bd. dirs. St. John's Well Child and Family Ctr., 2002—. Mem.: L.A. Children's Planning Coun., Calif. Profl. Soc. on Abuse of Children (founding, Recognition award 2002). Avocations: writing music, birdwatching, travel. Office: U So Calif 669 W 34th St Los Angeles CA 90089

GILLIGAN, CAROL, psychologist, writer; b. N.Y.C., Nov. 28, 1936; d. William Edward and Mabel (Caminez) Friedman; m. James Frederick Gilligan, June 12, 1960; children: Jonathan Mark, Timothy David, Christopher James. AB, Swarthmore Coll., 1958, hon. degree, 1985; AM, Radcliffe Coll., 1961; PhD, Harvard U., 1964; hon. degree, Regis Coll., 1983, Haverford Coll., 1987, Wesleyan U., 1992, Smith Coll., 1999. Instr. U. Chgo., 1965-66; lectr. Harvard U., Cambridge, Mass., 1967-69, rsch. asst., 1969-70, asst. prof., 1970-78, assoc. prof., 1978-86, prof., 1986—, now Patricia Albjerg Graham prof. gender studies Cambidge, Mass.; Laurie chair in Women's Studies Rutgers U., New Brunswick, N.J., 1986-87; Pitt Prof. U. Cambridge, Eng., 1992-93. Vis. prof. NYU Sch. Law, founding mem. Harvard Project on Women's Psychology and the Devel. of Girls, 1987—; co-dir., The Company of Women and Girls, 1991—. Author: In a Different Voice, 1982, Mapping the Moral Domain: A Contribution of Women's Thinking to Psychological Theory and Education, 1988, Making Connections: The Relational Worlds of Adolescent Girls at Emma Willard School, 1990, (with Lyn M. Brown) Meeting at the Crossroads: Women's Psychology and Girls Development, 1992, (with J. Taylor and A. Sullivan) Between Voice and Silence: Women and Girls, Race and Relationship, 1995; editor: Women, Girls and Psychotherapy: Reframing Resistance, 1991. Bd. dirs. Ms Initiative in Girls, Facing History & Ourselves. Sr. rsch. fellow Spencer Found., 1984—; Mellon Faculty fellow Bunting Inst.-Radcliffe Coll., 1982-83; recipient Grawemayer award U. Louisville, 1992, Heinz award, 1998. Mem.: APA, Assn. Women in Psychology, Nat. Acad. Edn. Democrat. Jewish. Avocations: music, piano, modern dance, theatre. Office: Harvard U Dept Human Devel-Psychology 503 Larsen Hall Appian Way Cambridge MA 02138-6502 also: NYU Sch Law 511 Vanderbilt House New York NY 10012 E-mail: carol-gilligan@harvard.edu.

GILLIGAN, MARY ANN, law librarian; b. Elizabeth, N.J., June 20, 1956; d. John Francis and Margaret Mary (Boyle) G. BA, Park Coll., 1977; MLS, Rutgers U., 1980. Asst. Time Inc., N.Y.C., 1981-83; law libr. Chubb & Son, Inc., Warren, N.J., 1985, Pennie & Edmonds LLP, N.Y.C., 1985—. Exec. committeewoman Monmouth County Dem. Party, 2000-02. Mem. ABA, Spl. Librs. Assn., Law Libr. Assn. Greater N.Y. (bd. dirs. 1998-2001), Preservation Red Bank, Red Bank Hist. Preservation Commn., Red Bank Women's Club. Democrat. Roman Catholic. Avocations: crafts, singing. Office: Pennie & Edmonds LLP Ste 1120 1155 Avenue Of The Americas Fl 17 New York NY 10036-2720

GILLIGAN, SANDRA KAYE, private school director; b. Ft. Lewis, Wash., Mar. 22, 1946; d. Jack G. and O. Ruth (Mitchell) Wagoner; m. James J. Gilligan, June 3, 1972 (div. June 1998); 1 child, J. Shawn Gilligan. BS in Edn., Emporia State U., 1968, MS in Psychology, 1971; postgrad., Drake U., 1976, U. Mo., St. Louis, 1977-79. Tchr. Parklane Elem. Sch., Aurora, Colo., 1968-69, Bonner Springs (Kans.) Elem., 1970; stewardess Frontier Airlines, Denver, 1969; grad. teaching asst. Emporia (Kans.) State U., 1970-71; lead tchr. Western Valley Youth Ranch, Buckeye, Ariz., 1971-74; staff mem. program devel., lead tchr. The New Found., Phoenix, 1974; ednl. therapist Orchard Pl., Des Moines, 1974-76; ednl. cons. Spl. Sch. Dist. of St. Louis County, 1976-79; founding dir. The Churchill Sch., St. Louis, 1978—. Instr. Webster Coll., Webster Groves, Mo., 1978-80; adj. prof. Maryville Coll., St. Louis, summer 1985; keynote spkr. Miss. Learning Disabilities Assn. Conv., 1991; site visitor blue ribbon schs. program U.S. Dept. Edn., 1992; mem. Evaluation Review Com. Indep. Sch. of Ctrl. States; cert. trainer Human Potential Seminars; presenter in field. Mem. Learning Disabilities Assn., Internat. Dyslexia Assn., St. Louis Jr. League. Avocations: gardening, painting. Office: The Churchill Sch 1035 Price School Ln Saint Louis MO 63124-1596 Office Phone: 314-997-4343.

GILLILAND, LUCILLE MARY, artist, writer; b. N.Y. d. Lincoln Xaviar Waters and Irene Cecelia Stawarz; m. Charles Gilliland; children: Stephen, Brian, Kevin, Kathryn. BA magna cum laude, Lehman Coll., Bronx, N.Y., 1995. Cons., tchr. Bronx Coun. on the Arts, N.Y., YMCA, N.Y., JASA, N.Y., NBWNRA, N.Y., Neighborhood S.H.O.P.P., N.Y. Author: (column) Art of Craft and Needlework, (poetry); artist: (paintings). Roman Catholic.

GILLILAND, MARCIA ANN, nursing administrator; b. Kansas City, Kans., Sept. 15, 1949; d. Robert Joseph and Mary Agnes (Paup) Caton; m. John Lee Gilliland, Mar. 28, 1974 (dec. Oct. 1983); children: Marcella Lyn, John Patrick, Devon Marie. ADN, Kansas City C.C., 1979; BSN, Webster U., 1990, M in Health Svc. Mgmt., 1999. RN, Kans. Staff nurse U. Kans. Med. Ctr., Kansas City, 1979-84, infection prevention and control coord., nurse clinician, 1984-2000, facilitator HIV/AIDS wellness group, 1991-2000, contract adminstr., 2000—. Cmty. health nurse Cath. Charities, Kansas City, 1980-82; pres., owner Kansas City Total Image, Overland Park, Kans., 1981-83. Active Rep. Precinct Committeewoman, Overland Park, Kans., 1994—; rep. candidate Overland Park City Coun., Kans., 1995; sec. Johnson County Rep. Commn., 2000; elected mem. Overland Park City Coun., Kans., 2001—; bd. dirs. Johnson County (Kans.) Rep. Party. Mem.: GOP Club Johnson County, Kans. (bd. dirs. 1999—). Republican. Avocation: reading. Home: 9430 Riggs St Overland Park KS 66212-1443 Office: U Kans Med Ctr 3901 Rainbow Blvd Kansas City KS 66160-0001 E-mail: mgilliland@kumc.edu., magillil@opkansas.org.

GILLIOM, JUDITH CARR, government official; b. Indpls., May 19, 1943; d. Elbert Raymond and Marjorie Lucille (Carr) G. BA, Northwestern U., 1964; MA, U. Pa., 1966. Feature writer, asst. women's editor Indpls. News, summers 1961-63; rsch. asst. cultural anthropology Northwestern U., 1963-64, asst. instr. freshman English, 1964; editorial asst. to dir. div. cardiology Phila. Gen. Hosp., 1965-67; asst. to ophthalmologist-in-chief Wills Eye Hosp., Phila., 1967-69; editor, writer Nat. Assn. Hearing and Speech Agencies, Washington, 1969-70; free-lance speech writer White House Conf. Children and Youth, 1969-70; free-lance editor, writer, abstractor, 1971-78; free-lance speechwriter President's Com. Mental Retardation, 1971-78; from dir. publs. to dir. comm. Nat. Assn. Hearing and Speech Action, Silver Spring, Md., 1972-77; editor Hearing & Speech Action mag., 1969-70, 72-77; program mgr. Interagy. Com. on Handicapped Employees, 1978, dep. exec. sec., 1979-83; mgr. disability program Dept. Def., 1983—. Cons. U.S. Archtl. and Transp. Barriers Compliance Bd., 1976-77, Office Ind. Living for Disabled, HUD, 1977-78, Office for Handicapped Individuals, HEW, 1978, Women's com. Pres.'s Com. Employment Handicapped, 1985-86. Mem. Nat. Spinal Cord Injury Assn., 1970-90, editor, pub. conv. jour., 1974-82, bd. dirs. D.C. chpt., 1975-81, 89-90, nat. trustee, 1975-81, nat. bd. dirs., 1978-79; bd. dirs. Nat. Ctr. for a Barrier-Free Environment, 1979-84, v.p., 1980-81, pres., 1981-82; nat. bd. dirs., treas. League Disabled Voters, 1980-85; local bd. dirs. Easter Seal Soc. Disabled Children and Adults, 1985-90; active Montgomery County Commn. on People with Disabilities, 1989-95; mem. Taxicab Svcs. Adv. Com., 1995-99. Recipient Geico Pub. Svc. award, 1996, Civilian Career Svc. award Office of Sec. of Def., 1997; Woodrow Wilson fellow, 1965. Mem. Phi Beta Kappa, Delta Delta Delta. Home: 901 Arcola Ave Silver Spring MD 20902-3401 Office: Dept Def The Pentagon Rm 3a272 Washington DC 20301-0001

GILLIS, RUTH ANN M. electric company executive; BS in Econs., Smith Coll.; MBA, U. Chgo. Formerly with U. Chgo. Hosps. and Health Sys., 1st Chgo. Corp.; sr. v.p., CFO Unicom Corp. (now Exelon Corp.). Office: Exelon Corp 37th Fl 10 S Dearborn St Chicago IL 60603

GILLISS, CATHERINE LYNCH, nursing educator; b. New Britain, Conn., Apr. 18, 1949; d. James A. and Lorraine Lynch; m. Thomas P. Gilliss, June 6, 1970. BS in Nursing, Duke U., 1971; MS in Nursing, Cath. U. Am., Washington, 1974; D of Nursing Sci., U. Calif., 1983; cert. adult nurse practitioner, U. Rochester, 1979. Staff and charge nurse Duke U. Med. Ctr., Durham, 1971, VA Hosp., Washington, 1971-72; asst. prof. U. Md., Balt., 1974-76, The Cath. U. Am., 1976-79; assoc. prof. U. Portland, Oreg., 1979-83; lectr. in nursing Sonoma State U., Rohnert Park, Calif., 1983-84; prof., chmn. dept. family health care U. Calif., San Francisco, 1984-98, prof. emeritus, 1999—; prof. Sch. Nursing Yale U., New Haven, Conn., 1998—, dean Sch. Nursing, 1998—. Chair NIH, Nat. Inst. Nursing Rsch. Study Sect., 1997-99. Co-author: Toward a Science of Family Nursing, 1989, The Nursing of Families, 1993; mem. editl. bd. Families, Systems and Health, 1994-98, jour. Family Nursing; contbr. articles to profl. jours. Bd. dirs. Com. Inst. for Child Health and Devel., Am. Acad. Nursing, U. Calif. San Francisco Ctr. for the Health Professions. Recipient Disting. Alumna award Duke U., 1991; Pres.'s fellow U. Calif., 1983; Se. fellow Ctr. for Health Professions, 1996-99, Primary Care Policy fellow USPHS, 1993; Regent U. Portland, Oreg., 1994-2000. Fellow Am. Acad. Nursing (bd. dirs. 1999-2006); mem. ANA, Nat. Coun. on Family Rels., Nat. Orgn. Nurse Practitioner Faculty (pres. 1995), Primary Care Fellowship Soc. (pres. 1996-97). Office: Yale U Sch Nursing PO Box 9740 New Haven CT 06536-0740

GILLMOR, HELEN, federal judge; BA, Queen's Coll. of CUNY, 1965; LLB magna cum laude, Boston U., 1968. With Ropes & Gray, Boston, 1968-69, Law Offices of Alexander R. Gillmor, Camden, Maine, 1970, Torkildson, Katz, Jossem, Fonseca, Jaffe, Moore & Hetherington, Honolulu, 1971-72; law clk. to Chief Justice William S. Richardson Hawaii State Supreme Ct., 1972; dep. pub. defender Office of Pub. Defender, Honolulu, 1972-74; dist. ct. judge per diem Family Ct. (1st cir.) Hawaii, 1977-83; per diem judge Dist. Ct., 1st circuit, 1983-85; pvt. practice Honolulu, 1985-94; district judge U.S. Dist. Ct. Hawaii, 9th circuit, 1994—. Counsel El Paso Real Estate Investment Trust, 1969; lectr. U.S. Agy. Internat. Devel., Seoul, South Korea, 1969-70, Univ. Hawaii, 1975. Office: Prince J K Kuhio Fed Bldg 300 Ala Moana Blvd Rm C-435 Honolulu HI 96850-0435

GILLMOR, KAREN LAKO, state agency administrator; b. Cleve., Jan. 29, 1948; d. William M. and Charlotte (Sheldon) Lako; m. Paul E. Gillmor, Dec. 10, 1983; children: Linda D., Julie E., Paul Michael, Connor W., Adam S. BA cum laude, Mich. State U., 1969; MA, Ohio State U., 1970, PhD, 1981. Asst. to v.p. Ohio State U., Columbus, 1972-77, spl. asst. dean law, 1979-81, assoc. dir. Ctr. Healthcare Policy and Rsch., 1991-92; asst. to pres. Ind. Cen. U., Indpls., 1977-78; rsch. asst. Burke Mktg. Rsch., Indpls., 1978-79; v.p. pub. affairs Huntington Nat. Bank, Columbus, 1981-82; fin. cons. Ohio Rep. Fin. Com., Columbus, 1982-83; chief mgmt. planning and rsch. Indsl. Commn. Ohio, Columbus, 1983-86; mgr. physician rels. Ohio State U. Med. Ctr., Columbus, 1987-91; cons. U.S. Sec. Labor, Washington, 1990-91; mem. Regional Bd. Rev./Indls. Commn., Ohio, 1991-92; state senator Ohio Gen. Assembly, 1993-97; vice-chair State Employment Rels. Bd., 1997—. Legis. liaison Huntington Bancshares, Ohio, Ohio State U., Columbus; trustee Heidelberg Coll., 1999—, Rutherford B. Hayes Presd. Ctr., 2002—. Mem. adv. coun. The Childhood League Ctr., 2003—; bd. dirs. Congl. Childcare Ctr., 2003—. Named Outstanding Freshman Ohio Legislator, 1994, Watchdog of the Treasury, 1994, 1996, Outstanding Nat. Freshman Legislator of the Yr., 1995; named to Rocky River HS Hall of Fame, 1998; recipient Pres. award, Ohio State Chiropractic Assn., 1994, Pub. Svc. award, Am. Heart Assn., 1995, Ctr. Advancement and Study of Ethics award, Capital U. and Trinity Luth. Sem., 1996, cert. of Achievement, U.S. Dept. of Army, 1997, Friend of Medicine award, Ohio State Med. Assn., 1997, Legis. Achievement award, Ohio chpt. Am. Acad. Pediat., 1997, Spirit of Women award, 1999; grantee, Andrew W. Mellon Found., 1978, Carnegie Corp., 1978. Mem.: DAR, Coun. Advancement and Support Edn., Am. Assn. Higher Edn., Ohio Fedn. Rep. Women, Women's Roundtable, Women in Mainstream, Phi Delta Kappa. Methodist. Office: 65 E State St Ste 1200 Columbus OH 43215-4209

GILLMOR, ROGENE GODDING, retired medical technologist; b. El Dorado, Kans., Jan. 25, 1939; d. Marc Antone and Verda May (Bogue) Godding; m. Charles Stewart Gillmor Jr, Nov. 28, 1964; children: Charles Stewart III, Alison Bogue. AA in Liberal Arts, Cottey Coll., 1958; BA in Biology, Stanford U., 1960; postgrad., Wesleyan U., U. Hartford, Foothills Coll. Rsch. asst. genetics Joshua Lederberg lab. Stanford U., 1960-62; assoc. scientist space biology/medicine Lockheed Missiles & Space Co., Palo Alto, Calif., 1962-64; rsch. asst. biology Princeton (N.J.) U., 1965-66, Wesleyan U., Middletown, Conn., 1967-69; lab. technician immunochemistry Hartford (Conn.) Hosp., 1978-84, instr. immunology clin. lab. edn. program, 1985-89, lab. supr. proteins/immunology dept. pathology/lab. medicine, 1986-99, ret., 1999. Researcher various labs France and Switzerland, 1984—85. Contbr. articles to profl jours. Leader Girl Scouts US, 1977—85; trustee, deacon Higganum Congregational Ch, Conn., 1980—. Recipient Achievement Award, Girl Scouts US, 1985. Mem.: Conn Hist Soc (secy 1970—72), Wesleyan Potters (pres 1982—84), Am Soc Clin lab Sci, Am Soc Clin Pathologists (cert immunology specialist), Am Asn Clin Chemistry, PEO Sisterhood, Haddam. Avocations: gardening, music, pottery. Home: 29 Spencer Rd Higganum CT 06441-4034 E-mail: rogenegillmor@hotmail.com.

GILLOM, JENNIFER, professional basketball player; b. Abbeville, Miss., June 13, 1964; Grad., U. Miss., 1986. Basketball player Italian League, Milan, 1987—91, Ancona, 1991—94, Messina, 1995—96, Athens, Greece, 1996—97, Phoenix Mercury, WNBA, 1997—2002, Los Angeles Sparks, WNBA, 2003—. Named an Sports Hall of Fame, U. Miss., 1999; named to All WNBA 2nd Team, 1997, All WNBA 1st Team, 1998, Inaugural WNBA All-Star Team, 2000; recipient Gold medal, Pan Am. Games, 1987, Olympic Games, 1988, Nat. Distinction award, U. Miss., 1998, Kim Perrot Sportsmanship award, 2002, USA Basketball World Championship Team, 2002. Office: Phoenix Mercury 201 E Jefferson St Phoenix AZ 85004-2412

GILLOOLY, EDNA RAE See BURSTYN, ELLEN

GILMAN, FRANCES M. genealogist, librarian; b. Cleve., Jan. 4, 1921; d. Christopher and Frances (Hitchcock) Magee; m. Stanley Hugh Gilman, Sept. 6, 1941 (div. May 1980); children: Robert Hugh, Wylie Burke, Andrew Magee, Kate Kane. BA, Sarah Lawrence Coll., 1941; MS in Libr. Sci., Columbia U., 1975. Libr. Clinton (Conn.) Hist. Soc., 1988—. Spkr. geneaol. issues to various groups including Friends of the Clinton Libr., DAR chpts., among others. Contbr. articles to profl. jours. Mem. Conn. Profl. Genealogists Coun., 2002—; orgn. chair Dem. Party, White Plaines, NY, 1986—87; bd. dirs. Godfrey Libr., Middletown, Conn., 1998—, Gov. Jonathan Trumbull House, Lebanon, Conn., 1998—2000. Mem. Westchester County Geneaol. Soc. (past pres.). Democrat. Avocations: tennis, work on family pedigrees. Office: Clinton Hist Soc PO Box 86 Clinton CT 06413

GILMAN, KAREN FRENZEL, legal assistant; b. Syracuse, N.Y., Jan. 11, 1947; d. Charles Henry and Cora Adell (Haith) Frenzel; m. Lawrence Sanford Gilman, June 5, 1970 (div. Feb. 9, 1977). AAS in Horticulture, SUNY, Morrisville, 1967; BS, Cornell U., 1969, MS in Floriculture and Ornamental Hort., 1971; attended, Syracuse Univ. Coll., 1983. Cert. legal asst. Floral designer Fortino of Fayetteville (N.Y.), 1965-69, 76-79, 81-84, Fallon's Florist, Raleigh, N.C., 1973-74; salesperson Finley Fine Jewelry, N.Y.C., 1979-80; legal asst. Agway, Inc., Dewitt, N.Y., 1984; legal asst. gen. legal Carrier Corp., Syracuse, N.Y., 1984-91, legal asst. intellectual property, 1992—. Mem. adv. bd. legal asst. program Syracuse U. Coll., 1986-90. Contbr. articles to profl. jours. Henry Strong Denison fellow, 1969. Mem. Pi Alpha Xi, Phi Theta Kappa. Avocations: gardening, biking. Office: Carrier Corp PO Box 4800 Carrier Pkwy Syracuse NY 13221

GILMARTIN, CLARA T. volunteer; b. East Stroudsburg, Pa., Jan. 23, 1922; d. Harry and Clarissa (Snearley) Treible; m. John Gilmartin, Jan. 18, 1945 (dec. Feb. 1956); children: Ronald, Donald; m. William Gilmartin, Sept. 8, 2002. BA, Rutgers U., 1961, MA, 1966. Elem. sch. tchr. Union Beach (N.J.) Pub. Sch., 1956-61; lang. arts tchr. Holmdel Village (N.J.) Intermediate Sch., 1961-82; Fulbright exch. tchr. New Zealand, 1973-74; mem. adv. bd. Juvenile Conf. Com., 1986—. Chair bd. trustees Grace Meth. Ch., Union Beach, 1997—. Mem. Monmouth County Ret. Educators Assn., Am. Legion (Post 321 Color Guard, scholarship com., trustee, chaplain), Triad. Democrat. Home: PO Box 143 Keyport NJ 07735-0143

GILMER, ELLEN LOUISE, writer, artist; b. East Rainelle, W.Va., June 21, 1949; d. James Wesley Gilmer and Margaret Wilmore Montgomery. BFA, U. N.C., Greensboro, 1971; student in liberal arts, Greenbrier Coll., 1965—67. Freelance writer, artist, N.Y.C., 1972—80; writing cons. publicity, 1980—90; promoter, publicist Pizzazz Clown & Party Svc., N.Y.C., 1990—93; pres. Crystal Clear Writing, N.Y.C., 1993—; dir. Ellen's Portraits, N.Y.C., 2000—. Author: (novels) La Belle Famille, 1997, (dramatic monologues) Free Style Run of the Heart, 2001. Vol. Met. Opera Assn., N.Y.C., 1995—. Mem.: ASCAP, NAFE, Theater Devel. Fund, Smithsonian Instn., Agora Internat. Press Corps, Internat. Platform Assn., Am. Woman's Econ. Devel. Assn. Avocations: dance, pantomime, swimming, reading. E-mail: elgilmer@earthlink.net.

GILMORE, BEVERLY J, retired journalist, gallery owner; b. Monroe, Mich., Mar. 7, 1933; d. James B. and Verna L. (Dahlke) G.; m. Richard J. Loftus (div. 1963); m. Irving B. Pearlman (div. 1974); m. Robert E. Huber (div. 1987); children: Richard G. Loftus, Laidainn M. Gilmore, Nicholas E.D. Gilmore. BA in Journalism, U. Wis., 1954, MA in Journalism, 1959; postgrad., NYU. Assoc. editor Elec. Info. Publs., Madison, Wis., 1954-55; reporter, editor Gainesville (Fla.) Sun, 1956-57; editor Office Editl. and Comms. Svcs. U. Wis., Madison, 1957-60; editor Grad. Coll. U. Ill., Champaign, 1962-63; asst. book rev. editor Libr. Jour., N.Y.C.; copy editor, reporter S.I. (N.Y.) Advance, 1971-72; trend editor, syndicated writer Newhouse News Svc., 1972-87; co-owner Glen Arbor (Mich.) City Limits, 1987-94; mgr. Molly Phinny Gallery, Glen Arbor, 1995. Mem. nat. nominating com. Coty Fashion Critics awards, Cutty Sark Menswear awards, 1974-86; juror sr. style projects Parsons (N.Y.) Sch. Design, 1975-85; judge features category Pa. Press Women's Ann. Contest, 1982. Co-founder Wis. Studies in Contemporary Lit., 1958; contbr. articles to profl. publs. Trustee Leelanau Hist. Soc., 1992-94; mem. steering com. Women Bus. Owners Leelanau, 1989-94; mem. Hudson River Environ. Group Clearwater, Inc., 1982—; mem. Friends of Crystal River Environ. Group, 1986—; mem. Integrated Liberal Studies alumni com. U. Wis., 1982-84, Daily Cardinal Alumni Assn. U. Wis., 1998—; mem. Mud Ln. Soc. for the Renaissance of Stapleton, 1979-87, co-chmn. 5th ann. house tour, 1981; mem., bd. dirs. Conf. House Assn. N.Y.C. Landmark, chmn., membership drive and benefit Evening with Letitia Baldrige, 1977-87; mem., bd. dirs. Preservation League of Staten Island, 1981-85. Recipient Nat. Fashion Journalism Lulu awards Men's Fashion Assn. Am., 1978-85, Cultured Pearl Assn. Am. and Japan Outstanding Media award, 1985, Outstanding Person of Grand Traverse Area-Traverse City (Mich.) Record-Eagle Picks of 1988. Mem. Fashion Group (N.Y. chpt.), Glen Lake-Sleeping Bear C. of C. (co-founder ann. holiday marketplace 1987), bd. dirs. 1988-90), Theta Sigma Phi, Alpha Chi Omega. Home: PO Box 4713 Santa Rosa Beach FL 32459-4713

GILMORE, CATHERINE RYE, arts administrator; b. Birmingham, Ala., Mar. 7, 1947; d. Thomas Aloyisius and Eva Catherine (Hydinger) Crawford; m. James William Rye, May 25, 1968 (div.); children: James William III, Susan Crawford Rye; m. Victor Alan Gilmore, May 23, 1986. BA in Theatre, Birmingham So. U., 1968; postgrad., U. Ala., Birmingham. Actress profl. cabaret theatre, Atlanta and Birmingham, 1970-80; talk show host WBMG-TV, Birmingham, 1980-82; exec. dir. Met. Arts Coun., Birmingham, 1996—. Instr. U. Ala., Birmingham, 1979-80. Stage appearances include Peter Pan, 1974, Sweet Charity, 1975, Wit's Other End Cabaret Theatre, 1976-80. Mem. The Women's Network, Birmingham; leadership class Birmingham C. of C., 1989; bd. dirs. Operation New Birmingham, Region 20/20. Recipient Silver Bowl award Festival of Arts, Birmingham, 1989, Obelisk award Arts Cmty., Birmingham, 1978; named one of Top 10 Corporate Women in Birmingham, Birmingham Bus. Jour., 1996. Episcopalian. also: Metropolitan Arts Council PO Box 370263 Birmingham AL 35237-0263

GILMORE, CONNIE SUE, director; b. Nashville, Sept. 3, 1951; d. Earl C. and L. Louise (Coleman) G. AA, Stephens Coll., 1971; BA, Vanderbilt U., 1973; MA, Cumberland U., 1992, postgrad., 1992—. Cert. tchr., Tenn. Tchr. Bellevue Presbyn. Ch., Nashville, 1980-83, dir., 1983-86; presch. tchr. St. Henry's Ch., Nashville, 1985-89, dir., 1986-90; comparative fin. analyst Vanderbilt U., 1998—. Tutor BellSouth Grant Reading Program, Lebanon, Tenn., 1990. Editor, author: Leadership, 1992. Mem. Nat. Assn. for Edn. Young Children, So. Assn. for Children Under Six, Tenn. Assn. for Young Children, Nashville Area Assn. for Young Children, So. Literacy Soc. (charter)., Kappa Delta Pi

GILMORE, JENNIFER A.W. computer specialist, educator; b. San Fernando, Trinidad, Jan. 12, 1954; came to U.S., 1972; d. Fitzroy Grant and Zelma (Williams) Oudkerk; m. Frederick R. Gilmore, June 17, 1983. BA, MA, Bklyn. Coll., 1984; BBA, MS, Baruch Coll., 1993; MBA, L.I. U., 1994; PhD, Walden U./Kennedy-Western U., 2001. COBOL programmer MetLife, N.Y.C., 1972-86; project mgr., human resources adminstrn. mgmt. info. sys. City of N.Y., 1990—. Adj. prof. N.Y.C. Coll. Tech., 1997, Kingsborough C.C., 1998, St. Francis Coll., Bklyn., 1998, Medgar Evers Coll., 1998, Borough of Manhattan C.C., 1998, Touro Coll., 1999—, Baruch Coll., 1999—2000, Monroe Coll., 1999—, U. Md., 2003—. Home: 47 Mckeever Pl Apt 16J Brooklyn NY 11225-2537 Office: NYC-HRA-MIS 15 Metrotech Brooklyn NY 11201 E-mail: jgilmore102716560@yahoo.com.

GILMORE, JUNE ELLEN, psychologist; b. Middletown, Ohio, Oct. 22, 1927; d. Linley Lawrence and Elizabeth Kathleen (Barker) Wetzel; m. John Lester Gilmore, July 6, 1945; children: John Lester Jr., Michael Edward. BS, Miami U., Oxford, 1961; MS, Miami U., 1964. Lic. psychologist, Ohio. Intern in psychology Hamilton (Ohio) City Schs., 1963-64; psychologist Talawanda, Shiloh, Trenton Schs., Butler County, Ohio, 1964-66, Franklin (Ohio) City Schs., 1966-72, Wapakoneta (Ohio) City Schs., 1972-76, Cin. City Schs., 1978-86; pvt. practice psychology, 1975-95; planner, evaluator Warren/Clinton Counties Mental Health Bd., Ohio, 1986-88; adj. instr. Wright State U., Dayton, Ohio, 1989-90. Co-author: Summer Children-Ready or not for School, 1986, The Rape of Childhood--No Time to be a Kid, 1990. Sec. Tri County Drug Coun., Lima, Ohio, 1975; chmn. Auglaize County Social Svcs., Wapakoneta, 1973-75; bd. dirs. Butler County Alcohol and Drug Addiction Svcs. Bd., 1990-97, sec., 1992-94. Mem. Ohio Sch. Psychologists Assn. (exec. bd. 1982-86), Southwestern Ohio Sch. Psychologist Assn. (pres.), Southwest Council Exceptional Children (Pres.), Nat. Assn. Sch. Psychologists, Ohio Psychol. Assn., Butler County Retired Tchrs. Assn. (newsletter editor 2002-04, pres. 2004), Butler County 648 Mental Health Bd. (bd. dirs. 1978-86, pres. 1983-84). Republican. United Methodist. Home and Office: 6120 Michael Rd Middletown OH 45042-9402

GILMORE, KATHI, state treasurer; b. Dec. 23, 1944; m. Richard Gilmore; children: Suzi, Barb, Jeff, Amy. Mem. N.D. Ho. of Reps. from Dist. 6, 1989-92; treas. State of N.D., 1993—. Mem. Bd. Tax Equalization, State Hist. Bd., State Investment Bd., Tchrs. Fund for Retirement Bd., State Canvassing Bd., Bd. of Univ. and Sch. Lands Mem.: Assn. Securities Profls. (hon. co-chair pension fund conf. 1994, Task Forces Orgnl. Planning and Coordinating Com. 1993), Retirement and Investment Office Internal Audit Com., Nat. Assn. State Treas. (pension com.). Democrat. Presbyterian. Office: State Treasurer 600 E Boulevard Ave Bismarck ND 58505-0660

GILMORE, LOUISA RUTH, retired nurse; b. Pitts., Oct. 31, 1930; d. Albert Leonard and Bertha Christina (Birch) Huber; m. William Norman II Kemp (div. 1975); children: Janyce Louise Kemp Lipson, Barbra Lea Kemp Bilharz, Robert William, Paul Lee, Charles Albert; m. Robert James Gilmore, Sept. 1, 1989; stepchildren: Robi Lynn Lee, Donna Elizabeth Singleton. Diploma in nursing, San Bernardino C.C., Needles, Calif., 1983. Office nurse Santa Fe Clinic, Needles, 1953-57; spl. duty nurse Needles Cmtys. Hosp., 1957-62; nurse supr. Santa Fe Clinic, 1962-79; staff nurse in surgery Needles Desert Cmtys. Hosp., 1979-90; Cell Tech ind. distbr. Reliv Products, Temple, Tex., 1991-95; with Fine Host Corp., 1996—2001; food or product demonstrator Sam's Club #6336, 2000-2001, demonstrator jewelry dept., door greeter, 2001—. Instr. CPR Needles Desert Cmtys. Hosp., 1987-90; med. officer San Bernardino County Fire Dept., Needles, 1980-83, pub. info. officer, 1983-85, vol. fire fighter, 1983-90; ind. distbr. Reliv Products, 1991-95, Cell Tech., 1996. Mem. Calif. State Fireman Assn., Needles Firefighters Assn. (treas. 1987, 88), Beta Sigma Phi-Zeta Gamma (treas. 1966, sec. 1967, v.p. 1968, pres. 1969, named Sweetheart Queen 1969), Order of Rose (life). Avocations: travel, painting and oil painting. E-mail: fireangel5318@yahoo.com., rgilmore@vvm.com., rolukg2@yahoo.com.

GILMORE, PHYLLIS, state legislator; m. Kenneth Gilmore. Social worker; mem. Kans. State Ho. of Reps. Dist. 27, 1994-99; exec. dir. regulatory bd. State of Kans., Topeka, 1999—. Office: State Kans Regulatory Bd Topeka KS 66601

GILMORE, VANESSA D. federal judge; b. St. Albans, N.Y., Oct. 26, 1956; BS, Hampton U., 1977; JD, U. Houston, 1981. Bar: Tex. 1982, U.S. Dist. Ct. (so. dist.) Tex. Fashion buyer Foley's Dept. Store, 1977-79; ptnr. Vickery, Kilbride, Gilmore & Vickery, Houston, 1981-85, 86-94; atty. Sue Schecter & Assocs., Houston, 1985-86; judge U.S. Dist. Ct. (So. dist.) Tex., Houston, 1994—. Spkr. ATLA, San Diego, 1990, ABA, Atlanta, 1991, N.Y.C., 1993, Leadership Tex., Austin, 1992, Hampton U. Alumni Assn., Dallas, 1992, Laredo Bus. and Profl. Women's Assn., 1993, XI Ann. Border Gov.'s Conf., Monterrey, Mex., 1993, Gov.'s Bus. Devel. Coun., Ausitn, 1993, Tex. A&M U., 1993, State Bar of Tex., Austin, 1993, Houston Bus. Coun., 1993, Minority Enterprise Devel. Week, Houston, 1993, Holman St. Bapt. Ch., 1994, Greater Houston Women's Found., 1994, The Kinkaid Sch., 1995, So. Meth. U., Dallas, 1996, South Tex. Coll. of Law, 1996, among others. Contbr. articles to profl. jours. Bd. dirs. Houston Ballet, Tex. So. Univ. Found., Neighborhood Recovery Community Redevel. Corp., 1992-95; chair African Am. Art Adv. Assn., Mus. Fine Arts; mem. scv. acad. nominations bd. Rep. Jack Fields, Tex., 1993, 94; active Texans for NAFTA; mem. Tex. Dept. Commerce, 1991-94, chairperson, 1992-94; mem. adv. bd. St. Joseph's Hosp.; mem. Leadership Tex. Named One of Houston's Black Achievers, Human Enrichment of Life Program, 1989; recipient Citizen of the Month award Houston Defender, 1990, YWCA award, 1991, Austin Met. Resource Bus. Ctr. award, 1991, Houston Bus. and Profl. Men's Club award, 1992, Disting. Svc. award Nat. Black MBA Assn., 1994, Cmty. Svc. award Holman St. Bapt. Ch., 1994. Mem. ABA, NAACP (chair chs. and orgns. com. Freedom Fund banquets 1989-93), ATLA, Am. Leadership Forum, Tex. Trial Lawyers Assn., Tex. Lyceum Assn., Houston Bar Assn., Houston Lawyers Assn., U. Houston Law Alumni (bd. dirs. 1993—), W.J. Durham Legal Soc., Links, Inc. (Mo. chpt., chair LEAD substance abuse and teen pregnancy prevention program 1990-91). Office: US Courthouse 515 Rusk Ave Rm 9513 Houston TX 77002-2605 E-mail: vanessa_gilmore@txs.us.courts.gov.

GILPATRICK, JANET, public affairs and public relations consultant; b. Seattle, Jan. 26, 1944; d. Donald Ernst Majer; children: Annie, Dawn. Dep. dir. Carter-Mondale Campaign, Wash. State, 1978-80; dist. dir. Spkr. of the House Thomas S. Foley, 1981-95; adminstr. asst. Office of Former U.S. Spkr. Thomas S. Foley, 1995-98; sr. cons. pub. affairs and pub. rels. Rockey-West Co., Spokane, 1998—2004; devel. dir. Inland N.W. Sci.-Tech., Spokane, Wash., 2004—. Bd. dirs. YWCA, Spokane, United Way, Women Helping Women, Mirabeau Point, Spokane Intercollegiate Rsch. Inst.; mem. Spokane Housing Commn.; mem. state bd. dirs. FEMA, Spokane. Office: Inland NW Sci-Tech S 129 Lincoln # 126 Spokane WA 99201 Office Phone: 509-984-1400.

GILPIN, DEBORAH J. museum administrator; b. Madison, Wis., Oct. 20, 1960; Exec. dir. Discovery Museums, Acton, Mass., 1994—. Office: Discovery Mus 177 Main St Acton MA 01720-3647

GILPIN, PERI, actress; b. Waco, Tex., May 27, 1961; m. Christian Vincent, 1999; 2 children, Ava, Stella. Former student, Dallas Theatre Ctr., U. Tex., Brit.-Am. Acad., London. Owner prod. co. (with Jane Leeves) Bristol Cities. Actress (TV series) Frasier, 1993-2004 (SAG award outstanding performance ensemble, 2000), The Lionhearts (voice), 1998; (TV guest appearances) 21 Jump Street, 1988, Matlock, 1990, Wings, 1992, Designing Women, 1993, Cheers, 1993, Pride & Joy, 1995, The Outer Limits, 1996, Early Edition, 1996, Superman, 1998, Hercules (voice), 1998, Baby Blues, 2000, The Chris Isaak Show, 2001, King of the Hill (voice), 2003, Justice League (voice), 2003, I'm With Her, 2003; (TV movies) Fight for Justice: The Nancy Conn Story, 1995, The Secret She Carried, 1996, Laughter on the 23rd Floor, 2001, (films) Spring Forward, 1999, How to Kill Your Neighbor's Dog, 2000, Finaly Fantasty: The Spirits Within (voice), 2001; guest appearance Later with Greg Kinnear, 1994, Early Edition, 1996, The Outer Limits, 1995, Superman, 1996, Pride & Joy, 1995, Talk Soup, 1991, Matlock, 1986, 21 Jump Street, 1987. Office: William Morris Agy One William Morris Place Beverly Hills CA 90212-2775*

GILPIN-GORDON, MARY ANN, retired educational association administrator; b. Spokane, Wash., July 21, 1948; d. Harrison William and Eva Francis Gilpin; m. Roger Stuart Gordon, Sept. 30, 2000. BA in Edn., Ea. Wash. U., 1970; MA, U. Wash., 1976. Specialist elem. music East Valley Sch. Dist., Spokane, 1970, tchr. jr. H.S. music and English, 1972—73; specialist elem. music Ctrl. Valley Sch. Dist., Spokane, 1970—72; prof. music and edn. Spokane C.C., Spokane, 1973—97, chmn. dept. humanities and social sci., 1990—97; assoc. prof. edn. Gonzaga U., Spokane, 1980—81. Mem., sec., treas. Wash. State Coll. Music Coun., 1973—81. Fellow Boeing, U. Wash., 1984—85. Mem.: ASCD, Music Tchrs. Nat. Conf., Music Edn. Nat. Conf. (chmn. C.C. N.W. divsn. 1975—85), Spokane Symphony Assocs. (vol. coord. 2002—03, pres.-elect 2004, Pres.'s award 2003), Spokane Club (mem. women's adv. coun.), Pi Lambda Theta (chpt. pres. Spokane 1986—88), Mi Phi Epsilon (v.p. Spokane alumnae 1970—76). Home: 5109 E 16th Ave Spokane WA 99212-3248

GILTON, DONNA LOUISE, library and information scientist, educator; b. Lynn, Mass., July 9, 1950; d. Rev. Charles Webster and Hattie Franklin Gilton. BA, Simmons Coll., 1972, MS, 1975; PhD, U. of Pitts., 1988. Pre-professional asst. Boston Pub. Libr., Boston, 1972—75, libr., 1975—79; head libr. Belize Teachers' Coll., Belize City, Belize, 1979—81; bus. reference libr. Western Ky. U., Bowling Green, Ky., 1984—88, Pa. State U., University Park, Pa., 1988—91; asst. prof. U. of RI, Kingston, RI, 1991—98, assoc. prof., 1998—. Mem.: ALA, R.I. Libr. Assn., Assn. of Libr. & Info. Sci. Educators. African Meth.Episcopal. Avocations: churchwork, reading, music. Office: University of Rhode Island 9 Rodman Hall Kingston RI 02881 Business E-Mail: dgilton@uri.edu.

GIMENES, SONIA REGINA ROSENDO, family therapist, psychologist; b. São Paulo, Brazil, Jan. 25, 1953; arrived in U.S., 1996; d. Joao Rosendo and Luzia Pragelis; m. Airton Jose Gimenes, May 7, 1976; children: Erika, Rodrigo. BS in Psychology, U. Mogi Cruzes, São Paulo, 1980; M in Sci. Psychology with honors, U. Americas, Mexico City, 1988; postgrad. in psychology; cert. in clin. psychology, U. Paulista, São Paulo, 1994. Registered family therapist intern Fla., lic. clin. psychologist Brazil. Family therapist intern Clinica Oira, Mexico City, 1987—88; psychologist intern Clinica Psicologia Objetivo, São Paulo, Brazil, 1994, Pontificia U. Cath., São Paulo, 1995; clin. psychologist Human Inst., São Paulo, 1995—96; family therapist Counseling and Hypnosis Inc., Miami, Fla., 1999—. Author: Domestic Violence, 2001; contbr. monography project Child Abuse, 1988, articles to profl. jours. Mem.: ACA, Am. Bd. Hypnotherapy, Am. Coll. Forensic Examiners, Am. Psychotherapy Assn., Rotary (chair new mems. 1998—, dir., chair found., vol. fight against domestic violence, Paul Harris medal of honor 1976). Avocations: music, dance, piano.

GIMMEL, MOLLY KAY, business executive; b. Baltimore, Md., May 25, 1968; d. Gerald K. and Carol S. Gimmel; m. James Froman, Oct. 11, 2003. BBA in mktg., Coll. of William & Mary, Williamsburg, Va., 1986—90; MS, Fla. Inst. Tech., Alexandria, Va., 1993—96. Cert. Profl. Contract Mgr. Nat. Contract Mgmt. Assn., 1998. Acquisition analyst Std. Tech. Inc, Falls Ch., Va., 1991—93; project adminstr. KPMG/Barents Group, Washington, 1993—95; contracts & pricing mgr. Arthur Andersen Office of Govt. Services, Washington, 1995—98, dir. proposal devel., 1998—2000; mgr., fed. program mgmt. office Deloitte Consulting, Reston, Va., 2000—01; exec. v.p. Design To Delivery Inc, Bethesda, Md., 2001—. Co-chairperson, govt. procurement spl. interest group NAWBO NOVA Chpt., Va., 2002—. Mem.: Nat. Assn. Women Bus. Owners, Nat. Assn. Female Exec., Gaithersburg-Germantown Chamber of Commerce, Assn. Procurement Mgmt. Professionals, Nat. Contract Mgmt. Assn. Office: Design To Delivery Inc 7910 Woodmont Ave Ste 800 Bethesda MD 20814 Personal E-mail: molly_kay@yahoo.com. E-mail: mgimmel@d2dinc.com.

GIMPELSON, LAURA J. environmental engineer, safety engineer; d. Stan J. and Beverly R. Gimpelson; m. John L. Norris, Oct. 10, 1982. B of Chem. Engring., Ga. Inst. of Tech., 1979. Registered profl. engr., Tex., Fla., Tenn. Environ. engr. U.S. EPA, Dallas, 1984—85; sr. engr. SQG Cons., Houston, 1985—87; staff engr. S & B Engrs. and Contractors, Inc., Houston, 1987—90; mgr. environment and safety Calabrian Corp., Houston, 1990—92; sr. process safety engr. Allstates Design, Houston, 1993; sr. engr. PSI, Inc., Houston, 1993—96; pres. LG Environ. Engring., Houston, 1996—. Chair archtl. control com. Oreg. Trace Homeowners Assn., Sanford, Fla., 2003—. Contbr. articles to profl. jours. Vol. Seminole County Libr., Sanford, Fla., 2002—03. Mem.: AIChE (pres. South Tex. chpt. 1997, Outstanding Young engr. South Tex. sect. 1992, Churchwell award for environ. programming South Tex. sect. 1995, Disting. Svc. award South Tex. sect. 2000), Fla. Engring. Soc., Soc. of Women Engrs. (sect. rep.Cen. Fla. chpt. 2002—03). Avocations: scuba diving, swimming, needlecrafts, travel. E-mail: lgenveng@aol.com.

GIN, SUE LING, retail executive; Chmn. Flying Food Co., Chicago. Mem. Womens Leadership Forum (bd. dirs.). Office: Flying Food Fare Inc 212 N Sangamon St Chicago IL 60607-1700

GINEVAN, ANNE V. state representative; b. Hazleton, Pa., Jan. 10, 1942; BA, U. Pitts., 1964, MEd, 1966, PhD, 1974. State rep. Vt. Ho. of Reps., 1996—. Mem. adv. com. Key Bank Vt. Moderator Middlebury ID#4, Middlebury Congregational Ch.; v.p. Addison County Transit Resources; bd. dirs. Middlebury Jr./Sr. H.S., chmn.; exec. dir., fundraiser United Way; past pres. Coun. Svc. Addison County; bd. dirs. Middlebury Cmty. House, Vt. Childrens Aid, Vt. Food Bank. Mem. Porter Med. Ctr. Aus. (past pres.). Home: 23 Gorham Ln Middlebury VT 05753-1001

GINGLES, MARJORIE STANKE, music educator, educator; b. Bklyn., Jan. 30, 1938; d. E.C. and E.L. (Lewthwaite) Stromberg; m. Charles Frederick Stanke, Aug. 27, 1960 (div. Nov. 8, 1976); m. William Glen Gingles, Sept. 29, 1984. BS in Music Edn., W. Chester U., formerly W. Chester State Tchrs. Coll., 1959; MA in Edn., W. Chester U., formerly W. Chester State Tchrs. Coll., mem, 1969. Elem. music tchr. George Gray Elem. Sch., Wilmington, Del., 1959-60, Penn-Delco Pub. Schs., Aston, Pa., 1960-61; pvt. piano tchr. home studio Berwyn, Norwood, Devon, Malvern, Pa., 1963—; choral dir. Coterie Singers, Wayne, Pa., 1975-84; music dir. St. Francis-in-the-Fields Ch., Malvern, Pa., 1981-88; piano tchr. Acad. Cmty. Music, Fort Washington, Pa., 1997—. Mem. music com. Main Line Unitarian Ch, Devon, 1970—, chair music com., 1978-79; mem. music com. Dorothy Taubman Inst. Piano, Amherst Coll., 1988-97, adjudicator Pa. Govs. Sch. Arts, 1986; music dir. Pro-Arte Chorale, 1980-86, dir. world and area premieres of new works; instr. several vocal workshops in field; clinician PMTA Convention, 1999. Piano concert artist, Pa. and N.Y. State; duo pianist with William Gingles; performances (in Gingles Duo) Pa. Music Tchrs. Conv. Taubman Piano Study grantee Pa. Music Tchrs. Assn., 2000. Mem. Main Line Music Tchrs. Assn. (chair adult recitals, chair Prime Time Players). Unitarian-Universalist. Avocations: reading, swimming, decorating. Home and Office: 27 Cypress Ln Berwyn PA 19312-1004 E-mail: msgingles@worldnet.att.net.

GINGOLD, HILARY WEINBERG, lawyer; b. Skokie, Ill., Aug. 25, 1969; d. Henry and Estelle (Cutler) Weinberg; m. Michael Gregg Gingold, Mar. 10, 2003; 1 child, Melissa Hailey. BA, Ariz. State U., 1991; JD, Calif. Western Sch. Law, San Diego, 1993. Law clk. Pima County Superior Ct., Tucson, 1994-95; asst. city prosecutor City of Tucson, 1995—99; dep. county atty. Maricopa County, 1999—. Mock trial coach Amphitheatre H.S., Tucson, 1994-99, Mountain Ridge H.S., 2000—; tutor Lawyers for Literacy, Tucson, 1994—. Vol. Hermitage Cat Shelter, Tucson, 1995—; girl's state mentor, 1996—. Mem. ABA, ATLA, Phi Alpha Delta. Republican. Jewish. Avocations: reading, playing trumpet. Office: 301 W Jefferson Phoenix AZ 85003

GINGRICH, MAUREE A. state representative; b. Balt., July 10, 1946; m. Calvin Gingrich; children: Julie, Katie, Adam, Michael. AS, Pa. Coll. of Med. Arts, 1967. Blood bank supr. M.S. Hershey Med. Ctr., 1973—86; mktg. rep. Omega Med. Labs., 1985—87; mktg. dir. Cornwall Manor, 1987—88; owner Mature Market Concepts, 1998—; Pa. state rep., 2003—. Mem. Palmyra Borough Civil Svc. Commn., 1987—90; pres. Palmyra Borough Coun., 1990—2001; personal chair Palmyra Pub. Libr., 1980—2002; mem. Palmyra Borough Planning Commn., 2002—. Steering com. chmn. Greater Harrisburg Sr. Outreach Svcs.; steering com. mem. Lebanon Valley Sr. Outreach Svcs.; bus. cons. Jr. Achievement, 1997—; chmn. Leadership Lebanon Valley, 1994—2000; mem. League of Women Voters of Lebanon County; bd. mem. Lebanon Valley C. of C., 2000—. Mem.: Pa. Women's Exch., Swatara Watershet Assn., Am. Mktg. Assn. Republican. Roman Catholic. Office: 412 Irvis Office Bldg Harrisburg PA 17120-2020 Home: 7 Sandalwood Dr Palmyra PA 17078 E-mail: maturemart@aol.com.

GINN, SHARON PATRICK, mechanical engineer; BSME cum laude, La. Tech. U., 1976; MBA, Fla. Inst. Tech., 1990. Sr. specialist engr. Dyn McDermott, New Orleans, 1987-93; cons., 1993-97; lead facility engr. Miss. Space Svcs./Johnson Controls, Bay St. Louis, Miss., 1997-2000; dir. facilities mgmt. Pacific U., Forest Grove, Oreg., 2000—. Tutor for Cmty. Literacy program, 1995. Mem.: ASME, Assn. Higher Edn. Facility Officers, Internat. Faclty Mgmt. Assn., Soc. Coll. and Univ. Planners. Office: Pacific U 2043 College Way Forest Grove OR 97116-1797 Home: 13385 NW Westlawn Ter Portland OR 97229-5543

GINORIO, ANGELA BEATRIZ, university research administrator, educator; b. Hato Rey, P.R., Jan. 30, 1947; d. Melquiades Alejandro and Juana del Carmen (Morales) G.; m. Charles H. Muller; 1 child, Emilia Beatriz Muller-Ginorio. BA, U. P.R., 1968, MA, 1971; PhD, Fordham U., 1979. Instr. U. P.R., Rio Piedras, 1970-71; asst. prof. Bowling Green (Ohio) State U., 1978-80; counselor Office of Minority Affairs, Seattle, 1981-82; dir. Women's Info. Ctr., Seattle, 1983-87; dir. N.W. Ctr. for Rsch. on Women and Women's Info. Ctr. U. Wash., Seattle, 1987-92, affiliate asst. prof. psychology, 1986-93, dir. N.W. Ctr. Rsch. on Women, 1993—99, asst. prof. women studies, adj. asst. prof. psychology, 1993—99, assoc. prof., adj. prof., 1999—. Cons. U. Hawaii, Honolulu, 1989, AAUW Rsch. Found., 1994—. Mem. editl. bd. Internat. Jour. of Intercultural Rels., Sex Roles, Signs; co-editor: (spl. issue) Women's Studies Quar., 1990; author: (monograph) Warming the Climate for Women in Academic Science, Si, se puede! Yes We Can! Bd. dirs. Mexican Am. Women Nat. Assn.-N.W., Seattle, 1988-89, Planned Parenthood, King County, Wash., 1991-93; mem. Wash. state com. Nat. Mus. Women in the Arts, 1989-92. Recipient Travel awards NIMH, 1979, APA/NSF, 1981; named Woman of Yr., Bus. and Profl. Women Campus chpt., 1986; grantee for evaluation Ford Found., 1989-91, grantee for summer sci. camp Discuren Found., 1992-93, NSF grantee, 1994-97. Fellow APA (bd. ethnic and minority affairs 1987-90); mem. Assn. for Women in Psychology. Office: Univ Wash Padel Ford Hall 35-4345 NW Ctr Rsch Women 35 110 Hall WA 98195-4345

GINSBURG, IONA HOROWITZ, psychiatrist; b. N.Y.C., Dec. 2, 1931; d. A. Eugene and Gertrude (Seidman) Horowitz; m. Selig M. Ginsburg, Aug. 15, 1954 (div. 1984); children: Elizabeth, Jessica. AB, Vassar Coll., 1953; MD, Columbia U., 1957. Diplomate Am. Bd. Psychiatry and Neurology. Pvt. practice, N.Y.C., 1961—; instr. psychiatry Columbia U., N.Y.C., 1961-81, asst. clin. prof. psychiatry, 1981-95, assoc. clin. prof. psychiatry, 1995—; psychiatrist student health svc. NYU, N.Y.C., 1978—2000. Cons.-liaison psychiatrist Columbia Presbyn. Med. Ctr., N.Y.C., 1982—. Contbr. articles to profl. jours. Med. adv. bd. Nat. Psoriasis Found. 1990-95. Recipient Josie Bradbury Travel award Psoriasis Assn. Gt. Britain. Mem. Am. Soc. Adolescent Psychiatry, N.Y. Soc. Adolescent Psychiatry (pres. 1986, cert. of appreciation 1986), Am. Psychiat. Assn., Am. Psychosomatic Soc., Met. Coll. Mental Health Assn. (pres. 1980), Assn. Psychocutaneous Medicine N.Am. (sec.-treas. 1994-95, v.p. 1995-98, pres. 1998-2000).

GINSBURG, RUTH, state representative; b. Bklyn., July 18, 1931; m. George S.; two children. Grad., Bklyn. Coll., 1954. Mem. Mayor's Adv. Com. for Social Svc. Funding; mem. dist. 26 N.H. Ho. of Reps., 1996—. Mem. sci., tech. and energy com., children and family law com. N.H. Ho. Reps. Former mem. Nashua Sch. Bd.; bd. dirs. Nashua Children's Assn.; mem. Nashua Ethnic Awareness Com. Jewish. Office: NH State Legis State House Concord NH 03301

GINSBURG, RUTH BADER, United States Supreme Court justice; b. Bklyn., Mar. 15, 1933; d. Nathan and Celia (Amster) Bader; m. Martin David Ginsburg, June 23, 1954; children: Jane Carol, James Steven. AB, Cornell U., 1954; postgrad., Harvard Law Sch., 1956—58; LLB Kent scholar, Columbia Law Sch., 1959; LLD (hon.), Lund (Sweden) U., 1969; LLD (hon.), Am. U., 1981, Vt. Law Sch., 1984; LLD (hon.), Georgetown U., 1985; LLD (hon.), DePaul U., 1985, Bklyn. Law Sch., 1987, Amherst Coll., 1991; LLD (hon.), Rutgers U., 1991; LLD (hon.), Lewis and Clark Coll., 1992, Radcliffe Coll., 1994, NYU, 1994; LLD (hon.), Columbia U., 1994; LLD (hon.), Smith Coll., 1994, L.I. U., 1994, U. Ill., 1995; LLD (hon.), Brandeis U., 1996, Wheaton Coll., 1997, Jewish Theol. Sem. of

Am., 1997; LLD (hon.), George Washington U. Law Sch., 1997; DHL (hon.), Hebrew Union Coll., 1988. Bar: N.Y. 1959, D.C. 1975, U.S. Supreme Ct. 1967. Law sec. to judge U.S. Dist. Ct. (so. dist.) N.Y., 1959—61; rsch. assoc. Columbia Law Sch., N.Y.C., 1961—62, assoc. dir. project internat. procedure, 1962—63; asst. prof. Rutgers U. Sch. Law, Newark, 1963—66, assoc. prof., 1966—69, prof., 1969—72, Columbia U. Sch. Law, N.Y.C., 1972—80; U.S. Cir. judge U.S. Ct. Appeals, D.C. Cir., Washington, 1980—93; assoc. justice U.S. Supreme Ct., Washington, 1993—. Phi Beta Kappa vis. scholar, 1973—74; fellow Ctr. for Advanced Study in Behavioral Scis., Stanford, Calif., 1977—78; lectr. Aspen (Colo.) Inst., 1990, Salzburg (Austria) Seminar, 1984; gen. counsel ACLU, 1973—80, bd. dirs., 1974—80. Author (with Anders Bruzelius): Civil Procedure in Sweden, 1965; author: Swedish Code of Judicial Procedure, 1968; author: (with others) Sex-Based Discrimination, 1974, Sex-Based Discrimination, supplement, 1978; contbr. numerous articles to books and jours. Fellow: Am. Bar Found.; mem.: AAAS, Coun. Fgn. Rels., Am. Law Inst. (coun. mem. 1978—93). Office: US Supreme Ct One First St NE Washington DC 20543*

GINSBURGH, JUDY CAPLAN, music specialist, vocalist, consultant; b. Alexandria, La., July 14, 1956; d. Edwin Joseph and Jacqueline Sonia (Segall) Caplan; m. Robert Howard Ginsburgh, Dec. 30, 1979; children: Rachel, Aaron, Jonathan. BM in Vocal Performance, Ind. U., 1978. Mgr., buyer Foley's, Houston, 1978-79; pers. adminstr. Lord and Taylor, Chgo., 1979-81; exec. sec. Beth El Hebrew Congregation, Alexandria, Va., 1982-85; profl. singer, 1982—; music cons., 1985—; founder, dir. Freelance Musicians Assn., Alexandria, La., 1990—; dir. Jewish Entertainment Resource Ctr., Alexandria, La., 1994; arts & healthcare coord. Arts coun. Ctrl. LA, Calif., 2003—. Cons., spkr. early childhood orgns., 1985—. Author, performer Shalom Yeladim/Hello Children (Parent's Choice award), 1994, Chanukah Favorites (Parent's Choice award), 1992, Smile (Nat. Parenting Ctr. Seal of Approval), 1997, Havdala Pajama, 1998 (Parents Choice award), Amazing Songs for Amazing Jewish Kids, 2000, (iParenting Media award), My Jewish World, 2002, (Childrens Music Web award). Pres. Rapides Arts & Humanities Coun., Alexandria, 1991-92; coord. Cmty. Concert, Alexandria, 1992—; chair Conf. for Alternatives in Jewish Edn., 1998. Recipient Mazel Tov award, 1989, Spl. Music award Religious Heritage Am., 1990, La. Artists Roster La. Divsn. Arts, 1989—, Seal of Approval, Nat. Parenting Ctr., 1996, Gov.'s Arts award Profl. Artist of Yr., 1999; named One of 10 Best Jewish Children's Performers in Country, Moment Mag., 1996, One of Top 10 Jewish Female Vocalists, 1997; 3rd place Just Plain Folks Song Contest. Mem. Nat. Assn. Rec. Arts and Scis., Coalition Advancement Jewish Edn. (bd. dirs., conf. chair 1998), Matinee Music Club, Nat. Assn. Edn. Young Children, So. Early Childhood Assn., Guild Temple Musicians, Women's Cantors Network, Children's Music Network. Avocations: needlework, genealogical research, composing, reading. Office: Ginsburgh PO Box 12692 Alexandria LA 71315-2692 Office Phone: 318-484-4474. E-mail: judyg@louisiana-arts.org.

GIORDANO, MARIE-CHRISTINE, choreographer, dancer, educator, performing company executive, director; b. Fribourg, Switzerland, Mar. 14, 1961; arrived in U.S., 1986; d. Francesco Giordano and Henriette Jeanine Tettamanti; m. Jeremy Todd Gentry, Mar. 16, 2000. Maturité, Lycée de Ste Croix, Fribourg, 1980; certificat d'études, Ecole Bénédict, Fribourg, 1981; completion fgn. student program, Alvin Ailey Am. Dance Ctr., 1989; cert. completion profl. level, Martha Graham Sch. Contemporary Dance, 1990. Dancer Martha Graham Dance Co., N.Y.C., 1993—94, instr. modern dance Broadway Dance Ctr., N.Y.C., 1996—99, New Dance Group Arts Ctr., N.Y.C., 1998—99; founder, artistic dir. Marie-Christine Giordano Dance Co., Bklyn., 1997—. Jury panel guest Assn. Action - Danse, Fribourg, 1998; invited guest New Europe Festival, 1999; creator outreach dance program in collaboration with Mentoring USA, N.Y.C., 2001—. Choreographer The Human Voice off Broadway Show, 1996, Transitional Pieces, 1998, Low Feed, 1999, Nouvelle Eve, 2001, Eve, Eros ef les autres, 2002. Recipient 2d prize dance competition, La Scene Français, 1982; scholar Merit, State of Fribourg, 1981—83, 1986, Martha Graham Sch. Contemporary Dance, 1990—93, Vienna Internat. Dance Festival, 1993. Avocations: movement research, psychology, ecology, reading. Office: Marie Christine Giordano Dance Co 220 25th St Ste 202 Brooklyn NY 11232 E-mail: mariechristineg@earthlink.net.

GIORDANO, PATRICIA A. music educator; d. Benjamin J. and Elma L. Del Tito; m. Joseph A. Giordano, June 22, 1974; 1 child, Joseph V. BS in Music Edn., West Chester (Pa.) U., 1972. Permanent tchg. cert. 1979. Music tchr. John B. Kelly Sch., Phila., 1972—81, Chichester Mid. Sch., Boothwyn, Pa., 1988—. Curriculum and instrn. chairperson Pa. Music Educators Dist. 12, Pa., 2003—. Mem.: Pa. Music Educators Assn., Music Educators Nat. Conf., NEA, Chichester Edn. Assn., Springfield Bus. and Profl. Women's Club (treas., corr. sec. 1980—84), Springfield Lioness Club, Philanthropic Ednl. Orgn. (PEO) (chaplain 2003). Avocations: cooking, travel, fitness, reading. Office: Chichester Middle Sch 925 Meetinghouse Rd Boothwyn PA 19061

GIOSEFFI, DANIELA (DOROTHY DANIELA GIOSEFFI), poet, writer, playwright; b. Orange, N.J., Feb. 12, 1941; d. Daniel Donato Gioseffi and Josephine Buzevska; m. Richard J. Kearney, Sept. 7, 1965 (div.); 1 child, Thea D. Kearney ; m. Lionel B. Luttinger, June 6, 1986. BA, Montclair State Coll., 1963; MFA, Cath. U. of Am., 1966. Cons., poet Poets-in-the-Schs., Inc., N.Y.C., 1972-85. Freelance writer, lectr. at numerous univs. throughout U.S. and Europe; appeared on Nat. Pub. Radio, CBC, BBC; spkr. on world peace and disarmament, 1979—; keynote spkr. Am. Forum for Global Edn. Nat. Conf., Miami, Fla., 1994, State Coun. Tchrs. English conf., Orlando, Fla., 1995, So. Edn. Found. Internat. Conf. of Tchrs. of English, Atlanta, 1997, IV Feminist Internat. Book Fair, Barcelona, 1989, Miami Internat. Book Fair, 1990. Author: The Great American Belly, 1977, The Great American Belly, 4th edit., 1979; author: (collections of poems) Eggs in the Lake, 1979, Word Wounds and Water Flowers, 1995, Going On, 2000, Symbiosis, 2002; author: Earth Dancing: Mother Nature's Oldest Rite, 1981, Women on War: International Voices for the Nuclear Age, 1988 (Am. Book award, 1990), rev. edit., 2003, On Prejudice: A Global Perspective, 1993—, Dust Disappears: Translations of Carilda Oliver Labra of Latin America, 1995—, (short stories) In Bed With the Exotic Enemy, 1997—, (novella) The Psychic Touch, 1996—; author: (play) The Golden Daffodil Dwarf, 1988—, Care of the Body, 1988—, The Sea Hag in the Cave of Sleep, 1988—; author: (radio play) Fathers and Children, 1988—, 1998—; author: (short stories) Daffodil Dollars, — (PEN Short Fiction award, 1990, Lifetime Achievement award Assn. Italian Am. Educators, 2003); contbr. numerous periodicals and anthologies;, performer (stage presentations throughout U.S. and Europe), composer (and lyricist), singer (many concert series) ; editor: PoetsUSA.com, —, NJ Poets.com, —; creator The First Bklyn. Bridge Poetry Walk, 1978; verses carved in marble: Penn Sta., 2002. Pres. Bklyn. Citizens for Sane Nuclear Policy, 1987—89; mem. exec. bd., chmn. media watch com. Writers and Pubs. Alliance for Nuclear Disarmament, 1978—91. Named Featured poet, The Peoples' Poetry Gathering: The Great Hall, Cooper Union, 2003; recipient World Peace award, Ploughshares Fund, 1989, 1999, Lifetime Achievement award, Assn. of italian Am. Educators, 2003; grantee poetry and fiction, Creative Artists' Pub. Svc. Program - N.Y. State Coun. on Arts, 1971—77, Thanks Be to Grandmother Winifred Found., 1996. Mem.: Poet's House, Nat. Book Critics Cir., Actors Equity Assn., Acad. Am. Poets, PEN Am. Ctr. Office: Box 8G 57 Montague St Brooklyn NY 11201-3356

GIPSON, GLORIA LORRAINE, social worker; b. Jersey City, Aug. 8, 1947; d. Wilmon and Mary (Castelberry) F.; m. Gordon Gipson Jr., Mar. 30, 1968; children: Leshante, Anthony, Lareesa, Natalie. Assocs., St. Peter's Coll., Jersey City, 1986, BS, 1987; Social Svcs. Competency Tng. cert., Montclair State Coll., 1990. Tutor, trainer Lit. Vols. of Am. Inc., Jersey City, 1993—. Author: Poems of Purpose, 1993. Avocations: sewing, decorating, ping pong/table tennis, writing, singing. Home: 131 Bidwell Ave # 2 Jersey City NJ 07305-3326

GIPSON, JULIET ANNETTE, real estate broker; b. Inglewood, Calif., June 3, 1961; d. Jessie L. Gipson and Jean Carrol Gipson-Jenkins; m. Claudius Karl Johannes Nanjo, Oct. 1990 (div. July 1991); m. Brian Donald MacDonald, July 27, 1995. BA in Polit. Sci., Calif. State U. Dominiguez Hills, 1982; MA in Adminstrn. and Leadership, Loma Linda U., 1984. C.A.R.E. broker license, notary public Calif., life creditial cmty. colls. Project coord. Archdiocese L.A., 1986—88; coun. commr. L.A. Redevelopment Agy. and Planning Commn., 1989—93; coll. adminstr., faculty mem. Miami-Dade C.C., 1993—95; sr. v.p. Realty World Corp., Irvine, Calif., 1996—98; real estate profl. Muller Comml. Real Estate, 1998—; real estate broker Pacific View Properties, San Juan Capistrano, Calif. Lectr., instr. UCLA, 1989—93; cons., bd. mem. Reality World Am., Newport Beach, Calif. Mem. Rep. Senatorial Inner Cir., Washington, 2002—. Mem.: Burbank C. of C., Toluca Lake C. of C., Women in Film (membership com. 1999—), Toluca Lake Tennis Club. Avocations: tennis, travel, reading, yoga. Home: Ste 428 10061 Riverside Dr Toluca Lake CA 91602

GIRA, CATHERINE RUSSELL, university president; b. Fayette City, Pa., Oct. 30, 1932; d. John Anthony and Mary (Stephen) Russell; m. Joseph Andrew Gira, July 17, 1954 (dec.); children: Cheryl Ann, Thomas Russell. BS, Calif. State U., 1953; M.Ed., Johns Hopkins U., 1957, M.L.A., 1972; PhD, Am. U., 1975. Tchr. Balt. County, Balt., 1953-60, head dept., 1958-60; writing cons. Md. State Dept. Edn., 1960-68; instr. Johns Hopkins U., Balt., 1964-65; from asst. prof. to prof. U. Balt., 1965-81, acting dean, 1981-82, provost, 1982-91; pres. Frostburg (Md.) State U., 1991—. Contbr. articles to profl. jours. Bd. dirs. Western Md. Health Sys., 1996—; chair bd. dirs. Leadership Md., 2004—. Inductee Md. Women's Hall of Fame, 1999; Am. U. scholar, 1973-75. Mem. Am. Assn. Univ. Adminstrs. (bd. dirs. 1984-87, pres.-elect 1987, pres. 1988-90), Fedn. State Humanities Couns. (bd. dirs. 1990-94, vice-chair 1993-94), Md. Humanities Coun. (chmn. 1989-90), Md. Assn. Higher Edn. (bd. dirs. 1983-85, pres. 1986-87), Shakespeare Assn. Am., Edgar Allan Poe Soc. (bd. dirs. 1982—). Methodist. Home: 106 Jones Ct Frostburg MD 21532-1415 Office: Frostburg State U 101 Braddock Rd Office of Pres Frostburg MD 21532-2302

GIRARD, ANDREA EATON, communications executive, consultant; b. N.Y.C., Oct. 16, 1946; d. Samuel Robert and Mimi (Eaton) Girard. Student, Syracuse U., 1964-66; BA cum laude, Finch Coll., 1968; MA, Columbia U., 1971. Talent coord./prodn. asst. Guber-Ford-Gross Prodns., NY, 1968-70; v.p. Charing Cross Press, N.Y.C., 1970-72; assoc. prodr., talent dir. TV shows "To Tell the Truth" and "Snap Judgement" Goodson Todman Prodns., N.Y.C., 1972-80; programming exec. David Letterman NBC, N.Y.C., 1980; dir. of talent, prodr. Daytime/Arts and Entertainment Networks (Hearst/ABC Video Enterprises), N.Y.C., 1981-84; dir. current programming acquisition, sr. prodr. Lifetime Network (Hearst/ABC/Viacom Entertainment Svcs.), N.Y.C., 1984-86; pres. Girard Comm., N.Y.C., 1986—, dir. med. comm. advantage internat., 1990-91; v.p. PRNY, N.Y.C., 1990-92; CEO Panache Comm. Inc., N.Y.C., 1992—. Judge Emmy Awards Internat. Film and TV Festival; spkr. pub. rels. coun. Sch. Continuing Edn. NYU, N.Y.C., media cons., 1987. Prodr., writer: (documentaries) Cave Dwellers of Crete, 1974; Sponge Divers of Kalymnos, 1979; Gypsies of the Camargue, 1983. Active fund raising bd. Jersey Wildlife Preservation Trust, NY; active hospitality com. UN, N.Y.C.; active Big Apple Com. Benefit of Image of N.Y. Mem.: NAFE, NATAS, Internat. Assn. Cooking Profls., N.Y. Women Film and TV, Delta Soc. Avocations: goldsmith, horseback riding, tennis. Office: Panache Comms 201 E 77th St Ste 7F New York NY 10021-2082 E-mail: panacheinc@aol.com.

GIRARD, NETTABELL, lawyer; b. Pocatello, Idaho, Feb. 24, 1938; d. George and Arranetta (Bell) Girard. Student, Idaho State U., 1957—58; BS, U. Wyo., 1959, JD, 1961. Bar: Wyo. 1961, D.C. 1969, U.S. Supreme Ct. 1969. Practiced in, Riverton, Wyo., 1963-69; atty.-adviser on gen. counsel's staff HUD; assigned Office Interstate Land Sales Registration, Washington, 1969-70; sect. chief interstate land sales Office Gen. Counsel, 1970-73; ptnr. Larson & Larson, Riverton, 1973-85; pvt. practice Riverton, 1985—. Condr. course on women and law; lectr. in field. Editor Wyoming Clubwoman, 1966-68; bd. editors Wyo. Law Jour., 1959-61; writer Obiter Dictum column Women Lawyers Jour., Dear Legal Advisor column Solutions for Seniors, 1988-94; featured in Riverton Ranger, 1994; also articles in legal jours. Chmn. fund dr. Wind River chpt., ARC, 1965; chmn. Citizens Com. for Better Hosp. Improvement, 1965; chmn. subcom. on polit. legal rights and responsibilities Gov.'s Commn. on Status Women, 1965—69, mem. adv. com., 1973—93; local chmn. Law Day, 1966, 1967, county chmn., 1994—97; mem. state bd. Wyo Girl Scouts USA, sec., 1974—89, bd. dirs., 2001—; state vol. adv. Nat. Found. March of Dimes, 1967—69; legal counsel Wyo. Women's Conf., 1977; gov. apptd. State Wyo. Indsl. Siting Coun., 1995—2001; rep. Nat. Conf. Govs. Commn., Washington, 1966. Recipient Spl. Achievement award HUD, 1972, Disting. Leadership award Girl Scouts USA, 1973, Franklin D. Roosevelt award Wyo. chpt. March of Dimes, 1985, Thanks Badge award Girl Scout Coun., 1987, Women Helping Women award Riverton Club Soroptimist Internat., 1990, Spl. award 27 yrs. svc. Wyo. Commn. for Women, 1964-92, Appreciation award Wyo. Sr. Citizens and Solutions for Srs., 1994, Arts in Action Pierrot award for outstanding musician, 1998, Disting. Svc. award Wyo. Music Edn. Assn., 2003. Mem. AAUW (br. pres., condr. seminar on law for layman Riverton br. 1965), Wyo. Bar Assn., Fremont County Bar Assn. (Spl. Recognition cert. 1997), DC Bar Assn., Women's Bar Assn. DC, Wyo. Trial Lawyers Assn., Nat. Assn. Women Lawyers (del. Wyo., nat. sec. 1969-70, v.p. 1970-71, pres. 1972-73), Wyo. Fedn. Women's Clubs (state editor, pres.-elect 1968-69, treas. 1974-76), Prog. Women's Club (pres.-elect. 1994-95), Riverton Chautauqua Club (pres. 1965-67, 2000-01), Riverton Civic League (pres. 1987-89), Kappa Delta, Delta Kappa Gamma (state chpt. hon.). Home: PO Box 687 Riverton WY 82501-0687 Office: 513 E Main St Riverton WY 82501-4440 Office Phone: 307-856-9339. E-mail: ngirard@tcinc.net.

GIRARD, SUSAN MARIE, manufacturing executive; b. Dennison, Ohio, Oct. 24, 1963; d. Vance Cy Smith and Agnes May (Moreland) Hursey; m. Paul Herbert Palmer Jr., July 7, 1990 (div. Oct. 1992); m. James D. Girard, Jr., June 26, 2000; 1 child, Jedediah James. BS in Chemistry, BS in Math., BSBA in Econs., Heidelberg Coll., 1986. Hostess Atwood Lake Resort, Dellroy, Ohio, 1984-87; asst. mgr. Ponderosa, Canton, Ohio, 1987-89; chemist, metals Wadsworth/Alert Labs., North Canton, Ohio, 1989-91; sr. chemist, metals Enseco/Wadsworth/Alert Labs, North Canton, 1991-94; group leader metals Quanterra, Inc., North Canton, 1994—97; sr. data automatin analyst STL, North Canton, Ohio, 1997—. Avocations: camping, reading, listening to music, plays. Home: 2967 State Route 212 NE Mineral City OH 44656-8800

GIRAUDO, SUZANNE MCDONNELL, psychologist; d. William and Theresa McDonnell; m. Louis John Giraudo, June 19, 1971; children: Bryan, Daniel, Denise, Izelle. BA, U. San Francisco, 1971, EdD, 1989; MA, San Francisco State U., 1981. Tchr. San Francisco Schs., 1978—79; learning specialist Archdiocese San Francisco, 1980—89; psychologist, dir. Calif. Pacific Med. Ctr., San Francisco, 1991—. Mem. adv. bd. Support for Families, San Francisco, 1998—; trustee U. San Francisco, 2002—; bd. dirs. Cmty. Alliance for Spl. Edn., San Francisco, 1999—. Contbr. chapters to books. Bd. dirs. Childrens Gardens Calif., San Rafael, 1990—96, Hamilton Family Ctr., San Francisco, 1993—99, Home Away From Homelessness, San Francisco, 1998—. Named Woman of the Yr., State Calif., 1998; recipient Knighthood of St. Gregory, Vatican Cath. Ch., 2000. Mem.: APA. Avocation: fitness. Office: Calif Pacific Med Ctr 3700 California St San Francisco CA 94118

GIRGUS, JOAN STERN, psychologist, university administrator; b. Albany, N.Y., Mar. 21, 1942; d. William Barnet and Louise (Mayer) Stern; m. Alan Chimacoff, Jan. 2, 1981; 1 child, Katherine Louise Stern. BA, Sarah Lawrence Coll., 1963; MA, The Grad. Faculty New Sch. for Social Research, 1965, PhD, 1969. Asst. prof. dept. psychology CCNY, N.Y.C., 1969-72, assoc. prof., 1972-77, assoc. dean div. social sci., 1972-75, dean, 1975-77; prof. psychology Princeton U., 1977—, dir. Pew Sci. Program Undergrad. Edn., 1987—2002, chair dept. psychology, 1996—2002. Contbr. articles and chpts. to profl. jours. and books. NSF fellow, NIH fellow; Research grantee CUNY, 1971-74; Nat. Inst. Child Health and Human Devel. research grantee, 1972-74; NSF grantee, 1975-79; NIMH grantee, 1985-91. Fellow APA, Am. Psychol. Soc.; mem. Eastern Psychol. Assn., Soc. Rsch. in Child Devel. Home: 1 Boudinot St Princeton NJ 08540-3007 Office: Princeton U Green Hall Princeton NJ 08544

GIRON, ANGELA, artist, educator; b. Phoenix, Ariz., Sept. 11, 1950; d. Carlos Longino Girón and Enriqueta Saldamando; m. James Richard Matz, Feb. 3, 1969 (dec. Mar. 29, 1979); 1 child, Felicia Anne Matz. BA in Theater, Ariz. State U., 2002, postgrad. Actress various locations, 1970—; writer, dir., actress Playwrights Workshop, Montreal, Canada, 1982—90; freelance photojournalist Toronto Star, Canada, 1986; photographic artist Le Cheval Blanc, Internat. Women's Day, Stagebrush Theatre, Montreal, Phoenix, and Scottsdale, 1990—; writing instr. Katauik Sch. Bd., Montreal, Canada, 1998. Film acquisitions dir. Trident Releasing, L.A., 1991—96; writer Big O Mag., Singapore and Malaysia, 1993—96. Actor: (films) The Moderns, 1987, (pub. svc. announcement) Amnesty Internat., 1985 (Venice Lion award, 1985); author: (children's book) Inside/Outside, 1994 (L.A.'s Best, 1994). Storybook reader Washington Sch. Dist., Phoenix, 1999; bd. dirs. Playwrights Workshop, Montreal, 1983—90. Recipient Mayor's Cert. of Recognition, City of L.A., 1991—, grad. tchg. fellowship in theater, Kenneth S. Smith Hispanic Scholarship Fund, 2003—04. Mem.: SAG (book pal 1991—), Grad. Women's Assn., Ariz. State U., Assn. Can. TV and Radio Artists (Jane Mallett award for best actress 2002—03). Democrat. Roman Catholic. Avocations: travel, language studies, cross-cultural cruising, wine, gardening. Office: Ariz State U Dixie Gammage PO Box 872002 Tempe AZ 85287 E-mail: angelagiron@aol.com.

GIRONE, JOAN CHRISTINE CRUSE, realtor, former county official; b. Kingston, Ont., Can., Aug. 30, 1927; d. Arthur William and Helen Wilson Cruse; m. Joseph MIchael Girone, June 26, 1954; children: Susan, Richard, William. Buyer Franklin Simon, Inc., N.Y.C., 1946-54; supr. Midlothian dist. Chesterfield County (Va.) Bd. Suprs., 1976-88, vice chmn., 1976-82; Founding mem. Capitol Area Agy. on Aging, 1973-89, Med. Coll. Va. Women's Health Adv. Coun., 1990-97, Chesterfield County Citizens for Responsible Govt., 1991—; comml. real estate agent Long and Foster Realtors, Richmond. Bd. dirs. Cen. Va. Ednl. TV Corp., 1989-94; commr., chmn. Richmond (Va.) Regional Planning Dist. Commn., 1976-88; Va. Power Consumer adv. bd.; chmn. cmty. edn. adv. com. Va. Bd. of Edn., 1972-79; mem. Va. Gov.'s Adv. Bd. on Aging, 1980-82; chmn. Richmond Met. Transp. Planning Orgn., 1981-88; bd. visitors Va. State U., 1980-84. Vice chmn., exec. com. Gateway Bus. Assn.; mem. Ctrl. Va. River Basin Com., 1985; mem. evaluation task force United Way of Greater Richmond, 1985; adv. bd. Chesapeake Bay Local Assistance Bd. Adv. Com. Midlothian YMCA, 2000; chmn. steering com. Bon Air Village Preservation, 1995—, mem. Coun. Advocates Va. Supportive Housing, 2001—; chmn. Chesterfield County Com. to elect John Warner and Paul Trible to U.S. Senate, 1979, 1982, 1984; Chesterfield chmn. Marshall Coleman for Gov., 1981—; chmn. Women for Reagen Bush, 1984; vice chair Rt. 288 Freeway Comm., 1996, exec. com.; mem. candidate recruitment com. Va. Fedn. Rep. Women, 1995; bd. dirs. Maymount Found., 1982—89, YMCA Greater Richmond Metro, ARC Va. Capital chpt.; bd. mgrs. Chesapeake Bay Local Assistance Bd. Adv. Com. Midlothian YMCA, 1999, bd. dirs., 1994—, Caucus Future Ctrl. Va., 1994—, Coalition for Greater Richmond. Recipient Good Govt. award Richmond First Club, 1985; Joan C. Girone Libr. named in her honor, Chesterfield County, 1995. Mem. Va. Assn. Counties (exec. bd. 1982-87), Richmond Metro C. of C. (bd. dirs. Chesterfield Bus. Coun. 1989—), Hugeunot Rep. Woman's Club (Rep. Woman of Yr. 1983). Home: 2609 Dovershire Rd Richmond VA 23235-2815 E-mail: joan.girone@longandfoster.com.

GIROUARD, PEGGY JO FULCHER, ballet educator; b. Corpus Christi, Tex., Oct. 25, 1933; d. J.B. and Zora Alice (Jackson) Fulcher; m. Richard Ernest Girouard, Apr. 16, 1954 (div. Mar. 1963); children: Jo Linne, Richard Ernest; m. James C. Boles, May 4, 1996. BS in Elem. Edn., U. Houston, 1970. Ballet instr. Emmamae Horn Studio, Houston, 1951-81; owner, dir. Allegro Acad. Dance, Houston, 1981—. Artistic dir. Allegro Ballet Houston, 1976—; asst. mgr. Sugar Creek Homes Assn., Sugar Land, Tex., 1979-90; coord. 1st Regional Dance Am. Nat. Festival, Houston, 1997. Choreographer (with Glenda W. Brown) Masquerade Suite, 1983, Sebelius Suite, 1983, Shannan, 1984, Papa Shamus, 1986, Silhouettes, 1987, Aspirations, 1989, Here Come the Clowns, 1990. Mem. Cultural Arts Coun. Houston; founding officer Regional Dance Am., 1988, bd. dirs., 1988-2001, sec., 1996-2001. Mem. Dance Masters Am. (dir. 1977-80), S.W. Regional Ballet Assn. (chmn. craft of choreography 1983-85, coord. to nat. assn. 1983-2003, Stream award 1986). Democrat. Home: 9945 Warwana Rd Houston TX 77080-7609 E-mail: pgirouard77080@yahoo.com.

GIROUARD, SHIRLEY ANN, nurse, policy analyst; b. New London, Conn., Jan. 16, 1947; d. Maxime Albert Girouard and Irene Barbara (Arnold) Reid. BA in Sociology, Ea. Conn. State Coll., 1972; MA in Sociology, U. Conn., 1974; MSN, Yale U., 1977; PhD in Policy Analysis, Brandeis U., 1988. Nurse Woodstock (Conn.) Pub. Health Assn., 1968-70; staff nurse Clinton (Conn.) Convalescent Ctr., 1970-72; ts. edn. coord. Middlesex Meml. Hosp., Middletown, Conn., 1973-75; clin. nurse specialist Dartmouth Hitchcock Med. Ctr., Hanover, N.H., 1977-83, staff nurse, 1983-84; legis. cons., lobbyist N.H. Nurses Assn., Concord, 1985-87; program officer Robert Wood Johnson Found., Princeton, N.J., 1987-92; exec. dir. N.C. Ctr. Nursing, 1992-93, Am. Nurse's Assn., 1993-94; health policy and nursing cons. pvt. and pub. sector orgns., Washington, 1994-95; v.p. child health and financing Nat. Assn. Children's Hosps. and Related Instns., Alexandria, Va., 1995-99; cons., 1999—; assoc. prof. So. Conn. State U., 2001—. Pvt. practice cons., 1983-87; profl. devel. cons., Lebanon, N.H., 1983-87; health policy and nursing cons. Author: (chpt.) Health Policy and Nurse Services, 1989, 98, others; mem. editorial bd. Clin. Nurses Specialist Jour., 1986—, others; contbr. articles to profl. jours. State rep. N.H. Legislature, Concord, 1982-84; counselor City of Lebanon Coun., 1984-87. Fellow Am. Acad. Nursing; mem. ANA (project dir. 1986), Sigma Theta Tau. Democrat. Office Phone: 203-392-6479.

GIROUARD, TANDY DENISE, special education educator, psychology educator; b. Ft. Worth, Tex., Aug. 25, 1960; d. Nolan Ray and Barbara Gale (Miller) Rutledge; m. Jan. 22, 1980 (div. Dec. 1995); children: Michael, Christopher, Kaneissa. BS in Generic Spl. Edn., U. of Mary Hardin-Baylor. Tchr. asst. spl. edn. Hurst-Euless-Bedford Ind. Sch. Dist., Bedford, Tex., 1988; tchr. asst. in spl. edn. McLennan County Dept. Edn., Waco, Tex., 1988-90; tchr. spl. edn. Moody Ind. Sch. Dist., 1991—94; tchr. resource reading LaVega Ind. Sch. Dist., 1994—95; tchr. life skills Waco Ind. Sch. Dist., 1996—98; tchr. 2d grade/tchr. spl. edn. Emma L. Harrison Charter Sch., 1998—99; tchr. resource Belton Ind. Sch. Dist., 1999—2000; tchr. spl. edn. Connally Ind. Sch. Dist., 2000—02; profl. scorer NCS Pearson Edn., 2003—04. Mem. Internat. Assn. of Pers. in Employment Security, Assn. Tex. Profl. Educators, PTA, Bedford-Euless Soccer Assn., Tex. State Edn. Assn., Pi Gamma Mu. Home: 500 Greenfield Dr Waco TX 76705-1705

GIROUARD, TINA, artist, curator; b. De Quincy, La., May 26, 1946; BFA, U. La. Established studio, N.Y.C., 1968—85, Cecilia, La., 1980—, Port-au-Prince, Haiti, 1991—. One-woman shows include Univ. Gallery, Lafayette, La., 1968, 1973, 1974, 112 Greene St. Gallery, N.Y.C., 1971—73, 1975, Vehicule, Montreal, 1975, Alfred (N.Y.) U. Gallery, 1975, Memphis Acad., 1975, Holly Solomon Gallery, N.Y.C., 1976, 1978, 1980, Alexandra Monet Gallery, Brussels, 1979, Forum Stadtpark Mus., Graz, Austria, 1979, Elmhurst Park Gallery, Lafayette, 1981, De Vleeshal, Middelburg, Holland, 1982, Zeeuws Kuntenaarscentrum, 1982, Arthur Roger Gallery, New Orleans, 1983, Museo Tamayo, Mexico City, 1983, Fabric Workshop, N.Y.C., 1984, World's Fair, New Orleans, 1984, PS 1, L.I., 1985, Arthur Roger Gallery, New Orleans, 1985, Artist's Alliance, Lafayette, 1986, Contemporary Art Ctr., New Orleans, 1987, Quebec Delegation Gallery, Lafayette, 1987, C.A.C., New Orleans, 1989, Mus. Art, Alexandria, La., 1989, one-man shows include Atlantic Ctr. Arts, 1990, one-woman shows include Lafayette Regional Airport, 1990, Contemporary Arts Ctr., New Orleans, 1990, exhibited in group shows at 112 Green St. Gallery, N.Y.C., 1972, Leo Castelli Gallery, 1974, UCLA Gallery, 1976, Cin. Art Mus., 1978, Mus. Modern Art, Oxford, Eng., 1980, Holly Solomon Gallery, N.Y.C., 1982, Arthur Roger Gallery, New Orleans, 1984, Inst. Contemporary Art, 1987, Contemporary Art Ctr., La., 1990, numerous others, commns. include, Contemporary Art Ctr., New Orleans, 1989, Lafayette Regional Airport, 1990, videography includes, Maintenance I, 1971, Maintenance II, 1972, Maintenance III, 1973, Maintenance IV, 1975, Six of Hearts, 1976, Maintenance V, 1976, WAWA, 1979, 2 C 3 T S, 1981, others. CAPS grantee, Art Matters, Inc. grantee, Nat. Endowment Arts grantee, La. Divsn. Arts fellow, Nat. Endowment Arts fellow, Creative Artists Pub. Svc. fellow, 1973, Internat. Comm. Agy. fellow, 1979, Lila Wallace Arts Internat. fellow, 1993, Gottlieb Fatn fellow, 1997. Office: Tina Girouard Art Projects PO Box 64 Cecilia LA 70521-0064

GIRTH, MARJORIE LOUISA, lawyer, educator; b. Trenton, N.J., Apr. 21, 1939; d. Harold Brookman and Marjorie Mathilda (Simonson) G. AB, Mt. Holyoke Coll., 1959; LLB, Harvard U., 1962. Bar: N.J. 1963, U.S. Supreme Ct. 1969, N.Y. 1976. Pvt. practice, Trenton, 1963-65; rsch. assoc. Brookings Instn., 1965-70; assoc. prof. law SUNY Law Sch., Buffalo, 1971-79, prof., 1979-91, assoc. dean, 1986-87; dean Ga. State U. Coll. Law, Atlanta, 1992-96, prof., 1992—. Vis. prof. U. Va. Law Sch., 1979-80; Southeastern Bankruptcy Law Inst. vis. prof. Emory Law Sch., spring 1991, vis. scholar, 1996; vis. legal educator W.Va. U. Coll. of Law Vis. Com., 1994-95; chancellor's search adv. com. Bd. of Regents, 1993-94. Author: Poor People's Lawyers, 1976, Bankruptcy Options for the Consumer Debtor, 1981, (co-author) Bankruptcy: Problem, Process, Reform, 1971. Bd. dirs. Buffalo and Erie County YWCA, 1972-76, Buffalo Unitarian-Universalist Ch., 1981-84, Feminist Women's Health Ctr., 1993-94, ACLU, Ga., 1995-2001, Unitarian-Universalist Congregation of Atlanta, 1999—2003; mem. commn. on peace, justice and human rights Internat. Assn. Religious Freedom, 1976-79; chmn. Erie County Task Force on Status of Women, 1985-87. Recipient award for pioneering achievements N.Y. State 8th Jud. Dist. Splty. Bar Assn. and Com. on Women in the Cts., 2000. Fellow Lawyers Found. Ga.; mem. ABA (mem. com. bus. law sect. 1985-89, chmn. consumer bankruptcy com. 1983-86), Am. Arbitration Assn. (comml. arbitration panel 1997—), Assn. Am. Law Schs. (profl. devel. com. 2002—, nominations com. 1996), Am. Law Inst., N.Y. State Bar Assn. (mem. exec. com. bus. law sect. 1980-91, chmn. bankruptcy law com. 1980-82, chmn. banking corp. bus. law sect. 1986-87, mem. ho. of dels. 1990-91), Ga. Supreme Ct. (commn. on racial and ethnic bias in ct. sys. 1993-95, commn. on equality 1995—2004, sec. 1998-2000, commn. on access and fairness in the cts. 2004—), Ga. Assn. Women Lawyers, Law Sch. Admissions Coun. (audit com. 1995-97, 1999—, fin. and legal affairs com., 1997-99), Mt. Holyoke Alumnae Assn. (centennial award 1972). Office: Ga State U Coll Law PO Box 4037 Atlanta GA 30302-4037 E-mail: mgirth@gsu.edu.

GIRVIN, LILA SHAW, artist; b. Denver, Aug. 20, 1929; d. Elmer Otto and Adah Grace Shaw; m. George William Girvin; children: Timothy, Robert, Jonathan, Matthew. BFA, U. Denver, 1951. Artist, Seattle and Spokane, Wash., 1953—. Represented in permanent collections N.W. Mus. Arts and Culture, Spokane, Wash., Jundt Art Mus., Gonzaga U., City of Spokane, bus. and pvt. collections. Mem. Spokane Cmty. Devel. Task Force, Wash., 1969—73, Spokane Arts Commn., Wash., 1976—80; bd. dirs. Cheney Cowles Mus., Spokane, Wash., 1962—70, Spokane Symphony Orch., Wash., 1982—86; mem. Spokane County Boundary Review, Wash., 1976—82; chmn. bd. dirs. Evergreen State Coll., Olympia, Wash., 1989—97. Mem.: Phi Beta Kappa. Avocations: music, reading, travel, sports. Home: 4203 S Perry Spokane WA 99203

GIRVIN, SHIRLEY EPPINETTE, retired elementary education educator, journalist; b. New Orleans, Apr. 16, 1947; d. Woodie Trevillion and Thelma Elizabeth (Axline) E.; m. Russell Robertson Girvin, Nov. 30, 1996. AA, East L.A. Coll., 1967; BA, Calif. State U., L.A., 1969, postgrad., 1969-70, U. So. Calif., 1982, Chapman Coll., 1983, Loyola Marymount U., L.A., 1986-87. Elem. tchr. Covina-Valley Unified Sch. Dist., 1970-74, San Gabriel (Calif.) Sch. Dist., 1974-75, Alhambra (Calif.) City Sch. Dist., 1976-78; elem. and program mentor tchr., faculty rep. L.A. City Unified Sch. Dist., 1978—2003; ret., 2003. Rewrite editor, staff writer San Gabriel Valley Newspaper Publs., 1975-76. Contbr. articles to profl. publs. Recipient TAP award Alhambra-San Gabriel dist. Soroptimist Club, 1975; Calif. State PTA scholar, 1981, Journalism Alumni Assn. scholar East L.A. Coll., 1967, Arthur J. Baum Journalism scholar Calif. State U., 1969. Mem. AAUW (mem. com. internat. rels. 1977-78, chmn. ednl. com. 1978-79), NEA, Calif. Tchrs. Assn., L.A. City Tchrs. Math. Assn., United Tchrs. L.A. (chpt. chairperson 1994-95), Women in Comm., Nat. Press Women, Humane Soc. U.S., Soc. for the Prevention of Cruelty to Animals, Handgun Control Inc., Sigma Delta Chi. Avocations: breeding, selling, and racing Thoroughbred race horses, gardening. Home: 8730 S East Ave Fresno CA 93725

GITECK, EVELYN B. poet, educator; b. Bklyn., Mar. 9, 1920; d. Max and Sophie Berman; m. Jack Bernard Giteck, Sept. 21, 1940; children: Anita Drujon Prager, Janice Susan, Sharon Phyllis Drujon. AA magna cum laude, L.A. City Coll., 1979; BA magna cum laude, Immaculate Heart Coll., 1980; MA in Humanities magna cum laude, Calif. State U., Dominiguez Hills, 1984. Office mgr. nursing dept. Cedars Sinai Hosp., L.A., 1968—70; office mgr. acad. dean's office L.A. City Coll., 1970—81; dir. program for women reentering the job market Assabet H.S., Marlboro, Mass., 1981—85; dir. lit. Friends of the Marlboro Libr., 1981—85; prodr. programs Santa Barbara (Calif.) Writers' Consortium, 1985—87, The Unquiet Woman; tchr. poetry continuing edn. Lexington, Mass., 1989—; tchr. poetry Bedford (Mass.) Pub. Libr., 2003—. Founder, dir. automobile resource conservation L.A. City Coll. Dist., 1973; founder, pres., program chair L.A. City Coll. chpt. Assn. for Women's Active Return to Edn., 1974—77; responsible for creation of women's and day care ctr. L.A. City Coll., 1974—78, coord. 50th anniversary celebration, 1979. Editor, contbr.: book of poetry Woven Word (Friends of the Libr. award, 1985); author: Everywhere There are Gardens, Everlasting Spirit, (poetry art) Santa Barbara's Writers' Consortium Anthology, The Writing Finger Moves, 1986, 1987. Pres. Brandeis U. Women, Santa Barbara, 1987—87. Recipient Minerva award, AWARE Assn., 1975—76, Cmty. Svc. to Lexington award for poetry film prodns., Comcast Cable Co., 2003. Mem.: Longfellow Poetry Soc. (life), Internat. Women's Writers' Guild (life). Avocations: writing, travel, swimming, reading, helping family. Home: Apt 16 425 Woburn St Lexington MA 02420

GITELSON, SUSAN AURELIA, business executive, civic leader; b. N.Y.C. d. Moses Leo and Miriam Evelyn (Silverman) G. BA, Barnard Coll.; MIA, Columbia Sch. Internat. Affairs; PhD, Columbia U.; student, Univ. Calif., Berkeley. Trainee Rockefeller Found.; asst. prof. internat. rels. Hebrew U., Jerusalem; rsch. assoc. Columbia U., N.Y.C.; dir. internat. affairs and third world World Jewish Congress, N.Y.C.; pres. Internat. Cons., Inc., N.Y.C., Magic Touch Icewares Internat. Corp., N.Y.C. Author: Multilateral Aid for National Development and Self-Reliance; editor, author: Israel in the Third World; contbr. articles to profl. jours., mem. edit. com. Jerusalem Papers on Peace Problems. Mem. nat. adv. coun., sponsor Gitelson Essay awards Ctr. for Study of Presidency, Washington; co-chair dean's coun. Columbia Sch. Internat. and Pub. Affairs; sponsor Dr. Susan Aurelia Gitelson Fund for Innovative Programs, Columbia Sch. of Internat. Pub. Affairs; pres. Dr. Susan Aurelia Gitelson Found. Inc.; mem. Columbia U. seminars; mem. bd. overseers Mus. Jewish Heritage--A Living Meml. to the Holocaust; sponsor Gitelson Lecture on Human Rights and U.S. Fgn. Policy, Columbia U., Gitelson award for human values in internat. affairs Columbia Sch. Internat. and Pub. Affairs, Gitelson-Meyerowitz Human Rights essay award Columbia Ctr. for Study of Human Rights, Gitelson Seminars on UN, City U. Grad. Ctr.; sponsor Gitelson Peace prize Truman Inst.; sponsor Gitelson Peace Papers and Publs., mem. bd. overseers Truman Inst. Hebrew U. Jerusalem; mem. internat. bd. govs. Hebrew U. Jerusalem; v.p. bd. dirs. Am. Friends of Hebrew U.; trustee Sutton Pl. Synagogue; mem. trustees Nat. Com. Am. Fgn. Policy; sponsor Gitelson-Meyerowitz Disting. Svc. award, Sutton Place Synagogue, Dr. Susan Aurelia Gitelson Fund Innovative Programs Columbia U. Faculty Arts and Scis. Recipient Outstanding Service award Columbia Sch. Internat. and Public Affairs; Alumni medal for conspicuous service Columbia U. Mem. Nat. Inst. Social Scis., Columbia Sch. Internat. and Pub. Affairs Alumni Assn. (pres. 1980-84), Columbia U. Alumni Fedn. (mem. exec. com.), Nat. Com. on Am. Fgn. Policy (mem. bd. trustees), Carnegie Coun. on Ethics and Fgn. Affairs, Fgn. Policy Assn., Am. Jewish Com. Home: 1201 Broadway Ste 1003 New York NY 10001 Office: 1201 Broadway New York NY 10001-7504 E-mail: susangitel@aol.com.

GITENSTEIN, DONNA M. academic administrator; b. Florala, Fla. m. Donald Hart; children: Pauline, Samuel. BA in English, Duke U.; PhD in English and Am. Lit., U. N.C., Chapel Hill. Asst. prof. English Ctrl. Mo. State U.; prof. English SUNY, Oswego, chair English dept., assoc. provost; provost Drake U., 1992—98, exec. v.p., 1997—98; pres. Coll. of N.J., Ewing, 1998—. Commr. Mid. States Commn. on Higher Edn. Author: (book) Apocalyptic Messianism and Contemporary Jewish-Am. Poetry; contbr. articles and reviews on Jewish and Am. Lit. Named Salute to Policy Makers, Exec. Women of N.J., 2002, Tribute to Women, YWCA of Princeton, N.J., 2003; recipient Woman of Distinction award, Girl Scouts of Del.-Raritan Coun., 2002. Mem.: Am. Coun. on Edn. (mem. commn. on minorities in higher edn., pres. sponsor (N.J. chapt.) network of women leaders in higher edn.). Office: Office of the Pres Coll of NJ PO Box 7718 Ewing NJ 08628*

GITMAN, LEDA VICTORIA, artist; b. Buenos Aires, Aug. 20, 1972; arrived in U.S., 1987; BA summa cum laude, BFA summa cum laude, Fla. Internat. U., 1996. Exhibitions include Mus. Art, Ft. Lauderdale, Fla., 1999, Tallahassee, Fla., 2000, Elite Fine Art Gallery, Miami, Fla., 2000, Fischbach Gallery, N.Y., N.Y., 2002, Miss. Mus. Art, Jackson, Miss., 2003, Daniel Weinberg Gallery, LA, Calif., 2003. Recipient Alumni Torch award, Fla. Internat. U., 2002; fellow Battel Stoeckel fellowship, Yale U. Sch. Art, 1994, South Fla. Cultural Consortium, 1999. Mem.: Coll. Art Assn. Jewish.

GITTENS, ANGELA, airport executive; Dep. dir. San Francisco Internat. Airport, 1983—93; gen. mgr. William B. Hartsfield Internat. Airport, Atlanta, 1993—98, regional dir. N.Am. for airport svcs., 1993—98; v.p. TBI Airport Mgmt., 1998—2001; dir. Miami Internat. Airport, 2001—. Office: PO Box 592075 Miami FL 33159

GITTLER, JOSEPHINE, law educator; b. Richmond, Va., May 13, 1943; d. Joseph and Lamie G. BA, Barnard Coll.; JD, Northwestern Coll., 1968. Bar: Conn. 1969. Law clk. U.S. Dist. Ct., New Haven, 1969-70, Conn. Supreme Ct., Hartford, 1970-71, U.S. Dist. Ct. Conn., 1971-72; from assoc. prof. Coll. Law to prof. Coll. Pub. Health U. Iowa, Iowa City, 1973—2002, prof. Coll. Pub. Health, 2002—. Chief counsel subcom. investigate juvenile deliquency jud. com. U.S. Senate, Washington, 1977-78; coord. U.S. Surgeon Gen.'s Conf., Washington, 1988; mem. exec. com. Consortium Ctrs. on Children Families & Law, 1989—2000; legis. cons. Nat. Assn. State and Territorial Maternal and Child Health and Crippled Children's Programs, 1982-86, recipient Pub. Svc. award 1982, 84; counsel interim study com. juvenile justice Iowa Gen. Assembly, Des Moines, 1975-77; vis. scholar Justice Ctr. of Atlanta, 1999; cons. in field. Contbr. articles to profl. jours. Chair Iowa Maternal and Child Health Adv. Coun., Des Moines, 1983-88; mem. Iowa Juvenile Justice Adv. Com., Des Moines, 1975—83, Iowa Crime Commn., Des Moines, 1974-75, interim com. Penal Reform and Correction, Des Moines, 1973-74. Office: U Iowa Coll Law Iowa City IA 52242

GITTLER, WENDY, artist, art historian, writer; b. Manhattan, N.Y. d. Lewis Frederic and Esther (Becker) G. Studied with George Grosz, Art Students League, N.Y., 1958-59; studied with Camillio Egas, N.Y.C., 1960; BS in Art History, Columbia U., 1963; MA in Art History, Hunter Coll., 1967; postgrad., NYU, 1968; MFA, Bklyn. Coll., 1973; postgrad., U. Paris, 1977-78. Lectr. art NYU, N.Y.C., 1966-68; lectr. art history Fairleigh Dickinson U., Teaneck, N.J., 1966-68; lectr., art history Hunter Coll., N.Y.C., 1968-80; lectr. art history Sch. Visual Arts, N.Y.C., 1979-86; lectr. Met. Mus., N.Y.C., 1988-89; lectr. art history Parsons Sch. of Design, N.Y.C., 1989-96; lectr. N.Y. Studio Sch., N.Y.C., 1991—. Instr. studio U. Haifa, Israel, 1971; curator First Street Gallery, N.Y.C., 1992; lectr. Brown U., R.I., 1993, South Fla. Art Ctr., 1990, Lowe Art Mus., U. Miami, Fla., 1984; moderator artists panels, bd. dirs. v.p. Artists Equity, N.Y.C., 1995-2003. One-woman shows include 1st Street Gallery, N.Y.C., 1976, 82, 88, 95, 99, 2002, Artists Equity, 1999, 2001, 2002; exhibited in group shows at Blue Mountain Gallery, Atlantic Gallery, N.Y.C., 1995-2001, 2002, 2003, N.Y. Studio Sch., 1996-2003, Savannah Coll. Art and Design, 1997,, S.E. Mo. State U. Mus., 1997, Fordham U., 1996, Ashawag Hall, East Hampton, N.Y., 1995, LeHigh U., Bethlehem, Pa., 1984, Gallery of Fine Arts, N.Y.C., 1976, N.Y. City C.C., 1975, McKee Gallery, N.Y.C., 1998, 1999-2003, N.Y. Studio Sch., 1999-2003; represented in permanent collections S.E. Mo. State U. Mus., Savannah (Ga.) Coll. Art and Design; contbg. author art jours., exhibit catalogues. Mem. Coll. Art Assn., Fedn. Modern Painters and Sculptors, Channel 13, Artist Equity (bd. dirs.), Internat. Assn. Art Critics. Avocations: archaeology, philosophy, travel. Home: 780 West End Ave New York NY 10025-5573

GITTMAN, ELIZABETH, education educator; b. NYC, Mar. 15, 1945; d. Kallman and Rebecca (Santcroos) Gittman; children: Stephen Loeb, Leslie Gulkis, Sherry Loeb. BS, NYU, 1966; MS, CUNY Queens Coll., 1969; PhD, Hofstra U., 1979, Cert. Advanced Study, 1987. Cert. ednl. adminstr., N.Y. Tchr. NYC Bd. Edn., Kew Gardens, NY, 1966-68; instr. New Sch. for Social Rsch., NYC, 1980-81; ind. cons., 1981-84; coord. instl. rsch. and evaluation Bd. Coop. Ednl. Svc. of Nassau County, Westbury, NY, 1984-94; assoc. prof. NY Inst. Tech., Old Westbury, NY, 1994-97, adj. assoc. prof., 2003; cons., 1997-98; dir. instrnl. support svc. Commack Pub. Sch., NY, 1998-2000; ind. cons., 2002—03. Adj. prof. L.I. U., Brookville, N.Y., 1987-93. Mem. high risk youth rev. com. Ctr. Substance Abuse Prevention, U.S. Dept. HHS, 1990-95; developer numerous ednl. programs. Recipient NYU Founders Day award, 1966; Hofstra U. Doctoral fellow, 1976. Mem.: ASCD, APA, Northeastern Ednl. Rsch. Assn. (membership com. 1989—90, program com. 1989—2003, nominating com. 1991—2003, program co-chair 1993, editor 1993—95, bd. dirs. 1993—98, treas. 1996—98, bd. dirs. 2003—), Nat. Coun. Measurement in Edn., Am. Evaluation Assn., Am. Ednl. Rsch. Assn., Phi Delta Kappa (rsch. rep. 1990—91, exec. bd. 1990—2003, sec. 1991—93, conf. co-chair 1992, v.p. 1993—94, pres. 1995—96, nominating com. 1996—2003, Svc. award 1998), Kappa Delta Pi. Republican. Jewish. Avocations: computer applications, reading, writing. E-mail: egittman@optonline.net.

GIULIANI, CRISTINA LYNN, broadcast technician, scriptwriter; d. Charles Fermo and Lynn Patricia (Cassidy) Giuliani; m. Tiago Lima Cruz, Feb. 21, 2002. BA in Sociology and Art, U. Calif., Santa Cruz, 1996; MA in Comm. Arts, N.Y. Inst. Tech., 2003. Location origination operator TCI of Colo. (now AT&T), Thornton, 1998—99; TV studio mgr. N.Y. Inst. Tech., N.Y.C., 2000—03; lighting dir. Atlantic Video, N.Y.C., 2003—. Bd. mem. Smart Girls Prodns., 2004—. Writer, dir. : (films) The Exchange, 1999; Donna Darling, 1999; Valentine's Day, 2003. Vol. Colo. AIDS Project, Denver, 1998—99; bd. mem. Bug Performance and Media Arts Ctr., Denver, 1998—99. Recipient Best of Show, Pallas Photography Womens Art Ctr. and Gallery, Denver, 1998. Mem.: Assn. Ind. Video and Filmmakers. Democrat. Avocations: photography, skiing, singing, songwriting. Office: Experimental Pictures 100 Remsen St #6F Brooklyn NY 11201 Office Phone: 917-918-0093.

GIULIANTI, MARA SELENA, mayor, civic worker; b. N.Y.C., June 3, 1944; d. Leon and Bertha (Jablonky) Berman; m. Donald Giulianti, May 29, 1966; children: Stacey Alexander, Michael Alan. BA, Tulane U., 1966. Social worker L.A. County Social Svcs., 1966-68; adminstrv. asst. neurosurg. cons. D. Giulianti, MD, Hollywood, Fla., 1980-83; campaign mgr. City Commr. Suzanne Gunzburger, Hollywood, 1982; mayor City of Hollywood, 1986-90, 92—. Vice chmn. Broward Employment and Tng. Adminstrn., 1987-89, 92-94, 96-2000, 01-02, chmn., 1989-90, 94-96, 2000-01, Work Force One chmn., 2002-04, chmn. pro tem, 2004—; mem. exec. bd. Fla. League Cities, Tallahassee, 1986-90, 92-94, bd. dirs., 1990-91, 94—; mem. econ. devel. pol. com. Nat. League Cities, Washington, 1987-90, human devel. policy com., 1992-94, fin., adminstrn. and intergovtl. rels. steering com., 1994-2002; mem. Broward County Met. Planning Orgn., 1986-90. Columnist The Digest, Hallandale, Fla., 2001-02, South Fla. Sun-Times, 2002—, Beach Digest, 2002-03; contbr. articles to local newspapers. Pres. Women in Distress, Broward County, 1982-83, bd. dirs., 1983-90, trustee, 1994-97; mem. exec. bd. Nat. Jewish Cmty. Rels. Adv. Coun., 1985-87; v.p. CHARLEE Family Care Homes, Broward County, 1986-88, bd. dirs., 1988-92; mem. Broward County Commn. on Status Women, 1984-86, Fla. Commn. on Drug and Alcohol Concerns, Tallahassee, 1984-85, Broward County Dem. Exec. Com., 1984-88; pres. Hills Dem. Club, 1991-94; trustee Graves Mus. of Archeol. and Nat. History, Dania, Fla., 1993-97; bd. dirs. Hollywood Econ. Growth Corp., 1994-95, 98-99; chmn. Hollywood Comty. Redevel. Agy., 1992—; v.p. South Broward unit Am. Cancer Soc., 1992-93, bd. dirs., 1993-99. Recipient Hannah G. Solomon award, 1983, Giraffe Stick Your Neck Out award Women's Advocacy--the Majority/Minority, 1986, Leadership award Leadership Hollywood Alumni, 1987, City of Peace award Israel Bonds, Broward County, 1987, Menorah award Histadrut, 1990, Juliette Gordon Low award Girl Scouts Broward County, 1997, Govt. Leadership award, ArtServe, 2002, Gracias award Hispanic Unity, 2000, Cmty. Covenant award, Broward Outreach Ctr., 2001, Breaking the Glass Ceiling award, Ziff Jewish Mus. of Fla., 2002, Spirit of Excellence award Am Bus. Women's Assn., 2003, Woman of Valor award Broward County Jewish Cmty. Ctr., 2003, Spirit Excellence award Am. Bus. Women's Assn., 2003, Founders award Chaminade-Madonna Coll. Prep., 2004; named Broward County Woman of Yr., Am. Jewish Congress, 1988, Woman of Yr. Women in Comms., Inc., 1990, Crystal Vision award Hollywood Art and Culture Ctr., 2000; Honoree Boys & Girls Clubs of Broward, 2001; inducted Broward County Women's Hall of Fame, 1996. Mem. Nat. Coun. Jewish Women (nat. bd. dirs. 1985-89), Jewish Fedn. So. Broward (chair community rels. com. 1981-82, bd. dirs. 1982-90), Broward County Med. Aux. (br. pres. 1977-78), Rotary. Democrat. Avocations: writing, volunteer work, travel. Office: PO Box 229045 Hollywood FL 33022-9045 Office Phone: 954-921-3321. Business E-Mail: mgiulianti@hollywoodfl.org.

GIUSTI, KARIN F. artist, educator; MFA in Sculpture, Yale U. Head sculpture dept. Bklyn. Coll., CUNY, 1995—. Selected exhbns., installations and projects, U. Mass. Fine Arts Ctr., Hartford, 1993, Sculpture Ctr., N.Y.C., 1993, Roosevelt Island, 1993, Real Art Ways, Hartford, 1994, La Quinta (Calif.) Open Air Mus., 1994, Bklyn. Coll. CUNY, Bklyn., 1995, Thread Waxing Space, N.Y.C., 1995, Socrates Sculpture Park, Queens, N.Y., 1995, Bklyn. Bridge, 1995, Conn. Commn. Arts, 1995, The Lytman Allyn Art Mus., 1995, Statewide Mus. Collaborative, 1995, Conn. Resource Recovery Authority, Hartford, 1996, Woodson Art Mus., Wis., 1998, Anya von Gosslen Gallery, N.Y.C., 1998, Trans Hudson Gallery, 1998, St. Mary's Cathedral, Limerick, Ireland, 1998, others, commns., PECO Energy Co., Phila., Excell Techs., Enfield, Conn., Bank of Boston, Western, Mass., others, pvt. collections. Named artis in industry resident, John Michael Kohler Arts Ctr., 1992, internat. artist's resident Lila Wallace-Reader's Digest, Givernyy, France, 1995; recipient award for innovation pub. art project Divsn. Capitol Planning and Ops., 1% for Arts Program, Boston, 1988; Guggenheim fellow, 1997—98, grantee, Conn. Commn. on the Arts, 1991, NEA, 1991, New Eng. Found. Arts, 1991. Studio: 82 Wall St Ste 1105 New York NY 10005-3600 Office: Bklyn Coll Sculpture Dept Whitehead Hall Rm 103 2900 Bedford Ave Brooklyn NY 11210-2814

GIVEN, MELISSA ANN, elementary school educator, educational consultant; b. Charleston, West Virginia, June 5, 1961; d. Robert Carl and Janet (Barnette) Rehe; m. Bruce Owen Given. BS, West Va. State Coll., 1983; MA, West Va. U., 1989. Cert. elem. edn., mental retardation K-12, preschool handicapped, severe,profound handicapped. Tchr. Kanawha County Sch., Charleston, 1984—91, Monongalia County Sch., Morgantown, W.Va., 1991—94, Gwinnett County Sch., Buford, Ga., 1995—98, Kanawha County Sch., Dunbar, W.Va., 1998—. Course grader W.Va. U., Morgantown, 1991—94; cons., cadre tchr. Office Spl. Edn. W.Va. Dept. Edn., Charleston, 1999—; qualified mental retardation profl. Braley & Thompson, St. Albans, W.Va., 2000—01; qualified mental retardation prof. cons., 1999—2002. Named Tchr. of the Yr., West Va. Fedn. Coun. Exceptional Children, 2001. Mem.: Coun. Exceptional Children, La Belle Garden Club (co-v.p. 2001—, pres. 2003—). Episcopalian. Avocations: boating, swimming, photography. Home: 848 Alta Rd Charleston WV 25314 Office: Kanawha County Sch Dunbar Middle Sch 325 27th St Dunbar WV 25064 Business E-Mail: Wvcatlover39@aol.com.

GIVENS, CHRISTINE JULIANO, music educator, elementary school educator; b. Abington, Pa., Mar. 11, 1960; d. Joseph Ernest and Mary Elizabeth Juliano; m. Barry Wallace Givens, June 10, 1990; children: Samantha, Alexandra, Robert. B in Music Edn., Fla. State U., 1983. Nat. bd. cert. music specialist, cert. tchr. Fla. Music specialist Mila Elem., Merritt Island, Fla., 1985—. Parental advisor Z88 Radio Positive Hits, Oviedo, Fla.; Brevard County chair steering com. Nat. Bd. Profl. Tchg. Stds.; lead tchr. music Brevard County Schs. Author, editor: curriculum guide Brevard County Music Curriculum, 1999, study guide Brevard County Symphony Guide, 1995—2003; editor: Brevard County Secondary Music, 2000. Judge Clavinova Piano Festival, Merritt Island, Fla., 1994—98; active Brevard County Foster Parents Assn., 2001—03. Exception Edn. grantee, Brevard Schs. Found., 2003. Mem.: Ctrl. Fla. Orff, Fla. Elem. Music Edn. Assn., Fla. Music Edn. Assn. Avocations: technology, music. Home: 2500 Long Sandy Cir Merritt Island FL 32952 Office: Mila Elem Sch 288 W Merritt Ave Merritt Island FL 32953

GIVENS, COURTNEY MICHELLE, finance company executive; b. Albemarle, Sept. 06; d. Robert and Constance Givens. BS, Western Ky. U., 1998; MBA, Thomas More Coll., 2002. Law clk. Stuart & Broz Attorneys at Law, Bowling Green, Ky., 1995—98; corp. devel. adminstrv. asst.

Western & So. Fin. Group, Cin., 1998—2000, market rsch. analsyt, 2000—03, product devel., market rsch. analyst, 2003—. Mem.: Am. Mktg. Assn. Roman Catholic. Avocations: running, travel. Personal E-mail: cmgivens@fuse.net.

GIVENS, FREDA D. school system administrator, musician; d. Leo and Mildred Givens. BS in Music Edn., Ala. State U.; degree in Edn., West Ga. U.; MusM in Edn., Jackson (Miss.) State U. Tchr. gen. music Northcutt Elem., College Part, Ga.; choral dir. Jonesboro (Ga.) Mid. Sch., 1998—2002, curriculum coord., 2002—. Min. of music Shekinah Ministries Internat., Atlanta, Ga., 2001—. Recipient Composition award, Met. Atlanta Rapid Transit Authority, 2001. Mem.: NAE, Ga. Music Educators Assn., Music Educators Nat. Conf., Internat. Reading Assn., Assn. for Supervision of Curriculum Devel. Office: Clayton County Public School 1058 Fifth Avenue Jonesboro GA 30236 Personal E-mail: fregr32@yahoo.com. E-mail: fgivens@clayton.k12.ga.us.

GIVENS, JANET EATON, writer; b. N.Y.C., July 5, 1932; d. Irving Daniel and Matilda (Schmelzle) E.; m. Richard Ayres Givens, Aug. 24, 1957; children— Susan Ruth, Jane Lucile. B.A., Queens Coll., 1953; M.A., Columbia U., 1955. Lic. tchr., N.Y. Tchr. pub. elem. schs., Silver Spring, Md., 1953-55, Mamaroneck, N.Y., 1955-59; supr. prospective tchrs., part-time lectr. Queens Coll., N.Y.C., 1959-68. Author: The Migrating Birds, 1964; Something Wonderful Happened, 1982; Just Two Wings, 1984; contbg. author: Tensions Our Children Live With, 1959. V.p. PTA, Pub. Sch. 219, Queens, N.Y., 1972-73, del. to United Parents Assn., 1971-72, editor PS 219 News, 1971-73. Home: 14711 68th Rd Flushing NY 11367-1332

GLACEL, BARBARA PATE, management consultant; b. Balt., Sept. 15, 1948; d. Jason Thomas Pate and Sarah Virginia (Forwood Pate) Wetter; m. Robert Allan Glacel, Dec. 21, 1969; children: Jennifer Warren, Sarah Allane, Ashley Virginia. AB, Coll. William and Mary, 1970, MA, U. Okla., 1973, PhD, 1978. Tchr. Harford County (Md.) Schs., 1970-71; tchr. Dept. Def. Schs., W.Ger., 1971-73; ednl. counselor U.S. Army, Germany, 1973-74; mgmt. cons. Barbara Glacel & Assocs., Anchorage, 1980-86, Washington, 1986-88; ptnr. Pracel Prints, Williamsburg, Va., 1981-85; sr. mgmt. tng. specialist Arco Alaska, Inc., 1984-85; gen. mgr. mgmt. programs Hay Systems, Inc., Washington, 1986-88; CEO VIMA Internat., Burke, Va., 1988-99, chmn. emeritus, 2000; 2d v.p., bd. dirs. Chesapeake Broadcasting Corp. Md.; prin. The Glacel Group, 2000—. Adj. prof. U. Md., 1973—74, Suffolk U., Boston, 1975—77, C.W. Post Ctr., L.I. U., John Jay Coll. Criminal Justice, N.Y.C., 1979—80, St. Thomas Aquinas Coll., N.Y.C., 1981, St. Mary's Coll., Leavenworth, Kans., 1981, Anchorage C.C., 1982; acad. adviser Ctrl. Mich. U., 1981—82; asst. prof. U. Alaska, Anchorage, 1983—85; mem. adj. faculty Ctr. for Creative Leadership, 1986—; guest lectr. U.S. Mil. Acad.; mem. U.S. Army Sci. Bd., 1986—90, U.S. Dept. Def. Sci. Bd. Quality of Life Panel, 1994—95, Def. Adv. Com. on Women in the Svcs., 2000—02, Consumer Rev. Bd. DOD Breast Cancer Rsch. Program, 2001—02; mem. adv. coun. Reves Ctr. for Internat. Studies Coll. William and Mary, 2001—; bd. dirs. The Fund for William and Mary, 2001—. Author: Regional Transit Authorities, 1983; (with others) 1000 Army Families, 1983, The Army Community and Their Families, 1989, Light Bulbs for Leaders, 1994, Hitting the Wall: Memoir of a Cancer Journey, 2001. Chmn. 172d Inf. Brigade Family Coun. Recipient Comdr.'s award for pub. svc. U.S. Dept. Army, 1984, U.S. Army Patriotic Civilian Svc. award 1991, U.S. Army Forscom Svc. award 1993, Dept. of Army Outstanding Civilian Svc. medal, 1999, Yellow Rose of Tex. award, 1999, Helping Hand Cmty. Svc. award, 1999, Coll. William & Mary Alumna medallion, 2001; AAUW grantee, 1977-78. Mem. ASTD (bd. dirs. Anchorage chpt.), APA, Soc. for Indsl. and Organizational Psychology, Instrnl. Systems Assn. (v.p. 1993-96), Soc. of Alumni Coll. of William and Mary (bd. dirs. 1992-98, v.p., 1997-98).

GLADDEN, VIVIANNE CERVANTES, healthcare consultant, writer; b. Brookhaven, Miss., Oct. 8, 1927; d. Thomas James Guillory and Edna Beatrice Torry; m. Garnett Lee Gladden; children: Mark Lee, Jeanne Sue Wood. Grad., Edwin Lester Sch. Musical Theater, 1976; LittD (hon.), Union U., 1979; BA, Golden State U., 1980, PhD, DHL, Honolulu U., 1993. Ordained to ministry Cmty. Ch. of the Best Way, 1985. Stage, film and TV actress, N.Y.C., Hollywood, 1950—64; model Harry Conover, N.Y.C., 1951; mannequin Jacques Heim, Paris, 1951; featured singer La Vien Rose, N.Y.C., 1951—52, Copa City, Fla., 1951—52; nutritional cons. Ctr. Holistic Health Cedars-Sinai Hosp., L.A., 1975—77; health and lifestyle counselor Beverly Hills and Newport, Calif., 1977—; lectr., cons. health sci. and products All Natural Products, Honolulu, Japan Life Inc., Tokyo. Radio ministry Sta. KIEV, Glendale, Calif., 1985—86; mem. adv. bd. Nat. Acad. Sports Medicine, Chgo., 1993—2002. Author (with Lee Gladden): (book) Heirs of the Gods, 1978 (Bronze Halo award So. Calif. Motion Picture Coun., 1982); author: (with Lee Gladden and Gary Couture) How to Win the Aging Game, 1979; author: Archeolinguistics, 1984. Chmn. Eco World, Hollywood, Calif., 1971; master of ceremonies Opening Ahmanson Theatre, L.A., 1976. Named to Hall of Fame, Oakwood Coll., Huntsville, Ala., 1956; recipient Gold award of merit, Martin Luther King Jr. Campaign Ctr., Port Arthur, Tex., 1988. Avocations: singing, piano, yoga, running.

GLAESER, BETSY, financial services company executive; BA in Fin., MBA in Fin., Columbia. Mgr. capital markets Mobile Corp.; dir. capital markets Deloitte and Touche LLP, N.Y.C. Mem. End Users of Derivatives Assn. (bd. dirs.), Fin. Execs. Inst. (com. corp. fin., derivatives disclosure task force). Office: Deloitte & Touche LLP 1633 Broadway New York NY 10019-6708

GLAESSMANN, DORIS ANN, former county official, consultant; b. Northampton, Pa., Feb. 18, 1940; d. Frank G. and Theresa (Fischl) Zwikl; m. Edward Glaessmann, Sept. 1, 1962; children: Edward Jr., Robert F. Grad. high sch., Northampton, 1958. Sec., bookkkeeper John F. Moore Agy., Inc., Allentown, Pa., 1958-64; ct. clk. Criminal div. Clk. of Cts. Office, Allentown, 1968-69, asst. dep. clk., 1969-76, chief dep. clk., 1976-82; clk. of cts., criminal and civil divsns. Lehigh County, Allentown, 1982-95; cons., 1995-2000; ret., 2001. Den mother, sec. Cub Scout Pack 140, Allentown, Pa., 1973-78; mem., past bd. dirs.; mem. coun. St. Peter's Evang. Luth. Ch., Allentown, 1984-89. Mem. Pa. Prothonotaries and Clks. Assn. (past pres., treas. 1993—), Pa. Elected Women's Assn. (past. sec.-treas. and pres. Lehigh Valley chpt.), Quota Internat. of Allentown (pres. 1997-99, 2d dist. lt. gov.). Democrat. Avocations: baking, reading, crocheting, walking. Home: 945 E Lynnwood St Allentown PA 18103-5250

GLANCY, DOROTHY JEAN, lawyer, educator; b. Glendale, Calif., Sept. 24, 1944; d. Walter Perry and Elva T. (Douglass) G.; m. Jon Tobias Anderson, June 8, 1979. BA, Wellesley Coll., 1967; JD, Harvard Law Sch., 1970. Bar: D.C. 1971, Calif. 1976, U.S. Dist. Ct. D.C. 1971, U.S. Ct. Appeals (D.C. cir.) 1972. Assoc. Hogan & Hartson, Wash., 1971-73; counsel U.S. Senate Judiciary Subcomm. on Constitutional Rights, Wash., 1973-74; fellow in Law & Humanities Harvard U., Cambridge, Mass., 1974-75; asst. to assoc. prof. law Santa Clara U., Calif., 1975-82, prof. law, 1984—; vis. prof. law U. Arizona, Tucson, 1979; asst. gen. counsel U.S. Dept. of Agr., 1982-83. Cons. Commn. Fed. Paperwork, Wash., 1976; dir. summer Law Study Program in Hong Kong, 1985-90; advisor Restatement, Third Property: Servitudes, 1986-97; mem. ct. tech. adv. com. Calif. Jud. Coun. Dir. legal rsch. project regarding privacy and intelligent trnsp. systems Fed. Hwy. Adminstrn., 1993-95; bd. dirs. Presidio Hts. Assn. Neighbors, 1990—. Fellow Wellesley Coll., Harvard U. Mem. ABA (chair ethics com. of sect. on natural resources, energy and environ. law, 1993-95, coun. mem. 1995-98), State Bar Calif. (mem. environ. law sect., adv. exec. com. 1993-96, advisor 1996—), Am. Assn. Law Schs. (chair environ. law sect. 1992-93, chair property sect. 1996-97), Am. Law Inst., Calif. Women Lawers, Soc. Am. Law Tchrs., Phi Beta Kappa. Democrat. Avocations: gardening, travel. Office: Santa Clara U Sch Law Santa Clara CA 95053-0001 Office Phone: 408-554-4075. E-mail: dglancy@scu.edu.

GLANCY, HELEN DIANE, literature educator; b. Kansas City, Mo., Mar. 18, 1941; d. Lewis and Edith (Wood) Hall; m. Dwane Glancy, May 2, 1964 (div. Mar. 1983); children: David, Jennifer. MFA, U. Iowa. Prof. English Macalester Coll., St. Paul. Author: (novels) The Only Piece of Furniture in the House, 1996, Pushing the Bear, 1996, Flutie, 1998, Closets of Heaven, 1999, The Man Who Heard the Land, 2001, The Mask Maker, 2002, Designs of the Night Sky, 2002, Stone Heart: A Novel of Sacajawea, 2003; contbr. short stories and essays to publs.; author: numerous poems. Named Edlestein-Keller Minn. Writer of Distinction, U. Minn., 1998; recipient Native Am. Prose award, 1991, Am. Book award, 1993, Prose-Playwriting award, Wordcraft Cir. Native Writers, 1997, Loft award of distinction, McKnight Fellowship, 1999, Cherokee medal of honor, Cherokee Honor Soc., 2001, Disting. Alumna award, U. Mo., 2003, NEA, 2003, Juniper Prize, U. of Mass. Press, 2003; fellow Many Voices, Playwrights Ctr., Mpls., 2001, Native Am. Screenwriter's fellow, UCLA, Sundance Inst., 1998. Office: Macalester Coll 1600 Grand Saint Paul MN 55105 E-mail: glancy@macalester.edu.

GLASBERG, LISA, radio personality; Disc jockey Sta. WQHT-FM, N.Y.C. Entertainment newscaster for various cable channels. Active in charity fundraisers. Avocation: jogging. Office: WQHT-FM/Emmis Broadcasting 395 Hudson St Fl 7 New York NY 10014-3600

GLASER, VERA ROMANS, journalist; b. St. Louis, Apr. 21, 1916; d. Aaron L. and Mollie (Romans); m. Herbert R. Glaser, Apr. 16, 1939; 1 dau., Carol Jane Barriger. Student, Washington U., St. Louis, George Washington U., Am. U., 1937-40. Reporter-writer Nat. Aero. mag., 1943-44; reporter Washington Times Herald, 1944-46; pub. relations specialist Great Lakes-St. Lawrence Assn., 1950-51; promotion specialist, writer Congl. Quar. News Features, 1951-54; writer-commentator radio sta. WGMS, Washington, 1954-55; mem. Washington bur. N.Y. Herald Tribune, 1955-56; press officer U.S. Senator Charles E. Potter, 1956-59; dir. pub. relations, women's div. Rep. Nat. Com., 1959-62; press officer U.S. Senator Kenneth B. Keating, 1962-63; Washington corr. N.Am. Newspaper Alliance, 1963-69, bur. chief, 1965-69; columnist, nat. corr. Knight-Ridder Newspapers, Inc., 1969-81; assoc. editor Washingtonian Mag., 1981-88, contbg. editor, 1988—; columnist Maturity News Svc., 1988-94. Mem. Pres.'s Commn. on White House Fellows, 1969, Pres.'s Task Force on Women's Rights and Responsibilities, 1970; judge 1981 Robert Kennedy Journalism Awards. Free-lance writer nat. publs.; radio and TV appearances on Stas. WTOP-TV, ABC, PBS, C-SPAN. Mem. nat. bd. Med. Coll. Pa., 1977-88; bd. dirs. Washington Press Club Found., 1986-88; bd. dirs. Internat. Women's Media Found., 1990-98. Mem. White House Corrs. Assn., Nat. Press Club (bd. govs. 1988, 89), Washington Press Club (pres. 1971-72), Cosmos Club. Unitarian Universalist. Home and Office: 4201 Cathedral Ave NW Apt 304E Washington DC 20016-4953

GLASGOW, CONSTANCE LENORE, pediatrician; b. N.Y.C., Jan. 31, 1934; d. Lester and Octavia Louisa Glasgow; m. Twitty Junius Styles, Aug. 11, 1962; children: Scott Peterson, Auria Octavia. BS, Hunter Coll., 1955; MD, SUNY Downstate, Bklyn., 1960. Pvt. practice physician, Clifton Park, NY, 1966—. Mem. ethics com. Ellis Hosp., Schenectady, NY, 1993—. Fellow: Am. Acad. Pediat.; mem.: Capital Dist. Links (co-chair nat. trends com. 1999—). Meth. Avocations: travel, music, walking. Office: Capital Care Pediat Clifton Park 942 Route 146 Clifton Park NY 12065

GLASGOW, KAREN, principal; b. N.Y.C., May 20, 1954; d. Douglas G. Glasgow. BS in Edn., U. Wis., 1976; MS in Spl. Edn., U. So. Calif., 1979; MA, Calif. State Univ., Los Angeles; PhD, Claremont Univ., 2001. Prin. Toluca Lake Elem. Sch., 2000—; adj. prof. Calif. State U. Northridge, Northridge, 2001—. Mem. Assoc. Adminstrs. L.A., Women in Ednl. Leadership, Assoc. of Calif. Sch. Adminstrn. of L.A.

GLASHAN, CONSTANCE ELAINE, retired nurse, civic worker; b. San Pedro, Calif., Oct. 15, 1932; d. Clyde Frizzell and Winifred Anne (Todd) Lapier; widow; children: Marilyn, Susan, Nanci, Linda. Dental and med. degrees, Lux Coll., San Francisco, 1953; student, Bryman Coll., San Jose, Calif., 1973; grad., Pacific Regional Staff Coll., 1998. With Family Practice Physician, 1974-80; pvt. home caregiver Carson City, Nev., 1980-91. Noon supr. Santee Sch., Franklin-McKinley Sch. Dist., San Jose, 1969-71; former leader Oak Hill 4-H Club; sec. Valley Glen Homeowner's Assn., 1967-70; exec. sec. Greater East San Jose Homeowners's Coun., 1969-82, del. to Calif. Met. Transp. Commn., 1972-82l exec. sec. UN Cultural Festival, Santa Clara County, Calif., 1969-75, exec. v.p., 1974-76; mem. Citizen's Cmty. Improvement Com., San Jose, 1969-82; former del. and mem. coordinating coun. on narcotics San Jose Police Dept., recorder for exec. bd. Anti-Crime Commn., from 1970; charter mem., exec. sec. Tchr.'s Day Com., 1970; citizen's coord. human rels. subcom. narcotics and cmty. rels. units San Jose Police Athletics League, 1971-72; former mem. bd. dirs. Pacific Neighbor's: San Jose's Sister Cities Program; formerly active Robert Smith Meml. Cultural Found.; charter mem. Performing Arts League, 1971—; charter mem. Coun. of Arts, City of San Jose; mem. Transp. Study Task Force, from 1972; former leader Brownies and Cadettes, Girl Scouts U.S.A.; formerly active San Jose C.C. Dist.; formerly active San Jose Mus. and Youth Sci. Inst., San Jose Hist. Mus., San Jose Zool. Soc.; formre mem. San Jose Mayor's Adv. Bd. Health.; vol. No. Nev. Healthfair, Carson City, 1982—, Make A Wish Found., 1984—; foster parent Spl. Olympics, 1984; nen, Advs. for Domestic Violence; lt., adminstrv. officer Carson Composite Squadron, CAP, Douglas County Composite Squadron, CAP; foster parent. Named Lady of Day, Sta. KARA, 1973. Mem. AAUW, Nat. Trust for Hist. Preservation, Beta Sigma Phi. Republican. Roman Catholic. Avocations: horseback riding, swimming, fly fishing, camping, fishing. E-mail: almabond@compuserve.com.

GLASS, DOROTHEA DANIELS, physiatrist, educator; b. N.Y.C. d. Maurice B. and Anna S. (Kleegman) Daniels; m. Robert E. Glass, June 23, 1940; children: Anne Glass Roth, Deborah, Catherine Glass Barrett, Eugene. BA, Cornell U., 1940; MD, Woman's Med. Coll. Pa., 1954; postgrad., U. Pa., 1960—61; DMS (hon.), Med. Coll. Pa., 1987. Diplomate Am. Bd. Phys. Medicine and Rehab. (guest bd. examiner 1978, 89). Intern Albert Einstein Med. Ctr., Phila., 1954-55, clin. asst. dept. medicine, 1956-59, attending phys. medicine and rehab., 1968-70, chmn. dept. phys. medicine and rehab., sr. attending, 1971-85; chief rehab. medicine VA Med. Ctr., Miami, Fla., 1985-95; clin. prof. dept. orthop. and rehab. U. Miami Sch. Medicine, 1985—. Lois Mattox Miller fellow preventive medicine Woman's Med. Coll. Pa., 1955-56, instr. preventive medicine, 1956-59, instr. medicine, 1960-62; resident phys. medicine and rehab. VA Hosp., Phila., 1959-62, chief phys. medicine and rehab., 1966-68, cons., 1968-82; asst. clin. dir. Jefferson Med. Coll. Hosp., Phila., 1963-66, Camden County Stroke Program, Cooper Hosp., Camden, N.J., 1963-66; gen. practice medicine, Phila., 1956-59; asst. med. dir., chief rehab. medicine and rehab. Moss Rehab. Hosp., Phila., 1968-70, med. dir., 1971-82, sr. cons., 1982[00bf] ; mem. active staff Temple U., Phila., 1968[00bf], asso. prof. rehab. medicine, 1968-73, prof., 1973-, dir. residency tng. rehab. medicine, 1968-82; program dir. Rehab. Rsch. and Tng. Ctr., 1977-80, chmn. dept. rehab. medicine, 1977-82; staff physician Hosp. Med. Coll. Pa., Phila., 1955-59, vis. assoc. prof. neurology, 1973-79, clin. prof., 1977-82, vis. prof., 1982-96; mem. cons. staff Frankford Hosp., Phila., 1968-82, Phila. Geriatric Center, 1975-82; mem. active staff Willowcrest-Bamberger Hosp., Phila., 1980-82; asso. phys. medicine and rehab. U. Pa. Sch. Medicine, Phila., 1962-66; asst. prof. clin. phys. medicine and rehab., 1966-68; asst. clin. dir. dept. phys. medicine and rehab. Jefferson Med. Coll., Phila., 1963-66; cons. Vols. in Medicine Clinic, Stuart, Fla., 1996—. Contbr. articles to profl. jours. Mem. profl. adv. com. Easter Seal Soc. Crippled Children and Adults Pa., 1975-82; active Goodwill Industries Phila., 1973-82, Cmty. Home Health Svcs. Phila., 1974-82, Ea. Pa. chpt. Arthritis Found., 1968-82. Recipient Humanitarian Svc. cert. Gov.'s Com. on Employment Handicapped, 1974, Outstanding Alumnae award Commonwealth of Pa. Bd., Hosp. Med. Coll. Pa., 1975, Humanitarian award Pa. Easter Seal Soc., 1981, John Eiselie Davis award Am. Kinesiotherapy Assn., 1988, Carl Haven Young Svc. award, 1994, Disting. Career award Moss Rehab. Hosp., 1997, Outstanding Svc. and Accomplishments award Fla. Soc. Phys. Medicine and Rehab., 2001, Susan B. Anthony award LWV of Martin County, 2002. Mem. AMA, Am. Acad. Med. Dirs., Am. Acad. Phys. Medicine and Rehab. (Disting. Clinician award 1995, Krusen award 2000), Am. Assn. Electromyography and Electrodiagnosis (assoc.), Am. Assn. Sex Educators, Counselors and Therapists, Am. Burn Assn., Am. Coll. Angiology, Am. Coll. Utilization Rev., Am. Congress Rehab. Medicine (bd. govs. 1979-85, pres. 1986-87, gold Key award 1989), Am. Heart Assn. (coun. on cerebrovascular disease), Am. Lung Assn. Phila. and Montgomery County (bd. dirs. 1977-79), Am. Med. Women's Assn., Assn. Acad. Physiatrists, Assn. Med. Rehab. Dirs. and Coordinators, Coll. Physicians Phila., Emergency Care Rsch. Inst., Gerontol. Soc., Internat. Assn. Rehab. Facilities, Internat. Rehab. Medicine Assn., Pan Am. Med. Assn., Fla. Med. Assn., Fla. Soc. Phys. Medicine and Rehab. (pres. 1975-77, Award for Outstanding Svc. in Rehab. Medicine 2001), Pa. Med. Soc. (phys. medicine and rehab. adv. com. 1975-82), Pa. Thoracic Soc., Delaware Valley Hosp. Coun. Forum, Phila. Med. Soc., Phila. PSRO (bd. dirs. 1975-82), Phila. Soc. Phys. Medicine and Rehab. (pres. 1968-69), Laennec Soc. Phila., Royal Soc. Health, Alpha Omega Alpha. E-mail: glassrd@earthlink.net.

GLASS, ELIZABETH L. social worker, literature educator; b. Louisville, Aug. 16, 1967; d. Joseph Gibbs and Nell Owen Glass. BA, U. Louisville, 1985, MEd, 1995; MA, Miami U., Oxford, Ohio, 1997. Editl. asst. Miami U. Press, Oxford, 1995—97; edn. coord. Tri-County Cmty. Action Agy., LaGrange, Ky., 1998—99; English prof. Jefferson C.C., Louisville, 1998—; social worker Seven Counties Svcs., Louisville, 1999—. Contbr. articles to profl. jours., short story, poem to jour., rev.; editor: Oxford Mag., 1996—97, Bachelor Bylines, 1996—97. Literacy tutor Oldham County Literacy Program, LaGrange, 1998—99. Avocation: fundraising for humane societies. Office: Seven Counties Svcs 3717 Taylorsville Rd Louisville KY 40220

GLASS, GLENDA JUNE, clinical microbiologist; b. Boise, Idaho, Oct. 8, 1950; d. James Myron and Elleen Grace (Heales) Glass; m. Tariq Khalidi, 1972 (div. 1998). BS in Med. Tech., U. Nev., Reno, 1973; grad., S.W. Sch. Bot. Medicine, 2003. Cert. clin. lab. technologist, Calif.; cert. med. technologist. Clin. microbiologist Biomed. Resources, Concord, Calif., 1976-78, M.D. Anderson Hosp., Houston, 1978-80; supr. microbiology Fong Diagnostic Lab., Sacramento, 1981-91, quality assurance technologist, 1991 92; clin. microbiologist St. Joseph's Regional Health System, Stockton, Calif., 1992—. Supporter Women Escaping a Violent Environment, Sacramento; mem. Planned Parenthood. Fleischman scholar, 1969; Doctor's Wives scholar, 1972. Mem. NOW, Am. Soc. Clin. Pathologists, Am. Herbalist Guild, Calif. Assn. Med. Lab. Technologists. Avocations: alternative energy, herbal and alternative medicine, various crafts. E-mail: sage@volcano.net.

GLASS, LAUREL ELLEN, gerontologist, developmental biologist, physician, retired educator; b. Selma, Calif., Oct. 1, 1923; d. Sydney L. and Marie (Domron) G. BA, U. Calif.-Berkeley, 1951; PhD, Duke U., 1958; MD, U. Calif., San Francisco, 1974. Teaching asst. zoology Duke U., 1953-56; rsch. assoc. Pathology Rsch. Lab. Med. Rsch. divsn. VA Hosp., Durham, N.C., 1957-58; instr. dept. anatomy U. Calif. Med. Sch., San Francisco, 1958-61, asst. prof., 1961-66, assoc. prof., 1968-72, prof., 1972-89, prof. emeritus, 1989—, prof. psychiatry, 1984-89, prof. emeritus, 1989—, dir. Ctr. on Deafness, 1984-89, adj. prof. family and community medicine, 1983-89; dir. project on adaptation to adult onset hearing loss Langley Porter Psychiat. Inst., U. Calif. Med. Sch., San Francisco, 1989-92. Mem. San Francisco adv. com. Child Health and Disability Prevention Program, 1974-79; mem. exec. com., bd. dirs. Mission Neighborhood Health Ctr., 1974-77; mem. med. adv. com. Coalition for Med. Rights of Women, 1974-87; mem. adv. bd. P.R. Orgn. Women Health Edn. Project, 1976-78; v.p. Developmental Disabilities Programs, Inc., 1976-87; Politzer vis. scholar Gallaudet U. Rsch. Inst., 1999; Powrie V. Doctor chair Deaf Studies Gallaudet U., 2000. Co-author: Beyond Refuge: Coping with Losses of Vision and Hearing in Later Life, 1989; co-editor: State of the Art: Research Priorities in Deaf-Blindness, 1985, Mental Health Assessment of Deaf Clients: A Manual, 1987, Mental Health Assessment of Deaf Clients: Special Conditions, 1989; contbr. articles to profl. jours. Mem. edn. commn. NAACP, Ocean View-Merced Heights Community Stblzn. and Improvement Project, exec. com. Ocean View-Ingleside Dist. Council, Bay Area Social Planning Council, 1969-73, adv. council Nat. Ctr. for Vision and Aging, 1986-94; bd. dirs. Service Com. on Pub. Edn., 1963-66, Constl. Rights Found., 1965-73, Deaf Counseling, Adv. and Referral Agency (DCARA), 1985-86, Hearing Soc. for the Bay Area, Inc., 1984-86, 93-96; trustee Self-Help for Hard of Hearing People, Inc., 1986-89, Glide Found., 1966-75, Gallaudet U., Washington, 1986-99; bd. govs. Pub. Advs. Inc., 1975-79; mem. San Francisco Bd. Edn., 1967-71, pres., 1969; regent Lone Mountain Coll., 1973-76; pres. United Meth. Congress of the Deaf, 1993-2001. Recipient Spl. Friend of Persons with Hearing Loss award, 1993. Mem. Am. Assn. Anatomists, Gerontol. Soc. Am., Am. Soc. on Aging, Self Help for Hard-of-Hearing People, Inc., Am. Deafness and Rehab. Assn., Phi Beta Kappa, Sigma Xi. Democrat. Methodist. Home: 1300 NE 16th Ave Apt 1408 Portland OR 97232-4405 E-mail: laurelglass@earthlink.net.

GLASS, M. SUSAN, principal; b. Johnstown, Pennsylvania, Sept. 8, 1947; d. Michael Angelo and Julia Lucy Nanna; m. Dennis Albert Glass, Sr., June 20, 1970; children: Tracy Lynn, Dennis Albert Jr. BS in Elem. edn., Indiana U., Ind., Pa., 1969; EdM, St. Francis U., Loretto, Pa., 2002. Third grade tchr. Ctrl. Cambria Sch., Ebensburg, Pa., 1969—73; second grade tchr. St. Aloysius Sch., Cresson, Pa., 1987—89; first grade tchr. All Saints Cath., Cresson, Pa., 1989—97, prin., 1997—. Sch. bd. mem. Bishop - Carroll High Sch., Ebensburg, Pa., 1999—2003; Diocesan sports com. Altoona - Johnstown Diocese, Ebensburg, Pa., 1999—2003, Misagna Challenge, Altoona, Pa., 2000—03. Pres. Little League Aux., Ebensburg, Pa., 1982—89; pres., athletics assn. Holy Name Sch., Ebensburg, Pa., 1987—90; homecoming Potato Festival Town of Ebensburg, Pa., 1197—2003. Recipient Target Scholarship, Target Stores, 2000, Outstanding Grad. Student Award, St. Francis U., 2002. Mem.: NCEA, PASCO. Avocations: reading, walking.

GLASS, NICOLE MARIE, music educator, musician; b. Colorado Springs, Colo., Oct. 4, 1969; d. Michele Marie Gutierrez and Lawrence James Saunders(Stepfather); m. Jawn Edward Glass, May 25, 1990; 1 child, Emily Elizabeth. MusB Edn., N.Mex. State U., 1999. Pvt. clarinet instr., Las Cruces, N.Mex., 1987—2002; prin. clarinetist Las Cruces Symphony Orch. N.Mex. State U., 1989—99; clarinetist El Paso (Tex.) Wind Symphony, 1993—94, Mesilla Valley Concert Band, Las Cruces, 1993—, El Paso Opera, 1998—99; student tchr. Las Cruces Pub. Schs., 1999—99, elem. music tchr., 1999—; 2nd clarinet El Paso Symphony Orch., 1999—2000; eb clarinetist El Paso Wind Symphony, 2002—. Clarinet master class instr. Onate H.S., Las Cruces, 1990—95, Artesia (N.Mex.) Ind. Sch. Dist., 1990—92, Las Cruces H.S., 1994—94; judge clarinet Gadsden (N.Mex.) Ind. Sch. Dist. Solo and Ensemble Festival, 1995—97, El Paso Ind. Sch. Dist. Solo and Ensemble Festival, 1998—, N.Mex Music Educators Assn. All-State Festival, Albuquerque, 1999—2001; clarinet master class instr. Mayfiield H.S., Las Cruces, 1996—97; officer Music Educators Nat. Conf., N.Mex State U. Collegiate Chpt., Las Cruces, 1998—99; com. mem. Las Cruces Pub. Schs. Elem. Music Curriculum Writing Com., 2000—00,

Character Counts Nat. Program, Las Cruces, 2001—; panel mem. music educators nat. conf. student session N.Mex Music Educators Assn. Ann. Conf., Albuquerque, 2000—00; new-tchr. selection com. mem. elem. music Las Cruces Pub. Schs., 2001—. Vol. Dona Ana County Youth Choir, Las Cruces, 1999—2002, Girl Scouts Am., Las Cruces, 2000—00, troop leader, 2001—02; musician local chs. Las Cruces, 1999—2003, pres. Dona Ana County Youth Choir, Las Cruces, 2002. Crimson scholar, N.Mex State U., 1999. Mem.: Music Educators Nat. Conf., N.Mex Music Educators Assn., Del Norte H.S. Phantom Knights Band (pres. 1986—87), N.Mex State U. Music Coun. (pres. 1988—90), N.Mex State U. Pride Marching Band (sec. 1988—90), N.Mex State U. Alumni Assn. (life). Liberal. Avocations: reading, music.

GLASSCOCK, HERLINDA MARTINEZ, dean; b. El Paso, Aug. 28, 1949; d. Raymond G. and Julia (Beltran) Martinez. BS, U. Tex., El Paso, 1971, MEd, 1976, EdD, 1996. Instr. El Paso C.C., 1972-78; learning specialist South Plains Coll., Lubbock, Tex., 1985-90, dean of instrn., 1991—, interim provost, 1992. Mem. com. of practitioners Tex. Higher Edn. Coordinating Bd., Austin, 1991-93. Bd. dirs. Lubbock Area Coalition for Literacy, Lubbock, 1990-93. Title VII grantee, 1975-76. Mem. Nat. Assn. Devel. Edn., Tex. Assn. Coll. Tech. Educators (exec. com. 1990—), Tex. Jr. Coll. Tchrs. Assn. Office: South Plains Coll 1302 Main St Lubbock TX 79401-3212

GLASSCOCK, JOYCE H. state official; BJ magna cum laude, U. Mo., 1985; postgrad., George Washington U., 1993. Adminstrv. asst. Bailey, Deardourff, Sipple Polit. cons., McLean, Va., 1986; legis. corr. U.S. Senator John C. Danforth of Mo., Washington, 1987; press sec. Danforth for U.S. Senate, St. Louis, 1988; field rep. Dole for Pres., St. Louis, 1988; comms. cons. Eisenhower Centennial Found., Washington, 1989; dir .pub. affairs Econ. Devel. Adminstrn., U.S. Dept. Commerce, Washington, 1989-93; press sec. Congress Dave Hobson of Ohio, Washington, 1993-94; campaign dir. Bill Graves for Gov., Topeka, 1994; chief of staff Kans. Gov. Bill Graves, Topeka, 1994—2001; Sec. of Adminstrn. State of Kans., Topeka, 2001—. Democrat. Office: Sec of Aminstrn Curtis Bldg Topeka KS 66612

GLASSER, LYNN SCHREIBER, publisher; b. Chgo., Sept. 19, 1943; d. Alexander Paul and Beatrice (Bollard) Schreiber; m. Stephen A. Glasser, Dec. 30, 1965; children: Susan, Laura, Jeffrey, Jennifer. BA, Chatham Coll., 1965. Publs. editor Inst. CLE U. Mich. Law Sch., Ann Arbor, 1966-68; asst. to dir. Practising Law Inst., N.Y.C., 1968-71; v.p., COO Law Jour. Press and Law Jour. Seminars, N.Y.C., 1971-78; exec. v.p., pub. Law & Bus./Harcourt Jovanovich, Inc., N.Y.C., 1978-86; co-pres. Prentice Hall Law & Bus., Englewood Cliffs, N.J., 1986-94; cons. Simon and Schuster, N.Y.C., 1994-95; pres. Glasser Publ. Inc., Little Falls, N.J., 1995—; co-pres. Glasser Legal Works, a Thomson Bus., 2003. Organizer, originator over 1000 CLE seminars, 1986—; organizer Woman Advt. Conf., N.Y.C., Chgo. and San Francisco, 1993-94; chmn. Woman Bus. Lawyer Conf., N.Y.C. and San Francisco, 1994. Trustee N.J. Chamber Music Soc., Montclair, 1989—, Montclair Art Mus., 1998—; Cmty. Found. of N.J., Morristown, 1995—; co-donor Lynn & Stephen Glasser Scholarship Fund, Colgate U., 1988—, Bloomfield Coll., 1993—. Office: 150 Clove Rd Little Falls NJ 07424-2138

GLASSER, PAMELA JEAN, musician, music educator; b. Livonia, Mich., June 26, 1953; d. Walter and Margaret Julia (Geersens) Glasser; m. Richard Barth Turner, Sept. 7, 1996. BEd in Music, Wayne State U., 1976; M of Music, Rice U., 1982. Prin. hornist Wyo. Symphony Orch., Casper, 1994—, Jackson Hole Symphony, 1999—2002; adj. prof. horn Casper Coll., 1998—2001; artistic dir. Casper Chamber Music Soc., 2001—; dir. music Fremont Sch. Dist. # 2, Dubois, Wyo., 2001—. Hornist music edn. programs Wyo. Arts Coun., 1993; hornist, solo performer Llangollen Eisteddfod North Wales, 1978. Mem.: SPLC, ACLU, NEA, Casper Chamber Music Soc. (ednl. liaison 1997—2001), Wyo. Edn. Assn., Am. Fedn. Musicians. Democrat. Episcopalian. Avocations: field and space science, organic gardening, cross country skiing, science fiction, crystal and mineral collecting, world music, religion. Home: PO Box 1357 Dubois WY 82513-1357 E-mail: pjglasser@yahoo.com.

GLASSMAN, CAROL, psychotherapist; b. Bklyn., Aug. 10, 1942; d. Seymour and Hilda (Lesser) Glassman; life ptnr. Susan N. Cook, May 15, 1978; 1 child, James Daniel Roberts. BA, Smith Coll., 1964; M in Social Sci., Montclair State U., 1971; MSW, SUNY Stony Brook, 1978; D of Social Work, Columbia U., 1991. LCSW. Cmty. organizer Newark Cmty. Union Project, 1964—68; supr. Vista Trinity Meth. Ch., Newark, 1969—75; exec. dir., tchr. Independence H.S., Newark, 1971—76; asst. prof. Rutgers U., New Brunswick, NJ, 1978—90; asst. prof. Sch. Social Work NYU, 1991—93, adj. prof. Sch. Social Work, 1999—; psychotherapist N.Y.C., 1978—. Contbr. articles to profl. jours. Mem.: NASW, So. Poverty Law Ctr. Democrat. Jewish. Avocations: horseback riding, running, gardening, sailing, photography. Home: 75 Bank St 2G New York NY 10014 Office: 6 Patchin Pl New York NY 10011*

GLASSMAN, CAROLINE DUBY, state supreme court justice; b. Baker, Oreg., Sept. 13, 1922; d. Charles Ferdinand and Caroline Marie (Colton) Duby; m. Harry Paul Glassman, May 21, 1953; 1 son, Max Avon. LLB summa cum laude, Williamette U., 1944. Bar: Oreg. 1944, Calif. 1952, Maine 1969. Atty. Title Ins. & Trust Co., Salem, Oreg., 1944-46; assoc. Belli, Ashe, Pinney & Melvin Belli, San Francisco, 1952-58; ptnr. Glassman & Potter, Portland, Maine, 1973-78, Glassman, Beagle & Ridge, Portland, 1978-83; justice Maine Supreme Judicial Ct., Portland, 1983-97. Lectr. Sch. Law, U. Maine, 1967-68, 80 Author: Legal Status of Homemakers in State of Maine, 1977. Mem.: ATLA, Russian Am. Rule of Law Consortium, Maine Trial Law Assn., Maine Bar Assn., Calif. Bar Assn., Oreg. Bar Assn., Am. Law Inst. Roman Catholic. Home: 56 Thomas St Portland ME 04102-3639

GLASSMAN, CYNTHIA A. commissioner; BA in econo., Wellesley Coll.; MA, PhD in econo., U. Pa. With Economists Inc., 1987—89; mng. dir. Furash & Co., Financial Svcs., 1989—97; prin. Ernst & Young, 1997—2001; commr. US SEC, 2002—. Mem.: Commn on Savings and Investment in Am., Women in Housing and Finance, Fed. Res. Bd Credit Union, Nat Economists Club. Office: US SEC 450 Fifth St NW Washington DC 20549

GLATZER, JENNA, writer; b. Bay Shore, N.Y., Nov. 27, 1975; d. Mark and Loretta Glatzer. BS in Comm., Boston U., 1997. Editor-in-chief Absolute Write.com, Rochester, NY, 1999—. Author: Taking Down Syndrome to School, 2002, Exploration of the Moon, 2002, Conquering Panic and Anxiety Disorders, 2002, greeting cards and slogans for gift products, Native American Festivals and Ceremonies, 2002; editor: Outwitting Writer's Block and Other Problems of the Pen, 2003, Words You Thought You Knew, 2003; contbr. numerous articles to profl.. jours. incl. Woman's World, Woman's Own, Writer's Digest, Salon.com, College Bound. Mem.: The Screenplayers (founding mem.), Nat. Writers Union. Episcopalian. Avocations: gardening, singing, reading, crocheting. Office: Absolute Write PO Box 93273 Rochester NY 14692

GLAVAN, DENISE LYNN, minister; b. Pueblo, Colo., Sept. 18, 1954; d. Joseph William and Anne Lyle Glavan; m. Edward Michael Wolgram, Aug. 1, 1973 (div. Apr. 22, 1982); children: Jeremy Albert, Nathan William, Luke Leon. AA in Computer Sci., U. So. Colo., 1984; MDiv, Phillips Sem., 1988. Clin. pastoral edn. Bapt. Med. Ctr. Chaplain Bapt. Med. Ctr., Oklahoma City, 1988—89; assoc. min. 1st Christian Ch., Edmond, Okla., 1989—94; dir. chaplaincy Comty. Hospice, Inc., Edmond, Okla., 1994—95; min. Nicoma Park Christian Ch. (now Faith Comty. Christian Ch.), Choctaw, Okla., 1995—. Disaster response leader Oklahoma City bombing, 1995; cons., trainer Clergy Response Inst., Oklahoma City, 1996—98, Interfaith Trauma Response Ch. World Svc., N.Y.C., 2000—. Author: (book) Hospice; A Labor of Love, 1999. Pres. Ministerial Alliance, Edmond, 1990—94; bd. dirs. Disciples Gen. Bd., Indpls., 1996—98. Democrat. Disciples Of Christ. Office: Faith Comty Christian Ch 100 S Choctaw Rd Choctaw OK 73020 E-mail: d.glavan@worldnet.att.net.

GLAVE, DIANNE D. education educator; PhD, SUNY Stony Brook, 1998; MA, SUNY Binghamton, 1992, BA, 1985. Tchg. asst. SUNY, Stony Brook, 1991—94, part time faculty, 1993—93, adj., 1993—94; asst. prof. Loyola Marymount U., L.A., 1996—. Mentor Keystone Club, Venice, Calif., 1995—96; women's leader Mt. Sinai Missionary Bapt. Ch., L.A., 1996—97; vol. Calif. African Am. Mus., L.A., 1996—97, Children's Nature Inst., Santa Monica, Calif., 1997—99; asst. Faithful Ctrl. Missionary Bapt. Ch., L.A., 1999—2003. Recipient Huggins-Quarles Award, Orgn. Am. Historians, 1995; scholar The Drusilla Dunjee Houston Meml. Scholarship, Assn. Black Women Historians, 1993; Grad. Fellowship, Smtihsonian Instn., 1994, Rsch. Grant, Rockefeller Archive Ctr., 1996, Archie K. Davis Fellowship, N.C. Soc., 1996, Andrew W. Mellon Rsch. Fellowship, Va. Hist. Soc., 1997, Study Grant, So. Bapt. Libr. and Archives, 2000.

GLAZA, MARY MARGARET, primary school educator; b. Appleton, Wis., May 8, 1951; m. Andrew Jerald Glaza, Dec. 27, 1971. BS, U. of Wis.-Stevens Point, 1969—74; MA, Lakeland Coll., 1998—2000. Tchr./ctr. dir. Head Start Preschool Program, Wood county, Wis., 1973—82; kindergarten tchr. Chilton Pub. Schools, Chilton, Wis., 1983—. Prodr./founder STAR Productions, Reedsville, Wis., 1992—2001. Dir.: h.s. and cmty. plays including Grease. Pres. Reedsville Lioness Club, Wis., 1984—2003. Recipient Citizen of the Yr., Reedsville Lions club, 1997. Mem.: Reedsville Lioness Club (pres. 1986—2003, President's Achievement award 1986, 1993, 1996). Roman Catholic. Avocations: gardening, acting, singing. Home: 412 Sunset Dr Reedsville WI 54230

GLAZE, LYNN FERGUSON, development consultant; b. Oakland, Calif., May 24, 1933; d. Kenneth Loveland and Constance May (Pedder) Ferguson; m. Harry Smith Glaze, Jr., July 3, 1957; children: Catherine, Charles Richard. BA, Stanford U., 1955, MA, 1966. Devel. dir. Greenwich Acad., Conn., 1982-84, Am. Lung Assn. of Del., 1988—89; devel. cons. St. Michael's Sch. and Nursery, Brandywine Mus., Opera Del., others, 1990—99. Author: Seasons of the Trail, 2000. Pres. Darien-Norwalk YWCA, Conn., 1973-76; sec. Darien Republican Town com., 1974-76; dist. chmn. Darien Rep. Meeting, 1974-76, mem. Rep. Nat. Conv. Platform Com., 1988; vestry St. Luke's Ch., Darien, 1979-82; justice of the peace, Darien, 1981-84; bd. dirs. Ingleside Homes, Inc., 1986-92, Henrietta Johnson Med. Ctr., 1994-97; pres. Del. ProChoice Med. Fund, 1997-99; mem. Gov.'s Small Bus. Coun., 1987, EEOC, New Castle County, 1991-94, Del. Common Cause, 1999-2004. Coro Found. fellow.

GLAZER, JANE, company executive; Pres., owner Home Trends, Inc. (formerly Quik-Cook, Inc.), Rochester, N.Y., 1983—. Active Jewish Cmty. Ctr., Rochester, v.p., chair pub. rels. com., chair pub. rels. Camp Seneca Lake com., chair pub. rels. children's com.; active Temple B'rith Kodesh; bd. dirs. Genesee Regional Health Care. Mem. Nat. Assn. Women Bus. Owners. Office: Home Trends Inc 1450 Lyell Ave Ste 106 Rochester NY 14606-2184

GLAZER, REA HELENE See KIRK, REA HELENE

GLEASON, CAROL ANN, mental health nurse, educator; b. Fairfield, Iowa, Mar. 6, 1945; d. Maurice Alvin and Geraldine (Cook) Crist; m. Michael Gleason Jr., Nov. 26, 1966 (div. Nov. 1980); children: Daniel Lee, Raymond Joe, Christopher John, Crystal Dawn. ADN, Indian Hills Coll., 1977; AS in Adminstrn., Des Moines Area Coll., 1982; BSPA in Health Care, St. Joseph's, 1985; cert. nurses aides edn., U. Iowa, 1989; BSN, Drake U., 1997; grad., Nat. Inst. Paralegal Arts Sci., 2002. Lic. nursing home adminstr., Iowa; cert. psychiat. and mental health, gerontology ANA. Staff night charge nruse Mahaska Manor Nursing Home, Oskaloosa, Iowa, 1977; dir. nursing Tower Park Nursing Home, Oskaloosa, 1977-78, Pleasant Park Nursing Home, Oskaloosa, 1978-85, adminstr., 1985-86; staff nurse ICU-CCU Ottumwa (Iowa) Regional Hosp., 1986; psychiat. nurse Knoxville (Iowa) Vets. Hosp., 1986—. Coord., instr. Iowa Ednl. inst., Oskaloosa, 1987—; cons. Tower Park Nursing Home, Oskaloosa, 1985-87, Siesta Park Nursing Home, 1985-87, Mahaska Manor, 1993-95. Mem.: NAFE, Am. Fedn. Govt. Employers. Democrat. Roman Catholic. Avocations: home bus./gifts, football games, walking, boating. Home: 220 Keomah Vlg Oskaloosa IA 52577-9671

GLEASON, HARRIET HALL, nurse; b. Otranto, Iowa, May 11, 1923; d. Roy Francis Sr. and Amy Ruth (Read) G. RN, Kahler Sch. Nursing, Rochester, Minn., 1947; BS, BA, Hartwick Coll., 1956. RN, N.Y. Office nurse Mayo Clinic, Rochester, 1947-53, various hosps., Oneonta, N.Y.C., 1953—56; instr. Fairview Hosp., Mpls., 1956-57; clin. instr. Swedish Hosp., Mpls., 1958-59; supr. sick children unit Mt. Sinai Hosp., 1959-60; ward nurse various temp. agys., N.Y.C., 1960-82; gen. and spl. duty nurse various vol. assignments, Morgantown, W.Va., 1982—. Author: (cookbooks) Therapeutic Diets, 1980, Be Brave, 1994, (essays) I Understand, 1994. Active ARC; membership com., vol. Rep. Party Caucus, Mpls., N.Y.C. and W.Va., 1960-82, 92, 93. Mem. AAUW, Tri Beta, Zeta Tau Alpha (Pan Hellenic rep.). Lutheran. Avocations: reading, spectator sports, volunteer work, music appreciation.

GLEASON, JEAN BERKO, psychology educator; b. Cleve., Dec. 19, 1931; d. Arthur E. and Alice (Gelberger) Berko; m. Andrew Mattei Gleason, Jan. 26, 1959; children: Katherine, Pamela, Cynthia. AB, Radcliffe Coll., 1953, AM, 1955, PhD, 1958. USPHS fellow MIT, 1958—59; research assoc. VA Med. Ctr., Boston, 1961—2000; vis. asst. prof. psychology Boston U., 1972—73, assoc. prof., 1973—76, prof., 1976—, chairperson dept. psychology, 1985—89, acting chair dept. psychology, 1997, dir. grad program devel. psychology, 1975—78, 1982—85, dir. grad. program human devel., 1997—2002; research assoc. edn. Harvard U., Cambridge, Mass., 1968—70, prin. research assoc. psychiatry, 1970—72. Rsch. scholar in residence Inst. Linguistics, Hungarian Acad. Sci., 1981, 83; mem. mental retardation rsch. com. Nat. Inst. Child Health and Human Devel., 1981-85; trustee Ctr. for Applied Linguistics, Washington, 1989-94. Author: The Development of Language, 1983, 4th edit., 1997, 5th edit., 2001, 6th edit., 2004, You Can Take It with You, 1989, Psycholinguistics, 1993, 2nd edit., 1998; mem. editl. bd. Child Development, 1971—77, Discourse Processes, 1982—2002, assoc. editor Language, 1997—2000; contbr. articles. Recipient Editors award Jour. Speech and Hearing Research, 1970. Fellow: APA, AAAS (coun. del. 2002—); mem.: ACLU, Internat. Assn. for Study of Child Lang. (pres. 1990—93), Soc. for Rsch. Child Devel., Linguistic Soc. Am. (chmn. program com. 1980—81, resolutions com. 2004), Radcliffe Alumni Assn. (bd. dirs. 1969—72), Radcliffe Grad. Soc. (past pres.), Gypsy Lore Soc. (exec. bd. 1983—87, 1992—2002, pres. 1996—99, exec. bd. 2003—), Acad. Aphasia, Phi Beta Kappa (pres. Radcliffe chpt. 1965—68). Home: 110 Larchwood Dr Cambridge MA 02138-4639 Office: Boston U Dept Psychology 64 Cummington St Boston MA 02215-2407 E-mail: gleason@bu.edu.

GLECKLER, LOIS EILEENE, occupational therapist; b. New Waterford, Ohio, Sept. 7, 1938; d. Russell Abner and Ella Catherine (Blazevich) Allmon; m. Donald LeRoy Gleckler, July 27, 1957; children: Sheryl Duerring, Mark B., Catherine Hubbs. Degree in Occupl. Therapy, Stark State Coll. Tech., 1999. Paraprofl. perception tchr. Salem City Schs., Salem, Ohio, 1972—86; vision therapist Walton & Bloom O.D., Hastings, Mich., 1986—93, Joel S. Riley O.D. Inc., Canton, Ohio, 1993—95; visual motor perception therapist Perry M. Lieberman O.D., Canton, 1995—. Cons. Hastings City Sch., 1987—89. Leader Campfire Girls Inc., Salem, Ohio, 1968—82; canvaser Am. Diabetes Assn., Louisville, Ohio, 1993—; den mother Boy Scouts Am., Salem, 1968—72. Mem.: Cath. Daughter of Americas #1021, Stark State Coll. Tech. Alumni Assn., Garden Study Club Salem (com. chmn. 1965—, pres. 1996—98, Best of Show 1st Place Flower Show award 1999). Avocations: square dancing, gardening, golf, bowling, bicycling. Office: Dr Perry M Lieberman OD 1340 Market St N Canton OH 44714 Home: 6488 Saint Augustine Dr NW Canton OH 44718-4039

GLEICH, CAROL S. health professions education executive; b. Kewanee, Ill., Jan. 18, 1935; d. Carl and Edna (Krause) Gleich. BA, U. Iowa, 1958, MS, 1967, PhD in Health Sci. Edn., 1972. Cert. clin. chemistry technologist, Nat. Registry Clin. Chemistry. From instr. to asst. prof. pathology U. Iowa Sch. Medicine, Iowa City, 1972-77, edn. specialist divsn. allied health, 1977-88, chief resource devel. sec., 1988-90, health manpower edn. officer, physician manpower and credentialing, chief spl. projects and data analysis br. divsn. medicine, 1991-95, exec. sec. coun. grad. med. edn., 1996-99; dir. area health edn. ctr. nat. program Bur. Health Professions, Health Resources & Svcs. Adminstrn., Rockville, Md., 1977—. Allied health cons. to Egypt; gov. cons. in internat. health profl. ed., Russia, 1993-99; dir. Geriatric Edn. Ctrs. PHS; adj. assoc. prof. U. Md. Sch. Medicine; mem. Iowa Health Manpower Com., 1972—; cons. U. Wis. System Acad. Affairs, 1974; panelist and participant workshops; presenter and U.S. chief del. internat. congress. Assoc. editor Am. Jour. Med. Tech., 1974-83, Jour. Allied Health, 1982-85; contbr. articles to profl. jours. Mem. Am. Soc. Clin. Pathologists (assoc., cert. med. technologist, sec. ASCP Bd. Registry 1975-77), Am. Soc. Clin. Lab. Sci., D.C. Soc. Med. Tech. (Outstanding Med. Technologist of Yr. 1975), Beta Beta Beta (Pub. Health Svc. award 1995), Alpha Mu Tau. Home: 14800 Rocking Spring Dr Rockville MD 20853-3635 E-mail: carolgleich@mindspring.com.

GLEN, NIKI, artist; b. Milw., Nov. 14, 1950; d. Alan and Janet (Marx) G.; children: Dana Alan Knops, Laramie Ann Glen. BS in Art Edn., U. Wis., 1973. Cert. in art edn. K-12. Pub. artist, muralist numerous orgns., various locations, 1973—; co-founder Madison (Wis.) Graphics, 1973-76; art educator various schs. various locations, 1973—; dir. S.W. Pub. Art Group, Phoenix, Ariz., 1996—. Exhibited in group shows Corcoran Gallery, Washington, 1986, Williams Ratliff Gallery, Sedona, Ariz., 1988, Veneble Neslage Galleries, Washington, 1989-92, Spirit of N.Mex. Art Exhbn., Washington, 1990, Marin-Price Galleries, Bethesda/Chevy Chase, Md., 1992, Am. Bank Gallery, Chevy Chase, 1994, Artisimo Gallery, Scottsdale, Ariz., 1995, Nat. Soc. Mural Painters Centennial Exhibit, N.Y.C., 1996, Exit Gallery, N.Y.C., 1996, 1st Internat. Pub. Art and Mural Congress, Mexico City, 1998, Exit Gallery, NYC, 2002, Sietz Gallery, Harrisburg, Pa., 2003 (art installation) Phoenix Coll., Ariz. Ctr. Blind and Visually Impaired, Phoenix Childrens Hosp.; featured in publs. including Community Murals, 1984, Street Murals: The Most Exciting Cities of America, Britain and Western Europe, 1982, The Art of Handmade Tile, also numerous covers and illustrations for textbooks and periodicals. Pres. Arts and Creativity in Early Chlidhood, 1993-96; bd. dirs. Gaynor Mus. and Found., 1993-95, Cmty. Built Assn., 2000-; mem. Ariz. Alliance for Art Edn., 1990-95. Recipient Orchid award City of Madison, 1975, Tempe Diablo award of excellence in edn., 1996, 97, Livable Cities award, 2001, Beautification award Art in Pvt. Devel.; Ariz. Artist Project grantee Ariz. Commn. on Arts, 1994, Phoenix Children's Hosp.; grantee numerous orgns. including Atlantic Richfield, City of Whitewater, The Mills Corp., Phoenix Arts Commn., Medtronics Inc., Phoenix (Ariz.) Coll., NEA, YMCA, City of Tempe. Mem. Nat. Soc. Mural Painters. Avocations: swimming, reading, sailing, dance.

GLENDENING, TERRY SKY, psychologist; b. Cin., Apr. 19, 1961; BA, Cornell U., 1983; MA, U. Cin., 1986, PhD, 1995. Lic. psychologist Ohio, Ky., cert. corrective thinking practitioner 1999. Dir. recreation Indian Hill Cmty. Edn., Cin., 1986—92; pvt. practice in clin. psychologist, psychotherapist, 1982—. Tchg. asst. Cornell U., Ithaca, NY, 1982—83; cons. IHHS Peer Counseling Program, Indian Hill, Ohio, 1987—96; lectr. in field. Author: (book) Thought Patterns in Depression and Somatization, 1986, Cognitive Specificity in Non-Clinical Depressive Manifestations of Distress, 1995, Timeless Parenting Techniques: Fair, Firm and Functional, 2002; author: (workshop series) Coping Skills for a New Millenium, 2000. Vol. recreation for disabled Camp Stepping Stones, Cin., 1997—98; vol. Spl. Olympics, Cin., 1997—98. Named Outstanding Young Woman of Am., 1986; recipient Sons and Daughters Am. Revolution award, 1974. Mem.: APA, Ohio Psychol. Assn., Psi Chi. Avocations: hiking, camping, art, sports, rock collecting.

GLENDON, MARY ANN, law educator; b. 1938; BA, U. Chgo., 1959, JD, 1961, M Comparative Law, 1963. Bar: Ill. 1964, Mass. 1980. Legal intern. EEC, Brussels, Belgium, 1963; assoc. Mayer, Brown & Platt, Chgo., 1963-68; prof. Boston Coll., 1968-86; vis. prof. Harvard U., 1974-75, prof., 1986—. Vis. prof. U. Chgo., 1983, 84, 86. Author: Rights Talk, 1991, A Nation Under Lawyers, 1994, A World Made New: Eleanor Roosevelt and the Universal Declaration of Human Rights, 2001. Foreign Law fellow U. Libre de Bruxelles, 1962-63, Ford Found. fellow, 1975-76. Mem. Am. Acad. Arts & Scis., Pres.'s Coun. Bioethics. Office: Harvard U Law Sch Cambridge MA 02138

GLENN, CONSTANCE WHITE, art museum director, educator, consultant; b. Topeka, Oct. 4, 1933; d. Henry A. and Madeline (Stewart) White; m. Jack W. Glenn, June 19, 1955; children: Laurie Glenn Buckle, Caroline Glenn Galey, John Christopher. BFA, U. Kans., 1955; grad., U. Mo., 1969; MA, Calif. State U., 1974. Dir. Univ. Art Mus. & Mus. Studies program, from lectr. to prof. Calif. State U., Long Beach, 1973—. Art cons. Archtl. Digest, L.A., 1980-89. Author: Jim Dine Drawings, 1984, Roy Lichtenstein: Landscape Sketches, 1986, Wayne Thiebaud: Private Drawings, 1988, Robert Motherwell: The Dedalus Sketches, 1988, James Rosenquist: Time Dust: The Complete Graphics 1962-92, 1993, The Great American Pop Art Store: Multiples of the Sixties, 1997, The Artist Observed: Photographs by Sidney B. Felsen, 2003; contbg. author: Encyclopedia Americana, 1995—, The Grove Dictionary of Art, 1989—, Double Vision: Photographs from the Strauss Collection, 2001, Carrie Mae Weems: The Hampton Project, 2000. Vice-chair Adv. Com. for Pub. Art, Long Beach, 1990-95; chair So. Calif. adv. bd. Archives Am. Art, L.A., 1980-90; mem. adv. bd. ART/LA, 1986-94, chair, 1992. Recipient Outstanding Contbn. to Profession award Calif. Mus. Photography, 1986, Disting. Scholarly and Creative Achievement award, Calif. State U. Long Beach, Women of Distinction award Soroptimist Internat., 1999. Mem. Am. Assn. Mus., Assn. Art Mus. Dirs. (trustee 2000-02), Coll. Art Assn., Art Table, Long Beach Pub. Corp. for the Arts (arts adminstr. of yr. 1989), Kappa Alpha Theta. Office: Univ Art Mus 1250 N Bellflower Blvd Long Beach CA 90840-0006 Office Phone: 562-985-5761.

GLENN, EVELYN NAKANO, social sciences educator; b. Sacramento, Aug. 20, 1940; d. Makoto and Haru (Ito) Nakano; m. Gary Anthony Glenn, Nov. 20, 1962; children: Sara Haruye, Antonia Grace, Patrick Alexander. BA, U. Calif., Berkeley, 1962; PhD, Harvard Coll., 1971. Asst. prof. sociology Boston U., 1972-84; assoc. prof. sociology Fla. State U., Tallahassee, 1984-86; prof. sociology SUNY, Binghamton, 1986-90; prof. sociology women's and ethnic studies U. Calif., Berkeley, 1990—. Mem. bd. scholars Am. Nat. Mus., L.A., 1989—; vis. rsch. scholar Murray Rsch. Ctr., Radcliffe Coll., 1989-90. Author: Issei, Nisei, Warbride, 1986, Unequal Freedom: How Race and Gender Shaped American Citizenship and Labor, 2002; editor: Mothering: Ideology, Experience and Agency, 1994; adv. editor Gender and Soc., 1986-90, Frontiers, 1991-93, Editl. Collective Feminist Studies, 1999-; dep. editor Am. Sociol. Rev., 1999-2003; contbr. articles to profl. publs. Named Japanese Am. of Biennum, Japanese Am.

Citizens League, 1994; recipient Article prize Assn. Black Women Historians, 1993. Mem. Am. Sociol. Assn. (mem. coun. 1990-94), Soc. for Study of Social Problems (pres. 1998-99, v.p. 1988-90, bd. dirs. 1984-87). Office: Univ Calif 2241 College Ave Berkeley CA 94720-1002

GLENN, IDELLA GOODSON, director; b. Darlington, S.C., May 9, 1962; d. James and Ruth Goodson; m. Michael Anthony Glenn, Dec. 24, 1983; children: Septima, Natalie. BS, Furman U., 1986; EdM, U. S.C., 1996. Adminstrv. asst. Wilson's Computer App., Simponsville, SC, 1985—86, software support/office mgr., 1986—88; computer specialist G&T Industries, Greer, SC, 1988, ops. mgr., 1989—90; records mgr., registrar Spartanburg (S.C.) Tech. Coll., 1991—96; dir. multicultural affairs Furman U., Greenville, SC, 1996—. Mem. diversity adv. coun. Greenville Hosp. Sys., 2001—; adv. bd. mentor Peace Ctr., Greenville, 2002—, S.C. Area Health Edn. Consortium, Greenville, 2002—. Vol. Ctr. for Ednl. Equity, Greenville, 2001—; bd. dirs. Urban League Upstate, Greenville, 1999—, Red Cross-Upstate S.C. Chpt., Greenville, 1999—. Mem.: S.C. Assn. for Access and Equity (pres. 2002—). Baptist. Home: 740 Meece Bridge Rd Taylors SC 29687 Office: Furman Univ 3300 Poinsett Hwy Greenville SC 29613

GLENN, ROSEMARY, writer; b. Haverhill, Mass., Apr. 26, 1932; d. Daniel Joseph Archetti and Helen Margaret Estill, Edward Leland Geissler (Stepfather), John James Estill (Stepfather); m. Richard Hall Ryan, Jan. 22, 1952 (div. Sept. 1955); 1 child, Richard Hall Ryan ; m. Michael Ohanian, Nov. 29, 1955 (div. May 1960); 1 child, Elena Louise Ohanian-Siegel ; m. Douglas Eugene Germain, June 1961; m. Maxwell Dewey Williams, Nov. 1963 (div. Nov. 1967); m. Gary Lloyd Glenn, Aug. 31, 1992 (dec.). Student, Glendale (Calif.) City Coll., 1959—60, L.A. City Coll., 1964—65, San Fernando Valley City Coll., Van Nuys, CA, 1979—81. Quality assurance engr. Am. Electronics, L.A., 1966—69, Rantec Corp., Calabasas, Calif., 1969—71; freelance tech. writer San Fernando Valley, Calif., 1971—73; programmer, analyst Lockheed-Calif. Co., Burbank, 1973—93; freelance writer, 1993—. Author: (novels) Holy Orders, 2001, Stalemate, 2003. Asst. Rep. Presdl. Campaign, L.A., 1963—64. Mem.: Am. Soc. Quality Control Engrs. (assoc.), Nat. Writers Union. Independent. Avocation: substance abuse counseling. Personal E-mail: rosemary@rmglenn.com.

GLENN, RUTH ESTHER MURPHY, counseling psychologist; b. Havana, Ala., Apr. 14, 1928; d. Willie and Olivia (Brown) Murphy; m. Ephriam Martin Sr., Apr. 7, 1947 (div. Nov. 1960); children: Ruth Taylor, Joyce Strickland, Ephriam Martin, Jr.; m. James Calvin Glenn, Mar. 29, 1962; children: Adrain Rozia, Andre Garnett. BA, Chgo. State U., 1974; MA, Govs.' State U., 1976. Diplomate Am. Psychotherapy Assn. Ammunition inspector Joliet (Ill.) Arsenal Ammunition Plant, 1951-53; mental health technician I, II, III, to supr. I Manteno (Ill.) Mental Health Ctr., 1954-64; social svc. aide II Manteno(Ill.) mental health ctr., 1971 74; social worker II, mental health specialist I, II Manteno (Ill.) Mental Health Ctr., 1974-81, psychologist II, III, 1981-85; social caseworker Dist. 259 Elem. Sch., Hopins Park, Ill., 1966-67; psychologist III Tinley Park (Ill.) Mental Health Ctr., 1985-92. Mem. reorganization and planning com. Tinley Park Mental Health Ctr., 1985-86; mem. libr. and med. record rev. bds., Manteno Mental Health Ctr., 1972-83; dir. of youth programs St. Anne Woods Chapel Comm. Ch., Ill., 1970-81; adv. bd. Pembroke Voters Civic League, Ill., 1964-72. Founder/editor: The Community Voice newsletter, 1955; co-author: Psychiatric Treatment Manual (Manteno Mental Health Ctr.), 1983. Vol. group counselor Thresholds(Ill.) Drug Abuse Program, Kankakee, Ill, 1974; trustee AFSCME, 1995; mem. exec. bd. dirs. #57/Retirees, Kankakee, Ill., 1999; classroom vol. Dist. #259 Elem. Sch., Hopkins Park, 1991; bd. dirs. Pembroke Voters Civic League, 1964; establisher and dir. Money Find for Coll., St. Anne, 1993. Named Key Lay Leader of the Yr., Internat. Coun. of Comm. Chs., Frankfort, Ill., 1993; recipient Vol. of Yr. Svc. award NAACP, Kankakee, 1995, Ill. Woman of Achievement award, 2000, others. Mem. AAUW, NAACP (life), ACA, Ill. Counseling Assn., Ill. Assn. for Assessment in Counseling, Nat. Coun. Negro Women, Ill. Mental Health Counselors Assn., Chgo. State U. Alumni Assn. (life), Govs. State U. Alumni Assn. Democrat. Avocations: reading, travel, gardening, writing. Home: 13334 E 6000 S Rd Saint Anne IL 60964-4562

GLENN, VICKI LYNN, mathematician, educator; d. Nolen E. and Virginia Buchanan; m. Steve Glenn, 0000; children: Jill Rene McDill, Steven Scott. BS, East Tex. State U., 1971, MS, 1981. Profl. Tchr. Tex., 1971, Counselor Tex., 1981, Supr. Tex., 1994. Tchr. Mesquite Ind. Sch. Dist., Tex., 1971—92, math coord., 1992—. Ad hoc com. mem., webccat Region 10 Ednl. Svc. Ctr., Richardson, Tex., 2000—; tnt com. Mesquite Ind. Sch. Dist., 1994—. Sound com. for worship svc. Shiloh Ter. Bapt. Ch., Dallas, 2001—03, worker with young adults, 1999—2003. Mem.: McMath, Mesquite Edn. Assn., Assn. Tex. Profl. Educators, Nat. Coun. Tchrs. Math. Baptist. Avocations: statistician for football sports broadcasts, reading, grandchildren.

GLESMANN, SYLVIA-MARIA, artist; b. Spardorf/Erlangen, Germany, June 8, 1923; arrived in the US, 1925; d. Rolf-Joseph and Auguste (Schultheiss) Hoffmann; m. John Brainerd Glesmann, Apr. 30, 1948; children: Glenn M., Eric B., Jonathan M. Degree, Acad. Fine Arts, Nurnberg, Germany, 1940, Acad. Fine Arts, Munich, 1944. Instr. Somerville Adult Edn. Exhibited in group shows at Carrier Clinic, 1993, Bergen Mus., 1993, Morris Mus., 1993, Nabisco Brands, 1993, Cultural and Heritage Gallery, Somerville, NJ, 1993-95, Salmagundi Club, 1994, Garden State Water Color Assn., Princeton, NJ, 1994, Barrons Art Ctr., 1993, Art on the Ave. Group Show of Flowers, 1991, Nat. Assn. Women Artists, NYC, 1991, 1994, SoHo, 1994, Bridgewater NJ County Libr., 1996, 2001-02, Nat. Assn. Women Artists New World Art Ctr., Soho, NY, 1999, Children's Specialized Hosp., Westfield, NJ, July 2002, Barrons Art Ctr, Woodbridge, NJ, 2002; others; one-woman shows include Childrens Specialized Hosp., Mountainside, NJ, 2002, N.U.I. Corp., Bridgewater, 1987, Salmagundi Club, NYC, 1995, 2000, Am. Artists Profl. League, 1995-97, Somerset County Libr., Bridgewater, 1996, 2001-02, Barrons Art Ctr., Woodbridge, NJ, 1997, Barrons Art Ctr., Bridgewater Mcpl. Bldg, 1999-2001, Nat. Assn. Women Artists (NYC), Balt. Conv. Ctr., Balt., 2000 (Editors Choice 2002), Bridgewater Libr., 2001, Nat. Assn. Women Artists, UN Visitors Lobby, 2002, Georgio Zikos Gallery, New Hope, Pa., 2002-03; others; author numerous poems. Recipient over 50 awards in water color, Editor's Choice award, 1998, Poetry Editors Choice award, 2002, Poetry award for poem, 2003. Mem. Am. Artists Profl. League (pres. NJ chpt. 1988-91), 2001, Bridgewater NJ Artists shows, 2002-2003, Nat. Assn. Woman Artists, Raritan Valley Arts Assn. (pres. 1976-78), Somerset Art Assn. (chairwoman 10th outdoor art show), Nat. Assn. Women Artists, Salmagundi Club, Nat. Mus. for Women in Arts (charter mem.). Lutheran. Avocations: sports, music, reading, poetry. Home and Office: 36 Twin Oaks Rd Bridgewater NJ 08807-2343

GLEUE, LORINE ANNA, elementary school educator; b. Lucas, Kans., Feb. 12, 1926; d. Otto Martin and Bertha Marie (Luker) Becker; m. Fred Christoph Gleue, June 12, 1947; children: David Jean, Steven Randolph, Paul Frederick. Assoc., Cloud County C.C., 1969; BS in Edn., Ft. Hays (Kans.) State Coll., 1971; MS in Elem. Edn., Ft. Hays State U., 1977; reading specialist degree, Kans. State U., 1984. Cert. tchr., Kans. Elem. tchr., Coffey County, Kans., 1944-47; libr. Belleville (Kans.) Pub. Libr., 1960-67, Carnegie Free Pub. Libr., Concordia, Kans., 1967-68; elem. tchr. Chester, Nebr., 1971-72, Washington (Kans.) Unified Sch. Dist. #222, 1972-75; Chpt. I program instr. Washington, Kans., 1975-87; tchr. Republic County Schs., Mankato, and USD #333, Concordia, 1987—. Producer, co-owner Gleue's-On-The-Go Shows, Flying Carpet Story Hours, Lorine's Letter Writing Svc. to Shut-ins and Small Fry, Mothers' Mender, Gleue-Gomoll Home-Loomed Rag Rugs; co-owner, developer Acres for Wildlife Resource Ctr., Belleville. Published poet; contbr. articles to profl. jours. Mem. book selection com. Kans. State Reading Cir., Topeka, 1979-81; mem. PTA, 1981-87; pres. Washington chpt. Tchrs. Assn., 1977-81. Recipient Golden Poet award, 3d Ann. Poetry Conv., Las Vegas, Nev., 1987, World of Poetry Golden Poet award, 1988, 1989, 1990, 1991, 1992, 3d pl. award, Poetry Rendezvous, 1991, Best of Fair award, 2000, 2001, Blue Ribbon award, 1990—2001, Celebrate Literacy award, Internat. Reading Assn., 1993, Kans. Gov.'s Leadership Commendation, 1979, 1981, Citation of Appreciation, Assn. Retarded Citizens, 1981, Kans. Nat. Edn. Assn., 1979, 1980. Mem. Kans. Authors Club, Kans. Reading Assn. (mem. thunderbird coun.), Internat. Soc. of Poets, Fort Hays Alumni Assn. (life), Washington Sign Lang. Club (charter). Avocations: reading, travel, originating scripts for 35mm slide presentation.

GLICK, CYNTHIA SUSAN, lawyer; b. Sturgis, Mich., Aug. 6, 1950; d. Elmer Joseph and Ruth Edna (McCally) G. AB, Ind. U., 1972; JD, Ind. U.-Indpls., 1978. Bar: Ind. 1978, U.S. Dist. Ct. (so. dist.) Ind. 1978, U.S. Dist. Ct. (no. dist.) Ind. 1981, U.S. Supreme Ct. 2000. Adminstrv. asst. Gov. Otis R. Bowen of Ind., 1973-76; dep. pros. atty. 35th Jud. Cir., LaGrange County, Ind., 1980-82, pros. atty., 1983—90; pvt. practice LaGrange, Ind., 1979—. Campaign aide Ind. Rep. State Ctr. Com., Indpls., 1972-73; chmn. La Grange County Rep. Ctrl. com. Named Hon. Spkr., Ind. Ho. of Reps., 1972, Sagamore of the Wabash, Gov. of Ind., 1974. Fellow Ind. Bar Found.; mem. ABA, Ind. State Bar Assn., LaGrange County Bar Assn. (pres. 1983-86), DAR, Order Eastern Star, Phi Delta Phi, Delta Zeta. Methodist. Home and Office: 113 W Spring St Lagrange IN 46761-1843 Office Phone: 260-463-7414.

GLICK, DEBORAH J. state legislator; b. N.Y.C. MBA, Fordham U. Formerly dir. gen. svc. Dept. Housing, Preservation and Devel., N.Y.C.; mem. N.Y. State Assembly, mem. children and families com., govt. employees com. Mem. environment conservation coms., gov. employment coms., ways and means com., chair social svcs. com., higher edn. com., N.Y. State Assembly. Mem. Greenpeace, N.Y. Zool. Soc., Defenders of Wildlife. Office: NY State Assembly LOB Rm 844 Albany NY 12248-0001

GLICK, JANE MILLS, biomedical researcher, educator; b. Memphis, Nov. 26, 1943; d. Albert Axtell Jr. and Mary Louise (Baynes) Mills; m. John Harrison Glick, May 25, 1968; children: Katherine Anne, Sarah Stewart. AB, Randolph-Macon Woman's Coll., 1965; PhD, Columbia U., 1971. Postdoctoral trainee NIH, Bethesda, Md., 1971-73; postdoctoral fellow Sch. of Medicine Stanford (Calif.) U., 1973-74; rsch. asst. prof. biochemistry Sch. Dental Medicine U. Pa., Phila., 1974-77; asst. prof. biochemistry Med. Coll. Pa., Phila., 1977-82, assoc. prof. biochemistry, 1982-90, prof. biochemistry, 1990-94; sr. rsch. investigator Inst. Human Gene Therapy, U. Pa. Sch. Medicine, 1994—2002; faculty adminstr. cell and molecular biology group Sch. Medicine U. Pa. Mem. metabolism study sect. NIH, 1993-97; adj. assoc. prof. U. Pa. Sch. Medicine, 1996—. Assoc. editor: Jour. Lipid Rsch., 1985-86, mem. editorial bd., 1987-99; contbr. articles to profl. jours. Trustee Episcopal Acad., Merion, Pa., 1989-95, Swarthmore Presbyn. Ch., 1995-97, pres. 1997. Recipient Rsch. Svc. award NIH, 1975-77, Young Investigator award, 1980-83, Teaching award Lindback Found., 1985. Mem. AAAS, AAUP (sec. 1990-92), Arteriosclerosis Coun. Am. Heart Assn. (program com. 1990-93), Am. Soc. for Biochemistry and Molecular Biology, Am. Soc. for Human Genetics, Phi Beta Kappa, Sigma Xi. Presbyterian. Office: U Pa Sch Medicine 632 BRB II/III 421 Curie Blvd Philadelphia PA 19104

GLICK, KAREN LYNNE, college administrator; b. Bucyrus, Ohio, Sept. 2, 1945; d. Phillip Dole and Bernice Grace Glick; children: M. Todd, K. Christine. BSJ, Bowling Green State U., 1967, MA, 1979. Editor Bowling Green (Ohio) State U., 1972-74; account exec. Howard E. Mitchell, Jr., Advt., Findlay, Ohio, 1974-77; asst. to dir. student devel. program Bowling Green State U., 1977-79; dir. pub. info. Bluffton (Ohio) Coll., 1980-83; asst. to v.p. for instl. advancement Findlay (Ohio) Coll., 1983-85; assoc. dir. devel. Bluffton Coll., 1985-90; assoc. dir. divsnl. support Miami U. Ohio, Oxford, 1990-93; sr. regional dir. devel. U. Ill. Found., Urbana, 1993—2003, assoc. campaign dir., 2003—. Bd. dirs. Provena Behavioral Health. Mem. Fla. Sea Kayaking Assn., Bowling Green U. Press Club (charter 1983). Anglican. Office: U Ill Found Harker Hall MC-386 1305 W Green St Urbana IL 61801-2945 E-mail: glick@uif.uillinois.edu.

GLICK, RUTH BURTNICK, author, lecturer; b. Lexington, Ky., Apr. 27, 1942; d. Lester Leon and Beverly (Miller) Burtnick; m. Norman Stanley Glick, June 30, 1963; children: Elissa, Ethan. BA, The George Washington U., 1964; MA, U. Md., 1967. Lectr. S.W. Writers Conf., Houston, 1984, Nebr. Writers' Guild, Omaha, 1985, Bouchercon, Balt., 1986, Triangle Romance and Fiction Writers' Conf., Raleigh, 1988, Romantic Times Booklovers Conf., San Antonio, 1990, Orlando, 2001, Kansas City, 2003, Malice Domestic, Bethesda, 1993, Howard C.C., 1995—. Author: (with Nancy Baggett) Dollhouse Furniture You Can Make, 1977, Dollhouse Lamps and Chandeliers, 1979, Soup's On, 1985, Oat Bran Baking, 1989, Skinny Soups, 1992, 100 Percent Pleasure, 1994 (US Today list of 12 best cookbooks of 1994), Skinny Italian, 1996, One-Pot Meals for People with Diabetes, 2002; (with Eileen Buckholtz, Carolyn Males and Louise Titchener) Love Is Elected, 1982 (named one of best romances 1982), Southern Persuasion, 1983, (with Titchener) In the Arms of Love, 1983 (Romance best seller list), Brian's Captive, 1983 (Romance best seller list), Reluctant Merger, 1983 (Romance best seller list), Summer Wine, 1984, Beginner's Luck, 1984, Mistaken Image, 1985, Hopelessly Devoted, 1985, Summer Stars, 1985, Stolen Passion, 1986, Indiscreet, 1988, (with Baggett and Gloria Kaufer Greene) Don't Tell 'Em It's Good for 'Em, 1984, Eat Your Vegetables!, 1985, (with Buckholtz) End of Illusion, 1984, Space Attack, 1984, Mission of the Secret Spy Squad, 1984, Mindbenders, 1984, Doom Stalker, 1985, Captain Kid and the Pirates, 1985, The Cats of Castle Mountain, 1985, Logical Choice, 1986, Great Expectations, 1987, A Place in Your Heart, 1988, Saber Dance, 1988, Postmark, 1988, Roller Coaster, 1989 (Young Adult Best Seller List), Silver Creek Challenge, 1989, Needlepoint, 1989, Life Line, 1990, Shattered Vows, 1991, Whispers in the Night, 1991, Only Skin Deep, 1992, Trial By Fire, 1992, Hopscotch, 1993, Cradle and All, 1993, What Child is This, 1993, Midnight Kiss, 1994, Tangled Vows, 1994, Till Death Us Do Part, 1995, Prince of Time, 1995, Face to Face, 1996, For Your Eyes Only, 1997, Father and Child, 1997 (Peregrine Connection series) Talons of the Falcon, 1986, Flight of the Raven, 1986, In Search of the Dove, 1986 (Lifetime Achievement award for romantic suspense series 1987), (with Kathryn Jensen) The Big Score, 1989 (Young Adult Best Seller List), Night Stalker, 1989 (Young Adult Best Seller List), (sole author) Dollhouse Kitchen and Dining Room Accessories, 1979, Invasion of the Blue Lights, 1982, More Than Promises, 1985, The Closer We Get, 1989, Make Me a Miracle, 1992, Bayou Moon, 1992, Skinny One Pot Meals, 1994, The Diabetes Snack, Munch, Nibble, Nosh Book, 1998, Simply Italian, 1998, Nowhere Man, 1998, Shattered Lullaby, 1999, Midnight Caller, 1999, Never Too Late, 2000, Amanda's Child, 2000, Fabulous Lo-Carb Cuisine, 2001, The Man from Texas, 2001, Never Alone, 2001, Lassiter's Law, 2001, Body Contact, 2002 (Waldenbooks Series Best Seller List), From the Shadows, 2002, Phantom Lover, 2003, Killing Moon, 2003 (Berkley Sensation Launch Book), Intimate Strangers, 2003, Edge of the Moon, 2003, Witching Moon, 2003, others; contbr. articles to profl. jours. U. Md. Am. studies fellow, 1964-65; recipient Romantic Times Career Achievement award for Romantic Mystery, 1994, Golden Leaf award for Best Long Contemporary novel and Best Novella N.J. Romance Writers, 2001, Best Selling Author, NY Times, USA Today, 2003; nominee Best Series Romance Book of the Yr. 1993-94 Romantic Times, 1995, 99, 2001, nominee Series Storyteller of Yr., 1996, nominee Best Harlequin Intrigue of Yr., 1998, nominee Best Series Romantic Suspense Writer of Yr., 2000. Mem. Author's Guild, Romance Writers Am. (lectr. Detroit, 1984, Atlanta 1985, Dallas 1987, 96, Boston 1989, San Francisco 1990, New Orleans 1991, 2001, Denver 2002, N.Y.C. 2003), Washington Romance Writers (bd. dirs.), Sisters in Crime, Novelists Inc., Md. Romance Writers.

GLICKMAN, BENITA, language educator, writer, poet; b. Bronx, N.Y., Oct. 21, 1952; d. Marcus and Esther Glickman. BA in Spanish magna cum laude, CCNY, 1973; MA in Spanish, Lehman Coll., 1976; postgrad., Manhattan Coll., 1980—84. Cert. tchr. Spanish 7-12 N.Y., tchr. ESL, tchr. jr. h.s. Spanish, bilingual common brs. grades 1-6. Tchr. Spanish and reading Gilbert Sch., Bklyn., 1973—74; adult edn tchr. Spanish and ESL William Howard Taft H.S., Bronx, 1974—75; bilingual tchr. P.S. 91, Bronx, 1975—78; tchr. ESL John F. Kennedy H.S., Bronx, 1978—91, Christopher Columbus H.S., Bronx, 1991—, Internat. House coord., 2003—; poet, writer, 2001—. Cons. Brown U.-The Edn. Alliance, N.Y.C., 2003. Contbr. short story Chicken Soup for the Sister's Soul, 2002 (Alice Minnie Hertz Heniger award for Children's Lit., 2001), poetry Wedding Blessings: Prayers and Poems Celebrating Love, Marriage and Anniversaries, 2003, poetry to 41 jours. Mem.: Tchrs. English to Students of Other Langs., Acad. Am. Poets, N.Y. State Writing Project, N.Y.C. Writing Project, Phi Beta Kappa. Avocations: reading, cooking, gardening, yoga, nature walking. Home: 55 Knolls Crescent Bronx NY 10463 Office: Christopher Columbus HS 925 Astor Ave Bronx NY 10469 E-mail: bgcchs@yahoo.com.

GLICKMAN, MARLENE, non-profit organization administrator; b. Evansville, Ind., May 13, 1936; d. Morris Jack and Sarah (Krawll) Foreman; m. Marshall Levi Glickman, Jan. 9, 1956 (dec. 2002); children: Cynthia Anne, Joseph Leonard. Student, Ohio State U., 1954-56. Area dir. Am. Jewish Com., Buffalo, 1981-2000; v.p. adminstrn. and fin. Network of Religious Cmtys., 2000—. Pres. Meals on Wheels of Buffalo and Erie County, 1981—83, Coun. Congl. Pres. Erie County, 1979—81; vice chair gen. campaign United Jewish Appeal, 1980, chair woman's divsn., 1979; pres. N.E. Lakes coun. Union Am. Hebrew Congregations, 1982—86; pres. Temple Beth Am, 1978—80, 2002—03, Sisterhood Temple Beth Am, 1969—71, 1976—77; agy. allocations com. United Way, chair Towns and Villages divsn., 1981; pres. Human Rights Adv. Coun. Western N.Y., 1988—96; bd. dirs. YWCA, Buffalo and Erie County, 1990—96, Buffalo Fedn. Neighborhood Ctrs., Inc., 1994—98; exec. com., sec. Sheehan Meml. Hosp., Inc., 1994—98; pres., bd. dirs. Western N.Y. Martin Luther King Jr. Commn., 1991—97, mem. Western N.Y. Vision for Tomorrow 2000 C. of C./Buffalo Partnership. Recipient Abraham Pugash Cmty. Rels. award for establishing Kosher Meals on Wheels, Jewish Family Svc., Buffalo and Erie County, N.Y., 1975, NAACP Human Rels. award, 1997, Cmty. Rels. award Am. Jewish Com. Western N.Y., 2001; Marlene Glickman H.S. Human Rels. Award of Western N.Y. named in her honor for Am. Jewish Com.; Am.-Pol Eagle Citizen of Yr., 1995. Mem. NAACP (life), Union Am. Hebrew Congregations (exec., bd. dirs. 1982-99, exec. com.), Commn. on Synagogue Music, Joint Cantorial Placement Commn., FRJ Admin. (budget and finance), New Congregations, Maintenance of Union Membership, Hadassah (life), Assn. Reform Zionists Am. (del. to Israel 1987), Brandeis Women's Com., Nat. Coun. Jewish Women (life, Hannah G. Solomon award 1985), Assn. Jewish Cmty. Rels. Workers, Jewish Communal Svc. Assn., Arza/World Union (bd. dirs. 1992-2000). Avocation: singing. Home: 94 Broadmoor Dr Tonawanda NY 14150-5532 Office: M&M Connections 94 Broadmoor Dr Tonawanda NY 14150 5532 also: PMB 361 425 Carr 693 Dorado PR 00646 E-mail: mglickman5@cs.com.

GLICK-WEIL, KATHY, library director; b. Milw., Jan. 11, 1950; d. Irving Robert and Janice Esther (Rosner) Glick; m. Gordon Weil, June 20, 1971; children: Jeffrey, Aaron. BA, Tulane U., 1971; MLS, U. Calif., Berkeley, 1972. Children's libr. Thayer Pub. Libr., Braintree, Mass., 1972-73; reference libr. Stoughton (Mass.) Pub. Libr., 1973-77; br. libr. Brockton (Mass.) Pub. Libr., 1977-78; asst. dir. Medford (Mass.) Pub. Libr., 1978-84; dir. Lincoln (Mass.) Pub. Libr., 1984-93, Newton (Mass.) Free Libr., 1993—. Mem. ALA, Mass. Libr. Assn. Home: 46 Acacia Ave Chestnut Hill MA 02467-1351 Office: Newton Free Library 330 Homer St Newton MA 02459-1429 Business E-Mail: kglickweil@mlnlib.net.

GLIER, INGEBORG JOHANNA, German language and literature educator; b. Dresden, Germany, June 22, 1934; came to U.S., 1972; d. Erich Oskar and Gertrud Johanne (Niese) G. Student, Mt. Holyoke Coll., 1955-56; Dr. phil. (Studienstiftung des deutschen Volkes), U. Munich, Germany, 1958; Dr. phil., Habilitation, 1969; MA (hon.), Yale U., 1973. Asst., lectr. U. Munich, 1958-69, universitätsdozentin, 1969-72; vis. prof. Yale U., 1972-73, prof. German, 1973—, chmn. dept., 1979-82, chmn. Medieval Studies, 1986-93, chmn. Women's Studies, 1995-96, sr. faculty fellow, 1974-75; vis. prof. U. Cologne, Germany, 1970-71, U. Colo., Boulder, spring 1983, U. Tubingen, summer 1984. Author: Struktur und Gestaltungsprinzipien in den Dramen John Websters, 1958, Deutsche Metrik, 1961, Artes amandi, Untersuchung zu Geschichte, Uberlieferung und Typologie der deutschen Minnereden, 1971; contbr. articles, book reviews to profl. jours. Mem.: Wolfram von Eschenbach Gesellschaft, Internat. Courtly Lit. Soc., Am. Assn. Tchrs. German, Medieval Acad. Am., MLA, Internat. Germanisten-Verband. Home: 111 Park St Apt 12T New Haven CT 06511-5421 Office: Yale Univ Dept Germanic Langs PO Box 208210 New Haven CT 06520-8210 E-mail: ingeborg.glier@yale.edu.

GLIMCHER, LAURIE H. immunology educator; MD, Harvard Coll., 1976. Irene Heinz Given prof. immunology Harvard Sch. Pub. Health; prof. medicine dept. immunology and infectious diseases Harvard Med. Sch. Contbr. articles to profl. jours. E-mail: glimche@hsph.harvard.edu.

GLISMANN, CLEMENTINE, elementary school educator, researcher; b. Oakland, Nebr., Aug. 4, 1917; d. Louis Martin Larson, Edvinna Josephine Young; m. Leonard William Glismann, Feb. 24, 1940 (dec. Feb. 1997). BA, Midland Luth. Coll., Fremont, Nebr., 1939; postgrad., U. Nebr., 1942—43, Weber Coll., Ogden, Utah, 1945—47, U. Utah, 1963—78. Tchr. 1st grade Bd. Edn., Norfolk, Nebr., 1939—40, secondary tchr. Madrid, Nebr., 1941—42, 3d grade tchr. Ogden, Utah, 1945—56, 4th grade tchr., 1957—63, Salt Lake City, 1964—79; ret., 1979. Traveling dealer Lenswood, 1977—91. Author: (TV program) Wheels, 1951; prodr.: (TV program) Wheels, 1951; author: (TV program) Paper, 1952; prodr.: (TV program) Paper, 1952; author: (TV program) Rubber, 1953; prodr.: (TV program) Rubber, 1953; author: (TV program) Clothes, 1954; prodr.: (TV program) Clothes, 1954; author: (TV program) Historical Masquerade (Great Americans), 1955; prodr.: (TV program) Historical Masquerade (Great Americans), 1955; author: (TV program) Mother Earth's Rock Family, 1962—63; prodr.: (TV program) Mother Earth's Rock Family, 1962—63. State chmn. Luth. Ch. Women, Utah, 1963. Mem.: Golden Spike Gem and Mineral Soc., Delta Kappa Gamma. Republican. Lutheran. Avocations: faceting gemstones, writing poetry.

GLOBUS, DOROTHY TWINING, museum director; b. Singapore, Aug. 31, 1947; d. Kinsley and Cynthia (Thébaud) T.; m. Stephen F. Globus, Sept. 9, 1973; children: Samuel Twining, Dorothy Schermerhorn. BA in Art History magna cum laude, Swarthmore Coll., 1969. Asst. to dir. Wilcox Gallery Swarthmore (Pa.) Coll., 1967-69; summer intern Smithsonian Instn., Washington, 1966-69, exhibits specialist Nat. Mus. Natural History, 1970-73, curator of exhbns. Cooper-Hewitt Nat. Mus. Design N.Y.C., 1973-92; mus. dir. Mus. at Fashion Inst. of Tech., N.Y.C., 1993—. Mem. trustees coun. Preservation N.Y. State, 1989—. Mem. Fashion Group, Artable. Office: Fashion Inst of Tech Seventh Ave at 27th St New York NY 10001-5992

GLODOWSKI, SHELLEY JEAN, administrator, writer, musician; b. Stoughton, Wis., Jan. 27, 1950; d. Rodney Keller and Janet Maude (Nelson) Peterson; m. Randolph Raymond Glodowski, July 31, 1976. BA, Hamline

U., 1972. Cert. secondary English tchr. Substitute tchr. Stoughton (Wis.) Schs., 1973-74; office worker Wis. Pharm. Assn., Madison, 1973-74; legal sec. Howard Hippman, Oregon, Wis., 1974-76; typist 3 dept. psychiatry U. Wis., Madison, 1976-78, supr., specialist fiscal affairs, 1978-79, grad. sec. dept. sociology, 1979-82, program asst. sch. music, 1982-84, dept. sec. sch. [illegible] office mgr. instructional materials ctr., 1987-91, chairs' sec. dept. sociology, 1991-94, adminstr. dept. philosophy, 1994—. Sound engr. Midwest Book Rev. program, Madison, 1986-89; organizer Wis. State Employees Union 2412 Clerical Union, Madison, 1990-91. Profl. musician Z.B.M. Band, Oregon, Wis., 1986-2003, (CD) Pay the Price, 1991, Z.B.M., 2000; book reviewer, Midwest Book Rev., 1975—; costume designer musical prodn. Godspell, Oregon Straw Hat Players, 1990; author: Murder on the Wrong Note, 2003. Canvasser Dem. Party, Stoughton, Wis., 1968; mem., organizer Wis. State Employees Union 2412 Clerical Union, Madison, 1990; vol. Wis. Libr. Assn., Madison, 1987-90; coord. fundraising cabaret Unitarian Ch., Madison, 1984-96; choir mem. Unitarian Universalist choir, Madison, 1979-96; mem. AFSME Union, to 1990. Mem. Letters and Sci. Adminstrs. Network (sec. 1998), Stoughton Fest. Choir, 2004. Avocations: reading, tennis, cross-country skiing, gardening, dogs. Home: 137 Washington St Oregon WI 53575-1548 Office: Instrnl Materials Ctr 225 N Miller St Oregon WI 53575-1610

GLOVER, ANN B. finance company executive; BA, St. Michael's Coll., Winooski, Vt.; MBA, Northeastern U., Boston. From exec. trainee to dir. customer mktg. PepsiCo., 1985—98; chief mktg. officer Hartford Fin. Svcs. Group, Hartford, Conn., 2000—02, sr. v.p. corp. rels. group, 2002—. Trustee St. Michael's Coll., Winooski, Vt.; bd. dirs. Greater Hartford YMCA. Office: Hartford Fin Svcs Group Hartford Plz 690 Asykum Ave Hartford CT 06115

GLOVER, JANE ALISON, conductor; b. Helmsley, Yorkshire, U.K., May 13, 1949; d. Robert Finlay and Jean (Muir) G. BA with honors, Oxford U., 1971, MA, DPhil, 1976; DLitt (hon.), Exeter, 1986; DUniv (hon.), Loughborough U. of Tech., 1988; DLitt (hon.), Open U., Eng., 1988, Huddersfield (Eng.) U., 1991, Bradford (Eng.) U., Eng., 1992, London U., 1992, City U., Eng., 1994, Brunel U., 1996. Musical dir. Glyndebourne Touring Opera, 1981-85, London Choral Soc., 1983—; artistic dir. London Mozart Players, 1984-91; prin. condr. Huddersfield Choral Soc., 1989-96. Fellow Royal Coll. Medicine. Office: care Lies Askonas Ltd 6 Henrietta St London WC2E 8LA England

GLOVER, JANET BRIGGS, artist; b. Allahabad, India, June 22, 1919; came to U.S., 1924; d. George Weston and Mary Ames (Hart) Briggs; m. Alan Marsh Glover, Feb. 5, 1949; children: Keith Terrot, John Carroll, Beth Marsh Glover Wittig. BA, Bennington Coll., 1943; postgrad., New Sch. Social Rsch., 1969-70. Artist, draftsman Chartmakers, Inc., N.Y.C., 1943-45; apprentice to Oscar Ogg Book of Month Club, N.Y.C., 1946; 2d grade tchr. Hartridge Sch., Plainfield, N.J., 1947-48, Country Day Sch., Lancaster, Pa., 1948-49; chmn. art dept. Women's Club Chatham, N.J., 1964-65, lectr. art, 1981-86; publicity chmn. N.J. Ctr. Visual Arts, Summit, 1980-81. One-man shows include Present Day Club, Princeton, N.J., 1967, Gallery 9 Upstairs, Chatham, 1978; group shows include Key Gallery, N.Y.C., 1980; contbg. editor N.J. Music and Arts Mag., 1970-71; art critic Madison Eagle, 1975-78. Recipient 1st prize Morris County Art Assn., 1966, Princeton Art Assn., 1969, Cmty. Art Assn., 1980. Mem. Chatham Twp. Art League (co-founder, 1st pres. 1988-90, editor Artist's Album 1993—, editor newsletter, 1996—), Drew U. Art Assn. (membership chmn. 1990-94, mem. directory illustrated 2000—). Democrat. Unitarian Universalist. Avocations: poetry, music. Home: 30 Oak Hill Rd Chatham NJ 07928-1552

GLOVER, KAREN E. lawyer; b. Nampa, Idaho, Apr. 14, 1950; d. Gordon Ellsworth and Cora (Frazier) G.; m. Thaddas L. Alston, Aug. 17, 1979; children: Samantha Glover Alston, Evan Glover Alston. AB magna cum laude, Whitman Coll., 1972; JD cum laude, Harvard U., 1975. Bar: Wash. 1975, U.S. Dist. Ct. (we. dist.) Wash. 1975. Assoc. Preston, Thorgrimson Ellis & Holman, Seattle, 1975-80; ptnr. Preston Gates & Ellis LLP, Seattle, 1981—. Bd. dirs. Adaptis, Inc., 2001—. Chmn. bd. dirs. United Way King County, Seattle, 1993-94; trustee Whitman Coll., Walla Walla, Wash., 1998—, King County Libr. Sys., Seattle, 1992-2001. Mem. Wash. State Bar Assn. (corp. and tax sects.), Seattle Pension Roundtable, Columbia Tower Club, Rainier Club. Episcopalian. Office: Preston Gates & Ellis 925 4th Ave Ste 2900 Seattle WA 98104-1158

GLOVER, KATHERINE DENISE, musician; d. Oscar Elwood and Cynthia Jane Glover; 1 child, Kristie Lyn Friesenhahn. MusM in Flute Performance, Midwestern State U., Wichita Falls, Tex., 1988. Cert. music tchr. Tex., 1985, secondary reading Tex., 1985, Orff level one AOSA, 2003. Music specialist Judson Ind. Sch. Dist., San Antonio, 1994—; adj. faculty Alamo C.C. Dist., San Antonio, 2002—; freelance flutist San Antonio and Austin; flute instr. Acad. of Fine Arts, St. Philip's Coll., San Antonio. Mem. San Antonio Wind Symphony, San Antonio, Austin Civic Orch., Austin, Tex., 1994—2000. Recipient Outstanding Educator of the Yr. award, Elolf Elem., Judson ISD, 2000; grantee, Judson Edn. Found. grantee, 2000. Mem.: Ctrl. Tex. Orff, Am. Orff Schulwerk Assn., Tex. Music Educators Assn., Nat. Flute Assn., Music Educators Nat. Conf. Avocations: travel, reading. Office: Olympia Elem Sch 8439 Athenian Dr Universal City TX 78148

GLOVER, LISA MARIE, transportation executive, consultant; b. Detroit, Oct. 14, 1963; d. Ronald and Denise (Wellons) Glover. BS, Tuskegee U., 1986; MS, Morgan State U., 1988. Cert. Microsoft profl. Summer intern IBM, Charlotte, NC, 1982, GM, Pontiac, Mich., 1983-85, Turner Constrn., Detroit, 1986; grad. intern State of Md., Dept. Transp., Balt., 1987-88; planner Dept. Transp., Detroit, 1988-90, asst. to dir., 1990-91, mgr. Office of Contract Compliance, 1991-93; transp. engr., cons. M2 Internat., Detroit, 1993-94; transportation cons. Trans. Svcs., Inc., 1994-95; asst. venue transp. mgr. Atlanta Com. Olympic Games, 1996; ind. contractor, 1997-2000; staff asst., sta. svcs. Met. Atlanta Rapid Transit Authority, 1998, bus. analyst, info. tech., 1998, rsch. asst., strategic planning, 1999, rsch. analyst, project mgr. transit rsch., 1999-2000; ind. contractor tech. support McDermott Sys., tech. support, 1999; sr. transp. planner Dekalb County Planning Dept., Decatur, Ga., 2000—04; transp. planning mgr. Henry County Bd. Commrs., Modonough, Ga., 2004—. Spl. events planner Von Creations, Inc., 1998; Dekalb County rep. Atlanta Regional Commn.-Transp. Coord. Com., 2000—04; mem. steering com. No. Sub-Area Study Ga. Regional Trans. Authority, 2001—04; mem. host com. RAIL-VOLUTION, Atlanta, 2001—03; mem. transp. coordinating com. Henry County rep. Atlanta Regional Commn., 2004—. Corr. sec. Metro Atlanta chpt. Nat. Congress Black Women, 2001—; math. tutor Ednl. Guidance and Tutoring Ctrs., Inc., 1995; nat. nominating bd. Outstanding Young Ams., 1995—96; mem. 14th Congl. Dist. Young Dems., spl. projects com., 1992; mem. Total Praise choir New Birth Missionary Bapt. Ch., Lithonia, Ga., 1997—, co-chair engrng. ministry, 1999—2000, vol. registrar Lay Inst. Equipping, 1999—2000. Recipient cert. of Merit, Mayor Coleman A. Young City of Detroit, 1980. Mem.: NAACP (young adults com. 1989—91), NAFE, Women Transp. Seminar (scholarship coord. 1988—2001, bd. dirs. 2003—), Conf. Minority Transp. Ofcls., Assn. Gen. Contractors Am. (pres. 1985—86), Morgan State U. Alumni Assn., Tuskegee Nat. Alumni Assn., Internat. Olympic Family, Morgan State Student Transp. Assn. (sec. 1986—87), Atlanta Regional Leadership Inst., Sigma Lambda Chi (charter), Delta Nu Alpha, Alpha Kappa Alpha (sponsor teen group 1989—95). Democrat. Baptist. Avocations: art, classical/jazz/gospel music, travel, remodeling projects. E-mail: gloveret@msn.com.

GLOVER, MAGGIE WALLACE, state legislator; b. Florence, S.C., Aug. 29, 1948; d. Fulton and Ethel (Greene) Wallace. 1 child, Marisa. BA, Fayetteville St. U., 1970; MEd, Marion Coll., 1982. Former mem. S.C. Ho. of Reps., dist. 62; mem. S.C. Senate. Active sch. bd. trustees, Florevce Sch. Dist., 1983-86, 86-89. With AUS 1974-77. Mem. NAACP. Democrat. Home: PO Box 910 Florence SC 29503-0910 Office: Senate House PO Box 142 Columbia SC 29202-0142

GLUBE, CONSTANCE RACHELLE, Canadian chief justice; b. Ottawa, Ont., Can., Nov. 23, 1931; d. Samuel and Pearl (Slonemsky) Lepofsky; m. Richard Hillard Glube, July 6, 1952 (dec.); children: John B., Erica D. Glube Kolatch, Harry S., B. Joseph. BA, McGill U., Montreal, Can., 1952; LLB, Dalhousie U., Halifax, Can., 1955, LLD (hon.), 1983, Mount St. Vincent U., 1998, St. Mary's U., 2000. Bar: N.S. 1956, created queen's counsel, 1974. Assoc. Kitz, Matheson, Halifax, 1964-66; ptnr. Fitzgerald & Glube, Halifax, 1966-68; sr. solicitor City of Halifax, 1969-74, city mgr., 1974-77; puisne judge Supreme Ct. of N.S., Halifax, 1977-82; chief justice Supreme Ct., Halifax, 1982-98, Nova Scotia, 1998—, Ct. Appeals, 1998—. Vice chair Can. Judges Conf.; interim bd. dirs. Nat. Jud. Ctr., 1987; bd. dirs. Nat. Jud. Inst., 1998—, Can. Inst. Adminstrs. Justice. Contbr. articles and papers to profl. publs. Co-chair Can. Coun. Christians and Jews; bd. dirs. Halifax Heritage Found., 1984—95, Internat. Commn. Jurists, Can. br., 2003—; chmn. bd. N.S. Archives, 1998—; chair (hon.) N.S. divsn. Can. Mental Health Assn., 1984—98; mem. adv. coun. Order N.S., 2001—. Recipient award of merit City of Halifax, 1977, Frances Fish award, 1997, N.S. Women Lawyers Achievement award, Justice award Can. Inst. for Adminstrn. of Justice, 2003. Mem.: Nat. Jud. Inst., Can. Jud. Coun. (adminstrn. of justice com. 1992—94, chmn. edn. com. 1986—88, equality com. 1994—99, jud. benefits com. 1994—99, fin. com. 1999—2002, chmn. edn. com. 2000—, exec. com. 2001—, vice chair jud. conduct com. 2001—), Can. Bar Assn., Golden Key Internat. Honor Soc. (hon.). Jewish. Avocations: swimming, gardening. Home: 5920 Inglewood Dr Halifax NS Canada B3H 1B1

GLUCK, CAROL, history educator; b. Newark, Nov. 12, 1941; d. David E. and Doris S. Newman; m. Peter L. Gluck, May 1, 1966; children: Thomas Edward, William Francis. Student, U. Munich, 1960-61, U. Tokyo, 1972-74; BA, Wellesley Coll., 1962; MA, Columbia U., 1970, PhD, 1977. Asst. prof. Columbia U., N.Y.C., 1975-83, assoc. prof., 1983-86, prof., 1986-88, George Sansom prof. history, 1988—. Vis. rsch. assoc. faculty law Tokyo U., 1978-79, 85-86, 92; vis. prof. Harvard U., Cambridge, Mass., 1991, Inst. Social Sci. Tokyo U., 1993, Ecole des Hautes Etudes en Scis. Sociales, Paris, 1995, 98; fellow Inst. for Advanced Studies in the Behavioral Scis., 1999-2000; publs. bd. Columbia U. Press, N.Y.C., 1991-96; co-dir. project on Asia in the core Curriuculm NEH, N.Y.C., 1987—; Am. adv. com. Japan Found., 1986-96, chair, 1991-96; disting. lectr. N.E. Area Coun., 1988, Japan Soc. for Promotion of Sci., 1989. Author: Japan's Modern Myths, 1985 (Fairbank prize 1986, Trilling award 1987); co-editor: Showa: The Japan of Hirohito, 1992, Asia in Western and World History, 1997; contbr. numerous articles to profl. publs. Mem. Coun. on Fgn. Rels., U.S.-Japan Friendship Commn., 1994—2001; mem. com. on rsch. librs. N.Y. Pub. Libr., 1987—, mem. humanities adv. coun., 1996—. Recipient Fulbright 50th Anniversary Disting. Fellow award, 2002; fellow, Woodrow Wilson Found., Fgn. Area fellow; grantee Fulbright grantee, 1985—86, Japan Found. grantee. Fellow: Am. Acad. Arts and Scis.; mem.: Am. Philos. Soc., Asia Soc. (trustee 1992—98, 2002—), Japan Soc. (bd. dirs. 1990—), Assn. Asian Studies (coun. 1981—84, nominating com. 1985—86, pres. 1996—97, bd. dirs. 1995—99), Am. Hist. Assn. (coun. 1987—90), Phi Beta Kappa. Home: 440 Riverside Dr New York NY 10027-6828 Office: Columbia U East Asian Inst 420 W 118th St New York NY 10027-7213

GLÜCK, LOUISE ELISABETH, poet, educator; b. N.Y.C., Apr. 22, 1943; d. Daniel and Beatrice (Grosby) G.; m. Charles Hertz (div.); 1 child, Noah Benjamin; m. John Dranow, 1977 (div.). Student, Sarah Lawrence Coll., 1962, Columbia U., 1963-65; LLD, Williams Coll., 1993, Skidmore Coll., 1995, Middlebury, 1996. Vis. poet Goddard Coll., U. N.C., U. Va., U. Iowa; Elliston prof. U. Cin., 1978; vis. faculty Columbia U., 1979; faculty M.F.A. program Goddard Coll., also Warren Wilson Coll., Swannanoa, N.C.; Holloway lectr. U. Calif., Berkeley, 1982; vis. prof. U. Calif.-Davis, 1983; Scott prof. poetry Williams Coll., 1983; Regents prof. poetry UCLA, 1985-88; faculty Williams Coll., 1984—, Preston Parrish 3d century prof., 1997—2003, Margaret Scott Bundy lectr., 2003—. Vis. prof. Harvard U., 1995; Hurst prof. poetry Brandeis U., 1996; delivered Phi Beta Kappa poem Harvard U. commencement, 1990; baccalaureate spkr. Williams Coll.; Hopwood lectr. U. Mich.; spl. cons. Libr. of Congress, 2000; judge younger poets competition Yale U. Press, 2003—. Author: Firstborn, 1968, The House on Marshland, 1975, Descending Figure, 1980, The Triumph of Achilles, 1985, Ararat, 1990, The Wild Iris, 1992 (Pulitzer Prize for poetry 1993), Proofs and Theories (collected essays), 1994, Meadowlands, 1996, Vita Nova, 1999, The Seven Ages, 2001. Grantee Rockefeller Found., Nat. Endowment for Arts, 1969-70, 79-80, 88-89, Guggenheim Found., 1975-76, 87-88, NEA, 1988-89; recipient lit. award Am. Acad. and Inst. Arts and Letters, 1981, award in poetry Nat. Book Critics Cir., 1985, Melville Cane award Poetry Soc. Am., 1986, Sara Teasdale Meml. prize Wellesley Coll., 1986, Bobbitt Natl prize Libr. Congress, 1992, Pulitzer prize, 1993, William Carlos Williams award, 1993, PEN/Martha Albrand award Non-Fiction, 1995, Lannan Found. award in poetry, 1999, New Yorker mag. award, 1999, Ambs. award English Spkg. Union, 1999, 50th Anniversary medal MIT, 2000, Bollingen prize, 2001; named Poet Laureate of Vt., 1994, U.S. Poet Laureate, 2003. Fellow Am. Acad. Arts and Scis.; mem. Am. Acad. Arts & Letters, Am. Acad. Poets (chancellor 1999—), Phi Beta Kappa (hon.). Office: Williams Coll Dept Engring Williamstown MA 01267

GLUECK, MARY AUDREY, retired psychiatric and mental health nurse; b. Bridgetown, Barbados; arrived in U.S., 1952; d. Hubert and Christina Cumming; m. Stephen G. Glueck (dec.). Grad. sch. nursing, St. Joseph's Mercy Hosp., Georgetown, Guyana; paralegal diploma, Profl. Career Devel. Inst., 2000. RN, Calif. Asst. nursing educator in new employee orientation San Mateo County Gen. Hosp., San Mateo, Calif., also facilitator video insvcs. for nursing staff, tchr. safety and emergency response procedures to staff, ret., 1998. Mem. Mid. Mgrs. Assn., Am. Psychiat. Nurses Assn. Home: 3692 S Desert Rd Tucson AZ 85735

GLUECK, SYLVIA BLUMENFELD, writer; b. Tulsa, Dec. 23, 1925; d. Maurice and Sina (Turk) Blumenfeld; m. Norton Shushan Glueck, June 15, 1947; children: Nancy Eisen, Milton. BJ, U. Mo., Columbia, 1949. Publicity dir. sta. WDSU, New Orleans, 1946-47; advt. copywriter Swiftway Direct Mail, New Orleans, 1961; freelance writer New Orleans, San Antonio, 1965—. Author book; contbr. articles to mags. and newspaper features, 1984—85, to mags. and newspaper features, 1990 (Golden Pro award, 1986). Mem.: AAUW. Home and Office: PO Box 12051 San Antonio TX 78212-0051

GLYNN, CARLIN (CARLIN MASTERSON), actress; b. Cleve., Feb. 19, 1940; d. Guilford Cresse and Lois Carlin (Wilks) G.; m. Peter Masterson, Dec. 29, 1960; children: Carlin Alexandra, Mary Stuart, Peter C.B. Student, Sophie Newcomb Coll., 1957-58. Prof. Columbia U. Grad. Film Sch., N.Y.C.; prof. MFA program Actors Studio at New Sch. for Social Rsch. Creative advisor Sundance Inst. Film Lab. Appeared in N.Y. as Miss Mona in: The Best Little Whorehouse in Tex., 1978-80; in London, 1981; starred in Pal Joey, Goodman Theatre, Chgo., 1988 (Joseph Jefferson award 1988), Cover of Life, Am. Place Theatre, N.Y., 1994, The Young Man from Atlanta, Signature Theatre Co., 1995 (Pulitzer prize for drama 1995), Amazing Grace, 1998, The Chemistry of Change, 1999, Frame 312, 2002, Safe, 2003; films include Three Days of the Condor, 1974, Resurrection, 1978, Continental Divide, 1981, Sixteen Candles, 1984, The Trip to Bountiful, 1985, Blood Red, Night Game, Convicts, 1989, Blessing, 1992, Judy Berlin, 1997, West of Here, 2001, Lost Junction, 2001; TV series Mr. President, 1987; dir. short film Love Divided By, 1993. Recipient Theatre World award, 1978, Antoinette Perry award, 1979, best actress award in musical Soc. West End Theatres, Lawrence Olivier award, London, 1981 Mem. SAG, AFTRA, Actor's Studio (bd. dirs.), Actors' Equity Assn. [illegible]

GLYNN, MARILYN, lawyer; Gen. counsel Office of Govt. Ethics, Washington. Office: Office of Govt Ethics 1201 New York Ave NW Ste 500 Washington DC 20005-3968

GOATES, PAT LANETTA, social worker, consultant; b. Waxahachie, Tex., Aug. 3, 1943; d. Elmer B. Owens, Bennie Inez Owens; m. Donald Ray Goates, June 7, 1963; children: Gretchen Brickhouse, Sunnae Hiler; 1 child, Donald Goates II. BMEd, Hardin-Simmons U., 1986, MEd, 1987; MSSW, U. Tex., Arlington, 1999. LMSW. Program adminstr. Tex. Dept. Protective and Regulatory Svc., Fort Worth, 1987—99; adj. prof. sociology Tarrant County Coll. and Weatherford Coll., Fort Worth, Tex., 1999—2001; v.p. BEACON Endeavors, Inc., Weatherford, Tex., 2000—. Trainer Ct. Apptd. Spl. Advocates, Fort Worth, 1996—99; cons. sexually abused children, Fort Worth, 1988—99; founder, CEO Counseling and Resource Endorsement, Inc., Fort Worth, 2000—; founder, pres. Social Svcs. Mgmt. Cons., Inc., Fort Worth, 2001—; music tchr. Tarver-Rendon Elem. Sch., Rendon, Tex. Contbr. Adoption Policy and Procedures Handbook, 1998. Presenter Tex. Legis. Sunset Commn., Austin, 1997—98; neighborhood chmn. Mother's March for March of Dimes, Fort Worth, 1988—91; selection com. bd. dirs. United Way of Tarrant County, Fort Worth, 1995—99. Mem.: NASW, Am. Bus. Women's Assn. (celebrity chpt.), Order of the Eastern Star. Baptist. Avocations: hunting, fishing, crocheting, music, cooking. Home: 7245 CR 1204 Cleburne TX 76031 Office: Counseling and Resource Endorsement, Inc 2944 Hemphill Fort Worth TX 76110 Home Fax: 817-373-2095. Personal E-mail: pogog@digitex.net. Business E-Mail: CareInc@digitex.net.

GOBEN, MIRELLA SEGALOTTO, real estate agent; arrived in U.S., 1964, naturalized, 1969; d. Palmiro Giovanni Segalotto and Clara Klara Stahl; children: Frank Palmiro Segalotto, Michael Jay Segalotto, Allen Floyd, Sherry Lorene. BA, Graceland U., 1998. Lic. Iowa, 1976; real estate Iowa, 1973. Pvt. real estate agt., Humeston, Iowa, 1973—; collections agt. Citigroup, Des Moines, 2000—. Author poetry. Republican. Avocations: painting, writing, travel, reading, gardening. Home: P O Box 269 Humeston IA 50123-0269

GOBES, LANDY, psychotherapist; b. Indpls., Oct. 12, 1933; d. Nathan Morr Beery and Mary Rebecca Decker; m. James Atherton Gobes, May 26, 1956 (div. May 1979); children: Catherine Elizabeth, James Atherton Gobes, Jr., Michael Edward, Anne Rebecca Gobes Arcata, Peter John, Mary Virginia. BA, Ind. U., 1955; MSW, U. Conn., 1979. Diploma clin. social work, LCSW Conn., lic. marriage and family therapist. Clin. social worker Family Svc., Inc., New Britain, Conn., 1979—83; pvt. practice psychotherapy West Hartford, Conn., 1979—; pvt. practice psychotherapy supr. and trainer, 1980—. Contbr. articles to profl. jours. Co-chair United Way Collection Campaign, West Hartford, 1966; organizer FISH of West Hartford, West Hartford, 1970—76; organist, choir dir. Bloomfield (Conn.) United Meth. Ch., 1963—2003. Fellow: Inst. Integrative Psychotherapy; mem.: NASW (mem. com. inquiry 1998—2003), Am. Group Psychotherapy Assn., Internat. Transactional Analysis Assn. (trustee 1987—89, chair transactional analysis cert. coun. 1989—93, tchg. and supervising transactional analyst). Democrat. Methodist. Avocations: piano, reading, travel, genealogy, hiking. Home: 1168 New Britain Ave West Hartford CT 06110

GOBI, ANNE, state legislator, lawyer; BS, Worcester State Coll.; JD, Mass. Sch. Law. Lawyer; state rep. Mass. House, 2001—. Mem. Exhange Club of Spencer. Mem.: W. Worcester Co. Bar Assn. Democrat. Office: Rm 146 State House Boston MA 02133

GOCEK, MATILDA ARKENBOUT (MRS. JOHN A. GOCEK), librarian; b. Hoboken, NJ, Feb. 18, 1923; m. Harry Francis Decker, May 15, 1939 (div. Nov. 1955); children: Ruth Ann Decker Robinson, Dianne Karen Decker McKinstrie; m. John A. Gocek, Nov. 18, 1956; 1 child, John Jacob. AA, Orange County CC, 1961; BA, SUNY, New Paltz, 1964; MLS, SUNY, Albany, 1967; PhD, Colo. State Christian Coll., 1973. Libr. dir. Monroe Free Libr., NY, 1958—61; dir. Tuxedo Pk. Libr., NY, 1963—76; historian Town of Tuxedo, 1973—76; dir. Suffern Free Libr., 1977—90; pres., CEO Libr. Rsch. Assoc., Inc., Monroe, NY, 1990—. Libr. cons. Tuxedo Union Free Sch., 1967—69. Editor: Libr. Rsch. Assoc., 1968; author: (weekly columnist) Times Herald Rec., 1977—80. Vice chmn. Montgomery Expdn. Meml. Observance, 1973; mem., publicist Monroe Hist. Soc., NY, 2002—; bd. dirs. Tuxedo Park Sch.; trustee, pres. Mus. Village of Orange County, NY, 1980—83. Mem.: Ramapo Catskill Libr. Sys. Assn. (exec. bd. 1986—88), Libr. Assn. Rockland County (goals com. 1977, exec. bd. 1980—83), Southeastern NY Libr. Ref. Resource Coun., NY Libr. Assn., Orange-Sullivan Pub. Libr. Assn. (pres. 1967—70). Home and Office: 3A Lamplighter Village Old Country Rd Monroe NY 10950

GOCKLEY, BARBARA JEAN, manufacturing executive; b. Pitts., July 26, 1951; d. William Ervin and Dorothy Marie (Wolf) Cain; m. William Lee Gockley, Mar. 29, 1975 (div. Aug. 1989); children: Ervin Cain, Marianne Cain, William Cain, Malinda Bellot; m. John W. Deaver, Dec. 27, 2002. BA in Bus. Mgmt. and Mktg. Mgmt., Alvernia Coll., 1993; MBA, Univ. Wis., 1997. Cert. in purchasing mgmt.; cert. prodn. and inventory mgmt. Asst. materials mgr. Redman Mobile Homes, Ephrata, Pa., 1972-75; mgr. inventory control Gym-Kin, Inc., Reading, Pa., 1975-77; supr. prodn./inventory control Wyomissing Converting, Reading, 1979-82; mgr. prodn./inventory control Doma Door Controls, Inc., Reamstown, Pa., 1982-85, project mgr., 1985-86; materials mgr. Powder Coatings Group-Morton Internat., Reading, 1986-94; dir. purchasing Dexter Corp., Waukegan, Ill., 1994-99; v.p. global strategic sourcing Spectrum Brands, St. Louis, 1999-2001; dir. global supply chain mgmt. The Falcon Cos., St. Louis, 2001—03; dir. supply chain mgmt. Elkay Mfg., Chgo., 2003—. Dir. programs Congress for Progress Inc., 1984-88, vice chmn., 1988-89, 99-2000, chmn., 1989-90, 2000-2001; dir. programs PRMS User Group Internat. Conf., 1991, 92; instr. Berks Campus, Pa. State U., Reading, 1985-86. Dir. Reinholds (Pa.) PTA, 1978-81; bd. dirs. Cocalico Sch. Bd., Denver, Pa., 1985-89. Mem.: Nat. Assn. Female Execs., Assn. Mfg. Excellence, Inst. for Supply Mgmt., Am. Prodn. and Inventory Control Soc. (cert. prodn. and inventory mgmt., treas. Schuylkill Valley chpt. 1981—82, pres. 1982—84, dir. membership region IX 1985—86, asst. v.p. 1987, v.p. 1988—89, Internat. Vol. Svc. award 1986). Republican. Presbyterian. Office: Elkay Mfg 2700 517th Ave Broadview IL 60155 E-mail: bjgockley@aol.com.

GODDARD, HAZEL BRYAN, religious organization administrator; b. Mineral, Ill., Aug. 17, 1912; d. Thomas Benton and Maude Carrie (Riley) B.; m. John Howard Goddard; children: David Bryan, Joan Kathryn. BA, Judson Coll., 1966; MS, No. Ill. U., 1973; LittD (hon.), Calif. Grad. Sch. Theology, 1981. Lic. Marriage and family therapist, Fla., Colo. Clin. counselor Warrenville (Ill.) Med. Clinic, 1958-78; pres. Christian Counseling Ministries, Buena Vista, Colo., 1978-99, lectr., cons., 1978—, pres. emeritus, 1999. Author: Can I Hope Again, 1971, Mama, Are You There?, 1996, Somebody Else's Girl, Connie, Bob Bronson; contbr. articles to jours. Mem. Am. Pychotherapy Assn. (diplomat), Am. Assn. Marriage and Family Therapists (clin.), Nat. Assn. Social Workers, Am. Assn. Counseling and Devel. Republican. Baptist. Avocations: writing, music, hiking, fishing, travel. Home: PO Box 1366 Buena Vista CO 81211-1366 E-mail: hazelg@chaffee.net.

GODDARD, JO ANN, investment advisor; BA in Math., Smith Coll.; JD, NY Law Sch. Mgr. treasury dept. Pacific Telesis Group, mgr. wholesale fins. and regulatory support Pacific Bell subs., dir. fed. regulatory rels., dir. investor rels. San Francisco; dir. investor rels. and shareholder svcs. So. Calif. Edison; with Edison Internat., Rosemead, Calif., 1996—, v.p. investor rels. Office: Edison Internat 2244 Walnut Grove Ave Rosemead CA 91770*

GODDARD, SANDRA KAY, elementary school educator; b. Steubenville, Ohio, Oct. 31, 1947; d. Albert Leonard and Mildred Irene (Hill) G. BS in Edn., Miami U., Oxford, Ohio, 1969; MEd, Miami U., 1973. Tchr. Gregg Elem. Sch., Bergholz, Ohio, 1969; tchr. elem. grades Springfield Mid. Sch., Bergholz, 1999—, media club advisor, 2002—; Praxis III assessor Ohio Dept. Edn., 2002—; spelling bee coord., co-coord. Edison Local Spelling Bee, 2003. Curriculum and textbook com. Jefferson County Schs., Steubenville, 1994-95, textbook com., 2002; cooperating tchr. Franciscan U., 1972-77, 2002; presenter Ohio Regional Tchrs. Workshop, 1998, County Tchrs. Workshops for ARC/Jefferson County Tchrs., 1992-97, Jefferson County coord. Presch./Kindergarten Workshop for ARC first aid course, 2000, 2002. Publicity chmn., rec. sec., box office chmn., lead actress, asst. dir. Steubenville Players, 1981-83; mem. Edison Local Adv. Coun. on Drug Edn., 1987-99; mem. Edison Local Curriculum Instrn. Com., 1993-99; state judge Ashland Oil Tchr. Achievement awards, 1988-90; regional and state judge Odyssey of the Mind, 1992-97, bd. dirs. Region XI, 1993-97, regional dir., chair governing bd., bd. dirs. Ohio chpt., 1994-97; exec. com. Gregg Elem. PTO, 1990-92; instr. 1st aid and CPR, ARC, 1990—, county disaster team, profl. rescuer status, 1997—, instr. trainer educator, 2002; instr. CPR for Profl. Rescuer, 2002—. Martha Holden Jennings scholar, 1972-73; mini-grantee Jefferson County Schs., 1991, 94. Mem. NEA (del. to rep. assembly 1979, 85-88), Ohio Edn. Assn. (exec. com. 1983-89, pres.'s cabinet 1985-87, appeals bd. 1994-2002), Ea. Ohio Edn. Assn. (pres. 1978-79, exec. com. 1983-89), Edison Local Edn. Assn. (pres. 1974-75, v.p. 1986-91, exec. com. 1991-94, negotiation's team 1987, 90, 93), Ohio Valley UNISERV Coun. (treas. 1986-92), Delta Kappa Gamma (legis. chair 1990-92). Democrat. Methodist. Avocations: singing, reading, theater, collecting hummels and bells, photography. Home: 200 Fernwood Rd Apt 11 Wintersville OH 43953-9200 Office: Springfield Mid Sch 4569 County Hwy 75 Bergholz OH 43908-9801 Office Phone: 740-768-2420., 740-282-1124. E-mail: sgoddard@eohio.net.

GODDEN, JEAN W. columnist; b. Stamford, Conn., Oct. 1, 1933; d. Maurice Albert and Bernice Elizabeth (Warvel) Hecht; m. Robert W. Godden, Nov. 7, 1952 (dec. Dec. 1985); children: Glenn Scott, Jeffrey Wayne. BA, U. Wash., 1974. News editor Univ. Dist. Herald, Seattle, 1951-53; bookkeeper Omniarts Inc., Seattle, 1963-71; writer editorial page Seattle Post-Intelligencer, Seattle, 1974-80, editorial page editor, 1980-81, bus. editor, 1981-83, city columnist, 1983-91, Seattle Times, 1991—. Author: The Will to Win, 1980, Hasty Put Ins, 1981. Communicator of the Yr. U. Wash. Sch. of Comm., 1995. Mem. LWV (dir. 1969-71), Wash. Press Assn. (Superior Performance award 1979), Soc. Profl. Journalists, Mortar-board, City Club, Phi Beta Kappa. Office: The Seattle Times PO Box 70 Seattle WA 98111-0070

GODDESS, LYNN BARBARA, commercial real estate broker; b. N.Y.C., Mar. 3, 1942; d. Eugene Daniel and Hazel Cecile (Kinzler) G.; divorced. BS, Columbia U., 1963, postgrad., 1964-66. Coord. John M. Burns Assembly Campaign, N.Y.C., 1963; dir. spl. events, projects Kenneth B. Keating Senatorial Campaign, N.Y.C., 1964; dist. dir. fund raising Muscular Dystrophy Assn. Am. Inc., N.Y.C., 1965-66; exec. acct. fund raising, pub. relations Victor Weingarten Co., N.Y.C., 1966-67, Oram Group (formerly Harold L. Oram Inc.), N.Y.C., 1967-70; dir. devel. City Ctr. Music Drama Inc., N.Y.C., 1970; sales person Whitbread-Nolan, N.Y.C., 1971-73; from asst. v.p. to sr. v.p. Cross and Brown Co., N.Y.C., 1973-1985; sr. dir., commercial real estate Cushman & Wakefield, Inc., N.Y.C., 1985—. Trustee Young Adult Inst.; founder, chmn. The Hazel K. Goddess Fund for Stroke Rsch. in Women., 2000—. Mem. Nat. Soc. Fund Raisers, Assn. Fund Dirs., Real Estate Bd. N.Y. (named Most Ingenious Broker Yr. 1975), Women's Forum (bd. dirs.). Office: Cushman & Wakefield Inc 51 W 52nd St Fl 11 New York NY 10019-6119 E-mail: lgoddess@cushwake.com.

GODENNE, GHISLAINE DUDLEY, physician, psychoanalyst, educator; b. Brussels; came to U.S., 1951; d. Pierre and Olive Dudley (Short) G. BS, Universite Catholique de Louvain, Belgium, 1948, MD, 1952. Intern Providence Hosp., Washington, 1951-52; resident in pediatrics, 1952-54; fellow in pediatrics Mayo Clinic, Rochester, Minn., 1954-57; fellow in pediatric research Johns Hopkins U., 1957-58, assoc. prof. mental hygiene, 1966-82, assoc. prof. psychiatry and pediatrics, 1966-82, psychoanalyst, 1972—, prof. psychology, 1973-90, prof. psychiatry, pediatrics, and mental hygiene, 1982—; resident in psychiatry Johns Hopkins Hosp., Balt., 1958-62, chief adolescent psychiat. service, 1964-73, dir. counseling and psychiat. services, 1973-90, dir. health svcs., 1978-88, dir. emeritus, 1990—; mem. staff various hosps. Balt., 1978-88; clin. prof. psychiatry U. Md., Balt., 1986—. Cons. psychiatrist Cylburn Children's Home, Balt., 1960-81, Catonsville (Md.) C.C., 1968-75, Good Shepherd Ctr., Balt., 1970-74, Assoc. Cath. Charity, Balt., 1970-77, Jewish Family of Children's Svcs., Balt., 1972-77, Mt. Washington Pediat. Hosp., Balt., 1974-81, Sheppard and Enoch Pratt Hosp., Balt, 1973-80, Loyola Coll., Balt., 1990-92. Mem. editorial bd.: Adolescent Psychiatry, 1978-83, Clinical Update Adolescent Psychiatry, 1982-85; contbr. articles to profl. jours. Bd. dirs. Balt. Girl Scouts Assn., 1958-60, 81-82, Met. Balt. Assn. Mental Health, 1965-69, Florence Crittendon Home, 1966-68; trustee McDonough Sch., 1975-83; pres. bd. Trustees Richmond Fellowship Md., 1975-77. Decorated Knight and Officer Order of Leopold (Belgium 1972-84), recipient Christophe Plantin prize (Belgium), 1989; awarded Nobility Concession with the title of Baroness (Belgium) 1991; recipient Career Teaching award NIMH, 1963-65, Schonfeld award Am. Soc. Adolescent Psychiatry, 1995; grantee Fulbright Found., 1951-52, Parke Davis Co., 1957-58, NIMH, 1961-63. Fellow ACP, Am. Psychiat. Assn. (life), APHA (life), Am. Orthopsychiat. Assn. (life), Am. Soc. Adolescent Psychiatry (life, pres. 1981-82), Am. Coll. Health Assn.; mem. AAUP, Am. Psycho-analytic Soc., Md. Soc. Adolescent Psychiatry (pres. 1968-69), Md. Psychiat. Soc. (past chmn. program com., co-chmn. women's com. 1991-96), Md. State Conf. Social Welfare (past mem. child welfare com.), Am. Soc. Adolescent Medicine (charter), Am. U. and Coll. Counseling Ctr. Dirs., Internat. Soc. Adolescent Psychiatry (v.p. 1989-92, sec.-gen. 1992-95, v.p. 1995-99, co-editor monograph 2000—), Women's Club of Johns Hopkins U. (pres. 1999-2000). Home: 15 Edgevale Rd Baltimore MD 21210-2215 E-mail: g_godenn@comcast.net.

GODFREY, JANET K, human resources specialist; d. Mable W. Godfrey; 1 child, Daryl. BA cum laude, W Va. State Coll., Institute, 1974; MA, Marshall U., Charleston/Huntington, W. Va., 1976; Ph.D.(abd), Kent (Ohio) State U., 1979. Asst. affirmative action officer CETA Program, Governor's Manpower Office, Charleston, W.Va., 1974—76; account executive-employee benefits adminstr. McDonough Caperton/Employee Benefits, Charleston, WV, W.Va., 1976—79; counselor-developmental services/resident dir. Kent State U., Kent, Ohio, 1979—82; counseling psychologist/internship-residency Ravenna Juvenile Detention Ctr., Ravenna, Ohio, 1982—83; comdr. State Area Command, Hdqs. Detachment, Kans. Army N.G., Topeka, 1991—94. Exec. dir. Office of the Asst. Sec. of Def., Employer Support of the Guard and Res., Topeka/Washington, DC, 1990—94; bd. of governors Assn. of the US Army, Topeka, 1994—99; federally employed womens com. U.S. Army N.G., Topeka, 1995—97. Chair; sec.-treas. Missionary Auxiliary, Shiloh Bapt. Ch., Topeka, 1995—2003; big sister Big Bros. and Big Sisters-Topeka Chpt., Kans., 2002—03; com. chair and worker(2001-visionary) Unity Coun. of Topeka, Kans., 2000—02. Decorated Armed Forces Res. Medal U.S. Army, Direct Congl. Commn., U.S. Army Reserves U.S. Congress, Pres. of the U.S., Dept. of Def., US Army, All County Band/W Va. Inst. of Technology's Ann. Concert Band Selectee Montgomery H.S., VAL Award U.S. Army, Army Res. Component Achievement Medal, Nat. Def. Medal; recipient Cum Laude, W Virgina State Coll., 1974, Academic Excellence/Dean's List, Dean, W Va. State Coll., 1971-1974, Nat. Honor Soc. Academic Achievement, Nat. Honor Soc. of the US, 1969, Miss Ivy, Alpha Kappa Alpha Sorority, Inc. (Nu Chpt.), 1972, Internat. Who's Who of Professionals, Bd. of Advisors, Internat. Who's Who, 1997, Tappee, Alpha Kappa Mu (Academic) Honor Soc., 1997, Who's Who Among Am. H.S. Students, Bd. of Advisors, Who's Who, 1971, Who's Who in Am. Colleges and Universities, 1974, VAL Award, Vol. Ctr. of Topeka, 2002, Outstanding Young Women of Am., Bd. of Advisors, Outstanding Americans, 1980, 1981, 1996, Two Thousand Notable Am. Women Nominee, Am. Biog. Inst., Inc., 1990, 2001, Women of Distinction-, KS MLK Meml. Com., 1997, Distinguish Grad. W Virgina State Coll., Black and Tribal Colleges and Universities, 1997; scholar Total Tuition, Alpha Omicron Omega Alumni Chpt., Alpha Kappa Alpha Sorority, Inc., 1972-1974. Mem.: N.G. Assn. of the US, Life Mem. (life mem. 1987), 5K Race Against Breast Cancer (assoc.), The Links, Inc. (immediate past pres.-2000-02, constn. and bylaws area-2000-03 2000—02), Alpha Kappa Mu, Alpha Kappa Alpha Sorority, Inc. (second vice pres./membership chair 2002—, Tuition award Alpha Omicron Omega chpt. 1972—74, Named Miss Ivy 1972). Achievements include first to First National Guard Officer, first African American, first female Commander, Adjutant General Corps, U.S. Army, Advance Course, Fort Benjamin Harrison, Jan. 1988- Jun.1988; First female, first African American to Command the approximately 350 soldier, Headquarters Detachment, State Area Command, Kansas Army National Guard; First female officer to serve as the Supervisory Management Specialist, Assistant to the Support Personnel Management Officer(Chief of Personnel/HR) & in the Fulltime Recruiting and Retention, KSARNG; First African American female Promoted to Field Grade Rank (MAJOR) in History of Kansas Army National Guard; highest ranking female on Active Guard/Reserve from '97-2000; First African American female in Kansas Army National Guard selected to the rank of Lieutanant Colonel, March 1999, Department of Army; Third female and first African American female to receive a Direct Congressional Commission to Lieutenant (U.S. Army Reserve Officer)-1976, W Virginia Army National Guard US.

GODIN, CHRISTINE C. library director; b. Boston, Oct. 7, 1946; d. Francis Brendan and Irene F. Crowley; m. Alan D. Godin, June 23, 1984; m. William J. Anderson III, Mar. 23, 1968 (div. June 1973). BA in English, U. Mass., Amherst, 1969; MA in Libr. Sci., U. Iowa, Iowa City, 1971. Libr. dir. Estherville (Iowa) Pub. Libr., 1971—72; pub. svcs. libr. Kans. City (Kans.) C.C., 1972—74, Johnson City C.C., Overland Pk., Kans., 1975—83; mktg. dir. Middlesex Office Supply, Inc., Newton, Mass., 1983—90; pub. svcs. libr. Johnson County C.C., Overland Pk., 1990—97; dir. of learning resources N.W. Vista Coll., San Antonio, 1997—. Contbr. articles to profl. jours. Artistic dir. Overland Stage Prodns., Overland Pk., 1993—97; program rev. vol. United Way of San Antonio, 2002—. Avocations: community theatre, mystery writing. Office: NW Vista Coll 3535 N Ellison Dr San Antonio TX 78251 Business E-Mail: cgodin@accd.edu.

GODOFF, ANN, book editor; b. N.Y.C., July 22, 1949; d. Boris and Marilyn (Rosenstock) G. BFA, NYU, 1972. Sr. editor Simon & Schuster, N.Y.C., 1980-86; editor in chief Atlantic Monthly Press, N.Y.C., 1986-91; exec. editor Random House Inc., N.Y.C., 1991-96, pres., editor-in-chief 1997—2003.

GODONE-MARESCA, LILLIAN, lawyer; b. Buenos Aires, June 9, 1958; d. Armand C.E. Godone-Signanini and E. Nydia Soracco-Godone; m. Paul Alexander Maresca-Lowell (dec.); children: Catherine Victoria, Gerard Frank, Warren Paul. BA, Cath. U. Buenos Aires, 1975, MA, 1977, JD summa cum laude, 1979, advanced tchg. degree in jud. sci., 1981. Bar: Dist. Ct. Buenos Aires 1980, Calif. 1995, U.S. Dist. Ct. (ea. dist.) Calif. 1995, U.S. Dist. Ct. (so. dist.) Calif. 1998; lic. real estate broker, Calif. Advisor Sub-Sec. of State for Fgn. Trade, Buenos Aires, 1982; pvt. practice law Buenos Aires, 1982-86; therapist Ocean Pkwy. Developmental Ctr., N.Y., 1992; pvt. practice law Sacramento, 1995-96, San Diego, 1997—. Asst. instr. Cath. U., Buenos Aires, 1983-86; adj. instr. U.S. Internat. U., San Diego, spring 1998. Contbr. articles to profl. jours.; author of poetry. Vol. San Diego Vol. Lawyer Program, 1993-94, Legal Svcs. No. Calif., Sacramento, 1995-96; catechist St. Ignatius, Sacramento, 1995-96, St. Michael's, Poway, Calif., 1997-98. Mem. Internat. Soc. Poets (disting.), State Bar Calif., Mothers Twins Club. Republican. Roman Catholic. Avocations: spending time with her children, the right to life, writing. Home: 202 Calle Florecita Escondido CA 92029

GODRIDGE, LESLIE V. bank executive; AB in History, Smith Coll.; MBA, NYU. Sr. exec. v.p. corp. banking Bank of NY, N.Y.C. Named one of 25 Women to Watch, US Banker Mag., 2003. Office: Bank NY 48 Wall St New York NY 10286

GODWIN, GAIL KATHLEEN, writer; b. Birmingham, Ala., June 18, 1937; d. Mose Winston and Kathleen (Krahenbuhl) G.; m. Douglas Kennedy, 1960 (div. 1961), m. Ian Marshall, 1965 (div. 1966). Student, Peace Jr. Coll., Raleigh, N.C., 1955-57; BA in Journalism, U. N.C., 1959; MA in English, U. Iowa, 1968, PhD, 1971, U. N.C., 1987, U. So.-Sewanee, 1994, SUNY, 1996. News reporter Miami Herald, 1959-60; rep., cons. U.S. Travel Service, London, 1961-65; editorial asst. Saturday Evening Post, 1966; instr. Univ. Iowa, Iowa City, 1967-71; lectr. Iowa Writer's Workshop, 1972-73, Vassar Coll., 1977, Columbia U. Writing Program, 1978, 81. Author: (novels) The Perfectionists, 1970, Glass People, 1972, The Odd Woman, 1974 (Nat. Book award nomination 1974), Violet Clay, 1978 (Am. Book award nomination 1980), A Mother and Two Daughters, 1982 (Am. Book award nomination 1982), The Finishing School, 1985, A Southern Family, 1987, Father Melancholy's Daughter, 1991, The Good Husband, 1994, Evensong, 1999, Evenings at Five, 2003; (short stories) Dream Children, 1976, Mr. Bedford and The Muses, 1983; editor: (with Shannon Ravenel) The Best American Short Stories 1985, 1985, Heart: A Personal Journey Through Its Myths & Meanings, 2001; librettist: (with Robert Starer) The Last Lover, 1975, Journals of a Songmaker, 1976, Apollonia, 1979, Anna Margarita's Will, 1981, Remembering Felix, 1987, Gregory The Great, 1996, The Other Voice: A Portrait of Hilda of Whitby in Words and Music, 1998, Magdalene At The Tomb, 1999, Abraham Remembers, 2000. Recipient Thomas Wolfe Meml. award Lipinsky Endowment of Western N.C. Hist. Assn., 1988, Janet Heidinger Kafka award U. Rochester, 1988; fellow Center for Advanced Study, U. Ill., Urbana, 1971-72; Am. specialist USIS, 1976; Nat. Endowment Arts grantee, 1974-75; Guggenheim fellow, 1975-76; recipient award in lit. Am. Acad. and Inst. of Arts and Letters, 1981 Mem. ASCAP, Authors Guild, Authors League. Home: PO Box 946 Woodstock NY 12498-0946*

GODWIN, MARY JO, editor, librarian consultant; b. Tarboro, N.C., Jan. 31, 1949; d. Herman Esthol and Mamie Winifred (Felton) Pittman; m. Charles Benjamin Godwin, May 2, 1970. BA, N.C. Wesleyan Coll., 1971; MLS, East Carolina U., 1973. Cert. libr., N.C. From libr. asst. to asst. dir. Edgecombe County Meml. Library, Tarboro, 1970-76, dir., 1977-85; asst. editor Wilson Library Bull., Bronx, N.Y., 1985-89, editor, 1989-92; dir. govt. sales The Oryx Press, Phoenix, 1993-95, dir. mktg. svc., 1995-96, dir. mktg., sales and promotional svcs., 1996-2000; sr. mktg. mgr. Oryx, Greenwood Pub. Group, Westport, 2000—02; dir. mktg. Scarecrow Press and Scarecrow Edn., Rowman & Littlefield Pub. Group, Lanham, Md., 2002—. Mem. White House Conf. on Librs. and Info. Svcs. Task Force; bd. dirs. Libr. Pub. Rels. Coun., 1992-95. bd. dirs. Friends of Calvert County Pub. Libr., 1994, Osborn Edn. Found., sec., 1997-98; mem. Ariz. Ctr. for the Book. Recipient Robert Downs award for intellectual freedom U. Ill. Grad. Sch. of Libr. Sci., 1992. Mem. ALA (3M/Jr. Mem. Roundtable Profl. Devel. award 1981), N.C. Libr. Assn. (sec. 1981-83), Info. Futures Inst., Ind. Librs. Exchange Roundtable (v.p., pres. elect 1994, pres. 1995-96). Democrat. Episcopalian. Office: Scarecrow Press 4501 Forbes Blvd Ste 200 Lanham MD 20706 E-mail: mjgodwin@comcast.net.

GODWIN, NAOMI NADINE, editor; b. Redfield, Iowa, Aug. 5, 1942; d. Dwayne Ivan and Emma Vernice Marie (Scott) G. BA, U. Iowa, 1964; MA, Columbia U., N.Y.C., 1972. Writer, copy editor Des Moines Register and Tribune, 1964-67; assoc. editor Travel Agt. Mag., N.Y.C., 1969-72; assoc. editor then sr. editor Travel Weekly, N.Y.C., 1972-92, mng. editor, 1992-96, editor Secaucus, N.J., 1996—, editor in chief. Author: Complete Guide to Travel Agency Automation, 1982, 2d rev. edit., 1987; contbr. articles to profl. jours.; speaker in field. Democrat. Mem. Christian Ch. (Disciples Of Christ). Avocations: reading history and biographies, sewing, cooking, traveling, photography.

GODWIN, PAMELA JUNE, financial services executive; b. Council Bluffs, Iowa, Mar. 29, 1949; d. Fred Norman and Carol Ethel (Hatfield) Humphrey; m. Wallace Gill Godwin, Dec. 20, 1970; 1 child, Christopher Humphrey. BA in French, Pa. State U., 1970; postgrad., West Chester (Pa.) State U., 1971-74. Tchr. various schs., Phila., 1971-74; various underwriting/tng. positions Colonial Penn Ins. Co., Phila., 1974-77, mgr., 1977-81, dir., 1981-84, v.p., 1984-86, Colonial Penn Group, Inc., Phila., 1986-87, sr. v.p., 1987-88; sr. v.p. customer mgmt. Nat. Liberty Corp., Valley Forge, Pa., 1988-93; pres., COO, Acad. Ins. Group, Frazer, Pa., 1993-95, Nat. Home Life Assurance Co., Frazer, Pa., 1993-95; pres. Change Ptnrs., Inc., Havertown, Pa., 1995—96, 2002—; acting pres. Womens Way, Phila., 1998-99; pres., COO agy. divsn. GMAC Ins. Personal Lines (formerly Integon Corp.), Winston-Salem, NC, 1999—2001; pres. Change Ptnrs., Inc., Havertown, 2001—. Bd. dirs. Wheels, Inc., J.F. Kennedy Vocat. Tech. Sch., Phila., 1987-88; bd. dirs. Gt. Valley Cmty. Edn. Found., 1991-95, past pres.; mem. Westgate Hills Civic Assn., Havertown, 1974—; mem. Wharton Exec. Edn. adv. bd.; chmn. adv. bd. Pa. State Great Valley, 1996-2000; bd. dirs. Winston-Salem C. of C., 1996-2001, Phila. Found., 2003—; mem. Com. of 200, 2000—. Named to Pa. Honor Roll of Women, 1996. Mem. Phila. Forum of Exec. Women (pres. 1998-99), Soc. Property and Casualty Underwriters (past pres. Phila. chpt. 1987-88), Phi Beta Kappa, Phi Sigma Iota. Democrat. Lutheran. Avocations: skiing, walking, reading. E-mail: changepartners@comcast.net.

GODWIN, SARA, writer; b. St. Louis, Feb. 18, 1944; d. Robert Franklin, Jr. and Annabelle Godwin; m. Charles D. James, May 1, 1990; children: Jane, Josh. BA, Calif. State U., 1967; postgrad., UCLA, 1968-70, U. Calif., Berkeley, 1970-71, W.I. Inst. Fairleigh Dickinson U., St. Croix, V.I., 1971-72; MA, Dominican Coll., 1974. Writer, editor Ortho Books, Std. Oil Calif., San Francisco, 1975-77; writer, editor Gannett Corp., San Rafael, Calif., 1977-79; sr. writer Shaklee Corp., San Francisco, 1979-88; freelance writer Marin County, Calif., 1988—. Featured spkr. Ask the Gardener Sta. KSFO, San Francisco, 1980—81; contbr., prodr. Raw Radio Travel, 1998—. Author: (book) Seals, 1990, Gorillas, 1990, The Angler's Companion, 1992, Hummingbirds, 1991, The Gardener's Companion, 1992 (N.Y. Times Rev., Garden Book Club selection), Landscaping Decks and Patios, 1994, Scott's See and Do: Lawns and Groundcovers, 1995; contbr. book Last Puff, 1990 (Lit. Guild selection), book The Sea, 1993; author (with others): (book) Smith and Hawken Book of Outdoor Gardening, 1996; author: (screenplays) Discover Canada, Discovering The USA; manuscript editor: All About Perennials, 1992, prin. lexicographer: Nat. Gardening Assn. Dictionary of Horticulture, 1994; scriptwriter, prodr. : China: The Middle Kingdom; contbr. CD ROM Microsoft Complete Gardening, 1996, CD ROM Frommer's Boston, 1996, articles to numerous U.S. and fgn. mags. Recipient 1st prize for personal column, Calif. Press Women, 1984. Mem.: PEN, Garden Writers Assn., Am. Soc. Journalists and Authors, Authors Guild. Avocations: reading, travel, gardening, fly fishing. Home: PO Box 1503 Ross CA 94957-1503

GOEHRING, MAUDE COPE, retired business educator; b. Persia, Tenn., Jan. 5, 1915; d. James Lawrence and Bobbie C. (Ross) Cope; m. Harvey John Goehring Jr., Aug. 12, 1950 (dec. Mar. 1992). Student, Lebanon Valley Coll., 1944-45; grad., Am. Inst. Banking, 1945; BS in Edn., Indiana U. of Pa., 1948; MEd, U. Pitts., 1950. Tchr. Penn Hills Sr. High Sch., Pitts., 1948-68, U. Pitts., 1959-60, ret., 1968; vol. chmn. ICU, operating rm. info. desk Margaret R. Pardee Meml. Hosp., Hendersonville, N.C., 1989-95; vol. Carolina Village Health Ctr., 1994-99. Coord. Henderson County Ct. House Vols., Hendersonville, 1983-89; cons., counselor tax aid program Am. Assn. Ret. Persons, Hendersonville, 1981-96. Neighborhood chmn. Girl Scouts U.S., Butler County Pa., 1976-79; bd. dirs. ARC, Hendersonville, 1986-91; sec.-treas., bd. dirs. Crime Stoppers of Henderson County, 1991-96; nat. bd. dirs. Second Wind Hall of Fame, 1991-95. Mem. AAUW (officer 1975-76), Gideon Internat. Aux. (pres., sec. 1969-70), Delta Pi Epsilon (life, Gamma chpt., pres., sec. 1956-59, nat. del. 1957). Republican. Lutheran. Avocations: gardening, crafts, sewing, reading.

GOEKEN, DEBORAH, editor; Reporter Rocky Mountain News, Denver, 1986, bus. editor, city editor, asst. mng. editor, mng. editor, 1999—. Office: Rocky Mountain Post 100 Gene Amole Way Denver CO 80204*

GOELLNER, SUSAN KITCHIN, nurse midwife; b. St. Louis, Mo., Mar. 14, 1948; d. William Joseph Kitchin, Doris (Goellner) Kitchin; children: Derek W.R. Becker, Robert Holmes Becker, Margaret Mirth Becker. BA in Art History, U. Md., 1972; ADN, Columbus State Coll., 1982; MSN, Case We. Res. U., 1998. Cert. nurse midwife WomenCare, Jeffersonville, Ind. Mem.: Birth Care Network, Am. Coll. Nurse Midwives, Sigma Theta Tau. Avocations: folk dancing, reading, walking, bicycling. Home: 2225 Blvd Napoleon Louisville KY 40205

GOERING, PAMELA JO, music educator, bank officer; b. Yankton, S.D., Apr. 13, 1958; d. Hugo Eugene and Donna Mae Milander; m. Kevin Lyle Goering, Aug. 9, 1980; children: Holly Jo, Amber Lynn, Heather Rae. BFA in Edn., Wayne State Coll., Nebr., 1980. Music tchr. Leigh Cmty. Sch., Nebr., 1980—83, Lakeview Cmty. Sch., Columbus, Nebr., 1986—89, Humphrey Pub. Sch., Nebr., 1990—93, 1994—98; family consumer sci. tchr. Columbus H.S., Nebr., 1999—2000; music tchr. St. Francis Schs., Humphrey, Nebr., 2000—02; bank teller Bank First, Columbus, Nebr., 2003—; music tchr. Immanuel Luth., Columbus, Nebr., 2003—. Mem. Lakeview Adv. Bd., Columbus, Nebr., 2003. Choir dir., organist St. John's Luth., Columbus, Nebr., 1986—. Mem.: Am. Choral Dirs. Assn., Music Educators Nat. Conf., 4-H Club. Avocations: sewing, quilting, music. Home: 25136 355th St Platte Center NE 68653

GOERLICH, SHIRLEY ALICE BOYCE, publishing executive, educator, media consultant; b. Oneonta, NY, May 17, 1937; d. John Orlo and Nella Virginia (Bartow) Boyce; m. Robert Frank Goerlich, Aug. 19, 1967; children: Robert John, Daniel Lee. AAS, SUNY, Cobleskill, 1957; BA, Parsons Coll., 1962. Cert. tchr. N.Y., bus. owner N.Y. Tchr. Milw. Pub. Schs., 1962-64, Huntington (N.Y.) Pub. Schs., 1964-67, Fairfax (Va.) County Adult Edn., 1970-76; pvt. practice Greene, NY, 1979-83; prin., owner RSG Pub., Sidney, NY, 1984—. Cons. Cemetery Bds. Trustees, Chenago, Delaware and Otsego counties. Author: Genealogy: A Practical Research Guide, 1984 (CSG award, 1987), 2d edit., 1995, At Rest in Unadilla, Otsego Co., N.Y., 1987 (CSG award, 1988, Otsego County Local History award, 1993), Etched in Stone in Sidney, Delaware County N.Y., 1997, East Guilford Cemetery, 1997, History of Unadilla, 4 vols., 1998, History of West Unadilla, 1999, Town of Guilford, Chenango County, N.Y., Book 2 (Guilford, Chenango County, N.Y.) Cemeteries and Burial Grounds, 2000, History of East Unadilla, 2000; pub.: Author Unknown, 2001, transcribed and pub.: N.Y. State Censuses for Guilford, Chenango County, N.Y., 1855, 1865, 1875, 1905, Sidney (Delaware County, N.Y.) 1850, Masonville (Delaware County, N.Y.) 1845 along with the Civil War Roster for this town, transcriber, pub.: N.Y. State censuses for Unadilla, N.Y., 1855, 1865, 1875, 1892, Civil War roster town of Franklin, Delaware County, N.Y. Historian Town of Unadilla, NY, 1909—90, trustee Evergreen Hill Cemetery Assoc., Unadilla, 1996—2000, advisor, 2001—; v.p. Prospect Hill Cemetery Assn., Sidney, NY, 2000, bd. dirs., 2001—, v.p. bd. dirs., 2001, pres., 2002—03, sexton, 2003—04. Recipient Nat. award, Nat. Soc. New Eng. Women, 1989, award for Excellence, Otsego County Local History Adv. Com., 1995, Civil War Re-enactors award, Bainbridge Hist. Soc., 2002. Mem.: Nat. Soc. New Eng. Women, N.Y. State Hist. Assn., Conn. Soc. Genealogists (Spl. Outstanding award 1989), Nat. Soc. Daus. Union Vets., Nat. Soc. DAR (chmn. 1989—91, organizing regent Gen. John Paterson chpt. 1978, Nat. Lineage Rsch. award 1987, 1988, 1989), Sidney Hist. Assn. (life). Republican. Presbyterian. Avocations: cooking, painting. Home: 217 County Highway 1 Bainbridge NY 13733-9307 Office: RSG Publishing 217 County Highway 1 Bainbridge NY 13733-3399 Home (Winter): PO Box 441 Sidney NY 13838-0441

GOERTZEL, GWENDOLYN MICHELE, painter, priest; b. Bklyn., July 25, 1967; d. Carroll Jean Yorgey and Donald Enix; m. Ben Goertzel, June 21, 1987; children: Zarathustra, Zebulon, Scheherazade. BA in Linguistics, Temple U., 1988; MS in Math., U. Nev., Las Vegas, 1992. Ordained zen priest Buddhist Order Hsu Yun. Exhibited in group shows at Vox Populi, Phila., 1988—89, Waikato Soc. Arts, Hamilton, New Zealand, 1995, New Century Artists, N.Y.C., 2002—03, one-woman shows include Local Artist, Las Vegas, Internat. Art Gallery, Perth, Australia, 1996, Riverview Arts Ctr., Phillipsburg, N.J., 1999, Intro Art Gallery, Jersey City, 2001; illustrator (book) Linus Pauling: A life in Science and Politics, 1995, designer Las Vegas Kardma (Alan Ackerman), 1994. Mem.: New Century Artists. Home: 4005 Delancy Dr Silver Spring MD 20906 Personal E-mail: garany@yahoo.com.

GOERTZEN, IRMA, hospital executive; BSN, U. Wash., 1967, MS, 1968, DS in Pub. Svc., 1998, D Humanities, 2000. Pres., CEO Magee-Women Hosp. and Rsch. Inst., 1989—2004; pres., CEO, Magee Women's Health Corp., 1998—. Office: 204 Craft Ave Pittsburgh PA 15213

GOERZ, MARY ELIZABETH LARSEN, civic worker; b. Mpls., Apr. 1, 1935; d. David Paul and Myrtle Mary (Grunnet) Larsen; m. David J. Goerz, Jr., Jan. 26, 1962; children: David J. III, Karen Goerz Preston, Julie Goerz Mulvaney. BA, Stanford U., 1957. Mem. pers. staff Hewlett-Packard Corp., Palo Alto, Calif., 1960—62. Bd. dirs. Packard Children's Hosp., Stanford, Calif., 1985-96, Ch. of the Pioneers Found., Menlo Park, 1991—, Lucile Packard Found. for Children's Health, Stanford, 1996-2001; founder Roth Aux. of Packard Children's Hosp., 1989, pres. Assn. of Auxs., 1986-89; pres. of corp. Menlo Park Presbyn. Ch., 1989-91, moderator women's ministries, 1989-91; pres. PTA, La Entrada Sch., Menlo Park, 1976-77; sec. Mid-Peninsula Access Corp., 1986-87. Mem. Stanford Alumni Assn., Stanford Club of Palo Alto (dir. 1971-73). E-mail: margrz@aol.com.

GOES, KATHLEEN ANN, secondary education educator, choral director; b. New Bedford, Mass., Jan. 13, 1951; d. Filento Andrade and Lillian (Cabral) G. BA in Psychology, U. Mass., North Dartmouth, 1976; postgrad., Ctrl. Conn. State U., 1987—98. Cert. K-8 elem. tchr., K-12 music tchr., Mass. Social worker Dept. Social Svcs., Cambridge, Mass., 1980-85; pvt. tchr. voice and piano, New Bedford, 1985-88; tchr. vocal music New Bedford Pub. Sch., 1985-90; tchr. music, choral dir. Fairhaven (Mass.) H.S., 1991—. Singer, actress, southeastern New Eng., 1974—; dir. music ministry St. Mary's Ch., South Dartmouth, Mass., 1988—; bd. dirs., sec. New Bedford Festival Theatre, 1990-97, v.p., 1997-99, mem. adv. bd., 1999—. Dir. musicals Me and My Girl, The Sound of Music, Cinderella, My Fair Lady, Bye, Bye Birdie, You're a Good Man Charlie Brown, How to Succeed in Business Without Really Trying, Little Shop of Horrors, The Boyfriend, Godspell, Jesus Christ Superstar; performed the mother in Amahl and the Night Visitors; actress, singer in musicals Fiddler on the Roof, Godspell, Phantom, The Sound of Music. Bd. dirs. New Bedford Symphony Orch., 1994-96. Named Promising Young Artist, Crescendo Club, Boston, 1981; recipient outstanding leadership award Fairhaven Assn. for Music Edn., 1995. Mem. NEA, Am. Choral Dirs. Assn., Nat. Pastoral Musicians Assn., New Eng. Theatre Conf., Drama League, Music Educators Nat. Conf., Mass. Tchrs. Assn., Mass. Music Educators Assn., Whale Hist. League. Roman Catholic. Avocations: cooking, crafts, computers, boating, scenic design. Home: 363 Maple St New Bedford MA 02740-1075 Office: Fairhaven HS 12 Huttleston Ave Fairhaven MA 02719-3122

GOESTENKORS, GAIL, basketball coach; b. Waterford, Mich., Feb. 26, 1963; m. Mark Simons. BA, Saginaw Valley State U., 1985. Grad. asst. Iowa State U., 1985-86; asst. coach basketball Purdue U., West Lafayette, Ind., 1986-92; head basketball coach Duke U., Durham, N.C., 1992—. Coach U.S. Jones Cup Team, taiwan; head coach Festival Trials, 1991, 95; coach 1994 ACC All-Star Team, Latvia, Lithuania. Named ACC Coach of the Yr., 1995-96, 97-98, 98-99, Nat. Coach of Yr. 1999. Office: Duke University Cameron Indoor Stadium PO Box 90555 Durham NC 27708-0555

GOETHE, ELIZABETH HOGUE, music educator; b. Balt., May 4, 1943; d. Paul Robert and Charlotte H. (Rigney) H.; m. Frederick Martin Goethe, June 30, 1973; children: Elizabeth Anne, Jonathan David. BS, Towson U., 1965; MEd in Music, U. Md., 1972. Cert. tchr. piano. Accompanist Vera Hax Dance Studio, Balt., 1962-66; music tchr. Balt. County Pub. Schs., 1965-74; ch. choir dir. Glyndon, Ellicott City, Md., 1976-79; class piano tchr. Balt. County Pub. Schs., 1980—83; piano tchr. Reisterstown, Md., 1978—; pvt. piano tchr., 1978—; music tchr. St. John's Episcopal Pre-Sch., Glyndon, 1978—2000. Mem. Choristers Guild, 1976-79. Mem. Music Tchrs. Nat. Assn. (ea. divsn. sec. 1996-98), Md. State Music Tchrs. Assn. (convention chair 1991-93, v.p. student activities 1993-97, cert. com. 1991-97), Greater Columbia Music Tchrs. Assn. (sec. 1996-98), Greater Balt. Music Tchrs. Assn. (treas. 1997—), Nat. Guild of Piano Tchrs. (adjudicator), Am. Coll. Musicians. Republican. Episcopalian. Avocations: family, teaching, profl. activities. Home and Office: 120 Nicodemus Rd Reisterstown MD 21136-3245

GOETZ, CECELIA HELEN, lawyer, retired judge; b. N.Y.C.; d. Isador and Sylvia (Cohen) G.; children: Matthew I. Spiegel, Robert Spiegel. BA cum laude, NYU, 1940, LLB, 1940, LLM in Taxation, 1957. Bar: N.Y. 1940, U.S. Dist. Ct. (so. and ea. dists.) N.Y. 1951, Fla. 1954, U.S. Ct. Appeals (2d cir.) 1958, U.S. Ct. Appeals (1st cir.) 1952, U.S. Ct. Appeals (9th cir.) 1967. Atty. claims div. (now civil div.) Dept. Justice, Washington, 1943-46; assoc. counsel Office Chief of Counsel for War Crimes, Nuremberg, Ger., 1946-48; ptnr. Goetz & Goetz, N.Y.C., 1949-51; asst. chief counsel Office Price Stblzn., Washington, 1951-52; spl. asst. to atty. gen., tax div., Dept. Justice, Washington, 1952-53; assoc. Weisman, Celler, Allan, Spett & Sheinberg, N.Y.C., 1953-58, Kaye, Scholer, Fierman, Hays & Handler, N.Y.C., 1958-64; ptnr. Herzfeld & Rubin, N.Y.C., 1964-78; judge U.S. Bankruptcy Ct., Eastern Dist. N.Y., Bklyn., 1978-93; of counsel Herzfeld & Rubin, P.C., N.Y.C., 1994-95. Mem. Assn. Bar City N.Y., N.Y. State Bar Assn., ABA, N.Y. County Lawyers Assn., NYU Law Rev. Alumni Assn., N.Y. Women's Bar Assn., Women's Bar Assn. State N.Y. Nat. Conf. Bankruptcy Judges, Nat. Assn. Women Judges, Assn. Women Judges State N.Y., Women's City Club N.Y. Office: 3400 N Ocean Dr West Palm Beach FL 33404-3220

GOETZ, REGINA M. research scientist, pharmacist; b. Freiburg im Breisgau, Germany, Sept. 16, 1964; arrived in U.S., 1996; d. Helmut Paul and Christine Emma Goetz. BSc in Pharmacy, Albert-Ludwigs U., Freiburg, Germany, 1988, PhD, 1995. Pharmacist various drugstores and univ. hosps., Freiburg, Germany, 1990—96; resident fellow Harvard Med. Sch., Boston, 1996—98, U. Coll. London, 1999; rsch. assoc. Meml. Sloan-Kettering Inst., N.Y.C., 1999—2002; assoc. rsch. scientist NYU Med. Sch., NYC, 2002—. Named Best Abitur of Germany, Govt. of Germany, 1984. Mem.: German Soc. Pharm. Scientists, Am. Heart Assn. (basic cardiovasc. sci. coun. 2001). Avocations: bicycling, sailing, hiking, photography. Home: 524 E 79th St Apt 5B New York NY 10021-1542 Personal E-mail: regina_m_goetz@hotmail.com.

GOFFEN, RONA, art educator, educator; b. N.Y.C., June 7, 1944; d. William and Stella (Friedman) G. AB cum laude, Mt. Holyoke Coll., 1966; MA, Columbia U., 1968, PhD with distinction, 1974. Lectr. dept. fine arts Ind. U., Bloomington, 1971-73; lectr. dept. art and archaeology Princeton (N.J.) U., 1973-74, asst. prof. art, 1974-78; asst. prof. dept. art and art history Duke U., Durham, N.C., 1978-80, assoc. prof. art, 1980-86, chmn. dept. art and art history, 1983—, prof. art, 1986-88; Disting. prof. Rutgers U., New Brunswick, N.J., 1988-98, chmn. dept. art history, 1990-96, bd. govs. prof., 1998—. Vis. assoc. prof. Barnard Coll. Columbia U., N.Y.C., 1980; vis. scholar Am. Acad. Rome, 1976, Inst. Advanced Study, 1999—2000; Robert Sterling Clark vis. prof. Williams Coll., 1997; vis. prof. UCLA, 2001, Ecole des Hautes Etudes, Paris, 2002. Author: Piety and Patronage in Renaissance Venice, 1986, Spirituality in Conflict, 1988, Giovanni Bellini, 1989, Titian's Venus of Urbino, 1997, Titian's Women, 1997, Masaccio's Trinity, 1998, Renaissance Rivals, 2002; co-editor: Life and Death in Fifteenth-Century Florence, 1989; co-editor/co-author: Il colore Ritrovato: Bellini a Venezia, 2000, bd. editors: Art History, Venezia Cinquecento; contbr. articles to profl. publs. Am. Philos. Soc. grantee, 1979, NEH grantee, summer 1986; Harvard U. Ctr. Italian Renaissance Studies fellow, Florence, Italy, 1976-77, Am. Council for Learned Socs. fellow, 1976-77, Nat. Humanities Ctr. fellow, Research Triangle Park, N.C., 1986-87, Guggenheim fellow, 1986-87. Mem. Coll. Art Assn., Renaissance Soc. Office: Rutgers U Dept Art History Voorhees Hall New Brunswick NJ 08901

GOGGIN, JOAN MARIE, school system administrator; b. Boston, Nov. 15, 1956; d. Richard and Florence Muriel (Stone) G. BS in Edn., Westfield State Coll., 1978; MS in Edn., Lesley Coll., 1981; Cert. Adv. Grad. Studies in Adminstrv. Leadership, U. Mass., 1999. Spl. needs tchr. Supervisory Union # 53, Pembroke, N.H., 1978-79; grad. intern, head tchr. Ednl. Collaborative Greater Boston, Brookline, Mass., 1979-80; vocat. counselor Charles River Assn. for Retarded Citizens, Needham, Mass., 1981-83; dir. vocat. svcs. Community Assistance Corp., New Orleans, 1983-84; tchr. of pre-sch. children with severe spl. needs St. Charles Parish Pub. Schs., Luling, La., 1985-88; career placement and tng. specialist Plymouth (Mass.) Carver Regional Sch. Dist., 1988-92; inclusion facilitator Plymouth Pub. Schs., 1992-98, asst. dir. spl. edn., 1999—. Cons. on self advocacy Mass. Assn. for Retarded Citizens, 1980-83; ednl. cons. Human Devel. Ctr., La. State U., New Orleans, 1984-85, D.K. Hollingsworth & Assocs., Metairie, La., 1984-88; vocat. cons. United Cerebral Palsy, Harahann, La., 1984-85; program coord. JTPA Project, Plymouth Sch. Dist., 1989-91, program. adminstr., 1991-93, exec. prodr. Bridging the Gap, We All Belong Together, 1991-93. Exec. prodr.: Bridging the Gap: Transition to Independence, We All Belong Together; author tng. program for paraprofls; curriculum devel. with adaptive modifications for learners with spl. needs, 1997. Active tadk force on criteria for spl. edn. svcs. Mass. Dept. Edn., 1992-93, mem. com. individual edn. plan, 1990-93, mem. com. on profl. devel., 2000—. Recipient Hon. Mention Tchr. of Yr. award Mass. Coun. Exceptional Children; grantee Mass. Dept. Edn., 1988—. Mem.: ASCD, NEA, Mass. Assn. Spl. Edn. Adminstrs., Assn. for Severely Handicapped. Democrat. Avocations: t'ai chi, yoga, travel, reading, gourmet cooking. Office: Pupil Personnel Svcs 253 S Meadow Rd Plymouth MA 02360-4739 E-mail: jgoggin@plymouth.k12.ma.us.

GOGGIN, MARGARET ENID (KNOX), librarian, educator; b. Nyack, N.Y., Feb. 24, 1919; d. Henry Julian and Eleanor (Green) Knox; m. John Mann Goggin, Nov. 22, 1962. AB, Maryville Coll., 1940; BS, Peabody Coll., 1942; MS, U. Ill., 1948, PhD, 1957. Tchr., librarian Flintville (Tenn.) High Sch., 1940-42; reference asst. Joint U. Library, Nashville, 1942-43, acting reference librarian, 1943-45; vis. instr. Peabody Library Sch., Nashville, 1943-45; readers adviser Youngstown (Ohio) Pub. Library, 1945-46; bibliographer, reference librarian Office Tech. Services Dept. Commerce, Washington, 1946-47; reference asst. U. Ill., 1948-49; asst. to dir. U. Fla. Libraries, asst. prof. library sci., 1949-50, head dept. reference and bibliography, asso. prof. library sci., 1950-62; asst. dir. U. Fla. Libraries (Readers Services), asso. prof. library sci., 1965-66, asst. dir. libraries, prof. library sci., 1966, acting dir. libraries, 1967-68; dean Grad. Sch. Librarianship, U. Denver, 1968-79, prof., 1979-84, prof. emeritus, 1984—. Vis. lectr. U. Okla. Libr. Sch., summer 1959, Emory U. Sch. Librarianship, 1965; dir. Satellite Libr. Info. Network, 1974-76; prin. investigator Telefax Libr. Info. Network, 1978-79; cons. U.S. Office Edn. divsn. Libr. Programs, 1968-69, 87, Aims C.C., Greeley, Colo., 1973, Wash. State Libr., 1978-79, Loretto Heights Coll., Denver, 1981; co-owner Book Seminars, Inc., 1986-95; interim dir. Collection Mgmt., Emory U., 1986-88; owner Margaret K. Goggin Books, 1994—. Recipient Colo. Libr. of Yr. award, 1979, Outstanding Svc. award U. Denver, 1985, Alumni citation Maryville Coll., 1987, Disting. Alumnus award Peabody Coll., 1987; Rockefeller Found. grantee, Haiti and Paris, 1958, 61-62, Fulbright grantee, 1972, OAS grantee for multi-nat. libr. edn. program, 1974-75 Mem. ALA (past div. pres.), Colo. Libr. Assn. (dir. 1978-79), Mountain Plains Libr. Assn. (dir. 1978-79), Assn. For Library and Info. Sci. Edn. (pres. 1977), Nat. League Am. Pen Women, Fla. Ctr. for the Book (mem. exec. bd. 1988—), Delta Kappa Gamma, Beta Phi Mu (past dir.), PEO. Clubs: Altrusa (bd. dirs. Denver 1974-76, 80-82, pres. 1983-84). Home: 1108 Camellia Rd Birmingham AL 35215-7208 E-mail: gog@gnv.fdt.net.

GOGGIN, WENDY, prosecutor; U.S. atty. mid. dist. Tenn., U.S. Dept. Justice, Nashville, prosecutor mid. dist. Tenn. Office: 110 9th Ave S Ste A961 Nashville TN 37203-3870 Fax: 615-736-5323.

GOH, CHAN HON, ballerina; b. Beijing, Feb. 1, 1969; arrived in Can, 1977; d. Choo Chiat and Lin Yee Goh. Dancer Goh Ballet Tng. Co., Vancouver, B.C., Can., 1986-87; corp de ballet dancer Nat. Ballet of Can., Toronto, 1988-90, second soloist, 1990-92, first soloist, 1992-93, prin. dancer, 1994—. Advisor in dance Met Toronto Arts Coun, 1992—94; guest artist Royal Danish Ballet, Hong Kong Ballet, Singapore Dance Theatre, Washington Ballet, Nat Ballet China, Suzanne Farrell Ballet, N.B.A. Ballet, Japan, Vail Internat. Dance Festival. Dancer The Sleeping Beauty, La Fille Mal Gardée, Don Quixote, Romeo & Juliet, The Merry Widow, The Nutcracker, Taming of the Shrew, Onegin, Swan Lake, Giselle, Cinderella, La Boutique Fantasque, Tales of Arabian Night, La Sylphide, Tristan and Isolde, Sylvia Pas de deux, Paquita, Dream Dances, Divertimento No. 15, Les Sylphides, Theme and Variations, Dèsir, The Four Temperaments, La Ronde, Dahnis and Chloe, Mozartiana, Song of the Earth, LaBayadere Act II, Etudes, Apollo, Chaconne, Serenade, Napolie Act 3, Firebird, Scotch Symphony, La Sonnombula, The Man I Love (pas des deux from Who Cares?), Afternoon of a Faun, Chaccoon, Can premieres include Madame Butterfly (Stanton Welch), Jewels (George Balanchine), Concerto for Flute and Harp (John Cranko), 1990, The Leaves are Fading (Anthony Tudor), 1990, Pastorale (James Kudelka), 1990, Musings (Kudelka), 1991, The Actress (Kudlka), 1993, Now and Then (John Neumeier), 1993, The Four Seasons (Kudelka), 1997, Terra Firma (Kudelka), Forgotten Land (Kylian), lead and organized stars of N.Am. Ballet, 2002, Meditations Pas de deux; author: Beyond the Dance: A Ballerina's Life, 2002. Nominee Norma Fleck award, for "Beyond the Dance, A Ballerina's Life", Tundra Books, 2002; recipient Prix de Lausanne, 1986, Solo Award, Royal Acad Dancing, 1987, Silver Medal, Adelene Genee Comp, London, 1988; grantee, Can Coun, 1987. Office: Nat Ballet of Canada 470 Queens Quay W Toronto ON Canada M5E 3K1

GOHEEN, JANET MOORE, counseling administrator, sales executive; b. Everett, Mass., Sept. 29, 1945; d. Franklin Pierce and Virginia Louise (Murphy) Moore; m. Peter Arthur Goheen, Apr. 2, 1967; children: Kevin Murphy Moore, Andrew Hudson Moore. BA, Ohio Wesleyan U., 1967; MS, U. Bridgeport, 1979. Cert. profl. guidance counselor Ohio. Tchr. English Nordinia Hills HS, Macedonia, Ohio, 1967-69, White Plains (N.Y.) HS, 1969-71, Hudson (Ohio) HS, 1982-83; tchr. emotionally disturbed Palisades Learning Ctr., Paramus, NJ, 1986-87; sales cons. Longaberger Co., Dresden, Ohio, 1983-84, br. advisor, 1984-90, regional advisor, 1990—2004, nat. sales leader, 2004—; counselor Hudson Midl. Sch., 1988—. Tchr. ESL Hitchcock Presbyn. Ch., Scarsdale, NY, 1976—79, Aurora (Ohio) City Schs., 1979—81, Hudson Local Schs., 1980—82. Mem. Jr. League Scarsdale, 1976—79, Jr. League Akron, 1979—82, Jr. League No. N.J., Ridgewood, 1983—85; trustee Am. Found. Suicide Prevention N.E. Ohio, 1997—; founder Anna Lee chpt. Questers, Hudson, 1981, Hudson Presbyn. Ch., 1980; mem. alumni bd. dirs. Ohio Wesleyan U., Delaware, 1990—93. Mem.: Ohio Sch. Counselors Assn., Am. Sch. Counselors Assn., Kappa Delta Pi, Kappa Kappa Gamma. Home: 97 Manor Dr Hudson OH 44236-3406 Office: Hudson Middle Sch 77 N Oviatt St Hudson OH 44236-3043

GOIN, SUZANNE, food company executive, chef; b. L.A., Sept. 25, 1966; BA in History, Brown U.; apprenticeship, Ma Maison, L.A. Line cook Chez Panisse, Berkeley, Calif., 1990-92, Arpege Brigade, Paris, 1993; sous chef Olives, Boston, 1993; exec. chef Alloro, Boston, 1994-96, Campanile, L.A., 1997-98. Named Best New Chef Boston mag., 1994. Office: Lucques 8474 Melrose Ave West Hollywood CA 90069-5313

GOIN-HARDING, CECILIA MARGARET, poet; b. Mansfield, Ohio, June 30, 1957; d. Cecil Eugene and Sara Jane Goin; children: Flora Emma, Beatrix Cessena. Student gen. equitation, St. John's Coll., Annapolis, Md., 1977—78; BA in English, Case Western Res. U., 1984; grad., Cleve. Sch. Ballet, 1984; postgrad., U. Geneva, 1984, postgrad., 1999—2000, Cornell U., 1985; diploma, Supérieure d'Etudes Françaises Modernes; student, Cleve. Inst. Music, 1980, Coconut Grove Ballet Sch., Miami, Fla., 2001—, Martha Mahr Sch. Ballet, 2003—, Miami-Dade Equestrian Ctr., Homestead, Fla., 2003. Governess pvt. family, Woody Creek, Colo., 1975; legis. aid Annapolis (Md.) Legislature, 1977; swimming instr. YMCA/YWCA, Mansfield, Ohio, 1979; proof reader Sun Press, Cleve., 1979; tchr. Am.-Nicaraguan Sch., Managua, Nicaragua, 1986, Cuyahoga C.C., Cleve., 1992, Cleve. State U., 1992. Model Parson's Sch. Design, N.Y.C., NY, 1975, Cleve. Inst. Art, 1988—92, Image Model and Talent Agy., Miami, 2003—; translator Adriana Schaked LLC, Miami, Fla., 2000—, ALS. Exhibitions include The Art Ctr., Mansfield, Ohio, 1977; author (poetry): Figures Of A Voyage: Collected Poems (1984-2000), 2002, numerous poems. Vol. Kingwood Ctr., Mansfield, 1981, NAMI, Miami, 1995. Named on Wall of Tolerance, So. Poverty Law Ctr. Montgomery Ala., 2003; recipient divisional medalist, U.S. Ski Assn., 1970. Mem.: Broadcast Music Inc., End Abuse Family Violence Prevention Fund, Fairchild Tropical Garden, Nat. Tropical Bot. Garden. Avocations: ice skating, soccer, learning to play new instruments, mathematics, prose writing. Home: 4060 Battersea Rd Miami FL 33133 Office Phone: 305-662-6806. Personal E-mail: ceciliamharding@yahoo.com.

GOINS, FRANCES FLORIANO, lawyer; b. Buffalo, Jan. 30, 1950; d. William and Anita (Graziano) Floriano; m. Gary Mitchell Goins; children: Matthew W., Mark W. MusB, Cleve. Inst. Music, 1971; MusM, Case Western Res. U., 1973, JD, 1977. Bar: Ohio 1977, U.S. Dist. Ct. Ohio 1978, U.S. Ct. Appeals (6th cir.) 1979, N.Y. 1984, U.S. Dist. Ct. NY 1984, U.S. Supreme Ct. 2002. Law clk to Hon. Frank J. Battisti U.S. Dist. Ct. (no. dist.) Ohio, Cleve., 1977-78; ptnr. Squire, Sanders & Dempsey, Cleve., 1986—. Mem. vis. com. bd. overseers Case Western Res. U., Cleve., 1984-2000; faculty Nat. Inst. Trial Advocacy, Cleve.; faculty, lectr. trial advocacy seminar Cleve. State U. Sch. Law, 1989-90. Editor-in-chief law rev. Case Western Res. Sch. Law, 1976-77. Trustee, chairperson devel. com. Lyric Opera Cleve., 1985-92, 2003—; founding trustee Shoreby Club Cleve.; v.p. bd. trustees Bay Village Montessori Sch., 1994-96; chmn. bd. trustees No. Ohio Breast Cancer Coalition, 2003—. Mem. ABA (bus. law sect., bus. lit. com., governance com. 1995—, fed. regulation of securities com., subcom. on civil litigation and SEC enforcement 1992—), Ohio Women's Bar Assn. (founding mem.), Ohio State Bar Assn. (ad hoc com. on bus. cts. 1994-99), Cleve. Bar Assn. (com. on women and the law 1987-2000, ethics com. 1988-90, securities law inst., jud. selection com. 1996-2001). Democrat. Roman Catholic. Office: Squire Sanders & Dempsey 4900 Key Tower 127 Public Sq Ste 4900 Cleveland OH 44114-1304

GOLBERT, SANDRA, artist; b. San Juan, PR, Nov. 9, 1937; d. Leonard and Hortensia (Portilla) G.; div.; children: Michelle, Jeanette, Pedro. Student, Haystack Sch. Workshops, Parsons Sch. Design. One-woman shows include Curacao Mus, Netherlands, 1974, Antilles, 1974, La Fortaleza Gov.'s Mansion, San Juan, PR, 1984, Origenes Origins, 1990, John Harms Ctr., Englewood, NJ, 1994, Art for Body and Wall, St. Thomas, VI, Curacao, San Juan, PR, 1994, Paper, Silk and Shadow, NYC, 1998, Art From My First 1000 Years, Franklin Lakes, NJ, 1999, exhibited in group shows at Centro de Amistad, Guadalajara, Mex., 1972, Art Ventures Gallery, Princeton, NJ, 1985, Citibank Gallery, Ateneo, San Juan, 1989, Ponce Mus., Puertorriqueno, San Juan, 1989, Women's Art Works II, Rochester, NY, 1992, Convergence '92, Washington, 1992, The Farrell Collection, 1992, Paramount Ctr. for Arts, Peekskill, NY, 1992, Lever House, NYC, 1992, America House, Piermont, NY, 1992, Barbara Gibson Gallery, Nyack, NY, 1993, Nat. Arts Club, NYC, 1993, Jacob K. Javits Fed. Bldg., 1994, West Broadway Gallery, Soho, NY, 1994, Johnson & Johnson HQ, New Brunswick, NJ, 1995, Old Ch. Cultural Ctr., Demerest, NJ, 1995, NAWA, Athens, 1996, Represented in permanent collections Jane Voorhees Zemmerli Mus., Rutger U., New Brunswick, NJ. Recipient fashion designs published, Vogue Mag., 1959, residency, Millay Colony for Arts, 1993; fellow, Weir Farm Trust, 2000; grantee NEA, 1991, grant, Pollock-Krasner Found., 1991, Empire State Craft, 1997. Mem.: Assn. Puerto Rican Women Artists, Arts Coun. Rockland, Nat. Assn. Women Artists, Salute to Women in Arts. Home: 12 Washington Ln Tappan NY 10983-2512

GOLD, ANNE MARIE, library director; b. N.Y.C., Feb. 24, 1949; d. James Raymond and Marion Rita (Magner) Scully; m. Steven Louis Gold, Aug. 9, 1974; 1 child, Lauren Z. BA in English, St. Lawrence U., 1971; MS in Libr. Svc., Columbia U., 1972. Libr. N.Y. Pub. Libr., N.Y.C., 1972-74, Oakland (Calif.) Pub. Libr., 1975-80, Solano County Libr., Fairfield, Calif., 1980-90, dir. libr. svcs., 1986-90; county libr. Contra Costa County Libr., Pleasant Hill, Calif., 1990-98; exec. dir. Stanford (Calif.) State Libr., 1998—. Mem. Lafayette Sch. Dist. Sch. Bd., 1993-97. Mem. ALA, Pub. Libr. Assn. (bd. dirs. 1992-93, mem. librs. sect., pres. 1992-93), Libr. Adminstrn. and Mgmt. Assn. (various coms.), Calif. Libr. Assn. (coun. mem. 1985-87, 90-92, exec. bd. 1991-92, co-chair legis. com. 1992-94, pres. 1998, Mem. of Year award, 1994), Calif. Inst. Librs. (v.p. 1990-91), Restructuring Calif. Pub. Librs. Task Force (1994-95). Office: Cecil H Green Libr Stanford U Stanford CA 94305-6004 E-mail: amgold@sulmail.stanford.edu.

GOLD, CALLA GISELLE, jewelry designer; b. L.A., Dec. 1, 1958; d. Robert Frederick Skeetz and Ruth Mary Connelly; m. Jeremy Peter Gold, July 15, 1979; 1 child, Daniel Jason. Grad. high sch., Berkeley, Calif. Sales rep. Fuller Brush, 1977-83; owner Cinderella Svcs., Santa Barbara, Calif.,

1979-82, Ceiling Cleaning Co., Santa Barbara, Calif., 1982-83, Calla Gold Jewelry, Santa Barbara, Calif., 1983—. Spkr. Profl. Jeweler Show and Conf., Las Vegas, 2000. Contbg. author Profl. Jeweler mag., 1997, 98, 99. Orchard to Ocean run food dir. Carpinteria (Calif.) Edn. Found., 1999; fundraiser Kinderkirk Presch., Carpinteria, 1996; specific event fundraiser Villa Majella, Santa Barbara, 1997-2002, Holderman Endowment for La Patera, Lompoc Aquarium, 2000-02, Santa Barbara Women's Health Coalition, Santa Barbara County Med. Soc. Alliance; bd. dirs. Leads Club, 1995. Recipient Leadership award, Leads Club, 1996. Mem. Am. Jewelers Assn., Calif. Jewelers Assn., Santa Barbara Event Profls., Santa Barbara Jewelers Guild, South Coast Bus. Network, Toastmasters (competent Toastmaster 1991). Avocations: hiking, horseback riding, reading, scrapbooking. Office: Calla Gold Jewelry PO Box 40102 Santa Barbara CA 93140-0102 E-mail: gold2@cox.net.

GOLD, CARLA CHRISTINE, commodities trader, director; b. Darby, Pa., Dec. 14, 1958; d. Marjorie Roberta Weisel and Edward Lee Goodman, Edmond Joseph Steel; m. Richard Barry Gold, Dec. 29, 1989 (div. July 10, 1998); 1 child, Ethan Ascher. BS in commerce and engring., Drexel U., 1976—81. Indsl. engr. Merck & Co., West Point, Pa., 1981—82; buyer Pratt & Whitney, East Hartford, Conn., 1999—2000, commodity integration mgr., 2000—; prodn. supr. Merck & Co., West Point, Pa., 1982—85; ops. analyst McNeil Consumer Products Co., Fort Washington, Pa., 1985—86, master scheduler, 1986—86, prodn. supr., 1987—88, buyer/planner, 1988—89; buyer/planner - spl. assignment Johnson&Johnson/Merck Joint Venture, Pasadena, Calif., 1990—90; spl. projects UTC - Pratt & Whitney, East Hartford, Conn., 1998. Newsletter editor Oak Grove Montessori Sch., Mansfield, 1997—99, Temple Beth Sholom, Manchester, 1992—93; v.p. Mt. Hope Montessori Sch., Mansfield, 1995—97. Jewish. Avocations: travel, knitting, gardening, wine, cooking. Home: 6 Lebanon Square Mansfield CT 06250 Office: Pratt & Whitney 400 Main Street East Hartford CT 06108 Office Phone: 860-557-3514. Personal E-mail: ethanmom@aol.com. E-mail: carla.gold@pw.utc.com.

GOLD, CAROL R. dean, nursing educator; PhD, Northwestern U. Assoc. prof., acting dean Marcella Nieff Sch. Nursing Loyola U., Chgo. Contbr. articles to profl. jours. Mem. ANA, Am. Acad. of Ambulatory Care Nursing, Ill. Nurses Assn., Sigma Theta Tau Internat. Office: Loyola U Chgo Niehoff Sch Nursing 6525 N Sheridan Rd Chicago IL 60626-5344

GOLD, CAROL SAPIN, international management consultant, speaker; b. N.Y.C. d. Cerf Saul and Muriel Louise (Fudin) Rosenberg; children: Kevin Bart Sapin, Craig Paul Sapin, Courtney Byrens Sapin. BA, U. Calif., Berkeley, 1955. Asst. credit mgr. Union Oil Co., 1956; with U.S. Dept. State, 1964-66; mem. dept. pub. rels. Braun & Co., L.A., 1964-66; corp. dir. pers. tng. Gt. Western Fin. Corp., L.A., 1967-71; pres. Carol Sapin Gold & Assocs., L.A., 1971—. Bd. dirs. Marathon Nat. Bank, L.A.; cons., profl. spkr., Bath, Eng., 1987-90; cons., Can., Mex., India, Australia, New Zealand; host radio program The Competitive Edge; mem. expdn. to Syria and Jordan, 1994, to Morocco, 1995; mem. WORID Bus. Acad.; instr. Learning Annex; presenter Expertise Forum Presentations, Malaysia, Bangkok, 1997; instr. Asian program U. So. Calif., 1998. Author: Solid Gold Customer Relations, Travel for Scholars, Paris, 1999; featured in tng. films Power of Words; Author: Cassette Libraries, Sound Selling. Bd. dirs. Ctr. Theatre Group, Town Hall, Music Ctr., Odyssey Theater; asst. dir. Dunhill Prodns., 1992—, Cabaret, Palisades Theatre; dir. Improv Corp.; vol. Exec. Svc. Corp., 1996—, CEO Leadership Forum. Mem. ASTD, Am. Film Inst. Assn., Sales and Mktg. Execs., Nat. Spkrs. Assn., Nat. Platform Assn., Women in Bus., KCET Women's Coun., Exec. Svc. Corps, World Affairs Coun., Blue Ribbon, Women in Arts, Women in Film, Manuscript Soc. Forum Scotland, Plato Soc., Brandeis Univ. Women, Sierra Club (Toure de Mt. Blanc), Supreme Ct. Hist. Soc., Dispute Resolution Svcs., Women of L.A., Marina Del Rey C. of C., DEO Exec. Forum. Avocations: collecting famous manuscripts, training public speakers. Office: PO Box 11447 Marina Del Rey CA 90295 Office Phone: 310-823-0202. E-mail: cconsult@aol.com.

GOLD, CHRISTINA A. cosmetics company executive; Grad., Carleton U., Ottawa; degree (hon.), U. Montreal, 1991. With human resources, sales, mktg., fin. and mgmt. depts. Avon Can., 1970-89, pres., CEO, 1989-93, head oper. bus. unit, 1993; sr. v.p., pres. Avon North Am., N.Y.C., 1993-98; exec. v.p. Global Direct Selling Devel., N.Y.C., 1997-98; co-CEO Teleglobe, Inc.; pres. Beaconsfield Group; chmn., pres., CEO Excel Comm., Inc., Dallas, Western Union Fin. Svcs. (subsidiary of First Data Corp.). Bd. dirs. Meredith Corp., 1999—2001, The Torstar Corp., The Conf. Bd., ITT Industries, N.Y. Life Investment Mgmt. LLC. Mem.: Direct selling Assn. (bd. dirs.), Conf. Bd. N.Y. and Can. (bd. dirs). Office: Western Union Financial Svcs 100 North Central Expwy Ste 600 Dallas TX 75201*

GOLD, DONNA LAUREN, writer; b. White Plains, N.Y., Apr. 24, 1953; d. Irving and Judy (Fleminger) G.; m. Bill Carpenter; 1 child, Daniel Carpenter-Gold. Student, Bennington Coll., 1971-72; BA, UCLA, 1975; MA, New Sch. for Social Rsch., N.Y.C., 1980. Various positions Friendly Publs., N.Y.C., 1977-80; v.p. Friendly Publs. Internat., Zurich, 1978-79; writer/producer Barry Howard Assocs., Larchmont, N.Y., 1983-84; art editor Kennebec Jour., Augusta, Maine, 1990-91; writer, journalist, 1981—; prin., owner Personal History, Stockton Springs, Maine, 1999—. Author: Country Roads of Maine, 1995, Country Towns of Maine, 1998; editor Maine Progressive 1987-89; author poetry; sculptor Sacred Spaces, 1993. Organizer, facilitator Peace and Justice in Cen. Am., Augusta, 1985-88; organizer June 12 Com./Photoshow, N.Y.C., 1982; v.p. founding bd. Paper Mus., Bucksport, Maine. Recipient 1st pla. arts criticism, Maine Press Assn., 1990. Mem. Maine Writers and Pubs. Alliance, Phi Beta Kappa. Democrat. Jewish. Avocations: art, literature, hiking, gardening, yoga, family, boating. Home: RR 1 Box 1297 Stockton Springs ME 04981-9766

GOLD, JANET NOWAKOWSKI, Spanish language educator; b. Torrington, Conn., Oct. 24, 1948; d. Peter S. and Virginia (Esseppi) Nowakowski; m. Hector Zamora, Dec. 1974 (div. Sept. 1978); m. Stephen Gold, June 28, 1981. BA, Albertus Magnus Coll., 1971; MEd, Worcester State Coll., 1981; PhD, U. Mass., 1990. Elem. sch. tchr., Tegucigalpa, Honduras, 1971-72; instr. English Centro Internat. de Idiomas, Cuernavaca, Mexico, instr. ESL, 1973; tchr. Spanish-English bilingual program Worcester (Mass.) Elem. Sch., 1974-82; tchg. asst. U. Mass., Amherst, 1984-88; instr. Spanish lang. and lit. Bates Coll., Lewiston, Mass., 1989-91; asst. prof. Spanish La. State U., Baton Rouge, 1991-95; assoc. prof. Spanish U. N.H., Durham, 1995—. Author: Clementina Suarez: Her Life and Poetry, 1995; contbr. books Reinterpreting the Spanish American Essay: Studies in Nineteenth and Twentieth Century Women's Essays, 1994, A Dream of Light and Shadow: Portraits of Latin American Women Writers, 1995; contbr. articles and revs. to Hispanic studies jours. Fulbright grantee, Honduras, 1988-89. Mem. MLA, Am. Assn. Tchrs. Spanish and Portuguese,Latin Am. Studies Assn., Millay Soc., Asociacion de Literatura Femenina Hispanica, Maine Writers and Publ. Alliance. Home: PO Box 357 Eliot ME 03903-0357 Office: U NH Dept Spanish Muriel Hall 209 Durham NH 03824*

GOLD, JUDITH HAMMERLING, psychiatrist; b. N.Y.C., June 24, 1941; d. James S. and Anne (Linder) Hammerling; m. Edgar Gold, June 27, 1965. MD, Dalhousie U., 1965; DHumL (hon.), Mt. St. Vincent U., 2002. Intern Victoria Gen. Hosp., Halifax, N.S., Can., 1964-65; resident Dalhousie U., Halifax, 1967-71; practice medicine specializing in psychiatry Halifax, 1971—2002; staff psychiatrist Dalhousie U. Student Health Clinic, 1971-73; vis. colleague U. Wales Med. Sch., 1973-75; asst. prof. dept. psychiatry Dalhousie U., Halifax, 1975-78, assoc. prof., 1978-80, part-time, 1980-87; pvt. practice Brisbane, 1998—. Vis. prof., reader in psychotherapy studies U. Queensland Dept. of Psychiatry, Brisbane, 1998-99. Editor: Clinical Practice Series, 1987-2001, 5 books; contbr. articles to profl. jours. Bd. govs. Mt. St. Vincent U., 1981-87, chmn., 1986-87. Med. Research Council Can. fellow, 1973-75; Health and Welfare Bd. Can. grantee, 1976-78 Fellow Am. Psychiat. Assn., Am. Coll. Psychiatrists (1st v.p. 1990-91, pres.-elect 1991-92, pres. 1992-93); mem. Can. Psychiat. Assn. (pres. 1981-82), Royal Coll. Phys. Surgeons Can. (exec. mem. 1992-94, coun. 1991-98), Order Can., Alpha Omega Alpha.

GOLD, JUDY ROSEN, psychologist; b. N.Y.C., N.Y., Nov. 14, 1943; d. Martin Lester Rosen and Shirley Furmansky; m. Arthur Lewis Gold, Feb. 6, 1966; children: Matthew, Samantha. BA, Syracuse U., 1964; MA, Hunter Coll., 1974; PhD, N.Y.U., 1983. Cert. in psychoanalysis & psychotherapy 1993. Sr. psychologist St. Vincents Med. Ctr., N.Y.C., 1981—96; pvt. practice N.Y.C., 1984—. Avocations: sculpture, oil painting, golf, travel. Office: 80 Fifth Ave New York NY 10011

GOLD, LOIS MEYER, artist; b. N.Y.C., June 2, 1945; d. Seymour Roy and Carol (Rubin) Meyer; m. Leonard Marshall Gold, Oct. 14, 1971 (dec. 1998); 1 child, Eric Marshall. BA, Boston U., 1967; MA, Columbia U., 1970. Tchr. Lenox Sch., N.Y.C., 1972-84, Columbia Grammar Sch., N.Y.C., 1975-76; artist, freelance N.Y.C., 1976—; represented by Lizan-Tops Gallery, Easthampton, NY, Canyon Ranch, Lenox, Mass., Martha Keats Gallery, Santa Fe, Karin Zatt, L.A., Ruzetti and Gow, N.Y.C. Prin. works include Canyon Ranch, Bristol Myers Squibb, Imperial Oil, Bed, Bath and Beyond, Boston U., others, exhibitions include juried selection Florence Biennial, 2003, Represented in permanent collections Herbert F. Johnson Mus. Art, Ithaca, N.Y., Boston U. Libr., corp. collections including Bklyn. Union Gas Co.; featured artist The Artists Mag., 1993, 2000 (Landscape award, 1993), Dan's Papers, 1999—2003, Pastel Artist Internat., 1999, Decor, 1999, Southwest Art, 2001, Pastel Jour., 2003, others, poster art represented in (films) My Fat Greek Wedding, Art International, 2003; various original posters, Romm Art; contbr. works to profl. jours., work to books including Pastel School, 1996, The pastel Painters Solution Book, 1996, Painting Shapes & Edges, 1997, The Best of Flower Painting, 1998. Recipient Artists Mag. Landscape award, 1991, 1993; scholar Pastel Soc. Am. Juried, 1994—95. Mem.: Studio Ctr. Artist's Assn., Cassatt Pastel Soc., Nat. Assn. Women Artists (Pauline Law award 1988, Works on Paper award 1988), Pastel Soc. Am., Internat. Assn. Pastel Socs. Avocations: bicycling, ballroom dancing, tennis, skiing, bicycling. Home: 45 E End Ave New York NY 10028-7953 Office Phone: 212-987-9693.

GOLD, MARI S. public relations executive; b. N.Y.C., June 17, 1940; d. George B. and Natalie (Machol) Sour; m. Joel S. Ullman, May 27, 1983. BA, Vassar Coll., 1962. Coord. Family Book Svc., Meredith Pub. Co., N.Y.C., 1962-64; assoc. producer Tanglewood Theatre, Lords Valley, Pa., 1966-68; producer CasperCitron Program, N.Y.C., 1968-70; free-lance publicist N.Y.C., 1970-74; with Lobsenz-Stevens Inc., N.Y.C., 1974—, exec. v.p., 1981—, assoc. gen. mgr., 1985-92; dep. press sec. N.Y.C. Health & Hosps. Corp., 1992-93, dr. mktg. and comm., 1993-95; dir. comm. MetroPlus Health Plan, N.Y.C., 1995— Office: MetroPlus Health Plan 11 W 42nd St Fl 2 New York NY 10036-8005 E-mail: goldm@nychhc.org.

GOLD, PHRADIE KLING See KLING, PHRADIE

GOLD, SARAE R. art educator; b. Mpls., Mar. 26, 1950; d. Samuel N. and Lillian Himmelfarb; m. Gary L. Nagel, Dec. 26, 1971 (div. Feb. 1991); children: Jill S. Nagel, Marcy B. Nagel; m. Herbert Arnold Gold, Feb. 18, 1996. BA in Art Edn., Northeastern Ill. U., 1970; MS in Art Edn., No. Ill. U., 1999; postgrad., Grand Valley State U., 2002, U. Nev. Las Vegas, 2003. Cert. tchr. Ill., Nev. Tchr. Chgo. Pub. Schs., 1970—74; sales rep. ARA Serve, Chgo., 1981—83; mgr. area ADIA Pers. Svcs., Chgo., 1983—84, NJ, 1984—86; pres. Photo Promotions Plus, NY and NJ, 1986—90; v.p. Olsten Profl. Acctg. Svcs., Chgo., 1990—93; pres. Photo Promotions Plus, Chgo., 1993—95; tchr. Chgo. Pub. Sch., 1995—99; dir. Fine Arts Grand Rapids Pub. Schs., Mich., 1999—2002; tchr. art Clark County Sch. Dist., Las Vegas, 2002—. Adj. art edn. prof. U. Nev., Las Vegas, 2004. Art Peoples Park, UNLV, 2003, Something Fishy in Grand Rapids, 2000, Santa Training School, N.J., 1987. Recipient Educator of Yr., Grand Rapids, 2002. Mem.: Nat. Art Edn. Assn., Art Educators So. Nev. (co-chair state conf. 2003, dir.-elect 2003—). Avocations: woodcarving, pastels.*

GOLD, SHARON CECILE, artist, educator; b. N.Y.C., Feb. 28, 1949; d. Henry Joseph and Betty (Kopan) G.; m. William McKay Watson III, July 12, 1992; 1 child, Miranda Cecile. Student, CUNY, 1967-68, Columbia U., 1968-70; BFA, Pratt Inst., 1976. Adj. prof. Art NYU, 1983; vis. artist SUNY, Purchase, 1985; assoc. prof. painting and critical theory Syracuse (N.Y.) U., 1986—; vis. artist The Art Inst. Chgo., Chgo., 1990. Lectr. in field; guest critic Sch. Visual Arts, N.Y.C., 1987, N.Y. Studio Sch., 1988. Solo exhibits include Stephen Rosenberg Gallery, N.Y.C., 1987, 89, 91, 55 Mercer St., N.Y.C., 1986, John Davis Gallery, Akron, Ohio, 1986, Pam Adler Gallery, N.Y.C., 1986; group exhibits include IRIS House, N.Y.C., 1992, Everson Mus. of Art, Syracuse, 1991, ARTSTAR, L.A., 1991, Stephen Rosenberg Gallery, N.Y., 1991, Rose Art Mus. Brandeis U., 1990, Robert Pardo Gallery, N.Y.C., 2001; performance/video works include A Video Tape 1990-1991 Stephen Rosenberg Gallery, 1991, North South Consonance St. Stephen's Ch., N.Y.C., 1984. Pratt Inst. Acad. fellow, 1974-76, NEA grantee, 1981, Penny McCall Found. grantee, 1988. Home: 10 Leonard St New York NY 10013-2929 E-mail: scgold@ix.netcom.com.

GOLD, SUSAN, conference educator; b. Phila., Sept. 30, 1948; d. Walter and Lillian Lena (Zimmerman) Gold; m. Harry Raymond, Mar. 22, 1970; children: Kimberly Dawn, Aviva Shayna, Leslie Steven. Tchr. Howard County Jewish Cmty. Sch., Columbia, Md., 1971—, prin., 1974-77; asst. prin. Balt. Hebrew Congregation, 1993—; conf. educator, 1971—. Author: Aleph Through Tav-Chalkboard Games, 1989, Reading Hebrew is Just a Game, 1992; co-author: World of Difference, 1991, Jewish Handbook for Group Discussion I, 1988, Jewish Handbook for Group Discussion II, 1989. Recipient Samuel Glasner award Bd. of Jewish Edn., 1990, Women of Distinction award Soroptimist Internat. of Howard County, 1997, Flame of Life award Jewish Fedn. of Howard County, 1997; named Most Inspiring Tchr. Hebrew Tchrs. Assn., 1990. Avocations: walking, racquetball, travel, reading. Home and Office: 9360 Dewlit Way Columbia MD 21045-5118

GOLDBACH, JENNIFER D. bank executive; b. Quarryville, Pa. married; 1 child. Degree in Computer Scis., Dickinson Coll. From v.p. and mgr. mortgage lending to sr. v.p. retail lending Sterlin Fin. Corp., Lancaster, Pa., 1995—2000, sr. v.p. retail lending, 2000—02; pres., CEO First Nat. Bank North East, Md., 2002—. Past pres. Child Abuse Prevention Com. Ctrl. Pa.; mem. mission outreach com. Salem United Ch. Christ; bd. dir. Am. Heart Assn. Named One of 25 Women to Watch, U.S. Banker Mag., 2003. Mem.: Mortgage Bankers Assn. Ctrl. Pa. (chmn. conf. 2000, 2001, past pres., past gov.). Avocation: golf. Office: First National Bank North East 14 South Main St North East MD 21901*

GOLDBERG, ANNE CAROL, physician, educator; b. Balt., June 12, 1951; d. Stanley Barry and Selma Ray (Freiman) G.; m. Ronald M. Levin, July 29, 1989. AB, Harvard U., 1973; MD, U. Md., 1977. Diplomate Am. Bd. Internal Medicine, Am. Bd. Endocrinolgy and Metabolism. Intern in medicine Michael Reese Hosp., Chgo., 1977-78, resident in medicine, 1978-80; fellow in endocrinology Washington U., St. Louis, 1980-83, instr. medicine, 1983-85, asst. prof. medicine, 1985-94, assoc. prof. medicine, 1994—. Fellow ACP, Am. Heart Assn.; mem. AMA, Am. Diabetes Assn., Am. Med. Women's Assn., Endocrine Soc., Alpha Omega Alpha. Democrat. Jewish. Avocation: needlepoint. Office: Washington U Med Sch Box 8127 660 S Euclid Ave Saint Louis MO 63110-1010 E-mail: agoldber@im.wustl.edu.

GOLDBERG, BARBARA M. consultant; b. Providence, Apr. 16, 1950; d. Bernard and Bertha Goldberg. BEd, Ithaca Coll., 1972; M Adult Edn., U. R.I., 1976, MBA, 1996. Cert. tchr., N.Y., R.I. Instr. Adult Correctional Instns., Cranston, R.I., 1972-73; dir. Providence Adult Edn., 1973-75; pres. Edn. Resource Assocs., Pawtucket, R.I., 1975-85; cons., mng. ptnr. Equine Resource Assocs., Cranston, 1981-90, Entelechy Resource Assocs., Cranston, 1990—. Bd. dirs. N.E. Ctr. for Orgnl. Efficiency, Boston, 1992-96; chair investment com. Profl. Investors II. Named Adult Educator of Yr., Nat. Assn. Adult Educators, 1981, R.I. Adult Edn. Assn., 1981. Mem. Cranston C. of C. (v.p. 1995-96), Exec. Round Table, Am. Horse Shows Assn., Cranston-Warwick Hadassah, Little Rhody Model A Ford Club. Jewish. Avocations: horses, photography, antique cars. Office: Entelechy Resource Assocs 6 Buttercup Rd Cranston RI 02920-3506

GOLDBERG, BETH SHEBA, artist, educator, art therapist; b. N.Y.C. d. Max and Hannah Segal; m. Benjamin Goldberg; children: Murray, Ilene, Gerald, Jeffrey. BA cum laude, Bklyn. Coll., 1955, MS in Guidance Sch. Counseling with honors, 1957; MA with distinction, Hofstra U., 1995. Tchr. Ohel Moshe Day Sch., Bklyn., 1954-55, N.Y. Bd. Edn., Bklyn., 1955-57, Amherst Sch. System, Snyder, N.Y., 1957-58, Farmingdale (N.Y.) Sch., 1959-60, Bd. of Edn. of Hebrew Acad. of Nassau, 1977-92; art therapy intern South Oaks, Amityville, 1994, South Nassau Hosp., Oceanside, 1995. Art therapy cons. L.I. State Vets. Home, 1998—2002. Exhibited in various one-woman shows and group exhibits including Salmagundi, Firehouse Gallery, Island Artists Gallery, Chelsea, Heckmans Mus., Sumner Mus.; represented in pvt. collections including Dupont Corp. Hon. trustee Farmingdale Jewish Ctr., 1992—; v.p. Ea. L.I. Women's League, 1982-86; pres. Lionesses, Farmingdale, 1973-74; pres. Sisterhood Farmingdale Jewish Ctr., 1969-70. Recipient award of excellence Ind. Art League, award of merit Salmagundi Juried Show, Grumbacher medallion Ind. Art Soc., 1996, 98, 99, Julia Cohn award for creativity, 1994, 95, 99, Am. Artist award East Islip Juried Show, 2000, Award of Excellence, Town of Oyster Bay, 2003, Suprs. award Babylon Arts Coun., 2001, various awards for art; named Woman of Distinction in Art, Town of Oyster Bay, 2000, Woman of Distinction in Civic and Cmty. Affairs, 2003. Mem. Art Circle 2100, Contemporary Art Soc., Pequa Art Assn. (pres.), Nat. League Am. Pen Women (exec. v.p. 1995-2000, pres. 2000-02, N.Y. State treas. 2000-02, award of excellence), Am. Art Therapy Assn., Clin. Art Therapy, Creative Art Therapist, Huntington Twp. Art League (Long Island), Visual Art Alliance League, Psi Chi (v.p.), Kappa Delta Pi (v.p.), Chi Sigma Iota. Avocations: painting, writing. Home: 23 Tanwood Dr Massapequa NY 11758-8548

GOLDBERG, BEVERLY, foundation administrator, consultant; b. N.Y.C., Sept. 29, 1940; d. Solomon and Bess Goldberg; m. Laurence Mark Janifer (div.); children: Meg Janifer, Seth Janifer. BA, Hunter Coll., N.Y.C., 1961; MA, CUNY, 1963. Cons. editor Washington Sq. Press, N.Y.C., 1964—66, sr. editor Funk & Wagnall's New Standard Reference Ency., N.Y.C., 1967—69; chief editl. svcs. Noble & Noble, a Divsn. of Dell Books, N.Y.C., 1969—72; v.p., dir. pubs. The Century Found., N.Y.C., 1972—; founding ptnr., exec. editor Brown Herron Pub., 2002—. Cons. Siberg Assocs., N.Y.C., 1989—99. Co-author: Dynamic Planning: The Art of Managing Beyond Tomorrow, 1994, Corporation on a Tightrope: Balancing Leadership, Governance, and Technology in an Age of Complexity, 1996; author: Overcoming High-Tech Anxiety: Thriving in a Wired World, 1999, Age Works: What Corporate America Must Do to Survive the Graying of the Workforce, 2000; contbr. articles to profl. jours. Office: The Century Foundation 41 E 70th St New York NY 10021 Office Phone: 212-535-4441. Business E-Mail: goldberg@tcf.org.

GOLDBERG, CHARLOTTE WYMAN, retired educator, retired travel company executive; b. Flint, Mich., July 3, 1914; d. Barney J. and Rose Wyman; m. Leo Goldberg, July 9, 1943 (dec.); children: Suzanne Goldberg Rosin, David, Edward. BS, Ea. Mich. U., 1936; MEd, Wayne State U., 1943. Cert. tchr., guidance counselor, Mass. Tchr. phys. edn. pub. schs., Muskegan Heights, Mich., 1936-37, Pontiac, Mich., 1937-44; asst. to dean Harvard Coll., Harvard U., Cambridge, Mass., 1967-68; guidance counselor Woburn (Mass.) H.S., 1968-72; travel agt. Travel Ctr., Tucson, 1978-97, ret. Pres. women's com. Brandeis U., Tucson, 1991. Mem. U. Ariz. Faculty Wives. Avocations: watercolor painting, lapidarist, golf, bowling. Home: 5700 E Rio Verde Vista Dr Tucson AZ 85750-1971

GOLDBERG, JACKIE, councilwoman; b. L.A. 1 child, Brian. Tchr. Compton and L.A. Unified Sch. Dists.; instr. Calif. State U.; city councilwoman City of L.A., 1993—2000; mem. Calif. Ho. of Reps., 2000—. Chairwoman Personnel Com.; vice chairwoman Intergovt. Rels. Office: PO Box 942849 Sacramento CA 94249

GOLDBERG, KIRSTEN BOYD, science journalist; b. San Bernardino, Calif., Oct. 29, 1963; d. Jerry Dock and Jewel Marie (Purkiss) Boyd; m. Paul Boris Goldberg, Aug. 25, 1985; children: Katherine, Sarah. BA, U. Calif., Berkeley, 1984. News editor Reston (Va.) Connection, 1985-86; reporter Edn. Week, Washington, 1986-88; assoc. editor Cancer Letter Inc., Washington, 1989-90, editor, pub., 1990—. Editor newsletter The Clin. Cancer Letter. Mem. Nat. Assn. Sci. Writers, Newsletter Pubs. Assn., Soc. Profl. Journalists (Washington Dateline award 1998), D.C. Sci. Writers Assn. Jewish. Office: Cancer Letter Inc PO Box 9905 Washington DC 20016-8905

GOLDBERG, LEE WINICKI, furniture company executive; b. Laredo, Tex., Nov. 20, 1932; d. Frank and Goldie (Ostrowiak) Winicki; m. Frank M. Goldberg, Aug. 17, 1952; children: Susan, Arlene, Edward Lewis, Anne Carri. Student, San Diego State U., 1951-52. With United Furniture Co., Inc., San Diego, 1953-83, corp. sec., dir., 1963-83, dir. environ. interiors, 1970-83; founder Drexel-Heritage store Edwards Interiors subs. United Furniture, 1975; founding ptnr., v.p. FLJB Corp., 1976-86; founding ptnr., sec., treas. Sea Fin., Inc., 1980; founding ptnr. First Nat. Bank San Diego, 1982. Den mother Boy Scouts Am., San Diego, 1965; vol. Am. Cancer Soc., San Diego, 1964-69; chmn. jr. matrons United Jewish Fedn., San Diego, 1958; del. So. Pacific Coast region Hadassah Conv., 1960, pres. Galilee group San Diego chpt., 1960-61; supporter Marc Chagall Nat. Mus., Nice France, U. Calif. at San Diego Cancer Ctr. Foun., Smithsonian Instn., Los Angeles County Mus., San Diego Mus. Contemporary Art, San Diego Mus. Art; pres. San Diego Opera, 1992-94. Recipient Hadassah Service award San Diego chpt., 1958-59; named Woman of Dedication by Salvation Army Women's Aux., 1992, Patron of Arts by Rancho Santa Fe Country Friends, 1993. Democrat. Jewish.

GOLDBERG, LOIS D. health facility administrator, disability analyst; b. Mar. 30, 1940; m. Gerald Allen Goldberg, Dec. 18, 1960; children: Sheri, Nancy, Karen. BS, U. Wis., Milw., 1961, MS, 1977. Cert. Am. Inst. Hypnotherapy and Psychotherapy, disability analyst. Health svcs. adminstr. Eastside Clinic, Milw., 1985—; acupuncture detox specialist, 1992-98. Pres. Fox Point PTA, Milw., 1980; bd. dirs. Close Encounters Chamber Music. Recipient Fighting Back Initiative cert. of recognition, Milw. County for Reduction of Substance Abuse and Improvement of Life of Milw. County Residents, 1995. Mem.: Pi Lambda Theta (assoc. v.p. 1982). Avocations: music, swimming, tennis. Address: 806 Cypress Blvd Apt 507 Pompano Beach FL 33069-4034 E-mail: LG507@aol.com.

GOLDBERG, LUELLA GROSS, corporation executive; b. Mpls., Feb. 26, 1937; d. Louis and Beatrice (Rosenthal) Gross; m. Stanley M. Goldberg, June 23, 1958; children: Ellen Goldberg Luger, Fredric, Martha Goldberg Aronson. BA, Wellesley Coll., 1958; postgrad. in philosophy, U. Minn., 1958-59. Dir. Reliastar Fin. Corp., 1978-2000, NRG Energy, Inc., Mpls., 2001—. Bd. dirs. Northwestern Nat. Life Ins. Co., Mpls. TCF Fin. Corp.,

Mpls., Hormel Foods Corp., Austin, Minn., Personnel Decisions Internatl., dir. Communications System, Inc., ING Group, Amsterdam, 2001—. Pres. Minn. Orch. Women's Assn., Mpls., 1972-74; bd. dirs. Minn. Orch. Assn., 1972—, chmn., 1980-83, Mpls. chpt. United Way, 1978-88, Ind. Sector, Washington, 1984-90; regent St. John's U., Collegeville, Minn., 1974-83; trustee U. Minn. Found., Mpls., 1970—, chmn. bd. trustees, 1996-98; mem. bd. overseers Sch. Mgmt., U. Minn., Mpls., 1980—; chmn. bd. trustees Wellesley (Mass.) Coll., 1985-93, acting pres., 1993; trustee Wellesley Coll., 1978-96, emerita, 1996—, Northwest Area Found., 1994—. Recipient Disting. Svc. award, Minn. Orch. Assn., 1983, Community Svc. Leadership award, Mpls. YWCA, 1986, Disting. Svc. to Higher Edn. award, Minn. Pvt. Coll. Coun., 1992, Humanitarian award, NCCJ, 1992, Regents award, U. Minn., 2000, Alumnae Achievement award, Wellesley Coll., 2002, Disting. Women's award, Northwoods U., 2001, Lifetime Achievement award as Outstanding Dir., Twin Cities Bus. Monthly, 2001. Mem. Minn. Women's Econ. Round Table, Cosmopolitan Club (N.Y.C.), Mpls. Club, Phi Beta Kappa. Avocations: water skiing, wind surfing, traveling. Home: 7019 Tupa Dr Minneapolis MN 55439-1643

GOLDBERG, MARCIA B. medical educator; b. Boston, July 29, 1957; AB in Biology summa cum laude, Harvard U., 1979, MD, 1984. Diplomate Am. Bd. Internal Medicine, Am. Bd. Infectious Diseases. Intern in primary care internal medicine Mass. Gen. Hosp., Boston, 1984—85, jr. and sr. resident in primary care internal medicine, 1985—87, clin. and rsch. fellow in medicine, 1987—90; rsch. fellow in medicine Harvard Med. Sch., Boston, 1987—90; rsch. fellow Unite de Pathogenie Microbienne Moleculaire, Inst. Pasteur, Paris, 1991—93; asst. prof. Dept. Microbiology and Immunology, Dept. Medicine divsn. Infectious Diseases Albert Einstein Coll. of Medicine, Bronx, NY, 1993—98, assoc. prof. dept. microbiology and immunology, 1998—99, assoc. dir. med. scientist tng. program, 1995—99; assoc. prof. medicine divsn. infectious disease Mass Gen. Hosp., Boston, 1999—. Contbr. articles and revs. to profl. jours. Recipient Rsch. award, Fundaciion para la Edn. Superior, 1981, Proctor-Wellington Fund award, 1987, Stuart Pharms. Travel award, Nat. Found. Infectious Diseases, 1990, Young Investigator award, Maxwell Finland, 1991, Intersci. Conf. on Antimicrobial Agents and Chemotherapy, 1991, Established Investigator award, Am. Heart Assn., 1996; fellow, Inst. Nat. de la Sante et de la Recherche Med., 1991, Moseley Traveling, Harvard Med. Sch., 1991—92; scholar Hon. Nat., Radcliffe Coll., 1975, Fulbright, 1991—92, Pew, 1994—98. Mem.: Infectious Diseases Soc. Am., Am. Soc. Microbiology, Phi Beta Kappa. Office: Mass Gen Hosp Divsn Infectious Disease 55 Fruit St Boston MA 02114-2696

GOLDBERG, MAUREEN MCKENNA, state supreme court justice; b. Pawtucket, R.I., Feb. 11, 1951; m. Robert D. Goldberg. Grad., St. Mary's Acad., 1969; AB cum laude, Providence Coll., 1973; JD cum laude, Suffolk U., 1978. Bar: R.I. 1978, Mass. 1978, U.S. Ct. of Appeals (1st cir.) 1979. Asst. atty. gen. Adminstr. of the Criminal Divsn., 1978-84; town solicitor South Kingstown, 1985-87, Town of Westerly, 1987-90, acting town mgr., 1990; spl. legal counsel R.I. State Police; apptd. assoc. justice Superior Ct., 1990-96; assoc. justice R.I. Supreme Ct., 1997—. Mem. ABA, R.I. Bar Assn., R.I. Trial Judges Assn., Pawtucket Bar Assn. Office: Rhode Island Supreme Ct 250 Benefit St 7th Fl Providence RI 02903-2719

GOLDBERG, NANCY G. business owner, community volunteer; b. Pitts., 1942; d. Henry and Rose Gross; m. Gerald Sanford Goldberg, 1966; children: Brian Michael (dec.), Sheri Goldberg Glickman. Student, U. Laval, Que., Can., 1962; BA, U. Pitts., 1963; MAT, Johns Hopkins U., 1965. French tchr. secondary schs., Balt., 1965, Arlington, Va., 1965-68; travel agt. with various agys., Plantation, Fla., 1984-94; interior decorator Nancy G. Goldberg, Interiors, Plantation, 1983-92; pres., owner Creative Inspirations, Inc., Plantation, 1992—. Owner, dir. Creative Inspirations Gallery, Fort Lauderdale, Fla., 1994—96; bd. dirs. Child Advocacy, 1978—81, Jewish Family Svcs., 1982; owner, dir. Creative Inspirations Gallery, Plantation, Fla., 1996—98, Delray Beach, Fla., 2001—02; owner ArtisticJewelry.com, DecoratorPaintings.com, Ci-Gallery.com. Chair for internat. health Broward County Med. Assn. Aux., 1982—83, mem., 1974—85; bd. dirs., chair for Broward County Mosaic, Jewish Life in Fla., Ft. Lauderdale, 1977—81; mem. Brandeis Univ. Women's Com., 1975—; numerous other civic activities; bd. dirs. Greater Ft. Lauderdale Sister Cities Internat., 1999—. Recipient awards for cmty. svc. Mem.: NOW, Women's Am. ORT, Nat. Coun. Jewish Women (various offices), Sigma Kappa Phi, Phi Beta Kappa. Democrat. Jewish. Avocations: art, gourmet cooking, gardening, world travel.

GOLDBERG, NIECA, cardiologist, educator; b. Bklyn., Oct. 21, 1957; BA, Barnard Coll., 1979; MD, SUNY, Bklyn., 1984. Diplomate Am. Bd. Internal Medicine. Resident in internal medicine St. Lukes-Roosevelt Hosp., N.Y.C., 1985-87; fellow in cardiology SUNY Health Sci. Ctr., Bklyn.; chief of cardiac rehabilitation and prevention ctr. Lenox Hill Hosp., N.Y.C.; asst. clin. prof. of medicine NYU Sch. Medicine. Nat. spokesperson Am. Heart Assn, adv. bd. Women's Day mag. Author: (book) Women Are Not Small Men: Life-Saving Strategies for Preventing and Healing Heart Disease in Women, 2003. Named to New York mag. Best Doctors issue, 1999, 2000, 2001. Mem. ACP, Am. Coll. Cardiology, Am. Heart Assn., Am. Soc. Echocardiography.$Dm. Coll. Physicians. Office: Lenox Hill Hosp Dept Med Divsn Cardiovasc Disease 177 E 87th St #503 New York NY 10128*

GOLDBERG, NORMA LORRAINE, retired public welfare administrator; b. South Bend, Ind., May 6, 1929; d. James Albert and Minnie Sylvia (Kaplan_ Seamon; m. Albert Goldberg, Apr. 19, 1959 (dec. Dec. 1976); children: Lisa Ann, Paul Ephraim. BS, Ind. U., Bloomington, 1950; postgrad., Ind. U., 1951-52. Social worker Indpls. Pub. Schs., 1951-53; with Marion County Dept. Pub. Welfare, Indpls., 1953-66, 71-73, asst. dir., 1961-64, dir., 1964-66, intake supr., 1971-73; asst. dir. Ind. Dept. Pub. Welfare, Indpls., 1973-79, dir., 1979-87, regional adminstr., 1987-91; spl. project officer Adminstrn. Children and Families, 1991-94, asst. regional adminstr., 1994-95. Steering com. Whitehouse Conf. on Children and Youth, Indpls., 1982-83; program com. Gov.'s Conf. on Children and Youth, Indpls., 1982-83. Founder Welfare Service League, Indpls., 1968, pres., 1968-71, mem., 1968—. Mem. steering com. Indpls. sect. Nat. Coun. Jewish Women, 1982-87; steering com. Guardian ad Litem Project; mem. Rep. Round Table, Indpls., 1983-87; city chmn. adult bd. B'nai B'rith Youth Orgn., 1985-86; mem. People of Vision, Indpls. Mus. Art, Social Action Com., Indpls. Hebrew Congregation, Indpls. Newcomers Club. Recipient Gov.'s Vol. Action Program Cmty. Svc. award Gov. Ind., 1980. Mem. Assn. Women Execs., Dallas Coun. World Affairs, Dallas Women's Found., Ind. Conf. on. Social Concerns (state coord. 1963-64), Network Women in Bus., Indpls. Coun. Women (program chmn. 1968-71), The 500 Club, Inc., Meridian Hills Kiwanis, Northside Investment Club. E-mail: gold@in.net.

GOLDBERG, PAMELA WINER, entrepreneurship educator, director; b. Boston, Oct. 14, 1955; d. Arthur Leonard and Marilyn (Miller) Winer; children from previous marriage: Frederick Warren, Alyssa Rachel, Meredith Hayley. BA, Tufts U., 1977; MBA, Stanford U., 1981. Day care dir. Cmty. Action Inc., Haverhill, Mass., 1977-79; lending assoc. Bankers Trust Co., N.Y.C., 1980-81; mgr., bank officer, corp. fin. dept. Citicorp, N.Y.C., 1981-82; assoc. dir., mergers and acquisitions group State St. Bank, Boston, 1983-85; ind. strategic cons. Wellesley, Mass., 1986-97; dir. bus. rels. Babson Coll., Wellesley, 1998—2002; prof., dir. Ctr. for Entrepreneurial Leadership Tufts U., 2002—. Exec. bd. friends Beth Israel Hosp., Boston, 1987—96; trustee Recuperative Ctr., Boston, 1988—95; mem. Hunnewell Sch. PTO Bd., 1991—96; mem. exec. bd. trustees Temple Beth Elohim, Wellesley, 1992—2000, treas., 1997—2000, Synagogue 2000 com., 2000—; bd. dirs. Wellesley LWV, 1995—98. Avocations: swimming, tennis, singing. Home: 34 Ivy Rd Wellesley MA 02482-4554 Office: Tufts University 4 Colby St Medford MA 02155 Business E-Mail: pamela.goldberg@tufts.edu. E-mail: pwg14@aol.com.

GOLDBERG, RITA MARIA, foreign language educator; b. N.Y.C., Oct. 1, 1933; d. Abraham Morris and Hilda (Weinman) G. BA, Queens Coll., 1954; MA, Middlebury Coll., 1955; PhD, Brown U., 1968. Mem. faculty Queens Coll., N.Y.C., 1956, Oberlin (Ohio) Coll., 1957; mem. faculty St. Lawrence U., Canton, NY, 1957—2001, Dana prof. modern langs., 1975—2000, emerita, 2001—, chmn. dept., 1972—75, 1983—91, 2000—01. Chmn. Regional Conf. Am. Programs in Spain, 1979-81; mem. Nat. Fulbright Selection Com., 1990-92; mem. advanced placement devel. com. for Spanish, Ednl. Testing Svc., 1993-2000, chair, 1996-99. Spanish Ministry of Fgn. Affairs scholar, 1954-56; Danforth grantee, 1960-62, 63-64; N.Y. State Regents scholar, 1954, Brown U. scholar, 1960-62. Mem. Am. Assn. Tchrs. Spanish and Portuguese, AAUP, MLA, Am. Council Teaching of Fgn. Langs., N.E. Modern Lang. Assn., N.Y. State Assn. Fgn. Lang. Tchrs., Phi Beta Kappa, Sigma Delta Pi. Roman Catholic. Office: St Lawrence U Dept Modern Langs Lits Canton NY 13617 Address: Maria Guilhou 2 28016 Madrid Spain E-mail: ritagoldberg@stlawu.edu.

GOLDBERG, SUSAN, editor; b. 1959; m. Gary Blonston (dec. Apr. 1999). Reporter Seattle Post-Intelligencer; asst. city editor Detroit Free Press, San Jose Mercury News, 1987—89, acting city editor, mng. editor, 1999—2003, v.p., 2001—, exec. editor, 2003—; dep. mng. editor USA Today, 1989—99. Chair mng. editors leadership and mgmt. com. AP. Mem. bd. visitors Northwestern U. Medill Sch. Journalism; bd. mem. Silicon Valley chpt. Am. Cancer Soc., 2003—. Mem.: Downtown San Jose Rotary Club. Office: San Jose Mercury News 750 Ridder Park Dr San Jose CA 95190-0001*

GOLDBERG, WHOOPI (CARYN ELAINE JOHNSON), actress; b. N.Y.C., Nov. 13, 1955; d. Robert and Emma (Harris) Johnson; m. Alvin Martin, 1973 (div. 1979); 1 child, Alexandrea Martin ; m. David Claessen, 1986 (div. 1988); m. Lyle Trachtenberg, 1994 (div. 1995). Mem. San Diego Repertory Theatre, 1975—80, Blake St. Hawkeyes, Berkeley, Calif., 1980—84. Author: Alice, 1992, Book, 1997; actor: (plays) Living on the Edge of Chaos, 1988 (Calif. theatre award outstanding achievement, 1988); (Broadway plays) A Funny Thing Happened on the Way to the Forum, 1996—98, Funny Girl, 2002; (films) Citizen, 1982, The Color Purple, 1985 (Golden Globe for best actress motion picture drama, 1986), Jumpin' Jack Flash, 1986, Burglar, 1986, Fatal Beauty, 1987, The Telephone, 1987, Clara's Heart, 1988, Homer and Eddie, 1989, Comicitis, 1989, The Long Walk Home, 1990, Ghost, 1990 (Acad. award for best supporting actress, 1991, Golden Globe for best supporting actress motion picture, 1991), Soapdish, 1991, Blackbird Fly, 1991, The Player, 1992, Sister Act, 1992, Sarafina!, 1992, Made in America, 1993, National Lampoon's Loaded Weapon 1, 1993, Sister Act 2: Back in the Habit, 1993, Naked in New York, 1993, (voice) The Lion King, 1994, The Little Rascals, 1994, Corrina, Corrina, 1994, Star Trek: Generations, 1994, (voice) The Pagemaster, 1994, Boys on the Side, 1995, Moonlight and Valentino, 1995, Theodore Rex, 1995, Bogus, 1996, The Ghost of Mississippi, 1996, Eddie, 1996, Tales from the Crypt Presents: Bordello of Blood, 1996, The Associate, 1996, (voice) A Christmas Carol, 1997, How Stella Got Her Groove Back, 1998, (voice) The Rugrats Movie, 1998, Alegria, 1998, Deep End of the Ocean, 1999, Jackie's Back!, 1999, Girl, Interrupted, 1999, (narrator) A Second Chance at Life, 2000, More Dogs Than Bones, 2000, Kingdom Come, 2001, Monkeybone, 2001, Rat Race, 2001, (narrator) Golden Dreams, 2001, Star Trek: Nemesis, 2002, Blizzard, 2003; (films, cameo) Beverly Hills Brats, 1989, House Party 2, 1992, Naked in New York, 1994; (TV films) My Past Is My Own, 1989, Kiss Shot, 1989, Defenders of Dynatron City, 1992, (voice) Yuletide in the 'hood, 1993, In the Gloaming, 1997, (voice) Mother Goose: A Rappin' and Rhymin' Special, 1997, Cinderella, 1997, A Knight in Camelot, 1998, Jackie's Back!, 1999, The Magical Land of the Leprechauns, 1999, Alice in Wonderland, 1999, (voice) Madeline: My Fair Madeline, 2002, It's a Very Muppet Christmas Movie, 2002, Littleburg, 2004; (TV series) Star Trek: The Next Generation, 1988—94, (voice) Captain Planet and the Planeteers, 1990, Bagdad Cafe, CBS, 1990, (voice) Happily Ever After: Fairy Tales for Every Child, 1997, (voice) Foxbusters, 1999, (voice) Liberty's Kids, 2002, (TV specials) Circus of the Stars #15, 1990, Tales from the Whoop: Hot Rod Brown, Class Clown, 1990; host : (TV series, talk show) The Whoopie Goldberg Show, 1992—93; actor, exec. prodr. (TV films) Call Me Claus, 2001, What Makes a Family, 2001, (TV series) Whoopi, 2003, actor, prodr. (TV films) Good Fences, 2003, (Broadway plays) Ma Rainey's Black Bottom, 2003; exec. prodr.: (TV films) Ruby's Bucket of Blood, 2001; (TV series) Strong Medicine, 2000; prodr.: Hollywood Squares, 1998—2002; (TV miniseries) Oh What A Time It Was, 1999; (Broadway plays) Thoroughly Modern Millie (Tony award for best musical, 2002); co-prodr.: (films) The Mao Game, 1999; dir., writer, performer (TV specials) Comic Relief, 1986, actor, writer (one-person show Broadway plays) Whoopi Goldberg on Broadway, 1984—85. Named Entertainer of the Yr., NAACP, 1990; recipient Grammy award for album of Broadway show, 1985, Hans Christian Andersen award for outstanding achievement by a dyslexic, 1987, Humanitarian of Yr. award, Starlight Found., 1989, Star on Hollywood Walk of Fame, 2001.

GOLDBERGER, BLANCHE RUBIN, sculptor, jeweler; b. N.Y.C., Feb. 2, 1914; d. David and Sarah (Israel) Rubin; m. Emanuel Goldberger, June 28, 1942 (dec. 1994); children— Richard N., Ary Louis. B.A., Hunter Coll., N.Y.C., 1934; M.A., Columbia U., 1936; Certificat d'Etudes, Sorbonne, Paris, 1936; postgrad. Westchester Arts Workshop Sculpture and Jewelry, White Plains, 1961-70, Silvermine Coll. Arts, 1962, Nat. Acad. Arts, N.Y.C., 1968. Tchr. French and Hebrew, N.Y.C. High Sch. System, Scarsdale Jr. and Sr. High Schs. One-woman shows include: Bloomingdale's, Eastchester, N.Y., 1975, Scarsdale Pub. Library, N.Y., 1976, Temple Israel, White Plains, N.Y., 1975, Greenwich Art Barn, Conn., 1972 Westlake Gallery, White Plains, N.Y., 1981; exhibited in group shows at Hudson River Mus., Yonkers, N.Y., 1978, Silvermine-New Eng. Ann., Silvermine, Conn., 1979; represented in permanent collection at Scarsdale High Sch. Library, N.Y.; sculpture commn. Jewish Community Ctr. White Plains, N.Y., 1988; commn. Manchester, Vt.; also pvt. collections. Recipient award Beaux Arts of Westchester, White Plains, N.Y., 1967, First Prize, White Plains Art Show, Holocaust Meml. Bronze Plaque for Synagogue Congregation Israel, Manchester, Vt.; various commns. for calli collis calligraphic collages. Mem. Nat. Assn. Women Artists, Nat. Assn. Tchrs. French, Scarsdale Art Assn. (bd. dirs.; first prizes for sculpture). Jewish. Avocations: lecturing on sculpture, reading contemporary lit. in Hebrew, the violin, classical music concerts, callicollies.

GOLDBERG-SCHAIBLE, JOCELYN HOPE SCHNIER, market research professional; b. NYC, Mar. 29, 1953; d. Alex and Eileen Rosalie (Firstenberg) Schnier. AB, Princeton U., 1974; MBA, Harvard U., 1977. Statis. technician John Hancock Inc., Boston, 1974-75; product mgr. Gen. Foods Corp., White Plains, N.Y., 1977-78; strategic and tactical bus. planning analyst Bausch & Lomb Corp., Rochester, N.Y., 1979-81; mgmt. assoc. Gordon S. Black Corp., Rochester, 1981-84; pres. Rochester Rsch. Group, 1985—. Dirs. adv. coun. M&T Bank. Bd. dirs. U. Rochester Med. Ctr., 1991-98, JCC Greater Rochester, 1998—; trustee Geva Theater, 1992-99; v.p. class of '74, Princeton U., 1999—. Recipient achievement award Wall Street Jour., 1977; nominee Athena award, 2001. Mem. Profl. Ski Instrs. Am. (cert.), Harvard U. Bus. Sch. Club (bd. dirs.). Home: 1666 Strong Rd Victor NY 14564-9133 Office: PO Box 22954 Rochester NY 14692-2954

GOLDBLATT, BARBARA JANET, sex therapist, educator; b. Denver, June 22, 1937; d. Robert and Esther Mae Gamzey; m. Arnold L. Goldblatt; children: Sheri, Neil. BA, U. Denver, 1958; MA, Goddard Coll., 1978. Tchr. Denver Pub. Schs., 1958—59; sex educator, therapist Denver, 1978—85; prin., owner Cultural Expeditions, Denver, 1985—90; CEO, founder Magnets for Health, Denver, 1997—2002. Founder Old Myths and New Realities workshop, 1977; spkr. Jewish Fedn., 1983, spkr. in field. Fund-raiser various cultural orgns.; planning com. Am. Jewish Com., 1977; bd. dirs., tchr., program developer Learning for Living, Met. State Coll., Denver, 1972—78; bd. dirs. Colo. Sex Therapists, Denver, 1978—85. Mem.: NARAL, Jewish Allied Fedn., Hadassah, Emily's List. Democrat. Jewish. Avocations: golf, bridge, concerts, opera, book club. Home: 3042 S Fillmore Way Denver CO 80210

GOLDEN, ELLEN FRANCES, economic development practitioner; b. Washington, Oct. 8, 1946; d. Gerald and Rose (Cohen) G.; m. Duane Alan Paluska, June 18, 1983. BA in Art History, Barnard Coll., 1968; MA in Pub. Policy and Mgmt., U. So. Maine, 1994. With Coastal Enterprises, Inc., Wiscasset, Maine, 1978—, comm. coord., ops. mgr., project developer, sr. program officer, sr. devel. officer. Bd. dirs., co-founder Women's Devel. Inst., Augusta, Maine, 1991-93, Women's Bus. Devel. Corp., Bangor, Maine, 1986-88; commr. Maine Commn. for Women, Augusta, 1988-92; bd. dirs. Maine Women's Lobby, Augusta, 1987-93; mem. Commn. on Women's Voices in the Economy Ctr. for Policy Alternatives, Washington, 1995-97; bd. trustees Maine Initiatives, Augusta, 1994-2000, former pres.; bd. dirs. Assn. for Enterprise Opportunity, Chgo., 1992-96, 1997-2002. Named Women Bus. Advocate of Maine U.S. SBA, 1987, Minority Bus. Advocate for Maine, 1994. Mem. Phi Kappa Phi. Avocations: dance, art, travel, music. Office: Coastal Enterprises Inc PO Box 268 Water St Wiscasset ME 04578

GOLDEN, JUDITH GREENE, artist, educator; b. Chgo., Nov. 29, 1934; d. Walter Cornell and Dorothie (Cissell) Greene; m. David T. Golden, Oct. 10, 1955 (div.); children: David T. Golden III, Lucinda Golden Rizzo. BFA, Art Inst. Chgo., 1973; MFA, U. Calif., Davis, 1975; PhD Art (hon.), Moore Coll. Art, 1990. Assoc. prof. art U. Ariz., Tucson, 1981-88, prof. art, 1989-96, prof. emerita, 1996—. NEA forum pub. grants panelist, 1987; project dir. U. Calif. L.A. NEA Lecture series, 1979, 84. One woman shows include Women's Bldg., L.A., 1977, G. Ray Hawkins Gallery, L.A., 1977, Quay Gallery, San Francisco, 1979, 81, A. Nagel Galerie, Berlin, 1981, Ctr. Creative Photography, U. Ariz., 1983, Colburg Gallery, Vancouver, Can., 1985, Etherton Gallery, Tucson, 1985, 89, 91, 95, Mus. Photog. Arts, San Diego, 1986, Friends of Photography, Carmel, Calif., 1987, Tucson Mus. Art, 1987, Mus. Contemporary Photography, Chgo., 1988, Visual Arts Ctr., Anchorage, Alaska, 1990, Temple Music and Art, Tucson, 1992, 97, Scottsdale (Ariz.) Ctr. Arts, 1993, Arte de Oaxaca, Mex., 1995, Etherton Gallery, Tucson, 1995, Columbia Art Ctr., Dallas, 1997, U. Arts, Phila., 2002; exhibited in group shows at Centre Georges Pompidou, Paris, 1981, Security Pacific Bank, L.A., 1985, Phoenix Mus. Art, 1985, L.A. County Mus. Art, 1987, Tokyo Met. Mus. Photography, 1991, Laguna Art Mus., 1992, U. N.M. Mus. Art, Albuquerque, 1993, L.A. County Mus., 1994, Hara contemporary Mus., Tokyo, 1995, Mus. Women in Arts, Washington, 1997, Santa Barbara Mus. Art, Calif., 1997, Mus. Cont. Photography, 1998, Tucson Mus. Art, 1999, Calif. Mus. Photography, 1999, Ctr. for Creative Photography, 1999, Santa Barbara Mus. Art, 1999, Mus. Fine Arts, Santa Fe, N.Mex., 2002, U. Ariz. Mus. Art, 2003, Akron (Ohio) Mus. Art, numerous others; represented in permanent collections at Art Inst. Chgo., Calif. Mus. Photography, Ctr. Creative Photography U. Ariz., Denver Art Mus., Fed. Reserve Bank San Francisco, Fogg Mus. Art, Grunwald Ctr. Graphic Arts, Internat. Mus. Photography George Eastman House, L.A. County Mus. Art, Mpls. Inst. Arts, Mus. Photographic Arts, San Diego, Calif., Mus. Fine Arts, Santa Fe, N.Mex., Newport Harbor Mus. Art, Oakland Mus. Art, Photography Mus. Osaka, Polaroid Corp., San Francisco Mus. Modern Art, Security Pacific Bank, Tokyo Met. Mus. Photography, Tucson Mus. Art, Weisman Found., L.A., Mus. Cont. Photography, Chgo., Seattle Art Mus., Wash., Akron (Ohio) Art Mus., Avon Collection, N.Y.C. Individual artist grantee Tucson Pima Arts Coun., 1987; faculty rsch. grantee U. Ariz., 1986-87, 93-94; Ariz. Found. grantee U. Ariz., 1984; fellow Ariz. Commn. Arts, 1984; individual photography fellow NEA, 1979; Regent's faculty fellow Creative Rsch. U.Calif. L.A., 1977. Achievements include appearance of works in archive of artists' works and other material established at Center for Creative Photography. E-mail: judithgolden@earthlink.net.

GOLDEN, KIMBERLY KAY, critical care nurse; b. Munich, July 31, 1961; arrived in US, 1961; d. Henry Davis and Mary Walker G. AA, Hinds Jr. Coll., Raymond, Miss., 1980, ASN, 1984; BSN, U. Miss., Jackson, 1987, AS in EMT-Paramedic, 1990; postgrad., U. Health Scis., Antigua, W.I., 1997—. Cert. ACLS, PALS provider and instr.; emergency nurse, crit. care RN; cert. paramedic, Miss., Tenn. Staff nurse neuro ICU U. Miss. Med. Ctr., 1984-85, staff nurse surg. ICU, 1985-87; staff nurse emergency rm. Rankin Gen. Hosp., Brandon, Miss., 1987-88; flight nurse Lifestar Helicopter Flight Svc., 1988-91; staff nurse emergency rm., ICU Nightingale Nursing, Jackson, 1988-91, Riveroaks Hosp., Jackson, 1990-91; staff RN emergency rm., Aerovesta flight Midland Meml. Hosp., Tex., 1991-93; flight nurse Hosp. Wing BTLS, Memphis, 1993-99, U. Health Sci. Med. Sch., Antigua, West Indies, 1997—; nurse Univ. Health Scis./Antigua Sch. Medicine, 1997—; emergency rm. staff nurse U. Nebr. Health Systems, 2001—. Examiner Nat. Registry EMT-P; advanced trauma life support station instr.; affiliate faculty paramedic program U. Miss. Faculty scholar Hinds Jr. Coll., 1983. Mem. AACN, Nat. Flight Assn., Emergency Nurses Assn. Baptist. Avocations: Karate, skiing, horse back riding, camping. Office: PO Box 140466 Austin TX 78714-0466 Home: 917 Reaves St Jackson MS 39204-5228

GOLDEN, LILY OLIVER, humanities educator; b. Tashkent, Uzbekistan, USSR, July 18, 1934; d. Oliver John and Bertha Alexander (Bialik) Golden; m. Abdulla Kassim Hanga, Mar. 13, 1960 (dec. 1966); 1 child, Yelena; m. Boris Vladimirovitch Yakovlev, Aug. 14, 1979 (dec. Mar. 1997). PhD, Soviet Acad. of Sci., 1966; LHD (hon.), Chgo. State U., 1992. Jr. rschr. Inst. of Oriental Studies Acad. of Sci., Moscow, 1957-59; sr. scientific rschr. Inst. of African Studies Acad. of Sci. of Russia, 1959-60; disting. scholar-in-residence Chgo. State U., 1992—. Vis. prof., lectr. Lumumba U., Moscow, Inst. of Asia and Africa, Moscow State U., Leningrad State U., Tbilici State U., History Inst. Tbilici State U., Columbia U., N.Y.C., NYU, Rutgers U., N.J., Peoria U., Ill., Loyola U., Chgo., Calif. State U., Cape Town U., South Africa, Libreville U., Gabon, Dakar U., Senegal, Zurich U., Switzerland, Benjinsu, China, Seoul, Republic of Korea, numerous others; presenter and lectr. in field. Author: Africans in Russia, 1966, The Tendencies of Development of African Music, 1967, Pan-Africanism, 1972, (with others) Trade Unions in Africa, 1964, Dr. Dubois-A Scholar Humanitarian and a Fighter for Freedom, 1971, USSR and Africa (also editor), 1977, Ideology of Revolutionary Democrats, 1981, Political Parties in Africa, 1964, Nationalism in Modern Africa, 1983, Marxism in Africa, 1987, African Musicology, 1984, others; editor: African Encyclopedia, Dr. Dubois-Scholar, Humanist, Fighter for Freedom, 1971, Presence Africain; contbr. articles to profl. jours. Bd. dirs. Internat. Intercultural Black Woman's Study Inst., Ctr. Am. Citizens, San Francisco, 1996—; chmn. Black-White Jews, Chgo., 1996—. Named hon. spkr. Black Caucuses U.S. Congress, Calif. State Congress; proclamation Lily Golden Day City of Mobile, Ala., City of Juno; recipient Award for Contbn. to Elimination of Racism Nat. Orgn. for Men Against Sexism, Internat. Achievement award Tau Gamma Delta; named to Educators Hall of Fame,Sacramento. Avocations: tennis, music. Home: 850 Happy Valley Cir Newnan GA 30263-7014 E-mail: lilygold@aol.com.

GOLDEN, MARITA, English language educator, foundation executive; b. Washington, Apr. 28, 1950; d. Francis Sherman and Beatrice Lee Golden; m. Joseph Butlar Murray, Aug. 23, 1991; 1 child, Akintunde Michael Kayode. BA, Am. U., 1972; MSc, Columbia U., 1973; LittD (hon.), U.

Richmond, 1998. Lectr. U. Lagos, Nigeria, 1975-79; asst. prof. Roxbury C.C., Boston, 1979-81, Emerson Coll., Boston, 1981-83; assoc. prof. George Mason U., Fairfax, Va., 1989-94; prof. English, Va. Commonwealth U., Richmond, 1994—2001. Author: Migrations of the Heart, 1983, A Woman's Place, 1986, Long Distance Life, 1989, And Do Remember Me, 1992, Wild Women Don't Wear No Blues, 1993, Saving Our Sons, 1995, Skin Deep, 1997, The Edge of Heaven, 1998, A Miracle Everyday, 1999, Gumbo, An Anthology of African American Writing, 2003, Don't Play in the Sun: One Woman's Journey Through the Color Complex, 2004. Pres. Hurston Wright Found., Hyattsville, Md., 1990—. Recipient Disting. Alumni award Am. U., 1994, Woman of Yr. award Zeta Phi Beta, 1997, Writers for Writers award Poets and Writers mag., 2001, Authors Guild Disting. Svc. award, 2002; named to Literary Hall of Fame, Chgo. State U., 2000. Mem. African Am. Writers Guild (pres. Washington 1986-90). Office: Hurston Wright Found Ste 531 6525 Belcrest Rd Hyattsville MD 20782*

GOLDEN, OLIVIA A. human service agency administrator; b. N.Y.C., May 23, 1955; BA in Philosophy and Govt., MPP, PhD, Harvard U. Budget dir. office human svcs. State of Mass., 1983-85; lectr. in pub. policy J.F. Kennedy Sch. Govt. Harvard U., Cambridge, Mass., 1987-91; dir. programs and policy Children's Def. Fund, Washington, 1991-93; commr. on children, youth and families HHS, Washington, 1993-97, prin. dep. asst. sec. for children and families, 1997, asst. sec. for children and families, 1997—2001; dir. D.C. Child and Family Svcs. Agy., 2001—. Mem. adv. com. children and youth City of Cambridge. Author: Poor Children and Welfare Reform, 1992. Candidate for senator, Mass. Office: Chid and Family Svcs Agy 400 6th St SW 5th Fl Washington DC 20024

GOLDENBERG, ELIZABETH LEIGH, editor; b. Dayton, Ohio, Oct. 29, 1963; d. Neal and Myrna (Gallant) G. AB in Philosophy and Politics, Mount Holyoke Coll., 1985. Intern, spokeswoman The White House, Washington, 1984; trainee Nat. Westminister Bank USA, N.Y.C., 1985-86, asst. to v.p. fin. and strategic planning ops. div., 1986-87; asst. dealer Toronto-Dominion Bank, N.Y.C., 1987-88, dealer money markets, 1988-90, sr. dealer money markets, 1990-91, sr. dealer, mgr. short term asset trading, 1991-93; sr. dealer, sr. mgr. short term loan participations TD Securities, Inc., N.Y.C., 1993-97, v.p., dir. short term money-market trading and origination, 1997-99; freelance journalist, author, 2000; reporter Bloomberg News, 2000—01, editor, team leader, 2001—02, mng. editor bonds, currencies and derivatives, 2002—. Econ. commentator, 1993-2000. Contbr. articles and photographs to mags. Bd. dirs. USA Rugby Met. N.Y., 1987-89, N.Y. Rugby Club, 1995-98; publicist, spokesperson, com. on image and mktg. USA Rugby, 1993; U.S.A. Eagles publicist USA Rugby, Colorado Springs, Colo., 1989-94; chair Youth Rugby for Harlem Devel. Com., 1994-95. Mem. Pub. Securities Assn. (chmn. money market com. 1990-92, bd. dirs. 1990-92, mem. polit. action com. 1990 92, program com 1990-92, awards com. 1991-93, chmn. money market com. 1997-99, bd. dirs 1997-99). Avocations: photography, rugby, cooking, baking, ballet. Home: 355 S End Ave Apt 20J New York NY 10280-1007 E-mail: egoldenberg2@bloomberg.net.

GOLDENBERG, KIM, academic administrator, internist; BS, SUNY, Stonybrook, 1968; MS, Polytech. Inst. N.Y., 1972; MD, Albany (N.Y.) Med. Coll., 1979. Test engr. lunar lander and naval jets, Grumman, NY, 1968—75; resident internal medicine Western Res. Care Sys., Youngstown, Ohio, 1979—82, dir. gen. internal medicine Wright State U. Sch. Medicine, Dayton, Ohio, 1983—89, vice chair medicine, 1988—89, assoc. dean for students and curriculum, 1989—90, dean, 1990—98, pres., 1998—. Office: Wright State U Office of Pres Dayton OH 45435

GOLDENBERG, MYRNA GALLANT, English language/literature and Holocaust educator; b. Bklyn., Mar. 8, 1937; d. Harry and Fay (Solomon) Gallant; m. Neal Goldenberg, Jan. 27, 1957; children: Elizabeth, David Brian, Eve Lisa. BS cum laude, CCNY, 1957; MA, U. Ark., 1961; PhD, U. Md., 1987. Prof. emerita dept. English Montgomery Coll., Rockville, Md., 1971—2003, chair dept., 1979-81, coord. gen. edn., 1981-90, coord. women's studies program, 1990-94, dir. Paul Peck Humanities Inst., 1997—2003. Lectr. Sch. Arts and Scis., Johns Hopkins U.; lectr. Holocaust and genocide studies, women's studies, Jewish women's studies, honors coll. English U. Md.; dir. project to integrate scholarship on women and minorities into the curriculum Ford Found., 1993-94; co-dir. project integrating scholarship of women in curricula of selected Md. C.C.s, FIPSE, 1988-90; chmn. Montgomery County Commn. on Humanities, 1984-91; chmn. Title IX adv. com. Montgomery County Pub. Schs., 1985-89; lectr. in field. Contbg. author/author: Common and Uncommon Concerns: The Complex Role of Community College Department Chairpersons/Enhancing Department Leadership, 1990, Different Horrors/Same Hell: Women Remembering the Holocaust, Thinking the Unthinkable: Human Meanings of the Holocaust, 1990, Writing Everybody In: Two-Year College English: Essays for a New Century, 1994, Testimony, Narrative and Nightmare: Experience of Jewish Women in the Holocaust: Active Voices/Women and Jewish Culture, 1995, Lessons Learned from Gentle Heroism: Women's Holocaust Narratives, 1995; The Beautiful Days of My Youth, 1997, Memoirs of Auschwitz Survivors: The Burden of Gender, 1998, Experience and Expression: Women, the Nazis, and the Holocaust, 2003; editor: Community College Guide to Curriculum Change, 1990, Experience and Expression: Women, the Nazis and the Holocaust; contbg. editor: Belles Lettres, 1989-98; editor C.C. Humanities Rev., 1990—; contbr. articles to profl. jours. Bd. dirs. Jewish Cmty. Coun., 1997-2002, Md. Humanities Coun., 1997-2003, Jewish Hist. Soc. Greater Washington, 1997—, Arts and Humanities Coun., 2000-02. Recipient Disting. Humanities Educator award C.C. Humanities Assn., 1989, Outstanding Faculty Mem. award Montgomery Coll., 1990, Teaching award Md. Assn. for Higher Edn., 1991; Acad. Adminstrn. fellow Am. Coun. on Edn., 1981-82; Lowenstein Wiener fellow Am. Jewish Archives, 1983; recipient William H. Meardy Faculty award Assn. of Comm. Coll. Trustees, 1996, Comcast Excellence in the Humanities award, 2002. Mem. MLA (sec.), Nat. Women's Studies Assn. (sec.), Assn. Jewish Studies, Nat. Coun. Tchrs. English, Jewish Hist. Soc. Greater Wash. (bd. dirs. 1997—2002, Phi Kappa Phi. Avocations: walking, travel, writing, reading, knitting. E-mail: myrnagoldenberg@hotmail.com.

GOLDENSTEIN, LISSA A. biotechnology company executive; B in Civil Engrng., Pa. State U. Registered Calif. From sales rep. to dir. comml. ops. McDonnell Douglas; sr. v.p. Molecular Simulations, Argonaut Technologies, Inc., Foster City, Calif., 1998—2001, pres., CEO, 2001—. Office: Argonaut Technologies Inc 1101 Chess Dr Foster City CA 94404-1102

GOLDFARB, IRENE DALE, retired financial planner; b. Newark, N.J., Jan. 13, 1929; d. Philip and Lucie (Mintz) Dale; m. Samuel Goldfarb, Jan. 28, 1951; children: Ruth Goldfarb Koizim, David Alan, Sally Fay, Judith Valerie. BS in Chemistry, Rutgers U., 1950; MBA, U. Pa., 1979. CFP. Asst. to assoc. provost Princeton (N.J.) U., 1968-70, asst. to provost, 1970-72, tech. staff, 1972-74, mgr. pers. svcs., 1974-75, asst. dir. pers. svcs., 1975-84; fin. planner, mgr. A.L. Herst Assocs., Inc., Princeton, 1984-86; pvt. practice Princeton, 1986-90; v.p. A.L. Herst Assocs., Inc., Princeton, 1990-92; fin. planner Glenmede Trust Co. N.J., Princeton, 1992—2001; ret., 2002. Cons. in field. Mem. Fin. Planning Assn. (founding officer Princeton-Western N.J. chpt. 1986-98, pres. 1988-89, chmn. 1989-90), Assoc. Alumnae Douglass Coll. (chmn. ann. fund 1982-84, v.p. adminstrn. 1988-94), Phi Beta Kappa. Avocations: music, gardening, travel. Home and Office: 69 Balsam Ln Princeton NJ 08540-5326

GOLDFARB, MURIEL BERNICE, marketing and advertising consultant; b. Bklyn., Mar. 29, 1920; d. Barnett Goldfarb and May (Steinberg) Goldfarb Oshman; BA, U. Miami, Coral Gables, Fla., 1942; postgrad. CCNY, 1950. Pub. info. asst. UNESCO, Paris, 1946-47; advt. mgr. Majestic Specialties Co., N.Y.C., 1947-50; retail promotion mgr. Glamour Mag., 1955-61; advt. dir. Country Tweeds Co., N.Y.C., 1961-65; advt. dir. S. Augstein & Co., N.Y.C., 1966-72, Feature Ring Co., Inc., Gotham Ring Co., Inc., Fidco Inc., N.Y.C., 1972-77; dir. advt. and promotion Wasko Gold Products Corp., N.Y.C., 1977-81; advt. and mktg. cons. specializing in promotions and sale of vintage jewelry and Bric á Brac. Lt. WAVES, 1943-46. Mem.Women's Jewelry Assn. (corr. sec. 1983-85). Jewish.

GOLDFARB, RUTH, poet, educator; b. Bklyn., Aug. 13, 1936; d. Nathan Alter and Florence Goldfarb. BA in Psychology, L.I. Univ., 1980; MA in Edn., NYU, 1984. Tchr. kindergarten N.Y.C. Bd. Edn., 1963-64, early childhood tchr., 1993-94, N.Y.C., Bklyn., 1970-84; tchr. common br. Bklyn. Bd. Edn., 1986-93; clk. Primary Health Care Ctr. North Broward Med. Ctr., Pompano Beach, Fla., 1998—. Author (poetry) Whispers and Chants, 1997; CD recs. include Christmas Memories, 1999, The Miracle of Christmas, 2000, Songs of Praise, 2000. Mem.: AARP, Gold Coast Poetry Group, Acad. Am. Poets, Internat. Soc. Poets. Avocations: poetry, music, sculpture, writing stories.

GOLDFEIN, IRIS, financial company executive; Vice chmn., human resources Coopers & Lybrand, Chgo.; leader of Price Waterhouse Coopers Kwasha HR Solutions, 1998—; group pres. HR Innovations. Office: Price Waterhouse Coopers 203 N La Salle St Chicago IL 60601-1210

GOLDIE, DOROTHY ROBERTA, retired suicide prevention counselor, educator; b. Phila., Apr. 7, 1922; d. Abe and Esther (Zupnick) Zafman; m. Ray Robert Goldie, Dec. 2, 1941 (dec. July 7, 2002); children: Deanne, Dale, Ron. MA in Humans Svcs., U. Calif., Riverside, 1976; postgrad., U. So. Calif. Bd. dirs. Family Svcs., San Bernardino, Calif.; counselor, instr. Suicide Crisis Hotline Inland Empire, San Bernardino; founder, counselor, instr., bd. dirs. Suicide Crisis Hotline Mountain Cmtys., Calif.; pres. Counsel of Mirage Inn, Rancho Mirage, Calif., 2004—. Mem. Amnesty Internat., Animal Samaritans SPCA, Inc.; charter mem. Women's Action Counsel Arthritis Found.; scholarship sponsor U. So. Calif. Law Sch., L.A., U. So. Calif. Keck Sch. Medicine, L.A., amb. to pres.; founder McCallum Theatre Bob Hope Cultural Ctr., Rancho Mirage, Eisenhower Hosp., Rancho Mirage; mem. Ctr. Sci. Pub. Interest, Jewish Family Svcs., Riverside Sheriff's Assn.; officer Sisterhood Temple Emanuel, San Bernardino, Sisterhood Temple Sinai. Mem.: AAUW, San Bernardino Lawyers Wives, B'nai B'rith (bd. dirs., pres.), U. So. Calif. Assocs. (life), U. So. Calif. Alumni Assn. (life), Rancho Mirage Calif. (life), Lake Arrowhead Country Club Women's Assn. (officer, bd. dirs.).

GOLDIN, CLAUDIA DALE, economics educator; b. N.Y.C., May 14, 1946; d. Leon and Lucille (Rosansky) G. BA magna cum laude with distinction, Cornell U., 1967; MA, U. Chgo., 1969, PhD, 1972; MA (hon.), U. Pa., 1985, Harvard U., 1990; DHL (hon.), U. Nebr., Lincoln, 1994. Asst. prof. econs. U. Wis., Madison, 1971-73; asst. prof. Princeton (N.J.) U., 1973-79, vis. fellow indsl. relations sec., 1987-88; vis. lectr. Harvard U., Cambridge, Mass., 1975-76, prof., 1990—; assoc. prof. U. Pa., Phila., 1979-85, prof., 1985-90; vis. fellow The Brookings Instn., 1993-94. Mem. Inst. Advanced Study, Princeton, 1982-83; rsch. assoc., project dir. Nat. Bur. Econ. Rsch., Cambridge, 1979—; vis. fellow Russell Sage Found., 1997-98. Author: Urban Slavery in the American South, 1976, Understanding the Gender Gap, 1990; editor: Strategic Factors in 19th Century American Economic History, 1992, The Regulated Economy, 1994, The Defining Moment: The Great Depression and the American Economy in the 20th Century, 1998, Jour. Econ. History, NBER Series on Long-Term Factors in Econ. Devel.; mem. editl. bd. Am. Econ. Rev., 1985-91, Quar. Jour. Econs., 1992—, Rev. Econs. and Stats., Jour. Interdisciplinary History; contbr. articles to profl. publs. Recipient NSF award, 1975-77, 79-81, 81-82, 84-86, 87-89, 92-93, 96-99, Spencer Found. rsch. award, 1996, 2001—; Guggenheim fellow, 1987-88. Fellow Econometric Soc.; mem. Am. Acad. Arts and Scis., Am. Econ. Assn. (v.p. 1990-91), Econ. History Assn. (pres. 1999-00, trustee 1984—, v.p. 1988-89). Avocations: aerobics, hiking, bird watching. Office: Harvard U Dept Econs Cambridge MA 02138 E-mail: cgoldin@harvard.edu.

GOLDING, CAROLYN MAY, former government senior executive, consultant; b. Essex County, N.J., July 1, 1941; d. Wesley Irwin and Florence Grace (Smith) G.; m. Gary Anthony Derosa, Oct. 18, 1975 (div. Sept. 1982). BA, Duke U., 1963, postgrad., 1965-66. English tchr. Parkersburg (W.Va.) H.S., 1963; asst. to registrar Duke U., Durham, N.C., 1963-65; mgmt. intern Dept. Labor, Washington, 1966-67, various other positions, 1967-72; dep. assoc. regional adminstr. Employment and Tng. Adminstrn., San Francisco, 1972-77, comptroller Washington, 1977-78, regional adminstr. San Francisco, 1979-82, dir. Unemployment Ins. Svc. Washington, 1982-87, adminstr. employment security, 1987-88, dep. asst. sec. employment and tng., 1988-96. Cons. on mgmt., labor force, long-range planning, workforce edn. issues and exec. coaching, 1996—. Recipient Disting. Career Svc. award Dept. Labor, 1979, Fed. Women's Career award Sec. Labor, 1983, Presdl. Meritorious rank, 1987, 95, Philip Arnow award Dept. Labor, 1988. Mem. Internat. Women's Forum, Women's Forum of Washington, Coun. for Excellence in Govt. (prin.). Episcopalian.

GOLDING, SUSAN G. former mayor; b. Muskogee, Okla., Aug. 18, 1945; d. Brage and Hinda Fay (Wolf) G.; children: Samuel, Vanessa. Cert. Pratique de Langue Francaise, U. Paris, 1965; BA in Govt. and Internat. Rels., Carleton Coll., 1966; MA in Romance Philology, Columbia U., 1974. Assoc. editor Columbia U. Jour. of Internat. Affairs, N.Y.C., 1968-69; teaching fellow Emory U., Atlanta, 1973-74; instr. San Diego Community Coll. Dist., 1978; assoc. pub., gen. mgr. The News Press Group, San Diego, 1978-80; city council mem. City of San Diego, 1981-83; dep. sec. bus., transp., housing State of Calif., Sacramento, 1983-84; county supr. dist. 3 County of San Diego, 1984-92; mayor City of San Diego, 1992—2000; pres. & CEO The Golding Group, Inc., San Diego, 2000—; head Homeland Security Office, Titan Corp., San Diego, 2000—. Chmn. San Diego Drug Strike Force, 1987-88, Calif. Housing Fin. Agy., Calif. Coastal Commn.; bd. dirs. San Diego County Water Authority; trustee So. Calif. Water Com., Inc.; founder Mid City Comml. Revitalization Task Force, Strategic Trade Alliance, 1993, Calif. Big 10 City Mayors, 1993; mem. Gov. Calif. Mil. Base Reuse Task Force, 1994; established San Diego World Trade Ctr., 1993, San Diego City/State/County Regional Permit Assistance Ctr., 1994; mem. adv. bd. U.S. Conf. of Mayors, 1994; chair Gov. Wilson's Commn. on Local Governance for 21st Century. Bd. dirs. Child Abuse Prevention Found., San Diego Conv. and Vis. Bur., Crime Victims Fund, United Cerebral Palsy, San Diego Air Quality Bd., San Diego March of Dimes, Rep. Assocs.; adv. bd. Girl Scouts U.S.; trustee So. Calif. Water Comm.; mem. Rep. State Cen. Com.; co-chair com. Presidency George Bush Media Fund, Calif.; chair San Diego County Regional Criminal Justice Coun., race rels. com. Citizens Adv. Com. on Racial Intergration, San Diego Unified Sch. Dist.; hon. chair Am. Cancer Soc's. Residential Crusade, 1988. Recipient Alice Paul award Nat. Women's Polit. Caucus, 1987, Calif. Women in Govt. Achievement award, 1988, Willie Velasquez Polit. award Mex. Am. Bus. and Profl. Assn., 1988, Catalyst of Chance award Greater San Diego C. of C., 1994, Woman Who Means Bus. award San Diego Bus. Jour., 1994, Internat. Citizen award World Affairs Coun., 1994; named One of San Diego's Ten Outstanding Young Citizens, 1981, One of Ten Outstanding Rep. County Ofcls. in U.S.A., Rep. Nat. Com., 1987, San Diego Woman of Achievement Soroptimists Internat., 1988. Mem. Nat. Assn. of Counties (chair Op. Fair Share, mem. taxation and fin. com.), Nat. Women's Forum. Republican. Jewish. Office: The Golding Group Inc 9276 Scranton Rd Ste 600 San Diego CA 92121 E-mail: commerce@golding.org.

GOLDMAN, ANNE L. ceramic artist; b. N.Y.C., July 10, 1935; d. Morris M. and Ethel (Aronow) Meislik; m. Donald L. Goldman, June 7, 1958; children: Nadine, Daniel. Attended, Ballet Arts Sch., N.Y.C., 1950-57, Santa Rosa Coll., Calif., 1974-76, Fairleigh Dickinson U., Hackensack, 1957-59, U. Calif., Berkeley, 1960-62. Sales dir. Assn. Calif. Ceramic Artists, San Francisco, 1974-86; workshop leader Oakland Visual Arts Program, 1987, J.F.K. Univ., Orinda, 1982, The Rossmoor Assn., Walnut Creek, 1991. One-Woman shows include Am. Craft Mus., N.Y.C., Everson Mus. Art, Syracuse, Crocker Mus., Sacramento, Oakland Mus.; numerous gallery shows including Hastings-on-the-Hudson Art Mus., Judah Magnus Mus., NCECA Shows, NEA Invitational, Univ. Utah, Salon Del Complemento De Arrido, Milan, others. Vol. Internat. Com. for Tibet, 1997—. Recipient Purchase award San Francisco Area Commn., 1984. Mem. Assn. Calif. Ceramic Artists, Am. Craft Coun. Avocations: international travel, river rafting, hiking, gardening. Office: 1972 Meadow Rd Walnut Creek CA 94595-2634

GOLDMAN, ELISABETH PARIS, lawyer; b. Pitts., Jan. 11, 1939; d. Harold H. and Silvia F. (Koenigsberg) Paris; m. Alvin Lee Goldman, Nov. 23, 1956; children: Polly, Douglas. BA, Queens Coll., 1964; JD, U. Ky., 1975. Bar: Ky. 1975, Calif. 1977. Chief law clk. Supreme Ct. Ky., Frankfort, 1975-76; pvt. practice Elisabeth Goldman PSC, Lexington, Ky., 1977—. Bd. dirs. ACLU Louisville, Ky., 1987-90, Hadassah, Chamber Music Soc., Fayette County Health Care Bd.; pres. Ctrl. Ky. Jewish Fedn., 1993-95, Ctrl. Ky. Civil Liberties Union, 1988-90, James Lane Allen PTA, Lexington, Ky., 1971-72. Recipient Pro-Bono Svc. award Ky. Bar Assn., Frankfort, 1994-2001. Mem. Am. Acad. Adoption Attys., Order of Coif, Phi Beta Kappa. Democrat. Avocations: skiing, hiking, dog training. Office: Elisabeth Goldman PSC 118 Old Lafayette Ave Lexington KY 40502-1704 E-mail: egoldman@adoptionattorneys.org.

GOLDMAN, FATIMA, social services administrator; BA, CUNY; MA, Bank St. Coll. Edn. With Human Resources Adminstrn., University Heights Day Care Ctr., Hartley Ho. Family Day Care, Graham-Windham Svcs. Families and Children; exec. dir. Brookwood Child Care, 1994—2002; v.p. Coun. Family and Childcare Agys., 2000—, exec. dir., CEO Fedn. Protestant Welfare Agys., N.Y.C., 2003—. Mem. adv. bd. Am. Cancer Soc., Resources Children with Spl. Needs. Office: 281 Park Ave S New York NY 10010

GOLDMAN, JANICE GOLDIN, psychologist, educator; b. Phila., Feb. 15, 1938; d. Samuel and Dorothea (Berenson) Goldin; m. Arthur S. Goldman, Aug. 31, 1958; children: Jill Ann Goldman-Callahan, Joshua N., Jennifer S. BA, U. Pa., 1960, MA, 1962; MS, Hahnemann Med. Coll., 1972, D in Psychology, 1975. Lic. psychologist, Pa. Chief psychologist Charles Peberdy Child Psychiatry Ctr. Hahnemann U., Phila., 1975-87, from clin. asst. to assoc. prof., 1985-87; pvt. practice Jenkintown, Pa., 1977—. Cons. Haverford (Pa.) State Hosp., 1982, Assn. for Mental Health Affiliates with Israel, 1984, 86; mem. profl. adv. bd. Pub. Radio Sta WHYY, Phila., 1984-86; workshop leader Women's Ctr. of Montgomery County, Jenkintown, 1982—. Contbr. articles to profl. jours. Board dirs. Assn. for Mental Health Affiliate with Israel, nationwide, 1984-88, Or Hadash Synogogue, Wyncote, Pa., 1989, 96-2000. Mem. APA, Am. Family Therapy Acad., Nat. Register Health Svc. Providers, Phila. Soc. Clin. Psychology (sec. 1977-79), Am. Amnesty Internat., Internat. Soc. for Study Dissociation, Greater Phila. Soc. Clin. Hypnosis, Phi Beta Kappa. Democrat. Avocations: tennis, biking, cooking, reading, writing. Office: The Plaza 1250 Greenwood Ave Jenkintown PA 19046-2901 Office Phone: 215-572-1355. Personal E-mail: jgold1222@aol.com

GOLDMAN, LYNN ROSE, medical educator; b. Galveston, Tex., Apr. 24, 1951; d. Armond Samuel and Barbara Jean (Bangert) G.; m. Douglas George Hayward. BS, U. Calif., 1976; MPH, Johns Hopkins U., 1981; MS, U. Calif., Berkeley, 1979; MD, U. Calif., San Francisco, 1981. Diplomate Am. Bd. Pediatrics; lic. physician, Calif. Resident in pediatrics Children's Hosp. Med. Ctr., Oakland, Calif., 1985; resident in preventive medicine U. Calif., Berkeley, 1985; pub. health med. officer Calif. Dept. Health Svcs., Berkeley, 1985-91, pub. health med. adminstr., 1991-93; asst. adminstr. Office of Prevention, Pesticides and Toxic Substances, EPA, Washington, 1993-98; prof. Sch. Hygiene and Pub. Health, Johns Hopkins U., Balt., 1999—. Democrat. Office: Johns Hopkins U Bloomberg Sch Pub Health 615 N Wolfe St Rm W8511 Baltimore MD 21205-1900 E-mail: lgoldman@jhsph.edu.

GOLDRING, ELIZABETH, environmental media artist, poet; b. Forest City, Iowa, Feb. 13, 1945; d. James C. and Vera (Farrington) Olson; 1 child, Jessica Tova Farrington Goldring. BA cum laude, Smith Coll., 1967; MEd, Harvard U., 1978. Art tchr. St. Louis Pub. Schs.; exhibits developer The Children's Mus., Boston, 1973-76; fellow Ctr. for Advanced Visual Studies MIT, Cambridge, Mass., 1977—96, exhibits and projects dir. Ctr. for Advanced Visual Studies, 1977—97, lectr. Dept. of Architecture, 1989—94; sr. fellow CAVS/MIT, 1996—. Co-dir. Sky Art Conf., CAVS, MIT, 1981—; mem. adv. coun. on art-sci. tech. MIT, 1994—; corr. mem. European Acad. Arts, Scis., Humanities; project dir. Desert Sun/Desert Moon, Lone Pine, Calif., 1986. Prin. works include with CAVS/MIT ICA, Boston, 1976, Documenta 6, Kassel, 1977, Smithsonian Institution, Washington, 1978, Secession, Vienna, 1979, Musee de l'art Moderne del la Ville de Paris, 1985, Eye/Sight interactive installations Lights/Orot, prin. works include Yeshiva U. Mus., N.Y.C., 1988, Kunstverein Karlsruhe, Fed. Republic Germany, 1988, Celebration of light, Savolinna, Finland, 1989, Washington Project for the Arts, 1989, MIT Mus., 1994, A Visual Language for the Blind und Retina Prints, 1991—; artist/producer (tapes with Vin Grabill) The Inner Eye-From the Inside Out, 1985, A Visual Language for the Blind, 1991, Interactive Cybervision Environments for the Blind, 1996, Eye Dance, 2000, (audiotapes) International Alarm, 1982, Der Hahnenschrei, 1983, Coyote, 1986, Kikeriki, 1989; co-author: (book) Sky Art Manifesto, 1996, (poetry books include) Laser Treatment, 1983, Without Warning, 1985, A Prairie Schooner Portfolio, 2001, EY-, 2002; exhibitions include Compton Gallery, MIT, 2003, Groton Sch., 2003; contbr. various pubs. Named one of Best and Brightest, Tech. Rev., 1998; named to Prix Arts Electronics honorable mention, 1996; recipient article New Eng. Jour. Optometry, 1990; fellow Charlotte Moorman, MIT, 1997; grantee NEA InterArts, 1985, Diabetes Rsch. and Edn., 1986, NASA, 2002, MIT Coun. for the Arts, 2002. Office: MIT Ctr Adv Visual Studies MIT N 52 265 Mass Ave Cambridge MA 02139-4312 Business E-Mail: goldring@mit.edu.

GOLDSCHEIDER, FRANCES K. sociologist, educator; b. Balt., June 12, 1942; d. George Hyde and Ida Thomas (Sledge) Engeman; m. David R. Kobrin, Sept. 23, 1961 (div. 1978); children: Sarah, Janet; m. Calvin Goldscheider, Aug. 18, 1983. BA, U. Pa., 1965, MA, 1967, PhD, 1971. Asst. prof. sociology Skidmore Coll., 1969-74, Brown U., Providence, 1974-86, prof., 1986—, chair dept. sociology, 1984-87, dir. Social Sci. and Data Ctr., 1984-85, dir. Population Studies and Tng. Ctr., 1989-92, 94-95, 2003—04; rsch. assoc. RAND Corp., 1980—, Inst. Social Rsch., U. Mich., Ann Arbor, 1989—. Vis. assoc. prof. demography The Hebrew U., 1983-84, vis. prof. sociology Stockholm U. Author: (with C. Goldscheider) The Ethnic Factor in Family Structure and Mobility, 1978, Ethnicity and the New Family Economy, 1989, (with Linda Waite) New Families, No Families: The Transformation of the American Home, 1991, (with C. Goldscheider) Leaving Home Before Marriage, 1993, (with C. Goldscheider) The Changing Transition to Adulthood: Leaving and Returning Home, 1999; editor: Demography, 1994-95; assoc. editor: Jours. of Gerontology, 1992-94, Am. Sociol. Rev., 1990-92, Jour. Marriage and Family, 1987—;contbr. articles to profl. jours. NEH grantee, 1973-74; Fulbright fellow, 1983-84, 2001-02. Mem. Am. Sociol. Assn. (chair population sect. 1988-89), Internat. Union for Sci. Study of Population, Population Assn. Am. (bd. dirs. 1987-90, 2nd v.p. 1991-92, chair Dorothy Swaine Thomas Award com. 1985-86). Home: 15 Fones Alley Providence RI 02906-3338 Office: Brown U Dept Sociology Providence RI 02912-0001

GOLDSCHMIDT, LYNN HARVEY, lawyer; b. Chgo., June 14, 1951; d. Arthur and Ida (Shirman) H.; m. Robert Allen Goldschmidt, Aug. 27, 1972; children: Elizabeth Anne, Carolyn Helene. BS with honors, U. Ill., 1973; JD magna cum laude, Northwestern U., 1976. Bar: Ill. 1976. Ptnr. Hopkins & Sutter, Chgo., 1976-2001, Foley & Lardner, Chgo., 2001—02; prin. D and G Cons. Group, 2002—. Articles editor Northwestern U. Law Rev. Mem. Airport Coun. Internat., N. Am., Order of Coif. Office: D&G Cons Grp 120 S LaSalle St Chicago IL 60603 E-mail: lhg@dg-cg.com.

GOLDSMITH, BARBARA, writer, historian, journalist; d. Joseph I. and Evelyn (Cronson) Lubin; children: Andrew Goldsmith, Alice Elgart, John Goldsmith. BA, Wellesley Coll., 1958; DLitt (hon.), Syracuse U., 1980; LHD (hon.), Pace U., 1982; DLitt (hon.), Lake Forest Coll., 1996. Contbr. N.Y. Herald Tribune, Esquire Mag., 1958—64; founder, contbg. editor N.Y. Mag., 1968—; sr. editor Harpers Bazaar Mag., N.Y.C., 1970-74. Lectr. NYU, 1969, 75. Spl. writer TV documentaries and entertainments; author: (novel) The Straw Man, 1975; (non-fiction) Little Gloria . . . Happy at Last, 1980, Johnson v. Johnson, 1987, Other Powers: The Age of Suffrage, Spiritualism and the Scandalous Victoria Woodhull, 1998, Obsessive Genius Marie Curie: A Life in Science, 2004. Pres. Com. for Preservation and Access, 1990—95; mem. Pres.'s Commn. on Celebration of Women in Am. History, 1998—2001; mem. jr. coun. Mus. Modern Art, N.Y.C., 1951—73; mem. acquisitions com. Friends of Whitney Mus. Art, 1964—; mem. pres.'s coun. Mus. City N.Y., 1970—; mem. exec. bd. PEN Am. Ctr., 1984—96; chmn. permanent paper com. PEN Freedom to Write Com., 1989—; founder Ctr. for Learning Disabilities, Albert Einstein Coll. Medicine; trustee N.Y. Pub. Libr., 1985—, mem. exec. com., 2003—; gubernatorial appointee N.Y. State Coun. on Arts, 1990; founder Barbara Goldsmith/PEN Freedom to Write awards, Barbara Goldsmith/N.Y. Pub. Libr. Conservation and Preservation Divsns., Barbara Goldsmith/NYU Preservation Lab., Am. Acad. in Rome Barbara Goldsmith Rare Book Rm.; bd. dirs. permanent paper task force Nat. Libr. Medicine, 1989—; bd. dirs. Parks Coun. N.Y.C., 1965—82, Nat. Dance Inst., 1979—, Goldsmith Found., 1981—. Recipient Brandeis U. Library Trust award, 1980, Albert Einstein Spirit of Achievement award, 1988, Permanent Paper citation N.Y. Pub. Libr., Lit. Lions award N.Y. Pub. Libr., 1988, Pubs. 1st Ann. award Lit. Market Place, 1990, Rome medal Am. Acad. in Rome, Nat. Libr. Medicine Lit. award, 1991, Nat. Archives award, 1991, NYU Presdl. Citation award, 1993, Lifetime Achievement award Guild Hall Acad. Arts, 1999, Poets and Writers Lit. award, 1999, Presdl. citation for pub. svc., 2000. Mem. Authors Guild, Century Assn., Am. Acad. Arts and Scis., Guild Hall Acad. Arts (Lit. Achievement award 1999). Office: Janklow & Nesbit Attn Ms Lynn Nesbit 598 Madison Ave New York NY 10022-1614

GOLDSMITH, CAROLINE L. arts executive; b. N.Y.C., Nov. 25, 1925; d. Reuben and Gladys (Garf) Steinholz; m. Mortimer M. Lerner, Dec. 1, 1946 (div. Nov., 1968); children: Lawrence, David; m. John F. Goldsmith, Dec. 1973. BA, Cornell U., 1946. Pres. dir. Gallery Passport Ltd., N.Y.C., 1960-66; sr. v.p. Ruder Finn Arts & Comm. Counselors, N.Y.C., 1966—; exec. dir. Arttable, Inc., N.Y.C., 1980-94. Mem. Cmty. Bd., N.Y.C., 1987-95. Mem.: Coll. Art Assn., Internat. Coun. Museums, Am. Fedn. Arts, Am. Assn. Museums, Internat. Women's Forum (bd. dirs.), The Century Assn., Smithsonian Inst. Democrat. Jewish. Avocations: theater, museums. Home: 375 W End Ave New York NY 10024-6568 Office: Ruder Finn Inc 301 E 57th St New York NY 10022-2900

GOLDSMITH, CATHY ELLEN, retired special education educator; b. NYC, Feb. 18, 1947; d. Eli D. and Gertrude A. G. BS, NYU, 1968, MA in Elem. Edn., 1971, MA in Ednl. Psychology, 1974. Cert. phys. handicapped, K-6 elem. edn. tchr., N.Y. 2d grade tchr. N.Y.C. Bd. Edn., 1968-69, tchr. learning disabled students (spl. edn.), 1969-86, tchr. emotionally disturbed learning disabled students, 1986-87, tchr. learning disabled students, 1987-88, tchr. trainable retarded students, 1988-2000, tchr. mixed disabilities class, 2000-01; ret., 2001. Represented in permanent collections Bobst Libr. NYU. Recipient Charles Oscar Maas Essay award in Am. History, 1968, Disting. Alumni Svc. award NYU, 1987. Mem. AAUW, Nat. Mus. Women in Arts, NYU Alumni Assn. (past rec. sec., v.p.), NYU Alumni Assn., NYU Alumnae Club (past v.p.), Pi Lambda Theta (past pres., past historian). Home: 418 Beach 133d St Rockaway Park NY 11694-1416

GOLDSMITH, DEBORAH, social studies educator; MA, U. Calif., Berkeley, 1981. Instr. San Francisco State U., 1981—83, City Coll. San Francisco, 1983—84, 1993—. Adviser Econs. Club City Coll. San Francisco, 1996—. Mem.: Internat. Assn. Feminist Econs., Am. Econ. Assn. Office: City Coll San Francisco 50 Phelan Ave San Francisco CA 94112

GOLDSMITH, DONNA, sports association executive; b. Long Island; Degree in comm., SUNY, Oswego. Worked at Swatch Watch USA, Revlon Inc.; v.p. licensing NBA; sr. v.p. consumer products World Wrestling Fedn. Entertainment Inc., Stamford, Conn., 2000—. Mem.: NY Women in Comm. Office: World Wrestling Fedn Entertainment Inc 1241 E Main St Stamford CT 06902 E-mail: donna.goldsmith@wwfent.com.*

GOLDSMITH, ETHEL FRANK, medical social worker; b. Chgo., May 31, 1919; d. Theodore and Rose (Falk) Frank; m. Julian Royce Goldsmith, Sept. 4, 1940; children: Richard, Susan, John. BA, U. Chgo., 1940. Lic. social worker, Ill. Liaison worker psychiat. consultation service U. Chgo. Hosp., 1964-68; med. social worker Wyler Children's Hosp., Chgo., 1968-98. Treas. U. Chgo. Service League, 1958-62, chmn. camp Brueckner Farr Aux., 1966-72; pres. Bobs Roberts Hosp. Service Commn., 1962; bd. dirs. Richardson Wildlife Sanctuary, 1988-2000; mem. Field Mus. Women's Bd., 1966—; bd. dirs. Hyde Park Art Ctr., 1964-82, Chgo. Commons Assn., 1967-77, Alumni Assn. Sch. Social Service Adminstrn., 1976-80, Self Help Home for Aged, 1985-2000, U. Chgo. Svc. League, 2002—; vol. Chgo. Found. for Edn.; mem. womens bd. U. Chgo., 1999—. Recipient Alumni Citation Pub. Service, U. Chgo., 1972. Mem. Phi Beta Kappa. Home: 5550 S Shore Dr Apt 1313 Chicago IL 60637

GOLDSMITH, JILL, scriptwriter, television producer; d. Stephen Goldsmith and Carol King. BA, U. Ill., 1984; JD, Washington U., 1987. Bar: Ill. 1987. Pub. defender Cook County Pub. Defenders Office, Chgo., 1989—96; writer, exec. story editor The Practice-David E. Kelley Prodns., Manhattan Beach, Calif., 1998—2001; writer, prodr. Law and Order-Wolf Films, Universal City, Calif., 2001—03. Spkr. Vis. Writer Program Writers Guild Found., L.A., 2000—. Scriptwriter : (TV series) NYPD Blue, 1998; The Practice, 1998—2001; Ally McBeal, 2000; Law and Order, 2001—03. Mem.: Writers Guild, Women in Film, Acad. TV Arts and Scis.

GOLDSMITH, JOCELYN STONE, retired state employment professional; b. Columbus, Ohio, Aug. 26, 1933; d. Roy J. Stone and Lillian Stone Frazin Alterman Friedland; m. Daniel J. Goldsmith, Mar. 15, 1953 (div. Nov. 1972); children: Debra Ann Goldsmith Wilson, Jeffrey Robert (dec.), David Michael; m. Chester G. Bandman, Sept. 20, 1992 (dec. Jan. 1995). BS in Bus., Frankin U., 1980, BS in Employee Assistance Counseling, 1989. User svcs. coord. R.G. Barry Corp., Columbus, 1974-82; claims mgr. Ohio Bur. Employment Svcs., Columbus, 1983-2001; ret., 2001. Adopt-A-Sch. coord. Columbus Pub. schs., Greater Columbus C. of C., 1979—. Mem. safe and drug-free schs. consortium Frnklin County Ednl. Coun. Recipient plaque Ohio Sch. Partnership, 1995. Mem. Internat. Assn. Personnel in Employment Security. Jewish. Avocations: reading, enjoying plays, concerts and ballet.

GOLDSMITH, KIMBERLEE BETH, special education educator; b. Highland Park, Ill., Aug. 31, 1978; d. Jay and Cindy Goldsmith. BS, Miami U., Oxford, Ohio, 2000. Cert. spl. edn. tchr. Cook County, Ill. Asst. lang. tchr. Takaoka (Japan) Bd. of Edn., 2001—03; spl. edn. tchr. Northbrook (Ill.) Jr. HS, 2003—. Spl. edn. tchr. PACTT Learning Ctr., Chgo., 2000—01. Home: 1100 Antique Ln Northbrook IL 60062

GOLDSMITH, NANCY CARROL, business and health services management educator; b. Conemaugh, Pa., May 11, 1940; d. John and Mary (Appley) Stinich; m. Sidney Goldsmith, Apr. 2, 1966. RN, Temple U., 1961; Assoc. summa cum laude, C.C. Phila., 1984; BS in Health Care Mgmt. summa cum laude, Phila. Coll. Textiles and Sci., 1986; MA in Health Care Adminstrn. summa cum laude, Antioch U., Yellow Springs, Ohio, 1988; PhD in Health Svcs. and Hosp. Adminstrn. summa cum laude, Southwest U., New Orleans, 1990. Nurse, head nurse to med. surg. supr. Temple U. Hosp., Phila., 1961-67; nursing rsch. assoc. Smith Klein & French, Inc. and Ames Med. Co., Phila. and Elkhart, Ind., 1967-69; sr. nursing rsch. assoc. NIH, Washington, 1969-75; adminstrv. supr. nursing svcs. Rolling Hill Hosp. and Diagnostic Ctr., Elkins Park, Pa., 1975-87, lectr. legal aspects nursing, 1980-90, dir. cost containment strategies, 1987-89, lectr. in health svcs. mgmt., 1989—, asst. dir. nursing svcs., 1988-89, nursing svcs. dir., 1989-90; prof. health svcs. adminstrn. and svcs. Phila U., 1991—, prof. bus. mgmt., 1992—, mem. adv. bd. health and wellness programs, 1993—, advisor, counselor, 1997—. Prof. managed care in health svcs. adminstrn. Ea. Coll., St. Davids, Pa., 1996—; lectr. Sr. Edn. League, 1992—; lectr. healthcare fin. and health svcs. adminstrn. Pa. State U., 1994; lectr. health svcs. reform C.C. Phila., 1993—, Free Libr. Phila., 1994—; instr. med./surg. nursing Sch. Nursing, Temple U., 1964-67, chmn. ann. fundraising, 1978-86. Author 2 books. Inventor use of dextrostix in hypoglycemic range, 1972 (Rsch. award 1974); co-patentee multipurpose biopsy needle, 1972; mem. editl. bd. Phila. U. Newletter, 1993—. Recipient Mayor's Liberty Bell award City of Phila., 1978, Legion of Honor award Chapel of Four Chaplains, 1981, Capitol award Nat. Leadership Coun., 1991; named to Hall of Fame, Internat. Profl. and Bus. Women's Assn., 1994. Mem. Am. Hosp. Assn., Am. Mgmt. Assn., Temple U. Nurse's Alumni Assn. (bd. dirs., v.p. 1991-92, pres. 1993-94, dir. continuing edn. com. 1986—), Temple U. Gen. Alumni Assn. (bd. dirs. 1980-88, 93—, Disting. Svc. award 1984), Downtown Club Temple U., Phi Beta Kappa, Phi Theta Kappa (pres. Delta of Pa. chpt. 1991-94, Honors Hall of Fame 1991). Jewish. Avocations: tennis, golf, home computing. Office: Phila U School House Ln Henry Ave Philadelphia PA 19144

GOLDSTEIN, DEBRA HOLLY, judge; b. Newark, Mar. 11, 1953; d. Aaron and Erica (Schreier) Green; m. Joel Ray Goldstein, Aug. 14, 1983; children: Stephen Michael, Jennifer Ann. BA, U. Mich., 1973; JD, Emory U., 1977. Bar: Ga. 1977, Mich. 1978, D.C. 1978, Ala. 1984. Tax analyst atty. Gen. Motors Corp., Detroit, 1977-78; trial atty. U.S. Dept. Labor, Birmingham, Ala., 1978-90; U.S. adminstrv. law judge office hearing and appeals Social Security Adminstrn., Birmingham, 1990—. New judge faculty U.S. adminstrv. law judges Social Security Adminstrn., 1991,93-. Mem. editl. bd. The Ala. Lawyer, 1994-99, The Addendum, 1995-99. Mem. Birmingham Bus. and Profl. Women Fedn., mem. steering com., 1995—2000; leader Girl Scout Troop, 1992—; bd. dirs. Cahaba Girl Scout Coun., 1996—2002; mem. Leadership Birmingham, 1997—98, Momentum, 2002—03; chmn. Success By 6 Blue Ribbon Adv. Com., 2003—; mem. Leadership Ala., 2004—; bd. dirs. Temple Emanu-El, 2000—03, United Way, Birmingham, 2004—, mem. vis. allocation team, 1998—, mem. planning com., 2001—; bd. dirs. YWCA, 2002—. Mem. ABA, Ga. Bar Assn., D.C. Bar Assn., Birmingham Bar Assn. (bd. dirs. women's sect. 1999—), Ala. Bar Assn., Zonta (co-pres. 1996-98), B'nai B'rith Women (chair S.E. region 1984-86, Women's Humanitarian award 1981), Hadassah (social action v.p. 2000-01). Jewish.

GOLDSTEIN, DORA BENEDICT, pharmacologist, educator; b. Milton, Mass., Apr. 25, 1922; d. George Wheeler and Marjory (Pierce) Benedict; m. Avram Goldstein, Aug. 29, 1947; children: Margaret E. Wallace, Daniel P., Joshua S., Michael B. Student, Bryn Mawr Coll., 1940-42, Stanford U., 1945; MD, Harvard U., 1949. Research assoc. Stanford U., 1955-70, sr. research assoc., 1970-74, adj. prof., 1974-78, prof. pharmacology, 1978-92, prof. pharmacology emerita, 1992—, co-dir. faculty mentoring program sch. medicine, 1994—2001. Author: Pharmacology of Alcohol, 1983; contbr. articles to sci. jours. Bd. dirs. Parents, Families and Friends of Lesbians and Gays, 2000—. Mem. Research Soc. Alcoholism (pres. 1979-81, award for excellence), Am. Soc. Pharmacology and Exptl. Therapeutics, Am. Soc. Biol. Chemists, Internat. Soc. Biomed. Research on Alcoholism, Intersex Soc. of N. Am. (adv. bd.). E-mail: dody@stanford.edu.

GOLDSTEIN, JACKIE LUTES, psychologist, educator; b. South Bend, Ind., July 31, 1942; d. John Rood and Marybelle Pearson Lutes; m. Lawrence Harold Goldstein, Dec. 17, 1967 (div. Jan. 0, 1981); children: Jennifer Rose Goldstein Decker, Lawrence Jonathan. Student, Western Mich. U., 1960—62; BA, Samford U., 1982; PhD, U. Ala., Birmingham, 1991. Seminar condr., coord. Smokenders, Inc., Birmingham, 1980—90; post-doctoral rsch. asst. Vision Sci. Rsch. Ctr., U. Ala., Birmingham, 1990—91; prof. Samford U., Birmingham, 1991—. Coord. faculty mentoring program Samford U., 2000—, sec. faculty senate, 1998—2000, mem. Instl. Rev. Bd., 2000—03. Contbr. articles to profl. jours. Founding pres. Compeer of Birmingham, Birmingham, 1993—2003; mem. edn. com. St. Luke's Episcopal Ch., Birmingham, 1996—2001. Recipient Spirit of Cmty. award, Mental Health Consumers of Ala., 2001; Faculty Mentoring grantee, Lilly Fellows Program, 2001. Mem.: APA, Am. Assn. Cmty. Psychiatrists. Office: Samford U 800 Lakeshore Dr SU #292308 Birmingham AL 35229-2308 E-mail: jlgoldst@samford.edu.

GOLDSTEIN, JILL M. psychiatric epidemiologist, clinical neuroscientist, psychiatry educator; b. New Haven, Sept. 18, 1954; d. Paul and Betty (M.) G.; m. Phillip S. Freeman, Sept. 23, 1984; children: Sonya, Eliana. AB with honors, Brown U., 1976; MPH, Columbia U., 1979, MPhil, 1984, PhD, 1985. Rsch. scientist N.Y. State Psychiat. Inst., N.Y.C., 1976-81, 81-84; rsch. fellwo Columbia U., N.Y.C., 1984-85; sr. rsch. assoc. Brandeis U., Mass., 1985-89; instr. psychiatry Harvard Med. Sch., Boston, 1986-89, cons. psychiat. rsch. project, 1987—, asst. prof. psychiatry, 1989-95, assoc. prof. psychiatry, 1996—; dir. rsch. on women's mental health Inst. Psychiat. Epidemiology and Geneticx. Mem. exec. com. Harvard Med. Sch./Mysell, Boston, 1992—; mem. NIMH sci. rev. com. Behavioral Sci. Track Awards for Rapid Transition, 1994—; exec. mem. rsch. com. Mass. Mental Health Ctr., Boston, 1995—. Reviewer, ad hoc jour. referee Am. Jour. Med. Genetics, Neuropsychiat. Genetics, Am. Jour. Psychiatry, Archives of Gen. Psychiatry, Biol. Psychiatry, Hosp. and Cmty. Psychiatry, Jour. Nervous and Mental Disease, Jour. Psychiat. Rsch., Psychiatry, Psychiatry Rsch., Schizophrenia Bull., Schizophrenia Rsch.; guest editor Schizophrenia Bull., 1990; contbr. articles to profl. jours. Grant reviewer Needham (Mass.) Edn. Found., 1992-94; fundraiser Countryside Sch., Newton, Mass., 1996—. NIMH fellow in psychiat. epidemiology, 1980-84; recipient Investigator award Nat. Alliance Rsch. on Schizophrenia and Depression, 1989, Investigator award Internat. Congress on Schizophrenia Rsch., 1989-91, NIMH Scientist Devel. award, 1992-94. Mem. AAAS, Phi Beta Kappa. Avocations: tennis, skiing, violin. Office: Harvard Med Sch/Mass Mental Health Ctr 74 Fenwood Rd Boston MA 02115-6113

GOLDSTEIN, JUDITH SHELLEY, reading and learning specialist; b. Bklyn., Mar. 5, 1935; d. Maurice and Mary (Goldstein) G. BA, Adelphi U., 1956; MA, Columbia U., 1957; EdD, Hofstra U., 1984. Cert. permanent tchr. in reading, spl. and elem. edn., N.Y. Early childhood tchr. N.Y.C. Sch. System, Bklyn., 1957-80; reading specialist Southampton (N.Y.) Unified Sch. Dist., 1981-87; spl. edn. tchr. Amagansett (N.Y.) Sch., 1987-88; mem. adj. faculty C.W. Post Campus, L.I. U., Brookville, N.Y., 1984-88, supr. clin. practice Southampton Campus, 1988-95. Exec. dir. nursery sch. Jewish Ctr. of Hamptons, East Hampton, N.Y., 1988-89; adj. assoc. prof. Southampton Campus L.I. U., 1989-94, Dowling Coll., 1990-92; chmn. edn. Hadassau, 2003-; adj. asst. prof. Suffolk County C.C., 1989-95, adj. assoc. prof. 1995—. Mem. Guild Hall, East Hampton, 1980—; v.p. edn. Hadassah, East Hampton, 1989-92, chmn. edn., 2003, chair Am. Affairs, 1993-96, Hadassah edn. chair 2002-03; tchr. religious ch. Jewish Ctr. of the Hamptons, 1990-98; vol. Bay St. Theatre, Sag Harbor, N.Y., Long House Res., East Hampton; mem., vol. Friends of Guild Hall, East Hampton. Mem. ASCD, AAUW (v.p. programming 1987-89, sec. 1993-99, 2003), Internat. Reading Assn. Democrat. Avocations: gardening, museums, theater. Home: 138 Windward Rd East Hampton NY 11937-3189

GOLDSTEIN, KATHERINE H. technology educator, computer consultant; b. N.Y.C., Oct. 17, 1968; d. Leon and Patricia (Chambers) G. BA, CUNY, 1991; MA, Columbia U., 1995. Lic. pub. h.s. tchr., N.Y.C.; lic. pub. h.s. tchr., N.Y. State. Acctg. asst. Biller & Schnyer, N.Y.C., 1984-89; salesperson retail electronics Crazy Eddie, N.Y.C., 1986-87; tchr. Hebrew sch. Larchmont (N.Y.) Temple, 1987-93; youth dir. United Synagogue Youth Forest Hills JCC, Kane St. and Town & Village Synagogue, N.Y., 1988—; computer tech. coord. Middle Coll. H.S. at LaGuardia Coll., Long Island City, N.Y., 1994—; computer tchr. Murry Bergtraun Adult Edn., N.Y.C., 1996—; computer instr. Monroe Coll., Bronx, 1996—. Adminstr. Camp Ramah, Nyack, N.Y., summer 1985-92, 96, 97; counselor, staff USY Pilgramage, Israel, and Poland sem. summer 1993-95; educator AIDS Ctr. Queens County, Queens, 1990-93; vol. Nat. Jewish Dem. Coun., N.Y.C., 1995—; vol., educator, mentor United Synagogue of Am., N.Y.C., 1987—. Mem. NOW, ACM, Coalition for Advancement of Jewish Edn., Delta Kappa Phi, Kappa Delta Phi. Democrat. Jewish. Avocations: rollerblading, swimming, traveling, woodworking. Office: Middle Coll HS at LaGuardia Coll Rm L101 31-10 Thomson Ave Long Island City NY 11101

GOLDSTEIN, LISA JOY, writer; b. L.A., Nov. 21, 1953; d. Harry George and Miriam (Roth) G.; m. Douglas Andrew Asherman, Jan. 12, 1986. BA, UCLA, 1975. Author: The Red Magician, 1982 (Am. Book award for best paperback 1983), The Dream Years, 1985, paperback edit., 1986, A Mask for the General, 1987, paperback edit., 1988, Tourists, 1989, paperback edit., 1994, Author's Choice Monthly: Daily Voices, 1989, Strange Devices of the Sun and Moon, 1993, paperback edit., 1994 (Sci. Fiction Book Club selection), Summer King, Winter Fool, 1994, paperback edit., 1995, Travellers in Magic, 1994, paperback edit., 1997, Walking the Labyrinth, 1996, paperback edit., 1998, Dark Cities Underground, 1999 (Sci. Fiction Book Club selection), paperback edit., 2000, The Alchemist's Door, 2002, paperback edit., 2003. Office: care Tor Books 175 5th Ave New York NY 10010-7703

GOLDSTEIN, MARCIA LANDWEBER, lawyer; b. Bklyn., Aug. 7, 1952; d. Jacob and Sarah Ann (Danovitz) Landweber; m. Mark Lewis Goldstein, June 3, 1973. AB, Cornell U., 1973, JD, 1975. Bar: N.Y. 1976, U.S. Dist. Ct. (so. and ea. dists.) N.Y., U.S. Ct. Appeals (2d, 3d, 5th, 7th and 9th cirs.). Assoc. Weil, Gotshal & Manges, N.Y.C., 1975-83, ptnr., 1983—, co-head, bus. fin. & restructuring devel. Adv. bd. Colliers on Bankruptcy, 15th edit.; vis. lectr. Yale Law Sch., 1986-88; lectr. Practicing Law Inst. ALI-ABA, Southeastern Bankruptcy Law Inst., NYU bankruptcy worksop. Mem. ABA (com. on creditors' rights, corp. counse. com.), Assn. of Bar of City of N.Y. (chair bankruptcy and reorgn. com.), Nat. Bankruptcy Conf. (chair legis. com.), Am. Coll. Bankruptcy. Office: Weil Gotshal & Manges LLP 767 5th Ave New York NY 10153 E-mail: marcia.goldstein@weil.com.*

GOLDSTEIN, MARGARET FRANKS, special education educator; b. Toledo, July 3, 1940; d. Ray E. and Esther R. (Drewicz) Franks; m. William D. Goldstein, July 30, 1961; children: Sheldon, Benjamin, Marshall, Rochelle. BS in Edn., Bowling Green (Ohio) State U., 1975; MEd, U. Toledo, 1984. Cert. spl. edn. and indsl. arts educator. Tchr. indsl. arts Toledo Pub. Schs., 1970-77, tchr. devel. handicapped/behavior disordered, 1980-86, tchr. devel. handicapped/transitional tchr., 1986—99, severe behavior disability career ladder tchr., 1987—2000, mem. state supt.'s spl. edn. adv. coun., 1988—, chair, 1999—. Mem. state supt.'s task force for preparing spl. educators Toledo Pub. Schs., 1986—. Mem. Am. Fedn. Tchrs. (conv. del.), Ohio Fedn. Tchrs. (exec. coun., publicity and svcs. com., elections com., chmn., conv. del.), Toledo Fedn. Tchrs. (bd. dirs.), NW Ohio Spl. Edn. Assn. Office: McTigue Jr HS 5537 Hill Ave Toledo OH 43615-4699

GOLDSTEIN, MARSHA FEDER, tour company executive; b. Chgo., July 7, 1945; d. Charles S. and Geraldine (Shulman) Feder; m. Michael Warren Goldstein, Dec. 26, 1966; 1 child, Paul Goldstein. BA, Roosevelt U., 1967. Tchr. art Chgo. Pub. Schs., 1967-68; freelance artist Chgo., 1968-71; tchr. arch. Brandeis U., Northfield, Ill., 1974-80; tour guide My Kind of Town Tours, Highland Park, Ill., 1975-79, owner, 1979—. Owner Tours at the Mart, 1992-95; art cons. Randall Pub. Co., Inc., 1984—. Editor: Highland Park by Foot or Frame, 1980; contbr. to book in field. Chmn., commr. Highland Park Hist. Preservation Commn.; bd. dirs. Roosevelt U., Chgo., Art Encounter, Parisian Salon Concerts; charter mem. Nat. Mus. Women in the Arts; mayoral appt. Sister Cities Com., 1998; chmn. Paris Sister Cities, 2000; mem. devel. bd. The Feltre Sch.; mem. adv. bd., benefit chmn. Gene Siskel Film Ctr. Recipient Cert. of Completion, Chgo. Arch. Found., 1975; named Disting. Alumni of Yr. Roosevelt U., 1997. Mem.: Meeting Profls. Internat., Chgo. Conv. and Tourism Bd. (devel. com.), Women's Exec. Network, Nat. Assn. Women Bus. Owners (bd. dirs. Chgo. chpt., pres.), Assn. Destination Mgmt. Execs. (founder), Internat. Spl. Events Soc. (bd. dirs.), Brandeis U. Nat. Women (v.p. 1977—, bd. dirs.), The Auditorium Bldg. Soc. (chmn. 1994, founder), Union League Club (standing com.). Jewish. Office: My Kind of Town 1585 Tara Ln Lake Forest IL 60045-1221 E-mail: info@mykindoftown.net.

GOLDSTEIN, MARY KANE, physician; b. N.Y.C., Oct. 24, 1950; d. Edwin Patrick and Mary Kane; m. Yonkel Noah Goldstein, June 24, 1979; children: Keira, Gavi. Philosophy degree, Columbia U., 1973, MD, 1977; MS in Health Svcs. Rsch., Stanford U., 1994. Resident Duke U. Med. Ctr., Durham, N.C., 1977-80; asst. prof. medicine U. Calif., San Francisco, 1980-84; clin. instr. dept. family and cmty. preventive medicine Stanford U., 1984-85; staff physician Mid-Peninsula Health Svc., Palo Alto, Calif., 1986-88; dir. grad. med. edn. divsn. gerontol. Stanford (Calif.) U., 1986-93, Agy. for Health Care Policy Rsch. fellow Sch. Medicine, 1991-94, asst. prof. medicine Med. Ctr. Line, 1996—99, assoc. prof. medicine Med. Ctr. Line, 1999—, Ctr. for Primary Care and Outcomes Rsch., 1998—, faculty fellow Inst. for Rsch. on Women and Gender, 2000—01; sect. chief for gen. internal medicine Palo Alto (Calif.) VA Med. Ctr., 1994-96, rsch. assoc. health svcs. R&D, 1996—2002; assoc. dir. clin. svcs. The VA Geriatric Rsch. Edn. and Clinical Ctr., Palo Alto, 1999—. Editor Computer Ctr. Pubs., N.Y.C., 1971-72; computer programmer Columbia U., N.Y.C., 1972-73; governing coun. evidence-based practice ctr. U. Calif., Stanford, 1998—. Author chpt. to book; contbr. articles to profl. jours. Recipient Clin. Practice Guidelines for Hypertension award, VA Health Svc. Rsch. & Devel., 1997, Practice Guidelines Multisite Study award, 2000, Intelligent Critiquing of Med. Records award, NIH/NLM, 2001, Disutility of Functional Limitations award NIH/NIA, 2001. Fellow: Am. Geriatrics Soc. (bd. dirs. 1997—2002). Office: VA Palo Alto Health Care Sys GRECC 182B 3801 Miranda Ave Palo Alto CA 94304-1207 E-mail: goldstein@stanford.edu.

GOLDSTEIN, MELISSA ANNE, writer; b. Silver Spring, Md., Sept. 11, 1969; d. Larry Joel and Sandra Goldstein. BA in English, U. Pa., 1992, MLA concentration in relationship between medicine and lit., 1995. Rschr. with Dr. Renée Fox, sociology dept. U. Pa., Phila., 1990—91, Charlotte Newcombe intern with Dr. Renée Fox, sociology dept., 1991, 1993, 1994, Writing Across the U. fellow for medicine and lit. seminar, sociology dept., 1992, 1995; ind. writer, scholar, pub. spkr. Phila., 1995—. Guest spkr. U.

Pa. Sch. Medicine, Phila., 1991, Phila., 2002; colloquium spkr. MLA program U. Pa., Phila., 1996; guest lectr. Quaker Mid. Sch., Horsham, Pa., 1998, Horsham, 2000; main spkr. 2000 Awareness Luncheon N.W. Fla. chpt. Lupus Found. Am., Pensacola, Fla., 2000; spkr. Cen. N.Y. chpt. Lupus Found. Am., Syracuse, NY, 2000; guest spkr. Everywoman Everywhere radio program, Syracuse, 2000; spkr. Alumni Vis. Series U. Pa., Kelly Writers House, Phila., 2001. Author: (book) Travels with the Wolf: A Story of Chronic Illness, 2000; contbr. essays, poetry and article to profl. publs. Vol. Lupus Found. Am., Phila., 1988—, Arthritis Found., Phila., 1988—, Am. Juvenile Arthritis Orgn., Phila., 1988—; founder Lupus Support Group, U. Pa., 1988. Mem.: Nat. Coalition of Ind. Scholars, Phi Beta Kappa, Philomathean Honor Soc. Democrat. Jewish. Avocations: traveling, swimming, attending ballets, jazz clubs, and modern dance performances. Home and Office: 1 Franklin Town Blvd Apt 2009 Philadelphia PA 19103 Office Phone: 215-567-4852.

GOLDSTEIN, PHYLLIS ANN, art historian, educator; b. Chgo., Apr. 27, 1926; d. Frederick and Belle Florence (Hirsch) Jacoby; m. Seymour Goldstein, Nov. 19, 1947 (dec. 1980); children: Arthur Bruce, Kathy Susan Goldstein Maultasch. BA, Hunter Coll., 1948; MA, Hofstra U., 1985. Tchr. home econs. Cin. Pub. Schs., 1948-50; nutrition instr. Brandeis U. Nat. Women's Com., Westbury, N.Y., 1975-78, instr. art history, 1984-91; lectr. art history Brandeis U./Nat. Women's Com., Westbury, N.Y., 1985-92; instr. art history Herricks Adult Cmty. Edn. Program, 1990-91. Camp counselor, troop leader Girl Scouts U.S., N.Y.C., Cin., 1942-51; cub leader Boy Scouts Am., Westbury, 1963-64; active Sisterhood of Temple Beth Avodah, Westbury, 1958-80, pres. 1964-65; active Sisterhood of Temple of Beth Am., Merrick, N.Y., 1980-91; life mem. Brandeis U. Nat. Women's Com., lectr. art history, 1992—, Meadowbrook chpt. pres., 1985-87, South Dade chpt., 1996-98, mem. Fla. regional bd., 1998-99; vol. Fairchild Tropical Gardens, 1994—. Mem. Williamsburg Mus., Mus. Art Ft. Lauderdale, Met. Mus. Art N.Y., Hadassah (life). Democrat. Avocations: sewing, swimming, needlework, quilting, travel.

GOLDSTEIN, SANDRA CARA, lawyer; b. Bklyn., May 12, 1964; BA, Barnard Coll., 1984; JD, NYU, 1987. Bar: N.Y. 1988. Office: Cravath Swaine & Moore LLP Worldwide Plz 825 8th Ave Fl 30 New York NY 10019-7475

GOLDSTEIN-ERICKSON, ELLIE, school librarian; b. Chattanooga, Tenn., Dec. 22, 1948; d. Louis Goldstein and Lillian Amlin; m. Clifton Carl Erickson, July 13, 1975; children: Jacob, Jonathan. BA, U. Conn., 1970; MLS, U. Calif., 1973. Cert. life tchg., Crosscultural Lang. and Academic Devel. credential. Head libr. Richmond (Calif.) H.S., 1973—83; libr. Piedmont (Calif.) Unified Sch. Dist., 1991—92, West Contra Costa Unified Sch. Dist., Richmond, 1992—96; libr. media tchr. Berkeley Unified Sch. Dist., 1996—. Contbr. articles to profl. jours. Bd. dirs. Congregation Beth El, Berkeley, 1991—98. Named Outstanding Educator, Berkeley Pub. Edn. Found., 2003. Mem.: Am. Assn. Sch. Libr., Am. Libr. Assn., Calif. Sch. Libr. Assn. (v.p. 1973, pres. 2002—, v.p./legis. 2002—). Jewish. Office: Berkeley High Sch Libr 2223 MLK Jr Way Berkeley CA 94704 E-mail: ellie@berkeley.k12.ca.us.

GOLDTHWAIT, JILL MURDOCH, state legislator; b. N.J., Jan. 5, 1946; m. Sheldon F. Goldthwait; three children. BA, U. New Hampshire; RN, Cabrillo Coll. Mem. Bar Harbor Town Council, Maine, 1985-94, chair., 1986-94; mem. Dist. 5 Maine Senate, Augusta, 1994—. Home: 22 Albert Mdws Bar Harbor ME 04609-1702 Address: Senate of Maine 3 State House Sta Augusta ME 04333-0003

GOLDWAY, RUTH Y. federal agency administrator; b. N.Y., Sept. 17, 1945; d. David and Mahilda G.; m. Derek N. Shearer; chldren: Casey, Anthony, Julie. BA, U. Mich., 1965; MA, Wayne State U., 1968; postgrad., UCLA, 1970-71. Asst. dir. Dept. Consumer Affairs, L.A., 1975-78; mayor City Santa Monica, Calif., 1979-83; dir. pub. affairs Calif. State U., L.A., 1984-91; mgr. pub. affairs Getty Trust, L.A., 1991-94; commr. postal rate commn., Washington, 1998—. Chair and founder Santa Monica Pier Restoration Corp., 1981-94; founding mem. Consumer Adv. Panel, GTE, San Francisco, 1974-76. Author: Letters From Finland, 1998; contbr. articles to profl. jours., 1994-97; actress in film Dave, 1992. Bd. dirs. So. Calif. Consumer Affairs Profls., 1986-92. Recipient Best Diplomatic Role Model, Helsinik City Mag., 1996. Avocations: biking, cooking, mystery novels. Office: Postal Rate Commn 1333 H St NW Ste 300 Washington DC 20268-0002

GOLDWEITZ, JULIE, lawyer; Assoc. counsel Reed Publishing USA. Office: 275 Washington St Newton MA 02458-1646

GOLEMBESKI, BEVERLY LONG, artist, art educator; d. Charles Wesley and Evelyn Mae (Hinchman) Long; m. Francis Gerald Golembeski, Feb. 24, 1962; children: Scott Fitzgerald, Cortlyn Elizabeth, Deidre Aleece, Tyler Gerard. BA in Fine Arts, Montclair (N.J.) State, 1962; studied watercolor with profl. artists, 1997—2003. Cert. art tchr. K-12. Art tchr. Ctrl. Regional High Sch., Bayville, NJ, 1962—66; recreation dir. Borough of Seaside Park (N.J.), 1963—67; art coord. Athletic Booster Club, Bayville, NJ, 1973—78. Adj. instr. Georgian Ct. Coll., Lakewood, NJ; profl. artist, instr., demonstrator, lectr., judge, 1980—2003; official artist U.S.C.G. Illustrator summer program booklets Borough of Seaside Heights, 1972—73, (yearly pamphlets) Toms River (N.J.) Soccer and Lavallette (N.J.) Little League, 1976—78, cons. on art articles Asbury Park (N.J.) Press, 1981—85; office designs, GTECH Corp., Mexico and Argentina, 1992—94, mural, Shore Cmty. Bank, Toms River, N.J., 1994, Brass Beds Antique Shoppe, Beachwood, N.J., 1995; illustrator various covers Jersey Shore Mag., Bayhead, N.J., 2000—03; exhibitions include N.J. Mus., Montclair, Monmouth Mus., Shrewsbury, N.J., Noyse Mus., Barnegat, N.J., John Hopkins U., Washington, Robertson Ctr., Delaware County, N.Y., Cooperstown (N.Y.) Mus. Activities coor; activities coord. Seaside Park Fire Co., 1970—76; asst. Girl Scouts U.S.A., Ocean County, NJ, 1977—82; pres., chair various activities Seaside Park Sch. PTA, 1975—85. Recipient awards, Garden State Juried Exhibit Trenton Mus., N.J., 2001, Jane Law's Art Gallery, Long Beach Island, Surf City, N.J., 2001, NJAAPL, 2000—03, combined exhibit Nat. Watercolor Soc. and Phila. Watercolor Soc. Pine Shores Art Assn. Manahawkin, N.J., 2002, Pine Shores Art Assn., 2002—03. Fellow: Nat. Am. Watercolor Soc.; mem.: N.J. Watercolor Soc. (bd. dirs.), Pa. Watercolor Soc., Am. Artists Profl. League (award Salmagundi Club 2002), Ocean County Artists' Guild (past pres.), Garden State Watercolor Soc., Phila. Watercolor Soc. (signature). Avocations: gardening, bicycling, cooking, snowmobiling, swimming. Home: 16 I St Seaside Park NJ 08752-1525 Office Phone: 732-793-8224. E-mail: Beviemae@aol.com.

GOLEMBIEWSKI, GAE S. gifted education educator; b. Erie, Pa., Nov. 13, 1951; d. Richard Leroy and Leona Louise (Volgstadt) Anderson; m. Wlater T. Golembiewski; 1 child, Leeanna Louise. BE, Edinboro (Pa.) U., 1973, MEd, 1977; EdD, U. Pitts., 1992. Cert. early childhood edn. tchr., elem. tchr., prin. Tchr., computer coord. Millcreek (Pa.) Twp. Sch. Dist., 1973-79, gifted specialist, 1979-89; headmistress Erie Day Sch., 1989-90; instr. U. Pitts., 1990-92; assoc. prof., coord. gifted programs Norfolk (Va.) State U., 1992—. Co-dir. Project eSS, 1992-97; advisor Olympian Soc., Norfolk State U., 1993—. Contbr. articles to profl. jours. Pres. Coun. Giftedness, Erie; past pres. Erie Summer Festival of Arts. Recipient Exec. Acad. Computer award Pa. Dept. Edn., 1991, Hollingworth award Intertel Found., 1994; Alumni scholar U. Pitts., 1993. Mem. NAGC (chair creativity divsn. 1997—). Avocations: travel, gardening, writing. Home: 2901 River Breeze Cv Virginia Beach VA 23452-7113 Office: Norfolk U # 204 Education Bldg Norfolk VA 23504

GOLIAN-LUI, LINDA MARIE, librarian; b. Woodbridge, N.J., Mar. 27, 1962; d. Joseph John Golian and Mary Grace (Juba) Rodriguez; m. Gary S. Lui, Oct. 6, 1988; 1 child, Katherine Jana Lui-Golian. BA, U. Miami, 1986; MLIS, Fla. State, 1988; EdS, Fla. Atlantic U., 1995, EdD, 1998; postgrad., Fla. Gulf Coast U., 1999—2002. Libr. tech. asst. U. Miami, 1981-86; serials control libr. U. Miami Law Sch., 1986-89; serials dept. head Fla. Atlantic U., Boca Raton, 1990-97; univ. libr. Fla. Gulf Coast U., Ft. Myers, 1997—2002, adj. instr. Coll. Arts and Scis., 1999—2002; dir. U. Hawaii, Hilo, 2002—. Adj. instr. Fla. Atlantic U. Coll. Continuing & Distance Edn., 1993-97, U. So. Fla. Coll. Libr. Sci., 1995-2002; program specialist Marriott Statford Ctr. Sr. Living Cmty., Boca Raton, 1994-96. Vol. storyteller Aid to Victims of Domestic Assault, Delray Beach, Fla., 1994-96. Mem. NOW, AAUW, NAFE, Spl. Libr. Assn., N.Am. Serials Interest Group (co-chair mentoring com. 1996-97), ASCD, Southeastern Libr. Assn., Assn. Libr. and Info. Sci. Educators, Am. Libr. Assn., Am. Assn. Higher Edn., Assn. Libr. Collection & Tech. Svcs., Libr., Adminstrn. & Mgmt. Assn., Reference & User Svcs. Assn. (continuing libr. edn. network & exch. round table, intellectual freedom round table, libr. instruction round table, new members round table, staff orgn. round table, women's studies sect. comm. com. 1994—, serials nomination com. 1993, Miami local arrangements com. 1994, chair libr. sch. outreach 1994—, pres. 1998-99, 3M profl. devel. grantee 1995), Assn. Coll. Rsch. Libr. (Lazerow rsch. fellow 1997), Laubach Literary Vols. of Am., Am. Assn. Adult and Continuing Edn., Fla. Libr. Assn. (serials libr. or yr. 1994, grantee 1987). Roman Catholic. Avocations: reading, fishing, ceramics, tennis. Office: U HI Hilo Edwin H Mookini Lib & Graphic Ser 200 W Kawili St Hilo HI 96720-4091 Office Phone: 808-933-3132.

GOLL, PAULETTE SUSAN, education educator; b. Cleve., June 5, 1947; d. Ferdinand Paul and Lillian Clarice (Mehalko) Goll. BA in English, Cleve. State U., 1969, MEd, 1974; MA in English, U. Bridgeport, Conn., 1979; PhD in English, Case Western Res. U., 1987. Cert. secondary tchr. Ohio, English tchr. Ohio, asst. supr. Ohio, secondary prin. Ohio. Part-time instr. U. Bridgeport, 1978-79, Case Western Res. U., Cleve., 1985-87, lectr., 2002—; tchr. English, Cleve. Pub. Schs., 1969—99, chmn. dept., coord. Ohio Proficiency Test, 1991—96; regional dir. Summer Inst. Gifted Midwest Region, Granville, Ohio, 2000—02. Adj. instr. English Case Western Res. U., Cleve. State U., 1999—2000; vis. assoc. prof. edn. Dickinson Coll., Carlisle, Pa., 2000; advisor Students Against Drunk Drivers, 1985—86; coord. project success Lincoln West HS, Cleve., 1987—90; ACT vis. tchr., 1999; external reviewer Bedford/St. Martins, 2003. Co-author: Shakespearean Comedies, 1985; external reviewer Reading Critically, Writing Well, textbook cons. McDougal Littel, 1999—2000. Mem. com. human rels. Cleve. Partnerships, 1989—92; co-chmn. High Schs. for Future, 1985—86; liaison Metrohealth/Lincoln-West Partnership, 1989—92. Named Master Tchr., Martha Holden Jennings Found., 1988; recipient Congl. Commendation Mary Rose Oaker, 1988, award of Excellence, Rotary, 1989, Tchr. of the Yr., Brit. Petroleum, 1997; NEH fellow, 1985, NEH Ind. Studies Humanities fellow, 1993, Jennings scholar, 1985, 1988. Mem.: ASCD (presenter), North Ctrl. Assn. (chair vis. team 1991, 1993), Nat. Assn. Gifted (presenter 2001), Phi Delta Kappa (v.p. programs 1993). Republican. Roman Catholic. Avocations: travel, music, needlepoint, writing, camping. Home: 11366 Clarke Rd Columbia Station OH 44028-9626 Personal E-mail: gollp@earthlink.net.

GOLLIN, SUSANNE MERLE, cytogeneticist, cell biologist; b. Chgo., Sept. 22, 1953; d. Harvey A. and Pearl (Reiffel) G.; m. Lazar M. Palnick; 1 child, Jacob Hillel . BA in Biology, Northwestern U., 1974, MS, 1975, PhD, 1980. Diplomate Am. Bd. Med. Genetics with cert. in clin. cytogenetics; cert. food protection specialist, 2002. Postdoctoral fellow U. Rochester (N.Y.) Med. Ctr., 1979-81; rsch. assoc. in cell biology Baylor Coll. Medicine, Houston, 1981-83, rsch. assoc. in genetics, 1983-84; asst. prof. dept. pathology and pediat. U. Ark. for Med. Sci., Little Rock, 1984-87; dir. cytogenetics lab. Ark. Children's Hosp., Little Rock, 1984-87; assoc. mem. Pitts. Cancer Inst., 1987-95, mem., 1995—; dir. U. Pitts. Cancer Inst. Cytogenetics Facility, 1989—; asst. prof. human genetics U. Pitts., 1987-95, dir. clin. cytogenetics lab., 1988-99, assoc. prof., 1995—2003, prof., 2003—, prof. human genetics, otolaryngology, pathology, 2003; dir. rsch., clin. cons. Pitts. Cytogenetics Lab., 1999—. Mem. pediat. oncology group, mem. exec. com. Ark. Genetics Program, 1984-87; mem. organizing com. Am. Cytogenetics Conf., 1990-2002; mem. Allegheny County Bd. Health, 1992—, vice chmn., 1997, 2000—; bd. dirs. Tobacco-Free Allegheny, 2002—; mem. clin. lab. improvement adv. com. Ctrs. Disease Control and Prevention, HHS, 1994-2000, mem. genetic testing subcom., 1997-2000; vis. sci. German Cancer Rsch. Ctr., Heidelberg, 1995; cons. med. devices adv. com. FDA, 1996—; mem. oral biol. med. I study sect. NIH, 1997; master gardener, 2000; mem. spl. emphasis panel Nat. Cancer Inst., 2000; mem. genetics spl. emphasis panel ZRG1-GEN-01S, NIH Ctr. for Sci. Rev., 2000, spl. emphasis panel Nat. Cancer Inst., Minority Instn./Cancer Ctr. Partnerships, 2000, mem. mammalian genetics study sect., 2002; lectr. U.S.-Japanese Cancer Rsch. Collaborative Conf., Tokyo, 2001. Contbr. articles to profl. jours. and encys. Mem. deans' adv. com. Pa. Sch. Excellence for Healthcare Profls., 1991-95; v.p. faculty senate U. Pitts. Grad. Sch. Pub. Health, 1994-95, mem. senate antidiscriminatory policies com., 1999-2002; vol. Lighthouse for Blind, Houston, 1983; vol. hort. dept. Pitts. Zoo, 2000-2001; chmn. med. ethics and civil liberties com. ACLU, Pitts., 1989-91; alt. del. Dem. Nat. Conv., 1992, 96, 2000. Fellow Am. Coll. Med. Genetics (founder); mem AAAS, Am. Assn. Cancer Rsch., Am. Soc. Human Genetics, Am. Soc. Cell Biology, Soc. Analytical Cytology, Pitts. Cancer Inst., Pitts. Cytogenetics Club (founder, coord. 1989-95), Phipps/Pitts. Garden Place, Western Pa. Conservancy, Rivers Club, Carnegie Museums, Pitts. Zoo, Sigma Xi. Avocations: mountain dulcimer, gardening, photography, pulled thread embroidery. Office: U Pitts Dept Human Genetics 130 Desoto St Pittsburgh PA 15213-2535 E-mail: sgollin@hgen.pitt.edu.

GOLON, MARYANNE, photojournalist; Picture editor Time Mag., NY, NY, 1983—99; coord. photographic coverage of the Olympic Games for Time mag., 1984—; photography editor of the Gulf War for Time and Life mag., Dhahran and Saudi Arabia, 1991—92; dir. of Photog. US News and World Report, 1999—2002; picture editor Time Mag., NY, NY, 2002—. Recipient Afred Eisenstaedt Award, Mag. Photgraphy; fellow On the Jury of Visa Pour L[00b0]Image, Pepignand. Mem.: Eddie Adams Workshop (Bd. of dir.). Office: Time 315 W End Ave New York NY 10023

GOLSTON, MAGGIE, small business owner, writer; b. Phoenix, Jan. 28, 1971; d. Rodger and Sydele Golston. BA, U. Ariz., 1995, MA, 1998. Mktg. specialist Ctr. for Creative Photography, Tucson, 1996—97; tchg. asst. U. Ariz., 1996—98, lectr., 2001—02; tchg. fellow U. UT, Salt Lake City, 1998—2001; owner, mgr. BIBLIO, Tucson, 2002—. Author: (poem) Ploughshares, 2001, Spork, 2002. Vol., instr. poetry ctr. U. Ariz., 1996—98, 2001—. Democrat. Jewish. Avocations: singing, songwriting. Office: BIBLIO 222 E Congress Tucson AZ 85701

GOLUB, SHARON BRAMSON, psychologist, educator; b. N.Y.C., Mar. 25, 1937; m. Leon M. Golub, June 1, 1958; children: Lawrence E., David B. Diploma, Mt. Sinai Hosp. Sch. Nursing, 1957; BS, Columbia U., 1959, MA, 1966; PhD, Fordham U., 1974. Head nurse Mt. Sinai Hosp., N.Y.C., 1957-59; contbg. editor RN Mag., Oradell, N.J., 1967-74; asst. prof. psychology Coll. New Rochelle, N.Y., 1974-79, assoc. prof., 1979-86, prof., 1986-98, prof. emeritus, 1998—, dir. women's studies, 1978-79, chmn. dept. psychology, 1979-82; pvt. practice individual and group psychotherapy Harrison, N.Y., 1976—. Adj. prof. psychiatry N.Y. Med. Coll., Valhalla, 1980-94. Editor: Menarche, 1983 (Assn. Women in Psychology Disting. Pub. award 1984, Book of Yr. award Am. Jour. Nursing 1984), Lifting the Curse of Menstruation, 1983, Health Care of the Female Adolescent, 1984, Health Needs of Women as They Age, 1984, PERIODS from Menarche to Menopause, 1992; (with Rita Jackaway Freedman) Psychology of Women: Resources for a Core Curriculum, 1987; editor Women and Health, 1982-86, mem. editorial bd., 1986—; mem. editorial bd. Psychology of Women Quar., 1989-2000. Grantee Nat. Libr. Medicine, 1983-84; NIH rsch. fellow, 1971-74. Fellow Am. Psychol. Assn. (chmn. task force on teaching psychology of women 1980-83), Am. Psychol. Soc.; mem. Soc. for Menstrual Cycle Rsch. (pres. 1981-83, bd. dirs. 1981-93), Assn. Women in Psychology, Westchester County Psychol. Assn. (pres. acad. divsn., Disting. Svc. award 2003), Phi Beta Kappa, Sigma Xi, Psi Chi. Office: Coll New Rochelle Dept Psychology New Rochelle NY 10805 E-mail: sgolubny@aol.com.

GOMBERG, EDITH S. psychologist, educator; b. N.Y.C., Jan. 14, 1920; d. Barnet and Dorothy (Resnick) Silverglied; m. Henry Jacob Gomberg, June 24, 1967; children: Stephen, Judith, Eugene, Richard, Robert. MA, Columbia U., 1940; PhD, Yale U., 1949. Lectr., rsch. asst., rsch. assoc. Center Alcohol Studies, Yale U., New Haven, 1949-67; assoc. prof. dept. psychology U. P.R., 1968-71; prof. Sch. Social Work, U. Mich., Ann Arbor, 1974-90; prof. psychology, dept. psychiatry U. Mich., Ann Arbor, 1988-99, prof. emerita, 1999—. Author: Gender and Disordered Behavior, 1979, Alcohol, Science and Society Revisited, 1982, Current Issues in Alcohol/Drug Studies, 1989, Drugs and Human Behavior: A Sourcebook for the Helping Professions, 1991, Women and Substance Abuse, 1993, Alcohol and Aging, 1995, Alcohol Problems and Aging, 1998; contbr. chpts. to books, articles to profl. jours. Mem. Rep. Town Meeting, Hamden, Conn., 1964-65; mem. Blue Ribbon Study Commn. on Alcoholism and Aging, Nat. Council on Alcoholism, 1979-82; chmn. panel on prevention, study to assess sci. opportunities of alcohol-related research Inst. Medicine, Nat. Acad. Sci.; mem. alcohol psychosocial research rev. com. Nat. Inst. Alcohol Abuse and Alcoholism, 1981-82. Mary E. Ives fellow, 1944; AAUW Elizabeth Avery Colten fellow, 1955 Mem. Psychonomic Soc., Sociedad Interamericana de Psicología, Rsch. Soc. on Alcoholism, Sigma Xi. Jewish. Home: 430 Hillspur Rd Ann Arbor MI 48105-1049

GOMBERG, SYDELLE, dancer educator; m. Ralph Gomberg. Student, Met. Opera Ballet Sch.; studies with Pierre Vladimiroff, Anatale Oboukoff, Edward Caton, Anatole Vilzak, Vincenzo Celli, Margaret Craske; student, Sch. Am. Ballet. Dir. Boston Ballet Sch., until 1993; faculty mem. Boston Converatory of Music; resident master teacher Walnut Hill School, Natick, Mass., 1993-96; guest tchr., mem. adv. bd. Walnut Hill Sch., Natick, Mass., 1996—. Performed with Met. Opera Ballet, Radio City Ballet; soloist (Broadway play) Lute Song starring Mary Martin and the Late Yul Brynner. Founder dance dept. All Newton Music Sch., Walnut Hill Sch., 1971-85, apptd. dean arts, trustee, adv. bd. mem.; regional sec. Royal Acad. Dancing; mem. dance panel Mass. Coun. on the Arts and Humanities; chmn. spl. com. Dance Edn. Home: 93 Pilgrim Rd Concord MA 01742

GOMES, SHIRLEY, state legislator; Mem. Harwich Bd. of Selectmen, 1987—95, Mass. Ho. of Reps., Boston, 1995—. Republican. Office: State House Rm 156 Boston MA 02133

GOMEZ, ANGELA GONZALEZ, art educator; b. Laredo, Tex., Oct. 29, 1953; d. Alberto and Aurora Benavides González; m. Albérico Michael Gómez, Aug. 7, 1982 (div. Feb. 1998); 1 child, Albérico Michael Gómez III. AA, Laredo (Tex.) Jr. Coll., 1973; BS in Art Edn., S.W. Tex. State U., 1975; M of Edn. in Art, Sul Ross State U., 1985. Cert. tchr. Tex. Art tchr. M.B. Lamar Jr. High, Laredo, 1975—83, United Mid. Sch., Laredo, 1989—. One-woman shows include Sal Ross State U., Alpine, Tex., Grad. Level Art Exhbn., 1984, Laredo Ctr. for the Arts., 1997—2002, United Mid. Sch., Laredo, 1989—2003. Adv., com. mem. Fine Arts Fiesta, Laredo, 1998—2003; com. mem. Youth Art Month, Laredo, 1976—83. Mem.: NEA, Tex. State Tchrs. Assn., Kappa Pi, Phi Theta Kappa. Avocations: art, travel, museums, movies, dance. Home: 1323 Kimberly Dr Laredo TX 78045 Office: United Mid Sch 700 E Del Mar Blvd Laredo TX 78045

GOMEZ, FABIOLA, marketing communications professional; b. Chgo., June 23, 1974; d. Ruben Gómez and Carmen Carmona. Cert. practique, U. Upper Brittany, Rennes, France, 1994; BA, Beloit Coll., 1996; MS, Northwestern U., 2004. Spanish tutor Learning Resource Ctr., Beloit (Wis.) Coll., 1993-95, telemarketer Office Admissions, 1995-96; Hispanic recruiter, admission counselor Office Admissions, Roosevelt U., Chgo., 1996—; asst. mktg. dir. The Princeton Rev., 1999—2001, outreach program mgr., 2001—02; mktg. dir. Kudan Group, Glenview, Ill., 2002—. Rsch. assoc. Cmty. Rsch. and Policy Studies Ctr., Beloit, 1996; tchr.'s and libr. aide Inst. Franco-Am., Rennes, 1994; presenter 10th Ann. Nat. Conf. for Undergrad. Rsch., 1996. Minority scholar Assoc. Colls. Midwest, 1995. Mem. Ill. Assn. for Coll. Admissions Counseling, Ill. Latino Coun. on Higher Edn., Profls. for Latino Recruitment in Higher Edn. Office: Kudan Group 1807 Glenview Rd Glenview IL 60025 E-mail: fabiolagomez@earthlink.net.

GOMEZ, PASTORA, medical/surgical nurse; b. Medellin, Colombia, Apr. 10, 1948; came to U.S., 1981; d. German and Lourdes (Escobar) G. Gen. nurse cert., U. Antioquia, Medellin, 1971, BSN, 1979. Cert. chemotherapist; RN N.Y., ACLS, cert. oncology nurse. Staff nurse, head nurse Inst. de Seguros Sociales, Medellin, 1972-81; LPN Parkway Hosp., N.Y.C., 1983-85, Elmhurst City Hosp., N.Y.C., 1985-87, staff nurse, 1987-90, asst. head nurse, 1990—. Bd. dirs. Queen Mary Anne Corp. Mem.: Oncology,Nursing Soc., Am. Nephrology Nurses Assn. Roman Catholic. Avocations: music, art, traveling, reading. Home: 88-02 35th Ave Flushing NY 11372-5710

GOMEZ, SYLVIA, newscaster; m. Jon Duncanson. BS in Mass Comm., U. Md., 1985. Field prodr. WRC-TV, Washington, 1983—88; weekend anchor KTSM-TV, El Paso, Tex., 1988—90; reporter and fill-in anchor KTVT-TV, Dallas, 1990—92, WMAQ-TV, Chgo., 1992—94, WBBM-TV, Chgo., 1994—96; weekend anchor WFLD-TV, Chgo., 1996—97; weekend evening anchor and reporter WBBM-TV, Chgo., 1998—. Office: WBBM-TV 630 McClurg Ct Chicago IL 60601

GOMEZ, TERRINE, school director; b. Trivandrum, India, Jan. 29, 1928; came to U.S., 1977; Tchr. Tng. Degree, Trinity Coll. Music, London, 1949; BA in History of Music, U. Ill., 1982. Licentiate in violin; assoc. in voice; Rolland specialist. Head dept. music Internat. Sch., India, 1959-72; head string dept. Am. Internat. Sch., India, 1972-77; asst. to artistic dir. Nat. Acad. of Arts and Conservatory of Champaign, Ill., 1983-89; major instr. violin CCI assisting Ian Hobson, 1983-89; dir. Young Artists' Studio, Champaign, 1989—. Condr. nat. and internat. workshops in preparation for Rolland Specialist category, Cambridge, Eng., 1976, Chichester, Eng. and Lausanne, Switzerland, 1977, Laval U., Que., 1981. Author: The Young Violinist (in 3 parts), 1985. Mem. European String Tchrs. Assn., Am. String Tchrs. Assn., Soc. Am. Musicians, Chamber Music Am. (Heidi Castleman award 1994). Roman Catholic. Avocations: languages, history, art, literature, shih-tzu dogs. Office: Young Artists Studio 1305 Mayfair Rd Champaign IL 61821-5023

GOMEZ, TRACY LYNN, psychologist, small business owner; d. Willie and Linda Joyce Gomez. BS, Liberty U., Lynchburg, Va., 1990; MA, Goddard Coll., Plainfield, Vt., 1993; MA in Bibl. Counseling, The Master's Coll., Santa Clarita, Calif., 2004. Cert. Masters Level Psychologist Mich., 1993; lic. Nat. Assn. of Nouthetic Counseling Mich.; Real Estate Agent Mich., 1990, Food Sanitation/Catering Mich., 2001. Access and utilization mgmt. dept. head Monroe Cmty. Mental Health Authority, Monroe, Mich., 1993—; real estate agt. Herbert Realty & Mgmt., Inc., Detroit, 1990—; owner Cent-Sational Catering, Lincoln Pk., Mich., 2001—. Dir./cons. L.G.

& Daughters Child Care Ctr., Melvindale, Mich., 2000—03; counselor Grace Bapt. Ch., Monroe, Mich., 2002—. Counselor/chaplain during 9-11 Red Cross, Detroit, Mich., 1993—2003. Mem.: Nat. Assn. of Nouthetic Counseling.

GOMEZ-FALCON, MARIAH ROSA, psychologist; arrived in U.S., 1971; d. Pedro Ernesto Gomez and Rosa Eugenia Medinilla; m. Juan Carlos Falcon, Aug. 15, 1992; children: Lianna Maria Falcon, Christian Elan Falcon. BA in Psychology, Calif. State U., Northridge, 1987, MA in Psychology, 1989; PhD in Psychology, Calif. Sch. Profl. Psychology, L.A., 1993. Lic. psychology Calif., Fla. Psychol. asst. Berta Ortiz, PhD, L.A., 1991—92, Sandra Fenster, PhD, Beverly Hills, Calif., 1992—93; predoctoral intern Verdugo Psychotherapy Inst., Glendale, Calif., 1992—93, registered psychologist, 1993; post-doctoral intern Glen Roberts Child Study Ctr., Glendale, 1993—94; psychologist County of Orange, Calif., 1993—96; pvt. practice psychologist Burbank, Calif., 1996—. Mem. disaster mental health team ARC, L.A., 1993—; cons. L.A. County Office Edn., 1997—, Archdiocese L.A., 2000—. Mem.: APA. Avocations: camping, reading. Office: Ste 201 905 S Lake St Burbank CA 91502

GOMEZ-VEGA, IBIS, humanities educator; b. San Antonio de los Baños, Cuba, Dec. 20, 1952;, U.S. d. Rodolfo Gómez-Oramas and Angela Vega-González. BA, U. Houston, 1976, MA, 1979, PhD, 1995. Lectr. U. Houston-Downtown, 1979—82, 1983—91, Houston C.C., 1982—95; tchg. asst. U. Houston, 1991—95; assoc. prof. No. Ill. U., DeKalb, 1995—. Author: Send My Roots Rain, 1991. Fulbright scholar, 2002, 2003. Mem.: PETA, AMIGA: Latina Lesbians. Democrat. Avocation: dogs. Home: 107 Andresen Ct Dekalb IL 60115 Office: No Ill U 1425 W Lincoln Hwy Dekalb IL 60115 Business E-Mail: ibis@niu.edu.

GONDEK, MARY JANE (MARY JANE SUCHORSKI), property manager; b. Milw, May 19, 1958; d. Zigmund Alexander and Felicia Theodore (Staszewski) Suchorski; children from previous marriage: Amy Lynn Seamars, Joseph Alexander, Christine Ann. Student, S.W. Tech. Coll., 1989, 94, Internat. Correspondence Sch., 1995. Cert. nursing asst., CPR. Nursing asst. Lancaster Living Ctr., 1988-89, 95-96, Franciscan Villa Nursing Home, South Mil., Wis., 1990-92; home care provider Homeward Bound, Inc., Lancaster, 1994-95; dietary aide St. Joseph's Convent, Milw., 1995-96; on-site mgr. Meridian Group, Inc., Middleton, Wis., 1997-98; home care provider Supported Home Care Options, Inc., Wauwatosa, Wis., 1999, Anew Home Care Options, Wauwatosa, Wis., 1999—; nursing asst. Allis Care Ctr., West Allis, Wis., 1998, 99-2000, VA Med. Ctr., Milw., 2000—; rep. and beauty cons. Avon, 2002—; owner Mary's Treasured Gifts, 2002—. Democrat. Roman Catholic. Avocations: gardening, canning. Address: 1232 S 46th St Milwaukee WI 53214 Personal E-mail: mjgcna@yahoo.com.

GONG, CAROLYN LEI CHU, real estate agent; b. Visalia, Calif., July 10, 1949; d. Robert C. and Lynn P. (Low) G. BA in Health Sci., Calif. State U., Long Beach, 1973; MA in Sociology, Calif. State U., L.A., 1980. Cert. jr. coll. tchr., Calif. Social worker County of L.A., El Monte, Calif., 1974-76, children treatment counselor, 1976-81, children svcs. worker Norwalk, 1981-89; real estate agt. Coldwell Banker, Diamond Bar, Calif., 1989-90, First Team Real Estate, Dana Point, Calif., 1991-92, Grubb & Ellis Real Estate, Dana Point, Calif., 1994—, 1994-95, San Clemente, Calif., 1995—. Active March of Dimes Walk-a-Thon, Toys for Tots, Sugar Plum Tree, Am. Cancer Soc., Am. Heart Assn., Disabled Vet., Easter Seal. Mem. Nat. Assn. Realtors (Mult-million Prodn. award, Relocation award 1995), Calif. Assn. Realtors, Tennis Connection, Orchid Soc. Republican. Avocations: tennis, piano, reading, traveling, theater.

GONG, GLORIA MARGARET, lawyer, pharmacist; b. Yreka, Calif., Oct. 12, 1953; d. Kenneth Wayne and Patricia Ann (Farley) McCain; m. Peter-Poon Ming Gong, Apr. 3, 1976; children: George-Wayne, Cynthia-May, Miranda-Lin. Pharmacist Degree, U. of the Pacific, Stockton, Calif., 1976; JD, Calif. Pacific Law Sch., Bakersfield, 1992. BAr: Calif. 1992, U.S. Dist. Ct. (ea., ctr. and so. dists.) Calif. 1992. Pharmacist Gong's Pharmacy, Tehachapi, Calif., 1978-93; atty. Gong & Hirsch, Bakersfield, 1994-97; pvt. practice, 1997—. Mem.: ATLA, ABA, Kern County Bar Assn., L.A. County Bar Assn., Lambda Kappa Sigma. Office: 6840 District Blvd Bakersfield CA 93313 E-mail: ggong@legalemail.com.

GONSALVES, JANE LOUISE, city councilor, claims adjuster; b. New Bedford, Mass., Nov. 3, 1958; d. Richard and Fernanda Pereira (Sousa) Gonsalves; m. Walter D. Moniz, July 4, 1998. BA in Econs., Providence Coll., 1980. Substitute tchr. City of New Bedford, 1981; claims adjuster Reliance Ins. Co., New Bedford, 1981-83, Firemans Fund Ins. Co., Middleboro, Mass., 1983-87; sr. claims adjuster Hanover Ins. Co., North Dartmouth, Mass., 1987-88, claims supr., 1988-96, claims adjuster, 1996—. Vol. United Way, New Bedford, 1992—; mem. City Coun., City of New Bedford, 1994—; pres. 1999City Coun., City of New Bedford; active Dem. City Com., New Bedford, 1995—; bd. dirs. YWCA Southeastern Mass., 1996—, New Bedford Prevention Partnership, 1996—99, Friends of Buttonwood Park, 1998—2001. Nat. Merit Commended scholar Nat. Merit Scholarship Assn., 1975. Mem.: Mass. Mcpl. Assn., Portuguese Am. Police Assn. (assoc.). Roman Catholic. Office: City of New Bedford 133 William St New Bedford MA 02740-6132

GONSALVES, MARGARET LEBOY, elementary school educator; b. Paia, Maui, Hawaii, Feb. 10, 1935; d. John Algarin and Antonia (Leboy) G. BS in Edn., Marylhurst U., 1959; elem. tchr. cert., U. Hawaii, 1971. Cert. elem. tchr., Hawaii. Nurses' aide St. Vincent Hosp., Portland, Oreg., 1956; office clk. Bur. Med. Econs., Honolulu, 1959; tchr. State of Hawaii Dept. Edn., Honolulu, 1959—, Benjamin Park Sch., Kaneohe, Hawaii, 1966-92. Tchr. ESEA-Title I Chpt. I reading and math. fed. program, 1979-92, coord. Parker Sch. Chpt. 1 reading and math. program. Vol. Am. Cancer Soc., Honolulu, 1979, Am. Diabetes Assn., Honolulu, 1992; reporter Nat. Data Corp.-Price Waterhouse, Springfield, Va., 1991-2002. Mem. NEA, Internat. Reading Assn., Hawaii State Tchrs. Assn. (faculty rep. 1960-62, 87-89, Golden Heart cert., 2003), Sigma Delta Pi. Roman Catholic. Avocations: reading, sweepstakes, fishing, gardening, traveling. Home: 1328 Maalahi St Honolulu HI 96819-1727

GONZALES, FRANCEEN MICHELLE, amusement facility executive; b. El Paso, Tex., June 6, 1972; d. Francisco Ruben and Gloria Gonzales. BS in Biol. Scis., Stanford U., 1995. Dir. ops. Volcanic Gardens Mgmt., Inc., El Paso, Tex., 1992—97; sales mgr. Golfland Entertainment Ctrs., Inc., Mesa, Ariz., 1997—98, dir. risk mgmt., 2000—, gen. mgr. Phoenix, 1998—. Mem. adv. bd. Jeff Ellis and Assocs., Kingwood, Tex., 2000—02. Mem.: Calif. Attractions and Parks Assn. (bd. dirs.), NSPI-9 Writing Com., Waterpark Best Practices Counc., Internat. Assn. Amusement Parks and Attractions, World Waterpark Assn. (bd. dirs., chair safety com.), ASTM (task group chair). Avocations: hiking, wine tasting, crossword puzzles, reading. Office: Golfland Entertainment Ctrs Inc 4243 W Pinnacle Peak Rd Glendale AZ 85310 Office Phone: 623-581-8446.

GONZALES, STEPHANIE, state official; b. Santa Fe, Aug. 12, 1950; 1 child, Adan Gonzales. Degree, Loretto Acad. for Girls. Office mgr. Jerry Wood & Assocs., 1973-86; dep. sec. of state Santa Fe, 1987-90; sec. of state, 1991-99; state dir. rural devel. U.S. Dept. of Agriculture, Albuquerque, 1999—; state liaison dept. energy Los Alamos Eviron. Mgmt. Site. Bd. dirs. N.Mex. Pub. Employees Retirement, N.Mex. State Convassing Bd., N.Mex. Commn. Pub. Records. Mem. exec. bd. N.Mex. AIDS Svc.; mem. Commn. White House Fellowships. Mem. Nat. Assn. Secs. State, United League United Latin Am. Citizens (women's coun.), Nat. Assn. Latin Elected and Appointed Ofcls. Office: Los Alamos Nat Lab PO Box 1663 Los Alamos NM 87545

GONZALEZ, CARMEN GRACIA, law educator; b. Havana, Cuba, Jan. 6, 1962; d. Francisco and Carmen (Bonachea) Gonzalez. BA, Yale U., New Haven, Conn., 1985; JD, Harvard Law Sch., Cambridge, Mass., 1988. Bar: Calif. 1988, DC 1989. Law clerk to Judge Thelton E. Henderson U.S. Dist. Ct. (no. dist.) Calif., San Francisco, 1988-89; atty. Pillsbury, Madison & Sutro, San Francisco, 1989-91, Pacific Gas & Electric Co., San Francisco, 1991-94; asst. regional counsel U.S. EPA, San Francisco, 1994—98; with ABA Ctrl. and East European Law Initiative, Ukraine, 1996-97; prof. Sch. Law Seattle U., 1999—. Fellow, Supreme Ct., 2004—; Fulbright scholar, 1998. Mem.: ABA, La Raza Lawyers Assn., Hispanic Nat. Bar Assn. Office: Seattle Univ School Law 900 Broadway Seattle WA 98122 Office Phone: 206-398-4067.

GONZALEZ, DIANA M. language educator; b. Spain, Dec. 21, 1964; MA, Columbia U., 1986; BA in Biology, Chemistry & Fine Arts, Bklyn. Coll., 1988; EdM, Columbia U.; postgrad., Fordham U., 2003—. TV anchorwoman World Television Cor., Whitestone, NY, 1972; theater asst. dir. Trinity Tabernacle Theatre Group, Bklyn., 1991; tutor Spanish lang. Tchg. Corps Program, Bklyn., 1992; tchr., governess Palermo, Italy, 1992; art instr. Chinese student Herald Summer Camp, NY, 1993; tchr. English Nanjing (China) Auditing Inst., 1993—94; tchr. English Nanjing Rwy. Med. Coll., 1994—95; liaison between sculptor and staff, tchr. English Tom Otterness Studio, Bklyn., 1996; tchr. Spanish NYU, N.Y.C., 1996; lang. instr. French, Italian and Spanish lang. divsn. Baruch Coll., N.Y.C., 1996; sci. chairperson Liberty H.S., 1996; instr. math. and English South Bronx Job Corps, 1997; art instr. for deaf and multiple handicapped J4 7 Sch. for the Deaf, 1998; itinerary lang. specialist of the hearing impaired Hearing Edn. Svcs., 1998—; tchr. Chinese culture and lang. N.Y.C. Police Dept. Dep. Commr., 1999—; note taker, transcriber of lectrs. for deaf students deaf edn. dept. Tchr.'s Coll., 2000—. Rep. Xunta Galicia, N.Y.C. Recipient Eleventh Inst. Children's Lit. award, Spanish Embassy, 1998; scholar Bd. Edn. scholar, Columbia U. Tchr.'s Coll., 1998. Achievements include speaking eight languages: Spanish, English, French, Italian, Cantonese, Mandarin, Am. Sign Language, German. Avocations: Chinese martial arts, dance, ping pong/table tennis, swimming, cartoon drawing. Address: Apt E-26 511 W 232 St Bronx NY 10463

GONZALEZ, IRMA ELSA, federal judge; b. 1948; BA, Stanford U., 1970; JD, U. Ariz., 1973. Law clk. to Hon. William C. Frey U.S. Dist. Ct. (Ariz. dist.), 1973-75; asst. U.S. atty. U.S. Attys. Office Ariz., 1975-79, U.S. Attys. Office (ctrl. dist.) Calif., 1979-81; trial atty. antitrust divsn. U.S. Dept. Justice, 1979; assoc. Seltzer Caplan Wilkins & McMahon, San Diego, 1981-84; judge U.S. Magistrate Ct. (so. dist.) Calif., 1984-91; ct. judge San Diego County Superior Ct., 1991-92; dist. judge U.S. Dist. Ct. (so. dist.) Calif., San Diego, 1992—. Adj. prof. U. San Diego, 1992; trustee Calif. Western Sch. Law; bd. visitors Sch. Law U. Ariz. Mem. Girl Scout Women's Adv. Cabinet. Mem. Lawyers' Club San Diego, Inns of Ct. Office: Edward J Schwartz US Courthouse 940 Front St Ste 5135 San Diego CA 92101-8911

GONZALEZ, IVETTE, biomedical engineer; b. N.Y.C., Dec. 25, 1964; d. Jesus and Isabelle Gonzalez. B, N.Y. Inst. Tech., Westbury, 1988. Master: GE Elfuns. Achievements include invention of (with others) hand-key glove. Avocations: hiking, photography, biking, travelling, volunteering. Home: 7450 NW 18th St Apt 206 Margate FL 33068-6879 Office: Cedars Med Ctr 1400 NW 12th Ave Miami FL

GONZALEZ, JUDITH R. psychologist, marriage and family therapist; b. Mex. d. Carlos Rodriguez and Eleazer Segura; m. Samuel Gonzalez, July 24, 1976; children: Misael, Joanna Carelli. EdB with honors, Universidad Nacional Autonoma de Mex.; B in Christian Edn., Seminario Teologico Bautista Mexicano; MA in Christian Edn., No. Bapt. Theol. Sem., Lombard, Ill.; D, Forest Inst. Profl. Psychology. Lic. marriage and family therapist Mo. Pres. Hand in Hand Ministries, Springfield, Mo., 2000—; faculty Forest Inst. Profl. Psychology, Springfield, 2003—. Prof. Ethnic Devel. Ctr., Jefferson City, Mo., Emmanuel Bapt. Theol. Sem., Guadalajara, Jalisco, Mexico, Seminario Teologico Bautista Mexicano, Mexico City; presenter in field. Translator: several books to Spanish; contbr. articles to profl. jours. Translator Med. Ctrs., Springfield; lang. cons. Women Mission Union, Jefferson City; mem. nat. coun. Convencion Nacional Bautista de Mex.; task force mem. Mo. Bapt. Conv., Jefferson City; pub. rels. Confraternidad Hispana de Mo., Jefferson City; mem. End of Life: Compassion, Springfield. Internat. scholar, No. Bapt. Theol. Sem. Mem.: APA, Internat. Family Therapy Assn., Am. Assn. Marriage and Family Therapy. Avocations: reading, music, writing, travel. Home: PO Box 1577 Springfield MO 65807 Office: Forest Inst Profl Psychology 2885 W Battlefield Rd Springfield MO 65807 Business E-Mail: jgonzalez@forest.edu.

GONZALEZ, NANCY BERGER, healthcare professional, educator; b. N.Y., Aug. 14, 1942; d. Jack and Ruth (Blierer) Berger; m. Rafael González; 1 child, Adam Matthew. BA in Edn., U. Toledo, 1964; Montessori degree, Fairleigh Dickinson U., 1966; MS in Anthropology and Education, Queens Coll., 1968. Prin. Escuelas Las Nereidas, San Juan, P.R., 1966-71, Montessori Sch., Brooklyn, N.Y., 1971-73; sch. dir. Associated YM-YWHAs of Greater N.Y., Brooklyn, 1972-78; mktg. and recruitment dir. Cmty. Blood Ctrs. South Fla., Ft. Lauderdale, 1991; dir., recruitment Am. Red Cross Blood Svc., 1992-94; patient svc. administrator Nat. Parkinson Found., 1995-98; dir. Rehab. Facility Nova SE Univ., Fort Lauderdale, Fla., 1999—. Mem. Am. Parkinson Disease Assn. Democrat. Avocations: travel, painting, attending interest classes, cultural anthropology. Office: Nova SE Univ Health Profl Divsn 3200 S University Dr Fort Lauderdale FL 33328-2018

GONZALEZ, ROSITA CHRISTINE, photographer; b. Seoul, Korea, Nov. 15, 1967; d. Enrique F. and Frances D. (Taylor) G.; m. Jonathan Mark Sleeman; 1 child, Noah Sol. BA, Austin Peay State U., Clarksville, Tenn., 1990; MS, U. Tenn., Knoxville, 1992. Tchr. photography Arnstein Jewish Cmty. Ctr., Knoxville, 1991; instr. photography U. Tenn., Knoxville, 1993, editor, graphic designer, 1992-95; freelance photographer Kigali, Rwanda, 1995—. Art dir. Almaden Mktg. Group, Ft. Collins, 1997-98; graphic designer City of Ft. Collins, 1998-2000.. Exhibitor photographs When May I Come?, 1990, When May I Come and Not Now, 1991, Restless Sleep, 1991, At Home in London, 1994. Vol., designer Planned Parenthood of East Tenn., 1994-95. Mem. AIGA, Soc. Newspaper Design (prs. 1991-92), Phi Kappa Phi, Omicron Delta Kappa, Kappa Tau Alpha. Democrat. Avocations: writing, photography, film, gardening, graphic designer. Office: PO Box 580 Fort Collins CO 80522-0580 Home: 1012 Glendale Rd Charlottesvle VA 22901-4014

GONZALEZ, TERESA ANN, academic administrator, psychologist, educator; d. Manuel Joaquin and Rita Anna (Albrecht) Gonzalez; m. Fred James Hoffmann, Apr. 5, 1975; children: Marta Jill Strand, Jennifer Tara Armstrong, Jamie Teresa Hoffmann. BA, Molloy Coll., 1968; EdM, PhD, Ohio U., 1975. Lic. profl. counselor Commonwealth Va., 1975. Asst. dir. admissions Molloy Coll., Rockville Centre, NY, 1968—70; resident dir. Ohio U., Athens, 1970—71, asst. coord. residence halls West Green, 1971—73, counseling intern Ctr. Psychol. Svcs., 1974—75; counseling psychologist James Madison U., Harrisonburg, Va., 1975—81, dir. counseling ctr., 1981—88, assoc. v.p. for student affairs, 1988—94, assoc. v.p. for academic affairs, 1994—. Mem. exec. com. Va. Assn. Student Pers. Administrs, 1983—87; coord. Va. Counseling Ctr. Info. Bank, 1985—89; pres. Southeastern Conf. Coll. Counseling Ctr. Pers., 1987; mem. nat. bd. and site visitor Internat. Assn. Counseling Svcs., 1987—89; coord. Va. Network Sr. Seminar, 1989—93, treas., 1994—; mem. ACE/OWHE Nat. Network, Washington, 1992—; advisor Chi Sigma Iota, JMU chpt., 1994—20.. Contbr. articles to profl. jours. [illegible] Augusta County Assn. for Gifted and Talented, 1995—99, treas., 1996—99; pres., v.p., membership chair Hugh K. Cassell PTA, 1990—93; mem., coord. religious edn. bd. St. John's Ch., Waynesboro, Va., lector; mem. Tender Heart Day Care Ctr., Harrisonburg, Va., 1986—88. Recipient award for U. Svc., James Madison U. Women's Caucus, 1986, George E. Hill Disting. Alumni award, Ohio U. Coll. Edn., 1995, Outstanding Profl. award, Va. Assn. Student Pers. Adminstrs. Mem.: Va. Network for Women Leaders (mem. exec. com. 1982—, chair exec. com. 1987—92), Am. Coun. on Edn./Nat. Network for Women Leaders, Am. Coll. Pers. Assn., Am. Counselors Assn., Phi Delta Kappa, Chi Sigma Iota, Golden Key Soc. (hon.). Roman Catholic. Avocations: gardening, running, cross stitch, reading. Office: James Madison University Msc 7503 Harrisonburg VA 22807 E-mail: gonzalta@jmu.edu.

GONZALEZ-CRESPO, TERESITA, art educator; b. Bridgeport, Conn., Oct. 8, 1960; d. Ramon Gonzalez-Perez and Luisa Crespo-Valle. BFA, Pontifical Cath. U., Ponce, P.R., 1996, MEd in Curriculum and instrn., 2003. Cert. tchr. art edn. P.R., 2002, profl. photography P.R., 1982, Mayaguez Vocat. Sch., 1982. Dance tchr. Dept. of Edn., Ponce, PR, 1996—97; curatorial asst. Ponce Mus. of Art, Ponce, 1996—99, mus. educator - dir. of edn. dept., 1999—2000; art specialist Dept. of Edn. Commonweath of PR, Villalba, 2001—; asst. libr. Children's String Program, PR Conservatory of Music, Hato Rey, PR, 1989—89; asst. dir. cultural outreach program Pontifical Cath. U., Ponce, PR, 1984—88; external resources oficial and stage mgr. Musical Theatre Ballet Co., Ponce, 1990—92; Spanish tchr./ tutor HS Equivalency Program -Pontifical Cath. U., Ponce, 1993—96. Vol. at curatorial dept. Ponce Mus. of Art, 1995—97; mus. collection's digitalization specialist various museums, PR, 2000—; art and drama workshop specialist various art orgns., PR, 1999—; dance tchr. Campionero Summer Camp, Pontifical Cath. U., Ponce, PR, 1995—. Actor(costume design, prop master,): (Luis Torres Nadal Theatre workshop) West Side Story, Dama del Alba, Bernarda Alba, Bella y la Bestia, Tiempo para una Historia, Ana Frank: Terror y Esperanza, Las Brujas de Salem (Best Tecnical Dir., 1984); singer: (opera chorus) Carmen, Cavalleria Rusticana, Il Pagliacci, Othello, La Gioconda, (chorus, Conservatory of Music) Beethoveen's 9th, Zarzuela Pieces, Faure's Requiem, Mozart's Requiem, etc.; actor(assistant dir., state mgr.): (producciones andromeda y artemisa) La Cueva del Indio, Cofresi, Aventuras en el Fondo del Caño, El Lazarillo de Tormes, Mala Nota; costumer (play, specialized sch. fine arts) La Bella y la Bestia, La Bella Durmiente. Recipient Most Outstanding Vol. Work award, Ponce Mus. of Art, 1997—98. Mem.: Nat. Art Edn. Assn.

GONZALEZ-HERMOSILLO, BRENDA, economist, researcher; b. Mexico City, Oct. 28, 1955; d. Jesus and Emilia (Gonzalez Watkins) G. BA in Econs., Inst. Tech. Autonomo de Mexico, Mexico City, 1979; MA in Econs., U. Western Ont., London, 1980, PhD in Econs., 1983. Rsch. asst. Bank of Mex., Mexico City, 1977; economist Banco Nacional de Mex., Mexico City, 1978, Min. of Fin., Mexico City, 1979, Bank of Montreal, Toronto, Ont., 1983-84, Bank of N.S., Toronto, 1985-89; sr. economist Bank of Can., Ottawa, Ont., 1989-94, Internat. Monetary Fund, Washington, 1994—. Contbr. articles to profl. jours. Recipient Govt. of Can. award to fgn. nationals, 1980-83; Inst. of Tech. scholar, 1976-78, U. Western Ont. scholar, 1979-80. Mem. Can. and Am. Econ. Assn. Achievements include research on financial crises, financial markets, monetary policy, medicare. Home: 4332 Leland St Chevy Chase MD 20815-6064 Office: Internat Monetary Fund 700 19th St NW Washington DC 20431-0001

GONZALEZ TRICOCHE, CYNTHIA MARIE, human resources specialist; b. Bayamon, Rio Piedras, Puerto Rico, Nov. 13, 1970; d. Mario González, Martina Tricoche; m. Michael Figgis; 1 child, Katie Liv Figgis. Student, Ind. U., Pa., 1990; B in Labor and Indsl. Rels., U. PR, 1994; postgrad., Capella U., 2003—. Cert. Cert. Hospitality Supr. Hotel and Motel Assn. Home: 13301 SW 24th St Miramar FL 33027 Office: 3700 Lakeside Dr Miramar FL 33027

GOOCH, AUDREY SMITH, retired education educator; b. St. Louis, July 7, 1925; d. James Irving and Mabel Dorthea (Higgins) Smith; m. Robert Thomas Gooch; children: Keith Ewing, Robert Kenneth. BA, Stowe Tchrs. Coll., 1947; MA in Tchg., Webster U., 1971. Cert. elem. tchr., reading specialist, coll. instr., child care. Elem. tchr. St. Louis Pub. Schs., 1947-66; edn. dir. Project Head Start, St. Louis, 1966-69, project dir., 1969-72; dir. Right to Read, St. Louis, 1972-74, Forest Park C.C., St. Louis, 1974-79; coord. Family Support Svcs., St. Louis, 1979-84; dir. Early Childhood Edn. Unit, St. Louis, 1984-90. Adj. faculty Harris Tchrs. Coll., St. Louis, 1972, Forest Park C.C., 1973; adv. bd. Learning Tree Day Care Ctr., St. Louis, 1991-97; cons. St. Louis Urban League, Right to Read Nat. Office, Washington, 1974, Mo. Vol. Accredition EOC, Jefferson City, 1989-90. Author: (booklet) A Guideline For Head Start Curriculum, 1967, Read On, 1973, Handbook for Reading Tutors, 1974. Mem. collections com. Mo. History Mus., St. Louis; mem. scholarship com. U. Mo., St. Louis; vice chmn. Kirkwood (Mo.) Human Rights Commn.; v.p. Kirkwood Hist. Soc., 2000; Oasis tutor Kirkwood Pub. Schs. Recipient Gateway medal City of St. Louis, 1972, Outstanding Vol. Svc. award at Mo. Hist. Soc., Union Electric and City of St. Louis, 1996, Woman of Achievement award St. Louis Globe Dem., 1985, Disting. Alumni award Harris-Stowe State Coll., 1992. Mem. Mo. Assn. for Edn. of Young Children (sec.), Gideon Internat. Aux. (v.p. 1993), Links Inc. (fin. sec. 1994), Delta Sigma Theta. Lutheran. Avocations: reading, volunteering. Home: 302 W Rose Hill Ave Saint Louis MO 63122-5942

GOOCH, CAROL ANN, psychotherapist consultant; b. Meridian, Miss., Apr. 17, 1950; d. James Tackett and Chris M. Page; (div.); 1 child, Aaron Patrick Gooch. BS, Fla. State U., 1972, DS, 1975; MS, Troy State U., 1974. Lic. profl. counselor Tex., chem. dependency counselor Tex., marriage and family therapist Tex., cert. chem. dependency specialist Tex., compulsive gambling counselor Tex., tobacco addiction counselor ACP Tex., bereavement counselor. Tchr. Okaloosa Sch. Dist., Fort Walton, Fla., 1972-77; counselor USAF, Osan AFB, Korea, 1977-79; sch. counselor Tomball (Tex.) Sch. Dist., 1983-90; cons. Montgomery (Tex.) Sch. Dist., 1992—; psychotherapist pvt. practice, Houston, 1990—; dir. cmty. rels. Cypress Creek Hosp., 1998—. Cons. school systems, Houston, 1990—; coord. sr. program Forest Springs Hosp., Houston, 1993—, Cypress Creek Hosp., 1994—. Vol. cons. PTO, Woodlands, Tex., 1990; life mem. Woodlands C. of C. Named Outstanding H.S. Counselor, Tomball Ind. Sch. Dist., 1989, Diplomat of Yr. for Woodlands C. of C., 2001, 2002; named to Leadership Montgomery County; recipient fellowship, Fla. State U., Tallahassee, 1973, Nat. Disting. Svc. award, Ex Coun. U.S. Pubs., N.J., 1989. Mem.: NAFE, ASCD, ACA, AAUW, Am. Bus. Women's Assn., Tex. Mental Health Counselors Assn., Am. Mental Health Counselors Assn., Tex. Sch. Counselors Assn., Fla. State U. Alumni Assn., Kappa Delta Pi. Avocations: travel, dance, boating. Home and Office: Carol A Gooch MS LPC PO Box 1308 Montgomery TX 77356-1308 Office Phone: 713-256-8002. E-mail: psychstages@aol.com.

GOOCH, NANCY EUGENIA SOUTH, secondary school educator, librarian; b. Big Spring, Tex., Sept. 21, 1945; d. James Lawton and Eugenia (Routh) South; m. James B. Gooch, Dec. 23, 1968; children: James Eric, Kim Hyo Eugenia. BA in Chemistry, Hardin-Simmons U., 1968; MLS, U. Tex., Austin, 1972. Cert. secondary tchr., Tex., nat. cert. chemistry/gen. sci. Tchr. Del Valle (Tex.) High Sch., 1979-82, Santa Anna (Tex.) High Sch., 1982-85, Mineral Wells (Tex.) High Sch., 1986-90; libr. Glen Rose (Tex.) Intermediate Sch., 1992-93; tchr. math. and phys. sci. Paradise (Tex.) Austin, 1993—99; libr. cons. Fairfield (Tex.) HS, 1998—, tchr. math and drama, 1999—. Mem. Am. Geneal. Soc., Assn. Tex. Profl. Educators (pres.

2003—), Tex. Tchrs. Assn. (pres. chpt. 1978-79), Tex. Libr. Assn., Amen Libr. Assn., Fairfield (Tex.) History Club, Ednl. Theatre Assn., Delta Kappa Gamma (corr. sec. 1990-92). Democrat. Presbyterian. Avocations: reading science history and science fiction, collect cats. Home: 410 Meadowbrook Ln Fairfield TX 75840-1829 E-mail: negooch@hotmail.com.

GOOD, EDITH ELISSA (PEARL WILLIAMS), writer; b. Hollywood, Calif., Jan. 10, 1945; d. Jack Brian and Rose Marie (Miller) Good; m. Michael Lawrence Black, Dec. 18, 1986 (dec.). BA in English, Calif. State U., Northridge, 1974; student, UCLA and U. Calif., Berkeley, 1962-92; student of ballet, Folklorico, Mex., 1963. Explorer Mayan ruins, Mex., 1963; author, pub. Gull Press, L.A., 1990-95. Participant numerous dance, art, music, lit., math. and sci. classes; dancer Hajde Dance Troop, Berkeley, Calif., 1962-66. One-woman shows, L.A., 1962-95; singer, various venues, L.A., 1986-96; author: (pseudonym Pearl Williams) The Trickster of Tarzana, 1992, Short Stories, 1995, Mad in Craft, 1995, Missives, 1995, others; author numerous poems; CDs, radio and internet broadcasts. Fundraiser, del. to local convs. Dem. clubs, Calif. and Mex., 1962—; supporter mental health orgns., 1962—; participant Consciousness raising groups, del. local convs., fundraiser, canvasser, office worker, driver, participant W.E.B. DuBois Club, Congress Racial Equality, San Francisco, Berkeley, L.A., and Oakland, 1965, Peace in Alliance for Survival, Berkeley, Oakland, L.A., 1964-80, women's rights Westside Women's Ctr., Woman's Bldg., L.A., 1974-80, Environment in Earth Day, L.A., 1977, phys. and mental health VA, cons. book reviewer, tutor, Mental Health Assn., L.A., 1962—. Recipient achievement prize, Internat. Biographical Ctr., Cambridge, Eng., 2000. Mem. Mensa, Am. Soc. Composers, Authors, and Pubs., Plummer Park Writers, Westside Writers. Achievements include writing chosen by a jury of experts for inclusion in the permanent collecton of the Library of Congress. Home: 1470 S Robertson Blvd Apt B Los Angeles CA 90035-3402

GOOD, ESTELLE M. minister; b. Charleston, S.C., Oct. 5, 1927; d. John Wesley and Minnie Estelle Hilton; divorced; children: Raymond L., Lee Good Sanders. BTh, Clarksville Sch. Theology, 1972, ThM, 1975, ThD, 1976, ThD, 1978, B in Sacred Music, 1980; PhD of Christian Psychology, Cornerstone U., 1992. Ordained to preach 1955; cert. hypnotherapist Internat. Assn. Counselors and Therapists, 1994. Organizer pastor Covenant Life Cathedral, Macon, Ga., 1962—. Pres. Lighthouse Bible Tng. Ctr., 1976—88. Fellow: Nat. Christian Counselors Assn. (diplomate 1993, lic. temperament therapist 1991, Christian counselor and therapist 1992); mem.: Women Preachers Coun. Am., Full Gospel Fellowship of Churches and Ministers Internat. Office: Covenant Life Cathedral 4543 Bloomfield Rd Macon GA 31203*

GOOD, JOAN DUFFEY, artist; b. Irvington, N.J., Apr. 8, 1939; d. Joseph Edmund and Mary Kathleen Duffey; m. Robert Whitney Meyers, Feb. 19, 1960; children: Robert Whitney Jr., Mary Kathleen; step-children: Alison H., Forrester H.; m. Allen Hovey Good, June 12, 1976. Student, Rosemont Coll., 1958-59, Summit Art Ctr., 1973-78; BA in Psychology and Studio Art, Drew U., 1987. Represented by Jain Marunouchi Gallery Soho, N.Y.C., 1991-92, Abney Gallery Soho, N.Y.C., 1992; exec. dir. New Jersey Ctr. Visual Arts, Summit, N.J. Interior designer Maytime Festival of Homes, 1985; freelance interior design cons., 1987-89; v.p. Atlantic Nat. Acquisition and Mergers, Inc., Short Hills, N.J.; bd. dirs. N.J. Ctr. for Visual Arts, Summit, curatorial assoc. gallery com., 1989-90, [illegible] curator exhbns., 1990-94, asst. gallery curator, 1991-92, gallery curator, 1992-94, pres. 1994-95, exec. dir., 1995—; archivist Oak Knoll Sch., 1988-95. One-woman show World Trade Ctr., N.Y.C., 1988; exhibited in group shows at Madison (N.J.) Pub. Libr., 1986, Chatham (N.J.) Pub. Libr., 1987, Korn Gallery, Drew U., 1986-87, 89-90, N.J. Ctr. for Visual Arts, 1987-90, Oak Knoll Sch. Alumnae Art Exhibit, 1989-90; represented in numerous private collections, Mass., Fla., Tex., N.J., N.Y., Calif. V.p., pres., membership chmn. PTO, 1966-69; homecoming com. mem. Oak Knoll Sch. Alumnae Bd., Summit, 1989-90, historian, 1988-94, archivist, 1988-95. Mem. N.J. Ctr. for Visual Arts, The Drew Art Assn., Chatham Fish & Game Assn., Mantoloking Yacht Club, Summit Tennis Club. Republican. Roman Catholic. Avocations: psychology, floriculture, photography, tennis. Subject of interview Inside N.J., 1993. Address: NJ Ctr Visual Arts 68 Elm St Summit NJ 07901

GOOD, LINDA L. music educator; b. St. Albans, Vt., May 4, 1952; d. Amos and Margaret Wilson; m. Vincent Robert Good, May 8, 1976; children: Heather Good Williams, Holly Good Schwider. MusB in Edn. with honor, Ea. Ill. U., 1974; MusM in Edn., Vandercook Coll. Music, 2002. Cert. tchr. Ill. Music tchr. ABL Sch. Dist., Broadlands, Ill., 1974—75, Libby Elem. Sch., Wheatland, Wyo., 1976—77, Ranchester (Wyo.) Elem. Sch., 1978—79, Morgan Pk. Acad., Chgo., 1986—87; elem. music tchr. Summit Hill Sch. Dist., Frankfort, Ill., 1987—. Dir. Walker 5th & 6th Grade Choir, Frankfort, 1987—, Julian Rogus Sch. 4th Grade Choir and Chime Choir. Mem. Tinley Park (Ill.) Cmty. Band, Tinley Park Cmty. Choir; dir. chime choir, dir. evangelism, mem. choir Savior Divine Luth. Ch., Palos Hills, Ill., 1979. Mem.: Music Educators Nat. Conf. Avocations: flute quartet, camping, bicycling, reading, hiking. Home: 7537 W 163rd Pl Tinley Park IL 60477 Personal E-mail: lgoodflute@aol.com.

GOOD, MARY LOWE (MRS. BILLY JEWEL GOOD), investment company executive, educator; b. Grapevine, Tex., June 20, 1931; d. John W. and Winnie (Mercer) Lowe; m. Billy Jewel Good, May 17, 1952; children: Billy, James. BS, Ark. State Tchrs. Coll., 1950; MS, U. Ark., 1953, PhD, 1955, LLD (hon.), 1979; DSc (hon.), U. Ill., Chgo., 1983, Clarkson U., 1984, Ea. Mich. U., 1986, Duke U., 1987; hon. degree, St. Mary's Coll., 1987, Kenyon Coll., 1988, Stevens Inst. Tech., 1989, Lehigh U., 1989, Northeastern Ill. U., 1989, U. S.C., 1989, N.J. Inst. Tech., 1989; hon. law degree, Newcomb Coll. of Tulane U., 1991; LLD (hon.), Coll. of William and Mary, 1992; DSc (hon.), Manhattan Coll., 1992, Ind. U., 1992, SUNY, Binghamton, 1994, Rensselaer Polytechnic Inst., 1994, Monmouth U., 1995, La. State U., 1995, Ill. Inst. Tech., 1997, Mich. State U., 1997, U. Mich., 1998; DEng (hon.), Mich. State U., 1997, U. Mich., 1998, Colo. Sch. Mines, 2000. Instr. Ark. State Tchrs. Coll., Conway, summer 1949, La. State U., Baton Rouge, 1954-56, asst. prof., 1956-58, assoc. prof. New Orleans, 1958-63, prof., 1963-80, Boyd prof. materials sci., divsn. engring. rsch. Baton Rouge, 1979-80; v.p., dir. rsch. UOP, Inc., Des Plaines, Ill., 1980-84; pres. Signal Rsch. Ctr. Inc., 1985-87; pres. engineered materials rsch. divsn Allied-Signal Inc., Des Plaines, Ill., 1986-88, sr. v.p.-tech. Morristown, N.J., 1988-93; under sec. of commerce for technology Dept. of Commerce, Washington, 1993-97; mng. mem. Venture Capital Investors LLC, Little Rock, 1997—; Donaghey Univ. prof., dean Coll. Info. Sci. & Systems Engr U. Ark., Little Rock, 1998—. Chmn. Pres.'s Com. for Nat. Medal Sci., 1979-82; adv. bd. NSF Chemistry Sect., 1972-76; com. medicinal chemistry NIH, 1972-76, Office of USAF Rsch., 1974-78, chemist divsn. Brookhaven and Oak Ridge Nat. Labs., 1973-83, chem. tech. divsn. Oak Ridge Nat. Lab., catalysis program Lawrence-Berkeley Lab.; catalysis program coll. engring. La. State U.; vice chair Nat. Sci. Bd., 1984, chair, 1988-90; bd. dirs. BiogenIdec, IDEXX Labs., Delta Bank and Trust, bd. chem. sci. and tech., Nat. Rsch. Council, 2003-, Govt. U., industry roundtable, NRC, 2000-, Ark. Sci and Tech. Authority, 1998-, Dialoge Com, Am. Chem. Coun., 2002-. Contbr. articles to profl. jours. Mem. Nat. Sci. Bd., 1980-91, chair, 1988-91; mem. Pres.' Coun. Advisors for Sci. and Tech., 1991-93. Recipient Agnes Faye Morgan rsch. award, 1969, Disting. Alumni citation U. Ark., 1973, Scientist of Yr. award Indsl. R&D mag., 1983, Delmer S. Fahrney medal Franklin Inst., 1988, N.J. Women of Achievement award Douglass Coll., Rutgers U., 1990, Indsl. Rsch. Inst. medal, 1991, Disting. Svc. award NSF, 1992, Roe award ASME, 1993, Gold medal SME, 1995, Earle Barnes award ACS, 1996, Priestley medal, 1997, UCLA Glenn T. Seaborg medal, 1996, Nat. Materials Advancement award Fedn. Materials Socs., 1996, Othmer medal award Chem. Heritage Found., 1998, Henry Michel award, Civil Engring. Rsch. Found., 1998, Heinz award for tech. The Economy and Employment, 2000, Vannevar Bush award NSF, 2004; AEC tng. grantee, 1967, NSF Internat. travel grantee, 1968, NSF rsch. grantee, 1969-80, Albert Fox Demers award, 1992. Fellow AAAS (Abelson award 1999, pres. 2000, chmn. bd. dirs. 2001), Am. Inst. Chemistry (Gold medal 1983), Chem. Soc. London, Royal Soc. Chemistry (hon.); mem. NAE, Acad. Arts and Scis, Am. Philos. Soc., Swedish Acad. Engring., Am. Chem. Soc. (1st woman dir. 1971-74, regional dir. 1972-80, chmn. bd. 1978, 80, pres. 1987, Garvan medal 1973, Herty medal 1975, award Fla. sect. 1979, Charles Lathrop Parsons award 1991), Internat. Union Pure and Applied Chmistry (pres. inorganic div. 1980-85),Alliance for Sci. and Tech. Rsch. in Am. (chmn. bd. dirs. 2000—), Zonta (past pres. New Orleans club, chmn. dist. status of women com. and nominating com., chmn. internat. Amelia Earhart scholarship com. 1978-88, pres. internat. Found. 1988-93, mem. internat. bd. 1988-90), Rotary Internat., Phi Beta Kappa, Sigma Xi, Iota Sigma Pi (regional dir. 1967-93, hon. mem. 1983), Ark. Women's Forum. Home: 13824 Rivercrest Dr Little Rock AR 72212-1521 Office: Venture Capital Investors LLC 400 W Capitol Ave Ste 1845 Little Rock AR 72201-4857 also: U Ark at Little Rock Coll Info Sci/Sys Engring 2801 S University Ave Little Rock AR 72204-1000 Office Phone: 501-569-8189. Personal E-mail: thegoods@aristotle.net. Business E-Mail: mlgood@ualr.edu.

GOOD, VIRGINIA JOHNSON, real estate executive; b. Onancock, Va., Mar. 1, 1919; d. Obed Wilbur and Sallie Mildred (Deyerle) Johnson; m. William Dennis Good, Jan. 14, 1941 (dec. Apr. 1970). Bus. cert., Elon College, N.C., 1937; real estate cert., U. Miami, 1973; student, Montgomery County Jr. Coll., 1974. Acct. Carolina Biol. Supply Co., Elon College, N.C., 1935-39, Sears Roebuck, Richmond, Va., 1939-40, Ritchie Electric, Charlottesville, Va., 1940-41; mgmt. investor Dr. & Mrs. William D. Good Real Estate, Washington and Gaithersburg, Md., 1941-70, Good Properties, Washington and Miami Beach, Fla., 1970-94, Dennis Apts., Miami Beach, Fla., 1972-94; owner Good Properties, Orlando, Fla., 1994—. Mem. D.C. Apt. Owners/Mgmt. Assn., Washington, 1970-84, Miami Beach Apt. Owners Assn., 1970-86, North Shore Apt. Owners Assn., Miami Beach, 1986-88. Exec. com. Anti Rock Quarry, Dawsonville, Md., 1959, Save Our Coast, Miami Beach, 1982-86; mem. Montgomery County Hist. and Geneal. Soc., Rockville, Md., 1977—, Nat. Geneal. Soc., 1980-95, Greater Miami Geneal. Soc., Miami, 1982-96, Va. Hist./Geneal. Soc. Richmond, 1988—, Bradley Blvd. Civic Assn., Bethesda, Md., 1989. Mem. La Gorce Country Club, Miami Beach, Columbia Country Club (Chevy Chase, Md.), DAR, Nat. Soc. So. Dames, United Daus. of Confederacy, Nat. Soc. Colonial Dames of XVII Century, Nat. Huguenot Soc. Mem. United Church of Christ. Avocation: genealogy. Home and Office: 3607 Lake Sarah Dr Orlando FL 32804-3425

GOODACRE, JILL, model; b. Lubbock, Texas, Mar. 29, 1965, m. Harry Connick, Jr., Apr. 16, 1994, 3 children. Model Elite Model Mgmt. Corp. Appearances include Victoria's Secret catalogues; (TV Series) Friends, 1994, Duckman, 1997, (films) Odd Jobs, 1984, Ladybird Ladybird, 1994, The Uninvited, 1997. Address: IMG 170 5th Ave New York NY 10010-5911

GOODALE, TONI KRISSEL, development consultant; b. N.Y.C., May 26, 1941; d. Walter DuPont and Ricka Krissel; m. James Campbell Goodale, May 3, 1964; children: Timothy Fuller, Ashley Krissel, Clayton A. (Ward). AB cum laude, Smith Coll., 1963; student, U. Geneva, 1962-63; postgrad., Hunter Coll., 1964-65. Congl. intern senator Keating U.S. Senate, Washington, 1963; broadcast analyst FCC, Washington, 1963-64; adminstrv. asst., dir. grant rsch. dept. Ford Found., N.Y.C., 1964-67, cons. pub. edn. dept., 1968-69; N.Y. rep. Smith Coll., N.Y.C., 1975-78, asst. dir. devel., 1978-79, pres. Goodale Assocs., N.Y.C., 1979-92, chmn., CEO, 1992—. Mem. NYC 2000 Millennium Coun.; vis. com. continuing edn. New Sch. Social; mem. bd. advs. First Women's Bank; bd. dirs. N.Y. Outward Bound., mem. exec. com., chmn. alumni com.; lectr., writer in field. Columnist Fund Raising Mgmt. Bd. dirs. N.Y. Pub. Libr.; bd. dirs., mem. exec. com. Pen Am. Ctr., chmn.; mem. Women's Fgn. Policy Group; mem. UNA Chmn. Coun.; lectr. U.S. Naval Acad.; mem. alumnae fund com. Smith Coll., v.p. class, chmn. 25th reunion, Women's Forum; univ. chmn.'s coun., trustee, alumnae fund chmn., mem. alumnae coun.; bd. dirs. Brearley Sch.; mem. exec. com. Parents' Assn., St. Bernard's Sch.; mem. benefit com. N.Y. Philharmonic; trustee, bd. govs. Churchill Sch.; co-chmn. spl. events com. Carnegie Hall, The Joffrey Ballet Opening Gala; chmn. Coro Benefit Dinners; trustee N.Y. Inst. Child Devel.; mem. women's divsn. Legal Aid Soc.; mem. N.Y. com. Joffrey Ballet; mem. benefit com. Grosvenor House; vice chmn. N.Y.C. Opera Benefit, Peir Ctr. Benefit; mem. com. Sch. Am. Ballet; active Women's Forum. Mem. Am. Coun. Arts (vice-chmn. bd., exec. com., chmn. nat. patrons commn., chair long range planning com.), Nat. Cultural Alliance (bd. dirs.), Am. Assn. Fund-Raising Counsel (bd. dirs. trust for philanthropy), Nat. Assn. Fund Raising Execs., Assn. Healthcare Philanthropy, Brearley Sch. Alumnae Assn., Smith Coll. Alumnae Assn., Cosmopolitan Club, Smith Club, Washington Club, Seventh Regiment Armory Club, Doubles Internat. Club, Women's Forum (Women's Leadership Forum select cir., transition team, NYC pub. adv.). Office Phone: 212-759-2999. E-mail: riowoman@aol.com.

GOODBERRY, DIANE JEAN (DIANE OBERKIRCHER), mathematics educator, tax accountant; b. Buffalo, June 24, 1950; d. Ralph Arthur and Muriel Carol (Glaeser) O.; m. Lawrence D. Goodberry, Sr. BS in Math. Edn., State Univ. Coll., Brockport, N.Y., 1972, MS in Ednl. Adminstrn., 1974; grad., Nat.Tax Tng. Sch., Monsey, N.Y., 2000. Cert. in secondary math. edn., N.Y. Uni-Pay clk. Marine Midland Bank, Buffalo, 1968-72; asst. registrar State Univ. Coll., Brockport, 1972-74; home instrn. tutor Clarence Ctrl. Sr. H.S., Sweet Home Sr. H.S., NY, 1974-75; part-time inst. Erie C.C., Buffalo, 1975-86; instr. math. Ednl. Testing Methods, Buffalo, 1984-90, Buffalo Pub. Sch. System, 1974—. Mem. curriculum devel. com. Buffalo Pub. Schs., 1988, 92—, yearbook advisor 1994—, math. intervention coord., 2002—; cooperating tchr. BRIET-U. Buffalo, 1990-96; owner Taxes by Diane; CEO, Larry's GrassRoots Landscaping Inc.; cons. Nat. Tax Tng. Sch., 1999—; AIS coord., Buffalo Pub. Sch. Sys., 2002—. Vol., World Univ. Games, Buffalo, 1993. Mem. AAUW, Nat. Assn. of Female Execs., Women Tchrs. Assn. (bd. dirs., v.p. 1993-94, pres. 1994-96, rec. sec. 1996-98, treas. 1998), Assn. Math. Tchrs. N.Y. State (conf. spkr.), Theodore Roosevelt Rough Riders, Nat. Coun. Math. (conf. spkr.), Assn. Curriculum Devel. and Supervision (Top 2000 scholar of 20th Century award, named one of 2000 Outstanding Scholars of 20th Century Winner in Math). Republican. Methodist. Avocations: crafts, reading, travel, sports. Home: 10644 Crump Rd Holland NY 14080-9303 Office: South Park HS 150 Southside Pkwy Buffalo NY 14220-1552

GOODE, ELIZABETH ANN, music educator; b. Cliffside, N.C., Jan. 9, 1932; d. Broadus B. Goode and Mary Elizabeth Hames. BA Duke U., 1954, MA Adelphi U., 1961, PhD U. of Cincinnati, 1978. Piano tchr. Kings Mountain Schs., NC, 1954—55; vocal music tchr. Plainview Schs., NY, 1956—61, Raleigh Schs., NC, 1961—63; choral dir. and music theory tchr. E. Meadow Schs., NY, 1963—92; ret., 1992. Adjudicator NY State Sch. Music Assn., 1966—92. Poll asst. and judge Rutherford Co. Bd. of Electors, Ellenboro, NC, 1994—2003. Mem.: United Daughters of the Confederacy, Daughters of Am. Revolution, Nassau Music Educators Assn., NY State Sch. Music Assn. (Piano Com. 1957—92, Manual Com. 1957—92), Music Educators Nat. Conf., Am. Choral Dir. Assn. (life), Iron Dukes, Pi Kappa Lambda, Delta Phi Alpha, Sigma Kappa (life). Republican. Methodist. Avocations: Genealogy, Reading. Home: 390 NC 120 Hwy Mooresboro NC 28114

GOODE, ERICA TUCKER, internist; b. Berkeley, Calif., Mar. 25, 1940; d. Howard Edwin and Mary Louise (Tucker) Sweeting; m. Bruce Tucker (div. 1971); m. Barry Paul Goode, Sept. 1, 1974; children: Adam Nathaniel, Aaron Benjamin. BS summa cum laude, U. Calif., Berkeley, 1962, MPH, 1967; MD, U. Calif., San Francisco, 1977. Diplomate Am. Bd. Internal Medicine. Chief dietitian Washington Hosp. Ctr., Washington, 1968; pub. health nutritionist Dept. Human Resources, Washington, 1969—73; intern Children's Hosp. (now Calif. Pacific Med. Ctr.), San Francisco, 1977—78, resident, 1978—80, chief med. resident internal medicine, 1979—80; pvt. practice internal medicine San Francisco, 1980—. Expert witness med.-legal issues, Calif., 1990—; lectr., tchr. med. house staff Calif. Pacific Med. Ctr. Hosp., 1982—; assoc. prof. medicine U. Calif., San Francisco, 1984—. Contbr. articles to profl. publs. Co-chair Physicians for Clinton, No. Calif., 1992, 96; mem. Calif. Commn. on Aging, 2003—. Mem. ACP, Calif. Med. Assn., Calif. Soc. Internal Medicine, San Francisco Med. Soc., U. Calif. Alumni Assn. (del.), Alpha Omega Alpha (named Best Doctor's list 1998-). Office: CPMC Inst for Health & Healing Clinic 2300 California St Ste 200 San Francisco CA 94115-2754 Office Phone: 415-600-3503.

GOODE, JANET WEISS, elementary school educator; b. Chattanooga, Tenn., Sept. 3, 1935; d. Albert H. and Dorothy E. (Crandall) Weiss; m. Gene G. Goode, June 11, 1961; children: Jennifer E., Amy V. BS in Biology, Carson-Newman Coll., 1957; MA in Botany, Vanderbilt U., 1959; MEd, Lynchburg Coll., 1980. Cert. postgrad. profl. tchr., Va. Instr. gen. biology, botany, zoology, animal ecology Carson-Newman Coll., Tenn., 1959-61; tchr. biology, chemistry Salem Acad., Winston-Salem, N.C., 1961-64; tchr. chemistry Wade Hampton High Sch., Greenville, S.C., 1964-65; tchr. sci. Va. Treatment Ctr. for Children, Richmond, 1966; tchr. biology Quantico (Va.) H.S., 1969-70; pvt. tutor Madison Heights, Va., 1980-85, James River Day Sch. and Seven Hills Sch., Lynchburg, Va., 1980-85; reading specialist Title I reading program Monelison Mid. Sch., Madison Heights, 1985-93; reading specialist Amherst County Adult Basic Edn. Program, 1992-94, 95—; reading specialist Title I reading and Reading Recovery Pleasant View Elem. Sch., Monroe, Va., 1993-96, Madison Heights (Va.) Elem. Sch., 1996—. Vis. instr. U. Chattanooga, summer 1960; mem. learning disabilities del. to Russia and Lithuania, Citizen Amb. Program, 1993; mem. mentor tchr. program Amherst County Pub. Schs., 1999-2000. Editor: (newsletter) Topics for Title I; author: Can You Read a Baseball Card?; co-author: Transitional Intervention Program. Sponsor sch. lit. mag. Monelison Mid. Sch., Pleasant View Elem. Sch.; organist, newsletter editor for Ptnr. Ch. com. First Unitarian Ch.; mem. Friends of Libr., Madison Heights Br. Libr., helper ann. book sale. Recipient Reading Tchr. of the Year Piedmont Va. Area Reading Coun., 1993-94. Mem. NEA, Nat. Coun. Tchrs. of English, Va. Edn. Assn., Amherst Edn. Assn., Internat. Dyslexia Assn., Piedmont Area Reading Coun. (past newletter editor, past treas.), Va. State Reading Assn., Internat. Reading Assn., Lynchburg Stamp Club. E-mail: jwgoode@worldnet.att.net.

GOODELL, KATHY SUSAN, artist, educator; d. Herbert Sumner and Celestine Goodell; m. Ralph James Rogers, June 30, 1996. BFA, San Francisco Art Inst., 1969—71, MFA, 1972. Instr. Calif. Coll. of Arts and Crafts, San Francisco, 1974—77, San Francisco (Calif.) State U, 1978—81, The San Francisco Art Inst., 1978—80; lectr. U Calif., Davis, 1981—82; assoc. prof. Moore Coll. of Art and Design, Philadelphia, 1984—91; instr. sculpture The Sch. of Visual Arts, N.Y.C., 1986—; prof. painting, drawing SUNY, New Paltz, 1993—. Juror sculpture fellowship N.Y. Found. For The Arts, N.Y.C., 1995; juror Nat. Scholastic Award Nat. Scholastic Soc., N.Y.C., 1999; lectr.,workshops at various colls.,univs., film festivals. lectr. in field. Contbr. video Unterbrochene Karrieren Hannah Wilke Berlin,Germany, 2000, video Crumb Sony Classics, 1994, book Art in the San Francisco Bay Area 1945-1980, 1985, book New Bay Area Painting and Sculpture, 1982, articles and reviews numerous mentions 1976-2003; one-woman shows include Queens Art Ctr., Queens,N.Y., 2000, Willoughby Sharp Gallery, N.Y.C., 2000, Calkins Gallery, Hofstra U, 1982, Gallery Paule Anglim, San Francisco,Calif., 1982, Atholl McBean Gallery, 1981, Axel Raben Gallery, N.Y.C., 2003, mid-Manhattan br. N.Y. Pub. Libr., 2004, Chappell Gallery, Boston, 2004, exhibited in group shows at The Chandler Gallery-Faculty Exhbn. SUNY, New Paltz,N.Y., 2002, Paul Morris Gallery, N.Y.C., 2001, Wake Forest U., Winston-Salem, N.C., 2000, Nicolai Fine Art, N.Y.C., 1999, The Islip Mus., East Islip, N.Y., 1998, Satellite, AT, Long Island,N.Y., 1997, URBANGLASS, N.Y.C., 1996, The Boise Mus., Boise,Id., 1994, numerous group shows at galleries and univs., 1977—, Represented in permanent collections DeSaisset Mus., Santa Clara,Calif., The Samuel Dorshy Mus., New Paltz,N.Y., Fortroyal Found., Fultonville,N.Y., Calif. Pacific Corp., San Francisco,Calif., The Oakland Mus., Oakland, Calif., The Albuquerque Mus., Albuquerque,N.M., The Inst. of Plastic Arts, Bucharest, Romania, The Ctr. for Visual Arts, Anchorage, AK. Recipient James D. Phelan Award, Internat. award to a Calif. born artist., James D. Phelan, 1983; grantee Fellowship, N.Y. Found. for the Arts, 1997, 1993, Pollock-Krasne Found. Grant In Sculpture, 1991, Artist In Residence, N.Y. Council for the Arts, 1985, Fellowship in Sculpture, Nat. Endowment for the Arts, 1983, 1979, Fulbright-Hays Fellowship - Romania, Fulbright-Hayes Foun. Mem.: Tribera Organ. of Artists, United Fed. of Tchrs. Home: 401 Washington St New York NY 10013 Office: SUNY 75 South Manheim Blvd New Paltz NY 12561 Office Phone: 212-431-0773.

GOODENBERGER, MARY ELLEN, literature educator; b. Trenton, Nebr., Aug. 4, 1923; d. George Andrew and Ida May (Stewart) Marshall; m. Marvin Eugene Goodenberger, Aug. 9, 1947; children: Daniel Marvin, Beverly Jane, Marshall Eric. BSEd, U. Nebr., 1947, MEd, 1963, PhD, 1976. Elem. tchr. Culbertson (Nebr.) Pub. Schs., 1940-41, 43-44; prin., tchr. English, libr. Trenton (Nebr.) Pub. Sch., 1957-58, 60-66; cons. in English Nebr. Dept. Edn., Lincoln, 1968-72; K-12 dir. instrn. McCook (Nebr.) Pub. Schs., 1973-80; coll. instr. U. Nebr. at Kearney, Lincoln, 1967-68, 80-85; county supt. Hitchcock County Schs., Trenton, 1984-90. Author: Ida May's Real People, 1985, Of Mice and Birds, 1986, Aedith's Fables, 1987, Letters for the Literate, 2002, (curriculum) Breakthrough in English, I, II, III, 1969-71. County chair Rep. Party, Red Willow County, 1950-54; Sunday sch. tchr. Youth Fellowship, leader, choir mem. local ch., McCook, Trenton, 1950-66; 4-H leader, Trenton, 1956-66; mem. Women's Fellowship, Trenton, 1980-90, pres. 1988-90. Regents scholar U. Nebr., Lincoln, 1940, 42, grad. study scholar Delta Kappa Gamma, Nebr., 1968, Disting. Educator award U. Nebr. at Omaha, 1980. Mem. Nebr. State Edn. Assn. (pres.-elect McCook and Holdrege 1966), Nebr. Coun. Tchrs. of English (pres. 1973), Nebr. Assn. for Supervision and Curriculum Devel. (bd. dirs. 1973-78), Nebr. Schoolmasters Club (pres. 1977), Delta Kappa Gamma (various offices), Phi Beta Kappa, Pi Lambda Theta. Methodist. Home: HC 2 Box 123 Trenton NE 69044-9744

GOODFELLOW, ROBIN, musician, educator, artist; b. Portland, Oreg., Jan. 25, 1940; d. Ted and Lois Goodfellow; m. Victor Wong, 1970 (div. 1977); m. Charles Hixson, Mar. 17, 1991. AA with honors, Merritt Coll., 1962; student, U. Calif., Berkeley, 1960—. 1st flute and piccolo Santa Rosa (Calif.) Symphony, 1958-60; dir. Queen's Ha' Penny Consort, Berkeley, Calif., 1960-80; dir., tchr. Mandala Fluteworks, Oakland, Calif., 1970—. Mem. adv. bd., illustrator Exptl. Music Inst. Mag., Nicasio, Calif.; performer, instr. and cons. in field. Author, illustrator in field. Avocations: curriculum development, drawing, chamber music, hiking, animation. E-mail: robingdfllw@earthlink.net.

GOODFELLOW, ROBIN IRENE, surgeon; b. Xenia, Ohio, Apr. 14, 1945; d. Willis Douglas and Irene Linna (Kirkland) G. BA summa cum laude, Western Res. U., Cleve., 1967; MD cum laude, Harvard U., 1971. Diplomate Am. Bd. Surgery. Intern, resident Peter Bent Brigham Hosp., Boston, 1971-76; staff surgeon Boston U., 1976-80, asst. prof. surgery, 1977-80; pvt. practice medicine specializing in surgery Jonesboro, La., 1980-81; practice medicine specializing in surgery Albion, Mich., 1984-87, Coldwater, Mich., 1987—. Bd. Overseers Case Western Res. U., 1977-82. AAUW fellow, 1970. Fellow ACS; mem. AMA, Phi Beta Kappa. Republican. Methodist.

GOODIN, EVELYN MARIE, writer; b. Fullerton, Calif. d. Theodore Hopper and Nellie Mary (Henger) DeWitt; m. Robert Delmer Goodin, Feb. 23, 1950; 1 child, Michael Warren. AA, Fullerton Jr. Coll., 1942; BA, U. Calif., Santa Barbara, 1946. Tchr. Bakersfield (Calif.) City Schs., 1947 50, Stockton (Calif.) City Schs., 1950-58, San Juan Unified Schs., Carmichael, [illegible] (poetry) The Young Heart Sings, 1940, (children's book) The Greatest Living Scientist, 1993; editor: (poetry anthology) First the Blade, 1942; writer radio show Uncle Punkle Show, 1951. Registrar Selective Svc. Sys., Bakersfield, 1948; vol. tchr. Sacramento Safety Ctr., 1985; sec. Suburban Writers Club, Sacramento, 1986-87; mem. Fremont Presbyn. Fremont Presbyterian Inspiration Recreation Svc., 1992-96; with Friendship Inspiration Recreation Svc. Recipient First Prize in Poetry, Creative Arts Coun. Fullerton Jr. Coll., 1942, Recognition award for extended profl. svc. San Juan Tchrs. Assn., 1982; named Disting. mem. Internat. Soc. Poets, 1998. Mem. Whitney Lunch Bunch, Calif. Ret. Tchrs. Assn. (mailing com. N.E. sect. 1994-96), Sports Leisure Travel Club. Avocations: music, reading, politics, decorating, travel. Home: 6017 Winding Way Apt 101 Carmichael CA 95608-1436

GOODIN, JULIA C. forensic pathologist, state official, educator; b. Columbus, Ky., Mar. 10, 1957; d. Vitus Jack and Geneva Goodin. BS, Western Ky. U., 1979; MD, U. Ky., 1983. Diplomate Am. Bd. Clin. and Anatomic Pathology, Am. Bd. Forensic Pathology. Intern Vanderbilt U. Med. Ctr., Nashville, 1983, resident in anatomic and clin. pathology, 1984-87; fellow in forensic pathology Med. Examiner's Office, Balt., 1987-88; asst. med. examiner Office of Chief Med. Examiner, Balt., 1988-90; dep. chief med. examiner State of Tenn., 1990-94; asst. med. examiner Nashville, 1990-93; chief med. examiner, 1993-94; asst. med. investigator State of N.Mex., Albuquerque, 1994-96; asst. prof. U. N.Mex., Albuquerque, 1994-96; clin. assoc. prof. U. of South Ala. Sch. Medicine, 1996-99; state med. examiner Ala. Dept. Forensic Scis., Mobile, 1996-99; chief state med. examiner State of Iowa, Des Moines, 1999—. Clin. prof. U. Md. Med. Sch., Balt., 1988-90, Vanderbilt U. Med. Ctr., 1990-94. Capt. USNR, 1985—. Mem. Am. Acad. Forensic Sci., Assn. Mil. Surgeons of U.S., AMA. Avocations: long-distance running, weight lifting, photography, studying french. Home: 100 Market St Unit 414 Des Moines IA 50309-4765 Office: 321 E 12th St Des Moines IA 50319-0075

GOODING, GRETCHEN ANN WAGNER, physician, educator; b. Columbus, Ohio, July 2, 1935; d. Edward Frederick and Margaret (List) Wagner; m. Charles A. Gooding, June 19, 1961; children: Gunnar Blaise, Justin Mathias, Britta Meghan. BA magna cum laude, St. Mary of the Springs Coll., Columbus, 1957; MD cum laude, Ohio State U., 1961. Diplomate Am. Bd. Diagnostic Radiology. Intern Univ. Hosps., Columbus, 1961-62; rsch. fellow Boston City Hosp., 1962-63, Boston U., 1963-65; with dept. radiology U. Calif., San Francisco, 1975—, assoc. prof. in radiology, 1981-85, prof., vice chmn., 1986—2003; asst. chief radiology VA Med. Ctr., San Francisco, 1978-87, chief radiology, 1987—2003, chief ultrasonography, 1975—. Chair com. acad. pers. U. Calif., San Francisco, 1993-94, bd. dirs. commn. accreditation vascular labs., 1993-96. Co-editor Radiologic Clinics of N.Am., 1993—; mem. editl. bd. San Francisco Medicine, 1986—, Applied Radiology, 1987-89, Current Opinion in Radiology, 1992-93, The Radiologist, 1993—, Emergency Radiology, 1993-2003, Jour. Clin. Ultrasound, 1997—; guest editor Emergency Radiology, 1999; contbr. articles to profl. jours. Recipient Recognition award Inter Societal Commn. for Accreditation of Vascular Labs., 1997, Disting. Alumna award, Ohio State U. Coll. Medicine and Pub. Health, 2001. Fellow Am. Coll. Radiology (mem. commn. on ultrasound 1984-2000, chair stds. com. commn. on ultrasound 2004), Am. Inst. Ultrasound in Medicine (bd. govs. 1981-84, chair conv. program 1986-88, Presdl. Recognition award 1984), Am. Soc. Emergency Radiology, Soc. Radiologists U.S.; mem. AMA, San Francisco Med. Soc. (chmn. membership com. 1992-94, bd. dirs. 1996—), RSNA (course com. 1984-88, tech. exhibit com. 1992-96), Bay Area Ultrasound Soc. (pres. 1979-80), Soc. Radiologists Ultrasound (chair membership com. 1991-93, chair corp. com. 1996-97), ARRS, AUR, CRS, Calif. Med. Assn., Am. Assn. Women Radiologists (pres. 1984-85, trustee 1991-94, Alice Ettinger Disting. Achievement award 2003), VA Chiefs of Radiology Assn. (pres.-elect, pres. 1994-95), San Francisco Radiol. Soc. (pres. 1990-91), Hungarian Radiol. Soc. (hon.), Pakistan Radiol. Soc. (hon.), Cuba Radiol. Soc. (hon.). Office: VA Med Ctr Radiology Svc 4150 Clement St San Francisco CA 94121-1545 E-mail: gretchen.gooding@radiology.ucsf.edu.

GOODKIN, DEBORAH GAY, corporate financial executive; b. Oceanside, N.Y., Dec. 8, 1951; d. Harold and Rose (Mostkoff) G.; m. Glenn Richard; children: Samuel Goodkin Richard, Sarah Goodkin Richard. BA, Syracuse U., 1972; M in Urban Planning, NYU, 1977. Planner Nassau-Suffolk Planning, Hauppauge, N.Y., 1972; asst. to treas. Nat. Assn. Savs. Banks, N.Y.C., 1973; planning aide Dept. City Planning, N.Y.C., 1973-79; planner, real property mgr. N.Y.C. Bd. Edn., 1979-81; dir. Capital Budget Bur., 1981-85; supervising mgmt. engr. Port Authority N.Y. & N.J., 1985-90, mgr. fin. sys., 1989-96; mutual funds ops. mgr. Tchrs. Ins. Annuity Assn., N.Y.C., 1997-99, tuition savs. program ops. mgr., 1999—2002; v.p. Citigroup Coll. Savs., 2002—. Cons. C Corp, L.A., 1983—. Author: (zoning law) Bay Ridge Zoning Dist., 1978; artist Show of Selected Works, Sireuil, France, 1983. Security cons. Dem. Nat. Com., N.Y.C., 1980; founder, pres. Allendale Opportunity and Enrichment Program. Recipient CEO Award of Excellence, 1987, 92. Mem. Women in Govt. (guest lectr. 1983), Syracuse U. Alumni Assn., NYU Alumni Assn. Office: Citigroup 300 1st Stamford Pl Stamford CT 06902

GOODMAN, CAROL HOCKENBURY, retired elementary school educator, consultant; b. Chgo., Nov. 12, 1943; d. Norman J. and Margaret Griffith Hockenbury; children: Kellie S., Krista L., Kirk A. BS, Lock Haven U., Pa., 1965; MEd, Shippensburg U., 1968. Cert. permanent tchg. cert. Pa. Elem. tchr. Wyalusing (Pa.) Area Sch. Dist., 1965—69, N.E. Bradford Sch. Dist., Rome, Pa., 1988—2004; adj. prof. Pa. State U., State College, 2001—, ret., 2004. Dir. Goodwriting Assocs., Wyalusing, 2002—. Dir., author, choreographer: elem. sch. musicals Broadway Dreams, American Pride, The Great American Vacation, others. Mem.: NEA (assoc.), Delta Kappa Gamma (state com. chair 2001—03). Avocations: writing, reading, travel, grandchildren. Home: PO Box 254 Wyalusing PA 18853 Personal E-mail: cgoodman@epix.net.

GOODMAN, ELIZABETH ANN, retired lawyer; b. Marquette, Mich., Aug. 11, 1950; d. Paul William and Pearl Marie Goodman; m. Herbert Charles Gardner, Sept. 24, 1977. Student, U. Munich, 1970-71; BA cum laude, Alma (Mich.) Coll., 1972; JD cum laude, U. Mich., 1977. Bar: Minn. 1978, Mich. 1978, U.S. Dist. Ct. Minn. 1979. Cert. real property law specialist, real property sect. Minn. Bar Assn. High sch. tchr. Onaway (Mich.) High Sch., 1973-74; assoc. Dorsey & Whitney LLP, Mpls., 1978-82; ptnr. Dorsey & Whitney, Mpls., 1983-99; v .p., chief gen. counsel Ryan Cos., 2000—03; ret., 2003.

GOODMAN, ELLEN HOLTZ, journalist; b. Newton, Mass., Apr. 11, 1941; d. Jackson Jacob and Edith (Weinstein) Holtz; m. Robert Levey; 1 dau., Katherine Anne. BA cum laude, Radcliffe Coll., 1963; hon. degrees, Mt. Holyoke Coll., Amherst Coll., U. Pa., U. N.H. Researcher, reporter Newsweek Mag., 1963-65; feature writer Detroit Free Press, 1965-67; feature writer columnist Boston Globe, 1967-74, assoc. editor, 1986—2001; syndicated columnist Washington Post Writers Group, 1976—; radio commentator Spectrum, CBS, 1978-80, NBC, 1979-80; commentator NBC Today Show, 1979-81. Vis. prof. Stanford U., 1995. Author: Close to Home, 1979, Turning Points, 1979, At Large, 1981, Keeping in Touch, 1985, Making Sense, 1989, Value Judgments, 1993, (with Patricia O'Brien) I Know Just What You Mean, 2000, Paper Trail, 2004. Trustee Radcliffe Coll.; judge Livingston Awards for Young Journalists, 1986—. Nieman fellow Harvard U., 1974, Lyndhurst fellow, 2000; named New Eng. Newspaper Woman of Year New Eng. Press Assn., 1968; recipient Catherine O'Brien award Stanley Home Products, 1971, Media award Mass. Commn. Status Women, 1974, Columnist of Year award New Eng. Women's Press Assn., 1973, Pulitzer Prize for [illegible], 1980, [illegible] column writing Am. Soc. Newspaper Editors, 1980, Hubert H. Humphrey Civil Rights award, 1988, William Allen White award 1995. Office: 5 JFK St Cambridge MA 02138 E-mail: ellengoodman@globe.com.

GOODMAN, ERIKA, dancer, actress; b. Phila. d. A. Allan and Laura (Baylin) G. Student, Sch. of Am. Ballet, 1961-63; BA in Theatre and Dance, Empire State Coll., 1993; master classes, Princeton Ballet, 1994, Hartford Ballet Co., 1995, Va. Intermont Coll., 1995—. Mem. faculty Actors and Dirs. Lab., N.Y.C., 1979—; founding mem. ensemble theater co. The Barrow Group, N.Y.C., 1986—; mem. dance faculty CCNY, 1990. Mem. dance faculty CCNY, 1990; guest tchr. ballet Balettakademein, Stockholm, 1986, 89; instr. master classes Rutgers U., East Carolina U., 1989, Hofstra U., U. Kans., 1990, Harvard U., summer 1993, Cornell U., Skidmore Coll., Vassar Coll., 1992—, Conn. Coll.; vis. prof. ballet, head ballet dept. CCNY, 1992—, lectr. world arts, 1993—. Dancer N.Y.C. Ballet Co., 1964-65, prin. dancer Joffrey Ballet, N.Y.C., 1966-75; performer (with Barrow Group) Seymour in the Heart of Winter, Perry St. Theatre, N.Y.C., 1986, When You Comin' Back Red Rider, 1987, Feather Hat, Three Sisters, 1989; casting dir. (films) Hazing in Hell, Neon Red; dir. ballet rehearsal Ballet Hispanico. Richard Porter Leach fellow, 1992-93.

GOODMAN, GAIL BUSMAN, small business owner; b. NYC, Feb. 8, 1953; d. Irving Laurence and Harriet (Topol) Busman; m. Laurence Goodman, June 17, 1979 (div. 1987). Student, Northwestern U., 1970-72; BS magna cum laude, Tufts U., 1975. Staff occupational therapist St. Joseph's Hosp., Yonkers, N.Y., 1975-77; sr. occupational therapist N.Y. Hosp., White Plains, 1977-79; chief occupational therapist Phelps Hosp., Tarrytown, N.Y., 1979-80; occupational therapy cons. Elmwood Manor Nursing Home, Nanuet, N.Y., 1982-83; from v.p. tng. to pres. Facelifters, Bklyn., 1981-86; pres. Visual Impact, Rye, N.Y., 1987—; owner, pres. ConsulTel, Inc., White Plains, N.Y., 1988—. Guest speaker Columbia U., N.Y.C., 1977, 78, 79, 82. Mem. Women in Sales (pres. Westchester chpt. 1989-91). Democrat. Jewish. Avocations: reading, movies, needlepoint, antique refinishing.

GOODMAN, GERTRUDE AMELIA, civic worker; b. El Paso, Tex., Oct. 24, 1924; d. Karl Perry and Helen Sylvia (Pinkiert) G. BA, Mills Coll., 1945. Pres. El Paso chpt. Tex. Social Welfare Assn., 1963-65, bd. dirs. 1965-70, state bd. dirs., 1965-70; state bd. dirs. Pan-Am. Round Table, El Paso, 1966—, bd. dirs. 1970-71, sec., 1973-74, life mem.; founder, 1st chmn. El Paso Mus. Art Mem. Guild, 1962-68; bd. dirs. Mus. Art Assn., 1962-69, also v.p.; chmn. dir. El Paso C. of C. women's Dept., 1976-77; bd. dirs. Rio Grande Food Bank, 1988-94; bd. dirs. El Paso Pub. Libr., 1972-80, pres. bd. dirs., 1978-80; pres. El Paso County Hist. Soc., 1981-82, bd. dirs., 1986-92; mem. planning com. El Paso United Way, 1953—; mem. El Paso Mus. Art Bd. Coun.; pres. Las Comadres, 2000-01. Recipient Hall of Honor award El Paso County Hist. Soc., Nat. Human Rels. award NCCJ, 1981, numerous awards for civic vol. work. Avocations: tennis, travel, art, books. Home: 905 Cincinnati Ave El Paso TX 79902-2435

GOODMAN, JOAN FRANCES, avionics manufacturing executive; b. N.Y.C., Oct. 25, 1941; d. Jack and Evelyn (Fine) G.; m. Stephen Gordon Glatzer, Oct. 2, 1982 (dec. Dec. 1987). BS, Alfred U., 1963; MA, NYU, 1967. RN, N.Y. Psychiat. liaison nurse Hosp. Albert Einstein Coll. Medicine, N.Y.C., 1968-73; nursing care coord. United Hosp., Port Chester, N.Y., 1974-80; asst. to pres. Glatzer Industries, New Rochelle, N.Y., 1980-87; pres., CEO Emergency Beacon Corp., New Rochelle, 1988—. Mem. ANA, Nat. League Nursing, Westchester Assn. Women Bus. Owners, Am. Women's Econ. Corp., Nat. Bus. Aviation Assn., Women in Aviation Internat. Office: Emergency Beacon Corp 15 River St New Rochelle NY 10801-4351

GOODMAN, JOY DUVALL, elementary school educator; b. Buford, Ga., Nov. 5, 1955; d. Clifton C. and Mary Allen Duvall; married, Aug. 23, 1980; children: Rachel, Rebecca. BS in bib. edn., Columbia Internat. U., 1977; BS in elem. edn., Shorter Coll., 1980; MEd in early childhood, Ga. So. U., 1998. Tchr. Reidsville (Ga.), 1985—. Pres. local chpt. Beta Sigma Phi, Reidsville, 2000—02. Recipient Mentoring cert., Ga. Dept. Edn., 1998. Mem.: Ga. Assn. Educators. Avocations: ch. pianist, scuba diving, travel, reading. Home: 2002 Sharward Ct Vidalia GA 30474 Office: Reidsville Elem Sch 147 Chandler Rd Reidsville GA E-mail: musicjoy@cybersouth.com.

GOODMAN, JULIE, nurse midwife; b. Dec. 14, 1937; m. Michael B. Goodman; children: Julia, Christopher, Jennifer. BAin Nursing, Coll. St. Catherine, 1960; MSN, U. Minn., 1975, PhDin Adult Edn., 1990. RN, Minn.; cert. nurse midwife. Staff nurse St. Joseph's Hosp., St. Paul, 1960-61; pub. health nurse Family Nursing Svc., St. Paul, 1961-63; instr. nursing U. S.D., Vermillion, 1963-66, Saint Mary's Sch. Nursing, Rochester, Minn., 1966-68, Rochester (Minn.) C. C., 1970-83; nurse practitioner Planned Parenthood, Rochester, Minn., 1978-81; dir. nursing cont. edn. Rochester (Minn.) C. C., 1983-88, dir. nursing, 1989-90, assoc. dean acad. affairs, 1994-95, dean of nursing and allied health, 1995—. Adv. bd. Family Consultation Svc., Rochester, Minn., 1983-86. Author, editor: Child and Family, 1982, 2nd edit. 1987; contbr. articles to profl. jours. Recipient Faculty Svc. award Mayo Med. Ctr., 1996, Main Achievement award, 1989. Mem. Am. Nurses Assn. (nat. del., Book of Yr. 1983), Nat. League Nursing, Minn. Orgn. Assoc. Degree Nursing (co-pres. 1994-96), Minn. Nurses Assn. (chair nursing edn. com. 1982-87, 87-89, bd. dirs. 6th dist.), Great Plains Perinatal Assn., Sigma Theta Tau Office: Rochester Cmty and Tech Coll 851 30th Ave SE Rochester MN 55904-4915

GOODMAN, KAREN LACERTE, financial services executive; b. Mesa, Ariz., Nov. 9, 1946; d. Howard Lee and Margaret (Duncan) G.; m. Grant A. Lacerte, Feb. 1, 1964; children: Arthur Grant Jr., Arcel Leon Rene. Student, George Washington U., 1974-76. Prodn. mgr. Data Corp. of Am., Reston, Va., 1967-73; pres. Transco Leasing Co., Washington, 1974-78; sec., treas. to v.p. Certa Data Corp., Orlando, Fla., 1989—; pres. Fin. Rsch. Assocs., Inc., Orlando, 1979—. Cons. in field, 1979—; dir. statis. seminars in field. Editor, pub.: Financial Studies of the Small Business (annual publ.), 1976—. Mem. Am. Heart Assn., Winter Haven, Fla., MADD, 1985—. Mem. Greater Orlando C. of C. Republican. Home: 6759 Winterset Gardens Rd Winter Haven FL 33884-3154 Office: 203 Ave A NW Ste 202 Winter Haven FL 33881-4503

GOODMAN, KIM, marketing professional, computer company executive; B in Polit. Sci., M in Indsl. Engring., Stanford U.; MBA, Harvard U., 1992. V.p. Bain & Co., Inc.; v.p. bus. devel., exec. asst. to the CEO Dell Inc., 2000, v.p., gen. mgr. for networking product group; v.p. mktg. Dell Americas Public Sector, Round Rock, Tex., 2003—. Office: Dell Inc One Dell Way Round Rock TX 78682*

GOODMAN, LILLIAN RACHEL, dean, nursing educator; b. Hanover, N.H., 1923; d. Benjamin and Anna (Tapper) G. RN, Peter Bent Brigham Hosp. Sch. Nursing, 1947; BS in Nursing, Boston U., 1950, MS, 1954, EdD, 1969; ScD (hon.), U. Mass., Worcester, 1991; PhD (hon.), Worcester State Coll., 1999. Dir. nurses Boston State Hosp., 1955-63; asst. chief supr. psychiat. nursing Mass. Dept. Mental Health, Boston, 1963-69; prof., acting dean U. Mass. Sch. Nursing, Amherst, 1970-73; prof., chmn. dept. nursing Worcester (Mass.) State Coll., 1973-91; dean, prof. U. Mass. Grad. Sch. Nursing, Worcester, 1991-99, dean emeritus, 2000—. Assoc. clin. prof. Boston U. Sch. Nursing, 1957-69; cons. VA Hosp., Brockton, Mass., 1960-67. Co-author: The Schizophrenic's Mother, 1963; mem. editl. bd. Nursing and Health Care, 1983-87, Perspectives in Psychiat. Care, 1961-76. Mem. Am. Nurses Assn., Mass. Nurses Assn. (leadership award 1970), [illegible] for Nursing, Vis. Nurses Assn. of Worcester (pres. 1982-85, v.p. 1979-82), Sigma Theta Tau.

GOODMAN, LULA CAROLYN, music educator; d. Daniel and Emma Grant; m. Floyd Goodman, Aug. 14, 1965; children: Delicia Goodman-Lee, Kennan. BS in Mus., Morris Brown Coll., Atlanta, Ga., 1964; MusD (hon.), Faith Coll., Birmingham, Ala., 1993. Cert. elem. tchr. Ga., 1969. Music tchr. Putnam County Sch. Sys., Eatonton, Ga., 1964—66, Liberty County Sch. Sys., McIntosh, Ga., 1966—67; elem. edn., music tchr. Chatham County Schools, Savannah, Ga., 1967—69; choral music specialist Atlanta Pub. Schs., 1969—. Mgr., asst. co-dir. Atlanta Schs. Prep. Chorus, 1995—98; music adv. team Atlanta Pub. Schs., 2000—02. Dir.: Recorder Instrument Ensemble Performance (Excellence in Tchg. grant, 1990), (music educators nat. conf.) Music In Our Schools Month TV Concert, 2003, (chorus performance) Ga. PTA Ann. State Conv., 2003, Mary McLeod Bethune Elem. Sch. Chorus (Most Outstanding Elem. Chorus, 2003). Parent vol. Atlanta Olympic Band, 1992—96; cherubs choir accompanist Ben Hill United Meth. Ch., Atlanta, 1982—2000. Named to, Atlanta Pub. Schs.' Hall of Fame, 1991; grantee Tchrs. for Excellence in Tchg., Apple Corps Inc., 1987—91. Mem.: PTA, NEA, Ga. Assn. of Edn., Music Educators Nat. Conf., Ga. Music Educators Assn. (dist. V elem. chair 1994—95, state chair Music in Our Schs. Month 1998—, Svc. award 2002, 2003), Heritage Valley Cmty. Club, Zeta Phi Beta, Zeta Phi Beta. United Methodist. Avocations: playing piano, performing in handbell choir, tennis, travel, listening to classical music. Home: 3487 Toll House Ln SW Atlanta GA 30331 Office: Mary McLeod Bethune Elem Sch 220 Northside Dr NW Atlanta GA 30314

GOODMAN, PHYLLIS L. public relations executive; b. N.Y.C., Sept. 7, 1946; d. Bernard Jacob and Claire (Rosenberg) Goodman. BS, Cornell U., 1967. Ext. home economist Nassau County Ext. Svc., Mineola, N.Y., 1967-68; editl. asst. Funk & Wagnalls, N.Y.C., 1968-69; sr. v.p. Glick & Lorwin, Inc., N.Y.C., 1969-80, Sci. and Medicine, N.Y.C., 1980-82; v.p. Hill and Knowlton, Inc., N.Y.C., 1982-85; assoc. v.p. comm. and pub. affairs St. Luke's-Roosevelt Hosp. Ctr., N.Y.C., 1985-92; owner Goodman Pub. Rels., Albuquerque, 1993-95; v.p. corp. comm. Sun Healthcare Group, Inc., Albuquerque, 1995-2000; v.p. mktg. and comms. St. Vincent Hosp., Santa Fe, 2000-01; v.p. mktg. and comm. Cin. Children's Hosp. Med. Ctr., 2001—. Mem. com. pub. affairs Greater N.Y. Hosp. Assn., 1988-92. Bd. dirs. Chamber Music Albuquerque, 1998-2001. Mem. Am. Soc. Health Care Mktg. and Pub. Rels. (treas. N.Mex. chpt. 1993-94), Pub. Rels. Soc. Am. (accredited, pres. N.Mex. chpt. 1996), Healthcare Pub. Rels. and Mktg. Soc. Greater N.Y. (pres. 1990-91), Westside C. of C. N.Y.C. (bd. dirs. 1986-92), Pi Lambda Theta. Office: Cin Childrens Hosp MLC 9102 3333 Burnet Ave Cincinnati OH 45229 Home: 3519 Traskwood Cir Cincinnati OH 45208-1809

GOODMAN, ROBYN S. communications educator; b. Long Beach, Calif., Jan. 24, 1961; d. Lawrence Howard and Sharlene Ellen Goodman. BA in Internat. Rels., Calif. State U., Chico, 1983; MA in Journalism, U. Mo., 1985; PhD in Mass Media, Mich. State U., 1997. Tchg. asst. U. Mo., Columbia, 1984; ESL instr. San Juan Capistrano (Calif.) United Sch. Dist., 1986—87; instr., cultural amb. Moscow Sch. #19, 1989; instr. Beijing Fgn. Studies U., 1988—90, Mich. State U., East Lansing, 1991—95; assoc. prof. comm. studies program Alfred (N.Y.) U., 1995—. Reporter and freelance writer for various newspapers including Simi Valley Enterprise, Orange County Register, Santa Barbara News-Press, Dem. Chronicle, Rochester, NY, 1982—. Contbr. articles to profl. academic jours. Mem.: Chinese Comm. Assn., Internat. Comm. Assn., Assn. for Edn. in Journalism and Mass. Comm. (editl. bd. mem. 2000—, internat. task force chair 2001—, head internat. divsn.). Avocations: travel, reading, writing, hiking, raising animals. Office: Alfred U Comm Studies Program Seidlin 009 Alfred NY 14802 Office Phone: 607-871-2387. E-mail: goodman@rochester.rr.com.

GOODMAN, SHERRI WASSERMAN, lawyer; b. N.Y.C., Apr. 9, 1959; m. John B. Goodman, Aug. 8, 1987. BA, Amherst (Mass.) Coll., 1981; JD, MPP, Harvard U., 1987. Bar: Mass. 1988, D.C. 1990. Analyst Sci. Applications, Inc., McLean, Va., 1981-83; counsel Senate Armed Svcs. Com., Washington, 1987-90; assoc. Goodwin, Procter & Hoar, Boston, 1990-93; dep. under sec. for env. security Dept. Def., Washington, 1993-2000; sr. fellow Ctr. for Naval Analyses, Alexandria, Va., 2001—. Cons. Def. Nuclear Facilities Safety Bd., Washington, 1990-92. Author: The Neutron Bomb Controversy, 1983, Weapons Acquisition, 1988; contbr. articles to profl. jours. Mem. Coun. on Fgn. Rels. Office: The CNA Corp 4825 Mark Center Dr Alexandria VA 22311

GOODMAN, SUSAN, curator; b. Phila. d. Maurice and Carolyn Kunst Tumarkin; m. Jerry Goodman, Oct., 1968; children: Micah, Nina. BA in Art History, U. Pa., 1956; MA in Art History, Columbia U., 1961. Editl., rsch. asst. The Solomon R. Guggenheim Mus., 1965-67; asst. curator The Jewish Mus., 1967-72, chief curator exhibns., 1972-98, sr. curator-at-large, 1999—. Fellow Meml. Found. Jewish Culture; grantee NEA, Trust for Mutual Understanding The Rockefeller Found. Mem. Am. Assn. Mus., N.E. Mus. Assn., N.Y. Assn. New Ams. (visual arts com.), Coll. Art Assn., Arttable. Address: 1140 5th Ave New York NY 10128-0806 Office: The Jewish Mus 1109 5th Ave New York NY 10128-0118 E-mail: sgoodman@thejm.org.

GOODMAN, SUSAN KATHLEEN, charitable organization administrator, educator; b. Seattle, Dec. 29, 1952; d. Robert S. and Barbara J. (Tseka) Campbell. BA with honors in Music, BA with honors in Elem. Edn., Wash. State U., 1976. Dir. St. Francis Episcopal Youth Brass Choir, Tex., 1976-79; pvt. music tchr. Bend, Oreg., 1979—; devel. assoc. St. Charles Med. Ctr. Found., Bend, 1992-96, dir. devel., 1997—. Music dir. Trinity Episcopal Church, 1979-89; adj. prof. French horn Ctrl. Oreg. C.C., 1979-89; substitute tchr. Bend LaPine (Oreg.) schs., 1980-82; team tchr. band Cascade (Oreg.) Jr. H.S., 1982; exec. dir. Cascade Festival Music, 1982-92; mgmt. cons. Oreg. Coast Music Festival, Coos Bay, 1989, Wash. Music Educators Assn., spkr. bd. dirs. retreat, 1993; project dir. Regional Arts Coun. Ctrl. Oreg., 1995; tutor Friends of Thompson Sch., 1992-94. Musician Houston Civic Symphony, 1976-79; prin. hornist, mgr. Ctrl. Oreg. Symphony; prin. hornist Brass and Woodwind Quintets, 1979-89; conductor, arranger, performer, then head coach orchestral ministries Westside Ch., Bend, Oreg., 1995—. Co-chair fundraising banquet, Young Life Ctrl. Oreg.; team leader Family Kitchen; music dir., choirmaster Trinity Episcopal Ch., 1980-89; juror touring programs Oreg. Arts Commn.; alumnus Leadership Bend, 1994—; bd. dirs. Ctrl. Oreg. Youth Choir, 1997—. Recipient Alumni of Yr. Woodway Sr. H.S., 1989, Cmty. Svc. award Ctrl. Oreg. Arts Soc., 1990. Mem. Cursillo Cmty. Ea. (rec. sec. 1995), Bend (Oreg.) C. of C. (mem. leadership com., ambassador 1995), Ctrl. Oreg. Avocations: pastoral music ministry, music performance, youth ministry. Office: St Charles Med Ctr Found 2500 NE Neff Rd Bend OR 97701-6015

GOODMAN, SYLVIA KLUMOK, volunteer; b. Moorhead, Miss., June 19, 1940; d. Sol Harry and Fannie Ida (Davidson) Klumok; m. Carl Gerald Goodman, June 5, 1960; children: Lisa Wynne Goodman Stone, Gary Steven, Jeffry David. BS in Zoology with honors, Newcomb Coll., 1962; M in Zoology, Tulane U., 1963; postgrad., Harvard U., summer 1990. Tchr. Midway Jr. H.S., Shreveport, La., 1963-68; instr. biology La. State U., Shreveport, 1967-68; instr. physiology, asst. coord. plans La. State U. Med. Ctr., Shreveport, 1970-74. Chmn. bd. dirs. Goldring Woldenberg Inst. So. Jewish Life, 2000-03. Mem. Shreveport Mayor's Women's Commn., 1986-90, C. of C. 100 Women of the Century; vice-chair La. State Mineral Bd., Baton Rouge, 1988-92; chmn. Food Project, Shreveport, 1990-92;

chair beautification com. Shreveport Regional Airport, 1990-94, So. Jewish Inst., 2000—; chmn. bd. dirs. Goldring/Woldenberg Inst. So. Jewish Life, 2000—; bd. dirs. Sci-Port Discovery Ctr., Shreveport, 1990—, pres., 1993-95; bd. dirs. La. Endowment Humanities, 1996-99; pres. Shreveport Jewish Fedn., 1982-83; trustee Shreveport-Bossier Cmty. Found., chmn., 1993—; bd. dirs. Meadows Art Mus., 1991-97, vice chmn., 1995; bd. dirs. La. Film Theater, 2003—, chair capital campaign, 2003; chancellor's adv. com. LSU-S, 1996—. Recipient Humanitarian award NCCJ, Humanitarian award Caddo Commn., 1991, Vol. Fundraiser award Nat. Fedn. Fundraising Execs., 1996, Angel award Blue Cross Blue Shield, 1998, award Point of Light Found., 1999, Friend of Edn. aard Caddo Assn. Educators, 2001; named Women Who Made a Difference Shreveport Celebration of Women Week, 1996, Best-Dressed Woman of No. La. Shreveport Times, 1998. Mem. Jr. League Shreveport (Sustainer of Yr. award 1995, Daily Point of Light 1999), Mensa, Phi Beta Kappa, Alpha Epsilon Phi. Jewish. Avocations: theater, piano, dance, taking courses, movies. Home: 409 Southfield Rd Shreveport LA 71106-2213 E-mail: gigigood@aol.com.

GOODMAN, VALERIE DAWSON, psychiatric social worker; b. Bluefield, W.Va., Feb. 2, 1948; d. Francis Carl and Lesly (Collett) Dawson; m. David William Goodman, June 9, 1985; 1 child, Amanda Lynn. BS, W.Va. U., 1970, MS, 1972; MSW, U. Md., 1980. Lic. clin. social worker, Md. Social worker Md. Children's Aide Family Svcs. Soc., Balt., 1972-78; social worker III Montgomery County Dept. Social Svcs., Rockville, Md., 1980-81; clin. social worker Johns Hopkins Hosp., Balt., 1981-83; pvt. practice Suburban Psychiat. Assoc. Hopkins at Greenspring Station, Balt., 1986—. Supr. Johns Hopkins Hosp., 1983-86, chair Brogden com., 1984-85, spl. events com. depression and related affective disorders dept. psychiatry, 1994; spkr. in field. Parent vol. Park Sch. Mem. Kappa Delta. Avocations: reading, piano, gourmet cooking, weightlifting. Home: 54 Bellchase Ct Pikesville MD 21208-1300 Office: Suburban Psychiat Svc Md Adult Ctr ADD Johns Hopkins at Greenspring Sta Falls Concourse Falls Rd Ste 306 Lutherville MD 21093

GODMAN-MILONE, CONSTANCE BETH, writer; b. Phila., Sept. 3, 1963; d. Marvin Joshua and Linda Goodman; m. David C. Milone, May 5, 2002. BA in Psychology, George Washington U., Wash., DC, 1985; MSW, Barry U., Miami Shores, Fla., 1999. Freelance writer, Phila., 1987—90, N.Y.C., 1990—96; social work intern Vets. Adminstrn. Med. Ctr., Miami, 1999; case mgr. Health South Drs. Hosp., Skilled Nursing, Coral Gables, Fla., 2000; freelance writer Miami, 2001—. Author: (poetry, photo) Medicinal Purposes Lit. Rev., 1995—2003, (poem, article, photos) Vitas Vital Signs, 2001—03, (poem) Today's Caregiver, 2002. Mem. Dem. Nat. Com., Washington, 1996—; hospice vol. Vitas Healthcare, Miami, 2000—; leadership coun. So. Poverty Law Ctr., Montgomery, Ala., 2002—; charter mem. Amnesty Internat. Women's Action Coun., N.Y.C., 2003; chair creative writing contest Jr. Orange Bowl Com., Coral Gables, Fla., 2003—. Mem.: Assn. for Death Edn. and Counseling South Fla. chpt. (cmty. pub. rels. 2002—), Nat. Writers Union, South Fla. Writers Assn. (v.p. mktg. 2003—, Bill Katzker Mem. of Yr. award 2003, Bereavement Vol. of Yr. Vitas Dade Program 2001), Soc. Social Work Leaders in Health Care (Fla. Chpt.), Nat. Assn. Social Workers, Nat. Assn. Poetry Therapy. Democrat. Jewish. Avocations: volunteering, photography, tennis, walking, books. Home and Office: 12920 SW 95 Ave Miami FL 33176 E-mail: cgmilone@bellsouth.net.

GOODSPEED, BARBARA, artist; b. Sept. 1, 1919; d. George Daniel and Bernice (Lucas) G. Diploma, Stoneleigh Coll., 1939, Famous Artist Schs., Westport, Conn., 1955. Freelance photographer, N.Y.C., 1941-52; Christmas card designer Sherman, Conn., 1952-69; oil and watercolor, fine arts artist, 1969—. Forever Flowers, 1979; contbr. Best of Oil Painting, Best of Watercolor-Light and Shadow, Landscape Inspirations, Best of Watercolor, Vol. 3, The Complete Best of Watercolor. Recipient Merit award Sheffield Arts League, 1979, 81, 83, others; named Artist of Yr., Art League of Harlem Valley, 1981. Fellow Am. Artists Profl. League (John Dole Meml. award, Parsons award 1991); mem. Salmagundi Club (Jane Peterson Meml. award, Samuel Shaw Meml. award 1997, Arthur Hill award 1998), Hudson Valley Art Assn. (bd. mem.), Acad. Artists, Nat. League Am. Pen Women, Allied Artist Am. (N.Y.C.), Butler Mus., Kent Art Assn. (trustee), Inc. (pres. 1970-72, 80-83, 85-88, 91-93, 97, 98, medal of Merit 1979, Grumbacher Gold medal 1989, 91, K.A.A. award 1995, 96, 97), Housatonic Art League (v.p., bd. dirs. 1977-83), Catharine Lorillard Wolfe Art Club (bd. dirs. 1990-93, 98-01, travel show 1996, Corp. award). Avocations: camping, crafts. Home: 11 Holiday Point Rd Sherman CT 06784-1624 E-mail: bgoodspeedb@aol.com.

GOODSPEED, KATHRYN ANN, pre-school educator; b. Elgin, Ill., Oct. 2, 1939; d. Earle Muller and Ruby Vera Curtiss; m. Robert Harrison Goodspeed, Feb. 4, 1961; children: Julie, Jill, Jerry, Jeff, Jennifer. BS, No. Ill. U., 1961. Tchr. spl. edn. Sch. of Hope, Rockford, Ill., 1962—65; home day care provider, 1971—78; tchr. presch., dir. Melrose DayCare Ctr., Iowa City, 1978—89, tchr. Blind Children's Learning Ctr., Santa Ana, Calif., 1989—92, dir. early childhood ctr., 1992—2001, asst. exec. dir., 2001—. Bd. pres. So. Calif. Network Serving Infants and Preschool Children with Visual Impairments, 1998. Co-treas. Joint Action Com. Visually Impaired, Calif., 1997—; co-chair Infant Vendor Com., Santa Ana, 2000; edn. commn. head Yorba Linda United Meth. Ch., 1998—2002. Named Laywoman of Yr., Yorba Linda United Meth. Ch., 2000. Mem.: Family Support Ntetwork Bd., Assn. for Edn. and Rehab. Blind and Visually Impaired, Coun. Exceptional Children, Calif. Transcribers & Educators Multihandicapped Specialist, Calif. First Chance Consortium (bd. dir., family support network com., mem. camp TLC). Avocations: reading, cooking, travel. Home: 856 Amber Ln Anaheim CA 92807

GOODSPEED, LINDA A. manufacturing executive; BSME, Mich. State U., 1984, MA in Bus. Adminstrn., 1989. Engr. Ford Motor Co., 1984—89; with R&D dept. Nissan, 1989—96; with GE, 1996—2001, range product devel. mgr., 1997, gen. mgr. Six Sigma divsn., 1999, product gen. mgr. GE Appliances, 1999—2001; pres., COO Partminer, Inc., 2001; chief tech. officer Lennox Internat., Richardson, Tex., 2001—. Office: Lennox Internat 2140 Lake Park Blvd Richardson TX 75080

GOODSPEED, MARGARET LOUISE, film editor; d. Raymond Ellis and Patricia Davey Goodspeed; 1 child, Gemma Goodspeed Allen. BA in Theatre Arts and Rhetoric, AB in English Lit., Occidental Coll., 1985. Freelance asst. film editor, LA, 1986—92; freelance film editor, 1992—. Assistant film editor (films) Bull Durham, Broadcast News; editor: (films) The Lizzie McGuire Movie, An American Rhapsody, Morgan's Ferry, Free Willy 3 The Rescue, The Spitfire Grill, (TV films) Snow White: The Fairest of Them All, If These Walls Could Talk II. Mem.: Motion Picture Editors Guild (bd. dir. 1990—92). Personal E-mail: bonyday@aol.com.

GOODSTEIN-SHAPIRO, FLORENCE (FLORENCE GOODSTEIN WALTON), art historian; b. N.Y.C., July 22, 1931; d. Philip and Cecelia (Pletchnow) Goodstein; m. Ivan Shapiro, June 24, 1951 (div. Jan. 1957); 1 child, Lisa Jean Shapiro; m. John A. Walton, Sept. 30, 1968. BS, CCNY, 1952; student, Cooper Union Inst., N.Y.C., 1950-52, Hans Hofmann Sch. Fine Arts, 1956-58, U. Calif., Long Beach, 1970-71; MA in Art History, U. Minn., 1973. Asst. prof. art history Lakewood Coll., White Bear Lake, Minn., 1971-72; lectr. art history Mpls. Inst. Art, 1973-74. Bd. dirs. Banfill-Locke Cmty. Art Ctr., Fridley, Minn., 1981. Exhibited in shows at Roko Gallery, N.Y.C., 1962, Smithsonian Inst., Washington, 1963, Aspects Gallery, N.Y.C., 1964, Loeb Gallery/NYU, 1966, Los Angeles County Art Mus., 1969, Bonython Gallery, Sydney, Australia, 1969, Peter M. David Gallery, Mpls., 1985, 91, Artbanque, Mpls., 1986, Coll. St. Catherine, St. Paul, 1988, McGallery, Mpls., 1994, Groveland Gallery, Mpls., 1998, Klevit Fine Arts Gallery, Silver Springs, MD, 1999, Johnson Heritage Post Art Gallery, Grand Marais, 1999, Mifa Artists Gallery, 2000; represented in collections at 3M Co., St. Paul, U. Minn. Mus., Martin Luther King Jr. Mus., Atlanta, Fairview Southdale Hosp., Mpls., Ctrl. Lakes C.C., Brainerd, Minn., Boyadjian Collection, Zurich, Ethan Coen, NYC, others. Mem. Cooper Union Alumni Assn. Democrat. Jewish. Avocations: camping, gardening, travel, sewing, reading. Office: Goodstein-Shapiro Studio 9983 Egret Blvd NW Coon Rapids MN 55433-6402 Office Phone: 763-767-2535. E-mail: goodsteinshapiro@aol.com.

GOODWIN, BECKY K. educational technology resource educator; Sci. tchr. USD 233 Sch. Dist., Olathe, Kans. Christa McAuliffe fellowship grantee State of Kans., 1992, 94, 97; named Kans. Tchr. of Yr., 1995; recipient Presdl. award for Excellence in Sci. and Math. Secondary Sci. for Kans., 1992, Outstanding Biology Tchr. award Nat. Assn. Biology Tchrs., 1992, Sci. Teaching Achievement Recognition Star award NSTA, 1993, Milken Nat. Educator award, 1995, Tandy Tech. Tchr. award, 1998. Office: USD 233 14090 Black Bob Rd Olathe KS 66063

GOODWIN, DORIS HELEN KEARNS, historian; b. Rockville Centre, N.Y., Jan. 4, 1943; d. Michael Alouisius and Helen Witt (Miller) Kearns; m. Richard Goodwin, 1975; children: Richard, Michael, Joseph. BA magna cum laude, Colby Coll., 1964; PhD, Harvard U., 1968. Intern Dept. State, D.C., 1963, Ho. of Reps., D.C., 1965; rsch. assoc. U.S. Dept. Health, Edn., and Welfare, D.C., 1966; spl. asst. to Willard Wirtz U.S. Dept. Labor, DC, 1967; staff asst. to President Lyndon B. Johnson, 1968; prof. govt. Harvard U., Cambridge, 1969—79; historian. Spl. cons. to President Johnson, 1969-73; hostess "What's the Big Idea", WGBH-TV, Boston, 1972; polit. analyst news desk, WBZ-TV, Boston, 1972; mem. Women's Polit. Caucus, Mass., 1972, Dem. Party Platform Com., 1972; reg. panelist News Hour with Jim Lehrer; commentator NBC, MSNBC. Author: Lyndon Johnson and the American Dream, 1976, The Fitzgeralds and the Kennedys: An American Saga, 1987, No Ordinary Time: Franklin and Eleanor Roosevelt- :The Homefront in World War II, 1994 (Pulitzer Prize for history 1995), Wait Till Next Year: A Memoir, 1997, numerous articles on politics and baseball; contbr.: Telling Lives: The Biographer's Art, 1979; forward: Mortal Friends: A Novel, 1992. Trustee Wesleyan U., Colby Coll., Robert F. Kennedy Found. Named Fulbright fellow, 1966, White House fellow, 1967, Mem. Am. Polit. Sci. Assn., Coun. Fgn. Relations, Women Involved, Group for Applied Psychoanalysis, Signet Soc., Phi Beta Kappa (outstanding young women of yr. award 1966), Phi Sigma Iota. Roman Catholic. Office: c/o Dori Lawson Soldier Creek Assoc PO Box 477 Rockport ME 04856*

GOODWIN, GRETA HALL, state legislator; m. James G. Goodwin. Legal asst., 1988—; mem. Kans. Ho. of Reps from 78th dist., Topeka, 1993-97, Kans. Senate from 32nd dist., Topeka, 1997—. Home: 420 E 12th Ave Winfield KS 67156-3721 Office: Kans Senate Chambers State Capitol Topeka KS 66612 E-mail: ggoodwin@ink.org.

GOODWIN, JEAN MCCLUNG, psychiatrist; b. Pueblo, Colo., Mar. 28, 1946; d. Paul Stanley and Geraldine (Smart) McClung; m. James Simeon Goodwin, Aug. 8, 1970; children: Laura (dec.), Amanda Harding Goodwin, Robert Caleb, Paul Joshua, Elizabeth Cronin Goodwin. BA in Anthropology summa cum laude, Radcliffe Coll., 1967; MD, Harvard U., 1971; MPH, UCLA, 1972. Diplomate Am. Bd. Psychiatry and Neurology, Am. Bd. Forensic Psychiatry; added qualifications in forensic psychiatry, psychoanalytic tng. Resident in psychiatry Georgetown U. Hosp., Washington, 1972-74, U. N.Mex. Sch. Medicine, 1974-76, asst. dir., dir. psychiat. residents tng., 1979-85; prof. Med. Coll. Wis., 1985-92, U. Tex. Med. Br., Galveston, 1992-98, prof. clin. psychiatry, 1998—; pvt. practice in gen. psychiatry, psychoanalysis. From instr. to assoc. prof. dept. psychiatry U. N.Mex. Sch. Medicine, 1976-85; cons. protective services Dept. Human Services, N.Mex., 1976-84; lectr. profl. groups; faculty Houston-Galveston Psychoanalytic Inst., 1999—; founding bd. mem. Houston-Galveston Trauma Inst., 2002—. Author: Effects of High Altitude on Human Birth, 1969, Sexual Abuse: Incest Victims and Their Families, 1982, 2d edit., 1989, Rediscovering Childhood Trauma: Historical Casebook and Clinical Applications, 1993, Mischief and Mercy, 1993; co-author (with Reina Attias) Splintered Reflections: Images of the Body in Trauma, 1999; mem. editl. bd. Jour. Traumatic Stress, 1985-93, Dissociation, 1988-98, Psychotherapy Rev., 1998-2000, Trauma and Dissociation, 2000—; contbr. numerous articles on child abuse to profl. jours. Chmn. work group on child sexual abuse Surgeon Gen.'s Conf. on Violence and Pub. Health, Leesburg, Va., 1985; mem. adv. bd. Nat. Resource Ctr. on Child Sexual Abuse, 1989-96. Recipient Esther Haar award Am. Acad. Psychoanalysis, 1990, Cornelia Wilbur award Internat. Soc. for Study of Dissociation, 1994; Nat. Cen. Child Abuse and Neglect grantee, 1979-82, Nat. Inst. Aging grantee, 1980-85. Fellow Internat. Soc. Study Dissociation (exec. com. 1991-96), Am. Psychiat. Assn. (dist. br. treas., sec. N.Mex. br. 1980-82, exhibits and programs subcoms. 1985-91); mem. Am. Profl. Soc. on Sexual Abuse in Children (bd. dirs. 1986-90). Democrat. Roman Catholic. Office: 4925 Fort Crockett Blvd Apt 510 Galveston TX 77551-5949 Office Phone: 409-762-1101. E-mail: jmgoodwin@aol.com.

GOODWIN, MARYELLEN, state legislator; b. Providence, Sept. 27, 1964; BS, R.I. Coll., 1988. mem. 12th Ward Dem. Com., R.I. Young Dems. Mem., Dist. 1 R.I. Senate, Providence, 1986—. Roman Catholic. Home: 325 Smith St Providence RI 02908-3759 Office: RI State Senate State House Rm 312 Providence RI 02903

GOODWIN, NANCY LEE, corporate executive; b. Peoria, Ill., Aug. 11, 1940; d. Raymond Darrell and Mildred Louise (Brown) G. BA (Nat. Meth. scholar, Nat. Merit scholar), MacMurray Coll., 1961; MA, U. Colo., 1963; PhD, U. Ill., 1971. Tchr. Roosevelt Jr. High Sch., Peoria, 1961-62; counselor U. Ill., Urbana, 1963-66, staff assoc., asst. prof. edn. measurement Chgo., 1967-71; asst. v.p., assoc. prof. stats. Fla. Internat. U., Miami, 1971-78; pres. Greenfield (Mass.) Community Coll., 1978-82, Arapahoe Community Coll., Colo., from 1982; corp. owner MTF Enterprises; prof. Nat. U.; owner C.A.T.S. Inc., 1987—; corp. mgr. DRM Enterprises. Dir. Cons. Mid-Am. Computer Corp., First Chance Network U.S. Office Edn., 1972-78 Mem. Com. on Ill. Govt., Higher Edn. Task Force; mem. Vol. Action Center, Miami, 1972-78; active Girl Scouts U.S.A.; mem. Franklin/Hampshire Area Service Planning Team, 1978; incorporator Franklin County (Mass.) United Way, Farren Meml. Hosp.; adv. Franklin County Public Hosp.; bd. dirs. Women's Inst. Fla., Franklin County Arts Council, Franklin County Devel. Corp., Western Welcome Week, Inc.; bd. dirs., mem. fin. monitoring com. New Eng. Soy Dairy, 1980. Recipient Merit award Chgo. Tchrs. Assn., 1969; citation Girl Scouts U.S.A., 1973 Mem. NEA, Am. Assn. Higher Edn., Am. Ednl. Research Assn., Assn. Instl. Research, Centennial C. of C. (dir. 1983) Home: 5228 Del Rey Ave Las Vegas NV 89146-1414

GOODWIN, NEVA R. economist; b. N.Y.C., June 1, 1944; children: David Kaiser, Miranda Kaiser; m. Bruce Mazlish. BA, Harvard Coll., 1962; MPA, Kennedy Sch. of Govt., 1982; PhD, Boston U., 1987; BA (hon.), Coll. of the Atlantic, Bar Harbor, Maine, 1990. Dir. Program for Study of Sustainable Change and Devel. Tufts U., Medford, Mass., 1991-94, co-dir. Global Devel. And Environment Inst., 1994—. Author: Social Economics: An Alternative Theory, 1991; series editor: (6 books) Frontier Issues in Economic Thought, 1995; editor: As If the Future Mattered: Translating Social and Economic Theory into Human Behavior, 1996; editor jour. spl. issue World Devel., 1991. Trustee Winrock Internat. Inst. for Agrl. Devel., 1986—; mem. task force on population and consumption Pres.'s Coun. on Sustainable Devel., 1995; mem. adv. coun. Coll. of the Atlantic, 1996—; vice chair bd. Coll. of the Atlantic, Bar Harbor, 1981-90. Avocations: gardening, cooking, bicycling, hiking. Office: Tufts U G-DAE Fletcher Sch Medford MA 02155

GOODWIN, SHARON ANN, academic administrator; b. Little Rock, May 19, 1949; d. Jimmy Lee and Eddie DeLois (Cluck) G.; m. Mitchell Shayne Mick, May 4, 1968 (div. Mar. 1973); 1 child, Heather Michelle; m. Raymond Eugene Vaclavik, June 24, 1974 (div. Aug. 1982); 1 child, Tasha Rae Vaclavik. BA in Psychology, U. Houston-Clear Lake, 1980; MEd in Higher Edn. Adminstrn., U. Houston, 1990. Various clerical positions Gen. Telephone Co., Dickinson, Tex., 1969-80; state dir. Challenge, Inc., Oklahoma City, 1980-82; gen. mgr. Mr. Fix It, Houston, 1982-85; assoc. dir. admissions U. Houston, Tex., 1985-92; adminstr. Inst. for the Med. Humanities U. Tex. Med. Br., Galveston, 1992—. Contbr. poetry to World of Poetry Anthology, 1986, 87, 90, 91, Nat. Libr. of Poetry Anthology, 1997, 99, 2001, SOL Mag., 1997-2000, Lucidity Jour., 1997, New Winds Jour., 1997, Galveston Writers Anthology, 1998-99, Nat. Poetry Guild Anthology, 1998; author (poetry exhibited) Moody Med. Libr., UTMB, 2003. Mem. legis. com. Comm. Workers, Dickinson and Austin, 1975; mem. centennial choir U. Tex. Med. Br., Galveston, 1992-2000; vol. Dickens on the Strand, Galveston, 1993-2000. Recipient award of merit World of Poetry Anthology, 1986, 91, Golden Poet award, 1987, Silver Poet award, 1990, rd 1990, Golden Poet award, 1991, hon. mention SOL Mag., 1997, 98, 1st pl., 1998, 2d pl., 1998; named to Internat. Poetry Hall of Fame, 1997. Avocations: travel, music, sports, books, movies. Office: Univ Tex Med Br Inst for the Med Humanities 301 University Blvd Galveston TX 77555-1311 Home: PO Box 1346 League City TX 77574

GOODWIN, STEPHANIE RUTH, art educator, finance educator; d. Ferlyn Wallace and Esther Ruth Korf; 1 child, Wade. BA, Ft. Hays State U., 1974. Instr. art edn. Lewis Pub. Schs., Kans., 1974—76; youth svc. worker Youth Ctr. At Larned, Kans., 1984—88; instr. art edn. USD 318, Atwood, Kans., 1988—2003; instr. bus. edn. USD 105, Atwood, 2003—. Pres and treas. Atwood Arts Coun., 1989—2003. Co-organizer Heartland Share, Atwood, 1997—2003. Mem.: Am. Legion, Theta Kappa. Avocations: gardening, needlecrafts, quilting. Home: 315 S 2d St Atwood KS 67730

GOODY, JOAN EDELMAN, architect; b. N.Y.C., Dec. 1, 1935; d. Beril and Sylvia (Feldman) Edelman; m. Marvin E. Goody, Dec. 18, 1960 (dec. 1980); m. Peter H. Davison, Aug. 11, 1984. BA, Cornell U., 1956; MArch, Harvard U., 1960. Registerd architect, Mass., Conn., Maine, Md., N.Y., R.I. Prin. Goody, Clancy & Assocs., Inc., Boston. Asst. prof., design critic Harvard U., Cambridge, Mass., 1973-80, Eliot Noyes vis. critic, 1985; faculty Mayors Inst. for Design, 1989—; lectr. in field. Mem. Boston Landmarks Commn., 1976-87; chair Boston Civic Design Commn.; bd. dirs. Historic Boston. Fellow AIA (hon. award 1980), Boston Soc. Architects (bd. dirs. 1983-85, design awards), Boston Archtl. Ctr. (hon.), Saturday Club, Tavern Club. Office: Goody Clancy & Assocs Inc 334 Boylston St Boston MA 02116-3866

GOOGINS, SONYA FORBES, state legislator, retired banker; b. New Haven, Nov. 9, 1936; d. Edward and Madeline Forbes; m. Robert Reville Googins, June 21, 1958; children: Shawn W. and Glen. R. BE, U. Conn., 1958. Tchr. Manchester (Conn.) High Sch., 1958-61; pres. Colonial Printing Co., Glastonbury, 1971-76; bank officer Conn. Nat. Bank, Hartford, 1982-89; mem. Conn. Ho. of Reps., 1994—. Mem. employment and tng. commn. Greater Hartford United Way, Conn., 1995—; vice-chair commerce Nat. Conf. State Legislatures; mayor Town of Glastonbury, 1983—85, 1987—91, 1993—95; mem. Town Coun., 1979—94, Rep. Town Com., Capitol Region Coun. Govts., 1983—94, chmn., 1989—94; chair Conn. Adv. Commn. Intergovtl. Rels., 1997—; chair fin. svc. com. Nat. Conf. of State Legislators, 2002—; advocacy com. Am. Diabetes Assn.; bd. dirs. Conn. Capitol Region Growth Coun., 1994—96, Conn. Audubon Soc., 1997—99, Hartford Symphony Orch., 1997—. Recipient Outstanding Svc. award Friends of Glastonbury Youth, 1990, Disting. Svc. award Capitol Region Coun., 1994; named Glastonbury Rep. of Yr., 1992. Mem. Hartford Cin. Auto Assn. Am. (bd. dirs. 1994—), Glastonbury Bus. and Profl. Women (past pres. and founder, Woman of Yr. 1988), Glastonbury C. of C. (past pres., bd. dirs. 1994—), Glastonbury Jr. Woman's Club. Roman Catholic. Avocations: golf, tennis, sailing. Home: 74 Forest Ln Glastonbury CT 06033-3918 E-mail: smya.googins@po.state.ct.us.

GOOLKASIAN, PAULA A. psychologist, educator; b. Methuen, Mass., Aug. 9, 1948; d. Paul K. and Sadie T. (Touma) G.; m. Francis C. Martin, July 29, 1978; 1 child, Christopher. BA, Emmanuel Coll., 1970; MS, Iowa State U., 1972, PhD, 1974. Asst. prof. U. N.C., Charlotte, 1974-79, assoc. prof., 1979-85, prof. psychology, 1985—, pres. faculty, 1989—. Cons. in field. Contbr. articles to profl. jours. NDEA fellow, 1971-74; grantee NSF, NIH, numerous others. Mem. AAAS, APA, Am. Psychol. Soc., Psychonomics Soc., Soc. for Computers in Psychology (sec.-treas. 1989-91, pres. 1994), Sigma Xi, Phi Kappa Phi. Home: 20125 River Chase Dr Cornelius NC 28031-7175 Office: U NC Dept Psychology Charlotte NC 28223 E-mail: pagoolka@email.uncc.edu.

GOOLSBY, MICHELLE, lawyer, food products executive; b. 1958; BBA, JD, U. Tex. Various positions Trammel Crow Co., Winstead Sechrest & Minick, 1988-98; ptnr., chair bus. sect., mem. compensation com.; exec. v.p., gen. counsel, sec. Suiza Foods Corp., Dallas, 1998—. Mem. ABA. Office: 2515 Mckinney Ave Ste 1200 Dallas TX 75201-1945

GOOREY, NANCY JANE, dentist; b. Davenport, Iowa, May 8, 1922; d. Edgar Ray and Glenna Mae (Williams) Miller; m. Douglas B. Miller, Sept. 12, 1939 (div. 1951); children: Victoria Lee, Nickola Ellen, Douglas George, Melahna Marie; m. Louis Joseph Roseberry Goorey, Feb. 22, 1980. Student, Wooster (Ohio) Coll., 1939-40; DDS, Ohio State U., 1955. Cert. in gen. anesthesiology. Mem. faculty coll. dentistry Ohio State U., Columbus, 1955-86, dir., chmn. div. dental hygiene coll. dentistry, 1969-86, asst. dean coll. dentistry, 1975-86, mem. grad. faculty colls. dentistry and medicine, 1980-86, asst. dean, prof. emeritus colls. dentistry, 1986—. Moderator, prodn. chmn. Lifesavers 40 Prodns., 1981—; mem. task force on sch. based-linked oral health project Ohio Dept. Health, 1999—. Producer, video program Giving Your Mouth a Sporting Chance, 1990, video Operation TACTIC. Chmn. State Planning Com. for Health Edn. in Ohio, Columbus, 1976-77, 87-88, 95-97; founder Coun. on Health Info., Columbus, 1980, del., 1981-85, chmn., pres., 1985-86, chmn. prodn. com., 1986-2003, chmn. mktg. com., 2003—, chmn. Capital Campaign; trustee Caring Dentists Found., Mayor's Drug Edn. and Prevention Program, Columbus, 1980—; mem. exec. com. Franklin County Rep. com., exec. com., 1993—; mem. human svcs. com. The Columbus Found.; pres. Worthington Arts Coun., 1998-2000, chmn. Capital Campaign, 2000-. Recipient Vol. of Yr. award Columbus Health Dept., 1988-89, Dental Hygiene Nancy J. Goorey award Ohio State U., 1988, Drug Free Sch. Consortium award, 1996, Champion of Children's Oral Health award Ohio Dept. of Health Dental Divsn., 1997, Disting. Alumnus award Ohio State U. Coll. Dentistry, YWCA Women of Achievement award, 2000, Disting. Svc. award Ohio Dental Assn., 2003-. Fellow: Internat. Coll. Dentists, Am. Soc. Dental Anesthesiology, Am. Coll. Dentists (chmn.-elect 1989—90, chmn. Columbus sect.); mem.: ADA (nat. consumer advisor 1975—78, coun. edn. and licensure 1997—), Cols. Med. Assoc. Mem. Sports Med. Comm., Ohio Dept. Health (sch. linked oral health project 1999), Ohio State Med. Assn. Alliance (chmn. state com. legis. affairs 1993—94, chmn. state health promotions com. 1994—95, v.p. 1995—97, pres.-elect 1997, pres. 1998), The Found. of the Acad. of Medicine (v.p. 1993—94), Columbus Dental Soc. (pres. bd. dirs. 1986—87, 1989—91, chmn. coun. on constn. and bilaws on jud. affairs 1989—2003, chmn. sports dentistry com. 1995—), Ohio Dental Assn. (cons. 1979—, mem. subcoun. on dentists concerned for dentists 1994—96, chmn. subcoun. chem. dependency, prin. investigator, chair smokeless tobacco rsch., Ohio Disting. Dentist 1983, Disting. Svc. award 2002, 2003), Am. Assn. Dental Schs. (pres. 1972—77, v.p.), Caring Dentists Found. (trustee), The Columbus Found. (human svcs. com.), Acad. of Medicine Aux. (pres. 1992—93, 1996—97, chair mouthguard project), Ohio State U. Faculty and

Profl. Womens Club (pres. 1971—72), Ohio State U. Starling Womens Club (pres. 1982—83), Omicron Kappa Upsilon. Republican. Episcopalian. Avocations: camping, travel, bridge, cooking, wine. Office: Ohio State U Coll Dentistry 305 W 12th Ave Columbus OH 43210-1267

GOOSEY, KARMEN EILEEN, nurse; b. Milan, Mo., Sept. 18, 1961; d. James Edward and Reta Lucille (Haley) Wohler; m. Rick Wayne Goosey, Nov. 4, 1989; children: Jacob Adam, Tara Ann. BSN summa cum laude, Avila Coll., 1983; MSN, U. Mo., Kansas City, 1997. RN, Mo.; cert. FNP Mo. State Bd. Nursing; cert. Am. Nurses Credentialing Ctr. Nurse North Kansas City (Mo.) City Hosp., 1982—, mem. policy and procedure com., 1988-89; nurse Richards Gebaur Tri Care Clinic Spectrum Healthcare Svcs., Kansas City, 1998-99, Garden City (Mo.) Med. Clinic, Cass Med. Ctr., 1999—. RN, dialysis nurse Cmty. Dialysis Svc., North Kansas City, 1984-89; RN, Lee's Summit (Mo.) Hosp., 1984-89, Liberty (Mo.) Hosp., 1988-91; flight nurse Spirit of Kansas City (Mo.) Life Flight, St. Joseph Health Ctr., 1989-91, policy and procedure chairperson, 1990-91; clin. nurse Northland Cardiology Dr. J. Miller, North Kansas City, 1992—; case mgr. Gini L. Toyne & Assocs., Inc., Kansas City, 1996—. Named Clin. Nurse of Yr., Greater Kansas City Chpt. Emergency Nurses Assn., 1994. Mem. Am. Acad. Nurse Practitioners (cert.), Nurse Practitioner Networking, Balloon Fedn. Am., Phi Kappa Phi, Sigma Theta Tau. Avocations: hot air ballooning, needlepoint, cross stitch, cooking, reading. Home: 16402 S Walnut Grove Rd Pleasant Hill MO 64080-8321

GOOTEE, TARA RENEE, independent kitchen consultant; b. Louisville, Jan. 11, 1973; d. Harry Ray Koons and Janice Marie Koons Tucker; m. John Phillip Gootee, July 1991; 1 child, Austin. BA in Psychology, Purdue U., West Lafayette, Ind., 1995; MS in Marriage and Family Therapy, Purdue U.-Calumet, Hammond, Ind., 1998. Introductory psychology tchr. Purdue U. Calumet, Hammond, Ind., 1995-97; marriage, family therapist Ill., 1996-98; acad. advisor Purdue U. Calumet, Hammond, 1997-98; ednl. counselor Kentuckiana Coll. Access Ctr., Louisville, 1998-2000. Ind. kitchen cons. Pampered Chef; spkr., presenter in field. Contbr. chpts. to books. Vol., blood donor ARC, North Vernon, Ind., 1990—93; vol. Floyd Meml. Hosp. and Health Svcs., 2000—; mem. Lanesville Jaycees, 2000—01. O. Bundrants and J. Eubanks ednl. grantee, 1991-97, Purdue U.-Calumet grant, 1997. Republican. Baptist. Avocations: arts and crafts, movies, reading.

GOOTMAN, PHYLLIS MYRNA, physiology, neuroscience and biophysics educator; b. N.Y.C., June 8, 1938; d. Albert and Ida (Krieger) Adler; m. Norman Gootman, June 1, 1958; children: Sharon Hillary, Craig Seth. BA cum laude, Barnard Coll., 1959; PhD, Yeshiva U., 1967. Rsch. assoc. dept. physiology and biophysics U. Wash., Seattle, 1963; instr. dept. physiology Albert Einstein Coll. Medicine, Bronx, N.Y., 1968-70, asst. prof., 1970-73, SUNY, Bklyn., 1973-75, assoc. prof., 1975-81, prof., 1981-98, prof. dept. pediatrics, 1997—, prof. dept. physiology and pharmacology, 1998—. Vis. asst. prof. dept. physiology Albert Einstein Coll. Medicine, Bronx, 1973-76, vis. prof. dept. Physiology and Biophysics, 1984-92; mem. clin. campus, 1989—. Contbr. articles to profl. jours.; mem. editl. bd. Jour. of Development Physiology, 1986-95, Jour. Sudden Infant Death Syndrome and Child Mortality, 1996-99, Clin. Autonomic Rsch., 1997—. Recipient Hendel Family award Brandeis U., 1957; John Miles Davidson fellow in physiology Albert Einstein Coll. Medicine, 1973; recipient numerous grants. Fellow Royal Soc. Medicine; mem. AAAS, Soc. for Neuroscis., Biophys. Soc., Am. PHysiol. Soc., Am. Heart Assn., Am. Inst. Biol. Scis., Am. Autonomic Soc. (exec. bd.), Microcirculatory Soc., Soc. for Exptl. Biology and Medicine, Am. Assn. Lab Animal Sci., Internat. Soc. for Devel. of Neuroscis. Office: SUNY Health Sci Ctr Bklyn Dept Physiology and Pharmacology Box 31 450 Clarkson Ave Brooklyn NY 11203-2056

GOOTNICK, MARGERY FISCHBEIN, lawyer; b. Rochester, N.Y., Oct. 24, 1927; d. Morris R. and Regina (Kroll) Fischbein; m. Lester T. Gootnick, Mar. 1, 1952; children— Jonathon, David, Amy. B.A., Harvard U., 1949; J.D., Cornell U., 1952. Bar: N.Y. 1952. Assoc. Stone & Hoffenberg, Rochester, N.Y., 1952-55; sole practice, Rochester, 1968—; permanent arbitrator Am. Airlines and Assn. Profl. Flight Attendants, NW Airlines and Teamsters Local 2000, Presbyn. Hosp.-N.Y. State Nurses Assn., U. Rochester and U. Rochester Security Guards Union, numerous others; chmn. Fgn. Service Impasse Disputes Panel, Washington, 1983-97; apptd. fgn. svc. grievance bd. U.S. State Dept., 1997; mem. exec. com. N.Y. State Bar, 1998. Mem. Rep. Jud. Screening Com., Rochester, 1976—. Mem. ABA, Fed. Bar Assn., Nat. Acad. Arbitrators (v.p. 1992-94, chair membership com. 1988-91, exec. com. 1987, bd. govs. 1983-86), N.Y. State Bar Assn. (labor and employment sect. chair elect 1994—, exec. com. 1982—), Soc. Fed. Labor Rels. Profls. (1st v.p. 1993—), Am. Arbitration Assn. (upstate N.Y. labor adv. panel). Office e-mail: mornings@ix.netcom.com. Home and Office: 46 Knollwood Dr Rochester NY 14618-3513

GOPMAN, BETH ALSWANGER, retired elementary school educator; d. Abraham Harry and Frieda (Lelowsky) Alswanger; m. Herbert Leon Gopman, Mar. 5, 1955; children: Paulette, Judith, Jonathan. BEd, U. Miami, Coral Gables, Fla., 1955; MS in Elem. Edn., Nova U., 1980. Cert. state cert. pre-sch., elem. edn. Fla. Tchr. kindergarten, 1st and 2d grades Dade County Pub. Sch., Miami; ret. Bd. dirs. Commn. on Status of Women, Miami Beach, Hearing and Speech Ctr., Miami. Author: (book) Siblings, 2002. Bd. dirs. Comty. Devel. Ch., Miami Beach. Mem.: United Tchrs. of Dade Retirees (bd. dirs. union), Dem. Women's Club (v.p.), Lions Club (bd. dirs.), Alpha Omicron, Alpha Delta Kappa. Avocation: musician. Home: 709 E DiLido Dr Miami Beach FL 33139-1239

GORA, JOANN M. university chancellor; BA, Vassar Coll.; M in Sociology, D in Sociology, Rutgers U. Various adminstrv. positions univ.-level, 1980—; dean Coll. Arts and Scis., sr. dean Madison campus Fairleigh Dickinson U.; provost, v.p. for acad. affairs, prof. sociology Old Dominion U., Norfolk, Va., 1992-01; chancellor U. Mass., Boston, 2001—. Author: The New Female Criminal: Empirical Reality or Social Myth?; co-author: Emergency Squad Volunteers: Professionalism in Unpaid Work; contbr. numerous articles to profl. jours. Office: U Mass Office of Chancellor 100 Morrissey Blvd Boston MA 02125-3393 E-mail: joann.gora@umb.edu.

GORA, SUSANNAH PORTER MARTIN, journalist, poet; b. New York, NY, Sept. 4, 1977; d. Joel Mark and Ann Ray Martin Gora. BA cum laude with high distinction in English, Duke U., 1995—99. Intern NY1 News, NYC, 1994, CBS News, NYC, 1996, Brillstein-Grey Entertainment, Beverly Hills, Calif., 1998; prodn. asst. ABC TV, NYC, 1999—2000; asst. to the editor Premiere Mag., NYC, 2000—01, assoc. editor, 2001—. Regular contbr. of entertainment coverage AP Radio, NYC, 2002—. Author: (book of poetry) Where Home Is; contbr. The Archive- Poetry Jour., The Ledge -Poetry Jour. The E. Blake Byrne scholarship for creative writing, Duke U., 1997. Mem.: NY Women in Comm., Inc., Phi Eta Sigma Nat. Honor Soc., Kappa Kappa Gamma Frat. (life; dir. of pub. rels. 1998—99). Office: Premiere Magazine 1633 Broadway 41st Floor New York NY 10019

GORAL, JUDITH ANN, language educator; b. Cleve., July 12, 1947; d. Chester and Elenore (Majka) C. BA, Cleve. State U., 1969; postgrad., Inst. Am., Guadalajara, Jalisco, Mex.; MAT, Marygrove Coll., 1998. Cert. Spanish, Eng. tchr., Ohio. Tchr. Spanish Wiley Mid. Schs., Cleveland Heights, Ohio; advanced courses coord. Inst. Cultural Mexicano Norteamericano de Jai, Guadalajara, tchr., bus.; tchr. Colegio Victoria, Guadalajara; tchr., Spanish Brecksville (Ohio) Sr. High Sch. Mem. Am. Assn. Tchrs. Spanish and Portuguese, MEs. Assn. Tchrs. Eng. to Speakers of Other Langs. (2d v.p. acad. programs and events 1985-86, pres. 1986-87), Ohio Fgn. Lang. Assn., Phi Beta Omicron. Office: Wiley Middle Sch 2155 Miramar Blvd University Heights OH 44118

GORDIMER, NADINE, author; b. Republic of South Africa, Nov. 20, 1923; d. Isidore and Nan (Myers) Gordimer; m. Reinhold Cassirer, Jan. 29, 1954; children: Oriane, Hugo. Ed., Convent Sch., Springs, Republic of South Africa. Author: (story collections) Face to Face, 1949, The Soft Voice of the Serpent, 1952, Six Feet of the Country, 1956, Friday's Footprint, 1960 (W.H. Smith and Son Literary award 1961), Not for Publication, 1965, Livingstone's Companions, 1971, Selected Stories, 1975, Some Monday for Sure, 1976, A Soldier's Embrace, 1980, Something Out There, 1984, Crimes of Conscience, 1991, Jump, 1991, Why Haven't You Written?, 1992; (polit. and lit. essays) The Essential Gesture, 1988, Three in a Bed, 1991, Living in Hope and History: Notes From Our Century, 1999; (literary criticism) The Black Interpreters, 1973, Writing & Being: Charles Eliot Norton Lectures, 1995; (essays) Living in Hope and History: Notes from Our Century, 1999; (novels) The Lying Days, 1953, A World of Strangers, 1958, Occasion for Loving, 1963, The Late Bourgeois World, 1966, A Guest of Honour, 1970 (James Tait Black Meml. prize 1973), The Conservationist, 1974 (Booker prize for fiction Eng. 1974), Burger's Daughter, 1979, July's People, 1981, A Sport of Nature, 1987, My Son's Story, 1991, None to Accompany Me, 1994, The House Gun, 1998, The Pickup, 2001, Loot, 2003; (other) On the Mines, 1973, Lifetimes Under Apartheid, 1986; editor: (with Lionel Abrahams) Southern African Writing Today, 1967. Decorated comdr. de l'Ordre des Arts et des Lettres (France), 1986; recipient Thomas Pringle award English Acad. South Africa, 1969, CNA award, 1974, 79, 81, 91, Grand Aigle d'Or, 1975, Disting. Svc. in Lit. Commonwealth award, 1981, MLA award, 1982, Nelly Sachs prize (Germany), 1985, Malaparte award (Italy), 1986, Bennett award, 1986, Internat. Premo Leui award, 2002, Mary McCarthy award, 2003; Benson medal, 1990, Nobel Prize for Literature, 1991; Neil Gunn fellow Scottish Arts Coun., 1981. Fellow Royal Soc. Lit.; mem. AAAS, Com. European Authors, Am. Acad. (hon.), Inst. Arts and Letters (hon.), PEN (v.p).

GORDLY, AVEL LOUISE, state legislator, community activist; b. Portland, Oreg., Feb. 13, 1947; d. Fay Lee and Beatrice Bernice (Coleman) G.; 1 child, Tyrone Wayne Waters. BS in Adminstrn. of Justice, Portland State U., 1974; Grad. John F. Kennedy Sch. Govt., Harvard U., 1995; grad., U. Oreg. Pacific Program, 1998. Phone co. clk. Pacific West Bell, Portland, 1966-70, mgmt. trainee, 1969-70; work release counselor Oreg. Corrections Divsn., Portland, 1974-78, parole and probation officer, 1974-78; dir. youth svcs. Urban League of Portland, 1979-83; dir. So. Africa program Am. Friends Svc. Com., Portland, 1983-89, assoc. exec. sec., dir. Pacific N.W. region, 1987-90; freelance writer Portland Observer, Portland, 1988-90; program dir. Portland House of Umoja, 1991; mem. Oreg. Ho. of Reps., Portland, 1991-96, mem. joint ways and means com., adv. mem. appropriations com., rules and reorgn. com., low income housing com., energy policy rev. com., others; mem. Oreg. Senate from 10th dist., Salem, 1997—; mem. crime and corrections com., trades econ. devel. com. Oreg. Senate, 1997, mem. joint ways and means com. on pub. safety, 1997, mem. joint ways and means com. on edn., 1999. Mem. joint ways and means com. on edn., mem. gov. drug and violent crime policy bd., mem. Oreg. liquor control commn. task force, mem. sexual harrassement task force, mem. Hanford waste bd., mem. Gov.'s Commn. for Women, Gov.'s Drug and Violent Crime Policy Bd.; originator, producer, host Black Women's Forum, 1983-88; co-producer, rotating host N.E. Spectrum, 1983-88. Mem. corrections adv. com. Multnomah Cmty.; mem. adv. com. Oregonians Against Gun Violence; mem. Black Leadership Conf.; treas., bd. dirs. Black United Fund; co-founder, facilitator Unity Breakfast Com.; co-founder Sisterhood Luncheon; past project adv. bd. dirs. Nat. Orgn. Victims Assistance; past citizen chmn. Portland Police Bur.; past mem. coordinating com. Portland Future Focus Policy Com.; past coord. Cmty. Rescue Plan; past vice chmn. internat. affairs Black United Front; past sec. Urban League Portland, past vice chmn. and exec. com.; past adv. com. Black Ednl. Ctr.; past vice chmn. Desegregation Monitoring; also past adv. com., past chmn. curriculum com., founder African Am. Leg. Issues Roundtable; founder Black Women Gathering; other past orgn. coms.; elected state senate First African Am. Woman, 1996. Recipient Outstanding Cmty. Svc. award NAACP, 1986, Outstanding Women in Govt. award YWCA, 1991, Girl Scout-Cmty. Svc. award, 1991, N.W. Conf. of Black Studies-Outstanding Progressive Leadership in the African-Am. Cmty. award, 1986, Cmty. Svc. award Delta Sigma Theta, 1981, Joint Action in Cmty. Svc.-Vol. and Cmty. Svc. award, 1981, Quality of Life Photography award Pacific Power & Light Co., 1986, Am. Leadership Forum Sr. fellow, 1988, Equal Opportunity award, Urban League, 1996, Outstanding Alumni, 1996, PSU, Causa '98 En Defensa de la Comunidad award, 1997, Matrix award Assn. for Women in Comm., 1999, Pres.'s award Portland Oreg. Visitors Assn., 1999, Legacy award Black United Fund, 2000, Leadership award Albina Ministerial Alliance, 2000 Mem. NAACP. Avocations: reading group, mentoring, photography, walking. Home: 6805 Ne Bradway St Portland OR 97213-5304*

GORDON, ALICE JEANNETTE IRWIN, secondary and elementary education educator; b. Detroit, Mar. 18, 1934; d. Manley Elwood and Jeannette (Coffron) Irwin; m. Edgar George Gordon, Feb. 4, 1967; children: David Alexander, John Scott. BA in Elem. Edn., Mich. State U., 1956; MA in Child Devel., U. Mich., 1959, EdS in Ednl. Psychology, 1967, MA in Reading, 1990; postgrad., Western Mich. U., 1990-97. Cert. K-12 tchr., Mich.; cert. K-12 reading specialist. Elem. tchr. Detroit Pub. Schs., 1956-67, reading tchr., 1967-68; secondary tchr. English and reading Parchment Pub. Schs., 1989-94; secondary reading specialist Kalamazoo Pub. Schs., 1994-96; jr. high reading specialist South Middle Sch., Kalamazoo, 1996-99; tchr. Milwood Elem. Sch., Mich., 1999-2001; ret. Reading therapist Western Mich. U., Kalamazoo, 1992-97; participant Ednl. Leadership Acad., 1998-99; bd. dir. U. Mich. Coll. Edn. Mem. alumni bd. Mich. State U. Coll. Edn., 1992-96; chmn. Century Ball, Nazareth Coll., Kalamazoo, 1987; co-chmn. Evening of Nte, Kalamazoo Symphony, 1989; precinct del. Kalamazoo Rep. Com., 1989, 92, 96, 99—; mem. Mich. Adult Edn. Practitioner Inquiry Project, 1994, 95, 96; docent Kalamazoo Inst. Art, 2002; bd. mem. Ready to Read, 2002, Literacy Coun., 2002; bd. dirs. U. Mich. Coll. Edn., 2003—, alumni bd. Coll. Edn. Western Mich. U., 2003—; bd. dirs. Ready to Read, 1998-, Kalamazoo Literacy Coun., 2002—; mentor, tutor Cmty. in Schs. Americorps, 2002—03, vista mem. 2003-04; docent Kalamazoo Inst. Arts, 2003-04. Recipient Crystal Apple award Mich. a., 1990, 2002, Excellence in Edn. grantee, 1997, Kalamazoo Pub. Edn. Found. grantee, 1997, 98, Arts Coun. Greater Kalamazoo minigrantee, 1997, 2000, State Dept. Arts grantee, 1997, Kalamazoo Pub. Edn. Found., 1998; Third Coast Writing fellow, 1998; MLPP grantee, 2001. Mem. Internat. Reading Assn., Mich. Reading Assn., Homer Carter Reading Assn., P.E.O. (pres. 2003—), Jr. League, Lawyers Wives Aux. (bd. dirs. 2002—, pres. 2003—), Phi Delta Kappa (pres. 1998-01, bd. dirs. 2002—), Alpha Omega Pi, Delta Kappa Gamma (bd. dirs. 2002—). Presbyterian. Avocations: miniatures, antiques, reading, genealogy, public education. Home: 4339 Lakeside Dr Kalamazoo MI 49008-2802 Office Phone: 269-337-0530.

GORDON, ANNE KATHLEEN, editor; m. Phillip L. Berman; 1 child, Aaron. BA speech pathology and audiology, U. Denver, 1979; postgrad., Columbia Grad. Sch. Journalism, 1983. Fin. writer Rocky Mountain Bus. Jour., Denver, 1981, Sun-Tattler, Hollywood, Fla., 1982-83, fin. editor, 1983; asst. bus. editor Ft. Lauderdale (Fla.) News, 1983-85; bus. editor The Denver Post, 1985-88, asst. mng. editor, 1988; news cons. Sta. KCNC-TV, Denver, 1988-89, assignment mgr., 1989-90; editor Jackson Hole News, 1990-92; editor Sunday Mag. The Plain Dealer, Cleve., 1993-99; arts and entertainment editor The Phila. Inquirer, 1999—2000, from assoc. mng. editor to dep. mng. editor arts and features, 2000—02, mng. editor, 2002—. Comm. dir. Colo. Dem. Party, Clinton presdl. campaign, 1992. Author: A Book of Saints, 1994. Recipient Best of Show award Colo. Press Assn., 1981, 86, Woman of Yr. award Broward County Bus. and Profl. Women's Assn., 1983, 1st Pl. Spot News award Colo. Associated Press, 1986, 1st Pl. Breaking News award Colo. Press Assn., 1986, Gen. Excellence award Wyo. Press Assn., 1991, Gen. Excellence award Nat. Newspaper Assn., 1992; Eisenhower fellow, 2000. Home: 149 Fairview Rd Narberth PA 19072-1330 Office: The Philadelphia Inquirer 400 N Broad St Philadelphia PA 19130-4015 E-mail: agordon@phillynews.com.*

GORDON, AUDREY KRAMEN, healthcare educator; b. Chgo., Nov. 18, 1935; d. Edward J. and Anne (Levin) Kramen; children: Bradley, Dale, Holly. BS with highest distinction, Northwestern U., 1965, MA, 1967, postgrad., 1971; MA, U. Chgo., 1970; PhD, U. Ill., Chgo., 1991. Cert. in clin. pastoral edn. Lectr. Northwestern U., Evanston, Ill., 1966-74; vis. asst. prof. Beloit (Wis.) Coll., 1974-75; research specialist U. Ill., Chgo., 1983-86, dir. continuing edn. Sch. Pub. Health, 1986-91, lectr. cmty. health scis., 1988-91, dir. coll. advancement Sch. Pub. Health, 1991-92, asst. prof., 1992—, sr. rsch. specialist Health Rsch. and Policy Ctr., 1992-2001, dir. instnl. rev. bd., 1998—, dir. human subjects rsch. Health Rsch. Policy Ctrs., 2001—; coord., counselor Jewish Hospice, Chgo., 1984-89. Lectr. Loyola U. Stritch Sch. Medicine, Maywood, Ill., 1982—90; pres. Rainbow Hospice Orgn., 1984—88, cons., 1988—92, rsch. cons., 2001—; project dir. S.E. Lake County Faith in Action Program, Highland Pk., 2003—. Co-author: (book) They Need to Know: How to Teach Children About Death, 1979; co-editor: Hospice and Cultural Diversity, 1995. Bd. dirs. AIDS Pastoral Care Network, 1999—2001. Recipient Merit award, Northwestern U. Alumni, 1993, Heart of Hospice award, Nat. Coun. Hospice Profls., 1997. Mem.: APHA, Nat. Hospice Orgn. (mem. ethics com. 1997—2000), Ill. Hospice Orgn. (pres. 1989—90, v.p. 1997—98), Ill. Pub. Health Assn., Delta Omega, Alpha Kappa Lambda, Alpha Sigma Lambda.

GORDON, DIANE, state legislator; b. Hemmingway, S.C. 4 children. Grad., N.Y.C. Tech. Coll.; BS, N.Y. City Tech. Coll., 1985. State rep. State of N.Y., 2000—; tchr. daycare, elem. students; former worker with sr. citizens. Mem. N.Y. State Black, Puerto Rican and Hispanic Legis. Caucus, Puerto Rican/Hispanic Task Force, Legis. Women's Caucus, Dem. Study Group, Bkln. Delegation of N.Y. State Assembly (Kings County); standing com. assignments include Aging, Alcoholism and Drug Abuse, Corps., Authorities and Comms., Correction. Founded Save Our Homes Orgn. of East N.Y., 1985. Democrat. Office: 669 Vermont St Brooklyn NY 11207

GORDON, DOROTHY K. silversmith, goldsmith; b. Boston, May 7, 1919; d. Barney and Sarah M. Kazer; m. Benjamin Gordon, Mar. 27, 1949; children: Judith, Ellis, William. Student, Mus. Sch. Art, Boston, Cath. U., Montgomery Coll. Tchr. metalsmithing D.C. Dept. Recreation, USDA Grad. Sch.; lectr. in field. Exhibited in group shows at YWCA, Washington, Smithsonian Instn. and Nat. Housing Ctr., St. John's Episcopal Ch., McLean, Va., Jewish Cmty. Ctr., Rockville, Md., Temple Micah, Washington, Crafts of the Synagogue touring exhbn, Plum Gallery, Kensington, Md., 1987, Nat. Mus. Am. Jewish History, Phila., 1990, Target Gallery, Alexandria, Va., 1993, B'nai B'rith Klutznick Nat. Jewish Mus., Washington, 1997, Washington Hebrew Congregation, 1998, 2000, Goldman Gallery, Jewish Cmty. Ctr., Rockville, 1999, television series, HGTV Modern Masters, 2003. Mem.: Soc. Am. Silversmiths (artisan mem.), Am. Art League, Washington Guild Goldsmiths. Avocation: painting. Home: 2856 Davenport St NW Washington DC 20008

GORDON, ELLA DEAN, health and nurse educator, women's health and orthopedic nurse; b. Chgo., Jan. 19, 1947; d. Ed and Mozelle (Jordan) Hall; m. Starling Alexander Gordon, Aug. 2, 1969; children: Gerald Alexander, Dana Rolean. Diploma, Grady Meml. Hosp., 1968; student, Ga. State U., 1969-75; BSN, Med. Coll. Ga., 1976; M in Health Sci., Armstrong State Coll., 1983. RN, Ga., Tex. Charge nurse pediatrics evenings Grady Meml. Hosp., Atlanta, 1968-71; staff nurse pediatrics Dr.'s Meml. Hosp., Atlanta, 1971; charge nurse Pediatricians Office, Decatur, Ga., 1971-72; staff nurse VA Hosp., Atlanta, 1972-76, nurse primary care med. ICU San Antonio, 1983; charge nurse, army nurse corps Eisenhower Army Med. Ctr., Ft. Gordon, Ga., 1976-79; staff nurse obstet. Noble Army Hosp., Ft. McClellan, Ala., 1984; instr. clin. nursing Jacksonville (Ala.) State Coll. Nursing, 1984-85; clin. nurse obstet. Gorgas Army Hosp., Republic of Panama, 1987-89; charge nurse oncology days Eisenhower Army Med. Ctr., Ft. Gordon, Ga., 1989-90; charge nurse obstet. Brooke Army Med. Ctr., Ft. Sam Houston, Tex., 1990-96; mem. labor & delivery Wilford Hall Air Force Med. Ctr., Lackland AFB, Tex., 1996; charge nurse orthopedics Brooke Army Med. Ctr., Ft. Sam Houston, Tex., 1996-99, health/nurse educator Health Promotion Ctr., 2000—. Cons. health edn. ETOWAH County Clinics, Gadsden, Ala, 1985; health educator Cardiovascular Coun. of Savannah, Ga., 1983, Parent/Child Devel. Svcs., Savannah, 1982. Contbr. articles to profl. jours. Instr. ARC, Ft. McClellan, 1985-86, chmn., vols., 1986-87. Capt. U.S. Army, 1976-79; col. USAR, 1991, ret., 1998. Named One of Outstanding Young Women in Am., 1979, 83. Mem. Ret. Army Nurse Corps Assn., Orthopaedic Nurses Assn., Officers Wives Club (publicity chmn. 1982-83), Sigma Theta Tau. Democrat. Avocations: cross-stitching, bowling, reading, ceramics. Home: 12810 El Marro St San Antonio TX 78233-5832 Office: Brooke Army Med Ctr Fort Sam Houston TX 78234 E-mail: satxella33@hotmail.com.

GORDON, ELLEN RUBIN, candy company executive; d. William B. and Cele H. (Travis) Rubin; m. Melvin J. Gordon, June 25, 1950; children: Virginia, Karen, Wendy, Lisa. Student, Vassar Coll., 1948—50; BA, Brandeis U., 1965; postgrad., Harvard U., 1968. With Tootsie Roll Industries, Inc., Chgo., 1968[00bf], corp. sec., 1970-74, v.p. product devel., 1974-76, sr. v.p., 1976-78, pres., COO, 1978—; v.p., dir. HDI Investment Corp. Mem. coun. on divsn. biol. scis. and Pritzker Sch. Medicine U. Chgo.; mem. med. sch. adv. coun. for cell biology and pathology Harvard U.; mem. bd. fellows Faculty of Medicine, Harvard Med. Sch. Mem. adv. coun. J.L. Kellogg Grad. Sch. Mgmt. at Northwestern U.; mem. univ. resources and overseers com. Harvard U.; mem. bd. advisors Women Inc. Recipient Kettle award, 1985. Mem. Nat. Confectioners Assn. (bd. dirs.). Office: Tootsie Roll Industries Inc 7401 S Cicero Ave Chicago IL 60629-5885

GORDON, FLORENCE IRENE, graphic artist, illustrator; b. L.A., Oct. 22, 1928; d. Harry and Etta (Goldstein) Gronoff; widowed; 1 child. Student, Chounard Art Inst., L.A., Santa Monica City Coll.; BA, Art Ctr., L.A. Graphic artist Ned North Enterprises, L.A.; artist Hawaii Newspaper, Oahu; tech. illustrator Northrop-Aircraft, L.A., McDonnell Douglas, L.A. Exhibited in group shows. Art scholar Chounard Art Inst., 1950. Home: 5166 Sepulveda Blvd Apt 208 Culver City CA 90230-5235

GORDON, IRENE MARLOW, radiology educator; b. White County, Tenn., May 21, 1943; d. Paul Terah and Mary Eva (Holloway) Marlow; m. Shigern Chino, July 14, 1969 (div.); children: Hatsuyo Mary Chino, Kazumi Elaine Chino, Junzo Paul Chino, Harold Carol Chino, Fumiko Catherine Chino; m. James Robert Gordon, Sept. 6, 1979. BS, U. Dayton, 1966; MD, Ohio State U., 1970, MS, 1974. Intern in medicine and pediat. St. Lukes Hosp., San Francisco, 1970-71; resident in gen. radiology Ohio State U. Hosp., 1971-74; fellow in radiation and oncology U. Calif., Irvine, Irvine; clin. instr. dept. radiology Ohio State U., Columbus, 1971-74; asst. clin. prof. divsn. radiation therapy U. Calif., Irvine, 1976-78, acting chief divsn. radiation therapy, 1976-77; asst. clin. prof. divsn. radiation therapy Harbor-UCLA Med. Ctr., L.A., 1981-82; clin. asst. prof. radiology, radiation oncology Ind. U. Med. Ctr., Indpls., 1992-95. Bd. dirs. Health Talents Internat., Sentinel Med. Rev. Orgn., sec., 1985-89, Hoosier Oncology Group, mem. exec. com., 1993-96; mem. staff St. Joseph & Children's Hosp., Orange, Calif., 1974-82, Long Beach Meml. Med. Ctr., 1979-82; dir. radiation oncology St. Elizabeth Hosp. and Med. Ctr. Regional Treatment

Ctr., Lafayette, Ind., 1982-2000; med. dir. Faith Hope and Love Cancer Care, Lafayette, 2000—. Translator for deaf Ouabache Ch. of Christ, Lafayette, 1993—; bd. dirs. Tippecanoe County chpt. ARC, 1992—. Mem. AMA, Am. Coll. Radiology (cert.), Am. Soc. Therapeutic Radiology and Oncology, Radiology Soc. N.Am., Am. Endocurie Soc., Am. Coll. Radiation Oncology, Am. Soc. Clin. Oncology, Tippecanoe County Med. Assn. (pres. 1994), Ind. 9th Dist. Med. Assn. (pres. 1994). Avocations: collecting japanese dolls, coins, stamps. Address: Faith Hope and Love Cancer Care 1425 Unity Pl Lafayette IN 47905

GORDON, JACQUELINE ALICIA, guidance counselor, protective services official; b. St. Catherine, Jamaica, Dec. 11, 1964; d. Winston Anthony and Phyllis Monica Gordon; children: Kerrianne Alicia Gordon-Davy, Augustus Jonathan Gordon-Davy. MS, CUNY, 1997. Cert. sch. counselor N.Y. Dept. Edn., 1998, tchr. N.Y. Dept. Edn., 1992. Mil. police officer U.S. Army Reserves, Uniondale, NY, 1984—; guidance counselor Western Suffolk BOCES, Dix Hills, 1998—. Mem. Copiague PTA. Decorated Army Achievement medal with 2 Oak Leaf Clusters USAR, Joint-Meritorius Unit award. Methodist. Avocations: travel, reading, exercising. Office: Western Suffolk BOCES Dix Hills NY 11746-5297 Personal E-mail: jacqueline.gordon@us.army.mil. E-mail: jgordon@wsboces.org.

GORDON, JASMINE ROSETTA, elementary school educator; b. Fort William, Westmoreland, Jamaica, Feb. 21, 1948; came to U.S., 1991; d. Terrence Gordon and Mavis Collins; children: Nigel Jordan, Marcia Muir. BSc in Middle Grade Edn., We. Carolina U., 1985; MA in Counseling and Psych. Svcs., Clark Atlanta U., 1993; EdD in Ednl. Leadership and Adminstrn., U. Sarasota, 1999; student, Atlanta Tech. Inst., 1999—. Cert. counselor, tchr. Ga. Tchr. Mt. Alvernia H.S., Montego Bay, Jamaica, 1980-87; tchr. lang. arts, social studies, religious edn. Anchovy H.S., St. James, Jamaica, 1987-88; instr., lectr. Bethlehem Tchr.'s Coll., St. Elizabeth, Jamaica, 1988-91; intern Inman Middle Sch., Atlanta, 1992-93; counselor Morris Brown Coll., Atlanta, 1994; sch. counselor Oakhurst Elem. Sch., Decatur, Ga., 1994-95; grad. asst. Sch. Edn. counseling and human devel. dept. Clark Atlanta U., 1994-96; tchr. 4th grade math. and lang. arts Cook Elem. Sch., 1995—; skill tchr. Atlanta Pub. Sch., Emory U., 1998—. Workshop facilitator Elem. Sci. Edn. Ptnrs. program Emory U., Atlanta, 1998—, mem., steering com. 1998—; facilitate staff devel. workshops Emory U., Atlanta Pub. Schs., 1999, tchr. in-service workshop Cook Elem. Sch., 1998-99, City Sch. Decatur, 1994-95, workshop ednl. profls. Savannah, Ga, 1994; substitute tchr. Atlanta Pub. Sch., 1992-94; spkr. Emory U., Atlanta Pub. Schs. ESEP Program, Assn. Village Pride, Fayetteville, Ga., U. Sarasota, 1999. Author rsch. papers. Vol. counselor Ga. Baptist Hosp., Atlanta, 1998—; contbr. various civic orgns. DeWitt Wallace-Reader's Digest scholar 1993-94; recipient Stanley Motor award Mico Tchrs. Coll., Jamaica, 1979-80. Mem. NEA, ABA (assoc.), Am. counseling Assn., Ga. Assn. Educators, Ga. Sch. Counselors Assn., Atlanta Assn. Educators, Atlanta Jamaican Assn. (edn. com. 1998—), Jamaica Tchrs. Assn., Jamaica Tchrs. Credit Union, Jamaica Assn. Tertiary Educators (profl. devel. com.). Methodist. Avocations: sewing, reading, crochet, travel, sports. Home: Clark Atlanta U PO Box 62 Atlanta GA 30301-0062 Office: Atlanta Bd Edn 210 Pryor St SW Atlanta GA 30303-3624 E-mail: jrgordon@acninc.net.

GORDON, JOAN IRMA, lawyer; b. N.Y.C., Nov. 1, 1945; d. Morris and Dora (Mittman) G. BA in Polit. Sci., Vassar Coll., 1967; MA in Polit. Sci., Brown U., 1969; JD, Am. U., 1974. Bar: Md. 1974, D.C. 1975, U.S. Dist. Ct. Md., 1976, U.S. Supreme Ct. 1978, N.Y. 1981. Intern N.Y. State Pub. Adminstrn., Albany, 1969-70; adminstrv. asst. to asst. commr. N.Y. State Health Dept., Albany, 1970-71; staff counsel Washington Suburban San. Commn., Hyattsville, Md., 1975-80; legal counsel and govt. affairs officer Montgomery C.C., Rockville, Md., 1980-84, gen. counsel, 1984—. Rsch. cons. Inst. Studies in Justice and Soc. Behavior, Am. U. Law Sch., Washington, 1974. Contbr. Maryland Criminal Jury Instructions and Commentary, 1975. Mem. prospective students com. Vassar Coll., Washington, 1975-83; vice-chmn. precinct Dem. Com. Montgomery County, 1976-82, Montgomery County coun. Task Force on Problems of Homeowners Assn., Condominiums and Cooperatives, 1989; mem. archtl control com. Redland Crossing Homeowners Assn., Derwood, Md., 1982-84, bd. dirs., 1984-88, pres. bd. dirs. 1986-87, v.p. 1987-88; mem. Montgomery County Commn. on Common Ownership Communities, 1992-95. Recipient Am. Jurisprudence award, 1972, 73. Mem. ABA, Am. Corp. Counsel Assocs., Nat. Assn. Coll. and Univ. Attys. (chair continuing legal edn. com. 1989-91, bd. dirs. 1987-90), Md. Bar Assn., N.Y. State Bar Assn., Montgomery County Bar Assn. Jewish. Home: 9192 Windflower Dr Ellicott City MD 21042-5630 Office: Montgomery CC 900 Hungerford Dr Rockville MD 20850-1740

GORDON, JUDITH, communications consultant, writer; b. Long Beach, Calif. d. Irwin Ernest and Susan (Perlman) G.; m. Lawrence Banka, May 1, 1977. BA, Oakland U., 1966; MS in Libr. Sci., Wayne State U., 1973. Researcher Detroit Inst. of Arts, 1968-69; libr. Detroit Pub. Libr., 1971-74; caseworker Wayne County Dept. Social Svcs., Detroit, 1974-77; advt. copywriter Hudson's Dept. Store, Detroit, 1979; mgr. The Poster Gallery, Detroit, 1980-81; mktg., corp. communications specialist Bank of Am., San Francisco, 1983-84, mgr., consumer pubs., 1984-86; prin. Active Voice, San Francisco, 1986—. Contbr. edit. The Artist's Mag., 1988-93; contbr. to book Flowers: Gary Bukovnik, Watercolors and Monotypes, Abrams, 1990. Vol. From the Heart, San Francisco, 1992, Bay Area Book Festival, San Francisco, 1990, 91, Aid & Comfort, San Francisco, 1987, Save Orch. Hall, Detroit, 1977-81, NOW sponsored abortion clinic project. Recipient Nat. award Merit. Soc. Consumer Affairs Profls. in Bus., 1986, Bay Area Best award Internat. Assn. Bus. Communicators, 1986, Internat. Galaxy awards, 1992, 95, 97, Internat. Mercury awards, 1995, Charles Schwab Excellence in Svc. award, 2000. Mem. AAUW, Nat. Writers Union, Editl. Freelancers Assn. Inc., Clarity, Achenbach Graphics Arts Coun., Women's Nat. Book Assn., Assn. for Women in Comms., Plain Lang. Assn., FIMA West (bd. dirs.), ZYZZYVA (bd. dirs.). Office: 899 Green St San Francisco CA 94133-3756 Personal E-mail: activvduo@msn.com.

GORDON, JULIE PEYTON, foundation administrator; b. Jacksonville, Fla., June 21, 1940; d. Robert Benoist Shields and Bessie (Cavanaugh) Peyton; m. Robert James Gordon, June 22, 1963. BA, Boston U., 1963; MA, Harvard U., 1965, PhD, 1969. Asst. prof. English Ill. Inst. Tech., Chgo., 1968-75, assoc. prof., 1975-77, asst. dean students, 1975-78; asst. dean acad. affairs Northwestern U., Evanston, Ill., 1978-80, lectr. English, Univ. Coll., 1978—, assoc. dean Univ. Coll., 1980-85, sec. Econometric Soc., 1975—, exec. dir. Econometric Soc., 1985—. Mem. nat. adv. com. ALA, Chgo., 1983-86. Author: Seasons in the Contemporary American Family, 1984. Grantee NEH, 1971-73; project scholar NEH, 1983-86. Mem. Phi Beta Kappa. Avocation: writing fiction and poetry. Home: 202 Greenwood Evanston IL 60201-4714 Office: Northwestern U Dept Econs Econometric Soc Evanston IL 60208-2600

GORDON, KELLY CAROLYN, theater educator, writer; d. Frank Woods Gordon and Judith Ann Bracken. BA, Ohio Wesleyan U., 1992; MA, Emerson Coll., 1994; PhD, U. Ga., 2001. Tchg. asst. Emerson Coll., Boston, 1993—94; theater mgr. U. Ga., Athens, 1994—95, tchg. asst., 1995—97, rsch. asst., 1999—2000; drama tchr. Chatham (Va.) Hall, 1998—99; vis. asst. prof. Ohio U., Athens, 2001—02; sr. lectr. U. Tex., Dallas, 2002—. Presenter Valdosta (Fla.) Women's Studies Conf., 2000; guest spkr. Dallas Mus. Art, 2003; presenter Hawaii Internat. Conf. on Arts & Humanities, 2004. Mem.: AAUW, Southea. Theatre Conf. (panel moderator 2002), Assn. Theatre in Higher Edn. Avocations: theater, films, cooking, kayaking.

GORDON, LANA G. state representative; b. Kansas City, Mo., Aug. 20, 1950; m. Arnold Gordon; children: Jennifer, Stacey, Jaime. BS in Edn., U. Kans., 1971. Subst. tchr., Mo., 1971—72; tchr. Lee's Summit (Mo.) Pub. Sch., 1972—73; test adminstr. State of Kans., 1978—80; sec., treas. Cardinal Bldg. Svcs., 1997—2001; office gen. Cardinal DBA/BG Svc. Solution, 2002—; mem. Kans. Ho. of Reps., 2001—. Sec. citizens adv. coun. USD 501 Dist., 1982—85; bd. dirs. USD 501 Sch. Found., 1994—97, Vol. Ctr. Topeka, 1998—, Jr. League Topeka, 2002—04, Topeka Conv. and Visitors Bur., 2004—. Republican. Jewish. Office: 181-W State Capitol 300 SW 10th Ave Topeka KS 66612 Address: 5820 SW 27th St Topeka KS 66614

GORDON, LISA DIANE, psychologist; b. Lower Merion Twp., Pa., May 25, 1960; d. Robert Bruce and Elinor Cloud G. BS in Psychology, Ursinus Coll., 1982; MA in Clin. Psychology, West Chester U., 1984; PhD in Counseling Psychology, Pa. State U., 1992. Lic. psychologist; cert. sch. counselor, Pa. Psychology intern USN/Nat. Naval Med. Ctr., Bethesda, Md., 1987-88; clin. psychologist Naval Hosp. Orlando, Fla., 1988-90; psychologist Delphic Mental Health Assocs., York, Pa., 1990-92; staff psychologist Reading (Pa.) Rehab. Hosp., 1992-94; psychologist Berks Counseling Assocs., West Lawn, Pa., 1994-97, PrimeCare Med., Harrisburg, Pa., 1994—2002; predoctoral intern supr. Pa. Coll. Osteopathic Medicine, Phila., 2001—02; psychologist Del. County Neurobehavioral Unit Riddle Health Care Ctr., Media, Pa., 2002—. Practicum supr. Millersville (Pa.) U., 1992. Lt. USNR, 1987-90. Fellow Pa. Psychol. Assn.; mem. APA, Mensa, Psi Chi. Republican. Episcopalian. Avocations: singing, reading, swimming, crafts, boating. Home: 6130 Pond View Dr Birdsboro PA 19508 Office: Delaware County Neurobehav Unit Riddle Health Care Ctr Ste 2205 1088 W Baltimore Pike Media PA 19063 E-mail: starry5@ptdprolog.net.

GORDON, MARJORIE, lyric coloratura soprano, opera producer, teacher; b. N.Y.C. d. Theodore and Minnie (Glantz) Fishberg; m. Nathan Gordon; children: Maxine, Peter Jon. BA cum laude, Hunter Coll. Nat. cert. voice tchr. Prof. voice Duquesne U., 1957-59, Wayne State U., 1961-91, Nat. Music Camp, Interlochen, 1963-65, Meadowbrook Sch. Music, 1966-71, U. Mich., 1970, Mich. State U., 1971; soloist, tchr. Am. U.-Wolf Trap Program, Washington, 1973. Spl. edn. cons. Detroit Grand Opera Assn.; adj. prof. Oakland (Mich.) U.; pres., gen. dir. Piccolo Opera Co., Inc. Solo debut N.Y. Philharm. Symphony, 1950, soprano soloist, N.Y.C. Opera, 1955-57, Chautauqua Opera Co., 1949-61, Pitts. Opera, 1956; dir. Detroit Opera Theatre, 1960-72, Piccolo Opera Co., 1961—; soloist with Chgo. Symphony, Phila. Symphony, Pitts. Symphony, other orchs., opera cos., summer stock, on radio and TV; recitals U.S., Greece, Europe, Can., Israel; editor: Opera Study Guide, 1968—. Mem. music adv. panel Mich. Arts Coun., 1993-; mem. Palm Beach County Cultural Coun.; opera producer Blue Lake Fine Arts Camp, 1993—. Recipient resolution honoring 25th Anniversary Piccolo Opera Co., Mich. Senate; established voice scholarship in perpetuity Nat. Opera Assn. Mem.: AFTRA, Nat. Assn. Tchrs. Singing, Met. Opera Guild, Ctrl. Opera Svc., Nat. Opera Assn., Music Tchrs. Nat. Assn., Am. Guild Mus. Artists, Mich. Music Tchrs. Assn. (voice chmn. 1970—76), Fla. Music Tchrs. Assn., Boca Delray Music Soc., Broward County Music Club, Mu Phi Epsilon. Avocations: handcrafts, swimming, reading, sketching. Fax: 561-394-0520. Office Phone: 800-282-3161. Personal E-mail: leejon51@msn.com.

GORDON, MARSHA L. dermatologist; b. Annapolis, Md., 1958; BA, Rutgers U., 1980; MD, U. Pa., 1984. Diplomate Am. Bd. Dermatology. Intern Cooper Med. Ctr., Camden, 1984—85; resident in dermatology Mt. Sinai Med. Ctr., N.Y.C., 1985—88, chief cons., 1988—, vice chair dermatology, 1996—. Asst. prof. Mt. Sinai Sch. Medicine, N.Y.C., 1988—97, assoc. clin. prof., 1997—. Office: Mount Sinai Med Ctr Box 1048 5 E 98th St New York NY 10029-6501

GORDON, MARY CATHERINE, writer; b. L.I., N.Y., Dec. 8, 1949; d. David and Anna (Gagliano) G.; m. James Brain, 1974 (div.); m. Arthur Cash, 1979; children: Anna Gordon, David Dess Gordon. BA, Barnard Coll., 1971; MA, Syracuse U., 1973. Tchr. English Dutchess Community Coll., Poughkeepsie, N.Y., 1974-78, Amherst (Mass.) Coll., 1979-80, Barnard Coll., 1988—. Author: (novels) Final Payments, 1978, The Company of Women, 1981, Men and Angels,1985, The Other Side, 1989, The Rest of Life, 1993, Spending, 1998, (short stories) Temporary Shelter, 1987, Good Boys and Dead Girls and Other Essays, 1991, The Rest of Life: Three Novellas, 1993, The Shadow Man, 1996, Seeing Through Places, 2000, Joan of Arc, 2000. Guggenheim fellow; recipient Kafka prize for Fiction, 1979, 82, Lila Acheson Wallace Reader's digest award. Roman Catholic. Office: Barnard Coll Dept English 3009 Broadway New York NY 10027-6501 Agent: Sterling Lord Literistic 65 Bleecker St Fl 12 New York NY 10012-2420*

GORDON, PAMELA ANN WENCE, pianist; b. Dayton, Ohio, Apr. 28, 1943; d. Arthur Elbert and Melva C. (Coleman) Wence (dec.); m. Clifford Elwood Gordon, Oct. 23, 1971. BS, Ind. State U., Terre Haute, 1966. Self-employed piano tchr., 1957—; round dance leader, 1973-98. Organist, Ctrl. Seventh Day Bapt. Ch., 1989—, choir dir. 2000—; Christmas carol pianist Williamsburg, Va., 2001–; mem. Greenbelt Astronomy Club, Md. Recipient Appreciation award Rock Eights, 1985. Mem. ROUNDALAB (charter mem., chair survey com. 1985-86, Maestro trophy 1998), Round Dance Tchrs. Assn. Greater D.C. Area (v.p.), Nat. Capital Area Sq. Dance Leaders Assn. (treas.), Washington Music Tchrs. Assn. (treas.). Avocations: camping, reading, caring for and playing with box turtles, indoor swimming, playing piano. Home: 219 Rainbow Dr # 11963 Livingston TX 77399-2019 E-mail: pcgordon@escapees.com.

GORDON, RITA SIMON, civic leader, former nurse, educator; b. Frederick, Md., Feb. 1, 1929; d. Jacob and Anna (Stein) Simon; m. Paul Perry Gordon, July 2, 1948; children: Stuart Yael, Hugh Ellis, Myla. RN, Frederick Meml. Hosp., 1949. RN, md surg. staff nurse Prince Georges Gen. Hosp., 1949-50; ped. staff nurse (part time) Frederick Meml. Hosp., 1950-54; surg. office nurse, 1960-62; nurse blood prog. ARC, 1954-83. Author: (with Paul P. Gordon) Textbook History of Frederick County, 1975, Playground of the Civil War, 1994, Never the Like Again, 1995. Mem. Frederick County Bd. Edn., 1975-85, pres., 1979-80, 83-84; mem. exec. com. Md. Assn. Bd. Edn., Annapolis, 1978-85, pres., 1983-84; bd. trustees, Jewish Mus. of Md. 1998—; bd. assocs. Hood Coll., Frederick 1985-94; mem. Md. Task Force on Ednl. Funding, Annapolis, 1983-84, Md. Values Edn. Com., Annapolis, 1979-83, Fed. Relations Network, Nat. Sch. Bd. Assn., 1978-82; bd. dirs. Community Commons, Frederick, 1983-85; area field rep. Am. Field Svc., Frederick, 1970-75; assoc. mem. adv. com. Vocat. Tech. Edn., publicity com. 1973 Snow Ball, Frederick Meml. Hosp. Aux.; past bd. dirs., vice pres. Beth Sholom Sisterhood; pres. Beth Sholom Congregation, 1988-90; past bd. dirs. Nat. Counc. Jewish Women, Frederick; vol. aide frederick Waverly Elem. Sch.; ofcr., chmn. fund raising North Market St. Sch.; active Girl Scouts U.S.A.; past pres., vice pres. Frederick Improvement Found., editor: Town Crier; trustee Community Found., Frederick County, 1991-1995. Named Woman of the Yr., Bus. and Profl. Woman's Club, 1975; Frederick's Outstanding Woman, Internat. Woman's Yr., 1975. Mem. Frederick Sect. Nat. Counc. Jewish Women (pres. 1986-88), C. of C. (Planned Growth-2000 com.), Md. Hist. Soc., Internat. Graphoanalysis Soc., Md. Jewish Hist. Soc., Frederick County Hist. Soc. Clubs: Rotary Inner Wheel (Frederick, Md.). Avocation: hist. rsch. Home: 202 Meadowdale Ln Frederick MD 21702-4036

GORDON, RONNI ANNE, journalist; b. N.Y.C., Aug. 24, 1954; d. Alfred O. and Lynne (Lewin) G.; children: Benjamin, Joseph, Katherine. BA in English, Vassar Coll., 1976; MS in Journalism, Boston U., 1979. Feature writer, reporter Holyoke (Mass.) Transcript-Telegram, 1979-80, editor, 1981; feature writer Springfield (Mass.) Union-News and Sunday Republican, 1982—. Office: The Republican Co 1860 Main St Springfield MA 01103-1000

GORDON, SUSAN JOAN, physician, educator; b. Atlantic City, Aug. 14, 1942; Student, Goucher Coll., 1959-62; MD, Jefferson Med. Coll., 1966. Diplomate Am. Bd. Internal Medicine, Am. Bd. Gastroenterology. Intern in medicine Hahnemann Med. Coll. and Hosp., Phila., 1966-67; resident in medicine Jefferson Med. Coll. Hosp., Phila., 1967-69; instr. Thomas Jefferson U., Phila., 1971-73, asst. prof., 1973-78, assoc. prof., 1978-87, clin. prof. medicine, 1987-97; jr. coord. medicine Jefferson Med. Coll., Phila., 1971-82; prof. medicine MCP-Hahnemann U., Phila., 1997—. Contbr. articles to profl. jours. Fellow ACP; mem. Am. Gastroenterol. Assn. (biliary sect., abstract reviewer, chairperson clin. biliary sect.), Am. Assn. Study Liver Disease, Pa. Med. Soc., Phil. Gastrointestinal Rsch. Forum, Sigma Xi. Office: Grad Hosp 1800 Lombard St Philadelphia PA 19146-1497

GORDON, THELMA STONE, retired audio-visual specialist, librarian; b. Boston; children: Emily, Richard, Daryl. BA, U. Bridgeport, 1969; MLS, So. Conn. State U., 1972; postgrad., Sacred Heart U., 1984. Freelance artist, Newton, Mass. and Tampa, Fla., 1955-65; exec. sec., bd mem. Associated Women Investors, Tampa, 1959-62; substitute art tchr., libr. Westport (Conn.) Bd. Edn., 1962-65; libr. asst. U. Bridgeport, Conn., 1964-65; art and music libr. Westport (Conn.) Pub. Libr., 1967-82, head audio-visual svcs., 1982-92; ret., 1992. Chmn. picture div. Spl. Librs. Assn., 1977-78, bd. dirs., 1980; chmn. adult svcs. sect. Conn. Libr. Assn., 1974; state rep. Art Librs. Assn. of N.Am., 1975. Contbg. author: Handbook of Picture Librarianship, 1981; contbr. chpts. to books, articles to mags., profl. newsletters. Bd. dirs. Friends of Music, Fairfield County, 1985—; mem. Westport-Weston Arts Coun., 1982—, Fairfield County, Mus. Modern Art, N.Y.C., 1984—; active audio visual task force State of Conn., panel mem. video workshop. Recipient award Conn. Assn. Libr. Bds., 1993. Mem. ALA, Home Cinema Soc., Edn. Film Library Assn., Spl. Librs. Assn. (chmn. picture div. 1977-78), Conn. Libr. Assn. (chmn. adult svcs. sect. 1974), Art Librs. Assn. (panelist at nat. conf. 1977), N.Y.C. Mus. Modern Art. Avocations: chamber music, theater, films, walking. Home: 32 Lincoln St Westport CT 06880-4201 Home (Winter): 1203 Peppertree Dr Sarasota FL 34242

GORDON, TINA, sculptor, art therapist; b. N.Y.C. d. Abraham and Rose (Scoff) Schapiro; m. Norman B. Gordon (div.); children: Jane, Judith, Marc. BA in Fine Arts, Goddard Coll., 1972; postgrad., NYU, 1978-80; student, Nat. Acad. Art, N.Y.C., 1981-83, Parsons Sch. Design, 1983-88. Art tchr. East River Montessori Sch., N.Y.C., 1969-72; instr. Nassau Cmty. Coll., 1973-76; art therapist Manhattan Psychiat. Ctr., N.Y.C., 1977-87. Curator ann. juried non-member exhbn. sculpture and photography; jury of awards for Wash. Square outdoor art club, 1995, 96. Exhibited in shows at Nat. Acad. Art, 1977, 78, 80, Nat. Art Club, N.Y.C., 1978, 79, 80, 83, 88, Thompson Gallery, N.Y.C., Salamagundi Art Club, N.Y.C., 1979-90, Pen and Brush, N.Y.C., 1984-89, L.I. Artists Guild, 1970, 71, 72, numerous others; commns. for Manhattan Psy. Ctr. Jury mem. Allied Artists Am., 1995-96, Pen and Brush Artists, 1995-96, Washington Sq. Outlook Artists, 1995-96, Salmagundi Art Club, 1996—. Recipient Philip Isenberg 1st prize in Sculpture, Salmagundi Art Soc., 1994, Riebman award for sculpture Salmagundi Club, 1997, Sculpture award Artists Guild, West Palm Beach, Fla., 1998. Mem. Salmagundi Art Soc. (curator, chmn. ann. open juries exhbn. 1994, jury of awards 1996—), Elliot Liskin award in sculpture 1984, 86, First Prize Sculpture award), Nat. Assn. Women Artists, Pen and Brush (bd. dirs., 1994, 96—, Merit award 1985, 87, 88, 89, jury of acceptance 1995, 96), Am. Soc. Contemporary Artists, Burr Artists, Allied Artists of Am. (elected as jury of acceptance 1995, 96), Knickerbocker Artists (Roman Bronze award 1981, 83), Nat. Sculpture Soc. (assoc.). Avocations: reading, music, poetry, bike riding, museums. Home: 24 5th Ave New York NY 10011-8858

GORDON-HARRIS, CASSANDRA I. curator, educator; b. New Orleans, Jan. 23, 1948; d. Kevin Michael Gordon and Mary Frances Roberts; m. Eugene L. Harris, June 6, 1977. A in Drawing, Casa de La Cultura, Guayaquil, Ecuador, 1964; BA in Art History, U. Fribourg, Switzerland, 1968. Mem. faculty The Arts Ctr., St. Petersburg, Fla., 1998—; curator Galleries at Salt Creek, St. Petersburg, 2000—03. Co-founder Santa Fe Multi-Cultural Artist Group, 1980—83; west coast mem. chair Fla. chpt. Womens Caucus for Art, 2001—03; co-designer, artist State N.Mex., Santa Fe, 1982; cons., designer, artist City St. Petersburg, 2000—01; designer, sponsor Ctr. Against Spousal Abuse, 2001; bd. dirs. Fla. Artist Group, 2002—. One-woman shows include Gallery One, Coconut Grove, Fla., Anna Sklar Gallery, Bal Harbour, Fla., 1986, DeMayo Gallery, Guayaquil, Ecuador, 1989—91, Synthesis Fine Arts, Tampa, 1999, Mahaffey Theatre, St. Petersburg, Fla., 2000, Avalon Island Gallery, Orlando, 2002, Confident Gallery, St. Petersburg, 2003, exhibited in group shows at Hilderbrand Gallery, New Orleans, La., 1995, 1996, Soho South Gallery, St. Petersburg, Fla., 1998, Fusion Gallery, 1998, Salt Creek Artworks, 1999, 2000, 2001, Rosemary Court Galleries, Sarasota, Fla., 2000, The Venice Arts Ctr., Fla., 2001, 2002, 2003, Big Arts Gallery, Sanibel Island, Fla., 2002, St. Augustine Art Assn., 2003, Confident Gallery, 2004. Mem. steering com. Pinellas County Arts for Complete Edn. Named Artist in Residence, Pinellas Arts Coun., 2001—04, Best of Bay 2001 Promoter of Women Artists, Weekly Planet Newspaper, 2001; recipient Cert. Spl. Recognition, Sociedad Amazonica, 1984. Mem.: AAUW, Nat. Assn. Women Artists, Artist Equity, Art Beyond Borders, Nat. Mus. Women in Art. Studio: 657 Central Ave Saint Petersburg FL 33701

GORE, GENEVIEVE WALTON, company executive; b. Salt Lake City, Mar. 23, 1913; d. Thaddeus and Ethel May (Arnold) Walton; m. Wilbert Lee Gore, Jan 1, 1935 (widowed July 1986); children: Robert, Susan, Virginia, David, Elizabeth. Student, U. Utah, 1933, Henninger Bus. Coll., 1935; HHD in Humanities, Westminster Coll., 1982; D in Bus. Adminstrn., Goldey-Beacom Coll., 1991. Co-founder W.L. Gore & Assoc., Inc., 1958—, sec., treas., 1958. Dir. W.L. Gore & Assoc., Scotland, West Germany, India, Del. State C. of C., Wilmington. Bd. counselors Goldey-Beacom Coll., Wilmington, Del., 1991; bd. govs. Winterthur (Del.) Mus., 1991. Recipient Medal Distinction, U. Del., Newark, 1983, Bavarian Order of Merit, Germany, 1988, Disting. Performance in Mgmt. award Widener U., Wilmington, 1986; named Del. Women's Hall of Fame, Dover, 1989, Del. Bus. Leaders Hall of Fame, 1991, (with husband Bob Gore) named to Nat. Bus. Hall of Fame, 2003. Mem. Girl Scouts Pres.Adv. Coun., Chesapeake Bay Girl Scouts, Independence Sch., Boy Scouts Am. Avocations: mountain climbing, swimming, music, world travel. Home and Office: WL Gore & Associates Inc PO Box 9329 Newark DE 19714-9329*

GORE, PATRICIA W. federal agency administrator; b. 1949; B, U. DC, 1973; grad. study, George Washington U. Dir. tchr. quality programs US Dept. Edn., Innovation and Improvement, Wash., 2002—; sr. exec. fellow Kennedy Sch. Govt., Harvard U., 1999. Office: US Dept Edn Off Innovation and Improvement 400 Maryland Ave SW Rm 5E121 Washington DC 20202

GORE, TIPPER (MARY ELIZABETH GORE), wife of the former vice president of the United States; b. Washington, Aug. 19, 1948; m. Albert Gore Jr., May 19, 1970; children: Karenna, Kristin, Sarah, Albert III. BA in Psychology, Boston U., 1970; MA in Psychology, Vanderbilt U., 1975. Freelance photographer. Mental health policy advisor to pres. Author: Raising PG Kids in an X-Rated Society, 1987, Picture This: A Visual Diary, 1996; co-prodr. (with Nat. Mental Health Assn.) Homeless in America: A Photographic Project. Co-founder Parents Music Resource Ctr., Arlington, Va., 1985; founder Tenn. Voices for Children, 1990; co-chair Am. Goes Back to Sch. Initiative, 1996—; chair Congl. Wives Task Force, 1978-79. Democrat. Office: 2100 West End Ave Nashville TN 37203*

GOREA, LUCIA-IOSEFINA, English educator, writer, poet; b. Oradea, Romania, Apr. 25, 1959; arrived in U.S., 1993; d. Joseph and Emilia Badea;

m. Simion Liviu Gorea, Apr. 22, 1989; 1 child, Alex Raoul. MA in Philology, U. Bucharest, Romania, 1986; secondary degree, U. Bucharest, 1989; PhD in English, Atlantic Internat. U., Miami, Fla., 2002. Notary pub. Oreg. English tchr. Maghcrani H.S., Mures, Romania, 1986—89; English prof. U. Mures, Romania, 1989—92; 2d grade tchr. Columbia Acad., Portland, Oreg., 1998—2000; English instr. Marylhurst (Oreg.) U., 2000—01, Portland C.C., 2000—, tchr. ESL, 2000—, Mt. Hood C.C., Portland, 2000—. Founder, leader Poetry Around the World, Beaverton, Oreg. Contbr. poetry to Echoes of the Century, Eternal Portraits, America at the Millennium, Mirrors (Hon. Mention, 1999), Sunrise and Soft Mist (Editor's Choice award, 1999), Gresham Outlook. Recipient Pres.'s award for lit. excellence, Nat. Authors Registry, 2000, Internat. Poet of Merit award, Internat. Soc. Poets, 2001, Silver award, 2002, Outstanding Achievement in Poetry Silver Cup award, 2003, Bronze Medallion Commemorative award, 2003, Cert. of Achievement in Poetry, 2004. Mem.: NEA, Internat. Libr. Poetry (Poet of Merit 2000), Oreg. Edn. Assn. Avocations: reading, writing, philosophy, performing arts, classical music, aquaerobics. Home: 6852SW 180th Ave Aloha OR 97007 E-mail: luciag_esl@yahoo.com.

GOREAU, ANGELINE WILSON, writer; b. Sept. 12, 1951; d. Theodore Nelson and Eloise (Keaton) G.; m. Stephen Jones McGruder, Mar. 19, 1983; 1 child, Keaton Angeline. BA, Barnard Coll., 1973. Hodder fellow Princeton (N.J.) U., 1982-83; lectr. Vassar Coll., Poughkeepsie, N.Y., 1980's. Judge for various prizes. Author: Reconstructing Aphra, 1980, The Whole Duty of a Woman, 1984; contbr. articles to mags., newspapers, essays to books. Fellow NEH, 1976, Nat. Endowment for Arts, 1981, Belgian Ministry of Culture, Hodder fellow, 1982-83. Mem. PEN, Book Critics' Cir., Authors' Guild. Office: c/o Georges Borchardt 136 E 57th St New York NY 10022-2707

GORELICK, JAMIE SHONA, lawyer; b. N.Y.C., May 6, 1950; d. Leonard and Shirley (Fishman) G.; m. Richard E. Waldhorn, Sept. 28, 1975; children: Daniel H., Dana E. BA, Harvard U., 1972, JD, 1975. Bar: D.C. 1975, U.S. Dist. Ct. D.C. 1976, U.S. Tax Ct. 1976, U.S. Ct. Claims 1976, U.S. Ct. Appeals (D.C. cir.) 1976, U.S. Ct. Appeals (5th cir.) 1977, U.S. Supreme Ct. 1979, U.S. Ct. Appeals (Fed. cir.) 1982, U.S. Ct. Internat. Trade 1984, U.S. Dist. Ct. Md. 1985, U.S. Ct. Appeals (4th cir.) 1986, U.S. Ct. Appeals (3d. cir.) 1988. With Miller, Cassidy, Larroca & Lewin, Washington, 1975-79, 80-93; asst. to sec., counselor to dep. sec. U.S. Dept. Energy, 1979—80; gen. counsel Dept. Def., 1993—94; dep. atty. gen. Dept. Justice, Washington, 1994-97; vice chair Fannie Mae, Washington, 1997—2003; mem. Nat. Commn. on Terrorist Attacks Upon the U.S., Washington, 2002—; ptnr. Wilmer, Cutler and Pickering, Washington, 2003—. Mem. chmn.'s adv. coun. U.S. Senate Jud. Com., 1988-93; tchr. Trial Advocacy Workshop Harvard Law Sch., Cambridge, Mass., 1982, 84; vice chair task force evaluation of audit investigative inspection components Dept. Def., 1979-80; mem. sec.'s transition team Dept. Energy, 1979; bd. dirs. United Technologies Corp., Schlumberger Ltd., Fannie Mae Found., John D. & Catherine T. MacArthur Found., D.C. Coll. Access, Am.'s Promise-Alliance for Youth, Nat. Park Found., Carnegie Endowment, 1989-93, Nat. Women's Law Ctr., 1991-93, Washington Legal Clinic for Homeless; bd. overseers Harvard Coll.; mem. nat. security adv. panel CIA; mem. internat. security adv. panel, 1997—, mem. Pres.'s Intelligence Rev. Panel, 2001-2002; mem. threat reduction adv. com. Dept. of Def.; mem. coun. Am. Law Inst., 1997-2000, D.C. Bar Found.; co-chair adv. com. Presdl. Commn. on Critical Infrastructure Protection, 1997-99; mem. Nat. Commn. Support Law Enforcement, Washington, 1995—; mem. Supreme Ct. Judicial Fellow. Selection Com. Mem. editl. bd. Corp. Criminal Liability Reporter, 1986-93, Destruction of Evidence, 1989; contbr. articles to profl. jours. Mem. bd. overseers Harvard Coll., 1989-93. Fellow Am. Bar Found.; mem. ABA (chair complex crimes litigation com. litigation sect. 1984-87, vice-chair complex crimes litigation com. 1983-84, Nat. Commn. to Support Law Enforcement, 1995—, sec. litigation sect. 1988-90, coun. mem. 1990-93, com. on profl. discipline, ho. of dels. 1991-93, 97—), D.C. Bar (pres. 1992-93, bd. govs. 1982-88, sec. bd. govs. 1981-92, bar found. advisors 1985-93, legal ethics com.), Womens Bar Assn., Am. Law Inst. (coun.), Coun. on Fgn. Rels. Office: Wilmer Cutler and Pickering 2445 M St NW Washington DC 20037

GORELIK, ALLA, piano educator; b. Chernobyl, Ukraine, Oct. 9, 1949; came to U.S., 1992; d. Simon and Eugena (Ben) Tsoiref; m. Roman Gorelik, June 16, 1971 (div. Apr. 1978); m. Valentin Stadnik, Dec. 26, 1979; children: Regina, Vladislav. BA, State Mus. Coll., Kiev, Ukraine, 1970. Piano and theory tchr. Music Sch. #5, Kiev, 1970-91; accompanist Fort Myers, Fla., 1992—; organist Temple Beth El, Fort Myers, 1993—; music instr. Learning Tree, Fort Myers, 1994—; piano and theory tchr. Fort Myers, 1992—. Children musical program dir. North Shore Child Care, Fort Myers, 1993-95; youth art dir. Music Sch. #5, Kiev, 1986-90. Vol., performer Jewish Fedn., Fort Myers, 1992—, Hadassah, Fort Myers, 1993—; vol., accompanist Temples Beth-El and Judea, Fort Myers, 1992—. Recipient Labor Merit medal Ministry of Culture, 1990. Mem. Nat. Music Tchrs. Assn. Avocations: travel, cooking, reading. Home: 18257 Huckleberry Rd Fort Myers FL 33912-5234

GORELOVA, LINDA M. elementary school educator; b. East St. Louis, Ill., Sept. 29, 1957; d. Winford and Mary Ellen Morris; 1 child, Nikolai. BA, Ind. U., Bloomington, 1983; MEd, Ohio U., Athens, 1995. Cert. tchr. Ohio, 1998. Tchr. Adina Local Schs., Frankfort, Ohio, 1998—2002, Circleville City Schs., Ohio, 2002—. Interpreter Russian-English State Dept., Washington; also New Eng. newspaper assn., Boston. Recipient Hon. mention, GlimmerFrain Literary Contest. Mem.: Delta Kappa Gamma.

GORENCE, PATRICIA JOSETTA, judge; b. Sheboygan, Wis., Mar. 6, 1943; d. Joseph and Antonia (Marinsheck) G.; m. John Michael Bach, July 11, 1969; children: Amy Jane, Mara Jo, J. Christopher Bach. BA, Marquette U., 1965, JD, 1977; MA, U. Wis., 1969. Bar: Wis. 1977, U.S. Dist. Ct. (ea. and we. dists.) Wis. 1977, U.S. Ct. Appeals (7th cir.) 1979, U.S. Supreme Ct. 1980. Asst. U.S. atty. U.S. Atty.'s Office, Milw., 1979-84, 1st asst. U.S. Atty., 1984-87, 89-91, U.S. Atty., 1987-88; dep. atty. gen. State of Wis. Dept. Justice, Madison, 1991-93; assoc. Ginbel, Reilly, Guerin & Brown, Milw., 1993-94; U.S. magistrate judge U.S. Dist. Ct. Wis., Milw., 1994—. Bd. dirs. U. Wis.-Milw. Slovenian Arts Coun., 1989—, treas., 1989—, Milw. Dance Theatre, 1993-98; bd. chair Bottomless Closet, 1999—. Recipient Spl. Commendation, U.S. Dept. Justice, 1986, IRS, 1988. Mem. ABA, Am. Law Inst., Nat. Assn. Women Judges, Fed. Magistrate Judges Assn. (cir. dir. 1997-2000), Milw. Bar Assn. (chair cmty. rels. com. 2000-03, Prosecutor of Yr. 1990, Disting. Svc. award 2003, Wis. Law Jour. Innovator of Yr. award 2003), State Bar Wis. (chair lawyer dispute resolution com. 1986—, chair professionalism com. 1988-2000, vice chair legal edn. commn. 1994-96, Pres. award 1995), 7th Cir. Bar Assn. (chair rules and practices com. 1991-95), Assn. for Women Lawyers, Profl. Dimensions (sec. 1998-2000, v.p. adminstrn. 2000-2002).

GORHAM, RAMSAY L. state legislator, political organization administrator; b. Rocky Mount, N.C., July 11, 1951; BA, Converse Coll., S.C. Artist; mem. N. Mex. Senate, Dist. 10., Sante Fe, 1996—; mem. edn. com., mem. rules com.; chmn. Republican Party N.Mex., 2003—. Republican. Office: 805 Salamanca St NW Albuquerque NM 87107-5619

GORING, RUTH ANN, editor, writer; b. Kansas City, July 4, 1954; d. Paul Goring and Alma Sue Harris; m. Daniel de la Pava, Apr. 5, 2003; children: Claire Elisa Stewart, Graham Benjamin Stewart. BA, U. of Kans., 1975. Editl. asst. Salem Press, Pasadena, Calif., 1987—89; assoc. editor World Christian Mag., Pasadena, 1989—90; freelance editor Wheaton, Ill., 1990—92; sr. copy editor InterVarsity Press, Westmont, Ill., 1992—. Minister campus InterVarsity Christian Fellowship, Glen Ellyn, 1996—2003; assoc. editor Target Earth Mag., Pleasanton, Calif., 1998—2000. Author: I Am Green, 1989, Environmental Stewardship, 1990, Heart Renewal, 1995, Holidays and Celebrations, 1995, Date Rape, 1996, The Creative Heart of God, 1997, Meeting God in Quiet, 1999, Meeting God in Relationships, 1999, Singleness, 2002, Adagio Penitento (ProCreation Poetry prize, 2000), Yellow Doors, 2004. Devel. coord. Chicagoans for a Peaceful Colombia, Chgo., 2003; internat. protective accompaniment Comisión Intereclesial de Justicia y Paz, Cacarica, Colombia, 2003. James B. Kennedy scholar, U. Kans., 1975. Avocations: painting, musician, gardening. Office: InterVarsity Press 430 W Plaza Drive Westmont IL 60559 Personal E-mail: ruth.goring@sbcglobal.net.

GORMAN, CHARLOTTE A. family and consumer sciences agent; b. Tuscaloosa, Ala., Apr. 12, 1945; d. Buster and Rosie Gorman; m. C. Curtis Trent, May 5, 1984. BS, Delta State U., 1970; MA, U. Tenn., 1973, Ball State U., 1977, EdD, 1978. Sci. tchr. West Boliver Elem. Sch., Rosedale, Miss., 1970—71; ext. home economist Miss. State U., Starkville, 1973—75; state ext. specialist U. Ark., Little Rock, 1978—84; pres. GT Assocs., Denton, Tex., 1985—93; ext. agt. U. Ark., Little Rock, 1993—97, Tex. A&M U. Sys., College Station, 1997—. Author: The Frugal Mind, 1990 (Book Club selection), The Frugal Mind rev. edit., 1998, The Little Book of Living Frugal, 2001; co-author: Speak for Yourself, 2002. Recipient Charlotte Gorman Day named in her honor, 1993. Mem.: Tex. Extension Assn. Family and Consumer Scis., Nat. Extension Assn. Family and Consumer Scis., Tex. Assn. Family and Consumer Scis., Am. Assn. Family and Consumer Scis., Cleburne C. of C. (program devel. com. 2001—), Epsilon Sigma Phi. Avocations: garage sales, piano. Home: 708 Meadowview Cleburne TX 76033

GORMAN, GAYLA MARLENE OSBORNE, consumer affairs executive; b. Owenton, Ky., Aug. 9, 1956; d. Frederick Clay and Helen Beatrice (Mason) O. AAS, No. Ky. U., 1982, BS, 1986; cert. in Chinese Mandarin, Def. Lang. Inst., 1975. Pers. clk. Dept. Edn. State Ky., Frankfort, 1974; sec. Dept. Health, Edn., Welfare Nat. Inst. Occupational Safety Health, Cin., 1977-79; specialist sales promotion U.S. Postal Svc., Cin., 1980, coord. customer liaison, task force pub. image, account rep., 1986-87, with stamp distbn. task force, 1993—; reservation sale agt. Delta Airlines, 1987-89. Councilmember Florence City Coun., Ky. 1984-87; vol. Children's Home, Covington, 1982, 87. With USAF, 1974-76. Named to Hon. Order Ky. Cols. Mem. Disabled Am. Veterans, No. Ky. U. Alumni Assn., Nat. Assn. Postmasters U.S., Boone County Fraternal Order Police, Ky. Assn. Realtors, Nat. Bd. Realtors, Women in Mil. Svc. for Am. (charter). Clubs: Fraternal Order Police. Democrat. Baptist. Avocations: horseback riding, travel, organizing seminars. Home: 8395 Juniper Ln Florence KY 41042-9279

GORMAN, JANE MARILYN, retired elementary school educator; b. Southampton, N.Y., Oct. 20, 1934; d. Joseph Alexander and Anna Clarabel (Maslin) Shott; m. Ronald Keith Gorman, Sept. 15, 1957; 1 child, Keith Owen. BS in Music Edn., SUNY, Potsdam, 1956. Music tchr. Liverpool (N.Y.) Ctrl. Schs., 1956-58; tchr. GED jr. high level U.S. Army, Saumur, France, 1959; substitute tchr. music Rochester (N.Y.) City Schs., 1959-60; elem. tchr. Simi Valley (Calif.) Unified Sch. Dist., 1963-91; ret. Mem. Calif. Ret. Tchrs. Assn., Sweet Adelines (pres. 1968-70), Order Ea. Star. Republican. Avocations: reading, golf, piano.

GORMAN, JOYCE J(OHANNA), lawyer; b. N.Y.C., Aug. 23, 1952; d. Peter J. and Jane M. (Kelly) G. Student, Williams Coll., 1972-73; BA, Smith Coll., 1974; JD with honors, U. Md., 1977. Bar: Md. 1977, D.C. 1988. Assoc. Miles & Stockbridge, Balt., 1977-84, ptnr., 1984-87, Washington, 1987-88, Ballard, Spahr, Andrews & Ingersoll, Washington, 1988-94, Piper & Marbury, Washington, 1994-98; spl. counsel Cadwalader, Wickersham & Taft LLP, Washington, 1998—. Bd. dirs. Va. Opera, 1994-98. Mem. Md. Bar Assn. (sec. corp. banking and bus. sect. 1983-84, vice chmn. 1984-85, chmn. 1985-86), Merchants Club (Balt. bd. dirs. 1980-87), City Club (Washington). Roman Catholic. Avocations: swimming, gourmet cooking, travel. Home: 9492 Lynnhall Pl Alexandria VA 22309-3064 Office: Cadwalader Wickersham & Taft LLP Ste 1100 1201 F St NW Washington DC 20004

GORMAN, KAREN MACHMER, optometric physician; b. Poughkeepsie, N.Y., June 4, 1955; d. James Andrew and Joan (Benton) Machmer; m. D.L. McCartney III, Aug. l6, l976 (div. June l982); m. N. David Gorman, Oct. l6, 1985; l stepchild, Danette Y. Gorman. BS in Optometry, U. Houston, 1976, OD, 1978; therapeutic pharm. lic., U. Mo., St. Louis, 1993. Diplomate Nat. Bd. Examiners Optometry; lic. optometrist, Colo., Mo., Tex. Pvt. practice, Dallas, 1978-83, 1984-85, Hurst, Tex., 1984-85, St. Joseph, Mo., 1986-2000; councilwoman, chmn. pub. safety com. City Coun., City of St. Joseph, 1997-98, chmn. landfill and water pollution com., 1998—; pvt. practice Maryville, Mo., 1999—. Charter mem. optometric adv. panel Pearle, Inc., 1991-93; lectr. on eyecare to community groups; free-lance journalist St. Joseph News-Press, Benson (N.C.) Rev., jazzreview.com, Jazz Amb. mag. Contbr. poetry to lit. jours. including Nat. Libr. of Poetry, Typo mag., Edge mag., articles to profl. jours. including St. Joseph News Press and Benson (N.C.) Review; lead actress (play) None Come Back Innocent, Robidoux Resident Theatre, St. Joseph, 1990, Hay Fever, 1991, The Best Man, 1992, Wedded But No Wife, 1993, Mousetrap, 1993, Diary of Anne Frank, 1994, Death and the Maiden, 1995, Veronica's Room, 1996, Plaza Suite, 1997, Dial M for Murder, 2000, The Laramie Project, 2002. Vol. Dallas Humane Soc., 1981, YWCA Women's Abuse Shelter; patron Robidoux Resident Theatre, St. Joseph, 1988-92, Ice House Theatre, St. Joseph, Kemper Albrecht Art Mus., St. Joseph, St. Joseph Animal Shelter; patron Second Harvest Food Bank, 1998-2003; sponsor, coach, cheerleader and drill team Mo. Western State Coll., St. Joseph, 1985-86; legis. corr. Humane Soc. U.S., 1990-92; mem. Nat. Soc. Newspaper Columnists; mem. St. Joseph (Mo.) City Coun., 1997—, chmn. landfill and water pollution com., chmn. pub. safety com. Recipient Optometric Recognition awards Pearle, Inc., 1986-90; U. Houston scholar, 1972-76 Mem.: DAR (Pony Express chpt.), Nat. Assn. Newspaper Columnists, U. Houston Alumni Assn., St. Joseph Lit. Guild, Tau Sigma. Avocations: jazz concerts, reading, writing, poetry, piano. Office: 1404 S Main Maryville MO 64468 E-mail: eyeDrKim@aol.com.

GORMAN, MARCIE SOTHERN, personal care industry executive; b. Feb. 25, 1949; d. Jerry R. and Carole Edith (Frendel) Sothern; m. N. Scott Gorman, June 14, 1969 (div.); children: Michael Stephen, Mark Jason. AA, U. Fla., 1968; BS, Memphis State U., 1970. Tchr. Memphis City Sch. Sys., 1970-73; tng. dir. Weight Watchers Palm Beach County, Weight Watchers So. Ala., West Palm Beach, Fla., 1973-97; pres. Weight Watchers Franchise Assn., 1999—. Pres. Markel Enterprises, LLC (formerly Markel Ads, Inc.). Cubmaster Boy Scouts Am. Hon. lt. col. a.d.c. Ala. Militia; bd. dirs. Crossroads Program, Palm Beach C.C., 2001—, Communities in Schs., West Palm Beach, 2003—. Mem. NAFE, NOW, Women Am. ORT (program chmn. 1975), Weight Watchers Franchise Assn. (chair mktg. com., advt./mktg. coun., chairperson region IV bd. dirs., treas., 2d v.p. 1991, 1st v.p., region IV co-chair 1998-99, bd. dirs., nat. pres. 1999—), Exec. Women of Palm Beaches, Am. Bus. Women's Assn., Women's C.of C., Zonta. Office: Weight Watchers Office 2435 10th Ave N Lake Worth FL 33461-3128 Office Phone: 561-964-8100.

GORMAN, MARGARET NORINE, probation officer, chemical dependency counselor; b. St. Louis, Aug. 28, 1945; d. Joseph Tarkington and Mary Jo Whitman; m. Thomas Edwin Gorman, Oct. 24, 1970; children: Mary Gorman Ray, Suzanne. BA, Ctrl. Meth. Coll., Fayette, Mo., 1967; student, Pan Am. U., Brownsville, Tex., 1985-90. Cert. alcohol and drug counselor; lic. chem. dependency counselor; cert. probation officer. Supr. Mo. Dept. Pub. Welfare, St. Louis County, 1968-71; child abuse investigator Tex. Dept. Child Welfare, Cameron County, 1974-84; adult probation officer, supr. substance abuse program Cameron County Cmty. Supervision and Corrections Dept., Brownsville, 1985—; instr. dept. continuing edn. U. Tex., Brownsville, 1999—2001. Bd. dirs. Palmer Drug Abuse Program, Brownsville, 1995-96. Mem. com. Brownsville Ind. Sch. Dist., 1994—; bd. dirs. Tip o' Tex. coun. Girl Scouts USA, Weslaco, 1980-82. Mem. AAUW. Avocation: tai chi. Office: Cameron County CSCD 854 E Harrison St Brownsville TX 78520-7121

GORMAN, MAUREEN J. lawyer; b. Rockford, Ill., Dec. 17, 1955; d. John William and Joanne Mary (Ollman) G.; m. Alan O. Sykes, 1980. BA, Coll. William and Mary, 1978; JD, Yale U., 1981. Bar: D.C. 1983, Ill. 1987. Law clk. to Hon. Warren W. Eginton U.S. Dist. Ct. Conn., 1981-82; assoc. Caplin & Drysdale, Washington, 1982-85; legis. atty. joint com. on taxation U.S. Congress, Washington, 1985-86; assoc. Mayer, Brown & Platt, Chgo., 1986-88, ptnr., 1988—. Mem. ABA (chairperson subcom. tech. corrections, employee benefits com., tax sect. 1987-91). Home: 343 E 1st St Hinsdale IL 60521-4241 Office: Mayer Brown & Platt 190 S La Salle St Ste 3100 Chicago IL 60603-3441

GORMAN, NANCY JANE, executive secretary; b. Riverton, N.J., Feb. 9, 1936; d. Albert and Florence Anstotz Gorman. Diploma with honors, Palmyra (N.J.) H.S., 1953; studied voice, piano and organ with, Amos Heacock; studied voice with, Robert Grooters, Temple U., Wayne Conner, Phila. Various stenographer positions Phila. Elec. Co., 1953—70, sec. to chmn. and CEO, 1970—88, sec. to asst. corp. sec., 1988—90; gen. asst., sec. William Knight, Burlington, NJ, 1991—. Singer (soloist): Acad. of Music, Carnegie Hall; singer: (mem.) Phila. Orch. Chorus, Acad. Chorale. Libr. chmn., program chmn., sec. Tri Boro Chorus, Riverton, NJ, 1960—75; vol. numerous human svc. orgns. NJ, 1978—; exec. sec. Am. Brittle Bone Soc., Cinnaminson, NJ, 1978—86; pres. Episcopal Ch. Women Diocese of N.J., 2003—, sec./treas. Burlington Convocation, 1990—; vestry sec. Christ Ch., Riverton, 1985—. Republican. Episcopalian. Avocations: classical music, church music singing, travel, cooking, needlework. Home: 402 Seventh St Riverton NJ 08077

GORMAN, PATRICIA JANE, editor; b. Oak Ridge, Tenn., Feb. 28, 1950; d. Joseph Francis and Ruth (Kommedahl) G.; m. Adrian Thomas Higgins, Apr. 22, 1978; children: Mary Catherine, Patrick Edward. BJ, U. Mo., 1972. Feature writer, copy editor Northamptonshire Evening Telegraph, Eng., 1972-76; asst. editor Am. Tchr. newspaper Am. Fedn. Tchrs., AFL-CIO, Washington, 1976-82, editor, 1982-2000; exec. editor editl. dept. Am. Fedn. Tchrs., Washington, 2000—. Mem. delegation of labor editors to Israel, AFL-CIO, Washington, 1983 Author TV study guides for tchrs., 1979-83 Mem. Internat. Labor Communications Assn. Democrat. Roman Catholic. Office: Am Fedn Tchrs 555 New Jersey Ave NW Washington DC 20001-2029

GORMAN, TARA ANN, music educator; b. Glen Ridge, N.J., May 29, 1975; d. Richard A. and Donna M. Gorman. MusB, Coll. of NJ., Ewing, 1998; MA, Columbia U., 2002. Cert. tchr. N.J. Gen. music tchr. Flocktown Rd. Sch., Long Valley, NJ, 1998—2001; choral dir. Long Valley (N.J.) Mid. Sch. North, 2001—. Treas. N.J. Sch. Music Assn., Stanhope, 2003—. Dir. children's choir Long Valley Presbyn. Ch., 1999—2000. Mem.: Music Educators Nat. Conf. Home: 76 Unger Ave Stanhope NJ 07874 Office: Long Valley Mid Sch North 51 W Mill Road Long Valley NJ 07853 Personal E-mail: tgorman@wtschools.org.

GORNICK, MELANIE DAWN, flight attendant, entrepreneur; b. Edina, Minn., Mar. 13, 1976; d. David Harlan and Dianne Alstrup; life ptnr. Timothy James Gornick; 1 child, Fletcher Alstrup. AA, Normandale C.C., Bloomington, Minn., 1995—98; BA, U. of Minn., Mpls., 2003. Owner Le Petit Cafe, Burnsville, Minn., 1999—2000; flight attendant NW Airlines, Bloomington, Minn., 1996—; pres. K.F. Jewelers, Bloomington, Minn., 2000—. Author: (book) "Mom, Where's My Dad?", 2001. Mem.: Nat. Soc. of Collegiate Scholars (life), Psi Chi. Achievements include invention of board game called I'll Drink to That. Avocations: golf, travel, yoga. E-mail: melaniealstrup@compuserve.com.

GORNIK, KATHY, electronics executive; Co-founder & pres. THIEL Audio, 1975—. Bd. dirs. Lexington Partnership for Workforce Devel., Econs. Am.-Ky. Named Top 40 Women in Bus., The Lane Report; recipient Ky. / So. Ind. Entrepreneur of Yr., Ernst and Young, Inc. Mag. and Merrill Lynch. Mem.: Electronics Industries Alliance (bd. govs.), Consumer Electronics Assn (co-vice chair, chair 2003, bd. dirs & exec. com., former chair, Audio Div. & Specialty Audio Sub-div.), Electronic Industries Found. Achievements include being the first women, the first executive of a small manufacturing company, and the first representative of the high-end audio cmty. to serve as Chair for the Consumer Electronics Assn. bd. dirs. Avocations: reading, skiing. Office: THEIL Audio 1026 Nandino Blvd Lexington KY 40511-1207*

GORON, MARA J. social studies educator, assistant principal; b. Jackson Heights, N.Y., Apr. 9, 1968; d. Stuart Platt and Joan (Arkin) Scolnick. BA, The George Washington U., 1990, MA, 1992; MEd, U. Md., 1995. Cert. secondary social studies and spl. edn. adminstrn. Resident asst., adminstr., supr. The George Washington U., Washington, 1989-92; tchr. religion Temple Sinai, Washington, 1990-96; peer tutoring coord. The George Washington U., 1991-92; adult edn. tchr. Montgomery County Pub., Rockville, Md., 1992; spl. edn. tchr. Alexandria (Va.) Pub. Schs., 1992, Prince Georges Pub. Schs., Upper Marlboro, Md., 1992-93; tutor Lab Sch. Washington, 1992—2002; spl. edn. tchr. Howard County Pub. Schs., Ellicott City, Md., 1993-96, social studies tchr., 1996-99; asst. prin. Centennial H.S., Ellicott City, 1999—2001; inaugural asst. prin. Reservoir H.S., 2001—02; asst. prin. Spanish River Cmty. H.S., Boca Raton, Fla., 2002—. Adviser Howard County Assn. Student Couns., 1997—99; pres. Howard County Coun. for Social Studies, 1997—99; adj. prof. Towson U., 1998, 99. Troop leader Girl Scouts of Am., 1994-95. Mem. ASCD, NAFE, Nat. Assn. Secondary Sch. Prins., Pi Kappa Phi, Omicron Delta Kappa. Avocations: walking, hiking, knitting, reading, scrapbooks. E-mail: goronm@palmbeach.k12.fl.us.

GORR, ELAINE GRAY, therapist, elementary education educator; b. Pitts., Oct. 3, 1949; d. Elmer and Elizabeth Gray; m. Joseph Charles Bonasorte, June 20, 1969 (div. 1972); 1 child, Leah Christine Bonasorte; m. Arthur Richard Gorr, Aug. 12, 1983; children: Matthew, Leah, Carl. BS in Psychology, U. Pitts., 1972; MA in Counseling/Psychology, Norwich U., 1993; PhD in Clin. Psychology, Walden U., 2000. Cert. elem. sch. counselor, Pa., elem. tchr., Pa. Tchr. Pitts. Pub. Schs., 1973-89; outpatient therapist Mercy Behavioral Health, Pitts., 1999—2003; pvt. practice clin. therapist Pitts., 1992—. Nat. bd. dirs. Children and Adults with Attention Deficit Disorders., 1997-2001. Mem. APA, PPA, Nat. Assn. Cognitive Behavioral Therapists, Greater Pitts. Psychol. Assn. Office: 615 Washington Rd Ste 302 Pittsburgh PA 15228

GORRELL, NANCY S. English language educator; b. N.Y.C., Mar. 6, 1946; d. Robert Morris Schwartz and Lillian Moskowitz; m. Joseph Gorrell, June 18, 1967; children: Sara Kate, Elizabeth Marie. BA summa cum laude, SUNY, Stony Brook, 1968, MA, 1970. Tchr. Harbor Country Day Sch., St. James, N.Y., 1970-72; English tchr. Morristown (N.J.) High Sch., 1972—. Tchr. summer training inst. Lincoln Ctr. Inst. for Arts in Edn. at Julliard, N.Y.C., 1983—; dir. Seeking Edn. Equity and Diversity, 1993—; project dir. Poem Pals Project, 1989—; active Geraldine R. Dodge Found. Poetry Coun., 1991. Contbr. articles to profl. jours. V.p. Temple Sholom, Bridgewater, N.J. A+ for Kids Tchr. Network grantee Sta. WWOR-TV, 1989, Dodge Found. Summer Opportunity grantee, 1991; recipient Innovative Teaching award Bus. Week Mag., 1990; named N.J. State Tchr. Yr., 1992.

Mem. Nat. Coun. Tchrs. English (mem. English tchrs. and sch. pub. com., state judge English lit. mag. ranking competition), Internat. Women's Writers Guild, Nat. Coun. Jewish Women. Office: Morristown High Sch 50 Early St Morristown NJ 07960-3898

GORSKE, MARGOT ELIZABETH, nurse administrator; b. Wilmington, Del., Oct. 7, 1955; d. Ronald Leander and Sandra Jean (Harstly) Smith; m. Wilton Scot Gorske, June 14, 1986; children: Wilton Benjamin, Alyson Elizabeth. BA, Beloit Coll., 1979; BSN with high honors, U. Tex., Austin, 1988; MS in Nursing, Troy State U., 1994. Nurse U.S. Army Nurse Corps., 1988-93; clin. nursing instr. U. Ga., Columbus, 1994-95, La Grange Coll., Ga., 1995; divsn. coord. psychol. nursing Svcs. Care S. Presenter in field. With U.S. Army Nurse Corps, 1988-93, res., 1993-96. U. Tex. scholar, 1985-88, Beloit Coll. scholar, 1974-79. Mem. Am. Psychiat. Nurses Assn., Sigma Theta Tau. Democrat. Mem. Soc. Of Friends.

GORSKI, HEDWIG IRENE, poet, writer; b. Trenton, N.J., July 18, 1949; d. Joseph and Irene (Bus) G.; m. Alfred Wishart Jr., Nov. 1, 1973 (div. 1979); m. D'Jalma Garnier III, Dec. 26, 1979. AA, Mercer County C.C., 1969; BFA, Nova Scotia Coll. Art Design, 1976; MA, U. Southwestern La., 1997; PhD, U. La., 2001. Program coord. Tex. Circuit Writers Svc. Orgn., Austin, 1981-83; exec. dir. Perfection Prodns., Lafayette, La., 1985—; fellow Wroclaw (Poland) U., 2003—. Performance poet East of Eden Band, audio tape, 1985, Charted Can. Radio; author: Snatches of the Visible Unreal, 1990, others. Recipient hon. resolution for poetry Tex. Senate, 1993; grantee New Orelans Contemporary Arts Ctr., 1996, Media Artist's fellowship La. Divsn. Arts, 2002-03, Fulbright fellow 2003-2004. Democrat. Roman Catholic. Avocation: films. Home: 100 Springfield Dr Carencro LA 70520-6016 E-mail: hig0162@louisiana.edu.

GOSFIELD, MARGARET, secondary school educator, school system administrator, consultant, editor; b. Marshall County, Minn., Mar. 9, 1942; d. William Jay and Evelyn Pearl (Anderson) Wayne; m. Amor Gosfield, Aug. 21, 1964. BA in History, U. Calif., Santa Barbara, 1966, secondary tchrs. credential, 1968, MA in Edn., 1976. Cert. tchr. Calif. Tchr. Ventura (Calif.) Unified Sch. Dist., 1969-89, coord. gifted and talented edn. program, 1982-97; cons. gifted edn. Author: (book) History of the Anderson Family, 1981, History of the Wayne Family, 1983, editor: Meeting the Challenge: A Guidebook for Teaching Gifted Students, 1996, Gifted Edn. Communicator, 1998—. Named Calif. Outstanding Educator, Johns Hopkins U., 1994; recipient Ednl. Achievement award, Phi Delta Kappa, 1997. Mem.: Calif. Assn. for the Gifted (regional rep. 1990—94, v.p. 1994—96, pres. 1996—98, Tchr. of the Yr. 1985), Santa Barbara Mus. Art. Avocations: travel, writing, family historical research, gardening. Home: 3136 Calle Mariposa Santa Barbara CA 93105-2775 Office: Calif Assn for Gifted 15141 E Whittier Blvd Ste 510 Whittier CA 90603 E-mail: gosfield@cox.net.

GOSINK, JOAN P. engineering educator; BS in Math., MIT, 1962; MS in Engrng., Old Dominion U., 1973; PhD in Mech. Engrng., U. Calif., Berkeley, 1979. Registered profl. hydrologist. NASA fellow Langley Rsch. Ctr., Hampton, Va., 1972—73; Fulbright-Hayes fellow U. Southampton, England, 1974—75; tchg. assoc. U. Calif., Berkeley, 1975—76, postdoctoral fellow Geophys. Inst., U. Alaska, 1979—81; asst. prof. geophysics U. Alaska, Fairbanks, 1981—86, geophysics coord. dept. geology and geophysics, 1986—88, assoc. prof. geophysics, 1986—91; program dir. chem. and thermal sys. NSF, 1990—91; prof., dir. divsn. engrng. Colo. Sch. Mines, Golden, 1991—. Mem. mech. engrng. dept. adv. bd. Carnegie Mellon U., 1992—. Treas., bd. dirs. Women in Crisis: Counseling and Assistance, Fairbanks, 1985—87; mem. Internat. Women's Forum. Recipient N.Y. State Regents scholarship in sci. and engrng., 1958, N.Y. State Regents scholarship, 1958, MIT scholarship, 1958—61, NASA fellowship, Langley Rsch. Ctr., 1972—73, Pacific Gas and Electric fellowship, 1976—78. Mem.: ASCE (rsch. com. of tech. coun. on cold regions rsch. 1986—), ASME (bd. on engrng. edn. 1999—, com. on low temperature and Arctic regions heat transfer K-18 1991—, com. on govt. rels. 1992—96), Women in Engrng. Programs Advocates Network, Am. Inst. Hydrology, Am. Soc. Engrng. Edn. Office: Colo Sch of Mines Divsn Engrng Golden CO 80401

GOSNELL, DAVINA J. dean, nursing educator; BSN, U. Pitts.; MS, PhD, Ohio State U. Dean Sch. Nursing, prof. Kent (Ohio) State U. Chair Ohio Pub. Health Coun. Recipient U. Pitts. Sch. Nursing Disting. Alumni award. Mem. ONA, NLN, STT, GSA, Delta Kappa Gamma. Office: Kent State U Sch Nursing PO Box 5190 Kent OH 44242-0001 E-mail: dgasnell@kent.edu.

GOSS, CYNTHIA LEE, tax accountant; b. Anderson, Ind., May 6, 1955; d. Ralph Samuel and Jacqueline Joyce LeMaster Ewell; m. George Gregory Goss, Sept. 17, 1977; 1 child, Cassandra Renee. Basic tax course H&R Block, Tenn. Receptionist Drs. Bridges Campbell & Woodall, Anderson, 1974-75, nurse's aide various orgns., Anderson, 1976-83; tax preparer, 1985-94; tax preparer, acct. Mayes & Assocs. Liberty Tax Svc., Chattanooga, 1995—2002; bank teller SunTrust Bank, Chattanooga, 2001—02. Tax instr. Liberty Tax Svc., Chattanooga, 1999—2002. Author: (poetry) Hearts Uplifted, 1997 (award winner Sure Truth, The Olive Garden and Lord Take Me, The Last Thing), Internat. Libr. Poetry, Led, Theatre of the Mind, One Thousand Great Americans; composer: (song) You're Still Here, 1991, (ch. choruses) I Am the One, John 10:28, My Prayer, My Plea, David's Song; author numerous poems. Mem. Neighborhood Watch, Highland Park, Chattanooga, 1990-93; rep. for neighborhood Am. Cancer Soc., Highland Park, Chattanooga, 1991-93. Recipient poetry awards; named Guard Dir. of Yr., Awana Ch. Orgn., Rossville, Ga., 1999. Republican. Baptist. Avocations: sewing, writing and singing music, writing poetry, walking, church activities. Home: 1000 School St Apt 313 Elk River MN 55330 Personal E-mail: cindybritches@aol.com.

GOSS, MARY E. WEBER, sociology educator; b. Chgo., May 8, 1926; m. Albert E. Goss, 1945; 1 son, Charles. BA in Sociology with distinction (Univ. Merit scholar 1946-47, Chi Omega Sociology prize 1947), U. Iowa, 1947, MA, 1948; PhD (Gilder fellow 1951-52), Columbia U., 1959. Rsch. asst. U. Iowa, 1947-48, Amherst Coll., 1949; instr. Smith Coll., 1949-50, U. Mass., 1950-51, 55-56, adj. mem. grad. faculty, 1961-66; rsch. assoc. Bur. Applied Social Rsch., Columbia U., 1952-53; cons. sociology, mem. rsch. staff, rsch. coord. N.Y. Hosp.-Cornell U. Med. Center, N.Y.C., 1957-66; mem. faculty dept. medicine Cornell U. Med. Coll., 1959-72, prof. sociology in pub. health, 1973-92, prof. emerita, 1992—. Author: Physicians in Bureaucracy, 1980; also numerous articles; editor: Jour. Health and Social Behavior, 1976-78; co-editor: Comprehensive Medical Care and Teaching: A Report on the N.Y. Hospital-Cornell Medical Center Program, 1967; mem. editorial bd. profl. jours. Fellow APHA, N.Y. Acad. Medicine; mem. AAAS, AAUP, Am. Sociol. Assn., Assn. Tchrs. Preventive Medicine, Acad. Health Svcs. Rsch., Internat. Sociol. Assn., Ea. Sociol. Soc., Phi Beta Kappa, Sigma Xi. Home: 25 Hillcrest Drive Piscataway NJ 08854 Office: Weill Med Coll Cornell Univ Dept Pub Health 411 E 69th St New York NY 10021-5608

GOSSELIN, TRACY KAREN, nursing administrator; b. Worcester, Mass., Dec. 21, 1970; d. Kenneth James and Karen Helen Gosselin; m. David Thompson Acomb, Sept. 5, 1998. BSN, Northeastern U., 1993; M of Nursing Sci., Duke U., 1997. Staff nurse Duke U. Med. Ctr., Durham, N.C., 1993-95, asst. nurse mgr., 1995-97, nurse mgr., 1998-2001; adminstrv. dir., 2001—. Spkr. MedImmune Inc., Gaithersburg, Md. Author: (book chpt.) A Nurse's Guide to Cancer Care, 2000; reviewer: Clin. Jour. of Oncology Nursing. Mem.: AOCN, Am. Coll. Surgeons Oncology Group, Triangle Oncology Nursing Soc. (sec. 1999—2001, pres.-elect 2001, pres. 2002), Oncology Nursing Soc. (contbg. editor monthly newsletter 1998—2002), Sigma Theta Tau. Avocations: cooking, reading. Office: Duke U Med Ctr Rm 005134 PO Box 3085 Durham NC 27710-0001 E-mail: gosse001@mc.duke.edu.

GOSSER-DRUMMOND, TARA O. counseling administrator, music educator; b. Louisville, Ky., Aug. 20, 1957; d. Wallace M. and O'Weida J. Gosser; m. Brian Drummond, July 16, 1988. B in Music Edn., Ea. Ky. U., 1979; EdM, U. Cin., 1984; cert. in adminstrn., Xavier U., 1999. Choral dir. Kenton County Schools, Taylor Mill, Ky., 1980—90; guidance counselor, music specialist Campbell County Schools, Alexandria, Ky., 1990—. Arts connections curriculum CET Edn., Cinn., 2003—. Steering com. tchr. leadership No. Ky. C. of C., Ft. Michell, 2001—; symphonic chorus singer Cinn. May Festival Assn., Cinn. Symphony Orch., 1982—; vol. Cinn. Arts Assn., 1997—. Named Ky. Elem. Counselor of Yr., Ky. PTA, 1991, Ky. Col., Hon. Order of Ky. Colonels, 2002; recipient Golden Apple (honorable mention), Ashland Oil, 1998. Mem.: NEA, Ky. Counseling Assn., No. Ky. Music Educators Assn. (gen. music chair k-5 1990—2003, choral divsn.), Ky. Music Educator's Assn. (state chair K-5 music 2002—04, dist. pres.), Music Educators Nat. Conf., Campbell County Edn. Assn. (bldg. rep. 1995—), Ky. Edn. Assn., Parent Tchr. Assn., Am. Orff Schulwerk, Phi Delta Kappa. Avocations: reading, travel. E-mail: tdrummon@campbell.k12.ky.us.

GOTLIEB, JAQUELIN SMITH, pediatrician; b. Washington, Oct. 20, 1946; d. Turner Taliaferro and Lois Barbara (Fisk) Smith; m. Edward Marvin Gotlieb, June 25, 1970; children: Sarah Ruth, Aaron Franklin, David Jacob. BS in Zoology, Duke U., 1968; MD, Med. Coll. Va., 1972. Diplomate Am. Bd. Pediat. Rotating intern Med. Coll. Va. Hosps.-Va. Commonwealth U., Richmond, 1972—73, resident in pediat., 1973—74; pvt. practice Richmond, 1974—75, Stone Mountain, Ga., 1976—86, 1987—; resident in pediat. U. Colo., Denver, 1975—76; med. dir., cons. CIGNA Healthplan Ga., Atlanta, 1986—87. Sch. physician Richmond City Schs., 1974-75. Bd. dirs. Ga. Health Found., Atlanta, 1985-95, vice chmn., 1995-99, chmn.. 1999—. Fellow Am. Acad. Pediat. (Ga. chpt. bd. dirs. 1996-99); mem. Med. Assn. Ga., Ga. Perinatal Assn. (bd. dirs. 1994-2002, pres. 1999-2000), DeKalb Med. Soc. (chmn. com. 1976). Office: Pediatric Ctr 5405 Memorial Dr Ste D Stone Mountain GA 30083-3236 Office Phone: 404-296-3800.

GOTO, MIDORI, classical violinist; b. Osaka, Japan, Oct. 25, 1971; Attended, Juilliard Sch. Music; grad., Profl. Childrens Sch., 1990. Performer worldwide, 1982—; founder Midori and Friends, 1992. Recordings on Philips, Sony Classical, Columbia Masterworks; performed with N.Y. Philharmonic Orch., Boston Symphony Orch.; worldwide performances include Berlin, Chgo., Cleve., Phila., Montreal, London; recordings include Encore, Live at Carnegie Hall; recordings (albums) Paganini: 24 Caprices, 1989, Encore!, 1992, Midori's 20th Anniversary CD, 2001. Named Best Artist of Yr. by Japanese Govt., 1988; recipient Dorothy B. Chandler Performing Arts award, L.A. Music Ctr., 1989, Crystal award Ashani Shimbun Newspaper contbn. arts, Suntory award, 1994. Office: Sony Classical Sony Music Entertainment Inc 550 Madison Ave New York NY 10022-3211 also: Midori and Friends 850 7th Ave Ste 1103 New York NY 10019-5230

GOTO SABAS, JENNIFER, state official; BA, U. Hawaii, 1983; JD, Georgetown U., 1986. Bar: Va. 1986. Legal rsch. and writing instr. Cath. U. Law Sch., 1986-87; legis. asst. Joint Chief of Staff-Office US Senator Daniel K. Inouye, Washington, 1987-90, dep. chief of staff, 1990-91, chief of staff Honolulu, 1993—. Adj. instr. legal rsch. and writing Am. U. Sch. of Law, 1988. Office: Office Sen Daniel K Inouye Prince Kuhin Bldg Fed Bldg Rm 7-212 Honolulu HI 96850

GOTSHALL, JAN DOYLE, financial planner; b. Pa., Nov. 5, 1942; d. Edward Albert and Rose M. (Leahy) Doyle; m. Ralph M. Gotshall Jr., Dec. 24, 1963; children: Rosemarie, Annmarie, Elizabeth Marie. AA, Neuman Coll., 1979; MSM, Am. Coll., Bryn Mawr, 1997. CFP; registered investment advisor. Co-founder Radnor Planning Assocs., Devon, Pa., 1979-82; fin. cons. Exeter Fin. Svcs. Co., Devon, 1982-85; owner, pres. GM Fin. Planners, Inc., Devon, 1985—. Minority-majority insp. Del. County Electorate, Broomall, Pa., 1973-83; mem. fin. bd. St. Pius X Ch., Broomall, 1988, Archbishop Prendengast H. Sch., Drexel Hill, 2003-. Mem. Inst. CFP (CFP, pres. 1986-87, chmn. 1987-89), Internat. Assn. Fin. Planners (v.p. 1980-88, pres. 1991-92, chmn. 1992-93), Nat. Assn. Ins. Women (cert. profl. ins. woman 1985, bd. dirs. local chpt. 1980-82), Del County Estate Planning Coun. (exec. com. 1989-90, 96—, v.p. 1991-94, pres. 1994-96, dir. 1996-98). Republican. Avocations: reading, golf, tennis. Office: GM Fin Planners Inc 49 Chestnut Rd Paoli PA 19301-1502 Office Phone: 610-644-0101.

GOTTERER, SHELLEY MCCULLOUGH, elementary school educator; b. Cleve., Ohio, Feb. 27, 1949; d. Oscar James McCullough and Marion Hattie Schuster; m. Gerald Saul Gotterer, June 22, 1978; children: Matthew Abraham, Jonathan Andrew stepchildren: Elizabeth Lauren, Rebecca Ruth. BA, Goucher Coll., Towson, Md., 1971; MA, Northwestern U., Evanston, Ill., 1982. H.S. English tchr. Bryn Mawr Sch. for Girls, Balt., 1973—78; storyteller, artist -in -residence St. Bernard Acad., Nashville, 1996—98, Napier Elem. Sch., Metro Pub. Sch., Nashville, 1996—99; adj. faculty, children's lit. and drama Vanderbilt Univ. Peabody Coll., Dept. of Tchg. and Learning, Nashville, 2002; story tchr. long term Artist-in-Residence, designing and tchg. storytelling curriculum, Currey Ingram Acad. (formerly the Westminster Sch. of Nashville), K-12 children with learning differences such as dyslexia, Brentwood, Tenn., 1989—. Radio feature reader, the children's corner Talking Libr. for blind and shut-in pub. listeners supported by the Metro Pub. Libr. and Local Pub. Radio, WPLN, Nashville, 2000—. Workshop leader Curriculum Design And Devel Performer, Retreat Leader, 1982—2003; contbr. articles to profl. jour.; performer: (short stories) (recording cd supplement) The Storyteller's Companion to the Bible. Mem.: Tenn. Assn. for the Preservation and Perpetuation of Storytelling (TAPPS) (pres. of tapps 2000—02), Nat. Storytelling Network (corr.; state liaison for tenn. 2003). Protestant Episc. Achievements include development of design and tchg. of an elem. sch. storytelling curriculum for children with learning differences, K-8. Avocations: travel, reading, walking. Home: 1604 Ash Valley Dr Nashville TN 37215 Office: Currey Ingram Acad 6544 Murray Ln Brentwood TN 37027 Personal E-mail: tales@comcast.net. E-mail: shelley.gotterer@curreyingram.org.

GOTTHARDT, MARY JANE, religious studies educator; b. Davenport, Iowa, Sept. 22, 1940; d. Harry Claus and Roseanne (Bealah May) Stoltenberg; m. Lawrence John Gotthardt, July 8, 1967; 1 child, Michael John. BA, DeLourdes Coll., 1987; MAT, Nat. Louis U., 1999. RN Ill. Nurse Resurrection Hosp., Chgo., 1960—70; chmn. pub. rels. Mark Hopkins Sch., Elk Grove, Ill., 1975—78, Transfiguration Night Train, Wauconda, Ill., 1980; tchr. religious edn. Transfiguration Sch., Wauconda, 1979—2002, tchr. and libr. aid, 1979—2000, tchr., 2000—; tchr. religious edn. St. Peter Ch., Volo, Ill., 1998—2002, dir. religious edn., 2002—. Co-owner Manheim Rental Equipment, Franklin Pk., Ill., 1968—. Sec. Homeowner's Assn., Wauconda. Mem.: AAAS, other ednl. orgns., Phi Delta Kappa. Roman Catholic. Avocation: travel. Office: Transfiguration Sch 316 W Mill St Wauconda IL 60084

GOTTLIEB, ALICE B. dermatologist; PhD, Rockefeller U., 1979; MD, Cornell U., 1980. Diplomate Am. Bd. Dermatology. Fellow in rheumatology Cornell U. Hosp. for Spl. Surgery, N.Y.C., 1982—84; intern in internal medicine N.Y. Hosp., N.Y.C., 1980—82, resident in dermatology, 1990—93; physician divsn. dermatology Robert Wood Johnson Med. Sch., New Brunswick, NJ, 1995—. Office: Robert Wood Johnson Med Sch One Robert Wood Johnson Pl PO Box 19 New Brunswick NJ 08903-0019

GOTTLIEB, LESLIE, geneticist, educator; BA in English Lit., Cornell U., 1957; PhD in Botany, U. Mich., 1969. Prof. genetics dept. evolution and ecology U. Calif., Davis. Contbr. articles to profl. jours. Recipient Merit award Bot. Soc. Am., 2000. Achievements include research on molecular genetics and evolution of phosphoglucose isomerase in plants, particularly in the wildflower Clarkia; research on genetic basis for large morphological differences between closely related plant species and subspecies. Office: U Calif Davis 5310 Storer Hall One Sheilds Ave Davis CA 95616 E-mail: ldgottlieb@ucdavis.edu.

GOTTSCHALK, SISTER MARY THERESE, nun, hospital administrator; b. Doellwang, Germany, June 21, 1931; arrived in U.S., 1953, naturalized, 1959; d. John and Sabina (Dietz) G. BS in Pharmacy, Creighton U., 1960; M.H.A., St. Louis U., 1970; DHL (hon.), U. Okla., 2001. Joined Sisters of the Sorrowful Mother, Roman Catholic Ch, 1952. Dir. pharmacy St. Mary's Hosp., Roswell, N.Mex., 1960-68, chief exec. officer, 1972-74; asst. adminstr. St. John Med. Ctr., Tulsa, 1970-72, pres., CEO, 1974-99, St. John Health Sys., Tulsa, 1982—; pres. Marian Health Sys., Tulsa, 1989—. Vol. ARC, United Way. Fellow: Am. Coll. Hosp. Adminstrs.; mem.: Cath. Health Assn. (bd. dirs. 1995—2001), Tulsa C. of C., Okla. Conf. Cath. Hosps. (past pres.), Tulsa Hosp. Coun., Okla. Hosp. Assn. (pres. 1984), Am. Hosp. Assn. (ho. of dels., regional policy bd.). Office: St John Med Ctr 1923 S Utica Ave Tulsa OK 74104-6502

GOTTSCHALL, JOAN B. judge; b. Oak Ridge, Tenn., Apr. 23, 1947; d. Herbert A. and Elaine (Reichbaum) G. BA cum laude, Smith Coll., Mass., 1969; JD, Stanford Univ., Calif., 1973. Bar: Ill. 1973. Assoc. Jenner & Block, 1973-76, 78-81, ptnr., 1981-82; staff atty. Fed. Defender Program, 1976-78, Univ. of Chgo., Office of Legal Counsel, 1983-84, magistrate judge U.S. Dist. Ct. (no. dist.) Ill., Chgo., 1984—96, judge, 1996—2002. Mem. vis. com., past chair Divinity Sch., U. Chgo., 1984—97. Bd. dirs. Martin Marty Ctr., U. Chgo. Div. Sch., Ill. Humanities Coun. Mem.: Divinity Sch. (vis. com.), Women's Bar Assn. Ill., Chgo. Bar Assn., Am. Bar Assn. Office: Everett McKinley Dirksen Bldg 219 S Dearborn St Ste 1978 Chicago IL 60604-1877 Office Phone: 312-435-5640.

GOUDY, JOSEPHINE GRAY, social worker; b. Des Moines, Nov. 30, 1925; d. Gerald William and Myrtle Maria (Brooks) Gray; m. John Winston Goudy, June 5, 1948; children: Tracy Jean, Paula Rae. BA, State U. Iowa, 1954, MSW, 1966; cert. in gerontology, U. Ill. LCSW, lic. ind. social worker Iowa, cert. social worker Iowa, Ill. Child welfare supr. Iowa Dept. Social Svcs., 1960-68; psychiat. social worker Cmty. Mental Health Ctr., Scott County, Iowa, 1966-71; social work instr. Palmer Jr. Coll., Davenport, Iowa, 1967-70; psychiat. social worker, chief social svcs. Jacksonville (Ill.) State Mental Hosp., 1971-74; coord. cmty. mental health outpatient svcs. McFarland Mental Health Ctr., Springfield, Ill., 1974; exec. dir. Macoupin County Mental Health Ctr., Carlinville, Ill., 1974-98, Youth Attention Ctr., Jacksonville, Ill., 1998-99; pvt. practice, 1999—. Chmn. Human Svcs. Edn. Coun., Springfield, 1979—81; bd. mem. Alzheimer's Disease and Related Disorders Assn., Springfield; past exec. Davenport Cmty. Welfare Coun.; adj. prof. dept. psychiatry So. Ill. U., Springfield. Mem.: AAUW (br. pres. 1964—66, state bar 1966—68, br. grantee 1975), NASW (del. to China 2000, Social Worker of Yr. Ctrl. Ill. area 1983), APA, Internat. Fedn. Univ. Women, Am. Psychotherapy Assn., Acad. Cert. Social Workers, Bus. and Profl. Women (Woman of Yr. 1983), U. Iowa Alumni Assn., Carlinville Women's Club (pres. 1975—77, 1996—98), Delta Kappa Gamma. Republican. Methodist. Home: 5347 Chapel Hill Rd Davenport IA 52802-9502

GOUGÉ, SUSAN CORNELIA JONES, microbiologist; b. Chgo., Apr. 18, 1924; d. Harry LeRoy and Gladys (Moon) Jones; student Am. U., Washington, 1942-43, La. Coll., 1944-45; BS, George Washington U., 1948; postgrad. Georgetown U., 1956-58, 66-69, Vt. Coll. of Norwich U., M.A. in Pub. Health, 1984, Walden U., 1996-2002, Kennedy We. U., 2003—; m. John Oscar Gougé, Aug. 7, 1943 (dec. Mar. 2003); children: John Ronald, Richard Michael (dec.), Claudia Renée Gougé Carr. Med. technician Children's Hosp. Research Lab., Washington, 1948-49; bacteriologist George Washington U. Research Lab., D.C. Gen. Hosp., 1950-53; med. microbiologist Walter Reed Army Inst. Research, Washington, 1953-61; research asst. Dental Research, Walter Reed Army Med. Ctr., 1961-62; microbiologist antibiotics div. FDA, 1962-63; supr. quality control John D. Copanos Co., Pharms., Balt., 1963-64; research tng. asst. infectious diseases and tropical medicine Howard U. Med. Sch., 1964-65; research assoc. Georgetown U. Lab. Infectious Diseases, D.C. Gen. Hosp., 1966-69; mycologist Georgetown U. Hosp. Lab., 1969-70; microbiologist Research Found. of Washington Hosp. Ctr., 1971-73; dir. quality control Bio-Medium Corp., Silver Spring, Md., 1973-76; microbiologist Alcolac, Inc., Balt., 1976-77; microbiologist div. labs., dept. human resources Community Health and Hosps. Adminstrn., Washington, 1978-79; microbiologist div. ophthalmic devices, Office Device Evaluation, Ctr. for Devices and Radiol. Health, FDA, Rockville, Md., 1979—, alt. contact on U.S. Pharmacopoeia Divsn. Stds. Devel. Microbiology subcom., 1996-2000, FDA observer on Nat. Com. Clin. Lab. Stds. com. abbreviated bacterial identification, 1994-98, alt. liaison to Assn. Advancement Med. Instrumentation sterilization stds. com., 1996—. Sec. to exec. bd. Bethesda Project Awareness, 1970-71; vol. lead poisoning detection testing project, D.C. Office Vols. Internat. Tech. Assistance, 1970-71; vol. Zacchaeus Free Clinic, Washington, 1979-84, Winchester Med. Ctr., 1994—. Mem. Nat. Capital Harp Ensemble, 1941-65; mem. parish social concerns com. Roman Cath. Ch., 1972-84; mem. Winchester Med. Ctr. Aux., 1994—. Recipient medal cmty. svc.; registered microbiologist Nat. Registry Microbiologists; specialist microbiologist Am. Acad. Microbiology. Mem. AAAS, VITA, IEEE (engrng. in medicine and biology soc.), LWV (v.p. Winchester-Frederick County chpt. 1997-98), Am. Soc. for Microbiology, Am. Inst. Biol. Scis., Am. Chem. Soc., Internat. Union Pure and Applied Chemistry, N.Y. Acad. Scis., Am. Pub. Heath Assn., Bus. and Profl. Women (Capital Club, rec. sec. 1973-74, 1st v.p. 1974-75, pres. 1975-76), Winchester Bus. and Profl. Women, Winchester-Frederick County League Women Voters (v.p. 1997-98), World Affairs Council of Washington D.C., Winchester-Frederick County Hist. Soc., Toastmasters Internat. (charter sec. BMD Club #3941 1979-80), Pi Kappa Delta, Phi Delta Kappa, Sigma Xi. Methodist. Office: FDA Div Ophthalmic Devices Office Device Evaluation 9200 Corporate Blvd Rockville MD 20850-3223

GOUGH, CAROLYN HARLEY, library director; b. Paterson, N.J., Sept. 23, 1922; d. Frank Ellsworth and Mabel (Harrison) Harley; m. George Harrison Gough, Sept. 21, 1944; children: Deborah Ann Gough Bornholdt, Douglas Alan. BA, Coll. William and Mary, 1943; MLS, Drexel U., 1966. Rsch. asst. Young and Rubicam, Inc., N.Y.C., 1943-44; libr. dir., asst. prof. Cabrini Coll., Radnor, Pa., 1966-81; chmn. Palm Beach County Libr. Bd., 1984-86. Mem. resources study com. Tredyffrin Twp. Libr., 1964-65; docent Henry Morrison Flagler Mus., 1982-92. Mem. AAUP, DAR (Palm Beach chpt.), Tri-State Coll. Libr. Coop. (v.p. 1973-74, pres. 1974-75), Assn. Coll. and Rsch. Librs. (dir. 1978-81), Questers, Inc. (1st nat. v.p. 1964-66), Atlantis Golf Club, Atlantis Women's Club (co-pres. 1982-83), Sir Robert Boyle Soc., Beta Phi Mu, Kappa Delta. Republican. Episcopalian. Home: 458 S Country Club Dr Lake Worth FL 33462

GOUGH, PAULINE BJERKE, magazine editor; b. Wadena, Minn., Jan. 7, 1935; d. Luther C. and Zita Pauline (Halbmaier) Bjerke; children: Mary Pauline, Sarah Elizabeth, Philip Clayton. BA, U. Minn., Mpls., 1957; BS, Moorhead (Minn.) State Coll., 1970; MS, Ind. U., Bloomington, 1972; EdD, Ind. U., 1977. Reporter women's page San Jose (Calif.) Mercury-News, 1957-58; with rsch. dept. Campbell-Mithun Advt., Mpls., 1958-60;

tchr. Univ. Elem. Sch., Bloomington, 1970-79; freelance writer Agy. Instrnl. TV, Bloomington, 1974-80; asst. editor Phi Delta Kappa, Bloomington, 1980-81, mem. profl. staff, 1981—, mng. editor, 1981-88, editor, 1988—. Mem. adj. faculty Ind. U.-Purdue U., Indpls., summers 1976, 77; leader insts. on writing for publ. Contbr. articles to profl. publs. Recipient Disting. Alumna award Moorhead State U., 1982. Mem. Phi Beta Kappa, Phi Delta Kappa. Office: Phi Delta Kappa PO Box 789 408 N Union St Bloomington IN 47405-3800 Home: 13611 Singletree Ct Carmel IN 46032-9435 E-mail: pgough@kiva.net.

GOUKER, JANE ANN, music educator; b. York, PA, Sept. 6, 1953; d. Ray Calvin and Freida Louise Gouker. B Music Edn., Ind. U., 1976, M in Music Edn., 1990. Elem. strings tchr. Fairfax (Va.) County Pub. Schs., 1976—77; elem./mid. sch. strings tchr. Manassas (Va.) City Pub. Schs., 1977—80; elem./mid. sch./h.s. orchestra dir., dept. chair Monroe County Cmty. Sch. Corp., Bloomington, Ind., 1980—; double bass tchr., ensemble dir. Ind. U. Summer Music Clinic, Bloomington, 1996—. Office Phone: 812-330-7714.

GOULD, BONNIE M(ARINCIC), realtor; b. Cleve., Sept. 3, 1947; d. Edward Louis and Frances (Dee (Pavlovich) Marincic. Student, John Carroll U. Asst. prodn. mgr. Nelson Stern Advt., Cleve., 1966-73; sec. acctg. S. James Dubin & Assocs., Eastlake, Ohio, 1976-78; sec., atty. James Todoroff, Andrews & Todoroff, Eastlake, 1977-78; realtor sales Century 21-Baur, Euclid, Ohio, 1978-82; relocations dir., mgr. Century 21, Euclid, 1979-82; realtor assoc., relocation dir. Century 21-Malone, Inc., Willowick, Ohio, 1982-83, Century 21-William T. Byrne, Cleve., 1983-84, Smythe, Cramer Co., Euclid, 1984-86; sr. v.p., treas., corp. mgr. Acacia Realty Profls. Inc., 1986-98; pres., treas., interior design coord. Acacia Design and Trade Profls. Inc. Gen. Contractors, 1990—; pres., CEO Acacia Design Fine Homes and Properties, 1999—. Mem. Realtors Polit. Action Com., Cleve., 1981—; vice chmn. local taxation and legislation com. Cleve. Area Bd. Realtors, 1983-84, vice chmn. polit. affairs, 1987—, chmn. home and flower 1986, mem. enlarged legis. com., 1986-97, internat. rules and fin. com., 1993-95, chmn. 1995; sec., trustee Euclid Gateway Found., 1987—. Recipient Disting. Svc. award Cleve. Bd. Realtors, 1983-87, 96, Woman of Yr. award 1990. Mem. Cleve. Bd. Realtors (dir. 1984-86, 93—, 2d v.p. 1994, treas. 1995, gov. No. Ohio multiple listings svc. 1992—, contract and fin. com., 1992—), Ohio Assn. Realtors (trustee 1981-97), Nat. Assn. Realtors Women's Coun. of Realtors (treas. Cleve. chpt. 1986-87, v.p. 1987-88, pres. 1989, chmn. nominating com. 1990, Woman of Yr. 1990), Lake and Geague Area Assn. Realtors (fin. com. 2001--, 2d v.p. 2004), North East Roundtable (sec. 1980, chair 1981). Republican. Roman Catholic. Office: Acacia Design Fine Homes & Properties 293 E 266th St Cleveland OH 44132-1552 E-mail: acaciadsgn@aol.com., acaciarelo@aol.com.

GOULD, CLAUDIA, museum director; BA in Art History, Boston Coll.; M in Mus. Studies, NYU. Curator, project dir., curator exhbns. Wexner Ctr. Arts, Ohio State U., 1989-91; ind. curator N.Y.C., 1992-94; exec. dir. Artists Space, N.Y.C., 1994-99, Inst. Contemporary Art, Phila., 1999—. Office: Inst Contemporary Art 118 S 36th St Philadelphia PA 19104-3289

GOULD, ELIZABETH, neuroscientist, educator; Asst. prof. dept. psychology Princeton U. Contbr. articles to profl. jours. Recipient Troland Rsch. award NAS, 2000. Office: Dept Psychology Princeton Univ Princeton NJ 08544-1010

GOULD, LILIAN, writer; b. Phila., Apr. 19, 1920; d. Reuben Barr and Lilian Valentine (Scott) Seidel; m. Irving Gould, Nov. 16, 1944; children: Mark, Scott, Paul, John. Student, U. Pa., Charles Morris Price Sch. of Advt. and Journalism, Phila. Copywriter, mgr. advt. agys., Phila. Author: Our Living Past, 1969, Jeremy and the Gorillas, 1977 (award 1977); freelance journalist mags. and newspapers. Mem. Authors Guild, Phila. Children's Reading Roundtable, Phila. Writers Orgn., Soc. of Children's Book Writers and Illustrators. Home: 772 Newtown Rd Villanova PA 19085-1121

GOULD, MARTHA BERNICE, retired librarian; b. Claremont, NH, Oct. 8, 1931; d. Sigmund and Gertrude Heller; m. Arthur Gould, July 29, 1960; children: Leslie, Stephen. BA in Edn., U. Mich., 1953; MS in Libr. Sci., Simmons Coll., 1956; cert., U. Denver Libr. Sch., 1978. Childrens libr. N.Y. Pub. Libr., 1956-58; adminstr. libr. svcs. act demonstration regional libr. project Pawhuska, Okla., 1958-59; cons. N.Mex. State Libr., 1959-60; children's libr. then sr. children's libr. L.A. Pub. Libr., 1960-72; acctg. dir. pub. svcs., reference libr. Nev. State Libr., 1972-74; pub. svcs. libr. Washoe County (Nev.) Libr., 1974-79, asst. county libr., 1979-84, county libr., 1984-94; ret., 1994. Cons. Nev. State Libr. and Archives, 1996—; part-time lectr. libr. adminstrn. U. Nev.; acting dir. Nev. Ctr. for the Book; chair, Presdl. appointee Nat. Commn. in Librs. & Info. Sci., 2000—03; mem. adv. coun. Nev. Coun. on Librs. and Literacy, 2001—; mem. adv. bd. Fleischmann Planetarium, 1999—2003. Co-editor: Nevada Women's History Project Annotated Bibliography, 1999; contbr. articles to jours. Exec. dir. Kids Voting/USA, Nev., 1996; trustee United Jewish Appeals, 1981; bd. dirs. Temple Sinai, Planned Parenthood, 1996-97, Truckee Meadows Habitat for Humanity, 1995-98; trustee RSVP, North Nevadans for ERA; No. Nev. chmn. Gov.'s Conf. on Libr., 1990; bd. dirs. Campaign for Choice, No. Nev. Food Bank, Nev. Women's Fund (Hall of Fame award 1989); mem. No. Nev. NCCJ, Washoe County Quality Life Task Force, 1992—, Washoe County Elections Taskforce, 1999—; bd. dirs. KUNR Pub. Radio, 1999-2000, chair bd. dirs., 2000-04; chair Nat. Commn. Librs. & Info. Sci., 2000-03; chair Sierra (Nev.) Cmty. Access TV; adv. bd. Partnership Librs. Washoe County; co-chair social studies curriculum adv. task force Washoe County Sch. Dist.; mem. Nev. Women's History Project Bd.; chair Downtown River Corridor Com., 1995-97; vice chair Dem. Party Washoe County; v.p. Nev. Diabetes Assn. for Children and Adults, 1998-2002, pres., 2002-04; chair devel. com. Planned Parenthood, 2002—; bd. dirs. Washoe Libr. Found., 2003-; mem. adv. Adv. Coun. on Edn./to the Holocaust, 2000—; chair Washoe County Dem. Women's Club, 2003—. Recipient Nev. State Libr. Letter of Commendation, 1973, Washoe County Bd. Commrs. Resolution of Appreciation, 1978, ACLU of Nev. Civil Libertarian of Yr. 1988, Freedom's Sake award AAUW, 1989, Leadership in Literacy award Sierra chpt. Internat. Reading Assn., 1992, Woman of Distinction award 1992, Cornerstone award Sierra chpt. Assn. Fundraising Profls., 2003. Mem. ALA (bd. dirs., intellectual freedom roundtable 1977-79, intellectual freedom com. 1979-83, coun. 1983-86), ACLU (bd. dirs. Civil Libertarian of Yr. Nev. chpt. 1988, chair gov.'s conf. for women 1989), Nev. Libr. Assn. (chmn. pub. info. com. 1972-73, intellectual freedom com. 1975-78, govt. rels. com. 1978-79, v.p., pres.-elect 1980, pres. 1981, Spl. Citation 1978, 87, Libr. of Yr. 1993). E-mail: mgould@powernet.net.

GOULD, MARY CHRISTA, small business owner; b. Chattanooga, Tenn., Dec. 20, 1977; d. Wallace Harry and Sandra Gayle Gould; children: Christian Charles, Grant Leighton. Co-owner Creative Minds Pub., Chattanooga, 1999—; proprieter True Worship Music, Chattanooga, 2000—; rep. A&R Fresh On Delivery Records, Chattanooga, 2000—. Composer: (songs) Fields of Life, 2000; author: Poems From the Heart, 2001. Mem.: ASCAP, BMI. Avocation: Avocations: public speaking against domestic violence, singing, writing, reading. Home: 1005 S Highland Park Ave Chattanooga TN 37404-4216

GOULDING, NORA See CLARK, SUSAN

GOULET, LORRIE, sculptor; b. Riverdale, N.Y., Aug. 17, 1925; Student, Inwood Potteries Studios, N.Y.C., 1932-36, Black Mountain Coll., N.C., 1943-44. Tchr. Mus. Modern Art, 1957, 64, Scarsdale Studio Workshop, 1959, 61, New Sch., 1961—75, Art Students League, 1981—. One-woman shows include Clay Club Sculpture Ctr., N.Y.C., 1948, 1955, Cheney Libr., Hoosick Falls, N.Y., 1951, Contemporaries Gallery, N.Y.C., 1959, 1962, 1966, 1968, Rye (N.Y.) Art Ctr., 1966, New Sch. Assocs., N.Y.C., 1968, Temple Emeth, Teaneck, N.J., 1969, Kennedy Galleries, N.Y.C., 1971, 1973, 1975, 1978, 1980, 1982, 1986, Carolyn Hill Gallery, 1988, 1991, Caldwell (N.J.) Coll., 1989, Nat. Mus. Women in the Arts, Washington, 1998, Harmon-Meek Galleries, Naples, Fla., 2000, David Findlay Jr. Gallery, 2001, 2002, exhibited in group shows at Mus. Natural History, 1936, Whitney Mus. Am. Art, N.Y.C., 1948—50, 1953, 1955, Met. Mus. Art, 1951, Detroit Inst. Art, 1960, Pa. Acad., 1950—52, 1954, 1959, 1964, AD, N.Y.C., 1966, 1975, 1977, Corcoran Gallery, Washington, 1966, Hofstra Mus., N.Y.C., 1990, The McNey Mus., 1990, The Copley Soc., Boston, 1991, The Spanish Inst., 1992, Lehigh U. Art Gallery, 1992, Iowa State U. Brunne Gallery, 1992, Paine Art Ctr., Oshkosh, Wis., 1992, Mitchell Art Gallery, St. John's Coll., Annapolis, Md., 1992, Erie (Pa.) Art Mus., 1995, Nat. Sculpture Soc., 2001, Art Students League, N.Y.C., 2003, Represented in permanent collections Hunter Mus., Chattanooga, N.J. State Mus., Wichita Mus. Art, Hirschhorn Sculpture Mus., Washington, The Philharm. Ctr., Naples, Fla., Art Students League, N.Y.C., Savannah Coll. Arts. Recipient Malvina Hoffman award Nat. Acad. Design, 2001, others; grantee Fhorsheim Art Fund, 1997. Fellow: Nat. Sculpture Soc. (coun.); mem.: NAD (academician 1989, mem. coun. 1994), Fine Arts Fedn. (pres. 1998—2002, hon. v.p. 2003), N.Y. Artists Equity Inc. (pres. 1998—2002), Visual Artists and Galleries Assocs., Sculptors Guild, Audubon Artists.

GOULETAS, EVANGELINE, investment executive; m. Hugh L. Carey, 1981. MA in Math, Northeastern Ill. State Coll. Formerly mem. faculty dept. Chgo. Bd. Edn.; prin. Am. Invsco Corp., Chgo., 1969—; ptnr. Electronic Realty Assn., IMB (Internat. Mcht. Banking), N.Y.C., 1969—. Formerly trustee DePaul U.; trustee Chgo. City Library, Com. for Thalassemia Concern; chairperson Combined Cardiac Research Women's Found., U. Chgo., N.Y. State Watch Com.; mem. exec. bd. Chgo. City Ballet, N.Y.C. Meals-On-Wheels, LaGuardia Community Coll. Recipient Great Am. award B'nai B'rith, 1977, Businesswoman of Yr. award Soc. of the Little Flower, 1979, Exec. Businesswoman of the Yr. Internat. Orgn. of Women Execs., 1980, Tree of Life Honor, Jewish Nat. Fund, 1981, Myrtle Wreath award, Nassau County Hadassah, 1981, Paedia award DePaul U., 1982, Eleanor Roosevelt Humanities award, State of Israel Bonds, 1983, humanitarian award Assn. for Children with Retarded Mental Devel., 1985, Woman of Distinction Pan Euboean Soc. of Am., 1985; two residences named in her honor Fedn. of P.R. Orgns., Bronx, United Cerebral Palsy, Staten Island; Evangeline Gouletas-Carey Leadership award presented annually in her name by LaGuardia Community Coll. of CUNY. Mem. Nat. Assn. Realtors, Inst. Real Estate Mgmt., Pres.'s Assn. of Am. Mgmt. Assn. Greek Orthodox.

GOUMNEROVA, LILIANA CHRISTOVA, physician, neurosurgeon, educator; b. Jakarta, Indonesia, Sept. 27, 1956; came to U.S., 1988; d. Christo Todorov and Jeanne Dimitrova (Petkova) G. BSc, Faculty of Medicine, Sofia, Bulgaria, 1977; MD, U. Toronto, 1980. Intern U. Toronto, 1980-81; resident in neurosurgery U. Ottawa, Can., 1981-86; fellow in pediatric neurosurgery Hosp. Sick Children, Toronto, 1987-88, assoc. staff neurosurgeon, 1987-88; assoc. staff surgeon Ottawa (Can.) Civic Hosp., 1986-87; Dana fellow in neurosurgery U. Pa., Phila., 1988-90; assoc. in neurosurgery Children's Hosp., Boston, 1990—, dir. clin. pediat. neurosurg. oncology, 1999—; assoc. in neurosurgery Brigham & Women's Hosp., Boston, 1990—; cons. neurosurgeon Dana Farber Cancer Inst., Boston, 1990—, dir. clin. pediat. neurosurg. oncology; asst. prof. surgery Sch. Medicine Harvard U., Boston, 1990—. Mem. Am. Assn. Neurol. Surgeons (Young Investigator award 1996). Office: Childrens Hosp 300 Longwood Ave Boston MA 02115-5737

GOURLEY, BRENDA, educational association administrator, academic administrator; married; 4 children. CTA (qualified accountant), MBL. From prof. acctg. and bus., dean faculty econs. and mgmt., dep. vice-chancellor to vice chancellor U. Natal, 1994; chmn. South African Univs. Vice-Chancellor's Assn., 1995—97; mem. bd. dirs. Internat. Assn. U., 2000—; vice-chancellor Open U., 2002—. Office: Open U Walton Hall Milton Keynes MK7 6AA England

GOURLEY, DIANE, music educator; b. N.Y.C., Apr. 12, 1952; d. Michael Alfred and Pauline Holcek; m. Robert Lee Gourley, June 19, 1971; children: Scott Michael, Daniel Lee. BS, Grand Canyon U., 1975. Music endorsement Ariz. Dept. Edn. Choral tchr. Independence H.S., Glendale, Ariz., 1980—83, Apollo H.S., Glendale, 1983—. Composer: (choral composition) Lord Walk With Me, 1978. Mem.: Ariz. Music Educators Assn. (tech. chmn. 1999—). Republican. Baptist. Avocations: singing, piano, web design, composing, painting. Office: Apollo HS 8045 N 47th Ave Glendale AZ 85302 E-mail: gourl@mindspring.com.

GOURLEY, HELEN ELIZABETH, physicist; b. Rochester, N.Y., Apr. 22, 1931; d. Karl Friedrich and Emma Christine (Kramer) Vogele; m. Edward Henry Gustafson, June 9, 1959 (div. Oct. 1968); 1 child, Rebecca Christine Gustafson-O'Hare; m. Darrell Lavonne Gourley, Apr. 18, 1973; children: Brandon Wayne, Lisa Amber. BS in Physics with hons., U. Rochester, 1953. Calif. state tchr.'s credential for electro-optics and electronics, gen. contractor's lic. Rsch. physicist U. Calif. Med. Ctr., San Francisco, 1953-55; project engr. Beckman Instruments, Richmond, Calif., 1955-60; sr. scientist Nuclear Rsch. Instruments, Berkeley, Calif., 1960-65; program mgr. Quantic Industries, San Carlos, Calif., 1965-70; owner, chief optical scientist System Scis. Group, San Francisco, 1971—. Dir., mem. Nat. Adv. Group for Nat. Tech. Inst. for the Deaf, Rochester Inst. Tech., Rochester, 1979-83; mem. nat. spkr.'s bur. Am. Phys. Soc., Washington, 1990—; lectr., seminar leader for various U. Calif. Physics Depts. Contbr. seminars and symposiums to various profl. meetings. Spkr. Lion's Club, "Women and Small Business", San Francisco, 1984, 86; presenter laser workshops for h.s. girls, San Francisco, 1983—; organizer, chmn. Tech-Net Consultant Group, San Francisco, 1992—. Recipient Bausch & Lomb Science award and scholarship Bausch & Lomb Optical Co., 1949, N.Y. State scholarship, 1949-53, Pres.'s award Internat. Soc. for Optical Engrg., 1964. Mem. Optical Soc. No. Calif. (pres. 1990-91), Optical Soc. of Am. (Nat. Edn. Coun. 1984-88), The Internat. Soc. for Optical Engring. (spkr. 1964—). Avocations: harp, orchid culture. Office: System Scis Group 389 Benito Way San Francisco CA 94127

GOURLEY, PAULA MARIE, art educator, artist, designer bookbinder, writer, publisher; b. Carmel, Calif., Apr. 29, 1948; d. Raymond Serge Voronkoff and Frances Eliseyvna (Kovtynovich) G.; m. David Clark Willard, Feb. 10, 1972 (div. Oct. 1973). AA, Monterey (Calif.) Peninsula Coll., 1971; BA, Goddard Coll., 1978; MFA, U. Ala., 1987; pvt. bookbinding study with, Donald Glaister, Roger Arnoult, Paule Ameline, Michelene de Bellefroid, Francoise Bausart, Sun Evrard, James Brockman. Radiologic technologist Cen. Med. Clinic, Pacific Grove, Calif., 1970-71, Community Hosp. of Monterey, 1972-75, Duke U. Med. Ctr., Durham, N.C., 1975-77; dept. head, ultrasound technologist Middlesex Meml. Hosp., Middletown, Conn., 1977-79; asst. prof. U. Ala., Tuscaloosa, 1985-93, assoc. prof., 1993-98. Established Pelegaya Press and Paperworks, 1978, Lilyhouse Studio Editions, 1999; asst. dir. Inst. for Book Arts U. Ala., 1985—88, coord., 1988—94, co-dir. MFA program in the book arts, 1994—97; U.S. rep. Les Amis de la Reliure d'Art, Toulousee, France, 1989—; founding dir. Southeastern chpt. Guild of BookWorkers, 1995—99; guest artist Marriott Libr. Book Arts Program U. Utah, 1999—; contbr. journalist for U.S. to Art et Metiers du Livre Revue Internat., Paris; adj. faculty Lane Micro Bus./Lane C.C., resource and edn. coord., 2002—; Saturday Market resource coord., Eugene, Oreg., 2001—; bd. dirs. Eugene (Oreg.) Saturday Mkt., Oreg. Micro Enterprise Network, Oreg. Coun. Bus. Edn. Editor First Impressions (newsletter), 1988-97; contbr. articles to profl. jours.; numerous nat. and internat. bookbinding exhbns., 1978—; contbr. editor Resource Corner, Saturday Market Newletter. Vol. PLUS Literacy Program, Tuscaloosa, 1991-96. U. Ala. grantee, 1988, 89, 90, 92; recipient Diplome of honneur Atelier d'Arts Appliques, France, 1986, Craft fellowship Ala. State Coun. on Arts, 1993-94. Mem. Am. Registry Radiologic Technologists, Am. Registry Diagnostic Med. Sonographers, Guild of BookWorkers (founder and bd. dirs. Southeastern regional chpt., editor, pub. newsletter True Grits, mem. exec. com.), Hand Bookbinders Calif., Bookbinders Internat. (v.p. U.S. 1989-92), Pacific Ctr. for the Book Arts, Am. Craft Coun., Ala. Craft Coun., Can. Bookbinders and Book Artists Guild, Nat. Mus. Women in Arts, Willamette Jazz Soc. (founding mem.). Avocations: photography, quilting, reading, cuisine, travel. Studio: 1936 W 34th Ave Eugene OR 97405-1709

GOUTHRO, BARBARA ANN, elementary school educator; d. Clarence Frederick and Hazel Josephine Norton; m. Kenneth Robert Gouthro, Jan. 28, 1983; m. Keith Paul Ronalter, Dec. 24, 1970 (div. May 10, 1982); children: Scott David Ronalter, Amanda Lori Ronalter. BS in music edn., Western Conn. State U., 1967—71; MS in music edn., Ctrl. Conn. State U., 1982—84. Music Educator Commonwealth of Mass., 1998. Elem. music tchr. Regional Sch. Dist. #10, Harwinton, Conn., 1971—78; music tchr. Torrington Christian Acad., Conn., 1985—86; supr./tchr./adminstr. Joy Christian Acad., Springfield, Mass., 1987—91; music tchr. Pioneer Valley Christian Sch., Springfield, Mass., 1991—99; choral dir. East Longmeadow H.S., Mass., 2000—01; fine arts tchr. Bellamy Mid. Sch., Chicopee, Mass., 2001—03. Pres./owner Hiz Biz Publications, Huntington, Mass., 1993—; bd. dirs., women's ministry Pioneer Valley Assembly of God, Huntington, music min., tchr.; pianist Cranwell Resort and Spa, Lenox, Mass.; women's worship tchg. ministry dir. Eighth Day, Huntington; pvt. piano tchr., 1971—; music facilitator Assn. of Christian Schools Internat., regional music coord.; lead women's cell network Pioneer Valley Assembly of God, Huntington, Mass., prayer counselor. Composer: (theme song) A Sure Foundation; author: (musical drama) The Gift, (books of poetry) A Collection; composer: (christian missions) Mountain of the Lord, (christian worship) In Thee, O Lord; Behold Him. Mem.: Western Mass. Writers Assn., Nat. Assn. of Music Educators, Mass. Teachers Assn.

GOUVELLIS, MARY C. utilities executive; b. Chester, Pa., Sept. 1, 1950; d. Nicholas Demitruis and Olga Gouvellis; m. Robert E. Zacconi, Dec. 25, 1976 (div. Sept. 30, 1999); 1 child, Kara. BA, U. Del., 1974; MBA, Ctrl. Mich. U., 1977. Mgr. PPG Industries, Inc., Pitts., 1975-90; mgr. pub. edn. and tng. Orange County Utilities, Orlando, Fla., 1990—. Co-chair Quality Clearing House, Orlando, 1997—. Contbr. articles to profl. jours. Mem. Assn. for Quality and Participation, Am. Water Works Assn., Water Environment Fedn. Home: 710 Terrace Blvd Orlando FL 32803-3241

GOUW, JULIA SURYAPRANATA, accountant; b. Surabaya, Indonesia, Aug. 22, 1959; came to U.S., 1978; d. Moertopo Suryapranata and Indira (Koelani) Suryapranata; m. Ken Keng-Hok Gouw, June 1, 1981. B.S. with highest honors, U. Ill., 1981. CPA, Ill. Acct., Texaco, Inc., Los Angeles, 1981-83; from asst. acct. to sr. audit mgr. KPMG Peat Marwick, LA, 1983-89; joined East West Bank as v.p., contr., San Marino, CA, 1989, exec. v.p., CFO, East West Bancorp Inc., 1994-, dir., 1997- . Bd. dirs. Huntington Meml. Hosp.; bd. visitors UCLA; bd. overseers LA Philharmonic; bd. govs. City Club; mem. Alexis de Tocqueville Soc. United Way. Named Philanthropist of Yr., United Way's Women Leaders for Giving and Nat. Assn. Bus. Owners, 2003, LA Bus. Jour. Women Making a Difference Awards, 2003; Named one of The Top 25 Most Powerful Women in Banking, US Banker mag., 2003. Mem. Chinese Am. CPA's, Nat. Assn. Female Execs., Beta Alpha Psi, Fin. Execs. Inst., Calif. Soc. CPA's . Office: East West Bank 415 Huntington Dr San Marino CA 91108*

GOVER, KATHLEEN ANN, dean, director; b. Rockville Center, N.Y., Sept. 10, 1949; d. Charles Lindsay and Kathryn Driscoll Gover. BA in Modern European History, St. John's U., 1971; MA in Higher Ednl. Adminstrn., Columbia U., 1972; MBA, L.I. U., 1976; cert. in coll. mgmt., budgeting and computer applications, Carnegie Mellon U., 1984. Instr. Bklyn. Coll., 1972—80, asst. to the provost, 1980—89, asst. dean, 1989—94, assoc. dean undergraduate studies and dir. freshman yr. coll., 1994—. Named Outstanding First Yr. Student Adv., Nat. Resource Ctr.; recipient Group Retention Excellence award, Noel-Levitz USA, 1999, Theodore M. Hesburgh award, 1998; Roth fellow, L.I. U., 1973—76. Avocations: painting, horseback riding, swimming, travel. Home: 531 Main St New York NY 10044 Office: Brooklyn Coll 2900 Bedford Ave Brooklyn NY 11210 Office Phone: 718-951-5771.

GOVERN, MAUREEN, information technology executive; B in computer sci., Northwestern U.; M in operations rsch., Stanford U. Sr. positions Bell-Northern Rsch., NYNEX Sci. and Tech.; joined Bell Labs., 1978; v.p. network architecture and tech. network sys. group Motorola Inc., v.p. advanced tech. devel., global telecom., solutions sector; chief tech. officer Convergys Corp., 2002—. Named one of Premier 100 Info. Tech. Leaders, Computerworld mag., 2004. Office: Convergys Corp 201 E 4th St Cincinnati OH 45202 Office Phone: 513-723-7000.*

GOWDEY, DOROTHY E. artist; b. Everett, Wash., Mar. 12, 1918; d. Albert N. and Gladys I. (Mallory) Smith; m. Dwight M. Gowdey, Dec. 4, 1945; children: Kathleen A. Hesseltine, Christine E., Sharon L. Art student, Cornish Sch., 1938-39, P. Camfferman, E. Zeigler, and others, 1941-46, Factory of Visual Arts, 1970-74, Janet Laurel, 1981-85; student nursing, Seattle Pacific Coll.; RN, Swedish Hosp. RN, Wash. Exhibited in shows including, Seattle Art Mus. N.W. Annual, 1943-45, Women Painters of Wash. Annual, 1946-2003, Providence Hosp., 1985, Internat. Snow Leopard Trus t Show, 1985, Nat. League of Am. Pen Women Biennial St. Exhbn., 1985-93, Churchill Club/Okayama, Japan, 1986, Eastside Assn. of Fine Arts, 1986, 89, 91, Mercer Island Visual Arts League, 1986, 87, 89, 90, Puget Sound Sumi Artists, Wash., 1987-98, Olympic Arts, Anacortes Arts and Crafts Festival, 1993, Bon Marche Gallery, 2002, Bellevue Unitarian Ch. Gallery, 2002; numerous others. Organizer, mem. Nellie Goodhue Group Homes for the Retarded, Seattle, 1970—; mem. ARC, Tex., 1963—, Down Syndrome Congress, Atlanta, 1971—. Recipient 1st prize Churchill Club, Okayama, Japan, 1986, Watercolor prize Western Wash. State Fair, 1990, numerous other art awards. Mem. Nat. League of Am. Pen Women (award of excellence 1987), Women Painters of Wash. (pres. 1984-86), Women in the Arts (charter, Washington), Seattle Art Mus., Puget Sound Sumi Artists, Olympic Arts (pres. 1992-93). Democrat. Presbyterian. Home: 11536 6th Ave NW Seattle WA 98177-4727

GOWING, PATRICIA M. retired elementary education educator; b. Hillsdale, Kans., Mar. 16, 1933; d. Carl Burton and Elsie Ida (Craven) White; m. Thomas Lee Gowing, June 10, 1956; children: Darrell Lee, Gerald Dean, Gregory Eugene. BS in Edn., Kans. State Tchrs. Coll., Pittsburg, 1955; MS in Edn., Kans. State Tchrs. Coll., Emporia, 1960; postgrad., Kans. State Tchrs. Coll., 1961-86. Cert. elem. tchr., jr. high subjects, counselor K-9. Tchr. grades 1-8 Dist. #11 Star Valley Rural Sch., LaCygne, Kans., 1951-54; tchr. McKinley Jr. High, Clay Center, Kans., 1955-56, Old Mission Jr. High, Shawnee Mission, Kans., 1956-61; tchr. grade 2 Prairie View Unified Sch. Dist. #362, Fontana, Kans., 1970-72, elem. counselor LaCygne, Parker, Fontana, 1972-74, Centerville, 1972-74, tchr., title I reading grades K-6 La Cygne, Fontana, Parker; ret., 1998. Kansas-China Exch. in Edn., 1986; People-to-People Amb. Reading Del. to Russia, Czech Republic, 1998. Mem. NEA (life), NEA Ret. (life), Kans. NEA Ret. (life), AAUW (life, sec., v.p., pres. 1970—), Kans. Ret. Tchrs. Assn., Miami County Area Kans. Ret. Tchrs. Assn., Pi Lambda Theta (study tours Australia, New Zealand, 1992, Scandinavian Countries, 1996, Orient, Manila, 1998, South AFrica 2000), Alpha Delta Kappa (rec. sec., v.p., pres.

1976—, South Ctrl. Regional scholar 1986, pres., corr. sec. Kans. Mu chpt.). Avocations: card ministry for church, traveling, reading, word finds, bird watching. Home: 23573 Brown Rd Parker KS 66072-9612

GOWLER, VICKI SUE, newspaper editor, journalist; b. Decatur, Ill., Apr. 16, 1951; d. Carroll Eugene and Audra Janet (Briggs) G. BS in Journalism, U. Ill., 1973. Reporter Iroquois County Daily Times, Watseka, Ill., 1973-75, Quincy (Ill.) Herald-Whig, 1975-78; from reporter to mng. editor Miami (Fla.) Herald, Stuart, Delray Beach, West Palm Beach, 1089-88; asst. news editor Knight-Ridder Washington Bur., 1988-93; exec. editor Duluth (Minn.) News-Tribune, Knight-Ridder newspaper, 1978—2001, editor and v.p., 1993—97, editor, 2001—; mng. editor Pioneer Press, Knight-Ridder newspaper, 1997—2001, editor, 2001—; sr. v.p. and editor St. Paul Pioneer Press, Knight-Ridder newspaper, 2001—. Recipient numerous awards for journalistic works, including RFK award, state AP awards in all categories. Mem. Am. Soc. Newspaper Editors. Methodist. Avocations: reading, tennis, playing clarinet, travel, visiting with her family.*

GOYAK, ELIZABETH FAIRBAIRN, retired public relations executive; b. Chgo., Oct. 7, 1922; d. Lewis Howard and Berenice Marie (Bowers) Fairbairn; m. Edward Anthony Goyak, May 20, 1951. BEd, So. Ill. U., 1943; MA, No. Ill. U., 1979. Reporter Internat. News Svc., Chgo., 1945-49, Chgo. Tribune, 1949-52; writer Gardner & Jones, Chgo., 1954-59, Aaron Cushman & Assocs., Chgo., 1959-60; v.p. Daniel J. Edelman, Chgo., 1960-76; mgr. pub. rels. Stone Container Corp., Chgo., 1976-82; pres. pub. rels. Firm Chgo. Connection, Matteson, Ill., 1982-98. Dir. pub. rels. Ill. Dem. Women for Adlai Stevenson, 1952; founder, pres. bd. dirs. Matteson Pub. Libr., 1958-87; chmn. Matteson Bicentennial Commn., 1973-76. Mem. Pub. Rels. Soc. Am. (accredited, Silver anvil award 1975), Publicity Club Chgo. (sec., bd. dirs. 1964-76, Golden Trumpet award 1965, 66, 75), Chgo. Press Vets. Mem. United Ch. Christ. Home: 9200 Lalique Ln Apt 1503 Fort Myers FL 33919-7408

GOYER, VIRGINIA L. accountant; b. Troy, N.Y., July 19, 1942; d. Clarence Archie and Edna Alice (Toussaint) G.; m. James Cobb Stewart, May 17, 1986. BS, Rochester Inst. Tech., 1975, MBA, 1976. Tax mgr. Deloitte Haskins & Sells, Rochester, N.Y., 1976-82, pres. Lamanna & Goyer, PC, CPAs, Rochester, 1982-89; owner Goyer & Assocs., CPAs, Rochester, 1989-93; pres. Virginia L. Goyer, CPA, P.C., Rochester, 1993—. Mem. adv. bd. Salvation Army, Rochester, 1985-88, Rochester Inst. Tech. Deferred Giving, 1988-89; mem. bd. Nat. Women's Hall of Fame, 1993-98; bd. dirs., treas. Friends of Women's Rights Nat. Park Inc., 2000—. Mem. AICPA (nat. coun. 1995-98), Fla. Inst. CPAs, N.Y. State Inst. CPAs (bd. dirs. 1990 93, v.p. 1994-95, 1st woman pres. Rochester chpt. 1988-89), Rochester Women's Network, Nat. Assn. Women Bus. Owners (bd. dirs. 1992-93), Estate Planning Coun. (bd. dirs. 1987-89), NOW, Century Club Rochester (bd. dirs., fin. chair 2001—). Office: 354 Westminster Rd Rochester NY 14607-3233

GOZEMBA, PATRICA ANDREA, women's studies and English language educator, writer; b. Medford, Mass., Nov. 30, 1940; d. John Charles and Mary Margaret (Sampey) Curran; m. Gary M. Gozemba, Sept. 4, 1967 (div. Feb. 1975). BA, Emmanuel Coll., Boston, 1962; MA, U. Iowa, 1963; EdD, Boston U., 1973. Tchr. Waltham (Mass.) H.S., 1962-64; prof. Salem (Mass.) State Coll., 1964—. Vis. fellow East-West Ctr., 1995; vis. prof. U. Hawaii, 1997-98; co-chair The History Project, Boston, 2000—; bd. dirs. Healthlink. Editor: New England Women's Studies, 1977—87; mem. editl. bd.: Thought and Action, 1990—93; contbr. articles to profl. jours.; author: Pockets of Hope: How Students and Teachers Change the World, 2002. Bd. dirs. Salem Alliance for the Environment, 2003—. Mem. NEA (standing com. 1982-93), NOW, NAACP, Nat. Women's Studies Assn. (gov. bd. 1977-89), Nat. Coun. Tchrs. English, Nat. Gay and Lesbian Task Force, Mass. State Coll. Assn. (editor 1982-90, 92-97), Herb Soc. Am. Democrat. Avocations: walking, tennis, gardening, photography. Home and Office: 17 Sutton Ave Salem MA 01970-5728

GRABER, MURIEL, music educator, lay worker; b. Yankton, S.D., May 1, 1949; d. Sollie and Nellie Kaufman; children: Karl, Kent. AA in Music, Freeman Jr. Coll., 1969; BA in Elem. Edn., Bethel Coll., 1971; postgrad., N.Am. Bapt. Sem., 1997—; MA in Christian Spirituality, Creighton U., 2002. Music tchr. Freeman (S.D.) Pub. Sch., 1971—75; piano and organ tchr. Freeman, 1975—94; music tchr. Montrose (S.D.) Pub. Sch., 1992—94, Freeman Pub. Sch., 1994—2002; intern Crestwood United Ch. of Christ, 2003—. Organist numerous chs., S.D., Kans., 1969—; co-founder Masterworks Chorus, Freeman, 1985—90; leader Children's Music Workshop, Freeman Arts Alliance, 1995. Pres. Freeman Area Arts Coun., 1976—80; chair conf., exec. and edn. coms. Mennonite No. Dist., 1986—92; pres., bd dirs. Wellspring Counseling Ctr., Freeman, 1992—. Mem.: Spiritual Dirs. Internat. Avocations: making jewelry, reading, playing piano, family activities, traveling. Home: Box 393 Freeman SD 57029

GRABER, SUSAN P. federal judge; b. Oklahoma City, July 5, 1949; d. Julius A. and Bertha (Fenyves) Graber; m. William June, May 3, 1981; 1 child, Rachel June-Graber. BA, Wellesley Coll., 1969; JD, Yale U., 1972. Bar: N.Mex. 1972, Ohio 1977, Oreg. 1978. Asst. atty. gen. Bur. of Revenue, Santa Fe, 1972—74; assoc. Jones Gallegos Snead & Wertheim, Santa Fe, 1974—75, Taft Stettinius & Hollister, Cin., 1975—78; assoc., then ptnr. Stoel Rives Boley Jones & Grey, Portland, Oreg., 1978—88; judge, then presiding judge Oreg. Ct. Appeals, Salem, 1988—90; assoc. justice Oreg. Supreme Ct., Salem, 1990—98; judge U.S. Ct. Appeals (9th cir.), Portland, 1998—. Mem. Gov.'s Adv. Coun. on Legal Svcs., 1979—88; mem. bd. visitors Sch. Law, U. Oreg., 1986—93; bd. dirs. U.S. Dist. Ct. of Oreg. Hist. Soc., 1985—, Oreg. Law Found., 1990—91. Mem.: Am. Inns of Ct. (master), Oreg. Appellate Judges Assn. (sec.-treas. 1990—91, vice chair 1991—92, chair 1992—93), Oreg. Jud. Conf. (edn. com. 1988—91, program chair 1990), Ninth Cir. Jud. Conf. (chair exec. com. 1987—88), Oreg. State Bar (jud. adminstrn. com. 1985—87, pro bono com. 1988—90), Phi Beta Kappa. Mailing: US Ct Appeals 9th Cir PO Box 193939 San Francisco CA 94119-3939 Office: US Ct Appeals 9th Cir 95 Seventh St San Francisco CA 94119*

GRABILL, VIRGINIA LOWELL, retired English educator; b. Hastings, Minn., Apr. 20, 1919; d. Charles S. and Dora May (Parker) Lowell; m. Paul E. Grabill, June 14, 1952 (dec. Feb. 1980); 1 child, Cynthia Maud. BA summa cum laude, Wheaton (Ill.) Coll., 1941; PhD, U. Ill., 1947. Asst. prof. English, Western Ill State Coll., Macomb, 1947-51; prof., head English dept. Taylor U., Upland, Ind., 1951, Bethel Coll., St. Paul, Ind., 1951-57; asst. prof. English and journalism Evansville Coll. (now U. of Evansville), Ind., from 1957; prof. English, women's counselor U. Evansville, 1957-89; ombudsman; chmn. senate, 1976-86; prof. Henderson (Ky.) Jr. Coll., 1990-92; ret., 1992. Named Hon. Alumna of Yr., U. Evansville, 1994. Mem. Delta Kappa Gamma. Avocations: tutoring through literacy center, shopping, eating, reading. Home: 905 S Spring St Evansville IN 47714

GRACE, BARBARA LEE, retail executive; b. Balt., Apr. 18, 1942; d. Edward Lawrence and Wanda Jane (Dembowski) G. BS, U. Md., 1970. Front office mgr., sales mgr. then dir. sales Hilton Hotelse, Annapolis, Md., 1969-75, asst. gen. mgr. Wilmington, Del., 1976-80; proprietor Charles-N-Us, Balt., 1980-89; gen. mgr. Harbor Club on the Severn, Herald Harbor, Md., 1989-92; dist. mgr. Royal Farms, Balt., 1993—2003; realtor ERA Deloach and Assoc., 2003. Mem. Nat. Assn. Profl. Women, Nat. Assn. Convenience Stores, Severna Park Racquet Club. Avocation: holistic medicine. Home: 8013 E Riverside Dr Pasadena MD 21122-3811 Office: Robinson Crossing Shpg Cntr 470 D Ritchie Hwy Severna Park MD 21146

GRACE, BETTE FRANCES, certified public accountant; b. Hanford, Calif., Apr. 16, 1957; d. Boyd Lowell Sharp and Janet Praria; m. Clyde Jon Nold, May 4, 1974 (div. 1987); children: Mandolin P., Christopher J.; m. Michael E. Grace, Feb. 14, 1996. AA in Bus., Gavilan Coll., Gilroy, Calif., 1992; BS in Bus./Acctg., San Jose State U., 1994, postgrad., 1994—. CPA, Calif. Fin. controller Hollister (Calif.) Disposal, Inc., 1984-92; owner, operator Hollister Bookkeeping and Tax Svc., 1985-98; acct. mgr. Ridgemark Golf & Country Club, Hollister, 1992-98; CPA, owner Grace & Assocs CPAs, Hollister, 1998—. Fin. controller John Smith Landfill, Inc., Hollister, 1986-92, Ajax Portable Svc., Hollister, 1987-92. Supporter Monterey County (Calif.) Symphony Guild, 1991—; parent mem. Calif. High Sch. Rodeo Assn., Hollister, 1991—; dir. 33rd Dist. Agrl. Assn., San Benito County Fair Bd., 1992-96; fin. chmn. AT&T Pebble Beach Nat. Pro-Am. Mem. AICPA, El Gabilan Young Ladies Inst. Republican. Roman Catholic. Avocation: water and snow skiing. Office: Grace & Assocs CPAs PO Box 1352 Hollister CA 95024-1352

GRACE, JULIANNE ALICE, retired investor relations firm executive; b. Riverdale, N.Y., Oct. 29, 1937; d. Arthur Edward and Julia May (McCarthy) Thompson; m. Daniel Vincent Grace, July 2, 1960; children: Daniel Vincent III, Deirdre Elizabeth Beck. BA, Marymount Manhattan Coll., 1959; MA, Fordham U., 1960. Dir. admissions Marymount Manhattan Coll., N.Y.C., 1966-72; mgr. human resources The Perkin-Elmer Corp., Norwalk, Conn., 1972-78, dir. human resources, 1978-81, asst. sr. v.p. semiconductor equipment, 1981-83, asst. pres., 1983-85, v.p., asst. to CEO, 1985-86, v.p. adminstrn., 1986-90, v.p. corp. rels., 1990-95; pres. The Jagcom Group, New Canaan, Conn., 1995—2004; ret., 2004. Bd. dirs. Norwalk and Wilton chpts. ARC, 1975—85, Metropool, 1991—98; pres., bd. dirs. Waveny (Conn.) Care Ctr., 1998—; bd. dirs. Waveny Network; trustee Norwalk YMCA, 1986—94; active Norwalk C.C. Found., 1986—90, Fairfield 2000; mem. corp. cabinet U. Conn. Downstate Initiative, 1995—98, mem. adv. com., lectr. exec. edn. program U. Conn., 1996—2001. Fellow Woodrow Wilson Nat. Found., 1959—60. Mem.: Fairfield Pub. Rels. Assn., Nat. Investor Rels. Inst. (sr. exec. roundtable), Econ. Soc. Conn., Saugatuck Harbor Yacht Club (bd. govs., flag officer fleet capt.), Wolfpit Running Club, Sports Car Club Am. Home and Office: 54 Louises Ln New Canaan CT 06840-2120

GRACE, MARCIA BELL, advertising executive; b. Pitts., July 29, 1937; d. Daniel Henry and Gertrude Margaret (Loew) Bell; m. Roy Grace, May 16, 1966; children: Jessica Bell, Nicholas Bell. AB, Harvard U., 1959. V.p., assoc. creative dir. Doyle Dane Bernbach, N.Y.C., 1964-77; sr. v.p., creative dir. Wells, Rich, Greene, Inc., N.Y.C., 1977-85, exec. v.p., creative dir., 1986-90; cons. Marcia Grace & Co., N.Y.C., 1990—. Represented in permanent collection Mus. Modern Art. Recipient 1st Pl. ANDY award Advt. Club N.Y., 1968, 70, 72, 75, 1st Pl. Gold award The One Show, 1973, 78, Hall of Fame award The Clio Show, N.Y.C., 1982, 86. Avocations: horseback riding, gardening.

GRACE, SUE, state legislator; b. Milw., Jan. 31, 1958; m. Vincent Grace. BA, Marquette U. Mem. Ariz. Ho. of Reps., 1991-96; mktg. specialist; mem. Ariz. Senate, Phoenix, 1996-. Named Legis. of Yr., Mental Health Assn., 1991. Mem., Paradise Valley Chamber of Commerce, United Fund Council, Phoenix Mountaineers. Republican. Office: Ariz State Senate Rm 303 1700 W Washington St Phoenix AZ 85007-2812 Address: 2102 E Redfield Rd Phoenix AZ 85022-1659

GRACE-CRUM, PHYLLIS VENETIA, military officer; b. Phila., Jan. 16, 1957; d. Philip Dean, Doris Eleanor Dean-Hagood; m. H. Ellis, Apr. 14, 2001. BS, Lincoln U., Oxford, Pa., 1979. Lic. ministry, 2003. Petroleum platoon leader 590th Combat Support and Combat Svcs. Support Co., Zebra Base, Saudi Arabia, 1991—91; chief billeting and housing Hdqrs. and Hdqrs. Co., 1st Area Support Group, Damman, Saudi Arabia, 1991—91; exec. officer Hdqrs. and Hdqrs. Co., 22nd Support Ctr., Dammam, Saudi Arabia, 1991—92; supply and svcs. platoon leader 226th Supply and Svcs. Co., Fort Stewart, Ga., 1992—93, platoon leader Ft. Stewart, Ga., 1992—93; with 632nd Maintenance Co. 87th Corps Support Bn., Ft. Stewart, Ga., 1993—94, asst. supply and svcs. officer, 1995—96; U.S. Army Recruiting Co. comdr. Pitts. Recruiting Bn., 1st Recruiting Brigade, 1996—99; co. comdr. 183rd Maintenance Co., 68th Corps Support Battalion, 43rd Area Support Group, Ft. Carson, Colo., 1999; logistics ops. officer 3/345th Regiment, 4th Brigade, 87th DIV (Tng. Support Divsn.), Forest Park, Ga., 2000—; promoted 2d lt., IMAR02 to major, 1991—. Environ. health specialist Ft. Devens, 1986—88. Contbr. The Logistician, 1996. Supt. ch. edn. Manna Missionary Baptist Ch., Chesapeake, Va., 2003; dir. tng. Word of Life Sch. Gifts, 2004. Decorated Army Achievement medal U.S. Army, Army Commendation medal, Nat. Def. medal, Joint Meritorious Unit award, Meritorious Svc. medal. Mem.: Am. Legion, Alpha Kappa Delta, Delta Sigma Theta. Avocations: horseback riding, ballroom dancing, reading, weightlifting. Office: 3/345th CS/CSS TS Bn Bldg 207B 4653 N First St Forest Park GA 30297-5000 Home: PO Box 61937 Virginia Beach VA 23466-1937 Office Phone: 757-788-2757. Personal E-mail: phylliscrum@hotmail.com.

GRACEY, JANET ENGLISH, church administrator; b. Wolcott, Ind., Aug. 11, 1937; d. Victor Floyd and Mae Avanelle (Norwood) English. Student, U. Mich., 1955-56, New Sch. for Social Rsch., 1960-62. Cons. Nat. Endowment for Arts, Washington, 1969; exec. asst. spl. studies project Rockefeller Bros. Fund, N.Y.C., 1963-70; dir. rsch. Associated Couns. of Arts, N.Y.C., 1970-73; dir. spl. projects Theatre Devel. Fund, N.Y.C., 1973-77, dir. program planning and rsch., 1978-83, dir. ops., 1983-90; dir. adminstrn. Ch. of the Holy Apostles/Holy Apostles Soup Kitchen, N.Y.C., 1991—. Panel mem. N.Y. State Coun. on Arts, 1985-86. Office: Ch of the Holy Apostles 296 9th Ave New York NY 10001-5703

GRAD, MAXINE J. state representative, law educator; b. Great Neck, N.Y., July 10, 1960; m. Ron Shems; 2 children. BA, MA, Clark U., 1982; JD, Vt. Law Sch., 1985; grad., Vt. Leadership Inst. State rep. State of Vt., 2001—. Mem. Gov.'s Commn. on Women, Moretown Action Planning Com., Bi-State Primary Care Vt., Women's Health Steering Com., Nat. Women's Health Network, 1988—96, Moretown and Ctrl. Vt. Regional Planning Commn., 1987; chair Moretown Dem. Com. Mem.: Northfield Bus. Profl. Assn., Rotary. Democrat. Office: 301 Paddy Hill Td Moretown VT 05660

GRADER, PATRICIA ALISON LANDE, editor; b. L.A., Mar. 23, 1960; d. Frederick and Irma Rose (Davidson) L.; m. Scott P. Grader, Feb. 11, 1995; 1 child, Louisa Frances Duo. Student, Washington U., St. Louis, 1977-79; BA with high distinction, U. Calif., San Diego, 1982. Editl. asst. Crown Pubs., N.Y.C., 1982-83; asst. editor St. Martin's Press, N.Y.C., 1983-84; editor Atheneum Pubs., N.Y.C., 1984-87; v.p., sr. editor Simon & Schuster, Inc., N.Y.C., 1987-91; v.p., dir. IMG-The Julian Bach Literary Agy., N.Y.C., 1992-95; exec. editor William Morrow, N.Y.C., 1995—. Mentor internship program Simon & Schuster, 1991; mem. adminstrv. com. IMG, 1992-95; speaker in field. Mem. Pi Beta Phi. Office: William Morrow 10 E 53d St New York NY 10022

GRADY, IRENE HART, reading specialist; b. Providence, R.I., Mar. 10, 1934; d. Hector Melvern and Mabel Hart; m. Harry E. Bay, July 26, 1958 (div. June 1969); children: Kathleen, Stephen. BA Brown U., Providence, R.I., 1955; MEd, Hood Coll., Frederick, Md., 1978. Cert. lifetime R.I., advanced prof. Md. Classroom tchr. Providence Pub. Schs., 1955—58, Portsmouth (R.I.) Pub. Schs., 1970—73, Montgomery County (Md.) Pub. Schs., 1976—77, reading specialist, 1978—2003. Mem.: AAUW (book sale chmn. 1959—65). Roman Catholic. Avocations: movies, reading, genealogy, law study, theater. E-mail: lggrinch310@aol.com.

GRADY, JOYCE (MARIAN JOYCE GRADY), psychotherapist, consultant; b. Riverside, N.J., Sept. 27, 1930; d. David and Agnes Marian (Conroy) Lawber; children: Andrea, Christine; m. James F. Moller, June 11, 1983. BA in Clin. Psychology, U. Penna, 1951; M in Social Work, certificate in alcohol studies, Rutgers U., New Brunswick, N.J., 1968; certificate in psychotherapy, Inst. Psychoanalytic Psychotherapy, 1973. Lic. clin. social worker, N.J. Caseworker Upward Bound Program, Rutgers U., New Brunswick, summer 1966; psychiat. social work supr., chief psychiat. social worker Roosevelt Hosp., Edison, N.J., 1968-92, in-svc. educator in nursing and social work, 1972-92, support group caregiver, 1970-92; nursing home cons. Abbot Manor Nursing Home, Plainfield, N.J., 1984-92; pvt. practice psychotherapy, Highland Park, N.J., 1975—. Adj. prof., field instr. grad. sch. social work Rutgers U., New Brunswick, 1970-92; guest lectr. depression and geriatrics Rutgers Sch. Social Work, New Brunswick, 1975-92; cmty. lectr. dying, aging, loss, and depression in long term care; outreach cons. personal assistance and homebound elderly, Middlesex County, N.J., 1975-78; mem. adv. bd., chmn. Middlesex County Adv. Coun. Aging, North Brunswick, N.J., 1973-95. Contbr. papers, panelist in field. Advocate, Middlesex County Adv. Coun. on Aging, North Brunswick, 1970-92; mem. Cmty. Outreach Adv. Coun.; participant seminars svc. providers, Middlesex County, N.J., 1995. Mem.: NASW (guest panel mem., guest spkr. psychotherapy confs.), Rutgers Club, Penn Club N.Y.C. Avocations: writing, decorating, music, computers, gardening. Office: 12 N 4th Ave Highland Park NJ 08904-2736

GRADY, KIMBERLY ANN, medical technician; b. St. Paul, Mar. 16, 1962; d. Paul William and Carol Ann Prokop; m. Michael Edward Grady Jr., Sept. 15, 1984; children: Amanda Carol, Joseph Michael. Med. Lab. Tech., Med. Inst. Minn., Mpls., 1980—82; BS bus. mgmt. with hon., U. Phoenix, 1999—2003. Cert. clinical lab. scientist Nat. Certifying Agy. for Clin. Lab. Pers., clin. lab. asst. Nat. Certifying Agy. for Lab. Pers., registered med. technologist Internat. Soc. for Lab. Tech. Pvt. practice, Wood Dale, Ill., 1996—; sr. med. technologist, safety officer Smith Kline Beecham Clin. Laboratories, Atlanta, 1988—96; med. technologist Memphis Clin. Lab., 1986—88; med. lab. technician Boyce & Bynum Pathology Lab., Columbia, Mo., 1984—86. Contbr. articles to profl. jours. Active Girl Scouts, Atlanta, 1995—96, Lady KC, Algonquin, Ill., 1996—2003; historian Theresians Internat., 1991—98; coord. Magnificat, Atlanta, 1994—96; leader Cursillo, Atlanta, 1994—96. Recipient Citizenship Medal, LEGIONARIES, 1976, Safety Award, Smith Kline Beecham, 1994. Mem.: Am. Soc. For Clin. Pathology (assoc.), Am. Soc. For Clin. Lab. Sci. (assoc.), Clin. Lab. Mgmt. Assn. (assoc.), The Nat. Assn. For Female Executives (assoc.). Republican. Roman Catholic. Avocations: golf, swimming, sewing, reading. Home: 3930 Wisteria Ct Lake In The Hills IL 60156 Office: Quest Diagnostics 1355 Mittel Blvd Wood Dale IL 60191 Office Phone: 630-595-3888. Personal E-mail: snoopykg1@aol.com. Business E-Mail: gradyka@questdiagnostics.com.

GRADY, PATRICIA A. health institute director, researcher; Diploma in nursing, St. Francis Hosp. Sch. Nursing, 1964; BSN, Georgetown U., 1967; MS, Sch. Nursing U. Md., 1968; PhD, Sch. Medicine U. Md., 1977; D of Pub. Svc. (hon.), U. Md., 1996; cert. in sr. mgrs. in govt., John F. Kennedy sch. Govt., Cambridge, 1994. Instr. Sch. Nursing Washington Hosp. Ctr., 1966-67; from instr. to rsch. asst. prof. Sch. Nursing U. Md., Bethesda, 1968-88, rsch. assoc., 1976-77; health sci. administrator Nat. Inst. Neurol. Disorders and Stroke NIH, Bethesda, 1988-92, asst. dir. Nat. Inst. Neurol. Disorders and Stroke, 1992-93, acting dir., dep. dir. Nat. Inst. Neurol. Disorders and Stroke, 1993-94, dep. dir. Nat. Inst. Neurol. Disorders and Stroke, 1994-95, dir. Nat. Inst. Nursing Rsch., 1995—. Cons., spkr., presenter in field. Contbr. articles to profl. jours., chpts. to books.; ad hoc reviewer SCIENCE; mem. editl. bd. STROKE. NIH fellow, 1973-76; NIN(C)DS grantee, 1976-88; recipient Sol Greenberg award for leadership ability and clin. excellence St. Francis Hosp., 1964, Rozella M. Schlottfeld Disting. Lecture award Case Western Reserve U., 1996, Centennial Achievement Medal, Georgetown U. Fellow Am. Heart Assn. Stroke Coun. (excellence in nursing lectr. award 1995); Mem. AAAS, ANA, Am. Acad. Nursing, Am. Lung Assn., Am. Soc. Profl. and Exec. Women, Am. Acad. Neurology (lectr. 1993-95), Am. Neurol. Assn., Soc. Neuroci., N.Y. Acad. Scis., Neurotrauma Soc., Sigma Theta Tau (award 1966), Inst. Medicine, 1999-. Office: Nat Inst Nursing Rsch NIH 31 Center Dr Bldg 31 Bethesda MD 20892-0001 Fax: (301) 594-3405.*

GRAEBNER, CAROL F. lawyer; b. 1954; BA in Intternat. Rels., Dickinson Coll.; JD, Am. U. Exec. v.p., gen. counsel Dynegy Inc.; sr. v.p., gen. counsel Duke Energy Internat., 1998; gen. counsel Conoco Global Power, Inc. Office: Office of Gen Counsel 1000 Louisiana Ste 5800 Houston TX 77002

GRAF, DOROTHY ANN, human resources specialist; b. Nashville, Mar. 21, 1935; d. Henry George and Martha Dunlap (Hill) Meek; m. Peter Louis Graf, Oct. 28, 1971; children: Sidney E. Pollard, Deborah Lynn Pollard, Robert George Pollard, Michelle Joy Graf. Student, Montgomery Coll., 1979—. Office mgr. Pa. Life Ins. Co., Miami and Dallas, 1957-72; exec. sec. to med. dir. Pitts. Children's Hosp., 1974; sec. GE/TEMPO, Washington, 1974-76; adminstrv. asst. to sr. v.p. Logistics Mgmt. Inst., Washington, 1976-81, dir. adminstrv. svc., 1981-97, dir. recruiting and tng., 1995-97, dir. human resources, 1997-99; cons. human resources specialist, 1999—2000. Dir. KHI Svcs., Inc. Mem. Washington Tech. Pers. Forum. Democrat. Baptist. Home: 1400 Newry Circle Ormond Beach FL 32174

GRAF, STEFFI, retired professional tennis player; b. Bruhl, Germany, June 14, 1969; d. Peter and Heidi Graf; m. Andre Agassi, 2001; 2 children. Founder Steffi Graf Marketing, 1996—; designer Steffi Graf Handbags, 2002—. Amb. World Wildlife Fund (WWF); founder Children of Tomorrow, 1998—. Winner numerous profl. women's tennis tournaments including The Golden Grand Slam (Australian Open, French Open, Wimbledon, U.S. Open, Olympics), 1988, Berlin Open, 1988, Wimbledon, 1989, 91, 92, 93, 95, 96, U.S. Open, 1989, 93, 95, 96, Australian Open, 1989, 1990, 94, French Open, 1993, 95, 96, 99, Olympic Gold Medal, 1988; ret. from competition, 1999; named WTA Player of Yr., 1987-90, 1993-96; recipient Olympic Medal of Honor, IOC, 1999, Female Sports Award of the Last Decade, Espy, 1999. Achievements include 107 Career Titles; finished WTA season ranked no. 1, 1987-90, 1993-96; ranked no. 1 in world for more consecutive weeks than any other player in tennis history; ranks 1st all-time in career proze money ($21 million); only person to win a Grand Slam on four different surfaces; only person to win a Golden Grand Slam. Office: Steffi Graf Sport GmbH Mallaustrasse 75 68219 Manheim Germany

GRAFF, PAT STUEVER, secondary school educator; b. Tulsa, Mar. 24, 1955; d. Joseph H., Sr. and Joann (Schneider) Stuever; m. Mark A. Rumsey; children: Earl, Jr., Jeremy. BS in Secondary Edn., Okla. State U., 1976; postgrad., U. N.M., 1976-87. Cert. tchr. lang. arts, social studies, journalism, French, N.Mex. Substitute tchr. Albuquerque Pub. Schs., 1976-78; tchr. Cleveland Mid. Sch., Albuquerque, 1978-86, La Cueva H.S., Albuquerque, 1986—, co-chair English dept., 1996—, chair sch. restructuring coun., 1999-2001. Adviser award winning lit. mag. El Tesoro, sch. newspapers The Edition, Huellas del Oso; instr. journalism workshops, N.Mex. Press Assn., Ind. U., Bloomington, Nat. Scholastic Press, Mpls., Kans. State U., Manhattan, Interscholastic Press League, Austin, Tex., St. Mary's U., San Antonio, Ala. Scholastic Press Assn., Wash.; keynote spkr. at numerous confs. in Ohio, Ind., Kans., S.C., Utah, La., Okla., Ala., N.Mex., Tex., Wash., Idaho, and N.Y.; reviewer of lang. and textbooks for several cos.; instr. Dial-A-Tchr., N.Mex., 1991—; textook evaluator Holt Pub., Inc., 1991; nat. bd. cert. tchr. adolescent/young adult English lang. arts, 2001—; mem. N.Mex. Network of Nat. Bd. Cert. Tchrs., 2002—, 2d v.p., 2003—; state bd. dirs. N.Mex. Coun. for the Social Studies, 1998—, chair state conf., 2001, state pres., 2002-03, state treas., 2003—; comm. officer, sec.

ABQ Tchrs. Fedn. 2003—. Author: Journalism Text, 1983; contbg. author: Communication Skills Resource Text, 1987, Classroom Publishing/Literacy, 1992; contbr. articles to profl. jours. Troop leader Girl Scouts U.S., 1979—90, coord. various programs, asst. program com. chmn. Chaparral Coun., 1988—89, chmn. adult recognition task force, 1991—96 bd. dirs., 1991—98; active PTA Gov. Bent Elem. Sch., 1983—86, v.p., 1985—86, Osuna Elem. Sch., 1986—92, N.Mex. PTA, 1994—2000; pub. various children's lit. mags., 1987—; pub. parent's newsletter, 1986—; newsletter layout editor Albuquerque Youth Soccer Orgn., 1985—88; active YMCA youth and govt. model legis.; faculty advisor La Cueva del., 1986—2002, press corps advisor, 1987—2001, asst. state dir., 2001—; asst. den. leader Boy Scouts Am., 1987—88, den leader, 1988—91. Recipient Innovative Teaching award Bus. Week mag., 1990, Svc. commendatin Coll. Edn. Alumni Assn., Okla. State U., 1990, Alumni Recognition award, 1993, Mem. Yr. Svc. award Bernalillo County Coun. Internat. Reading Assn., Thanks to Tchrs. award Apple Computers, 1990, Spl. Recognition Albuquerque C. of C., 1992; named Spotlighted Mem. Phi Delta Kappa, 1990, Spl. Recognition Advisor Dow Jones Newspaper Fund, 1990, Nat. H.S. Journalism Tchr. of Yr., 1995, Disting. Advisor, 1991, U.S. West Tchr. Yr. finalist, 1991, N.Mex. Pubs. Adviser of Yr., 1991, N.Mex. State Tchr. of Yr., 1993, finalist Nat. Tchr. Yr., 1993, finalist Am. Tchr. Awards, Disney, 1998; named USA Today All-Am. Tchr., 1999; grantee Phi Delta Kappa 1989, 91, Geraldine R. Dodge Found., 1990, 92, 95-97, Learn and Serve Am., 1999. Mem.: AAUW (chpt. newsletter editor 1995—2001, local v.p. 1997—99, state program v.p. 1997—99, state media chair 2000—), ASCD (editor newsletter 1991—92, focus on excellence awards com. 1992—94, state bd. dirs. 2002—, Focus on Excellence award 1990), N Mex. Coun. for Social Studies (mem. bd. 1999—, state v.p. 2001—02, pres. 2002—03), N. Mex. World Class Tchr. Network (state vice-pres. 2002—), N.Mex. Goals 2000 (panel mem. 1994—97), Quill & Scroll (adv. La Cueva chpt. 1986—, judge nat. newspaper rating contest 1988—97), Albuquerque Press Women (v.p. 1994, pres. 1995, Communicator of Achievement award 1993), N.Mex. Press Women (state scholarship chair 1994, publicity chair 1995—96, state treas. 1996—98, state v.p. 1998—99), N.Mex. Scholastic Press Assn. (state v.p. 1985—89, coord. workshop 1986, editor newsletter 1986—89, asst. chair state conf. 1988, 1989, state bd. dirs. 1991—2000, state v.p. 1992—95), N.Mex. Coun. Tchrs. English (regional coord. Albuquerque 1983—86, chair state confs. 1985—87, editl. bd. N.Mex. English Jour. 1986—88, state pres. 1987—88, chair facilities for Fall conf. 1988—93, chair English Humanities expo com. 1988—99, adv. mgr. 1989—90, editor N.Mex. English Jour. 1999—, Svc. award 1989, Outstanding H.S. English Tchr. N.Mex. 1991), Journalism Edn. Assn., Journalism Edn. Assn. (judge nat. contests 1988—, mem. nat. cert. bd. 1989—99, presenter nat. convs. 1989—, cert. journalism educator 1990, nat. bd. 1991—2002), Nat. Fedn. Press Women, Nat. Sch. Pub. Rels. Assn. (issues seminar planning com. 1990, chair 1991, master journalism educator 1991—, nat. conf. chmn. 1997—99, Zia chpt., contest winner 1991—94, Pres.'s award 1993), Nat. Coun. Tchrs. English (nat. chair com. English Tchrs. and Pubs. 1988—91, chair English Humanities Expo com. 1990—99, standing com. affiliates 1991—94, nat. chair 1995—98, chair English Humanities Expo com. 2001—03, nat. exec. com. 2001—03, nat. chair assembly for advisors of student pubs., regional rep. Tex., La., N.Mex., Disting. Svc. award 2002), Nat. Alliance High Schs. (tchr. rep. 1997—2000), Nat. Assn. Secondary Sch. Prins. (Breaking Ranks tchr. rep.), Phi Delta Kappa (pres. U. N.Mex. br. 2002—), Delta Kappa Gamma (state profl. affairs com. chair 2003—), Pi Lambda Theta (Ethel Mary Moore award Outstanding Educator 1993, Gov.'s Outstanding Women in N.Mex. 2004). Roman Catholic. Avocations: soccer, running, hiking, travel, skiing. Home: 8101 Krim Dr NE Albuquerque NM 87109-5223 Office: La Cueva H S 7801 Wilshire Ave NE Albuquerque NM 87122-2807 Fax: 505-797-2250. E-mail: pgraff@aol.com.

GRAFF, RANDY, actress; b. Bklyn., May 23, 1955; Grad., Wagner Coll. Profl. theater debut in Gypsy, Village Dinner Theater, Raleigh, N.C.; appeared in Godspell, Raleigh; other appearances include Pins and Needles, Roundabout Theatre, N.Y.C., 1978, Something Wonderful, Westchester Regional Theatre, Harrison, N.Y., 1979, Sarava, Mark Hellinger Theatre, N.Y.C., 1979, Coming Attractions, Playwrights Horizons, Mainstage Theatre, N.Y.C., 1980, Keystone, McCarter Theatre, Princeton, N.J., 1981, A...My Name is Alice, Village Gate Theatre, N.Y.C., 1984, Amateurs, Playhouse in the Park, Cin., 1985, Fiorello!, Goodspell Opera House, East Haddam, Conn., 1985, Absurd Person Singular, Phila. Drama Guild, Phila., 1986, Les Miserables, Broadway Theatre, N.Y.C., 1987, City of Angels, Va. Theatre, N.Y.C., 1989 (Drama Desk award Featured Actress in Musical 1989, Tony award Supporting of Featured Actress in Musical 1990), Falsettos, 1993, Laughter on the 23rd Floor, 1993, Moon Over Buffalo, Martin Beck Theatre, 1995-96, High Society, St. James Theatre, N.Y.C., 1998, A Class Act, Ambassador Theatre, N.Y.C., 2001, Fiddler on the Roof, Minskoff Theatre, 2004-; (TV shows) include Mad About You, Law & Order, Love & War, Pros & Cons; (films) Key's to Tulsa, 1995. Office: Peter Strain & Assoc Ste 2900 1501 Broadway New York NY 10036*

GRAFFEO, MARY THÉRÈSE, music educator, performer; b. Mineola, N.Y., Jan. 20, 1949; d. Michael Joseph and Florence Marie (Lonette) G. BA in Music Edn., Adelphi U., 1972; MusM in Vocal Performance, Kent State U., 1982. Cert. music tchr. N.Y. Tchr., therapist Nassau County Bd. Coop. Ednl. Svcs., Westbury, NY, 1972-85; tchr. music, developer curricula Great Neck (N.Y.) Pub. Schs., 1985-87; tchr. music Syosset (N.Y.) Pub. Schs., 1987-88, 89-90, Jericho (N.Y.) Pub. Schs., 1988-89; tchr. music, developer creative programs Lawrence (N.Y.) Pub. Schs., 1990-92; tchr. music Herricks Pub. Schs., New Hyde Park, N.Y., 1992-93, Hempstead (N.Y.) Pub. Schs., 1993—. Music dir. summer programs Friends Acad., Locust Valley, N.Y., 1989-95. Author: Creative Enrichment Programs/America: The First 300 Years in Song, 1990, (curriculum) Music for the Trainable Mentally Retarded, 1973, Music for the Early Childhood Center of Hempstead Public Schools, 2002; co-author: The Remediation of Learning Discrepancies Through Music, 1980; composer: (mus. play) Red Riding Hood's Day, 1993, The Bell of Atri, The Children's Song, 1995. Cultural adv. bd. Lawrence Pub. Schs., 1990-92, Hempstead Pub. Schs., 1993—; founding mem. United We Stand Am., Dallas, 1992-93. Scholar Adelphi U., 1968-72, Blossom Festival Sch., Kent, Ohio, 1978-79. Mem. NEA, Am. Fedn. Tchrs., Music Educators Nat. Conf., N.Y. State United Tchrs., N.Y. State Sch. Music Assn., Nassau Music Educators Assn. Democrat. Roman Catholic. Avocations: aviculture, needlework, travel, photography, concerts. Home: 18 Osborne Ln Greenvale NY 11548-1140 Office: Early Childhood Ctr 436 Front St Hempstead NY 11550-4212 E-mail: mgraffeo@optonline.net.

GRAFFEO, VICTORIA A. state appeals court judge; b. Rockville Centre, NY, Apr. 13, 1952; m. Edward E. Winders. BA, SUNY, Oneonta, 1974; JD Albany Law Sch., Union U., 1977. Pvt. practice, 1978—82; asst. counsel N.Y. State Div. Alcoholism and Alcohol Abuse, 1982—84; counsel to minority leader pro tempore Kemp Hannon N.Y. State Assembly, 1984—89, chief counsel to minority leader Clarence D. Rappleyea Jr., 1989—94; solicitor gen. State of NY, 1995—96; judge NY State Supreme Ct. (3d jud. dist.), 1996—98; assoc. justice Appellate div., 3d dept., 1998—2000; assoc. judge N.Y. State Ct. Appeals, Albany, 2000—. Office: 20 Eagle St Albany NY 12207

GRAFSTEIN, BERNICE, physiology and neuroscience educator, researcher; BA, U. Toronto, Ont., Can., 1951; PhD, McGill U., Montreal, Que., Can., 1954. Prof. physiology and biophysics Cornell U. Med. Coll., N.Y.C., disting. prof. neurosci. Office: Cornell U Weill Med Coll Dept Physiology New York NY 10021 E-mail: bgraf@med.cornell.edu.

GRAFTON, BETH P. music educator; b. Altoona, Pa., Dec. 16, 1957; d. Robert R. Reifsteck, Sally A. Reifsteck; m. Dirk S. Grafton; children: Christopher, Diana. MA in Music Edn., Indiana U. of Pa., 1994. Cert. Instrnl. II Pa., 1979. Tchr. music Indiana Area Sch. Dist., Indiana, Pa., 1979—; violist Altoona Symphony Orch., Altoona, Pa., 1975—94. Violist Johnstown Symphony Orch., Johnstown, Pa., 1979—99. Musician (condr., dir.): Indiana Area H.S. Pit Orch. V.p. Zion Luth. Ch. Coun., Indiana, 1998—2000. Mem.: Pa. State Edn. Assn., Pa. Music Educators Assn., Kappa Delta Pi (life), Delta Omicron (life). Lutheran.

GRAFTON, SUE, novelist; b. Louisville, Apr. 24, 1940; d. Cornelius Warren and Vivian Boisseau (Harnsberger) G.; children: Leslie, Jay, Jamie; m. Steven Humphrey, Oct. 1, 1978. BA, U. Louisville, 1961. Lectr. L.A. City Coll., Long Beach (Calif.) City Coll., U. Dayton (Ohio) Writers Conf., Midwest Writers Conf., Canton, Ohio, Calif. Luth. Coll., Thousand Oaks, Santa Barbara (Calif.) Writers Conf., L.A. Valley Coll., Antioch Writers Conf., Yellow Springs, Ohio, S.W. Writers Conf., Albuquerque, Smithsonian Campus on the Mall, Washington, and others. Author: (novels) Keziah Dane, 1967, The Lolly-Madona War, 1969, "A" is for Alibi, 1982 (Mysterious Stranger award 1982-83), "B" is for Burglar, 1985 (Shamus award 1986, Anthony award 1987), "C" is For Corpse, 1986, "D" is for Deadbeat, 1987, "E" is for Evidence, 1988 (Doubleday Mystery Guild award 1989), "F" is for Fugitive, 1989 (Doubleday Mystery Guild award 1990, The Falcon award 1990), "G" is for Gumshoe, 1990 (Doubleday Mystery Guild award 1991, Anthony award 1991, Shamus award 1991), "H" is for Homicide, 1991 (Doubleday Mystery Guild award 1992), "I" is for Innocent, 1992 (Doubleday Mystery Guild award 1992, Mystery Scene Am. Mystery award 1993), Kinsey and Me, 1992, "J" is for Judgement, 1994, "K" is for Killer, 1994 (Shamus award 1994), "L" is For Lawless, 1995, "M" is For Malice, 1996, "N" is for Noose, 1998, "O" is for Outlaw, 1999, "P" is for Peril, 2001, Q is for Quarry, 2002; editor: Writing Mysteries, 1992; author short fiction, short stories, screenplay, teleplay TV episodes. Mem. Writers Guild Am. West, Mystery Writers Am. Inc. (pres. 1994), Private Eye Writers Assn. (pres. 1989-90), Crime Writers Assn. Address: Penguin/Putnam 375 Hudson St New York NY 10014-3672

GRAHAM, ANNA REGINA, pathologist, educator; b. Phila., Nov. 1, 1947; d. Eugene Nelson and Anna Beatrice (McGovern) Chadwick; m. Larry L. Graham, June 29, 1973; 1 child, Jason. BS in Chemistry, Ariz. State U., 1969, BS in Zoology, 1970; MD, U. Ariz., 1974. Diplomate Am. Bd. Pathology. With Coll. Medicine U. Ariz., Tucson, 1974—, asst. prof. pathology, 1978-84, assoc. prof. pathology, 1984-90, prof. Pathology, 1990—. Fellow Am. Soc. Clin. Pathologists (bd. dirs. Chgo. chpt. 1993—, sec. 1995-99, v.p. 1999-2000, pres.-elect 2000-2001, pres. 2001-02), Internat. Acad. Pathology, Internat. Acad. Telemedicine, Coll. Am. Pathologists; mem. AMA (alt. del. Chgo. chpt. 1992-99, del. Chgo. chpt. 1999—), Ariz. Soc. Pathologists (pres. Phoenix chpt. 1989-91), Ariz. Med. Assn. (treas. Phoenix chpt. 1995-97). Republican. Baptist. Avocations: motorcycles, piano, choir. Office: Ariz Health Scis Ctr Dept Pathology Tucson AZ 85724-5108 E-mail: agraham@umcaz.edu.

GRAHAM, BARBARA S. electric power industry executive; Sr. v.p., treas., CFO Delmarva Power & Light Co. (now Connectiv), Wilmington, Del.; chief adminstrv. officer Connectiv, 1999—. Office: Connectiv PO Box 231 800 King St Wilmington DE 19899

GRAHAM, BETTY CAROL, community college administrator; b. Cow Pens, Ala., July 13, 1943; d. William Marvin and Lora Irene (Jones) Moody; m. Joel Wayne Graham; 1 child, Jeffery Wayne. BS in English, Jacksonville (Ala.) State U., 1971; MA in English, Montevallo (Ala.) U., 1975; AA in Secondary Edn., Auburn (Ala.) U., 1983, postgrad., 1993. Tchr. Tallapoosa County Bd. of Edn., New Site, Ala., 1972-89; with cmty. coll. pub. rels. Ala. Coll. System, Alex City, Ala., 1989-91; adminstrv. dir. Ctr. Ala. Cmty. Coll., Alex City, 1991-94, asst. dean students, 1994-96, dean students enrollment, 1996—. Bd. dirs. ARC, Alex City, 1993-96; judiciary health ednl. com. Ala. Legis., Montgomery, 1994—. Recipient Ala. State Support Workers Champion award ESPD, 1988. Mem. Ala. Edn. Assn. (pres. 1987-88, pres. post secondary edn. 1992-94), Lake Martin Area C. of C. (bd. dirs. 1992-96), Ala. Cattleman's Assn., Delta Kappa Gamma, Sigma Tau Delta. Democrat. Baptist. Avocations: reading, politics. Home: 3485 Cowpens Rd Alexander City AL 35010-7930 Office: Ctrl Ala Cmty Coll PO Box 699 Alexander City AL 35011-0699

GRAHAM, DEBORAH DENISE, minister, educator; b. Akron, Ohio, Dec. 15, 1961; d. Douglas Eugene Ward and Ruby Lucille (Head) Lockett; m. Curnell Graham, May 21, 1988; children: Shakira Denaé, Victoria Patrice. BA, U. Akron, 1984, PhD, 1998; MDiv, Duke U., 1987. Ordained elder East Ohio Conf. English tchr. Upward Bound Program, Akron, 1982—87, dormitory counselor, 1982—87; tchg. asst. Duke U., Durham, NC, 1984—87; rschr., tchr. U. Akron, 1987—94, adminstrv. asst. women's studies, 1987—94; sr. pastor Holy Trinity United Meth. Ch., Akron, 1987—. Bus. adminstr. Holy Trinity United Meth. Ch., Akron, 1987—; profl. counselor Juvenile Ct., Akron, 1987—; leadership trainer Akron Dist./Shirley Caesar, 1996—. Spkr. M. King Fed. Ctr., Battle Creek, 1999; expert in residence Kellog Found., Battle Creek, Mich., 1998; bd. mem. InterFaith Caregivers, Akron, 1999—2000. Named Most Loved Pastor, Gospel Today Mag., 2001; recipient Cmty. Leadership award, God First Ministries, 2002. Mem.: East Ohio Bd. Ordained Mins., Delta Sigma Theta. Democrat. Avocations: organ, reading, journaling, running, dining. Home: 1291 Morse St Akron OH 44320 Office: Holy Trinity UMC 1127 Copley Rd Akron OH 44320

GRAHAM, DIANE E. newspaper editor; b. Gary, Ind., June 29, 1953; d. William M. and Mary Jane (Shreve) Graham; m. Daniel Kevin Miller, Oct. 18, 1986. B, Drake U., 1974. Reporter Des Moines Tribune, 1974—78, Des Moines Register, 1978—84, bus. editor, 1984—86, dep. mng. editor, 1986—95, mng. editor, 1995—. Pres. Iowa Freedom of Info. Coun., Des Moines, 1992—93; chair adv. bd. Drake U. Sch. Journalism, Des Moines, 1995—. Recipient Davenport fellow for bus./econ. reporting, U. Mo., 1983. Avocations: playing pipe organ, gardening. Office: Des Moines Register 715 Locust St Des Moines IA 50309-3767

GRAHAM, FRANCES KEESLER (MRS. DAVID TREDWAY GRAHAM), psychologist, educator; b. Canastota, N.Y., Aug. 1, 1918; d. Clyde C. and Norma (Van Surdam) Keesler; m. David Tredway Graham, June 14, 1941; children: Norma, Andrew, Mary. BA, Pa. State U., 1938; PhD, Yale U., 1942; DSc (hon.), U. Wis., 1996. Acting dir. St. Louis Psychiat. Clinic, 1942-44; instr. Barnard Coll., 1948-51; research assoc. Sch. Medicine, Washington U., St. Louis, 1942-48, 53-57, U. Wis., Madison, 1957-64, asso. prof. pediatrics and psychology, 1964-68, prof., 1968-86, Hilldale research prof., 1980-86; prof. U. Del., Newark, 1986-89, prof. emerita, 1989—. Disting. faculty lectr., U. Del., Newark, 1989; cons. Nat. Inst. Neurol. Diseases and Blindness perinatal research br.; mem. exptl. psychology research review com. NIMH, 1970-74, NRC, 1971-74; mem. bd. sci. counselors NIMH, 1977-81, chmn., 1979-81; mem. Pres.'s Commn. for Study of Ethical Problems in Medicine and Biomed. and Behavioral Research, 1980-82 Mem. editorial bd. Jour. Exptl. Child Psychology, 1964-67, Child Devel., 1966-68, Jour. Exptl. Psychology, 1968-73, Psychophysiology, 1968-73; contbr. articles to profl. jours. Recipient Rsch. Scientist award NIMH, 1964-89, Disting. Alumna award Pa. State U., 1983, Wilbur L. Cross medal Yale U., 1992, Gold medal Am. Psychol. Found., 1995. Fellow AAAS (chmn. sect. psychology 1979, mem. nominations com. 1992-95), APA (coun. 1975-77, pres. div. physiol. and comparative psychology 1978-79, G. Stanley Hall award 1982, Disting. Scientist award 1990); mem. NAS, Am. Psychol. Soc. (William James fellow 1990), Soc. Rsch. Child Devel. (council 1965-71, pres. 1975-77, Disting. Sci. Contbns. award 1991), Soc. Psychophysiol. Rsch. (dir. 1968-71, 72-75, pres. 1973-74, Disting. Contbns. award 1981), Soc. Exptl. Psychologists, Soc. Neurosci., Fedn. Behavioral Psychol. and Cognitive Scis. (exec. com. 1991-94), Psychonomic Soc., Acoustical Soc. Am., Internat. Soc. Devel. Psychobiology, Phi Beta Kappa, Sigma Xi. Home: 311 Dove Dr Newark DE 19713-1211 E-mail: lkgraham@udel.edu.

GRAHAM, GLORIA FLIPPIN, dermatologist; b. Durham, N.C., Mar. 3, 1935; d. James Meigs and Ida Mae (Boyd) F.; m. Douglas Graham (div.); 1 child, Wayne Meigs; m. James Herbert Graham, July 29, 1989. BS, Wake Forest U., 1957; MD, Bowman-Gray Sch. Medicine, 1961. Diplomate Am. Bd. Dermatology. Intern Sch. Medicine Vanderbilt U., 1961-62; resident, dermatology U. Va. Med. Ctr., Charlottesville, 1962-65; pvt. practice Columbia, S.C., 1965-66; attending physician Crystal Coast Dermatology Svcs., P.A., Morehead City, N.C., 2000; physician, owner Wilson (N.C.) Dermatology Clinic, 1966-94; physician, pres. Grahams Dermatology Svcs., Morehead City, N.C., 1992-2000; attending physician Crystal Coast Dermatology Svcs., P.A., Moorehead City, N.C., 2000—. Cons. Carteret Gen. Hosp., Morehead City, 1986-2000; clin. attending prof. Bowman Gray Sch. Medicine, Winston-Salem, N.C., 1991-2000; adj. clin. prof. U. N.C. Sch. Medicine, Chapel Hill, 1995-2001; assoc. prof. dermatology Wake Forest U. Med. Sch., 2001-2004, bd. visitors, 2003—. Co-exhibitor: Two Hereditary Osseocutaneous Syndromes, Acad. Dermatology, 1965 (Silver award), So. Med. Assn. Exhibit Hereditary Acrokeratotic Poikiloderma, 1970 (Third Place award). Named Woman of Yr., Women's Residence Coun. Wake Forest U., 1982, Practitioner of Yr., Dermatology Found., 1998. Mem.: Internat. Soc. Cryosurgery (v.p. 2001—), Women's Dermatologic Soc. (pres. 1997—98, Rose Hirschler award 2001), Am. Dermatologic Assn. (elect), Am. Acad. Dermatology (bd. dirs. 1991—96, audit com. 1996—2000, ethics com. 1996—2001, nominating com. 2002—, chair nominating com. 2003, Fox award 2003), N.Am. Clin. Dermatologic Soc. (bd. dirs. 1995—2001), World Congress Dermatology (co-chmn. cryosurgical symposium 1997, 2001), Wake Forest U. Sch. Medicine Alumni Assn. (bd. dirs.). Avocations: travel, fishing. Home: 305 Cutty Sark Rd Winston Salem NC 27103 E-mail: ggraham@wfubmc.edu., ggfgraham@aol.com.

GRAHAM, HEATHER, actress; b. Milw., Jan. 29, 1970; Motion picture actress. Films include License to Drive, 1988, Drugstore Cowboy, 1989, I Love You to Death, 1990, Guilty as Charged, 1991, Diggstown, 1992, 6 Degrees of Separation, 1993, Don't Do It, 1994, Swingers, 1996, Boogie Nights, 1997 (MTV movie award 1998), Scream 2, 1997, Austin Powers: The Spy Who Shagged Me, 1999, Bowfinger, 1999, Kiss & Tell, 2000, Sidewalks of New York, 2001, From Hell, 2001, Killing Me Softly, 2002, The Guru, 2002, Alien Love Triangle, 2002, Hope Springs, 2003; T.V. series include Twin Peaks, 1990, 92. Recipient ShoWest award for Female Star of Tomorrow, 1999. Office: Creative Artists Agency 9830 Wilshire Blvd Beverly Hills CA 90211

GRAHAM, JANET C. former state attorney general; b. Salt Lake City, 1949; BS in Psychology, Clark U., Worcester, Mass., 1973; MS in Psychology, U. Utah, 1977, JD, 1980. Bar: Utah. Ptnr. Jones, Waldo, Holbrook & McDonough, Salt Lake City, 1979—89; soliciter gen. Utah Atty. Gen.'s Office, Salt Lake City, 1989—93; atty. gen. State of Utah, 1993—2001. Adj. prof. law U. Utah Law Sch.; bar commr. Utah State Bar, 1991; master of bench Utah Inns Ct. VII; mem. Utah Commn. on Justice in 21st Century; bd. dirs. Jones, Waldo, Holbrook & McDonough; bd. trustees, pres. Coll. Law U. Utah. Fin. devel. chair YWCA; chair Ctrl. Bus. Improvement Dist.; mem. Salt Lake City Olympic Bid Com. 1988 Games. Named Woman Lawyer of Yr., Utah, 1987. Mem.: Women Lawyers Utah (co-founder, mem. exec. com.), Am. Arbitration Assn. (nat. panel arbitrators). Democrat.*

GRAHAM, JANET LORRAINE, music educator; b. Halifax, NC, Jan. 15, 1947; d. Lloyd Cartez and Waline Wilkins; m. Aaron Richard Graham, June 21, 1969; children: Andrea Yvonne, Aaron Richard III. BA, NC Ctrl. U., 1969. Cert. music tchr. N.C., Ohio, N.J. 4th grade tchr., H.S. chorus dir. Scotland Neck (NC) Schs., 1969; elem./jr. high music tchr. Akron (Ohio) schs., 1969—71; gen. music tchr. grades K-6 Bergenfield (NJ) schs., 1971—. Bd. dirs. Bergen Philharm., Englewood, NJ, 1997—. Named Tchr. of Yr., State of NJ Dept. Edn., 1994. Mem.: NEA, No. NJ Orff Schulwerk Assn. (pres. 1999—2002), Bergenfield Edn. Assn., Tri-M Music Honor Soc. (life), Zeta Phi Beta. Achievements include featured in music textbooks on music methods. Avocations: travel, reading, dance. Home: 86 Church St Teaneck NJ 07666 E-mail: Janyvo@yahoo.com.

GRAHAM, JEWEL FREEMAN, social worker, lawyer, educator; b. Springfield, Ohio, May 3, 1925; d. Robert Lee and Lula Belle Freeman; m. Paul N. Graham, Aug. 8, 1953; children: Robert, Nathan. BA, Fisk U., 1946; student, Howard U., 1946-47; MS in Social Svc. Adminstrn., Case Western Res. U., 1953; JD, U. Dayton, 1979; LHD (hon.), Meadville-Lombard Theol. Sch., 1991. Bar: Ohio; cert. social worker. Assoc. dir. teenage program dept. YWCA, Grand Rapids, Mich., 1947-50, coord. met. teenage program Detroit, 1953-56; dir. program for interracial edn. Antioch Coll., Yellow Springs, Ohio, 1964-69, from asst. prof. to prof., 1969-92, prof. emeritus, 1992—. Mem. Ohio Commn. on Dispute Resolution and Conflict Mgmt., 1990-92. Mem. exec. com. World YWCA, Geneva, 1975-83, 87—, pres., 1983; bd. dirs. YWCA of the U.S.A., 1970-89, pres., 1979-85; bd. dirs. Antioch U., 1994-96. Named to Greene County Women's Hall of Fame, 1982, Ohio Women's Hall of Fame, 1988; named 1 of 10 Outstanding Women of Miami Valley, 1987; recipient Ambassador award YWCA of the U.S.A., 1993. Mem. ABA, Nat. Assn. of Social Workers (charter), Nat. Coun. of Negro Women (life), Alpha Kappa Alpha. Democrat. Unitarian Universalist. Avocations: bicycling, swimming, walking, needlework. Office: Antioch Coll Livermore 51 Yellow Springs OH 45387 E-mail: jewelg@aol.com.

GRAHAM, JORIE, writer, educator; b. N.Y.C., May 9, 1951; d. Curtis Bell and Beverly (Stoll) Pepper; m. James Galvin. BFA, NYU, 1973; MFA, U. Iowa, 1978. Asst. prof. Murray (Ky.) State U., 1978-79, Humboldt State U., Arcata, Calif., 1979-81; instr. Columbia U., N.Y.C., 1981-83; mem. staff U. Iowa, Iowa City, 1983—99, prof. English, dir. Writer's Workshop, 1999; Boylston Prof. of Oratory and Rhetoric Harvard U., 1999—. Poetry editor Crazy Horse, 1978-81; chancellor Acad. Am. Poets, 1997-2003. Author: Hybrids of Plants and of Ghosts, 1980 (Great Lakes Colls. Assn. award 1981), Erosion, 1983, The End of Beauty, 1987, Region of Unlikeness, 1991, Materialism, 1993, The Dream of the Unified Field: Selected Poems 1974-94, 1995, The Errancy, 1997, Swarm, 1999, Never, 2002; editor: Earth Took of Earth: 100 Great Poems of the English Language, 1996; co-editor: The Best American Poetry 1990. Recipient Am. Acad. Poets award, 1977, Young Poet prize Poetry Northwest, 1980, Pushcart prize, 1980, 82, American Poetry Review prize, 1982, Pulitzer prize in poetry, 1996, Lavan award Acad. Am. Poets, 1991, Martin Zaubel award Acad. and Inst. of Arts and Letters, 1992; Bunting fellow Radcliff Inst., 1982, Guggenheim fellow, 1983, John D. and Catherine T. MacArthur Found. fellow, 1990; grantee Ingram-Merrill Found., 1981. Office: Harvard U English Dept Barker Cntr 12 Quincey St Cambridge MA 02138

GRAHAM, K(ATHLEEN) M. (K. M. GRAHAM), artist; b. Hamilton, Ont., Can., Sept. 13, 1913; d. Charles and G. Blanche (Leitch) Howitt; m. J. Wallace Graham, Dec. 17, 1938; children: John Wallace, Janet Howitt. BA, U. Toronto, Ont., 1936. (one-woman shows) Carmen Lamanna Gallery, Toronto, 1967, Trinity Coll., U. Toronto, 1968, Founders Coll., York U., Toronto, 1970, Pollock Gallery, Toronto, 1971,73,75, Art Gallery Coburg, Ont., 1973, City Hall, Toronto, 1974, David Mirvish Gallery Gallery, Toronto, 1976, Klonaridis, Inc., Toronto, 1978, Watson-Willour Gallery, Houston, 1980, Downstairs Gallery, Edmonton, Alta., 1980, 82, Lillian Heidenberg Gallery, N.Y.C., 1981,86, Klonaridis, Inc., Toronto, 1981-85, 87, 88, 90, ELCA London Gallery, Montreal, Que., Can., 1983,

MacDonald-Stewart Art Centre, Guelph, Ont., 1984, Glenbow Mus., Calgary, 1984, Concordia Gallery, Montreal, 1984, Hart House Gallery, Toronto, 1985, Lillian Heidenberg Gallery, N.Y.C., 1986, Klondaridis Inc., Toronto, 1985, 87, 88, 90, 91, Feheley Fine Arts, Toronto, 1989, Douglas Udell Gallery, Vancouver, 1993, Meml. Art Gallery, St. Johns, N.F., 1994, Beaverbrook Gallery, Fredericton, N.B., 1994, Costin and Klintworth, Toronto, Ont., 1994, 95, The Art Gallery of Ont., 1997, The Moore Gallery, Toronto, 2000, 2001, (group shows) Montreal Mus. Fine Arts, 1976, Hirshhorn Mus., Washington, 1977, Edmonton (Alta., Can.) Art Gallery, 1977, Norman MacKenzie Art Gallery, Regina, Sask., Can., 1977, David Mirvish Gallery, Toronto, Watson De Nagy Gallery, Houston, Galerie Wentzel, Hamburg, Fed. Republic Germany, Beaverbrook Gallery, Fredericton, N.B., Associated Am. Artists, N.Y.C., 1986, 88, Elca London, Montreal, 1987, Klondaris Inc., Toronto, 1987, 91, Douglas Udell Gallery, Vancouver, 1987, Associated Am. Artists, N.Y.C., 1988, Feheley Fine Art, Toronto, 1989, (travelling shows) CanadaxTen, 1974, The Can. Canvas, 1975-76, Changing Visions, 1976-77, The Shell Canada Collection, 1977, The Fauve Heritage, 1997, 14 Canadians Hirschborn Mus., Washington, 1977, Certain Traditions, 1978, 79, Bolduc Fournier Graham, 1981, The Heritage of Jack Bush, 1981-82, Selections from the Westburne Collection, 1982-83, (permanent collections) Nat. Gallery Can., Ottawa, Edmonton Art Gallery, Art Gallery Ont., Art Gallery Hamilton, Ont., MacDonald-Stewart Art Gallery, Guelph, Ont., Toronto City Hall, The Brit. Mus., London, Art Gallery Vancouver, Agnes Etherington Art Centre, Kingston, Ont., Can., Musee d'Art Contemporarin Montreal, Beaverbrook Art Gallery, Frederickton, N.B., Art Gallery Nfld.and Labrador, Art Gallery, Peterborough, Ont., Robert McLaughlin Gallery, Oshawa, Ont., Kitchener Waterloo Art Gallery, McMichael Can. Art Gallery, Hart House Art Gallery, Toronto, also numerous corp. collections. Trinity Coll. fellow, U. Toronto, 1988. Mem. Royal Can. Acad.

GRAHAM, KIRSTEN RAE, computer scientist, educator; b. Inglewood, Calif., July 20, 1946; d. Ray Selmer and Ella Louise (Carter) Newbury. BS, U. Wis., Oshkosh, 1971; MS, U. Colo., 1980; postgrad., Army War Coll., 1987; EdD in Adult and Higher Edn., EdD, Mont. State U., 1998. Cert. flight instr. FAA. Chief info. svc. Mont. State Dept. Labor and Industry, Helena; dir., personal property and bus. lic. div. County of Fairfax, Va.; analyst officer U.S. Army Pentagon, Washington; battalion commdr. U.S. Army, Frankfurt, Germany, assoc. prof. West Point, NY; tchr. computer tech. Helena Coll. Tech., U. Mont., chmn. computer electronics tech. dept., 2002—03. Adj. prof. Western Mont. Coll., U. Mont.; del. People-to-People Women Computer Sci. Profls. program, China; coord. 1st statewide program for instrs. new to 2-yr. coll. sys.; faculty practitioner U. Phoenix; faculty fellow for svc. learning Mont. Campus Compact, 1999—2000, mentoring fellow, 2001—03. Del. to China Citizen's Amb. Program, 1993. Lt. col. U.S. Army, 1964—88. Faculty fellow, Mont. Campus Compact, 1999—2000, Mentoring fellow, 2001—02. Mem.: Am. Fedn. Tchrs., Assn. Computing Machinery.

GRAHAM, LAUREN, actress; b. Honolulu, Mar. 16, 1967; d. Lawrence Graham and Donna Grant. BA in English, Barnard Coll., Columbia U.; MFA in acting, So. Meth. U., 1992. Actor: (TV series) Good Company, 1996, Townies, 1996, Conrad Bloom, 1998, M.Y.O.B., 2000, Gilmore Girls, 2000—; (films) Nightwatch, 1997, Confessions of a Sexist Pig, 1998, One True Thing, 1998, Dill Scallion, 1999, Sweet November, 2001, Chasing Destiny, 2001, Bad Santa, 2003, Seeing Other People, 2004, Lucky 13, 2004, (guest appearance): (TV series) Caroline in the City, 1995—96, 3rd Rock from the Sun, 1996, Law & Order, 1997, Seinfield, 1997, NewsRadio, 1997; prodr.: (films) Something More, 2003. Office: ICM 8943 Wilshire Blvd Beverly Hills CA 90211-1934*

GRAHAM, LAURIE, editor, writer; b. Evanston, Ill., Nov. 22, 1941; d. Thomas Harlin and Mary Elisabeth (Stoner) Graham; m. George McKay Schieffelin, Dec. 12, 1980 (dec. Jan. 1988); m. Robert Dale Shearer, Apr. 6, 1994 (dec. Nov. 2002). Student, Mt. Holyoke Coll., 1959-61; BA, U. Colo., 1963. Editor Charles Scribner's Sons, N.Y.C., 1969-87. Originator, co-project dir. The Greater Pitts. Poem Chase, 2001. Author: Rebuilding the House, 1990, Singing the City, 1998; mem. editl. bd. Creative Nonfiction, 1994—, (press series) Emerging Writers in Creative Nonfiction, Duquesne U., 1994—; contbg. author: Pittsburgh Sports, 2000, Creative Nonfiction, 2003. Mem. PEN, N.Y. Jr. League, Colony Club. Home: 1000 Grandview Ave Pittsburgh PA 15211-1362

GRAHAM, MARGARET M. minister; b. Cleve., Feb. 16, 1939; d. Robert Newton and Jean Enloe McDowell; m. William Pierson Graham; children: Lisa Graham Mrozek, Heather Gray; 1 child, Jennifer Bennett. Bachelor of Edn., Nat.-Louis U.; Master of Theology, Va. Theol. Sem. Cert. clin. pastoral edn. Cons. dept. religion Lilly Endowment, Ind., 1981—86; founding mem., exec. dir. Nat. Alliance to End Homelessness, Washington, 1982—86; program dir. Ind. Sector, Washington, 1986—89; assoc. rector St. Margaret's Ch., 1991—95; rector St. John's Ch. Georgetown Parish, 1996—. Mem. standing com. Diocese of Washington, 1988—2000, mem. Commn. on Peace, 1991—93, dep. to gen. conv., 2000, 03; chair Bishop's Transition Com., 2001—02. Mem. UN Mid Decade Conf. for Women, Denmark, 1980; bd. dirs. Choral Arts of Washington, 1971—82; mem. adv. bd. Children's Hosp., Washington, 1979—81; pres. Prevent Child Abuse Am., Chgo., 1988—93; mem. adv. bd. Nat. Commn. Immigration Reform, 1981—85; bd. dirs. St. Francis Ctr., Washington, 1982—88, YMCA, Washington, 1984—86, Points of Light Found., 1988—90, Nat. Found. to Improve TV for Children, Boston, 1990—94, Bright Beginnings Homeless Day Care Ctr., Washington, 1992—97; mem. adv. bd. Children's Def. Fund, Washington, 1992—96; bd. dirs. Mt. Vernon Coll., 1994—96, Covenant House, Washington, 1996—2003. Recipient Alumnae Recognition award, Nat.-Lewis U., 1982. Mem.: Washington Clergy Assn. (pres. 2000—), Cosmos Club. Office: St John's Church Georgetown Parish 3240 O St NW Washington DC 20007

GRAHAM, PAMELA SMITH, artist, distributing company executive; b. Winona, Miss., Jan. 18, 1944; d. Douglas LaRue and Dorothy Jean (Hefty) Smith; m. Robert William Graham, Mar. 6, 1965 (div. 1974); children: Jennifer Courtney, Eric Douglas; m. Thomas Paul Harley, Dec. 4, 1976 (div. 2000). Student, U. Colo., 1962-65, U. Cin., 1974-76. Profl. artist, craft tchr., 1968—; property mgmt. and investor, 1972-77; acct., word processor Borden Chem. Co. divsn.. Borden, Inc., Cin., 1974-78; owner, pres. Hargram Enterprises, Cin., 1977-81; owner Sagebrush Studio, 1985—, Graham & Harley Enterprises, 1981-99; art tchr., dean of ceremonial art Coll. of Transformative Wisdom, 1999—2001; webpage designer dept. pharmacy U. Colo. Hosp., 1998-2000. Tchr.; cons. County committee-woman Bergen County, N.J., 1972, clk. of session, 1975-79, conv. chmn., 1981; campaign chmn. United Appeal, 1977; lifeline telephone counselor Suicide Hotline, 1985-90; coord. program svcs. and victim advisor Abusive Men Exploring New Directions, 1986-91, ann. donor by request of artowrk to P.B.S., 1990-. One woman shows include U. Colo. Health Scis. Ctr. Denison Libr., 1992—, Jefferson County Nature Ctr., 1990, Mt. Vernon Country Club, 1998-99, Colo. Symphony, 1998; exhibited in group shows at Colo. Audubon Soc., 1989, Evergreen Artists Assn. Fine Arts Fair, 1988-95, River Sage, 1989, Evergreen Naturalists Audubon Soc., 1988-91, Foothills Art Ctr., 1989, 93, Rocky Mountain PBS Annual Auction, 1991-, Gilpin County Arts Assn., 1989-94, Glenwood Springs Art Guild, 1989-90, Hilton Head Art League, 1999, Red Rocks Trading Post, 2004; featured in Spree mag., 1989, Weekend Arts sect. Denver Post, 1998; included in Ency. of Living Artists, 11th edit., 1999; represented in permanent collections at Univ. Hosp., AMEND, U. Colo. Health Scis. Ctr. Chancellor's Office, U. Colo. at Boulder Wardenburg Health Ctr., Willis Corroon Corp., Dean Witter Reynolds, Inc., others. Recipient awards for art exhibits including People's Choice award Evergreen Artists Assn. Mem. NAFE, Profl. Artists Assn., Nat. Assn. Fine Artists, Denver Art Mus., Denver Mus. Nature and Sci., Mus. Modern Art N.Y., United Sales Leaders Assn., Nat. Mus. Women in Arts, Colo. Artists Assn., Evergreen Artists Assn. (bd. dirs., pres. 1990-91, People's Choice award 1993), Hilton Head Art League, Ocean Journey Aquariaum, Colo. Calligraphers Guild, Gilpin County Arts Assn., Continental Divide Trail Alliance, Friends of Denver Pub. Libr. Assn., Foothills Art Ctr., Assn. Humanistic Psychology, Assn. of Rsch. Enlightenment, The Hemlock Soc., Mt. Vernon Country Club, Queen City Racquet Club, Alpha Gamma Chi, Kappa Kappa Gamma. Studio: Sagebrush Studio 818 Logan St # 903 Denver CO 80203-3123 E-mail: sagebrushstudio@yahoo.com., graham@sagebrushstudios.com.

GRAHAM, PATRICIA, information technology executive; With Prudential; dir. info. sys. Prudential Fin., Roseland, NJ. Past officer Data Mgmt. Assn. N.J.; presenter in field. Named one of Premier 100 Info. Tech. Leaders, ComputerWorld, 2003. Office: Prudential Group and Fin Svcs 55 Livingston Ave Roseland NJ 07068

GRAHAM, PATRICIA ALBJERG, education educator; b. Lafayette, Ind., Feb. 9, 1935; d. Victor L. and Marguerite (Hall) Albjerg; m. Loren R. Graham, Sept. 6, 1955; 1 child, Marguerite Elizabeth. BS, Purdue U., 1955, MS, 1957, DLett (hon.), 1980; PhD, Columbia U., 1964; MA (hon.), Harvard U., 1974; DHL (hon.), Manhattanville Coll., 1976; LLD (hon.), Beloit Coll., 1977, Clark U., 1978; DPA (hon.), Suffolk U., 1978, Ind. U., 1980; DLitt (hon.), St. Norbert Coll., 1980; DH (hon.), Emmanuel Coll., 1983; DHL (hon.), No. Mich. U., 1987, York Coll. of Pa., 1989, Kenyon Coll., 1991, Bank St. Coll. Edn., 1993; LLD (hon.), Radcliffe Coll., 1994, Salem State Coll., 1998. Tchr. high sch., Norfolk, Va., 1955-56, 57-58, N.Y.C., 1958-60; lectr., asst. prof. Ind. U., 1964-66; asst. prof. history of edn. Barnard Coll. and Columbia Tchrs. Coll., N.Y.C., 1965-68, assoc. prof., 1968-72, prof., 1972-74; dean Radcliffe Inst., 1974-77; also v.p. Radcliffe Coll., Cambridge, Mass., 1976-77; prof. Harvard U., Cambridge, Mass., 1974-79, Warren prof., 1979—2001, Warren Rsch. prof., 2001—; dean Grad. Sch. Edn., 1982-91; pres. Spencer Found., Chgo., 1991-2000. Author: Progressive Education: From Arcady to Academe, 1967, Community and Class in American Education: 1865-1918, 1974, S.O.S. Sustain Our Schools, 1992. Bd. dirs. Dalton Sch., 1973-76, Josiah Macy, Jr. Found., 1976-77, 79—; trustee Beloit Coll., 1976-77, 79-82, Northwestern Mut. Life, 1980—, Found. for Teaching Econs., 1980-87; bd. dirs. Spencer Found., 1983-2000, Johnson Found., 1983-2001, Hitachi Found., 1985—, Carnegie Found. for Advancement of Tchg., 1984-92, Ctrl. European U., Budapest, 2002—, Apache, 2002—. Mem.: AAAS (coun. 1993—96, v.p. 1998—2001), Ctr. for Advanced Study in the Behavioral Scis. (bd. dirs. 2001—), Am. Philos. Soc., Am. Hist. Assn. (v.p. 1985—89), Nat. Acad. Edn. (pres. 1984—89), Sci. Rsch. Assocs. (dir. 1980—89), Phi Beta Kappa. Episcopalian. Office: Harvard U Grad Sch Edn Cambridge MA 02138

GRAHAM, SUSETTE RYAN, retired English educator; b. Plattsburgh, N.Y., Aug. 31, 1929; d. Andrew Warren Ryan and Lillian Grace MacDougall; m. James H. Graham, July 1, 1950; children: Marguerite, Andrea, James Jr., Martha, Amy, Matthew. BA, Wellesley Coll., 1950; MA, U. Rochester, 1967, PhD, 1987. Prof. English Nazareth Coll., Rochester, N.Y., 1963-93, prof. emerita, 1993; ret. Contbr. articles, revs. to profl. jours. Fulbright sr. lectr., Poland, 1992-93. Mem. AAUW, MLA, Am. Acad. Poets. Democrat. Avocations: travel, reading, genealogical research. Home: 10 Arbor Ct Fairport NY 14450-1602 also: 603 Pipers Ln Surfside Beach SC 29575-5846 E-mail: jamesgraham@sc.rr.com.

GRAHAM, SYLVIA ANGELENIA, wholesale distributor, retail buyer; b. Charlotte, N.C., Mar. 27, 1950; d. John Wesley and Willie Myrl (Ray) White; m. James Peter Cleveland Fisher, Apr. 23, 1967 (div. Sept. 1972); 1 child, Wesley James Fisher; m. Harold Walker Graham, Sept. 14, 1972 (dec. June 1994); 1 child, Angelique Jane Graham. Cert., Naval Reserve Force Detachment Mgmt. Sch., 1985; air cargo specialist cert., Air U., 1987; grad., U.S. Naval Acad./Global Material Transp. Sch., 2003. Store owner Naval Air Terminal/Naval Transp. Support Unit, Norfolk, Va., 1985—; fleet liaison technician Naval Material Transp. Orgn., Norfolk, 1988-93; passenger svc. rep. Naval Transp. Support Unit Naval Material Transport Orgn., Norfolk, Va., 1996—; distbr. Blair Divsn. of Merchants, Lynchburg, Va., 1988—, Mason Shoe Co., Chippewa Falls, Wis., 1988—, mem. dealer adv. bd., 1997—; driver Greater Charlotte Transp. Co., 1988—, Watkins Products, Winona, Minn., 1992—, Citizens Def. Products, St. Joseph, Mo., 1993—; dealer Creative Card Co.ducts, Chgo., 1995—, Home Showcase Products, Lynchburg, 1995—; driver Carolina Transp., Charlotte, 2000—; distbr. Navy Leader Tng. Unit, Little Creek, Va., 2002. Jewelry dealer Merlite Industries, N.Y.C., 1994; dealer Creative Cards, Chgo., 1995—; mem. Nat. Safety Coun., Charlotte, 1988—, "C" team Watkins Products, Lincoln, Nebr., 1992—; sec. Popular Club Plan, Dayton, N.J., 1990—; pub. Citizens Def. Products, 1993—; sponsor The Paralyzed Vets. Am., Wilton, N.H., 1994—; mem. RBC Ministries, Grand Rapids, Mich., 1998—. Crusader Cancer Ctr. for Detection and Preventin Drive, Seattle, 1991—; block chmn. Easter Seal Soc., 1988—; census taker Census 2000, Charlotte, 2000—; active ARC. With USN, 1991, Persian Gulf; USNR, 1992, Somalian Relief Effort; USN, 1993-94. Named Top Dealer, Home Showcase Products, Lynchburg, Va. Mem. NAFE, Am. Assn. Ret. Persons, Nat. Enlisted Res. Assn., Naval Enlisted Res. Assn., First Class Petty Office Assn., Nat. Pk. and Conservation Assn., Nat. Trust Hist. Preservation, Direct Selling Assn., Navy League of the U.S., Libr. of Congress Assocs., Nature Conservancy, Nat. Audubon Soc., N.C. Sheriffs Assn. (hon. citizen mem. 2000-03), Handyman Club Am. (ofcl.). mem. Am. Red Cross United Response Citizen Corps, 2003. Employer Support of the Gaurd and Res., 2003. Democrat. Pentecostal. Avocations: stamp collecting, reading, bicycling, dance, painting. Home: PO Box 16066 Charlotte NC 28297-6066

GRAHAM, SYLVIA SWORDS, secondary school educator, retired; b. Atlanta, Nov. 15, 1935; d. Metz Jona and Christine (Gurley) Swords; m. Thomas A. Graham, Nov. 29, 1958 (div. 1970). BA, Mary Washington Coll., Fredericksburg, Va., 1957; MEd, W. Ga. Coll., Carrollton, 1980; SEd, W. Ga. Coll., 1981; postgrad., Coll. William and Mary, 1964-67. Tchr. Atlanta pub. schs., 1957-58, Newark County pub. schs., Newark, Calif., 1960-61; tchr. history Virginia Beach (Va.) pub. schs., 1964-75, Paulding County pub. schs., Dallas, Ga., 1976-97, ret., 1997. Tour dir. Paulding High Sch. trips, Far East, 1985, USSR, 1989, Australia, 1988-89. County chmn. Rep. Party, 1987-89, county chmn. for re-election of Newt Gingrich, 1982; mem. Gingrich edn. com., 1983, 88; 1st vice chmn. 6th Congl. Dist., 1989-90, chmn. 1989-90; chmn. 7th Congl. Dist., 1992-95; del. Nat. Rep. Conv., 1992. Named Star Tchr., Paulding County C. of C., Dallas, Ga., 1989, 97. Mem. Dallas Woman's Club (pres. 1982-84, 1st v.p. 1986-88, pub. affairs chmn. 1986—, treas. for Civic Ctr. fund 1984—), Phi Kappa Phi. Republican. Baptist. Avocations: travel, reading, piano, bridge. Personal E-mail: graham.sylvia@att.net.

GRAHAM, THERESA ANNE, art educator; d. Vincent Robert and Pearl Graham. BA, N.J. City U., 1976. Cert. tchr. N.J. Art educator Bayonne Bd. Edn., 1982—. Recipient Disney Am. Tchr. award, Disney Learning Partnership, 2001, N.J. State Best Practice award, State Dept. Edn. N.J., 2001, award, N.J. Suprs. and Prins. Assn., 2002. Mem.: Bayonne Hist. Preservation Commn. (commr. 2003), Art Educators N.J. Office: Bayonne Bd Edn 29th St & Ave A Bayonne NJ 07002

GRAHN, ANN WAGONER, retired scientific policy officer; b. Phila., Feb. 28, 1932; d. George and Marjorie Sharps (Jefferies) W.; m. Douglas Grahn, May 19, 1973. BA, Bryn Mawr Coll., 1953; MA, Middlebury Coll., 1954; MBA, Keller Grad. Sch., 1986. Asst. to dir. overseas programs Am. Coun. Edn., Washington, 1955-56; asst. to dir. mat. dist. div. Dem. Nat. Com., Washington, 1956; with geophysics and space sci. NAS, Washington, 1956-70, staff dir. coms. of space sci. bd., 1970-74; coord. Ctr. Policy Studies, assoc. dir. devel. U. Chgo., 1974-79; exec. officer Argonne Univs. Assn., Argonne Nat. Lab., 1979-82, U. Chgo. Office at Argonne Nat. Lab., Argonne, 1982-83. Spl. editor jour. Perspectives in Biology and Medicine, 1980; editor numerous books and reports. Bd. dirs., exec. dir. Community Found. of Madison and Jefferson County, 1992—96; mem. City of Madison Port Authority; adminstr. Christ Episcopal Ch., 1996-98, coord., Collaborative Mktg. Project of Jefferson Cty., 1999-2003, bd. Dirs., Madison-Jefferson Cty. Indsl. Devel. Corp. 1997-, chair, Info. Tech. Infrastructure Task Group, 2003-. Fulbright scholar, 1953-54, Cmty. Svc. award, C. of C., 2000. Mem. Jefferson County Hist. Soc. (bd. dirs. 1989-92). Republican. Episcopalian. Home: 218 Walnut St Madison IN 47250-3556

GRAHN, BARBARA ASCHER, retired publishing executive; b. Chgo., Mar. 26, 1929; d. Harry L. and Eleanor (Simon) Ascher; m. Robert D. Grahn, Dec. 23, 1952; children: Susan Grahn Gantz, Nancy Lee, Wendy Grahn O'Brien. BA, Miami U., Oxford, Ohio, 1950. Promotion dir. George Williams Coll., Chgo., 1950-52; sales mgr. Chatham Mfg., Chgo., 1952-54; research asst. Standard Rate and Data Service, Skokie, Ill., 1968-70, adminstr. editorial services, 1970-75, asst. editor, 1975-77, editor Wilmette, Ill., 1977-87; assoc. pub. Std. Rate and Data Svc., Wilmette, Ill., 1987-95, quality assurance mgr., 1995—2002; ret., 2002. Pres. Cmty. Club of Jewish Women, Skokie, 1958-60; bd. dirs., treas. North Shore Towers Condo Assn., Skokie, 1986-90, 93-99, 2002-. Mem. NAFE, Chgo. Ad Club, Alpha Epsilon Phi. Avocations: choreography, swimming, spending time with grandchildren, travel.

GRAINGER, MARY MAXON, civic volunteer; b. Arlington, Va., Apr. 14, 1957; d. Fred J. and Grace A. (Ziel) Maxon; m. Bradley R. Grainger, Aug. 18, 1979; children: Aileen, Maura, Erin. BS, Cornell U., 1979, MPS, 1987. Dir. pub. rels. Cazenovia (N.Y.) Coll., 1979-80; assoc. dir. admissions Cornell U., Ithaca, N.Y., 1980-85. V.p. Cornell Class of 1979, 1984-99, reunion chair, 1999—. Mem. devel. and mktg./pub. rels. com. Sciencenter, 1993-2000, mem. Gala com., 1996-2001; mem. comms. com. 1st Congl. Ch., 1985—; pres. Cayuga Heights PTA, 2001-02; newsletter editor Ithaca H.S. PTA, 2001—; leader Girl Scouts, 1991—; chair equity com. Boynton Mid. Sch. PTA, 1997-2001, chmn. comms. com., 2003—; adv. Cayuga Heights Sch., literary mag., 1996-2002; bd. dirs. Cornell Alumni Fedn., Ithaca Pub. Edn. Initiative; coun. rep. Ithaca PTA, 1996—.; mem. Cornell Coun., 2003—. Mem. AAUW (chair ednl. equity Ithaca br., event coord. Sister to Sister, 2000—), Tompkins Girls Hockey Assn. (v.p. bd. dirs.) Home: 421 Highland Rd Ithaca NY 14850-2215 Fax: 607-257-0483. E-mail: mmgithaca@aol.com.

GRAMBS, JENNIFER, writer; b. Apr. 5, 1945; d. Mary E. (Butler) Koser; m. Jeffrey Wood Grambs, Sept. 28, 1970; 1 child, Alison Rebecca. BA in English Lit., Hunter Coll., 1980, MA in English Lit., 1986. City editor The East Orange (N.J.) Record, 1965-67; asst. to fashion columnist Eugenia Sheppard, N.Y. Post Women's Wear Daily, 1967-73; bus. owner The Jennifer Grambs Collection, N.Y.C., 1985—. Author: Alaska, 1990, Texas, 1990, Florida, 1990; contbr. articles to profl. publs.; also theater, film and video work. Hotline vol. Self-Help for Women with Breast Cancer (S.H.A.R.E.), 1994—.

GRAMES-LYRA, JUDITH ELLEN, artist; b. Inglewood, Calif, Feb. 7, 1938; d. Glover Victor and Dorothy Margaret (Burton-Bellingham) Hendrickson and Carolyne Marie Carrick Hendrickson (stepmother); children: Nansea Ellen Ryan, Amber Jeanne Shelley-Harris, Carolyn Jane Angel Longmire, Susan Elaine Gomez, Robert Derek Shallenberger; m. Jon Robert Lyra, Feb. 14, 1997. Cert in journalism, Newspaper Inst. Am., N.Y.C., 1960; AA, Santa Barbara City Coll., 1971; BA, U. Calif., Santa Barbara, 1978, cert. in teaching, 1979. Cert. bldg. inspector, plumbing inspector, Calif. Editor, reporter, photographer Goleta Valley Sun Newspaper, Santa Barbara, 1968-71; editor, team asst. Bur. of Ednl. Rsch. Devel., Santa Barbara, 1971; bus. writer, graphics cons. Santa Barbara, 1971-77; art and prodn. dir. Bedell Advt. Selling Improvement Corp., Santa Barbara, 1979-81; secondary sch. tchr. Coalinga Unified Sch. Dist., Calif., 1981-83; bldg. insp. aide Santa Barbara County, Lompoc, 1983-88, from bldg. engrng. inspector I to III, 1988-99, asst. plans examiner, 1999—2003. Exhibited in group shows at Foley's Frameworks and Interiors, 1984, Grossman Gallery, 1984, 98, Lompoc Valley Art Assn., 1984— (numerous awards including Best of Show 1985, 1st Pl. 1984, 94, 2002, 2d Pl. 1984, 86, 88, 96, 97, 99, 3d Pl. 1987, 89, 97, 2003, Hon. Mention 1986, 90, 91, 97, 99, 2001, Judge's Choice award Mythic Mask Invitation, 2004), Brushes and Blues Invitational, 1998; featured artist Harvest Arts Festival, 1989, Cypress Gallery, 1994; contbr. poetry to anthologies. Mem. disaster response team Calif. Bldg. Ofcl., 1992-2003; exec. bd. dir. Lompoc Mural Soc., 1991-2003. Scholar, Delta Kappa Gamma. Mem. NOW, Nat. Abortion Rights Action League, Nat. Mus. of Women in the Arts (charter), Internat. Conf. Bldg. Ofcl., Engr. and Tech. Assn., Lompoc Valley Art Assn. (bd. mem.), Toastmasters Internat. (Outstanding Speaker awards 1991-93). Avocations: painting, stained glass, home improvement activities, illustrating note cards, writing children's stories.

GRAMM, WENDY LEE, economics educator, former government official; b. Waialua, HI, Jan. 9, 1945; d. Joshua and Angeline (AnChin) Lee; m. Phil Gramm, Nov. 2, 1970; children: Marshall Kenneth, Jefferson Philip. BA in Econs., Wellesley Coll., 1966; PhD in Econs., Northwestern U., 1971. Staff dept. quantitive methods U. Ill., 1969; asst. prof. Tex. A&M U., 1970-74, assoc. prof. dept. econs., 1975-79; research staff Inst. Def. Analyses, 1979-82; asst. dir. Bur. Econs. FTC, 1982-83, dir., 1983-85; adminstr. Office Info. and Regulatory Affairs, OMB, 1985-87; chmn. Commodity Futures Trading Commn., 1988-93; prof. econs. and pub. adminstrn. U. Tex., Arlington, 1993; chmn., regulatory studies prog. & disting. sr. fellow, Mercatus Ctr. George Mason U. Bd. dirs. Enron Corp., 1993—2002, Tex. Pub. Policy Found.; legal adv. bd. Nat. Fedn. Ind. Bus. Contbr. articles to profl. jours. Mem.: Ind. Women's Forum (bd. dirs.). Office: GMU Mercatus Ctr 3301 N Fairfax Dr, Ste 450 Arlington VA 22201*

GRAMMER, LESLIE CARROLL, allergist; b. St. Louis, Mo., 1952; MD, Northwestern U., 1976. Cert. internal medicine 1979, allergy and immunology 1981, diag. lab. immunology 1986, occupational medicine 1989. Intern Northwestern U., Chgo., 1976—77, resident, medicine, 1977—79, fellowship, allergy and immunology, 1979—81; allergist Northwestern Meml. Hosp., Chgo., 1981—; prof. medicine Northwestern U. Med. Sch., 1990—. Office: Northwestern U Feinberg Sch Medicine 303 E Chgo Ave Chicago IL 60611-3093

GRAMSTORFF, JEANNE B. retired farmer; b. Floydada, Tex., June 23, 1930; d. David Stephen Battey and Ruth Asbury Pitts; m. John C. Gramstorff, Feb. 14, 1951 (dec. Feb. 1993); children: Susan G. Gramstorff Fetzer, John C. BA, Tex. Tech U., 1951. Cert. tchr. Tex. Tchr. Perryton (Tex.) Mid. and HS's, 1951-66; farmer Gramstorff & Son, Farnsworth, Tex., 1951-2000; ret., 2000. Bd. dirs. Perryton Nat. Bank. Trustee, officer Perry Meml. Libr., Perryton, 1956—, pres., 2000—03; mem., officer Tex. Panhandle Libr. Sys. Coun., Amarillo, 1978—, chairperson, 2001—02; bd. dirs. Lydia Patterson Inst., 1993—2000; sec. Accord Agr., Inc., Farnsworth, 1995—; historian, v.p., pres. N.W. Tex. United Meth. Women; bd. dirs. N.W. Tex. Conf. United Meth. Ch., 1976—, dist. mission chair, 1996—, mem. ann. conf., 1976—2003. Avocations: reading, needlepoint. Home: PO Box 250 Farnsworth TX 79033-0250

GRANADE, CALLIE VIRGINIA SMITH S. lawyer, federal district judge; b. Lexington, Va., Mar. 7, 1950; d. Milton Hannibal and Callie Dougherty (Rives) Smith; m. Fred King Granade, Oct. 9, 1976; children: Taylor Rives, Milton Smith, Joseph Kee. BA, Hollins Coll., 1972; JD, U. Tex., 1975. Bar: Tex. 1975, Ala. 1976, U.S. Ct. Appeals (5th cir.) 1976, U.S.

Dist. Ct. (so. dist.) Ala. 1977, U.S. Supreme Ct. 1980, U.S. Ct. Appeals (11th cir.) 1981. Law clk. to chief judge U.S. Ct. Appeals (5th cir.), Montgomery, Ala., 1975-76; asst. U.S. atty. U.S. Dept. Justice, Mobile, 1977, sr. litigation counsel, 1987-90; chief criminal sect. U.S. Atty.'s Office, Mobile, 1990-97; 1st asst. U.S. Atty., 1997—2001; acting U.S. Atty., 2001, U.S. Dist. Judge Southern Dist. of Ala., 2002—, Chief Judge, 2003—. Mem. ABA, Fed. Bar Assn., Ala. State Bar Assn., Tex. State Bar Assn., Mobile Bar Assn., Am. Coll. Trial Lawyers. Presbyterian. Office: US Courthouse 113 St Joseph St Mobile AL 36602

GRANAHAN, ANDREA ELEANOR, editor, writer, construction executive; d. Walter Fred Rummel and Arvella Katie Cooper; children: Heather Alexandra, David James, Devin Scott. BA in psychology & expressive arts cum laude, Sonoma State U., MA in psychology, 1980—81. Calif. State Notary State of Calif., 2002. Pub./editor Meanderings Mag., Bodega, Calif., 2002—; owner Granahan & Sons Constrn., Occidental, Calif., 1974—; founding pub./editor Navigator -Weekly Newspaper, Bodega Bay, Calif., 1987—94; mng. editor Signal Weekly Newspaper, Bodega Bay, Calif., 1985—87; reporter The Paper, Monte Rio, Calif., 1979—85. Author: (book) Watermelons, Narwhales and Other Erotic Things. Pres. Sonoma County Press Club, Santa Rosa, Calif., 2000—01, dir., 1992—94. Recipient 1st Pl. Spot News Reporting, Calif. Newspapers Pub. Assn., 1986, 2nd Pl. Feature Writing, Calif. Newspaper Publishers Assn., 1986, 2nd. Pl. Reporting, Calif. Newspapers Pub. Assn., 1986, 2nd. Pl. Agrl. Reporting, Nat. Newspaper Publishers Assn., 1993, 3rd Pl. Agrl. Reporting, 1990, Lincoln Steffens Investigative Reporting, Sonoma State Univ./So9noma County Press Club, 1983, 1984, 1986, Menalli Meml. Lit. award, Santa Rosa Jr. Coll., 1979; Govtl. Studies grant, Nat. Newspaper Publishers Assn., 1993. Mem.: Bay Area Travel Writers (corr.), Sonoma County Press Club (corr.; pres. 2000—01). D-Liberal. Avocations: travel, anthropology, poetry, painting. Office: Granahan & Sons Construction Pob 302 Occidental CA 95465 Personal E-mail: navgal@earthlink.net. E-mail: navgal@earthlink.net.

GRANATA, DONNA ASSUNTA, photographer, educator; b. Encino, Calif., July 15, 1963; d. Charles Anthony Granata and Jo Ann (Thomas) Clark. AA, AS, Ventura (Calif.) C.C., 1990; BA, Brooks Inst. of Photography, Santa Barbara, Calif., 1993; MS in Photography (hon.), Brook Inst. Photography, Santa Barbar, Calif., 2003. Cultural arts instr. Comty. Svcs. Office of Cultural Affairs City of Ventura, Calif., 1988—; spl. programs asst. Office of Cultural Affairs City of Ventura, 1994—; owner, photographer Donna Granata Photography, Casitas Springs, Calif., 1989—; art studio intern Chiat Day Advt., Inc., Venice, Calif., 1990; docent, arts workshop instr. Carnegie Art Mus., Oxnard, Calif., 1990-93. Guest lectr., seminar and workshop presenter, statewide, 1988—; artists in the classroom resident Ventura County Unified Sch. Dist. Children's Outreach Program; ambassador to sub-saharan Africa, Rotary Internat. Found., 2000. Photographer: solo shows include The Creative Imagery of Donna Granata, Ventura City Hall, 1992, Brewhouse Grill, Santa Barbara, Calif., 1992, Images of Artists Agulars, Ventura, 1993, Transitions, A Fusing of Photography and Paint, Art City II, Ventura, 1993, The World of Art City (Audio visual slide documentary Ventura City Hall, 1995), The Beauty of Greece, Early World Restaurant, Brentwood, Calif., 1992—, Art & Soul: Donna Granata Carnegie Art Mus. Oxnard, 1998, Donna Granata Focus on the Masters Series Ventura City Hall West Wing Gallery, 1998, Ventura County Govt. Ctr., 1999, Ventura County Mus. History Art, 1999, Buena Ventura Art Assn., 2001, Ojai Ctr. Arts, 2002, The Laurel, 2003; selected group shows: Brooks Inst. of Photography, Santa Barbara, 1990, 93, Art City II, 1992, 93, 95, Ventura County Fair, 1991, 92, 94-96, Carnegie Art Mus., 1995, 96, 97, 98, Buenaventura Art Assn., Ventura, 1995, Calif. Luth. U., Thousand Oaks, 1996, 97, 98, Window to the World: Artist Eye, 3d Fl Gallery City Hall, Ventura, 1998, Window to the World: Figuratively Speaking, Cafe Banca D'Italia, Ventura, 1998, Remembrance: A memorial exhibit celebrating the life of Horace Bristol, Brooks Inst. Photography, 1997, Charles E. Probst Ctr. Performing Arts, 1996, The Brooks Inst. Photography, 1997, Cafe Banca D'Italia, Ventura, Calif., 1998, Gallery City Hall, Ventura, 1998; writer, dir. prodr. 17 minute slide show: The World of Art City, 1995; founder, writer, photographer, Focus on the Masters, 1995. Founding bd. dirs., mem. Kim Loucks Meml. Arts Edn. Scholarship Com., Ventura, Calif., 1995—; Artists in classroom residency-Focus on the Masters Ventura County Unified Sch. Dist., children's outreach prog., guest docent The J. Paul Getty Mus., Malibu, Calif., 1988-93; vol. Dia De Los Muertos Outreach Program, 1994. Recipient Betty Brooks Holt scholarship Brooks Inst. of Photography, 1992, Best of Coll. Photography Annual pub. finalist, 1987, 88, 90, 91, 92, 93, Best of Photography Annual pub. finalist, 1988, 89, 90, 91, 92, 93; 1994 Ventura County Fair 1st pl. Children, 1st pl. Creative; Best of Photography Annual 4th pl. color, Photographers' Forum, 1993, 2d pl. black and white (coll.), 1993; grantee City of Ventura, Office of Cultural Affairs, 1994-95, Ojai Studio Artists, 1996, Ventura County Arts Coun., 1997-98, 2d place photography, Santa Paula Soc. Arts, 1997-98; Artist fellow Ventura Office Cultural Affairs, 1998-2002. Mem. Advt. Photographers Am. (L.A. chpt.). Avocations: cooking, hiking, horseback riding. Office: PO Box 2619 Ventura CA 93002-2619

GRANATO, CAROL ANNE, writer; b. Phila., May 2, 1946; d. Leo Joseph De Stephanis and Margaret McLean; m. Robert Natale Granato, June 20, 1964; children: Robert Anthony, Stephen. Clk. typist Reliance Ins., Phila., 1963-65; receptionist Phila. Coll. Art, 1984-85; nursing office asst. Meth. Hosp., Phila., 1987; freelance writer, editor Garnet Pub., Phila., 1999—. Author, editor: The Universe and Beyond, 1999; contbr. poems to lit. jours. Asst. dir. Edward Rendell for Mayor, Phila., 1988, 92. Democrat. Roman Catholic. Avocations: paranormal research, gardening, cooking, educational reading. Home: 2506 S 18th St Philadelphia PA 19145-3701 Office: Garnet Pub PO Box 11955 Philadelphia PA 19145 E-mail: garnet1945@aol.com.

GRANATO, CATHERINE (CAMMI GRANATO), Olympic athlete; b. Downers Grove, Ill., Mar. 25, 1971; d. Natalie and Don Granato. Student, Providence Coll., R.I., 1989-93, Concordia U., 1994-97. Hockey player U.S. Nat. Team, 1992—. Recipient Gold Medal, Women's Ice Hockey, Nagano Olympic Games, 1998, Silver Medal, Sydney Olympic Games, 2002. Office: USA Hockey Inc 1775 Bob Johnson Dr Colorado Springs CO 80906-4090*

GRAND, CINDY, foundation director; BA in Humanities, Menlo Coll., 1989. V.p., CFO Richard Grand Found., San Francisco, 1987—. Bd. trustees Menlo Coll., Atherton, 1995—98. Mem.: AAUW.

GRANDGUIST, BETTY L. former director elder affairs; 5 children. Nursing, Mercy Hosp. Sch. Nursing, Des Moines; BA in Psychology, Drake U.; MA in Social Work, U. Iowa, 1976. Divsn. adminstr. Iowa Dept. Pub. Health, Des Moines; exec. dir. Iowa Dept. Elder Affairs, Des Moines, 1987—. Adj. instr. U. Iowa Sch. Social Work. Recipient Nat. Govs. Assn. award, 1992. Mem. Nat. Assn. State Units Aging (v.p.), Iowa Health Care Reform Council, Govs. Task Force Affirmative Action, Long Term Care Coordinating Unit (Issues Scanning Bd.), Drake U. Arts, Scis. Adv. Bd.

GRANDIN, TEMPLE, industrial designer; b. Boston, Aug. 29, 1947; d. Richard McCurdy and Eustacia (Cutler) G. BA in Psychology, Franklin Pierce Coll., 1970; MS in Animal Sci., Arizona State U., 1975; PhD in Animal Sci., U. Ill., Urbana, 1989; D (hon.), McGill U., 1999. Livestock editor Ariz. Farmer Ranchman, Phoenix, 1973-78; equipment designer Corral Industries, Phoenix, 1974-75; ind. cons. Grandin Livestock Systems, Urbana, 1975-90, Fort Collins, Colo., 1990—; lectr., asst. prof. animal sci. dept. Colo. State U., Fort Collins, 1990—. Chmn. handing com. Livestock Conservation Inst., Madison, Wis., 1976—; surveyor USDA. Author: Emergence Labelled Autistic, 1986, Recommended Animal Handling Guidelines for Meat Packers, 1991, Livestock Handling and Transport, 1993, 2nd edit., 2000, Thinking in Pictures, 1995, Genetics and the Behavior of Domestic Animals, 1998, Beef Cattle Behavior Handling and Facilities Design, 2000; contbg. editor Meat and Poultry mag., 1987-98; contbr. articles to profl. jours.; patentee in field. Named One of Processing Stars of 1990 Nat. Provisioner, 1990, Woman of Yr. in Svc. to Agr. Progressive Farmer, 1999; recipient Meritorious Svc. award Livestock Conservation, Madison, Wis., 1986, Disting. Alumni award Franklin Pierce Coll., 1989, Industry Innovators award Meat Mktg. and Tech. Mag., 1994, Brownlee award for internat. leadership in sci. publ. promoting respect for animals Animal Welfare Found. of Canada, 1995, Harry Roswell award Scientists Ctr. for Animal Welfare, 1995, Humane Ethics in Action award Geraldine R. Dodge Found., 1998, Forbes award Nat. Meat Assn., 1998, Founders award Am. Soc. Prevention Cruelty Animals, 1999, Humane award Am. Vet. Med. Assn., 1999, Joseph Wood Krutch award, Humane Soc. of U.S., 2001, Knowlton Innovation award in Meat Mktg. and Tech. Mag., 2001, 2002, Animal Welfare award, Brit. Soc. Animal Sci. and Royal Soc. Prevention Cruelty to Animals, 2002. Mem. Autism Soc. Am. (bd. dirs. 1988—, Trammel Crow award 1989), Am. Soc. Animal Sci. (Animal Mgmt. award 1995, Disting. Svc. award We. sect. 2003), Am. Soc. Agrl. Cons. (bd. dirs. 1981-83), Am. Soc. Agrl. Engrs., Am. Meat Inst. (supplier mem., Industry Advancement award 1995), Am. Registry of Profl. Animal Scis. Republican. Episcopalian. Achievements include design of stockyards and humane restraint equipment for major meat packing companies in the U.S., Canada and Australia; development of an objective scoring system used for monitoring animal welfare in slaughter plants. Home: Grandin Livestock Systems 2918 Silverplume Dr Apt C3 Fort Collins CO 80526-2402 Office: Colo State U Animal Sci Dept Fort Collins CO 80523-0001

GRANDIZIO, LENORE, social worker; b. N.Y.C., Apr. 20, 1952; d. Louis and Angelina (Prez de Garcia) G.; m. Lenny Mars Rothbart; 1 child, Angelica M. BA, SUNY, Geneseo, 1973; MSSW, Columbia U., 1978. Cert. social worker, N.Y.; cert. child psychiatry and child guidance; diplomate clin. social work. Assoc. staff mem. Child, Adolescent and Family Clinic Postgrad. Ctr. for Mental Health, N.Y.C., 1981-83, assoc. staff mem. Adult Clinic, 1984-87; social worker East Harlem Consultation Svc., N.Y.C., 1983-84; sr. worker Jewish Bd. Family and Children's Svcs., Bklyn., 1984-85; sch. social worker N.Y.C. Bd. Edn., 1985—. Co-chair regional staff devel. com. N.Y.C. Bd. Edn., 1996-98; presenter in field, N.Y.C., 1995-97. Mem. NAFE, NASW. Home: 229 W 105th St Apt 53 New York NY 10025-3918

GRANDY, JERILEE, research and evaluation consultant; b. Pitts., Oct. 22, 1942; d. George W. and Ada A. (Minnotte) Taylor. BA in Philosophy, U. Pitts., 1964; PhD in Psychometrics and Rsch. Methodologies, Union Inst., 1999. Rsch. asst. Bur. Rsch. in Neurology and Psychiatry, Princeton, N.J., 1965-66; programmer, numerical analyst Princeton U., 1968-70; programmer Mathematica Inc., Princeton, 1970-72; sr. statis. asst. Ednl. Testing Svc., Princeton, 1972-73, rsch. assoc., 1973-80, sr. rsch. assoc., 1980-83, assoc. rsch. scientist, 1983-87, rsch. scientist, 1987-96. Mem. proposal rev. coms. NSF, Washington, 1990—, U.S. Dept. Edn., Washington, 1993—; keynote speaker Math. Conf., Allentown, Pa., 1993; adj. faculty No. Ariz. U., 1998—. Contbr. numerous articles to profl. jours. Vol. instr., EMT; state coun. del. Pennington (N.J.) First Aid Squad, 1989-94, ARC, Flagstaff, Ariz., 1994—; mem. N.J. First Aid Coun., Mercer County, 1993, del., historian, 1991-94; docent Mus. No. Ariz., 1999—; bd. dirs. Grand Canyon Assn., 2003—. Rsch. grantee NEH, 1983, 94, NSF, 1988-90, 93, U.S. Dept. Edn., 1987. Mem. AAAS, APA, Am. Ednl. Rsch. Assoc. Achievements include research on women and minorities in science and engineering. Home and Office: 4540 Flintwood Ln Flagstaff AZ 86004-7533

GRANET, EILEEN, secondary school educator; AA, Palomar Coll., 1974; BA, San Diego State U., 1977, MA, 1983. Cert. social sci., math, history, spl. edn. tchr. Calif. and Wash., lang. devel. specialist, c.c. instr., tchr. handicapped. Circulation clk. San Diego Union-Tribune, Escondido, Calif., 1974-82; exec. sec. State Mutual Life, San Diego, 1978-79; basic skills & social skills tchr. Mira Costa Coll., Oceanside, Calif., 1984-86; spl. edn. tchr. Escondido Union Sch., 1979-85, tchr. 6th grade history and math, 1985-88, tchr. 7th grade math., 1988-91; tchr. 6th grad history, math., computers and drama cre, 1991-95; tchr. 7th and 8th grade history Escondido Union Sch. Dist., 1995—. Master tchr. student tchrs. Nat. U., Vista, Calif., San Diego State U., 1984—; dist. cons., tchr. coach Escondido Union Schs., 1987—, dist. mentor tchr./trainer, 1988-92, mem. dist. ednl. tech. planning com., 1996—; dept. chairperson Grant Mid. Sch., Escondido, 1988-93, 95—; presenter in field. Internat. conf. presenter Nat. Assn. Vocat. Edn. Spl. Needs Pers., Am. Vocat. Assn., Nat. Rehab. Assn., Chgo., 1983; conf. copresenter Northwest Regional Ednl. Lab., Oregon State U., 1991; conf. presenter San Diego County Partnership Symposium, Oceanside, Calif., 1998, Calif. Coun. Social Sci., Santa Clara, 1999. Fellow NEH, 1997, Calif. History/Social Sci. Project, Schs. Calif. Online Resources for Edn., 1997; named Tchr. of Yr., Escondido Elem. Educators Assn., 1984, 88. Mem. AAUW, NAFE, Nat. Tchr.'s Assn., Calif. Coun. Social Studies, Computer Using Educators, Phi Delta Kappa. Avocations: reading, travelling, photography, craft sewing, internet research. Home: PO Box 660 Escondido CA 92033-0660

GRANGER, KAY, congresswoman; b. Greenville, Tex., Jan. 18, 1943; children: John Dean, Chelsea, Brandon. BS, Tex. Wesleyan U., 1965, DHL. Mem. zoning com. City of Ft. Worth, 1981—89; mem. pvt. industry coun., 1988-89; councilwoman City of Ft. Worth, 1989-91, mayor, 1991-95; mem. 105th-108th Congress from 12th Tex. dist., 1997—; owner G&R Ins. Agy., Ft. Worth. Owner Kay Granger & Assocs. Recipient Woman of Yr. award, 1987, Bus. and Profl. Woman award, 1987; named Exec. of Yr., Ft. Worth Bus. Hall of Fame, 1999; inductee Tex. Women's Hall of Fame, 1999. Mem. Am. Planning Assn., Internat. Sister Cities Assn., Women's Policy Forum (bd. dirs.), East Ft. Worth Bus. and Profl. Assn. (bd. dirs.), Ft. Worth Bus. and Estate Planning Coun., Meadowbrook Bus. and Profl. Womens Assn., East Ft. Worth C. of C. (vice chmn.). Republican. Methodist.*

GRANHOLM, JENNIFER MULHERN, governor; b. Vancouver, B.C., Can., Feb. 5, 1959; arrived in U.S., 1962; d. Civtor Ivar and Shirley Alfreda (Dowden) Granholm; m. Daniel Granholm Mulhern, May 23, 1986; children: Kathryn, Cecelia, Jack. BA, U. Calif., Berkeley, 1984; JD, Harvard U., 1987. Bar: Mich. 1987, U.S. Dist. Ct. (ea. dist.) Mich. 1987, U.S. Ct. Appeals (6th cir.) 1987. Jud. law clk. 6th Cir Ct. Appeals, Detroit, 1987—88; exec. asst. Wayne County Exec., Detroit, 1988—89; asst. U.S. atty. Dept. Justice, Detroit, 1990—94; corp. counsel Wayne County, Detroit, 1994—98; atty. gen. State of Mich., 1999—2002, gov., 2003—. Gen. counsel Detroit/Wayne County Stadium Authority, 1996—98. Contbr. articles to profl. jours. Commr. Great Lakes Commn.; mem. bd. Cyberstate-.org YWCA. Mem.: Inc. Soc. Irish Lawyers, Women's Law Assn., Detroit Bar Assn. Democrat. Roman Catholic. Avocations: running, family, laughing. Office: Gov Office PO Box 30013 Lansing MI 48909*

GRANN, PHYLLIS, former publisher, editor; b. London, Sept. 2, 1937; d. Solomon and Louisa (Bois-Smith) Eitingon; m. Victor Grann, Sept. 28, 1962; children: Allison, David, Edward. BA cum laude, Barnard Coll., 1958. Sec. Doubleday Pubs., N.Y.C., 1958-60; editor William Morrow Inc., N.Y.C., 1960-62, David McKay Co., N.Y.C., 1962-70; sr. editor Simon & Schuster Inc., N.Y.C., 1970—74, editor-in-chief, Pocket Books paperbacks divsn., 1974—76; editor-in-chief G.P. Putnam's & Sons, N.Y.C., 1976—79, editor-in-chief, pub., 1979—84, pub., pres., 1984—86; pres. Putnam Berkley Group, N.Y.C., 1986—87, pres., CEO, 1987—91, chmn., CEO, 1991—96; pres., CEO Penguin Putnam, Inc., 1996—2001; vice chmn. Random House, 2002, sr. editor, Doubleday Broadway Publishing Co., 2003—. Adj. asst. prof. fin. and economics Columbia Bus. Sch., N.Y.C., 2003—. Co-founder Victor & Phyllis Grann Family Found.*

GRANSEE, MARSHA L. federal agency executive; b. Youngstown, OH, Sept. 26, 1952; BA in anthropology, Ohio State U., Columbus, 1974; JD, Cleveland Marshall Coll. Law, 1978. Bar: Va. 1978, Ohio 1979, D.C. 1987. Assoc. legal editor Pub. Utilities Fortnightly, 1979-83; clerk office admin. supv. law judges Fed. Energy Regularoty Commn., 1983-85; assoc. Rose, Schmidt, Chapman, Duff and Hasley, 1985-87; atty. adviser Electric Rates and Corp. Regulation, 1987-88, sr. trial atty. gas and oil litig., 1988—91, legal adviser commr., 1991—93, legal adviser chair, 1993—94, assoc. gen. counsel, 1994—99, dep. gen. counsel, 1999—. Contbg. author: Energy Law and Transactions. Mem. Fed. Energy Bar Assn. Office: Off Gen Counsel Fed Energy Reg Commn 888 First St Rm 10D-01 Youngstown OH 20426

GRANT, AMY, singer, songwriter; b. Augusta, Ga., Nov. 25, 1960; d. Burton and Gloria (Napier) Grant; m. Gary Chapman, 1983 (div. 1999); children: Matthew Garrison Chapman, Millie Chapman, Sarrah Cannon Chapman; m. Vince Gill, 2000; 1 child, Corinna. Student, Furman U., Vanderbilt U., Coll. Arts & Sci., 1982. Albums include Amy Grant, 1977, My Father's Eyes, 1979, Never Alone, 1980, Amy Grant in Concert, 1980, Amy Grant in Concert II, 1981, Age to Age (Grammy award), 1982, A Christmas Album, 1983, Straight Ahead, 1984, Unguarded (Grammy award), 1985, The Collection, 1986, Lead Me On, 1988, Heart in Motion, 1991, (with Vince Gill) House of Love, 1994, The Connection, 1993, Behind the Eyes, 1997, A Christmas to Remember, 1999, Legacy Hymns & Faith, 2002, Simple Things, 2003. Recipient 3 Dove awards Gospel Music Assn., Grammy award for contemporary gospel performance NARAS, 1982, for female gospel performance, 1983, 84, for female gospel vocal, 1985; Walk of Fame honoree, 2001. Office: Blanton Harrell Entertainment 25 Music Sq W Nashville TN 37203-3205*

GRANT, BARBARA, venture capitalist; PhD in Organic Chemistry, Stanford U., 1974. Rsch. scientist rsch. divsn. IBM, 1975-86; product mgr. IBM Sys. Printer Products, 1986-91; dir. IBM Storage Divsn. Magnetic Recording Head Bus. Unit, 1991-94; v.p. bus. devel. IBM Storage Sys. Divsn., 1994-95, v.p., gen. mgr. Removable Media Storage Solutions Bus. Unit, 1995—96; pres., CEO Siros Technologies, 1996—2004; exec.-in-residence Amer. River Ventures, 2004—. NSF fellow. Office: Amer River Ventures 2270 Douglas Blvd Ste 212 Roseville CA 95661

GRANT, BEATRICE, underwriter, consultant; b. Evanston, Ill., July 26, 1954; d. Roosevelt Lee and Mollie (Webb) Lee; m. David Grant, Oct. 6, 1973; children: Anton Lavon, Anita Leona Grant-Leigh. Student, Northeastern Ill. U., Chgo., 1972-74. Rating clk. Warner Ins. Group, Chgo., 1975-78, underwriter, 1981-85; underwriting technician CNA, Chgo., 1978-81, sr. underwriter, 1985-89; underwriting cons., br. bus. unit CNA Comml. Ins., Chgo., 1989—. Underwriting cons. Election judge Cook County, Country Club Hills, Ill., 1997—. Mem. Nat. Assn. Ins. Women, Chgo. Assn. Ins. Women (1st v.p. 1993-94, pres. 1995-96, 2000-01, Profl. Ins. Woman of Yr. 1996, state dir.-elect Ill. State Coun. 1999-2000, state dir. 2000-01, 04—, regional v.p. 2001-02). Office: CNA CNA Plz 37S Chicago IL 60685-0001 E-mail: beatrice.grant@cna.com.

GRANT, CATHERINE, music educator; b. Morehead City, N.C., July 23, 1952; d. Warren and Agnes Mae Grant. BM in Piano Pedagogy, East Carolina U., 1974, MusM in Piano Performance and Composition, 1983; MEd in Music Edn., Fla. State U., 1992; degree in Leadership and Adminstrn., Argosy U., 2003; student in Music Theory, Fla. State U., 1991. Music instr. Carteret Jr. Music, Morehead City, 1974—83, Carteret C.C., Morehead City, 1980—83; pianist Amelia Island (Fla.) Plantation, 1983—; music instr. Mandarin HS, Jacksonville, Fla., 1992—2000, Sugarmill Elem. Sch., St. Marys, Ga., 2000—. Composer: (songs) Beatitude, 1980, Canon for 2 French Horns, 1991. Mem.: MENC, Ga. Music Educators Nat. Convention, Phi Delta Kappa, Pi Lamda Theta. Home: 1337 South Fletcher Ave Fernandina Beach FL 32034

GRANT, COLLEEN, information systems specialist; b. Sunnyvale, Calif., Nov. 16, 1963; d. James Thomas and Hypatia May (Brierly) Walsh; m. Richard Michael Grant, May 30, 1999. Customs liaison Miami Valley Transportations Cons., Dayton, Ohio, 1984-8; sys. intergration coord. NCR Corp., Dayton, 1990-93; rsch. analyst Coding Svcs., Centerville, Ohio, 1993-94; office mgr. LaForsch Orthopedic, Dayton, 1994-95; office adminstr. CH2M Hill, Inc., Dayton, 1995-98; sr. adminstr. The Iams Co., Dayton, 1998-99, human resource info. specialist, 1999—. Mem. Phi Theta Kappa Internat. Republican. Avocations: boating, music, arts, travel. Office: The Iams Co 7250 Poe Ave Dayton OH 45414-5801

GRANT, CYNTHIA D. writer; b. Brockton, Mass., Nov. 23, 1950; d. Robert Cheyne and Jacqueline Ann (Ford) G.; m. Daniel Heatley; 1 child: Morgan; m. Erik Neel; 1 child, Forest. Author: Joshua Fortune, 1980 (Woodward Park Sch. annual book award 1981), Summer Home, 1981, Big Time, 1982, Hard Love, 1983, Kumquat May, I'll Always Love You, 1986, Phoenix Rising, 1989 (Mich. Libr. Assn. Young Adult Caucus best book of yr. 1990, PEN/Norma Klein award 1991, Detroit Pub. Libr. Author Day award 1992), Keep Laughing, 1991, Shadow Man, 1992, Uncle Vampire, 1993 (ALA best books for young adults list 1994), Mary Wolf, 1995, The White Horse, 1998, The Cannibals, Starring Tiffany Spratt, 2002. Recipient Book of Distinction award Hungry Mind Review, 1993, 94. Mem.: PEN (Norma Klein award 1991), Soc. Children's Book Writers and Illustrators. Avocations: reading, volunteer work, Cloverstock. Home: PO Box 95 Cloverdale CA 95425-0095 Office: Writers House LLC 21 W 26th St New York NY 10010

GRANT, DIANTHA HAWKES, not-for-profit administrator, educator; b. Portland, Maine, Feb. 6, 1952; d. Robert Charles and Rebecca Allen (Keith) Hawkes; m. Donald Edgar Grant, Aug. 2, 1986; children: David, Michael. BS, U. Maine, 1974; MS, U. Ill., 1979. Cert. therapeutic recreation splst., Nat. Coun. for Therapeutic Recreation Cert. Tchr. Livermore Falls (Maine) H.S., 1974-75; dir. Ind. Living Ctr., Bangor, Maine, 1975-77; grad. asst. U. Ill., Champaign, 1977-79; asst. prof. Slippery Rock (Pa.) U., 1979-89; edn., tng. coord. Alzheimer's Assn., Boca Raton, Fla., 1989-92; dir. cmty. rels. Hospice by the Sea, Boca Raton, 1993—98. Mem. adj. faculty Lynn U., Boca Raton, Fla., 1994-98. Bd. dirs. Coun. Human Svcs., Boca Raton, Fla., 1993-96. Named Woman of Distinction Soroptimist Club, 1996. Mem. Rotary (mem. group study exch. 1986, Rookie of Yr. 1996, sec. 1996-97, v.p. 1997-2000, pres. 2000-01). Democrat. Avocations: reading, swimming, sailing, pets, travel. Home: 3945 Octave Dr Jacksonville FL 32277-2148 Office: Alzheimer's Assn North Fla Regional Office Boca Raton FL

GRANT, FRANCES BETHEA, editor; b. Sumter, S.C., Jan. 25, 1932; d. Edward Samuel and Mildred (Ladson) Bethea; m. Victor Rastafari Grant, July 2, 1960 (div.); children: Christine Sharon, Pamela Ellen. BA, SUNY, Albany, 1954; postgrad., Temple U., summers 1955-59; MS, Coll. St. Rose, Albany, 1984. Cert. social studies tchr., N.Y. Tech. editor GE Knolls Atomic Power Lab., Schenectady, NY, 1976-89; tech. editor, writer Westinghouse Machinery Apparatus Operation, Schenectady, 1989-96. 1st black effective listening instr. GE Knolls Atomic Power Lab., Schenectady, 1988-89, Westinghouse Machinery Apparatus Operation, Schenectady, 1992; effective listening trainer Grant Enterprises, Albany, N.Y., 1988. Author, editor: Something to Believe In, 1973; author: (poetry) There's More to Tell, 1976, Waiting to Blossom, 2002; puppeteer, ventriloquist Puppet People, 1978-95; editor newsletter Jayncee, 1967-68. Founder, dir. Minority Women's Breast Cancer Network, Albany, 1992—; v.p. Empire State Black Arts and Cultural Festival Com., Albany, 1984-86; YWCA of Albany, 1986-92, YWCA of Schenectady, 1992-95; founder, 1st chairperson Diversity in Schenectady, AAUW Study Group, 1993-95; mem. nat. nominating com. YWCA/USA, Eastern states region, 1994-96; com. mem. Troy Conf. Ethnic Minority Scholarship Com., Latham, N.Y., 1990-96; vol. Reach to Recovery, Raleigh, 1997—, N.C. Assn. for Edn. of Young Children, 1998; bd. mem. Make a Joyful Noise, Raleigh, 1997-2002, Loaves and Fishes, Raleigh, 1998-2002, Nat. Coalition Bldg. Inst., Durham, N.C. Recipient Centennial award GE Knolls Atomic Power Lab., Schenectady, 1978, Scholar award First Reformed Ch., Albany, 1980, award of excellence Westinghouse Machinery Apparatus Operation Facility, Schenectady, 1994, Women of Note award, African Am. Cultural Complex, Raleigh, N.C., 2000, Disting. Alumni award, Coll St. Rose, Albany, NY, 2003. Mem. AAUW (life, chairperson internat. rels. 1973-74, chairperson vol. interpreters directory com. 2002, scholar award 1981, 83, cmty. action grant 1992, Edn. Found. grant honoree 1995), NAACP (life), Nat. Orgn. Black Chemists and Chem. Engrs. (copy editor newsletter 1995-97), Nat. Assn. Black Storytellers, Internat. Listening Assn. (life), Assn. Black Psychologists (life), Nat. Coun. Negro Women (life, co-founder Capital area sect. NC 1997), Nat. Story Telling Assn., N.Am. Assn. Ventriloquists, Puppeteers of Am., Fellowship of Christian Puppeteers, Nat. Women's History Mus. (charter mem.). Avocations: blues guitar, ventriloquist, poet, freelance writer, puppeteer.

GRANT, ISABELLA HORTON, retired judge; b. L.A., Sept. 24, 1924; d. John Daniel and Hannabelle (Horton) Grant. BA, Swarthmore Coll., 1944; MA, UCLA, 1946; JD, Columbia U., 1950; LLD (hon.), Molloy Coll., 1976. Jr. profl. asst. OSS, Washington, 1944-45; economist Inst. Indsl. Rels., UCLA, 1946-47, Office Price Stblzn., L.A., 1951-52; ptnr. Livingston, Grant, Stone & Kay, San Francisco, 1953-79; judge Mcpl. Ct., San Francisco, 1979-82, Superior Ct., San Francisco, 1982-97; ret., 1997. Bd. dirs. Kid's Turn, Pocket Opera. Fellow ABA; mem. Am. Arbitration Assn., San Francisco Ethics Commn. (chair 1999), San Francisco Bar Assn. (bd. dirs. 1978-79), Acad. Matrimonial Lawyers (pres. No. Calif. chpt. 1976), Assn. Family and Conciliation Cts. (pres. Calif. chpt. 1987-89), Nat. Coll. Probate Judges (William W. Treat award 2000), Queen's Bench (pres. 1964), Calif. Tennis Club, Phi Beta Kappa. E-mail: ihortongrant@cs.com

GRANT, JANETT ULRICA, medical/surgical nurse; b. Mavis Bank, St. Andrew, Jamaica, Jan. 15, 1956; came to U.S., 1990; d. John Edgerton and Daisy Ann (Sterling) Welsh; m. Aurnandy Alfanso Grant, Nov. 25, 1978; children: Avril, Adrian, Christophe. Grad., Kingston (Jamaica) Sch. Nursing, 1978, diploma in midwifery, 1988; BSN, N.J. City U., 1998. RN, N.J.; cert. med.-surg. nurse. Mem. staff med. surg. nursing Isaac Barrant Hosp., St. Thomas, Jamaica, 1978-79, Kingston Pub. Hosp., 1979-87, acting sister supr., 1988-90; mem. staff med. surg. nursing Newark Beth Israel Med. Ctr., 1990—, team leader Med.-Surg. Unit, 1995—97. Alt. unit rep. Coun. Nursing Practice, Newark Beth Israel Med. Ctr., 1994; pain resource nurse, 1996—. Mem. planning com. Salvation Army Basic Sch., Kingston, 1988-90. Mem. N.J. State Nurses Assn., Jamaica Nurses Assn. (N.J. chpt.). Methodist. Avocations: reading, sewing, cooking, gardening, craft work.

GRANT, JEAN TERRY, educational consultant; b. Apr. 27, 1930; d. Herbert Lewis and Flossie Mae (Stokes) Terry; m. Joseph Simeon Grant Jr., Oct. 22, 1955; children: Terry Von-Eric, Fricka Jeannine. BS, Howard U., 1953. Libr. asst. Howard U., Washington, 1953-59, Martin Luther King Libr., Columbus, Ohio, 1970-72; head of libr. Shepard Branch Libr., Columbus, Ohio, 1972; edn. cons. Ohio Dept. Edn., Columbus, 1972—. Creator performing exhibiting art shows Afroganza, Columbus Gallery of Fine Arts, 1972, 73, A Night to Remember, 1982-92. Creator performing/exhibiting art shows Afroganza, Columbus Gallery of Fine Art, 1972, 73. Bd dirs. YWCA, 1972-75, asst. treas. 1973-75; bd. dirs. Speech/Hearing Bd., 1989; mem. Govs. Coun. Genetic Diseases, 1975. Avocations: painting, reading, gardening, interior decorating. Office: Dept Edn 65 S Front St Rm 810 Columbus OH 43215-4183

GRANT, JOAN JULIEN, artist; b. Cornwall, Ont., Can., Apr. 15, 1934; d. John Duncan Julien and Winnifred Josephine McCormick; m. Douglas MacDougal Grant, Sept. 24, 1955; children: Stephen John, Ann Elizabeth, Abigail Jennifer, David King. AA, West L.A. C.C., 1975; BFA, Otis Art Inst., 1977, MFA, 1979. Instr. Plymouth (N.H.) State Coll., 1998; pvt. art instr. With works in nat. and internat. pvt. collections; author, editor: Terrestis, 1995, Flight of the Muse, 2002. Mem. CLCC Citizens for a Livable Culver City, 1998-2000. Avocations: reading, book discussion groups, walking, hiking. Home: 4274 LeBourget Ave Culver City CA 90232 E-mail: joan.grant@earthlink.net.

GRANT, KAY LALLIER, early childhood education educator; b. Leavenworth, Kans., Oct. 22, 1951; d. Leon Ernest and Retha Pearl (Poos) Lallier; m. Cary Benson Grant, Aug. 12, 1972; children: Shannon, Ryan. BA in Psychology, Human Devel. & Family Life, U. Kans., 1973; MA in Spl. Edn., U. Tulsa, 1982; EdD in Curriculum & Instrn., Okla. State U., 1990. Cert. early childhood and spl. edn.-mental retardation tchr. Kindergarten tchr. Muskogee (Okla.) Day Nursery, 1973; presch. tchr. Children's House Montessori Sch., Muskogee, 1974; kindergarten tchr. Haskell (Okla.) Pub. Schs., 1974-75; dir., tchr. presch. for handicapped Muskogee Pub. Schs., 1975-78; dir. child care ctr. Muskogee Gen. Hosp., 1982-84; instr. early childhood edn., field svc. coord. Northeastern State U., Tahlequah, Okla., 1985-88, program chair early childhood edn., 1988—92, asst. prof. early childhood Coll. of Edn., 1990—92, dir. early childhood edn. Muskogee Pub. Schs., 1992—99; asst. dean coll. edn. Northeastern State U., 1999—2001, interim dean, 2001—03, dean, 2003—. Reviewer Music and Child Devel., 1988, Total Learning: Curriculum for Young Child, 1987, The Boy Who Would Be a Helicopter, 1990; contbr. articles to profl. jours. Elder Bethany Presbyn. Ch., Muskogee, 1991—99. Recipient scholarship award Okla. Assn. on Children Under Six, 1988, Faculty Rsch. grant Northeastern State U., 1989. Mem. Okla. Assn. Childhood Edn. Internat. (pres. 1991-1999), Nat. Assn. Edn. Young Children, Okla. Assn. Early Childhood Tchr. Educators, So. Early Childhood Assn., Okla. Inst. Child Advocacy (bd. dirs. 1999-2001), Internat. Reading Assn., Phi Delta Kappa, Delta Kappa Gamma, Kappa Delta Phi, Okla. Assoc. Colls. Edn. Office: Northeastern State U Coll Edn Tahlequah OK 74464 E-mail: grantk1@nsuok.edu.

GRANT, LEE (LYOVA HASKELL ROSENTHAL), actress, television and film director; b. N.Y.C., Oct. 31, 1931; d. A.W. and Witia (Haskell) Rosenthal; m. Arnold Manoff (dec.); 1 dau., Dinah; m. Joseph Feury; 1 dau., Belinda. Student, Julliard Sch. Music, Neighborhood Playhouse Sch. Theatre, Met. Opera Ballet Sch. Stage debut as child in L'arocolo, Met. Opera House, N.Y.C., 1934; Broadway appearances include Detective Story (Critics Circle award 1949), Lo and Behold, A Hole in the Head, Wedding Breakfast; toured with The Maids (Obie award), Electra, Silk Stockings, St. Joan, Arms and the Man, Prisoner of Second Avenue; with road co. Two for the Seesaw, The Captains and the Kings, N.Y. Shakespeare Festival; motion pictures include Detective Story, 1952 (best actress Cannes Film Festival), Storm Fear, 1956, Middle of the Night, 1959, Affair of the Skin, The Balcony, 1963, Divorce American Style, 1967, Valley of the Dolls, In the Heat of the Night, 1968, Marooned, 1970, There Was a Crooked Man, 1970, The Landlord, 1970, Plaza Suite, 1971, Shampoo, 1975 (Acad. award for best supporting actress), Voyage of the Damned, 1976, Airport '77, 1977, The Swarm, 1978, The Mafu Cage, 1978, Damien-Omen II, 1978, When You Comin' Back, Red Ryder, 1979, Little Miss Marker, 1980, Charles Chan and the Curse of the Dragon Queen, 1981, Visiting Hours, 1982, Teachers, 1984, The Big Town, 1987, Defending Your Life, 1991, Under Heat, 1994, The Substance of Fire, 1996, It's My Party, 1996, The Amati Girls, 2000, Dr. T and the Women, 2000; TV series include Search for Tomorrow, 1953-54, Fay, 1975, Peyton Place (Emmy award for best supporting actres 1966), White Fang, 1993, Mulholland Drive, 1999; TV movies include Night Slaves, 1970, The respectfull Prostitute (BBC), Neon Ceiling (Emmy award), Ransom for a Dead Man, Lieutenant Shuster's Wife, 1972, Partners in Crime, 1973, What Are Best Friends For?, 1973, Perilous Voyage, 1976, The Spell, 1977, The Million Dollar Face, 1981, For Ladies Only, 1981, Thou Shalt Not Kill, 1982, Bare Essence, 1982, Will There Really Be A Morning?, 1983, The Highjacking of the Achille Lauro, 1989, She Said No, 1990, Something to Live For: The Allison Gertz Story, 1992, In My Daughter's Name, 1992, Citizen Cohn, 1992 (Emmy nomination, Supporting Actress - miniseries, 1993); dir. TV spl. Shape of Things, 1973; dir. play Private View, 1983; dir, (feature film) Tell Me A Riddle, 1980, Women of Willmar, 1982, Feature A Matter of Sex, 1983, Nobody's Child, 1986 (Dirs. Guild Am. award), Down and Out in America, 1987 (Acad. award), No Place Like Home, 1989, (feature comedy) Staying Together, 1989; dir. documentary Women on Trial, 1992, Breast Cancer Say it! Fight it! Cure it!, 1997; dir. TV film Season's of the Heart, 1994, Reunion, 1994, Sing Me The Blues, Lena, 1994. Recipient Congl. Arts Caucus award U.S. Govt., 1983, Lifetime Achievement award Women in Film, 1989.

GRANT, LINDA HESS, language educator; b. Cin., Aug. 17, 1949; d. Guy Cleveland and Mildred Moore Hess; m. James Benjamin Grant, Oct. 21, 1972; children: Mirrin Elizabeth, Lindsey Ann. BS in Speech Pathology, U. Cin., 1971, MA in Audiology, 1972. Clin. audiologist Mercy Hosp., Hamilton, Ohio, 1972-73; ednl. audiologist Davison Sch., Atlanta, 1973-77; ESL faculty Ga. Inst. Tech., Lang. Inst., Atlanta, 1979-96; asst. dir., faculty ESL program Emory U., Atlanta, 1998—2001. Adj. faculty applied linguistics grad. program Ga. State U., 1994—; cons. in field. Author: Well Said, 1993, (chpt.) Material Writer's Handbook, 1995. Chmn. bd. Bond Cmty. Fed. Credit Union, Atlanta, 1983—84; Olympic torchbearer, 2001; v.p. Candler Park Neighborhood Orgn., Atlanta, 1979—80; sec. Fernbank PTA, Atlanta, 1987—88; founding bd. dirs. Inman Park Parent Coop. Presch., Atlanta, 1974—84. Recipient Lee Foshay award, Cin. Speech and Hearing Ctr., 1971. Mem. Ga. Tchrs. English to Spkrs. of Other Langs. (newsletter editor 1986-87, v.p. 1987-89, Profl. Svc. award 1989, 92), Southeast Regional Tchrs. English to Spkrs. of Other Langs. (conf. chair 1991), Internat. Tchrs. English to Spkrs. of Other Langs. (chair interest sect. 2000), Phi Beta Kappa. Avocations: reading, writing, travel, gardening, pottery. E-mail: lhgrant@bellsouth.net.

GRANT, LINDA KAY (LINDA KAY SCOTT), small business owner, sales executive; b. Galesburg, Ill., Oct. 15, 1949; d. Claire Arline Tabb and Addie Mae (Smith) Stedman; m. James G. Scott, Feb. 20, 1968 (div. Dec. 1977); children: Angela Cristine, Aaron Cristopher; m. Daryl Quinn Grant, Sept. 20, 1986; 1 child, Rachael Jane. Student, Balckhawk East Coll., 1984-86. Sec. Flynn Beverage, Inc., Rock Island, Ill., 1972-76, Lee's Place, Inc., Rock Island, 1976-81; merchandising rep. Polaroid Corp., Boston, 1981-84; sales rep. Drawing Bd. Greeting Cards, Dallas, 1984-86; owner Card Creations, Galva, Ill., 1986-90; mktg. rep. Q.C. Metall. Labs., Davenport, Iowa, 1989-94; contract pharmacy rep. PDI Corp./Johnson & Johnson, Mahwah, N.J., 1994-96, Innoves Inc./Novartis Corp., Parsippany, N.J., 1996-2000; owner Spiritwood Farms, Kewanee, Ill., 2001—. Mem. Henry County Rural Revolving Loan Bd., 1994 . Mem. Dem. Women for Henry County, Cambridge, Ill., 1985—; pres. Galva/UA C. of C., 1988; advisor Galva/UA Econ. Devel. Com., 1989. Mem. NOW, Nat. Assn. for Female Execs. Methodist. Home: RR 1 Kewanee IL 61443-9801 Address: 10128 E 2300 St Kewanee IL 61443

GRANT, LINDA KAY, journalist; b. Peoria, Ill., May 24, 1940; d. Virgil and Esther (Lundberg) G.; m. Everett Martin, Jan. 19, 1966 (div.); m. Charles S. Ruby, Nov. 29, 1979 (div.); 1 child, Joshua Nathaniel Ruby. BS, Northwestern U., 1962; postgrad., New Sch. for Social Rsch., 1963, Tufts U., 1970. Asst. copy editor Ann Weekly, 1962; copy editor Saturday Evening Post, 1963-65; rschr. Newsweek Mag., 1965; freelance corr. Vietnam, 1966-68, 1968-70; econs. corr. South China Morning Post, 1968-70; reporter, rschr., assoc. editor Fortune Mag., N.Y.C., 1971-78, sr. writer, 1995—; from staff writer to sr. writer L.A. Times, 1978-84, sr. bus. corr., 1992-93; contbg. editor L.A. Times Mag., N.Y.C., 1991-93; sr. writer U.S. News and World Report, N.Y.C., 1993-95. Author: Face of Hong Kong, 1970. Recipient Best Mag. Reporting from Abroad award Overseas Press Club, 1967, writing award Aviation Space Writers Assn., 1981, Gerald Loeb award Disting. Bus. and Fin. Jour., 1982, 84. Home: 3024 E 6th St Tucson AZ 85716-4851

GRANT, LUCILLE, hospital administrator, social worker; b. N.Y.C., Aug. 29, 1942; d. Thomas Charles and Julia Mae Oliver; m. James Allen Grant Jr. (div.); children: Lucille Grant-Werts, James Allen Grant III. BSW, Adelphi U., 1976, MSW, 1977. LCSW, cert. Sr. addiction counselor Scant. Bd. of Edn., N.Y.C., 1971. Coord. social svcs. Julia Richmond H.S., N.Y.C., 1977—80; supr. social work, coord. Cmty. Mental Health Ctr., Queens Hosp. Ctr., Jamaica, NY, 1980—82, program dir. Teenage Pregnancy Program, 1982—99, program dir. Aspire program, 1999—2002. V.p. Laurelton Civic Assn., NY, 2001—; active mem. youth mentor program; pres. Queensboro Coun. Alcohol and Drugs, Queens, 2000—. Named Social Worker of Yr., N.Y.C. Health and Hosp. Corp., 1998, Mgr. of Yr., N.Y.C. Managerial Employee Assn., 2001, Lucille Grant Day proclaimed in her honor, Queens, N.Y.; recipient Outstanding Svc. award, NASW, 1993. Mem.: NAACP (life). Mem. African Meth. Episcopalian Ch. Avocations: reading, travel. Home: 4342 Cedar Lake Cove Conley GA 30288

GRANT, MARILYNN PATTERSON, secondary educator; b. Washington, Oct. 26, 1952; d. Rossie Lee and Mattie (Pringle) Patterson; m. David Michael Grant, Oct. 11, 1980; children: Karissa Joy, Jared David Michael. BA in History, U. Rochester, 1975, MS in Edn., 1982, postgrad; Cert. advanced studies, SUNY, Brockport, 1987. Cert. tchr., sch. adminstr., supr., N.Y. Jr. high coord. Rochester (N.Y.) City Sch. Dist., 1980-81, team tchr., 1981-83, skills cluster tchr., 1983-85, jr. high tchr., 1985-86, alternative to suspension, 1986-87, 89-90, dean of students, 1987-88, curriculum coord., 1988-89, acting house adminstr., 1990-91, social studies tchr., 1991—96, dir. of social Studies & multicultral edn., 1996—2002; prin. Joseph C. Wilson HS, Rochester, 2002—. Bd. dirs., allocations com. Rochester Monroe County Youth Bd., 1990-92; active Mt. Olivet Bapt. Ch., 1990—. Named one of Outstanding Young Women Am., 1984; recipient Volunteerism award Mayor of Rochester, 1991, Jack & Jill of Rochester Disting. Mother, 2000-01, RCSD Staff excellance award, 2001. Mem. Christian Visitor's Com. (chmn. 1990—), Rochester Urban League Guild (v.p. 1982-83), Jack & Jill of Am. (corr. sec. 1991-92, group leader 1992-93), Zeta Phi Beta (pres. 1985-87, parliamentarian 1985-87), Kappa Delta Pi. Democrat. Avocations: event planning, singing, drama, reading, writing. Home: 227 Genesee Park Blvd Rochester NY 14619-2459

GRANT, MICHELE BYRD, educator; b. Kansas City, Mo., Oct. 30, 1926; d. Ernest Louis and Violetta (Wallace) Byrd. B.S., Lincoln U., 1952; M.S. in Sci. Edn., U. Ill., 1955, advanced cert., 1964. Tchr., Unit 4, Champaign, Ill., 1956-66; tchr. sci. St. Louis Pub. Schs., 1966—, dept. head, 1978—, Mo. Outstanding Biology Tchrs. program dir., 1974— ; participant NSF Summer Inst., CCNY, 1968-69; instr. Webster Coll. Upward Bound Program, 1969-70; judge Monsanto-St. Louis Post Dispatch Sci. Fair, 1970— . Developer, edn. dir. Adventures in Medicine and Sci., 1992; coord., co-develpper Vashon Interdisciplinary Project for Edn. Reform, 1999-2000. Mem. Cath. Sch. Bd., St. Louis, 1982-83; mem. life aux. Barnes Hosp., 1968— ; trustee Meml. and Planned Funeral Soc., 1980. Recipient Mo. Outstanding Biology Tchr. award, Nat. Biology Tchrs. Assn., 1974, One of 50 Nationwide Unsung Heroes award Newsweek, 1987, Excellence in Leadership award Lincoln U., 1987, Newsweek Mag. Unsung Hero Satte Mo., 1987, Monsanto Sci. Tchg. award, 2001; named STARS Tchr., Solutia-NSF, 1999. Mem. ASCD, Nat. Sci. Tchrs. Assn., Nat. Assn. Biology Tchrs., Biology Tchrs. Assn., Mo. Sci. Tchrs. Assn., Mo. Acad. Sci., Alpha Kappa Alpha, Kappa Delta Pi. Roman Catholic. Office: 3405 Bell Ave Saint Louis MO 63106-1604

GRANT, NANCY MARIE, marketing professional, journalist; b. Tilden, Nebr., Jan. 2, 1941; d. William Gerald and Evelyn Marie (Baughman) Whitford; m. Marvin Ostberg, 1961 (div. 1969); children: Jill Marie Ostberg Bennett, Carrie Ostberg Chun; m. Richard Grant, 1973 (div. 1975). BA in Journalism, U. Nebr., 1963; postgrad., U. Oreg., 1968; MBA, Portland State U., 1978; postgrad., U. Wash., 1979-83; diploma, Bailie Sch. Broadcasting, Seattle, 1984; postgrad., Seattle Cen. C.C., 1992, Computer & Bus. Tng. Inst., Bellevue, Wash., 1993. Internship gen. assignment reporter Lincoln (Nebr.) Jour., 1962-63; asst. state editor Lexington (Ky.) Leader, 1963; freelance writer Shreveport Times, AP, Natchatoches, La., 1964; info. rep. 1 & 2 Univ. Oreg. News Bur., Old Oreg. Alumni Mag., Faculty Staff Newsletter, Eugene, 1965-70; dir. pub. rels. U. Portland, Oreg., 1971; info. rep. 3 Oreg. Hwy. Div. and Motor Vehicles, 1972-77; founder, bus. mgr. Grant Mktg., Seattle, 1979; exec. dir., founder Wash. Neurol. Alliance, Seattle, 1985—. Editor U. Oreg. Faculty-Staff Newsletter, 1969; editor, writer U. Portland Alumni Mag., 1970, Hwy Newsletter and film, 1971-77. Lobbyist, newsletter editor Wash. Neurol. Alliance; mem. Gov.'s Com. on Disaability Issues and Employment, 1983-86; bd. dirs. Wash. Assembly, 1983-86, Highland Community Ctr., Bellevue, Wash., 1984-86. Recipient Hearst award, 1963, No. 1 in country for hwy. pub. affairs event, 1973. Mem. NAFE, LWV (Seattle and Princeton, N.J.), Am. Assn. Women Bus. Owners (Seattle and Princeton), Internat. Platform Assn. Democrat. Unitarian Universalist. Avocations: hiking, climbing, bicycling, swimming. Home and Office: 221 NE 175th Ave Vancouver WA 98684-3738

GRANTHAM, CAMILLE RENEE THERIOT, high school librarian, media specialist; b. Lake Charles, La., Nov. 23, 1958; d. George Joseph Jr. and Pattia Jean (Hoppe) Theriot; m. John Steven Grantham, June 27, 1981; 1 child, Laura Lynn. BS, McNeese State U., Lake Charles, 1980, MEd, 1990; M in Libr. and Info. Sci., La. State U., 2003. Cert. tchr., La. Bus. tchr. St. Louis H.S., Lake Charles, 1980-84, Sulphur (La.) H.S., 1984-86; libr. A.A. Nelson Elem. Sch., Lake Charles, 1986-87, D.A. Combre Elem. Sch., Lake Charles, 1987-88, Gillis Elem. Sch., Lake Charles, 1988-89, Westlake (La.) H.S., 1989—; vis. libr. dept. tchr. edn. McNeese State U., 2000—. Mem. exec. bd. La. Assn. Student Couns., 1998. Bd. dirs. Children's Theatre Co., Lake Charles, 1996-98; provisional mem. Jr. League of St. Charles, 2003—. Named Libr. of Yr., Calcasieu Parish Reading Coun., 1994-95; named to Outstanding Young Women of Am., 1983; Ray Broussard grantee, 1993-94. Mem. ALA, La. Libr. Assn., Am. Assn. Sch. Librs., La. Assn. Sch. Librs., Profl. Educators of Reading (v.p.), Alpha Delta Kappa (chpt. pres., dist. chmn.). Roman Catholic. Avocations: reading, gardening. Home: 5705 Stonehaven Ln Lake Charles LA 70605-7177 Office: Westlake HS 1000 Garden Dr Westlake LA 70669-2502

GRANUM, DORIS R. music educator, director; b. Americus, Ga. d. Charles Wesley and Mary Winn (Greer) Rightmyer; m. Tom Warren Granum, Oct. 3, 1987; children: Margaret Eleanor, Mary Winn. B of Music Edn., Carson-Newman Coll., Jefferson City, Tenn., 1981; M of Music Edn., U. Ga., Athens, 1982, D of Music Edn., 2000. Cert. tchr. Ga. Tchr. music, pre-K Athens Acad., Ga., 1982—86; tchr. kindergarten David C. Barrow Elem., Athens, Ga., 1986—88, tchr. pre-K music, 1988—97, Oglethorpe Ave. Elem., Athens, Ga., 1998—; choral dir. Ga. Children's Chorus, U. Ga., Athens, 2003—. Pres., chorus mem. Athens Choral Soc., Ga., 1984—87; chorus mem. Atlanta Symphony Orch. Chorus, 1987—94, Robert Shaw Chamber Singers, 1987—99; choir mem., soloist First Presbyn. Ch., Athens, Ga., 1982—. Gene U. Simons scholarship, U. Ga., 1998. Mem.: Music Educators Nat. Conf., Am. Choral Dirs. Assn., Delta Omicron (state alumni rep. 1984—86). Democrat. Presbyn. Avocations: singing, gardening, reading, travel. Home: 270 Normal Ave Athens GA 30606 Office: Clarke County Sch Dist OAES 1130 Oglethorpe Ave Athens GA 30606

GRANVILLE, LAURA, professional tennis player; b. Chgo., May 12, 1981; d. Charles and Elizabeth. Student, Stanford U., 1999—2001. Profl. tennis player, 2001—. Named Coll. Player of the Yr., Tennis Mag./ITA, 2000, 2001, NCAA Singles Champion, 2000, 2001; recipient 2 Women's Circuit Singles Title, ITF. Office: WTA Tour Corporate Headquarters One Progress Plz Ste 1500 Saint Petersburg FL 33701*

GRANVILLE, PAULINA, independent music scholar and educator; b. Palmerton, Pa., Jan. 5, 1928; d. Paul Edward and Ethel (Hallock) Delp; m. Joseph Ensign Granville, July 11, 1950 (div. June 1980); children: Leslie, Blanchard, Leona, Sara (dec.), Paul (dec.), Mary, Johanna, John. BS, The Juilliard Sch., 1949; MA, Columbia U., 1950; PhD, Fla. State U., 1987. Cert. tchr., Fla. Theatrical organist, Lehighton, Pa., 1941-44; ch. organist, pianist, choir dir., 1938-88; voice accompanist Greenwich Village, N.Y.C., 1945-50; dir. pvt. piano studio for individual and group lessons, 1944-89; dir. gen. music studies, organist, choir leader St. James Episcopal Sch., Ormond Beach, Fla., 1967-72; elem. pub. sch. music specialist Volusia County, Fla., 1972-78; music specialist Bonner Elem. Sch., Daytona Beach, Fla., 1988-90; lectr./recitalist in Fla. and on cruise ships in the Caribbean, 1991-94; pvt. studio Ormond Beach, 1995—. Piano performances at internat. piano workshops in Salzburg, Austria, and Lausanne, Switzerland, 1979-80. Mem. Habitat for Humanity, Daytona Beach, 1993—, Symphony Soc., Daytona Beach, 1989—, Christian Med. Found. Internat., 1980—, Am. Fedn. Police and Concerned Citizens, Assn. Handicapped Artists, others, chairperson Social Ministry, Ormond Beach, Fla., 1999—. Mem. NEA, AAUW, Fla. Music Edn. Assn., Music Educators Nat. Conf., Nat. Music Tchrs. Assn., Fla. Music Tchrs. Assn., Volusia County Music Tchrs. Assn. (co-founder 1973), Pres.'s Club Fla. State U., Juilliard Alumni Assn., Am. Orff-Schulwerk Assn., Phi Kappa Phi, Pi Kappa Lambda. Republican. Lutheran. Avocations: reading, gardening, walking, swimming, traveling. Home: 40 Juniper Dr Ormond Beach FL 32176-2406

GRANZOW, POLLY, state representative, language educator; b. Eldora, Iowa, Sept. 29, 1941; BA, U. Iowa; MA, U. No. Iowa. Cert. tchr. Spanish. Tchr. Spanish; supr. Hardin County; state rep. dist. 44 Iowa Ho. of Reps., 2003—; mem. econ. growth com.; mem. natural resources com.; vice chair human resources com.; mem. health and human svcs. subcom. Mem.: Lions. Republican. Office: State Capitol Bldg East 12th and Grand Des Moines IA 50319

GRAPIN, JACQUELINE G. economist; b. Paris, Dec. 15, 1942; came to U.S., 1985; d. Jean and Raymonde (Ledru) G.; m. Michel Le Goc, June 4, 1971; children: Claire, Julien. Degree, Institut d'Etudes Politiques, Paris, 1966; Degree in Law, U. Paris, 1967; Auditeur, Inst. des Hautes Etudes de Def. Nat., Paris, 1980. Staff writer LeMonde, Paris, 1967-81; dir.-gen. Interavia Pub. Group, Geneva, 1982-86; pres. The European Inst., Washington, 1989—; assoc. prof. Am. U. Econ. corr. Le Figaro, Washington, 1987—; prof. Inst. d'Etudes Politiques, Paris, 1974-77. Author: Guerre Civile Mondiale, 1977, Radioscopie des Etats-Unis, 1980, Fortress America, 1984, Pacific America, 1987, Transatlantic Interoperability in Defense Industries, 2002; pub. European Affairs; contbr. articles to profl. jours. Trustee Aspen Inst. for Humanistic Studies, N.Y.C., 1981—96; bd. dirs. French Am. C. of C., Washington, Internat. Action Against Hunger. Recipient Prix Vauban Inst. des Hautes-Etudes, Paris, 1977, Officer in Order of Legion of Honor, 2001. Mem.: Internat. Inst. Strategic Studies, Cosmos Club, Nat. Press Club, Pen Club. Home: 4745 Massachusetts Ave NW Washington DC 20016-2345 Office: The European Inst 5225 Wisconsin Ave NW Ste 200 Washington DC 20015-2014

GRASMICK, NANCY S. school system administrator; b. Balt. m. Louis J. Grasmick. BS in Elem. Edn., Towson State U., 1961; MS in Deaf Edn., Gallaudet U., 1965; PhD in Communicative Scis. with distinction, Johns Hopkins U., 1979; LHD (hon.), Towson State U., 1992, Goucher Coll., 1992, U. Balt., 1996, Villa Julie Coll., 1998. Tchr. deaf William S. Baer Sch., Balt., 1961-64; tchr. hearing and lang. impaired children Woodvale Sch., Balt., 1964-68; supr. Office Spl. Edn. Balt. County Pub. Schs., 1968-74; prin. Chatsworth Sch., Balt., 1974-78; asst. supt. Balt. County Pub. Schs., 1978-85, assoc. supt., 1985-89; sec. juvenile svcs. Dept.

Juvenile Svc., Balt., 1991; spl. sec. children, youth and families Gov.'s Exec. Office, Balt., 1989-94; supt. schs. Md. Dept. Edn., Balt., 1991—. Mem., chmn. interagy. com. on sch. constrn. Gov.'s Subcabinet for Children, Youth and Families; mem. Gov.'s Workforce Investment Bd.; mem. profl. stds. and tchr. edn. bd. Md. Assocs. for Dyslexic Adults and Youth; mem. State Bd. Edn. profl. adv. bd. Met. Balt. Assn. Learning Disabled Children. Trustee Md. Retirement and Pension Sys.; active Women Execs. in State Govt.; mem. adv. coun. Scholastic, Inc. Recipient Medallion award Jimmy Swartz Found., 1989, Louise B. Makofsky Meml. award Md. Conf. Social Concern, 1990, Child Advocacy award Am. Acad. Pediat., 1990, Humanitarian award March of Dimes, 1990, Disting. Citizen's award Md. Assn. Non-pub. Spl. Edn. Facilities, 1991, Women of Excellence award Nat. Assn. Women Bus. Owners, 1991, Andrew White medal Loyola Coll., 1992, Nat. Edn. Adminstr. of Yr. award Nat. Assn. Ednl. Office Profls., 1992, Nat. award computing to asst. persons with disabilities Johns Hopkins U., 1992, Vernon E. Anderson Disting. Lecture award for outstanding leadership in edn. Coll. Edn., U. Md., 1992, DuBois Circle Award of Honor, 1992, Disting. Alumna of Yr. award Johns Hopkins U., 1992, Pub. Affairs award Md. C. of C., 1994, Educator of the Yr. award Am. Coun. on Rural Spl. Edn., 1992, Profl. Legal Excellence-Advancement of Pub. Understanding of Law award Md. Bar Found., Inc., Pressley Ridge award, Victorine Q. Adams Humanitarian award; named Communicator of Yr. by Speech and Hearing Agy., 1990, Marylander of Yr. by Advt. and Profl. Club of Balt., 1990, Marylander of Yr. by The Balt. Sun, 1997, Most Disting. Woman Girl Scouts Ctrl. Md., 1994, Cmty. Honoree 9th Ann. Heartfest Johns Hopkins Hosp., 1999; selected as one of Md.'s Top 100 Women, Warfields Bus. Record, 1996, 98. Fellow Nat. Assn. Pub. Adminstrs.; mem. Phi Delta Kappa (Excellence in Edn. award), Pi Lambda Theta. Office: Md Dept Edn 200 W Baltimore St Baltimore MD 21201-2595

GRASSELLI, MARGARET MORGAN, curator; b. Worcester, Mass., Mar. 1, 1951; d. Paul Shepard and Anne Piersol (Murray) Morgan; m. Nicholas Eugene Grasselli, May 24, 1981; children: James, Juliana, Anne Regina. AB magna cum laude, Radcliffe Coll., 1973; AM in Fine Arts, Harvard U., 1977, PhD, 1987. Curatorial asst. drawing dept. Fogg Art Mus., Cambridge, Mass., 1974-75, curatorial asst. print dept., 1977-78; asst. curator prints and drawings Nat. Gallery of Art, Washington, 1984-89, curator of Old Master Drawings, 1989—. Tutor fine arts dept. Harvard U., Cambridge, Mass., 1977; guest curator exhbn. Nat. Gallery of Art, Washington, 1980-84; professorial lectr. Georgetown U., Washington, 1988. Author: (exhbn. catalogs) Eighteenth-Century Drawings from the Collection of Mrs. Gertrude Laughlin Chanler, 1982, Colorful Impressions: The Printmaking Revolution in Eighteenth-Century France, 2003; co-author: (exhbn. catalogs) Renaissance and Baroque Drawings from the Collection of John and Alice Steiner, 1977, Old Master Drawings and Bronzes from the Cottonian Collection, 1979, Watteau 1684-1721, 1984-85, Master Drawings from the Armand Hammer Collection, An Inaugural Celebration, 1989, Art for the Nation, Gifts in Honor of the 50th Anniversary of the National Gallery of Art, 1991, Dürer to Diebenkorn: Recent Acquisitions of Art on Paper, 1992, Drawings from the O'Neal Collection, 1993, The Touch of the Artist: Master Drawings from the Woodner Collections, 1995, Mastery and Elegance: Two Centuries of French Drawings from the Collection of Jeffrey E. Horvitz, 1998, The Drawings of Annibale Carracci, 1999; mem. editl. bd. Master Drawings, 1994—; contbr. articles to profl. jours. Agnes Mongan Travelling fellow Harvard U., 1978-79, Samuel H. Kress Pre-doctoral fellow Samuel H. Kress Found., 1979-80, Ailsa Mellon Bruce Curatorial fellow Ctr. for Advanced Study in Visual Arts, 1989-90. Mem. Print Coun. Am. (bd. dirs. 1993-96). Office: Nat Gallery of Art 4th & Constitution Ave NW Washington DC 20565-0001

GRASSERBAUER, DORIS, computer scientist, mathematician, educator; Diplom-Ingenieurin, Vienna U. Tech., 2003. Hardware and software engr. Andronic Gmbh, Vienna, 1991—95; dir. of the multimedia ctr. CCNY, 2001—. Exhibitions include photographs, videos Www.dograba.com. Personal E-mail: doris@dograba.com.

GRASSIE, ANNE C. state legislator; b. Plymouth, N.H., Nov. 24, 1949; m. Charles W. Grassie; 5 children. Prodr. splty. foods, Rochester, N.H.; mem. N.H. Ho. of Reps. Mem. sci. tech. and energy com. N.H. Ho. of Reps. Seminar chairwoman, bd. dirs. Hugh O'Brien Youth Leadership, 1980—; leader Girl Scouts Am., 1986—. Mem. Rochester Jaycees. Address: 9 Central Ave Rochester NH 03867-2718

GRASSO, JULIA ALICE, nursing educator; b. N.Y.C., Nov. 23, 1948; d. William August and Ida K. Johnson; m. Thomas Francis Griffin, Sept. 7, 1968 (div. 1991); children: Steven, Heather, Shenon stepchildren: Pegi, Lynn; m. Robert Dennis Grasso, Feb. 28, 1997. Cert. in Nursing, Lewis A. Wilson Tech. Ctr., 1979; AS in Nursing, U. State N.Y., 1983; BSN, SUNY, 1995; MS in Natural Health, Clayton Coll. Natural Health, 2001. RN Fla., cert. CPR instr., Red Cross. Charge nurse Madonna Heights Convent Infirmary, Dix Hills, NY, 1979—81; staff nurse Good Samaritan Hosp., West Islip, NY, 1981—93; patient coord. GHI Homecare Inc., Rosedale, NY, 1993—95; staff developer and recruiter nursing svcs. Olsten Kimberly Quality Care, Ocala, Fla., 1995; supr. county immunization program Citrus County Dept. Health, Inverness, Fla., 1995—96; with Housecall Home Health, Crystal River, Fla., 1996; vis. nurse Ind. Home Health Svcs., Crystal River, 1997—99; instr. and program coord. Ctrl. Fla. C.C., Fla., 1997—99; insr. biology, phys. sci. med. skills Citrus County Schs., Crystal River, 1999—. Mem. Citrus County Pregnancy Prevention Coun. Grantee, Crystal River (Fla.) HS, Gulfcoast North Area Health Edn. Ctr., Inc., Citrus County Edn. Found. Mem.: Delta Kappa Gamma. Home: PO Box 395 Inverness FL 34451-0395

GRATZ, CINDY CARPENTER, dance educator, choreographer; b. Corpus Christi, Tex., Nov. 20, 1958; d. Regan and Sara (Medellín) Carpenter; m. Robert David Gratz, Dec. 30, 1995. BA, UCLA, 1980, MA, 1982; PhD, NYU, 1990. Adj. instr. dance NYU, N.Y.C., 1987-90, adj. asst. prof., 1990-91; asst. prof. dance Sam Houston State U., Huntsville, Tex., 1991-97, assoc. prof. dance, 1997—2003, prof. dance, 2003—. Artist-in-residence Dan-Ching Acad., Taiwan City, Taiwan, 1986, Brenau Coll., Gainesville, Ga., 1988, U. Nebr., Lincoln, 1989; dir. Washington Square Repertory Dance Co., N.Y.C., 1990-91; founder, dir. Janus Dance Projects, N.Y.C., 1986-91, Prime Time: Srs. in Motion Dance Co., Huntsville, 1992—, The Cindy Carpenter Dance Co., Huntsville, 1995-99, Tex. World Dance Co., Huntsville, 2001—. Choreographer, performer Afterimages, 1992, Gigglefeet Dance Festival, Ketchikan, Alaska, 2002; choreographer, dir. Post Post Dances: Another Artist Slips Away, 1995; dir., choreographer, performer (play) Stepping Out, 1995; choreographer Cheval, 1995, Prelude: Gathering of the Misfits, 1996, Starving, 1997, Excerpts from the Point, 1998, Requiem, 1999, Madwoman of Chaillot, 2001, Go, 2002, Bus Stop, 2003, Equus, 2003, Meatless Variations, 2004; performer Hula Halau Ohana Elikapeka, 1999-2000; elephant rider, showgirl Ringling Bros. and Barnum and Bailey Circus, 1977-78; guest artist, choreographer Stephen F. Austin State U., Nacogdoches, Tex., 2002; costume design and constrn. Cinderella, 2003. Founding mem. exec bd. World dance inst.; mem. exec. bd. Huntsville Cmty. Theatre, 1994-97, 98—. Grantee Chi Tau Epsilon, 1994, Huntsville Arts Commn., 1994-97. Mem. AAUP (pres. local chpt. 1994-97), AAUW (officer 1994-96), Sam Houston State U. Women (officer 1991-96), ACDFA (nat. bd. 2002—). Avocations: swimming, horses, Spurs fan. Home: 2223 Mustang Ln San Marcos TX 78666-1120 Office: Sam Houston State U PO Box 2269 Huntsville TX 77341-2269 Office Phone: 936-294-1311. E-mail: DNC_CLC@shsu.edu.

GRAU, MARCY BEINISH, real estate broker, former investment banker; b. Bklyn., Aug. 7, 1950; d. Joseph Beinish and Gloria (Rosenbaum) Bennett; m. Bennett Grau, Nov. 19, 1978; 3 children. AB with high honors, U. Mich., 1971; postgrad., Columbia U., 1972, N.Y. Inst. Fin., 1973. Asst. to chmn. Bancroft Convertible Fund, N.Y.C., 1973-75; precious metals trader J. Aron & Co., N.Y.C., 1975-81, mgr. metals mktg., 1981-83; v.p. Goldman, Sachs & Co/J. Aron, N.Y.C., 1983-88; investment banking cons. N.Y.C., 1988-90; real estate broker Fox Residential Group, 1998-99, Stribling & Assoc., N.Y.C., 1999—. Editor Precious Metals Rev. and Outlook, 1980—; contbr. article to profl. jours. Vol. worker pediatrics dept. Lenox Hill Hosp., N.Y.C., 1978-79; asst. The Holiday Project, The Hunger Project, N.Y.C., 1978-83; vol. Yorkville Common Pantry, N.Y.C., 1984; tutor Yorkville Neighborhodd Assn., N.Y.C., 1984; assoc. Child Devel. Ctr., N.Y.C.; trustee Congregation B'nai Jeshurun, 1989—, pres., 1991-94, chair, 1994-97; trustee Ethical Fieldston Fund, 1994-2000. Mem. Phi Beta Kappa. Avocations: interior design, fashion, cooking, piano. Home: 300 West End Ave New York NY 10023-8156 Office: 924 Madison Ave New York NY 10021-3577 Office Phone: 212-452-4361. E-mail: marcyg300@aol.com.

GRAU, NANCY AEREN, psychologist; b. Dallas, July 12, 1965; d. Aaron Grau and Jo Ann Feldman. BA in Polit. Sci. and Mass Comm., U. Denver; MA in Psychology, NYU; PhD in Counseling Psychology, N.Mex. State U. Lic. psychologist N.Mex. Clin. dir. La Casa, Inc., Las Cruces, N.Mex., 2001—02; exec. dir. Albuquerque Family and Child Guidance Ctr., 2002—. Adj. faculty U. N.Mex., Albuquerque, 2003—, N.Mex. State U., Las Cruces, 2000; internship Univ. Counseling Ctr. Tex. Tech U., Lubbock; trainer, presenter in field. Chairperson Erie County Coalition Against Domestic Violence, Buffalo, 1995—96; domestic violence cmty. coord. Haven Ho. Inc., Buffalo, 1994—96; vol. co-facilitator Batterers Intervention Program Cath. Charities, Buffalo, 1994—95. Recipient Outstanding Svc. award, Erie County Coalition Against Domestic Violence, 1996. Mem.: APA, N.Mex. State Psychol. Assn. Democrat. Jewish. Avocations: running, yoga, singing, music, travel. Personal E-mail: nancy_grau@qwest.net. E-mail: nancy_grau@qwest.net.

GRAU, SHIRLEY ANN (MRS. JAMES KERN FEIBLEMAN), writer; b. New Orleans, July 8, 1929; d. Adolph and Katherine (Onion) G.; m. James Kern Feibleman, Aug. 4, 1955; children: Ian, James, Nora Miranda, William, Katherine. BA, Tulane U., 1950. Author: (short stories) The Black Prince and Other Stories, 1955, The Hard Blue Sky, 1958, The House on Coliseum Street, 1961, The Keepers of the House, 1964 (Pulitzer prize for fiction 1965), The Condor Passes, 1971, The Wind Shifting West and Other Stories, 1973, Evidence of Love, 1977, Nine Women, 1986, Roadwalkers, 1994; writer publs. including Holiday, New Yorker, New World Writing, Mademoiselle, Saturday Evening Post, Atlantic, The Reporter, 1954—. Mem. Phi Beta Kappa. Office: PO Box 9058 Metairie LA 70055-9058 E-mail: shirleygrau@bellsouth.net.

GRAUER, SANDRA LEE, environmentalist, educator; b. Charleston, S.C., Jan. 30, 1950; d. William Jacob and Bella (Goldman) G. BS, U. S.C., 1972; BSN, Med. Coll. Ga., 1976; postgrad., Clemson U., 1983-86, Med. U. S.C., Charleston, 1987-90; MEd in Biology, The Citadel Evening Coll., Charleston, 1991. Charge nurse Eugene Talmadge Meml. Hosp., Augusta, Ga., 1977, Anderson (S.C.) Meml. Hosp., 1978-80; agrl. sci. asst. Clemson (S.C.) U., 1980-83, sci. rschr., 1983-86, tchg. asst. biology, 1985-86; sci. rschr. Med. U. S.C., Charleston, 1987-89; instr. biology and chemistry, anatomy and physiology Trident Tech. Coll., Charleston, 1988—95; instr. biology (environ.), gen. and environ. astronomy and chemistry Limestone Coll., Gaffney, SC, 1996—. Panelist Genetic Literacy, 2000—03. Vol. Sustainability Inst.; participant election campaign Cindy Floyd for Charleston County Coun., 1998—2002, Get Out the Vote, 2004. Elks state and local scholar Elks Lodge, 1968-71, Saul Alexander scholar, 1968-72; instnl. grantee Med. U. S.C., 1988, Coll. Charleston, 2004-. Mem. AAUW (membership chair 1995-97, participant women's polit. forum 1996), S.C. League Women Voters, Am. Soc. for Cell Biology, Nature Conservancy, S.C. Coastal Conservation League, Audubon Soc., Assn. for Women in Sci., Nat. Resources Def. Coun., Union Concerned Scientists, Sigma Xi, Gamma Sigma Delta. Jewish. Avocations: birdwatching, music, naturalist, stargazing, gardening. Home: 870 Colony Dr Apt 13 Charleston SC 29407-2404

GRAUMAN, NANCY, lawyer; b. Seattle, Nov. 4, 1968; d. David Willis and Joyce Marie Grauman. AB cum laude, Vassar Coll., Poughkeepsie, N.Y., 1991; JD cum laude, Loyola U., L.A., 1998. Bar: Calif. 1998. Summer assoc. White & Case, L.A., 1997; assoc. O'Melveny & Myers, L.A., 1998—2002, Gilchrist & Rutter Profl. Corp., Santa Monica, Calif., 2002—03, Piper Rudnick LLP, LA, 2003—. Recipient Am. Jurisprudence Bancroft-Whitney award for civil procedure and legal writing, Bancroft-Whitney, 1996. Mem.: Order of the Coif, Phi Alpha Delta. Avocations: cooking, travel, music. Office: Piper Rudnick LLP 1999 Ave of Stars Fl 4 Los Angeles CA 90067

GRAVER, SUZANNE LEVY, English literature educator; b. N.Y.C., Aug. 17, 1936; BA summa cum laude, CUNY, 1958; MA, U. Calif., Berkeley, 1960; PhD, U. Mass., 1976. Tchr. English Berkeley High Sch., 1960-61, Culver City High Sch., 1961-62; asst. prof. Berkshire Community Coll., 1966-72; vis. asst. prof. Tufts U., 1976-78; assoc. ind. study Empire State Coll., SUNY, 1978; lectr. Williams Coll., Williamstown, Mass., 1976, 78-82, coord. writing workshop, 1981-85, asst. prof., 1983-87, chair dept. women's studies, 1988-89, assoc. prof. English, 1988-91, assoc. dean faculty, 1990-91, prof., 1991—2002, John Hawley Roberts prof. English prof. emerita, 2002—, dean of faculty, 1991-94. Manuscript reader Ind. U. Press, Victorian Studiesm, A Victorian Periodicals Review, PMLA; fellowship and grants application reader NEH, Nat. Humanities Ctr., The Grad. Ctr., CUNY. Author: George Eliot and Community : A Study in Social Theory and Fictional Form, 1984, and numerous essays and revs. in Victorian lit. and culture. NEH fellow, 1985, 95, U. fellow U. Mass., Amherst, 1974-76, Am. Coun. Learned Socs. fellow, 1985-86, 89-90, Nat. Humanities Ctr. fellow, 1989-90. Fellow NEH; mem. AAUP, ACLU, NOW, Modern Lang. Assn. (rep. to del. assembly 1988-91), Amnesty Internat., Wilderness Soc., Northeast Modern Lang. Assn. (chair English novel sect. 1980). Office: Williams Coll Stetson Hall Williamstown MA 01267-0141

GRAVES, BRENDA VANESSA, small business owner; b. Jacksonville, N.C., Aug. 29, 1967; d. Charles Henry G. and Geraldine (Turner) Durham. Student, Cameron U., 1988-91, Oklahoma City C.C., 1993-94. Asst. mgr. Am. Eagle Outfitters, Oklahoma CIty, 1993-95; mgr. Added Dimensions, Oklahoma CIty, 1995-97; owner Tall Vicki's, Oklahoma CIty, 1997—. Republican. Mem. Ch. of Christ. Avocations: gardening, stamp collecting, repairing old cars, restoring old homes, dog training. Office: Tall Vicki's Womens Apparel 2209 SW 74th St Ste 307 Oklahoma City OK 73159-3929

GRAVES, HILLARY, marketing professional; With iVillage, N.Y.C., 1995—, v.p. online mktg. Office: 212 5th Ave New York NY 10010-2103

GRAVES, JO ANN, state legislator; b. Jan. 3, 1951; m. Bill Graves; children: Barrett, Daniel, Whitney. BS in Bus. Adminstrn., U. N.C., 1977. Mem. Tenn. Senate 100th Gen. Assembly, 1996—, speaker pro tem. Mem. Tenn. Commerce, Labor and Agr. Com., Edn. Com., Senate Environment, Conservation and Tourism Com., Fiscal Rev. Com., Tenn. Adv. Commn. Intergovtl. Rels. Past mem. Gallatin City Coun., past chair Pub. Works Com., past mem. Fin. Com., Safety Com.; active First United Meth. Ch., Meals on Wheels; trustee Ind. Sch.; curriculum chair Pub. and Pvt. Sch. Named Legislator of Yr., Cmty. Mental Health Orgn., Tenn. Sch. Bds. Assn., Tenn. Cattleman's Assn., Tenn. Psychol. Assn., County Clks. Assn., Sierra Club. Mem. BPW, Tenn. Leadership Assn., Sumner County Hist. Soc., Rotary Club, C. of C. Democrat. Office: 4 Legislative Plaza Nashville TN 37243-0218 E-mail: sen.joann.graves@legislature.state.tn.us.

GRAVES, LORRAINE ELIZABETH, dancer, educator, coach; b. Norfolk, Va., Oct. 5, 1957; d. Thomas Edward and Mildred Fayette (Odom) G. BS, Ind. U., 1978. Dancer, Regisseuse Dance Theatre of Harlem, N.Y.C., 1978—, ballet mistress, 1980—, prin. dancer, 1980, artistic asst., 1990—. Artistic advisor Va. Ballet Theatre, 1997—, tchr./coach Dance Theatre of Harlem, 1998-99, 2001, guest ballet mistress, 2001—; guest tchr. N.C. Sch. of Arts, Winston-Salem, 1987, 93, Gov.'s Sch. for Arts, U. Richmond, 1990—, Carlton Johnson Acad. of Dance, 1991-95, Okla. Summer Arts Inst., 1993-94, The Flint Sch. Performing Arts, Flint Youth Ballet, 2001—, Dance Theatre of Harlem, Kennedy Ctr. Residency Program, 1993-95, 98—, Worcester Sch. Performing Arts, 1997, Greenville Ballet, 2001; resident guest tchr. Gov.'s Sch. for Arts, Norfolk, Va., 1988-91, mem. faculty, 1996—; guest tchr. Worcester Sch. Performing Arts, 1997; resident guest tchr. S.C. Gov.'s Sch. for Arts, 1995-97; guest tchr. Va. Ballet Theatre, 1996—, artistic advisor, 1998—; guest tchr. Va. Sch. for the Arts, 1997—, resident guest tchr., 2003—; educator, judge Dance Olympus, 1997—; judge Internat. Dance Challenge, 1998—; guest faculty Mid-States Regional Dance Festival, 1999; mem. faculty SERBA Festival, Roanoke, Va., 2003. Dancer Dance Theatre of Harlem as Princess of Unreal Beauty in live TV prodn. of Firebird, 1982, as Myrta, Queen of the Willis in NBC prodn. of Creole Giselle, 1987, performed at White House, 1981, also at the closing ceremonies of the 1984 Olympics, toured with Dance Theatre of Harlem, USSR, 1988, South Africa, 1992, guest artist Young People's Concert series, N.Y. Philharm., 1988, Detroit Symphony, 1989, River City Ballet, Memphis, 1991, 1992, N.W. Fla. Ballet, 1994, prin. dancer Va. Ballet Theatre, Norfolk, 1996—, Dance Theatre of Harlem, 1999, guest ballet mistress, 1999—, regisseuse Dance Theatre of Harlem, 1989—96. Fellow Am. Guild Mus. Artists. Episcopalian. Avocations: modeling, teaching younger dancers.

GRAVES, MAUREEN ANN, self esteem and spirituality consultant; b. Sioux City, Iowa, July 10, 1946; d. Jack Milford and Elizabeth Mildred (St. George) Dryden; m. Thomas Darrel Graves, Oct. 9, 1965; children: Michael James, Lorrie Michelle. Grad. 1-yr. program, Gestalt Inst. Iowa, 1980. Cert. profl. asst., U. SD; cert. success in motivational coaching; cert. hypnotherapist, Wellness Inst., Seattle. Counselor Siouxland Coun. on Alcoholism and Drug Abuse, Sioux City, 1979-81; counselor, co-founder New Hope Alcohol and Addiction Ctr., South Sioux City, Nebr., 1981-98; Reiki practitioner, 1997—. Cons. St. Luke Hosp. Addiction Ctr., Sioux City, 1987—; trainer Va. Satir-Internat. Tng. Inst., Crested Butte, Colo., 1988-89. Vol. co-facilitator Siouxland Coun. on Alcoholism and Drug Abuse, Sioux City, 1976-79; exec. team couple World Wide Marriage Encounter, N.E. Nebr., 1979-82; trainer Va. Satir-Internat. Tng. Inst., Crested Butte, Colo., 1992; co-leader Satir Family Camp, 1992-03; active Avanta Faculty Governing Coun., 1994-04. Mem. Avanta Network, Moscow Inst. for Profl. Devel. of Psychologists and Social Workers (founding). Roman Catholic. Avocation: reiki master. Home and Office: 1814 N 155th Ave Omaha NE 68154-4123

GRAVES, NADA PROCTOR, retired elementary school educator; b. Kewaunee, Wis., Oct. 9, 1933; d. John and Martha Proctor; m. Harmon Sheldon Graves III, Dec. 28, 1958; children: Jessica, Gemont. BS, U. Wis., 1956. With TWA, Chgo., 1956-58; tchr. Denver Pub. Schs., 1959-61, Cherry Creek Schs., Englewood, Colo., 1980—99. Membership chmn. Denver Art Mus., 1966-68; treas. Glenmoor Homeowners, 1991-92; mem./vol. D.A.M., Mus. Nat. History, Ctrl. City Guild, The Guild Diabetes, Denver Lyric Opera Guild, Gathering Place., P.E.O., D. of the King Home: 17 Glenmoor Cir Englewood CO 80110-7121

GRAVES, PAMELA KAY, music educator; b. Cleve., Ohio, Oct. 29, 1953; d. Frank Michael and Harriet Gertude Duncan; m. Garry Thomas Graves, Aug. 17, 1979; 1 child, Tyler Logan. MusB, BE, Capital U., 1976. Bookkeeper McDonald Restaurants, Mayfield, Ohio, 1970—80; music tchr., instrumental dir. St. Joseph & John Sch., Stongsville, Ohio, 1985—2000; adj. music Ohio Music Educator Assn., Ohio, 1993—. Instrumental dir., tchr. Wickliffe Mid. Sch., Ohio, 1993—; freelance musician, Ohio, 1985—; guest conductor Ohio State Fair Band, Ohio, 1980—; piano tchr. Piano Turner Sch., Ohio, 1986. Contbr. articles to profl. jour., 2002. Mem.: Nat. Assn. of Music Edn., Levy Com., Wickliffe Parent and Tchr. Together (sec. 2001—03). Avocations: photography, crafts, gardening, family. Home: 1717 Robindale St Wickliffe OH 44092 Office: Wickliffe Mid Sch 29240 Eudid Ave Wickliffe OH 44092

GRAVES, RUTH PARKER, educational executive, educator; b. Port Arthur, Tex., Oct. 19, 1934; d. Thomas B. and Eunice Parker; m. Glenn R. Graves, Aug. 8, 1956; 1 child, Christopher. BA, Baylor U., 1956; MA, U. Tex., 1961; postgrad., George Washington U., 1963-64. Migrant labor advisor Tex. State AFL-CIO, Austin, 1959-61; pub. info. officer Pres.'s Com. on EEO, Washington, 1961-63; tchg. fellow George Washington U., Washington, 1963-64; labor desk coord. Dem. Nat. Conv., Washington, 1965-67; program analyst U.S. OEO, Washington, 1965-67, dir. migrant divsn., 1967-72; pres. emerita Reading is Fundamental, Inc., Washington, 1998. Nat. adv. coun. Ctr. for the Book, Libr. of Congress, 1977-97; adv. bd. Kidwave Radio Network, Phila., 1990-97; bd. advisors Ednl. Pub. Group, 1994-97; faculty Salzburg Seminar, 1998—; lectr. in field. Mem. editl. bd. Child Mag., N.Y.C., 1989-97; adv. coun. Ednl. Pub. Group, 1994-97; editor: The RIF Guide to Encouraging Young Readers, 1987; contbr. articles to profl. jours. Recipient William A. Jump award, U.S. Govt., 1971, Jeremiah Ludington Literacy Leadership award Ednl. Paperback Assn., 1982, Manhattan Literacy Coun. award, 1986, Internat. Reading Assn. Literacy award, 1987, As They Grow award Parents Mag., 1991; named Bookwoman of the Yr. Woman's Nat. Book Assn., 1987. Avocations: reading, theater, design and production of craft items.

GRAVES, VICKI LLOYD, retired mechanical engineer; b. Phoenix, Ariz., Aug. 5, 1935; d. Margarite Marie Hogue and Lonnie Hershal Lloyd, Ivan Burton and Dorothy Carol Lloyd; m. William S. Graves, June 24, 1966; stepchildren: Kay Levy, Lynn Neilson, Diane Graves-Dolk children: Darlene Ann Clow, Diane Jeanette Clow, Anthony Thomas Clow. Mech. Engring. Design, Marietta Cobb Tech., 1969. Cons. Engring. Cons. Designer, St. Petersburg, Fla., 1968—82; art designer Vicki Quail Run Art Studio, Mesa, Ariz., 1992—. Membership chmn. Scottsdale Artist League, Ariz., 1998—2000. Mem.: Scottsdale Artist League, Mesa Artist League. Address: 234 E Bakerview Rd Apt # 106 Bellingham WA 98226

GRAVOIS-MURR, ESTELLE, music educator; b. Baton Rouge, La., Nov. 19, 1970; d. Jerome Julius and Idalena Kelone Gravois; m. Raymond Dale Murr, July 10, 1999; children: Patrick Jerome, Evan Michael. BA, Northwestern State U., 1993; MEd, U. Tex., Arlington, 1998. Ins. sales NASE, La., 1993—94; band dir. Natchitoches (La.) Parish Schs., Camoti, La., 1994—95, Bridgeport (Tex.) Ind. Sch. Dist., 1995—97, Crowley (Tex.) Ind. Sch. Dist., 1997—99, Broward County/Deerfield Beach (Fla.) HS, 1999—2001, Joshua (Tex.) Ind. Sch. Dist., 2001—03, instr. Dept. Dance, 2003—. Chmn. Colorguard Solutions, Fort Worth, Tex., 2002—; judge Winterguard Internat., Ohio, 2001—02, V.S.S.B.A., NJ, 2000—. Recipient Bronze Congl. award, Senator/Pres., 1987. Mem.: Tex. Music Educators Assn., North Tex. Colorguard Assn. (parliamentarian 2003—), Sigma Alpha Iota (parliamentarian 1989—, Rose award 1991), Tau Beta Sigma (dist. v.p. 1990—). Republican. Roman Cath. Avocations: dance, colorguard, music, sewing, reading.

GRAY, ANN MAYNARD, broadcasting company executive; b. Boston, Aug. 22, 1945; d. Paul Maynard and Pauline Elizabeth MacFadyen; children: Richard R. Gray III, Dana Maynard Gray. BA, U. Mich., 1967; MBA, NYU, 1971. With Chase Manhattan Bank, N.Y.C., 1967-68, Chem. Bank, N.Y.C., 1968-73, asst. sec., 1971-73; asst. to treas., then asst. treas. ABC, Inc., 1974-76, treas., 1976-81, v.p. planning, 1979-86; v.p. Capital

Cities/ABC, Inc. (merged 1986), 1986—; sr. v.p. fin. ABC TV Network Group, 1988-91; pres. Diversified Pub. Group Capital Cities/ABC, Inc., 1991—; bd. dirs. Cyprus Empire Corp. Bd. dirs. Cyprus AMAX Minerals Co., Duke Energy Corp. Trustee Martha Graham Ctr. of Contemporary Dance, N.Y.C., 1989-92, Cancer Care, Inc., 1991—. Office: Cyprus Empire Corp PO Box 68 Craig CO 81626-0068

GRAY, ARLENE, music educator, musician; b. The Dalles, Oreg., Dec. 15, 1948; d. Irving Bernard and Sarah Grace (Adamson) Elle; m. David Leroy Gray, Oct. 20, 1972; children: Mark, Stephanie, Brian, Timothy. BS in Elem. Edn., Oreg. State U., 1970; BA in Music Performance, U. Mary, 1994. Tchr. kindergarten, Fairview, Mont., 1972; pvt. piano tchr. Mandan, ND, 1973—, Bismarck, ND. Coll. choir accompanist Bismarck State Coll., ND, 1994—2003, tchr. piano and organ, 1998—. Chair Piano Guild, Bismarck, 1987—; organist Presby. Ch., Mandan, 1982—98. Mem.: Jr. Fed. Music Club (chmn. The Playing Keys 1980—), ND Fed. of Music Clubs, Nat. Fed. of Music Clubs, N.D. Music Tchrs. Assn. (sec. 1996—98, chmn. state conv. 1997, co-chmn. 2003, chmn. state conv. 2003), Am. Coll. Musicians (chmn. 1987—, judge 1997—), Am. Guild Organists, Nat. Music Tchrs. Assn. (state bd. dirs.). Avocations: reading, gardening, swimming. Home: 4525 Camden Loop Bismarck ND 58503 Office: Bismarck State Coll 1500 Edwards Ave Bismarck ND 58501 Office Phone: 701-224-5510. Business E-Mail: Arlene.Gray@bsc.nodak.edu.

GRAY, BARBARA MAY, artist; b. N.Y.C., Apr. 29, 1934; d. Samuel David and Sadie Blum Ampolsey; m. Edward Gray, Aug. 29, 1954; children: Karen, Douglas. BA, CUNY, 1955; postgrad., Art Student League, 1965; MA, NYU, 1996. Graphics design Fred Kessler Collectors, N.Y.C., 1955; draftsman J. Rowland AIA, Kinston, N.C., 1955-57; art instr. Strathmore Sch., Matawan, N.J., 1963; instr. Guild of Creative Art, New Shrewsbury, N.J., 1965-66; art tchr. St. Mary's Town and Country Sch., London, 1967-68; lectr. Ctrl. Sch. of Art, London, 1975; art instr. Norwalk (Conn.) C.C., 1985-86, 95. Founder, dir. Westport (Conn.) Ctr. for Arts, 1984-86; cons. Colorful Art Gallery, Stamford, Conn., 1988-95. Creator Haiga-Haiku, 1982; collaborator (catalog) Five, 1979, Inner Eye, 1975; exhibns. in three cities in Europe; invited artist-in-residence Atelier A, Apricale, Italy, 1998. Mem. T's Women, Westport, Conn., 1997-99 Recipient Best in Graphics Fairfield U. Gallery, 1988. Mem. AAUW, Art/Place Gallery, Soc. of Am. Graphic Artists. Avocations: theatre, dining out, bicycling, writing poetry. E-mail: gray1@optonline.net.

GRAY, BONNIE ANN LAWRY, publishing executive; b. Bradford, Pa., Nov. 7, 1946; d. James Andrew Lawry, Helen Hipchen Lawry; m. Joe Wayne Gray; children: Jason, Matthew, Casey. Owner MusicBag Press, Plano, Tex., 1995—. Author: "Just The Facts" Music Theory Series, 1990, "Just The Facts II" Music Theory Series, 1998, "Just For Fun" Music Game Series, 2001. Mem.: Music Tchrs. Assn. Calif., Music Tchrs. Nat. Assn., Tex. Music Tchrs. Assn., Plano Music Tchrs. Assn. (pres. 1980—81, Life Membership award 1988). Avocations: reading, travel, piano, writing. Office: MusicBag Press PO Box 866953 Plano TX 75086-6953 Home Fax: 972-758-1179. Personal E-mail: annlawry@comcast.net.

GRAY, DAHLI, accounting educator and administrator; b. Grand Junction, Colo., Dec. 28, 1948; d. Forrest Walter and Mary (Crockett) G.; 1 child, Kimberly. BS, Ea. Oreg. State U., 1971; MBA, Portland (Oreg.) State U., 1976; D of Bus. Adminstrn., George Washington U., 1984. Instr. acctg. Portland State U., 1976-79, George Mason U., Fairfax, Va., 1980, George Washington U., Washington, 1981 82; asst. prof. Oreg. State U., Corvallis, 1983-86; rsch. fellow U. Notre Dame, South Bend, Ind., 1986-88; assoc. prof. Am. U., Washington, 1988-90; chair, Walpert, Smullian & Blumenthal prof. Towson (Md.) State U., 1990-92; chair Morgan State U., Balt., 1992-97, prof. acctg., 1997-2000, Wilson Coll., Chambersberg, Pa., 2000-2001, U. Md. Univ. Coll., Adelphi, 2001—03, Strayer U., 2000—. Contbr. articles to profl. jours. Named Tchr. of Yr., Alpha Lambda Delta, 1986; Peat Marwick Mitchell & Co. fellow, 1986-88. Mem. Internat. Assn. Acctg. Research and Edn., Am. Inst. CPA's, Nat. Assn. Accts. (Andrew Barr award 1982, 84, Cert. Merit 1982), Am. Acctg. Assn., Inst. Cert. Mgmt. Accts. Democrat. Home: 45 Timonium Rd Lutherville Timonium MD 21093-1206 E-mail: dgray@dahligrayconsulting.com.

GRAY, DAWN PLAMBECK, work-family consultant; b. Chgo., Aug. 23, 1957; d. Raymond August and Eunice Eve (Fox) Plambeck; m. Richard Scott Gray, Apr. 13, 1985; children: Zachary, Rae. BS, Northwestern U., 1979. Desk asst. Sta. WCFL, Chgo., 1979-80; writer UPI Internat., Chgo., 1980; asignment editor Cable News Network, Chgo., 1980-81; account exec. Aaron Cushman and Assoc., Chgo., 1981-83, Ruder Finn & Rotman, Chgo., 1983-84, account supr., 1984-86, dir. consumer group, 1986-87; dir. pub. rels. Tassani Communications, Chgo., 1987-90; v.p. Marcy Monyek & Assoc., Chgo., 1990; pres. Moments Inc., Chgo., 1991—. Avocation: dance. Office: Moments Inc 1028 W Monroe St Chicago IL 60607-2604

GRAY, DEBORAH DOLIA, business writing consultant; b. Elmo, Mo., Jan. 25, 1952; d. Gerald Lee and Rosalie (Thompson) G. BS in Music and Journalism cum laude, U. Nebr., 1976; MFA, Columbia U., 1988. Reporter Lincoln (Nebr.) Star, 1975-78; spl. writer, feature projects Ft. Lauderdale (Fla.) News, 1978-79; reporter Miami (Fla.) News, 1979-80; curriculum specialist John Jay Coll. Criminal Justice, CUNY, N.Y.C., 1980-84; tng. specialist Mgmt. Devel. Systems Inc., N.Y.C., 1985—. Writing cons. various non-profit agys. and corps. Contbr. articles to profl. jours. Hollingsworth fellow Columbia U., 1985. Avocations: songwriter, keyboard player, poet. Home: 900 W 190th St Apt 9R New York NY 10040 E-mail: ddgray@jonesday.com.

GRAY, DEBORAH MARY, wine importer; b. Sydney, N.S.W., Australia, Feb. 4, 1952; came to U.S., 1973; d. Anthony Eric and Mary Patricia (O'Mullane) Gray. Student, St. Petersburg Jr. Coll., 1973-85, Eckerd Coll., 1988-90. Fin. counselor Wuesthoff Meml. Hosp., Rockledge, Fla., 1973-75; admintrv. dir. Dresden & Ticktin, MDs, P.A., St. Petersburg, Fla., 1976-80; exec. dir., v.p. Am. Med. Mgmt., Inc., Clearwater, Fla., 1980-90; pres., dir. All Women's Health Ctr., Inc., various locations, Fla., 1980-90, Lakeland Women's Health Ctr., Fla., 1980-90, Ft. Myers Women's Health Ctr., Fla., 1980-90, Nat. Women's Health Svcs., Inc., Clearwater, Fla., 1983-90, Women's Ob-Gyn. Ctr. Countryside, Inc., 1984-90, D.M.S. of Ft. Myers, Inc., 1985-90; treas., v.p., dir. Birthing Mgmt. Inc., 1985-90; healthcare cons., 1990-92; N.Am. mgr. Cowra Wines, Australia, 1991-95; owner, sole proprietor The Australian Wine Connection, Carlsbad, Calif., 1992—; bd. dirs. Australian Trade Commn., N.Y., 1996—. Dir. Alternative Human Svcs., 1979; dir. Perinatal Ctr. Ga. Bapt. Med. Ctr., 1990-92. Mem. bd. agy. that facilitates hard to place children adoptions One Ch. One Child, 1990-94.

GRAY, ELIZABETH DODSON, theologian, writer, speaker; b. Balt., July 13, 1929; d. Fitzhugh J. and Lillian (Northam) Dodson; m. David Dodson Gray, July 2, 1957; children: Lisa, Hunter. BA, Smith Coll., 1951; BD, Yale U., 1954. Rsch. assoc. MIT Sloan Sch. Mgmt., Cambridge, 1974-76; vis. prof. Williams Coll., Williamstown, Mass., 1977; Theol. opportunities program coord. Harvard Divinity Sch., Cambridge, 1978—. Adj. faculty Boston Coll., Chestnut Hill, 1981-90, Antioch N.E. Grad. Sch., Keene, N.H., 1990-91. Author: Green Paradise Lost, 1979, Patriarchy as a Conceptual Trap, 1982, Sunday School Manifesto, 1994; co-author: Growth and Its Implications for the Future, 1974, Children of Joy, 1976; editor: Sacred Dimensions of Women's Experience, 1988. Film for TV, Adam's World, about her work and thoughts, Nat. Film Bd. Can., 1988. Mem. U.S. Assn. Club of Rome (co-vice chmn. 1979-82). Home: 4 Linden Sq Wellesley MA 02482-4709 Office: Harvard Divinity Sch 45 Francis Ave Cambridge MA 02138-1994 Office Phone: 781-235-5320. E-mail: rpol@comcast.net.

GRAY, ELIZABETH VAN DOREN, lawyer; b. Columbia, S.C., Jan. 3, 1949; d. Robert Lawson and Elizabeth Dacus (Gaines) Van Doren; m. James Cranston Gray, Jr., Apr. 30, 1982; children: James Cranston III, Elizabeth Gaines. BA in Internat. Studies, U. S.C., 1970, JD cum laude, 1976; student, St. Mary's Coll., Raleigh, N.C., 1966-67. Bar: S.C. 1977, U.S. Dist. Ct. S.C. 1977, U.S. Ct. Appeals (4th cir.) 1980, U.S. Ct. Appeals (6th cir.) 1989, U.S. Supreme Ct. 1998. Assoc. McNair Law Firm, PA, Columbia, 1977-82, shareholder, 1982-87; ptnr. Glenn Irvin Murphy Gray & Stepp, Columbia, 1987—2000; now ptnr. Sowell Gray Stepp & Lafitte, LLC, Columbia. Contbr. articles to profl. jours. Mem. ABA, Am. Coll. Trial Lawyers, John Belton O'Neal Inn of Ct., S.C. Bar (pres. 2001-02), S.C. Women Lawyers Assn. (bd. dirs. 1995-99, sec. 1997-98), Richland County Bar Assn. Episcopalian. Office: Sowell Gray Stepp & Lafitte LLC PO Box 11449 Columbia SC 29211 Home: 8 Mahalo Ln Columbia SC 29204-3380

GRAY, FRANCES BOONE, minister; b. Miami, Fla., Aug. 23, 1939; d. Roy and Willie Artis Boone; m. Joel A. Gray, Apr. 17, 1959 (dec. Nov. 2002); children: Linda Lamarsh, Joel A., Frances S. AA, Miami Dade Jr. Coll., Miami, 1959; BS, U. Miami, 1965; MDiv, Jacksonville Theol. Sem., Jacksonville, Fla., 1995; PhD, Jacksonville Theol. Sem., 1999. RN 1965. Nurse Jackson Meml. Hosp., Miami, 1954—65, Mt. Sinai Hosp., Miami, 1965—70, Miami Heart Hosp., 1970—77; minister Temple Missionary Bapt. Ch., Miami, 1988—95; pastor Jesus Christ Unltd. Ministry, Miami, 1995—. Tchr. Lindsey Hopkins Sch., Miami, 1966—67. Bd. dirs. United Way, Miami; asst. sec. SCIC, Miami, 1984—90; mem. NAACP. With USPHS, 1970—75. Mem.: Order Eastern Star (worthy matron 1981—88). Democrat. Avocations: reading, sewing, swimming, singing. Home: 1510 NW 114th St Miami FL 33167

GRAY, FRANCINE DU PLESSIX, author; b. Warsaw; came to U.S., 1941, naturalized, 1952; d. Bertrand Jochaud and Tatiana (Iacovleff) du Plessix; m. Cleve Gray, Apr. 23, 1957; children: Thaddeus Ives, Luke Alexander. BA, Barnard Coll., 1952; LittD (hon.), CUNY, Oberlin Coll., U. Santa Clara, St. Mary's Coll., U. Hartford. Annenberg fellow Brown U., 1997. Disting. vis. prof. CCNY, 1975; vis. lectr. Yale U., New Haven, 1981-82; Ferris prof. Princeton U., 1986; Disting. vis. prof. Vassar Coll., 1999. Author: Divine Disobedience: Profiles in Catholic Radicalism, 1970 (Nat. Cath. Book award), Hawaii: The Sugar-Coated Fortress, 1972, Lovers and Tyrants, 1976, World Without End, 1981, October Blood, 1985, Adam & Eve and the City, 1987, Soviet Women: Walking the Tightrope, 1989, Rage and Fire: A Life of Louise Colet, 1994, At Home with the Marquis de Sade: A Life, 1998, Simone Weil, 2001. Guggenheim Found. fellow, 1991-92. Mem. Am. P.E.N., Am. Acad. Arts and Letters. Democrat. Roman Catholic.

GRAY, GLORIA MEADOR, librarian; b. Marshall, Tex., Aug. 24, 1935; d. Alfred E. and Julia (Whitfield) Meador; m. Philip R. Gray, Mar. 23, 1955; children: Brian, David, Gordon. BA, U. North Tex., 1970, MLS, 1974. Libr. Richardson (Tex.) Ind. Sch. Dist., 1971-91. Vol. Dem. Com., Richardson, 1962—. Mem.: ALA, Tex. Libr. Assn. Democrat. Methodist. Avocations: reading, skiing, community volunteering.

GRAY, GWEN CASH, real estate broker; b. Cowpens, S.C., Oct. 24, 1943; d. Woodrow C. and Marie (Hamrick) Cash; m. Charles H. Gray, Oct. 24, 1987 ; children: Dianne Marie Young, Teena Michele Bulman. BS, Limestone Coll., Gaffney, S.C., 1984. Real estate sales rep., owner and broker-in-charge Southers Real Estate, Spartanburg, S.C. Bd. dirs. Bank of Am.; lectr. in field. Contbr. articles to profl. jours. Advisor S.C. Peach Festival, Gaffney, 1977—, Clemson U. Extension Svc., 1987—. Named Woman of Yr. Bus. and Profl. Women, 1979, Woman of Yr. S.C. Rural Electric Coop., 1984, Career Woman of Yr. Breakfast Club Spartanburg Bus. and Profl. Club, 1997. Mem. Am. Farm Bur., Nat. Bd. Realtors, S.C. Farm Bur., S.C. Bd. Realtors, Spartanburg Bd. Realtors (pres. 1998, Realtor of Yr. 1997), S.C. Hort. Soc. (bd. dirs.), S.C. Assn. Agr. Agts. (Friend of Extension award 1986), Spartanburg Multiple Listing Svc. Baptist. Republican. Avocations: reading, tech. coll. teaching. Office: Southers Real Estate 223 E Blackstock Rd Spartanburg SC 29301-2633 Office Phone: 864-576-9440. E-mail: GwenGray@teleplex.net.

GRAY, HANNA HOLBORN, history educator; b. Heidelberg, Germany, Oct. 25, 1930; d. Hajo and Annemarie (Bettmann) Holborn; m. Charles Montgomery Gray, June 19, 1954. AB, Bryn Mawr Coll., 1950; PhD, Harvard U., 1957; MA, Yale U., 1971, LLD, 1978; LittD (hon.), St. Lawrence U., 1974, Oxford (Eng.) U., 1979; LLD (hon.), Dickinson Coll., 1979, U. Notre Dame, 1980, Marquette U., 1984; LittD (hon.), Washington U., 1974; HHD (hon.), St. Mary's Coll., 1974; LHD (hon.), Grinnell (Iowa) Coll., 1974, Lawrence U., 1974, Denison U., 1974, Wheaton Coll., 1976, Marlboro Coll., 1979, Rikkyo (Japan) U., 1979, Roosevelt U., 1980, Knox Coll., 1980, Coe Coll., 1981, Thomas Jefferson U., 1981, Duke U., 1982, New Sch. for Social Research, 1982, Clark U., 1982, Brandeis U., 1983, Colgate U., 1983, Wayne State U., 1984, Miami U., Oxford, Ohio, 1984, So. Meth. U., 1984, CUNY, 1985, U. Denver, 1985, Am. Coll. Greece, 1986, Muskingum Coll., 1987, Rush Presbyn. St. Lukes Med. Ctr., 1987, NYU, 1988, Rosemont Coll., 1988, Claremont U. Ctr. Grad Sch., 1989, Moravian Coll., 1991, Rensselaer Poly. Inst., 1991, Coll. William and Mary, 1991, Centre Coll., 1991, Macalester Coll., 1993, McGill U., 1993, Ind. U., 1994, Med. U. of S.C., 1994; LLD (hon.), Union Coll., 1975, Regis Coll., 1976, Dartmouth Coll., 1978, Trinity Coll., 1978, U. Bridgeport, 1978, Dickinson Coll., 1979, Brown U., 1979, Wittenburg U., 1979, Dickinson Coll., 1979, U. Rochester, 1980, U. Notre Dame, 1980, U. So. Calif., 1980, U. Mich., 1981, Princeton U., 1982, Georgetown U., 1983, Marquette U., 1984, W.Va. Wesleyan U., 1985, Hamilton Coll., 1985, Smith Coll., 1986, U. Miami, 1986, Columbia U., 1987, NYU, 1988, Rosemont Coll., 1988, U. Toronto, Can., 1991; LDH, LHD, Haverford Coll., 1995; LDH (hon.), Tulane U., 1995; LLD, LLD, Harvard U., 1995; LHD (hon.), McGill U., 1993, Macalester Coll., 1993, Ind. U., 1994, Med. U. S.C., 1994, Haverford Coll., 1995, Tulane U., 1995; LLD (hon.), Harvard U., 1995, U. Chgo., 1996. Instr. Bryn Mawr Coll., 1953—54; tchg. fellow Harvard, 1955—57, instr., 1957—59, asst. prof., 1959—60, vis. lectr., 1963—64; asst. prof. U. Chgo., 1961—64, assoc. prof., 1964—72; dean, prof. Northwestern U., Evanston, Ill., 1972—74; provost, prof. history Yale U., 1974—78, acting pres., 1977—78; pres. U. Chgo., 1978—83, prof. dept. history, 1978—, Harry Pratt Judson disting. svc. prof. history, 1994—. Fellow Ctr. for Advanced Study in Behavioral Scis., 1966—67, vis. scholar, 1970—71; vis. prof. U. Calif., Berkeley, Calif., 1970—71. Co-editor (with Charles Gray): Jour. Modern History, 1965—70; contbr. articles to profl. jours. Mem. Nat. Coun.on Humanities, 1972—78; trustee Yale Corp., 1971—74; mem. bd. regents The Smithsonian Instn.; former chmn. bd. Andrew W. Mellon Found.; mem. Harvard Univ. Corp., 1986—; chmn. bd. Howard Hughes Med. Inst., Marlboro Sch. Music. Named Grosse Verdienstkreuz, Germany; recipient Grad. medal, Radcliffe Coll., 1976, Yale medal, 1978, Medal of Liberty award, 1986, Medal of Freedom, 1991, Frontrunner award, Sara Lee, 1991, Laureate Lincoln Acad. Ill., 1988, Charles Frankel prize, 1993, Centennial medal, Harvard U., 1994, Disting. Svc. award in edn., Inst. Internat. Edn., 1994, Medal of Distinction, Barnard Coll., 2000; fellow Newberry Libr., 1960—61, St. Anne's Coll., Oxford U., 1978—; scholar Fulbright scholar, 1950—51. Fellow: Am. Acad. Arts and Scis.; mem.: Coun. Fgn. Rels. N.Y., Coun. Fgn. Rels. Chgo., Nat. Acad. Edn., Am. Philos. Soc. (Jefferson medal 1993), Renaissance Soc. Am., Phi Beta Kappa (vis. scholar 1971—72). Office: U Chgo Dept History 1126 E 59th St Chicago IL 60637-1580 Business E-Mail: h-gray@uchicago.edu.

GRAY, HAZEL IRENE, retired special education educator, counselor, consultant; b. Van Nuys, Calif., July 2, 1921; d. Charles Clayton Cramer and Ida Mae (Leffler); m. Reed A. Gray; children: Mildred Lorene, Paul Charles; m. Neil Chapin Smith (dec.). BA, San Jose (Calif.) State Coll., 1964, MA, 1968; EdD, U. So. Calif., LA, 1977. Itinerant tchr. hearing impaired Santa Cruz County Office of Edn., 1964—66; resource specialist Santa Cruz Pub. Schools, 1966—68; psychologist Santa Cruz County Office of Edn., 1968—71; psychologist, cons. and parent counselor Project Idea, San Jose, 1971—72; dir. spl. edn. Live Oaks schs. Santa Cruz County Office of Edn., 1972—74; cons. Calif. State Dept. of Edn., Sacramento, 1975—76; adminstr. San Jose City Coll., 1976—78; dir. pupil pers. Campbell Union Sch. Dist., Calif., 1978; pvt. practice marriage counseling, 1971—. Cons. Catholic Pre-Sch., LA; lectr. Calif. State U, San Jose, U. Calif., Santa Clara, Santa Cruz; with Med. Info. Svcs. Co-author: (book) Behavior Modification, 1971. Mem. rescue Calif. Coast Guard, 1971—76; team mem. marriage family and child counseling license rev. Calif. State Dept. of Licensing, Sacramento. Mem.: San Jose Movie TC Club, Camera Club. Republican. Mem. Lds Ch. Achievements include vis. numerous countries Japan, So. Africa, Israel, Greece, Egypt, England, Can., Ireland, France and Portugal. Avocations: travel, photography, grandchildren.

GRAY, INA TURNER, fraternal organization administrator; b. Eagleville, Mo., July 25, 1926; d. Farris T. and Teloir (Anderson) Turner; m. Wallace G. Gray Jr., Dec. 18, 1948; children: Toni Jo, Tara Joy. BS with high honors, Cen. Meth. Coll., 1948; MA, Scarritt Coll., 1952; postgrad., U. Hawaii, 1969. Tchr. Rutherford-Met. Sch. Bus., Dallas, 1948-49; dir. Christian edn. 1st Meth. Ch., Lawton, Okla., 1953-54, Winfield, Kans., 1957-58; dir. religious life Southwestern Coll., Winfield, 1958-59; dir. commn. on archives and history Kans. West Conf., Winfield, 1960-78; exec. dir. Pi Gamma Mu, Winfield, 1976-96. English tchr. JoGakuin Jr. High, Hiroshima, Japan, 1971-72, Kitakyushu U., Japan, 1997-98. Mem. editorial bd. Fire on the Prairie, 1961-69; mem. editorial and pub. coms. The Lure of Kansas, 1990. Mem. Assn. Coll. Honor Socs. (del. 1986-96), Commn. Archives and History (local Ch. History award 1982—), Kans. State Assn. Parliamentarians (v.p. Walnut Valley unit 1991-92, 99-2000), Faculty Dames (pres. 1981-82). Republican. Avocations: travel, historical research, Japanese flower arranging. Home: 1701 Winfield Ave Winfield KS 67156-1919 Business E-Mail: gray@sckans.edu.

GRAY, JANET ETHEL, elementary school educator; b. Snyder, Tex., Dec. 15, 1942; d. James Lavern and Irene McClain (Brown) Cotton; m. Richard Lee Gray, June 24, 1960; children: Melinda, Eric, Heidi, Keith. BS in Edn., Abilene Christian U., 1964; degree in kindergarten-early childhood, Tex. Christian U., 1972. Tchr. Abilene (Tex.) Pub. Schs., 1964-67, Castleberry Ind. Sch., Fort Worth, 1967-84, Conroe (Tex.) Ind. Sch., 1984—2002. Tech Elem. Coord. Conroe ISD, 2002—03. Recipient Presdl. award for excellence in sci. and math. teaching NSF, 1994, Presdl. award for excellence in sci., Tex., 1994. Mem. Sci. Tchrs. Assn. Tex., Nat. Sci. Tchrs. Assn., Soc. Elem. Presdl. Awardees, Coun. for Elem. Sci. Internat., Tex. State Tchrs. Assn. (bldg. rep. 1992-95), ASCD. Home: 113 Chelsea Rd Conroe TX 77304-1705 Office: Anderson Elem Sch 1414 E Dallas St Conroe TX 77301-2100

GRAY, JENNIFER FRANCINE, photographer, illustrator; b. Kansas City, Oct. 20, 1956; d. James Franklin and Mary Jane (Stevenson) G.; m. Harold Whitehurst Jr., Dec. 26, 1981 (div. 1983); children: Jesse James Whitehurst, Stacy Parker. BA in Liberal Arts, The Evergreen State Coll., 1989. Portrait studio mgr. JC Penney Co., Seattle, 1989-91; owner, operator Cove Gallery, Shelton, Wash., 1991-93; photographer, illustrator Gray-Works, Lilliwaup, Wash., 1993—. Chmn. Shelton (Wash.) Arts Commn., 1991-94, 2001—. Mem. Peninsula Art Assn. (bd. dirs. 1991-95). Avocations: photography, illustration. Home and Office: PO Box 14 Hoodsport WA 98548-0014

GRAY, JONI NADINE, state agency administrator; b. St. Joseph, Mo., Mar. 24, 1959; d. Albert Benjamin and M. Nadine (Harris) G.; children: John Charles, Haley Brooke, Jordan Roselle Gray-DeKraai. BA in Psychology, U. Nebr., 1982, JD, MA in Psychology, 1990. Rsch. policy analyst Gov.'s Policy Rsch. Office, Lincoln, 1985-86; dir. trainee Lancaster Comty. Mental Health Ctr., Lincoln, 1987-88; policy analyst Ea. Nebr. Comty. Office of Mental Health, Omaha, 1989; sys. developer Ctr. for Children, Families and the Law, Lincoln, 1989-90; law and psychology instr. U. Nebr., Lincoln, 1987, 90-91; rschr., analyst Nebr. Advocacy Svcs., Lincoln, 1993-94; policy analyst Ctr. for Children, Families and the Law, Lincoln, 1993-94; mental health program specialist Dept. Pub. Instns., Lincoln, 1995-96; exec. dir. Nebr. Commn. on Status of Women, Lincoln, 1996—. Mem. adv. bd. Child Care and Early Childhood Edn. Coord. Com., Lincoln, 1996—, Nebr. Ctr. for Women, York, 1996—, Nebr. chpt. Nat. Mgr.'s Assn., Lincoln, 1996—. 1st author: Ethical and Legal Issues in AIDS Research, 1995; contbr. chpt. to book. Recipient Nat. Rsch. Svc. award NIMH, 1984-87, 92-93, Am. Jurisprudence award, 1989. Mem. Am. Psychology-Law Soc. (newsletter columnist 1984-85), Alpha Lambda Delta, Phi Eta Sigma. Office: Nebr Commn on Status of Women PO Box 94985 301 Centennial Mall S Lincoln NE 68508-2529

GRAY, JUDITH A. retired school librarian, educator; b. Pitts., Nov. 30, 1942; d. John and Helen Ondich; m. N. Gordon Gray, June 13, 1964; 1 child, Ameena. BS in Edn., Indiana U. Pa., 1963; MLS, U. Pitts., 1964. Cert. sch. libr., pub. libr., secondary tchr. English, N.Y. Peace Corps vol., libr. Tanzanian Nat. Libr., 1964-67; reference libr. Syracuse U., 1967; sch. libr. H.W. Smith Jr. H.S., Syracuse, N.Y., 1967-69; substitute tchr. Syracuse City Sch. Dist., 1971-72; sch. libr. Nottingham H.S., Syracuse, 1972—2001. Pres. coun. Good Shepherd Luth. Ch., Fayetteville, N.Y., 1988-89. Mem. Peoples Choice award for photography N.Y. State Fair, 1987. Mem. ALA, N.Y. Libr. Assn. (bd. dirs. sch. libr. media sect. 1988-92, pres. 1992-93), Am. Assn. Sch. Librs. (nat. guidelines revision com. 1995-98), Librs. Unltd. (sec. 1998-2000, pres. 2000-01), Syracuse Tchrs. Assn. (chair elections com. 1974-2001), Monday Evening Club (historian 1996—). Avocations: gardening, hiking and camping, knitting, photography, traveling. Home: 302 Pleasant St Manlius NY 13104-1816

GRAY, KARLA MARIE, judge; b. May 10, 1947; BA, MA in African History, Western Mich. U.; JD, Hastings Coll. of Law, San Francisco, 1976. Bar: Mont. 1976, Calif. 1977. Law clk. to Hon. W. D. Murray U.S. Dist. Ct., 1976-77; staff atty. Atlantic Richfield Co., 1977-81; pvt. practice law Butte, Mont., 1981-84; staff atty., legis. lobbyist Mont. Power Co., Butte, 1984-91; justice Supreme Ct. Mont., Helena, 1991-2000, chief justice, 2000—. Mem. Mont. Supreme Ct. Gender Fairness Task Force. Fellow Am. Bar Found., Am. Judicature Soc., Internat. Women's Forum; mem. State Bar Mont., Silver Bow County Bar Assn. (past pres.), Nat. Assn. Women Judges. Avocations: travel, reading, piano, family genealogy, cross-country skiing. Office: Supreme Ct Mont PO Box 203001 Helena MT 59620-3001*

GRAY, KATHERINE, marriage, family and child therapist, writer, educator; b. L.A., July 6, 1941; d. Edward David and Marjorie Ross; m. Daniel C. Gray, Feb. 5, 1965; children: Michael, Lisa. BA, Calif. State U., Sacramento, 1983; MS in Ednl. Cons. and Counseling, MS in Sch. Counseling, Calif. State U., 1987, EdD in Counseling Psychology, 1997. Lic. MFCT. Instr. Shasta Coll., Redding, Calif., 1965-69; owner Water Ojai (Calif.) Valley Chapel, 1971-77, Lipp & Sullivan, Marysville, Calif., 1978—. Instr. Yuba Coll., 1988—; pres. Interagy. Coun., 1988—; cons. and organizer various cmty. outreach programs in edn. Contbr. articles to profl. jours. and newspapers. County coord., bd. dirs. Am. Cancer Soc., Marysville, 1980—; mem. exec. com., bd. dirs., com. chairperson Gateway Projects, Yuba City, Calif., 1980—; bd. dirs. Mercy Guild, Yuba City, 1980—, Easter Seals; past bd. dirs., com. chairperson Campfire, Inc., Yuba City and Morro Bay, Calif., 1979-80; past pres. Ojai Valley-Oxnard

Symphony Orch. Assn., Ventura County, Calif., 1975; Sacramento focus program coord. 4-H, Yuba and Sutter Counties, 1985—; exec. officer, bd. dirs. Gateway Projects, 1985-87; pres. Interagy. Coun. of Yuba and Sutter Counties, 1988—. Recipient Presdl. Awd. for Outstanding Performance and Contribution of Svc., awds. granted for svc. on bd. and as an ofcr. on grad. stud. coun. and numerous univ. coms., Lipp & Sullivan. Mem. Calif. Funeral Dirs. Assn. (mem. legis. bd. com., edn., ethics and mem. bd. com.), Calif. Assn. for Counseling and Devel., Sacramento Area Gifted Assn., Children's Home Soc. (chpt. bd. sec.), Soroptimists (officer, bd. dirs.), Rainbow for Girls (pres., bd. dirs. 1985-87). Avocations: music, art, travel, historical studies. Home: PO Box 611 Yuba City CA 95992-0611 Office: PO Box 148 629 D St Marysville CA 95901-5527

GRAY, LINDA ALYN, artist, educator; b. Sacramento, Oct. 18, 1948; d. Jack Erwin Evans and Mary Louise Conner; adopted by Feorge Fiene, 1960; m. Gary Grover Gray, June 1, 1968; children: Nathan McMillen, Thaddeus Conner. Student, Am. Internat. Acad., Europe, 1968, 69, Fla. State U., Tallahassee, 1969-71; BA, Albertus Magnus Coll., New Haven, 1986. Cert. instr. art K-12, Fla. Designer, freelance artist, owner design bus., Fla., N.J., Okla., 1968-82; owner/mgr. retail operation, Wellington, Fla., 1981-83; adminstr. non-profit orgns., 1982-97; edn. coord. Old Sch. Sq. Cultural Arts Ctr., Delray Beach, Fla., 1990-93; dir. Glade Youth Discovery Ctr., Belle Glade, Fla., 1993-95; project adminstr. L.E.A.P., Palm Beach County, Fla., 1996-97; instr. Palm Beach County Schs., 1996—. Mem. ednl. panel Norton Mus. Art, West Palm Beach, 1996-97. Executed mural Palm Beach County Pub. Libr., 1994-95, H.L. Brumbach Health Clinic Pediatrics Wing, 1996, Migrant Edn. Bldg. Exterior, 1998. Supporter Nat. Arbor Day Found., Defenders of Wildlife, Nature Conservancy, Nat. Parks and Conservation. MacArthur Found. grantee, 1995-96, others. Mem. NEA, Palm Beach County Art Tchrs. Assn., Fla. Art Tchrs. Assn., Classrm. Tchrs. Assn. Palm Beach County, Fla. Tchg. Profls.

GRAY, LOIS HOWARD, construction company executive; m. James Norris Gray; children: Howard, Jim, Franklin, Stephen. Founder, chair James N. Gray Co., Lexington, Ky., 1960—. Office: James N Gray Co 10 Quality St Lexington KY 40507-1443

GRAY, LOIS SPIER, labor relations educator, consultant; b. St. Louis, Oct. 17, 1923; d. Charles and Mae (Imboden) Spier; m. Edward Franklin Gray (dec. July 1995). BA, Park Coll., 1943; MA, U. Buffalo, 1955; PhD, Columbia U., 1965; LLD (hon.), Park Coll., 1991. Economic analyst U.S. Mil Intelligence, Washington, 1944-45; field examiner Nat. Labor Rels. Bd., Buffalo, 1945-46; dir. we. dist. N.Y. State Sch. Indsl. and Labor Rels. Cornell U., 1947-56, dir. met. N.Y. State Sch. Indsl. and Labor Rels., 1956-76, prof. N.Y. State Sch. Indsl. and Labor Rels., 1974—, assoc. dean N.Y. State Sch. Indsl. and Labor Rels., 1976-88. Cons. ednl. instns. in U.S. and abroad on curriculum design and evaluation; chair N.Y. State Apprenticeship and Tng. Coun., 1975-2000. Author: Socio-Economic Profiles of Puerto Rican New Yorkers, 1976; author, editor: Under the Stars: Labor Relations in Arts and Entertainment, 1996; contbr. articles to profl. jours. Recipient Labor Edn. award N.Y. State AFL-CIO, 1995, Hispanic Labor Com., 1993, LIfetime Achievement award, 2000. Mem. Indsl. Rels. Rsch. Assn. (nat. exec. bd. 1980-84), Labor History Assn. (Labor Edn. award 1985, OSHA award 1988), Univ. and Coll. Labor Edn. Assn. (nat. pres. 1965-67), N.Y. Occupl. Safety and Health Assn., Ams. for Dem. Action (Social Justice award 1979), Wagner Archives (bd. dirs.). Avocations: drama, literature. Home: 3 Washington Square Vlg New York NY 10012-1836 Office: Cornell Univ 16 E 34th St New York NY 10016-4328

GRAY, MARGARET ANN, management educator, consultant; b. Junction City, Kans., Sept. 19, 1950; d. Carl Ray and Mayme Louise (Kopmeyer) G.; m. Dennis Wayne Stokes, June 9, 1973 (div. July 1981); m. Robert Frederick Carlson Jr., Nov. 21, 1987 (dec. Apr. 2003). BEd, Pittsburg State U., Kans., 1972; MBA, Wichita State U., 1981. Tchr., Sch. Dist. 1, Kansas City, Mo., 1972-73; tchr. Haysville Sch. Dist., Kans., 1974-81, dist. coord., 1979-81; instr. mgmt. Wichita State U., 1981-85; mgmt. devel. rep. Beech Aircraft Corp. a Raytheon Co., Wichita, 1985-87, mgr. mgmt. devel. and tng., 1988-91; tng. and devel. coord. MIT, Cambridge, 1991-96, mgr. tng. and devel., 1996-2000, dir. orgn. & employee devel., 2000—; cons. Dartnell Inst., Chgo., 1983—; assoc. dir. Ctr. for Entrepreneurship, Wichita State U., 1984-85. Bd. dirs. Kans. Found. for partnerships in Edn., 1986—; mem. speaker's bur. United Way, 1986—, vol. tng. dir., 1987—, tng. com.; 1987—, top leadership cabinet, 1989; bd. dirs. Kans. Literacy Group, 1989, Sedgwick County div. Am. Heart Assn., 1990; active Leadership 2000. Named Outstanding Young Alumnus Pitts. State U., 1991. Mem. ASTD (bd. dirs. Sunflower chpt.), Wichita C. of C. (bus. edn. success team 1988—), Rotary, Beta Gamma Sigma. Democrat. Roman Catholic. Club: Turnip (Wichita). Avocations: ballet, cross country skiing, classical music, hot air balooning. Home: 68 Thomas St Belmont MA 02478-2440

GRAY, MARY WHEAT, statistician, lawyer; b. Hastings, Nebr., 1939; d. Neil C. and Lillie W. (Alves) Wheat; m. Alfred Gray, Aug. 20, 1964. AB summa cum laude, Hastings Coll., 1959; postgrad., J.W. Goethe U., Frankfurt, Fed. Republic Germany, 1959-60; MA, U. Kans., 1962, PhD, 1964; JD summa cum laude, Am. U., 1979; LLD (hon.), U. Nebr., 1993; LHD (hon.), Hastings Coll., 1996. Bar: D.C. 1979, U.S. Supreme Ct. 1983, U.S. Dist. Ct., D.C. 1980. Physicist Nat. Bur. Standards, Washington, summers 1959-63; asst. instr. U. Kans., Lawrence, 1963-64; instr. dept. math. U. Calif., Berkeley, 1965; asst. prof. Calif. State U., Hayward, 1965-67, assoc. prof., 1967-68; assoc. prof. dept. math., stats. and computer sci. Am. U., 1968-71, prof., 1971—, chmn. dept., 1977-79, 80-81, 83—; statis. cons. for govt. agys., univs. and pvt. firms, 1976—. Vis. prof. King's Coll., London, 2004. Author: A Radical Approach to Algebra, 1970; Calculus with Finite Mathematics for Social Sciences, 1972; contbr. numerous articles to profl. jours. Nat. treas., dir. Women's Equity Action League, from 1981, pres., from 1982; bd. dirs. treas. ACLU, Montgomery County, Md.; mem. adv. com. D.C. Dept. Employment Services, 1983—; dir. Amnesty Internat. USA, 1985—, treas., 1988-93, chair, 1993—; mem. Commn. on Coll. Retirement, 1984-86; bd. dirs. Am.-Middle East Edn. Found., 1983—, chair, 1998–. Recipient U.S. Presdl. award for excellence in sci., engring. and math. mentoring, 2001; Fulbright grantee, 1959-60; NSF fellow, 1963-64, NDEA fellow, 1960-63 Fellow AAAS (chmn. com. on women, com. on investments, com. on sci. freedom and responsibility, Lifetime Mentoring award 1995); mem. AAUP (regional counsel 1984—, com. on acad. freedom 1978—, dir. Legal Def. Fund 1974-78, bd. dirs. Exxon Project on Salary Discrimination 1974-76, com. on status of women 1972-78, Georgina Smith award), Am. Math. Soc. (v.p. 1976-78, coun. 1973-78), Amnesty Internat. (internat. treas. 1995-2001, chair USA 1993-95), Conf. Bd. Math. Scis. (chmn. com. on affirmative action 1977-78), Math. Assn. Am. (chmn. com. on sch. lectrs. 1973-75, vis. lectr. 1974—), Assn. for Women in Math (founding pres. 1971-74, exec. com. 1974-80, gen. counsel 1980—), D.C. Bar Assn., ABA, Am. Soc. Internat. Law, London Math. Soc., Societe de Mathematique de France, Brit. Soc. History of Math., Can. Soc. History of Math., Assn. Computing Machinery, N.Y. Acad. Scis., Am. Statis. Assn., Phi Beta Kappa, Sigma Xi, Phi Kappa Phi, Alpha Chi, Pi Mu Epsilon. Home: 6807 Connecticut Ave Chevy Chase MD 20815-4937 Office: Am U Math & Stats Dept Washington DC 20016 Office Phone: 202-885-3121. E-mail: mgray@american.edu.

GRAY, MICHELE DIANE, psychotherapist, art gallery owner; b. Kathmandu, Nepal, Feb. 29, 1960; d. Clarence Cornelious Gray, III and Shirley Brown Gray. BA, Wellesley Coll., 1981; MSW, Smith Coll., 1991. Customer rep. Scudder, Stevens & Clark, Boston, 1982; adminstr. Bd. Govs. of the Fed. Res. Sys., Washington, 1987—90; psychotherapist Kennebec Valley Mental Health Ctr., Waterville, Maine, 1991—92; supr., psychotherapist Mid Coast Mental Health Ctr., Rockland, Maine, 1992—2002; pvt. practice psychotherapy Rockland, 1994—; owner Outsider Gallery, Rockland, 2003—. Bd. mem. Knox County (Maine) Coun. to Prevent Child Abuse and Neglect, 1995—97. Capt. USAF, 1982—92. Avocation: gardening.

GRAY, NANCY ANN OLIVER, college administrator; b. Dallas, Apr. 23, 1951; d. Howard Ross and Joan (Dawkins) Oliver; m. David Nelson Maxson, Oct. 5, 1985; children by previous marriage: Paul, Jeff, Scott. BA, Vanderbilt U., 1973; MEd, North Tex. State U., 1975; postgrad., Vanderbilt U., 1976-79; PhD (hon.), Presbyterian Coll., 2002. Cert. fund raising exec. Tchr. Highland Park High Sch., Dallas, 1973-75; chmn. drama dept. Harpeth Hall Sch., Nashville, 1975-77; assoc. dir. devel. Vanderbilt U., Nashville, 1977-78, assist. dean students, 1978-80; dir. spl. gifts U. Louisville, 1982-86; dir. major gifts Oberlin (Ohio) Coll., 1986-90; dir. capital programs The Lawrenceville (N.J.) Sch., 1990-91; v.p. devel. and univ. rels. Rider U., Lawrenceville, 1991-98; v.p. sem. rels. Princeton (N.J.) Theol. Sem., 1998-99; pres. Converse Coll., Spartanburg, S.C., 1999—. Trustee Princeton Theol. Sem., 2000—, Spartanburg Day Sch., 2000-2002, Vanderbilt U., Nashville, 1973-77; bd. dirs. Brevard Music Ctr., 1999—; mem. governing bd. Wye Faculty Seminar, 2000—. Home: 488 Connecticut Ave Spartanburg SC 29302-2158 Office: Converse Coll 580 E Main St Spartanburg SC 29302-1931 Office Phone: 864-596-9050. Business E-Mail: nancy.gray@converse.edu.

GRAY, PAMELA, screenwriter, educator; b. Bklyn., Feb. 28, 1956; d. Lawrence Maurice and Arlene Gloria G.; 1 child, Andrew Lowe, Feb. 19, 1983. BA in English, SUNY, 1978; MA in Creative Writing, Boston U., 1980; MFA in Screenwriting, UCLA, 1993. Prof. San Francisco State U., 1982-86, U. Calif. Berkeley Extension, Berkeley, 1988-89; screenwriter Miramax Films, N.Y.C., 1997-99, Paramount Pictures, L.A., 1998-99, Disney Studios, L.A., 1998-99, Universal Pictures, L.A., 1998—, Bedford Falls, L.A., 1999—. Guest spkr. Writers Guild Found., L.A., 1999, NOW Ann. Conf., L.A., 1999; keynote spkr. Catskills Inst. Conf., N.Y., 1999. Screenwriter: (feature films) A Walk on the Moon, 1999, Music of the Heart, 1999, (teleplays) Star Trek: The Next Generation, 1992, Calm at Sunset, 1996, The Love Letter, 1998, Once and Again, 1999. Vol. zookeeper for Exotic Feline Breeding Compound for endangered big cats. Recipient First Place Samuel Goldwyn Writing award Samuel Goldwyn Found., 1992, Scriptwriting Internship award Acad. TV Arts and Scis., 1991; chosen One of Ten Screenwriters to Watch Variety mag., 1999. Mem. Writers Guild Am. West, Dramatists Guild. Democrat. Jewish. Avocation: rare book collecting.

GRAY, PATRICIA B. retired librarian, information specialist; b. Lumberton, N.C., Feb. 10, 1938; d. Carl Webster and Gladys (Newman) Barbee; m. James William Gray, Jr., Sept. 2, 1961 (dec. Apr. 1987); children: Susanna Gray Lund, James William III. BA magna cum laude, U. N.C., 1960, MS in Libr. Sci., 1965. Cert. libr. N.C., Va. Bookmobile libr. Sheppard Meml. Libr., Greenville, N.C., 1958, 59; libr. asst. U. Miami Libr., Coral Gables, Fla., 1960; French tutor U. N.C., Chapel Hill, 1960-62; libr. Sch. Libr. Sci., Chapel Hill, 1960-62; govt. documents libr. Pub. Libr. Charlotte (N.C.), 1962-63; ref. libr. Norfolk (Va.) Pub. Libr., 1966-77, asst. dept. head ref. and adult svcs., 1990—; dir. Barron F. Black Libr., Norfolk, 1977-88, Larchmont Libr., Norfolk, 1988-90. Libr. dir. search com. Va. Wesleyan U., Norfolk, 1967-68. Contbr. articles to profl. jours., book revs. to newspaper. Mem. Friends of the Libr., Chesapeake, Va., 1977-81; chmn. United Way Campaign, Libr. Dept., Norfolk, 1984; vol. Tidewater coun. Boy Scouts Am., 1987-93; vol. driver ARC, DAV, 2003—. Mem. ALA, AAUW (bd. dirs. 1965, 66, 80, rsch. analyst 1966-70), Southeastern Libr. Assn., Va. Libr. Assn., Va. Assn. Law Librs., Tidewater Assn. Law Librs., Phi Beta Kappa, Beta Phi Mu, Phi Alpha Theta. Methodist. Avocations: travel, translating french, bowling, swimming, gardening.

GRAY, PHENESSA ANTOINETTE, not-for-profit developer; b. Warrington, Fla., Dec. 31, 1974; d. Carlond Ann Gray; 1 child, Hannah. AA in Liberal Studies, BA in English Lit., Fla. State U., 1996; MSLS, Clark Atlanta U., 2000. Accelerated acad. educator Landmark Mid. Sch., Jacksonville, Fla., 1996—97; site rep. technician BellSouth Corp. Libr., Atlanta, 1997—98, corp. resource mgr., 1998; rsch. analyst Atlanta Bus. Chronicle, 1998—99; prospect rsch. mgr. SE divsn. Am. Cancer Soc., Atlanta, 1999—2002; prospect rsch. analyst Children's Healthcare of Altanta, 2002—03. Author: (poetry) Sanctuary, 1997 (Homer Diamond award, 1998), (book) My Soul's Surrender, 2000; actor: (play) The Journey, 2000; author: What's This Prospect Research Thing?. Mem.: ALA, Assn. Profl. Rschrs. for Advancement, Spl. Libr. Assn., Alpha Kappa Alpha. Democrat. Avocations: poetry, art, cooking/baking, Scrabble, martial arts. Home: 60 Lakeview Trail Covington GA 30016

GRAY, ROBIN, stage manager; b. Newcastle, Ind., Oct. 30, 1956; d. Max F. and Shirley A. Gray; life ptnr. Kristin Tucker, Oct. 3, 1994. BFA, Kent State U., 1979. Stage mgr. Sacramento Opera Assn., 2000—, Sacramento Theatre Co., 2001—. Mem. People for the Am. Way. Mem.: Actors Equity Assn. (life), Amnesty Internat. D-Liberal. Non Denominational. Achievements include Worked with Jose Ferrer, actor/director; Toured with many broadway musical tours. Avocations: photography, travel. Home: 5516 2nd Ave Sacramento CA 95817 Personal E-mail: robinlgray@aol.com.

GRAY, SHEILA HAFTER, psychiatrist, psychoanalyst; b. NYC, Oct. 19, 1930; MD, Harvard U., 1958. cert. Washington Psychoanalytic Inst., 1969. Intern St. Elizabeths Hosp., Washington, 1958-59; resident McLean Hosp., Belmont, Mass., 1959-61; clin. and rsch. fellow Mass. Gen. Hosp., Boston, 1961-62; staff psychiatrist Chestnut Lodge, Inc., Rockville, Md., 1962-64; practice medicine, specializing in psychiatry and psychoanalysis Washington, 1964—; clin. asst. prof. psychiatry U. Md. Sch. Medicine, Balt., 1968-75, clin. assoc. prof., 1975-83, clin. prof., 1983-96; instr. Washington Psychoanalytic Inst., 1971-75, tchg. analyst, 1975-96, Balt.-Washington Inst. for Psychoanalysis, 1996—; clin. prof. psychiatry Uniformed Svcs. U. Health Scis., 1997-99, adj. prof. psychiatry, 1999—. Staff U. Md. Hosp., Balt., 1970-96; physician mem. Commn. on Mental Health, Superior Ct. of D.C., 1972-98; bd. govs. Nat. Capital Reciprocal Ins. Co., 1981-98; treas. NCRIC Physicians Orgn., 1994-97; cons. Walter Reed Army Med. Ctr., Washington, 1983—. Active Mayor's Adv. Com. on Mental Health Svcs. Reorgn., Washington, 1984; adv. panel Mayor's Environ. Design Awards Program, 1988-89; exec. com. D.C. Fedn. Civic Assns., 1984—, asst. rec. sec., 1985, rec. sec., 1986-88, 2d v.p., 1989-90, pres., 1991-92, del.-at-large, 1993—; v.p. programs Women's Equity Action League Met. D.C., 1986; commr. D.C. Adv. Neighborhood Commn., 1986-88; mem. Met. Washington Coun. of Govt.'s Partnership for Regional Excellence, 1992; trustee Accreditation Coun. for Psychoanalytic Edn., Inc., 2002—, sec., 2004—. Fellow: Am. Psychiat. Assn. (chair com. quality assurance and improvement, Coun. on Econ. Affairs, 1996—97); mem.: Washington Psychoanalytic Soc. (chmn. bd. dirs. psychoanalytic clinic and councillor ex officio 1987—90), Med. Soc. D.C. (exec. bd. 1982, ho. dels. 1992—97), Washington Psychiatric Soc. (councillor 1981—83), Am. Acad. Psychoanalysis (trustee 1996—99, pres.-elect 1999—2000, pres. 2000—01, editl. bd. jour. 2002—), Am. Psychoanalytic Assn. (diplomate Bd. Profl. Stds.), Palisades Citizens Assn. (bd. dirs. 1980—, treas. 1983—84, pres. 1984—86). Office: PO Box 40612 Palisades Sta Washington DC 20016 Office Phone: 202-338-1955.

GRAY, VICKI LOU PHARR, music educator; b. Orange, Calif., July 11, 1944; d. Kenneth E. and Louis Pauline (Wright) Pharr; m. Haskell H. Gray, Nov. 26, 1966; children: Jennifer, Justin, Juliette. B in Music Edn., Tex. Tech. U., 1966; MusM with high honors, So. Meth. U., 1989. Permanent profl. cert. Nat. Music Tchrs. Assn. Gen. music tchr. Richardson (Tex.) Ind. Sch. Dist., 1966-68; pvt. piano tchr. Gray Piano Studios, Dallas, 1968—. Owner, dir. Childrens Opera Workshop, Dallas, 1992—; owner Gray Piano Studios, Dallas, 1993—. Author: Music for Minors, 1989; writer, prodr. (childrens operas) Come Fly With Me, Mirror-Mirror, Dancing Princesses, H & G Go to Hollywood, Beauty. Mem. Tex. Music Tchrs. Assn., North Dallas Music Tchrs. Assn. (pres. 1993-2000), Dallas Music Tchrs. Assn. (pres. 1995—), Jr. Pianist Guild (pres. 1994), Steinway Soc. North Tex. (bd. dirs. 1998—, v.p. 1993-2000). Republican. Presbyterian. Avocations: gourmet cooking, traveling.

GRAY, VIRGINIA HICKMAN, political science educator; b. Camden, Ark., June 10, 1945; d. George Leonard and Ethel Massengale (Bell) Hickman; 1 child, Brian Charles. BA with honors, Hendrix Coll., 1967; MA, Washington U., St. Louis, 1969, PhD, 1972. Asst. prof. polit. sci. U. Ky., Lexington, 1971-73; from asst. prof. to assoc. prof. U. Minn., Mpls., 1973-83, prof., 1983-2000, chairperson dept. polit. sci., 1985-88; Winston Disting. prof. polit. sci. U. N.C., Chapel Hill, 2001—. Guest scholar Brookings Inst., Washington, 1977-78; vis. prof. U. Oslo, 1985, Nankai U., 1988, U. B.C., 1992, U. N.C., 1993-94; NSF vis. prof. for women, 1993-94. Co-author: The Organizational Politics of Criminal Justice, 1980, Feminism and the New Right, 1983, Politics in the American States, 1983, 8th edit., 2004, American States and Cities, 1991, 2d edit., 1997, The Population Ecology of Interest Representation, 1996, Minnesota Politics and Government, 1999. Bd. dirs. Health Ptnrs. Inc., 1992-2001, chair, 1999-2001. Fellow Woodrow Wilson Found., 1970, NDEA, 1969-70; grantee Swedish Bicentennial Found., 1985; recipient rsch. assistantship NSF, 1968-69, rsch. grant NSF, 1997-2001; scholar in residence Rockefeller Ctr., Bellagio, Italy; Investigator award Robert Wood Johnson Found., 2003-2005. Mem. Am. Polit. Sci. Assn. (coun. 1990-92), Midwest Polit. Sci. Assn. (coun. 1984-86, v.p. 1997-99, pres. 2003-2004), Policy Studies Orgn. (coun. 1977-79), So. Polit. Sci. Assn., Western Polit. Sci. Assn. Democrat. Unitarian Universalist. Home: 2 Heather Ct Chapel Hill NC 27517 Office: U NC Dept Polit Sci CB 3265 Hamilton Hall Chapel Hill NC 27599-3265 E-mail: vagray@email.unc.edu.

GRAYBEAL, BARBARA, editor, writer; b. Mountain City, Tenn., Sept. 21, 1935; d. Claude Harold and Ruby Lucille (Hodge) G.; m. Lewis N. Kremer, June 7, 1958 (div.); m. Charles L. Ring, May 8, 1982(div.). BA magna cum laude, Marietta Coll., 1957; grad. Pub. Procedures Course, Radcliffe Coll., 1957. With New Yorker mag., N.Y.C., 1957-58; assoc. editor Saturday Evening Post, Phila., 1958-62, Voter Registration in Mississippi, 1964, Episc. mag., Phila., 1962-69; asst. editor Luth. mag., Phila., 1971-72; instr. journalism Temple U., Phila., 1972-81; founding editor CGA World mag., 1980-82, sr. editor, 1982-83. Editor, writer: Fast and Fresh (by Julie Dannanbaum), 1981, The CGA Cookbook, 1984; editl. cons. Good Ideas for Decorating; contbr. articles, photographs and poetry to various publs. Mem. com. interpretation and promotion, dept. overseas missions Nat. Coun. Chs., 1966-68; mem. Phila. Dem. Com., 1968; bd. dirs., sec. Friends of Free Libr. Phila.; bd. dirs. N.C. Sch. Arts, The Assocs. of N.C. Sch. Arts, 1983-86; lay reader Episc. Ch.; vol. 1964 Miss. Freedom summer, Registration Project, Hattiesburg, Miss. Mem. AAUW (pres. br.), Women in Comms. (v.p. chpt.), Marietta Coll. Alumni Assn., Internat. Platform Assn., Phi Beta Kappa, Sigma Delta Chi, Alpha Xi Delta. Address: 1525 Woods Rd Apt 106 Winston Salem NC 27106-3135 Office Phone: 336-924-6913.

GRAYBIEL, ANN M. medical educator; AB magna cum laude, Harvard U., 1964; PhD, MIT, 1971. Woodrow Wilson fellow Tufts U., New Haven, 1965—66; Walter A. Rosenblith prof. neuroanatomy dept. brain and cognitive sci. MIT, Cambridge, Mass. Chair sect. neurobiology NAS; bd. neurosci. and behavioral health Inst. of Medicine; mem. nat. adv. mental health coun. NIMH. Recipient Williams and Wilkins award, Charles Judson Herrick award, McKnight qward. Mem.: Am. Acad. Arts and Sci., Inst. of Medicine of NAS, Royal Acad. Medicine (Spain) (hon.). Achievements include research in on cortico basal ganglia circuits and the role of these circuits in learning and the adaptive control of complex behaviors; on the structure of the brain has advanced the understanding of brain regions involved in neurological and neuropsychiatric disorders. Office: MIT Dept Brain/Cognitive Sci 45 Carleton St Bldg E25-618B Cambridge MA 02139-4307

GRAY-BUSSARD, DOLLY H. energy company executive; b. Wilmington, Del., July 29, 1943; d. Henry Odell and Dorothy (Knotts) Gray; m. Robert William Bussard, Mar. 17, 1981; stepchildren: Elise Bright, William Bussard, Robert L. Bussard, Virginia B. Barausky. BA in History and English Lit., U. Calif., San Diego, 1984; MA in History, Georgetown U., 1990. Coord. Orgn. Human Devel., San Diego, 1977-78; owner, prin. Hello Dolly, La Jolla, Calif., 1978-80; ptnr. Linda Chester Lit. Agy., La Jolla, 1978-80; owner, pres. Unicorn Literary Agy., La Jolla, 1980-85; pres., chmn. bd. Energy/Matter Conversion Corp., San Diego, Calif., 1988—. Vis. lectr. writers' confs. U. Calif., San Diego, 1979-81. Co-author: The Best of San Diego, 1981. Mem. adv. bd. Women's Voices; mem. majority coun. Emily's List; mem. nat. coun. Aspen Santa Fe Ballet; bd. dirs. Found. Santa Fe C.C. Mem. NAFE, Am. Hist. Assn., Phi Alpha Theta. Episcopalian. Avocations: book collecting, skiing, mountain climbing. Office: EMC2 Ste 103 9705 Carroll Center Rd San Diego CA 92126-6505

GRAY-LITTLE, BERNADETTE, psychologist, educator; b. Washington, N.C., Oct. 21, 1944; d. James and Rosalie (Lanier) Gray; m. Shade Keys Little, Nov. 21, 1971; children: Maura, Mark. Asst. prof. psychology U. N.C., Chapel Hill, 1971-76, assoc. prof., 1976-82, prof., 1982—, chair dept., 1993-98, assoc. dean, 1999—. NIMH fellow, 1967-68, Fulbright fellow, 1970-71, NRC fellow, 1982-83. Fellow Am. Psychol. Assn.; mem. Phi Beta Kappa. Office: U NC Psychology Dept Cb # 3270 Chapel Hill NC 27599-0001

GRAY-NIX, ELIZABETH WHITWELL, occupational therapist; b. Milton, Mass., Apr. 9, 1956; d. Roland and Susan (Brooks) Gray; m. Ronald Harding Nix; 1 child, Roger Harrison Nix. BS, Syracuse U., N.Y., 1978. Registered occupl. therapist. From occupl. therapist to clin. supr. Walter E. Fernald State Sch., Waltham, Mass., 1978-97; dir. occupl. therapy The Fernald Ctr., 1997—. Trustee Mass. Jaycees Charitable Trust, Mansfield, 1983-91; dir.-at-large South End Hist. Soc., Boston, 1983-85, fundraising dir., 1985-87; alumni rep. Beaver country Day Sch., Brookline, 1974-99, alumni sec., 1988-94. Recipient Baystater award #060, Mass. Jaycees, 1984, Armbruster Keyman award, 1981, Merit award, Maddak, Inc., 1991, 96, Jaycee Internat. Senatorship award, 1992, Mass. State Employee Svc. award, 1998, Paul Duhamel Svc. award, 2000. Mem. Mass. Occupational Therapists Assn., State Employed Occupational Therapists Assn. (union rep.), Am. Occupational Therapists Assn., World Fedn. Occupational Therapists, Mass. Nurses Assn.(bd. dirs. 2002), Jaycees Internat. (Mass. sec., pres. Riverside chpt. 1983, mem. coun. Newton chpt. 1979-82, state sec. 1994-95), Boston Ctr. for Arts (mem. coun. 1979-84). Home: 90 Pelham Island Rd Sudbury MA 01776-3132 Office: The Fernald Ctr 200 Trapelo Rd Ste 1 Waltham MA 02452-6302

GRAY-VENTRY, TINA L. minister; d. Charles H and Rosie L Gray; m. Sidney R.J. Ventry, 1994; children: Tier Gray, Adam Gray, Joseph Ventry. BS in Human Resource Mgmt., U. Nebr., Omaha, 1991. Contractor The Blackstone Group, Omaha, 1993—97; engr. Qwest Comm. (formerly US West), Omaha, 1995—2000; cons. Agape Christian Fellowship Ch., Omaha, 1996—2003; owner Tina At Your Svc., Inc., Omaha, 1997—; exec. asst. New Creations Transitional Housing Program, Omaha, 2003—. Asst. pastor Salvation Army North Corps, Omaha, 2002—. Contbr. biography I Married My Ex. Vol. min. York Correctional Facility, York, Nebr., 2000—; vol. Salvation Army, Nebr., 2002—. Recipient Am. Bus. Woman of the Yr., Omaha Bus. Women, 1991, Partnership with New Cmty. Devel. award, Today's Woman, 2002. Mem.: Omaha C. of C. Home and office: Tina At Your Svc Inc 4339 Fowler Ave Omaha NE 68111-2165 E-mail: taysinc@cox.net.

GRAY-VICKREY, PEG, nursing educator; BSN, SUNY, Plattsburgh, 1979; MSN, No. Ill. U., DeKalb, 1982; DNS, U. at Buffalo, 1993. RN Fla., 1979. Asst. prof. of nursing Lycoming Coll., Williamsport, Pa., 1986—96; prof. of nursing Fla. Gulf Coast U., Fort Myers, Fla., 1996—. Contbr. chapters to books. Adv. bd. chair Dubin Alzheimer's Disease Resource Ctr., Fort Myers, Fla., 2002—03. Recipient Prof. of the Yr., Fla. Gulf Coast U., 1999, Individual Faculty Svc. Excellence Award, 2003. Office: Florida Gulf Coast University 10501 FGCU Boulevard South Fort Myers FL 33965 Office Phone: 239-590-7508.

GRAZIANO, CATHERINE ELIZABETH, state legislator, retired nursing educator; b. Providence, Dec. 2, 1931; d. William J. and Catherine E. (Keegan) Hawkins; m. Louis W. Graziano, Oct. 9, 1954; children: Mary Lou, William F., Catherine E., Paul, Carol. BS, Salve Regina Coll., Newport, R.I., 1953, MS, 1984, Boston Coll., 1965; PhD, Pacific Western U., 1988. Instr. nursing Salve Regina U., 1953-66, asst. prof., 1966-74, assoc. prof., 1974-82, prof., 1982-97, chair dept. nursing, 1974-93, ret., 1997; staff-charge nurse St. Joseph's Hosp., Providence, 1953-93, part-time faculty, 1960, 65; mem. R.I. Senate, Dist. 5, Providence, 1992—2002. Mem. R.I. Bd. Nurse Registration and Edn., 1970-79, pres., 1977-79; charter mem., sec. R.I. Health, Sci. and Edn. Council, 1972-78; adj. asst. prof. Coll. Nursing U. R.I., 1986-2000; mem. R.I. Senate, Providence, 1992-2002, chairperson health, edn. and welfare com., 2001-02. Mem. adv. coun. John E. Fogarty Ctr./ARC, Fruit Hill Day Care Elderly Ctr., Ret. Sr. Vol. Program; mem. R.I. Commn. on Women, 1993—; active local and nat. senatorial campaigns. Named Outstanding RI Pro-Life Legislator, 2001; recipient Regina medal, Salve Regina U., 1997, Bishop's award, 2001. Mem. ANA, AARP (legis. chair, exec. coun.), R.I. Nurses Assn. (pres. 1969-71, 73-75), Women Educators (charter), Nursing Leadership Coun. R.I. (charter, chair 1981-82, sec. 1982—), Nat. League Nursing (accreditation site visitor 1990-96), R.I. Cancer Coun., R.I. Health Policy Coun., Shape Health Care Study, Silver Haired Legislature, Ret. Sr. Vols. (co-chair adv. coun.), Sigma Theta Tau. Roman Catholic. Home: 42 Rowley St Providence RI 02909-5521

GREALY, MARY R. medical association administrator; Sr. Washington counsel Am. Hosp. Assn., 1996—99; pres. Healthcare Leadership Coun., Washington, 1999—. Office: Healthcare Leadership Coun 1001 Pennsylvania Ave NW Ste 550 S Washington DC 20004 Business E-Mail: mgrealy@hlc.org.

GREASER, CONSTANCE UDEAN, automotive industry executive; b. Jan. 18, 1938; d. Lloyd Edward and Udean Greaser. BA, San Diego State Coll., 1959; postgrad., U. Copenhagen Grad. Sch. Fgn., 1963, Georgetown U. Sch. Fgn. Svc., 1967; MA, U. So. Calif., 1968; exec. MBA, UCLA, 1981. Advt., publicity mgr. Crofton Co., San Diego, 1959-62; supr. Mercury Publs., Fullerton, Calif., 1962-64; supr. engring. support svcs. divsn. Arcata Data Mgmt., Hawthorne, Calif., 1964-67; mgr. computerized typesetting dept. Continental Graphics, L.A., 1967-70; v.p., editl. dir. Sage Publs., Inc., Beverly Hills, Calif., 1970-74; head publs. RAND Corp., Santa Monica, Calif., 1974-90; mgr. svc. comms. Am. Honda Motors Co., Torrance, Calif., 1990—2002; ret., 2001. Co-author: Quick Writer-Build Your Own Word Procesing Users Guide, 1983, Quick Writer-Word Processing Center Operations Manual, 1984; editor: Urban Research News, 1971-74; mng. editor: Comparative Polit. Studies, 1971-74; contbr. articles to various jours. Mem. nat. com. Million Minutes of Peace Appeal, 1986, Nat. Info. Stds. Orgn., 1987-93, nat. com. Global Cooperation for Better World, 1988. Recipient Berber award Graphic Arts Tech. Found., 1989. Mem. Women in Bus. (pres. 1977-78), Graphic Comm. Assn. (bd. dirs. 1994-99), Soc. for Scholarly Pubs. (nat. bd. dirs.), Women in Comm., Soc. Tech. Comm., So. Calif. Women for Understanding (v.p. westside chpt. 2003-04).

GREAUX, CHERYL PREJEAN, federal agency director; b. Houston, July 30, 1949; m. Robert Bruce Greaux. BA, Tex. So. U., 1967; MA, U. Tex., 1973. Mgr. compliance programs Dept. Labor, N.Y.C., 1973-80; corp. human resources mgr. Allied Signal Inc., Morristown, N.J., 1980-85; account exec., sourcing specialist Dean Witter Reynolds, N.Y.C., 1986-88; dir. civil rights staff USDA Rural Devel., Washington, 1994—. Cons. Gen. Foods, White Plains, N.Y., 1985, Seagrams, N.Y.C., 1984. Author: Struggling Within or Success from Within? 1973. Lectr. Nat. Urban League, 1980—; cons. Nat. Urban Affairs Coun., N.Y., 1981-86; bd. dirs. Ednl. Opportunity Fund, N.J., 1985-87. Mem. Edges Group, Delta Sigma Theta. Office: Dept Agr 14th And Independence SW Washington DC 20250-0001 Office Phone: 202-692-0204. E-mail: cheryl.greaux@usda.gov.

GREAVER, JOANNE HUTCHINS, mathematics educator, author; b. Louisville, Aug. 9, 1939; d. Alphonso Victor and Mary Louise (Sage) Hutchins; 1 child, Mary Elizabeth. BS in Chemistry, U. Louisville, 1961, MEd, 1971; MAT in Math., Purdue U., 1973. Cert. tchr. Pres. Math Mentors Inc., 1962—. Part-time faculty Bellarmine Coll., Louisville, 1982-2002, U. Louisville, 1985—; project reviewer NSF, 1983—; advisor Council on Higher Edn., Frankfort, Ky., 1983-86; active regional and nat. summit on assessment in math., 1991, state task force on math., assessment adv. com., Nat. Assessment Ednl. Progress standards com.; charter mem. Commonwealth Tchrs. Inst., 1984—; mem. Nat. Forum for Excellence in Edn., Indpls., 1983; metric edn. leader Fed. Metric Project, Louisville, 1979-82; mem. Ky. Ednl. Reform Task Force, Assessment Com., Nat. Framework, Nat. Assessment Ednl. Progress Rev. Com.; lectr. in field. Author: (workbook) Down Algebra Alley, 1984; co-author curriculum guides. Named Outstanding Citizen, SAR, 1984; named to Hon. Order Ky. Cols.; recipient Presdl. award for excellence in math. tchg., 1983; grantee, NSF, 1983, Louisville Cmty. Found., 1984—86. Mem. Greater Louisville Coun. Tchrs. of Math. (pres. 1977-78, 94-95, Outstanding Educator award 1987), Nat. Coun. Tchrs. of Math. (reviewer 1981—), Ky. Coun. Tchrs. of Math. (pres. 1990-91, Jefferson County Tchr. of Yr. award 1985), Math. Assn. Am., Kappa Delta Pi, Delta Kappa Gamma, Zeta Tau Alpha. Republican. Presbyterian. Avocations: tropical fish, gardening, handicrafts, travel, tennis. Home: 11513 Tazwell Dr Louisville KY 40241 E-mail: jogreaver@aol.com.

GRECO, JANICE TERESA, psychology educator; b. N.Y.C., May 14, 1948; d. Joseph Ralph and Harriett May (McArdle) G.; m. Forlano, July 29, 1969 (div. Feb. 1993); children: Christopher, Jason, Jennifer. BS, MEd, U. Houston, 1975; PhD, U. Tex., 1992. Ins. clk. John Hancock Life Ins. Co., West Islip, N.Y., 1965-69; instr. San Jacinto Jr. Coll., Houston, 1976-77; with assessment & referral divsn. Employee Assistance Program, U. Tex., Houston, 1987-88; instr. psychology Houston C.C., 1977—, head behavioral stats.; adj. prof. HFH SCh. Social Work and Coll Pharmacy. Vol. Huppotherapy Group, Galveston, Tex., 1990-91, fellowshp., Automated Lectr., Instrl. Computing, 1998, web access to statistics course, 1998. Fellow Instructional Computing, 1998, Coll. Computer Program. Mem. ACA, Tex. Assn. Counseling and Devel., Tex. Jr. Coll. Tchr. Assn., Stats. for Behavioral Scis. (rsch. com.). Avocations: horse-back riding, travel, reading, billiards, lionel collector. Home: 5322 Dana Leigh Dr Houston TX 77066-1604

GRECO, MARGARET ELIZABETH, secondary school educator; b. Wheeling, W.Va., Feb. 23, 1951; d. Albert Carl and Marjorie Lucille Megale; m. Carman Michael Greco; 1 child, Jennifer Morgan. BA, West Liberty (W.Va.)State Coll., 1974. Tchr. Spanish Ohio County Schs., Wheeling, W.Va., 1974—2002. Mem.: Alpha Delta Kappa. Avocations: showing dogs, traveling with students to Spain.

GRECO, MARIE DANIELLE, advertising executive, director; b. Grand Rapids, Mich., June 17, 1976; d. Eugene Joseph and Betty Jane Greco; 1 child, Mason Dushawn Brown. Sales cons. Relcon, Grand Rapids, 1995—98; local advt. dir. Grand Rapids (Mich.) Mag., 1998—. Dir.: Grand Rapids (Mich.) Wedding Mag. Mem.: Am. Mktg. Assn. (assoc.; v.p. elect 2001—02, v.p. membership 2002—03, dir. large 2003—), Home and Bldg. Assn. Greater Grand Rapids (assoc.; pub. rels. com. 2001—), DECA (assoc.; region v.p. 1992—93), Alpha Kappa Psi (assoc.; sec. 1995—97). Office: Grand Rapids Magazine 549 Ottawa Avenue NW Grand Rapids MI 49503 E-mail: mgreco@geminipub.com.

GREDZENS, SANDRA MAY PILLSBURY, art educator; b. Mpls., Sept. 30, 1949; d. Robert Kinsey and Elizabeth Anne (Massie) Pillsbury; m. David Inesis Gredzens, Nov. 25, 1989; stepchildren: Tabatha, Alex. AA, Stephens Coll., 1971; BFA, U. Calif. Santa Cruz, 1980; MEd, Hamline U., 1995. Cert. elem. and secondary educator. Lay-out artist Monterey (Calif.) Peninsula Herald, 1973-75; tchr.'s aide spl. edn., substitute tchr. Pacific Grove (Calif.) Unified Sch. Dist., 1978-82; educator art Shattuck-St. Mary's Sch., Faribault, Minn., 1982-84; tchr. elem. Woods Acad., Maple Plain, Minn., 1986-87; tchr. elem. art, art cons. Anoka (Minn.)-Hennepin Ind. Sch. Dist., 1987-97; art tchr. Lake Superior Sch. Dist., Two Harbors, Minn., 1997—. Exhibited in group shows at Grant Marais Art Colony, 1986—98, 2001, Itasca Art Assn. Exhbn., 1996, 1999, 2001, 2003, Sally Brown Collaborative Art Exhbn., 1995, Union St. Gallery, Chicago Heights, Ill., 2000, Duluth (Minn.) Art Inst., 2002, 2003, Lake County Ct. House Atrium, 2002, Vanilla Bean Bakery and Café, 2003. Mem. Nat. Art Educators Am., Art Educators Minn., Delta Phi Delta. Republican. Lutheran. Avocations: painting, hiking, church activities, photography. Office: Two Harbors HS 405 4th Ave Two Harbors MN 55616

GREEN, ANGEL YVONNE, literature educator; b. N.Y.C., Oct. 24, 1955; d. Henry Arthur Moss and Lillie Vera Harris; m. Joseph Cecil Green, Nov. 18, 1975 (div. Feb. 1979); 1 child, Gabriel Veran. Baccalaureate English, U. R.I., 1986, Masters English, 1997, PhD English, 2001; Baccalaureate Psychology, Coll. Continuing Edn./U. R.I., Providence, 1995. On-call police matron Newport and Jamestown Police Depts., RI, 1986—95; tchg. asst. U. R.I., Kingston, 1995—2000, fellow Grad. Sch., 2000—01, adj. faculty, 2001—. Vol. Literacy Vol. Am., Newport, RI, 1995—2002; enrichment instr. Talent Devel., U. R.I., Kingston, 1996—2002. Author short stories. Bd. mem. Wahid, Newport, 1986—90, First Step Newport County, Newport, 1990—95. With USN, 1973, with USNR, 1976—98. Recipient MLK Scholarship award, Providence Pub. Schs., 1995—98. Mem.: MLA, NAACP, Mensa. Home: 21-E Rolling Green Rd Newport RI 02840 Office: Univ RI Feinstein Coll Continuing Edn 80 Washington St Providence RI 02903

GREEN, ANGELA LAVONNE, band director; b. Orrville, Ohio, June 3, 1974; d. Stephan Ernest and Shirley LaVonne Monigold; m. Aaron Lee Green, June 24, 2000. MusB, U. Akron, 1997. Cert. tchr. State Ohio Bd. Edn. Head band dir. Hoban H.S., Akron, 1997—98; music appreciation tchr. Massillon (Ohio) City, 1998—99; band dir. Musical Youth, Inc., Stark County, Ohio, 1999—. Sec. Cuyahoga Valley Brass, Akron, 1998—2003; cornet player Brass Band of Western Res., 2003—. Mem.: Kappa Kappa Psi, Golden Key. Avocation: reading. Home: 727 Matthias Ave NE Massillon OH 44646

GREEN, BARBARA MARIE, publisher, journalist, poet, writer; b. N.Y.C., Mar. 21, 1928; d. James Matthew and Mae (McCarter) G. BA, CCNY, 1951, MA, 1955; ABD, NYU, 1978. Adminstr., tchr. English, 1952-82; tchr. English Newtown High Sch., Elmhurst, Queens, N.Y., 1961; asst. prin. Jr. High Sch. 142, Queens, N.Y., 1963; founder, pub. The "Creative" Record, Virginia Beach, Va., 1988-92. Keynote speaker; pres. Bar 'JaMae Comm. Inc. Founder, publisher The Good News, East Elmhurst, N.Y., 1985-88; author: (book of poetry) Love Pain Hope, 1990, More Poetic Thoughts, 1993, Dreams and Memories, 1996, Spirit, 1997; contbr. poetry to publs. Ch. and cmty. reporter N.Y. Voice; mem. libr. action com. Corona (N.Y.)-East Elmhurst, Inc.; mem. Langston Hughes Cmty. Libr. and Cultural Ctr., Corona, Harpers Ferry Hist. Assn., Va. Symphony League; mem. Crispus Attucks Theater Restoration Com., Norfolk. Recipient Profl. award Nat. Assn. Negro Bus. and Profl. Women's Club Inc., 1964, Trophy "Career Woman of Yr.", County Line Guild of Career Women, 1967, Cert. of Appreciation Women's Equality Action League, 1978, First Lynnhaven Bapt. Ch., Virginia Beach, Va., 1982, Cert. of merit City of N.Y., 1982, Community Svc. award Arlene of N.Y., 1990, N.Y. State Resolution commemorating the "Good" News, 1985, participation award Coalition of 100 Black Women, Valuable Service citation Phi Delta Kappa, cert. of appreciation Houston C.C., 1998, plaque U.S. Army and USAF N.G. Bur., Ageless Hero for Creativity award Blue Cross/Blue Shield, 1998; named Star Among Stars, 1991, Keeper of the Flame, 1997, Hampton Roads Poet Laureate, 2002; named to African-Am. Biographies Hall of Fame, Atlanta, 1994; elected to Hunter Coll. Alumni Hall of Fame, 1997; named poet laureate-in-residence First Lynnhaven Bapt. Ch., Virginia Beach, Va., 1996—. Hampton Roads Poet Laureate, New Jour.-Guide Newspaper, 2002. Mem. Am. Bus. Women's Assn. (Elizabeth River Charter chpt.), Nat. Assn. Negro Musicians (life; bd. dirs. Chgo. 1984-91, ea. region dir. 1990-91), Harpers Ferry Hist. Assn., Poetry Soc. Va., Nat. Assn. Black Journalists, Zonta Internat., Va. Fedn. Bus. and Profl. Women's Clubs (corr. sec. 1992, 1st v.p. 1993, pres. 1993, chair coastal region pub. rels. com. state level 1994-95), N.Y.C. Ret. Suprs. Assn., Phi Delta Kappa, Alpha Kappa Alpha. Baptist. Office: PO Box 15442 Chesapeake VA 23328-5442

GREEN, BARBARA STRAWN, psychotherapist; b. Cleve., May 31, 1938; d. Charles Everard and Dorothy Haring (Strawn) G. BA, Pa. State U., 1960; MS, Columbia U., 1962; postgrad. in psychotherapy and psychoanalysis, Postgrad. Ctr. for Mental Health, N.Y.C., 1975. Ordained Dharma tchr., 2003; cert. social worker, N.Y.; cert. Rutgers Summer Sch. Alcoholism Studies, 1982. Social worker VA, N.Y.C., 1962-66; sr. psychiat. social worker in child psychiat. Downstate Med. Ctr., Bklyn., 1966-71; staff therapist Inst. for Contemporary Psychotherapy, N.Y.C., 1971-73; social worker Lower East Side Service Ctr., N.Y.C., 1975-77; intake coordinator alcoholism program Postgrad. Ctr. for Mental Health, N.Y.C., 1981-82; program coordinator Bowery Residents Com., N.Y.C., 1984—; pvt. practice psychotherapy N.Y.C., 1973—, Dingmans Ferry, Pa., 1994-2000; interpreter VAn Cortlandt Manor, Croton-on-Hudson, 2003—. Sec. alcoholism com. N.Y.C. chpt. NASW, 1987-89. Author: Jogging the Mind, 1995. Sec. Middle-Way Mediation Ctr., Danbury, Conn.; leader Buddhist meditation group Fed. Correctional Inst., Danbury, 2000—03; participant N.Y.C. Marathon, 1991, 1992. Mem. Social Workers Helping Social Workers (chmn. 1982-84). Avocations: pottery, travel. Office: 108 1/2 E 37th St New York NY 10016

GREEN, BETTY NIELSEN, education educator, consultant; b. Copenhagen, Apr. 30, 1937; came to U.S., 1979; d. Alfred Christian Josef and Lilly Nielsen; m. Philip Irving Green, Apr. 16, 1962; children: Ruth, Erik, Nils. AA in Fgn. Lang., Daytona Beach C.C., 1981; BA in Liberal Arts, U. Ctrl. Fla., 1986; MS in TESOL, Nova Southeastern U., 1988; EdD in Curriculum and Instrn., U. Ctrl. Fla., 1994. Cert. tchr., Fla.; cert. TESOL trainer, Fla. Tchr. TESOL, program mgr. English Lang. Inst. Daytona Beach C.C., Fla., 1986-91; tchr. TESOL, fgn. lang. specialist Volusia County Schs., Daytona Beach, 1991—; tchr. trainer, facilitator Nova Southeastern U., Ft. Lauderdale, Fla., 1991—. Cons. TESOL, Ormond Beach, Fla., 1991; adj. faculty, Daytona Beach, 1997—; chair Fla. Consortium of Multilingual-Multicultural Edn., 2001—. Author, editor Teaching Assistant Manual, 1987; editor Unitarian Universalist Soc. newsletter, 1987—, religious editl. dir., 1996—; eidtor Fla. Fgn. Lang. Assn. Newsletter. Pres. Unitarian Universalists, Ormond Beach, 1982-84, N.E. Cluster Unitarian Universalists, Volusia, 1982-86; pres., v.p. S.E. Unitarian Universalists Sem. Inst., Blacksburg, Va., 1985-89. Mem. TESOL, Sunshine State TESOL (mem.-at-large 1999—, 2d v.p., 1st v.p., pres. 2003—), N.E. Fla. TESOL (pres. 1995—, editor newsletter 1998—), ASCD, Nat. Coun. Tchrs. of English, Fla. Fgn. Lang. Assn. (membership bd., editor 2002—), Fgn. Lang. Adminstrn. and Mgmt. Edn. (sec. 1995-97, pres. 1998), Fla. Assn. Bilingual Edn. Suprs. (sec. 1995), Fla. Consortium on Multicultural Edn. (chair), Phi Kappa Phi, Kappa Delta Pi, Pi Delta Kappa. Democrat. Avocations: foreign languages, research on second language and multi-cultural educations, music, travel. Home: 771 W River Oak Dr Ormond Beach FL 32174-4641 Office: Volusia County Schs 729 Loomis Ave Daytona Beach FL 32114-4723 E-mail: drtesol@philgreen.org., drtesol@philgreen.org.

GREEN, CAROL H. lawyer, educator, journalist; b. Seattle, Feb. 18, 1944; BA in History/Journalism summa cum laude, La. Tech. U., 1965; MSL, Yale U., 1977; JD, U. Denver, 1979. Reporter Shreveport (La.) Times, 1965-66, Guam Daily News, 1966-67; city editor Pacific Jour., Agana, Guam, 1967-68, reporter, editl. writer, 1968-76, legal affairs reporter, 1977-79; asst. editor editl. page Denver Post, 1979-81, house counsel, 1980-83, labor rels. mgr., 1981-83; assoc. Holme Roberts & Owen, 1983-85; v.p. human resources and legal affairs Denver Post, 1985-87, mgr. circulation, 1988-90; gen. mgr. Distbn. Systems Am., Inc., 1990-92; dir. labor rels. Newsday, 1992-95, dir. comm. & labor rels., 1996-97; v.p. Weber Mgmt. Cons., 1997-98; v.p. human resources and labor rels. Denver Post, 1998—2000; v.p. human resources Denver Newspaper Agy., 2000—. 1985 speaker for USIA, India, Egypt; mem. Mailers Tech. Adv. Com. to Postmaster Gen., 1991-92. Recipient McWilliams award for juvenile justice, Denver, 1971, award for interpretive reporting Denver Newspaper Guild, 1979. Mem.: ABA, Soc. Human Resources Mgmt., Colo. and Internat. Women's Forum, Denver Bar Assn. (co-chair jud. selection and benefits com. 1982—85, 2nd v.p. 1986), Newspaper Assn. Am. (mem. human resources and labor rels. com.), Colo. Bar Assn. (bd. govs. 1985—87, chair BAR-press com. 1980), Leadership Denver. Episcopalian.

GREEN, CAROLE L. lawyer; b. Queens, N.Y., Mar. 17, 1959; d. Gerald Harry and Mary (Clark) G. AB cum laude with distinction, Dartmouth Coll., 1980; JD, Harvard Law Sch., 1983. Bar: N.Y. Congl. aide to rep. John Conyers U.S. House of Reps., Washington, 1980; assoc. real estate Kaye Scholer LLP, NY, 1983—85, Bingham McCuthen LLP, N.Y., 1985-87; gen. counsel Petrie Stores Corp., Secaucus, N.J., 1987-88; assoc. counsel JP Morgan Chase Bank, N.Y.C., 1988-91; v.p., asst. gen. counsel Chem. Bank (now JP Morgan Chase Bank), N.Y., 1991-96; contract atty. N.Y.C., 1996—; pub. arbitrator NASD Dispute Resolution, 1996—. Mem.: ABA, Met. Black Bar Assn., Practicing Attys. for Law Students, Inc. (founding mem. 1986—95), Assn. Bar City N.Y., N.Y. State Bar Assn., Black Alumni of Dartmouth Assn. Avocations: travel, swimming, jazz, cinema.

GREEN, CHARLENE, principal, speech pathology/audiology services professional; d. Winfred Muriel Green, Sr. and Pauline Henderson; m. Stephen G. McGowan, Mar. 4, 1988 (div. May 2002). BA in Communicative Disorders, U. of the Pacific, 1973; BS in Communicative Disorders, U. LaVerne, 1983; preliminary adminstr. credential, U.S. Internat. U., 1998; clear adminstrv. credential, Nat. U., 2001. Cert. clin. competence in speech/lang. pathology. Speech-lang. pathologist, Calif., 1974—2000; vice prin. San Diego Unified Sch. Dist., 2000—03, prin., 2003—. Mem.: PTA, Nat. Black Lang./Speech and Hearing Assn., Calif. Speech/Hearing Assn., Am. Lang./Speech/Heaering Assn. Democrat. Avocations: reading, horticulture, travel, exercise. Office: San Diego Unified Sch Dist 4100 Normal St San Diego CA 92103

GREEN, DARLENE, controller, municipal official; b. St. Louis; BSBA, Washington U. Budget dir. City of St. Louis, comptroller, chief fiscal officer, 1995—. Vol. St. Louis Pub. Schs., St. Louis Crisis Nursery, Big Bros. & Big Sisters, YWCA Greater St. Louis; mem. Airport Commn.; trustee City of St. Louis Retirement Sys.; bd. dirs. Employment Connection, St. Louis Cmty. Edn. Task Force. Mem.: NAACP, Govt. Fin. Officers Assn., Nat. Assn. Black Accts., Zeta Phi Beta. Office: City of St Louis 1200 Market St Rm 212 Saint Louis MO 63103-2805 Fax: 314-622-4026.

GREEN, ELEANOR MYERS, veterinarian, educator; b. Phila., Feb. 10, 1948; d. Wade Cooper and Eleanor Ruth (McWherter) Myers; children: George Ashby Jr., Stacy Elizabeth, William Wade. Student, U. South Fla., 1965-67, U. Fla., 1967-69; DVM, Auburn U., 1973. Diplomate Am. Coll. Vet. Internal Medicine, Am. Bd. Vet. Practitioners (pres. 1993-95, past pres. 1995-96). Ptnrship, owner Guntown (Miss.) Vet. Clinic, 1973-76; asst. prof. Miss. State U., Starkville, 1976-84; assoc. prof. U. Mo., Columbia, 1984-91; prof. U. Tenn., Knoxville, 1991-96; prof., chair dept. U. Fla., Gainesville, 1996—. Named Disting. Practitioner Nat. Acads. of Practice. Mem. Am. Assn. Equine Practitioners (bd. dirs. 1997-99), Fla. Vet. Med. Assn., Am. Vet. Med. Assn., Internat. Soc. Vet. Perinatology, Am. Assn. Vet. Clinicians (Faculty Achievement award 1999, pres. 1995-96, past pres. 1996-97), Nat. Acad.'s Practice (Disting. Practitioner 1998—), Fla. Thoroughbred Owners and Breeders Assn., Fla. Quarter Horse Assn. (bd. dirs.), Rotary Internat. Presbyterian. Avocations: horseback riding, tennis, painting. Office: U Fla Coll Vet Medicine Dept Large Animal Clin Scis Gainesville FL 32610-0136 E-mail: greene@mail.vetmed.ufl.edu.

GREEN, FLORA HUNGERFORD, lactation consultant, nurse; b. Mason City, Iowa, June 23, 1941; d. Mac Willard and Ethel Elizabeth (Hill) Hungerford; m. Ronald Eugene Green, Aug. 3, 1974 (div.); children: Elizabeth Jane, Marjorie Ann. Diploma, Meth-Kahler Sch. of Nursing, 1963; BS in Biology, Westmar Coll., 1964; BS in Nursing, Case Western Res. U., 1968; MA in Edn. Media, U. Minn., 1971. Cert. lactation cons. Internat. Bd. Cert. Lactation Cons., lamaze instr.; RN Idaho. Ednl. programmer U. Wis., Milw., 1970-72; asst. prof. nursing Idaho State U., Pocatello, 1972-76; dir. ins-svc. and patient edn. Bingham Meml. Hosp., Blackfoot, Idaho, 1976-77; staff nurse St. Agnes' Hosp., Fresno, Calif., 1979-81, Eden Hosp., Castro Valley, Calif., 1981-83; pvt. practice lactation cons. Fremont, Calif., 1985—91. Staff nurse high risk obstet. dept. Stanford U. Hosp., 1989—90; lactation cons., mother-baby nurse Kaiser Hosp., Hayward, 1991—99; lactation cons. St. Luke's Meridian (Idaho) Med. Ctr., 2001—; cons. media div. Lippincott Learning Systems, Nursing Media divsn. J.B. Lippincott Co., Phila., 1973—80; bd. dirs. Bay Area Lactation Assn., Daly City, Calif., 1985—88. Chmn. Blacow Sch. emergency and safety com., Fremont, 1987-88, 92-93; bd. dirs. Fresno Montessori Sch., 1980-81, Bannock County ARC, Pocatello, 1976-77; emergency svcs. disaster cons. Idaho State U., Bannock County Red Cross, Bannock County, Pocatello, Idaho, 1972-77. Mem.: Lamaze Internat., Internat. Lactation Cons. Assn. Lutheran. Avocations: skiing, reading.

GREEN, JEAN HESS, psychotherapist; b. Flushing, Mich., Aug. 10, 1930; d. Ozro Kline and Thelma Lucille (Cook) Hess; m. Warren Dale Sarley, Mar. 21, 1952 (div. 1971); children: Gaie Lee, Patton Garret, Erin Jessie; m. Peter B. Green, Jan. 4, 1972. BA, Mich. State U., 1955; MS, Columbia Pacific U., San Rafael, Calif., 1988, PhD, 1994. Cert. Rubenfeld synergist; diplomate Am. Psychol. Assn., 2000. Tchr. secondary English, Norwich (N.Y.) Pub. Schs., 1960-61; claims rep. Social Security Adminstrn., Rochester, N.Y., 1961-63; mgr. Maplewood Apts., Syracuse, N.Y., 1972-76; dir. overseas scholarships Episcopal Ch., USA, N.Y.C., 1979-81; dir. audio books N.Y. Pub. Libr., N.Y.C., 1987-89; pvt. practice psychotherapy, N.Y.C. and Mt. Vernon, N.Y., 1985—. Workshop presenter Mariandale Ctr., Ossining, NY., 1986—. Mem. Assn. for Humanistic Psychology, C.G. Jung Found., Analytical Psychology Club N.Y. (rec. sec. 1988-94, pres. 1994-96). Democrat. Roman Catholic. Avocation: writing poetry. Office: 222 E 5th St New York NY 10003-8564 Home and Office: PO Box 353 Denver NY 12421-0353

GREEN, JILL I. dance educator, researcher; b. Bklyn., June 19, 1954; d. Charles M. and Selma Z. (Stein) Green. BS summa cum laude, Bklyn. Coll., 1976; MA, NYU, 1981; PhD, Ohio State U., 1993. Lic. tchr. dance K-12,

N.C., tchr. Kinetic Awareness. Dance instr. NYU, N.Y.C., 1981; dance tchr. Pub. Sch. 46, Bronx, N.Y., 1981-83; dance and movement instr. Lee Strasberg Theatre Inst., N.Y.C., 1983-86; dance tchr. Sheepshead Bay H.S., Bklyn., 1985-89; movement and relaxation specialist Columbus (Ohio) Psychol. Ctr., 1989-92; tchg. assoc. Ohio State U., Columbus, 1989-92, [illegible], 1990-92; [illegible] mind and body awareness educator Columbus Somatics Ctr., 1992-93; asst. prof. dance U. N.C., Greensboro, 1993—, coord. dance edn. program, 1993—. Cons. for dance curriculum N.C. State Dept. Instrn., Raleigh, 1995-96; editl. cons. Ind. U. Press, 1995-96. Contbr. chpt. to book, articles to profl. jours.; co-editor Dance Rsch. Jours., 2003—. Vol. tchr. Very Spl. Arts Festival, Greensboro, 1994—, N.C. 4-H Coun., Greensboro, 1993—; demonstration classes N.C. Pub. Schs., 1993—; ednl. facilitator for homeless women WINGS Ctr. for SelfDiscovery, Columbus, 1992-93. New Faculty grantee, 1993-95; Dance Connections grantee Cmty. Found. Greater Greensboro, 1997; Ctr. for Study of Social Issues grantee, 1997—, U. N.C. Tchg. Excellence award, Sch. of Health and Human Performance, 1998. Mem. Nat. Dance Edn. Org., N.C. Dance Alliance (bd. dirs. 1996-98), Congress on Rsch. in Dance (bd. dirs. 1998—), The Somatics Soc., Natl. Dance Edn. Assn., Am. Ednl. Rsch. Assn. Office: U NC at Greensboro Dept Dance PO Box 26169 Greensboro NC 27402-6169 Office Phone: 336-334-4064. E-mail: jillgreen@uncg.edu.

GREEN, JOYCE HENS, federal judge; b. N.Y.C., Nov. 13, 1928; d. James S. and Hedy (Bucher) Hens; m. Samuel Green, Sept. 25, 1965 (dec.); children: Michael Timothy, June Heather, James Harry. BA, U. Md., 1949; JD, George Washington U., 1951, LLD, 1994. Practice law, Washington, 1951-68, Arlington, Va., 1956-68; ptnr. Green & Green, 1966-68; assoc. judge Superior Ct., D.C., 1968-79; judge U.S. Dist. Ct. for D.C., 1979—; judge presiding U.S. Fgn. Intelligence Surveillance Ct., 1988-95. Bd. advisors George Washington U. Law Sch., 1991-2001; jud. br. com. Jud. Conf. U.S., 1995-2001. Co-author: Dissolution of Marriage, 1986, supplements, 1987-89, Marriage and Family Law Agreements, 1985, supplements, 1986-89. Chair Task Force on Gender, Race and Ethnic Bias for the D.C. Cir. Recipient Alumni Achievement award George Washington U., 1975, Profl. Achievement award, 1978, Outstanding Contbn. to Equal Rights award Women's Legal Def. Fund, 1976, hon. doctor of Laws George Washington U., 1994, U.S. Dept. Justice Edmund J. Randolph award, 1995. Fellow Am. Bar Found.; ABA (jud. adminstrn. divsn., chair nat. conf. fed. trial judges 1997-98), Fed. Judges Assn., Nat. Assn. Women Judges, Va. Bar, Bar Assn. D.C. (jud. honoree of Yr. 1994), D.C. Bar, D.C. Women's Bar Assn., (pres. 1960-62, woman lawyer of yr. 1979), Exec. Women in Govt. (chmn. 1977), Woman's Forum of Washington D.C. Office: US Dist Ct E Barrett Prettyman US Courthouse 333 Constitution Ave NW Washington DC 20001-2802

GREEN, LAURA LORRAINE, foundation administrator; b. Denver, Nov. 23, 1924; d. Jack Wayne and Anna Laura (Cheney) Skiles; m. James Edward Green, Aug. 12, 1945 (dec. 1987); 1 child, Sharon Lee Payne. Grad. high sch., Santa Monica, Calif. Payroll Hanson Glove Factory, Milw., 1943-45; credit interviewer Broadway Dept. Store Orgn., Anaheim, Calif., 1956-57; sect. divsn. mgr. Hughes Aircraft Co., Fullerton, Calif., 1957-61; sec., payroll J.T. Murphy Carpet Co., San Jose, Calif.; owner 49er Trailer Ranch/RV & Mobile Home Park, Columbia, Calif., 1963-70; dir. adminstr. Sheriffs Aux. Vols., Tucson, 1988-92; retired. Mem. Ariz. County Attys. and Sheriffs Assn., Order of Ea. Star, Fraternal Order Police. Democrat. Methodist. Avocation: collecting stamps and antiques. Home: PO Box 1150 Marana AZ 85653-1150

GREEN, LAURIE, state agency administrator; Mgr. internat. and domestic programs State of Wash.; dep. dir. tourism Wyo. Bus. Coun., Cheyenne, 2000—01, dir. travel and tourism, 2001—. Mem.: Nat. Tour Assn. (DMO coun.). Office: Wyoming Business Council 214 W 15th St Cheyenne WY 28002

GREEN, LINDA C. education specialist administrator, researcher; b. Memphis, Nov. 21, 1947; d. Frank Allen and Mary Elizabeth (Hankins) Green; m. John Newton Osborne, Feb. 7, 1975 (div. June 1979); 1 child, Suzanne; m. Phillip Harold James, Oct. 17, 1980 (div. Aug. 2003); 1 child, Sarah Elizabeth. BA, U. Tenn., Martin, 1970; MA, Calif. State U., Long Beach, 1975; EdD in Higher Edn., U. Memphis, 1995. Instr. Memphis State U., 1979-85, dir. Wordsmith, 1984-85; asst. prof. Jackson (Tenn.) State C.C., 1985-90; adminstrv. intern State Tech. Inst. Memphis, 1990-91; asst. dir. Mid South Quality Productivity Ctr., Memphis, 1991-92; dir. acad. devel. State Tech. Inst. Memphis, 1992-93; edn. specialist Nat. Inst. Stds. and Tech., Gaithersburg, Md., 1993-94; systems mgmt. specialist U. Tenn., Martin, 1994-95; dir. assessment State Tech. Inst. Memphis, 1995-2000; v.p. acad. affairs The Nat. Grad. Sch., 2000—01. Bd. dirs., v.p. Greater Memphis Area Award for Quality; mem. adv. com. Nat. Govs. Conf. Edn., 1994; cons. City of Memphis Dept. Planning, 1993; mem. editl. bd. CQI Newsletter, 1994—; mem. adv. coun. Total Quality Learning Sys. Am. Soc. Quality, 1995—; trainer Koalaty Kids, 1996; bd. dirs. ASQ; Koalaty Kid Alliance, 1997—; mem. adj. faculty Nat. Grad. Sch., 1997—; bd. examiners Malcolm Baldrige Nat. Quality award, 1995-98, 99. Facilitator Leadership Memphis Diversity Program, 1993; vol. Girl Scouts, N.W. Tenn., 1986-89. Recipient grant Bell-South, 1991-93, fellow Tenn. Collaborative Acad., 1990-91. Mem. Am. Assn. Higher Edn., Am. Soc. Quality Control (assoc., Memphis sect. co-chair quality forum 1992-93), Tenn Assn. Devel. Educators, Phi Delta Kappa. Home: 30 Benjamin Nyes Ln North Falmouth MA 02556

GREEN, LINDA GAIL, retired international healthcare and management consultant, nurse educator; b. Kalamazoo, Nov. 29, 1951; d. Jesse Floyd and Mattie Dean (Fulcher) G. BS in Nursing, Fla. State U., Tallahassee, 1974; postgrad., Nova U., Ft. Lauderdale, Fla. Staff nurse med./surg. unit St. Mary's Hosp., West Palm Beach, Fla., 1974, staff nurse coronary care, 1974-75, relief charge nurse ICU, 1975-76, asst. nursing care coord. post anesthesia recovery rm., 1976-78, insvc. instr., 1978-81, asst. dir. staff devel. and edn., 1981-83; dir. insvc. H.H. Raulerson Hosp., Okeechobee, Fla., 1983-84; adminstr. Med. Personnel Pool, Palm Beach, Fla., 1984-90; regional exec. healthcare divsn. Interim Svcs., Inc. (formerly Pers. Pool of Am., an H&R Block Co.), Ft. Lauderdale, 1990-93; pres. L.G.I. Consulting/Cmty. Health Educator, West Palm Beach, 1993—2000. Dir. ednl. svcs., nurse educator Intracoastal Health Svcs., Inc., Good Samaritan Med. Ctr., St. Mary's Med. Ctr., West Palm Beach, Fla., 1998-2000; spkr. in field. Author: Sexual Harassment in Home Healthcare, 1993. Past bd. dirs. Vinceremos Therapeutic Riding Ctr., Inc. for Physically and Mentally Challenged, 1990-95; chair Helen K. Persson Endowment Scholarship, 1999-2000; mem. Palm Beach County Workshop Devel. Bus. Partnership Coun., 1999. Mem. ANA, AHA (heart walk industry leader 1994, 95), Palm Beach County Health Educators (past sec.), Palm Beach County Patient Educators (pres. 1989, Leadership and Spirit awards 1989), Royal Palm Beach Bus. Assn., Palms West C. of C. (v.p. 1987-88, Dedicated and Outstanding Svc. award 1989, Cert. of Appreciation 1986, 87), Zonta Internat. (pres. 1994-95, past v.p. Palms West chpt., del. to internat. conf., Hong Kong, 1992).

GREEN, LINDA LOU, systems analyst; b. Cape Girardeau, Mo., Sept. 12, 1946; d. Barney Oldfield and Opal (Jeffries) G. BA, East Carolina U., 1967, MA, 1969; postgrad., U. Utah, 1969-70; grad., Naval War Coll., Newport, R.I., 1985, Command and Staff Coll., Ft. Leavenworth, Kans., 1990. Cert. in collegiate teaching. Asst. prof. history Jackson (Miss.) State U., 1970-72, Va. State U., Petersburg, 1972-74; commd. 1st lt. U.S. Army, 1974, advanced through grades to lt. col., 1991, ret., 1996; logistics engr. land systems div. Gen. Dynamics Corp., Warren, Mich., 1983-84; systems analyst Raytheon Svc. Co., Huntsville, Ala., 1984-86; pres. Green & Assocs. Inc., Huntsville, 1985-86; logistics engr., cost analyst, br. mgr. Applied Rsch. Inc., Huntsville, 1986-90; sr. ILS analyst Native Am. Svcs. Inc., Huntsville, Ala., 1990; sr. systems analyst BDM Internat. Inc., 1990; pres. Green and Assocs., Inc., Huntsville, 1990-91; sr. logistics analyst Sigmatech Inc., 1991-95; pvt. cons., 1995—; sr. analyst Mastech Sys. Inc., 1997—98; engr. SAIC, 1998—. Instr. U. Md., Fed. Republic Germany, 1975-77, Calhoun Community Coll., Huntsville, 1990-91, [illegible]. Author: Study Guides for American History, 1969, The Family Tree, 1989, Logistics Engineering, 1991, The Town Crier: Descendents of Timothy and Elizabeth Trigg/Reagan, 1995, Town Crier: The Descendents of Archibald McCarver, 1996, Town Crier: The Ancestors of the Missouri Shrums, 1996. Mem. Rep. Nat. Com., Washington, 1986-91. Mem. LWV, Soc. Logistics Engrs. (bd. dirs. TVC chpt. 1992-93, chpt. Logistician of Yr. 1993, recipient Nat. Field award in Integrated Logistics Support 1994), Assn. U.S. Army (bd. dirs. Redstone, Huntsville chpt. 1988-91), Res. Officers Assn., Ret. Officers Assn., DAR, United Daus. of the Confederacy, Daus. of Union Vets. of the Civil War. Baptist. Avocations: horseback riding, raquetball, author.

GREEN, LISA CANNON, online editor; b. Marshall, Ky., May 7, 1962; d. Walter L. and Phyllis (Jones) Cannon; m. Bob Dale Green, May 31, 1980; children: Emily, Ethan. BA in Journalism and English, Murray State U., 1983. With The Post-Intelligencer, Paris, Tenn., 1983-84, The Jackson (Tenn.) Sun, 1984-90, The Tennessean, Nashville, 1990—. Office: The Tennessean 1100 Broadway Nashville TN 37203-3134 Office Phone: 615-259-8275. Business E-Mail: lgreen@tennessean.com.

GREEN, LYDA N. state legislator; b. Livingston, Tex., Oct. 16, 1938; m. Curtis Green; children: Shelton, Kristie, Brad. BBA, Sam Houston State U., 1959; Slingerland lang. cert., U. Alaska, 1988. Tchr. West H.S., 1962-63; adminstrv. asst. Pan Am. Petroleum, AMOCO, 1963-65; co-owner Anchorage Racquet Club, 1978-88; instrs. asst. U. Alaska, Anchorage, 1991; adj. instr. Mat-Su C.C., 1991-93; mem. Alaska Senate, Dist. N, Juneau, 1994—. Former mem. Gov.'s Coun. on Disabilities and Spl. Edn., 1991-94; mem. spl. edn. regulations task force Dept. Edn., 1993-94; active First Bapt. Ch. Recipient Defender of Freedom award NRA, Legislator Appreciation award 4-H; named Legislator of Yr., Alaska Farm Bur., 1996. Mem. Soroptimists, Palmer Pioneer Lions, C. of C. Republican. Avocations: reading, piano, tennis, sewing, dyslexia. Office: State Capitol 120 4th St Rm 125 Juneau AK 99801-1142 also: 600 E Railroad Ave Ste 1 Wasilla AK 99654-8135 Fax: 907-465-3805/907-376-3157. E-mail: green@legis.state.ak.us.

GREEN, MAE MAERA, artist; b. N.Y.C., Sept. 14, 1930; d. Phillip and Clara (Donnenfeld) Rabach; m. Sam Green, Feb. 1, 1953; children: Michelle, Tracy, Dori, Marshall. Student, Art Student League, 1947, Pratt Inst., 1951. Exhibited at Perspective Gallery, N.Y.C., 1949, State Mus. Art Gallery, Santa Fe, N.Mex., 1958, 59, 60, 72 (award), U. N.Mex. Jonson Gallery, 1972 (award), Malvina Miller Gallery, San Francisco, 1972, Meridian Gallery, Albuquerque, 1979; represented in permanent collections at Mus. of Albuquerque, City Albuquerque 1% for the Arts, Aetna Life Ins. Co., Mass., Temple Albert, Albuquerque. Recipient award Nat. Design Wallpaper/Fabric, 1950. Avocations: reading, travel, walking, gardening. Home: 1521 Sagebrush Trl SE Albuquerque NM 87123-4489

GREEN, MILLIE ANN, mathematician, educator; d. James Richard Caudle and Martha Grace Lewis; m. Charles Earl Irvin, June 14, 1964 (div. Aug. 1981); children: Karl Anne Irvin, Jan Richard Irvin; m. Kenneth M. Green, June 12, 1992. BSc, Calif. Polytech., 1979; tchr.'s credential, U. Redlands, 1988; postgrad., U. Calif., 1989—90; M in Adminstrn., Internat. U., 1999. Cert. in adminstrn., home econs., math., sci., and phys. sci. Tchr. math. Ladera Vista Jr. H.S., Fullerton, Calif., back up administr., 1993—; tchr. 6th grade Fontana, Calif., 1988—90. Mem. San Gorgonio Girl Scout Coun., Colton, Calif., 1984—88. Home: 25041 Acacia Ln Laguna Hills CA 92653-4961

GREEN, MONICA H. history educator; BA, Barnard Coll., 1978; MA, Princeton U., 1981; PhD in History of Sci., Princeton (N.J.) U. Fellow U. N.C., Chapel Hill; assoc. prof. history Duke U.; prof. history Ariz. State U., Tempe, 2001—. Author: (essays) Women's Helathcare and the Medieval West: Texts and Contexts, 2000; contbr. articles; editor, translator: The Trotula: A Medieval Compendium of Women's Medicine, 2001. Fellow, NEH, Inst. Advanced Study, Princeton U., Nat. Humanities Ctr., John Simon Guggenheim Meml. Found., 2003. Office: Ariz State U Dept History PO Box 872501 Tempe AZ 85287-2501

GREEN, NANCY LOUGHRIDGE, publishing executive; b. Lexington, Ky., Jan. 19, 1942; d. William S. and Nancy O. (Green) Loughridge. BA in Journalism, U. Ky., 1964, postgrad., 1968; MA in Journalism, Ball State U., 1971; postgrad., U. Minn., 1968; EdD, Nova Southeastern U., 2003. Tchr. English, publs. adv. Clark County H.S., Winchester, Ky., 1965-66, Pleasure Ridge Park H.S., Louisville, 1966-67, Clarksville (Ind.) H.S., 1967-68, Charleston (W.Va.) H.S., 1968-69; asst. publs., pub. info. specialist W.Va. Dept. Edn., Charleston, 1969-70; tchr. journalism, publs. dir. Elmhurst H.S., Ft. Wayne, Ind., 1970-71; adviser student publs. U. Ky., Lexington, 1971-82; gen. mgr. student publs. U. Tex., Austin, 1982-85; pres., pub. Palladium-Item, Richmond, Ind., 1985-89, News-Leader, Springfield, Mo., 1989-92; asst. to pres. newspaper divsn. Gannett Co., Inc., Washington, 1992-94; exec. dir. advancement Clayton State Coll., Morrow, Ga., 1994-96; v.p. advancement Clayton Coll. & State U., Morrow, Ga., 1996-99; v.p. comm. Ga. GLOBE U. Sys., 1999-2000; dir. circulation/distbn., sales & mktg. Lee Enterprises, Davenport, Iowa, 2000—02; v.p. circulation LEE Enterprises, 2002—. Dir. urban journalism program Harte-Hanks, 1984, various Louisville and Lexington newspaper pubs., 1976-82; pres. Media Cons., Inc., Lexington, 1980; sec. Kernel Press, Inc., 1971-82. Contbr. articles to profl. jours. Bd. dirs. Studen Press Law Ctr., 1975—, Richmond Cmty. Devel. Corp., 1987-89, United Way of the Ozarks, 1990-92, ARC, 1990-92, Springfield Arts Coun., 1990-91, Bus. Devel. Corp., 1991-92, Bus. Edn. Alliance, 1991-92, Caring Found., 1991-92, Cox Hosp. Bd., 1990-92, Springfield Schs. Found., 1991-92, Jr. League, Lexington, 1980-82, Manchester Ctr., 1978-82, pres., 1979-82; chmn. Greater Richmond Progress Com., 1986-87, bd. dirs., 1986-89; pres. Leadership Wayne County, 1986-87, bd. dirs. 1985-89; adv. bd. Ind. U. East, 1985-89, Richmond C. of C., 1987-89, Ind. Humanities Coun., 1988-89, Youth Comm. Bd., 1988-92, Opera Theatre No. Va., 1992-94, Atlanta chpt. AIWF, 1995. Recipient Coll. Media Advisers First Amendment award, 1987, Disting. Svc. award Assn. Edn. Journalism and Mass Comm., 1989; named to Ball State Journalism Hall of Fame, 1988, Coll. Media Advisers Hall of Fame, 1994. Mem. Student Press Law Ctr. (bd. dirs. 1975—, pres. 1985-87, 94-96, v.p. 1992-94), Assoc. Collegiate Press, Journalism Edn. Assn. (Carl Towley award 1988), Nat. Coun. Coll. Publs. Advs. (pres. 1979-83, Disting. Newspaper Adv. 1976, Disting. Bus. Adviser 1984), Columbia Scholastic Press Assn. (Gold Key 1980), So. Interscholastic Press Assn. (Disting. Svc. award 1983), Nat. Scholastic Press Assn. (Pioneer award 1982), Soc. Profl. Journalists, Internat. Newspaper Mktg. Assn. N.Am. (bd. dirs. 2002—), Newspaper Assn. Am. (postal com. 2001—, readership adv. group 2002—, diversity subcom. 1991—, circulation fedn. bd. 2002-), Clayton County C. of C. (adv. bd. 1995-99, chmn. internat. com. 1996-98). E-mail: nancy.green@lee.net.

GREEN, PATRICIA PATAKY, school system administrator, consultant; b. NYC, June 18, 1949; d. William J. and Theresa M. (DiGianni) P.; m. Stephen I. Green, Dec. 7, 1975. BS, U. Md., 1971, MEd, 1977, PhD, 1994. Tchr. Prince George's County Pub. Sch., Md., 1971-83; elem. instrnl. adminstrv. specialist Thomas Stone Sch., Mt. Ranier, Md., 1984-85, Glenridge Sch., Lanham, Md., 1984, Greenbelt Ctr. Sch., Md., 1983-84, Prince George's County Pub. Schs., 1985-91; prin. Columbia Pk. Sch., Landover, Md., 1985-91; asst. supt. Prince George's County Pub. Sch., 1991-95, assoc. supt., chief divsn. adminstr., 1995-99, assoc. supt. for pupil svc., 1999—2001, acting dep. supt. for instrn., 2000—02, fellow Broad Ctr. Supt., Bd. Found., 2002; supt. sch. North Allegheny Sch. Dist., Pitts., 2002—. Exec. dir. North Allegheny Found.; cons. nationwide sch. systems; presenter in field. Featured in numerous mag. and on TV shows; contbr. articles to profl. jour. Apptd. commr. Prince George's Commn. for Children, Youth and Families, bd. dir. Prince George's County Cmty. in Sch., 1998—2002; trustee North Allegheny Found., 2002, exec. dir., 2002—03. Recipient Nat. Sch. Recognition award US Dept. Edn., 1988, Outstanding Adminstr. award Prince George's County C. of C., 1990, Outstanding Rsch. award Md. Assn. Supervision and Curriculum Devel., 1995, Outstanding Educator award Prince George's County, 1983, Spotlight on Prevention award Md. State Atty. Gen., 1998, Disting. Achievement award North Allegheny Sch. Dist., 2002, Outstanding Profl. award U. Md. Coll. Edn., 2003. Mem. NAESP (Excellence of Achievement award 1988), ASCD, NEA, Am. Ednl. Rsch. Assn., Phi Kappa Phi. Kappa Delta Pi. Avocations: landscape gardening, photography, reading, writing, bicycling. E-mail: pgreen@northallegheny.org.

GREEN, RIVA LEE, social worker, minister; b. Denmark, S.C., May 18, 1953; d. Rious and Elizzillia (Banks) G.; m. George E. Collins, June 19, 1974 (div. June 1985); children: Corey E., Kevin L., Monique N. AAS, Cumberland County Coll., Vineland, N.J., 1992. Ordained to ministry Jamison Sch. Ministry, Phila., 1995. Caseworker Salem County Women's Svcs., Salem, N.J., 1992-97; family non-violence training U.S. Army, Ft. Dix, N.J., 1995—; family svc. specialist III State of N.J. Divsn. Youth and Family Svcs., Camden, 1997—. Pastor Strings of Faith ministry, Seabrook, N.J. Active NAACP (area coord. Bridgeton, N.J., 1995, 1st v.p. Cumberland County, 1995—); adv. bd. Maple Garden Tenant Assn., 1991-93; natural leader Martin Luther King Academy, 1995—; mem. C.O.R.E. Mem. C.O.R.E. Home: 32 Tower Ln Willingboro NJ 08046-4114

GREEN, RUTHANN, marketing and management consultant; b. Streator, Ill., July 14, 1935; d. John Joseph and Edna Marie (Peters) G. BS in Edn., U. Ill., 1957. Elem. tchr. Jefferson Sch., Davenport, Iowa, 1957-59; tchr. Hinsdale (Ill.) Jr. High Sch., 1959-62; ednl. cons. Harcourt Brace & World, Chgo., 1962-63; exec. sec. Everpure, Inc., Oakbrook, Ill., 1963-68; ednl. cons. Houghton Mifflin Co., Europe, 1968-69, 1969-77, sr. mktg. mgr. Boston, 1977-87; v.p., nat. sales mgr. Riverside Pub. Co., Chgo., 1987-89; v.p., dir. mktg. McDougal, Littell & Co., Evanston, Ill., 1990-92; v.p., gen. mgr. Open Court Pub. Co., Chgo., 1992-94; pres. Peters & Green, Inc. Seminars & Bus. Devel., Chgo., 1994—. Author: WSIL: Why Should I Listen, 1987, 93, A Garfield Memoir, 1995. Bd. dirs. Ritchie Tower Condo Assn. Recipient Svc. award Am. Arbitration Assn., 1987, Golden Reel of Excellence Internat. TV Assn., 1983. Mem. Am. Mktg. Assn., Nat. Assn. Women Bus. Owners, Internat. Reading Assn., People for Am. Way, Common Cause, Am. Arbitration Assn., Urban Gateways (bd. dirs.). Avocations: reading, fitness activities, travel, art. Home and Office: 1310 N Ritchie Ct Apt 21A Chicago IL 60610-8405 E-mail: petersgreen@att.net, rgreen3@att.net.

GREEN, SHARON ANNE, reading specialist, educator; b. Lackawanna, N.Y., May 20, 1951; d. Philip Kenneth Green and June Beatrice Witty; children: Andrew P. Przepasniak, Ellen L. Przepasniak. BA, SUNY, Fredonia, 1973; EdM, U. Buffalo, 1978. Cert. tchr. N.Y. Instr. ESL Pub. H.S. #1, Poznan, Poland, 1973—74, U. Buffalo, 1981—83, Summer Lang. Camp, Jaslo, Poland, 1996; tchr. grade 8 English St. Casimir Sch., Buffalo, 1976—78; instr. women's studies U. Buffalo, 1981—83, 1986—96; reading and writing specialist D'Youville Coll., Buffalo, 1986—98; reading coord. Niagara U., NY, 1998—. Author: (book) Sharon's Simple Study Strategies for College Success, 1998; contbr. articles to profl. jours. Bd. dirs. Buffalo Niagara chpt. NOW, 1997—99. Recipient Women Helping Women award, Buffalo/Niagara chpt. NOW, 1996. Mem.: Coll. Reading and Learning Assn., N.Y. Coll. Learning Skills Assn. (sec. 1998—2001, newsletter editor 2001—04, Outstanding Svc. to Profession award 2003). Roman Catholic. Avocations: reading, writing, gardening, home repairs, sewing. Home: 37 Devereaux Ave Buffalo NY 14214 Office: Niagara U Office of Acad Support Niagara University NY 14109 E-mail: sgreen@niagara.edu.

GREEN, SHARON JORDAN, interior decorator; b. Mansfield, Ohio, Dec. 14, 1948; d. Garnet and L. Wynell (Baxley) Fraley; m. Trice Leroy Jordan Jr., Mar. 30, 1968 (dec. 1973); children: Trice Leroy III, Caerin Danielle, Christopher Robin; m. Joe Leonard Green, Mar. 13, 1978. Student, Ohio State U., 1966-67, 75-76, U. St. Thomas, 2001, Rice U., 1998—. Typist FBI, Washington, 1968; ward clk. Means Hall, Ohio State U. Hosp., Columbus, 1970; x-ray clk. Riverside Hosp., Columbus, 1971; contr., owner T&D Mold & Die, Houston, 1988—; interior decorator, franchise owner Decorating Den, Houston, 1989-91; owner T&D Interior Decorator, Houston, 1992—; custom window designer The Great Indoors, 2001—. Tchr. aide Bedford Sch., Mansfield, Ohio, 1976-77, Yeager Sch., 1981-82; pres. N.W. Welcome Wagon, Houston, 1980-81, Welcome Club, El Paso, 1986-87; active North Houston Symphony, 1992—, North Houston Performing Arts, 1993—, Mus. Fine Arts, Houston, 1993—, Edn. and Design Resource Network, 1993—, The Wellington Soc. for Arts, 1994, Jr. Forum, 1995, Rep. Nat. Com., 1995—, The Heritage Soc., 1999—; vol. Harris County Juvenile Probation Dept., 1996; chmn. N.W. Houston Symphony Student Competition, 1998-99, founding mem. The Centrum Arts League, 1998-99, mem. Ptnrs. of the Woodlands Arts Ctr., 1998-99, mem. The Shepard Sch. Music, Rice U., 1998—, Heritage Soc., Houston. Mem. United Daus. of Confederacy. Home: 15114 Marlebone Ct Houston TX 77069

GREEN, SHAWNA MARIE, accountant; b. Great Bend, Kans., Dec. 9, 1978; d. Charles A. and Sharon Marie Satterfield; m. Brandon James Green. AAS with honors(hon.), Barton County C.C., Great Bend, Kans., 1998; B of Acctg. with honors, Ft. Hays State U., 2000. Asst. mgr. Wendy's, Great Bend, 1994—99; payroll, accts. payable RailWorks Neosho, Topeka, 2000; merch. distbn. analyst Payless Shoe Source, Topeka, 2001—02; computer technician Sykes, Hays, Kans., 1999, Koch Industries, 2002—. Vol. income tax assistance IRS, Hays, 1999—2000. Recipient Bronze Acad. award, Fort Hays State U., 1997, Excellence in Bus. award, 1997. Lutheran. Avocations: sports, physical fitness, crafts, art, auto racing. Home: 2549 Cambridge Ct Wichita KS 67219 Office: Koch Bus Solutions LP 4111 E 37th St North Wichita KS 67220

GREEN, SHIA TOBY RINER, therapist; b. N.Y.C.; d. Murray A. and Frances Riner; student CCNY; BA, Antioch Coll., MA, 1976; m. Gary S. Green, Sept. 4, 1957; children: Margot Laura, Vanessa Daryl, Garson Todd. Press. and legis. sec. U.S. Ho. of Reps., Washington, 1960-71; cons. Rehab. Services Adminstrn., Social and Rehab. Services, HEW, 1972-73; asst. dir. State of Md. Foster Care Impact Demonstration Project, 1977-78; therapist Alexandria (Va.) Narcotics Treatment Program, 1979-84, Assocs. Psychotherapy Ctrs., Gaithersburg, Md., 1984—; mem. treatment com. Alexandria Case Mgmt. and Treatment of Child Sexual Abuse. Mem. exec. bd. Children's Adoption Resource Exchange, Washington; vol. worker Girl Scouts U.S.A., also Boy Scouts Am., 1970-74. Diplomate Am. Coll. Forensic Examiners; mem. APA, Md. Psychol. Assn., Am. Assn. Marriage and Family Therapy. Co-author: Permanent Planning in Maryland— A Manual for the Foster Care Worker. Office: 8915 Shady Grove Ct Gaithersburg MD 20877-1308 Home: 21150 NE 38th Ave Apt 2804 Aventura FL 33180-4043

GREEN, SHIRLEY MOORE, retired public affairs and communications executive; b. Graham, Tex., Dec. 21, 1933; d. N. Edgar and Cora Day (Morrow) Moore; m. Paul M. Green, Aug. 26, 1967 (div. 1981); children: Ruth Lynn, Tracy Moore Anderson. Student, Midwestern U., Wichita Falls, Tex., 1952; BBA, U. Tex., 1956. Staff asst. Rep. Party, Austin, Tex., 1965-67; press asst. Bob Price U.S. Rep., Washington, 1967; coordinator Tex. and Ark. Bush for Pres. Campaign, Houston, 1979-80; dep. press sec.

V.p. Bush, Washington, 1980-85, acting press sec., 1983; dir. pub. affairs NASA, Washington, 1985-86, dep. assoc. adminstr. communications, 1987-89; spl. asst. to the Pres. White House, Washington, 1989-92, dep. asst. to Pres., 1992; dir. Pres. Bush Transition Office, Washington, 1993; dir. program support Internat. Rep. Inst., Washington, 1993-96; dir. corr. and constituent svcs. Gov. George W. Bush, Austin, 1996-2001; dir. comm. svcs. Atty Gen. John Cornyn, 2001—03. Local chmn. Jim Baker for Atty. Gen., 1978, Pres. Ford Com., San Antonio, 1976; trustee S.W. Found. Forum, San Antonio, 1974-78; bd. dirs. Child Welfare Bd. Bexar County, 1975-79. Recipient Exceptional Svc. medal NASA, 1989. Mem.: Tex. Fedn. Rep. Women (editor Partyline mag. 1969—72, one of 10 Outstanding Rep. Women Tex. 1979). Presbyterian. Avocations: reading, traveling. Home: 1513 W 30th St Austin TX 78703-1403

GREEN, SUZANNE LUNDY, music educator; b. Grants Pass, Oreg., May 27, 1965; d. Marvin Eugene and Maryann Lundy; m. Jonathan Samuel Green, Aug. 9, 2003; stepchildren: Matthew, Joshua. B in Music Edn., Willamette U., 1987; MusM, U. Ariz., 1993. Cert. tchr. Oreg., Wash. Choir dir. Roseburg (Oreg.) Pub. Schs., 1987—90, Banks (Oreg.) Sch. Dist., 1992—94; choir dir., program leader Jefferson Performing Arts, Portland, Oreg., 1993—96; choir dir. Scappoose (Oreg.) Sch. Dist., 1996—2003, Kent Sch. Dist., 2003—. Singer Counterpoint, 1996—. Music min. Epworth United Meth. Ch., Portland, 1993—2002. Tchg. grantee, U. Ariz., 1990—92, Collins scholar, Willamette U., 1984—87. Mem.: Music Educators Nat. Conf. (dist. 3 choir chair 2000—03), Oreg. Am. Choral Dirs. Assn. (membership chair 1999—2003), Oreg. Order of Amaranyth. Avocations: singing, reading, sewing, hiking. Home: 4011 S 181st St Seatac WA 98188

GREEN, TAMMIE, professional golfer; b. Somerset, Ohio, Dec. 17, 1959; Degree in recreation, Marshall U. Prol. golfer, 1986—. Mem. exec. com LPGA, 1992-94. Named Rookie of Yr. LPGA, 1987; 6 career wins including 1989 du Maurier Ltd. Classic, Healthsouth Palm Beach Classic, Rochester Internat., 1993, Youngstown-Warren LPGA Classic, 1994, Sprint Titleholder Champion, Gaintt Eagle LPGA Classic, 1997, LPGA Corning Classic, 1998. Avocations: fishing, gardening, horseback riding, sports. Home: 4990 Township Road 147 NE Somerset OH 43783-9753 Office: 3990 Twp Rd 147 Somerset OH 43783

GREENAWALD, SHERI, performing company executive; m. Alain Gourevitch (div.); 1 child, Madeline. Degree, U. No. Iowa; student in Profl. Studies, Juilliard Sch. Music. Vocal coach Santa Fe (N.Mex.) Apprentice Program, 1999, dir., 2000; prof. voice and opera Boston (Mass.) Conservatory, 2000—02; dir. San Francisco (Calif.) Opera Ctr., 2002—. Vis. artist U. Charleston; artist in residence U. No. Iowa. Singer: (Operas) San Francisco (Calif.) Opera, The Met. Opera, Lyric Opera Chgo., La Fenice, Munich State Opera, Welsh Nat. Opera, Netherlands Opera, Santa Fe (N.Mex.) Opera, LA (Calif.) Opera, others, (albums) Regina. Named Artist of Yr., Seattle (Wash.) Opera Assn., 1998; grantee, Rockefeller Found., NEA. Office: San Francisco Opera Center 301 Van Ness Ave San Francisco CA 94102-4509*

GREENAWALT, PEGGY FREED TOMARKIN, advertising executive; b. Cleve., Apr. 27, 1942; d. Bernard H. and Gyta Elinor (Arsham) Freed; m. Gary Tomarkin, Aug. 7, 1966 (div. 1981); children: Craig William, Eric Lawrence; m. William Sloan Greenawalt, Oct. 31, 1987; BS, Simmons Coll., 1964. Asst. account exec. Howard Marks/Norman, Craig & Kummel, Inc., N.Y.C., 1964-66; account exec. Shaw Bros. Advt. Co., N.Y.C., 1966-67; copywriter Claire Advt. Co., N.Y.C., 1967; ptnr. Copywriters Coop., Hartsdale, N.Y., 1970-73; copy chief Howard Marks Advt., N.Y.C., 1973-80; sr. copywriter Wunderman, Ricotta & Kline, N.Y.C., 1980-82; v.p., assoc. creative dir. Ayer-Direct (N.W. Ayer), N.Y.C., 1982-84; sr. v.p. creative dir. D'Arcy Direct (D'Arcy MacManus & Masius), N.Y.C., 1984-86; pres. Tomarkin/Greenawalt, Inc., N.Y.C., 1986—. Judge Echo Awards, Caples Awards, Fin. Comm. Soc. Awards. Author: Kiss, The Real Story, 1980. Dem. dist. leader. Mem. Direct Mktg. Assn., Women in Comms., Direct Mktg. Club N.Y., Westchester Assn. Women Bus. Owners (past pres.). Office: 24 Lewis Ave Hartsdale NY 10530 E-mail: pegdirect@aol.com.

GREENBERG, ARLINE FRANCINE, artist; b. N.Y.C. m. Sidney Greenberg. BA, Hunter Coll.; postgrad., NYU; AS, Parson Sch. Design, Pratt Inst. Ind. practice cons. firm in jewelry and design; v.p. Reliable Textile Co., N.Y.C.; fashion dir. Burlington Klopman Fabrics, N.Y.C., 1988-92. Guest lectr. AWED and Fashion Inst. Tech. Contbr. fashion articles to newspapers. Recipient Medal in Fine Arts; scholar NYU. Mem.: Citizens Union, Opera Guild, Smithsonian, Met. Mus. Art, Preservation Soc., Victorian Soc. N.Y.C. Avocations: travel, art, architecture, opera, music. Home: 555 Kappock St Apt 15D Bronx NY 10463-6458

GREENBERG, BARBARA LEVENSON, literature educator, poet; b. Boston, Aug. 27, 1932; d. Louis B Levenson, Esther Harrison Levenson; m. Harold L Greenberg; children: David A, Russell S. BA, Wellesley Coll., 1953; MA, Simmons Coll., 1973. Faculty MFA writing program Goddard Coll., Plainfield, Vt., 1976—80; faculty, mem. adv. bd. Warren Wilson MFA Program for Writers, Swannanoah, NC, 1981—83; faculty writing program MIT, Cambridge, Mass., 1988—90; sr. lectr. Suffolk U., Boston, 1998—2000; affiliated scholar Brandeis U. Women's Studies Rsch. Ctr., Waltham, 2000—. Author: (poems) The Spoils of August, 1974, The Never Not Sonnets, 1989, What Nell Knows, 1997, (short stories) Fire Drills, 1982.

GREENBERG, BONNIE LYNN, music industry executive; b. Roslyn Heights, N.Y., May 22, 1956; d. Morris U. Greenberg and Rozlyn (Wilner) Sadkin. BA, U. Denver, 1975; JD, Southwestern U., 1978. Bar: Calif. 1979, N.Y. 1980. Lawyer ABC Records, Inc., L.A., 1977-79; dir. bus. affairs MCA Records, Inc., Universal City, Calif., 1980-83, Paramount Pictures, 1984; co-chmn. Media MusiCons., L.A., 1988-93; CEO Ocean Cities Entertainment, Inc., Santa Monica, Calif., 1993—. Judge anti-drug video contest N.Y. Dept. Edn., 1988; prof. UCLA. Author: Negotiating Contracts in the Entertainment Industry, 1987, Music Volume; theatre prodr.: Getting Through the Night, 1985; music. supr. motion pictures include Hairspray, Book of Love, Menace II Society, The Mask, Corrina, Corrina, The Santa Clause, Flirting with Disaster, Dead Presidents, The Truth about Cats and Dogs, The Long Kiss Goodnight, My Best Friend's Wedding, Pleasantville, Parent Trap, The Muse, EdTV, How The Grinch Stole Christmas, What Women Want, Unconditional Love,Undercover Brother, Stuart Little 2. Atty. Bet Tzedek, L.A., 1987. Recipient Gov's. plaque N.Y., 1988. Democrat. Avocations: photography, sports, writing, languages, music.

GREENBERG, CAROL, poet; b. Yonkers, N.Y., June 8, 1927; married, June 17, 1951; children: Marc, Joel. Student, NYU, 1945—47. Design dir. Lenox Hill Industries, N.Y.C., 1947—53; fashion designer Rosenauch Bros. Cinderella, N.Y.C., 1960—71; fashion cons. A-Z Design, 1971—77; dir. women's div. ATA Textiles, Israel, 1979—83; dir. mktg. Allied Stores Internat., Israel, 1983—90; ret. Poet: In the Eye of the Jellyfish, 1982, Angels Knocking at the Back Door, 2002, Road to Recovery, 2003. E-mail: csoftah1@aol.com.

GREENBERG, CAROLYN PHYLLIS, anesthesiologist, educator; b. San Francisco, July 7, 1941; AB, Stanford U., 1962; MD, U. Calif., San Francisco, 1966. Diplomate Am. Bd. Anesthesiology. Rotating intern L.A. County Hosp., 1966-67; resident in anesthesiology Presbyn. Hosp., N.Y.C., 1967-69, vis. fellow in anesthesiology, 1969-70, asst. attending anesthesiologist, 1971-90, assoc. attending anesthesiologist, 1990-99, med. dir. ambulatory surgery, 1986-96, attending anesthesiologist, 1999; asst. attending anesthesiologist N.Y. Hosp., 1970-71; attending anesthesiologist N.Y. Presbyn. Hosp., 1999—. Instr. anesthesiology Cornell Med. Sch., 1970—71; assoc. anesthesiology Columbia U., N.Y.C., 1971—74, asst. prof. clin. anesthesiology, 1974—90, assoc. prof. clin. anesthesiology, 1990—99, prof. clin. anesthesiology, 1999, prof. emerita anesthesiology, 1999—; clin. prof. anesthesiology Cornell Med. Sch., 1999—. Contbr. book chpts., articles to profl. jours. Mem. Am. Soc. Anesthesiologists, N.Y. State Soc. Anesthesiologists (Media award 1992), Med. Soc. N.Y., Soc. Ambulatory Anesthesia (treas. 1994-98, 2nd v.p. 1998-99, 1st v.p. 1999, Ambulatory Anesthesia Rsch. Found. award 1992), Malignant Hyperthermia Assn. of U.S. (hotline cons. 1983-99, partnership award 1996). Jewish. Avocations: swimming, reading, piano, travel. E-mail: cgfcalvin@yahoo.com.

GREENBERG, ELINOR MILLER, university official, consultant; b. Bklyn., Nov. 13, 1932; d. Ray and Susan (Weiss) Miller; m. Manuel Greenberg, Dec. 26, 1955; children: Andrea, Julie, Michael. BA, Mt. Holyoke Coll., 1953; MA, U. Wis.-Madison, 1954; EdD, U. No. Colo., 1981; LittD (hon.), St. Mary-of-the-Woods, Ind., 1983; LHD (hon.), Profl. Sch. Psychology, Calif., 1987. Speech pathologist U. Colo., Denver, 1954—69, mem. faculty, 1967—69, exec. dir., 1969—71, Arapahoe Inst. for Cmty. Devel., 1969—71; founding dir. Univ. without Walls, Loretto Heights Coll., Denver, 1971—79, asst. acad. dean, 1982—84, asst. to pres., 1984—85; regional exec. officer Coun. for Adult and Experiential Learning, Chgo., 1979—91; founding exec. dir. US West Comm.-CWA, Pathways to the Future, 1986—91; rsch. assoc. Inst. for Rsch. on Adults in Higher Edn., U. Md., U. Coll., 1991; exec. dir. project leadership, 1986—. Project dir. Healthcare Seminars, Colo. Rural New Economy Initiative, 2000-02; pres., CEO EMG and Assocs.; sr. cons. US West Found., No. Telecom, Rose Found., Cogeoinfo., 1992-96; founding regional coord. Mountain and Plains Partnership, 1996-2002; adminstr. Visible Human Project-Undergrad. Edit., U. Colo. Health Scis. Ctr., 2002—04; cons. NEON Project, Western Interstate Commn. for Higher Edn., 2003—, NEAT Project, U. Wis., 2003—; cons. in field. Co-editor, contbr.: Educating Learners of All Ages, 1980; co-author: Designing Undergraduate Education, 1981, Widening Ripples, 1986, Leading Effectively, 1987, In Our Fifties: Voices of Men and Women Reinventing Their Lives, 1993, MAPP Online Voices, 2000; editor, contbr.: New Partnerships: Higher Education and the Nonprofit Sector, 1982, Enhancing Leadership, 1989, Liberal Education Journal, 1992; author: Weaving: The Fabric of a Woman's Life, 1991, Journey for Justice, 1994; guest editor Liberal Edn., 1992; gen. editor Seven MAPP Studies, 2002; feature writer Colo. Woman News, 1993-96, Women's Bus. News, 1995-96; contbr. Sculpting The Learning Organization, 1993; contbr. articles to profl. jours. Bd. dirs., exec. com. Anti Defamation League of B'nai B'rith, Denver, 1981-99, chair women's leadership com., 1991-93, bd. dirs., 1985-95; mem. Colo. State Bd. for C.C. and Occupl. Edn., 1981 86, vice-chair, 1984-85; bd. dirs. Internat. Women's Forum, 1986-88, Internat. Women's Forum Leadership Found., 1991-95, Griffith Ctr., Golden, Colo., 1982-86, Colo. Bd. Continuing Legal and Jud. Edn., 1984-96; pres. Women's Forum of Colo., 1986; v.p. Women's Forum Colo. Found., 1987; adv. bd. Anchor Ctr. Blind Child, Colo. Coalition Prevention Nuclear War, Mile Hi Girl Scouts, Nat. Conf. on Edn. for Women's Devel.; cmty. adv. bd. Colo. Woman News; adv. com. Colo. Pvt. Occupl. Sch., 1990-98, Colo. Cmty. Incentive Fund; co-chair Gov.'s Women's Econ. Devel. Taskforce, Women's Econ. Devel. Coun., 1988-96; bd. visitors U. Hosp., U. Colo., 1990-91, gov. apptd. Colo. Math., Sci. and Tech Commn. chair 1991-93 co-telecom, adv. commn. TAC 14, chair, 1993-95; founding steering com. Colo. Women's Leadership Coalition, 1988-96; mem. interdisciplinary telecomm. program, exec. bd. U. Colo., 1992-2003; U.S. Dept. Edn., mem. Tech. Panels, 1991—, mem. Expert Panel on Lifelong Learning, 1999—, Western AHEC Reg. Learning System, chair, coursework com., 1998; bd. dirs. Colo. Rural Tech. Program, 1996-2000, Housing for All/Metro Denver Fair Housing Ctr., 1999-2003, chair, 2002-03; chair Colo. Coalition for the Advancement of Telehealth, 2002-03; co-chair Colo. Coun. on Telehealth, 2003; mem. U. Physicians Inc. Task Force on Telehealth, 2003; mem. industry adv bd. MESA, 2002—. Named Citizen of Yr., Omega Psi Phi, Denver, 1966, Woman of Decade Littleton Ind. Newspapers, 1970; grantee W. K. Kellogg Found., 1982, Weyerhaeuser Found., 1986, Fund for Improvement of Post Secondary Edn., 1977, 80, Robert Wood Johnson Found., 1997-2002; recipient Sesquicentennial award Mt. Holyoke Coll. Alumni Assn., 1987, Minoru Yasui Cmty. Vol. award, 1991, Women of Excellence award Colo. Women's Leadership Coalition, 1996, Founding Mothers award, 1997, Woman of Dist., Mile High Girl Scouts, 1997, Martin Luther King Disting. Svc. award to Little Coun. for Human Rels., Arapahoe C.C., 2003, Arthur and Bea Branscombe Meml. award Housing for All: The Metro Denver Fair Housing Ctr., 2003. Mem. Am. Assn. for Higher Edn., Assn. for Experiential Edn. (editl. bd. 1978-80), Am. Speech, Lang. and Hearing Assn., Colo. Rural Devel. Coun., Nat. Conf. Women's Devel. Edn., Kappa Delta Pi. Democrat. Jewish. Home: 6725 S Adams Way Littleton CO 80122-1801 E-mail: ellie.greenberg@uchsc.edu.

GREENBERG, EVA MUELLER, librarian; b. Vienna, July 19, 1929; came to U.S., 1939; d. Paul and Greta (Scheuer) Mueller; m. Nathan Abraham Greenberg, June 22, 1952; children: David Stephen, Judith Helen, Lisa Pauline. AB, Harvard/Radcliffe Coll., 1951; MLS, Kent State U., 1975. Head reference McIntire Libr., Zanesville, Ohio, 1978; with Lorain (Ohio) Pub. Libr., 1978-81; head reference Elyria (Ohio) Pub. Libr., 1981-82; reference libr. adult svcs. Cuyahoga County Pub. Libr., Strongsville, Ohio, 1983-89; head adult svcs. Oberlin (Ohio) Pub. Libr., 1989—. Contbr. articles to profl. jours. Grantee Ohio Humanities Coun. for Pub. Programs; named Libr. of Yr., Ohio Support Svcs., 2000. Mem. ALA, Ohio Libr. Assn. (coord. community info. task force). Home: 34 S Cedar St Oberlin OH 44074-1520 Office: Oberlin Pub Libr 65 S Main St Oberlin OH 44074-1673

GREENBERG, HINDA FEIGE, library director; b. Bayreuth, Germany, Feb. 26, 1947; arrived in U.S., 1951; d. Samuel Leon and Sima (Schampagnere) F.; m. Joseph Lawrence, July 6, 1968; children: David Micah, Jacob Alexander. BA, Temple U., 1969; MLS, Rutgers U., 1981; PhD, Drexel U., 1999. Assoc. librarian Ednl. Testing Svc., Princeton, NJ, 1981-86; dir. info. ctr. Carnegie Found., Princeton, 1986-97, Robert Wood Johnson Found., Princeton, 1997—. Pres. Consortium of Found. Librs. Avocation: travel.

GREENBERG, JUDITH HOROVITZ, genetics and developmental biology administrator; b. Phila., Apr. 2, 1947; d. Monty B. and Evelyn (Cohen) Horovitz; m. Warren Greenberg, June 8, 1969; 1 child, Elyssa H. BS in Biology, U. Pitts., 1967; MA in Biology, Boston U., 1970; PhD in Biology, Bryn Mawr Coll., 1972. Rsch. assoc. ARC, Bethesda, Md., 1971—74; postdoctoral fellow NIH, Bethesda, 1974—75, sr. staff fellow, 1975—81, health scientist adminstr., 1981—88; dir. divsn. genetics and devel. biology NIH, Nat. Inst. Gen. Med. Scis., Bethesda, 1988—; acting dir. Nat. Inst. Gen. Med. Scis. NIH, Bethesda, 2002—03. Recipient Pub. Health Svc. Spl. Recognition award, 1991, Presdl. Meritorious Exec. award, 1999. Mem. Soc. Devel. Biology, Am. Soc. Cell Biology, Am. Soc. Human Genetics, AAAS, Sigma Xi. Office: NIGMS NIH 45 Center Dr Bldg 45 Bethesda MD 20892-6200 E-mail: greenbej@nigms.nih.gov.

GREENBERG, KATE, telecommunications industry executive; CFO Justice Tech. Corp., Culver City, Calif., Fastpoint Canon, L.A., 1999—. Office: Fastpoint Canon 5777 Century Blvd Ste 60 Los Angeles CA 90045 Fax: (310) 526-2100.

GREENBERG, LENORE, public relations professional; b. Flushing, N.Y. d. Jack and Frances Orenstein. BA, Hofstra U.; MS, SUNY. Dir .pub. rels. Bloomingdale's, Short Hills, N.J., 1977-78; dir. comms. N.J. Sch. Bds. Assn., Trenton, 1978-82; dir pub. info. N.J. State Dept. Edn., Trenton, 1982-90; assoc. exec. dir. Nat. Sch. Pub. Rels. Assn., Arlington, Va., 1990-91; pres. Lenore Greenberg & Assocs., Inc., 1991—. Adj. prof. pub. rels. Rutgers U. Freelance feature writer N.Y. Times. Mem. bd. assocs. McCarter Theatre, Princeton, N.J.; mem. Franklin Twp. Zoning Bd. Adjustment; mem. Franklin Twp. Human Rels. Commn.; chair Somerset County LWV; instr. Bus. Vols. for the Arts. Recipient award Am. Soc. Assn. Execs., award Women in Comms., award Internat. Assn. Bus. Communicators; Gold Medallion awrd Nat. Sch. Pub. Rels. Assn. Mem. Pub. Rels. Soc. Am. (accredited; pres. N.J. State chpt., nat. nominating and accreditation coms., Silver Anvil award), Nat. Health/Edn. Consortium. Home and Office: 30971 Carrara Rd Laguna Niguel CA 92677-2757

GREENBERG, LINDA I. education educator, volunteer, educator; b. Hanover, Pa., June 8, 1941; d. Richard Barnhart and Lillian (Shaffer) Garrett; m. Frederic Greenberg, Apr. 2, 1966; children: Timothy, Richard, Joshua. BA, Buckness Univ., Lewisburg, Pa., 1963; MA, Columbia Univ., NY, NY, 1964. Asst. prof., speech and theatre Montclair State Coll., Montclair, NJ, 1964—70; actor, children's theatre Pushcart Players, Caldwell, NJ, 1972—73; tchr. John Robert Power Sch., NYC, 1964—67, NY Bus. Sch., NYC, 1967—68; adj. prof. Fairleigh Dickinson Univ., Rutherford, NJ, 1991—93, Montclair State Univ., Montclair, NJ, 1993—99, ret., 1999. Singer: (oratorio) NY Oratorio Soc., 1964—69; performer: (plays) Caldwell Players, 1970—74; singer: (oratorio) NJ Oratorio Soc., 1970—74; performer: (plays) Caldwell Players, 1980, Glen Ridge Cmty. Players, 1991. Trustee Bucknell Univ., Lewisburg, Pa., 1995—, alumni bd. dir., 1991—95. Mem.: ednl. organizations (v.p.), Assn. of Gov. Bd. (AGB), Assn. of Univ. Women (AAUW), Turnip Theatre (bd. mem. 1990—2000), Arts Coun. of the Essex Area (v.p. 1973—80), Jr. League of Montclair (pres. 1976—78), art organizations (v.p.). Jewish. Avocations: singing, travel, reading, attending concerts and theatre, museums. Home: 17027 Flying Fish Lane Sugarloaf FL 33042 also: 45 E 89th St Apt 31E NY NY 10128

GREENBERGER, ELLEN, psychologist, educator; b. N.Y.C., Nov. 19, 1935; d. Edward Michael and Vera (Brisk) Silver; m. Michael Burton, Aug. 26, 1979; children by previous marriage[00bf] Kari Edwards, David Silver. BA, Vassar Coll., 1956; MA, Harvard U., 1959, PhD, 1961. Instr. Wellesley (Mass.) Coll., 1961—67; sr. rsch. scientist Johns Hopkins U., Balt., 1967-76; prof. psychology and social behavior U. Calif., Irvine, 1976—. Author: (with others) When Teenagers Work, 1986; contbr. articles to profl. jours. USPHS fellow, 1956-59; Margaret Floy Washburn fellow, 1956-58; Ford Found. grantee, 1979-81; Spencer Found. grantee, 1979-81, 87, 88-91. Fellow Am. Psychol. Assn., Am. Psychol. Soc.; mem. Soc. Rsch. in Child Devel., Soc. Rsch. on Adolescent Devel. Office: U Calif 3340 Social Ecology II Irvine CA 92697-7085 Office Phone: 949-824-6328. Business E-Mail: egreenbe@uci.edu.

GREENBERGER, MARSHA MOSES, sales executive; b. Lakewood, N.J., Mar. 15, 1943; d. Bernard David and Ethel (Gordon) Moses; m. Paul Edward Greenberger (div. 1969); 1 child, Nathan Scott. Student, Kent (Ohio) State U., 1961-62. Mgr. gen. sales Ellison Products, Fairfield, N.J., 1972-79; gen. mgr. Indsl. Maintenance Corp., Cherry Hill, N.J., 1979-83; co-owner corp. sect. Ven-Mar Sales, Inc., Blairstown, N.J., 1983-89; pres. MGM Sales, Inc., 1989—. Avocations: skiing, world travel, egyptology. Office: MGM Sales 29 High Ridge Rd Randolph NJ 07869 4567

GREENBLATT, MIRIAM, writer, editor, educator; b. Berlin; d. Gregory and Shifra (Zemach) Baraks; m. Howard Greenblatt (div.). BA magna cum laude, Hunter Coll.; postgrad., U. Chgo. Editor Am. People's Ency., Chgo., 1957-58, Scott Foresman & Co., Chgo., 1958-62; pres. Creative Textbooks, Chgo., 1972—. Tchr. New Trier (Ill.) HS, 1978—81. Author (with Chu): The Story of China, 1968; author: (with Cuban) (book) Japan, 1971; author: The History of Itasca, 1976; author: (with others) The American People, 1986; author: James Knox Polk, 1988, Franklin Delano Roosevelt, 1989, John Quincy Adams, 1990; author: (with Welty) The Human Expression, 1992; author: Cambodia, 1995; author: (with Jordan and Bowes) The Americans, 1996; author: Hatshepsut and Ancient Egypt, 2000, Alexander the Great and Ancient Greece, 2000, Augustus and Imperial Rome, 2000, Peter the Great and Tsarist Russia, 2000; author: (with Lemmo) Human Heritage, 2001; author: Genghis Khan and the Mongol Empire, 2002, Elizabeth I and Tudor England, 2002, The War of 1812, 2003, Iran, 2003, Charlemagne and the Early Middle Ages, 2003, Suleyman the Magnificent and the Ottoman Empire, 2003, Lorenzo de Medici and Renaissance Italy, 2003, Afghanistan, 2003; editl. cons. Peoples and Cultures Series, 1976—78, subject area cons. World Geography and Cultures, 1994; contbg. editor: A World History, 1979. Mem. nat. exec. coun. Am. Jewish Com., 1980—84, v.p. Chgo chpt., 1977—79; treas. Glencoe Youth Svcs., 1981—83. Mem.: Cliff Dwellers, Nat. Assn. Scholars. Jewish. Address: 2754 Roslyn Ln Highland Park IL 60035-1408

GREENE, ADELE S. management consultant; b. Newark; d. Adolph and Sara (Schubert) Shuminer; m. Alan Greene (div.); 1 child, Joshua. Student, Juilliard Sch. Music, 1942-44, NYU, 1942-44, New Sch. Social Research, 1944-47; diploma in mgmt., Harvard Bus. Sch., 1978. Account exec. Ruder and Finn Inc., N.Y.C., 1964-66, sr. assoc., 1966-68, v.p., 1968-72, sr. v.p., 1972-76; v.p. pub. affairs Corp. Pub. Broadcasting, Washington, 1976-78; pres., CEO TV Program Group, Washington, 1978-80; pres. Greene and Assocs., N.Y.C., 1981—. Exec. dir. Am. Friends of Brit. Mus., 1994—; instr. pub. relations and community affairs, NYU 1974-76; bd. dirs. Sci. Program Group, Washington 1976-81; treas., bd. dirs. Coliseum Park Apts. Co-author: Teen-Age Leadership, 1971. Advisor The Acting Co., Understudies, N.Y.C., 1987—; pres., CEO Am. Craft Coun., 1980-81, trustee, 1976-81; bd. dirs. Union Settlement, N.Y.C., 1987-90; trustee Duke Ellington Sch. Arts, Washington, 1977-81, Inst. for Cancer Prevention, 2002—. Mem. Pub. Relations Soc. Am. (silver anvil award 1971), Nat. Assn. Edn. Broadcasters, Am. Women Radio and TV. Home and Office: 30 W 60th St New York NY 10023-7902

GREENE, ANNIE LUCILLE, artist, retired art educator; b. Waycross, Ga. d. Henry William and Ella Mae (Hall) Tarver; m. Oliver Nathaniel Greene; children: Zinta LaRecia Greene Perkins, Oliver N. Greene, Jr. BS, Albany State Coll., 1954; MA, NYU, 1961. Art tchr. Thomasville (Ga.) Sch. Sys., 1954—55, Troup County Sch. Sys., LaGrange, Ga., 1955—89; ret., 1989. Apptd. mem. Ga. Humanities Coun., 2002—. 34 one-woman art shows, 1976—, 112 group exhbns., 1962— (numerous awards). Past mem. Neighborhood Housing Svcs. Pub. Rels. com.; Grand Marshall Sweet Land of Liberty July 4th Parade, LaGrange, 2001; pianist St. Paul African Meth. Episcopal Ch. and McGhee Chapel African Meth. Episcopal Ch., Hogansville, Ga., trustee, chmn. stewardship and fin. commn.; bd. dirs. March of Dimes, 1991—; bd. mem. Keep Troup Beautiful, 1997—2001; past bd. dirs. LaGrange Meml. Libr. Named one of Gracious Ladies of Ga., 1998; recipient Outstanding Svc., St. Paul A.M.C. Ch., 2000, Ch. Citizen of Yr. award, McGhee Chapel A.M.E. Ch., 1999. Mem.: LaGrange Symphony Guild, LaGrange Artist Guild, Chattahoochee Valley Art Mus. (past bd. mem.), Troup Ret. Tchrs. Assn. (past sect.), The Links, Inc. (Outstanding Svc. award 1987, parliamentarian 1999—2001, Presdl. award 2001, LaGrange chpt., Outstanding Svc. award 1987, Presdl. award 2001), Delta Sigma Theta (pres. 1991—93, LaGrange Alumnae chpt. Presdl. awards 1993—97, pres. 1995—97, Annie B. Singleton award 2000, fund raiser chair 2001—03, LaGrange Alumnae chpt. Presdl. awards 1993—97, Annie B. Singleton award 2000, numerous other awards). Avocations: music, crafts, reading, photography, travel. Home: 712 Pyracantha Dr Lagrange GA 30241

GREENE, AURELIA, state legislator; b. N.Y.C., Oct. 26, 1934; d. Edward Henry and Sybil Elaine (Russell) Holley; children: Rhonda, Russell; m. 2d, Jerome Alexander Greene, Apr. 18, 1975. B.A., Rutgers U., 1974. Dep.

exec. dir. Morrisania Community Corp., N.Y.C., 1969-76; exec. dir. Bronx Area Policy Bd. No. 6, N.Y.C., 1980-82; mem. N.Y. State Assembly, 1982—, now asst. majority leader, 77th assembly dist. chair Assembly Standing Com. on Banking. Dist. leader 76th Assembly Dist., Bronx, 1990-92; sec. Bronx County Dem. Party, 1980—, mem. exec. com.; exec. [illegible] Dem. Nat. Conv., 1984, mem. credentials com. Dem. Nat. Conv., Atlanta, 1988, N.Y.C., 1992, Chgo., 1996. Mem. Bronx NAACP (Woman of Yr. award 1974). Democrat. also: Legis Office Bldg Rm 939 Albany NY 12248-0001

GREENE, BERNADETTE, media specialist; d. Walter and Earlene Greene; 1 child, Arabihah Nicole Ali. BS, U. Montevallo, Ala., 1996; MS in Libr. and Info. Studies, U. Ala., Tuscaloosa, 2001. 5th grade tchr. Birmingham (Ala.) City Sch., 1997—2000, media specialist, 2000—.

GREENE, CLAUDIA, education associate; b. Orangeburg, S.C., Aug. 16, 1947; d. Joseph Elijah Randolph and Mazie Stephens; m. Kaponden McKinley, June 13, 1972; children: Karen Denise, Kory McKinley. BA in Elem. Edn., S.C. State U., Orangeburg, 1969, MA in Spl. Edn., 1973, EdD in Edn. Adminstrn., 1990. Notary pub., S.C. Tchr. Colleton County Schs., Walterboro, S.C., 1969-70, Dillon County Schs., Dillon, S.C., 1970-71, Orangeburg Dist. I, Branchville, S.C., 1971-73; tchr., supr. Calhoun County Schs., St. Matthews, S.C., 1973-83; tchr. Orangeburg Dist. 5, 1983-92; edn. assoc. S.C. State Dept. Edn., Columbia, 1992—. Vis. prof. S.C. State U., Orangeburg, summers 1984-86. Adminstr. TEAM program St. Paul Bapt. Ch., Orangeburg, 1993—. Mem. NAACP, Coun. for Exceptional Children (Spl. Educator award 1999), Am. Bus. Women;s Assn., Protection an Advocacy. Avocations: reading, gardening, fishing, tutoring, teaching. Home: 544 Rosemont Dr Orangeburg SC 29115-2137 Office: State Dept Edn 1429 Senate St Columbia SC 29201-3730 E-mail: csgreene@sde.state.sc.us.

GREENE, CYNTHIA BAIN, elementary school educator; b. Charlotte, N.C., July 3, 1946; d. James Britton and Kennon Pettus Bain; m. L. Thomas Greene, May 12, 1984; 1 stepchild, T. Jason. BS, Radford Coll., 1968; postgrad., George Mason U., U. Va., Shenandoah U. Tchr. Prince William County Schs., Woodbridge, Va., 1968—85, Haymarket, Va., 1985—2001. Avocations: antiques, interior decorating, reading, travel, singing. Home: 8385 Lunsford Rd Warrenton VA 20187

GREENE, DIANE, information technology executive; m. Mendel Rosenblum. BS in mech. engring., U. Calif., Berkeley; M in computer sci. and naval architecture, MIT. Joined Sybase, 1986; various tech. leadership positions Tandem, Silicon Graphics Inc.; co-founder, CEO Vxtreme (sold to Microsoft Corp.), Palo Alto, Calif., 1995—98; founder, pres. VMware (sub. of EMC), 1998—. Named one of 50 Most Powerful People in Networking, Network World mag., 2003. Office: VMware Inc 3145 Porter Dr Palo Alto CA 94304 Office Phone: 650-475-5000., 877-486-9273. Office Fax: 650-475-5005.*

GREENE, ELINORE ASCHAH, speech and drama professional, writer; b. Springfield, Mass., Oct. 14, 1928; d. Harry Joshua and Esther Gertrude (Cohen) Ziff; m. Kermit Greene, June 29, 1947; children: Clifford M., Laura L., William L. B of Lit. Interpretation, Emerson Coll., Boston, 1949. Dramatic interpreter Margaret E. Richardson Lect. Agy., Boston, 1950s, Flora Frame Lect. Bureau, Boston, 1960s; speech tchr. Academie Moderne, Boston, early 1970s, pvt. practice, Newton, MA, 1975-87, speech cons., 1985-89; writer, dir. Newton, 1989—. Presenter in field; voice-overs radio, TV, indsl. Author: (children's stories) AIM, Lollipops, Happiness, The Communique, Players, 1970—80, (poetry) Creative Urge, Dark Starr, Dreams; reviewer books: ; contbr. voice-overs. Brandeis women's com. and aid to speech therapy Emerson Coll. Mem. Aid to Speech Therapy Found. (pres. 1970s, bd. dirs. 1960s, Advocate Rose award 1975), Mass. Comm. of Boston, Am. Fedn. Theatre-Radio-TV Assns., Nat. Writers Orgn. (sr. mem.), Orgn. for Rehab. through Tng. (life), Hadassah. Avocations: family, music, composing greeting cards, reading, theater.

GREENE, ENID, retired congresswoman; b. San Rafael, Calif., Oct. 5, 1958; BS in Pol. Sci., U. Utah, 1980; JD, Brigham Young U., 1983. Caseworker, rsch. asst. U.S. Rep. Dan Marriott, R., 1980; atty. Ray, Quinney & Nebeker, 1983-90; dep. chief of staff Gov. Norman H. Bangerter, 1990-92; corp. counsel Novell, Inc., 1993-94; mem. 104th Congress from 2nd Utah dist., Washington, 1995-97; atty. Smith & Glauser, Salt Lake City, 1998—. Office: Smith & Glauser PC 7351 Union Park Ave #200 Midvale UT 84047-1870

GREENE, GAIL PURCHASE, medical/surgical nurse; b. Northampton, Mass., Dec. 17, 1951; d. Albion Francis and Helen Loretta (Golash) Purchase; m. Paul Franklin Greene, Sept. 2, 1972; children: Stephanie Lynn, Paul Franklin Jr. BSN cum laude, U. South Fla., 1982; AA, Greenfield C.C., 1971. Lic. LPN 1972, Internat. Bd. Lactation Cons. Staff nurse East Pasco Med. Ctr., Zephyr Hills, Fla., 1982—88, Humana Hosp. Pasco, Dade City, Fla., 1988, Hosp. Corp. Am. Raulerson Hosp., Okeechobee, Fla., 1988-89, Tucson Med. Ctr., 1989—2000, Meml. Med. Ctr., Savannah, Ga., 2000—. Office: Meml Hosp Univ Med Ctr Inc Mother Baby Unit 4700 Waters Ave Savannah GA 31403

GREENE, JANE, health educator; b. L.A., Apr. 14, 1954; d. Ben Louis and Julie Eisen Cohen; m. Russell Edward Greene, Jan. 3, 1981; children: Rachael, Lisa, Joshua. Student, UCLA, 1971-75, MSN, 1981-83; BSN, Calif. State U., Long Beach, 1978. Cert. pediat. nurse practitioner. Dietitian's asst. Century City Hosp., L.A., 1972-76; nurses aide Long Beach (Calif.) Cmty. Hosp., 1976-78; charge nurse oncology dept. Children's Hosp. Orange County, Orange, Calif., 1978-80; staff nurse Children's Hosp. Boston, 1980-81, Cedars Sinai Med. Ctr., L.A., 1981-83; pediat. instr. Washburn U. Sch. Nursing, Topeka, 1983-85; mem. fitness staff Popeyes Cardiofitness, Topeka, 1988-90; phys. edn. instr., tchr. Topeka Collegiate Sch., 1991—94; tchr. Pediatrics PA, 1990—96, nurse practitioner, 1990-96; teen health instr. Topeka Collegiate Sch., 1996—2001. Girls varsity basketball coach Bellflower (Calif.) H.S., 1975, 76; basketball boach Topeka Collegiate Sch., 1995-97, volleyball coach, 1996-98. Candidate for Kans. Legislature, 1994; asst. coach Woman's Jr. Nat. AAU, 1997; v.p. Temple Beth Sholom, 1997-99, pres., 1999; asst. varsity basketball and softball Tarbut V'Topah Sch., 2001. Named to U.S. Olympic Festival Team, Amateur Racquetball Assn., 1993; Allstate Ins. scholar, 1977-78, Auxilary of Garfield Hosp. nursing scholar, 1977-78. Mem. Nat. Assn. Pediat. Nurse Practitioners, Kans. Nurses Assn., Am. Amateur Racquetball Assn. (Kans. Women's Open State Champion 11 yrs.). Democrat. Jewish. Avocations: racquetball, tennis, jogging, biking, skiing. Home: 6800 SW Aylesbury Rd Topeka KS 66610-1442

GREENE, JUDY, elementary school educator; b. Pikeville, Ky., June 9, 1945; d. Patton and Ella Syck; m. David Keith Greene, Jan. 23, 1965; 1 child, Byron Keith. BS, Pikeville Coll., 1968; MA Morehead State U., 1978. Tchr. Pike County Schs., Pikeville, Ky., 1966—67, Zane Trace Schs., Chillicothe, Ohio, 1968—69, Huntington Schs., 1969—. Exec. com. Ohio Edn. Assn., Columbus, 1988—2002; bd. dirs. NEA, Washington, 1994—2002. Lobbyist NEA, Washington, 1994—2002. Mem.: Nat. Coun. Accreditation Tchr. Edn. (bd.examiners 2001—04). Democrat. Avocations: reading, gardening, travel, scrapbooks, writing. Home: 1256 Mingo Rd Chillicothe OH 45601 E-mail: jmg4nea@bright.net.

GREENE, KAREN SANDRA, actress, educator, singer; b. N.Y.C., Jan. 7, 1942; d. Nathan and Natalie (Barashick) Stein; m. Richard Greene, July 1, 1962 (div. 1980); children: Barry Randall, Lauren Jennifer. BA, U. Conn., 1988. Singer, dancer, Broadway actress, N.Y.C., 1960-62; pres., educator Karen Greene Studios, A Class Act, Tigre Prodns., Norwalk, Conn., 1962—; pres. Front Row Ctr. for Performing Arts, 1993—; pres., dir. voice On Stage Acad., Ltd., Westport, Conn., 1982-84; educator voice Norwalk Cmty. Coll.; dir., educator theater arts Westport YMCA, 1981-85. Educator Temple Shalom, Norwalk, 1977-87; dir. theater arts Bridgeport (Conn.) Jewish Ctr., 1985; dir. Norwalk Jewish Ctr., 1985, Wilton (Conn.) Children's Theater, 1988-90; educator music and drama St. Luke's Sch., New Canaan, Conn., 1989-90; educator voice, acting, adult edn. Norwalk and Westport (Conn.) Bds. Edn., 1974—; dir., educator Curtain Call, Stamford, Conn., 1996—. Voiceover artist nat. performing tours; dir., vocalist soc. band Shades of Greene. Founding mem., chmn. Norwalk Soc. for Arts, 1999; coord. Southwestern Conn. Women's Issues Conf., 1988; active women's equal rights, pro-choice, NOW, Women's Empowerment, Fairfield County, Conn.; active animal rights advocate; Conn. rep. Friends of Animals, others; founding mem., sec. The Greater Norwalk Coun. of the Arts, Conn., 1996—; dir., educator improvisation conquering stage fright program Norwalk H.s., 1999—; educator, dir. Westport (Conn.) Summer Teen Mus. Theater, 19990—, Greenwich (Conn.) Acad., 1997—. Mem. NOW, AFTRA, SAG, Actor's Equity Assn., Internat. Platform Assn., Internat. TV Assn., Women's Empowerment, N.E. Anti-Vivisect. Soc. (Conn. rep.), People for the Ethical Treatment of Animals (Conn. rep.), Greenpeace (Conn. rep.), Best Friends Animal Sanctuary. Avocations: art, animals, holistic healing, reiki ii, mariel. Home and Office: 4 Suburban Dr Norwalk CT 06851-1612

GREENE, LAURA HELEN, physicist; b. Cleve., June 12, 1952; d. Sam and Frances (Kain) G.; children: Max Greene Giannetta, Leo Greene Giannetta. BS cum laude in Physics, Ohio State U., 1974, MS in Physics, 1978; MS in Exptl. Physics, Cornell U., 1980, PhD in Physics, 1984. Mem. tech. staff Hughes Aircraft Co., Torrance, Calif., 1974-75; teaching asst. Ohio State U., Columbus, 1975-76, rsch. asst., 1976-77; teaching asst. Cornell U., Ithaca, N.Y., 1977-79, rsch. asst., 1979-83; postdoctoral mem. tech. staff Bellcore (formerly Bell Labs.), Red Bank, N.J., 1983-85, Murray Hill, N.J., 1983-85, mem. tech. staff Red Bank, N.J., 1985-92; prof. dept. physics U. Ill., Urbana, 1992—, Swanlund endowed chair, 2000, Ctr. for Advanced Study resident assoc., 2000—. Beckman assoc. Ctr. Advanced Study U Ill. at Urbana-Champaign, 1996-97, mem. provost's com. on sexual harassment edn., 1999-2000, mem. physics adv. com., 1999—; mem. McMillan award com. 1994-96, chair, 1995-97; co-chair Gordon Rsch. Conf., 1996, chair, 1998; mem.-at-large Coun. Gordon Rsch. Confs., 1999—, mem. schedule and selection com.; mem. Basic Energy Scis. Adv. Com., 2000; interim and founding bd. trustee Inst. for Complex and Adaptive Materials, Los Alamos and U. Calif.; mem. various rev. panels and workshops NSF and Dept. Energy; presenter in field; resident assoc. ctr. for advanced study U. Ill., Urbana, Ill., 2000-2001; review panel Can. Inst. Advanced Rsch., Superconductivity Review, 2002; mem. provost com. sexual harrassment edn. U. Ill., 1999-2001, oversight com. for vice chancellor rsch., U. Ill., 2001-2002, Sloan Found. Selection Com. for Physics, 2001—; adv. com. Sec. of Energy Bill Richardson, 2000—; chair external rev. panel, mem. bd. trustees Ctr. Integrated Nahotechnologies Nat. Lab., Los Alamos NAt. Lab., Sandia Nat. Lab. Contbr. over 200 articles to profl. jours.; presenter over 150 domestic and internat. invited talks. Mem. selection com. in physics Sloan Found. Recipient Beckman award U. Ill. Campus Rsch. Bd., 1993, E.O. Lawrence award Dept. Energy, 1999, 2001; rsch. grantee NSF, 1991—, ONR, 1995—, Dept. Energy, 1995—. Fellow AAAS (electorate nominating com. of sect. B physics 2000—, chmn. nominating com. for physics, 2001-02), Am. Acad. Arts and Scis., Am. Phys. Soc. (gen. councilor 1992—, congl. fellow screening com. 1993, exec. bd. 1995—, com. on coms. 1995—, chair 1997, search com. The Phys. Rev. 1996, nominating com. divsn. condensed matter physics 1998—, Maria Goeppert-Mayer award 1994, Centennial Spkr. 1997); mem. Materials Rsch. Soc. (symposium chair 1992), Am. Assn. Physics Tchrs., Internat. Union Pure and Applied Physicists (commr., U.S. liaison com. 1996—, U.S. del. to Low-Temperature Physics Commn. 1996—), Phi Kappa Phi. Avocations: children, physics, working out, music. Office: U Ill Loomis Lab Physics 1110 W Green St Urbana IL 61801-9013 E-mail: lhg@uiuc.edu.

GREENE, LILIANE, French language and literature educator, editor; b. Salonica, Greece, Oct. 10, 1928; came to U.S., 1941; d. Maurice and Daisy (Kohn) Massarano; m. Thomas McLernon Greene, May 20, 1950; children: Philip James, Christopher George, Francis Richard BA, Hunter Coll., 1948; MA, Columbia U., 1949; PhD, Yale U., 1969. Asst. in instrn. French Yale U., New Haven, 1964-65, instr., 1967-68, lectr., mng. editor Yale French Studies, 1980-94 (ret.); instr. Conn. Coll., New London, 1968-69, asst. prof., 1970-75. Contbr. articles to profl. jours. Fullbright fellow, 1949-50. Mem. MLA, Am. Assn. Tchrs. French, Ctr. Ind. Study (founding mem., pres. 1978-79, bd. dirs. 1977-89), Conn. Acad. of Arts and Scis. Democrat. Avocations: travel, theater. Home: 125 Livingston St New Haven CT 06511-2428

GREENE, LIZA M, creative services director, writer; b. Hartford, Conn. d. Walter L and Nancy R Greene; m. Robert A Pondiscio, Feb. 4, 1995. BFA, Carnegie Mellon U., Pittsburgh, Pennsylvania, 1976. Artist Nat. Conversational Software Systems, Westport, Conn., 1976—78; graphic designer Simon & Schuster, New York City, NY, 1978—79, People Mag., New York City, NY, 1979—89; art dir. Time Mag., New York City, NY, 1989—95, creative services dir., 1995—. Lectr. Cooper Union, New York City, NY, 1995—95. Author: New York for New Yorkers: A Historical Treasury and Guide to the Buildings and Monuments of Manhattan, 2001. Avocation: scuba diving.

GREENE, LYDIA ABBI JWUAN, elementary school educator; b. La Fayette, Tenn, Sept. 20, 1963; d. Thomas and Icy (Daniel) G. BSBA, Tenn. State U., 1985, M in Elem. Edn., 1993; MLIS, Trevecca NAzarene U., 2001. Customer svc. rep. JC Penney Telemarketing Ctr., Nashville, 1986-93; tchr. Paragon Mills Elem. Sch., Nashville, 1993—. Tchr. Youth Hobby Shop Camp, Nashville, 1981-83, Met. Nashville Edn. Assn., 1994—; mem. Faculty Adv. Com.; sci. facilitator Paragon Mills Elem. Mem. NEA, Nat. Sci. Tchr. Assn., Tenn. Edn. Assn., Fed. Aviation Assn. (educator 1995—), Tenn. Reading Assn., Nashville Inst. Arts, Libr. Congress, Title I (com. 1999—), MNEA (sch. rep 1999-2000). Mem. Ch. Christ. Avocations: personal computing, reading, travel. Office: Paragon Mills Elem Sch 260 Paragon Mills Rd Nashville TN 37211-4075

GREENE, LYNNE JEANNETTE, fashion designer; b. Albany, N.Y., Aug. 27, 1938; d. Zebulon Stevens and Helen Matilde (Maier) Robbins; m. Stanley E. Greene, Jan. 31, 1962 (dec. June 27, 1987); 1 child, Stuart Nathaniel; m. Michael Alan Karlan, Sept. 29, 1991. Student, Goucher Coll., 1956-57; BA with honors, Parsons Sch. Design, 1960. Asst. designer Haymaker Sportswear (David Crystal), N.Y.C., 1959-61; designer Craig Craely Sportswear and Dresses, N.Y.C., 1961-63, Flair Lingerie, N.Y.C., 1964-66; designer, owner Kaleidoscope Lingerie, N.Y.C., 1966-67; head designer Contessa/Monique/Fisher Lingerie, N.Y.C., 1967-71; creative dir. Eye of the Peacock Sportswear, N.J., 1968-72; head designer, owner Lynne Greene Designs Retail, Montclair, N.J., 1972-74; designer, pres. Little Greene Apples Inc., Montville, N.J., 1971—; designer, dir. mktg. Lady Lynne Lingerie, Guy Laroche Lingerie, N.Y.C. and Paris, 1973-93, Paris, 1973—93, Val Mode by Lynne Greene, N.Y.C., 1993-97; v.p. design and merchandising The Intapp Group/Go Figure, N.Y.C., 1997-99; pres. Vital Advantage LLC, 1999—, owner, 1999—. Lingerie critic Pratt Inst., 1984—. Patentee in field; illustrator books, pamphlets in fashion and packaging fields; comml. artist and illustrator Home & Office Design. Active participant Montville Soccer Assn, 1972-88, fund drives for Am. Heart Assn., Cancer Inc., March of Dimes. Recipient Humanitarian award, Polar Bear Project, Nikken Inc., 2003, honors in field. Mem.: The Fashion Group, 200 Club N.J., Kiwanis (pres. elect 2004, Kiwanian of Yr. 2002—03). Republican. Unitarian Universalist. Avocations: sketching, portraiture, cooking, sewing, painting. E-mail: maklynne@optonline.net.

GREENE, MARGARET H., telecommunications industry executive; b. Nebr. JD, U. Nebr., 1972; LLD (hon.), Georgetown Coll., 1975. Assoc. solicitor Dept. Energy, Washington; atty. pvt. practice; with legal dept. South Ctrl. Bell, 1983; pres. Bellsouth Corp., Ky., 1991—95; cabinet sec. Gov. Commonwealth Ky., 1996; v.p., gen. counsel Bellsouth Telecomm., 1996—98, pres. regulatory and external affairs Bellsouth Corp., Atlanta, 1998—. Mem. adv. com. rsch., devel. and tech. So. Govs. Assn.; bd. dors. High Mus. Art, Atlanta; mem. nat. bd. vis. U. Louisville Bus. Sch. Mem.: ABA, Nebr. Bar Assn., Ky. Bar Assn., D.C. Bar Assn., Ala. Bar Assn., U.S. Telecom Assn. (chair). Office: Bellsouth Corp 1155 Peachtree St NE Atlanta GA 30309-3610

GREENE, MONICA LYNN BANKS, recreational therapist, director; b. Washington, Sept. 24, 1963; d. John Thomas and Pricilla (Sneed) Banks; m. Edward Ray Greene, Sept. 12, 1991. BS in Microbiology and Therapeutic Recreation, Howard U., 1986; MBA, U. Md. Cert. therapeutic recreation specialist, activity cons. Therapeutic recreation specialist Dept. Human Svcs., Washington, 1986-91; dir. activities, vols., transp. Independence Ct. Hyattsville, Md., 1991-93; dir. therapeutic activity svcs. Asbury Meth. Village, Gaithersburg, Md., 1993—; dir. therapeutic activities and vol. svcs. Presdl. Woods Health Care Ctr., Adelphi, Md.; owner, pres. Excell Eldercare Mgmt., Inc.; asst. adminstr. St. Thomas More Nursing & Rehab. Ctr., Hyattsville, Md.; exec. dir. Morningside HOuse of St. Charles, Waldorf, Ind., 2003—. Democrat. Baptist. Avocations: swimming, reading, needlework, quilting. E-mail: edmonicathome@msn.com.

GREENE, REBECCA RACHEL, lawyer; b. Berlin, Nov. 14, 1947; parents U.S. citizens; m. Peter Alan Greene, June 22, 1969; children: Abraham, Ethan. BA, Barnard Coll., 1968; MA, Washington U., 1970; PhD, Columbia U., 1977; JD, Rutgers U., Newark, 1984. Bar: N.J. 1985, D.C. 1991, N.Y. 1992. Rsch. asst. Internat. Bank for Reconstrn. and Devel., Washington, 1970-71; rsch. fellow Cornell Med. Ctr., N.Y.C., 1974-76; vis. asst. prof. Colgate U., Hamilton, N.Y., 1979-80; staff atty. Union County Legal Svcs., Elizabeth, N.J., 1986-88; examiner N.J. Divsn. for Consumer Affairs, Newark, 1988—, regulatory officer, 1990—99; staff atty. Union County Legal Svcs., Elizabeth, NJ, 1999—2000, Passaic County Legal Aid, Paterson, NJ, 2000—01, Ctrl. Jersey Legal Svcs., Elizabeth, NJ, 2001—. Contbr. articles to profl. jours. Regents Coll. Tchg. fellow, 1968-69; Danforth fellow in history, 1968-69; Josiah Macy fellow, 1974-76; fellow in history of medicine NIH, 1978-80. Home: 246 Lenox Ave South Orange NJ 07079-1408

GREENE, STEPHANIE HARRISON, marketing executive; b. Lake Forest, Ill., June 20, 1950; d. Howard Harrison and Gloria Juliet (Christensen) Greene. BA in Journalism and Advt., Syracuse U., 1972; MBA in Mktg., Cornell U., 1975. With Weeden & Co., Boston, 1972-73; product rep. Allis Chalmers, Matteson, Ill., 1975-76; asst. product mgr. Midwest Am./Am. Hosp. Supply, Des Plaines, Ill., 1976-77; product mgr. Borden, Inc., Columbus, Ohio, 1977-80; product line mgr. John Sexton & Co./Beatrice, Chgo., 1980-82; product mgr. non-foods PYA/Monarch/Sara Lee, Greenville, S.C., 1982-84; mktg. mgr. Fuller Brush/Sara Lee, Winston-Salem, 1984-89; pres. Corbett Harrison Greene, Mundelein, Ill., 1984—; mktg. mgr. The Greehill Corp., Mundelein, Ill., 1989—, corp. sec.-treas., 2002—. Bd. dirs. Career Pub., Mundelein, v.p., 1993—. Editor: The Quotation Dictionary, 1968. Active Wilmette (Ill.) Chorus, 1993—95, Winnetka (Ill.) Theatre, 1992—2000, bd. govs., 1994—2000, v.p., 1995—96, pres., 1996—2000; mem. Chancel Choir, Libertyville, Ill., 1995—97. Mem.: Cornell U. Alumnae Assn. (pres. Class of 1975), Garden Clubs Ill. Inc. (conv. chmn. 2001—02, chmn. awards com. 2002—04, 2d v.p. 2004), Dist. 9 Garden Club Ill. (rec. sec. 1999—2000, properties 2003—04), Town and Country Garden Club (civic chmn. 1997—98, pres. 2003—), Holly Tree Garden Club (treas. 1983—84), Johnson Club (amb. 1990—91, pres. 1992—94), Serendipity Garden Club (treas. 1978—79), Pi Beta Phi. Republican. Episcopalian. Avocations: gardening, needlepoint, decorating, arts. Home: 408 Hampton Ter Libertyville IL 60048-3334 Office: Greenhill Corp 905 Allanson Rd Mundelein IL 60060

GREENE, WENDY SEGAL, special education educator; b. New Rochelle, N.Y., Jan. 9, 1929; d. Louis Peter and Anna Henrietta (Kahan) Segal; m. Charles Edward Smith (div. 1952); m. Richard M. Greene Jr. (div. 1967); children: Christopher S., Kerry William, Karen Beth Greene Olson; m. Richard M. Greene Sr., Aug. 29, 1985 (dec. 1986). Student, Olivet Coll., 1946-48, Santa Monica Coll., 1967-70; BA in Child Devel., Calif. State U., Los Angeles, 1973, MA in Elem. Edn., 1975. Cert. tchr., Calif.; cert. Specially Designed Acad. Instrn. in English, 1999. Counselor Camp Watitoh, Becket, Mass., 1946-49; asst. tchr. Outdoor Play Group, New Rochelle, 1946-58; edn. sec. pediatrics Syracuse (N.Y.) Meml. Hosp., 1952-53; with St. John's Hosp., Santa Monica, Calif., 1962-63; head tchr. Head Start, L.A., 1966-77; tchr. spl. edn. L.A. Unified Sch. Dist., 1977—, Salvin Spl. Edn. Ctr., L.A., 1976—85, Perez Spl. Edn. Ctr., L.A., 1986-. Instr. mktg. rsch. for motivational rsch. Anderson-McConnell Agy., 1966; mentor tchr. L.A. Unified Sch. Dist., 1992-99; mem. adv. com. for spl. edn. Tustin Unified Sch. Dist. Comty., 1994—. Contbr. to house organ of St. John's Hosp.; co-editor of newspaper for Salvin Sch., L.A.; contbg. reporter El Aquilar (The Eagle), Perez. Mem. coun. LEARN, Perez, 1996—; bd. dirs. Tustin Area Coun. for Fine Arts, 2002—, Richland Ave Youth House, L.A., 1960—63, Emotional Health Assn., L.A., 1961—66, Richland Ave. Sch. PTA, L.A., 1959—63. Mem.: AAUW, United Tchrs. L.A., Olivet Coll. Alumni Assn., Tustin Cmty. Chorus, Westside Singers (L.A.), Celebration of Life Singers, Kappa Delta Pi. Jewish. Avocations: music, writing, theater, travel, family. Home: 14291 Prospect Ave Tustin CA 92780-2316

GREENE LLOYD, NANCY ELLEN, retired infosystems specialist, physicist; b. Worcester, Mass., Nov. 4, 1947; d. William Arthur Greene II and Dorothy Goddard (Fuller) Greene; m. Stephen C. Lloyd, July 25, 1992; children: Ellen Dorothy, Gwyneth Tegan. BS in Physics, Ohio State U., 1969, MS in Physics, 1971. Instr. physics U. Colo., Colorado Springs, 1971-73; physics programmer U. N.Mex., Albuquerque, 1973-76; data analyst Los Alamos (N.Mex.) Nat. Lab., 1975-77, programmer, 1977-78, mem. tech. staff controlled thermonuclear reaction divsn., 1978-81, mem. tech. staff Accelerator Tech. div., 1981-84, mem. tech. staff adminstrv. data processing divsn., 1984-85, mem. tech. staff dynamic experimentation divsn., 1985-94, staff mem. supr., 1989-90, acting sect. leader, 1990-91, acting dep. divsn. leader, 1992, chief ops. explosives tech. and applications divsn., 1992-94, mem. tech. staff environ., safety, and health divsn. Instl. Affairs Office, 1994-97, with Environ., Safety and Health Divsn. Office, 1997-98, leader info. mgmt. team, 1997-98, mem. tech. staff info. mgmt. program, 1998—2002; ret., 2002. Speaker in field. Vol. Los Alamos Schs., 1980—88, Fountain Valley Sch., Colo., 1990—91; coord. nursery Christian Ch. Los Alamos, 1997—2000; foster parent State of N.Mex., 1998—; co-mgr. God's Pantry food bank, 1998—2002; children's ch. tchr. Christian Ch. Los Alamos, 1999—2002; liaison Hope Pregnancy Ctr.; Bldg. Blocks mentor Family Strengths Network, 2001—; vol. Calvary Christian Sch., 2002—; pres. Los Alamos Rio Arriba Foster Parent Assn., 2002—; nursery vol. Crossroads Bible Ch., 2004—. Nat. Merit scholar, Mich. State U., 1965, Nat. Defense Edn. Act Title IV fellow, Ohio State U., 1969. Mem. N.Mex. Digital Equipment Computer Users Soc. (exec. com. 1984-87, 88-90, registration chair computer conf. 1984-87, vice-chair 1988-89, publicity 1989-90), Nat. and N.Mex. Foster Parent Assn., N.Mex. Network for Women in Sci. and Engring., VAX Computer Local Users Group (chmn. 1981-82, sec. 1989-92), N.Mex. Square and Round Dance Assn. (dist. co-chair 1996-97). Avocations: reading, walking, dance, foster children. E-mail: nancy.lloyd@covad.net.

GREENE OSTER, SELMAREE, medical anthropologist, researcher; b. Phila., Feb. 17, 1949; d. Boisey and Elizabeth (Lewis) Greene; m. Gerald Oster, Apr. 11, 1973 (dec. Oct. 1995); 1 child, Alexander S. BS in Anthropology and Biology, U. Pa., 1969, CUNY, 1973, MSc, 1979, PhD, 1980. Cert. clin. lab. specialist N.Y. Dept. Health. Tchr. U.S. Peace Corps, Washington, 1975-77; med. rschr. Mt. Sinai Sch. Medicine, N.Y.C., 1978-88; pres., exec. officer Oster Children's Fund, N.Y.C., 1996—. Contbr. articles to sci. jours. Founder Gerald Oster Sch. for Peace Edn., Haiti. Tropical medicine grantee Friends of Children[ ]of Haiti, 1984-90. Mem. Am. Soc. Clin. Pathologists (lic. lab. pathologist and clinician). Democrat. Roman Catholic. Avocations: horseback riding, swimming. Home: PO Box 988 Village Sta New York NY 10014 Office: Peace Action Edn Rm 4050 866 United Nations Plz New York NY 10017 Fax: 609-871-5999.

GREENFIELD, LINDA SUE, nursing educator; b. Dover, Del., Aug. 5, 1950; d. Norman Raymond and Eleanor Henrietta (Harmon) Connell; m. Douglas Herman Greenfield, Dec. 27, 1976; children: Leah, Paige. BSN, Cath. U., 1972; MSN cum laude, Boston U., 1977; student, Met. Hosp. Sch. Nurse Anesthetists, 1979—81; postgrad., Coll. New Rochelle, 1986-88; PhD, Adelphi U., 1998. RN, N.Y. Staff nurse emergency rm. and ICU Washington Hosp. Ctr., 1974-75; operating rm. nurse Mass. Eye & Ear, Boston, 1975; ICU nurse Peter Bent Brigham Hosp., Boston, 1975-76; surg. nurse practitioner Kingsbrook Jewish Hosp., Bklyn., 1976-79; cert. registered nurse anesthetist Brookdale Hosp., Bklyn., 1981-92, Winthrop U. Hosp., Mineola, N.Y., 1992-94; adj. prof. Adelphi U., Garden City, N.Y., 1995-99; adj. prof. nursing N.Y. Inst. Tech., Old Westbury, 1998-99; clin. supr. Midtown Ctr. Complementary Care, N.Y.C., 1999-2000; clin specialist St. Francis Hosp., Roslyn, N.Y., 2000-01; asst. prof. nursing Adelphi U., 2001—. Bd. officer Manhasset Newcomers, N.Y., 1988-90; bd. dirs. Friends of Manhasset Libr., N.Y., 1990-94; mem. Make a Wish Found., Port Washington, N.Y., 1990—. Lt. U.S. Army, 1970-74. Mem.: ANA, Nat. Assn. U. Women, Nat. Assn. for Holistic Nurses, Nat. Assn. Homeopathy, Noetic Soc., Sch. Cmty. Assn., Am. Assn. Nurse Anesthetists, Sigma Theta Tau. Avocations: skiing, sailing, dance.

GREENFIELD, RACHEL, magazine executive; BA, Vassar Coll.; MBA, Harvard U. With Time Inc., N.Y.C.; sr. v.p. Ziff-Davis Pub.; gen. mgr. Martha Stewart Living Omnimedia, N.Y.C., 1995—, exec. v.p. Office: Omnimedia LLC 20 W 43rd St Fl D33 New York NY 10036

GREENHALGH, PATRICIA ELLEN DONOGHUE, marketing research consultant; b. Hempstead, N.Y., Aug. 30, 1958; d. Harold Edward and Lydia Ellen Donoghue; m. Paul Alan Greenhalgh, Mar. 19, 1983; children: Lauren, John. BS in Mktg., N.Y. State U., Albany, 1980, MBA, 1981. Rsch. project dir. NPD Group, Port Washington, NY, 1981—83; rsch. analyst Peter Paul Cadbury, Naugatuck, Conn., 1983—85; rsch. mgr. Heublein Inc./UDV, Inc., Hartford, Conn., 1985—98; regional brand strategist UDV, Inc., Stamford, Conn., 1998—99; pres. Greenhalgh Mkt. Rsch. & Cons. LLC, Cheshire, Conn., 1999—. Mem. strategic planning bd. Cheshire Pub. Schs., 2000; bd. dirs. Cheshire Interfaith Housing, 2003—; mktg. cons. Dem. Party, Cheshire, 2001, 2003. Mem.: Am. Mktg. Assn. Home: 25 N Pond Rd Cheshire CT 06410 Office: Greenhalgh Mkt Rsch & Cons 25 N Pond Rd Cheshire CT 06410 E-mail: greenhalghmktg@cox.net.

GREENHOUSE, LINDA JOYCE, journalist; b. N.Y.C., Jan. 9, 1947; d. Herman Robert and Dorothy Eleanor (Greenlick) Greenhouse; m. Eugene R. Fidell, Jan. 1, 1981; 1 child, Hannah Margalit Fidell. BA, Radcliffe Coll., 1968; M of Studies in Law, Yale U., 1978; D.H.L. (hon.) (hon.), Brown U., 1991; LLD (hon.) (hon.), Colgate U., 1993, Northeastern U., 1997, CUNY, 1997; LLD (hon.), U. Miami, 2004, Georgetown U., 2004. Asst. to James Reston The N.Y. Times, N.Y.C., 1968—69, met. reporter, 1970—74, state polit. reporter, 1974—77, supreme ct. corr. Washington, 1978—85, 1988—, congl. corr., 1986—88. Adv. com. Schlesinger Libr. on the History of Women in Am., Radcliffe Coll., 1995—2002; mem. Schlesinger Libr. Coun., 2003—; bd. dirs. Yale Law Sch. Fund, New Haven, 1984—91. Recipient Pulitzer prize in journalism for beat reporting, 1998, Carey McWilliams award, Am. Polit. Sci. Assn., 2002, Henry J. Friendly medal, Am. Law Inst., 2002, Golden Pen award, Legal Writing Inst., 2002, Goldsmith Career award, John F. Kennedy Sch. Govt., Harvard U., 2004. Fellow: Am. Acad. Arts and Scis.; mem.: Women's Forum of Washington (v.p. 2003—), Yale Law Assn. (exec. com. 1993—97), Am. Law Inst. (hon.), Am. Philos. Soc., Harvard Club of Washington (bd. dirs. 1989—92). Office: The NY Times 1627 I St NW Washington DC 20006-4007 Office Phone: 202-862-0371. E-mail: ligree@nytimes.com.

GREENLAW, MARILYN JEAN, education educator, consultant, writer; b. St. Petersburg, Fla., Apr. 1, 1941; d. Hinckley and Dorothy Rebecca (Ball) G. BA, Stetson U., 1962, MA, 1965; PhD, Mich. State U., 1970. Elem. tchr. Broward County schs., Ft. Lauderdale, Fla., 1962-64; ele. cons. Harper and Row Publs., Evanston, Ill., 1965-69; from asst. to assoc. prof. U. Ga., Athens, 1970-78; from assoc. to full prof. U. North Tex., Denton, 1978-87, regents prof., 1987—. Cons. Scholastic Publs., N.Y.C., 1978-87, Houghton Mifflin Co., Boston, 1984-94, Tex. Instruments, Dallas, 1981-85, Coordinating Bd., Austin, Tex., 1987-91. Author: Ranch Dressing: The Story of Western Wear, 1993, Welcome to the Stock Show, 1997; co-author: Storybook Classrooms, 1985, Educating the Gifted, 1988; editor book rev. column Jour. Reading, 1981-84, The New Adv., 1987-94. Mem. Friends of the Libr., Denton, 1984—, pres., 1995-97; bd. dirs. Denton Libr., 1992-97, chair, 1995-96. Recipient Arbuthnot award, 1992, Disting. Svc. award Tex. State Reading Assn., 1996, Pres.'s Coun. Disting. Svc. award U. North Tex., 1996. Mem. ALA (com. chairperson 1984-85), Nat. Coun. Tchrs. of English (com. chairperson 1980—, Outstanding Leadership in Edn. award 1976), Internat. Reading Assn. (com. chairperson 1980-90, Arbuthnot award 1992), Phi Delta Kappa (pres. 1982-83, Outstanding Young Educator award 1981), Phi Kappa Phi (v.p. 1986-87). Republican. Avocations: reading, gardening, photography. Home: 2600 Sheraton Rd Denton TX 76209-8620

GREENLEY, BEVERLY JANE, lawyer, educator; b. Cleve., Sept. 24, 1947; d. Gaylord H. and Joan C. (Gurklis) G. BA, Principia Coll., 1969; JD, U. Mo., 1976; LLM, Washington U., 1981. Bar: Mo. 1976, Ill. 1977, U.S. Tax Ct. 1979. Ptnr. McCarter & Greenley, St. Louis, 1976-81, McCarter, Snyder & Greenley, St. Louis, 1981-85; assoc. prof. law Stetson U. Coll. Law, St. Petersburg, Fla., 1981-85; ptnr. Gage & Tucker, St. Louis, 1985-87, Husch, Eppenberger, Donohue, Cornfeld & Jenkins, St. Louis, 1987-90, McCarter & Greenley, LLC, St. Louis, 1990—. Estate planning lectr. for CLE programs, 1997—; estate planning expert witness, 2000—. Co-author: Missouri Lawyer's Guide, 1984. Mem. Mo. Bar Assn., Ill. Bar Assn. Office: 1 Metropolitan Sq Ste 2100 Saint Louis MO 63102-2797 E-mail: bgreenley@mccartergreenley.com.

GREENMAN, JANE FRIEDLIEB, lawyer, human resources executive; b. N.Y.C., Sept. 9, 1950; d. Morton Jerome and Isabelle Irene (Bisgyer) F.; m. Charles P. Greenman, Nov. 23, 1975; children: Margot, Jaclyn, Danielle. BS, Cornell U., 1972; JD, NYU, 1975, LLM in Labor Law, 1981. Bar: N.Y. 1976. Assoc. Wolf Haldenstein, N.Y.C., 1975-79; faculty NYU Law Sch., 1979-81, Bklyn. Law Sch., 1981—82; assoc., counsel Hughes Hubbard & Reed, N.Y.C., 1982-91, ptnr., chair employee benefits dept., 1991-96; v.p., dep. gen. coun. human resources Honeywell Internat., Inc., Morristown, NJ, 1996—2003; v.p. compensation, benefits and labor rels. Tyco Internat., N.Y.C., 2003—. Bd. dirs. Women's Fund of N.J., Am. Benefits Counsel; vice chair bd. dirs. ERISA Industy com., N.J. Women's 300; adj. prof. Bklyn. Law Sch., 1982-92, 95, Hofstra U. Mem. Temple Sinai of Summit, Religious Action Ctr. Commn. for Social Action. Mem. ABA, N.Y.C. Bar Assn., N.Y. State Bar Assn. Jewish. Office: Tyco Internat (US) Inc 9 Roszel Rd Princeton NJ 08540

GREENMAN, PAULA S. lawyer; b. Putnam, N.Y., 1951; BA cum laude, Yale U., 1972; JD, Boston (Mass.) Coll., 1976. Bar: Conn. 1976, N.Y. 1995. Atty. Skadden, Arps, Slate, Meagher & Flom LLP, N.Y., ptnr., 2001—. Office: Skadden Arps Slate Meagher & Flom LLP Four Times Sq New York NY 10036*

GREENSIDES, CATHERINE MAY, poet; b. San Francisco, Calif., Nov. 17, 1927; d. Reginald David and Isabella Muir (Grant) Greensides. Studied, Coll. San Mateo, 1948—49; studied fine arts (voice), San Francisco Conservatory Music, 1939—51. Bookkeeper Bank of Am., San Mateo, Calif., 1945—46; office clk. Lowe & Zwerlein, San Mateo, Calif., 1946—47; note dept. First Interstate Bank, Burlingame, Calif., 1949—83; poet, 1997—. Author: (poetry) Chasing the Wind, 1997 (Editor's Choice, 1997), Reflections of the Heart, 1997, A Treasury of Famous Poems, 1997 (Award of Recognition, 1997), Richard Henry Wilde, 1997, Rainbow Rivulets, 1998, Best Poems of 1998, The Layers of Our Lives, 2002 (Editor's Choice, 2002), A Famous Poet, 1998 (Award of Recognition, 1998), The Best Poems and Poets of 2002, 2003, The Best Poems and Poets of 2003, 2004, Theatre of the Mind, 2003; composer: (songs) Song of Gratitude, 2001. Named a Famous Poet for 2001, Famous Poets Soc., 2002; nominee Poet of the Year, Internat. Poetry Soc. Poets, 2002; named to, Internat. Poetry Hall of Fame, 1998; recipient Commemorative Award Medallion, Internat. Poet of Merit Silver Award Bowl, 2002, Editor's Choice award, 2003. Mem.: No. Calif. Song Writers Assn., Internat. Soc. Poets. Avocations: gardening, japanese brush painting.

GREENSLADE, CINDY LOUISE, psychologist; b. Balt., Nov. 9, 1959; d. John Robert and Doris Ann Weeks; m. Ivor David Greenslade, Sept. 11, 1982. AA in Nursing, Catonsville (Md.) C.C., 1980; BS in Psychology cum laude, Liberty U., 1993; MA in Clin. Psychology, Biola U., 1997, PhD in Clin. Psychology, 2001. Lic. psychologist Calif.; RN Calif. Psychotherapist Deaf Journey Counseling Program, Orange, Calif., 1997—99; instr. West Coast Deaf Bible Coll., Long Beach, Calif., 1998—99; intern and staff psychotherapist St. John's Child and Family Devel. Ctr. and Deaf Program, Santa Monica, Calif., 1999—2001; staff psychologist deaf program Patton (Calif.) State Hosp., 2001—02; ednl. psychologist Calif. Sch. for the Deaf, Riverside, 2000; psychotherapist Meier Clinics, Long Beach, 2002—. Cons. forensic deaf mental health Patton State Hosp., 2001—, cons. deaf and hearing mental health Meier Clinics, 2002—. Mem.: APA, Adv. Coun. Abused Deaf Children, Nat. Assn. of the Deaf, Am. Deafness and Rehab. Assn. Achievements include co-establishment of the first deaf community counseling center in California. Avocations: backpacking, music, bicycling, stain glass. Office: Meier Clinics Ste 450 3545 Long Beach Blvd Long Beach CA 90807

GREENSPAN, DEBORAH, dental educator; 2nd BDS, U. London, 1960, BDS, 1964, DSc, 1991; fellow in Dental Surgery (hon.), Royal Coll. Surgeons, Edinburgh, 1994; LDS, Royal Coll. Surgeons, Eng., 1964; ScD (hon.), Georgetown U., 1990. Registered dental practioner, U.K.; diplomate Am. Bd. Oral Medicine. Vis. lectr. oral medicine U. Calif., San Francisco, 1976-83, asst. clin. prof., 1983-85, assoc. clin. prof., 1985-89, clin. prof., 1989-96, prof. clin. oral medicine, 1996—. Lectr. in oral biology, U. Calif., San Francisco, 1972, clin. dir. Oral AIDS Ctr., 1987—, active Sch. Dentistry coms, including admissions com., 1985—, chair task force on infection control, 1987—; cons. Joint FDI/WHO Working Group on AIDS, 1989—, EEC, 1990, WHO, 1990, 91, Dept. Health State Calif., 1991, others; ad hoc reviews Epidemiology and Disease Control Sect. Div. Rsch. Grants NIH, 1987—; mem. programs adv. com. Nat. Inst. Dental Rsch., 1989—, mem. spl. ad hoc tech. rev. panel, 1991, mem. panel Fed. Drug Adminstrn., 1991-94; other svc. to govtl. agys.; participant numerous sci. and profl. workshops, meetings, and continuing edn. courses, numerous radio, TV, and press interviews concerning AIDS and infection control in dentistry. Author: (with J.S. Greenspan, Pindborg, and Schiødt), AIDS and the Dental Team, 1986 (transl. German, French, Italian, Spanish, Japanese), AIDS and the Mouth, 1990, (with others) San Francisco General Hospital AIDS Knowledge Base, 1986, Dermatologic Clinics, 5th edit., 1987, Infectious Disease Clinics of North America, 2nd. edit., 1988, Oral Manifestations of AIDS, 1988, Contemporary Periodontics, 1989, Opportunistic Infections in AIDS Patients, 1990, AIDS Clinical Review, 1990, Oral Manifestations of Systemic Disease, 1990, others; mem. editl. bd. rev. Jour. Am. Coll. Dentists, 1991; mem. editl. bd. Oral Diseases, 1999; ad hoc referee Jour. Oral Pathology, 1983—, Cancer, 1985—, Jour. Acad. Gen. Dentistry, 1986—, European Jour. Cancer & Clin. Oncology, 1986, Archives of Dermatology, 1988—, Jour. AMA, 1988—, AIDS, 1991; contbr. numerous articles to profl. jours. Mem. dental subcom. of profl. edn. com. Calif. div. Am. Cancer Soc., 1982-90, profl. health care providers task force, 1991. Nat. Cancer Inst. fellow, 1978-79, Am. Coll. Dentists fellow, 1988; recipient Woman of Distinction award, London, 1986, Commendation cert. Asst. Sec. for Health, 1989; named Seymour J. Kreshover lectr. Nat. Inst. Dental Rsch., 1989, Hon. Lectr. United Med. and Dental Schs. of Guys and St. Thomas Hosps., U. London, 1991. Fellow AAAS, Royal Soc. Medicine, Royal Coll. Surgeons; mem. ADA (vis. lectr. speaker's bur. 1988—, cons. coun. on dental therapeutics 1988—, mem. coun. sci. affairs 1999—), Am. Assn. Dental Rsch. (session chair 1986-87, constitution com. 1988-91, chair 1990-91, pres. San Francisco sect. 1990—, treas. 1992—), Am. Acad. Oral Pathology, Am. Soc. Microbiology, Am. Assn. Women Dentists, Am. Acad. Oral Medicine, Am. Assn. Dental Schs., Internat. Assn. Dental Rsch. (pres. exptl. pathology group 1989-90, other coms. and offices), Internat. Assn. Oral Pathologists, Calif. Dental Assn., San Francisco Dental Soc., Internat. AIDS Soc., Inst. of Medicine. Achievements include rsch. on oral candidiasis in HIV infection, on HIV-associated salivary gland disease, on oral hairy leukoplakia, and on the prevalence of HIV-associated gingivitis and periodontitis in HIV-infected patients. Office: U Calif Sch Dentistry Dept Stomatology S 612 513 Parnassus Ave Box 0422 San Francisco CA 94143-0422

GREENSPAN, GLADYS, textile designer; b. N.Y.C., Sept. 14, 1923; d. Irving and Celia Appelbaum; m. Alex Greenspan, July 30, 1944; 1 child, Jeffrey. Doctor, Bklyn. Mus. Art Student, League, Queen's Coll. Textile designer Textile-Virgil Studio, N.Y.C., 1941-61, Ameritex, N.Y.C., Steintex, N.Y.C., Jane Albert Studios, N.Y.C. Active drawing with pastels, YMCA-YMHA, Queens, N.Y., 1976-78. Exhbns. include Roslyn Mus. Fine Arts, Long Beach Mus., Nat. Art League, Emil Leonard Gallery, Smithtown Twp. Art Coun., St. James, n.Y., Gaddard Ctr. for Visual Arts, Ardmore, Okla., Mus. of Southwest U. Mus., Midland, Tex., U. of the South, Tenn., Richmond (Ind.) Art Mus., Owtanna Arts Ctr., Minn., others; permanent collection in Jane-Voorhees-Zimmerli Mus. of Rutgers U. Awards include Best-in-Show Bayside Art League, Meml. award Jacob Javits Fed. Bldg., Paul Mellon Art Ctr., others. Mem. Pastel Soc. Am., Nat. Assn. Women Artists, Profl. Artist Guild Boco Mus./Fla., Artist Guilf of Norton Mus./Fla., Artist Network of Great Neck/L.I., N.Y. Home: 6080 Huntwick Ter Apt 307 Delray Beach FL 33484-1852

GREENSPAN-MARGOLIS, JUNE E. psychiatrist; b. NYC, June 28, 1934; d. Benjamin Robert and Theresa (Cooperstein) Edelman; divorced; 1 child, Alisa Greenspan; m. Gerald J. Margolis. AB, Bryn Mawr Coll., 1955; MD, Med. Coll. Pa., 1959; grad., Inst Phila Assn Psychoanalysis, Bala Cynwyd, 1975. Intern Albert Einstein Med. Ctr., Phila., 1959-60; pvt. practice medicine specializing in pediatrics Cinnaminson, N.J., 1961-67; psychiat. resident Hahnemann Med. Coll., Phila., 1967-71; practice medicine specializing in adult and child psychiatry, psychoanalysis Jenkintown, Pa., 1971—. Instr. U. Pa. Sch. Medicine, Phila., 1975—77, clin. assoc., 1977—81, clin. asst. prof., 1981—86, clin. assoc. prof., 1986—; tng. and supervisory analyst Phila. Ctr. for Psychoanalysis, Bala Cynwyd, Pa., 1986—. Fellow Am. Coll. Psychoanalysts, Am. Psychiat. Assn.; mem. AMA, Am. Psychoanalytic Assn. (cert. adult and child psychoanalysis), Am. Acad. Child Psychiatry, Ctr. for Advanced Psychoanalytic Studies (Princeton). Office: The Pavilion Ste 434 261 Old York Rd Jenkintown PA 19046 Office Phone: 215-887-5355.

GREENSPOON, IRMA NAIMAN, business executive; b. Washington, Oct. 18, 1920; d. Harry H. and Ada Marie (Himmelfarb) Naiman; m. Benjamin Greenspoon, July 10, 1960; children: Laurence, Julie. AB, George Washington U., 1942. Lic. tour guide, Washington, 1970-84; pres., CEO Guide Svc. of Washington, 1984-89. Bd. dirs. Washington Conv. and Visitors Assn., 1984-89, Am. Diabetes Assn., Washington, 1966-80; pres. Park View Citizens Assn., Chevy Chase, Md., 1986; Juvenile Justice Com. Montgomery County, Md., 1999—2003 Democrat. Jewish. Home: 3223 Park View Rd Chevy Chase MD 20815-5643 E-mail: birma01@comcast.net.

GREENSPUN, ADELE ARON, writer, educator, photographer; b. Phila., Dec. 22, 1938; d. Samuel and Eva Stern Aron; m. Steven Schwarz, Dec. 20, 1959 (div. Jan. 1985); children: Erica Schwarz Furman, Joanie Schwarz Rosenthal; m. Bertram Greenspun, Jan. 18, 1987. BS in Edn., U. Pa., 1960; postgrad., Wilkes Coll., 1974—79, U. Pa., 1987—88, postgrad., 1995. Author: Daddies, 1992 (one of 100 Most Noteworthy Childrens Book, 1992, Silver award Phila. Art Dirs. Club, 1993), Bunny & Me, 2000 (one of Best Childrens Books, Nick Jr. Mag., 2000), Ariel & Emily, 2003, Grandparents are the Greatest Because. . ., 2003, numerous poems; contbr. articles to popular mags.; one-woman shows include Art Gallery, 1981, exhibitions include Borowsky Gallery, 1994, exhibited in group shows at Art Inst., Phila., 1990, Millersville U., 1992, U. of the Arts, Phila., 1992—93. Mem.: Am. Soc. Media Photographers, Soc. Childrens Book-writers and Illustrators, Assn. Photographers and Media, Authors Guild. Democrat. Jewish. Avocations: cross country skiing, bicycling. Home: 1900 Rittenhouse Sq 9A Philadelphia PA 19103 Office Phone: 215-732-4392.

GREENSTEIN, LINDA R. assemblywoman; b. June 7, 1950; BA in Psychology, Vassar Coll.; MA in Psychology, Johns Hopkins U.; JD in Law, Georgetown U. Assemblywoman N.J. Gen. Assembly, 2000—; asst. majority leader, 2002—. Mem. West Windsor-Plainsboro Reg. Bd. of Edn., 1992—94, Plainsboro Twp. Com., 1995—2000. Democrat. Office: 7 Ctr Dr Ste 2 Monroe NJ 08831-1565 E-mail: AswGreenstein@njleg.org.

GREENSTEIN, MARLA NAN, lawyer; b. Chgo., Jan. 20, 1957; d. Charles Allen and Lenore Greenstein. Cert., Oxford U., Eng., 1978; AB, Georgetown U., 1979; JD, Loyola U., 1982. Bar: Ill. 1982, Alaska 1997, U.S. Dist. Ct. (no. dist.) Ill. 1982, U.S. Ct. Appeals (7th cir.) 1983. Sr. staff atty. Am. Judicature Soc., Chgo., 1982-85, Alaska Jud. Council, Anchorage, 1985-89; exec. dir. Ala. Commn. Jud. Conduct, Anchorage, 1989—. Cons. Com. on Cts. and Justice, Chgo., 1985. Author: Handbook for Judicial Nominating Commissioners, 1984. Mem. ABA (chair lawyers conf. jud. divsn. 1996-97), Assn. Jud. Disciplinary Counsel (bd. dirs. 1992—), Am. Judicature Soc. (bd. dirs. 1992-97, exec. com. 1997—2003), Pi Sigma Alpha. Avocations: photography, drawing. Office: Commn Jud Conduct 1029 W 3rd Ave 550 Anchorage AK 99501-1944 E-mail: mgreenstein@acjc.state.ak.us.

GREENSTEIN, RUTH LOUISE, research institute executive, lawyer; b. N.Y.C., Mar. 28, 1946; d. Milton and Beatrice (Zuity) G., m. David Seidman, May 19, 1972. BA, Harvard U., 1966; MA, Yale U., 1968; JD, George Washington U., 1980. Bar: D.C. 1980. Fgn. service info. officer USIA, Washington and Tehran, Iran, 1968-70; adminstrv. asst. Export-Import Bank U.S., Washington, 1971-72; asst. dean Woodrow Wilson Sch. Pub. and Internat. Affairs, Princeton U., 1972-75; budget examiner U.S. Office Mgmt. and Budget, Washington, 1975-79; budget coordinator U.S. Internat. Devel. Coop. Agy., 1979-81; dep. gen. counsel NSF, 1981-84; treas., then v.p. and gen. counsel Genex Corp., Gaithersburg, Md., 1984-90; v.p. fin. and adminstrn., gen. counsel Inst. for Def. Analyses, Alexandria, Va., 1990—. Mem. acad. adv. panel to tech. transfer intelligence com. CIA, 1983-90; mem. def. trade adv. group U.S. Dept. State, 1994-96; mem. com. for protection of human subjects ARC, 1996—; dir. VSA arts, 1998—, PLATO Learning Inc., 2002--. Mem. NAS (panel on future design and implementation of nat. security export controls 1989-91), AAAS (com. on sci. freedom and responsibility 1987-93), D.C. Bar Assn. Home: 2737 Devonshire Pl NW Apt 511 Washington DC 20008-3458 Office: Inst for Def Analyses 4850 Mark Center Dr Alexandria VA 22311-1882 Business E-Mail: rgreenst@ida.org.

GREENSTEIN, SHARON DIANE, health facility administrator, educator; b. Boston, May 18, 1962; d. George David and Barbara Evelyn (Bloom) G.; m. Robert Dean Sellers, Oct. 6, 1991; children: Bryan Jacob, Daniel Michael. BSN, U. Pa., 1984; MBA, U. Chgo., 1989. RN, Pa., Ill. Nurse Grad. Hosp., Phila., 1984-87, U. Chgo. Hosps., 1987-88; provider rels. cons. Pru Care Ill., Des Plaines, 1988; cons. Price Waterhouse, Chgo., 1989; dir. fin. svcs. Rush-Presbyn.-St. Luke's Med. Ctr., Chgo., 1990-96; dir. managed care Pediat. Faculty Found. Children's Meml. Hosp., Chgo., 1996—99; dir. managed care contracting Brigham and Women's Hosp., Boston, 1999—. Instr. Rush U., Chgo., 1990-97. Mem. Chgo. Health Execs. Forum. Jewish. Avocations: tennis, jogging. Home: 16 Olde Field Rd Newton MA 02459-2733 Office: Brigham and Womens Hosp 75 Francis St Boston MA 02115

GREENWALD, CAROL SCHIRO, professional services marketing research executive; b. Phila., Mar. 2, 1939; d. Sidney L. and Adele R. (Rosenheim) Schiro; children: David Bruce, William Michael. BA cum laude, Smith Coll., 1961; MA, Hunter Coll., 1965; PhD in Polit. Sci., CUNY, 1972. Instr. polit. sci. Queen's Coll., CUNY, 1970-73; asst. dir. Evaluation N.Y.C. Adminstrv. Decentralization Project, 1971-73; asst. prof. Richmond Coll., CUNY, 1973-76, Bklyn. Coll., CUNY, 1976-77; research assoc. Bunting Inst., Radcliffe Coll., 1977-79; project dir. Jobs in the 1980s Pub. Agenda Found., N.Y.C., 1979-81; assoc. dir. Grant Thornton acctg. firm, 1984-86; sr. mgr. Seidman and Seidman, 1986-87; market research mgr. KPMG Peat Marwick, 1988-90; cons., 1990-91, 2002—; mktg. dir. Haight, Gardner, Poor & Havens, 1991-92; dir. comm. Richard A. Eisner & Co., LLP, 1993-97; dir. mktg. Hamilton, HMC divsn. Kurt Salmon Assoc., 1997—, Whitman Breed Abbott & Morgan LLP, 1998-2000; cons. Market-Force, a divsn. of Hildebrandt, Internat., 2002; pvt. practice, 2002—. Author: Group Power: Lobbying and Public Policy, 1977; mem. editl. bd. Mktg. Rev., 1997—; contbr. articles on polit. sci. to profl. jours. Lilly Found. fellow Mem. Am. Mktg. Assn. (chair profl. devel. leadership coun. 1995—, mem. edtl. bd. 1996—), Common Cause (chmn. N.Y. 1981-83, nat. dir. 1978-84), Westchester Women in Comm. (treas. 1993-95). Home: 688 Forest Ave Larchmont NY 10538-1535 E-mail: greenwaldcarol@hotmail.com.

GREENWALD, SHEILA ELLEN, writer, illustrator; b. N.Y.C., May 26, 1934; d. Julius and Florence (Friedman) Greenwald; m. George E. Green, Feb. 18, 1960; children: Samuel Green, Benjamin Green. BA, Sarah Lawrence Coll., 1956. Author over 24 children's books, including Give Us a Great Big Smile Rosy Cole, 1980, Valentine Rosy, 1984, Rosy Cole's Great American Guilt Club, 1987, Write on Rosy, 1988, Rosy's Romance, 1989, Here's Hermione, 1991, The Mariah Delary Author of the Month Club, 1990, Rosy Cole Discovers America, 1992, My Fabulous NewLife, 1993, Rosy Cole, She Walks in Beauty, 1994, Rosy Cole: She Grows and Graduates, 1997, Stucksville, 2000, Mariah Delany Lending Library Disaster (The Mariah Delany Author of The Month Club 1999), Stucksville, 2001, The Hot Day reissued as Silver Mountain, 2002, Rosy Cole's Worst Ever, Best Yet Tour of New York City, 2003. Mem. PEN, Authors League.

Jewish. Office: Melanie Kroupa Books Ferrar Straus & Geroux 19 Union Sq W New York NY 10003 and: Orchard/Scholastic Inc 555 Broadway New York NY 10012 E-mail: sheilagreenwald@usa.net.

GREENWALD, THERESA MCGOWAN, medical administrator, nurse; b. Scranton, Pa., Feb. 8, 1950; d. Robert Bell and Agnes (Butler) McGowan; m. David Jeffrey Greenwald, Oct. 26, 1996; 1 child, Jennifer Emilie Nicole Drescher. Diploma in nursing, Hosp. U. Pa., Phila., 1970. RN, Ohio; cert. rehab. nurse, case mgr. Staff nurse, asst. head nurse Riddle Meml. Hosp., Media, Pa., 1971-80; rehab. nurse, mgr. Upjohn Rehab. Scvs., Phila. and Cin., 1980-85; cons., life care planner Occupl. Health Resources, Cin., 1985-87, Springfield, Va., 1987-88; dir. life care planning Rehab. Experts, Vienna, Va., 1988-89; program mgr., account exec. Comprehensive Rehab. Assocs., Cin., 1989-93; dir. managed care case mgmt. Sheakley Med. Mgmt. Sys., Cin., 1993-95; clin. program coord. Mayfield Clinic and Spine Inst., Cin., 1996—; dir. Nat. Bd. Certification Continuity of Care, 1998-99. Mem. cmty. adv. bd. Drake Ctr., Inc., 1998-2000. Mem. Nurse Case Mgrs. of S.W. Ohio (membership chair 1994-99). Office: Mayfield Spine Inst 506 Oak St Cincinnati OH 45219-2507

GREENWOOD, AUDREY GATES, librarian; b. Buffalo, Mar. 27, 1917; d. Marc Herbert and Genevieve Cecelia (Naab) Gates; BA, D'Youville Coll., 1939; BS in Library Sci., Cath. U. Am., 1940, MA, 1944; m. Clayton Edward Greenwood, Sept. 2, 1944; children— Mary Ellen, Nancy Jane, Susan Jean. Head librarian Gonzaga High Sch., Washington, 1940-45, Southeastern U. Evening Sch., 1941-45; reference librarian Cath. U. Am., evenings 1942-43; librarian St. Joseph's Collegiate Inst., Buffalo, 1945-46; head librarian Canisius High Sch., Buffalo, 1949-50; head librarian Eden (N.Y.) Central Schs., 1950-83, coordinator state and fed. funds, 1969-83, dir. adult edn., 1973-83. Recipient Frederica Hollinter award, 2002. Mem. Eden Tchrs. Assn. (past pres.), Erie County Ednl. Assn. (past v.p.), NEA, N.Y. State Tchrs. Assn., N.Y. State United Tchrs. (state del. 1992—, legis. chmn. Western zone, chmn. retirees of western N.Y. 1984-88, pres. retirees of western N.Y. 1989-96, mem. ROC com. 1985-88, mem. editl. bd. The Active N.Y. State United Tchrs. Retiree, pres. coun. II 1997—, mem. Commn. 100, retiree del. 1992—), N.Y. State Retired Tchrs. Assn. (pres. Southtowns chpt. 1987—, legis. commn. 1987—, historian western zone 1988-97, del. 1991—), Am. Fedn. Tchrs. (nat. del. 1984--), Sch. Librarians Assn. Western N.Y. (past pres.), N.Y. Educators Assn., Delta Kappa Gamma. (state legis. chmn., state fin. com. 1991—), Beta Zeta (v.p. 1986-89, pres. 1989-95). Democrat. Roman Catholic. Home: 5595 Armor Duells Rd Orchard Park NY 14127-3121

GREENWOOD, COLLETTE P. municipal official, finance officer; b. Summit, Ill. BA, Ea. Wash. U., 1980. With acctg. dept. Montgomerty Ward, Spokane, Wash., 1976-90; acctg. clk. water, hydro City of Spokane, 1979-93, budget acctg., 1993-96, dir. of office of mgmt. & bufget, 1996—. Recipient Class of 1998 award Leadership Spokane Spokane C. of C. Mem. Nat. Mgmt. Assn. (elected dir. 1999), Govt. Fin. Officers Assn., Wash. Fin. Officers Assn. Office: City Spokane 808 W Spokane Falls Blvd Spokane WA 99201-3333

GREENWOOD, HARRIET LOIS, environmental banker, researcher; b. Detroit, Oct. 4, 1950; d. Samuel H. and Elizabeth Ann (Bode) G.; m. Michael E. Carlson, Aug. 23, 1981 (div. Sept. 1986); m. Eric J. Halbeisen, Sept. 5, 1987 (div. Nov. 2003); 1 child, Robin Faith. BA in Biology, Antioch Coll., 1972; MS in Tchg., Antioch Coll. New Eng., 1975; postgrad., U. Mich., 1985-87. Dir. environ. studies Swanson Environ., Southfield, Mich., 1978-80; project mgr. ESEI, Ecol. Scis., Detroit, 1981-82; pres. Greenwood & Assocs., Detroit, 1982-83; mgr. environ. studies Environ. Rsch. Group, Ann Arbor, Mich., 1983-85; environ. policy specialist Clayton Environ., Southfield, 1985-91; pres. Environ. Tng. Svcs., Detroit, 1991-93; asst. v.p. Comerica Bank, 1993—. Part-time instr. Wayne State U., 1992—; rec. clk. Detroit Friends Meeting, 1985-88; bd. dirs. Friends Sch. Detroit, 1987-89. U. Mich. fellow, 1985-86. Mem.: S.E. Mich. Sustainable Bus. Forum, Mich. Bankers Assn. (environ. com.), Mich. Assn. Environ. Profls., East Mich. Environ. Action Coun., Environ. Bankers Assn., Nat. Trust Real Estate Assn. Mem. Soc. Of Friends. Avocations: english country dancing, cross country skiing, hand spinning. Office: Comerica Bank Trust Real Estate-3228 PO Box 75000 Detroit MI 48275-3228

GREENWOOD, HELEN MAXINE, retired office manager, executive assistant; b. Hoopeston, Ill., Oct. 20, 1916; d. Lloyd Earle and Eugenia Blanche (Evans) Gladding; m. James Condon, 1940 (div. 1957); children: Yvonne Condon Brosius, Marguita Condon Brown, Vivienne Condon Sargeant; m. James Raymond Greenwood, Sept. 11, 1970. BS in Journalism, U. Ill., 1938. Mem. display advt. staff Moline (Ill.) Daily Dispatch, 1938-41, book rev. columnist, 1939-41; legal sec. Moyer and Hiebert, Wichita, Kans., 1961-65; exec. sec. Learjet Corp., Wichita, 1965-70; adminstr. Camp Tapawingo, Alexandria, Va., 1971-73; exec. asst. Aerospace Cons., Green Valley, Ariz., 1985-98. Co-author: Stunt Flying in the Movies, 1982 (award Aviation Space Writers Assn. 1983); editor various publs. Life mem. pres. coun. U. Ill.; vol. Am. Red Cross, Wichita Art Mus. Bronze Tablet scholar U. Ill. Mem. AAUW (hon. life mem., pres. Wichita Branch, 1962-64, Svc. award 1988), Green Valley Women's Club, Aero Club Ariz., Ariz. Hist. Soc., Tubac Hist. Soc. Avocations: music, travel, hiking, reading, historical research. Home and Office: 435 E El Valle Green Valley AZ 85614-2924

GREENWOOD, JANET KAE DALY, psychologist, educational administrator, marketing professional; b. Goldsboro, N.C., Dec. 9, 1943; d. Fulton Benton and Kelminy Ethel Esther (Ball) Daly; 1 child, Gerald Thompson. AA, Peace Coll., 1963; BS in English and Psychology, East Carolina U., 1965, MEd in Counseling, 1967; postgrad., N.C. State U., 1967-69, U. London, 1969; PhD in Counseling and Higher Ednl. Adminstrn., Fla. State U., 1972. Tchr. English Kinston (N.C.) City Schs., 1965-66, Goldsboro City Schs., 1966-67; counselor and psychometrist primary and secondary schs. County of Wake, N.C., 1967-69; coord. Am. Inst. for Fgn. Study, 1969; supr. student tours in Eng., France, Switzerland, Italy, and Capri, 1969; counselor Fla. State U., Tallahassee, 1969-72; asst. dir. counseling Rutgers U., New Brunswick, N.J., 1972-73, cons. to v.p. for student svcs., 1973-74, lectr. in counseling psychology, 1972-74; coord. and assoc. prof. counselor edn. U. Cin., 1974-77, adviser to grad. students, 1974-77, vice provost student affairs, 1977-81; pres. Longwood Coll., Farmville, Va., 1981-87, U. Bridgeport, Conn., 1987-92; cons., ptnr., dir. Heidrick & Struggles, Washington, 1992-2000; v.p. A.T. Kearney, Inc., 2000—04; owner Greenwood & Assocs., Inc., 2004—. Guidance cons. South Plainfield Pub. Schs., 1973-76; adviser Parents without Ptnrs., 1976; bd. dirs. Hydraulic Co.; mem. Gov.'s Partnership To Prevent Substance Abuse in the Workforce, mem. audit com. and cmty. and govt. rels. com. Contbr. articles to profl. jours. Mem. Gov.'s Ad Hoc Edn. Com. on Tchr. Edn. and Counselor Edn., State of Ohio, 1975; mem. state planning commn. Nat. Identification of Women Project; chair Twin Rivers Tenants Rights Assn., 1972-74; bd. dirs. Bridgeport Hosp., Bridgeport Bus. Coun.; mem. adv. com. Bridgeport Pub. Edn. Fund; bd. dirs. Conn. Ballet Theatre, chair South End streeting com; mem. mgmt. adv. com. City of Bridgeport; mem. adv. com. United Way Tri-State; chair South End Partnership Com; mem. The Schiavone Steering Com./Downtown Bridgeport Project, YWCA Bd., Champion/United Way, United Way Community Human Svcs. Planning Coun., Bridgeport Symphony Bd., Bridgeport Opera Bd., Bridgeport Area Coll./Univ. Consortium, Conn. Conf. Ind. Colls., The Newcomen Soc. of U.S., The United Way Ea. Fairfield County; mem. adv. bd. Sacred Heart/St. Anthony Sch., Roosevelt Sch; mem. ct. com. Regional Plan Assn. Fairfield 2000; bd. dirs. Conn. Ballet Theatre; chair The Bridgeport Regional Bus. Coun. Brass Ring Task Force on Leadership; bd. govs. Fairfield County Study; mem. hon. bd. dirs. Conn. Earth Day 20, Inc.; chair L.I. Sound Western Regional Coun.; founding mem. L.I. Sound Assembly; mem. membership com., campus partnership subcom. Drugs Don't Work program, 1989-91. Recipient Spl. award Black Arts Festival, Meritorious Svc. award Am. Assn. State Colls. and Univs. Mem. AAUP, Am. Coll. Pers. Assn. (editor and chair media bd. 1975—), Am. Pers. and Guidance Assn., Cin. Pers. and Guidance Assn., Ohio Psychol. Assn., Clin. Psychol. Assn., Organizational Behavior Assn., Am. Sch. Counselors Assn., Ohio Sch. Counselors Assn., Assn. for Women Faculty, Ohio Counselor Edn. and Supervision Assn., Kappa Delta Pi.

GREENWOOD, JOAN, state representative; b. Glendale, Calif., Oct. 7, 1942; d. Oliver and Helen (Koleon) Bakken; m. Tom Greenwood; children: Laura, Douglas, Holly. BA in English, San Jose U. Tchr.; mem. Okla. Ho. of Reps., 1989—, vice chmn. pub. health com. Republican. Office: State Capitol 2300 N Lincoln Blvd Rm 507 Oklahoma City OK 73105

GREENWOOD, JOEN ELIZABETH, economist, consultant; b. Mineral Point, Wis., Aug. 29, 1934; d. John Edward and Lillian Laile (Rohr) G. BS, MA, U. Wis., 1956, 57; postgrad., U. Calif., Berkeley, 1957—61, Newnham Coll. Cambridge U., Eng., 1961-62; diploma in Advanced Mgmt. Program, Harvard Bus. Sch., 1983. Instr. econs. Wellesley (Mass.) Coll., 1962-68; sr. assoc. Charles River Assocs., Boston, 1968-79, v.p., 1979—2003, sr. cons., 2003—. Mem. bd. editors Energy Jour., 1979-83; mem. Nat. Coal Coun., 1993-2000. Co-author: Folded, Spindled and Mutilated: Economic Analysis and U.S. v. IBM, 1983; contbr. to profl. publs. Mem. Commonwealth of Mass. Pub. Health Coun., Boston, 1973—79; chairwoman Women's Philantropy Coun. U. Wis. Found., 2001—04, bd. dirs., 2001—04. Earhart fellow U. Calif.-Berkeley, 1960-61; Fulbright scholar U.K., 1961-62 Mem. Internat. Assn. Energy Economists (v.p. 1978-84, exec. v.p. 1981-84), U. Wis. Alumni Assn. (bd. dirs. 1987-93), Wis. Alumni Assn. Greater Boston (pres. 1987-89), Boston Club, Harvard Club, Phi Beta Kappa. Home: 130 Mt Auburn St Unit 304 Cambridge MA 02138 Office: Charles River Assocs 200 Clarendon St Fl 33 Boston MA 02116-5092 E-mail: jeg@crai.com.

GREENWOOD, M. R. C. college dean, biologist, nutrition educator; b. Gainesville, Fla., Apr. 11, 1943; d. Stanley James and Mary Rita (Schmeltz) Cooke; m. (div. 1968); 1 child, James Robert. AB summa cum laude, Vassar Coll., 1968; PhD, Rockefeller U., 1973; LHD (hon.), Mt. St. Mary Coll., 1989. Rsch. assoc. Inst. of Human Nutrition, Columbia U., N.Y.C., 1974-75, adj. asst. prof., 1975-76, asst. prof., 1976-78; assoc. prof. dept. biology Vassar Coll., Poughkeepsie, N.Y., 1978-81, prof. biology, 1981-86, dir. animal model, CORE Lab. of Obesity Rsch. Ctr., 1985-89, dir. undergrad. rsch. summer inst., 1986-88, dir. Howard Hughes biol. scis. network program, 1988, chmn. of biology dept., John Guy Vassar prof. natural scis., 1986-89; prof. nutrition and internal medicine, dean grad. studies U. Calif., Davis, 1989-96, chancellor Santa Cruz, 1996—2004; sr. v.p. academic affairs U. Calif. sys., 2004—. Mem. nutrition study sect. NIH, 1983-87; mem. NRC; assoc. dir. for sci. White House Office Sci. and Tech., 1993-95. Editor: Obesity, Vol. 4, 1983; contbr. over 250 articles and abstracts to profl. jours., 1974-89. Recipient Rsch. Career Devel. award NIH, 1978-83; Mellon scholar-in-residence St. Olaf Coll., Northfield, Minn., 1978; N.Y. State Regents fellow, 1968. Mem. Inst. Medicine of Nat. Acad. Scis. (chair food and nutrition bd., diet and health subcom. 1986—), N.Am. Soc. for Study of Obesity (pres. 1987-88), Am. Inst. Nutrition (BioServ 1982), Am. Physiol. Soc., The Harvey Soc., Am. Diabetes Assn., Internat. Assn. for Study of Obesity (treas. 1991—). Home: University House Santa Cruz CA 95064 Office: U Calif Chancellor Office 296 McHenry Libr Santa Cruz CA 95064-1077

GREENWOOD, MONIQUE, innkeeper, writer, restaurant owner; b. Wash., DC; m. Glenn Pogue. Grad. magna cum laude, Howard U. Lifestyle dir., style editor Essence mag., 1996—98, exec. editor, 1998—2000, editor-in-chief, 2000—01; owner, innkeeper Akwaaba Mansion Bed & Breakfast, Bklyn., 1995—, Akwaaba by the Sea, Cape May, NJ, 2001—; owner Akwaaba Cafe, Bklyn. Co-founder, pres. Go On Girl! Book Club. Author: Having What Matters: The Black Woman's Guide to Creating the Life You Really Want, 2001. Bd. mem. Bklyn. Urban League, Central Bklyn. Partnership, Bridge St. Devel. Corp. Recipient Points of Light award, Pres. Bush. Avocations: reading, antiques, travel, interior decorating. Mailing: Akwaaba Mansion Bed & Breakfast 347 MacDonough St Brooklyn NY 11233 Office Phone: 718-455-5958. Office Fax: 718-774-1744.*

GREENWOOD, PILAR FERNANDEZ-CAÑADAS, language and literature educator; b. Herencia, La Mancha, Spain, Feb. 26, 1940; came to U.S., 1965. d. Isidro Fernández-Cañadas and Maria Rosario González-Ortega; m. Davydd James Greenwood, June 19, 1965; 1 child, Alex David Greenwood. MA, U. Pitts., 1967, Cornell U., Ithaca, 1979, PhD, 1981. Head resident Grinnell (Iowa) Coll., 1963-64; lectr. Cornell U., Ithaca, N.Y., 1972-75, Wells Coll., Aurora, N.Y., 1987, vis. asst. prof., 1988-90, asst. prof., 1990-94, assoc. prof., 1994—. Author: Pastoral Poetics, 1983; contbr. numerous articles to profl. jours. Vol. CIVITAS, Ithaca, N.Y., 1983; mem. League of Women Voters, Ithaca, N.Y., 1987. Grantee Program Cultural Cooper, U. Minn., 1987. Mem. MLA, Assn. Cervantists, Feministas Unidas, Assn. Licenciados y Doctores Españoles en Estados Unidos, Phi Kappa Phi. Roman Catholic. Avocations: travel, music, performing arts, visual arts, gardening. Office: Wells Coll Rt 90 Aurora NY 13026

GREENWOOD LEVY, PHAEDRA JEAN, photojournalist, writer; b. Elmhurst, Ill., Aug. 24, 1942; d. Donald Gore and Joan Louise Barr; children: Alexander Bluesky Levy, Sara Kay Levy. Freelance writer, Taos, N.Mex., 2000—; columnist, staff reporter The Taos News, Taos, N.Mex., 1995—. Investigative reporter The Taos News, Taos, N.Mex., 1995—2000. Author: (short stories) Nimrod (Katherine Anne Porter Award, 1988). Sec. Com. to Save the Rio Hondo, Taos, N.Mex., 1977—82. Recipient PEN N.Mex, PEN, 1995, E.H. Shaffer awards, N.Mex Press Assn., 2000, Comm. Contest awards, N.Mex Press Women, 1997, 2001, Nikon Picture Am. Photo Contest, Nikon, Inc., 1998. Unitarian. Achievements include investigation of cattle mutilations. Avocations: writing, scuba diving, equestrian, photography. Home: PO Box 388 Arroyo Hondo NM 87513 Personal E-mail: phaedra@newmex.com.

GREER, CAROLYN A. guidance counselor; b. Dallas, Oct. 27, 1943; d. Billy Bryan and Estelle Catherine (Haney) Harris; m. Charles David Melton, Nov. 25, 1965 (div. Aug. 1991); 1 child, Melissa Gayle Melton Brydson; m. Robert S. Greer, Aug. 16, 1991. BA in English, U. North Tex., 1965, MEd in Counseling, 1971, mid-mgmt. cert., 1987, supt. cert., 1992, EdD, 1997; spl. edn. endorsement, Tex. Christian U., 1973. Lic. profl. counselor, Tex; approved supr. for lic. profl. counselors; cert. supt., Tex.; cert. mid-mgmt. adminstr., Tex.; cert. provisional secondary English, Tex.; cert. provisional secondary history, Tex. Tchr. English Carrollton-Farmers br. Ind. Sch. Dist., 1970-71, Onslow County Schs., NC, 1967, Dallas Ind. Sch. Dist., 1965-66, 68, 69; counselor Hurst-Euless-Bedford Ind. Sch. Dist., 1973-90; program dir. guidance and counseling Ft. Worth Ind. Sch. Dist., 1990-96; asst. prof. ednl. leadership and counseling dept. Sam Houston State U., 1996-98; instrnl. officer guidance and counseling Katy Ind. Sch. Dist., Tex., 1998—2001; cons. secondary assessment ACT, Inc., Austin, 2001—03; dir. enrollment Big Bros. Big Sisters Ctrl. Tex., 2003—. Adj. prof. U. H-Victoria, 1999-2000; part-time instr. psychology Tarrant County Jr. Coll., 1974-85; mem. Tex. Atty. Gen. Task Force on Sch. Violence Prevention, 1999-00; adv. mem. Tex. State Bd. for Educator Certification, 1998-2000; presenter workshops in field. Author: (books) Comprehensive Guidance Program—Ft. Worth, 1991, Administrv. Guide to Bias Free Classrooms, 1993; editl. adv. bd. Student Assistance Jour., 1989-91. Mem. women's issues com. Sam Houston State U., Huntsville, Tex., 1997-98; mem. zoning Commn., Bedford, Tex., 1990-92; mem. adv. for counselors Tex. Edn. Agy., Austin, Tex., 1998-99. Recipient Pub. Awareness award Tarrant County Mental Health Assn., 1995. Mem. ASCD, ACA (govt. rels. com. 1991-92, 99-2000), Am. Sch. Counselors Assn. (chair pub. rels. com. 1996-98), Assn. Counselor Educators and Supr. (chair sch. issues 1995-97), Nat. Career Devel. Assn. (chair sch. and bus. partnerships spl. interest group com. 1995-98), Tex. Counseling Assn. (senator 1985-88, sec. 1990-91, dir. region IV 1994-96, 1996 local conf. coord., pres.-elect 1997-98, pres. 1998-99, Rhoaine Fleming Outstanding Sch. Counselor award 1989, Molly Gerold Human Rights award 1995), Tex. Sch. Counselor's Assn. (pres. 1989-90), Tex. Assn. for Counselor Educators and Supr. (pres. 1995-96), Tex. Career Guidance Assn. (bd. dirs. 1993-96, pres. 1996-97), Tex. Assn. for Supervision and Curriculum Devel., Tex. Coun. Women Sch. Exec., North Cen. Tex. Counseling Assn. (pres. 1980-81, Outstanding Counselor award 1988, Caring Counselor award 1993). Avocations: walking, gourmet cooking, gardening. Home: 10018 Planters Woods Dr Austin TX 78730 Office: Big Brothers Big Sisters of Ctrl Texas 1400 Tillery Austin TX 78721 E-mail: greerc@act.org.

GREER, CAROLYN ARLENE, music educator, elementary school educator; b. Aberdeen, Wash., Apr. 29, 1961; d. Kenneth Junior and Alice Lorraine Linder; m. Ronald Keith Greer, Aug. 20, 1983; children: Tiffany Joy, Crystal Lynn, Brianna Nicole. AA in Gen. Studies, Grays Harbor Coll., 1982, N.W. Nazarene U., 1987; BA in Elem. Edn., St. Martin's Coll., 1999; student, Seattle (Wash.) Pacific U., 2002—. Cert. tchr. K-8; Music K-12 Wash., 1999. Med. records clk. Dr.s Morgan, Morgan & Worth Family Practice Ctr. of GH, Aberdeen, Wash., 1980—83; med. receptionist, bookkeeper Dr.s Magsalay, Caratao & Hutton (Pediat.), Aberdeen, 1988—96; elem. music tchr. Hoquiam (Wash.) Sch. Dist., 1999—, elem. band tchr., 1999—. Musician, worship leader, children's music ministries Immanuel Bapt. Ch., Hoquiam, 1994—; h.s. choir accompanist Hoquiam (Wash.) HS, 1996—97; accompanist all-state competition Hoquiam (Wash.) Sch. Dist., 1996—97, asst. elem. girls track coach, 2001—; judicator Ann. River Festival City Hoquiam, 2000—. Author: (plays) Christmas With Grandma, 1977;; editor: (plays) Christmas With Grandma; dir., prodr.: (plays) Christmas With Grandma. Mem.: NEA (assoc.), Wash. State Music Tchrs. Assn., Grays Harbor Chpt., Ret. Tchrs. Assn. (assoc.), Music Educators Nat. Conf. (assoc.). Republican. Avocations: kite festivals, camping, canoeing, singing, gardening, crafts.

GREER, CHERYL L. middle school educator; b. Hammond, Ind., Oct. 27, 1954; d. Roger R. and Margaret L. Potts; m. David E. Greer, June 8, 1974 (div. May 17, 2001); children: Kristen M., Jessica L. Student, Butler U., 1972—74; MusB, Wayne State U., 1976; MA in Edn., Western Ky. U., 1995. Asst. mgr., treas. Royal Oak Cmty. Credit Union, Royal Oak, Mich., 1977—82; note teller Farmer's Bank & Trust, Bardstown, Ky., 1982—85; owner, mgr. Sweets 'n Things, Bardstown, 1985—90; sub. tchr. Hardin County Pub. Schs., Elizabethtown, 1990—93; band dir., music tchr. Bullitt Lick Mid. Sch., Shepherdsville, 1993—. Musician 1st Christian Ch., Elizabethtown, 1992—95, Sunday Sch. tchr., 1992—95, Rineyville Bapt. Ch., Rineyville, Ky., 1996—97; musician Bardstown Meth. Ch., Bardstown, Ky., 2001—; mem. I.U.S. Concert Band, 2002—. Mem.: Ky. Educators Assn., Ky. Music Educators Assn. (sec., treas. 5th dist. 2001—), Music Educators Nat. Conf.

GREER, GERMAINE, author; b. Melbourne, Australia, Jan. 29, 1939; d. Eric Reginald and Margaret May Mary (Lafrank) G. BA with honors in English, French Lit., U. Melbourne, 1959; MA with honors in English, U. Sydney, Australia, 1961; PhD (Commonwealth scholar), Newnham Coll. of Cambridge U., Eng., 1967; Doctorate (hon.), U. Griffith, 1996, U. York, Toronto, 1999, Manchester Inst. Tech., 2000. Sr. tutor U. Sydney, 1963-64; lectr. English U. Warwick, Eng., 1967-72; prof. modern letters U. Tulsa, 1980-83; dir. Tulsa Ctr. for Study of Woman's Lit.; prof. English and comparative studies U. Warwick, 1998—. Vis. prof. grad. faculty modern letters U. Tulsa, fall 1979; founder-dir. Tulsa Centre for the Study of Women's Lit.; founder, editor Tulsa Studies in Women's Lit., 1981; dir. Stump Cross Books, 1988—; spl. lectr. and unofcl. fellow Newnham Coll., Cambridge, 1989-98; lectr. in N.Am. Am. Program Bur., 1973-78. Author: The Female Eunuch, 1969, The Obstacle Race: The Fortunes of Women Painters and their Work, 1979, Sex and Destiny: The Politics of Human Fertility, 1984, Shakespeare, 1986, The Madwoman's Underclothes, 1986, Daddy, We Hardly Knew You, 1989 (J.R. Ackerly Prize, Premio Internazionale Mondello), The Change: Women, Aging and the Menopause, 1991, Slip-Shod Sibyls: Recognition, Rejection and the Woman Poet, 1995, The Surviving Works of Anne Wharton, 1997; editor: (with Susan Hastings, Jeslyn Medoff, Melinda Sansone) Kissing the Rod: An Anthology of Seventeenth Century Women's Verse, 1988, The Uncollected Verse of Aphra Behn, 1989, The Change: Women, Aging and the Menopause, 1991, Slip-Shod Sibyls: Recognition, Rejection and the Woman Poet, 1995, The Whole Woman, 1999, The Whole Woman, 1999, John Wilmot, Earl of Rochester, 1999 The Boy, 2003; editor 101 Poems by 101 Women, 2001, Poems for Gardeners, 2003; selected journalism published as The Madwoman's Underclothes, 1986, columnist Sunday Times, London, 1971-73, broadcaster/journalist/reviewer various publs. 1972-79. Jr. Govt. scholar, 1952, Diocesan scholar, 1956, Sr. Govt. scholar, 1956, Commonwealth scholar, 1964, Teacher's Coll. Studentship, 1956, Hon. Doctorate Univ. of Griffith, 1996.

GREER, MIMI (MARTHA) EMILIE, language educator; b. Chicago, Ill., Dec. 4, 1947; d. John Robert and Jean Braunlich Greer. BA, U. Of Tex., 1967—69; MA, Drake U., 2003. Cert. Teacher Iowa, 1998, Tex., 1989. Mktg. mgr. AMLINGS, Chicago, Ill., 1985—88; spanish tchr. Ector Co. Isd, Odessa, Tex., 1989—98, Walcott Sch., Walcott, Iowa, 1998—. D-Liberal. Avocations: travel, golf. Home: 3000 E 32nd St #14 Davenport IA 52800 Office: Walcott School Walcott IA 52773 Personal E-mail: mimigreer222@aol.com.

GREETHAM, ELIZABETH M. health products executive; BSc, MA with honors, U. Edinburgh. Former cons. F. Eberstadt & Co.; former portfolio mgr. Weiss, Peck & Greer; bd. dirs. DrugAbuse Scis., Inc., Los Altos, Calif., 1998—, CFO, 1999—, CEO, 2000—. Bd. dirs. Guilford Pharms, Sangstat Med. Corp., PathoGenesis Corp., CliniChem Devel. Inc. Office: DrugAbuse Scis Inc 330 Distel Cir Ste 150 Los Altos CA 94022

GREEVER, JANET GROFF, history educator; b. Philadelphia, Sept. 12, 1921; m. William St. Clair Greever, Aug. 24, 1951; 1 child. BA, Bryn Mawr Coll., 1942, MA, 1945, Harvard U., 1951, PhD, 1954. Resident head grad. houses Radcliffe Coll., Cambridge, Mass., 1947-48; resident head undergrad. hall Bryn Mawr (Pa.) Coll., 1949-51, instr. history, 1949-50; asst. prof. history Wash. State U., Pullman, 1962-63, U. Idaho, Moscow, 1965-66; ind. rschr., lectr. history Moscow, Idaho, 1954—. Interim lectr. history Whitman Coll., Walla Walla, Wash., 1978; Idaho regional admissions cons. and interviewer Bryn Mawr COll., 1955-81. Author: Jose Ballivian y El Oriente Boliviano, 1987. Bd. dirs. U. Idaho Libr. Assocs., Moscow, 1979-81, pres. 1980-81. Pa. State scholar, 1938-42, History fellow Bryn Mawr (Pa.) Coll., 1944-45, Margaret M. Justin fellow AAUW, Washington, 1948-49; grantee Lucius N. Littauer Found., N.Y.C., 1948-49. Mem. Am. Hist. Assn. (life), Conf. on Latin. Am. History (life), Latin Am. Studies Assn., Soc. for Am. Archaeology (life), Archaeol. Inst. Am. (life), Phi Alpha Theta. Avocations: travel, photography. Home: 315 S Hayes St Moscow ID 83843-3419

GREGERSON, LINDA KAREN, poet, language educator, critic; b. Elgin, Ill., Aug. 5, 1950; d. Olaf Thorbjorn and Karen Mildred Gregerson; m. Steven Mullaney, 1980; children: Emma Mullaney, Megan Mullaney. BA, Oberlin Coll., 1971; MA, Northwestern U., 1972; MFA, U. Iowa, 1977; PhD, Stanford U., 1987. Actress Kraken Theater Co., 1972—75; asst. poetry editor The Atlantic Monthly Press, 1982—86; staff editor Atlantic Monthly, Boston, 1982—87; asst. prof. Dept. English U. Mich., 1987—91, William Wilhartz asst. prof. English, 1991—94, assoc. prof. Dept. English, 1994—2001, prof. Dept. English, 2001—03, Frederick G. L. Huetwell prof., prof. English, 2003—, dir. MFA program in creative writing, 1997—2000. Mem. usage panel Am. Heritage Dictionary, 1987—; vis. asst.

prof. creative writing program Dept. English Boston U., 1985—86; instr. lit. MIT, 1985—87; asst. editor Mich. Quarterly Rev., 1987—; editl. cons. Cambridge Univ. Press, 1989—, Harvard Univ. Press, 1989—, Oxford Univ. Press, 1989—, Wesleyan Univ. Press, 1989—, Ind. Univ. Press, 1989—, Bedford Books, 1989—, Univ. Mich. Press, 1989—, Wayne State Univ. Press, 1989—. Author: Fire in the Conservatory, 1982, The Reformation of the Subject: Spenser, Milton, and the English Protestant Epic, 1995, The Woman Who Died in Her Sleep, 1996, Negative Capability: Contemporary American Poetry, 2001, Waterborne, 2002, (poems) Illinois Again, 1975, Alone, 1977, Man Sitting in the Sun, 1979, To Albert Speer, 1980, (poetry) Ex Machina, 1982, Halfe a Yard of Rede Sea, 1983, Mother Ruin, 1984, Blazon, 1984, An Arbor, 1990, For the Taking, 1993, Fish Dying on the Third Floor at Barney's, 1996, Eyes Like Leeks, 2000, Pass Over, 2001, A History Play, 2002, Maculate, 2002. Recipient Levinson Prize award Poetry, 1991, Consuelo Ford award, Poetry Soc. Am., 1992, Isabel MacCaffrey award, Spenser Soc. Am., 1992, Pushcart prize, 1994, 2004, Acad. award in Lit., Am. Acad. Arts and Letters, 2002; fellow, Nat. Endowment Arts, 1985, 1992, Mellon, Nat. Humanities Ctr., 1991—92, Guggenheim, 2000; grantee Arts Found., Mich., 1994; Ingram Merrill grant, 1982—84. Mem.: MLA, Inst. Advanced Study (vis. mem. 1993—94), Milton Soc., Internat. Spenser Soc. (Isabel MacCaffrey award 1992), Renaissance Soc.Am., Shakespeare Assn. Am. Office: U Mich Dept English Lang and Lit 3147 Angell Hall Ann Arbor MI 48109-1045*

GREGG, CYNTHIA LOUISE, music educator; b. Charleroi, Pa., May 7, 1952; d. Michael Richard and Helen Marie Bucci; m. Thomas Lee Gregg, May 27, 1978; children: Ashley Marie, Tommy Lee. MusB, W.Va. U., 1974, MusM, 1976; postgrad., Duquesne U., 1993, Ind. U. Pa., 1994. Cert. tchr. Pa, Orff cert. level 1 Nat. Am. Orff Schulwerk, Orff cert. level 2 Nat. Am. Orff Schulwerk. Piano tchr. Trombino's Music, Belle Vernon, Pa., 1972—75; piano instr. W.Va. U. Prep. Dept., Morgantown, 1972—74; music tchr. Barbour County Schs., Phillippi, W.Va., 1974—75, Washington (Pa.) Sch. Dist., 1975—. Organist, choir dir. St. Anne, 1972—99. Nominee Am. Tchr. award, Disney, 2001. Mem.: Lions (dir. music necrology svc. 1998—99, pres. Rostraver Twp. 2002—, zone chmn. 2003). Roman Catholic. Avocations: travel, music, crafts, reading. Home: 1130 Willowbrook Rd Belle Vernon PA 15012 Office: Washington Park Sch 801 E Wheeling St Washington PA 15301 Personal E-mail: tomgregg1@earthlink.net.

GREGG, ELLA MAE, writer; b. Appalachia, Va., Sept. 29, 1949; d. James Andrew Weatherly and Jewel Audrey Ramey; div.; children: Jeanie Barnett, Marcella Grooms, Jimmie Blazer. Offset pressman, Morritown, 1983, beautician, Knoxville Sch. Beauty, 1985; ins. Liberty Nat., Knoxville Sch. Ins., 1990. Tax cons. Exact Tax, Newport, Tenn.; owner, operator Hair Unltd., Tootie Fruitie's Beauty Shop, Newport. Mem. Mystery Writers Am., Women Guild Am., Police Writers Am. Avocations: walking, dance, reading. Home: PO Box 1214 Newport TN 37822-1214 Office: 543 Freeman Ave Newport TN 37821-3840

GREGG, KATHY KAY, school system administrator; b. Washington, N.C., Aug. 26, 1956; d. Merwin Jack and Mary Elizabeth Gregg. BS, East Carolina U., 1978; MA, Appalachian State U., 1980; MEd, U. South Fla., 1993; PhD, Union Inst., Cin., 1998. Cert. educator Fla. Dept. Edn. Guidance counselor Waycross (Ga.) H.S., 1981—82; family life educator Family Svc. Ctrs., Clearwater, Fla., 1982—84; guildance counselor Pinellas County Schs., Largo, Fla., 1984—92, full svc. sch. coord., 1992—96, sch. adminstr., 1996—. Prof. Eckerd Coll., St. Petersburg, Fla., 1994—. Grantee Challenge Ropes Course, Jr. League St. Petersburg, 1997. Mem.: Assn. Experiential Edn. Avocations: reading, writing, sports, nature photography. Office: Northeast Cmty Sch 1717 54th Ave N Saint Petersburg FL 33714

GREGG, LAUREN, women's soccer coach; b. Rochester, Minn., July 20, 1960; BS in Psychology, U. N.C.; MS in Counseling and Consulting Psychology, Harvard U. Asst. soccer coach U. N.C., 1983; asst. coach Harvard U., Cambridge, Mass.; head coach U. Va., 1987-95; asst. coach U.S. Women's Nat. Soccer Team, 1996—. Named Coach of Yr. Nat. Soccer Coaches Assn. Am., 1990; recipient Gold medal Atlanta Olympics, 1996; Marie Jane postgrad. scholar. Office: US Soccer Fedn US Soccer House 1801 S Prairie Ave Chicago IL 60616-1319

GREGGS, ELANORA, social worker; b. Barnwell County, S.C., Nov. 10, 1933; d. Daniel and Georgia (Cobb) Young; children: John, Christopher, Paulette, Doris. BA, Coll. of New Rochelle, 1985; MSW, Yeshiva U., 1987. Para-profl. Bd. Edn., Bklyn., 1965—67; salesperson Tira Exclusive, Laurelton, NY, 1982—85, Mary Kay Cosmetics, Stanley Home Products; human svcs. supr. Cath. Charities, Bklyn., 1986—87, social work supr. Jamaica, NY, 1987—95, Jamaica Support Sys., 1995. Tchr. Maranatha Bible Inst., 2001—; grief cons., 2001—. Author: Broken Pieces, 1998. Alumni Coll. New Rochelle, NY, 1985—, Yeshiva U., N.Y.C., 1987—; pub. rels. Lake Arbor Found., Mitchellville, Md., 2000—; vol. in nursing homes, 1996—; active Christian Women of Faith, Mitchellville, Md., 2001—; acting min. Evangel Cathedral, 1995—. Avocations: reading, writing, walking, swimming, gardening.

GREGGS, ELIZABETH MAY BUSHNELL (MRS. RAYMOND JOHN GREGGS), retired librarian; b. Delta, Colo., Nov. 7, 1925; d. Joseph Perkins and Ruby May (Stanford) Bushnell; m. Raymond John Greggs, Aug. 16, 1952 (dec. 1994); children: David M., Geoffrey B., Timothy C., Daniel R. BA, U. Denver, 1948. Children's librarian Grand Junction (Colo.) Pub. Library, 1944-46, Chelan County Library, 1948, Wenatchee (Wash.) Pub. Library, 1948-52, Seattle Pub. Library, 1952-53, Renton (Wash.) Pub. Library, 1957-61, dir., 1962, br. supr. and children's services supr., 1963-67; area children's supr. King County Library, Seattle, 1968-78, asst. coordinator children's services, 1978-86; head librarian Valley View Library of King County Library System, Seattle, 1986-90. Cons., organizer Tutor Ctr. Library, Seattle South Community Coll., 1969-72; mem. Puget Sound (Wash.) Council for Reviewing Children's Media, 1974—, chmn., 1974-76; cons. to children's TV programs. Editor: Cayas Newsletter, 1971-74; cons. to Children's Catalog, Children's Index to Poetry. Chmn. dist. advancement com. Kloshee dist. Boy Scouts Am., 1975-78; mem. Bond Issue Citizens Group to build new Renton Libr., 1958, 59; mem. exec. bd. Family Edn. and Counseling Ctr. on Deafness, 1991-94; mem. children's lit. tour People to People, South Africa, 1996. Recipient Hon. Service to Youth award Cedar River dist. Boy Scouts Am., 1971, Award of Merit Kloshee dist., 1977, winner King County Block Grant, 1990. Mem. ALA (Newbery-Caldecott medal com. 1978-79, com. chmn. 1983-84; membership com. 1978-80, Boy Scouts com. children's svcs. div. 1973-78, chmn. 1976-78, exec. bd. dirs. Assn. for Libr. Svc. to Children 1979-81, mem. coun. 1985-92, chmn. nominating com. 1986-87, councillor 1989-92, exec. bd. 1989-92, exec. com. 1989-92, coun. orientation com. 1987-89), Wash. Libr. Assn. (exec. bd. children's and young adult svcs. div. 1970-78, chmn. membership com. 1983-90, publs. com. 1988-92, emeritus 1991, mem. elections com.), King County Right to Read Coun. (co-chmn. 1973-77), Pierce-King County Reading Coun., Wash. State Literacy Coun. (exec. bd. 1971-77), Wash. Libr. Media Assn. (jr. high levels com. 1980-84), Pacific N.W. Libr. Assn. (young readers' choice com. 1981-83, chmn. div. 1983-85, exec. bd. 1983-85). Methodist. Home: 11448 Rainier Ave S Seattle WA 98178-3940

GREGOIRE, CHRISTINE O. state attorney general; b. Auburn, Wash. m. Michael Gregoire; 2 children. BA, U. Wash.; JD cum laude, Gonzaga U., 1977. Clerk, typist Wash. State Adult Probation/ Parole Office, Seattle, 1969; caseworker Wash. Dept. Social and Health Scis., Everett, 1974; asst. atty. gen. State of Wash., Spokane, 1977—81, sr. asst. atty. gen., 1981—82, dep. atty. gen. Olympia, 1982—88; dir. Wash. State Dept. Ecology, 1988—92; atty. gen. State of Wash., 1992—. Chair States/B.C. Oil Spill Task Force, 1989—92, Puget Sound Water Quality Authority, 1990—92, Nat. Com. State Environ. Dirs., 1991—92. Bd. dirs. Wash. State Dept. Ecology, 1988—92. Named Woman of Yr., Am. Legion Aux., 1999; named one of 25 Most Influential Working Mothers, Working Mother mag., 2000; recipient Conservationist of Yr. award, Trout Unlimited/N.W. Steelhead & Salmon Coun., 1994, Gov.'s Child Abuse Prevention award, 1996, Myra Bradwell award, 1997, Wyman award, 1997—98, Bd. of Gov.'s award for professionalism, WSBA, 1997, Kick Butt award, The Tobacco Free Coalition of Pierce County, 1997, Wash. State Hosp. Assn. award, 1997, Citizen Activist award, Gleitsman Found., 1998, Woman of Achievement award, Assn. for Women in Comm. Matrix Table, 1999, Pub. Justice award, WSTLA, 1999, Excellence in Pub. Health award, Wash. State Assn. Local Pub. Health Ofcls., 1999, Women in Govt. award, Good Housekeeping, 1999, Spl. Recognition award, Wash. State Nurses Assn., 2000. Mem.: Nat. Assn. Attys. Gen. (consumer protection and environment com., energy com., children and the law subcom.). Democrat. Office: Attorney Generals Office 1125 Washington St SE PO Box 40100 Olympia WA 98504-6200*

GREGOR, DOROTHY DEBORAH, retired librarian; b. Dobbs Ferry, N.Y., Aug. 15, 1939; d. Richard Garrett Heckman and Marion Allen (Richmond) Stewart; m. A. James Gregor, June 22, 1963 (div. 1974). BA, Occidental Coll., 1961; MA, U. Hawaii, 1963; MLS, U. Tex., 1968; cert. in Library Mgmt., U. Calif., Berkeley, 1976. Reference libr. U. Calif., San Francisco, 1968-69; dept. libr. Pub. Health Libr. U. Calif., Berkeley, 1969-71, tech. services libr., 1973-76; reference libr. Hamilton Libr., Honolulu, 1971-72; head serials dept. U. Calif., Berkeley, 1976-80, assoc. univ. libr. tech. svcs. dept., 1980-84, univ. libr., 1992-94; chief Shared Cataloging div. Libr. of Congress, Washington, 1984-85; univ. libr. U. Calif.-San Diego, La Jolla, 1985-92, OCLC asst. to pres. for acad. and rsch. libr. rels., 1995—98; docent Asian Art Mus., San Francisco, 1997—, ret. Instr. sch. libr. and info. studies U. Calif., Berkeley, 1975, 76, 83; cons. Nat. Libr. of Medicine, Bethesda, Md., 1985, Ohio Bd. Regents, Columbus, 1987; trustee Online Computer Libr. Ctr., 1988-96; dir. Nat. Coordinating Com. on Japanese Libr. Resources, 1995-98; docent Asian Art Mus., San Francisco, 1997-. Mem. ALA, Libr. Info. Tech. Assn., Program Com. Ctr. for Rsch. Librs. (bd. chair 1992-93, Hugh Atkinson award 1994). E-mail: dgregor@mcn.org.

GREGORIE, CORAZON ARZALEM, operations supervisor; b. Bethesda, Md., Aug. 6, 1947; d. Faustino and Rosalina Arzalem. AA in Bus. Adminstrn., Palm Beach Coll., 1967; postgrad., Fla. Atlantic U., 1967; BA in Bus. Adminstrn., U. Fla., 1969. Mgmt. trainee Burdines Dept. Store, West Palm Beach, Fla., 1969; adminstrv. asst. divsn. econs. Nat. Food Processors Assn., Washington, 1970-71, statis. analyst divsn. econs. and stats., 1972-77, acting dir. divsn. econs. and stats., 1978; asst. editor Airfare Pub. Co., Washington, 1979-81; product specialist Arbitron Co., Beltsville, Md., 1982-83, tng. supr. Laurel, Md., 1984-87, night shift ops. supr. Columbia, Md., 1988—95, survey supr., 1996—. Collective mem., bd. dirs. Glut Food, Mt. Rainier, Md., 1973-78. Force vol. Nat. Park Svc., Washington, 1973-76; coord. College Park Food Coop., Md., 1970-72. Mem. Lotus Ltd. (bd. dirs. 1974—, treas., parts and tech. chmn., membership dir., corr. sec.). Avocations: photography, sports cars. Office: Arbitron Co 9705 Patuxent Woods Dr Columbia MD 21046-1572

GREGORY, BETTINA LOUISE, journalist; b. N.Y.C., June 4, 1946; d. George Alexander and V. Elizabeth Friedman; m. John P. Flannery, II, 1981 (div. 2001); 1 child, Diana Elizabeth. Student, Smith Coll., 1964-66; diploma in acting, Webber-Douglas Sch. Dramatic Art, London, 1968; BA in Psychology, Pierce Coll., Athens, Greece, 1972; PsyD, George Washington U., 2002; LittD (hon.), Susquehanna U., 1988, St. Thomas Aquinas U., 1992; LLD (hon.), Wilmington Coll., 1989; D in Journalism (hon.), U. Findlay, 1990; LittD (hon.), Bethany Coll., 2000. Reporter Sta. WVBR-FM, Ithaca, 1972-73, Sta. WCIC-TV, Ithaca, 1972; reporter, anchorwoman Sta. WGBB, Freeport, N.Y., 1973, Sta. WCBS, N.Y.; freelance reporter, writer AP, N.Y.C., 1973-74; freelance reporter N.Y. Times, 1973-74; with ABC News, 1974—2001, corr., 1977-79, White House corr., 1979, sr. gen. assignment corr., 1980, host The American Family, Goodlife TV Network, 1974—; pres. Sunshine State Telephone Co., Miami, Fla. Elected rep. for corrs. ABC News Women's Adv. Bd.; adj. prof. Robert H. Smith Sch. Bus.; adj. prof. exec. masters in bus. adminstrn. U. Md.; host Goodlife TV show "American Family." Reporter TV spl. Flaws in the Shield, 1989 (1st pl. Headliner award), A&E's Biography of Hillary Rodham Clinton, 1994 (Best Documentary ACE award 1994), Murder Trial O.J. Simpson (Edward R. Murrow award Best News Series 1996), Hannibal Lecter: the Honey in the Lion's Mouth, Am.Journal Psychotherapy, 2002. Recipient 1st Place award Nat. Feature News, Odyssey Inst., N.Y., 1978, Clarion award Women in Communications, Inc., 1979, hon. mention Nat. Commn. on Working Women, 1979, Media award for Am. Agenda segment on homeless World Hunger Found., 1990, Cable Ace Best Documentary award, 1995, Edward R. Murrow award for coverage of O.J. Simpson Murder trial, 1996; named one of top 10 investigative reporters, TV Guide, 1983. Mem. Radio TV Corrs. Assn., White House Corrs. Assn. Clubs: Newswomen's N.Y. (recipient Front Page award 1976); Nat. Press; Washington Press. Office: ABC News Washington Bur 1717 Desales St NW Washington DC 20036-4407 E-mail: bettinagre@aol.com.

GREGORY, CLAIRE DISTELHORST, television producer; b. Chgo., Mar. 6, 1926; d. Robert Henry and Genevieve (McCall) Distelhorst; children: Charles, Martha. Student, Cornell Coll., 1943-46; AB, Ind. U., 1947, MS, 1954. Tchr. pub. schs., Bismarck and Rossville, Ill., 1947-50, Helmsburg, Ind., 1950-51; grad. asst. Audio Visual Ctr. of Ind. U., 1953-55; dir. women's, children's/social svc. programs radio/TV, 1956-59; lectr., 1956-59; exec. dir. Cmty. Svc. Coun., Inc., Bloomington, Ind., 1971-75; asst. supr. instructional TV program devel. Ind. U. Radio and TV Svc., 1975-81, dir. spl. projects, 1982-92; chmn. Bloomington Telecomms. Coun., 1975-80. Writer, prodr: Russian Revolution and Arts, Parts I and II, 1976, Intro. to Immediate Access, 1977-80, Teleconference on Mass Transp., 1976, Transp. Briefing, 1977, videotapes on profl. devel. Internat. Devel. Inst., 1975-80, 16 videotapes on computer instrn., 1978-80, Getting There, 1980, Living Africa, 1979-82, Programming for Microcomputers, 1982, Negotiation, 1984, Ind. Collection, 1987, Joshua's Battle: The Story of Lyles Station, 1988, Charting New Courses teleconferences, 1988; prodr., videodisc instructional Clarity; prodr., dir., editor videotape SOUTH SHORE LINE: A Good Investment, 1990; prodr., editor Autism: Learning to Live, 1990 (Excellence award Autism Soc. Am. 1991), Autism: Stubborn to Love, 1991 (Excellence award Autism Soc. Am. 1992), Autism: Being Friends, 1991; TV advisor Mostly Moliere Troupe, 1981-89; lay reader A Moment of Silence prodn., 1996. Mem. United Way of Monroe County, 1982. Recipient Communication Industry Silver award Assn. Visual Communicators, 1989. Mem. Blue Ridge Assn. (treas. 1978-81), Univ. Club, Theta Sigma Phi, Psi Iota Xi.

GREGORY, DEIRDRE DIANNE, secondary educator; b. Fairview Park, Ohio, Feb. 12, 1958; d. Richard Whiting and Ruth Elizabeth (Moody) Mason; m. Thomas Bradford Gregory, July 15, 1995. BS, Ashland U., 1981; MS, Ohio State U., 1986; MEd, Ashland U., 1989, U. Dayton, 1993. Cert. tchr., Ohio; cert. vocat. family and consumer sci. sch. guidance counselor supr. Tchr. home econs. Mansfield (Ohio) City Schs., 1981-93, GRADS coord., 1993-99, guidance counselor, 1999—. Mem. adv. bd. Mansfield (Ohio) City Schs. Parents as Tchrs., 1993—, Pioneer Career and Tech. Ctr. GRADS Adv. Bd., Shelby, Ohio, 1993—; chair Children Family Health Svcs. Consortium, Mansfield, 1996-98; adj. prof. Ashland U., 2003-. Named one of Tw Thousand Notable Am. Women, 1993, Outstanding Young Woman, 1987-88, 88-89, 97-98. Mem. AAUW (pres. 1997-99), Mansfield Sch. Employee Assn. (pres. 1994-95), Am. Assn. Family and Consumer Sci., Order of Eastern Star, Kappa Omicron Phi, Phi Delta Kappa (pres. 1994-96, historian 1996-98). Republican. Presbyterian. Avocations: reading, singing, music, cross stitch, walking. Home: 411 Overlook Rd Mansfield OH 44907-1533 Office: Mansfield Sr H S 145 W Park Blvd Mansfield OH 44906-2621 Office Phone: 419-525-6369. Business E-Mail: DGregory@mansfield.k12.oh.us.

GREGORY, DOLA BELL, bishop, customer service administrator; d. Earl James Barnett and Wilda May Claspell-Barnett; 1 child, James DeWayne Gregory. Student, Frontier C.C., 1982—83, Kishwaukee C.C., 1987—88, Inst. Theology, 1995—97; min. lic., Full Gospel Chs. Internat., 1997. Supr. DDT Career Devel. Ctr., Fairfield, Ill., 1981—86; asst. tchr. DeKalb County Spl. Edn., Cortland, Ill., 1986—88; leadership Assembly of God/Full Gospel, Rochelle, Ill., 1988—99; sr. pastor, founder Rock House Ministries I and II, Rockford, Ill. and Demonte, Ind., 1999—, Forest Lake, Minn., 2003; customer rels. Credit Union, Rockford, 2001—. Coach Spl. Olympics, Bloomington, Ill., 1981—86; spiritual leader Tres-Dias, Rockford, 1997—98; fundraising chmn. PTA, Fairfield, 1984—86. Author: (audiotape) Spiritual Education, Spiritual Welfare, 2000. Referral sponsor Hope for Women, Rochelle, Ill., 1997—; vol. Rockford Rescue Mission, 1999—. Recipient Eunice Kennedy Spl. Olympics award, 1984. Mem.: Women's Aglow Internat. (educator 1993—95), Women in Ministry of Rockford (facilitator 2002—03). Avocations: reading, motorcycling, singing, sewing, remodeling. Office: Rock House Ministries 1325 7th St Rockford IL 61104 Office Phone: 815-962-5067.

GREGORY, JEAN WINFREY, ecologist, educator; b. Richmond, Va., Feb. 13, 1947; d. Thomas Edloe and Kathryn (McFarlane) Winfrey; m. Ronald Alfred Gregory, Dec. 13, 1973. BS in Biology, Mary Washington Coll., 1969; MS in Biology, Va. Commonwealth U., 1975, postgrad., 1982-90; MA in Environ. Sci., U. Va., 1983. Cert. fisheries sci. Lab. specialist A Cardiovascular Divsn. Med. Coll. Va., Richmond, 1969-70; pollution specialist State Water Control Bd. (now Dept. Environ. Quality), Richmond, 1970-77, pollution control specialist B, 1977-81, ecologist, 1981-85, ecology programs supr., 1985-88, environ. program mgr., 1988-2000, environ. mgr. II, 2000—. Adj. faculty Va. Commonwealth U., Richmond, 1978-93. Contbr. articles to profl. jours. Named One of Outstanding Young Women of Am., 1974; EPA fellow, Va., 1974-76. Mem. Am. Soc. Limnology and Oceanography, N.Am. Lake Mgmt. Soc., N.Am. Benthological Soc., Assn. Trad. Hooking Artists, Sisters in Crime. Democrat. Methodist. Avocations: herb gardening, walking, rug hooking, dalmation rescue. Office: Office Water Quality Programs PO Box 10009 Richmond VA 23240-0009 E-mail: jwgregory@deq.state.va.us.

GREGORY, MARILYN, primary school educator; b. San Marcos, Tex., Jan. 8, 1950; d. James F. and Mildred (Baker) Farmer; m. William Frederick Gregory III, June 2, 1973; children: William Frederick IV, James Patrick. BS, S.W. Tex. State U., San Marcos, 1972, MA in Edn., 1987. Kindergarten tchr. Luling (Tex.) Ind. Sch. Dist., 1972-73, Manor (Tex.) Ind. Sch. Dist., 1973-81, Lake Travis Ind. Sch. Dist., Austin, Tex., 1981—. Tchr. cons. State Seat Belt Program, Austin, 1978; student tchr. supr., tchr. tng. cons. S.W. Tex. State U., 1986. Co-author kindergarten curriculum guide and curriculum units, 1984. Vol. Am. Cancer Soc., Austin, 1992, Am. Heart Assn., Austin, 1994, Neighborhood Watch Program, Austin, 1994—, Muscular Dystrophy Assn., Austin, 1976. Recipient Sally Beth Moore award Austin Assn. Edn. of Young Chilodren, 1987; named Tchr. of Yr., Lake Travis Ednl. Found., 1987. Mem. AAUW, Am. Fedn. Tchrs., Classroom Tchrs. Assn., Tex. State Tchrs. Assn., Delta Kappa Gamma (Tex. Neurology chmn. 1997-99). Avocations: reading romantic novels, making craft items, computer, sports. Home: 11508 Quarter Horse Trl Austin TX 78750-1392

GREGORY, MYRA MAY, religious organization administrator, educator; b. N.Y.C., Sept. 21, 1912; d. Thomas and Anna (Collins) G. Diploma, Maxwell Tchrs. Tng. Sch., Bklyn., 1933; BS in Edn., Bklyn. Coll., 1940, MA in History, 1952. Cert. music tchr. Tchr. N.Y.C. Bd. Edn., Bklyn., 1943-75; social worker Berean Bapt. Ch., Bklyn., 1932-48, supr., 1932-94, fin. sec. Sunday sch., 1935-94. Bd. dirs. Berean-Vacation Bible Sch., Bklyn., 1935-86; tchr. Protestant Coun., N.Y.C., 1940-81; bd. dirs. Recreation Bedford-Stuyvesant Area Project Inc., Bklyn.; dir. seminar Christian Teaching, Bklyn., 1974-86, 1990—. Bd. mgrs. Bklyn. Sun. Sch. Union, 1974—; bd. dirs. Bklyn. Divsn. Coun. of Chs. 1935—, pres., 1984-86, bd. dirs. Bklyn. Sunday Sch. Union, 1974—. Named Tchr. of Yr. Cmty. Sch. Bd. Dist. 14 N.Y.C. Bd. Edn., Bklyn., 1973, Outstanding Tchr., Stuyvesand divsn., Bklyn. Sunday Sch. Union, 1977, Educator/Leader Berean Bapt. Ch., 1977; recipient Ecumenism citation Borough Pres.'s Office, Bklyn., 1985, Religious Educator citation Bklyn. Ch. Women United, Inc., 1993, Cmty. Svc. awrd Mayors Office, N.Y.C., 1993, Ecumenical Svc./Educator Honors Office the Coun. City of N.Y., 1994, Lifetime Achievement award Bklyn. Coll., 1995, Outstanding Svc. award Coun. Chs. the City of N.Y., 1995, Leadership/Educator Citation Borough Pres. Office, Bklyn., 1999, Educator/Svc. Citation Berean Baptist Ch., 2000. Mem. ASCD, Am. String Tchrs. Assn., Am. Viola Soc., Assn. Childhood Edn. Internat., Orgn. Am. Historians, Ctr. Study of Presidency, Music Tchrs. Nat. Assn., Nat. Orch. Assn., Schomburg Ctr. Rsch. Black Culture. Democrat. Avocations: string ensemble, drama, writing.

GREGORY, ROSAMUND ANN, actor; b. Battle Hastings, Eng., Nov. 18, 1947; arrived in U.S., 1960; d. Joseph Thomas and Margaret Celilia (Ervine-Andrews) Gregory; m. Craig Layton Manning, May 1966 (div. 1974). AA, West Valley Coll.; BA, Long Beach State U. Actor Santa Clara (Calif.) Players; asst. to dir. publicity Walt Disney Studios, Burbank, Calif., voice over artist; actor Glendale (Calif.) Ctr. Theatre; actor, tchr. Actor's Theatre, L.A.; pvt. tchr., dir. L.A. Cons. various theatres. Actor: (TV series) Wycliffe. Mem.: SAG, AFTRA, Brit. Actor's Equity. Avocations: gardening, painting, travel. Home: 1061 Peachwood Ct Medford OR 97501

GREGORY, STEPHANIE ANN, hematologist, educator; b. Vineland, N.J., June 23, 1940; d. Andonetta Gregory; m. Sheldon Chertow; children: Elizabeth Chertow, Jennifer Chertow, Daniel Chertow, Erica Chertow. BS cum laude, Boston Coll., 1961; MD cum laude, Med. Coll. Pa., 1965. Diplomate Am. Bd. Internal Medicine, subspecialty hematology, Am. Bd. Hematology. Intern in internal medicine Presbyn.-St. Luke's Hosp., Chgo., 1965-66, resident in internal medicine, 1966-68, fellow in hematology, 1968-69; chief resident Presbyn.-St. Lukes Hosp., Chgo., 1968-69; chief spl. morphology lab. sect. hematology Rush-Presbyn.-St. Luke's Med. Ctr., Chgo., 1972-76; from asst. prof. medicine to assoc. prof. medicine Rush Med. Coll., Chgo., 1972-86; sr. attending physician Presbyn.-St. Luke's Hosp., Chgo., 1982—; adminstr., dir. Rush-Presbyn.-St. Luke's Med. Ctr., Chgo., 1985—, dir. sect. hematol. divsn. hemat./oncology Rush Cancer Inst., 1994—, Elodia Kehm prof. medicine, dir. hematology, 1995—. Coord. continuing edn. sect. hematology Rush-Presbyn.-St. Luke's Med. Ctr., Chgo., 1970-76, dir. transfusion therapy svc. sect. hematology, 1972-76, asst. chmn. dept. medicine, 1972-76, clin. dir. Sheridan Rd. Pavilion, 1976-77, acting dir. sect. clin. hematology, 1980-81, assoc. dir. sect. hematology, 1993-94, asst. chairperson dept. medicine, 1993-94; co-dir. Lymphoma Ctr., Rush Cancer Inst., Chgo., 1992—; mem. UN Security Coun. Commn. Experts, 1994; mem. med. adv. bd. Leukemia Rsch. Found., 1996—, Leukemia/Lymphoma Soc. Am., Lymphoma Rsch. Found. Mentor Lean on Me support group for young adults with cancer Rush Cancer Inst., Chgo., 1992—. Recipient award Am. Women's Med. Assn., 1965, William B. Peck Sci. award for rsch. in hematopoietic stem cell studies Sci. Assembly of Interstate Postgrad. Med. Assn., 1973, Outstanding Alumni award MCP-Hahneman Med. Sch., 1998; grantee Schweppe Found. Rsch., 1969-72, NIH tng. grantee Nat. Heart, Lung and Blood Inst., 1974-79; Schweppe fellow, 1969-72. Fellow ACP (mem. Ill. coun. 1994—, mentor physician mems. for advancement to fellowship designation ann. meeting 1996, Ill. Laureate award 1996); mem. AMA, Internat. Soc. Hematology (Inter-Am. divsn.), Internat. Soc. Exptl. Hematology (charter), Leukemia Soc. Am. (bd. trustees Ill. chpt. 1987—, chmn.

patient aid com. Ill. chpt. 1988-90, treas. Ill. chpt. 1992-93, chairperson patient fin. aid com. Ill. chpt. 1992—, v.p. Ill. chpt. 1991-94, mem. med. adv. bd. Ill. chpt. 1996—), Am. Soc. Clin. Oncology, Am. Soc. Hematology, Cell Proliferation Soc., Ea. Coop. Oncology Group, Inst. Medicine Chgo., Chgo. Soc. Internal Medicine (exec. com. 1992—, sec.-treas. 1992-93, v.p. 1993-94, pres. 1994-96), Aplastic Anemia Found. Am. (hon. bd. trustees 1988—), Mark H. Lepper M.D. Soc. Tchrs. (elected), Alpha Omega Alpha, Sigma Xi. Office: Rush-Presbyn-St Luke's Med Ctr 1653 W Congress Pkwy Chicago IL 60612-3833*

GREGORY, VALISKA, writer; b. Chgo., Nov. 3, 1940; d. Andrej and Stephania (Lascik) Valiska; m. Marshall W. Gregory, Aug. 18, 1962; children: Melissa, Holly. BA cum laude, Ind. Ctrl. Coll., 1962; MA, Univ. Chgo., 1966; postgrad., Vassar Inst. Pub. Writing, 1984, Simmons Coll., 1986. Music and drama tchr. White Oak Elem. Sch., Whiting, Ind., 1962-64; tchr. Oak Lawn (Ill.) Meml. H.S., 1965-68; lectr. English U. Wis., Milw., 1968-74; adj. prof. English U. Indpls., 1974-83, Butler U., Indpls., 1983-85, writer-in-residence, 1993—; fellow Butler Writer's Studio, 1989-92. Founding dir. Butler U. Midwinter Children's Litf. Conf., 1989—; spkr., workshop leader schs., libr., confs., 1993—. Author: Sunny Side Up, 1986 (Chickadee Mag. Book of Month award 1986), Terribly Wonderful, 1986 (Grandparent's Mag. Best Book award 1986), The Oatmeal Cookie, 1987 (Best of Best Book list Chgo. Sun-Times), Riddle Soup, 1987 (Best of Best Book list Chgo. Sun-Times), Through the Mickle Woods (named Pick of List Am. Booksellers Assn. 1992, Parent's Choice award, 1992; State Ind. Read Aloud-List 1993), Happy Burpday, Maggie McDougal!, 1992 (State Ind. Read-aloud List 1993), Babysitting for Benjamin (Parent's Choice Honor award 1993), Kate's Giants, 1995, Looking for Angels, 1996, (named Picked of the List Am. Book Sellers Assn., 1996), When Stories Fell Like Shooting Stars, 1996, (Family Circle Mag. Critics Choice, 1996), A Valentine for Norman Noggs, 1999, Shirley's Wonderful Baby, 2002. Recipient Ill. Wesleyan U. Poetry award, 1982, hon. mention Billee Murray Denny Nat. Poetry Award Bilee Murray Denny Poetry Found., 1982, Hudelson award Children's Fiction Work-In-Progress, 1982, Artistic Excellence and Achievement award State Art Treasure Arts Ind., 1989; Individual Artist Master fellow Ind. Arts Commn. and Nat. Endowment for Arts, 1986. Mem. AAUW (Creative Writer's pres. 1984-86), Author's Guild, Authors League Am., Soc. Children's Book Writers and Illustrators, Nat. Book Critic's Circle, Children's Reading Round Table, Soc. Midland Authors. Democrat. Office: Butler U 4600 Sunset Ave Indianapolis IN 46208-3487*

GREGORY, YVONNE E. interior designer; b. The Hague, The Netherlands, Apr. 2, 1952; came to U.S., 1953; d. Joan Marinus Heyning and Johanna Alving; m. Hugh Martin Smith, Apr. 24, 1976 (div. Jan. 1990); 1 child, Erica Renee Smith; m. Walker Shelton Gregory, Aug. 8, 1992. AA, El Camino Coll., 1974; student, Harbor Coll., San Pedro, Calif., 1974-76, Torrance (Calif.) Art Ctr., 1976-79. Owner, designer HM Smith Constrn., San Pedro, 1981-90; owner, interior designer Nuhome Designs, Mt. Pleasant, S.C., 1991—. Comml. Designs, Mt. Pleasant, 1999—. Bd. dirs. Wild Dunes (S.C.) Cmty. Archtl. Rev. Bd., 1998—; v.p. Leads for Women, San Pedro, 1985-88. Recipient Best Model Home Merchandising award Charleston (S.C.) Homebuilders, 1998, Best Lobby Remodel award Clear Channel Comm., Charleston, 1999. Mem. Charleston Trident Homebuilders Assn., The Gibbs Art Mus. Democrat. Avocations: painting, reading, craft work, art work. Office: 3036 Intracoastal View Dr Mount Pleasant SC 29466-9022

GREGUS, LINDA ANNA, government official; b. Hartford, Conn., Mar. 24, 1956; d. Steven and Sylvia Christine (Ramunno) G. AB, Bowdoin Coll., 1978; MA in Law and Diplomacy, Tufts U., 1985. Vol. VISTA, Phoenix, 1978-79; research asst. Econ. Research Assocs., Boston, 1979; ops adminstr. CRT Inc., Hartford, Conn., 1980-82; program officer U.S. Dept. of State, Washington, 1986-90; intelligence officer CIA, Washington, 1990—2004, U.S. Dept. State, 2004—. Recipient Milo Peck Scholarship Town of Windsor, Conn., 1984. Home: 1904 Wilson Ln Mc Lean VA 22102-1958

GREIDER, CAROL WIDNEY, molecular biology educator; b. San Diego, Apr. 15, 1961; BA in Biology, U. Calif., Santa Barbara, 1983; PhD in Molecular Biology, U. Calif., Berkeley, 1987. Fellow Cold Spring Harbor (N.Y.) Lab., 1988-90, asst. investigator, 1990-92, assoc. staff investigator, 1992-94, investigator, 1994-97; assoc. prof. dept. molecular biology and genetics, Johns Hopkins U. Sch. Medicine, Balt., 1997—99, prof., 1999—2002, acting dir., 2002—03, Daniel Nathans prof. and dir., 2003—; prof., dept. oncology Johns Hopkins U. Sch. Medicine, Balt., 1999—. Contbr. numerous articles, revs., book chpts. Regents scholar U. Calif., 1981, Pew Biomed. Scis. scholar; recipient Allied Signal Outstanding Project award, 1992, Gertrude Elion Cancer Rsch. award Am. Assn. Cancer Rsch., 1994, Cornelius Rhoads award, 1996, Glenn Found. award Am. Assn. Cell Biology, 1995, Schering-Plough Sci. Achievement award, 1997, Ellison Medical Found. Sr. Scholar award, 1998, Gairdner Found. award 1998, Passano Found. award 1999, Rosenstiel award 1999, Harvey Soc. Lecture, 2000, Richard Lounsbery award, 2003. Mem. Phi Beta Kappa. Elected mem., Nat. Acad. Sciences, 2003, fellow, Am. Acad. Arts and Sciences, 2003. Office: Johns Hopkins U Sch Med 617 Hunterian Bldg 725 N Wolfe St Baltimore MD 21205-2105*

GREILICH, AUDREY, administrative assistant; b. Wayne, N.J., July 23, 1933; d. Kenneth J. Holmes and Majorie I. Paige; m. Gerald D. Thompson, June 23, 1956 (dec. 1980); children: Gerald D. Jr., Kerry O., Christopher K., Linda G., Jeffrey L., Bonnie J. Thompson; m. William H. Greilich, June 21, 1986. Cert. profl. sec., Office Profls. Internat., 1993. Statis. typist various CPAs, Paterson, N.J., 1951-52; svc. rep. Bell Telephone, Newark, N.J., 1952-57; compensatory aide Vernon (N.J.) Twp. Schs., 1979-83; sec. Jansen Real Estate, Vernon, 1977-79; adminstrv. asst. U.S. Army TACOM-ARDEC, Picatinny Arsenal, N.J., 1983—. Mem. Bus. Profl. Women Internat. (chmn. scholarship fund 1985—). Baptist. Avocation: church organist. Home: PO Box 113 Glenwood NJ 07418-0113

GREILING, MINDY, state legislator; b. Feb. 1948; m. Roger Greiling; 2 children. BA, Gustavus Adolphis Coll.; MEd, U. Minn. State rep. Minn. Ho. Reps., Dist. 54B, 1993—. Office: 100 Constitution Ave Saint Paul MN 55155-1232

GREIMANN, JANE, state representative, elementary school educator; b. Mason City, Iowa, Jan. 25, 1942; m. Lowell Greimann; children: Amy, Blair, Chad. BA, Iowa State U., 1964. Cert. tchr. Iowa. Tchr. Nevada, Iowa Mid. Sch., 1982—97; supr. student tchrs. Iowa State U., 1998—99; state rep. dist. 45 Iowa Ho. of Reps., 2000—; mem. edn. com.; mem. environment com.; mem. human svcs. appropriations com.; mem. natural resources com. Bd. hawk-i, 1996—99, CPTF Steering Com.; bd. dirs. Mid. Iowa Cmty. Action, 2001—02. Mem.: Family and Consumer Sci. Profl. Orgn., League Women Voters. Democrat. Presbyterian. Office: State Capitol East 12th and Grand Des Moines IA 50319

GREINER, SANDRA, state legislator; b. Washington, Iowa, Oct. 26, 1945; m. Terrence Greiner. Student, Stephens Coll. Mem. Iowa Ho. Reps., 1992-2000, Iowa State Senate, 2001—, vice chair bus. and labor rels. com., mem. agr. com., ways and means com., small bus., econ. devel. and tourism com. Mem. Agr. Coun. Am. (former exec. com. mem.), Am. Feed Industry Assn., Corn and Soybean Growers, Pork Prodrs., Am. Agri-Women (past pres.), Agrl. Women's Leadership Network, Animal Industry Task Force, Daus. Am. Agr. (bd. dirs.), Keokuk County, Wapello County and Mahaska County Rep. Women, Washington County Rep. Women, Washington County Rep. Ctrl. Com., Keota Unltd. Republican. Home: 1005 Hwy 92 Keota IA 52248 E-mail: sandra_greiner@legis.state.ia.us.

GREJDA, GAIL FULTON, dean; b. Clarion, Pa., Aug. 31, 1937; d. Ralph Jay and Virginia Agnew Fulton; m. Edward Stanley Grejda, Aug. 31, 1958; children: Richard Edward, Steven Douglas. BS, Clarion U., 1966, MEd, 1968; PhD in Instrnl. Sys. Design, Pa. State U., 1988. Cert. level 2 in elem. edn. and spl. edn., Pa. Tchr. Brookville (Pa.) Area Sch. Dist., 1966-69, Clarion (Pa.) Area Sch. Dist., 1969-87, dir. gifted programs, 1977-82; tchr. Beijing Internat. Embassy Sch., 1980-81; computer instr. Sch. of Am. Embassy, Bridgetown, Barbados, 1987-88; asst. prof. Clarion U., 1988-93, assoc. prof., 1993-97, prof., 1997-98, dean Coll. Edn. and Human Svcs., 1998—. Author: (book chpt.) Guidelines for Interpreting Educational Research, 1994; contbr. articles to profl. jours. Grantee U.S. Dept. Edn., 1999, Bell Atlantic Found., 1998, NSF, 1999-2003, 2003—. Mem. Am. Assn. Colls. for Tchr. Edn., Assn. Tchr. Educators (commn. on utilizing tech. for ednl. reform 1988—), Tchr. Edn. Coun. State Colls. and Univs., Assn. for Ednl. Comms. and Tech., Pa. Assn. Coll. Tchr. Educators (bd. dirs. 1988—), Phi Delta Kappa (v.p. 1982—), Pi Lambda Theta. Avocations: travel, reading, golf. Office: Clarion U 101 Stevens Hall Clarion PA 16214 E-mail: grejda@mail.clarion.edu.

GRENDELL, DIANE V. state legislator, nurse; m. Tim Grendell; children: James, Kate. Grad. in nursing, St. John's Coll.; JD, Cleve. Marshall Coll. Law; postgrad., Baldwin Wallace Coll. Bar: Ohio; RN, Ohio. Mem. Ohio Ho. of Reps., Columbus, 1993—. Recipient Seven Seals award, Wilson achievement award. Mem. Ohio Bar Assn., Ohio Nurses Assn., Chester C. of C., Chester and Geauga County Hist. Soc., Farm Bur. (chmn.), Sierra Club. Republican. Home: 7413 Tattersall St Chesterland OH 44026-2036 Office: OH House of Reps State House Columbus OH 43215

GRENZ, M. KAY, manufacturing executive; b. Minn., Dec. 1946; m. Rod Grenz; 1 child, Jenni. BA in Sociology, U. SD. Cord. 3M Co., 1969—71, salary adminstr., 1971—76, mgr., 1976—84, dir. human resources, 1984—96, v.p. human resources, 1996—98, sr. v.p. human resources, 1998—. Bd. dirs. Gillette Children's Specialty Healthcare. Mem.: Human Resource Planning Soc.*

GRENZIG, GAIL A. assistant principal, consultant; d. Daniel Tkatch and Virginia Mary Cosgrave; m. Edward W. Grenzig, June 23, 1990; children: Christopher Edward, Brittany Marie. Post Grad. Profl. Diploma, L.I. U., 1989; MS, Adelphi U., 1985, BS, 1983. Cert. SDA Ednl. Adminstrn. NY State Bd. of Regents, 1994. Asst. prin. Harry B. Thompson Mid. Sch. Syosset Ctrl. Sch. Dist., NY, 2002—; coord. of pupil pers. svcs. Mid. Country Ctrl. Sch. Dist., Centereach, NY, 1999—2002; tchr. spl. edn. Glen Cove City Sch. Dist., NY, 1985—94; ednl. cons. Grenzig Consulting, Nesconset, NY, 1993—; adj. prof. Dowling Coll., Oakdale, NY, 1994—94. Varsity coach Glen Cove City Sch. Dist., 1985—94. Vol. soccer coach Smithtown Kickers, NY, 1997—2003; editor - newsletter Nesconset Elem. PTA, 1996—2003; religion tchr. Parish of Holy Cross, Nesconset, 1999—2003. Mem.: ASCD, NASSP, Nat. Mid. Sch. Assn., Coun. of Exceptional Children (spkr., presenter N.Y. State Conf. 2002), L.I. Assn. of Spl. Edn. Adminstrs. Avocations: reading, travel, gardening, sports. Office: Syosset Central Sch Dist 98 Ann Dr Syosset NY Personal E-mail: gail@grenzig.com.

GRESS, DONNA MARY, health facility administrator; b. Nebraska City, Nebr., May 30, 1958; d. Henry Joseph and Verna Louise (Damme) G. Student, Rsch. Med. Ctr., Avila Coll., 1976-77, U. Nebr., 1981-83. Accredited record technician on patient care unit U. Kans. Med. Ctr., Kansas City, 1977-79; cancer registrar Archbishop Bergan Mercy Hosp., Omaha, 1979-84; cancer registry coord. Presbyn. Intercmty. Hosp., Whittier, Calif., 1984-90; supr. cancer registry St. Mary Med. Ctr., Long Beach, Calif., 1990—94, Parkview Cmty. Hosp., 1998—2001; cancer data mgr. South Coast Med. Ctr., Laguna Beach, Calif., 2001—. Mem. software beta testing divsn. C/Net, Sacramento, 1988—, mem. adv. bd., 1990-93; mem. spkrs. bur. comm. cancer ACS., Chgo., 1994—; lectr. in field. Author, asst. editor: (with others) Cancer Registry Management, 1996, 2nd edit., 2004; contbr. articles to profl. jours. Mem. Am. Health Info. Mgmt. Assn., Nat. Cancer Registrars Assn. (alt. liaison commn. cancer ACS 1995-98, sec. 1997-98, chmn. edn. com. 1996-97, chmn. edn. subcom. bldg. blocks data base mgmt. workshop 1995-96, mem. formal edn. subcom. 1995-96, sec. 1997-98, pres-elect 2002-03, pres. 2003-04, immediate past pres. 2004-05, chair Governance Planning and Evalution Com. 2004-05), Calif. Cancer Registrars Assn. (bd. dirs. del. 1989, v.p. 1992, pres. 1994-96, chmn. various coms.), So. Calif. Cancer Registrars Assn. (v.p. 1988, pres. 1989, chmn. various coms.). Roman Catholic. Avocations: sewing, crafts. Office: South Coast Med Ctr 31872 Coast Hwy Laguna Beach CA 92651 Office Phone: 949-499-7252. E-mail: dmgress@yahoo.com.

GREVILLE, FLORENCE NUSIM, secondary school educator, mathematician; b. Lynn, Mass., Nov. 19, 1913; d. Melach Joseph Nusim and Lillian Montrose; m. Thomas N.E. Greville (dec. Feb. 18, 1998). AB, Cornell U., 1935; MA, Columbia U., 1947. Sub. tchr Wis. Pub. Schs., Madison, 1975—80; tchr. math. Madison Area Tech. Coll., 1980—81; lectr. math. Piedmont C.C., Charlottesville, Va., 1982—84; sub. tchr. Charlottesville Pub. Schs., 1987—99. Instr. in math Oswego State Coll., 1947—48; tchr. Am. sch., Rio de Janeiro, 1953—54; program dir. AAUW, Monona, Wis., 1966—68, Charlottesville, Va., 2001—02. Author: (book) Computer Oriented Basic Math, 1970, Breakfast Gems, 2002. Fellow: AAAS; mem.: Math. Assn. Am. Avocation: playing classical piano. Home: 505 Pebble Hill Ct Charlottesville VA 22903-7873

GREW, PRISCILLA CROSWELL, university official, geology educator; b. Glens Falls, NY, Oct. 26, 1940; d. James Croswell and Evangeline Pearl (Beougher) Perkins; m. Edward Sturgis Grew, June 14, 1975. BA magna cum laude, Bryn Mawr Coll., 1962; PhD, U. Calif., Berkeley, 1967. Instr. dept. geology Boston Coll., 1967-68, asst. prof., 1968-72; asst. rsch. geologist UCLA, 1972-77, adj. asst. prof. environ. sci. and engring., 1975-76; dir. Calif. Dept. Conservation, 1977-81; commr. Calif. Pub. Utilities Commn., San Francisco, 1981-86; dir. Minn. Geol. Survey, St. Paul, 1986-93; prof. dept. geology U. Minn., Mpls., 1986-93; vice chancellor for rsch. U. Nebr., Lincoln, 1993-99, prof. dept. geoscis., 1993—, prof. conservation/survey divsn. Inst. Agr., 1993—, dir. U. Nebr. State Mus., 2003—; fellow Ctr. for Great Plains Studies, U. Nebr., Lincolm, 2003—; coord. Native Am. Graves Protection and Repatriation Act, 1998—. Vis. asst. prof. geology U. Calif., Davis, 1973-74; chmn. Calif. State Mining and Geology Bd., Sacramento, 1976-77; exec. sec., editor Lake Powell Rsch. Project, 1971-77; cons., vis. staff Los Alamos (N.Mex.) Nat. Lab., 1972-77; com. on minority participation in earth sci. and mineral engring. Dept. Interior, 1972-75; chmn. Calif. Geothermal Resource Task Force, 1977, Calif. Geothermal Resources Bd., 1977-81; earthquake studies adv. panel US Geol. Survey, 1979-83, adv. com., 1982-86; adv. coun. Gas Rsch. Inst., 1982-86, rsch. coord. coun., 1987-98, vice-chmn., 1994-96, chmn., 1996-98, sci. and tech. coun., 1998-2001; bd. on global change rsch. NAS, 1995-99, subcom. on earthquake rsch., 1985-88, bd. on earth scis. and resources, 1986-91, bd. on mineral and energy resources, 1982-88, Minn. Minerals Coord. Com., 1986-93, US nat. com. for internat. union of geological scis. (IUGS), 1985-93, US nat. com. for the internat. union of geodesy and geophysics 2001—, chmn., 2003—; mem. US Nat. Com. on Diversitas, 2000—; adv. bd. Stanford U. Sch. Earth Scis., 1989—, Sec. of Energy Adv. Bd., 1995-97; com. on equal opportunities in sci. and tech. NSF, 1985-86, adv. com. on earth scis., 1987-91, adv. com. on sci. and tech. ctrs. devel., 1987-91, adv. com. on sci. and tech. ctrs., 1996, adv. com. on geoscis., 1994-97; mem. State-Fed. Tech. Partnership Task Force, 1995-99, Fed. Coun. for Continental Sci. Drilling, 1992-98, Gt. Plains Partnership Coun., 1995-99; trustee Am. Geol. Inst. Found., 1988— (Ian Campbell medlist 1999). Contbr. articles to profl. jours. Bd. dirs. Abendmusik:Lincoln, 1995-97; trustee 1st Plymouth Congl. Ch., Lincoln, 1997-2000. Fellow NSF, 1962-66. Fellow AAAS (chmn. electorate nominating com. sect. E 1980-84, mem.-at-large 1987-91, chmn.-elect 1994, chmn. 1995, coun. del. 1997-98), Geol. Soc. Am. (nominations com. 1974, chmn. com. on geology and pub. policy 1981-84, audit com. 1988-90, chair 1990, com. on coms. 1986-87, 91-92, chmn. com. on coms. 1995, chair Day medal com. 1990, councillor 1987-91), Mineral. Soc. Am. (mem. Roebling medal com. 1999—2002), Geol. Assn. Can., Ctr. Great Plains Studies; mem. Am. Geophys. Union (chmn. com. pub. affairs 1984-89), Soc. Mayflower Descs., Nat. Parks and Conservation Assn. (trustee 1982-86), Nat. Assn. Regulatory Utility Commrs. (com. on gas 1982-86, exec. com. 1984-86, com. on energy conservation 1983-84), Interstate Oil and Gas Compact Commn. (mem. Petroleum Profls. Task Force, 2001-03), Cosmos Club, Country Club of Lincoln. Congregationalist. Office: U Nebr State Mus 307 Morrill Hall Lincoln NE 68588-0338 Office Phone: 402-472-3779.

GREWE, MARJORIE JANE, retired protective services official; b. Baltimore County, Md., Nov. 10, 1931; d. Wilbur Guy and Mary Alice (Stover) Gregory; m. Harold Henry, Oct. 31, 1954 (dec.); children: Dorothy Lee Gorkey, Eva-Maria Marjorie Shaeffer. Student, Essex County Coll., 1979-80, U. Md. Dep. sheriff Baltimore County Sheriff's Dept., Towson, Md., 1966-87; profl. interviewer U.S. Dept. Commerce, Phila., 1959-65; compiling stats., map making various orgns., Phila., 1959; profl. interviewer med. studies Johns Hopkins U., Balt., 1959; matron Balt. City Jail, 1957-58; demonstrator Tupperware, Balt., 1951-58; dep. area coord. civil def. City of Balt., 1956-59; ret., 1987. Freelance interviewer, 1959—65. Gossip columnist: local newspapers, 1959—65. Founder Md. Sheriff's Youth Ranch; activist Am. with Disabilities, EPA, Animal Rights; mem. Adv. for Wildlife; sec. Dem. Clubs, Baltimore County, 1959—66; mem. polit. action com., 1965. Mem.: Baltimore County Sheriff's Dept., Nat. Sheriffs Assn. (state dir. 1986—87), Md. State Sheriffs Assn. (life; sec.), Fraternal Order Police (life), Moose Aux. Presbyterian. Avocations: doll collecting, travel, gardening, cooking, genealogy. Home: Baldwin Hills Estates Der Palast at 115 Baldwin Ln Staunton VA 24401-8950

GREY, DEBORAH CLELAND, Canadian government official; b. Vancouver, B.C., Can., July 1, 1952; d. Mansell Caverhill Grey and Lilian Joyce (Russell) Levy; m. Lewis Larson, Aug. 7, 1993. Student, Burrard Inlet Bible Inst., 1973; student in Sociology and English, Trinity Western Coll., Langley, British Columbia, 1978; BA, U. Alta., Edmonton, Can., 1978, B of Edn. after degree, 1979. Tchr. Frog Lake (Alta.) Indian Res., 1979-80; tchr. jr. and sr. H.S. Dewberry (Alta.) Sch., 1980-89; M.P. Ho. of Commons, Ottawa, Ont., Can., 1989—. First mem. Reform Party Ho. Commons; Caucus chmn. Reform Party, 1993-2000, apptd. dep. parliamentary leader, 1995-2000, apptd. leader ofcl. opposition, 2000; dep. critic Human Resources Devel., 1998; caucus chair PC-DR Coalition Caucus, 2001; critic Aboriginal Affairs, 2001. Recipient Can. 125 medal, 1993, Alumni award of distinction Trinity Western U., 1996. Reform. Avocations: kayaking, gospel singing, motorcycles, drama, hiking. Office: House of Commons Parliament Bldgs Ottawa ON Canada K1A 0A6

GREY, RUTHANN E. communications specialist, management consultant; b. Buffalo, N.Y., May 13, 1945; d. Wilson Campbell and Rosalie (Briggs) Evege; m. Daine A. Grey, Aug. 25, 1990; children: Daine, Jr., Keenan, Nichole. BS, SUNY, Buffalo, 1966, MS, 1970, PhD, 1980; postgrad., Harvard U., 1988. Tchr. Bennett H.S., Buffalo, 1966-69; prof. Erie C.C., Buffalo, 1970-73; adminstr. No. Va. C.C., Annandale, 1975-76, Wayne State U., Detroit, 1978-80; dir. pub. affairs Burroughs Corp., Detroit, 1981-86; exec. asst. to chmn. bd. dirs. The Equitable, N.Y.C., 1986-89; mgr. pub. affairs N.Y. Times, N.Y.C., 1989-90; mgr. divsn. corp. rels. Pub. Svc. Corp. Colo., Denver, 1990-93; v.p. comm. and pub. affairs Hoechst Celanese, Bridgewater, NJ, 1993—; v.p. global media and external rels. Hoechst Marion Roussel, Bridgewater, NJ, 1996—; comm. chief Ednl. Testing Svc., Princeton, NJ; with The Caunos Group, Watchung, NJ, 1998—. Cons. A+ For Kids, Newark, 1989-90, Rockefeller Found., N.Y.C., 1989-90. Bd. dirs. Citizens Scholarship Found., Minn., 1990-94. Mem. Pub. Rels. Seminar, Arthur Page Soc., The Wisemen, Pub. Rels. Rsch. Found. Avocations: gardening, walking. Home: 28 Stonegate Dr Watchung NJ 07069-5471 Office: The Caunos Group 28 Stonegte Dr Watchung NJ 07069 Office Phone: 908-377-0180. E-mail: regrey@optonline.net.

GREY-BETHIEL, SHARI, artist, sculptress, jewelry designer; b. N.Y.C., July 27, 1959; d. Charles and Jean S. Grey; m. David Howard Bethiel, June 24, 1990; 1 child, Jonathan Blair. BFA with high honors, Pratt Inst., 1982; MA with high honors, NYU, 1993. Pres. Grey Originals, Inc., N.Y.C., 1999—. Sculptures in numerous corp. and pvt. collections including The Castle at Tarrytown, N.Y., Solid Ideas, Inc., Grand Prarie, Tex., N.W. Cmty. Hosp., Chgo. Avocations: skiing, music, writing, reading. Home: 12 Everett Pl Halesite NY 11743-2211

GRIBBON, DEBORAH, museum director; b. Washington, June 11, 1948; d. Daniel M. Gribbon and Mary Jane Retzler Gribbon; m. Winston Alt; children: Sarah Alt, Jane Alt. PhD, Harvard U., 1982, MA, 1971; BA, Wellesley Coll., 1970. Tchg. fellow Dept. Fine Arts Harvard U., Cambridge, Mass., 1972—74; curator Isabella Steward Gardner Mus., Boston, 1976—84; asst. dir. curatorial affairs The. J. Paul Getty Mus., L.A., 1984—87; assoc. dir. curatorial affairs The J. Paul Getty Mus., L.A., 1987—91, assoc. dir., chief curator, 1991—98, dep. dir., chief curator, 1998—2000, dir., 2000—. Instr. Ext. Sch. Harvard U., Cambridge, 1982—84; v.p. J.Paul Getty Trust, L.A., 2000—; bd. dirs. Courtauld Inst. Art, London. Co-author: The J. Paul Getty Museum and Its Collections: A Museum for a New Century, 1997; author (book): Sculpture in the Isabella Stewart Gardner Museum, 1978; contbr. articles to profl. jours. Recipient Plogsterth Prize for Art History, Wellesley Coll., 1970; fellow Theodore Rousseau Fellowship for Mus. Studies, Harvard U., 1982. Mem.: Assn. Art Mus. Dirs., Internat. Women's Forum. Office: The J Paul Getty Museum 1200 Getty Center Dr Los Angeles CA 90049

GRICE, LORRAINE E. finance educator; BS in Commerce and Bus. Adminstrn., U. Ala., Tuscaloosa, 1983, MA in Mktg., 1985. Cert. profl. educator Fla., 1989. Apparel mgr. Kmart Apparel Corp., Orlando, Fla., 1985—89; instr. Orange County Pub. Schools, Orlando, Fla., 1989—. Presenter on best practices. Mem. bd. dirs. Orlando Jaycees, Orlando, Fla., 1985—92. Recipient Innovative Classroom Practices, Walt Disney World, 1990, 1991, Tchr. of the Month, Palmetto Elem. Sch., 1992, Teacherrific Sch. Level Winner, Walt Disney World, 1993, 1995, 1998, Winning FFA Display, Ctrl. Fla. Fair, 1995, Tchr. of the Yr., Colonial HS, 1995-1996, Teacherrific Winner, Walt Disney World, 1998, Instrnl. Person of the Quin, Mid Fla. Tech, 2002. Mem.: FTP/NEA, OCBEA, CTA, Future Bus. Leaders of Am. (advisor 1989—99). Office: Mid Florida Tech - OCPS 2900 West Oak Ridge Rd Orlando FL 32809 Personal E-mail: gricel@ocps.net.

GRIDER, BARBARA JEAN, real estate broker, consultant; d. John and Ersell Pasadina; 1 child, Constance D. Grider-Miles. BA in Sociology, Marquette U., 1994. Lic. ins. agt. (health), notary pub. Owner, mgr. Aggressive Acctg. Svcs., Milw., 1978—79; adminstr. Juanita Virgil Acad., Milw., 1979—91; retail salesperson home-based bus. Home Care, 1991—99; loan broker Lifestyle Mortgage, 1995—2000; real estate broker Home Care Realty, Milw., 1995—. Mem.: Libr. of Congress, Habitat for Humanity Internat. Office: Home Care Realty 5634 N Green Bay Ave Milwaukee WI 53209 E-mail: hommtgins@aol.com.

GRIEB, ELIZABETH, lawyer; b. Chestertown, Md., Nov. 14, 1950; d. Henry Norman and Lillian (Ballard) Grieb; m. George Stewart Webb, Aug. 18, 1979 (div. 1990); children: Timothy Stewart, Margaret Elizabeth. BA English, Wells Coll., 1972; JD cum laude, U. Balt., 1977. Bar: Md. 1977. Assoc. Piper & Marbury, Balt., 1977-84, ptnr., 1984—. Adv. bd. U. Md. Sys. Downtown Ctr., Balt., 1990-92; bd. dirs., sec. Choice Jobs, Inc., Balt.,

1991-93; pres. U. Balt. Alumni Assn., 1994-95; bd. dirs. Balt. Zoo, 1995—, pres. bd. dirs., 1999—. Mem. Md. State Bar Assn. (chair securities laws com. 1990-92), Ho. of Ruth (bd. dirs. 1994-97), Ctr. Club. Episcopal. Office: Piper & Marbury 36 S Charles St Baltimore MD 21201-3020

GRIECO, MARIA TERESA, music educator; d. Andrea and Maria Grieco. BS in Edn., NYU, 1978, MA in Edn., 1981. Cert. tchr. N.Y., 1990. Tchr., dir. musical theater The Dalton Sch., N.Y.C., 1986—88; choral dir., music tchr. N.Y.C. (N.Y.) Pub. Schs., 1988—2000, Elmont (N.Y.) Sch. Dist., 2000—01, Malverne Pub. Schs., N.Y.C., 2002—. Musician: (songs) The Monster Concert with Eugene List; composer Remembrance 9-11, Lullaby in Wartime; musician NYU Choral Alumni Club; author: (poem (in italian) Silenzio published in Romanica; New York University's Romance Language magazine. Active ImagineN.Y. Mcpl. Art Soc. of N.Y., 2001—03; active Listening to the City Civic Alliance to Rebuild Downtown N.Y., N.Y.C., 2002—03; mem. Voice of the Civic Faithful, 2002—03. Scholar, NYU Sch. of Edn. Dept. of Music & Music Edn., 1978—80, 1984—86. Mem.: Music Educators Nat. Conf., Am. Choral Dirs. Assn., Mensa, Pi Kappa Lambda (hon.). Roman Catholic. Avocations: rabbits, poetry writing, meteorology, bicycling. Personal E-mail: mtgrieco@aol.com.

GRIEGO, LINDA, media executive; b. Tucumcari, N.Mex., 1949; m. Ronald C. Peterson. BA in history, U. Calif. Candidate for LA Mayor, 1993; LA dep. mayor Tom Bradley Adminstrn.; pres., CEO Rebuild LA Inc., 1994—97; interim pres. and CEO LA Cmty. Devel. Bank, 1999—2000; founder, mng. ptnr. Engine Co. No. 28, 1988—; pres., CEO Griego Enterprises (with Zapgo Entertainment Group), 1997—. LA bd. dirs. Federal Reserve Bank, San Francisco; bd. dirs. Southwest Water Co., Granite Construction Inc., 1999—, Blockbuster Inc., 1999—; bd. Taos Talking Pictures; mem. Thomas Rivera Policy Inst. Trustee Robert Wood Johnson Found.; mem. N. Am. devel. bank cmty. adjustment com. NAFTA, 1996—2000. Recipient numerous leadership and cmty. svc. awards. Mem.: LA Convention and Visitors Bureau. Achievements include developed TV programming aimed at young Latinos. Office: Griego Enterprises Inc 4245 Don Alanis Pl Los Angeles CA 90008*

GRIES, ROBBIE RICE, geologist, gas and petroleum company executive; Student, Del Mar Junior Coll., Corpus Christi, Tex.; BS in Geology, Colo. State U.; MS in Geology, U. Tex., Austin, 1970. Cert. petroleum geologist 1985. Geology tchr. Wichita State U.; with Texaco, Inc., Denver, 1973—76; staff geologist Reserve Oil Inc., 1976—80; ind. geologist, cons., 1980—92; founder Priority Oil & Gas, LLC, Denver, 1992—, pres., CEO, 1995—. Dir. Colo. Oil and Gas Assn. Mem. adv. coun. Geology Found., U. Tex., Austin. Named Leadership Honoree, Key Women in Energy awards, RaderEnergy, 2004; recipient Disting. Svc. award, Rocky Mountain Assn. Geologists. Mem.: Soc. Sedimentary Geology, Geol. Soc. Am., Am. Assn. Petroleum Geologists (hon.; sec. 1995—97, pres. 2001—02, A.I. Leverson award 1985, Disting. Svc. award 1991, named hon. mem. 1998). Achievements include First woman to serve as president of the Ammerican Association of Petroleum Geologists. Office: Priority Oil & Gas PO Box 27798 Denver CO 80227-0798*

GRIESER, ILSA ADELE, elementary school educator, music educator; b. Phila., June 24, 1958; d. George Robert and Ellen Adeline Bucher; m. James Allen Grieser, June 22, 1985; children: Josh, Kelsey. MusB, Heidelberg Coll., 1981. Cert. K-12 music tchr. specialist. Elem. music tchr. Liberty Center (Ohio) Elem. Sch., 1981—. Mem. Black Swamp Arts Coun. Bd., Archbold, Ohio, 2000—01. Recipient Artist-in-Residency, Ohio Arts Coun., 1988, 1989, 2000. Mem.: NEA, Ohio Edn. Assn., Nat. Assn. for Music Edn. Avocations: singing, cooking. Office: Liberty Center Elem Sch 103 Young St Liberty Center OH 43532

GRIFFEN, AGNES MARTHE, library administrator; b. Ft. Dauphin, Madagascar, Aug. 25, 1935; d. Frederick Stang and Alvilde Margrethe (Torvik) Hallanger; m. Thomas Michael Griffen (div. Nov. 1969); children: Shaun Helen Griffen D'Antoni, Christopher Patrick, Adam Andrew; m. John H.P. Hall, Aug. 26, 1980. BA cum laude in English, Pacific Luth. U., 1957; MLS, U. Wash., 1965; Urban Exec. cert., MIT, 1976; postgrad., Harvard U., 1993. Cert. librarian, Wash., Md., Ariz. Area children's libr. King County Libr. Sys., Seattle, 1965-68, coord. instl. librs., 1968-71, dep. libr. for staff and program devel., 1971-74; dep. libr. dir. Tucson Pub. Libr., 1974-80; dir. Montgomery County Dept. Pub. Librs., Rockville, Md., 1980-96; libr. dir. Tucson-Pima Pub. Libr., 1997—. Lectr. Grad. Libr. Sch., U. Ariz., Tucson, 1976-77, 79; vis. lectr. Sch. Librarianship, U. Wash., Seattle, 1983. Contbr. articles to library periodicals and profl. jours. Active Md. Humanities Coun., Balt., 1986-92, Ariz. Humanities Coun., Phoenix, 1977-80; charter mem. Exec. Women's Coun. of So. Ariz., Tucson, 1979-80; mem. coun. Nat. Capital Area Pub. Access Network, 1992-94, pres. bd., 1993-94, Ariz. Statewide Libr. Devel. Commn., 2000-02' mem. adv. coun. to Ariz. State Libr., 1998--. Recipient Helping Hand award Md. Assn. of the Deaf, 1985, Cert. Recognition Montgomery County Hispanic Employees Assn., 1985; Henry scholar U. Washington Sch. Librarianship, 1965. Mem. ALA (exec. bd. 1989-93, divsn. pres. pub. libr. assn. bd. 1981-82, councilor-at-large 1972-76, 86-93, chmn. com. on program evaluation and support 1987-88, legis. com. 1998-2002), Ariz. State Libr. Assn. (legis. com. 1997--), Md. Libr. Assn. Democrat. Home: 1951 N El Moraga Dr Tucson AZ 85745-9070 E-mail: agriffe1@ci.tucson.az.us.

GRIFFEY, LINDA BOYD, lawyer; b. Keokuk, Iowa, Aug. 6, 1949; d. Marshall Coulter and Geraldine Vivian (White) Boyd; m. John Jay Griffey, June 24, 1972. BS in Pharmacy, U. Iowa, 1972; JD, Duke U., 1980. Bar: Calif. 1980; lic. pharmacist, Iowa, N.C. Pharmacist Davenport (Iowa) Osteo. Hosp., 1972-75, Wagner Pharmacy, Clinton, Iowa, 1975-77, Durham (N.C.) County Gen. Hosp., 1977-80; assoc. O'Melveny & Myers, L.A., 1980-88, ptnr., 1988—. Spkr., writer in field of employee benefits and exec. compensation; former pres. L.A. chpt. Western Pension and Benefits Conf., 1998-99. Active L.A. Philharm. Bus. & Profl. Assn.; bd. dirs. Hillsides Home for Children, Pasadena Playhouse. Mem. ABA (employee benefits com. tax sect.), Am. Law Inst., L.A. County Bar Assn. (former chair employee benefits com. 1994-95), L.A. Duke Bar Assn. (pres. 1987-90, 91-92), Rotary (L.A. chpt. bd. dirs. 1995-97). Avocations: golf, reading, swimming. Office: O'Melveny & Myers 400 S Hope St Los Angeles CA 90071-2899 E-mail: lgriffey@omm.com.

GRIFFIN, BETTY JO, elementary school educator; b. Monroe, La., Jan. 12, 1947; d. Julia Odell (Foster) Calhoun; divorced; 1 child, James Odell Griffin, Jr. BA, So. U., 1969; MA, San Francisco State U., 1975; PhD, LaSalle U., 2000. Cert. elem. tchr., Calif. Tchr. lang. arts Oakland (Calif.) Unified Sch. Dist., 1970-73, Garfield Elem. Sch., 1973-77, 1977-96; splty. prep. libr. and lang. arts tchr. Webster Acad., 1996—. Trustee Allen Temple Bapt. Ch., Oakland, Calif., 1987—; lit. tutor Delta Sigma Theta, Oakland, 1990—; chairperson African Am. Chain Read In, 1995—. Recipient Libr. Protection Fund award State Dept. Edn., 1997, Leadership award Dem. Nat. Com., 1997. Mem. NAACP, NEA, Oakland Edn. Assn. (bd. dirs.), Calif. Tchrs. Assn. (coun. of edn. 1996), Nat. Alliance Black Sch. Educators, Delta Sigma Theta, Phi Delta Kappa. Democrat. Avocations: reading, helping others, public speaking. Home: 2559 Oliver Ave Oakland CA 94605-4820 E-mail: BettyJGri@aol.com.

GRIFFIN, DIANE EDMUND, research physician, virologist, educator; b. Iowa City, Ia., May 12, 1940; d. Rudolph William and Doris Irene (Swanson) Edmund; m. John Wesley Griffin, June 13, 1965; children: Christopher Todd, Erik Edmund. BA, Augustana Coll., Rock Island, Ill., 1962; MD, Stanford U., 1968, PhD, 1970. Diplomate Am. Bd. Internal Medicine, Am. Bd. Infectious Diseases. Resident in medicine Stanford (Calif.) U. Hosp., 1968-70; fellow Johns Hopkins U. Sch. Medicine, Balt., 1970-73, asst. prof., 1973-79, assoc. prof., 1979-86, prof., 1986—; prof., chair molecular microbiol. immunology Johns Hopkins U. Sch. Pub. Health, 1994—. Investigator Howard Hughes Med. Inst., Balt., 1973-79; mem. virology study sect. NIH, 1982-86; mem. adv. com. Nat. Multiple Sclerosis Soc., 1986-92; mem. microbiology and infectious diseases rsch. adv. com. NIH, 1989-92, chair, 1992-94. Author films and tapes; contbr. chpts. to books, articles to profl. jours. Grantee NIH, 1983—, Nat. Multiple Sclerosis Soc., 1986—, WHO, 1993—, Muscular Dystrophy Assn., 1996—. Fellow Infectious Diseases Soc. Am., AAAS; mem. Am. Soc. for Clin. Investigation, Am. Soc. for Virology (council 1987-89), Interurban Clin. Club. Democrat. Lutheran. Avocation: gardening. Office: Johns Hopkins Sch Pub Health 615 N Wolfe St Baltimore MD 21205-2103

GRIFFIN, ELEANOR, magazine editor; Exec. editor So. Living, Birmingham, 1993—. Office: Southern Living 2100 Lakeshore Dr Birmingham AL 35209-6721

GRIFFIN, GLORIA JEAN, retired elementary school educator; b. Emmett, Idaho, Sept. 10, 1946; d. Archie and Marguerite (Johnson) G. AA, Boise (Idaho) Jr. Coll., 1966; BA, Boise Coll., 1968; MA in Elem. Curriculum, Boise State U., 1975. Cert. advanced elem. tchr., Idaho. Tchr. music, tutor, Boise, Idaho; sec. Edward A. Johnson, atty., Boise, Idaho; tchr. Head Start, Boise, Idaho; elem. tchr. Meridian Sch. Dist., Idaho, 1968—2002, ret., 2002. Developer multi-modality individualized spelling program; co-developer program for adapting curriculum to student's individual differences. Author: The Culture and Customs of the Argentine People As Applied to a Sixth Grade Social Studies Unit. Sec. PTA. Named Tchr. of Yr., Meridian Sch. Dist., 1981. Mem. Actor's Guild, Alpha Delta Kappa (rec. sec.).

GRIFFIN, JANICE, political organization professional; Nat. chair Womens Leadership Forum Democratic Nat. Com., Washington. Office: Womens Leadership Forum Democratic Nat Com 430 S Capitol St SE Washington DC 20003-4024

GRIFFIN, JEAN LATZ, political strategist, writer; b. Joliet, Ill., Mar. 6, 1943; d. Carl Joseph and Helene Monica (Bradshaw) Latz; m. Dennis Joseph Griffin, Sept. 16, 1967; children: Joseph, Timothy, Peter. BS in Chemistry, Coll. St. Francis, Joliet, 1965; MS in Journalism, U. Wis., 1967. Clin. investigation coord. Baxter Labs., 1967-68; reporter Joliet Herald News, 1968-70, Raleigh (N.C.) Times, 1974-75, Suburban Trib, Hinsdale, Ill., 1976-78, regional edn. reporter, 1978-82; gen. assignment reporter Chgo. Tribune, 1982-84, edn. writer, 1984-88, pub. health writer, 1988-94, govt., politics, and pub. policy reporter, 1994-97, econ. devel. reporter, 1997; strategist The Strategy Group, Chgo., 1998—; owner CyberINK, 1998—; adj. journalism instr. Roosevelt U., Chicago, 2001—. Bd. dirs. Residents for Emergency Shelter, Chgo., 1978-82, Genesis House, Chgo., 1995-98, vol. cook, 1994-98; devel. com. mem. Hope Now, Inc., 1998-2000; membership chair Arlington Hts. C. of C., 2001-2002; vol. Taoist Tai Chi instr., 2001—, pres. Taoist Chi Soc., Ill., 2003—. Recipient Writing award Am. Dental Assn., 1969, Alumna Profl. Achievement award Coll. St. Francis, Joliet, 1985, First Prize in ednl. writing Edn. Writers Am., 1986, Grand prize, 1988, Benjamin Fine award Nat. Assn. Secondary Sch. Prins., 1988, Edward Scott Beck award for reporting Chgo. Tribune, 1988, Peter Lisagor award for pub. svc. Soc. Profl. Journalists, Chgo. chpt., 1990, Mark of Excellence Chgo. Assn. Black Journalists, 1992, Cushing award for Journalistic Excellence, Chgo. Dental Soc., 1992, Human First award Horizon Cmty. Svcs., Chgo., 1993, Robert F. Kennedy Grand Prize in Journalism, 1994, Editl. Excellence award Ill. Merchandising Coun., 1994; finalist Pulitzer Prize, 1994. Mem. Taoist Tai Chi Soc. USA-Ill. Office: CyberINK 621 N Belmont Ave Arlington Heights IL 60004 E-mail: jlgrif@earthlink.net.

GRIFFIN, KELLY ANN, public relations executive, consultant; b. Buffalo, May 20, 1964; d. Michael Gerald and Patricia Frances (Lippert) G.; m. Thomas Richard Kleinberger, Oct. 11, 1992. B in Polit. Sci., SUNY, Geneseo, 1986; postgrad., CUNY, Bklyn., 1994—. Legis. asst. to N.Y. State Assembly Spkrs. Stanley Fink and Mel Miller, Buffalo, 1986-87; acct. exec. Griffin Media Group, N.Y.C., 1987-88, acct. supr., v.p., 1988-90, pres., CEO, 1990-94; pub. rels. cons. N.Y.C., 1994—. Assoc. dir. N.Y. State Funeral Dirs. Assn., N.Y.C., 1992-94, Met. Funeral Dirs. Assn., N.Y.C., 1992-94, County Execs. of Am., N.Y.C. and Washington, 1993-2000; dep. exec. dir. County Execs. Am., 2000—; instr. remedial reading Cornell U. Sch. Industry/Lab. Rels., Buffalo, 1987; v.p. Fairfield Owners Cooperative, Riverdale, 1996-2000. Editor N.Y. State AFL-CIO Unity, 1988-90, County Execs. News, 1993—, N.Y. State Funeral Dirs. Assn./Met. Funeral Dirs. Assn. News, 1992-94, Amalgamated Transit Union News, 1988-90. Cons. Interfaith Assembly on Homelessness, N.Y.C., 1994-97, Voter Assistance Commn., N.Y.C., 1990-92; participant, cons. Erie County Dem. Party, Buffalo, 1985-87; mem. assocs. steering com. Children's Health Fund, N.Y.C., 1991-97; bd. dirs. Kingsbridge Hts. Cmty. Ctr., Bronx, 1999-2000, sec., 2000-01, chair, 2001—; mem. Parents' Assn., Frances Schervier Home and Hosp. Childcare Ctr., Bronx, 1997-2000, Support Our Schs. Com., Bronx, 1999-2000; class parent Prospect Hill Sch. PTA, Pelham Manor, 2001-03, rec. sec., 2003—; mem. fundraising com. Transition Learning Ctr., New Rochelle, NY. Recipient Acad. award DAR, 1978. Mem. Pub. Rels. Soc. N.Y.C., The Manor Club (Pelham Manor, N.Y.). Roman Catholic. Avocations: reading, swimming, bike riding, running. Home: 1061 Hunter Ave Pelham NY 10803-3409 Office: Griffin Media Group 3rd fl 1010 Massachusetts Ave NW Washington DC 20001-5402 E-mail: kgrif@optonline.net.

GRIFFIN, LAURA MAE, retired elementary and secondary school educator; b. Woodland, Calif., Aug. 14, 1925; d. George Everette Ramsey and Bertha (Storz) Ramsey Lowe; m. Roy J. Griffin, Nov. 19, 1944; children: Robert Eugene, Dennis Charles, Kathleen Ann. AA in Social Sci., Sacramento City Coll., 1969; BA in Geography, Calif. State U., Sacramento, 1972. Cert. elem. and secondary tchr., Calif.; Master Gardener. Sec. Alameda Naval Air, Alameda, Calif., 1944-45, Cal-Western Life Ins., Sacramento, 1945-47, Pacific Sch. Dist., Sacramento, 1956-57; substitute tchr. Sacramento Unified Sch. Dist., 1974-75; tchr. Mt. Diablo Unified Sch. Dist., Concord, Calif., 1976-91; ret., 1991. Dir. Heather Farm Garden Ctr., Walnut Creek, Calif., 1985-86, edn. chmn., 1986-87, pres., 1987-88, fin. sec., 1993-94; sec. investment group AAUW, Walnut Creek, 1978-79. Guardian Jobs Daus.-Bethel 325, Walnut Creek, 1978-79; leader Girl Scouts Am., Sacramento, 1971-72; den mother Boy Scouts Am., Sacramento, 1957-60; publicity chmn. membership Northgate Music Boosters, Walnut Creek, 1976-77; women's Bible study coord., 2003-04. Recipient Bert A. Bertolero Gardening award, 1996. Mem. Calif. Garden Clubs (life), Heather Farm Garden Club (pres. 1987-88, Outstanding Svc. award 1995), Walnut Creek Garden Club (pres. 1983-84, civic project chmn. 1994-95, 95-96), Order Ea. Star. Republican. Avocations: reading, travel, bowling, golf, music, gardening.

GRIFFIN, LUANNE MARIE, automotive corporation executive; b. Pitts., Dec. 19, 1961; d. Louis F. and Bernadette (Piekarski) Chapman; m. James E. Griffin, July 19, 1997. BA, Thiel Coll., 1983; MA, George Washington U., 1987. Sr. legis. asst. U.S. Rep. Thomas Ridge, Washington, 1983-87; English instr. Japan Min. Edn., Kagoshima, 1987-88; congrl. liaison Embassy of Japan, Washington, 1989-93; trade policy analyst Powell, Goldstein, Frazer & Murphy, Washington, 1993-95; corp. mgr. govt. affairs Nissan N.Am., Inc., Washington, 1995—. Mem. Women in Internat. Trade., Washington Internat. Trade Assn., Tenn. State Soc. (bd. dirs.). Republican. Roman Catholic. Office: 196 Van Buren St Ste 450 Herndon VA 20170-5337

GRIFFIN, MARY E. state representative; b. Boston, May 16, 1926; m. to Andrew J. Griffin. Grad., Pierce Secretarial, Boston. Legal sec., ret. 1975; sec. Windham Planning Bd., 1991-96; mem. dist. 27 N.H. Ho. of Reps., 1996—. Mem. mcpl. and county govt. com., N.H. House of Reps.; host/interviewer WCTV-51 Cable Access TV, 1986-96. State dir. N.H. Sr. Am. Pageant, 1993-96. Roman Catholic. Home: 4 Wynridge Rd Windham NH 03087-1628 Office: NH State Legis State House Concord NH 03301

GRIFFIN, MARY FRANCES, retired library media consultant; b. Cross Hill, S.C., Aug. 24, 1925; d. James and Rosa Lee (Carter) G. BA, Benedict Coll., 1947; postgrad., S.C. State Coll., 1948-51, Atlanta U., 1953, Va. State Coll., 1961; MLS, Ind. U., 1957. Tchr., libr. Johnston (S.C.) Tng. Sch., Edgefield County Sch. Dist., 1947-51; libr. Lee County Sch. Dist., Dennis High, Bishopville, S.C., 1951-52, Greenville County (S.C.) Sch. Dist., 1952-66; libr. cons. S.C. Dept. Edn., Columbia, 1966-87. Vis. tchr. U. S.C., 1977. Bd. dirs. Greater Columbia Lit. Coun.; mem. Richland County unit Assault on Illiteracy. Recipient Cert. of Living the Legacy award Nat. Coun. Negro Women, 1980. Mem. ALA, Assn. Ednl. Comms. and Tech., S.C. Assn. Curriculum Devel., AAUW (pres. Columbia br. 1978-80), Southeastern Libr. Assn. (sec. 1979-80), S.C. Libr. Assn. (sec. 1979), S.C. Assn. Sch. Librarians, Nat. Assn. State Ednl. and Media Pers. Baptist. Home: PO Box 1652 Columbia SC 29202-1652 also: 1100 Skyland Dr Columbia SC 29210-8127

GRIFFIN, MARY JANE RAGSDALE, educational consultant, writer, small business owner; b. Crawfordsville, Ind., Aug. 15, 1927; d. Ira Vincent and Sophronia Burdetti (Thompson) Ragsdale; m. Walter Wanzel Griffin, Jan. 20, 1951; children: Walter Vincent, Glenn Edwin, Edwin Wanzel. BS, U. Tenn., 1949, MS, 1970, doctoral student (hon.), 1975, EdS, 1976, EdD, 1980. Cert. math., sci., physics, chemistry, computer programming, elem. tchr., secondary and elem. adminstr., Tenn. Instr. physics lab., pianist, accompanist modern dance class U. Chattanooga (Tenn.), 1945-47; pvt. tchr. piano and violin Knoxville, Tenn., 1947-50, honorary captain airforce cadet, mil. sponsor Com. I U. Tenn., Knoxville, 1948-49; asst. dir. Sunshine Schoolette, Knoxville, 1954-69; tchr. sci. and math. Knox County Schs., Knoxville, 1970-74; tchr. math. methods U. Tenn., Knoxville, 1975-76; tchr. math. and computer programming Knox County Schs., Knoxville, 1977-88; freelance writer Knoxville, 1970—; real estate investor and mgr., 1975—; owner, pres. MIRG Enterprises, Knoxville, 1976—; freelance edn. cons. Knoxville, 1988—. Student asst. physics dept. head U. Chattanoga, 1945-47; asst. treas., historian, music chmn. U. Chattanooga, 1946-47; orientation leader U. Tenn., 1948; graduate asst. U. Tenn., Knoxville, 1975-76. Contbr. articles to various publs.; writer curriculum guides. Violinist Chattanooga Symphony, 1944-47; officer bd. dirs. Ossoli Circle, Knoxville, 1954-64, 89-90; poetry contest chmn. Fontinalis, 1993-96, fine arts chair, 1995-96; officer, bd. dirs. Girls Club Knoxville, Inc., 1962-70, charter signer, 1962; mem. Fountain City Town Hall, 1985—, Knoxville Symphony League, 1990—; tchr. adult Sunday sch., 1988-92; mem. chancel choir 1st Christian Ch., Knoxville, 1949-85, bd. dirs., 1982-85; mem. chancel choir Fountain City United Meth. Ch., Knoxville, 1985-91, bd. dirs., 1993-97, cert. 50 yr. mem.; pres. United Meth. Women, 1993-97, v.p. Knoxville Dist., 1996-98; mem. steering com. Just Older Youth, Fountain City, Tenn., 1998—. U. Chattanooga scholar, 1947; U. Tenn. fellow, 1968-70. Mem. NEA, ASCD, AAUW, DAR, Nat. Coun. Tchrs. Math. (life), Tenn. Edn. Assn. (workshop presenter 1980-88), East Tenn. Edn. Assn., Knox County Edn. Assn. (rep. 1980-85), East Tenn. Hist. Soc. (life), Ind. Hist. Soc. (life), Ky. Hist. Soc. (life), Va. Hist. Soc., Montgomery County (Ind.) Hist. Soc., Boone County (Ind.) Hist. Soc., Union County (Tenn.) Hist. Soc., Gen. Fedn. Womens Clubs, Tenn. Fedn. Womens Clubs, Appalachian Zool. Soc. (life), Soc. for Preservation Tenn. Antiquities (life), Nat. Corvette Mus., First Families of Tenn., U. Tenn. President's Club (life), Smoky Mountain Z-Car Club, Optimists (life, local bd. dirs. 1990-92, Tenn. dist. essay contest chmn. 1990-91, 1992-93, 1993-94, Tenn. dist. 1st lady 1990-91), Sigma Phi Sigma (life, chpt. pres. U. Chattanooga 1945-47), Nat. Corvette Mus., Delta Kappa Gamma (fin. com. 1980-91), Phi Delta Theta, Kappa Delta Pi (internat. voting del. 1982, 84, 86, conf. presenter 1982), Kappa Delta (life), Women's Athletic Assn. U. Chattanoga, Coed Colillion U. Chattanoga, Home Econs. Club U. Tenn., Women's Student Govt. Assn. U. Tenn. Avocations: nature walks and study, travel, photography, reading, public speaking. Home: 5213 Haynes Sterchi Rd Knoxville TN 37912-2816

GRIFFIN, MONICA VICTORIA, military officer, writer; b. Chgo., Aug. 5, 1968; d. Tomella Griffin; children: Paige Victoria Lloyd, Caleb Jamaal Lloyd. BA, Chgo. State U., 1991; MS, So. Ill. U., 2002. Advanced through grade to capt. U.S. Army, 1987, commd. 2d lt., 1991; pub. affairs officer 318th Press Camp Hdqs., Forest Park, Ill., 1993—96; platoon leader contr. observer 85th Tng. Divsn., Ft. Sheridan, Ill., 1996—99; ops. officer 648th Area Support Group, St. Louis, 1999—2002; pers. proponency integration officer USAR Pers. Command, St. Louis, 2002—. Freelance writer Suburban Jour., Belleville, Ill., 2003—, The Hub. Vision leadership team Deliverance Mission Christian Ch., Belleville, 2003. Recipient Editor's Choice award, Am. Libr. Poetry, 1999. Mem.: Greater St. Louis Assn. Black Journalists, Sigma Gamma Rho (life). Democrat. Baptist. Avocations: writing, tennis, kickboxing. Home: 5 Clinton Hill Dr Belleville IL 62226 Office: HRC St Louis 1 Reserve Way Saint Louis MO 63132 Office Phone: 314-592-0000 3606.

GRIFFIN, PENNI ONCKEN, dean, social worker; b. Cedar Rapids, Iowa, Nov. 11, 1945; d. Edward Charles and Rita Margaret Oncken; m. Walt Griffin, Dec. 6, 1980; children: Rebecca, Kathleen, Shawn, Megan. BA, Coe Coll., 1970; MSW, U. Cinn., 1992. LMSW S.C. Lead social worker Iowa Dept. Social Svcs., Cedar Rapids, 1975—79; dir. homemaker svcs. Family Svc. Agy., Cedar Rapids, 1979—80; investigator protective svcs. Iowa Dept. Social Svcs., Waterloo, Iowa, 1982—89; med. social worker S.C. Dept. Health and Environl. Control, SC, 1992—95; asst. prof. and dir. Social Work Program Limestone Coll., Gaffney, SC, 1995—2002, asst. dean and dir. Social Work Program, 2002—. Bd. dir. LinnHaven Home Retarded Adults, Cedar Rapids, 1976—78; mem. adv. bd. Make Today Count, Cedar Rapids, 1976—79, Cherokee County Alcohol and Drug Abuse Commn., Gaffney, SC, 2001—. Chmn. fin. Linn County Dems., Cedar Rapids, 1979—80, Steve Sovern U.S. Congress, Cedar Rapids, 1980; bd. dirs. Gaffney (S.C.) Little Theatre, 1994—2001. Mem.: NASW, Social Work Baccalaureate Program Dirs., Coun. Social Work Edn. Democrat. Avocations: reading, travel. Home: 1008 College Drive Gaffney SC 29340 Office: Limestone College 1115 College Drive Gaffney SC 29340 E-mail: pgriffin@limestone.edu.

GRIFFIN, SALLIE T. artist, photographer, sculptor, former radiologic technologist; b. Whiteville, NC, Sept. 2, 1940; d. Benjamin Oliver and Virginia Alma (Ponton) Thompson; m. C.H. Griffin, Dec. 26, 1964; children: A.F. Griffin, M.A. Griffin. Grad., St. Mary's High Sch. and Jr. Coll., Duke U. Med. Ctr., Sch. Radiological Tech. and Nuclear Medicine; student, Anson Tech. Coll., Ctrl. Piedmont C.C., 1976-80, Wingate U., 1976-91, 97; studied with Sally B. Miller. With Stanley Meml. Hosp., Albermark, N.C.; technician, tchr. Moses Cine Hosp. Founding mem. Union Co. Art Coun., Monroe, N.C., 1980-84., found. first libr. gallery Union Co. Libr., Marshville, NC, 1998. One woman shows include: Union County Pub. Libr., Monroe, N.C., 1980, 82, Wingate Coll., 1980, United Carolina Bank, 1981, Ivey's Southpark, Charlotte, 1985, Dove Pottery and Gallery, Monroe, 1990, Stanley County Libr., Albemarle, 1992, Artisan Ctr., Kannapolis, 1992, St. Mary's Coll., 1992, Union County Arts Coun., 1995, 50 piece show, 2000; Group shows include: Blooming Arts Festival (named Union County's Finest, 1981, 1st place winner, 1994), N.C. State U. Show, 1988, Dove Pottery and Gallery, 1991, Watercolor Soc. N.C., 1995, U. N.C. 1996, Myrtle Beach Convention Ctr., 1996, 22nd Nat. Show, Shelby, 1996, Greensboro Cultural Ctr., 1997, Mus. of York County, 1997, Shelby Nat. Show #23, 1997, Greenhill Gallery of N.C. Art, 1998, Taladega Mus., Ala.,

1998, Wingate U., 1998, Union County Libr., 1998, Weatherspoon Gallery, 1999, Fayetteville Mus. Art, 1999, 25th Ann. Art Show of N.W., Fla., 1999, Burroughs and Chapin Art Mus., Myrtle Beach, S.C., 1999, MOMA, N.Y.C., 2000; Fe-Mail E-Mail 2000. Bd. dirs. Wingate Coll. Libr., Wingate, NC, 1985-89, Union County Arts Coun., Monroe; founder Union County Arts Coun. NE N.C. Mem. The Marshville Rsch. Club, The Union Co. Art League (pres. 1986-87, 2000-01), The Watercolor Soc. N.C., Ariz., Ala., Conn., The Guild of Charlotte Artists, The Charlotte Art League, The Jaycettes (founder, bd. mem. 1965-75, pres. 1965-67). Democrat. Baptist. E-mail: salliegriffin@altel.com.

GRIFFIN, SYLVIA GAIL, reading specialist; b. Portland, Oreg., Dec. 13, 1935; d. Archie and Marguerite (Johnson) G. AA, Boise Jr. Coll., 1955; BS, Brigham Young U., 1957, MEd, 1967. Cert. advanced teaching, Idaho. Classroom tchr. Boise Pub. Sch., Idaho, 1957-59, 61-66, 67-69, reading specialist, 1969-90, 91-95, 98-2001, inclusion specialist, 1995-98, early childhood specialist, 1990-91. Tchr. evening Spanish classes for adults, 1987-88; lectr. in field; mem. cons. pool US Office Juvenile Justice and Delinquency Prevention, 1991—. Author: Procedures Used by First Grade Teachers for Teaching Experience Readiness for Reading Comprehension, The Short Story of Vowels, A Note Worthy Way to Teach Reading, The Little Black Schoolhouse, Hellside Elementary School, Reading, Righting, and Revenge, Memorandum: Murder, Once Upon a Trial. Advisor in developing a program for dyslexics Scottish Rite Masons of Idaho, Boise. Mem.: NEA, Actor's Guild, Idaho Edn. Assn. (pub. rels. dir. 1970—72), Boise Edn. Assn. (pub. rels. dir. 1969—72, bd. dirs. ednl. polit. involvement com. 1983—89), Alpha Delta Kappa. Avocations: music, creative writing. Home: 9948 W Sleepy Hollow Ln Boise ID 83714-3665

GRIFFIN, TAMMY LYNN, industrial engineer; b. Atlanta, Jan. 15, 1961; married July 30, 1999. BS in Indsl. Engring., Ga. Inst. Tech., 1982; MBA, Ga. State U. Registered profl. engr., Ga. Imagery scientist CIA, Washington, 1983-84; indsl. engr. N.Am. Philips, Little Rock, 1984-86; sr. quality assurance engr. Emerson Electric Co., Sanford, Fla., 1986-88; mgr. quality assurance J&J, Inc., Hampton, Ga., 1988-93; quality assurance mgr. Goody Products, Manchester, Ga., 1993-95. Asst. treas. Starr's Mill Bapt. Ch., Fayetteville, Ga., 1993—, mem. fin. com., 1994-95. Mem. Ga. Soc. Profl. Engrs. (treas. C-H-F chpt. 1992-93, v.p. 1993-94, pres. 1994-95, Young Engr. of Yr. award 1994). Avocations: golf, jazzercise. Home: 195 Grindstone Way Senoia GA 30276-1602

GRIFFIN, TERRI DUGGAN, media specialist; b. Albany, Ga., May 12, 1971; d. Henry Coleman and Pat Rose Duggan; m. Stephen Burt Griffin, Dec. 17, 1994; children: Elizabeth, Drew. BS in Early Childhood Edn., U. Ga., 1993, MEd in Instructional Tech., 1994. Media specialist Highland Magnet Sch., Albany, Ga., 1994—98; author, columnist Southwest Ga. Living Mag., 2001—. Author short stories; contbr. articles to mags. and local newspaper. Rec. sec. Jr. League Albany, 2001; vol. reader Libr. of Blind, 2002—03; mem. media com. First Bapt. Ch., Albany, 1999—2001. Recipient Ellen Raulerson Spirit of Commitment award, Jr. League, 2001. Republican. Avocations: guitar, reading, writing.

GRIFFIN-BURRILL, KATHLEEN R. F. See BURRILL, KATHLEEN R. F.

GRIFFITH, DOTTY (DOROTHY GRIFFITH STEPHENSON), journalist, writer; b. Terrell, Tex., Nov. 4, 1949; d. Edward Morrill and Dorothy (Koch) Griffith; children: Kelly, Caitlin Lee. BJ, U. Tex., 1972; MLA, So. Methodist U., 1980. Gen. assignment reporter Dallas Morning News, 1972—76, edn. writer, 1973—74, polit. writer, 1976—78, food editor, 1978—95; lifestyles editor, food columnist Design and Prodn., 1995—97, dining editor, restaurant critic, 1997—. Host In the Kitchen with Dotty KRLD Radio, 1992—94; guest host Warner-Amex, Qube Cable TV, Dallas, 1982—83. Author: Wild about Chili, 1985, Wild About Manchies, 1989, Gourmet Grains, Beans and Rices, 1992; editor: The Mansion On Turtle Creek Cookbook (Dean Fearing), 1987, Dallas Cuisine, 1994, The Texas Holiday Cookbook, 1997, Cooking with Days of Our Lives, 1997. Nutrition task force Am. Heart Assn., Dallas, 1981—87. Mem.: Newspaper Food Editor's and Writer's Assn. (v.p. 1984—86, pres. 1986—88), Les Dames d'Escoffier (founding mem. Dallas chpt.). Office: The Dallas Morning News Communications Ctr PO Box 655237 Dallas TX 75265-5237

GRIFFITH, ELIZABETH ANNA, communications executive, educator; BA, Trinity Coll., Washington, DC, 1978; MBA, U. Va., Charlottesville, 1985; MA in Liberal Studies, Georgetown U., 1995. Bus. mgr. Monticello, Charlottesville, Va., 1985—87; adminstr. Phillips Collection, Washington, 1987—91; various positions Nat. Pub. Radio, Washington, 1991—99; treas. Corp. for Pub. Broadcasting, Washington, 1999—. Adj. prof. Trinity Coll., Washington. Treas. Mary's Ctr. Maternal and Child Care, Washington. Mem.: Alumnae Assn. Trinity Coll. (pres.). Home: 5204 Western Ave Chevy Chase MD 20815 Office: Corp for Public Broadcasting 401 9th St NW Washington DC 20004

GRIFFITH, HURDIS M. dean; BSN, Jamestown Coll., N.D.; MSN, U. Washington; cert. adult, primary care nurse, PhD, U. Md. Fellow Robert Wood Johnson Health Policy, 1986-87; dean Coll. Nursing, prof. Rutgers U., Newark. Mem. Nat. Acads. Practice (pres.-elect). Office: Rutgers U Coll Nursing Ackerson Hall 180 University Ave Newark NJ 07102-1897 Fax: 973-353-1277. E-mail: griffith@nightingale.rutgers.edu.

GRIFFITH, JEWEL ANN, music educator; b. Bloomsburg, Pa., Dec. 23, 1942; d. Bruce M. and Bernice M. Bittner; m. Kenneth Carlton Griffith, July 22, 1967; children: Amy Sue Saylor, Lori Ann Grebner, Mindy Lynne. BS in Music Edn., Mansfield U., 1964; postgrad., Bloomsburg U., 1966, Potsdam Choral Inst., 1977—80. Vocal music tchr. Newark Valley (N.Y.) Ctrl. Schs., 1964—70, 1973, 1979—. Pvt. piano & vocal tchr., Newark Valley, 1964—74; vocalist chorus under Robert Shaw with Phila. Orch., 1978, 80; guest condr. choral festivals, N.Y., Pa.; choral dir. Am. Music Abroad Honor Choirs, 1992—2000; vocal soloist State Ea. Star Conv., Lake Placid, NY, 1995, Niagara Falls, NY, 99. Music dir. Meth. Ch., Newark Valley, 1965—95. Named Educator of the Week, Sta. WBNG-TV, 2001, Educator of the Yr., Sam's Club, 2002. Mem.: N.Y. State Sch. Music Assn. (mem. rural sch. music com. 1997—2003), Music Educators Nat. Conf., Am. Choral Dirs. Guild. Avocations: kickboxing, swimming, reading, gardening, dance. Home: 147 Gaskill Rd Owego NY 13827 Office: Newark Valley HS 64 Wilson Creek Rd Newark Valley NY 13811 Personal E-mail: jewelgriffith@yahoo.com.

GRIFFITH, KATHERINE SCOTT, librarian; b. Atlanta, Jan. 16, 1942; d. Robert Sherrill and Emily Howell (Reynolds) G.; m. Henry Armand Terjen, Sept. 4, 1970 (div. Nov. 1979); 1 child, Henry Foster Terjen (dec.); m. Michael Christopher Healy, May 20, 1995. AB, Sweet Briar Coll., 1964; Masters, Emory U., 1968. Editor South Today, So. Regional Coun., Atlanta, 1969-72; editor Phoenix, Bklyn., 1972-73; dir. comm. N.Y. C. of C. and Industry, N.Y.C., 1978-79; dir. pub. liaison N.Y.C. Dept. Ports and Terminals, 1979-80; sr. pub. affairs officer Citicorp/Citibank, N.Y.C., 1981-83; asst. v.p., pub. rels. mgr. Citicorp Diners Club Media Svcs., N.Y.C., 1983-84; asst. v.p., pub. rels. dir. Citicorp Pub., N.Y.C., 1985-86, asst. v.p. corp. comms., 1986-87; v.p. First Atlanta Corp., Atlanta, 1984; sr. mgr. Can. Imperial Bank of Commerce, N.Y.C., 1987-88, v.p. USA corp. comm., 1989-95; dir. mktg. and comm. Can. Imperial Bank Commerce Wood Gundy, N.Y.C., 1995-97; v.p., dir. corp. comm. Signet Banking Corp., Richmond, Va., 1997; comm. cons. Greenwich, Conn., 1998-99; pub. rels. supr. The Ferguson Libr., Stamford, Conn., 1999-2000; dir. comms. and external rels. N.Y. Regional Assn. Grantmakers, 2000—02, dir. comms. and govt. rels., 2002—03; libr. Bedford Free Libr., 2003—. Pres. 150 Joralemon Street Corp., Bklyn., 1987-89. Pres. 78th Precinct Cmty. Coun., Bklyn., 1977-78; mem. com. Cmty. Bd. 6, Bklyn., 1978-80; mem. coun. So. Regional Coun., Atlanta, 1984-98; bd. dirs. Atlanta Chamber Players, 1984; mem. Friends of Ferguson Libr., 2000—. Mem. Fin. Women's Assn. N.Y. (bd. dirs. 1995-96), Jr. League, Success by Six (mktg. com. 1999-2002), Beta Phi Mu. Democrat. Episcopalian. Home and Office: 472 Gramatan Ave Apt J2 Mount Vernon NY 10552-2941 E-mail: ksgriff@optonline.net.

GRIFFITH, LINDA MARIE (LYNNE), county government official; b. Helena, Mont., Sept. 22, 1949; d. Lawrence Eugene and Mary Ceona (Price) Smith; m. Dennis J. Willis Sr., July 6, 1968 (div. 1972); children: Dennis John Willis Jr., Andrew Bonnell Christian; m. Eugene Donald Griffith, Sept. 20, 1995. Cert. Paralegal, Kennesaw Coll., Marietta, Ga., 1986-88; Cert. Pub. Mgmt., U. Ga., 1991. Ga. state lobbyist. Reservations mgr. Guest Travel, Mpls., 1968-74; sales staff North Cen. Airlines, Mpls., 1974-76; dir. conv. and groupsales Summit Travel, Mpls., 1976-81; mktg. and sales mgr. Internat. Travel, Tampa, Fla., 1981-82; asst. dir. ops. and maintenance Cobb Community Transit, Marietta, Ga., 1989-95; legis. liaison office of fed. and state rels. Met. Atlanta Rapid Transit Authority, 1995-96, gen. supt. paratransit svcs., 1996—98; gen. supt. Perry Blvd., CNG fixed rate Ga. Regional Transp. Authority, Atlanta, 1998—2000, reg. mgr., 2000; exec. dir., CEO C-Tran, Vancouver, Wash., 2000—. Author (poetry): Battle of the Clouds, 1991 (Golden Poet award 1991). Civic leader E. Cobb Civic Assn./Alpine Lakes Homeowners, Marietta, Ga., 1983—89; legis. liaison Ga. Transit Assocs., 1995—96, Wash. State Transp. Assn., 2000—; mem. bi-state transp. com. Wash. Gov.'s I-5 Transp. and Trade Partnership Task Force, 2000—; pub. adminstrn. EXCEL-Cobb County; legis. com. chair Washington State Transp. Assn., exec. bd. officer, treas., 2003—; mem. Clark County R.R. Adv. Bd., 2003—; campaign mgr. com. to elect County Commr., Marietta, Ga., 1985—86; legis. liaison Cobb County Polit. Party, 1988—89, exec. com., 1988—89; bd. dirs. Columbia River Econ. Devel. Coun., 2000—, S.W. Wash. Regional Transp. Coun., 2000—; planning commr. Cobb County, Marietta, Ga., 1986—89; ofcl. spectator transp. sys. Centennial Olympic Games, 1996. Recipient Award for Service as Planning Commr. Cobb County Bd. Commrs., 1989. Mem.: Am. Pub. Transp. Assn. (bus. and paratransit ops. com.), Assn. County Commrs. (transp. and natural resource coms. 1986—89), Am. Planning Assn., Women's Transp. Seminar. Avocations: music, poetry. Home: 25704 NE 188th Ct Battle Ground WA 98604 Office: 2425 NE 65th Ave PO Box 2529 Vancouver WA 98668-2529 E-mail: lynneg@c-tran.org.

GRIFFITH, MARTHA, controller; b. Brockton, Mass., Sept. 9, 1945; d. Ishmael Hayes and Jettie L. (Dudley) Davis; m. Jack C. Griffith, May 29, 1965 (dec. June 1984); Michael S., David M.; m. Dan H. Fries, Nov. 5, 1994. Student, U. Ark., 1962-64; BA, Ball State U., 1967. Prin. Griffith Acctg. Co., Indpls., 1968-70; probate adminstr. Johnson & Weaver, Indpls., 1970-74; personnel adminstr. Hercules Inc., Houston, 1974-76; adminstr. Lapin Totz & Mayer, Houston, 1976-80; bus. mgr. Pasadena (Tex.) Citizen, 1980-84; contr. Houston Community Newspapers, 1984-88, DCI Pub., Alexandria, Va., 1989-90, Telescan Inc., Houston, 1990-93, Advolink, Inc., 1993-99, Suncoast Post-Tension, Inc., Houston, 1999—. Commr. Houston council Boy Scouts Am., 1983. Recipient Dist. Merit awards Boy Scouts Am., Houston, 1983. Mem. Internat. Newspaper Fin. Execs. (com. mem. 1986-89), Collier Jackson Users Group (moderator 1986-89), Nat. Assn. Female Execs. Democrat. Baptist. Avocations: dance, boating, traveling. Address: 14300 Ella Blvd #213 Houston TX 77014

GRIFFITH, MARY H. corporate communications executive; b. Ky. BA in English, Centre Coll., Danville, Ky. Sr. v.p., dir. pub. rels. 1st Nat. Bank Louisville, until 1990; with Nat. City Corp., Cleve., 1990—, sr. v.p. mktg. comm., 1992—. Bd. dirs. Centre Coll.; active numerous city and state civic orgns. Recipient Disting. Alumni award Centre Coll., 1991. Office: Nat City Corp Nat City Ctr 1900 E 9th St Cleveland OH 44114-3401

GRIFFITH, MELANIE, actress; b. N.Y.C., Aug. 9, 1957; d. Tippi Hedren; m. Steven Bauer (div.); 1 child, Alexander; m. Don Johnson, 1989 (div.); 1 child, Dakota; m. Antonio Banderas, 1996; 1 child, Stella. Student, Hollywood Profl. Sch., 1981; studied acting with, Stella Adler. Acting debut in Night Moves, 1975, other films include The Drowning Pool, 1975, Smile, 1975, One on One, 1977, Roar, Joyride, 1977, Underground Aces, Body Double, 1984, Fear City, Something Wild, 1986, Cherry 2000, 1988, The Milagro Beanfield War, 1988, Stormy Monday, 1987, Working Girl, 1988 (Acad. Award nominee), In the Spirit, The Grifters, Pacific Heights, 1990, Bonfire of the Vanities, Shining Through, Paradise, 1991, A Stranger Among Us, 1992, Born Yesterday, 1993, Milk Money, 1994, Nobody's Fool, 1994, Two Much, 1996, Mulholland Falls, 1996, Now and Then, 1996, Shadow of Doubt, Another Day in Paradise, Lolita, 1996, Celebrity, 1998, Crazy in Alabama, 1999, Cecil B. DeMented, 2000, Forever Lulu, 2000, Tart, 2001, Stuart Little 2 (voice), 2002, The Night We Called It a Day, 2003, Tempo, 2003, Shade, 2003; TV appearances include (series) Carter Country, (mini-series) Once an Eagle, Buffalo Girls, 1995, (TV movies) She's in the Army Now, 1981, Golden Gate, 1981, Alfred Hitchcock Presents, 1985, Women and Men: Stories of Seduction, 1990, Buffalo Girls, 1995, RKO 281, 1999, (pilots) Golden Gate; guest in Alfred Hitcock Presents; (Broadway plays) Chicago, 2003. Recipient Golden Globe award, 1989.*

GRIFFITH, NANCI, singer, songwriter; b. Austin, Tex., 1954; d. Griff and Ruelene G. BA Edn., U. of Tex., Austin. Former kindergarten & 1st grade teacher Austin SD; recording artist, 1978—. Albums include: There's a Light Beyond These Woods, 1978, Poet in My Window, 1982, Once in a Very Blue Moon, 1985, Last of the True Believers, 1986, Lone Star State of Mind, 1987, Little Love Affairs, 1988, One Fair Summer Evening, 1988, Storms, 1989, Late Night Grande Hotel, 1991, The MCA Years - A Retrospective, 1993, Other Voices, Other Rooms, 1993 (Grammy award Best Folk album), The Best of Nanci Griffith, 1993, Flyer, 1994, Country Gold, 1997, Blue Roses From the Moons, 1997, Other Voices, Too, 1998, The Dust Bowl Symphony, 1999, Wings to Fly and a Place to Be, 2000, The Millennium Collection, 2001, Clock Without Hands, 2001, From A Distance: The Very Best Of Nanci Griffith, 2002, Winter Marquee, 2002, Complete MCA Studio Recordings, 2003; appeared in Nanci Griffith on Broadway, 1994. Office: care Gold Mountain Entertainment 2 Music Cir S Ste 212 Nashville TN 37203-5708

GRIFFITH, NICOLA, writer; b. Leeds, Yorkshire, Eng., Sept. 30, 1960; life ptnr. Kelly Eskridge. Formerly ins. clk., waitress, singer, songwriter, tchr. self defense. Author: Ammonite, 1993 (Ga. and Atlanta Lit. prizes, Lambda Lit. award 1993, Tiptree Meml. award 1994), Slow River, 1995 (Lambda award, Nebula award), The Blue Place, 1999, Stay, 2002; co-editor: (short fiction series) Bending the Landscape. Office: care Shawna McCarthy Scovil Chichak Galen 381 Park Ave S Ste 1020 New York NY 10016*

GRIFFITH, PATRICIA KING, journalist; b. San Francisco, Jan. 20, 1934; d. Earl Beardsley and Frankie Mae (Kelly) King; m. Winthrop Gold Griffith, Oct. 4, 1958 (div. Jan. 1986); children: Kevin Winthrop, Christina Suzanne. BA, Stanford U., 1955. Copy asst., reporter Washington Post, 1956-57, 60-64; reporter San Francisco Examiner, 1957-59; Washington bureau chief Monterey Herald and Toledo Blade, Washington, 1979-81; investigative reporter Monterey (Calif.) Peninsula Herald, 1973-79, city editor, 1981-83, mng. editor, 1983-88; Washington bureau chief, White House corr. Toledo Blade and Pitts. Post-Gazette, Washington, 1988-99. Bd. dirs. Lyceum of Monterey Peninsula, 1977-79, All Sts. Episcopal Day Sch., Carmel, Calif., 1977-79, Monterey Coll. Law, 1978-79; sr. warden St. Dunstan's Episcopal Ch., Carmel Valley, Calif., 1983-84. Recipient Silver Gavel award ABA, 1978. Mem. Stanford Alumni Assn., Nat. Press Club, Gridiron Club, Stanford Club Washington, Stanford Cap and Gown Soc. Home: 103 Dockside Ln Belfast ME 04915

GRIFFITH, SIMA LYNN, investment banker, consultant; b. N.Y.C., Sept. 7, 1960; d. Morris Benjamin and Mary (Buberoglü) Nahum; m. Clark Calvin Griffith, Sept. 13, 1987. BA in English, Amherst Coll., 1982. Account exec. D.F. King & Co., Inc., N.Y.C., 1982-84, asst. v.p., 1984-86, v.p., 1986-88, Wells & Miller, Mpls., 1988; with Griffith, Levi Capital, Inc, Mpls., 1988-96; prin. Aethlon, Capital LLC, Mpls., 1996—. Co-chmn. PRSA, IR seminars, 1987; bd. adv. Pacer, Inc. Bd. dirs. Children's Hosps. and Clinics, 2004—; bd. govs. Children's Theater Co. Mem.: Pub. Rels. Soc. Am. (bod. govs., investor rels. sec. 1987—89), Assn. Bus. Communicators (bd. govs. 1987—88). Office: Aethlon Capital LLC 4920 IDS Ctr 80 S 8th St Minneapolis MN 55402-2100

GRIFFITHS, BARBARA LORRAINE, psychologist, marriage-family therapist, writer; b. Glendale, Calif., July 15, 1927; d. David William and Mabel Augusta (Gaarder) G.; m. Dale Elmo Rumbaugh, Mar. 28, 1948; 1 child, David Wynn. AA in Journalism, Valley C.C., 1958; BA in Psychology, U. Calif. Riverside, 1972; MS in Rehab. Counseling, Calif. State U., 1976; PhD in Clin. Psychology, Calif. Grad. Inst., 1984. Cert. Diplomate Am. Psychotherapy Assn., 1998, cert. addicition specialist, Marriage and Family Therapist 1979. Alcoholism counselor Kaiser Permanente, L.A., 1976-82; pvt. practice Hollywood, L.A., 1979-89, Glendale, Burbank, Calif., 1989-97, L.A., 1997—. Mem. State of Calif. Med. Diversion Evaluation Com., 1998—2003; screener 6th and 7th Prism awards Entertainment Industry Coun. Film, 2001—02; sci. expert reviewer 6th annual Prism Awards Entertainment Industry Coun., 2002—03; reviewer 6th and 7th Ann. PRISM awards Entertainment Industry Coun. Film, 2002; clinical psychologist Calif. Youth Authority, 2002—03. Editor (child abuse newsletter): Directions, 1976—86; writer, prodr. : (short film) Silver Bullet Kid, 2003; contbr. short stories, feature articles, columns to various mags., newspapers and profl. mags. Mem. Glendale Rotary, 1990-95, Verdugo BPW, 1988-91; Nat. Ski Patrolwoman #122, 1952-56. Recipient Editor's Choice award for poetry, 1997. Mem. APA (assoc.), L.A. County Psychol. Assn. Avocations: script writing, tennis, skiing, swimming and water sports, reading. Home and Office: 5159 Lakewood Dr San Bernardino CA 92407-2853 Fax: 323-660-7911. E-mail: griffiths7@aol.com.

GRIFFITHS, RACHEL, actress; b. Melbourne, Australia, June 4, 1968; m. Andrew Taylor, 2002; 1 child, Banjo Patrick. BEd in Drama and Dance, Victoria Coll. Actor: (films) Muriel's Wedding, 1994 (Best Supporting Actress Australian Film Critics award, Best Supporting Actress Australian Film Inst. award, 1995), Jude, 1996, To Have and To Hold, 1997, My Best Friend's Wedding, 1997, Hilary and Jackie, 1998 (nominee Best Supporting Actress Oscar, 1999), My Son, the Fanatic, 1998, Among Giants, 1998, Amy, 1998, Me Myself I, 1999, Blow, 2001, The Rookie, 2002, The Hard Word, 2002, Ned Kelly, 2003; (TV series) Secrets, 1993, Jimeoin, 1994, Six Feet Under, 2001— (Best Suppporting Actress Golden Globe award, 2001). Office: Tracey Jacobs United Talent Agy 9560 Wilshire Blvd Ste 500 Beverly Hills CA 90212 Address: Ann-Churchill-Brown Shanahan Mgmt 129 Bourke St Woolloomooloo NSW 2011 Australia also: David Lust Patricola Lust Pub Rels 8383 Wilshire Blvd Ste 530 Beverly Hills CA 90211*

GRIFFITHS, SYLVIA PRESTON, physician, educator; b. London, Dec. 25, 1924; d. Wheeler Bate and Dorothy (Hartley) Preston; m. Raymond B. Griffiths; 1 dau., Wendy Elizabeth. BA, Hunter Coll., 1944; MD, Yale U., 1948. Intern Grace-New Haven Community Hosp., 1948-49, resident, 1949-52; fellow in pediatric cardiology Yale U., 1952-54; asst. to prof. clin. pediatrics Columbia U., N.Y.C., 1955, prof. clin. pediatrics, 1977-90, prof. emeritus, 1990—. Recipient career scientist award Health Research Council, City of N.Y., 1963-69 Mem. N.Y. Heart Assn. (dir. 1977-83), Am. Acad. Pediatrics, Am. Pediatric Soc., Am. Heart Assn., Am. Coll. Cardiology, Babies Hosp. Alumni Assn. (pres. 1991-92). Office: Columbia Presbyterian Med Ctr 622 W 168th St New York NY 10032-3720

GRIGGS, BOBBIE JUNE, civic worker; b. Oklahoma City, Feb. 14, 1938; d. Robert Jefferson and Nora May (Green) Fish; m. Peter Harvey Griggs, Apr. 16, 1955; children: Diana (dec.), Terry, James. Grad. high sch., Salina, Kans. Commissary rep. Family Mag., Charleston AFB, S.C., 1976—; rep. Avon Corp., Charleston, S.C., 1976—; freelance demonstrator to USAF and USN orgns. Charleston, 1976—; rep. Salute Mag., Charleston AFB, 1986—; consumer edn. counselor Air Force-Navy exchs. Oster Kitchen Appliances, Charleston, 1987-90. Contbr. World's Largest Poem for Peace, 1991, Selected Works of our Best Poets, 1992, In A Different Light, 1992. Youth advisor, Charleston AFB, 1966-78; vol. doll distbn. program Salvation Army; clinic vol. ARC, Charleston AFB, 1967-75, chmn. family svcs. publicity and spl. projects, 1989; clinic vol. Clara Barton award, 1972; vol. Spoleto Festival, 1989—, Twin Oaks Retirement Ctr., 1992—, Chapel SUMMOM program, 1991—; asst. coord., publicity chmn. Family Svcs., 1967-83, named vol. of quarter, 1970, 72, 74, 76, named vol. of yr., 1970; active various scouting orgns., 1967—; asst. kindergarten Sunday sch. supt. Chapel I, 1966-68; active North Charleston (S.C.) Christian Women's Club, 1988—, hosp. chmn., mem. Charleston AFB Protestant Women's Club, 1965—; tchr. Bible sch., 1984-89; vol. tutor Lambs Elem., 1992, Trident Literacy Assn. (Laubach Literacy Action cert. 1992); coun. rep. Charleston AFB parish coun., 1988—; mem. Rocketeers Actors Group, Goals 2000 com. 1993—, Barnabas Outreach program, 1991—, Clown Ministry Charleston AFB, 1993—; chairperson Helping Hands Charleston AFB, 1991—, Voyagers Sunday Sch. Class Project, Summerville Homeless Shelter Charleston AFB, 1993—, Publicity Protestant Women, 1993—; vol. Lambs Elem., 1992—, Twin Oaks Retirement Ctr., 1992—, Barnabas Outreach Com., 1991—, Military Retirees, 1994—; counselor Jr. Achievement Program, 1994; mem. Charleston Raptor Ctr., 1996, S.C. Homeless Shelter Planning com., 1995-96, Am. Indian Heritage Coun., 1996; vol. tutor Lambs Elem., Charleston County, S.C., 1990—, jr. achievement counselor, 1992—, career day spkr., 1998 Recipient 1,000 Hours award Air Force Times, 1971, 1st Pl. award Designer Craftsman show, 1967-71, Dedicated Svc. award Charleston AFB, 1981, Hurricane Hugo Hero award, 1989, 1st Pl. award Bake-Off Contest YMCA, 1981, Hist. Charleston Trail Hike award Cub Scouts, 1988, Family Svcs. Vol. of Quar. award, 1990, Family Svcs. 6,000 Hour award, 1990, Golden Poet award, 1991, 1992, In a Different Light award Libr. Congress, 1991; named Enlisted Wife of Yr., Charleston AFB, 1974, Family Svcs. Vol. of Quarter Charleston AFB, 1990, Family Svcs. 6000 Hour award, 1991, Outstanding Vol. Svc. award Operation Desert Shield/Storm, 1991, Family Svcs. Spl. Recognition award, 1991, Appreciation acknowledgement Pres. of U.S., 1991, 98-99, First Lady Barbara Bush, 1992, Pres. of U.S., 1994, First Lady Hillary Clinton, 1994, Disting. Vol. award Charleston County Sch. Dist., 1995, Retiree Volunteer of the Quarter Charleston AFB, 1995, Vol. of Month Lambs Elem. Sch., 1995, Voting Slogan award Sec. Def., 1995, Family Svcs. Vol. of Quarter, 1996, Disting. Vol. award Lambs Elem., 1995-98, Family Mag. Poster/Display award Charleston Air Force Base, 1998, Disting. Vol. award Charleston County Sch. Bd., 1995-99, Vol. of Month Lambs Elem., 1998. Mem. Nat. Trust Hist. Preservation, Smithsonian Inst., Charleston AFB Non-Commd. Officers' Wives Club (pres. 1971-73, publicity chmn. 1969-70, wife of month 1967, wife of quarter 1973), Rocketeers Actors Group, Friends of Dock St.-Ushers. Avocations: cooking, sewing, collecting antiques, writing, decorating.

GRIGGS, NINA M. realtor; b. NYC, Sept. 21, 1932; d. John Malcolm Miller and Kathryn Ruth Wilenzick; m. Charles Guy Moseley, Aug. 28, 1954 (dec. Feb. 1970); children: Charles Edward Keeble Moseley, Kathryn Drew Moseley Kristofik; m. Bancroft Gerardi Davis, Dec. 31, 1971 (dec. Dec. 1980); m. Richard Curtis Miles, Feb. 5, 1983 (dec. Sept. 1987); m.

Northam Lee Griggs, Feb. 13, 1993 (dec. Mar. 2002). BA, Vassar Coll., 1954; MA, U. Va., 1956; postgrad., Columbia U. Exec. assoc., part-time rsch. assoc., 1961-63; founder, pres. Adventures Abroad, Ltd., 1964-71; also asst. to dir. profl. exams. divn. Psychol. Corp., N.Y.C., 1968-71; program officer Internat. Inst. Ednl. Planning/UNESCO, Paris, 1971-72; program adminstr. French and German lang. tchg. asst. prog. Inst. Internat. Edn., N.Y.C., 1973-85; dir. women's program Internat. Exec. Svc. Corps, 1988-91; real estate associate New England Land Co, Greenwich. Founder, dir. Women's Talent Corps, 1965-67; mem. N.Y. Jr. League; dir. Masters Nursery and Children's Ctr., 1962-81. Author: U.S. Citizenship Today, 1963; editor: (with Kertis, O'Driscoll) English Language and Orientation Programs in the United States, 1978, 80; contbr. articles to profl. jours. Trustee, chmn. nominating com. Dobbs Sch., 1968-71. Mem. Hyannisport Club, N.Y. Jr. League, Harvard Club of N.Y., Regency Club, Delta Delta Delta. Episcopalian. Home: 9 Country Rd Westport CT 06880-2524 Office: New England Land Co 783 North St Greenwich CT 06831-3105

GRIGSBY, AMANDA MOORE, special education educator; m. John Eric Grigsby, May 31, 2000; children: John Patrick, Catherine Elise. BS in Elem. Edn., Coll. Charleston, 1994; EdM in Spl. Edn.-Learning Disabilities, Converse Coll., 2001. Cert. tchr. elem. and spl. edn. S.C. Dept. Edn. Elem. edn. lang. arts grade 6 Cherokee County Sch. Dist., Gaffney, SC, 1994—96, elem. edn. tchr. 4th grade, 1996—97; learning disabilities tchr. grades k-8 Laurens (S.C.) Sch. Dist. #55, 1998—. Learning disabilities mentor Converse Coll. Learning Disabilities Camp, Spartanburg, SC, 1999; sch. intervention com. Waterloo (S.C.) Elem. Sch., 2001—; assessment report rsch. participant N.Mex State U., Las Cruces, 2003—; mem. PTO bd. Waterloo Elem. Sch., 2003—. Sponsor Hospice of Greenwood, SC; preschool tchr. Harris Bapt. Ch., Greenwood, SC, 2002—03. Mem.: S.C. Reading Assn., Palmetto State Tchrs. Assn., Coun. for Exceptional Children (divsn. learning disabilities), Coll. Charleston Alumni Assn. (life). Republican. Baptist. Avocations: travel, reading, computers, current events. Home: 1122 New Zion Rd Hodges SC 29653 Office: Waterloo Elem Sch 10457 Highway 221 South Waterloo SC 29384 Office Phone: 864-677-4670.

GRIM, ELLEN TOWNSEND, artist, retired art educator; b. Boone County, Ind., Nov. 1, 1921; d. Horace Wright and Sibyl Conklin (Lindley) Townsend; m. Robert Little Grim, Apr. 5, 1952; children: Nancy Ellen Grim Garcia, Howard Robert. Student, Our Lady of the Lake U., 1939-41, U. Tex., 1941-42; BA in Art, U. Wash., 1946; MA in Art, UCLA, 1950; postgrad., Otis Art Inst., L.A., 1970-71. Cert. secondary tchr., Calif. Art tchr., chairperson secondary Calif. and L.A. Unified Sch. Dist., 1947—82; retired, 1982; artist, 1975—. Guest speaker on art TV and cable, L.A., 1993. One-woman shows include Ventura County Mus. Art, 1982, Riverside Mcpl. Mus., 1984, Craft and Folk Art Mus., L.A., 1986, S.W. Mus., L.A., 1987, Calif. Heritage Mus., 1991, Brand Art Ctr., Glendale, 1996, Wurdemann Gallery, L.A., 1997, others; exhibited in more than 100 group shows. 1st lt. USMC, 1943-45. Recipient Purchase prize Gardena Fine Arts Collection, 1982, Watercolor West award San Diego Watercolor Soc. Internat., 1983, N.Mex. Watercolor Soc. award, 1989, 1st pl. award Fine Arts Fedn., 1987, 1st pl. award Art Educators L.A., 1988, 89, 1st pl. award Collage Artists Am., 1995, 2002, Brand Art Ctr. Watercolor West award, 1999, Painting award Valley Inst. of Visual Art, San Fernando Valley, 1999, 2001, Long Beach Arts painting award, 1999, 2000. Mem.: Alliance of Women Vets., Women Marines Assn., Collage Artists Am. (1st Place award 1995, 2002), Pasadena Soc. Artists (Painting award 1986, 1988, 1990, 1992, 1993, 1999, 2001, 2002), L.A. Art Assn. (bd. dirs. 1993—95), Women Painters West (membership chair, mem.-at-large 1983—89, Painting award 1985, 1986, 1989, 1992, 1993, 1995, 1999, Best of Show award 2000, Painting award 2000, 2001), Nat. Watercolor Soc. (historian 1989—90, Painting award 1984, 1999, 2000), Women in Mil Svc. for Am., Pi Lambda Theta, Alpha Phi. Avocations: Native American and Latin American culture, travel, Southwestern history.

GRIMBALL, CAROLINE GORDON, retail sales professional; b. Columbia, S.C., Dec. 21, 1946; d. John and Caroline Grimball. B.A. in Polit. Sci., Converse Coll., 1968; postgrad., S.C. Law Sch., 1968-69. Asst. buyer, buyer Rich's, Inc., Atlanta, 1971-78, spl. events fashion coordinator, Columbia, S.C., 1978-83; gen. mdse. mgr. Rackes, Inc., Columbia, 1983-84, Parasol Boutique, Columbia, 1984-86; retail cons. Retail Mdsg. Service Automation, Columbia, 1986-88; sales rep. Palmetto Promotions, 1989-93; retail mdse. supr. Riverbanks Zoo & Garden, 1993-94; retail mgr., buyer Riverbanks Zoo & Garden, 1994-2000; retail mgr. Aramark Entertainment, 2000-03. Pres. Columbia Action Coun., 1990-92; bd. dirs. Palmetto Leadership Coun., 1991-92, Palmetto State Orch. Assn., Columbia, 1979-89, Women's Symphony Assn., Columbia, 1985, Columbia Classical Ballet; com. chmn. Columbia Action Coun., 1984-85, exec. com., 1989-92. Named one of Outstanding Young Women Am., 1979, 80; recipient Community Service award Rich's, Inc., 1981. Mem. Nat. So. Colonial Dames Am., Columbia Jr. League, Columbia Drama Club. Democrat. Episcopalian. Avocations: bridge, reading, needlepoint, tennis. Home: 109 Walden Ct Columbia SC 29204-4043 E-mail: cgrimball@sc.rr.com.

GRIMES, DAPHNE BUCHANAN, priest, artist; b. Tulsa, Apr. 12, 1929; d. George Sidney and Dorothy Elnora (Dodds) Buchanan; m. Thomas Edward Grimes, Nov. 6, 1964 (dec. Oct., 1986). BFA, U. Houston, 1952; MA, Columbia U., 1954; MA in Religion, Episcopal Seminary of the Southwest, 1985. Ordained deacon Episcopalian Ch., 1982, priest, 1986. Tchr. history Rockland County Day Sch., Nyack, N.Y., 1959-61; dir. Am. Sch., Tunis, Tunisia, 1962-64; priest vicar St. Andrew's Ch., Meeteetse, Wyo., 1987-90; bd. dirs., pres. Thomas the Apostle Ctr., Cody, Wyo., 1990—; assoc. priest Christ Ch., Cody, 1994—. Stewardship chmn. Diocese Wyo., 1979-85, mem. bd. diocesan coun., 1987-90, chmn. social svcs., 1987-91. Author of poems. Chaplain West Park County Hosp., Cody, Wyo., 1981-84, West Park County Long Term Care Ctr., Cody, 1982—; bd. dirs. Park County Arts Coun., 1995-98. Mem. Cody Country Arts League, Cmty. of Celebration (spiritual adv. 1990—), Cmty. of the Holy Spirit (assoc.), Compass Rose Soc. (bd. dirs.), N.Am. Regional Coun., St. George Coll. Jerusalem (bd. dirs.) Avocations: reading science, theology, reading, writing, travel. Office: Thomas The Apostle Ctr 34 Thomas The Apostle Rd Cody WY 82414-9601

GRIMES, HEILAN YVETTE, publishing executive; b. Hamilton, Ohio, Sept. 16, 1949; d. J and Claudette (Hinkle) G. Grad., New Eng. Sch. Photography, 1987. Founder, pres. Dot & Line Graphics, 1975—, Color Computer Weekly, 1982—, Hollow Earth Pub., 1983—. Author: Norse Mythology, 1984, Legend of Niebelungenlied, 1984, Using QuarkXPress 3.3, 1994, Beginning Internet, 1994, Filemaker Pro Developer's Guide, 1997; founder Byte Mag., 1974, Macpower Mag., 1993. Recipient various photographic awards and grants. Democrat. Avocations: magic, juggling, hiking, traveling. Office: PO Box 51480 Boston MA 02205-1480 Office Phone: 617-249-0161. E-mail: yvettegr@hotmail.com.

GRIMES, MARGARET WHITEHURST, artist, educator; b. New Bern, N.C., June 5, 1943; d. Alan Pendleton and Margaret (Whitehurst) G. BA, Gov. State U., 1975, MA, 1976; postgrad., Notre Dame U., 1977; MFA, U. Pa., 1980. Instr. drawing and design Thornton C.C., Chgo., 1974-79; prof. painting and drawing Western Conn. State U., Danbury, 1980—, asst. chair, 1991-92, coord., master fine arts program, 2000—. Guest lectr./critic Vt. Coll. of Norwich U., Montepelier, 1995-96, Vt. Studio Ctr., Johnson, 1995, Tanglewood Inst., Lenox, Mass., 1997, S.V.A. Conf. on Liberal Arts and the Edn. of Artists, 1997, Ctrl. Conn. State U., New Britain, 1997, Weir Farm Nat. Hist. Site, Wilton, Conn., 1998, Gunn Mus., Washington, 2000; vis. artist Am. U., Corciano, Italy, 2001-02, Hendrix Coll., Conway, Ark., 2002, Chautauqua (N.Y.) Inst., 2003, Am. U., Wash. DC, 2004. Co-editor New Art Assn. Newsletter, 1971; one woman shows include Green Mountain Gallery, N.Y., 1979, (bieunally) Blue Mountain Gallery, N.Y., 1980-2003, Fischbach Gallery, N.Y., 1986, Moravian Coll., Bethlehem, Pa., 1990, Western Conn. State U., 1990, 98, Ctrl. Conn. State U., 1997, Washington Art Assn., 1990, 2000, Weir Farm Nat. Trust, Wilton, Conn., 2003, 100 Pearl Gallery, Conn., 2003, Hartford, Nat. Acad. Design, 2004, NAS, Washington, 2001; three-person show Provincetown Group Gallery, Mass., 1987; exhibited in group shows at Internat. Women's Art Festival, Walker Art Inst., 1976, Woodmere Mus., Phila., 1977, Provincetown Art Mus., Mass., 1978, Reading Mus., Pa., 1983, Queens Mus., N.Y., 1983, Rahr-West Mus., Manitowac, Wis., 1983, Columbus (Ohio) Mus. of Art, 1987, Katherina Rich Perlow Gallery, 1987, 88, 89, 76th Am. ann. show Newport (R.I.) Mus., 1988, Erector Sq. Gallery, New Haven, Conn., 1994, Kline Gallery, 1994, Creiger-Dane Gallery, Boston, 1995, Park Ave. Atrium, N.Y.C., 1995, Wilmington (Del.) Ctr. for Contemporary Art, 1996, Conn. State U. biennial, 1987-99, Blue Mountain Gallery, 1980-2001, Bachelier-Cardonsky Gallery, Kent, Conn., 1996, 97, 98, Philbrook Museum, Tulsa, Okla., Ringling Museum of Art, Sarasota, Fla., Davenport Museum, Iowa, 1999-2000, NAS, 2001-02; represented in permanent collections at Pitts. Plate Glass Co., Conn. Ins. Group, N.Am. Christian Sci. Ch. Ctr., Boston, U.S. Tobacco Co., Bellevue Hosp., N.Y., NAS, Washington, Nat. Acad. Sci. Recipient Disting. Lectureship award Henry Barnard Found., 1990; rsch. grantee in painting Conn. State U., 1985; named Univ. Prof. Conn. State U., 1992. Mem. AAUP (grantee 1986, 90, 91, 93, 95, 99, 2003), Coll. Art Assn. Home: 27 Wykeham Rd Washington CT 06793-1308

GRIMES, RUTH ELAINE, city planner; b. Palo Alto, Calif., Mar. 4, 1949; d. Herbert George and Irene (Williams) Baker; m. Charles A. Grimes, July 19, 1969 (div. 1981); 1 child, Michael; m. Roger L. Sharpe, Mar. 20, 1984; 1 child, Teresa. AB summa cum laude, U. Calif., Berkeley, 1970, M in City Planning, 1972. Rsch. and evaluation coord. Ctr. Ind. Living, Berkeley, 1972-74; planner City of Berkeley, 1974-76, sr. planner, 1983—2004, analyst, 1976-83. Bd. dirs. Vets. Asssistance Ctr., Berkeley, pres., 1978-93; bd. dirs. Berkeley Design Advocates, treas., 1987-94. Author: Berkeley Downtown Plan, 1988; contbr. numerous articles to profl. jours. and other publs. Bd. dirs. Berkeley-Sakai Sister City Assn., 1994—, pres., 1995-97, Ctr. Ind. Living. Honored by Calif. State Assembly Resolution, 1988; Edwin Frank Kraft scholar, 1966. Mem. Am. Inst. Cert. Planners, Am. Planning Assn., Mensa, Lake Merritt Joggers and Striders (sec. 1986-89, pres. 1991-93), Lions Internat. (bd. dirs. Berkeley club 1992-94, 2000-02, v.p. 1997-98, pres. 1998-99, chair membership com. 1999-2000), U. Calif. Coll. Environ. Design Alumni Assn. (bd. dirs. 1992-98, treas. 1994-96, disting. alumnus com. 1997-2003). Avocation: long distance running. Home: 1330 Bonita Ave Berkeley CA 94709-1925 Office: City of Berkeley 2118 Milvia St 3rd Fl Berkeley CA 94704 E-mail: ruthieg7@yahoo.com.

GRIMES, SUZANNE, publishing executive; With TV Guide, 1990—94, nat. advt. dir., 1994—95, sr. v.p., pub., 1995—97; pub. Women's Sports & Fitness, 1997—2000, Allure, 2000—01; pub., v.p. Glamour Mag., 2001—04. Office: Glamour Mag Conde Nast Bldg 4 Times Sq New York NY 10036-6522

GRIMES, TRESMAINE JUDITH RUBAIN, psychology educator; b. N.Y.C., Aug. 3, 1959; d. Judith May (McIntosh) Rubain; m. Clarence Grimes, Jr., Dec. 22, 1984; children: Elena Joanna, Elijah Jeremy. BA, Yale U., 1980; MA, New Sch. for Social Rsch., 1982; MPhil, PhD, Columbia U., 1990. Advanced tchg. fellow Jewish Bd. Family and Childrens Svcs., N.Y.C., 1980-82; tchg./rsch. asst. Columbia U. Tchrs. Coll., N.Y.C., 1983—84; rschr., historian Youth Action Program, N.Y.C., 1984-86; psychologist Hale House for Infants, N.Y.C., 1986-89; asst. rschr. Bank St. Coll., N.Y.C., 1988; addiction program adminstr. Harlem Hosp. Ctr., N.Y.C., 1989-91; asst. prof. psychology S.C. State U., Orangeburg, 1991-96, assoc. prof., 1996—2000, chmn. dept. psychology, 1998—2000, chmn. psychology & sociology, 1998-2000; asst. prof. psychology Iona Coll., 2001—02, assoc. prof., 2002—. Adj. prof. psychology Tchrs. Coll., Columbia U., N.Y.C., 1990-91; adj. prof. Iona Coll., New Rochelle, N.Y., 2000-01. Named one of Outstanding Young Women of Am., 1981. Mem.: APA, Soc. for Tchg. of Psychology, Assn. Black Psychologists, Ea. Psychol. Assn., Psi Chi, Kappa Delta Pi, Delta Sigma Theta. Democrat. Avocations: singing, drama. Office: Iona Coll 715 North Ave New Rochelle NY 10801 E-mail: newgrimes@yahoo.com.

GRIMMER, BEVERLEY SUE, consumer products company executive; b. Olathe, Kans., June 9, 1950; d. Edward Mathines Rice and Jessie LaVaun (Cade) Waymire; m. Danny Joe San Romani, June 4, 1977 (div. May 1991); 1 child, Justin (dec.); m. Gary G. Grimmer, June 21, 1992. Student, Kans. State Tchrs. Coll., 1968-71, U. Kans., 1975-77. Employee trainer, dept. mgr. T.G.&Y. Stores, Emporia, Kans., 1968-70; office mgr. Office of Staff Judge Adv. 3d Armored Div., Frankfurt, Fed. Republic of Germany, 1971-75, Don W. Lill, Atty. at Law, Emporia, 1976-77; instr., sub. tchr. Kodiak (Ala.) C.C. and Kodiak Pub. Sch. System, 1979-81, legal sec. Kaito & Ishida, Honolulu, 1983-84; adminstr. Alcantara & Frame, Honolulu, 1984-86; ind. contractor Hughes Hubbard & Reed, N.Y., Honolulu, 1986-88; paralegal Carlsmith, Ball, Wichman, Murray, Case, Mukai & Ichiki, Honolulu, 1988-91; spl. agt. Vanuatu (Hawaii) Maritime Agy., 1989—; ch. adminstr. Ctrl. Union Ch., Honolulu, 1991-94; owner Gentle Memories, Kailua, Hawaii, 1995—. Gubernatorial coun. appointee Juvenile Justice State Adv. Coun., 1993-94; mem. women's health week com. State of Hawaii, Commn. on Status of Women, 1994. 1st v.p. Christmas in April Oahu, 1995, bd. dirs., 1995-97; auction pub. chair Acad. Arts Guild, 1993; mem. Contemporary Arts Mus.; cmty. rels. and arrangements chairs for Tuxes 'n Tails Black and White Ball, Hawaiian Humane Soc., 1993, 94, silent auction Walkin in the Country, Boys & Girls Club; mem. Hawaii Lupus Found.; bd. dirs. Armed Forces YMCA, 1995-97; mem. vestry St. Christopher's Ch., 1995-98; chair silent auction Contemp '98, 100th Ann. Gala Honolulu Symphony, 1999. Recipient Order of Golden Swivel Shot award Comdt. USCG, 1981, 89, 1st Runner-up Maritime Week Maritime Employee award Propeller Club U.S., 1986, Letter of Appreciation, Dept. Navy, 1983, Cert. of Commendation, U.S. Army, 1975. Mem. Am. Heart Assn. (chair Celebrity Celebration 1994, silent auction co-chair 1996 Heart Ball, co-chair 1997 Heart Ball, Mary Lou Brogan award 1997), Coast Guard Officers' Spouses Club (nominating chair 1989, pres. 1982, 87, 88), Awa Lau Wahine (Coast Guard rep. 1988, 87, corr. sec. 1983, Boutiki chair 1982), Rotary (vice chair Friends of Foster Kids Picnic 1994, chair 1995), Jr. League (cmty. v.p. 1993, rec. sec. 1990, sustainer chair Honolulu 1999, sustainer chair 75th Gala 1999), Navy League, Propeller Club Port of Honolulu (bd. govs. alt. 1990), Hawaii Legal Aux. (v.p. 1994, pub./publs. chair 1994). Republican. Episcopalian. Avocations: golf, tennis, needlepoint, reading, community voluntarism. Home and Office: 159 Kakahiaka St Kailua HI 96734-3474

GRIMSLEY, JOY ELIZABETH, music educator; b. Atlanta, Ga., Dec. 11, 1973; d. Malcolm Walton and Rachel Wyland Barnes; m. James Braddock Grimsley, Oct. 10, 1975; 1 child, James Braddock. MusB in Edn., Troy State U., 1996, MS in Edn., 1997. Dir. of bands Lowndes Mid. Sch., Valdosta, Ga., 1998—2000, Irwin County Mid./High Sch., Ocilla, Ga., 2002; pre-kinderarten tchr. Coastal Plains Econ. Opportunity Authority, Valdosta, Ga., 2002—. Instrument repair technician M&M Music, Valdosta, Ga., 1999—2000. Mem.: Collegiate Music Educators Nat. Conf. (pres. 1995—96), Music Educators Nat. Conf., Ga. Music Educators Assn., Women Band Dirs. Internat. (Kathryn Siphers Meml. scholarship 1994), Kappa Delta Pi, Gamma Beta Phi, Alpha Lambda Delta, Omicron Delta Kappa (v.p. 1994—95), Tau Beta Sigma (life; sec., historian, warden 1993—95). Home: 1503 Pebblewood Dr Adel GA 31620 Personal E-mail: joybarnes@hotmail.com.

GRINDAL, MARY ANN, former sales professional; b. Michigan City, Ind., Sept. 9, 1942; d. James Paxton and Helen Evelyn (Koivisto) Gleason; m. Bruce Theodore Grindal, June 12, 1965 (div. Sept. 1974); 1 child, Matthew Bruce. BSBA, Ind. U., 1965. Sec. African studies program Ind. U., Bloomington, 1965-66; rsch. aide Ghana, West Africa, 1966-68; exec. sec. divsn. biol. scis. Ind. U., Bloomington, 1968-69; office asst. Dean of Students office Middlebury (Vt.) Coll., 1969-70; exec. sec. Remo, Inc., North Hollywood, Calif., 1974-76; sec., asst. to product mgrs. in cosmetic and skin care Redken Labs., Canoga Park, Calif., 1976-79; various sec. and exec. sec. positions L.A., 1979-81, 85-89; exec. sec. Sargent Industries, Burbank, Calif., 1981-85; sales asst. Chyron Graphics, Burbank, Calif., 1989-97; adminstrv. sec. divsn. instructional svcs. Burbank Unified Sch. Dist., 1998—. Author of poems and essays. Mem. U.S. Navy Meml. Found. Mem. DAR (chpt. registrar 1988-91, chpt. regent 1991-94, chpt. chmn. pub. rels. and pub. 1994-2001, chpt. chaplain 1994-2001, mem. spkrs. staff 1995-2001, state chmn. Am. Heritage 1994-96, state chmn. Calif. DAR scholarship com. 1996-98), Daus. of Union Vets. of Civil War, 1861-65, Inc., Ladies of the Grand Army of the Republic, Nat. Soc. Dames of the Ct. of Honor (state chaplain 1997-2001). Episcopalian. Avocations: travel, writing, genealogy.

GRINELL, SHEILA, museum director; b. N.Y.C., July 15, 1945; d. Richard N. and Martha (Mimiless) G.; m. Thomas E. Johnson, July 15, 1980; 1 child, Michael; stepchildren: Kathleen, Thomas. BA, Radcliffe Coll., 1966; MA, U. Calif., Berkeley, 1968. Co-dir. exhibits and programs The Exploratorium, San Francisco, 1969-74; promotion dir. Kodansha Internat., Tokyo, 1974-77; traveling exhbn. coord. Assn. Sci. Tech. Ctrs., Washington, 1978-80, exec. dir., 1980-82, project dir. traveling exhbn. Chips and Changes, 1982-84; assoc. dir. N.Y. Hall of Sci., 1984-87; pres., CEO Ariz. Sci. Ctr., Phoenix, 1993—. Cons. Optical Soc. Am., 1987, Nat. Sci. Ctr. Found., 1988, Interactive Video Sci. Consortium, 1988, Assn. Sci. Tech. Ctrs., 1988-89, Found. for Creative Am., 1989-90, Am. Assn. for World Health, 1990, Children's TV Workshop, 1991, Sciencenter, 1991, SciencePort, 1991, The Invention Factory, 1992, N.Y. Bot. Garden, 1992-93. Author: Light, Sight, Sound, Hearing: Exploratorium '74, 1974; editor A Stage for Science, 1979, A New Place for Learning Science: Starting and Running A Science Center, 1992, 2d edit., 2003, (with Mark St. John) Vision to Reality: Critical Dimensions in Science Center Development, Vol. I, 1993, II, 1994. Fulbright teaching asst., 1966; hon. Woodrow Wilson fellow, 1967 Fellow AAAS, mem. Am. Assn. Mus., Phi Beta Kappa. Office: Ariz Sci Ctr 600 E Washington St Phoenix AZ 85004-2303 Office Phone: 602-716-2010. E-mail: grinells@azscience.org.

GRISE, CHERYL, electric power industry executive; b. Eden, NC, June 30, 1952; BA, U. of NC, 1974; JD, Western State U., 1978. Atty. Hartford Ins. Group, Conn., 1979-1980; sr. v.p. & gen. counsel Northeast Utilities, Berlin, Conn., 1995—. Office: Northeast Utilities 107 Selden St Berlin CT 06037-1651

GRISON, DEBORAH D. publishing executive; b. Chicago, Ill., Dec. 1, 1972; d. Ricardo DePaul and Yvonne Grison. BS, Jackson State Univ., 1994; MS, Spertus Inst., Chgo., Ill.; PhD, Jackson State U., 2000—03. Founder & ceo Writes of Passage Pub. Group, Pearl, Miss., 2000—; rschr. Jackson State U., Jackson, Miss., 2000—03. Author: The Attic: Words From The Top. Mem. participant Habitat For Humanity, Jackson, Miss., 2001—02; cmty. organizer NAACP, Jackson, Miss., 1991—2003; youth leader Word of Faith Christian Ctr., Jackson, Miss., 2001—03. Named to Miss. State Artist Roster, Miss. Arts Commn., 2002—; fellow, Jackson State U., 2000-2003; grantee Project Momentum 125, 2001. Mem.: Delta Sigma Theta (life; jabberwock com. mem. 2002—03). D-Liberal. Christian. Achievements include Book Endorsement from renown poet Nikki Giovanni; Wrote and performed original poem at Walter Payton Memorial at Chicago's Soldier Field, 1999; Met and read for renown poets Gwendolyn Brooks and Sonia Sanchez; Published in the American Academy of Poetry Anthology, A Forgotten Paradise. Avocations: writing, singing, performing, teaching, travel. Office: Writes of Passage Publishing Group PO Box 97744 Pearl MS 39288 E-mail: dgcollage@aol.com.

GRITSCH, RUTH CHRISTINE LISA, editor; b. Duisburg, Germany, July 18, 1931; came to the U.S., 1941; d. Carl and Maria Augusta (von Schuman-Janssen) Sandman; m. Eric Walter Gritsch, June 4, 1955 (div. 1993); children: Deborah, Erika. BA, NYU, 1953. Assoc. Inst. for Internat. Edn., N.Y.C., 1953-55; sec. Zeigler Bros., Inc., Gardners, Pa., 1993—2003. Translator: (books) Liberty, Equality, Sisterhood, 1978, Office of the Ministry, 1981, Huldrich Zwingli, 1983, Unity of the Churches, 1984, I Am a Palestinian Christian, 1995, Violence, 1996; co-translator: Luther's Works, Vols. 39, 41, 1966, 67; editor: Roly, 1988; translator, editor: Justification of the Ungodly, 1968; editor, co-translator: Thomas Müntzer, A Tragedy of Errors, 1989. Active So. Poverty Law Ctr., Adams Co. Arts Coun. Mem.: LWV (bd. dirs., v.p. 1969—90, 1999—2001), Internat. Platform Assn. Democrat. Lutheran. Avocations: reading, collecting art. Home: 1 West St Gettysburg PA 17325-2130

GRIZZARD-BARHAM, BARBARA LEE, artist; b. Roanoke, Va., Apr. 4, 1935; d. Alton Lee and Mable (Jewell) Grizzard; m. Charles Thomas Barham, Sr., June 25, 1955; children: Charles Thomas, Christopher. BS, Va. Commonwealth U., 1971, postgrad. Educator Colonial Heights (Va.) Sch. Sys., 1971—88; represented by Agora Gallery, NYC, 1999—2001, Amsterdam Whitney Gallery, NYC, 2003—04. One-woman shows include Wakefield (Va.) Ctr. for Arts, 1992, 1993, 1994, Petersburg (Va.) Area Art League, 1993, 1995, 2000, Rappahannock Westminster-Canterberry Gallery, Va., 1995, Assn. for Visual Artists Gallery, Chattanooga, Tenn., 1999, Rappahanock Westminster Canterberry Gallery, Va., 1999, Williamsburg Regional Libr./Gallery/Theater Complex, 1999, exhibited in group shows at Richmond (Va.) Jewish Cmty. Ctr., 1991, 1993, Rappahannoc Art League Show, Va., 1995, Assoc. Artists Winston-Salem, N.C., 1991, 1992, 1996, Hoyt Inst. Fine Arts, Pa., 1998, Fredericksburg (Va.) Creative Ctr. Art, 1999, Richmond Shockoe Creative Ctr. Art, 1999, Richmond Women's Caucus for Art, 1999—2000, Shockoe Bottom (Va.) Art Ctr., 1999—2000, Agora Gallery, 1999, 2000, N.Y.C., 2001, 2002, Amsterdam Whitney Gallery, 2003, 2004, Limner Gallery, 2001. Recipient awards for art. Mem. Petersburg Area Art League, Shockoe Bottom Art League, Va. Mus. Art, Whitney Mus. Art, Mus. Modern Art. Republican. Episcopal. Avocations: judge and breeder Am. Cocker Spaniels champions, piano. Home: 701 Forestview Dr Colonial Heights VA 23834-1116

GRMEK, DOROTHY ANTONIA, accountant; b. Cleve., July 7, 1930; d. Louis and Antonia (Korosec) Lipanye; m. Charles Stelmach, June 13, 1953 (div. May 1977); children: Monica Doran Meade, Dwayne Alan Stelmach, Dale Richard Stelmach; m. William Edward Grmek, Aug. 18, 1978 (dec. Nov. 2003). BBA in Acctg., Fenn Coll., 1953. Chief acct. Pyromatics, Inc., Willoughby, Ohio, 1975-87; acct., exec. sec. Auctor Assocs., Inc., Cleveland Heights, Ohio, 1972-96; tax cons. Avon, Ohio, 1980—; contr., human rels. specialist Telefast Industries, Inc., Berea, Ohio, 1988-94; treas., buyer River Toy Box, Inc., Rocky River, 1990-2001. Mem.: Slovene Nat. Benefit Soc. (ins. agt. 1982—, charter mem., fin. sec. lodge 781 1982—, Cleve. Fedn. Lodges rec. sec. 1968—72, fin. sec. 1972—82). Home: 1925 Pembrooke Ln Avon OH 44011-1659

GROAH, LINDA KAY, nursing administrator, educator; b. Cedar Rapids, Iowa, Oct. 5, 1942; d. Joseph David and Irma Josephine (Zitek) Rozek; m. Patrick Andrew Groah, Mar. 20, 1975; 1 child, Kimberly; stepchildren: Nadine, Maureen, Patrick, Marcus. Diploma, St. Luke's Sch. Nursing, Cedar Rapids, 1963; student, San Francisco City Coll., 1976-77; BA, St. Mary's Coll., Moraga, Calif., 1978; BSN, Calif. State U., 1986; MSN, U. Calif., 1989. Staff nurse to head nurse U. Iowa, 1963-67; clin. supr., dir. oper. and recovery rm. Michael Reese Hosp., Chgo., 1967-73; dir. oper.

rms. Med. Ctr. Ctrl. Ga., Macon, 1973-74; dir. oper. and recovery rms. U. Calif. Hosps. and Clinics, San Francisco, 1974-90, asst. dir. hosps. and clinics, 1982-86; v.p. patient care svcs., dir. hosp. ops. Kaiser Found. Hosp., San Francisco, 1990—. Asst. clin. prof. U. Calif. Sch. Nursing, San Francisco, 1975—; cons. to oper. room suprs., to div. cdnl. [illegible] Med. Colls., 1970—; condr. seminars. Author: Perioperative Nursing Practice, 1983, 3d edit., 1996; contbr. articles to project jours. and textbooks; author, prodr. audio-visual presentations; author computer software. Mem. San Francisco C. of C. Fellow Am. Acad. Nursing; mem. ANA (vice chmn. oper. rm. conf. group 1974-76), Assn. Oper. Rm. Nurses (com. on nominations 1979-84, treas. 1985-87, 93-95, bd. dirs. 1991-93, pres.-elect 1995-96, pres. 1996-97, found. bd. trustees 1995-97, pres. found. 1992-95, Excellence award in Preoperative Nursing 1989), Nat. League for Nurses, Ctr. for Study Dem. Instns., San Francisco C. of C. Home: 5 Mateo Dr Belvedere Tiburon CA 94920-1071 Office: 3020 Bridgeway Ste 399 Sausalito CA 94965-2839 Office Phone: 415-833-3317. Personal E-mail: lindag1005@aol.com.

GROBMAN, HULDA GROSS (MRS. ARNOLD B. GROBMAN), retired health sciences educator; b. Phila., Aug. 2, 1920; d. Joseph and Dora (Abrahams) Gross; m. Arnold B. Grobman, Feb. 20, 1944; children— Marc Ross, Beth Alison Burruss. AB, U. Pa., 1940; MPA, U. Mich., 1941; EdD, U. Fla., 1958. Rsch. asso. Western Interstate Commn. on Higher Edn., Boulder, Colo., 1959-60; staff cons. Biol. Scis. Curriculum Study, Boulder, 1960-65, Joint Council on Econ. Edn., N.Y., 1965-66; prof. edn. N.Y. U., 1966-72, Bklyn. Coll., City U. N.Y., 1972-73; sr. rsch. assoc. ADA, Chgo., 1973-74; dir. edn./career mobility, area health edn. system, prof. med. edn. U. Ill. Med. Center, 1973-75; prof. health scis. edn. St. Louis U. Med. Ctr., 1975-88; prof. emeritus St. Louis U. Med. Center, 1988—. Cons. Sci. Edn. Center, U. Sao Paulo, Brazil; vis. prof. Asian Assn. Biol. Edn., Hebrew U. Jerusalem Inst. on Test Writing, 1972; cons. Fundacao Carlos Chagos, Sao Paulo, Brazil. Author: Developmental Curriculum Projects, 1970, Evaluation Activities of curriculum Projects, 1968, also articles; cons. editor Jour. Ednl. Rsch., 1973-80, Am. Ednl. Rsch. Jour.; mng. editor Serin Press. Bd. dirs. LWV Fla., 1950-55; candidate for City Commn., Gainesville, Fla., 1955; mem. Bd. State Dept. Children and Families, Dist. 15, 1997-2000. Recipient A-Individual Achievement award 3d Army Res. Command, 1956. Fellow AAAS (council 1967-73); mem. Asian Assn. Biology Edn. (charter hon. mem.), Am. Ednl. Research Assn. (sec. div. I 1979-81). Home: 5000-115 SW 25th Blvd Gainesville FL 32608 E-mail: agrobman@aol.com.

GROBSTEIN, RUTH H. health facility administrator; 3 children. BA, NYU, 1945; PhD in Biology, Yale U., 1957; MD, UCLA, 1976. Post-doctoral fellow Yale Med. Sch., Calif., mem. staff microbiology; prin. investigator U. Calif., San Diego, asst. prof. radiation oncology San Francisco, 1980—83; divsn. head radiation oncology Scripps Clin., La Jolla, Calif. Dir. The Ida M. and Cecil H. Green Cancer Ctr. Grantee Atomic Energy Commn., 1966, Nadonal Inst. Health, 1966. Office: Scripps Clinic Torrey Pines 10666 N Torrey Pines Rd La Jolla CA 92037-1092

GROCHOLSKI, BASIA (BARBARA) G. art director; b. Miami, June 28, 1972; d. Wlodzimierz and Magdalena Grocholski. BFA with honors, Sch. Visual Arts, 1998. Asst. art dir. Twoj Styl Mag., Warsaw, 1992—94; window display stylist Ralph Lauren, N.Y.C., 1995—98; art dir. Criterion Collection, N.Y.C., 1998—99; creative dir. 280:Design, N.Y.C., 1999—. Prof. Sch. of Visual Arts, 2000—01; adj. prof. Fashion Inst. of Tech., N.Y.C., 2001—03. Mem.: Art Dirs. Club. Office: 280:Design 280 E 10th St Store 1E New York NY 10009 E-mail: basia@280design.com.

GRODSKY, JAMIE ANNE, law educator; b. San Francisco; d. Gerold Morton and Kayla Deane (Wolfe) G. BA in Human Biology/Natural Scis. and History with distinction, Stanford U., 1977; MA in Econ. Geography, U. Calif., Berkeley, 1986; JD, Stanford Law Sch., 1992. Ednl. dir. Oceanic Soc., San Francisco, 1979-81; rsch. asst. Woods Hole (Mass.) Oceanographic Inst., 1983; analyst Office Tech. Assessment U.S. Congress, Washington, 1984-89; counsel Com. Natural Resources, U.S. Ho. of Reps., Washington, 1993—95; counsel to Com. on Judiciary U.S. Senate, Washington, 1995-97; jud. clk. with chief judge U.S. Ct. Appeals (9th cir.), 1997-98; sr. advisor to the gen. counsel U.S. EPA, Washington, 1999—2001; assoc. prof. law U. Minn. Law Sch., Mpls., 2001—. Articles editor Stanford Law Rev.; contbr. articles to profl. jours. Trustee Desert Rsch. Inst. Found. Mem.: D.C. Bar Assn., Calif. Bar Assn., Supreme Ct. Bar Assn. Home: 2900 Thomas Ave S Apt 2112 Minneapolis MN 55416-4106

GROFF, JOANN, organization administrator; b. Ft. Leonardwood, Mo., Oct. 10, 1956; d. Barry T. Groff and Ann (Ferry) Ragsdale. Student, Georgetown U., 1974-76; BS in Bus. Adminstrn., Babson Coll., Wellesley, Mass., 1978. Office mgr. Morgan Smith for Congress, Northglenn, Colo., 1978; fair and rodeo asst. Adams County Commrs., Brighton, Colo., 1979; mktg. devel. officer Columbine Title Co., Lakewood, Colo., 1979-80; express agt., loan officer Wells Fargo Credit Corp., Englewood, Colo., 1981-84; pub. banking rep. Cen. Bank of Denver, 1985-89; mem. Colo. Ho. of Reps., Denver, 1983-89, chmn. audit com., 1989; fin. com.; dir. Leadership Giving Mile High United Way, 1991-92; pres. Colo. Retail Coun., 1992—. Past pres. Westminster Cmty. Artist Series; mem. bd. Pub. Svc. Credit Union, Colo. State Dem. Com., 1980-93, Colo. State Exec. Com., 1988-93, del. Nat. Conv., 1980, 84, alt. del., 1976; bd. dirs. Westminster (Colo.) Cmty. Artist Series, Marycrest H.S.; apptd. mem. Colo. State Bd. Equalization, 1994—, Colo. Transp. Com., 1999—. Roman Catholic. Office: Colo Retail Coun 451 E 58th Ave Denver CO 80216-8412 E-mail: jag@coloradoretail.org.

GROGAN, PAULA CATALDI, newspaper editor; b. Syracuse, N.Y., May 8, 1950; d. Peter Paul and Gilda Sarah (Ingano) Cataldi; m. John Patrick Grogan, June 24, 1978. BA, Syracuse U., 1972. Reporter Syracuse (N.Y.) Post-Standard, 1972-75; feature writer Ft. Lauderdale (Fla.) News, 1975-78; successively copy editor, lifestyle editor, assoc. features Dayton (Ohio) Daily News and Jour. Herald, from 1978. V.p., bus. mgr. Atlanta Jour.-Constn., then pub., Atlanta, v.p. strategic mktg., 2000—; author column Paula Cataldi Grogan. Dir. Dayton YWCA. Mem. Ohio Newspaper Women's Assn. (2d place award 1983), Women in Communication. Office: Atlanta Journal-Constitution PO Box 4689 Atlanta GA 30302-4689

GROGG, ANN MARIE, director; b. Tacoma, Feb. 15, 1969; d. Joseph Anthony and Lynn Yurkiewicz; m. Curtis Lynn Grogg, Sept. 16, 1995; 1 child, Dayton Blane. BA in Interior Planning and Design, U. Idaho, 1993. Asst. mgr. Saucys Pizza, Tacoma, 1987—88; office mgr. Foodland, Glenville, Wash., 1993—94; asst. to assessor Gilmer County Ct. House, Glenville, 1994—99; program asst. Glenville State Coll., 1999—; asst. tng. workshops Glenville, 2001—03. Treas., sec. 4-H Club, Tacoma, 1985—87; active PTO, Troy, W.Va., 1997—99. Mem.: Coll. Leadership Coun., Classified Staff Coun. (v.p. 2001, pres. 2002, 2003). Avocations: crafts, sewing, painting, flowers. Office: Glenville State Coll 200 High St Glenville WV 26351

GROH, JENNIFER CALFA, law librarian; b. Patchogue, N.Y., Mar. 28, 1970; d. Anthony Bernard and Mary (Fogerty) C.; m. William Matthew Groh, May 10, 1997. BA in Social Sci., St. Joseph's Coll., 1992; MA in Internat. Edn., NYU, 1993; MSLS, Pratt Inst., Bklyn., 1996. Reference page Patchogue (N.Y.)-Medford Libr., 1986-93; from libr. asst. to sr. libr. Morgan & Finnegan, N.Y.C., 1994—. NYU grad. scholar, 1992, Law Libr. Assn. scholar, N.Y. 1995, Am. Assn. Law Librs. scholar, 1996. Mem. ALA, Spl. Librs. Assn., Law Libr. Assn. Greater N.Y. Home: 21 Mohawk Dr North Babylon NY 11703-3303 Office: Morgan & Finnegan 345 Park Ave New York NY 10154-0053

GROHSKOPF, BERNICE, writer; b. Troy, N.Y. m. Herbert Grohskopf (div.); 1 child, Margaret Ellen. MA, Columbia U., 1954. Writer-in-residence Sweet Briar (Va.) Coll., 1980—82; rsch. assoc. Work and Correspondence of William James, Charlottesville, Va., 1981-95; [illegible] of Button Hoo, 1970, 1973, 2000. Mem.: PEN, Nat. Book Critics Cir., Authors Guild. Home: Apt 11 116 Turtle Creek Rd Charlottesville VA 22901-6760

GRONAU, CRYSTAL LYNN, accountant; b. Newton, Kans., May 27, 1957; d. Albert Earl and Patricia Ann (Ulmer) G. BA, Tabor Coll., 1977; MBA, Golden Gate U., 1984. CPA, Calif., Kans. Sr. acct. Grant Thornton, Wichita, Kans., 1979-83; mgr. Price Waterhouse, San Jose, Calif., 1984-86, Palo Alto, 1987-88, sr. mgr., 1990-92, 94-97; Price Waterhouse GmbH, Frankfurt, Germany, 1992-94; mgr. taxation Geothermal Resources Internat., San Mateo, Calif., 1986-87; sr. mgr. Berger Lewis, San Jose, 1988-89; CFO ExpatEdge, 2000—. Dir. expatriate outsourcing svc. ctr, Price Waterhouse, San Jose, Calif., 1998-99. Mem. AICPA, Calif. Soc. CPAs.

GRONEMUS, BARBARA, state legislator; b. Nov. 21, 1931; d. Erwin J. and Irene (Resch) Barry; m. Lambert N. Gronemus, 1949; children: Michelle (Mrs. Jerome J. Carroll), Jacqueline (Mrs. Eric Baken), Margaret Susan (Mrs. David Williams). Former dir. nursing home activity; mem. from dist. 91 Wis. State Assembly, Madison, 1982—, mem. state affairs, small bus. coms., 1993, mem. agr. com., 1983—, vice chmn., 1985, chmn. subcom. on swing psuedorabies, 1985, vice chmn. commerce and consumer affairs, 1983, mem. excise/fees, tourism, recreation & forest productivity, 1985, mem. Minn.-Wis. boundary commn. legis. adv. com., 1983—, chmn. agr., forestry and rural affairs coms. Chmn. Trempealeau County Dem. Com., 1981-82, 3d Congl. Dist. Dem. Com., 1982-83. Mem. Am. Legion, Farmers Union, Whitehall Women's Club, Whitehall Rod and Gun Club, Trempealeau County Homemakers Club. Home: PO Box 676 36301 West St Whitehall WI 54773-8512 Office: Wis House of Reps Office Of House Mems Madison WI 53702-0001

GRONEWOLD, SUE ELLEN, history educator; b. Peoria, Ill., Apr. 18, 1947; d. Herman J. and Eleanor J. Gronewold; m. Peter Winn, May 22, 1976; children: Ethan, Sasha. BA, U. Wis., 1969, MA, 1973, Columbia U., 1980, PhD, 1996. Tchr. social studies, 1972—77; lectr. on Asia, Am. Mus. Natural History, N.Y.C., 1980-84; asst. prof. Marist Coll., Poughkeepsie, NY, 1993—2001, Kean U., Union, NJ, 2001—. Vis. lectr. Smith Coll., Northampton, Mass., 1984-85; project officer N.Y. Coun. for the Humanities, N.Y.C., 1985-86, 88; acad. co-dir China Identity Project, Am. Forum for Global Edn., N.Y.C., 1995-97. Author: Beautiful Merchandise: Prostitution in China, 1982; author revs. and articles on Chinese history, women in Asia, mission history, Asians in Am., world history. Mem. Am. Hist. Assn., Assn. for Asian Studies, Com. on Tchg. About Asian, China Mission Group. Avocations: cultural activities, jogging, bicycling, cooking, reading. Home: 315 W 106th St Apt 10C New York NY 10025-3446 Office: Kean U Dept History 1000 Morris Ave Union NJ 07083

GRONLUND, SALLY ANN, special education educator; b. Kansas City, Md., Dec. 15, 1955; d. John Richard and Barbara Ann Generaux; 1 child, Karen Elizabeth Conaway. BS in Elem. Edn., N.W. Mo. State U., 1979, MS in Elem. Edn., 1982. Cert. life tchr. Mo., Tex. Tchr. Liberty Pub. Schs., Mo., Lamkin Elem. Sch., Cypress, Tex., Hall-McCarter Mid. Sch., Blue Springs, Mo., Argentine Mid. Sch., Kansas City, Kans. Author: (article) Campfire Girls mag., 1985. Leader Weight Watchers, Overland Park, Kans. Mem.: Assn. Children with Learning Disabilties, Coun. Exceptional Children. Roman Catholic. Avocations: scuba diving, reading, travel. Home: 1166 Bluebird Ln Liberty MO 64068 Office Phone: 816-415-7180. E-mail: sgronlund@kc.rr.com.

GROPPE, LAURA, interactive software company executive; Asst. dir., co-prodr. feature films and music videos, Hollywood, Calif., 8 yrs.; pres., CEO, Girl Games, Inc., Austin, Tex. Bd. dirs. Teen People mag. Bd. dirs. Children's Info. Trust. Recipient Acad. award for best short Film Session Man, 1992, 4 MTV awards for co-producing R.E.M.'s music video Everybody Huarts, 1994, award for best cinematography as co-prodr. feature film Suture, Robert Redford's Sundance Film Festival, 1994. Mem. AAUW. Office: Girl Games Inc 523 Victoria Ave Venice CA 90291-4832 Fax: 512-478-2957. E-mail: info@girlgamesinc.com.

GROSCH, LAURA DUDLEY, artist, teacher; b. Worcester, Mass., Apr. 1, 1945; d. Daniel Swartwood and Edith Dudley (Taft) G. BA in Art History, Wellesley Coll., 1967; BFA in Painting, U. Pa., 1968. Solo exhbns. include Mint Mus. Art, Charlotte, N.C., 1974, Jerald Melberg Gallery, Charlotte, 1984, 87, Greenville (N.C.) Mus. Art, 1987, Greenville County Mus. Art, 1987, Christa Faut Gallery, Davidson, N.C., 1990, 93, 96, Rock Sch. Arts Found., Valdese, N.C., 2000, Millennium exhbn., Valdese, 2000, others; group exhbns. include Impressions Gallery, Boston, 1973, Rose Mus. Glenbow-Alberta Gallery, Can., 1974, New Orleans Mus. Art, 1975, Bklyn. Mus., 1976, Visual Arts Ctr. Alaska, 1978, Print Club, Phila., 1980, Palazzo Venezia, Rome, 1984, Syracuse U., N.Y., 1987, Wellesley (Mass.) Coll., 1997, Mint Mus. Art, Charlotte, N.C., 2002, Christa Faut Gallery, Cornelius, N.C., 2003, Charlotte Wine and Food, 2004; represented in pub. collections Boston Pub. Libr., Brit. Mus., London, Bklyn. Mus., Fla. State U., Manhattan Coll., Mus. Fine Arts, Boston, N.Y. Pub. Libr., Ringling Mus., Sarasota, Fla., Smithsonian Inst., Washington, UCLA, Newark Pub. Libr., Minn. Inst. Arts, Honolulu Acad. Arts, Dayton (Ohio) Art Inst., Carnegie Mellon U., Pitts., Free Libr. Phila., Victoria and Albert Mus., London, many others. Office: PO Box 10 Davidson NC 28036-8006

GROSE, ELINOR RUTH, retired elementary education educator; b. Honolulu, Apr. 23, 1928; d. Dwight Hatsuichi and Edith (Yamamoto) Uyeno; m. George Benedict Grose, Oct. 19, 1951; children: Heidi Diane Hill, Mary Porter, John Tracy, Nina Evangeline. AA, Briarcliff Jr. Coll., 1948; postgrad., Long Beach State U., 1954-55; BS in Edn., Wheelock Coll., Boston, 1956; MA in Edn., Whittier Coll., 1976. Cert. tchr., Mass., N.Y., Calif. Reading tchr. Cumberland Head Sch., Plattsburgh, N.Y., 1968-70; master tchr. Broadoaks Sch., Whittier (Calif.) Coll., 1971; reading tchr. Phelan/Washington Schs., Whittier, 1971-73; elem. tchr. Christian Sorensen Sch., Whittier, 1977-94, ret., 1994. Cons. Nat. Writing Projet, 1987—, South Basin Writing Project, Long Beach, 1987—; team tchr. first Young Writers' Camp, Long Beach State U., 1988. Author: Primarily Yours, 1987, Angel Orchid Watercolor, 1994. First v.p. Women's League of Physicians Hosp., Plattsburgh, 1970; photo historian of Acad. for Judaic, Christian and Islamic Studies at 6th Assembly World Coun. of Churches, Vancouver 1983, UCLA, 1994—, MIT, 1999—, Abraham Symposium, Istanbul, Turkey, 2000. Named Companion of the Order of Abraham, 1987. Mem. AAUW (assoc. in dialogue 1996—), NEA, Calif. Tchrs. Assn., Whittier Elem. Tchrs. Assn., English Coun. of Long Beach, Acad. Judaic, Christian and Islamic Studies (named companion Order of Abraham 1987), Orange County Soc. Calligraphy. Presbyterian. Avocations: travel, painting, gardening, gym. Home: Museum Heights 171 N Church Ln # 619 Los Angeles CA 90049-2000

GROSECLOSE, JOANNE STOWERS, special education educator; b. Bland, Va., Dec. 15, 1956; d. Claude Swanson and Josephine (Mustard) Stowers; m. John Vincent Groseclose, June 24, 1979; children: Jouette Nicole, Nicholas Vincent. BS, Radford Coll., 1979; MS, Radford U., 1983. Cert. tchr., Va. Tchr. kindergarten Bland (Va.) Combined Sch., Bland County Sch. Bd., 1979; tchr. 4th grade Marion (Va.) Intermediate Sch., Smyth County Sch. Bd., 1979-80, tchr. learning disabled 4th, 5th, 6th grades, 1980—. Instr. adult basic edn. Smyth County Schs., Marion, 1989-90. Technician Bland County Rescue Squad, 1975-78; bd. dirs. Am. Cancer Soc., 1985-88, Marion United Way, 1989-91, Smyth County Assn. for Retarded Citizens, 1982-85, Smyth County Cmty. Hosp., 1993-98; sec., vice chair Smith County Cmty. Found., 1998—; vol. Mt. Rogers Smyth House Group Home for Retarded Adults, 1983-85; mem. Hospice of Smyth County; mem. S.W. Va. Reading Coun., 1990-91, 91-[illegible] Smyth County Humane Soc.; mem. area Luth. ch. coun., 1996—. Named Outstanding Young Careerist Marion Bus. and Profl. Women, 1983, Outstand Young Woman of Am., Marion Bus. and Profl. Women, 1981, Radford U. Outstanding Alumi, 1990, Va. Tchr. of Yr. Ency. Britannica/Good Housekeeping/Coun. of Chief State Sch. Officers, 1991. Mem. NEA (del. conv.), Smyth County Edn. Assn. (rep. 1979, 82, 93—, treas. 1981-83, pres. 1985), Smyth County C. of C., Va. Edn. Assn. (del. conv.), Marion Book and Study Club, Phi Kappa Phi, Kappa Delta Pi. Avocations: reading, travel, camping, playing bridge, tennis. Home: 241 Magnolia St Marion VA 24354-4413 Office: Marion Intermediate Sch 820 Stage St Marion VA 24354-4000

GROSECLOSE, WANDA WESTMAN, retired elementary school educator; b. Clarks, Nebr., Oct. 5, 1933; m. B. Clark Groseclose; children: D. Kim, Byron C. Jr., Eric P., A. Glenn. B degree, Brigham Young U., 1976; M in Tchg., St. Mary's Coll., Moraga, Calif., 1981. Cert. tchr., Calif. 5th grade tchr. Brentwood (Calif.) Union Sch. Dist., 1977-97; ret. Art tchr., mentor tchr. Contra Costa County Program of Excellence. Author: American Music in Time, 1992, In the Shadow of Our Ancestors, vol. I, vol. II, 2003, The Lees of Southwest Virginia, 2003. Human rels. bd. dirs. City of Livermore, 1968—70. Republican. Mem. Lds Ch. Avocations: oil painting, sewing, gardening, genealogy. Home: 83 Payne Ave Brentwood CA 94513-4701 E-mail: grosclose@ecis.com.

GROSHNER, MARIA STAR, nuclear engineer; b. Las Vegas, Nev., Aug. 31, 1961; d. Robert Leroy and Stepheny (Higby) Groshner; m. Robert Clay Singleterry, Jr., May 18, 1984. BS in Nuc. Engring., U. Ariz., 1984; MBA, Averett U., 2003. Engr. in tng., Idaho; cert. pvt. pilot 2003. Reactor operator EG&G Idaho, Inc., Idaho Falls, 1985-89, engr., 1989-90, sr. engr., 1990-91; export control reviewer EG&G Idaho Inc., Idaho Falls, 1990-91; engr. III Westinghouse Idaho Nuc. Co., Idaho Falls, 1991-92, sr. engr. I, 1992-94; prin. engr., safety analyst Lockheed Martin Idaho Techs. Co., Idaho Falls, 1994-96, staff engr., 1996-97; prin. mem. Quantum Solutions LLC, 1995-96; sr. engr. BWX Techs., Inc., Lynchburg, Va., 1999—. Sci-by-mail mentor, 1998—2000. Mem. Citizen Energy Alert Network Nuc. Energy Inst., Washington, 1987—96; mem. Planned Parenthood, 1992—96; troop leader Girl Scouts; vol. Big Brothers Big Sisters, 2004—. Mem.: Soc. Women Engrs. (chpt. sect. rep. 1990—91, treas. 1993—96, v.p. southeastern Idaho chpt. 1989, coord. young women's conf. 1990), Am. Nuc. Soc. (media rels. chmn. Idaho chpt. 1990, comm. 2001), Toastmasters Internat. (chpt. pres. 1990, chpt. pres. Lynchburg unit 2000, adminstrv. v.p. Jack C. High unit 1989, v.p. pub. rels. 1995, Competent Toastmaster, Able Toastmaster), U.S. Golf Assn. Avocations: aviation, golf, camping, handcrafts, communications. Home: 407 Chadwick Drive Lynchburg VA 24502-Office: BWX Techs Inc PO Box 785 Lynchburg VA 24505-0785

GROSHOLZ, EMILY ROLFE, philosophy educator, poet; b. Phila., Oct. 17, 1950; d. Edwin DeHaven and Frances Skerrett Grosholz; m. Robert Roy Edwards, Jan. 2, 1987; children: Benjamin, Robert, William, Mary-Frances. BA, U. Chgo., 1972; PhD in Philosophy, Yale U., 1978. Fellow Nat. Humanities Ctr., Research Triangle Park, N.C., 1985-86; sr. rsch. fellow Inst. History & Philosophy of Sci. & Tech. U. Toronto, Can., 1988-89; assoc. Ctr. for Philosophy of Sci. U. Pitts., 1992—. Adj. assoc. prof. dept. philosophy U. Pa., Phila., 1992; prof. philosophy Pa. State U., University Park, 1993—, affiliate African and African-Am. studies, 1997—, fellow Inst. for the Arts and Humanities, 1995—; mem. poets' prize com. Nicholas Rsch. Mus., N.Y.C., 1993—. Author: Cartesian Method and the Problem of Reduction, 1991, Eden, 1992, The Abacus of Years, 2002; co-author: Leibniz's Science of the Rational, 1998; adv. editor: The Hudson Rev., 1984—, mem. editl. bd.: Jour. History of Ideas, 1998—, Studia Leibnitiana, 2001—. Fellow Nat. Humanities Ctr., 1985-86, Guggenheim Found., 1988-89, Am. Coun. Learned Socs., 1997, Nat. Endowment for Humanities, 2004-; Transatlantic Cooperation Rsch. grantee Alexander von Humboldt Found., 1994-97, NEH, 2004—. Mem. Am. Philos. Assn., Leibniz Soc. N.Am., Leibniz Assn., Clare Hall U. Cambridge (life), Philosophy Sci. Assn. Democrat. Episcopalian. Home: 116 Kennedy St State College PA 16801-7805 Office: Pa State Univ Dept Philosophy 240 Sparks Bldg University Park PA 16802 E-mail: erg2@psu.edu.

GROSKLOS, HOLLIE JO, music educator; d. Jack Louis and Carol Ann Grosklos. MusB, Tex. Christian U., 1986—91. BA in hist., MusM in flute performance, Tex. Christian U., 1991—93; D of musical arts, U. of North Tex., 1994—2001. Grad. fellowship in flute U. of North Tex., Denton, Tex., 1994—96; pvt. flute instr. Coppell Ind. Sch. Dist., Coppell, Tex., 1995—97; instrumental music buyer Pender's Music Co., Denton, Tex., 1996—98; asst. h.s. band dir. Putnam City Schools, Okla. City, Okla., 1998—99; h.s. asst. band dir. Duncan H.S., Okla., 1999—2001; mid. sch. band dir. Southlake Carroll Ind. Sch. Dist., Tex., 2001—. Music dir. Smithfield UMC, North Richland Hills, Tex., 2002—03, handbell dir., 2001—. Robert B. Toulouse Scholarship in Grad. Study, U. of North Tex., 1994—96, Tchg. Assistantship in Musicology, Tex. Christian U., 1992—93, Performance Scholarship, 1986—91, Academic scholarship, 1986—91. Mem.: Tex. Music Educator's Assn. (assoc.), Nat. Flute Assn. (assoc.), Pi Kappa Lambda (assoc.), Mu Phi Epsilon (v.p. 1989—90), Tau Beta Sigma (assoc.; parliamentarian 1989—90). Protestant. Avocations: travel, crafts, golf, reading, gardening. Office: Dawson Middle School 400 S Kimball Ave Southlake TX 76092

GROSS, ALICE BURTON, music educator; d. Emit Arvel and Mary D. (Herron) Burton; m. James Robert Francis Gross, Mar. 16, 1963 (div. May 1974). BS in Music Edn., Austin Peay State U., 1963, MA in Music Edn. with honors, 1966. Cert. profl. music educator Conn. Vocal music specialist Mollie E. Ray Elem. Sch., Orlando, Fla., 1963, Rolling Hills Elem. Sch., Orlando, 1963, Highland Elem. Sch., Hopkinsville, Ky., 1963—66, Millbrook Elem. Sch., Hopkinsville, 1963—66; choral dir. Christian County H.S., Hopkinsville, 1963—66; vocal music specialist Byrns Darden Elem. Sch., Clarksville, Tenn., 1966—67; choral dir. New Providence Jr. H.S., Clarksville, 1966—68; vocal music specialist Drs. Inlet Elem. Sch., Jacksonville, Fla., 1968—69, Middlebury Elem. Sch., Jacksonville, 1968—69; tchr. gen. music and choral dir. Kosciousko Jr. H.S., Enfield, Conn., 1969—70; vocal music specialist Enfield St. Elem. Sch., 1970—88, Enfield Intermediate Sch., 1970—71, Eli Whitney Elem. Sch., Enfield, 1970—, Nathan Hale Elem. Sch., Enfield, 1970—73, 1978—81, 1984—85, 1988—2000, Higgins Elem. Sch., Enfield, 1971—72, Noah Webster Elem. Sch., Enfield, 1972—73, 1973—74, Harriett Beecher Stowe Elem. Sch., Enfield, 2000—. Organist various chapels, Ft. Campbell, Ky., 1960—65, Valley Cmty. Ch., Feeding Hills, Mass., 1975—90. Mem.: Enfield Tchrs. Assn., Conn. Tchrs. Assn., Nat. Tchrs. Assn. Baptist. Avocations: tennis, dance, reading, travel.

GROSS, AMY, publishing executive; Features editor and spl. projects editor Vogue, 1978—88; founding editor Mirabella, 1988—93, editor-in-chief, 1996—97; editl. dir. Elle, N.Y.C., 1993—96; editor-in-chief O, The Oprah Mag., 2000—. Office: O The Oprah Mag 224 W 57th St New York NY 10019-6708

GROSS, ARIELA JULIE, law educator; b. San Francisco, Sept. 22, 1965; d. David Jonathan and Shulamith Pia Gross; m. Jon Edward Goldman, Sept. 2, 1990; children: Raphaela, Sophia. BA, Harvard U., 1987; JD, Stanford U., 1994, PhD, 1996. Bar: Calif. 1995. Acting asst. prof. law Stanford (Calif.) Law Sch., 1996; asst. prof. law U. So. Calif. Law Sch., LA, 1996—98, assoc. prof. law, 1998—2001, prof. law and history, 2001—. Steering com. Ctr. for Law, History & Culture, LA, 1999—; juror Frederick

Douglass Book prize Gilder Lehman Ctr., 2002—03. Author: Double Character: Slavery & Mastery in the Antebellum Southern Courtroom, 2000 (Phi Kappa Phi award, 2001); contbr. articles to profl. jours. Grantee Fgn. Lang. Area Studies scholar, US Dept. Edn., 1993; Littleton-Griswold grant, Am. Hist. Assn., 1995, Zumberge Rsch. Innovation grant, U. S.C., 1997—98, Guggenheim fellow, 2003—, Huntington fellow, NEH, 2003—, Burkhardt fellow, Am. Coun. Learned Socs., 2003—. Mem.: Law and Soc. Assn. (Willard Hurst prize com. 1999—), Am. Soc. Legal History (exec. com., bd. dirs., program chair 2001—). Office: Univ SC Law Sch Los Angeles CA 90089 Business E-Mail: agross@law.usc.edu.

GROSS, CAROL ANN, lawyer; b. St. Louis, Mo., May 25, 1951; m. William H. Gross. B in journalism, U. Mo., 1973; JD cum laude, Seton Hall U. Sch. Law, 1985. Bar N.J., 1985, Pa., 1985, N.Y., 1995, U.S. Dist. Ct., 1985. Law clerk N.J. office atty. gen., Trenton, 1983-85; assoc. Lowenstein, Sandler, Kohl, Fischer & Boylan, Roseland, N.J., 1985-90, Jones, Day, Reavis & Pogue, N.Y., 1990-96; ptnr. pvt. practice, Somerville, N.J., 1996—. Co-Author: (book) N.J. Environmental Law Handbook, 1989; contbr. Environmental Reporter's Handbook, 1988; co-editor (newsletter) Enviro-Notes, 1989-90; contbr. author: Legal Guide to Working with Environmental Consultants. Recipient Responsible Journalism award, N.J. Press Assn., 1982, Interpretive Writing award, N.J. Press Assn., 1980, Journalistic Excellence Under Deadline Pressure award, Soc. Profl. Journalists, 1979, Good Citizen award, Gannett Co., Inc., 1979, Merit award, Union Co. Civil Defense/Disaster Control, 1978. Mem. ABA, N.J. Bar Assn., Pa. Bar Assn. Avocations: gardening, guitar, cooking. Office: 79 Davenport St Somerville NJ 08876-1921

GROSS, CYNTHIA SUE, petrochemicals manufacturing executive; b. Palmyra, Mo., Aug. 14, 1959; d. Floyd Raymond and Carolyn Elizabeth (Howell) Mette; m. Edward Lee Gross, June 8, 1985; 1 child, Ray E.; stepchildren: Troy A., Christina M. BS in Metall. Engring., U. Mo., Rolla, 1980. Metallurgist Bryon Jackson Pump, Tulsa, Okla., 1981-82; metall. engr. Conoco, Inc., Ponca City, Okla., 1982-84, Vista Chem., Houston, 1984-89; staff maintenance engr. Hoechst Celanese, Clear Lake, Tex., 1989-92; instr. of welding metallurgy San Jacinto Coll., 1992; sect. leader maintenance engring. Hoechst Celanese, Bishop, Tex., 1992-93, sect. leader maintenance, 1993-95; prodn. supt. for polyester Hoechst Celanese, Trevira, Spartanburg, S.C., 1995-97; process hazards prevention leader Celanese, Clear Lake, 1997-98, methanol and maintenance mgr., 1999-2000, tech. and maintenance mgr., 2000—01, corp. reliability and maintenance dir., 2001—. Spkr. symposium Nat. Petroleum Refiners Assn., San Antonio, 1993, San Antonio, 2000, San Antonio, 02; instr. welding metallurgy San Jacinto Coll., Houston, 1992. Mem. quality mgmt. com. Houston Bus. Roundtable, 1990-92, chmn. Quality Day '91. Mem. NPRA (com. mem. 2001), Alpha Chi Sigma. Avocations: youth baseball, piano. Office: Celanese Clear Lake Plant 9502 Bayport Blvd Pasadena TX 77507-1402

GROSS, DONALYN ANN, counselor; b. Springfield, Mass., July 5, 1950; d. Harold Arnold and Estelle (Eisenstock) Gross. BS in Human Svcs./Social Work, U. Chattanooga, 1973; MEd in Counseling, Springfield Coll., 1979; PhD in Counseling/Thanatology, Columbua Pacific U., 1981. LCSW; cert. music practitioner/harpist. Thanatologist Conn. Dept. Corrections, 1991—95; activity dir. Genesis Eldercare, Heritage Woods Assisted Living Ctr., Agawam, Mass., 1997—98; social worker, dir. Good Endings Program SunBridge Care and Rehab. for East Longmeadow, 1998—. Adj. prof. Springfield Coll., Bay Path Coll., 1999; vol. coord. VNA and Home Care of Manchester, Conn.; workshop presenter Jewish Geriatric Svcs., 2000—01; dir. Good Endings program Heritage Hall West, Agawam, Mass., 2002—. Author: Dying in Prison - Counseling the Terminal Inmate, 1991, Voices of the Dying - Reflections of the Living, 1995, Good Endings - Caring for the Dying Resident - The Training Manual, 1999, Earth Angels - One Year of Vigil, 2000; contbr. articles to profl. publs.; musician: (CD) Remembering Music for Memorial Services. Harpist for dying; presenter, cons., spkr. on death and dying. Jewish. Avocations: professional musician, spinning wool. Home: 189 Porter Lake Dr Springfield MA 01106

GROSS, DOROTHY-ELLEN, library director, educator; b. Buffalo, June 13, 1949; d. William Paul and Elizabeth Grace (Hough) Gross. BA, Westminster Coll., 1971; MLS, Benedictine U., 1975; MDiv, McCormick Theol. Sem., 1975. Jr. cataloger McCormick Theol. Sem., Chgo., 1972-75; head tech. svcs. Barat Coll., Lake Forest, Ill., 1975-79, head libr., 1980-82; dir. coll. libr. North Park Coll. and Theol. Sem., Chgo., 1982-87, dir. coll. and sem. librs., 1987-96, assoc. dean, 1990-96, prof., 1991—. Cons. acad. librs.; spkr. various profl. meetings and confs. Author (with Karsten): From Real Life to Reel Life, 1993; editor: LIBRAS Handbook and Directory, 1982—96; co-editor: North Park Faculty Publs. and Creative Works, 1992; contbr. chpt. in book, articles, book reviews to profl. jours. Dir. rsch. United Way, Chgo., 1996—99; bd. dirs. Eldredge Libr., 2000—. Recipient Melvin R. George award, 1996. Mem.: LIBRAS (pres. 1983—85), ALA, Pvt. Acad. Librs. Ill. (pres. 1981—83, 1994—95, newsletter editor, contbr.), Assn. Coll. and Rsch. Librs. Presbyterian. E-mail: dottie@c4.net

GROSS, ELIZABETH ANNE, elementary school educator; b. Springfield, Mass., Oct. 8, 1974; d. George William III and Elise Lauziere Gross. AA, Brevard CC, Cocoa, Fla., 1994; BS in Communicative Disorders, U. Ctrl. Fla., Orlando, 1996, MA in Varying Exceptionalities, 1999, MA in Elem. Edn., 2002. Cert. Fla. Tutor Brevard CC, Melbourne, Fla., 1995—2000, adj. instr., 2000—; tchr. Brevard County Schs., Vera, Fla., 2000—. Pres. Backpack Buddies, Inc., Merritt Island, Fla., 2001—. Mem.: Coun. Exceptional Edn., Phi Kappa Phi, Golden Key, Pi Lambda Theta. Roman Catholic. Avocations: softball, collecting Coca-Cola, art. Home: 120 Marlin Dr Merritt Island FL 32952

GROSS, HARRIET P. MARCUS, religious studies and writing educator; b. Pitts., July 15, 1934; d. Joseph William and Rose (Roth) Pincus; children: Sol Benjamin, Devra Lynn. AB magna cum laude, U. Pitts., 1954; cert. in religious tchg., Spertus Coll. of Judaica, Chgo., 1962; MA, U. Tex., Dallas, 1990, postgrad., 1998—. Assoc. editor Jewish Criterion of Pitts., 1955-56; publs. writer B'nai B'rith Vocat. Svc., 1956-57; group leader Jewish Cmty. Ctrs. Met. Chgo., 1958-63; columnist Star Publs., Chicago Heights, Ill., 1964-80; pub. info. specialist Operation ABLE, Chgo., 1980-81; dir. religious sch. Temple Emanu-El, Dallas, 1983-86; freelance writer, 1986—; columnist Dallas Jewish Life Monthly, 1992-96, Dallas (Tex.) Jewish Week, 2000—04, Tex. Jewish Post, Dallas, 2004—. Lectr. U. Tex., DAllas, 1994-98; tchr. writing Homewood-Flossmoor (Ill.) Park Dist., Brookhaven Jr. Coll., Dallas; advisor journalism program Prairie State Coll., Chicago Heights, 1978-80; mem. adv. bd. The Creative Woman Quar. Publ., Gov.'s State U., Governors Park, Ill., The Mercury U. Tex., Dallas. Bd. dirs., sec. Family Svc. and Mental Health Ctr. of South Cook County, Ill., 1965-71; active Park Forest (Ill.) Commn. on Human Rels., 1969-80, chmn., 1974-76; bd. dirs. Ill. Theatre Ctr., 1977-80, Jewish Family Svc. of Dallas, 1982-95, Dallas Jewish Hist. Soc., 1995—; mem. Dallas Jewish Edn. Com., 1992-95. Recipient Humanitarian Achievements award Fellowship for Action, 1974, Honor award Anti-Defamation League of B'nai B'rith, 1978, Cmty. Svc. award Dr. Charles E. Gavin Found., 1978, 1st Ann. Leadership award Jewish Family Svc., 1990, Katie award Dallas Press Club, 2004; inducted into Park Forest (Ill.) Hall of Fame, 2000, Tex. Press Women State Writing award, 2003. Mem. Nat. Fedn. Press Women, Press Women of Tex., Ill. Woman's Press Assn. (named Woman of Yr. 1978), Intertel (pres. Gateway Forum of Dallas 1984-85), Nat. Assn. Temple Educators, Mensa, Soc. Profl. Journalists, Dallas Press Club, Nat. Soc. of Newspaper Columnists, Am. Jewish Press Assn., Phi Sigma Sigma. Jewish. Achievements include development of 1st community newspaper action line column, 1966. Office: 8560 Park Ln Apt 23 Dallas TX 75231-6312 Office Phone: 214-691-8840. Business E-Mail: hgross@utdallas.edu.

GROSS, IRIS LEE, not-for-profit association executive; b. Bklyn., Aug. 11, 1941; d. Frank and Anne (Schecter) Goodman; children: Michael, Henry. m. William E. Fullington. BA, Am. U., 1963. Cert. assn. exec. Field rep. mid-Atlantic region B'Nai Brith Women, Rockville, Md., 1973-76, dir. mid-Atlantic region, 1976-81; cen. svcs. dir. Nat. Coun. Jewish Women, N.Y.C., 1981-90, exec. dir., 1990—, Birmingham (Ala.) Internat. Festival, 1994—; pres. Nonprofit Resource Ctr. Ala., 1997-99. Leadership, Birmingham - Class of 98; Commr. Montgomery County Commn. for Women, 1980-81. Recipient Achievement Cert. City of Rockville, 1975, Cert. of Appreciation March of Dimes, 1980. Mem. Am. Soc. Assn. Execs., N.Y. Soc. Assn. Execs. (bd. dirs. 1987-90, Outstanding Com. Chair 1986), Soc. Non-Profit Orgns. Democrat. Avocations: reading, antiques, art history, archeology. Home: 1050 Highland Dr Birmingham AL 35244-3363 Office: Birmingham Internat Festival Frank Nelson Bldg Ste 423 205 20th St N Birmingham AL 35203-3609

GROSS, KAREN CHARAL, lawyer; b. N.Y.C., Nov. 25, 1940; d. Harry B. and Adele (Hook) Charal; m. Meyer A. Gross, Aug. 16, 1964; children: Dana Leslie, Jennifer P., Pamela A. AB, Barnard Coll., 1962; JD, NYU, 1965. Bar: N.Y. 1965. Atty. Wolder & Gross, N.Y.C., 1965-78, Wolder, Gross & Yavner, N.Y.C., 1978-86; sr. v.p. legal and bus. affairs GoodTimes Entertainment LLC, N.Y.C., 1986—. Editor NYU Law Rev., 1963-65. Parent liaison Ramaz Sch., N.Y.C., 1980-86; del. Dem. County Com., N.Y.C., 1988—; legal mentor to students Barnard Coll., N.Y.C. John Norton Pomeroy scholar NYU, 1963-65. Mem. Internat. Trademark Assn., Copyright Soc. USA. Avocation: travel. Office: GoodTimes Entertainment LLC 16 E 40th St New York NY 10016-0104

GROSS, LAURA ANN, marketing and communications professional, acupuncturist, herbalist; b. Kew Gardens, N.Y., July 11, 1948; d. Melvin Fredericks and Harriette (Levy) G. BA, Boston U., 1970; MA, Columbia U., 1974; MS, Pacific Coll. Oriental Medicine, 1996. Staff writer Am. Banker, N.Y.C., 1974-82, assoc. editor, 1982-88; dir. fin. svcs., instns., communications Am. Express Travel/Related Svcs. Co., N.Y.C., 1988-89; dir. sales promotion and pub. rels. Am. Express Travelers Cheque Group/Am. Express Travel Svcs., N.Y.C., 1989-92; dir. strategic bus. comm. Am. Express Travel Related Svcs., N.Y.C., 1992-93; pres. Strategic Comm. Cons., N.Y.C., 1993-2000; founder Alternative Ctr. for Natural Healing, 1997—; exec. v.p. mktg. Letsgotrade, Inc., 2000-01; sr. v.p. mktg./ebusiness Muriel Siebert & Co., Inc., 2001—. Spkr. fin. svcs. and Chinese medicine. Author, editor consumer surveys and articles. Recipient editorial awards Pannell Kerr Forster, 1984, N.E. Bus. Press Editors, 1986, N.Y. Bus. Press. Editors, 1987, first Boston U. Coll. of Liberal Arts Young Alumni award, 1985. Avocations: fiction writing, travel, snorkeling.

GROSS, LESLIE PAMELA, sales executive, consultant; b. N.Y., Aug. 23, 1952; d. Gerald Jay and Pearl (Meltzer) G., m. Ned T. Ashby (div. Mar. 1997); 1 child, James Warren Taylor Ashby; m. Russell A. Brown, Nov. 2003. AB, Cornell U., 1976. Ins. agt. Equitable Life, San Francisco, 1976-79; sales assoc. Digital Equipment Corp., San Francisco, 1979-81, from sales rep. to sales exec. Santa Clara, Calif., 1981-87, corp. acct. mgr. San Francisco, 1987-92; area mgr. WordPerfect Corp., Orem, Utah, 1992-94; sr. account mgr. Novell, Inc., Santa Clara, Calif., 1994-97; sr. client rep. IBM, Menlo Park, Calif., 1997—2001, client exec., 2001—. Missionary LDS Ch., Boston, 1973-75; jr. Sunday sch. tchr., Menlo Park, Calif., 1993-95, 1996-98, 2002—; pres. Women's Relief Soc., Stanford, Calif., 1986, counselor, Palo Alto, Calif., 1987-88, counselor, stake pres., Menlo Park, 1991-92, edn. com. 1999-2001; sec. Channing Pl. Homeowners Assn., Palo Alto, 1987-88, 90-91, pres., 1988-90. Avocations: travel, cinema, fitness. Personal E-mail: lpgross@us.ibm.com. Business E-Mail: lpgross@pacbell.net.

GROSS, LILLIAN, psychiatrist, educator; b. N.Y.C., Aug. 18, 1932; m. Harold Ratner, Feb. 4, 1961; children: Sanford Miles, Marcia Ellen. BA, Barnard Coll., 1953; postgrad., U. Lausanne, Switzerland, 1954-56; MD, Duke U., 1959. Diplomate Bd. Pediatrics, Am. Bd. Psychiatry and Neurology, Am. Bd. Child Psychiatry. Intern Kings County Hosp., Bklyn., 1959-60, resident, 1967-70, psychiatrist devel. evaluation clinic, 1970-72; resident Jewish Hosp., Bklyn., 1960-62; physician in charge pediatric psychiat. clinic Greenpoint (N.Y.) Hosp., 1964-67; pvt. practice pvt. practice, Great Neck, N.Y., 1970—. Clin. instr. psychiatry Downstate Med. Ctr., Bklyn., 1970-74, clin. asst. prof., 1974-99; lectr. in psychiatry Columbia U., 1974-99; psychiat. cons. N.Y.C. Bd. Edn., 1972-75, Queens Children's Hosp., 1975-96; mem. med. bd. Saras Ctr., Great Neck, N.Y., 1977—. Child psychiatry fellow Kings County Hosp., 1969-70, pediatric psychiatry fellow, 1962-63. Fellow Am. Acad. Pediatrics, Am. Acad. Child Psychiatry, Am. Psychiat. Assn. (life), N.Y. Soc. Clin. Hypnosis (pres.); mem. AMA, Nassau Pediatric Socs., Soc. Adolscent Psychiatry, N.Y. Coun. Child Psychiatry, Am. Med. Women's Assn. (Nassau, pres. 1985-86, 95-96), N.Y. Med. Socs., Internat. Soc. Study of Multiple Personality and Dissociation (founder, pres. L.I. component study group), Greater Long Island Psychiat. Soc. Home and Office: 55 Blue Bird Dr Great Neck NY 11023-1001 E-mail: drlillian@aol.com.

GROSS, ROBERTA LEE, inspector general; b. Dayton, Ohio, Mar. 11, 1947; m. Richard A. Gross; children: Edward, Eric. BA cum laude, Vassar Coll., 1969; MA in English, U. Mich., 1970; JD, Northeastern U., 1978. Tchr. Sharon, Newton (Mass.) jr. high sch. system, 1971-75; asst. district attorney Office of the District Attorney, Cambridge, Mass., 1978-79; from staff attorney to chief civil litigation section Office of the Corp. Counsel D.C., Washington, 1982-89; sr. dir. investigations, counsel Amtrak, Washington, 1990-95; insp. gen. NASA, Washington, 1995—. Office: NASA Office of the Inspector Gen 300 E St SW Washington DC 20546-0005

GROSS, ROSALIE-ETHELYN, secretary; b. N.Y.C., Feb. 24, 1914; d. Jacob Samuel Jr. and Julia Ethelyn Lavall; m. Charles Ray Gross, Sept. 20, 1942 (dec. July 1980); 1 child, Eunice Elaine. Grad., Washington Irving H.S., N.Y.C., 1932. Sec. Doles Sr. Citizens, Mt. Vernon, N.Y., 1987-95, Cmty. Sch. Initiative, Mt. Vernon, 1996-99. Sec. newsletter for srs., Mt. Vernon, 1987-95. Recipient 12 awards United Way, 1995—. Mem.: Nat. Coun. Negro Women (corr. sect. 1995—, Westchester sect. recording sec. 1987—95, 7 achievement awards 1992—98). Avocations: art, theater, museums, ice skating shows, soap operas.

GROSS, RUTH TAUBENHAUS, former pediatrician; b. Bryan, Tex., June 24, 1920; d. Jacob and Esther (Hirshenson) Taubenhaus; m. Reuben H. Gross, Jr., Aug. 22, 1942 (div. June 1952); 1 child, Carey E. BA Barnard Coll., 1941, MD Columbia U., 1944. Intern Charity Hosp., New Orleans, 1944; resident in pediat. Tulane U., New Orleans, 1945, Columbia U., N.Y.C., 1946—47; instr. Radcliffe Infirmary, Oxford, England, 1949—50; instr. pediat. Stanford (Calif.) U., 1950—53, asst. prof., 1953—56, assoc. prof., 1956—60, prof., 1973—92, prof. emerita, 1992, acting exec. pediat., 1957—59, assoc. dean student affairs, 1973—75, dir. divsn. gen. and ambulatory pediat., 1975—85, dir. Stanford-Children's Ambulatory Care Ctr., 1980—85. Nat. study dir. Infant Health and Devel. Program, 1983—92; assoc. prof. pediat., co-dir. divsn. human genetics Albert Einstein Coll. Medicine, Yeshiva U., N.Y.C., 1960—64, prof. pediat., 1964—66; clin. prof. pediat. U. Calif. Med. Ctr., San Francisco, 1966—73; dir. dept. pediat. Mt. Zion Hosp. and Med. Ctr., San Francisco, 1966—73. Contbr. articles to profl. jours. Fellow Commonwealth human genetics, Instituto de Genetica, Pavia, Italy, 1959—60. Mem.: Soc. Rsch. in Child Devel., Ambulatory Pediatric Assn., Am. Acad. Pediat., Soc. Pediatric Rsch., Am. Pediatric Soc., Am. Fedn. Clin. Rsch., Inst. Medicine NAS, Sigma Xi, Alpha Omega Alpha, Phi Beta Kappa. E-mail: rtgross@cox.net.

GROSS, SHARON RUTH, forensic psychologist, researcher; b. L.A., Mar. 21, 1940; d. Louis and Sylvia Marion (Freedman) Lackman; m. Zoltan Gross, Mar. 1969 (div.); 1 child, Andrew Ryan; m. Ira Chroman, June 1994. BA, UCLA, 1983; MA, U. So. Calif., L.A., 1985, PhD, 1991. Diplomate Am. Bd. Psychol. Spltys. Tech. Rytron, Van Nuys, Calif., 1958-60; computress on tetrahedral satellite Space Tech. Labs., Redondo Beach, Calif., 1960-62; owner Wayfarer Yacht Corp., Costa Mesa, Calif., 1962-64; electronics draftsperson, designer stroke-writer characters Tasker Industries, Van Nuys, 1964-65; pvt. practice cons. Sherman Oaks, Calif., 1965-75, 77-80; printed circuit bd. designer Systron-Donner, Van Nuys, Calif., 1975-76; design checker, tech. writer Vector Gen., Woodland Hills, Calif., 1976-77; undergrad. adv. U. So. Calif., L.A., 1987-89, rsch. asst. prof., rsch. assoc. social psychology, 1991—. Owner Attitude Rsch. Litigation and Orgn. Cons.; prof. Pierce Coll., Woodland Hills, Calif., 2000—. Contbr. articles to profl. jours., chpts. to books. Recipient Haynes Found. Dissertation fellowship U. So. Calif., 1990. Fellow Am. Coll. Forensic Examiners, mem. APA, AAAS, Computer Graphics Pioneers, Am. Psychol. Soc., Western Psychol. Assn. Democrat. Jewish. Office: 4570 Van Nuys Blvd #357 Sherman Oaks CA 91403 Office Phone: 818-905-1770. E-mail: sharonrgross@cs.com.

GROSSBARD-SHECHTMAN, SHOSHANA AMYRA, economist, educator; d. Henry and Anna Grossbard; children: Michal Hanna Shechtman, Zev Mordechai Shechtman, Haim Joshua Shechtman, Esther Eve Shechtman. PhD, U of Chgo., 1976. Prof. econs. San Diego State U., 1981—; vis. scholar Columbia U., N.Y.C., 2002—03. Author: On the Economics of Marriage; editor: (book) Marriage and the Economy, (journal) Rev. of Economics of the Household. Mem.: Am. Econ. Assn. Office: San Diego State U Dept Econs 5500 Campanile San Diego CA 92182-4485

GROSSET, JESSICA ARIANE, computer analyst; b. Paris, Aug. 31, 1952; came to U.S., 1970; d. Raymond Louis and Barbara Ann (Byrne) G.; m. Bruce Edward Kaskubar, May 23, 1986. AA, Berkshire Community Coll., Pittsfield, Mass., 1972; BS, SUNY, Potsdam, 1979; postgrad., Ariz. State U., 1980, U. Minn., 1980-81. Computer programmer Kay-Bee Toy and Hobby Shops, Lee, Mass., 1974-78; computer analyst Mayo Clinic, Rochester, Minn., 1981—. Voting staff Mayo Clinic, Rochester, 1996. Mem. Nat. Assn. Female Execs. Avocations: reading, sailing, travel, horseback riding, skiing. Office: Mayo Clinic 200 1st St SW Rochester MN 55905-0002

GROSSETETE, GINGER LEE, retired gerontology administrator, consultant; b. Riverside, Calif., Feb. 9, 1936; d. Lee Roy Taylor and Bonita (Beryl) Williams; m. Alec Paul Grossetete, June 8, 1954; children: Elizabeth Gay Blech, Teri Lee Maclennan. BA in Recreation cum laude, U. N.Mex., 1974, M in Pub. Adminstrn., 1978. Sr. ctr. supr., Office of Sr. Affairs, City of Albuquerque, 1974-77, asst. dir. Office of Sr. Affairs, 1977-96. Conf. coord. Nat. Consumers Assn., Albuqeruque, 1978-79; region 6 del. Nat. Coun. on Aging, Washington, 1977-84; conf. chmn. Western Gerontol. Soc., Albuqerque, 1983; N.Mex. del. White House Conf. on Aging, 1995; mem. adv. coun. N.Mex. Agy. on Aging, 1996-2002; mem. City of Albuquerque Affordable Housing Com., 2002—. Contbr. articles to mags. Campaign dir. March of Dimes N.Mex., 1966-67; pres. Albuquerque Symphony Women's Assn., 1972; exec. com. Jr. League Albuquerque, 1976; mem. Gov.'s Coun. on Phys. Fitness, 1987-91, chmn. 1990-91; bd. dirs. N.Mex. Sr. Olympics, 1995-2001; chmn. YWCA Alumnae Assn. for Women on the Move, 1999-2001. Recipient N.Mex. Disting. Pub. Service award N.Mex. Gov.'s Office, 1983, Disting. Woman on the Move award YWCA, 1986, Outstanding Profl. award N.Mex. State Conf. on Aging, 1995, Presdl. citation S.W. Soc. on Aging, 1995, Gov.'s award for Outstanding N.Mex. Women, 2001; inductee Albuquerque Sr. Citizens Hall of Fame, 1998. Fellow Nat. Recreation and Pk. Assn. (bd. dirs. S.W. regional coun. rep., bd. dirs. leisure and aging sect., pres. N.Mex. chpt. 1983-84, 97-98, bd. dirs. N.Mex. Sr. Olympics, 1994-2001, pres. leisure and aging sect. 1997-98, Outstanding profl. award 1982); mem. ASPA (pres. N.Mex. coun. 1987-88), S.W. Soc. on Aging (pres. 1984-85, bd. dirs., Outstanding Profl. award 1991, Presdl. citation 1996), U. N.Mex. Alumni Assn. (bd. dirs. 1978-80, Disting. Alumni award 1985), Las Amapolas Garden Club (pres. 1964), Phi Alpha Alpha, Chi Omega (pres. alumni 1959-60). Avocations: tennis, water skiing, snow skiing, racewalking, arts and crafts. Home: 805 Suzanne Ln SE Albuquerque NM 87123-4502 E-mail: alecg@flash.net.

GROSSETT, DEBORAH LOU, psychologist, consultant; b. Alma, Mich., Feb. 16, 1957; d. Charles M. and Margaret A. (Roethlisberger) G. BS, Alma Coll., 1979; MA, Western Mich. U., 1981, PhD, 1984. Lic. psychologist, Tex.; cert. in diagnostic evaluation, Tex.; bd. cert. behavior analyst, Tex. Grad. rsch. and teaching asst. Western Mich. U., Kalamazoo, 1979-84; asst. group home supr., cmty. outreach Residential Opportunities, Kalamazoo, 1982-84; psychologist Richmond (Tex.) State Sch., 1984-87, Shapiro Devel. Ctr., Kankakee, Ill., 1987-88; clin. coord. Monroe Devel. Ctr., Rochester, N.Y., 1988; chief psychologist Denton (Tex.) State Sch., 1989-90; dir. psychol./behavioral svcs. Ctr. for the Retarded, Houston, 1990—2002; psychologist Mental Health and Mental Retardation Authority of Harris County, Houston, 2002—. Behavioral cons. Ctr. for Developmentally Disabled Adults, Kalamazoo, 1984, Goodman-Wade Enterprises, Houston, 1987; instr. psychology Houston Community Coll., 1985-86, U. Houston-Clear Lake, 1987, 92, 95—. Contbr. chpt. to book, articles to profl. jours. Western Mich. U. fellow, 1984. Mem. Am. Psychol. Assn., Am. Assn. on Mental Retardation, Assn. for Behavior Analysis (chair Outreach Bd. 1989-91), Tex. Assn. for Behavior Analysis (bd. dirs. 1989-91, program chair 1996, pres. 1997). Democrat. Presbyterian. Avocations: golf, camping, gardening. Home: 9750 Ravensworth Dr Houston TX 77031-3130 Office: MHMRA Harris County 5901 Long Dr Houston TX 77087 E-mail: deb_grossett1@email.com.

GROSSINGER, CAROLINE, sales executive; b. Chgo., Dec. 16, 1967; d. Irwin and Sharon Grossinger; m. Scott Schiller, Aug. 29, 1992; children: Cameron, Grayson, Keaton. BA in Polit. Sci. and Econs., Wellesley Coll. Pres. Grossinger Motorcorp Inc., Lincolnwood, Ill., 1988—. Bd. dirs. First Bank and Trust of Evanston, Ill. Mem.: Chgo. Alumni Wellesley Club (sec. 1990—96), Lincolnwood C. of C (bd. dirs. 1992—96). Address: 6900 N McCormick Blvd Lincolnwood IL 60712-2788

GROSSMAN, ANN, professional tennis player; b. Columbus, Ohio, Oct. 13, 1970; Grad., Am. Sch., Chgo., 1989. Profl. tennis player; advanced to 2d round French Open, 1998. MVP U.S. Jr. Wightman Cup team, 1987; rep. U.S. on Maureen Connolly Brinker team and Nat. team, 1988, Ohio H.S. AAA State and Regl. champion, 1985; co-ranked No. 1 in U.S. 18 singles in 1987, winner Nat. Singles Title, 1987 Office: USTA 70 W Red Oak Ln White Plains NY 10604-3602

GROSSMAN, EDITH MARIAN, translator, critic, editor; b. Phila., Mar. 22, 1936; d. Alexander and Sally (Stern) Dorph; 1 child, Matthew Grossman. BA, U. Pa., 1957, MA, 1959; postgrad., U. Calif., Berkeley, 1960-62; PhD, NYU, 1972. Lectr. Spanish, CUNY, 1964-69; asst. prof. NYU, N.Y.C., 1969-72; prof. Dominican Coll., Orangeburg, N.Y., 1972-92. Translator: Love in Time of Cholera (Garcia Márquez), 1988, General in his Labyrinth (Márquez), Maqroll (Alvaro Mutis), 1992, Strange Pilgrims (Márquez), 1993, Of Love and Other Demons (Márquez), 1995, The Adventures of Maqroll (Mutis), 1995, Death in the Andes (Vargas Llosa), 1996; also others. Mem. PEN, Am. Lit. Translators Assn. Avocations: reading, music.

GROSSMAN, FRANCES KAPLAN, psychologist; b. Newport News, Va., May 28, 1939; d. Rubin H. and Beatrice (Fischlowitz) Kaplan; m. Henry Grossman, July 26, 1970; children: Jennifer, Benjamin. BA, Oberlin (Ohio) Coll., 1961; MS, PhD, Yale U., 1965. Diplomate Am. Bd. Profl. Psychology. Asst. prof. Yale U., New Haven, 1965-69, Boston U., 1969-71, assoc. prof. psychology, 1971-82, prof. psychology, 1982-2002, prof. emeritus, 2002—. Author: Brothers and Sisters of Retarded Children, 1971, Pregnancy, Birth and Parenthood, 1980, With the Phoenix Rising, 1999. Trustee Oberlin Coll., 1990-92, pres. Alumni Assn., 1979-80. Recipient Cert. of Appreciation Oberlin Coll. Alumni Assn., 1983. Fellow APA (mem. ethics com. 1994-97); mem. New Eng. Soc. for Study of Dissociation (bd. dirs. 1995—), Mass. Psychol. Assn. (chair ethics com. 1989-91, Career Contbn. award 1991), Sigma Xi, Phi Beta Kappa. Jewish. Office: Boston Univ Dept Psychology 64 Cummington St Boston MA 02215-2407 Office Phone: 617-332-6505. E-mail: frang@bu.edu.

GROSSMAN, JANICE, former magazine publishing company executive; b. Montreal, Que., Can., Nov. 3, 1949; m. Daniel Rubinstein, July 11, 1978; 1 child, Lauren Alexandra. MA, NYU, 1970; BA, New Sch. Social Research, 1971. Advt. sr. exec. recruiter Merrill, Lynch, Pierce, Fenner & Smith Inc., N.Y.C., 1976-78; advt. sales rep. Ms. mag., N.Y.C., 1978-80; N.Y. advt. mgr. Ms. Mag., N.Y.C., 1980-82, advt. dir., 1982-84, New Woman Mag., N.Y.C., 1984-86, assoc. pub., 1986-88, became pub., 1989, In Fashion Mag., N.Y.C., 1988, N.Y. Mag., 1991; pub. Seventeen mag., N.Y.C., 1992-96; v.p., group pub. PRIMEDIA Mags., N.Y.C., 1992-96; pres. Advt. & Mktg., N.Y.C., 1996—2000; exec. v.p. Primedia Consumer mags., N.Y.C., 1997—2000. Mem. Am. Mag. Conf. Com. Mem. adv. bd. Strang-Cornell Breast Ctr. Mem. Fragrance Found., Fashion Group, Advt. Women N.Y., Cosmetic Exec. Women, Advt. Club N.Y.

GROSSMAN, JOANNE BARBARA, lawyer; b. Brookline, Mass., Oct. 23, 1949; d. Bernard R. and Beatrice G. (Quint) G.; m. John H. Seesel, Dec. 30, 1973; children: Benjamin P., Rebecca A. AB, Radcliffe Coll., 1971; JD, U. Calif., Berkeley, 1975. Bar: Calif. 1975, D.C. 1976, U.S. Dist. Ct. D.C. 1976, U.S. Ct. Appeals (D.C. cir.) 1976, U.S. Supreme Ct. 1979. Assoc. Covington & Burling, Washington, 1975-83, ptnr., 1983—. Office: Covington & Burling PO Box 7566 1201 Pennsylvania Ave NW Washington DC 20044

GROSSMAN, JOYCE RENEE, pediatrician, internist; b. Bklyn., Nov. 15, 1951; d. Norman and Sydell (Rashbaum) Katz; m. Arthur Robert Grossman (div.); 1 child, Justin. BS, Bklyn. Col., 1973; MS, Cornell Med. Col., 1980; MD, Downstate Med. Col., 1986. Adj. prof. Downstate Med. Ctr., Bklyn., 1994—; attending physician N.Y. Hosp. Network, Bklyn., 1996-97, Beth Israel Med. Ctr., Bklyn., 1997; assoc. med. dir. Cigna of N.Y., N.Y.C., 1998—. Author: (with others) Pediatric Aspects of Tuberculosis & Clinical Handbook, 1995. Fellow Am. Acad. Pediatrics, Am. Acad. Physicians. Achievements include patents in field of gene therapy, antibiotics and chemotherapeutic agents.

GROSSMAN, MARY MARGARET, elementary school educator; b. East Cleveland, Ohio, Sept. 26, 1946; d. Frank Anthony and Margaret Mary (Buda) G. Student, Kent State Univ., 1965-67; BS in Elem. Edn. cum laude, Cleveland State Univ., 1971; postgrad, Lake Erie Coll., 1974-77, John Carroll Univ., 1978, 81, 82, 83, 85, Cleveland State Univ., 1985. Cert. elem. sch. tchr. grades 1 to 8, Ohio; cert. data processing, Ohio. Tchr. Cleve. Catholic Diocese, Cleve., Ohio, 1971-72, Willoughby-Eastlake Sch. Dist., Willoughby, Ohio, 1972—. Participant Nat. Econ. Edn. Conf., Richmond, Va., 1995. Eucharistic min. St. Christine's Ch., Euclid, 1988—, mem. parish pastoral coun., 1995-00. Recipient Samuel H. Elliott Econ. Leadership award, 1986-87, Consumer Educator award N.E. Ohio Region, 1986, 1st pl. award for excellence in tchg. Tchrs. in Am. Enterprise, 1984-85, 89-90; Martha Holden Jennings scholar, 1984-85. Mem. NEA, Ohio Edn. Assn. (human rels. award 1986-87, cert. merit 1987-88), N.E. Ohio Edn. Assn. (Positive Tchr. Image award 1988). Roman Catholic. Avocations: racquetball, softball, walking, tennis, bicycling. Home: 944 E 225th St Cleveland OH 44123-3308 Office: McKinley Elem Sch 1200 Lost Nation Rd Willoughby OH 44094-7324

GROSSMAN, MELANIE, dermatologist; AB in Biology, Princeton U., N.J., 1984; MD, NYU, 1988. Diplomate Am. Bd. Dermatology. Intern Yale U. Med. Ctr., New Haven, 1988—89; resident in dermatology Presbyn. Hosp./Columbia U., N.Y.C., 1989—92; fellow in laser dermatology and photodynamic therapy Mass. Gen. Hosp. and Wellman Labs., Boston, 1993—95; pvt. practice dermatology N.Y.C., 1992—. Asst. attending dermatology Presbyn. Hosp., N.Y.C., 1992—, Cornell U., N.Y.C., 1998—, N.Y. Hosp., N.Y.C., 1998—, St. Luke's Roosevelt Hosp. Ctr., N.Y.C., 1995—; attending physician dept. plastic surgery N.Y. Eye and Ear Infirmary, N.Y.C., 1996—; assoc. clin. in dermatology Columbia U., N.Y.C., 1992—; dir. clin. and laser rsch. studies Laser and Skin Surgery Ctr. of N.Y., N.Y.C., 1995; clin. affiliate dermatology N.Y. Hosp., N.Y.C., 1996—97; clin. instr. dermatology Cornell U. Med. Ctr., N.Y.C., 1996—97; clin. fellow dermatology Mass. Gen. Hosp.-Harvard Med. Sch., Boston, 1993—95. Contbr. articles to profl. jours. Fellow: Am. Soc. for Dermatologic Surgery, Am. Soc. for Laser Medicine and Surgery (socioecon. affairs com. 1997—2000, nominating com. 2000); mem.: Women's Dermatologic Soc., Women's Med. Soc. N.Y., Dermatologic Soc. Greater N.Y. (comm. com., exec. com.), Med. Soc. State of N.Y., Am. Acad. Dermatology (chair photobiology task force 1998—99, melanoma task force, comm. com. 1998—2000, comm. study group for 21st century, sports ad hoc com., chair socioecon. affairs com. 1999—2000). Office: 161 Madison Ave Ste 4 NW New York NY 10016

GROSSMAN, MELANIE DURAND, social worker, researcher; b. St. Martinville, La., Feb. 8, 1943; d. Howard J. and Genevieve Durand; m. William Grossman, Dec. 26, 1964; children: Jennifer, Edward, Jessica. BS in Edn., La. State U., 1965; MSW, Simmons Coll., 1980; PhD, Bryn Mawr Coll., 1999. LCSW Calif., 2000. Social worker N. Bennet St. Settlement House, Boston, 1965—66; psychiat. social worker Waltham Hosp., 1980—84; clin. social worker Vis. Nurses Assn., Westwood, Mass., 1984; social worker Cutler Counseling Ctr., Norwood, Mass., 1985—87; supr. sr. care Cutler Counseling, Norwood, Mass., 1987—93; instr. Bryn Mawr Coll., Bryn Mawr, Pa., 1996—97; rsch. assoc. UCSF Inst. Health and Aging, San Francisco, 1987—. Mem. planning com. Older Women's Health & Wellness Summit, San Franciscso, 1999. Vol. Peace Corp., New Delhi, 1966—68; bd. mem. New England Chamber Orch., Boston, 1990—94, Child Study Assn., Boston, 1976—80, Sinfonietta Orchertsa, San Francisco, 2002—, Network for Elders, San Francisco, 2002—. Recipient Certificate of Honor, City Bd. of Suprs., 2001, Cmty. Health award, Network for Elders, 2001, 2003. Mem.: Gerontol. Soc. Am., Nat. Assn. Social Workers, Older Women's League, Phi Kappa Phi. Democrat. Avocations: cooking, gardening, music, singing. Home: 33 Grenard Terrace San Francisco CA 94109 E-mail: melondg@aol.com., melaniegrossman@sbcglobal.net.

GROSSMAN, NANCY, artist; b. N.Y.C. d. Murray and Josephine G. BFA, Pratt Inst., 1962. Mem. jury sculpture N.Y. State Council on Arts, 1973, Prix de Rome fellowships Am. Acad. in Rome, 1974 Exhibited in one-woman shows, Krasner Gallery, N.Y.C., 1964, 65, 67, Cordier & Ekstrom, N.Y.C., 1968, 69, 71, 73, 75, 76, Church Fine Arts Gallery, U. Nev., Reno, 1978, Barbara Gladstone Gallery, N.Y.C., 1980, 82, Heath Gallery, Atlanta, 1981, 86, Terry Dintenfass Gallery, 1984, Exit Art, N.Y.C., 1991, Sculpture Ctr., N.Y.C., 1991, Hillwood Art Mus., Brookville, N.Y., 1991, Exit Art, N.Y.C., 1991, Hillwood Art Mus., Brookville, N.Y., 1991, Sculpture Ctr., N.Y.C., 1991, Artemisia, Chgo., 1992, Beacon St. Gallery, Chgo., 1992, Ark. Art Ctr., Little Rock, 1992, Contemporary Mus., Honolulu, 1992, Binghamton U. Art Gallery, 1992, Hooks-Epstein Galleries, Houston, 1993, 95, LedisFlam, N.Y.C., 1994, Weatherspoon Art Gallery, Greensboro, N.C., 1994, Greenville Cty Museum of Art, 2004; exhibited in numerous group shows, including, Whitney Mus. Am. Art, N.Y.C., 1968, 69, 69, 73, 80, 81, 93, 95, Fogg Art Mus., Cambridge, Mass., 1972, Am. Acad. Arts and Letters/Nat. Inst. Arts and Letters invitational, N.Y.C., 1974, 1987, New Mus. New American Painting exhbn., Hungary, Czechoslovakia, Poland, 1976, Bette Stoler, 1983, Whitney Mus. at Philip Morris, 1984, Exit Art, N.Y.C., 1991, Michael Rosenfeld Gallery, N.Y.C., 1996, Nat. Acad., N.Y.C., 1996, The Geffen Contemporary, L.A., 1999, Beacon Street Gallery, Chicago, 2001, George Adams Gallery, N.Y.C, 2003, Chelsea Art Museum, N.Y.C., 2004; represented in permanent collections, Whitney Mus. Am. Art, Hirshhorn Mus., Washington, Smithsonian Inst., Dallas Mus. Fine Arts, Balt. Mus., Mus. Boymans Van Beuningen, Rotterdam, Netherlands, U. Calif., Berkeley, Princeton U. Art Mus., N.J., Contemporary Arts Mus., Houston, Met. Mus. Art, N.Y.C., Va. Mus. Fine Arts, Richmond, Weatherspoon Art Gallery, Greensboro, N.C., Contemporary Mus., Honolulu. Recipient Inaugural Contemporary Achievement award Pratt Inst., 1966, award AAAL and Nat. Inst. Arts and Letters, 1974, Hassam, Spreicher, Betts and Symons purchase award Am. Acad. and Inst. Arts and Letters, 1989, Alumni Achievement award Pratt Inst., 1995, Joan Mitchell Found. fellowship, 1996; Ida C. Haskell scholar, 1962; Guggenheim fellow, 1965, fellow for sculpture Nat. Endowment for Arts, 1991; grantee Nat. Endowment for Arts, 1984. Mem. Nat. Acad. Address: 105 Eldridge St New York NY 10002-4405 Office: Michael Rosenfeld Gallery 24 W 57th St New York NY 10019-3918*

GROSSO, CAMILLE M. nurse; b. Geneva, N.Y., Sept. 28, 1938; d. Frank and Gaetana (Luongo) Balistreri; m. Gerard Michael Grosso, Apr. 8, 1961; children: Gerard II, Gina M. BS, George Mason U., 1976; MSN, Catholic U. Am., 1978; PhD, Case Western Res. U., 1995. RN. Staff nurse Project Hope, Saigon, Vietnam, 1961-62; head nurse Fairfax Hosp., Falls Church, Va., 1972-76; clin. specialist Arlington (Va.) Hosp., 1978-82; faculty Catholic U., Washington, 1982-89, U. Md., Balt., 1990-92; pvt. practice psychotherapist Annandale, Va., 1980—. Roman Catholic. Office: 7369 McWhorter Annandale VA 22003-5650

GROSSO, DEE, human resources executive; BA in Indsl. Rels., Temple U., 1979; MS in Dynamics of Orgns., U. Pa., 1998. Employee rels. and employment mgr. IMS Health, Plymouth Meeting, Pa., 1981—87, compensation and benefits dir., 1987—93, human resources I, bus. ptnr., human resources dir. II, sr. bus. ptnr., 1981—98; v.p. human resources Advanta Corp., Horsham, Pa., 1998—99; dir. human resources, sr. bus. ptnr. Astrazeneca Pharms., Wilmington, Del., 2000—. Mem.: World Future Soc., Human Resources Planning Group, Am. Mgmt. Assn., Orgnl. Devel. Network.

GROSSO, LISA THERESE, periodontist; b. Denver, Apr. 20, 1956; d. John and Agnes (Georgine) G. BSN cum laude, Loretto Hts. Coll., 1980; BS in Dentistry, U. Calif., San Francisco, 1993, DDS, specialty cert. in periodontology, MS in Oral Biology, U. Calif., San Francisco, 1996. RN oper. rm., Calif. Nurse oper. rm. Calif. Pacific Med. Ctr., San Francisco, 1988-89; periodontist pvt. practice, Concord, Calif., 1996—. Mem. ADA, Am. Acad. Periodontology, Calif. Dental Assn. Avocations: skiing, swimming, dog training, cooking. Office: 2425 East St Ste 16 Concord CA 94520-1926

GROSSO-PROULX, DEBORAH, medical/surgical nurse; b. New Brunswick, N.J., Aug. 4, 1952; d. Frank M. and Lydia Ann Grosso. BA in Psychology, Douglass Coll., 1974; ASN, St. Petersburg Coll., 1993. RN. Med. sec. Dept. Surgery R.I. Hosp., Providence, 1988—91; registrar ER Sun Coast Hosp., Largo, Fla., 1991—94; staff, charge nurse Columbia Northside Med. Ctr., St. Petersburg, Fla., 1994—97; staff, surg. oncology nurse Robert Wood Johnson Med. Ctr., New Brunswick, 1997—98; staff, med.-surg. nurse Somerset Med. Ctr., Somerville, NJ, 1998—2000; float, med.-surg. nurse St. Peter's U. Hosp., New Brunswick, 2000—. Mng. editor United Way News, 1978—80, assoc. editor Quest, 1980—84. Finalist Best of Photography Annual, Photographer's Forum Mag., 2001. Mem.: Internat. Freelance Photographers Orgn. Democrat. Avocations: photography, poetry, art.*

GROSZ, BARBARA JEAN, computer science educator; b. Phila., July 21, 1948; d. Joseph Eugene and Judith Phyllis (Zander) Gross. AB in Math., Cornell U., 1969; MA in Computer Sci., U. Calif., Berkeley, 1971, PhD in Computer Sci., 1977. Rsch. mathematician Artificial Intelligence Ctr., SRI Internat., Stanford, Calif., 1973-77, computer scientist, 1981-82, sr. computer scientist, 1981-82, program dir. nat. lang. and representation, 1982-83, sr. staff scientist, 1983-86; co-founder, mem. exec. com., prin. researcher Ctr. for Study of Lang. and Info. Stanford U. and SRI Internat., 1983-86; with divsn. engring. and applied scis. Harvard U., Cambridge, Mass., 1986—, interim assoc. dean for affirmative action, 1993-94, Higgins prof. natural scis., 2001—, dean of sci. Radcliffe Inst. Advanced Study, 2001—. Vis. faculty dept. computer sci. Stanford U., fall 1982, cons. assoc. prof. computer sci. and linguistics, 1984-85, computer sci., 1985-87; vis. scholar dept. computer and info. sci. U. Pa., Jan.-June 1982; conf. chair Internat. Joint Conf. on Artificial Intelligence (IJCAI-91), chair bd. trustees IJCAI Inc., 1989-91, mem. bd. trustees, 1987-97, program com. 1982; Harold Perlman vis. prof. faculty sci. Hebrew U., Jerusalem, 1992; invited spkr. numerous nat. and internat. profl. assns., confs., symposia; reviewer program proposals NSF; participant adv. meetings for rsch. and funding various govtl. agys. Author: (with others) Elements of Discourse Understanding, 1982, Understanding Spoken Language, 1982, Foundations of Cognitive Science, 1988, Intentions in Communications, 1988; editor: (with Sparck Jones, Webber) Readings in Natural Language Processing, 1986; assoc. editor: Ann. Rev. Computer Sci., 1982-1985; editl. bd.: Artificial Intelligence Jour., 1982—, Am. Jour. Computational Linguistics, 1981-83; contbr. articles and papers to profl. jours., workshops and conf. procs. Recipient Disting. Alumna award in computer sci. and engring., U. Calif., Berkeley, 1997, Donald E. Walker Disting. Svc. award, IJCAI, 2001. Fellow AAAS, Am. Assn. Artificial Intelligence (exec. coun. 1981-84, 86-89, pres.-elect 1991-93, pres. 1993-95, past pres. 1995-97, disting. svc. award, 1999); mem. NRC (computer sci. & telecom. bd. 1994-98), Assn. Computational Linguistics (exec. com. 1986-88), Assn. Computing Machinery (vice chair 1979-81, chair 1981-83, mem. SIGART), Am. Philos. Soc. Avocations: hiking, wildflower photography, snorkeling. Address: 33 Oxford St Rm 249 Cambridge MA 02138-2901

GROTA, BARBARA LYNN, academic administrator, educator; d. Jerome A. and Laura B. Grota; m. Charles Harrington Akin, May 24, 2003; m. James William Murphy, Apr. 30, 1988 (dec. Sept. 30, 1991). MS, Syracuse U., Syracuse, NY, 1980—82; BA, Southeastern Mass. U., North Dartmouth, MA, 1976—79. Orgnl. devel. cons. Carrier Corp., Syracuse, NY, 1980—81; social sci. - adj. faculty New Eng. Inst. of Tech., Warwick, RI, 1982—85, coop. edn. founder/coord., 1983—85; coop. edn. asst. dir. Roger Williams U., Bristol, RI, 1985—2000, social sci. adj. faculty, 1988—2000, asst. prof. of mgmt., 2000—, asst. dean, 2000—. Pres. New Eng. Assn. for Coop. Edn. and Field Experience, Boston, 1990—90; supervising editor NEACEFE newsletter, New Eng. Assn. for Coop. Edn. and Field Experience, Boston, 1991—92; mem. bd. of directors Riverwood Rehab. Services Inc., Bristol, RI, 1995—2000, co-president bd. of directors, 1997—99; strategic planning cons./facilitator Bristol Econ. Devel. Commn., Warren, RI, 2000—00; facilitator/trainer RI Probate Ct., West Greenwich, RI, 2002—02. Author (co-author): (rsch. article) Procs. of the 2002 Symposium for the Mktg. of Higher Edn. of the Am. Mktg. Assn., (pub. rsrch.) Procs. of the 1987 Nat. Coop. Edn. Assn. Conf. Canvas com. mem. Fairhaven Unitarian Universalist Ch., Fairhaven, Mass., 1999—99; exec. dir. evaluation com. mem. Riverwood Rehab. Services, Inc., Bristol, RI, 1995—2000; mem. Child and Family Services of Newport County, Newport, RI, 1999—99. Recipient The Excellence in Tchg. Award, Alpha Chi - Nat. Honor Soc., 1997, Psi Chi - Psychology Nat. Honor Soc., 2000, Honor Soc. Induction, Sigma Beta Delta - Internat. Honor Soc. in Bus., Mgmt., and Adminstrn., 2000, Outstanding Women On Campus award, Roger Williams U. Women's Ctr., 1998, 2002. Mem.: Am. Mktg. Assn., Am. Psychol. Assn. (APA), Roger Williams U. Dean's Diversity Coun., Nat. Academic Advising [illegible]. Avocations: hiking, gourmet cooking, reading. Office: Roger Williams University One Old Ferry Road Bristol RI 02809

GROTH, JENICE JOY, small business owner; b. Lapeer, Mich., Aug. 6, 1977; d. Bernard D. and Nancy Sue Hotchkiss; m. Aaron Joseph-Kenneth Groth, Aug. 12, 1995 (dec. Aug. 1, 1999); children: Samantha Marcia, Ashton Aaron. Cert., Lapeer (Mich.) County Vocational Tech. Sch., 1995; ABA, Detroit (Mich.) Coll. Bus., 1997. Sec. Lapeer (Mich.) Counseling Ctr., 1994—95; cons. Mary Kay Cosmetics, Mich., 1996—97; personnel dir. Hotchkiss Homes, Inc., Silverwood, Mich., 1996—98; office mgr. Profl. Counseling Ctr., Branoh-Lapeer, Mich., 1999—2001, Life Transitions Family Counseling Ctr., Imlay City, Mich., 2001—03; prin., owner Affordable Wedding Planning Inc., Lapeer, 2002—; contractor Vector Mktg., Branch-Lapeer, Mich., 2003—. Contbr. poetry to various pubs. Scholar, Detroit (Mich.) Coll. Bus., 1995, Lapeer (Mich.) County Vo-Tech., 1995. Mem.: PTA, Lapeer (Mich.) Area C. of C. Avocations: poetry, dance, writing, interior decorating.

GROTHEM, HELEN MARIE, occupational therapist, educator; b. Moorhead, Minn., Sept. 15, 1938; d. Marvin E. and Hilda Corrine Bystol; m. Frederick II Waldeman Bystol, Sept. 3, 1962 (div. June 6, 1968); children: Cynthia Bystol Lawson, Stacy Louise Poli, Frederick III Waldemar. BS in occupl. therapy, Milw.-Downer Coll., 1956—61; MS, Murray State U., 1998—2001. Cert. Occupational Therapist Nat. Bd. for Certification of Occupl. Therapy, 1961, lic. Ky. Bd. of Licensure for Occupl. Therapy, 1995. Occupl. therapist Milw. Children's Rehab. ctr., 1961—62, Mpls. Curative Workshop, 1962—64; occupl. therapy supr. Mpls. VA Hosp., 1964—66; program coord. St. Paul Assn. for Retarded Children, 1966—68; chief occupl. therapist St. Paul Ramsey Hosp., 1968—70; dir. of occupl. therapy Cmty. Meml. Hosp., Winona, Minn., 1970—80; cirector of occupl. therapy St. Francis Med. Ctr., LaCrosse, Wis., 1980—89; lead occupl. therapist Restorative Services, Inc., Hobart, Ind., 1990—95; occupl. therapy asst. program dir. Madisonville C.C., Ky., 1995—. Pres., bd. of dirs. Winona Day Activity Ctr., Winona, Minn., 1987—89; western dist. chair Ky. Occupl. Therapy Assn., 1999—2002, edn. chair, 2002—. Mem.: Ky. Occupl. Therapy Assn. (exec. bd. mem. 1999—2003), Am. Occupl. Therapy Assn. R-Consevative. Christian. Achievements include development of first occupational therapy assistant program in the state of Ky. Avocations: sewing, quilting, reading, bowling. Office: Madisonville Cmty Coll 750 North Laffoon St Madisonville KY 42431 E-mail: helen.grothem@kctcs.edu.

GROTTO, BETH ANNE, educational consultant; MusB, U. Mass., Lowell, 1992; MEd, U. Mass., Boston, 1997. Cert. music edn. K-12 Mass., 1992, early childhood edn. Mass., 1997. Tchr. Watertown (Mass.) Pub. Schs., 1992—98; cons. COMPASS Consulting, Jamaica Plain, Mass., 1996—2000, lead cons., 2000—. Vol. Kerry for Pres., Boston, 2003—03; mem. Centastage Theater, Boston, 2000—03. Paul Douglas Tchr. scholar, Commonwealth Mass. Bd. Higher Edn., 1988—92, Rappaport fellow for Law and Pub. Policy, Rappaport Found., 2003. Mem.: ASCD. Democrat. Roman Catholic. Avocations: French horn, skiing. Personal E-mail: beth.grotto@verizon.net.

GROTZINGER, LAUREL ANN, librarian, educator; b. Truman, Minn., Apr. 15, 1935; d. Edward F. and Marian Gertrude (Greeley) G. BA, Carleton Coll., 1957; MS, U. Ill., 1958, PhD, 1964. Instr., asst. libr. Ill. State U., 1958-62; asst. prof. Western Mich. U., Kalamazoo, 1964-66, assoc. prof., 1966-68, prof., 1968—, asst. dir. Sch. Librarianship, 1965-72, chief rsch. officer, 1979-86, interim dir. Sch. Libr. and Info. Sci., 1982-86, dean grad. coll., 1979-92, prof. univ. libr., 1993—. Author: The Power and the Dignity, 1966; mem. editl. bd. Jour. Edn. for Librarianship, 1973-77, Dictionary Am. Libr. Biography, 1975-77, Mich. Academician, 1990—; contbr. articles to profl. jours., books. Trustee Kalamazoo Pub. Libr., 1991-93, v.p., 1991-92, pres., 1992-93; pres. Kalamazoo Bach Festival, 1996-97, bd. dirs. 1992-98, exec. com. 1996-98. Mem. ALA (sec.-treas. Libr. History Round Table 1973-74, vice chmn., chmn-elect 1983-84, chmn. 1984-85, mem.-at-large 1991-93), Spl. Librs. Assn., Assn. Libr. Info. Sci. Edn., Mich. acad. Sci., Arts and Letters (mem.-at-large, exec. com. 1980-86, pres. 1983-85, exec. com. 1990-94, pres. 1991-93, vice chmn. libr./info. scis. 1996-97, chair 1997-98), Internat. Assn. Torch Clubs (v.p. Kalamazoo chpt. 1992-93, pres. 1993-94, exec. com. 1989-95), Soc. Collegiate Journalists, Phi Beta Kappa (pres. S.W. Mich. chpt. 1977-78, sec. 1994-97, pres. 1997-99), Beta Phi Mu, Alpha Beta Alpha, Delta Kappa Gamma (pres. Alpha Psi chpt. 1988-92), Phi Kappa Phi. Home: 2729 Mockingbird Dr Kalamazoo MI 49008-1626 Office Phone: 269-387-5418. E-mail: grotzinger@wmich.edu.

GROVE, DENISE WHITLOCK, accounting and financial professional; b. Marietta, Ga., July 5, 1959; d. J. Winston and Martha Josephine (Phillips) Whitlock. BSBA, Auburn U., 1981. CPA, Ga. Audit profl. KPMG, Dallas, 1982-85, with exec. office N.Y., 1985-86, audit mgr. Atlanta, 1986-87; fin. analyst Columbian Chem. Co. div. Phelps Dodge Corp., Atlanta, 1987-90; asst. v.p. acctg. policy Bank of Am. (formerly C&S/Sovran Corp.), Atlanta, 1990-91, v.p. acctg. policy, 1991-92; controller CryoLife, Inc., Marietta, 1992-94; sr. analyst N.W. Airlines, Inc., Atlanta, 1994-96, mgr. fin. projects, 1996-97; fin. mgr. Hewlett-Packard Co., Atlanta, 1997-98; CFO DBS Mfg., Inc., Atlanta, 1998; founder, owner Denise Whitlock Grove, CPA, Bus. and Fin. Cons., Peachtree City, Ga., 1998—, CFO Support, Inc., Atlanta, 1998—. Vol. CFO Cochran Mill Nature Ctr., 2000—. Treas., chmn. fundraising Atlanta Symphony Assn., 1987-89; bd. dirs., treas. Morningside Terrace Condominium Assn., Atlanta, 1987-90. Recipient Vol. of Yr. award, CFO Cochran Mill Nature Ctr., 2001. Mem.: AICPA (editl. advisor 1990—97), Ga. Soc. CPAs (continuing profl. edn. com. 1990—99, bd. dirs. 1994—, v.p. Atlanta chpt. 1997—98, pres. 1998—99, chmn. CPAs in industry, govt. and edn. com. 2000—02, coun. 1994—, leadership team industry sect.), Auburn U. Alumni Assn., U.S. Tennis Assn., Atlanta Lawn Tennis Club, Delta Gamma. Avocations: tennis, reading. Office: CFO Support Inc 1507 River Green Dr Atlanta GA 30327 E-mail: d.Whitlock@get.net.

GROVE, JANET E. retail executive; BS in Mktg., Calif. State U., Hayward, 1973. Exec. trainee Macy's West, San Francisco, 1973—74, from asst. buyer to gen. merchandise mgr., 1974—92; from sr. v.p. to exec. v.p. Broadway, Inc., 1992—96; sr. v.p. center core merchandising Federated Merchandising Group, Cin., 1996—97, exec. v.p. ready-to-wear and center core, 1997—98, exec. v.p. center core, cosmetics and home merchandising, 1998, CEO, exec. v.p. center core, cosmetics and home merchandising, 1999—; vice chair Federated Dept. Stores, Cin., 2003—. Recipient Humanitarian award, Nat. Jewish Med. and Rsch. Ctr., Denver, 2000, HUG award, Intimate Apparel Square Club, 2002. Office: Federated Dept Stores Inc 7 W Seventh St Cincinnati OH 45202

GROVE, MYRNA JEAN, elementary school educator; b. Bryan, Ohio, Oct. 24, 1949; d. Kedric Durward and N. Florence (Stombaugh) G. Student, Bowling Green State U., 1970-71; BA in Edn., Manchester Coll., 1971; postgrad., U. No. Colo., 1974-76, Purdue U., 1977, St. Francis Coll., Ft. Wayne, Ind., 1986, Coll. Mount St. Joseph, Ohio, 1986; MLS, Kent State U., 1999. Cert. elem. tchr., Ohio, 1971, permanent cert., 1999. Tchr. elem. sch. Bryan City Schs., 1972—. Author: Asbestos Cancer: One Man's Experience, 1995, Legacy of One-Room Schools, 1999; editor newspaper column Education Today, 1975-82, newsletter N.W. Ohio Emphasis, 1981-83 (award 1981). Dir., violinist Bryan String Ensemble, 1981—;

organist Trinity Episc. Ch., Bryan, 1979-89; active Lancaster Mennonite Hist. Soc., Hans Herr Found.; trustee Bryan Area Cultural Assn., 1984-89; bd. dirs. Williams County Cmty. Concerts; sec. Black Swamp Arts Coun., 2001—. Jennings scholar Martha Holden Jennings Found., Bowling Green State U., 1982-83. Mem. ALA, NEA (Ohio del., state contact 1986-87), Am. Booksellers Assn. (assoc. mem.), Ohio Edn. Assn. (presenter 1984, del. global issues 1986, sec. N.W. Ohio Tchrs. Uniserv. 1975-78), Bus. and Profl. Women Ohio (individual devel. com. 1986-90, speaking skills cert. 1987), Ohio Libr. Coun., Ohioana Libr. Assn., N.W. Ohio Manchester Coll. Alumni Assn. (past pres.), Bryan Edn. Assn. (exec. com., pres. 1985-86), Williams County Geneal. Soc., Williams County Hist. Assn., P. Buckley Moss Soc., Trees of Life (v.p. 1994-2001, region moss docent), Alpha Delta Kappa (pres. 1996-98), Alpha Mu. Avocations: collecting dolls, playing piano, organ and violin, reading, travel.

GROVE, PECOLIA J. social worker; b. Chadbourn, N.C., May 8, 1938; d. Robert Josey and Annie Bell (Spann) Edwards; 1 child, Phaedra Jo. BA, N.C. Ctrl. U., 1961. Counselor Leonard Tng. Sch., Raeford, NC, 1961—63; social worker dept. social svcs. Robeson County, Lumberton, NC, 1963—64, Cumberland County, Fayetteville, NC, 1964—69; counselor Juvenile Ct., Fayetteville, 1969—75; sch. social worker Cumberland County Bd. Edn., Fayetteville, 1976—95, 1996—98; substance abuse counselor Lee County Correctional Instn., Bishopville, SC, 1999—2000. Life mem. NAACP; v.p. Dem. Women, Fayetteville, 1994—96. With WAC, 1956—58. Mem.: Alpha Kappa Alpha. Democrat. Church Of Christ. Avocations: walking, gardening, reading. Home: 1013 Bentwood Rd Hartsville SC 29550-5080

GROVE, SHARI TAYLOR, librarian, educator; b. Norwalk, Conn., Sept. 5, 1942; d. Gabriel Szabo and Mary Olean Taylor; m. R. Bruce Grove, July 14, 1972 (div. Oct. 30, 1978). BA, Russell Sage Coll., 1964; MLS, So. Conn. State U., 1970; MA, Boston Coll., 1989. Libr. Anthropology Libr., Yale U., New Haven, Ctrl. Consol.Sch. Dist. 22, Kirtland, N.Mex., 1973—77; pub. svcs. libr. Tozzer Libr. Harvard U., Cambridge, Mass., 1978—81; collection devel. libr. Thomas P. O'Neill Jr. Libr. Boston Coll., Chestnut Hill, Mass., 1982—. Editor: American Indian Rock Art: Papers Presented at the 1974 Symposium. Mem. exec. bd. LWV, Farmington, N.Mex., 1974—77, Cambridge, 1978—81. Mem.: ALA (Am. Coll. and Rsch. Libr. coms. 1985—). Home: 295 Harvard St Apt 911 Cambridge MA 02139 Office: Boston Coll T P O'Neill Jr Libr 140 Commonwealth Ave Chestnut Hill MA 02467-3810 E-mail: grove@bc.edu.

GROVER, KATHRON CLAIRE, counselor, social worker; b. Chgo., Feb. 14, 1969; d. William A. and Marcia A. Grover. BA in Psychology, Kalamazoo Coll., 1991; M in Holistic Counseling, Salve Regina U., 1997. Registered social worker Mich. Bd. Social Work. Psycho-social counselor East Bay Mental Health, Barrington, RI, 1995—97; residential counselor Tzawapi Program Family Svcs., Inc., Providence, 1995—97; facilitator PREVENT Program Norfolk (Va.) Naval Sta., 1998; therapist Singing River Svcs., Gautier, Miss., 1998—2000; clinician mobile crisis response team Family and Children's Svcs., Kalamazoo, 2000—; counselor, victim advocate YWCA Sexual Assault Program, Kalamazoo, 2000—. Contbg. artist Women's Sacred Arts Festival, Newport, RI, 1996, Newport, 97. Author: (book) Book of Seasons, 1997 (NEHCA award hon. mention); editor: (anthology) Voices on the Line, 2003; editor, contbr.: sch. lit. mag. The Cauldron, 1990—91. Organizer sexual awareness mentor activities YWCA, Kalamazoo, 2001—03; vol. Comty. Advocates, Kalamazoo, 2000—03. Mem.: YWCA, Women's Action Coun., Phi Beta Kappa. Avocations: creative writing, yoga, letterboxing. Office: YWCA of Kalamazoo 353 E Michigan Kalamazoo MI 49007

GROVER, ROSALIND REDFERN, oil and gas company executive; b. Midland, Tex., Sept. 5, 1941; d. John Joseph and Rosalind (Kapps) Redfern;m. Arden Roy Grover, Apr. 10, 1982; 1 child, Rosson. BA in Edn. summa cum laude, U. Ariz., 1966, MA in History, 1982; postgrad. in law, So. Methodist U., Dallas. Libr. Gahr H.S., Cerritos, Calif., 1969; pres. The Redfern Found., Midland, 1982—; ptnr. Redfern & Grover, Midland, 1986—; pres. Redfern Enterprises Inc., Midland, 1989—. Chmn. bd. dirs. Flag-Redfern Oil Co., Midland. Sec. park and recreation commn. City of Midland, 1969-71, del. Objectives for Convocation, 1980; mem., past pres. women's aux. Midland Cmty. Theatre, 1970; chmn. challenge grant bldg. fund, 1980, chmn. Tex. Yucca Hist. Landmark Renovation Project, 1983, trustee, 1983-88; chmn. publicity com. Midland Jr. League, Midland, Inc., 1972, chmn. edn. com., 1976, corr. sec., 1978; 1st v.p. Midland Symphony Assn., 1975; chmn. Midland Charity Horse Show, 1975-76; mem. Midland Am. Revolution Bicentennial Commn., 1976; trustee Mus. S.W., 1977-80, pres. bd. dirs., 1979-80; co-chmn. Gov. Clements Fin. Com., Midland, 1978; mem. dist. com. State Bd. Law Examiners; mem. bd. visitors Hockaday, 2001—04; trustee Midland Meml. Hosp., 1978-80, Permian Basin Petroleum Mus., Libr. and Hall of Fame, 1989-98. Recipient HamHock award Midland Cmty. Theatre, 1978. Mem. Ind. Petroleum Assn. Am., Tex. Ind. Producers and Royalty Owners Assn., Petroleum Club, Racquet Club (Midland), Horseshoe Bay (Tex.) Country Club, Phi Kappa Phi, Pi Lambda Theta. Republican. Office: PO Box 2127 Midland TX 79702-2127 E-mail: rozgrover@aol.com.

GROVES, B C, educational consultant, writer; d. James Alvis Cowan and Jean Maxine Wilkinson; m. Winford E. Groves, Dec. 16, 1955; 1 child, Cheryl J. BA, North Tex. State U., 1962; MS, Okla. State U., 1976. Cert. tchr. Tex., Okla. Tchr. Carrollton (Tex.) ISD, 1966—74; supr. Right to Read, Stillwater, Okla., 1974—75; writing tchr. Dallas County Cmty., 1976—78, Dallas C.C., El Centro Coll., Tex. A&M, Coll. Sta., 1979—82; real estate broker self-employed, Dallas and Denton, 1982—90; mayor City of Lewisville (Tex.), 1991—93; author, cons. self-employed, Oreg., 1994—. Bd. dirs. Crimestoppers, Denton, Tex., 1989—91. Co-author: (book) Reflections on the Umpqua, 1999, Keeping Christmas, 2002; author: Heros of Lively County, 2003, various articles in periodicals and newspaper columns. Mem. Dallas Crime Commn., 1989—90; precinct chair Denton County Rep., Lewisville, Tex., 1990—93. Recipient Outstanding Woman, Dallas Times Herald, 1972. Mem.: DAR (com. chair 2003, 2nd vice regent Douglas County 2003—), Tex. State Tchrs. (life). Republican. Episcopal. Avocations: hiking, gardening, travel, volunteer. E-mail: pennypublications@hotmail.com.

GROVES, BERNICE ANN, retired elementary and secondary school coordinator, educator; b. Bklyn., Feb. 5, 1928; d. Charles and Mary (Silverman) Lichtenstein; m. Stuart Weiss, June 5, 1949 (div. June 1978); children: Joel Weiss, Patricia Weiss Levy; m. Sidney Groves, July 30, 1978 (dec. May 2000). MA, Adelphi U., 1971; MS in Edn., Coll. of New Rochelle, 1975. Cert. adminstr., supr., N.Y. K-6th grade tchr., reading tchr. Ossining (N.Y.) Schs., Byram Hills Schs., Armonk, NY, Bedford (NY) Schs., 1964—84; reading specialist The Hallen Sch., Mamaroneck, NY, 1984-88, coord. testing and curriculum New Rochelle, NY, 1988—2001; ret., 2002. Mgr. nutrition ctr. GNC, Scarsdale, NY, 1981—82; mem. curriculum adv. coun. Lower Westchester BOCES, 1988—2001. Pres. Mineola (N.Y.) Elem. Sch. PTA, 1962-63. Mem. ASCD, Lower Hudson Coun. Adminstrv. Women in Edn., Westchester Reading Coun., Orton Dyslexia Soc., Am. Mensa Ltd. Avocations: tennis, U.S.T.A., gourmet cooking, nutrition.

GROVES, LIZABETH A. accountant, local area network administrator; b. Muncie, Ind., June 21, 1964; d. Gary Michael and Pamela Kay Groves; m. Monti Klayman, Oct. 21, 1990. AA in Bus. Adminstrn., Brookdale C.C., Lincroft, N.J., 1993; BS in Acctg. summa cum laude, Kean U., Union, N.J., 1996. CPA, N.J. Bookkeeper Bonanza Motel, Wildwood Crest, N.J., 1982-83, Colts Head (N.J.) Vet., 1983-85; para-profl. Aronson & Thoma, Red Bank, N.J., 1985-94; acct. Withum, Smith & Brown, Red Bank, 1994-96, sr. acct., 1996-97, sr. acct., LAn adminstr., 1997—. Cons. AT&T Labs., Somerset, N.J., 1996-97; QuickBooks profl. advisor, 1999—. Mem. AICPA, N.J. Soc. CPAs, Assn. Cert. Fraud Examiners (assoc.), Phi Kappa Phi. Republican. Avocations: hiking, kayaking, travel. Office: Withum Smith & Brown 328 Newman Springs Rd Red Bank NJ 07701-5654 E-mail: lklayman@withum.com.

GROVES, MARTHA, newspaper writer; Computer writer L.A. Times, 1992-93, staff writer, 1985—. Office: LA Times Times Mirror Sq Los Angeles CA 90053

GROVES, SHARON SUE, elementary school educator; b. Springfield, Mo., Apr. 25, 1944; d. William Orin Jr. and Ruth M. (Jones) Hodge; m. Donald L. Groves, July 20, 1963. BA, Drury Coll., 1966, MEd, 1969. Cert. life elem. tchg.; Psychol. Examiners Cert. Adminstrn. Elem. tchr. Springfield Pub. Schs., 1966-96; asst. instr. individual testing Drury Coll., Springfield, 1969-76; asst. instr. enhancing math. S.W. Mo. State U., Springfield, 1991-94; parent resource educator Springfield Pub. Schs., 1998—. Sr. leader MAP 2000 (Mo. Assessment Project) Class I. Author: Modeling Effective Practices: Geometry and Computation. Active Springfield's Curriculum Coun.; mem. Tchg. Cadre, Strategic Planning Team; hon. life mem. PTA; chmn. adminstrv. coun. Hood United Meth. Ch.; children's coord., math. workshops.; sr. leader Mo. Assessment Project, 1993—. Recipient Extra Mile award, 1989; named Fremont Tchr. of the Yr., 1988, 93. Mem. ASCD, Internat. Reading Assn., Assn. for Childhood Edn., Nat. Coun. Tchrs. Math., Mo. Coun. Tchrs. Math., Mo. State Tchrs. Assn. (pres. S.W. dist. 1994-95, Educator of Yr. 1989), Springfield Edn. Assn. (pres. 1989-90, 93-96, Leader of Yr. 1990, pres. Scholarship corp. 1998-2000), Delta Kappa Gamma (1st v.p., pres. 2000-2002). Home: 8076 W Farm Road 144 Springfield MO 65802-8782

GROWE, JOAN ANDERSON, former state official; b. Mpls., Sept. 28, 1935; d. Lucille M. (Brown) Johnson; children: Michael, Colleen, David, Patrick. BS, St. Cloud State U., 1956; cert. in spl. edn., U. Minn., 1964; exec. mgmt. program State and local govt., Harvard U., 1979. Tchr. elem. pub. schs., Bloomington, Minn., 1956-58; tchr. for exceptional children elem. pub. schs. St. Paul, 1964-65; spl. edn. tchr. St. Anthony Pub. Schs., Minn., 1965-66; mem. Minn. Ho. of Reps., 1973-74; sec. of state State of Minn., St. Paul, 1975-98. Mem. exec. coun. Minn. State Bd. Investment. Mem. Women Execs. in State Govt., Women's Polit. Caucus, Minn. Women's Econ. Roundtable; candidate U.S. Senate, 1984; bd. dirs. Minn. Internat. Ctr.; mem. Nat. Commn. for the Renewal of Am. Democracy (Project Democracy); bd. dirs. Nat. Dem. Inst. for Internat. Affairs; mem. adv. bd. Hubert H. Humphrey Inst. for Pub. Affairs; bd. dirs. Mpls. Found. Recipient Minn. Sch. Bell award, 1977, YMCA Outstanding Achievement award, 1978, Disting. Alumni award St. Cloud State U., 1979, Charlotte Striebel Long Distance Runner award Minn. NOW, 1985, The Woman Who Makes a Difference award Internat. Women's Forum, 1991, Esther V. Crosby Leadership award Greater Mpls. Girl Scout Coun., 1992, Pathfinder award for Innovative Solutions, Ctr. for Policy Alternatives, 1996, Breaking the Glass Ceiling award Women Execs. in State Govt., 1998. Mem. Nat. Assn. Secs. of State (pres. 1979-80), Internat. Womens Forum. Roman Catholic.

GRUBAUGH, SALLY JO, automotive executive; b. Jemeppe-Sur-Sambre, Belgium, Aug. 29, 1946; Diploma Am. Registry of Radiological Tech., Mound Park Hosp, 1964—66. X-ray tech. Mound Park Hosp., St. Petersburg, Fla., 1964—67, Sparrow Hosp., Lansing, Mich., 1968—69; automotive worker General Motors, Lansing, Mich., 1978—. Home: 7691 W Mead Rd Saint Johns MI 48879

GRUBE, ELIZABETH, investment company executive; b. Indpls., 1917; d. Emery Warner and Jessie (Foster) Hanes; m. William F. Grube, Mar. 15, 1937; children: Carol Buck, F. William. Student, Consol. Bus. Coll., 1936, Ind. U.-Purdue U., Indpls., 1984. Pres. Prospect Investment Co. Bd. dirs. Indpls. Water Co., IWC Resources Corp., Indpls. Bd. dirs. Jameson Camp for Children, Indpls., 1981—, Greenwood Village South, Indpls., 1982—; mem. Rep. Senatorial Inner Circle, Washington, 1984. Methodist. Avocation: traveling. Home: 285 Celtic Cir Greenwood IN 46143-2458

GRUBER SPINKS, MELODY MITCHELL, protective services official; b. Columbus, Ga., Aug. 2, 1965; d. Johnnie Eldridge and Miriam Lucille (Mitchell) S.; m. Todd Charles Gruber, Apr. 6, 1998. AS in Criminal Justice, Columbus State U., 1989, BS in Criminal Justice, 1993, MS in Pub. Justice Adminstrn., 1995. Cert. peace officer, Ga., police instr., Ga. Ga. Police Officers Stds. Tng. Coun. Police officer patrol Atlanta Police Dept., 1989-94, police officer red dog/tactical narcotics team, 1994-95, investigator child molestation, 1995—, instr., 1995—. Mem. Fulton County Protocol Com. Mem. Ga. Coun. Battered Women, Atlanta, 1995-96. Named Outstanding Assistance in Fed. Investigations Violent Crimes no. dist. Ga. U.S. Atty.'s Office, 1997. Mem. Unitarian Ch.

GRUBIN, SHARON E. lawyer; b. Newark, Feb. 9, 1949; d. Harold and Blanche (Dultz) G. AB with honors, Smith Coll., 1970; JD with honors in Legal Writing and Analysis, Boston U., 1973. Bar: N.Y. 1974, U.S. Dist. Ct. (so. and ea. dists.) N.Y. 1974, U.S. Ct. Appeals (2nd cir.) 1974. Litigator White & Case, N.Y.C., 1973-84; judge U.S. Dist. Ct. (so. dist.) N.Y., N.Y.C., 1984-2000; gen. counsel Metroplitan Opera, N.Y.C., 2000—. Chair 2d Cir. Task Force on Gender, Racial and Ethnic Fairness in the Cts.; lectr. NYU Sch. Law, Yale Law Sch., Bklyn. Law Sch., N.Y. Law Sch.; dir., sec., exec. com. Lawyers' Com. on Violence, Inc. Author: (with others) Advocacy-The Art of Pleading a Cause, 1985, Removal, Federal Civil Practice, 1989, and supplement, 1993; spkr. seminars in field. Mem. ABA (chair spl. projects com. 1996-97, nat. conf. fed. trial judges, jud. adminstrn. divsn.), Nat. Assn. Women Judges (chair fed. gender bias com., publicity and pub. affairs com., newsletter com.), Fed. Bar Coun. (trustee, exec. com., chair nominating com. 1994, v.p. 1990-94, award com. 1988-94, com. on 2d cir. cts. 1982-96, long-range planning com. 1992-96), N.Y. State Bar Assn. (exec. com., nominations com., fed. cts. task force, comml. and fed. litig. sect.), N.Y. State Assn. Women Judges (bd. dirs.), Assn. of Bar of City of N.Y. (long-range planning com., chair nominating com. 1995—, chair spl. com. on legal history 1994-96, chair spl. com. on Orison S. Marden Meml. lectrs., chair 1994-96, exec. com. 1990-94, spl. com. on gender bias in fed. cts. 1991-94, coun. on jud. adminstrn. 1986-90, prof. and jud. ethics com. 1986-89, nominating com. 1984-85, 95-96, com. on jud. 1982-83, chair young lawyers com. 1979-81, com. on entertainment law, 2001-), Am. Judicature Soc. (editl. com. 1994-97). Office: Metropolitan Opera Lincoln Ctr New York NY 10023

GRUCCI BUTLER, DONNA, fireworks company executive; Pres. Grucci Fireworks, Brookhaven, NY. Prodr.: (firework prodn.) Six consecutive Presdl. Inaugurations; co-prodr.: Bklyn. Bridge, 1983, Centennial Celebration of Statue of Liberty, 1986; spokesperson for firework tours Wisk Bright Nights, Lever Brothers', Merit Harbor Lights, Philip Morris; prodr.: (firework prodn.) Wedding of Prince Abu Dhabi. Tchr. Cath. religious edn. classes to 1st graders; mem. local C. of C. events, local Head Start Programs; vol. fundraiser Am. Heart Assn.; established two scholarships Bellport H.S., 1992. Recipient Ellis Island medal of Honor for Outstanding Achievements in Arts and Entertainment Field, Nat. Ethnic Coalition Orgns., 1995. Avocations: gardening, reading. Office: Fireworks By Grucci 1 Grucci Ln Brookhaven NY 11719 E-mail: info@grucci.com.

GRUEN, MARGARET, actress; b. N.Y.C., July 24, 1949; d. Arno G. and Judith (Goldstein) Milenbach. Student, Yale Sch. Drama. Actress. Writer, performer (theatre) Tanya Talks: The Last Jew, 1997, The Young Sophisticate, 1994, What A Wonderful World, 1990, Dracula, 1970; one-woman show: Grenfell's Eccentric Characters; appeared in theatre, TV, and radio prodns., including Uncle Vanya, Garcia Lorca's New York; mem. comedy team The Chamansky Sisters. Mem. Am. Fedn. Television & Radio Artists, Actors Equity Assn., Screen Actors Guild. E-mail: gruen_margaret@yahoo.com.

GRUEN, MARSHA IRENE, marketing executive; b. Bklyn., Feb. 14, 1941; d. Harold and Adele (Brooks) Aisley; m. Peter Gruen, 1959 (div. 1977); children: Arthur, Kim; m. Bernard Berch, Sept. 8, 1985. Student, U. Calif., Berkeley, 1958-62. V.p. client svcs. Stratmar Sys., Port Chester, N.Y., 1977-93; dir. ops. Smart Demo, Wilton, Conn., 1993-94; v.p. ea. region Super Mktg., Mpls., 1994-95; dir. field promotion svcs. Mktg. Force, Detroit, 1995—96; v.p. nat. accts. Quality Mktg. Svcs., Fresno, Calif., 1996—. Vol. Bella Abzug Reelection Com., White Plains, N.Y. Mem. LVW, NOW, NAFE, Nat. Assn. Demonstration Cos. Avocations: gardening, politics, history. Home and Office: 15 Rita Rd Ridgefield CT 06877-2221

GRUHL, ANDREA MORRIS, librarian; b. Ponca City, Okla., Dec. 9, 1939; d. Luther Oscar and Hazel Evangeline (Anderson) Morris; m. Werner Mann Gruhl, July 10, 1965; children: Sonja Krista, Diana Krista. BA, Wesleyan Coll., 1961; MLS, U. Md., 1968; postgrad., Johns Hopkins U., 1970-71, U. Md., 1968, 71-73, Oxford U., 1996. Tchr. Broward County, Fla., U.S. Dept. Def. Montgomery County, Md., 1961-66; libr. Prince Georges County (Md.) Pub. Libr., 1966-68, 81-83, U. Md., College Park, 1970-72; art. history rschr. Joseph Alsop, Washington, 1972-74; libr. Howard County Pub. Libr., Columbia, Md., 1969-70, 74-79; European exch. staff Libr. of Congress, Washington, 1982-86; cataloger fed. documents GPO, Washington, 1986-93, supervisory libr., 1993—2001. Women's program adv. com., processing dept. rep. Libr. of Congress, 1983-86, mem. ofcl. Libr. of Congress delegation to Internat. Fedn. Libr. Assn. ann. conf., Munich, 1983, Chgo., 1985; state del. White House Conf. on Librs., 1978, 90. Indexer, editor: Learning Vacations, 3d edit., 1980; editor: Federal Librarian, 1994-99, NCA News & Notes, 2003-04; LCPA Index to Libr. of Congress Info. Bull., 1984. Trustee Howard County (Md.) C.C., 1989-95, Howard County Pub. Libr., Columbia, Md., 1979-87; publ. chmn. LWV Howard County, 1974, bd. dirs., 1996-97, sec., 2002-2004, co-pres., 2004—; bd. dirs. LWV Nat. Capital Area, 2002—; chair Homeland Security Com., 2003—; citizens rep. Howard County, exec. bd. Balt. Regional Planning Coun. Libr. com., 1976-79; Friends of Libr., Howard County, pres., 1976; vol. Nat. Gallery Art Libr., Washington, 1978-80. Mem.: ALA (govt. documents roundtable 1986—, fed. libr. round table 1988—, editor 1994—99, IFLA rep. 1996—, v.p. 1997—98, councilor 1997—2001, pres. 1998—99, co-chair coun. caucus 2000—01), Fed. and Armed Forces Librs. Round Table (chmn. constn. and bylaws com. 2001—, Disting. Svc. award 2001), Md. Libr. Assn. (pres. trustee divsn. 1982—83), Libr. Congress Am. Fedn. State, County and Mcpl. Employees Union (program chair 1984—86), Libr. Congress Profl. Assn. (coord. ann. staff art shows 1982—83, chair libr. sci. interest group 1985—87), Art Librs. Soc. N.Am. (coord. mems.' publ. exhbn. 1980—82), Internat. Fedn. Libr. Assns. and Instns. (sect. on cataloging, internat. std. bibliog. description/cartographic materials working gro), Assn. Coll. and Rsch. Librs., D.C. Libr. Assn. (co-chair mgmt. interest group 1996—97, v.p. 2001—02, pres. 2002—03, dir. 2004—), Libr. Adminstrn. and Mgmt. Assn. (planning and evaluation libr. svcs. 1996—97), Oxford U. Soc., Md. Assn. C.C. Trustees (sec. 1991—92, bd. dirs. 1992—93), UN Assn. Nat. Capital Area Chpt. (membership com. 1992, Md. tel. chair 1992—94, co-chair endowment com. 2004—), Md. Assn. C.C. (bd. dirs. 1992—95), Beta Phi Mu (v.p., pres.-elect Washington Area chpt. 2004—, Washington chpt. v.p., pres. elect 2004—). Democrat. Lutheran. Home: 5990 Jacobs Ladder Columbia MD 21045-3817

GRULING, KAY ANN, family physician; b. Merrill, Wis., Sept. 28, 1961; d. Robert Herman and Esther Martha (Schulz) G.; m. Timothy Charles Buttke, June 11, 1988; children: Calla Kay, Isaac Friedrich. Student, U. Wis., Wausau, 1982, U. Wis., 1984, Rheinische Frederick-Wilhelms U., Bonn, West Germany, 1984, U. Wis., 1988. Diplomate Am. Bd. Family Practice. Intern and resident in family medicine U. Wis. Wausau Program, 1988-91; family physician Marshfield Clinic,Wausau Med. Ctr., Wis., 1991—. Mem. edn. com., exec. com. Wausau Family Practice Ctr., 1988-91, bioethics com., 1989-91; mem. pediat. sedation task force Wausau Hosp., 1991-93, edn. com., 1992— (chairperson 1993-95, 98—); mem. physician extender task force Wausau Med. Ctr., 1991—, mktg. com., 1992-99, physician charging practices subcom., 1993-95, walk-in dept. task force, 1994, sect. head Family Practice dept., 2002—; mem. Shadowing Program U. Wis. Stevens Point, 1992-95; vol. faculty Residency Program Wausau Family Practice, 1991—; mem. domestic abuse task force, med. dir. Marathon County Med. Soc., 1993; v.p. U. Wis. Marathon Ctr. Found., 1994-95; bd. dirs. U. Wis. Marathon Ctr. Bd. dirs., mem. public edn. com. Marathon Unit Am. Cancer Soc., 1992-95; active Trinity Lutheran Ch., 1988—; active local and regional polit. campaigns, 1988—; mem., vol. Farm Bureau. Mem. Wis. Acad. Family Physicians, 1983— (publs. and pub. rels. com. 1991—, chairperson, 1992-95), legis. affairs com., 1991, women's task force, 1991-92, access to health care task force, 1992—, newsletter editor, 1992-95, Wis. Valley Dist., 1988—, pres. 1991—). Democrat. Lutheran. Avocations: walking, cooking, travel, decorating, sports. Home: 620 Hwy 0 Wausau WI 54401 Office: Marshfield Clinic Wasau Med Ctr 2727 Plaza Dr Wausau WI 54401-4129

GRULIOW, AGNES FORREST, artist, educator; b. Davenport, Iowa, July 5, 1912; d. James Lindsay and Agnes (Johnston) F.; m. Leo Gruliow, Sept. 25, 1945; children: Frank Forrest, Rebecca Agnes Lindsay. BA, Antioch Coll., Yellow Springs, Ohio, 1938; student, Art Students League, N.Y.C., 1963-66. Resident dir. Am. Peoples Sch., N.Y.C., 1937-41; asst. nat. sec. Nat. Fedn. Settlements, N.Y.C., 1941-43; assoc. pers. dir.,asst. prof. Antioch Coll. Extramural Sch., Yellow Springs, 1943-45; index designer-editor Current Digest of Soviet Press, Washington and N.Y.C., 1949-53; freelance editor N.Y.C., 1954-57; tchr. art City & Country Sch., N.Y.C., 1966-68; hostess Am. Friends Svc. Com. Internat. Seminar, Oestgeest, The Netherlands, 1960, Poughkeepsie, N.Y., 1961; sr. vis. fellow Woodrow Wilson Found., 1977-80; proprietor art studio N.Y.C., 1961-69, Worthington, Ohio, 1970-72; art therapy asst. Harding Hosp., Worthington, 1970-72. One-woman show at Antioch Coll., 1967; group shows Herndon Gallery, Yellow Springs, Ohio, 2000, Northwood Art Space, Columbus, Ohio, 2003. Pres. Columbia U. Greenhouse Nursery Sch., N.Y.C., 1954-59; bd. mem. Open Door Day Care Ctr., N.Y.C., 1954-59; mem. founding and adv. bd. East Harlem Tutoring Program, N.Y.C., 1965-73; mem. bd. Columbus Area Internat. Program, 1970-72, 79-87, edn. sec., 1981, pres., 1982-85, chair adv. bd., 1983-87; del. Nat. Bd. Coun. Internat. Programs, Cleve., 1981-83; mem. bd. Cmty. Svc., Inc., Yellow Springs, 1981-99. Mem. AAUW, Columbus Meml. Soc., Columbus Mus. Art, South Ctrl. Ohio Preservation Soc., UNA, UNICEF, World Federalist Assn. Ctrl. Ohio (membership sect. 1987-94), Crichton Club (Columbus), Order Eastern Star. Home: 163 E Lane Ave Columbus OH 43201-1212

GRUMMAN, CORNELIA, newswriter; B in Pub. Policy, Duke U.; M in Pub. Policy, Harvard U. Stringer Washington post News and Observer, Beijing, 1989; met., state, govt. and Internet reporter Chgo. Tribune, mem. editl. bd., 2000—. Recipient Casey medal for meritorious journalism, Studs Terkel award for coverage of disadvantaged communities, Herman Kogan award for editls. on death penalty, Peter Lisagor award for commentary, Pulitzer prize for editl. writing, 2003. Office: Chgo Tribune 777 W Chicago Ave Chicago IL 60610*

GRUNDBERG, BETTY, state legislator, property manager; b. Woden, Iowa, Feb. 16, 1938; d. Edwin and Eva Ruth Meyer; m. Arnie Grundberg, Dec. 31, 1960; children: Christine, Julie, Michael, Susan. BA, Wartburg Coll., 1959; MA, U. Iowa, 1969; postgrad., Drake U. Cert. tchr. Property mgr. and renovator, Des Moines, 1973—; with Des Moines Sch. Bd., 1975-90; legis. State of Iowa, Des Moines, 1993—. Chmn. edn. com.; mem. human resources com., labor com. Active LWV, Des Moines, 1972—. Republican. Home and Office: 224 Foster Dr Des Moines IA 50312 2540

GRUNDLER, MARY JANE LANG, business education educator; b. Wentworth, Mo., Oct. 26, 1919; d. Charles Fremont and Angeline Rose (Baker) Lang; m. Francis Edward Grundler, Dec. 26, 1963. BS in Edn., U. Mo., 1944, MEd, 1947, EdD, 1960. Tchr. Shiloh Sch., Carthage, Mo., 1940-41, Duenweg (Mo.) Elem. Sch., 1941-42; bus. tchr. Duenweg High Sch., 1942-43, Seneca (Mo.) High Sch., 1943-45, Lindenwood Coll., St. Charles, Mo., 1945-47; instr. bus. tchr. edn. U. Mo., Columbia, 1947-60, asst. prof., 1960-67, assoc. prof., 1967-76, prof., 1976-85, prof. emeritus, 1985—. Coord. bus. edn. Coll. Edn. U. Mo., Columbia, 1968-80. Contbr. articles to profl. bus. edn. jours. and yearbooks. Bd. dirs. Koinonia House, Columbia, 1988—. Recipient Disting. Svc. award U. Mo. Alumni Assn., 1986, Outstanding Alumnus award Mo. So. State Coll., Joplin, 1988. Mem. AAUW (state treas. 1988-90), Am. Vocat. Assn. (Outstanding Svc. cert. Divsn. Bus. Edn. 1980), Nat. Assn. Tchr. Educators Bus. Edn. (Recognition award 1984), Nat. Bus. Edn. Assn., Ret. Tchrs. Assn. Mo. (newsletter editor 1988-90), Mo. State Tchrs. Assn., Mo. Vocat. Assn., Mo. Bus. Edn. Assn. (Outstanding Bus. Educator 1979, Disting. Svc. award 1985, past pres., v.p., sec., charter inductee Who's Who in Mo., Bus. Edn. 1992), U. Mo. Alumni Assn. (life, sec. bd. dirs. 1972-86, historian 1994—), Pi Lambda Theta (sponsor Alpha chpt. 1989—, mem. nat. nominating com. 1992-93), Delta Kappa Gamma. Roman Catholic. Avocations: reading, music. Home: 1406 Business Loop 70 W #13 Columbia MO 65202-1324

GRUNNET, MARGARET LOUISE, pathologist, educator; b. Mpls., Feb. 20, 1936; d. Leslie Nels and Grace Harriet (Thomson) Grunnet; m. Irving Noel Einhorn, Mar. 10, 1972; stepchildren: Jeffrey Allan, Franne Ruth, Eric Carl, Stanley Glenn. BA summa cum laude, U. Minn., Mpls., 1958; MD, U. Minn., 1962; MS, Ohio State U., 1969. Resident in psychiatry U. Pa. Sch. Medicine, Phila., 1963-64; resident anatomic pathology Presbyn.-U. Pa. Med. Ctr., Phila., 1965-66; fellow neuropathology Phila. Gen. Hosp., 1967, Ohio State U. Hosp., Columbus, 1968-69; instr. Ohio State U., 1969; asst. prof. U. Utah Sch. Medicine, Salt Lake City, 1970-76, assoc. prof., 1976-80; assoc. prof. pathology U. Conn. Sch. Medicine, Farmington, 1980-90, prof., 1990—. Contbr. articles to profl. jours. Mem. Am. Med. Women's Assn., Internat. Soc. Neuropathology, Conn. Soc. Pathologists, World Muscle Soc., Am. Assn. Neuropathologists, Phi Beta Kappa, Alpha Omega Alpha. Mem. Ch. of Christ. Avocations: reading, music, travel. Home: 1550 Asylum Ave West Hartford CT 06117-2805 Office: U Conn Health Ctr Dept Pathology Farmington CT 06032

GRUNWALD, ILANA SHLOMIT, psychologist; b. N.Y.C., Feb. 14; d. Chaim and Mady Grunwald; m. Yoni Bardavid, Aug. 27, 1986. MA, Queens Coll., N.Y.C., 1990; MPhil, CUNY, N.Y.C., 1994, PhD, 1995. Lic. psychologist N.Y. Sr. psychologist Rusk Inst., N.Y.C., NY, 1994—. Contbr. articles to profl. jours. Mem.: APA, N.Y. Neuropsychol. Group, Phi Beta Kappa. Office: Rusk Inst NYU Med Ctr 400 E 34th St New York NY 10016

GRUOL, MARY CATHERINE SCHUETZ, human resources operations executive; b. Huntingburg, Ind., May 24, 1946; d. Hubert John Schuetz; m. Peter Raymond Gruol, Aug. 15, 1970; children: Michael, Jeffrey. Cert. x-ray tech., St. Mary's Sch. Nursing, 1965; student, IBM Edn. Ctr., 1967-70, Framingham State Coll., Northeastern Coll.; MEd, Cambridge Coll., 1994. Project mgr. MIS Barnett Computing Co., Jacksonville, Fla., 1971-75; sr. sys. analyst William Underwood Co., Westwood, Mass., 1975-80; co-owner Topside Properties, Chatham, Mass., 1985-89; pres. Bobbin Hollow Inc., Amherst, Mass., 1989-91; cons. Lighthouse Capital Mgmt., Boston, 1991-93; dir. ops. and human resources Bus. Matters, Inc., Waltham, Mass., 1993-96; pres., owner New Venture Solutions, Bedford, Mass., 1996-97; v.p. human resources MathSoft, Inc., Cambridge, Mass., 1997-00; chief adminstrv. officer, v.p. Mobile Internet Account., Bedford, Mass., 2000—02; chief oper. officer Mobile Internet Access, Inc., Bedford, Mass., 2002—. Mem. N.E. Human Resources Group, N.E. Human Resources Assn., 128 Venture Capital Group, Aero Club of New Eng. Home: 64 River Ridge Sudbury MA 01776-1428 E-mail: mgruol@aol.com.

GRUTMAN, JEWEL HUMPHREY, lawyer, writer; b. N.Y.C., Mar. 13, 1931; d. Robert and Gladys Humphrey; m. Robert W. Bjork, June 26, 1954 (div. Apr. 22, 1975); 1 child, Bruce Bjork; m. Roy Grutman, Oct. 30, 1975 (wid. 1994); m. Fredrick Yonkman, July 4, 1998. BA magna cum laude, Mt. Holyoke Coll., 1952; LLB, Columbia U., 1955. Bar: N.Y., U.S. Dist. Ct. (So. Dist.) N.Y. 1971, U.S. Dist. Ct. (ea. dist.) N.Y. 1974, U.S. Dist. Ct. Conn. 1984, U.S. Supreme Ct. 1984. Atty. Debevoise & Plimpton, N.Y.C., 1954-60; ptnr. Eaton Van Winkle, N.Y.C., 1976-79, Grutman Greene & Humphrey, N.Y.C., 1979—. Co-author: (with CD-ROM) The Ledgerbook of Thomas Blue Eagle, 1994 (Christopher award 1995, Internat. Reading Assn. award), The Sketchbook of Thomas Blue Eagle, 2001, (CD-ROM) The Journey of Thomas Blue Eagle, 1995 (Best Project award Intermedia, Asia, 1995, Creative NGee ANN Disting. award 1995, EMMA award best visual content 1996); asst. prodr., editor (ednl. film on art) Where Time is a River (1st prize Women's Film Festival); contbr. photograph illustrations: The Reforming Power of the Scriptures, 1996; developer series of designs based on Native Am. art; contbr. articles to mags. and newspapers. Dir. Inwood Ho., N.Y.C., 1970-80; past mem. various coms. Mt. Holyoke Coll.; mem. com. sr. advisors N.Y. Commn. for Internat. Bus. and UN, 1997; past chmn. com. to establish Barbara Black Fellowship at Columbia U. Law Sch.; past pres. 85th St. Playground Assn., N.Y.C.; active supporter The Children's Storefront, Harlem, N.Y.C., N.Y. Jr. League. Mem. Assn. Bar City N.Y., The Stanwich Club (Greenwich, Conn.). Avocations: opera, golf, tennis, poetry. E-mail: bijou203@optonline.net.

GRUVER, NANCY, publishing executive; Founder, pub. New Moon Pub., Dulath, Minn., 1992—. Produces (mag.) New Moon: The Magazine for Firls and Their Dreams, 1992—, New Moon: For Adults Who Care About Girls, —, (book series) Friendship, 1999, Sports, 1999, Money, Power and Independence, 1999, Writing, 1999. Office: New Moon Publishing 34 E Superior St #200 Duluth MN 55802-3003 E-mail: newmoon@newmoon.org.

GRYMES, ROSE, government agency administrator; PhD in Cancer Biology and Med. Microbiology, Stanford U., 1983. Cell biologist life scis. divsn. NASA, Ames, Calif.; assoc. dir. NASA Astrobiology Inst., Ames, Calif. Office: NASA Ames Rsch Ctr Bldg 240 Rm 107 Moffett Field CA 94035

GRZESIAK, KATHERINE ANN, primary educator; BS, Ctrl. Mich. U., 1968; MA in Tchg., Saginaw Valley State U., 1975; postgrad., various univs., 1975—. 6th grade tchr. Buena Vista Sch. Dist., Saginaw, Mich., 1968-69, 70-71; tchr. Carrollton Pub. Schs., Saginaw, 1972-80, St. Peter and Paul Elem. Sch., Saginaw, 1981-84, Sch. Dist. of City of Saginaw, 1984-90; instr. Ctr. for Innovation in Edn., Saratoga, Calif., 1989—; tchr. Midland (Mich.) Pub. Schs., 1991—; 5th grade tchr. Eastlawn Elem., Midland. Adj. faculty Saginaw Valley State U., University Center, Mich., 1976-80, 88-90; presenter in field. Contbr. articles to profl. jours. Recipient Presdl. award for Excellence in Sci. and Math. Tchg., 1994, Top Tchr. in Mich. Met. Woman mag., 1997, Nat. Educator award Milken Family Found., 1998; named Mich. Tchr. of Yr., 1998. Home: 3115 Mcgill St Midland MI 48642-3928 Office: Eastlawn Elem Sch 115 Eastlawn Dr Midland MI 48640-5561 E-mail: grzesiak@mindnet.org.

GUADARRAMA, BELINDA, computer company executive; B of Econs., Trinity U.; postgrad., U. Tex. Pres. CEO GC Micro Corp., 1986—. Chair NASA Minority Bus. Resource Adv. Com., 1997-99. Recipient Adminstrs. Excellence award U.S. Small Bus. Adminstrn., 1997; named 1 of 4 Women Who Could Be Pres., LLWV, San Francisco, 1998, U.S. Dept. Commerce NAt. Minority Female Entrepreneur of Yr., 1997. Mem. Hispanic Bus. CEO Roundtable, Calif. Hispanic C. of C. (Outstanding Bus. Mem. of Yr. award 1997). Office: GC Micro 25 Leveroni Ct Novato CA 94949-5726

GUAJARDO, ELISA, counselor, educator; b. Roswell, N. Mex., Nov. 13, 1932; d. Alejo Najar and Hortensia (Jiminez) Garcia; m. David Roberto Guajardo, Oct. 15, 1950; 1 child, Elsie Edith. BS, Our Lady of the Lake U., 1962, MEd, 1971; MA, Chapman U., 1977. Cert. tchr., adminstr., counselor, Calif. Elem. tchr. San Antonio (Tex.) Sch. Dist., 1962-63; tchr. social sci. Newport Mesa Sch. Dist., Costa Mesa, Calif., 1963-67, Orange (Calif.) Unified Sch. Dist., 1967-70, project dir., 1970-71, tchr. English, 1972-73, counselor, 1973—. Pres. Bilingual, Bicultural Parent Adv. Bd., Orange, Calif., 1971-72; reader bilingual projects Calif. State Dept. Edn., Orange, 1971-72; vis. lectr. We. Wash. Univ., Bellingham, 1972-73; mem. curriculum and placement couns., Orange Unified Sch. Dist., 1973-78, 95-96. Author: (Able)Adaptations of Bilingual/Bicultural Edn, Fed. Project Proposal. Mem. NEA, AAUW, Calif. Tchrs. Assn., Orange Unified Edn. Assn. Hon., Alpha Chi, Our Lady of Lake U., Tex. chpt. Democrat. Mem. Assemblies of God Church. Avocations: choir and solo singing, piano, marimba, organ. Home: 335 E Jackson Ave Orange CA 92867-5743 Office: Canyon HS 220 S Imperial Hwy Anaheim CA 92807-3945 E-mail: davielisa2@juno.com.

GUARD, PATRICIA J. federal agency administrator; b. Lafayette, Ind., June 9, 1948; BS, MS, Purdue U. Therapist speech, lang. and hearing Logansport Area Joint Spl. Svcs. Coop., 1974-76, supr. speech dept., 1976-78; dir. spl. edn. Boone-Clinton-NW Hendricks Count Joint Svcs. Spl. Edn. Coop., 1978-81; rsch. asst. U.S. Ho. of Reps., 1981-82; legis. specialist Office Legis. and Pub. Affairs, 1983-84; acting dir. Office Spl. Edn. Programs Dept. Edn., 1985-86, deputy dir. Office Spl. Edn. Programs, 1984-85, 86-87, sr. legis. analyst Office Legis. and Pub. Affairs, 1987-90, dir. policy and planning staff Office Spl. Edn. and Rehabilitative Svcs., 1990-92, dep. dir. Office Spl. Edn., 1992-93, acting dir. Office Spl. Edn. Programs, 1993-94; mem. sr. exec. svc. Office Edn. Programs, Washington, 1994—. Vice chmn., trustee Arlington Cmty. Residence, Inc., 1993, bd. dirs., 1989—. Fellow Inst. Ednl. Leadership, 1981; recipient Disting. Alumni award Purdue U., 1989, Mentor award Dept. Edn., 1994. Office: Spl Edn Programs 330 C St SW Washington DC 20201-0001

GUARDO, CAROL J. association executive; b. Hartford, Conn., Apr. 12, 1939; d. C. Fred and Marion (Biase) G. BA, St. Joseph Coll., 1961; MA, U. Detroit, 1963; PhD, U. Denver, 1966. Asst. prof. psychology Eastern Mich. U., Ypsilanti, 1966-68; assoc. prof., staff psychologist U. Denver, 1968-73; assoc. prof., dean coll. Utica Coll. of Syracuse U., Utica, N.Y., 1973-76; prof., dean Coll. Liberal Arts, Drake U., Des Moines, 1976-80; provost, prof. U. Hartford, 1980-85; pres. R.I. Coll., Providence, 1986-90, Great Lakes Colls. Assn., Ann Arbor, Mich., 1990—. Mem. Iowa Humanities Bd., 1976-80, pres., 1978-80; bd. dirs. Am. Coun. Edn., People's Bank. Author: The Adolescent As Individual: Issues and Insights, 1975; contbr. articles to profl. jours. Trustee St. Joseph Coll., Monmouth Coll., Colby-Sawyer Coll., Cabrini Coll. NSF fellow, 1964, NIMH fellow, 1964-66. Mem. Am. Assn. Higher Edn., Assn. Am. Colls. (vice chair 1987, chair 1988), Am. Psychol. Assn., Assn. Gen. and Liberal Studies (pres. 1979-81), Soc. Rsch. in Child Devel., Greater Providence C. of C., Phi Beta Kappa. Office: Great Lakes Colls Assn 2929 Plymouth Rd Ste 207 Ann Arbor MI 48105-3206

GUARNERE, JOANNE, protective services official; b. Rochester, N.Y., May 6, 1952; d. Paul and Betty Jane Guarnere. BSW, SUNY, Brockport, 1974; MS in Edn., Nazareth Coll., 1990. Cert. police instr., firearms cert. N.Y. State Bur. Mcpl. Police. Caseworker Monroe County Dept. Social Svcs., Rochester, N.Y., 1975-79; adminstrv. coord. City of Rochester, 1979-84; sr. probation officer County of Monroe, Rochester, 1984—; group facilitator Genesee Mental Health Ctr., Rochester, 1995—. Bd. mem. Domestic Violence Consortium, Rochester, 1994-96, Monroe County-City of Rochester Victims Task Force, 1994—; adj. prof. Monroe C.C., Rochester, 1996—. Literacy tutor Vols. Am., Rochester, 1999—; probation co-chair Heart Assn.-Heart Walk, Rochester, 1999. Mem. Am. Probation and Parole Assn., Civil Svc. Employees Assn. (pres. probation sect. 1996-99, v.p. 1999—), N.Y. State Probation Officers Assn., Monroe County Probation Officers Assn. Avocations: bicycling, hiking, photography, travel, literature. Office: Monroe County Office Probation 217 Main St W Rochester NY 14614-1101

GUARNIERI, ALBINA, Canadian government official, Canadian legislator; b. Faeto, Italy, June 23, 1953; BA, MA, McGill U. Solicitor Gen., Can., 1980; liberal leader1981 election; press sec. Mayor of Toronto, Ont., Can.; M.P. Ho. Commons, 1988—; parliamentary sec. to min. Canadian heritage Govt. of Can., Ottawa, 1993—96, assoc. min. nat. defense, 2003—, min. state (civil preparedness), 2003—. Office: House of Commons Rm 450 Confederation Bldg Ottawa ON Canada K1A OA6 also: Dept Nat Def Maj Gen George R Pearkes Bldg 101 Col By Drive 15 NT K1A 0K2 Ottawa ON Canada*

GUCIARDO, JOAN, family and consumer sciences educator; b. Centralia, Ill., Oct. 23, 1951; d. Ralph and Dorothy Margaret (Liszewski) Prusacki; m. John Edward Guciardo, Aug. 10, 1974. BS, Ea. Ill. U., 1973, MS, 1986. Tchr. family and consumer scis. Althoff Cath. H.S., Belleville, Ill., 1973-74, Assumption H.S., East St. Louis, Ill., 1974-75, O'Fallon (Ill.) Twp. H.S., 1975—. Mem. NAFE, Am. Assn. Family and Consumer Scis. (cert.), Ill. Career and Tech. Assn., Profl. Assn. Custom Clothiers, Profl. Dressmakers Assn. Roman Catholic. Avocations: reading, sewing. Home: 204 Ross Ln Belleville IL 62220-2843 Office: O'Fallon Twp H S 600 S Smiley St O'Fallon IL 62269-2316

GUCKERT, NORA JANE GASKILL, medical and surgical nurse, hospice nurse, holistic consultant; b. Pitts., June 17, 1945; d. James E. and Nora L. (McAllister) Gaskill; m. Ray H. Guckert, Aug. 1, 1964 (div. May 2001); children: Brian K. Sr., Bruce M., Brenda L. Jansen. LPN, C.C. Allegheny County, Pitts., 1976, AS in Nursing, 1982; BS, Clayton Coll. Holistic Med., 1998, MS, 1999, PhD, 2001. Staff nurse St. Margaret's Meml. Hosp., Aspinwall, Pa., 1976-86; vis. nurse Personal Touch Home Care, Pitts., 1986-87, Norfolk, Va., 1995-98; pvt. practice, 1988—; staff nurse Kimberly Quality Home Care/Portsmouth (Va.) Naval Hosp., 1988-90; liason Sentara Home Health, 1992; cons. Holistic Health of Tidewater, Inc., Va., 1995-99; dir. nursing Med. Staff Svcs., Inc., Va. Beach, 1997-98; hospice dir. Personal Tech Home Care, 1997—99; home health nurse Tender Loving Care/Staff Builders Inc., 2000—02; dir. nursing edn. Virginia Beach, Newport News and Richmond campsuses Med. Careers Inst., 2000—03; home health nurse Comfort Care Home Health, 2003—; cons. Holistic Health of Virginia Beach Cons. Svc., 1997—. Dir. 1st holistic conf. by profls., Virginia Beach, 1997; cons. Holistic Health of Va. Beach Cons. Svc., 1997—. Author materials on nutritional needs. Vol. Chesapeake Indigent Care Clinic. Home: 3280 Winterberry Ln Virginia Beach VA 23453-5910 E-mail: nonniejphd@cox.net., nguckert@comfortcarehomehealthstaff.com.

GUDE, NANCY CARLSON, lawyer; b. Kane, Pa., Aug. 5, 1948; d. Edward Walter and Theo Alberta (Herzog) Carlson. BA in History, Pa. State U., 1969; MS in Computer Sci., U. Central Fla., 1981; JD, Thomas M. Cooley Law Sch., 2001. Bar: Fla. 2001, U.S. Dist. Ct. (no. and so. dists.) Fla. 2003. Programmer Group Hospitalization, Inc., Washington, 1969-70; programmer analyst Space Age Computer Sys., Washington, 1970-73, Ky. Fried Chicken, Louisville, 1973-75; sys. analyst Sentinel Comm. Co., Orlando, Fla., 1975 77, programming supr., 1977-78, sys. and programming mgr., 1978-80, asst. dir. data processing, 1980, mgr. staff devel., 1981-82; mgmt. info. svcs. mgr. Sun-Sentinel Co., Ft. Lauderdale, Fla., 1982-83, v.p., dir. info. sys., 1983-94, sys. cons., 1994-98; assoc. atty. Walton Lantaff Schroeder & Carson, Ft. Lauderdale, 2002—. Adj. instr. U. Ctrl. Fla., Orlando, 1981—82. Participant Leadership Broward X; chair LBX Artserve Intervention Group. Recipient Thomas M. Cooley Leadership Achievement award, 2001. Mem.: Broward County Bar Assn., Fed. Bar Assn., The Fla. Bar, Pa. State U. Alumni Assn. (Ft. Lauderdale chpt., treas. 1990—92, v.p. 1992—93, pres. 1993—95). Presbyterian. Home: 1101 River Reach Dr Apt 216 Fort Lauderdale FL 33315-1177

GUDEA, DARLENE, publishing company executive; Group pub. Call Ctr./CRM group Advanstar Tech. Comms., Santa Ana, Calif., 2000—. Office: Advanstar Comms 201 Sandpointe Ave Ste 600 Santa Ana CA 92707-8700

GUDMUNDSON, BARBARA ROHRKE, ecologist; b. Chgo. d. Lloyd Ernest and Helen (Bullard) Rohrke; m. Valtyr Emil Gudmundson, June 14, 1951 (dec. Dec. 1982); children: Holly Mekkín Leighton, Martha Rannveig. BA, U. Tenn., 1950; MA, Minn. State U., 1965; PhD, Iowa State U., 1969. Microbiologist Hektoen Inst. & Ill. Ctr. Hosp., Chgo., 1950-52; immunologist Jackson Meml. Lab., Bar Harbor, Maine, 1952-54; dist. ecologist Corps of Engrs., St. Paul, 1971-72; sr. ecologist North Star Rsch. Inst., Mpls., 1972-76; staff engr. Met. Waste Control Commn., St. Paul, 1976-77; pres., prin. ecologist Ecosystem Rsch. Svc./Upper Midwest, Mpls., 1978-99. Pvt. practice as cons. ecologist, Des Moines and Mpls., 1968-70; mem. Citizens League Task Force on the Mississippi Riverfront, 1973-74; mem. adv. com. Mpls. Lakes Water Quality, Mpls., 1974-75; river ecologist Mississippi River Canoe Expdn., Coll. of the Atlantic, Bar Harbor, 1979. Author: V. Emil Gudmundson: Icelandic Canadian Unitarian, A Personal Biography, 1991; editor-in-chief The Icelandic Unitarian Connection, 1984; contbr. articles to profl. jours. Mem. from 61st dist. Dem.-Farmer-Labor Ctr. Com., Minn., 1978-80; mgr. Minnehaha Creek Watershed Dist., 1979-83, sec., 1982-83; mem. Capital Long-Range Improvements Com., Mpls., 1981; mem. steering com. Nokomis East Neighborhood Assn., 1995-97, bd. dirs. 1997-2003. Recipient Leadership award Izaak Walton League, 1982; River Basin Ecology grantee Iowa Acad. Scis., Cedar Falls, 1976, Mississippi River Ecology grantee Freshwater Biol. Rsch. Found., Navarre, Minn., 1979; Fulbright Sr. Rsch. grantee USA/Iceland Fulbright Commns., Washington, Reykjavik, 1986, 92. Mem. NOW (Minn. state bd. 1989-96, Anita Hill Courage and Justice award Twin Cities chpt. 1994, Minn.-NOW's Charlotte Striebel Long Distance Runner award 1998), Ecol. Soc. Am. (pres. Minn. chpt. 1971-75), Geol. Soc. Minn. (pres. 1981), Phycological Soc. Am., Internat. Assn. Diatom Rsch., Icelandic Am. Assn. Minn., Hekla Icelandic Club (pres. 1977), Fulbright Assn., Minn. Interfaith Campaign Climate Change, 2001—, Sigma Xi, Phi Kappa Phi, Sigma Delta Epsilon-Grad. Women in Sci. (nat. mem. com. 1990-93, chmn. 1991-93). Unitarian Universalist. Achievements include discovery of diatom genus Biddulphia in the state of Iowa; establishment of Diatom Herbarium of Iceland. Home: 5505 28th Ave S Minneapolis MN 55417-1957

GUDNITZ, ORA M. COFEY, secondary school educator; b. Crawforddsville, Ark., Jan. 24, 1934; d. Daniel S. and Mary (Oglesby) Cofey; children: Ingrid M. Hunt, Carl Erik, Katrina Beatrice. BA, Lane Coll., Jackson, Tenn., 1955; MEd, Temple U., 1969; student, U. Copenhagen, 1957; MA in Theol. Studies, Ea. Bapt. Theol. Sem., Pa., 1995, Eastern Bapt. Theol. Sem., 1995. Cert. permanent English, social studies and French tchr., Pa. Tchr. English, chmn. dept. Sayre Jr. High Sch., Phila.; tchr. English, Overbrook High Sch., Phila. Founder, exec. dir. Young Communicators Workshop, Inc.; lectr., Denmark. Contbr. articles to newspapers, poetry to anthologies. Recipient award Chapel of Four Chaplains, 1976, Women in Edn. award, 1988; grantee Haas Found., 1977, also others. Mem. Nat. Coun. Tchrs. English, Assn. for Ednl. Communication and Tech., Phi Delta Kappa, Delta Sigma Theta.

GUERRA, C. INES, real estate broker; arrived in U.S., 1969; d. Jose and Ines Guerra; children: Gloria Ines Toro, Ximena Romero. Diploma in early childhood edn., Colombia, 1965. Lic. real estate broker N.Y. Tchr. St. Tomas Aquino, Cali, Colombia, 1965—69; asst. mgr. St. Regis Hotel, N.Y.C., 1982—85, reservations mgr., 1985—88; front office mgr. UN Plaza Park Hyatt, N.Y.C., 1988—92, dir. ops., 1992—98; real estate broker Ines Guerra Realty, Rego Park, NY, 1999—. Sec. bd. dirs. Park City Estates, Rego Park. Recipient cert. recognition, U.S. Secret Svc., 1990, cert. appreciation, 1995. Avocations: travel, reading, theater. Home: 61-25 97th St # 9J Rego Park NY 11374 Office: Ines Guerra Realty Inc 63-26 99th St Rego Park NY 11374 Business E-Mail: iguerra@mlslirealtor.com.

GUERRA, EDNA, pharmacist; b. Kingsville, Tex., Dec. 4, 1952; d. Fidel and Rebecca Rodriguez; m. R. David Guerra, Aug. 16, 1975; children; Omar D., Sara Elena. BS in Elem. Edn., Tex. A&I U., 1975; BS in Pharmacy, U. Tex., 1981. Cert. tchr., Tex.; registered pharmacist, Tex. Tchr. Bishop (Tex.) Consol. Ind. Sch. Dist., 1975-76, N.E. Sch. Dist., San Antonio, 1976-77; cmty. pharmacist Laredo, Tex., 1981-90, McAllen, Tex., 1990-93. Mem. adv. bd. McAllen Internat. Mus., 1994—; bd. dirs. McAllen Ednl. Found., 1999—; co-chair United Way of Hidalgo County, McAllen, 1995, mem. allocation com., 1996, 98, 99; vol. Milam Elem. Sch. PTSA, McAllen, 1990, Gonzalez Elem. Sch. PTSA, McAllen, 1991-95; docent McAllen Internat. Mus., 1991-93, coll. fundraiser admittance chair, 1996, mem. com. 1997, coll. fundraiser, 1998-99; bd. dirs. Arthritis Found. Rio Grande Valley, McAllen, 1993-94, Rio Grande Valley Pharm. Assn., Mcallen, 1991-94; v.p. Young Women's Book Rev. League, McAllen, 1995-96; CCD instr. Our Lady of Sorrows Cath. Ch., McAllen, 1991; gala admittance chair Easter Seals Assn., McAllen, 1997; adminstr. Fidel Rodriguez Family Scholarships, Bishop Consol. Ind. Sch. Sch. Dist., 1996—; vol. Nat. Hispanic Scholarship Fund, McAllen, 1996, South Tex. Symphony Assn. fundraiser, McAllen, 1998, 99, Valley Alliance of Mentors for Opportunities and Scholarships, McAllen, 1998, Food Bank, Corpus Christi, Tex., 1999. Recipient Vol. of Yr. award Easter Seals, 1997. Mem. U. Tex. Ex-Students' Assn., Tex. Pharm. Assn. Roman Catholic. Avocation: reading. Home: 423 Nightingale Ave Mcallen TX 78504-1716

GUERRA, JUANITA PATRICIA, psychologist, educator; b. N.Y., N.Y., July 4, 1970; d. Jose Manuel Guerra and Patria Daza; m. Javier Ivan Duarte, June 19, 2000; 1 child, Izabella Natasha. BA, MA, City Coll., 1993; PhD, CUNY, 1998. Cert. psychologist N.Y., hypnotherapist Hypnotherapy Wellness Inst. Family therapist, supr. Puerto Rican Family Inst., N.Y., 1993—97; psychology intern Manhattan Psych. Ctr., N.Y., 1997—98; clin. psychologist Harlem Hosp., N.Y., 1999—. Prof. psychology Coll. New Rochelle, N.Y., 2002—; instr. Colombia Coll. Physicians and Surgeons, N.Y., 2003—; cons. Jackson Children's Reality House, N.Y., 2002—, supr., 2002—, mem. physician rev. bd., 2003—. Fellow Magnet fellowship, CUNY, 1993—97. Mem.: Am. Psychol. Assn., Golden Key, Phi Beta Kappa. Democrat. Avocations: meditation, journaling, reading, exercise. Home: 208 20 48 Ave Bayside NY 11364 Office: Harlem Hospital Ctr 530 Lenox Ave RBP 1085A New York NY 10037 E-mail: juanitapg@aol.com.

GUERRA, MAYRA, insurance company executive; b. N.Y.C., Aug. 3, 1968; d. Israel and Eloisa (Marquis) Anta; m. Jose Antonio Guerra, Feb. 8, 1992; children: Tony Scott, Elle Frances. Lic. prodr., Kovats Sch. Ins., Paramus, N.J., 1989. Customer svc. ins. rep. Muller Agy., Hoboken, N.J., 1988-90, Scirocco Assocs., North Bergen, N.J., 1990-96, Carle & Christie, Englewood Cliffs, N.J., 1996-99. Mem. Nat. Assn. Ins. Women No. (chair safety com. 1998-99). Office: Gulfshore Ins Inc 4100 Goodlette Rd N Ste 100 Naples FL 34103-3303 E-mail: mgu@gulfshoreinsurance.com.

GUERRERO, LISA (LISA GUERRERO-COLES), sports reporter; b. Chgo., Apr. 8, 1964; m. Scott Erickson. Cheerleader Los Angeles Rams; dir, choreographer Atlanta Falcons Cheerleaders, New England Patriots; reporter Extra, 1994; co-host Sports Geniuses, 2000; reporter The Best Damn Sports Show Period!, FoxSportsNet, 2000—03; sideline reporter Monday Night Football, ABC, 2003—04. Actress : (films) Batman Returns, 1992; Love Potion No. 9, 1992; Fire Down Below, 1997; (TV series) Wild West Showdown, 1994; Sunset Beach, 1998—99. Vol. Salvation Army, Cedar Sinai Med. Ctr. Achievements include appearing in over 200 commercials and the covers of Maxim and FHM. Office: 77 W 66th St New York NY 10023*

GUERRERO, MONICA ELAINE, judge; b. San Antonio, June 21, 1966; d. Ernesto R. and Ernestine P. Guerrero. BA in Polit. Sci., U. Tex., San Antonio, 1990; JD, U. Kans., 1994. Bar: Tex. 1994. Asst. dist. atty. Bexar County, San Antonio, 1995—2002; judge Bexar County Ct. # 7, San Antonio, 2003—. Mem.: Mex. Am. Bar Assn. Democrat. Roman Catholic. Office: Bexar County Ct # 7 300 Dolorosa Ste 2121 San Antonio TX 78205 Office Phone: 210-335-2002. E-mail: mguerrero@co.bexar.tx.us.

GUERRERO, OLIVE CIRIDON, retired educator, civic worker; b. Laoag City, The Philippines, May 5, 1922; came to US, 1971; d. Juan Rafael Ciridon and Maxima Burgos Castillo Ciridon; m. Vicente Guerrero, Aug. 24, 1946 (dec. Aug. 1992); children: Samuel, Jeremiah, Nehemiah. Elem. tchr.'s diploma, Ilocos Norte Normal Sch., Laoag City, 1946; BS in Edn., Northwestern Coll., Laoag City, 1951, MA, 1969; PhD in Edn., Honolulu U., 1991. Life gen. tchg. credential, Calif. Coord., treas. Star of the North, Hawaii, 1964-65; asst. mgr., treas. Merry Makers Club, Hawaii, 1971-72; tchr. Unified Sch. Dist., Compton and LA, 1973-79; head tchr., sch. nurse Assistance League so. Calif., LA, 1979-90; dir. brown bag program Internat. Sr. Orgn., LA, 1993-98; dir. nutrition program 1st United Meth. Ch., LA, 1993-2000; dir. ednl. and cultural affairs Philippine-Am. Cmty. of LA, LA, 1999—2001. Demonstrator Philippine cuisine Smithsonian Instn., Washington, 1975; demonstrator hand crafts and art Los Angeles County Mus., LA, 1980; coord. instrumental and mus. concerts Hollywood Seventh-day Adventist Ch., 1981-82. Contbr. articles to various periodicals. Pub. rels. officer so. lodges Legionarios del Trabajo in Am., LA, Upland, El Centro, Calif., 1983-87, gen. chmn. conv., Washington, Oreg., Calif., 1994-97; bd. dir. Filipino Am. Sr. Citizens, LA, 1995-96, auditor, 1997; dep. exec. dir. Media Breakfast Club, LA, 1997, dep. dir., 1998-99; treas. Sons and Daus. Paoay USA, LA, 1988-2000, Oriental Svc. Ctr., LA, 1997-98; corr. sec. Filipino Am. Cmty. LA, 1985-98, dir. ednl. and cultural affairs, 2000-01; pres. Telacu Plaza Cmty., LA, 1993-96. Recipient cert. of tribute City of LA, 1990, cert. of recognition Confedn. Philippine-US Orgn., 1990, Educator's plaque of honor Sons and Daus. Paoay USA, 1992, Outstanding Vol. Svc. award Downtown YMCA, LA, 1996, Cert. of Vol. Recognition LA Marathon, 1988, Top Personalities Appreciation award for tchr., folk dancer, 1999; Parangal Award, Pil-Am. Nat. Assoc., 2001; Ms Hawaii- Fil. Am. Svc. Grp., Inc. (FASGI), 2001; elec. Sec. of Phil Am. Nat. Assoc., 2001; Matron, LA Lodge 529 Legion, 2001; narios del Trabajo in Am., 2003; elected Sec. Gen., Fil. Am., 2002; Cmty. of LA (FACLA), 2003; Voted Pres. Bayanihan Sr., Inc., 2002; Voted as pres. Internat. Sr. Orgn. of LA (ISOLA), 2002. Mem. LA Sr. Citizens Assn., Lions (1st. v.p. LA chpt. 1998, Outstanding Svc. Sec. award 1990-92, Outstanding Svc. Treas. award 1993-94, President's medal LA 1993, named Outstanding Parent 1999—), Lions. Avocations: singing spiritual songs, folk and social dancing, dramatics, writing prose and poetry, cooking.

GUERRIERI, SISTER ANTONIA MARIA, ARCANGIOLINA VERONICA, sister; b. Stockbridge, Mass., Dec. 9, 1907; d. Antonio Biaggio Guerrieri and Anna Maria D'Andrea. BA, Mt. Holyoke Coll., 1929; MD, Marquette Sch. Medicine, 1934; PhD (hon.), Providence Coll., China. Lic. Physician NY State, 1935. Physician Maryknoll Sisters' Clinic and Rural Mobile Clinic, Kweialin, China, 1941—53, Maryknoll Sisters' Clinic, Pusan, Republic of Korea, 1953, Maryknoll Sisters' Gen. Medicine Clinic, Changhua, Taiwan, 1953—2001; retired, 2001. Vol. Phelp's Mem. Hosp., Sleepy Hollow, NY, 2001—03. Named Hon. Citizen of Taiwan, Taiwan, 2000. Home: Maryknoll Sisters of St Dominic PO Box 311 Maryknoll NY 10545-0311

GUERRIERO, CAROL MARIE, librarian; b. Sept. 10, 1963; BA in Radio/TV/Film, Wayne State U., 1985, MLS, 1988. Libr. Livonia (Mich.) Pub. Librs., 1991—. Office: Livonia Pub Libr 32777 Five Mile Rd Livonia MI 48154-3045

GUERTAL, ELIZABETH ANDERSON, agronomist, educator; BS, Ohio State U., 1984, MS, 1988; PhD, Okla. State U., 1993. Asst. prof. dept. agronomy & soils Auburn (Ala.) U., 1993—. Recipient Novartis Agronomy award Am. Soc. Agronomy, 1997. Office: Auburn U Dept Agronomy 202 Funchess Hall Auburn AL 36849-5412

GUESON, EMERITA TORRES, obstetrician, gynecologist; b. Angeles City, The Philippines, Jan. 4, 1942; came to U.S., 1964; d. Lina (Torres) Gueson. AA, U. Sto. Tomas, Manila, Philippines, 1958, MD, 1963. Resident in ob-gyn. Phila. Gen. Hosp., 1966-71; attending physician Nazareth Hosp., Phila., 1973—, Holy Redeemer Hosp., Meadowbrook, Pa., 1983—. Bd. dirs. Physicians Who Care; lectr. healthcare issues to consumer groups, Phila. Author: Doctors Under Fire, 1989, Scales of Justice: Exploring the Wilderness of Health Care and Society's Moral Conscience, 1992, Do HMO's Cut Costs...and Lives, 1997, Survival Guide for HMO Patients, 1997; pub. ThereseVision Publs.; also med. writer, screenplay writer, line dir., prodr. Hon. co-chair physicians adv. bd. Republican Nat. Com. Fellow ACOG, ACP; mem. AMA, Pa. Med. Soc., Philadelphia County Med. Soc., Pro-Life Ob.-Gynecologists (charter). Avocations: writing, painting, refinishing furniture. Office: 3336 Aldine St Philadelphia PA 19136-3802 E-mail: therese44@aol.com.

GUESS, AUNDREA KAY, accounting educator; b. Seth, W.Va., Feb. 7, 1953; d. Hobert and Inez Elizabeth (Howell) Adams; children: Renae, Rhonda. BBA, Baylor U., Waco, Tex., 1988; MBA, Auburn U., 1989; PhD, U. North Tex., 1993. CPA, Ala., Fla. Co-owner Stevenson (Ala.) All-Mart, 1967-94; grad. rsch. asst. Auburn (Ala.) U., 1988-89; teaching fellow U. North Tex., Denton, 1989-90, lectr., 1990-93; prof., dir. acctg. program Samford U., Birmingham, Ala., 1993—97, dir. new masters of acctg. degree program; prof. U. Tex., 1997—; dir. acctg. MBA profram St. Edwards U., Austin, Tex., 1998—. Cons. Kay Guess Cons., Birmingham, 1993—, activity based costing Coca-Cola; presenter Southwestern Bus. Adminstrn. Conf., 1994; discussant, 1995 track chair for acctg. and fin. Southwestern Case Rsch., pres. 2003—; owner Kay's Designer Dresses, Stevenson; prof. St. Edwards U., 2003; bd. dir. N.Am. Case Rsch. Assn. Contbr. pubs. to various jours. Recipient Fin. Execs. Inst. award, 1987, 89; Rsch. grantee Samford U.Heloise Brown Canter scholar Am. Women's Soc. CPA and Am. Soc. Women Accts., 1992. Mem. AICPA, Am. Acctg. Assn., Am. Soc. Women CPAs (South Birmingham chpt., Laurel scholar 1992, scholar 1989), Fla. Inst. CPAs, Inst. Mgmt. Accts. (bd. dirs. 1994—, dir. tech. meetings 1994—), Acad. Acctg. Historians, Inst. Internal Auditing, Phi Theta Kappa, Alpha Kappa Psi, Beta Alpah Psi (treas. Auburn chpt. 1989), Phi Kappa Phi, Beta Gamma Sigma. Baptist. Avocations: sewing, cake decorating, running. Home: 651 Martin Rd Dripping Springs TX 78620-3506

GUESS, GRETCHEN, state senator; b. Anchorage, Alaska, Sept. 5, 1969; BA in Econs., Carleton Coll., 1991; MS in Pub. Policy Analysis (magna cum laude), U. Rochester, 1996. Bus. analyst Alaska Comm. Sys.; spl. projects coord., fed. liaison Alaska Dept. Edn. and Early Devel.; mem. Alaska Ho. of Reps., 2000—02, Alaska Senate, 2002—. Cons. RAND Corp. Treas. Knowles/Ulmer Campaign; sr. warden's com. St. Mary's Ch.; mem. cmty. coun. Russian Jack; mem. elders coun. Mountain View; bd. dirs. Standing Together Against Rape. Democrat. Avocations: basketball, reading. Office: Rm 423 State Capitol Juneau AK 99801-1182 Address: 716 W 4th Ave Ste 240 A Anchorage AK 99501

GUEST, BARBARA, author, poet; b. Wilmington, NC, Sept. 6, 1920; d. James Harvey and Anna (Hetzel) Pinson; m. Lord Stephen Haden-Guest, 1948 (div. 1954); 1 child, Hon. Hadley; m. Trumbull Higgins, 1954 (dec.); 1 child, Jonathan van Lennep. AB, U. Calif., Berkeley, 1943. Editorial assoc. Art News, 1951-59. Author: (plays) The Ladies Choice, 1953, The Office, 1961, Port, 1965, (with Kevin Killian) Often, 2000; (poems) The Location of Things, 1960, Poems, 1963, The Blue Stairs, 1968, Moscow Mansions, 1973; (with Sheila Isham) I Ching: Poems and Lithographs, 1969, The Countess from Minneapolis, 1976, The Türler Losses, 1980, Biography, 1981, Quilts, 1981, Fair Realism, 1989; (with June Felter) Musicality, 1989; (with Richard Tuttle) The Altos, 1991, Defensive Rapture, 1993, Selected Poems, 1995, Stripped Tales, 1995; (novel) Seeking Air, 1978 (reprint 1997), (biography) Herself Defined, 2002, The Poet H.D. and Her World, 1984, (poems) Quill Solitary Apparition, 1996, Rocks on a Platter: Notes on Literature, 1999, If So, Tell me, 1999, The Confetti Trees: Motion Picture Stories, 1999, (with Laurie Reid) Symbiosis, 2000, Miniatures and Other Poems, 2002, (essay) Forces of Imagination: Writing on Writing, 2003, Dürer in the Window, 2003. Recipient Longview award Longview Found., 1960, Laurence Lipton prize in lit., 1990, San Francisco State U. award for poetry, 1994, Fund for Poetry award, 1995, The America award, 1996, Pen West Josephine Miles award, 1996, Robert Frost medal Poetry Soc. Am., 1999, Lifetime Achievement award Small Press Traffic, San Francisco, 2003; Yaddo fellow, 1958; Nat. Endowment for the Arts grantee, 1978. Address: 1301 Milvia St Berkeley CA 94709-1934 E-mail: barbguest@aol.com

GUEST, RITA CARSON, interior designer; b. Atlanta, Aug. 17, 1950; d. Walter Harold and Doris Rebecca Carson; m. John Franklin Guest Jr., Jan. 20, 1979. B of Visual Arts, Ga. State U., 1973. Registered interior designer Ga., Fla., D.C., Ala. Pres., dir. design Carson Guest, Inc., Atlanta, 1984—. Lectr. in field. Bd. dirs. Mus. of Design, Atlanta, 2002—. Recipient 5 1st place awards Gwinnett Home Show and Interior Design Expo, 1991. Fellow: ASID (Ga. chpt. dir. 1984, treas. 1985—86, nominating com. 1987, chmn. interprofl. devel. com. 1988—90, pres.-elect 1991—92, pres. 1992—93, nat. office coun. of pres.'s steering com. 1993—94, nat. dir. for region 14 1995—96, legis. adv. coun. 1997—98, mem. fellows coun. 1997—99, nat. bd. dirs. 2000—02, awards com. 2003, nat. nominating com. 2003, Comml. Design Project award 1983, Ga. chpt. Presdl. citation 1984, Residential Design award 1987, Ga. chpt. 1st place Office Design award 1987, Comml. Offices 1st place Project award 1989, Profl. Office Design award 1989, 1st place Libr. Design/1st place Comml. Offices award 1991, Pres. citation 1991, Designer of Yr. 1992, 2 Comml. Project awards 1992, 1st place Nat. Project award 1993, 1st place Instnl. Design award 1994, 1st place Healthcare Project award 1995, Ga. chpt. Silver Contract Design award 2000, Bronze Contract Design award 2001, Gold Instl. award 2002, Gold Comml. award 2003); mem.: Ga. Alliance Interior Design Profls. (pres. 1991—92, bd. advisors 1993—98), Atlanta C. of C. Presbyterian. Avocation: painting. Office: Carson Guest Inc 1720 Peachtree St NW Ste 1001 Atlanta GA 30309-2439 E-mail: ritaguest@carsonguest.com

GUEST, SUZANNE MARY, adult education educator, artist; b. Monroe, Mich., Sept. 24, 1935; d. Hubert George Guest and Lola Viola Anne Pfeffer. BA, Marygrove Coll., 1957; MFA, U. Notre Dame, 1969. Chmn. art dept. Marian H.S., Birmingham, Mich., 1960—66, St. Mary H.S., Akron, Ohio, 1966—68, Am. Sch., London, 1971—91; adult educator Wordens World of Art, Pompano, Fla., 1994—, Ft. Lauderdale (Fla.) H.S., 1994—, First Presbyn. Ch., Pompano, 1999—; mem. sisterhood Immaculate Heart of Mary, Detroit, 1957—69. Freelance artist Alan Kent Design Group, London, 1970; presenter workshops in field; calligraphy sabbatical Oreg. Sch. Arts and Crafts, Portland, 1988—89. Author: Calligraphy for Those Who Are Young at Heart, 1988; contbr. Ency. Calligraphy Techniques, 1990; exhibitions include various schs., restaurants, art stores, chs. Recipient Outstanding Svc. in Secondary Edn. award, European Coun. Internat. Schs., London, 1977—90, Calligraphy award, Soc. Scribes and Illuminators, London, 1991. Mem.: So. Fla. Watercolor Soc., Mus. for Women in Arts, Humane Soc. Democrat. Roman Catholic. Avocations: music, meditation, watercolor. Home: 3051 NE 48th St Apt 104 Fort Lauderdale FL 33308-4903

GUFFEY, BARBARA BRADEN, elementary school educator; b. Pitts., Aug. 10, 1948; d. James Arthur and Dorothy (Barrett) Braden; 1 child, William Butler Guffey III. BA in Elem. Edn., Westminster Coll., New Wilmington, Pa., 1970; MEd in Elem. Edn., Slippery Rock State Coll., 1973; postgrad., U. Pitts., Duquesne U., Westminster Coll. Cert. tchr., elem. and secondary history and govt. edn, elem prin. Tchr. Shaler Area Sch. Dist., Glenshaw, Pa., 1970—, lang. arts area specialist, 1988—91, 1992—93, grad. level chmn., 1991—92, curriculum support math./sci., 1994—, mem. instrnl. support team, 1995—. Mem. Shaler Area Stretegic Planning Core Team, 1992—; mem. A.S.S.E.T. Leadership Team, 1995—; condr. seminars and workshops in field. Pres. alumni coun. Westminster Coll., 1996—97, v.p., 1995—96, chmn. homecoming all-alumni luncheon, 1991—93, chmn. homecoming, 1995—96, trustee, 1999—, mem. sesquicentennial com., 2002, mem. enrollment mgmt., ednl. policy and student affairs com., vice chmn. instl. advancement com., 2003—; chairperson Westminster Fund, 2003; active Burchfield Elem. Sch. PTA; chmn. publicity Shaler Area Choir Parents Assn., 1996—2000; mem. Child Care Adv. Bd.; elder, chair Christian edn. com. Glenshaw Presbyn. Ch., 1995—2001, mem. Presbyn. Women. Mem.: NEA, Shaler Area Edn. Assn. (mem. at large, negotiator, former rec. sec., v.p., bldg. rep., editor newsletter), Pa. Edn. Assn., Nat. Geneal. Soc. (local arrangements chair Pitts. conf. 2003), Armstrong County Hist. and Mus. Soc., Ind. County Geneal. and Hist. Soc., Western Pa. Geneal. Soc. (bd. dirs. 1992—, chair 25th Anniversary 1999, pres. 1999—2000, publicity 2000—03, pres. 2002—03), Perry Historians, Juniata County Hist. Soc., First Families of Western Pa. (charter mem.), Westminster Coll. Women's Club Pitts. (pres. 1975—76, treas. 1994—99, pres. 2001—03, v.p., sec., chair ways and means), Kappa Delta Pi. Office: Burchfield Elem Sch 1500 Burchfield Rd Allison Park PA 15101-4099 E-mail: guffeyb@sasd.k12.pa.us.

GUFFEY, EDITH ANN, religious organization administrator; Asst. to dir. student records U. Kans., 1984-90, assoc. dir. admissions, 1990-91; sec. United Ch. of Christ, Cleve., 1991—. Office: United Ch of Christ 700 Prospect Ave E Cleveland OH 44115-1131

GUGGENHEIMER, JOAN, law administrator; BA, Binghamton Univ.; JD, Columbia Univ. Gen. coun. Citigroup's Global Corp. and Invest. Bank, Chgo.; head of diversity Smith Barney; Co-head of Anti-Money Laundering Citigroup, co-Gen. Coussel; assoc. Smith Barney, 1985; dep. gen. coun. for litig. Citigroup's Global Corp. and Investment Bank, Chgo., gen. counsel of the Inst. Bus., gen. coun.; clk. US Court of Appeals for the Second Circuit; litig. Davis Polk and Wardwell, 1980; chief legal officer Bank One - Former Gen. Coun. of Globil Corp. and Invest. Bank at Citigroup, Chgo. Editor: (tabloid) Law Rev./Columbia Univ. Ater joining Bank One in 2000, Christine Edwards successfully built Law, Compliance, and Gov. Rels. into a single dept.; helped establish strong working rels with regulators; significantly cut expenses and reduced reliance on outside coun.; established Bank Ones's Fed. Gov. Rels. Office in Wash. DC; and helped establish Bank One as a leader in corp. governance. Office: Office of Gen Coun Bank One Corp 1 Bank One Plz Chicago IL 60670

GUGLIUZZA, KRISTENE KOONTZ, transplant and general surgery educator; b. Siloam Springs, Ark., May 2, 1956; d. Lloyd Lawson Koontz Jr. and Helen Ruth (Camfield) Smith; m. Joseph Thomas Gugliuzza III, Sept. 3, 1989. AS, Lake Land Coll., Mattoon, Ill., 1977; BS with honors, Ea. Ill. U., Charleston, 1978; MD, U. Ill., Rockford, 1982. Diplomate Am. Bd. Surgery. Intern dept. surgery Tulane U. Med. Sch. and Affiliated Hosps., New Orleans, 1982-83, resident, 1983-87, fellow divsn. transplantation, 1987-89, instr. surgery, rsch. assoc. in surgery and transplantation, 1989-90; asst. prof. U. Tex. Med. Br., Galveston, 1990-97, assoc. prof., 1997—2003, prof., 2003—; spl. fellow in pancreas transplantation U. Minn., Mpls., 1989; courtesy staff St. Mary's Hosp., Galveston, 1991-96. Recovery surgeon La. Organ Procurement Agy., New Orleans, 1989-90, S.W. Transplant Alliance, 1990—; presenter in field. Contbr. articles to med. jours. Fellow ACS; mem. AMA, Am. Diabetes Assn., So. Surg. Assn., Galveston County Med. Soc., Tex. Med. Assn., Cell Transplant Soc., Assn. Women Surgeons, Singleton Surg. Soc., Assn. Acad. Surgery, Transplantation Soc., Tex. Transplant Soc., Tulane Surg. Soc., Am. Soc. Transplant Physicians, Tex. Surg. Soc., Alpha Omega Alpha. Avocation: reading. Office: U Tex Med Br Dept Surgery 301 University Blvd Galveston TX 77555-5302

GUHL, GABRIELLE V. music teacher; b. Bournemouth, Eng., Apr. 28, 1934; d. James Herbert and Eugenie Victoria (Biermer) Clegg; m. Hans Joachim Herzog, Mar. 15, 1962 (div. 1982); children: Teddy Michael Herzog, Karl Frederic Herzog, Heidi Elizabeth Herzog, Bruno Wilhelm Herzog; m. Gerhard Hermann Guhl, Apr. 15, 1988. AD in Musik, Mozarteum, Salzburg, Austria, 1950; BA in Music Performance, Conservatoire De Musique, Paris, 1952; MA in Music Performance, Musikhochschule, Hamburg, Germany, 1958; BS in Music Edn., Skidmore Coll., 1973. Cert. music tchr., N.Y. Music tchr. St. Peters Sch., Saratoga Springs, N.Y., 1969-76, ch. organist, choir dir., 1969-76; music tchr. St. Clements Sch., Saratoga Springs, 1976-80, ch.organist, folk group leader, 1976-79; ch. organist, choir dir. St. Matthews Ch., Greenwich, N.Y., 1979-80; chorus coach, tchr., dir. Herzog Music Sch., Del Mar, Calif., 1980-87; music tchr. St. John's Sch., Encinitas, Calif., 1982-85; music tchr., dir. Guhl Music Studio, Houston, 1987-90, Santa Barbara, Calif., 1990&. Trainer neuroassociative conditioning Robbins Rsch. Internat., San Diego, 1983-96; co-founder Saratoga Springs Suzuki Music Festival, 1972; co-founder, music dir. Schuylerville Cmty. Theater, 1976. Driver, caregiver Meals on Wheels, Barbados, W.I., 1961. Recipient priz a l'unanimité Conservatoire de Music, Paris, 1952, Best Spkr. award Toastmasters Am., 1984, Best Humourous Speech award, 1992. Mem. LWV, Nat. Assn. Investment Clubs (bd. dirs. Channel Islands chpt.), Vivace Investors of Santa Barbara (ednl. v.p. 1998-99, pres. 1996-98), Model Club. Avocations: exercise, yoga, playing the piano, making music in a group, family activities.

GUIDA, PAT, information broker, literature chemist; b. Highland Park, Mich.; d. Wilfred Bernard and Patricia Graham; m. Edward Silvio Guida, Aug. 29, 1965; chidren: Niels Bohr, Eric Bohr. Student, Regis Coll., 1946-48, Rutgers U., 1952-55; BS cum laude, Fairleigh Dickinson U., 1961. Asst. librarian Warner-Lambert Research Inst., Morris Plains, N.J., 1961-64; librarian Reaction Motors Div. Thiokol, Denville, N.J., 1964-69; mgr., info. ctr. Foster D. Snell Div., Booz Allen & Hamilton Inc., Florham Park, N.J., 1969-80; pres. Pat Guida Assocs., Fairfield, N.J. Mem. Sci. Adv. Bd. EPA, Washington, 1978-82, Library Com. Chemists Club, N.Y.C., 1983-89. Editor: Chemical Digest, 1971-74. Pres. PTA, Sparta, N.J., 1959-60. Avocations: theatre, West Highland white terriers, music, travel. Home and Office: 5 Cedar Tree Ln Sparta NJ 07871-2306 E-mail: vjrs@sys.uea.ac.uk .

GUILFORD, KIMBERLY SUE, music educator; b. Bethany, Mo., May 9, 1966; d. Raymond Eugene Boothe and Carol Jean McCoy; m. Michael Wayne Guilford, Dec. 11, 1993; children: Hannah Elizabeth, Rachel Marie. BS in Edn.-Music Edn., U. Mo., 1988, MS in Edn.-Music Edn., 1998. Tchr. music edn. grades K-12 Hale (Mo.) R-1 Sch., 1989—91, Brunswick (Mo.) R-2 Sch., 1991—93, Macon County R-4 Sch., New Cambria, Mo., 1994—. Choir mem. Ethel (Mo.) Cmty. Choir, 2001—, Crossroads Christian Ch., Macon, Mo., 2002—. Mem.: Mo. State Tchrs. Assn., Am. Choral Dirs. Assn., Music Educators Nat. Conf. (choral v.p. 1998—). Avocations: sewing, crafts, singing, scrapbooks, basket collecting. Home: 307 E Douglas Macon MO 63552 Office: Macon County R-4 Sch 501 S Main New Cambria MO 63558

GUILL, MARGARET FRANK, pediatrician, educator, medical researcher; b. Atlanta, Jan. 18, 1948; d. Vernon Rhinehart and Margaret N. (Tichenor) Frank; m. Marshall Anderson Guill III, July 6, 1974; children: Daniel Marshall, Laura Elizabeth. BA, Agnes Scott Coll., 1969; MD, Med. Coll. Ga., 1972. Diplomate Am. Bd. Pediatrics, Am. Bd. Pediatrics subbd. pulmonology, Am. Bd. Allergy and Immunology, Nat. Bd. Med. Examiners. Resident in pediatrics Kaiser Found. Hosp., San Francisco, 1976-78, fellow in allergy, 1978-79; staff physician Waipahu (Hawaii) Clinic, 1973-76; intern in internal medicine Med. Coll. Ga., Augusta, 1973, resident in pediatrics, 1974, fellow in allergy and immunology, 1979-80, from asst. prof. to prof. pediatrics, 1981—, also chief sect. pediatric pulmonology and dir. Asthma Ctr., dir. Cystic Fibrosis Ctr., 1990—, vice chair dept. pediat., 2000—, Dorothy A. Hahn chair pediats., 2001—. Pres. Physician Practice Group, 2001—04; pres. staff Childrens Med. Ctr. Hosp., 2000—01; spkr. in field. Host Healthwatch weekly program WJBF-TV, 1982-83; contbr. articles to profl. jours. Active Reid Meml. Presbyn. Ch.; vol. tchr. Episcopal Day Sch., 1982-85; career day participant Acad. Richmond County, 1982, 83; med. advisor Augusta Area Allergy and Asthma Support Group, 1984-86; adv. bd. East Cen. br. Am. Lung Assn. Ga., 1985—, program of work com., 1987—, bd. dirs., 1987—, program coordinating com., 1990-91, exec. bd., 1989-91; med. staff Camp Breathe Easy, 1985—, med. dir., 1996-98. Recipient Mosby Book award, 1973; grantee rsch. grantee, BRSG, 1981—86, Del Labs., 1982, Merrell-Dow, 1983—84, Elan Pharms., 1986, Am. Lung Assn. Ga., 1986—87, Hollister-Stier, 1986, Fisons Corp., 1989, 1991—93, 1995, Med. Coll. Ga., 1989, Am. Heart Assn., 1991, Genentech, 1991—, Miles, 1992, Clintrials, 1990—95, PathoGenesis, 1995—99, SmithKline Beecham, 1996, Kaleida Health, 2002, Chiron, 2002. Fellow Am. Acad. Pediat., Am. Coll. Chest Physicians, Am. Acad. Allergy, Asthma and Immunology, Am. Coll. Allergy, Asthma and Immunology, Am. Assn. Cert. Allergists; mem. Med. Assn. Ga., Richmond County Med. Soc., Allergy and Immunology Soc. Ga., S.E. Allergy Assn. (Hal Davison award 1985), Am. Assn. Clin. Immunologists and Allergists, Ga. Thoracic Soc. (Med. Profl. of Yr. 1998), Am. Thoracic Soc., Alpha Omega Alpha. Home: 2247 Pickens Rd Augusta GA 30904-4462 Office: Med Coll Ga Dept Pediatrics Augusta GA 30912 Office Phone: 706-721-2635. E-mail: mguill@mcg.edu.

GUILLAUM, MARSHA KAYE, information technology manager; b. Tell City, Ind., May 31, 1947; d. William and Anna Marie Richards; 1 child, Julie Lynn. OD, U. Evansville, 1969. Advt. mgr. The News, Tell City, Ind., 1971—76; advt. sales rep. The Messenger-Inquirer, Owensboro, 1976—86; advt. sales staff The Tampa (Fla.) Tribune, 1986—89; dir. mktg. and advt. The Legis. Gazette, Albany, NY, 1989—94; display mgr. Hoosier State Press Assn., Indpls., 1994—95; classified ad mgr. The Gleaner, Henderson, Ky., 1995—97; project and acquitions mgr. Village Profile, Elgin, Ill., 1998—. Recipient Advt. Design, Women's Press Club, 1979. Mem.: Perry County C. of C., Hoosier State Press Assn. (mem. advt. bd. 1972—76, Advt. Design award 1973), Ky. Press Assn. (mem. advt. bd. 1984—86, Advt. Design award 1974—86, v.p. sales goals awards 1998—2001). Independent. Evangelical. Avocations: reading, computers, graphic design, music, painting. Home: 509 13th St Tell City IN 47586

GUILLEN, ALITA (ALITA HAYTAYAN), newscaster; BA in English, U. N.H., 1992; MA in Broadcast Journalism, U. Miami, 1995. Anchor, prodr., reporter and host Dynamic Cable, Miami, Fla.; reporter and anchor

WABU-TV, Boston, 1995—96; reporter and substitute anchor WTSP-TV, Tampa, Fla., 1997—99; morning news anchor and reporter WFOR-TV, Miami, 1999—2002; co-anchor weekend news and reporter WBBM-TV, Chgo., 2002—. Office: WBBM-TV 630 N McClurg Ct Chicago IL 60601

GUILLERMO, LINDA SUE, clinical social worker; b. Chgo., July 4, 1951; d. Triponio Pascua and Helen Elizabeth (Moskal) Guillermo. BA, U. Ill., Chgo., 1973, MSW, 1975, postgrad., 1980, Jane Addams Coll. Social Work, 1980—82. Diplomate in clin. social work, lic. real estate broker Ill. Mktg. rsch. interviewer Rabin Rsch. Co., Chgo., 1970—73; mktg. rsch. interviewer, coder Marcor Mktg. Rsch., Inc., Chgo., 1973—75; social work intern Child and Family Svcs., Chgo., 1973—74, Chgo. Bd. Edn., 1974—75; social worker, therapist child abuse and neglect, case investigator, case planning cons., social svc. program planner Ill. Dept. Children and Family Svcs., Chgo., 1975—78; social svc. program planner, contract negotiator, monitoring agt. Ctrl. Resources Contracts and Grants, 1978—79; real estate sales person Sentry Realty, Chgo., 1976—; social worker, therapist, program coord., casework supr. of child abuse assessment and intervention program, proposal writer Casa Ctrl., Chgo., 1979—82, casework cons. of child abuse assessment and intervention program, proposal writer, program dir. and casework supr. of early intervention program, 1979—85; social worker, clin. supr. Chgo. Bd. Edn., 1985—. Tng. specialist City Coll. of Chgo., 1980; adj. assoc. rschr. Asher Feren Law Office, Chgo., 1980—81. Treas. Greenleaf Condominium Assn., Chgo., 1980—81, sec., 1987—88, interim pres., 1988; regional rep. North Ill. Assn. of Sch. Social Workers, 1986—87; active various polit. campaigns, Chgo. Mem.: Ill. Cert. Lic. Social Workers, Nat. Assn. Cert. Social Workers (register clin. social workers), North Side Real Estate Bd. Home: 7405 N Kenneth Ave Skokie IL 60076 Office Phone: 847-763-0865.

GUILLERMOPRIETO, ALMA, journalist, non-fiction writer; b. Mex., May 27, 1949; Journalist, 1978—. Dancer Ballet Co. of Mex. Author: (book) Samba, 1990, The Heart That Bleeds: Latin America Now, 1994. MacArthur fellow, 1995. Office: Random House Inc Publicity 11-6 201 E 50th St Fl 22 New York NY 10022-7703

GUILLILAND, MARTHA W. academic administrator; b. Pa. BS in Geology and Math., Catawba Coll., 1966; MS in Geophysics, Rice U., 1968; PhD in environ. engring./sys. ecology, U. Fla., 1973. Rsch. fellow sci. and pub. policy U. Mo., Kan. City, Mo., 1974—77; asst. prof. civil engring. and environment sci. U. Okla., 1975—77; exec. dir. Energy Policy Studies, Inc., El Paso, Tex., 1977—82; assoc. prof. civil engring. U. Nebr., Lincoln, 1988—90, dir. Ctr. Infrastructure Rsch., 1988—99; dean grad. sch. and asst. v.p. rsch. U. Ariz., 1990—93, vice provost academic affairs, 1993—95, academic v.p. info. and human resources, 1995—97, prof. hydrology and water resources, 1995—97; provost Tulane U., New Orleans, 1997—2000; pres. U. Mo., Kans. City, 2000—. Appointee Rsch. and Adv. Panel of Gen. Acctg. Office, Energy Engring. Bd. of Nat. Rsch. Coun., NAS Com. on Strategic Assessment of Dept. of Energy Coal Program, Nat. Inst. Global Change, Pres.'s Coun. of Advisors on Sci. and Tech., 2001. Author: (book) Energy Analysis: A New Public Policy Tool, co-author books; contbr. articles to profl. jours. Recipient Hubert H. Humphrey award, Policy Studies Orgn., 2002, Gov.'s award Excellence Total Qualty Efforts, Ariz.; fellow, W.K. Kellogg Found., 1985—88. Office: U Mo 5100 Rockhill Rd Kansas City MO 64110*

GUILMET, GLENDA JEAN, artist; b. Tacoma, Wash., Mar. 28, 1957; d. Cody Calvin Black and Maria Isabel Rivera; m. George Michael Guilmet, May 24, 1980; children: Michelle Rene, Douglas James. Student, Clover Park Vocat. Tech. Inst., 1982-83; BA in Bus. Adminstrn., U. Puget Sound, 1981, BA in Art, 1989. Freelance photographer, Tacoma and Blyn, 1976—; women's sports photographer U. Puget Sound, Tacoma, 1977-78, asst. photographer, 1978-79; visual artist Tacoma and Blyn, 1982—; photographic cons. Puyallup Tribe of Indians, Tacoma, 1984; on-call photographer Puyallup Tribal Health Authority, Tacoma, 1984-86. Instr. sculpture Tacoma Arts Commn., 1989; guest lectr. U. Puget Sound, 1990, 94; grants juror Artist Trust, Seattle, 1990; video festival juror Tacoma Mcpl. TV, 1990; photography competition juror Washington State PTA Reflections Com., 1995; art dir., Tacenda and Willo Trees Press, Marshfield, Mo., 1993. Contbr. photographs to various publs.; one-woman shows include, Stage Door Gallery, Tacoma Little Theatre, 1993, Seattle U. Women's Ctr., 1994, Inst. de Cultura Puertorriquena, Jayuya, Carolina and Caguana, P.R., 1994, 1995, Galleria on Broadway, Tacoma, 1996, 1998, Sacred Cir. Gallery of Am. Indian Art, Seattle, 1996, 1997, 1999, exhibited in group shows, Nat. Mus. of Women in the Arts, Washington, U. Puget Sound, Tacoma, 1989, Windhorse Gallery, Seattle, 1990, Chase Gallery, Spokane City Hall, 1990, Hanforth Gallery, Tacoma, 1990, 1991, Wash. State Capital Mus., Olympia, 1990, Foyer of the Okean Theater, Vladivostok, Russia, 1992, First Night Gallery, Tacoma, 1992, 1996, 1997, Sacred Cir. Gallery of Am. Indian Art, 1993, 1996, Cunningham Gallery U. Wash., 1993, Western Gallery, Western Wash. U., Bellingham, 1993, Seattle Art Mus., 1993, Bibliotheque Nat. de France, 1994, Street Level Photography Gallery, Glasgow, Scotland, 1995, Tacoma Art Mus., 1995, Park Ave. Armory, N.Y.C., 1995, Westfalische Mus. fur Naturkunde, Munster, Germany, 1995, 1996, Iverness (Scotland) Mus., 1997, Ione Gallery Highland Folk Mus., Kingussie, Scotland, 1997, U. Ariz. Mus. Art, 1997, Coos Art Mus., Coos Bay, Oreg., 1998, Pratt Fine Arts Ctr., Seattle, 2000, Wash. State Conv. and Trade Ctr., Seattle, 2000, Represented in permanent collections, Steilacoom (Wash.) Tribal Mus., Bibliotheque Nat. de France, U. Puget Sound, Chief Leschi Schs., Puyallup Tribe of Indians, also pvt. and corp. collections; art dir. Tacenda, Eureka, Calif., 2003. Recipient 1st Place Photography award, Crosscurrents Art Contest, 1988, Hedgebrook Invitational Residency, Hedgebrook Found., Langley, Wash., 2000. Mem. Artist Trust, En Foco, Atlatl, Women's Caucus for Art, Nat. Mus. Women in the Arts. Home and Studio: 652 Old Blyn Highway Sequim WA 98382-9695 E-mail: glendaguilmet@yahoo.com.

GUIN, CATHERINE, marketing professional, public relations executive, consultant; b. Albany, Ga. d. Bob Wayne and Eileen Ann Guin. BA, Fla. State U., 1982. With career svc. U. So. Fla., Tampa, Fla., 1982—88; mktg. and pub. rels. dir. Tampa (Fla.) Bay Performing Arts Ctr., 1988—95, Orlando (Fla.) UCF Shakespeare Festival, 1995—97, Atlanta (Ga.) Ballet, 1998—2001; dir. comms. Ala. Shakespeare Festival, 2001—02; prin., owner Catherine Guin and Assocs., Mary Esther, Fla., 2002—. Cons. Columbia Theatre Performing Arts, Wash., 2002, Alliance Theatre, Atlanta, 2003; mem. Theatre Comms. Group, 2000—. Named Marketer of Yr., Am. Mktg. Assn., 1995; recipient Best of Show award, Atlanta (Ga.) Advt. Fedn., 2000. Independent. Avocations: movies, art, reading.

GUINN, JANET MARTIN, psychologist, consultant; b. Rapid City, S.D., Aug. 16, 1942; d. Verne Oliver and Carolyn Yetta (Clark) Martin; m. David Lee Guinn, Oct. 27, 1962 (div. June 1988); children: Cynthia Gail, Kevin Scott, Garrett Lee. BS in Psychology, U. Alaska, 1980, MS in Counseling Psychology, 1983; PhD in Clin. Psychology, Calif. Sch. Profl. Psychology, 1988. Lic. psychologist, Alaska, Nev. Pvt. practice, Anchorage, 1988-93, Carson City and Reno, Nev., 1993—; clinician Behavior Medicine Cons., 1983-84; pvt. practice clinician, 1983-84; supr. Southcentral Counseling Ctr., Anchorage, 1984-85; cons. City/Borough of Juneau, Alaska, 1988; psychologist youth treatment program Alaska Psychiat. Inst., Anchorage, 1989-90; psychologist Nev. Mental Health Inst., Sparks, 1994-97. Cons. in field; cons. Alaska Small Bus. Coalition, Anchorage, 1990-92; reviewer Blors Corp. Contbr. articles to profl. jours. Active in politics. Mem. APA, Am. Coll. Forensic Examiners, Nev. Psychol. Assn., Internat. Neuropsychol. Soc., Rotary, Psi Chi. Republican. Avocations: skiing, gourmet cooking, dance.

GUINN, ROBERTA LOWTHER, not for profit organization administrator; b. Duquesne, Pa., June 6, 1946; d. William K. and Louise Perry Lowther; m. Robert K. Guinn, July 13, 1968; children: Christina L., Kathryn A. B in Elem. Edn., Fla. State U., 1985, EdM, 1995. Tchr. Covenant Christian Sch., Panama City, Fla.; program coord. Early Childhood Svcs., Panama City, 1991—96; program specialist Vols. of Am. North La., Alexandria, 1998, program mgr., 1998—99, program dir., 1999. Office: Vols of Am PO Box 2445 Jena LA 71342

GUINTHER, CHRISTINE LOUISE, special education educator; b. Chgo., Oct. 27, 1949; d. William Joseph and Olga (Sandul) Bacha; m. Paul H. Demper, July 22, 1972 (div. 1987); m. William Robert Guinther, June 25, 1988. BS in Edn., Ill. State U., 1971; MA in Exceptional Child Edn., Ohio State U., 1974. Cert. tchr., Mo. Resource tchr. for learning disabled students Palatine (Ill.) Community Consol. Sch. Dist. #15, 1971-72, Scioto-Darby City Schs., Hilliard, Ohio, 1972-76, Francis Howell Sch. Dist., St. Charles, Mo., 1976—. Mem. NEA (human rels. com. 1987-93, bd. dirs. 1993—), ACLU, ASCD, Nat. Staf devel. Coun., AAUW, Mo. NEA (bd. dirs. 1985-91, human rels. com. 1983—, exec. com. 1993—), Francis Howell Edn. Assn. (pres. 1981-82), NMSA, Delta Kappa Gamma. Methodist. Avocations: walking, music, needlework, reading, Scrabble. Home: 161 Castlewood Rd Ballwin MO 63021-7217

GUIRADO, TAMARA A. writer, educator; b. Bellflower, Calif., Aug. 5, 1968; d. Daniel Lewis Pope and Elyse Allison Guirado, John Goertzel (Stepfather) and Kumiko Sakai(Stepmother). BS in Social Sci., So. Oreg. State U., 1994; MFA in English and Creative Writing, Mills Coll., 1998. Creative writing and composition instr. Acad. of Art, San Francisco, Calif., 2000—01; tchg. assistent The Pl. For Writers, Mills Coll., Oakland, Calif., 1999—2000; tchg. asst. Stanford U., Palo Alto, 2001—01; mentor/tutor Stanford, U., Palo Alto, Calif., 2002—02; creative writing instr. ASA, Berkeley, Calif., 2002—02; intermediate and beginning fiction instr. U. of Wisconsin-Madison, Madison, Wis., 2002—03. Recipient Marion Hood Boess Haworth award for young adult fiction, Mills Coll., 1999; fellow Carl Djerassi fiction fellow, Wis. Inst. Creative Writing, U. of Wisconsin-Madison, 2002—03; Wallace Stegner Fiction fellow, Stanford U., 2001—02. Mem.: Phi Kappa Phi (hon.). Personal E-mail: greenmonkey68@earthlink.net.

GUISEWITE, CATHY LEE, cartoonist; b. Dayton, Ohio, Sept. 5, 1950; d. William Lee and Anne (Duly) G. BA in English, U. Mich., 1972; LHD (hon.), R.I. Coll., 1979, Eastern Mich. U., 1981. Writer Campbell-Ewald Advt., Detroit, 1972-73; writer Norman Prady, Ltd., Detroit, 1973-74, W.B. Doner & Co., Advt., Southfield, Mich., 1974-75, group supr., 1975-76, v.p., 1976-77; creator, writer, artist Cathy comic strip Universal Press Syndicate, Mission, Kans., 1976—. Author, artist: The Cathy Chronicles, 1978, What Do You Mean, I Still Don't Have Equal Rights??!!, 1980, What's a Nice Single Girl Doing with a Double Bed??!, 1981, I Think I'm Having a Relationship with a Blueberry Pie!, 1981, It Must Be Love, My Face Is Breaking Out, 1982, Another Saturday Night of Wild and Reckless Abandon, 1982, Cathy's Valentine's Day Survival Book, How to Live through Another February 14, 1982, How to Get Rich, Fall in Love, Lose Weight, and Solve all Your Problems by Saying "NO", 1983, Eat Your Way to a Better Relationship, 1983, A Mouthful of Breath Mints and No One to Kiss, 1983, Climb Every Mountain, Bounce Every Check, 1983, Men Should Come with Instruction Booklets, 1984, Wake Me Up When I'm a Size 5, 1985, Thin Thighs in Thirty Years, 1986, A Hand to Hold, An Opinion to Reject, 1987, Why Do the Right Words Always Come Out of the Wrong Mouth?, 1988, My Granddaughter Has Fleas, 1989, $14 in the Bank and a $200 Face in My Purse, 1990, Reflections (A Fifteenth Anniversary Collection), 1991, Only Love can Break a Heart, but a Shoe Sale Can Come Close, 1992, Revelations From a 45-Pound Purse, 1993; TV work includes 3 animated Cathy spls. (Emmy award 1987). Recipient Reuben award Nat. Cartoonists Soc., 1992. Office: Universal Press Syndicate 4520 Main St Ste 700 Kansas City MO 64111-7701

GUITARD, MARGARET MARY, elementary school educator; b. Lewiston, Idaho, Feb. 7, 1951; d. Ray Joseph and Genida Agnes Purcell; m. David William Guitard, May 5, 1984; 1 child, Patricia Ann. BA in Edn., Fort Wright Coll., 1973; MA in Spl. Edn., Mid. Tenn. State U., 1991, EdS in Curriculum and Instrn., 1999; PhD, Tenn. State U., 2003. Tchr. Lyle (Wash.) Pub. Schs., 1973—75; tchr. English Peace Corps., Kenifra, Morocco, 1976—78; tchr. gifted and talented Lewiston (Idaho) Pub. Schs., 1979—81; libr. Rutherford County Schs., Murfreesboro, Tenn., 1986—. Mem. transplant team Nat. Kidney Assn., Nashville, 1997—, vol., 1997—, Tenn. Donor Assn., Nashville, 1997—; Poinsettia chair Nat. Kidney Found., 1999, 2001; mem. ch. coun. bd. St. Lukes Cath. Ch., Smyrna, Tenn., 1998—99. Recipient Disting. Svc. award, Nat. Kidney Found., 2002. Mem.: Rutherford Edn. Assn. (rep. 1997—2002), Tenn. Edn. Assn. (mem. women in edn. com. 2001—03). Democrat. Roman Cath. Avocations: reading, gardening, sewing. Office: Rutherford County Stewartsboro 10479 Old Nashville Hwy Smyrna TN 37167

GUITRY, LORAINE DUNN, community health nurse; b. Bryan, Tex., Apr. 12, 1930; BS Elem. Edn., Paul Quinn Coll., 1954. Registered nurse U. Tex. Med. Br., Galveston, 1958—67, U.S. Pub. Health Svc., Galveston, 1967—. Home: 701 Chadley Ct Bryan TX 77803

GULAN, BONNIE MARION, writer, researcher; b. Kenosha, Wis., Feb. 27, 1922; d. Matthew and Elizabeth Ummy Thomas; m. Edward J. Gulan, Nov. 26, 1949; children: John, Michael, Kathryn. Beauty cons. Globe Dept., Kenosha, Wis., 1950—54; inventor & pitch artist Beauty Blush Cosmetic Line, Waukegan, Ill., 1954—56; creator & founder Felture's Inc., Brookfield, Ill., 1956—59; gen. mgr. & designer Eichling's Flowers Inc., Skokie, Ill., 1960—64; founder, dir. An-Oix-Is In-home Youth Ministry, Winnetka, Ill., 1965—75; founder & ceo The Christmas Tree Story Ho. Mus., Multiple Locations, Ill., 1970—90; author & rschr. Milwaukee, Wis., 1990—98; author Saukville, Wis., 1998—. Founder, pres. World-Wide Women's Inventor's Orgn., Libertyville, Ill., 1961—65; creator, lectr. Miracle Thinking Lecture Series, Mundelein, Ill., 1965—69; spkr. in field. Author: (book) Family Miracles, 1981, Stories From The Christmas Tree Story House, 1981, The Great Bible Dig, 2001, The House of the Seven Cats - An Adventure, 2001, Lost Adventures-House of the 7 Cats, 2001, 7 Cats Promised Land Adventure, 2001, Over the Fence Non-Sense Tales, 2001, Lamp Of Hope, 2001, Back Yard Critter Tales, 2001, A Collection Of Mrs. Claus' Christmas Stories, 2001, The Master Toy Maker, 2001, Adventures Down Nursery Rhyme Lane, 2001, A Collection Of Nodding Off Stories, 2001, Christmas In Our Town, 2002, The Great Journey in Pursuit of Jesus' Way, Truth & Life, 2002; composer: (albums) Sounds of The Christmas Tree Story House, 1975. Founder, pres. & lectr. T.H.E Anti-Drug Youth Program, Winnetka, 1971—75. Home: 1053 South Main Street Saukville WI 53080 Personal E-mail: bmgulan@aol.com.

GULBRANDSEN, NATALIE WEBBER, religious association administrator; b. Beverly, Mass., July 7, 1919; d. Arthur Hammond and Kathryn Mary (Doherty) Webber; m. Melvin H. Gulbrandsen, June 19, 1943 (dec. Feb. 23, 1991); children: Karen Ann Bean, Linda Jean Goldsmith, Eric Christian, Ellen Dale Williams, Kristin Jane Morgan. BA, Bates Coll., 1942, LLD (hon.), 1996; LHD (hon.), Meadville/Lombard Theol. Sch., Chgo., 1991. Social worker Bur. Child Welfare, Bangor, Maine. Leader Girl Scouts USA, Auburn, Maine, 1941—42, 1942—43, exec. dir. Belmont, Mass., 1943—45, leader, 1952—65, leadership trainer, 1946—63, bd. dirs. Wellesley, Mass., 1950—63, pres., 1960—63; mem. Wellesle Town Meeting, 1967—91; trustee Unitarian Universalist Women's Fedn., 1971—81, pres., 1977—81, mem. commn. on appraisal, 1981—85; moderator Unitarian Universalist Assn., U.S. and Can., Boston, 1985—93; bd. dirs. Unitarian Universalist Ch. of the Larger Fellowship, 1992—98, chairperson bd. dirs., 1996—98, ch. search com., 1998—99, chair ministerial rels. com., 1999—2001; bd. dirs. Unitarian Universalist Women's Heritage Soc., 1994—2002, ch. bd., 2001—02; chair denominational affairs Unitarian Universalist Soc. Wellesley Hills, 2002—; bd. dirs. Am. Field Svc., 1964—70; mem. permanent sch. accomodations com. Wellesley, 1970—76; mem. Wellesley Youth Commn., 1968—70, trustee Wellesley Human Rels. Svc., 1964—70, pres., 1973—76; bd. dirs. Newton Wellesley Weston Needham Area Mental Health Assn., 1975—78; co-chairperson METCO Program of Wellesley, 1965—69. Recipient Wellesley Ctr. Cmty. award, 1981, Unitarian Universalist Disting. Svc. award, 2002. Mem. AAUW, Boston Bates Alumnae Assn. (pres. 1966-69), Internat. Assn. Religious Freedom (mem. coun. 1981-90, v.p. 1990-93, pres. 1993-96, co-pres. U.S. chpt. 1997-2003, Clara Barton birthplace com. 1997-01). Unitarian Universalist. Home: 2251 Commonwealth Ave Auburndale MA 02466-1817

GULBRANDSEN, PATRICIA HUGHES, physician; b. May 9, 1940; d. Patrick Boland and Anne Hughes; m. Jon Alf Gulbrandsen, Mar. 6, 1972 (dec. Oct. 1984). BA, Cornell U., 1962; MD, U. Pa., 1967; MPH, Johns Hopkins U., 1980. Cert. Am. Bd. Disability Analysts; diplomate Am. Bd. Phys. Medicine and Rehab., Am. Bd. Occupl. Medicine. Rotating intern Chgo. Wesley Meml. Hosp., 1967-68; resident in neurology Pa. Hosp., Phila., 1968-69, Georgetown U. Hosp., Washington, 1972-74; fellow in gynecologic endocrinology Chelsea Hosp. for Women, London, 1969-71; resident in phys. medicine and rehab. Good Samaritan Hosp., Phoenix, 1974-76; commd. maj. U.S. Army, 1979, advanced through grades to lt. col., 1982; with Walter Reed Army Med. Ctr., Washington, 1979-81; occup. medicine officer U.S. Army/Army Environ. Hygiene Agy., Aberdeen Proving Ground, Md., 1981-83; resigned U.S. Army, 1983; med. dir. USN/Naval Surface Warfare Ctr., White Oak, Md., 1984-89, NASA Hdqs., Washington, 1990-93; acting chief med. officer Hdqs. FBI, Washington, 1995; med. officer Orgn. Am. States, Washington, 1999—2001; occupl. health phys., cons. Def. Intelligence Agy., Bolling AFB, Washington, 2001—03. Occuptl. medicine Profl. Occuptl. Health Svcs., 1997-98; staff physiatrist, head consultation svc. New Eng. Med. Ctr. Hosps., Boston, 1977-78; instr. neurology and phys. medicine and rehab. Tufts U. Sch. Medicine, Boston, 1977-78; med. cons. Fairfax County (Va.) Health Dept., 1990, Hummer and Assocs., Cleve., 1990-93, Allied Med. Cons., Inc., Washington, 1994-95, AspenMed Svcs., Inc., 1995-96, 2001-2003, Occu Save, Inc., Lanham, Md., 1996, staff privileges Drs. Cmty. Hosp., Lanham, Md., 1996-98, Hummer Whole Health Mgmt., 1998-99. Mem. Am. Coll. Preventive Medicine, Am. Coll. Occupl and Environ. Medicine, Montgomery County Med. Soc., Med. and Chirurg. Faculty Md. Fax: 301-585-6519. Office Phone: 301-585-6519. E-mail: mddocg@yahoo.com.

GULFO, ADELE MADELYN, pharmaceutical marketing executive; b. East Orange, N.J., Dec. 3, 1962; d. Felix Thomas and Adelaide (Balletti) Vitello; m. Joseph Vincent Gulfo, June 21, 1987. BS in Biology and Chemistry, Seton Hall U., 1984; MBA, Fairleigh Dickinson U., 1993. Analytical chemist Fisher Sci. Co., Fair Lawn, N.J., 1986-88, sr. rsch. chemist, 1988-90; mgr. sales and mktg. Spectra Tech. Co., Stamford, Conn., 1990-91; sr. med. writer Parke-Davis divsn. Warner Lambert, Morris Plains, Conn., 1991-94, internat. mktg. mgr., 1994-95, sr. dir. mktg., 1995-2000, Astra Zeneca v.p. cardiovascular therapy area, 2000—. Spkr. in field. Contbr. chpt. to book, articles to newspapers and profl. jours. Recipient Best Rx Product Launch award Fin. Times, 1999; named among Top 100 Marketers, Advt. Age, 1999. Mem. Healthcare Bus. Women's Assn. (Rising Star 1999), Healthcare MKtg. Coun., Am. Heart Assn. (pharm. round table). Roman Catholic. Avocations: fitness, golf, tennis. Office: Warner Lambert 201 Tabor Rd Morris Plains NJ 07950-2693 Home: PO Box 209 Rockland DE 19732-0209 E-mail: Adele.Gulfo@AstraZeneca.com.

GULLACE, MARLENE FRANCES, information engineer, systems analyst, consultant; b. Ft. Belvior, Va., Jan. 12, 1952; d. Amerigo Francis and Martha Arlene Guy; m. Gerald Lynn Tolley, June 26, 1970 (div. Nov. 1974); 1 child, Gerald Lynn Tolley Jr.; m. Salvatore Gullace, Nov. 19, 1976 (div. Apr. 1991). AA in Pre-Law, Cochise Coll., 1979; BA in Polit. Sci., U. Ariz., 1982; AA in Computer Sci., Bus., Chaparral Coll., 1985. Realtor, entrepreneur, inventor, Sierra Vista, Ariz., 1977-84; ADP instr. Chaparral Coll., Tucson, 1985; model Barbizon, Tucson, 1986-87; clk. HUD/FHA, Tucson, 1987-88; computer programmer DOD Inspector Gen., Arlington, 1988-89; programmer analyst U.S. Army Corps of Engrs., USAF, Washington, 1989-91, Calibre Systems Inc., Falls Church, Va., 1991; cons., systems analyst/programmer EDP, Vienna, Va., 1991-93; info. engr. Ogden/Anteon Corp., Vienna, 1993-96, Orkand Corp., 1996, SRA Internat., Inc., 1997-00, SRA Internat., 2000—01, SAIC, 2002—. Patented toy, registered trademark. Realtor assoc. Cochise County Bd. Realtors, 1977-84. Mem. IEEE, Fed. Women's Program at SBA (sec. 1976). Methodist. Avocations: art, design, crafts, sewing. Home: 7829 Piccadilly Dr Warrenton VA 20186-8623

GULLEDGE, KAREN STONE, educational administrator; b. Fayetteville, N.C., Feb. 3, 1941; d. Malcolm Clarence and Clara (Davis) Stone; m. Parker Lee Gulledge Jr, Oct. 17, 1964. BA, St. Andrews Presbyn. Coll., Laurinburg, N.C., 1963; MA, East Carolina U., 1979; EdD, Nova U., 1986. Social worker Lee County, Sanford, N.C., 1963-64; tchr. Asheboro (N.C.) City Schs., 1964-67, Winston-Salem (N.C.)/Forsyth County Schs., 1967-70; research analyst N.C. Dept. Pub. Instrn., Raleigh, 1971-76, sch. planning cons., 1976-89, dir. sch. planning, l989-95; dir. ednl. svcs. Peterson Assocs., Raleigh, 1995-98, The Roberts Group, PA, Raleigh, 1998-99; ret. Chmn. N.C. Elem. Commn. of So. Assn. Colls. and Schs., 1995; leader profl. seminars; spkr. in field. Trustee St. Andrews Coll. Recipient Outstanding Educator award East Carolina U., 1992. Mem. Am. Biographical Assn., So. Assn. Colls. and Schs. (Distinguished Educator award 1994), Coun. Ednl. Facility Planners (pres., chmn. 1995, Disting. Ednl. Achievement award 1994, Disting. Svc. award 1996, 98), The Order of the Long Leaf Pine, Five Hundred Leaders of Infullerence, Delta Kappa Gamma. Democrat. Avocations: reading, entertaining, travel. Home and Office: 9119 Carrington Ridge Dr Raleigh NC 27615-1000 E-mail: ksgulledge@nc.rr.com.

GULLESON, PAM, state legislator; Home: PO Box 215 Rutland ND 58067-0215 Office: ND Ho of Reps State Capitol Bismarck ND 58505

GULLETT, BRENDA B. state legislator; Mem. Ark. State Senate, Little Rock, 2001—, mem. joint budget com., mem. pub. health, welfare and labor com., mem. senate rules com., mem. tech. and legis. affairs com., others. Democrat. Baptist. Office: 28 Longmeadow Pine Bluff AR 71603 also: State Capitol Rm 320 Little Rock AR 72201 E-mail: bgullett@arkleg.state.ar.us.

GULLETTE, MARGARET MORGANROTH, cultural critic, writer; b. N.Y.C., May 13, 1941; d. Martin and Betty (Eisner) Morganroth; m. David G. Gullette, June 4, 1964; 1 child, Sean Morganroth. BA in English, Radcliffe Coll., 1962; MA in Comparative Lit., U. Calif., Berkeley, 1964; PhD in Comparative Lit., Harvard U., 1975. Vis. scholar Schlesinger Libr. Radcliffe Coll., Cambridge, Mass., 1988-89, 90-91; vis. scholar Harvard U, Cambridge, Mass., 1993-94, 95-96, Northeastern U., Boston, 1994-95; resident scholar women's studies Brandeis U., Waltham, Mass., 1996—. Asst. dir. Harvard-Danforth Ctr. for Tchg. and Learning, 1976-85; chair adv. com. Bunting Inst., Radcliffe, 1993-97; Charles A. Miller vis. prof. Ctr. for Advanced Studies, U. Ill., Urbana-Champaign, 2000; vis. scholar NYU, 1997, 2003. Author: Safe At Last In The Middle Years, 1988, Declining to Decline: Cultural Combat And The Politics of The Midlife, 1997; editor: Daughters of Danaaus (Mona Caird), 1989; co-editor Age Studies Series, Univ. Press Va., 1993-2000; contbg. editor N.Am. Rev.; author essays for numerous encyclopedias, mags. and anthologies. Bunting Inst. fellow, 1986-87, Am. Coun. Learned Socs. fellow, 1986-87, NEH fellow, 1991-92; recipient Emily Toth award Popular Culture/Am. Culture Assns., 1998. Mem. PEN Am. Home: 68 Pembroke St Newton MA 02458-2449 E-mail: mgullette@msn.com.

GULLETTE, VALENCIA DESHAE, counselor; b. Huntsville, Tex., Oct. 6, 1976; d. Henry L. and Myrtle Gullette. BS in Psychology, Prairie View A&M U., 1999; MS in Rehab. Counseling, So. U., 2001. Employment specialist Mental Health Assn., Baton Rouge, 2000—01; assoc. psychologist Tex. Dept. Criminal Justice, Huntsville, 2001—03; case mgr. Bayes Achievement Ctr., Inc., Huntsville, 2003—. Dir. adminstr., cons. Career Design, Huntsville, 2003. Mem.: Nat. Assn. Female Execs., Golden Key, Chi Sigma Iota, Alpha Kappa Alpha. Avocations: reading, bowling, time with children, decorating, softball. Office: Bayes Achievement Center Inc 7517 Hwy 75 South Huntsville TX 77340

GULLEY, JOAN LONG, banker; b. Balt., Sept. 10, 1947; d. Thomas F. and Florence (Waldron) Long; m. Philip Gordon Gulley, aug. 2, 1969; 1 child, Colin Jason. BA, U. Rochester, 1969; postgrad., Harvard U., 1985. Analyst U.S. Dept. Commerce, Washington, 1969-70, Fed. Res. Bd., Washington, 1970-74; sr. analyst 5, Washington, 1979-81; asst. v.p. Fed. Res. Bank Boston, 1975-79, v.p., 1981-83; sr. v.p. 5, 1983-86; exec. v.p. The Mass. Co., Boston, 1986-94, pres., CEO, 1994, also bd. dirs.; chmn., CEO PNC Bank New Eng., 1995-97; sr. v.p., mgr. strategic planning PNC Bank Corp., 1997-98, exec. v.p., dep. mgr. consumer bank, 1998—, dep. mgr. regional cmty. bank, 1999—2000; CEO PNC Bus. Banking, 2000—02, PNC Advisors, 2002—. Chmn. PNC Bank, New Eng., 1997-99. Mem. Allegheny Country Club, Nantucket Golf Club, Duquesne Club, Phi Beta Kappa. Office: PNC Bank Corp 1 PNC Plz 249 5th Ave Pittsburgh PA 15222-2709

GULLICKSON, BRANDY KLINGEL, conductor, music educator; d. Thomas Mark and Nina Elizabeth Klingel; m. Ross Dean Gullickson, Dec. 21, 2002. BS in Vocal and Classroom Music K-12, Mankato State U., 1997. Tchr. vocal and classroom music Mankato Area Cath. Schs., 1997; tchr. vocal music Waseca Pub. Schs., Minn., 1997—99; tchr. vocal & classroom music Janesville Pub. Sch., Minn., 1997—99; choir dir., tchr. vocal music Eden Prairie Pub. Schs., Minn., 1999—. Instr. pvt. lessons LaMusique, Minnetonka, Minn., 1999—2002, Klingel Music Studio, Eden Prairie, 2000—. Mem.: Minn. Am. Choral Dirs. Assn. (assoc.), Music Educators Nat. Conf. (assoc.), Minn. Music Edn. Assn. (assoc.), World Voices (assoc.). Office: Eden Prairie Central Middle School 8025 School Rd Eden Prairie MN 55344 E-mail: bklingel@edenpr.k12.mn.us.

GULLICKSON, NANCY ANN, art association administrator; b. Memphis, Jan. 7, 1942; d. Alfred John and Mildred Lucille (Houston) Bowen; m. John Charles Gullickson, June 25, 1966; children: Jay Weldon, Christine Lee. BFA, Miss. Univ. Women, 1964. Owner Yellow Awning Interiors, Lawrenceville, Ga., 1975-85; exec. dir. Gwinnett Coun. Arts, Inc., Duluth, Ga., 1983—. Pres. Ga. Assembly Cmty. Arts Agys., 1987, Alliance Children's Theatre, Atlanta, 1982-83, Lawrenceville Jr. Women's Club, 1977; trustee Woodruff Arts Ctr., Atlanta, 1982-83. Sec., bd. dirs. Gwinnett Conv. & Vis. Bur., 1992—; bd. dirs. Gwinnett Heart Assn., 1994—, Lawrenceville Downtown Devel. Authority, 1989-96; sustainer Gwinnett North Fulton Jr. League, 1985—. Recipient Gwinnett's Exceptional Women Leaders award League Women Voters, 1995. Avocations: boating, skiing, painting. Home: 373 Summit Ridge Dr Lawrenceville GA 30045-6041 Office: Gwinnett Coun Arts Inc 6400 Sugarloaf Pkwy Bldg 300 Duluth GA 30097-4091

GULLIVER, JEAN K. educational association administrator; m. John W. Gulliver; children: Peter, Kate, Elizabeth, Jean. BA in History, Wheaton Coll., 1974. Loan officer Conn. Bank & Trust Co., 1974—77; real estate, 1986—94; vice chair Maine State Bd. Edn., 1998—2000, chairperson, 2000—. Chair Educator Devel. Stakeholder Group, 1998—, Maine Edn. and Tech. Adv. Coun., 1998—99; mem. Maine Sci. and Tech. Bd., 1998—, vice chair, 2001—02; mem. Info. Svcs. Policy Bd., 1999—, Maine Learning Tech. Initiative Adv. Group, 2001—. Trustee Breakwater Sch., Portland, Maine, 1983—87, chair bd. trustees, 1985—86; trustee Portland Stage Co., mem. exec. bd., 1984—87; active classroom vol., com. mem. Falmouth Sch. Sys., 1985—; co-chair sesquicentennial capital campaign Maine Wheaton Coll., 1986—87; mem. Falmouth Bd. Edn., 1990—94, chair, 1992—94; Sunday sch. tchr. St. Mary's Ch., Falmouth, 1985—. Mem.: Nat. Assn. State Bd. Edn. (chair 2001—), Wheaton Coll. Club (pres. 1982—83). Home: 27 Thornhurst Rd Falmouth ME 04105

GULYAS, DIANE H. manufacturing executive; b. Chgo., 1956; BS in Chem. Engring., U. Notre Dame; advanced mgmt. program, Wharton Sch. Bus., 1994. Various sales, mktg., tech. and sys. devel. positions DuPont Polymers Bus. DuPont, Wilmington, Del., 1978, European bus. mgr. for Engring. Polymers Geneva, plant supt. Mechelen, Belgium, site, exec. asst. to chmn. bd. Wilmington, 1993—94, global bus. dir. Nylon Fibers New Bus. Devel. and Global Zytel Engring. Polymers, 1994—97, group v.p. DuPont Electronic and Comm. Techs. Platform, 2002—. Bd. dirs. United Way of Richmond; exec. com. Va. Bus. Coun. Office: DuPont Bldg 1007 Market St Wilmington DE 19898*

GUMINA, PAMELA RAY, municipal government administrator; b. Lamar, Colo., Nov. 2, 1954; d. James Dean and Elsie Ray Wilson; m. Kent B. Gumina, Dec. 16, 1978; children: Diane L., Anne E. AA, Lamar C.C., 1974; BA, Adams State Coll., 1977. Reporter, photographer Valley Courier, Alamosa, Colo., 1977-79; news editor Mid-Iowa Pub., State Center, Iowa, 1979-81; exec. dir. Sterling (Colo.) Urban Renewal Authority, 1983-90; cmty. devel. dir. City of Sterling, 1987-96, asst. to city mgr., 1996-2000, asst. city mgr., 2000—. Project mgr. depot renovation Sterling Downtown Improvement Corp., 1984-90; instr. non-profit grant writing, 1996; program mgr. mktg. campaign J. Harrigan Dialysis Ctr., 1995. Bd. dirs. cmty. edn. Northeastern Jr. Coll., Sterling, 1984-90; fundraiser St. Anthony's Sch., Sterling, 1991-96; mem. Colo. hist. grants com. Presbyn. Ch., Sterling, 1993-96. HUD grantee, 1995. Mem. Internat. City/County Mgmt. Assn., Am. Econ. Devel. Coun., Econ. Devel. Coun. Colo. (bd. dirs. 1994-97, Cmty. of Yr. award 1994)), Colo. Downtown Devel. Assn. (pres. 1990-91), Kiwanis (pres. 1990-91). Office: 421 N 4th St PO Box 4000 Sterling CO 80751-0400 E-mail: pgumina@ci.sterling.co.us.

GUMPERT, LYNN, gallery director; Student, Sorbonne, Paris, 1971-72; cert. completion first year, Ecole du Louvre, Paris, 1971-72; BA in History of Art with honors, U. Calif., Berkeley, 1974; MA in History of Art, U. Mich., 1977. Curatorial asst. The Jewish Mus., N.Y.C., 1978-80; curator The New Mus. Contemporary Art, N.Y.C., 1980-84, sr. curator, 1984-88; adj. curator Mus. Contemporary Art, L.A., 1988-89, We. States Arts Fedn., Santa Fe, 1988-89; coord. Eighth Biennale of Sydney Art Gallery N.S.W., Sydney, Australia, 1989-90; guest curator, adminstrv. dir. Amway (Japan) Ltd. and Setagaya Art Mus., Tokyo, 1989-91, Nat. Mus. Art, Osaka, Japan, 1989-91; cons. curator Gallery at Takashimaya, Inc., N.Y.C., 1992-95; guest curator, U.S. coord. ARC/Musée d'Art Moderne de la Ville de Paris, 1994-95; guest curator Grey Art Gallery, N.Y.C., 1996-97, dir., 1997—; interim dirl mus. studies program NYU, 1999-2000. Lectr. in field; juror in field; panelist in field; ind. curator/cons., 1988-97; mem. adv. com. Asia Soc. Galleries. Exhbns. include Grey Art Gallery, The New Mus. Contemporary Art, 1980, 81, 82, 84, 86, 89, Pitts. Ctr. Arts, 1983, Mus. Contemporary Art, Chgo., 1988, Galerie Ghislaine Hussenot, Paris, 1992, The Gallery at Takashimaya, N.Y.C., 1994, 95, numerous others; author: Christian Boltanski, 1993, reprint, 1996; editor: The Art of the Everyday: The Quotidian in Postwar French Culture, 1997. Decorated chevalier Order Arts and Letters (France); Univ. fellow U. Mich., 1975. Mem. Internat. Assn. Art Critics, ArtTable (N.Y.). Office: Grey Art Gallery NYU 100 Washington Sq E New York NY 10003-6688 Fax: 212-995-4024. E-mail: greygallery@nyu.edu.

GUND, AGNES, former art museum administrator; b. Cleve., Ohio; d. George Gund, Jr.; m. Daniel Shapiro, June 13, 1987; children: David, Catherine, Jessica, Anna. BA in art history, Conn. Coll., 1960; MA in art history, Fogg Mus., Harvard U., 1980; LHD (hon.), Case Western Reserve U., 1995, Brown U., 1996. V.p. Mus. Modern Art, N.Y.C., 1988—91, pres., 1991—2002, pres. emerita, 2002—; chair Mayor's Cultural Affairs Adv. Commn., N.Y.C., 2003—. Bd. trustees Wexner Ctr. Found., 1997—; trustee Mus. Modern Art, 1976—, Brown U., Aaran Diamond AIDS Rsch. Ctr., Inst. Advanced Study, Princeton, NJ, J. Paul Getty Trust, Malibu, Calif.; mem. mus. coun. Cleve. Mus. Art. Recipient Women in the Arts award, Coll. Art Assn., Art Table award for Disting. Svc. to Arts, 1994, Montblanc de la Culture award, 1997, Nat. Medal Arts, 1997, Arts Edn. award, Am. for the Arts, 1999, Evan Burger Donaldson Achievement award, Miss Porter's Sch., 2003, Centennial Medal, Harvard U. Grad. Sch. Arts and Sciences, 2003. Fellow: Am. Acad. Arts and Sciences; mem.: Studio in a Sch. Assn. (founder, Gov.'s Art award, N.Y. 1988, Dorothy Freeman award, N.Y.C. 1988). Office: care Museum Modern Art 11 W 53rd St New York NY 10019-5401*

GUNDECK, CAROLINE NYKLEWICZ, investment company executive; b. Paterson, NJ; BS econs., Marymount Coll. With Merrill Lynch, White Plains, NY, 1983, currently first v.p. investments, chair Adv. Com. to Mgmt. on Diversity, dir. Women's Bus. Devel., 2003—. Created No. NJ Women's Network for Financial Advisors. Mem. adv. com. Preservation and Use of Ellis Island appointed by Gov. Christine Todd Whitman; dir. Women Presidents' Orgn. Recipient Tribute to Women & Industry Award, YMCA, 1999, recognized for outstanding volunteerism, United Way of Passaic County, 2000. Office: 1300 Merrill Lynch Drive, 3rd Fl Pennington NJ 08534 E-mail: caroline_gundeck@ml.com.

GUNDERSEN, MARY LISA KRANITZKY, finance company executive; b. Schenectady, N.Y., July 20, 1955; d. Charles William Kranitzky and Shirley Ann (Thomas) Ballou. BS in Fin., U. Ala., 1982. Fin. specialist GE Co., Birmingham, Ala., 1981-83, supv. acctg. adminstrn. Atlanta, 1984-85, corp. auditor Schenectady, 1985-87; mgr. fin. analysis and auditing GE Constrn. Svcs., Burkville, Ala., 1988-90; mgr. fin. Manheim Auctions Inc., Atlanta, 1990-92; program fin. mgr. Latin Am. Sales Gen. Elec. Indsl. and Power Systems, Schenectady, 1992-94; dir. fin. GE Capital/PT Astra Sedaya Fin., Jakarta, Indonesia, 1995-97, GE Capital Asia Pacific, Hong Kong, 1997-99; comml. mgr. finance GE Energy Parts, Atlanta, 2000—. Bd. dirs. Birmingham Opera Theater, 1980—. Recipient Acad. Excellence medal Fin. Execs. Inst., 1982. Mem. Beta Gamma Sigma, Phi Kappa Phi, Omicron Delta Epsilon. Episcopalian. Avocations: music, water skiing, reading, travel. Home: 2920 Perrington Ct Marietta GA 30066-8717 Office: GE Energy Parts 4200 Wildwood Pkwy Atlanta GA 30339-8402 E-mail: lisa.gundersen@ps.ge.com.

GUNDERSON, JUDITH KEEFER, golf association executive; b. Charleroi, Pa., May 25, 1939; d. John R. and Irene G. (Gaskill) Keefer; m. Jerry L. Gunderson, mar. 19, 1971; children: Jamie L., Jeff S.; stepchildren: Todd G. (dec.), Marc W. Student pub. schs., Uniontown, Pa. Bookkeeper Fayette Nat. Bank, 1957-59, gen. leader bookkeeper, 1960-63; head bookkeeper 1st Nat. Bank, Broward, Fla., 1963-64; bookkeeper Ruthenberg Homes, Inc., 1966-69; bookkeeper, asst. sec.-treas. Peninsular Properties, Inc. subs. Investors Diversified, Mpls., 1969-72; conptr., pres. Am. Golf Fla., Inc. (doing bus. as Golf and Tennis World), Deerfield Beach, Fla., 1972-89, stockholder, 1972-92; sales assoc. Realty Brokers Internat., Inc., 1990; sec.-treas. Internat. Golf, Inc., 1974-89, stockholder, 1974-99; dir. Mary Kay Cosmetics, 1993-97; wellness cons. Nikken, Inc., 1997—; wellness cons., advisor USA+; assoc. Premier Travel Internat., 2002—.

GUNDERSON, SARAH CHLOE (SARAH CHLOE BURNS), historian, educator; b. Owensboro, Ky., Nov. 24, 1949; d. Robert Louis and Eleanor Lucille Burns; m. Dale William Denio, June 21, 1969 (div. May 1988); children: Krista Lynn Denio, Deborah Ann Denio, Matthew Justin Denio; m. Darryl Eugene Gunderson, Oct. 18, 1992. BA, Calif. State U., Bakersfield, 1994, MA, 1996. Tchg. intern Bakersfield Coll., 1995—96, prof. history, 1996—2002; instr. Porterville (Calif.) Coll., 1997; lectr. history dept. Calif. State U., Bakersvield, 2002—. Presenter Ancient to Modern Europe Athens (Greece) Ednl. Inst., 2003; lectr., presenter in field. Author: (book) Daughters of Juno, Chronicle One; Matilda of Argyll, 2004. Recipient Honorarium for book rev., Addison Wesley Longman Pubs., 1998. Mem.: AAUW (chmn. legal adv. fund 2000—01, v.p. ednl. found. 2001—02), Orgn. Am. Historians, Bodleian Libr., Phi Alpha Theta (del., presenter Oxford Roundtable 2003). Avocations: writing, piano, tennis, swimming, travel. Home: PO Box 20100 Bakersfield CA 93390-0100 Office Phone: 661-664-3009. E-mail: chloe@sarah4historyonline.com.

GUNDY-REED, FRANCES DARNELL, marketing executive; b. Muskegon, Mich., Aug. 19, 1947; d. Joseph Leo and Olaverne (Mathis) Merle; m. Russell Norman Gundy, Sept. 18, 1965 (div. 1985); 1 child, Raymond Joseph; m. Robert A. Reed, Aug. 26, 1995 (dec. 1997). AS, Aquinas Coll., 1980, BA, 1991; MLS, Wayne State U., 1993. Mktg. dir. Pine and Dunes coun. Girl Scouts Mich., Muskegon, Mich., 1999—. Active Mich. Strategic Planning Com., Muskegon Cmty. Health Project. Mem.: AAUW, ALA (specialized svcs. coordination com.), Muskegon Heights Alliance of Bus. and Edn. (pres.), Mich. Libr. Assn., Intellectual Freedom Roundtable, Am. Bus. Clubs (former dist. gov.), East Muskegon Heights Neighborhood Assn. (treas.). Home: 145 S Green Creek Rd Muskegon MI 49445-2272 E-mail: darnellgundy_reed@yahoo.com.

GUNN, JOAN MARIE, health facility administrator; b. Binghamton, N.Y., Jan. 29, 1943; d. Andrew and Ruth Antoinette (Butler) Jacoby; m. Albert E. Gunn, Jr., May 18, 1968; children: Albert E. III, Emily Williams Gunn Hebert, Andrew R., Clare M. Berchelmann, Catherine A.B., Philip D. Diploma, Binghamton State Hosp., 1966; BS summa cum laude, Tex. Women's U., 1983; MSN, U. Tex., Houston, 1989. RN, N.Y., Tex., Va., Gt. Britain. Staff nurse Columbia/Presbyn. Med. Ctr., N.Y.C., 1966-67; head nurse, ICU Montefiore Hosp. and Med. Ctr., N.Y.C., 1967-68; staff nurse Nat. Orthopedic and Rehab. Hosp., Arlington, Va., 1972-73, Woman's Hosp. of Tex., Houston, 1976-80; staff nurse geriatrics St. Anthony's Ctr., Houston, 1985-86; charge nurse gero psychiatry Bellaire Gen. Hosp., Houston, 1986; from head nurse gero psychiat. unit to dir. patient svcs. Harris County Psychiat. Ctr. U. Tex., Houston, 1986—2001, dir. patient svs. Harris County Psychiat. Ctr., 2001—. Mem. NRA, Nat. Soc. Colonial Dames of the XVII Century, Daus. of Union Vets. of Civil War, Sigma Theta Tau. Roman Catholic. Avocation: reading history. Home: 2329 Watts St Houston TX 77030-1139 Office: U Tex Harris County Psychiat Ctr 2800 S Macgregor Way Houston TX 77021-1032

GUNN, LUCY DAVIS, realtor; b. Lynchburg, Va., Aug. 19, 1922; d. James Thomas and Sue DuVal Davis; m. Richard E. Gunn, Oct. 5, 1946 (div. Oct. 1973); children: Sarah Otey, James Randolph, Sue Gunn Spooner; m. Charles E. Hackett, Mar. 25, 1977 (div. 1978). BS in Elem. Edn., Farmville State Tchrs. Coll., 1943; postgrad., Columbia U., U. Chgo., Va. Commonwealth U., William and Mary U. Accredited buyer rep., cert. residential specialist, grad. Realtors Inst. Elem. and art tchr. various pub. schs., Ashland and Richmond, Va., 1943—48; mgr., buyer, mktg. Toymaker of Williamsburg, Va., 1962—73; part-time tour guide Colonial Williamsburg, 1973—79; mgr. Charisma Florist, Williamsburg, 1980—83; realtor G.S.H. Real Estate, Williamsburg, 1984—. Mem. cmty. outreach com., ethics and stds. com. Williamsburg Area Assn. Realtors, 1984—2002. Docent Abby Aldrich Rockefeller Folk Art Collection, Williamsburg, 1962—72; bd. mem. Salvation ARmy, Williamsburg, 1986—; mem. altar guild, various other coms. Bruton Parish Ch., Williamsburg, 1980—. Recipient Bronze, Silver and Gold awards, Williamsburg Area Assn. Realtors, 1985—2003, Lifetime Achievement award, 2002. Mem.: Herb Soc. Am. (founding mem. Va. Commonwealth unit), Garden Club Va. (Williamsburg chpt.). Republican. Episcopalian. Avocations: herb gardening, travel, reading, flower arranging.

GUNN, MARY ELIZABETH, retired English language educator; b. Great Bend, Kans., July 21, 1914; d. Ernest E. and Elisabeth (Wesley) Eppstein; m. Charles Leonard Gunn, Sept. 13, 1936 (dec. Apr. 1985); 1 child, Charles Douglas. AB, Ft. Hays State U., 1935, BS in Edn., 1936, MA, 1967. Tchr. English Unified Sch. Dist. 428, Great Bend, 1963-80, Barton County C.C., Great Bend, 1977-84, tchr. adult edn., 1985-87, tchr. ESL, 1988-94; ret., 1994. Recipient Nat. Cmty. Svc. award, DAR, 1996; Conf. Am. Studies fellow, De Pauw U., 1969. Mem. AAUW (Outstanding Mem. 1991), NEA, Bus. and Profl. Women (Woman of Yr. 1974), Kans. Adult Edn. Assn. (Master Adult Educator 1986), Kans. Assn. Tchrs. English, PEO, Delta Kappa Gamma, Alpha Sigma Alpha. Democrat. Mem. United Ch. of Christ. Avocations: travel, driving, needlepoint, crossword puzzles, reading. Home: 3009 16th St Great Bend KS 67530-3705

GUNN, S. JEANNE, writer, natural healer; b. Janesville, Wis., Feb. 28, 1939; Grad. H.S., Evansville, Wis. Cert. Reiki master, massage therapy, aromatherapy, Ayurveda, iridology, healing arts, body wraps; ordained minister. Office mgr. constrn. co., 10 yrs; developer Bodywork & Co., Virginia Beach, Va., 1992, Sacred Earth Ctr., Virginia Beach, 1994. Author: Reiki and Beyond Healing Manual, 1994, also Reiki instrn. booklets, 1994, Natural Healing-Alternative Resources for Total Health, 1999, Calamity Coyote and Her Desert Friends series, 2000; also poems; editor several orgn. newsletters; contbr. articles to newspapers and tng. manuals; interior designer, painter greeting cards; designer wall hangings. Active PTA; troop leader Girl Scouts U.S.A.; den mother Boy Scouts Am.; girls softball coach; vol. hosp.; seminar developer Teen Imagines; founder Talk of Towne. Recipient award for outstanding media person in cmty. Mem.: Toastmistresses (past pres.). Avocations: writing poetry, gardening, walking, painting, quilting. E-mail: wddancer@yahoo.com.

GUNNERSON, DEBRA ANN, piano teacher; b. Detroit, Apr. 30, 1955; d. Robert James and Marjorie Jane (Page) Robinson; m. Gary Lee Gunnerson, May 22, 1976; children: Adam Lee, Julie Ann, Carrie Ann, Aaron Lee. BA in Piano Performance, George Mason U., 1976, MA in Piano Performance, 1991. Nat. cert. piano tchr. Music Tchrs. Nat. Assn. Pvt. tchr. piano, Chantilly, Va., 1971—. Asst. adj. prof. George Mason U., Fairfax, 1990-91; pianist Kennedy Ctr., Washington, 1973, Nat. Cathedral, Washington, 1973, McLean (Va.) Symphony, 1990. Scholar George Mason U., 1973. Mem. No. Va. Music Tchrs. (yearbook chmn. 1993-95, chmn. judged recital 1995-97, pres.-elect 1999-2001), Fairfax West Music Fellowship (historian 1996-97), Springfield Music Club (membership chmn. 1994-95, pres. 1997-99, historian 1999-2001); chmn. Chamber Music at Home Friday Morning Music Club, 1998—. Avocation: walking. Home: 4509 Hazelnut Ct Chantilly VA 20151-2415

GUNNING, CAROLYN SUE, dean, provost, nursing educator; b. Ft. Smith, Ark., Dec. 16, 1943; d. Laurence George and Flora Irene (Garner) G. BS, Tex. Woman's U., 1965; MS, U. Colo., 1973; PhD, U. Tex., Austin, 1981. RN, Tex. Clinician III Bexar County Hosp., San Antonio, 1968-71; instr. U. Tex. Sch. Nursing, San Antonio, 1973-74, asst. prof., 1974-83, asst. to dean, 1977-79, assoc. prof., asst. dean undergrad. programs, 1983-84, assoc. dean, 1984-88; dean Sch. Nursing Marshall U., Huntington, W.Va., 1988-90; dean Coll. Nursing Tex. Woman's U., Denton, 1991—2003, intern provost, v.p. academic affairs, 2003. Accreditation site visitor Commn. on Collegiate Nursing Edn. Contbr. articles to profl. jours. Active Leadership San Antonio, 1978-79, Leadership Tex., 1992. Served to capt. Nurse Corps, U.S. Army, 1965-68, to lt. col. Army N.G., 1980-88. Decorated Army Commendation medal. Mem. ANA, Sigma Theta Tau, Kappa Delta Pi, Phi Kappa Phi.

GUNNING, MONICA OLWEN MINOTT, elementary school educator; b. Jamaica, W.I., Jan. 5, 1930; came to U.S., 1948; d. Reginald Minott and Gwendolyn (Spence) Morgan; m. Elon S. Gunning, Feb. 2, 1957 (div. 1982); children: Michael Anthony, Mark Elon. BS in Edn., CUNY, 1957; M in Edn., Mount St. Mary's Coll., 1971. Elem. tchr., 1959-87; tng. tchr. UCLA, U. So. Calif., 1969-72; bilingual tchr. 10th St Sch., L.A., 1974-76; ESL tchr. Union Ave Sch., L.A.; dir. vacation ch. sch. Wilshire United Meth. Ch., L.A., 1977. Spkr. in field. Author: (poetry) Not A Copper Penny in Me House, 1993 (award 1994), Under the Breadfruit Tree, 1998 (Am. Studies award), Perico Bonito and the Two Georges, 1976. Active Friends of the Libr., 1974—; mem. So. Calif. Coun. of Lit. for Children and Young People, L.A., 1990—. Recipient Meritorious award Friends of the Libr., 1974—, Christian Edn. award Wilshire Meth. Ch., 1983. Mem. Soc. of Children's Book Writers and Illustrators, Toastmasters Beverly Hills Club (pres. 1990-91 Max Damm Outstanding Toastmaster 1995). Democrat. United Methodist. Avocations: gardening, traveling, shopping flea markets, continuing education classes. Home: 30731 Paseo Del Niguel Laguna Niguel CA 92677-2306

GUNTER, G. JANE, state legislator; 3 children. Grad. high sch. Rep. Dist. 7 N.D. Ho. of Reps., mem. human svcs. and polit. subdivsn. coms. Mem. Gov.'s Coun. Human Resources, Com. Children and Youth. Home: PO Box 449 Towner ND 58788-0449

GUNTER, NORMA, artistic director; Dance tchr., 1953-82; artistic dir. Parkersburg (W.Va.) Civic Ballet Co., 1982—, Mid Ohio Valley Ballet Co., Parkersburg. Office: Mid Ohio Valley Ballet Co PO Box 4204 Parkersburg WV 26104-4204*

GUNTER, WANDA BROCK, special education educator; b. New Bern, N.C., June 6, 1959; d. William H. and Carrie G. Brock; m. Willie D. Gunter, June 8, 1979; 1 child, Quincy A. Degree, N.C. Ctrl. U., Durham, 1979, Ctrl. Tex. Coll., Killeen, 1999, Profl. Devel. Career Inst., Atlanta, 1997. Cert. paraprofl. Tex. Bd. Edn., 1996, chess coach U.S. Chess Fedn., 2000, Kagan Coop. Learning Inst. 2001, Signing Exact English Profl. Staff Devel., Tex. Writer, 1977—; cashier AAFES, Fort Hood, Tex., 1981—83; cashier/lead cashier/ customer svc. Account and Fin. Office for Dept. Of Def., Wiesbaden, Germany, 1983—89; real estate videographer El Paso, Tex., 1991—93; dept. mgr. Armed Forces Youth Activities, Barstow, Calif., 1993—95, activities cons., 1993—95; ind. rep. Am. Fair Credit Assn., Killeen, Tex., 1995—97; substitute tchr. Killeen (Tex.) Ind. Sch. Dist., 1995—96; spl. edn. instrnl. aide Killeen Ind. Sch. Dist., 1996—; freelance writer Afrikan Posta Newspaper, Killeen, Tex., 1998—. Coach Mid. Sch., Killeen, Tex., 1996—; co-sponsor Diversity Club, Killeen, Tex., 2002—, African Am. Heritage Com., Killeen, Tex., 1995—2001; founder Broken Silence Books and Publs., Harker Heights, Tex. Exhibitions include Inside the Soul Cultural Arts Mus., 1997, San Bernardino County Libr. Genealogy, Barstow, Calif., 1995, Vive L'Arts Spl. Events Ctr., 1997, Manor Mid. Sch., 1998; author: June-June Calendar, celebrating Juneteenth. Founding mem. Nat. Campaign for Tolerance, Montgomery, Ala., 2002—03; mem. Nat. Urban League, Tex., Com. for Juneteenth, Killeen, Tex., 1997—2003; co-chair Noronha Networks, Killeen, Tex., 2002. Avocations: inventing, hiking, rock and fossil exploration, animal observation, gardening. Office: Broken Silence Books & Publications PO Box 2873 Harker Heights TX 76548

GUNTHER, BARBARA, artist, educator; b. Bklyn., Nov. 10, 1930; d. Benjamin and Rose (Lev) Kelsky; m. Gerald Gunther, June 22, 1949; children: Daniel Jay, Andrew James. BA, Bklyn. Coll., 1949; MA, San Jose State U., 1975. Instr. printmaking, drawing, painting Cabrillo Coll., Aptos, Calif., 1976-93. Instr. lithography Calif. State U., Hayward, 1978-79; instr. studio arts Calif. State U., San Jose, summer 1977, 78, 80; co-founder San

Jose Print Workshop, 1975. One-woman shows include include Palo Alto (Calif.) Cultural Ctr., 1981, Miriam Pearlman, Inc., Chg., 1984, D.P. Fong and Spratt galleries, San Jose, 1991—93, Branner/Spangenburg Gallery, Palo Alto, 1991, U. Calif., Santa Cruz, 1991, Cabrillo Coll., 1997, Frederick Spratt Galleries, San Jose, 1996, San Francisco, 2000, Triton Mus. of Art, Santa Clara, 2001; represented in permanent collections San Jose Art in Pub. Places Program, Triton Mus., Santa Clara, Calif., Mus. City NY, Santa Clara Law Sch., Found. Press, Chrysler Motors. Recipient Purchase award Palo Alto Cultural Ctr., 1975, Judges' Merit award Haggin Mus., 1988. Mem. Calif. Printmakers Soc., San Jose Inst. of Contemporary Art. Studio: 4000 Middlefield Rd Palo Alto CA 94303 E-mail: bgunther@sbcglobal.net.

GUNZBURGER, SUZANNE NATHAN, municipal official, social worker; b. Buffalo, July 12, 1939; d. Lawrence Emil and Ruth Lucille (Wohl) Nathan; m. Gerard Josef Gunzburger, Apr. 10, 1960; children: Ronald Marc, Cynthia Anne, Judith Lynn. BS in Edn., Wayne State U., 1959; MSW, Barry U., 1974. Tchr. pub. schs., Detroit, 1959-63, Trumbull, Conn., 1963-66, North Miami Beach, Fla., 1967-68, Broward County, Fla., 1968-72; pvt. practice clin. social work Hollywood, Fla., 1975—; vice mayor City of Hollywood, 1983-84, 85-87, city commr., 1982-92; commr. Broward County, 1992—, chair, 1994-95, 99-2000. Chmn. Met. Planning Orgn., Broward County, 1984—87, 1989, Statewide Human Rights Adv. Com., 1988—89; pres. Broward County Mental Health Bd., 1984; active Broward County Commn. Status Women, 1978—82, White House Conf. Families, Balt., 1980; del. Broward County League Cities, 1988—92; mem. adv. bd. Broward Homebound, 1991—; mem. Broward Children's Svc. Bd., 1988—92, Broward County Water Adv., 1992—94, 1997—98, Broward County Cmty. Redevel. Agy., 1992—, South Fla. Regional Planning Coun., 1992—94, 1998—99, treas., 1999; vice-chmn. Broward County Planning Coun., 1996—98, chair planning coun., 2000—01, Broward County Cultural Affairs Coun., 1996—; Broward chair Concert Assn. of Fla., Inc., 1996—; mem. Broward Children's Svc. Bd., 1998—; bd. dirs. Environ. Coalition Broward County, 1982—89, 1997—2000, Fla. Assn. of Counties, 1992—, Broward Alliance, 1992—2000, Broward Children's Svcs., 1997, Children's Svcs. Coun., 2001—. Named Broward County Woman of Yr., 1990, Humanitarian of Yr., David Posnack, Jewish Comty. Ctr., 1994, Environmentalist of Yr., Broward County Environ. Coalition, 1994, Polit. Leader of Yr., The Vanguard Chronicle, 1999, Woman of Valor, David Posnack JCC, 2003; recipient Woamn of Yr. in Govt. award Women in Comms., 1983, Disting. Achievement award Am. Jewish Congress, 1990, Fla. Philharm. Woman of Style and Substance, 1995, Woman of Distinction award March of Dimes, 1996, Heart award Children's Consortium, 1996, Disting. Alumni award Barry U., 1996, Jesse Portis Helms Dem. of Yr. award Dolphin Dem. Club, 1996, Gracias award Hispanic Unity, 1999, Polit. Alliance of Yr. award Dolphin Dem. Club, 1999; inductee Broward County Women's Hall of Fame, 1995, Woman of Distinction, City of Hollywood, 1997, Women's Polit. Caucus, 1997; Jewish Mus. Fla., Queen Esther Court Honoree, 2004. Mem. Nat. Assn. Social Workers (diplomate clin. social work), Internat. Acad. Behavioral Med., Counseling and Psychotherapy (diplomate profl. psychotherapy), Am. Acad. Behavioral Med. (clin. mem.), Nat. Coun. Jewish Women (pres. 1980-82, Hannah G. Solomon award 1989), Met. Planning Orgn., Israel Bond Coun., Hollywood C. of C. (leadership devel. 1990—), Kiwanis. Democrat. Avocations: reading, swimming, travel. Office: Office Bd County Commrs Govtl Ctr Rm 412 115 S Andrews Ave Fort Lauderdale FL 33301-1818

GUO, SU, science educator; BS Bioengring., Fudan U., 1991; PhD Genetics & Devel., Cornell U., 1996. Postdoctoral fellow Harvard Med. Sch., 1996—97, Genentech, 1997—2000; asst. prof. biopharm. scis. U. Calif., San Francisco. Office: Sch Pharmacy 513 Parnassus Ave Box 0446 San Francisco CA 94143

GUO, XIAOFENG, physicist; b. Fuzhou, China, Jan. 15, 1967; came to U.S., 1990; m. Jianwei Qiu, June 20, 1996. BS, Beijing U., 1988; PhD, Iowa State U., 1996. Postdoctoral rsch. scientist Columbia U., N.Y.C., 1996-98; postdoctoral rsch. fellow U. Ky., Lexington, 1998—. Contbr. articles to profl. jours. Mem. Am. Phys. Soc., Assn. Women in Sci.

GUOKAS, JOAN ELLEN (MRS. MATTHEW GUOKAS SR.), retired elementary school educator; b. New Rochelle, N.Y., Aug. 24, 1919; d. Homer Vincent and Mary Ellen Ann (Ivory) Burnham; widowed; children: Mary Tyrrell, Matthew Jr. BS in Edn., St. Joseph U., 1961; MEd, Temple U., 1970. Elem. sch. tchr. St. Timothy's Sch., Phila., 1950-53, St. Bernard's Sch., Phila., 1953-59, Vare Elem. Sch., Phila., 1961-68, McCall Elem. Sch., Phila., 1969-81; ret., 1981. Mem. fellowship award com. Emergency Aid, 1981—; mem. alumnae bd. Chestnut Hill Coll., Phila., 1990—; mem. Jefferson Hosp. Women's Bd., 1991; mem. election day voting panel Phila. Election Bd., 1981—; vol. Ocean City's Hist. Mus.; choir mem. Frances Cabrini Roman Cath. Ch., Ocean City. Mem. AAUW. Roman Catholic. Avocations: tutoring foreign students, mentoring, church activities. Address: 500 Bay Ave Apt 305N Ocean City NJ 08226-4809

GUPTA, TANYA, financial analyst; b. Calcutta, West Bengal, India, June 23, 1970; d. Gautam Gupta, Rupa Gupta; m. Abir Qasem. MBA, Bentley Coll., 1995. Lectr. North South U., Washington, 1995—97; ops. officer South Asia World Bank, Washington, 1997—99, resource mgmt. analyst L.Am., 1999—2003, resource mgmt. officer corp. resource mgmt., 2003—. Vol. Higher Achievement Program, Washington, 2001. Grantee, Bentley Coll., 1992, Internat. Student, 1994; scholar Mateo Ricci. Fellow: Am. Inst. Econ. Rsch. Office: World Bank (IBRD) 1818 H St Washington DC 20433

GUPTA, VINITA, communications executive; B Engring in electronics, U. Roorkee; MS in elec. engring., UCLA. Engr. GTE Lenkurt; engring. mgmt. Bell No. Rsch. Inc., 1978-85; chairperson Digital Link Corp., Sunnyvale, Calif., 1985—. Office: Quick Eagle Networks 217 Humboldt Ct Sunnyvale CA 94089-1300 Fax: 408-745-6250.

GUR, RAQUEL E. academic administrator; PhD, Mich. State U., 1974; MD, U. Pa., 1980. Dir. neuropsychiatry U. Pa., Phila. Contbr. articles to profl. jours. Mem.: Insat. of Medicine of NAS. Office: Univ Pa Dept Psychiatry 10 Gates Bldg Philadelphia PA 19104-4283

GURGIN, VONNIE ANN, social scientist, research; b. Toledo, Nov. 20, 1940; BA, Ohio State U., 1962; MA, U. Calif., Berkeley, 1966, D in Criminology, 1969. Rsch. asst. Calif. Dept. Mental Hygiene, San Francisco, 1962-64; rsch. sociologist U. Calif., Berkeley, 1964-66; dir. cons. svcs. Survey Rsch. Ctr., 1967-68, asst. prof. criminology, 1968-71; rsch. sociologist Social Sci. Rsch. Devel. Corp., Berkeley, 1966-67; sr. rsch. criminologist Stanford Rsch. Inst. (now SRI Internat.), Menlo Park, Calif., 1971-72; rsch. dir. Inst. Study Social Concerns, Berkeley, 1972—; asst. chief resource for cancer prevention and epidemiology sect. Calif. Tumor Registry, Calif. Dept. Health Svcs., Emeryville, 1981-86; dir. survey rsch. No. Calif. Cancer Ctr., Belmont, 1982-86, dir. SEER programs, 1986; mgr. dept. family and cmty. health Calif. Med. Assn., San Francisco, 1993-95; program dir. Calif. Immunization Partnership, Albany, 1995—; cons. to various rsch. orgns., 1996—; rsch. dir. Inst. for the Study of Social Concerns, Berkeley, Calif. Pres. bd. dirs. Inst. Study Social Concerns, Berkeley; cons. in field. Contbr. articles to profl. jours. Mem. AAAS, APHA, Am. Sociol. Assn. Address: 1099 Sterling Ave Berkeley CA 94708-1728

GURLEY, RHONDA JEAN, special education educator, consultant; b. Somerville, Mass., Sept. 20, 1967; d. Luther Dean and Dorothy Ann Gurley. Assoc. Degree in Acctg., Fisher Coll., 1987; BS in Bus. Adminstrn./Acctg., Salem State Coll., 1989; M in Spl. Edn., Wheelock Coll., 1992. CEIS L/T cert. Asst. tchr., billing coord., adminstrv. asst. Tri City Mental Health, Medford, Mass., 1987—92; spl. edn. tchr. Cambridge/Somerville (Mass.) Early Intervention, 1992—2002; asst. dir. Just A Start Corp., Somerville, 2003—. Adj. faculty Wheelock Coll., Boston, 1999—; cons. Cerebral Palsy Assn. Ea. Mass., Inc., Lynn, 2002—. Office: Just A Start 16 Butler Dr Somerville MA 02145

GURNO, MARY ANN, school system administrator; b. Jourdanton, Tex., Mar. 9, 1944; d. Leonard and Annie (Simmons) Ottinger. BS, Mary Hardin-Baylor U., 1967; MEd, S.W. Tex. State U., 1975, supervision cert., 1981, mid-mgmt. cert., 1984. Tchr. Killeen (Tex.) Ind. Sch. Dist., 1967-84, Burnet (Tex.) Consol. Ind. Sch. Dist., 1984-85, dir. curriculum/instrn., 1985-88, asst. supt., 1989—. Tech. advisor Lower Colo. River Authority, Austin, Tex., 1987-89. Named Educator of Month Rotary, 1982. Mem. Tex. Assn. Sch. Adminstrs./Tex. Assn. Sch. Bds., Tex. Assn. for Supervision and Curriculum Devel., Assn. for Compensatory Educators of Tex., Kiwanis (treas. 1996), Am. Legion Aux., Phi Delta Kappa. Republican. Methodist. Avocations: reading, gardening. Office: Burnet CISD 1201 N Main St Burnet TX 78611-1340

GURON, GUNWANT K. oncologist; b. Ludhiana, India, June 13, 1959; arrived in U.S., 1985; d. Manmohan Singh Guron and Mahinder Kaur Dishu; m. Marinder Gill, Mar. 28, 1987; children: Sukhmani K., Simirpreet. MB BChir, Gandhi Med. Coll., India. Resident in internal medicine Cook County Hosp., Chgo.; fellow in hematology/oncology Columbia Presbyn. Med. Ctr., N.Y.C.; clin. asst. prof. Seton Hall U. Sch. Grad. Med. Edn., NJ; dir. Comprehensive Hemophila Ctr. St. Michael's Med. Ctr., Newark, med. dir. hematology/oncology, 1998—. Office: St Michael's Med Ctr BRI 268 MLK Blvd Newark NJ 07102

GURWITZ-HALL, BARBARA ANN, artist; b. Ayer, Mass., July 7, 1942; d. Jack and Rose (Baritz) Gurwitz; m. James M. Marshall III, Mar. 12, 1966 (div. 1973); m. William D. Hall, May 3, 1991; 1 child, Amanda Posner. Student, Boston U., 1960-61, Katherine Gibbs Sch., Boston, 1961-62. Represented by Wilde-Meyer Gallery, Scottsdale and Tucson, Ariz., Courtyard Gallery, New Buffalo, Mich., Joanne Coia Gallery, Delray, Fla. Artist-in-residence Desert House of Prayer, Tucson, 1989—91. One-woman shows include Henry Hicks Gallery, N.Y.C., 1971, Karin Newby Gallery, Ariz., 1989—99, CCGV Artist of Month, 1997, Martin and Roll Gallery, Durango, 1998, others, exhibitions include CG Rein Gallery, Santa Fe, 1986, Data Mus., Einhod, Israel, 1987, exhibitions include juried show Santa Cruz Valley Art Assn., 1989—2000 (Best of Show award, 1989, award for excellence, 1992, Hon. Mention, 1990), exhibitions include SCV/aa 25 Anniversary Invitational, 1997, Scharf Gallery, Santa Fe, N.Mex., 1998, NLAPW/GV Juried Exhibit, 1997 (2d prize, 1997, hon. mention, 1998, 2d prize, 1999), exhibitions include juried exhibit U. Tampa, 1998 (award of Honor, 1998), exhibitions include Tucson Mus. of Art, 1998, 2000, 2002, 2004, Wilde-Meyer, Tucson, 2002, 2004, Los Cabaleros Mus., Wickerburg, Ariz., 2001, Craig Gall. Annual Christmas, 2003, Tohono Chul Mus., 2002, Ponies del Pueblo a Tucson Pima Arts Project, 2002—03, Thono Chul Mus., 2003—, Phippen Mus., 2002—, many others, Represented in permanent collections Nat. Mus. Women in The Arts, Washington, Tucson Mus. Art, Goldman Sachs and Co., N.Y.C., Diocese of Tucson, Data Mus., Israel, Haiku Mus., Japan, Nat. Haiku Archive, Calif., Tubac Elem. Sch., Phippen Mus., Prescott, Ariz., Sheraton Corp., Saguaro Ranch Corp. Mem. Tubac Village Coun., 1979-86; bd. dirs. Pimeria Alta Hist. Soc., Nogales, Ariz., 1982-84; creator Children's Art Walk, Tubac Sch. Sys. and Village Coun., 1980; set designer, choreographer DeAnza Ann. Pageant, Tubac Ctr. Arts, 1982-97; bd. dirs. Cath. Found., 2003—. Mem. Nat. League Am. PEN Women (pres. pro tem Sonora Desert br. 1999-2000, pres. 2000-02), Tucson Mus. Art, Nat. Mus. of Women in Arts Washington, Mus. Contemporary Art Tucson. Avocations: golf, theater, singing, travel.

GUSBY, KIM, newscaster; BS in Comm. Arts, Ga. So. U. News anchor WSAV-TV3, Savannah, Ga. Instr. "Legacy" Black history program King-Tisdell Cottage Found. Hon. chairperson Chatham County PTA Coun., 1998; mission work Savannah's Christian Revival Ctr., Haiti. Named one of Outstanding Young Ams., 1998. Office: WSAV-TV3 1430 E Victory Dr Savannah GA 31404

GUSKY, DIANE ELIZABETH, state agency administrator, planner; b. Orange, NJ, Mar. 4, 1948; d. Marvin Leonard and Mary Elizabeth (Frayne) Gusky; m. John Bertram Broster, May 21, 1983. B of Univ. Studies, U. N.Mex., 1981, M Cmty. and Regional Planning, 1984. Cert. cmty. planner. Cmty. planner Planning divsn. City Albuquerque, 1983-84; aviation planner Aeronautics office Tenn. Dept. Transp., 1985-88; chief planner Greater Nashville Regional Coun., 1988-90; sr. planner Buchart-Horn, Inc., 1990-92, Espey, Huston & Assocs. Inc., 1992-97; dep. dir. aeronautics divsn. Tenn. Dept. Transp., 1997-2000, asst. dir. Office Strategic Planning, 2000—03, dir. Office Strategic Planning, 2003—. Mem. Title VI adv. bd. Tenn. Dept. Transp., 1998—, vice chmn., 2001—. Co-author: Land Use Compatibility and Airports, A Guide for Effective Land Use Planning. Recreational therapist Assn. for Retarded Children, NJ and N.Mex., 1974-77; mem. Metro Greenways Citizens Adv. Com., Nashville, 1993—, chair planning and devel. com., 2000—; mem. Nat. Women's Polit. Caucus. Recipient So. Regional Adminstr.'s Top Flight award FAA, Atlanta, 1998; named to Outstanding Young Women of Am., 1983. Mem.: Am. Inst. Cert. Planners, Rebuild Tenn. Coalition (chmn. 1997—98). Office: Tenn Dept Transp Office Strategic Planning 505 Deaderick St Ste 300 Nashville TN 37243 Office Phone: 615-532-3560. E-mail: Diane.Gusky@state.tn.us.

GUSOFF, CAROLYN, reporter; married; 2 children. BA in Govt. and English, Cornell U., Ithaca, N.Y.; MA in Journalism, Columbia U., N.Y.C. Anchor-reporter WEVU-TV, Ft. Myers, Fla., 1985—87; reporter WIXI-FM. WLEQ-FM Radio, Ft. Myers, 1986—87; freelance reporter N.Y. Times, 1988—93; reporter Long Island Bur. NBC4, N.Y.C., 1993—. Corr. Internat. Cmty. Radio Taipei, Taiwan. Recipient 20 Long Island "Folio" awards, N.Y. Spot News award, Assoc. Press, 1991, Nat. award, Am. Women in Radio and TV, 1993. Office: NBC 30 Rockefeller Plz New York NY 10112

GUST, ANNE BALDWIN, retail apparel company executive; b. Grosse Pointe Farms, Mich., Mar. 15, 1958; d. Rockwell Thomas Jr. and Anne Elizabeth (Baldwin) G. BA, Stanford U., 1980; JD, U. Mich., 1983. Bar: Calif. 1983, U.S. Dist. Ct. (no. dist.) Calif. 1983, U.S. Ct. Appeals (9th cir.) 1983. Assoc. Orrick, Herrington & Sutcliffe, San Francisco, 1983-86, Brobeck, Phleger & Harrison, San Francisco & Palo Alto, Calif., 1986—91; assoc. gen. counsel The Gap, Inc., San Francisco, 1991—94, sr. v.p., gen. counsel, 1994—98, exec. v.p., human resources, legal & corp. adminstrn., 1998—99, exec. v.p., human resources, legal, global compliance & corp. adminstrn., 1999—2000, exec. v.p., chief adminstrv. officer, 2000—. Mem. bd. dirs., Jack in the Box Inc., 2003- Contbr. articles to labor trade jours. Mem. ABA (labor subcom.), Calif. Bar Assn. Office: The Gap Inc 1 Harrison St San Francisco CA 94105*

GUSTAFSON, ALICE FAIRLEIGH, lawyer; b. Houston, Dec. 1, 1946; d. William H. and Mary Davis (McCord) Bell; m. Charles R. Gustafson, May 30, 1971. BA in Econs., Wellesley (Mass.) Coll., 1968; JD, U. Puget Sound, 1976. Bar: Wash. 1976. Various positions U.S. Dept. HEW, various locations, 1968-75; assoc. Graham & Dunn, Seattle, 1977-83, ptnr., 1983—. Bd. dirs. King County Am. Cancer Soc., Seattle, 1983-85, Women & Bus., Inc., Seattle, 1984-87; mem. nominating com. YWCA Seattle-King County, 1985-88. Mem. ABA, Wash. State Bar Assn. (chair Bench-Bar-Press com. 1988-90), Seattle-King County Bar Assn. (trustee young lawyers divsn. 1980-83, treas. 1985-87), N.W. Comm. Lawyers, Met. Seattle Urban League (bd. dirs. 1991-93). Avocations: sailing, bicycling, skiing. Home: 13560 Riviera Pl NE Seattle WA 98125-3845 Office: Graham & Dunn 1420 5th Ave Fl 33 Seattle WA 98101-4087

GUSTAFSON, ANNE-LISE DIRKS, lawyer, foreign consul; b. Vejle, Denmark, Aug. 14, 1934; came to U.S., 1955; d. Hans and Edith Margerita Dirks; m. William L. Gustafson, June 23, 1958. BA cum laude, U. Miami, 1963, JD, 1971, LLM, 1973. Vice consul Nation of Denmark, Miami, Fla., 1973-76, consul, 1976—; assoc. atty. Aronovitz & Weksler, Miami, 1976-83; pvt. practice Miami, 1983—. Knighted by Queen of Denmark, 1976, 96. Mem. Fla. Bar Assn., Consular Corps Miami, Alpha Lambda Delta, Delta Phi Alpha, Kappa Delta Pi. Republican. Lutheran. Home and Office: 2655 S Le Jeune Rd Ph 1D Coral Gables FL 33134-5827 Fax: 305-448-4151, 305-448-9707.

GUSTAFSON, HOLLY BETH, psychologist; b. Rock Island, Ill., Nov. 12, 1960; d. Shirley Bessie Atkins and William Thomas Gustafson; m. Joseph Leonard Bargione, Sept. 16, 1989. BA, Western Ky. U., Bowling Green, 1982; MS, U. of So. Miss., 1987, PhD, 1989. Lic. psychologist Ky. State Bd. of Psychology, 1990, cert. sch. psychologist Ky. Dept. of Edn., 1989. Social worker asst. Miss. Welfare Dept., Hattiesburg, Miss., 1985; assoc. psychologist Ellisville State Sch., Miss., 1985; intern Ea. State Sch. and Hosp., Trevose, Pa., 1987—88; psychologist IV Seven Counties Services, Inc, Louisville, 1989—91; contract mental health cons. for cath. schs. Wayne Corp, Louisville, 1991—99; pvt. practice Louisville, 1991—. Practicum supr. Spalding U., Louisville, 1998—; adv. bd. mem. Learning Disabilities Assn. of Ky., Louisville, 1998—; bd. mem. Ky. Youth Advocates, Louisville, 1999—; adv. bd. mem. Crisis and Info. Ctr. of Seven Counties Svcs., Inc, Louisville, 1998—99, Com. of Edn. and Advocacy, Seven Counties Svcs., Inc., Louisville, 1999—2000. Co-editor: (newsletter) The Ky. Psychologist. Crisis vol. RESPOND Crisis Team, Louisville, 1990—94. Mem.: APA, Ky. Psychol. Assn. (Psychologist of the Yr. for the Jefferson Region 2001, Psychologist of the Yr. for the Jefferson Region 2001). Avocations: animal welfare, jewelry design and creation, reading, art.

GUSTAFSON, JUDITH, federal association administrator; b. Flint, Mich., May 16, 1938; d. Lorimer Bruce and Mildred Lucile (Carter) Gustafson. BA cum laude, Fairleigh Dickinson U., 1987. Asst. to dean of faculties and provost Columbia U., N.Y.C., 1958-65; adminstrv. sec. to exec. dir. Coun. on Fgn. Rels., N.Y.C., 1965-77, asst. to pres., 1977-87, asst. sec. of the corp., 1985-87, assoc. dir. studies, 1987-96, sec. of the corp., 1987—. Office: Coun on Fgn Rels 58 E 68th St New York NY 10021-5953 Home: 1 Corriedale Ln Cottekill NY 12419-5029

GUSTAFSON, KRISTEN, advertising executive; b. Norwood, Mass., June 22, 1976; d. Jeffrey Gustafson and Kimberly Belcher. Bachelors, Stonehill Coll., 1998. Cert. pub. U. Denver/The Pub. Inst., 1998. Publicity mgr. Internat. Pubs. Mktg., Sterling, Va., 1998—2003; advt. account exec. WABI-TV 5, Bangor, Maine, 2003—. Author: (nonfiction books) Graduate! Everything You Need to Succeed After College (Ronald G. Fraser Award for Excellence in Communication, 1997). Vol. Maine Discovery Mus., Bangor, 2001—03; big sister DownEast Big Bros./Big Sisters, Bangor, 2002—03. Mem.: NAFE, Maine Media Women, Maine Writers and Pubs. Assn. Republican. Methodist. Avocations: reading, gardening, travel, crafts, sports. Personal E-mail: kristen622@yahoo.com.

GUSTAFSON, MARDEL EMMA, secondary school educator, writer; b. Waukesha, Wis., June 10, 1922; d. Otto Robert and Emma Bertha (Steffan) Hoppe; m. Wayne Carroll Gustafson, Nov. 1, 1950; children: Faith, Keith, Richard, Wayne, John, Beverly. BE, U. Wis., Madson, 1946. Sec. Waukesha Motor Co., 1944—45, Wis. Gen. Hosp., Madison, 1945—46; tchr. Hannibal HS, Wis., 1946—49, St. John Pub. Sch., ND, 1949—50. Author: What Is Happening To Our Children?, 1993, Why A Role Mother?, 2001, All My Love, 2001. Mem.: Wis. Alumni Assn., TOPS Club (sec. 1978—83). Lutheran. Avocations: sewing, knitting, crocheting, gardening, walking. Home: W289 S2915 Hwy Dt Waukesha WI 53188-9581

GUSTAFSON, SANDRA LYNNE, retired secondary school educator; b. Phila., Mar. 8, 1948; d. William Henry Gustafson and Ruth Blossom (Berger) Watson. BS in Edn., Temple U., 1969. Tchr. Lincoln H.S., Phila., 1969—78, Germantown H.S., Phila., 1978—85, Lincoln H.S., Phila., 1985—88, Germantown-Lankenau Motivation H.S., Phila., 1988—98, dean of discipline, 1994—96; tchr. Germantown H.S., Phila., 1998—99, Saul H.S., Phila., 1999—2003; ret., 2003. Asst. to vice prin. Lincoln H.S., Phila., 1970-78; sponsor Nat. Honor Soc., Phila., 1989-92, 93-96, Peer Counselors and Peer Tutors, Phila., 1989-98, records mgr., testing coord. Germantown-Lankenau Motivation H.S., 1997-98; chaperone on choir's trip to Europe, Lincoln H.S., 1973, coord. Freshman Orientation Program, Phila., 1993-98. Sponsor Big Brother/Big Sister Program, 1994—98. Mem. MLA, Phila. Fedn. Tchrs. (del. to state conv. 1973, del. to nat. conv. 1973, 74), Phila. Area Spanish Educators, Sigma Delta Pi, Kappa Delta Epsilon. Democrat. Jewish. Avocations: theater, music, ballet, opera, reading. Personal E-mail: tigras503@verizon.net.

GUSTAVSON, CARRIE, museum director; Dir. Bisbee (Ariz.) Mining and Hist. Mus., 1992—. Office: Bisbee Mining & Hist Mus PO Box 14 Bisbee AZ 85603-0014

GUSTIN, ANN WINIFRED, psychologist; b. Winchester, Mass. d. Bertram Pettingill and Ruth Lillian (Weller) G.. BA in Psychology with honors, U. Mass.; MS (USPHS fellow), PhD, Syracuse U. Registered psychologist, Ga.; Diplomate Am. Bd. Med. Psychotherapists, Am. Bd. Psycho Diagnosticians, Am. Bd. Forensic Examiners. Rsch. asst., psychology trainee U. Mass., Tufts U., Harvard U., Syracuse U.; psychology intern VA, Canandaigua, N.Y.; asst. prof. psychology U. Regina, Sask., Can., 1969-74, assoc. prof. psychology, dir. counseling svcs., head tng. Saskatchewan, 1974-78; pvt. practice psychology Carrollton, Ga., 1978—, Atlanta, 1980—. Staff tng. cons. Frobisher Bay Dept. Social Services, N.W. Territories, Can., 1979-80; cons. staff Tanner Hosp.; ancillary staff West Paces Ferry Hosp., 1983-99; psychiat. cons. Social Security Adminstrn., Ga. Dept. Human Resources, 1980—. Contbr. chpt. to books. Membership chmn. Carroll County Mental H ealth Assn., 1979-81; nat. mental health disaster response team ARC. Fellow Ga. Psychol. Assn. (exec. divsn. lic. psychologists 1986-91, 92—, Nat. Red Cross disaster mental health team 1991); mem. Am. Psychol. Assn., Sask. Psychol. Assn. (mem. exec. coun. 1971-72, registrar 1972-73), Nat. Assn. Disability Examiners, Ga. Assn. Disability Examiners. Office: PO Box 548 Carrollton GA 30112-0548 Address: 107 College St Carrollton GA 30117-3136 Fax: 770-832-7818.

GUTENTAG, PATRICIA RICHMAND, social worker, family counselor, occupational therapist; b. Newark, Apr. 10, 1954; d. Joseph and Joan (Miller) Leflein; m. Herbert Norman Gutentag; children: Steven, Jesse. BS in Occupational Therapy, Tufts U., 1976; MSW, Boston Coll., 1979. Lic. family and marriage counselor, lic. clin. social worker, N.J.; diplomate Am. Bd. Examiners in Clin. Social Work; registered occupational therapist, N.J. Social worker Jewish Family Svc., Salem, Mass., 1979-82; pvt. practice family and marriage counselor Westfield and Red Bank, N.J., 1982—. Cons. high stress, Westfield and Red Bank, 1982—. Fellow N.J. Soc. for Clin. Social Work; mem. NASW, Am. Occupational Therapists Assn., Registered Occupational Therapists Assn., Soc. for Advancement Family Therapy in N.J., Am. Anorexia-Bulimia Assn., Am. Assn. Marriage and Family Therapy. Avocation: reading. Office: 200 Maple Ave Red Bank NJ 07701-1732

GUTH, CARYL JOY, retired anesthesiologist; b. Peoria, Ill., 1935; m. John Faistad, 1968 (dec. 2001). AA, Mars Hill Coll., 1955; BS, Wake Forest U., 1957, MD, 1962. Diplomate Am. Bd. Anesthesiology. Intern U. Kans. Med. Ctr., Kansas City, 1962-63; resident in anesthesiology U. Pa. Hosp., Phila., 1963-65; instr. dept. anesthesiolopgy Wake Forest U. Bapt. Hosp.,

Winston-Salem, NC, 1965; fellow in anesthesiology Queen Victoria Hosp., Sussex, Eng., 1966; former chmn. dept anesthesiology Mills-Peninsula Hosps., San Mateo, Calif., ret.; instr. U. Nijmegan, Netherlands, 1966; ind. Nikken wellness cons., 1996—; spl. interest-complementary medicine, 1998—. Bd. dirs. Mills-Peninsula Health Sys., Mills Hosp.; mem. bd. sci. and policy advisors Am. Coun. Sci. and Health, 2000—. Mem. AMA, Am. Soc. Anesthesiology (del. 1976-2000, chair com. on comms. 1987-90, chair com. profl. diversity 1995-97, ann. meeting program organizer 1983-84, 87-88, 94, 97), Calif. Med. Assn. (chair com. splty. socs. 1983-84), Calif. Soc. Anesthesiology (past pres., editor bull. 1976-79, asst. treas. 1979-81, pres.-elect 1981-82, pres. 1982-83), San Mateo County Med. Assn. (bd. dirs. 1984-86, chair med. staff affairs com. 1985-86), Coy C. Carpenter Soc., Wake Forest U. Soc. (pres. club Wake Forest U.), Wake Forest U. Med. Alumni Assn. (bd. dirs. 1999—, sec. 2003—, pres.-elect 2004, establisher, fundraiser endowed chair Holistic and integrative medicine 2002). Home: 105 Willowbrook Pl Advance NC 27006 E-mail: wellconsultant@5pillars.com.

GUTHRIE, DIANA FERN, nursing educator; b. N.Y.C., May 7, 1934; d. Floyd George and A. May (Moler) Worthington; m. Richard Alan Guthrie, Aug. 18, 1957; children: Laura, Joyce, Tammy. AA, Graceland Coll., 1953; RN, Independence (Mo.) Sanitarium, 1956; BS in Nursing, U. Mo., 1957, MS in Pub. Health, 1969; EdS, Wichita State U., 1982; PhD, Walden U., 1985. Cert. diabetes educator, bd. cert. advanced diabetes mgmt.; RN Mo., Kans., cert. holistic nursing, RN advanced practitioner; lic. profl. counselor Kans., cert. stress mgmt. edn., clin. hypnosis, healing touch, lic. marriage and family therapist. Instr. red cross U.S. Naval Sta., Sangley Point, Philippines, 1961-63; acting head nurse newborn nursery U. Mo., Columbia, 1963-64, birth defect nurse dept. pediat., 1964-65, nursing dir. clin. research ctr., 1965-67, research asst., 1967-73; diabetes nurse specialist Sch. Medicine U. Kans., Wichita, 1973—, asst. then assoc. prof. Sch. Medicine, 1974-85, prof. dept. pediat. and psychiatry Sch. Medicine, 1985-99, prof. emeritus, 2000; prof. dept. nursing Kans. U. Med. Ctr., Wichita, 1985-99, ret., 1999. Nurse cons. diabetes Mo. Regional Med. Program, Columbia, 1970-73; nat. advisor Human Diabetes Ctr. for Excellence, Lexington, Ky., 1982-90, Phoenix, 1983-92, Charlottesville, Ky., 1990-95; adj. prof. Sch. Nursing Wichita State U., 1985—. Author: Nursing Management of Diabetes, 1977, 5th edit., 2002, The Diabetes Source Book, 1990, 5th edit., 2003, Alternative and Complementary Diabetes Case, 2000; contbr. articles to profl. jours. Mem. health adv. bd. Mid-Am. All Indian Ctr., Wichita, 1978-80; bd. dirs. Wichita Urban Indian Health Clinic, 1980-82; bd. trustees Graceland Univ., Lamoni, Iowa, 1996-2001, bd. trustees emeritus, 2002—. Fellow: Am. Acad. Nursing; mem.: APHA, ANA, Am. Assn. Med. Psychotherapists (profl. adv. bd. 1985—), Am. Assn. Diabetes Educators (Kans. area Disting. Svc. award 1999), Am. Diabetes Assn. (Kans. area prof. edn. and youth com. 1988—, affiliate bd. dirs. 1979—83, pres. Kans. affiliate 1980—81, 1990—91, Outstanding Educator award 1979, Regional Outstanding Svc. award 1984), Sigma Theta Tau (Exemplary Recognition award Epsilon Gamma chpt. 1996). Democrat. Mem. Cmty. Of Christ Ch. Avocations: harp, piano, oil painting, crafts, reading. Office: 200 S Hillside Wichita KS 67211-2127 Office Phone: 316-687-3100. E-mail: dguthrie@kumc.edu.

GUTHRIE, HELEN A. nutrition educator, registered dietitian; b. Sarnia, Ont., Can., Sept. 25, 1925; d. David and Helen Andrews; m. George Guthrie, June 4, 1949; children: Barbara, Jane, James. BA, U. Western Ont., 1946, DSc (hon.), 1982; MS, Mich. State U., 1948; PhD, U. Hawaii, 1968; DSc, U. Guelph, 1996. Registered dietitian, Pa. From instr. to prof. Pa. State U., University Park, 1949-73, chair dept., 1974-89, endowed prof. nutrition, 1989-91, prof. emerita, 1991—. V.p. Heinz Inst. Nutrition Sci., 1993—; nutrition cons. to industry, govt. and academia. Chmn. Bd. of Health, State College, Pa., 1977-82. Recipient Borden award Am. Home Econs. Assn., 1976, W.O. Atwater award USDA, 1989, Pacemaker award Pa. Nutrition Coun., 1994. Fellow Am. Inst. Nutrition (councillor 1982—, pres. 1987—, Elvehjhem award for pub. svc. 1989), Soc. Nutrition Edn. (pres. 1978-79, fellow, 1992), Internat. Life Sci. Inst.-Nutrition Found. (trustee 1979-92, v.p. nutrition 1986-89, editor Nutrition Today 1987-97, Philippine Assn. Nutrition and Dietetics (hon.). Office: Pa State U S-125 S Human Devel University Park PA 16802 Home: 5260 S Landings Dr Apt 907 Fort Myers FL 33919-4677*

GUTHRIE, JANET, professional race car driver; b. Iowa City, Mar. 7, 1938; d. William Lain and Jean Ruth Guthrie. BS in Physics, U. Mich., 1960. Comml. pilot and flight instr., 1958-61; research and devel. engr. Republic Aviation Corp., Farmingdale, N.Y., 1960-67; publs. engr. Sperry Systems, Sperry Corp., Great Neck, N.Y., 1968-73; racing driver Sports Car Club Am. and Internat. Motor Sports Assn., 1963-86; profl. racing driver U.S. Auto Club and Nat. Assn. for Stock Car Racing, 1976-80; pres. Janet Guthrie Racing Enterprises Inc., 1978—. Highway safety cons. Met. Ins. Co., 1980-87. Named to Women's Sports Hall of Fame, 1980; recipient Curtis Turner award, Nat. Assn. for Stock Car Racing-Charlotte World 600, 1976, First in class award, Sebring 12-hour, 1967, 1970. Mem. Madison Ave. Sports Car Driving and Chowder Soc., Women's Sports Found., Les Dames d'Aspen, Internat. Wine and Food Soc., Nat. Spkrs. Assn. Achievements include being the first woman to qualify for and race in Daytona 500, 1977, Top Rookie; first woman to qualify for and race in Indpls. 500, 1977, finished 9th, 1978; North Atlantic Road Racing Champion, 1973.

GUTHRIE, JUDITH K. federal judge; b. Chgo., July 13, 1948; d. David Curtis and Kathleen McAfee G.; m. John H. Hannah, Jr., May 9, 1992 (dec. 2003). Student, Ariz. State U., 1966—68; BA, St. Mary's U., 1971; JD cum laude, U. Houston, 1980. Bar: Tex. 1981, U.S. Dist. Ct. (ea. dist.) Tex. 1982, U.S. Ct. Appeals (5th cir.) 1982, U.S. Dist. Ct. (no. dist.) Tex. 1983, U.S. Dist. Ct. (we. dist.) Tex. 1984. Editor Am. Coun. Edn., Washington, 1972-73; exec. asst. Tex. Ho. Reps., Austin, 1973-75; lobbyist Bracewell & Patterson, Austin, 1975-80, assoc. Houston, 1980-81; briefing atty. Tex. Ct. Appeals, Tyler, 1981-82; ptnr. Hannah & Guthrie, Tyler, 1982-86; magistrate judge U.S. Dist. Ct. (ea. dist.) Tex., Tyler, 1986—. Instr. legal asst. program, Tyler Jr. Coll., 1986-87; apptd. Tex. Jud. Coun., 1991-97, gender bias task force, 1991-92; lectr. in field. Contbr. articles to profl. jours. Adv. bd. Main St. Project; legal asst. adv. bd. Tyler Jr. Coll., 1986—, chmn. adv. bd., 1996—; mem. Citizens Commn. Tex. Jud. Sys., 1992—93; bd. dirs. Habitat for Humanity, 2003—; former Dem. chmn. Smith County; former bd. dirs. Found. Women's Resources, Leadership Am., Leadership Tex. Mem.: ABA (Fed. trial judges legis. com. 1991—93), Smith County Bar Assn. (chmn. law libr. com. 1985—2001), State Bar Tex. (dist. 2A grievance com. 1990—, chmn. 1995—96), 5th Cir. Bar Assn., Fed. Magistrate Judges Assn., Am. Judges Assn. Office: US Dist Ct 300 Fed Bldg & US Ct House 211 W Ferguson St Tyler TX 75702-7212

GUTHRIE, TERESA IRENE, pediatric nurse practitioner; b. Amityville, N.Y., Dec. 27, 1957; d. Anthony Arthur and Anita Gloria (Escorcia) Marino; m. Jay H. Guthrie, June 14, 1980; children: Derek Jay, Shannon Ashley. BSN, Adelphi U., 1980; MS, SUNY, Stony Brook, 1996. RN, N.Y. Staff nurse Sagamore Children's Hosp., Huntington, N.Y., 1980, Brunswick Hosp. Ctr., Amityville, 1980-85, charge nurse in orthopedic unit, 1985-90, staff nurse, 1990-94, Lewin Svcs., Inc., Riverhead, N.Y., 1994-95, West Sayville (N.Y.) Children's Med. Svcs., 1996—. Avocations: crafts, reading, outdoor sports. Home: 58 Newport Beach Blvd East Moriches NY 11940-1577

GUTIERREZ, JONI MARIE, landscape architect, political organization worker; BS in Horticulture, N.Mex. State U.; MLA in Landscape Arch., U. Ariz. Founder, prin. Gutierrez Borowski Assocs., Las Cruces, N.Mex.; vice chmn. Dem. Party, N.Mex., 2003, acting chmn., 2003. Office: Democratic Party Chmn 1301 San Pedro NE Albuquerque NM 87110

GUTIERREZ, YVONNE SOLIZ, school system administrator; b. Laredo, Tex., Apr. 6, 1951; d. Roberto and Estela (Segovia) Soliz; m. Juan F. Gutierrez, Jr., Oct. 30, 1971 (div. June 1992). BS in Edn. magna cum laude, Laredo State U., 1979, MS in Edn., 1982; postgrad., Our Lady of the Lake U., 1999—. Tchr. Laredo Ind. Sch. Dist., 1979-83, counselor, 1983-86, vice prin., curriculum facilitator, 1986-95, ctrl. office adminstr., 1995—. Mem. conduct site visits Tex. Sch. Improvement Initiative, Austin, 1996—. Contbr. Teen Forum Column Laredo News Newspaper, 1986, Parent to Parent Column Fed. Focus Parent Newsletter, 1996. Mem. Tchr. Corps U.S. Dept. Edn., Laredo, 1977; pres. Freedom's Found. of Valley Forge, Laredo, 1994; past sec. Laredo Commn. Women, 1995—; mem. Domestic Violence Coalition, 1998-99; bd. dirs. Casa de Misericordia Shelter for Battered Women, 1999—; mem. adv. bd. Safe and Drug Free Schs., Laredo, 1995—, Jr. Achievement, Laredo, 1998—. Recipient Paul Harris award Rotary Internat., 1995. Mem. AAUW, Laredo Adminstrs. and Suprs. Assn. (chaplain 1987-88), Princess Pocahontas Coun. (bd. dirs., sec. 1988—), A & M Mothers Club (v.p. Laredo 1993-95), Delta Kappa Gamma (Alpha Nu chpt.). Democrat. Roman Catholic. Avocation: writing. Home: 1309 Hibiscus Ln Laredo TX 78041-3320 Office: Laredo Ind Sch Dist 1702 Houston St Laredo TX 78040-4906 E-mail: yvonnesg@surfus.net.

GUTIN, MYRA GAIL, communications educator; b. Paterson, N.J., Aug. 13, 1948; d. Stanley and Lillian (Edelstein) Greenberg; m. David Gutin, Sept. 5, 1971; children: Laura, Sarah, Andrew. BA, Emerson Coll., 1970, MA, 1971; PhD, U. Mich., 1983. Asst. prof. comm. Cumberland County Coll., Vineland, N.J., 1972-80, Rider U., Lawrenceville, N.J., 1981-88, prof., 1989—. Adj. instr. Essex County Coll., Newark, 1971-72, Nassau C.C., Garden City, N.Y., 1972, Trenton (N.J.) State Coll., 1981-84; adj. asst. prof. Rider U., 1981-85; lectr. in field. Author: The President's Partner The First Lady in the 20th Century, 1989; contbr. articles to profl. jours. Officer Emerson Coll. Nat. Alumni Bd., 1994—2002, pres., 1998—2000; bd. dirs. Harry B. Kellman Acad., 1999—2002, vice chair bd. dirs., 1998—2000, chair bd. dirs., 2000—02; bd. dirs. Jewish Cmty. Relations Coun., 2003—. Recipient Alumni Achievement award, Emerson Coll., Boston, 1991. Mem. Ctr. for Study of the Presidency, Nat. Comm. Assn., Ea. Comm. Assn. Avocations: travel, theatre. Home: 119 Greenvale Ct Cherry Hill NJ 08034-1701

GUTMAN, LUCY TONI, school social worker, educator, counselor, b. Phila., July 13, 1936; d. Milton R. and Clarissa (Silverman) G.; divorced; children: James, Laurie. BA, Wellesley Coll., 1958; MSW, Bryn Mawr Coll., 1963; MA in History, U. Ariz., 1978; MEd, Northwestern State U., 1991, MA in English, 1992; postgrad., U. So. Miss., 1992—. Cert. sch. social work specialist, Nat. Bd. Cert. Counselor; diplomate in clin. social work; cert. secondary tchr., La.; cert. counselor, La.; cert. Acad. Cert. Social Workers, La. Bd. Cert. Social Workers. Social worker Phila. Gen. Hosp., 1963-65; sr. social worker Irving Schwartz Inst. Children and Youth, 1965-66; sr. psychiat. social worker Child Study Ctr. Phila., 1966-68; chief social worker Framingham (Mass.) Ct. Clinic Juvenile Offenders, 1968-72; dir. clinic, supr. social work Tucson East Cmty. Mental Health Ctr., 1972-74; coord. spl. adoptions program Cath. Social Svcs. So. Ariz., Tucson, 1974-75; social worker Met. Ministry, 1983; supr. social work Leesville (La.) Mental Health Clinic, 1984; sch. social worker Vernon Parish Sch. Bd., Leesville, 1984—. Cons. Nashua (N.H.) Cmty. Coun., 1969-72; adj. instr. English, sociology, Am. and European history Northwestern State U., Ft. Polk, La., 1984—; part-time counselor River North Psychol. Svcs., Leesville, 1989-92; presenter La. Sch. Social Workers Conf., 1986, 87, Ann. Conf. NASW, 1987, 88, La. Spl. Edn. Conf., 1988, La. Conf. Tchrs. English, 1991, 94, So. Assn. Women Historians, 1994, Mid-Am. Conf. History, 1997, Conf. Contemporary So. Women's Lit., 1997, La. Hist. Assn. Conf., 1998. Contbr. articles to profl. jours. Nat. Soc. Colonial Dames scholar, 1978-79; fellow Pa. State, 1961-62, NIMH, 1962-63. Mem. NASW (diplomate), La. Hist. Assn., So. Hist. Assn., So. Assn. Women Historians, Gamma Beta Phi, Phi Alpha Theta, Phi Kappa Phi. Home: 2004 Allison St Leesville LA 71446-5104 Office Phone: 337-239-1689.

GUTMANN, AMY, political science and philosophy educator, academic administrator; b. Bklyn., Nov. 19, 1949; 1 child, Abigail. BA, Radcliffe Coll.-Harvard U., 1971; MS in Polit. Sci., London Sch. Econ., 1972; PhD in Polit. Sci., Harvard U., 1976. Dir. grad. studies dept. politics Princeton (N.J.) U., 1986-88, dir. polit. philosphy program, 1987-89, dir. ethics and pub. affairs program, 1990-95, founding dir. Ctr. Human Values, 1990-95, 97-99, dean faculty, 1995-97, Laurance S. Rockefeller U. prof., 1990—. Tanner lectr., Stanford U., 1994-95; provost, Princeton U., 2001—. Author: Liberal Equality, 1980, Democratic Education, 1987, 2nd edit., 1999; co-author: (with Dennis Thompson) Democracy & Disagreement, 1996, (with Anthony Appiah) Color Conscious, 1996 (award N.Am. Soc. Social Philosophy), Identity in Democracy, 2003; editor: Democracy and the Welfare State, 1988, Multiculturalism, 1992, Freedom of Association, 1998, (with Dennis Thompson) Ethics and Politics, 3d edit., 1997. Bd. trustees Princeton U. Press, 1996—, Ctr. for Advanced Study in the Behavioral Scis., U. Calif., Stanford, 1998 ; mem adv. coun. Kennedy Sch. Govt.-Harvard U., 1996—. Recipient award AAAS, 1997, Ralph J. Bunche award Am. Polit. Sci. Assn., 1997. Mem. Assn. Practical and Profl. Ethics (bd. dirs.), Am. Soc. Political and Legal Philosophy (pres. 2000—). Office: Princeton U Three Nassau Hall Princeton NJ 08544-0001

GUTREUTER, JILL STALLINGS, financial consultant, financial planner; b. Chgo., Mar. 25, 1937; d. C.G. and Ann (Subject) Stallings; m. Robert L. Gutreuter, June 5, 1971; 1 child, Julia E. BA, U. Ill., 1967; postgrad., Chgo.-Kent, 1968-69, Coll. Fin. Planning, Denver, 1994. Staff dir. ABA, Chgo., 1969-71; trust officer Peoples Trust/Summit Bank, Ft. Wayne, Ind., 1980-87; fin. cons. Merrill Lynch, Ft. Wayne, Ind., 1987—2003; 2d v.p. investments Smith Barney, Ft. Wayne, Ind., 2003—. Fin. planning tchr., continuing edn. divsn. Ind. U.-Purdue U., Ft. Wayne, 1990—2000. Bd. dirs., mem. fin. com. YWCA, Ft. Wayne, 1997—2003; pres. Art League, Ft. Wayne Mus. Art, 1992—93; trustee Episcopal Diocese of North Ind. Found., South Bend, 1995—2000; Bd. dirs. Girl Scouts of the Limberlost, No. Ind., 1997—2000. Recipient Women of Achievement award YWCA, Ft. Wayne, 1994. Mem.: Inst. CFPs, Altrusa Internat. (pres. Ft. Wayne chpt. 1992—94), DAR, Rotary Internat. Episcopalian. Avocations: swimming, walking, painting, knitting. Home: 2312 Forest Park Blvd Fort Wayne IN 46805-3619 Office: Smith Barney One Summit Sq 20th Fl Fort Wayne IN 46869-3429

GUTTMAN, HELENE NATHAN, biomedical research consultant, transpersonal counselor, regression therapist; b. N.Y.C., July 21, 1930; d. Arthur and Mollie (Bergovoy) Nathan. BA, Bklyn. Coll., 1951; AM, Harvard U., 1956; MA, Columbia U., 1958; PhD, Rutgers U., 1960. Registered and cert. profl. past-life regression therapist; bd. cert. nutrition specialist; bd. cert. and registered hypnotherapist; registered and cert. transpersonal counselor; cert. and registered neurolinguistic therapist. Rsch. technician Pub. Health Rsch. Inst., N.Y.C., 1951-52; control bacteriologist Burroughs-Wellcome, Inc., Tuckahoe, NY, 1952-53; vol. rschr. Haskins Labs., N.Y.C., 1952-53, rsch. asst., 1953-56, rsch. assoc., 1956-60, staff microbiologist, 1960-64; lectr. dept. biology Queens Coll., N.Y.C., 1956-57; rsch. collaborator Brookhaven Nat. Labs., Upton, L.I., NY, 1958; guest investigator Botanisches Institut der Technisches Hochschule, Darmstadt, Germany, 1960; rsch. assoc. dept. biol. scis. Goucher Coll., Towson, Md., 1960-62; vis. asst. rsch. prof. dept. medicine Med. Coll. Va., Richmond, 1960-62; asst. prof., then assoc. prof. dept. biology NYU, 1962-67; from assoc. prof. to prof. dept. biol. scis. U. Ill.-Chgo., 1967-75, prof., 1969-75; prof. dept. microbiology U. Ill. Med. Sch., 1969-75; assoc. dir. for rsch. Urban Systems Lab. U. Ill., 1975; expert Office of Dir. Nat. Heart, Lung and Blood Inst., NIH, Bethesda, Md., 1975-77, coord. rsch. resources Office Program Planning and Evaluation, 1977-79; dep. dir. Sci. Adv. Bd., Office of Adminstr., EPA, 1979-80; program coord., post-harvest tech., food safety and human nutrition, sci. and edn. adminstrn. USDA, 1980-83, assoc. dir. Beltsville (Md.) Human Nutrition Rsch. Ctr., Agrl. Rsch. Svc., 1983-89; pres. HNG Assocs., 1983—; nat. animal care coord. Nat. Program Staff Agr. Rsch. Svc./USDA, Beltsville, 1989-95. Bd. advisors The Monroe Inst., 1993—. Sr. author: Experiments in Cellular Biodynamics, 1972; co-editor (procs.) First Joint USA-USSR Symposium on Blood Transfusion, Moscow, 1976, DHEW Publ. No. (NIH) 78-1246, 1978; editl. bd. Jour. Protozoology, 1972-75, Jour. Am. Med. Women's Assn., 1978-81, Methods in Cell Sci., 1994-2004; sr. editor: Science and Animals: Addressing Contemporary Issues, 1989; editor: Guidelines for Well-being of Rodents in Research, 1990, Rodents and Rabbits: Current Research Issues, 1994; (with others) Rodents and Rabbits: Addressing Current Issues, 1994; contbr. articles to profl. jours. Mem. edn. com. Ill. Commn. on Status Women, 1974-75; cons. EPA, sci. adv. bd., 1974-79; bd. dirs. Du Page County Comprehensive Health Care Agy., 1974-75. Andelot fellow Harvard U., 1956, Rutgers scholar Rutgers U., 1960; recipient Thomas Jefferson Murray prize Theobald Smith Soc., 1959; spl. award for work in Germany Deutscher Forschungs Gemeinschaft, 1960; Fellow Dazian Found., 1956; rsch. grantee. Fellow: AAAS, N.Y. Acad. Scis., Am. Acad. Microbiology, Am. Inst. Chemists (chmn. com.); mem.: Univ. and Coll. Women Ill. (past v.p.), Fed. Orgn. Profl. Women (past chmn. task force, past pres.), Assn. Women in Sci., Soc. Protozoology (past mem. exec. com., past com. chmn.), Am. Soc. Clin. Nutrition, Am. Soc. Cell Biology (past com. chmn.), Am. Soc. Microbiologists, Neuroscis. Soc., Am. Soc. Biol. Chemistry and Molecular Biology, Tissue Culture Assn. (com. chmn. Nat. Capital Area br. 1988—90), Soc. Sci. Exploration, Soc. for In Vitro Biology (chmn. constn. and bylaws com. 1994—2002, Disting. Svc. award 1995, 1999), Assn. for Transpersonal Psychology (profl. mem.), Soc. Am. Bacteriologists (pres.'s fellow), Internat. Assn. Regression Therapies (life profl.), Am. Running and Fitness Assn. (bd. dirs., mem. editl. bd., mem. bd. advisors 1993—95), Sigma Xi, Sigma Delta Epsilon (past coord. regional ctrs.). Home and Office: 5607 Mclean Dr Bethesda MD 20814-1021

GUY, DONNA S. artist; b. Brighton, Iowa, Apr. 6, 1933; d. Roy A. and Wilma E. (Farmer) Duttweilen; widowed; children: Debra Guy Greiner, Danny J. Grad. high sch., Brighton, 1951. Contbr. articles to jours. Recipient Excellence award World Orgn. China Painting, 1987, 1st Permanent Mus. Display award, 1995. Mem. Internat. Porcelain Artists and Tchrs., Internat. Porcelain Artists Inc. (master tchr.), Midwest Watercolor Soc., Iowa World Orgn. China Painting Tchrs., Iowa World Orgn. China Painting, Iowa Watercolor Soc. (signature mem.), Profl. Porcelain Artists Assn. Avocations: sewing, traveling, golf. Home: 300 Jefferson Brighton IA 52540

GUY, ELEANOR BRYENTON, writer; b. Pitts., Sept. 6, 1930; d. Lloyd Charles and Verda Eleanor (Hooper) Bryenton; m. Daniel Sowers Guy, Dec. 22, 1962; children: Stanley, Sharon. BA, Ohio Wesleyan U., 1953. Program dir. Lakewood Br. Cleve. Met. YWCA, Lakewood, Ohio, 1953-56, ctr. dir., 1956-57; residence dir., mem. faculty St. Luke's Hosp. Sch. Nursing, Shaker Heights, Ohio, 1957-59; pers. asst., counselor Acacia Mutual Life Ins. Co., Washington, 1959-62; admissions counselor Ohio No. U., Ada, 1963-64; freelance writer, photographer Kenton (Ohio) Times, 1984-88, Ada Herald, 1988-96; coord. external affairs, editor the Writ, Pettit Coll. of Law, Ohio No. U., 1995-96. Sec. bd. trustees, chmn. pub. rels. com. Ada Pub. Libr., 1982—86; mem. pub. rels. com., bd. dirs. Hardin County Alcohol and Drug Abuse Ctr., Kenton, 1989—92; chmn. publicity Town and Gown Planning Com., Ada, 1988; tchr., mem. co-chair edn. com., mem. missions com., mem., sec. adminstrv. coun., mem. centennial com., publicist local ch., 1985—, lay dist. del. to West Ohio Ann. conf., 1998—; dist. spiritual growth coord. Ch. United Meth. Women, 2000—03. Mem. AAUW (pres. local br. 1978-80), Ohio No. U. Women (parliamentarian, pub. rels. chair Christmas Arts Festival 1990-96), P.E.O. (v.p. 1994-96, sec. 1998-99), Twice Ten Art Club (pres. 1984-85, 90-91, 97-98, sec. 1988-89, 99-01, mem. v.p. 2003—). Methodist. Avocations: photography, travel, music.

GUY, JENNIFER LOUISE, nursing administrator; b. Ashtabula, Ohio, Oct. 17, 1948; d. Edward Frederick and Louise Arnoldia (Plagkais) Peterson; m. Donald File, Mar. 17, 1973 (div. Oct. 1978); m. Jerry Thomas Guy, Feb. 10, 1981; 1 child, Thomas Osler. BS, Ohio State U., 1970; diploma, Mt. Carmel Sch. Nursing, 1977. Lab. tech. Ashtabula (Ohio) Gene Hosp., 1964-65; rsch. specialist infectious diseases Ohio State U., Columbus, 1966-73, rsch. specialist oncology, 1973-77; dir. oncology Grant Med. Ctr., Columbus, 1977-88; adminstr. oncology Park Med. Ctr., Columbus, 1988-98; cons., 1998—. Adminstr. Columbus Cmty. Clin. Oncology Program, 1985-88; trustee Am. Cancer Soc., Columbus, 1995-96, v.p., 1995-96, pres. 1996—; pres. Assn. Cmty. Cancer Ctrs., Rockville, Md., 1991-92; grant reviewer NIH, Bethesda, Md., 1986-92. Contbr. articles to profl. jours, chpts. to books, CEu4u.com. Bd. dirs. Franklin County Unit Am. Cancer Soc., 1992—, pres., 1996—, Ohio Divsn. Am. Cancer Soc., 1998—; trustee Columbus Cmty. Clin. Oncology Program, 1990-94, Columbus Race for the Cure, 1994-99, Park Found. Columbus, 1995-98. Mem. Oncology Nursing Soc., One Ngy Soc. (bd. trustees Columbus (Ohio) chpt., 1999—, editor newsletter, 1999—), Oncology Nurses Network. Avocations: reading, travel, interior designs. Office: 711 S Mohawk St Columbus OH 43206-2108

GUY, MILDRED DOROTHY, retired secondary school educator; b. Brunswick, Ga. d. John and Mamie Paul (Smith) Floyd; m. Charles H. Guy, Aug. 18, 1956 (div. 1979); 1 child, Rhonda Lynn. BA in Social Sci., Savannah State Coll., 1949; MA in Am. History, Atlanta U., 1952; postgrad., U. So. Calif., U. Colo. Tchr. social studies L.S. Ingraham H.S., Sparta, Ga.; tchr. English and social studies North Jr. H.S., Colorado Springs, 1958-84, ret., 1984; cooperating tchr. Tchr. Edn. Program, Col. Coll., 1968-72. Fund raiser for Citizens for Theatre Auditorium, Colorado Springs, 1979; bd. dirs. Urban League, 1971-75; del. to County and State Dem. Conv., 1972, 76, 80, 84, 92, 96; mem. Pike's Peak C.C. Coun., 1976-83; mem. Colo. Springs Opera Coun. of 500, 1984-88; mem. nominating com. Wagon Wheel coun. Girl Scouts U.S.A., 1985-87; active Fine Arts Ctr., Pikes Peak Hospice; mem. St. John's Bapt. Ch., former sanctuary choir mem.; mem. Svcs. of Charity (local and nat.); life mem. Friends of Colorado Springs Pioneers Mus. Recipient Viking award North Jr. H.S., 1973, Woman of Distinction award Girl Scouts Wagon Wheel Coun., 1989, 94; Outstanding Black Woman of Colorado Springs award, 1975; named Pacesetter, Atlanta U., 1980-81, Outstanding Black Educator of Yr., Black Educators of Dist. II, Colorado Springs, 1984, Outstanding Ednl. Svc. award Colo. Dept. and State Bd. Edn., 1983, Dedicated Svc. award Pikes Peak C.C., 1983, Outstanding Cmty. Leadership award Alpha Phi Alpha, 1985, Action award Colo. Black Woman for Polit. Action, 1985, Sphinx award, 1986; named in recognition sect. Salute to Women, Colorado Springs Gazette Telegraph, 1986; Wall of Fame honoree Nat. Women's Hall of Fame, 1997. Mem.: AAUW, NEA, NAACP (life), LWV (Colo. chpt.), Women's Ednl. Soc. Colo. Coll. (bd. mgrs. 1992—98), Afro-Am. Life and History, Colo. Social Studies Assn., Women's Found. Colo., Negro Hist. Assn. Colorado Springs, Assn. for the Study of Afro Am. Life and History, Inc. (life), Colo. Springs Pioneers Mus. (life), Golden Heritage (life), Alpha Kappa Alpha (pres. Iota Beta Omega chpt. 1984—85, Chpt. Pres. award 1985), Alpha Delta Kappa. Home: 3132 Constitution Ave Colorado Springs CO 80909-2177

GUY, SANDRA, journalist, telecommunications writer; b. Bristol, Tenn., Jan. 7, 1961; d. William Clinton and Ruby Jeannette Guy. BA in Mass. Comms. cum laude, Emory & Henry Coll., 1983. Staff writer The Coalfield Progress, Norton, Va., 1983-84; Sullivan County bur. reporter Kingsport (Tenn.) Times-News, 1984-88; polit. writer The Times of N.W. Ind., Munster, Ind., 1988-93, West Lake editor, 1993-95; news editor Telephony mag., Chgo., 1995-98; news editor (mag. supplement) Internet Edge, 1997; bus. and tech. editor Am. Med. News, Chgo., 1998-99; freelance writer The Writing Experts, Chgo., 1999—; bus. writer Chgo. Sun-Times, 1999—. Child life vol. La Rabida Children's Hosp., Chgo., 1998-99. Mem. Art Inst. Chgo., 1988— Fellow Knight Ctr. for Specialized Journalism, 1996, recipient Meeman Found. award for Pub. Svc. Tenn. Press Assn., 1985, 1st pl. Best News Story, 1985, 2d Pl. In-Depth Writing award Va. Press Assn,. 1984, News Media award N.W. Ind. Jewish Fedn., 1994. Mem. NAFE, Assn. for Women Journalists (web site coord. 1998—), Soc. Profl. Journalists, Investigative Reporters and Editors, Chgo. Women in Pub., Nat. Mus. Women in the Arts. Lutheran. Avocations: tennis, tae bo, reading, volunteer work. Home: 3431 N Marshfield Ave Chicago IL 60657-1237 E-mail: sguy178525@aol.com.

GUY, SHARON KAYE, state agency executive; b. Nashville, Apr. 5, 1958; d. Dallas Hearold and Elizabeth Jean (Towns) Gregory; 1 child, Anthony Lee. Grad. high sch., Chgo. Clk. Pub. Health dept. State of Tenn., Nashville, 1979-84, office mgr. Health Facilities commn., 1984-92; asst. Legis. Svcs., Nashville, 1992-95; rep. State Ins., Nashville, 1995-98, mem. commerce ins. contractors bd., 1998-99; commerce and ins. adminstr. permits and license State Fire Marshal's Office, 1999-2000; bus. cons. State Dept. Econ. and Cmty. Devel., Nashville, 2000—. Acct. Bryant Guy Constrn., Nashville, 1984—. Blood drive coord. ARC, Nashville, 1984—; campaign vol. United Way, Nashville, 1984—; vol. State Community Coll., 1990—. Nashville Tech., 1991—. Baptist. Avocations: snow and water skiing, motor bikes. Home: 121 Candle Woods Dr Hendersonville TN 37075-4452 Office: Wm Snodgrass Bldg 8th Ave N Nashville TN 37243-0405 E-mail: sharon.guy@state.tn.us.

GUYARDO, GAYLE, newscaster; 2 children. Grad. in Comm., Auburn U., 1988; postgrad. in Theater and Comm., Northwestern U. Reporter WTOG, Tampa Bay, Fla., ABC Affiliate, Montgomery, Ala.; anchor New Channel 8, Sarasota, Fla., WFLA-TV, Tampa, Fla. Office: WFLA-TV PO Box 1410 Tampa FL 33601

GUYER, HEDY-ANN KLEIN, special education educator; b. Phila., Dec. 25, 1947; d. Edward Chuck Klein and Gladys Selma (Shapiro) Sussman; m. Eugene August Guyer, Aug. 24, 1980 (div. Mar. 2002). BS in Secondary Edn., St. Joseph's U., Phila., 1981; MEd in Spl. Edn., Arcadia Univ., 1996. Cert. in social studies, elem. edn., spl. edn. of mentally and/or physically handicapped, Pa. Tchr. spl. edn. Sch. Dist. Phila., 1996—. Mem. ASCD, Women in Edn., George Washington H.S. Alumni Assn., B'nai B'rith (educators unit), Coun. Exceptional Children. Home: 1033 Bloomfield Ave Philadelphia PA 19115-4829 Office: Sch Dist Phila William Penn HS Broad and Master Sts Philadelphia PA 19122-4097

GUYETTE, DIANA, minister; b. South Porcupine, Ont., Can., Oct. 18, 1942; d. Arthur and Marie Louise Doiron; 1 child, Susie Marie Florence Ordner. MDiv, Emory U., 1996. Ordained elder United Meth. Ch., 1998. Assoc. pastor Mulberry United Meth. Ch., Macon, Ga., 2000—02; dir. Hannibal (Ohio)-Clarington United Meth. Parish, 2002—. Chairperson Savannah (Ga.) Dist. Coun. on Ministries of the United Meth. Ch., 1998—99; mentor St. Clairsville Dist. of the East Ohio United Meth. Conf., Hannibal, 2003—. Literacy tutor Chatham County Libr., Savannah, 1985—87; lectr. Ga. Coun. on Child Abuse, Savannah, 1986—99; co-facilitator incest survivor group Army Cmty. Svc., Savannah, Ga., 1988—99; lectr. Candler Sch. Theology, Atlanta. Margaret Adger Pitts fellow, Andrew Coll., 1999. Methodist. Avocations: leading retreats, cross stitch, crocheting. Home: 40441 State Rte 7 PO Box 237 Hannibal OH 43931 Office: Hannibal-Clarington Parish PO Box 187 Hannibal OH 43931

GUYNES, DEMI See MOORE, DEMI

GUZAK, KAREN JEAN WAHLSTROM, artist; b. Cambridge, Mass., May 21, 1939; d. Ernest E. and Kathryn E. (Kemp) Wahlstrom; m. Steven V. Guzak, Aug. 29, 1959 (div. 1983); children: Gretchen, Christopher, Lauren. BS, U. Colo., 1961; BFA, Cornish Sch. Allied Arts, Seattle, 1976. Pres. Karen Guzak Inc., Seattle, 1982—. Owner Yoga Circle Studio, Snohomish, Wash. One-woman shows include Foster White Gallery, Seattle, 1981, 1984, 1987, 1989, 1991, 1994, 1996, 1998, 2000, Davidson Galleries, 1981, 1984, 1987, Tom Luttrell Gallery, San Francisco, 1981, Harris Gallery, Houston, 1982, Laura Russo Gallery, Portland, Oreg., 1987, 1989, 1991, 1996, Musee Hyacinth Rigaud, Perpignan, France, 1988, exhibited in group shows at Bklyn. Mus., 1981, Brentwood Gallery, St. Louis, 1982, Seattle Art Mus., 1983, San Francisco Mus., 1983, Portland Art Mus., 1985, Davidson Gallery, 1992, Stifel Fine Arts Ctr., Wheeling, W.Va., 1993, Bellevue Art Mus., Wash., 1988, 1990, 1995—96, DeCordova Mus., 1991, Purdue U., 1995, U. Brighton, Eng., 1997, Bronx Mus., 1987, Portland Art Mus., 1997, Ctr. on Contemporary Art, 2000, Tacoma Art Mus., 2002, Represented in permanent collections Portland Art Mus., Jundt Mus. Gonzaga U., Bklyn. Mus., NYC Libr., Pratt Inst., City of Seattle, King County Wash., pub. commns. include South Seattle C.C., So. Oreg. State Coll., King County Coun. Chambers, Overlake Ctr. for Sound Transit, Redmond, Wash. Bd. commrs. King County Arts Commn., Seattle, 1981—86, commr., 1984—85; arts adv. com. METRO Arts Program, Seattle, 1985—91; contemporary coun. Seattle Art Mus., 1990—96; pres., developer Sunny Arms Coop., Seattle, 1988—90; co-developer, pres. Union Arts Coop., Seattle, 1992—93; chair hist. design rev. bd. City of Snohomish, 2000—03; bd. dirs. Ctr. Contemporary Art, 1987—88; pres. bd. dirs. Artist Trust, Seattle, 1996—99; chair Historian Design Rev. Bd., 2004—. Boettcher scholar Univ. Colo., 1957-61; recipient Housing Designs that Work award Seattle Design Commn., 1991, Home of Yr. award Seattle Times and AIA, 1994. Democrat. Home and Office: Karen Guzak Inc 230 Avenue B Snohomish WA 98290-2841 Office: Yoga CircleStudio 707 Pine Ave 103 Snohomish WA 98290 Office Phone: 360-568-8595.

GUZE, PHYLLIS ARLENE, internist, educator, academic administrator; MD, U. So. Calif., 1971. Resident in internal medicine Harbor UCLA Med. Ctr., fellow; dean of edn. UCLA, 1991-95, prof. medicine, vice chair, 1985—; chief dept. medicine VA Greater LA Healthcare Systems, L.A., 1985—. Contbr. numerous articles to profl. jours. Recipient Disting. Tchr. award in clin. scis. Assn. Am. Med. Colls., 1995, Sherman M. Melinkoff Faculty award UCLA Sch. Medicine, 1995, Luckman Disting. Tchg. award, 1996, Disting. Tchr. award Alpha Omega Alpha, 1995. Mem. ACP, Am. Bd. of Internal Medicine (cert. com.), Assn. of Program Dirs. in Internal Medicine, Assn. of VA Chiefs of Medicine. Office: VA Greater LA Healthcare Sys West LA 11301 Wilshire Blvd # Mc111 Los Angeles CA 90073-1003

GUZMAN, CAROLE L. small business owner; b. Bklyn., N.Y., July 10, 1955; d. Carol Helen (Lipp) and Nicasio Guzman. Assoc. prodr. In The Life TV, N.Y.C., NY, 1992—93; asst. dir. pub. affairs Crosswalks TV, N.Y.C., NY, 1993; 2d asst. dir. 10 Benny, Montclair, NJ, 1994, Ed's Next Move, N.Y.C., NY, 1994; asst. dir. The Truth of Human Life, N.Y.C., NY, 1994, The Dinner Party, N.Y.C., NY, 1994; office mgr. September Music, N.Y.C., NY, 1995; exec. asst. New Sch. U., N.Y.C., NY, 1995—98; supr. Bus. and Legal Reports, Old Saybrook, Conn., 1998—2001; bus. owner Video Movietime, Westbrook, Conn., 2003—. Cons. Ms. Found. for Women, N.Y.C., NY, 1998. Author: (play) Pack My Bags . . . I'm Goin' to Heaven. Activist Act Up, N.Y.C., NY, 1982—92. Recipient IBM Means Svc., IBM Corp., 1988. Mem.: Women Make Movies.

GUZMAN, MARITZA, director; b. Canovanas, PR, Feb. 22, 1957; d. Antonio Guzman, Sara Vazquez; m. Victor Ramos, July 21, 1984. M in Guidance and Counseling, Interamerican U., 1985; BSW, U. Sagrado Corazon, 1978. Cert. social work 1978. Adminstrv. coord. U. Sagrado Corazon, San Juan, PR, 1995—, program dir., Vols. in Svc. to Am., 1990—95, program dir., tchr. tng., 1988—90, program dir., parents vol. program, 1987—88, counselor, 1986—87, Caribbean U., Bayamon, PR, 1985—86; therapist Against Addiction Svcs. Dept., San Juan, PR, 1983—85; social worker Family Dept. Municipality, San Juan, PR, 1978—83. Cons. Resources for Svc. & Engring. Ctr., San Juan, PR, 1998—99, Sports & Recreation Dept., San Juan, PR, 1999—2000; mem. adv. bd. SE Regional Ctr., San Juan, PR, 1992—93. Co-author: Learning To Be Better Parents, 1989. Recipient Svcs. Parent Vol.. Program award, Alcohol and Drug Prevention Program, 1990. Mem.: Am. Counseling Assn., Counselor Soc. Justice, Am. Coll. Counseling Assn., Puerto Rican Assn. Profl. Counseling (Excellence Labor During Presidency award 1999, Profl. Svcs. award 1999, 1991), Internat. Assn. Addictions Offender Counselor. Office: Univ Del Sagrado Corazon PO Box 12383 San Juan PR 00914-0383

GUZY, CAROL, photojournalist; b. Bethleham, PA, Mar. 7, 1956; ADN, Northampton County Area C.C., Pa., 1978; AAS in Photography, Art Inst. Ft. Lauderdale, 1980. Staff photographer The Miami Herald, 1980-88, The Washington Post, 1988—. Recipient Best Portfolio award Atlanta Seminar Photojournalism, 1982, 85, 90, Robert F. Kennedy award, 1984, Excellence citation Overseas Press Club, 1986, Pulitzer Prize in spot news photography, 1986, 95, Leica Excellence medal, 1994; named Newspaper Photographer of Yr. Nat. Press Photographer Assn., 1989, 92, 96, Photographer of Yr. White House News Photographers Assn., 1991, 93, 94, 95, 96, 97, 98, 2000, Pulitzer Prize in feature photography, 2000. Office: The Washington Post 1150 15th St NW Washington DC 20071-0002*

GUZZETTI, BARBARA JEAN, education educator; b. Chgo., Nov. 15, 1948; d. Louis Earnest and Viola Genevive (Russell) G. BS, No. Ill. U., 1971, MS, 1974; PhD, U. Colo., 1982. Title I reading tchr. Harlem Consolidated Sch. Dist., Loves Park, Ill., 1971-72; elem. classroom tchr. Rockford (Ill.) Pub. Schs., 1972-77; diagnostic tchr. Denver Pub. Schs., 1977-78; secondary reading tchr. Jefferson County Pub. Schs., Lakewood, Colo., 1979-81, secondary reading specialist, 1981—82; rsch. and program assoc. Mid-Continent Regional Ednl. Lab., Aurora, Colo., 1983-84; evaluation specialist N.W. Regional Ednl. Lab., Denver, 1984-85; assoc. prof. Calif. State U., Ponoma, 1985-88; prof. Ariz. State U., Tempe, 1988—. Chair tech. com. Nat. Reading Conf., 1994—97. Author: Literacy Instruction in Content Areas, 1996, Reading, Writing and Talking Gender in Literacy Learning; editor: Perspectives on Conceptual Change, Literacy in America: An Encyclopedia of History, Theory and Practice; mem. editl. bd. The Reading Tchr., Jour. of Reading Behavior, Nat. Reading conf. Yearbook; contbr. articles to profl. jours. Mem. Am. Ednl. Rsch. Assn., Nat. Reading Conf., Internat. Reading Assn. (chair studies and rsch. grants com. 1992-95). Democrat. Lutheran. Avocations: reading, oenology, raising a pot-bellied pig, piglet. Office: Ariz State U Coll of Edn Tempe AZ 85287-0411 Home: 1951 E Citation Lane Tempe AZ 85284 E-mail: guzzetti@asu.edu.

GWINN, MARY ANN, newspaper reporter; b. Forrest City, Ark., Dec. 29, 1951; d. Lawrence Baird and Frances Evelyn (Jones) Gwinn; m. Richard A. King, June 3, 1973 (div. Jan. 1981); m. Stephen E. Dunnington, June 10, 1990. BA in Psychology, Hendrix Coll., 1973; MEd in Spl. Edn., Ga. State U., 1975; MA in Journalism, U. Mo., 1979. Tchrs. aide DeKalb County Schs., Decatur, Ga., 1973—74, tchr., 1975—78; reporter Columbia (Mo.) Daily Tribune, 1979—83, Seattle Times, 1983—, internat. trade and workplace reporter, 1992—96, asst. city editor, 1996—98, book editor, 1998—. Instr. ext. divsn. U. Wash., Seattle, 1990; instr. journalism Seattle U., 1994. Recipient Edn. Reporting award, Charles Stewart Mott Found., 1980, Enterprising reporting award, C.B. Blethen Family, 1989, Pulitzer Prize for Nat. Reporting, 1990. Mem.: Newspaper Guild. Avocations: writing, gardening, reading, camping. Office: Seattle Times PO Box 70 Seattle WA 98111-0070*

GWINN, MARY DOLORES, business developer, philosopher, writer; b. Oakland, Calif., Sept. 16, 1946; d. Epifanio and Carolina (Lopez) Cruz; m. James Monroe Gwinn, Oct. 23, 1965; 1 child, Larry Allen. Student, Monterey Peninsula Jr. Coll., 1965. Retail store mgr. Consumer's Distbg. divsn. May Co., Hayward, Calif., 1973-78; mktg. rep. Dale Carnegie Courses, San Jose, Calif., 1978-79; founder, pres. Strategic Integrations, Ariz.'s Innovative Bus. Devel. Ctr., Scottsdale, 1985—, Gwinn Genius Inst., Scottsdale, 1998—. Speaker St. John's Coll. U. Cambridge, England, 1992, INC. Mag., U.S.A., 1996, Clemson Univ., 1996, Antelope Valley Coll., Lancaster, Calif., 1998; founder, pres. Internat. Inst. for Conceptual Edn., Scottsdale, 1993—; chairperson Keble Coll., Oxford (Eng.) U., 1997; spkr. Willard Internat. Hotel, Washington, 2000. Founder new fields of study Genestics and NeuroBus.; profiled the Thought Process of Genius; conceived Whole Brain Business Theory, 1985; author: Genius Leadership Secrets from the Past for the 21st Century, 1995; writer bus. column Gwinn on Bus., IMAGE Networker, Pa., 1996; contbr. articles to profl. jours. Chairperson Keble Coll., Oxford (Eng.) U. Republican. Avocations: reading, imagination games, playing with grandchildren. Home and Office: 5836 E Angela Dr Scottsdale AZ 85254-6410

GYAMFI, PHYLLIS, research scientist, researcher; b. Wurzburg, Germany, Apr. 20, 1968; d. Anthony and Mary Gyamfi; m. McGregor Ottley. BA, U. Miami, 1990; MA, Columbia University, 1995, PhD, 2001. Grad. rsch. fellow Ctr. Children and Families, N.Y., NY, 1995—2001; rsch. scientist ORC Macro, Atlanta, 2001—. Intern grad. rsch. Ednl. Testing Svc., Princeton, NJ, 1998. Recipient Outstanding Rsch. award, Soc. Social Work Rsch., 2000, 1st place winner grad. rsch. paper competition, APA, 1999, Dissertation Fellowship award, Woodrow Wilson Nat. Fellowship Found., 2001; fellow pre-doctoral fellow, Ednl. Testing Svc., 1998. Mem.: Soc. Rsch. in Child Devel. Office: ORC Macro 3 Corporate Sq NE Ste 370 Atlanta GA 30329 E-mail: phyllis.gyamfi@orcmacro.com.

GYER, JANE E. artist, educator; b. San Francisco, June 13, 1925; d. Raymond Bruce Linganfield and Amy Elizabeth Dunaway; m. Basil Eugene Judd, May 1949 (div. 1970); children: Kenneth Eugene Judd, Robin Judd Rodrigues. Artist in residence, Yosemite Nat. Park, 1981, 93, Rocky Mt. Nat. Park, 1985; BA, Emerson Inst., 1997, MS, 1999. Art editor Sierra Star, Oakhurst, Calif., 1957-69; freelance artist The Jays, Oakhurst, 1969—; art tchr. Vision Acad. Arts, Oakhurst, 1989—; art instr. Emerson Inst., Oakhurst, 1997—. Bd. dirs. Timeberline Gallery, Oakhurst; lectr. in field. Executed numerous murals, 1975—; illustrator Discovering Sierra Trees, 1972 (NPS Director's award); exhibited in numerous shows, including Kings Art Ctr., Hanford, 2002; represented in pvt. and pub. collections. Bd. dirs. Vision Acad. of Arts, Oakhurst, 1995—. Avocation: singing. Home: 50137 Sunset Dr # C Coarsegold CA 93614-9709 Office: The Jays PO Box 456 Oakhurst CA 93644-0456

GYLLENHAAL, MAGGIE, actress; b. N.Y.C., Nov. 16, 1977; d. Stephen Gyllenhaal and Naomi Foner. BA in English, Columbia U., 1999. Actor: (TV series) Shake Rattle and Roll: An American Love Story, 1999; (TV films) Shattered Mind, 1996, The Patron Saint of Liars, 1998, Resurrection, 1999; (films) Waterland, 1992, A Dangerous Woman, 1993, Homegrown, 1998, The Photographer, 2000, Cecil B. Demented, 2000, Pornographer: A Love Story, 2000, Donnie Darko, 2001, Riding in Cars with Boys, 2001, Secretary, 2002, 40 Days and 40 Nights, 2002, Adaptation, 2002, Confessions of a Dangerous Mind, 2002, Casa de los babys, 2003, Mona Lisa Smile, 2003. Office: Creative Artists Agy 9830 Wilshire Blvd Beverly Hills CA 90212*

HAAB, LUCILLE HELEN, primary school educator; b. Bakersfield, Calif., Sept. 11, 1943; d. Frank W. Haab and Lucy Haab Davis. BA, Calif. State U., San Jose, 1966, MA, 1992. Cert. kindergarten/primary tchr., Calif., gen. elem. tchr., Calif. Kindergarten tchr. Evergreen Sch. Dist., San Jose, 1966—, mentor tchr. Lectr./cons. Bur. of Edn. and Rsch., Bellevue, Wash., 1990-95; lectr./cons. Seminars for Early Childhood, San Jose, 1995—; pvt. lectr./cons. in field, 1988—. Author: The Developmentally Appropriate Classroom: A Children's Garden, 1990, Art Activities to Grow On, 1990. Mem. Saratoga Drama Group, 1974—. Democrat. Avocations: theater, travel, cooking.

HAAG, JANE, education educator; d. Dennis James Haag and Janet Marie Rooney. BA in Am. Studies and Art History, Fordham U., 1996; MA in Ednl. Tech. Leadership, George Washington U., 1999; postgrad., Walden U., 2003—. Ednl. program asst. Smithsonian Instn. Nat. Mus. Am. Art, Washington, 1996—98; instrnl. designer DMR Cons., Edison, NJ, 1998—2001; sr. instrnl. designer Maher & Maher, Neptune, NJ, 2001—. Mem.: Am. Ednl. Rsch. Assn., Assn. Ednl. Comm. in Tech., Phi Delta Kappa. Roman Catholic. Avocations: travel, wine tasting. Office: Maher & Maher 3535 Rte 66 Bldg 4 Neptune NJ 07753

HAAHEIM, PATRICIA JANE DANDO, pastor, consultant; b. Abington, Pa., May 29, 1947; d. Eion Ephraim and Jean Barbara (Wilson) Dando; m. Robert James Thompson, July 11, 1981 (div. July 26, 1994); 1 child, Zachary Eion Dando-Thompson ; m. Dale Robert Haaheim, Oct. 4, 1996. BA, U. Calif., Davis, 1969; tchg. credential, San Jose State U., 1970; MDiv, Bethel Theol. Sem., 1979; specialty in social change, Twin Cities Consortium of Sems., 1980. Tchg. credential Calif., Oreg. Tchr. McKenzie Elem. Sch., Blue River, Oreg., 1971—74; pvt. tchr., governess Selsdon Park Hotel, Sanderstead, England, 1974—75; pastor People's Congl. Ch., Bayport, Minn., 1981—84; missionary Nat. Assn. Congl. Christian Chs., Taiwan, 1985; founding pastor Promise Congl. Ch., Apple Valley, Minn., 1991—99; cons. revitalization pastor Nat. Assn. Congl. Christian Chs., Milw., 2000—. Adviser comty. edn Bldg. Youth Assets Dist. # 196 Comty. Edn., Apple Valley, 1992—95; comty. leader drug abuse prevention Searsport (Maine) Schs. and Comty., 1986—89; mem. adv. bd. Family Shelter Ministry S.O.M.E., Santa Rosa, Calif., 1989—91; co-founder Family Violence Network. Author: (booklet/Bible study guide) Saying Yes to God, 1987; contbr. articles to profl. jours. Recipient Founders award for prevention of family violence, Family Violence Network, 2001, Comty. Svc. award, Comty. Edn. Dist. # 196, 1995, Project award alcohol and drug prevention, Comty. Edn., 1988. Mem.: Internat. Congregation Fellowship (vice-chair youth commn. 2002—04), Minn. Fellowship Congregationalists (vice-chair 2002—03), Nat. Assn. Congl. Christian Chs. (mem. exec. com. 1999—2003). Congregationalist. Avocations: reading, travel, community work. Home: 13302 Ellice Ct Apple Valley MN 55124-8118 E-mail: revpatti@yahoo.com.

HAAR, ANA MARIA FERNANDEZ, advertising and public relations executive; b. Oriente Province, Cuba, Mar. 25, 1951; came to U.S., 1960; naturalized, 1970; d. Gilberto and Esmeralda Emiliana (Diaz) Fernández. Grad., Miami Dade C.C., 1971; student, Barry Coll., 1972-78. Adminstrv. asst. through asst. v.p. nat. accounts Flagship Bank, Miami Beach, Fla., 1971-77; v.p. comml. lending Jefferson Nat. Bank, Miami Beach, Fla., 1977-78; chmn., CEO, IAC Group, Inc., Miami, Fla., 1978—. Instr. Women in Mgmt. program Miami Dade C.C., 1980-81; hostess Sta. WPBT Program Viva; exec. com. World Trade Ctr., Miami; mem. Dade County Commn. on Status of Women, 1979-82; chmn. Econ. Devel. Task Force of Commn. on Status of Women, 1979-82; bd. dirs., chmn. Human Capital Group, New Am. Alliance; bd. dirs. Cuban Am. Nat. Found.; mem. adv. com. John S. and James L. Knight Found. Bd. dirs., vice-chmn. CAMACOL-Latin C. of C.; chmn. World Trade Ctr.; Miami dir. SCORE; mem. Exec. Assn. Greater Miami; vice chair New America Alliance; bd. dirs. Cuban Am. Nat. Found.. Recipient Gran Orden Martiana of Cuban Lyceum for excellence in community svc., 1976, Up and Comers award South Fla. Bus. Jour., 1988, Red Cross Spectrum award, 2000; named one of 100 Most Infulential Hispanics, Hispanic Bus. Mag., So. Fla. Leading Women Business Owners, 1990, Entrepeneur of the Yr. Inc. Mag. (natl. finalist), 1992. Mem. Advt. Fedn. Greater Miami, Greater Miami Advt. Fedn. (bd. dirs.) Asociación de Publicitarios Latino-Americanos (v.p.), Japan Soc. (bd. dirs.), Miami Beach C. of C. (hon. life, trustee), Greater Miami C. of C., Hispanic Heritage Festival Com., Cuban Women's Club (past pres.), Assn. Hispanic Advt. Agys. (pres. 1998-99), New Am. Alliance. Office: IAC Advt Group 2725 SW 3rd Ave Miami FL 33129-2335 E-mail: iac@iacadgroup.com.

HAAS, CAROLYN BUHAI, elementary education educator, publisher, writer, consultant; b. Chgo., Jan. 1, 1926; d. Michael and Tillie (Weiss) Buhai; m. Robert Green Haas, June 29, 1947 (dec. June 30, 1984); children: Andrew Robert, Mari Beth, Thomas Michael, Betsy Ann, Karen Sue. BEd, Smith Coll., Northampton, Mass., 1947; postgrad., Nat. Coll. Edn., Evanston, Ill., 1956-59, Art Inst. Chgo., 1958-59. Tchr. Francis W. Parker Sch., Chgo., 1947-49; tchr. art Glencoe (Ill.) Pub. Schs., 1967-68, substitute tchr., 1964-72. Co-founder PAR Leadership Tng. Found., Northfield, Ill., 1969-81; pres., editor CBH Pub., Inc., Northfield, 1979-92; cons., writer, adv. bd. The Learning Line; cons. presch. sci. program Mus. Sci. and Industry, Chgo.; adv. bd. My Own Mag.; cons. in field. Author: (with Ann Cole and Betty Weinberger) I Saw a Purple Cow, 1972, A Pumpkin In A Pear Tree, 1974, Children Are Children Are Children, 1976, Backyard Vacation, 1978, Purple Cow to the Rescue, 1982, Recipes for Fun and Learning, 1982, Recetas Para Divertirse, 1997; (with A.C. Friedman) My Own Fun, 1990, The Big Book for Recipes for Fun, 1979, Look at Me: Activities for Babies and Toddlers, 1985; co-editor: Know Your Town/East Hampton League Women Voters of the Hamptons, 1993; contbr. articles to profl. jours. Pres. West Sch. PTA, Glencoe, Jr. Bd. Scholarship and Guidance, Chgo.; bd. dirs. Family Counseling Svc. of Glencoe, Glencoe Human Rels. Com.; pres., sec, bd. dirs. Glencoe Pub. Libr.; pres. Friends of Glencoe Pub. Libr.; co-founder Glencoe Patriotic Days Com.; co-chair Frank Lloyd Wright Bridge Com., Glencoe; pres., bd. dirs. Chgo. League Smith Coll.; mem. women's bd. Northwestern U.; bd. dirs. Chgo. chpt. Am. Jewish Com.; mem. women's com. Chgo. Symphony Orch. Clubs; bd. dirs. Art Resources in Tchg.; vol. Parish Art Mus., The Retreat. Mem. AAUW, LWV (bd. dirs.), Internat. Reading Assn., Soc. Children's Bookwriters, Children's Reading Roundtable, Nat. Assn. Edn. Young Children, Assn. Childhood Edn. Internat., NEA, Artists Alliance of East Hampton (bd. dirs.), Ladies Village Improvement Soc. (bd. dirs.). Democrat. Jewish. Avocations: art, reading, sports, travel. E-mail: cbhpub@aol.com.

HAAS, EILEEN MARIE, homecare advocate; b. Pitts., Feb. 27, 1948; d. Michael Joseph and Bridget Agnes (Connolly) McNulty; m. Jerry Albert Haas, July 19, 1975; 1 child, Melissa. Student, York Coll. of Pa., 1975-78, Messiah Coll., Grantsville, Pa., 1978-80. Clk. Exch. Bur. Pitts., 1966-67; debt. collector Nat. Account Sys., Pitts., 1967-71; preadoptive advocate Hershey, Pa., 1983-84, Phila., 1984-85; homecare advocate Dillsburg, Pa., 1985-88, Deer Lodge, Mont., 1988-92, Gibsonia, Pa., 1992—. Interpreter svcs. St. Victors Ch., Bairdsford, Pa., 1992—; presenter Harrisburg (Pa.) Area C.C., 1985, Pa. Soc. Respiratory Therapy, Ctrl. Pa. chpt., 1985; co-presenter Coun. Exceptional Children, Salt Lake City, 1997; rschr. in pulmonary rehab. With USN, 1971-74. Mem. DAV, Am. Soc. Deaf Children, Coun. Exceptional Children, Assn. Severe Handicaps, Profl. Networking for Excellence in Svc. to Deaf and Hard of Hearing. Republican. Roman Catholic. Avocations: deaf education research, dysphagia research, writing, needlepoint, knitting. Home: 90 Kaufman Rd Gibsonia PA 15044-7950

HAAS, JUDITH, elementary school educator; b. New Rockford, N.D., Jan. 27, 1949; d. Norman E. Braaten and Audrey Nuella O'Hare; m. Duane Darryl Haas, Oct. 7, 1988. BS in Elem. Edn., Mayville (N.D.) State U.,

1971. Cert. tchr., N.D. 6th and 3d grade tchr. Minnewaukan (N.D.) Pub. Sch., 1971-76; 5th grade tchr. St. John (N.D.) Pub. Sch., 1976-87; 6th grade tchr. Little Flower Sch., Rugby, N.D., 1987-88. Pres. N.D. Tchr.'s Assn., 1985-87; vol. tchr. religious edn., Minnewaukan, 1974-76, St. John, 1980-82, Dunseith, N.D., 1995-99; leader Girl Scouts U.S.A., Minnewaukan, 1974-76 Republican. Roman Catholic. Avocations: reading, painting, drawing. Home: HC 2 Box 15A Saint John ND 58369-9712

HAAS, LU ANN, counselor; b. Waterloo, Iowa, Oct. 16, 1956; d. Leonard Edward and Naomi Lee (Binley) H.; divorced; children: Shauna Lee Haas, Nicholas William Smith. AAS, Ctrl. Tex. Coll., 1986; BA magna cum laude, Mt. mercy Coll., 1992; MA, U. Iowa, 1993. Cert. rehab. counselor; cert. lay spkr. Meth. Ch. Ind. truck driver, 1982-83; night supr. Four Oaks-John Mcdonald Residential Treatment, Monticello, Iowa, 1991-92; security officer RA-CO Security Co., 1993-94; substance abuse counselor Area Substance Abuse Coun., Anamosa, Iowa, 1993-94; counseling psychologist Dept. Vets Affairs, Cin., 1994-96, Dallas, 1996-97; mentor host program Fairfield Elem. Sch., Copperas Cove, Tex., 1994-97; ret., 1997. Spkr. in field; cons. in field. Unit sec. United Meth. Women. Sgt. U.S. Army, 1975-81, 83-87. Leonard A. Miller scholar, 1993. Mem. ACA, Nat. Rehab. Assn., Am. Rehab. Counseling Assn., Nat. Rehab. Counseling Assn. (sec./treas. 1997, 98, bd. dirs. 1995, 96, membership chmn. 1995-97), Tex. Rehab. Counseling Assn., Disabled Am. Vets. (life), U. Iowa Alumni Assn., Kappa Gamma Pi (liaison Mt. Mercy Coll.), Am. Legion, Vietnam Vets. Am. (assoc. Miami Valley (Ohio) chpt.). Democrat. Methodist. Avocations: crocheting, reading, writing. Home: 1404 Janet Ln Copperas Cove TX 76522-1228

HAAS, MARLENE RINGOLD, special education educator; b. Pitts., June 14, 1950; d. Rita Weisbrode and Irwin Mark Ringold; children: Melissa Beth, Ilyssa Meg, Seth Ringold. B in K-8 Elem. Edn. and K-12 Spl. Edn., Case Western Res. U., 1972; M in Spl. Edn., Duquesne U., 1975. Cert. spl. edn. K-12 Pa. Spl. edn. tchr. Pitts. Pub. Schs., 1972—. Home: 4244 Saline St Pittsburgh PA 15217 Office: Reizenstein Mid Sch 129 Denniston Ave Pittsburgh PA 15206

HAASE, PATRICIA ANN THOMPSON, retired nursing educator; b. Franklin, Ind., Dec. 8, 1931; d. Lawrence Edmond and Dorcas Rhea (Burton) Thompson; m. William C. Haase, Sept. 4, 1957 (div. Sept., 1972). BS in Nursing, Ind. U., 1956, MS in Nursing, 1957; PhD, Purdue U., 1972. RN, Ind. Project dir. nursing curriculum So. Regional Edn. Bd., Atlanta, 1972-75, 76-82; dir. grad. studies in nursing Ga. State U., Atlanta, 1975-76; dean Sch. of Nursing U. Tenn., Chattanooga, 1982-86, prof. nursing, 1986—96; ret., 1996. Asst. prof. De Pauw U., Indpls., 1965-66, asst. prof., dir. assoc. degree program in nursing, Ind. U., Indpls., 1966-72. Author: (books) The Origins and Rise of Assoc. Degree Nursing Edn., 1990, Assoc. Degree Nursing Edn.: An Historical Annotated Bibliography, 1942-88, 1990; also contbr. numerous articles to profl. jours., presented many papers at sci. and ednl. confs. Recipient Disting. Alumni award Ind. U. Sch. of Nursing, 1980. Avocation: Am. Civil War Lit. Home: 4016 Loch Highland Pass Roswell GA 30075-2032

HABACHY, SUZAN SALWA SABA, development economist, non profit administrator; b. Cairo, July 15, 1933; came to the U.S., 1952; d. Saba and Gameela (Gindy) H. BA, Bryn Mawr (Pa.) Coll., 1954; MA, Harvard U., Cambridge, Mass., 1956. Teaching fellow Ohio U., Athens, 1957-58; economist Mobil Oil Co., N.Y.C., 1959-64; reporter, editor Petroleum Intelligence Weekly, N.Y.C., 1964-65, McGraw Hill News Bur., London, England, 1965-68; program officer UN, N.Y.C., 1969-75, section chief, 1975-88; focal point for women UN Office of Pers., N.Y.C., 1988-93; exec. dir. The Trickle Up Program, N.Y.C., 1994-2001. Avocations: theatre, travel, reading. Home: 1056 5th Ave New York NY 10028-0112

HABEEB, HABEEBA HUSSAIN, library director; b. Male, Republic of Maldives, Sept. 9, 1930; d. Hussain Habeeb and Shahima Shamsuddin; m. Abdulla Zubair, May 18, 1923; children: Ibrahim, Shafeea, Shahida. Grad. High Sch. Urdu Medium, Osmania, Hyderabad, India, 1948, grad. High Sch. English Medium, Holy Family Convent, Colombo, Sri Lanka, 1952. Cert. librarian. Asst. prin. Govt. Service, Male, Maldives, 1956-62; sec. Prime Minister's Office, Male, 1962-67, Foreign Affairs, Male, 1968-70, Transp. Dept. Govt. Service, Male, 1974-78, Aid Dept. Ministry of Justice Govt. Service, Male, 1974-75; librarian Nat. Library, Male, 1978-86, deputy dir., 1986-90; dir., 1990-95; dir. gen., 1995—. Author: Mohammed Thakurufaan The Great, 1990; co-author: Innovation in Primary School Construction, 1986; translator: How to Write Short Stories, 1984, other lit. works from Urdu to Dhivehi and English to Dhivehi; editor Jour., Niru Libr. newsletter, Children's Club mag. including Faithoova mag.; contbr. articles to cultural publs. Recipient Pres.'s award Gold Pen, Presdl. award for 25 yrs. govt. svc., Presdl. Encouragement award transl. Mem. Nat. Ctr. for Linguistic and Hist. Rsch. (adv. mem.). Home: Mandoovilla 8 Bodufulah Str Male Machchangolhi 20-03 Maldives Office: Nat Libr 59 Majeedi Magu Galolhu Male 20-24 Maldives

HABER, MELISSA ANN, psychologist; b. Decatur, Ga., Sept. 6, 1974; d. Andrew Chalmers Doss and Debra Kay Thomas; m. Lawrence Gene Haber, Jan. 6, 1996; children: Taylor Madison, Ethan Cole. BS in Psychology, Trevecca Nazarene U., Nashville, 1997, MA in Counseling, 1999. Lic. psychol. examiner Tenn., 2000. Lic. psychol. examiner Dr. Jeri Lee & Psychol. Assoc., Gallatin and Goodlettsville, Tenn., 1999—2000; therapist Centerstone, Nashville, 2001—02, psychol. examiner, 2002—, Madison, Tenn., 2003—. Avocations: gardening, bicycling, walking, rollerblading. Office: Centerstone 315 Hospital Dr Madison TN 37115

HABERKORN, JUDITH R. former manufacturing executive; B Internat. Rels., Briarcliff Coll.; grad. Advanced Mgmt. program, Harvard Bus. Sch. Mem. exec. tng. program AT&T Co., 1968; gen. mgr. spl. svcs. New Eng. Tel., 1988—89, gen. mgr. access markets, mktg. and tech., 1989—90; v.p. materials mgmt. telesector resources group NYNEX Corp., 1990—92; v.p. mktg. and sales, 1992—93; v.p. consumer markets NYNEX Corp., N.Y.C., 1993—95, v.p. individual comm. svcs., 1995—97; pres. pub. and operator svcs. Bell Atlantic Corp., N.Y.C., 1997—98, pres. consumer sales and svc., 1998—2000; dir. Enesco Corp., Armstrong World Industries (chair nominating and governance com.), Lancaster, Pa., 1998—, WorldCom Group, 2003—. Adv. bd. Norfolk Southern. Author: (foreward) A Seat at the Table by Patricia Harrison. Adv. bd. Enterprise Found.; bd. dirs. Nat. Alliance Breast Cancer Orgns.; v.p. emerita alumni adv. bd. Harvard Bus. Sch., visiting com. Named one of N.Y.'s 100 Most Influential Women in Bus., Crain's N.Y.; recipient Dir.'s Choice award, Nat. Women's Econ. Alliance Found., 1995. Mem.: Com. of 200 (chair emerita), Internat. Women's Forum, Harvard Bus. Sch. Network Women Alumnae, Jr. League N.Y. Avocations: reading, movies, theater.*

HABERL, VALERIE ELIZABETH, physical education educator, company executive; b. N.Y.C., July 6, 1947; d. William Anthony and Rose Mary (Hoholecek) H. BS, So. Conn. State U., 1969, postgrad., 1979. Cert. elem. tchr., Conn. Tchr. phys. edn. West Haven (Conn.) Bd. Edn., 1969—. Pres. Creative Studio, 1992—; inventory control specialist, 1997-2001. Mem. Conn. Assn. Health, Phys. Edn., Recreation and Dance. Republican. Roman Catholic.

HABERMAN, LOUISE SHELLY, consulting company executive; b. N.Y.C. d. Harry Martin and Rebecca (Binstock) H.; m. Gordon Joel Schochet. BA, Cornell U., 1971; PhD, Princeton (N.J.) U., 1984. Mem. faculty numerous colls. and univs., 1975-84; researcher pub. policy U.S. Dept. Commerce, 1976; prin. investigator pub. policy study State of N.J., Trenton, 1979-80; pvt. practice cons. Highland Park, N.J., 1984-86; head regional bank svcs. Multinational Strategies, Inc., N.Y.C., 1986-90; pres. Haberman Assocs., Inc., Edison, N.J., 1990—. Author: (monograph) Regional Banks: International Strategies for the Future, 1987; editor: (with Paul Sacks) Ann. Rev. of Nations, 1988; contbr. articles to profl. jours. Issues advisor selected polit. candidates and civil liberties causes. Avocations: gardening, painting. Office: Haberman Assocs Inc 315 N 8th Ave Edison NJ 08817-2914

HABERMANN, HELEN MARGARET, plant physiologist, educator; b. Bklyn., Sept. 13, 1927; AB, SUNY, Albany, 1949; MS, U. Conn., 1951; PhD, U. Minn., 1956. Asst. botanist U. Conn., Storrs, 1949-51; asst. U. Minn., Mpls., 1951-53, asst. plant physiologist, 1953-55, head residence counselor, 1955-56; rsch. assoc. U. Chgo., 1956-57; rsch. fellow Hopkins Marine Sta. Stanford (Calif.) U., 1957-58; from asst. prof. to prof. biol. scis. Goucher Coll., Towson, 1958—82, chmn. dept. biology, 1963-66, 68, 78-79, Lilian Welsh prof. biol. scis., 1982-92; prof. emeritus, 1992—. Co-author Biology: A Full Spectrum, 1973, Mainstreams of Biology, 1977. NIH spl. rsch. fellow Rsch. Inst. Advanced Study, Balt., 1966-67. Fellow AAAS; mem. Phytochem. Soc. N.Am. (sec. 1987-93), Am. Soc. Plant Physiologists, Am. Soc. Hort. Sci., Soc. Devel. Biology, Am. Soc. Photobiology, Am. Inst. Biol. Scis., Scandinavian Soc. Plant Physiology, Internat. Soc. Plant Molecular Biology, Japanese Soc. Plant Physiology, Soc. Exptl. Biology and Medicine, Am. Camellia Soc., Pioneer Camellia Soc. (pres. 1994-95, sec. 2000-01), Am. Hort. Soc., Sigma Xi. Office: Goucher Coll Dept Biol Scis 1021 Dulaney Valley Rd Baltimore MD 21204-2753 E-mail: hhabermann@wans.net.

HABICH, ELIZABETH CHAMBERLAIN, librarian; b. Boston, Mar. 23, 1955; d. Eugene Randolph and Helen Howard Chamberlain; m. Michael Paul Habich, Sept. 10, 1977. BA in English, Wellesley Coll., 1977; MS in Libr. and Info. Sci., Simmons Coll., 1980; MBA, Northeastern U., 1990. Libr. asst., page Hingham Pub. Libr., 1971-78; circulation asst. MIT, Cambridge, 1978-80; reference libr. Saugus (Mass.) Pub. Libr., 1980-82; head res. svcs. Northeastern U. Libr., Boston, 1982-87, bldg. projects officer, 1986-91, adminstrv. svcs. officer, 1991—. Cons. in field. Author: Moving Library Collections: A Management Handbook, 1998; contbr. chpts. to books. Trustee North Reading (Mass.) Pub. Libr., 1992—; chair Libr. Orgn. and Mgmt. Sect. Fiscal and Bus. Officers Discussion Group, 2000-2002, mem., 2002—. Mem. ALA, Assn. Coll. Rsch. Libr., Libr. Adminstrn. Mgmt. Assn. (bldg. equipment sect. 1987—, vice-chair, chair-elect 1993-94, chair 1994-95, past chair 1995-96), program com. 1996-2000, fin. com. 2000-04, chair nominating com. 1997-98, Beta Phi Mu, Beta Gamma Sigma. Avocations: quilting, gardening, music. Office Phone: 617-373-4924. E-mail: e.habich@neu.edu.

HAC, LUCILE ROSE, biochemistry educator; b. Lincoln, Nebr., May 18, 1909; d. Peter F. and Carrie E. (Orinsky) H. BA, U. Nebr., 1930, MSc, 1931; PhD, U. Minn., 1935. Microbiologist Md. State Health Dept., Balt., 1935-36; rsch. assoc. dept. Ob-gyn. U. Chgo., 1936-43; rsch. dir. Internat. Minerals & Chem., Chgo., Calif., Tex. and, Fla., 1943-61; assoc. prof. biochemistry Northwestern U. Med. Sch., Chgo., 1961-77, emeritus prof., 1977—; job counsellor North Shore Sr. Ctr., Northfield, Ill., 1978-98. Patentee in field; contbr. articles to profl. jours. Bd. dirs. LWV, Wilmette, Ill., 1980-84. Recipient Kuppenheimer grant U. Chgo., 1936-45, Claude Pepper Disting. Svc. award, 1990, Clyde Murray Older Worker award Operation Able Chgo., 1991; named to Sr. Citizen Hall of Fame, Chgo., 1985. Mem. Am. Chem. Soc. (dir., bd. dirs. 1940-45), AAUW, Zonta Internat., Phi Beta Kappa, Sigma Xi, Iota Sigma Pi, Sigma Delta Epsilon. Republican. Avocations: music, flowers. Home: 6800 A St Apt 222 Lincoln NE 68510-5124 also: 6800 A St Apt 222 Lincoln NE 68510-5124

HACH-DARROW, KATHRYN, water testing company executive; m. Clifford Hach. Chair, CEO Hach Co., Ames, Iowa, 1947-98, chair, 1999—. Office: Hach Company Loveland CO 80538

HACKEL-SIMS, STELLA BLOOMBERG, lawyer, former government official; b. Burlington, Vt., Dec. 27, 1926; d. Hyman and Esther (Pocher) Bloomberg; m. Donald Herman Hackel, Aug. 14, 1949; children: Susan Jane, Cynthia Anne; m. Arthur Sims, Aug. 28, 1980. Student, U. Vt., 1943-45; JD cum laude, Boston U., 1948. Bar: Vt. 1948, Mass. 1948, D.C. 1979, Va. 1982. Individual practice law, Burlington, 1948-49, Rutland, Vt., 1949-59, 73—; city prosecutor City of Rutland, 1957-63; commr. Vt. Dept. Employment Security, 1963-73; treas. State of Vt., 1975-77; dir. U.S. Mint, Dept. Treasury, Washington, 1977-81. Chmn. Vt. Municipal Bond Bank, 1975-77 Mem. Vt. Adv. Com. on Mental Retardation, Interdept. Council on Aging, Commn. on Status Women, Human Resource Inter-Agency Com., Emergency Resource Priorities Bd., Info. Planning Council, Legis. Council Equal Opportunity Com., Vt. Indsl. Devel. Authority, Vt. Housing Fin. Agy., Vt. Claims Commn., Vt. Tchrs. Retirement Fund. Bd., Vt. Home Mortgage Guaranty Bd.; chmn. Vt. State Employees Retirement Fund; ex-officio mem. Nat. Manpower Adv. Com., 1971-72, Fed. Adv. Council on Unemployment Ins., 1971-72; Pres. Rutland Girl Scouts Leaders Assn., 1949-50, Rutland League Women Voters, 1951-52, Rutland Council Jewish Women, 1955-56; chmn. womens div. Rutland Community Chest Dr., 1952, Rutland County-Vt. Assn. for Blind, 1953-56; pres. Rutland County Democratic Women's Assn., 1956-63; treas. Rutland City Dem. Com., 1957-63; former rep. office women's activities Dem. Nat. Com., Regional Council I., Women's CD Councils; mem. Vt. bd. Girl Scouts U.S.A.; chmn. Arlington County Tenant-Landlord Commn., Va., 1986— . Mem.: LWV, AAUW (pres. Rutland County br. 1961—62), Interstate Conf. Employment Security Agys. (v.p. region I 1966—68, legis. com. 1969, sr. v.p. 1970—71, pres. 1971—72), Am. Soc. Pub. Adminstrn., Vt. Coun. Social Agys., Bus. and Profl. Women's Club, Rutland County Bar Assn. (pres. 1973), Vt. Bar Assn., Emblem (dir. 1960-63), Woodmont Country; Internat. (Washington), Moorings Country Club (Naples, Fla.), Emblem Club (dir. 1960—63), Delta Phi Epsilon.

HACKENBERG, BARBARA JEAN COLLAR, retired advertising and public relations executive; b. Venango County, Pa., Apr. 15, 1927; d. Guy Lamont and Marion Leona (Kingsley) Collar; m. George Richardson, June 13, 1953; children: Kurt Edward, Kim Ellen, Caroline Kingsley. BA, Grove City (Pa.) Coll., 1948; ML, U. Pitts., 1949. Advt. dir. The Halle Bros. Co., Erie, Pa., 1950-52, advt. and sales promotion dir. Pa. divsn., 1952-54; exec. dir. Wyomissing (Pa.) Inst. Fine Arts, 1970-74; dir. and cmty. liason Freedman Gallery, Albright Coll., Reading, Pa., 1976-78; selling supr. Pomeroy's Children's Dept., Wyomissing, Pa., 1981-83; pub. rels. account exec. Wentworth Assocs., Lancaster, Pa., 1983-84; exec. dir. World Affairs Coun., Reading, 1987—97; owner The WRITE Place, Reading, 1979—. Vice pres. Harrisburg (Pa.) Foreign Policy Assn., 1964-67; various fundraising activities, 1954-70; pub. rels.chmn. Erie World Affairs Ctr., 1957-60; mem. mil. affairs com. Berks County chpt. ARC, 1998—, mem. internat. com., 2003; apptd. to Parks and Recreation Bd., Twp. of Cumru, 1998—, sub-chair open and green spaces, 2003; mem. internat. com. YMCA, Berks County, Pa., 1999—, program chair, 2003. Mem. Women in Communications, Inc. (pub. relations chmn. ctrl. Pa. chpt., 1984-87, sec. ctrl. Pa. chpt., 1986-87). Avocations: writing, theater, art, concerts, bicycling. Home and Office: 1334 Welsh Rd Reading PA 19607-9334

HACKENJOS-BUTLER, GENIE MARIE, minister; b. Shreveport, La., Sept. 27, 1946; d. Reginald U. and Elizabeth Marie (Davis) Hackenjos; m. Sam Lennard Butler, Jr., Aug. 9, 1969 (div. Sept. 1981). BA in German, Southwestern U., Georgetown, Tex., 1969; MDiv, Iliff Sch. Theology, Denver, 1982. Lic. to preach 1977, Deacons Orders Rocky Mountain Conf. United Meth. Ch., 1978, Elder's Orders N.D. Conf., United Meth. Ch., 1983. Feature writer Houston Chronicle, 1969—70; substitute tchr. various locations Tex., 1970—75; ch. sec. United Meth. Ch., Glenwood Springs, Colo., 1972—75; bookkeeper Petre, Zimmerman & Shelton, P.C., Glenwood Springs, 1971—74; owner, mgr. Kwik Kopy Printing, Ft. Collins, Colo., 1977—80; tchr. German Langdon H.S., ND, 1993—94; pastor United Meth. Ch., Neche-Cavalier, ND, 1980—86, First United Meth. Ch., Lisbon, ND, 1986—92, Langdon, ND, 1992—98, Pierre, SD, 1998—. Vice-chmn. Bd. of Ordained Ministry, N.D. Conf. United Meth. Ch., 1985—97; pres. Pembina County Ministerium, Cavalier, ND, 1984—86, Cavalier County Ministerium, Langdon, 1996—98. Contbr. poetry to profl. jours. Leader Girl Scouts U.S., Lisbon, ND, 1988—92; mem. Acad. for Preaching United Meth. Bd. Discipleship, Nashville and Jerusalem, 1990—92; mem. Citizens Involvement Coun., Pierre, SD, 2000—. Grantee Study-Travel grantee, Wesley Ctr. of Religion, U. N.D., 1986. Mem.: AAUW (pres. 1983—84, N.Dak. state v.p. 1988—89, program v.p. 2001—), Pierre-Ft. Pierre Ministerial Assn. (chief chaplain, SD Legislature 2004). Methodist. Avocations: gardening, reading, travel, writing. Home: 320 W Capital Ave Pierre SD 57501

HACKETT, CAROL ANN HEDDEN, physician; b. Valdese, N.C., Dec. 18, 1939; d. Thomas Barnett and Zada Loray (Pope) Hedden; m. John Peter Hackett, July 27, 1968; children: John Hedden, Elizabeth Bentley, Susanne Rochet. BA, Duke U., 1961; MD, U. N.C., 1966. Intern Georgetown U. Hosp., Washington, 1966-67, resident, 1967-69; clinic physician DePaul Hosp., Norfolk, Va., 1969-71; chief spl. health svcs. Arlington County Dept. Human Resources, Arlington, Va., 1971-72; gen. med. officer USPHS Hosp., Balt., 1974-75; pvt. practice family medicine Seattle, 1975—. Mem. staff, chmn. dept. family practice Overlake Hosp. Med. Ctr., 1985-86; clin. asst. prof. Sch. Medicine U. Wash. Bd. dirs. Mercer Island (Wash.) Presch. Assn., 1977-78; coord. 13th and 20th Ann. Inter-profl. Women's Dinner, 1978, 86; trustee Northwest Chamber Orch., 1984-85. Fellow Am. Acad. Family Practice; mem. King County Acad. Family Practice (trustee 1993-96, pres.-elect 1997-98, pres. 1998-99), King County Med. Soc. (chmn. com. TV violence), Wash. Acad. Family Practice, Wash. State Med. Soc., DAR, Bellevue C. of C., N.W. Women Physicians (v.p. 1978), Seattle Symphony League, Eastside Women Physicians (founder, pres.), Seattle Yacht Club, Sigma Kappa. Episcopalian. Home: PO Box 3098 Bellevue WA 98009-3098 Office: 1414 116th Ave NE Bellevue WA 98004-3801 Fax: 425-462-5313. Office Phone: 425-454-8191.

HACKETT, KAREN L. medical association administrator; Exec. v.p., COO Am. Coll. Healthcare Execs., Chgo. Office: Am Coll Healthcare Execs One N Franklin St Ste 1700 Chicago IL 60606-3491

HACKLER, LISA MARGUERITE, minister; d. Thomas Theodore and Etta Marguerite Mintun; m. John Jefferson Hackler, Nov. 6, 1982; children: Sarah Marguerite, Teresa Ann. MDiv, Trinity Luth. Sem., 1985. Missionary Ctrl. African Rep. Evang. Luth. Ch. Am., Chgo., 1985—90; co-pastor Peace Luth. Ch., Pasadena, Tex., 1990—. Office: Peace Luth Ch 6435 Fairmont Pky Pasadena TX 77505 E-mail: lhackler@swbell.net.

HACKLER, RUTH ANN, retired educator; b. Rogers, Ark., Feb. 2, 1924; d. Ezekiel Burton and Effie Lena (Paschal) Ruddick; m. Eugene T. Hackler, Dec. 27, 1946; children: Amy E., Susan Hackler Fetsch, Nancy Hackler Beaver. BA, Washburn U., 1946. Cert. secondary tchr., Kans. Asst. registrar Washburn U., Topeka, 1947-49; tchr. bus. Washburn Rural High Sch., Topeka, 1949-50, Olathe (Kans.) High Sch., 1950-52; state rep. Kans. Ho. of Reps., Topeka, 1991-92; part-time legal sec. Hackler Law Firm, Olathe, 1949-90; ret. Mem. Gov.'s Edn. Cabinet, 1983-84; apptd. to Kansas. Interagy. Coord. Coun. on Early Childhood Devel. Svcs. Mem. Olathe Pub. Sch. Bd., 1969-91, pres., v.p.; mem. youth adv. bd. Johnson County Cmty. Corrections; former dir., mem. found. bd. Johnson County C.C.; mem. rsch. adv. com. League Kansas Municipalities, 1988—; treas., mem. ch. coun. St. Mark's Luth. Ch., Olathe; bd. dirs. Cedar House, Inc., 1969—2002; bd. dirs. Met. Kansas City United Cmty. Svcs., Inc.; organizer Olathe Children Initiatives, 1992; bd. dirs., sec., v.p. Olathe Pub. Libr.; mem. adv. coun. Olathe and Metro Parents as Tchrs.; bd. mem. Kans. Assn. Sch. Bds., 1978-85, pres., 1984; treas. St. Mark's Luth. Ch., 1993-94, pres., 1995-97. Recipient Lifetime Achievement award Johnson County Parks and Recreation, 1990, Friend of Edn. award Phi Delta Kappa. Mem. Met. Coun. on Child Care, Nat. Sch. Bds. Assn. (del. fed. rels. network, alternate nat. assembly del. 1982, del. 1983, 84, 85, Disting. Svc. award 1984), Kans. Assn. of Sch. Bds. (bd. dirs. 1977-82, chmn. sex edn./human sexuality/AIDS statewide com., chair state conf. on human sexuality/AIDS edn. 1988, past chmn. edn. PAC, pres. 1984), Olathe C. of C. (legis. com.), Chrysantas (past pres.), Delta Kappa Gamma. Democrat. Lutheran. Home: 685 W Cedar St Olathe KS 66061-4001

HACKNEY, VIRGINIA HOWITZ, lawyer; b. Phila., Jan. 11, 1945; d. Charles Rawlings and Edith Wrenn (Pope) Howitz; m. Barry Albert Hackney, Feb. 15, 1969; children: Ashby Rawlings, Roby Howison, Trevor Pope. BA in Econs., Hollins Coll., 1967; JD, U. Richmond, 1970. Bar: Va. 1970. Assoc. Hunton & Williams, Richmond, Va., 1970-77, ptnr., 1977—. Pres. Am. Acad. Hosp. Attys. Chgo., 1992-93. Mem. agy. evaluation com. United Way of Greater Richmond, 1981-86; sustainer Jr. League of Richmond; mem. Am. Health Lawyers Assn. (pres. 1992-93, bd. dirs. 1988-94). Named Outstanding Woman in field of law, YWCA, Richmond, 1981. Mem. ABA (bus. law sect. 1984—, forum com. on health law 1982—), Va. State Bar (long range planning com. 1985-90, chmn. standing com. lawyer discipline 1986-90, exec. com. 1988-90, Bar Coun. mem. 1984-90). Avocations: book tapes, reading, boating, jogging/walking. Office: Hunton & Williams Riverfront Plz East Tower 951 E Byrd St Richmond VA 23219-4074

HACKWOOD, SUSAN, electrical and computer engineering educator; b. Liverpool, Eng., May 23, 1955; came to U.S., 1980; d. Alan and Margaret Hackwood. BS with honors, DeMonfort U., Eng., 1976; PhD in Solid State Ionics, DeMontfort U., Eng., 1979; PhD (hon.), Worcester Poly. Inst., 1993; DSc (hon.), DeMontfort U., 1993. Rsch. fellow DeMonfort U., Leicester, Eng., 1976-79; postdoctoral rsch. fellow AT&T Bell Labs., Homdel, N.J., 1980-81, mem. tech. staff, 1981-83, supr. robotics tech., 1983-84, dept. head robotics tech., 1984-85; prof. elec. and computer engring. U. Calif., Santa Barbara, 1985-89, dir. Ctr. Robotic Systems in Microelectronics, 1985-89, dean Bourns Coll. Engring. Riverside, 1990-95; exec. dir. Calif. Coun. on Scis. and Tech., Riverside, 1995—. Editor Jour. Robotic Systems, 1983, Recent Advances in Robotics, 1985; contbr. over 100 articles to tech. jours.; 7 patents in field. Fellow AAAS, IEEE (sr.). Office: 5262 King St Riverside CA 92506-1623

HADAS, ELIZABETH CHAMBERLAYNE, editor; b. Washington, May 12, 1946; d. Moses and Elizabeth (Chamberlayne) H.; m. Jeremy W. Heist, Jan. 25, 1970 (div. 1976); m. Peter Eller, Mar. 21, 1984 (div. 1998). AB, Radcliffe Coll., 1967; postgrad., Rutgers U., 1967—68; MA, Washington U., St. Louis, 1971. Editor U. N.Mex. Press, Albuquerque, 1971-85, dir., 1985-2000, spl. acquisitions editor, 2000—. Bd. dirs. N.M. Endowment for the Humanities, 2001—. Mem. Assn. Am. Univ. Presses (pres. 1992-93). Democrat. Home: 2900 10th St NW Albuquerque NM 87107-1111 Office: U New Mexico Press 1720 Lomas Blvd NE Albuquerque NM 87106-3807 E-mail: ehadas@unm.edu.

HADAS, RACHEL, poet, educator; b. N.Y.C., Nov. 8, 1948; d. Moses and Elizabeth (Chamberlayne) H.; m. Stavros Kondilis, Nov. 7, 1970 (div. 1978); m. George Edwards, July 22, 1978; 1 child, Jonathan. BA in Classics, Radcliffe Coll., 1969; MA, Johns Hopkins, 1977; PhD, Princeton U., 1982. From adj. to assoc. prof. Rutgers U., Newark, N.J., 1981-92, prof., 1992—, Bd. Govs. Prof., 2002—; adj. prof. Columbia U., N.Y.C., 1992-93. Vis. prof. Hellenic studies program Princeton U., spring 1995. Author: (poetry) Slow Transparency, 1983, A Son From Sleep, 1987, Pass It On, 1989, Living in Time, 1990, Mirrors of Astonishment, 1992, Other Worlds

Than This, 1994, The Empty Bed, 1995, The Double Legacy, 1995, Halfway Down the Hall: New and Selected Poems, 1998, Indelible, 2001, Laws, 2004, (criticism) Merill, Cavafy. Poems and Dreams, 2001. Recipient award Am. Acad. Inst. Arts and Letters, 1990; Guggenheim fellow in poetry, 1988-89. Fellow Am. Acad. Arts and Scis.; mem. MLA, Poets, Essayists [illegible] Production. Reading. Home: 838 W End Ave Apt 3A New York NY 10025-5365 Office: Rutgers U Dept English Hill St Fl 5 Newark NJ 07102-2607 Business E-Mail: rhadas@andromeda.rutgers.edu.

HADDA, JANET RUTH, Yiddish language educator, lay psychoanalyst; b. Bradford, Eng., Dec. 23, 1945; came to U.S., 1948; d. George Manfred and Annemarie (Kohn) H.; m. Allan Joshua Tobin, Mar. 22, 1981; stepchildren: David, Adam. BS in Edn., U. Vt., 1966; MA, Cornell U., 1969; PhD, Columbia U., 1975. Prof. Yiddish UCLA; rsch. psychoanalyst So. Calif. Psychoanalytic Inst., L.A., 1988—, tng. and supervising analyst, 1995—, Inst. Contemporary Psychoanalysis, 1993—. Author: Yankev Glatshteyn, 1980, Passionate Women, Passive Men: Suicide in Yiddish Literature, 1988, Isaac Bashevis Singer: A Life, 1997, with New Introduction, 2003; mem. editl. bd.: Prooftexts, Yivo Ann; contbr. articles to profl. jours. Mem. MLA, Assn. Jewish Studies, Am. Psychoanalytic Assn., Inst. Contemporary Psychoanalysis, So. Calif. Psychoanalytic Inst., Phi Beta Kappa. Office: UCLA Dept English 1335 Rolfe Hl Los Angeles CA 90095-0001

HADDAD, COLLEEN, institutional marketing executive; b. Hackensack, N.J., Feb. 24, 1969; d. Charles Ross and Joan Chinni; m. Robert Edward Haddad, Sept. 9, 1995. BS, Northeastern U., Boston, 1992. Cert. NASD. Ops. mgr. Prudential Securities, N.Y.C., 1992-94, assoc. mgr. internal sales Newark, 1994-97; sr. regional sales PaineWebber, Inc., Weehawken, N.J., 1997-98; v.p. sales and mktg. Mitchell Hutchins, Weehawken, 1998—2000; v.p. mktg. The Dreyfus Corp., 2001—. Office: 200 Park Ave New York NY 10166 E-mail: Haddad.C@Dreyfus.com.

HADDAD, PATRICIA A. state legislator; BS, Bridgewater State Coll., 1972. Bd. dirs. Mody Dick Council Boy scouts; mem. Weir Econ. and Indsl. Revitalization Corp. Somerset Sch. Com., 1993—2001; mem. Health Access Collaborative. Mem.: Southcoast Bus. & Profl. Womens Assn. Democrat. Office: Rm 26 State House Boston MA 02133

HADDAWAY, JANICE LILLIAN, psychotherapist, consultant; b. Lexington, Ky., Oct. 26, 1941; d. James L. and Dalla A. (Mattingly) Evans; children: Chuck, Jennifer, Jeanni, Jim, Rich, Alex, Donna. BS, U. Ky., 1967; MA, We. Ky. U., 1981, Rank I, 1992. Cert. tchr. grades 6-12; lic. marriage and family therapist. Tchr. Ninth Bapt. Acad. and S.W. Christian Sch., Louisville, Ky., 1980-89; dir. guidance counseling S.W. Christian Sch., Louisville, 1983-92; pvt. practice Louisville, 1991—. Originator, developer support groups for children of incarcerated parents Jefferson County Pub. Schs., Louisville, 1995—, early childhood mental health cons. Ky. Head Start, South Ctrl. Ky., 1995—. Named Hon. Ky. Coll. for work with children State Govt. Mem. Am. Assn. Marriage and Family Therapists (clin.), Nat. Bd. Cert. Counselors (clin.), Ky. Assn. Marriage and Family Therapists (clin.). Republican. Baptist. Home: 8006 Rush Ct Hardwood Forest Louisville KY 40214

HADDEN, MARGARET (PEGGY HADDEN), writer; b. Roanoke, Va., July 29, 1944; d. Earl F. and Doris M. (Ratliff) H. Student, U. N.C., Greensboro, 1962-64, Parsons Sch. Design, N.Y., 1964-66. Tchr. Pratt Inst. Continuing Edn., Bklyn. and N.Y.C. Author: The Artist's Guide to New Markets, 1998, The Artist's Quest for Inspiration, 1999, The Quotable Artist, 2002; writer monthly column Art Calendar mag., bi-weekly column Art Job; contbr. articles to profl. jours.; represented in permanent collections Citicorp, Pricewaterhouse Coopers, First Interstate Bank, Calif., Ragu Foods Co. Mem. Authors Guild N.Y. Avocation: collecting McCoy pottery. Home: 61 Jane St New York NY 10014-5107

HADFIELD, TOMI SENGER, hospital administrator; b. Ft. Lee, Va., Dec. 8, 1954; d. Joseph Anthony and Vesta Ilene (Murray) Senger; m. Hal Burton Hadfield, June 6, 1975; children: Bradie Suzanne, Michael Burton, Evan Scott. Cert. in bus., U. N.D., 1975; BA in Bus., U. Calif., Riverside, 1979; M in Health Adminstrn., Chapman Coll., 1989. Project mgr. Control Data Corp., Mpls., 1980-84; asst. hosp. adminstr. Riverside Gen. Hosp., 1987—. Membership campaign cabinet Arthritis Found., Riverside, 1988, YWCA, Riverside, 1988, United Way, Riverside, 1988-89. Fellow Nat. Assn. Pub. Hosps.; mem. Calif. Assn. Pub. Hosps., So. Calif. Healthcare Mktg. Assn., Jr. League Riverside (v.p.), Medi-Trans (bd. dirs.), Riverside C. of C. (v.p. 1989—), Women in Healthcare. Avocations: travel, skiing, volunteer, family. Home: 1395 Rimroad Riverside CA 92506-5558 Office: Riverside Gen Hosp 26520 Cactus Ave Moreno Valley CA 92555-3911

HADLEY, JANE BYINGTON, psychotherapist; b. N.Y.C., Apr. 24, 1929; d. David and Ruth (Johnson) Millar; m. Arthur Twining Hadley, Feb. 24, 1979; children: Elisabeth Jane Wheeler, Caroline Anne Thies. BA, U. Va., 1951; MA, Columbia U., 1967; analytic tng., Met. Ctr. for Mental Health, 1970-73. Intern Queens Coll., 1969; pvt. practice psychotherapy N.Y.C., 1971—. Bd. mem. Am. Liver Found., Greater N.Y. Chpt. Mem. APA, Cosmopolitan Club, Century Assn. Democrat. Episcopalian.

HADLEY, LEILA ELIOTT-BURTON (MRS. HENRY LUCE III), writer; b. N.Y.C., Sept. 22, 1925; d. Frank Vincent and Beatrice Boswell Eliott Burton; m. Arthur T. Hadley, II, Mar. 2, 1944 (div. Aug. 1946); 1 child, Arthur T. III; m. Yvor H. Smitter, Jan. 24, 1953 (div. Oct. 1969); children: Victoria C. Van D. Smitter Barlow, Matthew Smitter Eliott, Caroline Allison F.S. Nicholson; m. William C. Musham, May 1976 (div. July 1979); m. Henry Luce III, Jan. 1990. MD, St. Timothy's Sch., 1943. Author: Give Me the World, 1958, reprinted, 1999, Give Me the World, 2003, How to Travel with Children in Europe, 1963, Manners for Children, 1967, Fielding's Guide to Traveling with Children in Europe, 1972, rev., 1974, 1984, Traveling with Children in the U.S.A., 1974, Tibet-20 Years After the Chinese Takeover, 1979; author: (with Theodore B. Van Itallie) The Best Spas: Where to Go for Weight Loss, Fitness Programs and Pure Pleasure in the U.S. and Around the World, 1988, rev., 1989; author: A Journey with Elsa Cloud, 1997, paperback edit. with afterword, 2003, Give Me the World, 1999; assoc. editor Diplomat mag., N.Y.C., 1964—65, Saturday Evening Post, 1965—67, contbg. editor ICON: World Monuments Mag.; contbg. editor: Tricycle, the Buddhist Rev., 1991—; editl. cons. TWYCH, N.Y.C., 1985—87, book reviewer Palm Beach Life, Fla., 1967—72, consulting editor Tricyle, The Buddhist Rev., 1991—, garden columnist Fishers Island Gazette; contbr. articles to various newspapers, mags. Bd. dirs. Wings Trust, Inc., Tibet House, 1995, Fishers Island Conservancy, 1995, Donald & Shelley Rubin Cultural Trust, 2001, Bd. Helike Found. Recipient Norman Vincent Peale award, 2002. Mem. Acad. Am. Poets, Soc. Woman Geographers (exec. council 1984—), Authors Guild, Nat. Writers Union, Nat. Press Club, PEN, Explorers Club, Central Park Conservancy, Ocean Conservancy (bd. dirs.), N.Y. Acad. Medicine (guest bd.), Nat. Arts Club, Lansdowne Club (Eng.). Home: 4 Sutton Pl New York NY 10022-3056 Office Phone: 212-759-8640. E-mail: leilahadleyluce1@aol.com.

HADLEY, NANCY LYNNE, management consultant, community foundation executive; b. Valhalla, N.Y., Mar. 1, 1951; d. Joseph and Emelia (Scavnicky) Nassetta; m. J. Dwight Hadley, May 13, 1978 (div. Aug. 1995); children: Stephen, Elizabeth. BA in Sociology and Urban Studies with honors, Manhattanville Coll., Purchase, N.Y., 1972. Asst. dir. Urban Renewal Agy., Ossining, N.Y., 1971-74; dir. cmty. devel. program Mayor's Office, Stamford, Conn., 1974-84; asst. commr. housing N.Y. State Divsn. Housing, Albany, 1984-91; dept. transportation commr. Conn. Dept. of Transportation, Newington, 1991-93; commr. Conn. Dept. of Motor Vehicles, Wethersfield, 1993-95; sr. program dir. Conn. multi-cities program Local Initiatives Support Corp., Hartford, 1995-96; exec. dir. Comty. Found. for Greater New Haven, Conn., 1996—2000; pres. Hadley Group LLC, Newington, 2000—. [illegible] Fellow Am. Leadership Forum (st.), mem. Nat. Assn. Housing and Redevel. Officials, Conn. Women's Coun., N.Y. State Assn. Housing and Redevel. Officials, Women Transportation Seminar (founding mem. Conn. Valley chpt.), Conn. Coun. Philanthropy (bd. mem., chair mem. comm. 1998). Office: Hadley Group LLC PO Box 310928 Newington CT 06131-0928

HADYK-WEPF, SONIA MARGARET, artist, real estate manager; b. May 30, 1931; d. Albert and Margaret (Rodriguez) Wepf; m. Walter Hadyk, Feb. 14, 1957 (div.June 1976); 1 child, W. Gordon Hadyk. BS in Art Edn., Pratt Inst., 1954. Tchr. art Midland Park (N.J.) Jr. H.S., 1954-55, Lyncourt (N.Y.) Pub. Sch., 1969-70; staff artist Norcross Greeting Cards, N.Y.C., 1955-56, Spencer Advt. Art, Union City, N.J., 1956-58, L.W. Peckham Advt., Syracuse, N.Y., 1958-59; freelance artist Syracuse, 1959-74; mgr. jewelry dept. Naum's, DeWitt, N.Y., 1974-75; owner Hadyk House of Gem Design, Syracuse, 1975—; mgr. Walter Hadyk Rental Homes, Syracuse, 1993—. Guest lectr. Carrier Women's Club, Syracuse, 1972, Nat. League Pen Women, Syracuse, 1972; juror Arts and Crafts Festival, Camillus (N.Y.) Hist. Soc., 1973. Designer, craftsman (cultured pearl necklace) Golden Claws, 1971, (bracelet) Bubbles, 1971, (ring) Elipses, 1983; designer, goldsmith numerous pieces including All Done With Mirrors, 1980 (Judges prize for Most Creative); designer, platinumsmith (earrings) Snowflake, 1982 (1st Runner-up). Recipient numerous awards Diamond Info. Ctr., N.Y.C., 1973, DeBeers Mines, N.Y.C., 1977, 1st prize award Jewelers' Circular Keystone, Radnor, Pa., 1979; finalist in color catalog of winning designs "Colored Gemstone Design award 2000,"; sponsored by Signity N.Y. Ltd., Stuller, Jewelers of Am., Nat. Jeweler Mag.; numerous others. Mem. Real Estate Investors Ctrl. N.Y., Gem and Mineral Soc. Syracuse Inc. Unitarian-universalist. Avocations: gem carving, gardening. Office: 102 Dewey Ave Fayetteville NY 13066-1607 Office Phone: 315-446-0184.

HAEBERLE, ROSAMOND PAULINE, retired music educator; b. Clearwater, Kans., Oct. 23, 1914; d. Albert Paul and Ella (Lough) H. BS in Music Edn., Kans. State U., 1936; MusM, Northwestern U., 1948; postgrad., Wayne State U., 1965-66. Profl. registered parliamentarian. Tchr. sch. dist., Plevna, Kans., 1936-37, Esbon, Kans., 1937-41, Frankfort, Kans., 1941-43, Garden City, Kans., 1943-44, music supr. Waterford Twp., Mich., 1944-47, tchr. Pontiac, Mich., 1947-80, ret., 1980. Pres. Pontiac Fedn. Tchrs., 1961-63. Bd. dirs. Pontiac Oakland Town Hall; adv. coun. Waterford Sr. Citizens, chmn., 1990-93; pres. Oakland County Pioneer and Hist. Soc., 1992-94. Recipient Tchrs. Day award, Mich. State Fair, 1963. Mem. AAUW (pres. Pontiac br. 1970-72, founds. chair Pontiac br.), Mich. Fedn. Music Clubs (state pres. 1993-95, chmn. state bylaws and citations, chair parliamentarian 2001—, pres. Tuesday musicale of Pontiac 1984-86, pres. S.E. dist. 1986-90, chmn. Music for the Blind Northeastern region 2000), Mich. Fedn. Bus. and Profl. Womens Club (Woman of Achievement award dist. IX 1994), Mich. DARS (state parliamentarian 1985-2002), DAR (Gen. Richardson chpt., regent 1983-85, libr. and parliamentarian, Excellence in Cmty Svc. award 1995), Waterford-Clarkston Bus. and Profl. Womens Club (bylaws and parliamentarian), Pontiac Area Ret. Sch. Pers. (parliamentarian, pres. 1981-84), Mich. Assn. Retired Sch. Pers. (Disting. Svc. award 1994), Mich. Bus. and Profl. Women's Club (dir. dist. 10 1965-67), Mich. Fedn. Music Clubs (Honored Recognition award 2000, Citations award 2000), Pontiac Bus. and Profl. Women (pres. 1959-61, Woman of the Yr. award 1974), Pontiac Area Fedn. Women's Clubs (pres. 1976-78, 81-84), Mich. Registered Parliamentarians, Louise Saks Parliamentary Unit (pres. 1990-92), Bloomfield Rep. Women's Club (parliamentarian 1999-2003), Detroit Women's Club, Eastern Star (60 Yr. award 2004), Mu Phi Epsilon, Beta Sigma Phi (life), Zeta Tau Alpha. Republican. Methodist. Avocations: travel, playing piano, reading, bell ringing, dance.

HAEGELE, PATRICIA, publishing executive; b. Wheeling, W.Va., Dec. 19, 1950; d. Thomas J. and Marcella (Kissell) Cook. Student, W. Liberty Coll., 1970-71, Brevard Community Bus. Coll., 1973-74, Rollins Coll., 1974-76. Retail advt. rep. Coca Today/Gannett Co., Cocoa, Fla., 1973-76, Tampa Tribune Co., Tampa, Fla., 1976-79; corp. advt. rep. Washington Post Co. Inc., Washington, 1979-82; corp. advt. mgr. USA Today/Gannett Co. Inc., N.Y.C., 1982-84, div. sales mgr., 1984-85, v.p., eastern sales mgr., 1985, v.p., advt. dir., 1985-86; pub. USA Weekend, N.Y.C., 1986-88; sr. v.p. advt. USA Today, N.Y.C., 1988—95; pub. Travel Holiday mag.; pres. gen. mgr. Newspaper Nat. Network, 1995—97; sr. v.p., pub. Good Houseeping, 1997—. Selected to YWCA's Acad. of Women Achievers, 1988; profiled On The Rise column Fortune mag., Aug., 1988. Mem. Am. Newspapers Pubs. Assn., Internat. Newspaper Advt. Mktg. Assn., Am. Mktg. Assn. Republican. Roman Catholic. Avocations: running, biking, body tng. Home: 510 E 80th St #6C New York NY 10021 Office: Good Housekeeping 959 Eighth Ave New York NY 10019

HAENSLY, PATRICIA ANASTACIA, psychology educator; b. Kronenwetter, Wis., Dec. 4, 1928; d. Paul Frank and Valeria (Woyak) Banach; m. William E. Haensly, 1954; children: Paul, Robert, Thomas, James, John, David, Mary, Katherine. BS, Lawrence U., 1950; MS in Genetics, Iowa State U., 1953; PhD in Ednl. & Devel. Psychology, Tex. A&M U., 1982. Histo technique specialist dept. vet. pathology Iowa State U., Ames, 1958-63; asst. prof. dept. ednl. psychology Tex. A&M U., College Station, 1982-97; instr. Blinn Jr. Coll., College Station; prin. Investigator Project Mustard Seed, U.S.D.O.E. Javits Grant, 1993-96; assoc. dir. programs Inst. for Gifted and Talented Tex. A&M U., College Station, dir. summer presch. program Minds Alive, 1987-95. Mem. adj. faculty psychology Western Wash. U., Bellingham, 1996—. Contbg. editor Roeper Rev., 1996—; mem. editl. bd. Gifted Child Quar., 1996—, Gifted Child Today, 1997—; guest editor: (spl. issues) Gifted Teachers/Teachers of Gifted Learners, Parenting the Gifted; contbr. articles to profl. jours., chpts. to books. Alt. U.S. del. World Coun. Gifted and Talented Children, 1997-99, 2001-02, del., 1999-2001; del. People to People amb. program Pacific N.W. Initiative to the People's Rep. of China., 1998. Recipient Outstanding Woman award AAUW, 1980, Govt. Rsch. Javits grante, 1993-96, Hon. Mention Hollingworth award Intertel Found., 1993. Mem. Tex. Assn. for Gifted and Talented (1st v.p. 1988, 89, editor news mag. 1988, 89), Nat. Assn. Gifted Children (co-chmn. rsch. and evaluation com. 1985-87, John Curtis Gowan Rsch. award 1981, program chair Conceptual Found. divsn. 1997-99, chair 2000-01), World Coun. for Gifted and Talented Children, Inc., Soc. for Rsch. in Child Devel., Coun. for Exceptional Children, Assn. for Childhood Edn. Internat., Am. Creativity Assn. (charter), Am. Psychol. Soc., Phi Kappa Phi. Home: 3384 Northgate Rd Bellingham WA 98226-9263 E-mail: haensly@cc.wwu.edu.

HAFER, BARBARA, state official; b. L.A., Aug. 1, 1943; m. Jack Pidgeon; 4 children, John, Kelly, Bethany, Regan. BS, Duquesne U., Pitts., 1969; postgrad., U. Pitts., U. London. Founder, exec. dir. Allegheny County Ctr. for Victims of Violent Crime, 1973—79; account exec. Sautel Agency, 1979—82; employee relations mgr. South Hills Health System, 1982—83; auditor gen. State of Pa., Harrisburg, 1989-96, state treas., 1997—. Commr. Allegheny County bd. commissioners, 1984—89; mem. Del. River Port Authority, 1989—, Pa Partnership for Econ. Edn., 1997—, Pa. Pub. School Employees Retirement System Bd., 1996—. Office: State of Pennsylvania Treasury Dept 129 Finance Building Harrisburg PA 17120-0018 E-mail: barbarahafer@patreasury.org.

HAFFEY, SUSAN M. treasurer; b. Cleve., May 14, 1958; d. Evelino William and Elizabeth (Benedictt) Mastrangelo. BS, Ohio State U., 1981. Auditor State of Ohio, 1981-84; treas. Wickliffe Bd. Edn., 1984—. Found. trustee, pres., v.p. Up With Kids, Inc., Cleveland Heights, 1993-97. Pres., sec. Wickliffe Rotary, 1988; treas. Citizens Against Retail Encroachment, 1996. Recipient Paul Harris fellow Rotary Found., 1996. Mem. Am. Payroll Assn., Am. Sch. Bus. Officials, Govt. Fin. Officers of America, Rotary Internat. Democrat. Roman Catholic. Avocations: performing arts, orchestra, gardening, baseball. Office: Wickliffe City [illegible] Wickliffe OH 44092-2020

HAFFORD, FAYE O'LEARY, writer; b. St. John Plantation, Maine, Apr. 27, 1925; d. Lee and Clara Mills O'Leary; m. Joseph Lee Hafford, Nov. 5, 1949 (dec. 1993); children: Michael Lee, Randi Lou. Student, Colby Coll., 1942—44; BS in Edn., U. Maine, 1965. Cert. elem. sch. tchr. Maine. Tchr. towns of Allagash, Limestone, Brunswick, Ft. Kent, Maine, 1951—76; ret. Author: 14 booklets on folklore of St. John Valleyl, 1986—. Contbr. curriculum guide Town of Brunswick; organizer, pres., vol. librarian Allagash Pub. Libr., 1998. Recipient County All Star award, Aroostook County, Presque Isle, Maine, 2000, Calendar award, Maine Ctr. for Women, 2000, Meritorious award, Nat. Coun. Geographic Edn., 1970, commendations for work on Allagash waterway, Gov. Maine, commendation, Maine Legis., Ken York award for work on Allagash Wilderness Waterway. Mem.: NEA, Aroostook Ret. Tchrs. Assn., Maine Ret. Tchrs. Assn., AARP. Republican. Congregationalist. Avocations: knitting, crocheting, fishing, camping, reading. Home and Office: Allagash Pub Libr 894 Allagash Rd Allagash ME 04774

HAFNER, GENEVIEVE, photographer; b. Saint-Galmier, Loire, France, June 20, 1961; came to U.S., 1986; d. André Jean Marius and Irène Marie (Massardier) H. CAP in Photography, EFET Sch. Photography, Lyon, France, 1983. Staff photographer La Tribune-Le Progres-Hebdo, Saint Etienne, France, 1984-86; photo corr. City Mag. Internat., N.Y.C., 1987-91; staff photographer News Comm., Inc., N.Y.C., 1991—2001; pub., photographer Concrete Jungle images, Inc., N.Y.C., 1990—. Photographer: New York: Metropolis of the American Dream, 1995, New York: A State of Mind, 1999, Les Editions Operae, Vitriol Factory, Paris, N.Y., 2003; photographer Herman Miller Ann. Report, 1993 (Merit award 1994). Office: Concrete Jungle Images Inc 65 Cooper Sq New York NY 10003-7116 Office Phone: 212-260-4488.

HAFNER, LAURINDA MARIE, minister; b. Indpls., May 9, 1954; d. Donald Warren and Colleen Marie (Wegener) Hafner; m. Richard Edward Walters, Oct. 8, 1983; 1 child, Ciana Marie Hafner-Walters. BA in Polit. Sci., Elon U., 1976; MDiv, Christian Theol. Seminary, 1979; DM, McCormick Theol. Seminary, 1984. Ordained United Ch. of Christ. Assoc. pastor Lakewood (Ohio) Congl. Ch., 1979—87; sr. pastor Pilgrim Congl. United Ch. of Christ, Cleveland, Ohio, 1990—. Hon. bd. mem. GLSEN, Cleveland, 1999—. Campaign mgr. Dist. 54-State Rep., St. Petersburg, Fla., 1988. Recipient Those Who Will Shape Our Lives in the New Millenium award, The Cleveland Plain Dealer, 2000. Democrat. United Ch. Of Christ. Avocations: hiking, films, basketball. Home: 3175 W 162nd St Cleveland OH 44111 Office: Pilgrim Congregational United Ch Christ 2592 W 14th St Cleveland OH 44113

HAFNER-EATON, CHRIS, health services researcher, medical educator, policy analyst; b. N.Y.C., Dec. 9, 1962; d. Peter Robert and Isabelle (Freda) Hafner; m. James Michael Eaton, Aug. 9, 1986; children: Kelsey James, Tristen Lee, Wesley Sean. BA, U. Calif., San Diego, 1986; MPH, UCLA, 1988, PhD Health Svcs. Rsch./Policy Analysis, 1992. Cert. health edn. specialist; internat. bd. cert. lactation cons. Cons. dental health policy UCLA Schl. Dentistry, 1989; grad. teaching asst. UCLA Sch. Pub. Health, 1987-92; health svcs. researcher UCLA, 1987-92; cons. health policy U.S. Dept. Health & Human Svcs., Washington, 1988—; analyst health policy The RAND/UCLA Ctr. Health Policy Study, Santa Monica & L.A., 1988-94; asst. prof. health care adminstrn. Oreg. State U. Dept. Pub. Health, Corvallis, 1992-95; pres. Health Improvement Svcs. Corp., 1994—; dir. rsch. rev. La Leche League Internat., 1996-99. Adj. faculty pub. health Linn-Benton Coll., 1995—; bd. dirs. Benton County Pub. Health Bd., Healthy Start Bd.; mem. Linn-Benton Breastfeeding Task Force, Samaritan Mother-Baby Dyad Team., Am. Public Health Assn. (sect. Council Med. Care). Peer reviewer for NIH jours., others; contbr. articles to profl. jours. including JAMA, Midwifery Today, Jour. Ambulatory Care Mgmt.; other numerous lay publs. such as Mothering Mag.. Rsch. grantee numerous granting bodies, 1988—. Mem. AAUW, NOW, Internat. Lactation Cons. Assn., La Leche League Internat. (area profl. liaison for Oreg.), Am. Pub. Health Assn. (med. care sect. coun., women's caucus), Am. Assn. World Health, Oreg. Pub. Health Assn., Oreg. Health Care Assn., Assn. Health Svcs. Rsch., Soc. Pub. Health Edn., Physicians for Social Responsibility, UCLA Pub. Health Alumni Assn. (life), Pub. Health Honor Soc., Delta Omega. Home: 27461 La Cabra Mission Viejo CA 92691-1005 E-mail: drmom@proaxis.com.

HAFT, GAIL KLEIN, pediatrician; b. N.Y.C., Mar. 5, 1938; d. Herbert and Pearl (Mittleman) Klein; m. Jacob I. Haft, Mar. 27, 1964; children: Bethanne, Ian. AB in Chemistry, Vassar Coll., 1959; MD, U. Rochester, 1963. Diplomate Nat. Bd. Med. Examiners, Am. Bd. Pediatrics. Intern Albert Einstein Coll. Medicine, N.Y.C., 1963-64, resident, 1964-65, Mt. Sinai Hosp., N.Y.C., 1967-68; pediatrician Dept. Health, Staten Island, N.Y., 1965-67, Head Start, Englewood, N.Y., 1969-71, Dept. Health, Hackensack, N.J., 1970-71; utilization rev. physician Hosp. Corp., N.Y.C., 1973-76; pediatrician Westchester County Health Dept., N.Y., 1974-76; sch. physician Bd. Edn., Yonkers, N.Y., 1974-76; bus. mgr. Heartronics, Newark, 1980-94; chief med. officer Bergen County Spl. Svcs., Paramus, N.J., 1984—; physician Tenafly (N.J.) Sch. Bd. Edn., 1990-94. Mem. Tenafly Bd. Edn., 1983-89, pres., 1986-88.

HAFTER, RUTH ANNE, library director, educator; b. N.Y.C., Apr. 18, 1935; BA in History and Econs. cum laude, Brandeis U., 1956; cert. Bus. Adminstrn., Harvard-Radcliffe U., 1957; MLS, Columbia U., 1963; PhD in Libr. and Info. Studies, U. Calif., Berkeley, 1984. Supr. sch. librs. Halifax County, N.S., Can., 1965-66; asst. edn. libr. Harvard U., Cambridge, Mass., 1967-68; univ. libr. St. Mary's U., Halifax, N.S., Can., 1969-75; libr. dir. Sonoma State U., Rohnert Park, Calif., 1978-86, San Jose (Calif.) State U., 1986-91, prof. div. libr. and info. sci., 1987-99, prof. emeritus, 1999—. Instr. St. Mary's U., 1972-75, Sonoma State U., 1982-85, U. Calif., Berkeley, 1975-78, 85-86; cons. Ministry of State Urban Affairs, Can., 1975, Sonoma County Hist. Records, 1979-80; coord. Geysers Info. Project., 1980-81; project humanist Calif. Coun. for Humanities, 1981-83; dir. Indochinese Cultures project Nat. Endowment for Humanities, 1983-84, Videodisc Work Shop Calif. State U., 1987—, Online Pub. Catalog Implementation, 1989; pres. Beethoven Ctr. San Jose State U., 1987-88. Author: Academic Librarians and Cataloging Networks: Visibility, Quality and Professional Status, 1986, (with George Rawlyk) Acadian Education in Nova Scotia, 1970; contbr. articles to profl. jours. Mem. Mayor Feinstein's com. on Teaching of Holocaust, San Francisco, 1986, adv. com. Foothill Coll. Libr. Tech. Asst. Program, 1987—, San Jose Pub. Libr. Found., 1987—, bd. govs. 1987-89, exec. bd. Friends of San Jose Pub. Libr., 1989—, Calif. State Libr. Networking Task Force, 1989—, adv. bd. dirs. Frances Gullard Child Devel. Ctr., 1990—; pres. alumni bd. Sch. Libr. and Info. Sci, U. Calif., Berkeley, 1993-94. Inst. Ethnography grantee Dept. Edn., 1994-95. Mem. ALA (com. on accreditation, field site vis. bd. 1982—, libr. career resource network 1987—, program com. reference and adult svcs. div. 1989—), Coop. Libr. Agy. Systems and Svcs. (bd. govs. 1988—, acad. librs. rep.), Calif. Acad. and Rsch. Librs. (pres. 1983-84), Calif. Libr. Assn. (legis. network 1988—, chair continuing edn. com. 1997), North Bay Coop. Assn. (exec. com. 1984-85), Phi Kappa Phi. Home: 177 19th St Apt 1E Oakland CA 94612-4653

HAGAN, JUDITH ANN, social worker; b. Chgo., May 7, 1943; d. Glenn Dean and Laura May Phillips; children: Stephen L. Curtis, Michael L.

Curtis; m. George Leonard Hagan, Nov. 13, 1993. AA with highest distinction, Scottsdale (Ariz.) C.C., 1978; BS magna cum laude, Ariz. State U., 1979, MSW, 1985. Cert. ind. social worker, Ariz.; cert. in critical incident stress mgmt., FEMA. Bus. assoc. Am. Express, Phoenix, 1980-89; client svcs. rep. Pharm. Card System, Scottsdale, 1986-87; case mgr. Child Protective Svcs., State of Ariz., Phoenix, 1985; dir. social svcs. S.W. Adoptions, Scottsdale, 1989-92; employee assistance profl. Ariz. Dept. Transp., Phoenix, 1992-96; pvt. practice psychotherapy; program and projects specialist with procurement staff Ariz. Dept. Transp., Phoenix, 1996—; owner, operator Complete Counseling Svcs., Phoenix; mobil therapist Terros Behavioral Health Agy., Phoenix, 2002—03; counselor II Valle Del Sol, Inc., 2003—. Presenter programs on reconstituted families, relationships and mental health, drug abuse, stress mgmt.; freelance writer, editor. Writer, editor Ariz. Dept. Transp. Women's Resource Group Newsletter; editor pub. newsletter Procurement Update, 1997-2002; author, dir., pub. tng. film Panorama of County Services for Managers, 1984; author Ariz. Dept. Transp. Intellectual Properties Drug Abuse Program, 1993; column writer Moon Valley Tattler, 1999-2003. Vol. in cmty. devel. Battered Women's and Children's Shelter Maricopa County, Phoenix, 1979; activist Civil Rights, Sumter, S.C., 1962, Green Peace, L.A., 1971, NOW, 1980, Citizens against Cockfighting, 1998, Yr. of the Humane Child, 2000. With U.S. Women's Army Corps, 1973-74. Recipient seal Acad. Cert. Social Workers, Washington, 1996-97. Mem.: Women in Mil. Svc. for Am. (charter), Ariz. Counselors Assn. (policy com., editor newsletter, editor newsletter 2003—), Phi Theta Kappa. Avocations: healthy gourmet cooking, yoga, public speaking. Address: 1209 S 1st Ave Phoenix AZ 85003 Office Phone: 602-291-4646. Personal E-mail: judith.hagan@cox.net.

HAGAN, KAY R. state legislator, lawyer; b. Shelby, N.C., May 26, 1953; married; 3 children. JD, Wake Forest U. Bar: N.C. Practiced in, Shelby, N.C.; mem. N.C. Senate, Raleigh, 1999— Mem. agr., environ. and natural resources com., appropriations on edn. and higher edn. com., appropriations/base budget com., children and human resources com., edn. and higher edn. com., health care com., vice chmn. judiciary II com. Democrat. Presbyterian. Office: NC Senate 300 N Salisbury St Raleigh NC 27603-5925

HAGAN, SHEILA B. corporate lawyer; b. 1961, BA, Coll. St. Thomas; JD, U. Minn. Bar: 1987. V.p., gen. counsel IBP, Inc., Dakota Dunes, S.D. Office: IBP Inc 800 Stevens Port Dr Ste 836 Dakota Dunes SD 57049-5005

HAGAN-HARRELL, MARY M. state legislator; b. Cape Girardeau, Mo. m. Stan Harrell. BS in Elem. Edn. and Fine Arts, Southeast Mo. State U.; MLS, George Peabody Coll. Tchr., libr. Riverview Gardens (Mo.) Sch. Dist., 1960-86; committeewoman Ferguson Twp., 1972-89; state rep. Dist. 75 Mo. Ho. of Reps., 1986—. Chmn. retirement com., state employees com.; mem. appropriations, edn. and pub. safety com., govt. ogrn. com., higher edn. com., elem. and secondary edn. com., labor com., joint coms. pub. employees retirement, workers compensation and employment security com., health care contbns. for state employees com.; sec. St. Louis County Dem. Ctrl. Com., 1976-89. Mem. NEA, Nat. Orgn. Women Legislators, Women Polit. Caucus, Mo. Orgn. Women Legislators, Mo. Sch. Librs. Assn., Downettes Charitable Club. Office: Mo Ho of Reps Rm 316 201 W Capitol Ave Jefferson City MO 65101-1556 E-mail: mhaganha@services.state.mo.us.

HAGBERG, VIOLA WILGUS, lawyer; b. July 3, 1952; d. William E. and Jean Shelton (Barlow) Wilgus; m. Chris Eric Hagberg, Feb. 19, 1978. BA, Furman U., Greenville, SC, 1974; JD, U. SC, 1978, U. Tulsa, 1978; honor grad. basic mgmt., def. acquisition, def. small purchase, advanced fed. acquisition regulation, DOD Army Logistics Sch., Ft. Lee, Va., 1981—82. Bar: Okla. 78, U.S. Ct. Appeals (4th cir.) 79. With Lawyers Com. for Civil Rights, Washington, 1979; pub. utility specialist Fed. Energy Regulatory Commn., Washington, 1979—80; contract specialist U.S. Army, C.E., Ft. Shafter, Hawaii, 1980—81; contract officer/supervisory contract specialist Tripler Army Med. Ctr., Hawaii, 1981—83; supervisoty procurement analyst and chief policy Procurement divsn. USCG, Washington, 1983; contracts officer and chief Avionics Engring. Contracting Br., 1984; procurement analyst office of sec. Dept. Transp., 1984—85; contracting officer Naval Regional Contracting Ctr., Long Beach, Calif., 1985—87; chief acquisition rev. and policy Hdqrs. Def. Mapping Agy., Washington, 1987—92, dir. acquisitions Fairfax, Va., 1992—93, dir. acquisition policy, 1994—96; dir. acquisition policy, tech. and legis. programs Nat. Mapping and Imagery Agy., 1996—97, Office of Gen. Counsel, Nat. Geospatial Intelligence Agy. Mem.: ABA (law student divsn. liaison 1977—78), Okla. Bar Assn., Va. State Bar Assn., Nat. Contract Mgmt. Assn., Kappa Delta Epsilon, Phi Alpha Delta. Home: 9810 Meadow Valley Dr Vienna VA 22181-3215 Office: Nat Imagery and Mapping Agy Office Gen Counsel 4600 Sangamore (MS D-10) Bethesda MD 20816

HAGEMAN, ANNA ROBBINS, writer; b. N.Y.C., May 24, 1920; d. Samuel Wolfe and Marie Lillian (Sassenhagen) Robbins; m. William Charles Hageman, July 7, 1956 (dec. Apr. 1978); children: Marie Dorothy, Anna Margaret. Student, U. Pa., 1937-38, Beaver Coll., 1939-40. Writer, rschr. coord. health and beauty aids advt. Sta. KYW, Phila., 1951-52; market analyst, asst. and acting rsch. mgr. promotion dept. Phila. Inquirer, 1952-56; assoc. rschr. Rsch. and Info. for Edn., King of Prussia, Pa., 1967-68; writer Rsch. for Better Schs., Phila., 1975; organizer, operator Robbins & Hageman Rsch., Glenside, Pa., 1956-59. Contbr. numerous articles to popular mags. and newspapers Former pres. bd. dirs. Contact Gloucester County, 1996&, former chmn. publicity and recruitment, tel. vol. support person, asst. chmn. on-going tng., vol. Contact Cape Atlantic; active United Meth. chs., 1945—; ecumenical chmn. 1st United Meth. Ch., Glassboro, N.J.; vol. Gloucester County Rep. Com.; del. CONTACT USA to Lifeline Internat. Conv., Sydney, Australia, 1996. Mem. South Jersey Writers, U. Pa. Alumnae Assn. (55th reunion com.). Democrat.

HAGEN, JOANNE R. elementary school educator; b. Sparta, Wis., Aug. 14, 1967; d. Maynard B. and Marie A. Hagen. Bachelor's degree, Coll. St. Scholastica, Duluth, Minn., 1989; Master's degree, Viterbo U., LaCrosse, Wis., 2003. Tchr. presch., primary child care Wee Welcome Inn Child Ctr., Sussex, Wis., 1989—95; substitute tchr. Sparta (Wis.) Area Schs., 1995—97, tchr. title I, 1997—99, tchr. 5th grade, 1999—. Nominee Disney Tchr. of Yr.; recipient 3d pl. WebFair Competition award, U. Wis.-Stout, 2002. Mem.: Delta Kappa Gamma Alpha Upsilon. Avocations: reading, walking, crocheting, sports, computers. Home: PO Box 34 Sparta WI 54656 Office: Sparta Area Schs 506 N Black River St Sparta WI 54656

HAGER, ELIZABETH SEARS, state legislator, social services organization administrator; b. Washington, Oct. 31, 1944; d. Hess Thatcher and Elizabeth Grace (Harper) Sears; m. Dennis Sterling Hager, Sept. 3, 1966; children: Annie Elizabeth, Lucie Caroline. BA, Wellesley Coll., 1966; MPA, U. N.H., 1979. Prin. Philbrook Ctr., Concord, N.H., 1970-71; rep. N.H. Gen. Ct., Concord, 1973-76, 85-94, 1996—; del. N.H. Constitutional Conv., Concord, 1974, 84; campaign coord. Anderson for Pres. Rep. Primary, N.H., 1980; mem. Concord City Coun., 1982-90; mayor City of Concord, 1988-90; exec. dir. United Way of Merrimack County, Concord, 1996—. Bd. dirs. Jefferson Pilot Funds, Concord, Bank of NH. Pres. Greater Concord United Way, 1980-81; campaign chair United Way of Merrimack County, Concord, 1986. Republican. Episcopalian. Office: 46 N Main St Concord NH 03301-4913 Home: 5 Pleasant View Ave Concord NH 03301-2555

HAGER, LOUISE ALGER, retired chaplain; b. Spokane, Wash., Dec. 15, 1923; d. Russel S. and Thelma Ella (Geib) Alger; m. Bernard Coe, Nov. 16, 1945 (dec. July 1965); children: Cynthia W., Marjorie L.; m. Onslow B. Hager, Jan. 16, 1970 (dec. Dec. 1983). BEd, Nat. Coll. Edn., 1946; M of Theol. Studies, St. Paul Sch. Theology, 1997. Kindergarten tchr. Edgewater Park Bd. Edn., Beverly, N.J., 1946-47, 59-83; pres. bd. mgrs. Cinnaminson (N.J.) Home, 1985-88; chaplain Rsch. Med. Ctr., Kansas City, Mo., 1986-88; assoc. chaplain John Knox Village, Lee's Summit, Mo., 1988-98; ret., 1998; vol. chaplain, psychogeriatric inpatient unit Sheppard Pratt Health Sys., 1999—; vol. chaplain Hollowell and Taylor Halls health care units Inpatient Nursing Svcs. at Broadmead Retirement Cmty., 1999—. Chaplain vol. Burlington County Hosp., Mt. Holly, N.J., 1987-88; lay minister. Recipient Disting. Alumni award, Nat. Louis U., 2002, Vol. Impact award for extraordinary svc., Sheppard Pratt Health Hosp., 2002. Mem. NEA, Lee's Summit Ministerial Soc., Coll. Chaplains, Am. Soc. on Aging, Mid-Am. Congress on Aging. Democrat. Mem. Soc. Of Friends. Avocations: reading, piano playing, singing, sewing, walking. Home: Broadmead 13801 York Rd Apt M1 Cockeysville MD 21030-1891

HAGER, SUSAN KULKA, public relations executive; b. Washington, Oct. 19, 1944; d. Joseph A. and Mary Margaret (Berry) Kulka; m. C. Eric Hager, Nov. 3, 1967; 1 child, Elizabeth Hager Finley. BA in Sociology, Brescia U., 1966. VISTA vol., vol. leader Office Econ. Opportunity, White Mountain, Alaska, 1966—67; VISA and Peace Corps recruiter, cons. Gale Assocs., Washington, 1968; program asst. Office Econ. Opportunity, Washington, 1969—70, program analyst, 1970—71; program dir. Nat. Ctr. for Voluntary Action, Washington, 1971—73; chair, CEO Hager Sharp, Inc., Washington, 1973—. Founder, first pres. Nat. Assn. Women Bus. Owners, Washington, 1974; chmn. U.S. Dept. Trustees Small Bus. Adv. Coun., Washington, 1980—82; pres. Nat. Small Bus. United, Washington, 1992; vis. prof., mentor Brescia U. Editor: (monthly column) Washington Bus. Jour., 1995—97. Bd. dirs. Greater Washington Bd. Trade, Washington, 1990—, Lab Sch. Washington, 1991—95, pres. bd. dirs., 1996—. Named Bus. Woman of the Yr., Nat. Assn. Women Bus. Owners, Washington, 1985, Small Bus. of the Yr., D.C. C. of C., Washington, 1995, Bus. Woman of the Yr., United Cerebral Palsy, Washington, 1998; named one of 25 Heroines and Heroes Whose Actions Over the Last Quarter Century Have Given Women in the Workplace a Better Shot, Working Women mag., 2001. Mem.: Leadership Washington (bd. mem. 1987—), Cosmos Club. Office: Hager Sharp Inc 1090 Vermont Ave NW Washington DC 20005

HAGERMAN, LANA LEE, reading educator; b. Evansville, Ind., Mar. 2, 1948; d. George Frederick and Hazel Marie (Walden) Ivy; m. Gary Wayne Hagerman, June 26, 1970; children: Edward, Carter, Misty, Justin, Brent. BS Elem. Edn., No. Ariz. U., 1970, MA Elem. Edn., 1975. 1st grade tchr. Flagstaff Sch. Dist., Ariz., 1970—73; kindergarten tchr. Palm Ln. Elem. Sch., Phoenix, 1984—88, 1st grade tchr., 1988—93; reading specialist Cartwright Sch. Dist., Phoenix, 1993— Citizen's adv. coun. Cartwright Sch. Dist., 1981—84; RIF program coord. Palm Ln. Elem. Sch., 1993—; exec. bd. Palm Ln. PTA, 1982—98. Vol. Barry Little League, Phoenix, 1977—85, Assn. Am. Youth Soccer, Phoenix, 1977—85; pres. Relief Soc., Avondale, Ariz., 1997—2000; Den Mother Den Mother Coach Coun. of Boy Scouts Am., 1983—84. Grantee edn. grants, Wells Fargo Bank, 1997—2000.

HAGERTHEY, GWENDOLYN IRENE, retired music educator; b. Sheffield, Eng., Sept. 28, 1937; arrived in U.S., 1938; d. Colin Clifford and Dorothy Abbott Oldfield; m. George Robert Hagerthey, June 23, 1962; children: Wendy Lee Hagerthey Canfield, Scot Edward. BS in Music, Trenton State Coll., 1959. Tchr. music Northfield Pub. Schs., NJ, 1959—64, 1971—74, Enfield Pub. Schs., Conn., 1974—78, Mt. Olive Twp. Pub. Schs., Budd Lake, NJ, 1978—99; ret., 1999. Organist, choir dir. various chs. including Stanhope (N.J.) Meth. Ch., 1950—98; camp music dir. Willow Lake Day Camp, Lake Hopatcong, NJ, 1985—97. Vol. Shore Meml. Hosp., Somers Pt., NJ, 1999—, Meadowview Nursing Home, Northfield, 1999—; dir. Atlantic County Hist. Soc., Somers Pt., 1999—. Named Rookie of Yr., Shore Meml. Hosp., 2000; recipient Govs. award for Outstanding Tchg., 1991. Mem.: AAUW (1st v.p. 1959—61). Home: 26 E Meyran Ave Somers Point NJ 08244

HAGERTY, POLLY MARTIEL, financial analyst, construction executive; b. Joliet, Ill., Aug. 17, 1946; d. George Albert and Gene Alice (Roush) Jerabek; m. Theodore John Hagerty, Feb. 12, 1972. BS in Elem. Edn., Midland Luth. Coll., 1968; MEd in Early Childhood Edn., U. Ill., 1977; MBA in Fin., U. Tex., 1986. Elem. tchr. Madison Heights (Mich.) Sch. Dist., 1968-70, Taft Sch. Dist., Lockport, Ill., 1970-72; systems clerk U.S. Army, The Pentagon, Washington, 1972-74; psychology aide Psychology Clinic U. Ill., Urbana, 1974-75; elem. tchr. Champaign (Ill.) Sch. Dist., 1975-77; with recruitment Standard Oil of Ohio, Cleve., 1977-78; v.p. NCNB Texas-Houston, 1981-88, Citibank, Tucson, 1988-92; substitute tchr. Austin (Tex.) Ind. Sch. Dist., 1993-94; project adminstr. Taylor Woodrow Comtys./Steiner Ranch, Ltd., Austin, 1994—; co-owner Hagerty Constrn. Co., Austin, 1994—. Pres. Christus Victor Luth. Ch., League City, Tex., 1985-88, Luth. Ch. of the Foothills, Tucson, 1990-92; treas. Holy Cross Luth. Ch., Austin, 1996—2002. Recipient Golden Circle Sales and Svc. award, 1991. Mem. NAFE, AAUW, U. Ill. Alumni Club. Republican. Lutheran. Avocations: jazzercise, skiing, needlework, spectator sports, gourmet cooking. Office: 3405 Grimes Ranch Rd Austin TX 78732-2141 Home: 22101 W Summit Dr Spicewood TX 78669 E-mail: polly.hagerty@us.taylorwoodrow.com.

HAGGARD, GERALDINE LANGFORD, primary school educator, adult education educator, consultant; b. Wellington, Tex., Dec. 12, 1929; d. Frank and Zelma Dell (Edmondson) Langford; children: Colby, Sarah, Mary. MEd, Tex. Women's U., 1973, EdD, 1980; Cert. in Reading Recovery, Ohio State U., 1989. Elem. sch. tchr. Denton County (Tex.) Schs., 1949-62, Plano (Tex.) Ind. Sch. Dist., 1963-69, reading tchr., reading dir., 1999-2001. Vis. prof. Tex. Woman's U. Editor and author lang. arts texts; contbr. articles to profl. jours.; author: Teaching and Assessing Comprehension Strategies, 2003. Sunday Sch. tchr. Prairie Creek Baptist Ch., Plano, 1994—; vol. facilitator Journey of Hope program for grief counseling. Named Hero Plano ISD centennial celebration, 1998. Mem. N.Am. Coun. Reading Recovery (bd. mem. 1995-99), Internat. Reading Assn., Tex. State Coun. Reading, Tex. Assn. Improvement of Reading, Coalition Reading English Suprs. Tex. (sec. 1994-97), Tex. Ret. Tchrs. Assn. (Plano chpt.), Alpha Delta Kappa, Delta Kappa Gamma, Phi Delta Kappa. Home: 2017 Meadowcreek Dr Plano TX 75074-4663

HAGGERTY, GRETCHEN R. accounting and finance executive; BS in Acctg., Case Western Reserve U., Cleveland; JD, Duquesne U., Pitts. CPA. V.p. acctg. and fin. U.S. Steel Group, Pitts., tax assist., 1977—80, leasing analyst, 1980—82, sr. financial analyst, 1982—84, corp. finance mgr., 1984—85, dir. plant and gen. acctg. USS Chemicals Div., 1985—86, gen. tax atty., dir. taxes, 1987—88, assist. treasurer corp. finance, 1988—89, assist. comptroller corp. acctg., 1989—91; v.p. and treasurer USX Corp., Pitts., 1991—98; v.p. acctg. and finance U.S. Steel Group, Pitts., 1998—2002, sr. v.p. and controller, 2002, sr. v.p. and treasurer, 2002—03, exec. v.p., treasurer, CFO, 2003—. Chmn. U.S. Steel and Carnegie Pension Fund. Mem.: Allegheny County Bar Assoc. Office: USX Corp 600 Grant St Ste 6100 Pittsburgh PA 15219-2805*

HAGGERTY, ROSANNE, entrepreneur; BA, Amherst Coll., 1982; post-grad., Columbia U. Coord. housing devel. Bklyn. Cath. Charities; founder, exec. dir. Common Ground, N.Y.C., 1990—. Bd. dirs. N.Y.C. Citizens Housing and Planning Coun., Ctr. Urban Cmty. Svcs., The Echorey Green Found., Fordham Preparatory Sch. Trustee Amherst Coll.; dir. Times Sq. Bus. Improvement Dist. MacArthur fellow, 2001. Office: Common Ground Cmty 505 8th Ave 15th Fl New York NY 10018

HAGGETT, ROSEMARY ROMANOWSKI, academic administrator; BA in Biology summa cum laude, U. Bridgeport, 1974; PhD in Physiology, U. Va., 1979. Postdoctoral fellow Northwestern U., Evanston, Ill., 1979-82; asst. prof. biology Loyola U. Chgo., 1982-87; asst. rsch. scientist zoology U. Md., College Park, 1987-88; from program dir. to divsn. dir. animals and nutrition USDA, 1988-94, dep. assoc. adminstr., 1988-94; prof. animal and vet. sci. W.Va. U., Morgantown, 1994—, dean Coll. Agr., Forestry and Consumer Scis., 1994-99, assoc. provost acad. programs, 1999—2003; dir. divsn. undergrad. edn. NSF, 2003—. Office: DUE NSF 4201 Wilson Blvd Ste 835 Arlington VA 22230 E-mail: rhaggett@nsf.gov.

HAGMANN, LILLIAN SUE, violin instructor; b. Fontana, Calif., Mar. 10, 1931; d. Riley Royston and Winifred Lillian (Humphry) Green; m. Armand P. Oueilhe, Dec. 17, 1950 (div. 1971); children: Ellen Lynne Oueilhe Keene, Karen Sue Oueilhe Stanton, A. Louis Oueilhe (dec. 1971), Gregoire Pierce Oueilhe; m. Rolf Hagmann, May 19, 1971. AA, Chaffey Coll., 1951; Travel Counselor, Internat. Travel Tng., Chgo., 1974; student, Suzuki Violin Tchr. Tng. Inst., Guelph, Can., 1992, Suzuki Violin Tchr. Tng. Inst., Forest Grove, Oreg., 1993, 97, Occidental Coll., Eagle Rock, Calif., 1994, Suzuki Violin Tchr. Tng. Inst., Stevens Point, Wis., 1995, Suzuki Violin Tchr. Tng. Inst., Aspen, Colol., 1998, Suzuki Violin Tchr. Tng. Inst., Chgo., 2000. Pricer MacNall Bldg. Materials, Santa Barbara, Calif., 1964-67; office mgr. Laguna Blanca Sch. Devel. Program, Santa Barbara, 1968; pub. rels. asst. to mgr. Goleta (Calif.) Savs. and Loan, 1969-71; travel counselor Around The World Travel, Palatine, Ill., 1974-77; travel mgr./dir. pub. rels. Newport Area Travel, Newport Beach, Calif., 1977-80; travel counselor Cresenta Valley Travel, La Crescenta, Calif., 1981; violin instr. Arise Acad. Arts, Pomona, Calif., 1989-94, U. Redlands (Calif.) Cmty. Sch. Music, 1994—2003, Arts Encounter, Rowland Heights, Calif., 1996—97. Del. 1st Stringed Instrument Edn. Del., China, 1997. Mem. The Fandango Chamber Group. Violinist Santa Barbara Symphony, 1962-70, Riverside (Calif.) City Coll. Symphony, 1990-97; judge Search for Talent contest Riverside Exch. Clubs, 2000-02; active Adams Sch. PTA, Santa Barbara, 1967—; bd. dirs. Calif. Congress PTA; organizer, pres. Assn. for Neurologically Handicapped Children, 1970-71; choir Corona Cmty. Ch., 1995-97; mem. five piece ensemble Evang. Free Ch. of Corona; organizer violin concerts for children including Master of Ceremonies, Orange County Suzuki Festival, 2002-03, 03-04. Democrat. Avocations: gardening, artist. Home: 1143 Via Santiago Corona CA 92882-3950 E-mail: mrbeethoven@prodigy.net.

HAGUE, ANGELA L. artist, gallery manager, art consultant; b. New Bedford, Mass., Mar. 16, 1941; d. Anthony and Alyce M. (Fraga) Perry; m. Ronald T. Hague, Sept. 29, 1962; children: Erica Hague MacNaught, Ronald J. Jr., Keith A., Ross J. Student, Cape Cod C.C., Barnstable, Mass., 1971-75, Cape Mus. Fine Arts, Dennis, Mass., 1986, R.I. Sch. Design, 1987, U. Mass., Brewster, 1988, Indian River C.C., St. Lucie, Fla., 1991; DFA (hon.), London Inst. Applied Rsch., 1994. Underwriter, claims mgr. Jacques Ins. Agy., New Bedford, 1959-62; underwriter, claims Frank Thacher Ins. Agy., Huannis, Mass., 1963-65; fin. mgr. The Hague Cos., Dennis, 1969-92; gallery sales Spectrum Gllaery Am. Art, Brewster, 1991-92; studio artist Create-A-Vision Studio Arts, Fla., also Dennis, 1991-95; art dir., tchr., art cons. Self Discovery Learning Ctr., Jensen Beach, Fla., 1994; art cons., mgr. Rose of Creede Art Gallery, Creede, Colo., 1995—; exec. dir., art workshop leader Adobe Artspace on the Silverthread, Colo., 2002—. Adj. faculty Indian River C.C., Port St. Lucie West, 1993. Curator art exhibits at galleries; display mgr. art shows and auctions; paintings and other artwork represented in pvt. collections in U.S. Mem. steering co. Earth Keeping Conf., 1989-90, rec. sec. Cape Mus. Fine Arts, 1988-89, Dennis Babe Ruth League, 1974-76; bd. dirs. Creede Repertory Theater, 1995-99; chair com. Bachelor Loop Audio Tour, 1998. Mem. Creede Arts Coun. (v.p. 1995-99), Creede-Mineral County C. of C. (bd. dirs.), Colo. Coun. on Arts, Western States Art Fedn. Avocations: interior and architectural design, floral arrangement and landscape design, theatre, horticulture. Home: PO Box 40 Creede CO 81130-0040

HAGY, TERESA JANE, elementary school educator; b. Bristol, Va., Nov. 1, 1950; d. Don Houston and Mary Garnett (Yeatts) Hagy. AA in Pre-Edn., Va. Intermont Coll., 1970, BA in Elem. Edn., 1972; MEd, U. Va., 1976, postgrad., Radford U. Cert. technology cert. U. Va., tchr. Va., Tenn. Tchr. 1st and 4th grades St. Anne's Demonstration Sch., Bristol, Va., 1972-75; tchr. 1st, 3d, 4th, 5th and 6th grades Washington Lee Elem. Sch., Bristol, 1975—. Clin. instr. edn. Va. Intermont Coll., Bristol, 1972-75; coordinator gifted and talented program Bristol Schs., 1980-82; condr. workshops; developer tests to evaluate reading progress. Pres. women's circle Cen. Christian Ch., Bristol, Tenn., also v.p. women's fellowship, libr. chmn., mem. ch. choir, dir. music for Bible Sch., Sunday sch. tchr. 3d and 4th grades, 1979—. Recipient numerous edn. awards; named Tchr. of Yr., S.W. Va. Reading Coun., 1994, Tchr. of Quarter, Bible Sch., 1992, Tchr. of Yr., Rotary, 2000. Mem.: AAUW (sec. 1976—79, v.p. 1981—86), NEA, Va. State Reading Assn., Internat. Reading Assn., Bristol Edn. Assn. (sec. 1978—80, chmn. Am. Edn. Week 1993, v.p. membership chair 1994—95, sch. renewal steering com. 1994—99, chair staff and personal com. 1994—99, comm. rep. 1995—97, faculty rep. 1996—98, comm. rep. 2000—, 2001—), Va. Edn. Assn., Nat. Trust for Hist. Preservation, U. Va. Alumni Assn., Va. Intermont Coll. Alumni Assn. (nat. pres. 1987—89), U. Va. Alumnae Assn., Phi Theta Kappa, Delta Kappa Gamma (chpt. v.p. 1986—88, pres. 1988—90, coordinating coun. chmn. 1990—92). Republican. Avocations: singing, piano, stitchery, walking, reading. Home: 820 Virginia Ave Bristol TN 37620-3935 Office: Washington Lee Elem Sch Washington Lee Dr Bristol VA 24201 E-mail: thagy@bristolvaschools.org.

HAHN, BEATRICE A. education educator; B, U. of Regensburg, W. Germany; MD, U. of Munich, Med. Sch., 1981. Post doctoral fellowship R.C. Gallo at the Nat. Cancer Inst., Bethesda, Md., 1982—85; prof. of medicine and microbiology U. of Ala., Dept. of Medicine, 1985—. Achievements include research in human retroviruses and associated diseases. Office: University of Alabama at Birmingham Dept of Medicine and Microbiology 720 20th St South Kaul 816 Birmingham AL 35294

HAHN, BESSIE KING, library administrator, lecturer; b. Shanghai, People's Republic of China, May 14, 1939; came to U.S., 1959; d. Jen Fong and Wei (Lok) King; m. Roger Carl Hahn, 1962 (div. 1983); children: Angela Yee-mei, Michael King-yau, Belinda Shee-wei; m. David Ware Duhme, 1989. BA, Mt. Marty Coll., Yankton, S.D., 1961; MSL.S., Syracuse U., 1972. Librarian Carrier Corp., Syracuse, N.Y., 1972; life sci. bibliographer Syracuse U. Libraries, 1973-75, head sci. and tech., 1975-78; asst. dir. reader services Johns Hopkins U. Library, Balt., 1978-81; dir. libraries Brandeis U., Waltham, Mass., 1981-96, asst. provost for libs., univ. libr., 1996-2000, nat. women's com. libr., asst. provost, 2000—03, univ. libr. emerita, 2003—. Cons. Shanghai Jiao Tong U. Library, Shanghai, 1983—, hon. prof., 1984 Editor Jour. Ednl. Media and Library Scis., 1983-99; contbr. articles to profl. jours. Bd. govs. Abraham Lincoln Brigade Archives, 1989-99; commr. New England Assoc. Schs. and Colls., Inc., 1991-97; exec. dir. Newton Symphony Orch., 2003—. Recipient Golden Cup award Johns Hopkins U. Class of 1980, 1980. Mem. ALA, Chinese-Am. Librarians Assn. (pres. 1982-83). Home: 148 Sudbury Rd Weston MA 02493-1351 Office: Brandeis U Libr 415 South St Waltham MA 02453-2728 E-mail: bhahn@brandeis.edu.

HAHN, BETTY, artist, photographer, educator; b. Chgo., Oct. 11, 1940; d. Eugene Joseph and Esther Josephine (Krueger) H.; widowed. AB, Ind. U., 1963, M.F.A., 1966. Asst. prof. photography Rochester (N.Y.) Inst. Tech., 1969-75; prof. art U. N.Mex., Albuquerque, 1976-97, prof. emeritus, 1997—. One-woman shows include Smithsonian Instn., Washington, 1969, Ctr. Photographic Studies, Louisville, 1971, Focus Gallery, San Francisco, 1974, Sandstone Gallery, Rochester, N.Y., 1978, Blue Sky Gallery, Portland, Oreg., 1978, Susan Spiritus Gallery, Newport Beach, Calif., 1977, 82, Witkin Gallery, N.Y.C., 1973, 79, Washington Project for the Arts, 1980, Ctr. Creative Photography, Tucson, 1981, Columbia Coll. Gallery, Chgo., 1982, Port Washington Pub. Library, N.Y., 1984, Mus. Fine Arts, Mus. N.Mex, Santa Fe, 1986, Lehigh U., 1988, U. Mass., Amherst, 1989, Andrew Smith Gallery, Santa Fe, 1991, U. N.Mex. [illegible] Albuquerque, 1991. Named Honored Educator, Soc. for Photog. Edn., 1984; Nat. Endowment Arts grantee, 1977-78, 82-83; N.Y. State Council Arts grantee, 1976 Mem. Soc. Photog. Edn., Coll. Art Assn., Evidence Photographers Internat. Council Office: Univ N Mex Art Dept Albuquerque NM 87131-0001

HAHN, CELIA FERNER, state representative, broadcaster; b. Sioux City, Iowa, Mar. 21, 1942; d. Arnold Erland and Celia Evelyn (Wright) F.; m. Curtis Henry Hahn, Feb. 6, 1966; children: Cathy Celia, Christopher Curtis. BA, State U. Iowa, 1964. Asst. to pres. Cranbrook Ednl. Cmty., Bloomfield Hills, Mich., 1972-78; owner WLDM Radio, Springfield, Mass., 1978-87, WNNZ Radio, Springfield, Mass., 1987-98; mem. Mass. Ho. of Reps., Boston, 1994—. Corporator Westfield Atheneum, WEstfield Boys and Girls Club, Woronoco Savs. Bank. Mem. Nat. Order Women Legislators (v.p. 1999—), Mass. Women's Polit. Caucus, Women's Legislators Lobby, Mass. Legis. Assn., Am. Legis. Exch. Coun., Greater Westfield C. of C. (pres. 1985), Zonta (charter), Westfield Woman's Club (program chmn. 1980-82), Western Mass. Bus. Women Bus. Owners Assn. Avocations: swimming, cars, travel, reading. Address: PO Box 1248 Westfield MA 01086-1248 Office: State House Rm 254 Boston MA 02133-2220

HAHN, HELENE B. motion picture company executive; b. N.Y.C. BA, Hofstra U.; JD, Loyola U., Calif., 1975. Bar: Calif. 1975. V.p. bus. affairs Paramount Pictures Corp., L.A., sr. v.p. bus. affairs, 1983-84; sr. v.p. bus. and legal Walt Disney Studios, Burbank, Calif., 1984-87, exec. v.p., 1987-94; with Dreamworks, 1994—. Recipient Frontrunner award in bus. Sara Lee Corp., 1991, Big Sisters Achievement award, 1992, Clairol Mentor award, 1993, Women in Bus. Magnificent Seven award, 1994.

HAHN, JESSICA FORTNER, lawyer; b. Long Beach, Calif., July 2, 1972; d. Raymond Griffith Fortner Jr. and Paula Bryant Fortner. BA Internat. Rels., U. So. Calif., 1994; JD, U. San Diego, 1998. Bar: Calif. 1998. Mem.: ABA.

HAHN, LORNA, political organization executive, author; b. Phila., June 16; d. Charles William and Belle Herman; m. Walter F. Hahn; 1 child, Randolph P. BA, Temple U.; MA, U. Pa., PhD in Internat. Rels., 1962. Instr. Temple U., Phila.; researcher Spl. Ops. & Rsch. Office, Washington; rsch. coord. Hist. Evaluation & Rsch. Orgn., Washington; dir. Masters program Am. U., Washington; exec. dir. Assn. Third World Affairs, Washington, 1968—. V.p. Internat. Fedn. for Protection of Religious, Linguistic & Ethnic Minorities, Washington, 1987—; pub. Third World Forum, 1976—; advisor Save Cambodia, Inc.,Washington, 1980—; lectr. Cath. U., Washington, 1965-66, Howard U., Washington, 1971-73, 82-83. Author: North Africa: Nationalism to Nationhood, 1960, Undergrounds in Insurgency, Revolutionary and Resistance Warfare, 1964, Morocco: Old Land, New Nation, 1966, An Historical Dictionary of Libya, 1981; author numerous monographs, articles and reviews; frequent guest on talk shows. Advisor Dem. candidates. Recipient Scholarship medal Phi Gamma Mu. Mem. Dems. 2000. Mem. Unitarian Ch. First woman to lecture at U.S. Nat. War Coll. and other mil. staff colls. Office: Assn Third World Affairs 1629 K St NW Washington DC 20006-1602

HAHN, MARY DOWNING, writer; b. Washington, Dec. 9, 1937; d. Kenneth Ernest and Anna Elisabeth (Sherwood) Downing; m. William Edward Hahn, Oct. 7, 1961 (div. 1977); children: Katherine Sherwood, Margaret Elizabeth; m. Norman Pearce Jacob, Apr. 24, 1982. BA in Fine Arts and English, U. Md., 1960, MA in English, 1969. Asst. libr. children's sect. Prince George's County (Md.) Meml. Libr. System, 1975-91; instr. English U. Md., College Park, 1970-74; free-lance illustrator PBS/WETA, Arlington, Va., 1973-75. Author: The Sara Summer, 1979, The Time of the Witch, 1982, Daphne's Book, 1983 (William Allen White Children's Choice award 1985-86), The Jellyfish Season, 1985, Wait Till Helen Comes: A Ghost Story, 1980 (11 Children's Choice awards), Tallahassee Higgins, 1987, Following the Mystery Man, 1988, December Stillness, 1988 (Book award Child Study Assn. 1989, Calif. Young Readers' medal 1990-91), The Doll in the Garden, 1989 (Md. Children's Book award 1990-91, 7 Children's Choice awards), The Dead Man in Indian Creek, 1990 (4 Children's Choice awards), The Spanish Kidnapping Disaster, 1991, Stepping on the Cracks, 1991 (Scott O'Dell Hist. Fiction award 1992, ALA notable 1991, Joan G. Sugarman award, Hedda Seisler Mason award, Children's Choice awards), The Wind Blows Backward, 1993 (ALA Best Books for Young Adults), Time for Andrew, 1994 (7 Children's Choice awards), Look for Me by Moonlight, 1995 (Yalsa Quick Picks for Reluctant Readers), The Gentleman Outlaw and Me-Eli, 1996, Following My Own Footsteps, 1996, As Ever, Gordy, 1998, Anna All Year Round, 1999, Promises to the Dead, 2000, Anna on the Farm, 2001, Hear the Wind Blow, 2003. Recipient Scott O'Dell award for hist. fiction, 1992, author's award Md. Libr. Assn., 1997. Mem. Soc. Children's Book Writers, Washington Children's Book Guild. E-mail: mdh12937@aol.com.

HAHN, VIRGINIA LYNN, reservations agent; b. Wharton, Tex., Oct. 27, 1951; d. Conrad E. and Verna Mae (Ammons) H. Student, Sam Houston State U., 1974. Reporter Pasadena (Tex.) Citizen Newspaper, 1975-97; reservations agt. Continental Airlines, 1997—. Mem. Tex. Press Women, 1976-86, Nat. Fedn. Press Women, 1976-86; condr. workshop Christian Writer's Conf., Pasadena, 1992. Bd. dirs. San Jacinto Day Found., Pasadena, 1990—; mem. pub. rels. com. Am. Cancer Soc., Pasadena, 1996—; vol. Restoration of USS Tex., Pasadena, 1992-94; former mem. Pasadena Rotary South, 1992-94, Am. Heart Assn., Pasadena, 1990-92; docent Houston (Tex.) Mus. Natural Sci., 1998—. Recipient awards Nat. Fedn. Press Women, 1985—, Tex. Press Women, 1985-90, Harris County Med. Soc., 1991-94. Mem. Am. Cancer Soc. (com. mem.), Pasadena Hist. Soc., Rotary, Pasadena Kiwanis Club (hon.), Alpha Rho (sec., pres. preceptor 1998), Beta Sigma Phi. Democrat. Mem. Church of God. Avocations: reading, visiting museums, cooking, embroidery.

HAHN WARANCH, HELENE, educational association administrator; b. Balt. m. Jeffrey H. Waranch; children: Andrew, David stepchildren: Andrew, Michelle. BS, U. Md., 1968; MEd, U. N.C., 1972. Owner, pres. Hahn Graphics Inc., 1981—96; prodn. coord. math. textbook series Whitmore Print and Imaging Inc., 1997—2000; v.p. comm., sales rep. Calvert Home Sch., 1997—2000; exec. dir. Literacy Works Inc., 1998—. Chair Premier Print Awards Printing Industries of Am. Inc., 1995—98, mem. long range planning, 1996—98; bd. chair Printing Industries of Md. Inc., 1996—97, treas., chair, fin., long range planning, 1994—96, sec., 1992—94, chair edn. com., 1990—96. Founding bd. dirs., various positions Literacy Works Inc., 1993—98; founding mem. Network 2000, 1992—94, Adv. Women's Inst., Coll. Notre Dame Com., 1992—95; Mem. Youth Coun. of Workforce Investment, Baltimore County, 1999—; mem. Sch. Partnership, Greater Balt. Com., 1989—93; mem. steering com. Enterprise Women's Network, 2003—; conv. program chair Women of Reform Judaism, Fedn. Temple Sisterhoods, 1989—91, treas., 1989—93, v.p., 1993—2001, nat. pres., 2001—; mem. task force on ethics Commn. on Social Action, inter-religious affairs com. Union Am. Hebrew Congregations, 1995—, v.p. Mid-Atlantic coun., 1998—2002; bd. dirs. World Union Progressive Judaism, 2000—, Md. Com. Children, 1992—94. Named one of Md.'s Top 100 Women, Daily Record, 1995, 1999; recipient Hannah B. Solomon award, Nat. Coun. Jewish Women, Balt., 2000, Naomie Berber Meml. award, Graphics Arts Tech. Found., 2000. Mem.: Advt. Assn. Balt., Md. Assn. Adult, Continuing and Cmty. Edn., Prodn. Club Balt. Office: # 303 9100 Franklin Square Dr Baltimore MD 21237

HAIDOSTIAN, ALICE BERBERIAN, concert pianist, volunteer, not-for-profit fundraiser; b. Highland Park, Mich., Sept. 21, 1925; d. Harry M. and Siroun Vartabedian Berberian; m. Berj H. Haidostian, Oct. 1, 1949; children: Cynthia Esther Haidostian Wilbanks, Christine Rebecca Haidostian Garry, Diran Berj. MusB, U. Mich., 1946, MM, 1949. Pvt. piano tchr., 1946-48; tchr. music Detroit Pub. Sch., 1953; dir. vocal trio The Haidostians, 1959—71; dir. youth choral group Cultural Soc. Armenians from Istanbul, 1965—72. Chmn. adv. coun. Armenian Studies Program, U. Mich., 1984-99. Initiator (Operas) Anoush, Mich. Opera Theatre, 1981—82, 2001—02, Transparent Anatomical Manikin exhibit, Detroit Sci. Ctr., 1976. Initiated Centennial Celebration U. Mich. Sch. Music, Detroit, 1980; mem. Armenian Gen. Benevolent Union Alex Manoogian Sch., 1981—91, Detroit chpt. core group com., 1992—; chmn. Marie Manoogian group Armenian Gen. Benevolent Union Alex Manoogian Sch, 1993—; active Detroit Women's Symphony Orch, Mich. Opera; bd. trustees Mich. Opera Theatre, 1982—; active Oakway Symphony Orch.; mem. Save Orch. Hall women's divsn.Project HOPE, 1964—, pres., 1995—96, Detroit Armenian Women's Club, 1957—; active women's chpt. Armenian Gen. Benevolent Union, Detroit, 1944—93; bd. dirs. Childhelp USA Greater Detroit Aux., 1998—; active Detroit Sci. Ctr., 1976—, bd. trustees, 1999—; organist, choir dir. Armenian Congl. Ch., Detroit, 1946—48; mem. Chancel Choir Westminster Ch. Detroit, 1965—80; bd. dirs. Detroit Symphony Orch., 1986—88. Recipient Spirit of Detroit award, 1980, Heart of Gold award United Found. City Detroit, 1981, Nat. Svc. citation U. Mich. Alumnae Coun., 1980, Disting. Alumni Svc. award U. Mich., 1981, Leadership plaque Detroit Symphony Orch., 1988, Magic Flute award Internat. Found. Mozarteum, Salzburg, Austria, 1989, Lifetime Achievement award Outstanding Woman Mich. Project HOPE, 1998, Cmty. Svc. award Wayne County Med. Soc. Alliance, 2000; named Armenian Mother of Yr., Internat. Inst. Detroit, 1981. Mem. Detroit Assn. Univ. Mich. Women (pres. 1969-71), Mich. Fedn. Music Clubs, Mich. State Med. Soc. Alliance, Wayne County Med. Soc. Aux. (pres. 1975-76), Pro Mozart Soc. Greater Detroit (pres. 1982-02, pres. emeritus 2002-, Cert. Appreciation 2002), Pro Musica Detroit (sec. 1969-90, 1st v.p. 1990—), Tuesday Musicale Detroit (pres. 1970-72), Univ. Mich. Alumni Assn. (chmn. alumnae coun. 1977-79), Univ. Mich. Sch. Music Alumni Soc., Women's Assn. Detroit Symphony Orch. (pres. 1986-88, vol. coun. Detroit Symphony Orch.), U. Mich. Alumni Assn. (bd. dirs.), U. Mich. Emeritus Club (pres. 1997-98). Avocation: piano. Home: 6838 Valley Spring Dr Bloomfield Hills MI 48301-2845

HAIG, SUSAN, conductor; BA in Music Theory and Composition, Princeton U.; DMA in Orchestral Conducting, MM in Orchestral Conducting, MM in Piano, State U. N.Y., Stony Brook; PhD in Humanities (hon.), U. Windsor, 1998. Coaching/conducting fellow Juilliard Am. Opera Centre, 1981—83; assistant conductor Minnesota Opera, 1983—84, New York City Opera, 1984—86, Santa Fe Opera, 1986; resident coach and conducting assistant Canadian Opera Co., 1986—88; resident staff conductor Calgary Philharmonic Orch., 1988—91; artistic dir. and principal conductor Windsor Symphony Orch., 1991—; music dir. designate S.D. Symphony Orch., 2000—. Recipient Heinz Unger Conducting award, 1992, Mayor's award for excellence in the performing arts, 1999. Office: SD Symphony Orch 300 N Dakota Ave Sioux Falls SD 57104*

HAIGHT, CAROL BARBARA, lawyer; b. Buffalo, May 3, 1945; d. Robert H. Johnson and Betty R. (Walker) Hawkes; m. H. Granville Haight, May 28, 1978 (dec. Nov. 1983); children: David Michael, Kathleen Marie. BSW summa cum laude, BA in Psychology summa cum laude, Widener U., Chester, Pa., 1980; JD cum laude, Widener U., Wilmington, Del., 1984. Assoc. Pepper, Hamilton & Scheetz, Phila., 1985-88, Hodgson, Russ, Andrews, Woods & Goodyear, Buffalo, 1988-90; pvt. practice Boca Raton, Fla., 1990—; corp. counsel Eilink Corp, Fremont, Calif., 2000. Arbitrator Am. Arbitration Assn., mediator, 1989—, mediation instr.; founding dir. Mediation Ednl. Svc., Fla. Supreme Ct. Cert. mediator and arbitrator, 1999-; vol. spkr. and coun. Hospice. Contbr. articles to profl. jours. Mem. Pa. Bar, Fla. Bar, Phi Kappa Phi Hon. Soc., Phi Alpha Delta, Phi Gamma Mu. Republican. Episcopalian. Avocations: scuba diving, skiing, tennis, sailing, ballroom dancing, flying. Home: 9385 E Maiden Ct Vero Beach FL 32967 Office Phone: 561-362-9100. Personal E-mail: cbhaight@yahoo.com.

HAILEY, V. ANN, retail executive; CFO The Limited Inc., Columbus, Ohio. Office: The Limited Inc 3 Limited Pkwy Columbus OH 43230-1467

HAIMBACH, MARJORIE ANNE, music educator; b. Abington, Pa., Feb. 9, 1927; d. Charles Albert and Laura Adeline (Hungerford) Haimbach. BA in Music, Ursinus Coll., Collegeville, Pa., 1948. Pvt. piano tchr., Langhorne, Pa., N.Y.C. Mem.: Soc. of Mayflower Descendants, Am. Coll. Musicians, Pa. State Music Tchrs. Assn., Nat. Guild of Piano Tchrs., Bucks County Assn. of Piano Tchrs. Home: 113 W Maple Ave Langhorne PA 19047

HAINES, CARYL, retired medical/surgical nurse; b. Addison, N.Y., Nov. 8, 1939; d. Carl Ward and Phoebe Anna (Cotton) Hamilton; m. Gale Swinter Haines, Dec. 31, 1964. Diploma, Arnot Odgen Meml. Hosp., Elmira, N.Y., 1960; student, Elmira Coll.; BS in Profl. Arts, St. Joseph's Coll., 2001. Cert. nurse adminstr. Staff nurse Arnot Ogden Meml. Hosp., unit dir. perinatal dept. and pediatric unit. Mem. ANA, N.Y. State Nurses Assn. Home: 62 Maple St Addison NY 14801-1124

HAINES, JOYBELLE, retired elementary school educator; b. Geronomo, Okla., Oct. 20, 1930; d. William Tommie and Ruby Dell Heffington; m. Meredith C. Haines, Aug. 22, 1953; children: Cynthia Elaine, Stephen Michael, Lisa Joy. Grad., Asbury Coll., Wilmore, Ky.; postgrad., Ball State Tchrs. Coll., Calif. State U. Missionary tchr., Seoul, Republic of Korea, 1954—56; tchr. Hartford City, Ind., 1956—65, Muncie, Ind., 1965—66, Stockton (Calif.) Unified Sch. Dist., 1966—2000; ret., 2001. Cons. new tchrs., tutor, Stockton, 1999—. Mem.: AAUW, Rep. Women's Club. Baptist. Home: 9530 Springfield Way Stockton CA 95212

HAINES, KATHLEEN ANN, pediatrician, educator; b. N.Y.C., July 28, 1949; d. George Raymond and Gertrude Ann (Driscoll) H.; m. Emil Claus Gotschlich, May 24, 1975; 1 child, Emily Claire. BA, CUNY, 1971; MD, Albert Einstein Coll. Medicine, 1975. Diplomate Am. Bd. Pediatrics, Am. Bd. Allergy and Immunology. Intern, resident N.Y. Hosp./Cornell U., N.Y.C., 1975-77, fellow in allergy/immunology, 1977-80; instr. in pediatrics NYU Sch. of Medicine, N.Y.C., 1980-84, asst. prof. pediatrics, 1984-91, asst. prof. medicine, 1989-91, assoc. prof. clin. pediatrics and medicine, 1991—; dir. pediat. rheumatology Hosp. for Joint Diseases/NYU Med. Ctr., 1994—2002; dir. clin. immunology lab. Hosp. for Joint Diseases, 1995—2002; sect. chief pediat. immunology Hackensack U. Med. Ctr., 2002—. Mem. rsch. coun. N.Y. Heart Assn., 1988-90; program com. Am. Coll. Rheumatology, 2000-03, vis. prof., 2001. Contbr. articles to profl. jours., chpts. to books in field. Med. and Scientific Com. N.Y.C. chpt. Arthritis Found., 1993-99. Grantee N.Y. Arthritis Found., 1990, 96, NIH, 1993-98. Fellow Am. Acad. Allergy and Immunology, Am. Acad. Pediatrics (mem. exec. com. rheumotology sect., 2003—); mem. Am. Fedn. Med. Rsch., Allergy, Asthma and Immunology Soc. of Greater N.Y. (sec. 1995-97, pres.-elect 1997-98, pres. 1998-99), Harvey Soc., Soc. Pediatric Rsch. Office: Hackensack U Med Ctr 30 Prospect Ave Hackensack NJ 07601 E-mail: mhaines@humed.com.

HAINING, JEANE, psychologist; b. Camden, N.J., May 2, 1952; d. Lester Edward and Adina (Rahn) H. BA in Psychology, Calif. State U., 1975; MA in Sch. Psychology, Pepperdine U., 1979; MS in Recreation Therapy, Calif. State U., 1982; PhD in Psychology, Calif. Sch. Profl. Psychology, 1985. Lic. clin. psychologist 1987, lic. ednl. psychologist 1982. Crisis counselor Calif. State U., Northridge, 1973-74; recreation therapist fieldwork Camarillo (Calif.) State Hosp.-Adolescent/Children's Units, 1974; Intern recreation therapist UCLA Neuropsychiatric Inst., L.A., 1975-76; substitute tchr./recreation therapist New Horizons Sch. for Mentally Retarded, Sepulveda, Calif., 1976-79; sch. psychologist Rialto (Calif.) Unified Sch. Dist., 1979-82, clin. psychologist field work San Joaquin County Dept. Mental Health, Stockton, Calif., 1982-83; intern clinical psychologist Fuller Theol. Sem. Psychology Ctr., Pasadena, Calif., 1984-85; clin. psychologist U.S. Dept. Justice, Terminal Island, Calif., 1985-86; cmty. mental health psychologist L.A. County Dept. Mental Health, 1987-89; clin. psychologist Calif. Dept. Corrections, Parole Outpatient Clinic, L.A., 1990—, Mary Magdeline Project, Commerce, Calif., 1992-2000. Adv. bd. Camarillo (Calif.) State Hosp., 1994-97, vice-chmn. adv. bd., 1996-97; examiner Lic. Ednl. Psychologist Oral Examinations, Calif. Bd. Behavioral Sci. Examinations, Sacramento, 1985. Recipient award Outstanding Achievement Western Psychology Conf., Calif., 1974. Mem. APA, Forensic Mental Health Assn. (con. planning com. 1993). Democrat. Lutheran. Avocations: rock climbing, skiing, skating, tennis, piano.

HAINSWORTH, MELODY MAY, information professional, researcher; b. Vancouver, B.C., Can., May 13, 1946; m. Robert John Hainsworth, Jan. 6, 1968; children: Kaleeg William, Shane Alan. BA with honors, Simon Fraser U., Vancouver, 1968; MLS, Dalhousie U., Halifax, N.S., Can., 1976; PhD, Fla. State U., Tallahassee, 1992. Libr. Dept. Edn. of Tanzania, Mbeya, 1969-72, Dept. of Edn. of Zambia, Mwinilunga, 1972-74; law libr., deptl. libr. Dept. of Atty. Gen. of N.S., Halifax, 1975-77; regional libr. Provincial Ct. Librs. Dept. of Atty. Gen. of Alta., Calgary, 1977-80, So. Alta. Law Soc. libr., 1980-89; dir. librs. Keiser Coll., Tallahassee, 1992-93; v.p. info. resources and svcs. Internat. Coll., Naples, Fla., 1993—. Adj. instr. Sch. Libr. and Info. Studies, Fla. State U., Tallahassee, 1990-91, libr. cons., 2004—; speaker in field; rschr. in law and info. sci.; co-founder Naples Free-Net, World Class Acad.; mem. faculty Practising Law Inst.; active Women's Polit. Caucus; co-founder Naples Free-Net; rschr. in law and info. sci. World Class Acad.; evaluator SACS/COC, 1999—; mem. external rev. panel ALA/COA, 1999—; spkr. Practising Law Inst. Author monographs; contbr. articles to profl. jours. Pres. Naples Free Net, 1993—; co-chair adv. com. com. on edn. and tech. Fla. State Bd. Ind. Colls. and Univs., 1993-2001; founding mem. Pub. Access to the Law of Fla., 1990—; mem. exec. bd. Calgary Legal Guidance, 1985-89, vice chmn., 1988-89, hon. life mem.; tech. grant com. Collier County Edn. Found., 1994-96, sec./webmaster World Class Collier; supt. search com., 1998; chair edn. com. East Naples Civic Assn., 1998; bd. dirs. Seacrest Country Day Sch., 1996-2002. Student Leader Bursaries Simon Fraser U. scholar, 1966-68; H.W. Wilson scholar Dalhousie U., 1974; recipient Woman of Distinction award AAUW, 1999. Mem. Spl. Librs. Assn (pres. 1994-95), Assn. Online Profls., Fla. State, Ct. and County Librs. Assn., Tallahassee Law Librs. Assn., Fla. Libr. Assn., Assn. Libr. and Info. Sci. Edn., Alta. Legal Archives Soc. (hon. life), Collier County Bar Assn., Women's Polit. Caucus (webmaster 1999—), Tempo Internat., bd. dirs. 2003—, Naples Press Club. Avocations: squash, hiking, travel. Office: Internat Coll 2655 Northbrooke Dr Naples FL 34119-5707

HAIR, JENNIE (M. VIRGINIA REPPERT), counseling administrator, poet; b. Philipsburg, Pa., Oct. 7, 1923; d. James Harold Reppert and Eleanor Rae Runk; children: John V. Wilmerding, James R. Wilmerding, Douglas C. Wilmerding. AB, Wellesley Coll., 1945; MA and profl. cert., Columbia U., 1967; diploma in ednl. adminstrn., L.I. U., 1987. Cert. sch. psychologist N.Y. Sch. psychologist BOCES Nassau County, NY, 1958—62, 1988—99, Commack Schs., NY, 1962—88. Poet (book) A Sisterhood of Songs, 1995, An Old Century, A New Testament, 1996. Mem. Northport Arts Coun., L.I. Philharmonic Chorus, Robert Shaw Collegiate Chorale. Mem.: L.I. Poetry Collective, Poets and Writers, Poetry Soc. Am., League Women Voters. Independent. Avocations: reading, gardening, choral singing, travel. Home: POB 190 Benson VT 05731

HAIRALD, MARY PAYNE, vocational education educator, coordinator; b. Tupelo, Miss., Feb. 25, 1936; d. Will Burney and Ivey Lee (Berryhill) Payne; m. Leroy Utley Hairald, May 31, 1958; 1 child, Burney LeShawn. BS in Commerce, U. Miss., 1957, M in Bus. Edn., 1963; postgrad., Miss. Coll., 1964, Miss. State U., 1970, U. So. Miss., 1986-88, 90, U. Calif., Davis, summer 1997, Babson Coll., summer 1998. Bus. edn. tchr. John Rundle High Sch., Grenada, Miss., 1957-59; youth recreation leader City of Nettleton, Miss., summers 1960-61; tchr. social studies Nettleton Jr. High Sch., 1959-70; tchr.-coord. coop. vocat. edn. program Nettleton High Sch., 1970—; area mgr. World Book, Inc., Chgo., 1972-84; local coord. Am. Inst. for Fgn. Study, Stamford, Conn., 1988—. Instr. bus. Itawamba C.C., Tupelo, 1975-80; with Cmty. Coord. for Program of Acad. Exch. (PAX), 1998—; advisor DECA, Nettleton, 1985—, state officers' advisor, 1995-01; apptd. adv. coord. mem. Miss. Coop. Edn.-State Dept. Edn. Editor advisor State DECA Newsletter, 1987-92; contbr. articles on coop. edn. to newspapers. Co-organizer Nettleton Youth Recreation Booster Club; fundraiser Muscular Dystrophy Assn.; Sunday sch. tchr. coll. and career class Nettleton United Meth. Ch. Recipient 1st place Nat. Newsletter award Nat. DECA, 1988, 89, 90, 92, Excellence in Supervision award Am. Inst. for Fgn. Study, 1992; named Star Tchr., Miss. Econ. Coun., 1978, 95, Dist. II DECA Advisor of Yr., Miss. Assn. DECA, 1990, 93, 00, also State DECA Advisor of Yr., 2000, hon. lifetime mem., Alumni Mem. of Yr., 1998; Nat. DECA Hall of Fame charter mem., 1996; named tchr. of yr. Wal-Mart, 1997; recipient award for excellence Pub. Edn. Forum, 1997; award finalist Miss. Mfrs. Assn., 1997, 98, 02. Mem. AAUW (charter), Am. Vocat. Assn. (Region IV New and Related Svcs. Tchr. of Yr. 1986, 96, Region IV Mktg. Edn. Tchr. of Yr. 1988, Region IV Outstanding Vocat. Tchr. of Yr. 1996, Nat. Tchr. of the Yr. 97), Coop. Work Experience Edn. Assn., Miss. Assn. Vocat. Educators (dist. sec., pres. 2001-02), Miss. Assn. Coop. Vocat. Edn. Tchrs. (v.p. 1980-83, pres. 1983-84, Miss. Tchr. of Yr. 1984, 87, 95), Miss. Assn. Mktg. Educators (Dist. II Tchr. of Yr. 1993, 94), Mktg. Edn. Assn., Jim Bowers/DECA Found. (charter, life), Nettleton Ladies Civitan Club (charter), Phi Delta Kappa (Phi Delta Kappa Kappan of Yr. 1998, found. rep.). Democrat. Methodist. Home: PO Box 166 Nettleton MS 38858-0166 E-mail: mhairald@hotmail.com.

HALABY, MARGARITA GONZALEZ, marketing professional, communications executive; m. Dominique Halaby; children: Austin C., Cameron R. BJ, U. Tex., 1997. Asst. placement dir., editor, photographer U. Tex. Grad. Sch. Libr. and Info. Sci., Austin, 1993—94; portrait photographer Lifetouch Portrait Studios, Austin, 1995—96; editl. asst. Constrn. Data News Constrn. Data Corp., Austin, 1996—97; staff writer The Brownsville (Tex.) Herald; Freedom Comm. Inc., 1997—98; reporter Valley Morning Star; Freedom Comm. Inc., Harlingen, Tex., 1998—99; mktg. comm. coord. Brownsville Pub. Utilites Bd., 1999—2000; mktg. and comm. mgr. Brownsville Pub. Utilities Bd., 2000—. Mktg. and pub. rels. cons. Importante Inc., Brownsville, 1998—2000. Bd. mem. BBB of South Tex., Weslaco, 2001—, Am. Cancer Soc. - So. Cameron County Chpt., Brownsville, 1999. Recipient Team award for Newspaper Series - Border Govs. Conf., Assn. Profl. Mng. Editors, 1999, Group Study Exch. to Finland, Rotary Internat., 2000, Ann. Report award of merit, Am. Pub. Power Assn., 2000. Mem.: Tex. Assn. Municipal Info. Officers Assn., Am. Mktg. Assn. (assoc.), Pub. Rels. Soc. Am. (assoc.), Tex. Pub. Power Assn. (mktg. and customer svc. com. mem.), Sunrise Rotary Club. Office: Brownsville Public Utilities Board 1425 Robinhood Dr Brownsville TX 78521-4230 E-mail: mhalaby@brownsville-pub.com.

HALAMICEK, TINA MARIE, special education educator; m. Gregory Joseph Halamicek, Dec. 6, 1975; children: Patrick Hennessy, Thomas Albert. BA(hon.), Chapman U., Orange, Calif., 1996—98. Specialist Instruction Credential Calif. State U. Bakersfield/Calif., 2002. Spl. edn. tchr. LA County Office of Edn., Downey, Calif., 1998—2000, Lancaster

Sch. Dist., Lancaster, Calif., 2000—. Polit. action com. mem. Teacher's Assn. of Lancaster, Lancaster, Calif., 2002—03, teacher's union rep., 2002—03. Mem.: Calif. Teacher's Assn. (assoc.), ASCD (assoc.), Coun. for Exceptional Children (assoc.).

HALAS, CYNTHIA ANN, business information specialist; b. Norristown, Pa., July 24, 1961; d. George and Maria (Mitrik) H. Student, Temple U., 1979-80; AS in Bus. Adminstrn., Montgomery County Coll., Blue Bell, Pa., 1993; student, Springhouse Computer Sch., Exton, Pa., 1994-95. Columnist, corr. The Recorder, Conshohocken, Pa., 1980-81; claims supr. Liberty Mut. Ins. Co., Blue Bell, 1980-84; claims svc. rep. Met. Property & Liability Ins. Co., Wayne, Pa., 1984-87; model Frank James Assocs., Phila., 1986-87; auditor/tng. coord. Coresource, Inc., Wayne, 1987-94; sys. support analyst Del. Valley Fin. Svcs., Inc., Berwyn, Pa., 1994-95; sys. support coord. Aetna-U.S. Healthcare, Blue Bell, Pa., 1995—. Active Nat. Arbor Day Found. Mem. NAFE, U.S. Fencing Assn. Byzantine Catholic. Avocations: golf, fencing, horseback riding, needlepoint, travel. Office: Aetna-US Healthcare 930 Harvest Dr Blue Bell PA 19422-1959

HALBER, DIANE, professional figure skater; b. Torrance, Calif., May 13, 1977; Competitive history include placing 19th in the Nat. Sr., 1997, 3rd place Pacific Coast Sr., 1997, 4th place Southwest pacific Sr., 1997, 5th place, 1996, 1st place Nat. Collegiate, 1996, others. Office: 20 1st St Colorado Springs CO 80906-3624

HALBERG, JEANNE, music educator; b. N.Y.C., June 25, 1949; d. Julius and Henrietta Newman; m. Howard Joel Halberg, July 24, 1983; children: Joshua, Jacob. BMusE, Fla. State U., 1972; MMus, U. Miami, Fla., 1978. State accredited judge Fla. Orch. Assn., 2001. Music tchr., dir. orchs. and choirs Silver Lakes Middle Sch., North Lauderdale, Fla., 1981—84; music specialist Pine Crest Sch., Ft. Lauderdale, Fla., 1985—87; music tchr., dir. orchs. and choirs Forest Glen Middle Sch., Coral Springs, Fla., 1990—96, Sawgrass Springs Middle Sch., Coral Springs, Fla., 1996—. Mem. mentorship orch. program Sawgrass Springs Middle and area HS, 1999—; adj. faculty Fla. Youth Orch., 2002—. Mem.: Broward County Music Educators Assn. (county bd. dirs. 2002—), Broward County Orch. Dirs. Assn. (county bd. dirs. 2002—), Fla. Vocal Assn. (orch. coord.), Fla. Orch. Dirs. Assn., Fla. Music Educators Assn. (state coord. All State 7-8 Honors Orch. 1999—, state bd. dirs. 1999—, Enrollment award 2002, Innovative Program award 2003). Home: 10142 NW 17 St Coral Springs FL 33071 Office: Sawgrass Springs Mid Sch 12500 W Sample Rd Coral Springs FL 33065

HALBERSTAM, MALVINA, law educator, lawyer; b. Kempno, Poland, May 2, 1937; came to U.S., 1947; d. Marcus and Pearl (Halberstam) H.; m. Wolf Z. Guggenheim (dec. 2002); children: Arye, Achiezer. BA cum laude, Bklyn. Coll., 1957; JD, Columbia U., 1961, MIA, 1964. Bar: N.Y. 1962, U.S. Dist. Ct. (so. dist.) N.Y. 1963, U.S. Ct. Appeals (2d cir.) 1965, U.S. Supreme Ct. 1966, Calif. 1968. Law clk. Judge Edmund L. Palmieri Fed. Dist. Ct. (so. dist.) N.Y., 1961-62; rsch. assoc. Columbia Project on Internat. Procedure, 1962-63; asst. dist. atty. N.Y. County, 1963-67; with Rifkind & Sterling, L.A., 1967-68; sr. atty. Nat. Legal Program on Health Problems of the Poor, L.A., 1969-70; prof. Sch. Law Loyola U., L.A., 1970-76; prof. Benjamin N. Cardozo Sch. Law Yeshiva U., N.Y.C., 1976—. Vis. prof. Gould Law Ctr., U. So. Calif., L.A., 1972-73, U. Va. Sch. Law, 1975-76, U. Tex. Sch. Law, summer 1974, Hebrew U., Jerusalem, 1984-85; counselor on internat. law U.S. State Dept. Office of Legal Adviser, 1985-86; cons., 1986-92. Author: (with De Feis) Women's Legal Rights. International Agreements An Alternative to ERA?, 1987; articles and rev. editor Columbia Law Rev., 1960-61; reporter Am. Law Inst. Model Penal Code Commentaries, 1977-81; contbr. articles, commentary, book revs. to profl. jours. Mem. Bklyn. Coll. Alumni Adv. Bd. on Women's Career Devel. and Leadership Program.; adv. com. to standing com. on law and nat. security, ABA; study group on shape Arab-Israeli settlement, humanitarian, and demographic issues Coun. on Fgn. Rels. Kent scholar (2x); Stone scholar; recipient Jane Marks Murphy prize. Mem.: Am. Assn. Law Schs. (chair sect. internat. law 2002—03, co-vice chmn. sect. nat. security law 2003—04), Am. Assn. Jewish Lawyers and Jurists (bd. govs.), Internat. Law Assn. (Am. br. exec. com., human rights com.), Assn. Bar City of N.Y. (coun. on internat. affairs), Am. Soc. Internat. Law, Am. Law Inst., Columbia Law Sch. Alumni Assn., Phi Beta Kappa. Home: 160 Riverside Dr New York NY 10024-2106 Office: Benjamin N Cardozo Sch Law Yeshiva U 55 Fifth Ave New York NY 10003-4391 E-mail: halbrstm@ymail.yu.edu.

HALDEMAN, KARIN TEUTSCH, music educator; b. Salt Lake City, Oct. 19, 1951; d. Walter S. and Gertrude O. Teutsch; m. Daniel Phillip Haldeman, Sept. 4, 1975; children: Jesse D., Rachel E. BA in Music summa cum laude, U.S. Internat. U., 1974; MS in Ednl. Psychology, Coll. St. Rose, 1999; postgrad., SUNY, 2003—. Tchr., adminstr. Hawthorne Valley Sch., Harlemville, NY, 1984—98; dir. string orch. Algonquin Mid. Sch., Averill Park, 1998—; adj. prof. Coll. St. Rose, 2003—. Tchr. cello pvt. practice, Harlemville, 1984—. Mem.: Anthroposophical Soc. Am., N.Y. State Sch. Music Assn., Music Educators Nat. Conf., Am. String Tchrs. Assn. E-mail: studystrings@hotmail.com.

HALE, CYNTHIA LYNETTE, religious organization administrator; b. Roanoke, Va., Oct. 27, 1952; BA, Hollins Coll., 1975; MDiv, Duke U., 1979; D in Ministry, United Theol. Sem., Dayton, Ohio, 1991; DD (hon.), Bethany Coll., N.W. Christian Coll. Ordained Disciples of Christ Ch., Va., 1977. Head resident Hollins (Va.) Coll., 1975-76; intern to minister St. Mark's United Meth. Ch., Charlotte, N.C., 1976; undergrad. counselor Office of Minority Affairs Duke U., Durham, N.C., 1976-77; intern to minister Staunton Meml. Ch., Pittsboro, N.C., 1977-78; coordinating counselor summer transitional program Duke U., Durham, N.C., 1978; chaplain Fed. Correctional Instn., Butner, N.C., 1978-83; chaplain, instr. staff tng. acad. Fed. Prison System, Glynco, Ga., 1983-85; pastor, developer Ray of Hope Christian Ch., Decatur, Ga., 1986—; 1st vice moderator Christian Ch. (Disciples of Christ), U.S. and Can., 1993—. Bd. dirs. Coun. on Christian Unity, 1978-81; bd. trustees Disciples Nat. Convocation, 1980-86, pres. 1982-84, pres. ministers' fellowship, 1990—; task force on Renewal and Structural Reform, Disciples of Christ, 1980-87, adminstrv. com. 1982-87, gen. bd., 1982-88; bd. dirs. Disciples Divsn. Higher Edn., St. Louis, 1986-89; bd. trustees Lexington (Ky.) Theol. Sem., 1990—; bd. dirs. Disciples' Nat. Evangelic Assn., 1991—. Mem. Project Impact-Dekalb, South Dekalb Ch. Coalition; bd. dirs. Beulah Heights Bible Coll., Destiny Atlanta.com; mem. governing bd. Nat. Coun. Chs., 1978—83, panel on bio-ethical concerns, 1980—82. Named Outstanding Ga. Citizen and Goodwill Amb., Sec. of State, 2001, Chaplain of the Day, Ho. of Reps., 2004; recipient Liberation award, Disciples Nat. Conv., 1984, Religion award, DeKalb Br. NAACP, 1990, Religious award for dedicated svc., Ninety-Nine Breakfast Club, award, Martin Luther King's Bd. of Preachers, 1993, Chosen award, Atlanta Gospel Choice, 1998, Profiles of Prominence award, Nat. Women Achievement, 2000, Gospel Honor award, 2000, Youth V.I.B.E. award for outstanding contbns. to the cmty., 2003, James H. Costen award in religion, 2004. Mem. Christian Ch. Office: Ray of Hope Christian Ch 2778 Snapfinger Rd Decatur GA 30034-2439 E-mail: kingdominfo@rayofhope.org.

HALE, HELENE H. state representative; b. Mpls., Mar. 23, 1918; children: Indira, William. BA, U. of Minn., 1938, MA, 1940. Supr. Hawaii County Bd. of Suprs., 1955—63; pres. Hawaii Isle Realty, Ltd., 1969—2000; rep. Hawaii State House, 2000—; tchr., lectr. Tenn. A&I State Coll., San Diego State Coll., Konawaena HS, U. of Hawaii-Hilo. Bd. suprs., mem. County of Hawaii, 1955—63, chmn., exec. officer, 1963—65; del. Hawaii State Constl. Conv., 1978; mem. Hawaii County Coun., 1980—84, 1988—92, 1992—94. Pres. Hawaii County YWCA Bd. of Dirs., 1973. Mem.: Hawaii County League of Women Voters (pres. 1995), Hawaii County Bd. of Realtors (pres. 1975), Hawaii State Fedn. of Women's Clubs (pres. 1999). Democrat. Office: State Capital Rm 331 415 S Beretania St Honolulu HI 96813 E-mail: rephale@Capital.hawaii.gov.

HALE, JANE ALISON, French and comparative literature educator; b. Washington, Sept. 29, 1948; BA in French magna cum laude, Coll. William and Mary, 1970; MST in Edn., U. Chgo., 1974; MA in French, Stanford U., 1981; postgrad., Ecole Normale Supérieure de Jeunes Filles, Paris, 1981-82; PhD with distinction, Stanford U., 1984. Student tchg. supr., counselor Peace Corps Tng. Program, Ft. Archambault, Chad, 1971; tchr. French, cross-cultural coord. Peace Corps Tng. Ctr., St. Thomas, V.I., 1972; Peace Corps vol., tchr. English as fgn. lang. Lycée Franco-Arabe, Abéché, Chad, 1970-72; tchr. 2d grade Pleasant Grove Union Elem. Sch., Burlington, N.C., 1974-77; tchg. fellow in French Stanford U., 1982-83; tchr. French Inst. Intensive French, U. Fla., 1986-88; asst. prof. French and comparative lit. Brandeis U., Waltham, Mass., 1985-91, assoc. prof. French and comparative lit., 1991—. Presenter Internat. Conf. on TV Drama at Mich. State U., 1985, Samuel Beckett at 80 at U. Stirling, Scotland, 1986, Internat. Colloquium on Raymond Queneau, Thionville, France, 1990, Internat. Vian-Queneau-Prévert Colloquium at U. Victoria, Can., 1992, Internat. Symposium on Beckett in the 1990s, The Hague, 1992, MLA, N.Y.C., 1992, West Africa Rsch. Assn. Internat. Symposium, Dakar, Senegal, 1997, African Literature Assn., Fès, Morocco, 1999, Internat. Colloquium on Feminist Rsch. in French, Dakar, Senegal, 1999. Author: The Broken Window: Beckett's Dramatic Perspective, 1987, The Lyric Encyclopedia of Raymond Queneau, 1989; contbr. chpts. to books and articles to profl. jours. French Govt. scholar, 1981-82, Fulbright Sr. scholar, Senegal, 1993-94; Whiting fellow in the humanities, 1983-84, Dana faculty fellow Brandeis U., 1985-90, Bernstein faculty fellow Brandeis U., 1989, Marion and Jasper Whiting fellow, 1994-98; NEH travel grantee, 1988, Mazer grantee for faculty rsch. Brandeis U., 1990; recipient Lerman-Neubauer prize for excellence in tchg. and counseling, 2001. Mem. Samuel Beckett Soc. (exec. bd. dirs. 1989-92), Les Amis de Valentin Brû, Phi Beta Kappa. Office: Brandeis U Dept Romance & Comp Lit MS 024 Waltham MA 02454 E-mail: jhale@brandeis.edu.

HALE, JANET, federal agency administrator; b. Buffalo, Apr. 2, 1949; d. Herman Haltom and Rachel (Townes) H. BS, Miami U., Oxford, Ohio, 1971; M.P.A., Harvard U., 1980. Adminstrv. asst. State Rep. Tom Gallagher of Fla., Washington, 1974-76; research asst. House Republican Com., Washington, 1976-77; spl. asst. Senator Edward Brooke, Boston, 1977-79; spl. asst. to sec., dir. exec. secretariat HUD, Washington, 1981-82, dep. asst. sec. for policy, fin. mgmt. and adminstrn., 1982-86; asst. sec. Dept. of Transportation, Washington, 1986—89; Asst. Sec. Budget, Tech., and Finance Dept HHS, Washington, 2002—03; Under Sec. Mgmt. Dept. Homeland Security, 2003—. Bd. dirs. Big Sisters Boston, 1978-80 Avocation: tennis. Office: Navel Security Station Nebraska & Massachusetts Ave NW Washington DC 20393

HALE, KAREN, state legislator; b. June 24, 1958; m. Jon Martin Hale. BS in Mass. Comm., U. Utah. Formerly pub. and editor; formerly vol. in neighborhood schs.; mem. Utah Senate, Dist. 7, Salt Lake City, 1998—; mem. trans. and pub. safety com., edn. com.; mem. pub. edn. appropriations com. Utah State Senate. Chair pub. rels. Sugarhouse Sesquicentennial Celebration, 1997; statewide edn. chair Earth Day Utah, 1990. Democrat. Home: 2564 Maywood Dr Salt Lake City UT 84109-1614

HALE, KAYCEE, research marketing professional; b. Mount Hope, W.Va., July 18, 1947; d. Bernard McFadden and Virginia Lucille (Mosley) H. AA, Compton Coll., 1965; BS, Calif. State U., Dominguez Hills, 1981. Fashion model O'Bryant Talent Agy., L.A., 1967-77; faculty mem. L.A. Trade-Tech. Coll., 1969-71, Fashion Inst., L.A., 1969-77, 1975—; pres. The Fashion Co., L.A., 1970-75; co-host The Fashion Game TV Show, L.A., 1982-87; exec. dir. Fashion Inst. Design and Merchandising Resource & Rsch. Ctr., L.A., 1975—, Fashion Inst. Design and Merchandising Mus. and Libr., L.A., 1977-98. Lectr. in field, internat., 1969—. Author: (brochure) What's Your I.Q. (Image Quotient)?; (tape) Image Builders; contbg. editor Library Management in Review; columnist The Public Image, 1990; contbr. Bowker Annual 1990-91, (newsletter) Northeast Library System, 1991. Adv. bd. Calif. State U., Long Beach, 1988-91. Mem. ALA, Spl. Librs. Assn. (pres. elect 1986—, pres. 1987-88, bd. dirs. So. Calif. chpt. 1985—), Spl. Librs. Adv. Coun. (pub. rels. com. 1987-89), SLA Libr. Mgmt. Div. (chmn.-elect 1987-88, chmn. 1988-89, pres.'s task force on image of libr./info. profl.), Textile Assn. L.A. (bd. dirs. 1985-87), Calif. Media and Libr. Educators Assn., Am. Mktg. Assn., Western Mus. Conf., Am. Mus. Assn., Costume Soc. Am. Office: Fashion Inst Design & Merchandising 919 S Grand Ave Los Angeles CA 90015-1421

HALE, MARGARET SMITH, insurance company executive, educator; b. Browning, Mont., May 10, 1945; d. Stephen Howard and Evelyn Sarah (Beer) Smith; m. Lawrence L. Hale, Apr. 25, 1970 (div. Jan. 1984); children: Katherine Moore, Laura Ellen. BSBA, Boston U., 1967; AS in Risk Mgmt., Ins. Inst. Am., 1986. Underwriter Chubb & Son, Inc., N.Y.C., 1967-70, br. mgr., asst. v.p. Boston, 1970-80; asst. v.p., account exec. Marsh & McLennan Inc., Boston, 1980-84; sr. v.p. Frank B. Hall, Boston, 1984-87; resident v.p. Warwick Ins. Co., Needham, Mass., 1987-90; pres. Smith & Hale Assocs., Inc., South Orleans, Mass., 1990—. Lectr. Risk and Ins. Mgrs. Soc., Boston, 1975-85; mem. fin. div. Babson Coll., Wellesley, Mass., 1987—. Bd. dirs. Lupus Erythematosus Assn., Boston, 1975-78, Parker Hill Med. Ctr., Boston, 1978-80; tchr. Congl. Ch. Sch., Needham, Mass., 1982—; chmn. ins. adv. com. Town of Needham, 1982-95; pres. Interfaith Coun. for the Homeless, 1999—. Mem. Ins. Mgrs. Assn. (treas. Boston 1971-80), Ins. Library Assn. (dir. 1980-82). Home: 76 Lienau Dr Chatham MA 02633-2118 Office: Smith & Hale Assocs PO Box 136 South Orleans MA 02662-0136

HALE, MARIE STONER, artistic director; b. Greenwood, Miss. Student in Piano, U. Miss., Hattiesburg; studied with Richard Ellis, Christine du Boulay, Jo-Anna Kneeland, David Howard. Tchr. Ellis/du Boulay Sch., Chgo., Jo-Anna Kneeland Imperial Studios, Palm Beach County, Fla.; co-founder Ballet Arts Found., West Palm Beach, Fla., 1973-86; co-founder, artistic dir. Ballet Fla., West Palm Beach, 1986—. Office: Ballet Fla 500 Fern St West Palm Beach FL 33401-5726*

HALE, MARSHA BENTLEY, real estate rehabilitator, song writer, mannequin historian; b. Santa Monica, Calif., Dec. 23, 1951; d. Marvin Addison Kempf and Margery Edith Hale; m. Douglas Eugene Marx. Student, UCLA, 1977-79; BFA in Film and Video, Calif. Inst. Arts, 1981; postgrad. Calif. Inst. Arts, 2003—. Co-owner Designer's Workshop, Beverly Hills, Calif., 1972-75, The Latticemakers, Westwood, Calif., 1975-76; owner Nat. Design Cons., 1976-86; mannequin historian, 1978—; CEO Vidi Vici, Inc., 1986-2003; contbg. writer FashionWindows.com, 2003—; animation archivist Amblin Entertainment, MCA Universal, 20th Century Fox, Dreamworks SKG, 1995-96; with Landworks Restoration & Design, Malibu, Calif., 1995-2000; songwriter Bentley Hale Prodns. (now Whirlwind Music LLC), 1996—; contbr. articles to profl. jours. Avocations: ocean, mountains, travel, cultural arts. Office: Vidi Vici II Inc PO Box 97493 Las Vegas NV 89193-7493 E-mail: writingpen@aol.com.

HALE, MIGNON S. PALMER-FLACK, elementary school educator, educator; b. Silver Spring, Md., July 09; d. Lawrence Henry and Dorothy Elizabeth (Still) Scott; m. Harley Eugene Flack (dec. Mar. 1998); children: Oliver S. Palmer II, Michael Scott Palmer; stepchildren: Harley E. II, Christopher F.; m. Frank W. Hale Jr., July, 2003. BS, D.C. Tchrs. Coll., 1966; MS, Johns Hopkins U., 1977. Cert. tchr., Md. Elem. tchr. D.C. Pub. Schs., Washington, 1968-71; dir. Home Day Care Ctr., Columbia, Md., 1973-77; from elem. tchr. to resource tchr. gifted and talented Howard County Pub. Schs., Columbia, Md., 1977-90; elem. tchr. Cherry Hill (N.J.) Pub. Schs., 1990-94. Lang. arts rep. Howard County Pub. Schs., Columbia, 1977-86, student tchr. coord., 1984-90, tchr. recruiter, 1986-90; cons., tutor Village Reading Ctr., Columbia, 1986-90. Bd. trustees Children's Mus. Dayton, Ohio, 1995—, Opera Guild Dayton, 1995—, Muse Machine, Dayton, 1995—, Dayton Mus. Natural History, 1996; planning com. Centennial Flight-Yr. 2003, 1995—; first lady of Wright State U., Dayton. Recipient Cmty. Svc. award United Way Ctrl. Md., 1982; named Outstanding Supt., Breath of Life Ch., 1981, First Lady of Wright State U., 1994-98. Mem. AAUW, Nat. Assn. State U. and Land Grant Colls., Am. Assn. State Colls. and U., Wright State Orgn. for Women, Phi Delta Kappa, Alpha Lambda Delta. Avocations: reading, travel, music, cooking, entertaining. Home: 9222 Snow Shoe Ln Columbia MD 21045-1826

HALE, PATRICIA S. state legislator; b. Durham, N.C., Jan. 9, 1937; m. Tom Hale; 5 children. Degree in mktg., U. N.C.; degree in econs., U. Richmond. Dir. strategic initiatives Fluor Daniel Hanford; mem. Wash. Senate, Dist. 8, Olympia, 1994—; majority whip Wash. Senate, Olympia, 1997—, Rep. caucus chair, 1999—. Bd. Tri-Cities Cancer Ctr. Found., United Way, Tri-Cities Vis. and Conv. Bur.; dir. Tri-Cities Indsl. Devel. Coun., Mid-Columbia Reading Found.; chair Econ. Devel. Com.; co-chair Mission Impossible com., March of Dimes, Walk Am. 96; fundraising co-chair Boys and Girls Club; campaign chair Benton/Franklin United Way, 1997; vice chair Pvt. Industries Coun. Recipient Total Quality Achievement award Westinghouse Hanford Co., 1989, Nat. Mgmt. award Westinghouse Electric Corp., 1990, Toastmasters Internat. Commns. and Leadership award, 2000, Top Notch award, Rockwell Internat., 2002, Citizen of Yr. award, Washington Asssn. Realtors, 2002, Legis. of Yr., Wash. Coun. of Police and Sheriffs, 2003. Mem. Wash. State Hist. Soc. (bd. mem.), Kennewick C. of C. (former dir.), Pvt. Indsl. Coun. (past vice chair and econ. devel. com. chair 1997), Richland Club, Rotary Club. Republican. Roman Catholic. Office: 303 Legislative Bldg Olympia WA 98504-0001 Home: 206 Irv Newhouse Bldg PO Box 40408 Olympia WA 98504-0408 E-mail: hale_pa@leg.wa.gov.

HALE, SHARON GILBERT, secondary school educator; b. Pine Bluff, Ark., Jan. 4, 1963; d. Melvin and Melba Gregory Gilbert; m. Jseph Denver Hale, Mar. 11, 1982; children: Sarah Joanne, Jonathan David. B.Music Edn., So. Ark. U., Magnolia, 1986. Music tchr. Mt. Holly Pub. Schs., Ark., 1986—91; choral dir., GIT coord. Harmony Grove Pub. Schs., Camden, Ark., 1991—. Mem.: Ark. Gifted and Talented Educators, Ark. Choral Dirs. Assn., Am. Choral Dirs. Assn. Baptist. Avocations: piano, singing. Office: Harmony Grove Public Schs 401 Quachita 88 Camden AR 71701

HALE, SUE A. editor; Reporter, metro editor, city editor, news editor Daily Oklahoman, Oklahoma City, asst. mng. editor, 1989—96, gen. mgr. Connect Okla., Inc. subs., 1996—2000, exec. editor, 2000—. Named one of Heroes of the 50 States, State Open Govt. Hall of Fame, Soc. Profl. Journalists/Nat. Freedom of Info. Coalition, 2003. Office: Daily Oklahoman 9000 N Broadway PO Box 25125 Oklahoma City OK 73125*

HALEY, JOHNETTA RANDOLPH, musician, educator, university official; b. Alton, Ill., Mar. 19; d. John a. and Willye E. (Smith) Randolph; children from previous marriage: Karen, Michael. MusB in Edn., Lincoln U., 1945; MusM, So. Ill. U., 1972. Cert. cons. 1995. Vocal and gen. music tchr. Lincoln H.S., E. St. Louis, Ill., 1945-48; vocal music tchr., choral dir. Turner Sch., Kirkwood, Mo., 1950-55; vocal and gen. music tchr. Nipher Jr. H.S., Kirkwood, 1955-71; prof. music Sch. Fine Arts So. Ill. U., Edwardsville, 1972—, dir. East St. Louis Campus, 1982—. Adjudicator music festivals; area music cons. Ill. Office Edn., 1977-78; program specialist St. Louis Human Devel. Corp., 1968. Interim exec. dir. St. Louis Coun. Black People, summer, 1970; bd. dirs. YWCA, 1975-80, Artist Presentation Soc., St. Louis, 1975, United Negro Coll. Fund, 1976-78; bd. curators Lincoln U., Jefferson City, Mo., 1974-82, pres., 1978-82; chairperson Ill. Com. on Black Concerns in Higher Edn.; mem. Nat. Ministry on Urban Edn. Luth. Ch.-Mo. Synod, 1975-80; bd. dirs. Coun. Luth. Chs. Stillman Coll.; pres. congregation St. Philips Luth. Ch.; bd. dirs. Girls, Inc.; mem. Ill. Aux. Bd., United Way; v.p. East St. Louis Cmty. Fund, Inc. Recipient Cotillion de Leon award for Outstanding Cmty. Svc., 1977, Disting. Alumnae award Lincoln U., 1977, Disting. Svc. award United Negro Coll. Fund, 1979; SCLC, 1981; recipient Cmty. Svc. award St. Louis Drifters, 1979, Disting. Svc. to Arts award Sigma Gamma Rho, Nat. Negro Musicians award, 1981, Sci. Awareness award, 1984-85, Tri Del Federated award, 1985, Martin Luther King Drum Maj. award, 1985, Bus. and Profl. Women's Club award, 1985-86, Fred L. McDowell award, 1986, Vol. of Yr. award Inroads Inc., 1986, Woman of Achievement in Edn. award Elks, 1987, Woman of Achievement award Suburban Newspaper of Greater St. Louis and Sta. KMOX-Radio, 1988, Love award Greeley Cmty. Ctr., Sammy Davies Jr. award in Edn., 1990, Yes I Can award in Edn., 1990, Merit award Urban League, 1994, Legacy award Nat. Coun. Negro Women, 1995, Diversity award Mo. ARC, 2001; named Disting. Citizen St. Louis Argus Newspaper, 1970, Dutchess of Paducah, 1973; the Johnetta Haley Scholars Acad. minority scholarship named in her honor So. Ill. U. Mem. AAUP, Music Educators Nat. Conf., Nat. Choral Dirs. Assn., Nat. Assn. Negro Musicians, Coll. Music Soc., Coun. Luth. Chs., Ill. Music. Educators, Jack and Jill, Inc., Women of Achievement in Edn., Friends of St. Louis Art Mus., The Links, Inc. (nat. parliamentarian, chair constnl. and by-laws com.), Las Amigas Social Club, Alpha Kappa Alpha (internat. parliamentarian, Golden Soror award 1995, Grad Svcs. award 2001), Mu Phi Epsilon, Pi Kappa Lambda. Lutheran. Home: 1926 Bennington Common Dr Saint Louis MO 63146-2555

HALEY, KATHLEEN M. communications executive; b. Boston, Dec. 30, 1970; d. Pierce J. and Marina A. Haley. BA in Comm., Romance Langs., 1993, MBA Boston Coll., 1997. Pub. rels. assoc., acct. rep. Lois Paul & Ptnrs., Burlington, Mass., 1994—95, acct. rep., 1995—96, sr. acct. rep., 1996—97; acct. mgr. C.H.E.N. PR, Wellesley, Mass., 1997; sr. acct. rep. Copithorne & Bellows PR, Grenoble, France, 1997—2000; Marcom mgr. Hewlett-Packard Inkjet Comml. Divsn., Barcelona, 2000—01; exec. comms. mgr. Hewlett-Packard Consumer Bus. Europe, Barcelona, 2001—02; internal comms. mgr., chief of staff Hewlett-Packard Imaging and Printing Group, Europe, Middle East and Africa, 2002—. Mem.: Boston Coll. Young Alumni Assn. (pres. 1996), Boston Coll. Alumni Assn. Avocations: photography, travel, reading. Office: Hewlett Packard Avda Graells 501 08190 Barcelona Spain

HALEY, PRISCILLA JANE, artist, printmaker; b. Boston, June 22, 1926; d. Arthur Benjamin and Jessamy (Fountain) H.; m. Tadeusz Bilous, May 21, 1961. BA, Oberlin Coll., Ohio, 1948; postgrad., Bklyn. Mus. Sch., 1955. Resident artist Yaddo Found., Saratoga Springs, N.Y., 1957. One-man show Village Art Ctr., N.Y.C., 1960; 3-man show Islip Art Mus., 1975; represented in permanent collection N.Y. Pub. Libr., Nat. Acad. Galleries, Bklyn. Mus., Libr. of Congress, Bowdoin Coll. Art Mus., Oberlin Coll., Addison Gallery art, Wesleyan U. Libr., Portland (Oreg.) Mus. Art, others; portfolio of prints and poems by Maine poets, The Island, 1961. Recipient Medal of Honor Audubon Artists, 1957, 1st prize Babylon Arts Coun. Juried Exhbn., 1992; Louis Comfort Tiffany Found. grantee, 1959. Mem. Soc. Am. Graphic Artists, York Art Assn. Home: 79 York St York ME 03909

HALEY, ROSLYN TREZEVANT, educational program director; b. Washington, July 23, 1955; d. Morti Trezevant and Sara Roslyn Kebe; m. Darrell D. Haley, July 30, 1988; children: Jessica, Darrell Jr., Donald, Anthony, Krystal. BA in History, S.C. State U., 1976; MPA, Calif. State U., L.A., 1983; EdD, UCLA, 1999. Faculty cert. U. Phoenix, 1996. Admissions evaluator UCLA, 1979-81, counselor Sch. Pub. Health, 1981-83, head counselor dept. theater, 1983-93; dir. student, counseling, and recruitment svcs. UCLA Sch. Theater, Film and TV, 1993—. Adult edn. tchr. L.A. Unified Sch. Dist., 1984-93; lectr. U. Phoenix, Woodland Hills, Calif., 1996—; bd. mem. Palmdale (Calif.) H.S., Visual and Performing Arts Acad., 1999. Author of poetry. March organizer March for Jesus, L.A., 1994, Antelope Valley, 1995-02; adminstr. Command Ctr., Convoy of Hope, [illegible] Elem. Sch., Palmdale, 1998-99, recruiter Boy Scouts Am. Western L.A. Coun. Bd., 1998-99; campaign chair Antelope Valley YMCA, 2001. Recipient Outstanding Svc. award March for Jesus, L.A., 1994, Outstanding Svc. award First Missionary Bapt. Ch., Littlerock, Calif., 1997, Outstanding Svc. award Jesus Day, Antelope Valley. Mem. Am. Assn. Ednl. Rsch. Avocations: reading, swimming, horseback riding, cycling. Home: 37518 Larchwood Dr Palmdale CA 93550-6037 Office: UCLA Sch TFT 405 Hilgard Ave Los Angeles CA 90095-9000 Fax: 310-825-3383. E-mail: rhaley@ucla.edu.

HALFVARSON, LUCILLE ROBERTSON, music educator; b. Petersburg, Ill., May 17, 1919; d. Harris Morton and Lucille (Fox) Robertson; m. Sten Gustaf Halfvarson, Aug. 8, 1946; children: Laura, Eric, Linnea, Mary. BA, Knox Coll., 1941; MusM, Am. Conservatory, 1969; DHL (hon.), Aurora U., 2000. Cert. tchr., Ill. Tchr. music and speech Freeman Elem. Sch., Aurora, Ill., 1941-44; choral dir. Galesburg (Ill.) Sr. H.S., 1944-46; dir. of music Our Savior Luth. Ch., Aurora, Ill., 1950-63; oratorio soloist, 1952-67; dir. of music Westminster Presbyn. Ch., Aurora, 1963-84; vocal instr. Merit Music Program, Chgo., 1982-93; ret., 1993. Choir dir. 1st Meth. Ch., Galesburg, 1944-46; choral-vocal instr. Waubonsee C.C., Sugar Grove, Ill., 1967-79; organizer Jr. Coll. Music Festival, Waubonsee Coll., Sugar Grove, 1972-73; pvt. vocal instrn., Aurora, 1979—. Conductor Messiah Concert Waubonsee Coll., Paramount Arts Ctr., 1968—, 25th Concert, 1992. Co-chair Citizens Adv. Com. Paramount Arts. Ctr., Aurora, 1977-78; founder United Arts Bd. Fox Valley, pres., 1977-82, Fox Valley Arts Hall of Fame, 2001; chair Paramount Celebration Arts, 1985-86; residency dir. Met. Life Affiliate Artist, Aurora, 1982-83; bd. dirs. YWCA, 1984-91, chair corp. award com., 1994-95; dir. New Eng. Congl. Ch. Bell Choir, 1997-99. Recipient Disting. Svc. award Cosmopolitan Club, Aurora, Ill., 1983; named Woman of Year YWCA, Aurora, 1976, Disting. Alumni Knox Coll., Galesburg, Ill., 1984; Paul Harris fellow Rotary Found. of Rotary Internat., 1999. Mem. AAUW, DAR, PEO, Music Educators Nat. Conf., Am. Choral Dirs. Assn., Aurora C. of C. (Image Maker 1992), Phi Beta Kappa. Avocations: needlecrafts, gardening, fishing, reading. Home: 1105 W Downer Pl Aurora IL 60506-4821

HALL, ADRIENNE A. international marketing executive, venture capitalist consultant; b. L.A. d. Arthur E. and Adelina P. Kosches; m. Maurice Hall; children: Adam, Todd, Stefanie, Victoria, Joe Hibbitt; adopted and foster children: Joe Kwan, Carlos Moreno. BA, UCLA. Founding ptnr. Hall & Levine Advt., L.A., 1970-80; vice chmn. bd. Eisaman, Johns & Laws Advt. Inc., L.A., Houston, Chgo., N.Y.C., 1980-94; pres., CEO The Hall Group, Beverly Hills, Calif., 1994—. Co-founder, chair, bd. dirs. Women, Inc.; chair, adv. bd., Women's Pres. Orgn., 1999—, co-chair, State Econ. Network, 2000—; chmn. Eric Bovy Inc., 1986-89, Hall Partnership, Venture Capital; bd. dirs. Calif. Mfrs. Assn., Calif. Life Corp., Inc.; mem. adv. bd. Global Asset Mgmt., The Edison Co., Sempra Energy. Trustee UCLA; bd. regents Loyola-Marymount U., 1990—, Natl. Bus. Counc., Wash. D.C.; mem. The Founders of Music Ctr., Save the Children, Vietnam and Haiti.; mem. women's leadership bd. Kennedy Sch. Govt., Harvard U.; commr. L.A. County Arts Commn.; commr. Calif. Gov.'s Commn. on Econ. Devel., task force Rebuild L.A.; chair, adv. bd. Leading Women Entrepreneurs of the World; bd. dirs. United Way, ARC, Exec. Svc. Corps, The Com. of 200, Shelter Partnership; trustee Nat. Health Found., Women's Enterprise Devel. Corp.; gov. Town Hall; mem. adv. coun. Girls' Clubs Am.; mem. adv. bd. Girl Scouts U.S., Asian Pacific Women's Adv. Bd., Coalition of 100 Black Women, Nat. Network of Hispanic Women, Women of Color, Women in Bus., Downtown Women's Ctr. and residence, Leadership Am., Washington, L.A., Food Bank; mem. exec. bd. Greater L.A. Partnership for Homeless, Recipient Nat. Headliner award Women in Comm., 1982, Profl. Achievement award UCLA Alumni, 1979, Award for Cmty. Svc., 1994, Asian Pacific Network Woman Warrior award, 1994, Woman of the Yr. award Am. Advt. Fedn., 1973, Ad Person of West award Mktg. and Media Decisions, 1982, Bus. Woman of Yr. award Boy Scouts Am., 1983, Women Helping Women award Soroptimists Internat., 1984, 1st ann. portfolio award for exec. women, 1985, Communicator of Yr. award Ad Women, 1986, Leader award YWCA, 1986, L.A. Women's Found. Mentor award, 1997, Leading Women Entrepreneurs of World award, 2003; named Bus. Leader of Yr., L.A. Bus. Coun., 1999, NAW Legal Defense/Edn. Fund. award, 2001; named NAWBO Hall of Fame, 2002. Mem. Internat. Women's Forum (Woman Who Made a Difference award 1987), Am. Assn. Advt. Agys. (bd. dirs. 1980, chmn. bd. govs. western region), Western States Advt. Agys. Assn. (pres. 1975), Hollywood Radio and TV Soc. (dir.), Nat. Advt. Rev. Bd., Overseas Edn. Fund, Com. 200 (western chmn.), Women in Communications, Orgn. Women Execs., Calif. Women's Forum (founder, chmn. The Trusteeship), Rotary (L.A. 5 chpt.), Internat. Bus. Fellows (mem. adv. bd.), Women's Econ. Alliance, Nat. Assn. Women Bus. Owners (adv. bd.), L.A. Area C. of C. (co-chair, alumni dir.). Clubs: Calif. Yacht; Stock Exchange, Los Angeles Advt. (pres.) (Los Angeles). Lodges: Rotary. E-mail: aahall@earthlink.net.

HALL, ANNA CHRISTENE, retired government official; b. Tyler, Tex., Dec. 18, 1946; d. Willie B. and Mary Christine (Wood) H. BA in Polit. Sci., So. Meth. U., 1969. Clk.-stenographer Employment and Tng. Adminstrn., U.S. Dept. Labor, Dallas, 1970, fed. rep., l970-80, program analyst Washington, l980-84, div. chief, l984-87, exec. asst., 1987-88, office dir. Dallas, 1988—2001; ret., 2002. Mem. Partnership for Employment and Tng., Nat. Honor Soc. Democrat. Presbyterian. Avocations: reading, theater, playing piano. Home: 603 Kingfisher Ln Arlington TX 76002-3456 E-mail: annachall@juno.com.

HALL, BARBARA, television producer; b. Danville, Va. d. Ervis and Flo Hall; m. Paul Karon; 1 child, Faith. BA summa cum laude in English, James Madison U., 1982. Author: Skeeball and the Secret of the Universe, 1987, Dixie Storms, 1990, Fool's Hill, 1992, House Across the Cove, 1995, A Better Place, 1994, Close to Home, 1997, Summons to New Orleans, 2000; Writer (TV series) include, Family Ties, Newhart, Anything But Love, Northern Exposure, I'll Fly Away, ER, Chicago Hope, New York News, Writer, prodr. Moonlighting, Writer, exec. prodr., developer Judging Amy, 1999—2002, cons. prodr. Northern Exposure, Chicago Hope, Judging Amy, 2002—, Creator, writer, exec. prodr. Joan of Arcadia, 2003—; singer: (band) The Enablers. Recipient Humanitas award, Golden Laurel, Prodrs. Guild of Am., awards, Am. Libr. Assn., award, Children's Def. Fund. Office: CBS/Sony Productions 10202 W Washington Blvd Tracy West Culver City CA 90232*

HALL, BARBARA LOUISE, interior designer, artist; b. Tulsa, Jan. 24, 1936; d. Paul Martin and Nell (Coy) Bolley; m. Denton Lee Richey, 1955 (div. 1970); m. William Volker Longmoor, 1971 (dec. 1981); m. Robert Leroy Hall, Sept. 11, 1984; 1 child, Christina Lee Edwards. BFA, U. Kans., 1975. Interior designer Pat O'Leary Assoc., Fairway, Kans., 1974-78, Jack Rees Interiors, Kansas City, Mo., 1978-83; interior designer, owner, pres. The Studio, Inc., Prairie Village, Kans., 1983-86; prin. Barbara Hall Interiors, Sun Lakes, Ariz., 1984—. Mem. Am. Soc. Interior Design (profl.), Ariz. Watercolor Assn. (juried mem.), Nat. Oil and Acrylic Painters Soc. Home and Office: 10915 E Twilight Dr Sun Lakes AZ 85248-7927

HALL, BETTY B. state legislator, manufacturing executive; b. Coblentz, Germany, Mar. 18, 1921; m. SIdney L. Hall, 1944; 5 children. Student, Barnard Coll.; BA, Columbia U., 1943; postgrad., U. N.H., Boston U. Pres. Milford Regional Counseling Svc., 1983-86, Harbor Homes Inc., 1984-86; v.p. Hall Mfg. Co., Inc., 1986—; mem. from dist. 20 N.H. State Ho. of Reps., mem. environ. and agr. coms. Chmn. Brookline Sch. Bd., 1963-71, bd. selectman, 1971-73, mem. fin. com., 1975-87. Mem. Common Cause (bd. dirs. 1975-86). Home: PO Box 309 18A Old Milford Rd Brookline NH 03033-2417 Office: NH State Senate State Capital Concord NH 03301

HALL, BETTY JEAN, public interest group executive, lawyer; b. Richmond, Ky., July 12, 1946; d. James Russell and Lillian (Guy) Hall; m. Thomas Michael Burke, Oct. 6, 1979; children: Tiffany Michelle Burke, Timothy Michael Burke. BA, Berea Coll., 1968; JD, Antioch Sch. Law, 1976. Bar: D.C. 1977, Va. 1977, Tenn. 1979, U.S. Dist. Ct. D.C. 1977, U.S. Ct. Appeals (D.C. cir.) 1977. Assoc. Law Offices of James Lawson, Washington, 1976—77; exec. dir. and gen. counsel Coal Employment Project, Dumfries, Va., 1977—88; dir. Women's Health and Safety Project Occupl. Safety Health Law Ctr., Washington, 1988—94; chief adminstrv. appeals judge and chair, Benefits Review Board Dept. of Labour, 1994—; chmn. bd. dirs. Highlander Ctr., New Market, Tenn. Named Ms. Mag. Woman to Watch in the 80's, 1980, John Hay Whitney fellow, 1978—80; recipient Rockefeller Pub. Service award, 1981, Berea Coll. Service award, 1985, Nat. Women's Health Network Health Advocate of Yr., 1980. Mem.: ABA, Tenn. Bar Assn., Va. Bar Assn., D.C. Bar Assn. Home: 6003 Saddle Horse Pl Fairfax VA 22030 Office: Benefits Rev Bd Dept of Labor PO Box 37601 Washington DC 20013-7601

HALL, BEVERLY ADELE, nursing educator; b. Houston, Aug. 19, 1935; d. Leslie Leo and Lois Mae (Pesnell) H. BS, Tex. Christian U., 1957; MA, NYU, 1961; PhD, U. Colo., 1974. RN, Tex., N.Y. With Ft. Worth (Tex.) Dept. Health, 1957-59; asst. prof. U. Mass., Amhurst, 1961-65; chief nurse N.Y.C. Med. Coll., 1965-67; asst. prof. U. Colo., Denver, 1967-70; assoc. prof. U. Washington, Seattle, 1974-80; prof., chmn. dept. U. Calif., San Francisco, 1980-84; Denton Cooley prof. nursing U. Tex., Austin, 1984-2001, prof. emeritus, 2001—, mem. grad. faculty Sch. Biomed. Sci. Galveston; disting. prof. Coll. Art & Scis., Akachi, Japan, 1999-2000. Pres. med. svcs. Bd. Dir. Project Transitions; disting. prof. Coll. Nursing, Arts and Scis., Hyogo, Japan; mem. NIH Study Group; cons. HIV/AIDS Internat. Coun. fo Nurses. Author: Mental Health and the Elderly, 1985 (Book of Yr.); mem. editl. rev. bd. Advances in Nursing, Archives Psychiat. Nursing, Qualitative Health Rsch., Rsch. in Nursing and Health, Nursing Outlook, Jour. Profl. Nursing, Jour. of the Am. Psychiat. Nurses Assn.; contbr. articles to profl. jours., chpts. to books. Served to capt. U.S. Army, 1962-66. Recipient Tex. Excellence Teaching award U. Tex. Ex-Students Assn., 1994. Fellow Am. Acad. Nursing (governing bd., mem. fellowship selection com.), Am. Coll. Mental Health Adminstrn.; mem. ANA (divsn. gerontological practice), Coun. Nurse Rschrs., Am. Inst. Life Threatening Illness and Loss, So. Nursing Rsch. Soc. Home: 23 Jackson Ct San Antonio TX 78230-2569 Office: U Tex 1700 Red River St Austin TX 78701-1412

HALL, BEVERLY JOY, police officer; b. St. Paul, Minn., Dec. 31, 1957; d. Kenneth Ray and Harriet Kathleen (Fuller) H.; m. Charles Alan Neuman, Feb. 14, 1956. AAS in Law Enforcement, North Hennepin C.C., Brooklyn Park, Minn., 1977; grad., FBI Nat. Acad., 1993; BA in Law Enforcement Mgmt., Met. State U., St. Paul, 1999. Lic. peace officer, Minn. Community svc. officer Brooklyn Park Police Dept., 1977-79; police officer St. Paul Police Dept., 1979-86, police sgt., 1986-95, police lt., 1995-2000, police comdr., 2000—. Hostage negotiator, St. Paul Police Dept., 1991-92, hostage negotiating team coord., 1992-96. Mem. Internat. Assn. Women Police (regional coord. 1988-94, bd. dirs.), Nat. Assn. Women Law Enforcement Execs. (2d. v.p. 2000-01), Minn. Assn. of Women Police (pres. 1982-86), Assn. Tng. Officers of Minn., FBI Nat. Acad. Assocs. Avocations: gardening, jogging, reading. Office: Saint Paul Police Dept 100 11th St E Ste 1 Saint Paul MN 55101-2296

HALL, BEVERLY L. school system administrator; b. Montego Bay, Jamaica; m. Luis Hall, Dec. 22, 1973; 1 child, Jason. BA in English, Bklyn. Coll., 1970, MA in Guidance and Counseling, 1973; PhD in Adminstrn., Fordham U., 1990. English tchr. Jr. H.S. 265, Bklyn., 1970—76; asst. prin. Satellite West Jr. H.S., Bklyn., 1977—83; prin. Pub. Sch. 282, Bklyn., 1983—87, Jr. H.S. 113, Bklyn., 1987—92; supt. Cmty. Sch. Dist. 27, Queens, NY, 1992—94; dep. schs. chancellor for instrn. N.Y.C. Pub. Schs., 1994—95; supt. Newark City Schs., 1995—99, Atlanta Pub. Schs., 1999—. Office: Atlanta Pub Schs 210 Pryor St SW Atlanta GA 30303

HALL, CAROL ANN, music educator; b. Lamar, Colo., Dec. 22, 1952; d. Raymond Dewey and Hazel Vera Morrow; m. Charlie Merle Hall, Apr. 21, 1979 (dec. Oct. 10, 2001); 1 child, Charlie Walter. AA, Lamar C.C., 1972; BA in Elem. Edn., BA in Music Edn. K-12, Adams State Coll., Alamosa, Colo., 1974. 4th grade tchr. Springfield Elem. Sch., 1974—75, tchr. K-6 music, 1990—; tchr. K-6 music Parkview Elem. Sch., Lamar, 1975—78; tchr. K-12 music Vilas Sch., 1986—88. Piano tchr., Vilas, 1986—88; voice tchr., Pritchett, Vilas and Springfield, Colo.; performer, recorded composed song Goldband records, 2002—03. Music leader, mem. Tri Ch. Trio Springfield Bapt. Chapel. Recipient award, Am. Women of Who's Who, 2002—03. Mem.: Springfield Elem. Tchrs. Assn., Music Educators Nat. Conf. Baptist. Avocations: bowling, composing. Home: 429 Monroe Box 85 Pritchett CO 81064

HALL, CAROL BETH, elementary school educator; b. Joliet, Ill., Jan. 9, 1947; d. Ellis Hugh and Elizabeth Edna (Corrigan) Jones; m. Alan Shelby Hall, June 8, 1969; children: Kevin William, Scott Ellis, Brian Patrick. BS in Edn., Ill. State U., 1970. Cert. Tchr. Ill. Tchr., Lisbon, Ill., 1969—71, Christian Learn & Care, Loves Park, Ill., 1981, Forrestville Valley Dist. 221, Leaf River, Ill., 1984—. Author: Autopsied Poems, 1996, Know Missteakes, 1999. Mem. Highland C.C. Chorale, Freeport, Ill., 1995—. Recipient 1st Place award, Phidian Art Club, 1992. Mem.: NEA, Northwest Writer's Assn., Nat. Assn. Music Edn., Internat. Educators Assn., Soc. Mayflower Descendants of Ill. Republican. Lutheran. Avocations: horseback riding, antiques, crocheting, knitting, singing. Home: 8602 W NW Rd Mount Morris IL 61054 Office: Forrestville Valley Sch Dist #221 PO Box 665 Forreston IL 61030

HALL, CHARLOTTE HAUCH, newspaper editor; b. Washington, Sept. 30, 1945; d. Charles Christian and Ruthadele Bertha (LaTourrette) H.; m. Robert Lindsay Hall, June 8, 1968; 1 child, Benjamin H. BA, Kalamazoo Co., 1966; MA, U. Chgo., 1967. Reporter, news editor The Ridgewood (N.J.) Newspapers, 1971-74; copy editor, news editor The Record, Hackensack, N.J., 1975-76; asst. mng. editor The Boston Herald Am., 1977-78; dep. met. editor The Washington Star, 1979-80; copy chief, met. editor, Nassau editor Newsday, Melville, NY, 1981—86, Washington news editor, 1986—88, asst. mng. editor for Long Island, 1988-94; mktg. dir. Newsday, Inc., Melville, NY, 1994-96, mng. editor, 1997-99, v.p., mng. editor, 1999—2003, v.p. planning, 2003—04; v.p., editor Orlando Sentinel, 2004—. Trustee Kalamazoo Coll. Recipient Robert G. McGruder Awards for Diversity Leadership award, Am. Soc. Newspaper Editors, 2003. Mem. Am. Soc. Newspaper Editors (bd. dirs.), Newspaper Assn. Am., Phi Beta Kappa. Office: Orlando Sentinel 633 N Orange Ave Orlando FL 32801-1349*

HALL, CINDY MAUREEN, internet consultant, educator, actress; b. Cedar Rapids, Iowa, Feb. 18, 1960; d. Earl Wilburn and Maureen (Lyness) H. BS in Comm., James Madison U., 1982; postgrad., Columbia Coll., Chgo., 1994—. Softwear specialist Loftus & O'Meara, Chgo., 1988-96; internet cons., Chgo., 1995—. Grad. asst. Columbia Coll., 1994-96, instr., part-time 1994—. Actress various theatres, Chgo., Washington, 1982-88, 1988—; performed in Second City Children's Theatre, 1991, Orpheus Descending, 1993, The Mighty Fergus, 1996-97; designer World Wide Web site Dicctionary for Arts Managers, 1997. Creator CompuKids program Honey Tree, Chgo., 1996. Mem. NAFE, Women in Tech., HTML Writers Guild. Avocations: rafting, needlework, reading.

HALL, CYNTHIA HOLCOMB, federal judge; b. Los Angeles, Feb. 19, 1929; d. Harold Romeyn and Mildred Gould (Kuck) Holcomb; m. John Harris Hall, June 6, 1970 (dec. Oct. 1980). AB, Stanford U., 1951, JD, 1954; LL.M., NYU, 1960. Bar: Ariz. 1954, Calif. 1956. Law clk. to judge U.S. Ct. Appeals 9th Circuit, 1954—55; trial atty. tax div. Dept. Justice, 1960—64; atty.-adviser Office Tax Legis. Counsel, Treasury Dept., 1964—66; mem. firm Brawerman & Holcomb, Beverly Hills, Calif., 1966—72; judge U.S. Tax Ct., Washington, 1972—81, U.S. Dist. Ct. for central dist. Calif., Los Angeles, 1981—84; cir. judge U.S. Ct. Appeals (9th cir.), Pasadena, Calif., 1984—, sr. judge, 1997—. Lt. (j.g.) USNR, 1951—53. Office: US Ct Appeals 9th Cir 125 S Grand Ave Pasadena CA 91105-1621

HALL, DAVIDA KAREN, art educator, elementary school educator; d. Alec Max and Pauline Michelson Margolis; m. David Douglas Hall, Jan. 11, 1972; children: Jason Neil, Jonathan Michael, Larisa Sharon, Joseph Daniel. AA, Montgomery Coll., 1968; BS, U. of Md., 1970; student in Edn., Towson (Md.) U., 2001—. Cert. tchr. Md., 2002. Field exec. Girl Scout Coun. of the Nation's Capital, Washington, 1972—75; coord. outdoor edn. program Girl Scouts of the USA, Potomac, Md., 1975—78; art specialist, spl. program coord. Montgomery County Dept. of Recreation, Silver Spring, Md., 1985—93; elem. sch. art tchr. Prince Georges' County Pub. Schs., Upper Marlboro, Md., 2001—. Chmn. Recreation Adv. Bd., Silver Spring, Md., 1983—85. Exhibited in group shows at Montgomery Coll., 1982, 1989, cover photograph, Utility Basenji, Basenji Mag., 1990. Treas. US Border Collie Club, White Post, Va., 1994—98; enrichment coord. PTA, Silver Spring, Md., 1980—83; newsletter editor Capital Dog Tng. Club, Silver Spring, Md., 1988—91. Mem.: NEA (assoc.), Nat. Art Edn. Assn. (assoc.), Alpha Epsilon Lambda (assoc.). Independent. Avocations: photography, travel, native american indian culture, art education. Home: 12813 Maple Street Silver Spring MD 20904-3004

HALL, DONNA MARIE, director; b. Monroe, La., Apr. 30, 1946; d. William James and Ida Smith McDonald; m. Teddy V. Hall (div.); children: Alecia P., Franchesta D. BS, Grambling State U., 1969, M in Basic Elem. Edn., 1985. Cert. tchr. elem. grades La., prin., parish or city supr. La. Democrat. Home: 3104 Barlow St Monroe LA 71201

HALL, DORIS SPOONER, music educator; b. New Orleans, Dec. 27, 1949; d. Henry and Geneva (Battley) Spooner; m. Morris D. Hall, Aug. 4, 1973; 1 child, Amy Evon. B of Music Edn., La. State U., 1971, M of Music Edn., 1972, postgrad., ALA A&M U., 1991. Cert. tchr. Ala., La. Band dir. Shreveport (La.) City Schs., 1972-73; asst. band dir. Ala. A&M U., Normal, 1973-74, asst. prof. music, 1974-79, aux. coord. marching units, 1979-87, prof. music, 1980—. Lectr. music U. Ala., Huntsville, 1980-89, Oakwood Coll., Huntsville, 1980-90; clinician Ala. Sch. System, Birmingham, 1989-92; cons. in field. Active Huntsville Sympjony Orch., 1975-79, 86-92; recitals U. Ala. and Ala. A&M U., 1990-92. Named Outstanding Young Women, 1982; recipient Outstanding Achievers awards, 1983. Mem. AAUP, Nat. Flute Assn., Nat. Woodwinds Assn., Music Educators Nat. Conf., Ala. Edn. Assn., Tau Beta Sigma, ALpha Kappa Alpha. Roman Catholic. Avocations: dance, reading, skating. Home: 12000 Bell Mountain Dr SW Huntsville AL 35803-3406 Office: Ala A&M U PO Box 258 Normal AL 35762-0258

HALL, ELLA TAYLOR, clinical school psychologist; b. Macon, Miss., Nov. 30, 1948; d. Essex and Mamie (Roland) Taylor; children: Banyikaai Monique (dec.), Motiqua Shante. BA, Fisk U., 1971, MA, 1973; PhD, George Peabody Coll., 1978. Mental health specialist behavioral sci. divsn. Meharry Med. Coll., Nashville, 1976-77; assoc. psychologist Bronx (N.Y.) Psychiat. tr., 1979; clin. psychologist Wiltwyck Residential Treatment Ctr., Ossining, N.Y., 1979-81; clin. cons. Abbott House, Irvington, N.Y., 1982-85; sch. psychologist Abbott Union Free Sch. Dist., 1985—. Cons. psychologist Youth Theater Interactions, Inc., N.Y.; rschr in the field. Author: (poetry) Double Twister, Somebody, Clinging Tears, 1994, Maple Tree at Dawn, 1995, Down My Three Rows, 1995, Mama Sis, 1995, These Times, 1995, Ordinary, 1996, Young Wilted Flower, 2000, Secret Garden, 2000, Blood Silence, 2000; (art) In My Mind, 1994, Picking Cotton, 1995. Lay reader, acolyte Episcopal Ch.; mem. Com. on Spl. Edn. NIMH tng. grantee, Kendall grantee; Crusade fellow. Mem. Schomburg Ctr. for Rsch., N.Y. State Psychol. Assn., N.Y. Bot. Soc., Wildlife Conservation Soc., Delta Sigma Theta. Avocation: photography.

HALL, GWEN MARIE, music educator; b. Crosby, N.D., Mar. 10, 1967; d. Mervin Arthur and Gail Selma Olsen; m. Randy Charles Hall, Aug. 7, 1993; children: Jesslyn Gail, Courtney Marie, Cameron Michael. BS in Music Edn., Minot State U., N.D., 1989. 4-12 vocal and instrumental music educator Edmore Pub. Sch., ND, 1989—92; 7-9 vocal music educator Grand Forks Pub. Schools, ND, 1992—93; k-6 elem. and 5-6 instrumental music educator Bismarck Pub. Schs., ND, 1993—. Children's music dir. First Luth. Ch., Washburn, ND, 1997—; west region rep. N.D. Music Edn. Assn., ND, 2001—; ednl. mentor Bismarck Pub. Schs., ND, 2002—03; children's honor choir - organizing chmn. N.D. Music Edn. Assn., ND, 2002—; marvelous music camp - organizing chmn. Prairie Winds Orff Chpt., Bismarck, ND, 2002—. Choir mem. First Luth. Ch. Choir, Washburn, ND, 1996—2003; girl scout leader Washburn Girl Scouts, Washburn, ND, 1999—2003. Profl. Devel. grant, N.D. Coun. on the Arts, 2001. Mem.: NEA, Music Educators Nat. Conf., N.D. Music Edn. Assn. (west region rep. 2001—03), N.D. Edn. Assn., Bismarck Edn. Assn. (bldg. rep. 1997—98), Am. Orff-Schulwerk Assn. (Gunild Keetman Scholarship 1999), Prairie Winds Orff Chpt. (pres., past pres., v.p., sec. 1995—2003). Home: 523 Main Ave Washburn ND 58577

HALL, JANE ANNA, writer, model, artist; b. New London, Conn., Apr. 4, 1959; d. John Leslie Jr. and Jane Dezzie (Green) H. Grad. model, Barbizon Sch., 1976; grad., Westbrook H.S., 1977. Model Barbizon Agy., New Haven, 1977; employed by dir. of career planning Wesleyan U., Middletown, Conn., 1985-86; free lance writer, poet, 1986—; artist, 1989—. Poetry contest judge Saybrook 25th Anniversary Celebration, Acton Pub. Libr., 1992; group poetry reader Literacy Vols. Valley Shore, Westbrook, 1995, Russell Libr., Middletown, Conn., 1999, 2000. Author: Cedar and Lace, 1986, Satin and Pinstripe, 1987, Fireworks and Diamonds, 1988, Stars and Daffodils, 1989, Sunrises and Stone Walls, 1990, Mountains and Meadows, 1991, Moonlight and Water Lillies, 1992, Sunsets and Beaches, 1993, New and Selected Poems 1986-94, 1994, Under Par Recipes, 1994, New and Selected Poems for Children 1986-95, 1995, Butterflies and Roses, 1996, Hummingbirds and Hibiscus, 1997, Swans and Azaleas, 1998, Damsel Flies and Peonies, 1999, Egrets and Cattails, 2000, Doves and Rhododendron, 2001, Bluebirds and Mountain Laurel, 2002, Beach Poems, Vol. I, 2002, Cardinals and Maples, 2003, Spring Poems Vol. I, 2003, Summer Poems Vol. I, 2003, Autumn Poems Vol. I, 2003, Winter Poems Vol. I, 2003, Sandpipers and Drift Wood, 2004; cover designer (books), 1986—, founder, editor (newsletter) Poetry in Your Mailbox, 1989—; contbr. poetry The Bell Bouy, Expressions I and II, The Pictorial Gazette, Conn. chpt. Romance Writers of Am. Newsletter, others; (one-woman shows) Westbrook (Conn.) Pub. Libr., 1989—99, Russell Libr., Middletown, 2000, Guilford (Conn.) Free Libr., 2001, Russell Libr., Middletown, 2002; one-woman shows include Deep River Pub. Libr., 2003, Russell Libr., 2003, Brainerd Meml. Libr., Haddam, Conn., 2003;, author poems, The Full Moon Looks Like, 2002; contbr. articles Conn. chpt. Romance Writers Am. Newsletter; reader (group poetry), Conn. Sunday sch. tchr. 1st Congl. Ch., Westbrook, 1977-90, asst. supt., mem. bd. Christian edn., 1979-84; poetry reader Congl. Ch., Broad Brook, Conn., 1988; vol. ch. fair

Westbrook Congl. Ch.; group poetry reader and displayer Westbrook Pub. Libr., 1989, 91, reader Night of Thousand Stars readathon, 1990; group poetry displayer Acton Pub. Libr., Old Saybrook, Conn., 1990, judge poetry contest 25th anniversary celebration, 1992; vol. 1st Congrl. Ch. Fair, Westbrook, Conn. Recipient 2d prize Conn. Poetry Soc., 1983-86, 3d hon. mention, 1996, chapbooks added to Soc. permanent archives at Housatonic Cmty. Tech. Coll., 1995; cert. of merit for disting. svc. to cmty., 1989, cert. world leadership, 1989. Mem. Internat. Platform Assn., Romance Writers Am. (book cover bd. designer Conn. chpt. 1991-93), Conn. Poetry Soc. (pres. Old Saybrook chpt. 1989-91, world poetry chmn. 1989; poetry reader 20th anniversary celebration at Russell Libr. Middletown, Conn. 1994, group poetry reader, Waterbury 2001). Avocations: interior decorating and design, fashion design, tennis, gardening, photography. Address: PO Box 629 Westbrook CT 06498-0629

HALL, JEAN QUINTERO, communications and history educator; b. Manila, July 28, 1946; came to U.S., 1963; d. Evan Drake Moody and Victoria (Quintero) Bombon; m. Edward Payson Hall. BA in Comm., U. Wash., 1978; MPA, U. Del., 1984. Faculty Kapiolani C.C., Honolulu, 1984-85; cmty. developer Cath. Social Svcs., Honolulu, 1985; adminstr. City & County of Honolulu, 1985-86; faculty New River C.C., Dublin, Va., 1986-90; adminstr. Radford (Va.) U., 1987-89, faculty, 1989-92; pres. Global Soc., Radford, 1989-92; ind. cons. Silver City, N.Mex., 1992-94; faculty Western N.Mex. U., Silver City, 1994—. Spkr. in field; columnist Filipino-Am. J., Phoenix, 1999—. Author: Desiderate Melodies, 1990, Rizal - Our Beloved Beacon, 1996. Grantee Commonwealth Va., 1991. Mem. Pacific & Asian Comm. Assn., Asian Studies/Philippine Studies Group, Filipino Am. Educators Assn., Filipino Cultural Heritage Soc., Filipino Am. Assn. N.Mex., Sigma Iota Epsilon. Avocation: writing. Home: 20 Vista Grande Silver City NM 88061-6613 E-mail: lysander@cybermesa.com.

HALL, JOAN M. lawyer; b. Inman, Nebr., Apr. 13, 1939; d. Warren J. and Delia E. (Allyn) McClurg; m. George J. Cotsirilos, Dec. 4, 1988; children: Colin Michael, Justin Allyn BA, Nebr. Wesleyan U., 1961; JD, Yale U., 1965. Bar: Ill. 1965, U.S. Dist. Ct. (no. dist.) Ill. 1965, U.S. Ct. Appeals (7th cir.) 1965. Assoc. Jenner & Block, Chgo., 1965-71, sr. ptnr., 1971—. Chmn. character and fitness Ill. Supreme Ct., 1988-89; mem. dist. admissions com. U.S. Dist. Ct. (no. dist.) Ill. Mem. exec. com. Yale Law Sch. Assn., 1976-86, treas., 1982-85; bd. dirs. Yale Law Sch. FUnd, 1978—, chmn., 1984-86; bd. dirs. Chgo. Lawyer's Com. Civil Rights Under the Law, 1978—, chmn., 1983-84; bd. dirs. Legal Assistance Found. Chgo., 1979-82; trustee Rush-Presbyn. St. Luke's Hosp., 1984—; mem. Gannon-Proctor Commn., 1982-84; trustee, bd. govs. Nebr. Wesleyan U., 1983—; bd. dirs. Goodman Theatre, Ill. Sports Facility Authority, 1986-96; mem. vis. com. Northwestern U. Sch. Law, 1987-92; mem. adv. coun. De Paul U. Sch. Law, 1987-94; bd. govs. Chgo. Lighthouse for the Blind. Fellow Am. Coll. Trial Lawyers; mem. ABA (chmn. litig. sect. 1982-83, fed. judiciary com. 1985-91, resource devel. coun. 1984-85, Ho. of Dels. 1991-93), Comml. Club (sec. 1995—), Econ. Club (Chgo., dir.). Office: Jenner & Block 1 E Ibm Plz Fl 4000 Chicago IL 60611-7603

HALL, JO(SEPHINE) MARIAN, editor; b. Aberdeen, S.D., July 12, 1921; d. Charles Martin Sykes and Deedie Mae (Keiser) Gruett; m. Winston Hall, Dec. 4, 1940 (dec.); children: Wendy Diane, Willis Edward. Student, U. Colo., 1958, U. S.D., 1976. With advt. dept. Mobridge (S.D.) Reminder, 1955-61, columnist, 1956-61; with advt. dept., columnist Mobridge Tribune, 1961-67, 93—, news editor, photographer, 1968-81, editor people page, 1981—. Airway observer U.S. Weather Bur., Mobridge, 1939-84, sec. bd. dirs. Klein Mus., Mobridge, 1976-80; chpt. pres. Am. Field Svc., 1972-82; vol. Mobridge Regional Hosp., 1990—; organist, dir. choir, sr. warden of vestry St. James Episcopal C., Mobridge; mem. S.D. Episcopal Diocesan Coun., 1993-99; grand marshal Sitting Bull Parade and Rodeo, Mobridge, S.D., 2003. Recipient numerous state and nat. awards for feature stories, news stories, columns, obituaries, photography, spl. sects. headlines, 1959—, including Herbert Bayard Swope award, 1978; 1st place award for newspaper editing Nat. Fedn. Press Women, 1979, for spl. edit., 1982; Golden Quill award S.D. Press Women, 1988; named S.D. State Homefront Hero of WW II, 2002. Democrat. Avocations: water aerobics, swimming, reading, cooking, gardening. Home: 910 3rd Ave W Mobridge SD 57601-1605 Office: Mobridge Tribune 111 3rd St W Mobridge SD 57601-2525

HALL, JUDITH YOUNG, nurse; b. Akron, Ohio, June 29, 1948; d. Frank Marshall and Dorothy Geraldine (Patterson) Young; m. Howard Rodney Hall, Mar. 21, 1970; children: Melissa Elyse, Simon Marshall, Elizabeth Grace. BA, U. Calif., 1971; BSN, U. Akron, 1983. RN. Dir. Perinatal Advisory Coun. of L.A. Comm., Encino, Calif., 1992-95; dir. clin. ops. and svcs. Olsten Kimberly Quality Care, San Mateo, Calif., 1995; dir. clin. devel. Natus Med., Inc., San Carlos, Calif., 1996—2002; HIPAA project coord. Stanford U. Sch. Medicine, 2002—03; sr. compliance specialist Stanford U. Med. Ctr., 2003—. Cons. Fetal Infant Mortality Review, L.A., 1993-94, Healthy Futures March of Dimes, L.A., 1993-94, Am. Belongs To Our Children, L.A., 1993-94, Ventura County Teen Pregnancy Coalition, 1993-94. Co-author, editor: Neonatal Protocols, 1992, Pre-Natal and Intrapartum Guidelines, 1994. Vol. nurse St. Paul's Episcopal Ch., Akron. 1983, lect. March of Dimes Speakers Bur., Burbank, Calif. 1993-94, Health Advisory Com. Early Intervention, L.A., 1993-94. Mem. Nat. Assn. Neonatal Nurses, Am. Assn. Women's Health Obstetrics and Neonatal Nursing, Am. Acad. Pediatrics, Sigma Theta Tau. Episcopal. Avocations: reading, travel, music. Home: 132 Panorama Ct Pacifica CA 94044-2148

HALL, KATHLEEN YANARELLA, financial executive; b. Beacon, N.Y., Feb. 21, 1957; d. Joseph R. and Mary Jane Reilley Yanarella; m. John Curtis Hall, Apr. 1, 1995. BS in Acctg., Marist Coll., 1979; MBA in Fin., Pace U., 1983. Acct. Alfa-Laval AB, Poughkeepsie, N.Y., 1979-81; bus. ops. mgr. IBM, Somers, Poughkeepsie, NY, 1981-96, fin. consol. mgr. Research Triangle Park, NC, 1996—2002, dir. fin. Somers, 2002—. Dir. Raleigh (N.C.) Ensemble Players. Recipient Salute to Women and Industry award YWCA, Dutchess County, N.Y., 1994. Mem. Inst. Mgmt. Accts. (cert. fin. mgr., cert. mgmt. acct., sec., dir. employment 1979-82). Avocations: theater, arts, reading. Home: 7532 Tynewind Dr Wake Forest NC 27587-4959 Office: IBM Rte 100 Somers NY 10589 E-mail: kyhall@us.ibm.com.

HALL, KATHRYN H. public relations executive; b. Douglas, Sept. 5, 1944; m. Steve Hall (div. 2003); children: Stephen, Scott, Stuart, Justin. Student, Casper Jr. Coll., Wyo., Nebr. Tchrs. Coll., Mesa State Coll., Grand Junction, Colo. Owner, v.p. Well Servicing Equipment and Supply, Grand Junction, 1979—85; dir. western office U.S. Sen. William Armstrong, Grand Junction, 1985—90, Sen. Hank Brown, Grand Junction, 1990—93; loan officer El Paso Mortgage Co., Grand Junction, 1993—95; br. mgr. Am. Rockies Mortgage Co., Grand Junction, 1995; commr. Mesa County Commn., Grand Junction, 1995—2003; owner Kathy Hall/Pub. Rels., Grand Junction, 2003—. Chair Dept. Human Svcs., Grand Junction, Cmty. Air Svc. Task Force, Grand Junction; chair legis. com. Colo. River Water Conservation Dist. Bd., Grand Junction, 1996—. Contbr. numerous articles to profl. jours. Co-chair United Way, Mesa County, 2003—; mem. Gov.'s Task Force on Welfare Reform, Gov.'s Task Force on Civil Justice Reform, Gov.'s Child Welfare Reform Task Force; chmn. legis. com. Colo. River. Conservation Dist.; mem. Colo. West Mental Health Adv. Com.; steering com. Colo. Benefits Mgmt. System; past chmn., treas. Assoc. Govts. of N.W. Colo.; mem. Riverfront Commn., Pvt. Industry Coun.; pres. Marillac Clinic; mem. Parks Improvement Adv. Bd.; active numerous other civic coms., subcoms., bds.; chmn. bd. Mesa County Commrs., Grand Junction, 1997—99, 2001—02. Recipient Elizabeth Prebich Disting. Leadership award, 2001. Republican. Methodist. Home: 2305 Pheasant Run Grand Junction CO 81506-4877 Office: Kathy Hall Pub Rels 743 Horizon Ct Ste 100C Grand Junction CO 81506

HALL, KATHRYN WALT, ambassador; m. Craig Hall; 2 children, 4 stepchildren. AB in Econs., JD, U. Calif., Berkeley. Asst. city atty., Berkeley, Calif.; with Safeway Stores; pres. Kathryn Hall Vineyards, Inc., Walt Mgmt., Inc.; mng. dir., ptnr. Hall Fin. Group, Inc.; amb. to Austria Vienna, 1997—. Mem. hunger adv. com. U.S. Ho. of Reps. Co-founder North Tex. Food Bank; mem. Nat. Adv. Coun. for Violence Against Women; trustee Woodrow Wilson Internat. Ctr. for Scholars; former bd. dirs., v.p. Tex. Mental Health Assn. Mem. Dallas Area C. of C., Comml. Real Estate Women, Tex. Retailers Assn. Office: The Honorable Kathryn Hall Amb Dept State 9900 Vienna Pl Washington DC 20521-9900

HALL, KATHY, nursing official; b. Covington, Ky., Feb. 15, 1953; d. Joseph B. and Mary Louise (Weindel) Dusing; m. Harold G. Hall, Oct. 6, 1973; children: Becky, Amy, Sarah. AA, Eastern Ky. U., 1973, BS in Nursing, 1978; MS in Nursing, Bellarmine U., 1989. Med.-surg. staff nurse Good Samaritan Hosp., Lexington, Ky., 1973; infection control nurse Pattie A. Clay Hosp., Richmond, Ky., 1975-93, orientation instr., 1978-82, quality assurance dir., 1982-93; nurse epidemiologist U. Ky. Chandler Med. Ctr., Lexington, 1993—99; edn. dir. Shriners Hosp. for Children, Lexington, 1999—2002; dir. continuing edu. devel. Coll. Health Sci. Ea. KY U. Mem.: NNSDO, KNA, ANA, Ctrl. KY Staff Devel. Group, Sigma Theta Tau. Office: CHS Continuing Edu & Devel 202 Perkins Bldg Ea KY U 521 Lancaster Ave Richmond KY 40475-3102

HALL, KATHY L. orchestra executive; b. Donnellson, Iowa; Prin. bassoonist Cedar Rapids (Iowa) Symphony Orch., exec. dir., 1992. Office: Cedar Rapids Symphony Orch 205 2nd Ave SE Cedar Rapids IA 52401-1213

HALL, LEILANI RAE, humanities educator; b. Marietta, Ohio, July 22, 1968; d. Alonzo Thomas Hall, Jr. and Madge Bailey Rauch, Donald Clarence Rauch (Stepfather). BA, Ohio U., 1989, MA, 1992; PhD, U. So. Miss., 2001. Lectr. Marietta (Ohio) Coll., 1994—96; dept. chair Colegio Franklin D. Roosevelt, Lima, Peru, 1996—98; lectr. U. So. Miss., Hattiesburg, 2001—02; asst. prof. English Calif. State U., Northridge, 2002—. Contbr. articles to jours., poetry to anthologies. Vol. poet in schs., L.A., 2002—; writer in social svc. U. So. Miss. Sch. Social Work Family Network Partnership, Hattiesburg, 2000—02; mem. So. Poverty Law Ctr., 2000—. Recipient Jane Kenyon prize, Waterstone Lit. Jour., 2003, Recognition for Tchg. Tolerance, So. Poverty Law Ctr., 2003. Mem.: Acad. Am. Poets, Toni Morrison Soc., Associated Writing Programs. Avocations: martial arts, animal rescue. Office: Calif State U Northridge 1811 Nordhoff St Northridge CA 91330 E-mail: leilani.hall@csun.edu.

HALL, LISA G. broadcast executive, lawyer; m. John Hall; 2 children. JD, Rutgers Law Sch., 1983. Atty. Debevoise & Plimpton, LLP; founding ptnr. Friedman, Kaplan & Seiler, LLP, N.Y.C.; co-founder Oxygen Media, Inc., N.Y.C., 1998, chief adminstrv. officer and gen. counsel, 1998—, COO, 1999—. Office: Oxygen Media Inc 7th Fl 75 9th Ave New York NY 10011*

HALL, LOIS BREMER, retired educator, volunteer; b. Oak Park, Ill., July 27, 1923; d. Frederick Statler and Mabel (Forbes) Bremer; m. Bruce Hall, Sept. 9, 1955 (dec. Mar. 1981); children: Donald, Richard, Barbara. B in Music Edn., U. Mich., 1946. Cert. elem., secondary tchr. Mich., Ky.; ordained elder Presbyn. Ch. Tchr. handbell ringing Elm St. Recreation Ctr., Atlantic Recreation Ctr. Handbell ringer AARP, Osprey Village and Quality Health, Bapt. Hosp., 1st Presbyn. Ch. Fernandina Beach; dir. Amelia Handbell Choir; singer Amelia Island Chorale, Meml. United Meth. Ch., Amelia Plantation Chapel, Amelia Bapt. Ch., St. Peter's Episcopal Ch., tenor Amelia Island Cmty. Corale. Mem. com. Peck Ctr.; founding mem., vol. coord. CROP Walk, 1989—99; vol. Michah's Place (abused women refuge); player Praise Band, 2003—04; hot line worker Abused Women Shelter, 2003—04; mem. exec. bd. Meml. United Meth. Ch.; vol. Church World Svc., Fernandina Beach, Synod of South Atlantic Coun., 1989; mem. Presbytery of St. Augustine Coun., 1984—97, music coord. of handbell and choral workshops, 1990—98; mem. hunger com. Presbyn. Gen. Assembly, 1992—96; vol.-in-mission New Hope Meth. Presbyn. Ch., N. Pole, Alaska, 1991—94, 1996; soloist, clarinet Ch. Choirs; bd. dirs. Amelia Arts Acad., 1994—2003, Ann. Fernandina Beach Talent Show, 2001—02. Recipient award for cultural enrichment, City of Fernandina Beach, 2001. Mem.: AARP (bd. dirs.), Woman's Club Fernandina Beach (pres. 1983—84, 1991—92), Outstanding New Mem. 1980—81, Cmty. Svc. award 1987—88), Rose Garden Club (treas. 1998—2002), Alpha Omicron Pi, Delta Omicron. Republican. Home: 607 Goldenrod Way Saint Marys GA 31558

HALL, LULA, retired special education educator; b. Eastman, Ga., Oct. 11, 1942; d. Lawrence and Lizzie Jackson Hall. BS, postgrad., Tuskegee U. Cert. spl. edn. tchr. Ga. Tchr. Ga. Dept. Juvenile Justice, Eastman, Dodge County Bd. Edn., Eastman; ret., 1997. Author poetry; contbr. articles to local newspaper. Sec. United Concerned Citizens of Dodge County, Eastman, 1994—99; vol. Dodge County Hosp. Aux./Pink Ladies, 1997—; actove civil rights projects and cmty. improvement. Recipient cert. of appreciation, Dodge County chpt. NAACP, Eastman, 1990. Baptist. Home: PO Box 844 Eastman GA 31023-0844

HALL, MADELON CAROL SYVERSON, elementary school educator; b. Kerkhoven, Minn., Dec. 27, 1937; d. Reuben C. and Hattie C. (Anderson) Syverson; m. Lewis D. Hall, June 13, 1959 (dec. 1984); children: Warren L., Charmaine D. BA, Trinity Bible Coll., Chgo., 1959; MEd, U.Cin., 1973. Cert. tchr., Ohio. Dir. admissions, asst. registrar Trinity Bible Coll., 1959-62; supr. elem. music edn. Dist. 80 Cook County Schs., Norridge, Ill., 1962-65; tchr. Rockford (Ill.) City Schs., 1966-67; tchr. music elem. grades Boone County Pub. Schs., Florence, Ky., 1970-72, Oak Hills Local Sch. Dist., Cin., 1972—. Also bldg. career coord., Jr. Achievement coord., safety patrol sponsor; mem. sch. improvement team. Composer: Seven Ways to Grow for Children's Mus., 1991. Dir. Summer Safety Village Program, 1987-91, Cin. May Festival Chorus, 1991-1993. Recipient Spl. Projects award Great Oaks Career Devel., 1992; named Tchr. of Yr. Oak Hills Sch. Dist, 1990-91, Ptnr. with PTA award, 2002-03. Mem. NEA, Ohio Edn. Assn., Music Educators Nat. Conf., Career Edn. Assn. (Tchr. of Yr. Ohio unit 1989-90), The Hunger Project, Just Say No Club. Methodist. Avocations: vocal music, piano, composing. Home: 456 Happy Dr Cincinnati OH 45238-5254 Office Phone: 513-922-1485.

HALL, MARCIA JOY, non-profit organization administrator; b. Long Beach, Calif., June 24, 1947; d. Royal Waltz and Norine (Parker) Stanton; m. Stephen Christopher Hall, March 29, 1969; children: Geoffrey Michael, Christopher Stanton. AA, Foothill Coll., 1967; student, U. Oreg., 1967-68; BA, U. Washington, Seattle, 1969. Instr. aide Glen Yermo Sch., Mission Viejo, Calif., 1979-80; market rsch. interviewer Rsch. Data, Framingham, Mass., 1982-83; adult edn. instr. Community Sch. Use Program, Milford, Mass., 1982-83; career info. ctr. coord. Milford High Sch., 1983-86; corp. rels. dir. Sch. Vols. for Milford, Inc., 1985-86; N.E. area coord. YWCA of Annapolis and Anne Arundel County, Severna Park, Md, 1987-89; exec. dir. West Anne Arundel County C. of C., Odenton, Md., 1989—2001, also exec. dir. Found., Inc., 1999—2001; coord. bus. and entrepreneurship continuing profl. edn. and outreach Anne Arundel C.C., Arundel Mills, Md., 2001—03, lead instr. nonprofit leadership devel., 2003—; pres., CEO Marcia Hall & Assocs., LLC, Severna Park, Md., 2003—. V.p. Corridor Transp. Corp., 1997-99; bd. dirs. Entrepreneur's Exch. Pres. PTO, Mission Viejo, 1979-80, Milford, 1981-84; consumer assistance vol., Calif. Pub. Interest Rsch. Group, 1977-78; chmn. grant com. 21st Century Edn. Found., Ann Arundel Pub. Schs., Leadership Anne Arundel. Mem.: Am. Assn. Women in C.C., Assn. Women in Comm., Md. Assn. C. of C. Execs. (pres. 1999—2000), Toastmasters (treas. 1988—, pres. 1989—). Avocations: piano, music composition, bridge, reading. Home: 507 Devonshire Ln Severna Park MD 21146-1017 Office Phone: 443-852-1415.

HALL, MARIAN M. retired music educator; b. York, Pa., June 22, 1932; d. Thomas Adrian and Olive Murray Martin; m. John H. Hall, June 1, 1953; children: Debra Grey, Cindy Dolen, Michael, Daniel. BA, Western Md. Coll., 1953; M Equivalence, Towson State U., 1972. Music tchr. Balt. City Schs., 1971—95; ret., 1995. Organist, choir dir. Rocklin Meth. Ch.; with Beth Ifiloh Summer Camp, Pikesville, Md.; piano tchr. Jason's Music Store, 1990—. Mem.: Suzuki Assn., Music Educators Nat. Conf. Avocations: music, camping, hiking, boating, swimming. Home: 4600 Lincoln Dr Baltimore MD 21227

HALL, MARNYE E. journalist, newswriter; b. Cicero, Ind., Dec. 14, 1976; d. C. Ronald and Tonekka Hall. BS, Butler U., 1999. Font operator/prodn. asst. WKRC-TV, Cin., 1999—99; master control operator WHMB-TV, Noblesville, Ind., 1999—2000; video journalist CNN, Atlanta, 2000; prodn. asst. CNN Newsource, Atlanta, 2000—01, writer, 2001—. Adult educator Girl Scout Coun. N.W. Ga., Atlanta, 2003; vol. Hist. Jonesboro, Ga., 2000; builder Habitat for Humanity, Atlanta, 2002. Recipient Gold award, Girl Scouts USA, 1994, Vol. Appreciation award, Hist. Jonesboro, 2003. Avocations: writing, reading, community service, French language, travel.

HALL, MARY HUGH, retired secondary school educator; b. Sumter, S.C., Apr. 15, 1937; d. Hughson Perry and Virginia Dare (Owens) Matthews; m. James Wallace Hall Sr., July 2, 1960; 1 child, James Wallace Jr. BA in Social Studies and French, Columbia Coll., 1959; postgrad., West Ga. Coll., 1975-79. Tchr. Arlington (Ga.) Schs., Inc., 1959-61; tchr., chair French dept. Douglas County H.S., Douglasville, Ga., 1965—97; ret., 1997. Mem. steering com. West Ga. Alliance, Carrollton, 1992—. Recipient Outstanding Officer award Jaycees, 1970, 71. Mem. NEA, Douglas County Assn. Educators, Ga. Assn. Educators. Avocations: dance, reading, cooking, wood crafts. Home: 4679 Bedford Pl Douglasville GA 30135-1805

HALL, MARY TAUSSIG, professional volunteer; b. St. Louis, Feb. 21, 1911; d. Frederick Joseph and Florence (Gottschalk) Taussig; m. Louis Benoist Tompkins, June 17, 1941 (dec. Oct. 1950); children: Frederick Kingsbury Tompkins, Mary Waterman Tompkins (Mrs. Neil Houghton); m. Thomas Steele Hall, Oct. 21, 1952 (dec. 1990). BA, Bryn Mawr Coll., 1933; MSW, Washington U., St. Louis, 1938; LHD (hon.), Lindenwood Coll., 1979. Cert. social worker. Caseworker New England Home for Little Wanderers, Boston, 1938-39. Editor: Stones for Bread, 1940. Pres., Mo. Assn. Social Welfare, 1942-44, bd. dirs., 1942-48; bd. dirs., chair industry com. Urban League Greater St. Louis, 1943-52; bd. dirs. Family and Children's Svcs., St. Louis, 1944-57; apptd. by gov. state commr. Children's Code Commn., 1945, Bd. Children's Guardians, 1946-55; apptd. by mayor bd. dirs. City Hosp. # 2 during racial integration; founding bd. dirs. Washington U. Med. Ctr. Child Guidance Clinic, St. Louis, 1948-52; chmn. bd. Divsn. Children's Svcs., St. Louis, 1955-66; nat. com. policy Child Welfare League Am., 1955-57; nat. coun. Internat. Social Svc., 1968-88; mem. world coun. YWCA, N.Y.C., 1963—; pres. St. Louis chpt. bd. UN Assn., 1977-80, nat. steering com. coun. chpt. pres., 1979-82, nat. bd. govs. UN Assn. USA, 1980-90; mem. nat. coun. UN Assn. USA, 1991—. Recipient alumni award Washington U., 1956, Woman of Achievement award for Social Concern, City of St. Louis, 1979, Arnold Goodman Nat. Leadership award UN Assn. U.S.A., 1994, Humanitarian award Planned Parenthood Assn. St. Louis, 2001. Mem. Cosmopolitan Club (N.Y.C.). Avocations: garden, travel. Home: 4969 Pershing Pl Saint Louis MO 63108-1220

HALL, NANCY CHRISTENSEN, publishing company executive, author, editor; b. N.Y.C., Nov. 14, 1946; d. Henry Norman and Elvira (Dugan) Christensen; m. John R. Hall Jr., June 12, 1968; children: Jonathan Scott, Kirsten Marie. BA, Manhattanville Coll., 1968; postgrad., Old Dominion U., 1970-71. Sr. assoc. editor Cahners Pub. Co., N.Y.C., 1972-74; freelance editor N.Y.C., 1974-78; sr. editor Grosset and Dunlap, N.Y.C., 1978-81; exec. editor, asst. v.p. Macmillan Pub. Co., N.Y.C., 1981-84; assoc. pub., v.p. Simon & Schuster Pub. Co., N.Y.C., 1984-85; founder, prin. Nancy Hall, Inc., juvenile book devel co., N.Y.C., 1986—; founder, ptnr. Hall Assocs., Inc., 1996—. Author: Monsters: Creatures of Mystery, 1980, Macmillan Fairy Tale Alphabet Book 1983; editor: Platt and Munk Treasury of Stories for Children, 1981, Favorite Tales from Hans Christian Andersen, 1988; prodr. series: Macmillan Jumbo Seasonal Patterns, Macmillan Manipulatives, Sesame Street Early Learning Games, Mickey's Young Readers Libr., Disney's Small World Libr., My First Hello Readers, and others. Office: Nancy Hall Inc 23 E 22nd St New York NY 10010-5304

HALL, NANCY K. college dean; b. Washington, July 7, 1947; Student, U. Ariz., 1965-67; BA in Med. Microbiology, Stanford U., 1969; NSF fellow in Marine Microbiology, U. Hawaii, 1969-70; student, U. Calif., Davis, 1970; MS in Med. Mycology, U. Okla., 1971; PhD in Vet. Pathology, Kans. State U., 1976; postdoctoral fellow, NIH, 1976-78. Rsch. assoc. dept. biochemistry Kansas State U., 1971; vet. diagnostician, virologist Kans. State U., 1972, instr. vet. diagnostic lab., 1973, assoc. prof. pathology, 1978-97; assoc. dean admissions U. Okla., Oklahoma City, 1997—. Dir. acad. programs dept. pathology U. Okla., 1978-85; disting. vis. prof. USAF Acad., 1994-95; lectr. in field; leader various workshops. Contbr. numerous articles to profl. jours. Trustee Leadership Oklahoma City, 1996-98, ARC, 1996—, Redlands Coun. Girl Scouts, 1997—; mem. adv. bd. Leadership Okla., 1993-95, 95-97. Mem. AAAS, Am. Soc. Microbiologists, Med. Mycol. Soc. Americas, Internat. Soc. Human and Animal Mycology, Am. Assn. Vet. Lab. Diagnosticians, Mycol. Soc. Am., am. Lung Assn., Soc. Exptl. Biology and Medicine, Am. Assn. Pathologists, Okla. Acad. Sci., Assn. Am. Med. Colls., Rsch. in Med. Edn. Office: PO Box 26901 Oklahoma City OK 73190-0001

HALL, NANCY KAY, music educator; b. Texas City, Tex., Mar. 29, 1951; d. Gerald Taylor and Modine (Griffith) Ramsey; m. David Earl Railey, July 20, 1974 (div. Sept. 1983); 1 child, Rachel Michal ; m. Michael Mabray Hall, Oct. 13, 1984. BS, Houston Bapt. U., 1973; postgrad., Southwestern Bapt. Theol. Sem., Ft. Worth, 1974. Pvt. piano tchr., Houston, 1970-73, Ft. Smith, Ark., 1977-84, Wharton, Tex., 1984-88, The Woodlands, Tex., 1988—; tchr. Kindermusik of Wharton, Tex., 1987-88, Kindermusik of The Woodlands, 1988—; studio and music store owner Hall's Family Musik, The Woodlands, 1994—. Mem. Nat. Assn. Music Tchrs., Nat. Guild Piano Tchrs. (cert., local chmn. 1997—), Am. Coll. Musicians, Early Childhood Music and Movement Assn. (Level 3 cert.), Kindermusik Educators Assn. (master tchr. cert., maestro 2000-), Conroe Music Tchrs. Assn. (v.p. 1994-96, pres. 1996-98, Tchr. of Yr. 1996). Republican. Avocations: boating, fishing, snorkeling. Home: 64 Eagle Rock Cir The Woodlands TX 77381-4343 Office: Hall's Family Musik and Kindermusik of The Woodlands 25210 Grogans Park Dr The Woodlands TX 77380-2175

HALL, PAMELA ELIZABETH, psychologist; b. Jacksonville, Fla., Sept. 10, 1957; d. Gary Curtiss and Ollie (Banko) H. BA, Rutgers U., 1979; MS in Edn., Pace U., 1981, PsyD in Psychology, 1984. Lic. psychologist, N.Y., N.J., Calif., Conn. Psychology extern St. Vincent's Med. Ctr., N.Y.C., 1981-82; intern in clin. psychology Elizabeth (N.J.) Gen. Med. Ctr., 1982-83, staff psychologist, 1983-85, J.F.K. Med. Ctr., Edison, N.J., 1985-87; pvt. practice Summit and Perth Amboy, N.J., 1985—; sr. supervising psychologist Muhlenberg Med. Ctr., Summit, N.J., 1987-90. Rsch. affiliate, internat. lectr. NIMH field trials on assessment of dissociative disorders Yale U., New Haven, 1990—; adj. prof. psychology Pace U., N.Y.C., 1979-99; exec. bd. dirs. Nat. Coun. on Alcoholism and Drug Dependence of Middlesex County, 2000-02. Active Mayor's Com. on [illegible] and Drug Dependence, 2000—. Named Henry Rutgers scholar, 1979. Mem. Am. Soc. Clin. Hypnosis, Internat. Soc. for Study of Dissociation (founder, pres. N.J. chpt. 1988—, dir. component socs.), Pace U. Alumni Assn., Rutgers U. Alumni Assn., Psi Chi. Avocations: crew, swimming, fine arts, weightlifting. Home: PO Box 1820 Perth Amboy NJ 08862-1820 Office: 12 Kent Place Blvd Summit NJ 07901-1907 Office Phone: 908-277-2383. E-mail: dr.pamelahall@comcast.com.

HALL, PAMELA S. environmental consulting firm executive; b. Hartford, Conn., Sept. 4, 1944; d. LeRoy Warren and Frances May (Murray) Sheely; m. Stuart R. Hall, July 21, 1967 (dec.). BA in Zoology, U. Conn., 1966; MS in Zoology, U. N.H., 1969, BS summa cum laude, 1982; student spl. grad. studies program, Tufts U., 1986-90. Curatorial asst. U. Conn., Storrs, 1966; rsch. asst. Field Mus. Natural History, Chgo., 1966-67; tchg. asst. U. N.H., Durham, 1967-70; program mgr. Normandeau Assocs. Inc., Portsmouth, N.H., 1971-79, marine lab. dir., 1979-81, programs and ops. mgr. Bedford, N.H., 1981-83, v.p., 1983-85, sr. v.p., 1986-87, pres., 1987—. Mem. Conservation Com., Portsmouth, 1977-90, Wells, Estuarine Rsch. Res. Rev.Commn., 1986-88, Great Bay (N.H.) Estuarine Rsch. Res. Tech. Working Group, 1987-89; trustee Trust for N.H. Lands, 1990-93; trustee N.H. chpt. Nature Conservancy, 1991—, chair 1995-99, chair emeritus, 1999—, trustee, 2000—, incorporator N.H. Charitable Fund, 1991-99; bd. advisors Vivamos Mejor, USA, 1990—; bd. dirs. Environ. Bus. Coun. New England, 1995—, treas. 1997—; bd. emeritus Ecosystems Inst., 1997—; commr. N.H. Land and Heritage Commn., 1998-99; bd. advisers N.H. Corp. Wetlands Restoration Partnership, 2003—. Recipient Environ. Leadership award Environ. Bus. Coun. New Eng., 1998; Graham Found. fellow, 1966; NDEA fellow, 1970-71. Mem. Women's Transp., The Nature Conservancy, Soc. of the Protection of N.H. Forests, The Nat. Audubon Soc., Audubon Soc. N.H., Phi Sigma, Sigma Xi. Home: 4 Pleasant Point Dr Portsmouth NH 03801-5275 Office: Normandeau Assocs Inc 25 Nashua Rd Bedford NH 03110-5500 E-mail: phall@normandeau.com.

HALL, PENELOPE COKER, writer, magazine editor; b. Charlotte, N.C., Mar. 19, 1932; d. James Lide and Elizabeth (Boatwright) Coker; m. William Parmenter Wilson, Sept. 6, 1964 (div. 1971); 1 child, Eliza Wilson Ingle; m. Mortimer Waddhams Hall, Dec. 8, 1972; stepchildren: Dorothy, Margaret, Mary Howland, Matthew. Student, Sarah Lawrence Coll., Bronxville, N.Y., 1954. Sr. editor, biographer Cleveland Amory's Celebrity Register, N.Y.C.; prodr., commentator Wrap-Up with Mike Wallace, N.Y.C.; co-prodr., interviewer for series of hr. long spls. NBC-TV, N.Y.C.; co-host 10 Around Town Channel 10 TV, Phila.; co-host The New Yorkers Channel 5 TV, N.Y.C., 1968-70; reporter, Sunday anchor 10 O'Clock News, Channel 5, N.Y.C., 1970-73; host cable cooking show Millbrook, NY, 1976—; editor-in-chief Dutchess Mag., N.Y.C., 1993—99, editor-at-large, columnist, 1998—. Contbr. numerous articles to profl. jours.; author: Fancy and the Cement Patch, 1966, The Wish Bottle, 1967, Riding High, 1990. Bd. trustees Spoleto Festival, Charleston, S.C., 1997—; Coker Coll., Hartsville, S.C., 2000— Mem. Authors League, Nat. Trust for Hist. Preservation Nat. Trust Coun., Sandanona Beagles, Millbrook Hounds, Century Assn., Millbrook Golf and Tennis Club (bd. dirs. 1989-93), Cosmopolitan Club. Democrat. Episcopalian. Avocations: painting, horseback riding, boating. Home: PO Box 516 Millbrook NY 12545-0516

HALL, RAMONA SHIELDS, art educator; b. Tuscaloosa, Ala., June 4, 1963; d. Donald Harrell and Ruth Elaine (Bonner) Shields; m. Gregory Linn Hall, Nov. 22, 1986; children: Anna Kathryn, Caroline Elizabeth. BS, U. Ala., 1985, MA, 1989. Tchr. art Albertville City Schs., Ala., 1985—. Exhibitions include Choctaw County Art Coun., 1990, Bank of Albertville, 1989. Pre-sch. choir dir. Mount Calvary Bapt. Ch., Albertville, 2001—; art judge Marshall County Schs., Guntersville, 1998—2000, 2002—03. Named Art Educator of Yr. Elem. divsn., Ala. Art Edn. Assn., 1999; named to Tchr. Hall of Fame, Jacksonville State U., 2000; recipient Young Careerist award, Albertville Bus. & Profl. Women's Club, 1999. Mem.: Mountain Valley Arts Coun. (bd. dirs. 1990—91, art instr.'s exhibitor 1996), Delta Kappa Gamma (corr. sec. Alpha Mu chpt. 2000—02), Kappa Kappa Iota (pres. Chi conclave 2003—). Baptist. Avocations: painting, walking, singing. Office: Albertville City Schs 107 W Main St Albertville AL 35950*

HALL, REBECCA ANN, executive secretary; b. Detroit, July 28, 1949; d. Henry August and Jeanne Maude (Plank) Isaacson; m. Gene Lawrence Hall, June 16, 1973; children: Mellany Anne, Leah Jayne. BS in Edn., Ctrl. Mich. U., 1971. Cert. tchr., Mich. Therapist speech and lang. Lapeer (Mich.) Cmty. Schs., 1971-77; clerical asst. Eaton Rapids (Mich.) Pub. Schs., 1991-2000, sec. to the prin. Lockwood Elem. Sch., 2000—. Parent involvement program coord. Lockwood Elem. Sch., Eaton Rapids, 1995-98. Mem.: AAUW (sec. Eaton Rapids br. 1989—91, chair Heritage com. 1989—91, 2d v.p. 1991—93, pres.-elect 1994—95, pres. 1995—98, 1st v.p. 1998—99, pres. 1999—2002). Avocation: reading. Home: 8175 5 Point Hwy Eaton Rapids MI 48827-9061 Office: Lockwood Elem Sch 810 Greyhound Dr Eaton Rapids MI 48827-2606

HALL, SHANNON, marketing professional, public relations executive, writer, photographer; BA in Comm., Mills Coll. Pub. rels. mgr. Ingres; ptnr., mng. dir. Horn Group, Inc., 1994—. Contbr. SF Atty. Mag.; freelance writer San Francisco mags., adv. assoc., photographer, San Francisco, 1999. Co-mgr. Calif. Minority Counsel program; mem. bd. dirs. Bay Area Video Coalition. Office: Horn Group Inc 612 Howard St San Francisco CA 94105 Business E-Mail: info@horngroup.com.

HALL, SHARON GAY, retired language educator, artist; b. Centralia, Ill., Oct. 2, 1942; d. Leon Lucene and Olyve Elizabeth Hall. BS, So. Ill. U., 1966, MS, 1984; postgrad., Ea. Ill. U., 1985—90. Cert. secondary tchr. Ill. English tchr. Webber Twp. H.S., Bluford, Ill., 1966—67, Mt. Vernon (Ill.) H.S., 1967—99, ret., 1999. Artist-in-residence Cedarhurst Art Guild, Cedarhurst Mus., 1974—. Treas. bd. dirs. Bus. and Profl. Women's Club, Mt. Vernon, 1966—76; mem. Jefferson County Hist. Soc., 2000—. Recipient Recognition award, Cedarhurst Mus., 2000. Mem.: NEA, AAUW, Ill. Edn. Assn., Mt. Vernon Edn. Assn. (sec., treas., bd. dirs. 1967—99), Phi Delta Kappa, Phi Theta Kappa, Alpha Delta Kappa. Republican. Avocations: raising exotic animals, handspinner, weaver, fiber artist, seamstress. Home: 11384 E Idlewood Rd Mount Vernon IL 62864

HALL, SUSAN LAUREL, artist, educator, writer; b. Point Reyes Sta., Calif., Mar. 19, 1943; d. Earl Morris and Avis Mary (Brown) H. BFA, Calif. Coll. Arts & Crafts, Oakland, 1965; MA, U. Calif., Berkeley, 1967. Mem. faculty Sarah Lawrence Coll., Bronxville, NY, 1972—75, Sch. Visual Arts, NYC, 1981—92, Skowhegan Sch. of Painting and Sculpture, Maine, 1981, Univ. of Colo., Boulder Co., 1981, Art Inst. of Chgo., Chgo., 1981, Univ. of Tex., Austin, Tex., 1993, San Antonio, 1995, San Francisco Art Inst., San Francisco, 1996. One-woman shows include San Francisco Mus. Art, 1967, Quay Gallery, San Francisco, 1969, Phillis Kind Gallery, Chgo., 1971, 1998, 98 Greene St. Loft, N.Y.C., Whitney Mus., Henderson Mus. U. Colo., Boulder, 1973, Nancy Hoffman Gallery, N.Y.C., 1975, U. R.I. Gallery, Kingston, 1976, Harcus Krakow Rosen Sonnabend Gallery, Boston, 1976, Hal Bromm and Getler-Pall Galleries, N.Y.C., 1978, Helene Shlien Gallery, Boston, 1978, Hamilton Gallery, N.Y.C., 1978—79, 1981, 1983, Ovsey Gallery, L.A., 1981—82, 1984, 1987, 1989, 1991, Paule Anglim Gallery, San Francisco, 1975—83, Ted Greenwald Gallery, N.Y.C., 1986, Trabia Macafee Gallery, 1988—89, Wyckoff Gallery, Aspen, Colo., 1990—92, Milagros Contemporary Art, San Antonio, 1995, Brendan Walter Gallery, L.A., 1995, U. Tex., San Antonio, 1996, Jan Holloway Gallery, San Francisco, 1997, San Francisco Mus. Art Gallery, 1998, Gail Harvey Gallery, L.A., 1999, 2001, Frank Lloyd Wright Civic Ctr., San Rafael, 1999, Jornigan Wicker Gallery, San Francisco, 1999, exhibited in group shows at Whitney Mus. Am. Art, San Francisco Mus., Oakland Mus., [illegible] Inst. Contemporary Art, Phila., Hudson River Mus., Bklyn. Mus., Nat. Mus. Women in the Arts, Mus. Fine Arts, Boston, Aldrich Mus. Contemporary Art, G.W. Einstein Gallery, Blum Helman Downtown, Leo Castelli Gallery Uptown, Graham Modern, N.Y.C., Kunstmus., Luzern, Switzerland, Landesmus., Bonn, Bolinas (Calif.) Mus., 2002, Ranches and Rolling Hills, Wicasio, Calif., 2001, 2002, 2003, 2004, Represented in permanent collections pub. collections Whitney Mus., San Francisco Mus., Bklyn. Mus., Carnegie Inst., St. Louis Mus., Nat. Mus. Women in the Arts, others; author: Painting Point Reyes, Susan Hall, 2003. Nat. Endowment Arts fellow, 1979-87, Adolph Gottleib Found. fellow, 1995; grantee: Pollack Krasner Found., N.Y. State Coun. on Arts; recipient Marin Arts Coun. Bd. Dirs. award, 1999.

HALL, TELKA MOWERY ELIUM, retired educational administrator; b. Salisbury, NC, July 22, 1936; d. James Lewis and Malissa (Fielder) Mowery; m. James Richard Elium III, June 20, 1954 (div. 1961); 1 child, W. Denise Elium Carr; m. Allen Sanders Hall, Apr. 15, 1967 (div. 1976). Student, Am. Inst. Banking, 1955-57, Mary-Hardin Baylor Coll., Waco, Tex., 1957; BA, Catawba Coll., Salisbury, 1967; MEd, Miss. U. for Women, Columbus, 1973; EdS, Appalachian State U., 1975; postgrad., U. N.C., Greensboro, 1977; EdD, U. N.C., Chapel Hill, 1990; postgrad., Ind. U., 1998. Cert. early childhood, intermediate lang. arts and social studies tchr., curriculum specialist, adminstr., supr., supt., NC; notary pub., NC; cert. in CPR and first aid and safety, ARC. Bookkeeper, teller Citizens & So. Bank, Spartanburg, SC, 1955-56; bookkeeper 1st Nat. Bank, Killeen, Tex., 1956-58; bookkeeper, savs. teller Exch. Bank & Trust Co., Dallas, 1958-61; acct. Catawba Coll., 1961-65; floater teller bookkeeping and proof depts. Security Bank & Trust Co., Salisbury, 1965-68, 71; tchr. Rowan County Sch. System, Salisbury, 1967-70, 71-72, 1973-82; asst. prin. North Rowan Elem. Sch., Spencer, NC, 1982-94, Rockwell Elem. and China Grove Elem. Sch., NC, 1994-96, ret., 1996; part-time asst. prin. of curriculum China Grove Elem., 1996-99, also part-time outside observer for Ctrl. Office, 1996, asst. prin. curriculum, 1996-99, ret., 1999. Receptionist H & R Block, Salisbury, 1979-83; Chpt. I reading tchr. Nazareth Children's Home, Rockwell, NC, 1979-81. Author: The Effect of Second Language Training in Kindergarten on the Development of Listening Skills. Mem. Salisbury Cmty. Chorus, 1951—52, Hist. Salisbury Found., Inc., Salisbury Concert Choir, 1981—83; foreperson Rowan County grand jury, 1991; cons. Dial HELP, Salisbury, 1981—83; charter mem. bd. dirs. Old North Salisbury Assn., 1980—2000; past mem. Children's Literacy Guild, ARC; mem. Harford-Dole chpt. ARC, 2002—, bd. dir., 2004—; pianist Franklin Presbyn. Ch., 1952—55, choir dir., 1975—87, adult class Sunday sch. tchr., 1979—80, nursery Sunday sch. tchr., 1996—99, substitute S.S. adult class tchr., 2002—03, pres., 2001—03, deacon, 1980—83, elder, 1991—92, 1996—99, 2001—04, clk. of session, 1992, 1996—98, 2002—, choir mem., 1947—, co-moderator women of ch., 1999—2003; mem. Magnify Christian Concert Choir, 1999—. Civitan Music scholar, 1954, Kiwanis Acad. scholar, 1966, Catawba Coll. Acad. scholar, 1965-67, Mary Morrow Ednl. scholar N.C. Assn. Educators, 1972-73. Mem. NEA, NCAE, AARP, AAUW (v.p. 1985-87, 91-93), AARP, ARC (vol.), NC Ret. Govtl. Employees' Assn., Rowan-Salisbury Ret. Pers., Salisbury Hist. Assn., Kappa Delta Pi, Theta Phi (pres. 1992-93). Avocations: photography, genealogy, calligraphy, singing, composing poetry. Home: 105 Sharon Ct Salisbury NC 28146-7241

HALL, TENNIEBEE M. editor; b. Bakersfield, Calif., May 21, 1940; d. William Elmer and Lillian May (Otis) Hall; m. Harold Robert Hall, Feb. 20, 1965. BA in Edn., Fresno State Coll., 1962; AA, Bakersfield Coll., 1960. Cert. tchr., Calif. Tchr. Edison (Calif.) Sch. Dist., 1962-65; substitute tchr. Marin and Oakland Counties (Calif.), Berkeley, 1965-66; engrng. asst. Pacific Coil Co., Inc., Bakersfield, 1974-81; editor United Ostomy Assn., Inc., Irvine, Calif., 1986-91. Co-author: Treating IBD, 1989, Current Therapy in Gastroenterology, 1989; author, designer: Volunteer Leadership Training Manuals, 1982-84; editor: Calif. Parliamentarian, 1999-2003; contbr. articles to Ostomy Quar., 1973—. Mem. Pacific Beach Town Coun., San Diego, 1977—; campaign worker Maureen O'Connor (1st woman mayor of city), San Diego, 1986; mem. Nat. Digestive Diseases Adv. Bd., NIH, Washington, 1986-91; mem. planning and devel. bd. Scripps Clinic and Rsch. Found. Inflammatory Bowel Disease Ctr., San Diego, 1993-2003; various vol. activities, 1966-74, 81-86. Recipient Outstanding Svc. award VA Vol. Svc., Bur. of Vets. Affairs, Washington, 1990. Mem. Nat. Assn. Parliamentarians, United Ostomy Assn. Inc. (regional program dir. 1980-84, pres. 1984-86, Sam Dubin award 1983, Industry Adv. award 1987), Crohn's and Colitis Found. Am. (nat. trustee 1986-95, nat. v.p. 1987-92). Avocations: travel, volunteerism. Home and Office: 8585 Via Mallorca Unit 7 La Jolla CA 92037-2585

HALL, TERESA JOANNE KEYS, manufacturing engineer, educator; b. Chanute, Kans., 1954; d. William Milton and Mary Joanne (Greve) Keys; m. Douglas Wayne Hall, Jan 31, 1986; 1 child, Benjamin Alan. BA in Industry, U. No. Iowa, 1988, MA in Tech., 1991; PhD in Indsl. Edn. and Tech., Iowa State U., 1997. Cert. mfg. engr. Dept. mgr. Cooks Inc., Waterloo, Iowa, 1974-76; grounds maintenance City of Waterloo, 1976-77; trades mechanic Deere & Co., Waterloo, 1977-79, foundry maintenance planner, 1979-82, metals analyst, 1982-84, sr. maintenance planner, 1984-87; pvt. practice Waterloo, 1988-91; instr. U. Northern Iowa, Cedar Falls, 1992-96, asst. prof., 1997-00, assoc. prof., 2001—03, mfg. program coord., 1998—2003; prof. S.D. State U., Brookings, 2003—, dept. head engring. tech. and mgmt., 2003—, dir. Polytechnic Ctr., 2003—. Expert witness mfg. fabrication and safety issues, 1999—2000; panel reviewer NSF, 1999—2000; dir. Polytech. Ctr. S.D. State U., Brookings, 2003—. Tech. editor, Am.Jour. Undergrad. Rsch., 2003—;contbr. articles to profl. jours. Grantee NSF, 1996, 98, Tchr. Edn. Alliance, 1997. Mem. AAUW, Soc. Mfg. Engrs. (faculty advisor 1993-2001, Region 9 exec. bd. 1998—, chair chpt.186, 2003, chmn. certification oversight and appeals bd. 2004—, President's award 2000, Internat. award of merit, 2003), Am. Mensa Ltd., Nat. Assn. Indsl. Technologists (Outstanding Prof. of Yr. for Region 2, reviewer Jour. Indsl. Tech.), Epsilon Pi Tau. Avocation: gardening. Office: SD State U Dept Engring Tech & Mgmt Brookings SD 57007-0092

HALLADAY, LAURIE ANN, public relations consultant, former franchise executive; b. Monroe, Mich., Aug. 18, 1945; d. Alvin John and Florence (Lowrey) Kohler; m. Edward L. Howell, Aug. 27, 1966; m. 2d Fredric R. Halladay, May 24, 1980. BJ, U. Mo., 1967. Reporter, staff writer Copley Newspapers, L.A., 1967-69; account exec. Furman Assocs., L.A., 1969-71, v.p., 1971-74; account supr. Bob Thomas & Assocs., L.A., 1974-76, v.p., 1976-78; v.p., sr. ptnr. Fleishman-Hillard, Inc., St. Louis, 1980-84; owner, operator McDonald's, Portland, Oreg., 1984-87, McDonald's McStop of Mid.-Mo., Kingdom City, 1988-92. Chmn. press ops. for Budweiser/G.I. Joe's Portland 200 Indy Car Race, 1984-87; mem. advt., promotions com. Hollywood Boosters, 1986. Bd. dirs. Waterman Place Assn., St. Louis, 1983; mem. pub. rels. com. Winston Churchill Meml., Fulton, 1988-92. Recipient Merit award Calif. Press Women, 1969, Lulu award Los Angeles Women's Ad Club, 1976, McDonald's Outstanding Store award, 1985, 86, 89, 90, 91. Mem. PRSA (Prism award 1977), Soc. Am. travel Writers (assoc. 1981-84), Women in Comm. (dir. St. Louis 1980-82), Nat. Tour Assn., Mo. Travel Coun., Delta Delta Delta (alumna adviser 1989, 90,, v.p. Delta Xi House Corp. 1991, collegiate dist. officer 1991, 94, regional program chmn. 1994, program resource team pub. rels. specialist 1995-96, nat. chmn. pub. rels. 1996, cons. pub. rels. chpt. 1998-2000). Home: 242 Hidden Bay Dr Unit 301 Osprey FL 34229-3107 E-mail: laurieh@comcast.net.

HALLAM, ARLITA WARRICK, quality of life administrator; b. Peoria, Ill., June 28, 1944; d. Jesse Edward and Hazel Winifred (McClister) Warrick; m. Donald Owen Hallam, Sept. 15, 1978. BS, Ill. State U., Normal, 1965; MS, U. Ill., 1968; PhD, U. Tex., Arlington, 1992. Dir. [illegible] instr. Ill. Ctrl. Coll., East Peoria, 1970-74; regional coord. Ill. Bicentennial Commn., Springfield, 1974-76; exec. dir. Ft. Crevecoeur, Creve Coeur, Ill., 1976-77; dir. sales and mktg. Group V Devel. Co., East Peoria, 1977-78; prin. libr. Abilene (Tex.) Pub. Libr., 1978-82; dir. North Richland Hills (Tex.) Pub. Libr., 1982-92, Clearwater (Fla.) Pub. Libr. Sys., 1992-98; quality of life adminstr. City of Clearwater, 1998—. Author articles. Grad. Leadership N.E., Ft. Worth, 1990, Exec. Fellows Program, Tampa, 1993, Leadership Pinellas, Clearwater, 1994. Named among Top Ten Women of Yr., Am. Bus. Women's Assn., Denver, 1974. Mem. ALA, Pub. Libr. Assn., Fla. Libr. Assn., Fla. Assn. Christian Librs., Rotary. Nazarene. Avocations: reading, travel, history, museums. Office: City of Clearwater 100 N Osceola Ave Clearwater FL 33755-4029 Home: 345 Dogwood Dr Grapevine TX 76051-3535

HALLAM, BEVERLY (BEVERLY LINNEY), artist; b. Lynn, Mass., Nov. 22, 1923; d. Edwin Francis and Alice (Linney) Hallam Murphy. BS in Edn, Mass. Coll. Art, 1945; postgrad., Cranbrook Acad. Art, Mich., 1948; MFA, Syracuse U., 1953. Chmn. dept. art Lasell Jr. Coll., Auburndale, Mass., 1945-49; assoc. prof. Mass. Coll. Art, 1949-62. Bd. dirs. Barn Gallery Assocs., Inc., Ogunquit, Maine. One-person shows include Joe and Emily Lowe Art Center, Syracuse U., 1953, DeCordova Mus., Lincoln. Mass., 1954, Shore Galleries, Boston, 1959, 62, 68, 73, 74, Witte Meml. Mus., San Antonio, 1968, U. Maine, 1969, Lamont Gallery, Exeter, N.H., 1969, Addison Gallery, Andover, Mass., 1971, Fitchburg Art Mus., 1972, Fairweather Hardin Gallery, Chgo., 1972, Hobe Sound (Fla.) Galleries, 1973, Inst. Contemporary Art, Boston, 1977, PS Galleries, Maine, 1981, Payson-Weisberg Gallery, N.Y.C., 1984, Farnsworth Mus., Rockland, Maine, 1984, 98, Midtown Galleries, N.Y.C., 1988, Francesca Anderson Gallery, Boston, 1988, Hobe Sound Galleries North, Portland, Maine, 1988, Evansville (Ind.) Mus. Arts and Sci., 1990, Sheldon Swope Mus., Terre Haute, Ind., 1990, Art Mus. S.E. Tex., Beaumont, 1990, Bergen Mus. Art and Sci., Paramus, N.J., 1990, Polk Mus. Art, Lakeland, Fla., 1991, Farnsworth Art Mus., 1998, Ogunquit Art Assn., 1999, Mass. Coll. Art, Boston, 2000, Univ. New England, 2000, Berkshire C.C., Pittsfield, Mass., 2003, River Tree Ctr. for the Arts, Kennebunk, Maine, 2003; two-person show, Inst. Contemporary Art, Boston, 1956, numerous group shows including Barn Gallery, 1954-2004, Busch-Reisinger Mus., Harvard U., 1956, 59, 60, Portland Mus., 1959, 84, 92, 93, 97, Mus. Fine Arts, Boston, 1960, Inst. Contemporary Art, Boston, 1960, 63, 68, 77, Pace Gallery, Boston, 1962, DeCordova Mus., 1963, 64, 68, 69, 70, 71, 75, Ward-Nasse Gallery, N.Y.C., 1971-72, Ogunquit (Maine) Mus. Am. Art, 1964, 70, 71, 78, 80, 84, 89, 91-93, 95, 98, 2000, 2003, R.I. Arts Festival, 1966, Smithsonian Instn., Washington, 1966, Am. Water Color Soc. Traveling Exhibition, 1967, Watercolor U.S.A., Springfield, Mo., 1968, Maine State Mus., 1976, Maine Coast Artists, 1974, 75, 77, 83, 89, 92, 93, Joan Whitney Payson Gallery of Art, Maine, 1980, Farnsworth Art Mus., 1982, 87, 92, 95, 96, Bowdoin Coll. Mus. Art, 1984, 92, Midtown Payson Galleries, N.Y.C., 1985, 87, 90, 92, Expo '92, Seville, Spain, Barbara Scott Gallery, Bay Harbor Island, Fla., 1993, Fitchburg (Mass.) Art Mus., 1994, Monmouth (N.J.) Mus., 1995, Evansville Mus. Arts and Sci., 1996, U. New England, 2000, Francesca Anderson Fine Art, Lexington, Mass., 2002; represented in permanent collections Rose Art Mus. Brandeis U., Fogg Art Mus., Cambridge, Mass.; Corcoran Gallery Am. Art, Washington, Witte Meml. Mus., San Antonio, DeCordova Mus., Lincoln, Addison Gallery, Andover, Bowdoin Coll. Mus. Art, Fitchburg Art Mus., Ogunquit Mus. Am. Art, Portland Mus., Colby Coll., U. Maine, Currier Gallery Art, Manchester N.H., Farnsworth Library and Art Mus., Rockland, Maine, U. N.H. Art Galleries, Durham, Everson Mus., Syracuse, First Nat. Bank, Boston, Ernst and Ernst, Chgo., Carnegie Corp., N.Y., Nat. Mus. Women in the Arts, Washington, Gouws Capital Mgmt., Inc., Portland, Maine, Marion Koogler Art Mus., San Antonio, Tex., others, also, pvt. collections, U.S. Can., Paris, Switzerland; Publ. Beverly Hallam, Paintings, Drawings and Monotypes, 1956-71, 1971; subject of book and video Beverly Hallam: The Flower Paintings, 1990, Beverly Hallam: An Odyssey in Art, 1998, (by Carl Little) One Hundred Works From the 20th Century at Colby College Museum of Art, 1996, Maine In America, 2000, On Paper: Masterworks From The Addison Collection, 2003, others. Recipient Pearl Safir award Silvermine Guild Artists, New Canaan, Conn., 1955, Painting prize Boston Arts Festival, 1957, Blanche E. Colman Found. award, 1960, Hatfield awards Boston Soc. Watercolor Painters, 1960, 64, 1st prize Edwin Webster award, 1962, Am. Artist Achievement award, 1993, Disting. Alumna award Mass. Coll. Art, 2000, Maine Coll. Art award for Visual Artist Achievement, 2001. Mem. Ogunquit Art Assn. (past pres.), Archives Am. Art. Avocations: photography, digital abstractions. Home: 30 Surf Point Rd York ME 03909-5053

HALLANAN, ELIZABETH VIRGINIA, federal judge; b. Charleston, W.Va., Jan. 10, 1925; d. Walter Simms and Imogene (Burns) H., U. Charleston, 1946; JD, W.Va. U., 1951; postgrad, U. Mich., 1964. Atty. Crichton & Hallanan, Charleston, 1952-59; mem. W.Va. State Bd. Edn., Charleston, 1955-57, Ho. of Dels., W.Va. Legis., Charleston, 1957-58; asst. commr. pub. instns. Charleston, 1958-59; mem., chmn. W.Va. Pub. Service Commn., Charleston, 1969-75; atty. Lopinsky, Bland, Hallanan, Dodson, Deutsch & Hallanan, Charleston, 1975-83; sr. judge U.S. Dist. Ct. for So. Dist. W.Va., Charleston, 1983—. Recipient Hannah G. Solomon award Nat. Coun. Jewish Women, 1997, Justitia Officium award W.Va. U. Coll. Law, 1997; named Woman of Achievement, YWCA, 1997, West Virginian of Yr., Charleston Gazette, 1997. Mem. W.Va. Bar Assn. Office: US Dist Ct PO Box 2546 Charleston WV 25329-2546 E-mail: Judge_Hallanan@wvsd.uscourts.gov.

HALLAREN, MARY, career officer, social service administrator; b. 1907; Enlisted WAACS (later WAACS), 1942, comdr. 1st batallion, 1943, dir., 1947-53. Dir. Women in Cmty. Svc.; primary exponent advocating permanent status for mil. women; instrumental in creation of Women in Mil. Svc. Meml., Arlington Nat. Cemetery.

HALLENBECK, LINDA S. elementary school educator; b. Iowa, 1948; m. Theodore R. Hallenbeck; children: Robert, Elizabeth. BS, Kent State U., 1974, MEd, 1976, postgrad. Cert. tchr. K-3, K-8, computer sci., math., Ohio; Nat. bd. cert.. Grad. asst. Kent (Ohio) State U., 1974-76; 3d grade tchr. Hudson (Ohio) Elem. Sch., 1976-77; 1st grade tchr. Evamere Sch., Hudson, 1977-86; 5th grade tchr. J.P. McDowell Elem. Sch., Hudson, 1986-92, East Woods Sch., Hudson, 1992—2001; tchr. Hudson Mid. Sch., 2001—03; rsch. assoc. NSF, 2002—03, Mich. State U., 2003—04. Cons. NSF, Washington, 1989-95, tchr. in residence, office of Gov. Bob Taft, 1999-2001, tchr., Presdl. Acad. for Excellence in Tchng. Mathematics at Princeton and Northwestern U., Middleschool Mathematics State Trainer, Math Acad., 2001-. Recipient Presdl. award for excellence in teaching sci. and math. NSF, 1993, Govs. Edn. leadership award, 1998, Ohio Pioneer in Edn award, 2000. Mem. Nat. Coun. Tchrs. Math., Ohio Coun. Tchrs. Math. (pres. 2004--), Ohio Math. Edn. Leadership Coun., PTO, Coun. for Presdl. Awardees of Math, Govs. Commn. for student success, Exec. Bd. of Ohio Math/Sci. Coalition. Avocations: snow skiing, gardening, sewing, decorating. Home: 7615 Oxgate Ct Hudson OH 44236-1877

HALLENBECK, POMONA JUANITA, artist; b. Roswell, N.Mex., Nov. 12, 1938; d. Cleve and Juanita Henriette (Williams) H.; children: Cheryl Ellis, Cynthia Ellis, Catherine Ellis. AA, Ea. N.Mex. U., 1965; BFA, Art Student's League, 1976; postgrad., Pan Am. Art Sch., 1976-77. Mgr. Paul Anderson Photography, San Antonio, 1951-54; tchr. Roswell (N.Mex.) Ind. Sch. Dist., 1960-64; dir., instr. Sketchbox Sch. Art, Galveston, Tex., 1965-71; monitor etching class Art Student's League, N.Y.C., 1975-77; dir., instr. Alleyworks Atlier, Austin, Tex., 1978-81; dir., proprietor, artist Sketchbox Studio, Roswell, 1982-94; instr. Elderhostel program Ghost Ranch, Abiquiu, N.Mex., 1984—2002, coord. Calender project, 1992—; owner, propr. Pomona's Accent Line, Roswell, 1986-94, cons., 1988-94. Artist, demonstrator Roswell (N.Mex.) Mus. and Art Ctr., 1981—90, Roswell Ind. Sch., 1982—90, Wonder of Watercolor Workshops, Austin, Tex., 1997—2001, Art After Sch., Bastrop, Tex., 1997—2001, Watercolor by Design U. Tex., Austin, 1999—, Fielding it with Watercolor, 2001—, Watercolor for Beginners continuing edn. programs, Bastrop and Elgin, Tex., 1998—, Painting Inside Out at U. Tex., Austin, 2001—; creator Marathon Watercolor workshop Stonypoint Conf. Ctr., NY, 2001; creator Marathon Watercolor Weekend, Austin; founder watercolor classes Elderhostels, Abiquiu and Santa Fe, 02. Illustrator: (book covers) Julian of Norwich, Nachman, Pseudo Dionysius, Classics of Western Spirituality, Naming the Powers, Unmasking the Powers, Engaging the Powers, Walter Wink, Ghost Ranch Cookbook, Savoring the Southwest Again, The Human Being: The Enigma of the Son of Man; one-woman shows Ghost Ranch Trading Post and New Arts Bldg., 2000-02, Laughing at the Sun Gallery, Austin, 2001, Depot Gallery, Austin, 2001-02, Trail of Ponies, Santa Fe, N.Mex., 2001, Zandoozi Gallery, 2004; (album cover) Smiling on the Inside; exhibited in Southwest Expressions Gallery, Chgo., 1990-91, Roswell Fine Art Mus., 1994, Artisan Gallery, Austin, 1995-, Cimmaron (N.Mex.) Art Gallery, 1995, Trading Post, 2001-, Bitzer & Johnson, Roswell, 1997, 2001-02, Potter's Guild Sho, 1997, Gallery Bunkhouse, Cypress Mill, Tex., 2002, Laughing at the Sun Gallery, Austin, 1996-2003, Rose Minn Gallery, Elgin, Tex., 2001-02, Blaire Carnehan Gallery, Santa Fe, N.Mex., 2001-. Mem. World Wildlife, 2000, Ghost Ranch Compadres, Santa Fe, 2000-, People for the Ethical Treatment of Animals, 2000-, Recos River Project, 1990-2000; arts convener silent auction, Ghost Ranch, 1995, New Art Bldg., 1998. Recipient purchase award Am. Artist, 1975, 2nd Place award Austin Art Guild, 1999; named Best of Show, Ghost Ranch Compadre Show, 1990, ALTRUSA Fashion Show, 1990; scholar Altrusa Club, 1973; grantee Whitney Enterprises, 1990, artist-in-residence grantee Ghost Ranch, 1992-, McKee grantee, 1995-96. Mem. Am. Watercolor Soc. (assoc.), Soc. Illustrators, Nat. Watercolor Soc., Western Colo. Watercolor Soc., Supts. Salon of Paris (Bronze medal 1988), Ghost Ranch Found. Ctr., Roswell Mus. and Art Ctr., U.S. Humane Soc., Tex. Watercolor Soc., Tex. Fine Arts Assn., Austin Contemporary Art Assn., Mus. Women Artists, Washington. Democrat. Avocation: photography. Office: Sketchbox Studio of Art 130 Old Austin Trail Elgin TX 78621-5744 E-mail: sketchbox130@aol.com.

HALLETT, CAROL BOYD, air transportation executive; b. Oakland, Calif., Oct. 16, 1937; married. Student, U. Oreg., San Francisco State Coll. Assemblywoman Calif. State Assembly, Sacramento, 1976-82, minority floor leader, 1979-82; cons., dir. Found. for Individual and Econ. Freedom, Sacramento, 1982-86; dir. of parks and recreation Calif., 1982-83; western regional dir. Citizens For Am., Sacramento, 1983-84; asst. to U.S. Sec. Interior, 1984-85; nat. field dir. Citizens For Am., Washington, 1985-86; amb. Am. embassy, Nassau, Bahamas, 1986-89; U.S. commr. of customs U.S. Customs Svc., Washington, 1989-93; sr. govt. rels. advisor Collier, Shannon, Rill & Scott, Washington, 1993-95; pres., CEO Air Transport Assn. Am., Washington, 1995. Head U.S. Presdl. del. for celebration St. Kitts and Nevis, 1983; mem. ofcl. U.S. Presdl. del. to observe Guatemalan presdl. election, 1985; cons. trade Clark Co., Paso Robles, Calif., 1993-95. Recipient Order of Merit King Juan Carlos I of Spain, 1994; named Woman of Yr., Bahamian Rev. mag., 1990, Paul Harris fellow Rotary, Nassau, 1980. Office: Air Transport Assn Am Ste 1100 1301 Pennsylvania Ave NW Washington DC 20004-1707

HALLETT, JUDITH PELLER, classical studies educator; b. Chgo., Apr. 4, 1944; d. Leonard and Celia (Stern) Peller; m. Mark Hallett, June 26, 1966; children: Nicholas, Victoria. BA, Wellesley (Mass.) Coll., 1966; MA, Harvard U., Cambridge, Mass., 1967, PhD, 1971. Lectr. classics Clark U., Worcester, Mass., 1972-74; asst. prof. classical studies Boston U., 1974-82; Blegen vis. rsch. scholar Vassar Coll., Poughkeepsie, N.Y., 1980; Mellon vis. asst. prof. Brandeis U., Waltham, Mass., 1982-83; assoc. prof. classics U. Md., College Park, Md., 1983-92, prof. classics, 1993—, acting equity adminstr. Coll. Arts & Humanities, 1988-89, chair classics, 1996—2004. Asst. to assoc. editor The Classical World, 1980—; founder, mem. steerng com. Women's Classical Caucus, 1972—. Author: Fathers and Daughters in Roman Society, 1984; co-editor: The Personal Voice in Classical Scholarship and Roman Sexualities, 1997; contbr. more than 50 articles to scholarly jours. Mem. Md. Humanities Coun., 2001—; bd. trustees Balt. Hebrew U., 2002—. Recipient various fellowships and grants NEH. Mem. AAUP (pres. chpt. 1994—), Am. Philological Assn. (dir. 1997-99), Assn. Ancient Historians, Classical Assn. Atlantic States (2d v.p. 1997-98, pres. 1999-2000), Md. Humanities Coun., Phi Beta Kappa (pres. U. Md. College Park chpt. 1996-98). Democrat. Jewish. Home: 5147 Westbard Ave Bethesda MD 20816-1413 Office: Dept Classics U Md College Park MD 20742-0001

HALLEY, DIANE ESTHER, artist; b. Jasper, Ind., May 14, 1939; d. John and Esther Margaret (Kruse) Darden; m. Norman B. Halley, May 21, 1966; 1 child, William Tull. BS in Elem. Edn., Ind. State U., 1961. Tchr. 4th grade, New Albany, Ind., 1961, Seymour, Ind., 1962-64, Westminster, Colo., 1964-68; portrait artist Arvada, Colo., 1979—. Juror fall exhbn. Colo. Watercolor Soc., 2002. Paintings included in books, Colo., 1990—, Denver Art Museum, Best of Watercolor-Painting Textures, 1997, Splash Six-The Magic of Texture, 2000; one-woman shows include Denver Nat. Bank, 1983, Foothills Art Ctr., Golden, Colo., 1984, Nat. Ctr. Atmospheric Rsch., Boulder, Colo., 1991, Colo. Christian U., 2000, exhibited in group shows at Lincoln Ctr., Ft. Collins, Colo., 2003, exhibitions include Challenge of Champions, Watercolor Art Soc. Houston, 2003, Artists Who Happen to be Women, Tex. A&M U., 2004, Watercolor Mo. Nat., Winston Churchill Meml. Lib., 2004, Tex. A&M Campus, 2004. Pres. Clear Creek Valley Med. Aux., Lakewood, Colo., 1973—74, 1991—92. Recipient Founder's award, Colo. Watercolor Soc., 1992, Pres.'s award, 1994, Grumbacher award, Pikes Peak Watercolor Soc., 1995, Cash award, Lakewood Arts Coun., 2001, Award of Distinction, Mo. Nat. Watercolor Exhbn., 2003, Westminster Cmty. Artist Series award, 2003. Mem.: Mo. Watercolor Soc. (signature mem.), Kans. Watercolor Soc. (Am. artist cash award 1999), Rocky Mountain Nat. Watermedia Soc., Catherine Lorillard Wolf Art Club (Adriana Zahn award 1985, Cynthia Goodgal award 1986), Nat. Watercolor Soc. (Del Mar Coll. award 1982), Nat. Assn. Women Artists (Cecil Shapiro Meml. award 1998). Avocations: Bible study, bridge, gardening. Home: 6631 Osceola Ct Arvada CO 80003-6426

HALLEY, GAIL RENEE, secondary school educator; b. Greeley, Colo., Aug. 16, 1976; d. Grant Gale and Linda Renee Rumsey; m. Alan A. Halley, July 31, 1999. BS, Colo. State U., 1998; MA, U. No. Colo., 2003. Lic. profl. tchr., instr. alt. coop. edn. program, agr. instr. Alternative coop. edn. tchr. Valley H.S., Gilcrest, Colo., 2000—. Mem.: Colo. Assn. Career and Tech. Educators (mem. spl. needs divsn.). Office: Weld County Sch Dist RE-1 1001 Birch St Gilcrest CO 80623 E-mail: halleyg@weld-re1.k12.co.us.

HALLINAN, MAUREEN THERESA, sociologist, educator; BA, Marymount Coll., 1961; MS, U. Notre Dame, 1968; PhD, U. Chgo., 1972. Prof. U. Wis., Madison, 1980-84; with U. Notre Dame, 1984—, now William P. and Hazel B. White prof. arts and letters, dept. sociology, dir. Ctr. for Rsch. on Ednl. Opportunity. Assoc. editor Social Forces, 1977-80; assoc. editor Sociology of Edn., 1979-81, editor, 1981-86, session organizer, 1980, 84, 89, 92; author: the Structure of Positive Setiment, 1974; editor: The Social Organization of Schools: New Conceptualizations of the Learning Process, 1987, Restructuring Schools: Promising Practices and Policies, 1995, Handbook of the Sociology of Education, 2000; co-editor: The Social Context of Instruction: Group Organization and Group Proceses, 1983, Change in Societal Institutions, 1990;co-editor Stability and Change in American Education: Structuce, Process and Outcomes, 2003; contbr. articles to profl. jours. Mem. Am. Sociol. Assn. (pres. sociology of edn. sect. 1993-94, sec.-treas. 1988-90, chairperson 1991-92, pres. 1995-96), Sociol. Rsch. Assn. (sec.-treas. 1999-2000, pres. 2000-01), Nat. Acad. of Edn., Phi Beta Kappa. Office: U Notre Dame Dept Of Sociology Notre Dame IN 46556 Office Phone: 574-631-8294.

HALLINGBY, JO DAVIS, lawyer, arbitrator; b. N.Y.C. d. Irwin and Ruth Davis; m. Paul Hallingby Jr., Nov. 17, 1994. BA, Boston U., 1966; JD cum laude, Bklyn. Law Sch., 1973. Bar: N.Y. 1974, U.S. Ct. Appeals (2nd cir.) 1974. Legal intern counsel to chmn. N.Y.C. Planning Commn., summer 1972; law clk. Hon. John R. Bartels U.S. Dist. Judge Ea. Dist. N.Y., 1973; law clk. Hon. William C. Conner U.S. Dist. Judge So. Dist. N.Y., 1974; staff atty. Criminal Appeals Bur., Legal Aid Soc., 1974-77; asst. U.S. atty. Ea. Dist. N.Y., 1978-83; assoc. Kass, Goodkind, Wechsler & Labaton, 1977-78; litigation counsel CBS, Inc., 1983-84; N.Y. counsel Kaye, Scholer, Fierman, Hays & Handler, 1984-93; arbitrator Nat. Assn. Securities Dealers, N.Y. Stock Exch., 1994—. Mem. U.S. Commn. on Civil Rights-N.Y. State Adv. Com., 1984-86; jud. com. Assn. of the Bar of the City of N.Y., 1984-90, fed. cts. com., 1990-94; dir. Riverside Park Fund, 1986-93; ct. adv. group com. on civil litigation U.S. Dist. Ct. Ea. Dist. N.Y., 1990-95; dir. Landmarks Preservation Found., 1995—; spkr. in field. Notes editor Bklyn. Law Rev., 1972-73. Office: Nat Assn Securities Dealers NY Stock Exch 1 Sutton Pl S New York NY 10022-2471

HALLMAN, CINDA A. management consultant; BSc in Math., U. So. Ark. With DuPont, 1981—2001; CEO Spherion Corp., Ft. Lauderdale, Fla., 2001—. Bd. dirs. Toys "R" Us, Catalyst, United Way Am., Christiana Care Health Sys.; bd. trustees Christiana Care. Named CIO of Yr., Info. Week, 1995; named one of Most Influential Info. Tech. Execs. of Decade, CIO Mag., 1997; recipient Visionary award, Comm. Week, 1996. Office: Spherion Corp 2050 Spectrum Blvd Fort Lauderdale FL 33309

HALLMAN, LYNDA, medical association administrator; BA in Music Education, Indiana U. CEO Am. Coll. Heathcare Adminstrs., Alexandria, Va.; dir. profl. svcs. Am. Coll. Healthcare Adminstrs., 1989—94, dir. member svcs., 1989—94; pres. Am. Hort. Soc., Alexandria, Va.; exec. dir. Am. Med. Women's Assn., Alexandria, Va., 2002—. Office: AMWA Ste 400 801 N Fairfax St Alexandria VA 22314

HALLOCK-MULLER, PAMELA, oceanography educator, biogeologist, researcher; b. Pierre, S.D., June 2, 1948; d. Graydon B. and Marjorie L. (Millard) H.; m. Robert Glenn Muller, Aug. 22, 1969. BA in Zoology, U. Mont., 1969; MSc in Oceanography, U. Hawaii, 1972, PhD in Oceanography, 1977. Asst. prof. earth scis. U. Tex. of Permian Basin, Odessa, 1978-83, assoc. prof. marine sci. U. South Fla., St. Petersburg, 1983-88, prof., 1988—. Participant Nat. Undersea Rsch. Ctr.-Fla. Keys, Saturation Mission, 1994. Assoc. editor Jour. Foraminiferal Rsch., Washington, 1985—; mem. editl. bd. Marine Micropaleontology jour., 1990—, Geology, 1996-98; contbr. articles to sci. jours., chpt. to books. Vol. speaker Pinellas County (Fla.) Schs. Speaker Bur., 1984—, U. South Fla.-St. Petersburg Speakers Bur., 1989-95; judge local, regional, and state sci. fairs, Fla., 1989—; vol. Pinellas County Dems., St. Petersburg, 1988, 92, 96. German Acad. Exch. Svc. rsch. fellow, Kiel, Germany, 1978; summer faculty fellow NASA Goddard Space Flight Ctr., 1987; NSF rsch. grantee, 1981, 85, 87, 89, 92. Fellow Cushman Found. for Foraminiferal Rsch. (bd. dirs. 1989—, v.p. 1992, 94, pres. 1995-96), Geol. Soc. Am. (W. Storrs Cole Rsch. award 1994); mem. Paleontol. Soc., Assn. Women Geoscientists (Outstanding Educator award 1999), Soc. Sedimentary Geology (v.p. Permian Basin sect. 1982-83, paleontology councilor 1997-98), ReefKeeper Internat. (sci. advisor Coral Reefs 1988—), N.Am. Micropaleontol. Soc., Am. Acad. Underwater Scis. Democrat. Avocations: scuba diving, canoeing, natural history. Office: U South Fla Dept Marine Sci 140 7th Ave S Saint Petersburg FL 33701-5016

HALLORAN, JEAN, advocate; BA with honors, Swarthmore Coll., 1967. Rsch. dir. INFORM, 1972-79; staff mem. Pres. Carter's Coun. Environ. Quality, 1979-80; dir. regulatory info. network project Consumer Policy Inst., Yonkers, N.Y., 1981-82, dir., 1982—. Office: Consumers Union 101 Truman Ave Yonkers NY 10703-1057

HALLSTRAND, SARAH LAYMON, denomination executive; b. Nashville, Oct. 25, 1944; d. Charles Martin and Lillian Christina (Stenberg) Laymon; m. John Peter Hallstrand, July 6, 1974; 1 child, Lillian Johanna. BA cum laude, Fla. So. Coll., 1966; ThM, Boston U., 1971; D of Ministry, McCormick Theol. Sem., 1985; grad., Coll. for Fin. Planning, Denver, 1990. Ordained Am. Baptist Ch., 1976; cert. ret. counselor, fin. counselor; CFP. Dir. Christian edn. Trinity United Meth. Ch., Bradenton, Fla., 1968-70, Univ. United Meth. Ch., Syracuse, N.Y., 1971-73; assoc. min. First Bapt. Ch., Syracuse, 1973-78; pastor Oneida (N.Y.) Bapt. Ch., 1978-80; midwest rep. Mins. and Missionaries Benefit Bd., Am. Bapt. Chs., Oak Park, Ill., 1981—2002; pastor First United Meth. Ch., Tellico Plains, Tenn., 2002—03; cons. MMBB, 2002—; interim exec. min. ABCCONN, 2004. Leader ret. planning seminars Am. Bapt. Assembly, Green Lake, Wis., 1985-2002, AutumnQuest Ret. Sems., Midwest Ministry Devel. Svc., 1994—, bd. dirs., 1987-2001, chair, 1993-96; mem. rep. Midwest Ministerial Leadership Commn., Valley Forge, Pa., 1985-2002; adj. prof., pastoral care McCormick Theol. Sem., Chgo., 1986-2001; adj. prof. retirement planning The Divinity Sch., Rochester, N.Y., 1994; vis. scholar Am. Bapt. Bd. Ednl. Ministries, Valley Forge, 1986-87; bd. dirs. The Gathering Place Retreat Ctr., Gosport, Ind., 1988-95; mem. program com. and women in ministry rep. Roger Williams Fellowship, 1988-95; mem. nat. continuing edn. team Am. Bapt. Chs., Valley Forge, Pa., 1991-98; conf. leader for women's spiritual renewal weekends; spkr. in field. Contbg. author: Songs of Miriam: A Women's Book of Devotions, 1994; contbr. articles to profl. jour. including The Inclusive Pulpit Jour., 2003-2004. Mem. Fin. Planning Assn., Alpha Gamma Delta. Democrat. Home and Office: 126 Santee Way Loudon TN 37774

HALM, NANCYE STUDD, retired academic administrator; b. Jamestown, N.Y., Mar. 26, 1932; d. Thomas Howerton and Margaret Hazel (LeRoy) Neathery; m. David Philip Mack, Aug. 25, 1951 (div. 1972); children: Margaret, Jennifer, Geoffrey, Peter; m. Loris L. Studd, July 6, 1974; m. James Richard Halm, Aug. 30, 1991. BS in Edn., SUNY, Fredonia, 1954, postgrad., St. Bonaventure U. Tchr. Morning Sun (Iowa) Consolidated Schs., 1956-57, Panama (N.Y.) Cen. Schs., 1958-65, Jamestown (N.Y.) Pub. Schs., 1967-69, Olean (N.Y.) Pub. Schs., 1969-72, Jamestown Pub. Schs., 1972-73; pers. mgr. F.W. Woolworth Co., Lakewood, N.Y., 1972-79; dir. Nat. Conf. Christians & Jews, Jamestown, 1979-86; counselor N.Y. State Div. for Youth, Jamestown, 1979-89; exec. rep. Am. Bapt. Found., Valley Forge, Pa., 1989-94; adminstr. New Castle Christian Acad., 1996—2002; ret., 2002. Pastor West Pitts. United Meth. Ch., 2003—. V.p. Chautauqua County Am. Bapt. Women, 1981—90; pres. Falconer Bapt. Women, 1986—90; love gift chmn. Pitts. Bapt. Assn., 1990—91; trustee, chair endowment fund Chautauqua Bapt. Union at Chautauqua Inst., 1982—; pres. ch. coun. Wesley United Meth. Ch., 2001—; pastor W. Pitts. United Meth. Ch., 2003—; mem. nat. bd. dirs. Am. Bapt. Chs. U.S.A., Valley Forge, Pa., 1988—89. Recipient Cert. of Merit Cassadaga Job Corp, 1984. Mem. Rebekah. Democrat. Avocations: quilting, reading, crafts. Home: 1702 W Washington St New Castle PA 16101-1360

HALPER, JUNE, medical center director; Pres. Consortium Multiple Sclerosis Ctrs., 1995—97, exec. dir., 1997—; found exec. dir. Internat. Orgn. Multiple Sclerosis Nurses; founder, exec. dir. Gimbel Multiple Sclerosis Ctr., 1989—. Editor: Comprehensive Nursing Care in Multiple Sclerosis, Advanced Concepts of Nursing Care in Multiple Sclerosis; co-editor: Staying Well with Multiple Sclerosis: A Self-Care Guide. Recipient First June Halper award for Excellence in Nursing Multiple Sclerosis, Inter. Orgn. Multiple Sclerosis Nurses. Fellow: Am. Acad. Nursing; mem.: Am. Acad. Nurse Practitioners. Office: Gimnel Multiple Sclerosis Ctr 718 Teaneck Rd Teaneck NJ 07666*

HALPERIN, KRISTINE BRIGGS, insurance sales and marketing professional; b. Pocatello, Idaho, July 25, 1947; d. Fergus and Shirley (Tanner) Briggs; m. Michael Lauren Halperin, Aug. 5, 1995; children: Anthony Ted Rojas, Nancy Kristine Rojas. Student, Idaho State U., 1965-66. Tech. coord. Farmers Ins. Group, Pocatello, 1971-81; svc. rep. All Seasons Ins. Agy., Ventura, Calif., 1982; sr. comml. underwriting asst. Royal Ins. Co., Ventura, 1982-85; sr. comml. lines underwriter Andreini & Co., Ventura, 1985-88; large comml. account unit coord. Frank B. Hall, Inc., Oxnard, Calif., 1988-93; mgr. comml. lines dept. Fox Ins. Agy. Inc., Camarillo, Calif., 1993-2001; acct. mgt. Venbrook Ins. Svcs., Woodland Hills, 2001—02, Brown & Brown of Calif. DSD Ins. Agy., Thousand Oaks, 2002—03; mgr. Dick Wardlow Ins. Brokers, Moorpark, Calif., 2003—. Editor (bulletin) News Waves, 1985—; artist various works specializing in charcoal portraits. Mem. NAFE, Ins. Women Ventura County (treas. 1987-88, v.p. 1988-90, 96-97, 2001—, pres. 1990-91, 97-98, corr. sec. 1991-92, bd. dirs. 1986, Woman of Yr. 1989-90, 99-2000), Nat. Assn. Ins. Women. Republican. Baptist. Avocations: belly dancing, gardening, reading, hiking, carpentry. Home: 2197 Brookhill Dr Camarillo CA 93010-2107 Office: 233 High St Moorpark CA 93021

HALPERN, CHERYL F. federal agency administrator; BA in Political Sci., Barnard Coll.; MBA in Finance, NYU. Prodr. news and classic music programs Sta. WKCR-FM, N.Y.C.; mem. Bd. for Internat. Broadcasting U.S. Info. Agy.; apptd. mem. bd. govs. Internat. Broadcasting Bur. U.S. Info. Agy., 1995—. Coalitions chair N.J. Rep. Com.; chair Nat. Jewish Coalition; bd. dirs. Washington Inst. for Near East Policy, N.J.-Israel Commn. Mem. Anti-Defamtion League (mem. N.J. adv. bd.), Ctr. for Pub. Policy. B'nai B'rith. Office: US Info Agy Internat Broadcasting Bur Independence Ave SW Ste 3360 Washington DC 20547-0001

HALPERN, DIANE F. psychology educator, professional association executive; b. Phila. BA in psychology cum laude, U. Penn., 1969; MA in psychology, Temple U., 1973, U. Cin., 1977, PhD in psychology, 1979. Tchg. assistantship U. Cin., 1977—78, cons. behavioral scis. lab., 1978—79; lectr., dept. psychology U. Calif., Riverside, 1979—81; asst. prof. dept. psychology Calif. State U., San Bernardino, 1981—84, assoc. prof. dept. psychology, 1984—86, prof. dept. psychology, 1986—2001, chair, dept. psychology, 1996—99; dir. Berger Inst. for Work, Family, and Children Claremont McKenna Coll., 2001—, prof. psychology, 2001—. Named Scholar-in-Residence, Rockefeller Found., 1995; recipient Prof. Yr. award, C. of C., 1986, Silver Medal, Coun. Advancement and Support Edn. (CASE), 1986, Ednl. Equity award, Assn. Black Faculty and Staff, 1987, Outstanding Alumni award, U. Cin., 1988, Birkett Williams Meml. Lecture award, Ouachita Baptist U., 1992, Fulbright Scholar award, 1994, Arthur Moorefield Meml. award, 1997, Disting. Vis. Scholar award, James Madison U., 1998. Fellow: Western Psychological Assn. (pres. 1999—2000, Outstanding Tchg. award 2002), Am. Psychological Soc. (charter mem.); mem.: APA (pres. 2004, named G. Stanley Hall Lecture 1991, Disting. Career Contbns. to Edn. and Training 1996—97, Eminent Women in Psychology 1998, Am. Psychological Found. award for disting. tchg. 1998—99, fellow divsn. 1, 2, 3, 35 1989), Psychonomic Soc., Am. Assn. Higher Edn. Office: Berger Inst Work, Family, and Children Claremont McKenna Coll Dept Psychology 850 Columbia Ave Claremont CA 91711 : APA Pres's Office 750 First St NE Washington DC 20002-4242 Office Phone: 202-336-6074. Office Fax: 909-607-9647., 909-607-9672., 202-336-6157. Business E-Mail: diane.halpern@claremontmckenna.edu.*

HALPIN, ANNA MARIE, architect, writer; b. Murphysboro, Ill., July 24, 1923; d. John William and Anna Christina (Weilmuenster) H. BS in Architecture, U. Ill., 1948. Designer, project architect various firms, San Francisco, Rome, N.Y.C., 1948-67; editorial dir. Sweet's div. McGraw-Hill, Inc., N.Y.C., 1967-88, ret. Sweet's div.; freelance cons., 1988-98. Rep. to Constrn. Industries Coordination Com., Am. Nat. Metric Council, 1974-80 Mem. AIA (treas., dir. N.Y. chpt. 1974-78, coll. fellows 1976, nat. dir. 1977-79, nat. v.p. 1980, dir. Found. 1980, Richard Upjohn fellow 1991), Women's Equity Action League (pres. N.Y. state orgn. 1976-77), Constrn. Specifications Inst., Alliance Women in Architecture. Home: 1404 NW 122nd St Apt 401 Oklahoma City OK 73114-8052

HALPIN, MARGARET RENEE, music educator; b. Natrona Heights, Pa., June 21, 1968; d. Nancy Jane and Joseph John Mellish; m. Martin David Halpin, June 29, 2002. MusB, W.Va. U., Morgantown, W.Va., 1986—89. Cert. Music Edn. K-12 W.Va., 1989, NC, 1990, Pa, 1991, Early/Middle Childhood Music Edn. Nat. Bd. for Profl. Tchg. Standards, 2002. Music tchr. Rockingham County Schools, Stoneville, NC, 1990; music tchr./choral dir. Monongalia County Schools, Morgantown, W.Va., 1990; pvt. music instr. Self-employed, Greensboro, NC, 1990—. Com. chair Stoneville Elem. Arts Com., Stoneville, NC, 1997—; dir. After Sch. Arts Enrichment Program, Stoneville, NC, 1997—; dept. chair Stoneville Elem. Leadership Team, Stoneville, NC, 2000—; co-chair Elem. All County Chorus, Eden, NC, 2003—. Dir.: (workshop) Integrating Art Into The Curriculum; editor: (publication) The Artribune, 2000—. Merit badge counselor Boy Scouts of Am., Stoneville, NC, 2002. Recipient Outstanding Young Educator Award Nominee, Stoneville Elem. Sch., 1995-1996, Tchr. of the Yr., 1997-1998, Who's Who Among America's Teachers, Ednl. Comm., Inc, 2002; grantee Grass Roots Grant, Rockingham County Arts Coun., 1994—2001. Mem.: NEA, NC Assn. of Educators, NC Music Educators Assn., Music Educators Nat. Conf. Avocations: piano, flute, scuba diving, skiing. Office: Stoneville Elementary School 203 Stone Street Stoneville NC 27048

HALPIN, MARY ELIZABETH, psychologist; b. Oak Park, ILl., June 4, 1951; d. Thomas Joseph and Rita Helen (Foley) H. BA, Marquette U., 1973, MEd, 1975, PhD, 1983. Lic. psychologist Ill., Calif., cert. sch. psychologist Ill. Staff psychologist Milw. Children's Hosp., 1975-83; postdoctoral intern El Dorado County Mental Health Ctr., Placerville, Calif., 1983-84; psychologist Inst. for Motivational Devel., Lombard, Ill., 1985-88; psychologist, founder, gen. ptnr. Assocs. for Adolescent Achievement, Deerfield, Ill., 1989-94; pvt. practice psychology, Deerfield, 1995—; sch. psychologist Winnetka (Ill.) Dist. 36, 2000—. Presenter Internat. Sch. Beijing, 1998. TV appearance Oprah Winfrey Show, 1995. Chmn., mem. peer rev. com. Charter Barclay Hosp., Chgo., 1991-93. Mem.: AAUW, APA, Ill. Psychol. Assn. (standing hearing panel ethics com. 1993, pub. rels. com. 1994, chair pub. rels. com. 1999—2002, area code rep. 1999—2002, pres.-elect 2002, pres. 2003). Office: 420 Lake Cook Rd Ste 109 Deerfield IL 60015-4914

HALPRIN, ANNA SCHUMAN (MRS. LAWRENCE HALPRIN), dancer; b. Wilmette, Ill., July 13, 1920; d. Isadore and Ida (Schiff) Schuman; m. Lawrence Halprin, Sept. 19, 1940; children: Daria, Rana. Student, Bennington Summer Sch. Dance, 1938-39; BS in Dance, U. Wis., 1943; PhD in Human Services (hon.), Sierra U., 1987; PhD (hon.), U. Wis., 1994, Santa Clara U.; student, Calif. Arts Coll., Calif., 2003; PhD (hon.), Art Instit. of San Francisco, Calif., 2003. Presenter opening invocation State of the World Forum by spl. invitation from Mikhail S. Gorbachev. Author: Moving Toward Life, Five Decades of Transformative Dance, Dance as a Healing Art, A Teachers' Guide and Support Manual for People with Cancer; performances at Kennedy Ctr., Washington, Yerba Buena Ctr. for Arts, San Francisco, Joyce Theatre, NYC, 2001-; 80th yr. retrospective performance Cowell Theatre, Returning Home Video - Moving with the Earth Body, Learning Lessons in Life, Loss & Liberation, 2003, Intensive Care, Reflections on Death and Dying, 2003, San Francisco, numerous other performances and publs. Bd. dirs. East West Holistic Healing Inst.; mem. Gov.'s Coun. on Phys. Fitness and Wellness. Recipient award Am. Dance Guild, 1980, Guggenheim award, 1970-71, Woman of Wisdom award Bay Area Profl. Women's Network, Tchr. of Yr. award Calif. Tchrs. Assn., 1988, Lifetime Achievement award in visual and performing arts San Francisco Bay Guardian newspaper, 1990, Women of Achievement, Vision and Excellence award, 1992, Balasaraswati/Joy Ann Dewey Bieneke chair for disting. tchg. Am. Dance Festival, 1996, Lifetime Achievement in Modern Dance award Am. Dance Festival, 1997, Lifetime Achievement award Calif. Arts Coun., 2000, Breast Cancer Watch, 2001, Dance Mag. N.Y.C. award, 2004; Person of Yr. in field of Dance award Ballet-ranz, Berlin; named to Isadora Duncan Hall of Fame, Bay Area Dance Coalition, 1986; Nat. Endowment Arts Choreographers grantee, 1976, NEA choreography grantee, 1977, San Francisco Found. grantee, 1981, Calif. Arts. Coun. grantee, 1990—; inductee Marin Women's Hall of Fame, 1998, lifetime achievement award Marin Arts Coun. Fellow Am. Expressive Therapy Assn.; mem. Assn. Am. Dance, Conscientious Artists Am., San Francisco C. of C. Home and Office: 15 Ravine Way Kentfield CA 94904-2713 E-mail: anna@annahalprin.org.

HALSBAND, FRANCES, architect; b. N.Y.C., Oct. 30, 1943; d. Samuel and Ruth H.; m. Robert Michael Kliment, May 1, 1971; 1 child, Alexander H. BA, Swarthmore Coll., 1965; MArch, Columbia U., 1968. Registered architect, N.Y., N.J., Mass., Conn., Ohio, Va., N.H., Pa., D.C., N.C., Ill., Miss., La., Fla.; cert. Nat. Coun. Archtl. Reg. Bds. Arch. Mitchell/Giurgola Archs., N.Y.C., 1968-72; ptnr. R.M. Kliment & Frances Halsband Archs., N.Y.C., 1972—. Vis. critic archtl. design Columbia U., 1975-78, 87, N.C. State U., 1978, Rice U., 1979, U. Va., 1980, Harvard U., 1981, U. Pa., 1981, U. Calif., Berkeley, 1997; dean Sch. Architecture, Pratt Inst., 1991-94; Freidman prof. U. Calif., Berkeley, 1997; Emens Disting. prof. Ball State U., 1998; Kea prof. U. Md., 2000; mem. N.Y.C. Landmarks Preservation Commn., 1984-87; lectr. U. So. Calif., U. Va., Temple U., Washington U., Tulane U., Harvard U., U. Oreg., U. Washington. Projects include: computer Sci. Bldg., Columbia U. (AIA Nat. Honor award 1987), Gilmer Hall addition U. Va., Town Hall, Salisbury Conn., Computer Sci. Bldg., Princeton U. (AIA Nat. Honor award 1994), Case Western Res. Adelbert Hall restoration (AIA Nat. Honor award 1994), Alvin Ailey Am. Dance Theater Found., N.Y.C., hdqs. Marsh & McLennan Co., Ind. Bank Hdqs., Bklyn. Coll. Master Plan, Entrance Pavillion L.I. Rail Rd. Penn Sta. (AIA Nat. award), U.S. Courthouse and Post Office, Bklyn., Yale Div. Sch., Dartmouth Roth Ctr. for Jewish Life, U.S. Courthouse, Gulfport, Miss.; works exhibited in Cooper-Hewitt Mus., Bklyn. Mus., Nat. Acad. Design, Deutsches Architekturmuseum, Frankfourt; author: Annotated Bibliography of Technical Resources for Small Museums, 1983. Trustee Nat. Inst. Archtl. Edn., 1988-93; mem. archtl. rev. panel Fed. Res. Sys., 1993—; mem. U.S. Dept. State Office Fgn. Bldgs. Ops. Archtl. Adv. Bd., 1998—; U.S. Gen. Svcs. Adminstrn. Nat. Register Peer Profls., 1998—. Fellow AIA (exec. bd. N.Y.C. chpt. 1979, pres. N.Y.C. chpt. 1991-92), Century Assn.; mem. Archtl. League N.Y. (exec. bd. 1975—, v.p. arch. 1981-85, pres. 1985-89), Assn. Collegiate Schs. Architecture (N.E. regional dir. 1993-95). Office: RM Kliment & Frances Halsband 255 W 26th St New York NY 10001-8001

HALSEY, MARTHA TALIAFERRO, Spanish language educator; b. Richmond, Va., May 5, 1932; d. James Dillard and Martha (Taliaferro) H. AB, Goucher Coll., 1954; MA, U. Iowa, 1956; PhD, Ohio State U., 1964. Asst. prof. Spanish, Pa. State U., Univ. Pk., 1964-70, assoc. prof., 1970-79, prof., 1979-95, prof. emeritus, 1995—. Vis. Olive B. O'Connor prof. lit. Colgate U., Hamilton, NY, 1983. Author: Antonio Buero Vallejo, 1973, Dictatorship to Democracy: the Recent Plays of Buero Vallejo (La Fundación to Música cercana), 1994; editor: Madrugada, 1969, Hoy es fiesta, 1978, Los inocentes de la Moncloa, 1980, El engañao, Caballos desbocaos, 1981, (with Phyllis Zatlin) The Contemporary Spanish Theater: A Collection of Critical Essays, 1988, Entre actos: Diálogos sobre teatro español entre siglos, 1999, Estreno, 1992-98; gen. editor Estreno Contemporary Spanish Plays, 1992-98, Estreno Studies in Contemporary Spanish Theater, 1998—; mem. editl bd. Modern Internat. Drama, 1968-75, Ky. Romance Quar., 1970-76, Annals Contemporary Spanish Lit., 1991—, Tesserae: Jour. Iberian and Latin Am. Studies, 1997—; contbr. articles to profl. jours. Grantee Am. Philos. Soc., 1970, 78, Inst. for Arts and Humanistic Studies, 1977, Program Cultural Coop. Between Spanish Ministry Culture and U.S. Univs., 1992, 94-95. Fellow Hispanic Soc. Am. (hon.); mem. MLA, N.E. MLA, Am. Assn. Tchrs. Spanish and Portuguese, Fellowship of Reconciliation, War Resisters League, Phi Beta Kappa, Phi Sigma Iota, Sigma Delta Pi. Democrat. Episcopalian. Home: 500 E Marylyn Ave Apt I-140 State College PA 16801-5248 Office: Pa State U Dept Spanish University Park PA 16802

HALSNE-BAARDA, ALANA MICHELLE, secondary school educator; b. Park Ridge, Ill., Nov. 18, 1971; d. Howard Osmund and Karen Diane Halsne; m. Brent Eric Baarda, May 31, 2002. BS, Ariz. State U., 1993; MA, Northeastern Ill. U., Chgo., 1998; EdD, Loyola U. Chgo., 2002. Cert. tchr., sch. adminstr. Ill. Tchr. Wickenburg H.S., Ariz., 1994—95; summer sch. tchr. Adlai E. Stevenson H.S., Lincolnshire, Ill., 1996—2002, Dist. 211/Palatine H.S., Ill., 2003; adj. prof. Am. Intercontinental U., Hoffman Estates, Ill., 2003—, Coll. of Lake County, Grayslake, Ill., 1997—; tchr. Warren Twp. H.S. #121, Gurnee, Ill., 1995—. Textbook reviewer Thomson Pub., Mason, Ohio, 2002—. Contbr. articles to profl. jours. Dance tchr. Granwood Pk. Dist., Gurnee, 1996—97; swim coach Gurnee Pk. Dist., 1996—; Sun. sch. tchr. St. Gilbert Ch., Grayslake, 2000. Mem.: ASCD, Nat. Bus. Edn. Assn., Phi Delta Kappa. Republican. Roman Catholic. Avocation: scuba diving. Office: Warren Twp High Sch 500 N O'Plaine Rd Gurnee IL 60031

HALSTEAD, TRAZANNA, newscaster; b. Heidleberg, Germany; BS Broadcast Journalism and English, Syracuse U. Reporter, anchor Jazz88 Radio, WEEK-TV, Peoria, Ill., KEYE-TV, Austin, Tex., 1997—99; reporter KPRC TV, Houston, 2000—. Spkr. in field. Fellow Michelle Carlk fellow for Minority News Profls., Radio and Television News Dirs. Assn., 1998. Avocations: exercise, dance, reading. Office: KPRC TV PO Box 2222 Houston TX 77252-2222

HALTEMAN HARWELL, BETH, state legislator; b. Norriwtown, Pa., July 24, 1957; married; 2 children. BA, David Lipscomb U.; MS, George Peabody Coll.; PhD, Vanderbilt U. Mem. Tenn. State Legis. Republican. Office: 107 War Meml Bldg Nashville TN 37243 also: 42 Wyn Oak Nashville TN 37205-5001

HALUPOWSKI, RACHEL ELIZABETH, fundraising campaign administrator; b. Berlin, Germany, Aug. 22, 1966; d. Sue and Paul Halupowski. BA in English, Oreg. State U., Corvallis, 1989. Cert. tchr. Oreg., Alaska. Logistics coord. Market Strategies, Inc., Portland, Oreg., 1997—98; adminstrv. asst., senate rules and elections and pub. affairs coms. Oreg. State Legislature, Salem, Oreg., 1999; adminstrv. asst. Dotten & Assocs., Portland, 1999—2000; fundraising campaign adminstr. Jewish Fedn. Portland, Portland, Oreg., 2000—. Contbr. poems to anthologies. Mem.: Women of Reform Judaism/Beth Israel Sisterhood (sec. and publicist 1997—2000, chair critical issues com. 2001—04), Epilepsy Found. Oreg. (bd. dirs. at large 2003—), Phi Eta Sigma. Democrat. Jewish. Avocations: singing, writing poetry, study, travel, volunteerism. Office: Jewish Fedn Portland 6680 SW Capitol Hwy Portland OR 97219 E-mail: rachelh@jewishportland.org.

HALVORSON, JUDITH ANNE (JUDITH ANNE DEVAUD), elementary school educator; b. Bethesda, Md., Apr. 28, 1943; d. Henri J. and Mary L. (Baumgart) Devaud; m. Peter L. Halvorson, Feb. 4, 1964; 1 child, Peter Chase. BS in Edn., U. Cin., 1965; MA in Edn., U. Conn., 1974, Cert. Advanced Grad. Study in Edn., 1980, postgrad. in French, 2003—. Tchr. Greenhills-Forest Park (Ohio) City Schs., 1965-67, Weld County Schs., Greeley, Colo., 1969-70, Chaplin (Conn.) Elem. Sch., 1970-2000; ret., 2000. Mentor Beginning Educator Support program State of Conn. and Chaplin Elem. Sch., 1988-2000; supr. student tchrs. East Conn. State U., U. Conn., U. No. Colo., 1969-2000. Past vice-chmn., past chmn., past sec. Coventry (Conn.) Bd. Edn., 1981-95; chmn. Coventry Sch. Bldg. com., 1981-92, Coventry Parks and Recreation Com., 1980-82, chmn., 1982; mem. Dem. Town Com. Coventry, 1973-98. Grantee, Nat. Sci. Edn. project, 1977-78; named Outstanding Elem. Tchr. Am., 1974; recipient Citation for Cmty. Leadership, Nat. Women's History Month, 1991; recognized for svc. to pub. edn. in Conn., Conn. Assn. Bds. of Edn., 1993, 94, 95, for contbns. to Conn., Beginning Educator Support and Tng. program Conn. State Dept. Edn., 1991-93, for svc. to cooperating tchr. programs Ea. Conn. State U., 1993, 95, for Outstanding Svc. to Pub. Edn., State of Conn., 1995. Mem. NEA (life), Conn. Edn. Assn. (life), Chaplin Edn. Assn. (past pres., v.p., chmn. negotiations 1970-2000), Assn. Ret. Tchrs. Conn., Pi Lambda Theta (past pres., v.p., chmn. membership Beta Sigma chpt. 1974—), Phi Delta Kappa. Episcopalian. Avocations: swimming, skiing, golf, leisure travel, French language and culture. Home: 90 David Dr Coventry CT 06238-1320 E-mail: jandphalvorson@msn.com.

HALVORSON, MARJORY, opera director; Pvt. studies with, Sister Marietta Coyle, Jerry Daniels, Dolores Ravich. Dir. vocal studies Whitworth Coll., Spokane; artistic dir. Spokane Opera, Spokane. Dir. vocal master classes iwth Thomas Hampson, Richard Miller, Dale Moore, John Shirley-Quirk, James Maddalena, Armen Guzlimien; tchr. pvt. lesons in voice, vocal pedagogy, diction and lit.; director opera workshop. Named Woman of Achievement in Arts and Culture, City of Spokane, 1996; recipient outstanidng cmty. svc. award Westminster United Ch. of Christ. Office: Spokane Opera 643 S Ivory St Spokane WA 99202-2362

HALVORSON, MARY ELLEN, education educator, writer; b. Salem, Ohio, Apr. 23, 1950; d. Robert J. and Betty June (Bear) Batzli; m. Thomas Henry Halvorson, June 10, 1972; children: Christine Lynn, Matthew Thomas, Rebecca Lynn. BS in Edn. with distinction, No. Ariz. U., 1972, postgrad., 1973-92, U. Ariz., 1974-76, Ariz. State U., 1975-76, U. Phoenix, 1989-90; PhD in Edn., Calif. Coast U., 2001. Cert. Supt. Ariz., 2001, elem. tchr. libr. Ariz. Tchr. Prescott (Ariz.) Unified Schs., 1972-77, dir. community nature ctr., 1978, reading tutor, 1985-88, family math. tchr., 1989-90, part-time libr., 1991-92; dir. Prescott Study Ctr., 1987-90; writer ednl. materials Herald House, Independence, Mo., 1994—; instr. Yavapai C.C., 1994-96; edn. coord. Yavapai Prescott Indian Tribe, 1996-98; tchr. Prescott Unified Sch. Dist., 1998—99; supt. Tri-City Prep. H.S., 1999—. Guest speaker Abia Judd Young Authors, Prescott, 1992; math. enthusiast instr. Ariz. Dept. Edn., Prescott, 1989-92; asst. instr. outdoor edn. Ariz. State U., Prescott, 1977-78; tutor English grammar No. Ariz. U., Flagstaff, 1971-72; presenter, U. Oxford (Eng.) Round Table, 2003. Co-author: Arizona Bicentenial Resource Manual, 1975; contbr. book rev. column to Prescott Courier, 1993, also articles to profl. publs. Cert. adult instr. Temple Sch., Independence, Mo., 1985—; sec., bd. dirs. Whispering Pines, Prescott, 1989-93; music docent Prescott Symphony Guild, 1982-85; state Christian edn. dir. Cmty. of Christ. Ch., Ariz., 1977-82, elder, counselor to pastor, 1993—; spokesperson Franklin Heights Homeowners, Prescott, 1985; leader Prescott Pioneers 4-H Club, 1989—, Christian Youth Group, 1985—; fundraiser Graceland Coll., 1993; craft demonstrator Sharlott Hall Mus.; master of ceremonies Prescott Summer Pops Symphony, 1995, 97. Recipient 4-H Silver Clover Svc. award, 1995; named Outstanding Young Educator, Prescott Jaycees, 1976, Outstanding Young Women of Am., 1985. Mem. Phi Kappa Phi, Kappa Delta Pi, Sigma Epsilon Sigma. Avocations: teaching piano, sewing costumes for school musical groups, oil painting. Home: 2965 Pleasant Valley Dr Prescott AZ 86305-7116

HALWIG, NANCY DIANE, banker; b. Rochester, NY, Sept. 17, 1954; d. Norman Charles and Elizabeth Marie (Callemyn) Graupman; m. John Michael Halwig, June 14, 1975; children: Courtney Elizabeth, John Christopher. BA in Elem. Edn. with honors, Goucher Coll., 1975; M. Mgmt. in Fin., Northwestern U., 1979. Br. adminstrv. mgmt. trainee Md. Nat. Bank, Balt., 1975-76; comml. banking officer Am. Nat. Bank Chgo., 1976-80; v.p. relationship mgr. Citicorp USA-Chgo., 1980-85; v.p., team leader Citicorp N.Am., Atlanta, 1985-89, v.p. region credit officer, 1986-90; v.p., regional mgr. Kredietbank-Atlanta, 1990-95; regional v.p. Bank of Am., FSB, Atlanta, 1995-96, sr. v.p., 1996-98; regional mktg. mgr., sr. v.p. Congress Fin. Corp., a Wachovia Co., Atlanta, 1999—2003. Contbns. com. Citicorp, Chgo., Atlanta, 1984-90; sec. S.W. Cobb Allergy and Asthma, P.C., 1989-97. Fin. com. Big Bros./Big Sisters, Atlanta, 1987-91; mem. leadership forum Scottish Rite Hosp., Atlanta, 1988-92; contbns. contact Scitrek Mus., Atlanta, 1988-90, mem. pres.'s coun., 1990-91; steering com. N.W. Ga. Girl Scouts Friendship Circle, 1993-94, active Friendship Circle, 1993—, Juliette Low assoc., 1998—; troop treas. Girl Scouts U.S., 1994-96; sustainer Atlanta Women's Fund, 1995-2003; co-chair Atlanta Women in Fin., 1999. Named one of Atlanta Women to Watch, Atlanta Bus. Chronicle, 1988, Women Looking Ahead News Mag.'s WLA 100's List of Ga.'s Most Powerful Women in Banking & Fin., 1999, 2000, 2001. Mem. Fin. Women Internat. (Paragon Cir., futures com. 1996-97, nominating com. 1997-98), Nat. Assn. Bank Women (found. trustee 1984-85, treas. found. 1985-86, bd. dirs. and chmn. fin. com. 1987-88, chmn. task force on child care financing alternatives, restructuring task force 1988-89, nat. conf. program chmn. 1991-92), Aux. Am. Coll. Allergy, Asthma and Immunology, Women's Fin. Exch. (founding bd. dirs.), Atlanta C. of C. (bd. advisors), Atlanta Venture Forum, Assn. Corp. Growth (bd. dirs. 2000—, chpt. pres. 2003-04, global awards chair 2004—), ACG Capital Connection Conf. (chair 2003, exec. planning com. 2004), Turnaround Mgmt. Assn., Comml. Fin. Assn. (bd. dirs. 2002-03), Northwestern U. Club Atlanta, Vinings Village Women's Club (pres. 2000-01), Phi Beta Kappa. Republican. Avocations: strength training, swimming, running. Home: 4400 Woodland Brook Dr NW Atlanta GA 30339-5365 Business E-Mail: ndhalwig@aol.com.

HAM, ARLENE H. state legislator; b. Belle Fourche, S.D., Aug. 1, 1936; widowed; 2 children. Owner, broker Real Estate bus.; chmn. S.D. Rep. Party, 1985-87; with Rep. Nat. Com., 1988-96; mem. S.D. Senate from 32nd dist., Pierre, 1996—. Bd. dirs. Luth. Social Svcs., U.S. West. Mem. 4-H Found., Wellspring. Mem. Nat. Realtors Assn., State Realtors Assn., Rapid City Realtors Assn. (bd. dirs.), Zonta Mental Health Assn., Vet. Bd. Examiners, S.D. Lottery Commn., S.D. Racing Commn., Rapid City C. of C. (Aethena award), Toastmistress. Republican. Lutheran. Home: 1116 Crestridge Ct Rapid City SD 57701-5381 Office: State Capitol Bldg Dist 32 500 E Capitol Ave Pierre SD 57501-5070

HAM, BONNIE DAVIS, state legislator; b. Woodstock, N.H., Oct. 5, 1947; d. Milton Alton and Doris (Baker) Davis; children: Jonathan A., Jarrett M. BE, Plymouth State Coll., 1969, MBA, 1982. Town clk. City of Woodstock, 1970-74, mem. budget com., 1974-86, mem. planning bd., 1974-92; pres., treas. Linwood Med. Ctr., 1976—; mem. budget com. Lincoln/Woodstock Coop. Sch. Dist., 1986—; pres. North Country Coun. (formerly Lincoln Woodstock Housing), 1989—, Jane's House, 1989—; mem. N.H. Ho. of Reps., 1993—. Mem. ways and means com. N.H. Ho. of Reps., 1993—, mem. sci., tech. and energy com. N.H. Ho. Reps.; bd. dirs. N.H. Assn. Regulated Planning Commn. Mem. N.H. Mcpl. Assn. (pres. 1986, bd. dirs. 1982-93), Bus. and Profl. Women's Club (Woman of Yr. 1987), Rotary Club (sec. 1987—). Republican. Address: PO Box 444 North Woodstock NH 03262-0444

HAM, KAREN, musician, music educator; b. Bklyn., Apr. 13, 1952; d. Irving and Eva (Walker) H. AA, Staten Island Coll., 1974; BA, CUNY, 1978; MA, NYU, 1983; student in piano, French Conservatory Music, N.Y.C., 19905. Tchr. Assn. Black Social Workers, Bklyn., 1978-85, Bklyn. Music Sch., 1985-87; tchr., condr. Holy Innocents Sch., Bklyn., 1985—. Dir. choir and music ensemble, keyboard classes. Roman Catholic. Avocations: research of american songwriters, american musical films. Office: Holy Innocents Sch 249 E 17th St Brooklyn NY 11226-4601

HAMAMOTO, PATRICIA, school system administrator, educator; b. Honolulu, Sept. 30, 1944; BA in History, profl. tchg. diploma, Calif. State Coll., Long Beach, 1967; education administrator's cert., U. Hawaii M, 1985. Social studies tchr. Fountain Valley (Calif.) H.S., 1967—72; social studies tchr., dept. chair Iiima Intermediate Sch., Ewa Beach, Hawaii, 1976—81; tchg. grad. asst. geography dept. U. Hawaii at Manoa, 1981—83; tchr. guidance/math. Pearl City H.S., Hawaii, 1985; vice prin. Maui H.S., Kahlui, Hawaii, 1983—85, Nanakul H.S. and Intermediate Sch, Nanakuli, Hawaii, 1985—87; prin. Pearl City Highlands Elem. Sch, Hawaii, 1987—89; pers. specialist ii Office Personnel Svcs. Contract Adminstrn., Honolulu, 1989—91; prin. Pres. William McKinley H.S., Honolulu, 1992—99; dep. supt. Hawaii Dept. Edn., Honolulu, 1999—2001, interim supt., 2001; supt. Hawaii Dept Edn., Honolulu, 2001—. Mem.: ASCD, Pacific Resources for Edn. and Learning, Coun. of Chief State Sch. Officers, Nat. Assn. Secondary Sch. Prins. Avocations: golf, reading, travel, walking. Home: 1767 Puowaina Dr Honolulu HI 96813 Office: Hawaiian Dept Edn 1390 Miller St #307 Honolulu HI 96813 Office Phone: 808-586-3310. E-mail: patricia_hamamoto@notes.k12.hi.us.

HAMARMAN, STEPHANIE, psychiatrist, educator; b. Phila., Jan. 23, 1964; d. Harry H. and Anne C. H.; m. Stuart Lee Goldberg, Aug. 16, 1998. BA, U. Pa., 1985, MD, 1993. Instr. psychiatry Hosp. U. Pa., 1993-96, Children's Hosp. Phila., 1996-98; med. dir. outpatient child & adolscent psychiatry N.J. Med. Sch., Newark, 1998—, asst. prof. psychiatry, 1998—. Co-author: (chpt.) Child Abuse, 2000; contbr. articles to profl. jours. Recipient Child Psychiatry award Group Advancement Psychiatry, 1997-98. Mem. Am. Acad. Child and Adolscent Psychiatry (prevention com. 2000—, task force child rsch. 1998-2000, Resident Leadership Achievement award 1995, scholar 1997-98, rsch. grantee for child rsch. 2001), Am. Acad. Psychiatry and Law (Rappeport com. 2000—), Am. Psychiat. Assn., Am. Profl. Soc. on Abuse of Children, Am. Assn. Acad. Psychiatry (Rappeport fellow 1996-97), Nat. Assn. Counsel for Children, N.J. Psychiat. and Child Psychiatris Assn. Office: NJ Med Sch 183 S Orange Ave UBHC C1404 Newark NJ 07103 E-mail: hamarmst@umdnj.edu.

HAMATY, JULIE ARMBRUSTER, secondary school educator; b. Denver, Apr. 16, 1962; d. Robert Joseph Armbruster and Margaret Ann Overholt; m. Jose M. Otero; 1 child, Amanda Ryan Otero. BA in Spanish cum laude, Rowan U., 1993. Cert. Spanish, elem. edn. tchr. N.J. ESL instr. C.E.E. Lang. Acad., Madrid, 1982—85, 1993—94; gifted and talented Spanish tchr. Vineland (N.J.) Pub. Schs., 1994—97; tchr. Vineland H.S. North, 1997—2001, Oakcrest H.S., Mays Landing, NJ, 2001—03, Atlantic City H.S., 2003. Mem. world lang. core curriculum adv. com. Vineland Pub. Schs., 1996—99; co-advisor Spanish Club Vineland H.S. North, 1997—99, AVID site team mem., 1998—2001, AVID program team lead tchr., 1999—2000, mem. World Lang.-spl. edn. adv. com., 2000—01, mem. pub. rels. com., 2000—01, mem. staff activities com., 2001. Leader Girl Scouts Am., Atlantic County, NJ, 1997—99; Sunday sch. tchr. Absecon (N.J.) Presbyn. Ch., 1996—97, 1999—2001; vacation Bible sch. advisor Cmty. Bible Sch., Absecon, 1998—. Fellow: Fgn. Lang. Educators N.J. Republican. Presbyterian. Avocations: travel, music, theater, reading. Home: 133 Sussex Pl Galloway NJ 08205-3655

HAMBLY, ANN ALLE, appliance company executive; b. Downey, Calif., June 26, 1957; d. William Bathe and Patricia (Tolzman) Ware; m. Stephen Ray Johnson, July 22, 1975 (div. 1984); children: Jeremy Johnson, Nicholas Johnson; m. Douglas Brent Hambly, Aug. 15, 1987. BA, La Salle U., 1984. Loan servicing agt. Director's Mortgage, Riverside, Calif., 1980-84; v.p. Cambridge Capital, Santa Ana, Calif., 1984-87; sr. v.p. Farwest Savings, Newport Beach, Calif., 1987-91, Bank of Am., L.A., 1991-95; chief operating officer GE, Houston, 1995—. Author: Trends in Commercial Real Estate Securitizations, 1997; contbr. article to profl. jour. Bd. dirs. Multi-family Housing Inst., 1997—. Mem. Comml. Securitization & Secondary Market Assn. (bd. dirs., gov. 1996—), Real Estate Capital Resources Assn. (chmn. 1994-96). Office: GE 363 N Sam Houston Pkwy E Houston TX 77060-2404

HAMBRECHT, PATRICIA G. retail executive; b. New Orleans; m. George A. Hambrect; children: Amanda, Elliot. B summa cum laude in History, Yale Coll., 1975; JD, Harvard U., 1978. Assoc. Hughes Hubbard and Reed; gen. counsel Christie's, 1988—95, mng. dir., 1995—97; pres. Christie's North and South Am., 1997—99, Harry Winston Inc., 2000—. Bd. dir. Internat. Found. of Art Rsch. Vol. Lawyers for the Arts; bd. dirs. N.Y.C. Ballet. Avocations: theater, ballet, opera, collecting 19th and 20th century drawings.*

HAMBRICK, ERNESTINE, retired colon and rectal surgeon; b. Griffin, Ga., Mar. 31, 1941; d. Jack Daniel and Nannie (Harper) Hambrick Rubens. BS, U. Md., 1963; MD, U. Ill., 1967. Diplomate Am. Bd. Colon and Rectal Surgery, Am. Bd. Surgery. Intern in surgery Cook County Hosp., Chgo., 1967-68, resident in gen. surgery, 1968-72, fellow colon and rectal surgery, 1972-73, attending surgeon, 1973-74, part-time attending surgeon, 1974-80; pvt. practice colon and rectal surgery Chgo., 1974-97; pres. med. staff Michael Reese Hosp., Chgo., 1990-92, chief surgery, 1993-95; founder, chmn. STOP Colon/Rectal Cancer Found., 1997—. Mem. Nat. Colorectal Cancer Round Table, 1997—, steering com. 2000—. Contbr. articles to profl. jours. Trustee Rsch. and Edn. Found., Michael Reese Med. Staff, Chgo., 1994-98, treas., 1994-98. Mem. ACS, Am. Soc. Colon and Rectal Surgeons (v.p. 1992-93, trustee Rsch. Found. 1992-98), Am. Coll. Gastroenterology. Avocations: travel, photography, scuba diving, flying, writing. Office: PMB 133 47 W Division St Chicago IL 60610 E-mail: ehcrsone@aol.com.

HAMBRICK, MYRA JEAN, musician, poet; b. Jan. 6, 1952; d. Frederick Levere and Ella Mae (Roberts) H. BA in English, Dillard U., 1974; MA in English, U. New Orleans, 1981. Scriptwriter for Fantastics, 1970-73; title I reading tchr. Pointe Coupee Sch. Bd., 1974-77; lit. music artist, cons. Rosenwald Elem. Sch., New Roads, 1998—. Cons. Dillard Writers Workshop; represented Dillard U. at Boston Poetry Symposium, 1972; guest lectr. So. U., New Orleans, 1978; television appearances Kutztown, Pa., 1973, New Orleans, 1973, 74. Contbr. poems to lit. publs. Recipient Deep South Writers and Artist Conf. Poetry and Fiction award, 1970-72, New Orleans br. Nat. Assn. Coll. Women Creative Writing awards, 1970-72. Mem. Acad. Am. Poets, NAACP (honored achievement), J.K. Haynes Found., Newman Club, Lambda Iota Tau. Democrat. Roman Catholic. Avocations: gardening, reading. Home: 108 St Jude St New Roads LA 70760-3720

HAMBURG, MARGARET ANN (PEGGY HAMBURG), public health administrator; b. Chgo., July 12, 1955; d. David Alan and Beatrix Ann (Mc Cleary) H.; m. Peter Fitzhugh Brown, May 23, 1992; children: Rachel Ann Hamburg Brown, Evan David Addison Brown. BA magna cum laude, Harvard/Radcliffe Coll., 1978; MD, Harvard, 1983. Diplomate Am. Bd. Internal Medicine, Nat. Bd. Med. Examiners. Intern, resident in internal medicine The N.Y. Hosp., Cornell Med. Coll., N.Y.C., 1983-86; spl. asst. to the dir., office of disease prevention and health promotion, office of the asst. sec. for health U.S. Dept. Health and Human Svcs., Washington, 1986-88; spl. asst. to the dir. Nat. Inst. Allergy and Infectious Diseases, NIH, Bethesda, Md., 1988-89, asst. dir., 1989-90; deputy commr. Family Health Svcs., N.Y.C. Dept. Health, N.Y.C., 1990-91; commr. of health N.Y.C. Dept. Health, N.Y.C., 1991-97; asst. sec. planning and evaluation U.S. Dept.

HHS, Washington, 1997—2001; v.p. biological programs Nuclear Threat Initiative, Washington, 2001—. Guest investigator The Rockefeller U., N.Y.C., 1985-86; clin. instr. dept. medicine Georgetown U. Sch. Medicine, Washington, 1986-90; asst. prof. clin. pub. health Columbia U. Sch. Pub. Health, N.Y.C., 1991-97; adj. asst. prof. medicine Cornell U. Med. Coll., N.Y.C., 1991-97; scholar Pub. Health Leadership Inst. Ctr. for Disease Control U. Calif., 1992; bd. dirs. N.Y.C. Health Systems Agy., Med. and Health Rsch. Assn., Health Hosps. Corp, Nat. Coun. on Women's Health, Primary Care Devel. Corp.; steering com. women and aids NIH, 1991; bd. govs. Greater N.Y. Hosp. Assn., 1991-97; mem. bd. sci. advisors. Nat. Pub. Radio, 1992-97; com. mem. on substance abuse mental health issues in aides rsch., 1993; advisory bd. mem. Medunsa Trust, Inc., Med. U. So. Africa, 1993-97; mem. defense sci. bd. task force on Gulf War Syndrome U.S. Dept. Defense, 1993—; bd. mem. sci. counselors Nat. Ctr. Infectious Diseases, U.S. Ctrs. for Disease, 1994-97. Editorial bd. mem. Jour. N.Y. Acad. Sci., 1992-97, The Bull. of N.Y. Acad. Medicine, 1992-97, Current Reviews in Pub. Health, 1993-97; contbr. to numerous profl. jours. Vol. attending physician The Washington Free Clinic, Washington, 1988-90; coun. fgn. rels. bd. overseers Harvard U., 1999—. Recipient commendation Pub. Health Svc., 1988, 90, Spl. Recognition award Pub. Health Svc., 1990, cert. of Honor The Women's Club of N.Y., 1993, N.Y. Rotary Club award, 1993, Robert F. Wagner Pub. Svc. award NYU, 1993. Fellow AAAS (med. scis. section com. 1989—), ACP; mem. APHA, Am. Med. Women's Assn., Nat. Acad. Scis., Coun. on Fgn. Rels., Health Care Exec. Forum, N.Y. Acad. Medicine, Pub. Health Assn. N.Y.C., Inst. Medicine, Soc. Social Biology, Women in Health Mgmt., Med. Office: Nuclear Threat Initiative 1747 Pennsylvania Ave NW 7th Fl Washington DC 20006

HAMBURGER, MARY ANN, medical management consultant; b. Newark, Aug. 25, 1939; d. Herman and Sylvia (Strauss) Marcus; div. June 1966; children: Bruce David, Marc Laurence. AA, U. Bridgeport (Conn.), 1960. Office mgr., Millburn, N.J., 1970-84; propr., mgr. Mary Ann Hamburger, Assocs., med. mgmt. cons. co., Maplewood, N.J., 1984-. Tchr. adult edn. South Orange Maplewood Bd. Edn., 1975-83; profl. physician recruiter, N.Y., N.J.; broker med. practices. Mem. NAFE. Democrat. Jewish. Avocations: reading, music, needlepoint, theatre, sports. Home and Office: 74 Hudson Ave Maplewood NJ 07040-1403

HAMBURGER, SUSAN, librarian; b. Newark, N.J., Feb. 22, 1949; d. Francis Leo Murphy, Mildred Marie Schultz; m. Joseph Victor Hamburger. AB, Rutgers U., 1975, MLS, 1976; MA, Fla. State U., 1985, PhD, 1994. Cert. archivist. Assoc. univ. libr. Fla. State U., Tallahassee, 1981—89; archivist, head description sect. Va. State Libr. and Archives now Libr. of Va., Richmond, 1989—92; manuscripts cataloger U. Va., Charlottesville, 1992—93, Va. Hist. Soc., Richmond, 1993—94; manuscripts cataloging libr. Pa. State U., University Park, 1994—. Contbr. Book A Guide to the History of Florida, 1989, Book The American Civil War, A Handbook of Research and Literature, 1996 (One of Choice's 625 Outstanding Academic Books of 1997, 1998), Book Encyclopedia of Rural America: The Land and People, 1997 (One of Library Journal's 30 Best Reference Sources 1997, 1998), Book American Book and Magazine Illustrators to 1920 (Dictionary of Literary Biography, vol. 188), 1998, Multi volume book American National Biography, 1999 (Dartmouth medal, 1999), Book Before the New Deal: Southern Social Welfare History, 1830-1930, 1999, Book Biographical Dictionary of Literary Influences: The Nineteenth Century, 1800-1914, 2001, Book Encyclopedia of New Jersey, 2004, Book Historical African Americans in Sports, 2004, Book Dictionary of Literary Influences: The Twentieth Century, 1914-2000, 2004. Mem.: Fla. Hist. Soc., N.Am. Soc. for Sport History (conf. co-mgr. 1998—99), Soc. Am. Archivists (liaison to ALA com. on cataloging: description and access 2000—04), Mid-Atlantic Regional Archives Conf. (chair publs. com. 1995—99, webmaster 1996—, Svc. award 2000, 1999), Phi Alpha Theta, Alpha Sigma Lambda. Avocations: organic gardening, guitar, selling vintage clothes, reading, cats. Office: Pa State Univ 126 Paterno Libr University Park PA 16802 Office Phone: 814-865-1755. Office Fax: 814-863-7293. Business E-Mail: sxh36@psulias.psu.edu.

HAMBY, SHERRY LYNNE, psychologist, researcher; m. Carl Albert Bardi, Apr. 1, 1995; children: Lynnaya, Julian. BS, Coll. William and Mary, 1985, MA, 1989; PhD, U. N.C., 1992. Registered Nat. Register Health Svc. Providers Psychology, lic. clin. psychologist N.C. Rsch. scientist U. N.H., Durham, 1998—99, rsch. asst. prof., 1999—2001; clin. & rsch. psychologist San Carlos (Ariz.) Apache Tribe, 1996—98; rsch. assoc. prof. U. N.C., Chapel Hill, 2002—. Co-author: (book) In Sickness and in Health: The Status of Women's Health in North Carolina, 1993, Out of the Darkness: Contemporary Rsch. Perspectives on Family Violence, 1997, Partner Violence: A Comprehensive Rev. of 20 years of Rsch., 1998, Violence Against Women: A Physician's Guide to Identification and Mgmt., 2003; contbr. articles to profl. jours.; co-author: (book) The Conflict Tactics Scales Handbook. Treas. People Helping People, San Carlos, 1998—99; sec. Domestic Violence & Rape Crisis Ctr. of Scotland County, Laurinburg, NC, 2002—03, v.p., 2003—. Recipient Alfred M. Wellner Meml. award, Nat. Register Health Svc. Providers Psychology, 1998; grantee, Office Environ. Health, Indian Health Svcs., U.S. Dept. of Interior, 1997, Nat. Ctr. Health Stats., Ctrs. Disease Control, 1998—99, L'Office Fédéral de la Formation Professionelle et de la Technologie, La Confédération Suisse, 2001—02, USAF and the Nat. Network Family Resiliency; Merit fellow, U. N.C., 1987—88, NIMH fellow, U. N.H., 1994—96. Mem.: APA, Nat. Coun. Family Rels., Soc. Psychology Women, Soc. Cmty. and Action (chair rural interest group 1998—2001). Avocations: genealogy, travel. Home: 12780 Stratford Dr Laurinburg NC 28352 Office: Possible Equalities P O Box 772 Laurinburg NC 28353

HAMED, MARTHA ELLEN, government administrator; b. Washington, Jan. 14, 1950; d. Rockford Norris and Dorothy Hope (Lough) Hamed. AA, George Washington U., 1985, BA in Psychology and Sociology, 1989; MS in Adminstrn., Ctrl. Mich. U., 1999. Command fed. women's program mgr. U.S. Atlantic Fleet, Norfolk, Va., 1978-79; fed. women's program mgr. Naval Ordnance Sta., Indian Head, Md., 1979-80; pers. mgr., Equal Employment Opportunity course dir. Naval Civilian Pers. Command, Arlington, Va., 1980-83; dep. Equal Employment Opportunity officer, site mgr. Ship R&D Ctr., Bethesda, Md., 1983-85, Naval Surface Weapons Ctr., Silver Spring, Md., 1985; command fed. women's program mgr. Naval Sea Sys. Command, Washington, 1985-87, mgr. command tng. programs, 19987-88, asst. dir. awards and performance appraisal programs, 1988-89; asst. mgmt. analysis Office of Insp. Gen., 1989-92; project mgr. Office of Under Sec. of Def., 1992—. Chief interagency bus process re-eng div Def Human Resource Activie Office Under Secy Def, 1998—. Comnr Anne Arundel County Women's Comn, 1990—92. Named to Oustanding Young Women Am, US Jaycees, 1983; recipient V P Hammer Award Bus Processing Re-Eng, 1995, Commendation Award, VA Vets Benefits Admin, 1996, Award and Medal, Pres's Comn Y2K, 2000, Commendation Award Y2K Transition, Secy Def, 2000. Mem.: NOW (life), Nat Asn Ret Fedn Employees, Federally Employed Women. Democrat. Avocations: natural history, cats, salt-water fishing. Office: Office of Undersec Def 4049 Fairfax Dr Arlington VA 22203

HAMERLE, JILL CHRISTINE, secondary school educator; b. St. Joseph, Mo., Nov. 12, 1961; d. Donald Richard and Carole Jane (Courtney) Vollintine; m. Scott Matthew Hamerle, Oct. 24, 1992; children: Adam, Courtney, Zachary, Jacob. BS in Elem. Edn., Mo. We. U., 1983; MA in Spl. Reading, U. Mo., 1986. Cert. speech, drama. 4th gr. tchr. Winnwood Elem., Kansas City, 1984—89; 7th gr. reading tchr. Maple Woods Elem., Kansas City, 1989—99; speech, psychology, sociology, current events tchr. St. Pius H.S., Kansas City, 2000—03. Spkr., presenter Ewing Kaufman Found., Kansas City; mem. Pleasant Valley (Mo.) Civic Orgn., 1984—91. Roman Catholic. Office: St Pius X HS 1500 NE 42nd Terr Kansas City MO 64116 E-mail: jhamerle@stpiusx-kc.com.

HAMID, SUZANNE L, academic administrator; d. B A and Helen Hamid. Ed. D (ABD), U. of Tenn., Knoxville, TN, 1997—2002. Dir., student events Lee U., Cleveland, Tenn., 1992—95, dir., first-year programs, 1996—. Workshop facilitator Wadsworth Pub. Co, Belmont, Calif., 2000—. Editor: (monograph) Peer Leadership: A Primer On Program Essentials. Supportor of fgn. missions. Grantee Strengthsfinder Project, Fipse In Conjunction With Cccu, 2001. Mem.: Aahe, Noda. Achievements include research in Peer Leadership. Home: 408 Barberry Drive Cleveland TN 37312 Office: Lee University 1120 N Ocoee St Cleveland TN 37312 Personal E-mail: shamid2leeuniversity.edu. E-mail: shamid@leeuniversity.edud.

HAMILTON, AMELIA WENTZ (AMY WENTZ), elementary school educator; b. Elizabethtown, Ky., Mar. 31, 1970; d. Willard Mason and Judith Parr Wentz; m. Brian Joseph Hamilton; children: Clinton, Levi, Samuel Jewell. B in Music Edn., Morehead State U., 1993, BA in Edn., 1994; MA in Edn., Western Ky. U., 1997. Rank I in edn. adminstrn. (elem. principalship). Music tchr. Flaherty Elem. Sch., Ekron, Ky., 1995—, extended sch. svc. tchr., 1995—. Testing cons. Ky. Instrnl. Results Info. Sys. Stewart Pepper Mid. Sch., Brandenburg, Ky., 1995; substitute tchr. Meade County Bd. Edn., Brandenburg, 1995; test scoring Ky. Instrnl. Results Info. Sys. Advanced Sys., Lexington, 1993—94; mem. scholarship com. Flaherty Elem. PTO, Ekron, 2001—. Named to All-Collegiate Band, Ky. Music Educators Nat. Conv., 1992, 1993; recipient 18 Outstanding Salesperson awards, The Castle, 1993—95. Mem.: Mothers of Preschoolers, Am. Orff-Schulwerk Assn., Meade County Edn. Assn., Ky. Edn. Assn., Ky. Music Educators Nat. Conf., Ky. Orff-Schulwerk Assn., Meade County Women's Dem. Club, Pi Kappa Phi, Gamma Beta Phi, Sigma Alpha Iota (life), Chi Omega (life). Baptist. Avocations: vocal music, reading. Home: 326 Homeview Dr Brandenburg KY 40108 Office: Flaherty Elem Sch 2615 Flaherty Rd Ekron KY 40117 Personal E-mail: brianamy@bbtel.com.

HAMILTON, ANN KATHERINE, artist; b. Lima, Ohio, June 22, 1956; d. Robert S. and Elizabeth B. H.; m. Michael John Mercil, Nov. 1993; 1 child, Emmett Moore Mercil. BFA in Textile Design, U. Kans., 1979; MFA in Sculpture, Yale Sch. of Art, 1985; PhD (hon.), R.I. Sch. of Design, 2002. Prof. Ohio State Univ., 2003—. Asst. prof. U. Calif., Santa Barbara, 1985-91. One woman shows include Santa Barbara Contemporary Arts Forum, Calif., 1985, The Mus. of Contemporary Art, L.A., 1988, San Diego Mus. of Contemporary Art, La Jolla, Calif., 1990, 21st Internat. São Paulo Bienal, 1991, Louver Gallery, N.Y.C., 1991, Tate Gallery, Liverpool, 1994, The Mus. of Modern Art, N.Y.C., 1994, Ruth Bloom Gallery, Santa Monica, Calif., 1994, Inst. Contemporary Art, Phila., 1995, Wexner Ctr. for the Arts, Columbus, Ohio, 1996, Veince Biennale, Italy, 1999, Akira Ikeda Gallery, Japan, 2001, Irish Mus. of Modern Art, Dublin., 2002, Wanas Found., Sweden, 2002 others. Exhibited in group shows at The Exit Gallery, Banff, Alberta, Can., 1981, The Walter Phillips Gallery, Banff, Alberta, Can., 1981, Twining Gallery, N.Y.C., 1983, 84, 90, The Oakland Mus., Cleveland Inst. of Art, 1987, Carl Solway Gallery, Cincinnati, 1987, Whitney Mus. of Am. Art, Philip Morris, N.Y., 1987, Santa Barbara Mus. of Art, Calif., 1988, The Nat. Mus. of Modern Art, Kyoto, 1990, The BMW Gallery, N.Y.C., 1990, New Orleans Mus. of Art, 1990, The Carnegie Mus. of Art, Pitts., 1991, Hayward Gallery, South Bank Centre, London, 1992, Stux Gallery, N.Y.C., 1992, Whitney Mus. of Am. Art at Equitable Ctr., N.Y., 1991, The Mus. of Modern Art, N.Y.C., 1993, Cleve. Ctr. for Contemporary Art, 1994, The Art Inst. of Chgo., 1995, others. Commissioned projects Mess Hall, Headlands Ctr. for the Arts, Sausalito, Calif., 1989-90, San Francisco Pub. Libr. Commn., The Arts Commn. of San Francisco, 1990-93; contrb. articles to profl. jours. Recipient Bessie award N.Y. Ann. award in the performing arts, creator category, 1988, Guggenheim Meml. Fellowship, 1989, Louis Comfort Tiffany Found. award, 1990, CAA Artist award, 1992, Skowhegan medal for Sculpture, 1992, NEA Visual Arts Fellowship, 1993, MacArthur Fellowship, 1993.

HAMILTON, BEVERLY LANNQUIST, investment management professional; b. Roxbury, Mass., Oct. 19, 1946; d. Arthur and Nancy Lannquist. BA cum laude, U. Mich., 1968; postgrad., NYU, 1969-70. Prin. Auerbach, Pollak & Richardson, N.Y.C., 1972-75; v.p. Morgan Stanley & Co., N.Y.C., 1975-80, United Techs., Hartford, Conn., 1980-87; dep. comptr. City of N.Y., 1987-91; pres., ret. ARCO Investment Mgmt Co, L.A., 1991-2000. Bd. dirs. Oppenheimer Funds, Mass. Mut. Investment Mgmt., Emerging Markets Growth Fund; trustee The Calif. Endowment, Monterey Inst. Internat. Studies; investment coms. Rockefeller Found., U. Mich., CSFB Sprout Venture Capital. Trustee Hartford Coll. for Women, 1981-87, Stanford Univ. Mgmt. Co., 1991-99; bd. dirs. Inst. for Living, 1983-87. Mem. NCCJ (bd. dirs. 1987-91), Conn. Natural Gas, 1982-2002, United Asset Mgmt. Corp., 1997-2000. Address: 5485 Quail Meadows Dr Carmel CA 93923-7971

HAMILTON, CANDIS LEE, religious organization administrator; b. Saratoga, NY, Apr. 8, 1942; d. Harry Lee Van Arnam and Lois Pickett; m. Woodbury Rogers Hamilton, Apr. 16, 1963; children: Sonya Ann Pacheco, David Sean, Lise Carey Hamilton-Hall, Paul Tate. Student, Brockport Coll., Tavistock Inst., Harvard U., Moreno Inst., 1976—80, U. Rochester, 1974—78, Sisters of St. Joseph Spirituality Ctr., Rochester, NY, 1986—90, St. Bernard's Inst., 1991—. Founder, co-pres. Penfield (NY) Learning Disabilities Assn., 1971—78; program designer, facilitator, instr. Designs for Anti- Racism, Rochester, 1973—81; program facilitator Sisters of St. Joseph Spirituality Ctr., Rochester, 1992—2000, spiritual dir., adj. staff, 1995—. Author: (anthology) Who am i; Who are U; Who are we?, learning courses. Facilitator Wellsprings, Rochester, 1991—96; facilitator, instr. Rochester Jungian Soc., 1990—98; team coord. Sisters of St. Joseph Spirituality Ctr., 1998—2001. Recipient certs. and letters of appreciation, various individuals and local ch. groups, 1971—2003. Democrat. Roman Catholic. Avocations: snorkeling, trampoline, recycling. Home: 844 Whalen Rd Penfield NY 14526

HAMILTON, DAGMAR STRANDBERG, lawyer, educator; b. Phila., Jan. 10, 1932; d. Eric Wilhelm and Anna Elizabeth (Sjöström) Strandberg; m. Robert W. Hamilton, June 26, 1953; children: Eric Clark, Robert Andrew Hale, Meredith Hope. AB, Swarthmore Coll., 1953; JD, U. Chgo. Law Sch., 1956, Am. U., 1961. Bar: Tex. 1972. Atty. civil rights divsn. U.S. Dept Justice, Washington, 1965-66; asst. instr. govt. U. Tex., Austin, 1966-71; lectr. Law Sch. U. Ariz., Tucson, 1971-72; editor, rschr. Assoc. William O. Douglas U.S. Supreme Ct., Washington, 1962-73, 75-76; editor, rschr. Douglas autobiography Random House Co., 1972-73; staff counsel Judiciary Com. U.S. Ho. of Reps., 1973-74; asst. prof. L.B. Johnson Sch. Pub. Affairs U. Tex., Austin, 1974-77, assoc. prof., 1977-83, prof., 1983—, assoc. dean, 1983-87. Interdisciplinary prof. U. Tex. Law Sch., 1983—; vis. prof. Washington U. Law Sch., St. Louis, 1982, U. Maine, Portland, 1992; Godfrey Disting. vis. prof. U. Maine Law Sch., 2002; vis. fellow U. London, QMW Sch. Law, 1987—88; vis. prof. U. Maine, Portland, 2002; vis. fellow U. Oxford Inst. European & Comparative Law, 1998. Contbr. to various publs. Mem. Tex. State Bar Assn., Am. Law Inst., Assn. Pub. Policy Analysis and Mgmt., Swarthmore Coll. Alumni Coun. (rep.), Kappa Beta Phi (hon.), Phi Kappa Phi (hon.). Democrat. Mem. Soc. Of Friends. Home: 403 Allegro Ln Austin TX 78746-4301 Office: U Tex LBJ Sch Pub Affairs Austin TX 78713 E-mail: dagmar.hamilton@mail.utexas.edu.

HAMILTON, HEATHER AMLIN, conductor, director; b. Bridgeport, Conn., Nov. 22, 1967; d. James Theodore and Gretchen Worley Hamilton; life ptnr. Nanette Teresa Raimondi. MusM in Solo Piano Performance, Manhattan Sch. Music, 1993, MusM in Orch. Piano, 1995. Dir. music 1st Ch. Congl., UCC, Fairfield, Conn., 1996—; artistic dir., condr., founder Meetinghouse Orch., Fairfield, 1998—. Mem. Manhattan Sch. Music Alumni Coun., N.Y.C., 2000—. Condr.: Brahms Requiem 5th Internat. Condrs. Inst. (conducting fellow, 2003), various choral and orch. pieces Dennis Keene Choral Festival (conducting fellow). Mem. Riverfield Improvement Soc., Fairfield, 2003; chair Renee B. Fisher competition Conn. Alliance for Music, Westport, 1990—93. Recipient full tuition scholarship, Manhattan Sch. Music, 1993, PTA Shield award, Roger Ludlowe H.S., 1985; scholar full tuition scholarship, Nat. Orch. Inst., 1993. Mem.: Am. Choral Dirs. Assn. (assoc.), Am. Symphony Orch. League (assoc.), Am. Guild of Organists (assoc.; bd. mem. 1991—93). Avocations: travel, sports, movies, theater, reading. Home: 28 Riverfield Dr Fairfield CT 06824 Office: 1st Ch Congregational UCC 148 Beach Rd Fairfield CT 06824 Personal E-mail: amlin@aol.com. E-mail: hhamilton@firstchurchfairfield.org.

HAMILTON, JACQUELINE, art consultant; b. Tulsa, Mar. 28, 1942; d. James Merton and Nina Faye (Andrews) H.; m. Richard Sanford Piper, Jan. 2, 1968 (div. June 1976). BA, Tex. Christian U., 1965; grad., Stockholm U., 1967; postgrad., Harvard U., 1972-73, Tufts U., 1971, Rice U., 1982-83, Houston C.C., 1986-87. Art cons. for corps., pvt. collectors and mus., Houston, 1979—. Expert witness in lawsuits regarding art. Contbr. articles to profl. publs. Bd. dirs. Opera in the Heights. Mem.: AIA (affiliate), Internat. Assn. Profl. Art Advisors, Rice Design Alliance, Assn. Corp. Art Curators, Assn. Fund Raising Professionals, French-Am. C. of C., Norwegian-am. C. of C., Swedish-Am. C. of C., Swedish Club, L'Alliance Francaise, The Forum Club, The Houstonian Club. Presbyterian. Office: PO Box 1483 Houston TX 77251-1483

HAMILTON, JANE, writer; b. 1957; Author: The Book of Ruth, 1988 (PEN/Ernest Hemingway Found. award, 1989), The Frogs Are Still Singing, 1989, A Map of the World, 1994, The Short History of a Prince, 1998 (Heartland prize for fiction), Disobedience, 2000, short stories. Office: Doubleday Pubs 1540 Broadway New York NY 10036*

HAMILTON, JEAN See CHAUDOIR, JEAN

HAMILTON, JEAN CONSTANCE, judge; b. St. Louis, Nov. 12, 1945; AD, Wellesley Coll., 1968; JD, Washington U., St. Louis, 1971; LLM, Yale U., 1982. Atty. Dept. of Justice, Washington, 1971-73, asst. U.S. atty. St. Louis, 1973-78; atty. Southwestern Bell Telephone Co., St. Louis, 1978—81; judge 22d Jud. Circuit State of Mo., St. Louis, 1982-88; judge Mo. Ct. Appeals (ea. dist.), 1988-90, U.S. Dist. Ct. (ea. dist.) Mo., 1990—, chief judge, 1995—2002. Office: US Courthouse 111 S 10th St Saint Louis MO 63102

HAMILTON, JOAN NICE, editor-in-chief; b. Chgo., 1948; d. William and Dorothy Nice. Grad., Pomona Coll., 1970. Former editor High Country News; editor Climbing Mag., editor-in-chief Sierra Mag., San Francisco. Contbr. articles to Audubon, Defenders, Nat. Wildlife Mags. Office: Sierra Mag 85 2nd St San Francisco CA 94105-3459

HAMILTON, LAURELL K. writer; b. Heber Springs, Ark. Author: Guilty Pleasures, 1993, The Laughing Corpse, 1994, Circus of the Damned, 1995, The Lunatic Cafe, 1996, Bloody Bones, 1996, The Killing Dance, 1997, Burnt Offerings, 1998, Blue Moon, 1998, Obsidian Butterfly, 2000, A Kiss of Shadows, 2001, Narcissus in Chains, 2002, A Caress of Twilight, 2003, Seduced By Moonlight, 2004. Office: Ballentine Publishing Group West Coast Pub Office 8950 W Olympic Blvd 383 Beverly Hills CA 90211

HAMILTON, LINDA HELEN, clinical psychologist; b. N.Y.C., Dec. 2, 1952; d. Peter and Helen (Casey) Homek; m. Terrence White, Aug. 10, 1974 (div. 1983); m. William Garnett Hamilton, Dec. 29, 1984. BA summa cum laude, Fordham U., 1984; MA, Adelphi U., 1986, PhD, 1989. Lic. psychologist, N.Y. Dancer N.Y.C. Ballet, 1969-88; clin. psychologist Fair Oaks Hosp., Summit, N.J., 1989-90, Miller Inst. for Performing Artists, N.Y.C., 1989-95; pvt. practice N.Y.C., 1991—. Rsch. assoc. Miller Inst. Performing Artists, N.Y.C., 1987-95; chair dance com. MedArt U.S.A., N.Y.C., 1990-92; cons. psychologist Sch. Am. Ballet, N.Y.C., 1991—, Alvin Ailey Am. Dance Ctr., N.Y.C., 1996—; wellness cons. N.Y.C. Ballet, 2003—; advice columnist Dance Mag., 1992—, sr. editor, 1997—; adj. assoc. prof. Fordham U., 1998-2002; co-leader Performing Arts Medicine Delegation to Russia and Ea. Europe, 1992; co-designer Wellness Program, N.Y.C. Ballet, 2001—. Author: The Person Behind the Mask: A Guide to Performing Arts Psychology, Advice for Dancers; featured in : (documentaries) by European Media Support; Dying to be Thin (Nova), 2001. Mem. exec. com. BFA Dance Program, Fordham U., 1997—. Miller Inst. Performing Artists grantee, 1987. Mem. APA (Daniel E. Berlyne award 1993), Internat. Assn. Dance Medicine and Sci. (mem.-at-large), Performing Arts Medicine Assn., Dance Profls. Assocs. (bd. dirs. 1997—2002). Avocations: travel, reading, opera, ballet. Office: 2000 Broadway New York NY 10023-5028 E-mail: lindahamilton1@msn.com.

HAMILTON, LISA GAY, actress; b. LA, Mar. 25, 1964; d. Ira and Tina. Grad., Juilliard Sch., 1988. Appeared in films: Reversal of Fortune, 1990, Naked in New York, 1994, Twelve Monkeys, 1995, Palookaville, 1995, Nick and Jane, 1997, Lifebreath, 1997, Jackie Brown, 1997, Drunks, 1997, Beloved, 1998, True Crime, 1999, The Sum of All Fears, 2002, The Truth About Charlie, 2002, Amanda America; TV appearances include Homicide, 1993, New York Undercover, 1994, Law & Order (Rebecca), 1995, Murder One, Chicago Hope, The Practice, 1997-2003, One Life to Live, 1996, The Defenders: Choice of Evils, 1998, Swing Vote, 1999, A House Divided, 2000, Hamlet, 2000; dir., prodr. Beah: A Black Woman Speaks, 2003; on Broadway plays include The Piano Lesson; (off Broadway) Measure for Measure, N.Y.C., Valley Song (Obie award, Clarence Derwent award, Drama Desk nominee). Office: Writers & Artists Agy 8383 Wilshire Blvd Ste 550 Beverly Hills CA 90211

HAMILTON, NANCY BETH, data processing executive; b. Lakewood, Ohio, July 22, 1948; d. Edward Douglas and Gloria Jean (Blessing) Familo; m. Thomas Woolman Hamilton, June 10, 1970; children: Susan Elizabeth, Catherine Anne. BA, Denison U., 1970. Cert. secondary edn. tchr., Fla. Tchr. Orange County (Fla.) Bd. Edn., 1970-71; registrar Jones Coll., Orlando, Fla., 1971-72; mgr. service dept. Am. Lawyers Co., Cleve., 1972-79, mgr. data processing dept., 1980-95, corp. sec.-treas., 1995—. Mem. bd. assoc. editors Comml. Law Jour., 1991—, vice chair, 2002—. Trustee, treas. Westshore Montessori Assn., Rocky River, Ohio, 1988—94; bd. dirs. Holly Lane PTA, Westlake, Ohio, 1988—94, treas., 1992—94; bd. dirs. Parkside PTA, Westlake, 1991—97, treas., 1994—96, Westlake Coun. PTAs, 1999—2001, Westlake H.S. PTA, 1995—98, pres., 1998—2000. Mem. Comml. Law League Am. (chmn. com. 1989-94, membership chmn. 1994-96, com. chair 1997—), Comml. Law League of Am. (Midwestern dist. rec. sec. 1997—), Assn. Law List Pubs. (treas. 1998—), Westwood Country Club, Alpha Phi (pres. Cleve. Westshore chpt. alumnae 1986-88). Republican. Methodist. Avocations: skiing, travel. Office: Am Lawyers Co 853 Westpoint Pky Ste 710 Cleveland OH 44145-1532

HAMILTON, PATRICIA ROSE, art dealer; b. Phila., Oct. 21, 1948; d. William Alexis and Lillian Marie (Sloan) Hamilton. BA, Temple U., 1970; MA, Rutgers U., 1971. Sec. to curator Whitney Mus., N.Y.C., 1971-73; sr. editor Art in Am., 1973; curator exhbns. Crispo Gallery, 1974-75; dir. Hamilton Gallery, 1976-84; artist's agt., 1984—2002; art dealer, 2002—. Democrat. Avocations: tennis, swimming, cooking. Home and Office: 6753 Milner Rd Los Angeles CA 90068-3214 E-mail: hamiltonpatricia@sbcglobal.net.

HAMILTON, REBECCA, state representative; b. Oklahoma City, Okla., Jan. 8, 1948; d. George and Betty (Cook) Hamilton; m. Rodney Hargrave; children: John, Hamilton. Writer; mem. Okla. Ho. of Reps., 1981—85, 2003—, chair commerce, industry and labor com. Democrat. Office: State Capitol 2300 N Lincoln Blvd Rm 301 Oklahoma City OK 73105

HAMILTON, RHODA LILLIAN ROSÉN, guidance counselor, language educator, consultant; b. Chgo., May 8, 1915; d. Reinhold August and Olga (Peterson) Rosén; m. Douglas Edward Hamilton, Jan. 23, 1936 (div. Feb. 1952); remarried, Aug. 1995 (dec. 1997); children: Perry Douglas, John Richard Hamilton. Grad., Moser Coll., Chgo., 1932-33; BS in Edn., U. Wis., 1953, postgrad., 1976; MAT, Rollins Coll., 1967; postgrad., Ohio State U., 1959-60; postgrad. in clin. psychology, Mich. State U., 1971, 76, 79, 80; postgrad., Yale U., 1972, Loma Linda U., 1972; postgrad. in computer mgmt. sys., U. Okla., 1976; postgrad. in edn., U. Calif., Berkeley, 1980. Exec. sect. to pres. Ansul Chem. Co., Marinette, Wis., 1934-36; pers. counselor Burneice Larson's Med. Bur., Chgo., 1954-56; adminstrv. asst. to Ernst C. Schmidt Lake Geneva, Wis., 1956-58; assoc. prof. fin. aid Ohio State U., 1958-60; tchr. English to spkrs. of other langs. Istanbul, Turkey, 1960-65; counselor Groveland (Fla.) H.S., 1965-68; guidance counselor, psychol. cons. early childhood edn. Dept. Def. Overseas Dependents Sch., Okinawa, 1968-85; instr./lectr. early childhood Lake Sumter Jr. Coll., Leesburg, Fla., 1986-88; pres. Hamilton Assocs., Groveland, Fla., Frederick, Md., 1986—. Vis. lectr. Okla. State U., 1980; co-owner plumbing, heating bus., Marinette, 1943-49; journalist Rockford (Ill.) Morning Star, 1956-58, Istanbul AP, 1960; lectr. Lake Sumter C.C., 1989—, Lake Sumter Jr. Coll., 1989. Author poetry on Middle East, 1959-64; Career Awareness, 1978; Listen Up, 1997-98. Vol. instr. U.S. citizenship classes, Okinawa, 1971-72; judge Gold Scholarships Okinawa Christian Schs., 1983, 84. Mem. Am. Fedn. Govt. Employees, Fla. Retired Educators, Order Ea. Star (organist; life mem. Shuri One in Okinawa and Trillium 208 in Wis.), Marinette Woman's Club (Wis., pres. 1949-51), Groveland Woman's Club (Fla.), Phi Delta Gamma. Episcopalian. Home: 2408 Ellsworth Way Apt 1A Frederick MD 21702-3124

HAMILTON, SARA DARLENE, special education educator; b. Greeley, Colo., Mar. 8, 1978; d. Robert Harold and Marilyn Ruth Hamilton. BA in Elem. Edn., Northwestern Nazarene U., Nampa, Idaho, 2000, MEd in Exceptional Child, 2001. Cert. profl. tchr. Colo. Dept. of Edn., 2002, tchr. Idaho Dept. of Edn., 2000. Spl. edn. tchr. Ctrl. Elem. Sch., Nampa, Idaho, 2001—02, Ridgeview Elem. Sch., Colorado Springs, Colo., 2002—. Mem.: Coun. for Exceptional Children. Independent. Avocations: family activities, travel, sports, exploring the outdoors.

HAMILTON, VALERIE MICHELLE, editor, administrative assistant; b. Memphis, Nov. 22, 1975; d. Larry Wayne Stafford and Paula Jean Mirestes; m. Brian O'Neal Hamilton, July 2, 2000; 1 child, Zora Michelle O'Neal. BA cum laude, U. Memphis, 1998; postgrad., Queens U., 2003—. Editor Metro Memphis Mag., 1997; intern childrens divsn. Chronicle Books, San Francisco, 1998; editl. asst. A Press Books, 1999; asst. to editor-on-chief Wired Mag., 1999—2001, editl. bus. coord., 2001—02; creative writing editor, copy editor Sensored Mag., Nashville, 2002—; adminstrv. asst. Stites & Harbison, 2002—. Author: Liberties, 2005. E-mail: vmhamilton1@yahoo.com.

HAMILTON, VIRGINIA VAN DER VEER, historian, educator; b. Kansas City, Mo., Sept. 7, 1921; d. McClellan and Dorothy (Rainold) Van der Veer; m. Lowell S. Hamilton, Aug. 4, 1946; children: Carol, David. AB, Birmingham (Ala.)-So. Coll., 1941, MA (Ford Found. Fund Adult Edn. fellow), 1961; PhD, U. Ala., Tuscaloosa, 1968; LittD, U. Ala., 1992. Staff writer AP, Washington, 1942—46, Birmingham News, 1948—50; asst. prof. history U. Montevallo, Ala., 1951—55; asst. prof., asst. to pres. pub. rels. Birmingham-So. Coll., 1955—56; lectr. in history U. Ala., Birmingham, 1965—68, asst. prof., 1968—71, assoc. prof., 1971—75, prof., 1975—87, prof. emerita, 1987—. Author: Hugo Black: The Alabama Years, 1972, Alabama: A History, 1977, The Story of Alabama, 1980, Your Alabama, 1980, Seeing Historic Alabama, 1982, rev. edit., 1996, Lister Hill: Statesman from the South, 1987, Looking For Clark Gable and Other 20th Century Pursuits, 1996; editor: Hugo Black and the Bill of Rights, 1978. Faculty Rsch. grantee U. Ala. at Tuscaloosa, 1969, U. Ala. at Birmingham, 1973-74, 74-75. Mem. So., Am. hist. assns., Orgn. Am. Historians, Soc. Am. Historians, Ala. Assn. Historians, Ala. Hist. Soc. Home: 2350 Montevallo Rd Apt 1602 Birmingham AL 35223-2342

HAMILTON, WENDY J. foundation administrator; b. N.Y. m. Lawrence Hamilton; children: Kaitlin, Ryan, Greer. Student, Genesee C.C., Batavia. Mem. Ind. chpt. MADD, 1984—, mem. nat. bd. dirs., 1995—, v.p. victim issues, v.p. field issues, nat. pres., 2002—, founder Ill. chpt., founder N.Y. chpt., N.Y. state chair, 1990—94, 1997—98, pub. policy liaison Md. chpt., 1998—2002. Office: PO Box 541688 Dallas TX 75354-1688*

HAMLIN, SONYA B. communications specialist; b. N.Y.C. d. Julius and Sarah (Saltzman) Borenstein; m. Bruce Hamlin (dec. 1977); children: Ross, Mark (dec. 1992), David. BS, MA, NYU; HLD (hon.), Notre Dame Coll., 1970. Host arts program Sta. WHDH-TV, Boston, 1963-65; host, prodr., writer (syndicated PBS program) Meet the Arts Sta. WGBH-TV, Boston, 1965-68; cultural reporter Sta. WBZ-TV, Boston, 1968-71, TV host, producer The Sonya Hamlin Show, 1970-75; host, producer Sunday Open House program Sta. WCVB-TV, Boston, 1976-80; host, producer, writer Speak Up and Listen program Lifetime Cable Network, N.Y.C., 1982-84; pres. Sonya Hamlin Communications, Boston and N.Y.C., 1977—, Different Drummer Prodns., N.Y.C., 1982-86. Pvt. comm. cons., U.S., Can., and Europe, 1977—; adj. lectr. Harvard Grad. Sch., Edn., Cambridge, Mass., 1974-76, Harvard Law Sch., 1977-81, Kennedy Sch. Govt., Harvard U., 1978-79; adj. asst. prof. Boston U. Med. Sch., 1977-80; mem. faculty Nat. Inst. Trial Advocacy, South Bend, Ind., 1977—, U.S. Dept. Justice, Washington, 1979-87, ABA, Chgo., 1979—; chmn. Law/Video Co., N.Y.C. and Waltham, Mass., 1987-92; comm. cons., weekly and weekend performer Today in NY (NBC), 1995—; daily panelist O.J. Today (Fox), 1995-96. Author: What Makes Juries Listen, 1985, How to Talk So People Listen, 1988, What Makes Juries Listen Today, 1998; prodr., dir., writer (films) China" Different Path, 1979 (Emmy nominee), Paul Revere: What Makes a Hero, 1976, others; contbr. articles to numerous profl. jours. Active Gov. Commn. Status of Women, Mass., 1973-83; campaign co-chair Mass. ERA Campaign, 1975-76; cons. Gov. Michael Dukakis, 1978, Dem. Nat. Party, Washington, 1979; bd. dirs. mem. Nat. Vol. Action com. United Way, Washington, 1986-91; bd. dirs. Taubman Ctr. Kennedy Sch. Harvard U., 1989-95; mem. Martha Graham Adv. Bd., 1997—; mem. Women's Leadership Bd., Kennedy Sch. Govt., Harvard U., 1999—. Recipient Best Program award for Meet the Arts Internat. Ednl. TV Assn., Tokyo, 1969, Ohio State Cultural Reporting award, 1970; named Outstanding Broadcaster New Eng. Broadcasters, Boston, 1973; Sonya Hamlin Day named in her honor Mayor of Boston, 1974.; archive of her works established Boston U. Library, 1983. Mem.: NATAS (two Emmy nominations), Internat. Women's Forum, Am. Fedn. TV and Radio Artists. Avocations: skiing, tennis, piano, dance, museums.

HAMM, CLAIRE ROSE, development information services administrator; b. Trenton, NJ, Aug. 10, 1957; d. Daniel Michael and Rose Mary Serinaldi; m. Kim Edward Hamm, Apr. 25, 1981; children: Dana Rose, Kristopher Edward. Cert. in French, baccalaureate, U. Besançon, France, 1978; BA in French magna cum laude, Rider U., Lawrenceville, N.J., 1979, MA in Ednl. Adminstrn. and Supervision, 1985; MA in Counselor Edn., Coll. N.J., 2003. Cert. prin., supr., N.J. Office asst. devel. Princeton (N.J.) U., 1979-81, dir. grad. admissions, 1985-87, mgr. grad. programs, 1997-99; dir. rsch. and records Rider U., Lawrenceville, 1981-85; prin. elem. sch. St. Ann Sch., Lawrenceville, 1994-97; founding sch. adminstr. Princeton Acad., 1999-2000; dir. devel. info. svcs., career counselor Rider U., Lawrenceville, NJ, 2001—. Recipient award Outstanding Achievement in German Culture Studies, German Consulate, 1979. Mem.: Nat. Career Devel. Assn., N.J. Career Devel. Assn., N.J. Counseling Assn., Am. Counseling Assn., Pi Delta Phi. Roman Catholic. Avocation: exotic birds. Home: 23 Clover Hill Cir Ewing NJ 08638

HAMM, MIA (MARIEL MARGARET HAMM), professional soccer player; b. Selma, Ala., Mar. 17, 1972; m. Christian Corry (div.); m. Nomar Garciaparra. BS in Polit. Sci., U. N.C., 1994. Forward U.S. Women's Nat. Soccer Team, Chgo., 1987—; profl. soccer player Washington Freedom, 2001—03. Author: Go for the Goal: A Champions Guide to Winning in Soccer and Life. Founder Mia Found. Named U.S. Soccer Female Athlete of Yr., 1994—98, MVP, U.S. Women's Cup, 1995, World Cup Champion, 1999; recipient Gold medal, Atlanta Olympics, 1996, Best Female Athlete of Yr., Espy, 1998, 1999, Soccer Player of Yr. award, 1999. Achievements include all-time leading international goal scorer for men and women; member of U. N.C. NCAA National Championship teams, 1989-93. Office: US Soccer Fedn US Soccer House 1801 S Prairie Ave Chicago IL 60616-1319

HAMMACK, JULIA KATHRYN, music educator; b. Tupelo, Miss., Aug. 30, 1950; d. James Marion and Lois Robbins Richey; m. Howard Crisler Hammack, Jan. 24, 1976; children: Stephen Crisler, Jill Annette. B in music edn., Miss. Coll., 1972, M in music, 1975, degree in ednl. specialist, 1988. Cert. education Yamaha Music Inst. Music therapist Jackson (Miss.) Pub. Schs., 1972—73; cons. Miss. Bapt. Convention Bd., Jackson, 1973—74; music specialist Canton (Miss.) Pub. Schs., 1974—77; choral dir. Canton (Miss.) Acad., 1977—84; dir. choral activities Jackson (Miss.) Acad., 1984—97; dir. music min. First United Meth. Ch., Canton, 1984—; music specialist Madison (Miss.) Sta. Elem., 1997—. Adjudicator Miss. Fed. Music Clubs, Jackson, 1987—; chmn. Madison (Miss.) Sta. Elem. Art Dept., 2000—. Recipient Thad Cochran Dist. Arts Educator award, Miss. Alliance Arts Edn., 2003. Mem.: Miss. Chpt. ACDA (bd. dir. 1992—96), Delta Omicron, Delta Kappa Gamma. Avocation: gardening. Home: 335 Glenfield Rd Canton MS 39046

HAMMARGREN, MARJORIE DOLORES, printing company executive; b. Watertown, S.D., July 06; d. Edward Richard and Elizabeth Christina (Mach) H. Student, U. Minn., 1983-85. Clk.-treas. City of Kilkenny, Minn., 1970-84; sec. Hammargren Printing Co., Kilkenny, 1956-70, gen. mgr., owner, 1970—. Designer floral arrangements Waseca (Minn.) Greenhouse, 1956-68. Author: History of Church of St. Canice, 1954; exhibited art, photography, crafts, 1968—, including Sister Kenny Internat. Arts Fair for People with Disabilities, Mpls., Le Sueur County Fair, Le Center, Minn. Del. Rep. county, dist. and state convs., Minn., 1976—; vice chmn. Le Sueur County Rep. Com., 1988—; mem. bd. Minn. Coun. on Disability, St. Paul, 1993—, Faribault deanery Coun. Cath. Women, 1964-75, S.W. deanery, 1975—; speaker on Ams. with Disabilities Act and spl. needs of people with disabilities. Recipient U.S. Bicentennial citation Gov. of Minn., 1976, leadership award St. Paul and Mpls. Archdiocesan Coun. Cath. Women, 1978, award S.W. Deanery Coun. Cath. Women, 1978, cert. and pin Minn. Clks. and Fin. Officers Assn., 1985, social justice disability award Archdiocesan Cath. Charities, 1994, Good Neighbor award Sta. WCCO, 1994; named one of 59 Minnesotan "Community Heros" Torchbearers for the Olympic Flame, Rochester, 1996. Mem. Am. Legion Aux. (pres. Kilkenny 1993-94), St. Canice Rosary Soc. (pres. 1988-89), Le Sueur County Old Settlers Assn., Le Sueur County Hist. Soc. (life), Daus. Union Vets. Civil War, Caths. United for Spiritual Action, Cmty. and Sportsman Club. Avocations: writing, singing, knitting, tatting, travel.

HAMMEL, ALICE MAXINE, music educator; b. Tampa, Fla., May 7, 1965; d. Nelson Dodge and Alice Maxine King; m. Bruce Ray Hammel, Feb. 6, 1993; children: Hannah Elizabeth, Hollie MaryAlice. BME, Shenandoah U., 1987; MME, Fla. State U., 1989; DMA, Shenandoah U., 1999. Band, choral dir. Trinity Cath. Sch., Tallahassee, 1987-89; choral dir. Hanover County Schs., Ashland, Va., 1990-93; ind. educator music Richmond, Va., 1989—; staff adjudicator Music Festivals, Birdsboro, Pa., 1989—; instr. U. Richmond, 1998—, dir. ednl. programs Musicate. Vis. asst. prof. U. Richmond; cons. and presenter in field; networking rsch. mentor Music Educators Nat. Conf., 2002—, nat. spokesperson. Musician (flutist): Music of Allan Blank, 1999; contbr. articles to profl. jours. Patriotic edn. chair Daus. Am. Colonists, Richmond, 1999—2001; dist. good citizens chair DAR, Richmond, 1998—2001, music chmn., 1997. Recipient Young Career Achievement award, Shenandoah U., 2000. Mem.: Coll. Music Soc., Va. Assn. Gifted, Am. Coun. Exceptional Children, Va. Music Educators Assn. (chamber music chair 1990—98, sight reading chair 1998—, spl. learners chair 1998—), Music Tchrs. Nat. Assn. (keynote spkr. 2001, woodwind rep. 2002), Music Educators Nat. Conf. (networking mentor rschr.), Sigma Alpha Iota (Nat. Leadership award 1987). Democrat. Baptist. Home: 5009 W Seminary Ave Richmond VA 23227-3407

HAMMER, BONNIE, broadcast executive; m. Dale Huesner. BA in Edn., MA in Media and New Tech., Boston U. V.p. current programs USA Networks, N.Y.C.; with WGBH, Boston; pres. Sci-Fi Channel (subsidiary of USA Networks), Universal City, Calif. Recipient Lillian Gish award, Women in Film. Office: Sci-Fi Channel c/o Vivendi Universal 100 Universal City Plaza Universal City CA 91608-1002

HAMMER, DEBORAH MARIE, librarian, paralegal; b. Bronx, N.Y., Nov. 16, 1947; d. Ben and Helen (Lorenz) Halprin; m. Mark Stewart Hammer, May 30, 1976; 1 child, Joshua Robert. BA, CCNY, 1968; MLS, Rutgers U., 1969. Cert. libr. N.Y. Gen. asst. info. tel. ref. divsn. Queens Borough Pub. Libr., Jamaica, NY, 1969-71, gen. asst. popular libr., 1972-80, asst. div. head history, travel & biography, 1972-81, divsn. head history, travel & biography, 1981-92, div. mgr. social scis., 1992-98; fee conciliation coord., computer systems mgr. Nassau County Bar Assn., Mineola, NY, 1999—. Democrat. Avocations: reading, cooking, handcrafts, camping. Office: 15th and West Sts Mineola NY 11501 E-mail: halimer@juno.com.

HAMMER, ELIZABETH CARTER BOWERS, art educator; b. Washington, Jan. 9, 1931; d. Walter Abraham and Sarah Cone Bowers; m. Lowell Varner Hammer; children: Sarah Elizabeth Haberl, Lowell Carter, Christopher Allen. BA summa cum laude, U. Md., 1981. Illustrator, editor U.S. Govt., Washington; editor US Embassy, Paris; tchr. Rabat (Morroco)-Am. Sch., Morocco. Exhibited in group shows at Salon Artistes Ind., Paris, 1982—85, Am. Embassy, 1982, 1983, Mayorie 11e, France1, 1983, Washington Women's Art Ctr., 1984—90, Avignon, France, 1991, Fairfax County Coun. Arts, 1992, 1993. Bd. dirs. Brain Tumor Found., Boca Raton, Fla. Mem.: Ind. Salon Artists Soc., Daughters 17th Century, Nat. Gavel Soc., Dacor-Bacon, Dames Loyal Legion (pres.), Phi Kappa Phi (award). Avocations: art history, genealogy, writing. Home: 1592 SE Ballantrae Ct Port Saint Lucie FL 34952

HAMMER, KATHERINE GONET, software company executive; b. Shreveport, La., Jan. 5, 1946; d. Joseph Peter and Bernice Evelyn (Post) Gonet; m. Gael Warren Hammer, May 25, 1965 (div.); children: Katherine Elizabeth, Evelyn Alice; m. Ronald R. Scott, Feb. 14, 1982 (div.). BA in English, U. Iowa, 1967, MA in Linguistics, 1969, PhD in English Linguistics, 1973. Asst. prof. Coe Coll., Cedar Rapids, Iowa, 1973-75; asst. prof. in linguistics Wash. State U., Pullman, 1975-80; vis. scholar Ctr. for Cognitive Sci. U. Tex., Austin, 1980-81; software devel. mgr. Tex. Instruments, Austin, 1981-84; mem. tech. staff Microelectronics and Computer Tech. Corp., Austin, 1984-90; pres., chief exec. officer Evolutionary Techs. Internat., Inc., Austin, 1991—. Avocation: sculpting. Office: Evolutionary Techs Internat 816 Congress Ave Ste 1300 Austin TX 78701-2646

HAMMER, LINDA See LINDROTH, LINDA

HAMMER, MARION PRICE, association executive; b. Columbia, S.C., Apr. 26, 1939; 3 children. Exec. dir. Unified Sportsmen of Fla., Fairfax, Va., 1978—; pres. NRA, Fairfax, Va.; bd. dirs. Tallahassee, Fla. Registered lobbyist for pro-gun issues. Recipient Harlon B. Carter Legis. Achievement award, 1992, SCOPE ann. 2d Amendment award, 1987, Roy Rogers Man of Yr. award, Outstanding Cmty. Svc. award Nat. Safety Coun., 1993, Nat. Edn. award Am. Legion, Sybil Ludington award. Mem. NRA (life, cert. firearm instr., chmn. legal policy com., chmn. task force on hunter safety legislation, vice chmn. women's policies com., mem. nominating com., pub. affairs com., ethics com., membership coms.). Office: Unified Sportsmen of FL PO Box 6565 Tallahassee FL 32314-6565

HAMMER, (BETH) MARY ELIZABETH, adult nurse practitioner; b. Eau Claire, Wis., June 23, 1964; d. Merlin Kenneth and Mary Catherine Hammer. BSN, Coll. St. Teresa, 1986; MSN Marquette U., 1996. RN Wis., 1987, cert. advanced practice nurse prescriber, Wis., 1997, adult nurse practitioner, 1997. Staff nurse med. telemetry Zablocki VA Med. Ctr., Milw., 1986—87, staff nurse ICU, 1987—98, staff nurse electrophysiology lab., 1990—2000, staff nurse cardiac cath. lab., 1990—2000, nurse practitioner cardiology, 1998—. Guest lectr. Concordia U. Coll. Nursing, Mequon, Wis., 2000—; clin. preceptor Marquette U. Coll. Nursing, Milw., 2002. Contbr. chapters to books. Mem., chair Teosinte, El Salvador Com., St. Sebastian Congregation, Milw., 1999—. Recipient Nursing Excellence award, Advancing the Profession, NurseWeek, 2003. Mem.: AACN, chpt. adv. team (Greater Milw. area chpt.v.p. 1997—98, pres. 2000—01, chpt. adv. team region 8 2002—, Mem. of the Yr. Excellence in Critical Care Nursing 1998), Sigma Theta Tau. Avocations: music, travel. Office: Zablocki VA Med Ctr 5000 W National Ave Milwaukee WI 53295

HAMMER, REBECCA ELAINE, secondary school educator; b. Decatur, Ga., Nov. 8, 1974; d. Carlton Leon Meeks and Suzanne Katherine Hamilton; m. Charles Robert Hammer, Aug. 28, 1994; 1 child, Abigail Rose. AS, Midland (Tex.) Coll., 1996; BA, U. Tex., Odessa, 1999. Cert. tchr. Ariz. Dept. Edn., Tex. Secondary sci. tchr. Ector County Ind. Sch. Dist., Odessa, 1999—2001, Gilbert (Ariz.) Unified Sch. Dist., 2001—. Named All-American scholar, U.S. Automobile Assn., 1998. Mem.: NEA. Democrat. Avocations: travel, coin collecting.

HAMMER, SUSAN W. educational foundation executive, former mayor; b. Altadena, Calif., Dec. 21, 1938; d. James Nathan and Katrine (Krutzsch) Walker; m. Philip Hammer, Sept. 4, 1960; children: Philip, Hali, Matthew. BA in History, U. Calif., Berkeley, 1960. Svc. rep. Pacific Telephone Co., Berkeley, 1960-61; staff asst. Peace Corps, Washington, 1962-63; councilwoman City of San Jose, Calif., 1980-81, 83-90, spl. asst. to mayor, 1981-82, vice mayor, 1985-87, mayor, 1991-99; CEO Synopsys Outreach Found. and Synopsys Silicon Valley Sci. and Tech. Championship, 1999—. Chair, pres. Adv. Com. on Trade Policy and Negotiations, 1994—. Bd. dirs. San Jose Mus. Art, 1971-90, pres., 1978-80; mem. governing bd. NCCJ, 1978—; mem. adv. bd. Cmty. Found. Santa Clara County, 1978—; mem. Santa Clara County Transp. Com., 1976-77, Santa Clara County Juvenile Justice Commn., 1980, Victim-Witness Adv. Bd., 1977-90, Children's Health Coun., San Jose, 1981-89, Santa Clara Valley Leadership Program, 1986-90, Childrens Shelter Project, 1991—, Am. Leadership Forum, 1992—; past chmn. parents adv. com. Trace Sch.; chair Pres.' Adv. Com. on Trade Policy and Negotiation; mem. San Jose Fine Arts Commn., 1980; v.p. Calif. Bd. Edn., 1999— Recipient Rosalie M. Stern Community Svc. award U. Calif., 1975, Disting. Citizen of San Jose award Exch. Club, 1979, Investment in Leadership award Coro Found., 1985, Tzedek award for honor, compassion and community svc. Temple Emanu-El, 1987, Recognition award YWCA, Santa Clara County, 1989, resolution of commendation Assn. for Responsible Alcohol Control, 1990, Woman of Achievement award The Women's Fund, 1990, Dox Quixote award Nat. Hispanic U., 1991, Friends of Bay Area Mcpl. Elections Com. award, 1991. Democrat.

HAMMERSTROM, BEVERLY SWOISH, state legislator; b. Mineral Wells, Tex., Mar. 28, 1944; d. William Graham and Marjorie Wirth (Lillis) Swoish; m. Don Preston Hammerstrom, June 25, 1966 (div. Oct. 1976); children: Todd Preston, Rory Scott. BA, Adrian Coll., 1966; MPA, U. Toledo, 1994. Cert. mcpl. clk. Tchr. Geneva (N.Y.) Pub. Schs., 1966-69; substitute tchr. Darien (Wis.) Pub. Schs., 1970-71; tchr. Bedford Coop. Nursery Sch., Lambertville, Mich., 1975; retail mgr., buyer Gallerie, Toledo, 1975-78, Personal Touch, Toledo, 1978-80; clk. Bedford Township, Temperance, Mich., 1980-92; mem. Mich. Ho. of Reps., Lansing, 1993-98, Mich. Senate from 17th dist., Lansing, 1999—. Bd. dirs. Family Med. Ctr., Temperance; emergency mgmt. bd. Washtenaw County, Ypsilanti, Mich., 1993—, Monroe (Mich.) County, 1993—. Mem. Internat. Inst. Mcpl. Clks. (bd. dirs. Found. 1996), Mich. Assn. Clks. (life, pres. 1990-91), Am. Legis. Exch. Coun. (transp. task force), Coun. State Govt. (med. policies com., del. 1995—), Women in Govt. (state dir. 1999—). Republican. Roman Catholic. Home: 1183 Oakmont Dr Temperance MI 48182-9563 Office: Mich Senate PO Box 30036 Lansing MI 48909-7536

HAMMICK, PATRICIA A. utilities company executive; BS in Chemical Physics and Math., Rice U.; MSc in Physics, U. Calif., Riverside; D in Math. Statistics, George Washington U. Former operating officer Natural Gas Supply Assn.; v.p. strategic planning Columbia Energy Group, Reston, Va., 1997-99, sr. v.p. strategy and corp. comms., 1998—. Office: Columbia Energy Group 12355 Sunrise Valley Dr Reston VA 20191-3458

HAMMOND, CHARLENE FOSTER, writer, choreographer, musician, artist, educator; b. Seattle, Wash., June 20, 1943; d. Charles Hopkins and Alta Rose (Boothe) Foster; m. William Boyd Hammond, May 1, 1970 (div. Jan. 27, 1996); children: William, Ruby, Stephen. BA English, Tenn. State Univ., Nashville, Tenn., 1990—95. Cert. ESL 1997. Theatre performer various locations, SC, Ga. Tenn., 1946—; legal sec. Greenville, SC, 1963—69, Atlanta, 1969—75, Nashville, 1975—81; instr., phys. fitness various locations, Nashville, 1981—; artistic dir. Priest Lake Dance, Nashville, 1981—98; freelance writer self directed from home, Antioch, Tenn., 1993—; tchr. Glencliff HS, Nashville, 1996—. Cmty. edn. instr. Cole Cmty. Edn., Nashville, 1988—98. Contbr. articles to profl. jours. and mags.; editor: TSU Today, 1994—95; author: Invisible Scars, 1997, Rubbers, 2001, Washlink, 2001, Music Row Surprise, 2001, Spaghetti Suede Shoes, 2001, Juvenile Justice Ctr., 2001. Coach for baseball, softball, and basketball acitivities Una Recreation Ctr., Nashville, 1979—93; Girl/Boy Scout Leader Girl/Boy Scouts of Am., Nashville, 1986—93; pres. Alpha Mu Gamma, 1994; vol. U.S. Forestry Svc., Santa Fe, 2003. Recipient Outstanding Jr. Lang., Lit., and Phil. Dept., Tenn. State Univ., 1993, Sigma Tau Delta, 1994, Alpha Mu Gamma, 1994, Phi Kappa Phi, 1994. Mem.: PTA (officer 1983—84), Profl. Educators Tenn., Internat. Women's Writing Guild, Final Draft, Author's Venue, Am. Screenwriters Assn., Internat. Dyslexia Assn., TESOL. Independent Thinkers. Cath. Avocations: crafts, home improvement, gardening, creative arts. Office: Glencliff HS 160 Antioch Pike Nashville TN 37211 Home: 417 Owendale Drive Antioch TN 37013 Office Phone: 615-333-5070. Personal E-mail: mspiggee@hotmail.com. E-mail: mspiggee@hotmail.com.

HAMMOND, DEBBIE JOHNSON, computer analyst; b. Shelbyville, Ky., June 21, 1957; d. Shirley De Rice Johnson and Charlotte Jane (White) Groves; m. Fred Franklin Hammond, June 27, 1987. BA in Polit. Sci., Ky. State U., 1987. Program coord. Commonwealth of Ky., Frankfort, 1976—2001; ret., 2001—. Mem. Ky. Human Svcs. Agy., Tenure (nominating com. 2001-02). Democrat. Baptist. Avocations: reading, travel, cooking. Home: 433 Inman St Harrodsburg KY 40330-8624

HAMMOND, DEBORAH D.J. school librarian, researcher; d. Karl Creller and Heather Mary Ashline; m. Bradley C. Hammond, Oct. 1, 1994; children: Samantha, Brett. BA, Gallandet U., 1988; MS, Western Md. Coll., 1993. Cert. Librarian U. Vt., lic. tchg. Vt. Residential advisor Austine Sch., Brattleboro, Vt., 1988—91, tchr. deag, 1995—97, libr., 1997—. Cons. ARDO Pub. Co., Edina, Minn., 2003—. Mem.: ALA, Am. Assn Sch. Librs. Avocations: writing, reading, cooking, sewing, walking. Office: Austine Sch Deaf 60 Austine Dr Brattleboro VT 05301 E-mail: debbie@austine.put.k12.vt.us.

HAMMOND, DEBORAH LYNN, lay worker; b. Olney, Md., Feb. 12, 1958; d. Cornelius Dennis Sr. and Beverly Laura (Dunn) H. AA in Gen. Studies, Catonsville C.C. Sec. Mt. Zion United Meth. Ch., Ellicott City, Md., 1980-95; data entry clerk Balt. Gas Electric Co., Pasadena, Md., 1994-95; sec. The Md. Correctional Instn. for Women, Jessup, Md., 1995-97; instr. computer & typing Milford Mill Acad., Randallstown, MD, 1995—; ch. sec. Trinity United Meth. Ch., Catonsville, MD, 1997—; adminstrv. ch. office mgr. Falls Rd AME Ch., Balt., 1996—; with Rees Sci. and Tech. Ltd., Balt., Md., 1997—. Chaplain, vol. activity coord. sec. Md. Correctional Instn. Women, 1995; choir dir. Falls Road AME Ch., 1995—; instr. adult edn. Milford Mill Acad., 1996—; bookkeeper Balt. Subway, 2002. Mem.: Order of the Eastern Star (Myra, Balt. chpt.). Home: 1 Sulky Ct Apt 101 Randallstown MD 21133-3149 Office: Trinity United Meth Ch 2100 Westchester Ave Catonsville MD 21228-4757 also: Falls Rd AME Ch 2145 Pine Ave Baltimore MD 21244-2827 E-mail: deborah5909@aol.com.

HAMMOND, JANE LAURA, retired law librarian, lawyer; b. nr. Nashua, Iowa; d. Frank D. and Pauline Hammond. BA, U. Dubuque, 1950; MS, Columbia U., 1952; JD, Villanova U., 1965, LHD, 1993. Bar: Pa. 1965. Cataloguer Harvard Law Libr., 1952-54; asst. libr. Sch. Law Villanova (Pa.) U., 1954-62; libr. Sch. Law, Villanova (Pa.) U., 1962-76; prof. law Sch. Law Villanova (Pa.) U., 1965-76; law libr., prof. law Cornell U., Ithaca, N.Y., 1976-93. Adj. prof. Drexel U., 1971-74; mem. depository libr. coun. to pub. printer U.S. Govt. Printing Office, 1975-78; cons. Nat. Law Libr., Monrovia, Liberia, 1989. Fellow ALA; mem. ABA (coun. sect. legal edn. 1984-90, mem. com. on accreditation 1982-87, mem. com. on stds. rev. 1987-95), PEO, Coun. Nat. Libr. Assn. (sec.-treas. 1971-72, chmn. 1979-80), Am. Assn. Law Librs. (sec. 1965-70, pres. 1975-76), Assn. Am. Law Schs. (exec. com. 1977). Episcopalian. Office: Cornell U Sch Law Myron Taylor Hall Ithaca NY 14853

HAMMOND, JANE PAMELA, adult education educator; b. Flint, Mich., Aug. 10, 1951; d. Duane Aurther and Norine Janet Moore; m. Larry Duane Hammond, June 22, 1974; children: Jason Duane, Joel Brady. BA in Sociology, Olivet Nazarene U., 1973; postgrad., U. Mich., 1973—74. Lic. real estate Mich. Line supr. Tex. Instruments, Lubbock, Tex., 1976—78; elem. tchr. United Meth. Ch. Sch., Tampa, Fla., 1979—80; adult edn. and substitute tchr. Mt. Morris (Mich.) Consol. Schs., 1981—85, substitute tchr., 1992—99; automobile sales person Hobson Ford Dealership, Clio, Mich., 1985—86, real estate salesperson Century 21, Clio and Flint, Mich., 1987—92; tchr. adult and alternative edn. Clio Area Schs., 1999—. Career pathways rep. Clio Area Schs. Cmty. Edn., 2000—. Mem. exec. com. Genesee County Reps., Flint, 2000—; sustaining mem. Mich. State and Nat. Rep. Coms., 2000—; Sunday sch. tchr. Ch. of the Nazarene, Mt. Morris, Flint, 1986—. Jr. Miss Vocal scholar, House of Harmony, 1967. Mem.: Clio Area C. of C. (Enhancement award 2002), Clio Common Grounds (lifelong learning and arts and recreation com.), Mich. Hist. Soc., Clio Hist. Soc., Mich. Farm Bur., VFW Ladies Aux. Avocations: interior decorating, flower arranging, antiques, camping. Home: 3105 E Dodge Rd Clio MI 48420

HAMMOND, KAREN T. writer, editor; b. Salem, Mass. m. Nathaniel T. Hammond; children: Emily, Gregory. BA, U. N.H.; MA, SUNY, Binghamton. Adj. faculty SUNY, Binghamton, 1988—97. Author: (book) From Vision to Excellence: A Popular History of Binghamton University, 1996; contbr. articles to mags. and newspapers. Mem.: Maine Writers and Pubs. Alliance, Editl. Freelancers Assn., Am. Soc. Journalists and Authors. Office: PO Box 154 South Bristol ME 04568

HAMMOND, LOU RENA CHARLOTTE, public relations executive; b. Muenster, Tex. d. Louis Martin and Regina L. (Schoech) Wolf; m. Christopher Weymouth Hammond, Sept. 6, 1964; 1 child, Stephen. BA, U. Houston, 1962. Rep. pub. rels. Pan Am. Airways, N.Y.C., 1968-76, mgr. pub. rels., 1977-79, dir. pub. rels., 1980-81, dir. pub. affairs, 1981; pres., ptnr. Taylor and Hammond, N.Y.C., 1981-84; prin., pres. Lou Hammond and Assocs., N.Y.C., 1984—. Mem. adv. bd. Ctr. for Tourism and Travel at NYU. Editor: (calendar) Avenue mag., 1976-79. Mem. Women's Bd. of Madison Sq. Boys and Girls Club, N.Y.C. Recipient Matrix award in pub. rels., 1992, Winthrop W. Grice award Hotel Sales and Mktg. Assoc. Internat., 1992, Inside PR Mag.'s All-Star award, 1992. Mem. Soc. Am. Travel Writers, Fashion Group, Assn. Better N.Y., Les DAmes de Escoffier, Women's Forum, Women Execs. in Pub. Rels., Doubles Club. Roman Catholic. Avocations: bridge, tennis, 18th century antiques. Office: Lou Hammond & Assocs Inc 39 E 51st St New York NY 10022-5916 E-mail: louh@lhammond.com.

HAMMOND, SUSAN MEEKS, elementary school educator; d. Willard H. and Wanda V. Meeks; m. Joseph E. Hammond, Dec. 22, 1973; 1 child, Joseph E. III. BMusEd in Piano and Clarinet (double major), James Madison U., 1971; MEd, Radford U., 1987, degree in Counseling, 1991. Cert. postgrad. profl. Va., 1987. Music tchr./guidance counselor Alleghany Highlands Pub. Schs., Covington, Va., 1985—91; dir. bands New Kent County Pub. Schs., New Kent, Va., 1991—2003, co-dir., creator sch. rels. policies-ROAR, pianist for New Kent choirs, 1991—, crisis intervention counselor, gifted performing arts dir., 1991—. Composer patriotic and religious piano/choir music. Dir. music SonShine Emmaus, Richmond, Va., 1998—2002; dir. cmty. music show Covington Music Shows, Covington, Va., 1986—87; instr./choreographer Dance Studio, Covington, Va., 1986—90. Recipient award, Va. Gov.'s Sch. For Medicine, 2002. Mem.: Emmaus Ministries (life). Methodist. Avocation: assisted living therapy dog border collies. Office: New Kent Co Pub Schs New Kent Hwy New Kent VA Personal E-mail: shammond2000@yahoo.com.

HAMMOND-BLESSING, DIANN A. elementary school educator; b. Cedar Rapids, Iowa, May 24, 1943; d. Russell Irving and Ola Arline (Leonard) Hammond; m. Dale Fredrick Blessing, June 10, 1979. BA in Edn., U. Wyo., 1966, MEd, 1973. Cert. elem. tchr., Colo. Tchr. German and social studies Deaver-Frannie Schs., Deaver, Wyo., 1966-68, Alliance (Nebr.) City Schs., 1968-70; tchr. elem. Jefferson County Schs., Arvada, Colo., 1971—. Del. Colo. Del. Assembly, 1974-79, 2000, 2001; sec. Argonauts Investment Group, 1986-87, v.p., 1989, pres., 1990, treas.-elect, 1993, treas., 1994. Co-author curriculum units Our Changing Langauge, 1978. Mem. Record Keeping Task Force, Jefferson County, Colo., 1974-75, 84; del. Dem. County and State Convention, Colo., 1976, 80; mem. polit. action com. Jefferson County Schs., 1979-80; precint chair Dem. Com., Colo., 1984. Mem. NEA, AAUW (editor newspaper 1985-87), PTA, Internat. Reading Assn. (Colo. coun., Colo. Edn. Assn., Colo. Reading Assn., Jefferson County Edn. Assn. (mem. com., rep. 1973-82, 94-95, 96-97, 97-98, 98-99, 99-2000, 2000-2001, bd. dirs. 1974-79), Jefferson County Internat. Reading Assn., Instrnl. Profl. Devel., Phi Delta Kappa. Avocations: special event and interior decorating, assembly and design of clothing, elegant crafts. Home: 6626 S Yukon Way Littleton CO 80123-3070 Office: Warder Elem Sch 7840 Carr Dr Arvada CO 80005-4420

HAMMOND-KOMINSKY, CYNTHIA CECELIA, optometrist; b. Sept. 1, 1957; d. Andrew and Angeline (Laorno) Kominsky; m. Theodore Glen Hammond, Sept. 21, 1985. Student, Oakland U., Rochester, Mich., 1976—77; OD magna cum laude, Ferriss Coll. Optometry, 1981. Lic. optometrist Mich., cert. diagnostic and therapeutic pharm. agt. Intern Optometric Inst. and Clinic of Detroit, 1980, Ferris State Coll., Big Rapids, Mich., 1980, Jackson (Mich.) Prison, 1981; assoc. in pvt. practice Warren, Mich., 1981—82; optometrist Pearle Vision Ctr., Sterling Heights, Mich., 1982—87, K-Mart Optical Ctr., Sterling Heights, 1982—87, Royal Optical, Sterling Heights, 1988—. Provided eye care to nursing homes, Mt. Clemens, Mich. Head vol. caregivers and organ donation programs St. Therese of Lisieux Ch., Shelby Twp., Mich. Achievements include invention of binocular low vision aid device. Avocations: music, sports, decorative painting, gardening, antique crystal. Home: 47626 Cheryl Ct Shelby Township MI 48315-4708 Office: Royal Optical Lakeside Mall 14300 Lakeside Cir Sterling Heights MI 48313-1326

HAMMOND-RECTOR, SUSAN GLYNN, illustrator, photographer, sculptor; b. Woodside, N.Y., May 12, 1947; d. René Embree and Virginia Hammond; m. Garrett Edward Rector, Oct. 22, 1994. Student, Joe Kubert Art Sch., 1992—94; AAS, Sussex County CC, Newton, N.J., 1997; student, Peter's Valley Ednl. Ctr., 1999—2001; BFA summa cum laude, postgrad., William Paterson U., 2000—. Illustrator U.S. Army, Dover, NJ, 1986—. Exhibitions include U.S. Army Rsch. and Devel. Ctr., Dover, 1997, William Paterson U., Wayne, N.J., 1998—2002, N.J. State Fair, Augusta, 2002, Printmaking Coun. N.J., North Branch Station, N.J., 2002, Brad Cooper Gallery, Tampa, Fla., 2002, Salmagundi Club, N.Y.C., 2003, Chgo. Fine Arts Gallery, 2003, Montclair (N.J.) State U., 2003; contbr. articles to profl. jours. Named Photographer of the Yr., William Paterson U., 2000; recipient Adolph Fassbender award for excellence in photography, N.J. State Fair, 2002, 1st pl. photography, 2002; Presdl. scholar, William Paterson U., 1997. Mem.: Provincetown, Mass., Art Assn. and Mus., Am. Assn. Mus., Printmaking Coun. N.J., Nat. Mus. Women in Arts, Internat. Ctr. Photography, N.Y., William Paterson U. Alumni Assn., Ctr. Photography Woodstock, Peters Valley Ednl. Ctr., City Without Walls Gallery, N.J., Pi Lambda Theta. Office: US Army LSED Bldg 1 Dover NJ 07801 Business E-Mail: shammond@pica.army.mil.

HAMMONTREE, MARIE GERTRUDE, writer; b. Jefferson County, Ind., June 19, 1913; d. Harry Clay and Hattie Agnes (Means) H. BA, Butler U., 1949. Sec. Bobbs-Merrill Co., Indpls., 1931-42, Ind. U. Med. Ctr., Indpls., 1942-48, Travel Enterprises, Inc., N.Y.C., 1949-50, U.S. Dept. Justice (FBI), Indpls., 1950-75; bookkeeper, purchasing agt. Office of William H. Hudnut, III/ Mayor of Indpls., 1978-92. Author: (children's books) Will and Charlie Mayo: Doctor's Boys, 1954, A.P.Giannini: Boy of San Francisco, 1956, Albert Einstein: Young Thinker, 1961, Mohandas Gandhi: Boy of Principle, 1966, Walt Disney: Young Movie Maker, 1969. Active in campaigns of Mayor William H. Hudnut, III and Ind. State Reps., Indpls., 1975-92. Mem. Nat. League Am. Pen Women (pres. Indpls. chpt. 1978-80), Women in Comms., Soc. of FBI Alumni, Inc. (treas. Indpls. chpt. 1990-98), Sigma Tau Delta, Phi Kappa Phi. Republican. Presbyterian. Avocations: travel, writing for children. Home: 8140 Township Line Rd Apt 5213 Indianapolis IN 46260-5866

HAMNER, EUGENIE LAMBERT, English educator; b. Darlington, Ala, May 24, 1936; d. Robert Eugene Jr. and Helen (Burford) Lambert; m. Gustavus O. Hamner, 1966 (div. 1988); children: Helen Gaussen, Nicholas Peagin. BA in English & history, Huntingdon Coll., 1958; MA in English, U. N.C., 1959, PhD in English, 1965. Instr. English, Winthrop Coll., Rock Hill, SC, 1959-60; instr. U. NC, Chapel Hill, NC, 1963-64; asst. prof. Huntingdon Coll., Montgomery, Ala., 1964-65, U. Ga., Athens, Ga., 1965-66; from asst. prof. to prof. U. So. Ala., Mobile, Ala., 1969-96, prof. emeritus, 1996. Co-editor: Ways of Knowing: Essays on Marge Piercy, 1991, (children's book) A Kitten for Julie and Christopher, 1997. Bd. dir. Mobile Mus. Art, 1984-88; mem. Mobile Hist. Devel. Commn., 1987-92; elem. sch. vol. Rolling Readers USA. Alpha Beta scholar, 1958, Sigma Sigma Sigma scholar, 1958. Mem. South Atlantic Modern Lang. Assn., Habitat for Humanity (pres.'s cir.), Mobile Opera Guild, Nat. Soc. Colonial Dames of Am., Omicron Delta Kappa. Democrat. Episcopalian. Avocations: reading, gardening, travel, children. Home: 3764 Mordecai Ln Mobile AL 36608-2007

HAMNER, SUZANNE LEATH, retired history educator; b. Ft. Worth, Feb. 29, 1940; d. Roland Martin and Mabel Lois (Hall) Leath; m. W. Easley Hamner, June 18, 1961; children: Janine Suzanne, Michael Edward. BA summa cum laude, Meredith Coll., Raleigh, N.C., 1961; MA, Tulane U., New Orleans, 1964. Tchg. asst. Tulane U., New Orleans, 1963-66; instr. history Coll. Liberal Arts Northea. U., Boston, 1966-71, lectr. history Univ. Coll., 1972-75; lectr. history Coll. Arts and Scis., Univ. Coll., Boston, 1985—2002, ret., 2002—. Sr. lectr. U. Coll., 1985-2002. Contbg. editor Reclaiming Our Global Heritage, Vol. I and Vol. II, 1990. Mem. adv. com. Follow Through Program, Cambridge (Mass.) Sch. Dept., 1977-79; treas., v.p. adv. bd. Parents Assn., Buckingham Browne and Nichols Sch., Cambridge, 1980-86; clk., bd. dirs., adv. bd. Cambridge Civic Assn., 1976-95; treas. Alice Wolf Election Com., City Coun., Cambridge, 1979-96; advisor Wolf Campaign for State Rep., 1996, 98; overseer Handel and Haydn Soc., Boston, 1989—; trustee Chorus pro Musica, 1993-95; adv. com. Meml. Ch., Harvard U., 1992-94; vice co-chair leadership com. United Way Cambridge, 1997, co-chair, 1998-2001; incorporator The Cambridge Homes, 1999—; mem. grants com. Meml. Ch., Harvard U., 1998-2000; reader Rec. for the Blind and Dyslexic, 2002—. Woodrow Wilson Found. fellow, Princeton, N.J., 1961-62; Tulane U. scholar, 1962-64. Mem. Am. Hist. Assn., New England Hist. Assn., Phi Alpha Theta. Democrat. Avocations: music, reading, travel, politics. Home: 3 Ellery Sq Cambridge MA 02138-4227

HAMOS, JULIE E. state representative; b. Budapest, Hungary, Jan. 29, 1949; m. Alan Greiman. BA, Wash. U., 1972; JD, George Washington U., 1975. Legis. dir. AFSCME Ill., 1979—81; legis. liaison Cook County State's Atty.'s Office, 1981—84; atty. child support divsn., 1984—88; pres. Julie E. Hamos & Assocs., Ltd., 1988—; mem. Ill. Ho. of Reps., 1998—. Resource bd. Met. Planning Coun., 1998—; adv. bd. Trilogy, 2001—; bd. dirs. Planned Parenthood, Chgo., 1995—. Democrat. Jewish. Office: 246-W Stratton Office Bldg Springfield IL 62706 Address: 820 Davis St Ste 103 Evanston IL 60201

HAMOUDA, AMY BICE, artist; b. Edinburg, Ind., Aug. 16, 1926; d. John Thomas Middleton and Rowene Elizabeth Baker; m. Abdel Mohsen Hamouda, 1952 (div. 1956); 1 child, Loubna Rowene ; m. John Avery Bice, Oct. 8, 1960; children: Juliet Elizabeth Bice, Warrick Vincent Bice. Student, Boston Mus. Sch., 1948—50; BFA, Ohio State U., 1952; MFA, L'Ecole de Beaux Art, Paris, 1959—60; postgrad., Instituto Allende, San Miguel Allende, Mex., 1952—54; M.Am. Studies, SUNY-Buffalo, 1984. Art mistress The English Sch., Cairo, 1953—55, English Mission Coll., Heliopolis, Egypt, 1955—56; art instr. Opportunity Sch., Denver, 1956—58, SUNY-Buffalo, Siena, Italy, 1969—70, instr. Am. Studies, 1982—84. Numerous one person and group exhbns. N.Y.C., Cairo, Buffalo, Boulder, Santa Fe, N.Mex., Seattle, Represented in permanent collections Metal Altar Cross, 1st Meth. Ch., Boulder, Kinetic Sound Sculpture, Buffalo, fountain sculpture, glass mosaic mural, Colo. State U., mural, Cairo, sound sculpture, Ctr. for the Performing Arts, SUNY, numerous others, Interactive Children's Sculpture, Austin, Tex., all artwork, welded nicel silver, Episcop. Ch., Worland, Wyo., mural, U. Wash., prin. works include Mural. Recipient CAPS for Sculpture, N.Y. State Coun. on the Arts, 1980; fellow MacDowell Colony, 1984; grantee Money for Women grantee, Money for Women Art Orgn., Fla., 1992. Mem.: AAUW, Austin Visual Arts Assn. Democrat. Avocations: travel, writing. Home: 2401 Crownspoint Dr Austin TX 78748 Office Phone: 512-280-2295.

HAMOY, CAROL, artist; b. N.Y.C., May 22, 1934; d. Morris David and Selma (Essex) Cohen. Student, Newark (N.J.) Sch. Fine Art, 1952-54, Art Students League, N.Y.C., various yrs. Lectr., spkr. in field. One-woman shows include USMA/West Point, N.Y., 1978, Katonah (N.Y.) Gallery, 1983, Lower Manhattan Cultural Coun., N.Y.C., 1986, May Mus./Lawrence, N.Y. Ceres, N.Y.C., 1992, MTA-Arts for Transit, N.Y.C., 1993, Robert Kahn Gallery, Houston, 1993, Temple Judea Mus., Elkins Park, Pa., 1993, Univ. Art Ctr., Shreveport, La., 1994, Ceres, N.Y.C., 1995, 98-99, 2001, Goldman Art Gallery, Rockville, Md., 1996, Nat. Mus. Am. Jewish History, Phila., 1996, Broadway Windows, N.Y.C., 1997, Ellis Island Immigration Mus., N.Y.C., 1997, Mizel Mus., Denver, 1997, Breman Heritage Mus., Atlanta, 1998, Eldridge St. Project, N.Y.C., 1998, Inter-Am. Gallery, Miami, Fla., 1998, Skirball Mus., Cincinnati, 1999, Franklin Marshall Coll., Lancaster Pa., 1999, Margolis Gallery, Houston, 1999, Lower East Side Tenement Mus., N.Y., 2000, The Neuberger Mus., Purchase, N.Y., 2000, Ceres, N.Y.C., 2001, Dacotah Prarie Mus., Aberdeen, S.D., 2002, Azarian/McCullough Gallery, Sparkill, N.Y., 2002, Futernick Gallery, Miami, 2003; exhibited in group shows at Pelham (N.Y.) Art Ctr., 1988, U. Ky., Lexington, 1989, HUC, N.Y.C., 1989, Kentuck Mus., Northport, Ala., 1989, Clough Hansen Gallery, Memphis, 1989, JRC Gallery, Evanston, Ill., 1992, Soho 20, N.Y.C., 1993, Charach-Epstein Mus., West Bloomfield, Mich., 1994, 97, Nat. Jewish Mus., Washington, 1995, Fine Arts Rosen Mus., Boca Raton, Fla., 1995, Right Brain Gallery, Atlanta, 1999, Miss. Univ. for Women, 1999, Skirball Mus., Cin., 1999, Neuberger Mus., Purchase, N.Y., 2000, Ellipse Arts Ctr., Arlington, Va., 2000, Contemporary Crafts, Pitts., 2000, Ceres, 2000, The Joseph Gallery Mus, N.Y.C., 2000-01, Moving On/Frauen Mus., Bonn, Germany, John Jay Coll., 2001—, Joseph Gallery, N.Y., 2000-01, Frauen Mus., Bonn, Germany, 2001-02, Detritus Show John Jay College, N.Y., 2001-02, Judaica Mus., Riverdale, N.Y., 2001-02, Kommunale Galerie Wilmersdorf, Berlin, 2001-02, Ctr. for Visual Art & Culture, Stamford, Conn., 2002, Am. Craft Mus., N.Y., 2002-03, Joseph Gallery, N.Y.C., HUC Mus., N.Y.C., 2003—, others; permanent collections include Nat. Mus. Women in the Arts, Nat. Jewish Mus., Washington, Frauen Mus., Bonn, others. Nominee, Joan Mitchell Found., 2000; grantee Va. Ctr. for Creative Arts, Sweet Briar, Va., 1980, Artists' Space, N.Y.C., 1981, Hillwood Art Mus., N.Y. State Coun. for Creative Arts, 1992, MTA-Arts for Transit, N.Y.C., 1993, Lucius N. Littauer Found. Bessemere Trust Co. N.A., 1997, Meml. Found./Jewish Culture fellow, Artists' Fellowship, Inc. of N.Y.C., 1999. Studio: 340 E 66th St New York NY 10021-6021 E-mail: hamoycar@aol.com.

HAMPLE, JUDY G. academic administrator; BA in Speech Comm. and Secondary Edn./French, David Lipscomb U.; MA and PhD in Comm., Ohio State U. Univ. fellow, asst. dir. intercollegiate debate Ohio State U.; faculty dept. speech comm. U. Ill., Champaign-Urbana; divsn. dir. dept. comm. arts and scis. Western Ill. U., assoc. dean for budget and pers. Coll. Arts and Scis.; dean Coll. Liberal Arts and Scis. Emporia (Kans.) State U., 1983—86; dean Coll. Arts and Scis. Ind. State U., 1986—93; sr. v.p. acad. affairs U. Toledo, 1993; chancellor Pa. State Sys. of Higher Edn., Harrisburg, 2001—. Cons.-evaluator North Cen. Accreditation Assn.; pub. cons.-evaluator ABA. Co-editor: Teaching in the Middle Ages, 3 vols.; editor: Studies in Medieval and Renaissance Teaching. Office: Pa State Sys of Higher Edn Dixon Univ Ctr 2986 N 2d St Harrisburg PA 17110

HAMPTON, ANGELA VAUGHN, music educator; b. Louisville, Ky., Nov. 12, 1970; d. Elvis and Donna Vaughn; m. Mark A. Hampton, Oct. 3, 1992. B in Vocal Music Edn., U. Louisville, 1992; M in Choral Conducting, U. Louisville, 1998. Music tchr. Floyd Ctrl. H.S., Floyds Knobs, Ind., 1995—. Asst. artistic dir. Voces Novae, Louisville, 1993—2002; handbell dir. Shively Bapt. Ch., Louisville, 1991—; free-lance musician, 1988—. Named Arts Educator of Yr., Arts Coun. So. Ind., 2003; recipient Excel award in Tchg., LG&E Energy and WHAS TV, 2002. Mem.: Am. Guild Eng. Handbell Ringers (ind. edn. coord. 1998—2003, Opening concert condr. - Area V Conf. 2003), Music Educators Nat. Conf. (Featured Condr. 2002 - Ind. State Conv. 2002), Am. Choral Dirs. Assn. (Featured condr. 2000 - Ctrl. Divsn. Conv. 2000). Avocations: piano, sewing, harp, theater.

HAMPTON, CAROL MCDONALD, priest, educator, historian; b. Oklahoma City, Sept. 18, 1935; d. Denzil Vincent and Mildred Juanita (Cussen) McDonald; m. James Wilburn Hampton, Feb. 22, 1958; children: Jaime, Clayton, Diana, Neal. BA, U. Okla., 1957, MA, 1973, PhD, 1984; cert. individual theol. study, Episcopal Theol. Sem. of S.W., 1998; MDiv summa cum laude, Phillips Theol. Sem., 1999. Ordained to Episcopal Transitional Diaconate, 1999, ordained priest, 1999. Tchg. asst. U. Okla., Norman, 1976—81; instr. U. Sci. and Arts Okla., Chickasha, 1981—84; coord. Consortium for Grad. Opportunities for Am. Indians U. Calif., Berkeley, 1985—86; trustee Ctr. of Am. Indian, Oklahoma City, 1981. Vice chmn. Nat. Com. on Indian Work, Episc. Ch., 1986; field officer Native Am. Ministry of Episc. Ch. (Nat.), 1986-94, sec., co-chmn., advising elder, prin. elder coun., 1994-96; field officer for Congl. Ministries of Episc. Ch. (Nat.), 1994-97; mem. nat. coun. Chs. Racial Justice Working Group, 1990-97, co-convenor, 1991-93, convenor, 1993-95; officer Multicultural Ministries of Episc. Ch. (Nat.), 1994-97; (hon.) canon of St. Paul's Cath., Oklahoma City, 2001—. Mem. editl. bd.: First Peoples Theology Jour.; contbr. articles to profl. jours. Trustee Western History Collections, U. Okla., Okla. Found. for the Humanities, 1983-86; mem. bd. regents U. Sci. and Arts Okla., 1989-95; bd. dirs. Okla. State Regents for Higher Edn., mem. adv. com. on social justice; mem. World Coun. of Chs. Program to Combat Racism, Geneva, 1985-91; bd. dirs. Caddo Tribal Coun., Okla., 1976-82; accredited observer Anglican Consultative Coun. UN 4th World Conf. on Women, 1995; v.p. Nat. Conf. Cmty. Justice, 1999-2002; bd. dirs. Ctrl. Okla. Human Rights Alliance, 1999—, Planned Parenthood, Oklahoma City, 2002—. Recipient Okla. State Human Rights awatrd, 1987; Francis C. Allen fellow Ctr. for the History of Am. Indian, 1983. Mem.: Okla. Conf. Chs. (bd. dirs. 2000—), Indigenous Theol. Tng. Inst. (bd. dirs. 2000—), Jr. League (Oklahoma City), Am. Assn. Indian Historians (founding mem. 1981—), Okla. Hist. Soc., Am. Hist. Assn., Orgn. Am. Historians, Western Social Sci. Assn., Western History Assn. Democrat. Episcopalian. Avocation: travel. Home: 1414 N Hudson Ave Oklahoma City OK 73103-3721 Office Phone: 405-235-3436. E-mail: cjchampton@aol.com, champton@stpaulscathedralokc.org.

HAMPTON, KYM, professional basketball player; b. Louisville, Nov. 3, 1962; Grad., Ariz. State U., 1984. Forward, Vigo, Spain, 1985—87, Barcelona, 1987—89, Valencia, Spain, 1989—91, Avellino, Italy, 1994—95, Pavia, Italy, 1995—97, Aix-en-Provence, France, 1993—94, Chanson, Japan, 1992—93, N.Y. Liberty, N.Y.C., 1997—. Named to, Italian League All-Star Team, 1992, 1995, 1996; recipient Street & Smith Hon. Mention, 1982, 1983, 1984. Avocations: jazz, R&B, travel, water sports, singing. Office: NY Liberty 2 Penn Plz New York NY 10121-0101

HAMRIC, CAROLYN MARIE, legal assistant, small business owner; b. Clarksburg, W.Va., Dec. 8, 1960; d. Russell Wade Kerns and Bernice Marie Linger; m. Richard Allen Hamric, Feb. 8, 1980; children: Nathan Scott, Lindsay Marie. Grad., Weston, W.Va. Legal asst. Law Offices Wilson & Bailey P.L.L.C., Weston, 1987—; owner Suds R Us Laundry, Weston, 1991—. Treas. Weston Circuit United Meth. Ch., 1994—2003. Mem.: Broad St. United Meth. Women. Republican. Methodist. Avocations: travel, health foods, reading. Home: 439 McCann's Run Jane Lew WV 26378 Office: Law Offices Wilson & Bailey PLLC 122 Court Avenue Weston WV 26452 Personal E-mail: rahamric58@aol.com. E-mail: wblawcmh@1stcounsel.com.

HAMURA, KAORI, artist; b. Fukuoka, Japan, Mar. 9, 1970; d. Shoei Yoh and Kimiko H. AA, Sophia Jr. Coll., Tokyo, 1990; BFA, Parsons Sch. Design, 1993. Character designer MTV Network, N.Y., 1993—, dir., animator, 1995; illustrator N.Y. Press, Interview, Timeout, Mademoiselle,

New Yorker, N.Y., 1995—, Clark Kent Co., Tokyo, 1988-90; artist Artist's Space, N.Y.C., 1992—, Drawing Center, N.Y.C., 1994—. Artist: Hotwired Pop Gallery, 1996. Recipient Poster Design award Harajuku Police Station, 1988; scholarship Parsons Sch. Design, 1990-93. Mem. N.Y. Found. Arts. Office: MTV Network 1633 Broadway Fl 31 New York NY 10019-6708

HAN, SOO J. governmental administrator; b. Suwon, Korea, Sept. 2, 1970; came to U.S., 1974. d. Hui Yul and Sung Ok (Kim) H. BA, BSBA, Boston U., 1992. Staff asst. Office of the V.P. of U.S., Washington, 1993-96; assoc. dep. dir. vice presdl. advance Clinton/Gore '96, Washington, 1996—; project mgr. U.S. Dept. State, 2003—. Dir. parade floats '97 Presdl. Inaugural Com., 1997; scheduler Sen. Edward M. Kennedy, 1997-99; project mgr. Internat. Joint Commn., 1999-2002.

HAN, SUE XU, marketing professional, application developer; b. Beijing, Dec. 27, 1968; arrived in U.S., 1990; d. Nian Guo Han and Mo Ju Li. BS, U. Tex. at Austin, 1993; MBA, So. Methodist U., Dallas, 2000. Software engr. Sprint, Las Colinas, Tex., 1994; sr. mem. scientific staff NORTEL, Richardson, Tex., 1995—98; global product bus. mgr. Ericsson, Richardson, 1998—99; sr. product mktg. mgr. Fujitsu Network Comm., Richardson, 2001; sr. global mktg. mgr. ADC Comm., 2002; wireless mktg. mgr. GE Med. Sys., Milw., 2002—. Founder, music and arts club NORTEL, 1996; spkr. in field. Stage mgr. Dallas Asian Festival, 2001—02. Mem.: NAFE, Am. Math. Soc., U. Tex. Alumni Assn. (mem. coun. 2002), Nat. Golden Key Honor Soc. Achievements include patent wireless frquency planning. Business E-Mail: suehan@alumni.utexas.net. E-mail: sue_han@yahoo.com.

HAN, WENGE, research scientist; arrived in U.S., 1999; m. Fuli Du, July 16, 1992; children: Bowen Du, Hannes Boen Du. BS, Tianjin (China) U., 1989, MS, 1992; PhD, U. Heidelberg, Germany, 1999. Lectr. physics Tianjin U., 1992—94; guest scientist German Cancer Rsch. Ctr., Heidelberg, 1995—95, predoctoral rschr., 1996—99; rsch. assoc. The Scripps Rsch. Inst., La Jolla, Calif., 1999—. Author: Comprehensive Coordination Chemistry II, Vol. 2 - Fundamentals, 2003; contbr. articles to profl. jours., German Cancer Rsch. Ctr. fellow, 1996—99. Mem.: Am. Chem. Soc., Biophysical Soc. Achievements include first to succesfully predicted the structure of N-Acetyl-L-alanine N'-Methylamide in water solution by DFT calculations. This structure was later approved by NMR experiments; first time to present the methodology to deduce the coupled redox potential for Mn(Fe)SOD from kinetic rate constants. This provides a valuable alternative to spectroelectrochemistry. Office: The Scripps Research Institute 10550 North Torrey Pines Road La Jolla CA 92037 E-mail: wengehan@scripps.edu.

HANABUSA, COLLEEN, state legislator, lawyer; b. Honolulu, 1952; m. June and Isao Hanabusa. BA in Econs. and Sociology, U. Hawaii, 1973, MA in Sociology, 1975, JD, 1977. Labor atty., Honolulu; legal rschr. Madison, Wis., 1978; mem. Hawaii Senate, Dist. 21, Honolulu; chair water, land and Hawaiian affairs com. Hawaii Senate, Honolulu, mem. commerce and consumer protection com., mem. govt. ops. and housing com. Advisor Arnold Morgado for Mayor Canmpaign, 1994. Recipient 2d runner-up Hawaii Jr. Miss Pageant, 1969. Avocation: reading murder mysteries. Office: State Capitol 415 S Beretania St Honolulu HI 96813-2407 Fax: (808) 586-7797.

HANAGAN, AUDREY JEANETTE, training services executive; b. Connersville, Ind., Oct. 19, 1968; d. Joseph J. and Patricia A. (Malinski) Hanagan; m. Eileen Marie Peterson, July 18, 1993. BS, U.S. Mil. Acad., 1990; MA, U. Ill., 1998. With U.S. Army, 1990—94; mgr. Russian Dream, Colo. Springs, 1994—95; adminstrv. asst. Jenner & Block, Chgo., 1995—97; unit mgr. Household Internat., Prospect Heights, Ill., 1997—2000, corp. trainer, 2000—. Democrat. Avocations: running, reading, gardening. Office: Household Internat 2600 Sanders Rd Prospect Heights IL 60070

HANAUER, LINDA, venture capitalist; BA, Aldelphi U.; MBA, Harvard Bus. Sch. CFO & chief adminstrv. officer, equity div. Credit Suisse First Boston Corp.; COO & CFO AEA Investors Inc.; CFO & chief adminstrv. officer Venrock Assoc., 2002—. Founding bd. mem. Private Equity CFO Assn., 2001—. Office: Venrock Assoc 30 Rockefeller Plaza, Rm 5508 New York NY 10112*

HANAWAY, ANDREA STEIN, emergency physician; b. Phila., Feb. 26, 1947; d. Raymond Oscar and Phyllis (Pomeranz) Stein; divorced; children: Jaime Karen, Stacy Alix. BA, U. N.C., 1969; MD, Med. Coll. Pa., 1973. Diplomate Am. Bd. Emergency Medicine, Nat. Bd. Med. Examiners; cert. ACLS provider and instr., BLS instr. Intern Med. Coll. Pa., Phila., 1973-74, resident in ob-gyn., 1974-75, resident, then chief resident emergency medicine, 1975-77; clin. instr. dept. medicine U. Pa. Med. Sch., Phila., 1977-79; attending physician emergency dept. Presbyn.-U. Pa. Med. Ctr., 1977-79; dir. emergency unit Albert Einstein Med. Ctr. Mt. Sinai-Daroff Divsn., 1979-85; clin. instr. dept. emergency medicine Thomas Jefferson U. Med. Sch., Phila., 1984—; dir. emergency dept. John F. Kennedy Meml. Hosp., Phila., 1985; 1989attending physician emergency medicine and indsl. medicine 1998St. Luke's Hosp., Bethlehem, Pa., 19988-89; attending physician emergency dept. Phoenixville U. Pa. Health System, 1998—; asst. dir. emergency dept. Phoenixville U. of Pa. Health Systems, 2002—. Co-chmn. med. panel Pa. Bd. Pensions and Retirement; small group seminar instr. dept. psychiatry Thomas Jefferson U. Med. Sch., 1982-85; adj. asst. prof. emergency Med. Coll. Pa./Hahnemann U., Phila., 1995; pres. med. staff John F. Kennedy Meml. Hosp., 1993-95, chair credentials com., 1995. Fellow Am. Coll. Emergency Physicians; mem. AMA, Pa. Emergency Physicians Soc., Phila. C. of C., Psi Chi. Office: Phoenixville U of Pa Health System Emergency Dept 140 Huff Rd Phoenixville PA 19460

HANAWAY, CATHERINE, state representative, lawyer; b. Schuyler, Nebr., Nov. 8, 1963; m. Christopher; children: Lucy, Jack. BA, Creighton U., 1987; JD, The Catholic U. of Am., 1990. Owner, atty. Hanamore Solutions, LLC; atty. Peper, Martin, St. Louis, 1990—93; campaign mgr. Bredemeier for Atty. Gen., 1996; dist. dir. Senator Kit Bond, 1993—96, 1996—98; polit. advisor Missourians for Kit Bond, 1998; rep. Mo. State Ho. of Reps., 1998—, spkr., 2002—; exec. dir. Mo. Bush/Cheney, 2002. Mem. Housing Adv. Bd.; bd. dirs. Hope House, Foster and Adoptive Care Coalition. Mem.: Mo. Bar Assn., St. Louis Junior League, St. Louis Jaycees (past pres.). Roman Catholic. Office: State Capital, Rm 308 201 W Capitol Ave Jefferson City MO 65101

HANCHETT, SUZANNE LORRAINE, anthropologist, consultant; b. Salinas, Calif., June 17, 1941; d. Edward Lorraine and Clara Louise (Walldow) H.-McDonald; m. Stanley Regelson, June 21, 1964 (div. May 1979); 1 child, Moira Ellen; m. Michael Munk, Nov. 27, 1992 (div. July 2001). BA, Reed Coll., 1962; PhD, Columbia U., 1970. Instr. anthropology Bard Coll, Annandale-on-Hudson, N.Y., 1969-70; asst. prof. Queens Coll. City Univ. N.Y., 1971-78; dir. govt. and found grants Bedford Stuyvesant Restoration Corp., Brooklyn, N.Y., 1979-83; dir. resource devel. Cmty. Family Planning Coun., N.Y.C., 1983-86; sr. planner Office Svcs. Planning, Human Resources Adminstrn. City of N.Y., 1986-88, project dir. cmty. planning for teens Bur. Maternity Svcs. and Family Plannig Dept. Health, 1988, coord. Office Adolescent Pregnancy and Parenting Svcs. Office of the Mayor, 1988-90, coord. kinship and foster care program N.Y.C. Child Welfare Adminstrn., 1990-91; devel. cons. Planning Alternatives Change, L.L.C., Portland, 1991—. Sr. adv. Bangaldesh Flood Action Plan U.S. Agy. for Internat. Devel., 1991-93, cons. tech. assistance program West Bank, Gaza, 1994; cons. World Bank Bangladesh, 1995; cons. water and sanitation planning, 1997—. Author: Coloured Rice: Symbolic Structure in Hindu Family Festivals, 1988; contbr. articles to profl. jours. Past mem. bd. dirs. Manhattan (N.Y.) Teen Pregnancy Network. Fellow Am. Inst. Indian Studies, 1977, rsch. fellow NIMH, 1966-67, Ogden Mills Fellow Am. Mus. Natural History, 1970-71; writing grantee Am. Coun. Learned Soc., Fulbright faculty rsch. abroad grantee, 1976. Fellow Am. Anthropol. Assn., Soc. Applied Anthropology; mem. Am. Pub. Health Assn., Nat. Coun. Internat. Health, Assn. Women in Devel., Soc. South India Studies (past pres.). Democrat. Jewish. Office: Planning Alternatives for Change PO Box 8952 Portland OR 97207

HANCOCK, BEVERLY J. counseling consultant, secondary school educator; b. Bridgeton, N.J., Dec. 16, 1943; m. J. Everett Hancock, Jr., Aug. 9, 1969; children: J. Michael, Faith Lynn. BE, Montclair (N.J.) State U., 1966; MEd in counseling, Temple U., Phila., 1972. Cert. Social Studies Tchr. N.J. Dept. Edn., 1966, Sch. Counselor N.J. Dept. Edn., 1972, Nat. Bd. Cert. Counselors, 1983, lic. Profl. Counselor Bd. of Marriage and Family Therapy Examiners of N.J., 1999. Tchr. English and social studies Burlington Twp. (N.J.) HS, 1966—69, Burlington County Inst. Tech., Westhampton, NJ, 1969—72, guidance counselor, 1972—93, student resource ctr. counselor, 1993—98, guidance counselor, 1998—2002, cons. counselor, English instr., 2002—04. Staff coord. Student-Supr. Liason Com., 1988—90; cons. N.J. Statewide Non-Traditional Career Assistance Ctr., 1992—. Author: Work Resource Handbook, 1986, Student Leadership Handbook, 1989; editor: The Source Guidance Bull. Co-developer Burlington County Job Fair for HS Srs. Mem.: NEA, N.J. Sch. Counselor Assn. (Counselor of Yr. 1990), N.J. Edn. Assn., Burlington County Sch. Counselors Assn., N.J. Sch. Counselor Assn., Am. Sch. Counselor Assn., Delta Kappa Gamma, Chi Sigma Iota. Episcopalian. Avocations: crafts, carpentry, reading. Home: 1419 Noreen Dr Burlington NJ 08016

HANCOCK, DONNA, secondary school educator; b. Crosset, Ark., Oct. 28, 1942; d. Mady Lee and Verna Marie (Hicks) Watts; m. James Weldon Hancock, Feb. 21, 1966; children: Terrence Ray, James Weldon. BS, Kent State U., 1965; MA, U. Louisville, 1975. Cert. tchr. secondary edn. English tchr. Gary (Ind.) Ind. Schs., 1965-69; English and bus. edn. tchr. Jefferson County Schs., Jeffersontown, Ky., 1970-71, 72-78; English tchr. Tyler (Tex.) Pub. Schs., 1978-81; counselor battered women Waukesha (Wis.) Women's Ctr., 1981-82; expeditor, buyer GE Co., Waukesha, 1982-85; English tchr., yearbook adv. South Milwaukee Pub. Schs., 1985-89; English tchr. Greenville County Schs., Greenville, S.C., 1989-99. Minority cons. S. Milw. Pub. Schs., 1987-89. Contbr. poetry to poetic jours. Rep. outstanding minority students in Wis. Minority Leadership Forum, 1985-86; mem. state bd. min. affairs com. Wis. State Tchrs. Assn., 1986-87; mem. bd., sec. NAACP, Waukesha, 1986-88. Mem. Greenville County Mus. Art, Am. Assn. Univ. Women (pub. policy chmn. 1996-98, bd. dirs. 1996—), Emrys Art Found. (bd. dirs. 1996—, sec. 1999—). Avocations: writing, playing the piano, theater, travel. Home: 109 Coventry Rd Greenville SC 29615-3203 E-mail: jimhancock@msn.com.

HANCOCK, ELLEN MARIE, communications executive; b. N.Y.C., Apr. 15, 1943; d. Peter Joseph and Helen Gertrude (Houlihan) Mooney; m. W. Jason Hancock, Sept. 17, 1971. BA, Coll. New Rochelle, 1965; MA, Fordham U., 1966. With IBM, 1966—, programmer, 1966-81, dir. communications programming sect., communication products div. Raleigh, N.C., 1981-83, v.p. communications programming sect., communication products div., 1983-84, asst. group exec. systems devel. info. systems and storage group Armonk, N.Y., 1985, v.p. telecommunication systems communication prodn. div., 1985-86, pres. communications products div., 1986-88, v.p., gen. mgr. communication system Somers, N.Y., 1988-91, v.p., gen. mgr. networking systems Staines, Eng., 1991-92, sr. v.p., group exec. networking systems, 1992—; v.p. technology Apple Computers, Cupertino, Calif., 1996-97. Bd. dirs. ARDIS Co., Lincolnshire, Ill., Colgate-Palmolive Co., N.Y.C., ROLM Co., IBM UK Holdings Ltd., London, Integrated Systems Solutions Corp.; adv. bd. Fireworks Ptnrs, IBM. Trustee Coll. of New Rochelle, N.Y., 1986—, Marist Coll., Poughkeepsie, 1988—. Roman Catholic. Home: PO Box 169 Ridgefield CT 06877-0169

HANCOCK, LONI, state legislator, former mayor; b. N.Y.C., 1940; children: Leita, Mara. BA, Ithaca Coll.; MA, Wright Inst. Mem. Berkeley City Council, 1971-79, Berkeley's Waterfront Adv. Commn., 1984-86; former mayor City of Berkeley; former region IX rep. US Dept. of Edn., San Francisco; mem. Calif. Ho. of Reps., 2003—. Mem. Bay Area Air Quality Mgmt. Dist., 1990—, Alameda County Congestion Mgmt. Agy., 1991—. Mem. Berkeley Parent Nursery Schs., 1964-68, Berkeley Citizens Action Com., 1975-93; mem., past pres. New Dem. Forum, 1982—; v.p. Berkeley Office of Econ. Opportunity, 1969-71, Local Gov. Commn., Literacy Vols. of Am., Youth Project; past regional dir. of ACTION, 1977-80; exec. dir. Shalan Found., San Francisco, 1981-86; mem., co-founder LeConte Neighborhood Assn,. 1969-71. Mem. Sierra Club, Nat. Women's Polit. Caucus. Office: PO Box 942849 Sacramento CA 94249

HANCOCK, SANDRA OLIVIA, secondary school educator, elementary school educator; b. Jackson, Tenn., Oct. 22, 1947; d. Carthel Leon and Thelma (Thompson) Smith; m. Jerome Hancock, Aug. 1, 1969; children: Casey Colman, Mandy Maria. BS, U. Tenn., 1969, MS, 1973; grad. safety seminar, Universal Cheerleaders Assn., 1989. Cert. educator. Educator Lexington (Tenn.) H.S., 1969-70, Clarksburg (Tenn.) H.S., 1970-78, 83-90, Dresden (Tenn.) Jr. H.S., 1994-95; instr. Camden (Tenn.) Elem. Sch., 1995—. Instr. Very Spl. Arts Festival, Carroll County, Tenn., 1994; GED instr. Contbr. poetry to various publs. Cub scout leader Boy Scouts Am., Clarksburg, 1982—84; assoc. mem. St. Labre Indian Sch. and Home Arrow Club, Ashland, Mont., 1988—89; vol. March of Dimes, Leukemia Soc. Am.; mem. fund raising com. Project Graduation Huntingdon H.S., 1992—95; art edn. asst. Huntingdon Spl. Sch. Dist., 1993—94; sec. Harbor Town Property Owners' Assn., 2001—; dir. presch. 1st United Meth. Ch., Huntingdon, 1992—93. Recipient various poetry awards. Mem.: NEA, Tenn. Reading Assn., Haiku Soc. Am., Benton County Tenn. Arts Coun., Poetry Soc. Tenn. (rec. sec. 1993—94, spkr. 1994), Am. Assn. Cheerleading Coaches and Advisors, Nat. Cheerleaders Assn. (Superior Advisor Performance award 1988), U.S. Olympic Assn., Tenn. Writers' Alliance, Nat. Fedn. State Poetry Socs., Benton County Reading Assn., Benton County Edn. Assn., Tenn. Edn. Assn., Phi Delta Kappa (N.W. Tenn. chpt. sec. 1993—94). Republican. Avocations: travelling, water skiing, snorkeling. Home and Office: 250 Branch Loop Rd Big Sandy TN 38221 also: Camden Elem Sch 208 Washington Ave Camden TN 38320-1130 E-mail: zywuvx@aol.com.

HAND, ANTOINETTE MARIE, accountant; b. St. Louis, Mo., Mar. 1, 1962; d. John Anthony and Patricia Ann Garanzini; m. William David Hand II, June 16, 1989; children: Gabriella Michelle, Krystal Alishia, Avery Tygre, Casey Orion. BS in Acctg. summa cum laude, Strayer U., 1999. Fin. officer Dept. State, Washington, 1989-98, CIA, Washington, 1983—88, 1998—, budget officer, dep. CFO, 1999-2000, CFO, 2000—. Mem., troop leader Girl Scouts Am., 1998—. Mem. Phi Beta Lambda (pres. Sierra Vista Chpt. 1981-82, state v.p. Ariz., 1982). Avocations: reading, needlecraft, walking, travelling. Home: 14529 William Carr Ln Centreville VA 20120

HAND, JONI MARIE, art educator; b. Bedford, Ohio, May 29, 1964; d. Vincent Michael Stenger and Sherry Ann Anulies; m. Scott Emory Garlock, June 3, 1989 (div. Sept. 1994); m. Kevin Curtis Hand, June 19, 2000. BA, Kent State U., 1989; MA, Bradley U., 1997; MA in Art History, Hunter Coll., 2004; PhD, CUNY, 2004. Chair art dept. Havana H.S., Ill., 1992—97; art instr. Homewood-Flossmoor H.S., Ill., 1997—2000, Tappan Zee H.S., Orangeburg, NY, 2000—; adj. prof. St. Francis Coll., Bklyn., 2004. Adj. art instr. Prairie State Coll., Chicago Heights, Ill., 1997—2000; set designer, instr. Summerstage, Orangeburg, NY, 2000. Co-author: Creating Democratic Classrooms, 1996. Mem.: Coll. Art Assn., N.Y. Road Runners Club. Home: 355 South End Ave #8K New York NY 10280

HAND, MARY JANE, artist; b. St. Cloud, Minn., Oct. 5, 1947; d. James E. Kelly and Margaret Hamm, Lloyd Arvid and Delores Cecelia (Hand) Wahlberg; children: Amy Beth, Emily Jane, Chelsea Jo. BS in Art Edn., U. Minn., 1972; MA in Human Devel., St. Mary's U., 2000. Cert. tchr. art edn., K-12 Minn. Adminstrv. asst. L.J. Graham Advt., N.Y.C., 1984—85, Augsburg Pub., Mpls., 1986, World Congress of Women, Moscow, 1987, Inst. Cultural Affairs; CNA Augsburg, Ebeneezer, Fairview, Mr. & Mrs. James Kelley E., Margaret Hamm and James E. Kelly Estate. Cons. in field. Fundraiser Mpls. Pk. and Recreation, Mpls. Pub. Schs., Minn. Project Leon, Nicaragua, Pine Ridge Reservation, SD, Minn. Orch., Minn. Sinfonia, Mpls. Children's Theatre Co.; vol. battered women and children's mental health issues. Home: 2110 Clinton Ave Apt 1 Minneapolis MN 55404-2649 Office Phone: 612-871-6169.

HAND, SHARON S. assistant principal; b. McPherson, Kans., Dec. 5, 1948; d. Marvin and Marge Rediker; m. James Hand, Nov. 21, 1970; children: Cynthia, Jeffrey. BS, Kans. State Tchrs. Coll., 1970; M Secondary Edn., Wichita State U., PhD Edn., 2001. Bus. tchr. Carlton Jr. High, Derby, Kans., 1970—82, Derby Jr. High, Derby, 1983—84; bus. & computer tchr., vocat. coord. Derby H.S., 1994—2000, asst. prin., 2000—. Mem.: United Sch. Adminstrn. (pres.-elect), Kans. Assn. for Career and Tech. Edn., Nat. Assn. Sec. Sch. Prins., Phi Delta Kappa.

HANDA, EUGENIE QUAN, graphic designer; b. Oakland, Calif., Oct. 18, 1957; d. Eugene Ernest and Ruby (Louie) Quan; m. Mark Richard Handa, Feb. 14, 1981; children: Sharice Quan, Chaz Quan. BFA in Graphic Design with distinction, Calif. Coll. Arts and Crafts, 1979. Graphic artist Bemis Corp., Union City, Calif., 1979-80; graphic designer Hubbert, Ltd. Advtsg., Santa Clara, Calif., 1980-81, Darien, Russell & Hill Advtsg., San Jose, Calif., 1981-82, KNTV, Inc.-Channel 11, San Jose, 1982-83; owner, graphic designer Quanda Design, San Jose and Danville, Calif., 1983—. Vol. graphic designer, cons. Sycamore Valley Elem. Sch., Danville, Calif., 1994-2003, Charlotte Wood Mid. Sch., Danville, 1999—, San Ramon Valley H.S., Danville, 2002—. Work includes design for No. Calif. Hyatt Hotels, 1983-88, Lifescan Quality Awards Program, 1984-87, Hewlett-Packard Collateral, 1987-2002, Jadtec Computer Group Collateral, 1987-95, Am. Med. Writer's Assn. Booklets, 1993-94, others. Art dir. fundraiser East Valley Ednl. Found., San Jose, Calif., 1986; adv. sch. bond Sycamore Valley PTA, Danville, Calif., 1995-98; legis. rep. San Ramon Valley Unified Sch. Dist., Sacramento, 1997-99, 2001-03; mem. standing com. PTA, newsletter and directory chmn., 1995-97; troop team mem., designer, coord. sibling care San Francisco Bay Coun. Girl Scouts USA, 1996-97; fundraiser com. chair Sycamore Valley Ball, 1997-2001, Charlotte Wood Charger Classic, 1999-2002; selected interview team mem. for middle sch. prin. San Ramon Valley Unified Sch. Dist. 2001. Recipient Sam Seagull award Advtsg. Club Monterey Peninsula, 1982, Outstanding Vol. award San Francisco Bay Girl Scout Coun., 1997, Charlotte Wood Mid. Sch. Svc. award, 2002. Mem. Calif. Coll. Arts and Crafts Alumni, PTA, So. Poverty Law Ctr. Tchg. Tolerance. Avocations: volunteering for children's education, providing senior citizen care. E-mail: quanda2@aol.com.

HANDELMAN, ALICE SAMUELS, public relations professional, writer; b. Bklyn., Mar. 17, 1943; d. Ned Harlan and Margaret (Isaacs) Samuels; m. Howard Talbot Handelman, Aug. 29, 1965; children: Karen, Patricia Handelman Bloom, Marjorie Lynn. BJ, U. Mo., 1965. Intern reporter Miami (Fla.) News, summer 1964; staff feature writer St. Louis Blues hockey club, 1968-77; freelance writer St. Louis, 1967—; cmty. rels. assoc. Jewish Ctr. for Aged of Greater St. Louis, Chesterfield, Mo., 1981-85, dir. cmty. rels., 1985-2000. Pub. rels. cons. Jewish Family and Children's Svc., St. Louis, 1983, 89; guest lectr. Maryville U., 1997. Author, photographer: LaSalle Street--A History of the St. Louis Wholesale Flower market, 1987; freelance writer, contbr. to St. Louis Globe-Dem., St. Louis Post-Dispatch, N.Y. Times, St. Louis Jewish Light, St. Louis Blues Goal Mag., Hockey News, Hockey World, Ladue News, Sporting News, Nat. Hockey League, Hockey Pictorial, Suburban Jour. Newspapers; writer copy for Knight's Catalogue, 1983. Instr. hockey for women Meramec C.C., St. Louis, 1976—77; adv. com. vis. prof. program JCA Assocs., 1981—83, Gerontol. Inst., St. Louis, 1981—83; pres. Weber Sch. PTA, Creve Coeur, Mo., 1982; mem. Women's Am. ORT, 1965; mem. ctrl. advancement team Pkwy. Ctrl. H.S., 1985—89; photographer Tour de Cure bicycle ride to benefit Am. Diabetes Assn., 1992, 1993; sec., bd. dirs. Gateway Elder Svcs., 1998—, pres., 1999—; chair devel. com. Mideast Area Agy. on Aging, 2001—03; mem. adult days svcs. adv. com. Jewish Cmty. Ctr., 2001—; mem. Shofar Soc. Congregation Temple Israel, 2000—; pub. rels. chmn. Nat. Coun. Jewish Women, 1981—83, publicity chmn. fashion sale, 1985; life mem. Jewish Hosp. Aux., 1965—, Jewish Ctr. for Aged Aux., 1986—, Nat. Coun. Jewish Women; pres. Young Women's Coun. on Edn. of Jewish Fedn. St. Louis, 1969; mktg./pub. rels. com. Reform Jewish Acad. St. Louis, 2000—01, Jewish Family and Children's Svc., 2000; mem. pub. rels. com. Temple Israel, 2000, 2001; bd. dirs. Am. Jewish Com., 2001—03; bd. dirs. women's divsn. Jewish Fedn. St. Louis; bd. dirs. Mideast Area Agy. on Aging, 1997—2003. Recipient William Randolph Hearst award Hearst Found., Columbia, Mo., 1965, United Way Graphic Design award, 1986, United Way Photography award, 1987, 89, 2d place award Guide to Jewish Life in St. Louis photo contest, 1989, 2d place award Jewish Hosp. St. Louis Generations of Women photo contest, 1989, Star Communicator comm. program award United Way Greater St. Louis, 1990, Bronze Photography award, 1995, 15 Yr. Svc. award Jewish Ctr. for Aged, 1997, Fred Goldstein Communal Svc. award Jewish Fedn. St. Louis, 1998; named St. Louis Woman of Achievement, 2002 (co-chair 50th Anniversary com.); Besse Marks Meml. scholar, 1964-65. Mem. Nat. Fedn. Press Women (1st place award comm. contest, 3d place photo feature 1989, 3d place award advt. photography 1993, hon. mention advt. photo, 2d place mktg. new svc. award, 2d place mag. advt., 1996, 3d place direct mail mktg. fundraising lit., 2d place direct mail advt.-fund raising Ann. NFPW Comm. Contest 1996, 3d place Color mag. advt. 1996, 1st place feature article 2003, St. Louis chpt. Quest award for disting. achievement in comm. 2000, 1st place award for personality profile 2002), Jewish Ctr. for Aged Aux., Fellows of Jewish Hosp., Mo. Press Women (1st place corp. newsletter category state feature writing comm. contest 1988, 93, 1st place advt. photography, 2d place feature article, 3 1st place awards 1994, 1st place not for profit newsletter 1994, 5 1st place comm. awards 1995, 2d pl. feature writing, 1st place newsletter award Mo. Assn. of Homes for the Aging 1994, planning com. Fair St. Louis Srs. Day 1995-98, planning com. Srs. Day VP Fair 1994), Mo. Assn. Homes for the Aging (publicity com., Outstanding 1st Place Newsletter award), Mo. Press Women (pub. chmn. 1994, 2000—), Women in Comm. (Ruth Philpott Collins award 1984, Best in the Midwest 2d place feature writing 1992), Press Club Met. St. Louis (bd. dirs. 2002, 1st v.p. 2003), Westwood Country Club. Jewish. Home: 12 Terry Hill Ln Saint Louis MO 63131-2422

HANDLER, ENID IRENE, health care administrator, consultant; b. N.Y.C., Oct. 17, 1932; d. Solomon and Fran S. (Bernstein) Ostrov; m. Murry Raymond Handler, Nov. 22, 1952; children: Lowell S., Lillian Handler Koch, Evan Elliott. BS, Queens Coll., 1968; MS in Adminstrv. Medicine, Columbia U., 1973. Adminstrv. dir. Phelps Mental Health Ctr., North Tarrytown, N.Y., 1973-85; cons. to health and human service agencies, 1986—. Bd. dirs. Orange County (N.C.) AIDS Svc. Agy., 1992-94, Inst. for Parapsychology; presenter to profl. orgns. Contbr. articles and book revs. to profl. jours. Mem. adv. bd. Marymount Coll., North Tarrytown, N.Y., 1983, Iona Coll., New Rochelle, N.Y., 1983; mem. adv. bd.; numerous bds. dir. in N.Y. and N.C.; pres. Westchester Assn. Vol. Agys., 1981-82; mem. Westchester County Community Svcs. Bd., 1980-86.

NIH fellow Columbia U., N.Y.C., 1971-72. Fellow Am. Orthopsychiat. Assn.; mem. Columbia U. Alumni Assn., N.C. Soc. for Ethical Culture (bd. dirs.). Avocations: music, travel. Home and Office: Enid Handler Cons 433 Fearrington Post Pittsboro NC 27312-8519

HANDLER, LAUREN E. lawyer; b. Jersey City, Mar. 13, 1953; BA cum laude, Tufts U., 1975; JD with honors, George Washington U., 1978. Bar: N.J. 1978, U.S. Dist. Ct. N.J. 1978, N.Y. 1984, U.S. Dist. Ct. (ea. and so. dists.) N.Y. 1986. Mem. Porzio, Bromberg & Newman PC, Morristown, N.J. Arbitrator U.S. Dist. Ct. N.J., 1985—. Fell. Am. Coll. Trial Lawyers; mem. ABA (sects. on torts and ins. practice, litigation, employment), Am. Bd. Trial Attorneys, N.J. State Bar Assn. (cert. trial attys. sect., mem. exec. com. civil trial bar sect. 1986-91, sec. 1989-91, vice chair 1992, employment law sect.), Trial Attys. N.J., Morris County Bar Assn. (chair med.-legal cooperation com. 1988-96, treas. 1996, 2nd v.p. 1997, 1st v.p. 1998, pres. 2000), Def. Rsch. Inst., Internat. Assn. Def. Counsel. Office: 163 Madison Ave Ste 6 Morristown NJ 07960-7324 E-mail: Lehandler@pbnlaw.com.

HANDLEY, MARGIE LEE, manufacturing executive; b. Bakersfield, Calif., Sept. 29, 1939; d. Robert E. and Jayne A. (Knoblock) Harrah; children: Steven Daniel Lovell, David Robert Lovell, Ronald Eugene Lovell; m. Leon C. Handley, Sr., Oct. 28, 1975. Grad. H.S., Willits, Calif. Lic. gen. engring. contractor. Owner, operator Shasta Pallet Co., Montague, 1969-70, Lovell's Tack 'n Togs, Yreka, Calif., 1970-73; v.p. Microphor, Inc., Willits, 1974-81; pres. Harrah Industries, Inc., Willits, 1981—. Gen. ptnr. Madrone Profl. Group, Willits, 1982—; pres. Hot Rocks, Inc., Willits, 1983-89; co-ptnr. Running Wild Ostriches, 1994—; bd. dirs. N-Tech, Nat. Bank of the Redwoods, NBR Mortgage Co., Howard Found., Willits Electronics Assembly, Inc., Redwood Empire Bancorp.; active State of Calif. Employment Tng. Panel, 1993-95, coord. State Calif. Timber Transition, 1994-95; apptd. mem. State of Calif. Econ. Strategy Panel, 1995-2000, mem. Selective Svc. Sys., Local Bd. State of Calif., 2002. Sec. Willits Cmty. Scholarships, Inc., 1962; trustee Montague Meth. Ch., 1966-73; sec. Montague PTA, 1969; clk. bd. trustees Montague Sch. Dist., 1970-73; del. Calif. State Conf. Small Bus., 1984; alt. del. Rep. Nat. Conv., Kansas City, Detroit, 1976, 80; 3d dist. chmn. Mendocino County Rep. Ctrl. Com., 1978-84; mem. Calif. State Rep. Ctrl. Com., 1985—; Rep. nominee for State Senate Calif. 2nd Senate Dist., 1990, 93; mem. Rep. Congl. Leadership Coun., 1980-82; Mendocino County chmn. Reagan/Bush, 1980, 84; Mendocino County co-chmn. Deukmejian for Gov., 1982; mem. Region IX Small Bus. Adminstrn. Adv. Coun., 1982-93; mem. Gov.'s Adv. Coun., 1983-90; Rep. nominee State Assembly 1st Assembly Dist.; del., asst. sgt. of arms Rep. Nat. Conv., Dallas, 1984, del., New Orleans, 1988, San Diego, 1996, Phila., 2000; vice chmn. Mendocino County Rep. Ctrl. Com., 1985; active Calif. Transp. Commn., 1986-90; state dir. North Bay Dist. Hwy. Grading and Heavy Engring. divsn., 1986; dir. Lit. Vols. Am.; mem. Calif. Rural Devel. Coun., 1998-2000, dir. Mendocino County Employer's Coun., 1999—; North Coast reg. chair George W. Bush for Pres., 1999-2000; bd. dirs. Mendocino Employers Coun., 1999—; mem. Calif. Rural Devel. Coun., 1998—; State vice-chair, Simon for Gov., 2001-2002. Named Mendocino 12th Dist. Fair Woman of the Yr. 1987. Mem. No. Coast Builders Exch., Soroptimist Internat., Rotary Internat. Willits (dir. 2001), Willits C. of C. (hon.), Rotary (dir. 2001-2002). Home: PO Box 1329 Willits CA 95490-1329 Office: Harrah Industries Inc 42 Madrone St Willits CA 95490-4206

HANDLEY, MARY ANN, state legislator; b. Manchester, Conn.; 2 children. BA, Conn. Coll.; MA, U. Conn. Tchr. history Manchester Cmty. Tech. Coll., 1967-97, ret., 1997; mem. Dist. 4 Conn. Senate, Hartford, 1996—. Co-chair legislature's human svcs. com. Conn. State Senate, vice chair edn. com., vice chair environ. com., vice chair select coms. on housing and aging. Mem. bd. dirs. Town of Manchester, 1987-89, dep. mayor, 1991-96; mem. Manchester's Human Rels. Commn., Cheney Hist. Dist. Commn., Martin Luther King Day Com., Substance Abuse Coun., Housing Rehab. Review Com., Spl. Olympics Com., World War II Commemoration Com., Manchester LWV, Unitarian Universalist Soc., Manchester Dem. Town Com.; chair Earth Day Com., Heritage Day Com., UN Day Com., Project Concern. Recipient Outstanding Legislator Svc. award Conn. Cmty. Devel. Assn.; named Legislator of Yr., NASW, 1988. Democrat. Home: 133 Prospect St Manchester CT 06040-6547 Office: State Capitol Legislative Office Bldg Rm 2000 Hartford CT 06106 E-mail: Handley@senatedems.state.ct.us.

HANDMAN, BOBBIE (BARBARA HANDMAN), foundation executive; V.p., N.Y. regional dir. People for the Am. Way Found., Washington. Organizer A Quiet Walk for the First Amendment. Recipient Nat. Medal of Arts, 1998. Office: People for the Am Way 2000 M St NW Ste 400 Washington DC 20036-3397 E-mail: pfaw@pfaw.org.

HANDRICH, HEIDI LEAH, speech pathology/audiology services professional; b. Green Bay, Wis., Feb. 7, 1976; d. Thomas John and Linda Francis Krouth; m. Troy Donald Handrich, Dec. 22, 2001; 1 child, Bennett Rae. BS, U. Wis., Stevens Point, 1998, MS, 2000. Speech lang. pathologist Howard Suamico Sch. Dist., Green Bay, 2000—. Cons., tutor, presenter in field. Vol. Head Start, Stevens Point, 1996—97; vol., mem. Nativity Parish, Green Bay, 2001—. Mem.: Am. Speech-Lang. Hearing Assn. (cert. clin. competence). Avocations: photography, piano, quilting, gardening. Office: Howard Suamico Sch Dist Green Bay WI 54313

HANDRICH, WENDY ELIZABETH, education educator, consultant; b. Berwyn, Ill., Feb. 8, 1953; d. Donald Frank and Alberta Elizabeth Slapak; children: Dustin Colin, Whitney Elizabeth. BS in Edn., Carthage Coll., 1975; MS in Edn., U. Wis., Whitewater, 1982; cert. elem./mid. level prin., U. Wis., Milw., 1990, specialist in adminstrv. leadership, 1994. Cert. dir. of spl. edn./pupil svcs. Early childhood spl. edn. tchr. Germantown (Wis.) Sch. Dist., 1975—77, Hartford (Wis.) St. #1 Sch. Dist., 1977—91; dist. adminstr. Rubicon (Wis.) St. #6 Sch. Dist., 1991—97; elem. sch. prin. Waukesha (Wis.) Sch. Dist., Waukesha, 1997—99, Wauwatosa (Wis.) Sch. Dist., Wauwatosa, 1999—2002; univ. slectr. U. Wis., Whitewater; ind. edni. cons. The Learning Curve of Wis., Inc., Oconomowoc, 2003—. Named Tchr. of Yr., Hartford Rotarian, 1990; recipient Women in Edn. award, Hartford AAUW, 1990. Mem.: CEC, Ill. Assn. Gifted Coun., Wis. Assn. for Talented and Gifted, Autism Soc. Wis. Avocations: bicycling, walking, reading, cooking. Home: 1463 St Andrews Dr Oconomowoc WI 53066 Office: The Learning Curv of Wis Inc 1463 St Andrews Dr Oconomowoc WI 53066 Office Phone: 262-567-9044. E-mail: learningcurvewi@charter.net.

HANEKE, DIANNE MYERS, retired education educator; b. San Francisco, Feb. 23, 1941; d. Wayne and Dorothy (Johnson) Myers; m. John Paul Haneke, Apr. 10, 1965; children: Mark, Debra, Julie. BA in Social Sci., Edn., So. Calif. Coll., 1964; MS in Edn., SUNY, Albany, 1971, cert. advanced studies, 1990, PhD in Reading, 1998. Cert. elem., social studies and reading tchr. N.Y. Reading specialist Greenville (N.Y.) Elem. Sch., 1971-72, 84-85, Durham (N.Y.) Elem. Sch., 1972-74, Cairo (N.Y.) Durham Schs., 1979-82, 86-89; counselor Capital Area Christian Counseling, Delmar, NY, 1980-81; instr. psychology Columbia Greene CC, Hudson, NY, 1982-83; reading specialist Hunter (N.Y.)-Tannersville Schs., 1985-86; instr. edn. and reading Mt. St. Mary Coll., Newburgh, NY, 1990-92; assoc. prof. reading edn. Concordia U., Austin, Tex., 1993—2001, dir. field work experiences, 1993—2001, prof. emeritus, 2001—. Author: A Woman After God's Own Heart, 1982, A View From the Inside: An Action Plan for Gender Equity in New York State Educational Administration, 1990, Improve Your Writing: A Workshop and Desktop Reference, 2001. Instr. water safety ARC, 1978—91; host parents Youth for Understanding, 1984—85, 1988—89; leader, resource person Girl Scouts U.S., 1978—90. Recipient Alumnus of the Yr. award, So. Calif. Coll., 1979, Disting. Contbr. award, 1988, Disting. Svc. award, So. Calif. Coll. Alumni Assn., 1994; Myers-Haneke Edn. endowed scholar, So. Calif. Coll., 1971—. Mem.: ASCD, Tex. State Reading Assn., Internat. Coun. Tchrs. English, Nat. Reading Conf., Coll. Reading Assn., Christian Educators Assn. Internat., Capital Area Reading Coun., Assn. Tchr. Educators, Am. Ednl. Rsch. Assn., Phi Delta Kappa, Delta Kappa Gamma. Republican. Avocations: swimming, tennis, music, travel, Special Olympics. E-mail: d.haneke@prodigy.net.

HANEY, MARLENE CAROL, music educator; b. Spokane, Wash., Dec. 10, 1952; d. Edward Nishan and Myrtle Anne (Jenkins) Getoor; m. Dennis Lee Haney, June 14, 1975; children: Mark Phillip, Stephanie Ann. BA, Whitworth Coll., 1975. Cert. Music Tchrs. Nat. Assn., 97, Wash. State Music Tchrs. Assn., 1998. Prin., owner Grand M Studio, Spokane, 1980—. Adv. bd. Music Fest N.W., Spokane, 1995—; adjudicator sonatina/sonata festival Ctrl. Wash. U., 2003. Adjudicator Sonatina/Sonatina Festival Ctrl. Wash. U., 2003. Mem.: Spokane Music Tchrs. Assn. (pres. 1995—97), Wash. State Music Tchrs. Assn., Music Tchrs. Nat. Assn., Mu Phi Epsilon. Nazarene. Avocations: rose gardening, travel.

HANFORD, GRAIL STEVENSON, writer; b. Far Rockaway, N.Y., Apr. 10, 1932; d. Warren Day and Agnes Beatrice (Kane) Hanford. BA, Smith Coll., 1954. Reporter Tustin (Calif.) News, 1955; newspaper editorial asst. The Register, Santa Ana, Calif., 1955; assoc. editor Am. Mercury Mag., N.Y.C., 1956-59; freelance writer N.Y.C., 1959-60; editor Royal Ins. Cos., N.Y.C., 1960-62; book editor/copy editor Am. Legion Mag., N.Y.C., 1962-75, sr. editor Washington and Indpls., 1976-82, asst. editor Indpls., 1982-83; sr. writer Writers For Bus., Indpls., 1983-88, Tampa, Fla., 1988—. Contbr. articles to profl. jours. Bd. dirs. Cathedral Sch. of St. Mary, Garden City, N.Y., 1967-71, pres. Alumna Assn., 1967-69; bd. dirs. Hort. Soc. Indpls. Mus. of Art, 1981-86; pres. Smith Coll. Club Indpls., 1982-84. Mem. Fla. Motion Picture and TV Assn., Nat. Book Critics Cir., Indpls. Press Club (bd. dirs. 1980), Am. News Women's Club, West Fla. Smith Coll. Club (v.p. 1992-94. pres. 1996-99), Ivy League Club of Tampa Bay (bd. dirs. 1989-96, sec. 1990, v.p. 1991). Republican. Roman Catholic. Office: Writers For Bus 4141 Bayshore Blvd Tampa FL 33611-1803

HANFT, RUTH S. SAMUELS, healthcare consultant, educator, economist; b. N.Y.C., July 12, 1929; d. Max Joseph and Ethel (Schechter) Samuels; m. Herbert Hanft, June 17, 1951; children: Marjorie Jane, Jonathan Mark. BS, Cornell U., 1949; MA, Hunter Coll., 1963; PhD, George Washington U., 1989; ScD (hon.), U. Osteo. Med & Health Scis., 1993. Cons. Urban Med. Econs. Project, Hunter Coll., N.Y.C. and D.C. Dept. Health, 1962—63; health economist Office of Rsch. and Stats., Social Security Adminstrn., Washington, 1964—66; chief grants mgmt. health div. Office Econ. Opportunity, Washington, 1966—68; sr. health analyst Office of Asst. Sec. Planning and Evaluation HEW, Washington, 1968—71, spl. asst., asst. sec. health, 1971—72, dep. asst. sec. for health policy, rsch. and stats. Office of Asst. Sec. for Health, 1977—79, dep. asst. sec. for health rsch., stats. and tech., 1979—81; health care cons., 1981—88; cons., rsch. prof. dept. health svcs. mgmt. and policy George Washington U., Washington, 1988—91, prof., 1991—95; cons., 1995—. Vis. prof. Dartmouth Med. Sch., 1976—; sr. rsch. assoc. Inst. Medicine NAS, Washington, 1972—76; adj. Ctr. for Bioethics, U. Va., 1999—. Contbr. articles to profl. jours. Mem. Med. Assistance Svc. Bd. Commonwealth Va., 1984—89; trustee Meharry Med. Coll., 1989—94. Fellow: Acad. Health Svcs. Rsch., Hastings Ctr., Nat. Acad. of Social Ins. (charter mem.); mem.: NAS, Inst. Medicine, Cosmos Club. Jewish. Home: 3340 Brookside Dr Charlottesville VA 22901-9566

HANKAMP, MARGARET, lawyer; b. Poughkeepsie, NY, Nov. 14, 1947; d. Joseph William and Winifred Estelle Hankamp; children: Forrest Matthew Addor, Kevin Andrew Addor. MLS, L.I. U., 1984; CAS, SUNY, New Paltz, 1989; JD, NY Law Sch., NYC, 2001. Bar: (N.Y.) 2002; cert. sch. dist. adminstr. N.Y., 1989, sch. libr. media specialist N.Y., 1989, pub. libr. N.Y., 1984. Libr. Arlington Ctrl. Sch. Dist., LaGrangeville, NY, 1987—2003; lawyer Pleasant Valley, NY. Pres. Sch. Libr. Media Specialists of Southeastern N.Y., Poughkeepsie, 1992—93. Mem.: ABA (assoc.), N.Y. Bar Assn. (assoc.), New York County Lawyers Bar Assn. (assoc.), Vanderbilt Garden Assn. (life; pres. 1995—96). Avocations: skiing, reading, gardening, travel, swimming. Home and Office: Margaret Hankamp PLLC PO Box 1320 241 Pine Hill Rd Pleasant Valley NY 12569-1320 Personal E-mail: mhankamp@juno.com.

HANKIN, LISA BUSH, art and architectural historian, consultant; b. Syracuse, N.Y., Feb. 16, 1960; d. Martin H. Bush and Elinor Seward Hall; m. Steven M. Hankin, Sept. 22, 1990. BA, Smith Coll., 1982; MBA, Dartmouth Coll., 1985; MA in Hist. Preservation, Goucher Coll., 1999. Cons. Sibson & Co., N.Y.C., 1985—91, 1993—96; dir. mktg. Adv. Bd. Co., Washington, 1991—93; rsch. Am. art Richard York Gallery, N.Y.C., 2001—. Contbr. exhibns. catalogues Paintings by Walter Beck, 2002, John Graham: Renaissance & Revolution, 2002, No Record So True: The Wildflower Photographs of Edwin Hale Lincoln, 2002. Chair design rev. Charlotte-Mecklenburg Hist. Landmarks Commn., Charlotte, NC, 1997—99; pro bono cons. Hist. Rosedale Plantation, Charlotte, 1997—99, Mcpl. AA Soc., N.Y.C., 1999—2001, Nat. Acad. Design, N.Y.C., 2001. Avocations: showing horses, travel.

HANKINSON, DEBORAH G. former state supreme court justice; BS with distinction, Purdue U.; MS, U. Tex., Dallas; JD, So. Meth. U. Bar: Tex., U.S. Ct. Appeals (5th cir.) 1995; cert. civil appellate law Tex. Bd. Legal Specialization. Spl. edn. tchr. Plano (Tex.) Ind. Sch. Dist.; assoc. Thompson and Knight, Dallas, 1983-95; judge U.S. Ct. Appeals (5th cir.), Dallas, 1996, Tex. Supreme Ct., Dallas, 1997—2003. Liaison Gender Bias Reform Implementation Com., family law sect. Dallas Bar. Editor-in-chief Southwestern Law Jour. Fellow Tex. Bar Found., Dallas Bar Found. Mem. ABA (litigation sect., com. appellate practice, judicial sect.), State Bar Tex. (judicial, litigation, appellate sects.), Dallas Bar Assn. (apellate law sect.), 5th Cir. Bar Assn., Coll. of State Bar Tex., Order of the Coif. Home: 3510 Turtle Creek Blvd Apt 2F Dallas TX 75219-5543

HANKLA, CATHY, English language educator, writer; b. Richlands, Va., Mar. 20, 1958; d. Alden Staley and Joyce Saunders Hankla. BA, Hollins Coll., Roanoke, Va., 1980, MA, 1982. Lectr. in theater arts and film Hollins Coll., 1982-83, lectr. in English, 1983-86, asst. prof. English, 1986-92, assoc. prof., 1993—. Lectr. in fiction writing U. Va., Charlottesville, 1985; writer-in-residence Randolph Macon Woman's Coll., Lynchburg, Va., 1987; vis. asst. prof. English Washington and Lee U., Lexington, Va., 1989-91. Author: Phenomena, 1983, Learning the Mother Tongue, 1987, A Blue Moon in Poorwater, 1988, Afterimages, 1991, Negative History, 1997, Texas School Book Depository, 2000, Poems for the Pardoned, 2002, Emerald City Blues, 2002, The Land Between, 2003, Last Exposures, 2004; contbr. Mondo Barbie, 1993, Mondo Elvis, 1994. Mem. adv. bd. Rockbridge Area Coalition Against Sexual Aassault, 1990-91. Mem. Acad. Am. Poets, Authors Guild, PEN Am. Ctr., Phi Beta Kappa, Omicron Delta Kappa. Office: Hollins Univ PO Box 9677 Dept English Roanoke VA 24020-1673

HANLEY, ROBERTA LYNN, alternative education coordinator, educator; b. Gary, Ind., May 4, 1953; BA, Purdue U., 1975; MS, Ind. U., Gary, 1982. Substitute tchr. Hobart (Ind.) High Sch., 1974-77, social studies tchr., 1977—, sophmore gifted/talented tchr., future problem solving coach, 1985-89, 90-91, coord./tchr. Challenge Program, Alternative Edn. Program, 1991-94; coord. Hobart (Ind.) Challenge Sch., 1994—. Faculty advisor Hobart Jr. High Sch. yearbook, 1978-80, 81-84. Choir libr. Hobart Presbyn. Ch., 1980-93, Sunday sch. sec., 1987-93, ch. historian, 1988-93. Recipient Tchr. of Yr. award Hobart Rotary Club, 1988, Tchr. of Yr. award Inland Steel-Ryerson Found., 1992. Mem. Nat. Coun. Social Studies, Ind. Coun. Social Studies. Office: Sch City Hobart 32 E 7th St Hobart IN 46342-5154

HANN, LUCY ELLEN, radiologist; b. 1946; MD, Harvard Med. Sch., 1971. Cert. diagnostic radiology 1977. Resident U. Pa. Hosp., Mass. Gen. Hosp.; assoc. prof., radiology Cornell U.; radiologist, dir. ultrasound Meml. Sloan-Kettering Cancer Ctr., N.Y.C. Office: Meml Sloan-Kettering Cancer Ctr 1275 York Ave Rm C278 New York NY 10021

HANNA, ANNE MARIE, artist; b. Bloomington, Ind., Mar. 16, 1938; d. August de Belmont Hollingshead and Carol Evaleen Dempsey; m. Gary E. Hanna, June 10, 1961; children: Haldee Calore, Mark H., Scot E. Student, Cen. Sch. Art, London, 1958—59; BA, BS, Ind. U., 1961. Mgr. art dept. Curry's Coll. Bookstore, Ind. U., Bloomington, Ind., 1961—65; nursery sch. tchr. Powder Mill Village, Beltsville, Md., 1965—67; art tchr. Prince Georges County Schs., Laurel, Md., 1973—89; dir. Savage Mill Galleries Savage Mill Corp., Savage, Md., 1989—96; artist Mid-Atlantic region, 1980—. Pres. Laurel Art Guild, 1973—74; lectr. art film series South Coastal Lab., Bethany Beach, Del., 2003—; grad. sculpture instr. Ind. U., 1960; chair vol. program JHES/Prince Georges County Schs., 1972—86; docent Rehobeth Art League, 1998—. Represented in permanent collections Am. Founders of Scouting, portaits, Boy Scouts Am. U.S. rep. Citizen Amb. Program to China, 1993; ofcl. portrait artist Nat. Capital Area Coun. Boy Scouts Am., Washington, 1984—2000; leader Girl Scouts Am., Prince Georges County, Md., 1968—76, Boy Scouts Am., Washington, 1974—94, leader Sea Scout, 1986—94, dist. tng. chair Patuxent dist., 1984—89, woodbadge instr., 1984—94. Recipient Best in Show award, Rehobeth Art League, 2002, Zwanfendael Art Gallery, Nat. Landscape Show, 2003, Silver Beaver award, Boy Scouts Am., 1986, Sea Badge award, 1992. Mem.: Nat. Portrait Soc., Potomac Valley Watercolorists, Balt. Watercolor Soc. (life Best in Show award 1995), DAR (historian Laurel chpt. 1981—95). Home: 208 Point Farm Dagsboro DE 19939 E-mail: artfoxag@msn.com.

HANNA, DEANNA, state senator; b. Flatonia, Tex. BS, Tex. Women's U.; MS, U. Colo. Clin. instr. Sch. Nursing, Tex. Woman's U., 1966-67; staff nurse Meth. Hosp., 1967-68; sch. nurse Denver Pub. Schs., 1968—; Dem. senator dist. 21 Colo. State Senate, 2000—. Appointed to Optometric State Regulatory Bd., 1983-88; mem. health, environ., children and families coms. Colo. State Senate, vice chair agr. and natural resources coms. Chair precinct Jefferson County, Colo., 1970—; bd. dirs. Kids in Need of Dentistry, 1980-86; trustee Denver Pub. Schs. Retirement Bd., 1990—; mem. cmty. budget steering com. Denver Pub. Schs., 1991-95. Mem. Colo. Assn. Sch. Nurses (chair/legis. chair 1986-92), Denver Classroom Tchrs. Assn. (polit. action chair 1997—). Office: 9536 W Ohio Pl Lakewood CO 80226 also: Colo State Senate 200 E Colfax Rm 332 Denver CO 80203 E-mail: deannahanna2000@yahoo.com.

HANNA, EMMA HARMON, architectural designer, business owner, official; b. Sharpsville, Pa., Apr. 29, 1939; d. James McKarney Supplee and Anne (Woods) Thompson; m. William Hayes Harmon, Sept. 1, 1962 (div. 1984); 1 child, James McKarney Harmon; m. Hugh Allen Hanna, Mar. 21, 1992. BArch, Kent (Ohio) State U., 1962. Drafter W.H. Harmon Architects, Orlando, Fla., 1970-73; pres., owner The Plan Shop, Inc., Orlando and Palm Bay, Fla., 1973-87, The Plan Place, Inc., Palm Bay, 1987-97; pres. Engring. & Design Concepts, Palm Bay, 1986-97; owner, pres. The Hanna Studio, Inc., 1997—. Vice chmn. Palm Bay Utility Corp.; vice chmn. substance abuse program Broken Glass, Valkaria, Fla. Mem. coun. City of Palm Bay, 1989-91, dep. mayor, 1991-92; treas. League of Cities, Brevard County, Fla., 1989-92, East Ctrl. Fla. Planning Coun., Orlando, 1989-90; mem. Federated Rep. Women, South Brevard County, 1989-91; mem. exec. com. Brevard County Reps.; mem. Panther Athletic Assn. bd. Fla. Inst. Tech., 1990—, pres., 1995-96, women's locker room bd., 1997-2000; mem. open campus adv. coun. Brevard C.C., Holmes Regional Hosp. Devel. Coun., 1991—, bd. dirs. 1998—; bd. dirs. Holmes Regional Found., 2002—; mem. Health First Women's Adv. Coun. Bd., 1997-2000, pres., 1999, found. bd. dirs. 2002—; mem. Brevard County Commn. on Aging, 2000—; chair devel. coun. Palm Bay Hosp., 2001-03; bd. dirs. Fla. Inst. Tech. Sch. Psychology, 2002—. Mem.: Greater South Brevard C. of C. (mem. govt. affairs com., bd. dirs. 1991—93, 1998—2001), Palm Bay C. of C., Bldg. Ofcls. Assn. Brevard County (assoc., Assoc. of Yr. 1989), Home Builder and Contractors Brevard County (assoc., bd. dirs. 1993—97, 2nd v.p. 1994—95, Assoc. of Yr. 1995), Drafters Guild (organizer), Zonta Club Melbourne (bd. 1997—2001, sec. 1999—2001, Zontian of Yr. 1998), Exch. Club (chpt. pres., charter pres.). Avocations: bridge, walking. Home and Office: The Hanna Studio 1482 Meadowbrook Rd NE Palm Bay FL 32905-5007 E-mail: hannastudio@telsurf.net.

HANNA, MARSHA L. artistic director; b. Tiffin, Ohio, Nov. 27, 1951; d. Willis Leondadis and Frances Lucille (Neeley) H. BS, Bowling Green State U., 1980. Drama specialist City of Dayton, Ohio, 1975-80; gen. mgr. Illumination Theatre, 1978-85, product analyst Mead Data Ctrl., 1980-86; instr. Sinclair C.C., 1986—; freelance stage dir., 1986—; resident dir. Human Race Theatre Co., 1986—, artistic dir., 1990—. Dir.: Equus, 1981, Beyond Therapy, 1983, The Diviners, 1984, Amadeus, 1985, The Fantasticks, 1986, Getting Out, 1987, Orphans, 1988, Fool for Love, 1989, A Shayna Maidel, 1990, A Christmas Carol, 1991, Steel Magnolias, 1992, The Elephant Man, 1993, Closer Than Ever, 1993, The Good Times Are Killing Me, 1994, Cloud Nine, 1995, Three Tall Women, 1996, The Cherry Orchard, 1996, Quilters, 1997, Taking Sides, Stonewall Jackson's House, 1998, On Golden Pond, 1999, Three Days of Rain, 1999, Art, 2000, Resident Alien, 2001, I Hate Hamlet, 2002, The Dazzle, 2003, Odd Couple, 2004. Office: The Human Race Theatre Co 126 N Main St Ste 300 Dayton OH 45402-1766 E-mail: Marsha@humanracetheatre.org.

HANNA, NOREEN ANELDA, retired adult education administrator, consultant; b. Napa, Calif., Nov. 28, 1939; d. Thomas James and Eileen Anelda (Jordan) H.; m. Leon O'bine Gotcher, Aug. 14, 1971 (div. Nov. 1980); children: John Allen, Tamara Kay. BA, San Francisco State U., 1963; postgrad., Sonoma State U., 1974-81, Ctr. for Leadership Devel., 1982-83; MA, U. San Francisco, 1989. Cert. gen. elem., specialist in reading, gen. adminstrv. svcs. Classroom tchr. Ullom Elem. Sch., Las Vegas, Nev., 1963, J. L. Shearer Elem. Sch., Napa, 1963-78, reading resource tchr., 1978-80; asst. prin. Napa Valley Adult Sch., Napa, 1980-81, acting prin., 1981-82; prin. El Centro Elem. Sch., Napa, 1982-83; adminstr. J.T.P.A./Gain Programs, Napa, 1983-90; prin. Napa Valley Adult Sch., Napa, 1983-99, retired, 1999; inst., curriculum for adult learners U.C. Berkley, 2001—. Commn. mem. Calif. Post Secondary Edn., 1987-89; cons. Calif. Dept. Edn., Sacramento, 1988—, Staff Devel. Inst., Sacramento, 1990-2001; adv. bd. dir. Ctr. for Adult Edn., San Francisco (Calif.) State U., 1988-95; adv. bd. mem. Immigration Reform & Control Act, Sacramento, 1989-92; presenter and cons. in field, cons. Am. Inst. Rsch., 2002. Exec. bd. dirs. Leadership Napa Valley, 1985-93; sec. Leadership Napa Valley Found., 1988-99. State Edn. scholar Calif. PTA, 1976, Grad. Edn. scholar Delta Kappa Gamma, Napa, 1977; recipient Cmty. Leadership award Napa Valley Unified Sch. Dist., 1988, George C. Mann Discing. Svc. award Calif. Coun. for Adult Edn., 1994; named Outstanding Adult Edn. Adminstr., Calif. Adult Edn. Adminstrs. Assn., 1998. Mem. ASCD, Am. Assn. for Adult and Continuing Edn., Assn. Calif. Sch. Adminstrs. (chair to state adult edn. com. 1988-1991, 93—95, state rep. assembly del. 1989-92, state adult edn. com. chairperson 1989-92, Adult Edn. Adminstr. of Yr. award 1992, others), Calif. Coun. for Adult Edn. (North Coast chpt. bd. dirs. 1988-99), Napa C. of C. (bd. dirs. 1985-88, edn./bus. com. 1985-99, others), Correctional Educators Assn., Soroptimist Internat. of Napa, Napa Valley Historical Soc. (pres. 1999-01), Napa Valley Geneological and Bio. Soc. (chart. mem.), Phi

Delta Kappa, Delta Kappa Gamma. Democrat. Roman Catholic. Avocations: needlepoint, reading, sailing, swimming, hot air ballooning. Office Phone: 707-252-7433. Personal E-mail: noreen@clanhannay.us.

HANNAFORD, JANET KIRTLEY, software administrative manager; b. [illegible] and Dorothy [illegible] Kirtley; m. Norman Kenneth Christie, July 1, 1960 (div. 1978); children: Linda Jean, Norman Bruce; m. Robert John Hannaford, Dec. 26, 1981. BA magna cum laude, U. Wash., 1984. Adminstrv. sec. Baylor Coll. of Medicine, Houston, 1976-78; asst. to pres. Weems & Co., Inc., Houston, 1978-79; adminstrv. asst. Seattle Trust & Savs. Bank, 1979-82; cons. Fred Hutchinson Cancer Rsch. Ctr., Seattle, 1985-88. Mktg. cons. Lifetime Learning Ctr., seattle, 1987. Editor newsletter AAUW Bull., 1987. Site dir., chmn. Expanding Your Horizons in Math. and Sci., Seattle Cen. Community Coll., 1990-92; founder, 1st pres. SMARTgirls, Inc., 1996-99. Mem. AAUW (1st v.p. 1989-90, task force chmn. 1990-92), Beta Gamma Sigma, Phi Beta Kappa. Avocations: creative needlework, folk dancing, reading, volunteering, electronic puzzles and card games. Home: 7550 40th Ave NE Seattle WA 98115-4926 E-mail: janhanna2@aol.com.

HANNAFORD, KARLA, college official; b. Kansas City, Mo., Sept. 19, 1944; d. Jim and Margaret (Stephens) Allison; m. Buddy Hannaford, July 27, 1968. BSE, Mo. Valley Coll., 1966. Cert. tchr., Mo. Tchr. Smithton (Mo.) Sch. Dist., 1966-68, Adrian (Mo.) Sch. Dist., 1968-69, Gallatin (Mo.) Sch. Dist., 1970-73; faculty sec. North Ctrl. Mo. Coll., Trenton, 1973—. Rschr.: Camp Counseling, 5th edit., 1977. Recipient Key to the City of Trenton City Coun., 1987. Mem. AAUW, Mo. C.C. Assn. Avocations: fishing, outdoor activities. Office: North Ctrl Mo Coll 1301 Main St Trenton MO 64683-1824

HANNAH, DARYL, actress; b. Chgo., Dec. 3, 1960; d. Don and Sue Hannah. Student, U. So. Calif., Goodman Theater Co., Chgo. Ind. actress, 1978—. Films include The Fury, 1978, The Final Terror, 1981, Hard Country, 1981, Summer Lovers, 1982, Blade Runner, 1982, Reckless, 1984, Splash, 1984, The Pope of Greenwich Village, 1984, The Clan of the Cave Bear, 1986, Legal Eagles, 1986, Roxanne, 1987, Wall Street, 1988, High Spirits, 1988, Steel Magnolias, 1989, Crimes and Misdemeanors, 1989, Crazy People, 1990, At Play in the Fields of the Lord, 1991, Memoirs of an Invisible Man, 1992, Grumpy Old Men, 1993, The Little Rascals, 1994, A Hundred and One Nights, 1995, The Tie that Binds, 1995, Grumpier Old Men, 1995, Two Much, 1996, The Last Days of Frankie the Fly, 1996, the Real Blonde, 1997, Gun, 1997, The Gingerbread Man, 1998, Hi-Life, 1998, Tripwire, 1999, Wild Flowers, 1999, Hearts and Bones, 1999, Speedway Junky, 1999, My Favorite Martian, 1999, Enemy of My Enemy, 1999, Dancing at the Blue Iguana, 2000, Diplomatic Siege, 1999, Cord, 2000, Cowboy Up, 2001, Jackpot, 2001, A Walk to Remember, 2002, Run for the Money, 2002, Bank, 2002, Northfork, 2003, The Job, 2003, The Big Empty, 2003, Casa de los babys, 2003, Kill Bill: Volume 1, 2003, Kill Bill: Volume 2, 2004; (TV films) Paper Dolls, 1982, Attack of the 50 Foot Woman, 1993, The Last Don, 1997, The Last Don II, 1998, Rescuers: Stories of Courage: Two Families, 1998, Addams Family Reunion (voice), 1998, Rear Window, 1998, Hard Target, 2000, Jack and the Beanstalk: The Real Story, 2001; prodr, dir.(feature films), Strip Notes, 2001; (short films) The Last Supper (Jury award for Best Short, Berlin Internat. Film Festival, 1994), 1994. Office: c/o UTA 9560 Wilshire Blvd #500 Beverly Hills CA 90212*

HANNAH, JUDY CHALLENGER, private education tutor; b. Balt., Oct. 8, 1948; d. John Thomas and Doris Rose (Etherington) Diehl; m. Brian Challenger, Apr. 15, 1968 (div. Dec. 1994); children: John Joseph, Jennifer Elizabeth; m. W. P. Hannah, Oct. 6, 2001. AA, Arlington Bible Coll., 1985; BS, Liberty U., 1991; M in Edn., Mt. St. Mary's Coll., 1996; Diploma, Inst. of Children's Lit., 1997. Cert. elem. tchr., Md., 1996. Tchr., K-4 Mill Valley Sch., Owing Mills, Md., 1984-85, Arlington Bapt. Sch., Balt., 1985-86, Mill Valley Sch., 1986-87; bookkeeper, sec. Challenger Engr., Inc., Finksburg, 1987-92; dir. B/A child care ABC Care Inc., 1992-95; tchr. internship Thurmont Elem. Sch., Md., 1995-96; tutor/office mgr. Learning Resources, Westminster, Md., 1996-97; pvt. tutor, owner A Lesson Learned, Inc., Union Bridge, Md., 1997—. Mem. delegation People to People Amb. Programs, China, 2001, Global Peace Mission, People to People Internat., Egypt, 2003. Vol. Crisis Hotline, Balt., 1972, leader/tchr. Pioneer Girls Internat., Arlington Bapt. Ch., 1975-78. Mem. Md. Emmaus, Internat. Dyslexia Assn., Smithsonian Inst., Vol. in Missions, Pi Lamba Theta, People To People Internat. Republican. Avocations: writing, hiking. Home: 48 Bucher John Rd Union Bridge MD 21791-9527

HANNAMAN, ALBERTA ANNA, artist; b. Passaic, N.J., Dec. 11, 1932; d. Henry George and Alice Edith Hanneman. Student, Newark Sch. Fine & Indsl. Art, 1950-53. Offset stripper Screenline Photo, N.Y.C., 1956-84, Verilen Graphics, N.Y.C., 1984-87; offset stripper inhouse printing dept. DDB Needham Worldwide, N.Y.C., 1987-88, Screen Images, N.Y.C., 1988-91. Poet, artist: Prince of Flowers, 1987; contbr. articles to poetry anthologies; exhibited in group shows at Del Bello Gallery, Toronto, Ont., Can., 1988-91, The Miniature Painters, Sculptors and Gravers Soc., Washington, 1990, 91, 98-2003, Long Beach Island Art Gallery, Surf City, N.J., 1990, 91, 98, 2003.

HANNAM-OOSTERBAAN, MARIA GERTRUDE, secondary school educator; b. The Netherlands, July 28, 1916;, U.S., 1948,arrived in U.S., 1948; d. Jan and Anna Geertruida (Vanderweg) O.; m. Aug 12, 1940. Tchr. Degree, Christian Coll., Amsterdam, 1936; Bachelor, Whittier Coll., 1953. Elem. tchr. Batavia Christian Sch. Dist., Java, Indonesia, 1937-38; tchr. Palembang, Sumatra, Indonesia, 1938-41; clandestine tchr. Concentration Camp, Semarang, Indonesia, 1942—46; tchr. Ranchito Sch. Dist., Pico., Calif., 1953—55, L.A. City Sch. Dist., 1955-77. Mem. Westminster Presbyn. Ch. Mem. AAUW, Calif. Ret. Tchrs. Assn., Order Eastern Star. Presbyn. Home: # G222 710 W 13th Ave Escondido CA 92025-5511

HANNEMAN, ELAINE ESTHER, salesperson; b. Waupaca, Wis., Aug. 28, 1928; d. Martin Fred Strey and Laura Rucks; m. Alfred Adam Hanneman, Feb. 14, 1948; children: Karen, Dale, Sally, Sandra. High sch. grad., 1946. Acct. AAL Life Ins. Co., Appleton, Wis., 1946-48; salesperson Cinderella Cosmetics, 1948-60; sales Artex Paint, Milw., 1960-74, Car Ins. and Memberships (AAA), Appleton, Wis., 1974-78, Am. Family Life, Columbus, Ga., 1979—. Mem. Gold Century Club, Pres. Club, Am. Family Life. Lutheran. Avocations: travel, reading, swimming, crafts. Home: 103 West St Weyauwega WI 54983 also: 8742 Edgewater Dr Amherst Junction WI 54407-9510

HANNER, ERIKA VARRICCHIO, museum program director; b. New Haven, Conn., Feb. 28, 1971; d. Frederick E. and Claudette G. Varricchio; m. Matthew R Hanner, Oct. 11, 2003. BA, Loyola U., Chgo., 1993. Assoc. dir. edn. Mus. of Contemporary Art, Chgo., 1994—. Website chairperson Kraft Art Discovery, Chgo., 2000—; bd. mem. Hyde Pk. Acad., Chgo., 2003—. Editor: MCA Collection Teacher Resource Book, 2003, (educational video and companion guide) Behind the Scenes in the Art World, 1998, Behind the Scenes at an Art Museum, 1997. Bd. mem. Chgo. Japanese Am. Hist. Soc., Chicago, Ill., 2002—. Recipient award, Ill. Alliance for Arts Edn., 2002. Mem.: Nat. Art Edn. Assn. Avocations: travel, reading. Office: Museum of Contemporary Art 220 E Chicago Ave Chicago IL 60611

HANNI, GERALDINE MARIE, retired therapist; b. Salt Lake City, Nov. 14, 1930; d. John Henry and Theresa Justine (Keirce) Gold; m. Kenneth J. Hanni, Mar. 14, 1951; children: Debra, Valerie, Kathleen, Cynthia, Kristine. BS, U. Utah, 1951, MSW, 1983. Lic. clin. social worker. Tchr. Hillside Jr. High Sch., Salt Lake City, 1970-73; intern Davis County Schs., Farmington, Utah, 1981-82, Westside Mental Health, Salt Lake City, 1982-83; group leader LDS Social Services, Salt Lake City, 1985; therapist ISAT, Salt Lake City, 1983-90, clin. dir., 1987-90; clin. instr. U. Utah, Salt Lake City, 1986-90; pvt. practice, 1990-97; ret., 1997. Mem. bd. Salt Lake County Sexual Abuse Task Force, Salt Lake City; cons. LDS Social [illegible] Salt Lake City, [illegible]. Contbg. author: Abuse and Religion, Confronting Abuse—an LDS Perspective. Sect. dir. Mortar Bd. Honor Soc., western U.S., 1970; pres. Highland High PTA, Salt Lake City, 1980; chairperson Highland High Community Sch. Orgn., Salt Lake City, 1981. Mem. Nat. Assn. Social Workers (Utah chpt.). Democrat. Mem. Lds Ch.

HANNIGAN, PAMELA S. economist, educator; b. Indpls., Aug. 12, 1955; d. Michael L. Hannigan and Bette J. Anderson. BS, MIT, 1975; MS, NYU, 2002; cert. appraiser fine art and antiquities, U. Md., 2001. Rschr. Harvard Inst. Econ. Rsch.-Martin Felstein, Cambridge, Mass., 1977—78; econ. analysis mgr. AT&T Anti-Trust Task Force, N.Y.C., 1977—78; energy economist Chase Manhattan Bank, N.Y.C., 1980—85; pres. Strategic Devel. Assn., N.Y.C., 2001—; assoc. prof. Real Estate Inst. NYU, N.Y.C., 2002—. Cons., rschr. Euopean Union, Brussels, 2001—02; adv. bd. Energy Independence Inst., N.Y.C., 1983—87; chair IPAA-Supply/Demand Com., Houston, 1986—87. Author: Retrospective Silhouette: One Century of Lithographic Posters, 1996, Rembrandt the Etcher, 1995, Policy Analysis and Crisis Management in New York City, 2002. Mem.: Internat. Soc. Appraisers, Wagner Rev. (editor 2000—), Am. Assn. Mus. (advocate, curator com. 1991—). Avocations: ballet, ancient civilizations, collecting art. Home: One Lincoln Plz New York NY 10023 Office: NYU Real Estate Inst 11 W 42d St New York NY 10036

HANNIGAN, PATRICIA C. prosecutor; b. July 1949; BA, U. Mass.; JD, Rutgers U. Bar: Del. 1982. With U.S. Atty. Office, Wilmington, Del. Mem.: Del. State Bar Assn. (pres. 2002). Office: US Attys Office Ste 1100 1201 Market St PO Box 2046 Wilmington DE 19899-2046

HANNON, PATRICIA ANN, library director; b. Passaic, N.J., Jan. 1, 1947; d. L. Robert and Frances Laurent Hannon. BA in Math., Caldwell Coll., 1968; MLS, L.I. U., 1972. Libr. Hackensack (N.J.) Pub. Libr., 1968-75; dir. Wood-Ridge (N.J.) Pub. Libr., 1975-81, Wanaque (N.J.) Pub. Libr., 1983-84, Oakland (N.J.) Pub. Libr., 1984-88, Emerson (N.J.) Pub. Libr., 1988—. Pres. St. Joseph's Parish Coun., E. Rutherford, N.J., 1979, Regency Pk. Condominium Assn., Ramsey, N.J., 1990-91. Named Outstanding Young Women of Am., 1977. Mem.: Highlands Regional Libr. Coop. (pres. 1999—2001), Bergen County Libr. Coop. Sys. (pres. 1997, 1988), N.J. Libr. Assn. (pres. 2003—), Emerson C. of C. (sec. 1992—94, 1997—), Beta Phi Mu. Avocations: guitar, needlepoint houses. Office: Emerson Pub Libr 20 Palisade Ave Emerson NJ 07630-1822 E-mail: Hannon@bccls.org.

HANNON, SHERRILL ANN, artist; d. Helen Lorraine Hartley and Frederick Henry White; m. Frederick Daniel Hannon Jr., July 21, 1973; 1 child, F. Daniel III. BA, U. N.H., 1972; student, Paul Ingbretson Studio of Drawing and Painting, Manchester, N.H., 1995—99. RN Mass. RN Newton-Wellesley Hosp., Newton Lower Falls, Mass., 1978—83; real estate salesperson Prudential, DeWolfe and Delta Real Estate, Westwood/Medfield, Mass., 1983—95; fine artist Tripp St. Studios, Framingham, Mass., 2000—. Artist demonstrator Everett (Mass.) Art Assn., 2003—. Exhibited in group shows at Salmagundi Club Grand Nat. Exhbn., 2000, Am. Artists Profl. League 73d Grand Nat. Exhbn., 2001, Am. Artists Profl. League 75th Grand Nat. Exhbn., 2003, Acad. Artists Assn. 52d Nat. Exhbn., 2002, Harvard Club, 2002, 2004, Boston Guild Artists Exhbn., 2002, 2004, Rockport Art Assn., 2003, 2004. Housing adv. mem. Greater Boston Interfaith Orgn., Boston, 2001; v.p. LWV, Westwood, 1986—87; local coord. Bread for the World, 1985—87. Recipient Ampersand Art award, Copley Art Soc., Boston, 1999, 1st prize, Neponset River Watershed Assn. Canton, Mass., 2000. Mem.: Portrait Soc. Am., Rockport Art Assn. (Francis S. Butler Meml. award 1998), Am. Artists Profl. League, Catharine Lorillard Wolfe Art Club (assoc.). Avocations: skiing, reading, gardening. E-mail: sherrillhannon@hotmail.com.

HANOUSEK, VICTORIA A. real estate broker; d. Lester A. and Thelma O. Day; children: Faith Renee, Brian Timothy. BS cum laude, Phillips U., 1982. Cert. residential specialist, master's cert. in grapho-analysis. Broker assoc. Landmark Real Estate, Enid, Okla., 1983—. Tchr. handwriting analysis OSU, CSU, Autry Vo-tech. Vol. Enid Symphony Aux., 2002—03. Mem.: Philanthropic Ednl. Orgn., Ambucs (social chmn. 2002—03). Conservative. Lutheran. Avocations: public speaking, race-walking, travel, piano. Office: Landmark Real Estate Co 706 W Maine Enid OK 73701 Personal E-mail: vickihanousek@hotmail.com. E-mail: vickihanousek@intercorp.net.

HANOVER, DONNA (DONNA ANN KOFNOVEC), actress; b. Oakland, Calif., Feb. 3, 1950; d. Bob and Gwen Kofnovec; m. Stanley Hanover (div.); m. Rudolph Guilani, 1984 (div. 2002); children: Caroline, Andrew; m. Edwin Oster, Aug. 2003. BA, Stanford U.; MA, Grad. Sch. Journalism, Columbia U. Host (TV series) House Beautiful; actor: (films) Power, 1986, Running on Empty, 1988, The Dream Team, 1989, The People vs. Larry Flynt, 1996, Ransom, 1996, Night Falls on Manhattan, 1997, Celebrity, 1998, The Siege, 1999, Just the Ticket, 1999, Superstar, 1999, Light it Up, 1999, The Intern, 2000, Keeping the Faith, 2000, Series 7: The Contenders, 2001, Someone Like You, 2001, Just a Kiss, 2002; (TV films) Another Woman's Husband, 2000, Jenifer, 2001; (TV series) Another World, 1997, As the World Turns, 1999, All My Children, 1999, One Life to Live, 2000, (guest appearances) Law & Order, The Practice, Ally McBeal, Family Law, Sex and the City.*

HANRATH, LINDA CAROL, librarian, archivist; b. Chgo., Aug. 22, 1949; d. John Stanley and Victoria (Fraint) Grzesiakowski; m. Richard Alan Hanrath, Nov. 1, 1980; 1 child, Emily. BA in History, Rosary Coll., 1971, MA in Library Sci., 1974. Tchr. social studies Notre Dame High Sch., Chgo., 1971-75; outreach libr. Indian Trails Pub. Libr., Wheeling, Ill., 1975-76, Arlington Heights (Ill.) Meml. Libr., 1976-78; corp. libr. William Wrigley Jr. Co., Chgo., 1978—. Mem. Spl. Librs. Assn. (chmn. libr. jobline com. 1981-83, 86-87, food agrl. and nutrition divsn. 1988-89, sec. Ill. chpt. 1984-86, pres.-elect 1993-94, pres. Ill. chpt. 1994-95, conf. bd. info. svcs. adv. coun. 1990—, winner outstanding achievement award 1997), Assn. Records Mgrs. and Adminstrs., Soc. Am. Archivists, Midwest Archives Conf., Beta Phi Mu. Avocations: needlework, skiing, reading, gourmet cooking. Home: 715 E Devon Ave Roselle IL 60172-1461 Office: William Wrigley Jr Co 410 N Michigan Ave Chicago IL 60611-4213 E-mail: lhanrath@wrigley.com.

HANRATTY, CARIN GALE, pediatric nurse practitioner; b. Dec. 31, 1953; d. Burton and Lillian Aleskowitz; m. Michael Patrick Hanratty, May 22, 1983; children: Tyler James, Alison Erin. BSN, Russell Sage Coll., 1975; postgrad., U. Calif., San Diego, 1980, St. Joseph's Coll., 2002—. Cert. CPR instr.; cert. NALS; cert. specialist ANA. PNP day surgery unit Children's Med. Ctr., Dallas, 1981-85; clin. mgr. pediatrics Trinity Med. Ctr., Carrollton, Tex., 1985-86; pediatric drug coord. perinatal intervention team for substance abusing women and babies Parkland Meml. Hosp., Dallas, 1990-97; sch. nurse practitioner Dallas Ind. Sch. Dist., 1997-98; head nurse Lewisville Ind. Sch. Dist. Colony H.S., 1998—2002. Guest talk show Morning Coffee, Sta. KPLX-FM, various TV programs. Rep. United Way, 1988-97, blood donor chair Parkland Hosp., 1990-97, chair March of Dimes, 1992-97; bd. dirs., med. cons. KIDNET Found. Mem. ARC (profl., life), Nat. Assn. PNPs (v.p. Dallas chpt. 1982-83), Tex. Nurses Assn. Avocations: sewing, swimming.

HANSCOM, MARINA, band director, musician; b. Warren, Pa., Feb. 17, 1964; d. Margot Pope; m. Jeff Hanscom, Mar. 16, 2001. BS, Ind. Univ., Pa., 1986. Cert. music educator K-12 Ind. Univ. Pa., 1986. Music tchr. K-8 McDowell County Schs., Welch, W.Va., 1989—96; tchr. elem. music Taylor [illegible] Sch., Sarasota, Fla., 1999—. Profl. musician clarinet Sarasota Concert Band, 1997—. Recipient Wal-Mart Tchr. of Yr., Venice, Fla., 1999. Mem.: NEA, Music Educators Nat. Conf. Home: 269 Alsace Ave Venice FL 34293 Office: Brookside Mid Sch 3636 S Shade Ave Sarasota FL 34239 Personal E-mail: marinach@comcast.net.

HANSEN, ANNE KATHERINE, poet; b. Coulter, Iowa, Oct. 29, 1928; d. Carl Christian and Else Katherine (Paulsen) H. BA, Chapman U., 1958; MA, U. Redlands, 1971. Life credential, Calif. Elem. tchr. Bloomington (Calif.) Schs., 1958-60, San Bernardino (Calif.) Unified Sch. Dist., 1960-87; ret., 1987. Contbr. poetry to anthologies. Recipient Golden Poet award World of Poetry, 1988, 89, 90, 91, 92, Poet of Merit award Internat. Soc. Poets, plaque, 1993, 94, 96, medallion, 1996. Home: 1371 Parkside Dr Apt 230 San Bernardino CA 92404-5356

HANSEN, BARBARA CALEEN, physiologist, science educator; b. Boston, Nov. 24, 1941; d. Reynold L. and Dorothy (Richardson) Caleen; m. Kenneth Dale Hansen, Oct. 8, 1976; 1 child, David Scott. BS, UCLA, 1964, MS, 1965; PhD, U. Wash., 1971. Asst. prof. then assoc. prof. U. Wash., Seattle, 1971—76; prof., assoc. dean U. Mich., Ann Arbor, 1977—82; assoc. v.p. acad. affairs and research, dean grad. sch. So. Ill. U., Carbondale, 1982—85; v.p. for grad. studies and research U. Md., Balt. and Balt. County, 1985—90, prof. physiology, dir. obesity and diabetes rsch. ctr., 1990—. Mem. adv. com. to dir. NIH, Washington, 1979—83; mem. joint health policy com. Assn. Am. U., Washington, 1982—86, Nat. Assn. State U. and Land-Grant Colls., Washington, 1982—86, Am. Coun. on Edn., Washington, 1982—86; mem. nutrition study sect. NIH, 1979—83; mem. program com. Inst. Medicine-NAS, Washington, 1982—84; mem. Armed Forces Epidemiology Bd., 1991—95; mem. bd. sci. counselors NIEHS, 1992—94, NIH, 1992—94, mem. nat. toxicology bd., 1992—94, NIEHS, 1992—94; mem. search com. Office of Rsch. Integrity, NIH, 1992—93. Author: The Commonsense Guide to Weight Loss for People with Diabetes, 1998, The Metabolic Syndrome X, 1999; co-editor: Controversies in Obesity, 1983, editor chpts. on physiology; contbr. articles to profl. jours.; co-editor: Insulin Resistance and Insulin Resistance Syndrome, 2002. Mem. adv. com. Am. Bur. Med. Advancement China, NYC, 1982—85; mem. adv. bd. African-Am. Inst., 1987—91; mem. adv. com. Robert Wood Johnson Found., Princeton, NJ, 1982—91. Fellow Nueroscis. fellow, U. Pa., 1966—68. Mem.: Internat. Assn. Study of Obesity (pres. 1986—90), Nat. Assn. State U. and Land Grant Colls. (chmn. coun. on rsch. policy and grad. edn. 1986—87), N.Am. Assn. Study of Obesity (pres. 1984—85, 1986—), Am. Soc. for Clin. Nutrition (pres.-elect 1994—95, pres. 1995—96, v.p.), Am. Soc. for Nutritional Scis., Inst. Medicine of NAS, Am. Physiol. Soc., Phi Beta Kappa (Arthur Patch McKinley scholar 1964). Republican. Presbyterian. Achievements include discovery of of periodic (10-14 min.) cycling pattern of pancreas insulin secretion; identification of the pattern of progressive defects in insulin secretion and insulin action preceeding overt clinical type 2 diabetes mellitus; showed prevention of obesity prevents most type 2 diabetes. Office: U Md-Balt Sch Medicine Obesity-Diabetes Rsch Ctr 10 S Pine St MSTF 600 Baltimore MD 21201-1116

HANSEN, CAROL LOUISE, English language educator; b. San Jose, Calif., July 17, 1938; d. Hans Eskelsen and Thelma Josephine (Brooks) Hansen; m. Merrill Chris Davis, July 17, 1975 (div.). BA in English, San Jose State U., 1960; MA in English Lit., U. Calif., Berkeley, 1968; PhD in English Lit., Ariz. State U., 1975. Asst. prof. English City Coll. San Francisco, Calif., 1985—, Coll. San Mateo, Calif., 1987—, De Anza Coll., 1998-99; lectr. expository writing U. San Francisco, 2001. Writing coord. Calif. State U., Monterey Bay, 1996; mem. rsch. com. Conf. on Coll. Composition and comm., 2001; presenter in field. Author: Woman as Individual in English Renaissance Drama, 1993, 2d edit., 1995, 3d edit., 2000, The Life and Death of Asham: Leonard and Virginia Woolf's Haunted House, 2000, Beyond Evil: Cathy and Cal in East of Eden, 2002; contbr. articles to profl. jours. Active Grace Cathedral, San Francisco. Fellow NDEA. Mem.: MLA (chair exec. com. discussion group on two-yr. colls. 1999), Virginia Woolf Soc. Episcopalian. Avocation: animal welfare. Office: City Coll San Francisco 50 Phelan Ave San Francisco CA 94112-1821 E-mail: carhansen1@aol.com.

HANSEN, ELAINE TUTTLE, academic administrator; m. Stanley Hansen; children: Emma, Isla. AB with greatest distinction cum laude, Mt. Holyoke Coll., 1969; MA, U. Minn., 1972; PhD, U. Wash., 1975. Asst. editor Mid. English dictionary U. Mich., 1975-77, assoc. rsch. editor, 1977—78; asst. prof. dept. English Hamilton Coll., NY, 1978—80, Haverford (Pa.) Coll., 1980—86, assoc. prof., 1986—90, chair, 1989—92, prof., 1991—2002, provost, 1995—2002; pres. Bates Coll., Lewiston, Maine, 2002—. Lectr. in field. Author: The Solomon Complex: Reading Wisdom in Old English Poetry, 1988, Chaucer and the Fictions of Gender, 1992, Mother Without Child: Contemporary Fiction and the Crisis of Motherhood, 1997; mem. editl. bd. Coll. Lit.; reader manuscripts for jours. and univ. presses; contbr. articles to profl. jours., also revs. and papers. NEH Summer stipendee, 1981; Mellon grantee for faculty devel. in humanities, 1983-84, Whitehead grantee for faculty in the humanities, 1987-88; Am. Coun. Learned Socs. fellow, 1993-94. Mem. MLA (mem. Chaucer divsn. exec. com. 1995-99, divsn. rep. to del. assembly 1996-99, com. on acad. freedom and profl. rights and responsibilities 1997-2000), Am. Coun. Learned Socs. (prescreener Cen. Fellowship Program), Medieval Acad., New Chaucer Soc., Nat. Women's Studies Assn., Soc. for Feminist Medieval Scholarship (pres. 1993-95). Office: Bates College Office of the Pres Lane Hall Rm 204 Lewiston ME 04240 E-mail: president@bates.edu.*

HANSEN, ELIZABETH (BETH) STEVENS, human resources consultant; b. Muskegon, Mich., Jan. 3, 1961; d. C. Leigh Stevens II and Ruth Stephens Stevens; m. J. Mark Hansen; children: Helen, Hannah. BS in Mgmt. Sci., So. Meth. U., 1983. Systems engr. Procter & Gamble, Dallas, 1982—89, customer svc. logistics mgr. Sherman, Tex., 1989—91; regional customer svcs. mgr. Procter & Gamble Distbg., Dallas, 1992—94; juice ops. mgr. Procter & Gamble, Sherman, 1994—99, site human resources mgr., 1999—2002; pres. HansenHR, Inc., Fairview, Tex. Founding pres. Found. Lovejoy Sch., Allen, Tex.; bd. dirs. Cross Timbers Youth Orch., McKinney, 2003—, Heard Natural Sci. Mus., McKinney, Tex., 1994—99, Dallas Symphony Innovators, Dallas, 1986—92, McKinney Symphony Orch., McKinney, Tex., 2000—02. Mem.: Texoma Human Resource Mgmt. Assn. (pres. 2001). Congregationalist. Avocations: swimming, gardening, music, travel. Office: HansenHR Inc 500 Lakewood Dr Mc Kinney TX 75069

HANSEN, EUGENIA S. lawyer; BS in Biochemistry magna cum laude, Tex. A&M U., 1977, MS in Biochemistry, 1979; JD, U. Houston, 1984. Bar: Tex. 1984, U.S. Dist. Ct. (no. dist.) Tex. 1985, U.S. Patent and Trademark Office 1985, U.S. Ct. Appeals (fed. cir.) 1988, U.S. Dist. Ct. (we. dist.) Tex. 1993. Ptnr. Sidley & Austin, Dallas. Spkr., presenter in field. Articles editor Houston Jour. Internat. Law, 1983-84. Mem. Am. Intellectual Property Law Assn. (chem. practice com., co-chmn. advanced biotech. and chem. practice seminar, mem. pub. appointments com., trademark com., biotech. com., past chmn. women in intellectual property law com.), Internat. Trademark Assn. (active Brand Name Edn. Found. and inauguration Pattishall medal for tchg. excellence), Licensing Execs. Soc., Dallas-Ft. Worth Patent Law Assn., Order of Barons, Phi Lambda Upsilon. Office: Sidley & Austin 717 N Harwood St Ste 3400 Dallas TX 75201-6534 Fax: 214-981-3400. E-mail: ehansen@sidley.com.

HANSEN, JANET M. bank executive; b. Sioux Falls, S.D., June 5, 1943; d. Edward Woodrow and Ruth Lillian Hansen. Student, Nettleton C.C., Sioux Falls, 1961; BS, U. Minn., 1983; JD, William Mitchell Coll. Law, 1987. Bar: Minn. 1988. Tchr. Nettleton Coll., 1961-65; dep. clk. U.S. Dist. Ct., Sioux Falls/Rapid City, S.D., 1965-78; paralegal East River Legal Svcs., Vermillion, S.D., 1978-80; legal sec. Faegre & Benson, Mpls., 1980-86, law clk., 1986-87; trust acct. mgr. Norwest Bank Minn., Mpls., 1987-91, trust dept. mgr., 1991-97; regional trust mgr. pvt. client svcs. Wells Fargo, Las Vegas, 1997—99; regional trust mgr. Wells Fargo Pvt. Client Svcs. Ctr., 1999—. Team capt. United Way, Mpls., 1996, Las Vegas, 1997-98. Recipient Leader Lunch award YWCA, 1986. Mem. Minn. Bar Assn., Hennepin County Bar Assn., Minn. Women Lawyers, Fin. Women Internat., So. Nev. Estate Planning Coun., Nev. Planned Giving Roundtable, So. Nev. Golf Assn. for Bus. Women (pres. 1999-2000), Women's So. Nev. Golf Assn. (v.p., 2002-03). Avocations: golf, reading, theater, movies, fishing. Office: Wells Fargo Ste 200 3300 W Sahara Ave Las Vegas NV 89102 E-mail: Hansenjm@wellsfargo.com.

HANSEN, JANICE ELIZABETH, psychologist; b. Wyandotte, Mich., Oct. 31, 1948; d. Robert Lewis and Wanda Elizabeth (Janice) Rutt; m. Lawrence Lee Lippitt, Jan. 1, 1980 (div.); 1 child, Eric Robert; m. Mark Allan Hansen, June 17, 1994. BA, Ea. Mich. U., 1971, MS, 1973; PhD, Kent State U., 1978. Lic. psychologist, Mich. Staging psychologist coord., staging psychologist ACTION, Peace Corps., Washington, 1973-74; univ. counselor U. Akron Counseling and Testing Ctr., 1977-79; psychologist for oncology program Akron Gen. Med. Ctr., 1979-81; clin. psychologist, dir. rehab. psychology Boulder (Colo.) Meml Hosp. PM&R, 1981-85; pvt. practice Sullivan, Nolan & Assocs., Ann Arbor, 1988-97; neuropsychologist, rehab. psychologist, phys. medicine/rehab Chelsea (Mich.) Cmty. Hosp., 1986-99; neuropsychologist, pvt. practice Saline, Mich., 1997—. Vol. fund raising Am. Cancer Soc., 1995, March of Dimes, Ann Arbor, 1997; den leader Cub Scouts/Boy Scouts Am., 1991-95. Mem. Am. Psychol. Assn., Mich. Psychol. Assn. Methodist. Avocations: bicycling, snow skiing, family history. Home: 3295 Rumsey Dr Ann Arbor MI 48105-1467 Office: 101 S Ann Arbor St Ste 203A Saline MI 48176-1360

HANSEN, JEAN MARIE, math and computer educator; b. Detroit, Mar. 8, 1937; d. Harvey Francis and Ida Marie (Hay) Chapman; m. Donald Edward Hansen, Aug. 29, 1968; children: Jennifer Lynn, John Francis. BA, U. Mich., 1959, MA, 1960. Cert. Secondary Sch. Tchr. Tchr. Detroit Pub. Schs., 1959-60, Newark (Calif.) Sch. Dist., 1960-65, Dept. Def., Zweibruken, Germany, 1965-67, Livonia (Mich.) Pub. Schs., 1967-69; instr. Ford Livonia Transmission Plant, 1990—. Trustee/pres. Northville (Mich.) Bd. Edn., 1981-97; trustee Northville Dist. Libr., 1999—, pres. bd., 2003. Author: California People and Their Government, 1965, Voices of Government, 1969-70. Named Disting. Bd. Mem., Mich. Assn. Sch. Bds., 1991, Citizen of Yr., Northville C. of C., 1991. Mem. AAUW (v.p. Northville bd. 1982-86, pres. 1987-89, Mich. chpt. Agt. of Change award, edn. area 1985), LWV, Kiwanis, Northville Women's Club. Republican. Avocations: weaving, basket weaving, skiing, golf, travel. Home: 229 Linden St Northville MI 48167-1426 E-mail: jhansen@comcast.net.

HANSEN, JO-IDA CHARLOTTE, psychology educator, researcher; b. Washington, Oct. 2, 1947; d. Gordon Henry and Charlotte Lorraine (Helgeson) H.; m. John Paul Campbell. BA, U. Minn., 1969, MA, 1971, PhD, 1974. Asst. prof. psychology U. Minn., Mpls., 1974-78, assoc. prof., 1978-84, prof., 1984—, dir. Ctr. for Interest Measurement Rsch., 1974—, dir. counseling psychology program, 1987—, dir. Vocat. Assessment Clinic, 1997—, prof. human resources and indsl. rels., 1997—. Author: User's Guide for the SII, 1984, 2d edit., 1992, Manual for the SII, 1985 2d edit. 1994; editor: Measurement and Evaluation in Counseling and Development, 1993-2000; editor Jour. Counseling Psychology, 1999—; contbr. numerous articles to profl. jours., chpts. to books. Recipient early career award U. Minn., 1982, E.K. Strong, Jr. gold medal, 1984. Fellow APA (coun. reps. 1990-93, 97-99, pres. divsn. counseling psychology 1993-94, chmn. joint com. testing practices 1989-93, com. to revise APA/Am. Ednl. Rsch. Assn. nat. coun. measurement evalation testing stds. 1993-99, exam. com. Assn. State Provincial Psychology Bds. 1996-99, bd. sci. affairs 2003-05, chair coun. of editors 2003-04; Leona Tyler award for rsch. and profl. svc. 1996); mem. ACA (extended rsch. award 1990, disting. rsch. award 1996), Assn. for Measurement and Evaluation (pres. 1988-89, Exemplary Practice award 1987, 90). Avocations: golf, theater, music, water and downhill skiing, spectator sports. Office: U Minn Dept Psychology Ctr Interest Measurement 75 E River Rd Minneapolis MN 55455-0280 Office Phone: 612-625-2081.

HANSEN, KAREN THORNLEY, accountant; b. Chgo., June 1, 1945; BA, Marycrest Coll., Davenport, Iowa, 1967. CPA, N.Y.; cert. med. technologist. Med. staff tech. Mercy Hosp., Davenport, Iowa, 1967-68, St. Joseph Hosp., Chgo., 1968, Spl. Hematology, Wilford Hall, USAF Hosp., Lackland AFB, Tex., 1973-78; staff acct. Lewittes & Co., Poughkeepsie, N.Y., 1980-81; sr. acct. Urbach, Kahn & Werlin, Poughkeepsie, 1981-82; ptnr. Hansen & Dunn, CPA's, Poughkeepsie, 1982-94, Hansen & Arnold, Poughkeepsie, 1995-2000, Sedore & Co., CPA, 2001—. Bd. dirs., sec. United Way Dutchess County, Poughkeepsie, 1988—94; mem. Jr. League Poughkeepsie, 1979—; mem. membership com. and econ. devel. com. Poughkeepsie Partnership, Inc.; trustee St. Martin de Porres Ch.; bd. dirs. YMCA Dutchess County, Girl Scouts U.S.A., 1983—87, Mid-Hudson Civic Ctr., Inc., 1993—95, Civic Properties, Inc., 1992—, Poughkeepsie Inst., 1999—. Am. Heart Assn. Dutchess and Ulster Counties. Mem. AICPA, N.Y. State Soc. CPAs, Greater Poughkeepsie Area C. of C. (bd. dirs. 1986—, 1st vice chair 1996, chair, 1997, sec. exec. com. 1991, Amrita Club (bd. dirs. 1982-92, pres. 1990), Poughkeepsie Tennis Club. Republican. Roman Catholic. Office: Sedore & Co CPA 309 Main St Poughkeepsie NY 12601-3116

HANSEN, LINDA MARIE, small business owner; b. Ottawa, Ill., June 5, 1953; d. Orville H. and Delphine M. (Waggoner) Smith; m. James D. Hansen, Oct. 8, 1970 (div. July 1994); children: Gary, Larry, Tyee. Student, Sauk Valley Coll., Dixon, Ill., 1988. Cert. cosmetologist, Ill. Stylist Total Look, Dixon, 1984, Ahead Time, Dixon, 1985-89; color technician ind. contractor, Dixon, 1989-94; owner, operator A Head of Times, Dixon, 1995—. Color cons., 1995—. Supporter girls athletic programs, Dixon, 1995—; fundraiser Muscular Dystrophy Assn., Dixon, 1997; make-up artist for drama group, Dixon, 1989. Mem. Am. Home Garden Club, Cath. Women's Club. Avocations: landscaping, flower gardening. Office: 1116 Carondelet Rd Dixon IL 61021-9368

HANSEN, MATILDA, former state legislator; b. Paullina, Iowa, Sept. 4, 1929; d. Arthur J. and Sada G. (Thompson) Henderson; m. Robert B. Michener, 1950 (div. 1963); children: Eric J., Douglas E.; m. Hugh G. Hansen (dec.). BA, U. Colo., 1963; MA, U. Wyo., 1970. Tchr. history Englewood (Colo.) Sr. H.S., 1963-65; dir. Albany County Adult Learning Ctr., Laramie, Wyo., 1966-78, Laramie Plains Civic Ctr., 1979-83; treas. Wyo. Territorial Prison Corp., Laramie, 1988-93, also bd. dirs. Bd. dirs. Wyo. Territorial Pk. Author: (textbooks) To Help Adults Learn, 1975, Let's Play Together, 1978, Clear Use of Power, A Slice of Wyoming Political History, 2002. Legislator Wyo. Ho. of Reps., Cheyenne, 1975-95, minority whip, 1987-88, asst. minority leader, 1991-92, 93-94; mem. mgmt. coun. Wyo. State Legislature, Cheyenne, 1983-84; chair Com. for Dem. Legislature, Cheyenne, 1990-94, Wyo. State Dems., 1995-99. GE fellow in econs. for high sch. tchrs., 1963; named Pub. Citizen of Yr., Wyo. Assn. Social Workers, 1980-81. Mem. LWV Wyo. (v.p. 1966-68), LWV Laramie (bd. dirs. 1966-72, Nat. Conf. State Legislators (vice chair human resources 1983, nat. exec. com. 1990-94), Laramie Area C. of C., Laramie Women's Club, Faculty Women's Club. Democrat. Mem. Soc. Of Friends. Avocations: gardening, quilting, mountaineering. Home and Office: 1306 E Kearney St Laramie WY 82070-4142

HANSEN, MEREDITH JANE, physician assistant educator; b. Fresno, California, June 7, 1955; d. William Bruce and Isabelle Ione (Misenheimer) H.; m. David Keith Watkins, June 15, 1991; children: David, Taylor. Student, U. Okla., San Antonio, 1983-85; BS summa cum laude, U. Okla., Norman, 1989; MPH, U. Tex. Health Sci. Ctr., 1995. Lic. physician asst., cert. EMT, Tex. Enlisted U.S. Army, 1975, advanced through grades to capt., 1992, pharmacy technician, 1976-83, physician asst. Fort Bragg, N.C., 1985-91, San Antonio, 1991-95; asst. prof. U. Tex. Health Sci. Ctr., San Antonio, 1995—. Author: Clinical Preceptors Handbooks, 1996; co-author: (with others) Primary Care for Physician Assistants, 1998; editor videotape Examination of the Musculoskeletal, 1993, The Neurological Examination, 1994. Decorated Bronze Star; recipient Saudi Arabian Military Med. Excellence award Saudi Arabian Dept. Defense, 1990, Young Faculty award Upjohn, 1995; grantee Area Health Edn. Ctr. of So. Tex., 1997. Mem. AAUW, Am. Acad. Physician Asst., Assn. Physician Assts. Programs, Tex. Assn. Allied Health Profls., Tex. Acad. Physician Assts., Tex. Public Health Assn. Republican. Avocations: gardening, reading, volunteer work.

HANSEN, PAULA J. academic administrator; b. Manitowoc, Wis., July 2, 1951; d. Paul and Anne (Reedy) H.; children: Megan, Benjamin, Molly. BS, U. Wis., 1972, MS, 1977, Adminstrv. Leadership Specialist, 1990. Title I adminstrv. asst. Coop. Svc. Agy. #9, Green Bay, Wis., 1974-75; dir. govt. programs West Bend (Wis.) Joint Sch. Dist., 1976-89; asst. supt. Sch. Dist. Rhinelander, Wis., 1989—. Evaluator Head Start program rev. U.S. Dept. HHS Region V, Dayton, Ohio, 1982; mem. com. pupil svcs. planning meeting Wis. Dept. Pub. Instrn., Madison, 1995; evaluator pub. sch. dist. consortium Sch. Edn. Consortium Rev. Sch. Dist., 1989. Contbr. articles to profl. jours. Active ad hoc zoning com. County of Oneida, Wis., 1997; bd. dirs., officer Lake Thompson Assn., Rhinelander, 1995—, Devel. Disabilities Svcs., Inc., Washington County, Wis., 1980-83; foster care parent Washington County Foster Care Program, 1982-85. Mem. Assn. Wis. Sch. Adminstrs., Assn. Sch. Dist. Rhinelander Adminstrs. (sec., exec. bd. 1995-97), Wis. Head Start Dirs. Assn. (sec. 1980-84), Wis. Coun. for Gifted and Talented, Rotary (pres., mem. exec. bd. 1990—), Lake Thompson Assn. Roman Catholic. Avocations: alpine and nordic skiing, sailing, playing various musical instruments. Office: Sch Dist Rhinelander 315 S Oneida Ave Rhinelander WI 54501-3422

HANSEN, ROBYN L. lawyer; b. Terre Haute, Ind., Dec. 2, 1949; d. Robert Louis and Shirley (Nagel) Wieman; m. Gary Hansen, Aug. 21, 1971 (div. 1985); children: Nathan Ross Hansen, Brian Michael Hansen; m. John Marley Clarey, Jan. 1, 1986; 1 child, John Zender Clarey. BA, Gustavus Adolphus, 1971; JD cum laude, William Mitchell Coll. Law, 1977. Bar: Minn. 1977, U.S. Dist. Ct. Minn. 1977. Atty. Briggs and Morgan P.A., St. Paul, 1977-93, Leonard, Street and Deinard, St. Paul, 1993—. Trustee Actors Theatre, St. Paul, 1980—88, Minn. Mus. Am. Art, 1994—97; mem. Minn. Inst. Pub. Fin., 1987—93, bd. dirs., 1993—95, pres., 1995; bd. dirs. St. Paul Downtown Coun., 1985—93, Met. State U. Found., 1993—, chair, 2000—02; bd. dirs. St. Paul Area Conv. and Vis. Bur., 1995—, chair, 1999—2001; bd. dirs. Capital City Partnership, 1997—, Pk. Sq. Theatre, 2003—. Mem. ABA, Minn. Bar Assn., Ramsey County Bar Assn., Nat. Assn. Bond Lawyers, St. Paul Area C. of C. (bd. dirs., exec. com. 1997-99). Office: Leonard Street and Deinard 380 St Peter St Ste 500 Saint Paul MN 55102 E-mail: robyn.hansen@leonard.com.

HANSEN, RUTH LUCILLE HOFER, business owner, consultant; b. Wellman, Iowa, Feb. 8, 1916; d. Harve Hiram and Frances Ada (Fitzsimmons) Hofer; m. Donald Edward Hansen, June 26, 1937 (dec. Feb. 1996); children: James Edward, Sandra Kaye. Student, Upper Iowa U., 1958, U. Northern Iowa, 1959. Co-founder, v.p. H & H Distbg. Co., West Union, Iowa, 1946-59, cons.; v.p., gen. ptnr., sec., treas. Don E. Hansen Family Partnership Ltd. Pres. United Presbyn. Women of Bethel Presbyn. Ch., West Union, Iowa, 1967—, mem. cmty. planning and devel. commn.; pres. Lakes & Prairies Presbyterial, Cedar Rapids, Iowa, 1972-75; elder Bethel Presbyn. Ch., West Union, 1960-63; v.p., program chmn., camp dir., leader Camp Wyo. Ch. Camp; dist. Wapsipinicon coun. Girl Scouts, 1972-75; tchr. Vacation Bible Sch., Ch. Sch. for Adults, 1970; rep. John Knox Presbytery. Mem. Bus. and Profl. Women (pres.). Avocations: community plays, sewing, dance, golfing, bridge. Home: 601 N Vine St West Union IA 52175-1033 also: 10101 Palmeras Dr Sun City AZ 85373

HANSHEW, LOUISA EMILY, fundraiser; b. Phila., Feb. 3, 1955; d. Joseph and Elizabeth (Morris) H.; 1 child, Chelsea. BS, Drexel U., 1976. Dir. individual giving Drexel U., Phila., 1982-86; dir. devel. Pa. Ballet, Phila., 1986-87; dir. corp. giving Hahnemann U., Phila., 1987-89; centennial coord. Drexel U., Phila., 1989-92; dir. devel. Albert Einstein Healthcare Found., Phila., 1992-93, Meth. Hosp., Phila., 1993-96; v.p. devel. The Devereux Found., Devon, Pa., 1996—; pres. Louisa Hanshew and Assocs., Maple Glen, Pa., 1997—. Mem. Nat. Soc. Fund-Raising Exec., Am. Mktg. Assn., Coun. for the Advancement and Support of Edn. Office: 1719 Rittenhouse Sq Philadelphia PA 19103-6109 Home: 1400 Comly Ct Maple Glen PA 19002-3148

HANSON, BARBARA JEAN, education educator; b. Pawtucket, R.I., June 4, 1940; d. Joseph Leo and Gladys May (Knowles) Wahl; m. Donald Roland Hanson, June 16, 1962 (div. 1996); children: Erika, Jake. B in Edn., R.I. Coll., 1962; MEd, Bridgewater State Coll., 1993. Tchr. Attleboro (Mass.) Sch. Sys., 1962-63, 68—, Pattonville (Mo.) Sch., 1965-67. Lectr. in field. Tchr. leader Ptnrs. for the Advancement Math and Sci. Mass. Tchr. fellow. Mem. NEA, Attleboro Tchrs. Assn., Attleboro Hist. and Preservation Soc., Order Eastern Star, Alpha Delta Kappa. Avocations: nature, arts, singing, crafts. Home: 41 Deerfield Rd Apt 13 South Attleboro MA 02703-7871

HANSON, DIANE CHARSKE, management consultant; b. Cleve., May 15, 1946; d. Howard Carl and Emma Katherine (Lange) Charske; m. William James Hanson, June 30, 1973. BS, Cornell U., 1968; MS, U. Pa., 1989. Home service rep. Rochester Gas and Electric, N.Y., 1968-70; home economist U. Conn., Storrs, 1970-72; job analyst personnel dept. State of Conn., Hartford, 1972-73; sales rep. Ayerst Labs., Waterbury, Conn., 1973-80, sales trainer, 1979-80; dist. sales mgr. Phila., 1980-87; pres. Creative Resource Devel., W. Chester, Pa., 1986—. Developer, pres. Womens Referral Network, West Chester, 1987-89. Vice-pres., bd. dirs., aux. pres. Chester County Soc. for Prevention Cruelty to Animals, 1986-97, pres. bd. dirs., 1992-94, mem. exec. com., 1994-95. Mem. ASTD (v.p. comm. Phila./Delaware Valley chpt. 1991-92, pres. Del. chpt. 1999-2002), Internat. Soc. for Performance Improvement (v.p. programs Great Valley chpt. 1993-94, pres.-elect 1995, pres. 1996), Pa. State Tech. Devel. Ctr. (bd. dirs. 1991-92), Assn. Quality and Participation, Phila. Soc. for Human Resources, Phila. Human Resources Planning Group, Phila. Orgn. Devel. Network, Chester County Human Resources Assn. (program chair 1991-92), Greater Valley Forge Human Resources Assn. (bd. dirs. 1993-94). Avocations: skiing, tennis, gardening, sailing, exercise. Home and Office: 824 W Strasburg Rd West Chester PA 19382-1927 E-mail: hanson@team-doctor.com.

HANSON, DORIS J. state legislator; b. Oct. 24, 1925; Student, U. Wis. Former bus. mgr., now v.p. real estate co.; mem. from dist. 48 Wis. State Assembly, Madison, 1992-98; exec. dir. Teach Wis., Madison, 1998—. Former sec., now pres. Village of McFarland, Wis.; former chairwoman Dane County Regional Airport Commn. Home: 4101 Monona Dr Apt 304 Monona WI 53716-1677 Office: 101 E Wilson St Madison WI 53702-0004

HANSON, HEIDI ELIZABETH, lawyer; b. Portsmouth, Ohio, Nov. 13, 1954; BS, U. Ill., 1975, JD, 1978. Bar: Ill. 1978, U.S. Dist. Ct. (no. dist.) Ill., U.S. Ct. Appeals (7th cir.). Atty. water, air and land pollution divs. Ill. EPA, Springfield, Ill., 1978-85, atty. water pollution div. Maywood, Ill., 1985-86; assoc. Ross & Hardies, Chgo., 1987-89, ptnr., 1990-94; founder H.E. Hanson Law Offices, Western Springs, Ill., 1994—. Named hon. Ky. Col., 2000. Mem.: Indsl. Water, Waste and Sewer Group, Air and Waste Mgmt. Assn., Chgo. Bar Assn., Chicagoland C. of C. Avocation: gardening. Office: 4721 Franklin Ave Ste 1500 Western Springs IL 60558-1720

HANSON, JANE, newscaster; married; 1 child. BA in Broadcast Journalism, U. Minn. Reporter Sta. KSFY-TV, Sioux Falls, Iowa; from gen. assignment reporter to anchor Sta. WMT-TV, Cedar Rapids, Iowa; corr., anchor WNBC, N.Y.C., 1979—, co-anchor Today in New York, 1988—2003, host Jane's New York, 2003—. Adj. prof. Stern Coll., L.I. Chmn. March of Dimes Walk-Am.; hon. chair Susan B. Koman Found.'s Race for the Cure, N.Y.C.; bd. dirs. Graham Windham, N.Y.C., NY. Named Corr. of the Yr., N.Y. Police Detectives, N.Y. Firefighters, Outstanding Mother of the Yr., Nat. Mother's Day Com., 1995; recipient Emmy Outstanding Morning News Program, 1996, 1997, 2000. Mem.: NATAS (trustee, bd. govs. N.Y. chpt.). Office: WNBC 30 Rockefeller Plz New York NY 10112*

HANSON, JANICE CRAWFORD, artist; b. Norwalk, Conn., Oct. 8, 1952; d. Arthur James and Jean Alice (MacKinnon) Crawford; m. Jeffrey Becker Hanson, May 29, 1976; children: Forrest James, Shane Crawford. BA, Wellesley Coll., 1974; MBA, U. Denver, 1979. CFA. Sec. to assoc. dean Yale Sch. of Music, New Haven, Conn., 1975-76; adminstrv. asst. to dir. of internships Inst. Policy Scis. Duke U., Durham, N.C., 1976-78; fiscal analyst Denver Water Bd., 1979-84; fin. analyst Englewood, Colo., 1984; part-time fin. analyst Jeffrey B. Hanson M.D., P.C., Granger, Ind., 1989-92; part-time watercolorist Englewood, Colo., 1989—. Exhibitions include group shows Watercolor West Exhbn., Riverside, Calif., 1995, 1999, Western Colo. Watercolor Soc. Nat. Juried Exhbn., Grand Junction, Colo., 1994—96, 2000, 2004, Rocky Mountain Nat. Watermedia Exhbn., Golden, Colo., 1996, 1998, 2002, Pikes Peak Watercolor Soc. Internat. Exhbn., Colorado Springs, Colo., 1997, 1998, 2000, exhibitions include group show, Colorado Springs, 2003, exhibitions include group shows Am. Women Artists Nat. Juried Competition, Taos, N.Mex., 1999, Nat. Watercolor Soc. Annual Exhbn., Brea, Calif., 2001, exhibitions include group show We. Fedn. Watercolor Soc., 2002, 2003. Vol. Denver Dumb Friends League, 1986-88, Cherry Creek Schs., Englewood, Colo., 1992—. Recipient Best of Show awards Nat. Greeley Art Mart, 1994, Steamboat Springs Art Coun. Summer Art, 2003; Platinum award, Nat. Greeley Art Mart, 1995, Dean Witter award for originality Colo. Watercolor Soc. State Juried Exhbn., 1996, WinsorNewton Merchandise award Am. Women Artists, 1999, Daler-Rowney award Pikes Peak Watercolor Soc. Internat. Exhbn., 2000, Betty Simpson award Rocky Mountain Nat. Watermedia Exhbn., 2002; Am. Women Artists scholar, 1999. Mem.: Denver Soc. Security Analysts, Western Colo. Watercolor Soc. (signature), Colo. Watercolor Soc. (signature), Watercolor West (juried assoc.), Assn. for Investment Mgmt. and Rsch., Nat. Watercolor Soc. (signature). Avocations: running, fiber arts, needlework, photography.

HANSON, JEAN ELIZABETH, lawyer; b. Alexandria, Minn., June 28, 1949; d. Carroll Melvin and Alice Clarissa (Frykman) H.; m. H. Barndt Hauptfuhrer, May 15, 1982; children: Catherine Jean, Benjamin Colman (twins). BA, Luther Coll., 1971; JD, U. Minn., 1976. Bar: N.Y. 1977, U.S. Dist. Ct. (so. dist.) 1977. Probation officer Hennepin County, Mpls., 1972-73; law clk. Minn. State Pub. Defender, Mpls., 1975-76; assoc. Fried, Frank, Harris, Shriver & Jacobson, N.Y.C., 1976-83, ptnr., 1983-93, 94—. Gen. counsel U.S. Treasury, Washington, 1993-94; mem. bd. regents Luther Coll.; mem. bd. visitors Law Sch. U. Minn. Recipient Disting. Svc. award Luther Coll., 1991, Outstanding Achievement award U. Minn., 1999. Mem. ABA, N.Y. State Bar Assn., Assn. of Bar of City of N.Y. (securities regulation com. 1991-98, mem. task force women in the profession 1995-98), U. Minn. Law Alumni Assn. Democrat. Lutheran. Office: Fried Frank Harris Shriver & Jacobson One New York Plaza New York NY 10004 Office Phone: 212-859-8198. E-mail: jean.hanson@friedfrank.com.

HANSON, JENNIFER RENEE, elementary school educator, music educator; b. Marion, Kans., Nov. 6, 1974; d. Carl Victor Hanson, Jr. and Margaret Elaine Pippin. B in Music Edn., Emporia State U., 1998. Music tchr. grades K-4 Unified Sch. Dist. 253, Emporia, Kans., 1998—. Named Outstanding Sr. in Edn., Rotary Club, Emporia, 1998. Mem.: Assn. Am. Educators, Music Educators' Nat. Conf., Nat. Guild Piano Tchrs., Phi Kappa Phi. Avocations: piano, reading, theater, music.

HANSON, JO, artist, lecturer, writer; b. Carbondale, Ill. d. Thomas A. and Carrie M. H. MA in Art, San Francisco State U.; MA in Edn, U. Ill. Past instr. sculpture U. Calif., Berkeley, Calif. Coll. Arts and Crafts, Oakland. Participant art panels Women's Caucus for Art and Coll. Art Assn., 1979, 81, 89, 91, 93, 99, Exploratorium Symposium, "Rising Above Our Garbage", San Francisco, 1994; co-curator Living in Balance, San Francisco Internat. Airport and Richmond Art Ctr., 1993, 94, Dear Mother Earth, Marin County Civic Ctr., 1998; moderator Bioneers Conf. panels on art and ecology, 1999-2002; presenter Soc. for Ecol. Restoration, 1999; subject of "Life Messages" book by Josephine Carleton, Andreus McMeel, 2002. Author: Artists' Taxes, The Hands-on Guide, 1987; co-prodr. Women Environment Artists Directory, 1996—; one-woman shows of sculpture and installations include, Corcoran Gallery Art, Washington, 1974, Pa. Acad. Fine Arts, Phila., 1976, Utah Mus. Fine Arts, Salt Lake City, 1977, San Francisco Mus. Modern Art, 1976, 80, Internat. Sculpture Conf., San Francisco, 1982, Internat. Conf. Healthy Cities, San Francisco, 1993, Dublin (Calif.) Civic Ctr., 1994, Fresno Art Mus., 1998; exhibited in group shows at San Francisco Mus. Modern Art, 1978, Museau de Arte Contemporanea da U. de São Paulo, Brazil, 1980, Pratt Manhattan Center, N.Y.C., 1981, Auckland City Art Gallery, N.Z., 1985, Municipal Art Soc., N.Y. 1990, John F. Kennedy U., San Francisco, 2001, Yerba Buena Ctr., San Francisco, 2002; represented in permanent collections including Herbert F. Johnson Mus. Cornell U., Fresno (Calif.) Art Mus., Mills Coll., Oakland, Calif., Oakland Mus. of Art, San Francisco Arts Commn., San Francisco Mus. Modern Art, numerous pvt. collections; contbg. author: Women, Art and Technology, 2003. San Francisco Arts commr., 1982-89; adv. bd. artist-in-residence Exploratorium, San Francisco, 1983-91; originator, advisor artist-in-residence program San. Fill Co., San Francisco, 1989—; advisor art and ecology Bioneers Conf., 1999—, EarthLight Mag., 1999—. Recipient citation San Francisco Bd. Suprs., 1980, San Francisco mayor, 1989, Honor award Bioneers Conf., 2000; named Disting. Woman Artist of Yr., Fresno (Calif.) Art Mus., 1998; Nat. Endowment for Arts fellow, 1977, grantee, 1980. Mem. Coll. Art Assn. (co-chair panel art and ecology 1999), Women's Caucus for Art (Regional Lifetime Achievement award 1992, Nat. Lifetime Achievement award 1997), Pacific Rim Sculptors Group.

HANSON, LINDA N. academic administrator, educator; d. Pierce R. Nesbitt and Miriam B. Brinson; m. J. Laird Hanson; 1 child, J. Pierce Hanson. B English, Speech, So. Nazarene U.; M Ednl. Adminstrn., EdD Ednl. Leadership, Seattle U. Tchr. Savannah Christian Prep. Sch.; English tchr. secondary sch. Atlanta pub. schs.; tchr. Sch. Edn. and Inst. Pub. Svc. Seattle U.; asst. provost exec. edn. Seattle U.; v.p. U. Rels. Seattle U.; pres. Coll. Santa Fe, 2001—. Pres. Ind. Colls. Wash.; v.p. devel. Tex. A&M U., Corpus Christi. With Assn. of Coll., U. and Cmty. Arts Adminstrs., Tex. Commn. on Arts Peer Rev., Rotary IV, others; mem. Santa Fe Chamber

Music Festival's Adv. Bd., Santa Fe C. of C., Pres.'s Leadership Group, Higher Edn. Ctr. Alcohol and other Drug Prevention; exec. dir. Paramount Theatre for Performing Arts. Mem.: N.Mex. Women's Forum, Nat. Assn. Ind. Colls. and Us., Roundtable. Office: Coll Santa Fe 1600 St Michael's Dr Santa Fe NM 87505

HANSON, MARIAN W. state legislator; b. Santa Maria, Calif., Jan. 17, 1933; m. Darrel Hanson; 4 children. Rancher, Ashland, Mont.; mem. Mont. Ho. of Reps., Helena, 1983-2000, spkr. of ho. pro tem, 1993-97. County mem. Local Govt. Study Commn. Republican. Office: Mont Ho of Reps State Capitol Helena MT 59620 Home: PO Box 575 Ashland MT 59003-0575

HANSON, NORMA LEE, farmer; b. Brainerd, Minn., Feb. 3, 1930; d. Fred Christian Kruckow and Lena Belle Sawyer; m. Lynn Curtis Hanson; 1 child, Michael Lynn. Student, Mpls. Sch. Bus., 1949—50; grad., Northland C.C., 1972. File clk. and predetermining mortgage payments Investors Diversified Svcs., Mpls., 1949—53; social reporter Thief River Falls Times, 1954—63; office mgr. Kiewel Products Co., 1963—70; lobbyist Minn. Farmers Union, St. Paul, 1970—72, columnist, 1973—76; asst. farm mgr. Good-Vue Ayr Farms, Goodridge, 1976—. Chmn. Senate Dist. 1, Minn., 1990—, Northwest Minn. Women's Fund, 2001—. Mem.: NW Minn. Dairy Assn. (sec., treas. 2000—), Am. Dairy Assn. (pres. 1986—2001), Midwest Dairy Assn. (bd. dirs. 1995—2000, sec., treas. N.W. Minn. chpt. 2000—), Am. Agrl. Women (chmn. dairy com. 1999—), Hort. Soc. (pres. 13th dist. 2000—), Goodridge Area Hist. Soc. (pres. 1980—, founder). Democrat. Lutheran. Avocations: horticulture, horseback riding, reading, writing, snowmobiling. Home: 21625 330th Ave NE Goodridge MN 56725

HANSON, PAULA, sports association executive; B.Journalism, U. Colo. Dir. promotions Denver Nuggets, v.p. mktg., v.p., asst. gen. mgr.; v.p. team svcs. NBA, 1985—96, sr. v.p. team ops., 1996—99; sr. v.p., COO WNBA, N.Y.C., 1999—2003, sr. v.p. Team Business Operations, 2003—. Office: WNBA Olympic Tower 845 Fifth Ave New York NY 10022*

HANSON, PAULA E. state legislator; b. Jan. 21, 1944; m. Jim Hanson; 3 children. Mem. Minn. State Senate, 1992—, mem. various coms. Democrat. Home: 2428 Bunker Lake Blvd NE Andover MN 55304-7129 Office: Minn State Senate 328 Capitol 75 Constitution Ave Saint Paul MN 55155-1601

HANSON, TAMARA SHIELDS, accountant; b. Lewiston, Idaho, Oct. 23, 1948; d. Brooks E. and Dona J. (Rogers) O'Kelley; m. Thomas J. Hanson Jr., 1 son, Stewart Alan. BBA cum laude, North Tex. State U., 1976. Securities lic., ins. lic.; cert. sr. advisor; CPA, Tex. Staff acct. James C. Beach CPA, Carrollton, Tex., 1972-76, Deloitte, Haskins & Sells, CPA, 1976-77; CFO Comm. Sys., Inc. (name changed to Scott Cable Comm. 1983), Irving, Tex., 1977-84; pvt. practice acctg. Dallas, 1984-93; treas., v.p. FTS Life Ins. Agy., Inc., 1993—. Lectr. in field; CPA. Author: Mastering the Dance, 2003. Bd. trustees local charity; active St. Andrews United Meth. Ch. Mem. AICPA, Tex. Soc. CPAs (former Dallas chpt. ethics com.), Beta Alpha Psi.

HANSON, VIRGINIA A. activities director; b. Mpls., Minn., Apr. 26, 1935; d. Edwin Fred Wahl, Elsie (Johnson) Wahl; m. Marshall Richard Hanson, Mar. 10, 1956; children: Bruce M., Christopher, Brian(dec.). Student, St. Olaf Coll., 1953—55, Mpls. Sch. Art, 1955—56, U. Cin., 1974. Cert. activity dir. Nat. Certification Coun. for Activity Profls. Fashion artist Daytons, Mpls., 1956—57, Maurice L. Rothchild-Young Quinlan, Mpls., 1957—58; activity dir. Beechknoll Woods, Cin., 1975—81; tchr. art, recreational counselor New Horizons for Developmentally Disabled, Millbrook, NY, 1983—91; tchr. therapeutic recreation art Waterside Retirement Estates, Sarasota, Fla., 1996—2001, Sarasota Bay Club, 2002—. Developed unique style archtl. gouache painting, 1984—. Recipient 1st pl. in Watercolor, Kent Art Assn., 2001, Critics Choice award, Pindar Art Gallery, 1990. Mem.: Womens Resource Ctr., Therapeutic Recreation Assn. (v.p. 1976—80), Women Contemporary Artists (Merit award 1982). Avocations: cooking, piano, painting, Scrabble, bridge. Home: 5172 Marshfield Ln Sarasota FL 34235

HANSON, WENDY KAREN, retired chemical engineer; b. Mpls., May 29, 1954; d. Curtis Harley Hanson and Patricia Lou (Vogler) Schweiger. BS, U. Minn., 1976; BA, U. Colo., Denver, 1984; postgrad., U. Calif., La Jolla, 1984-87. Chem. technician Shasta Beverages, Mpls., 1977-78, Conwed, Roseville, Minn., 1978-80; geologist Century Geophys. Corp., Grand Junction, Colo., 1980, Tooke Engring., Grand Junction, 1980-82; sr. scientist Sci. Ventures, San Diego, 1987-96; engr. Parker-Hannifin Corp., San Diego, 1996-97, ret., 1997. Patentee magnesium separation from Dolomitic phosphate by sulfuric acid leaching. Judge San Diego (Calif.) Sci. and Engring. Fair, 1987-96; leader, publs. editor San Diego (Calif.) Wilderness Assn., 1989-97. Avocations: backpacking, gardening, spitoon collecting. E-mail: packerwendy92117@yahoo.com., wkhanson@prodigy.net.

HANZALEK, ASTRID TEICHER, public information officer, consultant; b. N.Y.C., Jan. 6, 1928; d. Arthur Albin and Luise Gertrude (Funke) Teicher; m. Frederick J. Hanzalek, Nov. 11, 1955. A, Concordia Coll., 1947; BA, U. Pa., 1949. Cons., Suffield, Conn., 1960—; state rep. Conn. Gen. Assembly, Hartford, 1970-80, asst. majority leader, 1973-74, asst. minority leader, 1975-80. Corporator Conn. Childrens Med. Ctr., 1986—95; bd. dirs. Conn. Water Co., Clinton; mem. Conn. Nitrogen Credit Adv. Bd., 2001—. Contbr. articles to profl. jours. Mem. Conn. State Coun. Environ. Quality, Hartford, 1980—93; chmn. Conn. State Ethics Commn., Hartford, 1985—93; commr. New Eng. Interstate Water Pollution Control Commn., 1993—; mem. Conn. Greenways Commn., 1992—; mem., chair history com. Conn. Commn. on Arts, Tourism, Culture, History and Film, 2003—; trustee Priscilla Maxwell Endicott Scholarship Fund, 1972—; vice chmn. Bd. State Acad. awards, 1996—; chmn. Conn. Energy Found., Hartford, 1986—96; vice-chmn. Bradley Internat. Airport Commn., 1972—2002, Greater Hartford chpt. ARC, 1975—82; mem. Conn. Inter Agy. Libr. Planning Com., Hartford, 1975—85; bd. dirs. Riverfront Recapture, Inc., 1986—; chmn. Conn. River Watershed Coun., Easthampton, Mass., 1980—92; pres. Conn. Sr. Intern Program, Bridgeport, 1980—90; sec. Conn. Humanities Coun., Middletown, 1980—92. Named Panelist of the Yr., Auto. Consumer Action Panel, 1975—85; recipient Man of the Yr. award, Conn. Jaycees, 1972, Suffield Citizenship award, 1996. Mem.: Nat. Order Woman Legislators, Suffield Land Conservancy (bd. dirs. 1965—98, founder), Conn. Coun. Environ. Quality, Conn. Forest and Pk. Assn. (v.p., bd. dirs. 1975—), Antiquarian and Landmarks Soc. (v.p. 1974—95, pres. 1996—2002, bd. dirs.). Republican. Lutheran. Avocations: musical activities, sports, culinary arts. Home: 31 Abraham Ter Suffield CT 06078-2238

HANZEL, MIMI S. psychotherapist; b. Asheville, N.C., Aug. 28, 1941; d. James Andrew and Mary Athalinda (Wilmerding) Sutton; m. Charles J. Hanzel, June 1, 1963; children: Charles J., Mary Athalinda. BA, Calif. State U. L.A., 1984, MS, 1987; PhD, The Fielding Inst., 1995. Dual diagnosis coord. Pacific Clinics-El Camino, Santa Fe Springs, Calif., 1995—. Vol. Nat. Charity League, 1982-88, Assistance League of Pasadena, Calif., 1980-88. Recipient Outstanding Student Yr., The Fielding Inst., 1990-91; grantee L.A. Dept. Mental Health, 1997. Mem. San Gabriel Valley Psychol. Assn. (gov. affairs chair 1997), Am. Psychol. Assn., Calif. Psychol. Assn., Calif. Assn. Marriage and Family Therapists. Episcopal. Avocations: walking, reading, traveling. Office: Pacific Clins-El Camino 11721 Telegraph Rd Ste A Santa Fe Springs CA 90670-6835

HAPKA, CATHERINE M. Internet executive; BS, U. Minn.; MBA, U. Chgo. Gen. mgr. Gen. Electric, 1984-87; pres. Data Svcs., 1989-91; pres., COO Interprise, U.S. West Comms., 1991-94, exec. v.p., 1994-96; pres., CEO, chmn. and founder Rhythms NetConnections, Englewood, Colo., 1997—.

HAPNER, JOANNA SUE, humanities educator; b. Richmond, Ind., Mar. 30, 1956; d. Marne Dalton Fox, Martha Marie Yount; m. David Scott Hapner, June 19, 1976 (div.); children: Justin David, Clare Dennise. BA in English, U. South Fla., 1999. Tchr. pre-sch. Trinity Children's Ctr., Bradenton, Fla., 1985—95; tchr. Booker Mid. Sch., Sarasota, Fla., 2000—. Mem. youth bd. Trinity United Meth. Ch., Bradenton, 2000. Mem.: AAUW, Fla. Coun. Tchrs. English, Visual and Performing Arts Network. Avocations: reading, theater, art museums, fishing, hiking. Home: 708 30th St W Bradenton FL 34205 Office: Booker Mid Sch 2250 Myrtle Ave Sarasota FL 34234

HAPNER, MARY LOU, securities trader and dealer, writer; b. Fort Wayne, Ind., Nov. 9, 1937; d. Paul Kenneth Brooks and Eileen (Summers) H. BS with honors, Ariz. State U., 1966, MS, 1967. Stockbroker Young, Smith & Peacock, Phoenix, Ariz., 1971-76, v.p., 1976-89, Peacock, Hislop, Staley & Given, Phoenix, 1989-90, 1st v.p., 1990—. Author: Career Courage, 1984; (poems) The Power of Forgiveness, 1995, Take Someone's Hand, 1997, Cherubs, 1997, Self Portrait, 1998, Vision, 1999, Millenium, 2000, Walk with Me, 2001, Lullabies at Night, 2004. Chmn. March of Dimes, Sun City, Ariz., 1983; trustee St. Lukes, Phoenix, 1978; mem. fin. com. YWCA, Phoenix, 1975; mem. dean's coun. of 100, Ariz. State U. Coll. Bus., 2000-03; chair budget com. Ch. of Beatitudes, Phoenix, mem. exec. coun., 1991; bd. dirs. Ariz.'s Children Found., 1998; founder Ariz. Biltmore Country Club Women's Orgn., 1976, champion 1976-83. Recipient Spirit of Philanthropy award, 1997, Impact award for Enterprising Women, 2001, Arthritis Angel award, 2002, Rookie of Yr. award Arthritis Found., 2003. Mem. Charter 100 (chair membership 1979-81, pres. 1980, pres. 1982, v.p. 1981, treas., membership chair 1995, v.p. 2003—). Republican. Lutheran. Avocations: golf, singing with concert choirs, writing poetry. Office Phone: 602-952-6803.

HAQUE, MALIKA HAKIM, pediatrician; b. Madras, India; arrived in US, 1967; d. Syed Abdul and Rahimunisa (Hussain) Hakim; m. C. Azeez Haque, Feb. 5, 1967; children: Kifizeba Haque Akbar, Masarath Haque Khan, Asim Zayd Haque. MBBS, Madras Med. Coll., 1967. Diplomate Am. Bd. Pediatrics. Rotating intern Miriam Hosp. Brown U., Providence, 1967-68; resident in pediatrics N.J. Coll. Medicine Childrens Hosp., 1968-70; fellow in devel. disabilities Ohio State U., 1970-71; acting chief pediat. Nisonger Ctr., 1973-74; staff pediatrician Children and Youth Project Children's Hosp., Columbus, Ohio; clin. asst. prof. pediatrics Ohio State U., 1974-80, clin. assoc. prof. pediatrics, 1981-99, clin. assoc. prof. dept. internat. health Coll. Medicine, 1993-99, clin. prof. pediatrics and internat. health Coll. Medicine, 1999—. Pediatrician Children's Hosp. Physician Health Ctrs. Children's Hosp., Columbus, 1982—; dir. Pediat. Academic Assn., 1992-2002; cons. Ctrl. Ohio Head Start Program, 1974-79; med. cons. Bur. Rehab. and Devel. Disabilities for State of Ohio, 1990—. Contbr. articles to profl. jours. and newspapers. Charter founder Ronald Reagan Rep. Ctr.; trustee Asian Am. Health Alliance Network, Columbus, 1994-2001. Recipient Physician Recognition award, AMA, 1971—86, 1988—99, 2002—, 2003—. Gold medals in surgery, radiology, pediat. and ob-gyn., Presdl. medal of Merit, Pres. Ronald Reagan, 1982, Nat. Leadership award, Nat. Rep. Congl. Com., 2001, Physician of the Yr. award, 2003. Fellow Am. Acad. Pediatrics; mem. Islamic Med. Assn., Am. Assn. of Physicians of Indian Origin, Pediat. Acad. Assn. (dir. 1992-2002), Ambulatory Pediat. Assn., Ctrl. Ohio Pediatric Soc. Achievements include research on enuresis and tumors caused by human papilloma viruses. Home: 5995 Forestview Dr Columbus OH 43213-2114 Office: 700 Childrens Dr Columbus OH 43205-2664

HARADEN, MARY CLYDE, language educator, musician; b. Jacksonville, Tex., Feb. 27, 1935; d. Clyde Thomas Capps and Velma Pool; m. Emerson Haraden, Aug. 23, 1962 (dec. Aug. 4, 1997); children: Robert Parker, Mary Margaret. MusB in Music Theory, U. Tex., Austin, 1958, MusM in Lit., 1960; BA in English, U. Houston, Tex., 1967; MA in English, W. Tex. State U., Canyon, 1977. Cert. tchr. Tex., 1965. Mem. horn sect. Austin (Tex.) Symphony Orch., 1953—60; tchr. Alice Ind. Sch. Dist., 1960—62; mem. horn sect. Corpus Christi Symphony, 1960—63; tchr. Portland (Oreg.) Pub. Sch., 1965—67; writer U. news svc. W. Tex. State U., Canyon, Tex., 1974—75; tchr. Amarillo Ind. Sch. Dist., 1975—2000; instr. W. Tex. A&M U., Canyon, 2001—. Pronouncer local and regional Scrps - Howard Spelling Bee, Amarillo, Tex., 1975—82; faculty sponsor Nat. Honor Soc. Tascosa HS, Amarillo, 1979—2000. Author: (reader's theatre script) Amandla!, 1995. Vol. tchr. Amarillo Adult Literacy Coun., 2000—02. Recipient O'Brien award, 1993; Panhandle Tchrs. of English scholarship, 1987. Mem.: People Am. Way, Common Cause, Canyon Fine Arts Club. Democrat. Episcopalian. Avocation: music. Home: 1207 7th Ave Canyon TX 79015

HARA-ISA, NANCY JEANNE, graphic designer, county official; b. San Francisco, May 14, 1961; d. Toshiro and Masaye Hara; m. Stanley Takeo Isa, June 15, 1985. Student, UCLA, 1979-82; BA in Art and Design, Calif. State U., L.A., 1985. Salesperson May Co., L.A., 1981; svc. rep. Hallmark Cards Co., L.A., 1981-83; prodn. artist Calif. State U., L.A., 1983, Audio-Stats Internat. Inc., L.A., 1983; prodn. asst. Auto-Graphics Inc., Pomona, Calif., 1984-85, lead supr., 1985-86; art dir., contbg. staff writer CFW Enterprises, Burbank, Calif., 1987-88; graphic designer, prodn. mgr. Bonny Jularbal Graphics, Las Vegas, Nev., 1988-90; graphic designer Weddle Caldwell Advt., Las Vegas, 1990-92; owner Nancy Hara-Isa Designs, 1992—; graphic artist Regional Transp. Commn. of Clark County, Las Vegas, 1993-98; mgmt. analyst Clark County Dept. Aviation, Las Vegas, 1998—. Freelance designer Caesars Palace. Writer Action Pursuit Games mag. Parade asst., mem. carnival staff Nisei Week., L.A., 1980-84; asst. mem. Summit Orgn., L.A., 1987—; mem. selection com. United Way; alumni grad. Clark County Leadership Forum, 1996; mem. pub. policy com. Alzheimers Assn. So. Nev. Mem. NAFE, Women in Profl. Graphic Svcs. (acting 1st v.p. 1990, 2d v.p. 1991), Women in Comms., Green Valley Rep. Women's Club (1st v.p. 2000, treas. 2003), Am. Soc. Pub. Adminstrs. (coun. mem. 1998-99). Avocations: photography, swimming, horseback riding, shooting. Home: 1803 Dalton Dr Henderson NV 89014

HARALSON, LINDA JANE, communications executive; b. St. Louis, Mar. 24, 1959; d. James Benjamin and Betty Jane (Myers) N.; married. BA summa cum laude, William Woods Coll., 1981; MA, Webster U., 1982. Radio intern Stas.-KFAL/KKCA, Fulton, Mo., 1981; paralegal Herzog, Kral, Burroughs & Specter, St. Louis, 1981-82; staffing coord. then mktg. coord. Spectrum Emergency Care, St. Louis, 1982-85, mktg. mgr., 1985-87; dir. mktg. and recruitment Carondelet Rehab. Ctrs. Am., Culver City, Calif., 1987—. Mktg. dir. outpatient and corp. svcs. Calif. Med. Ctr., L.A., 1987-88; mktg. dir. Valley Meml. Hosp., Livermore, Calif., 1988-89; account exec. Laurel Comm., Medford, Oreg., 1989-91; cmty. rels. dir. Rogue Valley Med. Ctr., Medford, 1991-95; cmty. pub. rels. dir. Rogue Valley Manor, Medford, 1995-97; pvt. practice in comms. and mktg., 1997—. Party chmn. Heart Assn., St. Louis, 1982—; bd. dirs. Am. Lung Assn. Oreg. Recipient Flair award Advt. Fedn. St. Louis, 1984, Hosps. award Hagen Mktg. Rsch. and Hosps. mag., 1984; Presdl. Acad. scholar William Woods Coll., Fulton, 1977-81. Mem. AAUW, Britt Music Festivals, Alpha Phi Alumnae Assn. (pres. chpt. 1985-87). Republican. Avocations: running, travel, sports, french, needlepoint. Home and Office: 1550 NW Patrick Ct Albany OR 97321

HARANT, PATRICIA A. minister; b. San Francisco, Aug. 27, 1960; d. Mary Jo Robles; m. William M. Harant, Aug. 19, 1995; children: Rachel, Elijah. BA in History, San Jose State U., 1993; MDiv, Pacific Luth. Theol. Sem., 1997. Pastor Zion Luth. Ch., Roundup, Mont., 1998—. Chair Salvation Army, Roundup, 1999—. Mem.: Roundup Ministerial Assn. (chair 1999—2001). Lutheran. Office: Zion Luth Ch 401 6th Ave W Roundup MT 59072

HARARI, ZARALEYA KURZWEIL, psychologist, psychotherapist; b. Bklyn., Dec. 30, 1926; d. Phillip and Goldie (Simon) Kurzweil; m. Lawrence H. Strear, Aug. 24, 1947 (div. Sept. 1969); children: Peter Mark, Marcy Jana De Luca, Karen Jody Cucolo; m. Carmi Harari, Dec. 31, 1979; stepchildren: Karen Tarnofsky, Michelle Chino. BA, Bklyn. Coll., 1948; MS, CUNY, 1961; EdD, Yeshiva U., 1969. Lic. psychologist, sch. psychologist; nat. cert. sch. psychologist; nat. cert. health svc. provider psychology. Psychologist Wyandanch (N.Y.) Pub. Schs., 1961-63, Uniondale (N.Y.) Pub. Schs., 1963-69; pvt. practice N.Y.C. and Rockland County, 1969—; asst. prof. CUNY, 1970-75; mem. field faculty grad. program Goddard Coll., N.Y.C., 1977-78; consulting psychologist Greer-Woodycrest Children's Svcs., Pomona, NY, 1980-82; psychologist East Ramapo Ctrl. Sch. Dist., Spring Valley, NY, 1982-91. Lectr. Nassau C.C., Garden City, N.Y., 1967-69, Coll. of New Rochelle, N.Y., 1977-78, Rockland C.C., Suffern, N.Y., 1977-80; lectr. spkr.'s bur. Rockland County Mental Health Assn., Pomona, 1977—; cons. drug rehab. Topic House, L.I., N.Y., 1965-69; clin. dir. homosexual walk-in ctr. Identity House, N.Y.C., 1972-76; bd. dirs. women's issues divsn. Humanistic Psychology Ctr. of NY, N.Y.C.; pres. Women Unltd.; med. staff Nyack (N.Y.) Hosp., 1974—; presenter in field over 50 countries, 1972—. Editor: (Bklyn. Coll. Yr. Book) Brocklundian, 1947; contbr. articles to profl. jours., chapters to books; creator Zaraleya Psychoenergetic Technique, 1972, Zaraleya Semester Based Self-Actualization Psychotherapy; Exhibited in group shows at Arts Coun. Rockland (NY), 1997, 1999, Rockland Ctr. for Arts, 1998. Parent seminar leader New City (N.Y.) Libr., 1981; conf. presenter E. Ramapo Ctrl. Sch. Dist., 1982, 1984, 1987; newsletter editor Rockland Ctr. for the Arts, Nyack, NY, 1986—88. Recipient Gold Key award Bklyn. Coll., 1947. Mem.: APA (exec. bd. divsn. humanistic psychology, newsletter editor 1977—79, svc. award 1977), Internat. Assn. Cross-Cultural Psychology, Internat. Assn. Applied Psychology, Internat. Coun. Psychologists (chair com. libr. subscription devel.), Nat. Register Health Svc. Providers in Psychology, Nassau and Suffolk Psychol. Assn., Rockland County Psychol. Soc. (chairperson clin. com. 1981, 1982), N.Y. Soc. Clin. Psychologists, Nat. Assn. Sch. Psychologists. Avocations: writing, drawing, painting, travel. Office: PO Box 1363 Bellmore NY 11710-0991

HARASTA, CATHY ANN, journalist; b. Glens Falls, N.Y., July 1, 1952; d. Guy J. and Margaret C. (Daly) Luciano; m. Joe P. Harasta, Aug. 24, 1974; children: Lindsey Anne, Valerie M. BA in English, SUNY, Oswego, 1974; MA in English, SUNY, Binghamton, 1977. Cert. secondary tchr., N.Y. Ref. libr. asst. Dallas Times Herald, 1976-78, asst. ref. editor, 1978-81; sports copy editor Dallas Morning News, 1981-83, sports media columnist, 1983-85, sports writer, reporter, 1985-90, sports columnist, 1990—. Recipient Charles E. Green Journalism award, Headliners Found. Tex., 1994, 2d pl. award for column writing, Tex. Assoc. Press Mng. Editors Assn., 1993. Mem. Assn. Women in Sports Media. Office: Dallas Morning News PO Box 655237 Dallas TX 75265-5237

HARASYM, JEAN LOUISE, music educator; b. Lorain, Ohio, Jan. 16, 1956; d. Leonard Gustav and Margaret Ann Gutkowski; m. David John Harasym, Aug. 2, 1980; 1 child, Margaret Helen. B in Music Edn., Ohio State U., 1978. Instrumental music tchr. Cleve. Diocese Bd. Edn., 1978—84; salesperson Educators Music Corp., Lakewood, 1982—84; instrumental music tchr. St. William Sch., Euclid, Ohio, 1990—, gen. music tchr., 1995—. Bassoonist Euclid Civic Orch., 2003—04. Flutist, bassoonist St. William Folk Choir, Euclid, 1979—; bassoonist Lakeland Civic Orch., Mentor, 1979—96; leader Girl Scouts Am., Euclid, 1991—99. Recipient Father James P. O'Donnell award, Cleve. Catholic Diocesan Com. for Girls Religious Programs, 1994, Elizabeth Ann Seton award, 1996. Mem.: Ohio Music Educator's Assn. Roman Catholic. Avocations: sewing, arts and crafts, camping, walking, tai chi. Office: St William Sch 351 E 260th St Euclid OH 44132

HARBOUR, PAMELA JONES, lawyer; m. John Harbour; 3 children. BMus, Ind. U., Bloomington, 1981; JD, Ind. U., 1984. Asst. counsel N.Y. State Dept. Trans., Albany, NY; atty. antitrust bur. N.Y. State Atty. Gen., 1987—96, dep. atty. gen. pub. advocacy, 1997—99; ptnr. litig. dept. Kaye Scholer LLP, NY, 1999—2003; commr. Fed. Trade Commn., Washington, 2003—. Office: Fed Trade Commn 600 Penn Ave NW Washington DC 20580*

HARBUTT, SARAH, photographer, director; d. Charles Harbutt. Dir. of photography Newsweek, 2000; staff New York Times, NY, 1989—92, dep. picture editor, 1992—2000. Creator (exhibitions) "Our Grandmothers", collection, Parsons Sch. of Design and Maine Photographic Workshops, 1997. Recipient Publishers Award, New York Times, 1993, Mag. Picture Editor of the Yr., NPPA, 1999, Mag. of the Yr., Soc. of Mag. Designers, Editing Team of the Yr., World Press Photo, Canon Prize for Picture Editor of the Yr., Via Pour L'Image Internat. Photojournalism Festival at Perpignan, 2000. Office: Newsweek Dir of Photography 251 W 57th St New York NY 10019

HARCUM, LOUISE MARY DAVIS, retired elementary education educator; b. Salisbury, Md., May 1, 1927; d. E. Linwood and Dora Ellen (Shockley) Davis; m. W. Blan Harcum, Sr., Sept. 5, 1944; children: W. Blan, Jr., Angie E., Lee P., R. Linwood. BS, Salisbury State U., 1962, MEd, 1969; grad., Inst. Children's Lit., 1995. Cert. tchr. 9-10 English, Md. Tchr. Wicomico County Bd. Edn., Salisbury, Md., 1962—93, subs. tchr., 1994—96; tchr. English evening H.S. Bd. Edn. Salisbury, Md., 1995—. Columnist Daily Times, 1985-87; tchr. cons. Eastern Shore Md. Writing Project; ptnr., owner Beechnut Farms, Md. Co-author: Wicomico County History, 1981; author: Behavior Modification, 1989-92. Co-coord. Rep. Party Campaign, Wicomico County, Md., 1992; vice chmn. Zoning Appeals Bd.; pres. Wicomico County Farm Bur. Women, 1993, leader Olympians-Mardela 4-H Club, 1994-1997; mem. New Cmty. Singers, 1975-95, Sen. Richard Colburn's Scholarship Com., Wicomico County; chmn. senatorial com. for Colburn, 1996-2003. Mem. AAUW (pres. 1970-72, pres. Salisbury Branch 1994-96), Third Time Around-Salisbury Studio of Dance, County Rep. Women's Club (chmn. 1999-2001, state cmty. chmn. 2001, Rep. Fedn. 2000 Caring for Am. com. 1999-2001, established Cmty. Tutorial Ctr. in San Domingo 1998), Wicomico County Rep. Women (pres. 1998-2000), Wicomico Rep. Club, Ret. Tchrs. Wicomico County (pres. 1996-98). Republican. Methodist. Avocations: gardening, writing, dance. Home: 10720 Snethen Church Rd Mardela Springs MD 21837-2246

HARDAGE, PAGE TAYLOR, elementary school educator; b. Richmond, Va., June 27, 1944; d. George Peterson and Gladys Odell (Gordon) Taylor; 1 child, Taylor Brantley. AA, Va. Intermont Coll., Bristol, 1964; BS, Richmond Profl. Inst., 1966; MPA, Va. Commonwealth U., Richmond, 1982. Cert. tchr., Va. Competent toastmaster, dir. play therapy svcs. Med. Coll. Va. Hosps., Va. Commonwealth U., Richmond, 1970-90; dir. Inst. Women's Issues, Va. Commonwealth U., U. Va., Richmond, 1986-91; adminstr. Scottish Rite Childhood Lang. Ctr. at Richmond, Inc., 1991-99. Bd. dirs. Richmond Bus. Coun. Math. and Sci. Ctr. Found., Richmond, Emergency Med. Svcs. Adv. Bd., Richmond. Treas. Richmond Black Student Found., 1989—90, Leadership Metro Richmond Alumni Assn.; group chmn. United Way Greater Richmond, 1987; bd. dirs. Maggie L. Walker Hist. Found., Richmond YWCA, 1989—91, Capital Area Health Adv. Coun.; commr. Mayors Commn. of Concerns of Women, City of

Richmond. Mem.: ASPA, NAFE, Va. Assn. Fund Raising Execs., Va. Recreation and Park Soc. (bd. dirs.), Internat. Mgmt. Coun. (exec. com.), Adminstrv. Mgmt. Soc., Rotary Club of Hanover. Unitarian Universalist. Avocations: bridge, target shooting, aerobics, pub. speaking.

HARDCASTLE, MARCIA E. (MARCIA E. TEMME), retired journalist; b. Oakland, Calif., Nov. 28, 1945; d. Charles Frederick and Lillian Callita (Johnson) Temme; children: Glenn Arthur Hardcastle, Jason Roger Hardcastle. BA, San Jose State U. Society editor Los Altos (Calif.) News, 1967-70; reporter, lifestyle editor Santa Maria (Calif.) Times, 1979-82; adminstrv. asst. sr. Diablo Canyon Nuclear Power Plant, Calif., 1983-86; lifestyle editor 5-Cities Times Press Recorder, Arroyo Grande, Calif., 1987-98; arts and entertainment features editor Pulitzer Cmty. Newspapers, 1998-2000. Chair bd. dirs. publicity Am. Heart Assn., San Luis Obispo, Calif.; freelance photographer, writer, artist. Co-author: Reflections of The Soul, poetry.com. Press sec. Assemblyman Eric Seastrand, Calif., 1982; campaign mgr. Tris Colman for State Assembly, Calif., 1994; founder Five Cities Women's Network, 1987 Recipient Cmty. Svc. award Santa Maria Mental Health Assn., 1980, Media award Calif. Mental Health Assn., 1980, Hon. Mention award Nat. Newspaper Assn., 1989, 2d Place award Best Lifestyle/Family Life Pages Calif. Newspaper Assn., 1991. Mem.: Internat. Order Rainbow for Girls (worthy advisor). Avocations: photography, painting, piano, swimming, travel. E-mail: marcia_hardcastle@yahoo.com.

HARDEBECK, ANNE LYNCH, obstetrician, gynecologist; b. Inglewood, Calif., Jan. 14, 1960; d. James Lynch and Naomi Nilsen; m. James Robert Hardebeck, Aug. 8, 1981; children: Lisa, Krista, Mark. BS, Biola U., 1982; MD, Loma Linda (Calif.) U., 1989. Diplomate Am. Bd. Ob-Gyn. Resident Loma Linda U., 1989—93; ob-gyn. Friendly Hills, La Mirada, Calif., Kaiser Permanente, Anaheim Hills, Calif. Fellow: Am. Coll. Ob-Gyn.

HARDEN, ALICE V. state legislator; b. Magnolia, Miss., Apr. 17, 1948; m. Dennis Labert Harden. Student, Jackson State U. Tchr.; mem. Miss. State Senate. Mem. Hinds County Dem. Women. Mem. NAACP, various ednl. assns. Baptist. Home: 3247 Copperfield St Jackson MS 39209-6706 Office: Senate House New Capitol Jackson MS 39205

HARDEN, ANITA JOYCE, nurse; b. Jackson, Tenn., May 17, 1947; d. Percy Lawrence and Marjorie (Robinson) H.; 1 child, Brian Robinson Weir. BSN, Ind. U., 1968, MBA, 1989; MSN, Ind. U.-Purdue U., Indpls., 1973. Staff nurse Indpls. Hosps., 1968-71; instr. Ind. U. Sch. Nursing, 1973-75; dir. continuing care Gallahue Mental Health Ctr., Indpls., 1975-80; mgr. psychiatry Cmty. Hosp., Indpls., 1980-87, product line mgr. for psychiat. and mental health svcs., 1986—; dir. psychiat. svcs. Cmty. Hosp. North, 1987-89, v.p., 1990-94; exec. dir. mental health svcs. Cmty. Hosps. of Ind., Inc., 1989-90; exec. dir. mental health St. Vincent-Cmty. Health Network, 1994-96; exec. dir. behavioral care svcs. Cmty. Hosps. Indpls., 1996-2001, v.p. behavioral health, 2001—03; pres. Cmty. Hosp. East, 2003—. Clin. asst. prof. Ind. U., 1977-82, clin. assoc. prof., 1982—; clin. assoc., trainer Suicide Prevention Svc., Indpls., 1974-77; chmn. adv. bd. deinstitutionalization project Cen. State Hosp., Indpls., 1978-79; bd. dirs. Safe Sitter, Behavioral Sys. LLC, InteCare Contbr. articles to profl. jours. Mem. Ind. County Cmty. Mental Health Ctr., 1979-80; bd. dirs. Marion County Mental Health Assn., Indpls. Zoo; bd. dirs. Alternatives in Madison County, Jackson-Peoples Living Ctr. Recipient Outstanding Achievement in Professions award Ctr. Leadership Devel., 1981, Clin. Excellence award Ind. U. Sch. Nursing, 1989. Mem. Ind. U. Alumni Assn., Christian Women's Fellowship, 500 Festival Assocs., Greater Indpls. Orgn. Nurse Execs. (v.p.), Coalition 100 Black Women (bd. dirs.), Neal-Marshall Aumni Club, Alpha Kappa Alpha, Sigma Theta Tau, Chi Eta Phi. Mem. Christian Ch. Home: 7607 Newport Bay Dr Indianapolis IN 46240-3370 Office: 7150 Clearvista Dr Indianapolis IN 46256-1695 Office Phone: 317-355-5526. Business E-Mail: aharden@ecommunity.com.

HARDEN, MARCIA GAY, actress; b. LaJolla, Calif., Aug. 14, 1959; m. Thaddaeus D. Scheel; children: Eulala Grace Scheel, Hudson Harden Scheel, Julitta Dee Harden Scheel. BA in Theatre, U. Tex., 1980; MFA, NYU. Actor: (plays) Simpatico, 1994, Angels in America: Millennium Approaches/A Gay Fantasia on National Themes, 1993 (Tony nomination); (films) The Imagemaker, 1986, Miller's Crossing, 1990, Crush, 1992, Used People, 1992, Safe Passage, 1994, The Spitfire Grill, 1996, The Daytrippers, 1996, Spy Hard, 1996, The First Wives Club, 1996, Far Harbor, 1996, Flubber, 1997, Desperate Measures, 1998, Meet Joe Black, 1998, Curtain Call, 1999, Space Cowboys, 2000, Pollock, 2000 (Acad. award for best supporting actress, N.Y. Film Critics Circle award for best supporting actress), Gaudi Afternoon, 2001, Mystic River, 2003 (Acad. Award nomination for best supporting actress, 2004), Casa de los babys, 2003, Mona Lisa Smile, 2003, Just Like Mona, 2003, Welcome to Mooseport, 2004; (TV films) Kojak: None So Blind, 1990, In Broad Daylight, 1991, Fever, 1991, Sinatra, 1992, Talking with, 1995, Convict Cowboy, 1995, Path to Paradise: The Untold Story of the World Trade Center Bombing, 1997, Labor of Love, 1998, Spenser: Small Vices, 1999, Thin Air, 2000, See You In My Dreams, 2000, From Where I Sit, 2000, Walking Shadow, 2001, King of Texas, 2002, She's Too Young, 2003; (TV series) The Education of Max Bickford, 2001; (TV miniseries) Guilty Hearts, 2002. Office: Creative Artists Agy 9830 Wilshire Blvd Beverly Hills CA 90212-1825*

HARDEN, MARY LOUISE, human resources consultant, real estate broker, real estate appraiser; b. Natchez, Miss., Mar. 27, 1942; d. John Charles and Dorothy Louise (Reynolds) Brown; m. Billy Gene Redd, Mar. 12, 1957 (div. 1961); children: Andre Ranier, Allison Lawanda, Robin Yvette; m. Percy Lawrence Harden Jr., Aug. 31, 1968; children: Darrell Lawrence, Craig Robison. Student, Ball State U., 1975—76, Ind. U., Purdue U., 1983—88; BSBA, Ind. Wesleyan U., 1989; postgrad., U. S.C., 1990; MA, Ball State U., 1995; grad. in Diversity Leadership, Acad. Greater Indpls., 2003. Editor-in-chief U.S. Army Fin. and Acctg. Ctr., Indpls., 1974-81, pers. mgmt. specialist, 1981-87, pub. affairs officer, 1987-91; pers. mgmt. specialist Def. Fin. and Acctg. Svc., 1991-99; fed. women's program mgr. U.S. Army Fin. and Acctg. Ctr., Indpls., 1981-85. Minority advisor United Way of Ctrl. Ind., Indpls., 1985—2000; active Ind. Fever Adv. Team, 2001—; mem. Ind. Consortium to Eliminate Achievement Gaps, 2003; bd. dirs. Nat. Coalition of 100 Black Women, Indpls., 1986—, pres., 2002—03; bd. dirs. Urban Mission YMCA, 2002—, C.J. Walker Theatre Ctr., 2001—. Named Madame C.J. Walker Outstanding Woman of Yr., Ctr. for Leadership Devel. and Indpls. C. of C., 1988, Sarah Lewis Lifetime Achievement award, United Way Ctrl. Ind., 2003. Fellow: Dept. Def. Exec. Leadership Program; mem.: Am. Soc. Mil. Comptrs., Federally Employed Women. Presbyterian. Avocations: photography, real estate, flea markets, reading.

HARDEN, OLETA ELIZABETH, English educator, university administrator; b. Jamestown, Ky., Nov. 22, 1935; d. Stanley Virgil and Myrtie Alice (Stearns) McWhorter; m. Dennis Clarence Harden, July 23, 1966. BA, Western Ky. U., 1956; MA in English, U. Ark., 1958, PhD, 1965. Teaching asst. U. Ark., Fayetteville, 1956-57, 58-59, 61-63; instr. S.W. Mo. State Coll., Springfield, 1957-58, Murray (Ky.) U., 1959-61; asst. prof. English Northeastern State Coll., Tahlequah, Okla., 1963-65; asst. prof. Wichita (Kans.) State U., 1965-66; asst. prof. English Wright State U., Dayton, Ohio, 1966-68, assoc. prof., 1968-72, prof., 1972-93, asst. chmn. English dept., 1967-70, asst. dean, 1971-73, assoc. dean, 1973-74, exec. dir. gen. univ. services, 1974-76, pres. of faculty, 1984-85, prof. emerita, 1993—. Author: Maria Edgeworth's Art of Prose Fiction, 1971, Maria Edgeworth, 1984; editor: The Extension, 1999—. R & D grantee Wright State U., 1969, 78, Ford Found. grantee, 1971, Wright State U. sabbatical grantee Oxford U., Eng., 1978-79, 86-87; recipient Presdl. award for outstanding svc. Wright State U., 1986, Alumni Teaching Excellence award, 1993. Mem. MLA, AARP (impact alliance leader Ohio, 2001—), Coll. English Assn., AAUP, Women's Caucus for Modern Langs., Am. Conf. for Irish Studies (presenter 1989, 91, 94, 95). Office: Wright State U Dept English 7751 Colonel Glenn Hwy Dayton OH 45431-1674 Home: 2618 Big Woods Trl Dayton OH 45431-8704 Office Phone: 937-775-3136. E-mail: oharden@aol.com.

HARDENBURGER, JANICE, state legislator; m. William Hardenburger. Kans. state senator Dist. 21, 1993—; farm ptnr., 1996—. Home: 562 25th Rd Haddam KS 66944-9037

HARDER, ELAINE RENE, state legislator; b. Windom, Minn., Dec. 27, 1947; d. Russell Jacob and Eunice Rupp; m. Ronald Dale Harder, 1970; children: Graydon, Nicole. BS in Secondary Edn., Mankato State U., 1970. Tchr. secondary sch.; owner sml. bus.; sales rep.; rep. Dist. 22B Minn. Ho. of Reps., 1995—. Chair ethics com. Minn. Ho. of Reps., mem. agriculture policy com., agriculture and rural devel. finance com., taxes com., property tax divsn. com.; life and heatlh ins. profl. 4-H youth devel. agt. U. Minn. Ext. Svc. AAUW, Minn. Assn. Life Underwriters, Minn. Home Econ. Assn., Jackson C. of C., Kiwanis, Phi Upsilon Omicron, Delta Clovia. Office: 487 State Office Bldg Saint Paul MN 55155 Home: 96 Becky Dr Jackson MN 56143-1155 E-mail: rep.Elaine.Harder@house.leg.state.mn.us.

HARDER, WENDY WETZEL, communications executive; b. Oceanside, Calif., Feb. 14, 1951; d. Burt Louis and Marjorie Jean (Evans) W.; m. Peter N. Harder, Dec. 1, 1984; 1 child, Jonathan Russell. AA, Palomar Coll., 1971; BA in Communications, U. So. Calif., 1973; MBA, Pepperdine U., 1988. Pub. rels. dir. Orange County Community Devel. Coun., Santa Ana, Calif., 1975-76; assoc. producer Sta. KOCE-TV, Huntington Beach, Calif., 1976-77, reporter, 1977-79, anchor, assoc. producer, 1979-82; sr. adminstr. communications Mission Viejo (Calif.) Co., 1983-84, mgr. corp. affairs, 1984-85, dir. corp. affairs, 1985-91, v.p. corp. affairs, 1991-93, v.p. mktg. and corp. comm., 1993-97; dir. cmty. rels. Soka Univ. Am., 1998—. 1st v.p. Aliso Viejo (Calif.) Cmty. Found., 1988-93, 2003—, pres., 1993-97, Saddleback Coll. Found., Mission Viejo, 1989-94; co-chmn. The Ctr. on Tour-Schs. Com., Orange County, Calif., 1989-92; v.p. Found. for Vocat. Visions, 1996-2002, pres., 2000-03; bd. dirs. Dunaj Internat. Dance Ensemble, Orange County, 1985—2000; den leader Pack 709 Cub Scouts, 2001—; bd. dirs. Mt. of Olives Found., 2003—. Recipient Golden Mike award Radio & TV News Assn., 1981, co-recipient Best Spl. Event award, Pub. Rels. Soc. Am., 1986, Golden Mike award Radio & TV News Assn., 1979. Mem. Pub. Rels. Soc. Am., Aliso Viejo C. of C. (bd. dirs. 2002—), Orange County Press Club (Best Feature Release award 1983), Phi Beta Kappa. Republican. Lutheran. Avocations: folk dancing, reading. Office: Soka Univ Am 1 University Dr Aliso Viejo CA 92656 Office Phone: 949-480-4081. E-mail: wwharder@soka.edu.

HARDESTY, BARBARA LYNNE, revenue agent, auditor; b. Encino, Calif., Nov. 22, 1966; d. Charles Conrad Hardesty and Patricia Lynne (Weaver) Lane; m. Adrian Dale Haupt, Aug. 25, 1985 (div. May 1992); children: Nicholas Scott Haupt, Jeremy Julian Zavala; m. Jesus Jose Zavala, Jr., Mar. 18, 1994. BSBA with honors, U. Tex., El Paso, 1990. Revenue agent IRS, El Paso, 1991—. Security technician, computers, IRS, 1994—, outreach and small bus. workshop presenter, IRS, 1993—. Den leader Boy Scouts of Am., El Paso, 1994, 95; legis. com. chair, PTA Rosa Guerrero Elem. Sch., El Paso; tutor, mentor Helping One student to Succeed, Beall Elem. Sch., El Paso, 1993-95, team mother Am. Youth Soccer Orgn., El Paso, 1995—; vol. project graduation Franklin HS, 2003—. Recipient cert. of appreciation Vol. in Pub. Schs., 1993. Mem. Boy Scouts of Am., PTA. Home: 7253 Imperial Ridge Dr El Paso TX 79912-7217

HARDIN, BIANKA NICOLE, psychologist, educator; b. Lahnstuhl, Germany, Dec. 13, 1971; d. Ray Douglas and Eleonore Hardin; m. Carl Andrew Frye, June 28, 2002. BA, Miami U., 1994; MA in clin. psychology, PhD in psychology, Chgo. Sch. Profl. Psychology, 2000. Lic. clin. psychologist Ill. Dept. of Profl. Regulation, 2001. Predoctoral intern Adv. Family Care Network Childhood Trauma Treatment Cetner, Bolingbrook, Ill., 1999—2000; post doctoral fellow Village of Hoffman Estates, Ill., 2000—01, asst. dir., 2001—. Cons. Children's Advocacy Ctr., Hoffman Estates, 2002—03, Intellidyne-LLC, Falls Church, Va., 2002—03; asst. dir. Village of Hoffman Estates; presenter in field; affiliate prof. Chgo. Sch. Profl. Psychology, 2001—03, assoc. prof., 2003—. Mem. N.W. Suburban Com. on Domestic Violence Awareness, Elk Grove Village, Ill., 2003. Recipient Darwin award, Children's Advocacy Ctr., 2003. Mem.: APA (assoc.). Democrat. Avocations: exercise, travel, reading, soccer, cultural exploration. Office: Villageof Hoffman Estates-HHS 1900 Hassell Road Hoffman Estates IL 60195

HARDIN, ELIZABETH ANN, academic administrator; b. Charlotte, N.C., Nov. 21, 1959; d. William Gregg and Ann (Astin) H. BBA magna cum laude, U. Ga., 1981; MBA, Harvard U., 1985. Spl. project coord. NCNB Corp., Charlotte, 1981-82, investment officer, 1982-83; cons. Booz, Allen & Hamilton, Atlanta, 1985-86; asst. placement dir. Harvard U. Bus. Sch., Boston, 1986-87, dir. MBA program adminstrn., 1987-89, acting placement dir., 1988-89; mgr. employment Sara Lee Hosiery, Winston-Salem, N.C., 1990-92, mfg. mgr., 1992-93, dir. product devel., 1993-94; mng. cons. Info. Sci. Assocs., Charlotte, N.C., 1994-95; assoc. vice chancellor for bus. planning U. N.C., Charlotte, 1995—2002; exec. dir. Charlotte Inst. for Tech. Innovation, 2000—02, spl. asst. to chancellor, 2002—03; v.p. adminstrn. U. Wyoming, 2003—. Cons., developer adminstrv. policy guide Chelsea (Mass.) Pub. Schs., 1989-90. Mem. adv. bd. Harvard Non-Profit Fellowship, 1986—; chmn. Harvard Non-Profit Mgmt. Fellowship, 1989-96; active AIDS Action Com. Mass., Holy Comforter, Charlotte; mem. total quality edn. task force N.C. Bus. Com. on Edn., 1992-93; troop leader Girl Scouts U.S.A.; mem. Leadership Charlotte, 1996—, Leadership N.C., 1999-2000; mem. grant panel Arts and Scis. Coun., 1998, 99. Named one of 40 under 40, Charlotte Bus. Jour.; fellow State Farm Co. Found., 1980, Delta Gamma Found., 1983. Mem. Assn. for Corp. Growth (bd. advisors 1996-99), Harvard Bus. Sch. Assn., Phi Kappa Phi, Delta Gamma (pres. alumnae Charlotte 1982-83). Republican. Avocations: reading, writing, public policy, photography. Office: U of NC at Charlotte Charlotte NC 28223 Home: PO Box 778 Laramie WY 82073-0778

HARDIN, HEIDI, artist, educator; b. Oklahoma City, Aug. 24, 1953; d. Robert Scott and Ann Hardin; m. Richard Uchida, July 27, 1996. BA in Biology and Visual Arts, U. Calif., San Diego, 1976, MFA in Painting, 1979. Dir. in-schs. visual arts program Bayview Opera House, San Francisco, 1992—; mus. artist, supr. Fine Arts Mus. San Francisco, 1995—99. Exhibitions include Long Beach Mus., Triton Mus., LaJolla Mus., San Francisco Art Commn. Gallery, one-woman shows include SomArts Gallery, San Francisco, 2004, The Bayview Opera House, 2000, Metro Gallery, Reno, 2001, San Francisco Internat. Airport, 1995, others, exhibited in group shows at Andrew Shrine Gallery, L.A., 2003, The Second City Council Art Gallery, Long Beach, Calif., 2003, Santa Cruz Art League Gallery, Santa Cruz, Calif., 2002, WomanMade Gallery, Chgo., 2002, A.I.R. Gallery, NYC, 2002, Art Works Downtown, San Rafael, Calif., 2001, Lewis-Clark Center for Arts and History, 2001, others. Apptd. mem. Mayor's Citizens Adv. Com. for Re-Use Hunter's Point Shipyard, San Francisco, 1991—2003; commr. S.E. Cmty. Facility Commn., San Francisco, 1999—2003; bd. dirs. Businesses for Hunter's Point Shipyard, 1988—94. Recipient Commendation, Bayview Opera House, 2000, Cert. of Recognition, Calif. State Assembly and Senate State Calif., 2000, Environ. Achievement award, U.S. EPA Region 9, 2001, Cert. of Honor, Bd. Suprs., 2003. Mem.: Shipyard Trust for the Arts, ArtSeed. Avocations: reading, research, dog training, life-long learning. Home and Office: 1220 Ellis St #2 San Francisco CA 94109 Office Phone: 415-771-2198.

HARDING, MARIE, ecological executive, artist; b. Glen Cove, N.Y., Nov. 13, 1941; d. Charles Lewis and Marie (Parish) H.; m. John P. Allen, Jan. 29, 1965 (div. Oct., 1991); 1 child, Eden A. Harding. BA, Sarah Lawrence Coll., 1964; postgrad., Arts Students League, N.Y.C., 1965. Founder Synergia Ranch Ctr. for Wellness, Innovation, Retreats and Confs., Santa Fe, 1969; founding mem., actress Theater of All Possibilities, Santa Fe, 1971-86; founding mem., dir. Inst. Ecotechnics, Santa Fe, also London, 1974—; bd. dirs. Synopco Corp., N. Mex., 1974-81; bd. dirs., founding mem. Savannah Systems Pty., Ltd., Kimberly region, Australia, 1976—, Outback Sta. Pty. Ltd., Kimberly region, Australia, 1976-94; chair, dir. EcoWorld, Inc., Santa Fe, 1982-94; dir., founding mem., CFO Space Biospheres Ventures, Biosphere 2, Ariz., 1984-94; chair, CEO Oceans Expdns., Inc., 1986-92; pres. ecol. and biosphere R&D/implementation project Global Ecotechnics Corp., Santa Fe, 1994—; pres. Decisions Team, Inc. Ecol. Project Mgmt., Ariz., 1994—; pres., mng. mem. Synergia Ranch, LLC, retreats and confs., Santa Fe. Particpant in constrn. and fin. Capt. R. Heraclitus rsch. vessel, Oakland, Calif., 1974; bd. dirs. Hotel Vajra, Kathamdu, Nepal, 1976-94, Caravan of Dreams Performing Arts Ctr., Ft. Worth, 1983-94, Synergetic Press, London and Ariz., 1984—. Paintings shown in exhibitions San Francisco, Ft. Worth, Santa Fe, Biosphere 2, Ariz., 1979-93, Biosphere 2 Paintings Exhbn., London, 1996, San Marcos Studio Tour shows, 1999-2003, Berlin, 2003, London,2003, Peoples Bank N.Mex., 2003; project dir., artist mural project History of Jazz, Dance, Theater, Ft. Worth, 1982-83, San Marcos Studio Tours, 1999-2003; prodr., dir. (films) Bryon Gysin Loves ya, Project Charlie, The Search, Synergia History, Planet Earth Conf. Vol. Swallows, Madras, India, 1964, Project Concern, Vietnam, Hong Kong, 1964-65; artist, founder, trustee October Gallery Trust, internat. artists forum, London, 1979; mem. Planetary Coral Reef Found., Inc., 1993—. Avocations: ecological project implementation, endangered lifestyles/cultures, painting, landscape gardening, retreat facilitation. Home and Office: 26 Synergia Rd Santa Fe NM 87508-4438

HARDISON, DEE, former mayor; Tchr. spl. edn. Torrance Unified Sch. Dist., 1980-89, program specialist, 1989-94; mem. Torrance City Coun., 1986-94; mayor City of Torrance, 1994—2002. Office: Arc South Bay 1735 W Rosecrans Ave Gardena CA 90249

HARDMAN, ANGELA GAYLE BONTEMPS, social worker; d. Leon E. Bontemps and Barbara Ann Greene, Lynn Dale Greene (Stepfather); m. Herbert Lewis Hardman, Feb. 11, 1995; children: Houston Lauriel, Harrison Layne. B in Psychology and Sociology, Okla. State U., 1987; MSW, U. Okla., 1993. LCSW Okla. Resident asst. Okla. State U., Stillwater, 1986—87; customer svc. agt. Ea. Airlines, 1987—88, Braniff Airlines, 1988—89; night mgr., mem. on-call staff Domestic Violence Intervention Svcs., Tulsa, 1989—92; customer svc. agt. TWA, 1990, 1992—97; social work intern, adminstrv. social work intern Lloyd Rader Ctr., Dept. Human Svcs., State of Okla., Sand Springs/Tulsa, 1992—93; fostercare specialist, case mgr. The Bridge Therapeutic Fostercare, 1993—97; med. social worker Omega Home Health, Tulsa, 1997—99, Compassionate Heart, Tulsa, 1999; med. social worker, bereavement counselor Carter Healthcare and Hospice, Tulsa, 1999—. Mem. adv. bd. Dentists for the Disabled and Elderly, Tulsa, 1999—2003; bd. dirs. Ea. Okla. Charitable Dentists, Tulsa, 2003—. Mem.: NASW. Avocations: party planning, reading. E-mail: ahardman@carterhealthcare.com.

HARDMON, LADY, professional athlete; b. Sept. 12, 1970; Guard Utah Starzz, 1997-99, Sacramento Monarchs, 1999—. Named to All-SEC team, 1990, 92, SEC All-Tournament team, 1990, 92, Hon. Mention Kodak All-Am.; winner bronze medal World Univ. Games in Buffalo, 1993, gold medal, 1992; played in 1989 Jr. World Championship. Avocations: working out, speaking to young people at church. Office: Sacramento Monarchs Utah Starzz One Sports Pky Sacramento CA 95834

HARDON, IMOGENE M. elementary school educator; b. Ripley, Miss., Sept. 26, 1923; d. Theodore Clinton Mauney and Olivia Mae Mullikin; m. Jesse J. Hardon, Apr. 4, 1942 (dec. Aug. 17, 2001); 1 child, Patricia Hardon Collins. BS in Elem. Edn., Blue Mountain Coll., 1956; MS in Elem. Edn., U. Miss., Oxford, 1963, Cert. in Adminstrn. and Elem. Edn., 1979. 1st gr. tchr., prin. Dry Creek Elem. Sch., Booneville, Miss., 1946—55; 1st gr. tchr. Pine Grove Elem. Sch., Ripley, Miss., 1955—63, prin., 1963—86; elem. edn. instr. Blue Mountain (Miss.) Coll., 1986—2001, student tchr. supr., 1988—2001. Mem. scholarship com. Blue Mountain Coll., 1988—2001, mem. com. Staley Lecture Series, 1990—2001, faculty advisor, organizer campus Kappa Kappa Iota, 1993—2001, faculty sponsor freshman and sophomore classes, 1998, 2001, pres. faculty club, 1993; faculty advisor Bapt. Student Union, Blue Mountain. Cmty. corr. (news column) Southern Sentinel, 1996—2001. Mem. Tippah County Hist. Soc., Ripley, Miss., 1976—98; sponsor Tippah County 4-H Club, 1946—86. Mem.: NEA, AAUW (sec., v.p. 1995, Woman of Achievement award 1987), Miss. Ret. Tchrs. Assoc., Miss Ret. Public Employees, Nat. Ret. Tchrs. Assoc., Miss. Assn. Edn., Miss. Profl. Educators, Blue Mountain Coll. Local Alumnae Assn. (pres. 2001—02), Delta Kappa Gamma, Kappa Kappa Iota (chair 1982—2002, state pres. 1983—84, state scholarship 2002). Democrat. Baptist. Achievements include development of Imogene M. Hardon scholarship @ Blue Mountain Coll., 1988. Avocations: social work, church work, community service. Home: 2601 CR 601 Booneville MS 38829

HARDWICK, ELIZABETH, writer; b. Lexington, Ky., July 27, 1916; d. Eugene Allen and Mary (Ramsey) H.; m. Robert Lowell, July 28, 1949 (div. Oct. 1972); 1 child, Harriet. AB, U. Ky., 1938, MA, 1939; postgrad., Columbia U., 1939-41. Adj. assoc. prof. Barnard Coll. Author: (novels) The Ghostly Lover, 1945, The Simple Truth, 1955, Sleepless Nights, 1979, (essays) A View of My Own, 1962, Seduction and Betrayal, 1974, Bartleby in Manhattan, 1983, Sight Readings, 1998, Herman Melville, A Life, 2000; editor: The Selected Letters of William James, 1960; adv. editor: N.Y. Rev. Books. Recipient George Jean Nathan award for dramatic criticism, 1966, Gold medal for criticism Am. Acad. Arts and Letters, 1993; Guggenheim fellow, 1947. Mem. Am. Acad. and Inst. Arts and Letters, Acad. Arts and Scis. Home: 15 W 67th St New York NY 10023-6226

HARDWICKE, CATHERINE HELEN, motion picture production designer; b. Harlingen, Tex. d. John Benjamin III and Jamee Alberta (Bennett) H. BArch with highest honors, U. Tex., 1979; postgrad., UCLA. Prodn. designer for motion pictures. Prodn. designs include (for films) Tank Girl, Tombstone, Two Days in the Valley, Posse, Freeked, Passed Away, Car 54, Where Are You?, Mr. Destiny, I'm Gonna Git You Sucka!, Tapeheads (for TV) Sessions, Morton & Hayes, Trying Times, (for theatre) Carnage, Methusalem, Alagazam--After the Dog Wars; dir., producer live action short Puppy Does the Gumbo. Recipient Card Walker Animation award Disney Studios, 1984, Nissan Focus award, 1984, Joseph Jefferson award Chgo. Non-Equity Theatre, 1990, others.

HARDY, DEBORAH LEWIS, dean, educator, dental hygienist; b. Nov. 11, 1963; Student, Christopher Newport Coll., 1982-84; BS in Dental Hygiene, Old Dominion U., 1989, cert. in gerontol. studies, MS in Dental Hygiene, Old Dominion U., 1991; postgrad., U. Tex., Dallas, 1993. Cert. ADA Joint Commn. on Nat. Dental Exam.; lic. S.E. Regional Va., Tex., Va.; cert. in cardiopulmonary resuscitation. Assoc. prof. Caruth Sch. Dental Hygiene Baylor Coll., Dallas, 1991-95; assoc. dean health occupations-dental N.E. Wis. Tech. Coll., Green Bay, 1995-97, assoc. dean health and cmty. svc., 1997—. Dental asst. Dr. William Griffin, Newport News, Va., 1989; dental asst., dental hygienist Dental Power, Inc., Newport News, 1988-90; dental hygienist Dr. John Caudill, Virginia Beach, 1990-91, Drs. Cash and Weisburg, Norfolk, Va., 1990-91; dental hygienist, educator Riverside Regional Convalescent Ctr., Newport News, 1991; part-time dental hygienist East Dallas Clinic, 1992-95, Nelson-Tebedo Dental Clinic, Dallas, 1995, Oneida (Wis.) Dental Clinic, 1997; cons., educator Skilled

Nursing Facility, Collins Hosp., Baylor U. Med. Ctr., Dallas, 1992; lectr. and spkr. in field. Author: (book) Preventive Oral Health Services Provided by Nurses' Aides to Nursing Home Residents, 1991, (book chpt.) Oral Health and the Older Adult, 1995; editor: (newsletter) Oral Examiner, 1993-95; mem. editl. bd. Profl. Devel. Quar. PDQ, 1994-95; contbr. numerous articles and abstracts to profl. j[illegible] Operation Smile Internat., Ghana Med. Mission, Accra, 1989; vol. Ea. Va. Med. Sch.-Ea. Shore, 1988, Girls Inc., Dallas, 1992; coord. Spirit of Christmas Program, Caruth Sch. Dental Hygiene, 1991, Sr. Student Oral Health Edn., St. Philip's Episcopal Sch. and Comty. Ctr., Dallas, 1993, Health Fair, Dallas Marriott Quorum Hotel, 1993. Recipient Acad. Dentistry for the Handicapped award, 1989, award for phenomenal achievement and leadership Women Dentists' Awards Luncheon, 1993; fellow Old Dominion U., 1990; also numerous rsch. grants in field. Mem. Am. Vocat. Assn., Nat. Dental Hygienists' Assn., Am. Dental Hygienists' Assn., Am. Assn. Dental Schs., Student Nat. Dental Assn. (faculty facilitator 1992-95), N.E. Wis. African Am. Assn. (membership chair 1997), Dallas Dental Hygienists' Soc. (Mem. of Month 1993, 95), Sigma Phi Alpha. Office: NE Wis Tech Coll PO Box 19042 2740 W Mason St Green Bay WI 54303-4966

HARDY, DEBORAH WELLES, history educator; b. Milw., Nov. 2, 1927; d. Frank M. and Doris (Berger) Hursley; widowed; children: Scott, Jonathan, Bridget. Student, Swarthmore Coll., 1945-47; BA, Stanford U., 1949; MA, U. Calif., 1950; PhD, U. Wash., 1968. TV writer, 1964-72; mem. faculty U. Wyo., Laramie, 1967-93, prof. history, 1978-93, head dept., 1980-85, prof. emeritus, 1993—. Free-lance TV writer, 1964-74; mem. Wyo. Council Humanities, 1972-76. Author: Petr. Tkachev: The Critic as Jacobin, 1977, Wyoming University: The First Hundred Years, 1986, Land and Freedom: The Origins of Russian Terrorism, 1987; also articles. Grantee Social Sci. Research Council, summer 1971, Am. Philos. Soc., 1976; Internat. Research and Exchanges Bd. scholar, 1987. Mem.: Phi Beta Kappa. Home: 2450 E Park Ave Laramie WY 82070-4858 Office: U Wyo Dept History Laramie WY 82071

HARDY, DORCAS RUTH, business and government relations executive; b. Newark, N.J., July 18, 1946; d. C. Colburn and Ruth (Hart) H.; m. Samuel V. Spagnolo. BA, Conn. Coll., 1964-68; MBA, Pepperdine U., 1976. cert. sr. advisor. Legis. rsch. asst. U.S. Senator Clifford P. Case, Washington, 1970; spl. asst. White House Conf. Children and Youth, Washington, 1970-71; exec. dir. Health Svcs. Industry Commn., Cost of Living Coun., Washington, 1971-73; asst. sec. Calif. Dept. Health, Sacramento, 1973-74; assoc. dir. U. So. Calif. Ctr. Health Svcs. Rsch., 1974-81; asst. sec. human devel. svcs. HHS, Washington, 1981-86; commr. Social Security Washington, 1986-89; pres. Dorcas R. Hardy & Assocs., Spotsylvania, Va., 1989—; exec. v.p. Pub. Issue Mgmt., Washington, 2001—03. Chmn. bd. dirs., and CEO Work Recovery, Inc., Tucson, 1996-98; bd. dirs. First Coast Svc. Options, Inc., Options Clearing Corp., Wright Investors Svc. Managed Funds; Social Security Advisory Bd.; bd. visitors Mary Washington Coll.; VA Bd. of Rehabilitative Services; chmn. vocat. rehab. and employment task force Vets. Affairs, 2003-04. Author: Social Insecurity: The Crisis in America's Social Security System and How to Plan Now for Your Own Financial Survival, 1992. Mem. Girl Scouts USA, Va. Bd. Rehab. Svcs.; bd. dirs. Com. on Developing Am. Capitalism; former chmn. Pres.'s Task Force on Legal Equity for Women. Mem. Soc. Cert. Sr. Advisors. Office: Washington Metro Office 11407 Stonewall Jackson Dr Spotsylvania VA 22553-4608 E-mail: drhardy@worldet.att.net.

HARDY, JULIA IRENE, elementary school educator; b. Montrose, Iowa, Aug. 11, 1917; d. Carl Alfred Peterson, Achsa Leah LaDuke; m. Francis William Hardy, Oct. 12, 1940; children: Judith (Jeudi) Kay Vitale Eblin, Bruce William. BS in Edn., We. Ill. U., 1965, MS in Edn., 1970; postgrad., Colo. State U., Nat. Coll. Edn., U.S. Internat. U., U. Hawaii. Cert. Permanent profl. cert. Iowa, 1976. Clk. - typist Burlington Ordnance Plant, Iowa, 1941—45; tchr., counselor, reading specialist Keokuk Cmty. Sch. Dist., Keokuk, Iowa, 1957—81. Tchr. Lee County Pub. Schs., Montrose, Iowa, 1936—48; grad. asst. We. Ill. U., Macomb, 1967—68; bd. dirs., chmn. credit com. Keokuk Cmty. Sch. Employees Credit Union, 1986—2001; pvt. tutor, Keokuk, Iowa, 1969—89; presenter poetry programs and readings Christvision, Keokuk, Iowa, 1993—98; presenter poetry symposiums and convs., 1985—2003. Author: Theatre of the Wind, 2003—04, Colours of the Heart, 2003—04, (inspirational poetry) The Wonder of It All, 1996; composer: poems set to music for Emerald Records, 2000—. Tchr. Bethel Bible, 1970. Mem.: Internat. Soc. Poets (life Internat. Poetry Hall of Fame 1997), Internat. Reading Assn. (life Outstanding Achievement in Poetry award), Am. Legion Aux., Order Ea. Star (past matron, Grand page 1952), Kappa Delta Pi, Delta Kappa Gamma (com. mem. Alpha Epsilon chpt., Scholarship 1960), Internat. Beta Sigma Phi. Democrat. Lutheran. Avocations: art, reading, poetry, dramatics, family. Home: 2720 McKinley Ave Keokuk IA 52632-2250

HARDY, LINDA LEA STERLOCK, media specialist; b. Balt., Aug. 15, 1947; d. George Allen and Dorothy Lea (Briggs) Sterlock; m. John Edward Hardy III, Apr. 25, 1970; 1 child, Roger Wayne. BA in History, N.C. Wesleyan Coll., 1969; MEd in History, East Carolina U., 1972, MLS, 1990. Cert. tchr., N.C. History tchr. Halifax (N.C.) County Schs., 1972-83, learning lab tchr., 1983-91, computer lab tchr., 1990-95; media specialist Nash-Rocky Mount (N.C.) Schs., 1995—. Part-time history instr. Nash C.C., 1993. Mem. AAUW (pres. Rocky Mount br. 1993-95, sec. 1997-99, Named Gift award 1987), Bus. and Profl. Women (pres. Rocky Mount chpt. 1986-87, 90-91, 2003—, treas. 1992-97, 2000-03, sec.-treas. dist X 1989-90, state election chmn. 1989-90, 93-95, state credentials chmn. 1997-98, sec.-treas. dist. 6 1997-98, Girl Friday award 1981, 98, Woman of Yr. award 1986, 97, 2002, state found. fin. chair 1996-97, state treas. 1999-2001, state sec. 2001-02, dist. VI dir. 2002-03, state membership chair 2003—04, trustee 2003—), Nat. Assn. Educators, N.C. Assn. Educators, Nash/Rocky Mount Assn. Educators (faculty rep. 1995—), Phi Delta Kappa, Pi Gamma Mu. Methodist. Avocations: reading, travel, needlepoint, computers. Office: Red Oak Middle School 3170 Red Oak Battleboro Rd Battleboro NC 27809-9284 E-mail: llshardy@netscape.net.

HARDY, VICTORIA ELIZABETH, management educator; b. Marion, N.C., Feb. 26, 1947; d. Milton Victor Roth and Bertha Jean (Norris) R.; m. Michael Carrington Hardy, June 19, 1983 (div. 1993); 1 child, Christopher. BS in Edn., U. Mo., 1970; postgrad., So. Ill. U., 1974-75; postgrad. Mgmt. Devel. Program, Stanford U., 1980-81; MA in Mgmt., Aquinas Coll., 1999. Cert. facility mgr. Pub. sch. tchr. English and Theater, 1970-75; gen. mgr. Miss. River Festival, Edwardsville, Ill., 1975-77; dir. events and svcs. Stanford (Calif.) U., 1977-83; exec. dir. Meadowlands Ctr. for the Arts, Rutherford, N.J., 1983-87; pres., chief exec. officer Music Hall Ctr. for the Arts, Detroit, 1987-89; prin. AMS Planning & Rsch., Conn., 1989-94; prof. facility mgmt. Ferris State U., Big Rapids, Mich., 1994—2003; acad. dept. head Wentworth Inst. Tech., Boston, 2003—. Contbr. to various publs. Mem. USICA study team to China, 1981; bd. dirs. Internat. Facility Mgmt. Assn., 1994-97, standing coms. recognition and profl. devel.; mem. People to People facilities del. to Australia and New Zealand, 1996; bd. dirs., chair IFMA Found., 1998—. Named Disting. Educator of Yr., IFMA, 2001; named to Creativity in Business Doubleday, 1986; recipient Gold medal for Cmty. Programs, Coun. for Advancement and Support of Edn., Stanford, 1985. Mem. League of Hist. Am. Theaters (pres. bd. dirs. 1987-89). Democrat. Avocations: skiing, gardening. Office: Acad Dept Head Design & Facilities Wentworth Inst Tech 550 Hungtington Ave Boston MA 02115

HARE, DAWN MICHELLE ERVIN, alcohol/drug abuse services professional; b. Cin., Sept. 22, 1970; d. Gerald Lee Ervin and Barbara Ann Williams, Christine Ervin (Stepmother) and Wes Williams(Stepfather); m. Talliver J. Hare, May 18, 2000; children: Kendra Leigh, Graycelin Tate. Student, U. Phoenix, Reno, 2002—. Bada certified alcohol and drug counselor intern Nev. Bur. Alcohol and Drug Abuse, 2001. Drug and alcohol counselor Youth Recovery Ctr. Divsn. Colo. West Mental Health, Glenwood Springs, 1999—2001, China Spring Youth Camp, Minden, Nev., 2001—. Avocations: research, reading, travel, hiking. Office: China Spring Youth Camp PO Box 218 Minden NV 89423

HARE, ELEANOR O'MEARA, computer science educator; b. Charlottesville, Va., Apr. 6, 1936; d. Edward King and Eleanor Worthington (Selden) O'Meara; m. John Leonard Ging, Feb. 4, 1961 (div. 1972); 1 child, Catherine Eleanor Ging Huddle; m. William Ray Hare, Jr., May 24, 1973. BA, Hollins Coll., 1958; MS, Clemson U., 1973, PhD, 1989. Rsch. asst. cancer rsch. U. Va. Hosp., Charlottesville, 1957-58; rsch. specialist rsch. labs. engring. sci. U. Va., Charlottesville, 1959-64; tchr. Pendleton (S.C.) High Sch., 1964-65; vis. instr. dept. math. sci. Clemson (S.C.) U., 1974-79, instr. dept. computer sci., 1979-83, lectr. dept. computer sci., 1983-90, asst. prof. dept. computer sci., 1990-98, assoc. prof. dept. computer sci., 1998—. Contbr. articles to profl. jours. Bd. dirs. LWV of the Clemson Area, 1988-96; chmn. nursing home study LWV of S.C., 1988-92; oboe and English horn player Anderson (S.C.) Symphony, 1980—. Fellow Inst. Combinatorics and its Applications; mem. AAUP. Office: Clemson U Dept Computer Sci Clemson SC 29634-0001

HARE, ESTER ROSE, physician; b. St. Catherine, Jamaica, Apr. 15, 1952; came to U.S., 1979; d. Emcle and Lovina (Lee) H. BSc with honors, U. West, Indies, Jamaica, 1975; PhD in Biochemistry, Dalhousie U., Halifax, Can., 1984; MD, U. Conn., 1990. Diplomate Am. Bd. Internal Medicine. Intern U. Hosp. Cleve., 1990-91; resident Med. U. Hosp., Charleston, S.C., 1992-94; pvt. practice Orangeburg (S.C.) Med. Assn., 1994—. Mem. bd. health Women's Christian Orgn., Orangeburg, 1995—. Mem. ACP, AMA, Nat. Med. Assn., Am. Soc. Internal Medicine, S.C. Med. Assn., Sigma Psi. Avocations: gardening, aerobics. Office: Orangeburg Med Assocs 1291 Glen Gloria Orangeburg SC 29118

HARE, NORMA Q. retired school system administrator; b. Dadeville, Mo., July 10, 1924; d. James Norma and Mary Delia (Blakemore) Quarles; m. John Daniel Hare, June 27, 1944 (dec.); children: J. Daniel, Thomas C. BA, Calif. State U. Fresno, 1958, MA, 1963. Cert. tchr., sch. adminstr. Elem. tchr. Parlier Sch. Dist., Calif., 1956-57, Sanger Sch. Dist., Calif., 1958-66, S. San Francisco Schs., 1966-67, elem. edn. specialist, 1967, elem. sch. principal, 1967-81. Dir. Title I, Spruce Sch. ESEA, El Rancho Sch. Early Childhood edn. program, sch. dist. mgmt. negotiator, S. San Francisco Schs., 1977-79. Author: (books) Who is Root Beer, 1977, Wish Upon A Birthday, 1979, Mystery at Mousehouse, 1980, Puritans, Pioneers and Planters, 1995; co-author: (book) The Magatagans, 1998. Mem.: DAR, AAUW, Colonial Dames XVII Century (treas. 1995—98, pres. Sierra de Santa Lucia chpt. 2003—), Soc. Mayflower Descs. (gov. San Francisco/Peninsula colony 1983—86, govs. award 1988, 1992). Avocations: genealogy, travel. E-mail: nghare@aol.com.

HAREZI, ILONKA JO, medical technology research executive; b. Princeton, Ind., Jan. 17, 1949; d. Joseph and Helen Marie Fullop; m. John O. Schofield, Dec. 14, 1971 (div. Dec. 1982); 1 child, Franceska ; m. Courtland Reeves, Nov. 26, 1986; children: Bryan, Katharine. PhD, Chgo. Sch. Design, 1969. Mktg. ptnr. Fullop and Assocs., 1983-85; founder, sec., treas. Kinetic Energy Ltd., 1985-90; freelance set designer Ilonka Creative Environments, 1974-84; founder, v.p. Harezi Internat., 1980-84; founder, sec., treas. Elf Cocoon Corp., 1984-86; founder, pres., chmn. Elf Cocoon Internat. Ltd., 1985-92; founder, pres. Elfworks, Inc., 1991-94, Elfworks, Nev., 1994-96; pres., dir. Allied Fund for Capital Appreciation, Inc., 1994—98. Interviewed by radio, TV, and newspapers on design and extremely low frequency electromagnetic tech.; presenter tech. sems. on ELF and scalar phenomena. Author: The Resonance in Residence; contbr. articles to profl. jours. Bd. dirs. Inst. for Higher Human Learning Potential, Phila., 1979. Fellow N.Y. Acad. of Sci.; mem. NAFE, ACLU, AAAS, Am. Inst. Interior Designers, Women's Internat. League for Peace and Freedom, Nat. Assn. Against Health Fraud, Nat. Narcotics Officers Assns. Coalition, N.Y. Acad. Sci., UN-USA Bus. Coun., Knights of Malta (dame), Knights of Africa (dame), U.S. Acad. Polit. Sci., Am. Craft Coun. Achievements include patents pending for transdermal pump. Office: ELF Tesler St Rt 1 Saint Francisville IL 62460

HARF, PATRICIA JEAN KOLE, syndicated columnist, educational consultant, lecturer, clinical and behavioral psychologist, family therapist; b. Berea, Ohio, Oct. 14, 1937; d. Paul Frederic and Mena (Labordes) Kole. BS in Edn. with honors, Baldwin-Wallace Coll., Berea, Ohio, 1959; MS in Edn. with honors, U. Akron, 1966; D in Edn. cum laude, Ariz. State U., 1972; PhD, London Inst. Applied Rsch., 1995; HHD, World Acad., 1994; PhD, London Inst. Applied Rsch., 1995. Rsch. Edn1. Rsch. Coun. Am., 1967-69; tchr. Berea City Schs., Cleve. and Parma, Ohio, 1969-73; asst. prof. Cleve. State U., 1975—; corr., columnist, freelance writer, syndicated columnist Universal PressChronicle-Telegram, Elyria, Ohio, 1986-89; owner Harf Family Counselors, Berea, Ohio, 1993—. Ednl. cons. State of Ohio Bd. Edn. and Gov., 1997—; syndicated columnist Universal Press, Cleve. Plain Dealer; diagnostician of reading difficulties; trustee Coalition for Children's Media; cons. learning disabilities; guest lectr.; TV guest appearances; court appointed spl. cons. for juveniles, 1996-97; mem. Reading Enrichment for Adult Devel.; mem. Coun. of Higher Learning; cons., adult juror Kids First Coalition for Quality Children's Media; advisor, cons. to Juvenile Cts. of Clyahoga County. Author teaching materials and tchr. and children's texts; contbr. articles to profl. jours. ; also advisor to book pubs. and magazines. Pres. Berea Hist. Soc., World Found. Successful Women; mem. Cleve. Orch. Women's Com., Nat. Mus. Women in Arts, Coun. Exceptional Children, Ohio Town Forum, Ohio Arts Festival, com. 500 Project READ; advisor Cleve. Radio and TV Coun.; tutor Project Learn, Cleve.; mem. Berea Rep. Precinct Com.; founder Preventive Parenting; dep. senator Internat. Parliament Safety & Peace Italy; mem. Children's TV Workshop, 1995-96; trustee United Meth. Childrens Found. and Home, 1996-97, Berea Children's Home. Named Intellectual Woman of Yr., 1991-92, Emminent fellow in Universe of Mankind, 1994, Ohio Ednl. Woman of Yr., Ohio Educator of Yr. and Outstanding Educator, Outstanding Citizen Berea C. of C., Outstanding Berea High Grad. awd., 1997; Ohio Edn. Woman of Yr., 1991, Most Admired woman of Yr., 1993, Lifetime Fellow and Hon. Prof. Australian Inst. for Coordinated Rsch., 1995; recipient Women's Inner Cir. of Achievement award, 1992, Woman of Yr. commemorative medal Order of Internat. Fellowship, 1994, Excellence in Journalism award 1990-93, World Lifetime Achievement award, 1996, Gold Star award Am. Soc. for Outstanding Volunteerism, 1995; named baroness Royal Order Bohemian Crown, 1994. Mem. NEA, NOW, AAUW, LWV, Am. Writers Assn, Am. Women in Radio and TV, Inc., Soc. Profl. Journalists (Excellence in Journalism award 1990, Ohio Live, Woman Source directory 1998-00), Women in Journalism, Assn. Tchrs. of Learning Disabilities, Am. Assn. Women in Bus., Berea C. of C. (Outstanding Citizen 1965), Bus. Profl. Women Assn., Australian Inst. Coordinated Rsch. (fellow, hon. prof.), Berea Hist. Soc., Berea Bus. and Profl. Women, Women in Comm. Inc., Internat. Women's Media, Internat. Reading Assn. (cons. and writer for reading tchrs.), Ohio Edn. Assn. (Woman of Yr. in Comms. 1991), Internat. Platform Assn., World Found. of Successful Women, Nat. Assn. Women (Internat. Leaders in Achievement award 1996), Profl. Educators Assn., Learning Disability Assn., Nat. Assn. Psychologists, Ohio Assn. Psychologists, Nat. Assn. Women in the Arts, Western Res. Rep. Women's Assn., S.W. Women Rep. Assn., Kiwanis (sec., v.p.), Berea Rep. Club (Mayoral Volunteerism award 1987), Press Club of Cleve. (award 1996), Cleve. Women's City Club, Cleve. Orch. Women's Soc., U. Akron Alumni Assn., Berea H.S. Alumni Assn., Berea Town Forum, Berea C. of C., Baldwin Wallace Alumni Assn., Baldwin Wallace Women's Club, Berea Town Forum. Republican. Methodist. Avocations: reading, golf, flower arranging, politics, crafts. Home: PO Box 81720 Cleveland OH 44181-0720

HARGETTE, JULIE LYNN, social worker; b. Newport News, Va., Jan. 17, 1975; d. William Simuel Hargette, Janie Coleman Hargette. MSW, Va. Commonwealth U., 2001; BA, U.N.C., 1997. Social worker Va. Treatment Ctr. for Children, Richmond, 2001—; intern clin. social work Va. Treatment Ctr. for Children, Richmond, [illegible]—01; program counselor St. Mary's Hosp., Richmond, 1999—2000; intern Found. Social Work St. Mary's Wellness Ctr., Richmond, 1999—2000; counselor, Group Home Van Vleck House Teton Youth and Family Svcs., Jackson Hole, Wyo., 1997—99. Mem.: NASW. Home: 17 S Davis Ave Richmond VA 23220 Office: Virginia Treatment Ctr, Children 515 N 10th St Richmond VA 23298 Personal E-mail: JHargette@yahoo.com.

HARGIS, BARBARA LOUISE, artist; b. Painesville, Ohio, May 28, 1930; d. Ralph Frances and Claire Louise (Marquis) Fetterly; m. Henry Joseph Hargis Jr., June 4, 1956; children: Ben William, William John, Glenn D. AA, Citrus Coll., 1985. Artist Art Gallery, La Puente, Calif., 1984-94; gallery owner Hargis Chim Gregg Art Gallery, Pomona, Calif., 1994—. Grantee Millenn Prodn., Pomona, Calif., 1994-97. Mem. Carlsbad Oceanside Art League (life), DA Gallery Non Profit, Pomona Valley Art (dir. 1988, life), Corona Art Assn. (life), Women in Arts Mus. (charter mem.), Covina Arts and Crafts, Parks and Recreation (life). Republican. Baptist. Avocations: amateur radio, tennis, swimming, sewing, pool. Studio: BHUA El Cerrito CA 92881 E-mail: FINEART28@aol.com.

HARGITAY, MARISKA, actress; b. L.A., Jan. 23, 1964; d. Mickey Hargitay and Jayne Mansfield. Actor: (films) Ghoulies, 1985, Welcome to 18, 1986, Jocks, 1986, Mr. Universe, 1988, The Perfect Weapon, 1991, Bank Robber, 1993, Leaving Las Vegas, 1995, Hard Time Romance, 1998, Lake Placid, 1999, Perfume, 2001; (TV series) Downtown, 1986, Can't Hurry Love, 1995, Prince Street, 1997, Law & Order: Special Victims Unit, 1999—; (TV films) Finish Line, 1989, Blind Side, 1993, Gambler V: Playing for Keeps, 1994, The Advocate's Devil, 1997; (TV miniseries) Night Sins, 1997, (TV appearances include) Falcon Crest, 1984, In the Heat of the Night, 1988, Freddy's Nightmares, 1988, Baywatch, 1989, Wiseguy, 1990, Thirtysomething, 1990, Booker, 1990, Gabriel's Fire, 1990, Key West, 1993, Seinfeld, 1993, Hotel Room, 1993, All-American Girl, 1995, Ellen, 1996, The Single Guy, 1996, Cracker, 1997, ER, 1997, 1998. Office: Law and Order SVU NBC 30 Rockefeller Plaza New York NY 10112*

HARGRAVE, SARAH QUESENBERRY, consulting company executive; b. Mt. Airy, N.C., Dec. 11, 1944; d. Teddie W. and Lois Knight (Slusher) Quesenberry. Student, Radford Coll., 1963-64, Va. Poly. Inst. and State U., 1964-67. Mgmt. trainee Thalhimer Bros. Dept. Store, Richmond, Va., 1967-68; Cen. Va. fashion and publicity dir. Sears Roebuck & Co., Richmond, 1968-73, nat. decorating sch. coord. Chgo., 1973-74, nat. dir. bus. and profl. women's programs, 1974-76; v.p., treas., program dir. Sears-Roebuck Found., Chgo., 1976-87, program mgr. corp. contbns. and memberships, 1981-84, dir. corp. mktg. and pub. affairs, 1984-87; v.p. personal fin. svcs. and mktg. Northern Trust Co., Chgo., 1987-89; pres. Hargrave Consulting, 1989—. Spkr., seminar leader in field. Bd. dirs. Am. Assembly Collegiate Schs. Bus., 1979-82, mem. vis. com., 1979-82, mem. fin. and audit com., 1980-82, mem. task force on doctoral supply and demand, 1980-82; mem. Com. for Equal Opportunity for Women, 1976-81; chmn., 1978-79, 80-81; mem. bus. adv. coun. Walter E. Heller Coll. Bus. Adminstrn., Roosevelt U., 1979-89; co-dir. Ill. Internat. Women's Yr. Ctr., 1975. Named Outstanding Young Women of Yr. Ill., 1976; named Women of Achievement State Street Bus. and Profl. Woman's Club, 1978 Mem. ASTD, Eddystone Condominium Assn. (v.p. 1978-86), Profl. Women's Network. Home and Office: 34 Fairlawn Ave Daly City CA 94015-3425

HARGROVE, LINDA, professional basketball coach; m. Ed Hargrove; children: Brian, Tara. BS magna cum laude, Southwestern Coll., 1975; MEd, Wichita State U., 1985. Head coach Cowley County C.C. Tigers, 1972-89, Wichita State U. Shockers, 1989-98; head coach, dir. player pers. Colo. Xplosion, Am. Basketball League, Denver, 1998—; head coach Portland Fire, WNBA, 1999—. Asst. coach 1990 U.S. Sr. Nat. Women's Team, 1989, 1992 U.S. Olympic Team; cons. WNBA Orlando Miracle; mem. USA Basketball Sr. Nat. Team Com. Inductee Southwestern Coll. Athletic Hall of Fame, 1992. Mem. Women's Basketball Coaches Assn. (bd. dirs., Midwest divsn. I rep.). Office: Portland Fire One Center Ct Ste 150 Portland OR 97227

HARGROVE, SANDRA LEIGH, financial planner; b. Hillsboro, Oreg., Dec. 1, 1946; d. William Paul and Hazel Hannah Burgher; m. Larry Burke Hargrove, Nov. 25, 1977; m. John Anthony Coleman, July 13, 1964 (div. May 0, 1977); children: Tereasa Kay Taylor, Deborah Leigh Coleman. Student, Clatsop County C.C., Astoria, Oreg., 1983—85. Mgr. Columbia Ins., Knappa, Oreg., 1973—75; office supply and mail rm. staff Crown Zellerbach Corp Wauna Mill, Clatskanie, Oreg., 1975—76; switchboard operator/receptionist Crown Zellerbach Wauna Mill, Clatskanie, 1976—78, acct. #1 & 2 paper machines, 1978—80; gen. ledger acct. Crown Zellerbach/James River Corp. Wauna Mill, Clatskanie, 1980—84; fin. mgr. James River Corp. Wauna Mill, Clatskanie, 1984—89; co-owner S & K Images, Svenson, Oreg., 1996—98; relief postmaster USPS Oysterville (Wash.) Post Office, 2002—. Originator of project concept & manager (historical/genealogical research) The Lewis & Clark Descendant Project. Treas. Immanuel Luth. Ch., Knappa, 1986—98. Mem.: Pacific County Wash. Geneal. Soc. (pres. 1999—2001), Clatsop County Oreg. Geneal. Soc. (pres. 1998—2001). Democrat. Lutheran. Avocations: walking, genealogy. Personal E-mail: shargrov@pacifier.com.

HARING, ELLEN STONE (MRS. E. S. HARING), philosophy educator; b. L.A., 1921; d. Earl E. and Eleanor (Pritchard) Stone; m. Philip S. Haring, Dec. 1942 (div. June 1951). BA, Bryn Mawr Coll., 1942, MA, Radcliffe Coll., 1943, PhD (AAUW fellow), 1959. Adminstrv. worker ARC, Boston, 1943; mem. faculty Wheaton Coll., Norton, Mass., 1944-45, Wellesley Coll., 1945-72, assoc. prof., 1958-64, prof. philosophy, 1964-72, U. Fla., Gainesville, 1972-93, prof. emerita, 1993—, chmn. dept., 1972-80. Mem. Am. Philos. Assn., Metaphys. Soc. Am.

HARIRI, GISUE, architect, educator; b. Abadan, Iran, May 16, 1956; came to U.S., 1974; d. Karim Hariri and Behjat (Isphahani) Saboonchi. BArch, Cornell U., 1980. Apprentice Jennings and Stout, San Francisco, 1980-82; Paolo Soleri, Arcosanti, Ariz., 1982-83; apprentice Paul Segal Assocs. Architects, N.Y.C., 1983-85; ptnr. Hariri & Hariri, N.Y.C., 1986—. Lighting and furniture designer, 1993—; participant in Urban Housing Festival, The Hague, The Netherlands, 1991; lectr. in field. Work exhibited in Mus. Modern Art, 1999, Storefront for Art and Architecture, N.Y.C., 1988, Parson Sch. Design, N.Y.C., 1988, Princeton (N.J.) U., 1988, Archtl. League N.Y., 1990, Kent (Ohio) State U., 1991, Richard Anderson Gallery, N.Y.C., 1993, Cornell U., Ithaca, N.Y., 1993, Contemporary Arts Ctr., Cin., 1993, others, also in various profl. publs.; Monograph: Hariri & Hariri Work in Progress, 1996, Kliczkowski Casas Internat., 1997. Recipient Young Architects Forum award Archtl. League N.Y., 1990. Mem. Internat. Interior Design Assn. Media Stars, 1998. Office: Hariri & Hariri 18 E 12th St New York NY 10003-4458

HARITON, JO ROSENBERG, psychotherapist, educator; b. Albany, N.Y., June 12, 1948; d. Irving H. and Madeline P. Rosenberg; m. Frank J. Hariton; 2 children. BA, Goucher Coll., Towson, Md., 1970; MS, Columbia U., 1973; PhD, NYU, 1992; postgrad., Postgrad. Ctr. Mental Health, N.Y.C., 1979. Cert. psychoanalyst. With maternal and child health dept. Bronx (N.Y.) Mcpl. Hosp. Ctr., 1973-76, coord. emergency svcs. children's dept. child psychiatry, 1976-79; field work instr. NYU Sch. Social Work, 1977-79; sr. psychiat social worker divsn. child and adol. psychiatry Westchester divsn. N.Y. Hosp.-Cornell Med. Ctr., White Plains, N.Y.,

1979-82, social work coord., 1982-98; mem. faculty Cornell U. Med. Sch., 1982—; pvt. practice psychoanalysis and psychotherapy N.Y.C. Co-head ADHD Svc. Line, 1996—. Contbr. articles on group therapy to profl. jours. Fellow N.Y. State Soc. Clin. Social Work Psychotherapists; mem. NASW, Acad. Cert. Social Workers, Am. Orthopsychiat. Assn., Am. Group Psychotherapy Assn. Home: 1065 Dobbs Ferry Rd White Plains NY 10607-2212 Office: NY Presby Hosp Westchester Divsn 21 Bloomingdale Rd White Plains NY 10605-1596 E-mail: jhariton@med.cornell.edu.

HARITON, LORRAINE JILL, information technology executive; b. N.Y.C., Nov. 7, 1954; d. Martin and Barbara (Jaffee) H.; m. Stephen Alan Weyl; children: Eric, Laura. BS in Math Sci., Stanford U., 1976; MBA, Harvard U., 1982. Sales rep. IBM, N.Y.C., 1977-80, regional rep. San Francisco, 1982-84, sales mgr. Oakland, Calif., 1984-86; mgr. pricing Rolm, Santa Clara, Calif., 1986-87, adminstrv. asst. to v.p. sales, 1987-88, br. mgr., 1988-90, product line mgr., 1990-92; dir. mktg. Verifone, Inc., Redwood City, Calif., 1992-93; v.p. mktg. Network Computing Devices, Mountain View, Calif., 1993—99; pres., CEO Beatnik Inc., San Mateo, Calif., 1999—2003, chmn., 2003—; pres., CEO Apptera, Inc., San Bruno, Calif., 2003—. Office: Apptera Inc 1150 Bayhill Dr Ste 203 San Bruno CA 94066

HARKEN, SHELBY ELAINE, librarian; b. Minot, N.D., May 6, 1947; d. Albert Strand, Elaine Genevieve Strand; m. Stephen John Harken, Aug. 14, 1971; 1 child, Stephanie. MLS, U. N.D., 1971. Head cataloger Chester Fritz Libr., Grand Forks, ND, 1971—, head acquisitions, bibliographic control, 1991—. Author: (journal) Cataloging & Classification Quarterly, 1996, North Dakota Division of the American Association of University Women, 1964-1984, 1984, (newsletter) ODIN Information Notes, 1990, So This is How You Run a Media Center! Organizing, Administering, and Developing an Instructional Media Center - An Annotated Bibliography., 1971. Music leader Newman Cath. Ch., Grand Forks, 1980—99; sec. Red River Valley Gymnastics, Grand Forks, ND, 1985—, Roy Lake Assn., Mahnomen. Grantee, LSTA, 1999—2000, N.D. Dept. Pub. Instrn., 2000—01. Mem.: AAUW, ALA (subject analysis com. 1998—), Assn. Coll. and Rsch. Libr. (univ. sect. comm. com. 1991—93), Assn. Libr. Collections and Tech. Svcs. (MARBI com. 1991—96), Libr. and Info. Tech. Assn. (TESLA mem. 1996—98, com. cataloging and description and access liaison 2001—), Mountain Plains Libr. Assn. (tech. svc. sect. chair 1997—98), N.D. Libr. Assn. (tech. svc. roundtable 1991—92, govt. documents roundtable chair 1997—98), World-wide PALS Users Group (sec. 1996—2001). Roman Catholic. Avocations: swimming, crafts, gardening. Home: 1679 River Cove Manvel ND 58256-9789 Office: Univ ND Chester Fritz Libr Box 9000 Grand Forks ND 58202-9000 Office Phone: 701-777-4634. Office Fax: 701-777-3319. Business E-Mail: shelby-harken@und.nodak.edu.

HARKIN, ANN WINIFRED, elementary school educator, psychotherapist; b. Glasgow, Scotland, Oct. 14, 1951; came to US, 1956; d. John Joseph and Mary W. Leavy H.; 1 child, Julia A. Wilkinson. BA in Psychology cum laude, Immaculata Coll., 1973, MA in Counseling Psychology summa cum laude, 1999. Instrnl. II permanent cert. elem., secondary sch. tchr., Pa. Tchr. grade 3 St. Anastasia, Newtown Square, Pa., 1973-78; tchr. grade 1 Mother of Divine Providence, King of Prussia, 1979-89, St. Aloysius Acad., Bryn Mawr, Pa., 1989—; legal asst. Elizabeth R. Howard, Esquire, 2001—. Counselor Paoli Addictions Ctr., Pa. Mem. APA, ACA, Nat. Cath. Educators Assn., Diamond Rock Schoolhouse Assn., Donegal Soc. Phila., Chi Sigma Iota. Avocations: horticulture, animals, hiking, swimming, drawing. Home: 738 Cedar Dr Phoenixville PA 19460-3606

HARKIN, RUTH R. federal agency administrator, lawyer; b. Vesta, Minn. d. Walter Herman and Virginia (Coull) Raduenz; m. Tom Harkin, July 6, 1968; children: Amy, Jenny. BA in English, U. Minn., 1966; JD, Cath. U., 1972. With Dept. Army, Korea, 1966-67, Polk County Social Svcs., Des Moines, 1968; clk. Lawyers Com. Civil Rights under Law; elected county atty. Story County, Iowa, 1972-76; spl. prosecutor Polk County, 1977-78; dep. gen. counsel Dept. Agriculture, Washington, 1979-81, Akin, Gump, Strauss, Hauer & Feld, LLP, Washington, 1983-93; pres., chief exec. officer Overseas Pvt. Investment Corp., Washington, 1993—. Mem. Iowa Bar Assn., D.C. Bar Assn. Democrat. Lutheran. Office: Overseas Pvt Investment Co Office of the President 1100 New York Ave NW Washington DC 20527-0001

HARKINS, LIDA E. state legislator, educator; b. Jersey City, Jan. 24, 1944; d. Paul Vincent and Lida Cecelia (Higgins) McMahon; children: Michael, Julie, Joseph. BA, Regis Coll., 1966; cert. in pub. policy mgmt., Boston Coll., 1986. Tchr. Mass. Pub. Schs., 1966-68; dir. sch. bus. tng. partnership The Edn. Co-op., Wellesley, Mass., 1988-89; state legislator 13th Norfolk Dist., Needham, Dover and Medfield, Mass., 1989—. Bd. dirs. Charles River Workshop for Retarded Citizens, Needham, 1989. Mem. com. Needham Sch., 1976-82, chmn., 1979-80; mem. Needham Town Meeting, 1976—; chmn. Needham Dem. Town Com., 1983-85; bd. dirs. Needham area Boy Scouts Am., 1989. Recipient Alumnae Achievement award Boston Coll., 1989, Golden Donkey award Rendon Report Annual Polit. awards, 1989. Mem. Women Dems. of Dover and Needham. Roman Catholic. Avocations: reading, playing piano and flute. Home: 14 Hancock Rd Needham MA 02492-1926 Office: Room 234-State House Boston MA 02133

HARKLEROAD, ASHLEY, professional tennis player; b. Rossville, Ga., May 2, 1985; d. Danny and Tammy. Profl. tennis player, 2001—. Recipient Ranked #52, WTA, Ranked #9 Among U.S. Players, Winner Wimbledon Doubles Title, 2001, Highest Season Ending Single's Ranking #115, 2002, Top Ranked Am. Jr. Player at # 14 Internat., 2002, 2 Women's Circuit Singles Titles, ITF. Office: WTA Tour Corporate Headquarters One Progress Plz Ste 1500 Saint Petersburg FL 33701*

HARKLEROAD, JO-ANN DECKER, special education educator; b. Wilkes-Barre, Pa., Oct. 22, 1936; d. Leon Joseph Sr. and Beatrice Catherine (Wright) Decker; m. A. Dwayne Harkleroad; 1 child, Leon Wade. AS, George Washington U., 1960, BS in Health, Phys. Edn. and Recreation, minor in Spl. Edn., 1968, MA in Spl. Edn. and Ednl. Diagnosis and Prescription, 1969, postgrad., 1997-99. Recipient Appreciation cert. Fairfax County (Va.) Police Dept., 1987, Meritorious Svc. medal Pres. Com. on Employment of People with Disabilities, 1988. Instr. Cath. U. Am., Washington, 1960-61; tchr. Bush Hill Day Sch., Franconia, Va., 1961-63; ednl. diagnostician Prince William County Schs., Manassas, Va., 1969-71, supr. title I, 1971-72; writer, editor Sta. WNVT-TV, Fairfax, Va., 1980-82; dir. spl. edn. Highland County Schs., Monterey, Va., 1987-90. Author: (novel) Horse Thief Trail, 1981, 83, 86; columnist op-ed page The Recorder; radio broadcaster Sta. WVMR, Frost, W.Va. Ruling elder Presbyn. Ch., McDowell, Va., Clifton, Va.; mem. divsn. of Faith in Action Hunger com. Shenandoah Presbytery; dir. McDowell Presbyn. Ch. Choir; rotating dir. Highland County Cmty. Choir; past pres. Highland County Pub. Libr. Bd. Avocations: hiking, camping, rifleshooting, reading, gardening. Home: Windy Ridge Farm HC 33 Box 60 Mc Dowell VA 24458-9704

HARKNESS, MABEL GLEASON, retired librarian; b. Oil City, Pa., Jan. 20, 1913; d. Charles Wilcox and Mabel Amy (Fulton) Gleason; m. Benjamin Olney, Mar. 23, 1946 (dec. 1963); m. Bernard Emerson Harkness, Sept. 5, 1964 (dec. 1980). AB, U. Rochester, 1935, MA, 1962; LHD (hon.), Keuka Coll., 2003. Cert. libr., N.Y. Libr. Stromberg-Carlson Co., Rochester, N.Y., 1942-51, Garden Ctr. Rochester, 1953-67, Monroe County (N.Y.) Bookmobile, 1952-53; now ret. Vol. cataloger Geneva (N.Y.) Hist. Soc.; editor Gleam mag., Rochester Poetry Soc., 1945, Engr.'s Notebook, Stromberg-Carlson Co., 1946-50, Garden Ctr. Bull., 1955-67; co-founder, past pres. Western N.Y. chpt. Spl. Librs. Assn., 1945. Compiler: Harkness Seedlist Handbook 1986 (Worth award for bot./hort. writing Am. Rock Garden Soc.), 2d edit., 1993; contbr. articles on horticulture and local history to various publs. Trustee Keuka Coll., Keuka Park, N.Y., 1971-80, now emeritus. Mem. AAUW (life), Am. Rock Garden Soc. (life), Alpine Garden Soc. (Eng.), Scottish Rock Garden Club (life). Republican. Episcopalian. Avocations: musicology, architectural history. Home: 5169 Pre Emption Rd Geneva NY 14456-9736

HARKNESS, MARY LOU, librarian; b. Denby, SD, Aug. 19, 1925; d. Raleigh Everette and Mary Jane (Boyd) Barker; m. Donald R. Harkness, Sept. 2, 1967. BA, Nebr. Wesleyan U., 1947; AB in L.S, U. Mich., 1948; MS, Columbia U., 1958. Jr. cataloger U. Mich. Law Library, 1948-50; asst. cataloger Calif. Poly. Coll., 1950-52; asst. cataloger, then head cataloger Ga. Inst. Tech., 1952-57; head cataloger U. South Fla., Tampa, 1958-67, dir. libraries, 1967-87, dir. emeritus, 1987—. Cons. Nat. Library Nigeria, 1962-63. Bd. dirs. Southeastern Library Network, 1977-80. Recipient Alumni Achievement award Nebr. Wesleyan U., 1972 Mem. ALA, Fla. Library Assn., Athena Soc. Democrat. Presbyterian. Home: 13511 Palmwood Ln Tampa FL 33618-8409 E-mail: mharkne2@helios.acomp.usf.edu.

HARLAN, MEGAN, journalist, poet; b. Burlington, Vt., Jan. 1, 1970; d. Neal MacLaren and Sherry (Yandle) Harlan; m. Matthew Thomas Culligan, July 28, 2001. BA, Tufts U., 1991; MFA, NYU, 1993. Contbg. writer, book critic Entertainment Weekly, N.Y.C., 1995—; freelance book critic The N.Y. Times, N.Y.C., 1996—; freelance journalist Elle mag., N.Y.C., 1997—2000; freelance travel writer The N.Y. Times, N.Y.C., 1999—; freelance book critic The San Francisco Chronicle, 2001—. Contbr. poetry and short stories to anthologies (Pushcart Prize nomination, 1999, Short Short Competition, 1999). Recipient Writers fellowship, NYU GSAS, 1991—93. Mem.: PEN West (assoc.), Nat. Book Critics Cir. (assoc.). Liberal. Personal E-mail: meg@megharlan.com.

HARLAN, NANCY MARGARET, lawyer; b. Santa Monica, Calif., Sept. 10, 1946; d. William Galland and Betty M. (Miles) Plett; m. John Hammack, Dec. 1, 1979; children: Laryssa Maria Rebello, Leea Elyce. BS magna cum laude, Calif. State U., Hayward, 1972; JD, U. Calif., Berkeley, 1975. Bar: Calif. 1975, Fed. Bar, U.S. Dist. Ct. (ctrl. dist. 9th cir.) 1976. Assoc. Poindexter & Doutre, L.A., 1975—80; residential counsel Coldwell Banker Residential Brokerage Co., Fountain Valley, Calif., 1980—81; sr. counsel for real estate subs. law dept. Pacific Lighting Corp., Santa Ana, Calif., 1981—87; sr. v.p., gen. counsel The Presley Cos., 1987—. Bd. dirs. La Casa; exec. v.p. student body U. Calif., Berkeley, 1974—75. Mem.: NAFE, ABA, Bus. and Profl. Women, L.A. Women Lawyers Assn., Orange County Women Lawyers Assn., Calif. Women Lawyers Assn., Orange County Bar Assn. (dir. corp. counsel sect. 1982—), L.A. County Bar Assn., State Bar Calif. Office: William Lyon Homes Inc 4490 Von Karman Ave Newport Beach CA 92660-2008

HARLEM, SUSAN LYNN, librarian; b. L.A., Oct. 1, 1950; d. Frank Joseph and Esther Frances (Bomell) H.; m. Anthony Stephen Hacsi, Aug 31, 1990. BA, UCLA, 1972, MLS, 1976. Libr. U. Md., College Park, 1976-79, U.S. Dept. Edn., Washington, 1979-82, GSA, Washington, 1982-87, NLRB, Washington, 1988—. Tutor Washington Lit. Coun., 1992—. Co-author: Washington on Foot, 1984. Office: NLRB Libr 1099 14th St NW Washington DC 20570-0001 E-mail: susan.harlem@nlrb.gov.

HARLEMAN, ANN, English language educator, writer; BA in English, Douglass Coll., 1967; PhD in Linguistics, Princeton U., 1972; MFA in Creative Writing, Brown U., 1988. Asst. prof. dept. English, Rutgers U., New Brunswick, N.J., 1973-74, U. Wash., Seattle, 1974-79, assoc. prof., 1979-84; vis. assoc. prof., rsch. affiliate writing program MIT, Cambridge, 1984-86; vis. scholar program in Am. civilization Brown U., Providence, 1986—; Cole disting. prof. Wheaton (Mass.) Coll., 1992-93; prof. English, RISD, Providence, 1994—. Fulbright-Hays lectr., 1980-81. Author: Graphic Representation of Models in Linguistic Theory, 1976, (with Bruce A. Rosenberg) Ian Fleming: A Critical Biograhy, 1989, Happiness, 1994, Bitter Lake, 1996; translator: Mute Phone Calls, 1992; contbr. over 50 articles to scholarly publs., transls. and revs., poems and short stories to lit. mags. Recipient Raymond Carver prize, 1986, Nelson Algren runner-up award Chgo. Tribune, 1987, 3d prize Judith Siegal Pearson award, 1988, Chris O'Malley fiction prize Madison Rev., 1990, Judith Siegal Pearson award, 1991, syndicated fiction award PEN, 1991, Iowa short fiction award, 1993, spl. mention, Push Cart prize, 1998, Berlin Prize fellowship in Lit., 2000, Zoetrope Fiction Award, 2002, O'Henry Prize, 2003, Goodheart Prize, 2004; Guggenheim fellow, 1976-77, fellow Huntington Libr., 1979-80, MacDowell Colony, 1988, 99, 2004, Am. Coun. Learned Socs., 1992, Wurlitzer Found., 1992; sr. scholar Am. Coun. Learned Socs./IREX, 1976-77; grantee NEH, 1988, Rockefeller Found., 1989, Bogliasco Found., 1998, 2004; fellow R.I. Coun. Arts, 1989, 97. Mem. PEN Am. Ctr. Address: 18 Imperial Pl # 5! Providence RI 02903

HARLESS, KATHERINE J. telecommunications company executive; m. Skip Harless; children: Skip Jr., Ely, Bill. B in Acctg., U. Tex., 1972. With GTE, 1973—, regional pres. telephone ops., 1994-96, pres. airfone, 1996—. Bd. dirs. U. Tex. Bus. Sch., Skytel Comms. Mem. Com. of 200 (tres. com. 200 found. bd.), Chgo. Network, Internat. Women's Forum, Execs. Club Chgo., Barbara Bush Found. (mem. celebration of reading com.), Leadership Am. Office: GTE Airfone 2809 Butterfield Rd Oak Brook IL 60523-1151 Fax: 630-572-0506.

HARLEY, MARILYN M, music educator; b. Lakewood, Ohio, July 9, 1943; d. Sheldon Thomas and Nancy Elizabeth Henry; m. Laurence K Harley, Nov. 2, 1968; children: Christopher S, Elisa S, Stephen T, Cheryl L. MusB, Ohio Wesleyan U., Delaware, OH, 1965. Cert. K12 Music Teaching OH, 1965, Level 1 Technology In Music OH, 2000. Tchr. Painesville Twp. Local Schools, Painesville, Ohio, 1965—70; choir dir. Hope Ridge Ch., Mentor, Ohio, 1966—67, Painesville First Ch. Christ, Painesville, Ohio, 1967—68, Painesville First Ch. Of Christ, Painesville, Ohio, 1976, 1978—97; tchr. First Ch. Nursery Sch., Painesville, Ohio, 1984—88. Dir. Teen Choir, Painesville, Ohio, 1984—97, Found. Gospel Quartet, Painesville, Ohio, 1991—; tchr. Painsville Twp., 1988—. Performer, singer, dir. Many Organizations, Northeast, Ohio, 1965—2003. Mem.: Music Edn. Nat. Conf. & State & Locals, Ohio Edn. Assn. & Locals, Delta Kappa Gamma Edn. (music 1998—2004), Painesville Music & Drama Club. Christian. Avocations: singing, reading.

HARLEY, NAOMI HALLDEN, radiation specialist, environmental medicine educator; b. N.Y.C., Aug. 4, 1932; d. Carl Edward and Ida Wilson (Palmer) Hallden; m. John Henry Harley, Sept. 11, 1964. BS, Cooper Union U., N.Y.C., 1959; MS, NYU, 1967, PhD, 1971, Advanced Prof. Cert., 1983. Phys. scientist U.S. AEC, N.Y.C., 1951-65; rsch. prof. environ. medicine NYU, 1965—; coun. mem., sci. com. chmn. Nat. Coun. on Radiation Protection and Measurement, Washington, 1982—. Contbr. articles to profl. jours. Adviser to UN Sci. Com. on Effects of Atomic Radiation (UNSCEAR), 1989—. USPHS fellow, 1988. Fellow: AAAS, Health Physics Soc. Democrat. Office: NYU Sch of Medicine Dept Environ Medicine 550 1st Ave New York NY 10016-6402 E-mail: naomi.harley@med.nyu.edu.

HARLEY, RUTH, artist, educator; b. Phila. children: Peter Wells Bressler, Victoria Angela. Student, Pa. State U., 1941; BFA, Phila. Coll. Art, 1945; postgrad., U. N.H., 1971, Hampshire Coll., 1970. Former instr. Phila. Mus. Art, 1946-59; former art supt. Ventnor (N.J.) City Bd. Edn., 1959-61. Art tchr. The Print Club, Phila., Allens Lane Art Ctr., Phila., Suburban Ctr. Arts, Lower Merion, Pa., Radner (Pa.) Twp. Adult Ctr., 1949-59, Atlantic City Adult Ctr., 1959-60. One-woman shows include Dubin-Lush Galleries, Phila., 1956, Contemporary Art Assn., Phila., 1957, Vernon Art Exhbns., Germantown, Pa., 1958, Detroit Inst. Arts, 1958, Phila. Mus. Art, 1957, 59, Moore Inst., Phila., 1962-68, Greenhill Galleries, Phila., 1974, Phila. Civic Ctr., 1978, Natal Rio Grande du Norte, Brazil, 1979, Galerie Novel Esprit, Tampa, Fla., 1992-95, Mind's Eye Gallery, St. Petersburg, Fla., 1993, Ga. Tech. Art Ctr., 1998, Robert Ferst Ctr. for the Arts Ga. Inst. Tech., 1998-99; exhibited in group shows, including Group 55, Phila., 1955, Print Club, Phila., 1955, Nat. Tours 1956-59, Pa. Acad. Fine Arts, 1957, Vernon Art Exhbns., 1958, Detroit Inst. Arts, 1958, Phila. Mus. Art, 1959, Moore Inst., 1962, Phila. Civic Ctr. Mus., 1975, Galerie Nouvel Esprit Assemblage Russe, 1992, Kenneth Raymond Gallery, Boca Raton, 1992-93, Mind's Eye Gallery, 1993, Polk Mus. Art, Lakeland, Fla., 1993, Don Roll Gallery, Sarasota, Fla., 1994-95, Las Vegas (Nev.) Internat. Art Expo, 1994, Heim Am. Gallery, Fisher Island, Fla., 1996, McLean Gallery, Malibu, Calif., 1997, 98, 99, Robert Ferst Ctr. Arts, Ga. Tech. U., 1998, 99, Christina Gallery, Atlanta, 1999, 2000, Adrian Howard Gallery, St. Petersburg, 2000, 01, 02, 04, Melrose Bay Art Gallery, Melrose, Fla., 2001, Red River Valley Mus., Vernon, Tex., 2001, Kirkpatrick Mus., Okla., 2001, Airport, Gainesville, Fla., 2001, In Celebration of Art, 2004; represented in permanent collections at U. Villanova (Pa.) Mus., TemplU. Law Sch., Pa., Woodmere Mus., Phila.; included in Art in America Ann. Guide, 2000-01, 2002; photo sculpture commd. through Phila. Re-Devel. Authority. Contbr. art prize to Ventnor N.J. Sch. Sys. Home and Office: PO Box 433 Melrose FL 32666-0433 E-mail: harleyruth@aol.com.

HARLIN, MARILYN MILER, marine botany educator, researcher, consultant; b. Oakland, Calif., May 30, 1934; d. George T. and Gertrude (Turula) Miler; m. John E. Harlin II, Oct. 25, 1955 (dec. Feb. 1966); children: John E. III, Andrea M. Harlin Cilento. AB, Stanford U., 1955, MA, 1956; PhD, U. Wash., 1971. Instr. Am. Coll. Switzerland and Leysin, 1964-66; asst. prof. Pacific Marine Sta., Dillon Beach, Calif., 1969; asst. prof. marine biology U. R.I., Kingston, 1971-75, assoc. prof., 1975-83, prof., 1983-2000, prof. emerita, 2000—, chair botany dept., chair dept. biol. scis. Guest scientist Atlantic Regional Lab., Halifax, N.S., Can., 1973-78; hon. vis.prof. LaTrobe U., Bundoora, Victoria, Australia, 1984; resource person R.I. Coastal Resource Mgmt. Coun., 1980-2000, R.I. Dept. Environ. Mgmt., 1980; cons. Applied Sci. Assocs., Narragansett, R.I., 1988-98, Western Australia Water Authority, Perth, 1994; rsch. assoc. U. Calif., Santa Cruz, 1993. Co-editor: Marine Ecology, 1976, Freshwater and Marine Plants of Rhode Island, 1988. Bd. dirs. Westminster Unitarian Ch., East Greenwich, R.I., 1987; bd. govs. Women's Ctr., Kingston, 1989-90. Grantee NOAA, 1975-81, Dept. Environ. Mgmt./EPA, 1989-91, U.S. Fish and Wildlife, 1995. Mem. Internat. Phycological Soc., Phycological Soc. Am. (editor newsletter 1982-84, editorial bd. 1988-90), N.E. Algal Soc. (exec. com.), Sigma Xi (pres., sec. 1979-82). Avocations: yoga, hiking, reading, writing, gardening. E-mail: mharlinor@earthlink.net.

HARLOW, CAROL JEAN, prospect researcher; b. New Haven, Conn., Apr. 12, 1952; d. Frank J. and Aileen W. H., children: Anna, Lydia. BA, U. Conn., Storrs, 1974; MS, Southern Conn. State U., New Haven, 1978. Circulation librarian Atlanta Coll. of Art, Atlanta, 1980-83; registrar, 1983-85; admissions coord. Emory Univ. Sch. of Nursing, Atlanta, 1985-88; tech. writer TechData, Clearwater, FL, 1995-96; dir. prospect rsch. Univ. Tampa, Tampa, FL, 1996—. Mem.: Downtown Tampa Bus. and Profl. Women, Assn. Profl. Rschrs. for Advancement (track co-chmn. 16th ann. internat. conf.). Democrat. Avocations: reading, opera. Office: University of Tampa 401 W Kennedy Blvd Tampa FL 33606-1450 Fax: 813-258-7297. E-mail: charlow@ut.edu.

HARLOW, JUDITH LEIGH, educational institute executive, consultant; b. Denver, Aug. 11, 1943; d. Roy Afton and Virginia Lee (Whitehead) H. BA in Secondary Edn., U. N.Mex., 1966, MA in Counseling, 1973. Cert. in guidance and counseling, ednl. adminstrn., N.Mex.; lic. ednl. diagnostician, mediator. Tchr. Albuquerque Pub. Schs., 1966-79, ednl. diagnostician, 1979-80, adminstr. spl. edn., 1980-87, asst. prin., 1987-95; dir. Inst. for Behavior Intervention in the Schs. Ednl. Assessment Systems, Inc., Albuquerque, 1997—. Mem. adv. bd. Desert Hills Residential Treatment Ctr., Albuquerque, 1998—. Vol. N.Mex. Ctr. for Dispute Resolution, Albuquerque. Mem. Coun. for Exceptional Children (Disting. Svc. award N.Mex. 1992). Democrat. Avocations: golf, tennis. Home: 10920 Central Park Dr NE Albuquerque NM 87123-5426 Office: Inst for Behavior Intervention in the Schs 5200 Copper Ave NE Albuquerque NM 87108-1473

HARLOW, RUTH, lawyer; b. 1961; AB, Stanford U.; JD, Yale U. Bar: 1988. Atty. ACLU, NJ, Am. Civil Liberties Union, Lambda Legal Def. and Edn. Fund, 1996—2000, legal dir., 2000—03; atty. pvt. practice, 2003—. Recipient Lawyer of the Year, Nat. Law Journal, 2003. Office: 120 Wall St Ste 1500 New York NY 10005*

HARMAN, CAROLE MOSES, retired art educator, artist; b. Bklyn. BFA in Art Edn., R.I. Sch. Design, 1965, MA in Art Edn., 1969; PhD of Pedagogy (hon.), R.I. Coll., 2002. Tchr. art Fairfield (Conn.) Pub. Schs., 1965-68; chair dept. art Hope H.S., 1969—78, Central H.S., 1978—99; critic tchr., dept. art edn. R.I. Sch. Design, Providence, 1969—99, ret., 1999. Lectr. R.I. Inst. Secondary Edn., Brown U., 1989—; adj. tchr. art edn. dept. R.I. Coll., 1999—, coll. supr. art student tchrs., 1999—; cons. to the arts Providence Sch. Dept., 2000—; bd. dirs. New Urban Arts; trustee R.I. Sch. Design, 2002—. Exhbns. include Providence Art Club, Diva Gallery, Providence, R.I. Sch. Design, R.I. Art Educators, Salon de Refuse AS220, Providence, others. Active John Hope Settlement House; co-chair bus. edn. partnership Citizens Bank and Central H.S., 1989—; trustee R.I. Sch. Design, 2002. Recipient Proclamation citation and Key to the City awarded by Mayor Vincent Cianci for Outstanding Svc. to schoolchildren of Providence, Tchr. of Yr. award Providence Sch. Dept., 1982-83, Milken Family Found. Nat. Edn. award, 1993, Excellence in Edn. tchr. award Pub. Edn. Fund, 1998; grantee Pub. Edn. Fund, 1992-96. Mem. R.I. Sch. Design Alumni Assn. (pres. 1994-96, v.p. 1992), coun. exec. com. 1984—. Address: 158 10th St Providence RI 02906-2922

HARMAN, JANE, congresswoman; b. N.Y.C., June 28, 1945; d. A. N. and Lucille (Geier) Lakes; m. Sidney Harman, Aug. 30, 1980; children: Brian Lakes, Hilary Lakes, Daniel Geier, Justine Leigh. BA, Smith Coll., 1966; JD, Harvard U., 1969. Bar: D.C. 1969, U.S. Ct. Appeals (D.C. cir.) 1972, U.S. Supreme Ct. 1975. Spl. asst. Commn. of Chs. on Internat. Affairs, Geneva, 1969-70; assoc. Surrey & Morse, Washington, 1970-72; chief legis. asst. Senator John V. Tunney, Washington, 1972-73; chief counsel, staff dir. Subcom. on Rep. Citizen Interests, Com. on Judiciary, Washington, 1973-75; adj. prof. Georgetown Law Ctr., Washington, 1974-75; chief counsel, staff dir. Subcom. on Constl. Rights, Com. on Judiciary, Washington, 1975-77; dep. sec. to cabinet The White House, Washington, 1977-78; spl. counsel Dept. Def., Washington, 1979; ptnr. Manatt, Phelps, Rothenberg & Tunney, Washington, 1979-82, Surrey & Morse, Washington, 1982-86; of counsel Jones, Day, Reavis & Pogue, Washington, 1987-92; mem. U.S. Ho. of Reps. 103rd-105th, 107th-108th Congresses from 36th Calif. dist., 1992-98, 2001—; mem. nat. security com., intelligence com. 103rd-105th Congresses; mem. energy and commerce com., intelligence com. 107th Congress, 2001—; mem. Nat. Commn. on Terrorism, 1999—2000. Regents prof. UCLA, 1999-2000; mem. vis. coms. Harvard Law Sch., 1976-82, Kennedy Sch. Govt., 1990-96. Vice-chmn. Ctr. for Nat. Policy, Washington, 1981—90; trustee Smith Coll.; counsel Dem. Platform Com., Washington, 1984; chmn. Dem. Nat. Com. Nat. Lawyers' Coun., Washington, 1986—90; bd. dirs. Planned Parenthood, 1998—2000, Venice (Calif.) Family Clinic, 1998—2000. Mem. Phi Beta Kappa. Democrat. Office: 2400 Rayburn HOB Washington DC 20515-0536 also: 2321 Rosecrans Ave #3270 El Segundo CA 90245-4932*

HARMEL, HILDA HERTA See PIERCE, HILDA

HARMELINK, RUTH IRENE, marriage and family therapist, writer; b. Rock Valley, Iowa, Aug. 22, 1945; d. Gerritt Harmelink and Rena Miedema; m. John Bruce Kragt, Aug. 14, 1964 (div. June 1980); children: Daniel John, Thomas Dean, Michele Renae Kersten; m. Dennis Oliver Kaldenberg, May 23, 1982; 1 child, Sarah Ruth. AA, Iowa Lakes C.C., 1976; BA magna cum [illegible] Coll., Storm Lake, Iowa, 1978, MA, Drake U., Des Moines, 1983; PhD, Iowa U., 1985. Extension specialist Iowa State U., Ames, 1985—86; asst. prof. S.D. State U., Brookings, 1986—87, Oreg. State U., Corvallis, 1987—89; therapist pvt. practice Corvallis, 1985—86, 1989—96; prof., dir. marriage & family therapy masters program Northwest Christian Coll., Eugene, Oreg., 1991—96; therapist pvt. practice Ind., 1997—2000; adjunct prof. Notre Dame U., South Bend, 2000—01; part time therapist Chapin Street Clinic, South Bend, Ind., 2000—. Approved supr. Lutheran Family Svc., Portland, Oreg.; organizational cons. Tng. Inst., South Bend, 1997—. Author (and editor): (videotape) Lenders: Working Through the Farmer and Lender Crisis!, 1986. Elder Presbyn. Ch., Corvallis. Oreg. and South Bend, Ind., 1989—; bd. dirs., counselor Story County Sexual Assault and Care Ctr., Ames, Iowa, 1983—85. Recipient Pearl S. Swanson fellowship, Coll. Home Econs, Iowa State U., 1983. Mem.: Am. Assn. Marriage and Family Therapists. Democrat. Presbyterian. Achievements include organized first licensed marriage and family therapy graduate program in the state of Oregon. Avocations: gardening, knitting, reading, sewing, quilting. Home: 52471 Sunfield Loop Granger IN 46530

HARMENING, GAIL JOAN, craft pattern designer; Craft pattern designer www.quiltingoutlet.com, 1991-98; ind. NEWAYS distbr. www.havemoreincome.com/owner/gail1316, 1992—; entrepreneur craft patter designs; distbr. personal care products NEWAYS Internat., 1992—. Designer clown doll Clancey, (quilted wall-hanging patterns) Gail's Mini Quilt Patterns; author: Clancey the Clown Gets a New Look, children's stories; clown doll, bean bag bird. Recipient award for best original design, Del Mar (Calif.) Fair, 1995, Del Mar Fair, 1995. Republican. Avocations: reading, walking, swimming. Home: 5700 Baltimore Dr La Mesa CA 91942-1644 E-mail: hgail@handtech.com.

HARMON, ANGIE (ANGIE SEHORN), actress; b. Dallas, Aug. 10, 1972; d. Larry and Daphne Harmon; m. Jason Sehorn, 2001. Actress starring in TV series: Baywatch Nights, 1995, C-16: FBI, 1997, Law & Order, 1998-2001; appeared in Lawn Dogs, 1997; TV guest appearances include Renegade, 1995; TV films include Batman Beyond, (voice) 1999, Batman Beyond: Return of the Joker (voice), 2000, Video Voyeur: The Susan Wilson Story, 2002, Sudden Fear, 2002; appeared in films including Lawn Dogs, 1997, Good Advice, 2001, Agent Cody Banks, 2003. Office: c/o CAA 9830 Wilshire Blvd Beverly Hills CA 90212

HARMON, CAROLYN, adult education educator; d. Walter and Margaret Esserman; children: Andrew, Nathan. EdD, Nova Southeastern U., Ft Lauderdale, FL, 1998. Instr. Lincoln Land C.C., Springfield, Ill., 1986—; computer cons. Ctrl. Ill. Ednl. Svc. Ctr., Springfield, 1986—89; parent educator Parents as Teachers, Springfield, 1990—; dir., integrated child care project United Cerebral Palsy, Springfield, 1991—92; prof. U. of Ill.-Springfield, 2003—. Chair Kumler Neighborhood Ministries Bd., Springfield, Ill., 2001—, Local Interagency Coordinating Coun., 2000—; program chair Capitol Area Assn for the Edn. of Young Children, 1991—95; media appearances. Editor: (newsletters) Focus on FACES, Teen Parents Talk, the Adv.; contbr. articles to profl. jours. and periodicals. Mem. Voices for Ill. Children, Chgo., 1995—2003. Mem.: APA, Sangamon Area Literacy Coun. Avocations: travel, genealogy, music. Office: Parents as Teachers 2630 S Whittier Springfield IL 62704 E-mail: harmon@springfield.k12.il.us.

HARMON, CLARA CHOKENEA, public relations/marketing executive; b. Cleve., Feb. 5, 1953; d. Arthur Charles and Clara Ann (Sinagra) Chokenea; m. John Clifford Harmon, July 21, 1979; children: Anna Grace, Gail Frances. BS in Journalism, Bowling Green State U., 1975; MBA, Rochester Inst. Tech., 1979. Employee info. editor, news svcs. editor, sales rep. Eastman Kodak Co., Rochester, N.Y., 1975-79; mgmt. asst. South Ctrl. Bell/AT&T, Louisville, 1979-81; account exec. Caldwell Van Riper Inc., Indpls., 1981-82; editl. staff writer Sherman-Eckert Visual and Verbal Comms., Webster, N.Y., 1993; dir. comms. Pers. Works Inc., Pittsford, N.Y., 1993-95, dir. mktg., 1995-96; group leader corp. comm. Vis. nurse svc. Rochester and Monroe Coutny, 1996—98; dir. mktg. and pub. rels. U. New Haven, 1999—2000; dir. mktg. comms. Pitney Bowes Office Systems (spin-off Imagistics Internat.), 2000—02; cons. sales and mktg., property and casualty The Hartford, 2002—. Loaned exec. United Way, Rochester, 1979; chair cmty. rels. com., bd. dirs. Girls Clubs of Greater Indpls., 1982-84; mem. mktg./publ rels. com. ARC, Rochester, 1984-86; mem. bldg. mgmt. team, parent rep. shared decision-making team Thornell Rd. Elem. Sch., Pittsford, 1993-95; various com. chair positions Plank South Sch. PTSA, Webster, N.Y., 1991-92, chair family to family program, 1990-92; founder Plank Rd. South Pub. Ctr., Webster, 1991-92; dir. sch. program Mt. Rise United Ch. Christ, 1996-98; mem. bd. child and youth edn. First Ch. Congl., Fairfield, Conn., 2003—. Mem. Pub. Rels. Soc. Am. (bd. dirs. health acad.), Women in Comms. (pres. Rochester chpt. 1978-79, membership v.p. 1994-95, nat. nominations chair 1982-82), Soc. for Human Resource Mgmt. (newsletter editor 1994-96), Chi Omega. Mem. United Ch. of Christ. Avocations: crafts, quilting, sewing, gardening. Home: 66 Under Cliff Rd Trumbull CT 06611-2547 Office: The Hartford Hartford Plz 690 Asylum Ave Hartford CT

HARMON, JACQUELINE BAAS, librarian, infosystems specialist; b. Kalamazoo, Mich., Oct. 23, 1934; d. Jacob and Ethyl (Zuidema) Baas; m. Robert E. Davis, Aug. 21, 1955 (div. July 1979); children: Robert J., Sarah Jane, James E.; m. W. R. Harmon, Jan. 5, 1985 (dec. Nov. 2001). BS, Western Mich. U., 1955; postgrad., U. Iowa, 1961; MLS, U. Tex., Austin, 1978; MDiv, Asbury Theol. Sem., 1997. Cert. tchr., Mich., Tex., Iowa. Dir. info. svcs. Motorola, Inc., Austin, 1978-83; mgmt. and systems specialist Lockheed Missiles and Space Corp., Austin, 1983-84; corp. librarian Microelectronics and Computer Tech. Corp., Austin, 1984-98; pastor Lone Oak (Tex.) United Meth. Ch., 1998—2000, Keltys United Meth. Ch., Lufkin, Tex., 2001—. Contbr. articles to profl. jours. Pres. Austin Library Comm., City of Austin, 1978-89, Cen. Tex. Libr. Systems Bd., Austin, 1986-88, Sta. KLRN Adv. Bd., Austin, 1979; v.p. Internat. Hospitality Commn., Austin, 1976-88; mem. U. Tex. Adv. Coun. Libr. Sch., 1984-89, Meth. Children's Home Bd., Waco, Tex., 2003-; commr. Meth. Children's Home, Waco, Tex., 2003—. Mem. IEEE, Am. Assn. for Artificial Intelligence, ALA, Tex. Library Assn. Home: 508 McMullen St Lufkin TX 75904 E-mail: j_wr_harmon@juno.com.

HARMON, JANE, producer; With Jane Harmon Assocs., N.Y.C. Prodr. The Last Night of Ballyhoo (by Alfred Uhry), Tony award Best Play, Driving Miss Daisy (by Alfred Uhry, Pulitzer prize), also nat. and internat. tours and Broadway, Buried Child (by Sam Shepard), A Life in the Theatre (by David Mamet), The Robber Bridegroom (by Waldman/Uhry); co-prodr. Asinamali!, Beloved Friend. Bd. dirs. Young Playwrights Inc.; mem. League of Am. Theatres and Prodrs. Inc., Off Broadway Theatre League, League of Profl. Theatre Women. Office: Jane Harmon Assocs One Lincoln Plaza Ste 28-0 New York NY 10023

HARMON, KAY MADELON, occupational therapist; b. Galveston, Tex., Feb. 5, 1949; d. Roger Q. and Alma Faye (Hall) H.; m. Stanley Davis Mitchell, June 24, 1967 (div. Nov. 1968). BA in Sociology, East Tex. Bapt. U., Marshall, 1980; advanced cert. in Occupational Therapy, Tex. Woman's U., Denton/Dallas, 1989. Lic. occupational therapist, Tex., Ark. Staff occupational therapist N.E. Ark. Rehab. Hosp., Jonesboro, 1989-91; dir. clin. svcs. Marshall (Tex.) Phys. Therapy, 1991-93; staff occupational therapist Pro Care Rehab., Mountain Home, Ark., 1993, Premier Rehab., Texarkana, Ark., 1994-95, CMS Therapies Rehab., Longview, Tex., 1995-96; Rehab Works, Longview, Gladwater, Tex., 1996; regional occupational therapy supr. Sundance Rehab., Northeast, Tex., 1996; outpatient occupational therapist and home health Marshall (Tex.) Regional Med. Ctr., 1996-99. Cons. Rehab. Choice in local nursing homes, Marshall, 1997-99, Vencare Rehab Svcs. in nursing [illegible] Hot Springs, Ark., 1999-2000, Smith McGrew Clinic, Hot Springs, Glenwood, Hope and Arkadelphia, Ark., 2000—. Mem.: Am. Soc. Hand Therapists (assoc. Tex. chpt.), Ark.. Occupational Therapy Assn. (exec. bd., legis. chair), Am. Occupational Therapy Assn. (alt. rep. from Ark. to representative assembly), Shreveport Orchid Soc., Am. Orchid Soc., Phi Theta Epsilon. Baptist. Avocations: growing orchids, performance poetry. Home: 108 Old Brundage #25 Hot Springs National Park AR 71913 Office: 10121 N Rodney Parham Rd Little Rock AR 72227-5549 E-mail: kaymadelon@aol.com.

HARMON, MELINDA FURCHE, federal judge; b. Port Arthur, Tex., Nov. 1, 1946; d. Frank Cantrell and Wilma (Parish) Furche; m. Frank G. Harmon III, Oct. 16, 1976; children: Mary Elizabeth, Phelps, Francis. AB, Harvard U., 1969; JD, U. Tex., 1972. Bar: Tex. 1973, U.S. Dist. Ct. (so. dist.) Tex. 1974, U.S. Dist. Ct. (no. dist.) Tex. 1975, U.S. Dist. Ct. (ea. dist.) Tex. 1978, U.S. Ct. Appeals (5th and 11th cirs.) 1981, U.S. Supreme Ct. 1982, U.S. Ct. Claims 1987. Law clk. to presiding judge U.S. Dist. Ct. (so. dist.) Tex., Houston, 1973-75; atty. Exxon Co., Houston, 1975-88; judge 280th Jud. Dist. Ct. Tex. State Trial Ct., ctrl. jurisdiction, 1988-89; judge U.S. Dist. Ct. (so. dist.) Tex., Houston, 1989—. Mem. Tex. Bar Assn., Am. Inns of Ct., Houston Bar Assn., Harvard Radcliffe Club. Roman Catholic. Office: US Dist Ct 515 Rusk St Ste 9114 Houston TX 77002-2605

HARMON, MONICA RENEE, music educator; b. Greenville, Ohio, June 3, 1960; d. William Neil Harmon and Julie Ann Erk; m. Ronald Burk Lummis, Apr. 3, 1999. MusB magna cum laude, Morehead State U., 1983; BS, W.Va. State Coll., 1986; MusM, U. Miami, 1996. Profl. Tchr. Cert. Nat. Bd. for Profl. Tchg. Stds., 2002. Music dir. George Wash. Carver Mid. Sch., Miami, Fla., 1990—; music tchr. Coconut Grove Elem., Fla., 1988—90; permanent sustitute tchr. South Charleston Jr. High, W.Va., 1987—88. Children's choir dir. Coral Gables Congl. Ch., Fla., 1991—94, Plymouth Congl. Ch., Coconut Grove, 1995—96; vocalist Coral Gables Chamber Symphony and Opera Co., 2003—. Choir mem. St. Thomas Episc. Parish, 2002—. Mem.: Am. Choral Dirs. Assn., Fla. Orch. Assn., Fla. Vocal Assn., Fla. Bandmasters Assn., Music Educators Nat. Conf. Home: 9720 SW 146th St Miami FL 33176 Office: George Washington Carver Middle School 4901 Lincoln Dr Miami FL 33133 Personal E-mail: harmonlummis@yahoo.com. E-mail: harmonm@gwcm.dadeschools.net.

HARMON, PHYLLIS DARNELL, mortgage banker; b. Kingsport, Tenn., May 24, 1937; d. Kelly R. Darnell and Leah Viola Denny; m. John L. Harmon, Sept. 26, 1958; 1 child, Mark Darnell. Credit mgr. Givner's, Inc., Lorain, Ohio, 1955-59; traffic magr. Sta. WQTE-AM-FM, Monroe, Mich., 1959-61; accounts receivable mgr. Dundee (Mich.) Cement Co., 1961-65; owner, operator Grosse Pointe (Mich.) Mortgage Co., 1984—. Prospects and clerical chmn. United Found., Detroit, 1965-68; bd. dirs. Wayne County (Mich.) Spl. Edn. Adv. Bd., 1978-87, State Mich. Bd. Licensing and Regulation, Lansing, 1980-85; dir. corp. bd. dirs. United Cerebral Palsy Assn., Detroit, 1984-89. Office: Grosse Pointe Mortgage Co 1263 Berkshire Rd Grosse Pointe Park MI 48230-1034 Fax: 313-884-3131.

HARMON, SHARON GRANHOLM, special education educator; b. Sewickley, Pa., June 13, 1948; d. Walter Alex and Bertha Louise (Jones) Granholm; m. Charles Ellis Harmon, June 6, 1969; 1 child, Brad Vann. BS, Ga. State U., 1970, MEd, 1974; EdS, Valdosta State U., 2001. Cert. T6 spl. edn. tchr., K-12 mental retardation, learning disabilities tchr., spl. edn. leadership, Ga. Tchr. spl. edn. DeKalb County Bd. Edn., Decatur, Ga., 1970-75, Rockdale County Bd. Edn., Conyers, Ga., 1976-77, 82-93, Lowndes County Bd. Edn., Valdosta, Ga., 1993—2000, asst. dir. spl. edn., 2000—03, dir. spl. edn., 2003—. Cons. Gwinnett, Newton, Rockdale Early Intervention Program, summer 1993; mem. 21st Century Consortium for Edn., Athens, Ga., 1990. Co-chmn. host com. Friendship Force, Atlanta, 1977. Named Lowndes County Tchr. of Yr., 1995; fellow Am. Wilderness Leadership Sch., Granite, Wyo., 1988. Mem. NEA, Coun. for Exceptional Children, Ga. Assn. Educators, Lowndes County Assn. Educators. Baptist. Avocations: antiques, camping, history of american west. Home: 2600 Pebblewood Dr Valdosta GA 31602-1230 Office: Lowndes County Schs PO Box 1227 Valdosta GA 31603

HARMON, TERESA WILTON, lawyer; b. 1968; BS, U. Ala., 1990, MBA, 1991; JD, U. Chgo., 1994. Bar: Ill. 1994. Clk. for Hon. Phyllis Kravitch, U.S. Ct. Appeals (11th cir.), 1994; with Sidley Austin Brown & Wood LLP, Chgo., 1995—, ptnr., 2003—. Adj. prof. U. Ill. Coll. Law. Mem.: ABA (sect. bus. law and uniform comml. code com.), Chgo. Bar Assn. (co-chair comml. fin. and transactions com.). Office: Sidley Austin Brown and Wood LLP Bank One Plz 10 S Dearborn St Chicago IL 60603

HARMON BROWN, VALARIE JEAN, hospital laboratory director, information systems executive; b. Peoria, Ill., June 21, 1948; d. Donald Joseph and Frances Elizabeth (Classen) Harmon; m. James Roger Brown, Aug. 21, 1982 (dec. May 1994). BSMT, Northwestern U., Chgo., 1970. Med. tech. Evanston (Ill.) Hosp., 1970-71, chief tech., 1971-75; med. tech. II M.D. Anderson Hosp., Houston, 1975-76; dir. lab. Physicians Ref. Lab., Houston, 1978-81, Med. Ctr. Hosp., Conroe, Tex., 1981-91, Palo Pinto Gen. Hosp., Mineral Wells, Tex., 1993-94; sales mgr. Long Beach (Calif.) Meml. Med. Ctr., 1995-96; quality assurance/regulatory affairs mgr. Consol. Med. Labs., Lake Bluff, Ill., 1996-97; admissions dir. Bio-Diagnostics Labs., Torrance, Calif., 1997-2000; asst. dir. lab. Parkview Cmty. Hosp. Med. Ctr., Riverside, Calif., 2000—01; regional mgr. Memphis Antech Diagnostics, Southaven, Miss., 2001—03. Lab. cons. Texaco Chem. Wellness Program, Conroe, 1989; health career sponsor Willis Ind. Sch. Dist., Tex., 1989, 90; mem. adv. bd. Med. Lab. Technician program Weatherford Coll., 1994. Coord. blood drive Gulf Coast Region Blood Ctr., 1986-91; sponsor colon cancer screening Montgomery County Health Fair, 1986; sponsor Camp Sunshine/Lions Club, 1988; sponsor cholesterol screening Med. Ctr. Hosp. Health Fair, 1989. Mem. NAFE, Am. Soc. Clin. Pathologists, Am. Soc. Med. Technologists, Clin. Lab. Mgmt. Assn. Republican. Roman Catholic. Avocations: embroidery, reading, antiques. Home: 16 N William Street Mount Prospect IL 60056

HARMS, ELIZABETH LOUISE, artist; b. Milw., May 26, 1924; d. Frederick George and Veva (Sanderson) H.; m. Douglas Derwood Craft, Sept. 8, 1951. Diploma, Sch. Art Inst. Chgo., 1950, BFA, 1963, MFA, 1964. One-man shows: 55 Mercer St., N.Y.C., 1980, Fischbach Gallery, N.Y.C., 1975, Carnegie Inst. Mus. Art, 1969, Condeso/Lawler, 1982, 84, 85, 86, 90, 93, Gallery Jupiter, Little Silver, N.J., 1987, Jersey City Mus., 1988, Paul McCarron, N.Y.C., 2001, DVA, Narrowsberg, N.Y., 1996, 2002; group shows include Moravian Coll., Bethlehem, Pa., 1978, Jersey City Mus., 1980, 86, North of New Brunswick, South of N.Y., Rutgers-Newark, 1981, Coll. of New Rochelle, 1982, T. Bell Invitational, Condeso/Lawler, 1985, Montclair (N.J.) Art Mus., 1984, 86, Robeson Mus., Rutgers, Newark, 1988, Invitational Acad. & Inst. for Arts & Scis., N.Y.C., 1992, Skidmore Coll., Saratoga Springs, N.Y., 1993, So. Allegheny Mus. Art, Loretto, Pa., 1994, NAD Invitational, N.Y.C., 2004. Recipient Armstrong prize Art Inst. Chgo., 1962; Tiffany Found. grantee, 1977 Home: PO Box 245 Jeffersonville NY 12748-0245

HARMS, NANCY ANN, nursing educator; d. Orval M. and Ruth Marie (Nelson) H.; m. Gerhart J. Wehrbein. Diploma, Bryan Meml. Hosp., 1971; BS in Natural Sci., Nebr. Wesleyan U., 1971; BSN, U. Nebr., 1975, MSN, 1977, PhD, 1988. RN, Nebr. Staff nurse, asst. supr., ins. coord. Brewster Hosp., Holdrege, Nebr., 1971-72; instr. Immanuel Sch. Nursing, Omaha, 1972-75; coord. nursing care plan devel. Hosp. Info. Sys. U. Nebr. Med. Ctr., Omaha, 1975; asst. chair dept. Coll. St. Mary, Omaha, 1975-80; curriculum coord. Midland Luth. Coll., Fremont, Nebr., 1980-88, chair nursing divsn., 1988 . Mem. ANA [illegible] Nebr. Nurses' Assn. (Nurse Excellence award, Excellence in Writing award jour., adv. Nebr. Student Nurses Assn., mem. various coms.), Nat. League Nursing, Sigma Theta Tau (theta omega, gamma pi chpts.).

HARMSEN, DOROTHY, food products executive; b. Minneapolis; m. William Harmsen, 1939; children: William Jr., Robert, Michael. Student, U. Minn. Co-founder Jolly Rancher Candies, Wheatridge, Colo., 1942. Author: Two Comprehensive Western Art Volumes, 1972-79. Bd. dirs. Denver Art Mus., Arthritis Found., Salvation Army, Harmsen Mus. Art, Habitat for Humanity. Home: 3131 E Alameda Ave Denver CO 80209-3409

HARNEDY, JOAN CATHERINE HOLLAND, retired systems analyst; b. Hackensack, N.J., May 31, 1936; d. John Joseph and Marion Rita (Sexton) Holland; m. Edmund Richard Harnedy, Dec. 29, 1962; children: Richard J., Julia Ann. BS, Coll. New Rochelle, 1957. Adminstrv. asst. Ford Found. funded, Rockefeller Found. funded, 1957—59; systems analyst IBM, White Plains, NY, 1960—65; publicity chairperson YWCA, Vistas Comm., White Plains, NY, 1966—69; ret. Travel cons., photographer, White Plains, 1970—92. Supporter Am. Heart Assn., Am. Cancer Soc., Nat. Children's Cancer Fund. Mem.: AAUW (hospitality chair 1989—91), NAFE, LWV, Phi Chi. Avocations: writing, gardening, tennis, swimming, reading, art history.

HARNETT, LILA, retired publishing executive; b. Bklyn., Oct. 4, 1926; d. Milton Samuel and Claire S. (Merahn) Mogan; m. Joel William Harnett. BA, CUNY, 1946; postgrad., New Sch. for Social Rsch., 1950. Pers. exec. Walter Lowen Agy., N.Y.C., 1947-52; pub. Bus. Atomics Report, N.Y.C., 1953-63; weekly columnist N.Y. State Newspapers, 1964-74; fine arts editor Cue Mag., N.Y., 1975-80; founder, contbg. editor Phoenix Home & Garden mag., 1980—, assoc. pub., 1988—, editor, 1996-99. Pub. Scottsdale (Ariz.) Scene mag., 1992-98. Trustee Phoenix Art Mus., 1999—. Mem.: ArtTable, Inc. (founder 1979—). Home: 4523 E Clearwater Pkwy Paradise Valley AZ 85253 E-mail: lila.harnett@prodigy.net.

HARNEY, PATRICIA RAE, enviromental technical supervisor; b. Oklahoma City, Sept. 8, 1960; d. Donald R. Thompson and Donaleen L. Robinson; m. Timothy D. Harney, Dec. 2, 1997; 1 child, Adrian. AAS in Ct. Reporting, Mile Hi Coll. Ct. Reporting, 1985; AS in Environ. Sci., Front Range C.C., Westminster, Colo., 1999; BS in Environ. Sci., Americus U., 2003. Cert. in hazardous materials; cert. Dept. Transp.; cert. indsl. emergency responder. Pvt. practice ct. reporter, Denver, 1985-91; facility adminstr. Allen Bradley Co., Englewood, Colo., 1990-91; nuc. analyst Rocky Flats Environ. Tech. Site, Golden, Colo., 1991-95; tech. writer/analyst Y-12 Nuc. Plant, Oak Ridge, Tenn., 1995-96; nuc. safety sys. engr. Rocky Flats Environ. Tech. Site, Golden, 1996-99, tech. supr., 1999—2001, shift ops. mgr., 2001—. Com. mem. Pro Bono Com., Denver, 1989-91. Mem. Non-Profit Orgn. for Abused Children, Denver, 1984-86; vol. fundraiser Leukemia Soc., 2003. Recipient Productivity Improvement award for centralized waste storage facility EG&G Rocky Flats, 1994, 1st Pl. award Picasso Mgmt. Tng., 2000. Mem. Am. Nuc. Soc., Phi Theta Kappa. Avocations: reading, skiing, scuba diving, biking. Home: 8722 W Ute Dr Littleton CO 80128-6964

HARNISH, MARGARET ANN, music educator; b. Seattle, Sept. 21, 1941; d. Joe and Georgia Cornelia (Tipton) Harnish. MusB in Violin and Music Edn., Eastman Sch. Music, Rochester, N.Y., 1963; MusM in Violin and Music Lit., Eastman Sch. Music, 1964, postgrad., 1967—71. Strings tchr. Islip (NY) Pub. Schs., 1964—66; vis. instr. violin and theory Albion Coll., Mich., 1967—68; instr. violin/viola and theory Old Dominion U., Norfolk, Va., 1971—73; asst. prof. violin and theory Iowa State U., Ames, 1973—76; asst. prof. violin and viola Appalachian State U., Boone, NC, 1976—83; strings, orch. tchr. Enloe H.S., Raleigh, 1983—86; pvt. studio violin and viola tchr. Raleigh, 1986—. Adj. instr. violin/viola Meredith Coll., Raleigh, 1986—87, N.C. State U., Raleigh, 1987—88; recital violin Libr. of Performing Arts, Lincoln Ctr., N.Y.C., 1971; prin. 2d violin Norfolk Symphony, 1971—72; violinist numerous recitals. Grantee Emerging Artist grantee, Raleigh Arts Coun., 1988. Mem.: Am. Strings Tchrs. Assn. (life; N.C. chpt. pres. 1980—82, mem. nat. nominating com. 1982). Avocations: home maintenance and repair, gardening, sewing. Home: 3015 Mayview Rd Raleigh NC 27607-4051

HARNSBERGER, THERESE COSCARELLI, librarian; b. Muskegon, Mich. d. Charles and Julia (Borrell) Coscarelli; m. Frederick Owen Harnsberger, Dec. 24, 1962; 1 child, Lindsey Carleton. BA cum laude, Marymount Coll., 1952; MLS, U. So. Calif., 1953; postgrad, Rosary Coll., River Forest, Ill., 1955-56, U. Calif., L.A. Extension, 1960-61. Free-lance writer, 1950—; librarian San Marino (Calif.) High Sch., 1953-56; cataloger cons. San Marino Hall, South Pasadena, Calif., 1956-61; librarian Los Angeles State Coll., 1956-59; librarian dist. library Covina-Valley Unified Sch. Dist., Calif., 1959-67; librarian Los Angeles Trade Tech. Coll., 1972—. Mem. acad. senate, 1996—; med. librarian tumor registrar Alhambra (Calif.) Comty. Hosp., 1975-79; tumor registrar Huntington Meml. Hosp., 1979—; pres., dir. Research Unltd., 1980—; free lance reporter Los Angeles Best Bargains, 1981—; med. library cons., 1979—; reviewer various cookbooks, 1991—, Ten Speed Press, Berkeley, Calif., 1991—; columnist Cookbook Update, Citizen's Voice. Author: (poetry) The Journal, 1982, to Julia: In Memorian; author: (words to choral music by Lindsay C. Harnsberger) Haiku Poem for Vanigals, 1996; cookbook rev. columnist Citizen's Voice, 1997—; contbr. articles to profl. jours., poems to newspapers; Author numerous poems. Chmn. spirtual values com. Covina Corrdinating Coun., 1964-66; chmn. Neighborhood Watch, 1976—; Winner peotry contest Pasadena Star News, 1993. Mem. ALA, Internat. Women's Writing Guild, Calif. Assn. Sch. Librarians (chmn. legis. com.) Acad. Com Partimers Rep., 1996 Covina Tchrs. Assn., AAUW (historian 1972-73), U. So. Calif. Grad. Sch. Libr. Sci. (life), Am. Nutrition Soc. (chpt. Newsletter chmn.), Nat. Tumor Registrars Assn., Med. Libr. Assn., So. Calif. Libr. Libr. Assn. Law Libr., Book Publicists So. Calif., Am. Fedn. Tchrs. (exec. bd. part-timers 1994, alt. exec. bd. local #1521 coll. guild, acad. senate part timers rep., 1996—, reporter, co-editor Pen & Quill, 1997—), Coll. Guild, Calif. Libr. Assn., Assn. Poetry Bibliographers, Faculty Assn. Calif. Cmty. Colls., Immaculate Heart Coll. Alumnas Assn., Assistance League Pasadena, Loyola Marymount Alumnae Assn, (coord. 1986), Pi Lambda Theta. Office: 1407 Garfield Ave South Pasadena CA 91030-3923

HAROON, NASREEN, artist; b. Karachi, Pakistan, Dec. 10, 1952; came to U.S., 1980; d. Ahmad and Amina (Dada) Adaya; m. Haroon Haji Husein, Apr. 29, 1972; children: Omar, Sana. BA in Psychology, Philosophy and History, St. Josephs Coll., Karachi, 1972. Design cons. Shangri-La Hotel, Santa Monica, Calif., 1983—; spkr. on cultural, ethnic, religous diversity, 1991—. Exhibited oil paintings in numerous exhbns., 1992—; featured in premier issue Zarposh Mag., 1997; appears regularly on Adelphia Cable TV program God Squad; participant Muslim Jewish Dialogue; paintings selected for Art In Embassies program, displayed at U.S. Embassy, Pakistan, Senegal. Bd. dirs. Islamic Ctr. So. Calif., 1999-2002, pres. women's assn., 1991, Pakistan Arts Coun. of Pacific Asia Mus., Pasadena, Calif., 1994-96, v.p., 1997-99, Devel. in Literacy, L.A., 1996-97, Santa Monica (Calif.) Bay Interfaith Coun., 1994—; chmn. Muslim Jewish Dialogue. Recipient award for planning Youth Day, Westside Interfaith Coun., 1998. Democrat. Moslem. Avocations: reading, gardening, jewelry design, photography, travel. Office: Shangri-La Hotel 1301 Ocean Ave Santa Monica CA 90401-1010

HARP, TONI N. state legislator; b. San Francisco; m. Wendell Harp; three children: Djana, Jamil, Matthew. BA, Roosevelt U.; MEd, Yale U. Mem. New Haven Bd. Aldermen, 1988-92, Commn. Affirmative Action, 1990-92; mem. Dist. 10 Conn. Senate, Hartford, 1992—; chair pub. health com., 1997. Project coord. health svcs. Democrat. Office: Conn State Senate State Capitol Hartford CT 06106

HARPER, DIANE MARIE, retired communications retailer; b. Harrisburg, Pa., Oct. 22, 1938; d. Paull Harry Rineard and Berneice Marie (Westhafer) Gerhardt; m. William Irvin Harper, Nov. 17, 1957 (div. Aug. 1981); children: Dawn Michelle, Steven Lee, William Madison; 1 stepson: William Lee. Telephone operator United Telephone Pa., Carlisle, 1956-59, keypunch operator Harrisburg, 1960-61, Safety Sales & Svc., Harrisburg, 1967-70; keypunch operator, lead data entry operator Kinney Shoe Corp., Camp Hill, Pa., 1970-84; data entry operator First Health, Harrisburg, 1984-92; resolution analyst Electronic Data Systems, Camp Hill, 1992-97; comms. retailer Electronic Data Sys., Rossmoyne, 1997-99, ret., 1999. Part-time cashier KMart, 2000-01; Stephen min. of Evang. Luth. Ch., Stephen min. tng. leader, 2003; reporter, writer pubs. com. Electronic Data Systems, 1996-97, human resources coord. corrective action com., 1993-96, social coord. 2d shift Pa. XIX staff, 1993-96. Committeeperson 4th Ward, Carlisle, Pa., 1959-61, 1st Ward, Mechanicsburg, 1997—; minority insp. polls, Carlisle, 1959-61; pres. Mothers of DeMolay, Carlisle, 1976-78, Mechanicsburg Area Dem. Club, 1998-99, pres. emeritus, 1999, v.p., 2000; Halloween parade assoc. City of Mechanicsburg; mem. coun., chair witness and outreach com. St. Paul's Evang. Luth. Ch., Carlisle, Pa., 2000-, also lay minister, mem. choir, chaplain, 2004-. Mem. NOW, Nat. Abortion and Reproductive Rights Action League, Nat. Pks. and Conservation Assn., Nat. Resources Def. Coun., Nat. Arbor Day Found., Pa. Sheriff's Assn. (hon.), Pa. Chiefs of Police Assn., Mechanicsburg Mus. Assn., Legal Assts. Club, Friends Dauphin County Libr., Friends Mechanicsburg Libr., Little Theatre Mechanicsburg (v.p. 1962-63, pres. 1963-67), Nat. Trust for Hist. Preservation, Carlisle Women's Dem. Club (chaplain 2004), Mechanicsburg Dem. Club, Dem. Nat. Com., Blues Soc. Ctrl. Pa. Democrat. Avocations: theatre, reading, travel, cooking. Home: 306 S Market St Mechanicsburg PA 17055-6326

HARPER, DOREEN C. nursing educator; Student, Albertus Magnus Coll., 1966-68; BSN, Cornell U., 1971; MSN, Catholic U., 1974; PhD in Human Devel., U. Md., 1980. Cert. adult nurse practitioner ANA. Home care nurse Child Devel. Ctr. R.I. Hosp., Providence, 1971; pub. health nurse Fairfax County Health Dept., Fairfax, Va., 1971-72; charge nurse adolescent mental health unit The Bancroft Inst., Falls Church, Va., 1973; college health nurse Trinity Coll., Washington, 1973-84; asst. prof. nursing dept. nursing George Mason U., Fairfax, Va., 1974-77, assoc. prof. nursing dept. nursing, 1980-82, 1987—, project dir. adult and gerontological nurse practitioner trg. grant, 1988-91, adult nurse practitioner student health svcs., 1990—, coord. nurse practitioner program Coll. Nursing and Health Scis., 1991—; adult nurse practioner Kaiser/Georgetown Cmty. Health Plan, Springfield, 1979-81; chair RN to BSN program, asst. prof.Sch. Nursing U. Md., Catonsville, 1982-86; adult nurse practitioner OB-GYN Assocs., Alexandria, Va., 1987-1990; dir. nurse practitioner program Sch. Medicine and Health Scis. George Washington U., Washington, 1994—. Cons. in field; principal investigator Nat. Ctr. Nursing Rsch. NIH, 1989-92; presenter in field; mem. nursing task force Va. Area Health Edn. Ctrs., 1993—. Editor: Nursing Connections, 1987-89; editl. review bd. Advances in Nursing Sci., 1989-93; contbr. numerous chpts., articles to profl. jours. and books. Predoctoral rsch. fellow Nursing Rsch. Svcs. Adminstrn.U. Md., 1977-80; recipient: Nat. Inst. Mental Health traineeship award Dept. Health, Edn. and Welfare Catholic U. Am., 1972-74. Fellow Am. Acad. Nursing (nat. peer review com. 1980-88); mem. Va. Nurses Assn. (dist. VIII Outstanding Nurse of the Year award 1975, del. 1976, 81 conv., mem. joint med./nursing practice com. 1976-78, dist. 8 chmn. nominating com. 1981-82), Sigma Theta Tau (Kappa chpt. nominating com. 1978-79, Epsilon Zeta chpt. 1987—, nominating com. 1989-91). Office: George Mason U Nursing Graduate Program 4400 University Dr MSN 3C4 Fairfax VA 22030-4444 Home: 159 Robbins Rd Thompson CT 06277-2846

HARPER, JANET SUTHERLIN LANE, retired educational administrator, writer; b. La Grange, Ga., Apr. 2, 1940; d. Clarence Wilner and Imogene (Thompson); m. William Sterling Lane, June 28, 1964, (div. Jan. 1981); children: David Alan, Jennifer Ruth; m. John F. Harper, June 9, 1990. BA in English and Applied Music, LaGrange Coll., 1961; postgrad., Auburn U., 1963; MA in Journalism, U. Ga., Athens, 1979. Music and drama critic The Brunswick News, Brunswick, Ga., 1979-99; info. asst. Glynn County Schs., Brunswick, 1979-82; adj. prof. Brunswick Coll., Ga., 1981-87; dir. pub. info. and publs. Glynn County Schs., Brunswick, 1982-99, dir. grant writing and rsch., 1999-2000; ret., 2000. Contbg. editor Ga. Jour., 1981-84; editor, writer GAEL Conf. Jours., 1987-89. Mem. Golden Isles Arts and Humanities Bd., 1997—2000, sec., 1998—2000; organist St. Simons United Meth. Ch., 1981—; bd. dirs. Jekyll Island Music Theatre, 1994—2001, pres., 1994—97; bd. dirs. Am. Cancer Soc., 1998—2001. Recipient award of excellence in sch. and cmty. rels. Ga. Bd. Edn., 1984, 92, Edn. Leadership award, Ga., 1989, disting. svc. award Ga. Sch. Pub. Rels. Assn., 1991. Mem.: Ga. Sch. Pub. Rels. Assn. (exec. bd. 1981—87, pres. 1985—86, exec. bd. 1996—2000), Brunswick Press-Advt. Club (award of excellence in pub. rels. 1992), Ga. Assn. Ednl. Leaders (media rels. 1983—2001), Nat. Sch. Pub. Rels. Assn. (Golden Achievement award 1985, 2 awards 1988, 1990, 3 awards 1991, 1992, 1994, 1998), Mozart Soc. E-mail: harperss@bellsouth.net.

HARPER, KAREN J. medical writer; b. Nashville, Sept. 8, 1958; d. Jewel Benton and Josephine Cook Harper. BA, Duke U., 1980; MS, NC State U., 1982; PharmD, UNC Sch. Pharmacy, 1988. Lic. R.Ph. NC, 1988, Tenn., 2001. Asst. prof. U. Mo. Kans. City Sch. of Medicine, 1990—93; clin. rsch. scientist Anesta Corp., Salt Lake City, 1994—95; sr. asst. editor The Annals of Pharm., Cin., 1995—97; pres. Harper Med. Comm., Nashville, 1997—. Cons. various pharm. firms, N.Y.C., 1997—. Contbr. articles various profl. jours., chapters to books Attorney's Textbook of Medicine, 1997; exhibitions include 30 oil paintings Ctrl. So. Art Exhibition. Mem.: Nat. Mus. for Women in the Arts, Am. Med. Writers Assoc., The Chestnut Group, Cinn. Arts Club. Avocations: oil painting, sculpting, hiking, skiing.

HARPER, LINDA RUTH, disabilities educator, consultant; b. Wilson, N.C., Dec. 16, 1943; d. John Hoover and Mary Edna (Finch) Lamm; m. Thomas Oliver Harper, Sr., Aug. 12, 1962; children: Thomas O., John Walter, Stephen Timothy. BS in Home Econs., Bob Jones U., 1967; MEd, U. S.C., 1976. Tchr. S.C. Pub. Schs., Camden and Greenville, 1968-77; tchr., prin. Ga. Christian Sch., Union Point, 1979-86; asst. prin. N.C. Christian Sch., Goldsboro, 1986-87; tchr. AG & SP cons. program specialist N.C. Pub. Schs., Goldsboro, 1987—. Del., presenter Am. Assn. Mental Retardation, China, 1996; edn. cons. O'Berry Ctr., Goldsboro, 1990—. Author: Meal Preparation Teaching Individuals with DD to Cook, 1998, Frozen Foods, 1961. Co-founder Bethel Christian Sch., 1979; state historian 4-H Club, 1961, co-presenter4-H Demonstration Cooperative Program, 1959; Sunday sch. tchr., pianist, 1963—, women's club pres., 1996-2000, mission trips at various chs., 1992-2000, Rep. to Paraguay, 2000. Recipient Leadership Achievement award Nash County 4-H Club, 1961, Nat. Honor Club award, 1961, Nat. Key Club, 1962. Mem. NEA, Am. Assn. Mental Retardation (chair S.E. region 1997-99, exec. bd. 1997-99), N.C. Assn. Educators (pres. local chpt. 1998-2000), Coun. for Exceptional Children, State Employees Assn. Baptist. Avocations: sewing, piano, singing, flower arranging, food preparation. Office: O'Berry Ctr 400 Old Smithfield Rd Goldsboro NC 27530-8464

HARPER, LYNN D. biologist; BA, MS in Cell and Molecular Biology, U. Bridgeport. Tech. writer, asst. mgr. Bionetics Corp., Washington, 1982—83; tech. dir. space sys. divsn. Gen. Electric Mgmt. and Tech. Svcs. Co., Washington, 1983—86; program mgr. advanced missions and spl. projects space life scis. divsn. NASA, 1986—89; chief advanced life support divsn. NASA Ames Rsch. Ctr., 1990—93, acting chief advanced life support divsn., 1993—94, sr. sys. engr. space scis. divsn., 1994—96, lead, integrative studies. Office: NASA Ames Rsch Ctr MS 239-15 Bldg 244 Rm 148 Moffett Field CA 94035*

HARPER, MARY SADLER, financial advisor; b. Farmville, Va., June 15, 1941; d. Edward Henry and Vivien Morris (Garrett) Sadler; m. Joseph Taylor Harper, Dec. 21, 1968; children by previous marriage: James E. Hatch III, Mary Ann Hatch Czajka. Cert., Fla. Trust Sch., U. Fla., 1976. Registered securities rep., Fla., gen. securities prin., fin. and ops. prin., options prin., mcpl. securities prin., investment mgmt. advisor. Dep. clk. Polk County Cts., Bartow, Fla., 1964-67; rep. Allen & Co., Lakeland, Fla., 1967-71; with First Nat. Bank, Palm Beach, Fla., 1971-89, sr. v.p., 1984-86, S.E. Bank N.A., Palm Beach, 1986-89, 1st United Bank, 1997-98; pres., CEO Palm Beach Capital Svcs., Inc., 1986-88; mng. dir. Investment Svcs., Palm Beach Capital Svcs. Divsn., 1988; v.p. investments, trustee J.M. Rubin Found, Palm Beach, 1983—; v.p. sec., sr. v.p. investment divsn. Island Nat. Bank & Trust Co., 1989-97; chair, dir., pres., CEO Island Investment Svcs., Inc. (A Wachovia Co.), Palm Beach, 1989-98; also bd. dirs., mng. exec., sr. v.p. Wachovia Investments, Palm Beach, 1998-2000; sr. v.p. Wachovia Bank N.A., 1999-2000; sr. v.p., investment mgmt. advisor Wachovia Securities, Inc., 2000—; sr. v.p. investments Legg Mason, Wood, Walker, Inc., 2000—. Adv. coun. Nuveen, 1987-99, pres., 2001, chmn., 2002; adv. bd. Kedsanctuary, Inc. Adv. panel Palm Beach County YWCA, 1985, mem. endowment com., 1990—93; mem. Jupiter Med. Ctr. Found.; life mem. Juno Beach Civic Assn.; profl. endowment com. Rehab. Ctr. for Children and Adults, 1998—2002; chmn. Palm Beach adv. bd. Palm Beach Nat. Bank & Trust Co., 2000—01; dir., v.p. Friends of Abused Children, 2001—03; mem. Fla. History Mus.; dir. Ctr. for Family Svcs., 2003—, pres., 2004—; bd. dirs. Biomotion Found., 2002—, pres., 2004. Mem. Inst. CFPs (assoc.), Nat. Assn. Securities Dealers (dist. com. mem. 1995-98), Fin. Planners Assn., Fin. Women Internat., Fla. Securities Dealers Assn., Exec. Women of Palm Beaches (fin. com. 1985-92), Internat. Soc. Palm Beach (treas., trustee 1986—), Jupiter Hosp. Med. Ctr. Found. (pres.'s club 1989—), Loxahatchee Hist. Soc. (bd. dirs. 1991-93, chair devel. com. 1992-93), Sebring, Fla. Hist. Soc. (life), Jupiter/Tequesta C. of C. (assoc.), United Daus. of Confederacy, Gov.'s Club, Pub. Securities Assn. (exec. rep.), Jonathans Golf Club, Rotary (Palm Beach Found. com. 1990—, bd. dirs. 1992-94, co-chair, 1997, bd. dirs. 2000—, chair Rotary Internat. Found., Palm Beach 1998-2001), Lighthouse Ctr. for the Arts (life), Norton Art Mus. (patron), Old Port Yacht Club, Gov.'s Club, Palm Beach Yacht Club. Democrat. Baptist. Avocations: reading, history. Home: 800 Ocean Dr PH 4 Juno Beach FL 33408-1730 Office: Legg Mason 324 Royal Palm Way Ste 100 Palm Beach FL 33480 Fax: 561-626-7978. Business E-Mail: msharper@leggmason.com.

HARPER, MELISSA SUZANNE, music educator; d. Larry and Emma Harper. MusB in Music Edn. in Music Edn., MEd in Cmty. Counseling, Kent State U. Cert. music tchr. K-12 Ohio, 2001. Elem. music tchr. Rittman Exempted Village Schs., Rittman, Ohio, 2000—01; substitute tchr. Stark County Schs., Canton, Ohio, 2000—; choir dir., elem. music tchr. Marion C. Dulmer Bahn Clave., 2003. Vocalist in choir Holy Trinity Greek Orthodox Ch., Canton, Ohio, 2003—. Mem.: ACA (assoc.), Music Educator's Nat. Conf. (assoc.), Ohio Music Edn. Assn. (assoc.), Chi Sigma Iota, Golden Key.

HARPER, PATRICIA NELSEN, psychiatrist; b. Omaha, July 25, 1944; d. Eddie R. and Marjorie L. (Williams) Nelsen. BS, Antioch Coll., Yellow Springs, Ohio, 1966; MD, U. Nebr., 1975; grad., Topeka Inst. Psychoanalysis, 1997. Cert. psychiatrist. Psychiatric residency Karl Menninger Sch. of Psychiatry, Topeka, 1975-78; staff psychiatrist The Menninger Clinic, Topeka, 1978-98. Faculty mem. Karl Menninger Sch. of Psychiatry, Topeka, 1982-98. Program dir. Addictions Recovery Program C.F. Menninger Meml. Hosp., Topeka, 1987-98. Mem. Am. Psychiatric Assn., Am. Med Women Assn., Am. Psychoanalytic Assn. Office: Pk Nicollet Clinic 3800 Park Nicollet Blvd Minneapolis MN 55416-2527

HARPER, PEGGY SUE, music educator; b. Natchez, Miss., June 22, 1953; d. Paxton Raymond and Johnnie Jean Crosby; m. Charles Eddie Harper, May 26, 1979; children: April Lee, Christopher Austin, Charles Andrew. B of Music Edn. in Gifted and Spl. Edn., U. So. Miss., 1978. Drama supr. Ellisville (Miss.) State Sch.; drama supr., asst. coord. Ellisville State Sch.; music/recreation dir. Happy Times, Laurel, Miss.; gen. music tchr. Laurel, Jones County Schs., Laurel, Miss. Organizer Miss. Arts Fair for Handicapped, 1978—87; mem. adv. bd. BETA Club Shady Grove Elem. Sch., Laurel, 2000—; cons. in field. Dir. children's choir Sandhill Bapt. Ch., Ellisville, 1999—2002. Mem.: Music Edn. Nat. Com. Baptist. Avocations: reading, singing, playing piano, puzzles, collecting angels, music boxes, and lighthouses. Home: 58 Wade Davies Rd Ellisville MS 39437 Office: Shady Grove Elem Sch 4524 Hwy 15 N Laurel MS 39440 E-mail: eddieandpeggy@megagate.com.

HARPER, SANDRA STECHER, university administrator; b. Dallas, Sept. 21, 1952; d. Lee Roy and Carmen (Crespo) Stecher; m. Dave Harper, July 6, 1974; children: Justin, Jonathan. BS in Edn., Tex. Tech. U., 1974; MS, U. N. Tex., 1979, PhD, 1985; grad. mgmt. devel. program, Harvard U., 1992. Speech/reading tchr. Nazareth (Tex.) High Sch., 1974-75; speech/English tchr. Collinsville (Tex.) High Sch., 1975-77, Pottsboro (Tex.) High Sch., 1977-79; instr. comm. Austin Coll., Sherman, Tex., 1980-82; rsch. asst. U. N. Tex., Denton, 1982-84; vis. instr. comm. Austin Coll., Sherman, 1985; from asst. prof. to assoc. prof. comms. McMurry Coll., Abilene, Tex., 1985-95; dean Coll. Arts and Scis. McMurry U., Abilene, Tex., 1990-95; v.p. for acad. affairs Oklahoma City U., 1995-98; asst. dir. NEH univ. core curriculum project McMurry U., Abilene, Tex.; provost, v.p. for acad. affairs Tex. A&M, Corpus Christi, 1998—, prof. comms., 1998—. CIES mentor for Russian adminstr. from Moscow State U., Ulyanovsk, 1995-96; mem. adv. bd. Coll. Am. Indian Devel., 1995-98; critic judge Univ. Interscholastic League, Austin, 1980-93; mem. adv. bd. Univ. Rsch. Consortium, Abilene, 1990-95; mem. formula adv. com., mem. instrn. and operation formula study com. Tex. Higher Edn. Coordinating Bd., 1999—, mem. adv. com. AA in Tchg., 2003—; mem. working group Am. Assn. State Colls. and Univs. Am. Democracy Project, 2002—. Contbr. articles to profl. jours.; author: To Serve the Present Age, 1990; co-author U.S. Dept. Edn. Title III Grant; editl. bd. Soc. for the Advancement of Mgmt. Jour., 1999—. Planner TEAM Abilene, 1991; del. Tex. Commn. for Libr. and Info. Svcs., Austin, 1991; chair Abilene Children Today: Life and Cmty. Skills Task Force, 1994-95; del. Oklahoma City Ednl. TV Consortium, 1997-98; bd. dirs. South Tex. Pub. Broadcasting, 1998—, Leadership Corpus Christi; mem. gov.'s exec. devel. program Class XVIII, LBJ Sch. Pub. Affairs, U. Tex., Austin, 1999, S. Tex. Regional Leaders Forum, 2001-02. Named Outstanding Faculty Mem., McMurry U., 1988, Outstanding Adminstr., 1993; Media Rsch. scholar Ctr. for Population Options, 1989; recipient Corpus Christi YWCA Women in Careers Secondary Edn. award, 2000. Mem. Nat. Comm. Assn., Am. Assn. Higher Edn., Tex. Pub. Univ. Chief Acad. Officers Assn. (v.p. 2003—). Democrat. Roman Catholic. Office: Tex A&M 6300 Ocean Dr Corpus Christi TX 78412-5503 E-mail: sharper@falcon.tamucc.edu.

HARPER, SHIRLEY FAY, nutritionist, educator, consultant, lecturer; b. Auburn, Ky., Apr. 23, 1943; d. Charles Henry and Annabelle (Gregory) Belcher; m. Robert Vance Harper, May 19, 1973 (dec. Mar. 2000); children: Glenda, Debra, Teresa, Suzanna, Cynthia. BS, Western Ky. U., 1966, MS, 1982. Cert. nutritionist and lic. dietitian, Ky. Dir. dietetics Logan County Hosp., Russellville, Ky., 1965-80; cons. Western State Hosp., Hopkinsville, Ky., 1983-84, instnl. dietetic adminstr., 1984-88; dietitian Rivendell Children's Psychiat. Hosp., Bowling Green, Ky., 1988-90; instr. nutrition Western Ky. U., Bowling Green, 1990-92. Cons. Auburn (Ky.) Nursing Ctr., 1976-95, Belle Meade Home, Greenville, Ky., 1980—, Brookfield Manor, Hopkinsville, 1983—, Sparks Nursing Ctr., Ctrl. City, Ky., 1983—, Muhlenberg Cmty. Hosp., Greenville, 1989-2000, Russellville Health Care Manor, 1978-83, 92-, Westlake Cumberland Hosp., Columbia, Ky., 1993-, Franklin-Simpson Meml. Hosp., Franklin, Ky., 1993-2003, Lakeview Health Care Ctr., Morgantown, Ky., 2001-03, Morgantown Care and Rehab. Ctr., 2003-, Trigg County Personal Care Home, Cadiz, 2002-, Gainsville Manor, Hopkinsville, 2002-; nutrition instr. Madisonville (Ky.) C.C., 1995-98. Mem. regional bd. dirs. ARC of Ky., Frankfort, 1990-96; vice chair ARC of Logan County, 1992-93, chmn., 1993-96, 97—; bd. dirs. Logan County ARC United Way, 1993—; co-chair adv. coun. devel. disabilities Lifeskills, 1992-93, adv. coun. Lifeskills Residential Living Group Home, 1993-2000, human rights adv. coun., 1994-2000; chair Let's Build our Future Campaign; nutrition del. Citizen Am. Program to USSR, 1990; adv. chair for vocat. edn., Russellville; mem. adv. coun. for home econs. and family living, We. Ky. U., 1990-93; bd. dirs. ARC of Logan County for United Way, 1993—; del. 24th Internat. Congress on Arts and Comm., Oxford (Eng.) U., 1997. Recipient Outstanding Svc. award Am. Dietetic Assn. Found., 1993, Outstanding Svc. award Barren River Mental Health-Mental Retardation Bd., 1987, Svc. Appreciation award Logan-Russellville Assn. for Retarded Citizens, 1987, Internat. Woman of Yr. award for contbn. to Nutrition and Humanity, Internat. Biog. Assn., 1993-94, World Lifetime Achievement award Am. Biog. Inst., 1995; inaugurated Lifetime Dep. Gov., Am. Biog. Rsch. Bd., 1995, Pres.'s award ARC of Logan County, 1996, award of excellence Oxford, Eng. Internat. Congress on Arts and Comm., Internat. Sash of Acad., Am. Biog. Inst., 1997. Mem. Am. Dietetic Assn., Nat. Nutrition Network, Ky. Dietetic Assn. (pres. Western dist. 1976-77, Outstanding Dietitian award 1984), Bowling Green-Warren County Nutrition Coun., Nat. Ctr. for Nutrition and Dietetics (charter), Ky. Nutrition Coun., Logan County Home Economist Club (sec. 1994-95, 1999-2000, v.p. 1995-96, 2000-01, pres. 1996-97, 2001—), Internat. Biog. Assn., Internat. Platform Assn., Diabetes Care and Edn., Dietitians in Nutrition Support, Cons. Dietitians in Health Care, Phi Upsilon Omicron (pres. Beta Delta alumni chpt. 1994-96, Outstanding Alumni award 1997). Avocations: music, drawing and art, poetry, reading, cake decorating. Home and Office: 443 Hopkinsville Rd Russellville KY 42276-1286

HARPER, THELMA, state legislator; b. Williamson County, Tenn., Dec. 2, 1940; d. William and Clara (Thomas) Claybrooks; m. Paul Wilson Harper, 1957; children: Dylan Wayne, Linda Gail. Grad., Tenn. State U., 1978. Former commr. Davidson County, Tenn.; former councilwoman City of Nashville; entrepreneur Paul Harper's Convenience Markets, 1972—; mem. Tenn. State Senate, 1991—. Foreman Grand Jury Tenn. (5th cir.), 1977-79. Mem. YMCA, Nat. Hook-Up of Black Women, Davidson County Dem. Women's Club, Nashville Women's Pol. Caucus. Democrat. Mem. Church of Christ. First Black female elected to the Tenn. State Senate. Home: 714 Ringgold Dr Nashville TN 37207-3607 Office: 10A Legislative Plz Nashville TN 37243-0219

HARPHAM, HEATHER ELISE, performing arts educator; b. Oakland, Calif., May 16, 1967; d. Howard Charles Harpham and Jessica Flynn; m. Brian Morton; children: Amelia Grace, Gabriel. BA, World Coll. West, 1989; Masters Degree in theater arts, NYU, 1998, MFA in creative writing, 2000. Actor, tchr. creative arts team NYU, N.Y.C., 1994—2000, tchr. improvisation, 2000—. Editor: The Gallatin Rev., NYU, author short stories. Recipient Herbert Rubin award, 1998, prose prize, Brenda Veland, 2002; grantee ind. artist award, Warin Arts Coun., 2003. Home: 31 Webster Pl Brooklyn NY 11215-5507

HARP-JIRSCHELE, MARY, communications executive; Grad., St. Norbert Coll., 1976. Writer, reporter The Post-Crescent, Appleton, Wis.; media rels. specialist in corp. rels. Aid Assn. for Lutherans, Appleton, Wis., 1984-87, dir. pub. info., 1987-93, asst. v.p. media and mem. rels., 1993-95, 2d v.p. comms. products and svcs., 1995-97, v.p. comms., 1997-99, v.p. comms. and facilities mgmt., 1999—2001; v.p. comm. Aid Assn. for Lutherans/ Luth. Brotherhood, Mpls., 2001—02, Thrivent Fin. for Lutherans, 2002—. Mem. Pub. Rels. Soc. Am., Internat. Assn. Bus. Communicators. Office: Thrivent Fin for Luth 625 Fourth Ave S Minneapolis MN 55415

HARR, LUCY LORAINE, public relations executive; b. Sparta, Wis., Dec. 2, 1951; d. Ernest Donald Harr and Dorothy Catherine (Heintz) Harr Vetter BS, U. Wis., Madison, 1976, MS, 1978. Lectr. U. Wis., Madison, 1977-82; from asst. editor to editor Everybody's Money Everybody's Money Credit Union Nat. Assn., Madison, 1979-84, mgr. ann. report, 1984-92, v.p. pub. rels., 1984-93, sr. v.p. credit union devel., 1993-96, sr. v.p. consumer rels. and corp. responsibility, 1996-97; owner Providing Solutions, Stoughton, Wis., 1997—; ptnr. Fourth Lake Comm., LLP. Dir. consumer appeals bd. Ford Motor Co., Milw., 1983-87. Author: Credit Union Basic Guide to Retirement Planning, 1998. Bd. dirs. Madison Area Crimestoppers, 1982-84; Midwest coord. of ofcls. USA Triathlon, 2003. Recipient Clarion award, 1982. Mem. Women in Comm. (pres. Madison profl. chpt. 1982-83, nat. v.p. programs 1986-87, vice-chair/sec. nat. interim bd. 1996-97, chair nat. bd. dirs. 1997-2001), Internat. Assn. Bus. Communicators (program chair dist. meeting 1981), Am. Soc. Assn. Execs. (Gold Circle award 1984) Avocations: bicycling, reading. E-mail: lharr@providing-solutions.com.

HARRELL, CAROLYN LAWTON See KILGORE, CAROLYN HARRELL

HARRELL, ELIZABETH ANN, career officer; BA in History, Emory U., 1975; Grad., Officer Tng. Sch., 1976; MS in Human Resource Mgmt., Troy State U., 1986; Diploma, Air Command and Staff Coll., 1986, Air War Coll., 1993. Commd. 2d lt. USAF, 1976, advanced through ranks to brig. gen., 1999; various assignments to chief Infrastructure Panel Quadrennial Def. Rev., Hdqtrs. USAF/The Pentagon, Washington, 1996-97; exec. officer to vice-chief of staff Hdqtrs. USAF/The Pentagon, Washington, 1997-99; comdr. 81st Tng. Wing, Keesler AFB, Miss., 1999—. Decorated Legion of Merit with oak leaf cluster, Meritorious Svc. medal with three oak leaf clusters, Air Force Commendation medal. Office: 81 TRW/CC 720 Chappie James Ave Keesler AFB MS 39534-2600

HARREN, JULIE CATHERINE, marriage and family therapist; d. John Anthony and Charlene JoAnne Harren. BS, Tenn. Temple U., Chattanooga, Tenn., 1991; MS, Nova Southeastern U., Ft. Lauderdale, Fla., 1995, PhD, 1999. Lic. Marriage and Family Therapist Fla., 1999. Family tchr. South County Mental Health Ctr., Delray Beach, Fla., 1993—95; family therapist Children's Home Soc., West Palm Beach, Fla., 1995—98; adj. instr., grad. counseling program Palm Beach Atlantic U., West Palm Beach, Fla., 1999—2000; marriage and family therapist Spanish River Counseling Ctr., Boca Raton, Fla., 1998—2002; adj. instr., grad. counseling program Barry U., Miami, Fla., 2000; pvt. practitioner, marriage and family therapist Pvt. Practice, West Palm Beach and Boca Raton, Fla., 2002—; asst. prof., psycho. Palm Beach Atlantic U., Fla., 2004—. Admissions team Pl. of Hope, Palm Bech Gardens, Fla., 2001—; tchr., marriage classes Christ Fellowship, Palm Beach Gardens, Fla., 2002—; presenter, profl. workshops Health Care Dist., West Palm Beach, Fla., 2002; developer, tchr. marriage seminar. Chmn. Women's Issues com., NARTH, 2004—; provide seminars for sch. and ch. leaders Pvt. Practice, Palm Beach, Broward County, Fla., 2003—; bd. mem. Worthy Creations, Ft. Lauderdale, Fla., 2002—; cons.

Family Ties, Lake Worth, Fla., 2002—. Mem.: Am. Assn. of Marriage and Family Therapy (presenter profl. workshop), Fla. Assn. for Marriage and Family Therapy (presenter profl. workshop), Palm Beach Assn. for Marriage and Family Therapy (pres. elect 2001—02), Palm Beach Assn. of Marriage and Family Therapy (pres. 2003—04, Chpt. of the Yr. 2003). Christian. Achievements include research in qualitative study on how faith helps during times of crisis. Avocations: scuba diving, kayaking. Personal E-mail: drharren@hotmail.com.

HARRIETT, REBECCA, park director; BS in Park Mgmt., N.C. State U., 1981. With Nat. Park Svcs., 1981—; supt. Booker T. Washington Monument, Hardy, Va., 1995—. Mem. Rotary Internat., Assn. Nat. Park Rangers. Office: 12130 Booker T Washington Hwy Hardy VA 24101-3968

HARRIFF, SUZANNA ELIZABETH (BAHNER), advertising consultant; b. Vicksburg, Miss., Dec. 30, 1953; d. David S. and F. Suzanna (McElwee) Bahner; m. James R. Harriff, Sept. 10, 1977; 1 child, Michael James. BA summa cum laude, SUNY-Fredonia, 1976; postgrad., Cornell U. Law Sch., 1981; MDiv with distinction, Colgate Rochester Div. Sch., 1995. Ordained to ministry Am. Bapt. Chs. USA, 1995. Media asst. Comstock Advt., Syracuse, N.Y., Buffalo, 1976-77; media buyer/planner G. Andre Delporte, Syracuse, 1979-81; media dir. Roberts Advt., Syracuse, 1982; dir. media svcs. Signet Advt., Syracuse, 1982-84; owner, pres. MediaMarCon, Syracuse, 1984—. Interim dir. mktg. and comm. Onondaga C.C., 1998—99; pub. rels. cons. Syracuse Symphony Orch., 2000—01; adj. prof. Newhouse Sch. at Syracuse U., 2001—02. Pheresis donor ARC, 1987—; gen chair Sta. WCNY-TV, 1994; accompanist musicals and chorus Manlius-Pebble Hill Sch., 1991—96; resource devel. chair Winterfest, Syracuse, 1992; lead female vocalist Aspen Dreams, 1996—; cmty. liason Cmty. United Way, 2000—01; chair media divsn. Sta. WCNY-TV, 2004, vol. pub. TV auction drive, chair media divsn., 1986—97, 2004; music dir., pianist Manlius United Meth. Ch., NY, 1983—92, youth dir., 1983—85; dir. music First Bapt. Ch., Manlius, 1993—96; assoc. pastor Andrews Meml. United Meth. Ch., 1996—99; interim pastor Oswego First United Meth. Ch., 2000; pastor Apulia and Onativia United Meth. Chs., 2000—02; interim pastor Hannibal (NY) Cmty. Ch., 2003—; tchr. Am. Bapt. Chs. N.Y. state lay studies program Bethel Bible Inst., Syracuse; co-chair St. Nicholas Ecumenical Festival, 1992—98, Am. Bapt. Ch. Nat. Biennial Conf., 1995; workshop leader United Meth. Ch., 1997—. Recipient 500 Hour Svc. pin WCNY, 1996, Women in Bus. award, 2001, Bronze and Silver Paragon awards Nat. Coun. for Mktg. and Pub. Rels., 2000, Gold Medallion of Excellence, Upstate N.Y. dist., 1999. Mem. NAFE, Syracuse Advt. Club (dir. 1985-88, program chair 1986-88, pres. 1988-89), Irish-Am. Cultural Inst. Syracuse, Phi Beta Kappa. Democrat. Avocations: music, theatre. Home: 8180 Bluffview Dr Manlius NY 13104-9740 E-mail: mediamarco@aol.com.

HARRIGAN, ROSANNE CAROL, medical educator; b. Miami, Feb. 24, 1945; d. John H. and Rose (Hnatow) Harrigan; children: Dennis, Michael, John. BS, St. Xavier Coll., 1965; MS in Nursing, Ind. U., 1974, EdD in Nursing and Edn., 1979. Staff nurse, recovery rm. Mercy Hosp., Chgo., 1965, evening charge nurse, 1965-66; head nurse Chgo. State Hosp., 1966-67; nurse practitioner Health and Hosp. Corp. Marion County, Indpls., 1975-80; assoc. prof. Ind. U. Sch. Nursing, Indpls., 1978-82; nurse practitioner devel. follow-up program Riley Hosp. for Children, Indpls., 1980-85; chief nursing sect. Riley Hosp. Child Devel. Ctr., Indpls., 1982-85; prof. Ind. U. Sch. Nursing, Indpls., 1982-85; chmn., prof. maternal child health Loyola U. Niehoff Sch. Nursing, Chgo., 1985-92; dean Sch. Nursing U. Hawaii, Honolulu, 1992—2002; nurse practitioner Waimanalo (Hawaii) Health Ctr., 1998—; chair complementary and alternative medicine dept. John A. Burns Sch. Medicine, 2002—, prof. pediat., 2003—, Frances A. Matsuda Chair, Women's Health, 2000—. Lecturer Ind. U. Sch. Nursing, 1974-75, chmn. dept. pediatrics, family and women's health, 1980-85; adj. prof. of pediatrics Ind. U. Sch. Med., 1982-85; editorial bd. Jour. Maternal Child Health Nursing, 1984-86, Jour. Perinatal Neonatal, 1985—, Jour. Perinatology, 1989—, Loyola U. Press, 1988-92; adv. bd. Symposia Medicus, 1982-84, Proctor and Gamble Rsch. Adv. Com. Blue Ribbon Panel; scientific review panel NIH, 1985; mem. NIH nat. adv. coun. nursing rsch., 2000-, ; cons. in field. Contbr. articles to profl. jours. Bd. dirs. March of Dimes Cen. Ind. Chpt., 1974-76, med. adv., 1979-85; med. and rsch. adv. March of Dimes Nat. Found., 1985—, chmn. Task Force on Rsch. Named Nat. Nurse of Yr. March of Dimes, 1983; faculty research grantee Ind. U., 1978, Pediatric Pulmonary Nursing Tng. grant Am. Lung Assn., 1982-85, Attitudes, Interests and Competence of Ob-Gyn Nurses Rsch. grant Nurses Assn. Am. Coll. Ob-Gyn., 1986, Attitudes, Interests and Priorities of Neonatal Nurses Rsch. grant Nat. Assn. Neonatal Nurses, 1987, Biomedical Rsch. Support grant, 1988; Doctoral fellow Am. Lung Assn. Ind. Tng. Program, 1981-86. Mem. AAAS, ANA (Maternal Child Nurse of Yr. 1983), Assn. Women's Health, Obstetrical and Neonatal Nursing (chmn. com. on rsch. 1983-86), Am. Nurses Found., Nat. Assn. Neonatal Nurses, Nat. Perinatal Assn. (bd. dirs. 1978-85, rsch. com. 1986), Midwest Nursing Rsch. Soc. (theory devel. sect.), Ill. Nurses Assn. (comm. rsch. chmn. 1990-91), Ind. Nurses Assn., Hawaii Nurses Assn., Ind. Perinatal Assn. (pres. 1981-83), N.Y. Acad. Sci., Ind U. Alumni Assn. (Disting. Alumni 1985), Sigma Xi, Pi Lambda Theta, Sigma Theta Tau (chpt. pres. 1988-90).

HARRINGTON, ANNE WILSON, medical librarian; b. Phila., June 18, 1926; d. Edgar Myers and Jean Gould (DeHaven) Wilson; m. James Paul Harrington, June 11, 1948; children: Barbara Gould Harrington Murphy, Ian Edgar, Eric Bradley. BA, U. Pa., Phila., 1948; MS in Libr. Sci., Villanova U., 1977. Clk. Princeton U., 1948-51; CEO, ptnr. Teesdale Co., West Chester, Pa., 1954—; libr. asst. Franklin Inst., Phila., 1974-76; med. staff libr. The Chester County Hosp., West Chester, 1977-99. Mem., treas., chmn. sub-com. Consortium Health Info., Chester, 1977-99. Trustee, sec., com. chmn. Wilmington (Del.) Friends Sch., 1963—72, 1989; bd. dirs., subcom. chmn. cmty. bd. Kendal Corp. CCRC, Kennett Square, Pa., 1973—98; treas. com. on edn. Phila. Yearly Meeting Soc. Friends, 1980—91; mem., rep. Friends Coun. on Edn., Phila., 1991—96; overseer Quaker Info. Ctr., Phila., 1992—96, Phila. Yearly Meeting Soc. Friends, libr. svcs. group, 1999—, publ. working group, 2000—. Mem. Acad. Health Info. Profls. (sr.), Phila. Area Med. Library Assn., Lake Paupac Club (chmn. environ. com., bd. dirs. 1990-96), Friends Med. Soc. Democrat. Avocations: music, reading, walking, sailing, tennis. Home: 234 Crosslands Dr Kennett Square PA 19348 E-mail: libawh@aol.com.

HARRINGTON, BETTY BYRD, entrepreneur; b. Longview, Tex., July 11, 1936; d. William Henry Byrd and Minnie Lee Tidwell; 1 child, Randy Lee Harrington. AA, Cedar Valley DCCCD, Dallas, 1988. Actress, model, entertainer Kathy King Entertainment Agy., DeSoto, Tex., 1956—; owner Gateway to Success/Career Devel. & Outplacement Svc., DeSoto, Tex., 1981—, Resume Writing, Career Counseling & Outplacement Svc., DeSoto, 1987—. Author: The Dallas Dazzler, Job Search and Interview Techniques, (poetry) She Has Been Faithful, 1996, Pity the Children, 1996, My Dad, A Firm But Gentle Soul, 1999. Mem.: AGVA, SAG, AFTRA, Lions, Order of Eastern Star (past matron). Republican. Baptist. Home and Office: 1338 E Parkerville Rd Desoto TX 75115-6421 E-mail: resumewriting@aol.com.

HARRINGTON, BEVERLY, museum director; BS, Carnegie Mellon U., 1959; BAE, U. Wis., Oshkosh, 1967, MST, 1971; MSA, U. Wis., Milw., 1977. With art dept. U. Wis., Oshkosh, 1977-87; curator collections and exhibitions at arboretum Paine Art Ctr., Oshkosh, 1983-90; dir. Hearthstone Mus., Appleton, Wis., 1991—2004.

HARRINGTON, CAROL A. lawyer; b. Geneva, Ill., Feb. 13, 1953; d. Eugene P. and M. Ruth (Bowersox) Kloubec; m. Warren J. Harrington, Aug. 19, 1972; children: Jennifer Ruth, Carrie Anne. BS summa cum laude, U. Ill., 1974, JD magna cum laude, 1977. Bar: Ill. 1977, U.S. Dist. Ct. (no. dist.) Ill. 1977, U.S. Tax Ct. 1979. Assoc. Winston & Strawn, Chgo., 1977-84, ptnr., 1984-88, McDermott, Will & Emery, 1988—. Speaker in field. Co-author: Generation-Skipping Tax, 1996, Generation-Skipping Transfer Tax, Warren, Gorham & Lamont, 2000. Fellow Am. Coll. Trusts [illegible] (bd. regents 1999—), mem. ABA (chmn. B-1 generation skipping transfer com. 1987-92, coun. real property, probate and trust law sect. 1992-98), Ill. State Bar Assn., Chgo. Bar Assn. Chgo. Estate Planning Coun. Office: McDermott Will & Emery 227 W Monroe St Ste 3100 Chicago IL 60606-5096

HARRINGTON, CAROLYN MARIE, accountant, artist, jewelry designer; b. Pasadena, Calif., Oct. 19, 1938; d. Walter and Laina Hingula; m. William Harrington, July 12, 1971; 1 child, Christina. AA in Acctg., Bklyn. Coll., 1960; BS in Acctg., CUNY, 1962; MPA, L.I. Univ., 1991. Internal auditor Tchrs. Ins. and Annuities, N.Y.C., 1960-62; jr. acct. Goldfein & Goldfein, CPA, N.Y.C., 1962-63; field auditor Guardian Life Ins., N.Y.C., 1963-67; chief acct. Careers Inc., N.Y.C., 1967-69; sr. acct., dept. head Grolier Internat., N.Y.C., 1969-73; acct. Suffolk County Govt., Yaphank, NY, 1984—2002. Ptnr., artist Bellport Lane Art Galley, 1994—2001; v.p. Wet Paints Studio Group, Sayville, NY, 1992—94; treas. East of Broadway Show Group, East Islip, NY, 1982—83; ptnr., artist Phoenix Fine Arts Gallery, 2002—. Leader Girl Scouts of Am., East Islip, 1979-83. Recipient Holbein award of Excellence for Three Amigos painting, East Islip Arts Coun., 1998, Pub. Adminstrn. award, Long Island Univ., 1991, Spl. Opportunity stipend, N.Y. Found. for Arts and East End Coun., 1995, Special award for Contbrns to Pub. in World of Art, Town of Islip. Mem. South Bay Art Assn., Babylon Arts Coun., Huntington Twp. Art League, Smithtown Twp. Art Coun., N.Y. Plein Air Painters. Republican. Roman Catholic. Avocations: reading, writing, needlework, poetry. Home: 122 Keswick Dr East Islip NY 11730-3405

HARRINGTON, CHARLENE ANN, sociology and health policy educator; b. Concordia, Kans., Sept. 28, 1941; d. Lyman K. and Maxine (Boucher) Harrington; m. Ben Yerger, Aug. 28, 1976. BSN, U. Kans., Kansas City, 1963; MA in Cmty. Health, U. Wash., 1968; PhD in Sociology and Higher Edn., U. Calif., Berkeley, 1975. Staff nurse Good Samaritan Hosp., Portland, Oreg., 1963-64; sch. nurse U.S. Army Dependent Schs., Heilbronn, Germany, 1964-65; pub. health nurse Seattle King County and Group Health, Seattle, 1966-68; asst. prof., nursing program U. Kans., Kansas City, 1968-70; dep. dir., spl. asst. Calif. State Dept. Health, Sacramento, 1975-78; dir. Golden Empire Health Planning Agy., Sacramento, 1978-80; sr. rschr. Inst. for Health and Aging, U. Calif., San Francisco, 1980-83, asst. prof. Sch. Nursing, 1983-85, assoc. prof. dept. social and behavioral scis. Sch. Nursing, 1985-89, prof., vice chair dept. social and behavioral scis., 1989-93; chair dept. social and behavioral scis. U. Calif., San Francisco, 1994-96, prof. social and behavioral scis., 1997—. Assoc. dir. Inst. for Health and Aging, U. Calif., San Francisco, 1981-94; cons. Nat. Coalition for Nursing Home Reform, Washington, 1987—; com. on regulation nursing homes Inst. Medicine, 1984-86, com. on nursing staff, 1994-96. Author: Health Policy and Nursing, 3d edit., 2001; contbr. over 125 chpts. to books, articles to profl. jours. Fellow Am. Acad. Nursing (chair commn. on health policy 1991-93); mem. ANA, APHA, Nursing Econs. (bd. dirs. 1985-93), Inst. Medicine (com. nurse staffing 1995-96, roundtable of quality 1997-98, com. on quality in long-term care 1997—), Am. Sociol. Assn. (sect. coun. mem. 1992-94), Elected Inst. of Medicine (com. on longterm care quality 1998-2001, round table on quality 1997-98), Sigma Theta Tau. Democrat. Avocation: gardening. Office: U Calif Sch Nursing 3333 California St San Francisco CA 94143-0001

HARRINGTON, E.B. art dealer; b. N.Y., May 2, 1953; d. Robert Charles and Clarice (Garrett) Barbato.; m. Mark Garland Harrington, June 3, 1978 (div. May 1986); 1 child: Alexandra Harrington; m. Peter Ridgway Barker, June 5, 1992; 1 child: Robert Brinton Barker. BS, Finch Coll., 1975. Asst. dir. Richard L. Feigen & Co., N.Y., 1975-78; pres. E.B. Harrington & Co., N.Y., 1978—. Art cons. Procter & Gamble, Cin., Ohio, 1986—, James D. Wolfensohn, N.Y., Washington, D.C., 1988—, BT Wolfensohn, N.Y., 1997-99. Mem. (student) Appraiser's Assn. Am. Avocations: painting, drawing, tennis, cooking. Home and Office: 1600 Lexington Ave #B New York NY 10029-7359 E-mail: ebh-art@pipeline.com.

HARRINGTON, JEAN PATRICE, college president; b. Denver; d. James Michael and Katherine Ann (Holl) H. BA, Coll. Mt. St. Joseph, 1953; MA, Creighton U., 1958; PhD, U. Colo., 1967; LHD (hon.), Xavier U., 1983, Ohio Dominican Coll., 1988; LLD (hon.), St. Thomas Inst., Cin., 1985, Coll. Mt. St. Joseph, 1988, Hebrew Union Coll., 1990; D. Tech. Studies (hon.), Cin. Tech., 1988; LLD (hon.), No. Ky. U., 1996, U. Dayton, 1999. Joined Sisters of Charity of Cin., 1940; prin. St. Rose of Lima, Denver, 1953-56; tchr. Cathedral H.S., Denver, 1956-58, prin., 1958-68; dir. instl. rsch. Coll. Mt. St. Joseph, Cin., 1968-69, pres., 1977-87; exec. dir. Cin. Youth Collaborative, 1988-90; interim pres. Cin. State Coll., 1997. Bd. dirs. Penrose Hosp., Colorado Springs, 1976-86, St. Mary Corwin Hosp., Pueblo, Colo., 1972-80, Cin. Bicentennial Commn., 1982-89, Samaritan Health Resources, Inc., 1983-96, St. Rita Sch. for Deaf, 1983-86, United Appeal Cabinet, 1983, Cin. Cmty. Chest, 1988-95, Dan Beard coun. Boy Scouts Am., 1988-91; trustee Good Samaritan Hosp. and Health Ctr., Dayton, Ohio, 1978-80, 89-97, bd. dirs., 1989-96; trustee Miami U., 1989-97, chmn. 1994-97; bd. dirs. Coll. of Mt. St. Joseph, 1995-2002; trustee U. Dayton, 1999-2002. Recipient Disting. Svc. citation NCCJ, 1987, Women Helping Women award Soroptimist Internat., 1990, Statesman award Cin. Assn. Execs., 1988, St. Francis award Friars Club, 1994, Daniel Ransahoff Initiative award, 1994, Lincoln award No. Ky. U., 1994, Gt. Living Cincinnatian award C. of C., 1996, Svc. to Edn. award Ohiana Libr. Assn., 1998, Children's Advocate award Beech Acres; named Career Woman of Achievement YWCA, 1981, Disting. Bus. and Profl. Woman of Yr., 1982; inductee Hall of Excellence of Ohio Fedn. of Ind. Colls., 1990, Ohio Women's Hall of Fame, 2000, Pres.' award Children's Def. Fund, 2003. Mem. Nat. Assn. Ind. Colls. and Univs., Assn. Cath. Colls. and Univs. (bd. dirs.), Ohio Found. Ind. Colls., Greater Cin. Consortium Colls. and Univs. (vice chmn. 1980-82), Coun. Ind. Colls. (bd. dirs. 1981-85), Cin. C. of C. (bd. dirs. 1978-84, trustee 1981-85, sec. 1979-85). Roman Catholic. E-mail: jphsc@juno.com.

HARRINGTON, KATHLEEN M. federal agency administrator; BA, Colgate U.; MA in Psychology, The Cath. U. Am. Asst. adminstr. pub. affairs Fed. Aviation Adminstrn.; asst. sec. labor congrl. and intergovtl. affairs Sec. of Labor Elizabeth Dole; v.p. govt. rels. Aetna, Inc.; sr. v.p. pub. affairs and advocacy Health Ins. Assn. Am.; asst. sec. pub. affairs U.S. Dept. Labor, Washington. Office: US Dept Labor 200 Constitution Ave NW Washington DC 20210

HARRINGTON, KAY LORRAINE, executive secretary; b. Stockton, Calif., Jan. 27, 1947; d. Hal Hubert Van Da Griff, Ellen Louise (Carlson) Van Da Griff; m. Fredric T. Harrington, Aug. 23, 1987; children: Shannon Struik, Christopher Eckels, Jennifer Murray, Derek Eckels. BA in English, Regis Coll., 2003. Adminstrv. asst. Babson Coll., Wellesley, Mass., 1984—95, Regis Coll., Weston, Mass., 1995—2001. Recipient Grand prize, Poetry Guild, 1998, Editor's Choice award for Outstanding Achievement in Poetry, Nat. Libr. Poetry, 1998, Pres.'s award for Lit. Excellence, Iliad Press, 2002. Home: 5 Glen Rd Wayland MA 01778

HARRINGTON, LAMAR, retired curator; b. Guthrie Center, Iowa, Nov. 2, 1917; d. Arthur Sylvester and Anna Mary (Landkamer) Hannes; m. Stanley John Harrington, Jan. 1, 1938 (div. Jan. 1972); 1 child, Linda Harrington Chace. Student, Cornish Sch. Fine Arts, Seattle, 1945-50; BA in History of Art, U. Wash., 1979. Staff Henry Art Gallery, U. Wash., Seattle, 1957-75, assoc. dir., 1969-75; curator, rsch. assoc. Archives Northwest Art, U. Wash. Libr., 1975-77; dir., chief curator Bellevue Art Mus., Wash., 1985-90; cons. in arts, 1977—; founding curator art Univ. Ho., Seattle, 1997—2002. Mem. panel visual arts divsn. NEA, 1976—78; juror fellowship We. States Arts Fedn., 1989, Flintridge Found., Pasadena, 2001; pres. [illegible] 1998; trustee Pacific NW Arts Cn., 1971—74; exec. com. Living Treasures video series NW Designer-Craftsmen, 1996—99, Pacific NW Arts Coun. of Seattle Art Mus., 1976, mem. steering com. Photography Coun., 1977—78; participant 1st Symposium on Scholarship and Lang. Nat. Endowments for Humanities and Arts, 1981; mem. adv. com. NW Oral History Project Archives Am. Art, 1981; mem. adv. coun. Pilchuck Glass Sch., 1992—95, trustee, chmn. archives, 1981—87; v.p. Pottery Northwest, 1977—78; trustee, chmn. archives Internat. Coun., 1987—92; trustee Seattle bd. Santa Fe Chamber Music Festival, 1981—87, adv. bd. Santa Fe, 1988—89; trustee Puget Sound Chamber Music Soc., 1987—88; lectr. in field; organizer exhbns.; leader seminars; mem. art juries; appearances KCTS-TV, 1963—73; founder Archives of NW Art U. Wash., 1969; curator 3d Wyo. Biennial Exhbn., 1988—89; curator James W. Washington Jr.: The Spirit in the Stone Bellevue Art Mus., 1989, resident curator, mgr. Frank Lloyd Wright: In the Realm of Ideas, 1989—90; curator art collection, quar. exhbns. NW art Univ. House, Wallingford, 1995—2002; curator Between Night and Morning Work of Guy Anderson, 1990; curator Eternal Laughter: A Sixty-Yr. Retrospective of George Tsutakawa Bellevue Art Mus., 1990; founder changing exhbn. program Univ. House U. Wash., Wallingford, 1997, curator changing exhbn. program U. House, 1997—2002, founder experiments in art and tech. Seattle chpt. Henry Art Gallery, 1968. Author: Ceramics in the Pacific Northwest: A History, 1979, Washington Craft Forms: an Historical Perspective, 1981. Named LaMar Harrington Endowment, Bellevue Art Mus., 1991; recipient Friends of Crafts award, Seattle, 1972, Woman of Achievement award, Women in Comm., 1974, Gov. Writer's award, 1980, Arts Svc. award, King County Arts Commn., 1987, Arts award, Bellevue Art Commn., 1989, Cmty. Svc. award, Am. Inst. Interior Designers, 1990, Pyramid award, Corp. Coun. Arts, 1990. Fellow: Am. Crafts Coun. (hon.); mem.: AIA (hon.), Japan-Am. Soc. Wash. (trustee 1986—88), Allied Arts Seattle (trustee 1962—81), Pacific NW Arts and Crafts Assn. (pres. 1957—59), U. Wash. Retirement Assn. (exec. com. 1992—94). Office: 842 Washington St Ste 208 Port Townsend WA 98368-5777*

HARRINGTON, MARY EVELINA PAULSON (POLLY HARRINGTON), religious journalist, writer, educator; b. Chgo. d. Henry Thomas and Evelina (Belden) Paulson; m. Gordon Keith Harrington, Sept. 7, 1957; children: Jonathan Henry, Charles Scranton. BA, Oberlin Coll., 1946; postgrad., Northwestern U., Evanston, Ill., Chgo., 1946-49, Weber State U., Ogden, Utah, 1970s, 80s; MA, U. Chgo.-Chgo. Theol. Sem., 1956. Publicist Nat. Coun. Chs., N.Y.C., 1950-51; mem. press staff 2d assembly World Coun. Chs., Evanston, Chgo., 1954; mgr. Midwest Office Communication, United Ch. of Christ, Chgo., 1955-59; staff writer United Ch. Herald, N.Y.C., St. Louis, 1959-61; affiliate missionary to Asia, United Ch. Bd. for World Ministries, N.Y.C., 1978-79; freelance writer and lectr., 1961—; corr. Religious News Svc., 1962—. Prin. lectr. Women & Family Life in Asia series to numerous librs., Utah, 1981, 1981—82; pub. rels. coord. Utah Energy Conservation/Energy Mgmt. Program, 1984—85; tchr. writing Ogden Cmty. Schs., 1985—89; adj. instr. writing for publs. Weber State U., 1986—; instr. Acad. Lifelong Learning, Ogden, 1992—95, Eccles Cmty. Art Ctr., Ogden, 1993—94; dir. comm. Shared Ministry, Salt Lake City, 1983—97; chmn. comm. Intermountain Conf., Rocky Mountain Conf. Utah Assn. United Ch. of Christ, 1970—78, 1982—, Ind. Coun. Chs., 1960—63, United Ch. of Christ, Ogden, 1971—; dir. comm. United Chs., 1971—78, Christ Congl., Ogden,, 1980—; chmn. comm. Ch. Women United Utah, 1974—78, Ogden rep., 1980—, hostess Northern Utah, 1998. Editor: Sunshine and Moonscapes: An Anthology of Essays, Poems, Short Stories, 1994, (booklet) Family Counseling Service: Thirty Years of Service to Northern Utah, 1996; contbr. numerous articles and essays to religious and other publs. Pres. T.O. Smith Sch. PTA, 1976-78, Ogden City Coun. PTA, 1983-85; assoc. dir. Region II, Utah PTA, Salt Lake City, 1981-83, mem. State Edn. Commn., 1982-87; chmn. state internat. hospitality and aid Utah Fedn. Women's Clubs, 1982-86; v.p. Ogden dist., 1990-92, pres. Ogden dist., 1992-96, state resolutions com., 1996—; trustee Family Counseling Svc. No. Utah, Ogden, 1983-95, emeritus trustee, 1995—; Utah rep. to nat. bd. Challenger Films, Inc., 1986—; state pres. Rocky Mountain Conf. Women in Mission, United Ch. of Christ, 1974-77, sec., 1981-84, vice moderator Utah Assn., 1992-94; chair pastor-parish rels. com. United Ch. of Christ Congl., Ogden, 1999-2003, chmn. search com., 1995-96, Mission com., 2002-. Recipient Ecumenical Svc. citation Ind. Coun. Chs., 1962, Outstanding Local Pres. award Utah PTA, 1978, Outstanding Latchkey Child Project award, 1985, Cmty. Svc. award City of Ogden, 1980, 81, 82, Celebration of Gifts of Lay Woman Nat. award United Ch. of Christ, 1987, Excellence in the Arts in Art Edn. award Ogden City Arts Commn., 1993, Spirit of Am. Woman in Arts and Humanities award Your Cmty. Connection, Ogden, 1994, Heart and Hand award United Ch. of Christ, Ogden, 2001; Utah Endowment for Humanities grantee, 1981, 81-82. Mem. Nat. League Am. Penwomen (chmn. Utah conv. 1973, 11 awards for articles and essays 1987-95, 1st pl. news award 1992, 1st pl. short stories 1997, 3d pl. articles 1997), AAUW (state edn. rep. 1982-86, parliamentarian Ogden br. 1997—, membership v.p. Ogden br. 2003—), League of Utah Writers (Publ. Quill award 1998). Democrat. Avocation: building miniature world of peace each Christmas by family in the home. Home and Office: 722 Boughton St Ogden UT 84403-1152 E-mail: gkHarrington1@comcast.net.

HARRINGTON, NANCY D. college president; Pres. Salem (Mass.) State Coll., 1990—. Office: Salem State Coll Office Pres 352 Lafayette St Salem MA 01970-5348

HARRINGTON, NANCY O'CONNOR, volunteer; b. Chgo., Oct. 28, 1928; d. John Roland and Ethel Catherine (Constable) O'Connor; m. James Edward Harrington, Sept. 8, 1951; children: Mary Beth Grayson, Janet Gaines, Gail, Nancy Chartier-Jackson. BA in art edn., Rosary Coll., River Forest, 1946-50. Cert. art tchr., Ill. Artist Chgo. Park Dist., 1949; art tchr. Chgo. elem. schs., 1951-52; color coord. homes Palos Park (Ill.) Builder, 1957-58; vol. Art Inst. of Chgo., 1980-86. Exhibited in Loyola Ramble, 1970s, Wilmette, 1960s, Palos Park, Ill., Evergreen Park, Ill., Chgo., Osprey, Fla., 1990s, Glenview, Ill., 1980s, 1990s. Bd. mem. Acad. Our Lady H.S. Alumni Bd., 1960's; pres. Mothers Club, v.p. Parents Club Regina Dominican H.S., Wilmette, Ill., 1972-73; vol. Judge Robert Downing Dem. Party, Glenview, Ill., 1974; 1st forelady of criminal ct. Cook County Ct. Sys., Chgo., 1980s; assoc. mem. Art Inst. Chgo., 1990—; vol. Resurrection House Daycare Ctr. for Homeless, Sarasota, Fla., 1993-98, Juvenile Diabetes Found., 1998—; colleague Ringling Mus. Art, Sarasota, 1994—; gen. chair Beaux Arts Festival, The Oaks C.C., 1996; mem. women's bd. Rosary Coll., 1990-98; hostess Hist. Spanish Pointe Fla. Luncheon, 1998, 99; mem. women's bd. dirs. Dominican U., 1997—; decorating chmn., Bishop's Charity Ball at Chelsea Ctr., 2002, Bishop's Garnet Ball for Charity at St. Anne's Hall, Sarasota, 2003, Bishop's Charity Ball, 2004. Recipient medallion Regina Dominican H.S. Mothers Club, 1972-73, Kemeny Lion medallion Art Inst. Chgo., 1980s, Resurrection House medallion, 1999; Honored vol. Sarasota Arts Coun., 1992; named Artist of Class of 1950, Rosary Coll. Mem. AAUW, Natl. Heritage Soc., North Shore Country Club (gen. chairperson 9-hole golf 1986, gen. chairperson art festival, 1996), Oaks Country Club (mem. garden club, 1991—, ad hoc archtl. rev. bd., 1991-92, women's bd., 1993, Dominican Univ. Women's Bd., 1997—, vol. Juvenille Diabetes Found., Sarasota, Fla. 1998, 99, Hostess of Mrs. Potter Palmer Luncheon Historic Spanish Pointe, Osprey, Fla., Ringling Sch. of Art and Design Libr.; chair Art Seminar of 25th Internat. Congress on Arts and Comm., New Orleans, 1998; attendee, singer choir 26th Internat. Congress Arts and Commn., Lisbon, 1999; gen. chairperson art festival, 1995—, gen. chairperson Oaks Celebrates Arts, 1994, chairperson Art Club, 1993-94; founder Art Appreciation Club, 1993,

Artist of Month Column (author) 1994—); founding mem. Nat. Women's Art Museum. Roman Catholic. Avocations: travel, reading, aquacize, opera, bridge. Home: 210 Saint James Park Osprey FL 34229-9065

HARRIS, ANN BIRGITTA SUTHERLAND, art historian; b. Cambridge, Eng., Nov. 4, 1937; came to U.S., 1965, naturalized, 1996; d. Gordon B.B.M. and Gunborg Elizabeth (Wahlström) Sutherland; m. William Vernon Harris, July 13, 1965 (div. Oct. 1999); 1 son, Neil William Orlando Sutherland. BA with 1st class honours, Courtauld Inst., U. London, 1961, PhD, 1965. Asst. lectr. U. Leeds, 1964-65; asst. prof. art history Columbia U., N.Y.C., 1965-71, Hunter Coll., N.Y.C., 1971-73; asso. prof. SUNY, Albany, 1973-77; chmn. for acad. affairs Met. Mus. Art, N.Y.C., 1977-80; part-time faculty Juilliard Sch., N.Y.C., 1978-84; prof. U. Pitts., 1984—. Founder, 1st pres. Women's Caucus for Art, 1973-76; disting. vis. prof. U. Tex.-Arlington, fall 1982; Mellon prof. history of art U. Pitts., spring 1984; vis. prof. history of art So. Meth. U., Dallas, fall 1993. Author: Andrea Sacchi, 1977, Selected Drawings of Gian Lorenzo Bernini, 1977; co-author: Die Zeichnungen von Andrea Sacchi und Carlo Maratta, 1967, Women Artists: 1550-1950, exhbn. catalogue, 1977, Landscape Painting in Rome, 1575-1675, exhbn. catalogue, 1985, Italian, French, English and Spanish Drawings and Watercolors in the Detroit Institute of Arts, 1992, Seventeenth Century Art and Architecture, 2004. Fellow Guggenheim Found., 1971, Ford Found., 1975-76, NEH, 1981-82, rsch. fellow Getty Mus. Art, 1988. Mem. Coll. Art Assn., Women's Caucus for Art. Office: U Pittsburgh Dept History of Art Pittsburgh PA 15260

HARRIS, ANNE M. interior designer, educator; d. Fred David Harris and Florence Amelia Wickstrom; m. Howard Liss, July 5, 1952 (div. Nov. 4, 1974); children: Jodi Liss, Jennifer. AA, U. Minn., BA, 1978; M in Furniture Design and Interior Design, Hans Krieks Master Class, N.Y.C., 1978. Cert. Fed. Govt., N.Y.C. and N.Y. State. Art dir. Orion Pictures, Hollywood, Calif., 1948—49, Californian/Calif. Stylist Purl, L.A., 1946—49; fashion art dir. Pines Publs., N.Y.C., 1952—55; pres., designer Harris & Kate, N.Y.C., 1980—82; pres., interior designer Anne Harris Designs Ltd., N.Y.C., 1986—95, inventor, designer, pres., 1996—; tchr. interior design Sheffield Sch. Interior Design, N.Y.C., 1993—. Graphic mags., movies, newspapers, ad agys., interiors for vet. hosp., restaurants, yacht, penthouse, oth, furniture, tabletop, fabrics, rugs. Recipient awards for rug design, Edward Fields/A.S.I.D., 1st prize graphic design, Western Trade Editors. Mem.: Smithsonian Instn., Nat. Geographic Soc., Women in the Arts. Democrat. Achievements include patents for sofa bed mechanism and mattress; art table. Avocations: antique auctions, travel, museums, theater. Office: Anne Harris Designs 40 W 72d St New York NY 10023

HARRIS, BARBARA C(LEMENTINE), bishop; b. Phila., 1930; Grad., Charles Morris Price Sch. Advt. and Journalism, Phila.; student, Villanova U., Urban Theology Unit, Sheffield, Eng.; D in Sacred Theology (hon.), Hobart and William Smith Colls., 1981; DD (hon.), Gen. Theol. Sem., 1989, Episc. Div. Sch., 1989, Amherst Coll., 1989. Ordained to ministry Episcopal Ch. as deacon, 1979, as priest, 1980. Pres. Joseph V. Baker Assocs., Phila., 1958-68; sr. staff cons., mem. community rels. dept. Sun Oil Co.; priest-in-charge St. Augustine of Hippo, Norristown, Pa.; interim rector Ch. of the Advocate, Phila.; exec. dir. Episc. Ch. Pub. Co., 1984-88; suffragan bishop Episcopal Diocese of Mass., Boston, 1989—. Trustee Episc. Div. Sch. Address: Episc Diocese of Mass 138 Tremont St Boston MA 02111-1318

HARRIS, BARBARA S. publishing executive; BS in Phys. Edn., Fla. State U., 1978; Masters, N.E. Mo. State U. Editl. dir. Weider Publ., Woodland Hills, Calif., 1986—2003; exec. v.p. Am. Media, Woodlands Hills, Calif., 2003—. Past adviser Calif. Gov.'s Coun. on Phys. Fitness and Sports; past chmn. bd. dirs. Am. Coun. Exercise; mem. adv. bd. L.A. Commn. on Assaults Against Women, Melpomene Inst.; mem. adv. bd. Fitness Cert. program U. Calif., L.A.; instr. Omega Inst.; presenter in field. Appearances on Oprah, Today Show, CNN, MSNBC, Access Hollywood, Entertainment Tonight. Achievements include climbing 20,000 foot mountain in the Bolivian Andes, Mt. Rainier and Mt Kilimanjaro. Avocations: running, weightlifting, kayaking, photography, rock climbing. Office: Am Media 21100 Erwin St Woodland Hills CA 91367-3712 Business E-Mail: bharris@weiderpub.com.

HARRIS, BONNIE, psychological education specialist; b. Dayton, Ohio, Apr. 10, 1950; d. Joseph Boniface and Virginia May Myers; m. Gordon Harris, Oct. 17, 1978; children: Curtis, Hallie, Ashley. BS, Bowling Green State U., 1972, MS, 1974; postgrad., Wright State U., 1979, U. Dayton, 1974—76. cert. elem. edn, learning and behavior disorders. Tchr. Napoleon Schs., Ohio, 1972-74; psychol. edn. specialist Akron Child Guidance, Ohio, 1974-76; class therapist S. Cmty. MH, Dayton, 1976-78; psychol. edn. specialist Gordon A. Harris & Assocs., Dayton, 1978—. Spkr. numerous workshops. Mem. Councel Exceptional Children, Orton Dyslexic Soc. Home: 7320 Wastler Rd Clayton OH 45315-9777 Office: Gordon A Harris Assocs 5400 N Main St Dayton OH 45415-3453 E-mail: ionafarm@aol.com.

HARRIS, CARLA ANN, investment company executive; m. Victor Adrian Franklin, Aug. 11, 2001. BA in economics, Harvard U., 1984, MBA, 1987. Joined Morgan Stanley, N.Y.C., 1987, mergers, acquisitions, and restructuring dept., 1987—91, joined equity capital markets dept., 1991, mng. dir., head equity pvt. placements and retail capital markets. Singer: (albums) Carla's First Christmas, 2000. Funded Carla Harris Scholarship at Harvard U. and Bishop Kenny H.S., Jacksonville, Fla.; exec. bd. Food for Survival, N.Y.C. Food Bank, St. Charles Borromeo Cath. Sch., Sponsors for Ednl. Opportunities, A Better Chance Inc.; bd. dirs. Boy Scouts Am., Manhattan. Recipient Bethune Award, Nat. Coun. Negro Women, Ron Brown Trailblazer Award, St. John's U. Sch. Law, Women of Distinction Award, Girl Scouts of Greater Essex and Hudson Counties, Frederick Douglass Award, NY Urban League, 2003. Office: Morgan Stanley 1585 Broadway New York NY 10036

HARRIS, CELESTE ACQUANITA, vocational rehabilitation counselor; b. Brewton, Ala., Apr. 6, 1967; d. Robert Lee and Cleoline Johnson Harris. BS, Troy State U., 1989; MS, Jacksonville State U., 1999. Emergency instr. N.W. Regional Hosp., Rome, Ga., 1992; work coord. Floyd Tng. and Svc. Ctr., Rome, 1992—98; vocat. rehab. counselor Dept. Labor-Rehab. Program, Dallas, Ga., 1998—. Sec. adv. com. Enhancing Capabilities Inc., Rome, 2000—02. Tutor Child Adoption Planning, Rome, 2003; timer Job Corps, Atlanta, 1999—2002. Avocations: travel, fishing, gardening. Home: PO Box 314-2 Rome GA 30164 Office: Dept Labor-Vocat Rehab Ste 300 300 WI Pkwy Dallas GA 30132 E-mail: nscleoline1@aol.com.

HARRIS, CHRISTINE, dance company executive; b. Milw. Mktg. dir. Milw. Symphony Orch., 1984-90, head Arts in Cmty. Edn. program, 1990-95; with Inst. Music, Health and Edn., Mpls., 1996-97; exec. dir. Milw. Ballet, 1997—2002; pres. United Performing Arts Fund, 2002—. Office: United Performing Arts Fund 929 N Water St Milwaukee WI 53202

HARRIS, CORA LEE, science educator, small business owner; b. Huntsville, Ala., Apr. 26, 1939; d. Dnaiel and Orell (Draper) Barley; m. William Anderson Harris; children: William J., Coral A. BS, U. Memphis, 1969, MS, 1970; PhD, Goring Beauty Sch., 1999. Cosmetologist Goring Beauty Coll., Tenn., 1961; nailologist Mid-South Beauty Sch., Tenn., 1970; biology tchr. Memphis City Schs., 1967-84; owner Coral's Bazaar, Memphis, 1984—; biology and chemistry tchr. Shelby State C.C., 1993-96; biology tchr. Creigmont H.S., Memphis, 1999—. Mem. cosmetology bd. Hamilton H.S., Memphis; sci. fair coord. Memphis City Schs.; sales agt. Celebrity Fashion Gems; coord. trade shows, beauty pageants. Fashion editor Memphis City Newspaper; contbr. poetry to lit. publs. Bd. dirs. YWCA, Memphis, 1983; vol. food distbn. Dismas House, Memphis, 1989; judge city and state beauty pageants. Recipient Cert. of Appreciation, Sr. Svcs., 1996, Vol. Svc. award Girls Inc. Memphis, 1991, Cert. of Recognition Memphis Light Gas and Water Divsn., 1993; grantee Faith Brent U., 1999. Mem. NAACP (mem. Afro-Acad. cultural tech. sci. olympics 1979), Nat. Coalition of 100 Black Women (v.p.), Nat. Coun. Negro Women (fundraiser, social chair), Ladies of Distinction, Inc., Eta Phi Beta (pres.), Phi Delta Kappa, Delta Sigma Theta (social action chair, Delta of Yr. 1993, Cert. of Appreciation 1982). Democrat. Home: 4345 Hillbrook St Memphis TN 38109-5476 Office: Coral Bazaar 1515 Victor St Memphis TN 38106-5612

HARRIS, DALE HUTTER, retired judge, lecturer; b. Lynchburg, Va., July 10, 1932; d. Quintus and Agnes (Adams) Hutter; m. Edward Richmond Harris Jr., July 24, 1954; children: Mary Fontaine, Frances Harris Russell, Jennifer Harris Haynie, Timothy Edward. BA, Sweet Briar Coll., 1953; MEd in Counseling and Guidance, Lynchburg Coll., 1970; JD, U. Va., 1978; LLD (hon.), Wilson Coll., 1988. Bar: Va. 1978, U.S. Dist. Ct. (we. dist.) Va. 1978, U.S. Ct. Appeals (4th cir.) 1978. Admissions asst. Sweet Briar Coll. (Va.), 1953-54; caseworker Winchester/Frederick Dept. Welfare, Va., 1954-55; vis. lectr. Lynchburg Coll., Va., 1971; assoc. Davies & Peters, Lynchburg, 1978-82; substitute judge 24th Dist. Gen. Dist., Juvenile and Domestic Rels. Dist. Ct., Va., 1980-82; judge Juvenile and Domestic Rels. Dist. Ct., Lynchburg, 1982—2003. Judge Family Ct. Pilot Project, Va., 1990—91; lectr. law U. Va. Law Sch., 1986—98; pres. Va. Coun. Juvenile and Family Ct. Judges, 1994—96; mem. panel of experts and adv. com. Child Protection and Custody Resource Ctr., 1994—2001; mem. Commn. on Future of Va.'s Jud. Sys., 1987—89; mem. adv. bd. Hilton Project on Model State Laws about Family Violence. Vice chmn. bd. dirs. Sweet Briar Coll., 1976-86; vol. coord. vols. in probation with Juvenile and Domestic Ct., 1971-73; chmn. steering com. for establishment Youth Svc. Bur., Lynchburg, 1972-73; chmn. bd. dirs. Lynchburg Youth Svcs., 1973-75, mem. adv. bd. Juvenile Ct., 1957-60, 62-68, sec., 1966-68; bd. dirs. Family Svc. Lynchburg, 1967-69; Lynchburg Fine Arts Ctr., 1965-67, Seven Hills Sch., 1966-73, Greater Lynchburg United Fund, 1963-65, Lynchburg Assn. Mental Health, 1960-61, Miller Home, 1980-82, Lynchburg Gen.-Marshall Lodge Hosps., Inc., 1980-82; v.p. Lynchburg Mental Health Study Commn., 1966, bd. dirs. Lynchburg Sheltered Workshop for Mentally Retarded Young Adults, 1965-69; bd. dirs. Lynchburg Guidance Ctr., 1959-61, v.p., 1970, pres., 1961; bd. dirs. Hist. Rev. Bd. Lynchburg, 1978-82; adv. bd. study of effectiveness of civil protection orders Nat. Ctr. State Cts., 1994-97. Mem.: ABA, Am. Prosecutors Rsch. Inst., Nat. Coun. Juvenile and Family Ct. Judges (mem. child custody edn. com. 1993—98, chair family violence commn. 1998—2000, trustee 1998—2001, chair custody com. 1999—2001), Lynchburg Bar Assn., Va. State Bar (bd. govs. criminal law sect. 1988—90, bd. govs. family law sect. 1989—91), Va. Bar Assn., Phi Beta Kappa. Office: Juvenile and Domestic Relations Dist Ct PO Box 757 Lynchburg VA 24505-0757

HARRIS, DEANNA LYNN, special education educator, writer; b. Granite City, Ill., Feb. 25, 1948; d. Robert Eugene and Emma Lee Harris; m. George Thomas Aebel, May 6, 1967 (div. Apr. 28, 1983). BS, So. Ill. U., 1973, MS, 1986; degree, Inst. of Children's Lit., 1989. Cert. tchr. Madison County, Ill., 1973, Camden County, Mo., 1985. Adminstrv. sec. So. Ill. U., Edwardsville, Ill., 1966—69; elem. tchr. St. Boniface Sch., Edwardsville, 1973—77, Wolf Ridge Edn. Ctr., Bunker Hill, Ill., 1977—85; spl. edn. tchr. Camdenton (Mo.) R-III Sch. Dist., 1985—; propr. Heron Ho. Pub. Co., Linn Creek, Mo., 1996—. Pvt. tutor, Camdenton, 1985—. Author: God's Gift, 1995 (Editor's Choice award The Nat. Libr. of Poetry, 1995), Taters of the Ozarks, The Feud, 1996, 101+ Tater Jokes, 1996, The Man, 1998; editor: (newsletter) Foxtales, 1986—88. Recipient English award, St. Elizabeth Sch., 1962, Presdl. Sports award, President's Coun. on Phys. Fitness, 1988, 1993, 1996; grantee, State of Ill., 1972—73; scholar, 1969—73. Master: Red Hat Soc. (queen mother 2003); mem.: Coun. for Exceptional Children (assoc.), Learning Disabilities Assn. (assoc.), Mo. State Tchrs. Assn. (assoc.), Quill and Scroll Journalism, Holy Childhood Assn. Republican. Roman Catholic. Avocations: travel, gardening, water sports, pets, reading. Home: 22 Old Mine Drive Linn Creek MO 65052 Office: Camdenton R-III School District Old Township Road Camdenton MO 65020 Personal E-mail: tatertown@midmo.com. Business E-Mail: dharris@mail.camdenton.k12.mo.us.

HARRIS, DEBORAH A. counselor, consultant; d. Robert Lee and Adele Harris; m. Jonathan W. Sims, Mar. 14, 2003. BS in Psychology, Northwestern State U., Natchitoches, La., 1996; MS in Behavioral Sci. Psychology, Cameron U., 1998; MA in Counseling, Webster U., 2002. Clinically cert. behavior therapist Nat. Assn. Forensic Counselors, lic. profl. counselor I S.C. Exec. dir., founder Hopes for Higher Edn., Panama City Beach, Fla., 2001—; regional dir. Family Preservation Svcs., 2002—03. Cons. Midlands Counseling and Consulting Svcs., 2002—03. Mem. Richland County Child Health and Safety Coun., Columbia, SC, 2001—03, Richland County Citizens Rev. Panel, Columbia. Scholar, Sallie Mae/ USA Group, 2001, 2002, 2003. Mem.: APA, Am. Mental Health Counselors Assn., Alpha Kappa Alpha, Order Ea. Star, Psi Chi. Personal E-mail: dharris_aka@msn.com.

HARRIS, DEBORAH ANN, science educator; b. Jacksonville, Fla., Oct. 9, 1951; d. William Wendell and Rose Nell Neinast; m. John William Harris, Dec. 28, 1974; children: Andrew William, Brett Nelson. BS, Tex. Tech U., 1973. Registered microbiologist 1978, cert. tchr. 1995, mid. sch. sci. 2001. Quality control microbiologist Illes Co., Dallas, 1973—74; rsch. assoc. Baylor Coll. Medicine, Houston, 1975—84; tchr. Chapelwood Day Sch., Houston, 1989—95; tchr. sci. Houston Ind. Sch. Dist., 1995—2002, St. Francis Episc. Sch., Houston, 2002—. Mem. adv. bd. Academics Alive, Houston, 2001—. Recipient Lawrence Scadden award, N.Mex. State U., 2002, Crystal award of Outstanding Tchg., Houston Chronicle, 2001. Mem.: NSTA, Sci. for Students with Disabilities (adv. bd. 2002—), Am. Soc. Microbiologists. Methodist. Avocations: travel, reading. Office: St Francis Episc Day Sch 335 Piney Point Houston TX 77024*

HARRIS, DEBRA CORAL, physical education educator; b. Portland, Oreg., Feb. 4, 1953; d. Raymond Dale and Kathleen Caroline (Himpel) H. AA, Cen. Oreg. Community Coll., 1974; BS in Health and Phys. Edn., So. Oreg. State Coll., 1976, MST in Health Edn., 1982. Tchr. phys. edn., coach Franklin High Sch., Portland, 1976-79; instr. health, phys. edn., tennis coach Mt. Hood Community Coll., Gresham, Oreg., 1979-80; health and phys. edn. specialist, coach Inza R. Wood Middle Sch., Wilsonville, Oreg., 1980-86; tchr. health and phys. edn. West Linn (Oreg.)High Sch., 1986—. Mem. planning com. Seaside Health Conf., Oreg. Dept. Edn., 1985-87; writer AIDS curriculum, 1987-88; cons. health edn. textbooks Glencoe Pub. Co., 1987-88. Mem. AIDS subcom. ARC, Portland, 1988-89, safety svcs. com. 1988—, sex edn. coalition com. Planned Parenthood, Portland, 1988-90, com. women's sport leadership network U. Oreg., Eugene, 1988—. Recipient Vol. of Month award ARC, 1984, Profl. Leadership award Oreg. Gov's. Coun. for Health Phys. Edn. Fitness & Sport, 1986, Outstanding Health/Phy. Edn. award Portland State U., 1988, Nat. High Sch. Physical Educator of the Year award, 1993. Mem. Am. Alliance Health, Phys. Edn., Recreation & Dance (nat. pub. affairs & legis. com. 1987—), Oreg. Alliance Health, Phys. Edn., Recreation & Dance (pres. 1984-85), Oreg. Assn. Advanced Health Edn. (pres. 1987-89), AAUW, Oreg. Edn. Assn. (uniserv treas. 1985-86), Kappa Delta Pi. Avocations: swimming, skiing, tennis, traveling. Home: 7009 NE Broadway St Portland OR 97213-5339 Office: West Linn High Sch 5464 W A St West Linn OR 97068-3199

HARRIS, DIANA KOFFMAN, sociologist, educator; b. Memphis, Aug. 11, 1929; d. David Nathan and Helen Ethel (Rotter) Koffman; m. Lawrence A. Harris, June 24, 1951; children: Marla, Jennifer. Student, U. Miami, 1947-48; BS, U. Wis., 1951; postgrad., U. Oxford (Eng.), 1968-69. Advt. and sales promotion mgr. Wallace Johnston Distbg. Co., Memphis, 1952-54; welfare worker Tenn. Dept. Pub. Welfare, Knoxville, Tenn., 1954-56; instr. sociology Maryville (Tenn.) Coll., 1972-75, Fort Sanders Sch. Nursing, Knoxville, 1971-78, U. Tenn., Knoxville, 1967—; series editor Garland Pub., Inc., 1989—. Author: Readings in Social Gerontology, 1975, (with Cole) The Elderly in America, 1977, The Sociology of Aging, 1980, 2d edit., 1990; co-author: Sociology, 1984, Annotated Bibliography and Sourcebook: Sociology of Aging, 1985, Dictionary of Gerontology, 1988, Teaching Sociology of Aging, 1991, 4th edit., 1996, 5th edit., 2000; aging series editor Garland Pub., Inc., 1989—; contbr. articles to profl. jours. Chmn. U. Tenn. Coun. on Aging, 1979—; organizer Knoxville chpt. Gray Panthers, 1978; mem. Govnr.'s Task Force on Preretirement Programs for State Employers, 1973, White Ho. Conf. on Aging, 1981; bd. mem. Knoxville-Knox County Coun. on Aging, 1976, Sr. Citizens Info. and Referral, 1979, Sr. Citizens Home-Aide Svc., 1977; del. E. Tenn. Coun. on Aging, 1977. Recipient Meritorious award Nat. U. Continuing Edn. Assn., 1982, Pub. Svc. award Nat. Alumni Assn., 1992, Appreciation award Assn. Gerontology in Higher Edn., 1994, Appreciation award for excellent scholarly contbn. to ednl. gerontology lit. Ednl. Gerontology jour., 1996; grantee Retirement Rsch. Found., 1997—. Mem. Am. Sociol. Assn., AAAS, Gerontol. Soc. Am., Popular Culture Assn., So. Sociol. Soc., So. Gerontol. Soc. (pres.'s award 1984), N. Central Sociol. Assn., London Competitor's Club, Nat. Contest Assn., Knoxville Kontestars. Home and Office: U Tenn Dept Sociology PO Box 50546 Knoxville TN 37950-0546

HARRIS, DIANE CAROL, merger and acquisition consulting firm executive; b. Rockville Centre, N.Y., Dec. 25, 1942; d. Daniel Christopher and Laura Louise (Schmitt) Quigley; m. Wayne Manley Harris, Sept. 30, 1978. BA, Cath. U. Am., 1964; MS, Rensselaer Poly. Inst., 1967. With Bausch & Lomb, Rochester, N.Y., 1967-96, dir. applications lab., 1972-74, dir. tech. mktg. analytical systems divsn., 1974-76, bus. line mgr., 1976-77, v.p. planning and bus. programs, 1977-78, v.p. planning and bus. devel. Soflens divsn., 1978-80, corp. dir. planning, 1980-81, v.p. corp. devel., 1981-96; v.p. RID-N.Y. State, 1980-83; pres. Hypotenuse Enterprises, Inc., 1994—. Mem. adv. bd. Merger Mgmt. Report, 1986—92; internat. bd. dirs. Assn. Corp. Growth, v.p. corp. mem. affairs, 1993—94, v.p. internat. expansion, 1994—95, pres.-elect, 1996—97, pres., 1997—98, immediate past pres., 1998—99; bd. dirs. Flowserve Corp., chair audit com., 2001—; bd. dirs. Monroe Fund, Venture Capital Group. Contbr. articles to profl jours. Pres Rochester Against Intoxicated Driving, 1979—83, chmn polit action comt, 1983, 1986; bd dirs, chmn long range planning comt Rochester area Nat Coun Alcoholism, 1980—84; mem Stop DWI Adv Panel to Monroe County Legis, 1982—87, NY State Coalition for Safety Belt Use, 1984—85; mem. key exec. group Rensselaer Poly. Inst., 1993—96; mem. Com. 200, 1993—2002; mem ACG Speakers Bur, 1993—; mem adv comt Catalyst, 1995; bd dirs Rochester Rehab Ctr, 1982—84, Friends of Bristol Valley Playhouse Found, 1983—87. Named one of 50 Women to Watch in Corp Am, Bus Week Mag, 1987, 1992, 100 Women to Watch, Duns Bus Rev, 1988; recipient Distinguished Citizen's Award, Monroe County, 1979, Tribute to Women in Indust and Serv Award, YWCA, 1983, Pres's 21st Century Leadership Award, Women's Hall of Fame, 1995; grantee NSF, 1963. Mem.: Assn. Corp. Growth (Meritorious Svc. award 1995), Internat. Alliance Com. and Rochester Women's Network (com. of 200 1993—2002), Nat. Assn. Women Bus. Owners, Fin. Execs. Inst., Am. Mgmt. Assn., C. of C. (pub safety com. Rochester area chpt, task force on hwy safety and legi 1981—86, high technology Rochester adv. panel 1989—91, 1999—2000), Phi Beta Kappa, Delta Epsilon Sigma, Sigma Xi. Home: 60 Mendon Center Rd Honeoye Falls NY 14472-9363 Office: Hypotenuse Enterprises Inc 1545 East Ave Rochester NY 14610-1614 E-mail: harris@hypot.com.

HARRIS, DOLORES M. retired academic administrator; b. Camden, N.J., Aug. 5, 1930; d. Roland Henry, Sr. and Frances Anna (Gatewood) Ellis; m. Morris E. Harris, Sr., 1948 (div. 1987); children: Morris E. Jr., Sheila Davis, Gregory M. Sr. BS, Glassboro (N.J.) State Coll., 1959, MA, 1966; EdD, Rutgers U., 1983. Tchr., reading specialist Glassboro Bd. Edn., 1958-68, dir. aux. svcs., 1968-70; supr. adult edn. Camden Welfare Bd., summer 1968; head state dir. Glassboro SCOPE, summer 1969-70; assoc. dir. Jersey City State Coll., summer 1971; dir. adult edn. Glassboro State Coll., 1970-74, dir. continuing edn. dept., 1989-90, acting assoc. v.p. acad. affairs, 1989-91; ret., 1991. Cons. Mich. State Dept. Edn., Lansing, 1973; examiner N.Y. State Civil Svc. Commn., 1976—; chmn. adv. bd. Women's Ednl. Equity Comm. Network Project, San Francisco, 1977—78; cons. crossroads project Temple U., Phila., 1977; bd. dirs. Mgmt. Inst. Glassboro State Coll.; cons. corrections project Va. Commonwealth U., Richmond; mem., vice-chmn. comm. Accrediting Coun. Continuing Edn. and Tng., Richmond, 1985—89, chmn., 1989—; workshop/seminar chair Ea. Montgomery County chpt. SCORE, 1991—. Author: (book) How to Establish ABE Programs, 1972; author: (with others) Black Studies for ABE and GED Programs in Correction, 1975; founding editor: newsletter For Adults Only, 1970; contbr. articles to profl. jours. Founder, trustee, chair bd. trustees Glassboro Child Devel. Ctr., 1974—87; bd. dirs. Gloucester County United Way, NJ, 1977—, sec. bd. dirs., 1980, pres. bd. dirs., 1983—85; charter mem., bd. dirs. Glassboro Glass Mus., 1979—87; vice chair, chair, mem. Gloucester County Commn. Women, NJ, 1983—87; trustee Frederick Douglas Meml. and Hist. Assn., 2000—. Named Woman of the Yr., Gloucester County Bus. and Profl. Women's Club, 1985, Woman of Achievement, Gloucester County Commn. Women, 1987; named one of Outstanding Citizens, Holly Shores Girl Scouts U.S., 1987, 100 Most Influential Black Ams., Ebony Mag., 1989; named to Legion of Honor, Chapel of Four Chaplains, 1983; recipient Disting. Alumnae award, Glassboro State Coll., 1971, Disting. Svc. award, Camden County, 1974, N.J. Woman of Achievement award, 1991, Disting. Svc. award, Holly Shores Girl Scouts U.S., 1979. Mem.: AAUW (v.p. membership com. Gloucester County chpt. 1986—87), NEA, Montgomery County SCORE (chair seminars, workshop programs 2001—), N.J. Edn. Assn., Svc. Corps Ret. Execs., Women Greater Phila. (bd. dirs.), N.J. Assn. (life; pres. 1973—74), Soc. Docta (bd. dirs. 1987—), Links Club, Nat. Assn. Colored Women's Clubs, Inc. (pres. 1988—92), Northeastern Fedn. Women's Clubs (v.p.-at-large 1983—85, parliamentarian 1985—), N.J. State Fedn. Colored Women's Clubs (pres. 1976—80). Presbyterian. Avocations: reading, fitness exercises.

HARRIS, DUCHESS, social sciences educator; b. Newport News, Va., May 16, 1969; d. Frank and Miriam Mann Harris; m. Jon Vincent Thomas, Nov. 26, 1994; children: Austin Harris Thomas, Avril Noelle Thomas. BA in Am. History and African-Am. Studies, U. Pa., 1991; PhD in Am. Studies, U. Minn., 1997. Constituent adv. Sen. Paul Wellstone, St. Paul, 1993—94; rsch. fellow U. Minn. Law Sch., Mpls., 1996—97; assoc. prof. African-Am. studies and polit. sci. Macalester Coll., St. Paul, 1997—; policy fellow Hubert H. Humphrey Inst. Pub. Affairs, 1998—99. Contbr. articles and book revs. to profl. jours., chapters to books. Commr. Mpls. Commn. Civil Rights, 1996—98; bd. dirs. Genesis II for Women, St. Paul, 1996—99, Model Cities Family Devel., St. Paul, 1994—99, Minn. Women's Found., Mpls., 2000—. Named one of 30 Leaders under 30, Ebony Mag., 1997; fellow, Woodrow Wilson Found., 2001—02; grantee, Bush Course Devel., 2000, 2001. Mem.: Am. Studies Assn. (minority scholars com.), Nat. Conf. Black Polit. Scientist (exec. coun., chair women and politics sect.), Mensa. Democrat. Home: 401 Vadnais Lake Dr Saint Paul MN 55127 Office: Macalester Coll 1600 Grand Ave Saint Paul MN 55105

HARRIS, ELAINE K. medical consultant; b. N.Y.C., Mar. 17, 1924; d. Julius and Bertha (Wecker) Kirschbuam; m. Herbert Harris, Aug. 1, 1948; children: Gail, Linda, Geoffrey. AB Bus. Economics cum laude, Hunter Coll.; AM Bus. Edn., Columbia U. Lic. tchr. bus., N.Y. Founder, pres. Sjogren's Syndrome Found., 1983-91, exec. dir., 1991-94. Cons. in field; v.p. exec. bd. Nat. Alliance for Oral Health; developer Sjogren's Syndrome Ednl. Symposia for lay and profls., nat. and internat. support group network. Editor: Moisture Seekers Newsletter, 1984-94, Sjogren's Syndrome Handbook: An Authoritative Guide for Patients, 1989; editor: The New Sjogren's Syndrome Handbook, 1998; contbg. author: Sjogren's Syndrome: Clinical and Immunologic Aspects, 1987, Self-Help, Concepts and Applications, 1992; contbr. articles to profl. jours. Founded Nassau-Suffolk Chpt. Hunter Coll. Alumni Assn., 1949; treas. Youth Employment Svc., Great Neck (N.Y.) Pub. Schs., former chair of Broader Horizons Com., PTA, Great Neck Pub. Sch., others; active Jewish communal field. Recipient Women's Living Legacy, Women's Internat. Ctr., 1994, Third Internat. Conf. on Sjogren's Syndrome, Greece, 1991; elected to Hunter Coll. Hall of Fame, 1989. Mem. Pi Lambda Theta. Avocations: gardening, baking, photography.

HARRIS, E(LEANOR) LYNN(E), religious studies educator, literature educator, minister, writer; b. Villa Park, Ill., July 07; d. Robert Carl and Karin Elizabeth (Peterson) Karlström. BA, MA, U. Chgo.; MDiv, No. Bapt. Theol. Sem., 1975; D of Ministry, Chgo. Theol. Sem., 1980; PhD, NYU, 1980. Ordained min. United Ch. of Christ, 1987. Prof. U. Ill., Chgo., 1970—. Interim min. Union Congl. Ch., Moline, Ill., 1997; min. Glen Ellyn (Ill.) Congl. Ch., 1987-89; night ministry, Chgo., 1999, 2000, 01; adj. faculty religious studies Loyola U., Chgo., U. St. Francis; adj. faculty English Ind. U. Northwest, DePaul U., Ill. Benedictine U.; sec. Bd. Christian Witness in Soc., 1984-88; mem. seminaries com. Chgo. Met. Assn., United Ch. Christ, 2000-03; active Night Ministry, Chgo., summers 1999-2001; presenter, cons. adult edn. St. Pauls Ch., 2002; contbr. poetry to Kavya Bharati; presenter in field. Author: The Mystic Spirituality of A.W. Tozer, A Twentieth Century American Protestant, 1992; contbr. poems and articles to profl. jours. Recipient Lucia Queen of Light award City of Chgo., 1970. Mem. MLA, Am. Acad. Religion, Soc. Sci. Study Religion, Am.-Scandinavian Found., Chgo. Metro. Assn. (seminaries com.), Mensa. Avocations: art, music, travel, folk dancing, camping. Home: PO Box 412 Wheaton IL 60189-0412

HARRIS, ELLEN GANDY (MRS. J. RAMSAY HARRIS), civic worker; b. Spokane, Wash., Jan. 9, 1910; d. Lloyd Edward and Helen (George) Gandy; m. J. Ramsay Harris, Jan. 20, 1936; children: Sue Ellen, Hayden Henry. Student, U. Wash.; grad., Smith Coll., 1930. Mem. U.S. com. UNICEF, 1948-66; mem. Def. Adv. Com. Women in Service, 1951-54; nat. co-chmn. Citizens for Eisenhower, 1953-54; Republican candidate U.S. Congress from Denver, 1954; mem. Internat. Devel. Adv. Bd., 1955- 57; nat. co. chmn. Com. Internat. Econ. Growth, 1958-60; regional chmn. Met. Opera Council, 1958-66; mem. Gov. Colo.'s Local Affairs Commn., 1963-66; pres. Colo. Consumers Council, 1965-67; dir. Nat. Safety Council, 1958-60; mem. Nat. Adv. Council on Nurse Tng., HEW, 1969-73; pres. The Park People, 1975-79. Mem. Gov.'s Commn. on Status Women, 1970-75 Trustee 4 Mile Historic Park, The Park People. Mem. Assn. Jr. Leagues Am. (bd. dirs. 1947-50), Colonial Dames Am. Episcopalian. Home: 111 Emerson St Apt 1625 Denver CO 80218-3792

HARRIS, EMILY LOUISE, special education educator; b. New London, Conn., Nov. 16, 1932; d. Frank Sr. and Tanzatter (McCleese) Brown; m. John Everett Harris Sr., Sept. 10, 1955; children: John Everett Jr., Jocelyn E. (dec.). BS, U. Conn., 1955; MEd, Northeastern U., 1969. Cert. tchr. elem. spl. subject sci., Mass., spl. subject reading, secondary prin., elem. prin. Tchr. New Haven Sch. Dept., 1957-59, Boston Sch. Dept., 1966-68, Natick (Mass.) Sch. Dept., 1969-72; cert. nurse's asst. The Hebrew Rehab. Ctr., Roslindale, Mass., 1973-75; spl. edn. educator Boston Sch. Dept., 1975-76, 78—, support tchr., 1976-78. Site coord. Tchr. Corps., 1977-81; leader, co-leader Harvard U. Student Tchrs. at Dorchester H.S. Sem., 1995—; tchr. adviser Future Educators Am. Dorchester H.S. Editor, compiler: Cooking With the Stars, 1989. Mem.-del. Mass. Fedn. Tchrs., Boston, 1993-96; elected rep. AFL-CIO (Boston Tchrs. Union), 1986-96; registrar of voters Dorchester (Mass.) H.S., 1986—; adv. bd. New England Assn. Schs. and Colls., 1980-93; 1st v.p., bd. dirs. League of Women for Comty. Svcs., Boston, 1976-80, Cynthia Sickle-Cell Anemia Fund, Boston, 1976-80. Recipient Tchg. award Urban League Guild Mass., 1993. Mem. AAUW, Zeta Phi Beta (Zeta of Yr. 1994), Alpha Delta Kappa, Kappa Delta Pi, Order Ea. Star (past worthy matron Prince Hall chpt. 1983-84), Delta Omicron Zeta, Phi Delta Kappa. Baptist. Avocations: reading, sewing. Home: 36 Dietz Rd Hyde Park MA 02136-1134

HARRIS, EMMYLOU, singer; b. Birmingham, Ala., Apr. 2, 1947; d. Walter and Eugenia; children: Hallie, Meghann. Student, U.N.C.-Greensboro. Singer, 1967; assisted Gram Parsons on album GP, Grievous Angel, 1973; toured with Fallen Angels Band, performed across Europe and U.S.; recording artist on albums for Reprise Records, Warner Bros. Records., Electra/Asylum Records; appeared in rock documentary The Last Waltz, 1978; albums include The Gliding Bird, 1969, Pieces of the Sky, 1975, Elite Hotel, 1976 (Grammy award), Luxury Liner, 1977, Quarter Moon In A Ten Cent Town, 1978, Profile: Best of Emmylou Harris, 1978, Blue Kentucky Girl, 1979, Light of the Stable, 1979, Evangeline, 1981, Last Date, 1982, White Shoes, 1983, Profile II: Best of Emmylou Harris, 1984, The Ballad of Sally Rose, 1985, Thirteen, 1986, Trio (with Dolly Parton, Linda Ronstadt), 1987 (Grammy award), Angel Band, 1987, Bluebird, 1988, Duets, 1990, Cowgirl's Prayer, 1993, Songs Of The West, 1994, Wrecking Ball, 1995 (Grammy award 1996), Spyboy, 1998, The Horse Whisperer, 1998, Singin' with Emmy Lou Harris, Vol. 1, 2000, Vol. 2, 2003, Red Dirt Girl, 2000, Anthology: The Warner-Reprise Years, 2001, Nobody's Darling But Mine, 2002, Stumble Into Grace, 2003; co-writer, co-prodr.: (with Paul Kennerley) The Ballad of Sally Rose, 185. Pres. Country Music Found., 1983. Recipient of 11 Grammy awards, 1979, 80, 81, 84, 87, 92, 96, 98, 99, 2000, 2001, Orville H. Gibson Lifetime Achievement award, 1996, Patrick J. Leahy Humanitarian award-Americana Music awards Lifetime Achievement Performer, 2002; named Female Vocalist of Yr., Country Music Assn., 1980; co-recipient (with Dolly Parton and Linda Ronstadt) Album of Yr. award Acad. Country Music, 1987; named to Ala. Music Hall of Fame, 2003. Office: Vector Management 1607 17th Ave S Nashville TN 37212-2875*

HARRIS, EVA, molecular biology educator; b. N.Y.C., Aug. 6, 1965; BA, Harvard U., 1987; PhD in Molecular and Cell Biology, U. Calif., Berkeley, 1993. Dir. applied molecular biology/appropriate technol. transfer program U. Calif., San Francisco, 1993—, asst. adj. prof., 1997-98, asst. prof. Sch. Pub. Health Berkeley, 1998—. John D. and Catherine T. MacArthur Found. fellow, 1997. Mem. AAAS, Am. Soc. Microbiology. Office: U Calif Sch Pub Health 239 Warren Hl Berkeley CA 94720-0001

HARRIS, GRACE E. academic administrator; BS with highest honors, Hampton Inst., 1954; postgrad., Boston U., 1954-55; MA, U. Va., 1974, PhD, 1975; DHL (hon.), Va. Union U., 1995. Caseworker Dept. Pub. Welfare, Hampton, Va., 1955-57; caseworker, supr. Va. Dept. Welfare and Instns., Richmond, Va., 1957-63; exec. dir. Friends' Assn. Children, Richmond, Va., 1963-66; asst. dir. Richmond Cmty. Action Program, 1966-67; asst. prof. sch. social work Va. Commonwealth U., Richmond, 1967-76, dir. student affairs, 1975-76, assoc. prof. sch. social work, 1976-80, assoc. dean sch. social work, 1978-90, prof. sch. social work, 1981-90, dean sch. social work, 1982-90, vice provost continuing studies & pub. svc., 1990-93, provost, v.p. acad. affairs, 1993—, acting pres., 1995, 98. Bd. dirs. Richfood Holdings, Inc.; bd. trustees U. Richmond, 1992—; cons., presenter in field. Mem., trustee Coun. United Way Svcs., 1998, bd. dirs., 1982-89, 90-93; dir. Ctrl. Va. Ednl. Telecomm. Corp., 1997—, trustee World Affairs Coun. Greater Richmond, 1997—; mem. Richmond City Charter Commn., 1995, Richmond Cmty. Criminal Justice Bd., 1995—; bd. dirs. Christian Children's Fund, Inc.; vice chmn. State Bd. Family and Children's Trust Fund; mem. adv. com. spl. edn. Richmond Pub. Schs., 1981-86; mem. adv. bd. health professions Va. Union U., 1979-83; bd. dirs. Met. YMCA, 1979-82; mem. search com. Asst. City Mgr. Human Resources, 1979; mem. adv. bd. State Divsn. Volunteerism, 1979-83; Va. del. Rosalynn Carter's Cmtys. Plan Employment, 1978; bd. dirs. Womens Bank, 1976-84; active Cmty. Mental Health and Mental Retardation Svcs. Bd., 1976-82, chair, 1979; mem. task force Devel. Sch. Gifted/Disadvantaged Children, 1976; mem. com. Richmomd Area Cmty. Coun., 1972-73, day care com., 1971-72; client involvement com. State Dept. Weldare and Instns., 1971-72; bd. dirs. Young Women's Christian Assn., 1970-74; mem. adv. com. Richmond Redevel. & Housong Authority, 1967-69; bd. dirs. St. Gerard's Maternity Home, 1963-66. Recipient Alumna of Yr. award, Va. Comopnwealth U., 1989, Educator of Yr. award, Nat. Coalition 100 Black Women, 1990, Flame Bearer Edn. award, United Negro Coll. Fund, 1995, Va. Power Strong Men and Women Excellence in Leadership award, 1997, Coun. Va. Mus. Fine Arts Va. Women Style and Substance award, 1998, Presdl. award Cmty. Multicultural Enrichment and Riese-Melton award, Va. Commonwealth U., 1999; United Negro Coll. Fund fellow, Boston U., 1954-55, Phelps Stokes fellow U. Va., 1972-74, Ford Found. fellow, 1972-74, Am. Coun. Edn. fellow Am. Adminstrn. Va Commonwealth U., 1980-81; Va. Dept. Pub. Welfare grad. scholar, 1959-60. Mem. NASW (Knee/Whitman award 1991), Nat. Acads. Practice, Coun. Social Work Edn., Lychnos Hon. Soc., The Forum Club, Phi Beta Sigma, Alpha Kappa Mu. Office: Va Commonwealth U 901 W Franklin St PO Box 842527 Richmond VA 23284-2527

HARRIS, HARRIET, actress; b. Ft. Worth, Tex., Jan. 8, 1955; Grad., Juilliard. Actor: (TV series) The Five Mrs. Buchanans, 1994, Union Square, 1997—98, Stark Raving Mad, 1999, The Beast, 2001, It's All Relative, 2003; (plays) Hamlet, 1986—, Four Baboons Adoring the Sun, 1992, Jeffrey, 1993—, The Man Who Came to Dinner, 2000, (Broadway musical) Thoroughly Modern Millie, 2002— (Tony award, 2002); (films) Memento, 2000, Nurse Betty, 2000. Office: care Actors Equity Agy 165 W 46th St New York NY 10036*

HARRIS, HAZEL LYNN, medical/surgical nurse; b. Taylor, Tex., Apr. 29, 1953; d. L.B. Clark, Doris Evelyn Clark; m. James Paul Harris; 1 child, Jonathan. BSN, Tex. Woman's U., 1974. RN Tex., cert. orthopedic nurse. Student nurse Parkland Health & Hosp. Sys., Dallas, 1973—74, staff nurse, 1974—80, unit mgr., 1982—. Clin. instr. Am. Tng. Ctr., Dallas, 1988—90; mem. nursing peer rev. Parkland Health & Hosp. Sys., Dallas, 1999—99. Contbr. Book Decision Making in Medical / Surgical Nursing, 1990. Polit. action com. Am. Heart Assn., Dallas, 2000—03. Finalist Tex. Nurses Excellence award Cmty. Svc., Nurseweek, 2000; named one of Great 100 Nurses, Dallas/Ft. Worth Hosp. Coun. and Dists. Three and Four of Tex. Nurses Assn., 1998. Mem.: ANA, Tex. Nurses Assn., Nat. Assn. Orthopedic Nurses (treas. Dallas chpt. 1982—90), Nat. Coun. Negro Women (life; rec. sec. Greater Trinity sect. 1999—2003), Chi Eta Phi Sorority- Xi Phi Chapter (Tamiochus 2001—03, Basileus 2003). Methodist. Avocations: shopping, travel, walking. Home: 5606 Shady Crest Trail Dallas TX 75241-1803 Office: Parkland Health & Hosp Sys 5201 Harry Hines Blvd Dallas TX 75235 Home Fax: 214-374-0823. Personal E-mail: hazelharrisrn@aol.com. Business E-Mail: hlharr@parknet.pmh.org.

HARRIS, JEANNETTE FRANCES, artist; b. Mountain Grove, Mo., Nov. 17, 1938; d. Solon Francis and Mary Elizabeth (Roper) Manchester; m. James Partsch Harris, Mar. 18, 1965; children: James Patrick, Amy Elizabeth. BS in Edn. with honors, Southwest Mo. State U., 1962. Judge Sandbridge Art Show, Virginia Beach, Va., 1976-77; bd. mem. Textile Designer's Assn., 1978-79; founding bd. mem. Children's Art Ctr., Norfolk, Va., 1977; scholarship chmn. Marianas O'Wives, 1984, 85, 86, Kitsap Quilters Guild, 1993-98; mem. scholarship bd. North Kitsap Arts and Crafts, 1990-92, bd. mem., 1989-92; co-founder The Clay People, 1996. One-woman show Shoreline (Wash.) Coll., 1990, 91; exhibited in group shows at Virginia Beach (Va.) Art Ctr., 1975-76, Folk Arts Festival, Virginia Beach, 1975-76, Sandbridge Beach Art Show, Virginia Beach, 1976-77, Carlyle House, Alexandria, Va., 1978, Azalea Festival, Norfolk, Va., 1978, Textile Designer's Assn. Ann. Show, Norfolk, 1978, 79, Studio Northwest Mem. Shows, London, 1980-83, Guam Visual Arts Guild, Agana, 1984, Quad-A Guild Ann. Fine Art Show, Seattle, 1987, 88, Southwest Mo. State U. Alumni Art Show, 1988, Kitsap Arts and Crafts Show, Poulsbo, Wash., 1989-2002, Am. Assn. Cmty. and Jr. Colls. Nat. Conv., Seattle, 1990, Shoreline Arts Coun., Seattle, 1990, Artworks '92, Silverdale, Wash., 1992, Bainbridge (Wash.) Island Parks and Recreation Arts and Crafts Show, 1992, Hale Koa Internat. Christmas Fair, Honolulu, 1992, Artworks '93, 1993, Sidney Mus. and Arts Assn., Port Orchard, Wash., 1993, Cultural Arts Found., Poulsbo, 1993, Washington Potters' Assn., Seattle, 1993—, Seattle Pacific U., 1993, Arts Coun. of Snohomish County Gallery, Everett, Wash., 1993, 94, 95, Fiberworks '94, Port Townsend, Wash., 1994, Kenai (Alaska) Potters' Show, 1994, Kitsap Regional Libr., Bremerton, Wash., 1995, Kitsap Quilters' Ann. Show, Poulsbo, 1995, 96 (winner Art Quilt category 1997), The Clay People's Show, 1996, Cunningham Gallery, U. Wash., 1996, Weyrich Gallery, Albuquerque, 1996, Nine Potters Studio, Poulsbo, 1997, Best of the Northwest, Seattle, 1997, 2000, 2001, A Feast for the Eyes, Poulsbo, 1997, Edmonds Art Festival, Wash., 1998 (hon. mention); pub. art commn. bronze sculpture Arness Park, Kingston, Wash., 1992, stoneware sculpture Poolsbo Pub. Libr., Evergreen Hosp., Kirkland, 2003; contbr. author 500 Teapots. Recipient Hon. Mention award Edmonds (Wash.) Art Festival, 1998; included in 500 Teapots, 2002. Avocations: internet, genealogy, reading and research, photography, classical music.

HARRIS, JENNIFER A. aerospace engineer; b. Fostoria, Ohio, Aug. 1, 1968; BS in Aerospace Engring., MIT, 1990; postgrad., U. So. Calif., 1994—. Rschr. MIT Space Sys. Lab., 1989-90; subsys. engr. Jet Propulsion Lab., Pasadena, Calif., 1990-93, leader Mars Pathfinder Attitude and Info. Mgmt. Subsys., 1994—, leader Mars Pathfinder Surfact Ops. test program, flight dir.; H.S. and bus. sch. English tchr. Sevastopol, Ukraine, 1993-94. Office: Jet Propulsion Lab 4800 Oak Grove Dr M/S: T1722 Pasadena CA 91109-8099

HARRIS, JUDITH ANN WHITE, health occupations vocational educator, nurse; b. Springfield, Ohio, Mar. 6, 1939; d. Willis and Tennessee Belle (Poole) Martin; m. Allen G. Harris, Mar. 21, 1986; 1 child by previous marriage, Denise Marian Womble. Student, U. South Fla., 1978-85, BS/MS in Psychology, 2000. RN, Fla.; cert. tchr., Fla. Nurse Dr. Robert Tapogna, Springfield, Ohio, 1960-62, Springfield City Hosp., 1962-65, Dr. Robert Beam, Springfield, 1965-75; ednl. coord., instr. med. assisting Sarasota Vocat. Ctr., Fla., 1977-82, instr. med. assisting program, chmn. dept., 1982-84, 89-91, instr. health svc. occupations, placement coord. health occu, 1985-88; dept. chmn. Allied Health, 1989-95. Bd. dirs. Fla. Bd. Inc.; pres. J.W. Harris Pub. Co.; cruise ship lectr. for Princess, Royal Caribbean and Celebrity Cruise Lines; v.p., sec. Al Harris Pest Control, Inc. 1996-; dir. adv. & mktg., 2000-. Author: J.W. Harris Medical Assisting Review Manual, 1995, Templin, 2002; contbr. articles to profl. jours. Vol. Children's Breath Clinic, Sarasota, 1977-79, Kidney Found., Sarasota, 1982, ARC, Sarasota, 1976-88; dir. Spl. Care Unit, 1984-88; v.p. Sons of Norway, 1993-95; choir soloist Beneva Christian Ch., 1989—, deaconess, 1993-96, elder 1997—, chmn. Health Care Svcs. Dept., 1996—, vice chmn. bd. dirs., 2001-02, chmn. bd., 2002—; asst. state dir. Fla. Good Sons, 1993-94; bd. dirs. Fla. Bd. Camping Assn., Inc., sec., 1999--, newsletter editor, 1996—; chmn. FVA Leadership Forum, 1992—; parish nurse and chmn. health svcs. dept. Beneva Christian Ch., 1995—; pres. FVA Post Pres.'s Club, 1999—; 1st v.p. Sarasota Bay Republican Women's Club Federated, 1998-2001; mem. Sarasota Tiger Bay Club, 1999—, Sarasota Homebuilders Assn., 1999—; sec. Acorn Glass Bowling League, 2000—. Named Outstanding Vocat. Tchr. Sarasota County Sch. Bd., 1985, Woman of Impact for Edn., Sarasota County Commn. on the Status of Women, 1995. Mem. Am. Vocat. Assn. (Outstanding Vocat. Tchr. region II 1985, Vocat. Tchr. Yr. 1987), Health Occupations Educators (vice chmn. policy com. 1985-86), Nat. Assn. Health Occupations Tchrs. (v.p. region II 1984-86, pres. elect 1988, pres. 1989-91), Fla. Vocat. Assn. (bd. dirs. 1983-85, pres. 1987-88, Pres. award 1984, Outstanding Vocat. Educator region 23 award 1982, Sarasota Mayors award 1984, Gov.'s Proclamation for Outstanding Tchg. 1987, chmn. leadership forum 1993—), Health Occupations Educators Assn. Fla. (pres. 1983-84, chmn. legis. com. 1985-93, Outstanding Tchr. 1983), Sarasota County Vocat. and Adult Edn. Assn. (pres. 1978-80, editor newsletter 1978-83), Am. Assn. Med. Assts., Good Sams Inc. Fla. (asst. state dir. dist. 12 1993-95), Fraternal Order of Eagles Aux. (dist. 3 auditor 1995-96, eagle nurse 1995-97, chair health care dept. 1995—, condr. 1996—), Sarasota Bay Republican Women's Club (life; v.p. 1998—), Women's Coun. Realtors (ways and means chair 2002-, corr. sec. 2003, rec. sec. 2004), Sarasota Assn. Realtors, Sunrise Rotary Club (Paul Harris fellow, 2002-, Rotary Internat. Sustaining Mem. 2002-), Tiger Bay Club, Delta Kappa Gamma, Phi Kappa Phi. Avocations: swimming, camping, knitting, sewing, biking. Home: PO Box 7278 Sarasota FL 34278 Office: 6100 Palmer Blvd Sarasota FL 34232 E-mail: alharrispestcontrol@netzero.net.

HARRIS, JUDITH E. lawyer; b. Apr. 28, 1945; AB, Mount Holyoke Coll., 1967; JD, Howard U., 1970. Bar: Pa. 1971. City solicitor City of Phila., 1992-93; ptnr. Morgan, Lewis & Bockius LLP, Phila. Office: Morgan Lewis & Bockius LLP 1701 Market St Philadelphia PA 19103-2903

HARRIS, JULIE (JULIE ANN HARRIS), actress; b. Grosse Pointe Park, Mich., Dec. 2, 1925; d. William Pickett and Elsie (Smith) H.; m. Jay I. Julien, Aug. 12, 1946 (div. 1954); m. Manning Gurian, Oct. 21, 1954 (div. 1967); 1 child, Peter; m. Erwin Carroll, Apr. 1977, (div. 1982). Student, Perry Mansfield Theatre Work Shop, 1941-43, Yale Drama Sch., 1944-45. Theater debut in It's a Gift, N.Y.C., 1945; appeared in plays Playboy of the Western World, 1946, Oedipus, 1946, Henry IV-Part II, 1946, Alice in Wonderland, 1947, We Love A Lassie, 1947, Macbeth, 1948, Sundown Beach, 1948 (Theatre World award 1949), The Young and Fair, 1948-49, Magnolia Alley, 1949, Montserrat, 1949, The Member of the Wedding, 1950-51 (Donaldson award 1950), I Am a Camera, 1951-52 (Tony award 1952, Donaldson award 1952, Variety-N.Y. Drama Critics Poll 1952), Mademoiselle Colombe, 1954, The Lark, 1955 (Tony award 1956), The Country Wife, 1957, The Warm Peninsula, 1959, Little Moon of Alban, 1960, Romeo and Juliet, 1960, King John, 1960, A Shot in the Dark, 1961, Marathon 33, 1964 (Tony nomination 1964), Hamlet, 1964, Ready When You Are, C.B, 1964, The Hostage, 1965, Skyscraper, 1965 (Tony nomination 1969), A Streetcar Named Desire, 1967, Forty Carats, 1968 (Tony award 1969), The Women, 1970, And Miss Reardon Drinks A Little, 1971-72, Voices, 1972, The Last of Mrs. Lincoln, 1972 (Tony award 1973), The Au Pair Man, 1973 (Tony nomination 1974), In Praise of Love, 1974, Break a Leg, 1979, On Golden Pond, 1980, Mixed Couples, 1980, Under the Ilex, 1983, Tusitala, 1988, (nat. co.) Driving Miss Daisy, Love Letters, 1989, The Belle of Amherst, 1977 (Grammy award 1977, Tony award 1977), Currier Bell, Glass Menagerie, 1994, Ellen Foster, 1997, Love is Strange, 1999, Fossils, 2001; one-woman theater presentations include Lucifer's Child, 1991; film debut in The Member of the Wedding, 1952 (Acad. award nomination); other films include The East of Eden, 1955, I Am A Camera, 1955, The Truth About Women, 1958, Poacher's Daughter, 1960, Requiem for a Heavyweight, 1962, The Haunting, 1963, The Moving Target, 1966, You're a Big Boy Now, 1966, Reflections in a Golden Eye, 1967, The Split, 1968, Journey into Midnight, 1968, The People Next Door, 1970, The Hiding Place, 1975, Voyage of the Damned, 1976, The Bell Jar, 1979, The Prostitute, 1980, The Nutcraker: The Motion Picture, 1986, Gorillas in the Mist, 1988, Housesitter, 1992, The Dark Half, 1993, Little Surprises, 1995, Carried Away, 1996; TV series include Thicker Than Water, 1973, The Family Holvak, 1975, Knots Landing, 1979-87; TV movies include Wind From the South, 1955, The Good Fairy, 1956, The Lark, 1957, Johnny Belinda, 1968, Little Moon of Alban, 1958 (Emmy award 1959), A Doll's House, 1959, Victoria Regina, 1961 (Emmy award 1962), The Power and the Glory, 1961, Pygmalian, 1964, Hamlet, 1964, The Holy Terror, 1965, Anastasia, 1967, The House on Green Apple Road, 1970, How Awful About Alan, 1970, Home for the Holidays, 1972, The Greatest Gift, 1974, Backstairs at the White House, 1979, The Gift, 1979, The Christmas Wife, 1979, Too Good To Be True, 1988, Single Women, Married Men, 1989, They've Taken Our Children: The Chowchilla Kidnapping Story, 1993, When Love Kills: The Seduction of John Nearn, 1993, One Christmas, 1994, Scarlett, 1994, The Christmas Tree, 1996, James Dean: A Portrait, 1996, Carried Away, 1996, Bad Manners, 1997, Ellen Foster, 1997, The First of May, 1998, (voice) Frank Lloyd Wright, 1998; author: (with Barry Tarshis) Julie Harris Talks to Young Actors, 1971. Recipient Antoinette Perry award for best actress in Forty Carats, 1969, The Last of Mrs. Lincoln, 1973; Nat. Medal of the Arts, 1994, Tony award for lifetime achievement in Theater, 2002. Office: William Morris Agy c/o Samuel Liff 1325 Avenue of the Americas New York NY 10019*

HARRIS, KATHERINE, congresswoman; b. Key West, Fla., Apr. 5, 1957; m. Anders Ebbeson. Student, U. Madrid, 1978; BA in History, Agnes Scott Coll., 1979; MPA in Internat. Trade, Harvard U., 1996. Senator 24th dist. Fla. State Legislature, 1994—98; sec. of state State of Fla., 1999—2002; mem. U.S. Ho. of Reps from 13th Fla. dist., 2003—. Vice chmn. banking and ins. com. Fla. State Senate, vice chmn. govtl. reform and oversight com., chmn. commerce and econ. opportunities com. Congl. intern U.S. Senate and U.S. Ho. of Reps., 1978; vice chmn. Sarasota County Legis. Del.; mem. Supreme Ct. Gender Bias Commn.; vice chmn. Fla. Am. Legis. Exch. Coun.; mem. arts and tourism com. Nat. Conf. State Legislators; former mem. adv. coun. Mote Marine Lab., Women's Resource Ctr., Sarasota County Arts Coun.; mem. Leadership Sarasota, Leadership Tampa; former vice chmn. bd. trustees Ringling Mus.; mem. nominating com. Pub. Svc. Commn.; active Habitat for Humanity, New Coll., Fla. Rep. Exec. Com. Recipient Disting. Leadership Alumni award, Leadership Sarasota, 1994, Arts Advocacy award, Sarasota County Arts Coun., 1995, Best Govt. Ofcl. award, Sarasota Mag., 1995—2002, Legislator of Yr. award, Sarasota Opera, 1996, Ind. Funeral Dirs. of Fla., 1996, Fla. Optometric Assn., 1996, Legis. Appreciation award, Dept. Labor and Employment Security, 1996. Mem. Sarasota C. of C. (Disting. Leadership Alumni award 1994), Englewood C. of C., Charlotte C. of C., Venice C. of C., Jaycees. Republican. Presbyterian. Avocations: reading, sailing, painting, skiing, skeet shooting. Office: 116 Cannon Ho Office Bldg Washington DC 20515-0913*

HARRIS, KATHERINE SAFFORD, speech and hearing educator; b. Lowell, Mass., Sept. 3, 1925; d. Truman Henry and Katherine (Wardwell) Safford; m. George Harris, Oct. 2, 1952; children: Maud White, Louise. BA, Radcliffe Coll., 1947; PhD, Harvard U., 1954. Rsch. assoc. Haskins Labs., New Haven, 1952-85, v.p., 1985—; prof. CUNY, N.Y.C., 1970—, disting. prof., 1982—. Active U.S./Israeli Speech Program Littauer Found., N.Y.C., 1986. Author: (with Borden and Raphael) Speech Science Primer, 1970, 4th edit., 2002, (with Baer and Sasaki) Phonatory Control, 1986. Active U.S./Israeli Speech Program Littauer Found., N.Y.C., 1986. Nat. Inst. Deafness and Other Comm. Disorders grantee. Fellow AAAS, Acoustical Soc. Am. (pres. 2000-01), Am. Speech Hearing Assn., N.Y. Acad. Scis. Office: CUNY Grad Sch 415 5th Ave New York NY 10016

HARRIS, KATHLEEN RENEE, marketing professional; b. LA, Nov. 30, 1954; d. William Rogiere Harris and IdaBelle (Norman) Rivers. AA in Data Processing, Chabot Coll., 1980; BS in Bus. Mgmt., U. Phoenix, 2001. Gen. clk. sec. Western Girl Temp. Agy., San Leandro, Calif., 1973-75; mag card

II operator Bechtel Inc., San Francisco, 1975-76, data entry operator, 1976-79, office asst., 1979-80; adminstrv. asst. II Bechtel Power Corp., Walnut Creek, Calif., 1980-82; computer programmer I Bechtel Corp., San Francisco, 1982-86; ind. programmer/analyst, 1987—; project mgr. Clorox Co., 1998-99, info. systems super., 1999—. Database analyst Wollborg-Michelson; sys. support analyst Kraft Foods, 1990-92; LAN adminstr. So. Pacific Lines, 1992-93; sr. help desk specialist Triad Sys/Geoworks/Concord Gen., 1994-95; PC support tech. EDS/Blue Shield, 1995-96; LAN support mgr., Pacific Bell, 1996-97; project coord. Charles Schwab, 1997-98; project mgr., Clorox Co., 1998-99, info. tech. mgr. Clorox Svcs. Co., 1999-03; regional dir. First Class Benefits, Inc., 2003-; designer, seamstress, owner Feline Fit, Etc., Calif.; co-owner Next Generation Model Mgmt. Co., 1984. Mem. Better Bus. Bur. Avocation: licensed private pilot. Home: 894 Shelborne Dr Tracy CA 95377-8228 Office Phone: 209-833-6363.

HARRIS, KRISTINE, historian, educator; b. New York, July 10, 1964; d. Robert and Ingrid H.; m. Robert Polito, June 27, 1987. BA, Wellesley Coll., 1986; MA, PhD, Columbia U., 1997. Instr. New Sch. Social Rsch., N.Y.C., 1995; asst. prof. history SUNY, New Paltz, 1996—, dir. Asian studies program, 2000—. Contbr. articles to profl. jours. and books, collections. Fulbright Found. fellow, 1992-93, Am. Coun. Learned Socs. fellow, 1993, 98; grantee Pacific Cultural Found., 1994-95. Mem. Am. Hist. Assn., Assn. Asian Studies. Office: Dept History State U New York New Paltz NY 12561 E-mail: harrisk@newpaltz.edu.

HARRIS, LANI M. theater educator; b. L.A., June 8, 1951; d. Charles Edward and Lucy Rosetta McDonald; m. Thomas Lee Langkau, Sept. 30, 1980; children: Aeryn Paige Howard, Joseph Thomas Travis Langkau. AA, Coll. of the Redwoods, 1972; BA, Humboldt State U., 1976; MFA, U. So. Calif., L.A., 1980. Instr. Shasta Coll., Redding, Calif., 1983—90; lectr. Calif. State U., Chico, 1990—93, guest artist lectr. Bakersfield, 1993; asst. prof. U. Ala., Tuscaloosa, Ala., 1994—97; assoc. prof. U. Ctrl. Fla., Orlando, 1997—. Artistic dir. RCT Theatre, Redding, 1983—91. Contbr. chapters to books Stage Directions Guide to Auditions, 1998, 50 Great Directors of the Twentieth Century, 2003; prodr.: Air Born, 1995. Bd. mem. ACLU, Orlando, 1999—2002; chair, Coll. U. Divsn. Southeastern Theatre Conf., Greensboro, NC, 2001—04; v.p. Shasta County Arts Coun., Redding, 1986—91. Fulbright grant, Fulbright-Hays Grant Program, 2003. Mem.: Kennedy Ctr. Am. Coll. Theatre Festival (dir. of plays 1991—). Avocations: horseback riding, constitutional law. Office: U Ctrl Fla PO Box 162372 Orlando FL 32816-2372 E-mail: lharris@mail.ucf.edu.

HARRIS, LINDA RUTH, obstetrician and gynecologist; b. Clarkfield, Minn., June 22, 1954; d. Harold Francis Harris and Darlene Irene (Vik) Shaw. BA summa cum laude, Luther Coll., 1975; MD, U. Iowa, 1978. Diplomate Am. Bd. Ob-Gyn. Physician Feminist Women's Health Ctr., L.A., 1980-82, Eldonna Christine, M.D., Napa, Calif., 1983-85, Ob-Gyn. Health Ctr., Medford, Oreg., 1985—. Cons. Planned Parenthood, Medford, 1990-94; bd. dirs. Crossroads, Medford, 1985-87. Mem. ACOG (sect. chair 1982), AMWA, Oreg. Med. Assn., N.Am. Soc. of Pediatric and Adolescent Gynecology, Am. Soc. for the Study of Colposcopy and Cervical Pathology. Democrat. Avocations: skiing, biking, music. Office: Ob-Gyn Health Ctr 777 Murphy Rd Medford OR 97504-8425

HARRIS, MARCELITE JORDAN, retired career officer; b. Houston, Jan. 16, 1943; d. Cecil Oneal and Marcelite Elizabeth (Terrell) Jordan; m. Maurice Anthony Harris, Nov. 29, 1980 (dec. Jan. 1996); children: Steven Eric, Tenecia Marcelite. BA, Spelman Coll., 1964; postgrad., Ctrl. Mich. U., 1973-75, crwa. State U., 1975-76, Chapman Coll., 1979-80; BS, U. Md., Okinawa, Japan, 1986. Tchr. Head Start, Houston, 1964-65, commd. 2d lt. USAF, 1965, advanced through grades to maj. gen., 1965-97; student Squadron officers Sch., 1975; with Hdqrs. USAF, Pentagon, 1975; comdr. 39 Cadet Squadron, USAF Acad., Colorado Springs, Colo., 1978, Air Refueling Wing, McConnell AFB, Kans., 1980, Avionics Maintenance Squadron, McConnell AFB, 1981, Field Maintenance Squadron, McConnell AFB, 1982; dir. maintenance Pacific Air Forces Logistics Support Ctr., Kadena Air Base, Japan, 1982; student Air War Coll., 1983; dep. chief maintenance Tech. Tng. Ctr., Keesler AFB, Miss., 1986, wing comdr., 1988; student Harvard U.Sr. Officers Course, 1988, Capstone Flag and Gen. Officers Course, 1990; vice comdr. Oklahoma City Air Logistics Ctr., Tinker AFB, 1990-97; dir. tech. tng. USAF, Randolph AFB, Tex., 1993-97, dir. of maintenance, 1994, ret., 1997. Cabinet mem. United Way, Oklahoma City, 1991; mem. adv. bd. Salvation Army, Oklahoma City, 1991—; bd. dirs. U.S. Automobile Assn., 1993—, 5 Who Care, 1992, Urban League. Decorated Bronze star, D.S.M.; named one of Top 100 Afro-Am. Bus. and Profl. Women, Dollars and $ense Mag., 1989, named Most Prestigious Individual, 1991, One of Top 100 Most Influencial People, City News, N.J., 1997; recipient Ellis Island Medal of Honor award, 1996, Living Legacy award 1998. Mem. AAUW, Air Force Assn. (life), Tuskegee Airmen Inc. (life), Maintenance Officer Assn., Retired Officer Assn., Ret. Officer Assn., Delta Sigma Theta. Office: 771 Thrasher Dr Rockledge FL 32955-6305

HARRIS, MARCI W. psychologist; m. Thomas Harris, July 12, 1970; children: Jason Brandt, Kelsi An, Tiffany An. PhD, Ariz. State U., 1983—88. Licensed Psychologist Ariz., 1988. Psychologist Mario Mendoza Neuro Psychiat. Hosp., Tegucigalpa, Honduras, 1976—79; pvt. practice Scottsdale, Ariz., 1981—. Cons. US Peace Corp, Tegucigalpa, Honduras, 1976—79; mem. marriage and comm. skills commn. State Ariz., 2002—. Author: (resouce book) Tegus Con Gusto. Dir. Ariz. Psychol. Found., 2000—03. Mem.: Nat. Register of Health Svc. Providers in Psychology, Nat. Assn. of Sch. Psychologists, Am. Assn. for Marriage and Family Therapy, Ariz. Psychol. Assn. (comm. rep. 1996—99). Office: Marci W Harris PhD 6609 N Scottsdale Rd Ste 103 Scottsdale AZ 85250 Office Phone: 480-948-0119.

HARRIS, MARIAN S. social work educator; b. Tallahassee; d. Leo and Ida Mae Hoskin; 1 child, Trina S. Madison. BA, Fla. A&M U., 1964; MSW, Fla. State U., 1977; PhD, Smith Coll., 1997. Cert. social worker, diplomate in clin. social work, lic. ind. clin. social worker Wash., lic. clin. social worker Ill. Program dir. Ctrl. Bapt. Family Svcs., Chgo., 1990—93; postdoctoral fellow U. Wis.-Madison, 1997—99; rsch. adv. Smith Coll. Sch. for Social Work, Northampton, Mass., 1996—, adj. asst. prof., 1997—; asst. prof. U. Ill., Chgo., 1999—2002; faculty assoc. Chapin Hall Ctr. for Children U., Chgo., 2002—; asst. prof. U. Wash., Tacoma, 2002—. Cons. reviewer U.S. Children's Bur., Washington, 2002—; expert witness O'Callaghan & Colleagues, PC, Chgo., 2002—03; cons. FAST Program, Madison, 2003; commr. Coun. Social Work Edn., Alexandria, Va., 1999—2005. Cons. editor: AFFILIA Jour. Women and Social Work, 2003—08. Recipient SAMHSA Clin. Tng. award, Coun. Social Work Edn., 1994—97; postdoctoral fellow, NIMH, 1997—99, Founder's Endowment grantee, U. Wash., 2003. Mem.: Soc. Social Work and Rsch., Coun. Social Work Edn. (commn. role and status of women 1994—2005), Tacoma Urban League, Children's Home Soc. West Ctrl. Region, Alpha Kappa Alpha. Democrat. Roman Catholic. Avocations: tennis, swimming, jogging, travel, music. Office: U Wash 1900 Commerce St Tacoma WA 98402-3100 E-mail: mh24@u.washington.edu.

HARRIS, MARY COLE, counselor; b. Whitewood, Va., June 12, 1944; d. Sherman Cecil Cole and Virgie Mae Vance; m. Bobby E. Ratliff, June 30, 1962 (dec. Apr. 1973); children: Bobby Ratliff, Tamara Ratliff Allen; m. David R. Harris, Apr. 16, 1998. AAS, Chattahoochee Valley C.C., Phenix City, Ala., 1991; B in Applied Sci., Troy State U., Phenix City, 1995; MS, Troy State U., 1999. Nat. cert. counselor, lic. profl. counselor. Sr. adminstrv. asst. Columbus (Ga.) Bank & Trust Co.; tech. instr. Columbus Tech. Inst.; pastoral counselor Pastoral Inst., Columbus; counselor Children & Family Connection, Phenix City, parenting facilitator. Counselor Forensic Unit West Ctrl. Ga. Regional Hosp., Columbus, 2003—; counselor The Bradley Ctr., Columbus, 2003—. Mem. runaway task force Family Ct. of Russell County, Phenix City, 2001—. Mem.: Internat. Assn. Marriage and Family Therapy, Nat. Employment Counseling, Assn. Specialists in Grou work, Am. Counseling Assn. Republican. Presbyterian. Avocations: shelling, cooking, gardening. Home: 4823 Basswood Dr Columbus GA 31909

HARRIS, MARY HOWARD, finance educator; b. Riverside, N.J., Oct. 2, 1965; d. Henry Robert and Lois Jean (Frank) Howard; m. Stephen Andrew Harris, Nov. 7, 1992; children: Stephen Andrew, Jr, Shannon Lois, Darcy Robin. BA in Econs., Ursinus Coll., Collegeville, Pa., 1987; MBA in Acctg., St. Joseph's U., Phila., 1993; PhD in Econs., Lehigh U., Bethlehem, Pa. Cert. mgmt. acct., Pa. Mgmt. trainee Meridian Bank, Phila., 1987-88, asst./br. mgr., 1988-90, credit analyst, 1990-92, sr. auditor, 1992-94; sr. acct. Meridian Securities, Reading, Pa., 1994-95; staff acct. Rhone Poulenc Rorer, Inc., Collegeville, Pa., 1995—96; asst. v.p., underwriting analyst Corestates Bank, Allentown, Pa., 1996—99; asst. prof. fin. Cabrini Coll., Radnor, Pa., 2001—. Adj. prof. Alvernia Coll., Reading, 1994, Muhlenberg Coll., Allentown, 1995 Mem. Inst. Mgmt. Accts. Republican. Roman Catholic. Avocations: reading, swimming. Home: 1315 New Philadelphia Rd Pottstown PA 19465-8669 Office: Cabrini Coll 610 King of Prussia Rd Radnor PA 19087

HARRIS, MELBA IRIS, elementary education educator, secondary school educator, state agency administrator; b. Cullman, Ala., Aug. 8, 1945; d. Karl and Leona Christine (McDowell) Budweg; m. James Allen Harris, Apr. 17, 1965 (div. June 1981); 1 child, James Allen II. BS in Home Econs., U. Ala., 1970, MA in Elem. Edn., 1977, EdS, 1982; BS in Elem. Edn. magna cum laude, St. Bernard Coll., 1975. Instr. Cullman (Ala.) City Schs., 1966-68, Ft. Payne (Ala.) City Schs., 1974-99; curriculum developer Ala. State Dept. Edn., Montgomery, 1987-89; aerospace edn. coordinator Ala. State Dept. Aeronautics, Montgomery, 1987-89; instr. Gwinnett County (Ga.) Schs., 1999—. V.p. Ft. Payne Civettes, 1979. Recipient commendations Ala. Gov. George C. Wallace, 1985, 86, Gov. Guy Hunt, 1987, Ft. Payne City Coun., 1987, Ft. Payne City Bd. Edn., 1987, Civil Air Patrol Albertville Composite Squadron, 1987, Ala. State Bd. Edn., 1987, Ala. State Excellence in Edn. award Fed. Aviation Adminstrn., 1987, Stewart G. Potter award Nat. Aircraft Distbrs. and Mfrs. Assn., 1988, Nat. Frank G. Brewer Meml. Aerospace Edn. award Civil Air Patrol, 1989, Aviation Edn. Excellence award Nat. Gen. Aviation Mfrs. Assn., 1989, NEWEST award NASA, 1995, Achievement in Edn. award Optimist Club, 1999, Tchrs. as Leaders Inc. award, Gwinnett County Bd. Edn., 2001; named A. Scott Crossfield Nat. Aerospace Educator of Yr., 1987, The Nat. Aerospace Edn. Tchr. of Yr., 1987; Christa McAuliffe fellow, 1987, Tchr. of Yr. Meml. award, 1991; named to Ala. Aviation Hall of Fame, 1991. Mem. NEA, NSTA, Ala. Edn. Assn. (state aerospace edn. coord. 1992—), Ft. Payne Edn. Assn. (pres. 1985-86), Air Force Assn. (life), Ala. Aviation Assn., Exptl. Aircraft Internat. (maj. achievement award 1988), Exptl. Aircraft Chpt. 683 (sec., treas. 1987, pres. 1988), Internat. Ninety-Nines, Inc., Kappa Delta Pi. Home: PO Box 681174 Fort Payne AL 35968-1613 Office: Bethesda Sch 525 Bethesda School Rd Lawrenceville GA 30044-3509 Office Phone: 770-921-2000. E-mail: fflight@peoplepc.com.

HARRIS, MELISSA M. communications executive; d. Errol Romeo and Mildred M. Ritchie. BA in Comm., Edward Waters Coll., Jacksonville, Fla., 1991; MA in Mgmt., Webster U., 1997. Visual info. specialist USAF, San Antonio, 1994—2000, comm. coord. Dallas Employees' Retirement Fund, 2000—. With U.S. Army, 1987—95. Decorated NCO Profl. Devel. Ribbon U.S. Army, S.W. Asia Svc. medal with 3 bronze stars, Kuwait Liberation medal, Army Svc. Ribbon, Nat. Def. Svc. medal. Office: Dallas Employees' Retirement Fund 600 N Pearl St Dallas TX 75201 Office Phone: 214-580-7700. E-mail: mharris@dallaserf.org.

HARRIS, MERLE WIENER, college administrator, educator; b. Hartford, Conn., July 25, 1942; d. Irving and Leah (Glasser) Wiener; m. David R. Harris, June 23, 1963; children: Jonathan, Rebecca. BS, Ctrl. Conn. State U., 1964, MS, 1973; EdD, U. Mass., 1988. Clk., edn. com. Conn. Gen. Assembly, Hartford, 1971-72; career edn. coordinator Bloomfield (Conn.) Pub. Schs., 1973-78; asst. to commr. Dept. of Higher Edn., Hartford, Conn., 1978-82, asst. commr., 1982-88, deputy commr., 1988-89; pres. Charter Oak State Coll., New Britain, Conn., 1989—; exec. dir. Bd. for State Acad. Awards, New Britain, Conn., 1989—; interim pres. Cen. Conn. State U., 1995-96. Cons.on career edn. U.S. Dept. Edn., Washington, 1974; fellow Inst. for Ednl. Leadership, 1980; bd. dirs. Old State House, 1996—2003, Conn. Hist. Soc., 2003—, Conn. Literacy Vols., 1991—98, Conn. Humanities Coun., 1991—97, Conn. Acad. for Edn. in Math., Sci. and Tech., 2000—, vice chmn., 2002—; chmn. Joint Com. Ednl. Tech., 1991—98; mem. Conn. Commn. Ednl. Tech., 2000—. Mem. New Eng. Assn. Schs. and Colls. (bd. dirs. 1997-2003), Am. Coun. on Edn. (commr. on ednl. credit and credentials 1995-98). Democrat. Jewish. Avocations: gardening, cooking, teaching. E-mail: mharris@charteroak.edu.

HARRIS, MICALYN SHAFER, lawyer, educator, arbitrator, consultant, mediator; b. Chgo., Oct. 31, 1941; d. Erwin and Dorothy (Sampson) Shafer. AB, Wellesley Coll., 1963; JD, U. Chgo., 1966. Bar: Ill. 1966, Mo. 1967, U.S. Dist. Ct. (ea. dist.) Mo. 1967, U.S. Supreme Ct. 1972, U.S. Ct. Appeals (8th cir.), 1974, N.Y. 1981, N.J. 1988, U.S. Dist. Ct. N.J., U.S. Ct. Appeals (3d cir.) 1993. Law clk. U.S. Dist. Ct., Mo., 1967-68; atty. The May Dept. Stores, St. Louis, 1968-70, Ralston-Purina Co., St. Louis, 1970-72; atty., asst. sec. Chromalloy Am. Corp., St. Louis, 1972-76; pvt. practice St. Louis, 1976-78; atty. CPC Internat., Inc., 1978-80; divsn. counsel CPC N.Am., 1980-84, asst. sec., 1981-88; gen. counsel S.B. Thomas, Inc., 1983-87; corp. counsel CPC Internat., Englewood Cliffs, NJ, 1984-88; assoc. counsel Weil, Gotshal & Manges, N.Y.C., 1988-90; pvt. practice, 1991; v.p., sec., gen. counsel Winpro, Inc., 1991—. Arbitrator Am., Arbitration Assn., NYSE, NASD; adj. prof. Lubin Sch. Bus. Pace U.; mediator. Mem.: ABA (Ctr. Profl. Responsibility, bus. law sect., past chair corp. counsel com., past chair subcom. counseling the mktg. function, mem. securities law com., tender offers and proxy statements subcom., chair task force on e-mail privacy, task force on electronic contracting, task force on conflicts of interest, ad hoc com. on tech., profl. responsibility com.), Am. Law Inst. (mem. consultative groups, restatement of agy. 3d, UCC Arts. 1 & 2, internat. jurisdiction & judgements project), Computer Law Assn., N.J. Gen. Coun., Am. Corp. Counsel Assn. N.Y. (mergers and acquisitions com., corp. law com.), Mo. Bar Assn. (past chmn. internat. law com.), Bar Assn. Metro St. Louis (past chair TV com.), Assn. Bar City N.Y. (mediation coach), N.J. Bar Assn. (computer law com.), N.Y. State Bar Assn. (exec. com. bus. law sect., securities regulation com., chair internet and technology law com., past chair subcom. on licensing, task force on shrink-wrap licensing, electronic comm. task force). Address: 625 N Monroe St Ridgewood NJ 07450-1206

HARRIS, MILDRED CLOPTON, clergy member, educator; b. Chgo., May 27, 1936; d. Jordan and Willa Mildred Clopton; m. Herbert Curlee Harris, Feb. 4, 1928. BA, DePaul U., 1957; MA, Columbia U., 1963, Governors State U., 1975; MPS, Loyola U., Chgo., 1985; D in Min., Bible Inst. Sem., Plymouth, Fla., 1985. Ordained to ministry Ind. Assemblies of God. Tchr. Gary (Ind.) Pub. Schs., 1957-93; founder, pres. God First Ministries, Chgo., 1978—. Organizer Chgo. March for Jesus, 1995-97. Author: Traits of an Intercessor, 1991, Educating Your Child God's Way, 1991, The Productive Prayer Guide, 1991; exec. prodr. (cassette) tribe of Judah En Danse, 1995-96 (ASCAP award); host (TV show) Born Again, (radio show) WYCA 92.3, WCFJ 1470 AM. Bd. dirs. Midwestern U., Chgo., 1989-97, Goodman Theater, Chgo., 1994—, Make a Wish Found., Chgo., 1994-97, Windows of Opportunity, Chgo., 1997—; mem. exec. adv. com. Chgo. Housing Authority, 1995-99, commr., 1999—; overseer Gary (Ind.) Educators for Art, 1990—. Recipient CHANCE award Chgo. Housing Authority, 1998, Seniors-Gladys Reed award, 1998; Mary Herrick scholar Du Sable H.S. Alumni, 1998. Mem. ASCAP, Nat. Soc. Fundraising Execs., Religious Conf. Mgmt. Assn., Nat. Coun. Negro Women (life), Union League Club Chgo., Chgo. Ill. Links Inc. Avocations: traveling, interior decorating. Home: 7246 S Luella Ave Chicago IL 60649-2514

HARRIS, MILDRED STAEGER, retired broadcast executive; b. Newark, Oct. 18, 1917; d. Henry Ernest and Louise Sheffick Staeger; m. William Finlaw Harris, Oct. 20, 1945 (dec. Nov. 1963); children: Steven Alan, Sandra Louise, Douglas William. Prof. designation in bus. mgmt., UCLA, 1980. Mgr. fixed assets ABC, L.A., 1971-76, mgr. adminstrn., 1976-80, tech. mgr., 1980-85. Children's libr. counselor Kings County Literacy Coun., Hanford, Calif., 1990, bd. dirs., 1991—; coord. Am. Women in Radio and TV, L.A., 1979-84. Named Businesswoman of Yr., YWCA Coun., 1973; recipient Emmy award for Summer Olympics, NATAS, 1985. Mem. Calif. Sheriffs Assn., Literacy Vols. Am., Libr. of Congress. Avocations: history, language, reading, genealogy. Office: Kings Literacy Coun 505 W Cameron St Hanford CA 93230-3615

HARRIS, NAOMI LITORA, mental health services professional; b. Warm Springs, Ga., Apr. 3, 1975; d. James Lewis and Carolyn Jean Harris. BS psychol. and soc. work, La Grange Coll., La Grange, Ga., 1993—97; MS family therapy, Mercer Univ. Sch. of Medicine, Macon, Ga., 1999—2001. Social svc. case mgr. Dept. of Family and Children Services, Macon, Ga., 1998—2000; dir., counselor Residence Hall, Wesleyan Coll., Macon, Ga., 2000—01; mental health therapist Phoenix Ctr., Warner Robins, Ga., 2001—03; program coord. Women's substance abuse, Phoenix Ctr., Warner Robins, Ga., 2003—. Recipient Most Outstanding Sr. award, La Grange Coll. Psychology Dept., 1997, grad. Cum Laude, La Grange Coll., 1997. Mem.: Am. Assn. of Marriage and Family Therapy, Psi Chi (v.p. 1996—97), Pi Gamma Mu. Office: Phoenix Behavioral Health Ctr 202 No Davis Drive Warner Robins GA 31099 E-mail: naomiharris_2000@yahoo.com., naomiharris_2000@yahoo.com.

HARRIS, PATRICIA ANN BRADY, principal, educational consultant; b. Asheboro, N.C., Apr. 21, 1947; d. Joseph Graham and Mary Louetta (Coltrane) Brady; m. Norman Lee Harris, Feb. 17, 1968; children: Joseph Troy, William Chadwick. B in Music Edn., U. N.C., 1971, MusM, 1978, M in Edn. Adminstrn., 1985, D in Edn. Adminstrn., 1990. Tchr. Randolph County Schs., Liberty, NC, 1972—85; tchr., asst. prin. Chatham County Schs., Pittsboro, NC, 1985—90; prin. Nottaway (Va.) County Schs., 1990—96, Smithfield (N.C.) Mid. Sch., 1996—2001, W. Johnston HS, Benson, NC, 2001—. Adminstrv. mentor, evaluator cert., Va., 1992; cons., 1996—2003. Recipient Chatham 2000 Citizen award, Chatham County, N.C., 1989, Pub. Svc. award, VFW, 1994—96; grantee, U.S. Govt., 1991—95. Mem.: NSSE, ASCD (Lighthouse award 2001), NEA, N.C. Assn. Educators, Phi Delta Kappa. Avocations: bridge, flowers, reading. Home and Office: 314 W Horne St Clayton NC 27520

HARRIS, PATRICIA E. deputy mayor; BA in govt., Franklin and Marshall Coll. Asst. to Deputy Mayor Koch Admin., N.Y.C., 1979—83; exec. dir. N.Y.C. Art Commn., 1983—90; v.p. corp. and cultural mktg. Rogers and Cowan, 1990—92; v.p. of pub. rels. Serino Coyne Advertising, 1992—94; mgr. corp. comm. Bloomberg LP, 1994—2002; deputy mayor Bloomberg Admin., N.Y.C., 2002—. Office: City Hall New York NY 10007*

HARRIS, PAULETTE COLLIER, pre-school administrator, educator; b. Nashville, Nov. 5, 1956; d. Rogers Rayfield Collier and Lillie Elois (Waltower) Shannon; m. James Erwin Harris, June 17, 1989; children: Kenyada, Shannon, James Jr. BA in Behaviorial Sci., Shaw U., 1978. Cert. child devel. assoc. Replacement 5tchr. J. Enos Ray Elem. Sch., Takoma Park, Md., 1978; office mgr. Hawkins & Shannon Constrn., Bloomingdale, Ga., 1979-89; shift mgr. Eastern Airlines, Atlanta, 1989-91; bookkeeper Hair Palace Salon, Atlanta, 1989-91; tchr. Kindercare, Atlanta, 1991-94, Clark Atlanta U. Head-Start, 1994—, mem. adv. bd., 1995-96. Co-author curriculum materials. Mem. NAACP, Order of Ea. Star (Electra award 1997). Democrat. Baptist. Avocations: walking, reading, singing. Home: 381 Pine Valley Rd SW Mableton GA 30126-1621

HARRIS, PENELOPE CLAIRE, pre-school administrator, daycare administrator, consultant; b. Martinez, Calif., Aug. 20, 1952; d. John R. and Watrine (Spencer) H.; children: Sara A. Davidson, Rachel L. Harris. AA, Diablo Valley Coll., Pleasant Hill, Calif., 1973; BA, San Francisco State U., 1975; MA, Calif. State U., Hayward, 1993. Tchg. credential, cmty. colls. instr. credential, Calif. Tchr. spinning Albany (Calif.) Adult Sch., 1976; guest instr. U. Calif. Extension, Berkeley, 1978; tchr. Martinez Early Childhood Ctr., 1981-83, YWCA Child Care Ctr., Pacheco, Calif., 1986-87; co-dir. Martinez Parent Coop. Nursery Sch., 1983-87; program dir. YWCA of Contra Costa County, Pacheco, 1987-90; assoc. Internat. Child Resource Inst., Berkeley, 1988-92; dir. Escondido Children's Ctr., Stanford, Calif., 1990-92; coord. Sch. Age Parenting and Infant Devel. Program, Hayward, Calif., 1992—; teen pregnancy prevention coord. Helen Turner Children's Ctr., Hayward, Calif., 1995—, latchkey coord., 1998—. Textile arts cons. Judy Chicago's Through the Flower Corp., Benecia, Calif., 1986-87; instr. Chabot Coll., Hayward, Calif., 1996-97. Bd. dirs. Through the Flower, Belen, N.Mex., 1999—. Mem. AAUW, Calif. Assn. Concerned with Sch. Age Parents, Calif. School-Age Consortium, Delta Kappa Gamma. Office: Helen Turner Children's Ctr 23640 Reed Way Hayward CA 94541-7326

HARRIS, PENNY SMITH, fundraising consultant; b. Old Town, Maine, Apr. 6, 1941; d. Owen Halbert and Louise Marion (Whitten) Smith; m. Parker Fred Harris, June 22, 1963 (div. 1992); children: Susan Leslie, Nancy Lynne. BS in Sociology, U. Maine, 1963; MS in Bus. Mgmt., Husson Coll., 1984. Cert. fund raising exec. 2003. Social worker Elizabeth Lund Home, Burlington, Vt., 1964-65; pub. sch. tchr. Essex Junction, Vt.; asst. dir. devel., corp. support mgr. Maine Pub. Broadcasting Network, Bangor, 1985—89; dir. devel. Eastern Maine Healthcare, Bangor, 1989—94; dir. healthcare campaign N.E. Health, Rockland, Maine, 1994-97; sr. assoc. Copley Davenport Co., Inc., Wenham, Mass., 1997-98, M. Davenport Assocs., 1998—; pres. PS Harris Assocs., Portland, Maine, 2001—. Trustee Maine Pub. Broadcasting Corp., 1991—95, Ctr. for Maine Contemporary Art, 1993—, U. Maine Sys., 1991—2001; mem. task force on campaign fin. Senator George Mitchell, Augusta, Maine, 1983; mem. All Am. City selection award jury, Nat. Civil League, N.Y.C., 1987; chmn. bd. dirs. Ctr. for Maine Contemporary Art, 2003—; bd. dirs. Greater Bangor United Way, 1990—93. Mem. LWV (pres. Bangor-Brewer chpt. 1979-81, state pres. 1982-85, nat. bd. dirs. 1986-88, sec. nat. bd. dirs. 1988-90, project dir. TV polit. debates Bangor 1982, project dir. Nat. Security and You Conf., Portland, Maine 1983), U. Maine Alumni Assn. (v.p. bd. dirs. 1991-93), Greater Portland C. of C. Democrat. Methodist. Avocations: skiing, travel, hiking, biking. Home and Office: PO Box 2862 South Portland ME 04116 Office Phone: 207-741-9086.

HARRIS, RUBY LEE, real estate agent; b. Booneville, Miss., Mar. 5, 1939; d. Carl Jackson and Gladys (Downs) Hill; m. Lee Kelly Harris, Apr. 21, 1962; children: Lee Kelly Jr., Bradford William. Student, N.E. Miss. Jr. Coll., Booneville, 1957-58, U. Ala., Tuscaloosa, 1958-59. Lic. real estate agt., Calif. Agt. Forest E. Olson, El Toro, Calif., 1974-76, Coldwell Banker, Mission Viejo, Calif., 1976-78, Associated Realtors, Mission Viejo, 1978—. Mem. Children's Home Soc. Calif., Mission Viejo, 1985-88, Boys and Girls Club Am., San Clemente, Calif., 1989-91, Capistrano, 1994-95; mem. election com. Orange County, Mission Viejo, 1974—. Mem. Nat. Assn. Realtors, Calif. Assn. Realtors, Saddleback Valley Bd. Realtors (bd. dirs. 1989). Republican. Avocations: bicycling, gardening. Office: Associated Realtors 25350 Marguerite Pkwy Ste B Mission Viejo CA 92692-2993 Office Phone: 949-300-1332.

HARRIS, SHERELLE DENISE, journalist, librarian; b. Great Lakes, Ill., May 14, 1965; d. James Henry and Rosie Lee (Harris) H. BA in Journalism, Columbia Coll., 1989; cert. in children's lit., Inst. Children's Lit., 1993; MS in Libr. and Info. Sci., Pratt Inst., 1995. Freelance journalist, N.Y.C., 1992—; med. libr. NCI Advt., N.Y.C., 1996-97; young adult libr. South Norwalk (Conn.) Pub. Libr., 1997-99, dept. head children's libr., 1999—. Staff reporter The Hour, Norwalk, Conn., 1997-99, corr., 1999-2000. Contbg. author to mags. and children's books; prodr.: (play) 2020 B.C., Stamford Ctr. for the Arts, 2001; contbr. poetry to Nubian Gallery, 2003; columnist: Eagle View Press, 2003, contbg. editor: Conn. Librs. PUb., 2000—. Recipient 1st pl. juried poetry contest, Conn. Commn. on Arts, 2001; fellow for poetry and lit., Conn. Urban Artist Initiative, 1999—2002.

HARRIS, SHIRLEY, elementary, secondary and adult education educator; b. Chgo., Aug. 14, 1945; BA in Behavioral Sci., Nat. Louis U., 1985; MS in Edn., Chgo. State U., 1993. Cert. in curriculum and instr. Legal sec. Friedman/Rochester, Chgo. and Portland, Oreg., 1974; supr., clerical positions Model Cities, Chgo. and Portland, Oreg., 1973-75; bd. sec. Portland Comm., 1976-78; tchr., clerical positions Portland O.I.C., 1975-76; tchr., juvenile/youth counselor Yaun Youth Ctr., Portland, 1978-80; pres. Flexible Temps, Chgo., 1980—. Part-time prof. Wright Jr. Coll., 1999, Northeastern Ill. U., 1999—, Robert Morris Coll., 2000, DeVry Inst. Tech., 2000; cons. in field, Chgo., 1983; typing tchr., Chgo., 1983; pers. recruiter, Chgo., 1974-75. Contbr. poetry to anthologies. Bd. dirs. Operation Probe, Chgo., 1990-93. Mem. NAFE, ASCD, Internat. Platform Assn. Baptist. Home: 28 E Jackson Blvd Ste 1023-580 Chicago IL 60604

HARRIS, SKILA, government agency administrator; b. Bowling Green, Ky. d. Skiles Browning and Dorothy (Lester) Harris; m. Fred Graham. BS in Polit. Sci., Western Ky. U.; MS in Legis. Affairs, George Washington U. V.p. devel. and compliance Steiner-Liff Iron and Metal Co., Nashville, 1989—92; spl. asst. V.P. Al Gore, 1993—97; chief of staff Tipper Gore, 1993—97; with U.S. Dept. Energy, Washington, U.S. Synthetic Fuels Corp.; exec. dir. U.S. Sec. of Energy Adv. Bd., 1997—99; dir. TVA, Knoxville, 1999—. Bd. dirs. Nuclear Elec. Ins. Ltd.; vice chair2002 Consumer Energy Coun. Am.'s Forum on Energy Security and Electric Industry Restructuring. Grad. Leadership Knoxville, 2001. Office: TVA 400 W Summit Hill Dr Knoxville TN 37902-1499*

HARRIS, SUSAN LOUISE, financial services company executive; AB, UCLA, 1978; JD, U. So. Calif., 1981. Bar: Calif. 1981. Assoc. Lillick, McHose & Charles, 1981-85; sr. v.p., gen. counsel corp. affairs, sec. SunAmerica, Inc., L.A., 1985—.

HARRIS, SUSAN V. lawyer; b. 1961; BA, Oberlin Coll., 1983; JD, U. Chgo., 1992. Bar: Ill. 1992. With Sidley Austin Brown & Wood, Chgo., ptnr., 2000—. Mem.: ABA. Office: Sidley Austin Brown and Wood Bank One Plz 10 S Dearborn St Chicago IL 60603*

HARRIS, TERESA MARIA, visual artist; b. St. Louis, Dec. 20, 1957; d. Singleton Levi and Josie Bernice (Watkins) H. BFA, Washington U., St. Louis, 1975; MA, Fontbonne Coll., 1981; MFA, Pratt Inst., 1991. Cert. elem. and secondary sch. tchr., Mo. Art tchr. Christensted Bd. of Edn., St. Croix, V.I., 1975-76, St. Louis Bd. of Edn., 1976-87, 88-89; art tcht. Newark Mus./Rutgers U., 1995—96; prof. art N.J. City U., 1995—97, Passaic County Cmty. Coll., Paterson, NJ, 1996—2000, Katharine Gibbs Coll., 1999—2000, Jefferson Coll., Hillsboro, Mo., 2003—. Art tchr., cons. Jamaica Arts Ctr., 1992-95, Bronx Coun. on the Arts, 1992-94, Children's Arts Carnival, N.Y.C., 1991-92, Bklyn. Arts and Cultural Assn., Bklyn., 1990-91. One-woman shows include Sunshine Inn Restaurant, 1980, Vaughn Cultural Ctr., 1989, Teahouse Gallery at the N.Y. Open Ctr., N.Y.C., 1998; exhibited in group shows at Kimberly Gallery, 1976, Fontbonne Coll., 1981, U. Mo., 1982, Webster Coll., 1984, Florissant Valley Cmty. Coll., 1984, Ridge Street Gallery, 1991, L.I. City Artlofts, 1992, Citicorp Bldg., Cmty Showcase Gallery, 1992, Art in General, 1994, Serengeti Plains, 1999; contbr. articles to profl. jours. Individual artist grant N.Y. Dept. of Cultural Affairs, 1995; fellowship Nat. Endowment for the Humanities, 1980. Mem. Jamaica Co-op, Coll. Art Assn. Avocations: dance, reading, traveling, walking, researching and practicing natural living and eating methods. Home: 3543 Saint Henry Ln Saint Louis MO 63121-4135

HARRIS, VENITA VAN CASPEL, retired financial planner; b. Sweetwater, Okla. d. Leonard Rankin and Ella Belle (Jarnagin) Walker; m. Lyttleton T. Harris IV, Dec. 26, 1987. Student, Duke, 1944-46; BA, U. Colo., 1948, postgrad., 1949-51, N.Y. Inst. Fin., 1962. CFP. Stockbroker Rauscher Pierce & Co., Houston, 1962-65, A.G. Edwards & Sons, Houston, 1965-68; founder, pres., owner Van Caspel & Co., Inc., Houston, 1968—, Van Caspel Wealth Mgmt.; owner, mgr. Van Caspel Planning Svc., Van Caspel Advt. Agy.; sr. v.p. investments Raymond James and Assocs., 1987-95; ret., 1995. Moderator PBS TV show The Money Makers and Profiles of Success, 1980; 1st women mem. Pacific Stock Exchange. Author: Money Dynamics, 1978, Money Dynamics of the 1980's, 1980, The Power of Money Dynamics, Money Dynamics for the 1990's, 1988; editor: Money Dynamics Letter. Bd. dirs. Horatio Alger Assn., Robert Schuller Ministries; trustee Northwood U.; founding mem. Com. of 200. Recipient Matrix award Theta Sigma Phi, 1969, Horatio Alger award for Disting. Americans, 1982, Disting. Woman's medal, Northwood Univ., 1988, George Norlin award U. Colo. Alumni Assn., 1987. Mem. Internat. Assn. Fin. Planners, Inst. Cert. Fin. Planners, Phi Gamma Mu, Phi Beta Kappa. Methodist. Home: 4 Saddlewood Estates Dr Houston TX 77024-6841 Office: 6524 San Felipe St Ste 102 Houston TX 77057-2611

HARRIS, VICKI LEE, educational consultant; b. Indpls., Sept. 23, 1950; d. Carl Eugene and Mary Louise Ingels; 1 child, Andrea Kay Courtney. BS in Edn., Ball State U., 1972, MA in Edn., 1978. Lic. tchr. Ind., cert. total quality mgr. Quality Improvement Co., trainer for 4Mat learning style Excel Tng. Co. Statewide instrnl. specialist, regional program chairperson, indsl. trainer Ivy Tech. State Coll., Indpls., 1977—87; human resource specialist, instrnl. designer IN-Con divsn. Ball Corp., Muncie, Ind., 1991—92; statewide mgr. field ops. Green Thumb Program, Seymour, Ind., 1992—94; tchr. New Castle (Ind.) Cmty. Sch. Corp., 1995—; project developer/cons. Ind. Dept. Workforce Devel., Indpls., 1995—; project developer, cons. Ind. Dept. of Edn., Indpls., 2002—. Electronic portfolio project dir. Ind. Dept. of Workforce Devel., Indpls., 1995—2001; chmn. workforce assessment audit task force Henry County Econ. Devel., New Castle, 1998—2002. Author: (training package) Community Alliance Model (Telly, 2004); prodr.: (multimedia production) A Message for Educators - 1999 National Teacher of the Year (Telly, 2002, Axiom, 2003); composer: (multimedia documentary) A Multimedia Documentary Portfolio; dir.: (videotape production) Community Partnerships in Henry County, 1998; author: (electronic portfolio prototype, tutorial) Student Portfolio and Accreditation Reporting, 1997. Active Nat. Tchr. of Yr. Program, 1995—2004; facilitator East Ctrl. Collaborative Partnership, Ind., 1997—2003; vol. students with spl. needs I Can Work Program, Muncie, 1997—2004; student adv. Postsecondary Instns., Ind. Mem.: NAFE, ASTD, Ind. Staff Devel. Coun., Phi Delta Kappa Internat. Achievements include design of Community Alliance Model for use by communities meeting to address the needs of non-native speakers of English living and working within the United States; development of electronic portfolio prototype for individual and institutional reporting. Avocations: travel, cooking, reading. Office: Edn and Tng Cons PO Box 1187 Muncie IN 47308 Personal E-mail: harris_v_l@hotmail.com. E-mail: harris_v_l@hotmail.com.

HARRIS, VIRGINIA, religious organization administrator, publisher; m. G. Reed Harris; children: G. Richard, Donald Thomas, Steven Jeffrey. Postgrad., Mills Coll., 1964—66; BA in Polit. Sci. and Edn., Moorhead State U., 1967; C.S.B., Mass. Metaphys. Coll., 1982. Asst. to presdl. interpreter U.S. Dept. State, Washington, 1967-68; sec. sch. tchr. Fargo (N.D.) Pub. Schs., 1968-70; TV host, prodr. Pub. Broadcast Sys., Fargo, 1968-70; Christian Sci. practitioner, 1979—, Christian Sci. tchr., 1982—; Christian Sci. lectr., 1983-89. Bd. dirs. LWV, 1969-74; faculty mem. Healing & Spirituality Symposium Harvard Med. Sch. and Mind/Body Inst., Boston, 1995—; clk. The First Ch. of Christ Scientist, 1986-90; bd. dirs. The Christian Sci., 1990—, chmn. bd. dirs., 1992—; lectr., spkr. in field. Pub. The Writings of Mary Baker Eddy, 1992—; contbr. articles to profl. jours. Mem., treas., bd. dirs. Nat. Found. Women Legislators, Inc., Washington, 1994-2001; fellow George H. Gallup Internat. Inst., 1998-; chmn bd. trustees The Mary Baker Eddy Libr. for the Betterment of Humanity, 2000—, Dr.'s Coun. Harvard Divine Sch.'s women's studies religious progress, 2000— ; adv. bd. Drucker Found., 2001-; bd. overseers Boston Symphony Orch., 2003-. Mem. Coun. Women World Leaders Founders Fund Inaugural Cir., City Club Washington, Internat. Women's Forum (lectr., spkr., contbr. to profl. jours.). Avocations: skiing, reading, golf. Office: The First Ch of Christ Scientist 175 Huntington Ave # A253 Boston MA 02115-3117

HARRIS, ZELEMA M. academic administrator; b. Newton County, Tex., Jan. 12, 1940; d. James Robert and Gertrude Violet (Swearingen) Marshall; m. Manuel Holloway. BS, Prairie View A&M, 1961; MEd, U. Kans., 1972, EdD, 1976, U. Asst. dir. urban affairs U. Kans., Lawrence, 1970-72, asst. dir. Centennial Coll., 1970-72, dir. supportive edn. svcs., 1970-72; coord. curriculum evaluation Met. Community Coll., Kansas City, Mo., 1976-77, dir. curriculum evaluation, 1977-78, dir. edn. opportunity ctr., 1978-80, dir. dist. svcs., 1980; pres. Pioneer Community Coll., Kansas City, 1980-87, Pen Valley Community Coll., Kansas City, 1987-90, Parkland Coll., Champaign, Ill., 1990—. Co-author: Evaluation and Program Planning, 1978. Recipient Protestant award Kansas City Coun., 1987, Kansas City Spirit award Gillis Ctr. of Kansas City and Kansas City Star, 1987; named one of Women of Conscience, Panel of Am. Women, 1987. Mem. Nat. Inst. for Leadership Devel. Am. Assn. Women in Community Colls. (adv. bd.), Am. Assn. Community and Jr. Colls. (bd. dirs., Coun. on Black Am. Affairs), Black Women in Higher Edn., N. Cen. Assn. Colls. and Schs. (bd. dirs. N. Cen. region). Home: 7 Briar Hill Cir Champaign IL 61822-6137 Office: Parkland Coll Office of the President 2400 W Bradley Ave Champaign IL 61821-1806

HARRIS-OFFUTT, ROSALYN MARIE, counselor, consultant, mental health nurse, writer; b. Memphis; d. Roscoe Henry and Irene Elnora (Blake) Harris; 1 child, Christopher Joseph. RN, St. Joseph Cath. Sch. Nursing, Flint, Mich., 1965; student, Hurley Med. Ctr. Sch. of Anesthesia, 1970; BS in Wholistic Health Scis., Columbia-Pacific U., 1984, postgrad., 1985—. RN; cert. registered nurse in anesthesia; nat. bd. cert. addiction counselor; cert. psychiat. nursing Kalamazoo State Hosp.; lic. profl. counselor, N.C.; cert. detoxification acupuncturist; bd. cert. med.-legal nurse cons. Staff nurse anesthetist, clin. instr. Cleve. Clinic Found., 1981-82; pvt. practice psychiat. nursing and counseling; assoc. counselor human svcs., 1982-84; ind. contractor anesthesia Paul Scott & Assocs., Cleve., 1984, Via Triad Anesthesia Assocs., Thomasville, N.C., 1984-85; sec. Cons. Psychology Counseling, P.A., 1984-86; pvt. practice psychiat. nursing and counseling Greensboro, N.C., 1984-86; pvt. practice psychiat. nursing, counseling, psychotherapy UNA Psychol. Assocs., 1986—; staff cons. Charter Hills Psychiat. Hosp. in Addictive Disease, 1991—98. Nat. resource cons. Am. Assn. Nurse Anesthetists on Addictive Disease; cons. Ctr. for Substance Abuse Prevention, also advisor to assoc. and clin. med. dir. Ctr. Substance Abuse Prevention. Contbr. chpt. to book, also articles and columns in health field. Co-sponsor adolescent group Jack and Jills of Am., Inc., Bloomfield Hills, Mich., 1975; co-sponsor Youth of Unity Ctr., Clevelend Heights, Ohio, 1981-84; vol. chmn. hospitality Old Greensboro Preservation Soc., 1985; bd. dirs. Urban League, Pontiac, Mich., 1972; apptd. mem. gov's. coun. on alcohol and other drug abuse State of N.C., 1989—, gov's. coun. women's issues of addiction, 1991—; apptd. advisor to assoc. clin., med. dir. Ctr. for Substance Abuse Prevention, Dept. Health and Human Svcs. U.S., 1991—, nat. spkrs. bur., 1991—, cons.; apptd. legis. com., mental health study commn. on child and adolescent substance abuse State of N.C., 1992—; lay speaking min. United Meth. Ch.; mem. Triad United Meth. Native Am. Ch. Mission. Columbia-Pacific U. scholar, 1983. Fellow Soc. Prevention Nutritionists; mem. Am. Assn. Profl. Hypnotherapists (registered profl. hypnotherapists, adv. bd.), Am. Assn. Nurse Anesthetists (cert.), Nat. Alaska Native Am. Indian Nurses Assn., Assn. Med. Educators and Rsch. in Substance Abuse, Nat. Acupuncture Detoxification Assn., Am. Assn. Counseling and Devel., Assn. for Med. Edn. and Rsch. in Substance Abuse, Am. Assn. Clin. Hypnotists, Am. Assn. Wholistic Practitioners, Am. Acad. Experts Traumatic Stress, Am. Nurse Hypnotherapy Assn. (state pres. 1992-93), Am. Nurse Assn., Am. Holistic Nurses Assn. (charter mem.), Guilford Native Am. Assn., Negro Bus. and Profl. Women Inc. (v.p., parliamentarian 1961-83, 2001-03), Oakland County Coun. Black Nurses (v.p. 1970-74), Assn. Med. Educators (rschr. substance abuse, ad hoc com. mem. cultural diversity 1994—), Zeta Phi Beta (Nu Xi Zeta chpt. 2d anti-basilevs 1992-93, Beta Nu Zeta chpt. Greensboro). Republican. Avocations: music, nature, reading, egyptian history, metaphysics. Office: UNA Psychol Assocs and Prima Med-Legal Nurse Cons 620 S Elm St Ste 371 Greensboro NC 27406-1398 E-mail: rharrisoffutt@cs.com.

HARRISON, ANGELA EVE, manufacturing executive; b. Little Rock, Apr. 9, 1967; d. Stephen E. and Donie E. (Brown) H.; m. Petey King, Sept. 19, 1998; children: Haven Harrison King, Ashton Harrison King. BA in Psychology, U. Ark., 1989. Clin. specialist Nutri-Sys., Little Rock, 1990-91; sec., trea. Welsco, Inc., Maumelle, Ark., 1991-94, pres., CEO, 1994—. Co-chairperson Humane Soc., Pulaski County, Ark., 1996-98. Recipient Ark. Bus. Exec. Yr. Ark. Bus., 1997, named Top 100 Women Ark., 1996, 97, 98, 99, Top 500 Women Owned Cos. Working Women Mag., 1998, 99, 2000, 2001. Mem.: Internat. Oxygen Mfg. Assn. (bd. dirs. 1996—2000), Nat. Welding Supply Assn. (regional chmn. 1996—2000), Nat. Assn. Women Bus. Owners (Woman Bus. Owner of Yr., Ark. chpt. 1998), Young Pres.'s Assn. Avocation: golf. Office: Welsco Inc 9006 Crystal Hill Rd North Little Rock AR 72113-6693 E-mail: mail@welsco.com.

HARRISON, BETTY CAROLYN COOK, education educator, administrator; b. Cale, Ark., Jan. 11, 1939; d. Denver G. and Minnie (Haddox) Cook; m. David B. Harrison, Dec. 31, 1956; children: Jerry David, Phyllis Lynley. BSE, Henderson State Tchrs. Coll., Arkadelphia, Ark., 1961; MS, U. Ark., 1971; PhD, Tex. A&M U., 1975. Tchr. secondary schs., McCrory, Ark., 1962-64, Taylor, Ark., 1964069, Shongaloo, La., 1969-73, Minden, La., 1974-76, 77-80; adminstrv. intern La. Dept. Edn., 1974; cooperating tchr., supr. student tchrs. Grambling (La.) State U., 1974-76, La. Tech. U., Ruston, 1974-76, 78-80; asst. prof. vocat. edn. Va. Poly. Inst. and State U., Blacksburg, 1976-77; asst. prof. vocat. edn. Coll. Agr., La. State U., Baton Rouge, 1980-85, assoc. prof. Sch. Vocat. Edn., 1985-90, prov. vocat. edn., 1990—. Prof. career devel. specializing in instrnl. methodologies, edn. educator, sect. leader home econs. edn. La. State U., 1982-85, head dept. home econs. edn.and bus. edn., 1985-87, dir. La. Job Link Ctr., 1988-91; mem. La. State U. Grad. Coun., 1990-96, courses and curriculum sch. and coll., 1989-92. Contbr. articles to profl. jours. HEW fellow, 1973; grantee Future Homemakers Am., 1956, Coll. Acads., 1956, Ark. Edn. Assn., 1966-69, Internat. Paper Co., 1966-68, La. Dept. Edn., 1972, others. Mem. NEA (nat. assembly del.), ASTD (v.p. comm. 1991-92, sec. 1993-94), Am. Vocat. Assn., Nat. Assn. Vocat. Spl. Needs Pers., Am. Vocat. Edn. Rsch. Assn., Am. Home Econs. Assn., La Home Econs. Assn. (bd. dirs., pres.-elect), La. Vocat. Assn. (bd. dirs.), La. Assn. Vocat. Home Econs. Tchrs. (pres.), Nat. Assn. Vocat. Home Econs. Tchrs., Nat. Assn. Vocat. Home Econs. Tchr. Educators, (newsletter editor), Home Econs. Edn. Assn. (regional dir., nat. v.p., editor and chair publs. 1987-93), Family Rels. Coun. La. (edn. chmn. officer) Phi Delta Kappa, Delta Kappa Gamma (chpt. v.p., rsch. chair 1978-86), Gamma Sigma Delta (historian, sec., treas. 1984-93). Democrat. Baptist. Home: 2100 College Dr Apt 157 Baton Rouge LA 70808-1810 Office: La State U Sch Vocat Edn Baton Rouge LA 70803-0001 E-mail: bcharrison@worldnett.att.net

HARRISON, CAROL LOVE, fine art photographer; b. Washington, Mar. 4, 1950; d. Hunter Craycroft and Margaret Varina (Edwards) H.; m. Gregory Grady, Feb. 25, 1978; children: Olivia Love Harrison, Blake McGregor, Harrison Edwards. BS in Fgn. Svc., Georgetown U., 1973; MFA, U. Md., 1983. Guest lectr. art George Mason U., 1986, 87, Shephard Coll.,1987, 96, No. Va. C.C., 1986; participant creative program Fairfax County Coun. of Arts, 1990-92; participant artist workshop program Va. Mus. Fine Arts, Richmond, 1988-89. One-woman shows include Rizzoli Internat. Bookstore and Gallery, Washington, 1982, Arnold and Porter, Washington, 1983, Covington and Burling, Washington, 1983, Crowell and Moring, Washington, 1984, Nat. Strategy Info. Ctr., Washington, 1984, Swidler and Berlin, Washington, 1985, Reynolds Minor Gallery, Richmond, Va., 1987, Peninsula Fine Arts Ctr., Newport News, Va., 1989, Georgetown U., Washington, 1994; exhibited in group shows at Touchstone Gallery, 1999, Rockville Arts Place, 1999, Mus. Contemporary Art, Contemporary Mus., Balt., 1999—, Balt.'s Festival of the Arts, Rockville Arts Place, 1999, Photography Exhibit, 2001, Joan Kuyper Farver Art Gallery, Pella, Iowa, Art Gallery U. Md., Smithsonian Instn., Washington Women's Art Ctr., including Washington Project for Arts, 1981, Beijing Inst., 1985, Art Inst. Pitts., 1986, Kathleen Ewing Gallery, 1986-89, Mus. Contemporary Art, Washington, 1996, 98, 99, 2003, Dallas Mus. Art, 1997, Washington Arts Coun. Gallery, 1997, 98, 99, 2000, Snapshot, The Contemporary Mus., Balt., 1999—, Mus. Contemporary Art, Washington, 1998, 99, 2000, Aldrich Mus. Contemporary Art, Ridgefield, Conn., 2002, Arcadia U. Art Gallery, Glenside, Pa., 2002, Barrie Gallery Marymount U., 2003; represented in permanent collections at Corcoran Gallery Art, Washington, Va. Mus. Fine Arts, Richmond, Arnold and Porter, Williams Cos., Tulsa, Covington and Burling, United Va. Bank, Touchstone Gallery, 1999, Mus. of Contemporary Art, Washington, 1999-00, Artscape, Balt., 1999, U.S. Holocaust Meml. Mus., Am. Ctr. Polish Culture, Washington, Embassy of Poland, Washington, Nat. Gallery Art, Nat. Portrait Gallery, Addison Gallery Am. Art; pub. in Antietam Rev., Washington Rev., Photo Rev., Washingtonian, Profiles, Kalliope; Honorarium, Fla. Dept. Cultural Affairs, 1998; represented by Reynolds Gallery. Vol. Our Lady of Victory Sch., Washington, 1995—96, Westminster Sch., Annandale, Va., 1996—2003; mem. women's com. Nat. Symphony Orch., 1998—. Recipient honorarium Fla. Dept. Cultural Affairs, 1998, Cash award for black and white photography Westmoreland Art Nats., LaTrobe, Pa., 1998. Mem. Nat. Mus. Women in Arts (women's com. 1997—), No. Va. Fine Arts Assn. (artist mem.), Congl. Country Club, Langley Swim and Tennis Club. Episcopalian. Avocations: films, swimming. Home and Office: 666 Live Oak Dr Mc Lean VA 22101-1569 Personal E-mail: photoclh@aol.com.

HARRISON, CHRISTINE DELANE, company executive; b. Dearborn, Mich., July 22, 1947; d. Walter Frederick and Marguerite Elaine (Champagne) Hancock; m. Charles Richard Bashawaty, Aug. 31, 1968 (div. 1972); 1 child, Brett Charles; m. Andrew David Harrison, June 14, 1980; 1 child, Andrew David II. BS, Eastern Mich. U., 1969. Cert. early elem. tchr., Mich. Tchr. Westland Schs., Mich., 1969-71, Dept. Army, Ansbach, Germany, 1971-72; prin. sec. chemistry dept. U. Mich., Ann Arbor, 1973-78; word processing mgr. Great Copy Co., Ann Arbor, 1978-79; dir., v.p. Great Lakes Sch., Madison Heights, Mich., 1979-92; v.p. adminstrv. asst. Good Herbs, Inc., Troy, Mich., 1992—. Editor: Thorne's Guide to Herbal Extracts, 1992, A Practical Guide to Herbal Extracts, 1995-2002; mem. editl. bd. Herbal Extracts, 1984, Bull. Thermodynamics and Thermochemistry, 1973-78. Bd. dirs. Perry Nursery Sch., Ann Arbor, 1976-77. Recipient Prodn. award and Dedication award Los Feliz Apple Sch. Mem. Nat. Trust for Hist. Preservation, Greenpeace, Sierra Club. Avocations: reading, bicycling, aerobics, sailing. Office: Good Herbs Inc 1465 Combermere Dr Troy MI 48083-2745

HARRISON, ELZA STANLEY, medical association executive; b. Akron, Ohio, Apr. 10, 1938; d. Marshall Clayton and Elsie Helen Stanley; m. Ronald L. Davis, Feb. 4, 1961 (div. June 1979); children: Mark Davis, Lesley Davis; m. William Harrison II, May 29, 1989 (dec.); m. Michael Dunning, May 12, 2001. BA in English, U. Akron, 1963. Cert. assn. exec. Acting exec. dir., dir. pub. affairs, legis. rep. Med. & Chirurg. Facility, Balt., 1975-86; v.p. industry affairs Med. Mut. Liability Ins. Co., Hunt Valley, Md., 1986-87; exec. dir. Md. Dental Assn., Columbia, 1987—. Bd. dirs. Md. Found. Dentistry for Handicapped, Columbia, Dental Assn. Co., Columbia; mem. bd. visitors Nat. Mus. Dentistry, President Ctr. for Oral Health Studies. Mem. Am. Soc. Assn. Execs., Am. Soc. Constituent Dental Execs., Md. Soc. Assn. Execs. (pres. 1985-86). Democrat. Episcopalian. Office: Maryland Dental Assn 6410 Dobbin Rd Columbia MD 21045-5824 Office Phone: 410-964-2880. E-mail: elza@msda.com.

HARRISON, ESTHER M. elementary school educator, state representative; b. Columbus, Miss. Attended, Alcorn State U., Miss. State U. for Women. Tchr. Miss. State Schs.; adminstr. Minority Bus., Jackson, Miss.; rep. Ho. of Reps., Jackson, Miss., 2000—. Mem. Constitution, Edn., Juvenile Justice, Labor and Mil. Affairs coms. Ho. Reps., Jackson, Miss., 2000—. Mem.: Helping Hands, Lowndes County League of Voteers, NAACP (life), Zeta Phi Beta. Democrat. African Meth. Episcopalian. Home: 914 S 7th St Columbus MS 39701 Office: PO Box 1018 Jackson MS 39215-1018

HARRISON, GAIL G. public health educator; M in Nutritional Scis., Cornell U.; PhD in Biol. Anthropology, U. Ariz. Mem. faculty Coll. Medicine, founding dir. program in internat. health, prof. family and cmty. medicine U. Ariz., 1976—92; chair, prof. dept. cmty. health scis. UCLA Sch. Pub. Health; asst. program dir. program for health and at-risk populations UCLA/Jonsson Comprehensive Cancer Ctr. Mem. Food and Nutrition Bd., Nat. Acad. Scis./Inst. Medicine; cons. WHO, UNICEF. Mem.: Inst. Medicine. Office: UCLA Ctr for Health Policy Rsch 10911 Weyburn Ave Ste 300 Los Angeles CA 90024 Business E-Mail: gailh@ucla.edu.

HARRISON, HATTIE N. state senator; b. Lancaster, S.C., Feb. 11, 1928; d. Albert and Ester (Cunningham) Stewart; m. Robert Harrison, 1943; children: Robert, Philip. Student, J.C. Smith U., 1967, Antioch Coll. Tchr.; mem. Md. Ho. of Dels., Annapolis, 1973—, mem. legis. policy and econ. matters coms., mem. joint com. on protocol, mem. joint subcom. on unemployment ins. taxation/charging, chmn. rules and exec nominations com.; mem. Md. Senate, Annapolis. Mem. Md. State Dem. Ctrl. Com., 1970—; chairwoman 2d Dist. Dem. Ctrl. Com. Delegation; panelist Md. Conf. Social Welfare and Md. Commn. Higher Edn., 1973; apptd. to Md. Commn. on Status of Women, 1974; dir. Dunbar Neighborhood Facility, Balt. City Schs.; chairwoman Cmty. Sch. Adv. Coun., 1972; cons. Mott Found., Flint, Mich.; mem. Women's Com. for United Fund, Citizens for Fair Housing, Dunbar Cmty. Sch. Coun., Md. 4-C Com. on Day Care. Named Woman of the Yr., Alpha Zeta, 1974. Mem. NAACP, Nat. Lab. for Advancement Edn. Home: 3224 Belair Rd Baltimore MD 21213-1228 Office: Md Senate State Capital Bldg Annapolis MD 21401

HARRISON, HOLLY A. lawyer; b. 1958; BA, U. Denver, 1981; JD, Boston U., 1984. Bar: Mass. 1984, Ill. 1985. Law clk. to Hon. Raymond J. Pettine, U.S. Dist. Judge Dist. R.I., 1984—85; with Sidley Austin Brown & Wood, Chgo., 1985—, ptnr., 1992—. Office: Sidley Austin Brown and Wood Bank One Plz 10 S Dearborn St Chicago IL 60603*

HARRISON, JUDITH ANNE, human resources executive; b. N.Y.C., Aug. 15, 1954; d. William Russell and Lucille Kathlene Harrison; m. Brian Taylor Jarvis, Sept. 18, 1993. BA, CCNY, 1976. Bus. mgr. creative svcs. Burson-Marsteller, N.Y.C., 1976-80; creative ops. mgr. mktg. and comm. Arthur Young, N.Y.C., 1981-84; dir. collateral svcs. advt. and promotion CBS, N.Y.C., 1984-86; dir. mktg. comm. Media Gen., N.Y.C., 1986-87; pres. J.A. Harrison Comm., N.Y.C., 1988-92; v.p. The Fry Group, N.Y.C., 1992-96; v.p. human resources Ruder Finn, N.Y.C., 1997-99, s.r. v.p., 1999; chairwoman HR Roundtable/Coun. of Pub. Rels. Firms, 2000—. Mem.: World Studio Found. (bd. dirs. 1998—), Am. Women in Radio and TV (bd. dirs. N.Y. chpt. 1990—91), Soc. Human Resource Mgmt., Pub. Rels. Soc. Am., Women in Comms. Office: Ruder Finn 301 E 57th St New York NY 10022-2900

HARRISON, LOIS SMITH, hospital executive, educator; b. Frederick, Md., May 13, 1924; d. Richard Paul and Henrietta Foust (Menges) Smith; m. Richard Lee Harrison, June 23, 1951; children: Elizabeth Lee Boyce, Margaret Louise Wade, Richard Paul. BA, Hood Coll., 1945, MA, 1993, Columbia U.; LHD (hon.), Hood Coll., 1993. Counselor CCNY, 1945-46; founding adminstr., counselor, instr. psychology and sociology Hagerstown (Md.) Jr. Coll., 1946-51, registrar, 1946-51, 53-54, instr. psychology and orienta, 1954-56; registrar, instr. psychology Balt. Jr. Coll., 1951-54; bus. mgr., acct. for pvt. med. practice Hagerstown, 1953-2000; trustee Washington County Hosp., Hagerstown, 1975-97, chmn. bd., 1986-88, 95—; mem. bd. Washington County Health Sys. Inc., 1997—. Chmn. Home Fed. Savs. Bank, Hagerstown, 1997-99; chmn. acute care Health Sys. Bd., 1997—; chmn. bd. dirs. Home Fed. Savs. Bank, 1998-2000, emeritus, 2001—; spkr. ednl. panels, convs. hosp. panels and seminars. Author: The Church Woman, 1960-65. Trustee Hood Coll., Frederick, 1972—, chmn. bd., 1979-95; mem. Md. Gov.'s Commn. to Study Structure and Ednl. Devel. Commn., 1971-75; pres. Washington County Coun. Ch. Women, 1970-72; appointee Econ. Devel. Commn., County Impact Study Commn. Bd.; bd. dirs. Md. Hosp. Assn., 1988-98, Md. Chs. United, 1975—; chmn. bd. dirs. Md. Hosp. Edn. Inst., 1978-98; mem. Christ's Reformed Ch., 1935—; pres. Ch. Consistory; chmn. Chesapeake Healthcare Forum, 1995-97; chmn. Centennial Celebration, Washington County Hosp. Bd. Recipient Alumnae Achievement award Hood Coll., 1975, Washington County Woman of Yr. award, AAUW, 1984, Md. Woman of Yr. award, 1984, Md. Woman of Yr. award Francis Scott Key Commn. for Md.'s 350th Anniversary, 1984; named one of top 10 women Tri-State area, Herald-Mail Tri-State newspaper, 1990, Zonta Internat. Woman of Yr., 1994, Outstanding Woman of the Yr., Woman At the Table award, 2002. Mem. Hagerstown C. of C. Republican. Home: 12835 Fountain Head Rd Hagerstown MD 21742-2748 Office: Washington Cty Hosp Off Chmn Bd Hagerstown MD 21740 E-mail: lorichco@aol.com.

HARRISON, MARJORIE FREEMAN, secondary education educator, librarian; b. Yonkers, N.Y., Dec. 26, 1952; d. Burton Morton and Sandra (Firestone) Freeman; m. Fred Harrison, Mar. 31, 1974. Student, U. Rochester, 1970-72; BA cum laude, Barnard Coll., Columbia U., 1974; MLS, L.I. U., Greenvale, N.Y., 1975; postgrad., Columbia U., 1989—, MPhil, 1994, student, 2003—. Cert. tchr. secondary social studies, libr. media specialist, N.Y. Tchr., librarian Portledge Sch., Locust Valley, N.Y., 1975-77; tchr. history various L.I. high schs., 1977-82; tchr., libr. media specialist Lawrence High Sch., Cedarhurst, N.Y., 1982—. Contbr. chpts. in books and articles to mags. and newspapers. Vice chair N.Y. Dem. Com., N.Y.C. and Albany, 1982-94; mem. del. selection com. N.Y. State Dem. Com., N.Y.C., 1987, 91; bd. dirs. Citizen Action in N.Y., 1990—94; mem. Gov. Cuomo's Fact-Finding Panel on the Shoreham Nuclear Power Plant, 1983-84; chair L.I. Citizens in Action, 1978—; convenor L.I. Pub. Power Project, chair, 1980-88; mem. L.I. Studies Coun.; bd. dirs. L.I. Progressive Coalition, 1979-88. Named Citizen Activist of Month, Ralph Nader's Pub. Citizen, 1984; recipient Leadership award L.I. Progressive Coalition, 1987, others. Mem. N.Y. Hist. Soc., Lawrence Tchrs. Assn. (bldg. rep., press officer, local polit. action dir.), N.Y. State United Tchrs./Am. Fedn. Tchrs. (union del. 1988—92, mem. com., chmn. adv. coun. Nassau sch. libr. sys., 1997-2000), N.Y. Civil Liberties Union (mem. bd. Nassau chpt). Avocations: walking on long island beaches, travel, reading, community involvement, writing. Home: 62 Elinore Ave Merrick NY 11566-4214 Office Phone: 516-295-8015. E-mail: famh@optonline.net.

HARRISON, MONIKA EDWARDS, business development executive; b. Waiblingen, Federal Republic of Germany, July 31, 1949; came to U.S., 1957; d. Donnie Everette and Irmgard E. BA, Fla. State U., 1970, MS, 1977. Cabinet aide State Treas. Fla., Tallahassee, 1971-73; advisor to Pres. Fla. Senate, Tallahassee, 1973-74; legis. analyst U.S. Dept. Agr., Washington, 1975-76; dir. policy and planning U.S. Dept. Edn., Washington, 1976-85; dep. dir. Inst. Mus. Svcs., Washington, 1985-86; assoc. adminstr. U.S. SBA, Washington, 1986-89; assoc. dir. bus. devel. COLSA, Inc., Arlington, Va., 1989-92; assoc. adminstr. for small bus. devel. ctrs. U.S. SBA, Washington, 1992-93, assoc. adminstr. for bus. initiatives, 1993-2000, dep. ADA for enterpreneurial devel., 2000—02, chief human capital officer, 2002—. Commr. Cen. European Small Bus. Enterprise Devel. Commn., 1992-95; lectr. George Mason U., Fairfax, Va., 1985-86. Recipient Sr. Exec. Svc. award U.S. SBA, 1992-95, Presdl. Meritorius Exec. award, 2000. Office: US SBA 409 3rd St SW Washington DC 20024-3212

HARRISON, PATRICIA DE STACY, federal agency administrator; b. N.Y.C. m. Emmett Bruce Harrison; 3 children. BA, Am. U., 1968; MA, George Mason U. V.p. Holly Realty Co., Arlington, Va., 1965-69; co-founder, ptnr. E. Bruce Harrison Co., Washington, 1973—96; former pres. AEF/Harrison Internat., Washington; asst. sec. for educ. and cult. affairs U.S. Dept. State, Washington, 2001—. Keynote spkr. U.S. Dept. Labor del. to Israel and Greece, Indsl. Devel. Authority of Ireland Conf./Women Execs. in Mgmt., U.S. Info. Agy./WorldNET program for entrepreneurs via satellite to 7 countries, Export Expo '90, Seattle, Nat. Govs. Conf., U.S. SBA Fin. Mgmt. Conf. in 9 states, mgmt. and tng. program for women entrepreneurs Budapest, Hungary (Alliance Decade for Democracy series); guest lect. Thomas Colloquium on Free Enterprise, 1989; trustee Guest Svcs., Inc.; mem. adv. coun. Avon Products, Inc. Author: Inside and Out: The Story of a Hostage, 1981, (with Margaret Mason, editor) The Washington Post Pocket Style Plus, 1983-84, America's New Women Entrepreneurs, 1986. Bd. dirs. Med. Coll. Pa. Recipient Librs.' and Tchrs.' award for play produced at Kennedy Ctr., 1980, Del. award Insieme per La Pace, Rome, 1988, Disting. Woman award Northwood Inst., 1991; named Washington Woman of Yr., Washington Women Mag., 1985, Entrepreneur of Yr., Washington, Arthur Young Co. and Venture mag., 1988, Women of Enterprise award. Mem. Nat. Women's Econ. Alliance Found., Pres.'s Export Coun., SBA Nat. Adv. Coun. (co-chmn., exec. com.), SBA Women's Network for Entrepreneurial Tng. (adv. coun.), Nat. Coal Coun. (exec. com.), Women in Internat. Trade, Nat. Fedn. Press Women (ex-officio, communication award 1979, bus. communicator of yr. 1988), Capital Press Women (ex-officio, named bus communicator of yr. 1988, journalist award for non-fiction 1988), Pub. Rels. Soc. Am. (counsellors acad.), Internat. Pub. Rels. Assn. Office: US Dept State Educ & Cult Affairs Bureau 2201 C St NW Washington DC 20520

HARRISON, ROSLYN SIMAN, lawyer; b. Phila., Mar. 6, 1935; d. Max and Stella (Shapiro) Siman; m. Saul E. Harrison, June 12, 1955 (div. Mar. 1990); children: Dana Lynn, Julia Anne, Michael E. BA summa cum laude, Bryn Mawr Coll., 1956; LLB with honors, Rutgers U., Newark, 1977. Bar: N.J. 1977, U.S. Dist. Ct. N.J. 1977, U.S. Ct. Appeals (3rd cir.) 1981, N.Y. 1985, U.S. Dist. Ct. (ea. dist.) N.Y. 1985, U.S. Dist. Ct. (so. dist.) N.Y. 1987, U.S. Supreme Ct. 1987, U.S. Dist. Ct. (ea. dist.) Pa. 1988, U.S. Ct. Appeals (fed. cir.) 1994. Tchr. history Longmeadow (Mass.) High Sch., 1957-59; instr. polit. sci. Webster Coll., Webster Groves, Mo., 1964-66; assoc. McCarter & English, LLP, Newark, 1977-85, ptnr., 1986-2000, of counsel, 2000—. Social Sci. Rsch. Coun. grantee, 1955. Mem. ABA, N.Y. State Bar Assn., Assn. Fed. Bar State of N.J., N.J. Bar Assn. (mem. curriculum adv. com. Inst. for Continuing Legal Edn. 1990-96, chmn. N.J. bar intellectual property law sect. 1993-95), N.J. Intellectual Property Law Assn. (chmn. copyright com. 1993, chmn. trademark com. 1994-95), Internat. Trademark Assn. (internat. com., meetings com., ADR com. panel of neutrals), Am. Arbitration Assn., John J. Gibbons Am. Inn. of Ct. (mem. com. 1993—). Office: 4 Gateway Ctr 100 Mulberry St Newark NJ 07102-4056 E-mail: rharrison@mccarter.com.

HARRISON, SARAH K. music educator; b. Goleta, Calif., May 4, 1978; d. Donald Carl Branton and Constance Branton O'Connor; m. Keith Harrison, Dec. 21, 2003. MusB in Instrumental Edn., St. Olaf Coll., Northfield, Minn., 2000; MusB in Vocal Edn., St. Olaf Coll., 2000. Lic. tchr. K-12 Minn., Colo. Orch. tchr. Blaine H.S., Minn., 2001; choir tchr. Silver Creek Mid. Sch./H.S., Longmont, Colo., 2001—; music minister Westview Presbyn. Ch., Longmont, 2002—. Mem. Water On Mars A Capella Quartet, Boulder, Colo., 2002—. Mem.: Music Educators Nat. Conf., Am.. Choral Dirs. Assn. Avocations: hiking, rollerblading. Office: Silver Creek Middle Sch/High Sch 4901 Nelson Rd Longmont CO 80503

HARRISON, STEPHANIE A. language educator, director; b. Norman, Okla., Feb. 21, 1968; d. James L. Harrison and Linda K. Miskow. BA in English, U. Ga., 1989, MEd, 1991, EdS, 1997. Nat. Bd. cert. tchr. 2003. Tchr. English Madison County H.S., Danielsville, Ga., 1991—2001, South Forsyth H.S., Cumming, Ga., 2001—. Author (website): Journey to Japan, 2000. Alumni coord. Friends of Fulbright Meml. Fund, 2002—03. Mem.: NSDC, ASCD, Ga. Coun. Tchrs. English, Nat. Coun. Tchrs. English. Home: 165 Galecrest Dr Alpharetta GA 30004*

HARRISON, SUE ANN MCHANEY, writer; b. Lansing, Mich., Aug. 29, 1950; d. Charles Robert and Patricia Ann (Sawyer) McHaney; m. Neil Douglas Harrison Sr., Aug. 22, 1969; children: Koral(dec.), Neil Jr., Krystal. BA, Lake Superior State U., 1971. Author: Mother Earth Father Sky, 1990 (Best Book for Young Adults award Am. Libr. Assn., 1991), Cry of the Wind, 1998, Call Down the Stars, 2001. Methodist.

HARRISON, (HILDE), artist; b. Wallduern, Baden, Germany, Mar. 16, 1936; came to U.S., 1953; d. Heinz Lennartz and Hilde Lennartz-Klein; m. Charles E. Harrison Jr., Jan. 31, 1959; children: Charles, Marianne, Andrea, Pete, Bianca. Assoc. BS, Lord Fairfax Coll., 1989; BFA, Shepherd Coll., 1994; MA, NYU, Venice, 2001. Tchr. Pavan, Winchester, Va., 1998; pvt. lessons Front Royal, Va., 1999—; lectr. Frederick County Sch. Sys., Va., 1999—. Lectr. Culpeper (Va.) Art League, Manasas (Va.) Art League, Lurray (Va.) Art League. One-woman shows include Blue Ridge Arts Coun., Front Royal, 1984, Wallduern, Germany, 1992. Pres. Assn. for Children with Learning Disability, West Chester, Pa., 1972; founder, pres. Warren County Assn. for Children with Learning Disability, Front Royal, 1975; chair Warren County Sch. Bd. Spl. Edn., Front Royal, 1980, Vacation Bible Sch., Front Royal. Recipient Corning Glass award, 1980, Wheat Security award, 1984, 1st pl. Regional Show, Blue Ridge Arts Gallery, 2002, 2d pl., 2003. Mem. Women Arts, Va. Watercolor Assn., Blud Ridge Arts Coun. (docent), Shenandoah Valley Art Assn., Shenandoah Arts Coun. Avocations: reading, hiking, cooking, swimming, crafts. Home: 381 Windy Ridge Rd Front Royal VA 22630-7207

HARRISON-BRIDGEMAN, ANN MARIE, claims adjuster; b. St. Louis, Aug. 11, 1942; d. James W. and G. Marie Harrison; m. Loren JC Bridgeman, Apr. 10, 1961 (div. Feb. 1979); children: Michael, Mitchell, Michelle. AA, Belleville (Ill.) Area Coll., 1970; AS, San Antonio Coll., 1979; BS, S.W. Tex. State U., San Marcos, 1984, MS, 1999; postgrad., Okla. U., Norman, 1999—. Lic. sr. claims law assoc. Asst. chief acct. St. Mary's U., San Antonio, 1977-80; instr. acctg. and computers Reedley (Calif.) Jr. Coll., ABC Bus. Coll., Fresno, Calif., 1985; asst. to head acct. Hanford (Calif.) Cmty. Hosp., 1985-86; claims rep. acctg. USAA Ins. Co., San Antonio, 1980-85, policy svc. rep., 1987-99, 1980-82, acctg. tech., 1982-85, claims adjuster, 1987-96, total loss/salvage adjuster San Antonio & Okla. City, 1996-99; sr. total loss/slavage rep. U.S. Automobile Assn. Ins. Co., Oklahoma City, 1999—. Vol Olympic Games, 1993, others, 1990-96. With USN, 1960-62. Mem. AAUW, Smithsonian Instn., Nat. Geog. Soc., Am. Assn. Ret. Persons, Phi Theta Kappa. Roman Catholic. Office: USAA 212 S Quadrum Dr Oklahoma City OK 73108-1114

HARRY, ROBBIN NICOL, music educator; d. Asa Ray and Virginia Nadine Shaner; m. Kevin Edward Harry, June 12, 1993; children: Madison Nicol, Josiah Shane. BA in Music, Jacksonville (Ala.) State U., 1994, MusM in Edn., 1995. Dir. of bands Coosa Christian HS, Gadsden, Ala., 1996—98, White Plains HS, Anniston, Ala., 1998—. Music appreciation instr. Ayers State Tech. Coll., Anniston, Ala., 2000—02. Mem.: Ala. Edn. Assn., Calhoun County Band Directors Assn., Ala. Bandmasters Assn., Ala. Music Educators Assn., Music Educators Nat. Conf., Omicron Delta Kappa, Sigma Alpha Iota. Home: 1501 Kelsey Circle Jacksonville AL 36265 Office: White Plains High Sch 250 White Plains Rd Anniston AL 36207

HARRYMAN, KATHLEEN A. board administrator; b. Balt., Feb. 12, 1950; d. Michael A. and Catherine A. (White) Wagner; m. Steven L. Fader, Sept. 13, 1970 (div. Jan. 1976); m. Michael Andrew Harryman, July 17, 1981; 1 child, Tyler Andrew. Clk. typist Md. State Hwy. Adminstrn., 1968-71, stenographer, 1971-72, office sec., 1972-73, office sec. for met. dist./utility engr., 1973-76, exec. sec. for met. dist. engr., 1976-84, asst. MIS coord., computer divsn. Balt., 1984-90; asst. exec. dir. Md. State Bds. Barbers and Cosmetologists, Balt., 1990-92, adminstr., 1992—. Mem. task force on exam. process Md. Higher Edn. Commn., Annapolis; mem. cosmetology program adv. bd. Md. Divsn. Rehab. Svcs., Balt., 1992—. Chair clerical study com. Md. Classified Employees Assn., Balt., 1980; rep. Nat. Interstate Coun. Cosmetology. Avocations: crafts, writing poetry and children's stories. Office: Md State Bd Barbers and Cosmetologists 500 N Calvert St Baltimore MD 21202-3651 Home: 1707 Edgewood Rd Apt BT Baltimore MD 21234-5000

HARRYMAN, RHONDA L. education educator; b. Perry, Okla., Apr. 1, 1954; d. Otis Issac Jr. and Jeanette Roberta (Creacy) Shelley; m. Gilbert Wayne Harryman, Mar. 19, 1978. BS in Edn. cum laude, U. Ctrl. Okla., 1975, M in Spl. Edn., 1979; postgrad., Okla. State U., 1992—. Cert. learning disabilities, mentally handicapped, physically handicapped, emotional disturbance, elem. sch. adminstrs., Okla. Asst. workshop coord. for trainable mentally handicapped, physically handicapped Edmond (Okla.) ARC, 1974-76; instr. educable mentally handicapped, physically handicapped, emotionally disabled Edmond Pub. Schs., 1976-77, instr. spl. edn., emotionally disabled, educable mentally handicapped, physically handicapped, visually and hearing impaired, 1977-91; univ. coord., supr. practicums, instr. spl. edn. U. Ctrl. Okla., Edmond, 1992—. Edn. advisor tchrs. undrepresented populations in Shawnee, Okla. Three Feathers Assn., Norman, Okla. 1983; pvt. teaching, parent counseling learning disabilities, 1982-87; instr. spl. edn. Okla. Christian U., 1992—, mem. tchr. edn. adv. coun.; co-moderator New Eng. Joint Conf. Specific Learning Disabilities, Boston, 1991; edn. rep. Okla. Joint Conf. Juvenile Justice; edn. del. Okla. Japan-Am. Grassroots Coun., Tokyo, 1991; conducted workshops, presented insvcs., speaker in field. Editorial rev. bd. Teaching Resources, Dayton, Ohio. Counselor Edmond Youth Advocacy Bd.; mem. Gov.'s Round Table on Edn. and Bus., Edmond Juvenile Crime Commn.; sponsor Ala-Teen, Boys Ranch Town. Named Okla. Tchr. of Yr. by Okla. State Dept. Edn., 1992. Mem. Orton Dyslexia Soc., Coun. Exceptional Child, Kappa Delta Pi. Home: 3816 Deason Dr Edmond OK 73013-7742 Office: U Ctrl Okla Dept Spl Svcs 100 N University Dr Edmond OK 73034-5207

HARSANYI, JANICE, soprano, educator; b. Arlington, Mass., July 15, 1929; d. Edward and Thelma (Jacobs) Morris; m. Nicholas Harsanyi, Apr. 19, 1952; 1 son, Peter Michael. BMus, Westminster Choir Coll., 1951; postgrad., Phila. Acad. Vocal Arts, 1952-54. Voice tchr. Westminster Choir Coll., Princeton, N.J., 1951-63, chmn. voice dept., 1963-65; lectr. music Princeton Theol. Sem., 1956-63; voice tchr. summer sessions U. Mich., 1965-70; artist-in-residence Interlochen Arts Acad., 1967-70; voice tchr. N.C. Sch. Arts, Winston-Salem, 1971-78; music faculty Salem Coll., 1973-76; condr. voice master classes, choral clinics various colls., 1954—; prof. voice Fla. State U., Tallahassee, 1978—, chmn. dept., 1979-83. Concert singer, 1954—, debut, Phila. Orch., 1958; appearances with, Am., Detroit, Houston, Minn., Nat., Symphony of Air orchs., Bach Aria Group, 1967-68, maj. music festivals, U.S., 1960— ; toured with, Piedmont Chamber Orch., 1971-78, concerts and recitals, in major U.S. cities, also in Belgium, Eng., Ger., Italy, Switzerland and Sweden; rec. artist, Columbia, Decca, CRI records. Mem. Nat. Assn. Tchrs. Singing, Music Tchrs. Nat. Assn., Coll. Music Soc., Riemenschneider Bach Inst., Sigma Alpha Iota, Pi Kappa Lambda. Home: 2116 Trescott Dr Tallahassee FL 32308-0732 Office: Florida State Univ Sch Music Tallahassee FL 32306

HARSDORF, SHEILA ELOISE, state legislator, farmer; b. St. Paul, July 25, 1956; d. Ervin Albert and Eloise Vivian (Sodergren) H.; m. Vernon Clark Bailey, Nov. 18, 1989. BS in Animal Sci., U. Minn., 1978; grad., Wis. Rural Leadership Program, 1986. Loan officer Prodn. Credit Assn. River Falls, Wis., 1978-80; dairy farmer, Beldenville, Wis., 1980-88; mem. Wis. Assembly from 30th dist., Madison, 1988-98, Wis. Senate from 10th dist., Madison, 2001—. Part-time dairy farmer; mem. adv. coun. for small bus., agrl. and labor Fed. Res. Bank Minn., Mpls., 1988; mem. Wis. Agrl. Stblzn. and Conservation svc. Com., 1987-88. Mem., chairwoman Pierce County Dairy Promotion Com., 1986; mem. Congressman's Adv. Coun. on Agr., 1988—, First Covenant Ch., River Falls. Mem. Wis. Farm Bur. (co-treas. 1982-85, Discussion Meet winner 1986), Wis. Holstein Assn., Dairy Shrine. Republican. Home: N6627 County Rd E River Falls WI 54022-4036

HART, ANN WEAVER, educational administration educator; b. Salt Lake City, Nov. 6, 1948; d. Ted Lionel and Sylvia (Moray) Weaver; m. Randy Bret Hart, Sept. 12, 1968; children: Kimberly, Liza, Emily, Allyson. BS in History, U. Utah, 1970, MA in History, 1981, PhD in Ednl. Adminstrn., 1983. Tchr. pub. schs., Salt Lake City, 1970-73, 80-81; jr. high sch. prin. Provo (Utah) Pub. Schs., 1983-84; prof. ednl. adminstrn. U. Utah, Salt Lake City, 1984—98, assoc. dean Grad. Sch. Edn., 1991-93, dean Grad. Sch., 1993—98; provost, v.p. acad. affairs Claremont Grad. U., Calif., 1998—2002; pres. U. N.H., Durham, 2002—. Cons. various sch. dists., 1983—, regional ednl. labs., 1986—; bd. dirs. Citizens Bank N.H. Author: Principal Succession: Establishing Leadership in Schools, 1993, The Principalship, 1996, Designing and Conducting Research, 1996; editor: Ednl. Adminstrn. Quar., 1990-92; contbr. articles to profl. jours. Grantee U. Utah, State of Utah, U.S. Dept. Edn. Mem. Am. Ednl. Rsch. Assn., Am. Coun. on Edn., Phi Beta Kappa, Phi Kappa Phi. Avocations: skiing, backpacking, hiking, kayaking, bicycling. Office: Univ of New Hampshire Pres Office 201 Thompson Hall Durham NH 03824

HART, BRENDA REBECCA, retired gifted and talented educator; b. West Point, Ga., Aug. 29, 1941; d. Howard William Godfrey, Sarah Will Clegg; m. William Samuel Hart, Mar. 26, 1961 (dec. Oct. 1971); 1 child, Keith Samuel. BA in Social Studies, La Grange Coll., 1977, MEd in History, 1979. Tchr. gifted and talented State Dept. Edn., Atlanta, 1998—2003, ret., 2003. Collector data State Dept. Edn., Atlanta, 1985—, advance placement, 1998—. Home: 1702 Rosemont Ave West Point GA 31823 E-mail: KeithKeishart@yahoo.com.

HART, ELIZABETH ANN, foundation administrator; b. Moulton, Ala., Sept. 14, 1942; d. Maburn L. Bertie Hale and Julia Mae Evans; m. Bruce Burleson Hart, Dec. 19, 1964; 1 child, Alexandra Natasha Burleson Hart. Diploma in Nursing, Brigham & Women's Hosp., Boston, 1963; BA in Psychology and English, George Washington U., Washington, 1971; postgrad. in business, Le Tourneau U., Longview, Tex., 1999—. RN, N.Y. Co-therapist Psychiatric Inst., Washington, 1969—72; staff nurse NIMH, Bethesda, Md., 1966—67; instr. biology Vernon Ct. Jr. Coll., Newport, RI, 1965—66; chmn., CEO Susan G. Komen Breast Cancer Found., Dallas, 1994—95; pres., CEO Hart Internat., Dallas, 1995—, Easter Seals Rehab. Svcs., Dallas, 1999—, Easter Seals Greater Dallas, 2002. Instr. biology and gen. sci. Miramar Sch. Girls, Newport, R.I., 1965-66; cons. Nat. Cancer Inst., Bethesda, 1993—, Ctr. Non-Profit Mgmt., Dallas, 1995—, Cancer Cube, 1996—, Dept. Defense, Washington, 1997-99; cons. U.S. Army Breast Cancer Rsch. Program, 1993-97, consumer evaluation subcom., writing group, 1994, exec. com. integration panel, 1994-95, exec. com. liaison subcom., 1995-96; adv. coun. sch. nursing U. Tex., Austin, 1994-99; patient adv. com. NSABP/BCPT, 1995, subcom. clin. ctr. performance evaluation, 1995; bd. dirs. Nat. Cancer Policy Bd., Bethesda, 1997-99; data safety and monitoring com.. Internat. Breast MRI Consortium. Exec. prodr. (film) Women's Lives Dialogues on Breast Cancer, 1996; prodr. (video) Building for the Future, 2001. Pres. Women's Guild United Cerebral Palsy, 1985, Presbyn. Women, 1994-99; active Nat. Plan on Breast Cancer, Washington, 1995-2000; v.p. devel. Yellow Rose Found., 1996, v.p. cmty. outreach, 1997, Dallas Action Symphony Orch. League, Friends of Timberlawn. Recipient Vol. of Yr. award United Cerebral Palsy Assn. Met. Dallas, 1983, 101% Vol. award, 1983. Mem. Dallas-Ft. Worth Internat. Soc. Republican. Avocations: music, reading, mountain climbing, painting. Home: 9051 Oak Path Ln Dallas TX 75243 Office: Easter Seals Rehab Svcs 4443 N Josey Ln Carrollton TX 75010 E-mail: hart.elizabeth@worldnet.att.net., ehart@easterseals.com.

HART, KAREN ANN, advertising executive; b. Olean, N.Y., July 11, 1943; d. John Eugene and Lillian Lila (Gardner) H. BSN, D'Youville Coll., Buffalo, 1965. RN, Ohio, N.Y., Calif. Staff nurse, head nurse, supr. Montefiore Med. Ctr., Bronx, N.Y., 1965-77; nurse recruiter L.A. New Hosp., 1978-79, Midway Hosp., L.A., 1979-80; dir. nurse recruitment Akron (Ohio) City Hosp., 1980-87; exec. dir. Nat. Assn. Health Care Recruitment, Akron, 1987-96; sr. v.p. health care divsn. Bernard Hodes Group, N.Y.C., 1996—. Contbr. articles to profl. jours. Recipient Women in Comm. award Women Aware Program, 1986. Mem. Nat. Assn. Health Care Recruitment (past officer, Disting. Mem. award 1986, 87), Northeastern Ohio Assn. Health Care Recruitment (past officer), Sigma Theta Tau. Democrat. Roman Catholic. Avocations: traveling, writing, reading, swimming. Home: 201 N Hawkins Ave Akron OH 44313-6425 Office: 220 E 42nd St New York NY 10017 E-mail: khart@ny.hodes.com.

HART, KATHERINE MILLER, college dean; b. Hinsdale, Ill., Jan. 31, 1943; d. Donald William and Katherine (Hiatt) H. BA, DePauw U., 1965; MPH, U. Ill., 1976. Mem. staff 1st Nat. Bank Chgo., 1965-68; dir. phys. placement svcs. AMA, Chgo., 1968-75; from staff assoc. to assoc. dean U. Ill., Chgo., 1975-90, assoc. dean, 1990—. Mem. Chgo. Ill. Union bd., 1986-88. Mem. Assoc. Am. Med. Colls. (planning com. faculty affairs profl. dev. conference, 1998), U. ECOS Bus. Team. Office: Univ of Illinois Coll Medicine 1853 W Polk M/C 784 Chicago IL 60612

HART, KITTY CARLISLE, arts administrator; b. New Orleans, Sept. 3, 1917; d. Joseph and Hortence (Holtzman) Conn; m. Moss Hart, Aug. 10, 1946 (dec. 1961); children: Christopher, Cathy. Ed., London Sch. Econs., Royal Acad. Dramatic Arts; DFA (hon.), Coll. New Rochelle; DHL (hon.), Hartwick Coll.; LHD (hon.), Manhattan Coll., Amherst Coll. Chmn. emeritus N.Y. State Council on the Arts. Former panelist: TV show To Tell the Truth; actress on stage and in films including The Marx Brothers A Night at the Opera, 1936; Broadway theatre appearance in On Your Toes, 1983-84; singer, Met. Opera; one woman show on Great Performances My Broadway Memories, 1999; TV moderator and interviewer; author: (autobiography) Kitty, 1988; contbr. book revs. to jours. Assoc. fellow Timothy Dwight Coll. of Yale U., NYU, Skidmore Coll.; bd. dirs. Empire State Coll.; formerly spl. cons. to N.Y. Gov. on women's opportunities; mem. vis. com. for the arts MIT Recipient Nat. medal of Arts from Pres. Bush, 1991. Office: Arts Coun 915 Broadway Fl 8 New York NY 10010-7108

HART, MARIAN GRIFFITH, retired reading educator; b. Bates City, Mo., Feb. 5, 1929; d. George Thomas Leon and Beulah Winiferd (Hackley) Griffith; m. Ashley Bruce Hart, Dec. 23, 1951; children: Ashley Bruce Hart II, Pamela Cherie Hart Gates. BS, Ctrl. Mo. State Coll., 1951; MA, No. Ariz. U., 1976. Title I-chpt. I reading dir. Page (Ariz.) Sch. Dist.; Title I dir. Johnson O'Malley Preschool; dist. reading dir. Page Sch. Dist.; ret. Bd. dirs. Lake Powell Inst. Behavioral Health Svcs., sec., 1993-95, chmn. fin. com., 1995-96. Contbr. articles to profl. jours., childrens mags. Vol., organizer, mgr., instr. Page Cmty. Adult Literacy Program, 1986-91, Marian's Literacy Program, 1991-95; lifetime mem. Friends of Page Pub. Libr., sec. bd., 1990-91. Mem. Delta Kappa Gamma (pres. chpt. 1986-90, historian 1990-92, Omicron state coms., scholarship 1988-89, nominations 1991, Omicron State Comms. com. 1995-99, Tau chpt. nominations com. chair 1998), Beta Sigma Phi (pres. chpt., v.p. chpt., pvt. reading tutor 1997-2000). Home and Office: 66 S Navajo Dr PO Box 763 Page AZ 86040-0763

HART, MARY, television talk show host; b. Sioux Falls, S.D., Nov. 8, 1951; m. Burt Sugarman, Apr. 8, 1989; 1 child. BA, Augustana College, 1972. Co-host, prodr. Danny's Day, Oklahoma City, Iowa; co-host PM Mag., L.A., 1978, The Regis Philbin Show, N.Y.C., 1981-92, Entertainment Tonight, Hollywood, 1982—; co-owner Customer's Last Stand. Host: Tournament of Roses Parade, Macy's Thankgiving Day Parade; other TV appearences include (miniseries) Hollywood Wives, 1985, Circus of the Stars, Good Morning America, Blossom, Coach; exec. prodr., host Mary Hart Presents: Love in the Public Eye, 1990, Mary Hart Presents: Power in the Public Eye, 1990; musical debut Dolly, ABC-TV; headliner, dancer, singer, Las Vegas debut Golden Nugget, 1988, Resorts Internat., Atlantic City; videos include: Shape Up with Mary Hart, 1989, Mary Hart: Fit and Firm, 1990. Office: Paramount TV 5555 Melrose Ave Los Angeles CA 90038-3112

HART, MELISSA ANNE, congresswoman; b. Pitts., Apr. 4, 1962; d. Donald P. and Albina Simone Hart. BA, Washington and Jefferson Coll., 1984; JD, U. Pitts., 1987. Pa. state senator, 1990-2000; mem. U.S. Congress from 4th Pa. dist., 2001—; mem. fin. svcs. com., judiciary com., sci. com. Chmn. Sen. Fin. Com.; vice chmn. Sen. Urban Affairs & Housing Com.; bd. dirs. C.C. Allegheny County, Pitts. Cancer Inst., SWPA Vets. Home Adv. Coun. Bd. dirs. Vietnam Vets. Leadership Program; bd. trustees U. Pitts. Mem. Pa. Bar Assn., Allegheny County Bar Assn., North Suburban Builders Assn. Republican. Office: 1508 Longworth Ho Office Bldg Washington DC 20515-3804 also: 2525 Rochester Rd Ste 202 Cranberry Township PA 16066*

HART, PAMELA HEIM, banker; b. Chgo., July 14, 1946; d. Gordon Theodore and Leah Almira (Gardner) Heim; m. William Richard Hart, July 8, 1972 (div. 1979); 1 child, Elizabeth Alyson. BA, DePauw U., 1968; MA in Tchg., Washington U., St. Louis, 1970; M in Mgmt., Purdue U., 1982. Chartered bank auditor; cert. bank compliance officer. Tchr. history University City (Mo.) H.S., 1969-74; tchg. asst. Purdue U., Hammond, Ind., 1980-82, guest faculty, 1983-84; auditor Continental Bank NA, Chgo., 1984-86, legal and regulatory compliance specialist, 1986-88, asst. auditor, 1988-92, sr. portfolio risk analyst, 1992-94; with asset securitization group Bank of Am. (formerly Continental Bank NA), Chgo., 1994-98; v.p. capital raising products Bank of Am., Chgo., 1994-99, v.p. pvt. bank strategic planning and projects, 1999-2000, sr. audit mgr., 2001—. Trustee Forest Ridge Acad., Schererville, Ind., 1987-88, Wash. U. Eliot Soc.; mem. vestry St. Paul Episc. Ch., Munster, Ind., 1982-92, jr. warden, 1998, 99; active LWV. Mem. Chartered Bank Auditors Assn., Chicagoland Compliance Assn. (bd. dirs., treas. 1987-88), Cert. Bank Compliance Officer Assn. (exam. com. mem. 1992-96), P.E.O, Washington U. Eliot Soc. Avocations: needlework, travel, reading. Home: 910 Ridge Rd Munster IN 46321-1750 Office: Bank of Am 231 S La Salle St Chicago IL 60604-1407 E-mail: hartpamela55555@aol.com.

HART, PAMELA WALKER, artist, educator, writer; d. Frank Patton Jr. and Beatrice Caroline Cox Walker; m. Donald H. Hart, Feb. 12, 1972. BA in Fashion Merchandising, Fla. State U., 1965; BS in Art Edn. with honors, U. Nebr., 1978; MS in Edn. with honors, Elmira (N.Y.) Coll., 1989. Cert. tchr. art K-12, N.Y., Wis. Dept. mgr. Maas Bros., Tampa, Fla., 1965-67; regional office mgr. Cole of Calif., Atlanta, 1968-70; art tchr. grade K-12 various pub. schs., Rome, N.Y., Madison, Wis., 1979-88. Spkr., presenter Munson Williams Proctor Art Inst., Utica, N.Y., 2001, Rome (N.Y.) Club, 2001. One-woman shows include Gannett Gallery, SUNY, Marcy, 1989, 1992, Mohawk Valley Ctr. for Arts, Little Falls, N.Y., 1995, Library Gallery, Westernville, N.Y., 2001, Rome Club, N.Y., 2001, Art and Cmty. Ctr., Rome, NY, 2003, exhibited in group shows at Edith Barrett Gallery, Utica Coll. of Syracuse U., 2000, Ctrl. N.Y. Cmty. Arts Coun., 2001, exhibited in group shows, Art Assn., Cooperstown, N.Y., 2003, one-woman shows include Kirkland Art Ctr., Clinton, NY, 2003, exhibited in group shows at Everson Art Mus., Syracuse, 1997, Gannett Gallery, SUNY, Utica-Rome, 1997, Ctrl. N.Y. Cmty. Arts Coun., Utica, 2003, So. Vt. Art Ctr., Manchester, 1999, Allied Art Gallery, Richland, Wash., 1999, Nat. Acad. Mus., N.Y.C., 2000, Hiestand Gallery, U. Miami, Oxford, Ohio, 2001, Gallery of Contemporary Art, U. Colo., Colo. Springs, 2001, Van Vechten-Lineberry Art Mus., Taos, N.Mex, 2001, Nat. Arts Club, N.Y.C., 2001, Art Assn. Galleries, Cooperstown, 2001, Fifth Ave. Gallery, Nat. Assn. of Women Artists, N.Y.C., 2003, Represented in permanent collections Lib. Nat. Mus. Women in the Arts, book, Best of Sketching and Drawing, 1999. With USAF, 1970-74, col. USAFR, 1974-95. Recipient Golden Poet award World of Poetry, 1991, 1st prize SUNY, Marcy, 1995, 99, Spl. Recognition award Rome Art Assn., 1996, 3d prize Mohawk Valley Ctr. for the Arts, 1997, 98, Merit award East Wash. Watercolor Soc., 1999, Adolph and Clara Obrig prize Nat. Acad. Mus., N.Y.C., 2000, Watermedia prize Cooperstown Art Assn., 2001. Mem.: AAUW, Nat. Assn. Women Artists, Nat. Women's History Mus., Nat. Mus. Women in the Arts, Inst. Noetic Scis., Soc. for Layerists in Multi-Media, Ctrl. N.Y. Watercolor Soc. Office: LookGlas Images PO Box 337 Westernville NY 13486

HART, SARAH V. federal agency administrator; BS in Criminal Justice, U. Del.; JD, Rutgers U. Prosecutor Phila. Dist. Attys. Office; chief counsel Pa. Dept. Corrections, 1995—2001; dir. Nat. Inst. Justice U.S. Dept. Justice, Washington, 2001—. Vice chair legal affairs com. Am. Correctional Assn.; chmn. sentencing and corrections subcom. Federalist Soc.; bd. dirs. Crime Victims Law Inst.; mem. appellate procedural rules com. Pa. Supreme Ct.; trainer in field. Contbr. articles to profl. jours. Office: US Dept Justice Nat Inst Justice 810 7th St NW Washington DC 20531

HART-DULING, JEAN MACAULAY, clinical social worker; b. Bellingham, Wash. d. Murry Donald and Pearl N. (McLeod) Macaulay; m. Richard D. Hart, Feb. 3, 1940 (dec. Mar. 1973); children: Margaret Hart Morrison, Pamela Hart Horton, Patricia L. Hart-Jewell; m. Lawrence Duling, Jan. 20, 1979 (dec. May 1992); children: Lenora Daniel, Larry, Jayne Munch. BA, Wash. State U., 1938; MSW, U. So. Calif., 1961. Lic. clin. social worker, Calif.; accredited counselor, Wash. Social worker Los Angeles County, 1957-58; children's svc. worker Dept. Children's Svcs., L.A., 1958-59; program developer homemakers svcs. project Calif. Dept. Children's Svcs., L.A., 1962-64; developer homemaker cons. position State of Calif., L.A., 1964-66; supr. protective svcs. Dept. Children's Svcs., L.A., 1966-67; dep. regional svc. adminstrn. Dept. Los Angeles County Children's Svcs., 1967-76; adminstr. Melton Home for Developmental Disability, 1985-86; pvt. practice pro bono therapy Calif. and Wash. Therapist various pro bono cases. Mem. Portals Com., L.A., 1974, Travelers Aid Bd., Long Beach, Calif. 1969. Recipient Nat. award work in cmty., spl. award for work with emotionally disturbed Com. for Los Angeles, 1974. Mem. AAUW, NASW, Acad. Cert. Social Workers, Calif. Lic. Clin. Soc. Workers, Wing Point Golf and Country Club (Bainbridge Island, Wash.), Los Angeles County Retirement Assn. Republican. Congregationalist. Avocations: golf, bridge. E-mail: hart4942@aol.com.

HARTE, SHERRI JEAN, technical writer; b. Dallas, Mar. 17, 1954; d. Dalton Eugene and Margie Marie (High) Brockway; m. Larry J. Key, Oct. 6, 1972 (div. June 1991); 1 child, Jason J. BA in English, So. Meth. U., 1995. Tech. writer Pro Consultants, Dallas, 1994-95, Electronic Form Systems, Carrollton, Tex., 1995-96, Micrografx, Inc., Richardson, Tex., 1996—99, Macromedia, 1999—2002, Southwest Airlines, 2002—. Reading instr. Literary Vols. of Am., Dallas, 1991; vol. Genesis Women's Shelter, Dallas, 1995. Recipient numerous writing awards So. Meth. U., 1993-95, awards Lone Star chpt. Soc. for Tech. Comm., 1997-98. Mem. Phi Beta Kappa, Golden Key, Sigma Tau Delta. Avocations: yoga, reading, theater, symphony, lectures. Home: 5922 Martel Ave Dallas TX 75206-5708 Office: Southwest Airlines 2702 Love Field Drive Dallas TX 75235 Office Phone: 214-792-5435.

HARTEN, ANN M. relocation services executive; married; 1 child. BA in Indsl. Psychology, Indiana U. of Pa. With Boise Cascade, 1987—2000, dir. integrated supply, 1999—2000; v.p., chief info. officer US ops. SIRVA, Westmont, Ill., 2000—. Office: SIRVA 700 Oakmont Ln Westmont IL 60559*

HARTER, CAROL CLANCEY, university president, English language educator; m. Michael T. Harter, June 24, 1961; children: Michael R., Sean P. BA, SUNY, Binghamton, 1964, MA, 1967, PhD, 1970; LHD, Ohio U., 1989. Instr. SUNY, Binghamton, 1969-70; asst. prof. Ohio U., Athens, 1970-74, ombudsman, 1974-76, v.p., dean students, 1976-82, v.p. for adminstrn., assoc. prof., 1982-89; pres., prof. English SUNY, Geneseo, 1989-95; pres. U. Nev., Las Vegas, 1995—. Co-author: (with James R. Thompson) John Irving, 1986, E.L. Doctorow, 1990; author dozens of presentations and news columns; contbr. articles to profl. jours. Bd. dirs., mem. exec. com. NCAA, 2000—; mem. exec. com. Nev. Devel. Authority, 2001—; bd. dirs. Nev. Test Site Devel. Corp., 2000—; trustee Associated Western Univs., 2001—. Office: U Nev Office Pres 4505 S Maryland Pkwy # 1001 Las Vegas NV 89154-1001 E-mail: harter@ccmail.nevada.edu.

HARTER, LONNA, city manager; b. Bucyrus, Ohio, Oct. 15, 1940; d. Ernest Alfred and Letona Marie Rice; m. John Fredrick Harter, Mar. 14, 1969. BA cum laude, Ohio State U., 1995. Actuarial asst. Nationwide Ins., Columbus, Ohio, 1958-69; legal sec. Laughbaum & Assoc., Galion, Ohio, 1969-76; mayors adminstrv. sec. City of Galion, 1976-80, income tax mgr., 1980-91, dep. fin. dir., 1991-01. Sec. SSI, Inc.-User Group, Lebanon, 1994, v.p., 1995. Bd. sec. St. Mark's United Meth. Ch., 1981-83. Mem. Golden Key Nat. Honor Soc., Women of the Moose, Valley View Golf League (v.p. 1999—), New Winchester Golf League. Avocations: golf, painting, reading, pets, cooking. Home: 351 Portland Way N Galion OH 44833-1634 Office: City of Galion PO Box 790 115 Harding Way E Galion OH 44833-1902

HARTFORD, MAUREEN A. academic administrator; m. Jay Hartford. BA in French and History, MA in coll. tchg., U. N.C., Chapel Hill; EdD in higher edn. adminstrn., U. Ark. Dean of student affairs Case Western Res. U., Cleve., 1982—86; vice provost student affairs Wash. State U., 1986—92; v.p. student affairs U. Mich., Ann Arbor, 1992—99; pres. Meredith Coll., Raleigh, NC, 1999—. Faculty Ctr. Study of Higher and Post-Secondary Edn., Ann Arbor, Mich., 1992—99. Mem. governing bd. LeaderShape; bd. trustees Wake Edn. Partnership; bd. dir. Greater Raleigh C. of C., N.C. Triangle United Way; bd. of governors Capital City Club. Recipient Women in Bus., Bus. Jour.., 2002, Dist. Scholar award, N.C. Coll. Pers. Assn., 2002. Office: Meredith Coll 3800 Hillsborough St Raleigh NC 27607*

HARTIGAN, JACQUELINE RENEÉ, investigator; b. San Francisco, Mar. 10, 1961; d. Charles Allen and Lucille Avra (Miller) Ramsey; m. Daniel William Hartigan, Apr. 23, 1988; children: Daniel Albert, Rachel Aron. BS, Calif. State U., Chico, 1983. Cert. peace officer, Calif. Youth counselor Calif. Youth Authority, Chino, 1985-89; job developer Goodwill Industries, San Bernardino, Calif., 1989-90; licensing analyst Cmty. Care Licensing, Riverside, Calif., 1990-95; investigator Dept. Social Svcs., Carlsbad, Calif., 1995—. Pres. sch. site coun. Riverside Unified Sch. Dist., 1995-96; advisor Dayton-Hudson Target Family to Family Project, 1993-94. Vol. Children's Advocacy Coun., Riverside, 1994-96, Harrison Elem. PTA, Riverside; treas. St. Thomas Baseball, Riverside, 1995-96. Mem. Calif. Fraud Investigators. Jewish. Avocations: skiing, horseback riding, boating, hiking, sports. Office: State Dept Social Svcs 5900 Pasteur Ct Ste 125 Carlsbad CA 92008-8807

HARTIGAN, KARELISA DOROTHY, classics educator; b. Stillwater, Okla., Mar. 5, 1943; d. Charles Henry and Elsie Florence Voelker; m. Barry Hartigan, Apr. 21, 1966 (div. Feb. 1978); 1 child, Timothy Lawrence; m. Kevin Michael McCarthy, Dec. 22, 1992. BA in Classics, Coll. of Wooster, 1965; AM in Classics, U. Chgo., 1966, PhD in Classics, 1970. Asst. prof. St. Olaf Coll., Northfield, Minn., 1969-73; asst. prof., assoc. prof. Greek studies U. Fla., Gainesville, from 1973, prof., 1991—, co-dir. Ctr. for Greek Studies, 1980—, assoc. dir. honors program, 1989-95. Author: The Poets and the Cities, 1979, Ambiguity and Self-Deception, 1991, Greek Tragedy on the American Stage, 1995, Myths Behind Our Words, 1998, Muse on Madison Avenue, 2001; editor Text and Presentation jour., 1983-94; editor spl. issues Classical and Modern Lit.; Classical Reflections, 1980. Recipient Excellence in Tchg. award Am. Philol. Assn., 1985; Disting. Alumni Prof. award U. Fla., 1987-89, Univ.-Wide Tchg. award, 1990, Tchg. award, 1994, Disting. Prof. award, 2001. Mem. Modern Greek Studies Assn. (sec. 1983-1986), Classical Assn. Mid. West and South (pres. so. sect. 1986-88, nat. pres. 1992-93). Avocations: bicycling, swimming, travel, cooking, dogs. Office: University of Florida Ctr Greek Studies PO Box 117435 Gainesville FL 32611-7435 E-mail: kvhrtgn@classics.ufl.edu.

HARTLAND, CAROL D. real estate broker; d. Williard Barrett and Theresa Berry Brown; m. Lawrence F. Heuchert, June 30, 1998; m. Albert C. Hartland, Sept. 25, 1982 (dec. Apr. 15, 1991). BA, Vassar Coll., 1948. Broker assoc. Jim West Co., Houston, 1968—89; prin., owner RE/MAX Ctrl. West, Houston, 1989—. Office: RE/MAX Central West 8500 Hillcroft Houston TX 77096

HARTLEY, CELIA LOVE, nursing consultant, writer, retired nursing educator, nursing administrator; b. Colfax, Wash., Oct. 25, 1935; d. Thomas Warren and Ella Marie (Kerkman) Love; m. Lawrence Dosser (div.); children: Laurie Denise Draper, Byron Garth Dosser; m. Gordon E. Hartley, Dec. 17, 1972. Diploma, Deaconess Hosp. Sch. Nursing, Spokane, 1956; BSN, U. Wash., 1965, MSN, 1968. RN, Wash., Calif. Staff nurse Deaconess Hosp., Spokane, 1956-62; charge nurse Northgate Gen. Hosp., Seattle, 1963-65; hosp. supr. Stevens Meml. Hosp., Edmonds, Wash., 1965-66; prof. nursing Shoreline C.C., Seattle, 1967-73, dir. nursing edn., asst. div. chmn. health occupations, 1973-92; chair health sci. divsn. Coll. of the Desert, Palm Desert, Calif., 1992-99, prof. emerita, 1999—; nursing curriculum cons. Pres. Coun. on Nursing Edn. in Wash. State, 1992; adv. com. Antioch West and Seattle U., 1979-81, Nursing Edn. Com. Higher Edn. Coordinating Bd., 1990, Western Wash. U. Nursing, 1984, Seattle Pacific U. Nursing, 1992; other coms. various orgns., 1979—; presenter in field. Author: (with Janice Ellis) Nursing in Today's World; Challenges, Issues, and Trends, 1980, 8th rev. edit., 2004, Managing and Coordinating Patient Care, 1991, 4th edit., 2005, Fundamentals of Nursing, 1992; mem. editl. bd. Assoc. Degree Nurse, 1987-91, Jour. Nursing Edn., 1991—; contbr. articles to profl. jours. Mem. ANA, Nat. League of Nursing (bd. dirs. 1981-84, appeal panel Coun. AD Programs 1988-91, 95-98, chmn.-vice chmn. various com.), Wash. [illegible] 1984-87, chmn. nominating com. 1984-85, chmn. membership com. 1985-86), Calif. Nursing Strategic Planning Com., Sigma Theta Tau. Methodist. Home: 3234 Mabana Rd Camano Island WA 98282 E-mail: cegohart@aol.com.

HARTLEY, MARY, state legislator; b. Bronx, N.Y., Aug. 16, 1954; m. John Hartley; three children. Student, Air Force C.C. Mem. Ariz. Senate, Dist. 20, Phoenix, 1994—; mem. family svcs. com., mem. health com. Active Alhambra Elem. Sch. Dist. Governing Bd., DES Child Care Adv. Com., Ariz. State PTA, Kids Voting, Coalition for Tobacco Free Ariz. Recipient award of excellence All Ariz. Sch. Bd., 1995. Mem. MADD, Nat. Assn. for Partnership Edn. (award 1992), Sierra Club, Audubon Coun. Democrat. Office: State Capitol Bldg 1700 W Washington St Ofc 315 Phoenix AZ 85007-2812 also: 4118 W San Juan Ave Phoenix AZ 85019-2008 E-mail: mhartley@azleg.state.az.us.

HARTMAN, DEANNA MEARS, retired family counselor, addiction counselor; b. Norfolk, Va., Aug. 11, 1937; d. James Gordon Jr. and Sarah Talmadge (Johnson) Mears; m. David Luther Brinkley Jr. (div.); children: Kim Brinkley Hebebrand, David III, Jeffrey Lawrence Brinkley; m. Shirish Ramachandra Pandya, June 7, 1978 (dec.). AA, U. Akron, 1980; BA, Va. Wesleyan, 1983; MA, Antioch U., 1994. Cert. cognitive behavioral therapist; nat. cert. counselor. Dir. edn. svcs. Va. Coun. on Alcoholism, Drugs, Norfolk, 1985-87, exec. dir., 1990-93; outpatient program specialist Maryview Psychiat. Hosp., Portsmouth, Va., 1988-89; clin. therapist City of Portsmouth, 1988-89; educator, therapist City of Va. Beach, 1984-86, 93-95; mental health counselor Glasgow High Wellness Ctr., Newark, Del., 1995; family counselor, addiction specialist Williamsburg Pl., Farley Ctr., Williamsburg, Va., 1997—. Founder Survivors of Suicide, Virginia Beach, 1982-86, vol. educator AARP Bear, Del., 1995. Contbr. articles to profl. jours., various presentations. Bd. dirs. Hospice of Virginia Beach, 1983-85, Safe Place, 1988-90, Civitan Internat., 1990-92, cmty. adv. coun. for curriculum Coll. of Edn., Old Dominion U., Norfolk, 1991-92. Named Rookie of Yr., Civitan Internat., 1991; recipient Disting. Svc. award Va. Alcohol and Drug Abuse Counselors, 1992. Avocations: reading, writing, walking, birdwatching. E-mail: deannahartman@aol.com.

HARTMAN, JOAN EDNA, English educator; b. Bklyn., Oct. 5, 1930; d. H. Graham and Edna (Kuebler) H. Student, Mt. Holyoke Coll., 1951; postgrad., Duke U., 1952, Oxford U., 1958-59; PhD, Radcliffe Coll., 1960. Instr. Washington Coll., Chestertown, Md., 1952-54, Wellesley Coll., 1959-62, asst. prof., 1962-63, Conn. Coll., New London, 1963-66, CUNY-Queens Coll., Flushing, 1967-70, CUNY-S.I. C.C., 1970-72, assoc. prof., 1972-76; prof. CUNY-Coll. S.I., 1976-98, acting dean humanities and social scis., 1995-98. Vis. prof. Am. U. of Rome, 1991, 99, 2001, 03. Editor: Women in Print I, II, 1982, (En)Gendering Knowledge, 1991, The Norton Reader, 2000; contbr. articles to profl. jours. Fellow, AAUW, NEH, Mellon Found., Folger Shakespeare Libr. Mem. MLA, Soc. for the Study of Women in the Renaissance, Women's Caucus for the Modern Langs., Nat. Arts Club. Home: 201 E 21st St Apt 17C New York NY 10010-6423 E-mail: hartman@mail.csi.cuny.edu.

HARTMAN, LEE ANN WALRAFF, secondary school educator, consultant; b. Milw., Apr. 21, 1945; d. Emil Adolph and Mabelle Carolyn (Goetter) Walraff; m. Patrick James Hartman, Oct. 5, 1968; children: Elizabeth Marie, Suzanne Carolyn. BS, U. Wis., 1967; postgrad., U. R.I., 1972—73, Johns Hopkins U., 1990, Trinity Coll., 1996. Cert. tchr., Wis., Md. Secondary educator Port Wash. Bd. Edn., Wis., 1967-68; instr. ballet YWCA, Wilmington, Del., 1977-78; tutor Md. Study Skills Inst., Columbia, 1984-86; tchr. Howard County Bd. Edn., Columbia, 1985—. Contbr. articles to profl. jours. Bd. dirs. Columbia United Christian Ch., 1980-83; mem. Gifted and Talented Com., Columbia, 1980—, Lang. Arts Com., 1985—, USCG Officers Wives Club, 1970-72, Hosp. Aux. Bay St. Louis, 1970-72; troop leader Girl Scouts U.S., Columbia, 1980-91, Hospice; exec. bd. PTA, 1990-2000. Recipient Life Achievement award, Internat. Biog. Ctr., 1994, Woman of Yr. award, Am. Biog. Inst., 1994, Shirley Mullinex Tchr. of Yr. award, 1997, State of Md. Home/Hosp. Tchr. of Yr. award, 2001—02. Mem.: NAFE, AAUW (exec. bd. 1985—, v.p. Howard County br. 1990—92, pres. Howard County br. 1998—2000, chair membership 2003—), Internat. Platform Assn. (mem. citizen's adv. com. 1995—), Home Hosp. Tchrs. Assn. Md. (chair pub. rels., sec. 1994—98, v.p. 1998—99, pres. 1999—2002), Beaverbrook Homemakers Assn. (pres. 1995—97). Avocations: reading, swimming, skiing, ballet. Home: 5070 Durham Rd W Columbia MD 21044-1445 Office: Howard County Bd Edn Rte 108 Columbia MD 21044

HARTMAN, LENORE ANNE, physical therapist; b. Cleve., May 27, 1938; d. Howard Andrew and Emma Elizabeth (Beck) H. BS in Agriculture, Ohio State U., 1960, MS in Agriculture, 1963; postgrad., Kans. State U., 1963-67; cert. in phys. therapy, U. Kans., 1968. Staff phys. therapist R.J. Delano Sch. for the Handicapped, Kansas City, Mo., 1969-74; chief phys. therapist Children's Mercy Hosp., Kansas City, 1974-78; relief staff Mass Gen. Hosp., Boston, 1969-70; staff phys. therapist Menorah Med. Ctr., Kansas City, 1979-87. Clin. instr. phys. therapy St. Louis U., 1974-78, U. Ky., 1974-78, U. Mo., Columbia, 1973-78, U. Kans. Med. Ctr., Kansas City, 1974-87; mem. med. adv. com. Hospice Care of Mid Am., Kansas City, 1984-87; staff phys. therapist S.W. Gen. Hosp., 1992-2004; phys. therapy cons. Rocky River Riding Therapeutic Riding Program, 1994-97; chapel organist St. Luke's Hosp., Kansas City, 1978-87. Contbr. articles to profl. jours. Ohio del. Internat. Farm Youth Exch., Brazil, 1962. Mem. Internat. Farm Youth Exch. Assn. (life), Am. Phys. Therapy Assn. (del. to nat. 1975-76), Mo. Phys. Therapy Assn. (chmn. northwest dist. 1974-76), Am. Guild of Organists (chmn. profl. concerns com. Greater Kansas City chpt. 1983), Japan Am. Soc., Ohio State U. Alumni Assn. (life), Ohio Phys. Therapy Assn., Am. Morgan Horse Assn., U.S. Dressage Fedn., North Ohio Dessage Assn., Western Reserve Carriage Assn., Am. Driving Soc., Omicron Delta Epsilon, Phi Delta Gamma. Avocations: sketching, dog obedience training, gardening, dressage.

HARTMAN, MARILYN D. English and art educator; b. Denver, May 2, 1927; d. Leland DeForest Henshaw and Evelyn Wyman Henshaw; m. James Hartman, Oct. 7, 1949 (dec. Dec. 1989); children: Charles, Alice, Mary Hale. Student, U. Denver, 1947; BA, U. Colo., 1958; MA, UCLA, 1965, EdD in English Edn., 1972. Calif. life std. tchg. credential English and art, Colo. secondary English and art. Tchr. Denver Pub. Schs., 1959—65; asst. prof. San Fernando Valley State U., Northridge, Calif., 1970—72, San Diego State U. Mem., presenter Am. Ednl. Rsch. Assn., L.A., 1965-72; mem. Nat. Coun. Tchrs. English, L.A., 1965-72; officer Pi Lambda Theta-Alpha Delta chpt., L.A., 1970-72; with Ctr. for the Study Dem. Instns., L.A., 1970-72; tchg. asst., 1964, discussion leader linguistics; tchr. evaluator UCLA, 1970-72, Iliff Sch. Theology, Denver U.; cons. Dept Edn., Riley, 1992-2000, State Dept., 1992-2000, to Pres. Clinton, 1992-2000. Author: Linguistic Approach to Teaching English, 1965, Two Letters and Some Thoughts, 1968, Sound and Meaning of BE Speech, 1969, Teaching a Dialect, 1970, Contrastive Analysis: BE and SE Teaching, 1972, Touch the Windy Finger, 1980, Under the Hand of God, 2000; author: (with Bill Kirton) (short stories) O God, 1970, On Her Own: To Know and Not Know, 2002; author: The Luckiest People, 2002. Chmn. Denver Metro Area Food Drive, 1985, Interfaith Alliance; mem. Dem. Nat. Com., 1992—2002. Mem.: VFW, NOW, AAUW, Women in the Arts, Interfaith Alliance, Nat. Philatelic Soc., Am. Philatelic Assn., Common Cause, Sierra Club, Franciscan Missions, Natural Resources Def. Coun., Kempe Children's Found., Colo. Fedn. Dem. Women's Clubs, Inc. (officer 2001). Avocations: singing, painting, writing, teaching, counseling.

HARTMAN, MARY S. historian, educator; b. Mpls., June 25, 1941; married. BA, Swarthmore Coll., 1963; MA, Columbia U., 1964, PhD, 1970. From instr. to asst. prof. Rutgers U., 1968-75; from assoc. prof. to prof. history Douglass Coll., Rutgers U., 1975—; dean Douglas Coll. Rutgers U., 1982-94; dir. Inst. for Women's Leadership Douglass Coll., 1994—; prof. Rutgers U., 1994—. Author: Clio's Consciousness Raised, 1974, Victorian Murderesses, 1978; editor: Talking Leadership: Conversations with Powerful Women, 1999, The Household and the Making of History: A Subversive View of the Western Past, 2004. Office: 162 Ryders Ln New Brunswick NJ 08901-8555

HARTMAN, PATRICIA JEANNE, lawyer, educator; b. Redding, Calif., Apr. 24, 1956; d. Gary Mac and Rosemary Catherine (Aldrich) H. BS in Bus. Adminstrn., BA in Econs., Calif. State U., Sacramento, 1978, MBA with honors, 1979; JD with distinction, U. of Pacific, Sacramento, 1983. Bar: Calif. 1983, U.S. Dist. Ct. (ea. dist.) Calif. 1983. Adminstrv. analyst Dist. Attys. Office, Sacramento, 1976-80; assoc. prof. Calif. State U., Sacramento, 1979—; assoc. Van Camp & Johnson, Sacramento, 1983-85, Diepenbrock, Wulff, Plant & Hannegan, LLP, Sacramento, 1985-89, ptnr., 1989—98, Hunter, Richey, DiBenedetto & Eisenbeis, LLP, Sacramento, 1999—. Mem. County Bar Sects., Sacramento, 1983—. Contbr. articles to profl. jours. Trustee Sutter Hosps. Found., Sacramento, 1988-2002. Fellow AAUW; mem. ABA, LWV (steering com. 1994), Calif. State Bar, Women Lawyers of Sacramento, Med.Group Mgmt. Assn., Sacramento C. of C. Avocations: running, skiing, weightlifting, hiking. Office: Hunter Richey DiBenedetto & Eisenbeis LLP 801 K St Ste 2300 Sacramento CA 95814-3500

HARTMAN, RUTH CAMPBELL, director, educator; b. Galion, Ohio, Aug. 18, 1938; d. Richard Lewis and Florence Evelyn (Ireland) Campbell; m. Richard Louis Hartman, Jan. 14, 1956; children: Jeffery Lee, Marsha Elaine, Jerry Steven. BS, Ohio State U., 1970; MEd, U. LaVerne, 1976, postgrad., 1985—, U. Akron, 1977-85. cert. tchr., Ohio. Tchr. Willard (Ohio) City Schs., 1964-65; educator Mansfield (Ohio) City Schs., 1966—, home tutor, 1971-81, educator, 1977—, faculty advisory com., 1990-2001, young authors coord., 1991-92, co-coord. career edn., 1991-97; owner, dir. Hope Sch., Plymouth, Ohio, 2002—. Cons. Ohio State U., Ashland (Ohio) Coll., Mt. Vernon (Ohio) Nazarene Coll., 1976—. Co-author: Handbook for Student Teachers, 1983; contbr. to Norde News. Dir. of construction Hope School. Mem NEA, Ohio Edn. Assn., North Cen. Ohio Tchrs. Assn., Mansfield Edn. Assn. Republican. Methodist. Avocations: reading, traveling, tennis, music. Home: RR 1 Plymouth OH 44865-9801 Office: Hope School 4200≧ Opdyke Rd Plymouth OH 44865-

HARTMAN, SUSAN P(ATRICE), adult education administrator; Dir. adult edn. Front Range C.C., Westminster, Colo., 1995—. Recipient Regional Person of Yr. award, 1992. Office: Cmty Learning Ctr Front Range Community Coll Westminster CO 80031

HARTMAN-ABRAMSON, ILENE, medical educator; b. Detroit, Nov. 8, 1950; d. Stuart Lester and Freda Vivian (Nash) Hartman; m. Victor Nikolai Abramson, Oct. 21, 1971. BA, U. Mich., 1972; MEd, Wayne State U., 1980, PhD in Higher Edn., 1990. Cert. continuing secondary tchr., Mich. Program developer and instr. William Beaumont Hosp., Royal Oak, Mich., 1972—74; vocat. counselor for emigres Jewish Vocat. Svc. and Cmty. Workshop, Detroit, 1974—81; program developer and cons. Detroit Psychiat. Inst., 1982; instr. for foreign students Oakland C.C., Farmington Hills, Mich., 1983-99. Mem. adv. bd. Mich. Dept. Edn., Detroit, 1981; lectr. Internat. Conf. Tchrs. English to Speakers of Other Langs., 1981; guest presenter Wayne State U., Lawrence Tech. U., 1991, U. Mich. Anxiety Disorders Program, 1993; presenter rsch. presentations Nat. Coalition for Sex Equity in Edn., Ann Arbor, Mich.; presenter at seminar on learning anxiety Interdisciplinary Studies program Wayne State U., 1995; chair profl. stds. and measures com. Mich. Devel. Edn. Consortium, editor newsletter, 1997; mem. rehab. adv. coun. State of Mich.; guest lectr. med. edn./residency tng. initiatives Detroit Med. Ctr. Hutzel Hosp., Providence Hosp., Beaumont Hosp., Detroit Med. Ctr., Harper Hosp.; adj. faculty Wayne State U., 2000; adj. prof. internat. comms. Lawrence Tech. U., 2000—. Mem. editl. bd. Mensa Rsch. Jour.; contbr. articles to profl. jours. Mem. Am. Acad. on Physician and Patient, Am. Mensa (rsch. rev. com.). Jewish. Avocations: self-defense for women, Karate. Office: Lawrence Tech U 21000 W Ten Mile Rd Southfield MI 48075-1058 E-mail: abramson@ltu.edu., ihabramson@aol.com.

HARTMANN, HEIDI IRMGARD VICTORIA, economist, research organization executive; b. Elizabeth, N.J., Aug. 14, 1945; d. Henry Leopold and Hedwig (Bercher) H.; m. Frank Blair Cochran, June 17, 1967 (div. 1977); 1 child, Jessica Lee Cochran; m. John Varick Wells, July 15, 1979; children: Laura Cameron Hartmann Wells, Katharine Lina Hartmann Wells. BA in Econs. with honors, Swarthmore Coll., 1967; MPhil in Econs., Yale U., 1972, PhD in Econs., 1974; LLD (hon.), Swarthmore Coll., 1995. Computer programmer, researcher city planning dept. City of New Haven, 1969; acting instr. Yale U., New Haven, 1972-73; vis. asst. prof. econs. New Sch. for Social Rsch., N.Y.C., 1974-76; sr. rsch. economist Office of Rsch. U.S. Commn. on Civil Rights, Washington, 1976-78; rsch. assoc. Nat. Acad. Scis./Nat. Rsch. Coun., Washington, 1978-80, assoc. exec. dir. commn. on behavioral and social scis. and edn., 1980-83, study dir., 1984-86; Am. Statis. Assn.-NSF census fellow U.S. Bur. Census, Washington, 1986-87; founder, dir. Inst. for Women's Policy Rsch., Washington, 1987—; dir. women's studies program, prof. dept. sociology Rutgers U., 1988. Lectr. women's studies program George Washington U., Washington, 1978, dept. econs. U. Md., College Park, 1979; bd. dirs. Nat. Coun. Rsch. on Women; vis. scholar A. E. Havens Ctr. for Study of Social Structure and Social Change, U. Wis., Madison, 1987; numerous presentations in field; expert testimony before govtl. orgns. Author: (with others) Capitalism and Patriarchy: Report from a Seminar at Aalborg University Centre August 1982, 1983, Women, Households and the Economy, 1987, The Consequence of Economic Rhetoric, 1988, Handbook of Wage and Salary Administration, revised edit., 1983, Comparable Worth and Wage Discrimination, 1984, The Moral Foundations of Civil Rights, 1988, Gender in the Workplace, 1987, Ingredients for Women's Employment Policy, 1987, Winning America: Ideas and Leadership for the 1990s, 1988, Three Worlds of Labor Economic, 1988; editor: New Directions for Comparable Worth Research, 1985, (with B.F. Reskin) Women;s Work, Men's Work: Sex Segregation on the Job, 1985, (with D.J. Treiman) Women, Work and Wages: Equal Pay for Jobs of Equal Value, 1981; co-author: Welfare That Works: The Working Lives of AFDC Recipients, Economic Perspectives on Affirmative Action, Women's Access to Health Insurance, A Welfare Reform Based on Help for Working Parents, 1995; mem. editorial bd. Feminist Studies, 1974-88, Women and Work, Rev. of Radical Polit. Econs., 1972-74, Polit. Economy, 1972-73; referee Jour. Comparative Am. Sociol. Econs., Signs, Frontiers, Am. Jour. Sociology, U. Chgo. Press, NSF; contbr. numerous chpts. to books, articles to profl. publs. Mem. rsch. synthesis com. Russell Sage Found., 1987-94; numerous pub. svc. presentations in field. MacArthur Found. fellow, 1994. Mem. Am. Econs. Assn., Union for Radical Polit. Econs., Nat. Women's Studies Assn., Assn. for Pub. Policy and Mgmt., Internat. Assn. Feminist Econs. (co-chair econs. policy groups on women's issues). Democrat. Mem. Congregationalist Ch. Office: Inst for Women's Policy Rsch 1707 L St NW Washington DC 20036-4201 Fax: 202-833-4362.

HARTMAN TILLETT, COLLEEN, law educator; b. Harrisburg, Pa., Feb. 1976; d. Gregory Calvin Hartman; m. John William Tillett, Nov. 2, 2002. JD, Emory U., 2000. Bar: Ga. 2000. Atty. Troutman Sanders, LLP, Atlanta, 2000—02. Vis. prof. law Mercer U. Sch. Law, Macon, Ga., 2002—03. Scholar, Emory U., 1997—2000. Home: 1207 McLendon Dr Decatur GA 30033 Office: Mercer U Sch Law 1021 Georgia Ave Macon GA 31207 Personal E-mail: hartman_ca@mercer.edu. E-mail: hartman_ca@mercer.edu.

HARTNESS, SANDRA JEAN, venture capitalist; b. Jacksonville, Fla., Aug. 19, 1944; d. Harold H. and Viola M. (House) H. AB, Ga. So. Coll., 1969; postgrad., San Francisco State Coll., 1970-71; MA in Taxation, Golden Gate U., 1997. Rschr. Savannah (Ga.) Planning Commn., 1969, Environ. Analysis Group, San Francisco, 1970-71; dir. Mission Inn, Riverside, Calif., 1971-75; developer Hartness Assocs., Laguna Beach, Calif., 1976—. Ptnr. Western Neuro-Care Ctr., Tustin, Calif., 1983—89; pres. Asset Svcs., Inc., 1981—. V.p., mem. bd. dirs. Evergreen Homes, Inc., 1986-90; bd. govs. Human Rights Campaign, 2001—. Recipient numerous awards for cmty. svc. Democrat.

HARTNETT, ELIZABETH A. trade association administrator; b. Metuchen, N.J., June 28, 1952; d. John J. and Rita (Hackett) Kirwan; m. Raymond T. Hartnett, July 16, 1977; children: Kathleen E., John T. BS, Wheeling Coll., 1974. CPA, Pa. Jr. acct. Deloitte Haskins & Sells, Pitts., 1974-76, sr. acct. Washington, 1976-81, mgr., 1981-84; contr. Electronic Industries Assn., Washington, 1984-86, v.p. fin., 1986-98; contr. Am. Soc. Health Sys. Pharmacists, 1998—. Treas. Electronic Industries Found., Washington, 1984-98. Mem. Am. Soc. Assn. Execs., Greater Washington Soc. Assn. Execs., Pa. Inst. CPA's, D.C. Inst. CPA's. Republican. Roman Catholic. Office: Am Soc Health Sys Pharmacists 7272 Wisconsin Ave Bethesda MD 20814-4836

HARTSBURG, JUDITH CATHERINE, small business owner; b. Terre Haute, Ind., June 16, 1955; d. Ferris Lee and Mary Ann (Tully) Roberson; m. Donald Matthew Seprodi, Aug. 1, 1972 (div. Oct. 1994); children: Antoinette Seprodi, Jacob Seprodi, Brooklyn Seprodi; m. Joseph Wayne Hartsburg, Feb. 14, 1998. AA, Ivy Tech., 1990; grad., Dale Carnegie Course. Lic. property/casualty ins. agt.; notary pub. Sec. Equifax, Oklahoma City, 1975-76; ins. clk. Northside Family Medicine, Del City, Okla., 1976; office mgr. Dick Clark Ins., Terre Haute, 1981, Simrell's, Terre Haute, 1981-85, ADC acctg. clk./typist V Vigo County Welfare, Terre Haute, 1985-86, head ADC acctg., clk./typist IV, 1986-87; purchasing agt. Bruce Fox, Inc., New Albany, Ind., 1987-88; acctg. mgr. Terre Haute Coke and Carbon, 1988-96, acting sec. bd. dirs., 1989; ptnr., owner Thistlehare; office mgr. Terre Haute Truck Ctr., 1996; internet programmer, webmaster Advanced Microelectronics, Inc., Vincennes, Ind., 1997—2001; ptnr., entrepreneur Ceilings, Walls & All, 2000—. Ptnr., owner Thistlehare; bookkeeper Seprodi Constrn., Terre Haute, 1989—; grad. asst. Dale Carnegie Inst.; owner Take-A-Letter. Author: (poetry) Between Darkness and Light, In-Between Days. Coach, bd. dirs. Terre Haute Youth Soccer Assn., 1979—82; player N. Tex. Women's Soccer Assn., Plano, 1977—78. Recipient Dale Carnegie Highest award for Achievement. Mem.: AIPB, NAFE, Profl. Bookkeepers Assn., Am. Notary Assn., Vigo County Taxpayers Assn. Democrat. Roman Catholic. Avocations: gardening, camping, sewing, piano. Home: PO Box 323 Sandborn IN 47578-0323 E-mail: stocksnbears@tds.net., jhartsburg@hotmail.com.

HARTSHORN, BRENDA BEAN, elementary school educator; b. Randolph, Vt., June 23, 1962; d. David Anthony and Rita Mae (Jones) Boon; children: Tyler Anthony, Caitlyn Elizabeth. BA, Vt. Coll., 1985; MEd, St. Michael's Coll., 1990. Teaching prin. aide Moretown (Vt.) Elem. Sch., 1984-85, 1-3 grade tchr., 1985—. Cons. math. & assessment, Waitsfield, Vt., 1993—; assoc. in math. Inst. for Math. Mania, Montpelier, Vt., 1994—, specialist for Vt. Dept. Edn. and Univ. of Vt., Early Literacy Intervention, 1999-2001. Contbr. articles to jours. Forums with state legis., Vt. NEA, 1985—; Justice of the Peace, 1998-. Recipient Sallie Mae Outstanding First Yr. Tchr. award Sallie Mae, 1985-86, Outstanding Tchr. of Yr. award, 1993-94, Presdl. award in Math. Nat. Sci. Found., 1994-95. Mem. NEA, Nat. Coun. of Tchrs. Math., Vt. Coun. on Reading, Assn. Supervision & Curriculum Devel. Democrat. Avocations: quilting, reading, writing, outdoor sports, travelling. Home: 1192 Crossett Hill Waterbury VT 05676 Office: Moretown Elem Sch Rt 100B Moretown VT 05660

HARTSHORN, TERRY O. health facility administrator; b. 1944; Adminstrv. sec. Centinela Valley Hosp., Inglewood, Calif., 1965-68, adminstrv. asst., 1969; adminstr., cons. Community Health Svc., USPHS, L.A., 1969-71; adminstr. Luth. Hosp. Soc. So. Calif., L.A., 1971-73, Moore-White Med. Clinic, L.A., 1973-76; chmn. Pacificare Health Systems, Inc., Cypress, Calif., 1977—, chmn., pres., CEO Burbank, Calif., 1993—; chmn. bd., pres., CEO UniHealth Am., Inc., Burbank, 1993—. Office: Pacificare Health 3120 Lake Center Dr Burbank CA 92704

HARTSOCK, LINDA SUE, educational and management association executive; b. St. Joseph, Mo., Feb. 20, 1940; d. Waldo Emerson and Martha (Skelkop) H. BS, Ctrl. Meth. Coll., Fayette, Mo., 1962; EdM, Pa. State U., 1965, EdD, 1971. Cert. assn. exec. Am. Soc. Assn. Execs. Tchr. Jr. High Sch. (North Kansas City (Mo.) Pub. Sch. Sys.), 1962-63; sr. resident Pa. State U., 1963-64, asst. coord. residence halls, 1964-65, residence hall coord., 1965-66, asst. dean women, 1966-68, asst. dean students, 1968-71; rschr. Ctr. for Study Higher Edn., 1971, dir. new student programs, 1971-72; nat. dir. program AAUW, 1972-76; exec. dir. Adult Edn. Assn., 1976-80; now ret. CEO Integrated Options, Inc., assn., edn. and mgmt. svcs., Greenbackville, Va.; designer tng. and edn. programs for various orgns. and assns. V.p. fin. Com. for Full Finding Edn., 1979; mem. first adv. panel convened future directions of a learning soc. project Coll. Entrance Exam. Bd., 1978, mem. planning group for Course-By-Newspaper exam. project, 1979; bd. dirs. Coalition Adult Edn. Orgns., 1976; mem. White House Conf. on Aging Com., 1979; mem. nat. adv. bd. Nat. Ctr. Higher Edn. Mgmt. Sys. Project to Develop a Taxonomy for the Field of Adult Edn., 1978; nat. adv. coun. on adult edn. Futures and Amendments Project, 1977; adv. Collection of Census Data, Nat. Ctr. Ednl. Stats., 1977; mem. pub. policy com., program com. chmn. Adv. Coun. Nat. Orgns. to Corp. for Pub. Broadcasting, 1976; adv. devel. New Mediated Programs, Office Instructional Resources, Miami Dade C.C., 1976; mem. innovative awards com. Nat. Univ. Ext. Assn., 1977; field reader U.S. Dept. Edn. Title III Grants, 1981-83. Mem. editl. bd. Off to Coll. mag, 1972-74; contbr. articles to profl. jours. Mem. Greenbackville Va. Fire Dept. Women's Aux., 2000—; mem. aquatics com. Lower Shore YMCA, Pocomoke City, Md., 2002—. Recipient Disting. Alumni award Ctrl. Meth. Coll., 1978. Mem. Am. Soc. Assn. Execs. (individual membership coun. 1979-81, edn. com. 1985-88, 92-94, univ. affairs commn. 1989-92, awards com. 1991), Washington Women's Forum (budget, program and exec. coms. 1978-82), Alumni Soc. Coll. Edn. Pa. State U. (bd. dirs., chairperson strategic planning com. 1986, Outstanding Alumni award). E-mail: ioinc@dmu.com.

HARTSOUGH, CHERYL MARIE, nutritionist, director; b. Phila., Dec. 30, 1959; d. Edward Joseph and Anna Marie (Hansell) Hartsough; children: Katrina Raspa, Hannah Rose. BS in Dietetics, U. Fla., 1985. Dietitian U. South Fla., Tampa, 1985-87; lead nutritionist Doral Saturnia Internat. Spa, Miami, 1987-90; cons. nutritionist Turnberry Isle, Aventura, Fla., 1991-92; dir. nutrition PGA Resort & Spa, Palm Beach Gardens, Fla., 1991-96; dir. wellbeing Aspen (Colo.) Club, 1996-98; dir. wellness Nemacolin Woodlands Resort & Spa, Farmington, Pa., 1999-2000; spa dir. Gurney's Inn Resort & Spa, Montauk, NY, 2001—. Lectr. Gatorade Speakers Network, Chgo., 1991—; nutrition cons. YMCA, Tampa, Fla., 1985-87; instr. Hillsborough C.C., Tampa, 1986-87. Author: Anti-Cellulite Diet, 1991, Doral Cookbook, 1991; editor: Gov.'s Coun. of Sports, 1987. Sec. nutrition com. Am. Heart Assn., Tampa, 1986-87. Recipient Gov.'s award State of Fla., 1987. Mem. Am. Cancer Soc., Am. Dietetic Assn. Found. (chairperson 1988-90, chairperson southeast sports and cardiovascular nutrition 1987-91, Young Recognized Dietetian 1989), DAR. Democrat. Avocations: hiking, water and snow skiing. Office: Gurney's Resort & Spa 290 Old Montauk Hwy Montauk NY 11954 E-mail: cherylhartso@aol.com.

HARTSOUGH, GAYLA ANNE KRAETSCH, management consultant; b. Lakewood, Ohio, Sept. 16, 1949; d. Vernon W. and Mildred E. (Austin) Kraetsch; m. James N. Heller, Aug. 20, 1972 (div. 1977); m. Jeffrey W. Hartsough, Mar. 12, 1983; 1 child, Jeffrey Hunter Kraetsch Hartsough. BS, Northwestern U., 1971; EdM, Tufts U., 1973; MEd, PhD, U. Va., 1978. Vol. VISTA, Tenn., 1970-71; asst. tchr. Perkins Sch. for the Blind, Watertown, Mass., 1971-72; resource tchr. Fairfax (Va.) County Pub. Schs., 1972-76; asst. dir. ctr. U. Va., Charlottesville, 1976-78; sr. program officer Acad. for Edn. Devel., Washington, 1978-80; mng. cons. Cresap/Towers Perrin, Washington and L.A., 1980-86; pres. KH Consulting Group, L.A., 1986—. Mem. nat. adv. coun. Northwestern U. Sch. Speech, Evanston, Ill., 1992—; cons. in field. Contbr. more than 20 articles to profl. jours. Co-founder L.A. Higher Edn. Roundtable, L.A., 1987-94; mem. nat. adv. coun., coun. 100, Northwestern U., 1999-. Recipient Outstanding Woman of Achievement award Century City C. of C., 1991. Mem. Orgn. Women Execs. (past pres., bd. dirs. L.A. 1986-95). Home: 15624 Royal Ridge Rd Sherman Oaks CA 91403-4207 Office: KH Consulting Group 1901 Ave Of Stars Ste 1900 Los Angeles CA 90067-6020 Fax: 310-203-5419. E-mail: khcggak@aol.com.

HARTY, MAURA, federal agency administrator, former ambassador; m. James F. Larner. Grad., Georgetown U. With Fgn. Svc., 1981—, vice consul; consular assignments Bogota, Colombia; various consular assignments Madrid; staff officer Ops. Ctr., exec. secretariat Dept. State, spl. asst. to sec. state George P. Schultz, exec. asst. to sec. Warren Christopher, U.S. amb. to Paraguay, 1997-99, prin. deputy asst. sec., Bur. Consular Affairs, 2002—. Office: Dept State Washington DC 20520-0001

HARTZ, DEBORAH SOPHIA, editor, writer; b. Plainfield, N.J., July 11, 1951; d. Sylvester and Margaret (Buschart) H.; m. Thomas McDonald July 24, 1971 (div. Dec. 1976). BA, U. Pa., 1973; MS, U. Wis., 1977. Asst. editor Whitney Communications Corp., N.Y.C., 1978-79; lifestyles editor News Dispatch, Michigan City, Ind., 1979-80; food editor, restaurant critic Daily Herald, Arlington Heights, Ill., 1980-88; editor in chief Cook's mag., Bridgeport, Conn., 88-90; food Editor Sun-Sentinel, Ft Lauderdale, Fla., 1990—. Cons. newsletter, Cuisinart Corp., Greenwich Conn., 1985-88. Recipient Golden Carnation award, 1986, James Beard Journalism award. Mem. Am. Inst. of Wine and Food, Assoc. of Food Journalists, Les Dames d'Escoffier. Office: Sun-Sentinel 200 E Las Olas Blvd Ste 1000 Fort Lauderdale FL 33301-2293

HARTZ, JILL, museum director; b. Montreal, Que., Can., July 25, 1950; Undergrad. study, Oberlin U., 1969-71; MA in English Lang. and Lit. with honors, U. St. Andrews, Scotland, 1973; student, Cornell U., 1989-94. Mgr. Tompkins County Arts Coun., Ithaca, 1981-82, Grapevine Graphics, Ithaca, 1982-83; co-editor Grapevine Weekly Mag., Ithaca, 1983-84, Living Publs., Ithaca, 1984-86; coord. exhbns., asst. to dir. Herbert F. Johnson Mus. of Art, Cornell U., 1976-81, dir. pub. rels. and publs., 1986-93; asst. to chair, dept. of art Cornell U., Ithaca, 1993-94; coord. pub. rels. and spl. programs Coun. for the Arts, Cornell U., Ithaca, 1993-94; dir. comm. Arts & Scis. Devel. Office, U. Va., Charlottesville, 1994-97; interim dir. Bayly Art Mus., U. Va., Charlottesville, 1997, dir., 1997—. Co-curator Agnes Denes exhbn., 1991-92, editor monograph; co-founder, ptnr. LunaMedia pub. rels. co., Ithaca, 1993-94. Mem. Am. Assm. Museums, Nat. Cultural Alliance. Office: U Va Bayly Art Mus Rugby Rd Charlottesville VA 22903 Fax: 804-924-6321.

HARTZ, RENEE SEMO, cardiothoracic surgeon; b. Bessemer Twp., Mich., Dec. 7, 1946; d. Rita Ann Semo; children: Tyler Joseph, Colin Wilson. BA, Western Mich. U., 1969; MD, Northwestern U., 1974. Diplomate Am. Bd. Surgery, Am. Bd. Thoracic Surgery. Intern pediat. Children's Meml. Hosp., Chgo., 1974-75; intern gen. surgery Northwestern Meml. Hosp., Chgo., 1975-76, resident gen. surgery, 1976-79, chief resident cardiothoracic surgery, 1979-81; instr. dept. surgery Northwestern U. Med. Sch., Chgo., 1978-81, assoc. in surgery, 1981-85; asst. prof. surgery med. sch. Northwestern U., Chgo., 1985-87, assoc. prof. surgery med. sch., 1987-92; prof. surgery, chief divsn. cardiothoracic surgery U. Ill. Hosp. & Clinics, Chgo., 1992-97; prof. surgery dept. surgery divsn. of cardiothoracic surgery Tulane U. Sch. of Medicine, New Orleans, La., 1997—. Apptd. to Northwestern Meml. Hosp., Chgo., Children's Meml. Hosp., Chgo., VA Lakeside Hosp., Chgo., Evanston (Ill.) Hosp., Columbus Hosp., Chgo.; laser researcher Northwestern U. Med. Sch., 1984—, U. of Ill. Hosp., West Suburban Hosp., Ill. Masonic Hosp. Contbr. articles to profl. jours.; contbr. chpts. to Perioperative Cardiac Dysfunction II, 1985, General Thoracic Surgery, 1989, New Technology in Vascular Surgery, 1988; featured in Great Chgo. Stories. Mem. Am. Coll. Chest Physicians, Am. Coll. Surgeons, Am. Heart Assn., Am. Women's Med. Assn., Assn. for Acad. Surgery, Chgo. Heart Assn., Chgo. Surg. Soc., Ill. Surg. Soc., Laser Inst. Am., Soc. Thoracic Surgeons, Soc. Univ. Surgeons, Am. Assn. Thoracic Surgeons, Sigma Xi. Avocations: wind surfing, gourmet cooking, spending time with sons. Office: Tulane U Sch of Medicine 1430 Tulane Ave # Sl22 New Orleans LA 70112-2699

HARTZELL, IRENE JANOFSKY, psychologist; d. Leonard S. and Annelies Janofsky; 1 child, Mark Adam. BA, U. Calif., Berkeley, 1963, MA, 1965; PhD, U. Oreg., 1970. Psychologist Lake Washington Sch. Dist., Kirkland, Wash., 1971-72; staff psychologist VA Med. Ctr., Seattle, 1970-71, Long Beach, Calif., 1973-74; dir. parent edn. Children's Hosp., Orange, Calif., 1975-78; clin. psychologist Kaiser Permanente, Woodland Hills, Calif., 1979-94; clin. instr. pediats. U. Calif. Irvine Coll. Medicine, 1975-78. Author: The Study Skills Advantage; contbr. articles to profl. jours. Intern Oreg. Legis., 1974-75. U.S. Vocat. Rehab. Adminstrn. fellow U. Oreg., 1966-67, 69. Mem.: APA.

HARVARD, BEVERLY JOYCE BAILEY, protective service official; b. Macon, Ga., Dec. 22, 1950; d. Arcelious and Irene (Perkins) Bailey; m. Jimmy C. Harvard, 1972. BA, Morris Brown Coll., 1972; MS, Ga. State U., 1980. Cert. FBI Nat. Acad. Police officer Police Bur. City of Atlanta, crime analysis officer Police Bur., exec. protection officer Police Bur., dep. chief of police, spl. asst. to commr. dept. pub. safety, dir. pub. affairs dept. pub. safety, chief of police, 1994—. Commr. Commn. Accreditation for Law Enforcement Agys., 1991; bd. dirs. Coun. on Battered Women, 1991; trustee Leadership Atlanta, 1991;adv. bd. dir. Big Bros./Big Sisters, 1986—, Atlanta Victim/Witness Assistance Program, 1985—. Named Outstanding Atlantan, 1983, Alumna Yr., Morris Brown Coll., 1985, Bronze Woman Yr., Iota Phi Lambda, 1986, Woman Achiever Atlanta YWCA, YWCA Woman of Yr., 1996. City Govt. Woman of Yr., 1995, 100 Most Influential Georgians; recipient Trailblazer award for Law Enforcement City of Atlanta, TBS Trumpet award, 1999. Mem. Internat. Assn. Chiefs Police (tng. com. Ga. chpt.), Nat. Orgn. Black Law Enforcement (chmn. program), Bus. System Planning Team, Ga. State U. Alumni Assn. (bd. dirs. Atlanta chpt.), Delta Sigma Theta (parliamentarian). Office: Police Svcs City Hall 9th Fl 675 Ponce De Leon Ave NE Atlanta GA 30308-1829

HARVARD, RITA GRACE, real estate agent, volunteer; b. Aurora, Ill., June 28, 1929; d. Walter Scott Fredenhagen and Grace Lucille Towsley-Fredenhagen; m. Anton Castagnoli (div. Mar. 10, 1978); children: Susan G., Jodie A., Thomas A.; m. John Francis Harvard. BA, Monmouth Coll., 1951. Educator 5th grade Dixon (Ill.) Pub. Sch., 1951—53; real estate mgr. Naperville (Ill.) Prince Castles Co., 1972—85; sec.-treas. Naperville Creamery Co., 1985—2000. Part-time vol. asst. tchr. Naperville Pub. Sch. Sys., 1968. Trustee North Ctrl. Coll., 1982—; mem. instnl. rev. bd. Edward Hosp., Naperville, 1992—; active Bd. Fire and Police Commr., City of

Naperville, Ill., 1996—; trustee Naperville YMCA, 1996—; active Naperville Century Walk Bd., 1999—; trustee Monmouth Coll., Ill., 1974—81; hon. chmn. annual benefit Naperville United Way, 1988; bd. mem. Grace Meth. Ch. Found., 1993—, Naperville Heritage Soc., 1970—75, 1980—85, Grade Sch. and Jr. High Home and Sch. Assns., 1965—75, DuPage County [illegible], Original Naperville Recycling Ctr., 1970—75, Edward Hosp. Aux., 1955—61. Named Outstanding Woman Leader of DuPage County, YWCA/DuPage, 1995; recipient Disting. Svc. award, Naperville Jaycees, 1993, Gael D. Swing award for meritorious svc., North Ctrl. Coll., 1995, Naperville Family Spirit award, 1997, Crystal award, Citibank Naperville, 1997, Outstanding Alumna award, Naperville Ctrl. H.S., 1998. Mem.: LWV, AAUW (Woman of Yr. award Naperville br. 1988), PEO, Naperville Heritage Soc. (Outstanding Svc. award 1999—2000), Rep. Women's Club, Rotary Club Naperville (chmn. membership devel. 1992—2000, cmty. svc. and membership devel. com. 1998—2002, past pres. 1994—95, Rotarian of Yr. award 1995). Methodist. Home: 439 LeProvence Cir Naperville IL 60540

HARVEY, CANDI, professional basketball coach; Grad., Ouachita Baptist U., 1979. Coach women's basketball Ark. State U., Robert E. Lee H.S., Tyler, Tex.; asst. coach women's basketball Stephen F. Austin U., Nacogdoches, Tex., 1984—90; coach women's basketball Tulane U., New Orleans, 1990—94, Tex. A&M, College Station, 1994—98; coach women's basketball Nashville Noise Am. Basketball League, 1998; asst. coach Utah Starzz, 1999—2001; head coach Utah Starzz (now San Antonio Silver Stars), 2001—. Color analyst Fox Sports Net, 2002—. Office: 1 SBC Center San Antonio TX 78219*

HARVEY, CAROLE (KATE HARVEY), minister, church official; Grad., Andover Newton Theol. Sch. Co-pastor Ctrl. Bapt. Ch., Providence, 1st Bapt. Ch. Am., Providence; exec. dir. Ministers Coun. of ABC USA. Mem. regional and nat. mins. coun. and senate Am. Bapt. Chs.; v.p. Am. Bapt. Chs. USA, 1994-95; mem. state Senate ethics com. R.I. Legislature; pres. R.I. State Coun. Chs., 1987-89. Editor Minister, Am. Bapt. Chs., Into a New Day, 1997. Bd. dirs. Bapt. Today, 1995-98. Office: ABC in the USA PO Box 851 Valley Forge PA 19482-0851

HARVEY, CHRISTINE LYNN, publishing executive; b. Bklyn., Dec. 7, 1962; AS in Liberal Arts, Nassau C.C., 1982; BA in Comm. Arts, Adelphi U., 1985. Cert. EMT, 1983-86. Franchise mgr. N.Y. Daily News, Mineola, 1981-84; copywriter, vido prodr., 1984-85; pub. rels. assoc. King Features Syndicate, N.Y.C., 1986; account exec. Promotional Broadcasting Svc., Babylon, N.Y., 1986-87; sr. account mgr. L.I. Bus. News, Ronkonkoma, N.Y., 1987-91; sr. ptnr. Karen Saeger Assocs., Stony Brook, N.Y., 1990—; editor The Steuben News, Ridgewood, N.Y., 1992—; founder, pub., editor-in-chief New Living, Stony Brook, 1991—; pub. rels. cons. Am. Health Found., Valhalla, NY, 1994—96; radio prodr./dir./host New Living Prodns., Stony Brook, 1997—98. Clin. hypnotherapist, Reiki master, 1999; TV prodr. Outlook Mag., 1985; TV news reporter, field prodr. LI News Tonite, 1984. Avocations: running, swimming, cycling, hiking, golf. Office: New Living 1212 Route 25A Ste 1B Stony Brook NY 11790-1919

HARVEY, EDITH M. federal agency administrator; Bachelors Degree, Kans. State U.; M in Edn. Adminstrn. and Supervision, U. Nebr. Mgr., program specialist, contracting officer's rep. U.S. Dept. Edn., Washington, dir. improvement programs Office Innovation and Improvement. Office: US Dept Edn FOB-6 Rm 3E106 400 Maryland Ave SW Washington DC 20202

HARVEY, ELAINE, state representative; b. Lovell, Wyo., Sept. 18, 1954; m. Allen Harvey; children: Heather, Gretchen, Erin, Kristin. AS, Northwest Coll., 1993. Substitute tchr. Big Horn County Sch. Dist. # 2, 1993—; v.p. Children's Resource Ctr., 1996—; state rep. dist. 26 Wyo. Ho. of Reps., Cheyenne, 2002—, mem. govt. planning coun. for DD-shared visions. Republican. Lds Ch. Office: State Capitol Cheyenne WY 82002

HARVEY, ELEANOR JONES, museum curator; b. Washington, Sept. 20, 1960; d. Charles Roy Jr. and Margaret McChesney (Jeffries) Jones; m. Stephen Jay Harvey, Oct. 10, 1992. BA with distinction summa cum laude, U. Va., 1983; MA, Yale U., 1985, MPhil, 1987, PhD, 1998. Curatorial asst. Nat. Mus. Am. Art, Washington, 1985-89; asst. curator Am. paintings Mus. Fine Arts, Boston, 1989-91; assoc. curator Am. art Dallas Mus. Art, 1992-98, cons. curator Am. art, 1996—2003; cons. curator Nat. Mus. Wildlife Art, 1996—; curator Luce Foundation Center for American Art, Washington, 2003; chief curator Smithsonian American Art Museum, Washington, 2003—. Instr. art Yale U., 1985, 86, 87, mem. st. hall lecture series com., history of art dept., 1984-87, grad. student adv. com., 1985-87, grad. student rep., 1985-86, grad. and profl. student senate com. on libr. policy, 1985-88, alumni fundraising agt. for history of art dept., 1991—; lectr. in field. Co-author: Albert Pinkham Ryder, 1990, The Lure of Italy, 1992, Dallas Museum of Art: A Guide to the Collection, 1996; author: The Painted Sketch: American Impressions from Nature, 1830-1880, 1998; contbr. articles to profl. jours. Bd. dirs. Wood Turning Ctr., Phila., 1998—; mem. ann. giving adv. coun. U. Va.; mem. U. Va. Assocs. of Libr., 1998—. Henry S. McNeill fellow in Am. decorative arts Yale U., 1985-87, Smithsonian predoctoral fellow Nat. Mus. Am. Art, 1988-89; Henry Luce Found. grantee, 1987-88. Mem. Am. Assn. Mus., Am. Craft Guild, Coll. Art Assn. Avocation: dressage. Office: Nat Museum of American Art 750 9th St NW Washington DC 20001*

HARVEY, GLEN H. educational association administrator; BA in Psychology and Sociology, MA in Social and Philos. Founds. of Edn., U. Ky.; AM in Philosophy, PhD in Philosophy of Edn., Stanford U. With The NETWORK, Inc., Nat. Inst. Edn.; exec. dir. Learning Innovations WestEd and the Regional Lab. for Edn. Improvement of the N.E. and Islands; CEO WestEd Regional Edn. Lab., 1997—. Office: WestEd 730 Harrison St San Francisco CA 94107-1242

HARVEY, GLORIA-STROUD, physician assistant; b. Washington, D.C., Apr. 16; d. Robert W. and Ruth Elizabeth (Brown) Stroud; m. Jimmy Lawrence Harvey; children: Dana, Daman, Byron, Justin. BS, U. Md., 1968; physician asst. cert., Howard U., 1977. Physician asst. Weaver Clinic, Ahoskie, N.C., 1977-80, Western State Hosp., Staunton, Va., 1980-84, Walter Reed Army Med. Ctr., Washington, 1984-91, John Amsted Hosp., Butner, N.C., 1991—, U. N.C., Chapel Hill, 1991—. Physician asst. Aroyga, Durham, N.C., 1992—, Maria Parham Hosp., Henderson, N.C. Bd. dirs. Unique Builders, Henderson N.C., 1994-95, Cultural Initiatives, 1995. Mem. Am. Bus. Women's Assn., N.C. State-Employed Physician Assts.' Assn. (chmn. 1994), Triangle Assn. for Physician Assts., N.C. Assn. for Physician Assts. Methodist. Home: 2693 Hidden Spring Ln Oxford NC 27565-6146

HARVEY, JANE HULL, church administrator; BA with high honors, Scarritt Coll., Nashville, 1958; MA in Spl. Edn. with highest honors, Columbia U., 1972; grad., Tokyo Sch. Japanese Lang., 1966; Tchg. Cert., Sogetsu Japanese Ikebana Inst., Tokyo, 1969. Tchr. remedial English lang. arts Englewood (N.J.) Pub. Schs.; tchr. Head Start learning disabled children Ctrl. Harlem, N.Y.C.; person in mission United Meth. Ch., Korea, Japan, Okinawa, 1958-60, 64-69, 1975-80; office mgr. ednl. TV office Pub. Broadcasting Svc., Washington, 1980-81; program coord., asst. dir. dept. social/econ. justice Gen. Bd. Ch. and Soc. of United Meth. Ch., 1981-86, program coord. Justice for women project, 1986-88, dir. dept. human welfare, 1988-92, asst. gen. sec., 1992—. Lectr. in field. Contbr. articles to profl. jours.; asst. to editor Japan Christian Activity News, Tokyo, 1975-79; editl. asst. AMPO Mag., Tokyo, 1975-79. Chair bd. dirs. Interfaith IMPACT for Justice and Peace, 1995—; chair Washington Interreligious Staff Cmty., 1983-85, 89-91; co-chair Interreligious Coalition on Smoking or Health, 1992—; founding mem. World Alliance for Breast-feeding Action, Internat. Conf., Penang, Malaysia, 1990—; liaison to Gen. Commn. on Status and Role of Women, 1988—; chief staff Infant Formula Task Force, 1988-94; advisor Korean Legal Aid Ctr. for Family Rels., 1980-87; co-chair religion and [illegible] Dumbarton United Meth. Ch. [illegible]; founding mem., advisor Co-Madres, 1982; bd. dirs. Ptnrs. for Global Justice, 1982-87, Ctr. for Reproductive and Sexual Health, N.Y.C., 1973-75; co-founder Judson Health Project for Working Women, N.Y.C., 1973-75; adult counselor Youth March Against Hunger, Englewood, 1972-74; vol. adminstrv. asst. Greater Englewood Housing Authority, 1972-74; co-coord. United Farm Workers Boycott, Englewood, 1972-74; campaign coord., speech writer Dem. Mayoral Campaign, Englewood, 1972; co-dir. McGovern for Pres. campaign, Englewood, 1972. Office: United Meth Ch Gen Bd Ch Soc 100 Maryland Ave NE Washington DC 20002-5625

HARVEY, JUDITH GOOTKIN, elementary school educator, real estate agent; b. Boston, May 29, 1944; d. Myer and Ruth Augusta (Goldstein) Gootkin; m. Robert Gordon Harvey, Aug. 3, 1968; children: Jonathan Michael, Alexander Shaw. BS in Edn., Lesley Coll., Cambridge, Mass., 1966; MS in Edn., Nazareth Coll., Rochester, NY, 1987. Kindergarten tchr. Williams Sch., Chelsea, Mass., 1966-69; owner, tchr. Island Presch., Eleuthera, The Bahamas, 1969-70; substitute tchr. Brighton Cen. Sch., Rochester, NY, 1985-95; agt. Prudential Rochester Realty, Pittsford, NY, 1994—98. Author, dir. : (plays) The Parrot Perch, 1991. Bd. dir. in charge pub. rels. George Eastman Ho. Coun., mem. award steering com. honoring Lauren Bacall, 1990, chmn. gala celebration honoring Audrey Hepburn, 1992, mem. steering com. honoring Ken Burns, 1995; mem. art in bloom steering com. for fashion show Meml. Art Gallery, 1994; co-chmn. Fashionata, Rochester Philharm. Orch., 1990; mem. steering com. of realtors Ambs. to Arts; mem. Parrot Players Acting Group, 1990—; mem. steering com. Reels and Wheels Antique Car Festival, 1995, 1996; bd. dir. Birmingham Bloomfield Newcomers, 2000—03, in charge spl. events, 2000—02; com. mem. Birmingham Antiques Festival, 2000—02; co-chair World of James Bond Gala and the Spring Fashion Show, 2001, Saturday Night Fever...Live It! Gala and Spring Fashion Show, 2002; historian Birmingham Bloomfield Newcomers, 2002—03; mem. Dow Jones Investment Group, 2002—, recording ptnr., 2004—. Mem.: Genesee Valley Club, Chatterbox Club. Avocations: acting, directing, gardening, writing, bridge.

HARVEY, JULIE L. artist; d. Julian Tobey and Marie Teresa Harvey. BFA magna cum laude, Va. Commonwealth U., 1985; MFA, Parsons Sch. of Design, N.Y.C., 1987. Artist Featured artwork in films and TV shows such as Sex And The City and Spin City, N.Y.C., NY, 1992—; artist-lectr., series Governor's Magnet Sch. for the Gifted, Norfolk, Va., 1988; scenic painter for film,TV, and photography Harvey Backdrops, N.Y.C., NY, 1986—92; lectr. -sr. seminar lecture series Va. Commonwealth U., Richmond, Va., 1998. Prin. works include public art design Liberty Mural, N.Y.C. (First Pl., Wall St. Dist. Mural Competition, 1996), In the Garden, sculpture, Cubes (Mitsubishi Chem. Am. Project Grant, 1995), Red Hall (First Pl., Gallery '81, Norfolk VA, 1981). Grantee, ED Found., 2002, Mitsubishi Chem. Am., 1995—, 9-11 Arts Recovery Fund, 2002. Mem.: NOW, Guggenheim Mus., Whitney Mus. of Am. Art, Mus. of Modern Art, Soc. of Mayflower Descendents. Achievements include patents for bonding artist's material to archtl. panels. Avocations: dance, yoga, music, films. Office: Julie Harvey 174 Fifth Ave #201 New York NY 10010 Office Phone: 212-924-1992. E-mail: inquiries@julieharvey.com.

HARVEY, KATHERINE ABLER, civic worker; b. May 17, 1946; d. Julius and Elizabeth (Engelman) Abler; m. Julian Whitcomb Harvey, Sept. 7, 1974. Student, La Sorbonne, Paris, 1965-66; AAS, Bennett Coll., 1968. Asst. libr. McDermott, Will & Emery, Chgo., 1969-70; libr. Chapman & Cutler, Chgo., 1970-73, Coudert Freres, Paris, 1973-74. Adv., organizer libr. Lincoln Park Zool. Soc. and Zoo, Chgo., 1977-79, mem. soc.'s women's bd., 1976—; chmn. libr. com., 1977-79, sec., 1979-81, mem. exec. com., 1977-81; mem. jr. bd. Alliance Francaise de Chgo., 1970-76, treas., mem. exec. com., 1971-73, 75-76, mem. women's bd., 1977-80, 95—; trustee Chgo. Acad. Scis., 1986-88; adv. coun. med. program for performing artists Northwestern Meml. Hosp., 1986-94, mem. exec. com., 1992—, bd. treas., 1992—; pres., bd. dirs. William Ferris Chorale, 1988-89; mem. Fred Harvey Fine Arts Found., 1976-78, Phillips Acad. Alumni Coun., Andover, Mass., 1977-81, mem. acad.'s bicentennial celebration com. class celebration leader, 1978, co-chmn. for Chgo. acad.'s bicentennial campaign, 1977-79, mem. student affairs and admissions com., 1980-81. Mem. aux. bd. Art Inst. Chgo., 1978-88; mem. Know Your Chgo. com. U. Chgo. Extension, 1981-84; mem. guild Chgo. Hist. Soc., 1978—, bd. dirs., 1993—; mem. women's bd. Lyric Opera Chgo., 1979—, chmn. edn. com., 1980, mem. exec. com., 1980-84, 88—, treas. women's bd., 1983-84, 1st v.p. 1988-90; mem. women's bd. Northwestern Meml. Hosp., 1979—, treas., chmn. fin. com., 1981-84, 92-94, mem. exec. com., 1981-88, 92—, devel. com. 1995-97, 2d v.p. 1996-97, 1st v.p. 1997—, founding chair pres. com. 1993—, pres. 1999—, dir. Northwestern Meml. Hosp., 1999—, pres. women's bd. 1999—, 1st v.p. 1997-99; vis. com. Sch. Music Northwestern U., 1995—; bd. dirs. Found. Art Scholarships, 1982-83; bd. dirs. Glen Ellyn (Ill.) Children's Chorus, 1983-90, founding chmn. pres.'s com., 1983—; mem. women's bd. Chgo. City Ballet, 1983-84; bd. dirs. Grant Park Concerts Soc., 1986-92; chmn. pres. com. Chgo. Children's Choir, 1991-93. Mem. Antiquarian Soc. of Art Inst. Chgo. (life), Guild of Chgo. Historical Soc., Arts Club Chgo. (dir. 1996—), Chgo. Symphony Soc. (life), Friday Club (corre. sec. 1981-83), Casino Club (gov. 1982-88, sec. 1984-85, 1987-88, 1st v.p. 1985-86, 2d. v.p. 1986-87), Cliff Dwellers Club. Home: 1209 N Astor St Chicago IL 60610-2314

HARVEY, LYNNE COOPER, broadcasting executive, civic worker; b. near St. Louis; d. William A. and Mattie (Kehr) Cooper; m. Paul Harvey, June 4, 1940; 1 child, Paul Harvey Aurandt. DHL (hon.), Rosary Coll., 1996; D (hon.), Washington U., 1988. Broadcaster ednl. program KXOX, St. Louis, 1940; broadcaster-writer women's news WAC Variety Show, Ft. Custer, Mich., 1941-43; gen. mgr. Paul Harvey News ABC, 1944—. Pres. Paulynne Prodn., Ltd., Chgo., 1968—, exec. prodr. Paul Harvey Comments, 1968—; pres. Trots Corp., 1989—; editor, compiler The Rest of the Story. Pres. women's bd. Mental Health Assn. Greater Chgo., 1967-71, v.p. bd. dirs., 1966—; pres. woman's aux. Infant Welfare Soc. Chgo., 1969-71, bd. dirs., 1969—, benefits hon. chmn., 1994, 96; mem. Salvation Army Woman's Adv. Bd., 1967; reception chmn. Cmty. Lectures; women's com. Chgo. Symphony, 1972—; pres. Mothers Coun., River Forest, 1961-62; charter bd. mem. Gottlieb Meml. Hosp., Melrose Park, Ill.; mem. adv. bd. Nat. Christian Heritage Found., 1964—; mem. USO woman's bd., 1983, woman's bd. Ravinia Festival, 1972—; trustee John Brown U., 1980—; bd. dirs. Mus. Broadcast Comms., 1987—; adv. coun. Charitable Trusts, 1989—; mem. Joffrey Ballet Com.; chmn. Brookfield Zoo Whirl, 2000. Named to, Mus. Broadcast Comm.-Radio Hall of Fame; recipient Heritage of Am. award, 1974, Little City Spirit of Love award, 1987, Salvation Army Others award, 1989, disting. friend award, NCPCA, disting. alumni award, Washington U., Friske Meml. award, USO, 2000, Lynne Harvey scholarship named in her honor, Musicians Club of Women. Home: 1035 Park Ave River Forest IL 60305-1307

HARVEY, PATRICIA A. school system administrator; BS in elem. edn., Lincoln U.; MA in sch. admin., Roosevelt U. Prin. Hefferan Elem. Sch., Chgo., Idaho; exec. asst. to gen. supt. Chgo. Schs., 1994—95, chief accountability officer, 1995—97; sr. fellow dir. urban edn. Nat. Ctr. Edn. and Econ., Wash., DC, 1997—99; supt. Saint Paul Pub. Schs., Saint Paul, Minn., 1999—. Office: Saint Paul Pub Sch 360 Colborne St Saint Paul MN 55102

HARVEY, PATRICIA JEAN, special education administrator, retired; b. Newman, Calif., Oct. 27, 1931; d. Willard Monroe and Marjorie (Greenlee) Clougher; m. Richard Blake Harvey, Aug. 29, 1965; children: G. Scott Floden, Timothy P. BA, Whittier Coll., 1966, MA, 1971. Resource specialist Monte Vista High Sch. and Whittier (Calif.) High Sch., 1977-98; dept. chair spl. edn. Whittier (Calif.) High Sch., 1982-94; ret., 1998. Author: (tchrs. manual) The Dynamics of California Government and Politics, 1970, 90; co-author: Meeting The Needs of Special High School Students in Regular Education Classrooms, 1988. Active Whittier Fair Housing Com., 1972; pres. Women's Aux. Whittier Coll., 1972-73, sec., 1971-72; historian Docian Soc. Whittier Coll., 1963-64, pres. 1965-66. Democrat. Episcopalian. Home: 424 E Avocado Crest Rd La Habra Heights CA 90631-8128 Office: The Learning Advantage Ctr 13710 Whittier Blvd Ste 206 Whittier CA 90605-4407

HARVEY, SUSAN ANN, music educator, conductor, educator; b. Fairfax County, Va., Aug. 21, 1967; d. Ronald Lee and Rosalee Goins Harvey. BMEd, James Madison Univ., 1989; MEd, Va. Polytechnic Inst., 1995. Lic. postgrad profl. tchg. lic. music preK-12, dir. instrn., sec. sch. supr., and gen. supr. Band dir. mid. sch. and H.S. band Covington City Pub. Sch., Covington, Va., 1989—92; band dir. mid. sch. Rockbridge County Pub. Sch., Lexington, Va., 1992—2003; instr. adj. brass So. Va. Univ., Buena Vista, Va., 2000—; band dir. mid. sch., choir dir. H.S. Buena Vista City Pub. Sch., Va., 2003—. Music clinician, judge, lectr., guest conductor in field. Bugler Rockbridge County Ann. Relay for Life, Lexington, Va., 2001—, guest spkr. opening ceremonies, 2002; chairperson music curriculum writing com. Rockbridge County Pub. Sch., Lexington, Va., 1997; co-chairperson of dist. V festival judges and sight reading com. Va. Band and Orch. Dir. Assn. Dist. V, Va., 2000—; chairperson Ctrl. Highlands All Area Band, 2000—. Nominee Disney's Am. Tchr. Award, 1999, 2002; recipient Tchr. Recognition Day, Va. Govs. Sch. Visual and Performing Arts, 1995. Mem.: Nat. Edn. Assn., Music Educators Nat. Conf., Va. Music Educators Assn., Rockbridge Cmty. Symphony Orch. Non-Denom. Avocation: gardening. Office: Parry McCluer Middle Sch 2329 Chestnut Ave Buena Vista VA 24416 Office Phone: 540-261-7340.

HARVILL, MELBA SHERWOOD, retired university librarian; b. Bryson, Tex., Jan. 22, 1933; d. William Henry and Delta Verlin (Brawner) Sherwood; m. L. E. Harvill Jr., Feb. 2, 1968; children: Sherman T., Mark Roling. BA, North Tex. State Coll., 1954; MA, North Tex. State U., 1968, MLS, 1973, PhD, 1984. Tchr. Graham (Tex.) Ind. Sch. Dist., 1966-68; reference libr. Midwestern U., Wichita Falls, 1968—73; dir. librs. Midwestern State U., Wichita Falls, 1973-2000. Presenter in field. Vol. Boy Scouts Am., Wichita Falls, 1969—74, Wichita Falls Sr.-Jr. Forum, 1978—2000, mem. exec. bd. girls club, ways and means com., sec., asst. treas.; chmn. United Way Midwestern State U., 1975—76; mem. talent coordinating com. Wichita Falls Centennial Celebration; vol. Conv. and Vis. Bur., Lone Stars, 1993—; grad. Leadership Wichita Falls, 1990; pres. Southside Girls Club, 1997—98; auditor, budget com. chair Woman's Forum, 1997—99; ednl. programming chair Wichita Falls Arts Coun., 2001—04, bd. dirs., 2004—07; mem. U. North Tex. Advancement Adv. Coun.; bd. dirs. YWCA Wichita Falls, 1987—94, pres. bd. dirs., 1989—91, 1994—95; bd. dirs. River Bend Nature Works. Recipient Svc. award Sr.-Jr. Forum, Wichita Falls United Way Community Svc. award, 1975, Svc. award YWCA Bd. Dirs., 1991; named Met. BPW Woman of Yr., 1980. Mem. ALA, LWV (program v.p., pres. 1991-92), Tex. Libr. Assn. (mem. planning com., mem. membership com., mem. legis. com., mem. rsch. and grants com., chairperson dist VII, chairperson adminstrn. round table), Tex. Coun. State U. Librs. (sec.-treas. 1990-92), Wichita Falls Rotary North (sec. 1993-96), U. North Tex. Alumni Assn. (bd. dirs. 1992-94, 97-2002), Phi Alpha Theta, Pi Sigma Alpha, Phi Delta Phi, Gamma Theta Upsilon, Alpha Chi, Beta Phi Mu. Democrat. Avocations: spectator sports, swimming, music, reading, travel. Home: 4428 BUS 287J Iowa Park TX 76367 E-mail: mharvill@msn.com.

HARWELL, BETH H. political organization worker; b. Norristown, Pa., July 24, 1957; married; 2 children. BA, David Lipscomb U.; MS, George Peabody Coll.; PhD, Vanderbilt U. State legislator; mem. Tenn. State Legis., 1988—; chmn. Tenn. Republican Party, 2001—. Republican. Office: 1922 West End Ave Nashville TN 37203 also: 107 War Meml Bldg Nashville TN 37243 Address: 42 Wyn Oak Nashville TN 37205-5001

HARWELL, JOANNE BRINDLEY, music educator; b. Columbia, Tenn., June 29, 1935; d. Hugh Payne and Edna Doris (Bradford) Brindley; m. A. Brantley Harwell, June 18, 1957. BA in Music, Howard Coll., 1957; MEd in Elem. Edn., State U. West Ga., 1980, EdS in Mid. Grades, 1983, MusM in Voice Performance, 1986. Tchr. Pritchard (Ala.) Jr. High, 1957—58, Lamar County Schs., Barnesville, Ga., 1972—74; min. music 1st Bapt. Ch., Barnesville, 1973—76; tchr., choral dir. Carrollton (Ga.) City Schs., 1976—88; tchr. Clayton County Schs., Morrow, Ga., 1988—95; tchr., choral dir. Henry County Schs., McDonough, Ga., 1995—98; music dir. St. James Episcopal Ch., Clayton, Ga., 2001—, Tallulah Falls (Ga.) Sch., 2002—. Coun. mem. Cooperate Bapt. Fellowship, Macon, Ga., 2001—04, nominating com., 2004—, edn. com., 2000—, mem. nat. coun., 2004—. Mem.: Macon Morning Music Club, Am. Guild of English Handbell Ringers, Nat. Assn. for Music Educators, Macon Piano Tchrs. Guild (pres.), Ga. Bapt. Mins. Wives (pres. 1980, program chair, chair nominating com.), Ga. Music Edn. Assn., Chorister's Guild (mem. Atlanta chpt.), Kappa Delta Pi, Phi Kappa Phi, Phi Delta Kappa, Delta Omicron (life; pres. Omicron Gamma chpt., Sr. award Omicron Gamma chpt.). Democrat. Baptist. Avocations: hiking, travel, reading. Home: 143 Valley Croft Rd Otto NC 28763

HARWICK, BETTY CORINNE BURNS, sociology educator; b. L.A., Jan. 22, 1926; d. Henry Wayne Burns and Dorothy Elizabeth (Menzies) Routhier; m. Burton Thomas Harwick, June 20, 1947; children: Wayne Thomas, Burton Terence, Bonnie Christine, Beverly Anne Carroll. Student, Biola, 1942-45, Summer Inst. Linguistics, 1945, U. Calif., Berkeley, 1945-52; BA, Calif. State U., Northridge, 1961, MA, 1965; postgrad., MIT, 1991. Prof. sociology Pierce Coll., Woodland Hills, Calif., 1966-95, pres. acad. senate, 1976-77, pres. faculty assn., 1990-91, chmn. dept. for philosophy and sociology, 1990-95, co-creator, faculty advisor interdisciplinary program religious studies, 1988-95. Chmn. for sociology L.A. C.C. Dist., 1993-95; occasional cmty. guest lectr. religious studies and sociology, 1995—. Author: (with others) Introducing Sociology, 1977; author: Workbook for Introducing Sociology, 1978. Faculty rep. Calif. C.C. Assn., 1977-80. Alt. fellow NEH, 1978. Mem. Am. Acad. Religion, Soc. Bibl. Lit., Am. Sociol. Assn. Presbyterian. Home: 19044 Superior St Northridge CA 91324-1845

HARWOOD, BERNICE BAUMEL, artist, community volunteer; b. Bklyn., Mar. 6, 1923; d. Max and Mildred (Weinberger) Baumel; m. Daniel J. Harwood, Aug. 23, 1947; children: René Gordon, Felice Spodick. BS in Art Edn. cum laude, Hofstra U., Hempstead, N.Y., 1973; MS in Spl. Edn., Hofstra U., 1975; student, Ruth Leaf Studio, Douglaston, N.Y., 1980-87, Studio Camitzer, Valdottavo, Italy, 1983. Artist in residence Syosset (N.Y.) Sch. Dist., 1986. Pres. Graphic Eye Gallery, 1986-87. One-woman shows at Calkins Gallery, Hofstra U., 1985, Graphic Eye Gallery, Port Washington, N.Y., 1989; exhibited in group shows at Norton Gallery Art, Profl. Artists Guild, West Palm Beach, Fla., Coral Spring Mus., Fla., Hutchins Gallery, C.W. Post U., Greenvale, N.Y., Albrecht Mus., St. Joseph, Mo., Monmouth (N.J.) Mus. Art, Foxhall Gallery, Washington, Elaine Benson Gallery, Bridghampton, N.Y., 1989, Daruma Gallery, Woodmere, N.Y., 1991, Fla., Nat. Mus. Am. Jewish Mil. History, Washington D.C., 1999—, others; represented in pvt. and corp. collections including IBM, Bethlehem, Pa., Am. Stock Exchange, N.Y.C., Chase Manhattan (N.Y.) Bank, Sandoz, Nabisco; represented in permanent collection Queensborough C.C. Art

Gallery, N.Y.; illustrator: Five Towns, 1962. Chair LWV, Woodmere, N.Y., 1957-61; v.p. Nat. Coun. Jewish Women, Lawrence, N.Y., 1976-81; committeewoman Dem. Party, Woodmere, 1962-84; mem. bd. advisors Nassau County Mus. Fine Art, Roslyn, N.Y., 1981-88. With U.S. Navy (WAVES), 1944-46; painted artificial eyes for wounded servicmen. Recipient arts awards including Sally Carson award Norton Gallery of Art, West Palm Beach, Fla., 1993, 2d prize Emily Lowe Gallery, Hofstra U., 1984, award of excellence Long Beach (N.Y.) Art League, 1987, hon. mention Profl. Artists Guild, Coral Springs (Fla.) Civic Ctr., 1997, judges recognition Boca Raton Mus. Art Artists Guild, 2001. Mem. Nat. Assn. Women Artists (juror 1988-90, Leila Sawyer award 1983), Nat. Mus. of Women in Art (charter, Washington, DC.), Fla. Watercolor Soc., Palm Beach County Cultural Coun, Womens Vet. Meml. (charter), Arlington Cemetary. Democrat. Jewish. Avocations: golf, reading, traveling, music, theatre. Home: 41 Windsor Ln Boynton Beach FL 33436-6068

HARWOOD, ELEANOR CASH, librarian; b. Buckfield, Maine, May 29, 1921; d. Leon Eugene and Ruth (Chick) Cash; m. Burton H. Harwood, Jr., June 21, 1944 (div. 1953); children: Ruth (Mrs. William R. Cline), Eleanor, James Burton. BA, Am. Internat. Coll., 1943; BS, New Haven State Tchrs. Coll., 1955. Libr. Rathbun Meml. Libr., East Haddam, Conn., 1955-56; asst. libr. Kent (Conn.) Sch., 1956-63; cons. Chester (Conn.) Pub. Libr., 1965-71. Author: (with John G. Park) The Independent School Library and the Gifted Child, 1956, The Age of Samuel Johnson, LLD, Remember When, 1987, (essay) Growing Up in Chester, 1993, Moosley Yours, 1996, Chester, Years Ago, 2002. Mem. United Ch. Lt. (j.g.) USNR, 1944—46, WWII. Named Eleanor C. Harwood prize in her honor, Rev. Jacob Meml. Christian Coll., India, libr. named in her honor, 2003; recipient medal, Am. Theater-Victory. Mem. ALA, Conn. Libr. Assn., Chester Hist. Soc. (trustee 1970-72), DAV, Am. Legion, Am. Legion Aux., Soc. Mayflower Descs., Appalachian Mountain Club. Home: 10 Maple St # 255 Chester CT 06412-0255

HARWOOD, LYNNE, artist, book designer; b. Boston, Nov. 16, 1944; d. Reed and Faith (Garrison) H.; m. Roland Louis Gilbert, Aug. 1, 1979 (div. Aug. 1982); children: Curtis Gilbert, Sarah Gilbert. BA, Sarah Lawrence Coll., 1968. Self-employed artist, Anson, Maine, 1972—; pres. Union of Maine Visual Artists, 1988. Author, illustrator: Honeybees at Home, 1994. Maine Green Party. Avocations: gardening, beekeeping. Home: 608 Pease Hill Rd Anson ME 04911-9742

HARWOOD, PATRICIA L. judge; m. John Harwood; children: John Jr., Kylie, Lindsay, Olivia. BA, Boston Coll., 1982; JD, Suffolk Univ. Law Sch., 1985. Bar: R.I., (Federal). Chief judge City Pawtucket Municipal Police & Housing Court; law clerk R.I. Supreme Court, gen. magistrate. Mem.: R.I. Bar Assn. Office: Frank Licht Judicial Complex Providence RI 02903

HARWOOD, SANDRA STABILE, lawyer, state representative; b. June 25, 1950; BBA, Kent State U., 1988; JD, Univ. Akon Sch. of Law, 1991. State rep. dist. 65 Ohio Ho. of Reps., Columbus, 2002—, mem. juvenile and family law com., ranking minority mem. civil and comml. law, econ. devel. and tech., health, and judiciary coms., and children's healthcare and family svcs. subcom. Democrat. Office: 77 S High St Columbus OH 43215-6111

HARWOOD, VIRGINIA ANN, retired nursing educator; b. Lawrenceville, Ohio, Nov. 5, 1925; d. Warren Leslie and Ruth Ann (Wilson) H.; m. Kenneth Dale Juillerat, Dec. 21, 1946 (div. 1972); children: Rozanne Augsburger, Vicki Anderson, Carol Mann, Karen Albaugh. RN, City Hosp. Sch. Nursing, Springfield, Ohio, 1946; BSN, Ind. U., 1968; MS in Edn., Purdue U., 1973, PhD, 1982. Cert. psychiat./mental health nurse, ANA. Staff nurse various hosps., 1946-60; pub. health nursing supr. Whitley County Health Dept., Columbia City, Ind., 1960-65; nursing supr., coordinator staff devel. Ft. Wayne (Ind.) State Hosp., 1965-69; faculty sch. nursing Parkview Hosp., Ft. Wayne, 1969-74; faculty dept. nursing Ball State U., Muncie, Ind., 1974-77; dir. nursing program Thomas More Coll., Ft. Mitchell, Ky., 1977-79; faculty sch. nursing Purdue U., West Lafayette, Ind., 1979-80; dean sch. nursing Ashland (Ohio) Coll., 1980-83; retired, 1983-86; charge nurse admission psychiat. unit VA Med. Ctr., Marion, Ind., 1986-93, ret., 1994—. Active Rep. Nat. Com., 1978—, U.S. Senatorial Club, 1984—, Rep. Pres. Task Force, 1982—; mem. ch. coun. Grace Luth. Ch., Gas City, Ind., 1993-96; bd. dirs. Luth. Ctr., Ball State U., Muncie, Ind., 1994-96; bd. mgrs. Covington Creek Condominium Assn., 1997-2001; vol. Foellinger-Freeman Bot. Conservatory, 1993—. with Cadet Nurse Corps, 1944-46. With Cadet Nurse Corps, 1944—46. Mem. Am. Nurses Found., Ohio State Nurses Assn. (pres. Mohican dist. 1981-83), Mensa, Intertel, Sigma Theta Tau, U.S. Amateur Ballroom Dancing Assn. (bd. dirs. Ft. Wayne chpt. 1998-2001, v.p. 2000, pres. 2001), Ft. Wayne Woman's Club. Avocations: travel, reading, dance, orchid culture. Home: 6611 Quail Ridge Ln Fort Wayne IN 46804-2875

HASALONE EVE, ANNETTE LEONA, research and development company executive; d. Glenn Allen Greene and Betty Leona Palmer; m. Mark Joseph Eve, Sept. 24, 2002; m. Cipriano Ramirez, May 24, 1977 (div. Sept. 0, 1985); children: Elizabeth Leona Ramirez, Dominic Earl Ramirez, Jerrod Emmett Ramirez. D in Naturopathy, Trinity Coll. Natural Healing, Warsaw, Ind.ana, 2003. Pres. Elemental Rsch., LLC, Post Falls, Idaho, 1999—; R&D cons. Eniva Corp., Blaine, Minn., 1999—2003. Case mgr. Homeless Mental Health Program, Oroville, Calif., 1984—86; account clk. I GAIN, Woodland, Calif., 1986—88; drug and alcohol specialist Health and Human Svcs., Woodland, 1988—89; DUI edn. counselor AK Bean Found., Fairfield, Calif., 1988—89; mgr./cons. WaterOz, Grangeville, Idaho, 1997—99; radio talk show host WGTG, Ga., 1998—2000, WHJM, Knoxville, Tenn., 1998—2000. Author: (educational book) Mono-Atomic Minerals Information and Reference Guide, Off Balance, (educational booklet) Essential Information Booklet, (audio tape) Naturally Healthy With Mono-Atomic Minerals, (protocols for natural healing) Protocols Booklet. Campaign mgr. Ted Gunderson for Pres., Las Vegas, Nev., 1996—96. Recipient Outstanding Achievement in Poetry award, Internat. Libr. Poetry and Poetry.com, 2001, Outstanding Contbn. award, Enira Corp., 2001. Mem.: NAFE (assoc.), Internat. Ozone Soc. (assoc.). Republican. Achievements include invention of proprietary process for cell ready, ionic, liquid, water-soluble mineral supplements. Avocations: skiing, art, research and development, guitar, poetry. Office: Elemental Research LLC 4353 E Poleline Ave Post Falls ID 83854 Office Phone: 208-773-5264. Personal E-mail: hasalone@msn.com. Business E-Mail: annette@elementalresearchlls.com.

HASARA, KAREN A. mayor; b. Springfield, Ill., Oct. 17, 1940; m. Jerry Gott; 4 children. BA, Sangamon State U. Mem. Ill. Ho. of Reps., Springfield, 1986-91, 92-94, mem. appropriations I, elem. and sec. edn., counties and twps., agrl., children, aging, small bus., coal devel., mkt., fin. inst. and human svc. coms.; former spokesman on mental health Springfield; former vicespokesman on state govt. adminstrn.; mayor City of Springfield, 1995—. Office: City of Springfield 800 E Monroe St Ste 300 Springfield IL 62701-1699

HASELTINE, FLORENCE PAT, obstetrician, gynecologist, research administrator; b. Phila., Aug. 17, 1942; d. William R. and Jean Adele Haseltine; m. Frederick Cahn, Mar. 12, 1964 (div. 1969); m. Alan Chodos, Apr. 18, 1970; children: Anna, Elizabeth. BA in Biophysics, U. Calif., Berkeley, 1964; PhD in Biophysics, MIT, 1969; MD, Albert Einstein Coll. of Medicine, 1972. Diplomate Am. Bd. Ob-Gyn., Am. Bd. Reproductive Endocrinology. Asst. prof. dept. ob-gyn. and pediatrics Yale U., New Haven, 1976—82, assoc. prof. dept. ob-gyn. and pediatrics, 1982—85; dir. Ctr. for Population Research, Nat. Inst. Child Health and Human Devel. NIH, Bethesda, Md., 1985—; founder Haseltine System, Inc., Products for the Disabled, 1995—. Co-author: Woman Doctor, 1976, Magnetic Resonance of the Reproductive System, 1987; co-editor: 25 books on reproductive scis. Bd. dirs. Older Women's League, 1998—, Am. Women in Sci., 1998—. Fellow: AAAS (bd. dirs.); mem.: Soc. Cell Biology, Soc. for Advancement Women's Health Rsch. (founder, bd. dirs.), Soc. Gynecol. Investigation, Inst. of Medicine. Office: NIH/NICHD Ctr Population Rsch 6100 Executive Blvd Rm 8b07 Bethesda MD 20892-0001

HASELTON, MARY MICHELSON, retired foreign service officer, artist; b. Kansas City, Mo., May 15, 1920; d. Michael A. and Jeannette (MacFarlane) Michelson; m. George Harry Haselton, Sept. 4, 1964 (dec. Jan. 1995). Student, Washburn U., 1939-41, U. Tex., 1947-52; B in Liberal Arts, Harvard U., 2001. Rsch. sec. Mil. Intelligence U.S. Army, Econ. Def. Bd., Washington, 1941-43; statis. analyst Quartermaster U.S. Army Depot, San Antonio, 1943-44; office mgr. physicians San Antonio, 1944-46; sec. to dir. rsch. IMF, Washington, 1946-47; legis. asst. U.S. Senate, Washington, 1954-59; internat. rels. tchr. Simons Rock Coll., Great Barrington, Mass., 1966-72; fgn. svc. officer Dept. State, Washington, 1960-64, 74-79. Sr. assoc. mem. St. Antony's Coll., Oxford (Eng.) U., 1972—. Exhbns. include Tex. Watercolor Soc., Delgado Mus., New Orleans. Bd. dirs., exec. com. Austin Symphony Orch., 1947-53; mem. various coms. Tex. Fine Arts Assn., Austin, 1947-53; U.S. del. to world population conf. UN, Bucharest, Romania, 1974, Mexico City, 1975. Recipient numerous awards for paintings. Avocations: painting, music, philosophy, science, religion. Home: 85 S Main St Hanover NH 03755 E-mail: mhaselton@valley.net.

HASELWOOD, ALICIA JANE, photographer; b. Evanston, Ill., Nov. 9, 1962; d. Donald Eads Haselwood and Mary Elizabeth Weir; life ptnr. Patti L. Miller, Aug. 19, 1956. AA, St. Petersburg Coll., Clearwater, Fla., 1986—88. Photo lab tech Publix Supermarkets, Clearwater, Fla., 1987—92; color/bw printer Photo Am., Phoenix, 1993—95; custom color printer Image Craft, Phoenix, 1995—97; dupe, copy tech. Ivey Seright Pro Labs., Seattle, 1997—99; owner/artist AJ Haselwood Fine Art Photography, Tampa, Fla., 1999—. Lectr. photography. Prin. works include photography Running Water (Juried Water Impressions U. of South Fla., 2001), exhibitions include Haselwood & Linder, Snooty Judy's Fine Art Gallery, 2001, Spring Salon 2002 Limner Gallery Group Show, Surf's Up IV, Life's A Beach Ormond Meml. Art Mus. and Gardens Group Show, ISQ102 Windows Imaginestation.net Online Juried Gallery Show (Grand Prize Winner, 2002), exhibited in group shows at Tampa Gallery of Photographic Art Members Show, one-woman shows include A Sense of Memory, Joffery's Coffee House, 2000, il-lu-sion, 2002, Brooklyn: A Day in Our Life, 2003, A Touch of Red, Packing House Gallery, 2003, exhibited in group shows at Jasper Arts Ctr., 2004. Mem.: Tampa Gallery of Photographic Art. Independent. Avocations: photography/art, travel, music, golf, gardening. Home: 4630 W Euclid Ave Tampa FL 33629-8334 Office: AJ Haselwood Fine Art Photography 4630 W Euclid Ave Tampa FL 33629-8334 Personal E-mail: trudex@earthlink.net. E-mail: mail@ajhaselwood.com.

HASHE, JANIS HELENE, editor; d. James William and Arlene Florence (Houses) H. AA with honors, Cabrillo Coll., 1974; BA summa cum laude, San Francisco State, 1976; MA, San Jose State, 1982. Asst. editor Sunset Trade Publs., L.A., 1988 89, assoc. editor, 1989-90; editor Western Grocery News, L.A., 1990-95; sr. editor L.A. Parent Mag., Burbank, Calif., 1995—, nat. column editor. Author: (radio play) A Knot in the Heart, 1990; writer essays. Vol. Braille Inst., L.A., 1988—; block capt. Crime Watch Catalina, L.A., 1990-91. Scholar Am. Assn. U. Women, 1972. Mem. Nat. Writers Union, New One-Act Theatre Ensemble (artistic dir., 1985-88, pres., bd. dirs. 1995—). Democrat. Buddhist. Office: L A Parent Mag 443 Irving Dr Burbank CA 91504-2447

HASHIMOTO, CHRISTINE L. physician; b. Chgo., June 29, 1947; d. Shigeru and Kiyo (Sato) H. BA, Oberlin Coll., 1968; MD, Med. Coll. of Pa., 1973. Clin. instr. internal medicine, emergency medicine Med. Coll. and Hosp. of Pa., Phila., 1976-77; asst. prof. medicine Health Service Ctr. U. Colo., Denver, 1977-80, clin. asst. prof. medicine, 1980-87; staff physician emergency dept. St. Joseph Hosp., Denver, 1980-88, Rose Med. Ctr., Denver, 1988-91, Luth. Med. Ctr., Wheatridge, Colo., 1991—. Mem. Colo. Med. Soc., Denver Med. Soc., Am. Coll. Emergency Physicians. Office: Luth Med Ctr 8300 W 38th Ave Wheat Ridge CO 80033-6005

HASKELL, BARBARA, curator; b. San Diego, Nov. 13, 1946; d. John N. and Barbara (Freeman) H.; m. Leon Botstein; children: Clara Haskell Botstein, Maxim Haskell Botstein. BA, UCLA, 1969. Asst. registrar Pasadena (Calif.) Art Mus., 1969, curatorial asst., 1970, asst. curator, 1970, assoc. curator, 1970-72, curator painting and sculpture, 1972-74, Whitney Mus. Am. Art, N.Y.C., 1975—. Author: Arthur Dove, 1974, Marsden Hartley, 1980, Milton Avery, 1982, Blam! The Explosion of Pop, Minimalism and Performance 1958-64, 1984, Georgia O'Keefe: Works on Paper, 1985, Ralston Crawford, 1985, Charles Demuth, 1987, Red Grooms, 1987, Donald Judd, 1988, Burgoyne Diller, 1990, Agnes Martin, 1992, Joseph Stella, 1994, The Am. Century: Art and Culture 1900-1950, 1999, Edward Steichen, 2000, Elie Nadelman, 2002. Named Woman of Yr., Mademoiselle mag., 1973. Office: Whitney Mus Am Art 945 Madison Ave New York NY 10021-2701 E-mail: barbara_haskell@whitney.org.

HASKELL, MOLLY, writer; b. Charlotte, N.C., Sept. 29, 1939; d. John Haskell and Mary Clark; m. Andrew Sarris, May 31, 1969. BA, Sweet Briar Coll.; student, U. London, England, Sorbonne, Paris. Pub. rels. assoc. Sperry Rand; writer, editor French Film Office, N.Y.C.; film critic Village Voice, Viva, New York Magazine, Vogue, 1969-74, 74-80; film reviewer "Special Edition" Pub. TV; film reviewer "All Things Considered" Nat. Pub. Radio; assoc. prof. film Barnard Coll., N.Y.C., 1990; adj. prof. film Columbia U., N.YC., 1992—95; writer. Artistic dir. Sarasota French Film Festival. Author: From Reverence to Rape: The Treatment of Women in the Movies, 1973, rev. edit., 1987, Love and Other Infectious Diseases: A Memoir, 1990, Holding My Own in No Man's Land, 1997; (plays) The Last Anniversary, 1990; contbr. articles and essays to jours. Decorated chevalier Order Arts and Letters (France); recipient Nat. Bd. Review of Motion Pictures award, 1989, Disting. Alumna award Sweet Briar Coll., 1994. Mem. Nat. Soc. of Film Festival Selection Critics, N.Y. Film Critics Circle, N.Y. Film Festival Selection Com., N.Y. Inst. for the Humanities, Authors Guild (coun. 2000-03), The Century Club, Phi Beta Kappa.

HASKETT, DIANNE LOUISE, former mayor, lawyer, consultant; b. London, Ont., Can., Mar. 4, 1955; d. Allan Douglas and Frances Shirley (Crone) H.; m. Jack Kotowicz; 1 child, Annie. BA, U. Waterloo, Ont., 1974; LLD, U. Western Ont., 1977; LLM, London Sch. Econs., 1979. Lawyer Law Soc. of Upper Can., Canada, 1980—; founding ptnr. Haskett, Menear Assoc., Law Firm, 1980—94; speechwriter, internat. cons., and pub. rels. advisor Washington Contact, 2001—; immigration bus. coord. Law Offices of Lewis and Associates, Springfield, Va.; Senate and Congl. campaign advisor. V.p. London Urban Alliance on race rels. Contbr. articles to profl. jours. City councillor London City Coun., 1991-94; mayor, 1994-2000; founder Open Homes Can., London, Ont., 1992; founding mem. London Citizens Com., 1980-84; v.p. Ark Aid Street Mission Inc., London, On., 1986-88. Recipient Pericles award Am. Hellenic Ednl. Progressive Assn., 1999; Grad. scholar Rotary Internat., 1978-79; Paul Harris fellow Rotary Clubs London, 1998. Mem. Law Soc. of Upper Can. Avocations: journalism, collecting antiques and rare books, reading, speech making. Home: 2970 Kildare Ln Fairfax VA 22031

HASKINS, LINDA L. English educator; b. Beaver Falls, Pa., Aug. 31, 1947; d. Henry Griffin and H. Elizabeth Haskins. BA in English, Del. State U., 1969; MA in English, Seton Hall U., 1971; MA in Film, West Chester State U., 1983; postgrad., U. Del., 1988-91. Instr. Capitol Sch. Dist., Dover, Del., 1971-72, U. Del., Newark, 1972-75; asst. prof. Del. State U., Dover, 1975—. Contbg. editor: Succeeding Despite the Odds. Recipient NEH award, 1983. Mem. AAUP, AAUW, Nat. Coun. Tchrs. of English, NAACP, Alpha Kappa Mu, Alpha Kappa Alpha. Avocations: reading, gardening, singing, collecting african-americana. Office: Del State U 1200 N Dupont Hwy Dover DE 19901-2277 Office Phone: 302-857-6575.

HASLAR, PEGGY JO, elementary school counselor; b. Warsaw, N.Y., Aug. 17, 1957; d. Philip W. and Mary Jo Janowsky; children: Benjamin, Matthew. AA, Ctrl. Coll., 1977; BA, Adams State Coll., 1989, MA, 1999. Instr. English Adams State Coll., Alamosa, Colo., 1989—99; counselor Sanford (Colo.) Schs., 1999—2002; elem. counselor Monte Vista (Colo.) Schs., 2002—. Contbr. columns in newspapers. Mem.: Am. Counselors Assn., Colo. Sch. Counselors Assn. (region 4 rep. 2003). Office: Marsh Elem Sch 215 Lyell Monte Vista CO 81144 E-mail: phaslar@hotmail.com.

HASS, LISA M. freelance/self-employed counselor; b. Nashville, Sept. 4, 1953; d. Raymond Alonzo Palmer and Anne Michelle (Jones) Davies; m. Joseph Monroe Hass, Jr. BSBA, Belmont U., 1975; AA in Interior Design, Internat. Fine Arts Coll., 1977; postgrad., Tenn. State U., 1991-98; grad., Citizen Police Acad., 1997; postgrad., Westbrook U., 1998—. Interior designer Lisa Palmer Interior Designs, Nashville, 1977-84; sec. to pres. Hermitage Elect. Supply Corp., Nashville, 1981-83; sec. to dir. Tenn. Dept. Mental Health and Mental Retardation, Nashville, 1984-86; transp. planner Tenn. Dept. Transp., Nashville, 1986—99; pvt. practice wholistic lifestyle counselor Madison, Tenn., 1999—. Recipient cert. of appreciation Tenn. Dept. Mental Health and Mental Retardation, 1986; named Hon. Mem. Tenn. Ho. of Reps., 1990. Mem.: NRA, Mensa. Republican. Mem. Christian Ch. (Disciples Of Christ). E-mail: chachaqueen@comcast.net.

HASS, VICTORIA YUSIM, psychogeriatrics services professional, consultant; b. Chgo., Feb. 20, 1957; d. Sheldon Phillip Yusim and Sharon Friedman; m. Jeffrey Elliot Hass, Apr. 21, 1985; children: Matthew, Avi. BA in Polit. Sci., U. Wis., 1979; MA in Social Svc. Adminstrn., U. Chgo., 1983; PhD in Clin. Psychology, Northwestern U., 1995. Lic. clin. psychologist, Ill., clin. social worker, Ill. Cmty. supr. ret. sr. vol. program Hull House Assn., Chgo., 1979-81; social worker Coun. for Jewish Elderly, Lieberman Geriat. Health Ctr., Skokie, Ill., 1983-85; clin. psychologist Psychol. Assessments, Chgo., 1996-97; clin. dir. IN-PSYTE, Chgo., 1996-97; pvt. practice in psychogeriat. Wilmette, Ill., 1997—; mng. ptnr. Praxis Cognitive Rehab. Assocs., Skokie, 1999—. Psychol. cons. Coun. for Jewish Elderly Lieberman Ctr., Skokie, 1998—. Presenter at industry confs. V.p. Solomon Schechter Day Sch. Parent Orgn., Skokie, 1996—, Dorit chpt. Na'amat USA, Skokie, 1996—; v.p. ways and means Beth Hillel Synagogue, Wilmette, 1999—; bd. dirs. Bd. of Jewish Edn., Northfield, Ill., 1998—. Scholar Northwestern U., 1985-88. Mem. APA, NASW, Am. Group Psychotherapy Assn., Ill. Psychol. Assn., Internat. Psychogeriat. Assn. Avocation: psychology and religion in literature and film. Home: 720 Lamon Ave Wilmette IL 60091-2018 Office: 3612 Lake Ave Wilmette IL 60091-1000

HASSELBACHER, DARLENE M. human resources executive; b. Ill. Grad., Marycrest Coll., 1983; MBA, St. Ambrose U., 1985. Sr. v.p. Sears Mfg. Co., 1984 86; dir. human resources Lee Enterprises, Inc., 1986-97; v.p. human resources Aid Assn. for Luths., Appleton, Wis., 1997—. Vol. Emergency Shelter Bd.; mem. First English Luth. Ch.; bd. dirs. AAL Employee Credit Union. Mem. Media Human Resources Assn. (past pres.), Soc. for Human Resources Mgmt. Office: Aid Assn for Lutherans 4231 N Ballard Rd Appleton WI 54919-0001

HASSELBALCH, MARILYN JEAN, state official; b. Omaha, Jan. 2, 1930; d. Paul William and Helga Esther (Nodgaard) Campfield; m. Hal Burke Hasselbalch, June 13, 1954 (div. 1973); children: Kurt Campfield, Eric Burke, Peter Nels, Ane Catherine Hasselbalch McBride. BA with high distinction, U. Nebr., 1951. Cert. secondary tchr., Nebr. Pub. sch. tchr., Omaha and Long Beach, Calif., 1951-55; staff asst. U.S. Congressman Charles Thone, Lincoln, Nebr., 1973-78, Gov. of Nebr., Lincoln, 1978-82; exec. asst. Nebr. State Treas., Lincoln, 1983-86; sr. asst. Nebr. Gov. Kay A. Orr, Lincoln, 1987-91; exec. dir. Nebr. Appraiser Licensing Bd., Lincoln, 1991—. Mem. camp bd. dirs. YMCA, Nebr., 1969-70; mem. Nebr. Edn. Policies Commn., 1982; state conv. del. Rep. Party Nebr., 1986, 88; gov.'s rep. Nebr. State Hist. Soc., Lincoln, 1987-89; del. Edn. Commn. on States, Balt., 1988; participant strategic leadership for gubernatorial execs. Duke U., 1988; sec. Mission bd. Christ Luth. Ch., 1993—; treas. Danish Sisterhood #90, 1995—. Named to Outstanding Young Women Am., 1961, Woman of Yr., Rho Epsilon, 2000. Mem.: Assn. Appraiser Regulatory Ofcls. (bd. dirs. 1995—2002, publs. com. 1998—2002), Lancaster County Rep. Women (exec. bd. 1988), Nat. Fedn. Rep. Women, Danish Sisterhood Am., Am. Legion Aux., Phi Beta Kappa, Kappa Tau Alpha, Theta Sigma Phi. Lutheran. Avocations: reading, writing, travel, history, entertaining. Home: 4705 South St Lincoln NE 68506-1257 Office: Real Estate Appraiser Bd Nebr State Office Bldg Lincoln NE 68509 E-mail: mihass appraiser@dnr.state.ne.us.

HASSELL-THOMPSON, RUTH, state legislator; Mem. N.Y. Senate from 33d Dist., Albany, 2001—. Office: State Senate 413 Legislative Office Bldg Albany NY 12247

HASSELMEYER, EILEEN GRACE, medical research administrator; b. Bklyn., May 23, 1924; d. Edwin Allen and Margaret Grace (Cody) H. RN, Bellevue Sch. Nursing, 1946; BS, NYU, 1954, MA, 1956, PhD, 1963. Mem. staff Pediatric Metabolic and Nutritional Rsch. Svc., NYU Children's Med. Svc., Bellevue Hosp., N.Y.C., 1946-56, study coord., 1951-56; rsch. nursing supr. Met. Hosp., N.Y.C., 1951; lectr. pediatric nutrition rsch. U. Tex. Sch. Nursing, 1952-53; nursing dir. nutritional rsch. studies Children's Hosp. of John Seely Hosp. (U. Tex. Med. Br.), Galveston, 1952-53; lectr. and nursing rsch. assoc. nutritional svc. pediat. dept. Hosp. Infantile, Mexico City, 1953; nursing dir. rsch. unit Willowbrook State Sch., S.I., 1953-54; commd. USPHS, 1956, advanced through grades to asst. surgeon gen.-rear adm., 1981; ret. 1989; nurse cons. Divsn. Nursing Resources, Bur. Med. Svcs., USPHS, Washington, 1956-59; prin. investigator Handling and Premature Infant Behavior project, NYU, N.Y.C., 1961-63; sr. nurse cons. Div. Nursing, Bur. State Svcs., USPHS, Washington, 1963; spl. asst. for prematurity Office of Dir., Nat. Inst. Child Health and Human Devel., Bethesda, Md., 1963-66, acting dir. perinatal biology and infant mortality program, extramural programs, 1967-68, dir., 1969-74, asst. to dir. for perinatology, 1974-80; chief pregnancy and infancy br. Ctr. for Rsch. for Mothers and Children, 1974-79, acting chief clin. nutrition and early devel. br., 1979-80; assoc. dir. for sci. rev. Office of Dir., 1979-89; spl. asst. to dir. N.C. for Nursing Rsch., 1986-89; exec. dir. Uniform Svcs. U. Health Sci., Fed. Coll. Nursing Feasability Study Task Force, 1989-92. Annie W. Goodrich vis. prof. Yale U. Sch. Nursing, New Haven, 1968-69; asst. surgeon gen. USPHS, Dept. Health and Human Svcs., 1981-89, chmn. interagy. panel on sudden infant death syndrome, 1974-82, others. Contbr. articles to profl. jours. Recipient NICHD Recognition of Outstanding Performance, 1973, plaque for 25 yrs. dedicated svc., 1987, Chief Nurse Officer's medal USPHS, 1989; USUHS Commendable Svc. medal, 1990; USPHS Surgeon Gen.'s Cert. of Appreciation, 1990; HEW-USPHS Commendation medal, 1975; recipient Perinatal Research Soc. award, 1979; NYU Sch. Edn., Health, Nursing and Arts Professions Creative Leadership award, 1980; Achievement award Nat. Sudden Infant Death Syndrome Found., 1987, Eileen G. Hasselmeyer Disting. Sci. Achievement award Sudden Infant Death Syndrome Alliance, 1990; Outstanding Performance award NCNR, 1987, Meritorious Svc. medal HHS-USPHS, 1989; cert. appreciation NIH-NCNR, 1989; Nat. League for Nursing Commonwealth fellow, 1959-62; NIH fellow, 1962-63; Am. Nurses Found. grantee,

1962-63; State of Conn. Maternal and Infant Program grantee, 1969; Sigma Theta Tau research grantee, 1969-71; Yale U. Sch. Nursing developmental grantee, 1969; disting. alumnae award Bellevue Alumnae Assn., 1997. Mem. Pub. Health Svc. Commd. Officers Assn., Bellevue Alumnae Assn.

HASSELMO, ANN HAYES [illegible] college president, psychologist, educator; b. Baytown, Tex., Aug. 15, 1944; d. Robert L. and Dorothy Ann (Cooke) Hayes; 1 child, Meredith Anne. BS with highest honors, Lamar U., 1966; MEd, U. Houston, 1969; PhD, Tex. A&M U., 1977. Lic. psychologist. Asst. prof. dept. psychology Lamar U., Beaumont, Tex., 1977-82, assoc. prof., dir. Psychol. Clinic, 1982-86, dir. grad. programs in psychology, 1981-86, Regents prof. psychology, 1986, pres. faculty senate, 1985-86; pvt. practice clin. psychology Beaumont, 1979-87; prof. Tulane U., New Orleans, 1988-92, dean Newcomb Coll., 1988-92, assoc. provost, 1991-92; pres., prof. psychology Hendrix Coll., Conway, Ark., 1992-2001, pres. emerita, 2001—; v.p., ptnr. A.T. Kearney, Inc., higher edn. practice, Alexandra, Va., 2001—02; mng. dir. Acad. Search Consultation Svc., Washington, 2002—. Adminstr. adolescent residential unit Mental Health/Mental Retardation S.E. Tex., 1979-80, mem. cmty. adv. com., 1981-87; cons. in field; coordinating bd. Tex. Coll. and Univ. Sys. Internship, 1986, chair, bd. dirs. Ednl. and Instl. Ins. Adminstrs., 2000-02; bd. dirs. Nat. Merit Scholarship Corp., Acxiom Corp., Found. for Ind. Higher Edn., Air U., USAF. Contbr. articles to profl. jours. Mem. cmty. adv. com. Beaumont State Ctr. Human Devel., 1981-88; chair So. Collegiate Athletic Conf., 1996-97; participant Nat. Identification Program for Women, Am. Coun. on Edn., 1985, mem. govt. rels. commn., 1993-96, chmn., 1994-96, chmn. coun. of fellows, 1995-96, bd. dirs., 1997-2000; bd. dirs. Beaumont Civic Opera, Lamar U. Wesley Found., Tulane U. Wesley Found.; bd. govs. Isidore Newman Sch., 1991-92; trustee Robert Morris Coll., 1990-98, chmn. edn. com., 1990-94, chmn. pers. com., 1994-98; mem. univ. senate United Meth. Ch., 1993-01, chair commn. on instnl. rev., 1997-01; 1st v.p. Nat. Assn. Schs. & Colls. United Meth. Ch., 1996, pres. 1997-98; bd. dirs. Ouachita coun. Girl Scouts U.S., 1996-2000; mem. bd. visitors Air U., 1999—; mem. Internat. Women's Forum, 1995—, Ark. Women's Leadership Forum, 1999-02, pres. 2000-01; mem. Ark. Commn. to Streamline State Govt., 1996-98; mem. pres. commn. NCAA, 1997-01, chmn. div. III, 1999-2001, mem. exec. com. 1999-2001; chair Assoc. Coll. of the South, 1997-99; bd. dirs. Ark. Repertory Theatre, 2000-01, United Way of Faulkner County, 2000-01. Am. Coun. Edn. fellow Coll. William and Mary, 1986-87; recipient Regents Merit award, 1979, Coll. Health and Behavioral Sci. Merit award, 1982, Lamar U.; named one of Top 100 Women in Ark., Ark. Bus., 1995-99. Mem. APA, Southwestern Psychol. Assn., Family Svcs. Assn. (bd. dirs. 1988-89), Tex. Psychol. Assn. (dir. divsn. acad. psychologists 1986), S.E. Tex. Psychol. Assn. (treas. 1978-80, pres. 1983), Mental Health Assn. Jefferson County, Nat. Register Health Svc. Providers in Psychology, Nat. Assn. Ind. Colls. and Univs. (bd. dirs., vice chmn. 1995, chair 1996). Office: Acad Search Consultation Svc 1717 K St NW Ste 210 Washington DC 20036

HASSENBOEHLER, DONALYN, principal; Prin. McMain Magnet Secondary Sch. Evaluator FIRST grants U.S. Dept. Edn. Recipient U.S. Dept. Edn. Blue Ribbon award, 1990-91. Office: McMain Magnet Secondary Sch 5712 S Claiborne Ave New Orleans LA 70125-4908

HASSERT, ELIZABETH ANNE, transportation sales executive; b. Joliet, Ill., July 28, 1956; d. Wilbur Clarence and Frances Romayne (McLaughlin) H. BA, St. Mary's Coll., Notre Dame, Ind., 1978. Dept. mgr. Lord & Taylor, Aurora, Ill., 1978-79, Oak Brook, Ill., 1979-80; account exec. Cast (N.Am.) Ltd., Rolling Meadows, Ill., 1980-82; sales mgr. Cast (UK) Ltd., London, 1982-83, Sofati Container (UK), Birmingham, Eng., 1983-84; account exec. Sea-Land Svc., Inc., Rolling Meadows, 1984-88, sales mgr., 1988-90, sales exec., 1990-99; dir. strategic sales Maersk, Inc., Oak Brook, Ill., 1999—. Recipient of CSX award of Excellence, 1993. Mem. Hinsdale Jr. Women's Club, St. Mary's Coll. Alumnae Assn. Republican. Roman Catholic. Avocations: needlepoint, cross country skiing, travel, gardening, cooking. Home: 625 N County Line Rd Hinsdale IL 60521-2406 Office: Maersk Inc 2021 Spring Rd Ste 500 Oak Brook IL 60523-1859

HASSETT, VALERIE JANE, interior designer, architect, educator; b. San Diego, Calif., Dec. 22, 1962; d. Roger John and Cecealia Virginia (Cibrich) H. Student, U. Tenn., 1982-86; BFA in Interior Design, Va. Commonwealth U., Richmond, 1988; MArch, Va. Poly. U., Alexandria, 1993. Registered profl. interior designer, Va., cert. constrn. documents technologist, registered profl. architect, Va., cert. Nat. Coun. of Archtl. Registration Bds., Nat. Coun. for Interior Design Qualification (NCIDQ). Interior architect Washington Area Transit Authority, 1988-90, 91-92, Prince William County Va. Govt., 1993-96, RTKL, Balt., 1996-97; instr. Mt. Vernon Coll. at Georgetown U., Washington, 1997-99; project mgr., head interior design dept. Sharadan, Behm, Eustice and Assocs. Ltd., Arlington, Va., 1997—; assoc. prof. No. Va. C.C., 2000—04. Mem. professions fellowship rev. panel AAUW, 2003—. Exhibitions include Nat. Bldg. Mus., 1995, 1996. Chmn. women in architecture film festival Nat. Mus. Women in the Arts, 1998, 2000. Mem. AIA (bd. dirs., 1998-, v.p. 2003, chair women in architecture com. No. Va. chpt. 1993—), Internat. Interior Design Assn. (past pres. Mid-Atlantic chpt.), Neighborhood Design Ctr. Balt. Avocation: paper making. Office: Sheridan Behm Eustice & Assocs 3440 Fairfax Dr Arlington VA 22201-4431 E-mail: vjhassett@aol.com.

HAST, ADELE, editor, historian; b. N.Y.C., Dec. 6, 1931; d. Louis and Kate (Miller) Krongelb; m. Malcolm Howard Hast, Feb. 1, 1953; children: David Jay, Howard Arthur. BA magna cum laude, Bklyn. Coll., 1953; MA, U. Iowa, 1969, PhD, 1979. Rsch. assoc. Atlas Early Am. History Project, Newberry Library, Chgo., 1971-75; assoc. dir. Atlas Great Lakes Indian History Project, 1976-79, Hist. Boundary Data File Project, 1979-81; editor in chief Marquis Who's Who, Inc., Chgo., 1981-86; survey dir. Nat. Opinion Rsch. Ctr., U. Chgo., 1986-89; rsch. fellow Newberry Libr., Chgo., 1989-95, scholar in residence, 1995—; exec. editor St. James Press, Chgo., 1990-92; mng. editor Hist. Ency. of Chgo. Women U. Ill., Chgo., 1991-93, dir., editor Hist. Ency. of Chgo. Women project, 1993-2001, sr. rsch. assoc. Ctr. for Rsch. on Women and Gender, 1999—. Mem. faculty Newberry Libr. Summer Inst. Cartography, 1980. Author: Loyalism in Revolutionary Virginia, 1982, American Leaders Past and Present: The View from Who's Who in America, 1985; compiler: Iowa, Missouri, vol. 4 of Historical Atlas and Chronology of County Boundaries, 1788-1980, 1984; editor: International Directory of Company Histories, vols. 3-5, 1991-92, Women Building Chicago 1790-1990: A Biographical Dictionary, 2001; assoc. editor: Atlas of Great Lakes Indian History, 1987; curator exhibit on Chgo. history Spertus Inst. of Jewish Studies, 2002-03; contbr. articles to profl. jours. Mem. profl. adv. grad. program pub. history Loyola U., 1986—; treas., bd. dirs. Chgo. Map Soc., 1980-81, 93-95; mem. New Trier Twp. H.S. Bd. Caucus, 1972-74; mem. acad. coun. Am. Jewish Hist. Soc., 1985—; pres. Chgo. Jewish Hist. Soc., 1980-81, bd. dirs., 1977—. Recipient Alumna of Yr. award Bklyn. Coll., 1984, Colonial Williamsburg Found. grantee-in-aid, 1975, Brit. Acad. rsch. fellow, 1979; Am. Coun. Learned Socs. grantee-in-aid, 1980; NEH rsch. grantee, 1985, 87, 93-95, 97-98, fellow Women's Archive, 2003—. Fellow Royal Hist. Soc., Phi Beta Kappa, Kappa Delta Pi; mem. Am. Hist. Assn., Orgn. Am. Historians, Chgo. Area Women's History Conf. (sec., treas. 1994-2004, bd. dirs. 1990—), Caxton Club (coun. 1990-93, 2003—). Office: Newberry Library 60 W Walton St Chicago IL 60610-3380

HASTINGS, CYNTHIA LAMPROS, graphic artist, photographer; b. Lawrence, Mass., Mar. 21, 1942; d. Theodore and Imelda (Daigle) Lampros; m. Joseph MacAlphine Hastings, Aug. 8, 1963 (div. Oct. 1987); children: Lauren Smith, Sharon Castellanos, Joseph David. AAS, Westbrook Coll., Portland, Maine, 1962; BFA with Photo Concentration, Montserrat Coll. of Art, Beverly, Mass., 1998. Freelance designer CLH Graphics, Andover, Mass., 1989—. Computer illustrator: The Surface Plane, 1992. Home: 15 Avon St Andover MA 01810-1814 Office: 15 Avon St Andover MA 01810-1814

HASTINGS, DEBORAH, [illegible] b. [illegible], Ind., May 11, 1959; d. Mortimer Winthrop Hastings and Margaret Hooper (Smith) Zimmerman. Student music, U. Wis. Bass guitarist, N.Y.C. and Madison, Wis., 1975—; freelance photographer Madison, 1976-81; band leader Bo Diddley, 1992—; founder A/Prompt Computer Telepromting Svcs., Inc., 1994—. Featured bassist with Duck Dunn for Bush inauguration, performing with Billy Preston, Dr. John, Koko Taylor, Willie Dixon, Albert Collins, Joe Cocker, Carla Thomas, Eddie Floyd, Ron Wood, Steve Cropper, Bo Diddley, Jerry Lee Lewis, Chuck Berry, Joe Louis Walker; has also performed with Ben E. King, Little Anthony, Sam Moore, John Lee Hooker, Mick Fleetwood, Al Kooper, James Cotton; TV shows include Legends of Rock and Roll Live from Rome; appeared on David Letterman Show, 2003; subject of PBS Spl., 2003. Bass player TV shows Joan Rivers, 1987, Classsics of Rock and Roll, 1988, Gunslingers tour Live from the Ritz with Ron Wood & Bo Diddley, 1988, Live from the Ritz, 1989, Legends of Rock and Roll (live from Australia), Legends of Guitar from Seville, Spain, 1991, Showtime at the Apollo, 1992, N.Y. at Night, 1992; performed Into The Night, 1991 (TV show) Nashville Now, 1991, American Musicshop, 1991, Johnny Carson Show, 1990, Pat Sajak Show, 1990, Carla Thomas, 1991, Arts & Entertainment Revue, 1990, (Madison Sq. Garden) Tribute to John Lee Hooker, 1990, Richard Nader's 25th Anniversary Show, 1994, Conan O'Brien Show, 1996; recordings include Bo Diddley's Grammy Nominated Album "A Man Amongst Men", 1996; performer in concert video "A Man Amongst Men", 1996; tours in Europe, Australia and Japan; performed at inaugurations of Pres. George Bush, 1989, Pres. Bill Clinton, 1997; performed with Bo Diddley opening of Seattle Music Experience Mus., 2000, Edgar Winter, 2003, Buffy Saint-Marie, 2003. Fundraiser, bassist polit. campaigns, Madison. Recipient numerous awards for pottery, award Arts Coun., Madison, Arts Coun., Ann Arbor, Mich.; played at Rock and Roll Hall of Fame Mus. Johnnie Johnson in Buenos Aires, Argentina, 2003. Mem. Musicians Union (local 802). Democrat. Avocations: computers, photography, graphics design, video. Office: Talent Cons Internat 1560 Broadway Ste 1308 New York NY 10036-1518

HASTINGS, L(OIS) JANE, architect, architecture educator; b. Seattle, Mar. 3, 1928; d. Harry and Camille (Pugh) H.; m. Norman John Johnston, Nov. 22, 1969. B.Arch., U. Wash., Seattle, 1952, postgrad. in Urban Planning, 1958. Architect Boeing Airplane Co., Seattle, 1951-54; recreational dir. Germany, 1954-56; architect (various firms), Seattle, 1956-59, pvt. practice architecture, 1959-74; instr. archtl. drafting Seattle Community Coll., part-time 1969-80; owner/founder The Hastings Group Architects, Seattle, 1974—; lectr. design Coll. Architecture, U. Wash., 1975; incorporating mem. Architecta (P.S.), Seattle, 1980, pres., from 1980. Mem. adv. bd. U. Wash. YWCA, 1967—69; mem. Mayor's Com. on Archtl. Barriers for Handicapped, 1974—75; chmn. regional public adv. panel on archtl. and engrng. services GSA, 1976; mem. citizens adv. com. Seattle Land Use Adminstrn. Task Force, 1979—; AWIU guest of Soviet Women's Con., 1983; spkr. Pacific Rim Forum, Hong Kong, 1987; guest China Internat. Conf. Ctr. for Sci. and Tech. of the China Assn. for Sci. and Tech., 1989; mem. adv. com. Coll. architecture and urban planning U. Wash., 1993; mem. accreditation team U. Oreg. Coll. Architecture, 1991, N.J. Inst. Tech. Sch. Architecture, 1992; juror Home of the Yr. ann. award AIA/Seattle Times, 1996; mem. architect selection com. Wash. State capital carillon project, Pratt Art Ctr. new bldg., 2001. Design juror for nat. and local competitions, including Red Cedar Shingle/AIA awards, 1977, Current Use Honor awards, AIA, 1980, Exhibit of Sch. Architecture award, 1981; Contbr. to: also spl. features newspapers, articles in profl. jours. Sunset mag. Mem. bd. Am. Women for Internat. Understanding, del. to, Egypt, Israel, USSR, 1971, Japan and Korea, 1979, USSR, 1983; mem. Landmarks Preservation Bd. City of Seattle, 1981-83; mem. Design Constrn. Rev. Bd. Seattle Sch. Dist., 1985-87; mem. mus. con. Mus. History and Industry, 1987—; leader People to People del. women architects to China, 1990. Recipient AIA/The Seattle Times Home of Month Ann. award, 1968; Exhbn. award Seattle chpt. AIA, 1970; Environ. award Seattle-King County Bd. Realtors, 1970, 77,; AIA/House and Home/The American Home Merit award, 1971, Sp. Honor award Wash. Aggregates and Concrete Assn., 1993, Prize bridge Am. Inst. Steel Contrn., 1993; Honor award Seattle chpt. AIA, 1977, 83; Women Achievement award Past Pres. Assembly, 1983, Washington Women and Trading Cards, 1983; Nat. Endowment for Arts grantee, 1977; others; named to West Seattle High Sch. Hall of Fame, 1989, Woman of Achievement Matrix Table, 1994; named Woman of Distinction, Columbia River Girl Scout Coun., 1994. Fellow AIA (pres. Seattle chpt. 1975, pres. sr. coun. 1980, state exec. bd. 1975, N.W. regional dir. 1982-87, Seattle chpt. found. bd. 1985-87, Bursar Coll. Fellows 1989-90, Coll. of Fellows historian 1994—, internat. rels. com. 1988-92, vice chancellor 1991, chancellor 1992, Seattle chpt. medal 1995, Northwest & Pacific region Medal of Honor 2002, Leslie N. Boney Spirit of Fellowship award 2003, Richard Upjohn Fellows medal), Internat. Union Women Architects (v.p. 1969-79, sec. gen. 1985-89, del. UIA Congress, Montreal 1990), Am. Arbitration Assn. (arbitrator 1981—), Coun. of Design Professions, Assn. Women Contrs., Suppliers and Design Cons., Allied Arts Seattle, Fashion Group, Tau Sigma Delta, Alpha Rho Chi (medal).

HASTINGS, MELANIE (MELANIE JEAN WOTRING), television news anchor; b. Phila., May 9, 1955; d. Jean Athanase and Annabell (Snyder) Sayegh; m. Edmund Ross Wotring Jr., Apr. 19, 1980; children: Edmund Ross III, Allison Stewart. Attended, U. Nice, France, 1975; BA in Speech, Comm., U. Del., 1977. Anchor, reporter Sta. WOAY-TV, Oak Hill, W.Va., 1977-78, Sta. WSAZ-TV, Huntington, W.Va., 1978-79, 85-89, Sta. KTVI-TV, St. Louis, 1979-80; anchor ten o'clock news Sta. WTTV, Indpls., 1989-90; anchor (cable TV) NewsChannel 8, Washington, 1991—; anchor Sta. WDCA-TV, 1995-96. Mem. AFTRA, NATAS-DC, Am. Women in Radio and TV. Avocations: exercise, skiing. Office: 1100 Wilson Blvd Arlington VA 22209-2249

HATALOSKY, PAULETTE ANN, music educator; b. S.I., N.Y., Oct. 10, 1953; d. Paul Joseph Manzo and Loretta Laura Langere; m. George Thomas Hatalosky, June 28, 1986. BS in Music Edn., Hunter Coll., 1976; MA in Music Edn., NYU, 1981; cert. tchr. of handicapped, Keane Coll., 1987. Music tchr. Stella Maris H.S., Rockaway Park, NY, 1981—86, Trinity Christian Sch., Elizabeth, NJ, 1987—88; ins. claims staff Allstate Ins., Nashville, 1990—99; music tchr. Overbrook Sch., Nashville, 1999—. Mem.: Sweet Adelines Internat. (asst. dir. 1993—95).

HATCH, D. PATRICIA P. principal; Prin. Naubuc Sch. Recipient U.S. Dept. Edn. Elem. Sch. Recognition award, 1989-90, Women of the Year award Glastonbury Profl. Women. Office: Naubuc Sch 84 Griswold St Glastonbury CT 06033-1006

HATCH, PAMELA H. state legislator; Mem. from dist. 100 Maine State Ho. of Reps., 1993-95, mem. from dist. 98, 1995—. Office: Maine Ho of Reps State Capitol Augusta ME 04333-0001

HATCH, SALLY RUTH, foundation administrator, writer, consultant; b. Grand Rapids, Mich., Apr. 16, 1935; d. George and Evangeline (Boerma) Meyer; m. S. John Byington, Nov. 27, 1964 (div. Dec. 1988); children: Nancy Lee Rhodes, Barbara Ann Byington; m. Robert C. Hatch, Sept. 20, 2003. BA, Western Mich. U., 1957; MA, U. Md., 1962. Cert. tchr. K-8 Md. Grad. asst. U. Md., College Pk., 1959-60; tchr. U. Chgo. Lab. Sch., 1963-64, Grand Rapids, 1957-59. 64-65, Montgomery County Pub. Schs., Rockville, Md., 1961-63; learning specialist Endeavor Learning Ctr., Rockville, 1987-88; asst. to pres. Women in Mil. Svc., Arlington, Va., 1988-89; exec. asst. Korean War Vets. Meml. Adv. Bd., Washington, 1989-91; pub. safety cons., civic activist, 1991—2000. Cons. Children Early Edn. Program, Bur. Edn. Handicapped, Dept. Edn., Washington, 1975—80; pvt. practice diagnostician. Author: (book) Marriage Through Divorce and Beyond, Vol. Fairfax County Pub. Schs. Enrollment Study 1983, coord. Capital Hill Cmty. Policing Coun.; mem. MPD's Chief Police Citizens Adv. Coun.; project dir. Guns into Plowshares Sculpture Project; mem. Ward 6 Crime Task Force; mem. coun. Neighbors Who Care DC; exec. bd. dirs. MidNortheast Family Strengthening Collaborative; pres. Greater Springfield (Va.) Rep. Women's Club, 1980, v.p., 1980; dir. Fairfax County Rep. Com., 1988. Recipient Vol. Recognition award, Fairfax Pub. Schs., 1985; fellow, Metro Urban Concerns Ministry. Mem.: LWV (study rep. 1980), Capital Hill Restoration Soc. (pub. safety issues chair). Avocations: reading, writing poetry and music, active sports, church activities. Home and Office: 3406 Offutt Rd Randallstown MD 21133-3512 Office Phone: 410-521-8364.

HATCH, WILDA GENE, broadcast company executive; b. Ogden, Utah, Nov. 28, 1917; d. Abraham Lincoln and Edris Alida (Toombs) Glasmann; m. George Clinton Hatch, Dec. 24, 1940; children: Michell Arnow, Diane G. Orr, Jeffrey B., Randall C., Deepika Avanti. BA, Stanford U., 1939; HHD (hon.), Weber State U., 1981. Pres. The Std. Corp., Ogden, 1955-93; v.p. Sta. KUTV, Salt Lake City, 1956-94. Pres. Women's State Legis. Coun., Salt Lake City, 1967-69; active LWV, Salt Lake City, 1965—. Democrat. Avocations: hiking, rock art, fishing. Home: 1537 Chandler Dr Salt Lake City UT 84103-4220

HATCHELL, SYLVIA, basketball coach; b. Gastonia, N.C., Feb. 28, 1952; m. Sammy Hatchell; 1 child, Van. B.Phys. Edn. cum laude, Carson-Newman Coll., 1974; MS, U. Tenn., 1975. Coach jr. varsity women's team U. Tenn.; head coach Francis Marion Coll.; head women's basketball coach U. N.C., Chapel Hill, 1986—. Asst. coach U.S. World Univ. Games team, 1983, 85; ct. coach U.S. Olympic basketball try-outs, 1984, 92; basketball events taff Olympic Games, L.A., 1984; asst. coach U.S. team 1988 Olympic Games, Goodwill Games and World Championships; coach USA team World Univ. Games, Fukuoka, Japan, 1995, R. william Jones Cup, 1994. Named Nat. Coach of the Yr., USA Today, 1994, Coll. Sports Mag., 1994, Converse NAIA Reg. Coach of the Yr., 1986, AMFVoit Championship Coach, 1986, Coll. Basketball Coach of the Yr., Athletes Internat. Ministries, 1995, Carson-Newman Disting. Alumnus of the Yr., 1994; inductee Francis Marion U. Athletic Hall of Fame, 1993. Mem. Women's Basketball Coaches Assn. (pres. 1996-97, past bd. dirs.), Amateur Basketball Assn. of U.S. (women's games com.).

HATCHETT, GLENDA A. municipal judge; b. 1952; Former sr. atty., spokesperson Delta Air Lines; chief presiding judge, dept. head Fulton County Juvenile Ct., Atlanta. Bd. dirs. Gap Inc. Named Outstanding Jurist of Yr. Nat. Bar Assn. Office: Fulton Juvenile Court 395 Pryor St SW Atlanta GA 30312-2713

HATFIELD, C. MAILE, lobbyist; b. Exeter, N.H., Sept. 16, 1971; d. Harris Harding and Virginia Holmes (Brodhead) Hatfield. BA in English, William Smith Coll., Geneva, N.Y., 1993. Registered lobbyist, U.S. Congress. Rep. govt. affairs Grocery Mfrs. Am., Washington, 1995-98, mgr. fed. affairs, 1998—. Mem. Pub. Affairs Coun. Washington, 1998—. Chair United Way Campaign, Grocery Mfrs. Am., Washington, 1999; chair D.C. phonathon Emma Willard Sch., Troy, N.Y., 1999. Mem. The Food Group. Republican. Avocations: skeet/sporting clays, travel, music, philanthropy, architecture. Home: 1804 Bush St San Francisco CA 94109-5205 Office: Grocery Mfrs Am 1010 Wisconsin Ave NW Ste 900 Washington DC 20007-3673

HATFIELD, ELAINE CATHERINE, psychology educator; b. Detroit, Oct. 22, 1937; d. Charles E. and Eileen (Kalahar) H.; m. Richard L. Rapson, June 15, 1982. BA, U. Mich., 1959; PhD, Stanford U., 1963. Asst. prof. U. Minn., Mpls., 1963-64, assoc. prof., 1964-66; asso. prof. U. Rochester, 1966-68, U. Wis., Madison, 1968-69, prof., 1969-81; now prof. U. Hawaii, Honolulu, chmn. dept. psychology, 1981-83. Author: Equity: Theory and Research, 1978, Mirror, Mirror: The Importance of Looks in Everyday Life, 1986, Psychology of Emotions, 1991, Love, Sex and Intimacy, 1993, Emotional Contagion, 1994, Love and Sex: Cross-cultural Perspectives, 1996, Rosie, 2000; contbr. articles to profl. jours. Recipient Disting. Scientist award Soc. Exptl. Social Psychology, 1993. Fellow APA; mem. Soc. Sci. Study of Sex (pres., Disting. Scientist award 1996, Alfred Kinsey award 1998). Home: 3334 Anoai Pl Honolulu HI 96822-1418 Office: U Hawaii 2430 Campus Rd Honolulu HI 96822-2216 Office Phone: 808-956-6276. E-mail: elaineh@Hawaii.edu.

HATFIELD, JULIANA, vocalist; b. Duxbury, Mass., 1968; Student, Berklee Sch. Music. Recording and performing artist, 1987—. Singer, bass guitarist Blake Babies, 1987-91. Albums (solo) include Hey Babe, 1992, Become What You Are, 1993, Only Everything, 1995, Bed, 1998, (with Blake Babies) Nicely, Nicely, 1987, Earwig, 1989, Sunburn, 1990, (with Lemonheads) It's a Shame About Ray, 1992, Come On Feel the Lemonheads, 1993. Office: Atlantic Records Rm 203 1290 Avenue Of The Americas Fl Conc4 New York NY 10104-0199 also: 9229 W Sunset Blvd Los Angeles CA 90069-3402

HATFIELD, JULIE STOCKWELL, journalist, newspaper editor; b. Detroit, Mar. 22, 1940; d. William Hume and Ruth Reed (Palmer) Stockwell; m. Philip Mitchell Hatfield, Aug. 1, 1964 (div. 1979); children—Christian Andrew, Juliana, Jason David; m. Timothy Leland, Nov. 23, 1984; stepchildren— Christian Bourso, London Chamberlain BA, U. Mich, 1962. Staff reporter Women's Wear Daily, NYC, 1962-64; freelance feature writer Bath-Brunswick Times, Wis. State Jour., 1964-68, Quincy Patriot Ledger, Mass., 1968-77; freelance music critic, fashion editor Boston Herald, 1977-79; fashion editor Boston Globe, 1979-95, living/arts writer, 1995-96, soc. columnist, 1996-2001, travel writer, 2001; freelance travel writer, 2001—; fashion editor The Newbury St. and Back Bay Guide, Boston. Author: (with others) Guide to the Thrift Shops of New England, 1982, Felix, 2004. Recipient Lulu award Men's Fashion Assn., 1985, Atrium award for Outstanding Writing on Fashion U. Ga., 1987, 92; Nat. Endowment Arts grantee, 1973. Mem.: Soc. of Am. travel writers. Episcopalian. Avocation: piano. E-mail: juliestockwell@peoplepc.com.

HATFIELD, MARY LOU, flight nurse, paramedic; b. Kenosha, Wis., June 18, 1951; d. Jeanie (Galle) Hatfield; children: Anthony Bellantonio, Theresa Bellantonio. ADN, Gateway Tech. Coll., 1986. LPN, 1977-86; RN; cert. emergency nurse, Wis.; trauma nurse specialist; nat. registered emergency med. technician-paramedic. Staff nurse Kenosha Meml. Hosp., 1970-85, 87-89, St. Luke's Hosp., Milw., 1989-91; EMT I Arcadia (Wis.) Ambulance, 1991-97; flight nurse Gundersen Luth., La Crosse, Wis., 1991—; dep. med. examiner La Crosse County, 1993-2000; chief dep. med. examiner, 2000—; paramedic Tri-State Ambulance, La Crosse, 1996—. Mem. Internat. Forensic Nurse Assn., Air Surface Transport Nurse Assn., Emergency Nurse Assn., Air Surface Transport Nurse Assn. (edn. chair 1999-2000), Western Wis. Emergency Nurse Assn. (sec. 1995-97, pres. 1999-2000), North Ctrl. Nurse Assn. (Wis. rep. 1997-99, 2000—, pres.-elect 1999, pres. 2000), Wis. Coroners & Med. Examiners Assn. Avocations: cross-stitching, reading, biking, photography. Office: Gundersen Luth Med Ctr 1910 South Ave La Crosse WI 54601-5467 Home: 3832 Azalea Dr Las Cruces NM 88005-1027 E-mail: chopperRN@aol.com., mlhatfie@gundluth.org-w.

HATFIELD, RENEE S.J. music educator; b. Worcester, Mass., July 15, 1962; d. Raymond S.Y. and Ramona Mok Chin; m. Jeffery Allen Hatfield, Oct. 5, 1986; children: Aria Jenee, Tyler Allen. B in Music Edn.,

Campbellsville (Ky.) Coll., 1985. Lic. tchr. pre K-12 Mass. Gen. music tchr. Jacob Hiatt Magnet Sch. Blue Ribbon, Worcester, 1985—. Ch. pianist, worship leader, diversity leader First Bapt. Ch., Shrewsbury, Mass., 1970—; ch. pianist, worship leader Faith Bapt. Ch., Auburn, Mass., 2003—. Mem.: Orgn. Am. Kodaly Educators, Music Educators Nat. Conf. Home: 33 Neptune Rd Worcester MA 01605 Office: Jacob Hiatt Magnet Sch Worcester Pub Sch Systems 772 Main St Worcester MA 01610

HATFIELD, STACIE H. professional pianist; b. Shreveport, La., Mar. 12, 1967; d. Roger Dorion and Rita (Jasura) Haneline; m. Scott Andrew Hatfield, Aug. 14, 1993; children: Justin Edward, Veronica Cecilia. BMusic, Converse Coll., Spartanburg, S.C., 1989; MMusic, Manhattan Sch. Music, 1992. Dir. music St. Vincent's Acad., Savannah, Ga., 1991-93; pianist Honolulu Chorale, 1996-98; asst. pianist Hawaii Opera, Honolulu, 1996-98; pianist Hawaii Vocal Arts, Honolulu, 1996-98; tchr. Newport News, Va., 1998—. Freelance pianist; substitute organist Our Lady of Mt. Carmel, Newport News; accompanist, U. Norfolk, Christopher Newport U., Canberra, Australia; mem. Internat. Flabours Concert Series, Canberra. Mem. Va. Piano Tchrs. Assn., Am. Embassy Women's Assn. (co-chair hospitality), Women's Internat. Club. Home: 102 N Cromwell Rd Savannah GA 31410-3902 E-mail: Staciehh@bigpond.net.

HATHAWAY, LYNN MCDONALD, education advocate, administrator; b. N.Y.C., Mar. 28, 1939; d. William Douglas IV and Dorothy Edna (Homan) McDonald; m. Earl Burton Hathaway II, July 7, 1962; children: Earl Burton III, Amanda McDonald. BA, Bryn Mawr Coll., 1960. Editl. asst. Mademoiselle mag., N.Y.C., 1960-61; adminstrv. asst. Peace Corps office Nat. Coun. Chs., N.Y.C., 1961-62; vice chmn. cmty. rsch. N.Y. Jr. League, 1969-70; editor, chmn. N.Y. Entertains cookbook, 1973-74; edn. chair London Svc. League, 1979-80; pres., dir. London Svc. League, Jr. League, 1980-82; ind. writer, editor London, 1983. Bd. dirs Friends of Ferguson Libr., Stamford, Conn., 1988, mem., rec. sec., v.p., pres., 1988-95, trustee, 1996-01, sec. bd. trustees, 2000—, citizen adv., 2001—, continuing chair student life com.; trustee, mem. exec. com., chair student life com. Conn. State U. Sys., 1991—, sec. bd. trustees, 1999—. Mem. Bryn Mawr Alumnae Assn. (pres. London 1983-86, internat. councillor 1988-90). Episcopalian. Home: 7 Oakmont Dr Falmouth ME 04105-1157 Fax: 203-359-2511. E-mail: lynnhath@aol.com.

HATHCOCK, BONITA CATHERINE (BONNIE HATHCOCK), managed health care company executive; b. Chambersburg, Pa., Oct. 30, 1948; d. John McGillis Gentry and Lola Vaneda (Showaker) Wood; m. Lindsay Levoy Hathcock, Apr. 14, 1984. BS in Bus., Shippensburg State U., 1971; MBA, Nova U., 1989. Instr. bus. Cen. Pa. Bus. Sch., Summerdale, 1972-75; with Xerox Corp., various locations, 1975-84, product planning mgr. Dallas, 1982-84; dir. mktg. edn. Datapoint Corp., San Antonio, 1984-85, sr. dir. corp. edn., 1985, sr. dir. worldwide edn., 1985-87; dir. corp. tng. Siemens/Tel Plus, Boca Raton, Fla., 1987, joined Humana Inc., Louisville, 1999, now sr. v.p., chief human resources officer. Prin. bcG Enterprises (profl. awareness tng. co.) Dallas, 1982-84. Avocations: cooking, swimming, reading, walking, writing. Office: Humana Inc The Humana Bldg 500 W Main St Louisville KY 40202

HATHCOX, CATHY BRIZENDINE, special education educator; b. Roanoke, Va., Dec. 18, 1950; d. Sydnor Wells Brizendine, Jr. and Charlotte Scott Brizendine; m. Clarence Becton Hathcox, Aug. 10, 1984 (dec. July 1996). BA in Polit. Sci. cum laude, Duke U., 1972; AA in Bus. Adminstrn. summa cum laude, Nat. Coll. Bus. and Tech., 1978; initial lic. and endorsement in spl. edn., U. Va., 2003. Pers. dir. Caddo Parish Sheriff's Office, Shreveport, La., 1990—91; sales assoc. Dillards Dept. Stores, Shreveport, Bossier City, 1991—93; merchandising and asst. mgr. Burlington Coat Factory, Shreveport, 1993—94; customer svc. assoc. K-Mart Corp., Roanoke, Va., 1998—2000; spl. edn. instrnl. aide Roanoke City Pub. Schs., 1999—2000, learning disabilities tchr., 2000—02, substitute tchr., 2003, spl. edn. inclusion tchr. 9th Grade, 2003—. Mem.: NEA, Roanoke Edn. Assn., Va. Edn. Assn., Duke U. Alumni Assn. Democrat. Avocations: writing, travel, reading, fitness.

HATHORNE, GAYLE GENE, musician, family historian; b. Concordia, Kans., Sept. 3, 1953; d. Richard and R. Virginia (Huscher) Hathorne; 1 child, Amanda Kimberly. BMusic, Manhattan Sch. Music, N.Y.C., 1976; Artist's Diploma, Karajan Akademie, Berlin Philharm. Orch., 1980. Backstage hornplayer Bayreuth (Germany) Festival, 1977; 3d/1st solo hornist Stadt. Orch., Solingen, Germany, 1980-88; genealogy instr. Blue Ridge C.C., 1999—2002; dir. membership, office mgr. N.Y. Geneal. and Biog. Soc., 2002—. Substitute tchr. music and German, Henderson County Pub. Schs., 1988-98; pvt. horn tchr., Hendersonville, 1989—. Sr. editor Tarheel Tattler, 1994-96, River Ramblings, 1994-96; editor Kuykendall Gazette, 1996-97; performer on CDs/cassettes; extra in film 28 Days, 1999. Nat. Fedn. Music Clubs nat. scholar, 1971. Mem. DAR (state pub. rels. N.C. Soc. 1997-99, organizing regent Abraham Kuykendall chpt. 1996), Children of Am. Revolution (organizing sr. pres. French Broad River Soc. 1992, state libr. 1996-98). Democrat. Avocations: genealogical research, photography, travel, writing, listening to opera. E-mail: ghathorne@nygbs.org.

HATLER, PATRICIA RUTH, lawyer; b. Las Vegas, Nev., Aug. 4, 1954; d. Houston Eugene and Laurie (Danforth) Hatler; m. Howard A. Coffin II; children: Sloan H. D. Coffin, Laurie H. M. Coffin. BS, Duke U., 1976; JD, U. Va., 1980. Bar: Pa. 1980, Ohio 2002. Assoc. Dechert, Price & Rhoads, Phila., 1980-83; assoc. counsel Independence Blue Cross, Phila., 1983-86, sr. v.p., gen. counsel, corp. sec., 1987-99; exec. v.p., gen. counsel, corp. sec. Nationwide, Columbus, 1999—. Home: 17 N Parkview Ave Bexley OH 43209-1427 Office: Nationwide One Nationwide Plaza Columbus OH 43215 E-mail: hatlerp@nationwide.com.

HATTAN, SUSAN K. legislative staff member; b. Lincoln, Nebr., Jan. 11, 1951; d. Hubert Curtis and Margaret Marie H. BA summa cum laude, Washburn U., 1973; MA with distinction, Am. U., 1977. Legis. aide to Senator Robert J. Dole, Washington, 1973-77; policy analyst, special asst. Adminstrn. of Food Safety and Quality Svc., Dept. Agrl., Washington, 1977-78; legis. dir. to Senator Nancy L. Kassebaum, Washington, 1978-89; minority staff dir., sub-committee on edn., arts and humanities Senate Com. on Labor and Human Resources, Washington, 1989-92, minority staff dir., 1993-94, staff dir., 1995-96; dep. staff dir. Senate Com. Health, Edn., Labor and Pensions, Washington, 1997—. Mem. Phi Kappa Phi, Zeta Tau Alpha. Office: Health Education Labor Senate Hart Office Bldg Rm 835 Washington DC 20510-0001

HATTON, BARBARA R. academic administrator; b. La Grange, Ga., June 4, 1941; d. William H. and Katye (Tucker) H.; 1 child, Kera M. Washington. BS, Howard U., 1962; MA, The Atlanta U., 1966; MEA, Stanford U., 1971, PhD, 1976. Assoc. dir. Stanford (Calif.) U., 1970-72, asst. prof. edn. adminstrn. and policy studies, 1976-79; chair Dept. Adminstrn. & Supervision, acting assoc. dean The Atlanta U., 1979-80; dean, prof. Tuskegee U., Ala., 1984-88; dep. dir. The Ford Found., N.Y., 1988; scholar-in-residence So. Edn. Found., Atlanta, 1992—; pres. S.C. State U., Orangeburg, 1993—, Knoxville Coll., 1997—. Mem. adv. com. Tchr. Edn. Project Assn. Am. Colls.; mem. review panel Fifth Yr. Non-Trad. Edn. Programs Ala. Dept. Edn.; mem. futures task force Am. Assn. Colls. for Tchr. Edn.; noms. com. New Deans Orientation Com. Trainer New Dean's Inst. Am. Assn. of Colls. of Tchr. Edn.; commn. on ednl. quality So. Regional Edn. Bd.; mem. Math. Standardization Com. Atlanta Pub. Schs.; reader Jour. Ga. Ednl. Rsch. Assn.; chmn. subcommittee on provisional certification and reciprocity, exec. com. Bd. Regents and State Bd. of Edn., State of Ga. Mem. S.C. Humanities Coun., Orangeburg C. of C.; bd. dirs. Assn. Presbyn. Colls. and Univs., Tenn. Rsch. Valley, Knoxville Symphony; active Met. Drug Com., Coll. Bds. Equity 2000 Project. Fellow NDEA, EPDA; recipient The Rose award U. S.C., 1993, Drum Major for Justice awards, 1993. Mem. Am. Ednl. Rsch. Assn., Am. Assn. Sch. Adminstrs., Exec. Women's Assn., Rotary Knoxville, Alpha Kappa Alpha Sorority Inc., Phi Chi Hon. Soc., Phi Delta Kappa Hon. Soc. Office: Knoxville Coll 901 College St Knoxville TN 37921-4724

HATTON, JANIE R. HILL, principal; Formerly prin. Milw. Trade and Tech. H.S.; cmty. supt. Milw. Pub. Schs., 1989-91; dir. Dept. Leadership Svcs., 1996-97; dep. supt. Leadership Svcs., Milw., 1997-99; prin. Pulaski H.S., Milw., 1999—2001, N. Div. H.S., Milw., 2001—. Recipient Milw. Prin. Yr. award Alexander Hamilton H.S., 1986, Nat. Principal of the Year award Nat. Assn. Secondary Sch. Principals and Met. Life Ins. Co., 1993, It Takes a Whole Village Leadership award, 1999. Mem. Milw. Links Inc., Delta Sigma Theta. Office: 1011 W Center St Milwaukee WI 53206-3299

HAU, LENE, physicist, optics scientist; BS in Math. and Physics, U. Aarhus, Denmark, 1984, MS, 1986, PhD in Physics, 1991. Mem. sci. staff Rowland Inst., 1991; Gordon McKay prof. applied physics and prof. physics Harvard U., Cambridge, Mass., 1999—. MacArthur fellow, 2001. Office: Harvard U Dept Physics 17 Oxford St Lyman 229 Cambridge MA 02138

HAUBEGGER, CHRISTY, media consultant, publishing executive; b. Houston, Tex. d. David and Ann Haubegger. BA in philosophy, U. Tex., Austin, 1989; JD, Stanford U., 1992. Owner Alegre Enterprises, Inc.; founder, pub., CEO Latina Mag., N.Y.C., 1996—2001; bd. dirs. Latin Media Ventures, N.Y.C., 1996—; founder Latina Mag., N.Y.C., 2001—; cons. Hispanic-related initiatives Creative Artists Agy., 2003—. Assoc. prodr. (films) Chasing Papi, 2003. Bd. dirs. New Am. Alliance; mem. governing bd. Mgmt. Leadership for Tomorrow, Named to Am. Advt. Fedn. Advt. Hall of Achievement, 1999; David Rockefeller Fellow, N.Y.C. Partnership, 2002. Office: Latin Media Ventures 1500 Broadway Ste 700 New York NY 10036*

HAUCK, MARGUERITE HALL, broadcast executive; b. Bayside, N.Y., June 30, 1948; d. Carlyle Washington and Anzonette Marguerite (Asmussen) Hall; m. Harry Lennon, 1996. Student, Syracuse U., 1966-67; BA summa cum laude, Queens Coll., CUNY, 1974. Assoc. producer Animatic Prodns., Ltd., N.Y.C., 1968-72; mktg. analyst BBDO, Inc., N.Y.C., 1974-75, CBS, Inc., N.Y.C., 1975-76; dir. mktg. and research FM nat. sales, Radio div. CBS Radio, N.Y.C., 1976-85; dir. mktg. and research Christal Radio Sales div. Katz Communications, 1985-87; pres. Lennon Hall Antiques, Inc., 1986-94; v.p. research and mktg. Christal Radio Sales divsn., Katz Media, 1987-97; v.p., dir. sales mktg. KATZ Radio Group subs. of CLEAR Channel Media, N.Y.C., 1997—. Author: The 321 Billion Dollar Market, 1981, The Mid-Day Myth Exploded, 1982; columnist, TV-Radio Age mag., 1982, 89. Bd. dirs. Queens Coll. Student Services Corp., 1973-74. Recipient Queens Coll. Disting. Service award, 1974 Office: KATZ Radio Group 125 W 55th St New York NY 10019-5369

HAUGAN, GERTRUDE M. clinical psychologist; b. New Richland, Minn. d. Henry Albert and Ella Pauline (Gardson) H. BA, George Washington U., 1952, MA, 1956; PhD, U. Md., 1970. Lic. psychologist, D.C., Md. Research psychologist New Eng. Med. Ctr., Boston, 1959-62, intern clin. psychology Hall Psychiat. Inst., Columbia, S.C., 1968-69; fellow in pediatrics Sch. Medicine Johns Hopkins U., Balt., 1970-71; clin. psychologist adloescent program Devel. Services Ctr., Washington, 1971-72, chief children's unit, 1972-85; chief Devel Services Ctr., Washington, 1986-94. Cons. in psychology Ea. Shore State Hosp., Cambridge, Md., 1969-71, in child psychology Ctr. for Spl. Edn., Annapolis, Md., 1972-76; instr. in child psychology Montgomery Coll., Rockville, Md., 1977-78. Contbr. articles to profl. jours. Mem. profl. adv. council Easter Seal Soc. for Disabled Children and Adults, Washinton, 1987. Mem. APA, D.C. Psychol. Assn., Am. Assn. on Mental Retardation, Phi Beta Kappa. Home: 4720 S Chelsea Ln Bethesda MD 20814-3720

HAUGEN, JANET B. corporate financial executive; B in Econ. magna cum laude, Rutgers U. Ptnr. Ernst & Young LLP; corp. v.p., contr. Unisys Corp., Blue Bell, Pa., 1996—2000, corp. sr. v.p., CFO, 2000—. Mem.: Conf. Bd. Coun. of CFOs, Fin. Exec. Inst., Forum Exec. Women. Office: Unisys Corp Unisys Way Blue Bell PA 19424

HAUGEN, MARY MARGARET, state legislator; b. Camano Island, Wash., Jan. 14, 1941; d. Melvin Harry and Alma Cora (Huntington) Olsen; m. Basil Badley; children: Mary Beth Fisher, Katherine Heitt, Richard, James. Mem. Wash. Ho. Reps., Olympia, 1982-1992, past mem. natural resources com., transp. com., mem. joint legis. com. on criminal justice system; mem. Wash. Senate, Dist. 10, Olympia, 1993—. Chmn. govt. ops. com., transp. com., natural resource com., law and justice com. Wash. State Senate. Mem. LWV, Stanwood Camano Soroptomists. Lodges: Order Ea. Star. Democrat. Methodist. Avocations: fishing, reading, collecting antique clothing. Office: Wash Senate John A Cherberg Bldg Rm 435 PO Box 40482 Olympia WA 98504-0482

HAUGLAND, SUSAN WARRELL, education educator, consultant; b. Portland, Oreg., Aug. 29, 1950; d. George William and Commery Wallace (Coleman) Warrell; children from previous marriage: Charles, Michael. BS in Child Devel., Oreg. State U., 1972; PhD in Psychology, Saybrook Inst., 1976. Cert. family and consumer scis. Dir., head tchr. Lafayette Co-op Nursery Sch., Detroit, 1973-75; handicapped svcs. coord. OutWayne County Head Start, Wayne, Mich., 1975-76; asst. prof. child devel. Va. Poly. Inst. and State U., Blacksburg, 1976-79; prof. emeritus child devel. S.E. Mo. State U., Cape Girardeau, 1979-99, prof. emeritus, 1999—; pres. K.I.D.S. & Computers, Inc., Cape Girardeau, 1999—; prof. early childhood edn. The Met. State Coll. of Denver, 2000—. Dir. Ctr. for Child Studies, Cape Girardeau, 1979-99, Kids Interacting with Devel. Software, Cape Girardeau, 1985—; chair Human-Environ. Studies, Cape Girardeau, 1990-93; judge Developmental Software Awards, 1991—, Child Mag. Awards, 1992-99. Author: Helping Young Children Grow, 1980, Developmental Evaluations of Software for Young Children, 1990, Young Children and Technology: A World of Discovery, 1997, Haugland Developmental Software Scale, 1997, Haugland/Gertzog Developmental Scale for Web Sites, 1998; dept. editor Early Childhood Education Jour., 1992—; contbr. numerous articles to profl. jours. Grantee numerous orgns.; recipient Gov.'s award for Teaching Excellence, 1996. Mem. Assn. for Childhood Edn. Internat., Nat. Assn. for Edn. Young Children, Nat. Assn. for Early Childhood Tchr. Educators, Tech. and Young Children Caucus, Omicron Nu. Democrat. Methodist. Avocations: reading, travel, cooking, bicycling. E-mail: susanhaugland@hotmail.com.

HAUKENESS, HELEN, journalist, writer; b. Fortuna, N.D. d. O.J. and Ella Pauline (Norum) H.; m. James Byrne Ranck Jr.; 1 child, Mary Bolieu. AB, Augsburg Coll. Editl. asst. Am. Jour. Microbiology, Ann Arbor, Mich., 1964-67; editor Applied Dynamics News, Ann Arbor, 1969-72; reader, copy and line editor Avon Books, N.Y.C., 1976-80; copy editor Warner Publs., N.Y.C., 1980-84; freelance journalist, writer, 1984—. Contbr. travel essays to various newspapers, short stories and essays to periodicals. N.Y. Coun. for Arts fellow, 1995, MacDowell Colony fellow, 1971, 73, 75, 78, 82, Yaddo fellow, 1984, Va. Ctr. Creative Arts fellow 87, Millay Colony for Arts fellow, 1980. Mem. Am. Soc. Journalists and Authors, Authors Guild. Avocations: photography, watercolor, flute, piano. Home: 100 Bank St 4D New York NY 10014-2123

HAUNER-MORRIS, PHYLLIS MARIE, systems analyst; b. Bronx, N.Y., Feb. 1, 1954; d. William Joseph and Dolores E. Hauner. AAS in Bus. Adminstrn., N.Y. Inst. Tech., 1978, BS in Mgmt., 1981; MBA, Adelphi U., 1987. From inventory analyst to systems analyst Grumman Corp., Bethpage, N.Y., 1979-86; sr. systems analyst Grumman Aircraft, Bethpage, N.Y., 1986-89; from adminstr. III to adminstr. sr. GPU Nuclear Corp., Parsippany, N.J., 1989-95, staff mem., 1995-97; sr. bus. systems analyst (cons.), 1997—. Roman Catholic. Avocation: skiing. Home: 28 Laurel Ridge Rd East Stroudsburg PA 18301-8945

HAUPT, PATRICIA A. principal; Diplome du premier cycle, U. Strasbourg, France, 1969; dipome des etudes superieures, U. Montpellier, France, 1971; BA summa cum laude, St. Francis Coll., 1972; MA in French summa cum laude, Middlebury Coll., 1976; prin.'s cert. summa cum laude, Western Md. Coll., 1984; EdD in Adminstrn. and Leadership summa cum laude, Temple U., 1986. Cert. instrnl. II Pa., prin. Pa., asst. supt.'s letter of eligibility Pa., supt.'s letter of eligibility Pa. Die casting machine operator Doehler-Jarvis Internat., Pottstown, Pa., 1972—74; tchr. French Palmyra (Pa.) Area H.S., 1973—84; real estate agt. Jack Gaughen Realtor, Hershey, Pa., 1979—84; dir. pupil pers. svcs. K-12 So. Lehigh Sch. Dist., 1985—89; asst. prin. So. Lehigh Mid. Sch., 1984—89; prin. Fleetwood Area Mid. Sch., 1989—92, Bala Cynwyd (Pa.) Mid. Sch., Bala Cynwyd, 1992—. Lectr. and presenter in field; co-facilitator Lang. Immersion Program; coord. Tri-Dist. Consortium; mem. Gov.'s Task Force for Fgn. Langs.; ednl. liaison Kutztown Area C. of C. Recipient Leadership award, Am. Legion, ednl. scholarship for study abroad. Mem.: ASCD, Nat. Mid. Schs. Assn., Pa. Sch. Bds. Assn., Nat. Assn. Secondary Sch. Prins., Am. Assn. Sch. Adminstrs., Delta Epsilon Sigma, Delta Kappa Gamma (pres. Delta chpt.). Avocations: playing classical organ and piano, reading, swimming.

HAUPTLI, BARBARA BEATRICE, program administrator; b. Glenwood Springs, Colo., Sept. 20, 1953; d. Frederick James and Evelyn June (rood) Hauptli. BBA, Western State Coll., 1975. Contract specialist USA-TACOM, Warren, Mich., 1981-86; contract buyer Martin Marietta Orlando (Fla.) Aerospace, 1986; purchasing expediter Moog, Inc., Clearwater, Fla., 1986-89; subcontract adminstr. Olin Ordnance, St. Petersburg, Fla., 1989-91, sr. subcontract adminstr., 1991-93; reimbursement specialist Tod. K. Allen, Inc., 1993-96; program mgr. Nat. Rsch. Tech. Contract Mfg., Tallahassee, 1997-2000; payroll mgr. Worldwide Flight Svcs., Eagle, Colo., 2000—01; customer svc. rep. United Parcel Svc., Glenwood Springs, Colo., 2001—. Avocations: reading, sailing, travel.

HAUPTMAN, BETTY, hospital official, fundraiser; b. Bklyn., Nov. 26, 1936; d. Herman Paul and Regina (Greenberg) Holzman; m. Michael Hauptman, Nov. 28, 1957; children: James, William. BBA, CUNY, 1958. Dir. devel. Greenwich (Conn.) Libr., 1986-89, Ctr. for Non Profit Corps., Princeton, N.J., 1990-91, Windward Sch., White Plains, N.Y., 1992-93; dir. individual gifts Greenwich Hosp., 1993-97, dir. devel., 1997—2000, exec. dir. capital campaign, 2000—. Justice of peace, Greenwich, 1984—. Trustee, pres. Greenwich Libr., 1984-86; vice-chmn. Greenwich Bd. Health, 1981-84, ; co-chmn. cmty. forum United Way Greenwich, 1987-89; bd. dirs. Shelter for Homeless, Stamford, Conn., 1990-96; cmty. advisor, 1996-2000; chmn. Commn. on Aging, Greenwich, past vice-chmn.; mem. cmty. adv. bd. Greenwich Adult Day Care. Mem. Assn. Fund Raising Profls., LWV (pres. Greenwich 1974-76). Avocations: birding, hiking, reading. Home: 13 Carriage Rd Cos Cob CT 06807-1301 Office: Greenwich Hosp 5 Perryridge Rd Greenwich CT 06830-4697

HAUSE, EDITH COLLINS, college administrator; b. Rock Hill, SC, Dec. 11, 1933; d. Ernest O. and Violet (Smith) Collins; m. James Luke Hause, Sept. 3, 1955; children: Stephen Mark, Felicia Gaye Hause Friesen. BA, Columbia Coll., SC, 1956; postgrad., U. NC, Greensboro, 1967, U. SC, 1971—75. Tchr. Richland Dist. II, Columbia, 1971—74; dir. alumnae affairs Columbia Coll., 1974—82, v.p. devel., 1984—89, v.p. alumnae affairs, 1989—99, ret., 1999. Named Outstanding Tchr. of Yr., Richland Dist. II, 1974; recipient Disting. Svc. award, Columbia Coll. Alumae Assn., 2003, Columbia Coll. Medallion, 2003. Mem.: Nat. Soc. Fund Raising Execs., Coun. for Advancement and Support Edn., Columbia Network for Female Execs., SC Advocates for Women on Bds. and Commrs. (bd. dirs.), SC Assn. Alumni Dirs. (pres. 1996—98). Republican. Methodist. Home: 92 Mariners Pointe Rd Prosperity SC 29127-7674

HAUSELT, DENISE ANN, lawyer; BS, Cornell U., 1979, JD, 1983. Bar: N.Y. 1984, Ill. 1984, U.S. Dist. Ct. (we. dist.) N.Y. 1984, U.S. Bankruptcy Ct. 1984. Summer assoc. Wildman, Harrold, Allen & Dixon, Chgo., 1982; assoc. Nixon Peabody LLP, Rochester, N.Y., 1983-86; asst. counsel Corning (N.Y.) Inc., 1986-93, divsn. counsel, 1993-99, asst. gen. counsel, 1999-2000, asst. gen. counsel, asst. sec., 2000—01, corp. sec., 2001—. Bd. dirs. 171 Cedar Arts Ctr., The Rockwell Mus. Mem. adv. coun. Cornell Law Sch.; sec. Rockwell Mus., and Corning Inc. Found., Corning Mus. of Glass. Recipient Am. Jurisprudence Constl. Law prize, Cornell U., 1981. Mem.: ABA, Cornell Law Assn., Am. Corp. Counsel Assn. Republican. Avocations: sailing, skiing. Office: Corning Inc Riverfront Plz Mp Hq E2 Corning NY 14831-0001

HAUSER, JOYCE ROBERTA, marketing professional; b. N.Y.C. d. Abraham and Helen (Lesser) Frankel; divorced; children: Mitchell, Mark, Ellen BA, SUNY, 1976; PhD, Union Inst. and U., 1987. Editor Art in Flowers, 1956-58; pres. Joyce Advt., 1958-65; ptnr. Hauser & Assocs., Pub. Rels., 1966-75; dir. broadcasting Bildersee Pub. Rels., 1973-75; pres. Hauser & Assocs., Inc., Pub. Rels., 1975-78; COO, pres. Hauser-Roberts, Inc., Pub. Rels./Mktg., N.Y.C., 1978—85; pres. Mktg. Concepts & Communications Inc., N.Y.C., 1985-92; moderator show Perceptions Sta. WEVD, 1975-77, Speaking of Health Sta. WNBC, 1977-89, 97 Health Line, Sta. WYNY, 1980-83, Conversations with Joyce Hauser, Sta. WNBC, 1975-86, What's on Your Mind, Sta. WYNY, 1983-84, Talk-Net, 1983-90; entertainment critic Sta. NBC, 1986-92. Instr. Baruch Coll., CCNY, 1980—85; assoc. prof. NYU, 1987—, prof. edn., 1992—, developer pub. rels. specialization. Sr. editor Art & Leisure News Svc., 1988—; editor-in-chief N.Y. State Comms. Annual, 1999—; contbg. editor Alive, 1976-77; author: Good Divorces, Bad Divorces: A Case for Divorce Mediation, 1995; contbr. 70 articles to profl. jours., chpts. to books. Mem. Citywide Health Adv. Coun. on Sch. Health, 1970-88, treas., 1980-92; mem. adv. bd. degree programs NYU Sch. Continuing Edn.; mediator/arbitrator Victim Svcs. Agy., 1986-87, Inst. Mediation and Conflict Resolution, 1985-86. Named one of 10 Top Successful Women, Cancer Soc., 1976, Tchr. of Yr., Zeta Beta Tau, 1989-90, one of 20 Top Women in Pub. Rels., 1981, Prof. of Yr. Sch. of Edn., 1999, Prof. of Yr., NYU Sch. Edn., 1999-2000; recipient Professionalism award Sta. WNBC, 1980; John E. Wilson fellow, 1996-97. Mem. AFTRA, Pub. Rels. Soc. Am., Nat. Assn. Communicators, Nat. Assn. Scholars, N.Y. State Communicators (treas., v.p. 1996, pres. 1997), N.Y. State Comms. Assn. (editor annual 1998), Acad. Family Mediators, Soc. Profl. Dispute Resolutions, Drama Desk, Outer Critics Cir., N.Y. Press Club. Home: 115 E 82nd St New York NY 10028-0831

HAUSER, RITA ELEANORE ABRAMS, lawyer; b. N.Y.C., July 12, 1934; d. Nathan and Frieda (Litt) Abrams; m. Gustave M. Hauser, June 10, 1956; children: Glenvil Aubrey, Ana Patricia. AB magna cum laude, CUNY Hunter Coll., 1954; D in Polit. Economy with highest honors, U. Strasbourg, France, 1955; Licence en Droit, U. Paris, 1958; student, Harvard U., 1955-56; LLB with honors, NYU, 1959; LLD (hon.), Seton Hall U., 1969, Finch Coll., 1969, U. Miami, Fla., 1971, Colgate U., 1995. Bar: D.C. 1959, N.Y. 1961, U.S. Supreme Ct. 1967. Atty. U.S. Dept. Justice, 1959-61; pvt. practice N.Y.C., 1961-67; ptnr. Moldover, Hauser, Strauss & Volin, 1968-72; sr. ptnr. Stroock & Stroock & Lavan, N.Y.C., 1972-92, of counsel, 1992—; pres. The Hauser Found., N.Y.C., 1990—; presdl. apptd. mem. Pres.'s Fgn. Intelligence Bd. and Intelligence Oversight Bd., 2001. Handmaker lectr., Louis Brandeis Lecture Series, U. Ky. Law Sch.; lectr. internat. law Naval War Coll. and Army War Coll.; lectr. St. Anthony's Coll., Oxford (England) U., 2002; Mitchell lectr. in law SUNY, Buffalo; USIA lectr. constl. law Egypt, India, Australia, New Zealand; bd. dirs. The Eisenhower World Affairs Inst.; U.S. chmn. Internat. Ctr. for Peace in Middle East, [illegible], chair 1993—, U.S. pub. del. to Vienna follow-up meeting of Conf. on Security and Cooperation in Europe, 1986-88; mem. adv. panel in internat. law U.S. Dept. State, 1986-92, Am. Soc. Internat. Law Award to honor Women in Internat. Law; mem. Pacific Coun. on Internat. Policy, 1998-2000; bd. dirs. The Rand Corp; chair internat. adv. bd. The Internat. Crisis Group, 2004—. Contbr. articles to profl. jours. U.S. rep. to UN commn. on Human Rights, 1969-72; mem. U.S. del. to Gen. Assembly UN, 1969; vice chmn. U.S. Adv. Com. on Internat. and Cultural Affairs, 1973-77; mem. N.Y.C. Bd. Higher Edn., 1974-76, Stanton Panel on internat. info., edn., cultural rels. to reorganize USIA and Voice of Am., 1974-75, Mid. East Study Group Brookings Inst., 1975, 87-88, U.S. del. World Conf. Internat. Women's Yr., Mexico City, 1975; co-chair Com. for Re-election Pres., 1972, Presdl. Debates project LVW, 1976, Coalition for Regan/Bush; adv. bd. Nat. News Coun., 1977-79; bd. dirs. Bd for Internat. Broadcasting, 1977-80, Internat. Peace Acad., The Aspen Inst., The RAND Corp., U.S. Coun. Germany; trustee, exec com. N.Y. Philharm. Soc., 1982-2003; trustee Lincoln Ctr. Performing Arts; adv. bd. Ctr. For Law and Nat. Security, U. Va. Law Sch., 1978-84; vis. com. Ctr. Internat. Affairs Harvard U., 1975-81, John F. Kennedy Sch. Govt., Harvard U., 1992—, chair adv. bd. Hauser Ctr. for Non-Profit Orgns. at Harvard U.; co-chair dean's bd. advisors Harvard Law Sch., 1996—, vice-chair, nat. co-chair univ. fund-raising campaign, 1997-2000, vice chmn. com. on univ. resources, 2002-; bd. advisors Mid. East Inst., Harvard U.; bd. visitors Georgetown Sch. Fgn. Svc., 1989-94; chmn. adv. panel Internat. Parlimentatry Group for Human Rights in Soviet Union, 1984-86; mem. Lawyers Com. for Human Rights, 1995—; mem. spl. refugee adv. panel Dept. State, 1981; bd. fellows Claremont U. Ctr. and Grad. Sch., 1990-94; former trustee Internat. Legal Ctr., Legal Aid Soc. N.Y., Freedom House; mem. Lawyers Comm. Human Rights, 1996—. Fulbright grant U. Strasbourg, 1955; Intellectual Exch. fellow Japan Soc.; recipient Jane Addams Internat. Women's Leadership award, 1996, Women in Internat. Law award Am. Soc. Internat. Law, 1995, Fulbright award for Fulbright Alumni, 1997, Servant of Justice award, Legal Aid Soc. N.Y., 2000, Vanderbilt medal NYU Law Sch., 2004. Fellow ABA (life, mem. standing coms. on law and nat. security 1979-85, standing com. on world order under law 1969-78, standing com. on jud. selection, tenure, compensation 1977-79, coun. sect. on ind. rights and responsibilities 1970-73, advisor bd. jour. 1973-78); mem. Am. Soc. Internat. Law (v.p. 1988—, mem. exec. com. 1971-76), Am. Fgn. Law Assn. (bd. dirs.), Am. Arbitration Assn. (past bd. dirs.), Ams. Soc. (bd. dirs. 1988—), Coun. Fgn. Rels. (bd. dirs.), Internat. Inst. for Strategic Studies (London, bd. dirs. 1994—), Internat. Adv. Bd., Jaffee Ctr. for Strategic Studies, Tel Aviv Univ. (1999—), Am. Coun. on Germany, The Atlantic Coun. U.S., Friends of the Hauge Acad. Internat. Law (bd. dirs.), Assn. of Bar of City of N.Y., Catalyst (bd. dirs. 1989-96). Republican. Office: Stroock & Stroock & Lavan 180 Maiden Ln Fl 17 New York NY 10038-4937 also: The Hauser Found Office of Pres 712 5th Ave New York NY 10019-4108

HAUSERMAN, JACQUITA KNIGHT, management consultant; b. Donalsonville, Ga., Apr. 23, 1942; d. Lendon Bernard and Ressie Mae (Robinson) Knight; m. Mark Kenny Hauserman, July 8, 1978 (div. Mar. 1998). BS in Math., U. Montevallo, Ala., 1964; MA in Tchg. Math., Emory U., 1973; MBA in Fin., Ga. State U., 1978. Fin. analyst Cleve. Electric Illuminating Co., 1982-83, gen. supr. employment svc., 1983-85, sr. corp. planning advisor, 1985-86, dir. customer svc., 1986-88, v.p. adminstrn., 1988-90; v.p. customer svc. & cmty. affairs Centerior Energy Corp., Independence, Ohio, 1990-93, v.p. customer support, 1993-95, v.p. bus. svcs., 1995-97; v.p., chief devel. officer Summa Health Sys., Akron, Ohio, 1999-2000; prin. Arcadia Consulting, Pepper Pike, Ohio, 2000—. Bd. dirs. Cascade Devel. Corp., Am. Stone Industries; ind. cons. Trustee John Carroll U., U. Heights, Ohio. Home and Office: 2901 Greenflower Ct Bonita Springs FL 34134-4387 E-mail: jkh2clev@aol.com.

HAUSMAN, HARRIET SECELEY, administrator; b. Chgo., Apr. 8, 1924; d. Samuel and Lena Rubin; m. Martin C. Hausman, June 30, 1946 (dec. Apr. 1988); children: Daniel, Barbara. Student, U. Ill., 1941—42, Northwestern U., 1943—45; BS, Rosary Coll., 1972. Asst. tchr. Winfield (Ill.) Sch., 1945; psych testing Hines Vet. Hosp., Maywood, Ill., 1972-74; social worker Cook County Hosp., Chgo., 1973; pres. Power Parts Co., Chgo., 1947-87, CEO, 1987-92. Author: Reflections, A History of River Forest, 1975. Trustee River Forest (Ill.) Twp., 1978-90; bd. dirs. ACLU, 1988—, v.p.; bd. dirs. Jewish Childrens Bur., pres. 1970-92, v.p., 1992—; v.p., bd. dirs. Bldg. Better Futures (BBF), 1992-96, v.p. BBF Scholarship Bd., 1997-; vice chmn. scholarship com., 1998-. Named Woman Entrepreneur of Yr., 1992, U.S. Transp. Cmty. Svc. award Oak Park and River Forest, 1980, 96, 90, 92, 96, 99. Democrat. Jewish. Avocations: symphony, opera, drama, gardening, travel.

HAUVER, CONSTANCE LONGSHORE, lawyer; b. Abington, Pa., Oct. 9, 1938; d. Malcolm Rettew and Margaret Evans (Lyon) L.; m. Arthur R. Hauver, 1962 (div. Mar. 1979); 1 child, Sian; m. Giles Toll, 1990. BA with high honors, Swarthmore Coll., 1960; MA, UCLA, 1962; JD magna cum laude, U. Denver, 1967. Bar: Colo. 1968, U.S. Dist. Ct. Colo. 1968, U.S. Tax Ct. 1970. Libr. Friends Com. on Nat. Legis., Washington, 1960-61; lectr. U. Hawaii, Honolulu, 1963-64; assoc. Sherman & Howard, Denver, 1966-73, ptnr., 1973-91; vol. naturalist Lookout Mountain Nature Ctr., 1998—. Mem. grievance com. Colo. Supreme Ct., 1981-86. Co-contbr. legal articles. Trustee Rocky Mountain Women's Inst., Denver, 1987-90, Swedish Med. Ctr. Found., Denver, 1978-85; bd. dirs. Women's Forum Colo. Inc., Denver, 1988-89, Girls Count, Denver, 1995-2000, pres., 1996-97. Named New Vol. Naturalist of Yr., Lookout Mountain Nature Ctr., 1998, Vol. Naturalist of Yr., 2001; recipient Athena award, Alliance Profl. Women, 1987. Fellow Am. Coll. Probate Counsel; mem. Colo. Bar Assn. (chair probate and trust law sect. 1982-83), Denver Bar Assn. (del. to ABA Ho. of Dels. 1986-88), Rocky Mountain Estate Planning Coun. (pres. 1980-81). Democrat. Mem. Soc. Of Friends. Avocations: mountain climbing, kayaking, skiing, reading, learning Spanish.

HAVENS, CANDACE JEAN, planning consultant; b. Rochester, Minn., Sept. 13, 1952; d. Fred Z. and Barbara Jean (Stephenson) H.; m. Bruce Curtis Mercier, Feb. 22, 1975 (div. Apr. 1982); 1 child, Rachel; m. James Arthur Renning, Oct. 26, 1986; children: Kelsey, Sarah. Student, U. Calif., San Diego, Darmouth Coll., 1970-72, Am. U., Beirut, 1973-74; BA in Sociology, U. Calif., Riverside, 1977; MPA, Harvard U., 1994. Project coord. social svc. orgn. Grass Roots II, San Luis Obispo, Calif., 1976-77; planner City San Luis Obispo, 1977-86, city parking, spl. projects mgr., 1986-88; spl. asst. to city adminstr. City of San Luis Obispo, 1989, planning cons., mediator, 1991—; mgmt. rsch. specialist Bank of Boston, 1995-96; owner Office Suites, San Luis Obispo, Calif., 1997-2000, ADR Collaborative, 1997—. Past pres. Nat. Charity League, Riverside; mem. San Luis Obispo Med. Aux., 1986-93, San Luis Obispo Arts Coun., 1986—; pres. bd. dirs. San Luis Obispo Children's Mus., 1990-91, CFO, 1993; mediator in Newton (Mass.) Cts., 1996, San Luis Obispo, 1997; pres. Underwood Elem. PTO, 2000-2001; chmn. traffic coun., City of Newton, 2002—. Mem.: AAUW, Newton Transp. Task Force, Inst. Transp. Engrs., Mass. Assn. Mediation Profls. and Practitioners, Am. Planning Assn., Am. Inst. Cert. Planners, Assn. Conflict Resolution, Toastmasters (sec. 1986—87, v.p. 1987—88, pres. 1989—90, treas. 1991—92). Avocations: photography, running, arts, cooking, travel, languages. Office: 25 Hunnewell Ave Newton MA 02458-2214

HAVENS, CAROLYN CLARICE, librarian; b. Nashville, Sept. 11, 1953; d. Charles Buford and Iris Mae (Anderson) H.; m. Hilton Harris Huey, June 9, 1990; children: Heather Louise, Quentin Harris. AA, Sue Bennett Coll., 1973; BA in English, U. West Fla., 1974; MLS, U. Ky., 1981. Tchr. Escambia High Sch., Pensacola, Fla., [illegible], Pensacola, 1975-77; libr. tech. U. Ky., Lexington, 1978-82; libr. Auburn (Ala.) U., 1982—. Contbr. articles to profl. jours. and newspapers; editorial bd.: A Dynamic Tradition, 1991. Bd. dirs. Nat. Kidney Found. Ala., Opelika, 1986-89; active Conscientious Alliance for Peace, Auburn, 1989—. Clergy and Laity Concerned, Atlanta, 1991—. Mem. ALA, Southeastern Libr. Assn., Ala. Libr. Assn., North Am. Serials Interest Group, Ala. Assn. Coll. and Rsch. Librs., Studio 218. Democrat. Methodist. Avocations: painting, writing, photography. Office: Auburn U Ralph Draughon Libr Auburn AL 36849-5606

HAVENS, CHERYL CIANO, music educator; d. Rudolph Anthony and Grace Elsie Ciano; m. Shawn Havens, June 24, 1995. MusB magna cum laude, SUNY Potsdam, 1989; MS in Music Edn., We. Conn. State U., 1993. Dir. elem. orch. Mahopac Ctrl. Sch. Dist., NY, 1989—. Dir., co-founder Westchester/Putnam Youth Symphony, Mahopac, 1996—; musician pit orch. Brewster H.S., NY, 2002; dir. Mahopac Elem. Schs. Combined Orch., 1989—; gen. chairperson Putnam County All County Music Festival, Brewster, NY, 2002, orch. chairperson, Putnam Valley, NY, 01, Dutchess County All County Music Festival, Poughkeepsie, NY, 1999, Zone 10 Area All State Music Festival, Mahopac, 1994, Mahopac, 91; musician pit orch. Somers H.S., NY, 2003, 02. Editor: (state newsletter) NYASTA with NSOA Newsletter - The Bridge. Recipient Guest Condr., Nassau County All County Festival, 2000, Selected to conduct at NY State Sch. Bd. Conv., NY State Sch. Bd. Assn., 2002. Mem.: N.Y. State United Tchrs., Putnam County Music Educators Assn. (libr. 2001—03), N.Y. State Sch. Music Assn., Am. String Teachers Assn. with Nat. Sch. Orch. Assn. (editor 2001—03), Sons of Italy. Avocations: travel, gardening, ballroom dancing, foreign languages. Office: Austin Road Elementary School 390 Austin Road Mahopac NY 10541

HAVENS, JEANETTE LYNN, public relations executive; b. Jamestown, NY, Aug. 31, 1948; d. Mae Thompson Silverheels and Ira Tull Havens. BA, Syracuse U., Syracuse, NY, 1966—70; MS, Iona Coll., New Rochelle, NY, 1984—86. Mgr., pub. rels./product sales Girl Scouts of Westchester*Putnam, Inc., Pleasantville, NY, 1982—; adj. asst. prof. of communication arts Iona Coll., New Rochelle, NY, 1987—88; owner Pencil Point Productions, Mount Kisco, NY, 1983—87; prodn. editor, journals divsn. Pergamon Press, Elmsford, NY, 1982—82; publications editor World Assn. of Girl Guides & Girl Scouts, London, England, 1978—81; scriptwriter Seneca Nation of Indians TV Project, Allegany & Cattaraugus Indian Reservations, NY, 1976—77; coord. Title IV Program for Indian Edn., Gowanda, NY, 1975—76; home/sch. coord. Seneca Nation Edn. Program, Irving, NY, 1973—74. V.p. pub. rels. The Assn. for Women in Comm. - Westchester Chpt., NY, 2004—, pres., 1996—97, president-elect, immediate past pres., v.p. / comm., v.p. / profl. devel.; chair nominating com. The Assn. Girl Scout Exec. Staff sect. 1, NY, 2002—, chair referrals com., 2003; spring conf. chair Assn. Girl Scouts Exec. Staff, 2001—02; newsletter editor Assn. of Girl Scout Exec. Staff, Section I, 1996—99, pluralism chair, NY, 1993—96, pub. rels./promotion chair, nat. conv., Kansas City, Mo., 1998—99, nat. pluralism com. mem., Des Moines, 1993—96. Take it or leave it vol. Town of New Castle Recycling Ctr., Chappaqua, NY, 2001—; sec., comm. com. The Westchester County Assn., Inc., White Plains, NY, 1999—2003, comm. com. mem., 1997—2003. Recipient Matrix Award, The Assn. for Women in Comm. - Westchester Chpt., 2002, First Pl. Winner - Photography Contest, Old Sturbridge Village, Sturbridge, MA, 1998, First Prize (with teammate) - Westchester County Exec. Spelling Bee, Literacy Volunteers, 1995. Mem.: Am. Volkssport Assn., Hudson River Sloop Clearwater, Walkway Over the Hudson, Am. Mensa, Ltd., YWCA of White Plains (nominating com. mem. 1999—2000), Westchester Friends of UNICEF (coun. mem. 1999—2004), Walkabout Clearwater (chorus mem. 1988—2002), Walkabout Clearwater (newsletter editor - 2000—01), Walkabout Clearwater (coord., walkabout clearwater coffeehouse concert series 1990—98), Walkabout Clearwater Sloop, Inc. (pres. 1998—2001), AAUW - Westchester Br., AAUW - NY State (bd. mem. - nominating com. chair 1989—90), AAUW - NY State (br. leadership newsletter editor 1989—90), AAUW (see above) (Ednl. Found. Named Gift Honoree 1991), AAUW (bi-monthly newsletter editor - splinters 1990—2001), AAUW (legal advocacy fund chair 2000—01), AAUW (ednl. found. chair 2000—01), AAUW (co-v.p., programs 1998—99), AAUW (pres. 1999—2000), AAUW - Westchester Br. (newsletter editor 2001—), The Welsh Nat. Gymnafa Ganu Assn., Inc. (life), Girl Scouts of the USA (life). Avocations: travel, walking, singing, arts & crafts. Home: 40 Kisco Park Drive Mount Kisco NY 10549 Office: Girl Scouts of Westchester*Putnam Inc 2 Great Oak Lane Pleasantville NY 10570 Office Phone: 914-747-3080 221. Personal E-mail: jhavens@girlscoutswp.org. E-mail: jhavens@girlscoutswp.org.

HAVENS, PAMELA ANN, college official; b. Plattsburgh, N.Y., Nov. 30, 1956; d. Thomas L. and MaryAnn (Zalen) Romeo; m. Stephen L. Havens, Aug. 9, 1986; children: Stephanie Leigh, Skylar Lucas. BA, Eisenhower Coll., 1978; MA summa cum laude, SUNY, Plattsburgh, 1987; AAS summa cum laude, Cayuga C.C., 1999. VISTA vol. Retired Sr. Vol. Program, Plattsburgh, 1978-79; copywriter, newsperson Stas. WEAV-AM/WGFB-FM, Plattsburgh, 1979-83; traffic clk. Sta. WCFE-TV, Plattsburgh, 1983-84, pub. info. coord., 1984-85; coll. rels. officer Clinton Cmty. Coll., Plattsburgh, 1985-89; dir. publs. and comm. Cayuga C.C., Auburn, N.Y., 1989-2001; dir. stewardship Hamilton Coll., Clinton, N.Y., 2001—. Mem. adv. bd., vice-chair St. Mary's Sch. PTA, Clinton, NY, 2002—. Mem. adv. com. Cayuga C.C. Presch. Ctr., 1999-2001. Named Young Careerist Alternate Bus. and Profl. Women's Club, 1986; recipient award ACC/CCC Alumni Assn., 2000. Mem.: CASE, AAUW, Assn. Donor Rels. Profls. (ex-offico bd. mem. 2004), Nat. Coun. Mktg. and Pub. Rels. (Pro Devel. award 1999, Disting. Svc. award 2000), Eisenhower Coll. Aumni Assn. (bd. dirs. 1990—97, chmn. bd. 1992—95), Phi Theta Kappa. Avocations: fiction and poetry writing, doll and bear collecting, olympic pin collecting, tap dancing. Office: Hamilton Coll 198 College Hill Rd Clinton NY 13323 E-mail: phavens@hamilton.edu.

HAVER-ALLEN, ANN, communications director; d. Vivian Faye Haver; m. William Allen, June 21, 1986; children: Jason Allen, Summer Allen. AB in Journalism, Thomas Edison State Coll., Trenton, N.J. Reporter Angleton Times, Tex., 1985—86; mng. editor Princeton Packet Group, NJ, 1986—90, Engel Pub. Ptnrs., West Trenton, NJ, 1990—92; dir. engring. comm. Princeton U., NJ, 1992—. Dir., editor: mag. EQuad News. Commr. Red Heart Coastal Mvskoke Clan, Robertsdale, Ala., 2001—. Recipient APEX award for publ. excellence, 2002, 2003, Communicator award, 2002, Award of Merit, Internat. Assn. Bus. Communicators, 2002, 2004, Silver Quill award, Assn. Bus. Communicators, 2003, Crystal Award of Excellence, 2003, Clarion award, Assn. Women in Comm., 2003. Mem.: NAFE, Internat. Assn. Bus. Communicators (IRIS Award of Excellence 2002, IRIS award 2004), Women in Comm., Ednl. Press Assn. Am., Coun. for Advancement and Support of Edn. Personal E-mail: allen@princeton.edu.

HAVERLY, PAMELA SUE, nursing administrator; b. Huntingburg, Ind., Aug. 14, 1955; d. Robert Ray Reckelhoff and Shirley Ann Reister; children: Aaron, Madison. ADN, Grion Coll., Indpls., 1985; BSN, Ind. U., Indpls., 1994. RN Ind., cert. CLCP, CCRN, ACLS. Nurse various depts. Wishard Meml. Hosp., Indpls.; AIDS home nurse VA, Indpls.; liaison nurse Family Home Health, Indpls.; managed care specialist Rehab. Profls., Louisville, Ellis & Assocs., Chgo., Zurich North Am., Indpls.; clin. nurse cons. Venetec Internat., San Diego. Bd. dirs. Kid's Chance, Indpls. Vol. Gennerstreet Free Clinic, Indpls.; vol. trauma nurse Police & Firemen's Games, Indpls., 2000—01; active various other civic/charitable orgns.; del. to People's Republic of China Ind. U. Sch. Nursing, 1999. Mem.: Ind. Workmen's Compensation Inst., ANA, Ind. State Nurses Assn. (peer rev. com. 1986—99, del. 1985), Sigma Theta Tau, Kappa Kappa Sigma. Roman Catholic. Avocations: reading, [illegible]. Home: [illegible] Indianapolis IN 46250-1775 Office: Venetec Internat Ste 170 12555 High Bluff Dr San Diego CA 92130

HAVERSTOCK, LYNDA M. lieutenant governor; m. Harley Olsen; 4 children. MEd, PhD in Clin. Psychology, U. Saskatchewan. Pvt. practice clin. psychologist; lt. gov., 2000—. Instr. Sask. U., N.B. U., Canada; past radio talk show host. Author: (handbook) Fighting the Farm Crisis, (book) Safety and Health in Agriculture; contbr. articles to profl. jours. Recipient Triple E award, Gzowski award; Paul Harris fellow, Rotary Internat. Mem.: Army, Navy and Air Force Vets. Can. (life named hon. col.). Office: Govt House 4607 Dewdney Ave Regina SK S4P 3V7 Canada E-mail: lgo@ltgov.sk.ca.

HAVESON, BARBARA MARCIA, retired elementary education educator; b. Wharton, Tex., Aug. 4, 1934; d. Jack and Bertha (Kreitstein) Roth; m. Robert Franklin Haveson, Nov. 25, 1956; children: Celia Hannah (dec.), Judy. BS, U. Houston, 1956. Elem. edn. tchr. Fort Bend Ind. Sch. Dist., Sugarland, Tex., 1965-90; v.p. Fort Bend Tchr. Assn., 1972-73; pres. Fort Bend Tchrs. Assn., Sugarland, Tex., 1973-75; mem. exec. bd. region 4 Tex. State Tchrs. Assn., Houston, 1978-80; mem. Kinneret Group-Houston Chpt. of Hadassah, 1991—; pres. Kinneret Group, 1992-93. Mem. U.S. Holocaust Mus., Rep. Jewish Coalition. Recipient Hadassah Nat. Leadership award, 1996. Mem. Hadassah (pres. Kinneret Group/Houston chpt. 1992-95, co-pres. Anne Frank group 1998-99, Simcha of Aberdeen chpt., edn. co-v.p., 2001-03, exec. v.p. 2003—), Rep. Jewish Coalition, Delta Kappa Gamma, Lambda Delta (Sugar Land chpt.). Jewish. Avocations: knitting, travelling, volunteer work, reading, helping others. Home: 7211 Southport Dr Boynton Beach FL 33437-2974

HAVILAND, KAY LYNN (KADE HAVILAND), mental health services professional; b. Deer Lodge, Mont., July 16, 1952; d. Jackson C. and Juanita Maxine (Voelkel) Price; children: Jesse Jean, Kelsey Ann, Molly Claire. MA in Counseling Psychology, Adams State Coll., 1994. Cert. addictions counselor, counseling psychology. Cert. addictions counselor, outpatient therapist Arapahoe House Denver Outpatient Clinic, Denver, 1996—; addictions counselor, trainer State of Colo. Alcohol Drug Abuse divsn. Health and Hosps., Denver, 2001. Asst. therapist, CORE obesity project, Weight Choice Program dept. pediatrics U. Colo., 1998—2001. Author, editor: (mag.) Human Interest, 1987-88 (1st place award 1989); contbr. articles to profl. jours. Mem.: Eating Disorder Profls. of Colo. Avocations: calligraphy, cross-country skiing, reading. Office Phone: 303-825-0508 133.

HAWES, BESS LOMAX, retired anthropologist; m. Baldwin Hawes; children: Corey, Naomi, Nicholas. BA, Bryn Mawr U., 1941; MA, U. Calif., 1970; PhD (hon.), Kenyon Coll., 1994, U. N.C., 1995. With music divsn. N.Y. Pub. Libr.; prof. anthropology Calif. State U., Northridge, 1963—74, Smithsonian Instn., 1974—76; dir. Folk Arts Program Nat. Endowment for Arts, 1977—92; ret., 1992. Recipient Nat. Medal of Arts, Pres. Clinton, 1993. Home: 8136 Woodlake Ave Apt 284 West Hills CA 91304-3576

HAWES, GRACE MAXCY, retired archival specialist, writer; b. Cumberland, Wis., Feb. 4, 1926; d. Clarence David and Mabel Hannah (Erickson) Maxcy; student U. Wis., 1944-46; BA, San Jose State U., 1963, MA, 1971; m. John G. Hawes, Aug. 28, 1948 (dec.); children: Elizabeth, John D., Mark (dec.), Amy; m. E. Zumbrunnen, 1993. Library asst. NASA, Langley, Va., 1948-49; archival specialist Hoover Archives, Stanford U., 1976-80, adminstrv. asst., 1980-82; archival specialist Hoover Inst., 1982-89, rsch. archivist, 1989-93, 97-. Author: The Marshall Plan for China: Economic Cooperation Administration, 1948-1949, 1977. Address: 925 Ponselle Ln Capitola CA 95010 Home: 15864 NW Ryegrass St Portland OR 97229-9217

HAWK, CAROLE LYNN, retired insurance company executive, research analyst; b. Springfield, Ill., June 17, 1947; d. Warren Wesley and Mary June (Moore) Weiser; m. Charles Edward Hawk, Aug. 2, 1963; 1 child, Cynthia Jean Hawk-Lindzy. Student, Lincoln Land C.C., Springfield, 1970-75, Ind. U., South Bend, 1982-83. Cert. data processor, computer programmer, systems profl., assoc. in customer svc.; assoc. Ins. Regulatory Compliance. Systems analyst Office Ill. Sec. of State, Springfield, 1969-78; software specialist Clark Equipment Co., Buchanan, Mich., 1978-84; GC0S6 software analyst Contel Corp., Wentzville, Mo., 1984-87; tech. rsch. analyst The Horace Mann Cos., Springfield, 1988—2002; ret., 2002. Mem., vol. interpreter Dana-Thomas House Found.; adult literacy tutor; active Friends of the Fox Theatre, St. Louis; vol. usher Sangamon State Auditorium U. of Ill., Springfield; pres. Smedley Home Town Meml. chpt., 2000—. Fellow Life Mgmt. Assn.; mem. Assn. Info. Tech. Profls. (sec. Capital chpt. 1993-94, exec. pres. 1995, pres. 1996, exec. v.p. 2001), Ctrl. Ill. Life Mgmt. Inst. (co. rep. 1995-2000), Toastmasters (sec. Horace Mann chpt. 1992, pres. 1993, gov. area 1 1994-95, gov. dist. C 1995-97, v.p. edn. 1997-98, v.p. pub. rels. 1998-99, v.p. edn. 1999-2000, pres. 2002—).

HAWK, KATHLEEN PATRICIA, broadcast consultant; b. Butler, Pa., Feb. 12, 1945; d. Allen Clarence and Betty Ruth (Wilson) Pollock; m. Robert Ferdinand Hawk, Dec. 31, 1966; 1 child, Allen Robert. BSc, Parsons Coll., Fairfield, Iowa, 1966. Ind. internat. radiofrequency/microwave cons./personal wireless telecom./facilities siting cons., wireless facility siting cons., Butler, Pa., 1990—. Invited reviewer U.S. Congress, Office of Tech. Assessment, Wireless Technologies and the Nat. Info. Infrastructure, 1995; participant numerous seminars, confs., telecomms. adv. com.; mem. elec. sensitivity network. Author: Case Study in the Heartland, 1996; freelance writer Pitts. Post Gazette; contbr. articles to profl. jours. Worthy advisor Rainbow Girls, 1961; mem. Nat. Coalition of Citizens and Pub. Ofcls. for Local Control; founding mem., bd. dirs. Cellular Phone Task Force; bd. dirs. Delbert Parkinson Christian Cancer Coalition. Mem. Bioelectromagnetics Soc., Associated Bioelectromagnetics Technologists, Butler Natural Living Group, 1000 Club, Butler Country Club, 38 Year Card Club, Am. Legion Aux., Am. Golf Hall of Fame. Republican. Achievements include research on human and animal health in close proximity to telecomms. facilities. Avocations: gourmet cooking, crafts, sports, pub. speaking, politics. Home and Office: 122 Thornwood Dr Butler PA 16001-3442 E-mail: kathyhawk@webtv.net.

HAWK, PAULETTA BROWNING, student elementary school educator; b. Gilbert, W.Va., Aug. 10, 1952; d. Walter Browning and Gracie (Johnson) Tyner; children: Clifford Thompson III, Angie Thompson. AA, Cen. Fla. Community Coll., Ocala, 1988; BS in Elem. Edn., U. Cen. Fla., 1991; MEd in Curriculum and Instrn., Nat. Louis U., 1996. Med. receptionist Bluefield (W.Va.) Clinic, 1975-76; ins. clk. Bristol (Tenn.) Meml. Hosp., 1976-78; med. sec. Inter-Mountain Pathology Assn., Bristol, Tenn., 1978-80; substitute tchr. Citrus County Sch. Bd., Inverness, Fla., 1980-81, guidance sec., 1981-85, acct. I (on profl. leave of absence), 1990-91; office mgr. Victor Nothnagel, O.D., Inverness, 1985-87; tchr. Inverness Primary, 1991—99, Banyan Elem., Sunrise, Fla., 1999—2002; 'tchr. Brooksville (Fla.) Elem., 2002—. Vol. Nat. Arthritis Found., 1988-89, Inverness Primary Sch., Citrus County Sch. Bd., 1989. Mem. Phi Theta Kappa. Democrat. Baptist. Avocations: reading, swimming, cycling, gardening, clay modeling. Home: 5066 E Backner Ln Inverness FL 34452-8314

HAWKEN, PATTY LYNN, retired nursing educator, dean of faculty; b. Wheaton, Ill., July 13, 1932; d. Leonard William and Betty (Stock) H. BSN, U. Mich., 1956; MSN, Case Western Res. U., 1962, PhD, 1970. Instr. U.

Mich., Ann Arbor, 1956-57, Highland Hosp., Oakland, Calif., 1957-59; from instr. to assoc. prof., assoc. in adminstrn. Case Western Res. U., Cleve., 1960-71; assoc. prof. Emory U., Atlanta, 1971-72, prof., dir., 1972-74; dean, prof. U. Tex. Health Sci. Ctr. Sch. Nursing, San Antonio, 1974-97, ret., 1997. Contbr. articles to profl. jours. Bd. dirs. Wesley Cmty. Ctr., San Antonio, 1986, 89; mem. United Way Allocation Com., San Antonio, 1987; adv. com. Trinity U. Health Care Adminstrn., San Antonio, 1984-97, VA Dean's Com., San antonio, 1982-97. Recipient Nurse of Yr. award Tex. Nursing Assn., San Antonio chpt., 1985, Disting. Alumni award Case Western Res. U., 1991, U. Mich., 1995; named to Women's Hall of Fame. Mem. ANA (cabinet on edn. 1986-88), Nat. League Nursing (pres. 1989-91, Disting. Svc. award 1991), Am. Assn. Colls. of Nursing (com. on edn. 1986-88), Commns. Grads. Fgn. Nursing Schs. (trustee, pres. 1983-85), Am. Acad. Nursing (bd. govs. 1994-97), San Antonio 100 Club, Internat. Women's Forum (San Antonio pres. celebration, Hall of Fame 1994-97). Avocations: snorkeling, swimming. Home: 1826 Fallow Run San Antonio TX 78248-2000

HAWKES, CAROL ANN, academic administrator; b. N.Y.C. d. Howard N. and Lavinia M. (Lally) H. BA, Barnard Coll., 1943; MA, Columbia U., 1944, PhD, 1949. Dir. acad. English liberal arts div. Katharine Gibbs Sch., N.Y.C., 1950-57; prof. English, chmn. dept. English and comparative lit. Finch Coll., N.Y.C., 1957-75; v.p. for ednl. affairs, dean of coll. Hartwick Coll., Oneonta, N.Y., 1975-80; pres. Endicott Coll., Beverly, Mass., 1980-87; assoc. v.p. for acad. affairs Western Conn. State U., Danbury, 1987—. Trustee Norwich U., Hartwick Coll. Author: Master's Degree Programs and the Liberal Arts College, 1968. Harvard Sch. Dental Medicine fellow. Mem. MLA, LWV, Modern Humanities Rsch. Assn., Am. Assn. Higher Edn., Princeton Club (N.Y.C.), Columbia U. Club New Eng., Phi Beta Kappa. Office: Western Conn State U Academic Affairs Danbury CT 06810 Office Phone: 203-837-8851. E-mail: hawkesc@wcsu.edu.

HAWKINS, ANGELA, music educator; b. Murray, Ky., June 11, 1971; d. James Winston Houser and Sharon Kaye Filbeck; m. Roy Hawkins, May 25, 1996; 1 child, Nicolas. MusB in Edn. magna cum laude, Murray State U., 1994, M in Music Edn. summa cum laude, 2003. Music tchr. Paris (Tenn.) Spl. Sch. Dist., 1994—. Mem. exec. bd., newsletter editor Christian Student Ctr. Alumni and Friends, 2000—; sch. tech. coach Rhea Elem. Sch. Dir. family bible sch. U. Ch. of Christ, Murray, Ky., 2001—04. Mem.: Music Educators Nat. Conf., Sigma Alpha Iota (songleader Iota Beta chpt. 1993—94). Democrat. Avocations: computers, travel, collecting Disney memorabilia. Office: Paris Special School District 115 South Wilson Paris TN 38242 E-mail: hawkins@wgr.k12.tn.us.

HAWKINS, CYNTHIA, artist, educator; b. N.Y.C., Jan. 29, 1950; d. Robert D. Hawkins and Elease Coger; m. Steven J. Chaiken, Feb. 5, 1977 (div. Aug. 1985); m. John Edward Owen, Aug. 24, 1985; children: Ianna, Zachary. BA, Queens Coll., 1977; MFA, Md. Inst. Coll. Art, 1992. Tchg. asst. Md. Inst. Coll. of Art, Balt., 1990-92; adj. instr. Rockland C.C., Suffern, N.Y., 1993-96, Parsons Sch. Design, N.Y.C., 1996, The Coll. at New Paltz, SUNY, 1996-98, Ramapo Coll. of N.J., 1998-99; dir. galleries Cedar Crest Coll., Allentown, Pa., 2000—03; curator Rush Art Gallery, 2003—; ind. curator Lore Regenstein Gallery, 2003—. Mentor Empire State Coll., Nyack, N.Y., 1994; artist-in-residence The Studio Mus. Harlem, N.Y., 1997-98, Va. Ctr. for Creative Arts, Sweet Briar, Va., 1995-96; vis. artist Round House Press, Hartwick Coll., Oneonta, N.Y., 1994; curator Rockland Ctr. for Arts, art dept. Rockland C.C., Nyack, 1994-95, The Rotunda, 1994-95; vis. lectr. Forman Gallery, Hartwick Coll., Oneonta, 1994, Rockland C.C., Suffern, 1994-95; presenter in field. One-woman shows include, Paul Klapper Libr., Queens Coll., N.Y., 1974, Just Above Midtown/Downtown Gallery, N.Y.C., 1981, Frances Wolfson Art Ctr., Miami (Fla.)-Dade C.C., 1986, Cinque Gallery, N.Y.C., 1989, Essex (Md.) C.C., 1991, Queens Coll. Art Ctr., Benjamin S. Rosenthal Libr., Queens Coll., CUNY, Trinity Luth. Ch., New Milford, Conn., 1993, exhibited in group shows, Queens Coll. Gallery, N.Y.C., 1973, Emily Lowe Gallery, Hempstead, N.Y., 1979, Jamie Szoke Gallery, N.Y.C., 1984, Grace Borgenicht Gallery, N.Y.C., 1986, Aljira Gallery, Newark, 1989, Dome Gallery, N.Y.C., 1990, Decker Gallery, Balt., 1991, Kromah Gallery, Balt., 1992, Arts Alliance Haverstraw, N.Y., 1993, Nabisco Gallery, East Hanover, N.J., 1994, Artist Space, N.Y.C., 1993, Bronx Mus. Arts, 1994, U. Notre Dame at Balt., 1995, No. Westchester Ctr. for Arts, Mt. Kisco, N.Y., 1996, Hopper House, Nyack, 1996, Rush Art Gallery, N.Y., 1999, Foxglove Gallery, Stroudsburg, Pa., 2002, Represented in permanent collections, The Bronx Mus. of Arts, N.Y.C., Trinity Luth. Ch., New Milford, Dept. of State, Washington, The Printmaking Workshop, Chevron Corp., Calif., Cameron and Colby, N.Y.C., C.D. Walsh Assocs., Conn., Brooks Sausage Co., Kenosha, Wis., The Habitat Co., Chgo., Brown Mgmt., Balt.; art works featured in pubs. including N.Y. Times, Village Voice, 25 Years of African American Women Artist, Home Mag. Mem. com. Art in Pub. Places, Rockland County, 1999—2001. Recipient 2d pl. award for mixed media Atlanta Life Ins. Co. exhbn. and competition, 1984; fellow Va. Ctr. for Creative Arts, 1996, The Studio Mus. in Harlem, 1987-88, Patricia Robert Harris fellow U.S. Dept. Edn., 1990-92. Democrat. Episcopalian. E-mail: chawkins@cedarcrest.edu.

HAWKINS, ELINOR DIXON (MRS. CARROLL WOODARD HAWKINS), retired librarian; b. Masontown, W.Va., Sept. 25, 1927; d. Thomas Fitchie and Susan (Reed) Dixon; m. Carroll Woodard Hawkins, June 24, 1951; 1 child, John Carroll. AB, Fairmont State Coll., 1949; BS in Libr. Sci., U. N.C., 1950. Children's libr. Enoch Pratt Free Libr., Balt., 1950-51; head circulation dept. Greensboro (N.C.) Pub. Libr., 1951-56; libr. Craven-Pamlico Libr. Svc., New Bern, N.C., 1958-62; dir. Craven-Pamlico-Carteret Regional Libr., New Bern, N.C., 1962-92. Storyteller children's TV program Tele-Story Time, 1952-58, 63—; bd. dirs. Triangle Bank of New Bern. Mem. New Bern Hist. Soc., 1973—, Tryon Palace Commn., 1974—; mem. adv. bd. Salvation Army. Mem. N.C. Assn. Retarded Children, Pilot Club (pres. 1957-58, v.p. 1962-63). Baptist. Home: PO Box 57 Cove City NC 28523-0057

HAWKINS, EMMA B. humanities educator; b. Ardmore, Okla., July 28, 1946; d. Bernard C. and Occie E. (Morris) H. BA, Okla. Bapt. U., 1968; MDiv, Southwestern Bapt. Theol. Sem., 1976; MA, U. North Tex., 1990, PhD in English (Medieval), 1995. Instr. U. North Tex., Denton, 1990-95; lectr. Lamar U., Beaumont, 1995-97, asst. prof., 1997—2002, assoc. prof., 2003—. Chair program and arrangements South Cen. Conf. on Christianity and Lit., 1999, mem. exec. bd., 1999—; presenter numerous papers at profl. confs. Bus. mgr. Lamar Jour. Humanities; contbr. chpt. to book, articles to profl. jours. Recipient Go the Extra Mile award, 1997. Mem. MLA (sec. Old and Mid. English sect. South Ctrl. chpt. 1997, chair Old and Mid Eng. sect. chpt. 1998), Tex. Medieval Assn., Conf. on Coll. Tchrs. English (CCTE award best paper Brit. Lit., 2004), South Ctrl. Conf. Christianity and Lit. (chair various sessions, James Sims award 2000), Phi Kappa Phi, Sigma Tau Delta. Office: Lamar U PO Box 10023 Beaumont TX 77710-0023

HAWKINS, FRANCES PAM, business educator; b. Woodland, Ala., Dec. 2, 1945; d. Lowell M. and Bernice E. Mcmanus; children: Scott Cummings, Veronica Lovvorn. AS in Bus., Southern Union C.C., 1989; BS in Bus. Edn., Auburn U., 1990, MEd, 1992. Ptnr. C & S Pharmacy, Roanoke, Ala., 1974—90; bus. office tech. instr. West Ga. Tech. Coll., Lagrange, Ga., 1991—. Bus. tech., divsn. chair West Ga. Tech. Coll., Lagrange, 1999—2003, bus. office tech. adv. com. mem., 1992—, chairperson libr. com., 2001—; mem. tech. in edn. com. Ga. Dept. Edn., Atlanta, 2001—. Team leader March of Dimes, LaGrange, 1998—. Mem.: Ga. Bus. Edn. Assn., So. Bus. Edn. Assn., Nat. Bus. Edn. Assn. (com. mem. 2001), Auburn Alumni Assn., Phi Beta Lambda (sec. 1997—2001, nat. bd. dirs. future bus. leaders Am. 2001—, local advisor 1992—, state advisor 1999—, pres. Ga. Found. Inc. 1998—). Methodist. Office: West Ga Tech Coll 303 Fort Dr Lagrange GA 30240 Office Phone: 706-845-4323 ext. 5775. Business E-Mail: phawkins@westgatech.edu.

HAWKINS, GERI SUE, interior designer, jewelry designer, realtor; b. Kansas City, Mo., Sept. 4, 1940; d. William S. McCune and Verla J. (Kempter) McCune Stoll; m. LeRay D. Long, Oct. 12, 1958 (div. Dec. 1961); 1 chld, Lori Diane Long Seidl; m. Ray Eldon Hawkins, Oct. 9, 1964; children: Lynn M., John Ted; stepchildren: Celeste, Steve. Student, Kansas City Bus. Coll., 1961-62, U. Mo., Kansas City, 1974-75; AA, Maple Woods Coll., 1974; student, Wm. Jewel Coll. Interior designer Carpenter Bros. Inc., Kansas City, 1975-77; pres., designer Gerry Hawkins Interiors, Kansas City, 1977-81; interior designer R.D. Mann Inc., Kansas City, 1981-83; owner, designer Designs By Geri, Kansas City, 1983-89, 95-96, Interior Designs by Geri Inc., Parkville, Mo., 1989—, Greenstreet Interiors, 1993-94; realtor assoc. ERA Martin House, Platte City, Mo., 1984-85; sales rep. Don Wood Real Estate, 1987-88; with J.D. Reece Realtors, 1988—. Owner Designs By Geri, Inc., 2003—. Leader, Winding River coun. Girl Scouts U.S., 1966-71; mem. Grace Notes Singing Ensemble, Kansas City, 1980; trustee Park Hill Bapt. Ch., Parkville, 1983-85; trustee First Bapt. Ch., North Kansas City, Mo., 1998—, mem. choir, 1994—; mem. extension coun. Platte City, Mo. Mem. Platte County Bus. and Profl. Assn. (bd. dirs. 1980-81), Am. Soc. Interior Designers, Nat. Assn. Women Bus. Owners, Greater Kansas City, Platte County Women's Exch., Women in Bus., Northland Genealogy Soc. (bd. dirs. 1997—), Gen. Fedn. Women's Clubs, Patricia Club, Lions (hon.), Habitat for Humanity, Master Gardeners of Greater Kans. City Mo., Women's Missionary Soc., First Bapt. NKC. Mo. (dir.), Internat. Soc. Glass Bead Designers. Democrat. Baptist. Avocations: jewelry designing, swimming, golf, theatre, gardening. Home: 9203 NW 76th Ter Weatherby Lake MO 64152-1723 E-mail: redhen@gbronline.com.

HAWKINS, JACQUELYN, elementary and secondary education educator; b. Russell Springs, Ky., Apr. 30, 1943; d. J.T. Hawkins and Maudie Bell Crew. BS, Andrews U., 1969; MEd, Xavier U., 1976. Cert. elem. tchr., Ohio, reading tchr. elem. and high sch., Ohio. Tchr. Cin. Pub. Schs., 1969-99, Cummins Sch., Cin., 1971-81, Windsor Sch., Cin., 1982-83, 1983-89, acting contact tchr. chpt. 1 reading program, 1989-93, reading recovery tchr., 1993-99; ret., 1999; child care worker, 2002—. Rep. Cin. Coun. Educators, 1986-89, 91-92, 92-93, mem. book com.; mem. sch. improvement program Windsor Sch., 1982-84; mem. Sch. Improvement Program Cin. Chairperson United Way at Windsor Sch. Cin., 1986-89, 90-92, United Negro Coll. Fund Cin., 1986-89, ARC, Windsor Sch., Cin., 1986-89, 90-92; rep. Fine Arts Fund Cin., 1986-88; co-leader 4-H Club, Cin., 1987-88; leader Girl Scouts U.S., Cin., 1988-93; tutor Tabernacle Bapt. Ch., 1989; co-chairperson Windsor ARC, 1991-92. Recipient Cert. Achievement Cummins Sch. Cin., 1978 Democrat. Avocations: travel, reading, needlework.

HAWKINS, JOELLEN MARGARET BECK, nursing educator; b. Harvey, N.D., Dec. 15, 1941; d. Charles Joel and Gertrude Adelaide (Waits) Beck; m. Charles Albert Watson, June 27, 1964 (div. 1978); children: John Charles, Andrew Bruce; m. David Gene Hawkins, Oct. 4, 1978. Student, Oberlin Coll., 1959—61; diploma, Chgo. Wesley Meml. Hosp. Sch. of Nursing, 1964; BSN, Northwestern U., Chgo., 1964; MS, Boston Coll., 1969, PhD, 1977. Cert. women's health nurse practitioner. Staff nurse Sheboygan (Wis.) Meml. Hosp., 1964-65; instr., staff Boston Lying in Hosp., 1965-66, 68-69; staff nurse Brookline (Mass.) Vis. Nurse Assn., 1968, Guy's Hosp., London, 1968; campus nurse Roger Williams Coll., Bristol, RI, 1969-70; instr. Salve Regina Coll., Newport, RI, 1970-74; faculty Roger Williams Coll., Bristol, RI, 1974-75; prof. U. Conn., Storrs, 1978-83; asst., assoc. prof. William F. Connell Sch. Nursing Boston Coll., Chestnut Hill, Mass., 1975-78, prof., 1983—. Women's health nurse practitioner Crittenton Hastings House, 1984-2000, U. Conn. Student Health Women's Clinic, 1978-83, Sidney Borum Health Ctr., 2000—, Pine St. Inn Women's Clinic, 2000—. Author: Maternal-Newborn Nursing: Pretest Self-Assessment and Review, 1978, Clinical Experience in Collegiate Nursing Education: Selection of Clinical Agencies, 1981, Health Care of Women: Gynecological Assessment, 1982, Women and the Menopause, 1983, Linking Nursing Education and Practice: Collaborative Experiences in Maternal Child Health, 1987, Dictionary of American Nursing Biography, 1988, Nursing and the American Health Care Delivery System, 4th edit., 1993, Nurse-Social Worker Collaboration in Managed Care: A Model of Community Case Management, 1998, The Advanced Practice Nurse: Current Issues, 5th edit., 2000, Guidelines for Nurse Practitioners in Gynecologic Settings, 8th edit., 2004—; editor: Linking Nursing Education and Practice, 1987 (Book of Yr. award Am. Jour. Nursing, 1988), Clin. Excellence for Nurse Practitioners: Internat. Jour. of NPACE, 1996—, Diversity in Health Care Research: Strategies for Multisite, Multidisciplinary, and Multicultural Projects, 2003; contbr. articles to profl. jours., chapters to books. Recipient Disting. Alumni award North H.S., 1989, Miriam Manisoff award Planned Parenthood Fedn. Am., 1997, Disting. Alumna award Chgo. Wesley Meml. Hosp. Sch. Nursing, 1999; named Nurse Practitioner of Yr. Am. Acad. of Nurse Practitioners, 1995. Fellow Am. Acad. Nursing; mem. ANA, Mass. RNs Assn. (Disting. Nurse Rschr. award 1984, Lucy Lincoln Drown Nursing History award 1994), Internat. Coun. Women's Health, Nat. Acad. Practice, Am. Assn. for History Nursing (nominating chmn. 1989), Assn. Women's Health Obstetric and Neonatal Nurses, Sigma Theta Tau (Elizabeth Russell Belford Founder's award for excellence in edn. 1993). Democrat. Unitarian Universalist. Avocation: nursing history. Home: 151 Stanton Ave Auburndale MA 02466-3005 Office: Boston Coll William F Connell Sch Nursing 140 Commonwealth Ave Chestnut Hill MA 02467

HAWKINS, KATHERINE ANN, hematologist, lawyer; b. Teaneck, N.J., Oct. 25, 1947; d. Howard Robert and Helen Ann (Foley) Hawkins; m. Paul Jonathan Chrzanowski, June 29, 1974; children: Eric, Brian. AB, Manhattanville Coll., Purchase, N.Y., 1969; MD, Columbia U., 1973; JD, Fordham U., Sch. of Law, 2002. Intern Presbyn. Hosp., N.Y.C., 1973, Roosevelt Hosp., N.Y.C., 1974-75, resident, 1975-77; fellow NYU, 1977-79; attending hematologist Sickle Cell Ctr. St. Luke's Hosp., N.Y.C., 1985-87; assoc. attending physician St. Luke's - Roosevelt Hosp. Ctr., N.Y.C., 1989—; asst. clin. prof. medicine Columbia U., N.Y.C., 1987-94, assoc. clin. prof., 1994—96; assoc. dir. dept. medicine, dir. med. edn. St. Luke's Hosp., N.Y.C., 1991-96; assoc. residency program dir. Beth Israel Med. Ctr., N.Y.C., 1996—; assoc. prof. clin. medicine Albert Einstein Coll. Medicine Yeshiva U., N.Y.C., 1996—2002. Mem. attending staff Beth Israel Hosp., N.Y.C., St. Luke's-Roosevelt Hosp. Ctr., N.Y.C. Contbr. articles to profl. jours. Fellow ACP; mem. ABA, Am. Soc. Hematology, Am. Soc. Clin. Oncology, Am. Coll. Legal Medicine Roman Catholic. Office: Gair Gair Conason Steigman and Mackauf 80 Pine St New York NY 10005

HAWKINS, KATHLEEN L. writer, training services executive; b. Palo Alto, Calif., May 12; BA in Elem. Edn., Ea. Mich. U., 1968, MA in Reading Edn., 1969; MA in Creative Writing, San Francisco State U., 1973. Elementary Teaching Degree (K-9 for Life) Ea. Mich. U., Ypsilanti, MI, 1968, cert. elem. tchr. Mich. V.p. Nat. Mgmt. Inst., Flower Mound, Tex., 1976—, profl. spkr., 1976—, Effective Tng. Assocs., Los Gatos, Calif., 1976—. Adj. prof. U. Mich., Ann Arbor. Author: Test Your Entrepreneurial IQ, 1986, Time Management Made Easy, 1994, Spirit Incorporated: How to Follow Your Spiritual Path from 9 to 5, 1998; co-author: Reverse Speech: Hidden Messages in Human Communication, 1991; columnist: Success mag.; author and prodr. (audiocassette) How to Organize Yourself to Win, 1994, Speed Read to Win, 1995, author (video) Speed Reading Skills. Bd. dirs. Grapevine Lake Preservation Assn., Flower Mound, 2002—. Office: National Management Institute 3209 Lakewood Ln Flower Mound TX 75022-6802

HAWKINS, LINDA PARROTT, school system administrator; b. Florence, SC, June 23, 1947; d. Obie Lindberg Parrott and Mary Francis (Lee) Evans; m. Larry Eugene Hawkins, Jan. 5, 1946; 1 child, Heather Nichole. BS, U. S.C., 1969; MS, Francis Marion Coll., 1978; EdS in Adminstrn., U. S.C., 1994, PhD in Ednl. Adminstrn., 2002. Tchr. J.C. Lynch HS, Coward, SC, 1973—80; tchr., chair bus. dept. Lake City (SC) HS, 1980—89, assoc. prin., 1989—98; dir. Florence County Sch. Dist. 3, 1998—2003, sr. dir. accountability, 1980—89. Mem. Williamsburg Tech. Adv. Coun., Kingstree, S.C., 1985-90; adv. coun. Florence-Darlington (S.C.) Tech., 1981-87; co-chair Pee Dee Tech Prep consortia steering com.; co-chmn. allied health adv. com., 1990-93; spkr., presenter in field. Editor: Parliamentary Procedure Made Easy, 1983; contbr. articles to profl. jours. State advisor Future Bus. Leaders of Am., Columbia, S.C., 1978-86; treas. S.C. State Women's Aux., 1983-93; sec.-treas. J.C. Lynch Elem. Sch. PTO. Named Outstanding Advisor S.C. Future Bus. Leaders of Am., 1985, Tchr. of Yr., S.C. Bus. Edn. Assn., 1988-89, Secondary Tchr. of Yr., Nat. Bus. Edn. Assn., 1989-90, Educator of Yr. S.C. Trade & Indsl. Edn. Assn., 1993, S.C. Asst. Prin. of Yr., 1995, 2020 Vision Dist. Adminstr. award, 2000; Mary Eva Hite scholar, 2001. Mem. Profl. Secs. Internat., Nat. Bus. Assn. (S.C. chpt. membership dir. 1986-89, so. region membership dir. 1989-92, secondary program dept. dir. 1991-92), S.C. Bus. Edn. Assn. (jour. editor 1985-86, v.p. for membership 1986-87, treas. 1987-88, pres. elect 1988-89, pres. 1989-90), Am. Vocat. Assn., S.C. Vocat. Assn. (parliamentarian 1985-86, v.p. 1989-90, treas. 1991-92), SC Assn. of Title I Admin. (pres. elect 2003-2004), Internat. Soc. Bus. Educators, Lake City C. of C., Kappa Kappa Iota, Delta Kappa Gamma. Democrat. Baptist. Avocations: cross-stitching, reading, softball. Office: Florence County Sch Dist 3 PO Box 1389 Lake City SC 29560-1389 Office Phone: 843-374-8652. E-mail: lhawkins@florence3.k12.sc.us.

HAWKINS, LISA LYNNE, lawyer, municipal official; b. Washington, Mar. 15, 1971; d. Joseph Addison Jr. and Barbara Lynne (Brown) H. BA, Frostburg (Md.) State U., 1993; postgrad., Harvard U., 1995-96; JD, U. Calif., Berkeley, 1996. Bar: Md. 1996, D.C. 1998. Assoc. Patton Boggs, L.L.P., Washington, 1998—; polit. columnist Digital City Washington, Am. Online, Washington. Supervising editor Harvard Jour. on Legislation, Cambridge, Mass., 1995-96. Bd. dirs. Women Leadership Found., Washington, 1996-97; dir. fundraising Montgomery County (Md.) Young Dems., 1996-98; mem. city coun. Takoma Park, Md., 1997-98. Mem. ABA, Am. League of Lobbyists, Women in Govt. Rels., Bar Assn. D.C. Avocations: classic art, theater, mentoring. Office: Patton Boggs LLP 2550 M St NW Ste 400 Washington DC 20037-1301

HAWKINS, LORETTA ANN, retired secondary school educator, playwright; b. Winston-Salem, N.C., Jan. 1, 1942; d. John Henry and Laurine (Hines) Sanders; m. Joseph Hawkins, Dec. 10, 1962; children: Robin, Dionne, Sherri. BS in Edn., Chgo. State U., 1965; MA in Lit., Governor's State U., 1977, MA in African Cultures, 1978; MLA in Humanities, U. Chgo., 1998. Cert. tchr., Ill. Tchr. Chgo. Bd. Edn., 1968—2002; lectr. Chgo. City Colls., 1987-89; tchr. English, Gage Park H.S., Chgo., 1988—2002; ret., 2002. Mem. steering com. Mellon Seminar U. Chgo., 1990; tchr. adv. com. Goodman Theatre, Chgo., 1992, mem. cmty. adv. coun., 1996—; spkr. in field; creator 5-4-3-2-1- Essay Writing Method, 1997. Author: (reading workbook) Contemporary Black Heroes, 1992, (plays) Of Quiet Birds, 1993 (James H. Wilson award 1993), Above the Line, 1994, Good Morning, Miss Alex; contbr. poetry, articles to profl. publs.; featured WYCC-TV-Educate, 1996. Mem. Chgo. Tchg. Connections Network, DePaul U. Ctr. Urban Edn., 2001; mem. Chgo. Pub. Schs. Mentoring and Induction of New Tchrs. Program. Fellow Santa Fe Pacific Found., 1988, Lloyd Fry Found. 1989, Andrew W. Mellon Found., 1991, Ill. Arts Coun., 1993; grantee Cmty. Arts Assistance Program Award, Chgo. Dept. Cultural Affairs; recipient Feminist Writers 3d pl. award NOW, 1993, Zora Neale Hurston-Bessie Head Fiction award Black Writer's Conf., 1993, Suave Tchr. Plus award, 2002; numerous others. Mem. AAUW, Nat. Coun. Tchrs. English (spkr. conv.), Am. Fedn. Tchrs., Women's Theatre Alliance, Dramatists Guild of Am., Internat. Women's Writing Guild. Achievements include invention of 5-4-3-2-1 essay writing method. Avocations: films, coins, reading, walking. Home: 8928 S Oglesby Ave Chicago IL 60617-3047

HAWKINS, MARY ELLEN HIGGINS (MARY ELLEN HIGGINS), former state legislator, public relations consultant; b. Birmingham, Ala., Apr. 18, 1923; m. James H. Hawkins, Feb. 13, 1960 (div. 1971); children: Andrew Higgins, Elizabeth, Peter Hixon. Student. U. Ala., Tuscaloosa, 1945-47. Congl. aide to several mems. U.S. Ho. Reps., 1950-60; instr. art Sumter County Schs., Americus, Ga., 1971-72; staff writer Naples (Fla.) Daily News, 1972-74; prin. Daniels-Hawkins, Naples, 1982-84; mem. Fla. Ho. Reps., Tallahassee, 1974-94; vice chmn. BancFlorida Fin. Corp., Naples, 1979-91, pres., CEO, 1991-92, chmn., 1991-93, also. bd. dirs. Columnist, contbr. articles to local newspapers. V.p. Naples Philharm., 1984-91; life mem., vice chair Big Cypress Basin bd. South Fla. Water Mgmt. Dist., 1999—; mem. adv. com. Lower Gulf Coast Water Supply Plan, 1999—; trustee CREW Land and Water Trust, 2002—, treas., 2004—; vice chair Fla. Children's Campaign, 1997—; various offices Rep. Party Ga., Americus, 1965-71. Recipient numerous award for work in Fla. Legislature. Mem. Zonta Internat. Avocation: painting.

HAWKINS, NAOMI RUTH, nurse; b. Ft. Smith, Ark., Mar. 8, 1947; d. William Oscar and Sallie Inez (Reynolds) H. BS in Nursing, U. Cen. Ark., 1974. RN, Ark.; cert. pediatric nurse practitioner, Ark.; cert. family nurse practitioner. Nurse practitioner Booneville (Ark.) Med. Clinic, 1975-78; lic. practical nurse Greenhurst Nursing Home, Charleston, Ark., 1967-73, RN, 1973-75; pediatric nurse practitioner Ark. Dept. Health, Paris, Ark., 1978—. Fellow Nat. Assn. Pediatric Nurse Assocs. and Practitioners; mem. Ark. Assn. Pediatric Nurse Assocs. and Practitioners, Am. Assn. Christian Counselors, Pub. Health Nurses Assn. Ark., Ark. State Employees Assn. Democrat. Baptist. Avocations: photography, counted cross stitch. Home: 11111 Hwy 41 Charleston AR 72933-9418 Office: 102 E Academy St Paris AR 72855-4432

HAWKINS, PEGGY ANNE, veterinarian; b. Omaha, Dec. 9, 1956; d. Robert Leon and Karen Lynne Hawkins. BS, Iowa State U., 1982, DVM, 1991, MS, 1992. Vol., h.s. tchr. U.S. Peace Corps, Lesotho, 1982-85; lab. technician Iowa State U., Ames, 1986-87, tchg. asst., 1990-92; veterinarian, swine practitioner White Oak Mills/ProGenetics, Elizabethtown, Pa., 1992-94; tech. svcs. veterinarian Pfizer, Animal Health Group, Lee's Summit, Mo., 1994-96, product devel. vet. advisor N.Y.C., 1996—2001, vet. med. mgr., 2001—02; health svcs. vet. Monsanto Choice Genetics, St. Louis, 2002—. Vol. tchr. Jr. Achievement, N.Y.C. Pub. Schs., 1999. Recipient Swine Proficiency award Purina Mills, Inc., 1991; Iowa State U. scholar. Mem.: AVMA, Iowa Vet. Med. Assn., Am. Assn. Swine Veterinarians (Found. fellow 1998—). Avocations: travel, photography, hiking. Office: Monsanto Co 800 Lindbergh Blvd Saint Louis MO 63167

HAWKINS, SUSAN ANN, special education educator; b. Buffalo, Apr. 7, 1959; d. Robert M. and Ann M. MacGregor; m. Donald A. Hawkins, Oct. 27, 1984; children: Lindsay A., Joshua W. B, Boston U., 1983; M, SUNY, Buffalo, 1988. Tchr. spl. edn. Batavia High Sch., Batavia, NY, 1983—. Mem.: Phi Delta Kappa (Educator of the Yr. 2002). Avocations: swimming, walking. Office: Batavia High Sch 260 State St Batavia NY 14020

HAWKINS-SNEED, JANET LYNN, school psychologist, human resources administrator, small business owner; b. July 3, 1956; d. James Crawford Jr. and Oberia (Aiken) H. BS in Spanish and Psychology, Furman U., 1978; MEd in Secondary Edn., Converse Coll., 1981; EdS in Counseling and Sch. Psychology, Wichita State U., 1986. Tchr. Spartanburg Sch. Dist. 5, Duncan, S.C., 1979-80, Wichita (Kans.) Sch. Dist., 1982-85; psychology intern Mulvane (Kans.) Sch. Dist., 1985-86; sch. psychologist

Sch. Dist. Greenville (S.C.) County, 1986-93; with Dyslexia Resource Ctr., Greenville; with benefits dept. Suitt Constrn. Co., Greenville, 1997—98, human resources coord., 1998—99; owner, CEO Mystic Gifts, Williamston, SC. Presenter at profl. confs. Chancellor, Upstate S.C. Ch. of Wicca. Mem. NOW, Coun. Exceptional Children, Nat. Assn. Sch. Psychologists, Sierra Club, Nat. Wildlife Fedn., Phi Kappa Phi. Avocations: music, art, nature, equestrian, breeder of beagles. Home: 305 Hl Taylor RD Williamston SC 29697 Office: PO Box 455 Williamston SC 29697

HAWKS, SHIRLEY LYNN, manufacturing executive, writer; d. Robert Earl and Beatrice Josephine Anderson; m. Harvey Eugene Hawks, Oct. 28, 1989. BS in Bus. Mgmt. and Mktg., Ind. U., 1979; M in Indsl. Psychology, Purdue U., Ind., 1991. Second v.p Hawks Sales Corp. Rubber Products Distbrs., Indpls., 1984—2002; area merchandising purchasing mgr. Pulte Homes, Inc., Las Vegas, 2003—. Author: (poetry) Thank You, 2001 (3d Pl. Editor's Choice award). Commd. Ky. col. Hon. Order of Ky. Cols., 1990—. Mem.: Internat. Exec. Guild (life), Internat. Assn. Exec. Females (life), Phi Theta Kappa (life), Delta Omicron (life). Episcopal. Avocations: writing, working, counseling, gambling, travel. Home: 8350 W Dessert Inn Rd #2136 Las Vegas NV 89117

HAWLEY, ANNE, museum director; b. Iowa City, Iowa, Nov. 3, 1943; d. Marshall Newton and Leone Ardith (Wilson) Hawley; m. Bruce Ivor McPherson, Sept. 4, 1977; 1 child, Katherine Black. BA, U. Iowa, 1966; MA, George Washington U., 1969; LHD (hon.), Lesley Coll, 1987; LHD (hon.), Williams Coll., 1989, Babson Coll., 1990, sr. exec. prog., Kennedy Sch. Govt, Harvard Univ., Intern in edn., Washington, 1967-69; research assoc. Nat. Urban League, Washington, 1969-71, Ford Found. Study Leadership in Pub. Edn., Washington, 1971-73; exec. dir. Cultural Edn. Collaborative, Boston, 1974-77, Mass. Council Arts/Humanities, Boston, 1977-89; mus. dir. Isabella Stewart Gardner Mus., Boston, 1989—; resident Nat. Hist. Soc. 1993—; adv. com. Nat. Trust of Historic Preservation, 1993—; vis. com. Fitchburg Art Mus., 1992-94. Bd. dirs. New Eng. Found. for Arts, 1978-89, Nat. Assembly/State Arts Agencies, Washington, 1981-83, Greater Boston Arts Fund, 1984-89, Boston Archtl. Found., 1986-89, Nat. Art Stabilization Fund, 1990-95, Boston Fenway Program, 1990-93. Trustee Inst. Contemporary Art, Boston, 1990—, Old Sturbridge Village, 1991-94; vis. comm. Sch. Mus. Fine Arts, Boston, 1989—, adv. bd. Mass. Coll. Art, 1979-81. Fulbright scholar, 1986; recipient Design Travel Grant, Women's Travel Club, Boston, Mass., 1982, Polaroid travel grant, 1987, Fund for Mutual Understanding travel grant to USSR, 1988, Art award Mass. Coll. Art, 1987, Lyman Ziegler award Commonwealth of Mass., 1988. Mem. Nat. Endowment for Arts (mus. panel 1978-81, task force on trng. and devel. of artists and art edu., 1978, dance panel 1982-84, design panel 1978-81, 88—, Pres. Clinton's transition team for arts and humanities, 1992-93), Boston Soc. Architecture (hon. mem. 1989); Radcliffe Alumnae Career Svcs. (adv. comm. 1974). Office: Isabella Stewart Gardner Mus 2 Palace Rd Boston MA 02115-5807

HAWLEY, KIMRA, software company executive; BS in Psychology, Pitts. State U. Prin. MarketBound Assocs.; various mktg. mgmt. positions Amdahl Corp.; imaging mktg. dir. Action Point Software (formerly Cornerstone Imaging), 1992-96, gen. mgr. software divsn., 1996, now pres., CEO. Office: Actionpoint Software 1299 Parkmoor Ave San Jose CA 95126-3448

HAWLEY, LUCRETIA MARLENE, retired accounting educator; b. Stillwater, Okla., Nov. 19, 1932; d. Owen Hartman Schneider and Maudee Dessie (Callicoat) Bearg; m. Robert Paul Hawley, Nov. 27, 1955; children: James Owen, Kathleen Francis Jeschke, John Robert. BS in Econs., BSBA in Acctg., Ctrl. Mo. State U., 1955, MA in Acctg., 1970. CPA, cert. mgmt. acct. Payroll clk. Westinghouse, Kansas City, Mo., 1951; internal auditor Spencer Chem., Kansas City, 1955-56; bus. skills and Am. history tchr. J.C. Penney H.S., Hamilton, Mo., 1965-67; bus. skills and speech tchr. Breckenridge (Mo.) H.S., 1967-70; bus. skills and acctg. tchr. various bus. schs., 1972-77; instr., asst. prof. acctg. Mo. Western State Coll., St. Joseph, Mo., 1970-71, 77-95; ret., 1995. Mem. acad. computing com. Mo. Western State Coll., St. Joseph, 1988-95. Co-pastor, treas. Cmty. of Christ Ch. Mem. Inst. Mgmt. Accts. (bd. dirs., CMA dir., student dir.), Sr. Citizens Found. (treas., bd. dirs. 1980-95), Gen. Fedn. Women's Clubs Monday Club (pres.), Phi Delta Kappa, Delta Kappa Gamma (v.p. 1994-96, pres. 1996-98). Republican. Avocations: reading, travel, sewing, crafts, church work. Home: 1004 S Hughes Hamilton MO 64644

HAWLEY, NANCI ELIZABETH, association administrator; b. Detroit, Mar. 18, 1942; d. Arthur Theodore and Elizabeth Agnes (Fylling) Smisek; m. Joseph Michael Hawley, Aug. 28, 1958; children: Michael, Ronald, Patrick (dec.), Julie Anne. Pres. Tempo 21 Nursing Svcs., Inc., Covina, Calif., 1973-75; v.p. Profl. Nurses Bur., Inc., L.A., 1975-83; owner, CEO Hawley & Assocs., Covina, 1983-87; exec. v.p. Glendora (Calif.) C. of C., 1984-85; dir. membership West Covina (Calif.) C. of C., 1985-87; exec. dir. San Dimas (Calif.) C. of C., 1987-88; mgr. pub. rels. Soc. for Advancement of Material and Process Engrs., Covina, 1988-92; small bus. rep. South Coast Air Quality Mgmt. Dist., 1992-94; bus. counselor Commerce and Trade Agy., Small Bus. Devel. Ctr., 1994; exec v.p. Ontario (Calif.) C. of C., 1994-97; CEO, RMH Elec. Contractors, Colorado Springs, Colo., 1997-98; exec. v.p. Teen Resources, Inc., Colorado Springs, 1998; meetings mgr., registrar Am. Birding Assn., Colorado Springs, 1999—. V.p. Sangabriel valley chpt. Women in Mgmt. Recipient Youth Motivation award Foothill Edn. Com., Glendora, 1987. Mem. NAFE, Colo. Assn. Nonprofit Orgns., Pub. Rels. Soc. Am., Soc. Nat. Assn. Publs., Am. Soc. Assn. Execs., Nat. Assn. Membership Dirs., Profl. Communicators Assn. So. Calif., Profl. Conf. Mgrs. Assn., West End Bus. Assn. (pres. 1997-99), Western Assn. Chamber Execs. (Spl. merit award for mag. pub. 1995), Profl. Conv. Mgrs. Assn., Kiwanis (sec. 1989-90, pres. West Covina 1990-91, Kiwanian of Yr. 1989), Rotary. Avocations: reading, walking, painting, gardening, birdwatching. Office: PO Box 6599 Colorado Springs CO 80934-6599 Office Phone: 800-850-2473 x233. Personal E-mail: nanmick58@aol.com.

HAWLEY, SANDRA SUE, electrical engineer; b. Spirit Lake, Iowa, May 7, 1948; d. Byrnard Leroy and Dorothy Virginia (Fischbeck) Smith; m. Michael John Hawley, June 7, 1970; 1 child, Alexander Tristin. BSEE, U. Dayton, 1981; BS in Math. and Stats., Iowa State U., 1970; MS in Stats., U. Del., 1975. Rsch. analyst State of Wis., Madison, 1970-71; rsch. asst. Del. State Coll., Dover, 1972-73; asst. prof. math. and statis. Wesley Coll., Dover, 1974-81, chmn. dept. math. and computer sci., 1978-80; elec. engr. Control Data Corp., Bloomington, Minn., 1982-85; sr. elec. engr. Custom integrated Circuits, 1985-89; sr. lead engr. Cardiac Pacemakers, Inc., 1989-90; mgr. Tech. Rosemount Inc., 1990-94; prin. cons. Tri-Ess, Mpls., 1994—. Contbr. articles to profl. jours. Elder Presbyn. Ch. U.S.A., 1975—, mem. session Oak Grove Presbyn. Ch., Bloomington, 1985-88; moderator Presbytery of Twin Cities Area, 1996, chair Presbytery Coun., 1994, chair Coun. United Action, 1989-92, adminstrv. comm., 1989-91, chair com. on ministry, 1998—, commr. to Synod of Lakes & Prairies, 1990, Gen. Assembly Coun., 1992-98, com. on coun., 1992, commr. Gen. Assembly, 1991, chair Nat. Ministries divsn. Gen. Assembly, 1992-98; bd. dirs. Presbyn. Investment and Loan Program, gen. assembly coun. ch. growth strategy team, 1997-99; coun. advisors Dubuque Theol. Sem., 1999—; bd. dirs. Presbyn. Homes of Minn., 2002-. NSF scholar U. Dayton, 1981. Mem. IEEE, Soc. Women Engrs. Office: Tri-Ess 7724 W 85th St Minneapolis MN 55438-1382 E-mail: csshawley@aol.com.

HAWN, GOLDIE, actress; b. Washington, Nov. 21, 1945; d. Edward Rutledge and Laura (Steinhoff) H.; m. Gus Trinkonis, May 16, 1969 (div.); m. Bill Hudson (div.); children: Oliver, Kate, Wyatt. Student, Am. U. Profl. dancer, 1965; profl. acting debut in Good Morning, World, 1967-68; mem. company TV series Laugh-In, 1968-70; films include: The One and Only Genuine Original Family Band, 1968, Cactus Flower, 1969 (Acad. award best sup. actress, 1969, Golden Globe best sup. actress, 1969), There's A Girl In My Soup, 1970, $, 1971, Butterflies Are Free, 1971, The Sugarland Express, 1974, The Girl from Petrovka, 1974, Shampoo, 1975, The Duchess and the Dirtwater Fox, 1976, Travels with Anita, 1978, Foul Play, 1978, Seems Like Old Times, 1980, Lovers and Liars, 1981, Best Friends, 1982, Swingshift, 1984, Overboard, 1987, Bird on a Wire, 1989, Deceived, 1991, Housesitter, 1992, Death Becomes Her, 1992, Crisscross, 1992, The First Wives Club, 1996, Everyone Says I Love You, 1996, The Out of Towners, 1999, Town and Country, 1999, The Banger Sisters, 2002; exec. producer, actor Private Benjamin, 1980, Protocol, 1984, Wildcats, 1986; exec. prodr. My Blue Heaven, 1990, Something to Talk About, 1995 (TV films) When Billie Beat Bobby, 1991, The Matthew Shepard Story, 2002; exec. prodr., dir. (TV films) Hope, 1997; host TV spl. Pure Goldie, 1970, Goldie Hawn Special, 1978, Goldie and Liza Together, 1980, Goldie and Kids: Listen to Us!, 1982. Named Woman of the Year, Hasty Pudding Theatricals, 1999; recipient Women in Film Crystal award, 1997. Office: c/o ICM Ed Limato & S Dontanville 8942 Wilshire Blvd Beverly Hills CA 90211-1934*

HAWN, JUDITH RADY, medical/surgical nurse; b. Hartford, Conn., June 15, 1960; d. Thomas Francis Rady III and Dolores Pelczarski Rady; m. Benjamin Waters Hawn, May 1988 (div. Dec. 1997). BS, U. La., 1994, BSN, 1996. RN. Staff nurse Dauterive Hosp., NEw Iberia, La., 1996—97, Lafayette Gen. Med. Ctr., 1997, Supplemental Health Care, 1999—2000, Cross Country, 2000—02, TVL Health, 2002—. Reviewer Cert. Bd. Pre-oper. Nursing, Denver, 2003. Vol. litter cleanup and recycle, Bluffton, SC, 2000—; vet. asst. Spay/Neuter Clinic, 2003; vol. Jaspar County Animal Shelter, 2003—. With U.S. Army, 1984—87. Scholar, Assn. Oper. Rm. Nurses, 1993. Mem.: Am. Contract Bridge League (life), Phi Kappa Phi, Sigma Theta Tau. Avocations: gardening, reading. Office: JR Hawn PMB 246 20 Towne Dr Bluffton SC 29910 Personal E-mail: rhoderatt@aol.com.

HAWTHORNE, NAN LOUISE, Internet resources consultant, web site designer, writer; b. Hawthorne, Nev., Jan. 3, 1952; d. Louis Frederick Haas Jr. and Merle Forrest (Ohlhausen) Ritter; m. James Denver Tedford, Dec. 20, 1981. BS, No. Mich. U., 1981. Mng. dir. CyberVPM.com, Seattle, 1997—; content devel. eSight Careers Network, 1999—; mng. dir. nanhawthorne.com. Author: Loving the Goddess Within, 1990, Building Better Relationships with Volunteers, 1997, Managing Volunteers in Record Time, 1997, Recognizing Volunteers Right From the Start, 1998; contbr. articles to profl. jours. Mem. Assn. Vol. Adminstrs. (tech. com. 1998—), Soc. Profl. Journalists. Office: PO Box 1229 22833 Bothell-Everett Hwy 102 Bothell WA 98021-9366 E-mail: hawthorne@nanhawthorne.com.

HAWVER, CAROLYN DUNN, pharmaceutical production executive; b. Tarrytown, N.Y., Nov. 2, 1954; d. Robert Thomas and Carolyn Pamelia (McMichael) Dunn; m. Kenneth Flint Hawver, July 8, 1994; children: Andrew Eakins, Christian Eakins, Charles Eakins. BS in Chemistry and Math., Meredith Coll., Raleigh, N.C., 1976; MS, N.C. State U., Raleigh, N.C., 1984. Rsch. chemist Colgate-Palmolive, Piscataway, N.J., 1984-88, group leader, 1989-91, tech. mgr. N.Y.C., 1992-93, focused factory mgr. Jeffersonville, Ind., 1994-96; dir. Novartis Pharmaceuticals, Suffern, N.Y., 1997—. Office: Novartis Pharmaceuticals 25 Old Mill Rd Suffern NY 10901-4106 Home: 6 N Stone Edge Rd Bedminster NJ 07921-1645 Fax: 914-368-6934. E-mail: carolyn.hawver@pharma.novartis.com., hawver@earthlink.net.

HAY, ELIZABETH DEXTER, embryology researcher, educator; b. St. Augustine, Fla., Apr. 2, 1927; d. Isaac Morris and Lucille Elizabeth (Lynn) H. AB, Smith Coll., 1948; MA (hon.), Harvard U., 1964; ScD (hon.), Smith Coll., 1973, Trinity Coll., 1989; MD, Johns Hopkins U., 1952, LHD (hon.), 1990. Intern in internal medicine Johns Hopkins Hosp., Balt., 1952-53; instr. anatomy Johns Hopkins U. Med. Sch., Balt., 1953-56, asst. prof., 1956-57, Cornell U. Med. Sch., N.Y.C., 1957-60, Harvard Med. Sch., Boston, 1960-64, Louise Foote Pfeiffer assoc. prof., 1964-69, Louise Foote Pfeiffer prof. embryology, 1969—, chmn. dept. anatomy and cellular biology, 1975-93; prof. dept. cell biology, 1993—. Cons. cell biology sect. NIH, 1965-69; mem. adv. coun. Nat. Inst. Gen. Med. Sci., NIH, 1978-81; mem. sci. adv. bd. Whitney Marine Lab., U. Fla., 1982-86; mem. adv. coun. Johns Hopkins Sch. Medicine, 1982-96; chairperson bd. sci. counselors Nat. Inst. Dental Rsch., NIH, 1984-86; mem. bd. sci. counselors Nat. Inst. Environ. Health Sci., NIH, 1990-93. Author: Regeneration, 1966; (with J.P. Revel) Fine Structure of the Developing Avian Cornea, 1969; editor: Cell Biology of Extracellular Matrix, 1981, 2d edit., 1991; editor-in-chief Developmental Biology Jour., 1971-75; contbr. articles to profl. jours. Mem. Scientists Task Force of Congressman Barney Frank, Massach, 1982-92. Recipient Disting. Achievement award N.Y. Hosp.-Cornell Med. Ctrl. Alumni Coun., 1985, award for vision rsch. Alcon, 1988, Excellence in Sci. award Fedn. Am. Socs. Exptl. Biology. Mem. Soc. Devel. Biology (pres. 1973-74, E.G. Conklin award 1997), Am. Soc. Cell Biology (pres. 1976-77, legis. alert com. 1982—, E.B. Wilson award 1989, chair 40th anniversary 2000), Am. Assn. Anatomists (pres. 1981-82, legis. alert com. 1982—, Centennial award 1987, Henry Gray award 1992), Am. Acad. Arts and Scis., Johns Hopkins Soc. Scholars, Nat. Acad. Sci., Inst. Medicine, Internat. Soc. Devel. Biologists (exec. bd. 1977, keynote spkr. 1st Australian EMT conf. 2003), Boston Mycol. Club. Home: 14 Aberdeen Rd Weston MA 02493-1733 Office: Harvard Med Sch Dept Cell Biology 220 Longwood Ave Boston MA 02115-5701 Office Phone: 617-432-1651. E-mail: ehay@nms.harvard.edu.

HAY, SANDRA KAY GILLETTI, state agency administrator; b. Walsenburg, Colo., Jan. 6, 1947; d. Pete (Ghiglietti) and Violet A. (Pedron) Gilletti; m. James Wayne Hay, Sept. 9, 1967; 1 child, Quinn Michelle Hay-Falkner. BA, Adams State Coll., 1970, MA, 1971; Adminstr., U. No. Colo., 1989. Cert. tchr., adminstr., Colo. Elem./secondary tchr. Moffat (Colo.) Consol., 1968-70; elem. tchr. Alamosa (Colo.) Pub. Schs., 1970-89, dir., fed. state program, 1989-98; summer sch. tchr. Migrant Edn. Alamosa, 1972-86; summer sch. prin. Migrant Edn./Title I, Alamosa, 1986—98; middle sch. prin. Monte Vista (Colo.) Pub. Schs., 1998—2000; adj. prof. Adams State Coll., 2000—. Recipient Nat. Educator award for State of Colo., Milken Family Found. and Colo. Dept. Edn., 1990, Outstanding Comm. Contbn. award Alamosa C. of C., 1990, Outstanding Jr. Educator award Jaycees, 1977, others. Avocations: camping, fishing, reading, sewing, family.

HAY, SUSAN STAHR HELLER, museum curator; b. Mpls., Oct. 12, 1938; d. John Lewis and Suzanne Wallace (Finley) Heller; m. Edwin J. Anderson (div.); 1 child, Fletcher Scott Anderson; m. Edward Merrill Hay, July 20, 1984. BA in French Linguistics, Cornell U., 1960; MA in French Lit., Brown U., 1963; MA in Am. Civilization, U. Pa., 1981. From curatorial asst. to mus. curator Nat. Hist. Park, Phila., 1976-78; editor W. B. Saunders Co., Phila., 1978-79; asst. mng. editor Am. Quar., 1979-80; teaching fellow U. Pa., Phila., 1980-81; curatorial asst. costume and textiles Phila Mus. Art, 1981-82, asst. curator costume and textiles, 1982-85; curator costume and textiles Mus. Art R.I. Sch. Design, Providence, 1985—. Lectr. and presenter papers in field. Contbr. articles to profl. jours. Past v.p., trustee Coggeshall Farm Mus., Bristol, R.I.; past trustee Smith's Castle Historic Site, Wickford, R.I. Cooper-Woods Meml. Travel Study grant English Speaking Union, 1978. Mem. Am. Assn. Mus., Costume Soc. Am. Textile Soc. Am., Ctr. Internat. d'Etudes des Textiles Anciens., Tex. Soc. Am. Office: RI Sch Design Mus Art 224 Benefit St Providence RI 02903-2723

HAYASHI, MARIS LANI, librarian; b. Huntington Beach, Calif., July 19, 1973; d. Melvin Mitsuyoshi Hayashi and Eunice Naomi Hayashi Kishimoto. BA, U. Calif., Irvine, 1996; MA, U. Ariz., Tucson, 1999; MLS, U. Iowa, 2002. Info. arcade cons. U. of Iowa Librs., Iowa City, 2000—02; reference libr. Fla. Atlantic U. Librs., Boca Raton, Fla., 2002—. Author: (web tutorial) L.O.T. - Library Online Tutorial. Mem.: ALA, Assn.Coll. and Rsch. Librs., Soc. for Cinema and Media Studies, Internat. Communication Assn. Democrat. Avocations: web design, cooking. Office: Florida Atlantic U Librs 777 Glades Rd Boca Raton FL 33431 Business E-Mail: mhayashi@fau.edu.

HAYDEN, COLLEEN, advanced placement secondary school educator; b. Delano, Minn., June 13, 1940; d. F. Milton and Frances (Pianko) H. BA, Coll. St. Catherine, 1962. Tchr. Bloomington (Minn.) Pub. Schs., Xavier H.S., Appleton, Wis.; chair social studies dept. Jefferson H.S., Bloomington. Adult edn. tchr. SHAPE, 1978—. Dep. edn. state literacy trainer Literacy Minn.; mem. several coms., past-chairperson coun. adminstrn. and edn. Ch. of St. Joseph. Cert. tchr., Minn. Mem. ASCD, Nat. Coun. Social Studies, Minn. Coun. Social Studies, Minn. Hist. Soc., Pi Gamma Mu.

HAYDEN, DOLORES, author, architect, educator; b. N.Y.C., Mar. 15, 1945; d. J. Francis and Katharine (McCabe) H.; m. Peter Horsey Marris, May 18, 1975; 1 child, Laura Hayden Marris. BA, Mt. Holyoke Coll., 1966; diploma in English studies, Cambridge (Eng.) U., 1967; LHD (hon.), Mt. Holyoke Coll., 1987; MArch, Harvard U., 1972; MA (hon.), Yale U., 1991. Registered architect. Lectr. U. Calif., Berkeley, 1973; assoc. prof. MIT, Cambridge, 1973-79; prof. UCLA, 1979-91, Yale U., New Haven, 1991—. Author: Seven American Utopias, 1976, The Grand Domestic Revolution, 1981, Redesigning the American Dream, 1984 (notable book award ALA, 1984, award for outstanding publ. in urban planning Assn. Collegiate Schs. of Planning 1986), rev. edit., 2002, The Power of Place: Urban Landscapes as Public History, 1995 (Assn. Am. Pubs. award), Playing House, 1998, Line Dance, 2001, Building Suburbia, 2003, A Field Guide to Sprawl, 2004, American Yard, 2004; also articles (Best Feature Article award Jour. Am. Planning Assn. 1994). Guggenheim fellow, 1981, Rockefeller Humanities fellow, 1980, ACLS/Ford fellow, 1989, Nat. Endowment for the Humanities fellow; recipient Radcliffe Grad. Soc. medal, 1991, Preservation award L.A. Conservancy, 1986, Vesta award Woman's Bldg., L.A., 1985, Design Rsch. award Nat. Endowment for the Arts, Feminist scholarship in the arts. Mem. Am. Studies Assn., Orgn. Am. Historians, Am. Planning Assn. (Diana Donald award 1987, various awards L.A. and Calif. chpts.), Urban History Assn. (dir. 1991-93), Soc. Am. City and Regional Planning History. Avocations: travel, poetry. Office: Yale Univ Sch Architecture PO Box 208242 180 York St New Haven CT 06520-8242 E-mail: dolores.hayden@yale.edu.

HAYEK, CAROLYN JEAN, financial consultant, retired judge; b. Portland, Oreg., Aug. 17, 1948; d. Robert A. and Marion L. (DeKoning) H.; m. Steven M. Rosen, July 21, 1974; children: Jonathan David, Laura Elizabeth. BA in Psychology, Carleton Coll., 1970; JD, U. Chgo., 1973; webmaster cert., Lake Washington Tech. Coll., 2000. Bar: Wash. 1973. Assoc. Jones, Grey & Bayley, Seattle, 1973-77; pvt. practice Federal Way, Wash., 1977-82; judge Federal Way Dist. Ct., 1982-95; ret., 1995. Task force Alternatives for Wash., 1973-75; mem. Wash. State Ecol. Commn., 1975-77; columnist Tacoma News Tribune Hometown Sect., 1995-96; bus. law instr. Lake Washington Tech. Coll., 2000-2001; exec. dir. People's Meml. Assn., Seattle, 2002-03; owner Hayek Svcs., 2003-. Bd. dirs. 1st Unitarian Ch., Seattle, 1986-89, vice-chair 1987-88, pres. 1988-89; ch. adminstr. Northlake Unitarian Universalist Ch.; treas. Eastshore Unitarian Universalist Ch. Women's Perspective, 2001-2002; den leader Mt. Rainier coun. Boy Scouts Am., 1987-88, scouting coord., 1988-89; bd. dirs. Twin Lakes Elem. Sch. PTA; v.p. Friends of the Libr. Kirkland, 2000—; mem. Kirkland Planning Commn., 2002—. Recipient Women Helping Women award Federal Way Soroptimist, 1991, Martin Luther King Day Humanitarian award King County, 1993, Recognition cert. City of Federal Way Diversity Commn., 1995. Mem. AAUW (co-pres. Kirkland-Redmond br. 1999-2000, co-v.p. Lake Washington br. 2001-2003, pres. Federal Way br. 1978-80, 90-92, chair state level conf. com. 1986-87, diversity com. 1991-98, state bd. mem. 1995-97, dir. ESL project), ABA, Wash. Women Lawyers, Wash. State Bar Assn., King County Dist. Ct. Judges Assn. (treas., exec. com. 1990-93, com. chair, chair and rules com. 1990-94), Elected Wash. Women (dir. 1983-87), Nat. Assn. Women Judges (nat. bd. dirs., dist. bd. dirs. 1984-86, chmn. rules com. 1988-89, chmn. bylaws com. 1990-91), Fed. Way Women's Network (bd. dirs. 1984-91, 95-97, pres. 1985, program co-chair 1989-91, co-editor newsletter), Greater Fed. Way C. of C. (dir. 1978-82, sec. 1980-81, v.p. 1981-82), Sunrise Rotary (com. svc. chair, bd. dirs., membership com., Federal Way chpt. 1991-96, youth exch. officer 1994-95), Washington Women United (bd. dirs. 1995-97), Unitarian Universalist Women's Assn. (chair bylaws com. 1996), Eliot Inst. (bd. dirs. 1996-2000, vice-chair 1998-99, bd. chair 1999-2000, webmaster 1999-2002), Plaza on State Owners Assn. (bd. dirs. 1997-2000, pres. 1997-99, sec. 1999-2000, webmaster 2000—). E-mail: cjh@kirklandplaza.com.

HAYEK, SALMA, actress; b. Coatzacoalcos, Veracruz, Mexico, Sept. 2, 1968; d. Sami Hayek Domingues and Diana H. Television work includes: Un Nuevo amanecer, 1988, Teresa, 1989, The Sinbad Show, 1993, Roadracers, 1994, El Vuelo del aguila, 1996, The Hunchback, 1997, In the Time of the Butterflies (also exec. prod.), 2001; Television appearances: Dream On, 1992, Nurses, 1992, Action, 1999. Films include Mi Vida Loca, 1993, Four Rooms, 1995, Desperado, 1995, Fair Game, 1995, From Dusk Til Dawn, 1996, Fled, 1996, Fools Rush In, 1997, Follow Me Home, 1997, Breaking Up, 1997, Sister Diastole, 1997, The Velocity of Gary, 1998, The Faculty, 1998, 54, 1998, Dogma, 1999, Wild Wild West, 1999, No One Writes to the Colonel, 1999, Shiny New Enemies, 2000, Frida, 2000, Timecode, 2000, Chain of Fools, 2000, Living It Up, 2000, Traffic, 2000, Hotel, 2001, Frida (also prod.), 2002, Spy Kids 3-D: Game Over, 2003, Once Upon a Time in Mexico, 2003; dir, exec. prod.: The Maldonado Miracle, 2003.

HAYES, AILISH MAIRE, pediatrician; b. Limerick, Ireland, Feb. 1, 1951; arrived in U.S., 1984; d. Richard F. and Christina Beatrice (McDonald) H.; m. Haig Oghigian, Sept. 8, 1984 (div.). Grad., Univ. Coll., Dublin, Ireland, 1974, diploma in child health, 1976, diploma in obstetrics, 1978; MB, BCh, BAO, Nat. Univ. Ireland, Dublin, 1974. Bd. cert. in genetics. Intern in surgery Mater Miseriacordia Hosp., Dublin, Ireland, 1974-75; resident in pediatrics Children's Hosp., Crumlin, Dublin, 1975-77; fellow in neonatology Nat. Maternity Hosp., Dublin, Ireland, 1977-80; sr. resident in pediatrics Toronto Sick Children's Hosp., 1980-81; fellow in genetics Montreal Children's Hosp., 1981-84; instr. in pediatrics Med. Sch., Harvard U., Boston, 1984—; pediatrician Revere Pediatric Assocs., 1993—; asst. in pediatrics Mass. Gen. Hosp., Boston, 1990-93. Former attending physician Children's Hosp., Boston, Brigham and Women's Hosp., Boston, Beth Israel Hosp., Boston; cons. Nat. Birth Defects Ctr., Boston, 1986—; cons. in teratology Mass. Gen. Hosp., Boston, 1987-90; cons. pediatrics and genetics Retina Assocs., Boston, 1991-92; cons. Prenatal Diagnostic Ctr., Boston, 1994—; lectr. Harvard U. Med. Sch., Boston, 1989-91; presenter in field. Fellow Royal Coll. Physicians (Ireland), Royal Coll. Physicians (Can.). Home: 2 Stone Ter Marblehead MA 01945-1320 Office: Nat Birth Defects Ctr 40 2nd Ave Ste 460 Waltham MA 02451-1136

HAYES, ALICE BOURKE, academic administrator, biologist, researcher; b. Chgo., Dec. 31, 1937; d. William Joseph and Mary Alice (Cawley) Bourke; m. John J. Hayes, Sept. 2, 1961 (dec. July 1981). BS, Mundelein Coll., Chgo., 1959; MS, U. Ill., 1960; PhD, Northwestern U., 1972; DSc (hon.), Loyola U., Chgo., 1994; HHD (hon.), Fontbonne Coll., 1994; LHD (hon.), Mount St. Mary Coll., 1998; DSc (hon.), St. Louis U., 2002. Rschr. Mcpl. Tb San., Chgo., 1960-62; faculty Loyola U., Chgo., 1962-87, chmn. dept., 1968-77, dean natural scis. divsn., 1977-80, assoc. acad. v.p., 1980-87, v.p. acad. affairs, 1987-89; provost, exec. v.p. St. Louis U., 1989-95; pres. U. San Diego, 1995—2003, pres. emerita, 2003—. Mem. space biology program NASA, 1980—86; mem. adv. panel NSF, 1977—81, Parmly Hearing Inst., 1986—89; del. Bot. Del. to South Africa, 1984, to People's Republic of China, 1988, to USSR, 1990; reviewer Coll. Bd. and

Mellon Found. Nat. Hispanic Scholar Awards, 1985—86; bd. dirs. Pulitzer Pub. Co., Loyola U. Chgo., San Diego Found., Jack-in-the-Box, ConAgra. Co-author books; contbr. articles to profl. publs. Campaign mem. Mental Health Assn. Ill., Chgo., 1973-89; trustee Chgo.-No. Ill. divsn. Nat. Multiple Sclerosis Soc., 1981-89, bd. dirs., 1980-88, com. chmn., sec. to bd. dirs., vice chmn. bd. dirs.; trustee Regina Dominican Acad., 1984-89, Civitas Dei Found., 1987-92, Rockhurst Coll., Loyola U., Chgo., San Diego Found.; trustee St. Ignatius Coll. Prep. Sch., bd. dirs., 1984-89, sec., vice chmn.; bd. dirs. Urban League Met. St. Louis, St. Louis Sci. Ctr., 1991-95, Cath. Charities St. Louis, 1992-95, St. Louis County Hist. Soc., 1992-95, Cath. Charities San Diego, 1996—, San Diego Hist. Soc., 1996—, Old Globe Theater, 1996—, also trustee. Named to Tchrs.' Hall of Fame Blue Key Soc.; fellow in botany U. Ill., 1959-60; fellow in botany NSF, 1969-71; grantee Am. Orchid Soc., 1967; grantee HEW, 1969, 76; grantee NSF, 1975; grantee NASA, 1980-85. Mem. AAAS, AAUP (corp. rep. 1980-85), Am. Assn. for Higher Edn., Am. Assn. Univ. Adminstrs. (mem. program com. nat. meeting 1988), Am. Soc. Gravitational and Space Biology, Assn. Midwest Coll. Biology Tchrs., Am. Soc. Plant Physiology, Bot. Soc. Am., Am. Inst. Biol. Scis. Acad., Chgo. Network, Soc. Ill. Microbiologists (edn. com. 1969-70, Pasteur award com. 1975, pub. rels. com. 1974, chair speakers' bur. 1974-79), Chgo. Assn. Tech. Socs. (acad. liaison 1982-85, awards com. 1984-89), Am. Coun. on Edn. (corp. rep. higher edn. panel), Ctr. Rsch. Librs. (nominating com. 1986), North Ctrl. Assn. Colls. and Schs. (cons., evaluator Commn. on Higher Edn. 1984-95, commr.-at-large 1988-94), Mo. Women's Forum Club, Sigma Xi, Delta Sigma Rho, Sigma Delta Epsilon, Phi Beta Kappa, Alpha Sigma Nu. Roman Catholic. Home: 6801 N Loron Chicago IL 60646

HAYES, ALLENE VALERIE FARMER, government executive; b. Sept. 23, 1958; d. Thomas Jonathan and Allena V. (Joyner) Farmer; m. Thomas Gary Hayes; children: Tommia Chanel, Alle Victoria. Student, Richmond Coll., London, 1980; BA, Clark U., 1980; cert., U. Oxford, England, 1981; MLS, U. Md., 1986. Libr. asst. NUS Corp., Gaithersburg, Md., 1981-82; cataloger Libr. of Congress, Washington, 1982-84, copyright specialist, 1984-85; congl. fellow Ho. of Reps. Com. on D.C., Washington, 1985—. English tutor, writer Natural Motion, Washington, 1983-84; intern, archivist Howard U., Washington, 1985; intern Libr. Congress Intern Program, 1991-92. Compiler: Single Mother's Resource Directory, 1984; compiler, editor: Policy Research, 1985; author booklet: D.C. Statehood Issue, 1986. Mem. U. Md. Coll. Park Black Women's Coun., 1984; vol. Congl. Black Caucus Found., Washington, 1985 (fellow 1985). Recipient Fgn. Study award Am. Inst. for Fgn. Study, 1981. Mem. NAACP, ALA, Libr. of Congress Profls. Assn., Daniel A.P. Murray Afro-Am. Culture Assn. of Libr. of Congress (mem. exec. bd., newsletter editor, pres. 1994—), D.A.P. Murray African Am. Culture Assn. (pres. 1994-96), Delta Sigma Theta (tutor 1986). Avocations: travel, writing, dance, drama, tennis. Home: 2405 17th St NE Washington DC 20018-2051 Office: Libr of Congress 101 Independence Ave SE Washington DC 20540-0002

HAYES, CHERRY ANN, secondary school educator; b. Sacramento, Calif., Mar. 16, 1948; d. L.R. and Lillian Eleanor Blevins; m. Ted Warren Hayes, Apr. 24, 1948; children: Brandon Kelly, Christopher Martin. MEd, Lesley Coll., Cambridge, Mass., 1995; BA, Calif. State U., Sacramento, 1970. Cert. elem. tchr. Calif., 1971, secondary music tchr. Calif., 1999. Educator San Juan Unified Sch. Dist., Sacramento, 1971—80, Magnolia Intermediate Sch., Grass Valley, Calif., 1980—97, Bear River H.S., Grass Valley, Calif., 1993—. Dir. Pk. and Recreation Dist., Grass Valley, Calif., 2000—03. Entertainment dir. Pinesmen, Grass Valley, Calif., 1985—2003, Firebelles, Grass Valley, Calif., 1988—2003, Rotary Club, Grass Valley, Calif., 1993—2003. Named Educator of the Arts, May Martin Goyne Meml., 1997; named an Teachers Who Make a Difference, Assn. of Calif. Sch. Administrators, Nev. County, 2003; recipient Founders award, RAVES Festival, 1998, Disting. Svc. award, Barbershop Soc., 2002. Mem.: Calif. Tchrs. Assn. (assoc.), Am. Choral Dirs., Assn. (assoc.), Calif. Music Educators Assn. (assoc. Choral Music Educator of the Yr. 2003). Christian. Avocations: sewing, swimming, skiing, knitting, piano playing. Home: 14989 Stinson Dr Grass Valley CA 95949 Office: Bear River HS 11130 Magnolia Rd Grass Valley CA 95949 E-mail: chayes@nuhsd.k12.ca.us.

HAYES, COLLEEN BALLARD, writer, photographer; b. Kansas City, Mo. d. Charles Richard and Mary Frances (Ballard) Hayes. BA in English, U. Kans., 1972. Assoc. editor, reporter Johnson County (Kans.) Sun newspapers, 1967—68; editor, writer press releases and pub. rels. Met. Plan Agy., 1968-70; writer speeches, Freedom of Info. and other letters for Pres. U.S., U.S. Senators, U.S. Reps., midwest govs., EPA, 1972—82. Contbr. articles (with photography) Elle Mag., Travel-Holiday, Country Inns Mag., Archtl. Digest publs., Confederate Veteran Mag., The Boston Globe, The Phila. Inquirer, Chgo. Tribune, L.A. Times, The Balt. Sun, Odyssey, San Francisco Examiner, The Denver Post, Christian Science Monitor, The Detroit News, The Orlando Sentinel, St. Petersburg Times, St. Louis Post Dispatch, The Kansas City Star, San Jose Mercury News, N.Y. Daily News, The Plain Dealer, Chicago Sun-Times, Des Moines Register, Richmond (Va.) Times-Dispatch, Women's Sports and Fitness, The Calgary Herald, more than 70 others in U.S. and Can.; co-author: Anthology Am. Holidays; contbr. numerous nat. and regional poetry anthologies, Nat. Scholastic Mag. (recipient writing award), Mo. Hist. Rev., others; lead in drama prodns. at regional theaters and Topeka Civic Theater; commentator on WIBW-TV, performed role of Medea on KTWU Pub. TV, guest interview KCUR-FM, others. Named to honorary order, Ky. Cols.; recipient 1st Prize Bethany Coll. Creative Writing award, Key to City of St. Joseph, Mo., City and Regional Tennis awards, numerous others. Mem. Jackson County Hist. Soc., Quantrill Hist. Soc., Pony Express Hist. Soc., St. Andrew Scottish Soc., Woodside Racquet Club. Avocations: history, international and adventure travel, lap swimming, tennis, golf. E-mail: bcolin77@hotmail.com., bballard7@yahoo.com.

HAYES, CONSTANCE J. pediatric cardiologist; b. Cortland, N.Y., July 16, 1937; d. John Burns and Anna Marie (McGuire) H.; m. Edward William Lewison, Nov. 8, 1980. RN, BS, Coll. St. Rose, 1959; MD, Loyola U., Chgo., 1965. Diplomate Am. Bd. Pediatrics, Am. Bd. Pediatric Cardiology, Nat. Bd. Med. Examiners. Resident in pediat. St. Vincent's Hosp., N.Y.C., 1965-68; fellow in pediat. cardiology Columbia U., N.Y.C., 1968-71, assoc. pediat. coll. p. & s., 1971-72, asst. prof. clin. pediat., 1972-80, assoc. clin. prof. pediat., 1980-99, prof. clin. pediat., 1999—. Contbr. articles to profl. jours. Fellow Am. Acad. Pediatrics, Am. Coll. Cardiology; mem. Am. Heart Assn., N.Y. Heart Assn., Pediatric Cardiology Soc. Greater N.Y. (pres. 1987-88). Office: Columbia Presbyn Med Ctr 3959 Broadway New York NY 10032-1551

HAYES, CYNTHIA ANN (C.A. HAYES), writer; b. L.A., Sept. 11, 1954; d. Lafayette and Verna (O'Gee) H.; 1 child, LaLaunie Charisse. Student, U. Calif., L.A., 1972-75. Author: The My Family Collection, 1985, That Lovely Piece of Art, 1997, The Death of Lillie Maroe, 1998, The Night Aunt Ives Went to Sleep, 1999. Donor The Brotherhood Crusade, The Donor's Welfare Plan. Mem. U. Calif. L.A., The Duvall Found. Democrat. Baptist. Avocations: sewing, creating graphic designs, sailing, cycling, attending concerts and theater. Mailing: PO Box 922152 Sylmar CA 91392-2152

HAYES, JANET GRAY, retired business manager, former mayor; b. Rushville, Ind., July 12, 1926; d. John Paul and Lucile (Gray) Frazee; m. Kenneth Hayes, Mar. 20, 1950; children: Lindy, John, Katherine, Megan. AB, Ind. U., 1948; MA magna cum laude, U. Chgo., 1950. Psychiat. caseworker Jewish Family Svc. Agy., Chgo., 1950-52; vol. Denver Crippled Children's Service, 1954-55, Adult and Child Guidance Clinic, San Jose, Calif., 1958-59; mem. San Jose City Coun., 1971-75, vice mayor, 1973-75, mayor, 1975-82; co-chmn. com. urban econs. U.S. Conf. Mayors, 1976-78, co-chmn. task force on aging, mem. sci. and teck task force, 1976-80, bd. trustees, 1977-82; bd. dirs. League Calif. Cities, 1976-82, mem. property tax reform task force, 1976-82; chmn. State of Calif. Urban Devel. Adv. Com., 1976-77; mem. Calif. Commn. Fair Jud. Practices, 1976-82; client-community relations dir. Q. Tech., Santa Clara, Calif., 1983-85; bus. mgr. Kenneth Hayes MD, Inc., 1985-88; CEO Hayes House, Book Distbr., 1998—. Mem. Dem. Nat. Campaign Com., 1976; mem. Calif. Dem. Commn. Nat. Platform and Policy, 1976; del. Dem. Nat. Conv., 1980; bd. dirs. South San Francisco Bay Dischargers Authority; chmn. Santa Clara County Sanitation Dist.; mem. San Jose/Santa Clara Treatment Plant Adv. Bd.; chmn. Santa Clara Valley Employment and Tng. Bd. (CETA), League to Save Lake Tahoe adv. bd., 2000—; past mem. EPA Aircraft/Airport Noise Task Group; bd. dirs. Calif. Center Rsch. and Edn. in Govt, Alexian Bros. Hosp., 1983-92; bd. dirs., chmn. adv. council Public Tech. Inc.; mem. bd. League to Save Lake Tahoe, 1984-2000; pres. bd. trustees San Jose Mus. Art, 1987-89; founder, adv. bd. Calif. Bus. Bank, 1982-85; polit. advisor Citizens Against Airport Pollution, 2003—. AAUW Edn. Found. grantee. Mem. Assn. Bay Area Govts. (exec. com. 1971-74, regional housing subcom. 1973-74), LWC (pres. San Francisco Bay Area chpt. 1968-70, pres. local chpt. 1966-67), Mortar Bd., Phi Beta Kappa, Kappa Alpha Theta. E-mail: janetgrayhayes@sbcglobal.net.

HAYES, JOYCE MERRIWEATHER, secondary school educator; b. Bay City, Tex., Aug. 29, 1943; d. Calvin and Alonia (Harris) Merriweather. BS, Wiley Coll., Tex., 1967; postgrad., U. N.Y., Stony Brook, 1968; MS in Guidence Counseling, Ea. Mich. U., 1974; postgrad., Mercy Coll., 1991-92, Ea. Mich. U., 1991-92; MEd, U. Detroit, 1992. English tchr. Terrance Manor Mid. Sch., Augusta, Ga., 1968-69, Longfellow Jr. H.S., Flint, Mich., 1969-81, No. H.S., Flint, 1981—2002, chmn. English dept., 1992—2002; edn. cons. Ventures Edn. Systems Corp., N.Y.C., 2000—. English and speech tchr. Jordan Coll., Flint, 1989-91; adult edn. tchr. Mott Adult H.S., Flint, 1978-80, on-state content stds. com.; presenter workshops in field.; motivational spkr. Composer 3 gospel songs. Vol. Second Ward City Coun., Flint, 1989, Cmty. Coun., Flint, 1992-93, Cmty. Wide Assn. Coun., Flint, 1993; intercessory prayer warrior, 1995—; area dir. Home Ministry new mem. class tchr., Grace Emmanuel Bapt. Ch., co-coord. spl. svc. for Nat. Coun. Tchr. of Eng. Conv. Detroit, 1997. Named Saginaw Valley Tchr. of Yr., 2001, No. Alumni Tchr. of Yr., 2001. Mem. NEA, Nat. Coun. Tchrs. English (chair workshops 1992-93, mem. nominating com. 1994), Mich. Edn. Assn., United Tchrs. of Flint (in-svc com., Flares-English tchrs.), Phi Delta Kappa (Xinos advisor, del. to conf. 1999, past pres., textbook selection com.). Office: Ventures Edn Sys Corp 245 Fifth Ave Ste 802 New York NY 10016 Home: 1201 Dulles Ave Apt 6105 Stafford TX 77477-6105 E-mail: silverfoxhayes@aol.com.

HAYES, JUDITH, psychotherapist, educator; b. Lumberton, N.C., June 28, 1950; d. Eugene Lennon and Ada Margaret (Regan) Hayes; m. Jonathan Lafayette II Cutrell (div. Jan. 1979); 1 child, Jonathan L. Cutrell III; m. William Evans Hannon. BA, Augusta Coll., 1973; MA summa cum laude, U. N.C., Charlotte, 1996. Cert. tchr. midl sch. exceptional children. Tchr. Horry County (S.C.) Schs., 1973-77, Alexander County Schs., Taylorsville, N.C., 1978-83, Iredell County Schs., Statesville, N.C., 1983-94; with Charter Pines Behavioral Health, Charlotte, N.C., 1996-97; counselor Brawley Mid. Sch., Mooresville, N.C., 1997—. Bd. dirs. Statesville Dogwood Festival, 1981-82; ch. organist Fair Bluff (N.C.) Bapt., 1974-78. Fellow Phi Kappa Phi; mem. ACA (rep. N.C. Assn. Educators 1993-94), Mu Tau Beta chpt. Chi Sigma Iota. Avocations: reading, music, research.

HAYES, JUDITH M. music educator, elementary school educator, secondary school educator; b. Bayshore, N.Y., June 7, 1952; d. Henry G. and Mildred Marie Scordino; m. Dennis Michael Hayes, Oct. 9, 1976; children: Daniel, Jessica, Anthony. BS, Potsdam State U., 1974; M in Music Edn., C.W. Post U., 1978. Jr. high orch. dir. Lindenhurst (N.Y.) Pub. Schs., 1974—83; orch. dir., music theory educator West Islip (N.Y.) Pub. Schs., 1983—. Adjudicator N.Y. State Sch. Music Assn., L.I., new tchr. mentor, 2000—03, all-state symphonic orch. judge, 2002, 03. Charter mem. West Babylon (N.Y.) Civic Assn., 1998—2000. Grantee, Staff Devel. Ctr. of the Islips, 2002—03. Mem.: L.I. String Festival Assn., Suffolk County Music Edn. Assn., Music Educators Nat. Conf. Avocations: reading, swimming, cooking. Office: West Islip Pub Schs 1 Lions Path West Islip NY 11795

HAYES, MARY ANN, social studies educator; b. Princeton, Ind., Sept. 25, 1941; d. John W. and Mozelle Scott; m. Donald L. Hayes, Aug. 18, 1963; 1 child, Elizabeth Ann. BA, U. Evansville, Ind., 1963; MLS, Ind. U., 1968. Tchr. Greater Jasper (Ind.) Schs., 1963-99, dept. chair social studies, 1990-99. Alt. del. Rep. Nat. Conv., Kansas City, Mo., 1976; treas. North Dubois, Raintree Girl Scout Coun., 1995-98; pres. Dubois County Hist. Soc., 1997—; troop leader Girl Scouts, 1991-99; v.p. Dubois County Mus. Inc., 1998—. Recipient Appreciation award Raintree Girl Scout Coun., Evansville, 1996. Mem. NEA, Ind. State Tchrs. Assn., Jasper Classroom Tchrs. Assn., Jasper Bus. and Profl. Women's Club (Woman of Yr. 1979), Jasper Bus. and Profl. Women's Club (pres. 1974-76, Woman of Yr. 1979), Dubois County Hist. Soc. (v.p. 1979-97), Psi Iota Xi (pres. 1971-72, pres. Aux. 1982-84). Republican. Presbyterian. Avocations: history, archaeology.

HAYES, MARY DIANNE WIXTED, lawyer; b. Danbury, Conn., Jan. 4, 1942; d. Francis Joseph and Mary (Zwyner) Wixted; m. Paul P. Hayes, Jr., June 18, 1966. BA in Economics, Regis Coll., Weston, MA, 1961—64; JD, Suffolk U. Law Sch., Boston, 1968, LLM, 1968—70; MEd in Religious Edn., Boston Coll., Chestnut Hill, MA, 1989, MA in Theology, 1990—97; STL, Weston SJ Sch. of Theology, Cambridge, MA, 1997—2002. Bar: Mass. 1970, U.S. Dist. Ct. (Mass.) 1971, U. S. Supreme Ct. 1973, U.S. Ct. Appeals (1st cir.) 1979. Ptnr. Hayes and Hayes, Quincy, Mass., 1970—; volunteer atty. Irish Pastoral Centre, 1998—. Town meeting mem. Town of Milton, Milton, Mass., 1977—93; mem. Secular Franciscan Order, Boston, 1985—. Mem.: Am. Immigration Lawyers Assn., Real Estate Bar Assn., Mass. Assn. Women Lawyers (pres. 1993—94), Mass. Bar Assn. (chair probate law sect. coun. 1995—97), S. Shore Regis Club, Weston, Mass. (pres. 1973—75). Roman Catholic. Office: Hayes and Hayes 31 Newcomb Street Quincy MA 02169-4507 Business E-Mail: Wixtedhaye@aol.com.

HAYES, MARY ESHBAUGH, editor, writer; b. Rochester, N.Y., Sept. 27, 1928; d. William Paul and Eleanor Maude (Sievert) Eshbaugh; m. James Leon Hayes, Apr. 18, 1953; children: Pauli, Eli, Lauri Le June, Clayton, Merri Jess Bates. BA in English and Journalism, Syracuse U., 1950. With Livingston County Republican, Geneseo, N.Y., summers, 1947-50, mng. editor, 1949-50; reporter Aurora Advocate, Colo., 1950-52; reporter-photographer Aspen Times, Colo., 1952-53, columnist, 1956—, reporter, 1972-77, assoc. editor, 1977-89, editor-in-chief, 1989-92, contbg. editor, 1992—. Instr. Colo. Mountain Coll., 1979; Aspen corr. Reuters, 1997—. Author, editor: The Story of Aspen, 1996 (1st prize, 1996); contbg. editor: Destinations Mag., 1994—97, Aspen Mag., 1996—; editor: Aspen Pot Pourri, 1968 (1st prize, 1990), rev. edit., 2002 (1st prize, 2002). Recipient Living Landmark award, Aspen Hist. Soc., 2002. Mem.: Colo. Press Women's Assn. (writing award 1974—75, 1978—85, sweepstakes award for writing 1977—78, 1984—85, 1991—2003, 2d pl. award 1976, 1979, 1982—83, 1994—95, Woman of Achievement 1986), Nat. Fedn. Press Women (1st prize in writing and editing 1976—80, 1st prize in adv. photography 1998). Home: PO Box 497 Aspen CO 81612-0497 Office: Box E Aspen CO 81612

HAYES, MARY PHYLLIS, retired savings and loan association executive; b. New Castle, Ind., Apr. 30, 1921; d. Clarence Edward and Edna Gertrude (Burgess) Scott; m. John Clifford Hayes, Jan. 1, 1942 (div. Oct. 1952); 1 child, R. Scott. Student, Ball State U., 1957-64, Ind. U. East, Richmond, 1963; diploma, Inst. Fin. Edn., 1956, 72, 76. Teller Henry County Savs. and Loan, New Castle, 1939-41, loan officer, teller, 1950-62, asst. sec., treas., 1962-69, sec., treas., 1969-73, corp. sec., 1973-84; v.p., sec. Ameriana Savs. Bank (formerly Henry County Savs. and Loan), New Castle, 1984-91; exec. sec. Am. Nat. Bank, Nashville, 1943-44. Corp. sec. Ameriana Fin. Svcs., 1984-91. Treas. Henry County Chpt. Am. Heart Assn., New Castle, 1965-67, 76-87, vol. Indpls. chpt. 1980—; membership sec. Henry County Hist. Soc., New Castle, 1975-90; sec. Henry County chpt. ARC, New Castle, 1976-91; elected mem. Found. Inst. Fin. Edn., 1991—; mem. Internat. Platform Assn., 1974—, Woman's Club 1992—; vol. Ind. Basketball Hall of Fame, 1993—. Mem. Inst. Fin. Edn. (sec.-treas. East Ctrl. Ind. chpt. 1973-91), Ind. League Savs. Insts. (25 Yrs. award 1975, 40 Yrs. Cert. award 1988), Internat. Platform Assn., Henry County Cmty. Found., Ind. Hist. Soc., Heritage Found., Henry County Hist. Soc. (mem. sec.), Altrusa (past officer, bd. dirs. New Castle chpt.), PEO-CG (past chaplain, sec., past pres. 1994-95, v.p. 2001-03), Woman's Club (treas. 2000-01), Ind. Hist. Soc., New Castle Henry County C. of C., Guyer Opera House Guild, Art Ctr. of Henry County, Psi Iota Xi (past sec.-treas.). Mem. Christian Ch. Avocations: music, traveling, history, swimming.

HAYES, MARYLEE, editor, writer, nurse; b. Allegan, Mich., Nov. 14, 1949; d. Gay F. and Anna Marie (Swanty) H. Cert., Famous Writer's Sch., 1971; BA cum laude in English, U. Alaska, 1988; RN, Mercy Ctrl. Sch. of Nursing, Grand Rapids, Mich., 1970. RN, Colo., Wis., Wash., Mich., Alaska. Bedside nurse, Anchorage, 1970—; with Alaska Native Med. Assn., Anchorage. Author: (book) My Life is a Rainbow, 1977; mng. editor: (jour.) Alaska Women Speak, 1992-2002, Women's Feminist Jour., 1992-2002; contbr. articles to jours. and mags. Camp host Alaska State Park Svcs., Eagle River, 1993. Lt. USAF, 1975-77. Mem. NOW, Sierra Club, Greenpeace, Easter Seal Soc. Avocations: camping, hiking, guitar, piano. Home: 2611 Hiland Rd Eagle River AK 99577-9400

HAYES, NANCY EVEYLIN, anthropologist, geographer, researcher; b. N.Y.C., Jan. 8, 1940; d. Anatoli Nikolai Peres and Anna Katrina Rodrigues. BSED, U. Ga., 1970, postgrad., 1973. Elem. tchr. Kingsland (Ga.) Elem. Sch.; expense acct. Finlay, N.Y.C.; owner, mgr. S.D. Problem Shoppe, N.Y.C., 1990—; owner Second Dollar Group subs. S.D. Problem Shoppe. Sec. Internat. Students Orgn. U. Ga., Athens, 1968. Mem. NOW, N.Y. Acad. Scis., N.Y. State Archael. Assn., Nat. Writers Union, Internat. Healers, Gen. Inst. Semantics, Spiritual Frontiers Fellowship. Democrat. Jewish. Avocations: art, writing, archaeology, cooking, crafts, toy designing. Home: 100 Cooper St Apt 1B New York NY 10034-2311

HAYES, PATRICIA ANN, health facility administrator; b. Binghamton, N.Y., Jan. 14, 1944; d. Robert L. and Gertrude (Congdon) H. BA in English, Coll. of St. Rose, 1968; PhD in Philosophy, Georgetown U., 1974. Tchr. Cardinal McCloskey H.S., Albany, NY, 1966-68; tchg. asst. Georgetown U., Washington, 1968-71; instr. philosophy Coll. of St. Rose, Albany, 1973-75, instr. bus., 1981, adminstrv. intern to acad. v.p., 1973-74, dir. admissions, 1974-78, dir. adminstrn. and planning, 1978-81, v.p. adminstrn. and fin., treas., 1981-84; pres. St. Edward's U., Austin, Tex., 1984-98; exec. v.p., COO Seton Healthcare Network, Austin, 1998—2001, 2003—, interim pres., CEO, 2001—02. Trustee RGK Found.; bd. dirs. Tex. Assn. Pub. and Nonprofit Hosps., Topfer Family Found.; exec. bd. Austin Idea Network. Roman Catholic. Office: Seton Med Ctr 1201 W 38th St Austin TX 78705-1006 Office Phone: 512-324-1102. Business E-Mail: phayes@seton.org.

HAYES, PAULA FREDA, governmental official; b. Apr. 5, 1950; d. Ario Louis and Elena Marguerite (Gentile) Freda; m. Robert J. Hayes, Sept. 6, 1975; children: Brendan Michael, Lauren Ann. BA magna cum laude, R.I. Coll., 1972; MPA, Syracuse U., 1973. Criminal justice planner City of Syracuse, NY, 1973-75, asst. crime control coord., 1975-77; supervisory grants specialist Nat. Endowment Arts, Washington, 1977-78; criminal justice program analyst Dept. Justice, Washington, 1978-79, program mgr. arson discretionary grant program, 1979-80, sr. mgmt. analyst, 1980-81; dir. legis. and analysis divsn. Office of Insp. Gen., Dept. Agr., Washington, 1982-89, asst. insp. gen. for policy devel. and resources mgmt., 1989—2003, asst. insp. gen. for planning and spl. projects, 2003—. Roman Catholic. Office: USDA Office Insp Gen 1400 Independence Ave SW Rm 113W Washington DC 20250-0002

HAYES GLADSON, LAURA JOANNA, psychologist; b. Winnebeau, N.C., Mar. 26, 1943; d. Victor Wilson and Pansy Lorraine (Springsteen) Hayes; m. Jerry Allen Gladson, June 20, 1965 (div. Mar. 1992, remarried Dec. 27, 1997); children: Joanna Kaye, Paula Rae. BA, So. Coll., 1965; MEd, U. Tenn., Chattanooga, 1977; EdD, Vanderbilt U., 1985. Lic. psychologist, Ga. Psychol. intern Lakeshore Mental Health Inst., Knoxville, Tenn., 1985-86; counselor, psychologist Tara Heights Enterprises, Atlanta, 1986—; psychologist, owner Assoc. Psychol. Svcs., Inc., Ringgold, Ga., 1990—. Bd. dirs. Theraplay, Inc., Ringgold; founder Abused Children in Therapy, Inc., 1997. Mem. APA, Christian Assn. for Psychol. Studies, Ga. Psychol. Assn. Democrat. Home: 327 Homestead Cir Kennesaw GA 30144-1335 Office: Assoc Psychol Svcs Box 700 479 Cotter St Ringgold GA 30736-5149

HAYGOOD, ALMA JEAN, elementary school educator; d. John Thomas and Alma Perry Haygood. BS, Ala. A&M U., 1978; MA, George Mason U., 2001. Kindergarten tchr. Talladega (Ala.) County Pub. Schs., 1978—80; adult edn. tchr. Ft. Carson (Colo.) Mil. Base, 1980—82; day care ctr. tchr. KinderCare Learning Ctrs., Colorado Springs, Colo., 1982—84; child care ctr. dir. Open Hands Preschool, Colorado Springs, Colo., 1984—85; preschool tchr. Gum Springs Child Devel. Ctr., Alexandria, Va., 1985—87; tchr. Fairfax County Pub. Schs., Springfield, Va., 1987—. Cons., tutoring-mentoring program Lomax Ch., Arlington, Va., 1989—95. Sch. union rep. Fairfax Edn. Assn., Fairfax, Va., 2001—. Tchr. tng. grantee, Fairfax Edn. Assn., 2003. Mem.: Kappa Delta Pi (assoc.; mem. 2002—). Democrat. Baptist. Avocations: clarinet, aerobic exercise, piano, singing. Home: 5318 Harbor Court Dr Alexandria VA 22315-3934 Office: Mount Vernon Woods Elem Sch 4015 Fielding St Alexandria VA 22309 Personal E-mail: hhaggard86@aol.com. E-mail: Alma.Haygood@fcps.edu.

HAYMAN, CAROL ANNE, anthropology educator, photographer; b. Ft. Walton Beach, Fla., Feb. 18, 1953; d. William Paul and Thomasina Maude (Garbutt) Hayman; m. Robert Rayford White; 1 child, Brandon Paul White. BFA, U. Tex., 1975, BA, 1977, MA, 1989. Peace Corps vol., instr. Jamaica Sch. Art, Kingston, 1978-80; instr. Austin (Tex.) C.C., 1990—. Instr. Tex. Luth. U., 1994—; dir. Women Printmakers Austin. Recipient Arts Week Vol. award City of Austin, 1994. Avocation: weaving. Home: 1001 Eason St Austin TX 78703-4820 Office: Austin CC 1212 Rio Grande St Austin TX 78701-1710

HAYMAN, HELEN FEELEY, retired nursing director; b. Rahway, N.J., June 9, 1918; d. John J. and Margaret (Crahan) Feeley; 1 child, Richard J. Hayman. Nursing Diploma, All Souls Hosp., Morristown, 1939; BA, Trenton Coll., 1963. RN, N.J., Conn. Pvt. duty nurse Muhlenberg Hosp., Plainfield, N.J., 1939, staff nurse pediatrics, 1940-42, pvt. duty nurse, 1944-57; office nurse Westfield, N.J., 1939-40; indsl. nurse Nat. Pneumeonic, Rahway, N.J., 1942-44; dir. sch. nursing Bd. of Edn., Plainfield, N.J., 1957-67, dir. presch. health, 1967-73, dir. nurses health program, 1973-80, ret., 1980. Past mem. Town Coun.; vol. Jerry Lewis Labor Day Telethon Muscular Dystrophy; commr. Trumbull Sr. Citizens, Conn. State Dept. Aging; pres. Stern Village Residents Assn., 2000. Mem. Am. Cancer Soc. (Jail and Bail award), Nat. Assn. Ret. Educators, Trumbull Ct. (commr., chmn. vial of life), Greater Bridgeport Ret. Tchr. (exec. bd.), Trumbull Women's Club. Democrat. Roman Catholic. Home: 58 Hedgehog Cir Trumbull CT 06611-3940

HAYMAN, LINDA C. lawyer; b. Morgantown, W.Va., 1947; BS, Ohio State U., 1969; MA, U. Colo., 1973; JD, Capital U., 1979. Bar: Ohio 1979, N.Y. 1982. Ptnr. Skadden, Arps, Slate, Meagher & Flom, L.L.P., N.Y.C. Office: 4 Times Sq New York NY 10036-6522

HAYNES, APRIL MICHELLE, band director; b. Pomona, Calif., Apr. 1, 1972; d. Gary Lynn and Deborah Ann Haynes. MusS Edn., U. No. Colo., 1996. California Clear Credential, Single Subject (Music) Calif. Commn. Tchr. Credentialing, 2001. Band and orch. dir. Jefferson County Pub. Schs., Lakewood, Colo., 1996—98; band dir. Buckeye Union Sch. Dist., El Dorado Hills, Calif., 1998—2001; band and choir dir. Eureka Union Sch. Dist. (Cavitt Jr. High and Ridgeview Elem. Schools), Granite Bay, Calif., 2001—. Woodwind instr. Bear Creek H.S. Marching Band, Lakewood, 1997—97. Vol. ch. youth worker Bayside Covenant Ch., Granite Bay, 2000—01. Recipient Tchr. of Year, Rolling Hills Middle Sch., 1999—2000; Music scholar, Upland H.S. Band Boosters, 1990, Music Performance scholar, U. No. Colo., 1992—96. Mem.: Calif. Music Educators Assn. (assoc.), Music Educators Nat. Conf. (assoc.), Calif. Band Dirs. Assn. (assoc.), Golden Key Nat. Honor Soc., Pi Kappa Lambda. Avocations: scrapbooks, running. Home: 1020 Folsom Ranch Dr #105 Folsom CA 95630 Office: Cavitt Junior High School 7200 Fuller Dr Granite Bay CA 95746 Personal E-mail: april_haynes@msn.com. E-mail: ahaynes@eureka-usd.k12.ca.us.

HAYNES, DEBORAH GENE, physician; b. York, Neb., Feb. 18, 1954; d. Gene Eldridge and Margaret Lucille (Manchester) Haynes; m. Russell Larry Beamer, Mar. 3, 1979; children: Staci E. Beamer, Lindsay M. Beamer, Stephanie L. Beamer. BA in Biology cum laude, Wichita State U., 1976; MD, U. Kans., Wichita, 1979. Diplomate Am. Bd. Family Practice; cert. Added Qualifications-Geriatrics. Resident St. Joseph Hosp., Wichita, 1979-82; instr. dept. family and community medicine St. Joseph Family Practice Residency, U. Kans., Wichita, 1982-84, asst. prof. dept. family and community medicine, 1984-85; pvt. family practice Preferred Med. Assocs. - Northeast, Wichita, 1985—. Clin. asst. prof. U. Kans. Sch. Medicine, Wichita, 1985-99, clin. assoc. prof., 1999—; bd. govs. endowment assn. Wichita State U., 1995-96; bd. dirs. Via Christi Regional Med. Ctr., Am. Bd. Family Practice, Preferred Med. Assocs., chmn.. 1996-97, Wichita State U. Found. Trustee Wichita Collegiate Sch., 1993—. Recipient P.G. Czarlinsky award for Disting. Clin. Svc., U. Kans., 1979, Wichita State U. Gore scholarship, 1972. Fellow Am. Acad. Family Physicians (del. 1991—, commn. on edn. 1991-96, task force on procedures, Mead Johnson award 1990-91, chair COD credential com. 1994, bd. dirs. 1997-2000), Kans. Acad. Family Physicians (pres. elect 1988-89, pres. 1989-90), Kans. Med. Soc., Med. Soc. Sedgwick County (del. 1990-91, chair profl. investigation com. 1993-95), Alpha Omega Alpha. Presbyterian. Avocation: reading. Home: 1015 N Linden Cir Wichita KS 67206-4075 Office: 7111 E 21st St Wichita KS 67206 E-mail: dghaynes@cox.net.

HAYNES, KAREN SUE, academic administrator, educator; b. Jersey City, July 6, 1946; d. Edward J. and Adelaide M. (Hineson) Czarnecki; m. James S. Mickelson; children: Kingsley Eliot Mickelson, Kimberly Elizabeth Mickelson, David Mickelson. BA social work, Goucher Coll., 1968; MSW social work, McGill U., 1970; PhD social work, U. Tex., 1977. Dir., social work divsn., sociology dept. Mary Hardin-Baylor Coll., Tex.; faculty mem. S.W. Tex. State U., San Marcos, Tex.; cons. Inst. Nat. Planning, Cairo, 1977-78; asst. prof. Ind. U., Indpls., 1978-81, assoc. prof., 1981-85; prof. social work U. Houston, 1985-95, dean, 1985-95; pres. U. Houston-Victoria, Tex., 1995—2004, Calif. State U., San Marcos, 2004—. Founding presdl. sponsor Tex. Network Women Higher Edn.; formula adv. com. Tex. Coord. Bd. Higher Edn. Author: (book) Sage Publications, 1984, Longman, 1986, 1996, Springer, 1989, Allyn and Bacon, 2000, 2003; contbr. articles to profl. jours. Mem.: Leadership Houston, Leadership Tex., Leadership Am., Nat. Alliance Info. and Referral (pres. 1983—87), Internat. Assn. Schs. Social Work, Coun. Social Work Edn., Am. Coun. Edn. Network (mem. exec. bd. dirs.), Am. Assn. State Colls. and Univs. (sec.-treas., mem. exec. bd. dirs. 2003—), NASW. Avocation: poetry. Office: Calif State U 333 S Twin Oaks Valley Rd San Marcos CA 92096-0001

HAYNES, LINDA ROSE, medical/surgical nurse; d. Floyd George Hilbers, Sr. and Mildred Ann Hilbers; children: Jinny Marie Millican, Thomas Baird. ADN, Vernon Regional Coll. Am. Nurses Credentialing Ctr., RN Tex. Dir. of patient care Outreach Health Svcs., Wichita Falls, 2002—, RN case mgr., 1994—2002. Mem.: Am. Diabetic Assn. (diabetic educator), Phi Theta Kappa (Omega Kappa). Roman Catholic. Avocations: crafts, reading. Office: Outreach Home Health Ste 3 1411 13th St Wichita Falls TX 76301

HAYNES, MARCIA MARGARET, insurance agent; b. Bay City, Mich., June 28, 1931; d. Frederick O. and Margaret M. (Oakes) Rouse; m. N. Fred Haynes, July 20, 1957;children: Carol M. Krashen, David F. Haynes, Julie A. Beaty. BA, Denison U., Granville, Ohio, 1953. With advt.-sales dept. Birmingham (Mich.) Eccentric, 1953-55; tchr. Port Huron (Mich.) Area Schs., 1955-58; student tchr. coord. Mich. State U., Port Huron, Mich., 1967-70; insurance agent Northwestern Mut. Life Ins. Co., Port Huron, Mich., 1981—. Leader, Girl Scout U.S., Port Huron, 1956-57; treas. and bus. mgr., Port Huron Little Theater, Port Huron, 1959-1961; sec., v.p., and pres., Mus. of Arts and History, 1968-69, 74-80; sec., v.p. bd. dirs., Port Huron Hosp. Aux., 1960-70; trustee, Hist. Soc. of Mich., Ann Arbor, 1975-81; coord. of preservation Round Island Lighthouse, Straits Mackinac, Mich., 1972-76; pres. Friends Round Island Lightho., 1980-; chmn. Horizons, Port Huron Bicentennial Com., Port Huron, 1976; active in Rep. State Bicentennial Com, Lansing, Mich. 1976; trustee, St. Clair County C.C., Port Huron, 1981-2005, vice chmn., 1985-95; bd. dirs., Stuart House Mus., Mackinac Island, Mich., 1978, Internat. Symphony, Port Huron and Sarnia, Ont., Can., 1983-86; sec., treas., Blue Water Area Tourism Bur., Port Huron, 1985-87; adv. bd., Cmty. Found. of St. Clair County, Port Huron, 1986-91, 94-2001; vestry Grace Episcopal Ch., 1990-93; bd. dirs. Am. Heart Assn. St. Clair County, 1994-99; v.p. fin. Blue Water coun. Boy Scouts Am., 1995-99; exec. com. Port Huron/Marysville C. of C., 1997-99. Mem. Nat. Life Underwriters, Port Huron Estate Planning Coun. (pres. 1985-86), Mich. Mus. Assn. (bd. dirs. 1984-86), Rotary, Port Huron Golf Club.

HAYNES, REBA CAROL, media specialist, educator; d. John Edward and Elizabeth Walker Haynes. BS, Auburn (Ala.) U., 1980; MEd, State U. West Ga., 1992, EdS, 1995. Tchr. J.W. Stewart Mid. Sch., Douglasville, Ga., 1980—99; media specialist Chapel Hill HS, Douglasville, 1999—. Sch. sys. media resource tchr. Douglas County Sch. Sys., Douglasville, 1995—. Mem.: Ga. Libr. Media Assn., Ga. Assn. Instrnl. Tech., Kiwanis (key club advisor 2000—), Alpha Delta Kappa (scholarship chmn. 2003—04). Avocations: golf, travel. Office: Chapel Hill High School 4899 Chapel Hill Road Douglasville GA 30135

HAYNES, VICTORIA F. science administrator; Chief tech. officer, v.p. Advanced Tech. Group, BFGoodrich Co., 1992—99; pres., CEO Rsch. Triangle Inst., Research Triangle Park, NC, 1999—. Bd. dirs. Ziptronix Bd., Lubrizol Corp., Nucor Corp., MCNC, N.C. Biotech. Ctr., N.C. Bd. Sci. and Tech. Office: Rsch Triangle Inst Internat PO Box 12194 3040 Corwallis Rd Research Triangle Park NC 27709-2194

HAYNIE, BETTY JO GILLMORE, personal property appraiser, antiques dealer; b. Jackson, Ala., July 3, 1937; d. Joe McVey and Mary Elizabeth (Bolen) Gillmore; m. William T. Haynie Jr., Aug. 21, 1960; children: Virginia Elizabeth, Mary Allison. BA, U. Ala., 1959, MA, 1960, postgrad., U. So. Miss., U. Ala., Birmingham; grad. Paris program, Parsons Sch. Design, 1992; grad., Winter Inst., Winterthur, Del., 1994. Tchr. Demopolis (Ala.) Elem. Sch., 1960-61; instr. in history U. Livingston, Ala., 1961-64; tchr. history for jr. high Brooke Hill Sch. for Girls, Birmingham, Ala., 1965; instr. in history Jefferson State Jr. Coll., Birmingham, 1965-67; tchr. history and govt. Mt. Brook High Sch., Birmingham, 1970-71; instr. history U. Ala., Birmingham, 1971-72, Jefferson Davis Jr. Coll., Gulfport, Miss., 1978-81, Faulkner Jr. Coll., [illegible] South Ala., Mobile, 1988—2003, instr. Elderhostel programs, 1990—99. Owner Crown and Colony Antiques, Fairhope, Ala., 1982—92, Antiques and Fine Art, Fairhope, Ala., 1997—; co-owner Gillmore Plantation, Jackson, Ala., Ala., 1987—, and other properties. Contbr. articles to historical mags. Mem.: DAR, Internat. Soc. Appraisers, Clarke County Hist. Soc., Nat. Trust for Hist. Preservation. Presbyterian. Avocations: tennis, creative writing, traveling. Home: PO Box 485 Montrose AL 36559-0485

HAYS, ANNETTE ARLENE, secondary school educator; b. Dallas, Jan. 22, 1951; d. Ogle Winifred and Loretta Lavelle Hatfield; m. William Ned Hays, Aug. 7, 1971; children: Quincy Merritt, Gretchen Laurel. BS in Home Econ. Edn., U. Ark., Fayetteville, 1973. Office asst. dept. entomology U. Ark., Fayetteville, 1970—71; sales assoc. Hunt's Dept. Store, Fayetteville, 1971—72, Singer Sewing Co., Joplin, Mo., 1972—76, instr., 1974—76; home econ. tchr. Parkwood HS, Joplin, 1976—80; family & consumer sci. tchr. Acorn Sch., Mena, Ark., 1988—. Owner Hatfield, Honey & Sorghum, Pine Ridge, Ark., 1980—; Family, Career and Cmty. Leaders Am. advisor Acorn Sch., 1988—, mem. personnel policy com., developer tech-prep/transition program; trainer Ark. Workplace Readiness, 1993—; apptd. by gov. Ark. Workforce Commn., 1997—98; grantwriter; spkr. in field; bd. dirs., chair Healthy Connections, Mena, Ark., 2001—. Mem. Oden Sch. Bd., 1986—98, past sec., past v.p.; choir mem First Presbyn. Ch., Mena, del. to Peacemaking Conf., 1996. Recipient Tchr. of Yr., Ark. Assn. Family & Consumer Scis., 2003. Mem.: Ark. Assn. Family Consumer Scis. (bd. dirs. 2001—), Ark. Assn. Career and Tech. Educators (bd. dirs. 1999—2001), Asn. Career & Tech. Educators, Ark. Assn. Tchrs. Family & Consumer Scis. (pres. elect 1999—2000, pres. 2000—01, past pres. 2001—02, Polk County Tchr. of Yr. 2002, Tchr. of the Yr. 2003), Delta Kappa Gamma. Presbyterian. Avocations: hiking, reading, landscaping. Home: 38 Honey Bear Ln Pine Ridge AR 71966 Office Phone: 479-394-2101. E-mail: haysa@acorn.dmsc.k12.ar.us.

HAYS, DIANA JOYCE WATKINS, consumer products company executive; b. Riverside, Calif., Aug. 29, 1945; d. Donald Richard and Evelyn Christine (Kolvoord) Watkins; m. Gerald N. Hays, Jan 30, 1964 (div. Jan. 1970), 1 child, Tad Damon. BA, U. Minn., 1975, MBA, 1982; BS in Computer Sci. cum laude, Nat. U., 1997, MS in Software Engrng. magna cum laude, 1998. Microsoft cert. sys. engr.; cert. in C and C++ programming, visual C++ and visual basic programming; NCR Teradata cert. profl. engr. Dir. environ./phys. sci. Sci. Mus. Minn., St. Paul, 1972-76; dir. mktg. rsch. No. Natural Gas Co., Omaha, 1977-78; mktg. asst., asst. product mgr. Gen. Mills, Inc., Mpls., 1978-81; product mgr. ortho pharms. Consumer Products div. Johnson & Johnson, Raritan, N.J., 1981-82, product dir. home diagnostics, 1982-86; mktg. dir. new market devel. Consumer Products div. Becton Dickinson & Co., Franklin Lakes, N.J., 1986-90; dir. home diagnostics worldwide program Becton Dickinson Advanced Diagnostics Div. Becton Dickinson & Co., Balt., 1990-93; founder, pres. Exec. Computing Solutions, Inc., Vista, Calif., 1991-99; product mktg. mgr. Jostens Learning Corp., San Diego, 1994-95; mgr. MIS Circus Distbn., Inc., Vista, Calif., 1995-96; product mktg. mgr. St. Bernard Software, San Diego, Calif., 1997; software engr. NCR Corp., San Diego, 1997—; founder, prin. CodeCare, Vista, 2001—. Chmn. energy exhibit com. Assn. Sci.-Tech. Ctrs., Washington, 1974-75. Producer Ecologenie, 1975. Recipient Tribute to Women and Industry award YWCA, 1989. Mem. Am. Mktg. Assn., NAFE, Twin Mgmt. Forum, Am. Assn. of Health Svcs. Mktg., Capital PC User Group, Beta Gamma Sigma (life). Republican. Mem. Christian Ch. (Disciples Of Christ). Avocations: photography, travel. Office: NCR Corp 17095 Via del Campo San Diego CA 92127-1711

HAYS, KATHLEEN, news correspondent; B in Econs., M in Econs., Stanford U. Co-founder Market News Svc. Internat., served on NY bur., chief, mem. bd. dirs.; chief credit markets reporter Munifacts Fin. News; corr. Reuters' Money Desk, 1987—89; NY bur. chief, chief econs. corr. Investor's Bus. Daily, 1989—92; econs. editor, corr., commentator, segment host several CNBC programs, 1992—2001; joined CNN, 2001—; anchor CNN Money Morning and The Flipside; anchor, econs. corr. CNN Bus. News; contbr. Lou Dobbs' Moneyline; CNN Money contbg. columnist HaysWire. Office: CNN 5 Penn Plz Fl 20 New York NY 10001-1810*

HAYS, LOUISE STOVALL, retail fashion executive; b. Crenshaw, Miss., Aug. 30, 1916; d. Ernest Sydney and Anne Mary (Ray) Stovall; m. James Marion Klaer, June 30, 1938 (dec. Jan. 1962); m. Samuel Jackson Hays, Apr. 29, 1965 (dec. March 14, 2001); stepchildren: Elizabeth Razee, Samuel Jackson III, Carruthers Donelson. Grad., Memphis Sch. of Commrce; student, U. Memphis. Sec. Goldsmith's, Memphis, 1938, exec. sec., 1939, fashion coord., 1941-47, fashion dir., 1947-50, dir. fashion promotions and spl. events, 1950-74. Cons. Mademoiselle mag., 1964. Bd. dirs. Am. Heart Assn., 1960s, Memphis Arts Coun., 1964, Brooks Mus. Art, Memphis, 1989; chmn. Memphis Heart Gala, 1978. Named Vol. of Yr., Brooks Mus. League, 1987, Memphis Brooks Mus., 1989. Republican. Episcopalian. Avocations: art, poetry writing, travel. Home: 1701 Village Ridge Pl Collierville TN 38017-8700

HAYS, MARGUERITE THOMPSON, nuclear medicine physician, educator; b. Bloomington, Ind., Apr. 15, 1930; d. Stith and Louise (Faust) Thompson; m. David G. Hays, Feb. 4, 1950 (div. 1975); children: Dorothy Adele, Warren Stith Thompson, Thomas Glenn. AB cum laude, Radcliffe Coll., 1951; postgrad., Harvard U. Med. Sch., 1954; MD, UCLA, 1957; ScD (hon.), Ind. U., 1979. Diplomate Am. Bd. Internal Medicine, Am. Bd. Nuc. Medicine. Intern UCLA Sch. Medicine, 1957-58, resident, 1958-59, 61-62, USPHS postdoctoral trainee, 1959-61, USPHS postdoctoral fellow, 1963-64, asst. prof. medicine, 1964-68, SUNY-Buffalo, 1968-70, asst. prof. biophys. sci., 1968-74, assoc. prof. medicine, 1970-76, clin. assoc. prof. nuc. medicine, 1973-77; asst. chief nuc. medicine VA Med. Ctr., Wadsworth, Calif., 1967-68; chief nuc. medicine Buffalo VA Med. Ctr., 1968-74, assoc. chief of staff for rsch., 1971-74; dir. med. rsch. svc. VA Ctrl. Office, Washington, 1974-79, asst. chief med. dir. for R & D, 1979-81; chief of staff Martinez VA Med. Ctr., Calif., 1981-83; prof. radiology Sch. Medicine U. Calif., Davis, 1981-93, prof. medicine and surgery, 1983-91, assoc. dean, 1981; clin. prof. radiology Stanford U. Sch. Medicine, 1990—; assoc. chief of staff for rsch. Palo Alto (Calif.) VA Med. Ctr., 1983-97, staff physician, 1997-99, cons., 1999—2001. Vis. rsch. scientist Euratom, Italy, 1962-63; chmn. radiopharm. adv. com. FDA, 1974-77; co-chmn. biomedicine com. Pres.'s Fed. Coun. on Sci., Engrng. and Tech., 1979-81; mem. rsch. restructuring adv. com. Va. R & D Office, 1995-96, chair task group to restructure R & D Career Devel. Program, 1996-97; chmn. coop. studies evaluation com., Med. Rsch. Svc., VA, 1990-93; mem. sci. rev. and evaluation bd. Health Svcs. Rsch. and Devel. Svc., VA, 1988-91, chmn. career devel. com., 1991-99, chmn. career devel. com. Rehab. Rsch. and Devel. Svc., 1997-2003. Rsch. grantee VA, 1968-2003. NIH grantee, 1964-71; recipient Exceptional Svc. award Sec. Vets. Affairs, 2000. Fellow ACP; mem. Soc. Nuc. Medicine (chmn. publs. com., trustee, v.p. 1983-84), Am. Thyroid Assn. (bd. dirs. 1993-96), Endocrine Soc., Western Assn. Physicians. Home: 270 Campesino Ave Palo Alto CA 94306-2912 Office: 3801 Miranda Ave Palo Alto CA 94304-1207 E-mail: ritahays19@yahoo.com.

HAYS, RUTH, lawyer; b. Fukuoka, Japan, Sept. 20, 1950; d. George Howard and Helen Jincy (Mathis) H. AB, Grinnell Coll., 1972; JD, Washington U., 1978. Bar: Mo. 1978. Law clk. U.S. Ct. Appeals (8th cir.), St. Louis, 1978-80; assoc. Husch & Eppenberger, LLC, St. Louis, 1980-87, ptnr., 1987—. Articles editor Urban Law Annual, 1977-78. Bd. dirs. Childhaven, St. Louis, 1982-93, pres. 1987-88. Olin fellow Monticello Coll. Found., St. Louis, 1975-78; recipient Spl. Svc. award Legal Svs. Ea. Mo., 1993. Mem. ABA, Mo. Bar Assn., Bar Assn. Met. St. Louis, Employee Benefits Assn. (pres. 1995), Order of Coif, Phi Beta Kappa. Office: Husch & Eppenberger LLC 190 Carondelet Plz Ste 600 Saint Louis MO 63105

HAYS, SORREL (DORIS), composer; b. Memphis, Aug. 6, 1941; d. Walter Ernest and Christina Doris (Fair) Hays. MusB, U. Chattanooga, 1963; artist diploma, Munich Hochschule Music, 1966; MusM, U. Wis., 1968. Lectr. piano U. Wis., Madison, 1967-68; asst. prof. Converse Coll., Mt. Vernon, Iowa, 1969-70; asst. prof. music theory CUNY-Queens Coll., 1975-76; lectr. women's music New Sch. for Social Rsch., N.Y.C., 1976-77; concert pianist U.S. and Europe, 1971—; rec. artist Atlantic Records. Rec. artist other labels, including Folkways, Opus One, New World, Townhall Records and Tellus; cons. in field. Writer, composer (mus. theater prodns.) including Something (To Do) Doing, 1984, Love in Space, 1986, Sound Shadows, 1990, (operas) The Glass Woman, 1989, Mapping Venus, 1998, (opera for radio) Dream in Her Mind, 1995, (comic opera) Queen Bee-ing, The Bee Opera, 2003; audio art exhbn. Whitney Mus., 1990 (award); premiered Henry Cowell piano concerto in U.S.; keyboard rec. artist Dutch and German broadcasting orgns., 1971—; subject (documentary) Southern Voices: A Composer's Exploration, 1985. Lobbyist to Washington-and N.Y.-based instns. for equity and parity at nat. levels for women in music Nat. Music Coun., Rockefeller Found., Nat. Endowment for Arts. N.Y. Found. for Arts artist fellow, 1985, 98. Mem. ASCAP (ann. awards 1980—). Avocation: beekeeping. Home: 697 W End Ave New York NY 10025-6823 Office Phone: 212-663-6164. Personal E-mail: hays2ries@mindspring.com.

HAYTAYAN, ALITA See GUILLEN, ALITA

HAYWARD, OLGA LORETTA HINES (MRS. SAMUEL ELLSWORTH HAYWARD), retired librarian; b. Alexandria, La. d. Samuel James and Lillie (George) Hines; m. Samuel E. Hayward, July 12, 1945; children: Anne Elizabeth, Olga Patricia (Mrs. William Ryer). AB, Dillard U., 1941; BSLS, Atlanta U., 1944; MALS, U. Mich., 1959; MA in History, La. State U., 1977. Tchr. Marksville (La.) H.S., 1941-42; head libr. Grambling (La.) Coll., 1944-46; br. libr. br. nine New Orleans Pub. Libr. System, 1947-48; reference libr. So. U. Baton Rouge, 1948-73, libr. bus. and social scis. libr., 1973-84, libr. collection devel. consent decree program, 1984-86, chairwoman dept. reference, 1986-88, ret., 1988. Author: Graduate Theses of Southern University, 1959-71, A Bibliography of Literature By and About Whitney Moore Young Jr., 1929-71, 1972, The Influence of Humanism on Sixteenth Century English Courtesy Texts, 1977; also other bibliographies. Bd. dirs. La. Diocese Episcopal Cmty. Svcs., 1972-78; mem. banquet com. Baton Rouge chpt. Nat. Conf. Christians and Jews, 1981-2000, Nat. Conf. for cmty. and Justice, 2001-02. Recipient recognition, La. LIbr. Assn., 2003. Mem. life, La. Libr. Assn. (chair-elect subject specialists divsn. 1986-87, chairwoman subject specialists sect. 1987-88, Lucy B. Foote award subject specialists sect. 1990), Spl. Librs. Assn. (pres. La. chpt. 1978-79, Roll of Honor award 1995). Episcopalian. Home: 1632 Harding Blvd Baton Rouge LA 70807-5442 Office: 1632 Harding Bvd Baton Rouge LA 70807-5442

HAYWOOD, ANNE MOWBRAY, pediatrician, educator; b. Balt., Feb. 5, 1935; d. Richard Mansfield and Margaret (Mowbray) H. BA in Chemistry, Bryn Mawr Coll., 1955; MD, Harvard U., 1959. Cert. Am. Bd. Pediat. Intern U. Calif. Med. Ctr., San Francisco, 1959-60; fellow biochemistry dept. Columbia U., N.Y.C., 1961-62; fellow divsn. biology Calif. Inst. Tech., Pasadena, 1960-61, 62-64; asst. prof. microbiology, microbiology dept. Northwestern U. Med. Sch., Chgo., 1964-66, Yale U. Med. Sch., New Haven, 1966-73; resident in pediat. U. Wash., Seattle, 1974-75, pediat. infectious disease fellow, 1975-76, Vanderbilt U., Nashville, 1976-77; assoc. prof. pediat. and microbiology U. Rochester, N.Y., 1977—. Vis. asst. prof. Rockefeller U., N.Y.C., 1971-72; vis. scientist biophysics unit Agrl. Rsch. Coun., Cambridge, Eng., 1972-74, Inst. for Immunology and Virology, U. Zürich, Switzerland, 1987; vis. assoc. prof. dept. zoology U. Calif., Davis, 1986; vis. assoc. prof. McArdle Lab. for Cancer Rsch., U. Wis., 1999-2000. Co-author: Practice of Pediatrics, 1977, Infections in Children, 1982, Liposome Letters, 1983, Practice of Pediatrics, 1987, Molecular Mechanisms of Membrane Fusion, 1988, Membrane Fusion, 1991, Encyclopedia of Human Biology, 1991, 2d edit., 1997, Cell and Model Membrane Interactions, 1991. Fogarty Internat. Ctr. Sr. fellow NIH, 1987, European Molecular Biology Orgn. fellow, 1973-74, NIH Spl. fellow, 1971-73, Am. Cancer Soc. Postdoctoral fellow, 1960-62; Harvard Med. Sch. scholar, 1955-59, Harriet Judd Sartain scholar, 1955-59, N.Y. Alumnae scholar Bryn Mawr Coll., 1951-55. Mem. Biophys. Soc., Am. Soc. for Biochem. and Molecular Biology. Democrat. Office: U Rochester Med Ctr PO Box 777 Rochester NY 14642-8777 E-mail: ahyw@mail.rochester.edu.

HAYWOOD, B(ETTY) J(EAN), anesthesiologist; b. Boston, June 1, 1942; d. Oliver Garfield and Helen Elizabeth (Salisbury) H.; m. Lynn Brandt Moon, Aug. 29, 1969 (div. Aug. 1986); children: Kaylin, Kris Lee, Kelly, Kasy R. BSc, Tufts U., 1964; MD, U. Colo., 1968; MBA, Oklahoma City U., 1993; Grad., Air War Coll., 1997. Intern Wilford Hall AFB, San Antonio, 1968-69; resident in pediatrics U. Ariz., Tucson, 1971-72, resident in anesthesiology, 1972-74; dir. anesthesia dept. Pima County Hosp., Tucson, 1975-76; staff anesthesiologist South Community Hosp., Oklahoma City, 1977—, Moore (Okla.) Mcpl. Hosp., 1981-94, chief of anesthesia, 1990-94; staff anesthesiologist St. Anthony Hosp., Oklahoma City, 1982—; instr. dept. anesthesia U. Okla. Health Sci. Ctr., Oklahoma City, 1999—; col. USAF, active duty for Op. Enduring Freedom Wilford Hall Med. Ctr., Lackland AFB, Tex., 2001—02. Chief of ethics com. S.W. Med. Ctr., 1996. Bd. dirs. N.Am. South Devon Assn., Lynnville, Iowa, 1978—86; mem. med. com. Planned Parenthood Okla., 1992—; col. USAFR, 1968—. Mem. AMA, NAFE (co-dir. Oklahoma City chpt. 1996—), World South Devon Assn. (U.S. rep. 1985, 88), Tufts U. Alumni Assn. (rep.), Chi Omega (treas. 1963-64). Republican. Presbyterian. Avocations: skiing, sailing. Home: 705 NW 144th St Edmond OK 73013-1878 Office Phone: 405-271-8001 55120. E-mail: Beej1942@sbcglobal.net.

HAYWOOD, KATHLEEN MARIE, university educator, dean; b. St. Louis, Jan. 3, 1950; d. Eugene W. and Mildred Soric Haywood. PhD, U. Ill., Champaign, 1976. Prof., assoc. dean U. Mo., St. Louis, 2003—. Author: (book) Life Span Motor Development, Archery: Steps to Success. Recipient Mabel Lee award, Am. Am. Alliance Health, Phys. Edn., Recreation and Dance, 1984. Fellow: Am. Acad. Kinesiology and Phys. Edn.; mem.: North Am. Soc. Psychology Sport and Phys. Activity (pres. 1999—2000). Avocation: tennis. Office: U Mo-St Louis 8001 Natural Bridge Saint Louis MO 63121 Personal E-mail: kathleen_haywood@umsl.edu.

HAYWORTH, LAURA, bank officer, real estate analyst; b. Atlanta, July 28, 1948; d. Robert Edward Hayworth and Georgia Mabel Coffee; m. Randy Bruce Marrs, Feb. 19, 1977 (div. June 1980). BA in Psychology, Ga. State U., 1970, MS in Real Estate, 1984. Cert. property mgr. Asst. mgr. real property ops. Trust Co. Bank, Atlanta, 1978-80; 1st level officer real estate ops. So. Bell Telephone, Atlanta, 1980-81; v.p., trust officer C&S Nat. Bank, Atlanta, 1981-89; comml. loan workout officer FDIC, Atlanta, 1989-92; market analyst Mortgage Guaranty Ins. Corp., Atlanta, 1992; real estate and loan analyst Berkshire Mortgage Fin., Atlanta, 1993, contract real estate and loan analyst, 1994-97; asset mgr. retail portfolio Branch and Assocs., Atlanta, 1993-94; market rsch. assoc. Amresco Rsch., Atlanta, 1996-97; asst. v.p. and trust officer personal trust real estate ops. SunTrust Bank, Atlanta, 1997—. Pres. Emory Garden Condominium Assn., Decatur, Ga., 1984-86; bd. mem. Maple Bend Condominium Assn., Chamblee, Ga., 1987-93, Dunwoody (Ga.) Club Townhomes Condominium Assn., 1993—;

mem. Assistance League Atlanta, Chamblee, 1996—. Home: 4101 Dunwoody Club Dr Apt 41 Atlanta GA 30350-5215 Office: Sun Trust Bank Trust and Investment Svcs 25 Park Pl NE Atlanta GA 30303-2900

HAZAN, MARCELLA MADDALENA, writer, educator, consultant; b. Cesenatico, Italy, Apr. 15, 1924; d. Giuseppe and Maria (Leonelli) Polini; m. Victor Hazan, Feb. 24, 1955; 1 child, Giuliano. Dr. in Natural Scis., U. Ferrara, 1952, Dr. in Biology, 1954. Rschr. Guggenheim Inst., 1955-58; prof. math. and biology Italian State schs., 1963-66; founder Sch. of Italian Cooking, N.Y.C., 1969-94, Marcella Hazan Sch. of Classic Italian Cooking, Bologna, Italy, 1976-94, Master Classes in Classic Italian Cooking, Venice, Italy, 1986-98. Pres. Hazan Classic Enterprises, Inc., 1978-99. Author: The Classic Italian Cookbook, 1973, More Classic Italian Cooking, 1978, Marcella's Italian Kitchen, 1986, Essentials of Classic Italian Cooking, 1992, Marcella Cucina, 1997, Marcella Says, 2004. Roman Catholic. Address: 1212 Gulf Of Mexico Dr # 109 Longboat Key FL 34228 Fax: (941) 387-0183.

HAZARD, BARBARA WARD, writer, artist; b. Fall River, Mass., July 19, 1931; d. Albert Lincoln and Lillian Ward (Holland) Booth; m. Donald Thomson Hazard, Nov. 20, 1954; children: Steven Emerson, David Lincoln, Scott Winslow. BA in Advt. Design, RISD, 1953. Tech. editor Ginn & Co. Pubs., Boston, 1953—54; graphic artist Orr, Pope & Moulton, Concord, NH, 1954—56; freelance artist Chappaqua, NY, 1958—78; author Ballantine Fawcett Signet/NAL, N.Y.C., NY, 1980—. Author: 47 mass market paperback books, 1981—. Dir. pub. rels. Jr. League, Northern Westchester, 1969; bd. dirs. Chappaqua Libr., Chappaqua PTA, 1970—73, The Hostel, Hanover, NH, 2001—, Friends of the Hood Mus., 1998—99, Hopkins Ctr., Dartmouth Coll. Named Best Regency Author of Yr., Romantic Times Publ., 1985; named to Hall of Fame, Romantic Times Pub., 1988; recipient Best Short Hist. Suspense of Yr. award, Waldenbooks, 1986. Avocations: music, painting, quilting, reading, golf.

HAZARD, ROBERTA LOUISE, career officer; b. Boston, Nov. 8, 1934; d. Robert Louis and Louise Marie (Bourget) H. BS, Boston Coll., 1956, MA, 1957; grad., Nat. War Coll., 1978. Commd. ensign USNR, 1960; advanced through grades to rear adm. USN, 1988, adminstrv. asst. to chief naval ops., 1970-74, dir. women's career policy & guidance, 1978-80, comdg. officer Naval Tech. Tng. Command San Francisco, 1980-82, comdg officer Naval Tng. Sta. San Diego, 1983-85, comdr. Gt. Lakes Naval Tng. Ctr. North Chicago, Ill., 1985-87, dir. manpower & pers. for Joint Chiefs Staff Washington, 1987-89, dir. Navy personal readiness and community support, 1989-92. First USN female officer selected to rear admiral (upper half). Bd. dirs. Armed Forces YMCA, Springfield, Va., 1988—; trustee Boston Coll., 1984—. Decorated Def. D.S.M.; recipient Alumni Disting. Pub. Svc. award Boston Coll., 1983, Calif. Women in Govt. award, 1984, Disting. Svc. award Lake County (Ill.) YWCA, 1986, John Paul Jones Disting. Leadership award Navy League, 1987, J.B. Hancock Leadership award Navy League, 1987. Mem. Alpha Omega. Republican. Roman Catholic. Avocations: cooking, reading, traveling, music, entertaining. Office: Dir Navy Personal Readiness & Community Support Navy Annex Arl Va Washington DC 20380-0001

HAZBOUN, VIVECA, psychiatrist; b. Ramallah, Jordan, Nov. 2, 1949; arrived in U.S., 1966; d. Albert Anthony and Helen Hazboun. BS in Chemistry, Immaculate Heart Coll., L.A., 1970; MD, U. So. Calif., 1976. Diplomate in adult psychiatry Am. Bd. Psychiatry and Neurology, 1980, in child psychiatry Am. Bd. Psychiatry and Neurology, 82. Tchg. asst. Grad. Sch. U. So. Calif., L.A., 1970-72; intern in internal medicine Huntington Meml. Hosp., Pasadena, Calif., 1976-77; resident in adult psychiatry Los Angeles County U. So. Calif. Med. Ctr., 1977-79, fellow in child and adolescent psychiatry, 1979-81, chief child resident, 1980-81, asst. prof. clin. psychiatry, 1981-85, clin. instr., 1980-81; practice adult, child and adolescent psychiatry, L.A., 1980—; mental health supr. UN Relief and Work Agy., 1990-95; dir. adult and child psychiatry and neurology Guidance and Tng. Ctr., 1995—. Ward chief children's inpatient Los Angeles County-U. So. Calif. Med. Ctr. Psychiat. Hosp., 1981—85; cons. staff Edgemont Psychiat. Hosp., L.A., 1982—85; cons. Medecins sans Frontieres, Jerusalem, Medecins du Monde, Jerusalem; project dir. World Vision; founder Guidance and Tng. Ctr. for the Child and Family, 1994—, dir., 1994—. Contbr. chpts. to med. book. Recipient Papal award, Rome, 1968, recognition awards Child Guidance Clinic, 1980, Women in Data Processing, 1983; fellow Child Guidance Clinic, 1980. Mem. WHO (mem. steering com., thematic group, 2003—), Am. Acad. Child Psychiatry, So. Calif. Psychiat. Soc., So. Calif. Soc. Child Psychiatry, Internat. Assn. Child and Adult Psychiatry (sci. com.), Ea. Mediterranean Child and Adult Psychiatry Assn. (ethics com.), Am. Arab Univ. Grads. Office: PO Box 51399 Jerusalem Israel E-mail: gfc@p-ol.com.

HAZEKAMP, PHYLLIS WANDA ALBERTS, retired library director; b. Chgo. d. John Edward and Mary Ann (Demski) Wojciechowski. BA, De Paul U., 1947; MSLS, La. State U., 1959; postgrad., Santa Clara U., U. Chgo. Cert. tchr., Calif., Ariz. Libr. Agrl. Experiment Sta., U. Calif., Riverside, 1959-61; tech. libr. Lockheed Tech. Libr., Palo Alto, Calif., 1962-63; asst. law libr. Santa Clara (Calif.) U. Law Sch., 1963-72; libr. dir. Carmelite Seminary, San Jose, Calif., 1973-78; reference libr. San Jose State U., 1978-79; libr. dir. SAI Engrs., Santa Clara, 1980-81, Palmer Coll. Chiropractic, San Jose, 1981-90, Camp Verde (Ariz.) Cmty. Libr., 1990-98; ret., 1998. Mem. Cultural Commn., Santa Clara, 1968-72; pres. Santa Clara Art Assn., 1973-74; cons. various librs.; lectr. in field. Bd. dirs. Camp Verde Art Commn., 1994—; spkr. Ho. of Ruth, 2000—02; pres. Montezuma Chapel Ladies Guild, 1999—2001, 2003—04, book rev. chmn., 2003; bd. dirs. Beaver Creek Adult Ctr., 2000—02; vol. various orgns.; pres. Book Rev. Club, 2003—04; vol. Camp Verde Christian Sch. Avocations: writing articles, painting, teaching, giving talks to groups.

HAZEL, MARY BELLE, university administrator; b. Orange, N.J., May 30, 1932; d. Morris M. Sr. and Robena (Brinkley) Thomas; m. James H. Hazel, Sept. 28, 1958 (div. Sept. 1976); children: Sharon Marie Hazel-Griggs, James Thomas. BS in Bus. Adminstrn., Seton Hall U., South Orange, N.J., 1992, MA in Edn. cum laude, 1998. Publs. asst. advt. and pub. rels. dept. Foster Wheeler Corp., N.Y.C., 1969-87; ind. contractor, 1987-92; adminstrv coord. dean's office UMDNJ Sch. Health Related Professions, Newark, 1992—. Elder Elmwood United Presbyn. Ch. Mem. AAUW, NAFE, Smithsonian Nat. Assn., Soc. Allied Health Professions N.J., YWCA, N.J. Performing Arts Ctr., Jersey Ednl. Opportunity Fund Profl. Assn.

HAZELIP, EDWINA KAY, critical care nurse; b. Louisville, Jan. 25, 1952; d. Edwin O'Neil and Lorraine Esta (Nicols) H. Grad., High Point (N.C.) Meml. Hosp. Sch. Nursing, 1975. Day care ctr. worker Child's Kingdom, Wilkesboro, N.C.; nurses aide Wilkes Gen. Hosp., North Wilkesboro, N.C., 1971-72, head nurse coronary and ICU, 1972-82, pres. nurses' staff, 1976, 78, unit mgr. coronary and ICU, 1982-84; staff nurse Med. Pers. Pool of the Triad, Greensboro, N.C., 1982-88, mem. pers. com., 1984-87, chmn. pers. com., 1985-87; instr. cardiac defibrillation. Bd. dirs. Wilkes County unit Am. Heart Assn.; cert. instr. CPR, advanced life support; tchr. 2 yr.-old children Weekday Early Edn. of 1st Bapt. Ch., Jamestown, N.C., 1986-87, tchr. 3 yr.-old children, 1987, dir., 1988—, dir. summer day camp, chair weekday early edn. com.; dir. Weekday Early Edn. Presch., Summer Presch., Day Camp, dir. aftersch. program, handbell choir and solo handbell ringer, 1986—, mem. Chancel Choir, 1985—; Sunday sch. tchr., 1986, mem. sr. adult ministries com., chmn. children's coordinating com., 1989-93, dir. vacation Bible sch., 1998, 2000-02, asst. presch. choir, deacon, 2001-03; charter mem. Weekday Early Edn. Assn. N.C. Bapt. Conv., 1995; vol. cook area homeless shelter. Mem. ANA, N.C. Nurses Assn. (mem. bylaws com. 1991—, co-chair com. on coms. 1991-96, chmn. 1993-94), Greensboro Assn. Edn. of Young Child (mem. children's coordinating com. 1997—, chair, 1998—, Woman of Yr. 1997, 2000, 01). Home: 5112 Vickrey Chapel Rd Greensboro NC 27407-9737

HAZELIP, LINDA ANN, musician, small business owner, executive assistant; b. El Campo, Tex., Oct. 20, 1952; d. Al Gareth and Annabelle (Black) Braswell; m. Richard Chris Hazelip, July 28, 1972 (div. Aug. 30, 1984). Tchg. cert. in progressive series intermediate level piano, St. Louis Inst. Music, 1971; bus. diploma in computer programming and data processing, Massey Bus. Coll., 1972. Tchr. basic music and piano, 1971—79; bookkeeper Millar Instruments, Houston, 1973—74; sec. St. Andrew's United Meth. Ch., Houston, 1975—79; various positions as exec. asst., mgmt. asst., exec. sec., adminstr., and other adminstrv. positions Houston, 1979—; bus. owner, organist/choirmaster, pianist, vocalist sacred occasions, select secular spl. occasions Met. Area, Houston, S.E. Tex., 1986—; dir., exec. sec. Exponet Trading Co., Houston, 1983—86; exec. sec. InterFirst Bank Post Oak, Houston, 1986; sec., adminstr., mgmt. asst. Halliburton Energy Svcs., Houston, 1991—96; tchr. voice, organ, piano, 2000—. Organist, vocalist, pianist, children's music dir. Faith United Methodist Ch., South Houston, 1972—77; organist, vocalist, children's music dir. Old River Ter. United Methodist Ch., Channelview, Tex., 1978—80; organist, vocalist, music dir. St. John's United Methodist Ch., Baytown, Tex., 1980—84; organist, vocalist St. Stephens United Methodist Ch., Houston, 1983—85; organist, choir dir., vocalist Parker Meml. United Methodist Ch., Houston, 1984—85; choir dir., vocalist Covenant United Methodist Ch., Houston, 1985—86, Reid Meml. United Methodist Ch., Houston, 1985. Vocalist, pianist Open Door Mission, Houston, 1997—; mem. First United Meth. Ch., Houston, 1986—. Mem.: NAFE, Chorister's Guild, Houston Area League PC Users, Am. Bus. Women's Assn. (Skyscraper chpt., Woman of Yr. 1993—94), Am. Guild Organists. Methodist. Office Phone: 713-668-2248. E-mail: lhazelip@hal-pc.org.

HAZELTINE, JOYCE, former state official; b. Pierre, S.D. m. Dave Hazeltine; children: Derek, Tara, Kirk. Student, Huron (S.D.) Coll., No. State Coll., Aberdeen, S.D., Black Hills State Coll., Spearfish, S.D. Former asst. chief clk. S.D. Ho. of Reps.; former sec. S.D. State Senate; sec. of state State of S.D., Pierre, 1987—2003. Adminstrv. asst. Pres. Ford Campaign, S.D.; Rep. county chmn. Hughes County S.D.; state co-chair Phil Gramm for Pres., 1996. Mem. Nat. Assn. Secs. of State (exec. bd., pres.), Women Execs. in State Govts. (bd. dirs.). Republican.

HAZELTON, JUANITA LOUISE, librarian; b. Glendale, Calif., June 12, 1942; d. James Chester and Eddith Pearl (Henson) McCrain; m. Merrill Edward Hazelton, Apr. 27, 1968; children: Larry Scott, James Edward. BA in Arts and Letters, U. Oreg., 1964; MLS, U. Tex., 1970; tchg. cert., Tex. Woman's U., 1984. Cert. county libr., 1997. Librarian Dallas Pub. Libr., 1966 69; libr. asst. Austin Coll., Sherman, Tex., 1974-75; tchr., librarian Gunter (Tex.) Ind. Sch. Dist., 1984-94; librarian Plano (Tex.) Pub. Libr., 1994-95; libr. dir. Van Alstyne (Tex.) Pub. Libr., 1995—. Contbg. author: Telling Our Stories-Texas Family Secrets, 1997 (Gold Star award 1997); Bookshelf columnist Van Alstyne Leader, 1995—. Den leader, adv. coun. Cub Scouts, Gunter, 1984-88; club leader, adv. coun. 4-H, Gunter, 1988-95. Recipient Libr. of Yr., N.E. Tex. Libr. Sys., 1996; named Bus. Citizen of Yr. Van Alstyne C. of C., 1998, named to Tall Texans, 2003. Mem. Tex. Libr. Assn. (treas. dist. 5, 2000-01), TALL Tex., Toastmasters Internat., Van Alstyne Genealog. Assn., Tex. Storytelling Assn. Republican. Mem. Ch. of Christ. Avocations: collecting kachinas and folk tales, amateur storytelling, computers, genealogy, writing poetry and family history. Office: Van Alstyne Pub Libr PO Box 629 117 N Waco Van Alstyne TX 75495 E-mail: jhazelton@vanalstynepl.lib.tx.us.

HAZELTON, PENNY ANN, law librarian, educator; b. Yakima, Wash., Sept. 24, 1947; d. Fred Robert and Margaret (McLeod) Pease; m. Norris J. Hazelton, Sept. 12, 1971; 1 child, Victoria MacLeod. BA cum laude, Linfield Coll., 1969; JD, Lewis and Clark Law Sch., 1975; M in Law Librarianship, U. Wash., 1976. Bar: Wash. 1976, U.S. Supreme Ct. 1982. Assoc. law libr., assoc. prof. U. Maine, 1976-78, law libr., assoc. prof., 1978-81; asst. libr. for rsch. svcs. U.S. Supreme Ct., Washington, 1981-85, law libr., 1985, U. Wash., Seattle, 1985—, prof. law, assoc. dean libr. and computing svcs., 1985—. Tchr. legal rsch., law librarianship, Indian law; cons. Maine Adv. Com. on County Law Librs., Nat. U. Sch. Law, San Diego, 1985-88, Lawyers Cooperative Pub., 1993-94, Marquette u. Sch. Law, 2002. Author: Computer Assisted Legal Research: The Basics, 1993; author: (with others) Washington Legal Researcher's Deskbook, 3d edit., 2002; contbr. articles to legal jours.; gen. editor Specialized Legal Rsch. (Aspen). Recipient Disting. Alumni award U. Wash., 1992. Mem. ABA (sect. legal edn. and admissions to bar, chair com. on librs. 1993-94, vice chair 1992-93, 94-95, com. on law sch. facilities 1998—), Am. Assn. Law Schs. (com. law librs. 1991-94), Law Librs. New Eng. (sec. 1977-79, pres. 1979-81), Am. Assn. Law Librs. (program chmn. ann. meeting 1984, exec. bd. 1984-87, v.p. 1989-90, pres. 1990-91, program co-chair Insts. 1983, 95), Law Librs. Soc. Washington (exec. bd. 1983-84, v.p., pres. elect 1984-85), Law Librs. Puget Sound, Wash. State Bar Assn. (chair editl. adv. bd.), Wash. Adv. Coun. on Librs., Westpac. Office: U Wash Marian Gould Gallagher Law Libr William H Gates Hall Box 353025 Seattle WA 98195 Office Phone: 206-543-4089. Business E-Mail: pennyh@u.washington.edu.

HAZLETT-STEVENS, HOLLY, psychologist, educator; b. Phoenix, July 7, 1969; married, May 7, 1994. BA in Music and Psychology, U. So. Calif., 1993; PhD, Pa. State U., 1999. Psychology rsch. assoc. UCLA, 1999—2001; asst. prof. psychology U. Nev., Reno, 2002—. Author: New Directions in Progressive Relaxation Training: A Guidebook for Helping Professionals.; contbr. articles to profl. jours., chapters to books. Recipient Edwin B. Newman Grad. Rsch. award, Psi Chi/APA, 1998. Mem.: APA (Dissertation Rsch. award 1998), Assn. for Advancement of Behavior Therapy (winner Elsie Ramos Meml. Student Rsch. Competiton 1997). Avocation: orchestra performance. Office: U Nev Reno Dept Psychology 298 Reno NV 89557

HAZZARD, SHIRLEY, author; b. Sydney, Australia, Jan. 30, 1931; d. Reginald and Catherine (Stein) Hazzard.; m. Francis Steegmuller, Dec. 22, 1963 (dec. Oct. 1994). Ed., Queenwood Sch., Sydney, 1946. With Combined Services Intelligence, Hong Kong, 1947—48, U.K. High Commr. Office, Wellington, New Zealand, 1949—50, UN (gen. svc. category), N.Y.C., 1952—61. Boyer lectr., Australia, 1984, 88. Author: Cliffs of Fall and other stories, 1963; (novels) The Evening of the Holiday, 1966, People in Glass Houses, 1967, The Bay of Noon, 1970, The Transit of Venus, 1980, History Defeat of an Ideal: A Study of the Self Destruction of the UN, 1973, History Countenance of Truth, 1990; The Great Fire, 2003 (Nat. Book award, 2003); (memoir) Greene on Capri, 2000. Trustee N.Y. Soc. Libr. Named Hon. Citizen Capri, 2000; recipient Lit. Award, Nat. Inst. Arts and Letters, 1966, First prize, O. Henry Short Story Awards, 1976, Cir. Award for Fiction, Nat. Book Critics, 1981, Clifton Fadiman Medal for Lit., 2001, Nat. Book Award for Fiction, 2003, Medal of Honor, Nat. Arts Club Lit., 2004; Guggenheim Fellow, 1974. Fellow Royal Soc. Lit.; mem. AAAL, Nat. Arts and Sci., Century Club, N.Y.C.. Address: 200 E 66th St Apt C1705 New York NY 10021-9187

HEACKER, THELMA WEAKS, retired elementary school educator; b. Lakeland, Fla., Nov. 27, 1927; d. Andrew Lee and Stella Dicy (Hodges) Weaks; m. Howard V. Heacker, Aug. 21, 1947; children: Victor, Patricia, Paula, Jonathan, Johannah; m. V.L. Brown, Mar. 31, 1991. BA, Carson-Newman Coll., Jefferson City, Tenn., 1949; MA, Tenn. Technol. U., 1980; postgrad., U. Tenn. Cert. elem. and secondary tchr., Tenn.; cert. secondary tchr., Ga. Elem. tchr. Hamblen County Pub. Schs., Morristown, Tenn., 1949; secondary tchr. Morgan County-Coalfield High Sch., Coalfield, Tenn., 1986-87, Roane County-O. Springs High Sch., Oliver Springs, Tenn., 1949-71; elem. tchr. Morgan County-Petros-Joyner Sch., Oliver Springs, 1975-93. Vol. Keystone Elder Day Care, 2000—. Named Tchr. of Yr., 1986. Mem. NEA, Tenn. Edn. Assn., Ea. Tenn. Edn. Assn., Morgan County Edn. Assn., RCTA, HCTA Home: 102 Ulena Ln Oak Ridge TN 37830-5237 Office: Petros Joyner Elem Sch Petros-Joyner Rd Oliver Springs TN 37840-9700

HEAD, ELIZABETH, lawyer; b. Rochester, Minn., Dec. 17, 1930; d. Walter Elias and Ruth Winnogene (Evesmith) Bonner; m. C.J. Head, Dec. 30, 1950; 1 child, Alison Elizabeth. BA, U. Chgo., 1949, JD, 1952. Bar: Ill. 1952, Calif. 1955, N.Y. 1958, U.S. Supreme Ct. 1963, D.C. 1978. Atty. Nat. Labor Rels. Bd., Washington, 1953-54; assoc. Johnston & Johnston, San Francisco, 1954-56; atty. Aminoil Inc., San Francisco, 1956-57; teaching assoc. Law Sch. Columbia U., N.Y., 1957-58; assoc. Skadden Arps, N.Y., 1958-60; atty. The Coca-Cola Corp., N.Y., 1961-65; assoc. Kaye Scholer, N.Y., 1965-72, ptnr., 1973-82; mem. Hall & Estill, Tulsa, 1983-87; vis. fellow antitrust analysis Fed. Energy Regulatory Commn., Washington, 1987-89; gen. counsel Columbia U., N.Y.C., 1989-97. Arbitrator, mediator, 1998—. Trustee Mary Baldwin Coll., Staunton, Va., 1983-87. Mem. ABA (standing com. on dispute resolution 1983-90), Assn. of Bar of City of N.Y. (non-profit orgns. com. 1989-90, chair 1992-95, health law com. 1997-2000), Century Assn., Order of Coif, Phi Beta Kappa. Avocations: travel, music, art, theatre. Office: 303 E 57th St # 47F New York NY 10022-2947

HEAD, HELEN, state representative, management consultant; b. Griffin, Ga., May 12, 1953; m. Thomas Mercurio; 2 children. BA, U. N.H., 1975; MPA, U. Vt., 1989. Planning and develop cons.; state rep. State of Vt., 2003—. Parent vol. South Burlington Schs.; bd. trustees Vt. Ecumenical Coun. Mem.: Older Women's Legue. Democrat. Office: 65 East Terr South Burlington VT 05403

HEAD, MELVA ANN, artist; b. St. Louis, July 9, 1937; d. Melvin G. and Muriel J. (Hall) Irwin; m. Fred L. Head, Dec. 15, 1956; children: Allan L., Shawn M. Studied with, Thelma DeGoede Smith, 1973-83, Kwok Wai Lau, 1983—. V.p. gallery La Habra (Calif.) Art Assn., 1986-88, v.p. membership, 1988-89, v.p. programs, 1989-91, pres., 1991-92, dir., 1992-95. One person shows, including La Habra (Calif.) Art Assn., 1986, 90; exhibited in group shows at L.A. Art Assn., Chevron Oil and Field Rsch., La Habra, 1991, Long Beach (Calif.) Arts, 1994-2002, Palm Springs (Calif.) Desert Mus., 1994, 97, 2000, 02, 03, Gallery 825, L.A., 1995-2004, Pasadena (Calif.) Presbyn. Ch., 1995-97, Guggenheim Gallery, Chapman U., Orange, Calif., 1997, 98, Hollywood Los Feliz Jewish Cmty. Ctr., L.A., 1997, 36th Inland Empire Exhbn., San Bernardino County Mus., 2002, Women Painters West, 2001, 2004, Orange County Ctr. for Contemporary Art, Internat. Exhibit, 2001, San Diego Watercolor Soc. Internat. Exhibit, 2003 Mem. Artists Coun. Palm Springs, L.A. Arts, Long Beach Arts, La Habra Art Assn., Whittier Art Assn., Women Painters West. Avocations: sewing, reading

HEAD, TERESA RENA, electrical engineer; b. Dayton, Ohio, July 17, 1970; d. John Henry and Rudy Ima Gene (McIntosh) H. BSEE, U. Dayton, 1993. Electr. engr. co op Mead Corp., Chillicothe, Ohio, 1990-92; assoc. engr. Owens-Corning, Toledo, 1993-94, Granville, Ohio, 1994-95, project elec. engr. Newark, Ohio, 1995-98; engring. staff Hond of Am. Mfg., Inc., East Liberty, Ohio, 1998—. Life devel. coord., small group ministry co-leader New Salem Missionary Bapt. Ch., Columbus, Ohio, 1997; Jr. Achievement and tutoring Kettering Elem. Sch., Newark, Ohio, 1995-97. Mem. Ohio Soc. Profl. Engrs. Avocations: golf, pool, step aerobics, physical fitness training, tennis. Office: Honda of Am Mfg Inc 11000 State Route 347 East Liberty OH 43319-9471 Home: 2279 Woodduck Way Columbus OH 43229-9323

HEAD, WANDA KAY, elementary school educator; b. Monroe, La., Sept. 27, 1960; d. J. L. and Shirley Ann Manning; children: Jonathan Bernard Jr., Cassondra Kay. BS, S.W. Tex. State U., San Marcos, 1984; postgrad., Huston Tillotson Coll., Austin, Tex., 1989, Austin C.C. Physical edn. and 2d grade tchr. Edgewood Ind. Sch. Dist., San Antonio, 1985—87; 2d grade tchr. Del Valle (Tex.) Ind. Sch. Dist., 1987—89; K-1st grade tchr. Austin (Tex.) Ind. Sch. Dist., 1989—93; 1st grade tchr. Lockhart (Tex.) Ind. Sch. Dist., 1993—99; reading specialist Round Rock (Tex.) Ind. Sch. Dist., 1999—. Team leader Campus Performance Objective Com., Lockhart, Tex., 1996—97. Mem.: PTA, Soc. for Developmental Edn. Democrat. Baptist. Avocations: coin collecting, bible reading, interior decorating, leading youth groups, traveling. Office: Xenia Voigt Elem Sch 1201 Cushing Dr Round Rock TX 78664 E-mail: Wand_Head@rrisd.org.

HEADDEN, SUSAN M. editor; Formerly reporter Indpls. Star, Indpls.; now sr. editor U.S. News & World Report, Washington. Recipient Pulitzer prize for investigative reporting, 1991. Office: US News and World Report 2400 N St NW Washington DC 20037-1153

HEAD-HAMMOND, ANNA LUCILLE, retired secondary school educator; b. Providence, Ky., Dec. 16, 1924; d. Nathaniel A. and Nora D. (Martin) Rinehammer; m. Robert F. Head, Oct. 24, 1940 (wid. Apr. 1981); 1 child, Robert N. Head; m. Arthur G. Hammond, Aug. 24, 1995. BS, Oakland City U., Ind., 1955; MS, Ind. State Coll., 1964. Tchr. Princeton (Ind.) H.S., 1955-64; instr.. Oakland City U., 1964-77; owner, operator mobile home ct., Providence, 1973-78; real estate salesperson, appraiser Ball Real Estate, Providence, 1973-89; appraiser Frontier Properties, Okeechobee, Fla., 1973-89. Elected mem. Providence City Coun., 1972-73; adv. coun. Gulfstream Agy. on Aging, West Palm Beach, 1986-87; coun. mem. Cen. Fla. Regional Planning Coun., 1988-89. Mem. AAUW, Elks, Habitat for Humanity, Hospice, Alpha Phi Gamma. Republican. Presbyterian. Avocations: swimming, golf, walking. Home: 622 Delgado Ave Lady Lake FL 32159-8768

HEADLEY, CAROL ANN, elementary and secondary school educator; b. Butler, Mo., Oct. 4, 1937; d. William Harold and Fairy Anise (Hodges) Cain; m. Ralph Bruce Headley, Oct. 7, 1956; children: Kimberley Fritchie, Sandee McMillin. BS edn., Ctrl. Mo State Univ., Warrensburg, Mo., 1967—70, MS edn., 1971—75. Cert. Elem. Edn. K-8 1970, Remedial Reading K-12 1975, Learning Disabilities K-9 1975. Elem. tchr. Independence Sch. Dist., Independence, Mo., 1970—72, Lee's Summit Sch. Dist., Lee's Summit, Mo., 1972—95, substitute tchr., 1995—98, homebound tchr., 1995—97; reading tutor Laubach Literacy (K C Literacy), Kans. City, Mo., 1999—2000; adj. prof. Ctrl. Mo. State Univ., Warrensburg, Mo., 2000—01; substitute tchr. Lone Jack Sch. Dist., Lone Jack, Mo., 2002—03, Pleasant Hill (Mo.) Sch. Dist. Mentor Mother's Refuge - Home for homeless pregnant teens, Independence, Mo., 1997—2002; presenter com. chmn. for Parents Univ. Lee's Summit Cares, Lee's Summit, Mo., 2003—, bd. mem., 2003—. Bd. mem. Hazel Dell Cmty. Ctr., Greenwood, Mo., 1993—95; mentor Lee's Summit Cmty. Ch., Lee's Summit, Mo., 1996—2000; bd. mem. Mother's Refuge (Shelter for homeless pregnant teens), Independence, Mo., 1999—2002; past. pres. Lee's Summit Internat. Reading Assn. Nominee Reading Tchr. of the Yr., Lee's Summit Internat. Reading Assn., 1989—90, 1992—93, 1995. Mem.: Lee' Summit Ret. Tchr. Assn., Mo. State Tchr. Assn., Mo. State Ret. Tchr. Assn. (life), Daughters of the Am. Revolution (regent, treas., vice regent 1990—2000, Past Chpt. Regent 1998), Daughter of the Am. Colonists (libr., treas., v.p., chaplain 1990—2003), CMSU Kappa Delta Pi Soc. (hon.). Conservative. Christian. Avocations: travel, reading, genealogy, writing. Office: Lees Summit Sch Dist 600 Miller St Lees Summit MO 64063

HEADLEY, HEATHER A. actress; b. Trinidad, W.I., 1974; came to U.S., 1990; d. Iric and Hannah H. Student, Northwestern U., Evanston, Ill. Profl. acting roles include: (Broadway and other plays) Ragtime, 1996, The Lion King, 1997, Aida, 1998, 2000, (Tony nomination for 2000 performance,

Drama Desk award for Outstanding Actress in a Musical, Tony for Actress in a Musical), Do Re Mi, 1999; discography contbns. include: The Lion King/Disney Records, 1998, Return to Pride Rocke: Songs Inspired by 'The Lion King II: Simba's Pride, 1998, From the Soul of a Man, 1998, Do Re Mi: 1999 Original Cast Recording, 1999, Elton John and Tim Rice's Aida/Rocket Records, 1999.

HEADLEY, JENNIFER LYNN, art educator; b. Pitts., Aug. 31, 1973; d. Samuel Presley and Paulette Eileen Headley. AA, Art Inst. Pitts., 1996; BA, Point Pk. Coll., 1997; MFA, George Washington U., 2001; postgrad., George Mason U., 2001—. Adj. prof. Georgetown U., Washington, 2000—02, George Washington U., Washington, 2000—02; mem. faculty Art Inst. Washington, Arlington, Va., 2001—. Spkr. in field. Mem. Nat. Mus. Women in the Arts, 2002—. Grad. fellow, George Washington U., 1999—2001. Mem.: Coll. Art Assn., Omicron Delta Kappa. Democrat. Presbyterian. Avocations: running, camping. Office: Art Inst Washington Arlington VA 22209

HEAGARTY, MARGARET CAROLINE, pediatrician; b. Charleston, W.Va., Sept. 8, 1934; d. John Patrick and Margaret Caroline (Walsh) H. BA, Seton Hill Coll., 1957; BS, W.Va. Sch. Medicine, 1959; MD, U. Pa., 1961; DSc honoris causa, Iona Coll., 1989. Diplomate: Am. Bd. Pediatrics. Intern Phila. Gen. Hosp., 1961—62; resident in pediatrics St. Christopher's Hosp. for Children, Phila., 1962—64; dir. pediatric ambulatory care services N.Y. Hosp.-Cornell Med. Ctr., N.Y.C., 1969—78; dir. pediatrics Harlem Hosp. Ctr. Columbia U., N.Y.C., 1978—2000, prof. pediatrics coll. physicians & surgeons, 1987—2000, prof. emerita coll. physicians and surgeons, 2000—. Cons. Dept. HEW Promotion of Child Health, Washington; mem. Com. Community Oriented Primary Care Inst. Medicine, Washington; mem. Robert Wood Johnson Found. Program for Prepaid Managed Health Care, 1984; mem. governing council Inst. Medicine, Nat. Acad. Scis., 1986 Author: Changing the Medical Car System-Report of an Experiment, 1974, Medical Sociology: A Systems Approach, 1975, Child Health: Basics for Primary Care, 1980. Grantee Commonwealth Found., 1981, Robert Wood Johnson Found., 1983, Ctr. for Disease Control, 1985, Health Rsch. and Svc. Adminstrn., 1988, Nat. Inst. Allergy/Infectious Disease, 1988. Fellow Inst. Medicine (steering group for nat. forum on future of children and their families 1987—); mem. Ambulatory Pediatric Assn. (pres. 1976-77), Soc. Pediatric Research, Am. Pediatric Soc., Am. Acad. Pediatrics (com. on hosp. care 1988—), Assn. Pediatric Program Dirs., Nat. Bd. Med. Examiners. Home: 2520 Kingsland Ave Bronx NY 10469-6108 E-mail: mheagarty@aol.com.

HEAGY, LORRAINE MARY, office manager; b. Lancaster, Pa., Aug. 19, 1935; d. Ralph Long and Ella Ruth Shreiner; m. John Franklin Heagy, Oct. 15, 1960 (dec. 1979); children: John Franklin III, Loralie Leslie, Michael David. Grad. high sch., Lititz, Pa. Clk. typist Woodstream Corp., Lititz, 1953-54, Lititz Mut. Ins. Co., 1955-56; sec. Warner Lambert Co., Lititz, 1956-61; adminstrv. asst. Elam G. Stoltzfus, Jr., Lancaster, Pa., 1973-84; mgr. office support dept. Lancaster Labs., 1984-99; ret., 1999. Democrat. Avocations: reading, travel, sewing.

HEALEY, ANNE, state legislator; b. Scranton, Pa., Jan. 2, 1951; married; 2 children. BA, Marywood Coll., 1972; MA, Cath. U. Am., 1974. Del. Dist. 22 Md. State Delegation, 1991-94, del. Dist. 22A, 1995—, mem. ways and means com., 1991—, chair taxes and revenues subcom., 1994-97, vice-chair W & M com., 1998—. Councilwoman City of Hyattsville, Md., 1987-90; active Am. Cancer Soc. Mem. Prince George's County Pub. Rels. Assn. Home: 3920 Madison St Hyattsville MD 20781-1749 Office: 207 Lowe House Office Bldg 6 Gov Bladen Blvd Annapolis MD 21401-1529

HEALEY, KERRY MURPHY, lieutenant governor; b. Omaha, Apr. 30, 1960; d. Edward Morris and Shirley (Cumming) M.; m. Sean Michael Healey, Dec. 28, 1985; children: Alexander Edward, Averill Adair. AB in Govt., Harvard Coll., 1982; PhD in Law and Polit. Sci., Trinity Coll., Dublin, Ireland, 1991. Proctor freshman dean's office, vis. reseacher Law Sch. Harvard U., Cambridge, Mass., 1985—86; legal policy analyst ABT Assocs., Inc., Cambridge, 1986—87; pub. policy cons. Bklyn. and Boston, 1990—99; mem. Mass. Rep. State Com., 1999—; chmn. Mass. Republican Party, 2001—02; lt. gov. State of Mass., 2003—. Del. UN NGO assembly, 1994-95. Author: State and Local Experience with Drug Paraphernalia Laws, 1987, Victim and Witness Intimidation: New Developments and Emerging Responses, 1995; co-author: Compendium of Federal Justice Statistics, 1989, Handbook of Drug Control in the United States, 1990, Prosecutorial Response to Heavy Drug Case Loads, 1993. Bd. dirs., Mass. Women's Polit. Caucus, 1999-2001; bd. dirs., North Shore C.C. Found., Danvers, Mass., 1999-2002, Friends of Beverly (Mass.) Hosp., 1999-2001; co-chair North Shore United Way Campaign, Beverly, 2001, bd. dirs. YWCA, N.Y.C., 1992-95, mem. YWCA World Svc. Coun., 1992—. Grad. fellow Rotary Internat., 1983-84; rsch. grantee Mark DeWolfe Howe Fund of Harvard Law Sch., 1986. Mem. Harvard Club N.Y.C. (mem. schs. com. 1987-95), N.Y. Jr. League (rep. N.Y.C. ednl. priorities panel 1992-95), Cosmopolitan Club (N.Y.C.), Union Club (Boston). Office: State House Office of the Governor Room 360 Boston MA 02133 E-mail: khealey@romneyhealey.com.

HEALEY, LYNNE KOVER, editor, writer, broadcaster, educator; b. L.I., N.Y. d. R. Bascom and M Fuchs; div.; children: Christine Josepha, Lauren Teresa. BA in Comm., Rutgers U., 1983; MA in English, Drew U., 1987. Editor A.M. Best Co., Oldwick, N.J., 1985-91; communications cons. MetLife Ins. Co., 1992—2002; freelance writer, editor, 2002—. Adj. prof. English Middlesex County Coll., Edison, NJ, DeVry U., North Brunswick, NJ, Raritan Valley C. C., No. Branch, NJ. Bd. dirs. Women's Crisis Svcs. Mem. Meeting Planners Internat. (bd. dirs. N.J. chpt., co-chairperson com. for Give Kids the World project), Rutgers U. Alumni Assn. (exec. com.), Alpha Sigma Lambda (grad. sch. scholar 1986, bd. dirs. Rutgers chpt.). Avocations: photography, golf, dance, swimming, skiing.

HEALY, ALICE FENVESSY, psychology educator, researcher; b. Chgo., June 26, 1946; d. Stanley John and Doris (Goodman) Fenvessy; m. James Bruce Healy, May 9, 1970; 1 child, Charlotte Alexandra. AB summa cum laude, Vassar Coll., 1968; PhD, Rockefeller U., 1973. Asst. prof. psychology Yale U., New Haven, 1973-78, assoc. prof. psychology, 1978-81, U. Colo., Boulder, 1981-84, prof. psychology, 1984—. Rsch. assoc. Haskins Labs., New Haven, 1976—80; com. mem. NIMH, Washington, 1979—81; co-investigator rsch. contract USAF U. Colo., 1985—86, prin. investigator rsch. contract U.S. Army Rsch. Inst., 1986—; prin. investigator rsch. contract Naval Tng. Sys. Ctr., 1993—94; rsch. grant prin. investigator U.S. Army Rsch. Office U. Colo., 1995—2002; rsch. grant prin. investigator NASA, 1999—. Co-author: Cognitive Processes, 2d edit., 1986; editor: Memory and Cognition, 1986—89; co-editor (with S. M. Kosslyn and R. M. Shiffrin): (Essays in Honor of William K. Estes) From Learning Processes to Cognitive Processes Vol I, 1992; co-editor: (with S.M. Kosslyn and R.M. Shiffrin) From Learning Theory to Connectionist Theory: Essays in Honor of William K. Estes, Vol. II, 1992; co-editor: (with L.E. Bourne Jr.) Learning and Memory of Knowledge and Skills: Durability and Specificity, 1995, Foreign Language Learning: Psycholinguistic Studies on Training and Retention, 1998; co-editor: (with R. W. Proctor) Experimental Psychology, 2003; assoc. editor: Jour. Exptl. Psychology, 1982—84; contbr. articles to profl. jours. and chpts. to books. Recipient Sabbatical award, James McKeen Cattell Fund, 1987—88; grantee, NSF, 1977—86, 2003—, Spencer Found. Rsch., 1978—80. Fellow: AAAS (nominating com. 1988—91, chair nominating com. 1991, chair-elect psychology sect. 1994, chair psychology sect. 1995—96, retiring chair psychology sect. 1996—97), APA (exec. com. divsn. 3 1989—92, chair membership com. 1992—93, exec. com. divsn. 3 2001—, pres.-elect 2003—), Soc. Exptl. Psychologists; mem.: Soc. for Applied Rsch. in Memory and Cognition, Cognitive Sci. Soc., Rocky Mountain Psychology Assn. (pres.-elect 1993—94, pres. 1994—95, past pres. 1995—96), Soc. Math. Psychology, Psychonomic Soc. (governing bd. 1987—92, publs. com. 1989—93), Univ. Club, Sigma Xi, Phi Beta Kappa. Avocation: French pastries. Home: 840 Cypress Dr Boulder CO 80303-2820 Office: U Colo Dept Psychology 345 UCB Boulder CO 80309-0345 E-mail: ahealy@psych.colorado.edu.

HEALY, BERNADINE P. physician, educator, federal agency administrator, organization executive; b. N.Y.C., Aug. 2, 1944; d. Michael J. and Violet (McGrath) Healy; m. Floyd Loop, Aug. 17, 1985; children: Bartlett Anne Bulkley, Marie McGrath Loop. AB summa cum laude, Vassar Coll., 1965; MD cum laude, Harvard Med. Sch., 1970. Diplomate Am. Bd. Med. Examiners, Am. Bd. Cardiology, Am. Bd. Internal Medicine, lic. physician Md., Ohio. Intern in medicine Johns Hopkins Hosp., Balt., 1970—71, asst. resident, 1971—72; staff fellow sect. pathology Nat. Heart, Blood & Lung Inst., NIH, Bethesda, Md., 1972—74; fellow cardiovascular div. dept. medicine Johns Hopkins U. Sch. Medicine, Balt., 1974—76, fellow dept. pathology, 1975—76, asst. prof. medicine and pathology, 1976—81, assoc. prof. medicine, 1977—82, asst. dean postdoctoral programs and faculty devel., 1979—84, assoc. prof. pathology, 1981—84, prof. medicine, 1982—84, dean Coll. Med. and Pub. Health, 1995—99, prof. internal medicine, physiology, 1995—99; active staff medicine and pathology Johns Hopkins Hosp., 1976—, dir. CCU, 1976—84; pres. ARC, 1999—2001; advisor on weapons of mass destruction & bioterrorism White House, DC, 2001—; med. & healthcare columnist, sr. writer U.S. News & World Report, 2002—. Dep. dir. Office Sci. and Tech. Policy Exec. Office of Pres., White House, Washington, 1984—85; chmn. Rsch. Inst. The Cleve. Clinic Found., 1985—91, sr. health and sci. policy advisor, 1994—95; dean Med. Sch. Ohio State U., 1995—97; dir. NIH, Bethesda, Md., 1991—93; vice-chmn. Pres.' Coun. Advisers on Sci. and Tech., 1990—91; mem. Spl. Med. Adv. Group, Dept. Vet.'s Affairs, 1990—91, chmn. adv. panel for Basic Rsch. for 1990s, Office Tech. Assessment, 1990—91, mem. NHLBI Task Force on Atherosclerosis, 1990; mem. Vis. Com. Bd. Overseers Harvard Med. Sch. and Sch. of Dental Medicine, Boston, 1986—91; councillor Harvard Med. Alumni Assn., 1987—90; mem. Nat. Adv. Bd. Johns Hopkins Ctr. for Hosp. Fin. and Mgmt., 1987—91, Bd. Overseers Harvard Coll., 1989—; chmn. Office of Tech. Assessment Panel New Devels. in Biotech., U.S. Congress, 1986—87; mem. U.S.-Brazil Panel on Sci. and Tech., 1987, White House Sci. Coun., 1988—89; cons. Nat. Heart, Lung and Blood Inst., NIH, 1976—91; mem. adv. com. to dir. NIH, 1986—91; chmn. steering com. Post-CABG Clin. Triai, 1987—91; bd. dirs. Medtronic, Inc., Mpls., Nat. City Corp., Cleve., Nova Pharms., Balt.; mem. adv. bd. Bayer Fund for Cardiovasc. Rsch., N.Y.C., 1987—89; trustee Edison BioTech. Ctr., Cleve., 1990—; chmn. Ohio Coun. on Rsch. and Econ. Devel., 1989—91; bd. dirs. Nat. City Corp., 1989—90, 1995—2001, 2003—. Editl. cons. numerous jours.; abstract reviewer:, editl. bd.: Jour. Cardiovasc. Medicine, 1980—91, Am. Jour. Cardiology, 1981—82, Circulation, 1981—, Jour. Am. Coll. Cardiology, 1982—84, Am. Jour. Medicine, 1986—91; contbr. articles to profl. jours. Recipient Nat. Bd. Ann. award for Medicine, Med. Coll. Pa., 1983; fellow Eloise Ellery fellow, 1965—66, Stetler Rsch. fellow, 1976—77; scholar Matthew Vassar scholar, 1962—65, Harvard Nat. scholar, 1965—70. Mem.: ACP, Inst. Medicine NAS, Am. Bd. Internatl Medicine (bd. dirs. 1983—87, bd. govs. 1986—), Am. Soc. Clin. Investigation, Assn. for Women in Sci., Am. Med. Women's Assn., Internat. Acad. Pathology, Assn. Am. Med. Colls., Am. Coll. Cardiology (bd. govs. 1979—82), Am. Heart Assn. (fellow coun. on clin. cardiology, coun. on circulation, dir. 1983—84, pres. 1988—89, award 1983—84, 1990), Am. Fedn. Clin. Rsch. (pres. 1983—84), Johns Hopkins U. Soc. Scholars, Alpha Omega Alpha, Phi Beta Kappa.*

HEALY, CYNTHIA, pharmacologist, life scientist, researcher; BS in Chemistry, Coll. of White Plains; PhD in Pharmacology, N.Y. Med. Coll. Rschr. Roche Inst. Molecular Biology; mgr. drug discovery projects in inflammation CIBA-Geigy Corp.; dir. life sci. rsch. Kleiner, Perkins, Caufield & Byers, Menlo Park, Calif. Involved in beginning stage of privately held life scis. cos., inlcuidng Corixa, Georn, Pharmacopeia, and Signal Pharms.; bd. dirs. Argonaut Techs. Contbr. numerous articles on cellular immunology and inflammation to sci. jours. Office: Kleiner Perkins Caufield & Byers 2750 Sand Hill Rd Menlo Park CA 94025-7020 Fax: 650-233-0300.

HEALY, JANE ELIZABETH, newspaper editor; b. Washington, May 9, 1949; d. Paul Francis and Connie (Maas) H.; children: Randall, Kevin. BS, U. Md., 1971. Copy clk. N.Y. Daily News, Washington, 1971-73; met. reporter Orlando (Fla.) Sentinel, 1973-81, editorial writer, 1981-83, chief editorial writer, 1983-85, assoc. editor, 1985-92, mng. editor, 1993—2001, editl. page editor, 2001—. Recipient Pulitzer Prize, Columbia U., 1988, Sigma Delta Chi Disting. Service award, 1988. Mem. Am. Soc. Newspaper Editors. Office: Orlando Sentinel 633 N Orange Ave Orlando FL 32801-1349

HEALY, KAREN, automotive executive; B in Journalism, Mich. State U., 1976. With GM, 1976—95, staff pub. rels. fisher guide divsn., 1985—86, mgr. employee comm. Buick-Oldsmobile-Cadillac group, 1986, sr. adminstr. pub. affairs, dir. media comm. Delphi Corp. (formerly auto. components group worldwide), 1993—95; dir. comm. Delphi Corp., Troy, Mich., 1995—96, exec. dir. comm., 1997, v.p. corp. affairs, 1998—, v.p. mktg. comm. and facilities, 2000—. Trustee Music Hall Ctr. Performing Arts, Detroit; bd. visitors Oakland U. Bus. Sch.; bd. dirs. Forgotten Harvest, North Suburban Figure Skating Club. Named Businesswoman of Yr., Detroit News, 2000; named one of 100 Leading Women in Auto. Industry, Auto. News, 2000, Most Influential Women S.E. Mich., Crain's Detroit Bus., 2001. Mem.: Automotive Women's Alliance, Arthur Page Soc., Pub. Rels. Coun., Troy C. of C. (bd. dirs.). Office: 5725 Delphi Dr Troy MI 48098-2815*

HEALY, LAURA MARIE, editor; d. Frederick Louis and Carlyn Gay Falater(Stepmother); m. Brian Joseph Healy (div. Nov. 1, 1996); children: Brendan, Timothy, Sean, Genevieve. BSc, Ea. Ill. U., 1982, MS in Medicine, 1985. Cert. tchr. Ill. Manuscript editor Radiol Soc. N. Am., Oak Brook, Ill., 1986—87; freelance med. editor Montgomery, Ill., 1987—; prodr. FVTV, 2004. Project mgr. McGraw-Hill, Burr Ridge, Ill., 1999—2000; mng. editor Vet. Practice Pub., Irvine, Calif., 1999; project mgr. NursingCenter.com, Phila., 2000—02. Editor: (book) EMS Handbook, 2001, Disaster Medicine, 2002, MD Anderson Surgical Oncology Handbook, 2002, Runge/Netter: Internal Medicine, 2002, (jour.) Angiology, 2002, Clinical Pediatrics, 2002, author poems; editor: (jour.) Vascular Endovascular Surg. Founder/leader Cook County Bike Trl. Safety Sign Sys., Ill., 1992—93, Grassroots 40th and Glendenning Wetland Project, Downers Grove, Ill., 1995—99. Recipient Pet essay award, Suburban Life Newspapers, 1994. Mem.: Am. Med. Writer's Assn. Avocations: guitar, swimming, hiking, bicycling. Office: Med/Tech Editorial 2292 Stacy Cir Montgomery IL 60538 Office Phone: 630-966-0247. Personal E-mail: laurah40@juno.com.

HEALY, MARGARET MARY, retail marketing executive; b. Bklyn., Dec. 31, 1938; d. Nicholas Joseph and Margaret Marie (Ferry) H.; m. Robert L. Parker, 1979 (div. 1988); 1 child, Nicole Parker. BA, Manhattanville Coll., 1961; cert., NYU, 1967, Columbia U., 1971. Account exec. Geer, DuBois & Co., Inc., N.Y.C., 1965-71; dir. mktg. comm. Dry Dock Savs. Bank, N.Y.C., 1971-72; oper. v.p. Bloomingdales, N.Y.C., 1972-79; owner, pres. Healy & Pratts, Inc., N.Y.C., 1979-88; mgr. corp. pub. rels. J.C. Penney Co., Dallas, 1988-92; owner, pres. PH Network, Dallas, 1992—; co-owner, mng. dir. Network Assocs. Internat., Dallas, 1997-98. Mem. bd. advisors North Fork Bancorp, Melville, N.Y., 1997-99. Co-author: Salute to Italy Celebrity Cookbook, 1984, Salute to America Celebrity Cookbook, 1986; contbg. editor Dallas Home Mag. Bd. dirs. Dallas Children's Theater, 1989-2000. Recipient Cmty. Svc. award VFW, 1978. Roman Catholic. Avocations: Mexican culture, travel, reading Irish literature. Home and Office: PH Network 132 Tullamore Rd Garden City NY 11530-1139 E-mail. phnetwork@earthlink.net.

HEALY, MARY (MRS. PETER LIND HAYES), singer, actress; b. New Orleans, Apr. 14, 1918; d. John Joseph and Viola (Armbruster) H.; m. Peter Lind Hayes, Dec. 19, 1940 (dec. Apr. 1998); children: Peter Michael, Cathy Lind. Student parochial schs., New Orleans; hon. degree, St. Bonaventure U. With 20th Century Fox, Hollywood, Calif. Author: Twenty-five Minutes from Broadway, 1961; pictures and others, 1937-40; Broadway prodns. Around the World, 1943-46; (with husband) TV series Inside U.S.A, 1949, Peter and Mary Show, Star of the Family, 1952, Peter Lind Hayes Radio show, CBS, 1954-57; Broadway prodn. Who Was That Lady, 1957-58, Peter Lind Hayes show, ABC-TV, 1958-59, Peter and Mary, ABC-Radio, 1959—, Peter and Mary in Las Vegas; TV-film; Star (with husband) WOR radio show, 6 yrs; TV film series Fin. Planning for Women; (with husband) Film The 5000 Fingers of Dr. T, 1953; Appeared in: (with husband) Film Peter Loves Mary, 1960, When Television Was Live, 1975; films: You Ruined My Life, 1986, Looking To Get Out with Jon Voight, 1985. Mem. Pelham Country Club. Roman Catholic. Home: Canyon Gate 8641 Robinson Ridge Dr Las Vegas NV 89117-5807

HEALY, SONDRA ANITA, consumer products company executive; b. 1939; married; 3 children. BFA, Goodman Sch. Drama, 1963; MA, Nat. Coll., 1964. Owner, chair Turtle Wax, Chgo., 1973—. Office: Turtle Wax 5655 S 73rd Ave Chicago IL 60638

HEALY, SONYA AINSLIE, retired health facility administrator; b. Sudbury, Ont., Can., Apr. 7, 1937; arrived in U.S., 1949; d. Walter B. and Wilma A. Scott; m. Richard C. Healty, Jr., Dec. 16, 1961. Diploma, Good Samaritan Hosp., West Palm Beach, Fla., 1958; student, U. Mass., 1963—64, NYU, 1964—66; BS, Boston U., 1969, MS in Med.-Surg. Nursing, 1974. Various staff nursing, charge nurse positions, suprs., med.-surg. and obstet. nursing, 1958—69; chmn. jr.-sr. teaching team Sch. of Nursing Melrose (Mass.) Wakefield Hosp., 1969—73; asst. dir. nurses Boston State Hosp., 1973—74; asst. dir., DON Mt. Zion Hosp. and Med. Ctr., 1974—75; asst. dir. patient care svcs., DON St. Elizabeth's Hosp., Boston, 1975—80, St. Joseph's Hosp., Nashua, NH, 1980—82; adminstr. U. Calif. Med. Ctr., San Diego, 1982—91, corp. chief nursing officer, 1991, assoc. dir. hosp. and clinics, dir. patient care svcs., 1982—93; exec. mgmt. cons. Noyes & Assocs. Ltd., Bainbridge Island, Wash., 1993—. Mem. acad. affairs com., bd. trustees U. San Diego, clin. assoc., 1984—; mem. adj. faculty San Diego State U.; mem. clin. faculty UCLA Sch. of Nursing; presenter in field. Author: The 12-hour Shift: Is It Viable?-Nursing Outlook, 1984, (handbook) Human Resource Management Handbook, 1987, Human Resources Management Handbook, 1987, Nursing Economics, 1989; mem. editl. adv. bd. dirs. OR Nurse Today, 1989—96, editl. rev. Nursing Economics; contbr. articles to profl. jours. Mem.: San Diego Dirs. of Nurses (sec. 1982—83, pres. 1988—89), Calif. Soc. of Nursing Svc. Adminstrs. (task force on orgns. program com. 1984—85, bd. dirs. 1985—87, mem. com. 1987—88, long range planning com.), Mass. Soc. of Nursing Svcs. Adminstrs. (pres. 1977), Am. Orgn. Nurse Execs. (bd. dirs. 1990—92, by-laws com. 1990—92), ASNSA (nominations com. 1978, cert.), Sigma Theta Tau (Zeta Mu chpt.). Avocations: reading, golf.

HEALY, THERESA ANN, former ambassador; b. Bklyn., July 14, 1932; d. Anthony and Mary Catherine (Kennedy) H. BA, St. John's U., 1954, LLD (hon.), 1985. Tchr. elem. and secondary schs., N.Y.C., 1951-55; with U.S. Fgn. Svc., 1955-94, amb. to Sierra Leone, 1980-83; with Ctr. for Internat. Affairs, U. South Fla., Tampa, 1983-84; faculty Nat. Def. U., Washington, 1984-86; with pers. and mgmt. policy bur. U.S. Dept. State, 1986-92; with Office of Freedom of Info., 1992-94; ret., 1994. Cons. Dept. State, 1996—, Office of Freedom Info., 1997—; arbitrator dispute resolution Nat. Assn. Security Dealers, 1999—. Mem. Am. Fgn. Svc. Assn., Diplomatic and Consular Officers Ret. Roman Catholic. Home: 6800 Fleetwood Rd Apt 1002 Mc Lean VA 22101-3610

HEALY-SOVA, PHYLLIS M. CORDASCO, school social worker; b. Newark, Oct. 2, 1939; d. Carl and Mae (Seritella) Cordasco; m. James B. Healy, Dec. 22, 1966 (widowed); m. Peter J. Sova, Aug. 15, 2001. BA, Caldwell Coll., 1978; MS, Columbia U. Sch. Social Work, 1981; MA, Fairleigh Dickinson U., 1989. Cert. social worker, N.Y.; sch. social work specialist; diplomate in clin. social work; qualified clin. social worker; lic. clin. social worker, N.J. Social worker United Cerebral Palsy of North Jersey, East Orange, 1982-84, Cerebral Palsy Assn. Middlesex County, Edison, N.J., 1984-85; sch. social worker, mem. presch. child study team Newark Bd. Edn., 1985-92, social svcs. coord. N.J. Goodstarts prog. curr. svcs., 1992-96; sch. social work specialist Newark Bd. Edn., Office of Early Childhood, 1996—. Cons. in field. Founding mem. sr. citizen ctr. Borough of Caldwell, mem., past chair rent review bd. Recipient Alumna of Yr. award Caldwell Coll., 1985-86, Marion award, 1991, Veritas award, 1999. Mem. AAUW (legis. chair 1982-84), NASW, Nat. Assn. for the Edn. of Young Children, Acad. Cert. Social Workers, Coun. for Exceptional Children (N.J. divsn. early childhood pres. 1992-94, Mideast regional coord. for the internat. divsn. for early childhood 1994-98), Caldwell Coll. Alumni Assn. (scholar chair 1982-87), Columbia U. Alumni Assn. Roman Catholic. Office: Newark Pub Schs 2 Cedar St Newark NJ 07102-3015 Home: 12 Harkey Ct Roseland NJ 07068 E-mail: pandp12horkey@aol.com.

HEANUE, ANNE ALLEN, retired librarian; b. Ft. Oglethorpe, Ga., Feb. 7, 1940; d. James Edward and Mary (Dennean) Allen; m. Kevin E. Heanue, July 20, 1963; children: Mary, Brian, Patricia. BA cum laude, Dunbarton Coll., 1962; MA, Georgetown U., 1966; MS in Libr. Sci., Cath. U. Am., 1976. Libr. Deloitte Haskins and Sells, Washington, 1977-79; asst. to dir. Am. Libr. Assn., Washington, 1979-81, asst. dir., 1981-84, assoc. dir., 1984-98; ret., 1998. Bd. dirs. Alexandria (Va.) LWV, 1967-78; chmn. Alexandria Spl. Edn. adv. com., 1978-79; mem. Alexandria Gypsy Moth Control Commn., 1991-96; vol. White House, 1999—; trustee Freedom to Read Found., 2003—; mem. cancer care com. Inova Alexandria Hosp. Found., 2003—. Recipient Fed. Librs. Round Table Achievement award, 1988. Mem. ALA, Hist. Soc. Washington, D.C., Va. Hist. Soc., Rappahannock Hist. Soc., D.C. Libr. Assn. (bd. dirs. 1994-97), Beta Phi Mu, Pi Gamma Mu. Roman Catholic. Avocations: reading, travel, theater.

HEAP, SYLVIA STUBER, adult education educator; b. Clifton Springs, N.Y., Sept. 25, 1929; d. Stanley Irving and Helen (Hill) Stuber; m. Walker Ratcliffe Heap, June 9, 1951; children: Heidi Anne, Cynthia Joan, Walker Ratcliffe III. BA cum laude, Bates Coll., 1950; postgrad., U. Conn. Sch. Social Work, 1952-54, Boston U. Sch. Social Work, 1953-54, SUNY, Brockport, 1979, SUNY, Potsdam, 1980; MS in Adult Edn., Syracuse U., 1989. Dir. Y-Teens YWCA, Holyoke, Mass., 1950-51; social group worker West Haven (Conn.) Cmty. House, 1951-54; program dir. YWCA, Ann Arbor, 1954-55, part-time, 1955-59; mem. adv. bd. divsn. continuing edn. Jefferson C.C., 1965—, chmn. adv. bd., 1968-98. Pres. Jefferson County Med. Soc. Aux., 1971-72; bd. dirs. St. Lawrence Valley Ednl. TV, 1973-83, sec., 1976-80, treas., 1980-82; v.p., 1982-83, dir. Chem. People Project, 1983; bd. dirs. Watertown Lyric Theatre, 1973-83; bd. dirs. N.Y. State Med. Soc. Aux., 1974-85, 2d v.p. bd., 1979-80; fitness instr. Jefferson Community Coll., Watertown, 1977-86; chmn. health projects N.Y. State Med. Soc. Aux., 1981-85. Named Citizen of Yr., Greater Watertown C. of C., 1975, Friend of C.C., N.Y. State Bd. Trustees, 1988. Mem. AAUW, Bates Key, Alliance with the Jefferson County Med. Soc., Phi Beta Kappa. Unitarian Universalist (UN office envoy 1978—, St. Lawrence dist. envoy 1992—).

HEAPHY, JANIS BESLER, newspaper executive; b. Kalamazoo, Oct. 10, 1951; d. Elvin Julius and Margaret Louise (Throndike) Olson; m. Douglas R. Dern, Aug. 15, 1980 (div. Nov. 1985); m. Robert Thomas Heaphy, Feb. 11, 1989; 1 child, Tanner. BS, Miami U., 1973, MEd, 1976. Tchr. Edgewood Jr. H.S., Seven Mile, Ohio, 1973—75; acct. exec. L.A. Times, 1976—79, sr. acct. exec., 1986—87, ea. mag. mgr., 1987—89, nat. advt. mgr., 1989—92, retail advt. mgr. then sr. v.p.. advt./mktg., 1992—97; acct. exec. L.A. Mag., 1979—82; mgr. L.A. Omni Mag., 1982—86; pub. Sacramento Bee, 1997—. Co-editor: Secrets of the Master Sellers, 1987. Mem.: Advt. Club L.A. Avocations: home decorating, reading, swimming, music. Office: Sacramento Bee PO Box 15779 2100 Q St Sacramento CA 95852*

HEARN, BEVERLY JEAN, secondary education educator, librarian; b. Lexington, Tenn., Sept. 10, 1953; d. James Lawrence and Marie (Sparks) Kee; m. Larry Joseph Hearn, June 15, 1973; children: Matthew Joseph, David Andrew. BA, Union U., 1974; MLS, George Peabody Coll. for Tchrs., 1975; EdD, Memphis State U., 1991. Acqusitions librarian Union U., Jackson, Tenn., 1975-80, reference librarian, 1980-86; tchr. Madison County Bd. Edn., Jackson, 1986—. Instr. Memphis State U., 1990-95, Jackson State C.C., 1992-97; freelance cataloger, 1978-86. Grantee Fulbright Hayes Group Projects Abroad, US govt., 2000, 2002. TESOL, NEA, Internat. Reading Assn., Assn. for Curriculum Devel. Democrat. Baptist. Home: 558 Wallace Rd Jackson TN 38305-2839

HEARN, CYNTHIA ANN, education educator; b. Harrison, Ark., Sept. 6, 1962; d. Raymond Eugene Stills, Ann Etta Stills; m. Jeff Hearn, Aug. 9, 1980; children: Rebekah, Hannah. BA, Harding U., 1982, MEd, 1991; Ednl. Specialist, U. Ark., 2000, DEd, 2002. Cert. ednl. adminstr., Title I Specialist. Educator Harrison Pub. Schs., Harrison, Ark., 1984—2000, Title I Specialist, 2000—02; cons. Hearn and Assocs., Harrison, Ark., 1990—2002. Mem. Harding U. Pres.'s Devel. Coun. Author: (integrated ednl. program) MoveN'Learn, 1998, (ednl. program) KidNews, 1999; contbr. literacy program Camp Read-A-Lot, 2001. Recipient Roy G. Miller award, U. Ark., 2001; grantee, Harrison Pub. Schs. Found., 1998, 1999, Entergy, 2001. Mem.: AAUW, ASCD, NEA, Tchrs. Ark. Students Coun., Nat. Coun. Tchrs. English, Ozark Reading Coun., Internat. Reading Assn., Ark. Reading Assn., Harrison Edn. Assn., Ark. Edn. Assn., Phi Delta Kappa. Avocations: travel, music, literature, hiking, target/skeet. Office: Harrison Pub Schs 500 N Chestnut Harrison AR 72601 Personal E-mail: cynthia@alltel.net.

HEARN, JOYCE CAMP, retired state legislator, educator, consultant; b. Cedartown, Ga. d. J.C. and Carolyn (Carter) Camp; m. Thomas Harry Hearn; children: Theresa Hearn Potts Bailey, Kimberly Ann Johnson, Carolyn Lee Becker. Student, U. Ga.; BA, Ohio State U., 1957; postgrad., U. S.C. Former h.s. tchr.; dist. mgr. U.S. Census, 2d Congl. Dist., 1970; mem. S.C. Ho. of Reps., 1975-89. Asst. minority leader, 1976-78, 86-89; chmn., commn. alcohol beverage control, 1989-91; pres., cons. Hearn & Assocs., Columbia, S.C., 1995—. Mem. Richland County Planning Commn., 1974-76; bd. dirs. Meml. Youth Ctr. and Stage South; chmn. Sexual Assault Awareness Week; vice chmn. Dist. Rep. Com., 1968; Rep. chmn. 2d Congl. Dist., 1969; Rep. chmn. Richland County, 1972; del., platform com. Rep. Nat. Conv., 1980, 84; moderator Kathwood Bapt. Ch., 1979-80, former asst. Sunday Sch. tchr.; bd. dirs. Small Bus. Devel. Ctr., S.C., Columbia Coll. Bd. Vis., Columbia Urban League, Fedn. of Blind; trustee Columbia Mus. Art; apptd. to Alcohol Beverage Control Bd., 1989, apptd. chmn. commn., 1990-92, commr., 1991-94; bd. dirs. Lupus Found., 1990—; chair nat. adv. com. Occupl. Safety and Health, 1980-88. Recipient Outstanding Citizen award Columbia Rape Coalition, 1977, Disting. Svc. award Claims Mgmt. Assn., S.C., 1977, Nat. Fedn. Blind S.C., 1978, Columbia Urban League, 1983, MADD, 1985, Outstanding Legislator of Yr. award Alcohol and Drug Abuse Assn., 1980, Retarded Citizens Assn., 1982, S.C. Rehab. Assn., 1984, S.C. Assn. of Deaf, 1987, Legislator of Yr., Fedn. of Blind, 1988, Disting. Legislator, DAV, 1989; honoree Easter Seals, 1989; numerous other awards. Mem. Nat. Order of Women Legislators (v.p., pres.), Order of the Palmetto, S.C. Women's Club, Columbia Women's Club (bd. dirs.), Larkspur Garden Club.

HEARN, RUBY PURYEAR, foundation executive; b. Winston-Salem, N.C., Apr. 13, 1940; c. Mahlon Tasher H. and Ruby Mae (Hamilton) Puryear; m. Robert W. Hearn, Dec. 30, 1961; children: Janna E., Jennifer L. BA, Skidmore Coll., 1960; MS, Yale U., 1964, PhD, 1969. Postdoctoral rsch. assoc. Yale U., New Haven, 1968-69; dir. content devel. Children's TV Workshop, 1972-76; program officer Robert Wood Johnson Found., Princeton, N.J., 1976-80, sr. program officer, 1980-82, v.p., 1983-96, sr. v.p., 1996—. Trustee Meharry Med. Coll., 1981-86; bd. overseers Dartmouth Med. Sch., 1986-92. Recipient Outstanding Alumnae award Skidmore Coll., 197; Yale Corp. fellow, 1992-98. Fellow Yale Corp.; mem. AAAS, ABA (pub. mem. accreditation com. 1980-82), Inst. Medicine, Ambulatory Pediatric Assn., Periclean Honor Soc., Coun. on Fgn. Rels. Home: 7 Saint Johns Rd Baltimore MD 21210-2121 Office: Robert Wood Johnson Found PO Box 2316 Princeton NJ 08543-2316

HEARN, SHARON SKLAMBA, lawyer; b. New Orleans, Aug. 15, 1956; d. Carl John and Marjorie C. (Wimberly) Sklamba; m. Curtis R. Hearn. BA magna cum laude, Loyola U., New Orleans, 1977; JD cum laude, Tulane U., 1980. Bar: La. 1980, Tex. 1982; cert. tax specialist. Law clk. to presiding judge U.S. Ct. Appeals Fed. Cir., Washington, 1980-81; assoc. Johnson & Swanson, Dallas, 1981-84, The Kullman Firm, New Orleans, 1984—. Recipient Am. Legion award, 1970. Mem. ABA, La. State Bar Assn., Tex. State Bar Assn., Dallas Women Lawyers Assn. Democrat. Roman Catholic. Home: 106 Bordeaux St Metairie LA 70005-4231 Office: The Kullman Firm 1600 Energy Ctr 1100 Poydras St New Orleans LA 70163-1101

HEARNE, CAROLYN FOX, artist, historian, museum director; b. Brownwood, Tex., June 15, 1945; d. Marshal D. and Lena May (Parson) Fox; m. Roy Nicholas Hearne, Apr. 14, 1968; children: Jason Nicholas, Angela Della. BA in Spanish, Art, So. Meth. U., 1967; MA in Fine Arts, U. Tex., Tyler, 1985. Astrology lady, commls. K-BUY Radio, Ft. Worth, 1970-71; decorator, exec. dir. Holiday Inns, Inc., Houston, 1971-73; exec./bilingual sec. Kennecott Copper Corp., Houston, 1973-74; owner Fox-Hearne Studio, Kilgore, Tex., 1977—; art/music, history tchr. LeTourneau U., Longview, Tex., 1988—97; dir. Longview Art Mus., 1997—2000; art/art history tchr. Kilgore (Tex.) Coll., 2000—. Co-chmn. LeTourneau Fine Arts Week, Longview, 1992—; demonstrator, lectr. mus. and art groups, Longview and Tyler, 1979—; judge East Tex. art groups, Longview, Kilgore, and Henderson, 1990—; invited participant Master Artists Workshop, L.I. U., 1990. Prin. works include book cover, Gory Days, 1987, bronze sculpture, Frontier Spirit, 1983 (Citation 1983), sculpture for dedication, Gussie Nell Davis, 1983, commnd. A Race Against Time, 1978 (Spl. award 1978), model for catalogue, TV commls. for Strictly Petites, 1987—; exhbns. incl. Tex. Art Gallery, 1990-92. Bd. dirs. Kilgore Hist. Preservation Found., Kilgore, 1989—, past sec., past pres.; chmn. art fest Kilgore Improvement and Beautification Assn., 1981-86; chmn. Kilgore Civic Ball, 1980; decorator Jr. League Charity Ball, Longview, 1992; pres. Kilgore Garden Club, 1982-83; chmn. Theatre Restoration Kilgore, 1989-92; life mem. Tex. PTA, 1978—; bd. dirs., 1st v.p. Longview Art Mus., 1994—, exhbns. and acquisitions chmn., 1995-97; bd. dirs., chmn. exhbns. and acquisitions Longview Mus. Fine Arts, 2002-. Recipient 5 Citation awards East Tex. Classics, 1981, Outstanding Achievement award Artitudes mag., 1989. Mem. East Tex. Fine Arts Assn. (pres. 1981-83, Top Citation award 1984), Tex. Fine Arts Assn., LeTourneau Faculty Orgn., Coterie Club (pres. 1990). Republican. Presbyterian. Avocations: singing, gardening, cooking, volunteer work. Home: 8 Briar Ln Kilgore TX 75662-2201 Office: Kilgore Coll 1100 Broadway Kilgore TX 75662

HEARON, SHELBY, writer, lecturer, educator; b. Marion, Ky., Mar. 18, 1931; d. Charles Boogher and Evelyn Shelby (Roberts) Reed; m. William Halpern, Aug. 19, 1995; children from previous marriage: Anne Rambo, Reed. BA, U. Tex., 1953. Disting. vis. prof. U. Ill., Chgo., 1993, Colgate U., 1993, U. Miami, Fla., 1994, U. Mass., Amherst, 1994-96, Middlebury Coll., 1996-98. Author: Armadillo in the Grass, 1968, The Second Dune, 1973, Hannah's House, 1975, Now and Another Time, 1976, A Prince of a Fellow, 1978, Painted Dresses, 1981, Afternoon of a Faun, 1983, Group Therapy, 1984, A Small Town, 1985, Five Hundred Scorpions, 1987, Owing Jolene, 1989, Hug Dancing, 1991, Life Estates, 1994, Footprints, 1996, Ella in Bloom, 2001; contbr. articles, short fiction and book revs. to various publs. Pres. Tex. Inst. Letters, 1980; chair lit. panel Tex. Commn. on Arts, 1980; mem. lit. panel N.Y. Coun. on Arts, 1985. Recipient Syndication prize, NEA/PEN, 1984—85, 1985, 1987, 1988, Lit. award, Am. Acad. Arts and Letters, 1990; fellow, Guggenheim, 1982, Nat. Endowment Arts, 1983; grantee, Ingram Merrill, 1987. Mem.: PEN, Associated Writing Programs, Tex. Inst. Letters (Fiction award 1973, 1978), Poets and Writers Inc., Authors Guild. Democrat. Presbyterian. Home: 246 S Union St Burlington VT 05401-4514

HEARTT, CHARLOTTE BEEBE, university official; b. N.Y.C., Nov. 12, 1933; d. Stacey Kile and Charlotte Beebe; m. William Hollis Peirce, 1954 (div. 1960); children: Daniel Converse, William Kile; m. Stephen Heartt, 1962 (div. 1968); children: Thomas Beebe, Sarah Lincoln. BA, Wellesley Coll., 1954. Intern Office of V.p. Richard Nixon, Washington, 1953; asst. Computing Numerical Analysis Lab. U. Wis., Madison, 1954-56; dir. fund raising Boston Arts Festival, 1961; asst. to dean coll. rels. Radcliffe Coll., Cambridge, Mass., 1961-62; sec. to chmn. dept. city planning Harvard U., Cambridge, 1962; Fulbright program adviser, study abroad adviser Brandeis U., 1966-71, dir. office internat. programs, 1971-76, dir. found. and corp. rels., 1976-79; dir. corp. rels., asst. dir. devel. Smith Coll., Northampton, Mass., 1979-81, dir. devel., 1981-95, dir. prin. gifts, 1995-98; ind. cons., 1999—. Mem. Commonwealth Task Force on the Open Univ., 1973; bd. dirs. Coun. on Internat. Ednl. Exch., 1973-77, mem. exec. com., 1975-77; bd. dirs. Boston Area Seminar for Internat. Students, 1973-76; mem. adv. com. New England Colls. Fund, 1981-95; trustee Berkshire Sch., 1989-98, trustee emerita, 1999—; bd. dirs. Hampshire Cmty. United Way, 1996-2000; mem. devel. com. Belmont Day Sch., Belmont, Mass., 2000—, Boston (Mass.) Leadership Gift Cons. Wellesley Coll., 2002—. Mem. Sect. on U.S. Study Abroad (nat. sec., regional rep. 1972-74), Nat. Assn. Fgn. Student Affairs (nat. commr. liaison), Nat. Assn. Women Deans, Adminstrs. and Counselors (internat. students and programs com. 1974-76), Nat. Soc. Fund Raisers, Coun. for Advancement and Support Edn. Home: 11 Carver Rd Wellesley MA 02481-5351 E-mail: heartt@attbi.com.

HEATH, ALICE FAIRCHILD, retired mental health services professional; b. Normal, Ill., Jan. 18, 1931; d. Forrest Clark and Eunice Jane (Dooley) Fairchild; m. Robert Winfield Heath, June 14, 1952; children: Katharine Ann, Nancy Diane. BA in Sociology and Psychology, Ill. Wesleyan U., 1952; postgrad., Jane Addams Sch. Social Work, 1976—77; postgrad., No. Ill. U., 1990—91. Vol. svcs. coord. H.D. Singer Mental Health and Develop. Ctr., Rockford, Ill., 1979—99. Adv. curriculum com. human svc. dept. Rock Valley Coll., 1980—84; adv. com. student svc. learning Rockford Coll., 1993—98; mem. vol. svc. dept. human svc. State of Ill., 1990, policy manual rev. com. dept. human svc., 1995—97; steering com. Conf. Vol. Adminstrs., Ill., 1995—96. Steering com. Rockford Coalition for Homeless, 1985—86; co-chair planning com. Forward Rockford Congress, 1970; mem. Rockford Bd. Edn., 1972—75; mem. United Way, Rock River Valley, 1978—84; bd. dirs. YWCA, 1960—65, 1969—75; pres. Bloom Sch. PTA, Rockford, 1965—67; brownie leader Girl Scouts Am., 1960—66; mem. Winnebago County Bd. Health, 1990—99; co-chair fundraising event Rockford Area Lit. Coun., 1990, 1994; chair No. Ill. Cmty. Health Found., 1999—2001, vice-chair, 2001—; pres. Rockford chpt. Lyric Opera Chgo., 1991—93; steering com. Women's History Week, 1978—79, 1980; mem. Stephen minister Westminster Presbyterian Ch., Rockford, 1995—, former deacon & elder. Mem.: AAUW (edn. chair 1966—68), Ctr. for Learning in Retirement, Archaeology Inst. Am., Rockford Network, League Women Voters (pres. 1969—70), Winnebago-Boone Geneal. Soc., Alabet Temple Daughters of Nile, AARP, Kappa Kappa Gamma. Presbyterian. Avocation: community service. Home: 1017 Lundvall Ave Rockford IL 61107 E-mail: aheath1017@aol.com.

HEATH, ANGELA MARY, academic advisor; b. Detroit, Sept. 23, 1960; d. Robert Barry and Marilyn Ann Heath; 1 adopted child, Alexander Matthew. BS in Sociology cum laude, Ctrl. Mich. U., 1982; MA, Bowling Green State U., 1992. Corp. travel agt. Book Couzens Travel Agy., Southfield, Mich., 1985—87; head mgr. travel project Maritz Travel Co., Livonia, 1987—90; hall dir., Palmer, Davidson Halls Ball State U., Muncie, Ind., 1992—94; acad. advisor U. Mich. Athletic Dept., Ann Arbor, 1995—. Pet therapy Vol. Impact, Southfield, 2001; lectern, commentator St. Francis Cath. Ch., Ann Arbor, 2000—. Mem.: Nat. Assn. Acad. Advisors Athletes, Sigma Kappa (nat. officer 1990—94). Avocations: running, horseback riding, hiking, aerobics, needlecrafts. Office: U Mich Athletic Dept 1000 S State St Ann Arbor MI 48109

HEATH, AUDREY MARY, artist, jewelry designer; b. Providence, Mar. 1, 1956; d. Alfred Peter Venditto, Jr. and Loretta Ann Rice; m. Carmine Imbriglio III, Apr. 16, 1978 (div. July 1981); m. Michael Alfred Heath, May 4, 1998; one child, Michael Alfred II. Grad., C.C. R.I., 1983; BFA, Jewelry Inst. R.I., 1987. Cert. nursing asst. Artist and jewelry designer, R.I., 1987-98. Activity therapist, coord., psychiat. therapist R.I. State Med. Ctr. Pres. Jr. Achivement of R.I. Roman Catholic. Avocations: art, music, jewelry design. Home: 464 Water St Ellsworth ME 04605-2110

HEATH, BERTHANN JONES, education administrator; b. Dallas, May 4, 1938; d. James Lafayette and Allie Mae (Hudson) Jones; m. John Willie Heath, Jr., July 14, 1963 (div. 1975); 1 child, John William, III. BS cum laude, Pepperdine U., 1959; MS, UCLA, 1960. Nat. cert. family and consumer scientist. Tchr., dept. chair LA Unified Sch. Dist., Calif., 1960-69, dist. resource tchr., 1972-75; counselor LA HS, Calif., 1968-72; regional supr., home econ. edn. Calif. State Dept. Edn., 1975-85; program mgr., sch.-to-career transition San Diego City Sch., Calif., 1985-2000; cons., 2000—; owner Berthann's Enterprises, 2000—. Trustee Consumer Credit Counselors of San Diego and Imperial Counties, Calif., 1986-2000; mem. adv. com. Calif. State Dept. Edn. Home Econs. and Health Careers, Sacramento, 1985-98; mem. articulation team SDUSD and San Diego C.C.s, 1987-2000. Author, contbr. to curriculum guides, pamphlets and leaflets. V.p. San Diego chpt. The Links, Inc., 1995-97; presenter TV-8 Looks at Learning and Inside San Diego, 1985-95. Recipient Appreciation/Commendation award Calif. Dept. Edn., 1987, Nat. Gourmet Cook award Nat. Assembly, Links, Inc., 1996, Fin. Literacy Program Svc. award Consumer Credit Counselors of San Diego and Imperial Counties, 1996, Am. Assn. Family and Consumer Scis. Nat. Leader of Yr. award, 1998; named Woman of Distinction, Women, Inc., 1999. Mem. Am. Vocat. Assn. (bylaws chair family and consumer scis. edn. divsn. 1993-97), Nat. Assn. Local Suprs. of Family and Consumer Scis. (pres. 1992-93), Am. Vocat. Assn. (mem. policy and planning com. 1991-97), Calif. Assn. Family and Consumer Scis. (mem. San Diego chpt., chair secondary edn. 1985-95, state chair edn. com. 1989-90, ex-officio mem. articulation com. 1989-96), So. Calif. Biotech. Consortium (charter 1994-96), Links, Inc., Alpha Rho Tau, Delta Sigma Theta, Kappa Omicron Nu, Phi Delta Kappa. Avocations: food design and recipe experimentation, writing, elder care research and development. Office: Berthann's Enterprises PO Box 452934 Los Angeles CA 90045

HEATH, JINGER L. cosmetics executive; b. 1952; Homemaker, 1973-81; part-time interior decorator, cons., 1981; chmn. bd. Beauticontrol Cosmetics Inc., Carrollton, Tex., 1981—. Office: Beauticontrol Cosmetics Inc 2121 Midway Rd Carrollton TX 75006-5039

HEATH, JOSEPHINE WARD, foundation administrator; b. San Jose, Calif., Sept. 5, 1937; d. James Hugh and Adella Ward; m. Stratton Rollins Heath Jr.; children: Stratton, Kristin Heath-Colon, Joel. BS, Ea. Oreg. State U., 1959; MS, U. Wis., 1960. Commr. Boulder (Colo.) County, 1982-90; tchg. fellow John F. Kennedy Sch. of Govt., Harvard U., Cambridge, Mass., 1991; spl. asst. to the dir. White Ho. Office of Nat. Svc., Washington, 1993; pres. Jurismonitor, Boulder, 1993-95; tchr., project liberty John F. Kennedy Sch. Govt., Harvard U., Cambridge, 1994-98; pres. The Cmty. Found., Boulder, 1995—. Tchr. Bad Kreuznach, Germany, 1966-67, El Paso, Tex., 1963-64, Appleton, Wis., 1961-62; regional dir. ACTION, Denver, 1977-79. Editor: Alternative Work Patterns, 1977. Candidate U.S. Senate, Colo., 1992, 1990; commr. Met. Baseball Stadium Dist., Maj. League Colo. Rockies, 1991—; county commr. Boulder County, 1982-90; co-founder Women's Found. of Colo., 1987; trainer for elected offcls. in Ctrl. Europe, 1994-98. Named to Colo. Women's Hall of Fame, 2000; recipient William Funk award for Statewide Cmty. Leadership, Colo. Assn. Non Profits, 2004. Mem. Internat. Women's Forum (bd. dirs. 1986-89), Women's Forum of Colo. (pres. 1991). Democrat. Avocations: skiing, hiking, sports. Home: 2455 Vassar Dr Boulder CO 80305-5728 Office: The Cmty Found 1123 Spruce St Boulder CO 80302-4001 E-mail: JosieHeath@aol.com.

HEATH, MARTHA, state legislator; b. Newport, Vt., Dec. 21, 1946; m. Barry W. Heath; 3 children. BS, U. Vt., 1969. State rep. Vt. Ho. of Reps., 1993—. Active Westford Sch. Bd., Chittenden Ctrl. Sch. Bd.; trustee Camp Thorpe. Address: 342 Rollin Irish Rd Westford VT 05494-9519

HEATHCOTE, DIANA KAY, special education educator; b. Peru, Ind., Nov. 3, 1955; d. David Clark Spangler (dec.), Leland Bruce (Stepfather) and Norma Jean Gossett; m. Francis John Heathcote. BS in Mental Retardation, Ball State U., 1978, MA in Learning Disabilities/Neurologically Impaired, 1983. Tchr. Spl. Needs Logansport (Ind.) Cmty. Sch. Corp., 1978—. Instr. for homebound Logansport (Ind.) Cmty. Sch. Corp., 1983—. Sunday sch. tchr., liturgist, pastor/parish com. chmn. Wheatland Ave. United Meth. Ch., Logansport, 1987—; bd. dirs. Big Brothers/Big Sister, Logansport, 1987—92; tchr. sponsor Students Against Drunk Driving, Logansport, 1987—90; volunteer Special Olympics, Logansport, IN, 1996—now. Mem.: NEA.

HEATHCOTTE, TOBY FESLER, writer, retired educator; d. Howard Dale Fesler and Beulah Mae Crosley; children: Brandon, Brock. MAT, Ind. U., 1968. Lic. tchr. h.s. and coll. Tchr. speech, drama, English Phoenix Union H.S. Dist., 1969—94; writing tchr. Maricopa C.C. Dist., Glendale, Ariz., 1996—2000. Writer, prodr. plays Ariz. State U., Tempe, 1989—93. Author: Program Building: A Practical Guide for High School Speech and Drama Teachers, 2003 (San Diego Book Award, 1994); author: (with Betty Joy) Seeds for Fertile Minds: Eight Curriculum Integration Tools, 1995; author: (fiction) Alison's Legacy, 2000, Lainn's Destiny, 2004, Angie's Promise, 2004, Full Contact, 2004. Contest chair Ariz. Authors Assn., Phoenix, 2000—. Mem.: Inst. Noetic Scis. Unity Ch. Avocations: writing, theater. Home: 6145 W Echo Ln Glendale AZ 85302

HEATH-PSYD, PAMELA B. WASSERMAN, psychologist; b. Queens, N.Y., Nov. 20, 1967; d. Jerry A. and Donna L. Wasserman; m. Jeffrey A. Heath, Nov. 7, 1998; 1 child, Leah Heath. BA magna cum laude, L.I. U., 1989; D of Clin. Psychology, Ill. Sch. Profl. Psychology, 1995. Lic. clin. psychologist Ill., N.Y. Psychologist VA Med. Ctr., Denver, 1995; clin. supr. Greenwood Care, Inc., Evanston, Ill., 1995—97; clin. psychologist Evanston, 1997—99; clin. psychologist, dir. tng., clin. supr. St. Francis Hosp., Evanston, 1999—2000; psychologist Brookville, NY, 2001—. Assoc. faculty mem. Ill. Sch. Profl. Psychology, Rolling Meadows, 1996—99; cons. Greenwood Care, Inc., Evanston, 1995—99, Denver, 1993, Chgo., 92. Mem.: APA, N.Y. Psychol. Assn., Psi Chi. Republican. Jewish. Avocations: tennis, swimming. Office: 4 Quaker Ridge Rd Glen Head NY 11545*

HEATON, JANET NICHOLS, artist, art gallery director; b. Miami, Fla., May 27, 1936; d. Wilmer Elwood and Katherine Elizabeth (Rodgers) Nichols; children: Benjamin Nichols Heaton, Nancy Elizabeth Breedlove. Student, Fla. State U., 1954-56. Artist Heaton's Studio & Gallery, Lake Park, Fla., 1976—, dir., 1979—. One woman show Comercia Bank Trust, Palm Bch. Gardens, Fla., 1999; Exhibited in group shows at Leigh Yawkey Woodson Art Mus., Wausau, Wis., 1988-89, 91-93, 95-97, 99, Norton Gallery Art, West Palm Beach, Fla., 1989, 92, Mt. Kenya Safari Club, Kenya, East Africa, 1989, 92, Prestige Gallery, Toronto, Can., 1989, Kimball Art Ctr., Park City, Utah, 1990-91, Grand Cen. Gallery, N.Y.C., 1990, Gallery Fine Arts, Ft. Myers, Fla., 1990, Cornell Fine Art Mus., Winter Park, Fla., 1990, Cen. Park Zoo Gallery, N.Y.C., 1991, The Art League Marco Island, Fla., 1993, 96, Washington State Hist. Soc. Mus., Tacoma, 1993, Old Sch. Sq. Cultural Arts Ctr., Delray Beach, Fla., 1993, 94, The Salmagundi Club, N.Y.C., 1994, J.N. Bartfield Galleries, N.Y.C., 1994, Pt. Royal Gallery, Naples, Fla., 1994, Brookfield Zoo, Chgo., 1994, Ward Mus. Wildfowl Art, Salisbury, Md., 1995, Easton (Md.) Waterfowl Festival, 1995, Sarasota (Fla.) Visual Art Ctr., 1995, Shenandoah Art Ctr., North Wainsboro, Va., 1996, Village Gallery, Venice, Fla., 1997, The Hiram Blauvelt Art Mus., Oradell, N.j., The Mus. of Hounds and Hunting, Leesburg, Va., 1997, Nat. Arts Club Grand Gallery, N.Y.C., 1997, Fort Hayes Met. Edn. Ctr., Columbus, Ohio, 1997, Nat. Arts Club, N.Y.C., 1997, Leigh Yawkey Woodson Art Mus., Wausau, 1997, Wendell Gilley Mus., Southwest Harbour, Maine, 1996, Tampa (Fla.) Mus. Art, 1998, Village Gallery, Venice, Fla., 1998, 99, Disney's Animal Kingdom, Orlando, 1998, Smithsonian Instn.'s Conservation & Rsch. Ctr. & Noah's Network, Front Royal, Va., 1998, 99, Comercia Bank Trust, Palm Bch. Gardens, 1998, The Nature Gallery, West Boylston, Mass., 1998, Mus. Sci. and Scpace Transit Planetarium, Miami, 1998, Ambleside Gallery, Groose Points, Mich., Bigfork Art & Cultural Ctr., Bigfork, Mont., 1998, Holland and Holland Function, N.Y.C., 1999, Leigh Yawkey Woodson Art Mus., Wausau, Wis., 1999, John L. Wehle Gallery at Genesee County Mus., Mumford, Fla., 1999, Cleve. Mus. Natural Hist., Cleve., 1999, Comerica Bank & Trust, Palm Beach Gardens, Fla., 2000, Leigh Yawkey Woodson Art Museum, Wausau, Wisc., 2000-03, Feline Fine: Art of Cats Exhibition Tour, The Arts and Science Ctr., Pine Bluff, AR, 2002, Jouh D. MacArthur Beach State Park, North Plam Beach, Fla., 2003; numerous others; numerous exhbns. including most recently John D. MacArthur Beach State Pk., North Palm Beach, Fla., 2003, Ackley Hall Mus. Natural History, N.Y., 2003, Hiram Blauvelt Art Mus., Oradell, N.J., 2003, Geoffrey C. Smith Galleries, Stuart, Fla., 2003; represented in permanent collections Leigh Yawkey Woodson Art Mus., State House, Nairobi, Kenya, PGA Nat., Palm Beach Gardens, Fla., also numerous pvt. collections; subject numerous art jours.; represented by J.N. Bartfield Gallery, N.Y.C. Mem. Soc. Animal Artists (signature), Pastel Soc. Am. (signature), Fla. Watercolor Soc. (signature), Outdoor Writers Assn. Am., Catherine Lorillard Wolfe Art Club (signature). Avocation: photography. Office: Heatons Studio and Gallery 1169 Old Dixie Hwy Lake Park FL 33403-2311

HEATON, KATHLEEN HOGE, realtor; b. Flint, Mich., Mar. 3, 1948; d. Paul L. and Isabel Evelyn (Martin) Hoge; m. Joel Brion Heaton, Sept. 14, 1968; children: Paul Brion, Todd Erin. Student, Ohio U., 1966-67, U. Hawaii, 1969; grad., Realtors Inst. Va., 1987. Cert. residential specialist, 1991; lic. broker assoc., Va., 1990; cert. residential broker. Pub. rels. specialist USN Commissary and Exch., Pearl Harbor, Hawaii, 1969-71; asst. configuration mgr. Ball Rsch. Corp., Boulder, Colo., 1972; realtor assoc. Welbourne & Purdy Realty, Saratoga Springs, N.Y., 1979-82, Nancy Chandler Assocs., Norfolk, Va., 1982—2002. Bd. dirs. Little Theatre

Norfolk, 1985-90; mem. Maltese Cross Circle Children's Hosp. of Kings Daus., Norfolk, 1982-2002; pres. Lochhaven Civic League, 1998-2002; . Mem. Greater Hampton Rds. Realtors Assn. (mem. cir. excellence, 1995-2003, mem. grievance com., 2003), Navy League U.S. (treas. Norfolk Women's Coun. 1987-90), Lochhaven Civic League. Republican. [illegible] golf, bridge, travel. Home: 7451 Muirfield Rd Norfolk VA 23505-1753 Office: Nancy Chandler Assocs 701 W 21st St Norfolk VA 23517-1920 E-mail: kheaton@nancychandler.com.

HEATON, PATRICIA, actress; b. Cleve., Mar. 4, 1959; d. Chuck and Pat Heaton; m. David Hunt, 1992; 4 children BA in Theater, Ohio State U., 1980. Actress playing Debra Barone on Everybody Loves Raymond CBS-TV, 1996—. Appearances include (TV series) Room for Two, 1992-93, Someone Like Me, 1994, Women of the House, 1995, Everybody Loves Raymond, 1996— (Best Actress in Quality Comedy Viewers for Quality TV award 1998, Outstanding Lead Actress in Comedy Series Emmy award, 2000 and 2001); (TV episodes) Alien Nation, 1989, thirtysomething, 1990, (TV movie) Shattered Dreams: The Charlotte Fedders Story, 1990, (films) Beethoven, 1992, Memoirs of an Invisible Man, 1992, The New Age, 1994, Space Jam, 1996, (stage) The Johnstown Vindicator, 1987, Don't Get God Started, 1987-88, Miracle in the Woods, 1997, author (book): Motherhood and Hollywood, 2003. Hon. chairperson Feminists for Life. Recipient Emmy Award, 2000, 2001. Office: Internat Creative Mgmt 8942 Wilshire Blvd Beverly Hills CA 90211-1934

HEATWOLE, MARY PHYLLIS, lawyer; d. Mark Marion and Sarah Collier Heatwole. BA, Washington & Lee U., 1998; JD, Boston Coll., 2001. Bar: Mass. 2002, D.C. 2003. Assoc. Howrey Simon Arnold & White, Washington, 2001—03. Mem.: ABA, Mass. Bar, D.C. Bar. Home: 1322 N Wakefield St Arlington VA 22207

HEBEL, DORIS A. astrologer; b. Chgo., Jan. 1, 1935; d. Erich and Anna Dorothea (Hircy) H.; m. Leon L. Bram, Apr. 29, 1961 (div. Dec. 1973); 2 children. Libr. Campbell-Mithun, Chgo., 1958-61, Kenyon & Eckhardt, Chgo., 1961-64; pres. Astro-Technic Forecasting, Chgo., 1965—. Author: Contemporary Lectures, 1975, Celestial Psychology, 1985; contbr. various articles in astrological jours. and magazines. Mem. Am. Fedn. Astrologers (life), Nat. Coun. for Geocosmic Rsch. (life, nat. bd. dirs. 1975-80), Nat. Astrol. Soc., Assn. for Astrol. Networking, Internat. Soc. for Astrol. Rsch. Avocations: reading, singing, walking, metaphysical subjects, arts. Home and Office: 150 W Maple St Apt 1518 Chicago IL 60610-5433

HEBENSTREIT, JEAN ESTILL STARK, religion educator, practitioner; d. Charles Dickey and Blanche (Hervey) Stark; m. William J. Hebenstreit, Sept. 4, 1942; children: James B., Mark W. Student Conservatory of Music, U. Mo. at Kansas City, 1933-34; AB, U. Kans., 1936. Authorized C.S. practitioner, Kansas City, 1955—; bd. dirs. 3d Ch., Kansas City, 1952-55, chmn. bd., 1955, reader, 1959-62; authorized C.S. tchr. C.S. Bd., 1964—, bd. dirs., 1977-83, chmn., 1981—82. Mem. Christian Sci. Bd. of Lectureship, Christian Sci. Bd. Edn.; bd. trustees The Christian Sci. Pub. Soc., bd. dirs. First Ch. Christ.Scientist, 1977-83, chmn., 1981-82. Contbr. articles to C.S. lit. Pres. Mother Ch., The First Ch. of Christ, Scientist, 1999. Mem. Art of Assembly Parliamentarians (charter, 1st pres.), Pi Epsilon Delta, Alpha Chi Omega (past pres.), Carriage Club. Home: 310 W 49th St Ste A-2 Kansas City MO 64112-2425 Office: 310 W 49th St Apt A-3 Kansas City MO 64112-2425

HEBERLEIN, ALICE LATOURRETTE, healthcare educator, physical education educator, coach; b. L.A., Mar. 7, 1963; d. Louis and Jean Marie LaTourrette; m. Dave Heberlein, Mar. 20, 1993. BA, Idaho State U., 1985, MA, 1987. Tchr., coach Pocatello (Idaho) H.S., 1985—93; head women's volleyball coach Idaho State U., Pocatello, 1993—95; tchr., coach Pocatello H.S., 1995—99, Century H.S., Pocatello, 1999—, chair health dept., 2001—, chair phys. edn. dept., 2003—. Mem. nursing adv. bd. Vo-Tech H.S., Pocatello, 1995—2001; bd. dirs. Idaho Tennis Assn., Boise, 1998—99. Named Coach of Yr., Idaho H.S. Activity Assn., 1990—91, Jour. Coach of Yr., Idaho State Jour., 1999, Region 5 Coach of Yr., 1986—87, 1989—90, 1991—2000, Region 4-5-6 Coach of Yr., 2001. Mem.: Pocatello Edn. Assn. Achievements include coaching volleyball teams, 1989, H.S. state champions, 1990, 4th pl. State of Idaho, 2000, 2d pl. State of Idaho, 2001. Avocations: cross country skiing, hiking, tennis, snow shoeing, skate skiing. Home: 2934 Silverwood Pl Pocatello ID 83201 Office: Century HS 7801 Diamondback Dr Pocatello ID 83204

HEBERT, JANICE ELAINE, lawyer; b. Morgan City, La., Jan. 16, 1957; d. Earl Joseph and Nelwyn Elaine (Shepherd) H.; m. Arthur Joseph Cormier III, Oct. 2, 1987; children: Stephan Williams, Carlin Anne, Lillian Elaine. BA, U. Southwestern La., 1987; JD, La. State U., 1990. Bar: La., U.S. Ct. Appeals (5th cir.), U.S. Dist. Ct. (we. dist.) La. Law clerk Hon. Michael J. McNulty 16th J.D.C., La., 1990-92; sr. law clerk Hon. Richard T. Haik U.S. Dist. Ct., 1992-95; asst. U.S. atty. we. dist. La. U.S. Atty.'s Office, Lafayette, 1995—2002; atty. adv. and program coord. Exec. Office for U.S. Atty., Washington, 2002—03. Mem. faculty enhanced negotiations/mediation advocacy seminars U.S. Dept. Justice, 1996—; bd. dirs. Lafayette (La.) Pub. Libr. Found. Recipient John Marshall Alternate Dispute Resolution award U.S. Atty. Gen. Janet Reno, 1996. Mem.: Lafayette (La.) Parish Bar Assn. (bd. dirs.), Girl Scouts (Bayou coun. bd. dirs.). Office: US Attys Office 800 Lafayette St Ste 2000 Lafayette LA 70501-6942

HEBERT, KATHLEEN, information technology executive; Cons. Boston Cons. Group, Boston; from intern to corp. v.p. Microsoft, Redmond, Wash., 1988—2001, corp. v.p., 2001—. Office: One Microsoft Way Redmond WA 98052-6399

HEBERT, MARY OLIVIA, retired librarian; b. Nov. 11, 1921; d. Arthur Frederick and Clara Marie (Golden) Meyer; m. N. Hal Hebert, Sept. 9, 1943 (dec. Mar. 1969); children: Olivia, Stephen (dec. 1989), Christina, Deborah (dec. 1999), Beth, John, James. Secretarial positions in advt., 1942-43; v.p. Hebert Advt. Co., 1955-66; adminstrv. asst. comms. Blue Cross, St. Louis, 1966-69, libr., 1969-91; ret., 1991. Part-time archivist Cathedral Basilica of St. Louis, 1999. Mem. Spl. Librs. Assn. (pres. St. Louis Metro chpt. 1984), St. Louis Med. Librs., St. Louis Regional Libr. Network (coun. 1986-89). Roman Catholic.

HECETA, ESTHERBELLE AGUILAR, anesthesiologist; b. Cebu City, Philippines, Jan. 1, 1935; came to U.S., 1962, naturalized, 1981; d. Serafin Aquilar and Elsie (Nichols) Aguilar; m. Wilmer G. Heceta, Apr. 5, 1962; children: W. Cristina, W. Elgine, Wuela E. BS in Chemistry cum laude, Silliman U., Dumaguete City, Philippines, 1955, BS cum laude, 1956; MD cum laude, U. East Ramon Magsaysay, Quezon City, Philippines, 1961. Diplomate Am. Bd. Anesthesiology, Philippine Bd. Anesthesiology. Intern Youngstown (Ohio) Hosp. Assocs., 1962-63, resident in anesthesiology, 1963-66; anesthesiologist Salem (Ohio) City Hosp., 1967, St. Joseph's Hosp., Manapla, Philippines, 1967-72; instr. dept. anesthesiology U. Tenn., Memphis, 1972-74; staff anesthesiologist Ohio Valley Med. Ctr., Wheeling, W.Va., 1974—, Bellaire (Ohio) City Hosp., 1975—, East Ohio Regional Hosp., Martins Ferry, 1989—. Jt. conf. com. for profl. affairs, exec. com., sec.-treas. med. dental staff Ohio Valley Med. Ctr., 1992-96, pres.-elect, 1993-94, pres. med. dental staff, 1994-95; physician reviewer Anesthesiology W.Va. Med. Inst., 1992-96. Claims rev. panel W.Va. Med. Assn., 1990-95; vol. med.-surg. mission to Philippines, 1982-90. Fellow Am. Coll. Anesthesiology; mem. AMA, Am. Soc. Anesthesiologists, Ohio Valley Phillipine Med. Assn. (pres. 1988-90), Tri-State Phillipine-Am. Assn. (pres. 1991-92), Assn. Philippine Physicians in Am., Philippine Soc. Anesthesiologists in Am., W.Va. Soc. Anesthesiologists, Internat. Anesthesia Rsch. Soc., Am. Med. Womens Assn. (organizer, pres. 1983, regional gov. region IV 1987-89), W.Va. Med. Soc., Ohio County Med. Soc. Presbyterian. Home and Office: 15 Holly Rd Wheeling WV 26003-5656

[illegible] [illegible] Aurora, Ohio, May 2[illegible], 1969; d. Donald Heche; m. Coley Laffoon, 2001, 1 child. Appearances include (film) An Ambush of Ghosts, 1993, The Adventures of Huck Finn, 1993, A Simple Twist of Fate, 1994, Milk Money, 1994, I'll Do Anything, 1994, The Wild Side, 1995, Pie in the Sky, 1995, Walking and Talking, 1996, The Juror, 1996, Volcano, 1997, Donnie Brasco, 1997, Wag the Dog, 1997, I Know What You Did Last Summer, 1997, Return to Paradise, 1998, Six Days Seven Nights, 1998, Psycho, 1998, The Third Miracle, 1999, Auggue Rose, 2000, Prozac Nation, 2001, John Q., 2002, Timepiece, 2003; (TV movies) O Pioneers!, 1992, Girls in Prison, 1994, If These Walls Could Talk, 1996, Wild Side, 1996, One Kill, 2000, Gracie's Choice, 2004, (TV series) Another World, 1988-92, Murphy Brown, 1991-92, Ally McBeal, 2001 (TV spls.) Soap Opera Digest, 1989, The 16th Ann. Daytime Emmy Awards, 1989, (stage) Getting Away with Murder, 1991-92, (Broadway plays) Proof, 2002-03, Twentieth Century, 2004- (Tony nom. best actress in a play, 2004); author autobiography Call Me Crazy, 2001. Recipient Emmy award Another World.*

HECHT, MARION B. mental health counselor, mental health therapist; b. Bklyn., Nov. 21, 1966; d. Herman and Selma Sonnenblick; m. Ronald J. Hecht; 1 child, Henry. MA, Goddard Coll., Plainfield, Vt., 1991; postgrad., Goddard Coll., 1998, Hofstra U., U. Minn., U. Iowa, Montclair State U. Lic. profl. counselor, N.J., D.C.; registered art therapist Am. Art Therapy Assn.; cert. guidance counselor, tchr. of handicapped, N.J. Dept.Edn.; cert. cognitive behavioral therapist Nat. Assn. Cognitive Behavioral Therapists. Mental health specialist, gerontologist Bay Ridge Ctr. for Older Adults, Bklyn., 1989-90; art therapist, mental health therapist Rockaway Mental Health Svcs., Far Rockaway, N.Y., 1990-91, Coney Island Hosp., 1991—93; pvt. practice No. N.J. Counseling Svcs., 1996—; tchr. home instrn., spl. edn. Montclair & South Orange (N.J.) Pub. Schs., 1997-2000. Mem.: NJ Counseling Assn., NJ Mental Health Counselors Assn. Avocations: sports, reading, computer, drawing. Office: 15 Village Plaza South Orange NJ 07079 Office Fax: 973-597-1357. E-mail: rhecht2258@aol.com.

HECHT, MARJORIE MAZEL, editor; b. Cambridge, Mass., Dec. 21, 1942; d. Mark and Theresa (Shuman) Mazel; m. Laurence Michael Hecht, July 2, 1972 BA cum laude, Smith Coll., 1964; postgrad., London Sch. Econs., 1964-65; MSW, Columbia U., 1967. Dir. Forest Neighborhood Service Ctr., N.Y.C., 1967-70, Wiltwyck Sch. for Boys, Bronx Center, N.Y., 1970-73; mng. editor Fusion Mag., Washington, 1977-87, 21st Century Sci. & Technol. Mag., Washington, 1987—; sci. editor Exec. Intelligence Rev., Washington, 1997—. Co-author: Beam Defense: An Alternative to Nuclear Destruction, 1983 (Aviation and Space Writers award 1983); editor: Colonize Space! Open the Age of Reason, 1985, The Holes in the Ozone Scare: The Scientific Evidence That the Sky Isn't Falling, 1992. Press rep. LaRouche Campaign, N.Y.C., 1984 Democrat. Jewish. Avocation: astronomy. Office: 21st Century Sci & Technol Mag PO Box 16285 Washington DC 20041-6285 Office Phone: 703-777-7473. E-mail: tcs@mediasoft.net.

HECK, DEBRA UPCHURCH, information technology, procurement professional; b. Valparaiso, Fla., Nov. 4, 1956; d. Robert P. and Sallaine S. (Sledge) Upchurch; m. Robert J. Heck, May 31, 1980; children: Andrew W., Jennifer A. BS in Math., Purdue U., 1978, MS in Mgmt., 1980. Analyst mgmt. sci. Monsanto Corp. Mgmt. Sci., St. Louis, 1980-81; sys. analyst Monsanto Agr. Group, St. Louis, 1981-82, sr. sys. analyst, 1982-84; sr. analyst mgmt. sci. Monsanto Polymer Products Group, St. Louis, 1984-86; total quality fundamentals instr. Monsanto Co., St. Louis, 1985-86; project mgr. Monsanto Chem. Co., St. Louis, 1986-88; group leader Monsanto Corp. MIS, St. Louis, 1988-92, sr. group leader, 1992-95; info. tech. dir. Monsanto Bus. Svcs. Fin. & Procurement, St. Louis, 1995—97, dir. strategic sourcing procurement strategic initiatives, 1997—2000; exec. dir. global procurement Pharmacia, St. Louis, 2000—03; exec. dir. global sourcing Pfizer, 2003—04. Trustee, chair fall gathering, doubles, social com. Ethical Soc., St. Louis, 1982—; mem. sci. adv. com., PTO bd. Parkway Sch. Dist., St. Louis, 1992—; vol. St. Louis Assn. for Retarded Citizens, 1978-85. Recipient Leader award, YWCA Monsanto Corp., 1999. Mem. Nat. Assn. Purchasing Mgmt., Human Resource Sys. Profls., Leadership Am. Alumni (award 1994), Winning Women. Avocations: travel, sports, friends, family. Personal E-mail: debrauheck@aol.com.

HECK, MELISSA EILEEN, speech pathology/audiology services professional; b. New Hyde Park, N.Y., Jan. 19, 1975; d. Barry and Susan P. Heck. BA, Hofstra U., Hempstead, N.Y., 1997; MA in Speech Pathology, Hofstra U., 1999, MA in Audiology, 2001; candidate audiology, Pa. Coll. Optometry. Lic. speech and audiology N.Y. State. Speech pathologist Kessler Rehab., L.I., 2000—02; audiologist Park Ave. Acoustics, N.Y.C., 2000—02; speech pathologist, audiologist N.Y. Speech and Hearing, N.Y.C., 2001—; speech pathologist Mt. Sinai Hosp.-Elmhurst Ctr., NY, 2002—; chief speech pathology/audiology Wyckoff Hts. Med. Ctr., Bklyn., 2002—. Recipient Rsch. award, Saltzman Cmty. Svc. Ctr., 1999. Fellow: Am. Acad. Audiology; mem.: N.Y. State Speech and Hearing Assn., Am. Speech and Hearing Assn. (Award for Continuing Edn. 2002), Phi Beta Kappa. Avocations: fitness training, singing, dance, public speaking. Office: New York Speech and Hearing 200 E 15th St New York NY 10003

HECK, ROSE, state legislator; m. Raymond Heck; children: Nancy, Laury, Rosemary, Suzan. Attended, Seton Hall U. Assemblywoman dist. 38 N.J. State Assembly. Joint edn. com. N.J. State Assembly, regulated profl. com., past chair sr. citizens & social svc. com., environ com., chair joint adv. coun. women; mng. editor Hasbrouck Heights Publ. Co. Recipient alumna award Acad. Sacred Heart; named citizen of yr. Hasbrouck Heights Men's Assn. Mem. N.J. Press Assn., Hasbrouck C. of C., Lodi C. of C. Home: 2 Mercer St Ste 5A Lodi NJ 07644-1601

HECKEL, SALLY, independent filmmaker; b. Rochester, N.Y., Sept. 26, 1945; d. George Philip and Ethel Morley (Gage) H. MFA in Film, NYU, 1973. Ind. filmmaker, 1973—. Producer, adaptor, dir. editor: (film) A Jury of Her Peers, 1980 (Acad. Award nom. Best Dramatic Live-Action Short, 1981, Blue Ribbon Am. Film Festival 1981, Cine Golden Eagle 1981, Australian Tchrs. of Media award, 1982, Best Dramatic Film, Santa Fe Film Expo Judges award Sinking Creek Film Celebration 1982, Chris award Columbus Film Festival 1982, Best Language Arts Film Birmingham Internat. Edn. Film Festival 1982); prodr., dir., animator, editor: (film) The Bent Tree, 1979 (Judges award Sinking Creek Film Celebration 1980, Cine Golden Eagle 1980); co-dir., cinematographer, editor: (film) It's Not A One Person Thing, 1977 (Judges award Sinking Creek Film Celebration 1977); prodr., writer, dir., editor: (film) Ordinary Days, 1974 (Silver Hugo award Chgo. Internat. Film Festival 1974, 1st prize for narrative film womanview 1974, Judges award Wash. Nat. Student Film Festival 1974, Directing and Cinematography awards N.Y.U. Film Festival 1974, Cine Golden Eagle 1974). Recipient Abraham Schneider award N.Y.U. Grad. Inst. Film/TV, 1972, Leo Jaffe award, 1972, Film Prodn. awards N.Y.S. Coun. for the Arts, 1982, 86, 89; Post-Grad. Fellow in Film grant NYU Nat. Endowment For the Arts with NYU Grad. Inst. Film/TV, 1975; Artist grant Creative Artists Pub. Svc. N.Y.S. Coun. for the Arts, 1975, Film Prodn. grant Women's Fund-Joint Found. Support, 1977, Film Prodn. grant Beard's Fund & Cowan Found., 1978-80, Ind. FIlmmaker grant Am. Film Inst., 1981, Film Prodn. grantee Jerome Found., 1982, Film Prodn. grant Nat. Endowment For the Arts, 1990. Avocations: reiki, walking, reading, bicycle riding, mixed media art. Home: 52 E 1st St New York NY 10003-9391

HECKLER, MAUREEN KELLY, nursing home administrator; b. N.Y.C., Aug. 5, 1961; d. Henry James and Eileen (Kelly) Humphreys. BA in Psychology, Villanova U., 1983. Lic. nursing home adminstr.; cert. Am. Coll. Healthcare Adminstrs. [illegible] Manor, Inc., 1983-84, adminstr., 1984-85, Roslyn (Pa.) Nursing & Rehab., 1985-88; exec. adminstr. GraceCare, Inc., Plymouth Meeting, Pa., 1988—. Vol. Am. Cancer Soc. (Phila. divsn.). Mem. Am. Coll. Health Care Adminstrs. (cert.), Pa. Health Care Assn. (sec. 1985, 86, 88), Am. Coll. Health Care Execs., Villanova Alumni Assn. (sec. 1989-90), Soveregn Mil. Order. of the Knights of Malta Am. Assn. (exec. com.), Lourdes Pilgrimage Auxillary of Knights of Malta (co-chair). Republican. Roman Catholic. Avocations: travel, golf, reading, collecting historical memorabilia and autographs. Office: GraceCare Inc 2644 Bristol Rd Warrington PA 18976-1404

HECKMAN, CAROL A. biology educator; b. East Stroudsburg, Pa., Oct. 18, 1944; d. Wilbur Thomas and Doris (Betts) H. BA, Beloit (Wis.) Coll., 1966; PhD, U. Mass., Amherst, 1972. Rsch. assoc. Yale U. Sch. Medicine, New Haven, 1973-75; staff mem. Oak Ridge (Tenn.) Nat. Lab., 1975-82; adj. assoc. prof. U. Tenn.-Oak Ridge Biomed. Grad. Sch., 1980-82; assoc. prof. Bowling Green (Ohio) State U., 1982-86, prof. biology, 1986—. Cons. NSF, Washington, 1977-80, NIH, Rockville, Md., 1996-98; dir. EM facility Bowling Green State U., 1982—; NSF trainee, Amherst, 1967-70; vis. prof. Univ. Coll. London. Contbr. articles to profl. jours., chpts. to books. Internat. Cancer Rsch. Tech. fellow Internat. Union Against Cancer, 1980, Heritage Found. fellow, 1982, guest rsch. fellow, Uppsala, Sweden, 1989-90; grantee NSF, 1981-84, 90-92, NIH, 1987-88, 98-2001, Dept. of Def., 2000-02. Mem. AAAS, Am. Soc. Cell Biology, Microscopy Soc. Am., N.W. Ohio Microscopy (sec.-treas. 1986-90, pres. 1990-94), Soc. In Vitro Biology, Mid-Am. Drug Devel. (pres. 1999), Ohio Acad. Sci., Sigma Xi. Episcopalian. Achievements include research evaluation and development of in vitro anticarcinogens. Home: 861 Ferndale Ct Bowling Green OH 43402-1609 Office: Bowling Green State U Dept Biol Scis Bowling Green OH 43403-0001

HECKMAN, CAROL E. lawyer; b. Clinton, Iowa, Oct. 18, 1952; children: Tyler, Ethan. BA magna cum laude, Lawrence Univ., Wis., 1974; JD magna cum laude, Cornell Law Sch., 1977. Bar: N.Y., U.S. Supreme Ct., U.S. Tax Ct., U.S. Dist. Ct. (we. dist.) N.Y. Law clk. to Chief Judge John T. Curtin U.S. Dist. Ct. (we. dist.) N.Y., Buffalo, 1977-79, asst. U.S. atty., 1981-85, magistrate judge, 1992-2000; trial atty. Dept. of Justice, Civil Rights Div., D.C., 1979-81; assoc. Albrecht, Maguire, Heffern & Gregg, P.C., Buffalo, 1985-86, ptnr., 1986-89, Lippes, Kaminsky, Silverstein, Mathias & Wexler, Buffalo, 1989-92, Harter Secrest & Emery, 2000—. Mem. adv. com. for adminstrv. office U.S. Cts., 1996-99. Bd. dirs. Children's Hosp. Buffalo, 1995-97; mem. steering com., trustee Coun. Kaleide Hosp., 1997—; mem. adv. coun. Cornell U. Law Sch., 1997-2000; bd. dirs. Candle Beech Camp. Recipient Farley prize in philosophy Lawrence Univ., Fraser prize for outstanding scholarship and character Cornell Law Review, Achievement award N.Y. State Women's Bar Assn., 1992. Mem. Nat. Assn. Women Judges, Fed. Magistrate Judges Assn. (sec. 1996-97, treas. 1997-98, 2d v.p. 1998-99, 1st v.p. 1999-2000), Erie County Bar Assn., Women's Bar Assn. of the State of N.Y., Women Lawyers of We. N.Y., N.Y. State Bar Assn., Nat. Assn. of Women Judges. Office: One HSBC Ctr Ste 3350 Buffalo NY 14203-2884

HECKMAN, JYOTSNA (JO) L. bank executive; married; 2 children. With Denali State Bank, Fairbanks, Alaska, 1986—, pres., CEO, 2003—. Named One of 25 Women to Watch, U.S. Banker Mag., 2003. Office: Denali State Bank 119 N Cushman PO Box 74568 Fairbanks AK 99707-4568*

HECKMAN, LUCY T. librarian; b. Queens, N.Y., June 9, 1954; d. Charles and Ruth Heckman. BA in English, St. John's U., Jamaica, N.Y., 1976, MLS in Libr. Info. Sci., 1977; MBA, Adelphi U., 1981. Catalog libr. St. John's U. Libr., Jamaica, 1977—82, reference libr., 1982—2001, head reference, 2002—. Author: Franchising in Business, 1989, The New York Stock Exchange, 1992, Nasdaq, 2001, Damascus, 2004. Mem.: ALA (sec. bus. ref. and svcs. sect. 1998—2000), Beta Phi Mu. Avocations: photography, antiques. Home: 100-50 223 St Queens Village NY 11429

HEDDENS, LISA, state official; b. Rochester, Minn., June 6, 1964; AS, Des Moines Area C.C.; BS, Iowa State U. Cons.; family support coord.; disability rights advocate; substitute tchr.; state rep., 2003—. Mem. health and human svcs. appropriations subcom.; mem. pub. safety standing com.; mem. environ. protection standing com.; mem. human resources standing com. Leader Girl Scouts Am.; bd. dirs. Arc of Story County, Westory Vol. Fire Dept. Office: State Capitol E !2th and Grand Des Moines IA 50319

HEDGECOCK, JANE CLARKSON, secondary school educator; b. New Paltz, N.Y., Oct. 10, 1951; d. Robert Nelson and Laura Dawson Clarkson; m. Samuel Moore Hedgecock Jr., June 26, 1971; children: Greyson L., Pannill M., Hunter N. B in Architecture, Va. Polytechnic Inst. and State U., 1974; MS in Reading Edn., Old Dominion U., 2000. Registered architect, Va., 1980; lic. tchr. Va., 1995. Arch. project mgr. Morrisette, Cederquist, Bondurant, Norfolk, Va., 1976—81; architect Hargrove, Brockwell & Assoc., Va. Beach, Va., 1982—83; pvt. practice architect Norfolk, 1989—91; history tchr. Norfolk Collegiate Sch., Norfolk, 1997—. Leader Girl Scouts, Norfolk, 1985—99; vol. Norfolk Emergency Shelter Team, Norfolk, 1990—. Fellow, Va. Ctr. Tchg. Internat. Studies, 2002. Mem.: Nat. Coun. History Edn., Va. State Reading Assn., Internat. Reading Assn. Avocations: camping, reading.

HEDGES, JULIE ELAINE, photographer; b. Columbus, Ga., Jan. 22, 1974; d. Jerry Mitchell and Edith Lyle Ludy; m. Cary Shon Hedges, Oct. 21, 1995. Student, Columbus (Ga.) State U., 1992—94, Columbus Tech. Inst., 1994—95. Loma - Acs Aflac - Ga, 2003. Mgmt. AFLAC, Columbus, 1996—2004; owner J.E. Hedges Photography, Columbus, 2001—03; pvt. practice Columbus, 2004—. Mem.: Ga. Profl. Photographers Am. (assoc.), Profl. Photographers Am. (assoc.). Home: 4806 Sterling Dr Columbus GA 31909 Personal E-mail: julie@jehedges.com.

HEDGES, KAMLA KING, library director; b. Covington, Va. d. John Wilton and Rhoda Alice (Loughrie) K.; m. Harry George Hedges, July 24, 1988. AB, Coll. of William and Mary, 1968; MLS, Vanderbilt U., 1969. Law and legis. reference libr. Conn. State Libr., Hartford, 1969-74; dep. law libr. Steptoe and Johnson, Washington, 1974-78; law libr. Wilkinson, Cragun and Barker, Washington, 1978-83; corp. libr. The Bur. of Nat. Affairs, Inc., Washington, 1983-94, dir. libr. rels., 1995—. Compiler: (directories) BNA's Directory of State and Federal Courts, Judges, Clerks, 1995, BNA's State Administrative Codes and Registers, 1995; contbr. chpt. to law manual. Bd. dirs. Friends of the Law Libr. of Congress, 2000—. Mem. Am. Assn. Law Librs. (exec. bd. dirs. 1984-87), Spl. Libr. Assn. Episcopalian. Home: 4331 Embassy Park Dr NW Washington DC 20016-3607 Office: Bur Nat Affairs Inc 1231 25th St NW Washington DC 20037-1197

HEDIN, EDNA JENKS, musician, educator; b. Ft. Worth, Nov. 15, 1924; d. Edward Lee and Tressie (Jackson) Jenks; m. Alvin Morris Hedin, Apr. 1, 1947; children: John Alvin, Edward Morris, James Lee. AA, Ctrl. Coll. Women, Conway, Ark., 1945; BMus, Okla. Baptist U., 1948; MEd, Tex. Tech. U., 1972. Grad. asst. Ctrl. Coll. Women, Conway, Ark., 1946—47; pvt. tchr., piano, mus. dir., kindegarten Shawnee, Okla., 1948—49; dir. jr. high choir Crooked Oak Sch., Oklahoma City, 1950—51; music tchr. Norfolk Consol. Sch., Cushing, Okla., 1951—55, Artesia Pub. Schs., N.Mex., 1955—87; adj. instr. N.Mex. State U., Carlsbad. Organist First Bapt. Ch., Artesia, N.Mex., 1955—87. Mem.: Music Tchrs. Nat. Assn. (nat. cert. mem.), Nat. Guild Piano Tchrs., Delta Kappa Gamma, Kappa Delta Pi,

Sigma Alpha Iota, Phi Kappa Phi. Republican. Baptist. Home: 1 Cajun Ct Roswell NM 88201-3408 Office: Chapel at New Mex Mil Inst Roswell NM 88201 E-mail: studio1@cableone.net.

HEDLUND, ELLEN LOUISE, state agency administrator, educator; b. Omaha, Feb. 17, 1943; d. Edwin Hugo and Olga Josephine Parrish; m. Ronald David Hedlund, Aug. 22, 1964; children: Karen Marie, David Peter. BA, Augustana Coll., 1965; MA, U. Iowa, 1966; PhD, U. Wis. Milw., 1989. Cert. life cert. in guidance and counseling Wis. Dept. Pub. Instr., 1977. Counselor Clear Creek Cmty. Schs., Oxford, Iowa, 1966—67; counselor, tchr. Nicolet HS, Glendale, Wis., 1967—72, 1979; tchr. asst., project mgr. U. Wis., Milw., 1982—89, proposal writer, 1989; cons. R.I. Coll., Providence, 1990; adj. prof. U. R.I., Kingston, 1991; assessment coord. R.I. Dept. Edn., Providence, 1991—. Ptnr., cons. Wis. Pub. Opinion Mktg. Rsch., Milw., 1976—89. Adv. bd. U. Wis., Milw. Coll. for Kids, 1980—89; Sunday sch. supr. Bay Shore Luth., Whitefish Bay, Wis., 1987—89; congl. pres. Luth. Ch. of the Good Shepherd, Kingston, RI, 1996. Named Viking of Distinction, North HS, Omaha, Nebr., 2003. Mem.: Am. Edn. Rsch. Assoc., Assoc. for Supervision and Curriculum Devel., R.I. Assoc. Supervision and Curriculum Devel. Lutheran. Avocations: reading, gardening, home decor, stained glass. Office: RI Dept Elem Secondary Edn 255 Westminster St Providence RI 02903

HEDMAN, JANICE LEE, business executive; b. Elmhurst, Ill., Feb. 7, 1938; d. George Marion Hickman and Vera Beryl (Olsen) Sample; m. Daryl F. Hedman, Aug. 29, 1971 (div. Aug. 1983); children: Kevin G., Gregory Scott, Danny L., Shelly L. Wolanski-Bannon. Student, U. Puget Sound, 1970, Tacoma (Wash.) Community Coll., 1980. Head teller Puget Sound Nat. Bank, Tacoma, 1970-75; real estate agt. Shorewood Realty, Gig Harbor, Wash., 1975-80; mktg. rep. Western Fin. Planning, Inc., Tacoma, 1981-83; co-owner Schatz Avant Garde, Gig Harbor, 1984-86; asst. mgr. Classic Restaurant, Gig Harbor, 1984; co-owner Hedman Enterprises, Gig Harbor, 1976-93, owner, property mgr., 1993—; v.p. adminstrn. Teardrop Am., Inc., Wenatchee, Wash., 1986-90; pres. Teardrop N.W. Inc., Wenatchee, 1988-90; co-owner J&R Mktg., Wenatchee, 1989-90; mktg. specialist John L. Scott, Inc., Tacoma, 1991—2002; sr. mktg. rep. R & D, Excel Telecom., Gig Harbor, 1996-98, owner, mgr., 1993—; co-owner [illegible] Instruments, 1999—; owner Hedman Enterprises, 1993—; retired. Asst., Women's Task Force, Tacoma, 1980-81; asst. in fund raising events Am. Cancer Soc., 1992-95. Mem. Epsilon Sigma Alpha (pres. 1980-81, v.p. 1981-82).

HEDRICH, CLEDA POLLARD, real estate broker, writer; b. Richmond, Va., July 3, 1940; d. Herschel Newton and Frances Morton Pollard; m. Norman Hedrich, Mar. 27, 1967; children: Norman Lee, Bradley Charles. BA, U. of N.C., 1960—62. Real Estate Broker State of Fla., 1974. Exec. asst. to the pres. London & Cheshire Ins. Co., London, 1962—63; exec. asst. Eurofinance, Paris, 1963—64; psychiat. asst. Emory U. (Grady Hosp.), Atlanta, Ga., 1965—66; elem. tchr. City of Chgo. Sch. Sys., Chgo., 1967—67; book editor MacMillan Pub. Co., N.Y.C., 1967—69; editor Internat. Jour. of Psychiatry, Internat. Jour. of Child Psychotherapy, Internat. Jour. of Psychoanalytical Psychotherapy, N.Y.C., 1970—72; real estate broker/owner Pollard & Hedrich Realty Inc., Bonita Springs, Fla., 1976—; vice pres./owner Hickory Homes, Inc., Bonita Springs, 1976—. Author: (novels) A Pl. to Go Someday, (mystery novel) Threat of a Stranger, (novels) White Palm Mall, (screenplays) Threat of a Stranger. Personal E-mail: cleda@hedrichgroup.com.

HEDRICK, JOAN DORAN, writer, university educator; b. Balt., May 1, 1944; d. Paul Thomas and Jane (Connorton) Doran; m. Travis K. Hedrick, Aug. 26, 1967; children: Jessica, Rachel. AB, Vassar Coll., 1966; PhD, Brown U., 1974. Instr. Wesleyan U., Middletown, Conn., 1972-74, asst. prof. English, 1974-80; prof. history Trinity Coll., Hartford, Conn., 1994—, also dir. women's studies program, 1987-98. Vis. asst. prof. Trinity Coll., Hartford, 1980-81, vis. assoc. prof., 1981-82. Author: Solitary Comrade: Jack London and His Work, 1982, Harriet Beecher Stowe: A Life, 1994 (Pulitzer Prize for biography 1995); editor: The Oxford Harriet Beecher Stowe Reader, 1999. Mem. MLA, Am. Studies Assn., Org. Am. Historians, Soc. Am. Historians. Office: Trinity College Dept of History 300 Summit St Dept Of Hartford CT 06106-3186*

HEDWALL, PATRICIA GREGER, municipal assessor; b. New Britain, Conn., Aug. 26, 1948; d. John Anthony Greger and Dorothy Ann Thompson; m. Mark Alan Hedwall, June 27, 1975; 1 child, Adrianna. BS, Ctrl. Conn. State U., 1970, MS, 1976. CCMA, CCMC Conn. Tchr. Rham H.S., Hebron, Conn., 1970—78, East Hampton (Conn.) H.S., 1981—84; part-time instr. Ea. Conn. State U., Windham, 1986—90; asst. tax collector Town of Lebanon, Conn., 1984—86, assessor, 1987—91, Town of Madison, Conn., 1991—. Mem.: New Haven County Assn. Assessing Officers (pres. 2000—), Conn. Assn. Assessing Officers (instr. 1996—, v.p., sec., com. chair 1990—, spl. recognition 1995, Assessor of Yr. 2001), Internat. Assn. Assessing Officers (profl. designation advisor 1999—, CAE, Profl. Designee of the Yr. 2002). Home: 363 Randall Rd Lebanon CT 06249 Office: Town of Madison 8 Campus Dr Madison CT 06443

HEEG, PEGGY A. lawyer, former gas industry executive; b. Louisville, June 25, 1959; BA with honors, U. Louisville, 1983, JD, 1986. Bar: Ky. 1986, DC 1987, Tex. 1987. Various Tenneco Energy, El Paso Corp., Houston, 1996—97, v.p., assoc. gen. counsel regulated pipelines, 1997—2001, sr. v.p., dep. gen. counsel, 2001, exec. v.p., gen. counsel, 2002—04; ptnr. Fulbright & Jaworski L.L.P., 2004—. Legal advisor to commr. Charles Stalon Fed. Energy Regulatory Commn., 1988; bd. dirs. El Paso Tenn. Pipeline Co. Mem.: ABA, Interstate Natural Gas Assn. Am., DC Bar, State Bar Tex., Ky. Bar Assn., Energy Bar Assn. Office: Fulbright & Jaworski LLP 1301 McKinney Ste 5100 Houston TX 77010-3095*

HEEKIN, MARY ANN, oncology social worker; b. Cin., July 22, 1953; d. Herbert Joseph and Anna Jean (Hilberg) Heekin; children: John Patrick, Megan Hilberg, Anna Kathleen. BA in History with honors, Otterbein Coll., 1986; MSW, U. Cin., 1993. Lic. ind. social worker. Acct. coord. Miner Raymond Assn., Cin., 1987-89; oncology social worker Cancer Family Care, Cin., 1996—. Co-facilitator Wellness Cmty., Cin., 1997—. Parent campaign coord. Springer Sch., Cin., 1990; co-founder, past pres. bd. dirs., trustee First Step Home Inc., Cin., 1991—2001; vol. mediator Aring Inst. Beech Acres, Cin., 1993—; mem. cornerstone leadership com. Summit Country Day Sch., Cin., 1995, chair ann. alumni fund campaign, 1997; trustee Transitions, Newport, Ky., 1997—. Mem.: NASW (Jane Addams award 1993), Acad. Family Mediators, Social Work Oncology Group, Women's City Club, Phi Alpha Theta. Republican. Avocations: divorce mediation, family preservation. Office: Cancer Family Care 2421 Auburn Ave Cincinnati OH 45219

HEENEY, SUSAN WELCH, interior designer, educator; b. Nashville, Apr. 6, 1956; d. Glenn Thomas Welch, Sr., Georgia Hall Welch; m. Michael Patrick Heeney; children: Shea Patrick, Kevin Hall. B in Interior Design, O'More Coll. Design, 1991. Cert. Nat. Coun. for Interior Design Qualification, registered interior designer Tenn. Registered interior designer Susan Welch Heeney Interiors, Nolensville, Tenn., 1991—; assoc. prof. O'More Coll. Design, Franklin, Tenn., 1997—2003; owner, creator DecoratingStudio.com, Nolensville, 1998—, DecoratingBooks.com, Nolensville, Tenn., 2001—. TV/talk radio guest, 2000—; dir. O'More cultural sojourn O'More Coll. Design, Franklin, 2001—02; keynote spkr. Moen Nat. Interior Design Seminar, Las Vegas, Nev., 2000; guest spkr., cons. Author: (book) Choosing Color For Your Home, 1999, 60 Color Schemes, 1999; editor: (web site) www.DecoratingStudio.com, 1999; syndicated columnist: Your Home is Your Castle, 1999—. Coord. donation student interior design svcs. to various non-profit orgns., 1997. Recipient Recognition, Phenomenal Women of the Web, 1999. Mem.: Tenn. Coalition Interior Designers, Nat. Writers Union, Am. Soc. Interior Designers (cert.). Republican. Roman Catholic. Avocations: photography, travel, reading, gardening. Home: 9813 Sam Donald Rd Nolensville TN 37135 Office: DecoratingStudio dot com PO Box 455 Nolensville TN 37135 Office Phone: 615-776-2951. E-mail: swheeney@united.net.

HEERE, KAREN R. astrophysicist; b. Teaneck, N.J., Apr. 9, 1944; d. Peter N. and Alice E. (Hall) H. BA, U. Pa., 1965; MA, U. Calif., Berkeley, 1968; PhD, U. Calif., Santa Cruz, 1976. Rsch. assoc. NRC NASA Ames Rsch. Ctr., Moffett Field, Calif., 1977-79; rsch. astronomer U. Calif., Santa Cruz/NASA Ames Rsch. Ctr., 1979-86; assoc. prof. San Francisco State U., 1986-87; scientist Sci. Applications Internat. Corp., Los Altos, Calif., 1974-76, 87-93; rsch. specialist Sterling Software, Redwood City, Calif., 1993-98; sr. scientist Raytheon, Moffett Field, Calif., 1998—, mgr. space and earth sci., 2001—. Vis. scientist TATA Inst. for Fundamental Rsch., Bombay, India, 1984. Author numerous articles in field. Mem. Am. Astron. Soc. Avocations: hiking, birding, adventure travel. Home: PO Box 2427 El Granada CA 94018-2427

HEESTAND, DIANE ELISSA, internist, nephrologist, educator; b. Boston, Oct. 9, 1945; d. Glenn Wilson and Elizabeth (Martin) Heestand. BA, Allegheny Coll., 1967; MA, U. Wyo., 1968; edn. specialist, Ind. U., 1971, EdD, 1979. Asst. prof. communication Clarion (Pa.) State Coll., 1971; asst. prof. learning resources Indiana U. of Pa., 1971-72; asst. prof. communication U. Nebr. Med. Ctr., Omaha, 1972-74; assoc. prof. learning resources Tidewater Community Coll., Virginia Beach, Va., 1975-78; ednl. cons. U. Ala. Sch. Medicine, Birmingham, 1978-81; dir. learning resources, assoc. prof. med. edn. Mercer U. Sch. Medicine, Macon, Ga., 1981-88; asst. dean ednl. devel. and resources Ohio U. Coll. Osteopathic Medicine, 1989-90; assoc. prof. clin. med. edn., dir. biomed. communications U. So. Calif. Sch. Medicine, L.A., 1990-95, acting chair dept. med. edn., 1992-95; prof., dir. office ednl. devel. U. Ark. for Med. Scis., Little Rock, 1995—. Cons. Lincoln (Pa.) U., summer, 1975; vis. fellow Project Hope/China, Millwood, Va., summer, 1986. Author (teleplay) Yes, 1968 (award World Law Fund 1968); producer, dir. (slide tape) Finding a Way, 1980 (1st Pl. award HESCA 1981, Susan Eastman award 1981). Rsch. sect. chair So. Group on Ednl. Affairs, 1998-2000. Grantee, Porter Found., 1984, Ark. Dept. Higher Edn., 1996—97, UAMS Spl. Devel., 1997—99; Family and Preventive Medicine fellow, Health Resources and Svcs. Adminstrn., 2003—. Mem. Health Scis. Comm. Assn. (bd. dirs. 1982-86, pres.-elect 1987-88, pres. 1988-89, Spl. Svc. award 1990), Assn. Ednl. Comm. and Tech. (pres. media design and prodn. div. 1985-86), Assn. Biomed. Comm. Dirs. (bd. dirs. 1993-95), Soc. of Dirs. of Rsch. in Med. Edn. (steering com. 2000—, chair-elect 2002, chair 2003), Generalists in Med. Edn. (steering com. 1998-2001, chmn. 1999-2000). Democrat. Presbyterian. Avocations: tennis, gardening, golf.

HEFFERAN, COLIEN JOAN, economist; b. Mpls., May 13, 1949; d. Bernard and Rosemary Arnsdorf; m. Hollis Spurgeon Summers, Oct. 14, 1987; 1 child, Margaret Vimont Summers. BS, U. Ariz., 1971; MS, U. Ill., 1974, PhD, 1976. Asst. prof. Pa. State U., University Park, 1975-79; econ., rsch. leader Agrl. Rsch. Svc., USDA, Hyattsville, Md., 1979-88; adminstr. Coop. State Rsch., Edn. and Ext. Svc., 1988—. Adj. prof. U. Md., University Park, 1982-88; chmn. Ctr. for Family, Washington, 1985-87; vis. fellow Australian Nat. U., Canberra, NSW, 1989-91. Mem. editl. bd. Jours.-Family Econ. Issues, 1987—. Recipient Outstanding Citizen award U. Ariz., 1985, Outstanding Alumni award U. Ill., 1986, Presdl. Rank award as Disting. Fed. Exec., 2000. Mem. Am. Econ. Assn., Am. Coun. on Consumer Interests. Democrat. Roman Catholic. E-mail: chefferan@reeusda.gov.

HEFFERLIN, EARLINE DAWDY, retired writer; b. Kellogg, Idaho, Feb. 3, 1932; d. Earl Elmer and Gladys Stanton Dawdy; m. JB Lon Hefferlin, Aug. 6, 1955 (div. June 8, 1992); children: Amelia, Hilary. BA, Ea. Wash. Coll. Edn., 1954; MA, Stanford U., 1956; profl. diploma, Tchrs. Coll., N.Y.C., 1970. Tchr. TU Sch., Lloyd, Mont., 1953, Auburn (Wash.) Pub. Schs., 1954—55, E. Palo Alto (Calif.) Pub. Schs., 1956—57; rsch. asst. Stanford (Calif.) U., 1957—59; rsch., tchg. asst. Tchrs. Coll., N.Y.C., 1968—70; indexer Jossey-Bass Pubs., San Francisco, 1972—99. Mem.: AAUW (pres. 2000—01, gift honoree 1995—96). Home: 2632 Fenwick Ct Ann Arbor MI 48104-6726

HEFFERNAN, PATRICIA CONNER, management consultant; b. N.Y.C., Oct. 11, 1946; d. Arthur S. and Catherine (Center) Conner; m. John Joseph Heffernan, Sept. 13, 1969 (dec. June 1996). BA, U. Va., 1968; MBA, Suffolk U., 1980. Cert. mgmt. cons. Office mgr. Wobbly Barn, Killington, Vt., 1968-72; bus. mgr. Woodstock Country Sch., Vt., 1972-74; assoc. dean Vt. Law Sch., Royalton, Vt., 1974-83; mgmt. cons. Heffernan & Assocs., Killington, 1982-87; mgmt. cons., v.p. Sandage Inc., Burlington, Vt., 1987-92; mgmt. cons., ptnr. Mktg. Ptnrs., Inc., Burlington, 1992—. Vt. del. White House Conf. on Small Bus.; mem. region 1 adv. coun. SBA. Mem. Vt. Gov.'s Commn. on Women; bd. dirs. Rutland Regional Med. Ctr., 1986-91, New Eng. Bus. for Social Responsibility, 1990-93; trustee, pres. Killington Mountain Sch., 1978-85; mem. Killington Planning Commn., 1975-87, Killington Zoning Bd., 1979-84, Vt. Epilepsy Assn., 1977—, Vt. Telecom. Commn., Vt. Econ. Devel. Adv. Coun.; mem. Vt. steering com. for ACE Nat. Identification Program for Women in Higher Edn., 1978-83. Named Outstanding Leader, Vt. YWCA, 1985, Woman of Yr., Vt. Bus. and Profl. Women Found., 1986, Woman in Bus. Adv., SBA, 1993. Mem. Inst. Mgmt. Cons. (v.p. New Eng. region, nat. bd. dirs. 1991-93), Nat. Assn. Women Bus. Owners, Vt. Bus. Assn. for Social Responsibility (bd. dirs., pres. 1991—), Womwn Bus. Owners Vt. (founder, bd. dirs. 1983—, pres. 1984-86). Office: Mktg Ptnrs Inc 176 Battery St Burlington VT 05401-5296 E-mail: pheffernan@marketing-partners.com.

HEFLEY, LYNN A. state representative; b. Ruston, La., Apr. 30, 1940; m. Joe Hefley; children: Janna, Lori, Jules. Small bus. owner, ret. tchr.; state rep. dist. 20 Colo. Ho. of Reps., Denver, 1998—, chair judiciary com., mem. edn. com. and joint com. on legal svcs. Republican. Presbyterian. Office: State Capitol # 323 200 E Colfax Ave Denver CO 80203

HEFNER, CHRISTIE ANN, multi-media entertainment executive; b. Chgo., Nov. 8, 1952; d. Hugh Marston and Mildred Marie (Williams) H. BA summa cum laude in English and Am. Lit., Brandeis U., 1973. Freelance journalist, Boston, 1974-75; spl. asst. to chmn. Playboy Enterprises, Inc., Chgo., 1975-78, v.p., 1978-82, bd. dirs., 1979—, vice chmn., 1986-88, pres., 1982-88, COO, 1984-88, chmn., CEO, 1988—. Bd. dirs. Playboy Found.-Playboy Enterprises, Inc., Ill. chpt. ACLU, Mag. Pubs. Assn. Bd. dirs. Creative Coalition, Rush Med. Ctr., MarketWatch.com, Inc., Canyon Ranch Bus. Com. for the Arts, NCTA Diversity Com. Recipient Agness Underwood award, L.A. chpt. Women in Comm., 1984, Founders award, Midwest Women's Ctr., 1986, Human Rights award, Am. Jewish Com., 1987, Harry Kalven Freedom of Expression award, ACLU, Ill., 1987, Spirit of Life award, City of Hope, 1988, Eleanor Roosevelt award, Internat. Platform Assn., 1990, Will Rogers Meml. award, Beverly Hills C. of C. and Civic Assn., 1993, Champion of Freedom award, ADL, 2000, Bettie B. Port Humanitarian award, Mt. Sinai, 2001, John Wayne Cancer Ctr. award, 2001, Christopher Reeve 1st Amendment award, Creative Coalition, 2001. Mem. Nat. Cable and Telecomm. Assn. (Vanguard award 2002, Interlochen's Path of Inspiration award 2003), Mus. of TV and Radio Media Ctr., Brandeis Nat. Women's Com. (life), Com. of 200, Young Pres. Orgn., Chgo. Network, Voters for Choice, Sierra Club, Emilys List, Sierra Club, Phi Beta Kappa. Democrat. Office: Playboy Enterprises Inc 680 N Lake Shore Dr Chicago IL 60611-4455

HEFT, CAROL BETH, artist; b. Phila., Mar. 11, 1954; d. Charles B. and Leeba R. (Melmed) H.; m. William L. Warfield Jr., 1986. BFA, R.I. Sch. Design, 1976; MS Edn., Hunter Coll., N.Y.C., 1995. Artist, tchr. Studio in a Sch. Assn., N.Y.C.; tchr. art, drawing and art history Muhlenberg Coll., Cedar Crest Coll., Moravian Coll., Northampton C.C. One-woman shows include Gallery 120, N.Y.C., 1982, Ten Worlds Gallery, N.Y.C., 1989, Blue Mountain Gallery, N.Y.C., 1998, 2003, Washington Art Assn., Washington Depot, Conn., 2002; exhibited in group shows at Columbia Coll. and Mo. Arts Coun., 1992, PSA Art Showcase, 1994, St. Johns U. Gallery, 1996, Blue Mountain Gallery, 1995-96, St. Johns U. Nat. Exhbn., 1996. Mem. Coll. Art Assn., Am. Assn. Museums. Avocations: quiltmaking, knitting.

HEGEL, CAROLYN MARIE, farm bureau executive; b. Lagro, Ind., Apr. 19, 1940; d. Ralph H. and Mary Lucile (Rudig) Lynn; m. Tom Lee Hegel, June 3, 1962. Student pub. schs., Columbia City, Ind. Bookkeeper Huntington County Farm Bur. Co-op, Inc., Ind., 1959-67, office mgr., 1967-70; twp. woman leader Wabash County (Ind.) Farm Bur., Inc., 1970-73, county woman leader, 1973-76; dist. woman leader Ind. Farm Bur., Inc., Indpls., 1976-80, 2d v.p., bd. dirs., 1980—, chmn. women's com., 1980—, exec. com., 1988—. Farmer Andrews, Ind., 1962—; dir. Farm Bur. Ins. Co., Indpls., 1980—, exec. com., 1988—, audit com., 2000—, chmn. audit com., 2003—; bd. dirs., spkr. in field, bd. mem. Country Way Ins., 2002—. Women in the Field columnist Hoosier Farmer mag., 1980—. Mem. rural task force Gt. Lakes States Econ. Devel. Commn., 1987—88; mem. Ind. Farm Bur. Svc. Co., 1980—; active Leadership Am. Program, 1988; Sunday sch. tchr., bd. dirs. children's activities Bethel United Meth. Ch., 1965—; pres. Bethel United Meth. Women, Lagro, 1975—81; bd. dirs. Ind. Farm Bur. Found., Indpls., 1980—, Ind. Inst. Agr., Food and Nutrition, Indpls., 1982—, Ind. 4-H Found., Lafayette, 1983—86; mem. Ind. Rural Health Adv. Coun., 1993—96, Hoosier Homestead Award Cert. Com., Indpls., 1980—; organizer farm divsn. Wabash County Am. Cancer Soc. Fund Dr., 1974; bd. dirs. N.E. Ind. Kidney Found., 1984—, Nat. Kidney Found. of Ind., 1985—89. Named Big Sister of Yr., Wabash County, Ind., 2003; named one of Outstanding Farm Woman of Yr., Country Woman Mag., 1987; recipient State 4-H Home Econs. award, Ind. 4-H, 1960. Mem.: Am. Farm Bur. Fedn. (midwest rep. to women's com. 1986—93), Producers Mktg. Assn. (bd. dirs. 1980—94), Ind. Agrl. Mktg. Assn. (bd. dirs. 1980—94), Women in Comm., Inc. Republican. Home: 3330 N 650 E Andrews IN 46702-9616 Office: Ind Farm Bur Inc PO Box 1290 225 S East St Indianapolis IN 46202-4058 E-mail: chegel@infarmbureau.com.

HEGENDERFER, JONITA SUSAN, public relations executive; b. Chgo., Mar. 18, 1944; d. Clifford Lincoln and Cornelia Anna (Larson) Hazzard; m. Gary William Hegenderfer, Mar. 12, 1971 (dec. 1978). BA, Purdue U., 1965; postgrad., Calif. State U., Long Beach, 1966-67, Northwestern U., 1969-70. Tchr. English, Long Beach (Calif.) Schs., 1965-68; editl. asst. Playboy Mag., Chgo., 1968-70; comms. specialist AMA, Chgo., 1970-72; v.p. Home Data, Hinsdale, Ill., 1972-75, mktg. mgr. Olympic Savs. & Loan, Berwyn, Ill., 1975-79; sr. v.p. Golin/Harris Comms., Chgo., 1979-89; pres. JSH & A, Chgo., 1989—. Bd. dirs. Chgo. Internat. Film Festival, 1989, 90. Author: Slim Guide to Spas, 1984, (video) PR Guide for Chicago LSCs, 1991; editor: Financial Information National Directory, 1972; contbr. articles to profl. jours. Co-chmn. pub. rels. com. Am. Cancer Soc., Chgo., 1984; mem. com. March of Dimes, Chgo., 1986; mem. pub. rels. com. Girl Scouts Chgo., 1989-90, bd. dirs., 1994-95; bd. dirs. Greater DuPage Women's Bus. Coun., 1992-93, Girl Scouts U.S. DuPage County, 1994—; vol. ctr. adv. com. United Way, Chgo., 1990-93; mem. cmty. svc. com. Publicity Club Chgo., 1990. Recipient 5 Golden Trumpet awards Publicity Club Chgo., 1983, 96, 94, Silver Trumpet awards, 1984, 86, 88, Spectra awards Internat. Assn. Bus. Communicators, 1984, 85, 87, Gold Quill aard, 1985, Bronze Anvil award Pub. Rels. Soc. Am., 1985, award Nat. Creativity in Pub. Rels. award, 1995; named Influential Woman in Bus., 1998. Mem. Am. Mktg. Assn., Publicity Club Chgo., Pub. Rels. Soc. Am., Chgo. Women in Pub., Nat. Assn. Women Bus. Owners, DuPage Area Assn. Bus. Tech. (bd. dirs. 1997), Coun. on Fgn. Rels., Met. Women's Forum, Cinema Chgo. (bd. dirs. 1988-89). Avocations: travel, photography. Office: JSH & A Comms IS 450 Summit #320 Oakbrook Terrace IL 60181 E-mail: jonni@jsha.com.

HEGERTY, NANNETTE H. police chief; b. Milw. m. George Hegerty; stepchildren: Suzanne, Scott. BS in Edn., U. Wis., 1972; MS in Mgmt., Cardinal Stritch Coll., 1985; student, FBI Nat. Tng. Acad., 1988. From officer to chief police Milw. (Wis.) Police Dept., 1976—2003, chief police, 2003—; head Ea. Dist. Office U.S. Marshals Svc., 1994—2002. Office: Milwaukee Police Adminstrn Bldg 749 W State St Milwaukee WI 53233*

HEGGENESS, JULIE FAY, foundation administrator, lawyer; b. Long Beach, Calif., Nov. 9, 1959; d. Clark Richard Heggeness, June Lorraine Heggeness; 1 child, Thaddeus. BFA, U. So. Calif., 1982; JD, Western State U., 1998. Cert. specialist planned giving. Dir. Long Beach Meml. Med. Ctr., Long Beach, 1995—99, Meml. Med. Ctr. Found., Long Beach, 1999—. 1st v.p. Camp Fire U.S., Long Beach, 1999—2001; Leadership Long Beach Class of 2003 estate planning and trust coun., bd. mem. at large; mem. Nat. Coun. Planned Giving. Mem.: Long Beach (Calif.) Bar Assn., Assistance League Long Beach, Cameo Profl. Aux. Republican. Roman Catholic. Avocations: golf, gardening, skiing. Office: Meml Med Ctr Found 2801 Atlantic Ave Long Beach CA 90806 Personal E-mail: jheggeness@memorialcare.org.

HEGLER, ELLEN MARIE, business executive, retired educator; b. Dryden, Oreg., Dec. 16, 1916; d. George Westley Van Buskirk and Marie Frances Mineo; children: Brian Neils, Rollin Grant, Gary Mark. BA in English cum laude, So. Oreg. Coll., 1959, MA in English, 1963; postgrad., UCLA, 1969-70. Cert. secondary tchr., Calif., Oreg. Prodr., announcer Radio Program KYSC, Yreka, Calif., 1947-48; v.p., sec. Carl Hegler Logging Inc., Ashland, 1951-59; social worker Jackson County Pub. Welfare Commn., 1959-60; English tchr. Sr. H.S., Medford, Oreg., 1961-62; fashion editor May Co., L.A., 1963-64; asst. prof. English So. Oreg. Coll., Ashland, 1964-70, Calif. State U., L.A., 1971-72; owner Hegler Enterprises Ltd., Ashland, Medford, 1976—. Contbr. articles to profl. publs. Sec. Ashland Meml. Hosp. com., 1956-58; pub. rels. dir. Sch. Bond Issues, Ashland, 1958; sec., exec. bd. Ashland Hosp. Found., 1981-83; one of founders Nat. Literary Hon. Fraternity, 1958. Avocation: writing. Office: Hegler Enterprises PO Box 165 Ashland OR 97520-0006

HEGSTROM, JUNE, state legislator; m. Gerard D. Hegstrom; children: Tamara, Cameron. Grad., Ariz. State U. Paralegal; mem. Ga. Ho. of Reps., Atlanta, 1992—; mem. human rels. and aging, univ. sys. Ga. coms.; also legis. and congrl. reapportionment com. Active Cherokees of Ga. Intertribal Coun., Inc., Task Force on Am. Indian Concerns. Democrat. Office: Legis Office Bldg Rm 504 Atlanta GA 30334

HEGYELI, RUTH INGEBORG ELISABETH JOHNSSON, pathologist, government official; b. Aug. 14, 1931; came to U.S., 1963; d. John Alfred and Elsa Ingeborg (Sjogren) Johnsson; m. Andrew Francis Hegyeli, July 2, 1966 (dec. June 1982). BA in Scis., U. Toronto, 1958, MD, 1962. Intern Toronto Gen. Hosp., 1962-63; sr. rsch. pathologist Battelle Meml. Inst., Columbus, Ohio, 1967-69; med. officer Nat. Heart and Lung Inst., 1969-73; chief program devel. and evaluation Nat. Heart, Lung and Blood Inst., Bethesda, Md., 1973-76, acting dir. office program planning, 1975-76, asst. dir. internat. rels., 1976-86, assoc. dir. internat. rels., 1986—. Mem. sci. adv. bd. Giovanni Lorenzini Found., Inc., N.Y.C., Milan, 1982—. Coord. editor: Jour. Soviet Rsch. in Cardiovasc. Diseases, 1979-86; editor: Christopher Columbus Commemorative Book on Discovering New Worlds in Medicine, 1992, Internat. Position Paper: Women's Health and Menopause, A Comprehensive Approach, 2002, also 11 sci. books; contbr. poetry to nat. and internat. anthologies. Mem. nat. adv. bd. Nat. Mus. Women in Arts.

Named Hon. Mem. Eagle Tribe of Haida Indians, Queen Charlotte Islands, B.C., Can., 1961; named to, Internat. Poetry Hall of Fame, 1997; recipient German Friendship award, German Ministry Rsch. and Tech., 1988, Nicolaus Copernicus medal, Academica Medica, 1988, Superior Svc. award, HEW, 1975, DHHS, 1991, Outstanding Achievement award in Poetry, 2003. Fellow Acad. Medicine, Toronto; mem. Soc. Geriatric Cardiology, Am. Soc. Artificial Internal Organs, N.Y. Acad. Scis., Acad. Am. Poets, Interant. Soc. Poets, World Literary Acad., Fed. Exec. Alumni Assn. Republican. Avocations: poetry, fiction writing, art, music, travel. Home: 24301 Hanson Rd Gaithersburg MD 20882-3501 E-mail: hegyelir@nih.gov.

HEGYVARY, SUE THOMAS, nursing school dean, editor, nursing educator; b. Dry Ridge, Ky., Nov. 28, 1943; BSN, U. Ky., 1965; MN, Emory U., 1966; PhD in Sociology, Vanderbilt U., 1974. Asst. prof. nursing and sociology Rush U. Med. Coll., 1974, assoc. prof. med. nursing, chair dept., 1974-77, asst. prof. sociology, 1977-80; prof. nursing, assoc. v.p., assoc. dean Coll. Nursing Rush Presbyn. St. Luke's Med. Ctr., 1977—86; assoc. prof. sociology Rush U. Med. Coll., 1980—86; dean, prof. Sch. Nursing U. Wash., Seattle, 1986—98, adj. prof. Sch. Pub. Health and Cmty. Med. Mem. health care adv. com. Rep. Jennifer Dunn, 1993-96; vis. com. Bd. 50 Emory U. Sch. Nursing, Atlanta, 1990-92; mem. adv. panel outcomes rsch. Nat. Ctr. Nursing Rsch. NIH, 1990-91; external mem. Five Yr. Review com. Coll. Nursing U. Ky., 1989-90; mem. govtl. affairs com. Am. Assn. Colls. Nursing, 1988-92; chair planning com. Wash. State Conf. Nursing Shortage, 1989; mem. Wash. State Commn. Nursing, 1989; mem. adv. com. Child Devel. & Mental Retardation Ctr. U. Wash., 1986—; mem. task force nursing shortage Seattle Area Hosp. Coun., 1987-88; vis. prof., ann. lectr. Sch. Nursing U. Va., Charlottesville, 1988; vis. prof. U. Oulu, Finland, 1985; site visitor accreditation schs. nursing Nat. League Nursing, 1977-80; cons. VA Hosp., Miami, Fla., 1968-69, Vanderbilt U., Nashville, 1971-72, Area Health Edn. Sys., Rockford, Ill., 1975, Western Interstate Commn. Higher Edn., Denver, 1975, Andrews U., Berrian Springs, Mich., 1976, dept. nursing studies Nat. Hosp. Inst., Utrecht, The Netherlands, 1976-80, Haukeland Sykehaus, Bergen, Norway, 1976-77, Sch. Nursing Marquette U., Milw., 1977, Wayne State U., Detroit, 1978, Cath. U. Leuven, Belgium, 1980, Walter Reed Army Med. Ctr., Washington, 1979-83, Dalhousie U. Sch. Nursing, Halifax, N.S., 1981, U. Minn., Mpls., 1988, U. Mo., Columbia, 1992. Editl. adv. bd. Nursing Policy Forum, 1995-96; editl. cons. Nursing Care Guide Pfizer Corp., 1993; editl. bd. Jour. Nursing & Health, 1993—, Nursing Adminstrn. Quarterly, 1988—; mem. manucscript review panel Jour. Nursing Quality Assurance, 1986—, Nursing Outlook, 1983—, Jour. Rsch. Nursing & Health, 1981—, Nursing Rsch., 1979-89; contbr. chpts. to books and articles to profl. jours. Mem. ANA, Am. Acad. Nursing, Sigma Theta Tau. Office: U Wash Sch Nursing BNHS PO Box 357266 Seattle WA 98195-7266

HEICHEL, PAULA, investment company executive, financial consultant; b. Phila., Apr. 26, 1949; d. Francis Stephen Heichel and Dorothy Pauline O'Brien. BA in Bus., Rutgers U., Camden, N.J., 1971; MS in Consumer Econs., U. Mo., 1973. Vista vol. Neighborhood Legal Svc. Corp., Washington, 1973-75; dep. dir. Legal Svcs. for the Elderly/AARP, Washington, 1975-80; 1st v.p. investments, fin. cons. Smith Barney, Washington, 1981—. 1st soprano Alexandria (Va.) Singers, 1995—; mem. dean's coun. Rutgers U., Camden. Mem. Exec. Women Internat. (program dir. 1985-86). Avocations: dog training, scuba diving. Office: Smith Barney 1050 Connecticut Ave NW Ste 800 Washington DC 20036-5349 E-mail: paula.heichel@smithbarney.com.

HEIDELBERGER, KATHLEEN PATRICIA, physician; b. Bklyn., Apr. 13, 1939; d. William Cyprian and Margaret Bernadette (Hughes) H.; m. Charles William Davenport, Oct. 8, 1977. BS cum laude, Coll. Misericordia, 1961; MD cum laude, Woman's Med. Coll. Pa., 1965. Intern Mary Hitchcock Hosp., Hanover, N.H., 1965-66, resident in pathology, 1966-70; mem. faculty U. Mich., Ann Arbor, 1970—, assoc. prof. pathology, 1976-79, prof., 1979—2002; ret., 2002. Mem. Am. Soc. Clin. Pathologists, U.S.-Can. Acad. Pathology, Soc. for Pediatric Pathology, Coll. Am. Pathologists.

HEIDER, ANNE HARRINGTON, music educator; BA, Wellesley Coll., 1963; MA, NYU, 1965; DMA, Stanford U., 1981. Assoc. prof., resident choral condr. Roosevelt U.; artistic dir. Bella Voce Profl. Chamber Choir. Recipient Tempo All-Prof. Team, Humanities award, 1993. Office: Roosevelt U Coll Performing Arts 430 S Michigan Ave Chicago IL 60605

HEIDISH, LOUISE ORIDGE-SCHWALLIE, retired transportation specialist; b. Cin., May 21, 1938; d. Leslie Jacob and Louise (Oridge) Schwallie; m. William Edward Heidish, Sept. 2, 1961; children: Sara Louise Heidish-Hurst, Amy Jean. BA in History, Denison U., 1960; MA in History, Miami U., Oxford, Ohio, 1962; MS in Urban Studies, Ala. A&M U., 1994. Secondary tchr. Fox Chapel Sch. Dist., Pitts., 1962-69; part-time instr. U. Ala., Huntsville, 1976-78; substitute history tchr. City of Huntsville Schs., 1977-79; dir. comm. svcs. Heidish Enterprises, Huntsville, 1979-83; transp. specialist City of Huntsville, 1981—2004; ret., 2004. Regional 5 state coord. AAUW and NEH, Huntsville, 1981-83. Author: Biography: Alexander Long 1816-86, 1962, Marketing Ride Sharing, 1994; co-editor: Glimpses into Antebellum Homes, Huntsville, AL, 1999. Mem., project chair, bd. dirs. Huntsville Symphony Orch. Guild, 1974—; sec. Huntsville-Madison County Sr. Ctr., 1981, v.p., 1982, pres., 1983; v.p. Huntsville High Sch. PTA, 1985—86, pres., 1986—88; com. chmn. Panoply of the Arts Festival, Huntsville, 1985—87; mem. adv. bd. women's studies U. Ala., Huntsville, 1998—; mem. adv. bd. capital campaign Fantasy Playhouse, 1998—; publicity chair Huntesville-Madison County Libr. Benefit, 1999; 1st v.p. Huntsville Symphony Orch. Guild, 2001—02, pres., 2002—; mem. benefit com. Greater Huntsvile Humane Soc. Dog Ball, 2001; mem. Huntsville-Madison Co. Leadership Class, 2002—; bd. dirs. search com. Huntsville Symphony Orch. Assn., 2000—03. Mem.: AAUW (local pres. 1979—81, state v.p. 1981—83, regional coord. 1981—83, Outstanding Local Svc. award 1999), S.E. Assn. for Commuter Transp. (regional conf. chair 1995, chpt. treas. 1996, 1997, nat. conf. com. 2000), Pub. Rels. Coun. No. Ala. (newsletter editor 1993, conf. treas. 1994, coun. treas. 1995, coun. sec. 1996, v.p. profl. devel. 1997, v.p. membership 1998, 1999, v.p. projects 2000, pres. 2001, bd. dirs. 1993—, v.p. 1997—2000, pres. 2001, Sr. Practitioner Pub. Rels. award 2003), Kappa Kappa Gamma (regional officer 1958—, alumnae officer, local pres., Outstanding Kappa Kappa Gamma Svc. award 4 state region 1997). Presbyterian. Avocations: community arts volunteering, reading, swimming.

HEIGHT, DOROTHY I. association executive; b. Richmond, Va., Mar. 24, 1912; d. James Edward and Fannie (Burroughs) Height. BA, MA, NYU. Mem. nat. staff YWCA of the U.S.A., 33 yrs.; caseworker N.Y.C. Welfare Dept., 1934; dir. Ctr. Racial Justice YWCA, 1946; nat. pres. Nat. Coun. Negro Women Inc., 1957—97, pres. emeritus, 1998—. With Dept. Def. Adv. Com. Women, 1952—55; mem. N.Y. State Social Welfare Bd., 1958—68; bd. govs. ARC, 1964—70; pres.'s com. Employment Handicapped; mem. ad hoc com. Pub. Welfare Dept. Health Edn. and Welfare; dir. Ctr. Racial Justice YMCA. Pres. Nat. Coun. Negro Women, 1957—; hon. mem. nat. bd. dirs. YWCA of the U.S.A. Recipient Disting. Svc. award Nat. Conf. Social Welfare, 1971, William L. Dawson award, 1974, Citizens Medal award, 1989, CamilleCosby World Children award, 1990, Ambassador award YWCA of the U.S.A., 1993, Presdl. Freedom medal, 1994. Office: Pres Emerita Nat Coun Negro Women 633 Pennsylvania Ave NW Washington DC 20004*

HEIL, MARY RUTH, former counselor; b. Westerville, Ohio, June 8, 1921; d. George Walter and Bertha Ellen (Shrodes) H. BS in Edn., Ohio State U., 1944; MEd, Wayne State U., 1956; cert. advanced study, Western Carolina U., 1987; cert. theol. edn., U. South, 1987. Cert. counselor, tchr., Ohio, Ky., Mich., Fla., N.C. Tchr. 7th grade Cheshire (Ohio) Sch., 1942-43; tchr. biology, English Ohio Soldiers' and Sailors' Orphans' Home, Xenia, 1943-47; tchr. 7th grade Lakeview High Schs., Winter Garden, Fla., 1947-48; tchr. English, journalism Pine Mountain (Ky.) Settlement Sch., 1948-49, field and established camp dir. Columbus (Ohio) and Franklin County Girl Scouts, 1949-50; tchr. Mary Lyon Jr. High Sch., Royal Oak, Mich., 1950-56, 57-62, Coston Secondary Modern Girls' Sch., Greenford, Middlesex, Eng., 1956-57; tchr. English West Henderson High Sch., Hendersonville, N.C., 1962-65, guidance counselor, 1965-86. Chmn. Mayor's Com. Employment of Handicapped, Hendersonville, 1972-74; v.p. Mountain Ramparts Health Planning Bd., Asheville, N.C., 1972-76, Western Carolina Health Systems Agy. Bd., Morganton, N.C., 1976-82; bd. dirs., sec., com. chmn., Henderson County Dispute Settlement Bd., 1989-95; exec. com., bd. dirs. Western Carolina Presbyn. Retirement Com., 1987-94; active Henderson County Coun. Women, Hendersonville, 1994-96, treas.; mem.-at-large Pisgah coun. Girl Scouts U.S., 1994-98, chair fund devel. com., 1995-98, exec. com., 1997-98; bd. dirs. Henderson County Coun. on Aging, 1998-2001, chair nominating com., 1999. Named Woman of Achievement, Hendersonville Bus. and Profl. Women's Club, 1978, Civitan Citizen of Yr., Civitan Club, Hendersonville, 1986; named to Order Ky. Cols., 1988; recipient award, Galludent U., Washington, 1986, Thanks Badge, Pisgah Coun., Girl Scouts U.S., 1998, state degree of Style, Dignity, Title and Honor of Dame, Baron of Shalford, Eng., 2000, cert., Rt. Hon. Thomas de Shalford, 2000. Mem. NEA, ACA, Royal Oak Edn. Assn. (pres. 1954-56), N.C. Assn. Educators (pres. dist. 1970-72), Henderson County Mental Health Assn. (bd. dirs. 1965-74), Alpha Delta Kappa (N.C. 1st v.p. 1978-80, state pres. 1980-82, S.E. region grand v.p. 1987-89), Kappa Delta Pi. Democrat. Episcopalian. Avocations: golf, bowling, raising irish setters, classical music. Home: 726 Academy Rd Hendersonville NC 28792-9428

HEILMAN, MARY JOANNE, gifted education educator; b. Kansas City, Mo., Sept. 11, 1955; d. Norris Alger and Mary Jane (Brewster) Smith; m. James Heilman, Apr. 19, 1997; children: Jennifer Caruso, Angelia. AA, Miss. County Coll., 1985; BA, Gov.'s State U., University Park, Ill., 1988, MA in English, 1992. Cert. tchr, Ill., gifted students tchr., Ill. Tchr. Sch. Dist. #160, Country Club Hills, 1989-94; tchr., coord. gifted program Sch. Dist. #159, Mokena, Ill., 1994-96, Carroll County Middle Sch., Carrollton, Ky., 1997—, team leader, cluster leader writing portfolios, mem. middle sch. site based coun. Instr. Mississippi County C.C., summers 1993-96; instr. Joliet Jr. Coll., 1993-96, MOMS program; adj. instr. Jefferson C.C., 1997—; team leader, English dept. cluster leader; mem. site based decision making coun. Active NOW. Mem. NEA, Internat. Platform Assn. Avocation: reading. Home: 1 Wilson Way Carrollton KY 41008-9648

HEILMAN, PAMELA DAVIS, lawyer; b. Buffalo, July 2, 1948; d. George Henry and Natalie (Maier) Davis; m. Robert D. Heilman, June 27, 1970. AB, Vassar Coll., 1970; JD, SUNY, Buffalo, 1975. Bar: N.Y. 1976, Fla. 1980. Assoc. Hodgson, Russ, Andrews, Woods & Goodyear, Buffalo, 1975-84, ptnr., 1984—. Bd. dirs. United Way Buffalo, 1985-97, vice chmn., 1989-92, chair, 1993-97, gen. campaign chair, 1992; bd. dirs. D'Youville Coll., Buffalo, 2001—, WNY Internat. Trade Coun., Inc., Buffalo, 2001—, Fin. Instns., Inc., Warsaw, 2002—. Mem. ABA, N.Y. State Bar Assn. (vice chmn., exec. com., sect. on internat. law and practice 1988-90), Fla. Bar Assn., Erie County Bar Assn. Office: Hodgson Russ Andrews Woods & Goodyear LLP One M&T Plz Buffalo NY 14211-1638 E-mail: pheilman@hodgsonruss.com.

HEIM, ALBERTA JANE, publishing executive, writer; b. Davenport, Iowa, Jan. 23, 1947; d. Albert George Wieser and Marjorie May Myers; children: John Heim II, Jeffrey. BA, DePauw U., 1969. Pub. Touchstone Adventures, Paw Paw, Ill., 1996—; dir. organic edn. ctr. Oreg. Tilth, Inc., Salem, 1997—2000; pres. Ill. Tilth Organic Inst., Steward, 2001—. Vis. lectr. Coll. DuPage, Glen Ellyn, Ill., 1977; vis. spkr. Orgn. Govt. in Mgmt., Baton Rouge, 1982. Author: (book) The Directory of Working Women, 1982, What To Do When the Stock Market Falls, 1996, Car Living, 1999, Car Living Your Way, 2001. Vol. Menlo Orgn., Beaverton, Oreg., 1993—94, Rockford Area Literacy Coun., Ill., 2001—. Named Career Woman of the Month, Cosmopolitan Mag., 1982; recipient Outstanding Working Women's Exceptional Achievement award, The Woman's Adv., 1981; grantee Edn. Grant for Organic Edn. Ctr., Newman's Own Found., 1998, 1999. Mem.: Amnesty Internat. Office: Touchstone Adventures PO Box 177 Paw Paw IL 61353 Personal E-mail: ajarcher@earthlink.net.

HEIM, DIXIE SHARP, family practice nurse practitioner; b. Kansas City, Kans., Feb. 28, 1938; d. Glen Richard and Freda Helen (Milburn) Stanley; m. Theodore Eugene Sharp, Aug. 12, 1960 (dec. Apr., 1972); children: Diane Yvonne Price, Andrew Kirk, Bryan Scot; m. Roy Bernard Heim, June 14, 1979. Diploma nursing, St. Luke's Hosp. Sch. Nursing, Kansas City, Mo., 1959; family practice nurse clinician, Wichita State U., 1974. Cert. advanced registered nurse practitioner, Kans. Nurse surg. ICU Staff Kaiser Found. Hosp., San Francisco, 1959-61; oper. rm. supr. St. Luke's Hosp., Kansas City, Mo., 1962-63; emergency rm., oper. rm. supr. Lawrence (Kans.) Meml. Hosp., 1963-72; nurse clinician various doctors, Lawrence, 1973-81; nursing supr. spl. projects St. Francis Hosp. and Med. Ctr., Topeka, 1981-94; primary health care giver Health Care Access, Lawrence, 1992-94; nurse practitioner Dr. Glen Bair, Topeka, 1990-94; advanced registered nurse practitioner Dr. Jerry H. Feagan, Topeka, 1994, McLouth (Kans.) Med. Clinic, 1994—, Jefferson County Meml. Hosp., Winchester, Kans., 1995-96; family practice nurse practitioner Robert E. Jacoby II., M.D., Mathew Bohm M.D., Topeka, Kans., 1995-2000. Preceptor nurse practitioner program U. Kans., 1993-2001, registered nurse program Washburn U., 1996-2001; primary health care provider Jefferson County Law Enforcement Ctr., Oskaloosa, Kans., 1995-96. V.p. Am. Bus. Women. Assn. Lawrence chpt., 1969, sec. 1968; vol. Children's Hour, Lawrence, 1965-72, Comty. Resource for Career edn., 1975-76; adv. bd. E. Ctrl. Kans. Econs. Opportunity Corp., Lawrence, 1993-95; mem. Rep. Women Douglas County, Lawrence, 1994-2001. Recipient Nursing the Heart of Health Care award Kaiser Permanente, 1994. Mem. ANA, Am. Acad. Nurse Practitioners (cert.), Kans. State Nurses Assn. (v.p. 1958, chairperson fund raising campaign 1994, bd. dirs. 1996). Home: 540 Arizona St Lawrence KS 66049-2100 Office: Flannery & McBratney MDs PA 3550 S 4th St # 10000 Leavenworth KS 66048 E-mail: DKtrDixie@aol.com.

HEIM, HAZEL, nurse; b. Courtland, Miin. d. Frederick William H. and Augusta Marie Georgius. Diploma, Meth. Kahler Sch. Nursing, 1929. Charge nurse St. Mary's Hosp., Rochester, Minn.; vol. nurse Red Bird Mission Hosp., Beverly, Ky.; pvt. duty nurse Kahler Hosp., Rochester. Republican. Methodist.

HEIM, KATHRYN MARIE, psychiatric nurse, author; b. Milw., Sept. 29, 1952; d. Lester Sheldon Wilcox and Laura Dora (Corpie) Wilcox Sears; m. Vincent Robert Gouthro, June 30, 1970 (div. 1976); 1 child, Robert Vincent; m. George John Heim, Sept. 17, 1977 (div. 1988). AS in Nursing, Milw. Area Tech. Coll., 1983; BS in Nursing, NYU, 1986; MS in Mgmt., Cardinal Stritch Coll., 1988; PhD in Human Behavior, Newport U., 1997. Cert. psychiatric and mental health nurse, AMA. Staff geriatric nurse Clement Manor, Greenfield, Wis., 1983; nurse, health educator Milw. Boys Club, 1983-84; nurse mgr. Milw. County Mental Health Complex, 1984—2002, mem. gero-psychiat. inpatient adv. com., 1986-87, mem. joint practice com., guest rels. com., 1999-2001; hospitality com., 1999-2000; RN Psychiat. Acute Care Day Hosp., 1992—2002, cmty. support RN case mgr., 2002, Milw. County Dept. Aging, 2002—. Cons. Positive Perspectives, 1999-2000; rschr. on loneliness as it relates to mental health, 1989-92. Mem. wellness task force Milw. County Mental Health Complex, 1988-89, chairperson sensory deficit com. Geropsychiatry, 1989-90; active Boy Scouts Am., Milw., 1978-80. Mem. ANA (cert. gerontol. nurse), NAFE (network dir. Milw. chpt. 1982-92), Wis. Nurses Assn., NYU Alumni Assn., Cardinal Stritch Alumni Assn. (class rep. 1986-88), Milw. Area Tech. Coll. Alumni Assn. Avocations: yoga, jogging, reading, writing. Home: 226 N 63rd St Milwaukee WI 53213-4137 Office: Milwaukee County Dept ging 235 W Galena St Milwaukee WI 53212 Office Phone: 414-289-6110 Business E-Mail: kheim@wi.rr.com.

HEIM, MARCY LYNN SCHULTZ, foundation executive; b. Theresa, Wis., Nov. 15, 1957; d. Robert Julius and Irene Laura (Wecker) Schultz; m. Kenneth J. Heim; stepchildren: Carly, Elliott; children: Robert James, David Joseph. BS in Natural Scis. with distinction, U. Wis., 1979. Exec. asst. Wis. Phys. Therapy Svcs., Madison, 1975-80; dir. pub. rels. Wis. DHI Coop., 1980-83; sr. dir. devel. U. Wis. Found., 1983—. Pres. Marcy Heim Diversified Svcs., 1995—. Singer: (profl. group) Marcy & The Highlights, 1980—. Mem. Salvation Army, 1990—; vol. United Way of Dane County, Madison, Wis., 1987; treas. Van Hise Elem. PTO, 1994—95; grad. Leadership Greater Madison, 1997; bd. dirs. Middleton HS Choral Boosters, 2001—03, co chair musical fundraising event, 2001—03; bd. dirs. CTM Madison Family Theater, 2003—; mem. Jr. League of Madison, 2002—. Recipient Outstandng Svc. award, Wis. Agrl.Rsch. Sta., 2003. Mem.: CFRE (cert. 1998, 2002), Assn. Fundraising Profls. (Outstanding Fund Raising Execs. award 1997), Pub. Rels. Soc. Am., Nat. Agr. Mktg. Assn., Nat. Agr. Alumni and Devel. Assn. (edn. com. 1992—93, chair edn. com. 1994—96, bd. dirs. 1994—2002, pres. elect 1996—97, pres. 1998—2000, Nat. Profl. Achievement award 1997, Disting. Svc. award 2002), Women in Comm. Inc. (bd. dirs. 1988—91, pres. Madison chpt. 1990—91), Assn. Women Bus. Coalition (bd. dirs. 1988—91), Daus. of Demeter (bd. dirs. 1995—2000, pres. elect 1996, pres. 1997), Middleton Kiwanis Club, Kiwanis (chair,co-chair agr. conservation, environ. com., Downtown Madison chpt 1991—2002, bd. dirs. 1996—2000, found. bd. dirs. 2000—02), Alpha Zeta. Republican. Luth. Avocations: singing, dance, aerobics, scuba diving. Home: 471 Presidential Ln Madison WI 53711-1153 Office: U Wis Found PO Box 8860 Madison WI 53708-8860 Office Phone: 608-263-6669. E-mail: marcy.heim@uwfoundation.wisc.edu.

HEIM, MEGAN ALYSSA, biomedical engineer; b. Omaha, July 26, 1976; d. Thomas Anthony and Cheryl Ann Heim. BS in Biomedical Engring., Marquette U., 1999; MBA, U. Nebr., 2001. Engr. assoc. SCANMED, Omaha, 1999—2000; product engr. Avaya, Omaha, 2000—. Vol. Relay for Life Am. Cancer Soc., Omaha, 2002—. Mem.: NSPE, Tau Beta Pi (sec. 1998—99), Alpha Sigma Mu, Beta Gamma Sigma. Avocations: reading, running, skiing. Home: 1861 S 135th Ave Omaha NE 68144 Business E-Mail: heim@avaya.com.

HEIM, TONYA SUE, nurse, small business owner; b. Huntingburg, Ind., Nov. 9, 1948; d. Harold William and Marjorie Elouise (Buse) Rothert; m. James Frederick Heim, Sept. 6, 1969; children: Brian Christopher, Andrea Christine. Diploma, Deaconess Sch. Nursing, Evansville, Ind., 1969; BS in Mgmt., Oakland City U., 2001; MHA, U So. Ind., 2003. RN Ind., cert. HIV/AIDS instr., infection control, Healthcare Corp. Compliance Assn. From oper. rm. staff nurse to dir. corp. compliance St. Joseph's Hosp., Huntingburg, Ind., 1969—2003, dir. quality svcs., 2003—; owner, operator Holland (Ind.) Toning and Tanning Ctr., 1987—. Co-owner Heim Hardware, 1989—. Instr., trainer ARC So. Ind., 1970-92; chmn. health profl. adv. com., mem. exec. com. So. Ind./Ill. chpt. March of Dimes, 1978-92; v.p., chmn. program com., bd. dirs. So. Hills Counseling Ctr., Jasper, Ind., 1988-94—; event coord. Hoosiers fo Safety Belts, Dale, Ind., 1987; troop co-leader Girl Scouts Am., Holland, 1986-88; active Southridge Band Boosters, Huntingburg, 1986-91; mem. AIDS coun. S.W. Dubois County Sch. Corp., 1988—; mem. adv. coun. Prenatal Substance Use Prevention Program, 1989-93; mem. HIV prevention cmty. planning com., Ind. State Dept. Health, 1994-95; chmn. schs. com., chmn. Midwest AIDS Tng. and Edn. Ctr. com., founding co-chmn. Dubois County AIDS Cmty. Action Group, Huntingburg, 1991—; mem. S.W. Dubois County Sch. Bd., 1992—, pres., 1995-97; active March of Dimes, 1978-90; mem. perinatal adv. bd. S.W. Ind., 1997—. Mem. ANA (bd. dirs.), NAACOG, Ind. Coun. Nurse Mgrs., Assn. for Practitioners in Infection Control (Amelia K. Sloan lectureship Ind. 1992, pres.-elect 2002, pres. 2003), Assn. Oper. Rm. Nurses, Ind. Sch. Bds. Assn. (mem. legis. com., 1996-97, chmn. legis. com., 2000-01, mem. awards com. 2001—, chmn. awards com. 2002, region 9 dir., 2003—), Huntingburg C. of C., Beta Sigma Phi (v.p.). Republican. Lutheran. Avocation: reading. Home: PO Box 88 403 S 2nd Ave Holland IN 47541-9506 Office: St Josephs Hosp 1900 Medical Arts Dr Huntingburg IN 47542-9190 E-mail: theim@psci.net.

HEIMANN-HAST, SYBIL DOROTHEA, language arts and literature educator; b. Shanghai, May 8, 1924; came to U.S., 1941; d. Paul Heinrich and Elisabeth (Halle) Heimann; m. David G. Hast, Jan. 11, 1948 (div. 1959); children: Thomas David Hast, Dorothea Elizabeth Hast-Scott. BA in French, Smith Coll., 1946; MA in French Lang. and Lit., U. Pitts., 1963; MA in German Lang. and Lit., UCLA, 1966; diploma in Spanish, U. Barcelona, Spain, 1972. Cert. German, French and Spanish tchr., Calif. Assoc. in German lang. UCLA, 1966-70; asst. prof. German Calif. State U., L.A., 1970-71; lectr. German Mt. St. Mary's Coll., Brentwood, Calif., 1974-75; instr. French and German, diction coach Calif. Inst. of Arts, Valencia, 1977-78; coach lang. and diction UCLA Opera Theater, 1973-93, ret., 1993, lectr. dept. music, 1973-93; interviewer, researcher oral history program UCLA, 1986-93; dir., founder ISTMO, Santa Monica, Calif., 1975—. Cons. interpreter/translator L.A. Music Ctr., U.S. Supreme Ct., L.A., J. Paul Getty Mus., Malibu, Calif., Warner New Media, Panorama Internat. Prodn., Sony Records, 1986—; voice-over artist; founder, artistic dir. Westside Opera Workshop, 1986-94. Author of poems. Mem. KCET Founder Soc. UCLA grantee, 1990-91. Mem. AAUP, MLA, SAG, AFTRA, KCET Founder Soc., Sunset Succulent Soc. (v.p., bd. dirs., reporter, annual show chmn.), German Am. C. of C., L.A. Avocations: performing arts, literature, history, plants, designing and knitting sweaters. Home and Office: River's Edge 111 Dekoven Dr Apt 606 Middletown CT 06457-3463

HEIMBOLD, MARGARET BYRNE, publisher, educator, consultant; came to U.S., 1966, naturalized, 1973; d. John Christopher and Anne (Troy) Byrne; m. Arthur Heimbold, Feb. 26, 1984; children: Eric Thomas Gordon, Victoria Byrne Heimbold. BA, Queens Coll.; cert., Dale Carnegie, 1977, Psychol. Corp. Am., 1981, Wharton Sch., 1983, Stanford U., 1989; MA in Libr. Studies, Georgetown U., 2003. Group advt. mgr. N.Y. Times, N.Y.C., 1978-85; pub. Am. Film, Washington, 1985-86; v.p., pub. Nat. Trust for Hist. Preservation, Washington, 1986-90; pres. Summerville Press, Inc., Washington, 1990—. Pub. Metro Golf, 1992—; advisor Mag. Pubs.; mentor Women's Ctr. Va.; judge various publ. competitions; judge various mags. awards programs. Trustee Nat. Mus. Women in Arts, Choral Arts Soc. Washington. Office Phone: 703-622-3515.

HEIMBUCH, BABETTE E. bank executive; b. 1948; BS in Math Summa Cum Laude, U. Calif., Santa Barbara, 1972. Sr. v.p., CFO FirstFed. Bank Calif., Santa Monica, 1982—85, exec. v.p., CFO, 1985—87, dir., 1986—, FirstFed. Fin. Corp., 1987—; sr. exec. v.p., CFO FirstFed. Fin. Corp. & FirstFed Bank Calif, 1987—88, pres., COO, 1989—97, pres., CEO, 1997—2002, chmn., pres., CEO, 2002—. Bd. dirs. Water Pik Technologies Inc., 2002—, Scape Industries. Chair bd. advisors Santa Monica-UCLA Med. Ctr.; fin. oversight com. Santa Monica/Malibu Unified Sch. Dist. Named one of 25 Women to Watch, US Banker Mag., 2003. Office: First Fed Bank Calif 401 Wilshire Blvd Santa Monica CA 90401-1416*

HEIMBURGER, ELIZABETH MORGAN, psychiatrist; b. Atlanta, Apr. 23, 1932; d. Henry Durand and Lillian Elizabeth (Palmour) Morgan; div.; children: Elizabeth Morgan Whitaker, Homer Aggie Whitaker III, Margaret Diane Heimburger, Richard Ames Heimburger Jr., Katherine Durand Heimburger. BS, Ga. State U., 1963; MD, Med. Coll. Ga., 1967. Diplomate

Am. Bd. Psychiatry and Neurology. Intern in internal medicine Med. Coll. Ga., Augusta, 1967-68, resident in gen. psychiatry, 1968-70; fellow in child and adolescent psychiatry U. Tex., Galveston, 1970-72; asst. prof. dept. psychiatry U. Tex. Med. Br., Galveston, 1972-73, assoc. prof., dir. residency tng., 1980-87; asst. prof., assoc. prof., dir. psychosomatic svcs. U. Mo. Sch. Medicine, Columbia, 1973-80, clin. assoc. prof. dept. psychiatry, 1987-97; pvt. practice specializing in adolescent psychiatry Columbia, 1987-97, Atlanta, 1997—. Examiner Am. Bd. Psychiatry and Neurology, Chgo., 1977—; specialist, site visitor residency rev. Coun. Grad. Med. Edn., Washington, 1983—; exec. bd. Am. Assn. Dirs. Psychiat. Residency Tng., 1982-90; exec. coun. Tex. Psychiat. Soc., Austin, 1983-86; dir. confs., workshops on orgnl. and group dynamics. Editorial cons. bd. Am. Psychiat. Assn. Press., Inc., Washington,1 987-90; contbr. articles, scholarly papers to profl. publs. Bd. dirs. Mental Health Assn., Galveston, 1984-87, YMCA, Columbia, 1987-89. Grantee NIMH, 1978-80, 80-83. Fellow Am. Psychiat. Assn.; mem. Am. Soc. Adolescent Psychiatry, Am. Assn. Child and Adolescent Psychiatry (com.), A.K. Rice Inst. (bd. dirs. 1979-85, pres. Cen. States Ctr. 1979-88, bd. dirs. 1979-95), Am. Horticulture Soc. Episcopalian. Avocations: gardening, fitness, needlepoint. Home and Office: 686 Montana Rd NW Atlanta GA 30327-1536

HEIN, CONNIE L. real estate company officer, writer; b. Loveland, Colo., July 11, 1954; d. Travis L. Mimms and Leila F. Freeman; m. Edwin N. Hein; children: Trac, Kellie, Angie. Office adminstr. Hydro Constrn., Ft. Collins, Colo.; curriculum developer CIC, Cneeley, Colo.; adminstr. Hein Appraisals Inc., Windsor, Colo.; pub. Stillwater Pub., Windsor. Author: Touverin Time: For a Fourth of July Celebration, 2003. Mem.: Windsor C. of C. (bd. membership com. 2003). Office: Still Water Publishing Windsor CO 80550

HEIN, KAREN KRAMER, pediatrician, epidemiologist; b. NYC, Feb. 2, 1944; d. Irving W. and Ruth (Eisenberg) Kramer: m. Ralph Dell, Aug. 28, 1983; children: Ethan, Molly. BA, U. Wis., 1966; B of Med. Sci., Dartmouth Med. Sch., 1968; MD, Columbia U., 1970. Intern Bronx Mcpl. Hosp., Bronx Mcpl. Hosp. Ctr., 1970, resident, 1971-73; dir. adolescent AIDS program Montefiore Med. Ctr., NYC, 1987-94; prof. pediat. Albert Einstein Coll. Medicine, NYC, 1991—, prof. epidemiology and social medicine, 1993—, clin. prof. pediat., epidemiology and social medicine, 1995—; exec. officer Inst. Medicine NRC, Washington, 1995—98; pres. William T. Grant Found., NYC, 1998—2003. Cons. NYC Dept. Health, 1980-85, NYC Bd. Edn., 1987-93; bd. dirs. Dartmouth Med. Sch., Hanover, NH. Author: AIDS: Trading Fears for Facts Consumer Reports Books, 1989; contbr. articles to profl. jours. Named Outstanding Physician, Dept. Health and Human Svcs., 1989, Adminstrs. Citation award, 1993. Fellow Am. Bd. Pediat.; mem. Am. Pediatric Soc., Soc. for Pediatric Rsch., Am. Acad. Pediat., Soc. for Adolescent Medicine (pres. 1992-93). Address: Box 607 Jacksonville VT 05342

HEINDL, CHRISTINE, artist, educator; b. Rochester, N.Y., Feb. 24, 1960, BA in Art, Empire State Coll., 1992; MFA, Cornell U., 1994. Assoc. prof. Ohio U., Athens, 1994—. One-woman shows include White Columns, N.Y.C., 2000, Clementine Gallery, 2003. Fellow, Ohio Arts Coun., 2000, John Simon Guggenheim Found., 2001. Office: Ohio U Sch Art 528 Seigfred Hall Athens OH 45701

HEINE, KAREN MARIEKE, software development tutor, consultant; b. Washington, Sept. 18, 1972; d. Katherine J Heine, Warren F Heine. BA Systems Engrng., United States Naval Academy, Annapolis, MD, 1990—94; MA Electrical Engrng., Virginia Polytechnic Institute, Falls Church, VA, 1998—2000. Surface Warfare Officer United States Navy, Yokosuka, Japan, 1995—97; Associate Systems Engineer Raytheon, Falls Church, VA, 1997—98; Project Manager, Software Development Cayenta, Inc., Reston, VA, 1998—. Tutor Cayenta, Inc., Reston, 1998, Top Notch Tutoring, Reston, VA, 2000—. Lieutenant, Junior Grade United States Navy, 1994—97, Yokosuka, Japan. Mem.: American Association of University Women, Tau Beta Pi Engineering Honor Society (life), Phi Kappa Phi Honor Society (life), Navel Academy Alumni Association (life). Avocation: Aerobics, dance, reading, games, travel. Home: 2056 Headlands Circle Reston VA 20191 Office: Cayenta Inc 1900 Campus Commons Drive Reston VA 20191 Personal E-mail: kheine@1994.Usna.com.

HEINECKE, MARGARET THERESA, librarian; b. N.Y.C., Sept. 13, 1923; d. William and Mary Ellen (O'Callaghan) Brand; m. Heinrich Heinecke, Mar. 10, 1962 (div. Feb. 1991); 1 child, Fredrich Heinrich. BA, Coll. St. Elizabeth, 1945; MA in History, Columbia U., 1949, MLS, 1954. Instr. history, libr. Panzer Coll., East Orange, N.J., 1954-57; libr. Watchung Hills (N.J.) Regional H.S., 1957-59; libr. GS 11 USAF Europe, Germany, 1959-66; dep. county libr. San Diego Coutny, 1967-82. Vol. Proposition 13, San Diego, 1978, America's Cup, San Diego, 1992; puppeteer San Diego Opera, 1993-97, mem. outreach, 1995-97. Mem. AAUW. Avocations: rockhounding, travel, reading. Home: 3338 S Bonita St Spring Valley CA 91977-3020

HEINEMAN, HELEN L. provost; m. John L. Heineman; 4 children. BA summa cum laude, Queens Coll., 1958; MA in English, Columbia U., 1959; PhD, Cornell U., 1967. Prof., chair English Dept. Cardinal Cushing Coll., Brookline, 1964-73; fellow Bunting Inst. Radcliffe Coll., 1973-92; dept. chair Framingham State Coll., 1974, acad. v.p., interim pres., provost, 1996-99, pres., 1999—. Recipient Woodrow Wilson fellowship, AAUW fellowship. Office: Framingham State Coll 100 State St PO Box 9101 Framingham MA 01701-9101

HEINEN, JULIA MARGARET, music educator; b. Mankato, Minn., Mar. 11, 1960; d. Virgil Harry and Corinne Selly Rollings; m. Richard Lewis Kravchak, Dec. 16, 1989. MusB, U. Minn., 1982, D in Musical Arts, 1988; MusM, U. Mich., 1983. Asst. prof. Luther Coll., Decorah, Iowa, 1987—92; assoc. prof. Valdosta (Ga.) State U., 1992—95, Calif. State U., Northridge, 1995—. Profl. musician:. Home: 18001 Valerio St Reseda CA 91335 Office: Calif State U Northridge 18111 Nordhoff St Northridge CA 91330-8314 Business E-Mail: julia.heinen@csun.edu.

HEINEN, NANCY R. computer company executive; AB in Psychology and English with honors, JD, U. Calif., Berkeley. Pvt. practice, San Francisco & Palo Alto; group counsel, asst. sec. Tandem Computers Inc.; v.p., gen. counsel, sec. NeXT Software, Inc.; sr. v.p., gen. counsel Apple Computer, Inc., Cupertino, Calif., 1997—. Office: Mail Stop 301-4GC 1 Infinite Loop Cupertino CA 95014-2083

HEINONEN, ELANA RAE, elementary school educator; b. Cin., Oct. 11, 1976; d. Elmo Ray and Judy Ann Goodale; m. Erik Robert Heinonen, Aug. 7, 1999. BS in Human Ecology, Ohio State U., 1998, EdM in Elem. Edn., 1999. Std. profl. tchr. cert. Md., nat. bd. cert. tchr. 2003. Second grade tchr. Richland County Sch. Dist., Columbia, SC, 1999—2000; second grade tchr., team leader Balt. City Pub. Sch. Sys., 2000—. Tchr. adv. bd. mem. Balt. Zoo, 2003—. Mem.: ASCD, Internat. Reading Assn., Nat. Coun. Tchrs. Math. Roman Catholic. Avocation: reading.

HEINRICHS, APRIL, coach; b. Charlottesville, Va., Feb. 27, 1964; BA in Radio, TV and Motion Pictures, U. N.C., 1986. Lic. U.S. Soccer Federation "A" coaching license. Player U.S. Nat. Team, 1986—91; profl. soccer player Prato, Italy, 1987—92; head coach Princeton U., 1990, U. Md., 1991—95, U. Va., 1996—99; full time asst. U.S. Women's Nat. Team, 1995—97; mem. coaching staff 1995 Women's World Cup, 1995, 1996 Olympic Women's Soccer Team, 1996; head coach U.S. U-16 Nat. Team, 1997—2000; head coach, tech. dir. U.S. Women's Nat. Team, 2000—. Mem. NCAA Championship Team, 1983, 84, 86. Recipient U.S. Soccer Female Athlete of Yr. award, 1986, 89; voted female player of the 1980s Soccer America Magazine; first female inducted into Nat. Soccer Hall of Fame, 1998; named First Team All-American U. N.C. (3 times); inaugural recipient NSCAA Women's Com. award of Excellence, 2000. Achievements include coached U.S. Women's Soccer Team to Silver Medal, Sydney Olympic Games, 2000. Office: US Soccer House 1801-1811 S Prairie Ave Chicago IL 60616

HEINRICHS, MARY ANN, former dean; b. Toledo, Mar. 28, 1930; m. Paul Heinrichs, Jan. 26, 1952; children: Paul, John, Nancy, James. PhD, U. Toledo, 1973. Prof. English U. Toledo, Ohio, 1965-77, dean, 1977-93; prof. emeritus Coll. Edn. Contbr. articles to profl. jours. Mem. Cmty. Planning Coun. Rsch. Project Employed Women, Ohio, 1982-84; mem. Coun. Family Violence, Toledo, 1981—; com. chmn. St. Joseph Sch. Bd., Toledo. 1976-79. Recipient Outstanding Scholarship award U. Toledo, 1965; AAUW scholar, 1984, Hunanities scholar, 1987—; named One of Foremost Women 20th Century, 1987, Outstanding Woman U. Toledo, 1991; inducted into Notre Dame Acad. Hall of Fame, 1991. Mem. AAUW (corp. rep. 1978-84), Internat. Tech. Comm. Soc. (chmn. 1979-80), Zonta,, Pi Lambda Theta (chpt. pres., del. 1974-76), Phi Kappa Phi (chpt. pres, del. 1969). Roman Catholic. Avocations: hiking, traveling, music.

HEINS, ESTHER, botanical artist, painter; b. Bklyn, Nov. 10, 1908; d. Israel and Margaret (Brown) Berow; m. Harold Heins; Sept. 8, 1929 (dec. 1987); children: Marilyn Heins, Judith Leet. BS in Edn., Mass. Coll. Art, 1929. Freelance artist, Boston, 1930-60; bot. artist, illustrator plant introductions Arnold Arboretum, Boston, 1960—. Contbr. bot. illustrations to profl. jour.; one-woman shows include Graham Arader Gallery, NYC, Harvard Radcliffe Hilles Libr., Arnold Arboretum, Boston Pub. Libr., Schlesinger Libr., Cambridge, Mass.; group shows include Hunt Inst. for Bot. Documentation, Pitts., Arnold Arboretum, Munich, Germany, Smithsonian, Washington, Oakland, Calif., others; represented in permanent collections at Mus. Fine Arts, Boston, Hunt Inst. for Bot. Documentation, Schlesinger Libr., Radcliffe Coll., Arnold Arboretum, Boston Pub. Libr., Fogg Mus., Cambridge, and numerous others in pvt. collections; illustrator, contbr. essay: (book) Flowering Trees and Shrubs: The Botanical Paintings of Esther Heins, 1987; illustrator many covers Jour. AMA., the most recent 2002. Mem. Guild of Natural Sci. Illustrators. Avocations: attending concerts of Boston Symphony, gardening. Home: 8 Mitchell Rd Marblehead MA 01945-1130

HEINSEN, LINDSAY, newspaper editor; b. Berwyn, Ill., May 6, 1950; d. Henry Arthur and Mabel Scott (Witt) H. BA in French Lit., U. Ill., 1972, postgrad., 1972-76. Features editor D Mag., 1977-80; home and design editor Dallas Morning News, 1980-81, arts editor, 1981-89; freelance writer and editor Dallas, 1989-92; fine arts editor Houston Chronicle, 1992—2002, arts & entertainment editor, 2002—. Recipient Matrix award for Best Mag. Feature in Dallas, 1978; James scholar. Mem. Kappa Tau Alpha, Phi Kappa Phi. Office: Houston Chronicle 801 Texas Ave Houston TX 77002-2996

HEINZE, CHERYLL BOREN, state representative; b. Wewoka, Okla., Oct. 30, 1946; m. Harold Heinze. Diploma, East Ctrl. U.; BA, Alaska Pacific U. Art instr. UAA; co-owner His-N-Her Antiques; former dep. commr. natural resources; with Alaska Divsn. Tourism; mem. Alaska Ho. of Reps., 2002—; owner Adventure North Fishing & Guiding. Former pres. Anchorage Symphony League; bd. dirs. Breast Cancer Focus, Inc.; pres.'s steering com. Alaska Pacific U.; former rep. State C. of C., regional citizens adv. coun.; former bd. dirs. Pacific No. Acad., Anchorage Symphony Orch. Mem.: Alaska C. of C., Anchorage Women's Club. Republican. Avocations: music, art, poetry. Office: Rm 416 State Capitol Juneau AK 99801-1182 Address: 1336 Staubbach Cir Anchorage AK 99508

HEINZ KERRY, TERESA F. foundation administrator; b. Mozambique, Oct. 5, 1938; d. Jose Simoes Ferreira and Irene Thierstein; m. John Heinz (dec., 1991), children: John, Andre, Christopher; m. John Kerry, 1995. BA in Romance Langs., Lit., U. Witwatersrand, Johannesburg, South Africa, 1960; grad., U. Geneva, 1963; PhD (hon.), Beloit Coll., Wis., Bank ST. Coll. Edn., N.Y., Drexel U., Pa., Med. Coll. Pa. Cons. UN Trusteeship, N.Y.C.; chmn. Heinz Family Found., Pitts., Howard Heinz Endowment; trustee Vira I. Heinz Endowment; founder Women's Inst. for Secure retirement, 1996—. Endowed creation of professorship environ. mgmt. Harvard Bus. Sch., chair environ. policy John F. Kennedy Sch. Govt.; vice chair Environ. Def.; past mem. external adv. bd. Inst. Biospheric Studies, Yale U.; mem. adv. bd. Earth Comm. Office; founder Second Nature; co-founder, bd. dirs. Alliance to End Childhood Lead Poisoning; bd. dirs. Carnegie Corp., Family Comm.; trustee Brookings Inst.; former bd. dirs., trustee Phillips Exeter Acad., St. Paul's Sch., Georgetown U.; co-founder Nat. Coun. Families TV. Founding mem., co-chair Congl. Wives Soviet Jewry; trustee governing bd. Yale Art Gallery; mem. trustees coun. Nat. Gallery Art; bd. dirs. Carnegie Inst., Pitts. Women's Leadership award, Save the Children Found., 2003, World Ecology award, Internat. Ctr. for Tropical Ecology, U. Mo., 2003, Albert Schweitzer Gold medal for Humanitarianism, John Hopkins U., 2003. Avocation: art collecting. Office: Heinz Family Offices Ste 619 1201 Pennsylvania Ave NW Washington DC 20004-2401

HEISE, DOROTHY HILBERT, librarian, government official; b. Erie, Pa., June 17, 1945; d. George William and Annette Genevieve (Forrester) Hilbert; m. Charles W. Heise, June 29, 1968 BSL.S., Edinboro State U., Pa., 1968; postgrad., Catholic U., 1971-72; MLS, U. Md., 1987. Cert. sch. librarian, N.J., Va., Md. Librarian Toms River Intermediate Sch., N.J., 1968-70; librarian Prince George's County Schs., Md., 1970-72, Congl. Sch., Falls Church, Va., 1972-75, Consumer Product Safety Commn., Washington, 1976-77; tech. info. specialist Raytheon Service Co., Crystal City, Va., 1977-79, U.S. Dept. Agr., Washington, 1979—, head Econ. Research Service Reference Ctr., 1981—85; rsch. libr. Nat. Agr. Libr., 1985—. Recipient award for contbn. to Econ. Research Service Reference Ctr., U.S. Dept. Agr., 1985, award for contbn. to sci.gov website, 2001, award for contbn. to InvasiveSpecies.gov, 2001, award for NAL's Kids' Sci. website, 2001. Mem. ALA, Gamma Sigma Sigma. Lutheran. Avocations: needlecrafts; painting. Home: 8569 Tyrolean Way Springfield VA 22153-2241 Office: Nat Agrl Libr 1400 Independence Ave SW Washington DC 20250-7201

HEISE, KATHRYN ANN, music educator; b. Syracuse, Nebr., Oct. 13, 1957; d. Merlyn LaVerne and Donna Beth Saathoff; m. Theodore William Heise, June 24, 1993; children: Robert Allen, Michael Patrick, Aaron Jordan Robinson. BA, Midland Luth. Coll., 1980. Studio vocalist Sound Recorder Studio, 1977—81; asst. mgr. JL Brandies/Younkers, Omaha, 1982—89, J.P. Originals Bridal Shoppe, Omaha, 1989—93; music specialist Ashland (Nebr.)/Greenwood Pub. Schs., 1993—94; elem. music specialist Omaha Pub. Sch. Dist., 1994—98; music dir. Lafayette (Ind.) Sch. Corp., 1998—2002; music instr. Tippecanoe Sch. Corp., Battle Ground, Ind., 2002—03; rsch. asst. Children's Literacy and Sci. Project Purdue U., West Lafayette, Ind., 2002—. Miss Nebr., 1979; vocalist LNS Blues Band, Lafayette, Swing Tones Big Band, Omaha, 1993—97; dir. Star City Sweet Adelines, Lafayette, United States, 2000—02. Ch. coun. Our Savior Luth. Ch., West Lafayette, 1999—2002. Mem.: NEA (assoc.), Ind. Orff and Kodaly Assn. (assoc.), Music Educators Nat. Conf. (assoc.), Ind. State Tchr. Assn. (assoc.), Lafayette Edn. Assn. (assoc.; bldg. rep. 2000—03), Kappa Delta Phi. Avocations: long distance bicycling, hiking, reading, aerobics instructor, gardening. Home: 842 Kent Ave West Lafayette IN 47906

HEISE, MARILYN BEARDSLEY, public relations company executive; b. Cedar Rapids, Iowa, Feb. 26, 1935; d. Lee Roy and Angeline Myrtle Beardsley; m. John W. Heise, July 9, 1960; children: William Earnshaw, Steven James, Kathryn Kay Benninghoff. BA, Drake U., 1957. Prodn. mgr. Vend Mag., 1958—59; account exec. The Beveridge Orgn., Chgo., 1959—62; editor, pub. The Working Craftsman mag., Northbrook, Ill., 1971-78; columnist Chgo. Sun-Times, 1973-78; pres. Craft Books, Inc., Northbrook, 1978-84; v.p. Sheila King Pub. Rels., Chgo., 1984-87, Aaron D. Cushman, Inc., Chgo., 1987-88; pres. Creative Cons. Assocs., Inc., Glencoe, Ill., 1989—91, Heartfelt Charity Cards, 1991—. Mem. adv. panel Nat. Crafts Project, Ft. Collins, Colo., 1977; mem. adv. panel and com. Nat. Endowment for Arts, Washington, 1977; mem. editl. adv. bd. The Crafts Report, Seattle, 1978-86. Recipient achievement award Women in Mgmt., 1978. Mem. Pub. Rels. Soc. Am. (accredited). Office: Heartfelt 540 W Frontage Rd Ste 1060 Northfield IL 60093-1299

HEISEN, JOANN HEFFERNAN, health care company executive; b. Washington, Md., Jan. 25, 1950; d. Milton F. and Jeanne (Berger) Heffernan; childen: Douglas, Gregory, Cynthia, Courtney. BA, Syracuse U., 1972. Comml. lending officer Chase Manhattan Bank, N.Y.C., 1972-77; CFO Kenmill Textile Corp., N.Y.C., 1977-82; v.p. corp. affairs Primerica Corp., Greenwich, Conn., 1982-89; asst. treas. Johnson & Johnson, New Brunswick, N.J., 1989-90, v.p., mem. corp. staff, 1990-91, treas., corp. officer, 1991-94, contr., 1994-96, CIO, mem. exec. com., 1997—, v.p., CIO. Bd. trustees Princeton Med. Ctr. Bd. dirs. Women's Rsch. and Edn. Inst., Washington, 1990—. Recipient Women Achiever award YWCA N.Y., 1983, TWIN award Nat. YMCA, 1987, Dist. Alumni award Syracuse U., 1990. Mem. Fin. Women's Assn. (pres. 1980-81), Econ. Club N.Y. Office: Johnson & Johnson One Johnson & Johnson Pla New Brunswick NJ 08933

HEISER, NANCY E. freelance/self-employed writer, coach; b. Paterson, N.J., Sept. 24, 1953; d. William Henry Heiser and Joan Marie Muller; m. Jeffrey Louis Cohen, Aug. 12, 1979; children: Daniel Cohen, Jillian Cohen. BA, Colby Coll., 1975; MS in Libr. Sci., Columbia U., 1977. Reference libr. Hobart and William Smith Colls., Geneva, NY, 1977—79, L.I. U., Bklyn., 1979—80; reference specialist Congl. Rsch. Svc. Libr. of Congress, Washington, 1980—84; freelance writer Brunswick, Maine, 1984—; varsity tennis coach Brunswick H.S., 2001—. Corporator Mid Coast Hosp., Brunswick, 1996—; editl. cons., Brunswick, 1992—; founder Zipline Press, 2001—. Author, pub.: Seat-of-the-Pants Suppers, 2001; contbr. short stories and essays to various publs., articles to Portland Press Herald, Tennis Week, Brunswick Times Record, Libr. Jour., Port City Life, Bay Area Parent, Christian Sci. Monitor, others. Mem.: Maine Media Women (grantee 2000), Maine Writers and Pubs. Alliance (bd. sec. 1999—2000, bd. dirs. 1999—2001). Avocations: tennis, choral singing, piano. Office: Zipline Press PO Box 622 Brunswick ME 04011

HEISNER, ELLEN ANN, occupational health nurse; b. Kewanee, Ill., June 29, 1956; d. Joseph Francis and Margaret Mary Schmitt; children: Benjamin John Gerhardt, Lisa Mary Gerhardt. Diploma in Nursing, Franciscan Sch. Nursing, 1976; BS in Nursing, U. Ill., 1990. Cert. breath alcohol tech., CPR/AEb; occupl. health nurse, occupl. hearing conservationist, RN Ill., Iowa. Staff nurse East Moline (Ill.) Mental Health Ctr., 1976—79; staff nurse Regional Burn Ctr. Franciscan Med. Ctr., Rock Island, Ill., 1979—87, staff nurse Post Anesthesia Care Unit, 1987—94; staff nurse work Fitness Ctr., Bettendorf, Iowa, 1994—2001; staff nurse Work Fitness Ctr. Allcoa, Davenport, 2000—, City of Davenport, Iowa, 2001—. Mem. safety com. and wellness com. City of Davenport Occupl. Health, 2001—. Vol. nurse Scott County Bloodborne Pathogen Coalition, Davenport, Scott County Com. West Nile Virus, Davenport; mem. wellness com. St. Malachys Ch., Genseo, Ill. Recipient Leadership award, U. Ill. Coll. Nursing, 1990, Disting. Alumni award, 2003. Mem.: Quadcities Assn. Occupl. Health Nursing, U. Ill. Coll. Nursing Alumni Assn., Am. Assn. Occupl. Health Nurses. Avocations: fishing, travel, movies, family activities. Home: 635 North Aldrich St Geneseo IL 61254 Office: Occupational Health Service 1200 E 45th St Davenport IA 52807 E-mail: eah@ci.davenport.la.us.

HEISS, ALANNA, museum director; b. Louisville, Ky. married; 1 child. Degree, Lawrence U., Wis. Founder Inst. Art and Urban Resources (now Inst. for Contemporary Art), N.Y.C., 1971; dir. Clocktower Gallery, 1972—, PS1 Mus. (affiliate of Mus. Modern Art), N.Y.C., 1976—; dep. dir. Mus. Modern Art, 2000—; founder, exec. prodr. WPS1 online radio station, 2004—. Co-author (with John Wesley): Paintings: 1961-2000, 2001; co-author: (with Janet Cardiff) (foreward) A Survey of Works, Including Collaborations with George Bures Miller, 2002. Recipient award given by Mayor Koch, N.Y.C., 1980, Chevalier of Arts and Letters, France, 1987, Skowhegan award, 1989. Achievements include being knighted by the Swedish government in 1984; direction of over 500 shows. Office: PS1 Contemporary Arts Ctr 22-25 Jackson Ave Long Island City NY 11101*

HEISS, CLAIRE DEYOUNG, manufacturing executive; b. Oak Park, Ill., Dec. 1, 1946; d. Frederick H. and Ruth E. (DeYoung) H. BSIE, U. Ill., 1970. Quality mgr. X-Ray products GE, Milw., 1970-76, mfg. mgr. Home laundry Louisville, 1977-79, new plant start-up mgr. Aircraft Engine Wilmington, N.C., 1980-82, mfg. mgr. Aerospace Simulation Systems Daytona Beach, Fla., 1982-87, mfg. dir. X-Ray Bus./Med. Systems Milw., 1989-93; ops. dir. Motorola Tactical Electronics, Scottsdale, Ariz., 1987-89; v.p. consumer loans Bank Am., Brea, Calif., 1993-94; v.p., gen. mgr. cooking products Frigidaire Co., Springfield, Tenn., 1994—98; v.p, ops. Therasense, Inc., Alameda, Calif., 1999—2002; ops. cons. Thera Sense, Inc., 2002—. Mem. U. Ill., Alumni Bd. Dirs. Mech. and Indsl. Engrng., 2004—. Malcolm Baldrige Nat. Quality award Examiner, U.S. Dept. Commerce, 1992-93. Home and Office: 2921 Sea View Pkwy Alameda CA 94502-7450 Office Phone: 510-435-5647. E-mail: cdheiss@msn.com.

HEITKAMP, HEIDI, former state attorney general; b. Breckenridge, Minn. m. Darwin Lange; children: Althea Lange, Nathan Lange. BA, U. N.D., 1977; JD, Lewis and Clark Coll., 1980. Intern asst. Environ. Study Conf., Washington, 1976; legis. intern N.D. Legis. Coun., Bismarck, 1977; exec. dir. Northwestern Environ. Def. Ctr., Portland, 1978—79; rsch. asst. Nat. Resources Law Inst., Portland, 1979; atty. enforcement divsn. EPA, Washington, 1980—81; asst. atty. gen. Office of N.D. State Tax Commr., Bismarck, 1981—85, adminstrv. counsel, 1985—86, tax commr., 1986—92; atty. gen. State of N.D., Bismarck, 1993—2001. Del. Am. Coun. Young Polit. Leaders UK Internat. Def. Conf., 1988; trustee Fedn. Tax Adminstrs., 1991; presdl. appointee trade and environment policy adv. com. Office of Trade Reps., 1996. N.D. State Crusade chmn. Am. Cancer Soc., 1988—89. Named One of 20 Young Lawyers Making a Difference, ABA Barrister mag., 1990; recipient Young Achiever award, Nat. Coun. Women, 1987; fellow Toll fellow, Coun. State Govts., 1986. Mem.: Nat. Assn. Atty. Gens. Democrat. Office: 21 Captain Leach Dr Mandan ND 58554*

HEITKAMP, LYNN ELIZABETH, journalist; b. Saginaw, Mich., Oct. 2, 1979; d. Joseph Lawrence and Beverly (Collins) Heitkamp. BA magna cum laude, Ctrl. Mich. U., 1997—2001. Intern Cass City Chronicle, Cass City, Mich., 2000; editor-in-chief Ctrl. Mich. U. Chippewa Yearbook, Mt. Pleasant, Mich., 2000—01; editl. mgr. Builder/Arch. Mag., Saginaw, Mich., 2001—02; staff writer Twp. Times, Saginaw, Mich., 2002—. Mem. Ctrl. Mich. U. Student Media Bd., Mt. Pleasant, Mich., 1999—2001, Ctrl. Mich. U. Student Media Dir. Search Com., Mt. Pleasant, Mich., 2000. United Methodist. Avocations: writing fiction, music. Office: The Township Times 2089 Wieneke Saginaw MI 48603 E-mail: lynn@twptimes.com.

HEITSCH, LEONA MASON, artist, writer; b. Pontiac, Mich., Jan. 6, 1931; d. Russell Leonard and Margaret M. (Arnold) Mason; m. Charles Weyand Heitsch, July 5, 1952; children: Russell, Carrie, Grace, Charles, Irene. BA in chemistry, U. Mich., 1952. Ednl. asst. Spl. Sch. Dist., St. Louis County, Mo., 1969-81. Commentator Sta. KUMR, Rolla, Mo., 1996—.

Author: (pvt. printing) Echoes of the Ridge, 1985, Get Him to St. Louis, 1983; contbg. author: (poem anthology) Seasons of the Ozarks, 1998, Missourians Write About Reading, 2002, Apples, Apples Everywhere; contbr. poetry, articles to various publs. Sec., activist Mo. Assn. Children with Learning Disabilities, St. Louis, 1973-75; fundraising, writing Friends of [illegible] Breastfeeding Coalition, Lac du Flambeau, 1996—; activist Poets Against the War, 2003. Recipient honorable mention Mo. Writers Week award for poetry, 1992, 94, grand prize Artists Embassy Internat., San Francisco, 1997, Editors Challenge award Internat. Soc. Authors and Artists, Abilene, Tex., 1997, included in Memories and Memoirs, Anthology of Mo. authors, 2000; featured in Grandmother Earth IX, 2003, Grist, Mo. State Poetry Soc., 2003. Mem. St. Louis Poetry Soc., Rolla Area Writers Guild. Home and Office: Ridge Orchards HC 1 Box 66 Bourbon MO 65441-9305

HEIVILIN, DONNA MAE, government executive; b. Clear Lake, Iowa, May 12, 1937; d. Nels Oliver Ouverson and Nellie Bernice (Humphrey) Ouverson-Loats; m. Thomas Stuart Heivilin, Dec. 26, 1961 (div. Dec. 1971); children: Vincent Stuart, James Edward. Student, Iowa State U., 1956-57; BA, U. Minn., 1959; MPA, George Washington U., 1974, DPA, 1988. Assoc. dir. Navy issues, nat. security and internat. affairs U.S. Gen. Acctg. Office, Washington, 1985-88, dir. logistics issues, nat. security and internat. affairs, 1988-93, dir. def. mgmt., NASA issues, 1993-95, vice chair job process reengring. team, 1995-96, dir. planning & reporting, nat. security & internat. affairs, 1996-99, dir. quality and risk mgmt., 1999-2000, dir. applied rsch. and methods, 2000—. Pres. Nat. Coun. Assn.'s Policy Scis., Washington, 1980-83. Profiler editor Pub. Budget and Fin. Jour, 1985-98. Mem. Exec. Women in Govt. (pres. 1996-97), Am. Assn. Budget and Programming Analysts (bd. dirs. 1980-83, 98-99), Coun. Logistics Mgrs., Soc. Logistics Engrs., World Future Soc., Profl. Futurists Assn., The Internat. Alliance for Women (bd. dirs. 1997—, treas. 1998, 1st v.p. 1999, pres. 2000-01), Phi Kappa Phi. Avocations: recreational walking, plays, shakespeare, country music. Home: 5330 36th St N Arlington VA 22207-1816 Office: GAO 441 G St NW Rm 6105 Washington DC 20548-0001 E-mail: donna.heivilin@verizon.net., heivilind@gao.gov.

HEIZER, IDA ANN, retired real estate broker; b. Oxford, Colo., Mar. 14, 1919; d. Albert Henry and Ella (Engbrook) Ordener; m. Donald Heizer, Apr. 7, 1947; children: Robert John. Diploma, Brown's Bus. Coll., 1939; student Otero Jr. Coll., 1946-47, U. So. Colo., 1962; grad. Realtors Inst., Nat. Assn. Real Estate Bds., 1972. Cert. closer real estate, cert. residential specialist. Clk., Montgomery Ward Co., LaJunta, Colo., 1935-37; bookkeeper Colo. Bank & Trust Co., LaJunta, 1937-38; cashier/bookkeeper Fox Theatre, LaJunta, 1939-40; clk. Civil Service, LaJunta, 1940-45; steno/abstractor Deaf Smith Abstract Office, Hereford, Tex., 1948-50; sec. Otero County Agt. Office, Rocky Ford, Colo., 1953-55; real estate broker Pueblo Realty & Service Co., Inc., Colo., 1958-86; ret., 1988. Mem. Pueblo Bd. Realtors, Nat. Assn. Real Estate Appraisers, Nat. Assn. Realtors, Colo. Assn. Realtors, Women's Council Realtors, Daus. of the Republic Tex., Beta Sigma Phi. Home and Office: 331 Van Buren St Pueblo CO 81004-1807

HELBERG, KRISTIN VAUGHAN, artist; b. Syracuse, N.Y., Aug. 7, 1947; d. Burton Edward and Shirley Adelaide (Holden) H. Student, Boston U., 1965-67, Gerritt Rietvald Acad., Amsterdam, The Netherlands, 1969. Dress designer India Imports R.I., Providence, 1967-68, 70-71; costume designer Ctr. Stage, Balt., 1972; owner, pub. Rainy Day Press, Sausalito, Calif., 1972-84. Gallery artist Toad Hall Gallery ABC Home, N.Y., 1990—, Gallery Americana, Houston, 1991—, Frank Miele Gallery, N.Y.C., 1992—, Galerie Black, Lausanne, Switzerland, 1995—. One-woman shows include Toad Hall Gallery, Saratoga Springs, N.Y., 1991, Very Spl. Arts, Washington, 1993, NIH, Bethesda, Md., 1994, 96, Embassy of Switzerland, Washington, 1995, Children's Nat. Med. Ctr., Washington, 1996; exhibited in groups shows at Toad Hall Gallery, 1992, Gallerie Pro Arte Kaspar, Morges, Switzerland, 1994, NIH, Bethesda, Md., 1994, 96, 2003, Outsider Art Fair, N.Y.C., 1995-96, Am. Visionary Art Show, Balt., 1998; represented in permanent collections NIH, Children's Nat. Med. Ctr., Clinton Presdl. Libr., Little Rock. Ford Found. scholar, 1972; artist-in-residency grantee Md. State Arts Coun., 1989—, Howard County Arts Coun., 1993—, Montgomery County Arts Coun. grant, 1989-93. Avocations: playing piano, ballroom dancing, hiking. Studio: 221 S Chapel St Baltimore MD 21231-2619

HELBERG, SHIRLEY ADELAIDE HOLDEN, artist, educator; b. Solvay, NY; d. Isaac Edgar and Gladys Evelyn (Tucker) Holden; m. Burton Edvard Helberg; children: Keir Holm, Kristin Vaughan, Kecia Tucker Lau, Kandace Holden Mead, Kraig Brownlee. BE, Johns Hopkins U., 1969; MFA, Md. Inst. Art, 1975. Tchr. Norris Dam Govt. Sch., Tenn., 1945—46, various schs., N.J., Pa., N.Y., Bergenfield, Manchester (Pa.) Pub. Schs., 1965-84, Balt. City Schs., 1988-96; demonstration tchr. Balt. City Schs., O'Donnell Heights Sch., 1992. One-woman shows include U. Va. Charlottesville, 1974, Cayuga Mus. Art and History, Auburn, N.Y., 1974, Hist. Soc. York Mus., Pa., 1977, York Coll., 1984, Country Club York; represented in permanent collections Pres. Richard Nixon; author: (poetry) Chosen Few, 1998; author, illustrator: The Kitty Cat Who Wanted to Fly, 1999, The Jumping Frog of Calaveras County, 1999. Bd. dirs. York (Pa.) Arts Coun., 1964—66. Named Outstanding Tchr. Northeastern Sch. Dist. Bd. Edn. Mem. NEA, DAR, AAUW, Daus. of Union Vets., Nat. League Am. Pen Women (Pa. State art chmn. 1972-74, pres. Pa. orgn. 1974-76, nat. scholarship chair 1976-98, registrar 1986-88, 5th v.p. 1988-90, Disting. Svc. award 1978, 80, 82, 84, 86, 88, 90, 92, Disting. Achievement award 1988, 94), Pa. State Edn. Assn., Internat. Platform Assn., Harrisburg Art Assn., York Art Assn., Pa. Watercolor Soc., Johns Hopkins Faculty Club. Republican. Methodist. Home: 5433 Pigeon Hill Rd Spring Grove PA 17362-8854 also: 727 S Ann St Baltimore MD 21231-3402 Home: 727 S Ann St Baltimore MD 21231

HELD, NANCY B. perinatal nurse, lactation consultant; b. Winchester, Mass., Sept. 4, 1957; d. Ann and Laurence Babine; m. Lew Held, May 22, 1976; children: David, Jessica. BSN, NYU, 1979; MS, U. Calif., San Francisco, 1992. Cert. Internat. Bd. Lactation Cons. Examiners. Labor/delivery nurse Pascack Valley Hosp., Westwood, N.J., 1979-83; obstetrics educator Drs. Pinski, Wiener & Grasso, Westwood, N.J., 1982-85; ob/gyn office nurse Drs. Power Hagbom Holter & Clark, San Francisco, 1986-87; asst. to dir. maternity svcs. Women's Health Assn., Greenbrae, Calif., 1987-89; perinatal edn. and lactation ctr. clin. coord. Calif. Pacific Med. Ctr., San Francisco, 1989-99; owner North Bay Lamaze, 1988-96; co-owner Health Designs, San Rafael, 1997-98; exec. dir. Day One, LLC, San Francisco, 1999—. Speaker and cons. in field. Recipient Founders Day award, NYU. Fellow Am. Coll. Childbirth Educators; mem. Assn. Women's Health Obstetric and Neonatal Nursing (spkr. nat. con. 1993, nat. rsch. utilization team 1993), Am. Soc. Psychoprophylaxis (chpt. co-pres.), Nurses Assn. of Am. Coll. Ob/Gyn, Internat. Childbirth Educators Assn., Internat. Lactation Cons. Assn., Sigma Theta Tau. E-mail: nheld@dayonecenter.com.

HELDMAN, BETTY LOU FAULKNER, retired health facility administrator; b. Washington, N.C., June 3, 1937; d. Basil Frank Faulkner and Willie Mae Rose; m. Arthur Charles Heldman Jr., Aug. 23, 1959; children: Ruth Victoria, Andrew Basil. BS in Biology, Davis and Elkins Coll., Elkins, W.Va., 1959; MS in Med. Biology, C.W. Post Coll., 1978. Cert. eye bank technician Eye Bank Assn. Am. Lab. asst. Portsmouth (Va.) Gen. Hosp., 1954—58; lab. technician Johnson & Johnson Rsch., New Brunswick, NJ, 1959—62; med. assoc. Brookhaven Nat. Lab., Upton, NY, 1973—86; adminstrv. dir. Lions Eye Bank for L.I., Great Neck, NY, 1986—97; ret. Presenter in field; pres., v.p. exec. bd. Brookhaven Women in Sci., 1979—86; chairperson United Fund Brookhaven Nat. Lab., 1983—84; elected mem. lectr. com. Brookhaven Lab., 1978—84. Author, pub.: Faulkner, Cannon, Rose, Brickell-Families of Eastern North Carolina, 2003; contbr. rsch. papers to profl. jours. Recipient Outstanding Svc. in Sci. award, Town of Islip, 1985, Plaque of Appreciation, Lions and Lioness Clubs, 1991. Mem.: Assn. for Women in Sci. Home: 2146 Seaton Springs Rd Sevierville TN 37862

HELFER, RICKI TIGERT, banking consultant; b. N.C., Feb. 4, 1945; m. Michael S. Helfer; 1 child, Matthew. BA with honors, Vanderbilt U.; MA, U. N.C.; JD with honors, U. Chgo. Law clk. to hon. John Minor Wisdom U.S. Ct. Appeals; counsel to Jud. Com. U.S. Senate, Washington, 1978-79; assoc., ptnr. Leva, Hawes, Symington, Martin and Oppenheimer, 1979-83; sr. counsel internat. fin. Treasury Dept., Washington; chief internat. lawyer Fed. Reserve Bd., 1985-92; ptnr. Gibson, Dunn & Crutcher, Washington, 1992-94; chmn. FDIC, Washington, 1994-97; nonresident sr. fellow The Brookings Inst., Washington, 1998-99; prof. law, dir. fin. instns. program Washington Coll. Law, Am. U., Washington, 2000—; cons. Am. Cmty. Bankers, Washington, 2000—. Bd. govs., chmn. audit com. Phila. Stock Exch., 1997-99; cons. internat. banking and fin. regulation. Bd. dirs. Girl Scouts U.S., 1995-99, Life Pt. Hosps., Inc., 1999—; mem. vis. com. U. Chgo. Law Sch., 1989-92, 94-97. Mem. ABA (former chair internat. banking and fin. com.), Am. Law Inst., Coun. Fgn. Rels., Washington Fgn. Law Soc. (past pres.). Office: Am Cmty Bankers #400 900 19th St NW Washington DC 20006-2110

HELFERICH, CHRISTINE MARY, musician, music educator; b. Muskegon, Mich., June 13, 1970; d. Thomas John and Patricia Lee Helferich; m. Gerhard Kurt James Guter, June 12, 1999. MusB, Western Mich. U., Kalamazoo, 1993—98; MusM, U. Miami, Coral Gables, 1995—97. Prof. music Calif. State U. Long Beach, 2001—; prof. jazz voice Mt. San Antonio Coll., Walnut, Calif., 2001—. Dir. choral dept. Parchment HS, Parchment, Mich., 1993—95, Novato HS, Novato, Calif., 1997—2001. Mem.: Jazz Vocal Coalition, Am. Choral Director's Assn., Music Eductor's Nat. Conf., Internat. Assn. Jazz Educators. Catholic. Office: Calif State U Long Beach 1250 Bellflower Blvd Long Beach CA 90804 E-mail: chelferi@csulb.edu.

HELFGOTT, GLORIA VIDA, artist; b. NYC, May 25, 1928; d. Charles and Anna (Cohen) Wolff; m. Roy B. Helfgott; 1 child, Daniel Andrew. Grad. in fine arts, Cooper Union, 1948. Faculty mem. Ctr. for Book Arts, N.Y.C., 1989-98, San Francisco Ctr. for the Book, 1998-, Brookfield (Conn.) Craft Ctr., 1988—, Art New Eng. at Bennington (Vt.) Coll., 1992, Womens Studio Workshop, Rosendale, N.Y., 1992, Long Beach Art Mus., 1997-98. Solo and group exhbns. include P.S.I., L.I., N.Y., 1979, Handin Hand Gallery, N.Y.C., 1985, Grad. Ctr. for the Arts, W.Va. U., Morgantown, 1988, Berkshire Mus., Pittsfield, Mass., 1988, Ctr. for the Arts, Avado, Colo., 1989, Hoffman Gallery, Portland, Oreg., 1990, Granary Books, N.Y.C., 1990, Ted Cronin Gallery, N.Y.C., 1990, Boca Raton (Fla.) Mus., 1991, Sazama Gallery, Chgo., 1992, Harper-Collins Exhbn. Space, N.Y.C., 1993, 1998, 2000, Istvan Kiraly Mus., Hungary, 1994,1996, 1998, Meml. Art Mus., Ormond Beach, Fla., 1994, Brown U., 1995, Nexus Gallery, Phila., 1995, Ctr. for Book Arts, 1996, 2002, UCLA Art Libr., 1997; traveling exhbn. U.S. State Dept., 1996-98, San Francisco Libr., 1999, 2001; ; represented in permanent collections Ruth and Marvin Sackner Archive of Concrete and Visual Poetry, Miami Beach, Fla., Nat. Mus. Women in the Arts, Washington, Victoria and Albert Mus., London, Bklyn. Mus., Stanford U., UCLA, Swarthmore Coll., Oberlin Coll, U. of Alberta, LIU; curator, So Called Books, 1995-2002, San Francisco, NYC, Salt Lake City, Los Angeles; Beyond the Page, 1995, NYC; Metafiction, 1992, Kent, CT. Mem. Guild of Book Workers. Home: 1784 Palisades Dr Pacific Palisades CA 90272-2117

HELGANZ, BEVERLY BUZHARDT, counselor; b. Tampa, Fla., June 7, 1941; d. M. O. Buzhardt and Jeanne M. Buzhardt Crabb; m. Charles F. Helganz Jr., June 26, 1964 (dec. Dec. 1977). AA, Jacksonville U., 1962, BA, 1974; MEd, U. North Fla., 1993. Lic. mental health counselor; nat. cert. counselor; cert. addictions profl. Customer contact So. Bell, Jacksonville, Fla., 1959-66, supr., 1966—80, staff mgr., 1980—91; assessment counselor Charter Hosp., Jacksonville, 1995; sr. counselor River Region Human Svcs., Jacksonville, 1995—96; family link counselor Youth Crisis Ctr., Jacksonville, 1996—99; adult addictions counselor Clay County Behavioral Health Ctr., Middleburg, Fla., 1999—2000; therapist daniel, Jacksonville, 2000—01, Family Counseling Svcs., 2001—02, Biofeedback Assoc. of North East Fla. Inc., 2002—. Past pres. Am. Bus. Women's Assn., Jacksonville, 1969-70. Mem. women's aux. U. Med. Ctr., Jacksonville, 1994—98; 1st v.p. Aux. Hospice of N.E. Fla., Jacksonville, 1994—95; panel mem. foster care citizen's rev. bd. 4th Jud. Cir. Ct., Jacksonville, 1993—2002; docent Mus. Sci. and History, 1993—95; past pres. Jacksonville Alumnae Panhellenic Assn., 1982; mem., docent Jacksonville Mus. Contemporary Art; guardian ad litem 4th Jud. Cir. Ct., 2002—04; mem. Sheriff's Adv. Coun., 2001—; bd. dirs. N.E. Fla. Coun. on Alcoholism and Drug Abuse, 1997, treas. bd. dirs., 1999—2000; Baptist Med. Ctr. Auxiliary, 2002. Recipient Merit award Am. Bus. Women's Assn., 1966, Woman of Yr. award, 1969, Honor Ring Alumnae and cert of merit Zeta Tau Alpha, 1975, 76, Girl of Yr. award Beta Sigma Phi. Mem. ACA, Fla. Mental Health Counselors Assn., N.E. Fla. Mental Health Counselors Assn., Mental Health Assn., Telephone Pioneers of Am. (life), Pilot Club Jacksonville (bd. dirs., past pres.), Club Continental, Phi Kappa Phi. Avocations: collecting penguins, films, fine dining, art/museums. Home: 5000 San Jose Blvd Apt 97 Jacksonville FL 32207-7687

HELGENBERGER, MARG, actress; b. Nov. 16, 1958; m. Alan Rosenberg; 1 child, Hugh. BS, Northwestern U., 1982. Appeared in TV series Ryan's Hope, 1984-86, The Shell Game, 1987, China Beach, 1988-91 (Emmy award; named Primetime Programming Individual Outstanding Supporting Actress in Drama Series, 1990, 91), CSI:Crime Scene Investigation, 2000-; co-host of New Year's Rockin' Eve, 1988, Home, 1989, (TV movies) Blind Vengence, 1990, Death Dreams, 1991, In Sickness and In Health, 1992, Through the Eyes of a Killer, 1992, When Love Kills: The Seduction of John Hearn, 1993, Stephen King's The Tommyknockers, 1993, Where Are My Children?, 1994, Lie Down with Lions, 1994, Partners, 1994, Perfect Murder, Perfect Town: Jon Benet and the City of Boulder, 2000; appeared in films Always, 1989, After Midnight, 1989, Crooked Hearts, 1991, Desperate Motive, 1993, The Cowboy Way, 1994, Bad Boys, 1995, Species, 1995, Erin Brockovich, 2000.

HELIN, ELEANOR FRANCIS, astronomer, geologist; b. Pasadena, Calif. Rsch. asst. meteorite statistics Jet Propulsion Lab., Calif. Inst. Tech., 1960-61, rsch. asst. meteorite analysis, 1961-68, assoc. sci. asteroid rsch. and survey, 1969-76, sr. sci. asteroid survey and planetary sci., 1976-79, mem. profl. staff, 1979-80, mem. tech. staff, 1980—. Mem. Am. Astron. Soc., Inst. Astron. Union, Meteorol. Soc. Office: Jet Propulsion Lab Calif Inst Tech 4800 Oak Grove Dr # 183501 Pasadena CA 91109-8001

HELIN, JACQUELYN MAE, classical musician, music educator; b. Chgo., Sept. 24, 1951; d. Rudolph A. and Janet M. (Wallin) H.; m. Robert A. Glick, May 13, 1989; children: Kathryn Tyra Helin-Glick, William David Helin-Glick. MusB, U. Oreg., 1973; MA, Stanford U., 1976; D of Musical Arts, U. Tex., Austin, 1982. Tchg. musician Lincoln Ctr. Inst., N.Y.C., 1987-91; tchr. 92nd St Y Performing Arts Dept., N.Y.C., 1990-91; faculty mem. 92d St Sch. Music, N.Y.C., 1987-91; classical musician, tchr. N.Y.C., 1979-91, Santa Fe, 1991—. Cons. in field. Solo performer The Corcoran Gallery, Washington, 1982, Dumbarton Oaks, Washington, 1982, The Chagall Mus., Nice, France, 1984, Merkin Concert Hall, N.Y.C., 1986, the 92d St Y., N.Y.C., 1992, Caltech, Pasadena, 1993, On the Horowitz Piano, Los Alamos, N.Mex., 1993, On the Pianos of Horowitz, Paderewski & Cliburn, 1997, others; pianist Redwood Symphony, 1994, Santa Fe Symphony, 1994, Mesa Symphony, 1994, 98, Richmond Symphony, 1995, 97, Greenwich Symphony, 1996; live radio appearances include Performance Today on Nat. Pub. Radio WFMT, Chgo., WNCN, N.Y.C., WNYC, N.Y.C., WBAI, N.Y.C., WGBH, Boston, WGMS, Washington, numerous others. Recipient Lucy Moses award Outstanding Promise Yale U. Sch. Music, New Haven, Conn., 1974; named winner Artists in [illegible] (performing arts touring roster 1993-96), Northwest Arts Alliance, Western Alliance Arts Adminstrs., N.Mex. Touring & Residency Roster, The Bohemians. Avocations: scuba diving, skiing, hiking, film, opera. Home: 2327 Santa Barbara Dr Santa Fe NM 87505-5742

HELKE, CINDA JANE, pharmacology and neuroscience educator, researcher, academic administrator; b. Waterloo, Iowa, Feb. 27, 1951; d. Gerald and Lorna (Smith) Pieres; m. Joel Edward Helke, Aug. 10, 1974. BS in Pharmacy, Creighton U., 1974; PhD, Georgetown U., 1978. Staff fellow NIH, Bethesda, Md., 1978-80; asst. prof. dept. pharmacology Uniformed Svcs. Univ. of the Health Scis., Bethesda, 1980-85, assoc. prof. dept. pharmacology, 1985-88; prof. dept. pharmacology Uniformed Svcs. Univ. Health Scis., Bethesda, 1988—, prof. neurosci. program, 1991—2001, dir. neurosci. program, 1993—2002, assoc. dean for grad. edn., 2001—. Mem. adv. panel Am. Heart Assn., 1984-87, NIH, Bethesda, 1987-91; mem. oversight rev. panel NSF, 1986, pharmacology test com. Nat. Bd. Med. Examiners, 1992-94. Author chpts. in books; mem. editl. bd. Synapse, Pharmacology, Jour. Comparative Neurology; contbr. numerous articles to profl. jours. NIH grantee, 1981—. Mem. AAAS, Am. Soc. Pharmacology and Exptl. Therapeutics (sec.-treas. elect 2002—, Soc. for Neurosci. Women in Sci., Women in Neurosci., Soc. for Neurosci. (sec.-treas. Washington chpt. 1985-87). Avocations: piano and choral music, aerobics, photography, travel. Office: Uniformed Svcs U Health Sci 4301 Jones Bridge Rd Bethesda MD 20814-4712

HELLENBRAND, SHERRI, insurance company executive; b. Madison, Wis., May 2, 1969; MS in Fin. and Real Estate, U. Wis., Madison, 1995. Bus. analyst Goldman, Sachs & Co., N.Y.C., 1997—2001; ops. mgr. TitleVest Agy., Inc., N.Y.C., 2001—03; sole propr. Terra Abstract, N.Y.C., 2003—. Business E-Mail: shellenbrand@terra-abstract.com.

HELLER, AMANDA, editor; b. Washington, D.C., Apr. 6, 1946; d. Leo and Shirley (Stein) Young; m. Richard Benjamin Heller, Aug. 13, 1972; 1 child, Benjamin David. AB, Mt. Holyoke Coll., 1968. Editor Atlantic Monthly, Boston, 1969-76, Art New England, Boston, 1980-85; freelance editor, 1976—; book rev. columnist Boston Globe, 1980—. Co-author: Storm Across Asia, 1979. Mem. Dem. City Com., Newton, Mass., 1993—. Avocations: reading, crafts.

HELLER, BARBARA R. former dean, nursing educator; BS, Boston U., 1962; MS, Adelphi U., 1966; EdM, Columbia U., 1971, EdD, 1973; postgrad., U. Md., 1986-90. RN Md., Mass., N.Y., Pa., Va. Chmn. dept. nursing SUNY, Farmingdale; asst. dean acad. programs, Coll. Nursing Villanova U.; prof. and chair dept. edn., adminstrn. and health policy, Sch. Nursing U. Md., Balt., dean Sch. Nursing, 1990—2002, prof., 2002—. Dir. rsch. and edn. nursing dept., Clin. Ctr., NIH, 1983-84; congl. fellow in health policy and edn. Hon. Constance A. Morella, U.S. House of Reps., 1989-90; vice chair, mem. bd. dirs. Computer Based Patient Record Inst., 1992-94, So. Coun. on Collegiate Edn. for Nurses, So. Regional Edn. Bd., chmn. task force on telecomms., numerous others; cons. in field. Co-editor: (book) Information Management in Nursing and Health Care, 1995; contbr. chpts. to books, articles to profl. jours. Mem. bd. dirs. Paul's Place, Open Gates; chair adv. bd. Gov's. Wellmobile. Recipient Innovative Health Program award Md. Found. for Nursing, 1995, Outstanding Educator of Am. award, Alumni award for Nursing Excellence Boston U., Alumni award for Nursing Practice Tchr's. Coll. Columbia U.; numerous grants. Fellow Am. Acad. Nursing; mem. ANA, Am. Assn. Colls. Nursing, Am. Soc. Med. Informatics Assn., Am. Assn. Higher Edn., Nat. League Nursing, Md. Nurses Assn., Md. Assn. Higher Edn., Gerontological Soc., Nurses in Washington Roundtable, Women's Pol. Caucus Md., Exec. Women's Network Balt., Sigma Theta Tau, Phi Kappa Phi. Office: Univ MD Sch Nursing 655 W Lombard St Rm 725 Baltimore MD 21201-1506

HELLER, LOIS JANE, physiologist, educator, researcher; b. Detroit, Jan. 4, 1942; d. John and Lona Elizabeth (Stockmeyer) Skagerberg; m. Robert Eugene Heller, May 21, 1966; children: John Robert, Suzanne Elizabeth. BA, Albion Coll., 1964; MS, U. Mich., 1966; PhD, U. Ill., Chgo., 1970. Instr. med ctr. U. Ill., Chgo., 1969-70, asst. prof., 1970-71, U. Minn., Duluth, 1972-77, assoc. prof., 1977-89, prof., 1989—. Author: Cardiovascular Physiology, 5th edit., 2003; contbr. numerous articles to profl. jours. Mem. Am. Physiol. Soc., Am. Heart Assn., Soc. Exptl. Biology and Medicine, Internat. Soc. Heart Rsch., Sigma Xi. Avocation: birding. Home: 9129 Congdon Blvd Duluth MN 55804-0005 Office: Univ Minn Sch of Medicine Duluth MN 55812

HELLER, MARY WHEELER, photographer; b. Sterling, Ill., Mar. 4, 1928; d. LeRoy Coe and Gladys (Lawrence) Wheeler; m. Peter Seton Heller, June 30, 1956; 1 child, Kate Heller O'Reilly. B in Philosophy, U. Chgo., 1947; BA, U. Ariz., 1950; student, Internat. Ctr. Photography, N.Y.C., 1979-81, Maine Photographic Workshop, 1980. Editl. asst. The New Yorker, N.Y.C., 1951-56, reporter, 1957-60; art photographer N.Y.C., 1970—. Stock photographer Swanstock, Getty Images, 1985—; com. mem. Internat. Ctr. Photography, 1990—. One-woman shows include James Hunt Barker Gallery, Nantucket, Mass., 1979, Siasconset Bookstore, Nantucket, 1984, Studio Gallery, Siasconset, 1982, 1986—88, 1990, Ledel Gallery, N.Y.C., 1990, X Gallery, Nantucket, 1992—95, Lisa Steinmetz Gallery, Clayton, Mo., 1997, U.S. Embassy, Yemen, 1998, Old Spouter Gallery, Nantucket, 1998, New Gallery, 1999, Artists Assn. Nantucket, 2000, 2002, Century Assn., 2000, exhibited in group shows at Vision Gallery, San Francisco, 1987—88, Ledel Gallery, N.Y.C., 1987—88, Main St. Gallery, Nantucket, 1987—91, 1996—98, U.S. Embassy, Oman, 1997, Century Assn., N.Y.C., 1997—2002, One Pleasant St. Art Ctr., Nantucket, 1996—97, Artists' Assn. Nantucket, 1998, Gallery N., Setauket, N.Y., 1999, Photo Dist. Gallery, N.Y.C., 2003, others. Trustee N.Y.C. Sch. Vol. Program (now named Learning Leaders), 1961—, classroom tutor, 1961—62, chmn. bd. trustees, 1967—72, chmn. search com. for new exec. dir., 1976; bd. dirs. Pub. Edn. Assn., N.Y.C., 1966—74, pres. bd. dirs., 1972—74; co-chmn. edn. com. N.Y. Philharm, N.Y.C., 1970—80; bd. dirs. Chamber Music Soc. Lincoln Ctr., N.Y.C., 1975—91, chmn. exec. com., 1979—82, pres. bd. dirs., 1988—91; bd. dirs. Nantucket Land Coun., 1986—; v.p. bd. dirs. MacDowell Colony, Peterborough, NH, 1975—79, chmn. search com. for new dir., 1977. Mem.: Am. Soc. Media Photographers. Episcopalian. Avocations: reading, visual and performing arts, travel, golf, tennis.

HELLMANN, RENE BRAUN, English as a Second Language educator, elementary school educator; b. Hammond, Ind., July 13, 1967; d. Philip Leo and Suellen Ann (Thiel) Braun; m. Anthony Lawrence, June 29, 1991; children: Alexander, Nicholas, Benjamin. BA, Ind. U., 1989, MA, 1990. ESL tchr. Henry Abbott RVT Sch., Danbury, Conn., 1990-92, Danbury Adult Edn., 1990—96; tchr. Barnum Elem. Sch., Bridgeport, Conn., 1999—2000, Roberts Arc Elem. Sch., Danbury, Conn., 2000—. Adj. prof. Western Conn. State U., Danbury, 1991-99, Naugatuck Valley Cmty. Tech. Coll., 1996-99. Mem. TESOL. Home: 31 Pocono Ln Danbury CT 06810-4136

HELLON, TONI, state senator; 2 children. BA in Journalism, U. Ariz. Freelance writer, graphic artist; Rep. senator legis. dist. 12 Ariz. State Senate, Phoenix. Mem. appropriations, edn. and health coms. Ariz. State Senate, vice chmn. family svcs., mem. domestic rels. reform study subcom.; bd. dirs. Tucson Ariz. Boys Chorus; mem. pub. adv. bd. KUAT-TV, 2000—; mem. Pima County Trial Ct. Commn., 1992-2000; mem. gov.'s adv. bd.

Ariz. Film Commn., 1997—; polit. cons. Former editor-in-chief Tombstone (Ariz.) Epitaph. Vol. 88-rime, 1988-97; dir. Alliance to Save the Poison Info. Ctr., U. Ariz., Coll. Pharmacy, 1993-94; del. II Congreso De Mujeres Empresarias and Profesionistas, Sonara, Ariz., 1995-96; mem. Hispanic Profl. Action Com., Ariz. Women's Polit. Caucus; chmn. Pima County Rep. Party, Tucson, 1997, past pres.; past pres. Cactus Wren Rep. Women, Phoenix; former chmn. Rep. Legis. Dist. 13. Mem. Am. Diabetes Assn. (Ariz. chpt. gala chmn. 1999). Office: Ariz State Senate State Capitol Rm 304 1700 W Washington Phoenix AZ 85007 E-mail: thellon@azleg.state.az.us.

HELLWEGE, NANCY CAROL, special education educator; b. Bridgeport, Conn., Dec. 28, 1933; d. Emil and Dorothy Alma (Sell) Rosenoch; children: Michael, Christie, Patricia. BS with distinction, Ind. U., Ft. Wayne, 1972, MS, 1977; EdS, Ball State U., 1984. Tchr. 1st grade Luth. Schs., Ft. Wayne, 1962-66; coord. Head Start, Ft. Wayne, 1967-68; kindergarten tchr. Luth. Schs., Ft. Wayne, 1968-78; resource rm. tchr. East Allen County Schs., New Haven, Ind., 1978-81; cons. N.E. Colo. BOCES, Haxtun, 1982-84; strategist South Cen. BOCES, Pueblo, Colo., 1984-86; supr. Mt. BOCES, Leadville, Colo., 1986-87; coord. Broward Cunty Schs., Ft. Lauderdale, Fla., 1987-88; pres. Learning Power, Inc., 1988—; prin., owner Christi Acad., Sch. for learning disabled, 2000—. Author handbooks: Helping Children Reach Their Potential, 1991, Different Strokes/Different Folks, 1990. Mem.: NAFE, Phi Delta Kappa. Avocations: swimming, reading, camping. Office: Learning Power Inc PO Box 770253 Pompano Beach FL 33077-0253 Office Phone: 954-597-0645.

HELLWIG, MONIKA KONRAD, organization executive, theology educator; b. Breslau, Silesia, Germany, Dec. 10, 1929; came to U.S., 1955; d. Rudolf and Marianne (Blaauw) H.; adopted children: Ericka, Michael, Carlos. LLB, Liverpool (Eng.) U., 1949, C.S.Sc., 1951; MA, Cath. U. Am., 1956, PhD, 1968; LittD (honoris causa), St. Mary-of-the-Woods Coll., St. Mary-of-the-Woods, Ind., 1974, St. Mary's Coll., Notre Dame, Ind., 1985, Trinity Coll., Washington, 1986, St. Michael's Coll., Winooski, Vt., 1986; LLD (honoris causa), Our Lady of the Elms Coll., Chicopee, Mass., 1977, Loyola U., Chgo., 1990; STD (honoris causa), Immaculate Conception Sem., Darlington, N.J., 1980; DD (honoris causa), Jesuit Sch. Theology, Berkeley, Calif., 1987; LHD (honoris causa), Loyola Marymount U., 1989, Loyola U., New Orleans, 1989, Coll. St. Catherine, St. Paul, 1989; LHD, Fairfield U., 1990. Instr. St. Therese's Jr. Coll., Phila., 1956-62; ghostwriter, rsch. asst. Holy See, Vatican City, 1963-64; lectr. theology Georgetown U., Washington, 1967-68, asst. prof., 1968-71, assoc. prof., 1971-77, prof., 1977-90, Landegger Disting. prof., 1990-96; exec. dir. Assn. Cath. Colls. and Univs., Washington, 1996—. Vis. prof. DePaul U., Chgo., 1968, St. Norbert's Coll., Wis., 1974, St. Michael's Coll., Vt., 1975, U. San Francisco, 1976, Princeton (N.J.) Theol. Sem., 1977, 79, 83, St. John's U., Collegeville, Minn., 1978, 82, 85, St. Joseph's Coll., West Hartford, Conn., 1980, U. Notre Dame, 1986, U. Dayton, 1986, Boston Coll., 1987, Huntington (N.Y.) Sem., 1987-90; seminarist Ecumenical Inst. Advanced Theol. Studies, Jerusalem, 1975-76; mem. Nat. Com. on Social Justice and Peace, U.S. Cath. Conf., 1982-84, Nat. Cath.-Presbyn./Reformed Bilateral Consultation, 1982-85; theol. cons. Treehaus Publs., 1983—; mem. selection com. summer rsch. grants NEH, 1984, 86; mem. internat. selection com. Grawemeyer Award, 1991; mem. selection panel Theol. Book Award, Cath. Press Assn., 1989-91, Pax Christi Book Award, 1990-91. Author: What Are the Theologians Saying?, 1970, The Meaning of the Sacraments, 1972, the Christian Creeds, 1973, Tradition: The Catholic Story Today, 1975, The Eucharist and the Hunger of the World, 1976, Death and Christian Hope, 1978, Understanding Catholicism, 1981, Whose Experience Counts in Theological Reflection?, 1982, Sign of Reconciliation and Conversion, 1982, Jesus the Compassion of God, 1983, Christian Women in a Troubled World, 1985, Gladness Their Escort: Homiletic Reflection, Years A, B and C, 1987; also articles; author: (with others) Community of Character, 1988, Faithful Witness: Foundations of Theology for Today's Church, 1989, Catholic Perspectives on Medical Morals, 1989, The Best in Theology, Vol. 4, 1990, Handbook of Faith, 1990, Christianity and the Wider Ecumenism, 1990, Christian Uniqueness Reconsidered, 1990, The Universal Catechism Reader, 1990, Georgetown at Two Hundred, 1990, The Catholic Church and American Culture, 1990, Death or Dialogue?, 1990, The Way of Ignatius Loyola, 1991, A Spirituality for Today's World, 1991, Individuality and Cooperative Action, 1991, Systematic Theology: Roman Catholic Perspectives, 1991, others; contbr. to: Encyclopedia of Religion, 1987, The New Dictionary of Theology, 1987; gen. editor: (book series) Sacraments Series, Zachaeus Doctrinal Series; assoc. editor Jour. Ecumenical Studies, 1973—; mem. editorial bd. Theol. Studies, 1981-91; editorial cons. Religious Studies Bull., 1983—. Bd. dirs. Woodstock Theol. Ctr., 1985-91; mem. bd. visitors Sch. Religious Studies, Cath. U., 1989—; mem. disting. women's adv. coun. St. Catherine's Coll., St. Paul, 1990— Recipient award Cath. U. Am. Alumni Assn., 1986; named D.C. Prof. of Yr., Coun. for Advancement and Support of Edn., 1988; fellow Ecumenical Inst. Advanced Theol. Studies, 1975-76, Woodrow Wilson Internat. Ctr. for Scholars, 1985-86; Hesbergh award, Aswsn of Cath. Coll. & Univ., 1994. Mem. AAUP, Cath. Theol. Soc. Am. (v.p. 1984-85, pres.-elect 1985-86, pres. 1986-87, John Courtney Murray award 1984), Coll. Theology Soc. Democrat. Roman Catholic. Home: 9211 Mintwood St Silver Spring MD 20901-3519 Office: Assn Cath Colls and Univs 1 Dupont Cir NW Ste 650 Washington DC 20036-1134

HELLYER, CONSTANCE ANNE (CONNIE ANNE CONWAY), writer, musician; b. Puyallup, Wash., Apr. 22, 1937; d. David Tirrell and Constance (Hopkins) H.; m. Peter A. Corning, Dec. 30, 1963 (div. 1977); children: Anne Arundel, Stephanie Deak Cunningham; m. Don W. Conway, Oct. 12, 1980. BA with honors, Mills Coll., 1959. Grader, rschr. Harvard U., Cambridge, Mass., 1959-60; rschr. Newsweek mag., N.Y.C., 1960-63; author's asst. Theodore H. White and others, N.Y.C., 1964-69; freelance writer, editor Colo., Calif., 1970-75; writer, editor Stanford (Calif.) U. Med. Ctr., 1975-79; comm. dir. No. Calif. Cancer Program, Palo Alto, 1979-82, Stanford Law Sch., Palo Alto, 1982-97; mgr., vocalist, pianist String of Pearls Band, 1991—, co-leader China tours, 1999, 2001, 2002. Founding editor (newsletters) Insight, 1978-80, Synergy, 1980-82, Stanford Law Alum, 1992-95; editor (mag.) Stanford Lawyer, 1982-98; contbr. articles to profl. jours. and mags. Recipient silver medal Coun. for Advancement and Support Edn., 1985, 89, award of distinction dist. VII, 1994. Mem. Nat. Assn. Sci. Writers, Phi Beta Kappa. Democrat. Home: PO Box 828 Cannon Beach OR 97110

HELM, JOCELYN B. retired gerontologist; b. Boston, Sept. 20, 1928; d. George Warrin and Helen Elizabeth (Nathan) Bird; m. Carl Edward Helm, June 10, 1950; children: Carla Jean, Curtis Warrin, Christopher Evan, Kimberly. BA in Edn., Duke U., 1950; MA in Edn., NYU, 1974. Asst. dir. phys. edn. YWCA, Detroit, 1951-53; tchr. phys. edn. Stuart Sch. Secred Heart, Princeton, N.J., 1969-73; intern St. Vincent's Hosp., N.Y.C., 1973-74; exec. dir., founder Princeton Sr. Resource Ctr., 1974—96, ret., 1996. Adj. asst. prof. Stockton State Coll., Pomona, N.J., 1975. Mem. Princeton Cmty. Housitn, 1983—; mem., sec. Mercer City Alcohol & Drug Abuse Adv. Com., Trenton, 1990—; bd. dirs. Am. Heart Assn., Princeton, 1994; transp. com. ARC, Princeton, 1991—; chair Salvation Army Svc. Group, Princeton, 1986—. Recipient Delta Phi Rho Alpha Athletic award Duke U., 1950; Woman of Yr. Soroptimist Internat., 1996, Ethical Svc. award Ethical Humanist Soc., 1996, Cmty. Svc. award Princeton (N.J.) Area Cmty. Found., 1999. Mem. Am. Dance Therapy Assn., Am. soc. Aging, Older Women's League, Inst. Sr. Ctrs., Sigma Phi Omega. Avocations: cooking, reading, dance, swimming, walking. Home: 207 Mount Lucas Rd Princeton NJ 08540-2714

HELM, MONICA M. elementary school educator, mental health therapist; b. Edgemont, Ill., Sept. 3, 1967; d. Eddie and Mildred Helm. BA in Comm., Ea. Ill. U., 1990. Comm. cons. Bd. Edn., East St. Louis, Ill., 1990—92, tchr., 1992—96, mental health therapist, 1997—98, tchr. Cahokia, 1998—99; mgr. customer rels. ATT, Manchester, Mo., 1999—2001; tchr. Bd. Edn., Cahokia, 2001—. Cons. in field, Belleville, Ill., 2001—. Mem.: NAFE. Republican. Avocations: reading, aerobics, tennis, bowling, writing.

HELM, PHALA ANIECE, physiatrist; b. Ft. Worth, 1931; MD, U. Tex., Dallas, 1966. Diplomate Am. Bd. Phys. Medicine and Rehab. Intern Baylor U. Med. Ctr., Dallas, 1966-67, resident in phys. med. and rehab., 1967-70; mem. staff Parkland Meml. Hosp., Dallas, 1973—; prof. physiatry U. Tex. S.W. Med. Ctr., Dallas, 1973—. Mem. ABA, Am. Diabetes Assn., Am. Acad. Phys. Medicine and Rehab., Am. Congress Phys. Medicine and Rehab. Office: U Tex Southwestern Med Ctr Sprague Clin Sci Bld CS1104 5323 Harry Hines Blvd Dallas TX 75390-7208

HELMAN, IRIS BARCA, elementary school educator, consultant; b. Kenosha, Wis., May 21, 1930; d. Alphonse and Rosalie (Russo) Barca; divorced; 1 child, Gabriel Heidi. BS in Edn., U. Wis., 1955; MS in Edn., U. Wis., Milw., 1971; Student, U. Wis., Kenosha, 1980-82, Carthage Coll., 1972-74. Cert. elem. tchr. Wis. Sec. USN, Great Lakes, Ill., 1950-53; tchr. Kenosha Unified Sch. Dist. #1, 1955—92; student tchr. supr. U. Wis. Sys. Cons. in field. Author: Now What Do I Do?, 1980, Primer on Gifted Education, 1982; co-author: Shapers of Wisconsin, 1998; contbr. articles to profl. jours. Chmn. Democratic Com., Kenosha, 1977; legisl. chmn. City of Kenosha, 1979-80, harbor commr., 1987-90; pres. Wis. Orgn. for Gifted and Talented, 1977-79; chmn. Wis. Coun. for Gifted and Talented, 1979-80; bd. dirs. AFL-CIO Coun., Kenosha, 1980—; vice-chmn. City Plan Commn., 1992-98, 2000—. Named Outstanding Labor Person, City of Kenosha, 1989, County of Kenosha, 1989. Democrat. Roman Catholic. Avocations: reading, skiing, sailing, tennis, politics. Home: 6207 7th Ave Apt 22 Kenosha WI 53143-4565

HELMER, M(ARTHA) CHRISTIE, lawyer; b. Portland, Oreg., Oct. 8, 1949; d. Marvin Curtis and Inez Bahl (Corwin) H.; m. Joe D. Bailey, June 23, 1979; children: Tim Bailey, Bill Bailey. BA in English magna cum laude, Wash. State U., 1970; JD cum laude, Lewis & Clark Coll., 1974; LLM in Internat. Law, Columbia U., 1998. Bar: Oreg. 1974. Assoc. Miller Nash, Portland, 1974-81, ptnr., 1981—. Adj. prof. Lewis & Clark Law Sch., 1999—; guest lectr. Xiamen U. Law, China, 1995; mem. Oreg. Bd. Bar Examiners, Portland, 1978-81; del. 9th Cir. Jud. Conf., 1984-87, mem. exec. com., 1987-90. Author: Arrest of Ships, 1985, Has China Adopted the UCC?, 1999. Mem.: ABA (internat. and litig. sections), Internat. Bar Assn., Maritime Law Assn., Oreg. Bar Assn. (bd. govs. 1981—84, treas. 1983—84, ho. of dels. 2003—), World Affairs Coun. (chair bd. dirs.), Multnomah Athletic Club, Phi Beta Kappa. Avocations: antiques, travel, fashion. Office: Miller Nash 111 SW 5th Ave Ste 3500 Portland OR 97204-3699 E-mail: chris.helmer@millernash.com.

HELMETAG, DIANA, music educator; b. Bryn Mawr, Pa., 1965; d. Charles and Ruth Helmetag; m. Steven Glanzmann, 1993. BS in Music Edn. cum laude, Duquesne U., 1987; MusM, Pa. State U., 1990. Instr. Sch. Music Pa. State U., University Park, 1988, 90, lectr. Delaware County campus Media, 1991-95; music tchr. Radnor (Pa.) Twp. Sch. Dist., 1993-94, 95, 96; piano accompanist Villanova (Pa.) Voices Villanova U., 1995-99; instr. Delaware County C.C., Media, 1996; orch. dir. Upper Merion Area Sch. Dist., King of Prussia, Pa., 1996—, subject area leader, 1997—2001, pit orch. dir., 1997, 1998, 2001—; choir dir. and children's orch. dir. Strings Internat. Music Festival Bryn Mawr (Pa.) Coll., 2001— . Pianist, violinist Mu Phi Epsilon recitals, Phila., 1991, 92, 94; orch. dir. Schuylkill Valley Area Orch. Festival, Wayne, Pa., 1996—; founding mem. Montgomery County Honors String Orch. Festival, Plymouth Meeting, Pa., 1999—; music dir. King of Prussia Players, 2000. Orch. dir., pianist, violinist Narberth (Pa.) Cmty. Theatre, 1997—. Recipient grad. assistantship Pa. State U., 1987-90. Mem. Am. String Tchrs. Assn. with Nat. Sch. Orch. Assn., Music Educators Nat. Conf., Music Tchrs. Nat. Assn., Coll. Music Soc., Pa. Music Educators Assn. (host. dist. 11 orch. festival 1998, orch. dir. and presiding chair in-svc. conf. 2001, host all-state orch. festival 2002), Phi Kappa Phi, Pi Kappa Lambda. Office: Upper Merion Area Sch Dist 435 Crossfield Rd King Of Prussia PA 19406 E-mail: dhelmetag@umasd.org.

HELMS, KATIE MAE, artist; b. N.C., Dec. 10, 1939; d. Tirzia Lillan Hagler; m. Willie Joe Helms; children: Joe Jr., Frank, Pheobe, Nathneal. Home: 469 Clontz Long Rd Monroe NC 28110-8252

HELMS, SUSAN JANE, astronaut; b. Charlotte, N.C., Feb. 26, 1958; d. Patrick Gibson and Doris Ann (Platt) H. BS in Aero. Engring., USAF Acad., 1980; MS in Aero./Astronautics, Stanford U., 1985. Commd. lt. USAF, 1980, advanced through grades to lt. col., 1980—; weapons separation engr. USAF Armament Lab., 1980-82, lead engr. weapons separation, 1982-84; asst. prof. aero. USAF Acad., 1985-87; student USAF Test Pilot Sch., Edwards AFB, Calif., 1988; F-18 flight test engr. Aero. Engring. Test Establishment, CFB Cold Lake, Alta., Can., 1989-90; astronaut trainee NASA, 1990-91; astronaut NASA, Johnson Space Ctr., Houston, 1991—; space shuttle crew mem. STS-54 USAF, 1993. Mem. AIAA, Women Mil. Aviators, USAF Acad. Assn. Grads., Stanford Alumni Assn. Avocations: jazz, piano, jogging, computers, reading, travel. Office: NASA/Code CB Johnson Space Ctr Houston TX 77058

HELMS GUBA, LISA MARIE, nursing administrator; b. Sioux City, Iowa, Nov. 24, 1962; d. Dean Edward and Betty Lou Victora (Guenther) H. BA in Nursing, Carroll Coll., Helena, Mont., 1986; postgrad., Calif. State U., Sacramento, 1990-92; MSN, Incarnate Word Coll., 1996. Cert. pediatric nurse. Enlisted U.S. Army, 1981, advanced through grades to maj., 1999, nurse, 1986-90, Calif. Nat. Guard, San Francisco, 1990-92, Rio Linda (Calif.) Union Sch. Dist., 1990-92; enlisted USAF, 1992; mem. A.F. Nurse Corps Wilford Hall Med Ctr., Lackland AFB, Tex., 1992-96; asst. nurse mgr. and critical care aeromed. transp. team nurse dir. Malcolm Grow Hosp., Andrews AFB, Md., 1996-2000; dir. Nurse Triage Ctr., 2001—03; nursing exec. Internal Medicine and Women's Health, Dover AFB, 2003—. Deployed to Guantanamo Bay, Cuba, July to Oct. 1994 for Operation Sea Signal, Operation Safe Haven; provider med. care to Haitian/Cuban migrants. Vol. Big sister/Big brother program United Way. Mem. AACN, Emergency Nurses Assn., Nat. Assn. Flight Nurses. Roman Catholic. E-mail: lisaguba@sprintmail.com.

HELMSLEY, LEONA MINDY, hotel executive; b. N.Y.C. m. Harry B. Helmsley, Apr. 8, 1972 (dec. Jan., 1997). Vice pres. Pease & Elliman, N.Y.C., 1962-69; pres. Sutton & Towne Residential, N.Y.C., 1967-70; sr. v.p. Helmsley Spear, N.Y.C., 1970-72, Brown, Harris, Stevens, N.Y.C., 1970-72; pres., CEO, chmn. bd. Helmsley Hotels, Inc., N.Y.C., 1980—. Named Woman of Yr. N.Y. Council Civic Affairs, 1970; named Woman of Yr. Town & Country Condos & Coops., 1981; recipient Service award Ort Sch. Engring., 1981, Profl. Excellence award Les Dames d'Escoffier, 1981, Spl. Achievement award Sales Execs. Club N.Y., 1981, Woman of Yr. award Internat. Hotel Industry, 1982 Home: 36 Central Park S New York NY 10019-1600 Office: Helmsley Hotels Inc 230 Park Ave New York NY 10169-0005

HELMS-VANSTONE, MARY WALLACE, anthropology educator; b. Allentown, Pa., Apr. 15, 1938; d. Samuel Leidich and Mary (Wallace) Helms; divorced. BA, Pa. State U., State College, 1960; MA, U. Mich., 1962, PhD, 1967. Instr. Wayne State U., Detroit, 1965-67; asst. prof. Syracuse (N.Y.) U., 1967-68; lectr. Northwestern U., Evanston and Chgo., Ill., 1969-79; prof. U. N.C., Greensboro, 1979—, head dept. anthropology, 1979-85. Author: Asang: A Miskito Community, 1971, Middle America, 1975, Ancient Panama, 1979, Ulysses' Sail, 1988, Craft and the Kingly Ideal, 1993, Creations of the Rainbow Serpent, 1995, Access to Origins, 1998, The Curassow's Crest, 2000; contbr. articles to profl. jours. Fellow: Am. Anthrop. Assn.; mem.: Medieval Acad. Am., So. Anthrop. Soc. (pres. 1980—81, procs. editor 1982—94), Am. Ethnological Soc., Am. Soc. Ethnohistory (pres. 1976). Avocations: travel, painting, musical activities, crafts. Office: Univ NC Dept Anthropology PO Box 26170 Greensboro NC 27402-6170

HELOISE, columnist, writer; b. Waco, Tex., Apr. 15, 1951; d. Marshal H. and Heloise K. (Bowles) Cruse; m. David L. Evans, Feb. 13, 1981. BS in Math. and Bus, S.W. Tex. State U., 1974. Owner, pres. Heloise, Inc. Asst. to columnist mother, Heloise, 1974-77, upon her death took over internationally syndicated column, 1977; author: Hints from Heloise, 1980, Help from Heloise, 1981, Heloise's Beauty Book, 1985, All-New Hints from Heloise, 1989, Heloise: Hints for a Healthy Planet, 1990, Heloise from A to Z, 1992, Household Hints for Singles, 1993, Hints for All Occasions, 1995, In The Kitchen With Heloise, 2000, Heloise Conquers Stinks & Stains, 2002, Get Organized with Heloise, 2004; featured on radio show Ask Heloise, Liberty Broadcasting; contbg. editor Good Housekeeping mag., 1983, Speaker for the House; co-founder, 1st co-pilot Mile Pie in the Sky Balloon Club. Mem. Good Neighbor Coun. Tex.-Mex.; sponsor Nat. Smile Week. Recipient Mental Health Mission award Nat. Mental Health Assn., 1990, The Carnegians Good Human Rels. award, 1994. Mem. AFTRA, SAG, Women in Comm. (Headliner 1994), Tex. Press Women, Internat. Women's Forum, Women in Radio and TV, Confrerie de la Chaine des Rotisseurs (bailli San Antonio chpt.), Ordre Mondial des Gourmets De'Gustateurd de U.S.A., Death Valley Yacht and Racket Club, Zonta. Home: PO Box 795000 San Antonio TX 78279-5000

HELPERN, JOAN (JOAN MARSHALL), designer, business executive; b. N.Y.C., Oct. 10, 1926; d. Edward and Ethel (Tilzer) Marshall; m. David M. Helpern, Aug. 14, 1960; 1 child, Elizabeth Joan. BA, Hunter Coll., N.Y.C., 1947; MA, Columbia U., 1948; PhD, Harvard U., 1967. Psychologist, author, educator, lectr., 1948-68; dir. child guidance N.Y.C. Bd. Edn., sch., Lexington, Mass.; founder, owner, pres., CEO, chief designer Joan and David (footwear, sportswear, accessory design/mfg.), N.Y.C., 1968-2000; fashion designer, pres. Joan Helpern Designs, Inc., N.Y.C. Author: Guidance of Children in the Elementary Schools. Recipient Coty award Am. Design, 1978, FFANY Footwear Designer award, 1992, Fairchild Footwear Designer award, 1992, Fairchild Hall of Fame award, 1993, Michelangelo Footwear Design award, 1993, Female Bus. Owners award, 1993-94, Athena award Hunter Coll., 1996; Columbia U. grantee, 1947-48; named one of 50 Leading Female Entrepreneurs of World, 1998, 50 Leading Bus. Women of World, Working Woman, 1995, 96, 97, 98. Mem. Com. of 200 (founding mem.).

HELSEL, ELSIE DRESSLER, retired special education educator; b. Butler, Pa., July 10, 1915; d. Adolph and Nelle Simpson Dressler; m. Robert Griffith Helsel, Sept. 2, 1939, children: William Griffith Waring, Robert Griffith Helsel, Jr., Marjorie Lynn. AB in Biology and Pre-Medicine magna cum laude, Chatham Coll., 1937; MS in Genetics, U. Pitts., 1939, PhD in Genetics, 1942; MA in Spl. Edn., Ohio State U., 1962. Biology tchr. Wilkinsburg (Pa.) H.S., 1937—41; instr. human genetics dept. zoology Ohio State U., Cole, 1951—53; cons. med. and sci. dept. United Cerebral Palsy Assn., N.Y.C., 1955, dir. Washington, 1968—74; coord. spl. edn. Ohio U. Coll. Edn., Athens, 1974—77, prof. emeritus, 1981—; dir. Ohio U. Affiliated Ctr. for Human Devel., 1975—81. Asst. dir. divsn. spl. studies Am. Assn. Mental Deficiency, 1964—68; project coord. Protective Svcs. Project Ohio Dept. Mental Health and Mental Retardation, 1967—69; chairperson Ohio Devel. Disabilities Planning Coun., 1993—98; mem. govs. vision com. Dept. Mental Retardation and Devel. Disabilities, 1997—99. Contbr. articles to profl. jours. Mem. govtl. activities com. United Cerebral Palsy Assn., 1965—97, bd. dirs., 1976—94, mem. cmty. svcs. com., 1995—97; Ohio coun. rep. Nat. Assn. Devel. Disabilities Couns., 1985—87, mem. policy com., 1995—97; bd. dirs. United Cerebral Palsy Ohio, 1955—76, 1990—96, v.p., 1977—83, vol. exec. dir., 1991—97; chairperson cmty. svcs. programs Ohio U. Coll. Medicine, 1995—98. Home: 188 Longview Heights Athens OH 45701-3340

HELSTEIN, IVY RAE, communications executive, psychotherapist, writer; d. Harold and Celia Weintraub Markowitz; children: Hilary, Eden, Flyn. BA, Queens Coll., 1958; MA in Human Behavior, Goddard Coll., Plainfield, Vt., 1979. Founder, pres. Comm. Dynamics, Great Neck, N.Y., 1973—. Creator Practical Spiritualism; instr., lectr. classroom mgmt. skills various sch. dists., N.Y., 1976; instr. assertiveness tng., conflict mgmt., adult continuing edn. Hofstra U., Hempstead, N.Y., 1976, C.W. Post U., Brookville, N.Y., 1979; adj. faculty Nassau C.C., Garden City, 1977—. Author: Great Persuaders: Sales Training, 1984, Great Communicators II, 1987, Infinite Abilities: Living Your Life on Purpose, 1999. Trainer N.Y. State Child Protective Svcs., 1995—, Suffolk County (N.Y.) Dept. Labor, 1997. Mem. Nat. Spkr. Assn. (profl., past pres., Chpt. Mem. of the Yr. award 1986), Tri-State Nat. Spkrs. Assn. (pres. 1985-86), Authors Guild, Inc. Avocation: world travel. Home and Office: 27 Georgian Ln Great Neck NY 11024-1615 E-mail: IHelstein@aol.com.

HELTERLINE, MARILYN, sociology educator; b. Syracuse, N.Y., Oct. 18, 1947; d. Frederick William and Mary Ellen (Gaffney) Helterline; m. Charles J. Buehler, June 14, 1969 (div. Dec. 1976); m. Peter Friedman, Oct. 9, 1981; children: Willa Helterline Friedman, Samuel Helterline Friedman. BA, LeMoyne Coll., 1969; MA, U. Notre Dame, 1971, PhD, 1974. Prof. sociology SUNY, Oneonta, 1973—. Contbr. articles to profl. jours. Mem. Am. Sociol. Assn. Democrat. Home: 69 Maple St Oneonta NY 13820-1523 Office: SUNY College at Oneonta Oneonta NY 13820

HELTON, PATRICIA BETH, realtor; b. Paintsville, Ky., Sept. 5, 1954; d. Oscar Jr. and Chloteen (McFarlan) Wheeler; m. John Keith Helton, Mar. 8, 1975. BS in Edn., Ea. Ky. U., 1975; MS, St. Cloud State U., 1983; grad. realtors inst., Nat. Realtors Inst., 1991. Cert. residential specialist. Med. sec. Willard (N.Y.) State Psychiat. Ctr., 1975-76; adminstrv. asst. Leo Payne Automotive Plaza, Denver, 1976-77; tchr. elem. edn. Aroka (Minn.)-Hennepin Schs., 1977, Naperville (Ill.) Sch. Dist., 1983-85; realtor, real estate instr. Coldwell Banker Real Estate, Westlake Village, Calif., 1985—, estates dir., 1988—, corp. property specialist, 1989—. Co-author: (history book) Profiles of Women, 1993. Trustee St. Matthews Meth. Ch., Newbury Park, Calif., 1987; mem. Nat. Women's Polit. Caucus, Thousand Oaks, Calif. Mem. AAUW (dir. univ. rels. 1993-94, v.p. edn. found. 1985-94, Gift Honoree 1991), Calif. Assn. Realtors, Women's Coun. Realtors (speker 1985-92), Order of Ea. Star. Republican. Methodist. Avocations: snow skiing, biking, canoeing, hiking, swimming. Office: Coldwell Banker Real Estate 171 E Thousand Oaks Blvd Thousand Oaks CA 91360-5712

HELTON, SANDRA LYNN, telecommunications industry executive; b. Paintsville, Ky., Dec. 9, 1949; d. Paul Edward and Ella Rae (Van Hoose) H.; m. Norman M. Edelson, Apr. 15, 1978. BS, U. Ky., 1971; MBA, MIT, 1977. Capital budget adminstr. Corning (N.Y.) Glass Works, 1978-79, fixed assets mgr., 1979-80, contr. electronics divsn., 1980-82, mgr. customer fin. svcs., 1982-84, dir. fin. svcs., 1984-86, asst. treas., 1986-91, v.p., treas., 1991-94, sr. v.p., treas., 1994—97; exec. v.p. fin., CFO TDS Telecom, Chgo., 1998—2000, exec. v.p., CFO, 2001—. Bd. dirs. U.S. Cellular Corp., The Prin. Fin. Group. Vol. Mass. Gen. Hosp., Boston, 1976; treas. Corning Mus. of Glass; treas pres. bd. dirs. Chemung Valley Arts Coun., Corning, 1981-87; bd. dirs. Corning Summer Theatre, 1987-91, Arnot Hosp. Found., 1988—; mem. fin. com. Clemens Performing Arts Ctr., Elmira, N.Y., 1985-92; mem. adv. bd. Chase Lincoln, 1988-91; mem. bus. com. Met.

Mus. Art, 1992—; pres. bd. dirs. Rockwell Mus., 1992—; mem. Regional Cultural Adv. Com., 1992—; mem. FEI com. on Corp. Fin., 1995—; bd. dirs. Arnot Ogden Meml. Med. Ctr., Arts of the So. Finger Lakes. Mem. Nat. Assn. Corp. Treass., Fin. Women's Assn., Soc. Internat. Treas., Fin. Execs. Inst. Avocations: music, tennis.

HELVESTON, EUGENE MCGILLIS, pediatric ophthalmologist, educator; b. Detroit, Dec. 28, 1934; d. Eugene McGillis and Ann (Fay) H.; m. Barbara Hiss, June 15, 1959; children: Martha Hiss, Lisa Hiss. BA, U. Mich., 1956, MD, 1960. Intern St. Joseph Hosp., Ann Arbor, Mich., 1960-61; resident Ind. U. Hosps., Indpls., 1961-66; dir. pediatric opthalmology Ind. U. Sch. Medicine, Indpls., 1967—, asst. prof., 1967-72, assoc. prof., 1972-76, prof., 1976—, chmn., 1981-83, dir. sect. pediatric ophthalmology, 1967—. Fellow in opthalmology Wilmer Inst., Balt., 1966-67 Author: Pediatric Ophthalmology Practice, 1973, Atlas of Strabismus Surgery, 4th edit., 1993, Strabismus: A Decision Making Approach, 1994; chief editor; Am. Orthoptic Jour., 1976-82; contbr. articles to profl. jours. Mem. med. adv. bd. Project Orbis, 1989—. Kellogg scholar, 1959; grantee Heed scholar Heed Found., Chgo., 1966; recipient Outstanding Heed Fellow award, 1975 Fellow ACS, Am. Acad. Ophthalmology, Am. Orthoptic Coun. (pres. 1976-80), Am. Assn. Pediat. Ophthalmology and Strabismus (pres. 1990), Internat. Strabismus Assn. (sec.-treas.). Office: Ind U Sch Medicine 702 Rotary Cir Indianapolis IN 46202-5133

HELWICK, CHRISTINE, lawyer; b. Orange, Calif., Jan. 6, 1947; d. Edward Everett and Ruth Evelyn (Seymour) Hailwood; children: Ted C., Dana J. BA, Stanford U., 1968; MA, Northwestern U., 1969; JD, U. Calif., San Francisco, 1973. Bar: Calif., U.S. Supreme Ct. U. S. Ct. Appeals (9th cir.), U.S. Dist. Ct. (no., ctrl., so. and ea. dist.) Calif. Tchr. history New Trier Twp. High Sch., Winnetka, Ill., 1968-69; sec. to the producer Flip Wilson Show, Burbank, Calif., 1970; assoc. Crosby, Heafey, Roach & May, Oakland, Calif., 1973-78; asst. counsel litigation U. Calif., Oakland, 1978-84, mng. univ. counsel, 1984-94, counsel Berkeley campus, 1989-94; gen. counsel Calif. State U. Sys., 1994—. Lectr. in field. Mem. instnl. rev. bd. Devel. Studies Ctr., Oakland, 1990—; mem. Alameda County Fee Arbitration Panel. Mem. Nat. Assn. Coll. and Univ. Attys. (bd. dirs. 1995-98, 2000—, pres. 2002-03), Nat. Assn. Coll. and Univ. Bus. Officers (bd. dirs. 2002—), State Bar Calif. (exec. com. 1980-83, Leadership Calif. 1998), dirs. 1977), Alameda County Bar Found. (adv. trustee 1988-90, bd. dirs. 1991), Order of Coif. Episcopalian. Office: Calif State U 401 Golden Shore 4th Fl Long Beach CA 90802-4275

HELWIG, ANNETTE L. retired elementary school educator; b. Burlington, N.J., Dec. 18, 1926; d. William and Jesselyn V. Cox; m. Edward O. Helwig, Aug. 20, 1949; children: Lyn M., Keith W. BS in Edn., SUNY, Buffalo, 1948. Elem. tchr. North Tonawanda (N.Y.) Bd. Edn., Cedar Grove (N.J.) Bd. Edn.; ret., 1993. Cooperating tchr. for student tchrs. William Paterson State Coll., Caldwell Coll. Named N.J. Tchr. of Excellence, 1986, 90. Mem. NEA, N.J. Edn. Assn., Essex County Edn. Assn., Cedar Grove Edn. Assn. (sec., 2d v.p., chmn., rep.). Home: 20 Pine Dr Cedar Grove NJ 07009-1036

HEMANN, PATRICIA A. federal judge; b. 1942; BA summa cum laude, U. Ill., 1964; JD summa cum laude, Cleveland Marshall Coll. Law, 1980. Law clk. to hon. William K. Thomas U.S. Dist. Ct. (no. dist.) Ohio, 1980-82; assoc. Hahn Lowser & Parks, 1982-93; magistrate judge U.S. Dist. Ct. (no. dist.) Ohio, Cleve., 1993—. Summer intern strike force organizad crime divsn. U.S. Dept. Justice, Cleve., 1979; mem. vis. com., hon. trustee Cleveland Marshall Coll. Law. Mem. ABA, Fed. Bar Assn., Nat. Assn. Women Judges (membership chair dist. 7), Ohio Women's Bar Assn., Greater Cleve. Bar Assn. (trustee). Office: US District Courts 801 W Superior Ave Cleveland OH 44113-1829 Fax: (216) 522-2000.

HEMANN, PHYLLIS A (NN), public relations executive; d. Charles A. Hemann, Jr. and Elaine C. Hemann. B.Liberal Arts, U. of Ark., Little Rock, 1996; MFA, Antioch U., Marina del Rey, Calif., 2001. Layout artist Falcon Pubs., Little Rock, 1991—93; writing intern UALR's U. Writing Ctr., Little Rock, 1992—94; assoc. prodr./show sec. Farkleberry Follies, Little Rock, 1997—99; adminstrv./broadcast asst. CJRW, Little Rock, 1999—2001; reporter KDC Comm., North Little Rock, Ark., 1994—2002; pubs. coord. Ctrl. Ark. Radiation Therapy Inst., Little Rock, 2001—. Webby awards site reviewer Internat. Acad. of Digital Arts and Scis., San Francisco, 2000—03. Editor: (magazine) Focus, (newspaper) CancerAnswers!; author: (nonfiction) The Times, The Maumelle Monitor, The Chronicle, (poetry manuscript) Vernacular, (screenplay) The Painted Lady; teacher (writing workshop) MuseMe Online Writing Workshop;, author short story, essay, poem; actor: (one-act play) The Golden Door, (variety skits) Farkleberry Follies; author: (variety skits) Farkleberry Follies; photography exhibition, Door to the Past; editor: (magazine) Perspective. Vol. Susan G. Komen Race for the Cure, Little Rock, 2000—03, CARTI Aux. Festival of Trees, Little Rock, 2001—, CARTI Kids, Little Rock, 2001—03; mem. Cath. Daughters of the Americas, North Little Rock, Ark., 1991—. Recipient Diamond Award for feature writing, Ark. Hosp. Assn., 2002—03, Diamond Award for external publ., 2002, Bronze Quill Award of Merit for mags., Internat. Assn. of Bus. Communicators Ark. Chpt., 2001—03, Bronze Quill Award of Merit for newsletters and tabloids, 2001. Mem.: Poet's Roundtable of Ark., Nat. Fedn. of Poetry Societies, Am. Acad. of Poets, HTML Writer's Guild, Popular Culture Assn., Golden Key. Roman Catholic. Avocations: ceramic pottery, drama, reading, travel, web design. Personal E-mail: phemann@reporters.net. E-mail: phemann@carti.com.

HEMING, CAROL PIPER, historian, educator; b. Modesto, Calif., July 1, 1945; d. Richard Stanley and Eva Mae Weston (Sturtevant) Piper; m. Dwight Arthur Heming, May 1, 1965; 1 child, Valerie Ann. BA, Ctrl. Mo. State U., 1982, MA, 1986; PhD, U. Mo., 2000. Lectr., instr., asst. prof. Ctrl. Mo. State U., Warrensburg, 1989—2003, assoc. prof., 2003—. Judge Mo. History Day, Columbia, 1999—2003. Author: Protestants and the Cult of the Saints in German-Speaking Europe: 1517-1531, 2003. Friend Trails Regional Libr., Warrensburg, 2002—. Mem.: NOW, AAUP, Am. Hist. Assn., Phi Alpha Theta, Phi Beta Delta. Democrat. Unitarian. Achievements include research on Mo. Germans; research on women and the Luth. Ch.-Mo. Synod; research on translantic aspects of Mo. German history; research on German Reformation. Avocations: cooking, gardening. Home: PO Box 961 Warrensburg MO 64093 Office: Dept History and Anthropology Ctrl Mo State Univ Warrensburg MO 64093*

HEMISH, CAROL MARIE, liturgist/spiritual director, musician; b. Canby, Minn., June 12, 1950; d. Richard Joseph and Mathilda Rose (Mihm) H. BA in Music Edn., Piano Performance, Mt. Mary Coll., Milw., 1973; MA in Liturgical Studies, St. John's U., Collegeville, Minn., 1985; MA in Human Developmental Biospirituality, St. Mary's U. of Minn., 2000. Cert. spiritual dir. Dir. music, liturgy and spiritual renewal St. Mary's Parish, Willmar, Minn., 1981-84; dir. music ministries Epiphany Parish, Coon Rapids, Minn., 1984-87; liturgy dir. Marquette U., Milw., 1987-90, St. Benedict Ctr., Madison, Wis., 1990-92; assoc. dir. Archdiocesan Spirituality Ctr., New Orleans, 1992-93; coord. Ctr. for Liturgy at St. Louis U., 1994—. Retreat dir. Sacred Heart Retreat House, Sedalia, Colo., 1989—; liturgy cons. various religious congregations, dioceses, parishes, 1980—. Mem. Sch. Sisters Notre Dame, Nat. Pastoral Musicians, Assn. Contemplative Sisters, Spiritual Dirs. Internat. Avocations: vegetarian cooking, creative sewing. Home: 3933 Fillmore St Saint Louis MO 63116-3115 Office: Ctr for Liturgy at St Louis U 3837 W Pine Blvd Saint Louis MO 63108-3307

HEMKIN-KAVANAUGH, SUE, music educator; b. Brainerd, Minn., Aug. 27, 1956; BS, Bemidji State U., 1978. Elem. music specialist Harrison Sch. Dist., Brainerd, Minn., 1999—; pvt. piano and trumpet instr. Brainerd, 1984—; restaurant mgr., resort owner Kavanaugh's, Brainerd, 1985—; music tchr. and accompainist Ctrl. Lakes Coll., Brainerd, 1996—. Home: 11711 Pine Beach Dr East Gull Lake MN 56401

HEMLOCK, ROBERTA LEIGH, veterinary technician; b. Chgo., Aug. 24, 1946; d. John Nolan and Gertrude Mathilda (Lahti) Hemlock. AA, Chgo. City Coll., 1966; BFA, Art Inst. Chgo., 1970; AAS, Bel-Rea Inst., Denver, 2001. Intelligence analyst State Dept., England, 1972—73; pres. Hemlock, Hemlock & Others, Chgo., 1973—80; design dir. Hemlock, Hemlock & Others, Chgo., 1973—80; prof. Colo. Inst. of Art, Denver, 1980—93; vp. ops. & design Design Prodns., Inc., Denver, 1993—94; v.p. ops. & editor Syber Media Group, Denver, 1994—96; pvt. practice tech. grantwriter Denver, 1996—2000; vet. technician Huron Animal Hosp., Denver, 2001—03; vet. technician/surgery Erie (Colo.) Animal Hosp., 2003—; ednl. cons., clin. adv. Dr. Joel Stone Prod., 2004—. Cons. AAUW, 2001—, IAUW, 2001—; mem. adv. bd. CCD of Denver, 2001—. Mem.: NAVTA, Colo. Assn. Cert. Vet. Technicians (cert., state pub. rels. dir. 2001—), Denver Botanic Gardens. Avocations: photography, conceptual writer, publisher. Home: 10648 Huron St # 412 Northglenn CO 80234-4022

HEMMINGER, PAMELA LYNN, lawyer; b. Chgo., June 29, 1949; d. Paul Willis and Lenore Adelaide (Hennig) H.; m. Robert Alan Miller, May 14, 1979; children: Kimberly Anne, Jeffrey Ryan, Eric Douglas. BA, Pomona Coll., 1971; JD, Pepperdine U., 1976. Tchr. Etiwanda (Calif.) Sch. dist., 1971-74; law clerk Gibson Dunn & Crutcher, Newport Beach, Calif., 1974-76, assoc. L.A., 1976-84, ptnr., 1985—. Contbg. author Sexual Harassment, 1992, Employment Discrimination Law, 3d edit. and supplements, 1996; contbr. articles to profl. jours. Mem. Comparable Worth Task Force Calif., Sacramento, 1984, Pepperdine U. Sch. of Law Bd. Visitors, 1990—, Calif. Law Revision Commn., 1998-99; mem., bd. dirs. Dispute Resolution Svcs., 1998—. Named alumnus of yr. Pepperdine Sch. Law, 1996; listed in Best Lawyers in Am., 1998--. Mem. L.A. County Bar Assn. (chair, labor and employment sect. 1996-97), Calif. C. of C. (employment rels. com. 1984—). Republican. Lutheran. Office: Gibson Dunn & Crutcher Ste 4921 333 S Grand Ave Los Angeles CA 90071-3197

HEMMINGS, MADELEINE BLANCHET, management consultant, media consultant, not-for-profit fundraiser; b. Bryn Mawr, Pa., Aug. 14, 1942; d. Wilfred Loyola and Feroline (Sissenere) Blanchet; m. Richard B. Hemmings, Mar. 14, 1970; 1 child, Laurie Cornwall Hemmings Stull. Cert. in lang. and linguistics, U. Fribourg, Switzerland, 1961; BS in Indsl. and Labor Rels., Cornell U., 1976. Owner Hallmark Pers. of Pa., Harrisburg, Pa., 1964-70; assoc. dir. human resources Cornell U., Ithaca, NY, 1972-77; policy dir. employee benefits NAM, Washington, 1977-79; policy dir. edn., employment and tng. C. of C. U.S., Washington, 1979-83; v.p. policy Nat. Alliance Bus., Washington, 1983-85; pres. W.Va. Roundtable, Charleston, 1985—96; exec. dir. Nat. Assn. State Dirs. Vocat. Tech. Edn., Washington, 1987-96; mng. dir. Nat. Telelearning Network, Inc., Washington, 1996-98; pres. Hemmings Assocs., Inc., 1998—2002; grants coord. Wayne-Finger Lakes Bd. of Coop. Edn. Svcs., Newark, NY, 2002—. Select adv. com. to asst. sec. edn., 1989—93; pres. adv. com. Fed. Office Vocat. Edn. Performance Stds., 1992—95; ant. adv. bd. Ctr. Edn. and Work, U. Wis., 1992—96, Nat. Ctr. Rsch. Vocat. Edn., Berkeley, Calif., 1993—96. Author: (book) The New Job Training Partnership Act, 1982, Economic Development Plan, State of West Virginia, 1987, Education for a Working America, 1994, (newsletter) The Techocrat, 1988—95. Exec. dir. Nat. Vocat. Tech. Edn. Found., 1987—96; campaign mgr. Connie Cook for Congress, Ithaca, 1984; sponsor U.S. Pony Club, Olney, Md., 1987—96. Mem.: Greater Washington Soc. Assn. Execs. (chief exec. coun. 1989—98), U.S. C. of C. (edn. com. 1987—96), Cornell Pres.' Club. Avocations: thoroughbred breeding and racing, combined training, oil painting. Home: 111 Lea Dr Newark NY 14513 Office: Wayne-FInger Lakes BOCES 131 Drumlin Ct Newark NY 14513 Fax: 301-570-9104. E-mail: mhemming@rochester.rr.com.

HEMMINGSEN, BARBARA BRUFF, microbiologist, educator; b. Whittier, Calif., Mar. 25, 1941; d. Stephen Cartland and Susanna Jane (Alexander) Bruff; m. Edvard Alfred Hemmingsen, Aug. 5, 1967; 1 child, Grete. BA, U. Calif., Berkeley, 1962, MA, 1964; PhD, U. Calif., San Diego, 1971. Lectr. San Diego State U., 1973-77, asst. prof., 1977-81, assoc. prof., 1981-88, prof., 1988—. Vis. asst. prof. Aarhus U., Denmark, 1971—72; cons. AMBIS, Inc., San Diego, 1984—85, Woodward-Clyde Cons., 1985, 1987—91, Novatron, Inc., 2000—. Author (with others): (book) Microbial Ecology, 1972; contbr. articles to profl. jours. Mem. Planned Parenthood, San Diego. Mem.: AAAS, San Diego Assn. Rational Inquiry (sec. 1998—2001, treas. 2002—), Am. Women Sci., Am. Soc. Microbiology, Phi Beta Kappa (corr. sec. Nu chpt. Calif. 1994—2002, past pres., historian 2003—), Sigma Xi. Democrat. Office: San Diego State U Dept Biology San Diego CA 92182-4614

HEMPERLY, REBECCA SUE, publishing manager; b. Reading, Pa., June 17, 1966; d. Kenneth Jay and Ann Rebecca (Riehl) H. BA, Wheaton Coll., 1988; MA, Emerson Coll., 1992. Editl. asst. Coll.-Hill Press/Little, Brown, Boston, 1988-90, Little, Brown and Co., Boston, 1990, contracts coord., 1990-92, asst. mgr. contracts, 1992-96, mgr. contracts, 1996-98; paralegal WGBH Ednl. Found., Boston, 1998-99, pub. contracts cons., 1998-99, v.p. client svcs., 2000; client svcs. mgr. Database Pub. Group, Cambridge, Mass., 1999-2000; contracts mgr. Candlewick Press, Cambridge, 2000—. Del. 1st Amendment Congress, 1997; spkr. rights and permissions Assn. Am. Pub., Washington, 1996; mem. diversity task force Little, Brown and Co., Boston, 1993-98. Contbr. essays: The Book Group Book, 3d edit., 2000, Teaching Contemporary Theory to Undergraduates, 1995. Team capt. AIDS walk-a-thon Little, Brown and Co./AIDS Action Com., Boston, 1995-97; phone coord. GLOW, Watertown, Mass., 1989-98; mem. Rails to Trails Conservancy, 1995—. Mem. Women in Publishing, Nat. Writers' Union, Bookbuilders of Boston, Phi Beta Kappa (scholar 1988). Avocations: gardening, cycling, Karate, photography.

HEMPFLING, LINDA LEE, nurse; b. Indpls., July 28, 1947; d. Paul Roy and Myrtle Pearl (Ward) H. Diploma, Meth. Hosp. Ind. Sch. Nursing, 1968; postgrad., St. Joseph's Coll. Cert. medical audit specialist, 2000. Charge nurse Meth. Hosp., Indpls., 1968; staff nurse operating rm. Silver Cross Hosp., Joliet, Ill., 1969; charge nurse operating rm. Huntington (N.Y.) Hosp., 1969-73; night supr. oper. rm., post anesthesia care unit Hermann Hosp., Houston, 1973-76, unit mgr., purchasing coord. oper. rms., 1976-83; RN med. auditor, quality improvement and tng. coord. Nat. Healthcare Rev., Inc., Houston, 1984—98; RN med. auditor Integra Solutions, 1999—. Future Nurses Am. scholar, 1965, Nat. Merit scholar, 1965. Mem.: Am. Assn. Med. Audit Specialists, Tex. Med. Auditors Assn., Assn. PeriOperative Registered Nurses. Office: 9401 SW Freeway # 631B Houston TX 77074

HEMPHILL, DIANE EILENE, music educator; b. Rochester, Pa., June 20, 1949; d. John Lester and Ruth Elinor (Moore) Neely; m. Ricky Dean Hemphill, June 8, 1991; 1 child, Andrea Taylor. BFA, Carnegie Mellon U., 1971; postgrad., Duquesne U., 1973. Tchr. music Blackhawk Sch. Dist., Beaver Falls, Pa., 1972—81; tchr. music, choral dir. Blackhawk High Sch., 1981—. Pianist worship team Beaver Assembly of God, 2000—; accompanist Slippery Rock U., 2000—. Mem. Polit. Action Com. for Edn., Pa. Mem.: Blackhawk Edn. Assn., Music Edn. Nat. Conf., Pa. Music Educators Assn. Democrat. Home: 938 Achortown Rd Beaver Falls PA 15010 Office: Blackhawk Sch Dist 500 Blackhawk Rd Beaver Falls PA 15010

HEMPHILL, JEAN HARGETT, college dean; b. Pollocksville, N.C., Aug. 21, 1936; d. Robert Franklin and Frances (Hill) Hargett; m. Raymond Arthur Hemphill, Feb. 28, 1964; 1 child: Gerald Franklin. BS, East Carolina U., 1958; MEd, U. Nev., Las Vegas, 1968; student, N.C. State U., 1993. Sec.-treas. Five Points Milling Co., Inc., New Bern, N.C., 1968-77; instr. Craven C.C., New Bern, 1973-80, dean svc. techs., 1980—. Mem. mgmt. team New Bern-Craven County Coll. Tech. Prep., 1990—; mem. Craven County Schs. Sch.-to-Work Curriculum com., 1996—; internat. rep. NC Cmty. Coll. Improvment Projects, 1992—96, 2002—. Scholarship chmn. continuing edn. divsn. Woman's Club, New Bern, 1981—, treas. continuing edn. divsn., 1986—; instnl. rep. N.C. C.C. Sys. Curriculum Improvement Projects, 1992-96, 2002-2003. Achievement award Woman's Club, New Bern, 1999. Mem. N.C. Assn. C.C. Instrnl. Adminstrs., Phi Kappa Phi. Democrat. Methodist. Office: Craven Community Coll 800 College Ct New Bern NC 28562-4900

HEMPHILL, MARGARET AYARS, priest, artist; b. San Francisco, Oct. 8, 1931; d. David Preston and Margaret Taylor Ayars; m. James Drain Hemphill, Jan. 2, 1951; children: Greg, Kimberleigh, Ayars, Scofield, Chapin, Ashley. Student, Northwestern U., 1949-51; BA, Mundeline-Loyola U., 1980; M Div., Seabury Western Theol. Sem., Evanston, Ill., 1986, DMin, 2003. Assoc. priest St. James the Less, Northfield, Ill., 1997-99; pastoral affiliate Kenilworth (Ill.) Union, 1995-99; asst. rector St. Thomas Ch., Hanover, NH, 2001. One-woman shows include: All Chgo. U. Club, 1998, Tavern Club, 1973, Clausen Gallery, 1980; group-shows include: Winnetka Women's Club, Evanston Women's Club, North Shore Art League, Tavern Club, Evanston Art League. Episcopalian. Achievements include 1st ordained woman clergy to deliver sermon St. Andrews Ch., Zurich, Switzerland, 1987. Office: St Thomas Episcopal Ch 9 W Wheelock St Hanover NH 03755-1710 E-mail: jdhemp@aol.com.

HEMPLEMAN, BARBARA FLORENCE, archivist; b. Bellevue, Pa., Mar. 3, 1925; d. Warren Wilson and Florence Permelia (Firth) Hampe; m. David William Hempleman, Aug. 4, 1956; children: Warwick, Terence. BA, Coll. of Wooster, 1947; MA, NYU, 1953; MLS, Atlanta U., 1973. Dir. Christian edn. Calvary Reformed Ch., Reading, Pa., 1951-52; libr. asst. Duke U., Durham, N.C., 1957-59; asst. prof. history Warren Wilson Coll., Asheville, N.C., 1948-51, 54-56, 66-69, libr. dir., 1978-86, archivist, 1986-98, adj. prof. women's history, 1983-96; vis. prof. libr. sci. Emory U., Atlanta, 1973-74; adj. prof. libr. sci. Atlanta U., 1973, 78, reference libr., 1974-78. Contbr. numerous articles to Owl and Spade mag. Bd. dirs. YWCA, Asheville, 1978-79; libr. developer, adminstr. Black Mountain (N.C.) Correctional Ctr. for Women, 1997—. Nat. Assn. Fgn. Student Affairs grantee, 1975. Mem. Women's History Club Asheville (historian 1996—). Democrat. Presbyterian. Avocations: travel, reading.

HEMSTREET, PAMELA S. real estate broker; b. Jackson, Mich., Jan. 22, 1957; d. Ronald C. Jacobs, Sr. and Sharon K. Jacobs; m. Garry L. Hemstreet, Aug. 11, 1983; stepchildren: Rick, Lisa, Chris, John, Sherrey. Real estate sales assoc. C-Z1 Home Towne Realty, Lansing, Mich., 1986—90; real estate broker Trinity Realty, Jackson, Mich., 1990—. Mem. women of world Bethel Family Worship Ctr., Jackson, 1990—, tchr., 2002—03, facilitator Relay for Life, 2002—03. Mem.: Jackson (Mich.) Area Assn. Realtors, Greater Lansing (Mich.) Assn. Realtors, Mich. Assn. Realtors, Nat. Assn. Realtors. Pentecostal. Avocations: time with family, church, volunteering.

HENARD, ELIZABETH ANN, controller; b. Providence, Oct. 9, 1947; d. Anthony Joseph and Grace Johanna (Lokay) Zorbach; m. Patrick Edward Mann, Dec. 18, 1970 (div. July 1972); m. John Bruce Henard Jr., Oct. 19, 1974; children: Scott Michael, Christopher Andrew. Student, Jacksonville (Fla.) U., 1966. Sec. So. Bell Tel. & Tel., Jacksonville, 1964-69; office mgr. Gunther F. Reis Assocs., Tampa, Fla., 1969-71; exec. sec. Ernst & Ernst, Tampa, 1971-72; exec. sec. to pres. Lamalie Assocs., Tampa, 1972-74; exec. sec. Arthur Young & Co., Chgo., 1975; adminstrv. asst. Irving J. Markin, Chgo., 1975; contr., v.p., corp. sec. Henard Assocs., Inc., Dallas, 1983-92; realtor Coldwell Banker Residential Real Estate, Tampa, 1999—; contr. Meridian Ptnrs., Tampa, 2003—. Mem. Dallas Investors Group (treas. 1986-91), Tampa Palms Country Club. Republican. Roman Catholic. Avocations: photography, crafts, golf, reading. Home: 5014 Wesley Dr Tampa FL 33647-1375 E-mail: eahenard@aol.com.

HENCE, JANE KNIGHT, designer; b. Pitts., June 27, 1937; d. Luther and Doris (Ayers) Knight; m. Carleton Campbell Hence, May 12, 1962 (div. 1975); children: Kyle Fitz-Randolph Hence, Maxson Bentley Hence, Juliellen Hence Casey. Grad., Emma Willard Sch., Troy, N.Y., 1955; student, Skidmore Coll., Saratoga Springs, N.Y., 1955-58; Grad., Traphagen Sch. of Design, N.Y.C., 1960; student, Yale U., 1986-90, R.I. Sch. of Design, 1988-90. Owner various bus. ventures including Bed and Breakfast, catering bus., free-lance interior design, 1982—; owner, prin. JKH Design, 1989—; consulting assoc. and designer Michael McKinley & Assocs., Stonington, Conn., 1993—2001. Mem. Westerly Sch. Facilities Com., Westerly, R.I., 1993-96, Westerly Sch. Bldg. Com., 1992-93; mem. Bd. S.E. Mus., Brewster, N.Y., 1970-74. Designer over 45 bldgs., renovations and additions in New Eng., 1987—; co-designer more than 40 bldgs. in R.I. and Conn., 1989-99; interior designer, 1998—; painter various media in collections in Midwest, South, N.Y. and New Eng. Alt. Westerly Zoning Bd., RI, 2000—02. Avocations: travel, reading, opera, theatre. also: 946 Burgundy St New Orleans LA 70116-3004 Home and Office: 73 Washington St Newport RI 02840-1533

HENDERSHOT, CAROL MILLER, physical therapist; b. Lancaster, Pa., July 24, 1959; d. Richard Horace and Joan Marie (Nonnenmocher) Miller; m. Richard A. Hendershot, Dec. 29, 1989; 1 child, Scott Michael. BS in Phys. Therapy, Quinnipiac U., 1981. Staff phys. therapist Easter Seal Rehab. Ctr., Lancaster, 1981-85, phys. therapy dept. head, 1986-89; staff phys. therapist Community Hosp. of Lancaster, 1985-86, Guilds' Sch. & Neuromuscular Ctr., 1990—. Dir. publicity and pub. rels. Lancaster Dist. United Meth. Women, 1988—89; chmn. ch. and soc. com. Covenant United Meth. Ch., 1987, 1988, mem. chancel choir, 1981—89, mem. adminstrv. bd., 1975—88; trustee Audubon Pk. United Meth. Ch., 1990—93, mem. chancel choir, 1990—92, mem. staff parish rels. com., 1993—94, mem. Jubilee Bell Choir, 1990—, mem. worship com., 1996—, chair worship com., 2003—, dir. Bethlehem and Joy Bells Handbell Choirs, 1994—96, dir. Jubilee Handbell Choir, 1996—. Mem.: Lancaster County Vis. Nurse Assn. (prof. adv. com. 1987—89), Neuro-Devel. Treatment Assn., Beta Beta Beta. Democrat. Methodist. Avocations: sewing, music, cooking, needlework, gardening, stamping. Home: 6007 W Hopi Ct Spokane WA 99208-9046

HENDERSHOTT LOVE, ARLES JUNE, television community relations director; b. Rockford, Ill., Oct. 22, 1956; d. Eugene Bourden and Rose Marie (Erickson) Hendershott; m. Joseph William Love, Sept. 20, 1986. BS with high honors, Ill. State U., 1979; postgrad., U. Mo., Columbia, 1992. Reporter Sta. WTVO-TV, Rockford, 1979-82, news prodr., 1982-83; news assignment editor Sta. WIFR-TV, Rockford, 1983-86, news dir., 1986-97; dir. cmty. rels. Benedek Broadcasting Corp./WIFR-TV, 1997—. Speaker Rockford Pub. Schs., 1980-83, 97—. Producer news story Pee Wee Explosion, 1985 (AP award 1986). Bd. dirs. Rockford Airshow, 1994-95; mem. com. YWCA, Rockford, 1987, Westminister Presbyn. Ch., Rockford, also tchr. Sunday Sch., 1983-2000; bd. dirs. No. Ill. chpt. March of Dimes, 1980-84, NW Ill. chpt. Spl. Olympics, Rockford, 1986—, Discovery Ctr. Mus., Rockford, 1987-90, N.W. Ill. Alzheimer & Related Disorder Assn., 1991, Rockford CrimeStoppers, 1992—; active YWCA Leader Luncheon Coun., 1992-93, leader Lunch Coun., 1994-95; bd. dirs. YWCA Rockford, 1997-99, Am. Lung Assn. Winnebago County, 1997—, Rockford Boys and Girls Club, 1997—; pres. bd. dirs. Am. Hearth Assn. Winnebago County 1999—, bd. dirs. 1997—. Recipient Leadership award Ken-Rock Cmty. Ctr., Rockford, 1980, Presdl. award of honor Rockford Jaycees, 1986, Dist. award Zonta Pub. Rels. Campaign, 1990, Leader Luncheon award YWCA,

1991, Recognize the Abilities Cmty. Svc. award, 1999, Congl. Cert. for Cmty. Svc., 1999, Midwest Affiliate Am. Heart Assn. Spl. Heart award, 1999, Crimestopper of Yr. award Rockford, 1996, 2000, Disting. Svc. award Am. Heart Assn., 2000, award of merit Ill. Pub. Health Assn., 2000, Kiwanis Touch A Life award, 2003. Mem. AAUW (bd. dirs. 1982-84), NAFE, Radio-TV News Dirs. Assn. (TV state coord. for Ill. 1989-96), Ill. News Broadcasters Assn., Soc. Profl. Journalists, Am. Mgmt. Assn., Archeology Inst. Am., Rockford C. of C. (pres. club 1993—, public policy com. 1997—, amb. 1997—), Univ. Chgo. Oriental Inst., Ill. Assoc. Press (exec. com. 1989—, pres.-elect 1990, pres. 1991), Lens & Shutter Club (pres. 1983-85, others), Zonta. Avocations: traveling, photography. Office: Sta WIFR-TV 2523 S Meridian Rd Rockford IL 61102 E-mail: jwl-ajh@worldnet.att.net.

HENDERSON, ALMA, religious studies educator; b. Milw., Mar. 19, 1920; d. Gotthieb and Matilda (Zielke) Siewert; m. George Henderson, Sept. 28, 1946 (dec. May. 1997); adopted many African and Chinese young people. Grad., Flight Sch., 1945; BA, Tocoa Falls Coll., 1946; MA, U. Ga., 1973. Missionary tchr. N.Am. Bapt., Cameroon, West Africa, 1947-70; tchr. Athens (Ga.) Christian Sch., 1973-83, U. Ga., Athens, 1983-99. Baptist. Avocations: african and chinese culture, foreign student affairs, theological studies. Home: 7 Sleepy Holw Athens GA 30601-5543

HENDERSON, CATHERINE LYNN, retired secondary education educator, writer; b. Charleston, W.Va., Oct. 19, 1946; d. Raymond Anis Frame and Alma Madalene Green; m. W. Elliott Henderson, Apr. 12, 1978 (dec. 1985). BA in English, Morris Harvey Coll., 1968; MA in Journalism, Marshall U., 1976. Tchr. Kanawha County Bd. Edn., Charleston, W.Va., 1968—2001; ret., 2001. Stringer Offcl. Detective Group. Author: Fairs, Festivals & Funnin' in West Virginia, 1996; co-author: Essential Strategies for School Security, 2001, contbr. to Wonderful W.Va. Mag., Charleston City Mag. Mem. Nat. Writers Assn., Mystery Writers of Am., Am. Crime Writers League, Sisters in Crime, Soc. of Profl. Journalists. E-mail: murdermostfoul@charter.net.

HENDERSON, CHERYL LYNNE, retail executive; b. Duluth, Minn., Sept. 20, 1960; d. Gene Robert Henderson and Patricia Anne (Young) Smith; children: Holly Lynne, Cristina Joelle. Student, Phx. Coll., 1976-77. Talk show host Sta. KFI, L.A., 1994-95; dir. Creative Resources, Glendale, Calif., 1996—2000; recycling coord. L.A. Police Dept., 1991—2000; v.p. The Blvd. Entertainment, Inc., Burbank, Calif., 1997—2001; gen. mgr. Ted's Music Co., Chatsworth, Calif., 2000—; officer SSK Game Enterprises and Diamond Game Enterprises, Chatsworth, 2002—. Cons. Youth Escaping the Streets, Glendale, 1992—2001. Vol. Ams. for Free Choice in medicine; voter registrar Los Angeles County, 1993—. Mem. Ayn Rand inst. Avocations: coin collecting/numismatics, interior decorating, stamp collecting/philately, art, travel. Home: 626 N Howard St Apt 4 Glendale CA 91206-5302 Office: Ted's Music Co 9817 Variel Ave Chatsworth CA 91311 Office Phone: 818-727-1690. E-mail: chenderson@diamondgame.com.

HENDERSON, CONNIE CHORLTON, city planner, artist and writer; b. Cedar Rapids, Iowa, July 16, 1944; d. Robert Brown and Lorraine Madeline (Marquardt) Chorlton; m. Dwight Franklin Henderson, Dec. 24, 1966; 1 child, Patricia. BA, Anderson U., 1966; MA in Edn., St. Francis Coll., Ft. Wayne, Ind., 1972; MPA, U. Tex. San Antonio, 1987. Art coord. Ft. Wayne Comty. Schs., 1966-67; art tchr. East Allen County Schs., New Haven, Ind., 1968-71, 74-79; instr. Manchester Coll., N. Manchester, Ind., 1971-72; rsch. assoc. Tremar Real Estate Rsch., San Antonio, 1983-84; planning asst. (vol.) City of San Antonio, Tex., 1985-88, planner I, 1988-89, project mgmt. specialist, 1990, conservation edn. coord., 1990-91; planner II San Antonio Water Sys., 1991-96, 2003—, water edn. coord., 1996-97, spl. events. coord., 1998—2002; youth edn. specialist, 2003—. Docent (vol.) San Antonio Mus. Assn.; rsch. mgr. N. San Antonio C. of C., 1988. Artist: numerous paintings and fiber sculptures in juried and invitational shows, 1966-80; poetess: (2d prize Iowa Poetry Day Assn., 1961). Bd. dirs. Tex. Soc. to Prevent Blindness, San Antonio, 1981-83; v.p. U. Tex. at San Antonio Women's Club, 1981-82, pres. 1983-84; mem. San Antonio Conservation Soc., 1985—, mem. Assistance League of San Antonio, 1988—, liason Thrift House, San Antonio, 1995-96; co-pres. River Gardens Family and Friends, 1993-94, sec., 1995-96. Mem. Am. Planning Assn. (cert. planner, asst. dir. San Antonio sect. 1990, dir., 1991-93, Am. Water Works Assn., Univ. of Tex. at San Antonio Alumni Assn. Avocations: travel, reading, landscape design, swimming, mus. visits. Bus. Home: 2410 Shadow Cliff St San Antonio TX 78232-4010 Office: San Antonio Water System PO Box 2449 San Antonio TX 78298-2449 Office Phone: 210-704-7254. Business E-Mail: chenderson@saws.org.

HENDERSON, CYNTHIA ANNE, theater educator, actress; b. Mobile, Ala., May 11, 1966; d. Geraldine D. P. Henderson and Bobbie R. Henderson, Sr.; 1 child, Justin C. Baldessare. BS, Troy State U., 1994; MFA, Pa. State U., 1997. Asst. prof. Ithaca (N.Y.) Coll., 1999—. Actor: stage, film and TV (Best Supporting Actress in Musical, European Tournament of Plays, 1991). Demonstrator, Washington, 2003. Fulbright Scholar, CIES - Fulbright, 2003—. Mem.: Actor's Equity Assn. Avocations: hiking, camping, poetry, pastels, travel. Office: Ithaca Coll Dept Theatre 201 Dillingham Ctr Ithaca NY 14850 Personal E-mail: chenderson@ithaca.edu.

HENDERSON, DEIRDRE HEALY, foundation administrator; b. Chgo., Nov. 10, 1942; d. Laurin Hall and Patricia (Kelly) H.; m. Duncan Yeandle, Sept. 27, 1969; children: Allison Dow, Duncan Dylan. AA, Briarcliff Coll., 1962; BA, Conn. Coll., New London, 1964. Editorial asst. Commerce Clearing House, San Francisco, 1964-65; tchr. Harris Sch., Chgo., 1966-67; stockbroker Dominick and Dominick, E.F. Hutton, Chgo., 1968-70; ptnr. Park West Interiors, Chgo., 1976-88; founder, pres. Franklin and Copley, Ltd., Chgo., 1987-98; coord. gun control com. San Francisco Gen. Hosp. Trauma Found., 1998—. V.p., bd. mem., Com. for Handgun Control, Chgo., 1976-84, organizer G.A. Ranney for U.S. Senate, Donald Haider for Mayor, Chgo., 1985-87. Mem. events com. Coro No. Calif., 1997—, San Francisco Gen. Hosp. Found., 1998—2000; trustee Chgo. Hist. Soc., 1990—93, Westover Sch., Middlebury, Conn., 1990—96; officer, bd. dirs. Women's Bd. Rehab. Inst., Chgo., 1073—1985, Women's Bd. Rush-Presbyn., St. Luke's Hosp., Chgo, 1973—84; mem. steering com. U. Chgo. Women's Bd., Field Mus. Women's Bd., 1989—93, Antiquarian Soc. of the Art Inst.; mem. bd. dir. The Trauma Found., San Francisco, 2003—; devel. com. bd. dir. The Bell Campaign; bd. trustees Penobscot Marine Mus., Searsport, Maine, 1998—, officer, 2001—; bd. dir. Coro No. Calif., 2000—02. Mem. Chgo. Hist. Soc. Guild (officer, bd. dirs., chmn. 1985-93), Chgo. Acad. of Scis. (bd. dirs. 1984-93), Chgo. Found. for Edn. (bd. dirs. 1985-92), Friends of Lincoln Park (bd. dirs. 1985-92), Seven Seas Cruising Assn. (transatlantic sailor), Woman's Athletic Club (officer bd. dirs. 1975-81), Friday Club (officer bd. dirs. 1985-91), Children's Theatre Assn. (bd. dirs. 2000-02), Calif. Tennis Club, San Francisco Golf Club. Episcopalian. Avocations: tennis, sailing, golf, photography, biking.

HENDERSON, E. SUZANNE, elementary school educator; b. Champaign, Ill., Nov. 18, 1947; d. Donald Albert Fackler and Fiana B. Warfel Hardig; m. William Arthur Henderson, Aug. 17, 1968; children: Holly Janel, Rachel Eileen. BS, So. Ill. U., 1968; MEd, U. Ill., 1976. Tchr. grade 4 Pulaski County Spl. Sch. Dist., Jacksonville, Ark., 1968-70; tchr. grade 5 Tuscola Cmty. Unit Sch. Dist., Tuscola, Ill., 1970—. Recipient Presdl. Award for Excellence in Teaching of Math. and Sci., 1994. Mem. NEA, Ill. Edn. Assn., Tuscola Edn. Assn. (v.p. 1994-95), Nat. Coun. Tchrs. Math., Ill. Coun. Tchrs. Math. Avocations: flower gardening, golf. Home: 105 E Scott St Tuscola IL 61953-1834 Office: Tuscola Sch Dist 409 S Prairie St Tuscola IL 61953-1770

HENDERSON, ELIZABETH ANN, farmer; b. N.Y.C., Jan. 13, 1943; d. Sydney and Laura (Rosenbaum) Berliner; m. Harry Brinton Henderson III, Sept. 23, 1966 (dec. Jul. 1972); 1 child, Andrew Melville. BA, Barnard Coll., 1964; MA, Yale U., 1966, PhD, 1975. Asst. prof. Russian lit. Boston U., 1975-81; organic farmer Unadilla Farm, Gill, Mass., 1981-88, Rose Valley Farm, Rose, N.Y., 1988-98, Peacework Organic Farm, Newark. Adminstrv. coun. N.E. Sustainable Agr. Rsch. and Edn. Program, Burlington, Vt., 1993-97, mem. tech. com., 1990-93; mem. adv. coun. to dean Coll. Agr. and Life Scis., cornell U., Ithaca, N.Y., 1995—; lectr. in field. Author/editor: The Real Dirt: Farmers Tell About Organic and Low-Input Practices, 1994; author: Food Book for a Sustainable Harvest, 1994, Sharing the Harvest. A Guide to Community Agriculture, 1999, Whole Farm Planning Manual, 2003; contbr. articles to profl. jours. Mem. exec. com. Nat. Sustainable Agr. Coord. Coun., Washington, 1993-97; chmn. Wayne County Agrl. and Farmland Protection Bd., N.Y., 1993—; adv. com. Farming Alterantives Program, Cornell U., 1993—; bd. dirs. Genesee-Finger Lakes Food Sys. Project, 1994-97. Named Conservation Farm of the Yr., Wayne County Soil and Water Conservation Disst., 1991, Honoree of the Yr., North Rose Wolcott Profl. Bus. Women's Assn., 1994; AAUW Jr. Faculty grantee, 1978. Mem. N.E. Organic Farming Assn. (founding pres. 1982-84, governing coun. 1988—, Outstanding Mem. Yr. 1990), N.Y. Sustainable Agr. Working Group (steering com. mem. 1992-2002), N.Y. Grange (gatekeeper 1995-96). Avocations: theatre, modern dance, travel. Home and Office: 2218 Welcher Rd Newark NY 14513-9308

HENDERSON, FLORENCE (FLORENCE HENDERSON BERNSTEIN), actress, singer; b. Dale, Ind., Feb. 14, 1934; d. Joseph and Elizabeth Elder H.; m. Ira Bernstein, Jan. 9, 1956 (div.); children: Barbara, Joey, Robert Norman, Elizabeth; m. John Kappas, Aug. 4, 1987. Attended, St. Francis Acad., Owensboro, Ky.; studied at, Am. Acad. Dramatic Arts. Broadway and stage debut in Wish You Were Here, 1952; on tour in Oklahoma!, 1952-53, at N.Y.C. Ctr., 1953, Fanny, 1954, The Sound of Music, 1961, in revival of Annie Get Your Gun, 1974; appeared in The Great Waltz, Los Angeles Civic Light Opera Assn., 1953, on Broadway in The Girl Who Came to Supper, 1963, in revival of South Pacific, 1967, in revival The Sound of Music, Los Angeles Civic Light Opera Assn., 1978, Bells are Ringing, Los Angeles Civic Light Opera Assn., 1979; appeared in Oldsmobile indsl. shows, 1958-61, actress: (movies) Song of Norway, 1970, Shakes The Clown, 1991, Naked Gun 33 1/2: The Final Insult, 1994, The Brady Bunch Movie, 1995; appeared on TV in Sing Along, 1958, The Today Show, 1959-60, The Brady Bunch, 1969-74, The Brady Bunch Hour, 1977, The Brady Girls Get Married, 1981, A Very Brady Christmas, 1988, The Bradys, 1990, Fudge-A-Mania, 1995, (host) Bradymania, 1993; numerous other TV appearances include The Love Boat, 1976, 83, The Brady Brides, 1981, Hart to Hart, 1981, Fantasy Island, 1981, 83, Alice, 1983, Murder She Wrote, Dean Martin TV Series; hostess Country Kitchen; appeared in TV spl. Just a Regular Kid, guest appearances It's Garry Shandling's Show, Wil Shriner Show, Jay Leno Family Spl.; first female host of The Tonight Show; co-host: Later Today, 1999—; writings, A Little Cooking, A Little Talking, and A Whole Lotta Fun; films include: Holy Man, 1998, Get Bruce, 1999. Recipient Sarah Siddons award Office: The Blake Agency 1327 Ocean Ave Ste J Santa Monica CA 90401-1024

HENDERSON, HARRIET, librarian; b. Pampa, Tex., Nov. 19, 1949; d. Ervin Leon and Hannah Elizabeth (Yee) H. AB, Baker U., 1971; MLS, U. Tex., 1973. Sch. libr. Pub. Sch. Sys., Pampa, 1971-72; city libr. City of Tyler, Tex., 1973-80, City of Newport News, Va., 1980-84, dir. librs. and info. svcs., 1984-90; dir. Louisville Free Pub. Libr., 1990-97, Montgomery County (Md.) Pub. Librs., 1997—. Del. White House Conf. Librs. and Info. Svcs., 1991; mem. Leadership Louisville, 1991—97, Alliant Health Sys. Adult Oper. Bd., 1991—97; mem. adv. com. dept. edn. Spalding U., 1991—95; mem. Md. Adv. Coun. on Librs., 2001—; diaconate Hiddenwood Presbyn. Ch., Newport News, 1983—85; bd. dirs. Tex. Libr. Sys. Act adv. bd., 1979—80, Peninsula Women's Network, Newport News, 1983—85. Recipient Tribute to Women in Bus. and Industry, Peninsula YWCA, Newport News, 1984. Mem.: ALA (councillor 2001—), Pub. Libr. Assn. (v.p. 1998, pres. 1999), Va. Libr. Assn. (chmn. legis. com. 1981—84, v.p. 1985, pres. 1986), Ky. Libr. Assn. (chair pub. libr. sect. 1995, Outstanding Pub. Libr. Svc. award 1997). Office: Montgomery County Pub Librs Office of Dir 99 Maryland Ave Rockville MD 20850-2330

HENDERSON, HAZEL, economist, writer, lecturer; b. Bristol, Somerset, U.K., Mar. 27, 1933; came to U.S., 1957, naturalized, 1962; d. Kenneth and Dorothy May (Jesseman) Mustard; m. Carter Henderson (div. 1981); 1 child, Alexandra Leslie Camille Henderson Cassidy. Baccalaureate, Clifton Sch., Bristol, U.K., 1950; ScD (hon.), Worcester (Mass.) Poly. Inst., 1975; ScD (hon.), Soka U., 2000, U. San Francisco, 2001. Freelance writer, various locations, 1967—. Vis. regent's lectr. U. Calif., Santa Barbara, 1979; Horace Allbright chair dept. forestry, U. Calif., Berkeley, 1982; adviser, cons., lectr. for founds., non-profit agys., govt. agys. and corps. in over 30 countries; dir. Worldwatch Inst., 1975-2001; advisor Calvert Social Investment Funds.; ptnr. Calvert-Henderson Quality of Life Indicators; guest on over 300 radio and TV programs including Today Show, AM Am., Bill Moyer's Jour.; prodr. Sunrise Semester series, CBS, 1977, 78, informative series, PBS, 1984; founder Ethical Marketplace LLC; mem. commn. on globalization; presenter seminars. Author: Creating Alternative Futures: The End of Economics, 1978, 2d edit., 1996, The Politics of the Solar Age: Alternatives to Economics, 1981, 2d edit., 1988, Paradigms in Progress, 1991, 2d edit., 1995, Building a Win-Win World, 1996, Beyond Globalization, 1999; editor: The United Nations: Policy and Financing Alternatives, 1996; syndicated columnist InterPress Svc., L.A. Times-Mirror Syndicate; contbr. articles to C.S. Monitor, U.S. News and World Report, Time, N.Y. Times, InterPress Svc.; contbr. to anthologies; editorial bd. Futures U.K., Foresight U.K., Futures Rsch. Quar., Future Survey, Resurgence. Adv. coun. U.S. Congress Office Tech. Assessment, Washington, 1974-80; adv. Com. on Future Fla. State Legislature, Tallahassee, 1984-86; mem. Commn. on Globalization, World Commn. on Global Consiousness; internat. adv. bd. Forum 2000, Prague. Named Citizen of Yr. N.Y. Med. Soc., 1967; awardee UN Environ. Program; co-winner Global Citizen award, 1996. Fellow World Bus. Acad., World Futures Study Fedn., Findhorn Found., Global Edn. Assn., Club of Budapest (hon.). Avocations: cycling, gardening, swimming. Office: PO Box 5190 Saint Augustine FL 32085-5190

HENDERSON, HELENA NAUGHTON, legal association administrator; b. New Orleans, Mar. 19, 1956; d. John Francis and Helen Naughton; div.; children: William Henry Henderson, Kevin Richard Henderson. BS in Psychology, Harvard U., 1976, Newcomb Coll, 1978; postgrad., Tulane U., 1990—. Exec. dir. New Orleans Bar Assn. Mem. La. Commn. on Policy and Rsch., 1999-2001, chair Juvenile Law Conf. for La., 1999. Bd. dirs. La. Ctr. for Law-Related Edn., New Orleans, 1992—, New Orleans Police Found., 1996—, Voices for Children, 1997—. Mem. ABA (assoc.), Am. Soc. Assn. Execs., Nat. Assn. Bar Execs. (chair strategic planning com. 1996-98), Nat. Ctr. for Nonprofit Bds. Office: New Orleans Bar Assn 228 Saint Charles Ave Ste 1223 New Orleans LA 70130-2643

HENDERSON, JANET E. lawyer; b. 1956; BA, U. Okla., 1978; JD, Columbia U., 1982. Bar: Okla. 1982, U.S. Dist. Ct. (no. dist.) Okla. 1982, Ill. 1986, U.S. Dist. Ct. (no. dist.) Ill. 1986. With Sidley & Austin, Chgo., 1985—, ptnr., 1990—. Lectr. on lender liability issues and bankruptcy to legal orgns., including Midwest Assn. Secured Lenders. Harlan Fiske Stone scholar Columbia U., 1982. Mem. ABA, Chgo. Bar Assn., Am. Bankruptcy Inst., Phi Beta Kappa. Office: Sidley & Austin Bank One Plz 10 S Dearborn St Chicago IL 60603 Fax: 312-853-7036.*

HENDERSON, JANET LYNN, small business owner; b. Chgo., Sept. 14, 1943; d. Howard Charles and Lucille Laura (Lambrecht) Harris; m. Todd Dierks Nelson, Jan. 30, 1965 (div. May 1997); children: Erik Nelson, Brooks Nelson, Jessica Nelson, Jillian Nelson; m. Phil M. Henderson, Dec. 26, 1997. BS in Bus. Adminstrn., Elmhurst Coll., 1966. Lic. real estate broker. Career counselor Employee Svcs., Inc., Chgo., 1966-67; acctg. mgr. Ins. Mgmt., Inc., Milw., 1967-70, Hosp. Coun. Greater Milw., 1970-84; broker assoc. Klein & Heuchan, Inc., Clearwater, Fla., 1994-99; pres., owner Weddings On Water, Clearwater, Fla., 2003—. Mem. leadership tng. coun. Nat. League Cities, Washington, 1999—2002; mem. internat. com. Fla. League Cities, Tallahassee, 1999—2002. Pres. Dunedin Youth Guild, 1993—; city commr. City of Dunedin, Fla., 1997—2002, vice mayor, 1999, 2002; chair Relay for Life, 2003; chmn. Pinellas County Heart Ball, 2000; bd. dirs. Childrens Svc. Soc., 1983—86, Ruth Eckerd Hall Found., Clearwater, Fla., 1998—2004, chair spl. events com., mem. Leading Ladies Bd.; bd. dirs. Pinellas Planning Coun., Clearwater, Fla., 1998—2002, Watson Ctr., 1999—2004, Pinellas County Cmty. Found., Bowman Meml. Scholarship Fund Com., 2003—04; v.p. Dunedin Hist. Soc.; bd. dirs. Dunedin C. of C., 2003—04, Women in Philanthropy Steering Com., 2004, Leadership Pinellas, 1993—. Ill. State scholar, 1962. Mem.: Dunedin Hist. Soc. (2d v.p.), Friends Libr., Rotary. Republican. Office: Weddings on Water Inc 200 Seminole St Clearwater FL 33755 E-mail: jlh1464@aol.com.

HENDERSON, JERRIE, realtor; b. Rockcastle, Ky., Jan. 19, 1929; d. Jason and Okla Martin Cox; m. David Lucas Henderson, Dec. 6, 1947 (dec.); children: Mark Steven, Marcia Renee Henderson Brewer, Kathy. BS Ea. Ky. Univ., 1951. Cert. Real Estate Ohio Real Estate Com., 1966. Elem. tchr. Ft. Campbell Army Base, Ky., 1951—53, Dayton Ohio Pub. Schs., 1953—85; realtor assoc. C.W. Moore Realty, Dayton, Ohio, 1963—66; realtor/broker Jerrie Henderson Realty, Dayton, Ohio, 1966—85, Century 21 Dampier, Lexington, Ky., 1985—90, Jerrie Henderson Realty, Lexington, Ky., 1990—. Vol. Inner-City Day Care, Lexington, Ky., 2000—; com. mem. Nursing Home Ombudsman Agency, Lexington, Ky., 1985—89. Recipient Four Star Pace Setter, Century 21 Dampier, 1988. Mem.: Lexington-Bluegrass Assn. of Realtors, Ky. Assn. of Realtors, Nat. Assoc. Realtors, DEA, OEA, NEA. Democrat. Bapt. Avocations: photography, antiques, Ladies Sunday Sch.. Home and Office: 600 Vincent Way No 1104 Lexington KY 40503

HENDERSON, KAREN LECRAFT, federal judge; b. 1944, BA, Duke U., 1966; JD, U. N.C., 1969. Ptnr. Wright & Henderson, Chapel Hill, NC, 1969—70, Sinkler, Gibbs & Simons, P.A., Columbia, SC, 1983—86; asst. atty. gen. Columbia, 1973—78; sr. asst. atty. gen., dir. of spl. litigation sect., 1978—82; deputy atty. gen., dir. of criminal div., 1982; judge U.S. Dist. Ct. S.C., Columbia, 1986—90, U.S. Ct. Appeals (D.C. cir.), Washington, 1990—. Apptd. Dist. Ct. Adv. Com. Mem.: ABA (litigation sect. and urban, state and local government law sect.), S.C. Bar (government law sect., trial and appellate practice sect., fed. judges assn.), N.C. Bar Assn. Office: US Ct Appeals 333 Constitution Ave NW Washington DC 20001-2802*

HENDERSON, KAREN SUE, psychologist; b. Bloomington, Ill., Mar. 25, 1946; d. Charles Lewis and Faye Lanore (Wantland) Henderson; m. David Thomas Biggs, Dec. 2, 1967 (div. 1972); m. Dean Eugene Dixon Jr., Jan. 13, 1973 (div. 1995); children: Christopher, Matthew; m. William Wayne Riggs, May 19, 1998. BA, U. Calif., Berkeley, 1966; MS, San Jose (Calif.) State Coll., 1971; PhD, Union Inst., 1991. Lic. clin. psychol., Alaska; cert. C.C. tchr.; registered play therapist and supr. Psychologist pvt. practice, Anchorage, 1980—2001; cons. Alaska Youth and Parent Found., Anchorage, 1989—2001, Kenai Peninsula Counseling Svcs., 1995-2000, Parents United, Anchorage, 1989; mental health cons. Rural Alaska Community Action Program, Anchorage, 1988; cons., mem. adolescent treatment team Charter North Hosp., Anchorage, 1985-88; cons. Infant Impaired Hearing Program, Anchorage, 1984-85, Parent Tng. Ctr., Anchorage, 1980-82; psychiat. social worker Langdon Psychiat. Clinic, Anchorage, 1976-80; instr. in psychology U. Alaska Community Coll., Anchorage, 1974-81; parole agt. narcotic outpatient program State Dept. Corrections, Oakland, Calif., 1972-74; group counselor II, caseworker Alameda County Probation Dept., Oakland, Calif., 1971-72; adj. prof. U. Alaska, Anchorage, 1999-2000, Tex. A&M Internat., 2002—; cons. psychologist pvt. practice, 2002—. Adj. prof. U. Alaska, Anchorage, 1994-95; cons. psychologist Alviso (Calif.) Econ. Devel. Program, 1971-72; instr. psychology Coll. of Alameda, 1973; faculty adv. for coop. edn. U. Alaska C.C., 1975-76. Sec., liaison to bd. Susitna Sch. PTA, Anchorage, 1983-84; co-chmn. optional bd. Susitna Sch., 1984-85, chmn., 1985-86, vol. coord., 1988-89; mem. adv. bd Steller Alt. Sch., 1992-95. Mem. APA, Alaska Psychol. Assn. Democrat. Avocations: running, reading, camping, travel, bridge.

HENDERSON, L(EONA) HARRIETTE, retired social work administrator, consultant; b. Phila., Mar. 8, 1934; d. Luther and Leona (Wilson) Highsmith; m. Charles Leon Henderson, 1958; children, Victor Parks, Craig Lamarr. BA, Fisk U., 1955; MS in Edn., Temple U., 1958; MSW, Adelphi U., 1973. Lic. social worker, N.Y. From caseworker dep. commr. Human Resources Adminstrn./Dept. Social Services, N.Y.C., 1961—86, dep. commr. family svcs., 1986—89, ret., 1989. Social work cons. region 2 Head Start, N.Y.C., 1990—. Trustee Fisk U., Nashville, 1984-87, recruiter, 1984—; music dir. children's choir Good Shepherd Ch., West Hempstead, N.Y., 1970—; alto Carr-Hill Singers, 1983—. Recipient pub. svc. award Fund for City N.Y., 1985, recognition Human Resources Adminstrn.-Women's Advisors, 1989. Mem. Managerial Assn. N.Y.C., Social Work Mgrs. Nat. Network (Exemplar award 1988), NAACP (Social Svc. award 1987), Delta Sigma Theta. Home: Apt 1613 3600 Conshohocken Ave Philadelphia PA 19131-5330

HENDERSON, MADELINE MARY (BERRY HENDERSON), chemist, researcher, consultant; b. Merrimac, Mass., Sept. 3, 1922; d. Burton B. and Irene R. (Murphy) Berry; m. Richard S. Henderson, Nov. 5, 1957; children: Anne M., Matthew R., Katherine M., Laura J. AB in Chemistry, Emmanuel Coll., Boston, 1944; MPA, Am. U., Washington, 1977. Chemist E.I. DuPont, Gibbstown, N.J., 1944-45, MIT, Cambridge, Mass., 1946-52; info. specialist Battelle Meml. Inst., Columbus, Ohio, 1953-55; rsch. assoc. NSF, Washington, 1956-62; computer specialist Nat. Bur. Standards, Washington, 1964-79; cons. Bethesda, 1980—. Chmn. Gordon Rsch. Conf. on Sci. Info. Problems, 1972. Author, co-author, editor books on info. sci.; co-author, author papers, articles on info. sci., standards, and libr. automation. Dept. of Commerce Sci.-Tech. fellow, 1971-72; Am. U. Key Exec. scholar, 1975-77. Fellow AAAS (sec. sect. info. scis. 1978-85); mem. Am. Chem. Soc., Am. Soc. Info. Sci. & Tech. (mem. publs. com. 1983-87, chmn. pub. affairs com. 1987-89, Watson Davis award 1989), Pi Alpha Alpha (nat. honor soc. pub. adminstr.). Office: 7401 Willow Rd #425 Frederick MD 21702-2500

HENDERSON, MARY R. (NINA), food/consumer products executive; BS, Drexel U. With Bestfoods, 1972—; various gen. mgmt. and sr. mktg. mgmt. positions; v.p. mktg. S.B. Thomas Inc. subsidiary Bestfoods, 1982-86; v.p. N.Am. divsn., pres. bestfoods specialty markets group Bestfoods, 1986-97, corp. v.p., pres. Bestfoods grocery, 1997—. Bd. dirs. AXA Fin. Inc. (formerly Equitable Cos. Inc.), The Equitable Life Assurance Soc., Pactiv Corp. (former Tenneco Packaging), Hunt Corp. Trustee Drexel U. Office: Best Foods 700 Sylvan Ave Englewood Cliffs NJ 07632-9976

HENDERSON, MAUREEN MCGRATH, medical educator; b. Tynemouth, Eng., May 11, 1926; arrived in U.S., 1960; d. Leo E. and Helen McGrath Henderson. MB BS, U. Durham, Eng., 1949, DPH, 1956. Prof. preventive medicine U. Md. Med. Sch., 1968—75, chmn. dept. social and preventive medicine, 1971—75; assoc. epidemiology Johns Hopkins U. Sch. Hygiene and Pub. Health, 1960—75; prof. epidemiology and medicine U. Wash. Med. Sch., 1975—96, prof. emeritus epidemiology and medicine, 1996—, asst. v.p. and assoc. v.p. health scis., 1975—81, head cancer prevention rsch. program Fred Hutchinson Cancer Rsch. Ctr., 1983—94; mem. Nat. Inst. Environ. Health Scis. Adv. Coun., 1994—97. Chmn. epidemiology and disease control study sect. Nih, 1969—82; chmn. clin. trial rev. com. Nat. Heart Lung and Blood Inst., 1975—79; mem. Nat. Cancer Adv. Bd., 1979—84; mem. bd. Robert Wood Johnson Health Policy fellowship [illegible] rated Order of Brit. Empire; recipient John Snow award, Am. Pub. Health Assn., 1990; scholar Luke-Armstrong, 1956—57, John and Mary Markle, Acad. Medicine, 1963—68. Mem.: Nat. Rsch. Coun. (mem. com. rsch. priorities for airborne particulate matters 1998—2000, mem. report rev. com. 1996—), Am. Epidemiol. Soc. (pres. 1990—91), Internat. Coun. Cancer Rsch. (sci. adv. bd. 1989—92), Soc. Epidemiol. Rsch. (chmn. 1969—70), Assn. Tchrs. Preventive Medicine (pres. 1972—73), Am. Coll. Epidemiology, Inst. Medicine N.A.S. Home: 5309 NE 85th St Seattle WA 98115-3915

HENDERSON, MAXINE OLIVE BOOK (MRS. WILLIAM HENDERSON III), foundation executive; b. Rush, Colo., Apr. 22, 1924; d. Jesse Frank and Olive (Booth) Book; m. William Henderson III, Apr. 10, 1948 (dec. May 1983); children: William IV, Meredith. BA, U. Colo., 1945. Personnel adminstr. GE Co., Schenectady, N.Y.C., 1945-54; asst. dir. placement Katherine Gibbs Sch., N.Y.C., 1967-70; v.p., dir. William Henderson Cons., Inc., N.Y.C., 1969-83, pres., dir., 1983-86; dir. recruitment Girl Scouts U.S.A., N.Y.C., 1973-78, dir. human resources, 1978-82, dir. career devel., 1982-91, adminstr. human resources, 1991-93; pres., adminstr. World Found., 1993-2000. Pres. Goddard-Riverside-Trinity Sch. Thrift Shop, N.Y.C., 1964-65, Trinity Sch. Mothers' Orgn., N.Y.C., 1965-66, Trinity Sch. Parents Assn.; treas. Brearley Sch. Parents Assn., N.Y.C., 1966-67; mem. L.I. Mus., Smithtown Arts Coun., Met. Mus. Art, N.Y.C. Mem. North Suffolk Garden Club, Nissequogue Beach Club. Episcopalian. Home: 606 W 116th St New York NY 10027-7011

HENDERSON, MOLLY, academic administrator, educator; BA in Comm., U. Sci. and Arts Okla., 1993; MA in Political Sci., U. Ctrl. Okla., 1996. Coord. high sch., coll. rels. U. Sci. and Arts Okla., Chickasha, 1996—98; coord. cmty. outreach Oklahoma City C.C., 1998—2000, adminstr. acad. programs, 2000—04, dir. coop. edn., 2004—. Adj. instr. U. Sci. and Arts Okla., Chickasha, 1996—98, Oklahoma City C.C., 1999—. Candidate liaison Okla. Rep. Party, Oklahoma City, 1994—96. Recipient Proclamation Recognition Outstanding Acheivement, Okla. State Legislation, 1996; scholar Mosier Leadership Higher Edn. Adminstrn., Okla. State U., 2003; President's Leadership scholar, U. Sci. and Arts Okla., 1987. Mem.: Phi Kappa Phi. Office: Oklahoma City C C 7777 South May Ave Oklahoma City OK 73159

HENDERSON, NANCY GRACE, marketing and technical documentation executive; b. Berkeley, Calif., Oct. 23, 1947; d. John Harry and Lorraine Ruth H. BA, U. Calif., Santa Barbara, 1969; MBA, U. Houston, 1985; teaching credential, UCLA, 1971; MLA, Naropa U., 2002. Chartered fin. analyst. Tchr. Keppel Union Sch. Dist., Littlerock, Calif., 1969-72, Internat. Sch. Prague, Czechoslovakia, 1972-74, Sunland Luth. Sch., Freeport, Bahamas, 1974-75; tchr., dept. head Internat. Sch. Assn., Bangkok, 1975-79; exec. search Diversified Human Resources Group, Houston, 1979-82; data processing analyst Am. Gen. Corp., Houston, 1982-83, personnel and benefits dept., 1983-85, investment analyst, 1985-86, equity security analyst/quantitative portfolio analyst, 1986-87; dir. mktg. and communications Thomson Corp., San Francisco, 1987-90, dir. technical writing, 1990—. Tchr. English as Second Language program Houston Metro. Ministries, 1980-81. Pres., bd. dirs. Home Owners Assn., Walnut Creek, Calif., 1988-90; tchr. English to refugees Houston Metro Ministries, 1982; exec. dir. Internat. Child Abuse Prevention Found., 1989; ch. choir, session, fundraising and com. chmn. Presbyn. Ch.; active Crisis Hotline, 1978-79, 92-93; dir. project Working in Networks for Good Shelter, 1993-95. Named a Notable Woman of Tex., 1984-85. Mem. Assn. for Investment Mgmt. and Rsch., Toastmasters (pres. Houston chpt. 1983, v.p. 1982-83). Avocations: tennis, skiing, hiking, photography, writing short stories and essays. Office: Thomson Vestek 425 Market St Fl 6 San Francisco CA 94105

HENDERSON, RITA BEATRICE, county official; b. CLinton, S.C., May 23, 1952; d. William D. and Mattie D. (Williams) Taylor; m. Curtis Henderson, Apr. 6, 1974; 1 child, Tori Rodshida. AS, Piedmont Tech. Coll., 1990; student, So. Wesleyan U., 1997—. Billing clk. Ithaca, Inc., Clinton, S.C., 1973-86; adminstrv. asst. United Way Laurens County, Clinton, S.C., 1990-91; head payroll dept. B.F. Shaw Fabricating Co., Laurens, S.C., 1991-92; dir. Laurens County Registration/Elections, 1993—. Screener Good Shepherd Free Clinic, Laurens, 1994-98. Methodist. Avocations: reading, piano, cooking, travel. Home: 118 Paul St Laurens SC 29360-7544 Office: Laurens County Registration/Elections 3 Catherine St Laurens SC 29360-1745

HENDERSON, ROBBYE ROBINSON, library director; b. Morton, Miss., Nov. 10, 1937; d. Robert and Aljuria (Myers) R.; 1 child, Robreka Aljuria. BA in Lang. Arts, Tougaloo Coll., 1960; MSLS, Atlanta U., 1968; PhD in Ednl. Leadership, So. Ill. U., 1976. Librarian Patton Lane High Sch., Basteville, Miss., 1960-66, Utica (Miss.) Jr. Coll., 1966-67, Miss. Indsl. Coll., Hollysprings, 1967-68; acquisition librarian Miss. Valley State U., Itta Bena, 1968-72, acting librarian, 1972-73, dir. James Herbert White Library, 1973—. Cons. Office of Health Resources Opportunity, Washington, 1977-79, Miss. Assn. of Colls., Jackson, 1970-79. Vol. Teen Parenting Project State of Miss., 1987. Mem. Miss. Library Assn., Alpha Kappa Alpha (pres. Kappa Alpha Omega chpt. 1984-86, coordinator 1987, Baseilus award 1985). Home: MVSU Box 5042 14000 Highway 82 W Itta Bena MS 38941-1400 Office: Mississippi Valley State U James Herbert White Libr Itta Bena MS 38941

HENDERSON, ROBYN LEE, project manager; b. Hastings, Nebr., Apr. 3, 1960; d. Darrel Franklin and Bonnalynne Beulah Henderson. BS, Nebr. Wesleyan U., 1982; MHS, Johns Hopkins U., 1996. Aide to spkr. Nebr. Legis., Lincoln, 1981-82; program instr. Close Up Found., Arlington, Va., 1982-84; legis. aide Sen. Jim Exon, Washington, 1984-91; legis. rep. Am. Thoracic Soc., Washington, 1991-94; rsch. assoc. Nat. Health Policy Forum, Washington, 1994-96; govt. policy analyst Nat. Rural Electric Coop. Assn., Arlington, Va., 1996-98; v.p. program svcs. Nat. Rural Health Assn., Kansas City, 1998—2003; project mgr. U. Nebr. Pub. Policy Ctr., Lincoln, 2003—. Chair govt. rels. Affinity Group Nat. Health Coun., Washington, 1993-94, Rural Renaissance Network, Washington, 1996-98. Recipient Young Alumna Loyalty award Nebr. Wesleyan U., 1980; named Outstanding Young Women of Am., 1984, 87. Mem. APHA, Am. Soc. Assn. Execs., Nat. Rural Health Assn., Kansas City Soc. Assn. Execs., Phi Alpha Theta. Avocations: reading, history, golf, music. Home: 6409 Boxelder Dr Lincoln NE 68506 Office: U Nebr Pub Policy Ctr 121 S 13th St # 303 Lincoln NE 68588-0228 E-mail: rhenderson@nebraska.edu.

HENDERSON, ROGENE FAULKNER, toxicologist, researcher; b. Breckenridge, Tex., July 13, 1933; d. Philander Molden and Lenoma (Rogers) F.; m. Thomas Richard Henderson II, May 30, 1957; children: Thomas Richard III, Edith Jeanette, Laura Lee. BSBA, Tex. Christian U., 1955; PhD, U. Tex., 1960. Diplomate Am. Bd. Toxicology. Research assoc. U. Ark. Sch. Med., Little Rock, 1960-67; from scientist to sr. scientist and group supr. chemistry and toxicology Lovelace Inhalation Toxicology Research Inst., Albuquerque, 1967—; deputy dir. Nat. Environ. Respiratory Ctr. Lovelace Respiratory Rsch. Inst., Albuquerque, 1998—. Mem. adv. com. Burroughs Wellcome Toxicology Scholar award, 1987-89, NIH toxicology study sect., 1982-86, Nat. Inst. Environ. Health Scis. adv. coun., 1992-95, EPA scientific adv. bd. environ. health commn., 1991-95; mem. bd. sci. counselors EPA, 2002—; mem. Com to Assess the Sci. Base for Tobacco Harm Reduction, adv. group Am. Cancer Soc.on Cancer and the Environment, 1999—, Health Effects Inst. Rsch. Com., 1997—, USEPA Bd. of Sci. Counselors, 2001— Assoc. editor Toxicology Applied Pharmacology, 1989 95, Jour. Exposure Analysis and Environ. Epidemiology, 1991-95; contbr. articles to profl. jours. Named Woman on the Move YWCA Albuquerque, 1983; grantee NIH, 1958-60, 1960-62, 1986—. Mem. AAAS, NAS (bd. on environ. studies and toxicology 1998—), Am. Chem. Soc. (chmn. ctrl. N.Mex. sect. 1981), Soc. Toxicology (pres. Mountain-West Regional chpt. 1985-86, pres. inhalation specialty sect. 1989—), N.Y. Acad. Scis., Nat. Acad. Scis. (com. toxicology 1985-98, chair 1992-98, com. epidemiology of air pollution 1983-85, com. biol. markers 1986—, com. on risk assessment methodology 1989-92, bd. environ. studies and toxicology 1998—), Nat. Acad. (nat. assoc.). Presbyterian. Home: 5609 Don Felipe Ct SW Albuquerque NM 87105-6765 Office: Lovelace Respiratory Rsch Inst 2425 Ridgecrest Ave SE Albuquerque NM 87108 E-mail: rhenders@lrri.org.

HENDERSON, SALLY KATHLEEN, advertising, communications and marketing executive; b. Dallas, Dec. 13, 1942; d. Charles Edward and Lexie Mary (Edmundson) Shelton; m. John Joseph Henderson; children: Rebecca, Mary. Student, U. Calif., Berkeley, 1960-62; BA, Antioch U., L.A., 1973. Profl. cert. advt. UCLA. Dir. product devel. The Walt Disney Co., Burbank, Calif., 1976-79; nat. comm. dir. Vivitar Corp., Santa Monica, Calif., 1979-81; creative dir. Sweeney & Assocs., L.A., 1981-83; v.p. Doremus & Co., L.A., 1983-90; exec. v.p., creative dir. Christiansen & Fritsch, Seattle, 1990-93; pres. The Clarion Group, Vashon, Wash., 1993—. Bd. dirs. ElderHealth N.W., Seattle. Office: 22215 Wax Orchard Rd SW Vashon WA 98070-6923

HENDERSON, (RUEJENUIA) SECRET, social worker; d. Johnnie Henderson, Sr. and Mary Lula Henderson; children: Steven O'Neal, Reginald Patrick. BA in Social Work, Tex. So. U., 1994. LCSW; cert. state cert. HIV antibody testing counselor, state cert. HIV ptnr. elicitation and notification counselor, AIDS/HRAP adolescent tng. trainer, Assn. Drug Abuse Prevention and Treatment, Facing HIV/AIDS in the Deaf Cmty., Toward Healthy Sexuality, Montrose Clinic HIV Update Conf., Regional VII Client Coun. Clk. social work dept., chemistry dept. Tex. So. U., Houston, 1986—89; sec. State of Tex. Client Coun. and Regional VII Client Coun., Austin, Tex., 1988—; case mgr., HIV counselor, st. outreach worker Montrose Clinic, Houston, 1989—98; case mgr. Donald R. Watkins Meml. Found., Houston, 1999—2000; outreach case mgr. St. Hope Found., Houston, 2001; HIV case coord. Harris County Sheriff's Office, Houston, 2001—. Pres. State of Tex. Client Coun., 2001; v.p. Lone Star Legal Svc., 2002. Vol. client coun. mem., sec., pres., bd. dirs. Gulf Coast Legal Found., Houston, 1972—. Mem.: NASW, Assn. Black Social Workers (Outstanding Student award 1992), Tex. State U. Social Work Club, Tex. State U. Sociology Club. Democrat. Church Of Christ. Avocation: helping others. Home: PO Box 8454 Houston TX 77088-8454 Office: Harris County Sheriff's Office 1200 Baker St Houston TX 77002

HENDERSON, SHIRLEY ELIZABETH, minister; b. Phila., Apr. 13, 1954; d. Clyde Elinwood Wright and Ellen Smith; m. Harry Warren Henderson (dec. July 4, 2001). Gen. equivalency diploma, Internat. Corr. Sch., Scranton, Pa., 1988. Lic. min. Emmanuel Tabernacle Bapt. Ch. of the Apostolic Faith, Ohio, 1968, ordained apostle Deliverance Temple of Truth, Fla., 1994, ordained min. Tabernacle of the Enlightened Ch. of God, Fla., 1989. Electronic assembler Western Electric, Roanoke, Va., 1973—75; min. of music E. C. Cannon Evangelistic Crusade, Inc., Charlotte, NC, 1975—83; founder and pastor Praise Ministries Deliverance Ctr. Inc., Raleigh, NC, 1994—; religious instr. Pilgrim Assemblies of the World, Bklyn., 1985—88; founder and pastor Praise Ministries Inc., Orlando, Fla., 1989—94. CEO Praise Ministries Deliverance Ctr., Inc., Raleigh, NC, 1995—; chief exec. officer/dir.CEO, dir. Project Help Cmty. Devel. Ctr., Inc., Garner, NC, 1995—, cons., 1995—. Author: The Power of Worship and Praise, 1986 (Spl. Recognition award, 2000), Victory, 1989, Who's Doing the Talking, 2001, Male and Female Created He Them, 2003; composer: Apostle Shirley E. Henderson Presents the PMI Apostolic Co., 2000; prodr.: (songs/live recording) LaNore's Music (Trophy, 1997); composer: (songbook) The Power of Worship and Praise for Ch. Services, 1996, The Power of Worship and Praise Songbook for Choirs, 1999. Dir. Praise Ministries Inc. Food Bank, Orlando, Fla., 1990—94; cmty. involvement vol. Project Help Cmty. Devel. Ctr., Inc., Garner, NC, 1996—99, interior decorator/painter, 1995; presenter/supporter N.C. Assn. of Educators-Education Rally, Raleigh, NC, 2003; dir./presenter of music entertainment Nat. Computer Tech. Conf., Orlando, Fla., 1993. Recipient Letter of Recognition, City of Raleigh, 2001. Democrat. Avocations: cooking, interior decorating, painting, singing, writing. Home: 1319 Cross Link Rd Raleigh NC 27610 Office: Project Help Cmty Devel Ctr 118 East Main St Garner NC 27529 Personal E-mail: apostlepmdc@yahoo.com. Business E-Mail: projcthelp@yahoo.com.

HENDERSON HALL, BRENDA FORD, computer company executive; d. Frances Long and Johnny Dell Ford, William Alfred Randall; m. Joseph Aubrey N/A, Jan. 1, 2001. BSc, U. of NC, 1974—81, MBA, 1982—85. Six Sigma Green Belt 2003. Bookkeeper, transit operator Wachovia Bank, Wilmington, NC, 1968—73; cost acctg. technician, staff reliever E I du Pont de Nemours and Co., Inc., Wilmington, NC, 1973—86; acctg. instr. Shaw U., Wilmington, NC, 1985—86; systems engr. Electronic Data Systems, Dallas, 1986—87; edp mgr. Potomac Savs. Bank, Silver Spring, Md., 1987—88; v.p. Fin. Comm. Sys. Services Inc., Clinton, Md., 1987—89; sr. systems analyst The Maxima Corp., Lanham, Md., 1988—94; adj. acctg. instr. Prince George CC, Largo, Md., 1990—93; pres. Your Efficient Tax Service, Oxon Hill, Md., 1992—93; sr. mem. of the tech. staff Computer Sciences Corp., Falls Church, Va., 1994—95; account mgr., developer, analyst The Maxim Group, Reston, Va., 1995—97; prin. cons. Computer Sciences Corp., Falls Church, Va., 1997—2002; team leader, developer, analyst The Maxim Group, Reston, Va., 1997; sr. mem. of the exec. staff Computer Sciences Corp., Lanham, Md., 2002—, acct. exec. - fed. sector, 2003—. Charter mem. Williston Alumni Assn., Wilmington, NC, 1974—78; pres. -master of bus. adminstrn. assn. U. of NC, 1983—85; bd. mem. DuPont's Cape Fear Employees' Credit Union, Wilmington, NC, 1979—80; charter mem. nat. assn. of accountants U. of NC, 1980—81. D-Liberal. Baptist. Achievements include facilitated the effort that resulted in the achievement of the first software acquisition capability maturity model level 3 rating. Avocations: travel, swimming, reading, philanthropic activities, writing. Office: Computer Scis Corp 7900 Harkins Rd Lanham MD 20706 Personal E-mail: jhallz71@comcast.net. E-mail: bhall25@csc.com.

HENDERSON ROLLYSON, TONYA RENE, artist; b. Flint, Mich., Apr. 12, 1962; d. Eugene Ralph and Opal Joan Henderson; m. Brooks Earl Rollyson, Nov. 25, 1989 (div. July 9, 1998); children: Zachary Jordan, Katie Lynn. AA, Colo. Inst. Art, 1987. Graphic designer WJRT-TV 12, Flint, 1986—89; designer DWB Design, Flint, 1990—92; graphic artist Concept Three Advt., Davison, Mich., 1985—87, 1990—; art instr., acrylic painter Gaines, Mich., 1997—; freelance artist, designer, 1998—2001; graphic designer RL Fisher & Co. Mktg., Fenton, Mich., 1999—2001.

HENDLEY, EDITH DI PASQUALE, physiology and neuroscience educator; b. N.Y.C., Sept. 5, 1927; d. Michael and Rose (Parillo) Di Pasquale; m. Daniel Dees Hendley, Apr. 21, 1952; children: Jane Alice, Joyce Louise, Paul Daniel. AB, Hunter Coll., N.Y.C., 1948; MS, Ohio State U., 1950; PhD, U. Ill., Chgo., 1954. Instr. U. Chgo., 1954-56; asst. lectr. U. Sheffield, England, 1956-57; instr., rsch. assoc. Johns Hopkins U. Sch. Medicine, Balt., 1963-72; sr. investigator Friends Med. Sci. Rsch. Ctr., Balt., 1972-73; from assoc. prof. to prof. U. Vt. Coll. Medicine, Burlington, 1973-94, prof. emeritus, 1994—. Co-author: 6 books; contbr. articles to profl. jours. Rsch. grantee NIH, 1974-95, NSF, 1986-98, Vt. affiliate Am. Heart Assn., 1982-83, The Sugar Assn. Inc., 1984-85. Mem. AAAS, Am. Physiol. Soc., Am. Soc. Pharmacology and Exptl. Therapeutics, Soc. for Neurosci. (exec. com., treas. Vt. chpt. 1978-84), Assn. for Women in Sci. (treas. 1972-74, exec. com., long range planning com. 1974-79) [illegible] opera, theatre, cinema. Home: 10 Highland Ter South Burlington VT 05403-7601 Office: U Vt Coll Medicine Dept Molecular Phys Bi Burlington VT 05405-0001

HENDRA, BARBARA JANE, public relations executive; b. Watertown, N.Y. d. Frederick R. and Irene J. H. BA, Vassar Coll., 1960. Publicity dir. Fawcett World Library, N.Y.C., 1961-69; v.p., dir. publicity and pub. relation Pocket Books-Simon & Schuster, N.Y.C., 1969-77; corp. dir. publicity and pub. relations Putnam Pub. Group, N.Y.C., 1977-79; pres. Barbara J. Hendra Assocs., Inc., N.Y.C., 1979-91, The Hendra Agy. Inc, Bklyn., 1991—. Adj. prof. NYU, 1981. Contbg. author: Trade Book Marketing, 1983, The Encyclopedia of Publishing, 1995. Mem. Pubs. Publicity Assn. (bd. dirs. 1977-81, pres. 1979-81), Publicity Club N.Y., Soc. Profl. Journalists, Women's Media Group, Book Critics Cir., Vassar Club, Regency Whist Club. Home: 140 Sterling Pl Brooklyn NY 11217-3307 Office: The Hendra Agy Inc 142 Sterling Pl Brooklyn NY 11217-3307

HENDREN, MERLYN CHURCHILL, investment company executive; b. Gooding, Idaho, Oct. 16, 1926; d. Herbert Winston and Annie Averett Churchill; m. Robert Lee Hendren, June 14, 1947; children: Robert Lee, Anne Aleen. Student, U. Idaho, 1944-47; BA with honors, Coll. of Idaho, 1986. With Hendren's Furniture Co., Boise, 1947-69; co-owner, v.p. Hendren's Inc., Boise, 1969-87, pres., 1987—. Bd. dirs. Idaho Law Found., 1978-84; chmn. Coll. of Idaho Symposium, 1977-78, mem. adv. bd., 1981—; bd. dirs. S.W. Idaho Pvt. Industry Coun., 1984-87; pres. Boise Coun. on Aging, 1959-60, mem. adv. bd., 1986—; mem. Gov.'s Commn. on Aging, 1960; Idaho del. to White House Conf. on Aging, 1961; trustee St. Luke's Regional Hosp., 1981-92; mem. adv. bd. dirs. Boise Philharm. Assn., Inc., 1981—, Ballet Idaho; bd. dirs. Children's Home Soc. Idaho, 1988; founding pres. Idaho Congl. Award Program, 1993—; sustaining mem. Boise Jr. League. Mem. Boise C. of C. (bd. dirs. 1984-87), Gamma Phi Beta. Episcopalian. Home: 3504 Hillcrest Dr Boise ID 83705-4503 Office: PO Box 9077 Boise ID 83707-3077 E-mail: rhendren@albertson.edu.

HENDRICK, ZELWANDA, drama and psychology educator; b. Rusk, Tex., Nov. 28, 1925; d. Lloyd Irvin and Viola Alice (McGuire) Hendrick; A.A., Lon Morris Coll., 1945; B.S., N. Tex. U., 1947; M.A., So. Meth. U., 1958. Tchr. theatre arts Overton (Tex.) High Sch., 1947-49, Nacogdoches (Tex.) High Sch., 1949-50, Boude Storey Sch., Dallas, 1950-53, Kimball High Sch., Dallas, 1953-62; tchr. theatre arts H. Grady Spruce High Sch., Dallas, 1962-78, chmn. fine arts dept., 1963-77, ret., 1978; drama and psychology tchr. Alexander Sch., 1978— ; substitute tchr. Highland Park High Sch., Dallas, 1980— ; part-time tchr. John Robert Powers Finishing Sch., 1951— ; teaching fellow N. Tex. U., 1964-65; ptnr. Adventure II Miniature Horse Ranch, Rusk, Tex., 1985—; co-dir. Adventure II Miniature Horse Show, Lufkin, Tex., 1987—. Active, Tyler (Tex.) Civic Symphony, 1949-50, Tyler Civic Theatre, 1949-50, Dallas Theatre Center, 1960-61; guest dir. Cherokee Civic Theatre, Rusk, 1983, pres. 2002—; mem. adv. com. Smithsonian Instn., 1975; co-sponsor U.S. Inst. Tech. Theatre; del. Democratic Dist. Conv., 1980; candidate Tex. State Legislature, 1980; chmn. Dallas County Transp. Bd., 1982— ; life mem. First United Meth. Ch., Rusk. Mem. Internat. Thespians (state dir.), Tex. Speech Assn. (sec. 1973—), Am. Assn. Ednl. Theatre, Am. Miniature Horse Registry, Friends of the Railroad, Dallas Ednl. Drama Assn. (governing bd.), Tex. Tchrs. Assn., Nat. Forensic League, AAUW, Classroom Tchrs. Dallas, Internat. Platform Assn., Ednl. Arts Assn., Tex. Congress Parent Tchr. Assn. (hon. life), DAR, Daus. Republic of Tex., N. Texas Collie Club, Nat. Assn. Royalty Owners, Tex. Ind. Producers and Royalty Owners Assn., Tex. Farm Bur., Am. Miniature Horse Assn., Paws of E. Tex., Delta Kappa Gamma. Club: Order Eastern Star. Contbr. to A Guide to Student Teaching in Music, 1968-70. Home: 204 E 4th St Rusk TX 75785-1308 Office: Adventure II Miniature Horse Ranch Hwy 84 W Rusk TX

HENDRICKS, SUSAN MCCURDY, art educator, artist; b. Buffalo, Jan. 12, 1941; d. Robert C. and Gladys C. (Deel) McCurdy; m. Thomas C. Hendricks, June 17, 1961; children: Jennifer Ann, Julie Lynn. AA, Montgomery Coll., 1987; BS, U. Md., 1989, MA, 1992, PhD, 1995. Cert. K-12 art edn. tchr., Md. Proprietor Ceramic Studio, Olney, Md., 1970-85; art specialist Howard (Md.) Bd. Edn., 1989-97; grad. asst. edn. program U. Md., College Park, 1992-95; instr. art Montgomery Coll., Rockville, Md., 1995—; coord. art edn. program U. Md., College Pk., 1997—. Cons. in field. Author: A Cross Discipline Approach for Developing Cultural Literacy in the Arts, 1990, Convergence on the Roles and Guidelines for Designing, Implementing and Teaching a Multicultural Elementary Art Education Curriculum, 1995; contbr. articles to profl. jours. Chairperson Williamsburg Civic Assn., 1973—; active Md. Multicultural Coalition. Mem. NAEA, MAEA, Seminar for Rsch. in Art Edn., Golden Key, Phi Theta Kappa. Avocations: ceramics, oil painting. Home: 3601 John Carroll Dr Olney MD 20832-2216

HENDRICKSON, ANITA ELIZABETH, biology educator; b. LaCross, Wis., Feb. 20, 1936; d. Walter V. and Alno (Larkin) Schnell; m. Morris N. Hendrickson, June 8, 1957; children: Lisa, Karin, Gordon. BA, Pacific Luth. Coll., 1957; PhD, U. Wash., Seattle, 1964. Instr. anatomy Northwestern Med. Sch., Chgo., 1964-65; rsch. assoc. Children's Meml. Hosp., Chgo., 1964-65; rsch. instr. dept. biol. structure U. Wash., Seattle, 1965-67, instr. dept. ophthalmology, 1967-69, asst. prof. dept. ophthalmology, 1969-73; affiliate/assoc. prof. dept. ophthalmology Reg. Primate Ctr./U. Wash., 1972—, 1973-81; affiliate Child Devel. & Mental Retardation Ctr., U. Wash., 1975; prof. dept. opthalmology U. Wash., 1981-97, prof. dept. biol. structure, 1984—, chair dept. biol. structure, 1994—, adj. prof. ophthalmology, 1997—. Vis. assoc. prof. neuropathology Harvard Med. Sch., Boston, 1975-76; adj. assoc. prof. dept. psychology U. Wash., 1975-78; mem. NIH VisB study section, 1976-80. Editorial bd. Jour. of Neurosci., 1982-88, Investigative Ophthalmology, 1977-82, Vision Research, 1990-95; contbr. articles to profl. jours. Dolly Green rsch. grantee, 1981; named Alumnus of the Yr., Pacific Luth. U., 1982. Mem. AAAS, Am. Assn. Anatomists, Soc. for Neurosci. (mem. nat. coun. 1982-86), Internat. Soc. for Eye Rsch., Assn. for Rsch. in Vision and Ophthalmology (prog. chmn. 1983-84, trustee 1993—), Cajal Club. Home: 1029C NE 120th St Seattle WA 98125-5003 Office: U Washington Dept Biol Structure Box 357420 Seattle WA 98195-7420

HENDRICKSON, ELIZABETH ANN, retired secondary school educator; b. Bismarck, N.D., Oct. 21, 1936; d. William Earl and Hilda E. (Sauter) Hinkel; m. Roger G. Hendrickson, Apr. 18, 1960; 1 child, Wade William. BA, Jamestown Coll., 1958; postgrad., U. Calif., Davis, 1962, Calif. State U., Sacramento, 1964, U. San Diego, 1985-88, Ottawa U., 1986-88. Cert. tchr., Calif. Tchr. Napoleon (N.D.) High Sch., 1958-59, Kulm (N.D.) High Sch., 1959-61, Del Paso Jr. High Sch., Sacramento, 1961, Mills Jr. High Sch., Rancho Cordova, Calif., 1961-97; ret., 1997. Mem. sch. attendance rev. bd. Folsom-Cordova Unified Sch. Dist. Mem.: AAUW, NEA, Sacramento Area Gifted Assn., Folsom Cordova Ret. Tchrs. Assn. (sec., mem. steering com., mem. newsletter com.), Calif. Ret. Tchrs. Assn., Calif. Tchrs. Assn., Calif. Assn. for Gifted, N.G. Aux., Sgt. Maj. Assn. of Calif. Aux. Enlisted Assns., Soroptimists (news editor Rancho Cordova 1985). Democrat. Lutheran. Home: 2032 Kellogg Way Rancho Cordova CA 95670-2435

HENDRICKSON, LOUISE, retired association executive, retired social worker; b. Lansdowne, Pa., Sept. 14, 1916; d. Norman and Gertrude (Powers) H. AA, Long Beach Jr. Coll., 1936; BA, U. Calif., Berkeley, 1938, gen. secondary tchr.'s cert., 1939; MS in Social Work, Columbia U., 1952. Cert. secondary tchr., Calif.; registered social worker, Calif. Dir. young adult program YWCA, Oakland, Calif., 1944-48, dir. group work and informal edn. svcs. Bklyn., 1948-53, exec. dir. Spokane, Wash., 1953-58; field cons. Nat. Bd. YWCA, Chgo., 1958-63, assoc. exec. community divsn. N.Y.C., 1963-66, exec. community divsn., 1966-71, dir. orgn. devel., 1971-74, dep. exec. dir., 1974-82, ret., 1982. Contbr. articles to profl. jours. Pres. Cmty. Welfare Coun., Spokane, 1956-57; mem. majority coun. Emily's List, Washington; mem. Common Cause, LWV. Mem. NASW (charter 1958-62).

HENDRIE, ELAINE, public relations executive; b. Bklyn. d. David and Pearl Kostell; m. Joseph Mallam Hendrie; children: Susan, Barbara. Asst. acct. exec. Benjamin Sonnenberg Pub. Rels., N.Y.C., 1953-57; pub. rels. cons., writer, editor, dir. pub. rels. and media Religious Heritage of Am., Washington, 1973-75; nat. media coord. NOW, Washington, 1978; media dir. Am. Speech-Lang.-Hearing Assn., Washington, 1979-80; pub. info. officer, head media and mktg. Dept. Navy, Washington, 1980-81; pres. Hendrie & Pendzick, 1982-92, Elaine Hendrie Pub. Rels., 1992—. Prodr., interviewer radio program, sta. WRIV, WALK AM/FM, L.I., N.J., Westchester County, N.Y., Conn., 1974-77; exec. dir. Women in New Directions, Inc., Suffolk County, N.Y., 1974-77, cons., 1981—; resource person for media Nat. Commn. on Observance of Internat. Women's Yr., 1977; cons. Multi-Media Prodns. Inc., N.Y.C., 1978—; adv. bd. Women's Edn. and Counseling Ctr., SUNY, Farmingdale. Mem. Bellport-Brookhaven Hist. Soc. (trustee 1999—). Home: 50 Bellport Ln Bellport NY 11713-2736

HENDRIX, CHRISTINE JANET, retired government agency administrator, retired small business owner, volunteer; b. Corry, Pa., Dec. 3, 1939; d. Merle Alvin and Janet May Besson; m. Alfred E. Hendrix, Mar. 27, 1965; 1 child, Lee Andrew. BS in Edn., Clarion (Pa.) State Teacher's Coll., 1961. Tchr. Montour Schs., McKees Rocks, Pa., 1961—62, Newcomerstown (Ohio) Exempted Schs., 1962—65; welcome wagon hostess Welcome Wagon Internat., Newcomerstown, 1965—71; mgr. Amos Placement Bur., New Phila., Ohio, 1972—75; paralegal Pros. Atty.'s Office, New Phila., 1976—79; small bus. coowner Child Care Alternatives, New Phila., 1980—85; dir. Tuscarawas County Sr. Ctr., Dover, Ohio, 1985—89; relocation agt. Ohio Dept. of Transp., Fairlawn, Ohio, 1989—98; assignment commr. Mcpl. Ct., New Phila., 1998—2000, ret., 2000. Editor: Child Care Alternatives Newsletter, 1980—85. Vol. Cats N Us, Dover, Ohio, 2002, Ret. Sr. and Vol. Program, New Phila., 2003; ctr. and exec. com. Tuscarawas County Dem. Party, New Phila., 1980; various offices New Phila. (Ohio) Dem. Club, 1994—2001; mem. Bd. of Zoning Appeals, New Phila., 1979—89; rep. sr. citizens United Way, New Phila., 1983—85; mem. Domestic Violence Orgn., New Phila., 1987—89; various offices NOW, New Phila., 1974—79; vol. COMPASS Inc., New Phila., 2000. Democrat. Protestant. Avocations: genealogy, antiques. Home: 183 Wabash Avenue NW New Philadelphia OH 44663 Personal E-mail: cjhendrix@wilkshire.net.

HENDRIX, JACQUELYN MCINTYRE, elementary music educator; b. Atlanta, Dec. 9, 1946; d. James Jackson and Stella Martha (Hinson) McIntyre; m. David Richard Hendrix, June, 4, 1966. B of Music Edn., Ga. State U., 1968, postgrad., 1976, 90—. Customer svc. rep. Ga. Power Co., Atlanta, 1965, receptionist W.M. Hinson Co., Atlanta, 1966-67; elem. music specialist Atlanta Pub. Schs., 1968-81, Gwinnett County Schs., Lawrenceville, Ga., 1982—, mid. sch. choir dir., 1981-82. Author, composer W.S.B.-TV Spl. theme song, 1995; composer Egleston Hosp. Campaign theme music, 1985; writer, editor county music curriculum Gwinnett County Elks, Lawrenceville, 1995—; contbr. articles to profl. jours. Ch. choir dir. children, youth Stewart Ave. Meth. Ch., Atlanta, 1967—, coord. children & youth, 1979—; dir.'s staff opening ceremonies Atlanta Com. Paralympic Games, 1995-96; cast asst. dir. opening ceremonies Centennial Olympic Games Atlanta Olympic Com., 1995-96; fund raiser Meth. Children's Home Aux., Decatur, Ga., 1990—; mem., co-block capt. Peachtree Hills Civic Assn., Atlanta, 1979—. Recipient Super Tchr. award Turner Broadcasting/Ga. Bus. Forum, Atlanta, 1995, Resolution Commendation Senate State Ga., Atlanta, 1993, 94, 95, Commendation award State & Nat. "Just Say No" Campaign, Ga., 1986, 88, 89, 90, 91, Gwinnett Clean & Beautiful, 1985, 90. Mem. NEA, Music Educators Nat. Conf., Ga. Citizens Arts, Ga. Assn. Educators, Ga. Music Educators Assn., Alpha Delta Kappa. Avocations: reading, travel, swimming, boating. Home: 2103 Fairhaven Cir NE Atlanta GA 30305-4314 Office: Gwinnett County Pub Schs PO Box 343 Lawrenceville GA 30046-0343

HENDRIX, SUSAN CLELIA DERRICK, civic worker; b. McClellanville, S.C., Jan. 19, 1920; d. Theodore Elbridge and Susan Regina (Bauknight) Derrick; m. Henry Gardner Hendrix, June 5, 1943; children: Susan Hendrix Redmond, Marilyn Hendrix Shedlock. BA, Columbia Coll., 1941; MA, Furman U., 1961; EdD (hon.), Columbia Coll., 1985. Cert. tchr. SC. Tchr. Whitmire Pub. Schs., 1941-43, Greenville (S.C.) Pub. Schs., 1944-46, 58-63, dir. Reading Clinic, 1965-68; counselor Greenville County Sch. Dist., 1965-68, dir. pub. rels., 1968-83; grad. instr. Furman U., 1967-69. Cons. Nat. Seminar on Desegregation, 1973. Author (with James P. Mahaffey): Teaching Secondary Reading, 1966, Communicating with the Community, 1979, History of Robert Morris Class, 1995; editor: Communique, 1968—83, Celebrating Our Legacy--Oral Interviews, 2001; mem. United Meth. Gen. Conf. editl. and revision com.: Book of Discipline, 1996, 2000; contbr. articles to profl. jours. and mags. Trustee Columbia Coll., 1958—70, chmn., 1968—70, Greenville County Rehab. Bd., 1974—76; vice chmn. bd. Jr. Achievement, Greenville, 1978—79; mem. S.C. Commn. on Women, Columbia, 1979—88, chmn., 1982—88; pres. United Meth. Women Buncombe St. Ch., Greenville, 1956—57; mem. adminstrv. bd. Buncombe St. Ch., 1968—, trustee, 1980—88, endowment fund bd. trustees, 1994—, chmn., 2001—03, co-chair ch. bldg. com., 1999, lay del. to S.C. Ann. Conf., 1986—2003, mem. commn. on Archives and History, 2001—; mem. United Meth. Ch. Southeastern Jurisdictional Coun. on Ministries, 1980—88, Southeastern Jurisdictional Commn. on Archives and History, 1984—88; chmn. S.C. Conf. Coun. on Ministries United Meth. Ch., 1980—88, del. gen. conf., 1980, 1984, 1988, 1992; mem. S.C. Conf. Commn. Com., 1995—97; chmn. S.C. Conf. Budgeting Task Force, 1996—97; mem. S.C. Conf. Ann. Fund Com. Camps and Retreats, 1998—2001; mem. strategic planning com. Columbia Coll., 1996—97, class agt., 2000—, mem. com. of 150, 2003, mem. Sesquicentennial com., 2003—; mem. Bd. Global Ministries United Meth. Ch., 1972—80, chmn. fin. com., 1976—80; mem. gen. ch. commn. study of ministry United Meth. Ch., 1984—92, mem. gen. ch. coun. ministries, 1988—96, mem. gen. conf. agys. staff and site location com., 1988—96, rschr. missions project West Africa, 1986, chmn. gen. ch. com. legis., 1992—96, chmn. gen. ch. com. on inter-agy. legis., 1992—96, gen. ch. mission agy. site location com., 1993—96, gen. ch. structure com., 1992—96; mem. S.C. Conf. Africa U. Task Force, 2000—01; charter mem. Nat. Mus. Women in Arts, 1978—. Recipient medallion, Columbia Coll., 1980, Alumnae Disting. Svc. award, 1983, Disting. Achievement award, Women's History Week, Greenville, 1984, S.C. Woman of Achievement award, 1988, Clelia D. Hendrix endowment Archives and History at Buncombe St., United Meth. Ch., 2000; established Clelia D. Hendrix Endowed Scholarship, Columbia Coll., 1988. Mem. S.C. PTA (life), Columbia Coll. Alumnae Assn. (life), Dem. Women, S.C. Women in Govt. (bd. dirs. 1985-87), Alpha Delta Kappa (pres. 1970-72, 90-91). Home and Office: 309 Arundel Rd Greenville SC 29615-1303 E-mail: cleliahendrix@aol.com.

HENES, DONNA, celebration artist, ritualist, writer; b. Cleve., Sept. 19, 1945; d. Nathan and Adelaide (Ross) Trugman. Student, Ohio State U., 1963-66; BS, CCNY, 1971, MS in Art Edn., 1972. Prodr. series pub. participatory celebratory events in parks, museums and univs., 100 cities in 9 countries, 1970—. Designer Olympic Medalist Tickertape Parade, N.Y.C., 1984; ednl. cons. New Wilderness Foundation, N.Y.C., 1985; judge Jane Addams Peace Assn. Children's Book Award, N.Y.C., 1983-89; ritual cons. Mama Donna's Tea Garden. Author, designer: Dressing Our Wounds in Warm Clothes, 1982, Noting the Process of Noting the Process, 1977, Celestially Auspicious Occasions, 1996, Moon Watcher's Companion, 2004, The Queen of Myself, 2004; author, performer (CD) Reverence to Her: Part I Mythology, the Matriarchy & Me, 1998; pub., editor quar. Always in Season: Living in Sync with the Cycles; author (with others): Peace: Piece by Piece; editor: Celebration News, 1986-92; internationally syndicated columnist; contbr. numerous articles to profl. jours. Co-founder, pres. STAND (Stand Together Affirmative Neighborhood Devel.), N.Y.C.; composer Chants for Peace/Chance for Peace, Sta. WNYC, first peace message in space, 1982. Fellow Nat. Endowment for Arts, 1982, interarts, 1983, N.Y. Found. for Arts, 1986, 90; grantee N.Y. State Coun. on Arts, N.Y.C. State Bicentennial Commn., Com. for Visual Arts, Money for Women, Beard's Fund, Jerome Found., Ctr. for the Media Arts; recipient Citation award Mayor of N.Y.C. David Dinkins. Mem. Internat. Ctr. for Celebration (bd. dirs., co-founder). Avocations: dance, travel, reading, walking, swimming. E-mail: cityshaman@aol.com.

HENG, SIANG GEK, communications executive; b. Singapore, Dec. 4, 1960; came to U.S., 1984. m. G.J. Sturgis, 1991. BSEE with honors, Nat. U. Singapore, 1983; MSEE in Computer Engring., U. So. Calif., 1985; MS in Engring. Mgmt., Nat. Technol. U., 1993. Cisco cert. design profl., cert. network assoc. Rsch. engr. Nat. Univ. Singapore, 1983-84; sys. mgr. LinCom Corp., L.A., 1985-87; fin. planner N.Y. Life Ins. Co., L.A., 1987-88; mem. tech. staff AT&T Bell Laboratories, Holmdel, N.J., 1988-96; sr. mem. tech. staff AT&T, N.J., 1996-2000, prin. tech. staff mem., 2000—. Freelance computer and comm. cons., N.J., 1987-94. Contbr. articles to profl. jours.; patentee in field. Avocations: music, kickboxing, swimming, reading, weightlifting. Office: AT&T Rm A2-2F34 200 S Laurel Ave Middletown NJ 07748-1998

HENIG, SUZANNE, retired educator, writer, editor; b. N.Y.C., Jan. 12, 1936; d. Samuel G. and Gicia (Gottesdiener) Henig. BA, NYU, 1957, MA, 1961, PhD, 1968. V.p. Am. Heritage Soc., Washington, 1975-80; editor Va. Woolf Quar., San Diego, 1976-79; pres. India Expo, San Diego, 1976-81; mng. dir. Aeolian Press, San Diego, 1976—. Pres. Genesis Prodns. of Hollywood, San Diego, 1990-96. Editor Internat. Jour. Medicine, 1996; contbr. articles to profl. jours. V.p. N.Y. Young Reps., N.Y.C., 1953-54. Recipient Thomas Wolfe award for poetry NYU, 1957; grantee ACLS, Leopold Schepp Found., Am. Philos. Soc. Address: 5303 La Jolla Hermosa La Jolla CA 92037

HENINGTON, CARLEN, psychologist, educator; d. Carl Frank and Betty Jean Votapka; m. William Leonard Henington, 1978; children: Blake Leonard, Robin Leonard, Brianne Marie. PhD, Tex. A&M U., Coll. Sta., Tex., 1991—96. Cert. Sch. Psychol. NASP, 1996. Asst. prof. Miss. State U., 1996—2000, assoc. prof., 2000—. Cons. Miss. Early Intervention Program, Jackson, Miss., 1997—2003. Children's adv. Statewide Sch. Districts, Miss., 1994—2003. Mem.: APA, Behavior Spl. Interest Group - NASP (sec. 1999—2001), Nat. Assn. Sch. Psychol. Office: Mississippi State University 508 Allen Hall Box 9727 Mississippi State MS 39762 Office Phone: 662-325-7099. E-mail: cdh@colled.msstate.edu.

HENIN-HARDENNE, JUSTINE, professional tennis player; b. Liège, Belgium, June 1, 1982; d. Jose and Francoise Henin. Winner, Roland Garros French Open Grand Slam, 2003, US Open, 2003, German Open, 2003 Office: WTA Tour 1 Progress Plz Ste 1500 Saint Petersburg FL 33701-4335

HENKE, JANICE CARINE, educational software developer and marketer; b. Hunter, N.D., Jan. 28, 1938; d. John Leonard and Adeline (Hagen) Hanson; children: Toni L., Tom L., Tracy L. BS, U. Minn., 1965; postgrad., misc. schs., 1969—. Cert. elem. tchr., Minn., Iowa. Tchr. dance, 1953-56; tchr. kindergarten Des Moines Pub. Schs., 1964-65; tchr. elem. Ind. Sch. Dist. 284, Wayzata, Minn., 1969-93; pvt. bus. history Wayzata, 1978—; marketer, promoter health enhancement Jeri Jacobus Cosmetics Aloe Pro, Am. Choice Nutrition, Multiway, KM Matol, Wayzata, 1978—; developer ednl. software, marketer of software Computer Aided Teaching Concepts, Excelsior, Minn., 1983—; Edn. Minn. authorized rep. with Midwest Benefit Advisers, Excelsior, 1993—. Developer, author drug edn. curriculum, Wayzata, 1970-71; mem. programs com. Health and Wellness, Wayzata, 1988-93; chmn. Wayzata Edn. Assn. Ins. Com., 1991-93; mem. Staff Devel. Adv. Bd., Wayzata, 1988-93; coach Odyssey of the Mind, 1989-93. Author, developer computer software; contbr. articles to newspapers. Fundraiser Ind. Reps. Wayzata, 1976-79; mem. pub. rels. com. Lake Minnetonka (Minn.) Dist. Ind. Reps., 1979-81, fundraising chmn., 1981-82; chmn. Wayzata Ind. Reps., 1981-82; sec. PTO, Wayzata, 1981-82. Mem. NEA, Minn. Edn. Assn., Wayzata Edn. Assn. (bd. mem., ins. chairperson). Lutheran. Avocations: swimming, skiing, traveling, reading, learning. Office: Henke Services Inc 20380 Excelsior Blvd Excelsior MN 55331-8733 E-mail: jhenke8464@hotmail.com.

HENKEL, KATHRYN GUNDY, lawyer; b. West Columbia, Tex., Oct. 16, 1952; d. Louis Ory Jr. and Patricia Dolores (Fields) Gundy. BA cum laude, Rice U., 1973; JD cum laude, Harvard U., 1976. Bar: Tex. 1976, U.S. Dist. Ct. (no. dist.) Tex. 1982, U.S. Ct. Appeals (5th cir.) 1994, U.S. Tax Ct. 1981, U.S. Supreme Ct. 1983; bd. cert. estate planning and probate law, Tex. Bd. Legal Specialization. Ptnr. Hughes & Luce, L.L.P., Dallas, 1982—. Author: Estate Planning and Wealth Preservation: Strategies and Solutions, 1997; mem. editl. bd. Estate Planning mag. Mem. adv. coun. Cmtys. Found. Tex. Inc., 1982—; mem. planned giving adv. com. Children's Med. Ctr., Dallas; trustee, chmn. bd. advisors to found. com. Dallas Opera. Fellow Am. Coll. Trust and Estate Counsel; mem. ABA (vice chair sect. real property, probate and trusts com. on generation-skipping transfers 1992-95, chair sect. of taxation com. on estate and gift taxes 1993-95, coun. dir. sect. taxation 1996-99, co-chair sect. real property, probate and trust law estate planning study com. on law reform), State Bar Tex. (chair sect. taxation 1992-93), Dallas Bar Assn. (past chair sect. taxation), Tex. Bar Found. Roman Catholic. Avocations: reading, travel. Office: Hughes & Luce LLP 1717 Main St Ste 2800 Dallas TX 75201-4685 E-mail: henkelk@hughesluce.com.

HENLEY, DEBORAH S. newspaper editor; City editor New York Newsday, N.Y.C.; exec. editor The News Journal, New Castle, Deleware, currently. Office: The News Journal 950 W Basin Rd New Castle DE 19720-1006

HENLEY, JODY DALE HARTIG, music educator, consultant; b. Burlington, N.C. d. Donald Clarence and Jane Evelyn (Johnson) Hartig; m. Daniel Gary Henley, June 19, 1984; children: Megan Dale, Weston Daniel. MusB, U. N.C., Greensboro, 1979, MusM, 1982, postgrad., 1983—84. Cert. music tchr. grades K-12 N.C. Choral dir. grades 7-12 N.W. Guilford H.S., Greensboro, 1984—95; music educator grades K-5 Brooks Global Studies Magnet, Greensboro, 1995—. Presenter, cons. N.C. Ctr. for the Advancement Tchg., Cullowhee, NC, 1991; presenter Guildford County Assn. Elem. Music Educators, 2003; cons., presenter State Collegiate N.C. Music Educators Conf., Greensboro, 2003. CPR instr., vol. Am. Heart Assn., Greensboro, 1984—98; bd. mem. The Grand Staff/Grimsley H.S., Greensboro, 2002—03. Grantee, Ayers Endowment Fund, 2002; Tchr. Art grantee, United Arts Coun., 2002—03, Enrichmnet Fund grantee, Guilford County Enrichment Fund, 2002—03. Mem.: Music Educators Nat. Conf. (dist. pres. 1984, mini-grant 1999—2000), Alpha Delta Kappa (chpt. pres. 1998—99), Pi Kappa Lambda. Republican. Evangelical. Avocations: basket weaving, needlecrafts, herb gardening, travel. Home: 215 Green Valley Rd Greensboro NC 27403

HENLEY, KATHERINE I. human resources specialist, consultant; d. Charles and Loraine Smith; m. Tommy Henley; children: Trent, Chandra. BBA, U. Houston, 1979, postgrad., 1979—80. Cert. ERISA Regulations PPS, 1999, Compensation Am. Compensation Assn., 1993, benefits adminstrn. Nat. Benefits Assn., 1998. Cons./educator T. A. Henley & Assoc., Pearland, Tex., 1985—2003; human resource ops. mgr. U. Tex.-HCS, Galveston, 1998—2001. Dir. human resources Woman's Hosp. Tex., Houston, 1979—98. Contbr. articles to mags. and newspapers. Beautification bd. City of Pearland, Tex., 1980—82; vol. Mayor's Commn. for Elderly, Houston, 1986—95; human resource cons. Sheltering Arms, Houston, 1985—90; educator Head Start, Houston, 1978—82; treas., v.p. LWV, Houston, 1980—90. Mem.: Soc. for Human Resource Mgmt., Houston Human Resource Assn. (membership chmn. 1981—82), Houston Hosp. Assoc. (v.p., v.p. mktg., treas. 1979—96), Internat. Benefits Assn.

HENLEY, MARIE SUZANNE, accountant, consultant; b. North Little Rock, Ariz., Feb. 10, 1976; d. Michael Fred and Gina Marie Henley. BBA, Baylor U., 1997, M of Taxation, 1998. CPA. Tax assoc., Dallas, 1998—2000; tax sr. Arthur Andersen, Miami, Fla., 2001—02; tax mgr. Embraer Aircraft Corp., Ft. Lauderdale, Fla., 2002; internat. tax mgr. DeLoitte & Touche, Dallas, 2002—03. Voter dep. registrar State of Tex., 1996—2000; mem. Jr. Achievmeent, Tex., 2002—03. Avocations: writing, reading, running, diving. Office: Deloitte & Touche LLP Chase Tower 2200 Ross Ave Denton TX 76201 Home: 6265 Anita St Dallas TX 75214-2614

HENLEY, PATRICIA JOAN, principal; b. Harrison, Ark., Dec. 30, 1944; d. Durward Milford and Nola V. (Foresee) Ellis; m. Robert Lee Henley; children: Robert, Kevin, Laura. BA, Wichita State U., 1968; MS, Pittsburg (Kans.) State U., 1973, EdS, 1976; PhD, Kans. State U., 1980. Tchr. Wichita (Kans.) Pub. Schs., 1968-70; tchr. Oswego (Kans.) Pub. Schs., 1970-73; elem. prin. Aurora (Mo.) Schs., 1973-77; grad. teaching asst. Kans. State U., Manhattan, 1977-78; asst. supt. Turner Unified Sch. Dist. #202, Kansas City, Kans., 1978-82; supt. Platte County Schs., Platte City, Mo., 1982-89; dep. supt. Kansas City (Mo.) Schs., 1989-91; elem. prin. Ft. Osage Schs., Independence, Mo., 1991—. Instr. grad. courses U. Mo. Kansas City; assessor, supt. mem. Mo. Dept. Elem. and Secondary Edn. Spl. Edn. Panel. Recipient Outstanding Leadership award Jackson County Inter-Agy. Coun., 1995, Heroes in Edn. award Reader's Digest, 1995; named Bus. Woman Yr. Townsend Publs., 1989. Mem. Nat. Assn. Elem. Sch. Prins. (Nat. Disting. prin. 1994), Mo. Assn. Elem. Sch. Prins., Kansas City Suburban Assn. Elem. Sch. Prins., Rotary. Office: Cler-Mont Cmty Sch 19009 Susquehanna Rdg Independence MO 64056-3103

HENN, CYNTHIA, artist, educator; b. Passaic, N.J., July 19, 1969; d. William Arthur and Elsie Ann Henn. BA in Fashion, Montclair State U., 1992, MA in Tchg./Art Edn., 1996. Cert. tchr. N.J., supr. N.J. Store mgr. Claires Stores, Inc., Paramus, NJ, 1991—96; fashion instr. Berkeley Bus. Coll., West Paterson, NJ, 1996; tchr. art Hanover Twp., NJ, 1996—97, Westwood (N.J.) Regional Sch. Dist., 1997—2001, Millburn Twp. (N.J.) Schs., 2001—. Instr. art Sussex County CC, Newton, NJ, 2002, Newton, 03. Contbr. articles to profl. jours. Artist Artists Collective Social Change, Englewood, NJ, 2001—03; del. Stanhope (N.J.) Environ. Commn., 2003—04. Named to Earthwatch expdn., Va. McNear Found., 2001; recipient Hands Across the Water Tchr. Exch., Dodge Found., 2003; Artists Edn. grantee, N.J. Arts Consortium, 2002—03. Mem.: Art Educators N.J. (grants coord. 2002—04, comms. coord.), Nat. Art Edn. Assn. Avocations: gardening, kayaking, skiing, Bavarian dancing, artwork. Office: Millburn Twp Schs Glenwood Sch 325 Taylor Rd S Short Hills NJ 07078

HENNAGAN, MONIQUE, Olympic athlete; b. Columbia, S.C., May 26, 1976; Degree in psychology, U. N.C., 1998. Co-winner 4X400 meter relay U.S.A. Track and Field Team, Sydney, 2000; part time human resources supr., recruiter for hub ops. UPS. Recipient 400 meter champion, USA Indoor, 2003, Bronze medalist 4x400 meter, World Indoor, 2nd pl. at Adidas Boston Indoor Games, US Indoor 400m, 2002. Office: USA Track and Field Team One RCA Dome Ste 140 Indianapolis IN 46225

HENNEBERGER, JUDITH NOLEN, retired music educator; b. Bassett, Va., Mar. 13, 1942; d. Aaron Dove Nolen, Gladys Young Nolen; m. John Edwin Henneberger; 1 child, John. BS in Music Edn., Bridgewater Coll., 1964; MA in Edn., Va. Tech, 1987. Cert. Orff Schulwerk tchr. Min. music Ch. of the Brethren, Arlington, Va., 1966—78; tchr. Fairfax County Pub. Schs., 1971—90, music supr., 1990—98; univ. supr. James Madison U., Harrisonburg, Va., 1999—; writer music curriculum McGraw-Hill Pub., 2004—. Music cons. Kennedy Ctr. Performing Arts, Washington, 1998—; presenter regional, nat. music edn. confs.; guest condr. choral festivals. Author: (book) Musical Games and Activities to Learn By, 1976, Stepping Stones Choral Curriculum, 1997; editor: (music book) The Little Music House, The Giant Music House, (book) The High School Music Sampler, (book) The Middle School Music Curriculum. Mem.: Music Educators Nat. Conf., Va. Music Educators Assn., Am. Choral Directors Assn., Am. Orff-Schulwerk Assn. (mem. adv. bd.), Choristers Guild (bd. dirs. 1993—99), Bridgewater Coll. Alumni Assn. (bd. dirs. 1996—) Avocations: travel, gardening. Personal E-mail: hennberg@aol.com.

HENNESSEY, AUDREY KATHLEEN, computer researcher, educator; b. Fairbanks, Apr. 4, 1936; d. Lawrence Christopher and Olga Virginia (Strandberg) Doheny; m. Gerard Hennessey, Mar. 10, 1963; children: Brian, Kate. BA, Stanford U., 1957; HSA, U. Toronto, Ont., Can., 1968; PhD, U. Lancaster, Eng., 1982. Asst. dir. European sales Univ. Soc., Heidelberg, Germany, 1959—61; landman's asst. Union Oil Co. Calif., Anchorage, 1962; sys. analyst No. Telephones, New Liskeard, Canada, 1962—63; adminstr. group pension Mfgs. Life Ins., Toronto, 1963—65; instr. office systems Adult Edn. Ctr., Toronto, 1965—68; lectr. office sys. Salford Coll. Tech., Lancashire, England, 1968—70; sr. lectr. data processing Manchester (Eng.) Met. U., 1970—79; lectr. computation U. Manchester Inst. Sci. and Tech., 1979—82; assoc. prof. computer sci. Tex. Tech. U., Lubbock, 1982—86, assoc. prof. info. sys., 1987—94, prof. info. sys., 1994—2001; pres., CEO ISOA Inc., 1994—2002; dir. Internat. Ctr. Informatics Rsch., 1996—2000; v.p., gen. mgr. YMG/Rudolph Tech. Inc., 2002—03; pres., CEO, ICIR Inc., Richardson, Tex., 2002—; mng. dir. Konsult Europe Ltd., Stourport, England, 2002—. Dir. Inst. for Studies of Orgn. Automation/Tex. Tech. U., Lubbock, 1987-95; vis. instr. Fed. Law Enforcement Tng. Ctr., Glynco, Ga., 1984-88; adj. prof. West Tex. A&M U., Canyon, 1994-95, U. Alaska, Anchorage, 1995, U. Tex., Dallas, 1995-98; mem. NATO panel of experts on visualization of massive data sets, 1996-98. Author: Computer Applications Project, 1982; contbg. author: Semiconductor International, 1998, 2002; editor (procs.) Office Document Architecture Internat. Symposium, English version, 1991; contbr. articles to profl. jours.; 14 patents in field. Organizer Explorer Scouts Computer Applications, Lubbock, 1983-85. Recipient various awards, Tex. Instruments, 1982—86, 1994, Xerox Corp., 1985, Halliburton, 1986, Sys. Exploration, 1987, State of Tex., 1988—93, 1996—99, Knowledge-based Image Analysis award, USN Tencap, 1991—96, Immunization Tracking Sys. award, Robert Wood Johnson Found., 1993, Sematech S77 award, 1994, award, Leica GmbH, 1994—2001. Mem.: IEEE (contbg. author Systems Man Cybernetics 1984), Assn. Info. Tech. Profls. (chpt. pres. 1989, Disting. Info Sci. award 1992), Assn. Computing Machinery, Soc. Mfg. Engrs., Spl. Interest Group for Artificial Intelligence (JEDEC working group ISO semiconductor defect data stds. 1999—2002), Sigma Xi Rsch. Soc. (chpt. pres. 1996—97). Office: Konsult Europe/ICIR Ste 141 1221 W Campbell Rd Richardson TX 75080 Office Phone: 972-690-3398. E-mail: icirinc@aol.com.

HENNESSY, ELLEN ANNE, lawyer, benefits compensation analyst, educator; b. Auburn, N.Y., Mar. 3, 1949; d. Charles Francis and Mary Anne (Roan) H.; m. Frank Daspit, Aug. 27, 1974. BA, Mich. State U., 1971; JD, Cath. U., 1978; LLM in Taxation, Georgetown U., 1984. Bar: D.C. 1978,

U.S. Ct. Appeals (D.C. cir.) 1978, U.S. Supreme Ct. 1984. Various positions NEH, Washington, 1971-74; atty. office chief counsel IRS, Washington, 1978-80; atty.-advisor Pension Benefit Guaranty Corp., Washington, 1980-82, assoc. Stroock & Stroock & Lavan, Washington, 1982-85, Willkie Farr & Gallager, 1985-86, ptnr., 1987-93; dep. exec. dir. and chief negotiator Pension Benefit Guaranty Corp., Washington, 1993—98; sr. v.p. and dir. Actuarial Sci. Assoc. Holdings Inc., 1998—2000; sr. v.p. Aon Cons. Inc., Washington, 2000—03; pres. Fiduciary Counselors, Inc., 1999—. Adj. prof. law Georgetown U., Washington, 1985—; mem. com. on continuing profl. edn. Am. Law Inst./ABA, 1994—97. Mem. ABA (supervising editor taxation sect. newsletter 1984-87, mem. standing com. on continuing edn. 1990-94, chair joint com. on employee benefits 1991-92), Worldwide Employee Benefits Network (pres. 1987-88), D.C. Bar Assn. (mem. steering com. tax sect. 1988-93, chair continuing legal edn. com. 1993-95), Am. Coll. Employee Benefits Counsel (bd. govs. 2000—).mem. standing com. on tech. and info. sys. 2002—, mem. task force on corp. responsiblity, 2002—. Democrat. Avocation: whitewater canoeing. Home: 1926 Lawrence St NE Washington DC 20018-2734 Office: South Bldg Ste 900 601 Pennsylvania Ave NW Washington DC 20004-2601 E-mail: nell.hennessy@fiduciarycounselors.com.

HENNEY, JANE ELLEN, health facility administrator, educator, oncologist; b. Kendallville, Ind., Mar. 26, 1947; d. Harry H. and Jeanette (Park) H.; m. J. Robert Graham, June 6, 1975. BS, Manchester Coll., North Manchester, Ind., 1969; MD, Ind. U.-Indpls., 1973. Intern St. Vincent's Hosp., Indpls., 1973-74; with Nat. Cancer Inst., Bethesda, Md., 1976—85, dep. dir., 1980—85; assoc. prof. medicine U. Kans. Med. Ctr., Kansas City, Kans., 1985—92, assoc. vice chancellor, acting dir. Mid Am. Cancer Ctr., 1985—92; prof. medicine, v.p. for health svcs. U. N.Mex., 1994—98; dep. commr. for ops. U.S. FDA, 1992—94, commr. food and drugs, 1998—2001; sr. v.p, provost for health affairs U. Cin., 2003—. Scholar in residence Assoc. Acad. Health Ctrs., 2001—03. Served with USPHS, 1976-86. Recipient commendation USPHS, 1979, 81, Sec.' Recognition award HHS, 1985. Mem.: Inst. Medicine. Office: U Cin Health Professing Bldg Rm 250 Cincinnati OH 45202

HENNING, RONI ANITA, printmaker, artist; b. Bklyn., Mar. 19, 1939; d. Margaritis George Michos and Jane Eliza Duggan; m. John Henry Henning, Dec. 28, 1958 (dec. May 18, 1992); children: Dawn, Diane. Cert. in fine art, Cooper Union Sch. Art and Arch., 1970. Dir., masterprinter, tchr. screen-print workshop N.Y. Inst. Tech., Old Westbury, NY, 1977—95; dir., masterprinter Henning Screenprint Workshop, Bklyn., 1994—. Leader screened monotype workshop Rutgers U., New Brunswick, NJ, 1998, New Brunswick, 2000, Lower Eastside Printshop, N.Y.C., 1998—2003, Hunterdon Art Mus., Clinton, NJ, 1999—2001; cons. Photographys Changing Image Frontiers of Photography, Time Life Book, N.Y.C., 1972; cons. waterbased screen printing U. of the West of Eng., Bristol, 1999; leader children's printmaking workshop Goddard-Riverside Cmty. Ctr., N.Y.C., 1990. Author: Screenprinting: Water-based Techniques, 1994; exhibitions include The Art of Women Printmaker, The Womens Mus., Washington, 1991, Represented in permanent collections Lang Comm., NIH, Bethesda, Md. Active print project for Save the Children Columbia Tchrs. Coll., N.Y.C., 1985. Scholar, Cooper Union Sch. Art and Arch., N.Y.C., 1966—70. Achievements include development of quality non-toxic water-based screenprinting system as an alternative to the traditional solvent-based one. Avocations: gardening, travel, protecting wildlife and their environment. Home: 7908 Ridge Blvd Brooklyn NY 11209 Office: Henning Screenprint Workshop 7908 Ridge Blvd Brooklyn NY 11209

HENNINGS, DOROTHY GRANT (MRS. GEORGE HENNINGS), education educator; b. Paterson, N.J., Mar. 15, 1935; d. William Albert and Ethel Barbara (Moll) Grant; m. George Hennings, June 15, 1968. AB, Barnard Coll., 1956; EdM, U. Va., 1959; EdD, Columbia U., 1965. Tchr. Pierrepont Elem. Sch., Rutherford, NJ, 1956-58, Thomas Jefferson Jr. H.S., Fair Lawn, NJ, 1959-64; prof. edn. Kean U. of N.J., Union, 1965-99, disting. prof. edn., 1999—2002, disting. prof. emeritus, 2002—. Author citation N.J. Inst. Tech., Divsn. Continuing Edn., 1982; author: (with B. Grant) Teacher Moves, 1971; Content and Craft: Written Expression in the Elementary School, 1973; Smiles, Nods and Pauses: Activities to Enrich Children's Communication Skills, 1974; Mastering Classroom Communication: What Interaction Analysis Tells the Teacher, 1975; (with G. Hennings) Keep Earth Clean, Blue and Green: Environmental Activities for Young People, 1976; Words, Sounds, and Thoughts: More Activities to Enrich Children's Communication Skills, 1977; Communication in Action: Teaching the Language Arts, 1978, 8th edit. 2002 (with D. Russell) Listening Aids Through the Grades, 1979; (with G. Hennings) Today's Elementary Social Studies, 1980, 2d edit., 1989; Written Expression in the Language Arts, 1981; Teaching Communication and Reading Skills in the Content Areas, 1982; (with L. Fay) Star Show, 1989, Grand Tour, 1989, Previews, 1989, Reading with Meaning: Strategies for College Reading, 1990, 6th rev. edit., 2004, Poets Journal, 1991, Beyond the Read Aloud: Learning to Read Through Listening to and Reflecting on Literature, 1992, Vocabulary Growth: Strategies for College Word Study, 2001, Words Are Wonderful: An Interactive Approach to Vocabulary, books 1 and 2, 2003, book 3, 2004; contbr. articles to Edn., The Record, Lang. Arts, Sci. Tchr., The Reading Tchr., Jour. of Adolescent & Adult Lit., Jour. of Reading, Tchr. to Tchrs., Sci. and Children, Early Years, Reading Rsch. and Instrn., New Eng. Jour. of History, Jour. Reading Edn., others. Mem. Unitarian Ch., Summit, NJ. NSF Acad. Yr. Inst. grantee, 1959, Field Enterprise grantee Columbia U., 1965; recipient Edn. Press award, 1974, Outstanding Article award, 1999. Mem. Nat. Coun. Tchrs. English, N.J. Reading Assn. (Disting. Svc. to Reading award 1993), Internat. Reading Assn. (Outstanding Tchr. Educator in Reading award 1992), Suburban Reading Coun., Phi Beta Kappa, Phi Delta Kappa, Phi Kappa Phi, Kappa Delta Pi. Home: 21 Flintlock Dr Warren NJ 07059-5014 E-mail: hennings@verizon.net.

HENNINGSEN, JACQUELINE VINCENT, civilian military official; BS in Math. Edn., N.W. Mo. State U., 1966; MS in Math. Edn. and Ednl. Psychology, 1973; MS in Indsl. and Mgmt. Sci. Engring., U. Nebr., 1982, PhD in Indsl. and Mgmt. Sci. Engring., 1987; postgrad., Harvard U., 1992; cert. in alt. dispute resolution, Justice Ctr., Atlanta, 1996. Tchr. math.-psychology, Title IV program dir., ednl. cons., Omaha, also other cities, 1966-80; instr. ops. rsch. and stats., indsl. and mgmt. sys. U. Nebr., Lincoln, 1981-85; mgmt. cons. Wells Engrs., Omaha, 1984-85; ops. rsch. analyst for sci. and rsch. Hdqs. SAC, Offutt AFB, Nebr., 1985-88, dir. combat analysis group, 1988-89, chief capability assessments divsn., 1990-92; chief assessments U.S. Strategic Command, Offutt AFB, 1990-92; sr. analyst force and infrastructure cost analysis divsn. Office Sec. Def., Washington, 1992-94, sr. analyst regional assessment amd modeling divsn., 1994-98; assoc. dir. for modeling, simulation and analysis Hdqs. USAF Air and Space Ops., Washington, 1998—. Mem. Chancellor's Commn. on Status of Women, U. Neb., 1982-84. Recipient Disting. Alumni award North H.S., Omaha, Meritorious Civilian Svc. award; fellow NSF. Fellow Mil. Ops. Rsch. Soc. (exec. bd. 1991-96), Alpha Pi Mu. Office: Hdqs USAF Air and Space Ops 1630 Air Force Pentagon Washington DC 20330-1630

HENNION, CAROLYN LAIRD (LYN HENNION), investment executive; b. Orange, Calif., July 27, 1943; d. George James and Jane (Porter) Laird; m. Reeve L. Hennion, Sept. 12, 1964; children: Jeffrey Reeve, Douglas Laird. BA, Stanford U., 1965; grad. Securities Industry Inst., U. Pa., 1992. CFP, fund specialist; lic. ins. agt.; registered gen. securities prin. Portfolio analyst Schwabacher & Co., San Francisco, 1965-66; adminstrv. coord. Bicentennial Commn., San Mateo County, Calif., 1972-73; dir. devel. Crystal Springs Uplands Sch., Hillsborough, Calif., 1973-84; tax preparer Household Fin. Corp., Foster City, Calif., 1982; freelance, 1983-87; sales promotion mgr. Franklin Distbrs., Inc., San Mateo, 1984-86, v.p. and regional sales mgr. of N.W., 1986-91, v.p. Mid-Atlantic, 1991-94; v.p. Viatech, Inc., 1986-92; propr. Buncom Ranch, 1990—; v.p. Keypoint Svcs. Internat., 1992—2002; pres. Brock Rd. Corp., 1993—; v.p. Strand, Atkinson, Williams & York, Medford, Oreg., 1994—2004, sr. v.p., 2004—; asst. treas. Allamar Techs., Inc., 2004—. Editor: Lest We Forget, 1975. Pres. South Hillsborough Sch. Parents Group, 1974—75; sec. Vol. Bur. San Mateo County, Burlingame, Calif., 1975; chmn. Cmty. Info. Com., Town of Hillsborough, 1984—86, mem., subcom. chmn. fin. adv. com., 1984—86; mem. adv. com. Rogue Valley Internat. Airport, 1996—2003, vice-chair, 1999—2001, chair, 2001—03; mem. coun. Town of Buncom, Oreg., 1990—; chmn. Jackson County Applegate Trail Sesquicentennial Celebration, 1995—97; founding dir. So. Oreg. Hist. Soc. Found., 1995—, v.p., sec., 1995—98, pres., 1998—2001; trustee Oreg. Shakespeare Festival Endowment Fund, 1996—2000, sec., treas., 1997—98, pres., 1998—2000; dir. Rogue Valley Manor Cmty. Svcs., 1996—, vice-chair, 1997—; dir. Craterian Performances Co., 1997—, chmn. mem. com., 1998—2001, pres., 2001—03; dir. So. Oreg. Estate Planning Coun., 1997—2003, pres., 1998—99; dir. Oreg. Cmty. Found., 2002—; chmn. Oreg. Cmty. Found., So. Oreg. Leadership Coun., 2002—; bd. dirs. Pacific N.W. Mus. Natural History, 1995—96, Providence Cmty. Health Found., 1996—2003, chmn. planned giving com., 1997—2000, sec., 1998—2000, v.p., 2000—01, pres., 2001—02; bd. dirs. Chamber of Medford, Jackson Co., 1997—2000, v.p., 1999—2000; bd. dirs. Oreg. Shakespeare Festival, 2002—. Recipient awards Coun. for Advancement and Support of Edn., 1981, Exemplary Direct Mail Appeals Fund Raising Inst., 1982, Golden Mic award Frederic Gilbert Assocs., 1993, White Rose award March of Dimes, 2004; named Wholesaler of Yr., Shearson Lehman Hutton N.W. Region, 1989, among Top 300 Fin. Advisors, Worth Mag., 1998, Top 250 Fin. Advisors, 1999, 2001, Among 10 Outstanding Brokers Registered Rep. Mag., 2000. Mem. So. Oreg. Estate Planning Coun., Buncom Hist. Soc., Oreg. Shakespeare Festival, Britt Festivals, So. Oreg. Hist. Soc., Jr. League, Medford Rogue Rotary, Craterian Performances Co. Republican. Home: 3232 Little Applegate Rd Jacksonville OR 97530-9303 Office: Strand Atkinson Williams & York 2495 E Barnett Ste A Medford OR 97504 E-mail: lhennion@strandatkinson.com.

HENRETTA, DEB, consumer products company executive; m. Sean Murray; 3 children. Grad., St. Bonaventure U., 1983; MA, Syracuse U. Brand asst. Procter & Gamble, Cin., 1985, v.p., gen. mgr. baby care, pres. global baby care, 2001—. Mem. adv. com. Newhouse Sch. Pub. Comm., Syracuse U. Named one of 50 Most Powerful Women in Bus., Fortune, 2002. Office: Procter & Gamble Procter & Gamble Plaza Cincinnati OH 45202*

HENRICKS, MARY SIGRID, retired elementary school educator; b. Milw., Jan. 14, 1939; d. Gunahr Bruhn and Luella Kathryn Henricks. BSc in Edn., Mount Mary Coll., 1960; MEd, Marquette U., 1968. Tchr. Milw. (Wis.) Pub. Schs., 1960—68, reading specialist, 1968—96, ret., 1996. Tutor Maple Tree Sch., Milw., 1998—. Docent Milw. (Wis.) Symphony Orch., 1997—; vol. Milw. (Wis.) County Zoo, 1998—. Mem.: Zoo Pride, Zool. Soc. Avocations: travel, reading, photography, needlepoint.

HENRICKSON, BONNIE, college basketball coach; BS in Phys. Edn., St. Cloud (Minn.) U., 1986; MS in Phys. Edn., Western Ill. U., 1988. Asst. coach U. Ia., 1995-97, Big 10 regular season conf. champions, 1995-96, Big 10 tournament conf. champions, 1996-97; asst. coach Va. Poly. U. Hokies, Blacksburg, Va., 1988-95, head coach, 1997—, Atlantic 10 tournament champions, 1997-98; ranked 14th in NCAA, 1998-99. Office: c/o Athletic Dept Womens Basketball Va Poly Inst State U Blacksburg VA 24061

HENRIKSEN, EVA H. former anesthesiology educator; b. Petaluma, Calif., Jan. 1, 1929; d. Peder Henrik Boas and Karen (Nielsen) Henriksen; m. Daniel Edward MacLean, Aug. 25, 1957 (dec. Dec. 1981); children: Elizabeth, Mary Ann. AA, U. Calif., Berkeley, 1948, BA, 1950; MD, Yale U., 1954. Diplomate Am. Bd. Anesthesiology. Intern, resident Los Angeles County Hosp., L.A., 1954-57; from instr. to asst. prof. anesthesia Loma Linda U. (formerly Coll. Med. Evangelists), L.A., 1957-68; from instr. to assoc. prof. surgery anesthesiology Sch. Medicine U. So. Calif., L.A., 1957-94, assoc. prof. anesthesiology emeritus, 1994—. Anesthesia cons. L.A. Coroner's Office, 1992—2004. Mem. governing coun. Angelica Luth. Ch., 1992—2000, 2002—04. Democrat. Avocation: patchwork quilt making. Home: 957 Arapahoe St Los Angeles CA 90006-5703

HENRIKSON, LOIS ELIZABETH, photojournalist; b. Lytton, Iowa, Nov. 10, 1921; d. Daniel Raymond and Cora Elizabeth (Thomson) Wessling; m. Arthur Allen Henrikson, July 3, 1943; children: Diane Elizabeth Henrikson Russell, Janet Christine, Michele Charlene Henrikson Smetana. BS, Northwestern U., 1943. Adminstrv. asst. to v.p., dir. ops. bus. comm. divsn. ITT Telecommunications Co., Des Plaines, Ill., 1980-82; adminstrv. asst. to exec. v.p. Wholesale Stationers' Assn., Des Plaines, 1982-84, membership svcs. coord., editor membership roster, 1984-88; field editor Office World News, BUS Publ. Group, Jericho, N.Y., 1988-92. Contbg. editor: Home World Bus. ICD Publs., Today's Office, FM Bus. Publs., Inc., Office Tech. Mgmt., Bus. Tech. Comms. Inc.; project editor: Dyna Search, Inc., Wallace Offutt Cons.; pub. rels. photographer 1995—; contbr. and appeared on ABC 7 News investigative reports Signed, Sealed and Swindled, 1996, Fraud From Afar, 1998; copy editor for author Jan Henrikson, 2000—. Chair safety com. Cumberland Sch. PTA, Des Plaines, 1957-58, publicity 1960-61; bd. dirs. Maine West High Sch. Music Boosters, Des Plaines, 1967-69; capt. fin. dr. YMCA, Des Plaines, 1964; mem. diaconate bd., visitation coord., growth and membership bd. 1st Congl. Ch., Des Plaines; mem. Art Inst. Chgo., Peale Ctr. for Christian Living. Mem. NAFE, AAUW (chair social com. 1983-84, editor newsletter 1984-85, 88-94, newsletter 1st pl. award 1993, membership com. 1988-94, N.W. Suburban Ill. br. Ednl. found. contbn. made in honor 1992, 95), DAR, Am. Soc. Assn. Execs. (cert. membership mktg. 1986), Am. Soc. Profl. and Exec. Women, Am. Assn. Editl. Cartoonists Aux., Chgo. Soc. Assn. Execs. (registrar 1984-85), Soc. Profl. Journalists, Am. Bus. Editors and Writers, Nat. Soc. Magna Charta Dames, Am. of Royal Descent, Northwestern Univ. Guild, Northwestern U. Club Chgo., Northwestern U. Half Century Club, Alpha Gamma Delta. Avocations: theater, music, art, traveling. Home and Office: 27 N Meyer Ct Des Plaines IL 60016-2243 Office Phone: 847-296-1309. E-mail: LAHENRKSON@aol.com.

HENRIKSON, VICKIE L. social worker; b. Chokio, Minn., Aug. 31, 1943; d. Paul R. and Frieda L. Asmus; children: Paul, Kristin, Nathan. BA, Concordia Coll., 1965; MSW, U. Minn., 1994. Tchr. Dubuque H.S., Iowa, 1965—67, Rock Falls H.S., Ill., 1967—68, Dubuque H.S., 1968—69; dir. Vol. Svcs. Cmty. Med. Ctr., Rugby, ND, 1984—89, Bethany Homes, Fargo, ND, 1989—92, Chris Jensen Health and Rehab. Ctr., Duluth, Minn., 1992—95, dir. Social Svcs., 1995—. Recipient Performance Recognition award, St. Louis County, 1997, Individual Excellence award, 2001, Performance Recognition Group award, 2003. Democrat. Avocation: music. Home: 108 Mitchell Cir Duluth MN 55811 Office Phone: 218-720-1568.*

HENRION, ROSEMARY P. nurse; b. Greenville, Miss., Oct. 2, 1930; d. Vincent and Camille (Portera) Provenza; BSN, U. Tex. Med. Br., Galveston, 1963; M.S.N. (NIMH fellow 1971), Vanderbilt U., 1972; M.Secondary Edn., U. So. Miss., 1974; RN, Tex.; cert. logotherapist (diplomate); m. Albert Joseph Henrion, Sept. 8, 1956 (dec.); 1 child, Albert Joseph. Staff nurse St. Mary's Hosp., Galveston, 1951-52; office nurse and pvt. duty surg. nurse, Galveston, 1952-53; head nurse Ob and med.-surg. nursing, Greenville (Miss.) Gen. Hosp., 1953-54, supr. obstetrical nursing, 1954-56; nursing instr. Providence Hosp. Sch. Nursing, Waco, Tex., 1957-59; dir. inservice edn. Meml. Hosp., Gulfport, Miss., 1966-67, from asst. dir. to dir. nursing service, 1966-68; psychiat. clin. nurse specialist Biloxi (Miss.) VA Med. Center, 1972-89; assoc. chief Nursing Svc. Biloxi VA Med. Ctr., Gulfport divsn. psychiatry, 1989—, in-house cons., 1975—; participant rsch. projects So. Region Edn. Bd., 1973-75; asst. clin. prof. psychiat.-mental health nursing Grad. Sch. Nursing, La. State U., New Orleans, 1975, asst. clin. prof. psychiat. mental health Grad. Sch. Nursing, U. So. Miss., 1983-92; mem. Miss. Bd. Nursing, 1973-79, pres., 1976-78; bd. dirs., faculty Viktor Frankl Inst. Logotherapy, Abilene, Tex.; co-founder Ednl. Ctr. for Meaningful Living, 2002. Co-author: The Pwer of Meaningful Intimacy: Key to Successful Relationships, 2004. Charles F. Menninger Soc. fellow, 1978—. Mem. Am. Nurses Assn., Dist. Nurses Assn. (membership com., 1964-66, chmn., 1966-67), Miss. Nurses Assn. (vice-chmn., program chmn. spl. interest group 1972-75, Nurse of Yr. 1988), Vanderbilt U. Alumni Assn., U. So. Miss. Alumni Assn., Pope John Paul II Cultural Ctr., Leadership Am. Alumnae Assn., Mus. for Women (charter), Wellsley Club for Women, Sigma Theta Tau. Roman Catholic. Club: Officers. Researcher, speaker, panelist profl. confs., contbr. articles to profl. jours. Home and Office: 19 Wenmar Ave Pass Christian MS 39571-3144 E-mail: ahenrion@cableone.com.

HENRIQUES, DIANA BLACKMON, journalist; b. Bryan, Tex., Dec. 17, 1948; d. Lawrence Ernest and Pauline (Webb) Blackmon; m. Laurence Barlow Henriques, Jr., June 7, 1969. BA with distinction, George Washington U., 1969. Editor Lawrence Ledger, Lawrenceville, N.J., 1969-71; reporter Asbury Park (N.J.) Press, 1971-74; copy editor Palo Alto (Calif.) Times, 1974-76; investigative reporter Trenton (N.J.) Times, 1976-82; bus. writer The Phila. Inquirer, 1982-86; writer Barron's Fin. Weekly, N.Y.C., 1986-89, The New York Times, 1989—. Vis. fellow, cons. Woodrow Wilson Sch., Princeton U., N.J., 1981-82, Guggenheim Found., N.Y., N.J., 1981-82. Author: (books) The Machinery of Greed, 1986, Fidelity's World, 1995, The White Sharks of Wall Street, 2000; contbr. articles to profl. jours. Mem. internat. coun. Elliott Sch. Internat. Affairs George Washington U. Recipient Bell Prize N.J. Press Assn., 1977, Investigative Reporting prize Deadline Club, 1997; co-recipient Loeb award Deadline Reporting, 1999. Mem. N.Y. Fin. Writers Assn., Phi Beta Kappa, Lectr. Am. Press Inst. Avocations: walking, reading. Office: The New York Times 229 W 43rd St New York NY 10036-3959

HENRY, BARBARA A. publishing executive; b. Oshkosh, Wis., July 23, 1952; d. Robert Edward and Barbara Frances (Aylesworth) Henry BJ, U. Nev., 1974. With Gannett Co., 1974—; reporter Reno Gazette-Jour., 1974—78, city editor, 1978-80, mng. editor, 1980-82; asst. nat. editor USA Today, Washington, 1982-83; exec. editor Reno Gazette-Jour., 1981-86; editor, dir. Rochester (N.Y.) Dem. and Chronicle and Times-Union, 1986—91; pub. Great Falls (Mont.) Tribune, 1992-96; pres., pub. Des Moines Register, 1996—2000, The Indianapolis Star, 2000—; pres. Ind. Newspaper Group, 2002—. Recipient Publisher of the Year, Gannett Newspaper Group, 2001. Mem. Soc. Profl. Journalists, Associated Press Mng. Editors, Am. Soc. Newspaper Editors Avocation: skiing. Mailing: Indianapolis Star PO Box 145 Indianapolis IN 46206-0145*

HENRY, CATHERINE ANN, health science association administrator; MD, Wis. State U., 1985. Staff physician Cleve. Clin. Found.; clin. asst. prof. Pa. State U.; asst. prof. Clin. Found. Health Sciences Ctr. Ohio State U.; pres. Am. Med. Women's Assn. Mem. Physicians for Social Responsibility (chpt. pres., Detroit), Wis. State U. Alumni Assn. (bd. dirs.). Office: AMWA 801 N Fairfax St Ste 400 Alexandria VA 22314-1757

HENRY, ELAINE OLAFSON, artist, educator; b. Marshall, Minn., Aug. 25, 1945; d. Norman Jonas and Isfold Sigurdur (Josefson) Olafson; m. James Edward Henry, Sept. 30, 1967 (div. Dec. 1978); children: Julie Lynn, Cheryl Anne Henry Fields; m. Richard Story Garber, July 25, 1992. BFA, U. Wyo., 1992; MFA, So. Ill. U., 1995. Mktg. coord. Cannon Design, Inc., Grand Island, N.Y., 1978-82; mktg. cons. Mpls., 1982-83; mktg. dir. Campbell City C. of C., Gillette, Wyo., 1983-86; owner J&J Awards and Ad Concepts, Gillette, 1986-89; grad. asst. So. Ill. U., Carbondale, 1992-95; asst. prof. Emporia (Kans.) State U., 1996—2002, chair dept. art, 2000—, assoc. prof., 2002—. Pres. Nat. Coun. on Edn. for the Ceramic Arts, Erie, Colo., 2002—; pres. Emporia Arts Coun., 1997-99; pres. Kans. Artist Craftsman Assn., 1999-2000. Featured artist/sculptor Ceramics: Mastering the Craft, 2001, Studio Potter Mag., 1999, Ceramic Design Book, 1998; featured artist and author Ceramics Monthly Mag., 1996. Emporia State U. grantee, 1997, 99; recipient awards. Mem. Kans. Artist Craftsmen Assn. (pres. 1999). Avocations: travel, books, music. Office: Emporia State U Campus Box 4015 1200 Commercial St Emporia KS 66801-5087

HENRY, FRANCES ANN, journalist, educator; b. Denver, July 23, 1939; d. Lewis Byford and Betsy Mae (Lancaster) Patten; m. Charles Larry, June 28, 1963 (div. May 1981); children: Charles Kevin, Tracy Diane. BA in English, Carleton Coll., 1960; MA in Social Sci., U. Colo., Denver, 1988; MA in Journalism, Memphis State U., 1989. Cert. tchr. Lang. arts tchr. Rolla (Mo.) Pub. Schs., 1963-66; journalism/English tchr. Douglas County Pub. Schs., Castle Rock, Colo., 1976-99, retired, 1999, chmn. English dept., 1992-98; asst. prof. Memphis State U., 1991-92; mng. editor Douglas County News-Press, Castle Rock, 1986-87; editor Fourth World Bulletin, 1988; exec. editor Daily Helmsman Memphis State U., 1988-89, gen. mgr. Daily Helmsman, 1991-92; sole proprietor The Editor's Desk, 1997—. Contbr. articles to profl. jours. Recipient Gov.'s award for excellence in edn. Colo. Endowment for Humanities, 1997. Mem. ACLU, Colo. H.S. Press Assn. (sec. 1981-83, pres. 1983-91, bd. dirs., named Colo. Journalism Tchr. of Yr. 1985), Mensa, Kappa Tau Alpha. Democrat. Episcopalian.

HENRY, JANICE K. construction materials company executive; BS, Columbia Union Coll.; MBA, George Washington U. Various fin. mgmt. positions Martin Marietta Corp. (now Lockheed Martin Corp.), 1974-94, corp. sec.; CFO Martin Marietta Materials, Raleigh, N.C., 1994—, sr. v.p. Trustee Peace Coll., Raleigh. Office: Martin Marietta Materials Inc 2710 Wycliff Rd Raleigh NC 27607

HENRY, KAREN LEE, writer, lecturer; b. Grand Rapids, Mich., Feb. 20, 1944; d. Leo John and Mary Alice (Mallick) Henry. AS with high honors, Davenport Coll., 1983; BA, U. Mich., 1989. Writer Palestine Human Rights Campaign, Chgo., 1984-85; journalist Al Fajr, Jerusalem, 1985-86; dir. activities Villa Maria Retirement Cmty., Grand Rapids, Mich., 1990-93; libr. asst. Grand Rapids Pub. Libr., 1994—2000; freelance writer, lectr. Grand Rapids; exec. dir. dept. justice Weed & Seed, 2000—. Ednl. cons. on Mid. East Inst. for Global Edn., Grand Rapids, 1983—, bd. dirs., 1995—. Contbr. articles to profl. jours. Apptd. Housing Bd. Appeals, Grand Rapids, 1984; spl. projects dir. Econ. Devel. Corp., Grand Rapids, 1983; active Grand Rapids AIDS Task Force, 1986-92, Coop Am., Feminist Majority, Am. Ednl. Trust, New Jewish Agenda, Am. Arab Anti-Discrimination Com., YWCA, Nat. Humane Soc., Expressions for Women; bd. dirs. YWCA, Grand Rapids, 1996-97, Am. Friends Svc. Com. of Great Lakes Region, 1996-2002; pres., founding mem. Women's Action Network, Grand Rapids, 1993—; mem. pediat. oncology resource team Butterworth Hosp., 1998—, Racial Justice Inst., 1999-, Grand Rapids Inst. Info. Democracy, 1998—; chmn. task force Project Safe Neighborhood, 2002; bd. dirs. Pediat. Oncology Resource Team, 2003—; gov. appointee Arab Am. Affairs Commn.; U.S. atty. appointee Bldg. Respect in Diverse Groups to Enhance Sensitivity; founder Women's Empowerment Network, 2003. Recipient Appreciation cert. Econ. Devel. Corp., 1983, Housing Appeal Bd., 1985, Chicago House, 1987. Mem. AAUW, Nat. Assn. Arab Am. Women, Nat. Mus. Women in Arts, Am. for Mid. East Understanding, Union Palestinian Women's Assn., Progressive Women's Alliance, Gilda's Club. Avocations: hiking, discussing books. Home and Office: 29 Wallinwood Ave NE Grand Rapids MI 49503-3719

HENRY, KATHLEEN MARIE, marketing executive; b. Stillwater, Okla., Sept. 24, 1950; d. Irl Wayne and Hulda Mary Henry. BS, U. Cen. Okla., Edmond, 1972. Community relations dir./account exec. Lowe Runkle Advt., Oklahoma City, 1972-74, account coordinator, 1975; sales promotion cons. McDonald's Corp., Houston, 1974, regional advt. supr. Southfield, Mich., 1975, regional advt. mgr., 1976-78, local store mktg. mgr. Oak Brook, Ill., 1978-80, staff dir., store mktg./sales promotion, 1980-82, home office dir. store mktg./sales promotion, 1982-83, dir. nat. sales promotion, 1983-84, internat. mktg. dir., 1984-85; mktg. dir. McDonald's System France, 1985-86, McDonald's System Europe, 1985-88, v.p. mktg., 1988-97; pres. Henry Jamieson Assocs., Tulsa, Okla., 1997—. Publicity chmn. Keep Okla. Beautiful, 1973-74; publicity chmn. Muscular Dystrophy Assn. Am., Okla. chpt., 1973-74; bd. dirs. Southfield Arts Coun., Mich., 1976-78; commr. Lake Keystone Planning and Zoning Commn., 1999—; bd. dirs. Perry High Sch. Alumni Assn., 1999-; bd. dirs. sec. Keystone Peninsula Property Owners Assn., 1998-. Recipient Chgo. YWCA Leadership award, 1978, Disting. Former Student award U. Ctrl. Okla., 1979, Bronco award U. Ctrl. Okla. Centennial, 1991; named Outstanding Sr. Woman U. Ctrl. Okla., 1972, Outstanding Greek Woman, 1972. Mem. U. Ctrl. Okla. Alumni Assn. (dir. 1974, 1998-2002, found. bd. dirs. 1999—), U. Ctrl. Okla. Centennial Commn., Sigma Kappa. Office: Henry Jamieson Assocs Rte 3 Box 150A Cleveland OK 74020

HENRY, LOIS HOLLENDER, psychologist; b. Phila., Jan. 19, 1941; d. Edward Hubert and Frances Lois (Nesler) Hollender; m. Charles L. Henry, Oct. 24, 1964 (div. 1971); children: Deborah Lee, Randell Huitt, Andrew Edward. BA, Thomas A. Edison Coll., 1979; MSW, Fordham U., 1981; PhD in Indsl. Psychology, City U. L.A., 1992. Diplomate cert. neurofeedback provider; cert. social worker, Ariz., N.Y., N.J., EEG Biofeedback Practitioners; lic. svc. profl., career counselor, Ariz. Pers. asst., sec. IBM, Paterson, N.J., St. Louis, 1964-66; min.'s asst. Grace Luth. Ch., St. Cloud, Fla., 1966-68; adminstr., tchr. Fla. Finishing Acad., St. Cloud, 1968-70; adminstv. asst. Newark Book Ctr., 1972-77; intern, med. social worker Jersey City Med. Ctr., 1979-80; intern, psychiat./med. social worker VA Med. Ctr., Lyons, N.J., 1980-81; sch. social worker Lakeview Learning Ctr., Budd Lake, N.J., 1981-82; mgr. human resources Terak Corp., Scottsdale, Ariz., 1982-85; v.p. counseling and bus. devel. Murro & Assocs., Phoenix, 1985-88, exec. v.p. cons., 1988-91; prin. career cons. Henry & Assocs., Scottsdale, 1982-97; staff psychologist Nelson O'Connor & Assocs., Phoenix, 1993-97; v.p. dir. profl. svcs. Lee Hecht Harrison, Phoenix, 1997-98; cert. neurotherapist Forensic Psychol. Svcs., Phoenix, 1995-96; career cons., individual/family counselor/psychotherapist/neurotherapist, spkr. Henry & Assocs., Scottsdale, 1982-97. Adj. prof. Ottawa U.; mem. employers com. Ariz. Dept. Econ. Security; cons. in field. Coord.-vol. Job-A-Thon, Phoenix, 1983. Fellow Am. Orthopsychiat. Assn., Internat. Assn. Outplacement Profls. (treas. Ariz. region 1992-95, assoc. editor Internation Jour. Neuronal Regulation), Nat. Registry of Soc. Neuronal Regulation (diplomate, charter mem.); mem. NASW, Soc. Human Resource Mgmt., Am. Assn. Psychophysiology.

HENRY, LORETTA MARRIE, writer; b. Gould, Mich., May 21, 1942; d. Sigvard Strom and Florence Loretta (McNeill) Tremblay; m. Richard Lee Denton, Jan. 20, 1980 (wid. Mar. 1985); stepchildren: Dale Carter Henry, Brian Henry; m. Delbert Lee Henry, July 4, 1989. Grad. H.S., Lansing, Mich. Color print technician Van's Camera and Processing, Lansing, Mich., 1960-64, Lynn's Processing Lab., Lansing, Mich., 1964-66; color movie film technician Capitol Film Svcs., Lansing, 1966-68; part-time photographer Olan Mills, Lansing, 1960-73; real estate broker Graham Realty, Lansing, 1973-84; owner coin laundry Laundry Mat, Haslett, Mich., 1974-83; owner rental units, flooring store, D&D Plumbing, Lansing, 1973-85, D&D Mechanical, Lansing, 1976-85, Denton Harbor Marina, Haslett, 1979-87, Denton Harbor Amusements, Haslett, 1979-85; pres. Denton Swartz Investments, 1980-87, Foxden, Inc., Haslett, Mich. and, Ky., 1985—. Author: (craft book) Braided Wire Jewelry, The Art of Recycling, 1995, Nobody's Child, 1998. Mem. Moose, Eagle's. Avocations: photography, art, inventing, pocket billiards. Office: Foxden Inc 3721 Vanover Rd Utica KY 42376-9737 Address: 34408 SR 54 West Zephyrhills FL 33543

HENRY, MARGARET ROSE, state legislator; b. Rayne, La., June 20, 1944; BA, Tex. So. U.; MA, Springfield Coll. Mem. Dist. 2 Del. Senate, Dover, 1994—, mem. joint fin. com., children, youth and their families, mem. health and social svcs., chmn. pub. safety coms.; chmn. Combat Drug Abuse Coms. Trustee Med. Ctr. Del.; exec. dir. of Girls, Inc., Del. Mem. Brandywine Profl. Assn. E-mail: mrh9220@aol.com.

HENRY, PAULA LOUISE (PAULA LOUISE HENRY COOVER), academic administrator; b. White Plains, NY, Mar. 5, 1947; d. Raymond Francis and Carolyn Louise (Landis) Henry; m. John David Coover, Nov. 18, 1967 (div. Jan. 1992); children: Jeffrey Darren, Robert Benson, Jennifer Danielle (dec.). AA in Psychology, Monmouth U., 1967; student, Pace U., 1972-76; BA in Psychology, Monmouth U., 1993. Chair gifted and talented com., then pres. Hunterdon County (N.J.) Coun. PTAs, 1980-86; chmn. county pres. group, nat. conv. del., gen. conv. chmn. N.J. Congress Parents & Tchrs., Trenton, 1985-87, field svc. chmn., 1985-89, pres., 1989-91, immediate past pres., 1991-93, hon. v.p., 1991—; asst. to dean Rutgers Bus. Sch., Newark and New Brunswick, 1995—2002; campus adviser Office Student Jud. Affairs, Rutgers U., Newark and New Brunswick, 1996—, sr. exec. asst. univ. rel. New Brunswick, 2002—. Sch. bd. Union Twp. Bd. Edn., N.J., 1983-86, assembly del., 1984-86, legis. chmn. 1984-86, policy chmn. 1986, edn. chmn. 1984-85; trustee Jennie M. Haver Scholarship Fund, 1984-89; active Hunterdon County Edn. Coalition, 1984-88, Child Abuse and Missing Children Com., Hunterdon, 1987-98, Hunterdon County Youth Svcs. Commn., Flemington, 1987-98, N.J. Gov.'s Commn. on Quality Edn., 1991-93; treas. Fannie B. Abbott Student Loan Found., 1985-90, trustee, 1985-80; v.p. Hunterdon County Child Assault Protection Program, 1986-90; strategic planning com. United Way of Essex and West Hudson, 1994-95; trustee Good News Home for Women, 1997-2002, sec., 1999-2002; governing bd. Quality Edn. N.J., 1998—, co-chair, 2000-02, immediate past chair 2002; bd. dirs. Recordings for the Blind and Dyslexic, NJ, 2001-02, Bus. and Edn. Partnership Somerset/Hunterdon Counties, 2002—; mem. Raritan Millstone Heritage Alliance Bd., 2002—. Democrat. Methodist. Home: PO Box 5228 Clinton NJ 08809-0228 Office: Rutgers Univ Univ Relations New Brunswick NJ 08901-1281 Office Phone: 732-932-4299. E-mail: pauhen@yahoo.com., phenry@oldqueens.rutgers.edu.

HENRY, PHYLLISS JEANETTE, marshal; AA in Law Enforcement, Des Moines Area C.C., 1972; B Gen. Studies, U. Iowa, 1984, MA in Comm. Studies, 1986, PhD in Comm. Rsch., 1988. Police officer Des Moines (Iowa) Police Dept., 1972-82; state adminstrv. dir. Roxanne Conlin for Gov. campaign, Iowa, 1982; intern Police Found., Washington, 1984; comm. rsch. analyst Starr and Assocs., 1985; mgr. support svcs. Dept. Pub. Safety Iowa State U., 1990-94; U.S. marshal so. dist. Iowa, apptd. by Pres. Clinton U.S. Dept. Justice, 1994—. Adv. com. Dirs. Marshals, 1995-97. Named Woman of Yr., Metro. Woman's Network, 1991, Officer of Yr. Internat. Assn. of Women, 1991. Mem. Iowa Assn. Women Police (co-founder, Officer of Yr. 1991), Fed. Exec. Coun. Policy Com., Nat. Ctr. for Women and Policing (adv. bd.). Office: Office US Marshal US Courthouse 123 E Walnut St Rm 343A Des Moines IA 50309-2035 E-mail: Phylliss.Henry@usdoj.gov.

HENRY, SALLY, assistant principal; b. Elyria, Ohio; d. Robert A. and Dorothy M. Eskins; m. James M. Henry (dec.); children: Ronald, Gregory, Mark, Tammy, Gary. A in Liberal Arts, Lorain County C.C., Elyria, 1978; B in Elem. Edn., U. Ky., 1980, M in Elem. Edn., 1981, EdD, 1987. Cert. tchg. and leadership Ky., tchg., leadership and ESOL Fla. Tchr. mid. sch. St. Peter Sch., Lexington, Ky., 1983—85; adj. instr. Lexington C.C., 1985—88; grad. asst. U. Ky., 1985—87; curriculum cons. Harcourt Brace, Orlando, Fla., 1988—89; tchr., educator Polk County Schs., Bartow, Fla., 1989—95; program specialist Collier County Schs., Naples, Fla., 1995—99, asst. prin., 1999—. Facilitator, chair Sch. Adv. Coun., Everglades City, Fla., 1995—; coord. vol. program, Everglades City, 1995—, Ptnrs. in Edn., Everglades City, 1995—. Recipient Kids Count award, First Union Bank, Naples, 1996, Environ. award, Dept. Environ. Edn., Tallahassee, Fla., 1997—2001; grantee Great Gator Reading grant, Collier County Edn. Found., Naples, 1996, Creative Writing grant, United Arts Coun., Naples, 2000. Mem.: AAUW, Fla. Reading Coun., Phi Beta Kappa. Avocations: reading, rose gardening, decorating, shopping, collecting manatee memorabilia. Home: 348 Nassau Ct Marco Island FL 34145

HENRY, SALLY MCDONALD, lawyer; b. Durham, N.C., Aug. 1, 1948; d. John Frederick and Mary Frances (McDonald) Henry. BA, Duke U., 1970; MA in Anthropology, SUNY, Binghamton, 1973; JD, NYU, 1982. Bar: U.S. dist. ct. (ea. dist.) N.Y. Tchr. Endicott (N.Y.) Pub. Schs., 1971-75, Monticello (N.Y.) Pub. Schs., 1975-79; clk. U.S. Bankruptcy Ct., Bklyn., 1982-83; assoc. Skadden, Arps, Slate, Meagher & Flom L.L.P., N.Y.C., 1983-91, ptnr., 1991—. Author: Ordin on Contesting Confirmation, 1998; editor articles Rev. Law and Social Change, 1981-83; contbr. numerous articles to profl. jours. Mem. rules com. Ea. dist. N.Y. bar, Bklyn, 1984. Home: 395 Riverside Dr Apt 6A New York NY 10025-1843 Office: Skadden Arps Slate Meagher & Flom 4 Times Sq Fl 24 New York NY 10036-6595

HENRY, SHERRYE P. former political advisor; b. Memphis, July 13, 1935; Grad. magna cum laude, Vanderbilt U.; MBA, Fordham U. Asst. adminstr. Office Women's Bus. Ownership SBA; sr. adv. to congresswoman Louise M. Slaughter, 2000—. Vice-chair interagy. com. on women's bus. enterprise. Author of 2 books including The Deep Divide: Why American Women Resist Equality; contbr. numerous articles to nat. mags.; creator, host Woman! program on Sta. WCBS-TV, N.Y.C.; ind. prodr., broadcaster Sherrye Henry Program WOR Radio, N.Y.C. Active Group for the South Fork, eastern end of L.I., N.Y., Fedn. Protestant Welfare Agys. N.Y., The Retreat, East Hampton, N.Y. Mem. Women's Forum N.Y. (founding mem.).

HENRY, SUE, social worker, educator; b. Marion, Ind., Aug. 25, 1934; d. William Floyd and Mildred Ethel (Schwark) H. AB, Earlham Coll., 1956; MSc in Social Adminstrn., Western Res. U., 1964; DSW, U. Denver, 1972. Teenage program dir. YWCA, Lima, Ohio, 1956-62; br. exec. YWCA Met. Cleve., 1964-67; spl. svcs. dir. YWCA Met. Denver, 1967-70; asst. prof. U. Pa., Phila., 1972-76; assoc. prof. U. Denver, 1976-82; faculty fellow Colo. Divsn. Mental Health, Denver, 1984-85; adj. faculty Met. State Coll., Denver, 1985-89; prof. U. Denver, 1982-99, prof. emerita, 2000—. Cons. Denver Internat. Program, 1977—; rsch. assoc. Applied Social Sci. Cons., Denver, 1982-87. Author: Group Skills in Social Work, 1981, revised edit., 1992; sr. editor: Social Work with Groups Mining the Gold, 2002; mem. editl. bd. Social Work with Groups, 1981—; contbr. articles to profl. jours. Com. chair Am. Friends Svc. Com., Phila., 1972-76; mem. Planning Commn., Gilpin County, Colo., 1985 88, chair Citizen Adv. Bd. Health and Human Svcs., 1997-2002; bd. pres. Columbine Family Health Ctr., 1988-92. W.T. Grant fellow YWCA of U.S.A., N.Y.C., 1962-64, doctoral tng. grantee Children's Bur., U.S. Govt., 1970-72; recipient Contbn. to Profl. Lit. award Assn. Social Group Workers, 1986, Contbn. to Profl. Lifetime Achievement award Assn. Social Group Workers, 2001. Mem. AARP (mem. nat. legis. coun. 2002—), Coun. Social Work Edn. (ho. of dels. 1981-83), Assn. for Advancement Social Work with Groups. Democrat. Avocations: international cuisine cooking, travel, skiing, weaving. E-mail: shenry@du.edu.

HENSCHEL, SHIRLEY MYRA, licensing agent; b. N.Y.C., Dec. 18, 1932; d. Joseph and Leah Rose (Cooper) H. BA, Barnard Coll., 1954. Pub. rels., sales promotion exec. Louis Marx & Co., Inc., N.Y.C., 1954-59; acct. exec. Harold J. Siesel Co., N.Y.C., 1959-62; pres. U.S. Motor Sport Promotions, Inc., N.Y.C., 1962-66; v.p. Flora Mir Candy Corp., N.Y.C., 1966-71, Marden-Kane, Inc., N.Y.C., 1971-79; pres. Alaska Momma, Inc., N.Y.C., 1979—. Mem. Sch. and Home Products Assn. (assoc.), Licensing Industry and Merchandisers Assn. (charter mem. Achievement award 1988, nominee Hall of Fame 1994, 98, 99, 2000), Women Inc., Women in Toys (charter mem.). Democrat. Jewish. Avocations: cooking, travel, reading, theatre, investing. Office: Alaska Momma Inc 303 5th Ave Rm 2009 New York NY 10016-6652 Office Fax: 212-696-1340. Business E-Mail: licensing@alaskamomma.com.

HENSCHKE, CLAUDIA INGRID, physician, radiologist; b. Berlin, Mar. 3, 1941; d. Ulrich Konrad and Gisela Franziska H. BA in French, So. Meth. U., 1962, MS in Math. Stats., 1966; PhD in Stats., U. Ga., 1969; MD, Howard U., 1977; Radiologist, Harvard U., 1981. Diplomate Am. Bd. Radiology. Internship, residency dept. radiology Harvard Med. Sch./Brigham and Women's Hosp., 1977-81, clin. fellow in radiology, 1977-81; rsch. fellow in radiology Brigham and Women's Hosp., 1981-82, Harvard Med. Sch., Boston, 1981-82; rsch. fellow in epidemiology Harvard Sch. of Pub. Health, 1981-82; assoc. radiologist Brigham and Women's Hosp., 1982-83, co-dir. Thoracic Divsn., 1983; asst. attending radiology to assoc. radiologist The N.Y. Hosp. - Cornell Med. Ctr., 1983-87, 87-92, sect. chief, chest imaging to chief of divsn., 1988-92, 92-95, attending radiologist, 1992—, chief, Divsn. of Health Care Policy and Tech. Assessment, 1995—, chief, Divsn. of Chest Imaging, 1995—. Various acad. positions to prof. radiology, Cornell U. Med. Coll., 1992—; cons. Rockefeller U., 1986—, Med. Billing Program Devel. and Med. Computer Systems Planning, 1986—; lectr. in field; mem. numerous coms. in field; vis. prof. numerous univs., including Columbia U., 1999, Roy Castle Internat. Ctr. for Lung Cancer Rsch., Liverpool, Eng., 1999, Washington U., 1999, Clinica U., Pamplona, Spain, 1999, U. Rochester, N.Y., 1999, others. Mem. editl. bd. Complications in Surgery, 1995—, Investigative Radiology, 1990-94, Clin. Imaging, 1988—, Acad. Radiology, 1994—, others; reviewer Am. Jour. Cardiology, 1982—, Chest, 1992—, Radiology, 1993—, Jour. of Computed Assisted Tomography, 1995—, Am. Jour. of Radiology, 1995—, others; contbr. numerous books, including: Women's Complete Handbook, 1994, Introduction to Statistics and Computer Programming, 1975, Instructions for General Purpose Program Package, 1971, First and Second Biomedical Computing Symposium 1965 and 1966, 1967; contbr. numerous articles to profl. jours. and publs. Named Ky. Col. by Gov. of Ky., 1963; grantee in field. Mem. Am. Statis. Soc., Am. Assn. Women Radiologists (Marie Curie award/2d place 1994), Radiol. Soc. N.Am., Am. Coll. Radiology, Soc. Thoracic Radiology, Sigma Xi, Phi Kappa Phi. Office: New York Hosp/Dept Radiol Cornell Med Ctr New York NY 10021 E-mail: chensch@med.cornell.edu.

HENSEL, NANCY H. academic administrator; 1 child. BA, MA, Calif. State U., San Francisco; EdD, U. Ga., 1973. Prof. early childhood edn., Calif.; dean coll. of edn., health and rehab. U. Maine, Farmington, 1992—95, provost and v.p. academic affairs, 1995—99; pres. U. Maine at Presque Isle, 1999—. Named to Fourteenth Maine Women's Hall of Fame, 2003. Office: U Maine at Presque Isle 181 Main St Presque Isle ME 04769-2888*

HENSELER, SUZANNE MARIE, state legislator, social studies educator, majority whip; b. Brookline, Mass., Dec. 7, 1942; d. Paul R. and Evelyn (Warren) McGoldrick; m. John L. Henseler, June 26, 1965; children: Sean Patrick, Warren Paul, Timothy Brian. BS in History Edn., Boston Coll., 1964. Tchr. Pilgrim High Sch., Warwick, 1964-66; clk. house labor com. R.I. Ho. Reps., Providence, 1977-82; tchr. St. Rocco Sch., Johnston, R.I., 1984—; mem. R.I. Ho. of Reps., Providence, 1982, majority whip, 1992—. Former mem., bd. mem. North Kingstown (R.I.) Soccer Assn., 1974-89; mem. North Kingstown Dem. Town Com., 1974—; mem. sch. com., Kingstown, 1974-76; co-chair pay equity commn., 1995—; co-chair Legis. Women's Health Commn., 1995—; chmn. R.I. Mobile Home Commn., 1988-93; chmn. Legis. Commn. to Study the Solid Waste Mgmt. Corp.; mem. leg. com. study Dept. of Environmental Mgmt. Named Outstanding Young Women of Yr., North Kingstown Jaycetes, 1977, Nat. Environ. award 1993. Mem. Nat. Orgn. Women Legislators, Women in Govt. Home: 210 Edmond Dr North Kingstown RI 02852-2416 Office: Majority Whip State House # 303 Providence RI 02903

HENSELMEIER, SANDRA NADINE, retired training and development consulting firm executive; b. Indpls., Nov. 20, 1937; d. Frederick Rost Henselmeier and Beatrice Nadine (Barnes) Henselmeier Enright; m. David Albert Funk, Oct. 2, 1976; children: William H. Jr. Stolz, Harry Phillip II Stolz, Sandra Ann Stolz. AB, Purdue U., 1971; MAT, Ind. U., 1975. Exec. sec. to dean Ind. U. Sch. Law, Indpls., 1977—78; adminstrv. asst. Ind. U.-Purdue U., Indpls., 1978—80, assoc. archivist, 1980—81; program and comm. coord. Midwest Alliance in Nursing, Indpls., 1981—82; tng. coord. Coll./Univ. Cos., Indpls., 1982—83; pres. Better Bus. Comms., Indpls., 1983—. Adj. lectr./lectr. U. Indpls. Ctr. Continuing Mgmt. Devel. and Edn., Indpls., 1984—. Author: Successful Customer Service Writing, Winning with Effective Business Grammar, Successful Telephone Communication and Etiquette, Management Writing; contbr. articles to profl. jours. Mem.: Econ. Club of Indpls. Republican. Presbyterian. Avocations: travel, walking, reading, learning new ideas.

HENSLEY, ELIZABETH CATHERINE, nutritionist, educator; b. Mpls., Feb. 27, 1921; d. Erich Christian and Lulu Mabel (Elliott) Selke; m. Eugene B. Hensley, June 10, 1954 (dec. 1992). BS in Edn., U. N.D., 1942; MS, Cornell U., 1944, postgrad., 1950-51. Instr. food and nutrition U. Del., 1944-47; asst. prof. Okla. A&M U., 1947-50; mem. faculty U. Mo., Columbia, 1951—, prof. food and nutrition, 1954-84, prof. emeritus, 1984—, chmn. dept. home econs., 1954 55, head dept. food and nutrition, 1955-65, co-chmn. dept. human nutrition, 1973-76. Author: Basic Concepts of World Nutrition, 1981. Mem. Am. Home Econs. Assn., Nutrition Today Soc., Mo. Home Econs. Assn., Boone County Hist. Soc., PEO, Pi Lambda Theta, Omicron Nu, Phi Upsilon Omicron, Gamma Sigma Delta, Kappa Alpha Theta Mem. Christian Ch. (Disciples Of Christ). Home: 802 Greenwood Ct Columbia MO 65203-2841

HENSLEY, MARY KAY, dietician; b. Dodge, Nebr., June 2, 1946; d. Joseph Leo and Sally H. (Fangman) Klitz; m. Charles Hensley, Feb. 4, 1978 (div. Dec. 30, 1985). BSc, Coll. of St. Mary, 1967, U. Nebr., 1970; MSc, Gov.'s State U., 1982. Registered dietician Am. Dietetic Assn., cert. specialist in renal nutrition. Therapeutic dietician ARA Hosp. Food Mgmt., Omaha, 1968—75, food prodn. mgr., 1975—77, renal dietician Hammond, Ind., 1977—92, Comprehensive Renal Care, Gary, Ind., 1992—99, Total Renal Care/Davita (now Davita), Gary, 1999—. Chmn. Coun. Renal Nutrition, 1986, 89. Editor: CRN Quarterly, 1983—85; contbr. articles to profl. jours.; mem. editl. bd.: Jour. Renal Nutrition, 1990—95. Named Outstanding Nephrology Profl., Tri-State Renal Network, 1990, Dietitian of Yr., Ill. Coun. Renal Nutrition, 1999; recipient Recognized Renal Dietitian award, Coun.on Renal Nutrition, 1990. Mem.: Am. Dietetic Assn. (specialty cert. panel 1997—), Nat. Kidney Found. Ind. (sec. 1991, 1998—2000, pres. 1993—95). Roman Catholic. Home: 20 Spruce Ct Schererville IN 46375 Office: Comprehensive Renal Care Davita 4802 Broadway Gary IN 46408

HENSLEY, PATRICIA DRAKE, principal; BLS in Liberal Studies, MA in Edn., PhD in Edn. Adminstrn., St. Louis U., Mo. Cert. use of tech. in sch. setting Tech. Leadership Acad. Tchr. grades 7 and 8 math. and sci., 1976—82; prin. St. Mary Magdalen, St. Louis, 1982—86; vice-prin. St. Elizabeth Acad., St. Louis, 1986—91; prin. St. Francis of Assisi, St. Louis, 1991—95; acad. adviser grad. programs Webster U., St. Louis, 1990—2002; prin. Ursuline Acad., St. Louis, 1995—. Adj. instr. math. and computer sci. Webster U., St. Louis, 1986—; nat. media cons. FM radio stas.; fellow St. Louis Prin. Acad., 1994; state prin. assessor NASSP, 1994; grant reviewer U.S. Dept. Edn., 2002. Mem. Archdiocesan Com. for Rev. of H.S. Admissions, 1997—99; bd. dirs., co-chair ednl. policies com. DeSmet Jesuit H.S., 1998—; bd. dirs. Vianney H.S., 1999—.

HENSON, ANNA MIRIAM, retired otolaryngologist, retired medical educator; b. Springfield, Mo., Nov. 7, 1935; d. Bert Emerson and Esther Miriam (Crank) Morgan; m. O'Dell Williams Henson, Aug. 1, 1964; children: Phillip, William. BA, Park Coll., Parkville, Mo., 1957; MA, Smith Coll., 1959; PhD, Yale U., 1967. Instr. Smith Coll., Northampton, Mass., 1960-61; rsch. assoc. Yale U., New Haven, 1967-74; instr. U. N.C., Chapel Hill, 1975-78, rsch. asst. prof., 1978-83, rsch. assoc. prof., 1983-86, prof. Sch. Medicine dept. otolaryngology, 1986—2001; ret., 2001. Mem. study sect. on hearing rsch. NIH, Bethesda, Md., 1990-93. Contbr. articles to profl. jours. Fulbright scholar, Australia, 1959-60; NIH grantee, 1975—2003. Mem. Assn. for Rsch. in Otolaryngology, Sigma Xi. E-mail: mmhenson@med.unc.edu.

HENSON, GLENDA MARIA, newspaper writer; b. Marion, N.C., June 17, 1960; d. Douglas Bradley and Glenda June (Crouch) H. BA in English cum laude, Wake Forest U., 1982. Reporter Ark. Dem., Little Rock, 1982-84; bur. reporter Tampa Tribune, Crystal River, Fla., 1984; statehouse reporter Ark. Gazette, Little Rock, 1984-87, bur. chief Washington, 1987-89; editl. writer Lexington (Ky.) Herald-Leader, 1989-94; editl. writer, columnist The Charlotte (N.C.) Observer, 1994-98; dep. editl. page editor Austin (Tex.) American-Statesman, 1998-2001, asst. mng. editor enterprise, 2001—. Lectr. journalism, Indonesia, 2001; juror Nat. Headliner Awards, 2002—04, ASNE Writing Awards, 2001—03; mem. Nieman Selection Com., 2004. Mem. Wake Forest Presdl. Scholarship Com., Ky., 1992, Wake Forest Bd. Visitors, 1995-99; Pulitzer Prize juror, 1994, 95, 99, 2000. Recipient Pulitzer prize, 1992, Walker Stone award Scripps Howard Found., 1992, award Ky. Press Assn., 1992, N.C. Press Assn., 1995, 96, Leadership award Duke U., 1995, Nat. Headliner award, 1996; named Wake Forest Woman of Yr., 1992; Nieman fellow Harvard U., 1993-94; Found. Am. Comm. Econs. fellow, 1997. Mem. Soc. Profl. Journalists (Sigma Delta Chi award 1991, Green Eyeshade award Atlanta chpt. 1992), Nat. Conf. Editorial Writers, Investigative Reporters & Editors Assn., Am. Soc. Newspaper Editors, Omicron Delta Kappa. Avocations: skiing, bicycling, swimming, travel, rafting. Home: 6506 Santolina Cove Austin TX 78731-2806 Office: Austin Am-Statesman 305 S Congress Ave Austin TX 78704-1200 Office Phone: 512-445-3965.

HENSON, PAMELA TAYLOR, secondary education educator; b. Mobile, Ala., Aug. 31, 1958; d. Richard Dowdy and Martha Jo (Hanson) Taylor; m. Thomas Baird Henson III, Mar. 7, 1987; 1 child, Joshua Taylor. BS in Secondary Edn./Biology, U. South Ala., 1983; MS in Secondary Edn./Biology, U. Mobile, 1989, Adminstrv. Cert., 1990; Edn. Specialist Adminstrn., Ala. State U., 1995; postgrad., U. West Fla. Cert. secondary edn. educator. Sci. tchr. Fairhope (Ala.) Middle Sch., 1984-91, Foley (Ala.) H.S., 1991-97; sci. supr., grant writer Baldwin County Schs., 1994—. Christa McAuliffe fellow State Dept. of Edn., 1994, Outstanding Biology tchr. Nat. Assn. Biology Tchrs., 1994, Outstanding Instr. in Environ. Edn., Legacy Found., 1995, Outstanding Sci. Supr. award, 2002, Mobile Bay NEP award, 2002, YWCA Woman of Profl. Achievement award, 2002; recipient Presdl. award NSTA, 1994, Melvin Paul Jones award Tuskegee U., Outstanding Svc. to Edn. award. Mem. NSTA, Nat. Assn. Biology Tchrs., Ala. Sci. Tchrs. Assn., Nat. Marine Educators Assn., Baldwin County Assn. Profl. Educators (pres. 1994—), Alpha Delta Kappa (treas. 1994-96). Republican. Baptist. Avocations: travel, walking, outdoor summer sports. Home: PO Box 1676 810 Juniper Ct Daphne AL 36526-4358

HENSON SCALES, MEG D(IANE), artist, writer, publisher; b. Portland, Oreg., Oct. 16, 1953; d. Kenneth Jack and Jessie Louise (Mott) Henson; m. Jeffrey Charles Henson Scales, Dec. 16, 1985; 1 child, Coco Tigre Roja. Student, San Francisco State U., 1972-73, 74-75, Friends' World Coll., Guatemala, 1974. Founding mem. Black Edn. Ctr., Portland, Oreg., 1970-71 [illegible] editor Woman's [illegible] Kleinbauer Investigations, L.A., 1981-83; tchr. CUNY, N.Y.C., 1987-89, Mindbuilders, Bronx, NY, 1987-89; painter, writer, strategist Henson Scales Prodns., N.Y.C., 1989—; founder Com. for Rational African Americans Against the Parade, N.Y.C., 1995; pub., editor The Harlem Howl, N.Y.C., 1995—; freelance photographer N.Y. Times, The Oregonian, The Internat. Herald Tribune, The LA Weekly, 2001—; freelance writer N.Y. Times, 2001—. Commn. Sacred banners for Grace Methodist Ch., Wilmington, Del., 1997; spkr. in field. Author: The Book of Love, 1988, Melisma, 1989 (Deming award 1989); co-creator, performer Tragedy in Black and White/A Race Record in One Act, 1981; dir., prodr. video documentary Class, 1989, Action/Reaction, 1998; prodr., dir. videos Who's Your Daddy, 2003, You Slay Me, 2004; author essays Tenderheaded; Man, God and the Okey-Doke; Be/Held; contbg. author: Divine Mirror: The Maddonna Revealed, 2001, Tenderheaded, 2001, Internat. Rev. of African Am. Art, 2001, Davis Mus./Wellesley Coll., 2000; one-woman show U. Fla. at Gainesville Univ. Gallery, 1998, Smithsonian Anacostia Mus. and Ctr. for African Am. History and Culture, 1999. Founding mem. African Am. Against Violence, N.Y.C., 1995. Recipient N.Y. Found. Arts fellowship, N.Y.C., 1989, honorable mention Dorothea Lange/Paul Taylor prize in photojournalism, 1993. Avocations: creation myths, prayers, piano, flute. E-mail: mhensons@yahoo.com.

HENTGES, HARRIET, not-for-profit developer; m. Wayne Allan Koonce, 1985. BS, Coll. St. Catherine, St. Paul; MS in Internat. Rels. and Econs., Am. U., Washington; PhD in Internat. Econs., Johns Hopkins U., Balt. Aide Sen. Mark O. Hatfield; spl. asst. Dep. Spl. Rep. for Trade Negotiations; economist policy planning staff U.S. Dept. State, Washington; exec. dir. LWV, 1978—81; v.p. planning and rsch. Sears World Trade, Inc.; mng. ptnr. Clifton Investment Group LP, Arlington, Va.; chair Balkans Initiative U.S. Inst. of Peace, Washington, 1994—99, exec. v.p., COO, 1999—. Trustee Coll. of St. Catherine, St. Paul. Office: US Inst of Peace 1200 17th St NW Washington DC 20036*

HENTZ, SUSAN MARIE, special education educator, consultant, trainer; b. Somerset, N.J., May 2, 1961; d. Donald George and Susan Elizabeth Hentz. BA, Glassboro State Coll., 1983; MA, U. So. Fla., 1995; EdS in Ednl. Leadership, Nova Southeastern U., 2001. Cert. tchr. Fla., 2001. Exceptional student edn. tchr. Sarasota (Fla.) Bd. of Edn., 1989—2004; pres., owner Valuable Innovative Ednl. Wisdom (VIEW), Inc., Sarasota, 2003. Contbg. author: (textbooks) Early Childhood Education Today, Teaching in America, 2004. Mem. Adv. for Better Hearing, Inc.; bd. dirs. Sarasota County Leadership Acad. Named ESE Model Demonstration Classroom Tchr., 1993, Sarasota County Model Classroom Tchr., 1997, Tchr. of the Year, Sarasota County Coun. for Exceptional Children, 2002; recipient PRSE Recognition award, 2000. Mem.: Fla. Spkrs. Bureau, Coun. for Exceptional Children (pres. 1998—99, named Marjorie Crick Tchr. of the Yr., Fla. br. 2002, Award of Excellence 1999). Achievements include development of exceptional student education training modules. Home and Office: VIEW Inc 750 N Tamiami Trail Ste 902 Sarasota FL 34236

HENTZ-POLK, NICEY, secondary school educator; b. Lambert, Miss. d. Fred and Daisy E. Hentz; children: Billy, Caroline, Rasheda. AA, Coahoma Jr. Coll., Clarksdale, Miss., 1969; BS, Jackson State U., 1971; MA, Ohio State U., 1973. Tchr. Columbus (Ohio) City Schs., 1973—. Mem.: ASCD, Nat. Coun. Tchrs. English. Democrat. Baptist. Avocations: reading, travel, photography, gardening. Home: 6205 Sharon woods Blvd Columbus OH 43229

HEPBURN, JEANETTE C. home health nurse; b. Provo, Utah, Nov. 7, 1952; d. George Blaine Clay, Sr. and E. Joan Clay; m. David Smiley, Feb. 15, 1975 (div. Aug. 1991); children: Peter David, Paul William, Adam George; m. Moller Boon, June 10, 1994 (dec. Sept. 1994); m. Charles Raymond Hepburn, June 3, 2000. Nursing diploma, Crouse Irving Meml. Hosp. Sch. Nursing, Syracuse, N.Y., 1972; BSN, Rockhurst Rsch. Coll., Kansas City, Mo., 1997; postgrad., Bowie State U. RN, cert. tech., ARC Disaster Health Svcs. Nursing asst. Crouse-Irving Meml. Hosp., Syracuse, NY, 1970—72; nurse RR, emergency rm., ICU Tompkins County Hosp., Ithaca, NY, 1972—75; ICU staff nurse II George Washington Hosp., Washington, 1975—78; ICU staff nurse Prince William Hosp., Manassas, Va., 1978—79; office nurse Romaker & Assocs., Kansas City, Mo., 1992—95; home health nurse Glen Burnie, Md., 1995—; served with disaster relief Pentagon Anne Arundel County, 2001, Am. Red Cross disaster nurse, 1998—2003, served with disaster relief Pentagon Hyattsville, Md., 1998—2003. Com. mem. to implement primary nursing George Washington Hosp., Washington, 1976. Sem. tchr. Ch. LDS, Adelphi, Md., 1999—2000, relics soc. counselor Adelphi, Glen Burnie, Md., 1996—98, relief soc. counselor, 2000—01. Scholar Senatoral scholar, Md., 2001—03. Mem.: Bowie Student Nurses Assn., Phi Sigma Tau. Mem. Lds Ch. Avocations: cross stitch, dog training, swimming. Home and Office: 312 Oak Manor Dr Glen Burnie MD 21061 E-mail: crhepburn@msn.com.

HEPPE, KAROL VIRGINIA, lawyer, educator; b. Vinton, Iowa, Mar. 14, 1958; d. Robert Henry and Audry Virginia (Harper) Heppe. BA in Law and Society, U. Calif., Santa Barbara, 1982; JD, People's Coll. Law, 1989. Cmty. organizer Oreg. Fair Share, Eugene, 1983; law clk. Legal Aid Found. L.A., summer 1986; devel. dir. Ctrl. Am. Refugee Ctr., L.A., 1987-89; exec. dir. Police Watch-Police Misconduct Lawyer Referral Svc., L.A., 1989-94; instr. People's Coll. Law, L.A., 1992-94; dir. alternative sentencing project Ctr. Juvenile and Criminal Justice, 1994-95; cons. Bay Area Police Watch, 1996; investigator Office Citizen Complaints City and County of San Francisco, 1998—. Vol. law clk. Legal Aid Found. L.A., 1984—86, Lane County Legal Aid Svc., Eugene, 1983. Editor: (newsletter) NLG Law Students Action, 1986, Ctrl. Am. Refugee Ctr., 1986—89, Prison Break, 1994. Mem. Coalition Human Immigrants Rights, 1991—92, So. Calif. Civil Rights Coalition, 1991—92; bd. dirs. Nat. Police Accountability Project Adv. Bd., 1999—2003, People's Coll. Law, 1985—90, Law Student Civil Rights Rsch. Coun., N.Y.C., 1986. Scholar, Kramer Found., 1984—88, Law Students' Civil Rights Rsch. Coun., 1986, Davis-Putter Found., 1988, Assn. Cmty.-Based Edn. Prudential, 1988. Avocations: reading, travel. E-mail: karol_heppe@ci.sf.ca.us.

HEPPER, IONA LYDIA, retired gallery owner; b. Eureka, S.D., Mar. 10, 1918; d. Emanuel E. and Lydia (Koerner) Voll; m. Kenneth Melvin Hepper, May 1, 1938 (dec. Feb. 1998); children: Judy, Rod. Student, Calif. Sch. Arts & Crafts, 1936-37. Owner Flair Gifts & Interiors, Stockton, Calif., 1951-81, tchr. art, 1965—, designer, 1971—; owner GAlerie Iona, Stockton, Calif., 1993-99. Cover designer (book) The Concepts of Bodily Objects, 1997. Named Millennium Artist of Yr. Haggin Mus., 2000. Mem. Nat. Watercolor Soc., Pastel Soc. Am., Pastel Soc. West Coast, Stockton Art League. Republican. Presbyterian. Avocations: painting, travel, reading. Home: 5469 Covey Creek Cir Stockton CA 95207-5329

HEPPLER, ROBIN LEE, project manager; b. Detroit, Aug. 12, 1953; d. Warren G. and Maurida (Tillie) Heppler. Student, Glendale CC, 1971-74, 82, Ariz. State U., 1975, 81, U. Wis., 1981. Various positions Valley Nat. Bank, Phoenix, 1971-78; project bus. regional dir. Jr. Achievement, Inc., Phoenix, San Jose, Atlanta, 1978-81; asst. v.p., ctr. mgr. 1st Tenn. Bank, Memphis, 1981-83; customer svc. mgr., ops. analyst Wells Fargo Credit Corp., Phoenix, 1983-84; officer Citibank, Ariz., Phoenix, 1984-85; ops. mgr., asst. v.p. MeraBank, Phoenix, 1985-89; lending officer, policy analyst 1st Interstate Bank, Phoenix, 1989; project mgr. Colo. Nat. Bank, 1991-93; project mgr. Ctr. of Excellence for Project Mgmt. US West Techs., Denver, 1993—2000; lotus notes developer and project mgr. EDS at Western Union, Englewood, Colo., 2000—. Active Fiesta Bowl Parade Com., 1983—92; sec. bd. dirs. Ariz. Easter Seal Soc., Phoenix, 1989—90, Human Svcs. Inc., Denver, 1991—95; bd. dirs. Ctrl. Ariz. Arthritis Found., Phoenix, 1989—90, chmn. jingle bell run, 1989; chmn. jail-athon Am. Cancer Soc., 1989; fundraiser Fiesta Bowl Com., Tempe, Ariz., 1990—92; chmn. Festival of Kites, Denver, 1992; chmn. champagne and chocolate black tie silent auction, 1994; chmn. Denver Jr. League, 1994—2000, chair holiday mart solicitations, 1996; coporate teams chair Safehouse Denver 5K Run, 1994, 1995; precinct bd. Maricopa County Election Dept., Phoenix, 1990; coord. Andre Ho. Diocese of Phoenix, 1987—90. Named one of Outstanding Young Women Am., 1979; recipient award for outstanding contbn., Arthritis Found., 1990, award for outstanding achievement, Am. Cancer Soc., Phoenix, 1989. Mem.: Soc. Tech. Comm., Fin. Women Internat. (bd. dirs. 1988—90). Avocations: calligraphy, guitar, skiing, hot air ballooning. Home: 3635 S Carr St Denver CO 80235-1801

HEPPNER, GLORIA HILL, medical science administrator, educator; b. Gt. Falls, Mont., May 30, 1940; d. Eugene Merrill and Georgia M. (Swanson) Hill; m. Frank Henry Heppner, June 6, 1964 (div. 1975); 1 child, Michael Berkeley. BA, U. Calif., Berkeley, 1962, MA, 1964, PhD, 1967. Damon Runyon postdoctoral fellow U. Wash., Seattle, 1967—68; asst. and assoc. prof. Brown U., Providence, 1969-79, Herbert Fanger meml. lectr., 1988; chmn. dept. immunology, dir. labs., sr. v.p. Mich. Cancer Found., Detroit, 1979-91; dir. breast cancer program Karmanos Cancer Inst., 1991—2003, dep. dir., 1994—2003; assoc. chair for rsch. dept. internal medicine Wayne State U. Sch. Medicine, Detroit, 1991—2001, asst. dean cancer program, 2002—03, pres. Karmanos Cancer Inst., spl. asst. to dean, 2003, assoc. v.p. rsch., 2003—. Mem. external adv. com. basic sci. program M.D. Anderson Hosp. and Tumor Clinic, Houston, 1984-94; mem. external adv. com. Case Western Res. U. Cancer Ctr., Cleve., 1988—, Roswell Park Meml. Inst., Buffalo, 1991-98; Sarah Stewart meml. lectr. Georgetown U., Washington, 1988; bd. sci. counselors Nat. Inst. Dental Rsch., 1993-97. Editor: Macrophages and Cancer, 1988; mem. editl. bd. Cancer Rsch., 1989-93, Jour. Nat. Cancer Inst., 1988, Sci., 1988-92; contbr. over 200 articles to sci. jours. Bd. dirs. Lyric Chamber Ensemble, 1996-99. Recipient Mich. Sci. Trail-Blazer award State of Mich., 1987; fellow Damon Runyon-Walter Winchell Found., 1967-69. Mem. AAAS, Am. Assn. for Cancer Rsch. (bd. dirs. 1983-86, chmn. long-range planning com. 1989-91), Am. Assn. Immunologists, Metastasis Rsch. Soc. (bd. dirs. 1985-89), Women in Cancer Rsch. (nat. pres.), Internat. Differentiation Soc. (v.p. 1990-92, pres. 1992-94), LWV (bd. dirs. Grosse Pointe, Mich. 1989-95). Democrat. Avocations: music, theater. Office: 4047 FAB 656 W Kirby Detroit MI 48202 Office Phone: 313-577-8848. E-mail: heppnerg@wayne.edu.

HEPWORTH-WOOLSTON, CONNIE JO, choreographer; Dancer Ririe-Woodbury Dance Co.; choreographer U. Utah; bd. govs. AAHPERD. Dancer educator, chair dance dept. East H.S., Salt Lake City; artistic dir. East H.S. Dance Co.; cons. U. New Mex. Contbr. Discover Dance: A Guide to Modern Dance in Secondary Schools. Achievements include Connie Jo Hepworth-Woolston scholarship awarded to East H.S. Grad. outstanding in dance. Office: AAHPERD 1900 Association Dr Reston VA 20191-1598

HERALD, CHERRY LOU, research educator, research director; b. Beeville, Tex., Dec. 23, 1940; m. Delbert Leon Herald, Jr., July 31, 1964; children: Heather Amanda, Delbert Leon, III. BS, Ariz. State U., 1962, MS, 1965, PhD, 1968. Faculty rsch. assoc. Cancer Rsch. Inst. Ariz. State U., Tempe, 1973-74, sr. rsch. chemist Cancer Rsch. Inst., 1974-77, asst. to dir. and sr. rsch. chemist Cancer Rsch. Inst., 1977-83, asst. dir., assoc. rsch. prof. Cancer Rsch. Inst., 1984-88, assoc. dir., rsch. prof. Cancer Rsch. Inst., 1988—. Co-author: Biosynthetic Products for Cancer Chemotherapy, vols. 4, 5, & 6, 1984, 85, 87, Anticancer Drugs from Animals, Plants & Microorganisms, 1994, sci. jours. Mem. Am. Soc. Pharmacognosy, Am. Chem. Soc. Office: Ariz State U Cancer Rsch Inst Tempe AZ 85287-2404 Office Phone: 480-965-6756. E-mail: cherald@asu.edu.

HERBERT, CHERYL SUE CHAPMAN, music educator; b. Beloit, Kans., Feb. 11, 1946; d. Donovan Otis Chapman and Elizabeth Aileen Wooster Chapman; m. Charles Douglas Herbert, Dec. 27, 1969; children: Charles Douglas II, Katrina Noelle, Abigail Carolina. B in Music Edn., Wichita State U., 1969; MS in Edn. with honors, U. Kans., 1996. Cert. music tchr. grades K-12, classroom tchr. grades K-8. Vocal music tchr. El Dorado Pub. Schs., El Dorand, Kans., 1969—71, Killeen (Tex.) Pub. Schs., 1971—72, Shawnee Mission (Kans.) Pub. Schs. #512, 1974—. Vol., chair Bible Sch. and soup kitchen Presbyn. Ch., Overland Park, Kans., 1987—2002. Mem.: NEA, Music Educators Nat. Conf. (treas. Wichita State U. 1968), Alpha Delta Kappa, Mu Phi Epsilon. Avocations: tennis, swimming, painting, gardening. Home: 8030 W 115th St Overland Park KS 66210 Office: Shawnee Mission Pub Schs 75 Antioch Shawnee Mission KS 66204

HERBERT, KATHY, retail executive; MBA, Lake Forest Grad. Sch. Mgmt. Dir. personnel tng. Jewel-Osco, 1996—98, v.p. human resources, 1998—2001; exec. v.p. human resources Albertson's, Inc., Boise, 2001—. Chair Jewel-Osco United Way Campaign; bd. dirs. Chgo. Sinfonietta, Kohl's Childrens Mus. Office: Albertsons Inc 250 Parkcenter Blvd Boise ID 83726

HERBERT, MARY KATHERINE ATWELL, writer; b. Grove City, Pa., Dec. 9, 1945; d. Stewart and Luella Irene (Brown) Atwell; m. Roland Marcus Herbert; children: Stephen Todd, Amy Elizabeth, Jill Anne. BA, Ariz. State U., 1968, MA, 1973; film cert., U. So. Calif., 1978. Film writer Scottsdale Daily Progress, 1976-79; dir. pub. relations Phoenix Theatre, 1980-85; script analyst, 1985-86; exec. asst. to v.p. prodn. DeLaurentiis Entertainment Group, 1986; producer's assoc. film TRAXX, 1986-87; dir. of devel. Devin/DeVore Prodns., 1988-89; free-lance script analyst and writer Glendale, Calif., 1989-97. Chmn. motion picture TV dept. Scottsdale (Ariz.) Coll., 2000—. Script writer: (TV shows) Trial By Jury, Dick Clark Prodn., (feature films) Dry Heat, Blind Desire, others; author: Writing Scripts Hollywood Will Love, 1994, 2d edit., 2000, Selling Scripts to Hollywood, 1999. Mem. bd. mgrs. Hollywood-Wilshire YMCA, 1992-96. Mem. Kappa Delta Pi, Pi Lambda Theta.

HERBERT, TIFFANY AMBER, marketing professional; b. Hartford, Conn., June 16, 1975; d. Robert and Carol Herbert. BBA, U. Tex., 1997; MBA, Am. Grad. Sch. Internat. Mgmt., 2003. Intern, cast mem. Walt Disney World, Orlando, Fla., 1994—2000; mgmt. devel. program GE, various locations, 1998—2001; stratetic mktg. intern The Coca-Cola Co., Atlanta, 2002; product mktg. mgr. GE Global Consumer Fin., Melbourne, Australia, 2003—. Project leader Thunderbird Corp. Cons., Taipei, Taiwan, 2002—03, Brand Mgmt. Cons., Glendale, Ariz., 2002—03. Mem.: Thunderbird Mktg. Club (chair alumni rels. 2001—03), Am. Mktg. Assn., Thunderbird Cmty. Svc. Club, Beta Gamma Sigma, Phi Sigma Iota. Avocations: travel, scuba diving. Office: GE Consumer Fin 1600 Summer St Stamford CT 06902

HERBRAND, KRISTINE M. music educator; b. Dodgeville, Wis., Dec. 13, 1952; d. Leslie and Elnora Elizabeth Forseth; m. Daniel H. Herbrand, July 2, 1977; children: Danielle, Kristopher. B.Music Edn., U. Wis.-Eau Claire, 1975; BA in Edn., Viterbo Coll., LaCrosse, Wis., 1995. Elem. music tchr. Sch. Dist. of Barron, Wis., 1976—77; elem. music tchr., h.s. vocal tchr. Sch. Dist. of Neillsville, Wis., 1977—. Music leader 4-H, Clark County, Wis., 1988—; officer, treas. Booster Club of Neillsville, 1995—. Named Tchr. of the Yr., Neillsville Schs., 1998. Mem.: Philanthropic Ednl. Orgn. (recording sec., treas. 1990—), Music Educators Nat. Conf. Lutheran.

[illegible] psychologist; BA in Psychology magna cum laude, U. Calif., 1985; MA in Clin. Psychology, Calif. Sch. Profl. Psychology, 1990, PhD in Clin. Psychology, 1994. Diplomate Am. Bd. Psychol. Specialties, 2000. Counselor, clin. coord. Vista Hill Treatment Ctrs., San Diego, 1987—97; lic. clin. psychologist Hess & Assocs., Summit Behavioral Partners, Las Vegas, 1997—99, pvt. practice, Las Vegas, 1999—. Author: (sci. paper) Age Difference in the Adaptive Behavior of Institutionalized Down Syndrome Individuals, 1984, Effects of Age on the Adaptive Behavior on Institutionalized and Non-Institutionalized Individuals with Down Syndrome, 1988. Mem.: Nev. State Psychol. Assn., APA, Pi Gamma Mu. Avocation: dance. Office: Diane Herbs PhD LLC 1771 E Flamingo Ste 112B Las Vegas NV 89119 Office Phone: 702-641-2422.

HERBST, PATRICIA CARLISLE, lay worker; b. Pitts., July 21, 1933; d. Burton Samuel and Katherine (Schiffhauer) Carlisle; m. Richard Joseph Herbst Sr.; children: Patricia Rae, Tracy Lynn, Karen Kay, Gregory Paul, Richard Joseph Jr. BA in Theology, Allentown Coll. St. Francis deSales, 1993; MA in Holistic Spirituality/Spiritual Direction, Chestnut Hill Coll., 1994. Dir. of vols. Presbyn. Homes We. N.Y., 1978-82; dir. religious edn. Holy Ghost Ch., Bethlehem, Pa., 1982-89; pvt. practice spiritual dir. Bethlehem, Pa., 1986—; pastoral minister Ch. Assumption Blessed Virgin Mary, Bethlehem, Pa., 1990—; spiritual dir. Ch. Renewal Ctr., Allentown, Pa., 1993—. Cons. Diocesan Exec. Youth Bd., Allentown, Pa., 1985-89; chair, bd. Ea. Pa. Dir. Religious Edn. Conf., Allentown, 1983-89; chair vol. seminar U. Buffalo, 1980; organizer charter office Vol. Adminstrs. We. N.Y., 1979-82. Judge elections GOP, Chgo., 1960-64; bd. dirs. Mesh Cmty. Exchange, ShareCare Bethlehem, 2000—. Mem. Am. Counseling Assn., Assn. Transpersonal Psychologists, Spiritual Dirs. Internat. Roman Catholic. Avocations: tennis, bridge, reading. Home: 1290 Sycamore Ave Bethlehem PA 18017-1040

HERBSTREITH, YVONNE MAE, primary education educator; b. Wayne County, Ill., Aug. 18, 1942; d. Daniel Kirby and Rizpah Esther (Harvey) Smith; m. Bobbie L. Cates, Oct. 18, 1964 (div. 1969); 1 child, Shawn L.; m. Jerry Carrol Herbstreith, Sept. 15, 1979. BS, So. Ill. U., 1964. Cert. elem. tchr., Ill. Kindergarten tchr. Beardstown (Ill.) Elem., 1964-65, Pekin (Ill.) Pub. Schs. # 108, 1966-94. V.p. Pekin Friends of 47, 1986-91, pres. 1991-93, pres. Rebecca-Sarah Cir. 1st United Meth. Ch., Pekin, 1988—; trustee Sta. WTVP-TV, Peoria, Ill., 1990-91; active PTA, 1965-94, treas. 1992-93. Recipient Louise Alloy award Sta. WTVP, 1995. Mem. NEA (life), AAUW, Ill. Edn. Assn., Pekin Edn. Assn., Pekin Friends of Libr., Tazewell County Ret. Tchrs., Alpha Delta Kappa, Alpha Theta (chpt. pres. 1986-88, state sgt. at arms 1990-92, state chaplain 1992-94, state pres.-elect 1994-96, state pres. 1996—). Democrat. Methodist. Avocations: mystery books, reading, ceramics, crafts, photography, traveling. Home: 1922 Quail Hollow Rd Pekin IL 61554-6351

HERERA, SUE, television host; BA in Journalism, Calif. State U., Northridge. Anchor, reporter Fin. News Network CNBC, Ft. Lee, N.J., 1989, credit and futures market reporter The Money Wheel, co-anchor The money Wheel, Market Wrap, anchor The Edge, Host Bus. Tonight; anchor CNBS The Edge; co-anchor Market Wrap I. Author: Women of The Street: Making it on Wall Street-The World's Toughest Business, 1997. Office: CNBC Nat Broadcasting Co 2200 Fletcher Ave Fort Lee NJ 07024-5005

HERGENHAN, JOYCE, public relations executive; b. Mt. Kisco, N.Y., Dec. 30, 1941; d. John Christopher and Goldie (Wago) H. BA, Syracuse U., 1963; MBA, Columbia U., 1978. Reporter White Plains Reporter Dispatch, 1963-64; asst. to Rep. Ogden R. Reid Washington, 1964-68; reporter Gannett Newspapers, 1968-72; with Consol. Edison Co. of N.Y., Inc., N.Y.C., 1972-82, v.p., 1977-79, sr. v.p. pub. affairs, 1979-82; v.p. corp. pub. relations General Electric Co., Fairfield, Conn., 1982-98; pres. GE Found., 1998—. Trustee Syracuse U., 1996-; bd. dirs. Civilian Pub. Affairs Coun., U.S. Mil. Acad. at West Point, 1990-, Jackie Robinson Found. 2001, Conn. Audubon Soc., Inner City Found. for Edn. and Charity; past chmn. Pub. Rels. Seminar. Recipient Lifetime Achievement award, Women in Communications, 1999. Office: GE 3135 Easton Tpke Fairfield CT 06431-0002

HERGO, JANE ANTOINETTE, piano educator, composer; b. Dayton, Ohio, Apr. 16, 1946; d. Frank Gustav and Antoinette Rosalyn (Jean) Hergo. BMus, U. Dayton, 1968, BS in Music Edn., 1975; MMus, Wright State U., 1980. Cert. music tchr., Ohio. Kindergarten tchr., Englewood, Ohio, 1971-73; elem. tchr. Dayton, Ohio, 1976-77, 78-81; class piano instr. Sinclair C.C., Dayton, Ohio, summer 1981, piano accompanist for ballet and modern dance, 1983-84; ind. piano tchr. Dayton, Ohio, 1964—. Composer (book) Five Finger Frolics, 1988, Keyboard Confections, 1992 (sheet music) Gems on the Lake, 1991 (Ohio Music Tchrs. Assn. award 1990), Skeleton Skedaddle, 1993 (hon. mention award composition contest), Forest in the Rain (hon. mention award composition contest), Jazz Spooks (hon. mention award composition contest), Ghostly Gatherine, 1991, Chilipeppers, 1998, Snowswirls, 2002 (hon. mention award composition contest). Piano soloist Dayton Philharm. Designer Show House, 1985, 87; adjudicator Jr. Music Club Festivals, Dayton, 1989—. Recipient Jr. Composer award Ohio Fedn. Music Club, 1998, Piano Compositions awards Key Piano Mag., 1990, 93, Merit award Nat. Fedn. Music Clubs, 1990. Mem. ASCAP, Music Tchrs. Nat. Assn. (nat. cert.), Ohio Music Tchrs. Assn. (officer student composition sect. Western dist. 1988-90, composition panel 1989, state conv. 1992), Jr. Music Club, Dayton Music Club (composer), Sigma Alpha Iota. Avocations: emboidery, drawing, sewing, reading, flower gardening.

HERING, DORIS MINNIE, dance critic; b. N.Y.C., Apr. 11, 1920; d. Harry and Anna Elizabeth (Schwenk) H. BA cum laude, Hunter Coll., 1941; MA, Fordham U., 1985. Freelance dance writer, 1946-52; assoc. editor, prin. critic Dance mag., N.Y.C., 1952-72; exec. dir. Nat. Assn. for Regional Ballet, N.Y.C., 1972-87; adj. assoc. prof. dance history NYU, 1968-78; freelance dance writer, lectr., cons., 1987—. Mem. dance panel NEA, 1972-75, cons., 1991—; mem. dance panel N.Y. State Coun. Arts, 1992-96, program auditor, 1997—; bd. dirs. Walnut Hill Sch., 1975—, Internat. Ballet Competition, 1981—; hon. bd. dirs. Phila. Dance Alliance, 1980—; cons. Regional Dance Am.; adj. assoc. prof. dance history NYU Grad. Sch. Ed. Author: 25 Years of American Dance, 1950, Dance in America, 1951, Wild Grass, 1965, Giselle and Albrecht, 1981; sr. editor Dance mag., 1989—. Howard D. Rothschild Rsch. fellow Harvard U., 1991-93; recipient 33d ann. Capezio Dance Found. award for lifetime svc., 1985, Award of Distinction Dance mag., 1987, Sage Cowles Land Grant chair in dance U. Minn., 1993, Sr. Critics tribute Dance Critics Assn., 2002, Annual award, Martha Hill Dance Fund, 2002; named to Hunter Coll. Alumni Hall of Fame, 1986. Mem. Dance Critics Assn., Assn. Dance History Scholars, Phi Beta Kappa, Chi Tau Epsilon (hon.). Office Phone: 212-787-3834.

HERLIHY, MAURA ANN, psychology technician; b. Yokohama, Japan, July 13, 1953; d. Joseph Brendan and Margaret Cecilia (Corrigan) H. AA in Liberal Arts, Middlesex Community Coll., 1973; BA in Elem. Edn., Rivier Coll., 1975, MA in Counseling, 1986. Sub. tchr. Bedford (Mass.) Pub. Schs., 1975-76; sec. Instrumentation Labs., Lexington, Mass., 1976-77, Electronized Chems. Corp., Burlington, Mass., 1977-78, Digital Equipment Corp., Bedford, Mass., 1978-80; sales clk. Lord and Taylor, Burlington, 1979-81; sec. Dept. VA, Bedford, 1980-89, psychology technician, 1989—. Mem.: DAV Aux, Women Affirming Life, Inc., Nat. Right to Life Assoc., North Am. Bluebird Soc., Mass. Audubon Soc., Feminists for Life of Am., Mass. Bluebird Assoc., Am. Birding Assoc., Sierra Club, Applachian

Mountain Club. Roman Catholic. Avocations: reading, sewing, piano, music. Home: 426 Great Elm Way Acton MA 01718-1005 Office: Dept Vet Affairs 200 Springs Rd Bedford MA 01730-1114

HERMAN, ALEXIS M. former secretary of labor; b. Mobile, Ala., July 16, 1947; BA, Xavier U., New Orleans, 1969. Founder, CEO A.M. Herman & Assocs., Washington; nat. dir. Minority Women's Employment Program, Washington, until 1977; dir. Women's Bur. Dept. Labor, Washington, 1977-81; chief staff, then dep. chair Dem. Nat. Conv. Com., Washington, until 1991, CEO, 1991-92; dep. dir. Clinton-Gore Presdl. Transition Office, Washington, 1992-93; asst. to President U.S., Pub. Liaison dir. White House, Washington, 1993-96; sec. labor U.S. Dept. Labor, Washington, 1997-2001; chmn. & CEO New Ventures, Inc., DC, 2001—; chairperson Coca-Cola Human Resources Diversity Task Force, Ga., 2001—; chmn. Toyota North Amer. Diversity Bd., 2002—. Mem. bd. dirs. Entergy Corp., 2003—, Cummins Inc., President Life Insurance Co., MGM Mirage. Recipient Sara Lee Front Runner award, 1999. Mem. Nat. Coun. Negro Women, Delta Sigma Theta. Democrat.*

HERMAN, ANDREA MAXINE, newspaper editor; b. Chgo., Oct. 22, 1938; d. Maurice H. and Mae (Baron) H.; m. Joseph Schmidt, Oct. 28, 1962. BJ, U. Mo., 1960. Feature writer Chgo.'s Am., 1960-63; daily columnist News Am., Balt., 1963-67; feature writer Mainichi Daily News, Tokyo, 1967-69; columnist Iowa City Press-Citizen, 1969-76; music and dance critic San Diego Tribune, 1976-84; asst. mng. editor features UPI, Washington, 1984-86, asst. mng. editor news devel., 1986-87; mng. editor features L.A. Herald Examiner, 1987-91; editor/culture We/Mbl Newspaper, Washington, 1991—. Recipient 1st and 2d prizes for features in arts James S. Copley Ring of Truth Awards, 1982, 1st prize for journalism Press Club San Diego, 1983. Mem. Soc. Profl. Journalists, Am. Soc. Newspaper Editors, AP Mng. Editors, Women in Communications. Avocations: music, art. Office: We Mbl Newspaper 1350 Connecticut Ave NW Washington DC 20036-1722 Office Phone: 858-459-3265.

HERMAN, EDITH CAROL, journalist; b. Edgewood, Md., July 1, 1944; d. Herbert R. and Thirza E. (Simmons) H.; m. Leonard Wiener. BA, Purdue U., 1966. Reporter Hollister Newspaper Chain, Wilmette, Ill., 1966-68, Chgo. Tribune Newspaper, 1968-79, edn. editor, 1971-74, feature writer, 1976-79; sr. editor TV Digest Inc., 1980-83; pub. rels. mgr. AT&T, 1983-90; pub. rels. cons. Bethesda, 1990—93, Warren Comm., 1994—, assoc. mng. editor, 2001—. Bd. dirs. Sigma Delta Chi Found. of Washington, 1990-92. Recipient Journalism award Ill. Edn. Assn., 1969-70; Editorial award Ill. Automatic Merchandising Council, 1977 Mem. Soc. Profl. Journalists. Home: 5501 Burling Ct Bethesda MD 20817-6309 E-mail: eherman@warren-news.com.

HERMAN, ELIZABETH MULLEE, elementary school educator; b. N.Y.C., May 1, 1939; d. Raymond Garrett and Theresa (Lang) Mullee; m. Paul Herman, Feb. 10, 1962; children: Susan DeAlejos, Christina Cylwik, Andrew, Marianne Schell, Jane (dec.). BA, Manhattanville Coll., Purchase, N.Y., 1960; MA, Columbia U., 1962; Cert. Advanced Study, Sacred Heart U., Fairfield, Conn.; Pimms scholar, Wesleyan U., 1990-93. Tchr. Birch Wathen Sch., N.Y.C., 1960-61, Madison Jr. High Sch., Trumbull, Conn., 1978-79, Holy Rosary Sch., Bridgeport, Conn., 1979-82, St. Theresa Sch., Trumbull, 1982-88, Roosevelt Sch., Bridgeport, 1988-94, Maplewood Annex Sch., Bridgeport, 1994-99. Mem. Secular Order Franciscans. Mem. NEA, APA, Bridgeport Ret. Tchrs. Assn. Roman Catholic. Avocations: ancient ruins, swimming, sheltering abused and abandoned cats. Home: 144 Plymouth Ave Trumbull CT 06611-4152

HERMAN, JAYNE E. music educator; b. Huntington, N.Y., Jan. 20, 1951; d. Alice M. and Frank W. Thurber; m. Nicholas R. Herman, II, June 30, 1973; children: Scott Alan, Matthew Frank. MusB in Music Edn., Bowling Green State U., 1972, MusM, 1992. Elem. music specialist Mason Consol. Schs., Erie, Mich., 1992—; adj. faculty Monroe C.C., Monroe, Mich., 2000—03. Assessment cons. Milw. Symphony ACE Project, 1990—2000. Regional coord. Region 17 Sweet Adelines, Ohio, 1999—2003. Mem.: Music Educators Nat. Conf., Sweet Adelines Internat. Roman Catholic. Avocations: aviation, barbershop music, needlecrafts, reading. Home: 6508 Black Diamond Lane Lambertville MI 48144 Office: Mason Consolidated Schs 2400 Mason Eagles Dr Erie MI 48133 Personal E-mail: jnherman@att.net.

HERMAN, JOAN ELIZABETH, healthcare company executive; b. N.Y.C., June 2, 1953; d. Roland Barry and Grace Gales (Goldstein) H.; m. Richard M. Rasiej, July 16. 1977. AB, Barnard Coll., 1975; MS, Yale U., 1977. Actuarial student Met. Life Ins. Co., N.Y.C., 1978-82; asst. actuary Phoenix Mut. Life Ins. Co. (now Phoenix Life Ins.), Hartford, Conn., 1982-83; assoc. actuary, dir. underwriting rsch. Phoenix Mut. Life Ins. Co., Hartford, 1983-84, 2d v.p., 1984-85, v.p., 1985-89, sr. v.p., 1989-98; pres. splty. bus. WellPoint Health Networks, Woodland Hills, Calif., 1998, group pres., 1999—2001, pres., sr. splty. and state sponsored programs divsn., 2002—. Bd. dirs. PM Holdings, Inc., Phoenix Group Holdings, Inc., Phoenix Am. Life Ins. Co., Emprendimiento Compartido, S.A., v.p., BC Life & Health Co., Profl. Claims Svcs Inc., Proserv., MEDIX. Contbr. articles to profl jours. Capt. fundraising team Greater Hartford Arts Coun., 1986; bd. dirs. Hadassah, Glastonbury, Conn., Temple Beth Hillel, South Windsor, Conn., 1983-84, Children's Fund Conn., 1992-98, My Sister's Place, Shelter, Hartford, 1989-94, Western Mass. Regional Nat. Conf. Conn., 1995-98, Greater Hartford Arts Coun., 1997-98; bd. dirs. Hartford Ballet, 1989-95, corporator, 1995-98; bd. dirs. Leadership Greater Hartford, 1989-94, chmn. bd. dirs., 1993-94, bd. dirs. Health Ins. Assn. Am., 2002-03, So. Calif. Leadership Network, 2003—; mem. bd. founders Am. Leadership Forum of Hartford, 1991-98; corporator Hartford Sem., 1994-98. Fellow Soc. Actuaries (chairperson health sect. coun. 1994-95); mem. Am. Acad. Actuaries (bd. dirs. 1994-97), Am. Leadership Forum. Jewish. Avocations: reading, swimming, bicycling, jogging, aerobic dancing, hiking. Office: Wellpoint Health Networks 1 Wellpoint Way Thousand Oaks CA 91362-3893 Office Phone: 805-557-6333. E-mail: joan.herman@wellpoint.com.

HERMAN, MARY MARGARET, neuropathologist; b. Plymouth, Wis., July 26, 1935; d. Elmer Fredolein and Esther Lydia (Bross) H.; m. Lucien Jules Rubinstein, Jan. 31, 1969. BS in Med. Sci., U. Wis., 1957, MD, 1960. Diplomate Nat. Bd. Med. Examiners, Am. Bd. Anatomic Pathology, Am. Bd. Neuropathology. Intern Mary Hitchcock Meml. Hosp., Hanover, N.H., 1960-61; resident in neurology U. Wis. Hosps., 1961-62; intern in pathology Yale U., New Haven, 1962-63, asst. resident in pathology, 1963-64, fellow neuropathology, 1964-65, rsch. assoc. pathology, 1967-68; fellow neuropathology Stanford U., Palo Alto, Calif., 1965-66, fellow, acting instr. neuropathology, 1966-67, asst. prof. pathology, 1967-74, assoc. prof., 1974-81; prof., co-dir. divsn. neuropathology U. Va. Sch. Medicine, Charlottesville, 1981-91, prof. clin. pathology, 1991-92; spl. expert neuropathology in clin. brain disorders br. NIMH, Washington, 1991-96, sr. staff scientist, 1996—; neuropathologist NIMH Brain Collection, 1992—, Stanley Fund Brain Collection, 1992—2002. Vis. asst. prof. Albert Einstein Coll. Medicine, Bronx, NY, 1971—72; mem. program project rev. com. Nat. Inst. Neurol. and Communicative Diseases NIH, 1973—77; cons. lab. svc. VA Hosp., Salem, Va., Ctrl. Va. Tng. Ctr., Lynchburg, 1982—92, ad hoc mem. pathology A study sect., 1986—91; cons. neuropathologist D.C. Med. Examiner's Office, Washington, 1992—, Med. Examiner's Office, No. Va. Dist., Fairfax, 2000—, D.C. Gen. Hosp., 1992—2002; mentor scientist NIH Intramural Rsch. Tng. award, Fogarty Fellows, Howard Hughes Med. Inst./MCPS/NIH student and tchr. internships program, Stanley Found. scholar's program. Mem. editl. bd.: Jour. Neuropathology and Exptl. Neurology, 1989—93, 2001—; contbr. over 190 articles to profl. jours. Recipient Rsch. Career Devel. award, NIH, 1967—72, Staff Recognition award, 2000—02, Faculty Devel. award, Merck Found., 1969. Mem. AAAS, AMA, Am. Assn. Anatomists (trust fund com.), Soc. Biol. Psychiatry, Am. Assn. Neuropathologists (Weil award 1974), Am. Soc. for Investigative Pathology, Soc. for Devel. Biology, Internat. Soc. Neuropathology, Am. Soc. Cell Biology (rsch. fellowship program, mentor scientist summer tchr. 1994), Internat. Acad. Pathology, Soc. In Vitro Biology, Soc. Neurosci. Achievements include research in neuropathology of serious mental disorders, neurodegeneration and aluminum neurotoxicity, and embryonal tumors of the CNS. Avocations: tennis, gardening, music. Home: 10008 Stedwick Rd Apt 304 Montgomery Village MD 20886-3718 Office: Clin Brain Disorders Br NIMH NIH Msc 4091 Bethesda MD 20892-4091 Office Phone: 301-480-0042. E-mail: mh230t@nih.gov.

HERMAN, MINDY, broadcast executive; d. Leonard and Flora Herman. BS in Economics, Warton Sch. Bus., U. Penn, 1982; JD, MBA, UCLA; student, London Sch. Economics. With News Corp., 1990—98; v.p. bus. affairs Twentieth Century Fox, 1990—93; sr. v.p. bus. affairs FX Networks, 1993—95; exec. v.p. bus. ops. Tele-TV, 1995—97; exec. v.p. Fox Television Studios, 1997—99; pres., CEO Viewer's Choice (renamed In Demand, 2000), 1999—2000, E! Networks, N.Y.C., 2000—. Recipient Women of Vision in Cable award, 2002, Larry Stewart Leadership and Inspiration award, Prism Awards, The Entertainment Industries Coun., 2004. Office: E! Networks 11 W 42d St Fl 19 New York NY 10036*

HERMAN, REBECCA LYNN, human resources specialist; b. Evansville, Ind., Apr. 30, 1960; d. Randy (Stepfather) and Sandra Goin, Richard Admire; 1 child, Trevor Laine. BSBA, U. Evansville, 1982; MA in Orgnl. Mgmt., U. Phoenix, 1997; postgrad., Capella U., 2003—. Quality control mgr. TJ Maxx, Evansville, Ind., 1985—91; facility mgr. Clayton's, 1991—93; gen. mgr. Laine's People Mover, San Diego, 1993—96; mgr., recruitment Maintenance Warehouse, 1998—2002, sr. mgr., human resources, 2002—. Adj. faculty Oakland City U., Evansville, 1991—93, Nat. U., San Diego, 1998—2000. Mem.: Employment Mgmt. Assn., Acad. Mgmt., Soc. Human Resources Mgmt., Alpha Omicron Pi (found. scholar 2003—, Rose award 1995, 2001, Presdl. citation 1981, Outstanding Svc. award 1996). Office: Maintenance Warehouse 10641 Scripps Summit Ct San Diego CA 92131

HERMANN, MILDRED L. artist; b. Bklyn., Mar. 8, 1920; d. Philip and May Atkin Lipskin; m. Arthur E. Hermann, June 27, 1942; children: Laurie Schwartzer, Elizabeth Schoenfeld, Jane Simons. Student, Bklyn. Coll., 1937—40, Artists in Am. Sch. Painting. One-woman shows include over 21 solo shows, Represented in permanent collections Albright-Knox Gallery, Buffalo, N.Y., Norton Mus. Art, West Palm Beach, Fla. Recipient Childe Hassam Purchase award, Am. Acad. Arts and Letters, 1978. Mem.: Audubon Artists (Mixed Media Painting award 1981), Nat. Assn. Women Artists. Address: Denise Bibro Fine Art 529 W 20th St 4th Fl New York NY 10011

HERMES, KATHERINE ANN, historian, history educator; b. Cin., 1959; d. William Anthony and Rose Helen Hermes. BA cum laude, U. Calif., Irvine, 1985; JD, Duke U., 1992; PhD, Yale U., 1995. Adj. prof. N.C. Ctrl. U., Durham, 1989-90; lectr. U. Otago, Dunedin, New Zealand, 1992-97; assoc. prof. Ctrl. Conn. State U., New Britain, 1997—, interim chair dept., 2001, interim coord. Polish studies, 2001—02. Editor: Australasian Jour. Am. Studies, 1995 (Fulbright Issue), Am. Jour. Legal History, 1999, Polish American Studies. The Many Legalities of Early America, 2001, Communities of Women, 2002, (with A. Maravel) (CD) The Litigious Scipio Brown, 2003; (book) Conn. History, rev. edit., 1999; exhbn. sculpture Moray Place Gallery, 1995; contbr. essays and papers to profl. publs. Election judge State of Calif., Orange County, 1984. Mem. AAUP (exec. coun. 2002—), Am. Hist. Assn., Assn. Study Conn. Hist. (bd. dirs. 2003), Orgn. Am. Historians. Office: Ctrl Conn State U 1615 Stanley St New Britain CT 06053-2439

HERMINGHOUSE, PATRICIA ANNE, foreign language educator; b. Melrose Park, Ill., Mar. 13, 1940; m. 1964; 2 children. BA, Knox Coll., 1962; MA, Washington U., 1965, PhD in German, 1968. Asst. prof. German U. Mo.-St. Louis, 1966-67, vis. lectr., 1968-69; asst. prof. Washington U., St. Louis, 1967-78, assoc. prof. German, 1978-83; Fuchs prof. German studies U. Rochester, NY, 1983—, chmn. dept. fgn. langs., lits. and linguistics, 1983—89. Lectr. German, Fontbonne Coll., 1965-66. Internat. Research & Exchanges Bd. ad hoc grantee, 1976. Editor or co-editor: Literatur der DDR in den siebziger Jahren, 1983, Literatur und Literaturtheorie in der DDR, 1976, Frauen im Mittelpunkt, 1987, Gender and Germaness, 1997, Ingeborg Bachmann and Christa Wolf, 1998, German Feminist Writings, 2000; editor GDR Bull., Newsletter Lit. and Culture in German Dem. Republic, 1975-83; co-editor: Women in German Yearbook, 1994-2002. Recipient Susan B. Anthony Lifetime Achievement award, 2003; sr. fellow, NEH, 1991. Mem. MLA, Am. Assn. Tchrs. German (exec. coun. 1979-81), German Studies Assn. (exec. com., v.p./pres. 2001-02, pres. 2003-04), Coalition Women German (coord. 1974-75, nat. steering. com. 1976-79, 94-2002), Assn. Depts. Fgn. Langs. (exec. com.). Address: U Rochester Dept Modern Lang and Cultures Rochester NY 14627 E-mail: pahe@troi.cc.rochester.edu.

HERNANDEZ, AILEEN C(LARKE), urban consultant; b. Bklyn., May 23, 1926; d. Charles Henry and Ethel Louise (Hall) Clarke; divorced. AB in Sociology and Polit. Sci. magna cum laude, Howard U., 1947; MA in Pub. Adminstrn. with honors, Calif. State U., L.A., 1961; LHD (hon.), So. Vt. Coll., 1979. From organizer to dir. edn. and pub. rels. Internat. Ladies' Garment Workers' Union, Calif., 1950-61; asst. chief Calif. div. Fair Employment Practices, 1962-65; appointed commr. U.S. EEOC, Washington, 1965-66; prin. Aileen C. Hernandez Assocs., San Francisco, 1966—. Rsch. asst. dept. govt. Howard U., 1948; specialist in labor edn., lectr. U.S. Dept. State, 1960; mem. internat. conf. on minorities and the metropolis Konrad Adenauer Found./U.S. Dept. State, 1975; mem. Nat. Commn. on Study of People's Republic of China, 1978, Nat. Commn. on Am. Fgn. Policy Towards South Africa, 1981; advisor BART impact study com. Nat. Acad. Engring.; commr. Bay Vision 2020, 1990-93; vice chair San Francisco 2000; lectr. polit. sci. U. Calif., Berkeley, UCLA, San Francisco State U. Columnist Washington Tribune, 1946-47; contbr. commn. report South Africa: Time Running Out, 1981. Coord. Senator Alan Cranston's campaign for State Controller of Calif., 1961; chair Working Assets Money Fund; co-chair Nat. Urban Coalition, bd. dirs. Death Penalty Focus; vice chair nat. adv. couns. ACLU; coord. San Francisco African Am. Agenda Coun.; mem. adv. bd. Program for Rsch. on Immigration Policy; mem. nat. adv. coun. Nat. Inst. for Women of Color; bd. dirs. Ctr. for Women Policy Studies; mem. Citizens Commn. on Civil Rights; treas. Eleanor R. Spikes Meml. Fund; active San Franciscans Seeking Consensus, 1982—; founding mem., chair Coalition for Econ. Equity; chair Sec's. Adv. Com. on Rights and Responsibilities of Women; officer, bd. dirs. Mt. Zion Hosp.; bd. dirs. Westside Community Mental Health Ctr.; chair Calif. Coun. Humanities; founding mem. Nat. Women's Polit. Caucus, Black Women Organized for Action, Bay Area Black Women United, Nat. Hook-Up of Black Women; bd. dirs., project dir. Nat. Com. Against Discrimination in Housing; mem. housing com. Assn. Bay Area Govts.; chmn. Ctr. Common Good, Calif. Women's Agenda; bd. dirs. Wellesley Ctrs. for Rsch.; bd. Ctr. Govtl. Studies. Named Woman of Yr., Cmty. Rels. Conf. So. Calif. 1961, One of Ten Most Disting. Women in the San Francisco Bay Area, San Francisco Examiner, 1969, One of Ten Women Who Make a Difference, San Francisco LWV, 1985; recipient Disting. Postgrad. Achievement award Howard U., 1968, disting. svcs. to urban cmtys. award Nat. Urban Coalition, 1985, Bicentennial award Trinity Bapt. Ch., 1976, humanitarian svcs. award Glide Meml. United Meth. Ch., 1986, appreciation awards Nat. Inst. for Women of Color, 1987, Western Dist. Conf. of Nat. Assn. Negro Bus. and Profl. Women's Clubs, 1988, San Francisco Conv. and Visitors Bur., Parren J. Mitchell award San Francisco Black C. of C., 1985, Silver Spur award, Wise Woman award Ctr. for Women Policy Studies, Women of Achievement award, Vison and Excellence award, Earl Warren Civil Liberties award ACLU, 1989, others. Mem. NAACP (life), NOW (past nat. pres.), Ms. Found. for Women (bd. dirs.), Bay Area Urban League (past bd. dirs.), Urban Inst. (life trustee), Gamma Phi Delta (hon.), Alpha Kappa Alpha. Office: Aileen C Hernandez Assocs 818 47th Ave San Francisco CA 94121-3208 Personal E-mail: aileenfem@aol.com.

HERNANDEZ, ANN MARGARET, education educator; b. Williamsport, Pa., Feb. 19, 1939; d. Adam E. and Helen A. (McMunn) Sieminski; m. Jorge E. Hernandez, June 20, 1970; children: James, Natalia, David. BS in Edn., Ohio U., 1961; MEd in Adminstrn., Pa. State U., 1969; EdD in Instrnl. Leadership, U. Ala., 1984. Tchr. Greenwich (Conn.) Sch. Sys., 1961-65, L.A. (Calif.) City Schs., 1965-66, Colegio Bolivar, Cali, Colombia, 1966-68, elem. prin., 1968-88; dir. early childhood and lower sch. Canterbury Sch., Ft. Wayne, Ind., 1988-95; assoc. prof. edn. U. St. Francis, Ft. Wayne, Ind., 1995—. Adj. prof. Ind. Vocat. Tech. Coll., Ft. Wayne, 1989-95, Ind. U.-Purdue U., Ft. Wayne, 1993-95; bd. dirs. WFWA-TV Pub. Broadcasting, Ft. Wayne, 1995-97; presenter and cons. in field. Bd. dirs. Found. Art & Music in Elem. Schs., 1997-2003. Named Nat. Disting. Prin., U.S. Dept. Edn., 1987. Mem. ASCD, So. Assn. Colls. and Schs. (evaluator for overseas schs.), Phi Delta Kappa, Kappa Delta Pi. Home: 7012 Blake Dr Fort Wayne IN 46804-1016 Office: Univ of St Francis 2701 Spring St Fort Wayne IN 46808-3939

HERNANDEZ, ANTONIA, lawyer; b. Torreon, Coahuila, Mexico, May 30, 1948; came to U.S., 1956; d. Manuel and Nicolasa (Martinez) H.; m. Michael Stern, Oct. 8, 1977; children: Benjamin, Marisa, Michael. BA, UCLA, 1971, JD, 1974. Bar: Calif. 1974, D.C. 1979. Staff atty. Los Angeles Ctr. Law and Justice, 1974-77; directing atty. Legal Aid Found., Lincoln Heights, Calif., 1977-78; staff counsel U.S. Senate Com. on the Judiciary, Washington, 1979-80; assoc. counsel Mexican Am. Legal Def. Ednl. Fund, Washington, 1981-83, employment program dir., 1983-84, exec. v.p., dep. gen. counsel Los Angeles, 1984-85, pres., gen. counsel, 1985—. Bd. dirs. Golden West Financial Corp., Automobile Club of So. Calif., Am. Charities. Contbr. articles to profl. jours. Active Inter-Am. Dialogue Aspen Inst., Nat. Com. Innovations in State and Local Govt., Nat. Endowment for Democracy, Pres.'s Commn. White House Fellowships. AAUW fellow, 1973-74. Mem. ABA, State Bar Calif., Washington D.C. Bar Assn., Mexican-Am. Roman Catholic. Avocations: gardening, outdoor sports. Office: Mexican Am Legal Def Ednl Fund 634 S Spring 11th Fl Los Angeles CA 90014-3921

HERNANDEZ, CHRISTINE, educational consultant; b. San Antonio, July 23, 1951; d. Joe and Aurora (Zapata) H. BA, Our Lady of the Lake Coll., 1973; MA, U. Tex., 1981. Cert. elem. tchr. Tchr. San Antonio Ind. Sch. Dist., 1973-83; pres. San Antonio Fedn. of Tchrs., 1983-86; ednl. cons. Bexar County Fedn. Tchrs., San Antonio, 1986-90; regional dir. U.S. Dept. Health and Human Svcs., Dallas. Dir. Southwest Policy Leaders Forum, Ctr. Policy Alternatives, 1999—. Mem. Dist. 124 Tex. Ho. of Reps., 1991-99, mem. legis. budget bd., 1994-99, select. com. on revenue & pub. edn. funding, 1997-99, calendars com., 1997-99, mem. appropriations com., 1993-99, mem. pub. edn. com., 1993-99; bd. edn. San Antonio Ind. Sch. Dist., 1986-91; pub. mem. bd. dirs. State Bar Tex., 1989-92; bd. dirs. So. Regional Coun., 1990-98, mem. exec. com., 1993-95, v.p., 1995-98; bd. dirs. Target '90 Goals for San Antonio, 1987-91, Providence High Sch., 1987-90; bd. dirs. Tex. Lyceum, 1990-97, sec., 1991-93, v.p. 1993-94; exec. com. San Antonio River Corridor com., 1987-89, Govs. Commn. for Women, 1985-87, Tex. Task Force on Indigent Health Care, 1983-84; bd. mgrs. Bexar County Hosp. Dist., 1982-84; bd. review Hist. Dists. and Landmarks, 1981-82; task force Southland Corps. Coll. Program, 1985; mem. San Antonio Commn. on Literacy, 1987-89; trustee United Way, 1988—; founder, pres. La'Tina Found., 1997—, San Antonio-Mex. Found. for Edn., 1997-99; mem. nat. adv. bd. Found. for Women's Resources, 1993-95. Named Hispanic Woman of Yr., 1984, Young Woman of Promise, Good Housekeeping Mag., 1985, Sunday's Woman, S.A. Light, 1985, Alumnus of Yr., U. Tex., San Antonio, 1992, Friend of Bus., Tex. C. of C., 1994, San Antonio Women's Hall of Fame, 1992; recipient Outstanding Leadership award YWCA, 1989, Spirit of the Am. Woman award J.C. Penney Co., 1992, Pacesetter award Stennis Ctr. for Pub. Svc., 1998. Mem. Tex. Assn. Sch. Bds. (bd. trustees 1989-90), Leadership Am. Alumnae Assn., Hispanic Women's Network of Tex. (bd. dirs.), Leadership San Antonio Alumni Assn., Tex. Women's Forum, Any Baby Can Alliance, Leadership Tex. Alumnae Assn., San Antonio 100 (charter), Am. Fedn. Tchrs. (v.p. 1978-81, treas. 1981-83, pres. 1983-86). Democrat. Roman Catholic. Avocations: traveling, reading novels and biographies. Office: US Dept Health and Human Svcs 1301 Young St Ste 1124 Dallas TX 75202-5433

HERNANDEZ, IRIS N. clinical specialist; b. Arecibo, P.R., June 1, 1953; d. Israel Hernandez and Dolores Rodriguez; divorced; children: Zobeida Despiau, Jessica Despiau. ADN cum laude, Arecibo Regional Coll., 1972, BSN cum laude, 1982; MSN, U. P.R., 1985. RN, P.R., Md. Dir. nursing Manati (P.R.) Dr. Ctr. Hosp., 1985-87; emergency rm. nurse Md. Health Care Sys., Balt., 1987-88, clin. specialist in medicine, 1988-89, case mgr. medicine, 1989-90, nurse mgr., 1990-92, clin. specialist oncology, 1992—. Instr. UIC, Guatemala/Honduras, 1998, 2000. Instr. youth group Edgewood (Md.) Army Post, 1996—. Maj. U.S. Army, 1989—. Mem. NAFE, ANA, Nat. Oncology Nurses Assn. (membership award 1995), Greater Balt. Oncology Nurses. Avocations: dance, running, reading, friends, cooking. Home: 410 Sugarberry Ct Edgewood MD 21040-3555 Office: Md Health Care Sys 10 N Green St Baltimore MD 21201

HERNANDEZ, JO FARB, music director, consultant; b. Chgo., Nov. 20, 1952; BA in Polit. Sci. & French with honors, U. Wis., 1974; MA in Folklore and mythology, UCLA, 1975; postgrad., U. Calif., Davis, 1978, U. Calif., Berkeley, 1978-79, 81. Registration Mus. Cultural History UCLA, 1974-75; Rockefeller fellow Dallas Mus. Fine Arts, 1976-77; asst. to dir. Triton Mus. Art, Santa Clara, Calif., 1977-78, dir., 1978-85; adj. prof. mus. studies John F. Kennedy U., San Francisco, 1978; grad. advisor arts adminstrn. San Jose (Calif.) State U., 1979-80; dir. Monterey (Calif.) Peninsula Mus. Art, 1985-93, cons. curator, 1994—2000; prin. Curatorial and Mus. Mgmt. Svcs., Watsonville, Calif., 1993—. Cons.SPACES (Saving and Preserving Art and Cultural Environ.), 2000—; nominator Creative Works Fund, 2001; adj. prof. gallery mgmt. art dept. U. Calif., Santa Cruz, 1999—; cons. Archives Am. Art., 1998—2000; dir. Thompson Gallery, San Jose State U., 2000—; lectr., panelist, juror, panelist in field USIA, Calif. Arts Coun., Calif. Confedn. for Arts, Am. Assn. Mus., Western Mus. Assn., Am. Folklore Soc., Calif. Folklore Soc., Internat. Coun. on Mus., others; vis. lectr. U. Wis., 1980, U. Chgo., 1981, Northwestern U., 1981, San Jose State U., 1985, UCLA, 1986, Am. Cultural Ctr., Jerusalem, 1989, Tel Aviv, 89, Binational Ctr., Lima, Peru, 1988, Daytona Beach Mus. Art, 1983, UCLA, 1986, Israel Mus., 1989, Mont. State U., 1991, Oakland Mus., 1996, High Mus. Art, Atlanta, 1997, Mus. Am. Folk Art, NY, 1998, San Francisco Mus. Modern Art, 1998, U. Calif., 1998, Grinnell Coll., Iowa, 1999, Arts Coun. Silicon Valley, 2000, U. Calif., Santa Cruz, 2000, ICOM, Barcelona, 2001, Intuit Gallery, Chgo., 2004, Chgo., 04; guest curator San Diego Mus. Art, 1995—98; guest on various TV and radio programs. Author: (mus. catalogs) The Day of the Dead: Tradition and Change in Contemporary Mexico, 1979, Three from the Northern Island: Contemporary Sculpture from Hokkaido, 1984, Crime and Punishment: Reflections of Violence in Contemporary Art, 1984, The Quiet Eye: Pottery of Shoji Hamada and Bernard Leach, 1990, Alan Shepp: The Language of Stone, 1991, Wonderful Colors: The Paintings of August Francois Gay, 1993, Jeannette Maxfield Lewis: A Centennial Celebration, 1994, Armin Hansen, 1994, Jeremy Anderson: The Critical Link/A Quiet Revolution, 1995, A.G. Rizzoli: Architect of Magnificent Visions, 1997 (one of 10 Best Books in field Amazon.com), Misch Kohn: Beyond the Tradition, 1998, Fire and Flux: An

Undaunted Vision/The Art of Charles Strong, 1998, Mel Ramos: The Galatea Series, 2000, Holly Lane: Small Miracles, 2001, Irvin Tepper: When Cups Speak/Life with the Cup, 2002; co-author: Sam Richardson: Color in Space, 2002, Marc D'Estout: Domestic Objects, 2003; mem. internat. editl. bd. Raw Vision Mag., 2001—; contbr. articles to profl. publs. [illegible] of San Jose, 1981-83, Santa Clara Arts and Hist. Consortium, 1985, Non-Profit Gallery Assn., 1979-83, v.p., 1979-80; mem. nat. adv. bd. The Fund for Folk Culture, Santa Fe, 1995-98; mem. founding and exec. bd. Alliance for Calif. Traditional Arts, 2002—; mem. founding internat. adv. bd. Friends of Fred Smith, 2002—. Recipient Golden Eagle award, Coun. Internat. Non-theatrical Events, 1992, Leader of Decade award, Arts Leadership Monterey Peninsula, 1992, merit award, N.Y. Book Show, 1997; Rsch. grantee, Calif. State U., 2001, 2002, 2003, Dean's grantee, 2001, Lottery Fund grantee, 2000, 2004. Mem.: Nat. Coun. for Edn. in Ceramic Arts, Western Mus. Conf. (bd. dir., exec. com. 1989—91, program chair 1990), Am. Folklore Soc., Art Table, Calif. Assn. Mus. (bd. dirs. 1985—94, v.p. 1987—91, chair nominating com. 1988, chair ann. meeting 1990, chair nominating com. 1990, pres. 1991—92, chair nominating com. 1993), Am. Assn. Mus. (lectr. 1986, mus. assessment program surveyor 1990, nat. program com. 1992—93, mus. assessment program surveyor 1994), Phi Beta Kappa. Office: Curatorial Mus Mgmt Svcs 345 White Rd Watsonville CA 95076-0429 E-mail: jfh@cruzio.com.

HERNANDEZ, MADELINE, mental health services professional; b. Havana, Cuba, July 3, 1973; d. Mercedes and Luis Ramon Hernandez. M in Psychology with distinction, Carlos Albizu U., 1997, PhD in Clin. Psychology, 2001. Licensed Mental Health Counselor Fla. Dept. of Health and Med. Quality Assurance, 1999. Pres. South Fla. Psychol. Ctr., Inc., Hialeah, Fla., 2002—; psychotherapist GreenCross Health Systems, Inc, Coral Gables, Fla., 2000—; lic. clinician, assessment Citrus Health Network, Inc., Hialeah, Fla., 1999—; treatment plan coord. Palmetto North Health Ctr., Inc., Hialeah, Fla., 1996—99; psychotherapist Geriatric Services South Fla., Inc., Hialeah, Fla., 1993—96. Pres. South Fla. Psychol. Ctr., Inc., Hialeah, Fla., 2002—. Mem.: APA (licentiate). Achievements include correlational research on women's body image, performance and test-anxiety. Office: South Florida Psychological Center Inc 1800 West 49 St Suite 230 Hialeah FL 33012 Personal E-mail: mhernandezpsyd@yahoo.com. E-mail: mhernandezpsyd@yahoo.com.

HERNANDEZ, ROBIN RENEE, artist, graphics designer; b. Casablanca, Morocco, Sept. 19, 1959; d. Jerry Edward Jamison and Jamison-Sowers Betty, Tom Sowers (Stepfather); m. David William Hernandez, Sept. 9, 1998; children: Shannon Alissa Smith, Erica Renee Smith. Student, No. Va. C.C., 2002, George Mason U., 2003. Ticket and freight acctg. Air Midwest Airlines, Wichita, Kans., 1985—86; acctg. and bus. mgr. DDB Needham Worldwide Advt., McLean, 1986—90; owner Litho Lab, Inc., McLean, 1990—97; artist Robin Hernandez Art, McLean, Va., 1998—. Painting, A Fly on the Wall (First Pl., 2001), sculpture, Grandpa's Time Machine (Hon. Mention, 2001), Betula Nigra: A Memorial (Hon. Mention, 2002). COMPEER vol. Psychiat. Rehab. Svcs., Falls Church, Va., 1999—2000; election officer Bd. of Elections, Fairfax, Va., 1999—99; historian Alpha Beta Rho chpt. Phi Theta Kappa, Annandale, Va., 2000—01. Recipient Margaret Dellert scholarship, No. Va. Handcrafters Guild, 2002. Mem.: Nat. Mus. of Women in the Arts (assoc.), Corcoran Mus. of Art (assoc.). Liberal. Taoist. Avocations: ceramics, sculpting, painting, photography, foreign films. Personal E-mail: robin@robinhernandez.com. E-mail: robin@robinhernandez.com.

HERNDON, ALICE PATTERSON LATHAM, public health nurse; b. Macon, Ga., Dec. 18, 1916; d. Frank Waters and Ruby (Dews) Patterson; m. William Joseph Latham, July 21, 1940 (dec. Apr. 1981); children: Jo Alice Latham Miller, Marynette Latham Herndon, Lauruby Latham Herndon; 1 adopted child, Courtney Marie Herndon; m. Sidney Dumas Herndon, Apr. 26, 1985. Diploma, Charity Hosp. Sch. Nursing, New Orleans, 1937; student, George Peabody Tchrs. Coll., 1938-39; BS in Pub. Health Nursing, U. N.C., 1954; MPH, Johns Hopkins U., 1966. Staff pub. health nurse assigned spl. venereal disease study USPHS, Darien, Ga., 1939—40; county pub. health nurse Bacon County, Alma, Ga., 1940—41; USPHS spl. venereal disease project Glynn County, Brunswick, 1943—47, county pub. health nurse, 1949—51, Ware County, Waycross, 1951—52; pub. health nurse surp. Wayne-Long-Brantley-Liberty Counties, Jesup, 1954—56; dist. dir. pub. health nursing Wayne-Long-Appling-Bacon-Pierce Counties, Jesup, 1956—70; dist. chief nursing S.E. Ga. Health Dist., 1970—79, organizer mobile health svcs., 1973—. Founder, exec. dir. Wayne County Home Health Agy., 1968—80; exec. dir. Ware County Home Health Agy., 1970—79, mem. exec. com., 1978—85; mem. governing bd. S.E. Ga. Health Sys. Agy., 1975—82; organized and mem. governing bd. Health Dept. Home Health Agy., 1978—, also author numerous grant proposals; governing bd. Brunswick Civic Orch., 1993—97. Contbr. to state nursing manuals. Mem. adv. coun. Ware Meml. Hosp. Sch. Practical Nursing, Waycross, Ga., 1958; mem. Altar Guild St. Paul's Episc. Ch., 1979—86, vestrywoman, 1981—82; mem. Altar Guild St. Marks Episcopal Ch., Brunswick, Ga., 1994—2001; bd. dirs. Wayne County Mental Health Assn., 1959—61, 1981—82, Wayne County Tb Assn., 1958—62, a non-alcoholic organizer Jesup group Alcoholics Anonymous, 1962—63. Recipient recognition Gen. Svc. Bd., Alcoholics Anonymous, Inc. Fellow APHA; mem. ANA, 8th Dist. (pres. 1954-58, sec. 1958-60, dir. 1960-62, 1st v.p. 1962), Ga. Nurses Assn. (exec. bd. 1954-58, program rev. continuing edn. com. 1980-86, Dist. 21 Excellence in Nursing award 1994), Ga. Pub. Health Assn. (chmn. nursing sect. 1956-57), Ga. Assn. Dist. Chiefs Nursing (pres. 1976). Home: 192 Bluff Dr Brunswick GA 31523-6225

HERNDON, MERLE PUCKETTE, principal; b. Lynchburg, Va., Jan. 5, 1954; d. Walter William and Marion (Layne) Puckette; m. William Robertson Herndon III, June 19, 1976; children: William Robertson IV, Stuart Thomas, Caroline Whitney. BS in Elem. Edn., Averett Coll., 1974; MEd in Reading, Lynchburg Coll., 1977, EdS, 1986; EdD in Ednl. Leadership, U. Va., 1993. Cert. elem. tchr., prin., supt., reading specialist, devel. reading tchr., Va. Remedial math. and reading tchr. T. C. Miller Elem. Sch., 1974-75; remedial math. and reading tchr., reading specialist Dearington Elem. Sch.; reading specialist Linkhorne Elem. Sch., Lynchburg, Va., 1975-86, unit leader, 1984-86, staff devel. specialist, 1986-87, prin., 1987—; staff devel. specialist Lynchburg City Schs., 1986-87. Coord. partnership programs with bus. and Linkhorne Elem. Sch.; presenter in field. Mem. Madeline Hunter Inst., Williamsburg, Va., 1987; active Brookneal Elem. PTA, William Campbell Mid. Sch. PTA, Staunton River Hist. Soc.; past pres. Red Hill Garden Club; mem. adminstrv. coun. Brookneal Meth. Ch.; den leader Cub scouts Boy Scouts Am., Brookneal, 1986-89. Mem. ASCD, Piedmont Area Reading Coun., Va. Assn. Elem. Prins. (chmn. grand session 1992, mem. conf.), Nat. Assn. Elem. Prins. (Va. state del. to conv. 1992, session presider), Lynchburg Assn. Elem. Sch. Prins. (chair supt. and legislators forum 1989), Lynchburg Coll. Alumni Assn., Averett Coll. Alumni Assn., Optimist Club (chmn. youth essay contest 1988-90, project designer youth recognition program 1989—, children at risk ct. project 1988), Phi Delta Kappa, Kappa Delta Pi, Delta Kappa Gamma. Office: Linkhorne Elem Sch 2501 Linkhorne Dr Lynchburg VA 24503-3398 Home: 2286 Swinging Bridge Rd Brookneal VA 24528-2598

HERNREICH, NANCY, federal official; b. State College, Miss., July 27, 1946; d. Bernard Francis and Nancy Davis (Martin) McAvoy; m. Robert Eastman Hernreich, Sept. 21, 1968 (div. 1979); 1 child, Ashley Proulx. BA, Webster Coll., 1968; postgrad., Ark. State U. Social worker Jonesboro (Ark.) Sch. Dist., 1970-76; scheduling sec. Gov. of Ark., Little Rock, 1985-92; dep. asst. to pres., dir. Oval Office White House, Washington, 1993—. Mem. Ft. Smith Jr. League, Little Rock Jr. League; chmn. bd. Ft. Smith Pride; social worker, Jonesboro; bd. dirs. Big Bros./Big Sisters Ft. Smith, Spl. Olympics; mem. state steering com. Mondale for Pres.; mem. state Dem. Exec. Com.; del. Dem. Nat. Conv., 1980; election commr. Sebastion County; coord. Sebastion County Clinton Campaign, 1980, 82, 84; dir. March of Dimes Telethon, 1985; head state pub. affairs com. Jr. League. Democrat. Avocations: running, [illegible] 1600 Pennsylvania Ave NW Washington DC 20500-0004

HERNSTADT, JUDITH FILENBAUM, city planner, real estate executive, broadcasting executive; b. N.Y.C., Nov. 18, 1942; d. Alex and Ruth Selena (Silberman) Filenbaum. BA, NYU, 1964, M Urban and Regional Planning, 1966; cert. smaller co. mgmt. program, Harvard Bus. Sch., 1977. With Office Planning Coordination, State of N.Y., 1966-68; ptnr. Devel. Planning Assocs., N.Y.C., 1967-68; with engring. scis. dept. Svc. Bur. Corp., N.Y.C., 1968-69; planning cons. Llewelyn-Davies Assocs., N.Y.C., 1969-71, Arlen Realty & Devel. Corp., N.Y.C., 1971-73; ptnr. Planning & Devel. Team, N.Y.C. and Las Vegas, 1974—; v.p. Sta. KVVU-TV Nev. Ind. Broadcasting Corp., Las Vegas, 1974-75, pres., 1976-77, Hernstadt Broadcasting Corp., 1978-81. Chmn. adv. bd. Internat. Film and TV Exch., Inc.; mem. coun. Rockefeller U., 1998—. Condr. TV interview programs. Bd. dirs. Nat. Com. on Am. Fgn. Plicy, Decorative Arts Trust, 1980—98, Eastside Internat. Cmty. Ctr., 1988—96; bd. advisors ACORN Found.; mem. fine arts com. U.S. Dept. State, 1976—; del. Fine Arts Fedn. N.Y., 1970—90; mem. Hudson Inst., 1980—92. Mem. Internat. Film and TV Exch. (bd. dirs.), Harvard Club (N.Y.C.), Hadji Baba Soc., Lotos Club, Explorers Club. Home: 927 5th Ave New York NY 10021-2650

HEROLD, ROCHELLE SNYDER, early childhood educator; b. Bklyn., Oct. 6, 1941; d. Abe and Anna (Chazen) Snyder; m. Frederick S. Herold, May 7, 1966; children: David Marc, Caryn Michele. BA, Bklyn. Coll., 1963; MS, CCNY, 1968. Cert. tchr., N.Y.; cert. child-care provider, Fla. Tchr. N.Y.C. Pub. Schs., 1963-68; tchr., adminstr. Chanute AFB Pvt. Sch., Rantoul, Ill., 1970-72; dir. early childhood edn. Temple Solel, Hollywood, Fla., 1974-99, dir. social and ednl. programs for young couples, families and singles, 1995-99. Cons. bd. dirs. Temple Solel, 1982-99; nursery sch. com. PTO, 1982-89; lectr., coord. at tchr. seminars, parenting lecture series; freelance writer parenting mags. Author, illustrator: A Family Seder Through a Child's Eyes, 1984, Celebrating Shabbat in the Home, 1992, Choosing Chessie, 2000, Baby Bear Learns to Share, 2001, A Bear in the Brook, 2001, Seven Secrets of P-E-R-F-E-C-T Parenting, 2004. Mem. AMA Aux., Fla. Med. Assn. Aux., Temple Solel Sisterhood. Avocations: ventriloquism, arts and crafts, interior design, directing children's musical productions. E-mail: rsherold@aol.com.

HERR, PAMELA STALEY, writer, historian; b. Cambridge, Mass., July 24, 1939; d. A. Eugene and Phyllis (Parker) Staley; children: Christianna, Robin Elizabeth. BA magna cum laude, Harvard U.-Radcliffe Coll., 1961; MA, George Washington U., 1971. Writer, historian Field Ednl. Publs., Palo Alto, Calif., 1973; editor Sullivan Assocs., Palo Alto, 1973-74; project mgr. Sanford Assocs., Menlo Park, Calif., 1974-76; mng. editor Am. West mag., Cupertino, Calif., 1976-79; author, historian, 1980—. Author: Jessie Benton Frémont, 1987, paperback edit., 1988 (Spur award for best western nonfiction book Western Writers Am. 1987); editor: (with Mary Lee Spence) The Letters of Jessie Benton Frémont, 1992; bd. editors Western Hist. Quar., 1993-96. Grantee Nat. Hist. Publs. and Records Commn., Nat. Archives, 1989-91. Mem. Western History Assn., Phi Beta Kappa. Home: 559 Seale Ave Palo Alto CA 94301-3830

HERR, SHARON MARIE, librarian; b. St. Cloud, Minn., June 23, 1950; d. Lawrence James and Avis Christina (Klein) Blenkush; m. Dennis Wilfred Herr, June 8, 1985. BA cum laude, Coll. St. Benedict, 1972; MA in LS, U. Mich., 1974. Scheduling asst. South Jr. H.S., St. Cloud, 1968; asst. to libr. Coll. of St. Benedict, St. Joseph, Minn., 1972-73; sci. libr. Ohio No. U., Ada, 1974-78, cataloging libr., 1978—. Mem. univ. coun. Ohio No. U., Ada, 1989-91, 97-2001, mem. pers. com., 1979-80. Author essay. Judge elections Hardin County Bd. Elections, Kenton, Ohio, 1995-2001. Recipient Betty Crocker Homemaker award Gen. Mills, 1968. Mem.: ALA, Assn. Libr. Collections and Tech. Svcs., Assn. Coll. and Rsch. Librs., Ohio Hist. Soc., Smithsonian Instn. Democrat. Avocations: antiques, gardening, christmas tree ornament collecting, investing. Home: 822 S Johnson St Ada OH 45810-1521 Office: Ohio No U Ada OH 45810

HERRANEN, KATHY, artist; b. Zelienople, Pa., Dec. 22, 1943; d. John and Helen Elizabeth (Sayti) D'Biagio; m. John Warma Herranen, Dec. 31, 1974 (div. Feb. 1994); 1 child, Michael John. Student, Scottsdale (Ariz.) C.C., 1990—. Cert. tchr. art, State Bd. Dirs. for Cmty. Coll. of Ariz. Horseback riding instr. Black Saddle Riding Acad., Lancaster, Calif., 1960—65; tel. company supr. Bell Tel., Bishop, Calif., 1965; reporter, part-time photographer Ellwood City (Pa.) Ledger, 1967—70; back-country guide and cook Mammoth Lakes (Calif.) Pack Outfit, 1970; motel mgr. Mountain Property Mgmt., Mammoth Lakes, 1970—72; reporter, bookkeeper Hungry Horse (Mont.) News, 1973—74; pig farmer Columbia Falls, Mont., 1973—75; fine artist, illustrator, graphic designer Mont., Calif., and Ariz., 1980—; fine arts cons. Collector's Gallery, Galleri II, Yuma, Ariz., 1983—84; wind chime designer, creator Phoenix, 1995—; represented by Backstreet Furniture and Art, Phoenix, 1995—2001, Marcella's Ariz. Collection, Phoenix, 1995—2003, Hohn Gallery Fine Arts, Ltd., Scottsdale, Ariz., 1997—, Magickal Paths, Tempe, Ariz., 2003—04, Coomers Mall, Phoenix, 2003—, Wilson's Antiques, Coraopolis, Pa., 2003—. Guest lectr. Paradise Valley Tchrs Acad., Phoenix, 1993, Sr. Adult Edn. Program, Scottsdale (Ariz.) Cmty. Coll., 1994, pastel painting instr., 1996—; guest demonstrator Binder's Art Ctr., Scottsdale, 1995, Backstreet Furniture and Art, Phoenix, 1995-96; guest lectr., demonstrator Summer Edn. Program Paradise Valley Sch. Dist., 1996, 99, 2000; guest demonstrator Phoenix Artists Guild, 2000, Paradise Valley Artists, 2000. Solo shows include Pinnacle, Phoenix, 1993, Villas of Sedona, Ariz., 1995. Sec. Young Dems., Ellwood City, Pa., late 1960's, Vistas Home Owners Assn., Phoenix, 1995—; troubleshooter Maricopa County Elections Dept., Phoenix, 1994-96, 2000, 02, 03. Recipient 1st place award, Potpourri Artists, Yuma, Ariz., 1981, Subscriber award, Butte (Mont.) Arts Coun., 1981, 2d place award, Desert Artists, Yuma, 1982, hon. mention, Yuma County Fair, 1983, Wildlife Painting Exhibit, Scottsdale, 1993, Fountain Festival Juried Competitive exhbn. Fine Arts, 1993, Scottsdale Studio 13, 1991, 1992, Spl. award, 1993, Merit award, 1993, 2 Merit awards, 1994, 1st Pl. award, Phoenix Ctr. for the Arts, 2003. Mem. Nat. Assn. Sr. Friends Fine Artists (chair 1995-2003, honorable mention 1993, People's Choice award 1996, 1st place award, hon. mention, 2001), Women's Caucus for Art, Phoenix Artists Guild (hon. mention 2003), Ariz. Pastel Artists Assn. (charter mem., juried mem., membership chair 1995-96, 2002—, 2d v.p., show chair 1996, guest demonstrator 1995, guest lectr. 1998, Merit award 1995), Ariz. Art Alliance (juried mem., publicity chmn. 2000—), Artists and Craftsmen of Flathead Valley Mont. (founder, charter mem., pres. 1981-82), Desert Sage Artists (charter mem., juried mem., v.p. 2003-), Phi Theta Kappa. Republican. Lutheran. Avocations: public speaking and acting, dance, stamp collecting, photography, interior decorating. Office Phone: 602-569-6209. E-mail: kathyherranen@aol.com.

HERRERA, ANA LUISA, news anchor, journalist, writer; b. Lima, Peru, Dec. 1, 1956; came to U.S., 1986; d. Alberto and Luisa (Jefferson) H.; m. Bruce Michael Baur, Sep. 12, 1993; children: Ana Jadira, José Alfredo. Masters in Journalism, Catholic U., Lima, 1975. Radio producer and anchor CIEN-FM, Lima, 1986; cultural reporter La Prensa newspaper, Lima, 1976-80; free-lance columnist El Comercio, Lima, 1984-86; news anchor Panamericana T.V., Lima, 1980-86; reporter El Nuevo Herald, Miami, Fla., 1987, Sta. WSCV, Miami, Fla., 1987-89; corr. Latin Am. and Carribbean Telemundo Network, Miami, Fla., 1989-91; news anchor Sta. KVEA, Los Angeles, 1992; news anchor internat. NBC Canal de Noticias, Charlotte, NC, 1993—98; Spanish sr. editor ZD Net LatinAm., 2000-2001; freelance Latin Am. corr., 2001—; editor Crystal Mag., Miami, 2002; assoc. editor El Sentinel Newspaper, 2002—. Avocations: tennis, classical music, theatre, writing. E-mail: ana_luisa_herrera@hotmail.com.

HERRERA, CAROLINA, fashion designer; b. Caracas, Venezuela, Jan. 8, 1939; d. Guillermo and Maria Cristina Pacanina; m. Reinaldo Herrera, 1968. Founder, head designer Carolina Herrera, 1981—, launched bridal collection, 1987; opened Carolina Herrera / New York boutique, N.Y.C., 2000. Recipient Red Cross, 1979, Best Design Hall of Fame, 1980, Latin Am. Designer "Fashion award", 1987, Pratt Inst., 1990, Mary Ann Magnin awards, 1994, Special Distinction to a Career in the World of Design, Internat. Fashion Ctr. de New York, 1995, Reward to an enterprising spirit, Women's Div., Albert Einstein Coll. of Med. of Yeshiva U., 1996, Women with Heart award, Am. Aevet Assn., 2001. Office: 501 7th Ave Fl 17 New York NY 10018-5903

HERRERA, CHARLOTTE MAE, medical office administrator; b. Walla Walla, Wash., Dec. 15, 1945; d. Paul Donald and Doris Jean (Wells) Leonard; m. Hector Raul Herrera, Feb. 26, 1940; children: Elisa, David. A in Nursing, Monroe C.C., Rochester, N.Y., 1965. RN, N.Y. Nurse Rochester Gen. Hosp., 1965-72, head nurse, 1972-74; office mgr. Plastic Surgery Assoc., Rochester, 1981—. Pres., co-founder PTO Holy Trinity Sch., Webster, N.Y., 1985-87; pres. Aux. Monroe County Med. Soc., Rochester, 1990-92, 97-98, Coun. Meml. Art Gallery, 1994-96, chmn. numerous projects, 1985—, mem. bd. mgrs., 1997—. Home: 1195 Gatestone Cir Webster NY 14580-9142 Office: 1445 Portland Ave Rochester NY 14621-3036

HERRERA, CLARITA, medical association administrator; Rsch. fellow in cardiopulmonary physiology Manhattan Veterans Adminstrn. Med. Ctr., NYU Med. Ctr.; pvt. practice in internal medicine N.Y.C.; faculty mem. N.Y. Med. Coll., Office of Primary Care Edn., Lenox Hill Hosp.; past pres. Women's Med. Assn. of N.Y.C.; chair Health Planning Com., N.Y. County Med. Soc.; pres. Am. Med. Women's Assn., 1997—. Office: Am Med Womens Assn 801 N Fairfax St Ste 400 Alexandria VA 22314

HERRERA, LINDA R. pharmacist; b. Pennington Gap, Va., June 7, 1957; d. Dudley and Alice Juliet Gilliam; 1 child, Pamela Roberson. Cert. pharmacy tech. Va., 2002. Pharmacy tech. Lakeside Pharmacy, Richmond, Va., St. Mary's Hosp., Colonial Pharmacy, Mechanicsville, Advanced Pharmacy, Sandston. Mem.: Order of Moose. Baptist. Avocations: camping, swimming, sewing, dance. Office: Advanced Pharmacy Solution 2512 Lewis Rd Sandston VA 23150

HERRERA, MARY CARDENAS, education educator, music minister; b. Sugar Land, Tex., Feb. 21, 1938; d. Jose Chavez and Juanita (Lira) Cardenas; m. Saragosa Martin Herrera, Sept. 20, 1960 (dec.); children: Michael (dec.), Patricia Ann Zagrzecki, Aaron Martin Herrera, Katherine Ann Nava. Grad., Sugar Land (Tex.) High Sch., 1957, Patricia Stevens Bus. Modeling Sch., 1960; student, Houston C.C., 1991, 92. Sec. William Penn Hotel, Houston, 1959-66; payroll clk. Peakload, Inc., Houston, 1967-69; acctg. clk. Am. Gen., Inc., Houston, 1970-73; nurse asst. Ft. Bend Ind. Sch. Dist., Sugarland, Tex., 1973-88, tchr.'s asst., 1988—2001; ret., 2001. Numerous offices Holy Family Cath. Ch., Missouri City, Tex., 1981-90, Hispanic choir dir., 1981-89; Hispanic choir dir. Notre Dame Cath. Ch., 1990-91; Hispanic del. Galveston-Houston Diocese, 1987-89; regional del. Encuetro Diocesceno Conf., San Antonio, 1983, 84, 85; dir., coord. Diocesan Hispanic Choir, 1982-86, music workshops, 1982-88. Songwriter in field. Mem. Holy Family Hispanic Com.; mem. choir Iglesia del Pueblo, Pasadena, Tex., 1991, 92, asst. Sunday sch. tchr., 1992-93, coord. monthly Women's Praise Gathering, 1994-97; music min. local prayer groups Houston area, 1990—; music min. King of Kings Prison Ministry, Texas City, Tex., 2000-, Casa Oracion, South Houston, Tex., 1998-, S.E. region Texas City Women's Prison, 2000--. Mem. Women's Aglow (praise and worship music min. Pasadena chpt. 1988-90). Democrat. Avocations: jogging, playing guitar. Home and Office: 1809 Crestwood Ln Pasadena TX 77502-3233

HERRERA, PALOMA, dancer; b. Buenos Aires, Dec. 21, 1975; d. Alberto Oscar and Diana Lia (Rube) H. Attended, Olga Ferri Studio, 1982, Ballet Sch. of Minsk, 1987, English Nat. Ballet, London, 1990, Sch. Am. Ballet, N.Y.C., 1991; diploma, Inst. Superior Art at The Colon Theatre, Buenos Aires, 1991. Soloist Am. Ballet Theatre, N.Y.C., 1992-95, prin. dancer, 1995—. Dancer (ballets) Don Quixote, 1987, 88, soloist La Bayadere, The Sleeping Beauty, Don Quixote, Met. Opera, N.Y.C., 1992, Études, The Sleeping Beauty, Swan Lake, Symphonic Concertante, Voluntaries, 1993, prin. Symphonie Concertatne, Symphonic Variations, 1993; prin. Peasant Pas de Deux in Giselle, Colon Theatre, Buenos Aires, 1992, La Bayadere, 1993; prin. Don Quixote, soloist Etudes, Voluntaries, Theme and Variations, Kennedy Ctr., Washington, 1993; prin. The Nutcracker, Dorothy Chandler Pavilion, L.A., 1993, Palace Theatre, Stamford, Conn., 1993; repertoire Met. Opera House Symphonic Variations, Theme and Variations, The Nutcracker, Cruel World, Symphonic Concertante, Gala Performance, 1994, La Bayadera, Don Quixote, Paquite, How Near Heaven, Les Sylphides, Cruel World, Tchaikovsky Pas de Deux, Romeo and Juliet, 1995; guest artist Ballet Gala, Toronto, 1993, Colon Theatre, Buenos Aires, 1993, Gala Ballet of Aix-En-Provence, France, 1993, New Generation Ballet, Moscow, Gala Tribute to Nureyev, Toronto, Le Gala des Etoiles, Montreal, Internat. Evenings of Dance, Vail, Colo., Don Quixote, Kremlin Palace, Moscow, 1995. Recipient First prize Latino Am. Ballet Contest, Lima, Peru, 1985, Coca-Cola Contest of Arts and Scis., 1986, Finalist diploma XIV Varna (Bulgaria) Internat. Competition of Ballet, 1990; scholar Colon Theatre Found., 1989; Dance scholar Antorchas Found., 1991. Home: One Lincoln Plz 20 W 64th St Apt F New York NY 10023-7129 also: Billinghurst 2553 10 Piso Dto CP 1425 Buenos Aires Argentina Office: American Ballet Theatre 890 Broadway Fl 3 New York NY 10003-1278

HERRERIAS, CARLA TREVETTE, epidemiologist, health policy analyst; b. Chgo., Apr. 8, 1964; d. Ludvik Frank and Carlotta Trevette (Walker) Koci; m. Jesus Herrerias, Feb. 25, 1989; children: Elena Mikele, Coco Trevette. BS in Med.Tech., Ea. Mich. U., 1987; MPH in Molecular and Hosp. Epidemiology, U. Mich., 1991. Med. clk. hydramatic divsn. GM, Ypsilanti, Mich., 1983-86; rschr., support staff dept. human genetics U. Mich., Ann Arbor, 1987-91; program mgr. Am. Acad. Pediat., Elk Grove Village, Ill., 1991-99, sr. health policy analyst, 1999—2003; clin. rsch. analyst Am. Coll. Chest Physicians, Northbrook, Ill., 2003—. Project mgr., contbr.: Clinical Practice Guideline: Otitis Media with Effusion in Young Children, 1994. Mem. APHA, Ill. Pub. Health Assn., Acad. Health Svcs. Rsch. and Health Policy, U. Mich. Alumni Soc., U. Mich. Club Chgo. Avocations: reading, biking, needlework, horseback riding. Office: Am Acad Pediat 141 NW Point Blvd Elk Grove Village IL 60007-1019 E-mail: cherrerias@aap.org.

HERRICK, KATHLEEN MAGARA, social worker; b. Mpls., Oct. 18, 1943; d. William Frank and Mary Genevieve (Gill) Magara; m. John M. Herrick, Feb. 5, 1966; children: Elizabeth Jane, Herrick-Chapman, Kathryn Mary. Grandchildren: Kate Margaret Chapman, John Nicolas Chapman. BA in Social Work and French, Coll. St. Benedict, St. Joseph, Minn., 1965; MSW (Mildred B. Erickson fellow), Mich. State U., 1976. Cert. diplomate Am. Psychotherapy Assn., 1998; cert. Acad. Cert. Social Workers. Social worker II Carver County Social Svcs., Chaska, Minn., 1965-70; therapist St. Lawrence Cmty. Mental Health Ctr., Lansing, Mich., 1974-75; sch. social worker Ingham Intermediate Sch. Dist., Mason, Mich., 1975-76; home/sch. coord. Eaton Intermediate Sch. Dist., Charlotte, Mich., 1976-81; sch. social worker, 1994—. Caseworker St. Vincent Home for Children, Lansing, 1979-80; tchr. cons. for severely emotionally impaired, 1981-83; behavior disorder cons., 1983-85; sch. social work cons., 1985-87, prevention splst. profl. and program svcs., 1987-94. Chmn. bd. dirs. Eaton CountyChild Abuse and Neglect Prevention Coun., 1986—; Dem. precinct del.; bd. dirs. Cath. Socia Svcs., Lansing; splst. substance abuse prevention region XIII SAPE, 1987-94. Recipient Eaton County Svc. to children award Eaton County Child ABuse and Neglect Prevention Coun., 1997. Mem.: NOW, NEA, NASW, Am. Psychotherapy Assn. (diplomate), Am. Orthopsychiat. Assn., Mich. Assn. Emotionally Disturbed Children, Mich. Assn. Sch. Social Workers, Mich. Edn. Assn., Nat. Women's Health Network, Amnesty Internat., Glasser Inst. Reality Therapy & Choice Theory, Mich. Assn. Suicidology, Phi Alpha, Phi Kappa Phi. Democrat. Home: 2113 Long Leaf Trl Okemos MI 48864-3210 Office: 1790 Packard Hwy Charlotte MI 48813-9717 E-mail: kherrick@eaton.k12.mi.us.

HERRICK, SYLVIA ANNE, health service administrator; b. Minot, N.D., Oct. 5, 1945; d. Sylvester P. and Ethelina (Harren) Theis; m. Michael M. Herrick, Nov. 8, 1969; children: Leo J., Mark A. BSN, U. N.D., 1967; MS in Pub. Health Nursing, U. Colo., Denver, 1970; sch. nurse credential, San Jose State U., 1991; postgrad., Golden Gate U. RN, Calif.; cert. pub. health nursing, health svc., profl. healthcare quality, 2003. Pub. health nurse Dept. Pub. Health City of Mpls.; instr. nursing San Francisco State U., 1975-88; cons. exec. search Med-Power Resources, Alameda, 1988; coord. health svcs. Alameda Unified Sch. Dist., 1988-91; team mgr. home care nursing and program devel. coord. Vis. Nurse Assn. and Hospice of No. Calif., 1991-99; mgr. disease mgmt. and health awareness East Bay Med. Network, Emeryville, Calif., 1999-2000, interim dir. med. mgmt., 2000; dir. utilization and quality mgmt. Children First Health Network, Oakland, Calif., 2001—. Spkr. in field. Mem. Nat. Nurses Bus. Assn., Calif. Sch. Nurses Orgn. (bd. dirs., chair edn Bay Coast sect.), Delta Kappa Gamma. Home: 1711 Encinal Ave Alameda CA 94501-4020 Fax: (510) 450-5868. E-mail: sherrick@mail.cho.org.

HERRIN, LORETTA RASBERRY, physical education educator; d. Rubin Rasberry and Mattie Rumph; m. Ellis John Herrin, Dec. 20, 1969 (dec. Sept. 10, 1976); 1 child, Eldridge Denae. BS, S.C. State U., 1959; MEd, Tenn. State U., 1963; Assoc. in Bus., Columbia Jr. Coll., 1983. Tchr. health and phys. edn. Anderson (S.C.) City Sch. Dist. 5, 1959—66, Tuskegee (Ala.) Inst., 1966—70, Richland Sch. Dist. 5, Columbia, SC, 1970—71; dir. Project Upward Bound Benedict Coll., Columbia, SC, 1973—95, asst. prof. health, phys. edn., recreation, 1971—. Sec. Southeastern Assn. Spl. Programs Region 4, Ridgewood Found., Columbia, 1993—95; pres. S.C. Assn. Spl. Program Pers., Columbia, 1990—93. Mem.: Charmettes, Inc. (pres.-treas. 1993—97), Phi Delta Kappa, Alpha Kappa Alpha. Avocations: travel, shopping, watching TV, reading, word search puzzles. Home: 416 Portchester Dr Columbia SC 29203 Office: Benedict Coll 1600 Harden St Columbia SC 29204 E-mail: herrin1@benedict.edu.

HERRIN, STEPHANIE ANN, retired aerospace engineer, astrobiotical engineer; b. Oakland, Calif., May 13, 1950; d. Thomas Edgar Herrin and Mary Teresa Silva; m. Este Stovall, May 20, 1989. BSc, U. Pacific, 1976; MSc, Columbia Pacific U., 1978; PhD in Engring. & Applied Scis., U. Bradford, West Yorkshire, U.K., 1994. Reliability engr. Applied Tech. Litton Industries, Sunnyvale, Calif., 1979-80; sr. reliability engr., reliability project mgr. ESL, Inc., Sunnyvale, 1980-84; sr. reliability and quality assurance engr. Martin Marietta, Balt., 1984-85, lead, sr. reliability engr. Los Alamos Tech. Assn., Albuquerque, 1985-86; sr. reliability engr. Boeing, Houston, 1987-89; sr. sys. engr., knowledge capture engr. Astrobiology Inst. NASA-Ames Rsch. Ctr., Moffett Field, Calif., 1988-99; marine capt. pvt. personal yacht, 1999—; sr. systems/astrobiotical engr. biology lab. Space Sta. Freedom. Cons. Lawrence Livermore Labs., Livermore, Calif., 1985-87; failure analysis engring. radiographer, analyst Ford Aerospace & Comm. Corp., Palo Alto, Calif., 1973-79; owner, analyst Fail Safe Radiography, Palo Alto, 1975-81. Contbr. articles to profl. jours. Recipient U.S. govt. Manned Flight Awareness award, 1994, 96-97, 2000 Outstanding Scientists of 20th Century medal, Cambridge, Eng., 2000, Cambridge U. Sch. Honor Scientist of Yr., Queen Elizabeth II; named Internat. Scientist of Yr. Cambridge U., 2001; NASA grantee, 1987-89, 90-93, 94-95; recipient numerous fellowships and lifetime awards. Mem.: AAUW, IEEE (reliability and maintainability soc., engring. in medicine and biology computer soc., info. theory, sys., man and cybernetics, oceanic engring. soc.), Nat. Assn. Ret. Fed. Employees. Achievements include patent for Real-time Automated Diagnosis and Intelligent Utility for Maintainability (RADIUM).

HERRING, SUSAN WELLER, dental educator, oral anatomist; b. Pitts., Mar. 25, 1947; d. Sol W. and Miriam (Damick) Weller; m. Norman S. Wolf, May 27, 1995. BS in Zoology, U. Chgo., 1967, PhD in Anatomy, 1971. NIH postdoctoral fellow U. Ill., Chgo., 1971-72, from asst. prof. to prof. oral anatomy and anatomy, 1972-90; prof. orthodontics U. Wash., Seattle, 1990—. Vis. assoc. prof. biol. sci. U. Mich., Ann Arbor, 1981; cons. NIH study sect., Washington, D.C., 1987-89; sci. gov. Chgo. Acad. Sci., 1982-90; mem. pub. bd. Growth Pub. Inc., Bar Harbor, Maine, 1982—. Mem. editl. bd. Cells, Tissues, Organs, 1989—, Jour. Dental Rsch., 1995-98, 2003—, Jour. Morphology, 1997—, Integrative Biology 2000—; Archives of Oral Biology, 2003-; contbr. articles to profl. jours. Predoctoral fellow NSF, 1967-71; rsch. grantee NIH, 1975-78, 81—, NSF, 1990-92, 94-95. Fellow AAAS; mem. Internat. Assn. Dental Rsch. (dir. craniofacial biology group 1994-95, v.p. 1995-96, pres.-elect 1996-97, pres. 1997-98, Craniofacial Biology Rsch. award 1999), Soc. Integrated Comp. Biol.(chmn. vertebrate zoology 1983-84, exec. com. 1986-88), Am. Soc. Biomechanics, Am. Assn. Anatomists (chmn. Basmajian com. 1988-90), Soc. Vertebrate Paleontology, Internat. Soc. Vertebrate morphology (convenor 4th congress 1994, pres. 1994-97), Sigma Xi. Avocation: semi-profl. violin. Office: U Wash Box 357446 Seattle WA 98195-7446 E-mail: herring@u.washington.edu.

HERRINGER, MARYELLEN CATTANI, lawyer; b. Bakersfield, Calif., Dec. 1, 1943; d. Arnold Theodore and Corinne Marilyn (Kovacevich) C.; m. Frank C. Herringer; children: Sarah, Julia. AB, Vassar Coll., Poughkeepsie, N.Y., 1965; JD, U. Calif. (Boalt Hall), 1968; Exec. Program, Stanford Grad. Sch. Bus., 1994. Assoc. Davis Polk & Wardwell, N.Y.C., 1968-69, Orrick, Herrington & Sutcliffe, San Francisco, 1970-74, ptnr., 1975-81; v.p., gen. counsel Transamerica Corp., San Francisco, 1981-83, sr. v.p., gen. counsel, 1983-89; ptnr. Morrison & Foerster, San Francisco, 1989-91; sr. v.p. gen. counsel APL Ltd., Oakland, Calif., 1991-95, exec. v.p., gen. counsel, 1995-97; gen. counsel allied bus. Littler & Mendelson, San Francisco, 2000. Bd. dirs. Golden West Fin. Corp., World Savs. Bank, ABM Industries Inc. Author: Calif. Corp. Practice Guide, 1977, Corp. Counselors, 1982. Regent St. Mary's Coll., Moraga, Calif., 1986—, pres., 1990-92, trustee, 1990-99, chmn., 1993-95; trustee Vassar Coll., 1985-93, The Head-Royce Sch., 1993-2002, Mills Coll., 1999—, The Benilde Religious & Charitable Trust, 1999—, Alameda County Med. Ctr. Hosp. Authority, 1998-2002, Univ. Calif. Berkeley Art Mus., 2001—; bd. dirs. The Exploratorium, 1988-93. Mem. ABA, State Bar Calif. (chmn. bus. law sect. 1980-81), Bar Assn. San Francisco (co-chair com. on women 1989-91), Calif. Women Lawyers, San Francisco C. of C. (bd. dirs. 1987-91, gen. counsel 1990-91), Am. Corp. Counsel Assn. (bd. dirs. 1982-87), Women's Forum West (bd. dirs. 1984-87). Democrat. Roman Catholic. E-mail: mherringer@aol.com.

HERRINGTON-BORRE, FRANCES JUNE, sign language school director; b. Austin, Tex., June 14, 1935; d. George Wilmas Neill and Mildred Lucille (Alexander) Williamson; m. Harold M. Herrington, June 6, 1953 (dec. Dec. 1978); children: Harold M.(dec.), Cheryl Anne Calhoun; m. Thomas Raymond Borre, Apr. 5, 1985. Student, U. Tex., 1967-71. With Tex. Dept. Human Svcs., Austin, 1961-90, adminstrv. technician, 1967-71, field rep., 1971-81, asst. pers. dir., 1981-88, labor rels. dir., 1988-89, judge adminstrv. law, 1989-90; freelance profl. interpreter for deaf, 1964—; dir. Austin Sign Lang. Sch., 1964—. Gov.'s appointee Joint Adv. Com. on Ednl. Svcs. to Deaf, Austin, 1977—79; project dir. Gov.'s Office, 1980; chmn. Tex. Commn. for Deaf Bd. Evaluation of Interpreters, 1981—84, Tex. State Agy. Liaisons to Gov.'s Commn. for Women, 1985; legis. liaison Symposium Deaf and Hard-of-Hearing Texans, 1991—99; cons. in field. Co-recipient Lyndon B. Johnson award, Tex. Assn. of the Deaf and the Gallaudet U. Regional Ctr., 1992; named Person of the Week for Outstanding Cmty. Svc., Fox 7 KTBC-TV, Austin, 2000; named an Outstanding Woman Ctrl. Tex., AAUW, 1982; recipient Tex. Rehab. Commn. Merit award, 1977, Gov.'s citation, 1978, Significant and Meritorious Svc. to Mankind award, Capitol Sertoma Club, 1976, Disting. Svc. as Adv. and Interpreter award, Dal-Tar Lions Club, 1977. Mem. Nat. Assn. of Deaf (Golden Hand award 1987), Tex. Assn. of Deaf (Svc. citation 1967, Vol. Svc. award 1971, 91-93, Presdl. citation 1989, Friendship award 1995, Gratitude for Vol. Svcs. award 1993-95, Appreciation award 1996), Tex. Soc. Interpreters for the Deaf (Interpreter of Decade award 1981, Bob Alcorn award 2000), Austin Interpreters for Deaf. Mem. Ch. of Christ. Home: 2404 Laramie Trl Austin TX 78745-3664 Office Phone: 512-462-2052. E-mail: franhborre2@cs.com.

HERRMAN, MARCIA KUTZ, child development specialist; b. Boston, June 16, 1927; d. Cecil and Sonia (Schneider) Kutz; m. Bayard F. Berman, July 23, 1949 (div. 1960); m. William H. Herrman, June 23, 1961; 1 child, Fred. BA, Smith Coll., 1949; MA, Pacific Oaks Coll., 1974. Credentialed tchr., Calif. NIMH intern Cedars-Sinai Med. Ctr., L.A., 1966-67; ednl. therpist L.A. Child Guidance Clinic, 1967-69, Child and Family Study Ctr., Cedars-Sinai Med. Ctr., 1969-71; dir. tng., asst. project dir. handicapped early edn. program Dubnoff Ctr., North Hollywood, Calif., 1972-76; child devel. cons. schs., agys. and families L.A. Co., Calif., 1969—. Cons. L.A. Child Guidance Clinic, Head Start, Child Care and Devel. Svcs., 1969-73; cons. child and parenting program St. Joseph's Ctr., Venice, Calif., 1992-98; profl. expert L.A. Unified Sch. Dist., 1976-80; vis. faculty Pacific Oaks Coll., Pasadena, Calif., 1970-76. Vol. Alliance for Children's Rights, 1992-94, Child Advocate's Office, Superior Ct., L.A., 1983—; mem. Dependency Ct. Com., 1988-92, Task Force on Rep. of Children in Dependency Ct., Superior Ct., L.A. County, 1994; mem. oversight and resource coms. Placement Project, joint com. of program policy adv. com. Dept. Children and Family Svcs., 1995-98; steering com. Cmty. Based Placement Project, Joint Effort of Youth Law Ctr., L.A. Dept. Children & Family Svcs. and Calif. Dept. Social Svcs., 1995; mem. L.A. Foster Care Network, 1987-94, L.A. County MacLaren Children's Ctr. Task Force, 1990-95, cmty. mem., 1996—; cmty. adv. com. St. Joseph's Ctr., 1992-96; policy and implementation coms. Cmty. of Care Integration Project, 1998—, L.A. County bd. suprs., policy and implementation coms.; bd. chair Keeping Families Together, L.A., 1987-88; trustee Ruth Pearce Fund for Therapeutic Companions, 1994—. Recipient Vol. of Yr. award L.A. County Bd. Supr., 1986, Commendation for Dedicated Svc. to Cmty., 1991, Recognition award for Outstanding Svc. to Children L.A. County Inter-Agy. Coun. on Child Abuse, 1991; Sophia Smith scholar, 1949. Fellow Am. Orthopsychiat. Assn. (life); mem. N.Y. Acad. Scis., Assn. Child Devel. Specialists, Nat. Ct. Appointed Spl. Advocate Assn. Democrat. Jewish. Avocations: music, theater, hiking, travel. Home and Office: 3919 Ethel Ave Studio City CA 91604-2204

HERRMAN, MARGARET SUSAN, university official, sociologist; b. Columbia, S.C., Nov. 4, 1944; d. Henry and Frances (Smith) H.; m. Eugene Carl Bianchi, May 1, 1993. BA, Emory U., 1966, MA, PhD, 1977. Lectr. dept. sociology Ga. State U., Atlanta, 1971-77; lectr., temp. asst. prof. dept. sociology U. Ga., Athens, 1978-83, from pub. svc. asst. to assoc., 1983-93, sr. pub. svc. assoc. Carl Vinson Inst. Govt., 1993—. Cons. Carter Ctr., Emory U., Atlanta, 1985; founder, exec. dir. Nat. Conf. on Peacemaking and Conflict Resolution, Washington, 1979-87, chmn. bd. dirs., 1987-89; keynote spkr. nat. confs.; participant numerous nat. and statewide profl. meetings. Contbr. articles to profl. jours., chpts. to books. Recipient numerous grants. Mem.: Assn. Conflict Resolution, Alpha Kappa Delta. Avocations: gardening, travel, family. Home: 400 Red Fox Run Athens GA 30605-4476 Office: U Ga Carl Vinson Inst Govt 201 N Milledge Ave Athens GA 30602-5027 E-mail: herrman@cviog.uga.edu.

HERRMANN, DEBRA MCGUIRE, chemist, educator; b. Ft. Benning, Ga., Dec. 28, 1955; d. Delbert Wayne and Twyla Pauline (Moran) McGuire; m. David Read Herrmann, Aug. 2, 1980; children: Adam James, Jesse Read, Aaron Matthew. BS in chemistry, U. Tex., 1979, U. Ark., 1989. Rsch. chemist Dow Chem., Oyster Creek, Freeport, Tex., 1980-84; chemist Aluminum Co. Am., Bauxite, Ark., 1984-87; tchr. Little Rock (Ark.) Sch. Dist., 1987-90; tchr. chemistry and integrated physics and chemistry Carroll Ind. Sch. Dist., Southlake, Tex., 2002—. Pres., bd. dirs. Little Peoples Acad. Sch. Montessori, Ottumwa, Iowa, 1990-93; den leader Cub Scouts. Mem. PEO, Phi Beta Kappa. Democrat. Presbyn. Avocations: walking, watercolor, dogs, sailing, gardening. Home: 1100 Harbor Haven St Southlake TX 76092-2811

HERRNKIND, HILDA MARIE, writer, military volunteer; b. Miami, Fla., Jan. 6, 1974; d. Jeanette Marie Herrnkind. A of Bus Admin.(hon.), Mt. Wachusett C.C., 1999. Cert. computer asst. acctg., Mt. Wachusett C.C., 1999; small bus. mgmt. Mt Wachusett C.C., 2000. Sales and svc. assoc. Bankboston, Gardner, Mass., 1996—99; writer Ind., 1999—. Coord. first investment seminar for customers Bankboston, Gardener, Mass., 1998, coord. first how-to banking program for H.S. students, 98. Contbr. (photos) A Moment in Time, In Enduring Textures, 2000, At the End of a Rainbow, In Chasing Dreams, 2000, Internat. Libr. Photography. Vol. USNG, Gardner, Mass., 2001, asst. to commdg. officer, 2001—02, asst. for N.Y. relief drive, 2001, mng. unit raffle, 2001—02. Decorated Unit Coin Vol. Svcs. USNG; recipient many Svc. Stars for Intergrity and Teamwork, Bankboston, 1997-1998. Mem.: USNG (hon.; auxliary mem. 2001), Alpha Beta Gamma (life Nat. Bus. Honor Soc. Cert. 1994). Avocations: reading, singing, travel, sports. Personal E-mail: star39_97@yahoo.com.

HERRON, CINDY, actress, vocalist; b. San Francisco, Sept. 26, 1965; m. Glenn Braggs; 1 child, Donovan Andrew. Vocalist En Vogue, Atco/Eastwest Records, N.Y.C. Albums include Born to Sing (Platinum 1990), Funky Divas, Remix to Sing, Runaway Love, The Best of En Vogue, 1999; actress (motion picture) Juice, 1992. Recipient Soul Train Music award, 1991; nominated Grammy award, 1990. Office: care En Vogue Atco Eastwest Records 75 Rockefeller Plz New York NY 10019-6908

HERRON, ELLEN PATRICIA, retired judge; b. Auburn, N.Y., July 30, 1927; d. David Martin and Grace Josephine (Berner) H. AB, Trinity Coll., 1949; MA, Cath. U. Am., 1956; JD, U. Calif.-Berkeley, 1964. Bar: Calif. 1965. Asst. dean Cath. U. Am., 1952-54; instr. East H.S., Auburn, 1955-57; asst. dean Wells Coll., Aurora, N.Y., 1957-58; instr. psychology and history Contra Costa Coll., 1958-60; dir. row Stanford, 1960-61; assoc. Knox & Kretzmer, Richmond, Calif., 1964—65; ptnr. Knox & Herron, Richmond, 1965-74, Knox, Herron and Masterson, Richmond, 1974-77; judge Superior Ct. State of Calif., Contra Costa, Calif., 1977-87; pvt. judge, 1987—90, JAMS, Walnut Creek, Calif., 1990—2002. Ptnr. Real Estate Syndicates, Calif., 1967-77; owner, mgr. The Barricia Vineyards, 1978—. Active numerous civic orgns. Home: 15700 Sonoma Hwy Sonoma CA 95476-3025 also: 51 Western Dr Point Richmond CA 94801 Fax: 707-938-0544. Office Phone: 707-938-3782. Personal E-mail: patherron@vom.com.

HERRON, FLORINE PERNELL, retired music educator; b. Pitts., Mar. 14, 1951; d. Samuel Melvin and Sadie Leah Herron. BA in Music Edn., Duquesne U., Pitts., 1973; MA in Music Edn. and Performance, Ill. State U., 1975. Cert. tchr. Pa., Fla., Miss., La., Kans., Ill. Prof. music, chmn. dept. Donnelly Coll., Kansas City, Kans., 1983—84; min. music, clinician AME Ch., La., 1973—, chaplain Eighth Episcopal Dist., 2004—. Cons./clinician AME Ch., La., 1973—2003. Author: (piano/organ book) Harmonic Praise, (songbook - sacred and polit. music) In Thee O Lord Do I Put My Trust, (guitar method book) ProgressiveGuitar Melodies. Mem. La. Women's Legis. Caucus, La., 2003. Mem.: Am. Fedn. Of Tchrs., Nat. Coun. Of Negro Women, Connectional Music Com. (assoc. dir., keyboards 2000—03), Music Educators Nat. Conf., Women's Missionary Soc., Mu Phi Epsilon. African Methodist Episcopal. Avocation: raising birds. Office: Florimusic Studios PO Box 1420 Slidell LA 70459 Personal E-mail: florineflorimusic@juno.com.

HERRON, GAYLE ANN, forensic psychologist, mental health consultant, psychotherapist, health facility administrator, columnist; b. L.A., Sept. 21, 1953; d. Robert Owen Sr. and Rachel Rebecca (Lemley) Colvin; m. Curtis William Sr. Herron, Feb. 14, 1997. AA in Psychology, Okla. City C.C., Oklahoma City, 1986; BS in Sociology, Okla. State U., 1989, BS in Psychology, 1990, MS in Counseling, 1992; postgrad., U. Okla., 1994—95, U. Nev., Las Vegas, 1995—96. Lic. profl. counselor N.C., Mo., Nebr., cert. master psychologist, forensic clin. counselor Nat. Bd. Cert. Forensic Counselors. Adminstr., fin. cons. Security Fin. Cons., Oklahoma City, 1980-88; case worker Big Bros./Big Sisters, Stillwater, Okla., 1988-89; counselor Payne County Family Practices, Stillwater, 1989; social worker Dept. Human Svcs. Child Welfare, Stillwater, 1990-91; asst. to v.p. bus. and fin. Okla. State U., Stillwater, 1990-91; adj. instr. Langston (Okla.) U., 1992; counselor Christian Counseling Assocs., Stillwater, 1993-95; social worker U. Nev. Las Vegas Health Ctr., 1995, Clark County, Las Vegas, Nev., 1995—96; counselor Payne County Health Dept. Child Guidance Clinics, Stillwater and Cushing, Okla., 1992—95; clin. dir., clin. psychotherapist New Beginnings Clin. Svcs. Corp., Las Vegas, 1995—2003; clin. dir., master psychologist/psychotherapist New Beginnings Diagnostic and Clin. Svcs., Brunswick City, NC, 1997—2003, clin. dir., psychotherapist Branson, Mo., 1999-2001; forensic master psychologist, clin. dir. Crisis Intervention Svcs., Branson, Mo., 2001—02; cons. master psychologist Tri-Lakes Primary Care, Hollister, Mo., 2001—02; dir., forensic clin. counselor, masters psychologist Ozark Child, Adolescent and Adult Counseling, Branson, 2002—. Vol. mental health clinician Crisis Incident Response Team, S.W. Mo., 2001-03. Columnist Brunswick County News, 1997-98. Disaster vol. ARC, Oklahoma City, 1987-88; vol. disaster inquiry team, Oklahoma City, Las Vegas, 1995; vita site coord. IRS, Oklahoma City, 1982-84; emergency room EMT Hillcrest Hosp., Oklahoma City, 1994; EMT/intermediate paramedic Amcare Ambulance Svcs., 1994. Mem. ACA, APA, NASW, Am. Assn. for Christian Counselors, Nat. Assn. Social Workers, Okla. Psychol. Assn., Okla. Assn. Counseling and Devel., Assn. for Humanist Psychology, N.C. Assn. Lic. Counselors and Therapists, Golden Key Soc., Phi Theta Kappa, Psi Chi. Democrat. Mem. LDS Ch., Roman Catholic. Avocations: traveling, drafting, hiking, flying, sports. Address: PO Box 1855 Hollister MO 65673-1855 Office: 574 State Hwy 248 Ste A Branson MO 65616 E-mail: gayleannherron@wmconnect.com., ozarkcounseling@earthlink.net.

HERRON, JANET IRENE, industrial manufacturing engineer; b. Zanesville, Ohio, Oct. 14, 1949; d. Lincoln and Freda Louise (Nolan) Estep; m. Wade Harold Herron, June 10, 1967; children: Toni Renee, Dawnise Renee. AAS, Muskingum Area Tech. Coll., 1978; BS, Ohio U., 1990. Elec., mech. designer Nat. Cash Register, Cambridge, Ohio, 1978-83; restructuring engr. Cooper Ind., Zanesville, 1983-87; sr. product engr., quality mgr. Tomkins Ind., Malta, Ohio, 1990-93; pres., owner Herron Engring., Ltd., Chandlersville, Ohio, 1993—; co-owner Herron Renovations, Ltd., 1999—. Engring. instr. Mid-East Ohio Joint Vocat. Sch., 1987-88, Ctrl. Ohio Tech. Coll., 1987-88, Muskingum Area Tech. Coll., 1990—; mfg. outreach engr. Edison Welding Inst. Columbus, Ohio, 1996-98. Mem. NAFE, AAUW, Am. Soc. Quality, Am. Soc. Home Inspectors, Inst. Indsl. Engrs., Soc. Mfg. Engrs., Soc. Engrs. in Mfg., Soc. Women Engrs., Mid-East Ohio Women's Entrepreneurs. Democrat. Presbyterian. Avocations: hosting foreign exchange students, attending concerts, travel, home restoration. Home: 9945 Claysville Rd Chandlersville OH 43727-9765

HERRON, SHERRY SHELTON, biology educator; b. Hattiesburg, Miss., Sept. 4, 1954; d. John Joseph III and Alice English Shelton; m. John Larkin Herron, June 1, 1974; children: Alicia Hope, John Lark, Forrest Boyd, Lauren Guess. BS, U. South Ala., 1975, MEd, 1988; PhD, U. So. Miss., 1999. Sci. tchr. Baldwin County Sch. Sys., Fairhope, Ala., 1975-80, Bayside Acad., Daphne, Ala., 1981-83, Baldwin County Sch. Sys., Bay Minette, Ala., 1983-93; freshman biology program coord. U. So. Miss., Hattiesburg, 1993-2000, dir. Biol. Scis. Freshman Ctr., 1995-2000; staff biologist Biol. Scis. Curriculum Study, Colorado Springs, Colo., 2001—. Author: General Biology Laboratories: Investigations Into the Unity and Diversity of Life, 1998, 2nd edit., 2000, Investigations Into the Issues of Human Biology, 1998, Inquiries into Introductory Biology, 1999. Officer Alpha Delta Gamma, Bay Minette, Ala., 1984-95. Recipient award USM Coll. Discovery, Inst. Higher Learning, 1993-95, award Using Constructivist-Based Investigations and Cooperative Learning in Introductory Coll. Biology, NSF, 1999-2001. Mem. AAAS, Nat. Assn. for Rsch. in Sci. Tchg., Miss. Acad. Sci. (corp. coord. 2000), Sigma Xi, Gamma Beta Phi. Methodist. Avocations: piano, organ. Office: Biol Scis Curriculum Study 5415 Mark Dabling Blvd Colorado Springs CO 80918-3842 Office Fax: 719-531-9104. E-mail: sherron@bscs.org.

HERSCHER, PENNY, company executive; BA in Maths. with honors, Cambridge U., England. R&D engr. Tex. Instruments, England; mgr. Daisy Sys. Corp. ASIC Program; from v.p. mktg., gen. mgr. to dir. product mktg. Design Environ. Group Synopsys Inc.; pres., CEO Simplex Solutions Inc., 1996—. Office: Simplex Solutions Inc 521 Almanor Ave Sunnyvale CA 94085-3512 Fax: 408-774-0285. E-mail: info@simplex.com.

HERSH, KRISTIN, vocalist, musician; b. Atlanta, 1965; Represented by 4AD, 1985-91, Sire Records, 1987—. Lead singer Throwing Muses, late 1970s—; solo vocalist, 1994—. Albums include Throwing Muses, 1986, The Fat Skier, 1987, House Tornado, 1988, Hunkpapa, 1989, The Real Ramonoa, 1991, Red Heaven, 1992, Hips and Makers, 1994, Strings, 1994, University, 1995, Sky Motel, 1999. Address: Summit Entertainment 1630 Stewart St Ste 120 Santa Monica CA 90404-4058

HERSHAFT, ELINOR, space planner, interior designer; b. N.Y.C., Aug. 12, 1940; d. Solomon and Rose (Cohen) Klausner; m. Arthur Hershaft, June 21, 1959 (div. 1983); children: Karin, Peter; m. Alan J. Hoffman, Sept. 2, 1990. Student, Skidmore Coll., 1956-58; BA, N.Y.U., 1960; postgrad., N.Y. Sch. Interior Design, 1977-78. Lic. home improvement contractor, Conn. Interior designer Elinor Hershaft Interiors, Greewich, Conn., 1979—. Major projects house constrn. with interior design, 1985-87, additions, 1982—; projects pub. in House Beautiful, 1988, Tile News, 1988, Kitchen and Bath Concepts, 1989; numerous comml. and residential interior design projects in Fairfield, Conn. and Westchester, N.Y. Counties, Mass., So. Fla., Boulder, Colo., Wilmington, N.C.; also custom furniture design and fabrication. Creative dir. Greenwich Jewish Fedn., 1983—86; creator logo Bobbie Silverman Inst. for Jewish Culture, Greenwich, Conn., 2001; developer design format, logo and calligraphy spl. fund raising campaign Temple Sholom, Greenwich, 1994—95; pro bono office design and space planning Jewish Cmty. Svcs. Recipient Svc. award Jewish Community Svcs. of Greenwich, 1985, Greenwich Jewish Fedn., 1983, 84, 85. Mem. ASID (allied mem.), Allied Bd. Trade, AIA (allied individual), AAF (allied individual). Jewish. Avocations: calligraphy, reading, swimming, piano. Studio: 115 Old Mill Rd Greenwich CT 06831-3015

HERSHENSON, MIRIAM HANNAH RATNER, librarian; b. Springfield, Mass., July 23, 1944; d. David and Thelma (Wasserman) Ratner; children: Trent M., Scott D. AB, Syracuse U., 1966; MS, Simmons Coll., 1967; postgrad., Nova U., 1987-89. Cert. tchr./librarian, Mass. Media specialist Quincy (Mass.) Pub. Schs., 1967-71, Virginia Beach (Va.) Pub. Schs., 1982-84, Portsmouth (Va.) Pub. Schs., 1984; regional children's coord. Broward County Libr., Ft. Lauderdale, Fla., 1985-88, br. liaison, 1988-89, br. librarian, 1989-93, regional br. supr., 1993-2001; head pub. svc. Nova Southeastern U./ Broward County Libr., 2001—03; pub. svc. adminstr. Broward County Libr., 2003—. Mem. ALA, Pub. Libr. Assn., Fla. Libr. Assn. (caucus chair 1990-91), Broward County Libr. Assn. (pres. 1994-95), Hadassah (life, chpt. pres. 1983-84), Nat. Coun. Jewish Women (life), Jewish Women Internat. (life), Brandeis Univ. Women (life). Office: Broward County Libr 100 South Andrews Ave Fort Lauderdale FL 33301 Office Phone: 954-357-7335. E-mail: mhershen@browardlibrary.org.

HERSHEY, BARBARA (BARBARA HERZSTEIN), actress; b. Hollywood, Calif., Feb. 5, 1948; d. William H. Herzstein; 1 child, Tom; m. Stephen Douglas, Aug. 8, 1992 (div. 1995). Student public schs., Hollywood. Appearences include (TV series) The Monroes, 1966-67, From Here to Eternity, 1979, (mini-series) A Man Called Intrepid, 1979, Return to Lonesome Dove, 1993, Abraham, 1994; other TV appearances include Gidget, 1965, The Invaders, 1967, Daniel Boone, 1967, Love Story, 1973, Bob Hope Chrysler Theatre, 1967, High Chaparral, 1967, Kung Fu, 1973, CBS Playhouse, 1967, (TV movies) Flood, 1976, In the Glitter Palace, 1977, Just a Little Inconvenience, 1977, Sunshine Christmas, 1977, Angel on My Shoulder, 1980, The Nightingale, 1985, My Wicked, Wicked Ways... The Legend of Errol Flynn, 1985, Passion Flower, 1986, Killing in a Small Town, 1990 (Emmy award 1990, Golden Globe award 1991), Paris Trout, 1991 (Emmy award nomination), Stay the Night, 1992, Abraham, 1994, (films) With Six You Get Egg Roll, 1968, Last Summer, 1969, Heaven with a Gun, 1969, The Liberation of L.B. Jones, 1970, The Baby Maker, 1970, The Pursuit of Happiness, 1971, Dealing, 1971, Boxcar Bertha, 1972, Angela (Love Comes Quietly), 1974, The Crazy World of Julius Vrooder, 1974, Diamonds, 1975, You and Me, 1975, Dirty Night's Work, 1976, The Stunt Man, 1980, Take This Job and Shove It, 1981, The Entity, 1982, The Right Stuff, 1983, Americana, 1983, The Natural, 1984, Hoosiers, 1986, Hannah and Her Sisters, 1986, Tin Men, 1987, Shy People, 1987 (Best Actress Cannes Film Festival, 1987), A World Apart, 1988 (Best Actress Cannes Film Festival, 1988), The Last Temptation of Christ, 1988, Beaches, 1988, Tune in Tomorrow, 1989, Defenseless, 1991, The Public Eye, 1992, Falling Down, 1993, Swing Kids, 1993, Splitting Heirs, 1993, A Dangerous Woman, 1993, Last of the Dogmen, 1995, Portrait of a Lady, 1996 (nominated Golden Globe Best Supporting Actress, nominated Academy award Best Supporting Actress), The Pallbearer, 1996, A Soldier's Daughter Never Cries, 1998, Frogs for Snakes, 1998, The Staircase, 1998, Breakfast of Champions, 1999, Passion, 1999; (theatre, Broadway) Einstein and the Polar Bear, 1981. Recipient Golden Palm award for best actress Cannes Film Festival, 1987, 1988. Office: CAA care Jenny Rawlings 9830 Wilshire Blvd Beverly Hills CA 90212-1804 also: Bymel O'Neill Mgmt care Suzan Bymel N Vista Los Angeles CA 90046

HERSHMAN, LYNN LESTER, artist; b. Cleve. 1 dau., Dawn. BS, Case-Western Res. U., 1963; MA, San Francisco State U., 1972. Prof. U. Calif., Davis, 1984—. Vis. prof. art U. Calif., Berkeley, Calif. Coll. Arts and Crafts, San Jose State U., 1974-78; assoc. project dir. Christo's Running Fence, 1973-76; founder, dir. Floating Mus., 1975-79; ind. film/video producer and cons., 1979— Author works in field; one-man shows include Santa Barbara Mus. Art, 1970, Univ. Art Mus., Berkeley, Calif., 1972, Mills Coll., Oakland, Calif., 1973, William Sawyer Gallery, 1974, Nat. Galleries, Melbourne, Australia, 1976, Mandeville Art Gallery, U. Calif., San Diego, 1976, M.H. de Young Art Mus., 1978, Pallazo dei Diamonte, Ferrara, Italy, 1978, San Francisco Art Acad., 1980, Portland Center Visual Arts, 1980, New Mus., New Sch., N.Y.C., 1981, Inst. Contemporary Art, Phila., 1981, Anina Nosai Gallery, N.Y.C., 1981, Contemporary Art Center, Cin., 1982, Toronto, Los Angeles Contemporary Exhibits, 1986, Univ. Art Mus. Berkeley, 1987, Madison (Wis.) Art Ctr., 1987, Intersesction for the Arts, San Francisco, Pacific Film Archive, A. Space, "Guerilla Tactics" Toronto, Can., Venice Bienalle Global Village; group exhbns. include Cleve. Art Mus., 1968, St. Paul Art Ctr., 1969, Richmond (Calif.) Art Ctr., 1970, 73, Galeria del Sol, Santa Barbara, Calif., 1971, San Francisco Art Inst., 1972, Richard Demarco Art Gallery, Edinburgh, Scotland, 1973, Laguna Beach (Calif.) Art Mus., 1973, Univ. Art Mus., Univ. Calif., Berkeley, 1974, Bronx (N.Y.) Mus., 1975, Linda Ferris Gallery, Seattle, 1975, Madenville Art Gallery, San Diego, Contemporary Arts Mus., Houston, 1977, New Orleans, 1977, Ga. Mus. Art, Athens, 1977, New Mus., N.Y., 1981, Calif. Coll. Arts and Crafts, 1981, San Francisco Mus. Modern Art, 1979, 80, 90, Art-Beaubourg, Paris, 1980, Ars Electronica, 1989, Am. Film Inst., 1989, Mus. Moving Image Internat. Ctr. for Photography, 1989, Kitchen Ctr. for Video-Music, N.Y., 1990, Robert Koch Gallery, San Francsico, 1990, Inst. Contemporary Art, London, 1990, Frankfurt (Germany) Art Fair, 1990, Inst. Conteporary Art, Boston, 1991, Oakland (Calif.) Mus., 1991, La Cite des Arts et des Nouvelles Technologies, Montreal, 1991, Richard F. Brush Art Gallery, Canton, N.Y., 1992, Jack Tilton Gallery, N.Y., 1992, Southeastern Ctr. for Contemporary Art, Winston-Salem, N.C., 1992, Bonner Kunstverein, Bonn, Germany, 1992, Chgo. Ave. Armory, 1992, Retrospective, Tribute, 1994, Nelson Gallery, Paris, 1994, Hess Collection, 1994. Bd. dirs. San Francisco Art Acad., Spectrum Found., Motion a Performance Collective. Western States Regional fellow (film/video), 1990; grantee Nat. Endowment for the Arts, (2) Art Matters Inc., San Francisco Found., N.Y. State Coun. for the Arts, Zellerbach Family Fund, Inter Arts of Marin, Gerbode Found., The Women's Project; recipient Dirs. Choice award San Francisco Internat. Film Festival, 1987, tribute 1987 Mill Valley Video Festial, Exptl. Video award 1988, 1st prize Montbelliard, France, 1990, 2d prize, Vigo, Spain, 1992, 1993 Ars Electronica, Austria, WRO Poland, Nat. Film Theatre, London, Gerber award Seattle Art Mus., 1994, ZKM/Siemans award, 1995, Golden Nica, Ars Electronica, 1999, Flintridge award Lifetime Achievement in the Arts, 1999. Mem. Assn. Art Pubs. (dir., Annie Gerber award 1995). Office: 1201 California St San Francisco CA 94109-5001

HERSON, ARLENE RITA, television producer, journalist, television personality, commentator; b. N.Y.C. d. Sam and Mollie (Friedman) Hornreich; m. Milton Herson, June 16, 1963; children: Michael, Karen. Student, Queens Coll., 1957, New Sch. for Social Rsch., N.Y.C., 1960. Exec. sec. Tex McCrary, Inc., N.Y.C., 1958-60; asst. to William L. Safire, Safire Pub. Rels., N.Y.C., 1960-62; columnist The Advisor, Inc., Middletown, NJ, 1974-78; prodr., host The Arlene Herson Show, N.Y.C., 1978—. Syndicated on Tempo TV, 1988, Channel Am., 1989-93; spokesperson Storer Cable TV, Monmouth County, 1989-91, Nutri/Systems, Monmouth and Ocean Counties, 1989-90; news anchor Nostalgia Cable TV Network at Rep. Nat. Conv., 1993; cons., talent coord. Super Annuities, 1993-94; moderator debate on capital punishment, 1998; moderator panel on assisted suicide, 1999; panelist, interviewer The Am. Sr. Side-WXEL-Nat. Pub. Radio, 1999-2004; panelist radio program Fla. Forum NPR, 2004; co-host radio sta. WJNA, Lunch Bunch; entertainment chmn. Polo Club, 2001—; master of ceremonies Calvacade of Stars, 2002—; mem. grievance com. Fla. Bar, 2003—; invited mem. U.S. Holocaust Meml. Coun., 2004; lectr., spkr. in field. Contbg. writer The Washington/Hampton Connection Dan's Papers, 1993-98, The Hill Newspaper, 1994-98; exec. producer The Magic Flute, conductor Victor Borge, DAR Constitution Hall, Washington, 1995, 1776, 1997; exec. producer, casting dir. (musical) 1776, DAR Constitution Hall, Washington, 1996, encore prodn., 1998; prodr. 1776 (featuring current mems. of Congress), 1998; interviewer Steven Spielberg's Shoah Found., 1997-99; co-host radio program Changing Times, 1999; host WXEL-TV Pledge Drive, 2000. 92d St. Y benefit com. Variety-The Children's Charity; active Women's Project and Prodns., 1992; com. mem. Children's Psychiat. Ctr., 1971-90, Monmouth Park Charity Fund, 1980-90; corp. exec. bd. Family and Childrens Svcs., 1985—90; life mem. N.Y. chpt. Brandeis U. Libr. Fund; dir.'s resource coun. Nat. Women's Econ. Alliance; social com. Westbridge Condominium; fin. chmn. Mike Herson for Congress, 1994, fin .com. March of Dimes, 1995; profl. women's coun. Nat. Mus. of Women in the Arts, 1994; com. mem. Vicent T. Lombardi Cancer Rsch. Ctr., 1994-98, Parkinson's Action Network, 1996; publicity chmn.exhbn. for Israel Tennis Ctrs. Excalibur Soc. of Lyn U., 1996—; adv. coun. to co-chmn, Rep. Nat. Com., 1997—2000, active Power of Women Effecting Renewal, 1997, 2d decade coun. Am. Film Inst., 1998; bd. dirs. A Healing Among Nations, 1999; active Soc. of 100, Fla. Philharm. Orch., 1999; benefit com. Caldwell Theatre, 1999; bd. dirs. Miami City Ballet, 1999—2000; founder Israel Children's Ctrs., 2000; bd. dirs. Fla. Film and Entertainment Adv. Coun., 2001—; mem. com. Shaare Zedek Med. Ctr., 2001; honors bd. dirs. Miami City Ballet, 2000—; com. mem. Ctr. for the Arts, 2001—, Palm Beach Cultural Coun., 2001—03; corp. exec. com. Ctrl. Park Conservancy, Women of Washington; corp. exec. com. mentor program Women's Econ. Devel. Coun.; gubernatorial appointee, bd. dirs. Miami City Ballet Sch., 2001—03; exec. com. Cmty. Rels. Coun., 2001—; leadership coun., exec. com. Rep. Jewish Coalition, 2002—; mem. Carnet Soc. PBS, NPR, 2004; life mem. Boca Raton cancer unit Papanicolau Corps for Cancer Rsch., 2002—; mem. Boca Raton Mus. Art, 2002, coun. trustees, 2001—03; Boca Raton Rep. Club; adv. coun. Take Pride in Am., 1993; bd. dirs. women's activities campaign Sen. Jacob J. Javits, N.Y.C., 1968, Monmouth (N.J.) Mus., 1982—86, Will Rogers Inst., 1992—, Washington Symphony Orch., 1994—98, v.p., 1994; bd. dirs. Boca Raton Ednl. TV, 2001—, Palm Beach Internat. Film Festival, 2000. Recipient CAPE award for best talk show on Cable TV Network, 1984-93, Woman of Achievement in Comm. award Adv. Commn. on Status of Women, 1986, Cable Ace awards Best Talk Show nationwide Arlene Herson Show, 1987, Pub. and Leased Access (PAL) award for best talk show Paragon Cable TV, N.Y.C., 1988, spl. resolution N.J. Assembly, 1988, Willie award for outstanding svc. Will Rogers Inst., 1992; named Disting. Alumni mem. Waldorf Astoria, 1998. Mem. NAFE, NATAS, Nat. Acad. Cable Programming, Nat. Assn. Profl. Women, Women in Comm., Women in Cable, Women in Film and Video, Am. Women in Radio and TV, Power Women Effecting Renewal, Internat. Radio and TV Soc., Internat. Newswoman's Assn., Rep. Gov's Assn., Nat. Press Club, Friends for Life, Friars Club (house com. 1993, admissions com. 1994—), Bethesda Country Club, Lotos Club, East River Tennis Club, Excalibur Soc. of Lynn U., Seagate Beach Club, Polo Club (cmty. rels. com. 1998-99, social com. 2000, entertainment chmn. 2001), Palm Beach Rep. Club, Profl. Bus. Forum, Boca Raton Roundtable. Avocations: tennis, swimming, reading. Fax: 561-998-4776. E-mail: aherson123@aol.com.

HERTEL, SUZANNE MARIE, training and development specialist; b. Hastings, Neb., Aug. 8, 1937; d. Louis C. Hertel and W. Lenore (Cross) Budd. BA, Doane Coll., Crete, Neb., 1959; MSM, Union Theol. Sem., 1961; postgrad., U. Hartford, 1966, U. Conn., 1975; MA, Merrill Palmer Inst., 1977; EdD, Boston U., 1982. Tchr. music Pub. Sch., Wethersfield, Conn., 1962—63; libr. serials Hartford Sem. Found., 1963—64; tchr. elem. Pub. Sch., Glastonbury, Conn., 1965—79; asst. prof. U. No. Iowa, Cedar Falls, 1979—81; tng. mgr. Focus Rsch. Sys. Inc., W. Hartford, Conn., 1982—89; pers. adminstr. City of Hartford, 1989—99; cons., 1999—2002. Mem. leadership educators program John F. Kennedy Sch. Govt., Harvard U., 1999; mem. Human Resource Mgmt. Del., Russia and Estonia, 1992, Initiative Edn., Sci. and Tech., South Africa, 1995. Recipient Maria Miller Stewart award, 1992. Mem.: Am. Guild Organists. Democrat. Personal E-mail: smher82@aol.com.

HERTENSTEIN, MYRNA LYNN, publishing executive; b. Detroit, July 19, 1937; d. Bernard Franklin and Alice Agnes (Stewart) Aller; m. George Ronald Hertenstein, June 21, 1958 (div. July 1979); children: Dale Ronald, Robert Mark. AS in Bus., Wayne State U., 1957; student, Huntingdon Coll., 1980-84. Departmental sec. Sch. of Bus. Wayne State U., Detroit, 1957-59; county and vol. coord. Montgomery (Ala.) Area Coun. on Aging, 1977-80; admissions counselor Coastal Tng. Inst., Montgomery, 1981-83; rural volunteerism coord. State of Ala., Montgomery, 1983-84; account exec. Ala. Bus. Rev., Montgomery, 1984-85, Sta. WRJM-FM, Montgomery, 1985-86; asst. local sales mgr. Sta. WCOV-TV Fox Affiliate, Montgomery, 1986-90; owner, assoc. pub. TRAVELHOST of Cen. Ala., Montgomery, 1990—2003; owner, assoc. pub., editor TRAVEL Quest Mag., 2004—. Mem. Dirs. of Vols. in Agys., Montgomery, 1978-82, Montgomery County Health Coun., 1979-81, Area Agy. on Aging Adv. Coun., Montgomery, 1981-83, Pres.' Coun. Montgomery, 1983, 84; asst. to instr. Dale Carnegie & Assocs., Montgomery, 1978-83. Editor (newsletter) Montgomery Area Coun. on Aging, 1978-80; dir., writer (commls.) Sta. WCOV-TV, 1986-90; writer (commls.) Sta.WRJM-FM, 1985-86. Mem. adminstrv. coun. Whitfield United Meth. Ch., Montgomery, 1977, coord. Meals-on-Wheels, 1978-86; mem. pub. rels. coun. First United Meth. Ch., Montgomery, 1992-94, mem. comms. com. 1995—, vice chmn., 1997, chmn., 1998, mem. coun. of ministries, 1998, mem. adminstrv. bd., 1998; den leader coach Boy Scouts Am., Bellevue, Nebr., 1969-71; editor Capitol Jr. Woman's Club, Montgomery, 1975-82; pres. Parents Without Ptnrs., 1983-85; bd. dirs. Arthritis Found., 1992-2003, vice chair, 1995, chair, 1996, mem. Ala. chpt. exec. com., 1996; dance com. Ala. Dance Theatre, 1996-2000; bd. dirs. Montgomery chpt. Am. Cancer Soc., 1998-2000, Hospice of Montgomery, 1999—, mem. exec. com., 2000—. Recipient Emerging 30 award Montgomery Area C. of C., 1992, small business of yr. award, 1994, corp. vol. of yr. award Voluntary Action Ctr., Montgomery, 1992, award Montgomery Com. for Arts, 1993, Spl. Achievement award U.S. Small Bus. Administrn., 1995, Silver Medal award Montgomery Advt. Fedn. and Am. Advt. Fedn., 1996. Mem. Pub. Rels. Coun. Ala., Ala. Travel Coun., Montgomery Restaurant Assn., Montgomery Hotel/Motel Assn. (bd. dirs. 1992-94, 99—), Sales and Mktg. Execs. (editor newsletter 1995-98, bd. dirs. 1998-99), Montgomery Assn. Bus. Communicators, Montgomery Advt. Fedn. (bd. dirs. 1985-92, 96-2001, newsletter editor 1996-97), Montgomery C. of C. (vice chmn. ambs. 1992, chmn. ambs. 1993, chmn. advt. promotions and publs. 1994, hospitality devel. and mktg. task force 1995-2000, chmn. spl. projects com. 1996), Montgomery Civitans. Avocations: ballroom dancing, photography, ceramics. Home: 3005 Baldwin Brook Dr Montgomery AL 36116-3803 Office: Travelhost of Cen Ala PO Box 20666 Montgomery AL 36120-0666

HERTWECK, ALMA LOUISE, sociology and child development educator; b. Moline, Ill., Feb. 6, 1937; d. Jacob Ray and Sylvia Ethel (Whitt) Street; m. E. Romayne Hertweck, Dec. 16, 1955; 1 child, William Scott. AA, Mira Costa Coll., 1969; BA in Sociology summa cum laude, U. Calif., San Diego, 1975, MA, 1977, PhD, 1982. Cert. sociology instr., multiple subjects tchg. credential grades k-12, Calif. Staff rsch. assoc. U. Calif., San Diego, 1978-81; instr. sociology Chapman Coll., Orange, Calif., 1982-87; instr. child devel. Mira Costa Coll., Oceanside, Calif., 1983-87, 88-89; instr. sociology U.S. Internat. U., San Diego, 1985-88; exec. dir., v.p. El Camino Preschools, Inc., Oceanside, 1985—. Author: Constructing the Truth and Consequences: Educators' Attributions of Perceived Failure in School, 1982; co-author: Handicapping the Handicapped, 1985. Mem. Am. Sociol. Assn., Am. Ednl. Rsch. Assn., Nat. Coun. Family Rels., Nat. ASsn. Edn. Young Children, Alpha Gamma Sigma. Avocations: foreign travel, sailing, bicycling. Home: 2024 Oceanview Rd Oceanside CA 92056-3104 Office: El Camino Preschs Inc 2002 California St Oceanside CA 92054-5693 E-mail: ahertweck@cox.net.

HERTZ, DAWN LESLIE, lawyer; b. Michigan City, Ind., June 15, 1946; d. Wilbur Tracy and Norma (Elaine) Scrivnor; m. Ted Torpo Phillips, July 7, 1969 (div. Dec. 1988); 1 child, Kristin Ann; m. Roger Helmut Hertz, Aug. 5, 1989. BA, U. Mich., 1968, JD, 1971. Bar: Mich. 1971. Law clerk U.S. Dist. Ct., Detroit, 1971-73; assoc. Dickinson, Wright, Detroit, 1973-78; ptnr. Keywell and Rosenfeld, Troy, Mich., 1978-90; pvt. practice Ann Arbor, Mich., 1990—. Gen. counsel Mich. Press Assn., Lansing Mich., 1980—. Author: Michigan Media Law, 1998. V.p. Mich. Edn. Trust, Lansing, 1991—; pres. Creative Arts Center, Pontiac, Mich., 1993—. Fellow Mich. Bar Found.; mem. ABA (co-chair com. 1997-99), Mich. Bar Assn., Women In Comm. Methodist. Avocations: golf, travel. Home: 7844 Fischers Way Dexter MI 48130-9405 Office: 301 E Liberty St Ste 250 Ann Arbor MI 48104-2266 E-mail: dlph@lawyers.com.

HERTZEL, DOROTHY, librarian; b. Cleve., Aug. 5, 1915; d. Walter and Helen (Metz) Hoffstetter; m. Franklin William Hertzel, July 22, 1944 (dec. May 1987); children: Franklin Dale, Brian James. BS, Baldwin-Wallace Coll., 1938; MLS, Case Western Res. U., 1965, DPhil, 1985. Tchr. math. Garfield Heights High Sch., 1939-49; asst. children's libr. Cuyahoga County Pub. Libr., Parma, Ohio, 1960-64, children's libr., 1964-65, Brooklyn, Ohio, 1965-66, libr. mgr., 1966-79. Founder Friends of Bklyn. Br. Cuyahoga County Pub. Libr., 1973—, trustee; vol. Brooklyn Sr. Ctr., 1979—; mem. Bklyn. City Sch. Vol. Tutor com., 1980-88; mem. Bklyn. City Sch. Bd. Edn., 1990-93, v.p., 1992, pres., 1993; mem. Brooklyn City Sch. Fin. com., 1993-97, Cmty. Edn. Adv. Com., 1987-90. Mem. Ohio Libr. Coun., Brooklyn Hist. Soc. (co-founder 1970, v.p. 1970-73, corr. sec. 1973-78), Soc. Ohio Archivists, Mid-Atlantic Regional Archives Conf., Greater Cleve. Genealogical Soc., Ohio Hist. Soc., Cleve. Archival Roundtable, Brooklyn Genealogical Soc. (founder 1996, pres.1996-2001, program chair 2003).

HERVIEUX-PAYETTE, CÉLINE, Canadian senator; b. L'Assomption, Quebec, Can., Apr. 22, 1941; JD, U. Montreal, 1973. Cert.: Can. Investment Dealers Assn. Parlimentary sec. Solicitor Gen. Can., Min. State for Fitness and Amateur Sports, Min. State for Youth, 1979—85; senator The Senate of Can., Ottawa, 1995—. Dir. projects Premier Bourassa's Cabinet, 1973—78; dir. pub. rels. Steinberg Inc., 1978—79; v.p. bus. ventures SNC Group, 1985—89; exec. v.p., assoc. Donancy Ltd., 1990; v.p. pub. affairs Medycis, 1991; v.p. regulatory and legal affairs Fonorola Inc., 1991—95; counsellor Fasken, Martineau, Dumoulin, Montreal, 1995—. V.p. Can. br. Commonwealth Parliamentary Assn., 2001; pres. Can. Club Montreal, 2001, Can.-Mex. Friendship Group, 1996—. Named Woman of Yr., 1984; recipient Commemorative medal, Confederation of Can., 1993. Mem.: FRAPPE, Interparliamentary Forum of the Ams. (pres. 2001—), Quebec Bar Assn., Can. Bar Assn. Liberal. Office: 361-E Centre Block The Senate of Canada Ottawa ON Canada K1A 0A4

HERZECA, LOIS FRIEDMAN, lawyer; b. July 7, 1954; d. Martin and Elaine Shirley (Rapoport) Friedman; m. Christian S. Herzeca, Aug. 15, 1980; children: Jane Leslie, Nicholas Cameron. BA, SUNY-Binghamton, 1976; JD, Boston U., 1979. Bar: N.Y. 1980, U.S. Dist. Ct. (so. and ea. dist.) N.Y. 1980. Atty. antitrust div. U.S. Dept. Justice, Washington, 1979-80; assoc. Fried, Frank, Harris, Shriver & Jacobson, N.Y.C., 1980-86, ptnr., 1986—. Editor: Am. Jour. Law and Medicine, 1978-79. Mem. ABA, N.Y.C. Bar Assn. Office: Fried Frank Harris Shriver & Jacobson 1 New York Plz Fl 22 New York NY 10004-1980

HERZENBERG, CAROLINE STUART LITTLEJOHN, physicist; b. East Orange, N.J., Mar. 25, 1932; d. Charles Frederick and Caroline Dorothea (Schulze) L.; m. Leonardo Herzenberg, July 29, 1961; children: Karen Ann, Catherine Stuart. SB, MIT, 1953; SM, U. Chgo., 1955, PhD, 1958; DSc (hon.), SUNY, Plattsburgh, 1991. Asst. prof. Ill. Inst. Tech., Chgo., 1961-66, research physicist ITT Research Inst., 1967-70, sr. physicist, 1970-71; lectr. Calif. State U., Fresno, 1975-76; physicist Argonne (Ill.) Nat. Lab., Ill., 1977-2001. Prin. investigator NASA Apollo Returned Lunar Sample Analysis Program, 1967-71; producer and host TV sci. series Camera on Sci.; disting. vis. prof. SUNY, Plattsburgh, 1991; mem. final selection com. 1993 Bower award and Prize for Achievement in Sci., 1993-94; bd. adv. the Bower award and Prize for Achievements in Sci.; mem. nat. panel of advisors PBS TV sci. series Bill Nye the Sci. Guy, 1991-95; steering com. mem. Midwest Consortium for Internat. Security Studies, 1994-95. Author: Women Scientists from Antiquity to the Present: An Index, 1986; co-author: (with R.H. Howes) Their Day in the Sun: Women of the Manhattan Project, 1999; contbr. articles to profl. jours. Candidate for alderman, Freeport, Ill., 1975; past chmn. NOW chpt., Freeport Am. Phys. Soc. Congl. Scientist fellow finalist, 1976-77; recipient award in sci. Chgo. Women's Hall of Fame, 1989. Fellow AAAS, Am. Phys. Soc. (past chmn. com., past sec.-treas. forum on Physics and Soc., past exec. bd. Forum on the History of Physics, panel pub. affairs), Assn. Women in Sci. (nat. sec. 1982-84, pres. 1988-90); mem. Sigma Xi. Home and Office: 1700 E 56th St Apt 2707 Chicago IL 60637-5092 E-mail: carol@herzenberg.net.

HERZIG, PHYLLIS GLICKSBERG, social worker; b. Cin., June 16, 1941; d. Daniel and Molly Shokler Glicksberg; m. David Jacob Herzig, Sept. 2, 1962; children: Michael A., Pamela J., Roberta L., Karen B. Ajsel. BA, U. Cin., 1963; MSW, Specialist in Aging Cert., U. Mich., Ann Arbor, 1981. LCSW Mich., 1981, cert. apprentice counselor in substance abuse Mich., 1986, employee assistance profl. Employee Assistance Professionals Assn., 1988. Social worker, vol. coord. Hebrew Home for the Aged, Washington, 1963—65; social worker, discharge coord. Twin Oaks Nursing Ctr., Morristown, NJ, 1975—77; social worker, in-home counselor Child and Family Svcs., Ann Arbor, Mich., 1981—86; substance abuse counselor Adult Recovery Ctr., Ann Arbor, Mich., 1985—88; social worker U. Mich. Communicative Disorders Clinic, Ann Arbor, 1986—88; employee assistance profl. counselor Employee Assistance Assocs., Ann Arbor, Mich., 1988—97; dir. older adult programs Jewish Cmty. Ctr. of Washtenaw County, Ann Arbor, Mich., 1997—. Bd. dirs. Jewish Fedn. of Washtenaw County, Ann Arbor, Mich., 1985—91; mem. adv. bd. U. Mus. Soc., Ann Arbor, Mich., 2003. Jewish. Avocations: travel, aerobics, gardening. Home: 3540 Windemere Dr Ann Arbor MI 48105 Office: Jewish Cmty Ctr 2935 Birch Hollow Dr Ann Arbor MI 48108 Personal E-mail: djph_herzig@msn.com. E-mail: phyllisherzig@jccfed.org.

HERZIG, RITA WYNNE, critical care nurse, soprano; b. N.Y., May 12, 1928; d. William and Pearl Edna Wynne; m. William Fred Herzig, June 29, 1950 (dec. Sept. 24, 2002). RN, Beth Israel Hosp., N.Y.C., 1951. RN N.Y., 1951. Singer Met. Opera, N.Y.C.; nurse Beth Israel Hosp., N.Y.C. Exec. dir. Doctors Orch., 1989—95. Contbr. poetry to jours.; prodr.: (TV series) Manhattan Cable Network; author: Final Exam, 2004. Vol. Mayoral Campaign, N.Y.C., 1990. Recipient Cable TV Silver award, Manhattan Cable, 1989. Avocations: animal welfare, producing shows for elderly, poetry. Home: One Gracie Terrace New York NY 10028

HERZLINGER, REGINA, economist, educator; b. Palestine, Dec. 5, 1943; came to U.S. 1952; d. Alexander and Ella (Joffe) E.; m. George Herzlinger, Jan. 27, 1966. BS, MIT, 1965; Doctorate, Harvard Bus. Sch., 1971. Economist, Washington, 1966-67; v.p. Various Cons. Firms, Cambridge, 1967-71; asst. sec. Gov. Commonwealth Mass., 1971; prof. Harvard Bus. Sch., Boston, 1971—. Vis. com. MIT; audit com. Town of Belmont, Mass. Avocations:art, literature, tennis, aerobics. Office: Harvard Bus Sch Soldier's Field Cambridge MA 02163

HERZOG, VALERIE WIRTH, computer company executive; d. Edward Dewey and Mary Litton Wirth(Stepmother); m. Timothy Allan Herzog, July 4, 1999. MEd - Athletic Tng., U. Va., Charlottesville, VA, 1996; B.S. Athletic Tng., Alderson-Broaddus Coll., Philippi, Wv, 1993; doctoral student, Marshall U. Cert. CPR/AED/First Aid Instructor ARC, 1994, Lifesaving ARC, 1992; Certified Athletic Trainer Nat. Athletic Trainers' Assn. Bd. of Certification, 1993. Pres. Higher Level Thinking, LLC, South Charleston, W.Va., 2002—; asst. prof. U. of Charleston, Charleston, W.Va., 1996—2001; head athletic trainer Va. Episcopal Sch., Lynchburg, Va., 1993—95. Author: (conference speaker) Nat. Athletic Trainers' Assn., (journal manuscript) Jour. of Athletic Tng., (journal article) Athletic Therapy Today, (journal manuscript) Advance for Directors in Rehab., (conference speaker) West Virginia Athletic Trainers' Association, (journal manuscript) Jour. of Sport Rehab. Mem. Kanawha Valley Civitans, Charleston, W.Va., 1999—2003; mentor/mem. Women in Athletic Tng. Com., Dallas, Tex., 2003—03; pres. W.Va. Athletic Trainers' Assn., Charleston, W.Va., 2003—. Scholar Post-grad. scholarship recipient, Nat. Athletic Trainers' Assn. Rsch. and Edn. Found., 1995. Mem.: W.Va. Athletic Trainers' Assn. (membership chairperson 2001—02, pres. 2003—), Nat. Athletic Trainers' Assn. Democrat-Npl. Christian. Achievements include development of Educational Software - SimWriter Software. Avocations: hiking, camping, ballroom dancing. Home: 754 Echo Road South Charleston WV 25303 Office: Higher Level Thinking LLC 754 Echo Road South Charleston WV 25303 Personal E-mail: vherzog@charter.net. E-mail: valerieherzog@higherlevelthinking.com.

HERZSTEIN, BARBARA See **HERSHEY, BARBARA**

HESLIN, CATHLEEN JANE, artist, designer, entrepreneur; b. Bklyn., Feb. 24, 1929; d. Charles Jenkins and Katherine (Bauer) Hunter; m. John Thomas Heslin, June 24, 1950. AA, Packer Collegiate Inst., Bklyn., 1950; postgrad., Duke U., 1952, Pratt Inst., 1952. Sr. artist, designer Klopman Mills, Rockleigh, N.J., 1966-72; free-lance designer, 1972-90; propr. Quilters Corner, Tappan, N.Y., 1978-90. Author: History of Rockleigh, N.J., 1648-1973, 1973, Old Order Amish-The People and Their Quilts, 1988; inventor Quilters Quarter measuring device. Councilwoman Borough of Rockleigh, 1973-85, 90-92, pres. coun., 1983-85, historian, 1973-90, chmn. anniversary dedication com., 1973, environ. com., 1974, action com., 1974-75, borough hall com., 1975, acquisition com., 1975, chmn. bicentennial com., 1974-76, chmn. fin. com., 1977-78, chmn. hist. adv. com., 1977-86, liaison to Bergen County hist. programs, 1978, pub. safety com., 1979-84, chmn. bldg. com., 1983-85, housing commn., 1984, Hist. Preservation Commn., 1987-90, ins. com., 1990, liaison to planning bd., 1990, designs for Rockleigh Commons; mem. Rockleigh Planning Bd., 1973, 87-89; Rep. mayoral nominee Borough of Rockleigh, 1988; founder Cathleen Heslin Found., 1990; trustee Abram Demaree Homestead, 1982-84; established Rockleigh Wildlife Sanctuary and Land Preserve. Recipient various certs. of appreciation. Mem. Tappantown Hist. Soc. (dir.), Soc. Archtl. Historians, Am. Soc. Planning Ofcls., Bergen County Hist. Soc. (trustee 1984-90), Historic Homes Assn. N.J. Achievements include being obtained State and Nat. Historic Dist. status for Borough of Rockleigh, 1976. Home and Office: PO Box 115 Northvale NJ 07647-0115

HESLOP, HELEN E. physician, educator, health facility administrator; MB, ChB, Otago U., New Zealand. Fellow dept hematology Royal Free Hosp., London; prof. dept. pediats. Baylor U.; dir. adult bone and marrow and stem cell transplant program Meth. Hosp., Houston. Contbr. articles to profl. jours. Fellow RACP, RCPA. Office: 6621 Fannin St # Mc33320 Houston TX 77030-2303

HESS, DARLA BAKERSMITH, cardiologist, educator; b. Valparaiso, Fla., June 4, 1953; d. James Barry and Irma Marie (Baker) Bakersmith; m. Leonard Wayne Hess, July 20, 1988; 1 child, Ever Marie. BS, Birmingham So. Coll., 1975; MD, Tulane U., 1979. Diplomate Am. Bd. Internal Medicine, Am. Bd. Cardiovascular Disease. Commd. ensign USNR, 1979, advanced through grades to lt. comdr., 1988; resident in internal medicine Portsmouth (Va.) Naval Hosp., 1979-82, cardiologist, head non-invasive cardiology, 1986-88; fellow in cardiology San Diego Naval Hosp., 1982-84, cardiologist, head med. officer in charge ICU Camp Lejeune (N.C.) Naval Hosp., 1984-85; asst. prof. medicine U. Miss. Med. Ctr., Jackson, 1988-91, asst. prof. ob/gyn., 1990-91; dir. noninvasive sect. cardiology, dir. fetal echocardiography U. Mo., Columbia, 1991—99, co-dir. Adult Cogenital Heart Disease Clinic, 1991—99, assoc. prof. medicine, assoc. prof. ob/gyn., 1998—2001. Author: (with others) Obstetrics and Gynecology Clinics, 1992, Clinical Problems in Obstetrics & Gynecology, 1993, General Medical Disorders During, 1991; co-editor: Fetal Echocardiography, 1999; contbr. articles to So. Med. Jour., Ob/Gyn. Clinics N.Am., Soc. Perinatal Obs., Jour. Reproductive Medicine, others. Fellow Am. Coll. Cardiology, Fellow Am. Heart Assn. (fellow stroke coun.), Fellow Am. Soc. Echocardiography; mem. Am. Assn. Nuclear Cardiology, Phi Beta Kappa, Alpha Omega Alpha. Republican. Episcopalian. Home: 7945 Springhouse Rd New Tripoli PA 18066

HESS, EVELYN VICTORINE, medical educator; b. Dublin, Nov. 8, 1926; arrived in U.S., 1960, naturalized, 1965; d. Ernest Joseph and Mary (Hawkins) H.; m. Michael Howett, Apr. 27, 1954. MB, B.Ch, BAO, U. Coll., Dublin, 1949; MD, Univ. Coll., Dublin, 1980. Intern West Middlesex Hosp., London, Eng., 1950; resident Clare Hall Hosp., London, 1951-53, Royal Free Hosp. and Med. Sch., London, 1954-57; rsch. fellow in epidemiology of Tb Royal Free Med. Sch., London, 1955; fellow U. Tex. Southwestern Med. Sch., Dallas, 1958—59, asst. prof. internal medicine, 1960-64, assoc. prof. dept. medicine U. Cin. Coll. Medicine, 1964-69, McDonald prof. medicine, 1969—, dir. div. immunology, 1964-95. Sr. investigator Arthritis and Rheumatism Found., 1963-68; attending physician Univ. Hosp., VA Hosp.; cons. Children's Hosp., Cin., 1967—, Jewish Hosp., Cin., 1968—; mem. various coms., mem. nat. adv. coun. NIH; mem. various coms. FDA, Cin. Bd. Health. Contbr. articles on immunology, rheumatic diseases to jours., chpts. to books. Active Nat. Pks. Assn., Smithsonian Instn., others. Recipient Arthritis Found. award, 1973, 78, 83, Am. Lupus Soc. award, 1979, Am. Acad. Family Practice award, 1980, award for AIDS work State of Ohio, 1989, Spirit of Am. Women award, 1989, Daniel Drake medal U. Cin., 2001; travel fellow Royal Free Med. Sch., Scandinavia, 1956, Empire Rheumatism Coun., 1958-59. Master ACP (gov. Ohio chpt. 1999-2003, Master Tchr. award 1995); fellow AAAS, Am. Acad. Allergy, Royal Soc. Medicine, ACR (master, Disting. Rheumatologist award 1996); mem. Heberden Soc., Am. Coll. Rheumatology, Pan-Am. League Assns. for Rheumatology (Gold medal), Ctrl. Soc. Clin. Rsch., Am. Fedn. Clin. Rsch., Am. Assn. Immunologists, Am. Soc. Nephrology, Am. Soc. Clin. Pharmacology and Therapeutics, Transplantation Soc., N.Y. Acad. Scis., Soc. Exptl. Biology and Medicine, Rheumatological Soc. Colombia (hon.), Rheumatological Soc. Peru (hon.), Rheumatological Soc. Italy (hon.), Clin. Immunol. Soc. Japan (hon.), Cuban Soc. Rheumatology (hon.), Alpha Omega Alpha. Home: 2916 Grandin Rd Cincinnati OH 45208-3418 Office: U Cin Med Ctr ML 563 ML 563 MSB Cincinnati OH 45267-0001 Office Phone: 513-558-4701. E-mail: hessev@email.uc.edu.

HESS, FRANCES ELIZABETH, retired secondary school educator, retired director; b. Trenton, N.J. d. George Alfred and Frances Randall Hess. BS in Edn., Temple U., 1956, MS in Edn., 1964. Tchr. Bd. Edn., Trenton, 1956—60, Fallsington, Pa., 1960—93, aquatics dir., 1981—97; ret., 1997. Instr., trainer ARC, Levittown, Pa., 1983—2003, mem. health & safety, 1981—2003; tech. v.p. U.S. Synchronized Swimming, Indpls., 1999—2003. Named to Hall of Fame, Temple U., 1983; recipient Lillian Mackillae Disting. Svc. award, 2003. Avocations: swimming, jigsaw puzzles, gardening. Home: 718 S Olds Blvd Fairless Hills PA 19030

HESS, MARCIA WANDA, retired secondary school educator; b. Cin., Mar. 15, 1934; d. Edward Frederick Lipka and Rose (Wirtle) Lipka Stanley; m. Edward Emanuel Grenier, Aug. 9, 1952 (div.); m. Thomas Benton Hess, Mar. 25, 1960; children: Kathleen Ann, Cynthia Jean, Thomas Allen. Grad. high sch., Cin. Instr. asst. Cin. Pub. Schs., 1970-95, also mem. staff desegregation workshop and unified K-12 reading communication arts program staff tng. com.; ret., 1995. Contbr. tchr.-instr. asst. handbook, instr. asst. tng. film. Mem. Winton Place Vets of World War II Women's Aux. (pres. 1982-84, bd. dirs. 1982-86, 89-91, v.p. 1997-99). Republican. Roman Catholic. Avocations: travel, reading, collecting first editions, needlepoint, photography. Home: 157 Palisades Pt Apt 4 Cincinnati OH 45238-5660

HESS, MARGARET JOHNSTON, religious writer, educator; b. Ames, Iowa, Feb. 22, 1915; d. Howard Wright and Jane Edith (Stevenson) Johnston; m. Bartlett Leonard Hess, July 31, 1937; children: Daniel, Deborah, John, Janet. BA, Coe Coll., 1937. Bible tchr. Cmty. Bible Classes, Ward Presbyn. Ch., Livonia, Mich., 1959-96, Christ Ch. Cranbrook (Episcopalian), Bloomfield Hills, Mich., 1980-93, Luth. Ch. of the Redeemer, Birmingham, Mich., 1993-99. Co-author (with B.L. Hess): How to Have a Giving Church, 1974, The Power of a Loving Church, 1977, How Does Your Marriage Grow?, 1983, Never Say Old, 1984; author: Love Knows No Barriers, 1979, Esther: Courage in Crisis, 1980, Unconventional Women, 1981, The Triumph of Love, 1987, Lessons from Life's Journey, 2003; contbr. articles to profl. jours. Home: 15191 Ford Rd Apt 302 Dearborn MI 48126-4696

HESS, MARILYN ANN, state legislator; m. Dennis J. Hess; children: Christine, Craig. AA, NYU, 1977; BBA in Mgmt. cum laude, Pace U., 1980. Assoc. Merrill Lynch, N.Y.C., 1972-77; home improvement contractor Conn., 1982-90; mem. Conn. Ho. of Reps., 1993-2001; rep. 150th Assembly Dist., Conn., 1993—2001. Dir. Rep. Town Com., 1989—2001; mem. Conn. Reps. for Choice, 1992—, Rep. Roundtable of Greenwich, 1993—2001, Amb. Roundtable, 1994—2001; chmn. Conn. Internat. Trade Coun., 1995—2001. Organizer pack 516 Boy Scouts Am., N.Y.C., 1976; alt. Greenwich Planning and Zoning Commn., 1990—93; bd. dirs. Friends of the Byram Shubert Libr., 1989—93; founding trustee Byram Scholarship Fund, 1991—; bd. dirs. YMCA, Greenwich, 1997—; fund raiser, chmn. Lewisboro Neighbor's Club, South Salem, 1979; sec. Ridgefiled Hist. Dist. Commn., 1984—85, Greenwich Hist. Dist. Commn., Greenwich, 1988—90; del. Parents Together, 1980; underwriting com. Bruce Mus. Ball, 1990—91; co-founder Byram River Watershed Alliance, 1995—. Named Mother of the Yr., Town and Village Newspaper, 1974. Home: 660 Lake Ave Greenwich CT 06830-3854

HESS, PATRICIA ANN, dietician; b. Washington, June 28, 1954; d. Robert Bruce Sr. and Kathryn Irene (Thomas) Black; m. Amos Christ Hess II, May 17, 1989; children: Hannah Ashley, Kenneth Andrew; stepchildren: Stephanie, Joshua. BS, U. Ky., 1978; MEd, U. Hartford, 1981. Registered dietician; cert. diabetes educator; bd. cert. advanced diabetes mgmt. Clin. dietician St. Joseph Hosp., Lancaster, Pa., 1989-99; dietician York Wellspan Endocrinology, York, Pa., 2000—. Cons. Nat. Nutrition, Inc., Lancaster, 1997. Sunday sch. tchr. St. Paul Ch., Millersville, Pa., 1990-93, Sunday sch. supt., 1992-93; mem. spkrs. bur. Lancaster Diabetes Assn., 1992—. Mem. Am. Dietetic Assn., Am. Soc. Parenteral and Enteral Nutrition, Am. Assn. of Diabetes Educators, Am. Nurse Credentialing Coun., Pa. Assn. of Diabetes Educators, Lancaster Assn. of Diabetes Edn. Lutheran. Avocations: teddy bear making, crosstitch, quilting, rollerblading, bicycling. Home: 9 N Duke St Millersville PA 17551-1601 E-mail: ThessRD@aol.com.

HESS, SUZANNE HARRIET, newspaper publisher, photographer; b. Steubenville, Ohio, Nov. 8, 1941; d. Roswell J. and Ruth R. (Feuer) Caulk; m. Richard Robert Hess, Aug. 28, 1960 (div. Oct. 1989); children: Richard, Rebecca. Student, Lane C.C., 1961. Cert. radiologist, Oreg.; cert. ofcl. nat. level USA Track and Field, 1992-2002. Med. asst. Dr. John Burket, Medford, Oreg., 1970-72; sec. receptionist Dr. Paul Saarinen, Eugene, Oreg., 1982-84; office mgr. Europcar Internat., Sicily, Italy, 1989-91; visitor svcs. mgr. Conv. and Visitors Assn. Lane County, Eugene, Oreg., 1991-94; office mgr. Nat. Masters News, Eugene, Oreg., 1994-97, adminstrv. editor, 1998—2001; pub. Nat. Masters News, 2002—. Bd. dirs. U.S. Amateur Track and Field, Oreg., Photographer Nat. Masters News; nat. sec. USA Track and Field-Masters Com., 1997-98, 99—, vice-chair master's com. Sec. Oreg. Track Club, Eugene, 1993-96, com. person for preservation of Prefontaine Rock, 1995; protester Preservation of Old Growth Timber, Eugene, 1994; elected nat. sec. USA Track and Field Masters Com., 1996, elected vice chair, 2000-. Recipient Appreciation award Oreg. Track Club, 1995, 2 Nat. Championship awards U.S. Amateur Track and Field, 1995, Silver medal 16# and 25# weight throw U.S. Amateur Track and Field Nat. Masters Indoor Championship, 1995, Bronze medal discus and hammer U.S. Amateur Track and Field Nat. Masters Outdoor Championships, 1995, Gold medal 16# weight throw and 25# superweight throw U.S. Amateur Track and Field Nat. Masters Weight and Superweight Championships, 1995, Gold medal U.S. Amateur Track and Field Nat. Masters Weight Pentathlon, 1995, Bronze medal 16# weight throw, Silver medal 25# super weight throw U.S. Amateur Track & Field Indoor Nat. Championships, Boston, 1997, Gold medals 16# and 25# superweight U.S. Amateur Track and Field Indoor Nat. Championships, Boston, 1998; named All Am. U.S. Amateur Track and Field, 1995, 97-99, 2000, 2001, 2002, 2003, Adminstr. Yr., U.S. Amateur Masters Track and Field, 1999, Silver medals 16# weight, 25# superweight Indoor Nat. Championships, Boston, 2000, Bronze medal, Seattle. Democrat. Avocations: track and field, bicycling, golf, travel. Office: Nat Masters News Ste 5 2791 Oak Alley Eugene OR 97405 E-mail: natmanews@aol.com., suzyhess@aol.com.

HESS, TERRY LEE, writer, educator, logistician; b. Balt., July 22, 1954; d. Lee Hess Ray and Ruth Carol Smith, Iva Estelle Teague (Stepmother). MA in English Creative Writing Nonfiction, U. Ctrl. Fla., 2002, postgrad. Program mgr., logistic engr. TRW Aerospace, Redondo Beach, Calif., 1982—89; sr. logisitics engr. Boeing/McDonnell Douglas, Kennedy Space Ctr., Cape Canaveral, Fla., 1990—97; mng. editor Fla. Rev., Orlando, 1999—2002, non-fiction editor, 2001—02; sr. proposal specialist Johnson Controls, Inc., Cape Canaveral, 2003, proposal mgr., 2003—. Instr. U. Ctrl. Fla., 2001—03. Author: (Memoir) Bellingham Review, 2002 (AWP Intro Award for Creative Nonfiction, 2001), Cypress Dome, 2000, 4th edit., 2003. Fin. advisor 53rd Assembly Dist., 27th Congl. Dist., Rep. Party, L.A., 1985—87. With USAF, 1972—76, with USMC, 1978—82. Recipient United Arts Emerging Writers award, First Place Nonfiction and Second Place Fiction, United Arts, Orlando, Fla., 1999. Home: 3242 Angelica St Cocoa FL 32926 Office: Johnson Controls Inc 7315 N Atlantic Ave Cape Canaveral FL 32926 Personal E-mail: hes1of6@bellsouth.net.

HESS, WENDY K. art curator, researcher, writer; b. Cleve., Aug. 9, 1961; d. Robert Sheldon and Linda Ruth Kendall; m. Julius Lewis Hess, Aug. 30, 1987; children: Maxwell Harrison, Theodore Lawrence. B in Philosophy, Miami U. of Ohio, 1983; MA, U. Minn., 1987. Art reviewer Rochester (Minn.) Post-Bull., 1988-89; asst. curator Akron (Ohio) Art Mus., 1989-95; art reviewer Cleve. Plain Dealer, 1996; freelance curator, writer Akron Art Mus., Acme Art Co. Gallery, 1996, Greater Columbus Arts Coun., 1996. Lectr. Cleve. Artists Found., Cleve., 1999, symposium discussant, presenter, 1993, 96; grant panelist Ohio Art Coun., Columbus, 1998; juror Women's Caucus for Art, Ohio chpt., Akron, 1993; vol. grant writer Revere Sch. Dist., 2000—. Author: Ohio Perspectives: Architectural Graphic and Industrial Design, 1991, The Art of William Sommer, 1993, (with others) Akron Art Museum: Art Since 1850, An Introduction to the Collection, 2000; contbr. articles to profl. jours. Vol. Children's Hosp. Doggie Brigade, Akron, 1995-99; vol. benefit com. Akron Zool. Park, 1992-95; com. chair City of Akron Holocaust Arts and Writing Competition, 1990-93. Recipient Achievement citation Ohio Gov. George Voinovich, 1994, Mus. Excellence award No. Ohio Live Mag., 1994. Mem. Am. Assn. Mus., Am. Craft Coun., Western Res. Kennel Club (com. chair 1999—). Avocations: travel, skiing, raising and showing dogs, collecting contemporary ceramics, reading.

HESS-BENISH, JENIFER, protective services official, real estate agent; d. David Eugene Hess and Jayann Sue Michael; m. Robert Charles Benish, Mar. 18, 2000. BS in Psychology and Justice Studies, Grand Canyon U., 1996. Lic. realtor Ariz., cert. probation officer Ariz. Inst. Probation. Office mgr. That Door Co., Gilbert, Ariz.; real estate sales Prudential Real Estate, Tempe, Ariz.; juvenile intensive probation officer Juvenile Ct., Mesa, Ariz. Leader cmty. activities Juvenile Ct., Ariz., 1997—. Mem.: S.E. Valley Regional Assn. Realtors. Office: Maricopa County Juvenile Ct 1810 S Lewis Mesa AZ 85210

HESSE, CAROLYN SUE, lawyer; b. Belleville, Ill., Jan. 12, 1949; d. Ralph H. Hesse and Marilyn J. (Midgley) Hesse Dierkes; m. William H. Hallenbeck. BS, U. Ill., 1971; MS, U. Ill., Chgo., 1977; JD, DePaul U., 1983. Bar: Ill. 1983, U.S. Dist. Ct. (no. dist.) Ill. 1983. Rsch. assoc. U. Ill., Chgo., 1974-77; tech. adviser Ill. Pollution Control Bd., Chgo., 1977-80; environ. scientist U.S. EPA, Chgo., 1980-84; assoc. Pretzel & Stouffer, Chartered, Chgo., 1984-87, Coffield Ungaretti Harris & Slavin, Chgo., 1987-88; ptnr. McDermott, Will & Emery, 1988-99; pvt. practice Chgo., 1999-2001; with Barnes & Thornburg, 2001—. Frequent spkr. seminars on environ. issues. Contbr. articles on environ. sci. to profl. jours. Mem. ABA, Chgo. Bar Assn. Office: Barnes & Thornburg 1 N Wacker Dr #4400 Chicago IL 60606-2807 E-mail: chesse@btlaw.com.

HESSE, KAREN (KAREN SUE HESSE), writer, educator; b. Balt., Md., Aug. 29, 1952; d. Alvin Donald and Frances Broth Levin; m. Randy Hesse; children: Kate, Rachel. BA, U. Md., 1975. Reference libr. U. Md., 1973-75, leave benefit coord., 1975-76; advt. sec. Country Journal mag., 1976-77, typesetter, proofreader, 1978-88; mental health care provider, 1989-91; children's lit. reviewer, 1993-94. Author: (children's books) Wish on a Unicorn, 1991 (Hungry Mind Rev. Children's Book of Distinction 1992), Letters From Rifka, 1992 (Nat. Jewish Book award 1993, IRA Children's Book award 1993, Christopher award 1992, Sydney Taylor Book award 1992, ALA Notable Book 1992, ALA Best Book for Young Adults 1992, Sch. Libr. Jour. Best Book of Yr. 1992, Horn Book Outstanding Book of Yr. 1992, Booklist Editors' Choice 1992, NY Pub. Libr. 100 Titles for Reading and Sharing 1992), Poppy's Chair, 1993 (Am. Booksellers Assn. Pick of List 1993), Lester's Dog, 1993 (Best Book of Yr. Sch. Libr. Jour. 1993, Notable Children's Trade Book in Field of Social Studies 1993), Lavender, 1993, Sable, 1994 (Sch. Libr. Jour. Best Book of Yr. 1994, NY Pub. Libr. 100 Titles for Reading and Sharing 1994, Boston Globe 10 Best Trade Books 1994, Parenting Mag. 40 Outstanding Children's Books 1994), Phoenix Rising, 1994 (Sch. Libr. Jour. Best Book of Yr. 1994, IRA Tchr.'s Choice 1995, NY Pub. Libr. Books for the Teenage 1995, Best Book for Young Adults ALA 1995, Notable Book, 1995, Wilson Libr. Bull. 33 Favorite Reads 1994 (S.C. Jr. Book award, 1996, 97, others), A Time of Angels, 1995 (IRA Tchr's Choice 1996, IRA Young Adults' Choice, 1997, NY Pub. Libr. Books for the Teenager 1995), The Music of Dolphins, 1996 (Pub.'s Weekly Best Book of Yr. 1996, Best Book of Yr. Sch. Libr. Jour. 1996, Book Links, 100 Titles for Reading and Sharing NY Pub. Libr. Children's Book 1996, Best Books for Young Adults ALA, 1997, Golden Kite Honor Book, 1997), Out of the Dust, 1997 (Newbery medal 1998, Scott O'Dell award 1998), Just Juice, 1998 (100 Titles for Reading and Sharing NY Pub. Libr. 1998, Notable Children's Trade Book in the Field of Social Studies 1998), Come On, Rain!, 1999 (BCCB Blue Ribbon Book, NYPL 100 Books for Reading & Sharing, Jr. Library Guild selection, Book of the Month Club selection, Hon. Mention award, Columbus Internat. Film Fest., ALA Notable Video, 2004); contbr. When I Was Your Age, Vol. II, 1999 (2000 Books for the Teen Age), A Light in the Storm, 1999 (Notable Children's Trade Book in the Field of Social Studies 1999, Kennedy Ctr. Stage Adaptation, 2001), Stowaway, 2000 (SLJ Book of Yr., 2001, Capitol Choice Noteworthy Books for Children (10-14), 100 Titles for Reading and Sharing NY Pub. Libr., 2000, Jr. Libr. Guild Selection), Witness (NY Pub. Libr. 100 Books for Reading and Sharing, ALA Notable Children's book, LA 100 Best Books 2001, 2002 IRA Notable 2002, CBC Choice 2002, Myers Award 2002, NCTE Notable 2002, Christopher award 2002, Parents Guide to Children's Media award); Aleutian Sparrow (Jr. Libr. Guild selection 100 Titles for Reading and Sharing), The Stone Lamp (Assn. Jewish Librs. Notable 100 Titles for Reading and Sharing); contbr. articles to profl. jour. Chmn. Sch. Bd., 1989; sec. bd. dirs. Moore Free Libr., 1989-91; active Hospice, 1988—. MacArthur fellow, 2003—. Mem. Soc. Children's Book Writers and Illustrators, So. Vt. Soc. Children's Book Writers (leader 1985-92), Ctr. for Children's Environ. Lit., Author's Guild. Avocations: reading, hiking, cultivating friendships, music. Office: Scholastic 555 Broadway New York NY 10012-3919

HESSE, MARTHA O. gas industry executive; b. Hattiesburg, Miss., Aug. 14, 1942; d. John William and Geraldine Elaine (Ossian) H. BS, U. Iowa, 1964; postgrad., Northwestern U., 1972-76; MBA, U. Chgo., 1979. Research analyst Blue Shield, 1964-66; dir. div. data mgmt. Am. Hosp. Assn., 1966-69; dir., chief operating officer SEI Info. Tech., Chgo., 1969-80; assoc. dep. sec. Dept. of Commerce, Washington, 1981-82; exec. dir. Pres.' Task Force on Mgmt. Reform, 1982; asst. sec. mgmt. and adminstrn. Dept. of Energy, Washington, 1982-86; chmn. FERC, Washington, 1986-89; sr. v.p. 1st Chgo. Corp., 1990; CEO Hesse Gas Co., Houston, 1990—2003. Bd. dirs. Pinnacle West Capital Corp., Ariz. Pub. Svc. Co., Mut. Trust Life, AMEC plc, Terra Industries, Enbridge Energy Prnrs. Home: 4171 Autumn Hills Dr Winnemucca NV 89445

HESSELBEIN, FRANCES RICHARDS, foundation executive, consultant, editor; b. South Fork, Pa. d. Burgess Harmon and Anne Luke (Wicks) Richards; widowed, 1978; 1 child, John Richards. DHL(hon.), Buena Vista Coll., 1987, Juniata Coll., 1990, Hood Coll., 1991; D Mgmt. (hon.), GM Inst., 1990; LLD (hon.), Wilson Coll., 1991; LHD (hon.), Marymount-Tarrytown Coll., 1993; DHL (hon.), Boston Coll., 1994, U. Nebr., Kearney, 1994, Lafayette Coll., 1995, Carroll Coll., 1996, Fairleigh Dickinson U., 1996, Muhlenburg Coll., 1996; LLD (hon.), Moravian Coll., 2000; D in Pub. and Internat. Affairs, U. Pitts., 2001; DHL (hon.), Mt. Mary Coll., 2002, Union Inst. and Univ., 2003, U. Cin., 2003. CEO Talus Rock Girl Scout Coun., Johnstown, 1970-74, Penn Laurel Girl Scout Coun., York, Pa., 1974-76, Girl Scouts U.S., N.Y.C., 1976-90; pres., CEO Peter F. Drucker Found. Nonprofit Mgmt., N.Y.C., 1990-99, chmn., 1999—2003, Leader To Leader Inst., N.Y.C., 2003—. Chmn. Nat. Bd. Vols. Am.; bd. dirs. Mut. of Am. Ins. Co., N.Y.C.; nat. bd. visitors Peter F. Drucker Grad. Mgmt. Sch. Claremont (Calif.) Grad. Sch., 1987—; chmn. bd. govs. Josephson Ethics Inst., 1989-99; adv. com. to bd. dirs. N.Y. Stock Exch., 1988-91; bd. govs. Ctr. for Creative Leadership, Greensboro, N.C., 1992-98; adv. bd. Harvard Bus. Sch.'s Initiative on Social Enterprise, Harvard's Kennedy Sch. Hauser Ctr. Nonprofit Policy and Leadership Program; chmn. Vols. Am., 2002-, Leader to Leader Inst., 2003—. Editor-in-chief Leader to Leader; co-editor The Leader of the Future, The Organization of the Future, The Community of the Future, Drucker Found. Future Series, Leader to Leader Book, 1999, Leading Beyond the Walls, 1999; author: Hesselbein on Leadership, 2002. Trustee Juniata Coll., Huntingdon, Pa., 1988—, Allentown (Pa.) Coll., 1988-97; mem. Pres.'s Adv. Com. on Points of Light Initiative Found., 1989; bd. dirs. Nat. Exec. Svc. Corps., N.Y., Commn. on Nat. and Cmty. Svc., 1991-94; adv. bd. The Leadership Inst., U. So. Calif., 1991, Harvard U.'s John F. Kennedy Sch. Govt. Nonprofit Policy and Leadership Program. Recipient Outstanding Achievement award Inter-Svc. Club Coun., Johnstown, 1976, Entrepreneurial Woman award Women Bus. Owners of N.Y., 1984, Nat. Leadership award United Way of Am., Washington, 1985, Disting. Cmty. Svc. award Mut. of Am. Ins. Co., 1985, Dir.'s Choice-award Nat. Women's Econ. Alliance, 1989, Pa. Soc. Disting. Citizen award, 1991, Wilbur M. McFeeley award Internat. Mgmt. Coun. YMCA, 1993, U. Pitts. Legacy Laureate award, 2000, Internat. Leadership award Athena Found., 2001, Henry Russo award Ind. U. Ctr., 2001, Dwight D. Eisenhower Series Nat. Security award, 2002, Leadership Devel. award, Boston U., 2003, Juliette award Women of Distincton Girl Scouts USA, 2004, Visionary award Am Soc. Assn. Execs., 2004; named to Bus. Hall of Fame, Johnstown, 1995; named Outstanding Exec., Savvy Mag., 1985, Disting. Alumni Fellow U. Pitts., 1999, Disting. Dau. of Pa., Gov. Ridge, 1999, Woman of Yr., Boy Scouts of Greater N.Y., Legacy Laureate, U. Pitts., 2000; on cover BusinessWeek, 1990, Presdl. Medal of Freedom, 1998;

featured in Chief Exec. mag., 1995, Fortune, 1995-96, Chapel of Four Chaplains Gold Legion of Hon. medal, 1999, Athena Found.-Internat. Leadership award, 2001, Henry Rosso award for lifetime ethical fundraising Ind. U. Ctr., 2001-02, Marion Gislason award Boston U., 2003, Juliette award Girl Scouts U.S., 2004, Visionary award [illegible] Hesselbein How To Be leadership award for ethical leadership established at Jur. Achievement, 2003. Mem. Sky Club, Pa. Soc. Office: Leader to Leader Inst 320 Park Ave 3d Fl New York NY 10022-6815 Office Phone: 212-224-1174. Office Fax: 212 224-2508. E-mail: frances@leadertoleader.org.

HESSELINK, ANN PATRICE, financial executive, lawyer; b. Tokyo, July 20, 1954; d. Ira John Jr. and Etta Marie (Ter Louw) H.; 1 child, Katherine Marie Hesselink Hicks. AB in Psychology, Hope Coll., 1975; JD, St. Johns U., 1980; advanced profl. cert. in fin., NYU, 1983. Bar: N.Y. 1981; CPA, N.Y. Tax mgr. Coopers & Lybrand, N.Y.C., 1980-82; asst. v.p. Bankers Trust Co., N.Y.C., 1982-83; dir. internat. taxes PepsiCo, Inc., Purchase, N.Y., 1983-85; sr. v.p., dir. taxes Young & Rubicam Inc., N.Y.C., 1986-94; v.p. taxes, tax counsel AT&T Capital Corp., Morristown, N.J., 1994-97; cons., 1997—2002; dir. taxation Gentek Inc., Parsippany, NJ, 2002—. Trustee, v.p. Blue Rock Sch., Palisades, N.Y., 1987-89; treas., bd. dirs. Plays for Living, 1991-98; trustee New Brunswick Sem., 1993-98; bd. trustees Ctrl. Coll., 1999—. Mem. ABA, N.Y. State Bar Assn., AICPA, Am. Sch. in Japan Alumni Assn. (chmn. N.Y. region). Democrat. Presbyterian. Home: 27 Ballantine Rd Mendham NJ 07945-3004 E-mail: ahesselink@gentek-global.com.

HESSER, LORRAINE M, special education educator; d. Joseph V. Scolari III, Agnes E. McGovern; m. George W. Hesser III, June 1, 1979; children: Stephanie M., Matthew G. BA in Spl. Edn., Rowan U., 1996; AAS in Bus. Adminstrn., Mktg., Camden County Coll., 1977. Cert. Tchr. of Handicapped N.J., 1996, elem. tchr. N.J., 1997. Tchr. spl. edn. Vineland Pub. Schs., Vineland, NJ, 1998—, Ind. Child Study Teams, Jersey City, 1996—98. Mem. Salem County Bd. of Sch. Estimates, 2003—; chairperson Salem County Mental Health Bd., Salem, NJ, 1995—2003; bd. dirs. Salem County Spl. Svcs. Sch. Dist. Bd. Edn., Woodstown, NJ, 1996—, v.p., 2004—; parent adv. Phila. Child Guidance Ctr. Children's Hosp., 1994; organizor Girl Scouts Am., Medford, NJ, 1985—88. Mem.: NEA, Statewide Parent Adv. Network, N.J. Edn. Assn., Coun. for Exceptional Children (Learning Disabilities divsn., Culturally and Linguistically Diverse Exceptional Learners divsn., Spl. Educator award 2000). Avocations: music, travel, photography, gardening, reading. Home: 1065 Rainbow Cir Pittsgrove NJ 08318 Office: Vineland Board of Education 625 Plum St Vineland NJ 08360 Personal E-mail: lmhesser@aol.com.

HESSINGER, JILL A. art educator; b. Niagara Falls, N.Y., June 6, 1958; d. George and Janet A. Gunzelman; m. Philip M. Hessinger, Sept. 1, 1984; children: Kelly, Austen. AS in Fine Arts, Niagara County C.C., Sanborn, N.Y., 1990; BS in Art Edn., Buffalo State Coll., 1996, MS in Art Edn., 1999. Cert. art tchr. N.Y. Customer svc. rep. Marine Midland Bank, Niagara Falls, NY, 1979—93; art tchr. Kenmore (N.Y.) Ctrl. Sch. Dist., 1997—98, Niagara Wheatfield Ctrl. Sch. Dist., Sanborn, NY, 1998—. Contbr. articles. Grantee Niagara Orleans BOCES, 1999, 2000, 2001, Kenan Ctr., 1999, 2001. Mem.: N.Y. State Art Tchrs. Assn. Democrat. Avocations: painting, travel, visiting museums.

HESTER, JULIA A. lawyer; b. L.A., Nov. 14, 1953; d. Robert William and Bertie Ella (Gilbert) Hester; children: Allison Hester-Haddad, Nancy Hester-Haddad. BA, Fla. Atlantic U., 1984; JD, Nova U., 1990. Bar: Fla. 1990, U.S. Dist. Ct. (mid. dist.) Fla. 1993. Asst. pub. defender Broward Pub. Defender, Ft. Lauderdale, Fla., 1990-93; atty., ptnr. Haddad & Hester, Ft. Lauderdale, 1993-95, 97—. Bd. dirs. St. Anthony Found., Ft. Lauderdale, Ft. Lauderdale Billfish Tournament, 1992—96; bd. dirs., mem. exec. bd. St. Thomas Aquinas Found.; mem. Sunrise Intercoastal Bd., Ft. Lauderdale, 1995; bd. dirs., officer Kids Inn Distress Aux., Ft. Lauderdale, 1984—87. Office: 1 Financial Plz Ste 2612 Fort Lauderdale FL 33394-0061

HESTER, LINDA HUNT, retired dean, counseling administrator, sociology educator, physical education educator; b. Winston-Salem, NC, June 16, 1938; d. Hanselle Lindsay and Jennie Sarepta (Hunt) H. BS with honors, U. Wis., 1960, MS, 1964; PhD, Mich. State U., 1971. Lic. ednl. counselor, Wis. Instr. health and phys. edn. for women U. Tex., Austin, 1960—62; asst. dean women U. Ill., Urbana, 1964—66; dean of women, asst. prof. sociology and phys. edn. Tex. Woman's U., Denton, 1971—73. Rsch. assoc. bur. higher edn. Mich. Dept. Edn., Lansing, 1969-70; vol. counselor Dallas Challenge and Dallas Ind. Sch. Dist., 1989-90 Bd. dirs. Dallas Opera, Dallas, 1986—; Stradivarious mem. Dallas Symphony, 1991—; assoc. mem. Dallas Mus. Art, 1991—; friend of Kimbell Art Mus., com. of 1000 Philharmonic Ctr. for Arts, Naples, Fla.; founder Women's Mus., Dallas; mem., donor Naples Mus. Art; bd. dir. Disting. Svc. Registry in Counseling and Devel. Fellow coll. edn. Mich. State U., 1968; listed in Texas Women, 2003. Mem. ACA, Am. Coll. Pers. Assn., Nat. Assn. Women in Edn., Brookhaven Country Club, Wyndemere Country Club, Delta Kappa Gamma, Alpha Lambda Delta. Republican. Presbyterian. Avocations: golf, reading, sailing, cooking, travel. Home: 7606 Wellcrest Dr Dallas TX 75230-4857

HESTER, NANCY ELIZABETH, county government official; b. Miami, Fla., Jan. 20, 1950; d. George Temple and Lorraine Patricia (Cluney) Hester. BA, Bucknell U., 1972; MIA, Columbia U., 1974; MBA, Fla. Internat. U., 1979. Treasury rep. Westinghouse Elec. Co., N.Y.C., 1974-76; adminstrv. officer serving in bldg. and zoning, gen. svcs. and corrections and rehab. depts. Metro Dade County, Fla., 1979-2000, bur. comdr. corrections and rehab. dept., 1990-2000. Adj. prof. Fla. Internat. U., Miami, 1980-83. Bd. dirs. YWCA Greater Miami, 1988-92, LWV Dade County, 1993-98; pres. bd. dirs., pres. bd. trustees edn. fund, 1994-96; mem. adv. bd. SafeSpace, 1995-2001, v.p. adv. bd., 2000.

HESTON, RENATE, nursing administrator; b. Gross-Strehlitz, Germany; came to U.S., 1960; d. Guenter and Elisabeth (Englich) Paetzold; m. Leonard Lancaster Heston; children: Barbara and Ardis (twins). BS in Human Svcs., U. Minn., 1987. RN bd. cert. gerontolog. nurse., Minn., Iowa, Oreg. Staff nurse, asst. head nurse; head nurse psychiat. unit Oreg. State Hosp., U. Oreg., U. Iowa Med. Sch.; nurse supr. The Wilder Found., New Brighton, Minn. Cons. in field. Co-author: The Medical Casebook of Adolf Hitler. Bd. dirs., dir. vol. svcs. U. N.A. Minn., 1973-88. Mem. AAUW, U. Minn. Alumni Assn. Avocations: classical music, reading, gardening, visual arts, gourmet cooking. Home: 128 Windsor Ct New Brighton MN 55112-3372

HESTON, SARA SMITH, art educator, artist; b. Altoona, Pa., June 9, 1946; d. Charles Bernard Smith and Virginia Louise Bolger; m. Newton Heston, July 4, 1970; children: Heather S., Todd N. BS in Art Edn., cum laude, Ind. U. Pa., Ind., Pa., 1968; Med hons., U. Pitts., Pitts., Pa., 1974. Cert. permanent tchg. Pa., 1974. Art tchr. Norristown Area Sch. Dist., Pa., 1968—70, Savannah/Chatham County Sch., Savannah, Ga., 1970—71, Chartiers Houston Sch. Dist., Houston, Pa., 1971—76, Peters Twp. Sch. Dist., McMurray, Pa., 1984—2001; instr. Va. Marti Coll. of Art and Design, Lakewood, Ohio, 2002—. Mentor tchr. Peters Twp. Sch. Dist., McMurray, Pa., 1997—2000. Prin. works include Goodbye to Summer (inclusion in SPLASH 8: Watercolor Discoveries book, 2003, first Pl. - Women's Art League of Akron juried exhibit, 2002), Watercolor Paintings (5 - Eat'n Pk. Golden Sable Awards), exhibitions include watercolor painting/poster, Nat. Assn.of State and Local Garden Clubs (First Pl. Award - Nat. Level, 1992), watercolor painting, Patriotic Gazebo (first Pl. -Paint Hist. Medina(Ohio-)contest, 2003). Deacon and elder Ctr. Presbyn. Ch., McMurray, Pa., 1980—96; moderator Presbyn. Women- Ctr. Ch., McMurray, Pa., 1990—2000; mem. Hobbitt's Nursery Sch., Richfield, Ohio, 2002—03; group leader La Leche League Internat., McMurray, Pa., 1977—85; pres. McMurray Art League, Pa., 1992—93. Recipient Lifetime membership, Presbyn. Women, 1994; scholar Tchr. Inst. Attendee, Nat. Gallery of Art, 1995 [illegible] Hall Floor (coll.), Crooked River Gang of Artists (assoc.), Women's Art League of Akron(Ohio) (assoc.), Pitts. Watercolor Soc. (assoc.), Ohio Watercolor Soc. (assoc. painting selected for ann. juried exhibit 2003), Delta Phi Delta (life), Alpha Omicron Pi (life; pres. -collegiate chpt. 1966—67). Protestant. Achievements include Electronic Imagery course curriculum designed and implemented in 1993. Avocations: travel, gardening, photography, art. Home: 2008 McClaren Ln Broadview Heights OH 44147 Office: Va Marti Coll of Art and Design Detroit Ave Lakewood OH 44107

HETHERINGTON, EILEEN MAVIS, psychologist, educator; b. Nov. 27, 1926; BA, U. B.C., 1947, MA, 1948; PhD in Psychology, U. Calif.-Berkeley, 1958. Clin. psychologist B.C. Child Guidance Clinic, 1948-51, sr. psychologist, 1951-52; clin. internship Langley Porter Clinic, 1956-57; instr. psychology San Jose State Coll., 1957-58; asst. prof. Rutgers U., 1958-60; from asst. prof. to prof. U. Wis., 1960-70; prof. psychology U. Va., Charlottesville, 1970-99, James Page prof. psychology, 1976-99, prof. emeritus, 1999—, dept. chmn., 1980-84. Editor Child Devel., 1971-77; rschr. in personality devel. and childhood psychopathology, the role of family process and parent characteristics on normal and deviant behavior in children, the effects of divorce and remarriage on families, parents and children. Bd. dirs. Found. for Child Devel. Recipient Disting. Scientist award Am. Assn. for Marriage and Family Therapy, 1988, Am. Family Therapy Assn., 1992, Burgess award Nat. Coun. on Family Rels., 2000. Mem. APA (pres. divsn. 7, 1978-79, Stanley Hall Disting. Scientist award 1987, Disting. Scientist award 1993), Soc. Rsch. in Child Devel. (pres. 1985-87, Disting. Scientist award 1995), Soc. Rsch. in Adolescents (pres. 1986-88, Disting. Scientist award 1988, William James Disting. Scientist award 1994), Am. Psychol. Soc. Office: U Va Dept Psychology Gilmer Hall PO Box 400400 Charlottesville VA 22904-4400

HETHERINGTON, NANCY, state legislator; MDiv, Andover Newton Theol. Sch., 1981; MSW, R.I. Coll., 1992. Ordained to ministry, United Meth. Ch. Dir. social svcs. Dorcas Place Adult Literacy Ctr., Providence; vice chair health, edn. & welfare; R.I. state rep. Dist. 28. Address: 122 Westwood Ave Cranston RI 02905

HETRICK, JOAN WILLETTE, critical care nurse, administrator; b. Oct. 14, 1959; d. Wilbert D. Sproul and Lois Diane (Wilson) Pinette Anderson; m. Charles Vance Frum, May 4, 2002. B in Health Scis., Fla. Atlantic U., 1996; ASN, Miami-Dade Med. Ctr., 1998. RN, Fla., Ga. Adminstrv. asst., cons. Holiday Prime Foods, 5 Star Mktg. Group, Davie, Fla., 1996—2002; RN critical care Aventura (Fla.) Hosp., 1999; RN Meml. Reg. Hosp., Hollywood, Fla., 1999, Hollywood Med. Ctr. Telemetry and Prog. Care, 1998-99; charge nurse Hallandale Rehab. Ctr., 2000—02; ER nurse Plantation Gen. Hosp., 2001—02; RN specialist Agy. for Health Care Adminstrn., Fla., 2001—02; RN Agy., 2002—03; oncology nurse Kennestone Hosp., Ga., 2003—. Health instr. Miami Book Fair Internat., Miami-Dade C.C., 1997; health care rschr. for 104th Congress, 1995. Mem. Oncology Nurses Soc., Internat. Thespian Soc., Fla. Nurses Assn., Oncology Nursing Soc., Kappa Delta Pi, Alpha Phi Omega. Republican. Avocations: critical care nursing studies, business studies, real estate studies, pets, surfing the internet. Home: 282 Hood Pkwy Kennesaw GA 30152-

HETTMANSPERGER, SUE, artist; b. Akron, Ohio, Nov. 20, 1948; d. Hilton E. Hettmansperger and Dorothy E. Stone. Student, Yale U., summer 1971; BFA in Lithography and Drawing cum laude, U. N.Mex., 1972, MA in Lithography and Drawing, 1974. Grad. tchg. asst. U. N.Mex., 1972-74; instr. lithography, intaglio and drawing Pa. State U., State Coll., 1974-75; prof. painting and drawing U. Iowa, Iowa City, 1977—. Vis. lectr. U. N.Mex., Albuquerque, 1985; invited artist in residence in painting and drawing Roswell Art Mus., N.Mex., 1990; artist in residence in drawing U Cross Found., Wyo., 1992; curator of prints Tyler Graphics, Bedford Village, N.Y., 1976; nat. affiliate A.I.R. Gallery, N.Y.C., 1989—; lectr. in field. One-woman shows include, Frumkin & Struve Gallery Chgo., 1981, A.I.R. Gallery, NYC, 1990, 1994, 1999, 2003, CSPS Alternative Space, Cedar Rapids, Iowa, 1992, U. No. Iowa Gallery, Cedar Falls, 1994, Artemisia Gallery C, Chgo., 1995, exhibited in group shows, Artemisia Gallery, Chgo., 1996, Arts Iowa City Gallery, Iowa, 1998, Galeria Article 26, Carer de Ferlandina, Barcelona, Spain, 1999, U. Tex. San Antonio Gallery, 2002, Faulconer Gallery, Grinnell Coll., 2003, numerous others, represented in pub. and pvt. collections. MacDowel Colony Drawing fellow, 1977; NEA fellow in drawing, 1983; recipient Faculty Scholar award U. Iowa, 1997-99; arts and humanities interdisciplinary grantee U. Iowa, 2001. Office: U Iowa E 100 AB Riverside Dr Iowa City IA 52242

HEUBUSCH, LOUISE MADELINE, physical therapist, educator; b. Buffalo, N.Y., Jan. 18, 1948; d. Alphonse John Heubusch and Louise Frances Ellman. BS, SUNY, Buffalo, 1970, MS, 1984. Lic. phys. therapist N.Y., 1970, N.J., 1975, cert. neurodevel. treatment 1972. From staff to sr. phys. therapist Helen Hayes Hosp., West Haverstaw, NY, 1970—77; coord. rehab. West Essex Nursing Svc., West Caldwell, NJ, 1977—78; asst. prof., coord. clin. edn. dept. phys. therapy SUNY, Buffalo, 1978—89; coord. rehab. Deaconess Skilled Nursing Facility, Buffalo, 1989—98; phys. therapy asst. instr. Villa Maria Coll., Cheektowaga, NY, 1998—; contract phys. therapist Diversified Rehab. Svcs., Kenmore, NY, 1998—2002; staff phys. therapist Home Care divsn. Univera Health Care, Buffalo, 2002—. Profl. adv. bd. Red Cross Multiple Home Care Agys., Buffalo, 1989—90; cons. in field; profl. adv. bd. mem. Diversified Rehab. Svcs., Kenmore, 1998—2002. Contbr. articles to profl. jours. Vol. various theater groups, Buffalo, 1966—; participant in China People to People Program, 1992; mem. Buffalo Choral Arts Soc., 1978—. Grantee, Kaleida Health, Buffalo, 1998. Democrat. Roman Catholic. Avocations: world travel, singing, reading, hiking, skiing.

HEUER, BETH LEE, music educator, composer, arranger; b. Rockford, Ill., May 13, 1957; d. Stanton Lee and Gladys Mae Heuer. BA in Music, 1980, BFA in Music Edn., 1981, M in Music Edn., 2001. Vocal music tchr. Boylan Cath. H.S., Rockford, Ill., 1981—82, Pecatonica (Ill.) H.S., 1982—83; band dir. Boylan Cath. H.S., 1983—, chmn. dept. music, 1987—. Pvt. music tchr., Rockford, 1982—. Music arranger, composer, 1985—. Mem.: Ill. Music Educators Assn., Music Educators Nat. Conf., Internat. Jazz Educators Assn. Avocations: gardening, reading, traveling. Office: Boylan Cath HS 4000 St Francis Dr Rockford IL 61103

HEUER, CATHERINE ANN, music educator; b. Oshkosh, Wis., Jan. 9, 1959; d. Walter Richard Dugolenski and Ruth Elizabeth Knaggs; m. William Michael Heuer, July 18, 1992. B in Music Edn., U. Wis., Oshkosh, 1981; Kodaly cert., Silver Lake Coll., 2002. Music tchr. Sts. Peter and Paul Sch., Kiel, Wis., 1982—84, St. Joseph Sch., Stratford, Wis., 1985—88, St. John Sch., Marshfield, Wis., 1988—2001, Marshfield Area Cath. Schs., 2001—. Music min. St. John the Bapt. Cath. Ch., Marshfield, 1994—; dir. Marshfield Area Recorder Ensemble, 1993—; mem. Ctrl. Chamber Chorale, Marshfield. Mem.: Am. Recorder Soc., Music Educators Nat. Conf., Wis. Choral Dirs. Assn., Am. Choral Dirs. Assn., Orgn. Am. Kodaly Educators, Assn. Wis. Area Kodaly Educators (treas. 2002). Avocation: aerobics.

HEUER, MARGARET B. retired microcomputer laboratory coordinator; b. Juneau, Alaska, Sept. 12, 1935; d. William George and Flora (Rusk) Allen; m. Joseph Louis Heuer; children: Leilani, Joseph (dec.), Daniel, Suzanne, Karen, Mark, Jerina. AA, San Bernardino Valley Coll., 1980. Cert. data processing, computer repair and maintenance, microcomputer support specialist. Coord. microcomputers lab. Oakton Community Coll., Skokie, Ill., 1981-93, ret., 1993, switchboard oper. Coll. Am. Pathologists, 2000—.

HEUKESHOVEN, JANET KAY, music educator; b. Mpls., Mar. 11, 1957; d. Burton O. and Bertha I. Norby; m. A. Eric Heukeshoven, Mar. 20, 1986; children: Hans, Max. BS in Music Edn., U. Minn., 1979; MusM, Boston Conservatory, 1984; DMA, U. Wis., 1994. Asst. music prof., dir. band and orch. Coll. of St. Teresa, Winona, Minn., 1982—87; assoc. prof. instrumental music and music edn., band dir. St. Mary's U. of Minn., Winona, 1994—, chmn. dept. music, 1998—. Soloist, performer Minn. Amb. of Music, 2000—; performer, sect. leader Winona Mcpl. Band; flute musician St. Mary's U. Faculty Ensemble, 1990—; performer, soloist recitals and chamber ensembles, 1984—; guest condr. various regional clinics and concerts, 1990—. Charter mem. Winona Fine Arts Commn., 1996—2002. Recipient R. Church Meml. Conducting award, U. Wis., 1994, Performance award, Sigma Alpha Iota, 1979. Mem.: Minn. Coll. and Univ. Chairs of Music (pres.), Coll. Band Dirs. Nat. Assn. (chpt. sec. 2000—03), Minn. Music Educators Assn. Avocations: gardening, reading, cross country skiing. Office: Saint Mary's Univ of Minn 700 Terrace Heights #58 Winona MN 55987

HEUMANN, JUDITH, bank executive; m. Jorge Pineda. BA Speech and Theatre, Long Island U., 1969; MPH, U. Calif., Berkeley, 1975. Spl. edn. and 2d grade tchr. N.Y.C. Pub. Schs., 1970-73; legis. asst. to chair Senate Com. Labor and Pub. Welfare, Washington, 1974; sr. dep. dir. Ctr. Independent Living, Berkeley, 1975-82; spl. asst. to exec. dir. State Dept. Rehab., Sacramento, 1982-83; v.p., co-founder, dir. Rsch. Tng. Ctr. Pub. Policy in Independent Living, Berkeley, Calif., 1983-93; co-founder World Inst. Disability, Berkeley, Calif.; U.S. asst. sec. U.S. Dept. Edn., Washington, 1993—2001; also chair, vice chair, bd. mem. Archtl. & Transp. Barriers Compliance Bd., Washington, 1998—2001; adv. disability and devel. World Bank, Washington, 2002—. Office: World Bank 1818 H Street NW Washington DC 20433

HEWITT, EMILY CLARK, judge, minister; b. Balt., May 26, 1944; d. John Frank and Margaret Genevieve (Gray) H. AB, Cornell U., 1966; MPhil, Union Theol. Sem., 1975; JD, Harvard U., 1978. Bar: Mass. 1978, U.S. Dist. Ct. Mass. 1979, U.S. Ct. Appeals (1st cir.) 1984, U.S. Ct. Appeals (fed. cir.) 1999, U.S. Supreme Ct. 2003; ordained priest Protestant Episcopal Ch. 1974. Adminstr. Upward Bound Programs Cornell and Hofstra U., N.Y.C., 1967-69; asst. min. St. Mary's Episcopal Ch., Manhattanville, NY, 1972-73; lectr. Union Theol. Sem., N.Y.C., 1972-73, 74-75; asst. prof. Andover Newton Theol. Sch., Newton Centre, Mass., 1973-75; assoc. Hill & Barlow, Boston, 1978-85, ptnr., 1985-93; gen. counsel GSA, 1993-98; judge U.S. Ct. of Fed. Claims, Washington, 1998—. Co-author: Women Priests: Yes or No?, 1973; contbr. works in field. Bd. dirs. Mass. Found. for Humanities and Pub. Policy, South Hadley, 1983-89. Mem.: Mass. Conveyancers Assn. (exec. com. 1990—93), New Eng. Women in Real Estate (dir. 1985—89), ABA (vice chair Bid Protest com. sect. pub. contract law 2000—02). Office: National Courts Bldg 717 Madison Pl NW Washington DC 20005

HEWITT, JACQUELINE N. astronomy educator; AB in Econs., Bryn Mawr Coll., 1980; PhD in Physics, MIT, 1986. Prof. physics MIT, 1989—; dir. Ctr. Space Rsch. 2002MIT. Recipient Annie Jump Cannon award in Astronomy, 1989, David and Lucille Packard fellowship, 1990, Alfred P. Sloan rsch. fellowship, 1990, Henry G. Booker prize award, 1993, Maria Goeppart-Mayer award Am. Phys. Soc., 1995. Office: MIT Dept Physics Room 37-241 Cambridge MA 02139 E-mail: jhewitt@mit.edu.

HEWITT, JENNIFER LOVE, actress, singer; b. Waco, Tex., Feb. 21, 1979; d. Danny and Pat. Appeared in films, including Munchies, 1992, Little Miss Millions, 1993, Sister Act 2: Back in the Habit, 1993, House Arrest, 1996, Trojan War, 1997, I Know What You Did Last Summer, 1997, Can't Hardly Wait, 1998, Telling You, 1998, I Still Know What You Did Last Summer, 1998, The Suburbans, 1999, Bunny, 2000, Breakers, 2000, Adventures of Tom Thumb and Thumbelina (voice), 2000; television appearances include Kids Inc., 1989-91, Shaky Ground, 1992, The Byrds of Paradise, 1994, McKenna, 1994, Party of Five, 1995-99, The Senior Prom, 1997, Time of Your Life, 1999—, The Audrey Hepburn Story, 2000; albums include Love Songs, 1992, Let's Go Bang, 1995, Jennifer Love Hewitt, 1996. Office: William Morris Agy 151 S El Camino Dr Beverly Hills CA 90212-2775

HEWITT, MAUREEN GILGORE, scholarly book publishing executive; b. Waukegan, Ill., July 16, 1943; d. Rolland Robert Gilgore and Marguerite Annabelle Terrien McHale; m. Terry Ned Trobec, June 8, 1968 (div. Oct. 1983); children: Kerry Morgan Trobec, Justin John Trobec; m. John Douglas Hewitt, July 28, 1985. BA, Lake Forest (Ill.) Coll., 1966; MA, La. State U., 1971. Test adminstr. Abbott Labs., North Chicago, Ill., 1966-67; editor Rand McNally, Lincolnwood, Ill., 1967-69, La. State U. Press, Baton Rouge, 1969-72; freelance editor Libertyville, Ill., 1972-75; devel. editor AHM Pub. Co., Arlington Heights, Ill., 1975-78; mng. editor Harlan Davidson, Inc., Arlington Heights, Ill., 1978-84; editor-in-chief Harlan Davidson, Ic., Arlington Heights, Ill., 1984-86; v.p., editor-in-chief Harlan Davidson, Inc., Wheeling, Ill., 1986—, also bd. dirs.; asst. dir., editor-in-chief La. State Univ. Press, Baton Rouge, 1996-99, assoc. dir., editor-in-chief, 1999—. Mem. mktg. com. Lake County LEARNS, Libertyville, 1992-96. Mem. NOW (pres. Baton Rouge chpt. 1970, pres. Lake County chpt. 1972), Women in Comms., Inc. (pres.-elect 1994-95, programming cons. North Shore chpt. 1993-94), Chgo. Women in Pub. (chair mgr.'s roundtable, mem. bd. dirs. 1989-91, mem. exec. adv. bd. 1994-95), Chgo. Book Clinic, So. Hist. Assn., Am. Hist. Assn., Orgn. of Am. Historians, Baton Rouge Early Risers Kiwanis, Internat. Hospitality Found. (bd. dirs. 1999—). Unitarian Universalist. Avocations: biking, dance and outdoor roller-skating, book discussion groups, piano playing, studying japanese, spanish and american sign language. Office: La State U Press PO Box 25053 Baton Rouge LA 70894-5053 E-mail: mhewitt@lsu.edu.

HEWITT, PATRICIA HOPE, English government official, political scientist, researcher, broadcaster; b. Canberra, Australia, Dec. 2, 1948; arrived in U.K., 1967; d. Lenox and Hope (Tillyard) Hewitt; m. Julian Gibson-Watt, Aug. 8, 1970 (div. 1976); m. William Birtles, Dec. 17, 1981; children: Alexandra, Nicholas. BA, Newnham Coll., Cambridge, 1970; MA, Cambridge (Eng.) U., 1974, Oxford (Eng.) U., 1992. Gen. sec. Nat. Coun. Civil Liberties (now Liberty), England, 1974-83; press sec. to Leader of Opposition (Neil Kinnock), England, 1983-87; policy coord. Leader of Opposition, England, 1987-89; dep. dir. Inst. for Pub. Policy Rsch., England, 1989-94; dir. rsch. Andersen Consulting (now Accenture), England, 1994—97; mem. House of Commons, Parliament, 1997—, Sec. of State for Trade and Industry and Min. for Women, 2001—. Author: About Time: The Revolution in Work and Family Life, 1993. Bd. dirs. Internat. League for Human Rights, N.Y.C., 1983—; public relations officer, Age Concern, 1971-74, women's rights officer, 1973-74. Mem. Brit. Labour Party. Avocations: art history, gardening, cooking. Office: Dept Trade & Industry 1 Victoria St London SW1H OET England

HEWITT, VIVIAN ANN DAVIDSON (MRS. JOHN HAMILTON HEWITT JR.), retired librarian; b. New Castle, Pa., Feb. 17, 1920; d. Arthur Robert and Lela Luvada (Mauney) Davidson; m. John Hamilton Hewitt, Jr., Dec. 26, 1949; 1 son, John Hamilton III. AB with honors, Geneva Coll., 1943, LHD, 1978; BSLS, Carnegie Mellon U., 1944; postgrad., U. Pitts., 1947-48. Sr. asst. libr. Carnegie Libr., Pitts., 1944-49; instr., libr. Sch. Libr. Sci. Atlanta U., Atlanta U., 1949-52; with Readers Reference Svc., Crowell-Collier Pub. Co., N.Y.C., 1953-55; libr. Rockefeller Found., N.Y.C., 1955-63; librarian Carnegie Endowment Internat. Peace, N.Y.C., 1963-83; librarian Mexican Agrl. Program, Rockefeller Found., summer 1958; dir. libr. and info. svcs. Katherine Gibbs Sch., N.Y.C., 1984-86; reference asst. Coun. on Fgn. Rels., 1986-89. Lectr. spl. librarianship at grad. schs. of L.S. and info. throughout U.S. and Can., 1968-88; condr. profl. seminars Am. Mgmt. Assn., 1968-69, UN Inst. Tng. and Rsch., 1973, 74, Grad. Sci. Libr. and Info. Sci., Rutgers U., 1986; mem. faculty Grad. Sch. Libr. and Info. Sci., U. Tex., Austin, summer 1985; SLA rep. to Internat. Fedn. Libr. Assns., 1970-73, 73-75, 75-77; mem. nat. adv. com. Ctr. for the Book, Libr. of Congress, 1979-84; mem. adv. bd. Who's Who Among African Ams., 1975—. Contbr. chpt. to: The Black Librarian in America, 1970, What Black Librarians Are Saying, 1972, New Dimensions for Academic Library Service, 1975, A Century of Service, 1976, Handbook of Black Librarianship, 1977, 2d edit., 2000, The Black Librarian in America Revisited, 1994, Notable Black American Men, 1999. Bd. dirs. Graham-Windham, 1967, sec., 1980-87; bd. dirs. Laymen's Club, Cathedral Ch. of St.John the Divine, 1975-82, sec., 1986-93. Recipient Outstanding Cmty. Svc. awards, United Fund N.Y., 1965—77, Disting. Alumna award, U. Pitts.-Carnegie Mellon U. Alumni Assn., 1978, Merit award, Carnegie Mellon U. Alumni Assn., 1979, Leadership award, Carnegie Mellon U. Black Alumni, 2001. Mem.: ALA (Disting. Svc. to Librarianship award Black Caucus 1978, Leadership in Profession award Black Caucus 1992), Jack and Jill Am., Inc. (ea. regional dir. 1967—69), Spl. Librs. Assn. (rep. to Pacem in Terris Convocation 1965, rep. to White House Conf. Internat. Coop. Yr. 1965, pres. N.Y. chpt. 1970—71, nat. pres. 1978—79, Hall of Fame 1984, Leadership award 2001), Am. Soc. Order of St. John, Pierians, Inc. (hon.), Alpha Kappa Alpha, Tower Soc. Geneva Coll. Democrat. Episcopalian. Home: 862 West End Ave New York NY 10025-4959 E-mail: jhh2nyc@aol.com.

HEWLETT, ELIZABETH M. county official; b. N.Y.C., Apr. 4, 1955; BA in Polit. Sci., Tufts U., 1976; JD, Boston Coll., 1979; postgrad., Harvard U., 1998. Legal intern Dist. Attys. Office Queen's County, N.Y.C., 1978; legis. aide Prince George's County Coun., 1980—82; law clk. Prince George's County Atty.'s Office, 1982—84; litigation atty. Legal Aid Bur., Inc., 1984—86; assoc. Meyers, Billingsley, Shipley, Curry, Rodell and Rosenbaum, 1986—88; chairwoman Prince George's County Planning Bd. Md. Nat. Capital Park and Planning Commn., 1995 . Apptd. mem. Gov.'s Drug and Alcohol Abuse Commn., 1989—95, Charter Com. of the Ct. Appeals Md., 1989—95, Md. State Bd. Law Examiner, 1995; appt. chmn. Census Partnership in Prince George's County, 1999; bd. dirs. Greater D.C. Cares, Inc., 1991—93, Pennvision, YMCA Met. Washington, 1999—. Mem.: Nat. Coun. Negro Women, Doctor/Lawyer Edn. Partnership Program, Prince George's County Women Lawyers Caucus, Prince George's Bar Assn., Women's Bar Assn. Md., Md. State Bar Assn., Nat. Bar Assn. Office: Md Nat CapitalPk and Planning Commn 14741 Governor Oden Bowie Dr Upper Marlboro MD 20772

HEWLETT, GLORIA LOUISE, rancher, retired educator, civic volunteer; b. Clifton, Tex., Nov. 28, 1930; d. Dock Simpson and Leona Martha (Fricke) Martin; m. Robert Eckhart Hewlett, Jr., Sept. 3, 1950; children: Robert Eckhart, III, Jeffrey Martin Hewlett. BS, Tex. A&M, Corpus Christi, 1962; MEd, Northwestern State U., Natchitoches, La., 1974; DEd, East Tex. State U., 1988. Tchr. Terrebonne Parish Sch. Dist., Houma, La., 1962-69, Natchitoches (La.) Parish Sch. Dist., 1970-76, Mesquite (Tex.) Sch. Dist., 1977-91; ret., 1991. Author: A Descriptive Study of Textbook Preparation Programs and State Level Textbook Adoption in Texas, 1988. Mem. sr. affairs commn. Dallas City Coun., 1995-97, Bosque County Armed Forces, 2003; pres. Eta Zeta chpt. of Delta Kappa Gamma, Dallas, 1992-94. Named Gift to the Ednl. Found. of AAUW, 1992-93, 94-95. Mem. AAUW (pres. Dallas br. 1991-93, v.p. Tex. 1994-96), Dallas Ret. Tchrs. Assn. (pres. 1997-99), The Women's Coun., Am. Legion Aux., Dallas County Hist. Soc. Avocations: reading, genealogy, gardening. Home and Office: 9402 Mill Hollow Dr Dallas TX 75243-6338 E-mail: gloriamh28@earthlink.com.

HEWLETT, SANDRA MARIE, clinical consultant; b. Chgo., Jan. 28, 1959; d. Stanley Vincent and Angeline Sajkiewicz. BS, Rush U., 1988, MS, 1989; postgrad., U. Ill., Chgo., 1992-95, Tex. Woman's U., 1997—. RN, Ill.; cert. BLS instr. Am. Heart Assn.; cert. breast health awareness instr.; cert. advanced oncology nurse; cert. rehab. RN and advanced cardiac life support certification. Acct., comptr. McKinsey Steel Co., Inc., Forest Park, Ill., 1976-79; exec. dir. Adolescent Youth Svcs., Village of Stone Park, Ill., 1979-81; coord. Midwest Therapeutic Assocs., Morton Grove, Ill., 1981-83, adminstr., 1983-86; in-outpatient oncology nurse Rush North Shore Med. Ctr., Skokie, Ill., 1988-89; oncology resource nurse West Suburban Hosp. Med. Ctr., Oak Park, Ill., 1989-90; oncology clin. nurse specialist Holy Family Hosp., Des Plaines, Ill., 1990-92; oncology clin. specialist, dir. autologous transplant program N.W. Oncology, Hematology S. C., Elk Grove Village, Ill., 1992-95; dir. Breast Ctr. The Dr.'s Hosp., Dallas, 1996-97; cons. Schering Plough Pharms., Mansfield, Tex., 1997—2002; dir. patient care svcs. Healthsouth Rehab. Hosp., 2002—. Asst. prof. Wright Coll., Chgo., 1990 95; mem. profl. adv. bd. Rainbow Hospice, Park Ridge, Ill., 1990-93; profl. educator Ill. Cancer Pain Initiative, N.W. Suburban Cook County, Ill., 1991—. Author: (ednl. program) AIDS-Facts & Myth, 1988, (audio cassettes-patient edn.) Chemo-Induced Sequelae, 1989, Lymphoscintigraphy and Sentinel Lymph Node Biopsy, 1999. Bd. dirs. Am. Cancer Soc. Unit 113, 1992—. Rush U. scholar, 1987-88; recipient Luther Christman award and scholarship Rush U./Rush Presbyn. St. Lukes Med. Ctr., 1988, Excellence in Gerontol Nursing award, 1988, Spl. Project award, 1988. Mem. Oncology Nursing Soc. (pres. elect local chpt., chmn. mem. com., continuing edn. approval panel bd. dirs. 1999—), Am. Cancer Soc. (mem. nurses ednl. com. 1990—, profl. educator 1990—, Grad. scholar 1988-89, bd. dirs. unit 113 1992—), Soc. Otolaryngology and Head-Neck Nurses (treas. 1990-93, legis com. 1991, editor newsletter 1991), Gamma Phi chpt. Sigma Theta Tau. Republican. Roman Catholic. Avocations: reading, writing, travel, classical and jazz music. Home and Office: 9745 Corral Dr Keller TX 76248-5522 Office Phone: 817-289-3394.

HEWLETT-KIERSTEAD, NANCY CARRICK, psychologist, educator; b. Schenectady, Feb. 19, 1927; d. Clarence Wilson and Mary Stephens (Carrick) Hewlett; m. Andrzej T. Romer, June 19, 1952 (div. 1969); children: Jan Edward, Anna Louise, Mary Helena; m. Henry A. Kierstead, July 26, 1981 (dec. Feb. 1990). BFA, Cornell U., 1949; MA (univ. fellow), U. Mich., 1952; PhD (univ. fellow), U. Conn., 1972. Registered clin. psychologist. Tchr. art Thomaston (Conn.) H.S., 1960-63; freelance artist, potter, 1962-67; assoc. prof. psychology Eastern Conn. State U., Willimantic, 1969-84, ret., 1984; clin. psychologist Effective Coping Strategies, Ill., Conn., 1982-91; writer, 1987—. Author: The Green Ribbon, 1997. Asst. clk. Storrs (Conn.) monthly meeting Soc. of Friends, 1978-80, clk., 1980. Mem. ACLU, ADL, Hemlock Soc., Choice in Dying, Framingham (Mass.) Friends Mtg. Home: PO Box 185 Waban MA 02468-0002

HEWSON, MARY MCDONALD, civic volunteer; b. Larned, Kans., Nov. 5, 1922; d. William Michael and Bernice Ulata (Gregory) McDonald; m. Kenneth Dean Hewson, June 21, 1946; children: Rebecca Hewson Lewis, Roberta Hewson Grogan, Margaret Hewson Smith. BS in Edn. cum laude, BS in Psychology, Kans. State U., 1948. Cert. secondary edn. tchr. Freshman counselor Kans. State U., 1948-49; substitute tchr. Larned Unified Sch. Dist., 1958—, tchr. gifted program, 1988, vol. gifted tchr., 1997—, vol. grief counselor for secondary students, 1996—. At home tutor, 1938—; spkr. Nat. Fraternity Blue Key Kans. State U., 1995-1998; gifted coord. vol. secondary level., 1997—; bd. mem. Kans. State U. Trustee Kans. State U. Found., Manhattan, 1980—, trustee planning and funding com., 1996—; mem. Kans. Farmers Union, McPherson, 1982—, Help Eliminate Abuse Locally, Larned, 1982—, Mental Health Assn., Larned, 1982—; spokesperson 8 counties Pawnee County Health Resource, Kans., 1992—, Ctrl. Kans. Environ. Resource Planning Group, 1992—; chmn. Swim for Kids; mem. growth com. Pawnee County Fair, 1995, mem. bldg. com., 1996—; vol. gifted tchr. aide, 1996—; mem. exec. bd. 4-H Co., mem. completed 4-H Bldg; pres. Golden Key Club Kans State Univ. Alums, 1998; spkr. Kans. State U. Alums Family Weekend, 1998. Recipient Medallion award Kans. State U., 1986, Nat. Vol. of Yr. award Coun. for Advancement and Support of Edn., 1983; named to Nat. Women's Hall of Fame, 1996, Ret. Bus. Woman of Yr., 2001. Mem. AAUW (charter), DAR (officer), Kans. Press Women (life mem., patron ednl. support 1988), Patron Menninger Found., 1990—, YMCA (bd. dirs.), Philanthropic Ednl. Orng., Kans. State U. Alumni Assn. (bd. mem., strategic planning com., student rels. com.), Wildcats for Higher Edn. Program, Golden K Club (pres. 1998, spkr. family weekend 1998), Phi Alpha Mu. Avocations: reading, collecting antiques, collecting sports cards, writing, geneaology. Home: PO Box 102 Larned KS 67550-0102

HEYD, EVA, photographer; b. Prague, Czech Republic, Aug. 26, 1953; came to U.S., 1985; naturalized, 1989; d. Otto Anthony Heyd and Miluska (Sindelarova) H.; m. Jan Mach, June 3, 1975 (div. June 1979); 1 child, Kristyna; m. Vaclav Victor Krakora, Aug. 13, 1985 (div. June 1999); 1 child, Thomas. M in Journalism, Charles U., Prague, 1977. Freelance journalist, Prague, 1974-77; freelance photographer, 1977-79; editor Horizon Pub. Ho., Prague, 1979, Architekt mag., Prague, 1979-85; freelance photographer N.Y.C., 1985—. Lectr. Faculta Zurnalistiky Fotoklub, Strahovsky Fotoklub, Prague, 1975; juror photog. competitions, Prague, 1976-78. Illustrator: A Sort of Life (Graham Green), 1974, Photographer (Pierre Boulle), 1982; artist multimedia project (with dancer, painter Lisa Pilot), Jean Gibson Gallery, N.Y., 1991, Paula Cooper Gallery, N.Y., 1992; exhibited in group shows at Silver Image Gallery, Seattle, 1990, Gallery Manes, Prague, 1993, Heller Gallery, N.Y., 1995, Smithtown Arts Coun., 1996, Barret Ho. Galleries, Poughkeepsie, N.Y., 1997, Bohemian Gallery, N.Y., 1997, City Hall, N.Y.C., 1997, Cast Iron Gallery, N.Y.C., 1998, A Center for Photography, Woodstock, 2000, Chappell Gallery, 2001, 2004, Mostly Glass Gallery, Engelwood, 2002; one-woman shows include Gallery USM Rubin, Prague, 1979, Gallery Sztuky Wspolcesnej, Warsaw, 1982, Gallery Fotochema, Prague, 1982, Thermal, Karlovy Vary, Czech Republic, 1985, Gallery Junge Kunstler, Berlin, 1985, Ekazent Gallery, Vienna, 1987, UMPRUM Mus. Expresso, Prague, 1994, New Horizon Gallery, Prague, 1994, Bohemian Gallery, N.Y., 1998; represented in permanent collections at UMPRUM Mus., pvt. collection; contbr. articles and revs. to mags. and jours., Czech Republic and U.S. Home: 84-28 63rd Rd Middle Village NY 11379 Office Phone: 718-426-2192. E-mail: evaheyd@yahoo.com.

HEYDE, MARTHA BENNETT (MRS. ERNEST R. HEYDE), psychologist; b. New Bern, N.C., Jan. 31, 1920; d. George Spotswood and Katherine (McIntosh) Bennett; m. Ernest R. Heyde, Aug. 17, 1946. AB, Columbia U., 1941, MA, 1949, PhD, 1959. Instr. psychol. founds and svcs. Tchrs. Coll., Columbia U., N.Y.C., 1957-59, rsch. assoc., 1960-70, cons., 1970-73. Contbg. author: (rsch. monograph) The Vocational Maturity of Ningh Grade Boys, 1960, Floundering and Trial After High Sch., 1967, co-author: Vocational Maturity During the High School Years, 1979. Mem. Barnard Coll. alumnae coun. Columbia U., 1956-61, 69—, pres. class, 1956-61, trustee, 1974-79, hon. vice chmn. Barnard Coll. Centennial, 1987-89. Mem. APA, Sigma Xi, Kappa Delta Pi, Pi Lambda Theta. Home: 530 E 23rd St Apt 8E New York NY 10010-5030

HEYEN, BEATRICE J. psychotherapist; b. Chgo., June 23, 1925; d. Carl Edwin and Anna W. (Carlson) Lund; m. Robert D. Heyen, June 16, 1950 (dec. Feb. 1981); children: Robin, Jefferson, Neil; m. Robert Christiansen, Nov. 24, 1984. BS, U. Chgo., 1949. Instr. Boone (Iowa) Jr. Coll., 1959-64, Rochester (Minn.) Jr. Coll., 1967-68, Winona (Minn.) State Coll., 1965-68; dir. social svc. State Clinic, Kirksville, Mo., 1968-71; supr., dir. Family Counseling Agy., Joliet, Ill., 1971-85; pvt. practice Muskegon, Mich., 1985—. Cons. Homes for Aged, Programs for Aged, Winona, 1965-68, Spl. Programs and Individuals in Psychotherapy, Muskegon, 1984—; dir. Christiansen Fine Art Gallery, North Muskegon. Mem. Gov.'s Com. on Status of Women, Iowa, 1957-62, Gov.'s Com. on Aging, Minn., 1966-68; bd. mem. Mission for Area People, Muskegon, 1998. Grantee for Pilot Projects in Svc. to Women 1971-84. Mem. AAUW, NASW, Acad. Cert. Social Workers, C.G. Jung Inst. (Chgo.). Methodist. Avocations: ecological interests, day lily gardening, contemporary art. Home: 1610 N Weber Rd North Muskegon MI 49445

HEYER, CAROL ANN, illustrator; b. Cuero, Tex., Feb. 2, 1950; d. William Jerome and Merlyn Mary (Hutson) H. BA, Calif. Luth. U., 1974. Freelance artist various cos., Thousand Oaks, Calif., 1974-79; computer artist Image Resource, Westlake Village, Calif., 1979-81; staff writer, artist Lynn-Davis Prodns., Westlake Village, Calif., 1981-87; art dir. Northwind Studios Internat., Camarillo, Calif., 1988-89; illustrator Touchmark, Thousand Oaks, 1989—. Cons. art dir., writer Lynn-Wenger Prodns., 1987-89; guest spkr. Ariz. Kidney Found. Children's Art and Lit. luncheon 2000, Thousand Oaks Libr., Author's Faire, Calif. Luth. U., Soc. Children's Book Writers and Illustrators, Illustrators Day, Ventura County Reading Assn.'s Author's Faire; guest artist/spkr. Oxnard Libr.; booksignings/appearances Anaheim Conv. Ctr., L.A. Conv. Ctr., Am. Booksellers Assn.; guest 1996 Readout, grand opening Barnes and Noble, Thousand Oaks; represented by Art Works, N.Y.C.; invited artist Ann. Art Show, Chemers Gallery; spkr. in field. Illustrator (children's books) Down the Grand Canyon Harcourt, A Star in the Pasture, 1988, The Dream Stealer, 1989, The Golden Easter Egg, 1989, All Things Bright and Beautiful, 1992, Rapunzel, 1992, The Christmas Carol, 1995, Prancer, Gift of the Magi, Black Beauty, Dinosaurs Strange and Wonderful, Down the Great Unknown, 1999, Abraham Lincoln, 2002, Teacher of the Year, Two Fridas, Down the Grand Canyon, The First Easter, 2003, The First Christmas, 2003, Flame and Clay (teachers' big book) 1998, 3 Repeat Jobs for Hampton/Brown (teacher's big book), (illustrator) Night Journey, 1999, Here Come the Brides, (adult book) The Artist's Market, also L.A. Times, Daily News, The Artist's Mag., News Chronicle; also cover art for Troll Assoc., Top Secret, The Loveless Cafe (cookbook), Ellery Queen's Mystery Mag., Frontispiece Collectors Leather Bound Edition, Crippen and Landru Mystery Covers, Dragon mag., Dungeon mag., Aboriginal Sci. Fiction mag., Wizards of the Coast, (game covers) F.X. Schmid - Puzzle Wizards of the Coast (fantasy collector cards, Dune and Hobbit), 4 covers, frontspieces and chpt. headings for Henry Winkler's Hank Zipzer series, Georgw W. Bush Scholastic, 2003, also various novels, books and games; illustrator Bugs Bunny Coloring Book, Candyland Work Book. The Dragon Sleeps Step Ahead Workbook, City of Sorcers, CD-ROM cover for Memorex/Roaring Mouse Prodns., George W. Bush Scholastic; interior art for various publs. including (mags.) Amazing Stories two covers, Interzone, Aboriginal Sci. Fiction Mag., Alfred Hitchcocks Mystery Mag., Ideals mag., Ellery Queen's Mystery mag. two covers, Realms of Fantasy mag., Sci. Fiction Age mag., Tomorrow mag., (book) Tome of Magic, Spider Magazine, (book) Top Secret, (book, interiors) Star Trek Next Generation, (also art for game cards), (repeat covers) Crippen and Landru, (game book cover) Wizards of the Coast; writer (screenplay) Thunder Run, 1986; illustrator, writer (children's books) Black Beauty, Beauty and the Beast, 1989, The Easter Story, 1989, Excalibur, Robin Hood, 1993, Sleeping Beauty in the Wood, 1996, The Christmas Story, 1996, Down the Great Unknown, 1999, Flame and Clay, 1998, Black Beauty, The First Easter, 2003, The First Christmas, 2003; paintings for line of Fantasy Art Prints, Scafa/Tornabene, religious art prints; rep. by Every Picture Tells a Story Gallery, Worlds of Wonder; cover art/bookmark for Antioch Pub.; new cover for Baen Books; art for Maruri USA Corp.; 2 covers for young adults Hyperion/Disney Press; one-woman show Adventures for Kids Gallery; illustrator poster for motion picture and TV fund; writer Disney ednl. prodns., others; freelance artist Disney Interactive. Guest spkr. Ariz. Kidney Found. Recipient Lit. award City of Oxnard Cultural Arts Commn. and Carnegie Art Inst., 1992, Best Cover Art Boomerang award, 1989, Cert. of Merit, Career Achievement award Calif. Luth. U., 1993, Cert. of Excellence Alumni Career Achievement award, 1993, Print's Regional Design Ann. award, 1992, Best Paper Backs award Internat. Reading Assn. Children's Book Coun. Joint Com., 1994, Spectrum Internat. Competition for Best in Contemporary Fantastic Art, Spectrum 7 award, Spectrum 9 Art Competition award, award Ventura Soc. of Children's Bookwriters and Illustrators, 2002. Mem. Soc. Children's Book Writers (judge 1990, Mag. Merit award 1988, Keynote spkr.), Assn. Sci. Fiction and Fantasy Artists (nominated for Chelsey award), Soc. Illustrators (Cert. of Merit 1990-92, winner Ann. Illustration West show, award L.A. chpt. 1998). Achievements include being featured in articles. Home and Office: Touchmark 925 Ave Arboles Thousand Oaks CA 91360

HEYER, LAURA MIRIAM, special education educator; b. L.A., Jan. 6, 1967; d. William Ronald and Miriam Harriet (Muedeking) Heyer. BA, M of Tching., U. Va., 1990; EdM, George Mason U., 2001. Lic. tchr. Va. Asst. tchr. Sch. for Contemporary Edn., Annandale, Va., 1991-93, classroom tchr. Phillips Programs, 1993—2003, program supr., 2003—. Support group facilitator, Sexual Minority Youth Assistance League, Washington, 1995-96. Mem. Coun. for Children with Behavioral Disorders, Coun. for Exceptional Children. Avocation: playing sports. Office: Phillips Programs 7010 Braddock Rd Annandale VA 22003-6006

HEYER, MARILEE, illustrator; b. Long Beach, Calif., May 7, 1942; d. Arthur Henry and Esther Mae Heyer. BA, Art Ctr. Sch. of Design, L.A., 1966. Scene planer Format Prodns., L.A., 1966—67, Filmation Prodns., L.A., 1967—70; fashion illustrator Liberty House Dept. Store, Oakland, Calif., 1970—77, I. Magnin Dept. Store, San Francisco, 1977—87; illustrator story bds. Lucas Film, Industrial, Light & Magic, San Raphael, Calif., 1985; owner, illustrator Heyer Studios, Los Osos, Calif., 1987—. Lectr. in field. Illustrator (children's books) The Weaving of a Dream, 1986, Forbidden Door, 1990, (children's book) The Girl, The Fish and the Crown, 1994, (book) We Goddesses, (music posters) for L.A. Opera, Oregon Bach Festival, Godiva Chocolates, (book covers) Tamora Pierce's Song of the Lioness, The Immortals. Mem.: Children's Book Writers and Illustrators, Graphic Artists Guild.

HEYMAN, SALLY ANNE, state legislator, crime/loss prevention specialist; b. Balt., Nov. 10, 1954; BA in Criminal Justice, U. Fla., 1975, MS in Criminal Justice, Nova U., 1981; JD, U. Miami, 1992. Bar: Fla. 1993. Crime/loss prevention splst.; owner, cons. CRIME: Gopher It Inc., 1981—; mem. Fla. Ho. of Reps., Tallahassee, 1994—. Vice chair Com. on Crime and Punishment Justice Coun., 1996-97; mem. Com. on Health Care Svcs. Govt. Svcs. Coun., 1996-97, Com. on Regulated Svcs. Econ. Impact Coun., 1996-97. Mem. Adv. Com. for Disabled Individuals, N. Miami Beach Commn. on Status of Women, Friends of Libr., Women's Polit. Caucus, Fla. Breast Cancer Coalition, Dade Ptnrs. for Safe Neighborhoods, Crime Watch; active City of North Miami Beach Coun., North Miami Beach Police Dept., Miami Police Dept., Fla. Commn. on Status of Women, local charitable, civic, polit., women's orgns. Mem. Am. Cancer Soc., NOW, North Miami Beach C. of C., North Dade C. of C., North Miami C. of C., Fla. Assn. Women Lawyers, Voters Coun., North Miami Beach Homeowners Assn., Ives Estates Homeowners Assn., United Dems. Dade, All Peoples Democratic Club, Aventura Mktg. Coun., Winn Dixie Hope Lodge. Jewish. Avocations: biking, water sports, snow skiing, hiking, football. Address: 1100 NE 163rd St Ste 303 North Miami Beach FL 33162-1616 Office: Fla Capitol 402 S Monroe St Tallahassee FL 32399-6526

HEYWOOD, ANNE, artist, educator, author; b. Newport, RI, Sept. 15, 1951; d. Albert Paul and Eileen Frances (Laforest) Boretti; m. Ciro DiGiovanni, May 24, 1969 (div. 1980); 1 child, Carlo; m. Henry Robert Heywood, Nov. 9, 1985. BA in Art summa cum laude, Bridgewater (Mass.) State Coll. Tchr. drawing and pastels Silver Lake Reg. H.S. Adult Edn., Kingston, Mass., 1991—95; art educator pastels, drawing South Shore Art Ctr., Cohasset, Mass., 1996—; art educator pastels Fuller Mus. Art, Brockton, Mass., 1996—2003, Pastel Painters Soc. Cape Cod, Barnstable, Mass., 1997; art educator drawing Swinburne Sch., Newport, RI, 1995, Round Top Ctr. for Arts, Damariscotta, Maine, 1996; workshop instr. Northwest Pastel Soc., Gig Harbor, Wash., 2002. Pastel demonstrator, spkr. in field; artist residency Carillon Beach Inst., Panama City, Fla., 2002; juror Renaissance in Pastel, 1999; juror N.W. Pastel Soc., 2002, workshop instr., Wash., 02. Author: Pastels Made Easy, 2003; contbg. artist: Best of Pastel, 1996, Landscape Inspirations, 1997, Best of Sketching and Drawing 1999; one-woman shows include East Bridgewater (Mass.) Pub. Libr., 1992, 95, Mass. Audubon Soc., Marshfield, 1992, South Shore Natural Sci. Ctr., Norwell, Mass., 1993, Marion (Mass.) Art Ctr., 1994, Fuller Art Mus., Brockton, Mass., 1995, 2000, Passage Gallery, South Shore Art Ctr., Cohasset, Mass., 1996, 98, Sparrow House, Plymouth, Mass., 1997, 2000, Landmark Bldg., Boston, 1999; exhibited in group shows at Duxbury Art Assn., Mass., 1993, Trenton (N.J.) State Coll., 1994, Bridgewater State Coll., 1994, Zullo Gallery, Medfield, Mass., 1995, 99, 2001, Maine Art Gallery, Wiscasset, 1995, Pastel Soc. Am., N.Y.C., 1995, 97, Internat. Assn. Pastel Socs., 1997, 99 (Convention Image award), Left Bank Gallery, Wellfleet, Mass., 1997, Gallery at C3TV, South Yarmouth, Mass., 1997, Salmagundi Club, N.Y. 1999 (George Inness Jr. Meml. award for pastel), Nat. Biennial Exhbn. Degas Soc., La. (La. Watercolor Soc. award of merit), Colo. History Mus., Fla. Pastel Soc., Soc. Western Artists, Mass., 1999, Pastel Soc. of the West Coast, 2001, Audubon Artists Exhbn., 2001, Newington-Cropsey Found., N.Y., 2001, Attleboro Mus. Ctr. for Arts, 2003; pvt. collections; contbr. articles to profl. jours.; editor Pastel Painter's Soc. Cape Cod newsletter, 1998-99, bd. dirs. Sec. East Bridgewater Arts Coun., 1992-97, Artists Ctr. at Fuller Mus., Brockton, Mass., 1995-97; juror Renaissance in Pastel, 1999, Northwest Pastel Soc., Harbor, Wash., 2002. Recipient 1st pl. drawing East Bridgewater Art Festival, 1991, 1st pl. awards Wickford (R.I.) Art Assn., 1992, Taunton (Mass.) Art Assn., 1993, South Shore Art Ctr. Blue Ribbon Members Show, Cohasset, 1994, Fuller Art Mus., Brockton, 1994, 1st pl. pastels Plymouth Guild May Members Show, 1994, award Providence Art Club, 1996, award of distinction All New Eng. Color Show, Cohasset, 1996; Vt. Studio Ctr. Residency fellow, 1999. Mem.: Nat. Assn. Women Artists (D.Wu and Elsie Jeck-Key Meml. award 2000), Oil Pastel Assn./United Pastellists Am. (signature mem.), Pastel Soc. Am. (Holbein award 1995), Conn. Pastel Soc. (signature mem.), Pastel Painters Soc. Cape Cod (signature mem., Canson-Talens award 1997), Allied Artists of Am., Associated Pastelists on Web (signature mem.), Am. Artists Profl. League, Internat. Assn. of Pastel Socs., Salmagundi Club. Roman Catholic. Avocations: reading, walking, biking, choir. Home: 85 Ashley Dr East Bridgewater MA 02333-1703 E-mail: aheywood@anne-heywood.com.

HEYZER, NOELEEN, international organization official; BS, U. Singapore; PhD in social scis., Cambridge U. Exec. dir. UN Devel. Fund for Women, 1994—. Sociology tutor U. Singapore; keynote spkr. for numerous univs. and orgns. Named Woman of Distinction, NGO Com. on the Status of Women, 2003; fellow, Inst. Devel. Studies U. Sussex. Mem.: Isis Internat., Asia Pacific Women in Law and Devel., Devel. Alternatives with Women for a New Era. Office: UNIFEM 304 E 45th St 15th fl New York NY 10017

HEZEL, AMY R. librarian, educator; b. Buffalo, N.Y., Dec. 10, 1976; d. George M. and Sally (Clough) Hezel; m. Graham W. Foust, Aug. 31, 2002. MLS, U. Buffalo, 2002, BA magna cum laude, 2000. Adj. faculty libr. Drake U., Des Moines, 2002—; libr. Pub. Libr. of Des Moines, 2002—; libr. asst. Albright-Knox Art Gallery, Buffalo, 2000—02. Lectr. U. Buffalo, 2002—, tchg. asst. Women Studies Tchg. Collective, 1999—2000. Bd. mem. Housing Opportunities Made Equal, Buffalo, 1998—2002. Mem.: ALA, Iowa Libr. Assn., Beta Phi Mui.

HIAR, DANIELLE MARIE, graphics designer, educator; d. Stella Marie Hiar. MEd. Higher Edn. Adminstrn., Grand Valley State U., 1998, BFA Graphic Design, 1996; A.A.S. Comml. Art, Northwestern Mich. Coll., Traverse City, MI, 1991—93. Graphic design coord. Ctrl. Mich. U., Mt. Pleasant, Mich., 1999—; area coord. Davidson Coll., Davidson, NC, 1998—99. Regional conf. coord. Nat. Assn. for Campus Activities, 2003—. Recipient Outstanding New Profl., NACA Gt. Lakes Region, 2001. Mem.: NASPA. Office: Central Michigan University Bovee University Center 100 Mount Pleasant MI 48859-0001

HIATT, JANE CRATER, arts agency administrator; b. Winston-Salem, N.C., May 26, 1944; d. Howard Rondthaler Jr. and Irene (Sides) Crater; m. K.W. Everhart Jr. (div. June 1973); m. Wood Coleman Hiatt, May, 1978; 1 child, Jonathan David. BA, U. N.C., 1966; MA, Wake Forest U., 1972. Eng. tchr. Winston-Salem (N.C.)/Forsyth County Schs., 1966-70; exec. dir. Tenn. Com. for the Humanities, Nashville, 1973-77; cons. various ednl. and cultural agys. Ocean Springs, Miss., 1978-80; asst. dir. Miss. Humanities Coun., Jackson, Miss., 1981-85; exec. dir. Arts Alliance of Jackson and Hinds County, Miss., 1985-89, Miss. Arts Commn., Jackson, 1989-95; interim dir. Miss. Mus. Art, 2001. Participant Arts Leadership Inst. of Humphrey Inst. for Pub. Affairs, Mpls., 1986, Leadership, Jackson, 1987; interim exec. dir. Miss. Mus. Art, 2001. Co-editor Peoples of the South, 1976; exec. producer (TV series) The South with John Siegenthaler, 1976; host, reporter Miss. Ednl. TV, Jackson, 1981-87. Mem. Miss. Econ. Coun., 1986—87, Miss. R&D Coun., 1984—88; pres. Mental Health Assn. of Hinds County, Jackson, 1986; treas. Miss. for Ednl. Broadcasting, 1987, 1988, 1989, Premier Class Leadership, Jackson, 1987, 1988; mem. cmty. adv. coun. Jr. League of Jackson, 1995—2004; mem. representing Miss. Friends of Art and Preservation in Embassies Millennium Com.; bd. dirs. Miss. Mus. Art, 2000—, Friends of Univ. Press, 2004—; bd. dirs. Miss. state com. Nat. Mus. Women in Arts. Recipient Heritage award City of Biloxi, 1984. Mem.: Greater Jackson Found. (bd. dirs. 1996—, chmn. 2002—03), Pub. Edn. Forum (bd. dirs. 1993—), Miss. Ctr. for Nonprofits (vice chmn., bd. dirs. 1993—96, adv. bd. 1997—), So. Arts Fedn. (bd. dirs. 1989—95), Nat. Assembly State Arts Agys. (bd. dirs. 1992—95, 2d v.p. 1995), Nat. Coun. on Arts, Nat. Assembly Local Arts Agys., Phi Beta Kappa. Home: 4 Waterstone Pl Jackson MS 39211-5987 E-mail: hiattw@bellsouth.net.

HIBBARD, JUDITH USHER, obstetrician; b. Chgo. m. Mark C. Hibbard. Studied, Edgewood Coll., Madison, Wis., 1966—68; BS in Secondary Edn., Gen. Sci. & History, MS in Sci. Edn., U. Wis., Madison, 1968—72; studied, Coll. of DuPage, Glen Ellen, Ill., 1977—78, Ill. Benedictine Coll., Lisle, 1978—79; MD, Loyola U., Maywood, Ill., 1979—82. Diplomate Nat. Bd. Med. Examiners, 1983, Am. Bd. Ob-Gyn., 1990, in Maternal-Fetal Medicine 1991. Sci. tchr. Verona Mid. Sch., Wis., 1970—72, Toledo Jr. H.S., Oreg., 1972—74; sci. and math. tchr. Mesquite H.S., Ridgecrest, Calif., 1975—77; resident, ob-gyn. U. Chgo., 1982—86, fellow, instr., maternal-fetal medicine, 1986—89, asst. prof., maternal-fetal medicine, 1989—96, acting dir., ob-gyn. ultrasound, 1999—2000, assoc. prof., clin. ob-gyn., 1996—2001, fellowship dir., maternal-fetal medicine, 2001—, prof., maternal-fetal medicine, 2001—, sect. chief, maternal-fetal medicine, 2003—. Reviewer for various jours. Recipient Hon. Sci. award, Bausch and Lomb, 1968, Scholastic Achievement award, Am. Med. Women's Assn., 1982, Young Investigator's award, Am. Diabetes Assn., 1988, Faculty Devel. Tng. award, Berlex Found., 1991, Young Investigator's Travel award, NIH, 1994. Mem.: Chgo. Soc. Perinatal Obstetricians, Chgo. Gyn. Soc., Ill. Perinatal Assn., Ctrl. Assn. of Ob-Gyn., Internat. Soc. of Ultrasound in Ob-Gyn., Internat. Soc. for Study of Hypertension in Pregnancy, Nat. Perinatal Assn., Soc. Obstetric Medicine, Soc. Maternal Fetal Medicine, Am. Coll. Ob-Gyn., Pi Lambda Theta, Alpha Omega Alpha. Office: Dept Ob-Gyn Univ Chgo 5841 S Maryland Ave MC2050 Chicago IL 60637

HIBBS, DAWN WILCOX, elementary school educator; b. Buffalo, Sept. 30, 1940; d. Alfred and Helena Pavone; m. Leroy Wilcox, July 18, 1964 (div. June 1981); children: Brett Alan, Dana Lee; m. Harold Keith Hibbs, Dec. 27, 1986. Tchr. 5th grade North Tonawanda (N.Y.) Schs., 1961-63, Los Alamos (N.Mex.) Schs., 1963-64; tchr. 6th grade Kenmore (N.Y.) Schs., 1965-69; caseworker Erie County Dept. Social Svcs., Buffalo, 1980-84; elem. tchr. Lynwood (Calif.) Schs., 1986-88, Santa Ana (Calif.) Schs., 1988-96, intermediate tchr., 1996—2002, textbook advisor, grant writer, 1996-97. Mentor new tchrs. Santa Ana Schs., 1991-92, instr. Reading to Learn programs, 1999-2000, tchr. cabinet rep., 1998-2000, mem. sch. site coun., 2000-2001, mem. Oreg. project, 2000-02. Patentee eyewear identification labels and design. Pres. Parents Without Ptnrs., Tonawanda, 1983. Mem. AAUW (treas. 1995-96, EF fund prize chmn. 1997, membership v.p. 1997-2000, mem. membership com. Calif. 1998-2001, co-pres. Orange County Interbr. 1999—, tech. trek coord., 1999-2001, v.p. Mission Viejo-Saddleback Valley br. LAF 2000-2001, pres. 2003-), Class Act Investors (treas. 1999—).

HICKCOX, LESLIE KAY, health educator, consultant, counselor; b. Berkeley, Calif., May 12, 1951; d. Ralph Thomas and Marilyn Irene (Stump) H. BA, U. Redlands, 1973; MA in Exercise Physiology, U. of the Pacific, 1975; MEd in Curriculum Teaching, Columbia U., 1979; MEd in Health Edn., Oreg. State U., 1987, MEd in Guidance & Counseling, 1988, EdD in Edn., 1991. Cert. Calif. State C.C. instr. (life). Phys. edn. instr., dir. intramurals SUNY, Stony Brook, 1981-83; instr. health edn. Linn-Benton C.C., Oreg., 1985-94; instr. human studies and comm. studies Marylhurst U., Portland, 1987-96, 2002—; edn. supr., instr. Oreg. State U., Corvallis, 1988-90; health and phys. edn. instr. Portland C.C., 1994-95, 2003—; instr. health edn. U. Auckland, New Zealand, 1991; instr., coord. dept. health, phys. edn. and recreation Rogue C.C., Grants Pass, Oreg., 1995-97; assoc. prof., coord. health and phys. edn. Western Mont. Coll., Dillon, Mont., 1997-99; asst. prof. health edn. Northeastern Ill. U., Chgo., 1999—2002; health and phys. edn. instr. Portland C.C., 2003. Founder Experiential Learning Inst., 1992—, found., Lilly N.W. High Edn. Tchg. Conf., 1996; founding v.p. Home Health Diagnostics, Portland, Oreg., 1996, dir. health info., 1996-2003. Contbr. articles to profl. jours. Mem. ASCD, Am. Pub. Health Assn., Am. Sch. Health Assn., Am. Assn. Health Edn., Higher Edn. R&D Soc. Australasia, Coun. for Adult and Experiential Learning, Adult Higher Edn. Alliance, Kappa Delta Phi, Phi Delta Kappa. Office: 2635 N Baldwin St Portland OR 97217 E-mail: lesliekayh@aol.com.

HICKEY, CATHERINE JOSEPHINE, school system administrator; b. N.Y.C., Mar. 14, 1936; d. John James and Delia Bridget (Finnegan) Tighe; m. Stephen M. Hickey, Mar. 30, 1959; children: Catherine, Marie, Joanne, Clare, Geraldine, Margaret. BS, Fordham U., 1958, PhD, 1983; MS, CUNY, 1974; LHD (hon.), Mercy Coll., 1990, Iona Coll., Kings Coll., Wilkes-Barre, Pa. Prin. Sacred Heart Sch., Dobbs Ferry, N.Y., 1977-89; instr., adj. prof. Mercy Coll., Dobbs Ferry, 1983-87, Long Island U., Dobbs Ferry, 1984-87, Fairfield (Conn.) U., 1984-87; supt. schs. Archdiocese of N.Y., N.Y.C., 1989—, sec. of edn., 2000—. Roman Catholic. Home: 415 Marlborough Rd Yonkers NY 10701-6709 Office: Archdiocese NY 1011 1st Ave New York NY 10022-4106

HICKEY, DELINA ROSE, retired education educator; b. N.Y.C., Mar. 25, 1941; d. Robert Joseph and Marie (Ripa) Hickey; m. David Andrews; 1 child, Jon Robert. BS in Edn., SUNY, Oneonta, 1963; MA, Manhattan Coll., 1967; EdD in Counselor Edn. and Psychology, U. Idaho, 1971; postgrad., Harvard U., 1995. Sch. tchr., counselor pub. schs., Westchester, NY, 1963-68; part-time instr. psychologist St. Thomas Aquinas Coll., Sparkhill, NY, 1971-72; asst. prof. edn. Nathaniel Hawthorne Coll., Antrim, NH, 1972-75; mem. faculty Keene (N.H.) State Coll., 1975—2000, assoc. prof. edn., 1978-87, prof., coord. faculty, 1987-2000, interim dean profl. studies, 1887, v.p. student affairs, 1990-2000; ret., 2000. Mem. adv. coun. Title IV, 1979—82; assoc. in edn. Harvard U., 1984—85, Inst. Ednl. Mgmt., 1995; chmn. curriculum Acad. Life Long Learning U. S.C., Aiken, SC, 2003—; presenter in field. Contbr. Bd. trustees Hist. Aiken Found., 2002—, Smart Growth Aiken, 2000—; pres., co-founder HMS Assocs. Ednl. Cons., 2002—; mem. N.H. Ho. of Reps., 1981—85, trustee Big Bros.-Big Sisters, Keene, 1978—80, Family Planning Svcs. S.W. N.H., 1976—85, Monadnock Family Svcs., 1995—97, Monadnock Hospice, 1994—96, chmn. pers. com.; mem. N.H. Juvenile Conf. Com., 1976—81; bd. dirs. Cheshire Med. Ctr.; trustee Cheshire Med. Assn., 1996—2001; pres. bd. dirs. CHESCO; trustee Home Health Care, 1998—2001. Fellow, Nat. Ctr. Rsch. in Vocat. Edn., 1984—85; grantee, Marion Jasper Whitney Found. Mem.: AAUW (vice chmn. programs 2002—), N.H. Assn. Student Pers. Adminstrs. (adv. bd.), N.H. Pers. and Guidance Assn., New Eng. Rsch. Orgn., New Eng. Assn. Tchrs. and Educators, Am. Vocat. Assn., Nat. Assn. Student Pers. Adminstrs. (adv. com. region I, editor, chief Net Results electronic mag. 1997-99), N.H. Order Women Legislators. Office: HMS Ednl Cons Aiken SC 29801 E-mail: delhickey@bellsouth.net.

HICKEY, MARISA SORRENTINO, music educator; b. Queens, N.Y., Feb. 25, 1977; d. Enrico R. and Patricia A. Sorrentino; m. Robert L. Hickey, June 28, 2003. BS in Music Edn., Pa. State U., State College, 2000. Choir dir. Williamsport (Pa.) Area Sch. Dist., 2000—. Mem.: Am. Choral Dirs. Assn. Pa. (women's r&s chair 2003—), Pa. Music Educators Assn. Personal E-mail: marisa164@cs.com.

HICKEY, SHARON MARIE, councilman, elementary school educator, Mayoral aide; b. Leon, Iowa, Nov. 25, 1953; d. Clarence Joseph Ross and Marie Florence Page; m. Thomas Patrick Hickey, June 26, 1976; children: Melissa, Christine, Patrick, Matthew. AA, Iowa Central CC, Ft. Dodge, Iowa, 1974; BA, Buena Vista Univ., 1976. Sec. Dr. McDonald, Ft. Dodge, Iowa, 1975—76; substitute tchr. Ft. Dodge Cmty. Sch., Iowa, 1978—94; tchr. Corpus Christi, Ft. Dodge, 1994—95; substitute tchr. Ft. Dodge Cmty. Sch., 1995—2001. Sch. improvement bd. Ft.Dodge Cmty. Sch., Iowa, 2001; coun. mem. City of Ft. Dodge, Iowa, 1992—2001, mayor pro tem, 1993—2001. Recipient Gov.'s Leadership award, State of Iowa, 1991, Hillcrest Neighborhood award, 1985—2001. Roman Catholic. Home: 304 2nd St NW Fort Dodge IA 50501 E-mail: shickey@mchsi.com.

HICKEY, WINIFRED E(SPY), former state legislator, social worker; b. Rawlins, Wyo. d. David P. and Eugenia (Blake) Espy; children: John David, Paul Joseph. BA, Loretto Heights Coll., 1933; postgrad., U. Utah, 1934, Sch. Social Svc., U. Chgo., 1936; LLD (hon.), U. Wyo., 1991. Dir. Carbon County Welfare Dept., 1935—36; field rep. Wyo. Dept. Welfare, 1937—38; dir. Red Cross Club, Europe, 1942—45; commr. Laramie County, Wyo., 1973—80; mem. Wyo. Senate, 1980—90; dir. United Savs. & Loan, Cheyenne; active Joint Powers Bd. Laramie County and City of Cheyenne. Pub. Where the Deer and the Antelope Play, 1967; pres. Meml. Hosp. of Laramie County, 1986—88, Wyo. Transp. Mus., 1990—92; pres. county and state mental health assn., 1959—63; trustee U. Wyo., 1967—71; active Gov. Residence Found., 1991—93, Wyo. Transp. Mus., 1993—; trustee St. Mary's Cathedral, 1986—; active Nat. Coun. Cath. Women; pres., bd. dirs. U. Wyo. Found., 1986—87; chmn. adv. coun. div. cmty. programs Wyo. Dept. Health and Social Svcs.; chair Am. Heritage Assocs. of U. Wyo., 1992—96. Named Outstanding Alumna, Loretto Heights Coll., 1959, Woman of Yr., Commn. for Women, 1988, United Med. Ctr., Cheyenne, 1998, Legislator of Yr., Wyo. Psychologists Assn., 1988, Family of the Yr., U. Wyo., 1995, Person of Yr., United Med. Ctr., Cheyenne, Wyo., 1998. Mem.: Altrusa Club (Cheyenne).

HICKMAN, ELIZABETH PODESTA, retired counselor, educator; b. Livingston, Ill., Sept. 30, 1922; d. Louis and Della (Martin) Podesta; m. Franklin Jay Hickman, Mar. 17, 1944 (dec.); children: Virginia Hickman Hellstern, Franklin. BE summa cum laude, Ea. Ill. State U.; MA, George Washington U., 1966, EdD (Exxon Found.-Raskob Found. grantee), 1979; postgrad., U. Chgo., 1945, U. Va., 1964-66; postgrad. (fellow), Northeastern U., 1967-68. Lic. counselor, Va. Tchr. pub. schs., Ill., Ohio, 1944-64; dir. coll. transfer guidance Mayrmount Coll. Va., Arlington, 1964-67, dir. Counceling Ctr., 1974-81, assoc. dean counseling and residence life, 1981-84; cmty. counselor Divsn. Mass. Employment Security, Newton, 1968-69; tchr. English conversation, Fuchu, Japan, 1969-73; placement dir., career counselor Coll. of Gt. Falls, Mont., 1973-74; assoc. rschr. George Washington U., Washington, 1986. Lectr. Far East divsn. U. Md., Fuchu, 1971-73; spl. advisor Internat. Ranger Camps, Denmark and Switzerland, 1974-81; spl. cons. Internat. Quaker Sch., Werkhoven, The Netherlands, 1959-63; mem. steering com. Pres.'s Com. on Employment of Handicapped, 1974-95. Vol., ARC, 1967-68, Family Svcs., 1954-75, White House Agy. Liaison, 1986—, Kennedy Ctr. Adminstrn., Washington, 1984—, Arlington Free Clinic, 2000—. With WAVES, 1943-44. Recipient Disting. Alumnus award Ea. Ill. U., 1984. Mem. Brent Soc., Rose Soc., Potomac (Ill) Soc., Italian Am. Soc., Marymount U. Angels Soc., Women's Com. Nat. Symphony Orch., Washington Opera Guild, Delta Epsilon Sigma, Pi Lambda Theta. Roman Catholic. Home: 4708 38th Pl N Arlington VA 22207-2915

HICKMAN, LUCILLE, physical therapist; b. Chgo., July 21, 1949; d. Louis Melvin and Edna (Edwards) H. BA in Sociology, Lake Forest Coll., 1972; BS in Physical Therapy, Chgo. Med. Sch., 1975; MS in Health Sci., Gov.'s State U., 1985. Staff phys. therapist Michael Reese Hosp., Chgo., 1975-79; dir. phys. therapy Provident Med. Ctr., Chgo., 1979-83; instr. phys. therapy Chgo. State U., 1983-87; pres. adminstrv. dir. R.O.C. Phys. Therapy Svcs., Chgo., 1985—93; founder, pres. PhysioCare Ltd., Chgo., 1988—93. Pvt. practice therapy cons., Chgo., 1983—93. Mem. Am. Phys. Therapy Assn., Nat. Soc. Allied Health. Democrat. Episcopalian. Achievements include patents for exercise machine, 1998. Avocations: piano, composing, cooking, writing.

HICKMAN, MARGARET CAPELLINI, advertising executive; b. Hartford, Conn., Sept. 21, 1949; d. Anthony Serafino Capellini and Mary Magdelan (Budash Capellini) Zanardi; m. Richard Lonnie Hickman, Nov. 6, 1982; children: Wilder A., Langdon B. BA, U. Conn., 1971. Mktg. asst. Advo Sys., Inc., Hartford, Conn., 1971-72, mktg. analyst, 1972-75; mktg. asst. Cinamon Assocs., Inc., Brookline, Mass., 1975-77, profn. supr., 1977-81, v.p. prodn., 1981-84, v.p. client svcs., 1984-85, 86; dir. client svcs. Bozell, Jacobs, Jenyon & Eckhardt, Boston, 1985-86; ptnr. Hickman & Hickman, Merritt Island, Fla., 1987; prodn. mgr. Direct Mktg. Aty., Stamford, Conn., 1988-90; v.p. prodn. Martin Direct, Glen Allen, Va., 1990-96, Martin Agy., Richmond, Va., 1996—. Mem. Direct Mktg. Assn. (past sec., treas., v.p.), Cape Ann Child Devel. Programs (past dir.), Am. Legion Aux. Democrat. Roman Catholic. Home: 10717 Wellington St Fredericksburg VA 22407-1272

HICKMAN, PATRICIA, artist, craftswoman; BA, U. Colo., 1962; MA in Design and Textiles, U. Calif., Berkeley, 1977. Prof., head fiber program art dept. U. Hawaii at Manoa, Honolulu. One-woman shows include U. Hawaii, 1991, Contemporary Mus., Honolulu, 1995—96, Banker Gallery, San Francisco, 1996, San Francisco Craft and Folk Art Mus., 1998—99, exhibitions include, Kanezawa, Japan, 1982, Kassel, Germany, 1985, Galerie de Sluis, Leidschendam, The Netherlands, 1984, Maya Behn Gallery, Copenhagen, 1986, Zurich, Switzerland, 1985, Kyoto, Japan, 1987, N.D. Mus. Art tour in Far East, 1988—90, Bradford, Eng., 1990, Philharm. Gallery, Liege, Belgium, 1991—93, Am. Embassy, Warsaw, 1991—93, Africa tour, 1992—94, Represented in permanent collections Contemporary Mus., Honolulu, State Found. Culture and Arts, Honolulu Acad. Art, Ark. Arts Ctr., Little Rock, Am. Craft Mus., N.Y.C., Erie (Pa.) Art Mus., Oakland (Calif.) Mus., Wadsworth Atheneum, Hartford, Conn., Savaria Mus., Smithsonian Instn., Washington, also corp. collections, commns., Maui Arts and Culture Ctr., Kahului, Hawaii, 1991—94, work represented in various publs.; contbr. essays to exhbn. catalogs. Individual artist visual arts fellow, Hawaii State Found. on Culture and Arts, 1998, grantee, NEA, 1986—87.

HICKMAN, SHIRLEY ANNA, secondary school educator; b. Gunnison, CO, Apr. 16, 1936; d. Steven Joseph and Mary Rose Skufca; m. Joe A. Hickman, Dec. 29, 1962; 1 child, Joseph Steven. BA, Western State Coll., 1958; MA, Calif. State U., Fresno, 1966, Calif. State U., Bakersfield, 1990. Cert. Gen. secondary life tchg. credential, preliminary ednl. adminstrn. Tchr. Tulare (Calif.) Union H.S., 1958—60, Porterville (Calif.) Union H.S., 1960—65, Calif. Poly U., San Luis Obispo, 1965—68, Kings River Coll., Reedley, Calif., 1968—69; tchr., adminstr. Monache H.S., Porterville, Calif., 1970—94; tutor, self-employed Porterville, 1994—; writer, 1994—.

HICKMAN, TERRIE TAYLOR, administrator; b. Rapid City, S.D., Dec. 2, 1962; d. William Adrian and Carolyn Gene (Habben) T.; children: Matthew, Kalie. BS, Okla. State U., 1985; MEd, Cen. State U., 1988. Cert. elem tchr., presch. tchr., Okla. Mktg. dir. Tealridge Manor, Edmond, Okla., 1989-90; owner Oxford Pointe Jazzercize, Edmond, Okla., 1989-90; adminstr. Retirement Inn at Quail Ridge, Oklahoma City, 1991-92, Country Club Square, Edmond, 1992-93; planner Areawide Aging Agency, Oklahoma City, 1992-97; tchr. John Ross Elem. Sch., 2003—. Mem. adv. coun., co-chmn. Okla. Bus. and Aging Leadership Coalition, newsletter Networker editor; presenter in field; adv. coun. sr. companion planning com. State of Okla. Conf. on Aging; mem. Oklahoma City Reading Coun. Co-editor Sage Age; contbr. articles to various pubs. Co-chmn. media hosting party Olympic Festival, Norman, Okla., 1989; co-coord. jazzercize for hope Benefit for Hope Ctr., Edmond, The McGruff Safe House Program, Stillwater, Okla.; com. chmn. Coalition for Elderly Concerns, Oklahoma City; vol. Stillwater Domestic Violence Shelter, Payne County Employment Svcs., Stillwater; mem. renter's adv. bd. Okla. State U. Student Senate. Mem. ASCD, Women in Bus., Edmond Area C. of C., Okla. Bus. and Aging Leadership Coalition, Phi Kappa Delta, Alpha Gamma Delta, Sigma Phi Omega, Kappa Delta Pi. Republican. Lutheran. Avocation: biking. Personal E-mail: cityfarmer@att.net.

HICKMAN, TRAPHENE PARRAMORE, retired library director, storyteller, library and library building consultant; b. Dallas, Jan. 31, 1933; d. Redden Travis and Stella (Moore) P.; m. John Robert Hickman, June 9, 1950; children[00bf] Lynn Kleifgen, Laurie Ward AA, Mountain View C.C.; BA, U. Tex-Arlington; MLS, U. North Tex. Cert. libr., Tex. Libr. Cedar Hill (Tex.) Pub. Libr., 1959-77; dir. Dallas County Libr. Sys., Dallas, 1977-93; libr. cons. Dallas County, 1993-95; libr. High Pointe Elem. Sch., 2003—. Chair leadership coun. and family ministries FUMC of Cedar Hill. Editor: History and Directory of Cedar Hill, 1976; editor News and Views newsletter Dallas county Employees, 1986-92. Chmn. Bicentennial Com., Cedar Hill, 1976; del. Dem. Nat. Conv. 9th Senate Dist., Tex., 1976; chmn. Sesquicentennial Com., Cedar Hill, 1984-86; Dallas County Dem. Forum; mem. Electoral Coll., 1988; chairperson Women's Bd. Northwood Inst., Cedar Hill; active Dallas County Sesquicentennial Com., 1996-; lay speaker United Methodist Ch., 2004. Recipient Newsmaker of Yr. award Cedar Hill Chronicle, 1976; named Amb. of Goodwill, State of Tex., 1976 Mem. ALA, Tex. Libr. Assn. (legis. com. 1984-95, councillor 1982-83, trustee com. 1987-95, pub. info. com. 1987-95), Pub. Libr. Adminstrs. of North Tex. (sec., v.p., pres. 1980, 87), Dallas County Libr. Assn., N.E. Tex. Libr. Sys. (legis. commn. 1978-95, Libr. of Yr. 1987), U. North Tex. Sch. Libr. and Info. Scis. Alumni Assn. (pres. 1987-88), Cedar Hill C. of C., Cedar Summit Book Club (officer), Dallas Area Storytelling Guild (pres. 1995-99), Librn. CHISD (mem. 2003-2004). Democrat. Methodist. Avocations: writing, reading, storytelling, gardening, bridge, travel, square dancing. Home and Office: 421 Lee St Cedar Hill TX 75104-2697

HICKOK, SISTER ALICE MARIE, special education educator; b. Green Bay, Wis., Oct. 27, 1939; d. Marlyn Ashley and Mary Alice (McLaughlin) Hickok. BA in Latin and English, Holy Family Coll., Manitowoc, Wis., 1969; MA in Elem. Edn., Clarke Coll., 1970. Tchr. grades 1-4, 3-5 St. James Sch., Cooperstown, Wis., 1961—63; tchr. grades 3-4 St. Peter Indian Mission Sch., Bapchule, Ariz., 1963—66; tchr. grade 2 St. Anthony Indian Mission Sch., Topawa, Ariz., 1966—68; tchr. grades 3-5 San Xavier Indian Mission Sch., Tucson, 1968—69; reading specialist, title I coord. Indian Oasis Pub. Sch. Dist., Sells, Ariz., 1970—74; instr. reading workshop Silver Lake Coll., Manitowoc, 1971—72, dir. spl. edn. clinic, 1973—, instr. child growth and devel., 1973; tchr. lang. arts grades 6-8, grade 3 Cathedral Sch., Honolulu, 1974—81; reading specialist, ESL tchr. Immaculate Conception Sch., Yuma, Ariz., 1983—91; reading specialist St. Christopher Sch., West Covina, Calif., 1991—92. Mem. adv. coun. Hawaii Right to Read Coun., Honolulu, 1978—81; mem. editl. bd. Ariz. Reading Jour., Phoenix, 1987—91; instr. readingand oral lang. Majunto, Marshall Islands, Wis., 1979; coord. Am. Reads, Am. Counts, 1996—, dir. spl. edn. clinic, 1996—. Recipient NDEA Fellowship grant, U.S. Edn. Dept., Clarke Coll., 1969—70, NEH grant, NEH, Wayne State U., 1987, Ronald McDonald House Charities grant, 2001. Mem.: CEC, Hawaii State Reading Assn. (bd. dirs. 1976—81), Internat. Reading Assn. Roman Catholic. Avocations: reading, swimming, crossword puzzles, designing materials and games for clinic use. Office: Silver Lake Coll 2406 S Alverno Rd Manitowoc WI 54220

HICKS, ANN NEUWIRTH, clinical social worker; b. Columbus, Ohio, Nov. 8, 1932; d. Willis A. and Luella (Knowlton) Neuwirth; children: Malcolm Lee, Geoff Cody. BA, Ohio State U., 1954; MA, West Tex. State U., 1980. Cert. social worker, Tex. Clin. social worker Amarillo State Ctr.; adoption and foster care social worker CAth. Family Svc., Amarillo, Tex.; social worker N.Mex. Health and Social Svcs., Clovis. Active community actitives. Mem. NASW (Nat. Assn. of Social Workers), League of Women Voters, Wildcat Bluff Nature Ctr. Home: 6301 Bayswater Rd Amarillo TX 79109-6503

HICKS, BETHANY GRIBBEN, judge, commissioner, lawyer; b. N.Y., Sept. 8, 1951; d. Robert and DeSales Gribben; m. William A. Hicks III, May 21, 1982; children: Alexandra Elizabeth, Samantha Katherine. AB, Vassar Coll., 1973; MEd, Boston U., 1975; JD, Ariz. State U., 1984. Bar: Ariz. 1984. Pvt. practice, Scottsdale and Paradise Valley, Ariz., 1984-91; law clk. to Hon. Kenneth L. Fields Maricopa County Superior Ct. S.E. dist., Mesa, 1991-93; commr., judge pro tem domestic rels. and juvenile depts. Maricopa County Superior Ct. Ctrl. and S.E. Dists., Phoenix and Mesa, Ariz., 1993-99; magistrate Town of Paradise Valley, Ariz., 1993-94; judge ctrl. dist. domestic rels. dept. Maricopa County Superior Ct., Phoenix, 1999-2000, presiding judge family ct. dept., 2000—02, judge S.E. dist. civil dept., 2002—. Mem. Jr. League of Phoenix, 1984-91; bd. dirs. Phoenix Children's Theatre, 1988-90; parliamentarian Girls Club of Scottsdale, Ariz., 1985-87, 89-90, bd. dirs., 1988-91; exec. bd., sec. All Saints' Episcopal Day Sch. Parents Assn., 1991-92, pres., 1993-94; active Nat. Charity League, 1995-99, Valley Leadership Class XIX, 1997-98; vol., Teach for Am., 1997—. Mem.: ABA, City Scottsdale Jud. Adv. Bd., Nat. Assn. of Women Judges, Assn. Family Ct. Conciliators (bd. dirs. 2001—), Ariz. Women Lawyers' Assn. (steering com. 1998—), Maricopa County Bar Assn., State Bar Ariz. Republican. Episcopalian. Office: 222 E Javelina Ave Mesa AZ 85210- Office Phone: 602-506-2139. E-mail: bhicks@superiorcourt.maricopa.gov.

HICKS, BETTY HARRIS, real estate agent, real estate company executive; b. Tellico Plains, Tenn., May 5, 1946; d. Ellis Fay Harris and Dellie Elizabeth Lynn; m. Roy Edward Hicks, Oct. 8, 1981. Student, Hiwasse Coll., 1982; cert., Trees Real Estate Sch., 1983. Sewing machine operator Colonial Garments, Tellico Plains, 1965—79; owner, operator Garner's Beauty Salon, 1980—81; sec. Monroe County C. of C., Madisonville, Tenn., 1981—82; salesperson Norman Lee Real Estate, Madisonville, 1982—83, Wattenbarger Real Estate, Loudon, Tenn., 1983—84; broker, owner AApple Realty Co., Loudon, Tenn., 1984—91, Anchor Properties, Loudon, Tenn., 1992—; prin., owner Anchor Mortgage Co., Loudon, 2003—. Tchr. Tenn. Real Estate Sch., Knoxville, 1998; pres. Loudon County Bd. Realtors. Pres. Loudon C. of C., Loudon. Named Realtor of Yr., 1987; recipient Cert. of Appreciation, Loudon C. of C., 1988, City of Loudon, 1988. Mem.: Loudon County C. of C. Republican. Avocations: genealogy research, gardening, cooking, reading, bird watching. Office: Anchor Properties 811 Mulberry St Loudon TN 37774

HICKS, CAROL ANN, small business owner, educator; b. Danville, Ill., Mar. 14, 1943; d. Hughie Jay Johnson and Doris N. Jean Bostwick; m. T. Keith Hicks, June 6, 1975; children: Beverly, Bobbi Ann, Sandra, Michael. AS, Danville (Ill.) Area C.C., 1985, AS in Desk Top Publ., 1996; B in Elem. Edn., Ea. Ill. U., 1988. Grain technician Danville Grain Inspection, 1981-91; tchrs. aide reading and phonics Honeywell Sch., Hoopston, Ill., 1985-88; substitute tchr. Hoopeston (Ill.) Area Cmty. Schs., 1988—; mgr., asst. mgr. Casey's Gen. Store, Hoopeston, Gifford, Ill., 1994-98; owner, mgr. Carol's Corner and Genealogy Plus, Hoopeston, 1998—. Cons. Pape Meml. Home, 2001—, Gardens Funeral Home, 2001—; ct. reporter The Neighbor, Attica, Ind.; reporter The Chronicle, Hoopeston, Ill. Author: The Presley Family History, 1993, (newsletter) Presley Research Assn., 1993-99; contbr. columns to newspapers, 2000-. Grant Twp. com. chmn. Dem. Party, Hoopeston, 1997—2000; hospice vol. USMC Logan Campus, Danville, 1991-96. Mem. NSDAR (past pres., historian 1991-95), Am. Legion Aux. (pres. 1993-95, historian), Barbara Standish NSDAR (historian, pres. 1991-95), VFW Aux., Kappa Delta Pi (Beta Pi chpt.). Mem. Ch. LDS. Avocations: genealogy, research history, bowling, reading, travel. Home: PO Box 97 Hoopeston IL 60942-0097 Office: Carols Corner and Genealogy Plus PO Box 97 Hoopeston IL 60942-0097

HICKS, DOROTHY JANE, obstetrician and gynecologist, educator; b. Cleve., Apr. 18, 1919; d. Arnell R. and Marvel M. (Hale) H. AB, Case Western Reserve U., 1941; MD, Temple U., 1944. Diplomate Am. Bd. Obstetrics and Gynecology. Asst. prof. dept. ob-gyn. U. Miami, 1967-85, prof., 1985—. Bd. dirs. rape treatment ctr. Jackson Meml. Hosp., Miami, med. dir., 1974-93, cons., 1993—; dir. pedigyn clinic Jackson Meml. Hosp. Contbr. articles to profl. jours. Fellow Am. Coll. Ob-Gyn., N.Am. Soc. Pediatric and Adolescent Gynecology, South Atlantic Ob-Gyn. Soc., Fla. Soc. Ob/Gyn, Miami Ob/Gyn Soc. Avocations: dog training, golf. Office: U Miami Sch Medicine Dept Ob-Gyn PO Box 16960 Miami FL 33101-6960

HICKS, HERALINE ELAINE, environmental health scientist, educator; b. Beaufort, S.C., Sept. 27, 1951; d. Heral and Ophelia Lillie (Albergottie) H. BA, Ohio Wesleyan U., 1973; MS, Atlanta U., 1978, PhD, 1980; postgrad., U. N.C., 1980-84. Rsch. assoc. Chapel Hill Dental Rsch. Ctr. U. N.C., 1980-81; NIH postdoctoral fellow Chapel Hill Dental Rsch. Ctr. Chapel Hill Dental Rsch. Ctr. and Dept. Surgery, 1982-84; guest scientist Naval Med. Rsch. Inst., Bethesda, Md., 1985-87; asst. prof. Chapel Hill Sch. Dentistry U. N.C., 1985-88; prof., dir. electron microscopy Morris Brown Coll., Atlanta, 1988-90; sr. environ. health scientist, dir. Cts. for Disease Control and Prevention/Agy. for Toxic Substances and Disease Registry, Atlanta, 1990—; program dir. Gt. Lakes Human Health Effects Rsch. Program, Agy. for Toxic Substances and Disease Registry. Mem. health profls. task force adv. bd. Internat. Joint Commn., Washington, 1995—. Author: (chpt.) Development and Diseases of Cartilage and Bone Matrix, 1987, Birth Defects and Reproductive Disorders, 1993; contbr. articles to profl. jours. Predoctoral traineeship NIH, 1977-79, Barnett F. Smith award for outstanding achievement Atlanta U., 1978; Acad. scholar Ohio Wesleyaan U., 1969-73, Josiah Macy Jr. scholar Woods Hole Marine Biol. Lab., 1979, Tuition scholar Atlanta U., 1979-80; postdoctoral fellow NIH, 1982-84, Notable Alumnus of Clark U., 1995; named one of Outstanding Young Women of Am., 1980. Mem. Am. Soc. for Cell Biology (Young Investigator fellowship 1990), Teratology (Young Investigator fellowship 1987), Microscopy Soc. Am., Biology Honor Soc., Beta Kappa Chi. Presbyterian. Avocations: reading, exercise, playing chess. Office: Ctrs for Disease Control and Prevention Mail Stop E29 1600 Clifton Rd NE Atlanta GA 30329-4018

HICKS, JOCELYN MURIEL, laboratory medicine specialist; b. Leamington Spa, Warwickshire, Eng., Aug. 17, 1937; arrived in U.S., 1965; d. Harold Archie and Muriel Ellen (Cumberland) Bingley; m. John Geoffrey Hicks, Aug. 15, 1959 (div. Nov. 1965); m. Melvin Blecher, May 1, 1973. BS, U. London, 1959, MSc, 1962; PhD, Georgetown U., 1971. Fellow Georgetown U. Med. Ctr., Washington, 1969-71; dir. clin. chemistry Children's Hosp. Nat. Med. Ctr., Washington, 1971-75, chmn. dept. lab. medicine, 1975-90, chief of lab. medicine and pathology, 1990—2001, dir. clin. support svcs., 1995-99; asst. prof. George Washington U. Med. Ctr., Washington, 1972-74, assoc. prof., 1975-81, prof., 1981—2002, prof. emeritus, 2002—; mem. profl. staff The Hosp. for Sick Children, Washington, 1984—2001; exec. dir. Ctr. Complex Diseases, 1999-2001; exec. dir. emeritus Children's Nat. Med. Ctr., 2002—; COO genetics divsn. Genetics and IVF, Fairfax, Va., 2002—. Pres. Children's Faculty assocs. Children's Hosp., Washington, 1989—90, chmn. bd. dirs., 1990—93, chmn. exec. com., 1994—95; clin. affiliate Cath. U. Am., Washington, 1982—94; cons. Johnson and Johnson Clin. Diagnostics, Bayer Diagnostics, i-Stat Corp. Author: Selected Analyses of Clinical Chemistry, 1984, Textbook of Clinical Chemistry, 1984, Directory of Rare Analyses, 1986, 1987, 1990, 1992, 1994, 1997, 1998, 2000, The Neonate, 1974, Pediatric Reference Ranges, 1995, 1997; co-author: Biochemical Basis of Pediatric Disease, 1992, Biochemical Basis of Pediatric Disease, 2d edit., 1995; co-editor: Point-of-Care Testing, 1999; contbr. articles to profl. jours. Recipient Kone award, Assn. Clin. Biochemists, 1987. Fellow: Royal Coll. Pathologists U.K.; mem.: Internat. Fedn. Clin. Chemistry and Lab. Medicine (treas. 2003—), Acad. Clin. Lab. Physicians and Scientists, Portuguese Soc. Clin. Pathologists (hon.), Assn. Clin. Biochemistry (hon.), Israeli Soc. Clin. Biochemistry (hon.), Egyptian Soc. Lab. Medicine (hon.), Am. Assn. Clin. Chemistry (bd. dirs. 1978—81, pres. 1981—82, chmn. publs. commn. 1982—87, Joseph H. Roe award 1976, Bernard Gerulat Meml. award 1983, Fisher award 1984, Van Slyke award 1988, Miriam Reiner award 1991, Outstanding Contbns. to Clin. Chemistry 1993, Outstanding Spkr. award 2002, Roger Boeckx Meml. lectr. 2002, Cert. of Honor). Home: 4329 Van Ness St NW Washington DC 20016-5625 Office: Genetics and IVF Genetics Divsn 3022 Javier Rd Fairfax VA 22031 E-mail: jhicks@givf.com.

HICKS, JUDITH ANN, systems analyst; b. Sulphur Springs, Tex., Dec. 11, 1962; d. Lynn Dearl and Roberta Arlene Hicks. BA, Trevecca Nazareen U., 1998. Software quality analyst EDS, Plano, Tex., 1999—2002, bus. analyst, 2002—. Mem. Prestonwood Bapt. Ch., Plano, 1998—2003. Conservative. Baptist. Avocations: hockey, reading, movies.

HICKS, LOIS ROSA, personal care industry executive, educational assistant; b. Indpls., Dec. 1, 1953; d. Harold and Margaret Lantz Lambertus; m. Dale Lynn Hicks, Jan. 29, 1977; children: Rosa Lynn Salzman, James Robert. BS, U. Wyo., 1975. Site supr. Wackenhut Corp., Gillette, Wyo., 1984—98; compensatory tchr's. asst. Campbell County H.S., South Campus, Gillette, 1998—. Sales rep. Avon Products, Gillette and Casper. Dist. commr. Boy Scouts of Am., Gillette, 1988—2003. Named Alen Micklelson Scouter of Yr., Troop 64, Boy Scouts of Am., Gillette, 1999; recipient Dist. Award of Merit, Chocadewakoa Dist., Boy Scouts of Am., 2001. Personal E-mail: jrlh@vcn.com.

HICKS, NANCI ANN, minister, marketing professional; b. Burlington, Vt., Oct. 29, 1961; d. Jessie Brittain and Betty Jane McNeil; m. Steven Bradley Hicks, Apr. 25, 1984; children: Steven Atticus, Annie Elizabeth. EdM, U. Ga., 1986; MDiv, Emory U., 1997; postgrad., Drew U. Assoc. pastor of youth ministries Mt. Carmel United Meth. Ch., Norcross, Ga., 1989—97; assoc. pastor Roswell (Ga.) United Meth. Ch., 1997—99; program and mktg. dir. Simpsonwood Conf. and Retreat Ctr., Norcross, 2000—. Bd. mem. Norcross H.S. Touchdown Club, 2003. Mem.: Christian Educators Fellowship. Democrat. Avocations: reading, writing, working out, outdoor activities. Home and Office: Simpsonwood Conf and Retreat Ctr 4511 Jones Bridge Cir Norcross GA 30092 E-mail: nhicks@simpsonwood.org.

HICKS, RITCHIE B. physical education educator; b. Tallahassee, Fla. d. Frank Evans and Isabella (Lawrence) Stewart; m. Eddie Jay Hicks; children: Eddie Darrell, Jay Freeman, Michele Dianne. AA, Howard Coll.; BS in Edn., Fla. A & M Univ.; MA in Secondary Sch. Adminstr., N.E. Mo. State Univ. Cert. health and phys. edn. tchr., secondary sch. adminstr. Phys. edn. tch. Scott Jr. High Sch., Savannah, Ga., Florissant Jr. High Sch., Mo.; head track coach Berkeley Sr. High Sch., Mo.; phys. edn. tchr. Airport Elem. Sch., Berkeley, Mo., Berkeley Jr. High Sch., Mo.; phys. edn. and health tchr. Ferguson Middle Sch., Mo.; basketball, volleyball and track coach McCluer North Sr. High Sch., Florissant, Mo.; chairperson, dept. phys. edn. Cross Keys Middle Sch., Florissant, Mo. Mem. sch. and dist. curriculum and instrn. coms., 1995; mem. Bldg. Improvement Com.; dir. Sch. Intramural Program, 1995. Writer guidelines for Cross Keys Mid. Sch. phys. edn. students. Apptd. to Youth Adv. Commn. City of Florissant, Mo.; coach Mo. State H.S. Basketball, Track and Field Championship Teams; bd. trustees Ward Chapel AME Ch., 1995, dir. Richard and Sarah Allen Summer Acad., 1995; coord. bldg. Ferguson-Florissant Scholarship Run/Walk Program, 1995. Recipient Tchr. of Yr. award State of Mo., 1992, Mid. Sch. Phys. Edn. Tchr. of Yr. Nat. Assn. Sport and Phys. Edn., 1993, Mo. Coach of Yr. for track and field, 1982, Salute to Am. Tchr. Walt Disney, 1993; named to Nat. Women's Hall of Fame. Mem. Nat. Edn. Assn., Am. Assn. Univ. Women, Mo. AAHPERD (middle and secondary sch. phys. educator award of 1993), AAHPERD (middle sch. phys. edn. tchr. award of 1993), Am. Running and Fitness Assn., Phi Delta Kappa. Avocations: fitness walking, reading, weight training, golf, dance.

HICKS, SHIRLEY E. director; b. St. Louis, Nov. 9, 1936; d. Joseph Alonzo and Thelma Elizabeth Hill; m. Sharon Lavert Hicks (div. Aug. 1978); children: Beth Ann Hargrove, Lynne Marie Catching. BA, Notre Dame Coll., Lemay, Mo., 1975; MA, Webster U., 1980. Program specialist/in-house coord. St. Louis Housing Authority; MEGASKILLS regional trainer Cooperating Sch. Dist., St. Louis; pres. S.E. Hicks and Assocs.; spl. svcs. educator Sch. Dist. City of Ladue, St. Louis. Chmn. mktg. and pub. rels. Mo. Coun. Women's Econ. Devel. Tng., State of Mo., 1988—93. Contbr. articles to profl. jours. Mem., com. chmn. Mo. Coun. on Women's Econ. Devel. and Tng., Jefferson City, St. Louis, 1988—93; mem. Grad. Class 13 Coro Found.-Women in Leadership, St. Louis. Recipient Leadership award, Chums, Inc., 1986, Excellence in Tchg. award, Urban League Met. St. Louis, 1993. Mem.: ASCD, Mo. State Tchrs. Assn. (pres. Ladue chpt. 1993—95), Chums, Inc. (nat. pub. rels. officer 1988—90, nat. v.p. 1990—94, Leadership award 1986), Zonta Internat. (St. Louis chpt.), Phi Delta Kappa (pres. 1992—94, Washington U.-Maryville chpt.). Avocations: travel, concerts, painting, reading. Home: Apt 217 3915 Olive St Saint Louis MO 63108-3157

HICKS, VIRGINIA BUCHHOLZ, secondary school educator; b. El Paso, Tex., Feb. 25, 1947; d. Oscar T. and Miriam M. Buchholz; m. Jack H. Hicks Jr., May 31, 1969; children: Virginia, Jordan. BA, U. S.C., 1969; MEd, Lesley U., 2001. Cert. tchr., Nat. Bd. Cert. Tchr. Richland County Sch. Dist., Columbia, SC, 1969; freelance model Knoxville, Tenn., 1970—76; tchr. Brunswick Jr. Coll., Brunswick, Ga., 1977, Pickens County Sch. Dist., Easley, SC, 1992—, dist. honor roll tchr., 2002—03. Mem. dist. grant bd. Sch. Dist. Pickens County, Easley, 2002; mem. outreach faculty S.C. Gov. Sch. for Arts, Greenville, 1993—2002; bd. dir. Ctr. for Creative Learning, Greenville; mem. steering com. dist. small learning communities grant, 2003—04. Contbr. chapters to books The Fire That Forged My Steel; editor: Jocassee Valley, 2003. Recipient Internat. Educator Yr. award, 2004, Chapel of the Four Chaplains Legion of Honor award, 2004; grantee, SC Dept. Edn., 2000—04. Mem.: Nat. Art Edn. Assn., S.C. Art Edn. Assn. (award 2001). Avocations: painting, horseback riding, travel. Office: Pickens High School 111 Blue Flame Drive Pickens SC 29671

HIDAY, VIRGINIA ALDIGÉ, sociologist educator; b. New Orleans, Jan. 28, 1939; d. Robert Joseph and Mary Boagni (Anding) A.; m. L.L. Hiday, Sept. 5, 1970 (div. June 2, 1997). AB, U. N.C., 1960, MEd, 1961, PhD, 1973. Asst. prof. U. Colo., Boulder, 1972-75; postdoctoral fellow Duke U. Med. Ctr., Durham, N.C., 1975-76; asst. prof., prof. N.C. State U., Raleigh, 1976—. Vis. prof. U. N.C., Chapel Hill, 1974-75; referee for various sci. jours. in sociology, law, psychiatry; cons. N.C. Divsn. Mental Health, Raleigh, 1986, 89, Nat. Health Svc., London, 1999, Ont. Ministry of Health, Toronto, 2000. Mem. editl. bd. Contemporary Sociology, 1986-91, 98-2000, Rose Monograph Series, 1982-88, Jour. Health and Social Behavior, 2000—, Internat. Jour. Law and Psychiatry, 2000; contbr. numerous articles to profl. jours. Mem., com. AAUP, Boulder, Colo., 1972-75; worker Campaigns for local, state, nat. offices, Chapel Hill, 1966—, Habitat for Humanity, Chapel Hill, 1996-97; bd. dirs. Orange County Mental Health Assn., Chapel Hill, 1995-99. Named NIMH Postdoctoral fellow, Popultion Predoctoral fellow NICHD. Mem. APA, Am. Sociol. Assn. (coun. mem. med. sect., sec., treas. mental health), So. Sociol. Soc. (coun. mem.), Internat. Acad. Law & Mental Health (coun. mem. 1993—), Soc. for Study of Social Problems, Phi Kappa Phi, Sigma Xi. Democrat. Episcopalian. Avocations: tennis, skiing, dance. Office: NC State U Dept Sociology/Anthropology PO Box 8107 Raleigh NC 27695-0001

HIDSON, PATRICIA DIANE, artist, educator; b. Edmonton, Alta., Can., Nov. 20, 1948; arrived in U.S., 1974; d. Albert John Hidson and Patricia Florence Ryland; m. James Wilfred Brozek, Feb. 14, 1991; m. Brian Peter Bentz, Jan. 16, 1974 (div. Oct. 1985); children: Paul Bentz, Meighan Bentz, Brian Bentz. B, U. Alta., Edmonton, 1975; postgrad., U. Wis. Ext., Milw., 1978—81, Cape Sch. Art, Provincetown, Mass., 1982—84, Milw. Inst. Art and Design, 1983—84. Dir., tchr. The Hidson Art Sch. and Studio, Milw.; prin., owner Pat Hidson Art Gallery, Milw., 2003—. Lectr., spkr. in field. One-woman shows include Regional Art Ctr., LaCrosse, Wis., 1998, Grace Chosy Gallery, Madison, Wis., 1998, 1995, 1993, Gruen Gallery, Chgo., 1997, 1990, Madison U. Med. Hosp., 1993, Tory Folliard Gallery, Milw., 1993, others, exhibited in group shows at Door County, Wis., 2001, Tory Folliard Gallery, 2000, 1999, 1998, Art Resources Gallery, St. Paul, 1998, Edmonton Art Gallery, 1997, Gallerie Stephanie, Chgo., 1995, Wustum Mus., Racine, Wis., 1985—97, Carolyn Ruff Gallery, Mpls., 1993, Banaker Gallery, San Francisco, 1993, San Miguel Allende, Mex., 1993, others, Represented in permanent collections Walt Disney Corp., Quadracci Corp. Collection (Milw.), Associated Bank (Milw.), Marine Bank (Milw.), numerous others; featured and reviewed (numerous publs.). Episcopalian. Avocations: yoga, reading, wildlife rehabilitation. Home: 5730 N river Forest Dr Glendale WI 53209 Office: Hidson Art Sch Studio and Art Gallery 303-133 W Pittsburgh Ave Milwaukee WI 53204

HIEATT, CONSTANCE BARTLETT, English language educator; b. Boston, Feb. 11, 1928; d. Arthur Charles and Eleonora (Very) Bartlett; m. Allen Kent Hieatt, Oct. 25, 1958. Student, Smith Coll., 1945-47; AB, Hunter Coll., 1953, AM, 1957; PhD, Yale U., 1959. Lectr. City Coll., CUNY, 1959-60; from asst. prof. to assoc. prof. English Queensborough C.C., CUNY, 1960-65; from assoc. prof. to prof. St. John's U., Jamaica, N.Y., 1965-69; prof. English U. Western Ont., London, Can., 1969-93, prof. emeritus, 1993—. Author: (with A.K. Hieatt) The Canterbury Tales of Geoffrey Chaucer, 1964, rev. edit., 1981, Spenser: Selected Poetry, 1970; The Realism of Dream Visions, 1967, Beowulf and Other Old English Poems, 1967, rev. edit., 1983, Essentials of Old English, 1968, The Miller's Tale By Geoffrey Chaucer, 1970; (with Sharon Butler) Pleyn Delit: Medieval Cookery for Modern Cooks, 1976, rev. edit., 1979; (with Brenda Hosington) rev. 2d edit., 1996, Karlamagnus Saga, Vols. I and II, 1975, Vol. III, 1980; (with Sharon Butler) Curye on Inglysch, 1985; An Ordinance of Pottage, 1988; (with Robin F. Jones) La Novele Cirurgerie, 1990; (with Minnette Gaudet) Guillaume de Machaut's Tale of the Alerion, 1994; (with Brian Shaw and Duncan Macrae-Gibson) Beginning Old English, 1994; (with Rudolf Grewe) Libellus de Arte Coquinaria, 2001; also children books (with Hieatt) The Canterbury Tales of Geoffrey Chaucer, 1961, Sir Gawain and the Green Knight, 1967, The Knight of the Lion, 1968, The Knight of the Cart, 1969, The Joy of the Court, 1971, The Sword and the Grail, 1972, The Castle of Ladies, 1973, The Minstrel Knight, 1974. Yale U. fellow, and Lewis-Farmington fellow, 1957-59, Vis. fellow Yale U., 1985-86, 89-93; Can. Council and Social Sci. and Humanities Rsch. Coun. grant. Fellow Royal Soc. Can.; mem. MLA, Medieval Acad. Am., Internat. Soc. Anglo-Saxonists, Can Soc. Medievalists. Episcopalian. Home: 335 Essex Mdws Essex CT 06426-1526 Personal E-mail: constance.hieatt@yale.edu.

HIEBNER, AIDA CECILIA, secondary school educator, education educator; b. Quito, Ecuador, Aug. 18, 1946; arrived in U.S., 1975; d. Carlos Humberto Padilla Salazar and Zoila Amada Vallejo Diaz; m. Lauren Wayne, June 2; children: Andrey Johann, Diego Ryan. Elem. edn., Normal for Tchrs., 1965; BA in ESL, Ctrl. U. Quito, 1972, U. Nebr., 1987, MEd, 2001; postgrad., Inst. Children's Lit., 2001. Typist Dept. Civil Registry, Quito, 1965—69; exec. sec. Ecuadorian Ins. Co., Quito, 1969—73; sec. Def. Dept., Quito, 1973—75; tchr. Pvt. Sch., Quito, 1974—75; tchr. aide O'Neill Elem. Sch., Nebr., 1978—80; tchr. Page Pub. Sch., Nebr., 1989—92; tchr. art O'Neill Pub. Sch., 1993—. Tchr. art St. Mary's H.S., O'Neill, 1988—89, tchr. Spanish, 1993—; instr. Spanish I North East C.C., O'Neill, 2000—. Author (poem): Nat. Libr. Poetry, 1998 (Editor's Choice, 1998); Hispanic Art Show, Kearney, Nebr., 1986 (1st Pl., 1986), State Art Clubs, 1988 (Hon. Memtion), Ranchland Art Group, 1981—89 (Best of Show). Mem.: O'Neill Edn. Assn., Nebr. Assn. Art Clubs, Nebr. State Edn. Assn., Alpha Delta Kappa. Avocations: painting, travel, reading, photography, writing. Office: O'Neill Pub Sch PO Box 230 Oneill NE 68763*

HIGDON, LINDA HAMPTON, congressional staff; b. Athens, Tenn., Mar. 14, 1951; d. Lula Sue (Stiles) Hampton; a m. Donald Wayne Higdon, Dec. 20, 1973. BA, Tenn. Wesleyan Coll., Athens, 1973; MPA, U. Tenn., 1985. Cert. Am. Soc. Pub. Adminstrs., Knoxville, Tenn. Tchr. McMinn Co. Schs., Etowah, Tenn., 1973-75; dist. staff asst. U.S. Rep. John Duncan Jr., Athens, Tenn., 1975—. Adj. instr. Tenn. Wesleyan Coll., Athens, 1985-86. Former pres., McMinn Co. Young Rep., Athens, Tenn., McMinn Co. Rep. Women's Club; former GOP chmn. McMinn Co. Rep. Party, Athens, Tenn.; area 2 vice-chmn. Tenn. Fedn. Rep. Women State Bd.; program leader Athens Area C. of C. Leadership McMinn Program. Named Miss Tenn. Young Rep. State Yr-Fed, Nashville, 1972; recipient Lincoln award McMinn Co. Young Rep. Club, Athens, Tenn., 1992. Mem. ASPA. Republican. Methodist. Avocations: boating, gardening. Home: Kirkwood Est Englewood TN 37327 Office: US Rep John Duncan Jr 6 E Madison Ave Athens TN 37303-3697

HIGDON, PAMELA LEIS, writer; b. San Bernardino, Calif., Sept. 2, 1943; d. Stella Doss and Raymond Ellsworth Leis; m. Sherman Robert Higdon Jr., Aug. 29, 1964 (dec.); 1 child, Mary Katherine Christian. BS in Edn., Tex. Technol. U., Lubbock, 1966. Cert. tchr. Tex., 1966. Elem. sch. tchr., sci. coord. for elem. sch., dist. lang. arts com. mem., after sch. computer instr. Arabian Am. Oil Co., Ras Tanura, Saudi Arabia, 1978—86; editor/writer, Bird Talk Mag. and Birds USA Fancy Publications, Irvine, Calif., 1987—90; writer/editor, product developer, project mgr., acquisitions editor Ednl. Insights, Carson, Calif., 1990—94; freelance writer and editor PLH Writing/Editing, Castroville, Tex., 1994—. Author: (children's educational book) Science Notes. How Things Move; author, editor (pet care book) The Essential Cockatiel, The Essential Zebra Finch; editor: (prehospital medical booklet) The Life You Save: Community Defibrillation Programs & the Emergency Care Responder; author: (monthly newsletter Can. Paramedics) Jour. Emergency Med. Svcs.; editor (monthly periodicals) Journal of Emergency Medical Services, Fire Rescue Magazine, Clarity, EMS Insider, EMS M&S, EMS Best Practices, Caring for the Ages-for Long-Term Care Practitioners; author (with Julie Mancini): (bird watching book) Watching Backyard Birds; author: (children's educational book) Pattern Blocks (math series); author, project manager (computerized educational games) Geosafari & Geosafari Jr., assorted; author (with Katherine Christian): (educational book) Third Grade Review; writer, Nat. Wildlife Fedn. (interactive, wildlife, educational) Insects, Exotic Animals, Sea Life, Wild Animals, Dinosaurs; author (with Dr. David McCluggage): (animal care book) Holistic Care for Birds: A Manual of Wellness and Healing; author: (pet care book) Bird Care and Training, (bird care book) Happy Healthy Pets: The Quaker Parrot; writer, editor (pet care book) The Essential African Grey. Vol. writer of cmty. newsletter Mills Br. Village Bd. Dirs., Kingwood, Tex., 1996—2000; vol. writer, designer, pub. town newsletter Castroville, Tex., 2001—03; exec. bd., rec. sec. Meth. Ch., Castroville, 2003—; chair Landmark Hist. Preservation Commn., 2004—. Recipient Cmty. Svc. award, Mills Br. Village Bd. Dirs., 1997. Mem.: Exec. Bd., Meth. Ch., Castroville, Tex., DAR (life), Daughters of the Republic of Tex. (rec. sec. 2002—). Democrat. Avocations: mentoring children, quilting, reading, swimming, birdwatching.

HIGDON, POLLY SUSANNE, federal judge; b. Goodland, Kans., May 1, 1942; d. William and Pauline Higdon; m. John P. Wilhardt (div. May 1988); 1 child, Liesl. BA, Vassar Coll., 1964; postgrad., Cornell U., 1967; JD, Washburn U., 1975; LLM, NYU, 1980. Bar: Kans. 1975, Oreg. 1980. Assoc. Corley & Assocs., Garden City, Kans., 1975-79, Kendrick M. Mercer Law Offices, Eugene, Oreg., 1980-82; pvt. practice law Eugene, 1983; judge U.S. Bankruptcy Ct., Eugene, 1983-95, Portland, Oreg., 1995-97, chief judge, 1997—. Active U.S. Peace Corps, Tanzania, East Africa, 1965-66. Mem. Am. Bankruptcy Inst., Nat. Conf. Bankruptcy Judges, Oreg. Women Lawyers. Office: US Bankruptcy Ct 1001 SW 5th Ave Fl 7 Portland OR 97204-1147

HIGGINBOTHAM, EDITH ARLEANE, radiologist, researcher; b. New Orleans, Sept. 14, 1946; d. Luther Aldrich and Ruby (Clark) H.; m. Terry Lawrence Andrews (div. 1979); m. Donald Temple Ford (div. 1989). BS, Howard U., 1967, MS, 1970, MD, 1974. Diplomate Am. Bd. Radiology, Am. Bd. Nuclear Medicine. Intern St. Vincent's Hosp., N.Y.C., 1974-75, resident in diagnostic radiology, 1975-78, resident in nuclear radiology, 1978-79; asst. prof. radiology, chief nuclear medicine Howard U., Howard U. Hosp., Washington, 1979-82; assoc. prof. clin. radiology, dir. nuclear medicine U. Medicine and Dentistry N.J., Newark, 1982-90; locum tenens radiologist Sterling Med., Cin., 1991-94, Med. Nat., San Antonio, 1990-91; diagnostic radiologist Diagnostic Health Imaging Systems, Lanham, Md., 1994-95; locum tenens radiologist, 1995-97; radiologist, dir. radiology N.E. Wash. Med. Group, Colville, Wash., 1997—99; radiologist Mount Carmel Hosp., Colville, 1997-99, Barstow (Calif.) Cmty. Hosp., 1999, Queen of Peace Hosp., Mitchell, SD, 1999—2002, New Ulm Med Ctr., Minn., 2002—03, dir. radiology, 2003; radiologist Albert Lea (Minn.) Med. Ctr., Mayo Health Sys., 2003. Cons. Biotech. Rsch. Inst., Rockville, Md., 1989-94; profl. assoc. Ctr. for Molecular Medicine and Immunology, Newark, 1984-90; asst. prof. radiology George Washington U., Washington, 1990; presenter in field. Contbr. articles to profl. jours. Named Outstanding Working Woman, Glamour mag., 1981, Hon. Dep. Atty. Gen., State of La., 1982. Mem. Am. Coll. Radiology, Radiol. Soc. N.Am., Soc. Nuclear Medicine, Sigma Xi, Phi Delta Epsilon. Roman Catholic. Avocations: aerobics, reading, self-improvement, music. travel.

HIGGINBOTHAM, ELIZABETH REBECCA OSBORNE, special education educator; b. Jacksonville, Fla., May 4, 1975; d. Albert Thomas Osborne II and Carolyn Elizabeth Moore Osborne; m. Kenneth James

Higginbotham, June 20, 1998; children: Keithen James, Kyle Benjamin. A, Fla. C.C., 1995; BA in Spl. Edn., U. No. Fla., 1997, M in Pre-K Handicap, 2000. Cert. tchg. Fla. Tchr. phys. impaired Duval County Sch. Bd., Jacksonville, 1998—. Mem. Coun. For Exceptional Children, Jacksonville, 1995—; co-leader Girls Scouts Am., 1995—. Mem.: Duval Tchrs. Union. Avocations: photography, travel.

HIGGINBOTHAM, EVE JULIET, ophthalmologist, educator; b. New Orleans, Nov. 4, 1953; d. Luther Aldrich and Ruby Edith (Clark) H.; m. Frank Christopher Williams, June 7, 1986. BSChE, MS in Engring., MIT, 1975; MD, Harvard U., 1979. Intern Pacific Med. Ctr., San Francisco, 1979-80; resident La. State U. Eye Ctr., 1980-83; fellow Mass. Eye and Ear Infirmary, Boston, 1983-85; asst. prof. U. Ill., Chgo., 1985-90; assoc. prof. U. Mich., Ann Arbor, 1990-94; prof., chair dept. ophthalmology U. Md., Balt., 1994—. Co-editor: Management of Difficult Glaucoma, 1994, Clinician's Guide to Comprehensive Ophtholomology, 1998; contbr. articles to profl. jours; mem. editl. bd. Jour. of Glaucoma, 1990-93, Archives of Ophthalmology, 1994—; sect. editor: Glaucoma in Principles and Practice of Ophthalmology. Bd. dirs. Prevent Blindness Am., Schaumburg, Ill., 1990-97, chair publs. com., 1990-95, chair scientific adv. com., 1995—. Fellow Am. Acad. Ophthalmology (trustee 1992-95); mem. Women in Ophthalmology (bd. dirs. 1990-99), Assn. Univ. Profs. Ophthalmology, Assn. in Rsch. in Vision and Ophthalmology, Inst. Medicine, Md. Soc. Eye Physicians and Surgeons (v.p. 1997-99, pres. 2000—), Balt. City Med. Soc. (treas. 1999-00, v.p. 2000—). Avocations: golf, piano. Office: U Md 419 W Redwood St Baltimore MD 21201-1734

HIGGINBOTHAM, JOAN E. astronaut; b. Chgo., Aug. 03; BSEE, So. Ill. U., 1987; M in Mgmt., Fla. Inst. Tech., 1992, M in Space Sys., 1996. Payload elec. engr. divsn. ele. and telecomm. sys. NASA, Kennedy Space Ctr., Fla., 1987, lead orbiter experiments space shuttle Columbia, 1987, exec. staff asst. to dir. shuttle ops. and mgmt., backup orbiter project engr. space shuttle Atlantis, lead orbiter project engr. space shuttle Columbia; astronaut, mission specialist NASA, Johnson Space Ctr., Houston, 1996—. Named Disting. Alumni, Fla. Inst. Tech., 1997, So. Ill. U.; named one of 50 Disting. Scientists and Engrs., Nat. Tech. Assn.; recipient Key to City of Cocoa, Fla., Key to City of Rockledge, Presdl. Sports award in bicycling and weight training, Outstanding Woman of Yr. award, Exceptional Svc. Medal, NASA. Mem.: Links, Inc., Bronze Eagles, Delta Sigma Theta. Avocations: weightlifting, cycling, music, motivational speaking. Office: Astronaut Office/CB NASA Johnson Space Ctr Houston TX 77058*

HIGGINBOTHAM, WENDY JACOBSON, political adviser, writer; b. Salt Lake City, Oct. 23, 1947; d. Alfred Thurl and Virginia Lorraine (LaCom) Jacobson; m. Keith Higginbotham, July 12, 1969; children: Ann Elizabeth Morley, Ryan Keith, Laura Carol Hoopes. Student, Occidental Coll., 1965—66, U. Grenoble, France, 1967; BA cum laude with highest honors, Brigham Young U., 1969. Tchg. instr. Brigham Young U., Provo, Utah, 1969-70, editor univ. press, 1970-71; freelance editor Camarillo, Calif., 1971-78; freelance newspaper writer Vienna, Va., 1983-85; mem. profl. staff U.S. Senate Labor Com., Washington, 1985-86; exec. asst. U.S. Senator Orrin G. Hatch, Washington, 1986-88, legis. dir., 1988-91, chief of staff/adminstrv. asst., 1991-94, chief policy adviser, 1994-95; polit. adviser, freelance writer Washington, 1996—. Mem. Profl. Rep. Women, Phi Kappa Phi. Republican. Mem. Lds Ch. Avocations: traveling, hiking. Home: 2022 Willow Branch Ct Vienna VA 22181-2972

HIGGINS, DIANE W. music teacher; b. Troy, N.Y., Jan. 19, 1949; d. Harris Arthur and Mary Agnes (Cochrane) Ward; m. Charles Royden Higgins, Jr., June 5, 1971; children: David Royden, Carolyn Ward. BMus, Salem Coll., 1971. Treas. N.C. Music Tchrs. Assn., 1986-89, v.p./scholarship, 1989-91, chair state piano tchrs., 1995-97, conv. chair, 1997-99, pres., 1999-2001; v.p. Charlotte Piano Tchrs. Forum, N.C., 1995-97, pres., 1997-99. Violinist Winston-Salem Symphony, 1967—71; founder, dir. Charlotte Music Career Fair, 1999—; piano instr. U. N.C.-Greensboro Summer Music Camp, 1996—2001. Solo pianist ASID Home Tour, Charlotte, N.C., 1986-2001, Holiday House Tour, Charlotte, 1989-2001, Fourth Ward Christmas Tour, Charlotte, 1989-99, Presbyn. Hosp., Charlotte, 1986-2001; mem. Salem Coll. Friends of Music, 2001; pres. Queens Coll. Friends of Music, 2001. Recipient violin scholarship Salem Coll., Winston-Salem, 1967-71. Mem.: Nat. Guild Piano Tchrs., Charlotte Music Tchrs. Assn. (sec. 1999—2001), Charlotte Piano Tchrs. Forum (pres. 1997—99), N.C. Music Tchrs. Assn. (pres. 1999—2001), Music Tchrs. Nat. Assn., Friends of Music at Salem Coll., Friends of Music at Queens Coll., Charlotte Civic Orch. (violinist 1987—), N.C. Fedn. Music Clubs (dist. chair 1981—84), Charlotte Music Club (sec. 1984—85). Home: 4625 Mullens Ford Rd Charlotte NC 28226-5040

HIGGINS, DOROTHY MARIE, dean, educator; b. Lawrence, Mass., May 1, 1930; d. John Daniel and Mary Jane (Herbertson) H. AB, Emmanuel Coll., 1951; MS, Cath. U., 1961; PhD, Boston Coll., 1966. Assoc. prof. chemistry Emmanuel Coll., Boston, 1966-88, chair chemistry dept., 1974-85; div. chair math., sci., tech. Roxbury Community Coll., Roxbury Crossing, Mass., 1988-90; dean arts and scis. Teikyo-Post U., Waterbury, Conn., 1990-97; part-time instr. organic chemistry & genl. chemistry Naugatuck Valley C.C., 1998—, rsch. assoc., 1999—, instr. intro. to engring., 1998—. Grant cons. N.E. coll. Optometry, Boston, 1986; faculty cons. Zymark Corp., Hopkinton, Mass., 1982; rsch. assoc. U. Mass., Boston, 1975-84. Editor: (workbook) Geometry: Development Students, 1989; editor sci. newsletter, 1989; editorial adv. bd. Jour. Coll. Sci. Teaching, 1984-88, 2001-2005 Instrumentation grantee NSF, 1985, Chautauqua grantee NSF, 1981-82, Instrumentation grantee George Alden Trust, 1985, Boston Globe Found., 1985, Extramural Assoc. grantee NIH, 1984. Mem. Am. Chem. Soc., Nat. Sci. Tchrs. Assn., New Eng. Chem. Tchrs., Soc. Coll. Sci. Tchg. Democrat. Roman Catholic. Avocations: needlework, crocheting, cross-country skiing. E-mail: dhiggins@snet.net.

HIGGINS, HARRIET PRATT, investment advisor; b. Cortland, N.Y., Dec. 18, 1950; d. Edward Frances and Adeline (Bostelmann) Higgins; children from previous marriage: John Higgins MacDonald, Peter Brewster MacDonald. BA, Wells Coll., 1972; MA, Middlebury Coll. Grad. Sch. Langs., 1973; MBA, Columbia U., 1977. Corp. fin. officer Bank Am., N.Y.C., 1978-80; asst. v.p. J. Henry Schroder Bank and Trust Co., N.Y.C., 1980-82; mgr. Royal Bank Can., N.Y.C., 1982-84, sr. mgr., 1984-94; v.p. pvt. client svcs. TCW Group, N.Y.C., 1994-99; mng. dir. Auda Advisor Assocs. LLC, 1999—2000; mgr., CEO Alyssa LLC, 1999—2000; pres. Mayflower Capital, 2000—; mng. dir., ptnr. Fin. Net Boston, 2001—; regulatory rep. Winston, Evans & Crocher, Boston, 2001—. Adj. prof. econs. Pace U., N.Y.C., 1979—80, NYU, N.Y.C., 1983—84; chmn., CEO, pres. McGraw, NY, 1987—95; alumni bd. Columbia Bus. Sch., 1982—87; trustee, chair investment com. Wells Coll., 1998—. Trustee Boston Police Found.; mem. Commonwealth of Mass. Ctrl. Artery and Tunnel Commn.; vol., contbr. Rep. Nat. Com., N.Y.C., 1980—; trustee Boys and Girls Club, Newport County, 2000—. Fellow Carnegie Found., 1974—75. Mem.: Fin. Womens Assn., Preservation Soc. Newport County, Newport Hist. Soc., Desc. of the Mayflower Soc. Republican. Episcopalian. Avocations: skiing, tennis, violin. Office: PO Box 1311 Newport RI 02840 : Easton's View 236 Eustis Ave Newport RI 02840 E-mail: hhiggins@mayflowercapital.net.

HIGGINS, ISABELLE JEANETTE, librarian; b. Evanston, Ill., Dec. 13, 1919; d. Frank LeRoy and Ada Louise (Wilcox) Heck; m. George Alfred Higgins, Jan. 23, 1945 (dec. Sept. 1994); children: Alfred Clinton, Donald Quentin, Heather Higgins Aanes, Laura Higgins Palmer, Carol Higgins. BS, Northwestern U., 1940; MLS, U. Md., 1971. Cert. libr., Md. With Liebermann Waelchli Co., Tokyo, 1940-41, Shanghai Evening Post, 1941-42; editl. asst. Newsweek mag., N.Y.C., 1944; wire editor FBIS/FCC, Washington, 1944-46; rsch. and analysis China desk CIA, Washington, 1946-49; supr. library vols. Westbrook Sch., Bethesda, Md., 1965-69; reference libr. Montgomery County Pub. Librs., Bethesda, 1969-83; libr. Brooks Inst. Photography, Santa Barbara, Calif., 1984-96, ret., 1996. Treas. Friends of Santa Barbara Pub. Libr., 1987-88. Mem. AAUW (bd. dirs. Santa Barbara br. 1988-94, del. nat. conv. 1989), Spl. Librs. Assn., Calif. Libr. Assn., Santa Barbara Little Gardens Club (pres. 1987-89), Floriade Garden Club (pres. 1990-91). Congregationalist. Avocations: reading, swimming, gardening. Home: Apt 203 3775 Modoc Rd Santa Barbara CA 93105 E-mail: ijhiggins@netzero.net.

HIGGINS, KATHRYN O'LEARY, consulting firm executive; b. Sioux City, Iowa, Oct. 11, 1947; d. Paul C. and Mary Kathryn (Callaghan) O'Leary; widowed; children: Liam James, Kevan Paul. BS, U. Nebr., 1969. Manpower specialist U.S. Dept. Labor, Washington, 1969-78; asst. dir. employment policy White House Domestic Policy, Washington, 1978-81; staff dir. minority U.S. Senate Labor & Human Resources Com., Washington, 1981-86; chief of staff U.S. Representative Sander Levin, Washington, 1986-93, Sec. of Labor Robert Reich, Washington, 1993-95; cabinet sec. White Ho. Cabinet Affairs, Washington, 1995-97, dep. sec. of labor, 1997-99; v.p. pub. policy Nat. Trust for Hist. Preservation, Washington, 1999—2003; pres. TATC Cons. Firm, 2004—. Bd. dirs. Charles Carroll House, Surface Transp. Dept. Policy Project Bd.; cabinet mem. Balt. Basilica; bd. dirs. Londontown Found.; bd. dirs. project children young leaders U. Md.. Sch. Pub. Affairs; bd. dirs. Bridges to Peace Ignatian Lay Vol. Corps, Video Action; adv. coun. Historic Annapolis. Democrat. Roman Catholic. Avocations: cooking, antiques, book club. Home: 151 Duke Of Gloucester St Annapolis MD 21401-2504 Office: TATC Consulting 2409 18th St NW Washington DC 20009

HIGGINS, LARKIN MAUREEN, artist, poet, educator; b. Santa Monica, Calif. d. DuWayne and Mary Jean (Sampson) H. BA, Calif. State U., Long Beach, 1976; MA, Calif. State U., Fullerton, 1983; MFA, Otis Coll. Art and Design, 1995. Artist/poet resident Dorland Mountain Arts Colony, 2000, 2001, 2002; prof. art Calif. Luth. U., Thousand Oaks. Represented in numerous collections; exhibited nationally in group and one-woman shows; art reviewed/ pub. in various pubs. including L.A. Times, Artweek, The Boston Globe, Genre, Antiques & The Arts Weekly, U-TURN, others; poetry pub. in Blue Satellite, Beyond Baroque mag., Saturday Afternoon jour., others; 3 anthologies: Matchbook, Jitters: The Best of Southern California Coffee House Fiction and Poetry, So Luminous the Wildflowers: Anthology of California Poetry. Past. bd. dirs., past chairperson nat. photography exhbn. com. Westwood (Calif.) Ctr. for the Arts; past chairperson lecture com. L.A. Ctr. for Photographic Studies; founding mem. Women in Photography, L.A. Recipient cash award ASA Gallery, U. N.Mex., 1982, Purchase award Erie (Pa.) Art Mus., 1984; Hewlett Found. Ind. Artist grantee, 1987-88, Jones grantee, 1986. Mem. Coll. Art Assn., Beyond Baroque Lit. Arts Ctr., Women's Caucus Art.

HIGGINS, LINDA I. state legislator; b. Mpls., Nov. 11, 1950; AA, Iowa Lakes C.C.; BS, Mankato State Coll. Mem. Minn. Senate from 58th dist., St. Paul, 1996—. Home: 1715 Emerson Ave N Minneapolis MN 55411-3226 Office: 226 Capitol 75 Constitution Ave Saint Paul MN 55155-1601

HIGGINS, MARY CELESTE, lawyer, researcher; b. Chgo., Feb. 9, 1943; d. Maurice James and Helen Marie (Egan) H. AB, St. Mary-of-the-Woods Coll., Ind., 1965; JD, DePaul U., 1970; LLM, John Marshall Law Sch., Chgo., 1976; postgrad., Harvard U., 1981—82, MPA, 1982; MPhil, U. Cambridge (Eng.), 1983. Bar: Ill. 1970, U.S. Dist. Ct. (no. dist.) Ill. 1970. Pvt. practice, Chgo., 1970—72, 1979—80; atty. corp. counsel dept. Continental Bank, Chgo., 1972—76; asst. sec., asst. counsel Marshall Field & Co., Chgo., 1976—79; sr. atty. Mattel, Inc., Hawthorne, Calif., 1980—81; rsch. in revitalization and adjustment of U.S. Industries in U.S. and world markets, 1981—83; legal cons., 1983—85; Midwest regional officer Legal Svcs. Corp., 1985—87, assoc. dir., 1986, acting dir. office of field svcs., 1986—87, dir., 1987—89, Meridian One Corp., Alexandria, Va., 1990—. Recipient Am. Jurisprudence awards for acad. excellence, 1966-70. Mem.: Ill. Bar. Assn. Home: 203 Yoakum Pky Apt 508 Alexandria VA 22304-3711 Office Phone: 703-461-5200. E-mail: mch@meridianone.com.

HIGGINS, MARY ELLEN See HAWKINS, MARY ELLEN HIGGINS

HIGGINS, OLEDA JACKSON, retired medical and surgical nurse; b. Thibodaux, La. d. Tillman and Bessie (Charles) Jackson; m. Samuel J. Higgins; 1 child, Sterling J. BSN, Dillard U., 1958. From staff nurse to nursing dir. Flint-Goodridge Hosp., New Orleans, 1958-78; staff nurse Jo Ellen Smith Med. Ctr., New Orleans, 1979-95; ret., 1995. Nursing home cons. Bapt. Faith Home, New Orleans, 1968-72. Mem. ANA, Nat. League for Nursing, Dillard U. Profl. Orgn. Nurses, Order Ea. Star, Chi ETa Phi (basileus Rho Chi chpt., chaplain 1976). Baptist. Avocations: singing, soft music, operas. Home: 4321 Macarthur Blvd New Orleans LA 70131-6843

HIGGINS, ROBIN L. federal agency administrator; B in English, SUNY, Oneonta; M in English, Long Island U.; postgrad., Hebrew U., Jerusalem. Commd. USMC, advanced through grades to lt. col., ret.; dep. asst. sec., acting asst. sec. Vet.'s Employment and Tng. U.S. Dept. Labor; exec. dir. Fla. Dept. Vet.'s Affairs, 1999—2001; under sec. meml. affairs Dept. Vet. Affairs, Washington, 2001—. Author: Patriot Dreams - The Murder of Colonel Rich Higgins. Recipient Dickey Chapelle award, Marine Corps League, Pub. Spirit award, Am. Legion, Vets. Caucus award, Am. Acad. Physician Assts. Mem.: Marine Corps League, AmVets, Jewish War Vets., Retired Officers' Assn., Disabled Am. Vets., Gold Star Wives, Am. Legion. Office: US Dept Vet Affairs Nat Cemetery Adminstrn 810 Vermont Ave NW Washington DC 20420

HIGGINS, ROXANNE SNELLING, educational consultant; b. Ft. Eustis, Va., Aug. 17, 1954; d. William Rodman and Anne Louise (Kurtz) Snelling; m. Vincent James Elliott, Oct. 1, 1983 (div.); children: Brian William, Lauren Elizabeth; m. Robert K. Higgins, June 16, 2001. BA, Denison U., 1976; MBA, Syracuse U., 1978. Internat. loan officer First Pa. Bank, Phila., 1978-82; ins. assoc. Ind. Sch. Mgmt., Wilmington, Del, 1982-83, dir. mgmt. insts., 1983-87, cons., exec. dir. consortium, 1984—, v.p., 1986-90, pres., 1990—. Office: Ind Sch Mgmt 1316 N Union St Wilmington DE 19806-2594

HIGGINS, RUTH ELLEN, theatre producer; b. Streator, Ill., Jan. 23, 1945; d. Thomas Francis and Mary Madeline (Ahearn) H.; m. Byron L. Schaffer, Oct. 17, 1975 (dec. May 1990); 1 child, Kareth Madeline Schaffer. BS in Edn. and Theater, No. Ill. U., 1967; MA in Theater Arts, U. Nebr., 1968; postgrad., No. Ill. U., 1970-74. Instr. Glenbrook North H.S., Northbrook, Ill., 1968-69; dir. theatre Highland C.C., Freeport, Ill., 1969-73; co-prodr. Dinglefest Theatre Co., Chgo., 1972-77; arts cons. Chgo. Cmty. Trust, 1973-74; exec. dir., founder Chgo. Alliance for the Performing Arts, 1974-79; prodr. New Tuners Theatre, Chgo.; exec. dir., co-founder Chgo. Coalition for Arts in Edn., 1979-83; gen. mgr. Theatre Bldg., Chgo., 1981-97, North Shore Ctr. Performing Arts, Skokie, Ill., 1997-99; dir. MBA arts mgmt. Roosevelt U., Chgo., 1999—. Cons. Office Cook County Assessor, Chgo., 1980, Donors Forum, Chgo., 1981, Paramount Fine Arts Ctr., Aurora, Ill., 1979-81, North Park Village, Chgo., 1982; mem. theatre adv. panel Ill. Arts Coun., 1992; bd. dirs. Nat. Alliance Mus. Theatre.; mem. theatre creation and presentation panel Nat. Endowment for Arts, 1992, 97; bd. mem. Nat. Alliance for Mus. Theatre, 1996-2000; co-chair New Works Panel 2000, Commn.'s Com., 1998-2000. Co-prodr. over 90 world premieres, plays and musicals, 1972—; host (TV program) Arts & The Community, NBC's Knowledge, 1978. Mem. Chgo. Coun. on Fine Arts, 1976-79; panel mem. Dance Adv. Panel/Ill. Arts Coun., Chgo., 1979; mem. Ill. Arts Coun. theatre adv. panel 1992; mem. Nat. Endowment for the Arts, Opera Musical Theatre New Am. Works Panel, 1993; bd. dirs. Community TV Network, Chgo., 1980-84, Performance Community, Chgo., 1974-2000; mem. adv. bd. Gospel Arts Workshop, Chgo., 1979-85. Recipient Svc. to Arts & Edn. award Ill. Alliance for Arts in Edn., Chgo., 1984, 1st place award for direction Readers Theatre Nat. Competition Jr. Colls. Avocation: sailing. Office: New Tuners Theatre Theatre Bldg 1225 W Belmont Ave Chicago IL 60657-3205

HIGGINS, SISTER THERESE, English educator, former college president; b. Winthrop, Mass., Sept. 29, 1925; d. James C. and Margaret M. (Lennon) H. AB cum laude, Regis Coll., 1947; MA, Boston Coll., 1959, DHL, 1993; PhD, U. Wis., 1963; DHL, Emmanuel Coll., 1977, Lesley Coll., 1991; postgrad. in lit. and theology, Harvard U., 1965-66; LLD (hon.), Northeastern U., 1982, Bentley Coll., 1992, Regis Coll., 1994. Joined Congregation of Sisters of St. Joseph, Roman Cath. Ch., 1947; asst. prof. English, Regis Coll., Weston, Mass., 1963-65, asst. prof., 1965-67, assoc. prof. English lit., 1968—, pres., 1974-92, also trustee, v.p. devel., 2003—. Book reviewer Boston Globe, 1965—. Trustee Waltham (Mass.) Hosp., 1978-85, Cardinal Spellman Philatelic Mus., 1976-92; mem. Mass. Gov.'s Commn. on Status Women, 1977-79, Nat. Com. Ecclesial Role Women, Archdiocesan Fin. Coun., 1991—. U. Wis. research grantee Eng. Mem. Nat. Cath. Ednl. Assn., AAUW, MLA, AAUP, Assn. Ind. Colls. and Univs. Mass. (exec. com.), New Eng. Colls. Fund, NEASC (commn.). Office: Regis Coll 235 Wellesley St Weston MA 02493-1505 E-mail: therese.higgins@regiscollege.edu.

HIGGS, MARY PHIL EGERTON, editor; b. Richmond, Va., July 14, 1928; d. William Graham Egerton and Rebecca Crenshaw White; m. Barnie Allen Higgs, June 14, 1948; children: Janet Anne, Graham Egerton, David Allen, Mary Virginia Higgs Beach Higgins. BA with highest honors, U. Tenn., 1973. Missionary United Meth. Ch., 1949; tchr., adminstr. Rhodesia Ann. Conf. (now Zimbabwe Ann. Conf.), 1949—66; Rhodesia editor Africa Christian Advocate, 1951—64; program dir. Rhodesia Ambassadors Quartet tour to U.S., 1958—60; assoc. editor Vanderbilt U. Publs., Nashville, 1968—78, editor, dir., 1978—93. Democrat. Episcopalian. Home: 4040 Woodlawn Dr Nashville TN 37205-1908

HIGH, MARIA LOUISE, artist; b. Bristol, Pa., Oct. 31, 1970; d. Frederick George Fischer and Maria Louise Fassano; m. Brian Anthony High, May 27, 1995; children: John Frederick, Brian Anthony Jr. BA, Shippensburg U., Pa., 1988—93. Exhibitions include Inaugural Nat. Conf. on Coastal and Estuarine Habitat Restoration, The Big Show!; featured artist Silver Monkeyz, Balt., 2003. Mem.: Creative Alliance, Alpha Omicron Pi (alumnae chpt. pres. 2003). Liberal. Roman Catholic. Avocations: travel, reading. Home: 221 E Biddle St Baltimore MD 21202 Personal E-mail: marialouisehigh@hotmail.com.

HIGHTOWER, NANCY ELIZABETH, literature educator; b. Phila., Pa., July 22, 1970; BA in English Lit., Ft. Lewis Coll., 1992; MA in English Lit., U. Denver, 1997. Grad. tchg. asst. U. Denver, instr., 1995—, Women's Coll., U. Denver, 2000—, DU Summer Link to Coll., Denver, 2000—, Daniels Fund Coll. Prep. Program, Denver, 2003—, Rocky Mountain Talent Search, Denver, 2003—. Mem. faculty adv. com. The Women's Coll., Denver, 2000—01; advisor Kuwait Student Orgn., Denver, 2001—02; grad. tchg. asst., adj. instr. DU, Women's Coll. Author poetry in publs. Tchg. fellow, U. Denver, 1995—99, Weil Summer fellow, 2000. Home: 238 W 2nd Ave #1 Denver CO 80223

HIGUCHI, SHIRLEY A. lawyer; Grad., Georgetown U., 1984. Atty. Epstein, Becker & Green, PC; asst. exec. dir. legal and regulatory affairs APA, Washington. Mem.: Asian Pacific Am. Bar Assn. (bd. dirs.), D.C. Bar Assn. (treas. 1993, bd. govs. 1994—2000, pres. 2003—04, pub. svc. activities com., co-chair health law sect.'s steering com.). Office: Am Psychol Assn 750 First St NW Washington DC 20002

HIITOLA, BETHANY, writer, consultant; b. Reed City, Mich., Aug. 22, 1975; d. Paul and Joan Haara; m. Matthew Hiitola, Sept. 4, 1999. BS in Sci. and Tech. Comm., Mich. Technol. U., 1997; MS in Human Computer Interaction, DePaul U., 1999. Software testing engr. intern X-Rite Inc., Grandville, Mich., 1997; tech. writer level I and II U.S. Robotics/3Com Corp., Mt. Prospect and Rolling Meadows, Ill., 1997—2000; curriculum mgr. 3Com Corp., Rolling Meadows, Ill., 1999—2000, sr. tech. writer, 2000—01; sr. content developer Motorola, Inc., Schaumburg, Ill., 2001—02; sr. cons. CGN & Assocs., Inc, Oakbrook Terrace, Ill., 2002—. Team lead 3Com Corp., Rolling Meadows, 2000—01; presenter in field. Mem.: IEEE (assoc.), Scientfic and Tech. Commn., Internat. Profl. Commn. Conf., STC (assoc.). Office: CGN & Assocs 18 W 140 Butterfield Rd Oakbrook Terrace IL 60181 Personal E-mail: bethany@hiitola.com. E-mail: bhiitola@cgn.net.

HILAS, MARY ELIZABETH (BETTY HILAS), civic volunteer; b. Polson, Mont., Oct. 31, 1918; d. Fredrick Thomas and Elizabeth (Patterson) Turner; m. Frank Lorenzo Brown, July 30, 1936 (div. 1954); children: Frank L. Jr., Thomas M., James D., Timothy L.; m. George Hilas, Mar. 29, 1975. AA, East L.A. Jr. Coll., 1963. Group supr. Calif. Youth Authority Reception Guidance Ctr., Norwalk, 1963-64; women's correctional supr. I Calif. Rehab. Ctr. for Drug Addicts, Corona, 1964-65, 66-71, Calif. Dept. Corrections Outpatient Ctrl. Testing clinic, L.A., 1965-66; correctional officer Calif. Dept. Correctons, Soledad Prison, 1971-72, Calif. Med. Facility for Men, Vacaville, 1972-74, correctional program supr. I, 1974-76, ret., 1976. Staff rep. Calif. Med. Facility Equal Employment, Vacaville, 1974-76. Active affirmative action, Friends Outside; pres. East Montebello Coord. Coun., 1950; adv. com. L.A. County Fedn. Cmty. Coord. Couns., 1951; mem. Sr. Citizens, Georgetown, Calif., 1983—, LWV of the Divide, Garden Valley, 1991—. Mem. ACLU, PTA (life), Calif. State Retirees, VFW Aux., Ret. Officers Assn. Aux., Friends of the Libr. Democrat. Unitarian Universalist. Avocations: politics, reading, cards.

HILB, JEANE DYER, community volunteer; b. Hutchinson, Kans., Apr. 8, 1921; d. Howard Emmons and Clara Riner Dyer; m. Frank Markel Swirles Jr. Oct, 24, 1942 (div. 1950); 1 child, Jeane Swirles MacClyment; m. Justin Mitchell Hilb, Oct. 6, 1979. BA, U. So. Calif., L.A., 1942; postgrad., Radcliffe Coll., 1943-45. Lifetime cert. tchr., Calif. Pres. Palm Springs Friends of Philharm., 1998—; mem. Coll. of the Desert Found., 1982—; founding pres. Coll. of the Desert Found. Aux., 1984-87, Ballet Guild of the Desert, 1985—. Recipient Disting. Svc. award Bd. Suprs. County of Riverside, 1998, day named in honor, 1998. Mem. Harvard-Radcliffe Club of So. Calif, Phi Beta Kappa. Avocations: travel, theatre, bridge. Home: 911 Juarez Ave Palm Springs CA 92262-4121

HILBERG, ROSEMARY HELEN, retired human resource specialist; b. Elmhurst, Ill., Feb. 28, 1922; d. Michael and Gertrude H. (Heegard) Kross; m. Albert W. Hilberg, Aug. 22, 1944; children: Jeffrey, Eric, David, Kristin, Susan. BS in Biology, Elmhurst Coll., 1944; MA in Developmental Clin. Psychology, Antioch U., Columbia, Md., 1978; LLD (hon.), Elmhurst Coll., 1971. Lab. asst. Kegerreis Med. Clinic, Elmhurst, Ill., 1946-47; substitute tchr. Montgomery County (Md.) Pub. Schs., 1965-66; elected mem. Montgomery County Bd. Edn., 1966-74; legis. aide Md. Ho. of Dels., Annapolis, 1976-77; employee assistance specialist Montgomery County Pub. Schs., 1979-97. Planner/dir. 1st Network Symposium on Family Therapy Practice, D.C. Met. Area, 1978; adult edn. instr. Montgomery County Pub. Schs., 1981. Author: Shifting Gears For Eighty Years, 2003. Editor voters guide/bd. dirs. LWV of Montgomery County, 1950-54, 1st v.p., sec. Montgomery County Coun. of PTAs, 1964-66, elected precinct chair Dem. Party of Montgomery County, 1964-66. Recipient Life Membership award Md. Congress of Parents and Tchrs., 1976. Democrat. Unitarian Universalist. Avocations: reading, music. Home: 12512 Davan Dr Silver Spring MD 20904-3501

HILBERN, SANDRA J. library director; b. Vallejo, Calif., July 2, 1945; d. Curtis Tom Sr. and Pauline Stout (Daniels) Hamilton; m. James W. Hilbern Sr., Nov. 27, 1970 (div. Aug. 1993); 1 child, James William Jr. BSE, Northeastern Okla. State U., 1970, MS, 1973; postgrad., U. Tex., Dallas, 1977, So. Ill. U., 1978, Northeastern Okla. State U., 1976-89. Cert. tchr., libr., Okla.; cert. for the blind/visually impaired. Elem. tchr. Okay (Okla.) Pub. Schs., 1970-75; sr. vocat. rehab. counselor State Okla. Dept. Rehab., Muskogee, 1975-98; prof. Connors State Coll., Muskogee, 1989-2000, mem. gerontol. consumer adv. com., 1999-2000; libr. media specialist Okla. Sch. for Blind, Muskogee, 2000—. Unit commr. Boy Scouts Am., Muskogee, 1984-86; coach, team mother Green County Soccer League, Muskogee, 1979-81; publicity dir. single living bd. Christ Ch., Tulsa, 1998—, Phoenix Singles pres., v.p., 1996-99. Sgt. U.S. Army, 1966-69. Recipient Outstanding Recognition award for Outstanding Svc., U.S. Ho. of Reps., 1998, Pres.'s award for Outstanding Svc. Okla. Rehab. Counselors Assn., 1984, Starfish Recognition award Connors State Coll., 2000. Mem. Okla. Rehab. Soc. (sec. 1978-84), Okla. Assn. C.C.'s., Am. Libr. Assn., Okla. Libr. Assn., Assn. Libr. Media Specialists. Democrat. Avocations: silk and dried floral arranging, organizing fine arts and cultural tours. Office: Okla Sch for the Blind 3300 Gibson St Muskogee OK 74403

HILBERT, RITA L. librarian; b. Orange, N.J., Nov. 1, 1942; d. Ralph P. LaSalle and Arlene (Julian) Strobel; children: Toby Gayle Buchanan, Stacey Giordano, Joseph, Matthew. AA, NYU, 1988, BA, 1990; MLS, Rutgers U., 1992. Merchandising rsch. analyst Burrelle's, Livingston, N.J., 1975-82; teaching asst. Montessori Sch., Millburn, N.J., 1982-84; outreach specialist Rockwood Meml. Libr., Livingston, 1984-90, head spl. svcs., 1990-92; libr. dir. Lincoln Park (N.J.) Pub. Libr., 1992-94, Mount Olive Township Pub. Libr., 1994—. Mem. Adult Sch. Bd., Livingston, 1990—, Lincoln Pk. Bd. of Edn., 1995-98, chair policy com., 1997-98, negotiations com., 1997-98. Member Livingston Adv. Com. for the Handicapped, 1985—, Livingston Coun. for Sr. Citizens, 1985—, Region III Com. for Svcs. to Spl. Populations, sec., 1987-88, elected mem. Lincoln Park Bd. Edn., 1995-98, chair policy and negotiations coms., 1995-98; trustee Lincoln Park Libr., 1997-98. Recipient Founder's Day award NYU, 1990. Mem.: AAUW (scholarship 1987), ALA, Morris Automated Info. Network (sec. 1993—94, v.p. 1995, pres. 1996), NJ Assn. Libr. Assts. (pres. 1989—90, scholarship in her name 1994), NJ Libr. Assn. (scholarship 1990), Mt. Olive C. of C. (rec. sec. 2002—), Mt. Olive Twp. Hist. Soc. (founding and charter mem.), Kiwanis (bd. dirs. 1999—), Alpha Sigma Lambda. Avocations: walking, painting, traveling. Office: Wolfe Rd Budd Lake NJ 07828

HILDEBRAN, FRANCES ELAINE, municipal clerk; b. Shelby, N.C., Nov. 8, 1954; d. James Pinkney and Margaret Ellen (Mull) Sain; m. Dennis Alan Hildebran, June 26, 1976; 1 child, Curtis Alan. AAS, Western Piedmont C.C., 1975. Cert. mcpl. clk., N.C. Adminstrv. sec. Burke County Health Dept., Morganton, N.C., 1975-80; adminstrv. asst. to city mgr. City of Valdese, N.C., 1980—. Loaned exec. Burke County United Way, Morganton, 1990, bd. dirs., 1991—; mem. Burke County Libr. Bd., Morganton, 1995—; mem. indsl. adv. bd. Valdese Gen. Hosp., 1994—; sec., advocate Heritage Mid. Sch. Advocates, 1996; pres. Rutherford Coll. Elem. Sch. PTO, 1993; mem. Leadership Burke, Burke County C. of C., Morganton, 1991. Mem. Internat. Inst. Mcpl. Clks., N.C. Assn. Mcpl. Clks., Valdese Pilot Club (pres. 1981). Baptist. Avocations: reading, walking, cooking, travel. Office: City of Valdese 121 Faet St NW Valdese NC 28690-2315 Home: PO Box 184 Rutherford College NC 28671

HILDEBRAND, KAYE, music educator; b. Elk City, Okla., June 22, 1958; d. Raymond Ernest and Theresa Orlean (Taylor) Hildebrand. B in Music Edn., Southwestern Okla. State U., 1980, M in Music Edn., 1981. Tchr. elem. vocal music Pioneer Pleasant Vale Sch., Enid, Okla., 1981—. Mem.: NEA, Okla. Music Educators Assn., Okla. Edn. Assn., Nat. Assn. Music Educators, Alpha Phi Sigma. Baptist. Avocation: Avocations: piano, singing, guitar, dulcimer. Home: 1522 Beverly Dr Enid OK 73703-7715

HILDEBRAND, VERNA LEE, human ecology educator; b. Dodge City, Kans., Aug. 17, 1924; d. Carrell E. and Florence (Smyth) Butcher; m. John R. Hildebrand, June 23, 1946; children: Carol Ann, Steve Allen. BS, Kans. State U., 1945, MS, 1957; PhD, Tex. Women's U., 1970. Tchr. home econs. Dickinson County H.S., Chapman, Kans., 1945-46; tchr. early childhood Albany (Calif.) Pub. Schs., 1946-47; grad. asst. Inst. Child Welfare U. Calif., Berkeley, 1947-48; tchr. kindergarten Albany Pub. Schs., 1948-49; dietitian commons and hosp. U. Chgo., 1952-53; instr. Kans. State U., Manhattan, 1953-54, 59, Okla. State U., Stillwater, 1955-56; asst. prof. Tex. Tech U., Lubbock, 1962-67; from asst. prof. to prof. Mich. State U., East Lansing, 1967-97, prof. emeritus, 1997—. Legis. clk. Kans. Ho. of Reps., Topeka, 1955. Author: Introduction to Early Childhood Education, 1971, 6th edit., 1997, Guiding Young Children, 1975, 6th edit., 1998, Parenting and Teaching Young Children, 1981, 90, Management of Child Development Centers, 1984, 5th edit., 2002, Parenting: Rewards and Responsibilities, 1994, 2d edit., 1997, 6th edit., 2002; co-author: China's Families: Experiment in Societal Change, 1985, Knowing and Serving Diverse Families, 1996, 2d edit., 1999. Mem. Nat. Assn. for the Edn. Young Children (task force 1975-77), Am. Home Econs. Assn. (bd. dirs., Leader award 1990), Women in Internat. Devel., Nat. Assn. Early Childhood Tchr. Edn. (award for meritorious and profl. leadership 1995).

HILDEBRANDT-WILLARD, CLAUDIA JOAN, banker; b. Ingelwood, Calif., Feb. 12, 1942; d. Charles Samual and Clara Claudia (Palumbo) Hildebrandt; m. I. LeRoy Willard, Nov. 5, 1993 (dec. Oct. 2001). BBA, U. Colo. Head teller First Colo. Bank & Trust, Denver, 1969—70; asst. cashier First Nat. Bank, Englewood, Colo., 1975—79, asst. v.p., 1979—83, v.p., 1983—92; owner CJH Enterprises, Inc., Breckenridge, Colo., 1980—, Garden Tea Shop, Georgetown, Colo., The Gifted Swan, Georgetown, Colo., 1982—92, Laudiac, Inc., Breckenridge, 1993—, Mgmt. for Ministry, 1993—. Mem.: Am. Inst. Banking, Am. Soc. Pers. Adminstrn., Fin. Women Internat. (pres.-elect 1989—92), Nat. Assn. Bank Women, Mile High Group. Roman Catholic. Home: PO Box 665 Georgetown CO 80444-0665 Office: 410 3d St Georgetown CO 80444

HILER, MONICA JEAN, reading and sociology educator; b. Dallas, Sept. 3, 1929; d. James Absalom and Monica Constance (Farrar) Longino; m. Robert Joseph Hiler, Nov. 1, 1952; children: Robert, Deborah, Michael, Douglas, Frederick. BA, Agnes Scott Coll., Decatur, Ga., 1951; MEd, U. Ga., Athens, 1968; EdS, U. Ga., 1972, EdD, 1974. Social worker Atlanta Family and Children's Svcs., 1962-63; tchr. Hall County pub. schs., Ga., 1965-67; mem. faculty Gainesville Jr. Coll., Ga., 1968-87, prof. reading and sociology, 1975-87, chmn. devel. studies program, 1973-85, acting chmn. divsn. social scis., 1986-87, prof. emeritus reading and sociology, 1987—. Cons. So. Regional Edn. Bd., 1975-83, Gainesville Coll., 1987-95; apptd. spl. advocate Juvenile Ct. Union County, Ga., 1994-96; ch. organist, pianist, choir dir., 1964-82, 1988—. Pres. Ch. Women United, N.E. Ga., 1992-94. Named Ch. Woman of Yr, N.E. Ga., 2001, Woman of Yr., St. Francis of Assisi Ch., Blairsville, 1996. Mem. ASCD, Internat. Reading Assn., Ga. Sociol. Assn., Gainesville Music Club, Phi Beta Kappa, Phi Delta Kappa, Phi Kappa Phi. Avocations: piano, painting, sewing. E-mail: jeannbob@brmemc.net.

HILFSTEIN, ERNA, science historian, educator; b. Krakow, Poland; arrived in U.S., 1949, naturalized, 1954; d. Leon and Anna (Schornstein) Kluger; m. Max Hilfstein; children: Leon, Simone Juliana. BA, CCNY, 1967, MA, 1971; PhD, CUNY, 1978. Tchr. secondary schs., N.Y.C., 1968-84, 86-92; collaborator Polish Acad. Scis., 1968-85. Vis. prof. Queens Coll., 1973; affiliate Grad. Sch./Univ. Ctr., CUNY. Author: Starowolski's Biographies of Copernicus, 1980; collaborator English version of Nicholas Copernicus Complete Works, vol. 1, 1972, vol. 2, 1978, vol. 3, 1985, vols. 2 and 3, 2d edit., 1992; co-translator: The Leviathan in the State Theory of Thomas Hobbes: Meaning and Failure of a Political Symbol, 1996; editor: Science and History, 1978, Copernicus and His Successors, 1995, Sebastian Petrycy, A Polish Renaissance Scholar, 1997; contbr. articles and revs. to profl. jours. Recipient Rector's medal, Univ. M. Kopernik, Torun, 1989, medal, Towarzystwo Naukowe Torun, Poland, 1990, Dom Kopernika in Torun medal, 1989, Order of Merit Silver medal, Rep. of Poland, 1991, Scholar of Polish Descent medal, 1989; grantee, NEH, 1984—85. Mem. History Sci. Soc., Polish Inst. Arts and Scis. in Am., CUNY Acad. for the Humanities and Scis., N.Y. Acad. Scis., Kosciuszko Found., United Fedn. Tchrs. (chpt. chmn. 1978-84, 86-92, del. 1980-92), Am. Mus. Nat. History, Libr. Congress,Nat. Commn. Am. Fgn. Policy, New Cracow Friendship Soc. (bd. dirs. 1998—). Home: Woodheaven Estate 375 Westwood Dr Hurleyville NY 12747-5506 also: 22 Beech St Nanuet NY 10954-1308

HILGERT, ARNIE, management and marketing educator; b. Detroit, Feb. 24, 1944; d. Norris Bersford and Romayne Catherine (Kent) Clarke; m. Jeffrey L. Hilgert, Dec. 21, 1964 (div. Dec. 1981); children: Michele Leanne, Tracy Lee. BA, U. Redlands, 1982; MBA, Peter F. Drucker Sch. Mgmt., 1984; MA Ctr. Ednl. Studies, The Claremont Grad. U., 1991, PhD Ctr. Ednl. Studies, 1992. Ptnr. Durawood Shasta Pacific Industries, Chico, Calif., 1971-78; mgr., owner Homefront Home Improvement Stores, Chico, Calif., 1975-78; rsch. assoc. exec. mgmt. program The Claremont (Calif.) Grad. Sch., 1984-85, adminstr. exec. mgmt. program, 1985-89; sponsored rsch. analyst Calif. State U., L.A., 1989-90; assoc. prof. mgmt. and mktg. No. Ariz. U., Yuma, 1992-98, 1998—. Mem. faculty devel. in internat. bus. U. S.C., 1993; mem. faculty devel. in internat. mktg., Thunderbird, 1989; participant Global Learning Day; participant in nat. and internat. profl. confs.; rschr. in multimedia and distance learning, implementation of ADA Act; Peernet reviewer MCB U. Press, Jour. Mgmt. Devel. Mem. editl. bd. Jour. Bus. Adminstrn., 1988—; textbook reviewer McGraw Hill Pubs.; contbr. articles to profl. jours. Participant Rio Colorado Commn., Yuma, 1993—, dedication Nonquit St. Green, Boston, 2002, A Dragon for Dorchester, Boston, 2003. State of Calif. Grad. fellow, Claremont, 1982-84; Econs. scholar John Randolph Haynes and Dora Haynes Found., 1981, Elizabeth Malpass scholar Zonta Club Redlands, 1980. Mem.: Acad. Internat. Bus., Acad. Mgmt., Ariz. Distance Learning Assn. (membership chmn 2002—), Acad. Bus. Adminstrn. (Tchg. Excellence award 1998), Friends of the Nonquit St. Neighborhood Assn. and Land Trust Inc., Claremont U. Sch. Womans Scholars, Ctr. for Study of Intellectual Devel. Home: 11843 E Calle Del Cid Yuma AZ 85367-7216 Office: No Ariz U PO Box 6236 Yuma AZ 85366-6236

HILL, BARBARA BENTON, healthcare executive; b. Balt., May 28, 1952; d. George Stock and Charlotte (Russ) Benton; m. Charles David Hill, June 4, 1970 (dec. Oct. 1980); children: Gregory George, Douglas Charles; m. Ancelmo E. Lopes, May 9, 1987. BA, John's Hopkins U., 1973, MS, 1976. Counselor Planned Parenthood of Md., Balt., 1975-76, Hillcrest Clinic, Balt., 1977, dir. community rels., 1977-78, adminstr., 1978-80, exec. dir., 1980-83; pres. Hill & Ward Constrn. Co., Balt., 1980-81; exec. dir. East Balt. Med. Plan, Balt., 1983-84, v.p. John's Hopkins Health Plan, Balt., 1984-85, pres., 1985-91, Hopkins Preferred Network, Balt., 1986-91; v.p. mid-atlantic group ops. Prudential Ins. Co., Balt., 1991-93, v.p. health care policy Newark, 1993-94; pres. Aetna Health Plans of Midwest, Chgo., 1994-96, Rush Prudential Health Plans, Chgo., 1996—. Treas. Greater Balt. com., 1993-94, bd. dirs., 1991-94; mem. Mayor's Econ. Adv. Coun., 1993-94. Named Businessperson of the Yr., Balt. Bus. Jour., 1989. Mem. Ill. Assn. HMOs (v.p. 1994-96, pres. 1996—), Md. C. of C. (bd. dirs. 1993-94), Phi Beta Kappa. Office: Rush Prudential Health Plans 233 S Wacker Dr Ste 3900 Chicago IL 60606-6324

HILL, BETTI CHRISTIE, government executive; b. Bozeman, Mont., Feb. 11, 1954; d. Douglas P. and Ruth M. (Bristow) Christie; m. Rick Hill; children: Todd, Corey, Mike. BA, Western Mont. Coll., 1976. Sch. tchr., Chester and Townsend, Mont., 1976-78; pub. info. officer Office of Pub. Instrn., Helena, Mont., 1980-84; with Hill Pub. Rels., Helena, 1984-89; field rep. U.S. Sen. Conrad Burns, Helena, 1989-91; chief of staff Lt. Gov.'s Office, Helena, 1991-95; transition dir. Gov. Judy Mantz, 2000, spl. projects dir., 2001—02. Fin. dir. County Rep. Party, Helena, 1991-95; mem. WMC Found. Bd., Dillon, 1989-93, Mont. House Bd., Helena, 1989-92, Florence Crittenton Three Bd., Helena, 1997—, Mont. Arts Coun., Helena, 2003—. Home: PO Box 4717 Helena MT 59604-4717

HILL, BEVERLEY JANE, physician assistant; b. Balt., May 19, 1938; d. Isaac Corbert Hill and Grace Vivian Bryant. BS in Phys. Edn., Western Md. Coll., Westminster, 1960, MEd, 1968; postgrad., Johns Hospkins Univ., 1972; cert. in physician asst., Essex Cmty. Coll., Balt., 1991. Lic. physician asst. Md., Va., Del., N.C. Tchr. phys. edn. Balt. County Sch. Sys., Towson, Md., 1960—65; tchr. John Carroll Sch., Bel Air, Md., 1965—86, dean of students, 1965—86, dir. of athletics, 1965—86; physician asst. Beebe Gen. Hosp., Lewes, Del., 1991—94, Johns Hopkins Hosp., Balt., 1992, San Carlos (Ariz.) Hosp., Apache Reservation, 1992; physician asst. Indian Health Svcs., Supai Indian Reservation, Grand Canyon, Ariz., 1992; physician asst. St. Agnes Hosp., Balt., 1993—94, EMSA, Ltd., Pax River, Md., 1994; ambulatory care Md. State Penitentiary, 1992—96; physician asst. Ft. Belvoir/Dewitt Army Hosp., 1996—97, Coastal Govt. Svcs., 1994—97, Profl. Occupl. Health, Lanhan, Md., 1997—98, Dept. of Def., Womack Army Med., Ft. Bragg, NC, 1998—, USN Acad., Annapolis, Md., 2001—02. Contbr. articles to profl. jours. Named to, Western Md. Coll. Sports Hall of Fame. Mem.: Phi Theta Kappa (mem. Nat. Deans list). Democrat. Avocations: running, walking, reading, writing.

HILL, BEVERLY ELLEN, health sciences educator; b. Albany, Calif., May 20, 1937; d. Bert E. and Catherine (Doyle) H. BA, Coll. Holy Names, 1960; MS in Edn., Dominican Coll., 1969; EdD, U. So. Calif., 1978. Producer, dir. Health Scis TV U. Calif., Davis, 1966-69, coordinator Health Scis. TV, 1969-73; asst. dir. IMS U. So. Calif., Los Angeles, 1973-76, asst. dir. continuing edn., 1976-80, dir. biocommunications, 1976-80; dir. Med. Ednl. Resources Program Ind. U. Sch. Medicine, Indpls., 1980—, acting asst. dean continuing med. edn., 1991-95. Presenter Cath. U. Nijmegen, Netherlands, 1980, 81, European Symposium on Clin. Pharmacy, Brussels, 1982, Barcelona, Spain, 1983. Contbr. articles to profl. jours. Pres. Indpls. Shakespeare Festival, 1982-83; mem. subcom. Ind. Film Commn., Indpls., 1984—. Recipient first place in rehab. category 4th Biannual J. Muir Med. Film Fest., 1980. Mem. Assn. Biomed. Communications (bd. dirs. 1985—), Health Scis. Com. Assn. (bd. dirs. 1976-79, First Place Video Festival, 1979), Assn. for Edn. Communications and Tech. Avocations: painting, travel, archeology, music, tennis, swimming. Office: Med Ednl Resources Program BR 156 1226 W Michigan St Indianapolis IN 46202-5212 Home: 849 Michigan Blvd Pasadena CA 91107-5734

HILL, BONNIE GUITON, consulting company executive; b. Springfield, Ill., Oct. 30, 1941; d. Henry Frank and Zola Elizabeth (Newman) Brazelton; m. Walter Hill Jr.; 1 child, Nichele Monique. BA, Mills Coll., 1974; MS, Calif. State U., Hayward, 1975; EdD, U. Calif., Berkeley, 1985. Adminstr. asst. to pres.'s spl. asst. Mills Coll., Oakland, Calif., 1970-71, adminstrv. asst. to asst. v.p., 1972-73, student svcs. counselor, adv. to resuming students, 1973-74, asst. dean of students, interim dir. ethnic studies, lectr., 1975-76; exec. dir. Marcus A. Foster Ednl. Inst., Oakland, 1976-79; adminstrv. mgr. Kaiser Aluminum & Chem. Corp., Oakland, 1979-80; v.p., gen. mgr. Kaiser CTR Inc., Oakland, 1980-84; vice chair Postal Rate Commn., Washington, 1985-87; asst. sec. for vocat. and adult edn. Dept. Edn., Washington, 1987-89; sec. State and Consumer Svcs. Agy. State of Calif.; spl. adv. to Pres. for Consumer Affairs, dir. U.S. Office Consumer Affairs, 1989-90; pres., CEO Earth Conservation Corps, Washington, 1990-91; sec. State and Consumer Svcs. Industry, State of Calif., 1991-92; dean McIntire Sch. Commerce U. Va., Charlottesville, 1992-97; v.p. The Times Mirror Co., 1997-2000; pres. B. Hill Enterprises, LLC, 2001—; COO Iconblue, Inc., LA Times, 2001—. Sr. v.p. comm. and pub. affairs L.A. Times, 1998—2001; pres., CEO The Times Mirror Found., 1997—2001; bd. dirs. The Home Depot Co., Hershey Foods Corp., AK Steele Corp., Yum Brands, Inc., Albertsons Inc., Calif. Water Svc. Co. Office: B Hill Enterprises LLC Ste 600 5670 Wilshire Blvd Los Angeles CA 90036

HILL, CARLA LARSEN, physical education educator, gymnastics judge; b. Washington, May 28, 1951; d. Charles Arne and Clara (Kemp) Larsen; m Ronald Franklin Hill. Aug. 4, 1973; children: Michael Eric, Erin Michelle. AB in Math., Lenoir Rhyne Coll., 1973; MS in Computer Sci., Union Coll., 1979. Tchr. Wappingers Ctrl. Sch. Dist., Wappingers Falls, N.Y., 1974-75, substitute tchr., 1989-99; women's gymnastics judge USAG-N.Y. State, 1997—. Adj. lectr. Dutchess C.C., Poughkeepsie, N.Y., 1980—, Marist Coll., Poughkeepsie, 2000—. Troop leader Dutchess County coun. Girl Scouts U.S., 1984—; first aid instr. Dutchess County Red Cross, Poughkeepsie, 1978—; mem. com. Hudson Valley coun. Boy Scouts Am., 1984-99. Mem. AAUW, Girl Scouts U.S.A. (life; Nat. Appreciation award 1993, Nat. Honor pin 1997, 35-Yr. Pin 2003), Nat. Assn. Women's Gymnastics Judges. Lutheran. Avocations: reading, needlework. Home: 28 Bowdoin Ln Wappingers Falls NY 12590-3921 Office: Dutchess CC Pendell Rd Poughkeepsie NY 12601 E-mail: cmlhill@att.net.

HILL, CAROL KOELLING, library director; BS, Mo. Western State, 1974; MLS, Emporia State U., 1980. Libr. dir. City of Fort Walton Beach, Fla., 1995—. Office: 185 Miracle Strip Pkwy SE Fort Walton Beach FL 32548-6614 E-mail: chill@fwb.org.

HILL, CATHARINE B. provost, economics educator; BA, Williams Coll., 1976; BA with 1st class honors, Oxford U., 1978; PhD, Yale U., 1985. Former Arthur Okun Rsch. fellow Brookings Instn., Washington; formerly with Econ. Devel. Inst., Ministry of Fin., Zambia, World Bank; former chair dept. econs. and Ctr. for Devel. Econs. Williams Coll., Williamstown, Mass., provost, John J. Gibson prof. econs. Contbr. articles to profl. jours.; co-editor: Public Expenditure in Africa. Grantee, NSF, Coun. on Fgn. Rels., Am. Coun. Learned Socs. Office: Williams Coll Provost Office 880 Main St Hopkins Hall 3d Fl Williamstown MA 01267

HILL, CHRISTINE MARIE, voice educator, music educator; d. James Howard Ellis and Ruby Carol (Van Beek) McBride; m. Shawn Devin Hill; 1 child, Laura. BMus, Western Wash. U., 1983, MMus, 1986. Cert. music tchr. Wash., Music Tchrs. Nat. Assn. Applied music voice prof. Grays Harbor Coll., Aberdeen, Wash., 1992—; pvt. practice Montesano, Wash., 1990—. Vocal dir. musical theatre Grays Harbor Coll., Aberdeen, 1998—99, dir. concert choir, music appreciation instr., music theory and ear tng. instr., 1998—2000. Mem.: Wash. State Music Tchrs. Assn. (pres. Grays Harbor chpt. 1995—98, dist. IV v.p. 1997—99, state fin. com. 1999—2001, sec. Gray Harbor chpt. 2001—03, pres. Grays Harbor chpt. 2003—, state membership chair 2001—). Democrat. Methodist. Avocations: singing, writing. Office: Grays Harbor Coll 1620 Edward P Smith Dr Aberdeen WA 98520

HILL, CLARA EDITH, psychology educator; b. Shivers, Miss., Sept. 13, 1948; d. Fletcher Von and Anna (Teich) H.; m. James Gormally, May 25, 1974; children: Kevin, Katherine. BA, So. Ill. U., 1970, MA, 1972, PhD, 1974. Lic. psychologist, Md. Asst. prof. dept. psychology U. Md., College Park, 1974-78, assoc. prof. dept. psychology, 1978-85, prof. dept. psychology, 85—. Author: Therapist Techniques and Client Outcomes, 1989, Working with Dreams in Psychotherapy, 1996, Helping Skills: Facilitating Exploration, Insight and Action, 1999, Dream Work in Therapy: Facilitating Exploration, Insight and Action, 2003, Helping Skills: The Empirical Foundation, 2001, Working with Dreams in Therapy, 2003; editor: Jour. Counseling Psychology, 1994—99, Psychotherapy Rsch., 2004—. Grantee NIMH, 1983-92. Fellow APA (Leona Tyler award, divsn. 17 2002, Disting. Psychologist award, divsn. 29, 2003); mem. Soc. Psychotherapy Rsch. (pres. N.Am. chpt. 1990, pres. internat. orgn. 1994-95), Assn. Study of Dreams, Soc. Exploration of Psychotherapy Integration. Avocations: reading, dining out, walking. Office: U Maryland Dept Psychology College Park MD 20742-0001 E-mail: Hill@psyc.umd.edu.

HILL, DARLENE, newscaster; b. Cleve. m. Bernard Murray, 1996; 2 children. B, Ohio State U. Gen. assignment reporter CBS affiliate, Monterey, Calif.; anchor and reporter KJRH-TV, Tulsa, Okla., WFLD-TV, Chgo., 1994—. TV Journalist The Expt. in Black and White, 2002 (Nat. Emmy award cmty. svc., regional Emmy award, AP award, Edward R. Murrow award, Scripps Howard Found. award, Nat. Assn. Black Journalists award, Soc. Profl. Journalists award). Mem.: Chgo. Assn. of Black Journalists, Nat. Assn. of Black Journalists, Alpha Kappa Alpha. Office: WFLD-TV 205 N Mich Ave Chicago IL 60601

HILL, DEBORA ELIZABETH, writer, journalist, screenwriter; b. San Francisco, July 10, 1961; d. Henry Peter and Madge Lillian (Ridgeway-Aarons) H. BA, Sonoma State U., 1983. Talk show host Rock Jour. Viacom, San Francisco, 1980-81; interviewer, biographer Harrap Ltd., London, 1986-87; editor North Bay Mag., Cotati, Calif., 1988; guest feature writer Argus Courier, Petaluma, Calif., 1993-95; concept developer BiblioBytes, Hoboken, N.J., 1994-95; feature writer The Econs. Press, 1996-97; film cons., editor United Film Prodns. Internat., 2003—. Assoc. prodr. White Tiger Films, 1995—; concept developer Star Trek: Voyager and Star Trek: Deep Space Nine, 1997—98; mem. MedioCom, 2001—; script cons. Shadowhawk Prodns., Ireland, 2003—. Author: CUTS from a San Francisco Rock Journal, 1982, Punk Retro, 1988, Gale Research-Resourceful Woman, 1994, St. James Guide to Fantasy Writers, 1996, St. James Guide to Famous Gays and Lesbians, 1997, (sequel) Jerome's Quest, 2003; co-writer, cons. prodr. The Danger Club, contbr. (anthologies) Between Darkness and Light, 2000, Best Poets of 2000, Eyes of the World, 2001, Poetry's Elite, 2001, Hidden Frontiers, 2002, Celebrations Book Series, 2002—03, Best Poets of 2001, Best Poets of 2002, Theatre of the Mind, 2003, Death of a Shining Star, 2004; contbr. stories and articles to profl. jours. Democrat. Avocations: clothing design, cooking, internet, reading, interior design. Home and Office: Lost Myths Ink 8312 Windmill Farms Dr Cotati CA 94931-4570 Personal E-mail: debhill@att.net.

HILL, DEBORAH NIXON, elementary school educator, minister; b. Norfolk, Va., Apr. 8, 1955; d. Joe Dancy and Gladys Jones Nixon; m. Fred Eugene Hill, July 4, 1975; children: Marcus Donnell, Calvin Dwayne, Alexis Evon. BS in Bus. Adminstrn. and Fin., Norfolk State U., 1973; M in Elem. Edn., Regent U., 1998. Operator/trainer AT&T Co., Norfolk, Va., 1978—92; tchr., child care coord. Norfolk Pub. Schs., 1992—. Lang. art tchr./coord. HOST, 1995—99; mem. Norfolk Pub. Sch. Tchr. Mentor Corp., Norfolk, 1998; site coord. Comer-Zigler, 1998—2003; mem. adv. bd. Ida Gray Yes 2 Children-Before/After Sch. Care, Norfolk, 2003. Mem.: NEA, Va. Edn. Assn. (state del. 2001—02), Internat. Reading Assn. (chaplain Alpha Chi chpt.), Nat. Coun. Negro Women, Iota Phi Lambda. Democrat. Apostolic. Avocations: reading, singing, walking. Home: 2121 Burnside Pl Chesapeake VA 23325 Office: Norfolk Pub Schs 1300 Marshall Ave Norfolk VA 23504

HILL, DONNA MARIE, writer, retired librarian; d. Clarence Henry and Emma Charlotte (Wirthlin) Hill. Student, Phillips Gallery Art Sch., 1940—43; BA, George Washington U., 1948; MS, Columbia U., 1952. Code clk. U.S. Embassy, Paris, 1949—51; asst. to librarian NY Pub. Libr., N.Y.C., 1952—59; instr. Hunter Coll., CUNY, N.Y.C., 1970—75, head tchrs. ctrl. lab., 1974—84, asst. prof., 1975—79, assoc. prof., 1980—84, prof. emeritus, 1984—. Established Donna Hill Collection Marriott Libr., U. Utah, Salt Lake City, 1994. Author: First Your Penny, 1985, Murder Uptown, 1992, Shipwreck Season, 1998 (Christopher award, 99); Exhibited in group shows at Paris, Washington, world tour, 1950—51. Recipient Cert. of Distinction, Alumni Assn. Ctrl. H.S., 1984. Mem.: Women's Nat. Book Assn. (membership chmn. N.Y.C. chpt. 1991—93), Am. Recorder Soc. (nat. sec. 1959—61, editor-in-chief 1962—63), Delta Kappa Gamma (Ruth Mack Havens award 1991), Phi Beta Kappa. Mem. Lds Ch. Avocations: opera, Baroque music, recorder playing, drawing, painting.

HILL, DORA ANN (DOUFFAS), language educator, writer; b. Monmouth, Ill., Dec. 31, 1943; d. Gust John and Ruth Ida (Baker) Douffas; m. Ronald Ernest Naedele, Feb. 3, 1966 (dec. Sept. 30, 1966); 1 child, Ronnann Naedele-Risha. BA in English, Milligan Coll., 1966; MA in English, E. Tenn. State U., 1974. Cert. tchr. Miss., Tenn., N.C., Md., Fla. Editor/asst. editor Courier And Gateway Newspapers, Suitland, Md., 1966—69; English tchr. Long Beach (Miss.) HS, 1969—74, Garinger HS Night Program, Charlotte, NC, 1974—76; curriculum specialist, English instr. Ctrl. Piedmont CC, Charlotte, 1976—81; mgr. tng. and devel. Control Data Corp. and Comml. Credit Corp., Charlotte, Balt., 1980—87; program designer, rschr. Rutledge Coll. Sys., Charlotte, 1987—88; assoc. prof. Daytona Beach (Fla.) CC, 1990—. Lead tchr. adult HS English Daytona Beach CC, 1998—. Co-author: Ecology: The Living World, 1996; author: English All Around Us, vols. 1-4, 1999—2003. Assoc. mem. Seaside Music Theater; singles' lay min. South Daytona Christian Ch., 1990—2001. Named Lay Person Of The Yr., Kiwanis Port Orange And South Daytona, 1996. Mem.: Fla. Assn. CCs, Nat. Coun. Tchrs. English. Avocations: photography, theater, writing, crafts, movies. Office: Daytona Beach CC Adult Edn 1200 International Speedway Blvd Daytona Beach FL 32114 Personal E-mail: hollyhilla@aol.com. Business E-Mail: hilld@dbcc.cc.fl.edu.

HILL, DOROTHY BENNETT, community activist; b. Union Springs, Ala., Nov. 6, 1955; d. William Davis and Carrie Lou Bell Davis-Cody; m. Simon James Hill I, Dec. 15, 1976; children: Angela Elizabeth, Carrie LaVonna Denise, Simon James II. BA in Human Resource Adminstrn., St. Leo Coll., 1992. Asst. tchr., bus driver Econ. Opportunity Authority, Savannah, Ga., 1978-84; paraprofl. Chatham County Bd. Edn., Savannah, 1984-86; owner, dir. Hill's Daycare and Preschool, Savannah, 1986-89; suspense tech. Aetna Medicare, Savannah, 1989-93; family support coord. Youth Futures Authority, Savannah, 1993-94, finance specialist family resource ctr., 1994-95; cmty. campaigner Ga. Campaign for Adolescent Pregnancy Prevention, Savannah, 1996-98; owner, dir. Lesye-Anye Scholastic Inst. of Achievement, Savannah, 1998—. Cons. Daycare Home Providers The La Nourriture Co., Decatur, Ga., 1989—. V.p. Windsor Forest High Sch. PTA/PTO; mem. parent adv. team to supt. Savannah-Chatham Bd. Edn.; bd. dirs. Neighborhood Improvement Assn.; citizen rev. panelist Juvenile Ct. Chatham-Savannah Youth in Foster Care; mem. family to family steering com. Alternative Placement to Foster Care; bd. dirs. Healthy Start Initiative Male Involvement; exec. com. Youth Crime Watch of Savannah; mem. neighborhood coun. Cmty. Change for Youth Devel., youth advisor; sec. Eastside Concerned Citizens; mem. adv. com. Summer Youth Roundtable; vol. Meml. Med. Ctr.; founder, advisor Chatham-Savannah Youth Action Team; pres. stewardess bd. #2 St. Philip A.M.E. Ch., mem. pulpit aid bd., usher bd. # 1, communication com.; troop leader Girl Scouts U.S.A.; den mother Cub Scouts. Mem Savannah State U. Alumni Assn., St. Leo Coll. Alumni Assn. Avocations: sewing, horticulture, reading, travel. Home: PO Box 15132 Savannah GA 31416-1832

HILL, DOROTHY MONROE, retired educator; b. Portsmouth, Va., Oct. 8, 1923; d. Elmer Sylvester and Dorothy Fleet (Barkley) Monroe; m. Gladstone Middleton Hill, June 19, 1945; children: Dorothy Fleet Hill, Robert M. Hill, Brooke Hill, Thomas Wyatt Hill. BA, Westhampton Coll., 1944; MA, U. Va., 1973. Cert. tchr. K-12, Va. H.s. tchr. Va. Beach (Va.) Pub. Schs., 1944-45; elem. and middle sch. tchr., dept. head Ports Pub. Schs., Portsmouth, Va., 1969-90, ret., 1990. Mem. strategic action com. Portsmouth Pub. Schs., 1993-94, grant writer John Tyler Sch., 1994. Bd. dirs. Planned Parenthood of S.E., Va. 1992-96, Cmty. Concert Assn., 1988-2003, Va. Coun. of Chs., 1992-96; com. Portsmouth Dem. Com., 1991-93; resource mother Child and Family Svc., Portsmouth, 1991-92. Recipient Outstanding Social Studies Tchr. Va. Coun. for Social Studies, 1985l; named Strong, Smart and Bold, Girls, Inc. Ctr. Youth, 2002. Mem. AAUW (pres., v.p., mem. state bd. dirs., Ednl. Found. Named grant 1985), The Students Club (pres. 1994-96), World Affairs Coun., Nat. Woman's Polit. Caucus, Internat. Assn. Torch Clubs (pres.2002—), Delta Kappa Gamma. Democrat. Methodist. Avocations: travel, art, gardening. Home: Admiral's Landing #706 475 Water St Portsmouth VA 23704-3819

HILL, ELEANOR JEAN, lawyer; b. Miami Beach, Fla., Dec. 19, 1950; d. Elbert Cray and Florence Louise (Strzycki) Hill; m. Thomas Paul Gross, April 7, 1990; 1 child, Bryan Michael Gross. BS, Fla. State U., 1972, JD, 1974. Bar: Fla. Asst. atty. U.S. Atty's Office, Tampa, Fla., 1975-78; spl. atty. Organized Crime Strike Force, U.S. Dept. Justice, Tampa, Fla., 1978-80; asst. counsel U.S. Senate Permanent Subcommittee on Investigations, Washington, 1980-82, chief counsel to minority, 1982-87, staff dir., chief counsel, 1987-95; inspector gen. U.S. Dept. Defense, Arlington, Va., 1995-99; ptnr. King & Spalding, Washington, 1999—. Mem. Fla. Bar Assn., Phi Beta Kappa, Phi Kappa Phi. Office: King & Spalding Ste 1100 1730 Pennsylvania Ave NW Washington DC 20006-4795

HILL, ELIZABETH ANNE, academic administrator, lawyer; b. N.Y.C., Dec. 29, 1942; d. Harry Gerald and Grace Marie (Byrne) H. BA, St. Joseph's Coll., Bklyn., 1964; MA, Columbia U., 1965; JD, St. John's Law Sch., Jamaica, N.Y., 1978. Bar: N.Y. 1979, U.S. Dist. Ct. (ea. dist.) N.Y. 1979; cert. tchr. English and social studies K-12, N.Y. H.s. tchr. Acad. St. Joseph, Brentwood, N.Y., 1967-70, Bishop Kearney H.S., Bklyn., 1970-71; co-dir. formation program Sisters of St. Joseph, Brentwood, 1971-76; atty. Cath. Migration Office, Bklyn., 1978-80; exec. asst. to pres. St. Joseph's Coll., Bklyn., 1980-97, pres., 1997—. Bd. dirs. Brookhaven (N.Y.) Hosp., L.I. Assn., Commn. Independent Colls. and Univs.; mem. bd. trustees L.I. Reg. Adv. coun. Higher Edn. Mem. Bishop's Commn. on Pub. Policy, Bklyn., 1978-81; mediator Diocesan Mediation and Arbitration Panel, Bklyn., 1981—. Mem. Nat. Assn. Coll. and Univ. Attys., Bklyn. C. of C. (bd. dirs.). Office: St Joseph's Coll 245 Clinton Ave Brooklyn NY 11205-3602

HILL, ELIZABETH GOODWIN, legislative analyst; b. Modesto, Calif., Jan. 16, 1950; d. Judson Norton Stone Jr. and Beverly Jean (Goodwin) Winger; m. Laurence Arden Hill, June 22, 1974; children: Erik G., Kristina M. BA with honors, Stanford U., 1973; M in Pub. Policy, U. Calif., Berkeley, 1975. Program analyst Legis. Analyst's Office, Sacramento, 1976-79, prin. program analyst, 1979-86, legis. analyst, 1986—. Adv. bd. Ctr. for Calif. Studies, Sacramento, 1988—, Pub. Policy Inst. Calif., San Francisco, 1995—; mem. Calif. Constn. Revision Commn., Sacramento, 1994-96. Author: (newsletter) Ballot-Box Budgeting, 1990; contbr. chpt. to book. Legis. chair United Way Campaign, Sacramento, 1988, 96; leader Boy Scouts Am., Sacramento, 1990-93. Fulbright scholar Royal Inst. Tech., Stockholm, 1976; Pub. Ofcl. of Yr., Governing Mag., 1997; recipient Disting. Svc. award Calif. Assn. of Counties, 1995. Mem. Nat. Assn. Legis. Fiscal Officers, Western States Legis. Fiscal Officers Assn. (pres. 1990, 98), Assn. for Pub. Policy and Mgmt. (v.p. 2000-01) (policy coun. 1986-90, 1998-2000), Stanford Alumni Assn., Calif. Alumni Assn. Avocations: golf, photography, gardening, genealogy, cooking. Office: Legis Analysts Office 925 L St Ste 1000 Sacramento CA 95814-3762 Office Phone: 916-445-4656.

HILL, ELIZABETH MARIE, research scientist; b. Tuscaloosa, Ala., Oct. 26, 1954; d. William Taylor and Kathleen (Jordan) H. AB in Psychology, U. Mich., 1977; MS in Exptl. Psychology, Tulane U., 1979, PhD in Exptl. Psychology, 1983; MS in Biometry, La. State U., 1986. Instr. dept. psychology Furman U., Greenville, S.C., 1981-82; rsch. fellow dept. psychiatry Albert Einstein Coll. Medicine, N.Y.C., 1982-84; rsch. fellow dept. biometry and genetics La. State U. Med. Ctr., New Orleans, 1985-87; rsch. fellow dept. psychiatry U. Mich., Ann Arbor, 1987-88, asst. rsch. scientist dept. psychiatry, 1990-97; assoc. prof. dept. psychology U. Detroit Mercy, 1997—. Dir. biometrics divsn. dept. psychiatry U. Mich., Ann Arbor, 1989-94; dir. data mgmt. and analysis U. Mich. Alcohol Rsch. Ctr., Ann Arbor, 1989-97. Contbr. articles to profl. jours. Grantee Nat. Inst. on Alcoholism and Alcohol Abuse, 1995, 96. Mem. Rsch. Soc. on Alcoholism, Human Behavior and Evolution Soc. (treas. 1989-90, newsletter editor 1992-97), Animal Behavior Soc. Avocations: tennis, softball, dogs. Office: U Detroit Mercy Dept Psychology 8200 W Outer Dr Detroit MI 48219-3580

HILL, ELLEN ANNETTE, artist; b. Madisonville, Tex., Feb. 16, 1940; d. Thelma Clyde and Pauline Ellen (Black) Keefer; m. William Robert Hill, Aug. 29, 1958; children: Shaun Anthony, Stanton Alan, Shannon Kathleen. BS, Sam Houston State U., 1960; postgrad., Southwestern Sch. Art, 1982—84; BFA magna cum laude, U. Albuquerque, 1986. Owner Mariposa Studio, Albuquerque, 1980—86, Mariposa Art Gallery and Studio, North Zulch, Tex., 2002—. Art tchr. Mariposa Art Gallery, North Zulch, Tex., 2002—; mem. arts coun. Madison County. Author poetry; exhibitions include N.Mex. Art League Gallery, Albuquerque, 1980—85, Tumbleweed Gallery, 1985—88, Galleries of Anastasia, 1989—90, Treetop Gallery, Oak Ridge, Tenn., 1991—93, La Scala, San Antonio, 1995, Mariposa Art Gallery, North Zulch, Tex., 2001—, others, —. Sec. Cmty. Devel. Coun., North Zulch, 2002—03. Recipient 2nd pl., Auroria Art Club Show, 3rd pl., Coral Gables Art League Show. Mem.: Nat. Mus. Women in the Arts (charter), Brazos Valley Art League, Oil Painters Am. Republican. Mem. Church Of Christ. Avocations: gardening, reading, photography, writing. Home: PO Box 112 North Zulch TX 77872

HILL, EMITA BRADY, academic administrator, consultant; b. Balt., Jan. 31, 1936; d. Leo and Lucy McCormick (Jewett) Brady; children: Julie Beck, Christopher, Madeleine Vedel. BA, Cornell U., 1957; MA, Middlebury Coll., 1958; PhD, Harvard U., 1967. Instr. Harvard U., 1961-63; asst. prof. Western Reserve U., 1967-69; from asst. prof. to v.p. Lehman Coll. CUNY, Bronx, N.Y., 1970-91; chancellor, grad. faculty Ind. U., Kokomo, Ind., 1991-99, chancellor emerita, 1999—. Vis. advisor Salzburg Seminar Univs. Project; cons. in field. Trustee Am. U. in Central Asia; mem. Women's Forum of NY. Mem.: Internat. Assn. Univ. Pres., Phi Beta Kappa. Avocations: music, scuba diving, tennis. E-mail: ehill@indiana.edu.

HILL, EMMA, apparel executive; b. Eng. Grad., Ravensbourne Coll. Design and Comm., London. Accessories designer Marc Jacobs; sr. designer for men's and women's accessories Calvin Klein, N.Y.C.; accessories designer Burberry, London; v.p. men's and women's accessories The Gap, Inc., San Francisco, 2002—. Office: Gap Inc Two Folsolm St San Francisco CA 94105*

HILL, EMMA LEE, education educator; b. Crane, Tex., Jan. 13, 1949; d. Howard Lee and Eddie Marie (Gill) H. BS, Hardin-Simmons. U., 1970; MEd, Abilene Christian U., 1974, postgrad., 1979. Cert. provisional elem. mentally retarded, lang./learning disabilities, bilingual tchr., profl. supr., profl. midmgmt., tchr. appraiser, Tex. Tchr. Kileen (Tex.) Ind. Sch. Dist., Harker Heights, 1970-71, Winters (Tex.) Ind. Sch. Dist., 1971-73, Abilene (Tex.) Ind. Sch. Dist., 1973—. Bldg. rep. Supt.'s Task Force on Schs. 5-Yr. Plan, Abilene, 1990-91; tchr. leader/dir. Coll. Connections, McMurray U., 1991—; sch. rep. Cleannn/Proud program. Illustrator: (book) Richard the Great, 1967. Mem. local election com. Tex. Tchrs. for Gov., Abilene, 1988; sec. Abilene PTA, 1980-82, Tex. PTA, 1980-82. Scholar Abilene C. of C., 1967-69. Mem. Assn. for Supervision and Curriculum Devel., Internat. Reading Assn., Tex. Assn. Bilingual Educators (pres. Abilene 1988-89), Tex. Classroom Tchrs. Assn., Assn. Tex. Profl. Educators (bldg. rep. 1980—, Outstanding Tchr. award 1989), AAUW, Internat. Soc. Poets (life), Nat. Honor Soc., Delta Kappa Gamma (treas. Abilene 1990-91). Avocations: watching professional sports, playing basketball and baseball, running, walking, movie classics. Home: PO Box 266 Tye TX 79563-0266 Address: 801 G Ave E Apt 3 Alpine TX

HILL, FAITH, musician; b. Jackson, Miss., Sept. 21, 1967; d. Ted and Edna Perry; m. Daniel Hill, 1988 (div. 1991); m. Tim McGraw, Oct. 6, 1996; children: Gracie, Maggie, Audrey. Grad., McLaurin H.S. With Warner Bros. Records, 1993—. Musician: (recordings) Take Me As I Am, 1993, It Matters To Me, 1995, Faith, 1998, Breathe, 1999 (ACM Video of YR., 2000, Billboard Hot 100 Airplay Track of Yr., 2000, Best Female Country Vocal Performance Grammy, 2001, Best Country Album, 2001, Top Selling Album, Can. Country Music Assn., 2001), Cry, 2002 (Best Female Country Vocal Performance Grammy, 2003, Hottest Female Video of Yr., CMT Flameworthy Video Music Awards, 2003); contbr. to sound tracks: Pearl Harbour, How the Grinch Stole Christmas, Prince of Egypt, Practical Magic, Maverick, contbr. to TV sound track: King of the Hill. Frounder Faith Hill Family Literacy Project, 1996. Named New Female Vocalist of Yr., ACM, 1993, Top Country Female Artist, Billboard, 1994, Female Star of Tomorrow, TNN/MCN, 1995, Female Vocalist of Yr., ACM, 1999, TNN/MCN, 2000, Female Country Artist of Yr., Country Weekly, 2000, Hot 100 Singles Female Artist of Yr., Billboard, 2000, Favorite Female Artist Country Music, AMA, 2001, Favorite Pop-Rock Female Artist, 2001, Female Vocalist of Yr., ACM, 2001, TNN/CTM Country Weekly Music Awards, 2001, Favorite Female Artist Country Music, AMA, 2002; recipient Single of Yr., Song of Yr., Video of Yr. for It's Your Love, ACM, 1998, Video of Yr. for This Kiss, CMA, 1998, Single of Yr. for This Kiss, ACM, 1999, Video of Yr. for This Kiss, 1999, Vocal Event of Yr. for Just To Hear You Say You Love Me, 1999, GNN/MCN, 1999, Song of Yr. for Just to Hear You Say That You Love Me, TNN/MCN, 1999, Sigle of Yr. for This Kiss, 1999, Video of Yr. for This Kiss, 1999, Best Country Collaboration with Vocals for Let's Make Lofe, Grammy Awards, 2001, Favorite Female Mus. Performer, People's Choice Awards, 2001, Favorite Country Album, AMA, 2001, 5 Platinum awards, Can. Rec. Industry Assn., 2001, Favorite Female Artist Country, AMA, 2003, Favorite Female Mus. Performer, People's Choice Awards, 2002, 2003. Office: c/o Creative Artists Agy 3310 West End Ave 5th Fl Nashville TN 37203*

HILL, FAY GISH, retired librarian; b. Rensselaer, Ind., Sept. 19, 1944; d. Roy Charles and Vergie (Powell) Gish; m. John Christian Hill, May 20, 1967; 1 child, Christina Gish. BA, Purdue U., 1967; MLS, U. Tex., 1971. Asst. libr. basic reference dept. Tex. A&M U., College Station, 1972, assoc. libr. sci. ref. dept., 1972-74, acting head libr. sci. reference dept., 1975; reference libr. Ctrl. Iowa Regional Libr., Des Moines, 1984—2003. Troop leader Girl Scouts U.S., Ames, Iowa, 1983—88; bd. dirs. Friends of Fgn. Wives, Ames, 1982—86, Iowa Questers, 2000—. Mem.: ALA, Iowa Libr. Assn. Found. (bd. dirs. 1990—95), Iowa Libr. Assn. Presbyterian. Avocation: antiques. Home: 5604 Thunder Rd Ames IA 50014-9448

HILL, FELICITY JANE, editor; b. Bath, England, 1964; arrived in U.S., 1986; d. John Clifford Bradley and Jayne Marian Hill; children: Tristan, Miles. BA with honors, U. Fla., 1990, MA, 1994. Reporter & columnist Sun Newspapers, Cleve., 1995—96, corr., 1996—2000; asst. editor Shaker Mag., Shaker Heights, 2001—03, editor, 2003—. Mem. faculty adv. com. U. Fla., Gainesville, 1989—90, mem. grad. adv. com., 1993—94. Coun. rep. PTO, Shaker Heights, 2001—02; chair internat. families Lomond Sch., 2000—. Mem.: Soc. Profl. Journalists, Phi Kappa Phi. Home: 19000 Oxford Rd Shaker Heights OH 44122-2530 E-mail: felicityjh@aol.com.

HILL, GRACE LUCILE GARRISON, education educator, consultant; b. Gastonia, N.C., Sept. 26, 1930; d. William Moffatt and Lillian Tallulah (Tatum) Garrison; m. Leo Howard Hill, July 24, 1954; children: Lillian Lucile, Leo Howard Jr., David Garrison. BA, Erskine Coll., 1952; MA, Furman U., 1966; PhD, U. S.C., 1980. Lic. sch. psychologist, S.C. Tchr. Bible, Clinton (S.C.) Pub. Schs., 1952-53; tchr. English Parker High Sch., Greenville, S.C., 1953-55; elem. tchr. Augusta Circle Sch., Greenville, 1955-57; tchr. homebound children Greenville County Sch. Dist., Greenville, 1961-64, psychologist, 1966-77; adj. prof. grad. studies in edn. Furman U., Greenville, 1977—, U. S.C., Columbia, 1982—; ednl. cons. Ednl. Diagnostic Svcs., Greenville, 1980—. Exec. dir. Camperdown Acad., Greenville, 1986-87; cons. learning disability program Erskine Coll., Due West, S.C., 1978—; Disting. lectr. Erskine Coll., 1999. Contbr. articles to profl. jours. Pres. Lake Forest PTA, Greenville, 1970-71; pres. of Women A.R. Presbyn. Ch., Greenville, 1973-75, adult Bible tchr., 1978—; sec. bd. trustees Erskine Coll., 1982-88; bd. dirs. Children's Bur. S.C., Columbia, 1981-87, YWCA, Greenville, 1984-88; bd. advisors for adoption S.C. Dept. Social Svcs., Columbia, 1987-92. Recipient Order of the Jessamine, Greenville News award, 1994-95, Sullivan award Erskine Coll., 2000. Mem. Am. Edn. Rsch. Assn. (southeastern rep. 1982-84, editor newspaper for SIG group 1982-83), Jean Piaget Soc., Assn. for Supervision and Curriculum Devel., Orton Dyslexia Soc. (pres. Carolinas br. 1984-88), Ea. Ednl. Rsch. Assn., S.C. Psychol. Assn., Order of the Jessamine, 21st Century Learning Initiative, Delta Kappa Gamma. Democrat. Avocations: travel, writing. Home and Office: 28 Montrose Dr Greenville SC 29607-3034

HILL, HELEN MOREY WILLIAMS, English literature educator; b. Bklyn., Mar. 26, 1915; d. Arthur Herbert and Sophie Weston (Baker) Williams; children: Rebecca, Anthony, Richard, Alan. AB, Wheaton Coll., Norton, Mass., 1936; AM, Brown U., Providence, R.I., 1937. Grad. tchg. asst. U. Ill., Urbana, 1939-42, 1945-48; editl. asst. U. Mich., Ann Arbor, 1959-63; instr., prof. English Ea. Mich. U., Ypsilanti, 1963-83. Co-editor: New Coasts and Strange Harbors: Discovering Poems, 1974, Straight on Till Morning: Poems of the Imaginary World, 1977, Dusk to Dawn: Poems of Night, 1980; (author) A Proud and Fiery Spirit: Journals of Captain Edward Baker, 1846-1895; Memoirs of Crooked Lane, Duxbury and Marshfield, Massachusette, 1995; editor: The Man Who Easts Snakes and other Tales, 2002, Reminiscences of the Twentieth Century, 2002; contbr. articles to profl. jours. Founder Alliance For the Mentally Ill Washtenaw County, 1984, Trailblazers of Washtenaw, Ann Arbor, 1989. Rsch. grantee Nat. Hist. Records and Publs. Commn. (Nat. Archives), 1972. Home: 928 Olivia Ave Ann Arbor MI 48104-3535

HILL, HOLLY TRAYNHAM, choral director, music minister; b. Simpsonville, S.C., May 21, 1976; d. Carolyn Garrett Traynham, Howard William Traynham, Jr.; m. Brian Patrick Hill. BA in Music, North Greenville Coll., 1998. Office mgr. Ft. Wayne Pools Distbn. Greenville, SC, 1995—2000; music min. Beulah Bapt. Ch., Fountain Inn, SC, 1999—2000; choral dir. Bryson Middle Sch., Simpsonville, SC, 1999—; music min. New Hope Bapt. Ch., Simpsonville, 2000—01. Pres. Music Etude Soc. Tigerville, SC, 1995—98; alto sect. leader North Greenville Choral Dept., Tigerville, 1995—98; tchr. edn. rep. North Greenville Edn. Dept., Tigerville, 1996—97; team leader Joyful Sound-Bapt. Student Union Ensemble, Tigerville, 1997—98, Bryson Middle Exploratory Team, Simpsonville, 1999—. Mem.: Am. Choral Dirs. Assn., S.C. Music Eduators Assn., Music Educators Nat. Conf. Baptist. Avocations: singing, skiing, travel, cooking, movies. Home: 206 Flagstar Ct Fountain Inn SC 29644 Office: Bryson Middle Sch 3657 S Industrial Dr Simpsonville SC 29681 Office Fax: 864-967-1843. Personal E-mail: hollyh47@charter.net. Business E-Mail: hollyh47@charter.net.

HILL, IDA JOHNSON, education consultant, technologist, administrator; b. Mecklenburg, Va. d. Mack H. and Hattie H. (Hardy) Johnsn; m. Russell Langston Hill (dec.). BS, Va. State U., 1957, MS, 1962; EdD, U. Va., 1981. Cert. reading specialist. Reading cons. Richmond (Va.) Schs., 1961-68; TV tchr., specialist Sta. WCVE/WNVT-TV, Richmond, 1968-78, v.p. programming, 1978-86; dir. reading clinic Va. State U., Ettrick; instr. Va. Commonwealth U., Richmond, Va. Union Univ., Richmond, Va. State U., Petersburg; dir. of tech. Henrico County, Richmond, 1987-88; dep. supt. Va. Dept. of Edn., Richmond, 1990-94, asst. supt. for tech., 1988-97. Editl. adv. bd. Acad. Therapy/Intervention, Austin, 1985—; contbr. articles to profl. jours. Pres., bd. chair Literacy Coun. of Metro. Richmond, 1987; adv. bd. Robert E. Lee Boy Scouts, Richmond, 1997, U. Va. Continuing Edn., Charlottesville; bd. chair Richmond Cmty. H.S., 1987; bd. dirs. Richmond New Cmty. Sch., 1997. Recipient Presdl. Citation Nat. Assn. of Equal Opportunity in Higher Edn., 1991, Outstanding Accomplishments in Edn. award Zeta Phi Beta, 1997; named Outstanding Educator YWCA, 1996, Honor award Ida J. Hill Tech. Ctr. Va. Dept. Edn., 1997. Mem. ASCD, Va. Soc. for Tech. in Edn. (award for excellence in performance, hon., bd. dirs. 1987-97), Satellite Edn. Resources Consortium, (bd. dirs. 1995-97), Altrusa Club (bd. dirs. 1995-97, Ida Hill scholarship for literacy 1993). Avocations: travel, community service, reading. Home: PO Box 906 Chesterfield VA 23832-0013

HILL, JACQUELYN LOUISE HARRISON, secondary school educator; b. Summerville, S.C., July 26; d. Joe and Pearl Geneva (Tucker) Harrison; m. George Rutledge Hill, Jr., Sept. 28, 1969; children: George Rutledge III, Brian Desmond Harrison. BS in Biology, Benedict Coll., 1969; MEd in Elem. Edn., Coll. of Charleston, 1978; EdS in Adminstrn., The Citadel, 1989; postgrad., Nova U., 1993—. Tchr. biol. R.B. Stall High Sch., Charleston, SC, 1969-70; tchr. sci. and math. Givhans Elem. Sch., 1970—2003; tchr. sci. DuBose Mid. Sch., Summerville, 1985—. USDA summer food coord. Berkely, Dorchester and Colleton County Community Action Agy., summers 1977, 79; tchr. biology Morningside Mid. Sch., Charleston, summer 1986; tchr. adult edn. Garrett High Sch., 1991. Lay speaker Murray Meth. Ch., Summerville, pres. United Meth. Women, 1988-91, now v.p., mem. stewardess bd., 1989—; layman Bethel A.M.E. Ch., 1988-91. Music scholar Benedict Coll. 1965-68. Mem. NEA, S.C. Edn. Assn. (Outstanding Pres. award 1983), Summerville Edn. Assn. (pres. 1988-89), Zeta Phi Beta (pres. Lambda Nu Zeta chpt. 1985-91, coor.d S.C. Archotte 1991—). Avocations: assisting and volunteering with elderly, writing articles for community newspapers and newsletters, sewing, physical fitness. Home: 307 S Railroad Ave Ridgeville SC 29472-6306

HILL, JUDITH DEEGAN, retired lawyer; b. Chgo., Dec. 13, 1941; d. William James and Ida May (Scott) Deegan; children: Colette M., Cristina M. BA, Western Mich. U., 1960; cert., U. Paris, Sorbonne, 1962; JD, Marquette U., 1971; postgrad., Harvard U., 1984. Bar: Wis. 1971, Ill. 1973, Nev. 1976, D.C. 1979. Tchr. Kalamazoo (Mich.) Bd. Edn., 1960-62, Maple Heights (Ohio) Bd. Edn., 1963-64, Shorewood (Wis.) Bd. Edn., 1964-68; corp. atty. Fort Howard Paper Co., Green Bay, Wis., 1971-72; sr. trust adminstr. Continental Ill. Nat. Bank & Trust, Chgo., 1972-76; atty. Morse, Foley & Wadsworth Law Firm, Las Vegas, 1976-77; dep. dist. atty., criminal prosecutor Clark County Atty., Las Vegas, 1977-83; atty. civil and criminal law Edward S. Coleman Profl. Law Corp., Las Vegas, 1983-84; pvt. practice law, 1989-99; ret., 1999. Bd. dirs. YMCA, Highland Park, 1973-75, Planned Parenthood of So. Nev., 1977-78, Nev. Legal Svcs., Carson City, 1980-87, state chmn., 1984-87; bd. dirs. Clark County Legal Svcs., Las Vegas, 1980-87, St. Jude's Ranch for Children, 1999-2001; mem.

Star Aux. for Handicapped Children, Las Vegas, 1986-96, Greater Las Vegas Women's League, 1987-88; jud. candidate Las Vegas Mcpl. Ct., 1987, New Symphony Guild, Variety Club Internat., 1992-93; mem. Nat. Conf. for Cmty. and Justice, So. Nev., 1998-2000; mentor in Clark County Sch., 1999-2002. Auto Splties. scholar, St. Joseph, Mich., 1957-60, St. Thomas More scholar Marquette U. Law Sch., Milw., 1968-69; juvenile law internship grantee Marquette U. Law Sch., 1970; honored as one of first 100 Women Attys. in the State of Nev., Oct. 1999. Children's Village Club (pres. 1980). Home: 521 Sweeney Ave Las Vegas NV 89104-1436 Fax: 702-384-4167.

HILL, JUDITH SWIGOST, business analyst, information systems engineer; b. Harvey, Ill., Dec. 31, 1942; d. J.W. and M.J. (Kuczaik) Swigost; m. Wallace H. Hill, May 16, 1982; stepchildren: Scott, Amy, Molly, Elizabeth. BA in Theater, U. Ill., 1964; postgrad., Am. U., 1967-69, New Sch. U., N.Y.C., 1977-85. Vol. U.S. Peace Corps, Philippines, 1964-66, recruiter, 1966-67, program mgr. Micronesia, 1968, dir. corr. Washington, 1969; editor, prin. Congl. Monitor, Inc., Washington, 1970-76; legis. analyst Philip Morris, Inc., N.Y.C., 1976-77; tech. analyst, writer Jesco, Inc., N.Y.C., 1978-79; assoc. pub. Thomas Pub. Co., N.Y.C., 1980-84; bus. analyst AGS, Inc. Ind. Cons., N.Y.C., 1984-93; dir. MIS N.Y.C. Sch. Constrn. Authority, 1993-94; ind. cons. in project mgmt. N.Y.C., 1994—. Ind. cons. info. engring. and tech. orgn., N.Y.C., 1987—. golf instr., 2002-. Editor, contbr. Golf for Women newsletter, 1999—; golf instr., 2003-, contbr. articles to profl. jour. Mem. Internat. Women's Writing Guild, Nat. Assn. Returned Peace Corps Vols. Greater N.Y., Nat. Peace Corps. Assn. Avocations: golf, writing, banjo, piano. E-mail: joodgolf@yahoo.com.

HILL, KAREN CAECILIA, education educator; b. LaCrosse, Wis., Apr. 23, 1961; BA, U. Ark., 1984; MEd, U. So. Miss., 1996. Instr. in writing Hartnell Coll., Salinas, Calif., 2000—. Author: One Bird, 2001. Home: PO Box 279 Marina CA 93933

HILL, KATHLEEN BLICKENSTAFF, lawyer, mental health nurse, nursing educator; b. Greenville, Ohio, Oct. 24, 1950; d. Donald Edward and Mary Ann (Subler) Berger; children: Benjamin Arin, Amanda Marie, Kathryn Megan; m. David M. Hill, Sr., Sept. 27, 2002. BS, Ohio State U., 1972, MS, 1973, sch. nurse cert., 1990; JD, Capital U. Law Sch., 1998. Cert. sch. nurse grades K-12. Cons. cmty. educator S.W. Cmty. Mental Health Ctr., Columbus, 1973-77; patient and cmty. educator Daniel E. Blickenstaff, DDS, Inc., Columbus, 1977-86; staff nurse Riverside Meth. Hosp., Columbus, 1986-90; clin. instr. Columbus (Ohio) State C.C., 1989; from asst. to assoc. prof. Capital U., Columbus, 1989-2000, prof., 2000—01, adj. prof., 2001—03; assoc. Porter, Wright, Morris & Arthur LLP, Columbus, 2000—. Mem. cmty. svcs. com. Mid Ohio Dist. Nurses Assn., Columbus, 1990—2001, bd. dirs., 1991—94, mem. legis. com., 2002—. Leader Girl Scouts, Grandview Heights, Ohio, 1989-93; bd. dirs. H.S. PTO, Grandview Heights (Ohio) City Schs., 1990-93, treas. H.S. PTO, 1990-92, co-chair oper. levy, 1991. Mem.: ANA, ABA, Columbus Bar Assn. (health law com.), Ohio State Bar Assn. (health and disability law com.), Ohio Nurses Assn., Am. Health Lawyers Assn., Sigma Theta Tau. Avocations: quilting, sewing, gardening. Home: 1935 Marblecliff Crossing Ct Columbus OH 43204-4968 Office: Porter Wright Morris & Arthur LLP 41 S High St Ste 2900 Columbus OH 43215-6194 Office Phone: 614-227-2147. Personal E-mail: kbhill@porterwright.com. Business E-Mail: kblicken@columbus.rr.com.

HILL, KATHLEEN JOY, administrative assistant; b. Joliet, Ill., July 7, 1952; d. Phillip Craig and Gloria Dianne (Novy) Bock; m. Gregory Robert Hill, June 25, 1983; 1 child, Lyndsay Joy Surman. BS in Mgmt. cum laude, Olivet Nazarene Coll., 1995. Tech. sec. Johnson & Johnson Co., Wilmington, Ill., 1979-94, adminstrv. asst., 1994-96; bd. dirs., sec.-treas. Van-Mack Electric Co., Joliet, 1996—. Elder, ch. session Presbyn. Ch. Mem. NAFE, Joliet C. of C. Avocations: travel, home decorating, water sports. Office: Van-Mack Electrical 2433 Reeves Rd Joliet IL 60436-9538

HILL, LARKIN PAYNE, real estate company operations administrator; b. Oct. 30, 1954; d. Max Lloyd and Jane Olivia (Evatt) H. Student, Coll. Charleston, 1972-73, U. N.C., 1973. Lic. real estate broker, N.C. Sec., property mgr. Max L. Hill Co., Inc., Charleston, S.C., 1973-75, sec., data processor, 1979-82, v.p. adminstrn., 1982—; ops. mgr. Shorline Internat. Real Estate, 2003—04; v.p. adminstrn. Max L. Hill Co., Inc., Mt. Pleasant, SC, 2004—. Resident mgr. Carolina Apts., Carrboro, N.C., 1975-77; sales assoc., Realtor, Southland Assocs., Chapel Hill, N.C., 1977-78; cons. specifications com. Charleston Trident Multiple Listing Service, 1985. Bd. dirs. Charleston Area Arts Coun., 1992-93; co-chair Beaux Arts Ball, Sch. Arts. Mem. Royal Oak Found., Scottish Soc. Charleston (bd. dirs. 1989-91), Preservation Soc., Charleston Computer Users Group, N.C. Assn. Realtors, Spoleto Festival USA (chmn. auction catalog com. 1990-92). Republican. Methodist. Avocations: reading, crossword puzzles, American Staffordshire Terriers. Home: 7 Riverside Dr Charleston SC 29403-3217 Office: Max L Hill Co INc 824 Johnnie Dodds Blvd Mount Pleasant SC 29464 E-mail: larkinhill@charleston.net.

HILL, LAURYN, vocalist, actress; b. South Orange, N.J., May 25, 1975; Student, Columbia U. Teamed with Prakazrel "Pras" Michel and Wyclef Jean as the Fugees while still in H.S.; trio produced 2 albums: Blunted on Reality, 1994, and The Score, 1996 (17 million copies sold). Solo albums: The Miseducation of Lauryn Hill, 1998, MTV Unplugged No. 2.0, 2002; wrote and produced On That Day for gospel artist CeCe Winans; wrote A Rose is Still a Rose for Aretha Franklin album, also directed song's accompanying video. Actress: (films) Sister Act 2: Back in the Habit, 1993, King of the Hill, 1993, Rhyme & Reason, 1997, Hav Plenty, 1997, Restaurant, 1998; television appearances As the World Turns, 1991, Daddy's Girl, 1997. Founder non-profit The Refugee Youth Camp Youth Project. With Fugees received 2 1996 Grammy awards--Best Rap Album for The Score and Best R&B Performance by a Duo or Group With Vocal (Killing Me Softly). Recipient 1999 Grammy awards for Album of Yr., Best New Artist, Best R&B Song, Best R&B Album, Best Female R&B Vocal Performance. Nominated for several awards at 13th Annual Soul Train Music Awards in L.A. Recipient 4 awards (Outstanding New Artist, Outstanding Female Artist, Outstanding Album and NAACP President's award) 30th Annual NAACP Image Awards, Pasadena, Calif., 1999. Other awards include Favorite New Soul/R&B Artist (26th Annual Am. Music Awards), Best New Artist (Danish Grammy Awards), Entertainer of Yr. (Entertainment Weekly), #1 Album of Yr. (Time mag., N.Y. Times), Best R&B Album of 1998 (USA Today), Artist of Yr. (Spin mag.), Artist of Yr. (Details mag.), 3 Rolling Stone Music Awards. Office: Sony Music 550 Madison Ave New York NY 10022-3211

HILL, LEDA KATHERINE, librarian; b. Bklyn., Feb. 16, 1952; d. David and Leda Louise (Jones) H. BA, Bklyn. Coll., 1974, MS in Edn., 1989; MLS, Queens (N.Y.) Coll., 1995. New bus. coord. INAC Corp., Cranford, N.J., 1974-80; paralegal Orgn. Women for Legal Awareness, Inc., East Orange, N.J., 1980-83; tchr. Roselle (N.J.) Bd. Edn., 1983-84; libr., tchr. N.Y.C. Bd. Edn., Bklyn., 1985—. Mem. ALA, Bklyn. Reading Coun., N.Y.C. Sch. Librs. Assn., N.Y. Libr. Assn., Am. Assn. Sch. Librs. Office: Middle School 2 655 Parkside Ave Brooklyn NY 11226-1505 Office Phone: 718-462-6992. E-mail: lhill4@2nycboe.net.

HILL, LORIE ELIZABETH, psychotherapist; b. Buffalo, Oct. 21, 1946; d. Graham and Elizabeth Helen (Salm) H. Student, U. Manchester, Eng., 1966-67; BA, Grinnell Coll., 1968; MA, U. Wis., 1970, Calif. State U., Sonoma, 1974; PhD, Wright Inst., 1980. Instr. English U. Mo., 1970-71; adminstr., supr. Antioch-West and Ctr. for Ind. Living, San Francisco, Berkeley, 1975-77; dir. tng. Ctr. for Edn. and Mental Health, San Francisco, 1977-80, exec. dir., 1980-81; pvt. practice Berkeley and Oakland, Calif., 1976—; instr. master's program in psychology John F. Kennedy U., Orinda, Calif., 1985, 94—. Founder group of psychotherapists against racism; spkr. on cross-cultural psychology; creater Jump Start, a violence prevention and unlearning racism program for youth; trainer for trainers 3rd Internat. Conf. Conflict Resolution, St. Petersburg, Russia; sr. facilitator Color of Fear. Organizer against nuclear war; founding mem. Psychotherapists for Social Responsibility; psychologist Big Bros. and Big Sisters of the East Bay, 1986-88; vol. instr. City of Oakland Youth Skills Devel. Program; active Rainbow Coalition for Jesse Jackson's Presdl. Campaign, Ron Dellums Re-election Com.; campaigner for Clinton-Gore; founder, dir. Providing Alternatives to Violence; creator JumpStart program; co-founder Wellstone Progressive Dem. Club, 2003. Mem. Calif. Psychol. Assn. (chairperson pub. interest divsn. 1997, Helen Margulies Mehr Pub. Svc. award 1996, chair social issues 1996—, Silver Psi award 1999), Wellstone Dem. Renewal Club (co-founder). Democrat-Socialist. Avocations: sports, travel, music, reading. Office: 2955 Shattuck Ave Berkeley CA 94705-1808

HILL, MARIE See DAVIS, MAGGIE

HILL, MARILYNN IRENE REYNOLDS, secondary school educator; d. Merle Raymond and Vivian Helen Gordon Reynolds; m. Barry Edward Hill, Nov. 9, 1968. BA, U. Maine, 1968. Cert. profl. tchr. Maine. Tchr. Lake Region Sch. Dist., Bridgton, 1968—. Head tchr. Bridgton Jr. High and Lake Region Mid. Sch., Bridgton and Naples, Maine, 1982—87. Named Educator of Yr., Holocaust Human Rights Ctr. of Maine, 2000. Mem.: Delta Kappa Gamma (pres. 1994—96). Methodist. Avocations: nature study, Holocaust study, reading. Office: The Learning Ctr Skillins Cir Bridgton ME 04009

HILL, MARTHA N. community health nurse; b. Boston, July 14, 1943; d. Paul Lawrence Norton and Margaret M. Hagerty; m. Gary S. Hill, June 18, 1966; children: Paul, Justin. Diploma, Johns Hopkins Hosp., Balt., 1964; BSN, The Johns Hopkins U., 1966, PhD, 1987; MSN, U. Pa., 1977. From instr. to assoc. prof. Johns Hopkins Hosp. Sch. Nursing, Balt.; nurse specialist in hypertension Hosp. of U. Pa., Phila.; now dean Johns Hopkins Univ. Sch. of Nursing, Balt., 2002—. Contbr. articles to profl. jours. Recipient Malcolm Alderfer Schweiker award, 1985, Ruth B. Freeman award 1987; fellow Am. Acad. Nursing, 1989. Mem. ANA (rep. to NIH high blood press coord. com.), Am. Heart Assn. (vice chmn. coun. cardiovasc. nursing 1989-91, pres. 1997-98), Inst. of Medicine.

HILL, MARY LOU, accountant, business consultant; b. Phila., July 8, 1936; d. Norman Findlay and Gladys Louise (Weigand) Tompkins; m. Ernest Clarke Hill Jr., Mar. 15, 1958; children: Sally, Holly, Randy, Dave, James. Student, U. Miami, 1954-55, U. Okla., 1955-57; BBA, Portland State U., 1979, M in Taxation, 1982. CPA, Oreg. Staff acct. Fordham & Fordham, Hillsboro, Oreg., 1982-84; instr. Portland (Oreg.) State U., 1984-85; owner The Bookshelf, Sunriver, Oreg., 1985-88; instr. Cen. Oreg. Community Coll., Bend, 1986, 88-89; small bus. cons., 1988—; staff acct. Richard Rocci CPA, Portland, Oreg., 1990-91, Scribner & Scribner, PC, Portland, 1992-94, Alten & Sakai & Co., Portland, 1994-95, Napier & Co., Tigard, Oreg., 1996—, Rox Ann Strong, CPA, PC, Tigard, Oreg., 2000—. Mem. AAUW, Oreg. Soc. CPAs, Kappa Kappa Gamma. Democrat. Christian Scientist. Avocations: travel, reading, swimming, computers. Home and Office: 9172 SW Wilshire St Portland OR 97225-4050

HILL, MAY BRAWLEY, art historian; b. Salisbury, N.C., Dec. 10, 1942; d. Boyden and Marguerite Brawley; m. Frederick David Hill, July 12, 1967; children: Marguerite Boyden, Nathaniel. BA, Salem Coll., 1963; MA, Inst. Fine Arts, NYU, 1967; postgrad., CUNY, 1985. Curator Am. Soc. Art Gallery, N.Y.C., 1968-73. Author: Women: An Historical Survey of Women Artists, 1972, Three American Purists: Mason, Miles, von Wiegand, 1975, Dance Image: A Tribute to Serge Diaghelev, 1979, Fidelia Bridges, American Pre-Raphaelite, 1981, The Woman Sculptor: Malvina Hoffman and Her Contemporaries, 1984, Grez Days: Robert Vonnoh in France, 1987, Joellyn Duesberry, 1988, Edward Gobbi: Representative Works 1953-1993, 1994; Grandmother's Garden: The Old-Fashioned American Garden, 1865-1915, 1995, Furnishing the Old-Fashioned Garden: Three Centuries of American Summerhouses, Dovecotes, Fences, Privies, and Pergolas, 1998. Bd. dirs. Warren (Conn.) Land Trust, 1989—; mem. Friends of Hort., Wave Hill, N.Y., 1993—. Mem. Hort. Soc. N.Y. (bd. dirs. 1997—), Ft. Ticonderoga Assn., Garden Conservancy Fellows, Century Assn. Avocation: gardening. Home: 184 Brick School Rd Warren CT 06754-1424 Office: 103 E 86th St #3B New York NY 10026-1058

HILL, PATRICE SUSAN, journalist, economist; b. Taipei, Taiwan, Oct. 27, 1954; parents Am. citizens; d. Robert John Jr. and Gladys (Evers) H.; m. Donald F. Tatum, Dec., 2002. BA, Oberlin Coll., 1976. Reporter Inside Washington, 1982-85, Bond Buyer, Washington, 1986-93; chief econs. corr. Washington Times, 1993—. Mem. Nat. Press Club. Avocations: piano, singing. Home: 1206 Clement Pl Silver Spring MD 20910-1642 Office: Washington Times 3600 New York Ave NE Washington DC 20002-1996

HILL, RUTH FOELL, language consultant; b. Houston, Sept. 13, 1931; d. Ernest William and Florence Margaret (Kane) Foell; children: Linden Ruth, Andrea Grace. Student, Principia Coll., 1950; BA, U. Calif., Berkeley, 1952; postgrad., San Diego State, 1955, Cen. Piedmont, 1981. Cert. tchr., Calif. Owner, dir. Art Gallery of Chapel Hill (N.C.), 1966-75; ecumenical bd. Campus Ministry, Charlotte; with referral svc. Charlotte (N.C.) Bed and Breakfast Registry, 1980-90; lang. cons. Berlitz Internat., Raleigh, N.C., 1988-91; ESL tchr. Albemarle Elem. Sch., 2000—. Cert. cons. Performax Internat.; rep. UN Decade for Women Conf., NGO Forum, Nairobi, Kenya, 1985, Women and Global Security Conf., 1986; rep. emerging issues forum N.C. State U., 1987-93; presenter Southeastern Women's Studies Conf. Author: (poetry) Noble House, 2003; contbr. poetry to Nat. Libr. of Poetry Internat. Hall of Fame. Bd. dirs., chmn. natural resources com. LWV; coord. USIA grant region 6, Internat. Exch. Network; mem. N.C. Leadership Forum, N.C. Citizens Assembly, 1989; chmn. Week of Edn. Pub. Forum on Energy, Union Concerned Scientists, 1990-93; bd. dirs. Nat. Women's Conf. Commn., 1994—; mem. edn. subcom. Mayor's Internat. Cabinet, 1995; mem. Congress House Spkr.'s Citizen Task Force, 1995—; mem. Rep. Platform Com. and Nat. Presdl. Task Force, 1999, Rep. Inner Cir., 1995; mem. edn. com. Charlotte/Mecklenberg Historic Properties, 1986-88; mem. groundwater subcom. Mecklenburg County Commrs., 1987. Named Outstanding Athlete Women's Athletic Assn., Woman of the Yr., Am. Biog. Inst., 1994, Internat. Poetry Hall of Fame, 1998; Hewlett Found. scholar. Mem. AAUW (v.p. membership com., bd. dirs.), Ams. for Legal Reform (adv. bd.), Am. Farm Land Trust, UN Assn. U.S.A. (chpt. pres. 1991-93, co-chair UN Day Queens Coll. 1992, N.C. divsn. sec. 1993-94, UN50 chair 1995, So. Summit Queens Coll. 2002), Am. Biog. Inst. Rsch. Assn. (nominated to bd. govs.), Am. Biog. Inst. (aptd. adv. bd.), Carolina Coun. on World Affairs, Chapel Hill-Carrboro Sch. Art Guild (pres.), Midwest Acad., World Wide Women in Environment, N.Y. Acad. Sci. Republican. Christian Scientist. Avocations: travel, environmental issues, international exchange networking. Office: PO Box 220802 Charlotte NC 28222-0802 E-mail: rhill37901@aol.com.

HILL, SUSAN SLOAN, safety engineer; b. Quincy, Mass., June 1, 1952; d. Ralph Arnold and Grace Elenore (Sloan) Crosby; m. William Loyd Hill, Dec. 16, 1973 (div. July 1982); m. William Joseph Graham, Sept. 10, 1983 (div. Feb. 1985). AS in Gen. Engring., Motlow State C.C., Tullahoma, Tenn., 1976; BS in Indsl. Engring., Tenn. Technol. U., 1978. Intern, safety engr. Intern Tng. Ctr., U.S. Army, Red River Army Depot, Tex., 1978-79, Field Safety Activity, Charlestown, Ind., 1979, sys. safety engr. Comm.-Electronics Command Ft. Monmouth, N.J., 1979-84, gen. engr., 1984-85; chief sys. safety Arnold Air Force Sta., USAF, Tullahoma, 1984; sys. safety engr. U.S. Army Safety Ctr., Ft. Rucker, Ala., 1985-91; medically ret.; ind. cons. sys. safety, 1991—. Founder Fibromyalgia Support Group; leader Arthritis Found. Support Group; active Arthritis Found. Recipient 5 letters of appreciation, U.S. Army, letter of appreciation, Arthritis Found. Mem. NAFE, Assn. Fed. Safety and Health Profls. (regional v.p. 1980-84), Soc. Women Engrs., Nat. Safety Mgmt. Soc., Am. Soc. Safety Engrs., Sys. Safety Soc., Order Engr. Republican. Episcopalian. Avocations: reading, gardening, walking, cooking, golf. Home and Office: 1307 Bel-Aire Dr Tullahoma TN 37388

HILL, TERRI, diversified financial services company executive; BA in Orgnl. Comm., Ariz. State U.; cert. in human resources, Cornell U. With Am. Express, 1984—96, Nationwide Mutual Ins. Co., 1996—, sr. v.p. human resources and ops. Scottsdale Ins. Co., exec. v.p., chief adminstrv. officer, 2003—. Office: Nationwide Mutual Ins Co One Nationwide Plaza Columbus OH 43215-2220*

HILL, TESSA, president non profit environmental group; BA in Edn., Park Recreation Adminstrn., U. Minn., 1968. Tchr. elem. schs., 1970; founder Kids For Saving Earth Worldwide, Mpls., 1989—. Adv. com. U.S. Environ. Protection Agy., Dept. Health Human Svcs. Agy. Toxic Substances Disease Registry. Editor CHEC Report, Kids for Saving Earth News/Programs. Bd. dirs. Children's Health Environ. Coalition, Nat. Coalition Against Misuse Pesticides. Home and Office: Kids for Saving Earth Worldwide 5425 Pineview Ln N Minneapolis MN 55442-1704 E-mail: KSEWW@aol.com.

HILL, VALERIE CHARLOTTE, nurse; b. Shaftsbury, Vt, Dec. 2, 1932; d. William Henry Harrison and Angeline Margaret Stella (Fuller) Hill; m. Edward Joseph Klanit (dec. July 1984); 1 child, Joyce Ellen Klanit Artadi. Grad., Mt. Sinai Hosp. Sch. Nursing, 1955. RN, NY. Nurse The Jack Martin Respiratory Ctr. of The Mt. Sinai Hosp., N.Y.C., 1955-57; v.p. Chauffeurs Unlimited, Inc., N.Y.C., 1957-77; nurse Rusk Inst., N.Y.C., 1957-58, Beth Israel Med. Ctr., N.Y.C., 1978-79; owner, mgr. Powers Fish Market, Inc., N.Y.C., 1977-84; tchr. Tech. for Creating, Albany, 1983-97, Techs. for Creating, Snohomish, Wash., 1997—2002; nurse Doctors Hosp., N.Y.C., 1984-86; pvt. duty nurse Personal Health Care Svcs., Albany, N.Y., 1987-88; nurse Albany Med. Ctr. Hosp., 1987-95; real estate sales assoc. Century 21-Stanley Major Ltd., West Sand Lake, N.Y., 1988, Century-21 Home Towne Properties, Albany, 1989-92. Author numerous poems. Organizer Class 1955 Reunion Mt. Sinai Hosp. Sch. Nursing, 2000; mentoring two children. Recipient Outstanding Svc. to Cmty. award Mayor Koch City of NY, 1983. Mem. Alumnae Assn. Mt. Sinai Hosp. Sch. Nursing (bd. dir. 1968). Democrat. Avocations: reading, writing poetry, home videos, piano, still photography, painting. Home: 7618 129 Dr SE Snohomish WA 98290-6248

HILL, VICKI KAUFMAN, civil rights investigator; b. Quincy, Mass., June 29, 1941; d. Edwin Manuel and Althea Beatrice (Cohen) Kaufman; m. Robert J. Carolan, June 1, 1963 (div. Sept. 25, 1970), children: Wendy Katherine Badger, Amy Elizabeth Speer; m. Kenneth H. Hill, Mar. 28, 1992. BA, Boston U., 1963. Tchr. Sch. Dists. of Rye, N.H. and Sumter, S.C., 1964-68; curriculum libr. U. Tenn., Nashville, 1969-71; sales/office mgr. The Jaques Co., Inc., Boston, 1972-88; civil rights investigator DHHS, Boston, 1989—. Site coord. Serve, Inc., Derry, N.H., 1992—; founder, pres., bd. dirs. South Shore Coalition for Human Rights, Quincy, 1977—, pres., bd. dirs. Cmty. Ch. Boston, 1985-89, Dove, Inc., Shelter for Abused Women, Quincy, 1981-2001; ward 3 chair, bd. dirs. Quincy Rep. Com., 1975-89. Recipient Drylong-so award Cmty. Change, 1993, Regional award NCCJ, 1981. Mem. ASPA (bd. officer, treas. 1993—), Boston U. Alumni Assn. (pres. 1982-85, bd. dirs.). Avocations: reading, music, community service. Home: 4 Fairview Ave Derry NH 03038-2730 Office: Office for Civil Rights Dept Health and Human Svcs JFK Bldg Rm 1875 Boston MA 02203

HILLARD, CAROLE, former lieutenant governor; b. Deadwood, S.D., Aug. 14, 1936; m. John M. Hillard (dec.); children: David, Sue Ellen, Todd, Eddie, Lornell. BA in Edn., Univ. of Ariz., 1957; MA in Edn., S.D. State Univ., 1982; MA in Polit. Sci., Univ. of S.D., 1984. State rep. State of S.D., 34th dist., 1991-95; lt. gov. State of S.D., 1995—2003. Dir. Mich. Nat. Bank., Black Hills Regional Eye Inst., YMCA; mem. exec. bd. Nat. Crime Prevention Coun. Active Rapid City Common Coun., Rapid City C. of C., S.D. Bd. of Charities and Corrections, McGruff Crime Prevention Coun. (exec. bd.), S.D. Corrections Commn., Cmty. Care Ctr., S.D. Children's Home Soc., S.D. Assurance Alliance, Nat. Child Protection Partnership, First United Methodist Ch. (exec. bd.), Rapid City Econ. Devel. Partnership, F.L.A.G.S. Found.; mem. exec. bd. Bog Bros./Big Sisters; chair bd. trustees Heifer Internat. Found. Recipient Pub. Svc. award, 1987, Gov.'s Outstanding Citizen award, 1988, George award Rapid City C. of C., 1994; named Outstanding Chirperson, United Way, 1986, S.D. Guardian Small Bus., 1991. Mem. LWV, Women's Network, Mt. Rushmore Soc., Indian-White Coun., Toastmasters, Ninety-niners, Rapid City Fine Arts Coun. Republican. Methodist. Avocations: flying (lic. pvt. pilot), snow skiing, scuba diving, reading.*

HILLARD, WONDA YVETTE, art educator, artist; b. Phila., Nov. 20, 1958; d. Richard Hillard and Angela McFadden Watkins; m. J. B. Utsey, Sept. 5, 1982 (div. May 1996); children: Jasmine A. Utsey, Jared B. Utsey. BA in Art Edn., S.C. State U., 1981, MEd, 1988. Educator art Bowman Elem. Sch., SC, 1981—88, St. George Elem. Sch., St. George, 1988—96, Tri County Sch.s, Walterboro, 1992—98, Brook Glenn Elem. Sch., Taylors, 1996—98, Oakview Elem. Sch., Simpsonville, 1996—2002, Phillis Wheatley Ctr., Greenville, 2003, Bell's Crossing Elem. Sch., Simpsonville, 2002—. Presenter Intergrating Art in Curriculum, Simpsonville, SC, 2002; pub. rels. Kenny Smith Basketball Camp, St. George, 1995; pres. St. George Elem. Sch. PTA, 1993—95. One-woman shows include Moja Arts Festival, 2002, Claflin U., 2002, murals, Instr. mag., 1984. Grantee, Alliance Quality Edn., Greenville, 2002. Mem.: S.C. Alliance Art Educators, S.C. Educators Assn., S.C. Art Educators Assn., Nat. Art Educators Assn. Avocations: drawing, painting, kickboxing, aerobics, dance.

HILLEGASS, CHRISTINE ANN, psychologist; b. Lancaster, Pa., July 13, 1952; d. Michael and Ann Christine (Wolf) Hillegass; m. F. Thomas Shellenberg, 1998. BA, Bard Coll., 1975; MA in Forensic Psychol., John Jay Coll. Criminal Justice, 1979; PsyD, Rutgers U., 1993. Lic. psychologist N.J., Mont. Staff psychologist Adult Diagnostic Treatment Ctr., N.J. Dept. Corrections, Avenel, 1979-84; dir. Monmouth County Sexual Abuse Treatment and Prevention Program, Ocean, N.J., 1984-87; staff various mental health, social svc., correctional and law enforcement agencies, 1987—99; pvt. practice Livingston, Mont., 1999—. Mem. Monmouth County Sexual Abuse Coalition, 1983—, chair, 1986-87, co-chair, 1987-88; mem. N.J. Statewide Sexual Abuse Network, 1984-89, Monmouth Prosecutor's Task Force on Child Abuse, Freehold, N.J., 1985-86. Bd. dirs. Park County Red Cross, 1999—, Tri-County Network Against Domestic and Sexual Violence, 1999—. Recipient Woman of Achievement award Monmouth County Adv. Commn. on Status of Women, 1987. Mem. APA, Mont. Psychol. Assn., Am. Profl. Soc. on Abuse of Children, Nat. Adolescent Perpetration Network. Office: 320 N Main St Ste 5 Livingston MT 59047-2000

HILLENBRAND, LAURA, writer; b. Fairfax, Va., 1967; Student, Kenyon Coll. Editor: Equus Mag., 1989—; contbr. articles to mags.; author: Seabiscuit: An American Legend, 2001 (finalist Nat. Book Critics Cir. award). Office: Ballantine Books Random House 1745 Broadway New York NY 10019

HILLERT, GLORIA BONNIN, anatomist, educator; b. Brownton, Minn., Jan. 25, 1930; d. Edward Henry and Lydia Magdalene (Luebker) Bonnin; m. Richard Hillert, Aug. 20, 1960; children: Kathryn, Virginia, Jonathan. BS, Valparaiso (Ind.) U., 1953; MA, U. Mich., 1958. Instr. Springfield (Ill.) Jr. Coll., 1953-57; teaching asst. U. Mich., Ann Arbor, 1957-59, instr. [illegible], Ill., 1958-59, asst. prof. Concordia Coll., River Forest, Ill., 1959-63; vis. instr. Wright Jr. Coll., Chgo., 1974-76, Ill. Benedictine Coll., Lisle, 1977-78, Rosary Coll., River Forest, 1976-81; prof. anatomy and physiology Triton Coll., River Grove, 1982-92, prof. emeritus, 1992—; vis. asst. prof. Concordia U., 1993—. Vis. instr. Wheaton (Ill.) Coll., 1988; advisor Springfield Jr. Coll. Sci. Club, 1953-57, Concordia Coll. Cultural Group, 1959-62; program dir. Triton Coll. Sci. Lectr. Series, 1983-87; participant Internat. Educators Workshop in Amazonia, 1993. Dem. campaign asst., Maywood, Ill., 1972, 88; vol. Mental Health Orgn., Chgo., 1969-73, Earthwatch, St. Croix, 1987, Costa Rica, 1989, Internat. Med. Care Team, Guatemala, 1995, Earthwatch End of Dinosaurs, 1997. Mem. AAUW, Ill. Assn. Community Coll. Biol. Tchrs., Nat. Assn. Biol. Tchrs. Lutheran. Avocation: traveling. Home: 1620 Clay Ct Melrose Park IL 60160-2419 Office: Triton Coll 2000 N 5th Ave River Grove IL 60171-1907

HILLERY, MARY JANE LARATO, columnist, television personality, television producer, writer, military officer; b. Boston, Sept. 15, 1931; d. Donato and Porzia (Avellis) Larato; m. Thomas H. Hillery, Feb. 25, 1961; 1 son, Thomas H. Assoc. Sci. (scholar), Northea. U., 1950; BS, U. Mass. Harvard Extension, 1962; grad., Command and Gen. Staff Coll., 1982. Sales agt., linguist Pan Am. Airways, Boston, 1955-61; interpreter Internat. Conf. Fire Chiefs, Boston, 1966; tchr. Spanish YWCA, Natick, Mass., 1966-67; cmty. rels. cons., adv. bd. dirs., lectr. for migrant edn. project divsn., Mass. Dept. Cmty. Affairs, Boston, 1967-69; editor-in-chief Sudbury (Mass.) Citizen, 1967-76; assoc. editor The Beacon, 1976-79, contbg. editor, 1979-83; area editl. adviser Beacon Pub. Co., Acton, Mass., 1970-80, editor, 1976-80; columnist Town Crier, 1987—; contbg. editor Towne Talk, 1975-79, Citizens' Forum, 1975-81; editor Spl. Forces Ann. History, 1989-90; dir. pub. affairs Mass. Dept. Environ Quality Engring., 1981-83; prodr., host TV interview show For the Record, 1985—. Pub. affairs officer Fed. Emergency Mgmt. Agy., 1995-2003; women vets. spkr. State House Mass. ofcl. Vets. Day observances, ceremonies, 1999. Editor Hansconian, 1983-85. Mem. Bus. Adv. Com., 1972-77, Sudbury Sch. Com., 1976-77; mem. Meml. Day Celebration Com., 1972—, master of ceremonies, 1973—, parade marshal, 1997, 2003; chmn. Sudbury WWII Commemorativ e Cmty., 1992-96; chmn. Sudbury Korean War 50th Anniversary Commemorative Com., 2000—; mem. Sudbury Town Report, 1967-72, 85-88, chmn., 1969-72; chmn. Sudbury Vets. Adv. Com., 1986-92; panelist Internat. Women's Year Symposium, 1975, Women in Politics, 1987, Women in Mil., 1987; mem. congl. 5th dist. Mass. nomination bd. West Point, apptd. mil. aide-de-camp to Mass. Gov. Wm. Weld, 1992—; Veterans' agt. Town of Sudbury, 1992—. With USN, 1950-54; lt. col. USAR; Persian Gulf, 1991-92; liaison officer U.S. Mil. Acad. West Point, 1976-89, 93—; pub. affairs officer 94th USAR Command, 1982-83, Office of Sec. of Def., The Pentagon, Washington, 1989-93; dir. pub. rels. Mission One, Employer Support Guard and Res., Dept. of Def.; parade marshall Sudbury Meml. Day Parade, 2003. Decorated Meritorious Svc. medal, 1985, Joint Svc. Achievement medal, 1991, Nat. Def. medal-Bronze Star, 1991, Outstanding Svc. award Sec. Def. Pub. Affairs, 1992, Joint Meritorious unit award, 1992, Def. Superior Svc. medal, 1993, Employer Support Guard and Res. Mission One award, 1999; named Editor of Yr., Beacon Pub. Co., 1970; recipient medal of appreciation Internat. Order DeMolay, 1969, cert. of appreciation U.S. Def. Civil Preparedness Agy., 1975, Mass. Bicentennial Commn., 1976, Appreciation award U.S. Mil. Acad., 1976-86, citations Mass. State Senate, 1979, 82, Newswriting award Media Contest Air Force Sys. Command, 1984, Outstanding Svc. award Sec. Def. Pub. Affairs, 1991, Cmty. Citizen award Citizen of Yr., Sudbury Grange, 1999, Cmty. Svc. award DAR, 2000, George Washington Honor medal Bay State chpt. Freedoms Found. at Valley Forge, 1998. Mem. LWV (dir. 1964-68), Nat. Editl. Assn., Nat. Newspaper Assn., Nat. Press Club, Rotary Internat. (mem. Sudbury chpt. scholarship chmn. 1993—, bd. dirs. 1994-95, 96-97, 97—, pub. rels. chmn. 1995-97, assoc. editor The Bull., 1996-97, Found. chmn. 1997-99, pres.-elect 2000-01, pres. 2001-02), New Eng. Press Assn., Internat. Platform Assn. (Silver Bowl award for poetry 1997), Bus. and Profl. Women's Club (Sudbury 1st v.p. 1973, pres. 1973-76, parliamentarian 1978-88, 90-92, legis. chair 1990-92, state bylaws com. 1977-78, 79-81, 86-88, state legis. chmn. 1979-81, 86-88, state polit. action com. chmn. 1988-89, Woman of Yr. 1979, Woman of Achievement 1982), Nat. League Am. Pen Women (exec. bd. Boston 1974-76, 78-88, pres. Boston br. 1976-78, 94-98, 2000—, state exec. bd. 1994-1998, publicity chmn. 1979-80, chmn. bylaws com. 1979-80, 86-88, parliamentarian 1978-80, 82-88, auditor 1980-82, 84-88, 1st v.p. 1988-92, nat. editor Achievements, The Pen Woman 1992-94, nat. protocol chairperson 1998, nat. scholarship chmn. 1998—, nat. 4th v.p. 2000-02, nat. 3d v.p. 200204), Res. Officers Assn. (life, dept. sec. 1978-79, dept. army v.p. 1992-95, pres. Boston chpt. 1986-88, dept. pres.-elect 1995-96, dept. pres. 1996-97, army v.p. 1995-96, army coun. rep. 1989-92, 1999—, budget com., 1990-91, dept. publicity chmn. 1988-92, editor Advisor 1991-95, Outstanding Svc. award 1978-79, co-chair Nat. Conv. 1995-98), Spl. Forces Assn. (Green Berets, asst. to chmn. nat. conv. 1999-2000), Am. Legion (post comdr. 2000-01, exec. bd. 1996—, chaplain 1996-2000, 2002-, vet. svc. officer 2001—), Korean War Vets. Mass. (life), Omega Sigma. Home: 66 Willow Rd Sudbury MA 01776-2663

HILLERY, SUSIE MOORE, retired elementary school educator; b. Lunenburg County, VA, Feb. 25, 1928; d. William Edward and Sarah Anderson Moore; m. Herbert Vincent Hillery, June 17, 1956 (div. Jan. 1969); children: Vincent, Nathan. BA, Lynchburg Coll., 1950; MA, U. Ky., 1955; student, Lexington Sem., Ky.; student, U. Va., U. Tex. Youth min. Christian Ch. Disciples of Christ, Clarksville, Tenn., 1950—52; tchr. religious edn. Martinsville (Va.) Pub. Sch., 1952—53; elem. sch. tchr. Lynchburg (Va.) Pub. Schs., 1953—54, Austin (Tex.) Pub. Schs., 1956—58, 1964—69, Henrico County Pub. Schs., Richmond, Va., 1969—91; youth min. Colonial Christian Ch., Richmond, 1983—86; pastor/min. Christian Ch., Gordonsville, Va., 1993—98, Bella Grove Christian Ch., Louisa, Va., 1998—2000; vol. chaplain Henrico Drs. Hosp., Richmond, 1999—. Rep. Interfaith Coun., 1993—; with Ch. Women United, 1998—.

HILLGREN, SONJA DOROTHY, journalist; b. Sioux Falls, SD, May 17, 1948; d. Ralph Oliver and Priscilla Adaline (Mannes) Hillgren; m. Ralph Lee Hill (dec.). BJ, U. Mo., 1970, MA, 1972; postgrad., Harvard U., 1982—83. Washington corr. Ohio-Washington News Svc., 1972-73; reporter UPI, Annapolis, Md., 1974-76, reporter, editor Washington, 1976-78, farm editor, 1978-88; Washington corr. Knight-Ridder, Washington, 1988-90; Washington editor Farm Jour., 1990-95, editor, 1995—2004, sr. v.p., 2000—. Exec.-in-residence U. Mo., 1997; campaign steering com. U. Mo. Sch. Journalism, 2003—. Chair bd. dirs. Nat. Press Bldg. Corp., 1997; bd. dirs. Winrock Internat., Philabundance, 2000—. Named Old Master, Purdue U., 1992, Agrl. Communicator of Yr., Nat. Agri-Mktg. Assn., 1996; recipient J.R. Russell award, Newspaper Farm Editors Am., 1985, Reuben Brigham award, Agrl. Comms. in Edn., 1988, Oscar in Agr. for Excellence in Agrl. Reporting, U. Ill., 1998, Recognition of Excellence in Print Media award, Ill. Soybean Assn., 2002, Prodr. Comms. award, United Soybean Bd., 2003; Nieman fellow, Harvard U., 1982—83, Woodrow Wilson vis. fellow, 1993—94. Mem.: AAUW, Coun. on Fgn. Rels., Farm Found., Nat. Agri-Mktg. Assn., Am. Agrl. Editors' Assn., Am. Soc. Mag. Editors, Soc. Profl. Journalists, N.Am. Assn. Agrl. Journalists (pres. 1987—88), Congl. Country Club, Nat. Press Club (bd. govs. 1991—96, chair 1993—94, v.p. 1995, pres. 1996), Alpha Zeta, Pi Beta Phi (Carolyn Helman Lichtenberg Crest award 1999). Lutheran. Avocations: sports, reading. Home: 315 S 18th St Philadelphia PA 19103-6619 Office: Farm Jour 1818 Market St Fl 31 Philadelphia PA 19103-3654 E-mail: shillgren@farmjournal.com.

HILLIARD, CELIA, writer, educator; b. Chgo., May 9, 1942; d. Carl Franz Schmid and Isabelle Grossman; m. David Craig Hilliard, Feb. 16, 1974. BA, Northwestern U., Evanston, Ill., 1964. Contbr. chapters to books, articles to profl. jours.; author: Providing a Home-A History of the Old People's Home of the City of Chicago, [illegible], Then and Now-Thirty Years of the Newberry Library Associates, 1995, The Woman's Athletic Club of Chicago-A History, 1999. Trustee The Poetry Found., Chgo.; mem. Northwestern U. Women's Bd., Evanston, Ill., Chgo. Hist. Soc. Guild, Antiquarian Soc., Chgo., Textile Soc., Chgo. Mem.: The Casino, Woman's Athletic Club Chgo., The Caxton Club. Home: 1320 N State Pky Chicago IL 60610

HILLIARD, LIL, sales executive; b. Montgomery, Ala, Sept. 30, 1955; d. Louis C. and Laura M. Brewington; (div. Feb. 1, 1992); 1 child, Jeremiah Brewington. AA, So. Jr. Coll., 1974; student, Ala. State U. Sales rep. Lucky Heart Cosmetics, Memphis, Vulcan Svc., Birmingham, Ala. Avon rep., 1998-2001. Sec. Gibbs Village Cmty. Ctr., Montgomery, 1996-97; pres. Levi Watkins Libr. Club Ala. State U., 1999-2000. Recipient Golden Poet award, Poetry Guild, Calif., 1990. Mem. Custom Clothier Assn., Xperte Profl. Orgn. Democrat. Home: 2001 Terminal Rd Apt B Montgomery AL 36108-3136

HILLINGER, EDITH, artist; b. Berlin, Nov. 12, 1933; arrived in Turkey, 1937,arrived in U.S., 1948; d. Franz and Margaret (Griegoleit) Hillinger; m. Laurence Singer, 1974 (div. 1993). Cert. in painting, Cooper Union Sch. Art, 1964; BA, NYU, 1976. One-woman shows include Pro Arts-East Bay Open Studios, 1996, America House Gallery, Munich, Germany, 1986, Bluxome Gallery, San Francisco, Calif., 1983, Shirley Cerf Gallery, San Francisco, 1981, Electro Arts Gallery, 1981, Caravan House Gallery, N.Y.C., 1976, First Nat. City Bank, 1974, exhibited in group shows at Bklyn. Mus., 1975, Birmingham (Ala.) Mus. Art, 1975, Silvermine Guild of Artists, New Canaan, Conn., 1975, Chatham Coll., Pitts., 1976, NYU Gallery, 1976, Braithwaite Fine Arts Gallery, National, Utah, 1977, 1979, Minn. Mus. of Art, St. Paul, 1977, 24 Sather Gate Gallery, Berkeley, Calif., 1978, Kaiser Ctr., Oakland, Calif., 1979, Berkeley (Calif.) Art Ctr., 1979, Glyptok Mus., Copenhagen, Denmark, 1980, Reese Bullen Gallery, Arcada, Calif., 1980, 1982, Richmond (Calif.) Art Ctr., 1980, Library of Congress, High Art Tech., Washington, D.C., 1981, Capricorn Asunder Gallery, San Francisco, 1981, Bluxome Gallery, 1981, Alta Bates Cmty. Art Gallery, Berkeley, Calif., 1982, Humboldt State U., Arcada, Calif., 1982, Chevron Gallery, San Francisco, 1982, Sun Gallery, Hayward, Calif., 1983, Walnut Creek (Calif.) Art Gallery, 1983, Princeton U. Art Mus., 1983, Electrostatics Internat., Cleve., 1984, Cleve. State U. Gallery, 1984, Watercolor Gallery, Berkeley, Calif., 1985, Riverside (Calif.) Art Mus., 1986, All Calif. Biennial Juried Exhbn., 1986, Pyramid Art Gallery, Rochester, N.Y., 1986, Collage at N.A.M.E., Chgo., 1988, Pro Arts, Oakland, Calif., 1989, 1991, Gallery Imago, San Francisco, 1990, North Berkeley Frame Gallery, 2000, exhibitions include Pro Arts 2000 Juried Annual, 2000, Gallery Route One, 16th Ann. Juried Exhbn., 2001, Calif. Small Works 2001, 2001, Berkeley Art Ctr. Ann. Member Exhbn., 2001, Laguna Art Mus., Sales and Rental Gallery Exhbn., 2001, Women Made Gallery, Chgo., 2001, Nexus Gallery, 5th Nat. Juried Exhbn., N.Y.C., 2001, Pro Arts Juried Ann., Oakland, Calif., 2001—02, Claudia Chapline Gallery, Stenson Beach, Calif., 2002; contbr. articles to profl. catalogs, jours. Avocations: reading, travel, gardening. Home and Studio: 1711 9th St Berkeley CA 94710

HILLMAN, CAROL BARBARA, communications executive, consultant; b. Sept. 6, 1940; d. Joseph Hoppenfeld and Elsa (Spiegel) Hoppenfeld Resika; m. Howard D. Hillman, May 25, 1969. BA with honors, U. Wis., 1961; postgrad., U. Lyon, France, 1961-62; MA, Cornell U., 1966. Asst. editor Holt Rinehart & Winston Pubs., 1965-66; staff assoc. pub. rels. Ea. Airlines, N.Y.C., 1966-74; pub. affairs mgr. Squibb Corp., N.Y.C., 1974-75; asst. dir. corp. pub. rels. Burlington Industries, N.Y.C., 1975-77, dir. corp. pub. rels., 1977-80, v.p. pub. rels., 1980-82; v.p. corp. comms. Norton Co., Worcester, Mass., 1982-89, sr. cons., 1989-90; nat. dir. pub. rels. and comms. Deloitte & Touche, Wilton, Conn., 1990-91; v.p. univ. rels. Boston U., 1991-95; prin. Hillman & Kersey Strategic Comms., 1995-2000, CB Hillman & Assocs., 2000—. Mem. pub. affairs coun. Machinery and Allied Products Inst., 1982-89; mem. dep. policy com., agenda com. Mass. Bus. Roundtable, 1982-89, vice-chair; trustee Mass. Econ. Stblzn. Trust, 1986-2003; bd. dirs. Commonwealth Corp., 1995—, vice chair, 2003—. Mem. Cornell Coun., Ithaca, 1981—85, pub. rels. com., 1981—88; mem. adv. coun. Coll. Human Ecology, Cornell U., Ithaca, 1982—84; mem. bd. visitors coll. letter sci. U. Wis., 1996—99; mem. adv. bd. Ct. Apptd. Spl. Advocates, Worcester, 1983—87; bd. dirs. Planned Parenthood League Mass., 1986—90, pub. affairs com., 1991—2002; trustee Quinsigamond C.C., Worcester, 1987—98; mem. exec. com. Save America's Treasures: Preserving Eleanor Roosevelt's Home at Val-Kill, 2000—; voting mem. Wis. Union Trustees, U. Wis., Madison, 1982—, trustee, 1990—; mem. Clark U. Assocs., Worcester, 1983—89. Fulbright scholar, U. Lyon, 1961—62, Cornell grad. fellow, 1962—63. Mem. Internat. Women's Forum, Mass. Women's Forum, The Wisemen, Phi Beta Kappa, Mortar Bd., Phi Kappa Phi. Home: 299 Belknap Rd Framingham MA 01701-4716 Office: CB Hillman & Assocs 299 Belknap Rd Framingham MA 01701-4716 Office Phone: 508-877-2916. E-mail: chillman96@aol.com.

HILLMAN, CAROL DOROTHY MARY, editor, genealogist, small business owner, artist; d. Geraldine Sophia Dorothea Hillman. BS in Design, U. of Mich., 1957; MA in Art, Mich. State U., 1962. Asst. editor, rsch. assoc., libr. The Med. Letter on Drugs and Therapeutics, N.Y.C., 1965—76, assoc. editor, 1976—93; prin., owner KINFO, Kerhonkson, 1990—; freelance sci. copy editor Kerhonkson, NY, 1993—. Graphics designer Sullivan County Cmty. Chorus, Loch Sheldrake, NY, 2000—. Editor: (book) The Medical Letter Handbook of Drug Interactions, 6 edits.; author: Index to the Parish Register of Drung and Larah, Diocese of Kilmore, Co Cavan, Ireland., 1995, Abstracts and index to guardianship Letters, Westchester Co, NY 1802-1896, 1995, Handwritten Comments in the Margins of the Twelve Decisive Battles of the Civil War, by William Swinton, 1997, Christ Lutheran Church and 2nd Dutch Reformed Church, Ellenville, NY, 1995; one-woman shows include Pub. Libr. Gallery, Ellenville, N.Y., 2001, exhibitions include Orange County Annual Juried Art Exhbn., Sugar Loaf, N.Y., 2000—. Vol. Mid. Sch., Ellenville, NY, 2000—03; active Ulster County Arts Coun.; election insp. Ulster County Bd. of Elections, Rochester, NY, 1997—2003, Sullivan County Bd. Elections, Mamakating, NY, 1993—97. Mem.: Nat. Geneal. Soc., Marbletown Arts Assn., Sullivan County Cmty. Chorus (bd. mem. 1999—2003). Democrat. Lutheran. Avocations: singing, bowling, study.

HILLMAN, JENNIFER ANNE, commissioner, ambassador, trade negotiator; b. lawyer, Toledo, Jan. 29, 1957; d. Charles Winchell and Anne Sylvia (Mossberg) H.; m. Mitchell Rand Berger, Oct. 20, 1990; children: Benjamin Stanley Berger, Daniel Charles Berger. BA, Duke U., 1978, MEd, 1979; JD, Harvard U., 1983. Bar: D.C., U.S. Ct. Internat., U.S. Mil. Appeals. Asst. to chancellor Duke U., Durham, N.C., 1979-80; freshman Proctor Harvard U., Cambridge, Mass., 1981-83; assoc. Patton, Boggs & Blow, Washington, 1983-87; legis. asst. Senator Terry Sanford, Washington, 1987-88, legis. dir., 1988-92; dep. cluster coord. for fin. instns. U.S. Presdl. and Vice Presdl. Transition Team, Washington, 1992-93; ambassador, chief textile negotiator Office of U.S. Trade Rep., Exec. Office of Pres., Washington, 1993-95; gen. counsel Office of the U.S. Trade Rep., 1995-97; commr. Internat. Trade Commn., Washington, 1998—; vice-chmn. U.S. Internat. Trade Commn., 2002—. Trustee Duke U., 1977-80. Adviser Terry Sanford for Senate Campaign, 1986, 1992; Trinity Coll. bd. visitors Duke U., 1999—; commr. Stoddert Youth Soccer, 2000—; mem. N.C. Dems., Raleigh, 1986—, Georgetown Presbyn. Ch., 1988—; tchr. adult learning Sacred Heart, Washington, 1983—92. Mem. Coun. on Women's Studies Duke U., Phi Beta Kappa. Avocations: running, scuba diving, traveling, reading. Office: Internat Trade Commn 500 E St NW Washington DC 20436-0001

HILLMAN, KATHY ROBINSON, librarian; b. Sonora, Tex., Aug. 5, 1951; d. Thomas Payne and Mary Allie (Barton) Robinson; m. John Royce Hillman, Dec. 22, 1973; children: John Marshall, Michael Thomas, Holly Michelle-Marie. BA summa cum laude, Baylor U., 1973, postgrad., 1976-80; MLS, U. North Tex., 1976. Cert. tchr., Tex. Tchr./libr. Eldorado (Tex.) H.S., 1974-76; asst. acquisitions libr. Baylor U., Waco, Tex., 1976-79, assoc. prof. acquisitions libr., 1980—. Co-author: Devotions from the World of Sports, 1998, Devotions from the World of Women's Sports, 2000; contbr. articles to profl. jours. Adv. bd. Heart O' the Hills Camp, Hunt, Tex., 1993—, Camp Stewart for Boys, Hunt, 1993—; bd. dirs. Paisano Bapt. Encampment, Alpine, Tex., 1996—; vol. Jr. League, Waco, 1985-89, 92—; bd. dirs. Baylor Bear Found., 1995-96; promotional v.p. Tex. Woman's Missionary Union, Dallas, 1988-92, pres., 2000—; v.p. Woman's Missionary Union SBC, 2000—; mem. com., house bd. Hist. Waco Found., 1976—; mem. Waco Symphony Coun., 1988—. Named Outstanding Alumni Mortar Bd., 1989, Outstanding Young Alumni, Baylor U., 1989. Mem. Tex. Libr. Assn. (life, chair acquisitions roundtable 1984-85), So. Bapt. Libr. Assn. (rec. sec. 1996-98, v.p. 1999-2000, pres. 2000-01), Baylor Alumni Assn. (life, sec. Class of 1973, 1973—), Waco Alumnae Panehllenic (pres. 1986-87), Delta Delta Delta. Avocations: writing, spectator sports, drama, photography. Home: 8505 Oakdale Dr Waco TX 76712-3557 Office: Baylor Univ PO Box 97151 Waco TX 76798-7151 E-mail: kathy_hillman@baylor.edu.

HILLMAN, MARGUERITE AGNES, literary agent, consultant; b. Oshkosh, Wis., Nov. 12, 1948; d. William C.J. Hillman and M. Joan Hastings; children: Kristen, Matthew, Sara, Tarla. BA in Lit., San Diego (Calif.) State U., 1970, MA in Am. Studies, 1977. Mgr. Anderson Consulting, San Diego; dir. Jostens Learning, San Diego; v.p. Lightspan, Inc., San Diego; prin. Hillman Consulting, San Diego; CEO Cosmos Literacy, Inc., San Diego. Mem. adv. bd. Ad Hoc, San Francisco. Author: Kazmanee, 1998, Felipe The Frog, 2001. Mem. com. North Coast Repertory Theatre, San Diego, 2003—. Democrat. Avocations: writing, boxing, travel.

HILLMAN, SANDRA SCHWARTZ, public relations executive, marketing professional; b. Chester, Pa., 1941; m. Robert S. Hillman, Apr. 1964; children: Pamela Hillman Loeb, Allison Buchalter. BA, Pa. State U., 1962. Assoc. editor McFadden-Bartell Pub., N.Y.C., 1963-64; pub. rels. account exec. Edward M. Meyers & Assocs., N.Y.C., 1964-66; info. officer Nat. Tchr. Corps, U.S. Office Edn., Washington, 1966-68, Balt. Dept. Housing and Cmty. Devel., 1968-71; prin., CEO Trahan, Burden & Charles, Inc., 1984—. Mktg., pub. rels. cons. to cities of Pitts., San Diego, Buffalo, Niagara Falls, N.Y., N.Y.C., Miami, Milw., Curacao, Netherlands Antilles, Charleston, Chattahooga, Edinburg; mem. bd. Gov.'s Tourism Task Force; presenter, lectr. in field. Bd. dirs. Balt. Symphony Orch., World Trade Ctr. Inst., Balt. City Found., Boy Scouts Am., Md. Film Commn., The Nat. Aquarium, Jr. League Cmty. Coun., Urban League; pres. Balt. Ctr. for Performing Arts, 1976-92. Recipient Lifetime Achievement award Balt. Pub. Rels. Soc., 1996. Fellow Pa. State U. (Disting. 1991); mem. Gov.'s World Trade Ctr. Inst. (mem. bd., coms.), Md. C. of C. (strategic planning com.), Children's Theater Assn. Office: Trahan Burden & Charles 1030 N Charles St Baltimore MD 21201-5442

HILLMER, LOIS MARGURITE, retired receptionist; b. Vick, Ark., June 2, 1917; d. Thomas Oscar and Effie Ellen (Sledd) Clanton; m. Robert Carrol Owen, Dec. 8, 1933 (div. Nov. 1965); stepchildren: Armin Reid Hillmer, Terry Morphew; m. Armin F. Hillmer, Nov. 2, 1966; children: David Owen, Kathy Driski, Randi Midgley. Student, Monticello A&M, 1936. Saleswoman Hardin Stockton Realtors, Prairie Village, Kans., 1965-73; lobby receptionist Shawnee Mission (Kans.) State Bank, 1973-78. Mem. women's coun. Nat. Real Estate Bd., Chgo., 1963-73; precinct committeewoman Republican Party, Overland Park, Kans., 1967—; mem. Bd. Zoning Appeals, Overland Park; charter mem. Republican Presdl. Task Force, Washington. Lutheran. Avocations: porcelin dolls, golf, gardening, horses.

HILLMER, MARGARET PATRICIA, library director; b. Cirencester, Gloucestershire, Eng., Mar. 17, 1936; came to U.S., 1960; naturalized, 1973; d. John Albert and Margaret Evelyn (Richardson) Hall; m. Max Lorraine Hillmer, Mar. 24, 1962; children: Felicity Margaret, Jennifer Anne. ALAM, London Acad. Music Dram. Art, London, 1955; AB magna cum laude, Heidelberg Coll., 1976; AM in Libr. Sci., U. Mich., 1977. Cert. libr. Ohio. Speech and ballet tchr., Cirencester, 1955-58; governess, 1959-60; ballet instr., choreographer Heidelberg Coll., Tiffin, Ohio, 1969-73, adminstrv. asst. pub. rels. Water Quality Lab., 1978-79; head reference dept. Tiffin-Seneca Pub. Libr., 1979-80, libr. dir., 1980—. Contbr. articles to profl. publs. Chair Take Our Daughters to Work Day, 1993-2000; bd. dirs. Tiffin-Seneca Teen Ctr., 1992—; mem. Tiffin City Schs. Bd. Edn., 1991—, pres., 1995-96; mem. Seneca County Dept. Human Svcs. Bd., 1984-91, pres., 1987-89. Recipient Liberty Bell award Seneca County Bar Assn., 1990, People's Law Sch. award Ohio Acad. Trial Lawyers, 1993, Athena award Tiffin Area C. of C., 1999. Mem. ALA, AAUW, LWV (pres. Tiffin chpt. 1980-82, chair internat. rels. Ohio 1975-76), Ohio Libr. Assn. (legislation com. 1985-89, chair legis. network 1989-93, chair awards and honors com. 1995-96, seminar spkr. 1985—), Pub. Libr. Assn., Freedom to Read Assn., Tiffin Rotary Club (pres. 2001-02), Beta Phi Mu. Democrat. Episcopalian. Avocations: reading, theater, classical music. Home: 25 Southview Pl Tiffin OH 44883-3312 Office: Tiffin-Seneca Pub Libr 77 Jefferson St Tiffin OH 44883-2339 E-mail: hillmepa@oplin.org.

HILLS, CARLA ANDERSON, lawyer, former federal official; b. Los Angeles, Jan. 3, 1934; d. Carl H. and Edith (Hume) Anderson; m. Roderick Maltman Hills, Sept. 27, 1958; children: Laura Hume, Roderick Maltman, Megan Elizabeth, Alison Macbeth. AB cum laude, Stanford U., 1955; student, St. Hilda's Coll., Oxford (Eng.) U., 1954; LLB, Yale U., 1958; hon. degrees, Pepperdine U., 1975, Washington U., 1977, Mills Coll., 1977, Lake Forest Coll., 1978, Williams Coll., 1981, Notre Dame U., 1993, Wabash Coll., 1997. Bar: Calif. 1959, DC 1974, US Supreme Ct. 1965. Asst. US atty. civil divsn., LA, 1958-61; ptnr. Munger, Tolles, Hills & Rickershauser, LA, 1962-74; asst. atty. gen. civil divsn. Justice Dept., Washington, 1974-75; sec. HUD, 1975-77; ptnr. Latham, Watkins & Hills, Washington, 1978-86, Weil, Gotshal & Manges, Washington, 1986-88; US trade rep. Exec. Office of the Pres., 1989-93; chmn., CEO Hills & Co. Internat. Cons., 1993—. Chair Nat. Com. for US-China Rels.; bd. dir. Inst. for Internat. Econ., CSIS, Asia Soc., Am. Internat. Group, AOL-Time Warner, Lucent Tech., Inc., Chevron Texaco Corp., TCW Group, Inc.; mem. adv. bd. Calif. Coun. on Criminal Justice, 1969—71; adj. prof. Sch. Law UCLA, 1972; mem. corrections task force LA County Sub-Regional; mem. standing com. discipline US Dist. Ct. for Ctrl. Calif., 1970—73; mem. Adminstrv. Conf. US, 1972—74; bd. councillors U. So. Calif. Law Ctr., 1972—74; mem. at large exec. com. Yale Law Sch., 1973—78; mem. exec. com. law and free soc. State Bar Calif., 1973; trustee Pomona Coll., 1974—79; mem. com. on Law Sch. Yale U. Coun.; mem. Sloan Commn. on Govt. and Higher Edn., 1977—79, Internat. Found. for Cultural Cooperation and Devel., 1977—89, Am. Com. on East-West Accord, 1977—79, Trilateral Commn., 1977—82; mem. adv. com. Princeton U., Woodrow Wilson Sch. of Pub. and Internat. Affairs, 1977—80; mem. Fed. Acctg. Std. Adv. Coun., 1978—80; Gordon Grand fellow Yale U., 1978; trustee Brookings Instn., 1985, Am. Productivity and Quality Ctr., 1988; coun. mem. Calif. Gov. Coun. Econ. Policy Adv., 1993—98, Coun. Fgn. Rels., 1993—; mem. Trilateral Commn., 1993—; vice-chair bd. dir. Inter-Am. Dialogue, 1999—; vice chair Coun. Fgn. Rels., 2001—. Co-author: Federal Civil Practice, 1961; co-author, editor: Antitrust Adviser, 1971, 3d edit., 1985; contbg. editor: Legal Times,

1978-88; mem. editorial bd. Nat. Law Jour., 1978-88. Trustee U. So. Calif., 1977-79, Norton Simon Mus. Art, Pasadena, Calif., 1976-80; trustee Urban Inst., 1978-89, chmn., 1983-89; co-chmn. Alliance to Save Energy, 1977-89; vice chmn. adv. coun. on legal policy Am. Enterprise Inst., 1977-84; bd. visitors, exec. com. Stanford U. Law Sch., 1978-81; bd. dir. Am. Coun. for Capital Formation, 1978-82; mem. exec. com. Inst. for Internat. Econ., 1993—; mem. adv. com. MIT-Harvard U. Joint Ctr. for Urban Studies, 1978-82. Fellow Am. Bar Found.; mem. Am.'s Soc. (bd. dir.), LA Women Lawyers Assn. (pres. 1964), ABA (chair publ. com. antitrust sect. 1972-74, council 1974, 77-84, chair 1982-83), Fed. Bar Assn. (pres. LA chpt. 1963), LA County Bar Assn. (fed. rules and practice com. 1963-72, chair issues and survey 1963-72, chair sub-com. revision local rules for fed. cts. 1966-72, jud. qualifications com. 1971-72), Am. Law Inst., Am.-China Soc. (bd. dir. 1995—), Am. Soc. (bd. trustees), Asia Soc. (bd. trustees), Yale of So. Calif. Club (bd. dir. 1972-74), Yale Club. Clubs: Yale of So. Calif. (dir. 1972-74); Yale (Washington). Office: Hills & Co 901 15th St NW Ste 400 Washington DC 20005

HILLS, PATRICIA GORTON SCHULZE, curator; b. Baraboo, Wis., Jan. 31, 1936; d. Hartwin A. Schulze and Glennie Gorton Baker; m. Frederic W. Hills, Jan. 17, 1958 (div. Feb. 1974); children: Christina, Bradford; m. Guy Kevin Whitfield, Jan. 3, 1976; 1 child, Andrew. BA, Stanford U., 1957; MA, Hunter Coll., 1968; PhD, NYU, 1973. Curatorial asst. Mus. Modern Art, N.Y.C., 1960-62; guest curator Whitney Mus. Am. Art, 1971-72, assoc. curator 18th and 19th Century art, 1972-74; vis. asst. prof. art dept. Hunter Coll., 1973; adj. assoc. prof. fine arts Inst. Fine Arts NYU, 1973-74; assoc. prof. fine arts and performing arts York Coll. CUNY, 1974-78; assoc. prof. dept. art history Boston U., 1978-88, prof., 1988—, chmn. dept., 1995-97. Adj. assoc. prof. Grad. Sch. Arts and Scis., Columbia U., 1974-75; adj. curator Whitney Mus. Am. Art, 1974-87. Author: Eastman Johnson, 1972, The American Frontier: Images and Myths, 1973, The Painters' America. Rural and Urban Life, 1810-1910, 1974, Turn-of-Century America: Paintings, Graphics, Photographs, 1890-1910, 1977, Alice Neel, 1983, Social Concern and Urban Realism: American Painting of the 1930s, 1983, John Singer Sargent, 1986, Stuart Davis, 1996, Modern Art in the USA: Issues and Controversies of the 20th Century, 2001; co-author: The Figurative Tradition and the Whitney Mus. Am. Art, 1980, Jacob Lawrence: Thirty Years of Prints: 1963-1993, Eastman Johnson: Painting America, 1999. Danforth Found. grad. fellow for women, 1968-72, John Simon Guggenheim Meml. Found. fellow, 1982-83, Charles Warren Ctr. for Studies in Am. History fellow, 1982-83, W.E.B. DuBois Inst. for Afro-Am. Rsch. fellow, Harvard U., 1991-92, NEH fellow, 1995. Mem. Coll. Art Assn., Women's Caucus for Arts, Am. Studies Assn., Am. Assn. Mus. Home: 238 Putnam Ave Cambridge MA 02139-3767 Office: Boston U Dept Art History Boston MA 02215 E-mail: pathills@bu.edu.

HILLS, REGINA J. journalist; b. Sault Sainte Marie, Mich., Dec. 24, 1953; d. Marvin Dan and Ardithanne (Tilly) H.; m. Vincent C. Stricherz, Feb. 25, 1984. BA, U. Nebr., 1976. Reporter UPI, Lincoln, Nebr., 1976-80, state editor, bur. mgr., 1981-82, New Orleans, 1982-84, Indpls., 1985-87; asst. city editor Seattle Post-Intelligencer, 1987-99, online prodr., 1999—2001, mng. prodr., 2001—. Panelist TV interview show Face Nebr., 1978-81; vis. lectr. U. Nebr., Lincoln, 1978, 79, 80; columnist weekly feature Capitol News, Nebr. Press Assn., 1981-82 Recipient Outstanding Coverage awards UPI, 1980, 82 Mem. U. Nebr. Alumni Assn., Zeta Tau Alpha. Office: Seattle Post Intelligencer 101 Elliott Ave W Ste 200 Seattle WA 98119-4295 Office Phone: 206-448-8000.

HILLSMAN, JOAN RUCKER, music educator; b. Anderson, S.C., Mar. 25, 1943; d. William Isaiah and Elizabeth Gilliard Rucker; m. Horace Jerome Hillsman (dec. Mar. 2002); 1 child, Quentin Jerome. B in Music Edn., Howard U., 1964, M in Music Edn., 1969; PhD in Musicology, Union Inst., 1978. Music tchr. St. Mary's County Pub. Schs., Leonardtown, Md., 1964—67, D.C. Pub. Schs., Washington, 1967—88, supr. music, 1988—96; ret.; prof. music Bowie (Md.) State U., 1996—. Owner, music cons., talent promoter Joan Hillsmans Music Network, Suitland, Md., 1996—; adj. music prof. Union Inst., Cin., Shenandoah Conservatory and Union Inst. Cmty. and Civic awards; organizer nation's Capitol 1st Gospel Homeless Choir. Author: Gospel: An African American Art Form, 1990, 1992, poetry. Vol. music for the elder various nursing homes, 2000—; vol. Prince George County Dems., 2002. Recipient Key to City of Detroit; Joan Hillsman's Day in the Nation's Capital named in her honor. Mem.: Music Educators Nat. Conf. (D.C. pres. 1996—2000, Outstanding Educator award 1996), Black Urban League, Top Ladies Orgn., Phi Delta Kappa, Alpha Kappa Alpha. Baptist. Avocations: music, poetry, bowling, research. Home: 3706 Stonecliff Rd Suitland MD 20746 Office: Bowie State Univ Fine and Performing Arts 14000 Jericho Park Rd Bowie MD

HILTABRAND, LINDA MAE, state official; b. La Salle, Ill., Jan. 7, 1953; d. Lyndon Dean and June Catherine (Schafer) H. AS, Illinois Valley C.C., Oglesby, Ill., 1973; BS in Agr., U. Ill., 1975. County mgr. Ill. Farm Bur., Greenville, 1975-78; reclamation specialist Ill. Dept Mines and Minerals, Springfield, 1978-95; environ. protection specialist Ill. Dept. Natural Resources, Ottawa, 1995—. Mem. Nat. Assn. State Reclamationists (pres. 1989-90, 96-97), Ill. Fedn. Bus. and Profl. Women (pres. 1992-93), Ill. Fedn. Square and Round Dance Clubs (pres. 1996-97), Ill. Square Dance Assn. (rec. sec. state coun. 1995-97, pres. 1997-99, corr. sec. 2002—), Peoria Area Square Dance Assn. (pres. 1993-95), U. Ill. Agrl. Alumni (country coord. 1988-90), Zonta (pres. La Salle-Peru 1983-85, area bd. dirs. 1986-88, parliamentarian dist. VI 1988-90, internat. environ. com. 1992-94, rec. sec. 2000-02, chmn. status of women 2002-2004). Avocations: square dancing, travel, photography. Home: 1825 Baker Ln Peru IL 61354-1834 Office: Ill Dept Natural Resources Office Mines and Minerals 424 W Main St Ottawa IL 61350-2802

HILTON, CHERYL CELESTE, music educator; d. Phinehas G. and Rebecca R. Valenti; m. Robert Allan Hilton; 1 child, Robbie. BS in Music Edn., Cen. Conn. State U., 1982; Kodaly Mus. Tng. Inst. cert., U. Hartford, 1986, Master's equivalent, 1987. Cert. profl. tchg. cert. Conn. Tchr. elem. music Martin Elem., Manchester, Conn.; choir dir. Bennet Mid. Sch., Manchester, Conn. Dir. Comty. Choir Manchester. Mem.: Am. Choral Dirs. Assn., Conn. Music Edn. Conf., Music Edn. Nat. Conf. (choral chair 2003—04). Republican. Evangelical Covenant. Avocations: gardening, reading. Office: Bennet Mid Sch 1151 Main St Manchester CT 06040

HILTON, JEAN BULL, musician; b. Northampton County, Va., Sept. 29, 1926; d. Charles Russell and Margret Davis Bull; m. Ellis Baker Hilton Jr., July 3, 1948 (dec. Mar. 1988); children: Jeffery Allan, Ellis Baker, William Russell, Andrew Douglas. BA, Randolph-Macon Woman's Coll., 1947; MSc, Old Dominion U., 1974. Music tchr. Norfolk Pub. Schs., Norfolk, Va., 1947—48, Radford Pub. Sch., Radford, Va., 1948—49; minister of music First Luth. Ch., Portsmouth, 1951—91; tchr. Portsmouth Pub. Sch., Portsmouth, Va., 1961—68, music supr., 1969—91; minister of music First Luth. Ch., 1998—. Composer songs. Recipient 1st Place award, Va. Fedn. Music Clubs, 2000. Mem.: AAUW, Va. Gateway Ctr. for the Arts, Portsmouth Cmty. Concerts, Inc., Va. Fedn. Music Clubs, Nat. Fedn. Music Clubs, Va. Music Educators Conf., Music Educators Nat. Conf., Daughters of Am. Revolution, Jamestowne Soc., Delta Kappa Gamma (Gamma chpt.). Lutheran. Avocations: reading, genealogy, exercise.

HILTON, LINDA D. academic administrator; d. Charles W. and Delores R. Neary; m. Richard D. Hilton, Nov. 23, 1973; children: Guinevere Boston, Julia. BA, Villanova Univ., Villanova, Pa., 1985—87; MS, Drexel Univ., Phila., Pa., 1987—90. Libr. The Hill Sch., Pottstown, Pa., 1985—90; dean of adminstrn. The Haverford Sch., Haverford, Pa., 1990—98; chief tech. officer Lyndon State Coll., Lyndonville, Vt., 1999—2003; chief info. officer Vt. State Coll., Waterbury, Vt., 2003—. Recipient David H. Clift Scholarship, Am. Libr. Assn., 1997. Mem.: Datatel User Group Governing Bd. (bd. mem. 2003—06). Office: Vermont State Collegtes POBox 359 Waterbury VT 05676

HILTON, NICHOLAI OLIVIA See HILTON, NICKY

HILTON, NICKY (NICHOLAI OLIVIA HILTON), apparel designer; b. Oct. 5, 1983; d. Rick and Kathy Hilton. Designer Samantha Thavasa, Tokyo, 2001—. Actor: (films) Wishman, 1991. Contbr. Free Arts for Abused Children Found. Achievements include appeared on cover of numerous mag. including Maxim, GQ, FHM, Vanity Fair, others; heiress and great-grand daughter of Conrad Hilton, founder of Hilton Hotel Chains; modeled for Anand Jon.*

HILTON, PARIS, actress; b. NYC, Feb. 17, 1981; d. Rick and Kathy Hilton. Designer Samantha Thavasa, Tokyo, 2001—. Actor: (films) Wishman, 1991, Sweetie Pie, 2000, Zoolander, 2001, QIK2JDG, 2002, Nine Lives, 2002, Wonderland, 2003, The Cat in the Hat, 2003, L.A. Knights, 2003, Raising Helen, 2004, The Hillz, 2004; (TV series) The Simple Life, 2003, (guest appearances) Saturday Night Live, 2003, Las Vegas, 2003, The O.C., 2003. Contbr. Toys for Tots. Achievements include appeared on cover of numerous mag. including Maxim, GQ, FHM, Vanity Fair, others; heiress and great-grand daughter of Conrad Hilton, founder of Hilton Hotel Chains; modeled for designers March Bouwer and Catherine Malandrino; worked on ad campaign for Italian label Iceberg.*

HILTON, SHIRLEY SHIN SIL, controller; b. Honolulu, Aug. 29, 1960; d. Harry M. H. and Sook Ja (Lee) Pai; m. Joseph F. Hilton. BBA, U. Hawaii-Manoa, Honolulu, 1983, MA, 1992. CPA, Hawaii. Acct. GA Pacific Holdings, Honolulu, 1986-87; contr. ASE Enterprises, Honolulu, 1987—99; dir. fin. Phiana Pacific, Honolulu, 1999—2001; sr. v.p. fin. and bus. devel. Convergence CT, Pleasanton, Calif., 2001—. Mem. fundraising com. Ronald McDonald House, Honolulu, 1992-94; dir., treas., v.p. Honolulu Chinese Jaycees, 1991-95, pres., 1995-96; dir. United Chinese Soc., Honolulu, 1996-98; treas. Orgn. Chinese Ams., Honolulu, 1996-97, v.p., 1998—. Recipient Miyamura Meml. award Hawaii Jaycees, 1992, Akaka award, 1994, Nakano award, 1995. Home: 3722 Keanu St Honolulu HI 96816-3840 Office: Convergence CT 6130 Stoneridge Mall Rd Ste 115 Pleasanton CA 94588 Office Phone: 808-398-7724.

HILTZ, STARR ROXANNE, sociologist, educator, computer scientist, writer, lecturer, consultant; b. Little Rock, Sept. 7, 1942; d. John Donald and Mildred V. Smyers; m. Murray Turoff, 1985; children: Jonathan David, Katherine Amanda. AB, Vassar Coll., 1963; MA, Columbia U., 1964, PhD, 1969. Prof. sociology Upsala Coll., 1969-85; info. sys. N.J. Inst. Tech., 1985-93, disting. prof. computer sci., 1993—. Cons. social impacts of computer systems. Author: Creating Community Services for Widows, 1976, (with M. Turoff) The Network Nation, 1978, 2d edit., 1993, (with E. Kerr) Computer-Mediated Communication, 1982, Online Communities, 1984, The Virtual Classroom, 1994, (with L. Harasim, L. Teles and M. Turoff) Learning Networks, 1995, (with Ricki Goldman) Learning Together Online, 2004. Recipient N.J. Woman of the Millennium for Ednl. Tech., 2000. Mem.: Assn. for Info. Sys., Assn. Computing Machinery. Unitarian Universalist. Home: 19 Meadowbrook Rd Randolph NJ 07869-3808 Office: NJ Inst Tech Info Systems Newark NJ 07102

HILYARD, VERONICA MARIE, education administrator; b. Phila., May 5, 1946; d. John Joseph and Antoinette M. (Gentile) H.; m. John W. Paquet, Mar. 25, 1972 (div. Feb. 1988); 1 child, Christopher Hilyard; m. Harley Mitchell Smith, Apr. 13, 1996. BS in Edn., Gwynedd Mercy coll., 1974; MA, Maryville U., 1991; postgrad., St. Louis U., 1997—. Elem. sch. rincipal Immaculate Conception Sch., Daidenne, Mo., 1982-87; tchr. Wentzville (Mo.) Mid. Sch., 1988-91; tchr. gifted Maryville University summer program, St. Louis, 1991, Rockwood Sch. Dist., Eureka, Mo., 1991-92, Clayton (Mo.) Sch. Dist., 1992-93, Northeast Ind. Sch. Dist., San Antonio, 1993-94; coord. gifted programs parkway Sch. Dist., St. Louis, 1994—. Adj. prof. Maryville U., St. Louis, 1997; mem. Mo. Improvement Team Dept. of Elem. and Secondary Edn. Mem. AAUW, NAGC, SAGE,Gifted Assn. of Mo., Women in Ednl. Leadership, St. Louis Metro Coun., Phi Delta Kappa (pres. 1997—). Avocations: music, reading, travel. Office: Parkway Sch Dit 12657 Fee Fee Rd Saint Louis MO 63146-4481

HIMBURG, SUSAN PHILLIPS, dietician, educator; b. Norfolk, Va., May 17, 1946; d. Claude Ralph Jr. and Sarah Ann (Gilbert) Phillips; m. James Donald Himburg, Feb. 9, 1968; 1 child, Karlene Susan. BS, Fla. State U., 1968; M in Med. Sci., Emory U., 1972; PhD, U. Miami, Fla., 1979. Dietetic intern Emory U., Atlanta, 1971; clin. dietitian Emory U. Hosp., Atlanta, 1972-73; from instr. to prof. Fla. Internat. U., Miami, 1973—, dir. coordinated program in dietetics, 1979-99, dir. health scis. recruitment and retention program, 1985—, chmn. dietetics and nutrition, 1992-97, self-study dir., 1997-2000. Grant reviewer disadvantaged assistance program HHS, Rockville, Md., 1989—; site visitor So. Assn. Colls. and Schs., Atlanta, 1987—. Author: (tng. manual) ADA Self-Study, 1988, 91, 95; contbr. articles to profl. jours. Fellow Am. Dietetic Assn. (site visitor 1985—, chairperson commn. on accreditation 1992-93, medallion 1996); mem. Soc. Nutrition Edn., Fla. Dietetic Assn. (del. 1990-2000, Disting. Dietitian 1995), Miami Dietetic Assn. (mem. nominating com. 1989, Disting. Dietitian 1994), Phi Kappa Phi, Kappa Omicron Nu. Office: Fla Internat Univ Ch 201 Dietetics & Nutritio Miami FL 33199-0001 Home: P O Box 560847 Miami FL 33256-0847 E-mail: himburgs@fiu.edu.

HIMES, BARBARA ALISON (SYDNEY KENDALL), writer; b. Cincinnati, OH, June 19, 1954; d. Albert Kendall Himes, Ruth Mary Himes., University of Cincinnati, Cincinnati, Ohio, 1973—75. Author: (Novel) A Turn for DeWurst, 2000. Mem.: Society of Children's Book Writers and Illustrators. Avocation: acting, ballroom dancing, drawing, poetry writing, playgoing, reading, jewelry design, philosophy .

HIMES, DIANE ADELE, buyer, fundraiser, actress, lobbyist; b. San Francisco, Aug. 11, 1942; d. L. John and Mary Louise (Young) H. BA, San Francisco State U., 1964. Rep. west coast home furnishings Allied Stores, nationwide; gift buyer Jordan Marsh, Miami; buyer The Broadway Stores; west coast sales mgr. Xmas divsn. Vincent Lippe Corp., L.A.; midwest sales mgr. Vincent-Lippe Chgo. Actress Nine 'O Clock Players, 1995, short film The Traveling Companion, 1998. Statewide co-chair Californians Initiative No On #102, 1988; founding co-chair Life AIDS Lobby, 1985—88; mem. Beverly Hills rent control bd., 1984; co-chair Californians Against Proposition #64, 1986; co-chmn. Mcpl. Elections Com., L.A.; co-chmn. bd. dirs. L.A. Women's Shakespeare Group, 1992—94. Named Woman of Yr. of L.A., ACLU, 1987, Christopher Street West, 1988. Avocations: acting, appearing in short films.

HIMM, EMILIE GINA, administrative analyst, records and information manager, consultant; b. Huntington, N.Y., July 12, 1946; d. Joseph Pratte and Constance Delores (Carioli) Walker; m. Thomas Robert Himm, Apr. 23, 1966; 1 child, Thomas Francis II. Student, Thomas Edison State Coll., 1990-93, 96—. Cert. Pub. Mgr., Rutgers State U., 1992. Acct. corr. McGraw Hill, Inc., Hightstown, N.J., 1966-68; supervisory and adminstrv. positions various state agencies, Trenton, N.J., 1973-85; mcpl. court adminstr. Pemberton (N.J.) Twp., 1985-86; records and info. mgr. N.J. Dept. Transp., Trenton, 1986-97, supr. records and info. mgmt., 1997—. Co-chair State Govt. Industry Action Com., Prairie Village, Kans., 1989, chair, 1990-92, 95-96, chmn. industry specific group-transp., 1996-98; mem. impact study group N.J. Dept. State, Trenton, 1991; co-chair programs Princeton ARMA, 1997-98; mem. govt. rels. com. GRECO, 1999—, chair, 2000-01; mem. N.J. State Task Force on Imaging Tech. Best Practices Methodology, 1998, state govt. advisor content mgmt., U.S. Govt Group, 2003-; spkr. at nat. and internat. seminars and confs. Contbg. writer various local govt. publs, including N.J. Dept. Transp. Records Control and Preservation Tng. Workbook and Essential Elements of Local Govt. Records Mgmt. Legis. Bd. dirs. Soroptimists Internat., 1986-88; publicity chair Little League Aux., Pemberton Twp., 1982-84; post-prom com. Bordentown (N.J.) Residents Against Drugs, 1991-93; mem. Prin.'s Adv. Coun., Bordentown, 1992; co-leader Girl Scouts Am., 1971-73; mem. N.J. Image Enabled Document Processing Storage, Retrieval and Workflow Taskforce. Mem. ASPA, Nat. Assn. State Info. Resource Execs., Assn. Records Mgrs. and Adminstrs. (co-founder so. N.J. chpt., sec. 1981, 82, bd. dirs. ctrl. N.J. chpt. 1990-92, pres. 1993-95, program chair 1997—, spkr. internat. seminars, chpt. ISG liaison 1995—, legis./regulatory liason, 1998—, chmn. U.S. govt. rels. com. 1999—), Assn. Imaging and Info Mgmt. Democrat. Roman Catholic. Avocations: native american studies, gardening, travel, reading. Office: NJ Dept of Transportation PO Box 600 Trenton NJ 08625-0600 E-mail: emiliehimm@dot.state.nj.us.

HIMMEL, LESLIE WOHLMAN, real estate manager; d. Robert Wohlman; m. Jeffrey Steven Himmel, July 14, 1984. Degree, U. Penn.; MBA, Harvard Bus. Sch., 1978. With Integrated Resources, Inc., 1979—84; mng. ptnr. Himmel and Meringoff Properties, N.Y.C., 1984—. Mem.: Young Presidents Org., Real Estate Bd. NY (bd. gov. 2000, exec. com. 2004). Office: Himmel and Meringoff Properties 30 W 26th St Fl 8 New York NY 10010*

HIMMELHEBER, EVE, theater educator, theater director, actor; b. Garden Grove, Calif., Oct. 20, 1960; d. Joseph John Himmelheber and Imelda Delores Bozorgmehr; 1 child, Joseph Daniel. BFA in Musical Theatre, U. Ariz., 1995; MFA in Theatre, Calif. State U., Fullerton, 1995. Asst. dir. mktg. theatre and dance dept. Calif. State U., Fullerton; instr. Cypress (Calif.) Coll., 1995—99; asst. prof. musical theatre Iowa State U., Ames, 1999—2001; asst. prof. acting and directing U. Ariz. Sch. Theatre Arts, Tucson, 2001—. Adj. instr., dir. Rio Hondo Coll., Whittier, Calif., 1995—96; prodn. and performance adjudicator Kennedy Ctr., Am. Coll. Theatre Festival, Regions V and VIII, 1995—; adj. lectr. Calif. State U., Fullerton, 1995—98; exective bd. mem. at large Kennedy Ctr., Am. Coll. Theate Festival Region VIII, 1999—; coord. Irene Ryan scholar competition Kennedy Ctr., Am. Coll. Theatre Festival, Region VIII, 2003—; Ariz. coord. Next. Step Audition, Calif. Ednl. Theatre Assn., 2002—. Dir.: (plays) Guys & Dolls, Black Boy, The Grapes of Wrath, Rags, Inspecting Carol, A Piece of My Heart, Kiss Me Kate, Oklahoma, The Music Man, The Heidi Chronicles, (co-choreographer) The Fantasticks; (plays, industrial fund raiser) Theatrical Threads, (choreographer); (plays) Lucky Stiff, Into the Woods, (producer): (TV series) Cypress College Americana Awards, : (plays) Ghosts; (plays) The Good Times are Killing Me, asst. dir., voice & text coach The Taming of the Shrew, asst. dir., voice & dialect coach (musical theatre hist. pageant plays) Capistrano!; singer: (concert) The Hollywood Bowl Concert Version of The Music Man, (hollywood bowl orchestra concerts) Broadway '97 & Broadway '98; actor(singer): (plays) A Shakespearean Christmas, (musical theatre historical pageant) Capistrano!, (producer) (independent film) Escape Velocity (Best Narrative Film award BEA, 2002), : (plays) Scaramouche, Vanishing Point, As You Like It, Henry V, Tartuffe (Best Comedic Performance of Yr. award OC Weekly, 1996), Macbeth, Richard III, A Midsummer Night's Dream, The Best Little Whorehouse in Texas, And a Nightingale Sang. (LA Times Critic's Pick for Individual Performance, 1994); (plays) The Threepenny Opera, co-dir., choreographer Working, text/voice coach A Midsummer Nights Dream; text, vocal coach: plays Twelfth Night. Theatre badge workshop leader Boy Scouts of Am., Ames, Iowa, 2000—01. Mem.: Theatre Comm. Group, Assn. Theatre in Higher Edn., SAG, Actors Equity Assn., Theta Alpha Phi (life; faculty advisor 2002—03). Avocations: reading, gardening, cooking. Office: Univ Ariz Sch Theatre Arts PO Box 210003 Tucson AZ 85721-0003 E-mail: eve@email.arizona.edu.

HINCKLE, PIA JEANNE, journalist, editor; b. Petaluma, Calif., Jan. 2, 1965; d. Warren James H. III and Denise Ann (Libarle) McCarthy; m. Christian Mittlestaedt, July 20, 1996; 1 child, Lucien Samuel Mittelstaedt. BA in Liberal Arts, Sarah Lawrence Coll., 1986; MS in Journalism, Columbia U., 1997. Writer, researcher Calif. Coastal Conservancy, Oakland, 1986-87; reporter Associated Press, Rome, 1988-89; news reporter Vatican Radio, 1989-90; spl. corr. Newsweek, Rome, 1989-92; mng. editor Argonaut Press, San Francisco, 1992-93, San Francisco Bay Guardian, San Francisco, 1993-96; bus. editor San Francisco Examiner, 1997—. Knight-Bagehot fellow bus. and econs. Columbia U., 1996-97; recipient Disting. Achievement award Ednl. Press. Assn. Am., 1992, First Place News Peninsula Press Club, 1996. Mem. Soc. Profl. Journalists (bd. dirs. no. Calif. chpt. 1995—), N.Y. Fin. Writers Assn., Investigative Reporters and Editors, Assn. Stampa Estera. Avocations: travel, bay swimming, cooking, sand collecting, languages. Office: San Francisco Examiner 110 5th St San Francisco CA 94103-2918

HINDLE, MARGUERITA CECELIA, textile chemist, consultant; b. Providence, Nov. 26, 1928; d. Joseph and Elsie Cecelia (Johnson) Lombardo; m. Robinson J. Hindle, June 17, 1950. BS in Chemistry, U. R.I., 1949, DSc, 1993. Textile chemist Kenyon (R.I.) Industries, 1950-88, lab. dir., 1960-88, R&D dir., 1968-88, v.p. R&D/tech., 1978-88; ind. textile cons., 1988—. Mem. textile adv. com. U. Mass., Dartmouth, 1979—; mem. textile adv. bd. U. R.I., Kingston, 1991—; environ. com. chair Am. Textile Mgrs. Inst., Washington. Mem. Am. Assn. Textile Chemists and Colorists (nat. pres. 1987-88). Home and Office: TCE Consulting Svcs 15 Belle Rose Dr Westerly RI 02891-3917

HINDLE, PAULA ALICE, nursing administrator; b. Cambridge, Mass., Feb. 26, 1952; d. Edward Adam and Geraldine Ann (Donahue) H. BSN, Fitchburg State Coll., 1974; MSN, Duke U., 1980; MBA, Simmons Coll., 1988. Staff nurse Mt. Auburn Hosp., Cambridge, Mass., 1974-75, U. Hosp., Boston, 1975-77, head nurse, 1977-79; staff nurse Duke U. Med. Ctr., Durham, N.C., 1979-80, clin. instr., 1980-81, area mgr., 1981; nurse leader, clin. dir. New Eng. Med. Ctr., Boston, 1981-87; cons. Ctr. for Nursing Case Mgmt., Boston, 1984-87; v.p. nursing Faulkner Hosp., Boston, 1987-94; v.p. nursing and support svcs. Alexandria (Va.) Hosp., 1994-97; v.p. for patient care, chief nurse exec. Loyola U. Med. Ctr., Maywood, Ill., 1997—. Mem. adv. com. Regis Coll. Nursing, 1993; mem. planning and resource com. Simmons Coll., 1993-94; mem. affiliate faculty George Mason U., 1994-95. Active Am. Heart Assn. Mem. Am. Orgn. Nurse Execs., Va. Orgn. Nurse Execs., Mass. Orgn. Nurse Execs. (treas. 1991-93), Humane Soc., Simmons Coll. Grad. Sch. Mgmt. Alumni Assn. (bd. dirs. 1991-93, pres. 1992-93), Sigma Theta Tau. Democrat. Roman Catholic. Avocations: ballroom dancing, reading, theatre, music. Home: 1123 Mistwood Ln Downers Grove IL 60515-1284 Office: Loyola U Med Ctr 2160 S 1st Ave Maywood IL 60153-3304

HINDS, SALLIE ANN, retired township official; b. Saginaw, Mich., June 8, 1930; d. Alex W. and Elsie E. (Letourneau) Chriscaden; m. James F. Hinds; children: Amy Lynn Hinds-McLean, Jennifer L. Hinds-Wanner. Student, MacMurray Coll. for Women, Jacksonville, Ill., 1948-49. Rsch. sec. Lufkin Rule Co., Saginaw, Mich., 1949-51; traffic mgr. WKNX-TV, Saginaw, 1953-59; treas. Sims Twp., AuGres, Mich., 1980-92; clk. Sims Twp. Water Dept., AuGres, 1990-91; mem. East Tawas (Mich.) Planning Com., 1993—. Bd. mem. Sims-Whitney Cemetary/Landfill, AuGres, 1980-92; cons. Sims-Whitney Water Bd., AuGres, 1982-92. Author: Bits and Pieces of Nature's Seasons, 1986, Simple Words...Quiet Thoughts, 1994, Halcyon Days, 1999; participating author: Best Poems of the 90's (Editors Choice award 1996), Best Poems of 1996 (Editors Choice award 1996, 98). On The Edge of Woods and Water, 2002. Instr. USCG Aux., AuGres, 1982-83; mem. Tawas St. Joseph Hosp. Samaritan Club, Aux. Vol., 1993—,

East Tawas, 1980—; election inspector East Tawas Elections Bd., 1994—. Named Homemaker of Yr. award, Arenac County, Mich., Standish, Mich., 1980, Mrs. Mich. 60's, Beauties of Am., Orlando, Fla., 1990, Ms. Sr. Mich. rep. City of East Tawas, 1997; recipient Logo Winner, Vets. Meml. Honor Roll, VFW Post 8275, AuGres, Mich., 1987, Golden Poet award World of Poetry, Calif., 1987-92, Mrs. Scottish Am. Achievement 2001, Mrs. Universal Gem, 2002. Silver Cup and Poet of Merit Medallion award, Internat. Soc. of Poets, 2002-03. Mem. Internat. Soc. Poets (life), Acad. Am. Poets, N.E. Mich. Arts Coun. (bd. dirs. 1984), Arenac County Hist. Soc. (pres. 1981-84), Ladies Lit. Club (treas. 1995-2002, Club Woman of Yr. 1997-98); Gen. Federated women's Club (N.E. dist. treas. Mich. 2002—). Avocations: writing, needlework, artwork, nature and environmental study.

HINE, BETTY DIXON, design consultant; b. San Francisco, May 9, 1920; d. Reginald Stanley and Sarah Elizabeth (Evey) Dixon; married; children: Charles Henri Hine III, Holly Elizabeth Hine Suich. BA, U. Pacific, 1941. Tchr. Calif. Pub. Schs., 1941-45; comm. svc. worker San Francisco Bay Area, 1950—; antiques and design cons., 1975—. Sec./treas. bd. dirs. Hine, Inc., San Francisco; mem. adv. bd. St. Mary's Coll. Art Mus.; bd. dirs. Achievement Rewards for Coll. Scientists. Bd. dirs. U. Calif. San Francisco Hosp., 1960—; trustee Calif. Coll. Arts and Crafts, Oakland, 1970—; life mem. Women's Bd. Oakland Mus., Calif., 1971—. Mem. Calif. Assn. of Mus. (founding mem.), The World Trade Club, The Villa Taverna/San Francisco. Office: Hine Inc 490 Bosphorous Ave Tampa FL 33606-3608

HINER, CHERYL LYNN, adult nurse practitioner; b. Minneapolis, Feb. 23, 1952; B in Nursing, U. Minn., 1976; M in Pub. Health, 1982. Cert. RN. Nurse practitioner and fin. mgr. Neurologic cons., Maplewood, Minn., 1979—2003; v.p. and fin. mgr. Hiner Devel., St. Paul, 1984—2003; CFO Mulligan Masters Golf Ctr., 2002—.

HINER, ELIZABETH ELLEN, pharmacist; b. Balt., Aug. 11, 1943; d. Samuel Joseph and Zola Mae (Hedrick) Bracken; m. William O. Hiner (div.); children: Christine Ellen, Oliver Joseph; m. Ray Danforth Crossley, Aug. 3, 1985. BS in Pharmacy, W.Va. U., 1966; postgrad., Johns Hopkins U., 1984-87; cert. in pub. health pharmacy, Royal Soc. Health, London, 1996; PharmD (hon.), U. Okla., 2002. Registered pharmacist, W.Va., Md., Va. Staff pharmacist U. Va. Hosp., Charlottesville, 1965-66; pharmacy supr. Andrew Rader Army Health Clinic, Ft. Meyer, Va., 1977; pharmacist NIH, Bethesda, Md., 1977-78; consumer safety officer Bur. Biologics FDA, Bethesda, 1978-80, freedom of info. officer, 1980-81, biologics adverse reaction coord., 1981-84, sr. regulatory officer divsn. bacterial products, 1984-92, dir. health promotion fed.-state rels. Rockville, Md., 1992—. Mem., chair pharmacy adv. com. USPHS, Rockville, 1991—; ad hoc mem. Bur. Voluntary Compliance, Nat. Assn. Bds. of Pharmacy, Chgo., 1993-98; mem. faculty Food and Drug Law Inst., 1996-97. Contbr. articles to sci. jours. Mem. parent adv. bd. Beaver Coll., Glenside, Pa., 1993-2000; mem. Olney (Md.) Women's League, 1986—. Capt. USPHS, 1978—. Recipient Cert. of Recognition, Nat. Assn. Bds. of Pharmacy, 1993, 94, 95, 96, 98, 99. Mem. Am. Pharm. Assn., Am. Soc. Health Sys. Pharmacists, Commd. Officers Assn., Lambda Kappa Sigma Alumni. Avocation: sailing.

HINERFELD, RUTH G. civic organization executive; b. Boston, Sept. 18, 1930; m. Norman Hinerfeld, children: Lee, Thomas, Joshua. AB, Vassar Coll., 1951; grad. Program in Bus. Adminstrn., Harvard-Radcliffe Coll., 1952. With LWV, 1954—, UN observer, 1969-72, chairperson internat. rels. com., 1972-76, 1st v.p. in charge legis. activities, 1976-78, pres., 1978-82. Dir. LWV Overseas Edn. Fund, 1975-76, trustee, 1975-86; chair LWV Edn. Fund, 1978-82; mem. White House Adv. Com. for Trade Negotiations, 1975-82; sec. UN Assn. of U.S., 1975-78, vice chmn., 1983—, bd. govs., 1975—, mem. econ. policy coun., 1976-93; bd. dirs. Overseas Devel. Coun. 1974-2000; trustee, vice chair Inst. of Internat. Edn., 1997—; mem. U.S. del. auspices of Nat. Com. on U.S.-China Rels. and Chinese People's Inst. Fgn. Affairs, 1978. Mem. coun. Nat. Mcpl. League, 1977-80, 83-86; del.-at-large Internat. Women's Yr. Conf., Houston, 1977; mem. exec. com. Leadership Conf. on Civil Rights, 1978-82; trustee Citizens Rsch. Found., 1978-2000; mem. Nat. Petroleum Coun., 1979-82; mem. U.S. del. to World Conf. on UN Decade for Women, 1980; mem. adv. com. Nat. Inst. for Citizen Edn. in the Law, 1981-91; mem. North South Roundtable, 1978-88; mem. nat. gov. bd. Common Cause, 1984-90; vice chmn. U.S. com. UNICEF, 1986-90, treas., 1990-91; mem. vis. com. Harvard U. Bus. Sch., 1984-90; bd. dirs. Com. for Modern Cts., 1993-96. Recipient Disting. Citizen award Nat. Mcpl. League, 1978; Outstanding Mother award Nat. Mother's Day Com., 1981; Aspen Inst. Presdl. fellow, 1981. Mem. Coun. on Fgn. Rels., Phi Beta Kappa. Office: 11 Oak Ln Larchmont NY 10538-3917

HINES, ALIDA N. marketing professional, researcher; d. Roosevelt Delano Hines and Verdell Lett Dawson. Student, Duke U., 1994—95; BA magna cum laude in Econs., Spelman Coll., 1998; MA with hons. in Mktg. Rsch., U. of Ga., 2000. Bus. rsch. intern Eastman Kodak Co., Atlanta, 2000, bus. rsch. analyst, 2001—03; market rsch. analyst The Home Depot, Atlanta, 2003—. Tutor Mt. Olivet Bapt. Ch., Rochester, NY, 2001—02; mentor Big Brothers Big Sisters, Atlanta, 2003—. Recipient, Nat. Merit Scholarship Corp., 1994; scholar, Armstrong World Industries, 1994, Motorola, 1997, UNCF scholarship, Quaker Oats Co., 1997, Coca-Cola Found., 1999—2000. Mem.: Nat. Assn. Female Execs. Office: The Home Depot 2455 Paces Ferry RD Atlanta GA 30329 E-mail: alida_hines@homedepot.com.

HINES, CHERYL, actress; b. Miami Beach, Sept. 21, 1965; m. Paul Young, Dec. 30, 2002; 1 child, Catherine Rose. BA in radio and TV, U. Cent. Fla. Mem. The Groundlings Theater, star Cheryl Hines' One Woman Show; actor: (TV series) Curb Your Enthusiasm, 2000— (Emmy nomination best supporting actress, 2003), (voice) Father of the Pride, 2003, : (TV films) Double Bill, 2003; (films) Cheap Curry and Calculus, 1996, (guest appearances): (TV series) Unsolved Mysteries, 1997, Suddenly Susan, 1998, Wayans Brothers, 1998, Friends, 2000, Everybody Loves Raymond, 2002, Reno 911, 2003. Office: Internat Creative Mgt 8942 Wilshire Blvd Beverly Hills CA 90211-1934 Office Phone: 310-550-4000.*

HINES, DAISY MARIE, freelance/self-employed writer; b. Hanna City, Ill., Dec. 31, 1913; d. Frank W. and Edith Earl (Folger) Humphrey; m. Herbert Waldo Hines, Jr., Dec. 20, 1958; children: Grace Consuelo, Ruby Marie. Student, Western Ill. U., 1955-57, So. Ill. U., 1956. Mem. staff advt. dept. Macomb Daily Jour., Ill., 1943-47; writer, exec., dir., promoter McDonough County Tb Assn., 1949-58; sec. U.S. Dept. Agr., Macomb, 1955-58; rschr., writer 1st Nat. Bank, Springfield, 1963, adminstrv. asst. to state legislator, 1964-69; with Sentinel Printing Co., Illiopolis, Ill., 1965; newspaper columnist, free-lance writer, mem. survey staff Prairie Farmer Pub. Co., Decatur, Ill., 1965-79, Successful Farming, Des Moines, 1982; freelance corr. Automotive News divsn. Crain Comm., Inc. Active Altar Soc. Blessed Sacrament Cath. Ch., Springfield; freelance writer Springfield Cath. Times newspaper, 1991, Decatur (Ill.) Herald and Rev. newspaper, 1991; corr. Ill. State Jour.-Register, Springfield; chmn. Illiopolis unit Univ. Ill. Home Extension; pub. rels. dir. Springfield chpt. Am. Cancer Soc., 1961-68; 2d v.p. Ill. Conf. Tb Workers, 1952-53; mem. Sangamon County Farm Bur., women's com., chmn. health and safety, St. John's Hosp. Aux., Ill. Traffic Safety Leaders. Mem. Nat. League Am. Pen Women (pres. Springfield chpt. 1972-73, sec. Ill. br. 1974), Ill. Traffic Safety Leaders, Western Ill. U. Alumni Coun. (sec., Disting. Alumni award 1982, com. mem. Coll. Applied Scis. Agr. rep. Alumni Coun.), Illiopolis Am. Legion (aux. unit 521), Ill. Press Assn. USAF Air Def. Team (hon. life), Ill. Women for Agr., Civil War Round Table, Sangamon County Hist. Soc., Republican Women's Club. Address: PO Box 310 Canton IL 61520-0310

HINES, DEBORAH SUE, special education educator; b. Duncan, Okla., Sept. 13, 1956; d. Clinton Dale Thacker and Rebecca Sue Hollingsworth; m. Melvin Lee Mayo, Aug. 16, 1976 (div. Dec. 1984); 1 child, Dorinda Sue Elwood ; m. Richard Lynn Hines, Oct. 25, 1991; stepchildren: Jeff, Crystal, Austin. BS in Edn., East Ctrl. Okla. State U., 1978, M in Edn., 1988. Elem. edn. educator Graham (Okla.) Pub. Sch., 1978—80, kindergarten tchr., 1980—81; multi-handicapped students (severe and profound) educator Stephens County Coop. Sch., Marlow, Okla., 1985—89; K-12 spl. edn. tchr. and coord./dir. Ctrl. HS, Marlow, 1989—. Recipient Tchr. of Today award, Masons, Marlow, 1995—96. Democrat. Baptist. Avocations: sewing, walking, fishing, baking, grandchildren. Home: PO Box 484 Duncan OK 73533 Office: Ctrl HS Rt 3 Box 249 Marlow OK 73055

HINES, JOANN R. professional association executive and consultant; b. Balt., Dec. 16, 1948; d. Donald Reed Russell and Marjorie Louise Heller Scott; m. Rex Michael Hines, Apr. 5, 1980. Student, Temple U., 1971-75. Sales rep. Union Camp Corp., Atlanta, 1976-79; market devel. Crown Zellerbach, Atlanta, 1979-83; bus. devel. mgr. Advanced Design and Packaging, Atlanta, 1983-86; market devel. mgr. Chesapeake Display and Packaging, Winston-Salem, N.C., 1986-88; ind. packaging cons., pres. Globalpak (formerly Hines & Assocs), Acworth, Ga., 1988—; pres. Global Assn. Mgmt. (formerly Hines & Accos.), 1988—; founder, exec. dir. Women in Packaging, Inc., Acworth, 1993—. Judge for CorrPak '92, '93, AmeriStar Packaging Competition, Package Printing and Converting's Excellence Awards, 1992, 93, Drummer Merchandising and Promotion Award; chmn. First Internat. Packaging Symposium; lectr. in field; chmn. Large Events Planning Packaging Coun.; cons. to Ga. So. U. to develop packaging curriculum; sr. cons. to Pub. Affairs Group. Contbg. author: Board Converting News; contbr. articles to profl. jours.; editl. adv. bd. The Profl. Jour. of Packaging; exec. editor: Packaging Horizons Mag., 1996-99. Mem. TAPPI (mktg. chmn. mktg. adv. com. internat. corrugated container dir.), Western Packaging Assn. (bd. dirs. 1999—), Soc. Competitive Intelligence, Internat. Assn. Design and Package Printing Industry (founding bd. dirs. 1994—), AICC, Nat. Inst. Packaging, Handling, and Logistics Engrs., Inst. Packaging Profls. (packaging cons. coun.), Internat. Packaging Cons. Avocations: sewing, fishing, reading, travel, knitting, gourmet cooking.

HINES, MARY SUSAN, musician, educator; b. Longview, Tex., Oct. 14, 1953; d. Herbert and Mary Jerome Smith; m. Gary Don Hines, June 10, 1978; 1 child, Erin Marie. MusB, N. Tex. State U., 1976. String tchr. Houston Ind. Sch. Dist., 1977—79; string tchr. 5 schs. Williamsburg (Va.)/James City Schs., 2002—; pvt. cello instr. Houston, 1977—93, Newport News, Va., 1993—; cellist Stowehaven String Quartet, Newport News, 1995—, Va. Symphony, Norfolk, 1998—. Suzuki method clinician, Tex., 1978—98; guest lectr. Old Dominion U., Norfolk, 1999—2003; founder Tidewater Suzuki Cello Ensemble, 1999—; adj. prof. Christopher Newport U., Newport News, 2001—03. V.p. bd. dirs. Peninsula Youth Orch., Newport News, 1995—98; founder Sagemont Orch. Sagemont Ch., Houston, 1986. Mem.: Suzuki Assn. Am. Republican. Baptist. Avocations: tennis, reading, camping, white-water rafting. Home: 107 Spring Trace Ln Newport News VA 23601 Office Phone: 757-595-8588.

HINES, ROBERTA LEIGH, medical educator; b. Manchester, N.H., Sept. 18, 1952; BA, U. N.H., 1974; MD magna cum laude, Dartmouth U, 1978. Diplomate Am. Bd. Anesthesiology, critical care cert.; lic. physician, Conn. Intern surgery Yale-New Haven Med. Ctr., 1978-79, asst. resident surgery, 1979-81, asst. resident anesthesiology, 1981-83, chief resident, 1982-83, cardiovascular fellow, 1983-84, assoc. physician, 1983-84, attending physician, 1984—, dir. recovery rm., 1984-87, dir. cardiothoracic ICU, 1984—, chief dept. anesthesiology, 1995; instr. anesthesiology Yale U. Sch. Medicine, 1982-83, asst. prof., 1984-90, assoc. prof., 1990-94, acting chair, 1994, prof., chmn. dept. anesthesiology, 1994—. Assoc. examiner Am. Bd. Anesthesiologists, 1991—; lectr., vis. profs. various univs. and hosps. Mem. editl. bd. Soc. Cardiovascular Anesthesia, 1985-89, Jour. Clin. Anesthesia, 1992, 93, 94, 95, Seminars in Anesthesia, 1995; editor Heart Failure, 1988-92; editl. cons. Anesthesia and Analgesia, 1992, 93, 94, 95, Anesthesiology, 1992, 93, 94, 95, Am. Soc. Obstetrics and Gynecology, 1993, 94, 95; reviewer, editl. cons. Clin. Anesthesia, 1993, 94, 95; reviewer Critical Care Medicine, 1992, 93, 94, 95, Jour. Clin. Monitoring, 1992, 93, 94, 95; editor: (with C. Blitt) Monitoring in Anesthesia and Critical Care, 1994; contbr. articles to profl. jours., chpts. to books. Mem. Soc. Edn. in Anesthesia, Internat. Anesthesia Rsch. Soc., Am. Soc. Anesthesiologists (clin. circulation subcom. 1990, 91, critical care medicine subcom. 1991), Soc. Critical Care Medicine (program chair 1994, 95), Soc. Cardiovascular Anesthesiologists (program com. 1990, 91, 92, editl. bd. 1983-88), Assn. Univ. Anesthesiologists, Am. Soc. Critical Anesthesiologists, Conn. State Soc. Anesthesiologists (bd. dirs. 1991-95). Office: Yale U Sch of Medicine PO Box 208051 333 Cedar St New Haven CT 06520-8051

HINES, TINA LOREE, video producer, writer, publicist, photographer; b. Orlando, Fla., Apr. 26, 1955; d. William and Dorothy Virginia (Martin) H.; m. Stephen Lynn Collins, June 21, 1994; stepchildren: Kevin Lynn, Tracy Edward. Student, U. Nebr., 1973-76; BA in Journalism, Ea. Wash. U., 1988; Cert. in Film and Video, U. Wash., 1989; MS in Mass Comm., Miami U., Oxford, Ohio, 1995. Race horse exerciser Ak-sar-Ben Race Track, Omaha, 1973-77, Belmont Park Race Track, Elmont, N.Y., 1978-83; jockey Hialeah, Gulfstream, Calder, Miami, 1983-85; pub. asst. Playfair Race Track, Spokane, Wash., 1986-88, Longacres Park, Renton, Wash., 1988-92; sr. staff writer Turfway Park, Florence, Ky., 1992-95; pub. asst. Keeneland Racing Assn., Lexington, Ky., 1993-95; prodn. support ABC Sports, N.Y.C., 1995—; owner, prodr. Fast Horses Prodns., Burlington, Ky., 1995—; prodn. specialist Sta. WCET-TV, Cin., 1997—; assoc. prodr. Winner Comms./ESPN, 1997—. Mem. notes team Jim Beam Stakes Turfway, Florence, Ky., 1993-95, Preakness Pimlico, Balt., 1993-94; media asst. Ky. Derby Churchill Downs, Louisville, 1993-94; dir. sta. rels. Breeders' Cup Newsfeed, Louisville, 1994; freelance photographer, writer. Prodr.: (video documentary) Five Women Jockeys, 1995, Faulkner's Old Colonel, 1995; prodr., writer (video/book) Women Jockeys History, 1996—; writer (screenplay) Sand Tracks, 1995—. Vol., asst. leader Boy Scouts, Burlington, Ky., 1993-97. Recipient Grad. assistantship Miami U., Oxford, Ohio, 1994. Mem. Women in Comms., Inc., Turf Publicists of Am. (bd. dirs.), Ky. Thoroughbred Media, Cin. Film Commn. (vol. 1993—), Ky. Film and Video Profls. Avocations: equine sculpture, photography, sailing, camping, riding horses. Office: Fast Horses Prodns 5873 Green Acres Burlington KY 41005-9480

HINES, VONCILE, special education educator; b. Detroit, Dec. 1, 1945; d. Raymond and Cleo (Smith) H. AA, Highland Park Community Coll., 1967; BEd, Wayne State U., 1971, MEd, 1975; MA, U. Detroit, 1978. Tchr. primary unit Detroit Bd. Edn., 1971-79, spl. educator, 1979-94; self-employed ednl. rsch. edn. co-creations. Tchr. trainee Feuerstein's Instrumental Enrichment, 1988—; cons. Queen's Community Workers, Detroit, 1977—; evaluator Teen Profl. Parenting Project, New Detroit Inc., 1986-87; guest educator, critic "Express Yourself", Sta. WQBH 1400 AM, 1989; advisor to home sch. educators. Author: I Chose Planet Earth, 1988; inventor in field. Recipient cert. of merit State of Mich., 1978, 88, cert. of appreciation Queen's Cmty. Workers, 1980, Wayne County Bd. Commrs., 1988, award of recognition Detroit City Coun., 1984, 88. Mem. Assn. for Children and Adults with Learning Disabilities, Assn. Supervision and Curriculum Devel., Nat. Thinking Skills Network, NAFE, Nat. Council Negro Women (presenter 1987), Met. Detroit Alliance of Black Sch. Educators. Democrat. Avocation: travel.

HINES-MARTIN, VICKI PATRICIA, nursing educator, researcher; b. Louisville, Aug. 18, 1951; d. William Adolphus Hines and Myra Iris Bailey; m. Kenneth Wayne Martin, Dec. 30, 1978; 1 child, Michelle Hines Martin. BSN, Spalding Coll., 1975; MA in Edn., Spalding U., 1983; MSN, U. Cin., 1986; PhD, U. Ky., 1994. Cert. clin. specialist in adult psychiat. mental. Staff nurse Norton Hosp., Louisville, 1978-81, instr. critical care Sts. Mary & Elizabeth Hosp., Louisville, 1981-82; asst. chief nursing svcs. VA Med. Ctr., Cin., 1983-85; nursing instr. Jefferson Community Coll., Louisville, 1985-87; head nurse mgr. VA Med. Ctr., Louisville, 1987-88; asst. prof. nursing Ind. U. S.E., New Albany, 1989-95, U. Ky., Lexington, 1995-98, U. Louisville, 1998—. Bd. dirs. Seven Counties Mental Health Svcs., 1995-2000; mem. steering com. on practice parameters Ky. Health Policy Bd., 1996. Contbr. articles to profl. jours. Chmn. bd. dirs. West Louisville Area Health Edn. Ctr., 1997-2000; mem. African-Am. Health Edn. Leadership Program com. Jefferson County Health Dept., 1997-98, African-Am. Health Initiative, African-Am. Strategic Planning Group, 1998-2000; bd. dirs. Ky. Nurses Found., 1998-2001. Nurses Scholar/Fellow, Lucy Zimmerman scholar, 1982, Estelle Massey Osborne Meml. scholar, 1983-84, trainee U. Cin., 1983, grad. scholar, 1983; named to Outstanding Young Women of Am., 1986; Elizabeth Carnagie scholar, 1991, Am. Nurses Found. scholar, 1992; Fellow U. Ky., 1988, grad. fellow, 1992; recipient Rsch. award Ky. Nurses Found., 1992, Nursing Excellence award Jefferson County Ky., 1995, Psychiatric Mental Health Nurse of the Year Ky. Nurses Assn., 1995, Rsch. in Minority Health award So. Nursing Rsch. Soc., 1999, Emerging Nursing Star Health Disparities Rsch. award Howard U. Sch. Nursing, 2004; postdoctoral fellow in Health Policy ANA Ethnic Minority fellowship program, 1996; Louisville Courier Jour. Forum fellow, 1997. Mem.: ANA (minority clin. fellow 1991—93, ethnic racial minority fellow 1997), Internat. Soc. Psychiat. Nurses (mem. rsch. coun., chair diversity task force), So. Nurses Rsch. Soc., Nat. Black Nurses Assn., Kyanna Black Nurses Inc. (co-founder, past pres.), Ky. Nurses Assn. (mental health coun. sec. 1986—88, editl. bd. 1994—97), Am. Psychiat. Nurses Assn. (chair coun. African Am. nurses 2000—02), Sigma Theta Tau. Office: Univ Louisville 3038 Bldg K 555 S Floyd St Louisville KY 40202-3801 E-mail: vphine01@louisville.edu.

HING, BARBARA LIM, elementary school educator, assistant principal, data processing executive; b. Jan. 06; arrived in U.S., 1973; d. Amado K. H. and Bee-chu Tan Lim; m. Y. Ray Hing, Oct. 11, 1975; children: Abigail Hing Wen, Byron Lim, Colleen Lim. BA, Maryknoll Coll., Quezon City, The Philippines, 1971; MA, Ea. Mich. U., 1975; prin. cert., Cleve. State U., 1994. Cert. tchr. Ohio, Ill., adminstr. Ohio, Ill. Instr. St. Claire Coll., Windsor, Canada, 1975; substitute tchr. Shawnee Local Schs., Lima, Ohio, 1980-84, Solon (Ohio) City Schs., 1984-86; tchr. Cleve. Pub. Schs., 1986-95, title I tchr., 1995—2000; asst. prin. Buhrer Elem. Sch., Cleve., 2000—02, data mgr., 2003—. Contbr. strategic planning com. Solon Schs., 1989—91; chairperson Fundraising Com., Cleve., 1995—98, Attendance Com., Cleve., 1995—. Author: (book) Joy the Spider, 1975; writer, editor, pub.: Harvey Rice Attendance Newsletter, 1996—99, Harvey Rice Newsletter, 1999—2000. Mem., supporter Heritage Found., Washington, 1991—, Cmty. Action Team, 1993—94, Concord Coalition, Washington, 1996; chairperson scholarship com. Solon Acad. Boosters Club, 1995—97; sustaining mem. Rep. Nat. Com., Washington, 1994—. Named Outstanding Leader, Health Den, Mentor, Ohio, 1999; recipient Outstanding award, Charities of Choice, Cleve., 1995—97. Mem.: Orgn. Chinese Ams. Greater Cleve. (supporter, v.p. 1998—2003, bd. dirs. 1999—, Outstanding Citizen award 1999, 2002), Chinese Womens Club Cleve. (founder, treas. 1999—2001).

HINIKER, LUANN, management consultant, educator, researcher, grants consultant; b. Mankato, Minn., Sept. 30, 1956; d. Christopher Joseph Hiniker and Phyllis C. Krier; m. Donald George Olson, June 27, 1992. AS, Minn. State U., 1985, BS in Spanish summa cum laude, 1991, MS in Ednl. Adminstrn., 1995; PhD, So. Ill. U., 2002. Admissions recruiter Minn. State U., Mankato, 1979-91, coord. Rsch. Enterprise, 1991-93, rsch. adminstr., 1991-96, dir. Info. Scis. Inst., 1997—; dist. dir. U. Minn. Ext. Svc. Heintz Ctr., Rochester, Minn., 2003—. Rsch. adminstr. Minn. State U., Mankato, 1991-96; mem. adv. coun. S. Ctrl. Minn. Tech. Coun., 1993-96, Region Nine Small Bus. Devel. Ctr., 1993-96; grants cons. Housing Authority Murray State U., 1998-99; instr. multimedia devel. Workforce Edn. and Devel. So. Ill. U., Carbondale, 1999-2000, rschr. videoconferencing technologies, 1999-2000; mem. bd. dirs. Minn. Tech., Inc., 1997-96. Presdl. scholar Minn. State U., 1994-95. Mem. AAUW, NAFE, Am. Ednl. Rsch. Assn., Phi Kappa Phi, Phi Delta Kappa, Omicron Tau Theta. Avocations: guitar, parrots, scuba diving, gardening. Office: U Minn Ext Svc Heintz Ctr Rochester MN 55904 E-mail: luannh@umn.edu.

HINKELMAN, RUTH AMIDON, insurance company executive; b. Streator, Ill., June 4, 1949; d. Olin Arthur and Marjorie Annabeth (Wright) Amidon; m. Allen Joseph Hinkelman, Jr., Oct. 28, 1972; children: Anne Elizabeth, Allen Joseph III. AB in Econs., U. Ill., 1971. Underwriter Kemper Ins. Group, Chgo., 1971-75; acct. exec. Near North Ins. Agy., Chgo., 1975-76; underwriter Gen. Cologne Reinsurance Corp., Chgo., 1976-78, asst. sec., 1978-79, asst. v.p., 1979-83, 2nd v.p., 1983-87, v.p., 1987—. Home: 133 Linden Ave Wilmette IL 60091-2838 Office: Gen Colongne Reinsurance Corp 1 N Wacker Dr Ste 1700 Chicago IL 60606 E-mail: rhinkelm@genre.com.

HINKENS, KAY L. social services association executive; Student, U. Wis., Oshkosh. With Aid Assn. for Luths., Appleton, Wis., 1971—, with employee credit union, 1971-85, co-founder, mgr. lending and mktg., Member Credit Union, 1986-91, v.p. Member Credit Union, 1991-94, pres. Member Credit Union, 1994—. Past tchr. Sunday sch. Mem. Mkt. Coun., Luth. Missionary Soc. (past pres.), Fox Cities Chpt. Credit Unions (past pres., treas.), Credit Union Exec. Soc. Office: Aid Assn for Lutherans 4321 N Ballard Rd Appleton WI 54919-0001

HINKLE, CHRISTINA NICOLE, primary school educator; d. Ronald William and Karol Daughn Mueller; m. Christopher Lee Hinkle, Aug. 31, 1996; 1 child, Mackenzie Paige. BS in Elem. Edn., So. Ill. U., 2000. Lic. elem. educator Ill., early childhood elem. educator Mo. Centerville tchr. Sch. Dist. of Cahokia, Ill., 2000—01; kindergarten tchr. Sch. Dist. of University City, St. Louis, 2001—. Lang. arts curriculum writer Sch. Dist. of University City, 2002; jewelry designer Peace, Love and Beads, 2001—. Spl. needs counselor Camp Roxy, Roxanna, Ill., 1998. Mem.: University City Edn. Assn. Republican. Avocations: tennis, jewelry making, camping, golf, singing. Office: Sch Dist of University City Nathaniel Hawthorne 1351 N Hanley Saint Louis MO 63130

HINKLE, ERIKA GALVÃO, art educator, digital artist; b. Uberlândia, Brazil, Feb. 15, 1961; d. Wilson and Ismalita César Galvão; m. Andrew Ralph Hinkle, Sept. 9, 1995. B in Art Edn., U. Federal Uberlândia, 1979, BFA, 1981; M in Art Edn., Ohio State U., 1991, PhD in Art Edn., 1995. Prof. ESEBA-U. Fed. Uberlândia, 1981-86, vis. prof., 1995-97; prof. Universidade de Uberaba, 1996—. Digital art work printed in Advocate Jour., 1990; one-woman shows include It's An Art Gallery, 1994, Barley's Restaurant, 1994, Fort Hayes Sch. Visual Arts, 1994, D'Alberto Investments Inc., 1995; contbr. articles to profl. jours. Recipient Crabbie award Calendar Mag., 1995. Avocations: reading, Tae Kwon Do. Home: 6308 Wyler Ct Dublin OH 43016-8275 Office: U Fed Uberlândia Av João Naves Avila Uberlândia 38400 Brazil E-mail: erika@nanet.com.br.

HINKLE, JANET, project leader; b. Groton, Conn., Mar. 26, 1958; d. David Randall and Muriel (Nelson) Hinkle; m. Richard Alden Wilcox, Oct. 1, 1983 (div. Mar. 1991); 1 child, Lillian Marie Hinkle. AA in Fashion Design cum laude, Endicott Jr. Coll. for Women, Beverly, Mass., 1978; BA in Psychology, Conn. Coll., 1981. Project leader Sonalysts, Inc., Waterford, Conn., 1983—. Corporator Lawrence and Meml. Hosp., New London, Conn., 1995—, mem. planned giving com., 1998—99; mem. gift com. adv. Cmty. Found., New London, 1998—.; mem. curriculum com. planned sci.

and tech., Magnet H.S., 2003-. Named to Outstanding Young Women of Am., 1997. Mem. Thames Club. Republican. Avocations: training horses, ballet dancing, rollerblading, skiing, painting. Home: 221 Elm St Stonington CT 06378-1165 Office: Sonalysts Inc 215 Parkway N Waterford CT 06385-1209 E-mail: jlhinkle@sonalysts.com.

HINKLE, MURIEL RUTH NELSON, naval warfare analysis company executive; b. Bayonne, N.J., Mar. 17, 1929; d. Andrew and Florence Martha Ida (Nuber) Nelson; m. David Randall Hinkle, June 5, 1954; children: Valerie Nelson, Janet Lee, Sally Ann. Student, Md. Coll. for Women, 1947-49; BA, U. Md., 1951. Mgr. Wildacres Thoroughbred Horse Farm, Waterford, Conn., 1960-70; illustrator naval warfare predictions/computer simulated naval engagements Analysis & Tech., Inc., North Stonington, Conn., 1970-73; pres. Sonalysts, Inc., Waterford, Conn., 1973-88, 94-98, CEO, 1973-2001, pres., CEO emerita, 2001—; also founder, past dir. Command Engring. & Tech. Svcs. Co.; pres., CEO, chmn. Stonington Farms Inc. (now Mystic Valley Hunt Club), 1983. Adv. bd. Conn. Nat. Bank, 1988-92; chmn., CEO Angiers Assocs., 1989-96, S.I. Devel. Corp., 1989-2001; cons. Def. Nuclear Agy. for Tactical Nuclear Effects in anti-submarine warfare, 1974-75; spl. edn. substitute tchr. Waterford Pub. Schs., 1968-74. Co-author: Scope of Acoustic Communications Systems in Naval Tactical Warfare, 1974, Non-Acoustic Anti Submarine Warfare, 1974, Nuclear Weapons Effects in Anti Submarine Warfare, 1974, Measures of Effectiveness, Naval Tactical Communications, 1975, Destroyer ASW Barrier, 1977. Bd. trustees Thames Sci. Ctr., 1979-82. Recipient commendation for svcs. to submarine force Comdr. Submarine Squadron Ten, 1973, SBA New Eng. Contractor of Yr. award, 1986, SBA Adminstr.'s award for excellence, 1985, 86, bus. assoc. of yr. award Naval Inst., 1999, Disting. Cmty. Svc. award Mitchell Coll., 2001, William Crawford Disting. Svc. award C. of C., 2002. Mem. Am. Horse Shows Assn., Nat. Audubon Soc., Submarine Devel. Group Two Wives Club (pres. 1968), Sigma Kappa (pres. Senesk chpt. 1987-89), Navy Wives Club. Republican. Baptist. Home: 9 Cove Rd Stonington CT 06378-2304 Office: Sonalysts Inc PO Box 280 215 Parkway N Waterford CT 06385-1209

HINKLEY, CAROLINE LAWSON, dean; b. Pasadena, Calif., Oct. 8, 1940; d. Thurman S. Wilkins and Mary Katherine Moore; m. Todd K Hinkley, June 11, 1964 (div. 1981); children: Andrew Moore, Alexander Sasha. MFA, Calif. Inst. of Arts, 1975, Claremont Grad. U., 1969; BA, Occidental Coll., Calif., 1963—63. Lectr. design and photography U. Colo., Boulder, 1982—88, adj. faculty photography, 1997—2000; dean Naropa U., Boulder, Colo., 2000—. Bd. mem. Dragon Mt. Zen Ctr., 2001—. Contbr. book Clarence King: A Biography, 1988, book Thomas Moran: Artist of the Mountains, 1998, articles publ. New Am. Photographies; Exhibited in group shows at San Francisco Camerawork. Fundraiser Rocky Mt. Peace & Justice Ctr., Boulder, Colo., 1994—96. Recipient Phelan Photography award, San Francisco Camerawork, 1994. Democrat. Buddhist. Avocations: hiking, photography. Office: Naropa U 2130 Arapahoe Ave Boulder CO 80302 E-mail: caroline@naropa.edu.

HINKLEY, NANCY EMILY ENGSTROM, foundation administrator, educator; b. St. Louis, Jan. 3, 1934; d. Sigfrid E. and Ida C. (Stenstrom) Engstrom; children: Karen Elizabeth, Christine Marie, Catherine Andrea. BA, Augustana Coll., 1955; MA, U. Fla., 1956; EdD, N.C. State U., 1975. Adult edn. specialist Nationwide Long Term Care Edn. Ctr., Raleigh, N.C., 1975-77, dir., 1977-78; owner, pres. Aging and Long Term Care Ednl. and Cons. Svcs., Raleigh, 1978-82; dir. edn. Beverly Found., South Pasadena, Calif., 1983-84; dir. tng. and mgmt. devel. Care Enterprises, Anaheim, Calif., 1984-87; pres. The Hillhaven Found., Tacoma, 1987-93; dir. employment & tng. divsn. Kitsap Cmty. Resources, 1997-99; pres. AJM Assocs., 1993—. Bd. dirs. Tacoma Community Coll. Found.; mem. editorial bd. Nursing Homes, 1988—; mem. editorial bd. Aspen Rsch. Pub. Group, 1989-93. Author: (with others) A Time and Place for Sharing: A Practical Guide for Developing Intergenerational Programs, 1984; mem. editorial bd. Jour. Univ. Programs, 1988-93; contbr. articles to profl. jours. Vol. Big Bros./Big Sisters, Tacoma, 1989-90; bd. dirs. Jessie Dyslin Boy's Ranch, Tacoma, 1988-90. Mem. ASTD, Am. Med. Dirs. Assn. (assoc.), Am. Assn. Homes for the Aging (assoc.), Am. Coll. Health Care Adminstrs. (assoc.), Am. Soc. on Aging, Gerontol. Soc. Am., Phi Kappa Phi, Phi Alpha Theta, Alpha Kappa Delta, Alpha Psi Omega, Sigma Phi Omega. Home and Office: PO Box 64190 Tacoma WA 98464-0190

HINMAN, EVE CAISON, retired academic administrator; b. Charleston, S.C., May 17, 1951; d. Robert Lee Jr. and Ella Louise (Cross) Caison; m. William DeLeon Thrasher, June 9, 1972 (div. 1997); 1 child, Beverly Ann Thrasher Varner; m. Charles Steven Hinman, Feb. 27, 1998. Student, Francis Marion Coll., 1974-78, Trident Tech. Coll., 1990-91. Adminstrv. asst. to dean, acad. v.p. Francis Marion Coll., Florence, S.C., 1973-78; bus. mgr. dept. neurology Med. U. S.C., Charleston, 1978—2001; ret., 2001; part-time fiscal analyst Med. U. S.C., 2001—02; call desk rep. Universal Data Solutions, Charleston, SC, 2002—. Mem. Friendship United Meth. Ch., Cross, SC, chairperson worship com., 1993. Mem.: Southeastern Bluegrass Assn. Avocations: bluegrass guitar and bass, singing and performing. Office Phone: 843-556-5565. E-mail: hinmane@universaldata.net.

HINOJOSA, LETICIA See HINOJOSA, TISH

HINOJOSA, MARIA L. news correspondent; b. Mexico City, July 2, 1961; d. Raul and Berta (Ojeda) H.; m. German E. Perez, July 20, 1991. BA magna cum laude, Barnard Coll., 1984. Reporter Enfoque Nacional, San Diego, 1985, prodr., 1987; asst. prodr. weekend edit. NPR, Washington, 1986, freelance reporter, prodr. N.Y.C., 1989, correspondent, 1990—; prodr. CBS News Radio, N.Y.C., 1988; asst. prodr. CBS This Morning, N.Y.C., 1988; reporter Sta. WNYC Radio, N.Y.C., 1990; host radio Latino USA, N.Y.C., 1993—; host TV show Visiones Sta. WNBC, N.Y.C., 1993-95; urban affairs corr. CNN, N.Y.C., 1995—, N.Y. bur. corr., 1997—. Lectr. in field. Author: CREWS—Gang Members Talk to Maria Hinojosa, 1995, Raising Raul—Adventures Raising Myself and My Son, 1999; mem. editl. bd. NACLA, N.Y. Bd. dirs. Columbia U. Coun. on Urban Affairs, N.Y.C., 1994. Recipient Unity award for radio feature Lincoln U., 1992, Cindy award Assn. Visual Communicatoes, 1993, Best Radio Feature award Soc. Profl. Journalists, 1993, Robert F. Kennedy Journalism award, 1995; named one of Women of Yr. 2000, Glamour Mag., one of 100 Most Influential Latinos in U.S., Hispanic Bus. Mag., 2000, one of 25 Most Influential Working Mothers in Am., Working Mother Mag., 1999. Mem. Nat. Assn. Hispanic Journalists (Best Radio Report 1992), Nat. Alliance Third World Journalists, Newswoman's Club of N.Y. Avocations: reading, writing, dance, hiking, yoga. Office: CNN 5 Penn Plz Fl 20 New York NY 10001-1810

HINOJOSA, TISH (LETICIA HINOJOSA), vocalist; b. San Antonio, Dec. 6, 1955; d. Felipe and Maria H.; m. Craig Barker, 1982; children: Adam, Maria, Christina. Singer Mel Tillis Prodn. Co., Nashville, 1983-85. Performer locally and on radio, 1973, gubernatorial inauguration Ann Richard's, 1991, presdl. inauguration Bill Clinton, 1993. Albums: Taos to Tennessee (self-released cassette), 1985, Homeland, 1989, Aquella Noche, 1991, Memorabilia Navidenia, 1991, Culture Swing, 1992, Destiny's Gate, 1994, Frontéjas, 1995, Dreaming from the Labyrinth, 1996, Cada Nino, 1996, Sonar Del Labertino, 1997, Sign of Truth, 2000, From Texas for a Christmas Night, 2003; TV appearances include CBS This Morning, 1993; radio appearances include Prairie Home Companion, All Things Considered, 1994. Recipient First prize Kearville Folk Festival, 1979. Office: Manazo Music Mgmt PO Box 3304 Austin TX 78764-3304

HINSCH, CATHLEEN LOFFREDO, press secretary; b. Milford, Conn., Feb. 1, 1964; d. Eugene E. and Pearl (Chidiac) Loffredo; m. Kenneth W. Hinsch; 1 child, Laura Rose. AA, South Ctrl. C.C., New Haven, 1984; BA, Ctrl. Conn. State U., New Britain, 1986. Studio asst. WFSB-TV, Hartford, Conn., 1985—86; prodn. engr. WTNH-TV, New Haven, 1986—88; staff writer Branford (Conn.) Rev., 1988—90, Middletown (Conn.) Press, 1990—92; press sec. House Rep. Office, Conn. Gen. Assembly, Hartford, 1992—96; asst. dir. coll. rels. Conn. Coll., New London, 1996—99; press sec. Office of Lt. Gov. M. Jodi Rell, Hartford, 1999—. Program co-host Conn. Radio Info. Sys., Wethersfield, 1994—97; reader Recording for the Blind, New Haven, 1989—92; mem. Middlefield (Conn.) Rep. Town Com., 1999—; mem., past chmn. Cromwell (Conn.) Rep. Town Com., 1995—97. Mem.: Rotary Club of Cromwell (past pres.). Episc. Avocations: bicycling, hiking, reading, knitting, cooking. Office: Office of Lt Governor M Jodi Rell State Capitol Rm 304 Hartford CT 06106

HINSDALE, STEPHANIE M. social worker; b. Reading, Pa., Sept. 11, 1975; d. Glenn William Krick, Joyce Krick; m. Lyle R. Hinsdale. BA, Coll. of William and Mary, 1997; MSW, Va. Commonwealth U., 1999. Cert. sch. social worker 1999. Intensive in-home counselor Interstate Corp. Ctr. Family Preservation Svcs.-Tidewater Region, 2004—. Office: Family Preservation Svcs Tidewater Region Interstate Corp Ctr #20 Ste 249 Norfolk VA 23502 Home: 173 Swanson Rd Norfolk VA 23503-4729 E-mail: sswskrick@msn.com.

HINSHAW, ADA SUE, dean, nursing educator; b. Arkansas City, Kans., May 20, 1939; d. Oscar A. and Georgia Ruth (Tucker) Cox; children: Cynthia Lynn, Scott Allen Lewis. BS, U. Kans., 1961; MSN, Yale U., 1963; MA, U. Ariz., 1973, PhD, 1975; DSc (hon.), U. Md., 1988, Med. Coll. of Ohio, 1988, Marquette U., 1990, U. Nebr., 1992, Mount Sinai Med. Ctr., NY, 1993, U. Medicine and Dentistry N.J., 1995, Grand Valley State U., 1995, U. Toronto, Can., 1996, St. Louis U., 1996, Georgetown U., 1998. Instr. Sch. Nursing U. Kans., 1963-66; asst. prof. U. Calif., San Francisco, 1966-71; prof. U. Ariz., Tucson, 1975-87; dir. nursing rsch. U. Med. Ctr., Tucson, 1975-87; dir. Nat. Inst. Nursing Rsch. Pub. Health Svc., Dept. Health and Human Svcs., NIH, Washington, 1987—94; dean, prof., Sch. Nursing U. Mich., Ann Arbor, 1994—. Contbd. articles to profl. jours. Recipient Kay Schilter award U. Kans., 1961, Lucille Petry Leone award Nat. League for Nursing, 1971, Wolanin Geriatric Nursing Rsch. award U. Ariz., 1978, Alumni of the Yr award Sch. Nursing U. Kans., 1981, Disting. Alumni award Sch. Nursing Yale U., 1981, Alumni Achievement award U. Ariz., 1990, Disting. citation Kans. Alumni Assn., 1992, Health Leader of the Yr. award Pub. Health Svc., 1993, Centennial award Columbia Sch. Nursing, 1993, Presdl. Meritorious Exec. Rank award, 1994. Mem. ANA (Nurse Scientist of Yr. Award 1985, Salute to Nurses award 1994), Inst. Medicine Coun., Coun. Nurse Rschrs. (Nurse Scientist of Yr. Award 1985), Md. Nurses Assn., Western Soc. for Rsch. in Nursing, Am. Acad. Nursing, Inst. Medicine, 1989-, Sigma Xi, Sigma Theta Tau (Beta Mu Chpt. award of Excellence in Nursing Edn., 1980, Elizabeth McWilliams Miller Excellence in Rsch. Award, 1987), Alpha Chi Omega. Avocations: hiking, camping, bicycling. Office: U Mich Sch Nursing 400 N Ingalls St Ann Arbor MI 48109-2003*

HINSHAW, JUANITA, electric distributor executive; CFO Graybar Elec., St. Louis, 2000—, sr. v.p., 2000—. Bd. dirs. Ipsco Inc. Office: Graybar Electric PO Box 7231 Saint Louis MO 63177

HINSON, CLAUDIA BURNS, elementary school educator; b. Dallas, July 2, 1921; d. Claude L. and Madge I. Burns; children: Kathleen D. Hinson Baillargeon, C. Daniel Hinson. BA, Baylor U., 1943; MA, Pepperdine U., 1977. Cert. elem. and spl. edn. tchr., Calif. Copywriter Moody Bible Inst., Chgo.; dir. youth program Cen. Tex. Conf., Meth. Ch., Waco, Tex.; tchr. Corona (Calif.)-Norco Unified Sch. Dist. Dir. seminars on religious edn.; freelance writer; artistic dir. musical theater; mem. Colleagues Pepperdine U. Contbr. articles and poetry to profl. publs. Recipient hon. svc. award Calif. PTA. Mem. Nat. Coun. Tchrs. English, Corona-Norco Tchrs. Assn. (rep.), Instrnl. Improvement Coun., Tchrs. and Writers Collaborative, Poetry Soc. Am.

HINSON, CYNTHIA THOMAS, minister; b. Charlotte, N.C., Jan. 26, 1951; d. Frealon Ed Thomas and Frances Elizabeth Love; m. Yancy Gerald Hinson, Dec. 22, 1973; children: Y. Jerry Hinson, III, William Thomas, Elizabeth Anne. BA in English Linguistics, U. Houston, 1994; MDiv cum laude, So. Meth. U., 1998; Beeson Doctoral fellow in Ministry, Asbury Theol. Sem., 2001—. Lic. pastor The United Meth. Ch., Houston, Tex., 1996, ordained deacon The United Meth. Ch., Houston, Tex., 1997, ordained elder The United Meth. Ch., Houston, Tex., 2000, cert. pastoral care specialist Krist Samaritan Ctr. for Couseling and Edn., Clear Lake, Tex., 2000; lic. real estate broker Real Estate Licensing Bd., North Carolina, 1971. Guitar instr. YWCA, Charlotte, NC, 1966—72; lab. technician The ARC, Charlotte, 1972—74; mgr. Headen and Co., Charlotte, 1974—76, Jetero Properties, Houston, 1977—79; property mgr. Krupp Co., Houston, 1979—81; english tchr. Houston Ind. Sch. Dist., Bellaire, Tex., 1994—95; sr. pastor St. Paul United Meth. Ch., Conroe, Tex., 1995—. Registrar com. on ordained ministry Houston (Tex.) North Dist. United Meth. Ch., 2001—; divsn. of edn. Tex. Ann. Conf. United Meth. Ch., Houston, 2000—, mentor pastor Com. Rules and Structure, 2000—; bd. of trustees Montgomery County Interfaith Hospitality Network, Conroe, Tex., 2000—02; spiritual dir. Houston North Emmaus Cmty., Tex., 1999—; page Gen. Conf. 2000 of the UMC, Cleveland, Ohio, 2000—00; v.p. Friends of Bellaire (Tex.) Parks, 1985—92; faith-based initiative Montgomery Co. Dept. of Corrections and St. Paul United Meth. Ch., Conroe, 2001—; instr. Lay Spkr. Sch. United Meth. Ch., Houston, 1996—2002; spkr. in field. Russ Pitman Park Playground. Supervising pastor Clowns for Christ, Conroe, 1999—2003; trustee Mont. County Interfaith Hospitality Network, Conroe, 2000—02. Recipient Vision award, Friends of Bellaire (Tex.) Pks., 1996; fellow, Beeson Internat. Sch. for Bibl. Preaching, Asbury Theol. Sem., 2001—. Mem.: Renewal Network, Sam Houston State U. Parents' Assn. (bd. dirs.), Houston Emmaus Cmty. (spiritual dir. 1999—), The Confessing Movement United Meth. Ch., Ea. Star, Sigma Tau Delta. Republican. United Meth. Office: St Paul United Methodist Church 1100 W Semands / P O Box 506 Conroe TX 77305

HINSON, KAREN RENEE, mental health services professional; b. Tampa, Fla., Oct. 17, 1973; d. Earlston Eugene and Linda Voncille Hinson. BA, U. South Fla., 1995, MA, 1997. Lic. mental health counselor. Clin. therapist Personal Enrichment through Mental Health Svcs., Largo, Fla., 1997—, Hector R. Corzo and Assoc., Pinellas Park, Fla., 2002—. Avocations: reading, volleyball, writing, gem collecting. Office: PEMHS 1614 Palm Way Largo FL 33771

HINSON, SHIRLEY ROGERS, state representative; b. Aug. 22, 1949; d. Rhodes Leon and Betty M. Rogers; 1 child, Trey. Grad., Trident Tech. Coll., 1992; BS, Coll. Charleston, 1994. Realtor Prudential Carolina; mem. SC Ho. of Reps., 1997—. Mem. Berkeley County Sch. Bd., 1988—96, Sch. Improvement Coun., 1984—96; mem. strategic planning com. Stratford H.S., 1996—; adv. bd. Trident Health Sys.; vice chmn. Berkeley County Legis. Del.; bd. dirs. Charleston Coun. Govt., Berkeley Coun. Govt., Dorchester Coun. Govt. Recipient Silver Knight award, Berkeley County Vol. award, 1996. Mem.: Berkeley County C. of C. (bd. dirs.), Nat. Fedn. Rep. Women, SC Fedn. Rep. Women, Berkeley County Rep. Women. Republican. Office: State Capitol 308 D Blatt Bldg Columbia SC 29211

HINTHORN, DAWN ROSA, elementary and secondary school educator; b. Huntington, Ind., May 5, 1966; d. Robert Gene and Martha Lucille Smith; m. Douglas James Hinthorn, June 3, 1995; children: Jessica Dawn, Branden David. MusB, Huntington Coll., 1984—89. Bookkeeper Smith Furniture, Huntington, Ind., 1980—92; substitute tchr. Various K-12 schools, Various, Ind., 1989—90; mid. sch. and h.s. choral dir. Whitko Mid. Sch. and Whitko H.S., Larwill and South Whitley, Ind., 1990—. Ch. choir dir. Etna Ave. Wesleyan Ch., Huntington, Ind., 1988—94. Mem. of ch. worship band Coll. Pk. Ch., Huntington, Ind., 1996—. Recipient Walmart Tchr. Of The Yr., Warsaw Area Walmart, 2002, Dekko Excellance In Tchg. award, Dekko Found., 2001, Heart Of Gold award, Whitley County, Ind., 2002. Mem.: ACDA (licentiate), MENC (licentiate). Protestant. Office: Whitko High School 1 Big Blue Ave South Whitley IN 46787 E-mail: dawn.hinthorn@whitko.org.

HINTON, KAROLYN KAY, retired elementary school educator; b. Fairview, Okla., Mar. 9, 1945; d. Albert Lowell Woods and Jewell Deloria Bromlow-Woods; m. Patricia Jeanne Woods. AA, Frank Phillips Coll., 1965; BS, West Tex. State U., 1968; MEd, West Tex. A&M. Cert. profl. certification in English, Speech Tex. State Bd. Edn., provisional certification in Spanish. Tchr. Friona (Tex.) Ind. Sch. Dist., 1967—2000. Tchr. GED and ESL classes, Friona. Contbr. poetry Internat. Book of Poetry Washington, 2000, poetry Internat. Book of Poetry Fla., 2001. Mem.: OES (Worthy Matron 1968—). Democrat. Baptist. Avocation: needlework, painting, writing.

HINTON, PAULA WEEMS, lawyer; b. Gadsden, Ala., Dec. 5, 1954; d. James Forrest and Juanita (Weems) H.; m. Steven D. Lawrence, Mar. 31, 1984; 1 child, David Hinton Lawrence. BA, U. Ala., 1976, MPA, JD, U. Ala., 1979. Bar: Ala. 1979, Tex. 1982, U.S. Dist. Ct. (so. dist.) Ala. 1980, U.S. Dist. Ct. (so. dist.) Tex. 1981, U.S. Dist. Ct. (no. dist.) Tex. 1988, U.S. Dist. Ct. (ea. and we. dists.) Tex. 1989, U.S. Dist. Ct. (no. and mid. dists.) Ala. 1993, U.S. Ct. Appeals (5th and 11th cirs.) 1981, U.S. Supreme Ct. 1998. Law clk. to magistrate U.S. Dist. Ct. Ala., Mobile, 1979-80; assoc. Vinson & Elkins, LLP, Houston, 1981-88; ptnr. Akin Gump Strauss Hauer & Feld, L.L.P., Houston, 1989—2001, Vinson & Elkins, Houston, 2001— Mem. Supreme Ct. Gender Bias Reform Implementation Com., 1998—, co-chair, 2000—, chmn., 2002-. Bd. dirs. Planned Parenthood Houston and S.E. Tex., Inc., 2000-03. Rotary fellow U. Sevilla, Spain, 1980-81. Mem.: ABA (mem. ligation sect., internat. law sect., antitrust and bus. litigation sect., women andthe law sect., alternate dispute resolution sect.), ATLA, Tex. Bar Found. (nominating co-chair 2002, co-chmn. nominating com. 2002), London Ct. of Internat. Arbitration, Internat. Bar Assn., Houston Bar Assn., Greater Houston Partnerships, Exec. Women's Partnership (steering com. 2002, Ma'at Justice award 2001), U. Houston Law Found. (adv. bd,), Houston Bar Found. (bd. dirs. 1994—96, chmn. 1996—97, bd. dirs. 2002—), State Bar Tex. (chair women in the profession com. 1996—98, mem. disciplinary rules of profl. conduct com. 2000—01, bd. dir. 2002—, mem. litigation sect., internat. law sect., antitrust and bus. litigation sect., alternative dispute resolution sect., women and law sect.). Office: Vinson and Elkins LLP 2300 First City Tower 1001 Fannin St Houston TX 77002-6760 Business E-Mail: phinton@vclaw.com.

HINTON, SUSAN FRAZIER, secondary school educator; b. Lebanon, Tenn., Dec. 13, 1951; d. Henry Edward and Frances (Fuston) Frazier; m. Jerry Lee Hinton, 1993; children: Troy E. Hinton, David L. Hinton, Rance Kelly Jr. BS, Belmont U., Nashville, 1972; Master's degree, Ala. A&M U., 1974, EdS, 1976. Cert. elem. tchr., Ala.; reading specialist, Ala.; cert. adminstrn. supr. schs. Dir. migrant edn. Morgan County Sch. Sys., Decatur, Ala., 1986-89, elem. tchr., 1972-86, 1989-98; lang. arts tchr. DeKalb Mid. Sch., Smithville, Tenn., 1998-2000; dir., tchr. Dekalb County H.S., 2000—. Cons., chmn. So. Assn. Colls. and Univs., 1993—. Vol. Hospice of Am., Huntsville, Ala., 1992—, 4-H Clubs of U.S., Morgan County, 1989-96; pianist Smithville (Tenn.) First Bapt. Ch., 1995-96, asst. choir dir., pianist Kingdom Kids; active DeKalb Art League, 1998—; mem. Southern Gospel Singing Group-The Harmoneers, 1998—; mem., asst. pianist DeKalb Cmty. Chorus. Mem.: NEA (del. 1986, mem. pub. rels. com., pianist, Ala. Educator of Yr. 1986, Morgan County Tchr. of Yr. 1996), Morgan County Edn. Assn. (pres. 1972, 1976), Ala. Edn. Assn. (del., mem. various coms.), Nat. Coun. Tchrs. English, Smithville Study Club (music chmn.), Smithville Bus. and Profl. Women's Club (pres. 2003—). Democrat. Home: PO Box 622 Smithville TN 37166-0622 E-mail: hinton@dtccom.net.

HINTON-HYSMITH, ANTOINETTE, social services administrator; d. Hudy Henry and Othur Aselena (Williams) Hysmith. BS in Criminal Justice, Tex. Christian U., Fort Worth, 1976—79; M in Human Rels., U. Okla., Norman, 1987—89. Cert. Practicuum Instr. U. Okla., 1998. Counselor Women's Haven of Tarrane County, Fort Worth, Tex., 1979—81; sta. dir. ARC, Tinker Air Force Base, Okla., 1981—84; dir., social svcs. & corrections The Salvation Army, Okla. City, 1989—91, social svcs. casework supr., 1989—91, exec. dir., social svcs. & disaster svcs., 1994—; exec. dir. L.M. Tolliver Alternative Care Ctr., Okla. City, 1991—92; therapist JBN Mental Health Svcs., Okla. City, 1997—98. Social services casework supr. The Salvation Army, Oklahoma City, 1989—91, dir. of social services & corrections, 1989—91; exec. dir. L.M. Tolliver Alternative Care Ctr., Oklahoma City, 1991—92; therapist JBN Mental Health Services, Oklahoma City, 1997—98; exec. dir. of social services & disaster services The Salvation Army, Oklahoma City, 1994—. Founder, pres. Oakcliff Neighborhood Assn., Okla. City, 1989—2003; founder, chairperson of food pantry Fairview Bapt. Ch., Okla. City, 1999—2003. Mem.: Task Force for TB for the Homeless, Okla. Coalition for the Homeless & Needy, NASW (assoc.), Alpha Kappa Delta, Delta Sigma Theta (assoc.). Baptist. Avocations: computers, music, exercise, reading, home decorating. Personal E-mail: antoinethinton@cox.net.

HINTZKE, TERESA ANNA, illustrator; b. Bydgoscz, Poland, Aug. 1, 1934; arrived in U.S., 1953; d. Stanislaw Mikosz and Anna Reysowska; m. Edward Stanley Hintzke, Dec. 7, 1973; children from previous marriage: Richard A. Sobilo, Barbara M. Sobilo. PhB, Northwestern U., 1981. Tech. illustrator GM Corp., Detroit, 1969—73; chief tech. illustrator Apeco, Inc., Evanston, Ill., 1975—77, Telemedia, Inc., Chgo., 1977—79; pvt. practice Winnetka, Ill., 1979—. Author: (memoir) Six Years Til Spring, 2001. Docent Oriental Inst. Mus., U. Chicago, 1975—. Mem.: Pan Pacific and S.E. Asia Womens Assn. (nat. pres. 1997—2001), Internat. Women Assocs. Inc. Avocations: collecting antique maps, Mid.-East archaeology.

HIPP, KRISTINE KIEFER, adult education educator; b. Duluth, Minn., Sept. 17, 1949; d. Neil Timothy Sullivan and Evelyn Marie (Chartier) Kiefer; m. John A. Hipp, Nov. 25, 1972 (dec.). BS, U. Wis., Whitewater, 1971, MS, 1975; PhD, U. Wis., Madison, 1995. Tchr. spl. edn. Janesville (Wis.) Sch. Dist., 1971-80, 80-90; edn. cons. pvt. practice, Wis., Ind., 1987—; coord. staff devel. Janesville Sch. Dist., 1988-92; rsch. assoc. U. Wis., Madison, 1992-95; asst. prof. Ball State U., Muncie, Ind., 1995-97; assoc. prof. Cardinal Stritch U., Milwaukee, Wisc., 1997—. Adj. grad. instr. U. Wis., Whitewater, 1975-90. IDEA fellow, 1990. Mem. NOW, AAUW, ASCD, Am. Ednl. Rsch. Assn., Nat. Staff Devel. Coun., U. Wis. Alumni Assn. Democrat. Avocations: tai chi, swimming, travel. Office: Cardinal Stritch U Grad Edn Coll of Edn 6801 N Yates Rd Milwaukee WI 53217-3945

HIRAHARA, PATTI, public relations executive; b. Lynwood, Calif., May 10, 1955; d. Frank C. and Mary K. Hirahara; m. Terry K. Takeda, Sept. 1995. AA, Cypress Coll., 1975; BA, Calif. State U., Fullerton, 1977. Pub. affairs dir. United TV, L.A., 1977-80; v.p. Asian Internat. Broadcasting Co., L.A., 1980-81; mktg. cons. Disneyland, Anaheim, Calif., 1982; pub. rels. agt. Japan External Trade Orgn., L.A., 1982-86, 87-92; owner, pres. Prodns. By Hirahara, Anaheim, 1982—. Comml. photographer Hirahara Photography, Anaheim, 1977-83; publicist Tokyo Met. Govt., 1981, World Trade Week So. Calif., 1997, 98, 99; advisor State Colo. Trade Mission to Japan, 1986, State Ariz. Trade/Investment Mission to Japan, 1987, County

Riverside, Calif. for Japanese trade, investment, tourism, 1986-88; coord. JETRO's Bus. Study Series, L.A., 1988; advisor Japan External Trade Orgn., 1987-88, TV Prodr./Host: Images, 1980, Expressions, 1994. Mem. reader panel Golf for Women Mag. Bd. dirs. Nisei Week Japanese Festival, L.A., 1980-81; mem. Anaheim H.S. 20 Yr. Reunion Com., 1993, Nat. [illegible] Mag. Youth Adv. Coun., 1973; named Orange County Nisei Queen, Suburban Optimist Club, Buena Park, Calif., 1974, nat. semi-finalist Outstanding Working Women Competition Glamour Mag., 1975; recipient svc. award Suburban Optimist Club of Buena Park, 1975. Mem. NAFE, Soc. Profl. Journalists (bd. dirs. 1980-81), World Trade Ctr. Assn. Orange County, Japanese Am. Citizens League, Am. Women in Radio and TV (bd. dirs. So. Calif. chpt. 1980-82, vice-chair western conf. 1981), So. Calif. Golf Assn., Pub. Rels. Soc. Am. (Orange County chpt. 1990), Adelaide Price Elem. Sch. (30 yr. reunion chair 1997), Suburban Optimist Club of Buena Park (bd. dirs. 1993-96, chairperson 30th Anniversary Celebration 1996, Optimist of Yr. 1995-96), Alpha Gamma Sigma.

HIRANO, IRENE ANN YASUTAKE, museum director; b. L.A., Oct. 7, 1948; d. Michael S. and Jean F. (Ogino) Yasutake; 1 child, Jennifer. BS in Pub. Adminstrn., U. So. Calif., 1970, MPA in Pub. Adminstrn., 1972. Project adminstr. U. So. Calif., 1970-72; assoc. dir. Asian Women's Ctr., 1972-73; nat. project coord., Japanese site supr. Nat. Asian Am. Field Study, L.A., 1973-75; cons. U.S. Dept. Health, Edn. and Welfare, Adminstn. on Aging, San Francisco, 1975; exec. dir. T.H.E. Clinic for Women, Inc., L.A., 1975-88; exec. dir., pres. Japanese Am. Nat. Mus., L.A., 1988—. Lectr., spkr. in field. Mem. L.A. Ednl. Alliance for Restructuring Now, 1993—, Pres's. Com. on Arts & Humanities, 1994—, Commn. on Future of Smithsonian Inst., 1993—, L.A. Coalition, 1993—; trustee Malborough Sch., 1993—; co-founder Leadership Edn. for Asian Pacifics, 1983, pres. 1983-86, v.p. 1986-90; pres., bd. dirs. Asian Pacific Am. Support Group, U. So. Calif., 1984-88; bd. dirs. Liberty Hill Found., 1984-88, community funding bd., 1981-84, chairperson Calif. Commn. on the Status of Women, 1981-82, commn. mem., 1976-83; many others. Recipient Nat. Outstanding Asian/Pacific Islander award NEA, 1983, Outstanding Women of the '90's, Robinson's Corp., 1992, Outstanding Svc. award Nat. Women's Polit. Caucus, 1986, Nat. Inst. Women of Color, 1984, Outstanding Alumni award U. So. Calif., 1994, So. Calif. Hist. Soc. Cmty. award, 1995. Office: Japanese Am Nat Mus 369 E 1st St Los Angeles CA 90012-3901

HIRONO, MAZIE KEIKO, former lieutenant governor; b. Fukushima, Japan, Nov. 3, 1947; arrived in U.S., 1955, naturalized, 1959; d. Laura Chie (Sato) H. BA, U. Hawaii, 1970; JD, Georgetown U., 1978. Dep. atty. gen., Honolulu, 1978-80; Shim, Tam, Kirimitsu & Naito, 1984-88; mem. Hawaii Ho. of Reps., Honolulu, 1980-94; lt. gov. State of Hawaii, 1994—2002. Chair Hawaii Policy Group, Nat. Commn. on Tchg. and Ams. Future, Govs. Task Force on Sci. and Tech. Bd. dirs. Nuuanu YMCA, Honolulu, 1982-84, Moiliili Cmty. Ctr., Honolulu, 1984; dep. chair Dem. Nat. Com., 1997. Mem. U.S. Supreme Ct. Bar, Hawaii Bar Assn., Phi Beta Kappa. Democrat. E-mail: ltgov@exec.state.hi.us.*

HIRSCH, ANNE, dean; BSN, Wash. State U., 1974; MNin, U. Wash., 1978; DNS, U. Ind., 1983. Cert. family nurse practitioner. Nurse Ialdn Hosp., Anacortes, Providence Med. Ctr., Seattle, St. Luke's Hosp., Spokane; faculty Pacific Luth. U. Sch. Nursing, Tacoma, interim dean, assoc. dean for undergrad. nursing; assoc. dean for acad. affairs Wash. State U. Coll. of Nursing, 1998—. Lt. USN Nurse Corps. Res. Office: Wash State U Coll Nursing 2917 W Fort George Wright Dr Spokane WA 99224-5202

HIRSCH, BETTE G(ROSS), college administrator, foreign language educator; b. N.Y.C., May 5, 1942; d. Alfred E. and Gladys (Netburn) Gross; m. Edward Raden Silverblatt, Aug. 16, 1964 (div. Feb. 1975); children: Julia Nadine Silverblatt, Adam Edward Silverblatt; m. Joseph Ira Hirsch, Jan. 21, 1978; stepchildren: Hillary, Michelle, Michael. BA with honors, U. Rochester, 1964; MA, Case Western Res. U., 1967, PhD, 1971. Instr. and head French dept. Cabrillo Coll., Aptos, Calif., 1973-90, 2003—, divsn. chair fgn. langs. and comms. divsn., 1990-95, interim dir. student devel., 1995-96, dean of instrn., transfer and distance edn., 1996—2003. Mem. steering com. Santa Cruz County Fgn. Lang. Educators Assn., 1981-86; mem. liaison com. fgn. langs. Articulation Coun. Calif., 1982-84, sec., 1983-84, chmn., 1984-85; workshop presenter, 1982—; vis. prof. French Mills Coll., Oakland, Calif., 1983; mem. fgn. lang. model curriculum stds. adv. com. State Calif., 1984; instr. San Jose (Calif.) State U., summers 1984, 85; reader Ednl. Testing Svc. Advanced Placement French Examination, 1988, 89; peer reviewer for div. edn. programs, NEH, Washington, 1990, 91, 93; grant evaluator, NEH, 1995; mem. fgn. lang. adv. bd. The Coll. Bd., N.Y.C., 1986-91. Author: The Maxims in the Novels of Duclos, 1973; co-author (with Chantal Thompson) Ensuite, 1989, 93, 98, 2003, Moments Litteraires, 1992 (with Chantal Thompson and Elaine Phillips) Mais Oui! workbook, lab. manual, video manual, 1996, 2000; contbr. revs. and articles to profl. jours. Pres. Loma Vista Elem. Sch. PTA, Palo Alto, Calif., 1978-79; bd. dirs. United Way Stanford, Palo Alto, 1985-90, mem. allocations com., 1988, bd. dirs. Cabrillo Music Festival, 1996-2003, sec., 1998, v.p., 2000-2002; bd. dirs. Cmty. TV of Santa Cruz County, 1997-99, vice chair, 1997-98. Grantee NEH, 1980-81, USIA, 1992; Govt. of France scholar, 1982, 2003. Mem.: MLA (mem. adv. com. on fgn. langs. and lits. 1995—2000, chair 1999—2000, com. on info. tech. 2001—, chair 2003—), Am. Assn. Tchrs. of French, Assn. Depts. Fgn. Langs. (exec. com. 1985—88, pres. 1988), Assn. Calif. C.C. Adminstrs. Democrat. Jewish. Avocations: traveling, reading, antique collecting, gourmet eating and cooking. Home: 4149 Georgia Ave Palo Alto CA 94306-3813 Office: Cabrillo College 6500 Soquel Dr Aptos CA 95003-3194 E-mail: behirsch@cabrillo.edu.

HIRSCH, CALLIE CLARK, instructional facilitator; b. Memphis, Oct. 15, 1951; d. Wallace Jr. and Ossie Nell (Pugh) Clark; m. Arnett Sebastian Hirsch Jr. (dec. Oct. 1983); children: Wayne Morris, Sean. BS in Sociology, LeMoyne-Owen Coll., Memphis, 1976; MEd, Memphis State U., 1978. Mental health trainee N.E. Mental Health Ctr., Memphis, 1975-76; tchr. Memphis City Schs., 1978-95, instrnl. facilitator, 1995—. Program coord. Jackson Sch., Memphis, 1983-88; chairperson Leadership Coun., Memphis, 1994-95; staff devel. chairperson A.B. Hill Sch., Memphis, 1995—, lead staffer, 1997; fashion model Ebony Bridal Showcase, 1992—. Cub Scout leader Boy Scouts Am., 1997; vol. Memphis Interfaith Assn., 1992; coord. City Beautiful, Memphis, 1996; rep. Pan Hellenic Coun., Memphis, 1997. Recipient Svc. award Memphis Edn. Assn., 1987, Plaque, Jr. Achievement, Memphis, 1994; named Zeta of Yr., Zeta Phi Beta, Memphis, 1983. Mem. Tenn. Ednl. Assn. (rep. 1979—, Svc. award 1997), bd. dirs. MANDCO. Avocations: canoeing, hiking, horseback riding, reading, skeet shooting. Home: 1820 Fairmeade Ave Memphis TN 38114-5814 also: 1560 Florida St Memphis TN 38109-1902

HIRSCH, GILAH YELIN, artist, writer; b. Montreal, Quebec, Can., Aug. 24, 1944; came to US, 1963; d. Ezra and Shulamis (Borodensky) Y. BA, U. Calif., Berkeley, 1967; MFA, UCLA, 1970. Prof. of art Calif. State U., Dominguez Hills, L.A., 1973—. Adj. prof. Internat. Coll., Guild of Tutors, LA, 1980-87, Union Grad. Sch., Cin., 1990. Founding mem. Santa Monica (Calif.) Art Bank, 1983-85; bd. dir. Dorland Mountain Colony, Temecula, Calif., 1984-88. Recipient Disting. Artist award Calif. State U., 1985, Found. Rsch. award, 1988-89, 97-98; grantee Nat. Endowment for the Arts, 1985; Dorland Mountain Colony fellow, 1981-84, Banff Ctr. for the Arts fellow, Can., 1985, MacDowell Colony fellow, NH, 1987, Dorland Mountain Arts Colony fellow, 2003; named artist-in-residence RIM Inst., Payson, Ariz., 1989-90, Tamarind Inst. Lithography, Albuquerque, 1973, Rockefeller Bellagio Ctr., Italy, 1992, Tyrone Guthrie Ctr. for Arts, Annamahkerrig, Ireland, 1993, Creative Rsch. award Sally Canova Rsch. Scholarship and Creative Activities awards program, 1997-99, 2003; Class Found. grant, 2003, 2004. Office: Calif State Univ Dominguez Hills 1000 E Victoria St Carson CA 90747-0001

HIRSCH, IRMA LOU KOLTERMAN, retired nurse; b. Clay Center, Kans., June 11, 1934; d. Arthur Henry and Mildred (Peterson) Kolterman; m. William A. Hirsch, June 8, 1958; children: David William, Brian Duane. BSN, U. Kans., 1957; M Nursing, U. Wash., 1961. RN, Mo. Instr. Duke U., Durham, N.C., 1961-64; nurse clinician U. Kans. Med. Ctr., Kansas City, 1968-70; project dir., cons. Mo. Regional Med. Program, Kansas City, 1970-74; project dir., program coord. ANA, Kansas City, 1974-79, policy developer, 1981-92; supr. VA Med. Ctr., Kansas City, 1979-81, dept. dir., 1981-83. Cons. nursing edn. Joint Commn. on Accreditation of Hosps., Chgo., 1973; cons. for project devel. Am. Nurses Found., Kansas City, 1974; cons. nursing stds. Health Stds. Directorate, Ottawa, Ont., Can., 1978, Mid-Am. Coalition on Health Care, 1993-98; mem. affiliate faculty U. Mo. Sch. Nursing, Kansas City, 1995-98. Editor: Guidelines for Review of Nursing Care at the Local Leval, 1976, Nursing Quality Assurance Management/Learning System, 1982, Peer Review in Nursing, 1982, Issues in Professional Practice, 1985, Classification Systems for Describing Nursing Practice. Mem. Friends of Art, Kansas City, 1975—, Internat. Rels. Coun., Kansas City, 1980—; chpt. pres. Am. Field Svcs., Kansas City, 1978—79; mem. adv. com. Nancy Whalen Nursing Found., 1992—97; mem. evaluation com. Heart of Am. United Way, 1993—97, chmn., 1996—97; chmn. adv. com. Kansas City Presbyn. Manor, 1985—98; trustee Nursing Heritage Found., 1993—98, pres., 1994—97; deacon, elder, chmn. strategic planning, pers. chmn. 2d Presbyn. Ch., Kansas City, 1996—97; trustee Presbyn. Manors Mid-Am., 1967—86, 1998—, chmn. quality assurance com., 1999—; bd. dirs. Adolescent Resource Corp., 1995—97. Mem. ANA (pres. Mo. dist. 1980-81), U. Kans. Nurses Alumni Assn. (pres. 1964-66), Sigma Theta Tau. Home: 1035 W 57th Ter Kansas City MO 64113-1163

HIRSCH, LYNN CHRISTY, elementary school educator, art educator; b. Springfield, Minn., Nov. 7, 1951; d. LaVern Wallace and Joan Elizabeth Bredeson; m. Gary Lee Hirsch, Dec. 18, 1971; children: Nealie Kim Hill, Kelly Lynn. Postgrad., U. No. Iowa, 1969—72; BA, Marycrest Coll., 1973. Lic. tchr. Iowa. Tot lot and pk. bd. dir. Cedar Rapids (Iowa) Pk. Bd., 1970, 1971, Bettendorf (Iowa) Pk. Bd., 1973—75; elem. art tchr. Bettendorf Cmty. Schs., 1973—75, 1982—; pvt. childcare provider Bettendorf, 1976—82. Com. mem., vol. Davenport (Iowa) Mus. Art, 1995—; tchr. mentor Bettendorf Cmty. Schs., 2000—03. Leader, spkr. Christ in Others Retreat, Davenport and Bettendorf, 1976—83, Pre-Cana, Davenport, 1978—90; pres., mem. St. Joan of Arc Cir., Bettendorf, 1977—2000. Recipient First in Nation Edn. award, Tchrs. Assistance Team Gov. Iowa, 1999. Mem.: Behavioral Initiative Team (co-chair), Art Inst. Chgo., Nat. Mus. Women in the Arts. Democrat. Roman Catholic. Avocations: crafts, boating, tennis, reading, walking. Home: 4200 Apple Valley Dr Bettendorf IA 52722 Office: Bettendorf Cmty Schs 3311 Central Ave Bettendorf IA 52722

HIRSCH, ROSEANN CONTE, publisher; b. N.Y.C., Feb. 5, 1941; d. Frank and Anna (Burzycki) Conte; m. Barry Jay Hirsch, Oct. 1, 1967; children: Brian Christopher, Nicholas Benjamin, Jonathan Alexander. Student, Boston U., 1958-61. Editorial asst. Grolier, Inc., 1962-64; editor Ideal Pub. Corp., N.Y.C., 1968-74; editorial dir. Sterling's Mags., Inc., N.Y.C., 1975-78, Hearst Spl. Publs., Hearst Corp., N.Y.C., 1978-84; v.p. Ultra Communications, Inc., N.Y.C., 1984-89; pub., pres. Dream Guys, Inc., N.Y.C., 1986-93; pres. Lamppost Press, Inc., N.Y.C., 1989-. Author: Super Working Mom's Handbook, 1986; editor: Young & Married Mag., 1976-77, 100 Greatest American Women, Good Housekeeping's Moms Who Work; contbr. articles to various mags. Home and Office: Lamppost Press Inc 710 Park Ave # 19B New York NY 10021-4944

HIRSCH, TINA, film editor, educator; d. John and Adelaide Kugel; m. Karl Epstein, Sept. 10, 1989. BA, Boston U., 1966. Freelance film editor. Adj. prof. U. S.C. Cinema Sch., 2004—. Editor: (pilot) Party of Five, 1994, The West Wing, 1999 (Emmy nomination, 2000, Eddy award, 2000), (films) Macon County Line, 1974, Big Bad Mama, 1974, Death Race 2000, 1975, Eat My Dust!, 1976, The Driver, 1978, More American Graffiti, 1979, Heartbeeps, 1981, Gremlins, 1984, Explorers, 1985; dir.: (films) Munchies, 1987; editor: (films) Mystery Date, 1991, Captain Ron, 1992, Steal Big, Steal Little, 1995, Dante's Peak, 1997, (TV films) Saved By The Light, 1995, Labor of Love, 1998, Behind the Mask, 1999 (Eddy nomination, 1999), Stealing Sinatra, 2003, The One, 2003, Plainsong, 2003, (TV miniseries) Tom Clancy's Op Center, 1995 (Eddy nomination, 1995), A Will of Their Own, 1998. Mem.: NATAS, Am. Cinema Editors (v.p., pres. 2000—, bd. dirs.), Am. Acad. Motion Picture Arts and Scis. Avocations: travel, yoga, pottery, painting.

HIRSCHFELD, ARLENE F. civic worker, homemaker; b. Denver, Apr. 6, 1944; d. Hyman and Gertrude (Schwartz) Friedman; m. A. Barry Hirschfeld, Dec. 17, 1966; 2 children. Student, U. Mich., 1962-64; BA, U. Denver, 1966. English tchr. Abraham Lincoln High Sch., Denver, 1966-70. Pres. Jr. League of Denver, 1986-87, v.p. ways and means, 1985-86, v.p. mktg., 1982-83, chmn. Colo. Cache cookbook mktg. com., 1978-79, chair holiday mart, 1981, 85-87, participant in Nat. Jr. League Mktg. Conf.; trustee Graland Country Day Sch., 1988-97, bd. sec., 1990-95, chmn. edn. com., 1989-95, pres. parent coun., 1982-83, auction chmn., 1980, 81; bd. dirs. Allied Jewish Fedn., 1988-96, 98—, women's campaign chair, 1993; bd. dirs. Allied Jewis Fedn. Colo., 1999-03, bd. chair 1999-2001; co-chmn. collector's choice event Denver Art Mus., 1989, 94, trustee, 1995—, co-chair mktg. com.; co-chair ann. dinner Inst. Internat. Edn., 1997; co-chmn. benefit luncheon Pub. Edn. and Bus. Coalition, 1990, mini grants selection com., 1985-87; mem. bd. Minoru Yasui Comty. Vol. award, 1986-87; mem. Greater Denver C. of C. Leadership Denver, class of 1987-88; bd. dirs. Women's Found. Colo., 1992-97, hon. trustees coun., 1997—, annual event co-chair, 2001; bd. dirs. Anti-Defamation League, 1996-, Colo. Spl. Olympics Coun. Advisors, 1995-98, Mizel Ctr. for Art, Film and Culture, 1996-2003; bd. dirs. Mizel Mus., 2003—; trustee Rose Cmty. Found.(chair child and family com.), 2000—; mem. Jewish Life com., Mile High coun. Girl Scouts U.S, 1998—; dean's coun. Harvard Div. Sch., 1992—, nat. leadership com. Harvard Women's Studies in Religion Program, 1994—; exec. com. Children's Diabetes Found., Denver, 1993—; appointee to exec. endemic bd. Gov. Roy Roman, 1989-99, residence bd. Gov. Bill Owens, 1999—; gov. appointee mem. Colo. Women's Econ. Devel. Coun., 1989-99. Named Humanitarian of Yr., Nat. Jewish Ctr., 1988, Sustainer of Yr., Jr. League, 1992, Collectors Choice honoree, Denver Art Mus., 2002, Outstanding Vol. Fundraiser, Nat. Philanthropy Day in Colo., 2003; recipient Colo. Chpt. award, Nat. Women's Mus. of the Arts, 1991, Alumni Cmty. Svc. award, U. Denver Founder's Day, Woman of Distinction award, Rocky Mountain News and Hyatt Beaver Creek, 1993, Colo. I Have A Dream Found. award, 1992, Vol. award, Denver br. AAUW, Golda Meir award, Allied Jewish Fedn. Colo., 1999, Intermountain Jewish News Feature, 1999, Martin Luther King Bus. Social Responsibility award, 2002, Mizel Mus. Cmty. Cultural Enrichment award, 2001, Rex Morgan award, Sci. and Cultural Facilities Dist., 2002, Collectors Choice Honoree, Denver Art Mus., 2002, Outstanding Jewish Woman award, Rocky Mountain Jewish Hist. Soc., 2004, Heritage award, 2004. Mem. Colo. Women's Forum. Avocations: aerobics, snow and water skiing, golf. Office: 5200 Smith Rd Denver CO 80216-4525

HIRSCHHORN, ROCHELLE, genetics educator; b. Bklyn., Mar. 19, 1932; d. Hyman and Anna Reibman; m. Kurt Hirschhorn; children: Melanie D., Lisa R., Joel N. BA, Barnard Coll., 1953; MD, NYU, 1957. Intern NYU-Bellevue Med. Divsn., N.Y.C., 1958—59; rsch. fellow, teaching asst. NYU Sch. Medicine, N.Y.C., 1963—65, assoc. rsch. scientist, 1965—66, instr. medicine, 1966—69, asst. prof. medicine, 1969—74, assoc. prof. medicine, 1974—79, prof. medicine, 1975—, head divsn. med. genetics, 1984—, prof. medicine and cell biology, 1986— . Hon. fellow [illegible] Human Genetics & Biometry Univ. Coll., London, 1971—72; assoc. attending physician in medicine Beffevue Hosp., N.Y.C., 1969—80, Univ. Hosp., NYU Sch. Medicine, 1974—81; attending physician Bellevue Hosp., 1980—, Univ. Hosp., 1981—; mem. numerous coms. & study sects. NIH, 1973—; vis. prof. Harvard U., 1995, U. Calif., San Francisco, 1995. Trustee AIDS Med. Found./AMFAR; judge Westinghouse Nat. Sci. Talent Search; founding mem. Village Cmty. Sch.; senator NYU Senate, mem. pediatrics search com., 1987—89, human subjects instl. rev. bd., 1989—94, co-dir. second year med. genetics course, 1989—93, NYU appts. and promotions com., 1995—2002. Named Disting. Alumna, Barnard Coll. Fellow: AAAS, Hero Arthritis Found., Am. Coll. Med. Genetics (founder), Am. Coll. Rheumatology; mem.: Inst. of Medicine of NAS, Harvey Soc. (coun. 1989—92), Soc. for Inherited Metabolic Diseases, Peripatetic Soc., Interurban Clin. Club (pres. 1987—88), Am. Soc. Human Genetics (cert. 1987), Am. Assn. Immunologists, Assn. Am. Physicians, Am. Soc. for Clin. Investigation, Alpha Omega Alpha (councillor Delta of N.Y. 1982—2002). Achievements include elucidation of pathophysiologic mechanisms, delineation of molecular and biochemical defects of genetic disorders including adenosine deaminase and glycogen storage disease type II. Office: NYU Med Ctr 550 1st Ave CD612 New York NY 10016-6402 Office Phone: 212-263-6276. Business E-Mail: hirscr01@med.nyu.edu.

HIRSH, CRISTY J. principal; b. Dallas, Oct. 3, 1952; d. Bernard and Johanna (Cristol) H. BS in Early Childhood and Elem. Edn., Boston U., 1974; MS in Spl. Edn., U. Tex., Dallas, 1978; MEd in Counseling and Student Svcs., U. North Tex., 1991. Cert. counselor, sch. counselor; lic. profl. counselor, Tex.; cert. tchr., Tex., Mass.; cert. prin., Tex. Dir., learning specialist Specialized Learning, Dallas, 1981—93; counselor, mem. adj. faculty Eastfield Coll., Mesquite, Tex., 1992—95; counselor Grapevine-Colleyville Ind. Sch. Dist., Tex., 1995—2000, alternative sch. prin., 2000—. Mem. adj. faculty Richland Coll., Dallas, 1991—92. Mem. ACA, ASCD, Am. Sch. Counselor Assn., Coun. for Exceptional Children, Coun. for Children with Behavior Disorders, Tex. Assn. for Alternative Edn., Pi Lambda Theta, Phi Delta Kappa. Avocations: travel, theater, film, cooking, reading. Office: VISTA Alternative Campus 3051 Ira E Woods Ave Grapevine TX 76051-3817

HIRSH, CYNTHIA, food service executive; Caterer various TV shows, L.A., Calif.; prin., owner Cynthia's Restaurant, L.A. Guest KNX "Food News Notebook". Office: Cynthias Restaurant 8370 W 3rd St Los Angeles CA 90025

HIRSHFIELD, JANE B. poet; b. NYC, Feb. 24, 1953; d. Robert L. and Harriet Esther (Miller) H. AB magna cum laude, Princeton U., 1973. Lectr. U. San Francisco, 1991—; vis. assoc. prof. U. Calif. Berkeley, 1995. Adv. bd. Marin Arts Coun., San Rafael, Calif., 1988—; steering com. Pen Am . Ctr. West Coast br., Berkeley, 1991-94; adj. prof. No. Mich. U., Marquette, 1994, U. Minn., Duluth, 1995, U. Calif., Berkeley, 1995; vis. prof. U. Cin., 2000; faculty writing seminars Bennington (Vt.) Coll., 1998-2004. Author: Alaya, 1982, Of Gravity & Angels, 1988, The October Palace, 1994, The Lives of the Heart, 1997, Nine Gates, 1997, Given Sugar, Given Salt, 2001; editor: The Ink Dark Moon, 1988, Women in Praise of the Sacred, 1994. Recipient Poetry medal Commonwealth Club Calif., 1988, 94, Poetry Ctr. Book award San Francisco State Poetry Ctr., 1994, Bay Area Book Reviewers award, 1994, 2001, finalist Nat. Books Critics Ctr. award 2001; Guggenheim fellow, 1985, Rockefeller Found. Bellagio fellow, 1995. Office: care of Steven Barclay Agy 12 Western Ave Petaluma CA 94952

HIRSHTAL, EDITH, retired concert pianist, educator, chamber musician; b. Bregenz, Austria, May 31, 1950; d. Izak and Sabina (Silbershein) Hirschthal; 1 child, Jessica Elise. B of Music, Temple U., 1973, M of Music, 1975; artist diploma, Peabody Conservatory, 1983; studied with Leon Fleisher, studied with Adele Marcus, studied with Harvey Wedeen. Adj. faculty mem. Temple U., Phila., 1973-83, Bryn Mawr (Pa.) Conservatory, 1980-83; pianist, mem. faculty Downeast Summer Chamber Inst., 1983, Dobbs Ferry Chamber Inst., 1984; prof. piano emeritus Calif. State U., Long Beach, 1984—2001, ret., 2002. Collaborations with Phila. Opera Co., Sequoia Quartet, Joanne Faletta, Mostovoy Concerto Soloists, Stephanie Chase, Jonathan Mack, Antoinette Perry, Peter Marsh, Michael Carson, Dudley Moore. Musician: (compact discs) Impromptu, Despite the Odds; performed at Weill Recital Hall, N.Y.C., Carnegie Hall, Lincoln Ctr., Alice Tully Hall, co-prodr., co-artistic collaborator, music supr. (documentary) The Phoenix Effect, Nat. Holocaust Meml. Mus., Washington, D.C., 2003. Recipient Galica prize Paderewski Found., Phila., 1970. Democrat. Jewish. E-mail: hirshtal@earthlink.net.

HIRVELA-ABERLE, HELEN DEREE, lawyer; b. Jesup, Ga., Apr. 6, 1952; d. David Andrew and Glenna DeRee (O'Quinn) Hirvela; m. Robert Kenneth Aberle, Aug. 21, 1982 (div. Feb. 1995); children: Alexis DeRee, Julianne Allocca. BS, Ga. So. U., 1974; JD, John Marshall Law Sch., 1979. Bar: Ga., 1979; U.S. Dist. Ct. (so. dist.) Ga. 1980. Econ. devel. specialist Altamaha Ga. So. Area Planning and Devel. Commn., Baxley, 1974-76; paralegal Gibbs, Leehart & Smith, P.C., Jesup, Ga., 1976-79, assoc., 1979-81; sr. ct. clk. State Ct. of Fulton County, Atlanta, 1981-83; caseworker II S.D. Dept. Social Svcs., Rapid City, 1983-85; paralegal instr. Barclay Career Sch., L.A., 1986-88; dir. of adminstrn. Broadcast Tng., Inc./Columbia Sch. Broadcasting, Hollywood, Calif., 1990-91; adminstrv. atty. Nev. Pub. Svc. Commn., Las Vegas, 1991-93; asst. adminstr. State of Nev./Dept. Bus. Industry, Divsn. Indsl. Rels., Las Vegas, 1993-97; asst. dist. atty. Brunswick Jud. Cir., Jesup, Ga., 1997—. Contbr. various Altamaha Ga. So. Area Planning and Devel. Commn. publs. Mem. Comm. Leadership Class, Wayne County C. of C., 1987; panel speaker Emerging Leadership Conf., South Ga. Coll., Douglas, 1973. Qem. DAR, Bus. and Profl. Women, Kiwanis, Zeta Tau Alpha, Pi Kappa Phi. Methodist. Avocations: reading, antiques, art collector. Office: Dist Atty's Office Brunswick Jud Cir PO Box 1157 Jesup GA 31598

HIRZEL, KATHERINE RENEE, communication strategist, geographer, photographer; b. Toledo, Oct. 2, 1962; d. Alfred Ernest and Eleanor Theresa Hirzel; m. Evan Mark Rosen. BBA in Econs., Ohio U., 1984; MA in Geography, San Francisco State U., 1996. Internat. telecom. cons. AT&T, San Francisco, 1993—99; sr. strategist Impact Video Communication, San Francisco, 1999—. Photo historian East Marin Island Archaeol. Project, Marin County, Calif., 1992; field supr. Sunol Archaeol. Project, 1993; photo curator San Francisco State U. Bayside Archaeology, 1992, 99. Photo editor: (book) Personal Videoconferencing, 1996; author: Plant Use Among the Maroons of Accompong, Jamaica, A Key to Cultural Survival. Mem. Assn. Am. Geographers, Soc. for Calif. Archaeology. Office: 1750 Montgomery St San Francisco CA 94111 E-mail: khirzel@impactvid.com.

HISCAVICH, MICHELLE, music educator, consultant; b. Suffern, N.Y., July 14, 1962; d. Lawrence John and Rose Marie Hiscavich. MusB, Univ. Miami, Fla., 1984; MEd, Univ. Mo.-Columbia, Mo., 1986; sixth yr. degree ednl. leadership, So. Conn. State Univ., New Haven, Conn., 1994. Cert. initial educator adminstr./supr. Conn., profl. educator music preK-12 Conn. Orch. dir. Ridgefield Pub. Sch., Conn., 1987—88, Newtown Pub. Sch., Conn., 1988—, dir. music, 1995—. Best portfolio scorer Conn. State Dept of Edn., Hartford, Conn., 2002—03, best assessor, 1995—97; asst. condr. Ridgefield Youth orch., Conn., 1988—91. Bd. dirs. Danbury Music Ctr., Conn. Mem.: Assn. for Supr. and Curriculm Devel., Music Educators Nat. Conf., Kappa Delta Pi. Avocations: music, outdoor activites.

HISEY, LYDIA VEE, educational administrator; b. Memphis, Tex., July 10, 1951; d. Murray Wayne Latimer and Jane Kathryn (Grimsley) Webster; m. Gregory Lynn Hisey, Oct. 4, 1975; children: Kathryn Elizabeth, Jennifer Kay, Anna Elaine. BS in Edn., Tex. Tech U., 1974, MEd, 1990. Cert. tchr., mid-mgmt., Tex.x. Tchr. phys. edn. Lubbock (Tex.) Ind. Sch. Dist., 1975-79, tchr., 1982-91, asst. prin., 1991-95, prin., 1995-2000, assoc. H.S. prin., 2000. Recipient Way-To-Go award Lubbock Ind. Sch. Dist., 1989, Impact II grantee, 1991. Mem. Tex. Assn. Secondary Sch. Prins., Tex. Elem. Prins. and Suprs. Assn., Lubbock Elem. Prins. and Suprs. Assn. (v.p. 1997-98, pres. 1998-99), Delta Kappa Gamma, Phi Delta Kappa. Baptist. Avocation: gardening. Home: 4417 87th St Lubbock TX 79424-4231 E-mail: veehisey@lubbock.k12.tx.us.

HISLE, LINDA BETH See **FRYE, LINDA BETH**

HITCH, ELIZABETH, academic administrator; Dir. higher edn. Ctrl. Mich. U., assoc. dean Sch. Edn., Health and Human Svcs., prof. dept. human environ. studies; mgr. instrn. design Sch. Medicine U. Mich., Ann Arbor; dean Coll. Edn. and Profl. Studies Ea. Ill. U., Charleston, Ill.; provost, vice chancellor U. Wis., LaCrosse, 2002—. Office: U Wis LaCrosse 145 Main Hall 1725 State St La Crosse WI 54601

HITCH, MELANIE AUDREY, orthopaedics nurse; b. Chgo., Sept. 19, 1947; d. Alden Edwards and Frances (Gillette) Snell; m. David C. Hitch, Sept. 2, 1972; children: Charles Joseph, Kathryn Elizabeth Frances. AA, Va. Intermont, Bristol, Va., 1967; BSN, U. Va., 1969; MS, U. Okla., 1982. Head nurse U. Va. Hosp., Charlottesville, 1969-73; clin. nurse specialist Sunnybrook Med. Ctr., Toronto, Ont., Can., 1973-75; staff nurse Bapt. Hosp., Memphis, 1975; head nurse Porter Meml. Hosp., Denver, 1976-78; physician's asst. Kaiser Permanente, Denver, 1978; clin. nurse specialist Okla. Children's Meml. Hosp., Oklahoma City, 1978-82, instr. Cazonovia (N.Y.) Coll., 1983; clin. nurse specialist Onondaga County Health Dept. Long Term Health Care, Syracuse, NY, 1983-89; supr. Montgomery County Combined Health Dist., Dayton, Ohio, 1990—. Preceptor Syracuse U., 1986-89; mem. affiliate faculty Sch. Medicine, Wright State U., Dayton, 1990—; adj. asst. prof. Sch. Nursing, SUNY, Syracuse, 1988-89. Co-author: An Introduction to Orthopaedic Nursing: An Orientation Module, 1991; editor: (video) Total Hip Replacement-Patient Edn. (1st pl. Am. Jour. Nursing Patient Edn. Media award 1994). Recipient Otto Au Franc award The Hip Soc., New Orleans, 1982; named for Neonatal Intensive Home Care, Nat. Assn. Counties, 1987. Mem. Nat. Assn. Orthopaedic Nurses (com. chairperson 1991, nominating com., 1998-2001, nominating com. chair 2000-01), Orthopaedic Nurses Assn. (v.p. 1977-78, sec. 1978-80, bd. dirs. 1974-75, mem nat. nominating com. 1975-77), Dayton Area Orthopaedic Nurses (pres. 1992 93, 2004-). Episcopalian. Avocations: skiing, gardening, sailing. Home: 4962 Walther Rd Kettering OH 45429-1944 Office: 117 S Main St # 230 Dayton OH 45402-2005

HITCHCOCK, JOANNA, publisher; b. London; BA, Oxford (Eng.) U., 1960, MA in Modern History, 1965. Asst. publicity dept. Oxford U. Press, London, 1962-66; asst. promotion mgr. Princeton (N.J.) Univ. Press, 1966-68, advt. and exhibits mgr., 1968-69, staff editor, 1970-72, mng. editor, 1972-80, exec. editor, 1980-84, asst. dir., 1985-87, exec. editor for humanities, 1988-92, dir. U. of Tex. Press, Austin, 1992—. Mem. Princeton U. Libr. Coun., 1986-95; adv. com. Tex. Book Festival, 1996-. Mem. Am. Assn. Univ. Presses (bd. dirs. 1984-87, chair equal opportunities com. 1985-86, ann. program planning com. 1986-87, pres. 1997-98, past pres. 1998-99). Home: 1507 Preston Ave Austin TX 78703-1903 Office: Univ of Texas Press PO Box 7819 Austin TX 78713-7819

HITCHCOCK, KAREN RUTH, biology educator, university dean, academic administrator; b. Feb. 10, 1943; d. Roy Clinton and Ruth (Wardell) H. BS in Biology, St. Lawrence U., 1964; PhD in Anatomy, U. Rochester, 1969. Postdoctoral fellow in pulmonary cell biology Webb-Waring Inst. Med. Rsch., 1968-70; asst. prof. dept. anatomy Tufts U. Sch. Medicine, Boston, 1970-75, assoc. prof. dept. anatomy, 1975-80, assoc. prof., acting chmn. dept. anatomy, 1978-80, prof., chmn. dept. anatomy and cellular biology, 1980-82, George A. Bates prof. histology, 1982-85, chmn. dept. anatomy and cellular biology, 1982-85; prof. dept. cell biology and anatomy Tex. Tech. U. Health Scis. Ctr.; assoc. dean Tex. Tech. U. Sch. Medicine, Lubbock, 1985-87; vice chancellor rsch., dean grad. coll. U. Ill., Chgo., 1987-91, prof. cell biology, anatomy and biol. scis., 1987-91; v.p. acad. affairs, prof. biol. scis. U. at Albany, SUNY, 1991-95, interim pres., 1995-96, pres., 1996—. Mem. nat. adv. rsch. resources coun. NIH, 1992-96, Nat. Bd. Med. Examiners, 1987-95; bd. dirs. N.Y. Capital Region Ctr. Econ. Growth, 1996—; mem. steering com. Assn. Colls. & Univs. State N.Y., 1995—; mem. N.Y. State Senate Higher Edn. com. adv. com., 1995—; pres., bd. dirs. Capital Region Info. Svc., N.Y., 1995—; bd. dirs. Charter One Bank F.S.B., 1999. Mem. exec. com. Gov.'s Sci. Adv. Com., Ill., 1991; pres. Albany-Colonie C. of C., 1999. Mem. Am. Assn. Anatomists (exec. com. 1981-85, v.p. 1986-88, pres. 1990-91), Nat. Assn. for Biomed. Rsch. (bd. dirs. 1990-92), Nat. Assn. State Univs. and Land-Grant Colls. (chair coun. acad. affairs com. 1994-95), Ill. Soc. Med. Rsch. (pres. 1988-91). Home: 5 Englewood Pl Albany NY 12203-1042 Office: U at Albany Office of Pres Room UAB 430 1400 Washington Ave Albany NY 12222-0100

HITCHCOCK, SUSAN Y. school administrator, city council member; b. South Gate, Calif., Oct. 3, 1948; d. Ralph Wayne and Evelyn Angela Hitchcock; m. David Michael Akin, July 21, 1972 (div. 1989); 1 child, David Michael Akin Jr. ; m. Jerry Lee Glenn, July 1, 1995. BS in Bus. Adminstrn., Calif. State U., Sacramento, 1979; MA in Edn., U. Pacific, 1997. Cert. tchr., Calif., adminstr. svcs. credential Calif. Loan officer Bank of Am. NT&SA, Mountain View, Calif., 1967-74; tchr. St. Anne Sch., Lodi, Calif., 1981-92, Lodi Mid. Sch., 1992-97, Morado Middle Sch., 1997—99, vice prin., 1999—2001; prin. Clairmont Elem. Sch., Stockton, 2001—. Spkr. on urban land use planning League Calif. Cities, Sacramento, 1985-95. Mem. City Coun., City of Lodi, 1998—, planning commr., 1981-95, Mayor, 2002—; grand juror San Joaquin County, Stockton, 1979-80. Mem. AAUW (pres.). Roman Catholic. Avocation: travel. Home: 2443 Macarthur Pkwy Lodi CA 95242-3252 Office: Clairmont Elem Sch 8282 LeMans Ave Stockton CA 95210

HITE, CATHARINE LEAVEY, orchestra manager; b. Boston, Oct. 1, 1924; d. Edmond Harrison and Ruth Farrington Leavey; m. Robert Atkinson Hite, Aug. 28, 1948; children: Charles Harrison, Patricia Hite Barton, Catharine Hite Dunn. BA, Coll. William and Mary, 1945. Restoration guide Williamsburg Restoration, 1944-45; asst. edn. dept. Honolulu Acad. Arts, 1945-46; sec., tour guide edn. dept. office chief curator Nat. Gallery Art, 1946-48; opera liason/coord. Honolulu Symphony, 1972-73, asst. to gen. mgr., 1973-75, community devel. dir./opera coord., 1975-77, dir. ops./opera prodn. coord., 1977-79, orch. mgr., 1979-84, mem. exec. com., 1965-69, pres. women's assn., 1965-66; com. chmn., opera assn. chmn. Hawaii Opera Theatre, 1966-69. Mem. W. R. Farrington Scholarship Com., 1977—, chmn., 1982-94; mem. community arts panel State Found. Culture and the Arts, 1982, State Found. Music and Opera, 1984; docent Iolani Palace, 1990—; docent Honolulu Acad. Arts, 1996—. Mem. Jr. League, Alliance Française, Hawaii Watercolor Soc. Mem. Phi Beta Kappa. Episcopalian.

HIXON, EMILY EARL, artist, educator; b. Auburn, Ala., July 30, 1919; d. Charles Robert and Hassie Earl (Terrell) Hixon; m. Paul David Sturkie, June 19, 1940 (div. Oct. 1962); children: David Paul Sturkie, Margaret Anne (Sturkie) Mitchell; m. Frank Beasley Gunter, July 4, 1974 (dec. July 1979); m. George Arthur Taplin, Aug. 15, 2001. BA, Auburn U., 1940; MA, Rutgers U., 1966. Illustrator Ala. Ext. Svc., Auburn, 1942-44; art dir. Rutgers Prep., Somerset, NJ, 1961-74; founding, exhibiting mem. Amos Eno Gallery, NYC, 1974—. One-woman shows include, Edinburgh, Scotland, Princeton, NYC, New Brunswick, NJ, exhibited in group shows, Coburg, Germany, Windsor, Can., Phila., exhibitions include exhibitions, Boston, exhibited in group shows, Calif., Chgo., East Hampton, Sag Harbor, Montclair Coll., NJ, Montclair Mus., NJ State Mus., Trenton, NJ, Represented in permanent collections Bristol-Meyers Squibb, Johnson & Johnson, Rutgers U., Monmouth Coll., Himalayan Inst. . Mem. HS Task Force, Franklin Twp., NJ, 1968, mem. human rels. commn., 1968—72; bd. dirs. Hamilton Pk. Youth Devel., Franklin Twp., 1970—74, Intercounty Cmty. Devel. Corp., Franklin Twp., 1975—82. Recipient 1st prize in oils, Monmouth Coll., 1964, Printmaker's prize, NJ Painters and Sculptor's Soc., 1965, Purchase prize, Monmouth Coll., 1973. Mem.: Amos Eno Gallery, Parrish Art Mus., Guild Hall, Artists Alliance East Hampton. Democrat. Avocations: playing piano, cats.

HIXSON, ALLIE CORBIN, retired adult education educator, advocate; b. Columbia, Ky., May 28, 1924; d. Alfred B. Corbin and Emma Triplett-Corbin; m. William Forrest Hixson, Aug. 16, 1945; children: Mary Emma, Clarence Hervey, Walter Lawrence. BA in English, Okla. A&M Coll., 1949; MA in Humanities, U. Louisville, 1961, PhD in English, 1969. Sec.-bookkeeper Ky. Farm Bur., Louisville, 1942-45; tchr. English Pub. H.S., Stillwater, Okla., 1949, various secondary schs., Louisville, 1957-64, Ind. U. S.E., Jeffersonville, 1965-69, Bellarmine Coll., Louisville, 1970; head English dept. Collegiate Prep. Girls Sch., Louisville, 1970-74; tchr. Began All-Vol. Feminist Advocacy, 1975-95; ret., 1995. Author: A Critical Study of Edwin Muir, 1977, (with Riane Eisler) ERA Facts and Action Guide, 1986 (Sally Bingham award, grant 1986), (with Martha Grise) Survey of Rural Displaced Homemakers, 1980 (nat. funding AAUW, 1979). Lobbyist women's issues Ky. Women Advs., Frankfort, 1975-78; co-organizer, chmn. Ky. Pro-ERA Alliance-Statewide, 1975-95; chmn. coordinating com. Ky. Internat. Women's Year, 1977; co-chmn. Internat. Women's Yr. continuing com. Houston Conf., 1985-89; state rep. Nat. Women's Polit. Caucus, Louisville, 1978; charter mem., State and Nat. Older Women's Leagues, Louisville, 1980; founder, chmn. Nat. ERA Summit, Washington, 1991-97. Recipient ERA Advocacy award Ky. Pro ERA Alliance, 1996, Women's Equity Action League, 1997, Celebration of Svc. Women of Distinction award, 2003; named Feminist of Yr. Ky. NOW, 1999, One of Most Prominent Feminist leaders in Ky., 2001; named to Ky. Women Remembered permanent exhibit. Mem. AAUW (pres. Ky. Divsn. 1980-84, Predoctoral U. Louisville Coll. Faculty award 1964-65), Campbellsville Bus. and Profl. Women (past pres., nat. ERA chmn. 1975-76; Ky. Woman of Distinction 1991, 2001, 2003), Kappa Delta Gamma (hon.). Democrat. Unitarian Universalist. Avocations: reading, writing memoir, caring for pets, bird watching, taking walks. Home: 3318 Hunsinger Ln Louisville KY 40220

HIXSON, SHEILA ELLIS, state legislator; b. L'Anse, Mich., Feb. 9, 1933; divorced; children: Denise, Lynn, Andy, Todd. AB, No. Mich. U., 1953. Tchr. Head Start; campaign mgr., aide Congressman William Ford, Mich., 1963-64; adminstrv. aide to state senator, 1965-66; legal aide to sec. of Dem. Nat. Conv., 1966-76; mem. Md. Ho. of Dels., Annapolis, 1976—, mem. ways and means com., environ. matters com., budget and audit com., house rules and exec. nominations com., procurement com., lottery com., others, chair joint com. fed.-state rels., chair task force on child abuse and neglect; chmn. Ways and Means com. Mem. Gov. Work Force Investment Bd. Mem. Montgomery County Dem. State Cen. Com. Mem. Nat. Assn. Sunday Sch. Instrs., Nat. Profl. and Bus. Women's Orgn., Women's Polit. Caucus, Plowmen and Fishermen, NOW. Home: 1008 Broadmore Cir Silver Spring MD 20904-3108 Office: Md Gen Assembly Ways and Means Com Rm 100 Lowe House Office Bl Annapolis MD 21401-1991

HLAVAY, SARAH INEZ, fundraising executive; b. Corvallis, Oreg., Dec. 10, 1942; d. Samuel Sidney and Mary Eleanor (Grantham) Wood; m. Joseph Francis Hlavay, Aug. 3, 1985. BS, U. Ga., 1964; MA in Tchg., Emory U., 1965; MBA, Pepperdine U., 1979. Social studies coord. Holy Innocents Parish Day Sch., Atlanta, 1965-68; adminstrv. asst. Dorothy Freedman & Assoc., N.Y.C., 1969; regional sales mgr. Milliken, Inc., L.A., 1969-74; acct. exec. Clinique Labs., Inc., L.A., 1974-75; area mgr. Orlane, L.A., 1975-79; ESL tchr. Beverly Hills (Calif.) Adult Sch., 1980-81; regional rep. St. Jude Childrens Rsch. Hosp., Arlington, Va., 1982-83; assoc. dir. alumni rels. Emory U., Atlanta, 1983-85; mgmt. cons. S.I. Wood and Assoc., Calgary, Can., 1979—. State treas. Nat. Soc. Fund Raising Execs., Atlanta, 1984-85; bd. dirs. Learning Ctr., Calgary, 1988-94, Juvenile Diabetes Found., L.A., 1979-81; state ctrl. com. Calif. Rep. Party, L.A., 1973-75; mem. Nat. Charity League, L.A., 1978—. Ford Found. fellow Emory U., 1964. Mem. N.S. Daus. of the Am. Revolution (past regent), Colonial Dames of Am., Colonial Dames XVII Century (internat. chpt., organizing pres. 1968—), N.S. Daus. of Colonial Wars (state pres. Ariz. 1993—, treas.), N.S. Sons and Daus. of the Pilgrims (nat. chair 1995-2003, state gov.), Alpha Gamma Delta (internat. ext. com. 1960—). Episcopalian. Avocations: reading, travel, golf. Home: 94 Willow Park Green SE Calgary AB Canada T23 3 LI Office: Chief Constrn Co Ltd Calgary AB Canada

HLEDE, KORIE, professional basketball player; b. Mar. 29, 1975; BS in Psychology and Comm., Duquesne U. Guard Montig, Croatia; guard Detroit Shock WNBA, 1998—99, guard Utah Starzz, 1999—. Named 1995 Atlantic 10 Rookie of the Yr., 1997-98 Atlantic 10 Player of the Yr. Achievements include becoming first athlete in Duquesne history to have jersey number retired; ranks second in Atlantic 10 history in career points; Duquesne's all-time leading scorer, male or female, with 2,631 points. Avocations: tennis, travel, reading. Office: Utah Starzz 301 W South Temple Salt Lake City UT 84101-1216

HLOZEK, CAROLE DIANE QUAST, finance company executive; b. Dallas, Apr. 17, 1959; d. Robert E. and Bonnie (Wootton) Quast. BS, BBA, Tex. A&M U., 1982. CPA Tex. Internal auditor Brown & Root Inc., Houston, 1982-84; asst. contr. Wilson Supply Co., Houston, 1984-86; sr. acctg. supr. Hydro Conduit Corp., Houston, 1986-87; fin. analyst Am. Capital, Houston, 1989-94; dir. adminstrn. Am. Gen. Securities, Inc., Houston, 1994-98; CFO 1st Fin. Group Am., Houston, 1998-2000; contr. Clearworks, 2000-01; dir. Ornate Holdings Inc., Houston, 2001—02; full time cons. Robert Half Internat., 2002—03; contr., v.p. finance eLinear Technologies, 2003—04, cons., 2004—. Chmn. bd. dirs. On Our Own, Inc., 1987-91; mentor CPA's Helping Schs.; treas. Sampson Elem. PTO, 2002-04; contr. eLinear Techs., 2003-. Mem. Mensa, Houston Livestock Show and Rodeo. Home: 13527 Greenwood Manor Cypress TX 77429-4840

HO, BETTY JUENYÜ YULIN, physiological educator, researcher; b. Nanking, China, Nov. 20, 1930; came to U.S., 1947; d. William Tien-Hu and Gwei-Hsin (Wang) Ho; m. Lajos Rudolf Elkan, Feb. 27, 1958 (div. Aug. 1967); children: Amanda, Anita, Julien (dec.), Raoul. Student, Western Coll., Oxford, Ohio, 1947-48; BS, Columbia U., 1952; postgrad., piano studies with Maurice Perrin, Lausanne, Switzerland, 1956-58, CCNY, 1966-67, 72-74. Lab. technician Columbia U., N.Y.C., 1953-54; ct. report typist Palais de Justice, Lausanne, Switzerland, 1956-57; pianist, accompanist Ecole de Ballet Mara Dousse, Lausanne, Switzerland, 1958-60; English tchr. Montcalme Inst., Lausanne, Switzerland, 1960-61; piano tchr. Le Manoir Inst., Lausanne, Switzerland, 1960-61, N.Y.C., 1964-65. Rsch. dir. Juvenescent Rsch. Corp., N.Y.C., 1963—. Author: The Living Function of Sleep, Life & Aging, 1967, The Origin of Variation of Races of Mankind & The Cause of Evolution, 1969, A Scientific Guide to Peaceful Living, 1972, How to Stay Healthy A Lifetime Without Medicines, 1979, A Chinese & Western Daily Practical Health Guide, 1982, Immediate Hints to Health Problems, 1991, 101 Ways to Live 150 Years Young and Healthy, 1992, Una Guia Unica para la salud, la juventud y la longevidad, 1994, A Unique Health Guide for Young People, 1994, How To Live a Long Life, 2003, In Preparation: Live 150 Years Young, 2003. Named Citizen of Yr. Principality of Hutt River Province, Queensland, Australia, 1994, awarded royal patronage status for life, 1995, XXth Century Achievement award; recipient Cert. of Merit award Dictionary Internat. Biography dedication, 1998, Internat. Award of Merit, 1999. Mem.: The Order Internat. Fellowship (life). Home and Office: Juvenescent Research Corp 807 Riverside Dr Apt 1F New York NY 10032-7352

HO, DOREEN WOO, bank executive; b. Australia; married; 3 children. BA, Smith Coll.; MA, Columbia U. Corr. Time Mag., Phnom Penh, Democratic Peoples Republic of Korea, 1972—73; various sr. level positions Citibank, 1973—98; pres. nat. home equity Wells Fargo Home Mortgage, Inc., San Francisco, 1998—. Mem. exec. com. Wells Fargo Diversity Coun. Bd. dir. San Francisco (Calif.) Opera. Office: Wells Fargo Home Mortgage Inc 420 Montgomery St San Francisco CA 94163*

HO, WEIFAN LEE, merchandise executive; Student, Middlebury Coll.; BA, CCNY, 1972. Furniture buyer Gimbels East, N.Y.C., 1972-86; sr. buyer Carson Pirie Scott, Chgo., 1986-89; buyer Bloomingdales, N.Y.C., 1989-92; divsnl. mdse. mgr. Conran's-Habitat, N.Y.C., 1992-93; buyer Abraham and Straus/Jordan Marsh, N.Y.C., 1994, Macy's East, N.Y.C., 1995—. Mem.: WITHIT. Office: Macy's East 151 W 34th St New York NY 10001-2180

HO, YINHSIN, retired mathematician, artist; m. Chungwu Ho, June 20, 1964; children: Minnie, Ronald. BS, U. Wash., 1964; MS, Northeastern U., 1967; postgrad., St. Louis U., 1972—76. Lectr. U. Mo., St. Louis, 1974—76, So. Ill. U., Edwardsville, 1976—81; engr., sr. engr. McDonnell Douglas Inc., St. Louis, 1981—91; instr. Belleville (Ill.) Area Coll., 1991—97. One-woman shows include Chinese Cultural Ctr., St. Louis, 1999, exhibitions include East Meet West, 2000; actor: Chinese Arts Assn., 2002; painting included in, 20th Anniversary Art Book of Chinese Art Assn. Pres. St. Louis Chinese Painting Club, 1991; mem. South Bay Chinese Opera Group, San Jose, Calif., 2001. Recipient 3d place award, Gateway East Artist Guild, Belleville, 1997, award of excellence, Asian Pacific Art Inst., N.Y.C., 1999, medal, Asian Pacific Art Inst., 1999. Mem.: Chinese Art Assn. Avocations: Chinese opera singing, erhu, writing. Home: 3261 Falls Creek Dr San Jose CA 95135

HOAG, TAMI, writer; b. 1959; Author: McKnight in Shining Armor, 1988, The Trouble with J.J., 1988, Straight from the Heart, 1989, Mismatch, 1989, Man of Her Dreams, 1989, Rumor Has It, 1989, Magic, 1990, Tempestuous, 1990, The Rainbow Chasers: Heart of Gold, 1990, The Rainbow Chasers: Keeping Company, 1990, The Rainbow Chasers: Reilly's Return, 1990, Heart of Dixie, 1991, Sarah's Sin, 1991, Magic, 1991, The Restless Heart, 1991, The Last White Knight, 1992, Taken by Storm, 1992, Lucky's Lady, 1992; : Still Waters, 1992, Cry Wolf, 1993, Dark Paradise, 1994, Night Sins, 1995, Guilty as Sin, 1996, A Thin Dark Line, 1997, Ashes to Ashes, 1999, Dark Horse, 2002, Lucky's Lady, 2004. Office: Andrea Cirillo Jane Rotrosen Agency 318 East 51st St New York NY 10022

HOAGLAND, CHRISTINA GAIL, occupational therapist, industrial drafter; b. Long Beach, Calif., July 18, 1954; d. Joseph Richard and Dorothy Marian (Bell) H. BS in Occupl. Therapy, Loma Linda U., 1975; AS in Indsl. Drafting Tech., Mt. San Antonio Coll., 1985. Registered occupl. therapist. Occupl. therapist Yuka Mission Hosp., Zambia, Africa, 1976-77; staff occupl. therapist Glendale (Calif.) Adventist Med. Ctr., 1978-79; indsl. drafter Amerex Co., Riverside, Calif., 1985-88; re-entry occupl. therapist Rancho Los Amigos, Downey, Calif., 1989-90; staff occupl. therapist Corona (Calif.) Cmty. Hosp., 1990-92; occupl. therapist Linda R. Brown, Visalia, Calif., 1992; floating staff occupl. therapist Hilltop Rehab. Hosp., Grand Junction, Colo., 1992-94, St. Mary's Rehab. Ctr., Grand Junction, 1995—97, Interim Home Health Care, 1998—, Grand Junction Cmty. Hosp., 2000—. Mem. Am. Occupl. Therapy Assn., Occupl. Therapy Assn. Colo. Nat. Mus. Women in Arts, Western Colo. Ctr. for the Arts. Democratic Socialist. Seventh-Day Adventist. Home and Office: 578 N 26th St Grand Junction CO 81501-7961

HOAK, CAROLYN CLARKE, physician assistant; b. Balt., Sept. 4, 1963; d. Edward Owen Clarke, Jr. and Pearl Rhea Clarke; children: Robert Ryan, Lauren Rebecca. B in Med. Sci., Alderson Broaddus Coll., 1985. Physician asst. cert. Physician asst. migrant health cmty. edn. Shenandoah Cmty. Health Ctr., Martinsburg, W.Va., 1987—90, physician asst. family practice, 1987—90; physician asst. neonatology San Bernardino (Calif.) Med. Ctr., 1990—91; physician asst. Pediat. Assn. Winchester, Va., 1991—92, Tri State Cmty. Health Ctr., Hancock, Md., 1992—97; physician asst. internal medicine Winchester Med. Cons., 1997—. Elder Sunnyside Presbyn. Ch., Winch, Va., 1992—95. Fellow: Am. Acad. Physician Asst. Avocations: sewing, baking, painting, music. Office: Martinsburg VA Med Ctr 510 Butler Ave Martinsburg WV 25401

HOARD, HEIDI MARIE, lawyer; b. Mt. Clemons, Mich., Feb. 8, 1951; d. Duane Jay and Elizabeth Hoard; m. John B. Lunseth II, Jan. 11, 1980; children: John B. III, Steven J. BA, Macalester Coll., 1972, JD cum laude, U. Minn., 1976. Bar: Minn. 1976, U.S. Dist. Ct. Minn. 1976. Assoc. Faegre & Benson, Mpls., 1976-83, ptnr., 1984-93; sr. legal counsel Medtronic, Inc., 1993-95; v.p., gen. counsel, corp. sec. The Musicland Group, Minnetonka, 1995—. Mem. State Bd. Women in the Legal Profession Task Force, State Bd. Legal Cert., 1986-88, pres. Tel-Law, Bar Assn. Com., Mpls., 1978-80; bd. dirs. Fund for Legal Aid Soc. Mem. Minn. Region G, Law Enforcement Assistance Assn. Com., 1971-72; vol. aide U.S. Senate Nursing Home Investigation and Hearing, Mpls., 1971-72; student dir. Legal Aid Clinic, U. Minn., Mpls., 1975-76. Mem. Am. Soc. Corp. Secs. (bd. dirs. Minn. sect.), Am. Corp. Counsel Assn., Minn. Bar Assn., Phi Beta Kappa. Democrat. Office: Musicland Group 10400 Yellow Circle Dr Hopkins MN 55343

HOBAN-MOORE, PATRICIA A. federal agency administrator; b. Detroit, Jan. 31, 1949; m. Charles Harrison Moore, Feb. 10, 1974; 2 children. BA, Wayne State U., 1973; M in Pub. Adminstrn. and Mgmt., U. Ga., 1976. Neighborhood rep. Detroit Model Cities Program Model Neighborhoods Bur., 1972-74; dep. ombudsman Office of the Ombudsman, Atlanta, 1974-76; dir. adminstrn. Aviation Dept. Hartsfield Internat. Airport, Atlanta, 1976-77; spl. asst. Dept. HUD, Birmingham, 1977-80, dir. NVACP, acting dep. mgr., 1980-83, dir. adminstrn., 1983-85; assoc. mem. Jefferson County (Ala.) Pers. Bd., 1985-90; chief op. officer Jefferson County (Ala.) Housing Authority, 1989-90; dir. dept. housing and cmty. devel. City of Pensacola, Fla., 1990-93; dep. dir. divsn. housing and cmty. devel. City of Memphis, 1993-94, urban revitalization demonstration dir. Memphis Housing Auth, 1994-95; plans and grants analyst Dept. Econ. and Cmty. Devel. City of Jackson, Miss., 1995, exec. dir. Greater Jackson Found., 1995; state coord. Miss. State Office Southeast-Caribbean Dept. HUD, Jackson, Miss., 1995—. Contbr. articles to profl. jours. Mem. Young Women's Christian Assn. (bd. dirs.), Leadership Birmingham Alumni Assn., Am. Soc. Pub. Adminstrn., Mayor's Commn. on Status of Women, Downtown Rotary. Methodist. Avocation: soccer. Office: Dept HUD Dr A H McCoy Fed Bldg 100 W Capitol St Ste 910 Jackson MS 39269-1602

HOBART, BILLIE, education educator, consultant; b. Pitts., Apr. 19, 1935; d. Harold James Billingsley and Rose Stephanie (Sladack) Green; m. W.C.H. Hobart, July 20, 1957 (div. 1967); 1 child, Rawson W. BA in English, U. Calif., Berkeley, 1967, EdD, 1992; MA in Psychology, Sonoma State U., 1972. Cert. tchr. Calif., Irlen screener 2003. Asst. prof. Coll. Marin, Kentfield, Calif., 1969-78; freelance cons., writer, 1969—; asst. prof. Contra Costa Coll., San Pablo, Calif., 1986-99, Santa Rosa (Calif.) Jr. Coll., 1999—. Author: (cookbook) Natural Sweet Tooth, 1974, (non-fiction) Expansion, 1972, Purposeful Self: Coherent Self, 1979, 2002, (non-fiction) Talking to Dead People, 1996, On the Subject of Prayer, 2000, (biography)

Captain Granville Perry Swift, California Pioneer and Sonoma Bear, 1999, (fiction) Last Days of Gifted Light, 2000, Timethinner, 2001, Getting to Start, 2001, Clearing to Core, 2002; contbr. articles to profl. jours. Served with WAC, 1953-55. Mem. No. Calif. Coll. Reading Tchrs. Assn. (pres. 1996-98), Mensa, Commonwealth Club San Francisco, Phi Delta Kappa. Home and Office: PO Box 1542 Sonoma CA 95476-1542

HOBBY, ZOE ELAINE, musician, educator, composer; b. Tifton, Ga., Aug. 4, 1966; d. Elvin (Buck) and Joyce McDuffie Hobby. MusB in Edn., Shorter Coll., Rome, GA, 1984—88. Cert. tchr. Ga. Profl. Tchg. Standards Commn., 1988, Orff, level one Western Carolina U., 1989. Choral dir. A.S. Clark Mid. Sch., Cordele, Ga., 1988—92; tchr. mid./high sch. Coffee Co. Bd. of Edn., Douglas, Ga., 1992—96, fine arts coord., 1996—97; HS choral dir. N.E. campus HS Tift Co. Bd. of Edn., Tifton, Ga., 1999—. Clinician Tift Co. H.S. Choral Dept., 1989—2000; accompanist and pianist First Bapt. Ch., Douglas, Ga., 1993—2001; pianist Irwinville (Ga.) Bapt. Ch., Irwinville, 2002—; composer-arranger Tift County HS. Composer 3 dozen vocal/choral works; performer: (musical theater) Most Happy Fella, The Devil and Daniel Webster; accompanist: musical theater Man of La Mancha, Bye, Bye, Birdie, soloist: choral performances Mozart Requiem, Beethoven Te Deum, Handel's Messiah. Vol. scheduler All-State Chorus Auditions, 2000—; accompanist and soloist comty. orgns. Recipient Tchg. Excellence award, Tift Co. Found. for Ednl. Excellence, 2003, Hon. Mention, Billboard Songwriting Contest, 1995. Mem.: Ga. Music Educators Assn., Mu Phi Epsilon. Office: NE Campus Tift Co HS 3021 Fulwood Rd Tifton GA 31794 Personal E-mail: ticklish@innocent.com. E-mail: zhobby@tiftschools.com.

HOBDY, JERRILYN, nurse midwife; b. Nashville, Apr. 24, 1952; BSN, U. Miss. Med. Ctr., Jackson, 1975; MS in Maternal-Child Nursing/Midwifery, Columbia U., 1978. Registered gen. nurse and midwife, U.K.; registered nurse-midwife, Pa. Educator Childbirth Edn. Assn., Jackson, 1974-75; staff nurse, charge nurse in obstetrics Roosevelt Hosp., N.Y.C., 1975-77; from instr. to asst. prof. maternal-newborn Yale U., New Haven, 1979-82; staff midwife Rosie Maternity Hosp., Cambridge (Eng.) Area Health Authority, 1984-85; pvt. practice clin. midwifery Buffalo, 1986-89; clin. midwife Woman Nurse-Midwifery Svcs. Inc., Pa. Hosp., Phila., 1989-94; mem. faculty, nurse-midwifery program U. Pa. Sch. Nursing, Phila., 1990-94; acad. adminstr. nurse midwifery program Frontier Sch. Nursing and Midwifery, Phila., 1994-96; assoc. dir. Inst. Midwifery, Women and Health, 1996-97, sec., 1996—, program dir., 1997—. Assoc. editor Jour. Nurse Midwifery, 1982, internat. editor, 1982-85; contbr. numerous articles to profl. jours.; presenter in field. Mem. Am. Coll. Nurse-Midwives. Office: Phila U Hayward Hall Inst Midwifery Women Health Schoolhouse Ln and Henry Av Philadelphia PA 19144

HOBERECHT, REYNOTTA JAHNKE, school system administrator, educator; b. Mattoon, Wis., Mar. 26, 1938; d. Laurence Herman and Magdalena Evelina (Waidelich) Jahnke; m. Hal G. Hoberecht, Sept. 19, 1970; 1 child, Marc. BS, U. Wis., 1961; MA, U. San Francisco, 1978, EDD, 1998. Tchr. Travis (Calif.) Unified Schs., 1971-99, adminstrv. asst., 1995—. Participant Unidad de Paleontologia Expdn., Las Hoyas, Spain, 1992. Ecosystems project award Travis Sch. Bd., 1993. Mem. Calif. Tchrs. Assn. (treas. 1994-99, sec. 1967-68).

HOBERMAN, MARY ANN, author; b. Stamford, Conn., Aug. 12, 1930; d. Milton and Dorothy (Miller) Freedman; m. Norman Hoberman, Feb. 4, 1951; children: Diane, Perry, Charles, Meg. BA, Smith Coll., 1951; MA, Yale U., 1984. With advt. dept. Gimbel's Dept. Store, N.Y.C., 1951-52; newspaper reporter Harrisburg, Pa., 1952; editor N.Y. Graphic Soc., Greenwich, Conn., 1963-64. Poetry cons.; lectr. in field; program coord. C.G. Jung Ctr., N.Y.C., 1981; adj. prof. Fairfield (Conn.) U., 1980-83; instr. Yale U., New Haven, 1989; founder, mem. The Pocket People, 1968-75; founder, performer Women's Voices, 1983-93. Author: All My Shoes Come in Two's, 1957, How Do I Go?, 1958, Hello and Good-by, 1959, What Jim Knew, 1963, Not Enough Beds for the Babies, 1965, A Little Book of Little Beasts, The Raucous Auk, 1973, The Looking Book, 1973, Nuts to You and Nuts to Me, 1974, I Like Old Clothes, 1976, Bugs, 1976, A House Is a House for Me, 1978, Yellow Butter, Purple Jelly, Red Jam, Black Bread, 1981, The Cozy Book, 1982, Mr. and Mrs. Muddle, 1988, A Fine Fat Pig and Other Animal Poems, 1991, Fathers, Mothers, Sisters, Brothers, 1991; editor: My Song is Beautiful, 1994, The Cozy Book, 1995, The Seven Silly Eaters, 1997, One of Each, 1997, Miss Mary Mack, 1998, The Llama Who Had No Pajama, 1998, And to Think that We Thought We Would Never Be Friends, 1999, The Cozy Book, 1999, The Eensy Weensy Spider, 2000, the Two Sillies, 2000, Michael Finnegan, 2001, It's Simple, Said Simon, 2001, You Read to Me, 2001, The Looking Book, 2002, The Marvelous Mouse Man, 2002, Right Outside My Window, 2002, Bill Grogan's Goat, 2002, Mary Had a Little Lamb, 2003, You Read to Me, I'll Read to You II, 2003, Whose Garden Is It?, 2003, Yankee Doodle, 2003. Bd. dirs. Greenwich Libr., 1988-91, Literacy Vols., 1997-2003, Conn. Ctr. for the Book, 2003—. Recipient Nat. Book award, 1984, Poetry for Children award Nat. Coun. Tchrs. of English, 2003. Mem. Authors Guild. Avocations: dance, gardening, hiking, tennis. Home: 98 Hunting Ridge Rd Greenwich CT 06831-3134

HOBSON, ALESA, medical/surgical nurse; b. Brigham City, Utah, Feb. 29, 1960; d. Clifford James and Berniece (Tanner) H. BSN, U. Utah, 1983. RN, Utah. Staff nurse cardiovascular-thoracic unit, nurse care mgr. LDS Hosp., Salt Lake City, 1988-99, cardiovascular-thoracic clin. nurse eductor, 1998—, instr. and dir. EKG course, preceptor, 1986—. Academic, scholarship advisor Xi Alpha chpt. Chi Omega Fraternity, U. Utah. Youth group leader/advisor Ch. of Jesus Christ of Latter-Day Saints, 1992-98, Sunday sch. tchr., 1998—; alumni amb. U. Utah; 4-H leader, 1988-94. Mem.: Nat. Nurse Staff Devel. Orgn., Utah Orgn. Nurse Leaders, Am. Assn. Critical Care Nurses, Utah Nurses Assn. Democrat. Avocations: family, reading, needlepoint, waterskiing, music.

HOBSON, DIANE MARIE, social worker; d. Robert Eugene and Victoria Irene Hobson; m. Mohamed Ahmed; children: Zack, Ali. BA, Ind. U., Ft. Wayne, 1983; MSW, U. Ky., 1985. Child welfare worker Summit County Children's Svc., Akron, Ohio, 1985—87; foster care worker Family and Children's Svc., Midland, Mich., 1987—89, foster care supr., 1989—92, outpatient therapist, 1992—94, Mich. Psychiat. Svcs., Bay City, 1996—97, List Psychol. Assocs., Bay City, 2003—. Big sister Big Bros./Big Sisters, Midland, 1997—; bd. mem. Am. Heart Assn., Midland, 1995—97.

HOBSON, MELLODY, investment company executive; b. Chgo., Apr. 3, 1969; BA, Woodrow Wilson Sch. Internat. Rels., Princeton U., 1991. Joined mktg. team Ariel Capital Mgmt., Inc., 1991—94, sr. v.p., dir. mktg., 1994—2000, pres., 2000—. Bd. mem. Tellabs, Inc., 2002—; fin. corr. ABC's Good Morning Am. Bd. dir. Chgo. Pub. Edn. Fund, Chgo. Pub. Libr., Field Mus.; bd. trustees Princeton U. Named a Global Leader Tomorrow, World Econ. Forum, Davos, Switzerland, 2001; named one of 30 Leaders of Future, Ebony, 40 under 40, Crain's Chgo. Bus. Office: Ariel Capital Mgmt LLC 200 E Randolph Dr Ste 2900 Chicago IL 60601 Office Phone: 312-726-0140. Office Fax: 312-612-2702.*

HOCHBERG, FAITH S. US district court judge; BA summa cum laude, Tufts U., 1972; JD magna cum laude, Harvard U., 1975. Law clk. to Hon. Spottswood W. Robinson III U.S. Ct. Appeals (D.C. cir.), 1975-76; pvt. practice Washington, Boston, Roseland, N.J., 1977-83; asst. U.S. atty. Dist. N.J., Newark, 1983-87; ptnr. Cole, Schotz, Bernstein, Meisel & Forman, Hackensack, NJ, 1987-90; sr. dep. chief counsel Office Thrift Supervision, U.S. Treasury Dept., Jersey City; dep. asst. sec. law enforcement U.S. Treasury Dept., Washington; U.S. Atty. Dist. of N.J., 1994-99; judge U.S. Dist. Ct., 1999—. Office: US Courthouse and PO Bldg Newark NJ 07102

HOCHBERG, JENNIFER ANNE, counselor; b. Conn., May 4, 1974; d. David Keith and Carol Janice Hochberg. BS in Speech Pathology-Audiology, Ithaca (N.Y.) Coll., 1997. Residential counselor Kennedy Ctr Inc., Trumbull, Conn., 1997—. Vis. scholar Modern Music Masters [illegible] Fairfield N.Y. [illegible], 1999. [illegible] Jewish. Avocations: writing, reading, music, cooking, dance. Home: 232 Church Hill Rd Fairfield CT 06825 Office: Kennedy Ctr Inc 2440 Reservoir Ave Trumbull CT 06611

HOCHLERIN, DIANE, pediatrician, educator; b. N.Y.C., Feb. 4, 1942; d. William J. and Bertha Hochlerin. BS, U. City of N.Y., 1958; MD, Med. Coll. Pa., 1966. Diplomate Am. Bd. Pediats. Intern Albert Einstein Hosp., Phila., 1966-67; resident Phila. Gen. Hosp., 1967-69; attending pediatrician St. Luke's Roosevelt Hosp., N.Y.C., 1969—; clin. assoc. prof. pediats. Columbia U., N.Y.C., 1969—; asst. attending physician Cath. Med. Ctr., N.Y.C., 1993-99. Faculty advisor Adelphi U., N.Y.C., 1994. Fellow Am. Acad. Pediats.; mem. N.Y. State Med. Soc., County Med. Soc. Office: 241 Central Park W New York NY 10024-4530

HOCHMAN, NAOMI LIPSON, special education educator, consultant; b. Bklyn. d. William Lipson and Tillie Silverstein-Beech Lipson; m. Elihu Hochman (div. Mar. 1978); children: Richard, Lisa, Lauren. BA cum laude, Bklyn. Coll., 1956; MA, William Paterson U., 1973. Cert. spl. edn. tchr., N.Y., learning disability cons., N.J. Tchr. Bd. Edn., N.Y.C., 1956-58, spl. edn. tchr. Wayne, N.J., 1968-73; instr. edn. William Paterson U., Wayne, N.J., 1973-74; learning disability cons. Wayne Bd. Edn., 1973-2000; cons. Assocs. Ednl. Consulting, 2000—. Mem. Thorough & Efficient Steering Com., N.J., 1975-80, Adv. Panel Spl. Edn., 1985-93; spkr. Literacy Vols. N.J. Passaic C.C., 1991—; bd. dirs. Wayne Counseling Youth, 1987-90. Mem. LWV, Wayne, 1965-73, Wayne Arts League, 1968-72. Recipient Honors Edn. award Bklyn. Coll., 1956, Anita McKeon award, 1998, N.J. Sch. Psychologists award, 2004. Mem. N.J. Edn. Assn., Profl. Svcs. Coun. N.J., N.J. Assn. Learning Cons. (pres. 1989-91). Avocations: tennis, bldg. doll houses. Home: 201 Zeppi Ln West Orange NJ 07052-4130 Office: Assocs Ednl Cons PO Box 1829 Clifton NJ 07015-1829

HOCHSCHILD, ANN, molecular biologist; b. Urbana, Ill., Jan. 20, 1955; d. Gerhard P. and Ruth Hochschild; m. James Oliver Schwartz, Aug. 26, 1978; children: Eli N., Daniel A. AB, Radcliffe Coll., 1978; PhD, Harvard U., 1986. Asst. prof. Harvard Med. Sch., Boston, 1989-95, assoc. prof., 1995—. Recipient Established Investigator award Am. Heart Assn., 1996. Office: Harvard Med Sch Dept Microbiology 200 Longwood Ave Boston MA 02115-5701

HOCHSCHILD, CARROLL SHEPHERD, computer company and medical equipment executive, educator; b. Whittier, Calif., Mar. 31, 1935; d. Vernon Vero and Effie Corinne (Hollingsworth) Shepherd; m. Richard Hochschild, July 25, 1959; children: Christopher Paul, Stephen Shepherd. BA in Internat. Rels., Pomona Coll., 1956; Teaching credential, U. Calif., Berkeley, 1957; MBA, Pepperdine U., 1985; cert. in fitness instrn., U. Calif., Irvine, 1988. Cert. elem. tchr., Calif. Elem. tchr. Oakland (Calif.) Pub. Schs., 1957-58, San Lorenzo (Calif.) Pub. Schs., 1958-59, Pasadena (Calif.) Pub. Schs., 1959-60, Huntington Beach (Calif.) Pub. Schs., 1961-63, 67-68; adminstrv. asst. Microwave Instruments, Corona del Mar, Calif., 1968-74; co-owner Hoch Co., Corona del Mar, 1978—. Rep. Calif. Tchrs. Assn., Huntington Beach, 1962-63. Mem. Alta Bahia com. Orange County Philharm., 2002. Mem. AAUW, P.E.O. (projects chmn. 1990-92, corr. sec. 1992-94, 98-99, 99-2003, chpt. pres. 1994-95), NAFE, ASTD (Orange County chpt.), Internat. Dance-Exercise Assn., Assistance League Newport-Mesa, Orange County Philharm. Soc. (assoc., Alta Bahia chpt.), Toastmistress (corr. sec. 1983), Jr. Ebell Club (fine arts chmn. Newport Beach 1966-67). Republican.

HOCHSTEDLER, LISA INEZ, educational association administrator; b. El Dorado Springs, Mo., Oct. 25, 1970; d. Gary Lee and Barbara Helene Messick; m. Bernard LeRoy Hochstedler, Aug. 16, 1989; children: Garren Machquade, Gunnar Levi. AS, Drury U., 2002. Child Development Associate (CDA) Wash., 2002. Vol. West Ctrl. Mo. Cmty. Action Agy., Head Start, Stockton, Mo., 1996—98; substitute West Ctrl. Mo. Cmty. Action Agy., Head Start, Stockton, Mo., 1998—2000, co-teacher/driver-head start, 2000—03; ctr. director-head start West Ctrl. Mo. Cmty. Action Agy., El Dorado Springs, Mo., 2003—. Treas. Jerico Springs Picnic Com., Mo., 2003—. Christian. Avocations: cooking, sports, scrapbooks. Home: 307 East Logan Jerico Springs MO 64756 Office: El Dorado Springs Head Start 210 E Fields Blvd El Dorado Springs MO 64744 Personal E-mail: latergator647562000@yahoo.com.

HOCK, JOANNE MEANS, film director, cinematographer; b. Charlotte, N.C., Sept. 11, 1958; d. William Edward and Bonnalyn (Means) H. BA, U. N.C., 1981. Promotions dir. WCHL Radio, Chapel Hill, NC, 1981—82; creative dir. Highland Advt., Winston Salem, NC, 1982—83; prodr., dir. WCNC-TV - Group W, Charlotte, NC, 1983—87, Archdale Advt., Charlotte, NC, 1987—90, creative dir., 1990—92; dir., cinematographer Bridge Prodns., Charlotte, NC, 1993—2002, Emulsion Arts, Charlotte, NC. Recipient Addy award Advt. Club, Charlotte, 1989, Telly award TV Advt., 1994. Mem. Charlotte Film and Video Assn. (bd. dirs., info. dir. 1993—). Avocations: sailing, scuba diving, running, photography. Office: Emulsion Arts 1111 Hawthorne Lane Charlotte NC 28205

HOCKLESS, MARY FONTENOT, educational consultant; b. New Iberia, La., July 23, 1954; d. Gill B. and Thelma Fontenot; m. Jospeh W. Hockless; children: Kellie, Amie, Marcus. BA in Speech Pathology, U. La., 1978, EdM, 1984, postgrad., 2003—. Cert. speech pathology, early intervention guidance & counseling K-12, family svc. coord. Speech therapist Iberia Sch. Dist., New Iberia, La., 1977, presch. tchr., early interventionist; coord. La. Dept. Edn., 1992, regional coord., 1992—2000; rsch. U. Ark., Little Rock, 2000—03; pvt. practice First Steps Referral and Cons. LLC, New Iberia, 2003—. Contbr. articles to profl. jours.; author: (manual) Challenging Behavior Support, 2002, Perfect Rhythm, 2003. Named Tchr. of Yr., Jaycees, New Iberia, 1985, Outstanding Alumni, U. Southwestern La., 2003. Home: PO Box 12213 New Iberia LA 70562 Office: First Steps Referral & Cons LLC 810 Center St New Iberia LA 70560

HODAL, MELANIE, public relations executive; Pres., CEO Dennis Davidson Assocs., Inc., L.A. Office: Dennis Davidson Assocs Inc US Divsn DDA Ltd London 5670 Wilshire Blvd Ste 700 Los Angeles CA 90036-5607

HODARA, SUSAN MINA, writer; b. Washington, Nov. 7, 1953; d. Bernard and Selma Wenesky Rubin; m. Paul Sterling Hodara, Oct. 9, 1983; children: Sofie Elana, Ariel Marissa. BFA, Harvard U., 1975; MFA, Columbia U., 1979. Editor in chief Big Apple Parent, N.Y.C., 1991—2000; consulting editor Westchester Parent, No. White Plains, NY, 2000—; freelance writer. Tchr. Young Writers Workshop, Chappapua, NY, 1997—, Gilda's Club, White Plains, NY, 2002—03, No. Westchester Ctr. for the Arts, Mt. Kisco, NY, 2003—; pub. reader Hudson Valley Writers Ctr., Sleepy Hollow, NY, 2001. Author: Animation: The Art and The Industry, 1984; contbr. articles to profl. jours. and mags. Recipient Editl. Excellence award, Parenting Publs. Am., 1993. Home and Office: 204 Croton Ave Mount Kisco NY 10549

HODEL, MARY ANNE, library director; b. St. Louis, Aug. 12; d. William George and Florence Marie (Betz) H.; children: Courtney Hodel Denham, Christian Hodel Denham. BA, U. Wis., 1972; MLS, Catholic U., 1973. Project libr. TRACOR-JITCO, Rockville, Md., 1973-74; from project mgr. to database mgr. Nat. Resources Libr. U.S. Dept. of Interior, Washington, 1974-77; cataloger USAF Base Libr., Ramstein, Germany, 1977-79; from project libr. to automation libr. Law Libr. Georgetown U., Washington, 1984-85, automation libr. Law Libr., 1985-91; chief state libr. resource ctr. Enoch Pratt Free Libr., Balt., 1991-95; dir. Ann Arbor (Mich.) Dist. Libr., 1995—2001, Orange County (Fla.) Libr. System, 2002—. Network coord. [illegible] Coun. Md. Librs., 1991-93, mem. Sailor implementation group, 1992-95, grants and devel. task force liaison, 1993-95; v.p. Mich. Libr. Consortium, 1998-99, bd. pres., 1999-2000, bd. dirs. Mem. exec. com. Ann Arbor Hands On Mus., 1998—2001. Recipient Libr. of Yr. award Libr. Jour., 1997-98. Mem.: ILAMA, ALA, ALA (Libr. of Yr. award 1997—98), Law Librs. Soc. Washington (program coord. 1989, 1990, chair innovative interfaces users workshop 1989, pres. acad. spl. interest sect. 1988—89, rec. sec. 1989—91), Md. Libr. Assn. (del. to ALA legis. day 1992, co-chair tech. interest group 1994, conf. planning com. 1993, 1994, program coord. 1994), Md. Assn. Profl. Libr. Adminstrs., Pub. Libr. Assn. (sys. sect. v.p./pres.-elect 1994—95, pres. 1995—, chair Leonard Wertheimer award com. 2000—01), Mich. Libr. Consortium (v.p. 1999, pres. 1999—2000), Am. Assn. Law Librs. (program coord. ann. meeting 1987, chair innovative interfaces users com. 1988—89, editor innovative interfaces users com. 1989), Mich. Libr. Assn. (chair pub. libr. divsn. 2001—). Avocations: travel, photography. Home: 9152 Pinnacle Cir Windermere FL 34786 Office: 101 Central Orlando FL 32801

HODGE, KATHERINE RHODES, retired school guidance counselor; b. Norfolk, Va., Oct. 17, 1928; d. E. Weldon and Mary (Eaton) Rhodes; m. Kenneth D. Hodge, June 13, 1949; children: Jeffrey M., Judith M. BA, Coll. William and Mary, 1948; MEd, SUNY, Buffalo, 1970. Cert. secondary tchr., Va.; cert. secondary tchr. guidance counselor, N.Y. Tchr. French and English, Norfolk County Schs., Norfolk, 1948-53; tchr. English Clarence (N.Y.) Sch. Sys., 1966-68, guidance counselor, 1969-86; ret., 1986. Co-writer Western N.Y. Vocat. Guidance Program, Buffalo, 1982-84; mem. first in Am. com. Moore County Schs., 2001-02. Vol. guardian ad litem Moore County, 1989—; clk. of session West End (N.C.) Presbyn. Ch., 1994-96; bd. dirs. Ruth Pauley Lecture Series, 1995-2001, Moore County Libr., 2003-; mem. Moore County Welfare Reform Com., 1997-2002, Pub. Edn. Found. Moore County, 2004-; bd. sec. Seven Lakes Civic Group, 2002—. Recipient Vol. Svc. award, N.C. Gov., 1998, Human Values award, Moore County Kiwanis, 1999. Mem. AAUW, LWV (edn. dir., observer chmn. 1988—, pres., 1991-93, budget chmn., 1994, v.p. 2003—), Moore County Hist. Assn., PEO, Phi Beta Kappa, Pi Beta Phi. Avocations: reading, gardening, bridge. Home: 1066 7 Lks N West End NC 27376-9754

HODGE, KATHLEEN O'CONNELL, academic administrator; b. Balt., Dec. 26, 1948; d. William Walsh and Loretto Marie (Wittek) O'Connell; m. Vern Milton Hodge, Apr. 8, 1972; children: Shea, Ryan. BS, Calif. State U., Fullerton, 1971, MS, 1975; EdD, U. So. Calif., 2002; postgrad., U. Calif., Irvine, 1977-84. Cert. marriage and family therapist. Counselor Saddleback Coll., Mission Viejo, Calif., 1975-87, prof. of psychology, speech, 1975—2002, dean of continuing edn., cmty. svcs., dean emeritus inst., 1987-95, vice chancellor, 1995—, acting chancellor, 1998-99. Accreditation liaison officer Saddleback Coll., 1986; mem. adv. bd. Nat. Issues Forum, Calif., 1985, 87, Saddleback Coll. Community Services, 1984, Access and Aspirations U. Calif., Irvine, 1979. Author: (workbook) Assessment of Life Learning, 1978; editor emeritus: Flavors in Time Anthology of Literature, 1992. Mem. Calif. Community Coll. Counselors Assn. (region coord. 1987), Calif. Tchrs. Assn., Am. Assn. Women Community and Jr. Colls., Assn. Marriage Family Therapists, C.C. Educators of Older Adults (pres. 1990-92). Democrat. Roman Catholic. Avocations: skiing, reading, political advocacy. Home: 4011 Calle Juno San Clemente CA 92673-2616 Office: South Orange County C C Dist 28000 Marguerite Pky Mission Viejo CA 92692-3635

HODGE, MARY, state representative; b. Kans., Dec. 17, 1946; m. Richard Hodge; children: Andrew, Jeffrey, Michael. BA in Elem. Edn., U. No. Colo. Elem. sch. tchr., owner, mgr. rental property; state rep. dist. 30 Colo. Ho. of Reps., Denver, 2002, mem. agr. livestock and natural resources, bus. affairs and labor, and local govt. coms. Precinct com. co-capt. Rep. Party, Adams County exec. ctrl. and outreach coms.; mem. ctrl. and fin. coms. Colo. Dem. Party. Democrat. Office: State Capitol # 307 200 E Colfax Ave Denver CO 80203

HODGE, SUSAN, oil industry executive; BS in Acctg., Iowa State U., 1979; MBA, U. Tex., 1993. CPA, Tex. From mem. staff to treas. Shell Oil Co., Houston, 1979-97, treas., 1997—; mem. staff Bankers Trust Co., N.Y.C., 1986-89; v.p. The First Nat. Bank Chgo., Houston, 1989-95; from asst. treas. to deputy treas. Enron Corp., Houston, 1995-97; leader global bus. line, 2000—; CFO Coral Energy (sub. of Shell Oil Co.), Houston. Bd. dirs. Interfaith Ministries Greater Houston, Theater Under the Stars, Houston. Office: Royal Dutch Shell Group Carel Van Bylandtlaan 16 2596 The Hague Netherlands also: Shell Oil Co One Shell Plaza 900 Louisiana St Houston TX 77002-4901

HODGES, ANN, retired television editor, newspaper columnist; b. McCamey, Tex., Sept. 7, 1928; d. Ernest Cornelius and Margaret Isabel (Wood) Haynes; m. Cecil Ray Hodges, July 2, 1954 (div. Nov. 1974); children: Craig McNeley, Elizabeth Ann. BJ, U. Tex., 1948. Reporter Houston Chronicle, 1948-51; soc. editor The News, Mexico City, 1951-52, TV editor, columnist, TV critic, 1962—2003; ret., 2003. Mem. adv. bd. U. Miami TV Ctr. for Advancement of Modern Media, 1994—; U.S. juror Banff TV Festival, 1995. Mem. Critics Consensus (dir. 1965-75), TV Critics Assn. (founder, exec. bd., v.p., pres.), Houston Press Club (pres. 1967-78).

HODGES, ANN, actress, singer, dancer; b. Elizabethtown, Ky., June 24; d. Henry Lavely and Margaret Rhodes (Lewis) H.; m. Richard Angleine; 1 child, Michael Christian Angleine; m. Barry C. Tuttle, Sept. 16, 1969 (div. 1972). Cert., registered yoga alliance tchr.; ordained min. Congl. Ch. Practical Theology. Yoga instr., Tampa, St. Petersburg, Safety Harbor, Clearwater, Fla., Under the Live Oak, Casa Bella Vista. Pvt. instr. Yoga, Fla. Appeared in (Broadway shows) No Strings, The Rothchilds, Heathen, (off-Broadway shows) The Boys From Syracuse, There Goes The Old Ballgame, Bella, (TV shows) The Jackie Gleason Show, The Steve Allen Show, The Ed Sullivan Show, Bell Telephone Hour, Ellery Queen, Omnibus, The Vic Damone Show, The Big Record, (TV spls.) Once Upon A Mattress, The G.M. Spectacular, The Esso Spectacular, (motion pictures) The Cardinal, The New Life Style, Oldsmobile, (plays) Applause, The Best Little Whorehouse in Texas, Gypsy,(leading roles in plays) Hello Dolly!, Sugar Babies, Chicago, Can Can, Sweet Charity, Mame, Damn Yankees, See How They Run, Catch Me If You Can., Legends!, I Ought to Be in Pictures, How the Other Half Loves, Pajama Tops, The Last of the Red Hot Lovers, Pal Joey, Cole Porter Reveiw, Gone with the Wind (role of Belle Watling in American Premiere Production), The Greenwich Village Scandals of 1923; also many commls., voice overs and indsls.; performer numerous charities including Am. Cancer Soc., Am. Heart Assn., Handicapped, Abused Wives and Children; star performer Gasparilla Coronation, 1991, guest performer Fla. Orch. at Clearwater Jazz Festival. Yoga instr. Safety Harbor Spa, Don CeSar, Harbour Island Athletic Club, Casa Bella Vista. Named the Queen of Mus. Theatre by the Press, one of Tampa Bay's top achievers. Mem.: Suncoast Yoga Tchrs. Assn. (past pres., bd. dirs.). Avocations: yoga, swimming, horse back riding, piano playing, embroidery.

HODGES, ELIZABETH SWANSON, educational consultant, tutor; b. Anoka, Minn., Apr. 7, 1924; d. Henry Otto and Louise Isabel (Holiday) Swanson; m. Allen Hodges, June 27, 1944; children: Nancy Elizabeth, Susan Kathleen, Jane Ellen, Sara Louise. BA cum laude, Regis Coll., Denver, 1966; postgrad., U. No. Colo., 1966-79, Valdosta State U., 1979-81. Cert. secondary edn., hosp./homebound, learning disabilities, Colo., Ga., Ariz. Vol. emergency St. Anthony's Hosp., Denver, 1960-64; v.p., tutor St. Elizabeth's Adult Tutorial, Denver, 1964-69;

hosp./homebound tchr. Liberty County Sch. System, Hinesville, Ga., 1979-87; ednl. tutor Colo. River Indian Tribes, Parker, Ariz., 1986-87; vol. Twin Cities Community Hosp., Templeton, Calif., 1987-89, Guardian Ad Litem Cir. Ct. 5th Dist. Fla., 1992—, Munroe Regional Med. Ctr., Ocala, Fla., 1991-92; cons., tutor Sylvan Learning Ctr., Ocala, 1990—. Vol. tutor Blessed Trinity Sch., Ocala, 1996—. Democrat. Roman Catholic. Avocations: swimming, reading, sewing, piano, gardening. Home and Office: # 6-314 11295 N 99th Ave Peoria AZ 85345-5409

HODGES, KATHLEEN MCGILL, art educator; b. Mpls., Oct. 9, 1964; d. John Michael and Marilyn (Gore) McGill; m. Garry Allen Hodges, Dec. 28, 1991. BFA, U. North Tex., 1987; MEd, Tex. Woman's U., 1991. Elem. art specialist Garland (Tex.) Ind. Sch. Dist., 1988—. Illustrator Cooper Inst. Aerobics Rsch., Dallas, 1995—98, Garland ISD, 1988—, Med. Health Group Credit Union, 1988, Tex. Assn. Landscape Contractors, 1996; campus improvement team Walnut Glen Acad., Garland, 1991—2003, creator pet patrol, 1995—. Art and design com. Dallas Area Rapid Transit, 2000; creator ann. paper towel drive Rogers Wildlife Rehab. Ctr., Hutchins, Tex., 1996—; mem. PTA, Garland, 1988—, hon. life mem., 2003—. Named Tchr. of Yr., Wal-Mart, 2001; Garland ISD grantee, 2001. Mem.: Tex. Art Edn. Assn., Nat. Art Edn. Assn., Pi Beta Phi. Avocations: skiing, antiques, travel. Office: Walnut Glen Acad Excellence 3101 Edgewood Dr Garland TX 75042

HODGES, MARGARET MOORE, author, educator; b. Indpls., July 26, 1911; d. Arthur Carlisle and Anna Marie (Mason) Moore; m. Fletcher Hodges, Jr., Sept. 10, 1932; children: Fletcher III, Arthur Carlisle, John Andrews. AB with honors, Vassar Coll., 1932; MLS; Carnegie Libr. Staff scholar, Carnegie Inst. Tech., 1958. Lectr. U. Pitts. Grad. Sch. Library and Info. Services, 1964-68, asst. prof., 1968-72, assoc. prof., 1972-75, prof., 1975-77, emeritus, 1977— (Children's libr., radio and TV storyteller) Carnegie Library Pitts., 1953—64, (story specialist) Pitts. Pub. Schs., 1964—68, (storyteller) WQED Schs. Svcs. Dept NIT network., 1965—; author: (juvenile books) One Little Drum, 1958, What's for Lunch Charley?, 1961, Club Against Keats, 1962, Tell It Again, 1963, Secret in the Woods, 1963, Wave, 1964, Hatching of Joshua Cobb, 1967, Constellation, a Shakespeare Anthology, 1968, Sing Out, Charley!, 1968, Lady Queen Anne, 1969, Making of Joshua Cobb, 1971, Gorgon's Head, 1972, Hopkins of the Mayflower, 1972, Fire Bringer, 1972, Persephone and the Springtime, 1973, Baldur and the Mistletoe, 1974, Freewheeling of Joshua Cobb, 1974, Knight Prisoner, The Tale of Sir Thomas Malory and His King Arthur, 1976, The High Riders, 1980, The Little Humpbacked Horse, 1980, The Avenger, 1982, If You Had a Horse, 1984, Saint George and the Dragon, 1984, Making a Difference, 1989, The Voice of the Great Bell, 1989, The Arrow and the Lamp, 1989, The Kitchen Knight, 1990, Buried Moon, 1990, Brother Francis and the Friendly Beasts, 1991, Saint Jerome and the Lion, 1991, Hauntings, 1991, Don Quixote and Sancho Panza, 1992, Of Swords and Sorcerers, 1993, St. Patrick and the Peddler, 1993, The Hero of Bremen, 1993, Hidden in Sand, 1994, Gulliver in Lilliput, 1995, Comus, 1996, Molly Limbo, 1996; co-editor: Elva S. Smith's The History of Children's Literature, 1980, The True Tale of Johnny Appleseed, 1997, Silent Night, the Song and Its Story, 1997, Up the Chimney, 1998, Joan of Arc, the Lily Maid, 1999, The Boy Who Drew Cats, 2002, The Legend of St. Christopher, 2002. Mem. ALA (Newbery-Caldecott com. 1960), Pa. Library Assn., Am. Assn. Library Schs., Pitts. Bibliophiles, Zonta Internat., Distinguished Daus. Pa. Republican. Episcopalian. Home: Longwood at Oakmont 48 Garden Ct Verona PA 15147-3852 Office: U Pitts Bellefield Ave Pittsburgh PA 15260

HODGES, MARY BOZEMAN, literature educator; b. Jefferson City, Tenn., July 1, 1944; d. Paul L. Bozeman, Charlie Mae Bozeman; m. James Albert Hodges; children: James Boyd, Amy. BA, Washington U., St. Louis, Mo., 1966; MEd in English, U. Tenn., 1971. Tchr. English St. Andrews Jr. H.S., Charleston, SC, 1967—68; tchr. Latin/English Jefferson County H.S., Jefferson City, Tenn., 1974—76; tchr. English Orange Park H.S., Orange Park, Fla., 1976—78; tchr. English LeJardin Acad., Kailua, Hawaii, 1978—83; sec. Emmaus United Ch. of Christ, Vienna, Va., 1984—88; instr. English Carson-Newman Coll., Jefferson City, 1988—. Author: (short stories) (collection) Tough Customers and Other Stories, 1999, reprinted, 2002, Plastic Santa and Other Stories, 2003; author: (short story) The Mis-Conception, 1998; author: (critical article) T.R. Pearson: Debatable Hereos, 1997; author: (short stories) "The Fall and The Pot-Bellied Stove", 1996, Trulla's Beauty Shop, 1994, In Memory, 1998; author: (book) Structures of Faith, 1990; author: (book rev.) Lost, But Not Found, 1995. Elder First Presbyn. Ch., Jefferson City, 2000—; workshop leader New Opportunities for Women, Berea, Ky., 2001—; pub. readings Pub. Sch. Sys., 1994—; keynote spkr. African-Am. Appalachain Arts Soc., Knoxville, 2000, Annual Storytelling Festival, Wytheville, 2000, Abingdon H.S. Tchrs., Abingdon, Va., 1999; lectr., keynote spkr. SE Va. Libr. Assn., Abingdon, 1999; keynote spkr. First Lady of Morristown Banquet, Morristown, Tenn., 2000; original readings of Christmas ALPS, Morristown, 2000; original readings Seedtime in the Cumberlands Festival, Whitesburg, Ky., 1999—2001; reading short stories Holston-Chilowee Acad., Knoxville, 1999; readings Hindman Settlement Sch., Hindman, Ky., 1993—2002; tchr. Short Stories Hindman Writers Workshop with writer Lee Smith, Hindman, 2000; keynote spkr. Jefferson County Bicentennial Celebration, Dandridge, Tenn., 1996; mem. libr. com. Carson-Newman Coll., 1992—94, mem. tchr. edn. com., 1994—96. Recipient Denny C. Plattner Writing Excellence award, Appalachian Heritage Jour., 1994, Creative Faculty award, Carson-Newmwn Coll., 1998, Outstanding Tchr. award of Am., 1994, 1996; grantee PEW Grant, Carson-Newman Coll., Spring 2001, Summer 1999, Fall 1998, Spring 1998, ACA Grant, Berea, Ky., Spring 1998, PEW Grant, Carson-Newman Coll., Spring 1997, ACA Grant, Berea, Ky., Spring 1997, Acad. Enrichment, Carson-Newman Coll., Spring 1995, Faculty Scholars Program Grant, U. Ky., Summer 1994; scholar Faculty Scholars, Spring 1995. Mem.: Knoxville Writers Guild (reading 2000), So. Appalachain Writers Coop., Tenn. Mountain Writers, Nat. Coun. Tchrs. English, So. Women Writers, Appalachain Studies Assn. (readings 1994—2001), So. Appalachain Writers Coop. (co-chmn. 1999—2000), Sigma Tau Delta (life; faculty sponsor 1996—). Avocations: writing, gardening. Office: Carson-Newman College CNC Box 72057 Jefferson City TN 37760 Personal E-mail: mhodges@cn.edu. Business E-Mail: mhodges@cn.edu.

HODGES-ROBINSON, CHETTINA M. nursing administrator; b. Roosevelt, N.Y., Mar. 12, 1963; d. Clifford and Janice (Revis) Hodges-Jones; m. Darrell K. Robinson, Mar. 17, 1991. BSN, NYU, 1986; postgrad., C.W. Post U. Cert. med.-surg. nurse basic life support and advanced cardiac life support. Staff nurse NYU Med. ctr., N.Y.C., 1986-87, Christ Hosp., Jersey City, 1986-87; cardiothoracic recovery rm. and post-anesthesia nurse, staff nurse Lenox Hill Hosp., N.Y.C., 1987-94; asst. nurse mgr. critical care/intensive/coronary care unit Good Samaritan Hosp., West Islip, L.I., N.Y., 1994—; staff nurse cardiovasc. ICU U. Hosp. at Stony Brook, N.Y., 1995—; field nurse Staff Builders, Medford, N.Y., 1995—; asst. head nurse, sub-acute, rehab. unit Jewish Home and Hosp., Bronx, NY, 1996—2003; staff nurse North Shore Univ. Hosp., Manhasset, Long Island, NY, 2003—. Mem. Luth. Ch. of the Good Shepherd, Roosevelt, N.Y. Mem. ANA, N.Y. State Nurses Assn., N.J. Nurses Assn., Black Nurses Assn. (L.I. chpt.), Zeta Alpha Beta (bd. election Suffolk County inspector). Home: 119 S 28th St Wyandanch NY 11798-2813 E-mail: Chettina@msn.com.

HODGKINSON, GRETA, dancer; b. Providence, R.I. Grad., Nat. Ballet Sch., 1990. Mem. Nat. Ballet of Can., Toronto, Canada, 1990—96, prin. dancer, 1996—. Dancer (ballets) Swan Lake, 1999, Romeo and Juliet, The Merry Widow, The Sleeping Beauty, The Taming of the Shrew, La Bayadère, Giselle, Manon, The Four Seasons, Herman Schmerman Pas de Deux, Sphinx, the Rubies Variation; internat. guest artist Can., U.S., Europe, Australia. Office: Walter Carsen Ctr Nat Ballet of Canada 470 Queens Quay West Toronto ON Canada M5V 3K4

HODGSON, BARBARA CAROLINE, music educator; b. Delaware, Ohio, Aug. 31, 1947; d. Floyd Merrick O'Keefe and Phyllis Jane Johnson; m. Edward Charles Hodgson, Nov. 8, 1986; children: Stephanie Caroline Gilmore, Thomas Louis, Douglas Merrick DeWitt, Nicole Ann Bebiak. BS in Music, Ohio State U., 1969; MusM in Edn., No. Ill. U., 1993. Profl. soloist, 1967—; organist and dir. of music Augsburg (Germany) Mil. Base Chapel, 1969—71, Hilltop United Meth. Ch., Columbus, Ohio, 1971—77; instrumental specialist Ward Mid. Sch., Bolingbrook, Ill., 1978—87; dir. of music Friendship United Meth. Ch., Bolingbrook, Ill., 1979—91; pvt. music instr. Delaware, Ohio, 1964—69, Columbus, Ohio, 1971—78, Bolingbrook, Ill., 1978—93; music specialist Westmont (Ill.) Elem. Schs., 1987—, elem. choral dir., 1990—. Musical cons. Grove City (Ohio) Prodns., 1971—72; presenter Ill. State Conf. Music Edn. Named one of Top Educators, State of Ill. Mem.: NEA (life), Ill. Music educator's Assn. (life), Music Educators Nat. Conf. (life). Methodist. Achievements include research in Computer Based instruction within the Music Classroom. Avocations: photography, travel, technology, literature, crafts. Home: 21221 Barth Pond Lane Crest Hill IL 60435 Office: Westmont Schs 200 N Linden Ave Westmont IL 60559 Personal E-mail: bhodgson@westerncom.net. E-mail: bhodgson@westmont.dupage.k12.il.us.

HODGSON, HARRIET W. non-fiction writer; b. Flushing, N.Y., Sept. 27, 1935; d. Alfred Earnst and Mabel Clifton Weil; m. C. John Hodgson, Aug. 10, 1957; children: Helen Anne, Amy Jeanne. BS in Early Childhood Edn., Wheelock Coll., 1957; MA in Art Edn., U. Minn., 1960. Former tchr. (12 yrs.). Editor, newsletter of The Minn. Med. Assn. Alliance Alliance E News. Author: Smart Aging: Taking Charge of Your Physical and Emotional Health, 1999, The Alzheimer's Caregiver: Dealing with the Realities of Dementia, 1998, Alzheimer's: Finding the Words, a Communication Guide for Those Who Care, 1995, Heart Surgery and You: An Activity Book for Preschoolers, Heart Surgery and You: An Activity Book for Gradeschoolers, Heart Surgery and You: a Guide for Teens, Powerplays: How Teens Can Pull the Plug on Sexual Harassment, 1993, Powerplays Leader's Guide, When You Love a Child, 1992, Rochester: City of the Prairie, 1989, Parents Recover Too: When Your Child Comes Home from Treatment, 1988, A Parent's Survival Guide: How to Cope When Your Kid is Using Drugs, 1986, Contraptions, Toyworks, Gameworks, Artworks, My First Fourth of July Book, 1987, "I Made It Myself!", E is for Energy, M is for Me, Just for You; contbr. articles to websites, reports, columns, and profl. jours.; author: Food Label Detective: An Activity Book, 2002; co-author: AMA Alliance Comm. Guide. Mem. Walden Hill Vocal Ensemble; vol. McGruff House; past mem. regional devel. bd. Minn. Pub. Radio; mem. Olmsted County Coordinated School Health Coun., Minn. Takes Action for Healthy Kids, Adolescent Health Com., Zumbro Valley Med. Soc., Minn. Med. Assn. Commn. Com. Mem.: AAUW, Assn. Health Care Journalists, Wing of the Aerospace Med. Assn. (pres.), Zumbro Valley Med. Assn. Alliance (bd. dirs., past pres., v.p., sec., newsletter editor), Minn. Med. Assn. Alliance (pres.), Am. Med. Assn. Alliance (integrated mktg. comm. com.), Minn. Manx Assn., N.Am. Manx Assn., The Study Club. Avocations: cooking, art projects. Home and Office: 1107 Foxcroft Ln SW Rochester MN 55902

HODGSON, HELEN, writer; AB in English, U. Mich.; MA in English, PhD in English, U. Denver, postgrad., Yale U., Oxford U., Eng. Freelance med. writer; prof. comm. Westminster Coll., New Wilmington, Pa., dir. Masters of Profl. Communication Program, dir. Communications and the Arts. Condr. seminars in field; tech. pubs. editor U.S. Geol. Survey; cons. in field; food editor Salt Lake Mag. Contbr. numerous articles to profl. jours. Mem.: Internat. Assn. of Bus. Communicators, Coun. for Programs in Tech. and Sci. Comm., Am. Med. Writers Assn. (pres. 2001—02), Assn. of Tchrs. in Tech. Writing (life), Soc. for Tech. Comms. (sr.). Office: Am Med Writers Assn 40 W Gude Dr Ste 101 Rockville MD 20850-1192 Address: Westminster College Dept Comm Market St New Wilmington PA 16172

HODGSON, IRENE BELLE, language educator, translator; b. Saint Charles, Mo., May 14, 1950; d. Dale L. and Sarah Larowe Hodgson. BA in English, Purdue U., 1971; MA in Spanish Lit., NYU, 1974; PhD in Spanish and Latin Americana, Purdue U., 1986. Instr. The Ohio State U., Columbus, Ohio, 1981—84, Calif. State U., Chico, Calif., 1985—86; prof. Xavier U., Cin., 1986—. Advisor Voices for Solidarity Xavier U., 1989—. Election observer Global Exchange, Nicaragua, 2001, Christians Peace in El Salvadore, El Salvador, 1994, 1999, bd. dir., 2001—. Mem.: Modern Lang. Assn., Am. Coun. Fgn. Lang. Tchrs., Am. Assn. Tchrs. Spanish and Portuguese, Latin Am. Studies Assn., Alpha Sigma Nu (Bishop Fenwick Tchg. award 2001). Office: Dept Modern Langs Xavier Univ 3800 Victory Parkway Cincinnati OH 45207-5784

HODGSON, JANE ELIZABETH, obstetrician, gynecologist, consultant; b. Crookston, Minn., Jan. 23, 1915; d. Herbert and Adelaide (Marin) H.; m. Frank Walter Quattlebaum, Feb. 22, 1940; children: Gretchen, Nancy. BS, Carleton Coll., 1934, DSc (hon.), 1994; MD, U. Minn., 1939, MS in Ob-Gyn., 1947. Diplomate Am. Bd. Ob.-Gyn. Fellow Mayo Clinic, Rochester, Minn., 1941-44; pvt. practice in ob-gyn. St. Paul, 1947-72; med. dir. Preterm Clinic, Washington, 1972-74; med. dir. fertility control clinic St. Paul Ramsey Med. Ctr., 1974-79; med. dir. Planned Parenthood Minn., St. Paul, 1980-82, Midwest Health Ctr. Women, Mpls., 1981-83, Women's Health Ctr., Duluth, Minn., 1981-84, mem. staff, 1986—, also bd. dirs.; ostetrician/gynecologist Project Hope, Grenada, West Indies, 1984; vis. prof. ob-gyn. project hope Zheijiang Med. Sch., Hangzhou, People's Republic of China, 1985-86; clin. assoc. prof. ob-gyn. U. Minn., Mpls., 1986—. Vis. med. educator Project Hope, Cairo, 1979-80; vis. prof. dept. ob-gyn. U. Calif., San Francisco, 1983. Editor: Abortion & Sterilization, 1981; contbr. numerous articles to profl. jours. Bd. dirs. Genesis II Women, Mpls., 1988—, Pro Choice Resources, Mpls., 1991—, Wellstone Alliance, Mpls., 1992—, Ctr. for Reproductive Rightsy, N.Y.C., 1995—. Recipient Ann. Humanitarian award Nat. Abortion Fedn., 1981, Woman Physician of Yr. award Med. Women Minn. Med. Assn., 1983, Ann. Jane Hodgson Reproductive Freedom award Nat. Abortion Rights Action League, 1989, Hanah G. Solomon award Nat. Coun. Jewish Women, 1990, Margaret Sanger award Planned Parenthood Fedn. of Am., 1995, Harold Swanberg award Am. Med. Writer's Assn., 1996. Fellow Am. Coll. Ob-Gyn. (founding); mem. Am. Med. Women's Assn. (E. Blackwell award 1992, Reproductive Health award 1994), Minn. Ob-Gyn. Soc. (pres. 1967), Minn. Med. Assn. (So. Minn. Med. award 1952), Minn. Women's Polit. Caucus (16th Ann. Founding Feminist award 1988), Mayo Clinic Alumni Assn. Home and Office: 2211 3rd St NW Apt 1405 Rochester MN 55901-2895

HODNICAK, VICTORIA CHRISTINE, pediatrics nurse; b. Detroit, Dec. 29, 1960; d. Roderick Lewis and Beverly Caroline (Backus) Turner; m. Mark Michael Hodnicak, Sept. 20, 1986; children: (twins) Christopher Alan and Matthew Lewis (dec.). ADN, Henry Ford C.C., Dearborn, Mich., 1982. RN, Mich., Tenn. Charge nurse, surg. nurse Harper Grace Hosp., Detroit, 1982-86; neonatal nurse St. John Hosp., Detroit, 1986; home care nurse, coord. med. mgmt. Bloomfield Nursing Svcs., Clawson, Mich., 1986-88; coord. pediat. endocrine growth study So. Health Sys., Memphis, 1988-92; nurse specialist, growth study coord. U. Tenn. Med. Group/St. Jude Children's Rsch. Hosp., Memphis, 1992-98; care coord., educator Pediat. Svcs. Am., Memphis, 1998-99; edn. coord. of nursing Meth. Alliance Healthcare, Memphis, 2001—02, clin. nurse educator, developer home care nurse tng. program, 2002—. Home care pediat. nurse Personal Pediat. Nursing Profls., Pontiac, Mich., 1987-88; staff nurse Nancy Kissick's Profl. Nursing Svc., Mt. Clemens, Mich., 1988; website cons. Family Pathfinder Resource Ctr. of Tenn.; parent advisor TIPS; mem. Project DOCC. Inventor Growth Hormone new dose form, 1991, Hydrocortisone dose and stress dosing card, 1990; contbr. articles to profl. jours.; inventor equipment cart for vent. patients. Mem. tng. com. Ctr. for Devel. Disabilities, 2000—. Mem. Pediat. Endocrinology Nursing Soc. (membership com. 1992), Endocrine Nursing Soc., Human Growth Found., Neurofibromatosis Found., Turner Syndrome Soc., MAGIC Found., Alexander Graham Bell Assn. for Deaf, Project DOCC. Lutheran. Avocations: crafts, doll collecting, travel. E-mail: vnumber1survivor@aol.com.

HODNICKI, JILL ANN, historian, researcher; b. Holyoke, Mass., June 22, 1957; d. Edward and Mona H. (Peterhansel) H. BA, Coll. Our Lady of Elms, 1979; MA, U. Mass., 1981. Prospect researcher Mount Holyoke Coll., South Hadley, Mass., 1981-92, dir. prospect resch., 1992-97, curator South Hadley Canal at 200 Yrs./Art Mus., 1996; dir. devel. rsch. U. Hartford, West Hartford, Conn., 1997—. Instr. art history U. Mass., Amherst, 1981. Active Holyoke Hist. Commn., 1991-2003, chmn., 1992-2000; mem. Holyoke Master Plan Com., 1997-2000. Mem. Soc. Archtl. Historians, New England Soc. Archtl. Historians, New England Devel. Rsch. Assn., New England Historic Geneal. Soc., Assn. Profl. Rschrs. Advancement. Roman Catholic. Avocations: local history, genealogy. Office: U Hartford Alumni House West Hartford CT 06117

HODSDEN, SARA MARIE, minister; d. Charles and Deanna Blanche Bontempo; m. James Michael Hodsden, July 6, 1996; 1 child, Thomas Alexander. BA, Ashland U., Ohio, 1991; MDiv, Louisville Presbyn. Theol. Sem., 1998. Min. of Word and Sacrament Muskingum Valley Presbytery Presbyn. Ch. USA, 1999. Radio announcer WBZW FM, Loudonville, Ohio, 1991—94; student chaplain Ky. Correctional Psychiat. Ctr., LaGrange, 1994—95; supply pastor Lexington (Ind.) Presbyn. Ch., 1995—99; pastor New Harrisburg Presbyn. Ch., Carrollton, Ohio, 1999—2003; assoc. for christian edn. First Presbyn. Ch., Vernon, Tex., 2003—. New ch. devel. task force Muskingum Valley Presbytery, New Phila., Ohio, 1999—2002, chair of representation, 2000—03, vice-moderator, 2003—03; mem. confessing ch. planning team Confessing Churches of the PCUSA, 2001—03; participant pastor-theologian consultation on youth ministry and sacraments Lilly Found. Avocations: reading, writing, travel. Office: First Presbyterian Church 2001 Yucca Lane Vernon TX 76384

HOEFFKEN, REBECCA LYNN, private school educator; b. Belleville, Ill., Mar. 16, 1976; d. Theodore John and Patricia Marie Hoeffken. BS, So. Ill. U., 2001, postgrad. Dance instr. Becky Kern's Dance Studio, Belleville, 1993—2001; tutor Americorps, Belleville, 1999—2000; tchr., tutor The Churchill Sch., St. Louis, 2001—. Presenter The Churchill Sch. Outreach Program, 2002—. Author: (children's picture book) The Princess and the Turtle. Mem.: Coun. Exceptional Children, Alpha Sigma Tau (pres. 2000—01, Officer of Yr. 2001). Office: The Churchill Sch 1035 Price School Ln Saint Louis MO 63124 Personal E-mail: bhoeffken@churchillschool.org.

HOEHN, MARGARET MAIER, neurologist; b. San Francisco, Nov. 24, 1930; d. Peter Paul and Eva Till Maier; children: Robert Anthony Till, Margaret Eve Maier Hanan. BA, U. Sask., Saskatoon, Can., 1950; MD, U. B.C., Vancouver, Can., 1954; postgrad., U. B.C. and Nat. Hosp. Neurol. Diseases, London, 1954—60. Asst. in neurology Boston U., 1961-62; asst. prof. Columbia U., N.Y.C., 1963-70; clin. prof. U. Colo., Denver, 1970—, dir. Parkinson's disease and movement disorder clinic, 1984—. Clin. rschr. Parkinson's Disease and other movement disorders; cons. in clin. rsch., lectr. in field. Contbr. over 100 articles to profl. jours.; developer Hoehn and Yahr Scale as a measure of severity of Parkinson's disease. Fellow ACP, Royal Coll. Physicians Can., Am. Acad. Neurology; mem. Am. Neurol. Assn., Movement Disorder Soc., Colo. Soc. Clin. Neurology, Alpha Omega Alpha. Avocations: travel, bridge, swimming, reading, theater. Office: 3851 S Xanthia St Denver CO 80237-1602

HOELL, VICTORIA ANN, special education educator; b. Green Bay, Wis., Sept. 25, 1951; d. Frederick G. Smith Sr. and Alyce L. Smith; m. William H. Hoell, June 21, 1979; children: Jessica, Gregory, Allison. BS, U. Wis., Eau Claire, 1973, Designated Vocat. Instr., 1983. Spl. edn. educator grades 1-8 Lincoln Elem. Sch., Hartford, Wis., 1973—74; instr. spl. edn., work study coord. West DePere (Wis.) H.S., 1974—, designated vocat. instr., 1983—. Mem. vocat. adv. panel Dept. Pub. Instrn., Madison, Wis., 1986; evaluator, cons. West DePere Area, 1974—90. Named Brown County Educator of Yr., 1985. Mem.: Wis. Edn. Assn. (bldg. rep. 1982—84), United Northeastern Educators (rep. 1997—2003), Green Bay Jr. Women's Club (officer 1982—98). Methodist. Office: West DePere High Sch 665 Grant St De Pere WI 54115

HOELZEL, SALLY ANN, lawyer; b. Knoxville, Iowa, Apr. 5, 1962; d. Clement C. and Helen J. (Falck) H.; m. Peter M. Eckblad, Oct. 11, 1986. BS, U. Wis., 1984, JD, 1987. Bar: Wis. 1987, U.S. Dist. Ct. (we. dist.) Wis. 1987. Assoc. McBurney, Perina, Wyngaard, Wilson & Raymond, Madison, Wis., 1987-88; staff atty. Office of State Pub. Defender, Racine, Wis., 1988-96; pvt. practice Racine, 1996—. Mem.: NOW, ACLU, Ctr. for Reproductive Law and Policy, Racine County Bar Assn., State Bar Wis., Planned Parenthood. Office: 201 6th St Ste 300 Racine WI 53403-1264 Office Phone: 262-638-9945.

HOERING, HELEN G. elementary school educator; b. Liberty, N.Y., Mar. 27, 1946; d. Lewis J. and Charlotte (Huggler) Gerow Sr.; m. Rudolf O. Hoering, Dec. 23, 1968; children: Otto, Katrina. BS, SUNY, Oneonta, 1968; MSEd, SUNY, 1971. Elem. tchr. Liberty Cen. Sch. at WSS, Liberty, N.Y. Mem. N.Y. State Reading Assn., Sullivan County Reading Coun., Alpha Delta Kappa (past pres.). Home: RR 1 Box 543 Jeffersonville NY 12748-9706

HOEY, RITA, public relations executive; b. Chgo., Nov. 4, 1950; d. Louis D. and Edith M. (Finnemann) Hoey; m. Joseph John Dragonette, Sept. 4, 1982 (dec.). BA in English and History, No. Ill. U., 1972. Asst. dir. Nat. Assn. Housing and Human Devel., Chgo., 1975; pub. rels. account exec. Weber Cohn & Riley, Chgo., 1975-76; publicity coord. U.S. Gypsum Co., Chgo., 1976-77; with Daniel J. Edelman, Inc., Chgo., 1977-84, sr. v.p., 1981-84; exec. v.p. Dragonette, Inc., Chgo., 1984-91, pres., 1991-99, GCI Dragonette, Chgo., 1999—. Mem. Pub. Rels. Soc. Am. Home: Ste 2200 680 North Lake Shore Dr Chicago IL 60611 Office: GCI Dragonette 205 W Wacker Dr Ste 2200 Chicago IL 60606-1215

HOFBAUER, MICHELE PACE, illustrator, writer; b. Bridgeport, Conn., May 19, 1953; d. Michael F. and Theresa A. Pace; m. John Alfred Hofbauer, July 22, 1978; 1 child, Michael. BS in Spl. Edn., So. Conn. State U., 1975, MS in Spl. Edn., 1982. Spl. edn. tchr. Chalk Hill Mid. Sch., Monroe, Conn., 1976—83; freelance illustrator, author Trumbull, Conn., 1984—; assoc. pub. Green Bark Press, Inc., Bridgeport, 1996—. Edn. cons. Monroe Bd. Edn., 1984—85; spkr., lectr. in field. Author, illustrator: children's book All the Letters, 1993, Couldn't We Make A Difference, 2000, illustrator: children's book The Bug and the Slug in the Rug, 1995. Mem. first day book selection com. Bridgeport Edn. Fund., 2001. Mem.: Conn. Classic Artists, Nat. League Am. Pen Women (v.p. Fairfield County chpt.). Republican. Roman Catholic. Home: 111 Williams Rd Trumbull CT 06611

HOFF, ANN MARIE, sales professional; b. Morrison, Ill., June 12, 1958; d. Elmer Boyed and marion (Grill) H. BS in Studio Art, U. Wis., Platteville, 1980; MS in Animal Sci., U. Ariz. Asst. tchr. U. Wis., Platteville, 1978-80; rsch. asst. U. Ariz., Tucson, 1980-83; pharm. salesperson Bristol Myers-Squibb, Tucson, 1983-86; exec. sales rep. Smith Kline Beecham, Tucson, 1986—2001; hosp. account salesperson Pharmacia, 2001—02; ind. territory mgr. GWR Med., 2003—. Staff Primavera Fundraiser, Tucson, 1995; chmn. So. Ariz. Ceramic Artists, Tucson, 1995; main instr. East Side Tae Kwon

Do. Ceramics sculptor with numerous exhbns., including: juried shows by So. Ariz. Ceramics Assn., Impressions Gallery, Tucson, 1991 (1st place award), 1992, and 1995; group shows: Invisible Theater, Tucson, 1995, Phoenix Ctr. Visual Arts Gallery, 1995, Art Forms Gallery, Tucson, 1994, 95, Alamo Gallery, Tucson, 1994, 95, U. Ariz. Student Union Gallery, 1992, So. Ill. U., 1991, Shemer Ceramic Art State (Ariz.) show (spl. merit award), others. Awards include riding the Res. World Champion Am. Paint Horse, Ft. Worth, 1993, 94, named 6th Novice Amatuer for 1993, Ft. Worth, 1993. Mem. Am. Paint Horse Assn., So. Ariz. Ceramic Artists. Democrat. Presbyterian. Avocations: snow skiing, arts, tae kwon do (3d degree black belt), horses, reading. Home: 9142 E Indian Hills Rd Tucson AZ 85749-9359 Office: Casa de Artistas of Scottsdale 7058 E Main St Scottsdale AZ

HOFF, JOAN WHITMAN, philosophy educator, women's studies coordinator, director; PhD, The Am. U., Washington, DC, 1977—82. Prof. of philosophy Lock Haven U. of PA, Lock Haven, Pa., 1990—. Author: (book) Philosophies for Living. Chmn. ethics com. Lock Haven Hosp., Lock Haven, Pa., 1996—2003. Recipient Outstanding Scholarship award, 2003; grantee Faculty Enrichment Grant and Rsch. Grant, Can. Embassy, 1999, 1995, 1990, 1989, NEH, 1988—93. Mem.: Pa. Canadian Studies Consortium, The Am. Philos. Assn. Achievements include 2002 LHU Woman of Distinction. Home: PO Box 23 Castanea PA 17745 Office: Lock Haven Univ of PA Lock Haven PA 17745 Office Phone: 570-893-2642. Business E-Mail: jhoff@lhup.edu.

HOFF, MARY ELLEN, educational consultant; b. Highland Pk., Mich., Mar. 23, 1951; d. Jean Clair and Mary Anne (Ronan) Hoff; 1 foster child, Geoffrey A. Menko. Cert. in Interior Design, Fairfield (Conn.) U., 1979; BA in Humanities, Charter Oak Coll., 1983; MEd in Spl. Edn., N.C. State U., 1994. Hort. therapist Green Chimney's Sch., Brewster, NY, 1987—88; coord. svcs. for students with learning disabilities & attention deficit disorder Wake Tech. C.C., Raleigh, NC, 1992—96; pvt. practice Mindsmatter Inc., Apex, NC, 1995—. Interim dir. Wake Tech. C.C., Raleigh, 1996; mem. ethics and stds. com. Nat. Coaching Network, Lafayette, Pa., 1995—98. Mem.: Phi Kappa Phi. Democrat. Avocations: gardening, floral basket design, weaving.

HOFFER, ALMA JEANNE, nursing educator; b. Dalhart, Tex., Sept. 15, 1932; d. James A. and Mildred (Zimlich) Koehler; m. John L. Hoffer, Oct. 7, 1954; children: John Jr., James Leo, Joseph V., Jerome P. BS, Bradley U., 1970; MA, W. Va. Coll. Grad. Study Inst., 1975; EdD, Ball State U., 1981, MA, 1986. Reg. Nurse. Staff nurse St Joseph Hosp., South Bend, Ind., 1958-59, Holy Cross Cen. Sch., St Joseph Hosp., South Bend, 1959-63; sch. nurse South Bend Sch. Corp., 1970-72; faculty staff Morris Harvey Coll., Charleston, W.Va., W.Va. Inst. Tech., Montgomery, 1975-76; asst. prof. Ball State U., Ind., 1976-77, Ind. U.-Purdue U., Ft. Wayne, 1977-81; assoc. prof. U. Akron, Ohio, 1981-83, 91-95, asst. dean, grad. edn., 1983-90, assoc. prof., 1991-93; prof., chair Dept. of Nursing St. Francis Coll., Fort Wayne, Ind., 1993-95; prin. investigator rsch. project Well Begun is Well Done Children's Med. Ctr. Women's Bd. Akron, 1995-96; coord. parish nurse St. Hilary Ch., 2001—. Trustee Akron Child Guidance, 1983-88, 89-95, chair planning com., 1988; nursing Blick Clin., Akron, 1988; rsch. cons. St. Joseph Hosp., Ohio, 1989; cons. Health Sense, 1996-98; rschr., presenter in field. Contbg. author: Family Health Promotion Theories and Assessment, 1989, Nursing Connections, 1992. Task force mem. Gov. Celeste's Employee Assistance Program for State U. Campuses, Ohio, 1983-84, del. People to People Citizen Amb. Program to Europe, 1988; mem. health and wellness com., coord. St. Hilary Parish. Mem. ANA, Nat. League for Nursing, Midwest Nursing Rsch. Soc., Transcultural Nursing Soc. (chair certification and recertification com. 2000—, Leininger Leadership award 2002), Portage Country Club, Cleve. Country Club, Sigma Theta Tau. Republican. Roman Catholic. Avocations: tennis, golf, skiing. bus. Office: PO Box 794 Bath OH 44210-0794 E-mail: ajhoffer@earthlink.net., ajh1@uakron.edu.

HOFFER, DEBRA HUMES, educational association administrator; Exec. dir. Louisville Ballet, 1991—99; pres. Jr. Achievement Kentuckania Inc., 2000—. Office: Louisville Ballet PO Box 24403 Louisville KY 40224-4403

HOFFHEIMER, MINETTE GOLDSMITH, community service volunteer; b. Cin., May 1, 1927; d. Philip Hess and Cecile (Crager) Goldsmith; m. Arthur Hoffheimer Jr., June 16, 1948; children: Craig R., Roger Steven, James Martin, Mark Todd. Student, Conn. Coll. for Women, New London, 1945-48. Editor, prodr. (book in braille) Lilias Yoga and You, 1974, (poems) Marjorie's Book, 1974; editor: Lilias Yoga and Your Life, 1981; contbr. short story: (anthology) Cincinnati Short Story Winners, 1985. Trustee, sec. Cin. chpt. Nat. Coun. Jewish Women, 1966-73, chmn. and developer Large Type Program of Aid to Visually Handicapped, 1964-75, chmn. Angel Ball, 1968, on Angel Ball com. 1964-69, treas. thrift shop, 1965-67, auditor, mem. budget, ways and means, survey and evaluation coms., 1971; trustee Clovernook Home and Sch. for Blind, Cin., 1980-87; founder, 1st pres. Clovernook Assocs., Cin., 1981-85; trustee, chmn. edn. com., Boca Raton (Fla.) Mus. Art, 1996—; program developer, tchr. of Yoga to Blind, Cin., 1973-87 Named Vol. of Yr. Clovernook Home and Sch. for Blind, 1976, Woman of Yr. Cin. Enquirer, 1983. Mem. Brandeis, Nat. Braille Assn. (After 4000 hours svc. award 1971, 30 yr. cert. svc. 2001), Cin. Yoga Tchrs. Assn., Life Long Learning Soc. Fla. Atlantic U., Friends of Boca Raton Mus. Art., others. E-mail: mghno1@aol.com.

HOFFLICH, FRANCINE K. network architect; b. Hollywood, Calif., Dec. 15, 1966; d. Morton and Bessie Lee (Ani) H. BS in Computer Info. Systems, DeVry Inst. Technology, City of Industry, 1988. Systems analyst Lockheed Aeronautical, Burbank, Calif., 1988-90; PC specialist Farmers Ins. Group, L.A., 1990-94; network architect Countrywide Home Loan, Calabasas, Calif., 1994—. Mem. Appaloosa Horses Club. Avocations: horses, running, biking. Office: Countrywide Home Loan 26541 Agoura Rd # Ac132 Calabasas CA 91302-1958

HOFFMAN, ADA JEAN, music educator; b. Youngstown, Ohio, July 13, 1952; d. James Laurence and Elva Jean Hoffman. MusB, Westminster Coll., 1974, MEd, 1977. Tchr. choral music Wilmington Area Schs., New Wilmington, Pa., 1974—79, Villa Maria HS, 1979—89, Sharpsville Area Schs., 1989—90, West Middlesex Area Sch. Dist., 1991—, coord. gifted edn., 1997—. Organist First Presbyn. Ch., Ford City, Pa., 1976—, choir dir., 1978—. Dir. Heritage Cmty. Choir, Ford City, 1989—; music dir. Vacation Bible Sch., Ford City, 2000—. Named to Hall of Fame, Ford City, 1999. Mem.: NEA, Pa. State Educators Assn., Music Educators Nat. Conf., Pa. Music Educators Assn., Delta Kappa Gamma (chmn. membership 2000—01, chmn. scholarship com. 2002—, named to Pa. Album of Distinction 2000), Kappa Delta Pi. Avocations: travel, sewing, reading, crafts. Office: West Middlesex Area School Dist 3591 Sharon Rd West Middlesex PA 16159

HOFFMAN, ALICE, writer; b. N.Y.C., Mar. 16, 1952; m. Tom Martin; children: Jake, Zack. BA, Adelphi U., 1973; MA, Stanford U., 1975. Author: Property of, 1977, The Drowning Season, 1979, Angel Landing, 1980, White Horses, 1982, Fortune's Daughter, 1985, Illumination Night, 1987, At Risk, 1988, Seventh Heaven, 1990, Turtle Moon, 1992, Second Nature, 1994, Practical Magic, 1995, Local Girls, 1999, Fireflies: A Winter Tale, 1999, Horsefly, 2000, The River King, 2000, Blue Diary, 2001, Aquamarine, 2001, Indigo, 2002, Green Angel, 2003, The Probable Future, 2003, (screenplay) Independence Day, 1983. Mirelles fellow Stanford U., 1975, Breadloaf fellow, 1976. Office: c/o Putnam Berkley 200 Madison Ave New York NY 10016-3903*

HOFFMAN, BRENDA JOYCE, gastroenterology educator; b. Madisonville, Ky., Sept. 4, 1957; d. John Willis and Lavada Fae (Baxter) H. BS, Murray State U., 1979; MD, U. Ky., 1983. Diplomate Am. Soc. Gastroenterology and Internal Medicine. Resident Med. U. S.C., Charleston, 1983-86, chief med. resident 1986-87, gastroent./internal medicine fellow, 1987-89, therapeutic fellow, 1989-90, clin. instr. medicine, 1990-91, asst. prof. medicine, 1991-95, assoc. prof. medicine, 1995-2000, prof. medicine, 2001—, chief endosonography, clin. dir., 1993—. Contbr. articles to profl. jours. Fellow ACP, Am. Coll. Gastroenterology; mem. Am. Gastroent. Assn., Am. Soc. Gastrointestinal Endoscopy. Avocations: soccer, sailing, reading. Office: Med U SC 171 Ashley Ave Charleston SC 29425-0001

HOFFMAN, DARLEANE CHRISTIAN, chemistry educator; b. Terril, Iowa, Nov. 8, 1926; d. Carl Benjamin and Elverna (Kuhlman) Christian; m. Marvin Morrison Hoffman, Dec. 26, 1951; children: Maureane R., Daryl K. BS in Chemistry, Iowa State U., 1948, PhD in Nuclear Chemistry, 1951; D (hon.), U. Bern, Switzerland, 2001; PhD (hon.), Clark U., 2000. Chemist Oak Ridge (Tenn.) Nat. Lab., 1952—53; staff radiochemistry group Los Alamos (N.Mex.) Sci. Lab., 1953—71, assoc. leader chemistry-nuclear group, 1971—79, leader chem.-nuclear divsn., 1979—82, leader isotope and nuclear chem. divsn., 1982-84; prof. chemistry U. Calif., Berkeley, 1984—91, prof. emeritus, 1991—93, prof. grad. sch., 1993—; faculty sr. scientist Lawrence Berkeley Lab., 1984—; dir.'s fellow Los Alamos Nat. Lab., 1990—; dir. G.T. Seaborg Inst. for Transactinium Sci., 1991—96. Spkr. in field; subcom. on nuclear and radiochemistry NAS-NRC, 1978—81, chmn. subcom. on nuclear and radiochemistry, 1982—84, bd. on radioactive waste mgmt., 1994—99; titular mem. commn. on radiochem. and nuclear techniques Internat. Union of Pure and Applied Chem., 1983—87, sec., 1985—87, chmn., 1987—91, assoc., 1991—93; organizer of symposiums in field; com. mem. Internat. Symposium on Nuclear and Radiochemistry, 1988; organizing com. Actinides, 1993, nat. adv. com., 2001; planning panel Workshop on Tng. Requirements for Chemists in Nuclear Medicine, Nuclear Industry, and Related Fields, 1998; radionuclide migration peer rev. com., Las Vegas, 1986—87; steering com. Advanced Steady State Neutron Source, 1986—90; steering com., panelist Workshop on Opportunities and Challenges in Rsch. with Transplutonium Elements, Washington, 1983; energy rsch. adv. bd. cold fusion panel Dept. Energy, 1989—90, nuclear energy rsch. adv. com, 2000—01; separations subpanel of separations tech. and transmutation systems panel NAS, 1992—94; mem. steeering com. Accel. Transmutation Waste Roadmapping Study, 1999; mem. ANTT subcom. subcom. NERAC, 2002—04; mem. NAS-NRC Russian-Am. Commn., 2001—02; Welch Found. lectr. Tex. univs., 2000. Author: The Transuranium People, 2000; contbr. articles to profl. jours. Named Disting. Lectr., Inst. Phys. Rsch and Tech., Ames Lab., 1998, Welch Found. lectr., 2000; named to Women in Tech. Internat. Hall of Fame, 2000; recipient Alumni Citation of Merit, Coll. Scis. and Humanities, Iowa State U., 1978, Disting. Achievement award, Iowa State U., 1986, Berkeley citation, U. Calif., 1996, U.S. Nat. Medal Sci., 1997, Leonard A. Ford Lectureship, Mankato State U., 1998, Frontiers Sci. award, Soc. Cosmetic Chemists, 1998; fellow, Guggenheim Found., 1978—79; Sr. postdoc.fellow, NSF, 1964—65. Fellow: AAAS (coun. mem. 1995—97), Am. Acad. Arts and Scis., Am. Phys. Soc., Am. Inst. Chemists (pres. N.Mex. chpt. 1976—78); mem.: Radiochem. Soc. (Lifetime Achievement award 2003), Norwegian Acad. Sci. & Letters, Am. Chem. Soc. (John Dustin Clark award 1976, Nuc. Chemistry award 1983, Francis P. Garvan-John M. Olin medal 1990, Priestley medal 2000, Mosher award 2001), Alpha Chi Sigma (Hall of Fame 2002), Sigma Delta Epsilon, Pi Mu Epsilon, Iota Sigma Pi, Phi Kappa Phi, Sigma Xi Rsch. Soc. (Procter prize for sci. achievement 2003). Methodist. Home: 2277 Manzanita Dr Oakland CA 94611-1135 Office: Lawrence Berkeley Nat Lab MS70 R0319 NSD Berkeley CA 94720

HOFFMAN, ELIZABETH, academic administrator; b. Bryn Mawr, Pa. BA in history, Smith Coll., 1968; MA in history, U. Pa., 1969, PhD in history, 1972; PhD in econs., Calif. Inst. of Tech., 1979. Academic and adminstrv. positions U. Fla., Northwestern U., Purdue U., U. Wyo., U. Ariz., Iowa State U.; prof. econs., history, polit. sci. and psychology U. Ill., Chgo., 1997—2000, prof. Inst. of Govt. and Pub. Affairs, 1997—2000, provost and vice chancellor, 1997—2000; pres. U. Colo. Sys., Boulder, Colo., 2000—. Appointee Nat. Sci. Bd., 2002. Author books; contbr. articles to profl. jours. Named one of 100 women making a difference, Today's Chgo. Woman, 1999; recipient Ronald H. Coase prize, Electronic Intelligence citation, ANBAR. Office: 35 SYS 914 Broadway Boulder CO 80309-0035*

HOFFMAN, ELIZABETH PARKINSON, librarian; b. Pitts., Mar. 23, 1921; d. William Sterrett P. and Elizabeth Helen Hill; m. James William Hoffman, Apr. 2, 1944; children; W. Sterrett, Elizabeth, Charles, Lloyd. BA, Dickinson Coll., 1942; MLS, Drexel U., 1961. Libr. coord. Haverford (Pa.) Twp. Sch. Dist., 1958-65; dir. divsn. libr. Pa. Dept. Edn., Harrisburg, 1965-75; chair dept. libr. sci. Villanova (Pa.) U., 1975-78; dir. Havertown (Pa.) Twp. Free Libr., 1979-91. Cons. in field. Author 7 books. 8Mem.L-lamerch Women's Club. Republican. Presbyterian. Avocations: travel, writing, needle work. Home: 805 Beechwood Rd Havertown PA 19083-2621

HOFFMAN, FAITH LOUISE, social worker; b. Buffalo, June 7, 1944; d. William George Hoffman, Louise Caroline Hoffman; children: Donald Louis, Louis William, Christopher Robert. BS magna cum laude, Medaille Coll., 1983—87; MSW, SUNY, Buffalo, 1991—93. LCSW 1993. Case mgr. N.Y. Crime Victim's Assistance Program, Buffalo, 1987—88; dir. domestic violence program YWCA of Tonawanda's, 1988—90; dir. family support program Concerned Ecumenical Ministry, Buffalo, 1990—92; social worker Dept. Veteran's Affairs Med. Ctr., Buffalo, 1993—95, women veteran's program mgr., 1995—. Dir., founder Hopegivers, Buffalo, 1991—; dir. VA Domestic Violence Program, Buffalo, 1995—; field faculty SUNY, Buffalo, 1996—; domestic violence cons. Erie County Dept. Health, Buffalo, 2000—02; spkr. in field. Named cmty. hero, torchbearer Western N.Y. Olympic Torch Relay, Atlanta Olympic Com., 1996—96; recipient Svc. to Mankind award, Sertoma Greater Buffalo, 1998—98, ann. leadership award, YWCA Western N.Y., 2001—01, Joan A. Levine award, Woman Focus, 2002, Fed. Woman of Yr. award, Buffalo (N.Y.) Fed. Exec. Bd., 2003. Office: VA Western NY Healthcare Sys 3495 Bailey Ave Buffalo NY 14215 Office Phone: 716-862-8675. E-mail: faithhoffman@va.gov.

HOFFMAN, HELENE, lawyer; b. Cleve., Aug. 7, 1952; d. Martin and Gitta Hoffman; m. Ronald B. Loewe, Nov. 1, 1987; children: Maya, Brandon. BA, U. Wis., 1974; JD, DePaul U., 1982, LLM, 1991. Bar: Ill., Miss. Staff atty. Prairie State Legal Svcs., Waukegan, Ill., 1982—87; atty. Ill. Dept. Profl. Regulations, Chgo., 1990—2000, Helene Hoffman Assoc., Starkville, Miss., 2001—. Contbr. articles various profl. jours., poetry Beyond Lament: Poets of the World Bearing Witness to the Holocaust, 1998, poetry Anthology of Midwest Poetry, 1987, poetry American Poetry Annual, 1990; author: (short stories) Bridges, 1995. Recipient 2nd and 3rd prize, Ray Bradbury Poetry Contest, 1985—87, 1st prize, Joanne Hirschfield Poetry Contest, 1987, Ragdale Found. Residency, Ragdale Found., 1999. Mem.: Nat. Lawyers Guild, Nat. Org. Women (v.p. 2002—03). Avocations: writing, holocaust edn.. Office: Helene Hoffman and Assoc 203 E Main St Starkville MS 39759

HOFFMAN, JENNIFER ANNE, vascular technician, director; b. Bklyn., Aug. 29, 1971; d. Louis Frank Marchese and Carol Maryann Sclafani; m. Brian David Hoffman, Sept. 24, 2000. BS, SUNY, Bklyn., 1997. Registered vascular technologist, cert. EMT N.Y. Office mgr. Maimonides Med. Ctr., Bklyn., 1996—98, clin. vascular specialist, 1998—99; tech. coord. St. Luke's-Roosevelt Hosp. Ctr., N.Y.C., 1999—2001, tech. dir., 2001—03, Duke U. Med. Sch., Durham, NC, 2003—. Instr. SUNY Health Sci. Ctr., Bklyn., 1998—99; vascular ultrasound tng. dept. radiology St. Luke's-Roosevelt Hosp. Ctr., N.Y.C., 2001—03. Contbr. articles to profl. jours.; spkr. in field. Recipient Musical Achievement award, N.Y. State Bd. Edn., 1989, Am. Venous Found. Beiersdorf-Jobst Rsch. fellowship, 1999. Mem.: Soc. Vascular Tech., Am. Registry Diagnostic Med. Sonographers. Avocations: flute, saxophone, poetry, travel. Office: Duke U Med Ctr Box 2990 Durham NC 27710 Personal E-mail: vascsono@aol.com.

HOFFMAN, JETHA L. piano and vocal teacher, musician; b. New Orleans, Oct. 2, 1948; d. Jether Anthony and Dorothy Carmen (Adriani) Hübsch; m. James Tyre Dennis, Oct. 6, 1965 (div. Jan. 1972); 1 child, James Tyre Dennis; m. Gary William Hoffman, Oct. 2, 1988. Grad. h.s., New Orleans, 1966. Performer, soloist, entertainer, concert pianist, 1962—; prof. accompanist all opera and theatre, New Orleans; piano tchr., vocal tchr. New Orleans, Cathedral City, Calif., 1994—; performed in numerous bands, 1967—. Piano/vocals, entertainer Pete Fountain Enterprises, New Orleans, 1979-86, performed throughout U.S. Composer piano solos; arranger and editor for piano, vocals. Recipient numerous awards and trophies. Mem. Music Tchrs. Nat. Assn., Calif. Assn. Profl. Music Tchrs. Roman Catholic. Home: 68590 Tachevah Dr Cathedral City CA 92234-3879 Fax: 760-325-1220.

HOFFMAN, JOY YU, harpist, pianist; b. Nanjing, Jiangsu, People's Republic of China, Mar. 28, 1952; came to U.S., 1984; d. Zhong Hai and Xing Huang Yu; m. Paul Franklin Hoffman, July 16, 1988. Diploma in music, Shenyang Conservatory of Music, China, 1981; MusB, Roosevelt U., 1988; MusM, Northwestern U., 1991. Opera coach Harbin (China) Opera, 1970-83; piano, harp tchr. Morton Grove, 1989—; harpist Fox Valley Symphony, Aurora, Ill., 1993—, Ill. Chamber Symphony, St. Charles, Ill., 1996—. Adj. prof. harp Roosevelt U., Chgo., 1993-98; harpist Harbin Opera Co., 1980-83, concert pianist, 1970-83. Performer, composer (CD) Ballad, 1999; author: What is the Kong Hou Chinese Harp?, 1999, Chinese Folk Music and Kong Hou, 1995. Recipient 1st prize Young Artists Competition City Govt., 1982. Mem. Hist. Harp Soc., Great Lakes Harpers, Am. Harp Soc., Ill. Music Tchrs. Assn., Am. Fedn. Musicians. Avocations: photography, painting, garden design. Home: 8826 Menard Ave Morton Grove IL 60053-2461

HOFFMAN, JUDY GREENBLATT, preschool director; b. Chgo., June 12, 1932; d. Edward Abraham and Clara (Morrill) Greenblatt; m. Morton Hoffman, Mar. 16, 1950 (div. Jan. 1983); children: Michael, Alan, Clare. BA summa cum laude, Met. State Coll., Denver, 1972; MA, U. No. Colo., 1976, MA in Spl. Edn. Moderate Needs, 1996. Cert. tchr., Colo. Pre-sch. dir. B.M.H. Synagogue, Denver, 1968-70, Temple Emanuel, Denver, 1970-85, Congregation Rodef Shalom, Denver, 1985-88; tchr. Denver Pub. Schs., 1988—. Bilingual tchr. adults in amnesty edn. Denver Pub. Schs., 1989-90. Author: I Live in Israel, 1979, Joseph and Me, 1980 (Gamoran award), (with others) American Spectrum Single Volume Encyclopedia, 1991. Coord. Douglas Mountain Therapeutic Riding Ctr. for Handicapped, Golden, Colo., 1985—; dir. Mountain Ranch Summer Day Camp for Denver Pub. Schs., 1989-91. Mem. Nat. Assn. Temple Educators. Democrat. Avocations: riding, writing, music. E-mail: jhoff3@earthlink.net.

HOFFMAN, KARLA LEIGH, mathematician, educator; b. Paterson, N.J., Feb. 14, 1948; d. Abe and Bertha (Guthaim) Rakoff; m. Allan Stuart Hoffman, Dec. 26, 1971; 1 child, Matthew Douglas. BA, Rutgers U., 1969; MBA, George Washington U., 1971, DSc in Ops. Rsch., 1975. Ops. rsch. analyst IRS, Washington, 1970-72; rsch. asst. George Washington U., 1972-75, assoc. professional lectr., 1978-85; NSF postdoctoral rsch. fellow NAS, Washington, 1975-76; assoc. prof. sys. engring. dept. George Mason U., Fairfax, Va., 1985-86, assoc. prof. ops. rsch. and applied stats., 1986-89, prof. ops. rsch., 1990—, disting. prof., 1989, interim dept. chmn., 1996-97, chmn., 1997-98, chmn. sys. engring. and ops. rsch., 1998—2000. Mathematician Nat. Bur. Stds., Washington, 1976—84; vis. assoc. prof. ops. rsch. U. Md., 1982; mng. ptnr. Optimization Software Assocs.; cons. Govt. Agys., Airline, Telecomm. and Def. Industries. Contbr. articles to profl. jours. Recipient Applied Rsch. award, Nat. Inst. Stds. and Tech., 1984, Silver medal, U.S. Dept. Commerce, 1984, Disting. Prof. award, 1989. Fellow: Inst. Ops. Rsch. and Mgmt. Sci. (treas. 1995—96, exec. com. 1995—99, pres. 1998); mem.: Math. Programming Soc. (editor newsletter 1979—82, chmn. com. algorithms 1982—85, coun. 1985—88, exec. com., chmn. membership com. 1988—89), Ops. Rsch. Soc. Am. (sec.-treas. Computer Sci. Tech. sect. 1979—80, vis. profl. lectr. 1980—, vice chmn. sect. 1981, chmn. sect. 1982, chmn. tech. sect. com. 1983—86, coun. 1985—88, chmn. Lanchester Prize com. 1989, treas. 1993—94). Home: 6921 Clifton Rd Clifton VA 20124-1525

HOFFMAN, LINDA M. chemist, educator; b. N.Y.C., Dec. 18, 1939; d. Theodore and Esther (Schaeffer) Weiss; m. Robert G. Hoffman, Feb. 2, 1958; 1 child, Samuel A. BS in Chemistry, Queens Coll., 1959; MS, NYU, 1967, PhD in Organic Chemistry, 1970. Rsch. assoc. Kingsbrook Jewish Med. Ctr., N.Y.C., 1973-77; asst. prof. Baruch Coll., CUNY, N.Y.C., 1977-79, assoc. prof., 1979-82, prof., 1982—, chair dept. natural scis., 1995-98. Reviewer grant proposals NIH. Contbr. articles on Tay-Sachs disease and glycosphingolipids to profl. jours. Mem. edn. com. UN Internat. Sch., N.Y.C., 1981-84; bd. dirs. Forest Hills Gardens Corp., 1993-2000. Recipient Moore award Am. Soc. Neuropathologists, 1981, 84, Founders Day award NYU, 1971, 112th Precinct Cmty. Coun. award, 1993; postdoctoral fellow Sloan Kettering Inst. Cancer Rsch., N.Y.C., 1972-73. Mem. AAAS, Am. Chem. Soc., Sigma Xi. Office: Baruch Coll Dept Natural Scis One Bernard Baruch Way New York NY 10010-5518 E-mail: linda_hoffman@baruch.cuny.edu.

HOFFMAN, LINDA R. social services administrator; b. New Haven, July 23, 1940; d. Bernard Harry and Sylvia (Paul) Rosenfield; m. Peter A. Hoffman, Sept. 25, 1965; 1 child, Tracie Hoffman Cohen. BA, Russell Sage Coll., 1962; MSW, U. Mo., 1968. Cert.,social worker, N.Y. Case worker Conn. Dept. Welfare, New Haven, 1962-63, N.Y.C. Bur. Child Welfare, N.Y.C., 1963-65, supr., 1965-66; asst. to commr. program planning N.Y.C. Dept. Social Svcs., N.Y.C., 1968-70; spl. asst. to commr. N.Y.C. Spl. Svc. for Children, N.Y.C., 1972-79; pres. N.Y. Found. Sr. Citizens, N.Y.C., 1979—. Cons., USIA, Teheran, Iran, summer 1975; adj. prof., mem. dean's adv. coun. Columbia Sch. Social Work. Mem. Cmty. Bd. # 8, N.Y.C., 1982—, YWCA/N.Y.C. Acad. Women Achievers, 1995—; bd. dir., Grosvenor Neighborhood House, 2003; mem. Women's Forum, 1998—. Recipient, Presdl. Recognition award for Community Svc., 1983, East Manhattan C. of C., award for Disting. Civic Svc., 1990, The Mcpl. Art Soc. of N.Y. award, 1997; named to Columbia U. Sch. Social Work Hall of Fame, 2000. Mem. Nat. Assn. Social Workers (cert.), Women's City Club of N.Y. Avocations: boating, fishing, and thoroughbred race horses. Office: NY Found Sr Citizens Ste 1416 11 Park Pl Rm 1416 New York NY 10007-2801

HOFFMAN, M. KATHY, graphic designer, packaging designer; b. Sidney, Nebr., Aug. 30, 1956; d. Norman and Irline (Dillon) Barnica; m. Jeffrey W. Hoffman, Apr. 16, 1988. BA, U. Nebr., Kearney, 1978, BFA, 1984, MA, 1987. Product quality assurance Baldwin Filters, Kearney, Nebr., 1978-88, product technician, 1988-90, product devel. technician, 1990-92, product identification coord., 1992—, packaging and graphics designer, 1993—. Mem. Inst. Packaging Profls., Assn. Corel Artists and Designers, Women in Packaging. Avocations: collect cat figures, reading, movies. Office: Baldwin Filters 4400 Highway 30 E Kearney NE 68847-0724

HOFFMAN, MARGARET ANN HOVLAND, artist, activist; b. Seattle, Feb. 20, 1930; d. Harold Kenneth and Gertrude Anne (Maxson) Hovland; m. Don Lee Hoffman, Apr. 2, 1955 (div.); children: Lori, Lee. Student, U. Wash., 1948-51; B Profl. Arts, Art Ctr. Coll. Design, 1955. Interior designer Bon Marché, Seattle, 1948-49; interior designer, coord. Paul Siegal, Seattle, 1949-51; asst. designer Seattle Design Ctr.; indsl. designer Olsen/Spencer,

L.A., 1955-57; freelance artist L.A., 1957-61, 85—; designer, asst. Don Hoffman Jewelry, Beverly Hills, Calif., 1975-85; activist, creator, founder Oceanside Beach Restoration Assn., San Diego County, Calif., 1988—. Mem. grad. adv. bd. Art Ctr. Sch. Coll. Design, L.A. and Pasadena, Calif., 1956-80. Designer logos and pamphlets for Shell Oil, 1953, AEC, 1953-55, Owl/Rexall Drugs, 1954, Pegasus/Tidewater Oil, 1955-57, AEC; commd. Oceanside Beach Protection Com., 1996-98. Mem. Women in Arts (charter). Avocations: watercolor artist, decorating, riding horses, swimming, travel. Home: 270 Tavistock Ave Los Angeles CA 90049-3229

HOFFMAN, MARY ANN HARTMAN, principal; d. Buddy McHenry and Shirley Arlene Hartman; children: Jennifer Lynn, Brandy Thomas. BS in Elem. Edn., Bloomsburg U., 1972; MEd in Early Childhood Edn., Coll. Charleston, 1982. Cert. elem. tchr. Pa., elem. edn., early childhood edn., and supervision Va. Tchr. gifted and talented Ctrl. Columbia Sch. Dist., Bloomsburg, Pa., 1977—78, Marrington Mid. Sch., Charleston, SC, 1978—82; tchr., dir. summer spl. programs Norfolk Acad., Va., 1984—94; prin. Heathwood Hall Episcopal Sch., Columbia, SC, 1994—. Cons. Vertex Innovation, Stone Mountain, Ga., 2001—02. Author: The Parents Guide to Navy Life, 1982, A New Adventure, 1982, A Special Family, 1982; contbg. author: Looking Ahead: Independent School Issues and Answers. Chair edn. com. Edventure Children's Mus., Columbia, 2000—02. Mem.: Phi Delta Kappa. Avocations: reading, writing, photography, yoga, walking. Office: Heathwood Hall Episcopal Sch 3000 S Beltline Rd Columbia SC 29201

HOFFMAN, MARY CATHERINE, retired nurse, anesthetist; b. Winamac, Ind., July 14, 1923; d. Harmon William Whitney and Dessie Maude (Neely) H. RN, Meth. Hosp., Indpls., 1945; cert. obstet. analgesia and anesthesia, Johns Hopkins Hosp., 1949; grad., Cleve. Sch. Anesthesia, 1952. Staff nurse Meth. Hosp., 1945-49; rsch. asst., then staff anesthetist Johns Hopkins Hosp., 1949-62; staff anesthetist Meth. Hosp., 1962-64, U. Chgo. Hosps., 1964-66; chief nurse anesthetist Paris (Ill.) Cmty. Hosp., 1966-80; staff anesthetist Hendricks County Hosp., Danville, Ind., Ball Meml. Hosp., Muncie, Ind., 1981-86. Mem. Am. Assn. Nurse Anesthetists, Am. Heart Assn., Ind. Fedn. Bus. and Profl. Women's Clubs (Ill. dist. chmn. 1977-78, state found. chmn. 1978-79, Found. award 1979). Republican. Presbyterian. Home: 1700 N Maddox Dr Muncie IN 47304-2674

HOFFMAN, MERLE HOLLY, political activist, social psychologist, author; b. Phila., Mar. 6, 1946; d. Jack Rheins and Ruth (Dubow) H.; m. Martin Gold, June 30, 1979. BA magna cum laude in Psychology, Queens Coll., 1972; postgrad., CUNY, 1972-75. Founder, pres. Choices Women's Med. Ctr., Long Island City, N.Y., 1971—; family planning cons. Health Ins. Plan, N.Y.C., 1973-85; founder, pres. Ctr. for Comprehensive Breast Svcs., N.Y.C., 1979-82, Merle Hoffman Enterprises, N.Y.C., 1986—, Choices Mental Health Ctr., 1993—. Speaker, debator on women's rights and polit. issues; founder, pres. Nat. Liberty Com., 1981; active Choices East Project, Moscow, 1992—; provider of Project Liberty Svc., Sept. 11, 2001. Cons. editor Female Health Topics and Diagnostic Reporter, 1979-81; editor, pub. On The Issues: The Progressive Woman's Quarterly, contbr. articles in field to various publs.; producer documentary film Abortion A Different Light; founder N.Y. Pro-Choice Coalition; host cable TV series MH: On the Issues, 1986. Recipient Women's Equality award, L.I. (N.Y.) NOW, 1995, Woman of Power and Influence award, N.Y. Chpt. NOW, 1998, Lifetime Svc. award, Vet. Feminists Am., 2000. Mem. APPA (bd. dirs.), Nat. Assn. Abortion Facilities (co-founder, pres. 1976-77), Nat. Abortion Fedn. (co-founder, sec. 1977-78), Vet. Feminists of Am., Nat. Adv. Bd., Phi Beta Kappa, Achievements include papers in Sallie Bingham Ctr. Women's History, Duke U. Office: Choices Women's Med Ctr Inc 29-28 41st Ave Long Island City NY 11101-3303 Office Phone: 718-349-9100 x 880. Personal E-mail: Mhoti@aol.com.

HOFFMAN, NANCY, art gallery director; b. N.Y.C., 1944;, Wellesley Coll., 1964, Columbia U., 1966. Asst. registrar Asia House Gallery, N.Y.C., 1964-69; dir. Contemporary Gallery French & Co., N.Y.C., 1969-72; owner Nancy Hoffman Gallery, N.Y.C., 1972—. Lectr., jury exhibitor throughout U.S. Contbr. chpt. to text. Office: Nancy Hoffman Gallery 429 W Broadway New York NY 10012-3799

HOFFMAN, RITA MARY, counselor, cosmetics executive, consultant; b. Albany, N.Y., Nov. 29, 1949; d. William L. Hoffman, Jr. and Margaret C. (Clark) Hoffman. BA in Sociology, Coll. St. Rose, 1971; MS in Pub. Adminstrn. Human Svcs., Russell Sage Coll., 1980, MS in Addiction and Addicted Family Counseling, 1988. Credentialled alcoholism and substance abuse counselor N.Y. Cons. Jafia Cosmetics, Inc., Nassau, NY, 1980—, mgr. Yankee Heritage Brand, 1982—88; advt. dir. Plaza Mag., Kinderhook, NY, 1982—86; addictions counselor intern Samaritan Hosp. Detox, Troy, NY, 1987—88, addictions counselor I, 1988—89; addictions counselor II Conifer Park Inpatient Rehab., Glenridge, NY, 1989—90, Hudson Mohawk Recover Ctr. Day Treatment Program, Troy, 1991; addictions counselor III Crossroads Outpatient Clinic, Delmar, NY; dir., counselor Late Bloomers Counseling, Selkirk, NY, Delmar. Reading tutor Jumpstart Elsmere Sch., Delmar, NY; literacy vol., 1997—98; active Albany Tricentennial Com., Dem. Party. Mem.: Bethlehem Hist. Assn. (membership chair), Delmar Progress Club. Avocations: swimming, reading, travel, jigsaw puzzles, painting. Home: 18 Bedell Ave Delmar NY 12054 Office: Late Bloomers Counseling 18 Bedell Ave Delmar NY 12054

HOFFMAN, ROBYN BROWN, lawyer; b. N.J., July 29, 1948; d. Robert Gwinn and Elizabeth Jane Brown; m. Stephen B. Hoffman, May 11, 1980; children: Russell, Robert. BA, Mt. Holyoke Coll., 1971; JD, U. Conn., 1975. Bar: Ariz. 1975, N.Mex. 1991, U.S. Supreme Ct. 1995. Asst. atty. gen. State of N.Mex., Santa Fe, 1992—97; gen. counsel N.Mex. Dept. Health, Santa Fe, 1997—2002. Mem. Southwestern Coll., Santa Fe, 1991—94, chair, 1992—94; mem. Med. Rev. Commn., Albuquerque, 1996—; founder Urban Indian Law Program Phoenix Indian Ctr., Ariz., 1977. Mem.: Nat. Assn. State of Mental Health Attys. (chair class actions com. 1996—98), N.Mex. Women's Bar Assn. (founding mem.). Avocation: opera. Home: 98 Lagarto Rd Tijeras NM 87059

HOFFMAN, SHARON LYNN, adult education educator; b. Chgo. d. David P. and Florence Seaman; m. Jerry Irwin Hoffman, Aug. 25, 1963; children: Steven Abram, Rachel Irene. BA, Ind. U., 1961; M Adult Edn., Nat.-Louis Univ., 1992. High sch. English tchr. Chgo. Pub. Schs., 1961-64; tchr. Dept. of Def. Schs., Braconne, France, 1964-66; tchr. ESL Russian Inst., Garmisch, Fed. Republic Germany, 1966, 67; tchr. adult edn. Monterey Peninsula Unified Schs., Ft. Ord, Calif., 1977-79; tchr. ESL MAECOM, Monmouth County, N.J., 1979-80; lectr., tchr. adult edn. Truman Coll./Temple Shalom, Chgo.; tchr. homebound Fairfax County Pub. Schs., Fairfax, Va., 1976; entry operator Standard Rate & Data, Wilmette, Ill., 1986-87; rsch. editor, spl. projects editor Marquis Who's Who, Wilmette, 1987-92; mem. adj. faculty Nat.-Louis U., Evanston and Wheeling, Ill., 1993-99, tutor coord., then coord. learning specialist, 1993-99; pres. Cultural Transitions, Highland Park, Ill., 1992—. Mem.: TESOL, ASTD, Nat. Coun. Tchrs. English. Home and Office: 3071 El Toro Rd Pebble Beach CA 93953-2942 E-mail: culturaltrans1@aol.com.

HOFFMAN, SUE ELLEN, retired elementary school educator; b. Dayton, Ohio, Aug. 23, 1945; d. Cyril Vernon and Sarah Ellen (Sherer) Stephan; m. Lawrence Wayne Hoffman, Oct. 28, 1967. BS in Edn., U. Dayton, 1967; postgrad., Loyola Coll., 1977, Ea. Mich. U., 1980; MEd, Wright State U., 1988. Cert. reading specialist and elem. tchr., Ohio. 5th grade tchr. St. Anthony Sch., Dayton, Ohio, 1967-68, West Huntsville (Ala.) Elem. Sch., 1968-71; 6th grade tchr. Ranchland Hills Pub. Sch., El Paso, Tex., 1973-74; 3rd grade tchr. Emerson Pub. Sch., Westerville, Ohio, 1976, St. Joan of Arc Sch., Aberdeen, Md., 1976-78, Our Lady of Good Counsel, Plymouth, Mich., 1979-80; 5th grade tchr. St. Helen Sch., Dayton, 1980—2002; ret., 2002. Selected for membership Kappa Delta Pi, 1988. Mem. Internat. Reading Assn., Ohio Internat. Reading Assn., Dayton Area Internat. Reading Assn., Nat. Cath. Edn. Assn. Roman Catholic. Home: 2174 Green Springs Dr Kettering OH 45440-1120

HOFFMAN, SUSAN TALBOT, chemist, printmaker; b. Thibodaux, La., Mar. 14, 1955; d. John Kenneth Talbot and Joycelyn Theresa Gros; m. Andrew Hoffmann III, Aug. 29, 1981. BS in Chemistry, Nicholls State U., 1976; MS in Pathology, La.State U., 1979; PhD in Pathology, La. State U., 1981; BFA, Nicholls State U., 1999. Rsch. asst. Tulane Med. Ctr., New Orleans, 1973—81, NIH, Bethesda, Md., 1981—86; asst. prof. Tulane Med. Ctr., 1986—96; printmaker Seven Oaks Studio, Schreiver, La., 1999—. Grant rev. Terrebonne Arts and Humanities Coun., Houma, La., 2000—. Represented in permanent collections WVES Pub. TV, New Orleans, La., The Haven, Houma, La., Food Bank, New Orleans, La., Thibodaux, La., Houma, La., Bank One, Offshore Oil, Morgan City, La., Brit. Petroleum, Houston, Tex., others, prin. works include Beauty is Truth, 2000, exhibitions include numerous; contbr. articles to profl. jours. Grantee, NIH, 1983—86. Mem.: Am. Color Print Soc., La. Agr. Ctr. (master gardener 2002—), Bayou Jr. Womens Club, Phi Kappa Phi, Kappa Pi. Avocations: cooking, gardening, art. Home and Studio: Seven Oaks Art Studio 110 St George Rd Schriever LA 70395

HOFFMAN, VALERIE JANE, lawyer; b. Lowville, N.Y., Oct. 27, 1953; d. Russell Francis and Jane Marie (Fowler) H. Student, U. Edinburgh, Scotland, 1973-74; BA summa cum laude, Union Coll., 1975; JD, Boston Coll., 1978. Bar: Ill. 1978, U.S. Dist. Ct. (no. dist.) Ill. 1978, U.S. Ct. Appeals (3rd cir.) 1981, U.S. Ct. Appeals (7th cir.) 1983. Assoc. Seyfarth Shaw, Chgo., 1978—87, ptnr., 1987—. Adj. prof. Columbia Coll., 1985. Contbr. articles to legal publs. Dir. Remains Theatre, Chgo., 1981-95, pres., 1991-93, v.p., 1991-95; dir. The Nat. Conf. for Cmty. and Justice, Chgo. Region, 1993—, nat. trustee, 1995—; trustee bd. advisors Union Coll., 1996-99, trustee, 1999—, trustee and sec., Grad. Coll. Union U., 2003—; dir. AIDS Found. of Chgo., 1997—, exec. com., 1999-2003. Mem. ABA, Chgo. Bar Assn., Univ. Club Chgo. (bd. dirs. 1984-87), Phi Beta Kappa. Office: Seyfarth Shaw 55 E Monroe St Ste 4400 Chicago IL 60603-5713

HOFFMANN, ANNE MARIE, health facility administrator; d. Charles J. and Josephine C. Hoffmann; children: Danielle M. Cost-Robinson, Damien F. Cost. BA, Marymount Manhattan, 1996. Mgr. emergency medicine NYU./Bellevue Hosp., N.Y.C., 1989—2002, N.Y. Presbyn., N.Y.C., 2002—. Mem.: Emergency Medicine Assn. Residency Coords. (chmn exec. com. 2003—). Avocations: painting, reading, travel. Home: 817 Ave C Bayonne NJ 07002 Office: New York Presbyterian 525 East 68th St New York NY 10021

HOFFMANN, ELINOR R. lawyer; b. N.Y.C., Apr. 18, 1954; BA magna cum laude, NYU, 1974, LLM in Antitrust and Trade Regulation, 1984; JD cum laude, Bklyn. Law Sch., 1977. Bar: N.Y. 1978, U.S. Dist. Ct. (so. and ea. dists.) N.Y. 1978, U.S. Supreme Ct. 1982, U.S. Ct. Appeals (2nd cir.) 1991, U.S. Ct. Appeals (5th cir.) 1994, U.S. Tax Ct. 1996. Ptnr. Coudert Bros. LLP, N.Y.C., 1986—; mediator U.S. Dist. Ct. (so. dist.) N.Y., 1994—. Mng. editor Bklyn. Law Rev., 1976-77; contbr. articles to profl. jours. Mem. ABA, Internat. Bar Assn., N.Y. State Bar Assn., Assn. Bar City NY, Phi Beta Kappa. Office: Coudert Bros LLP 1114 Avenue Of The Americas New York NY 10036-7710 E-mail: hoffmanne@coudert.com.

HOFFMANN, JOAN CAROL, retired academic dean; b. Cedarburg, Wis., Feb. 20, 1934; d. Frank Ernst and Althea Wilhelmina (Behm) H. Nursing diploma, Michael Reese Hosp., 1955; BS in Zoology, U. Wis., Madison, 1959; PhD in Physiology, U. Ill., Chgo., 1965. RN, Wis., Ariz. Sci. instr. Michael Reese Hosp., Chgo., 1959-62; USPHS trainee U. Ill., Chgo., 1962-64; NSF postdoctoral fellow Coll. de France, Paris, 1964-65; asst. prof. U. Rochester, N.Y., 1965-70; assoc. prof., prof. U. Hawaii, Honolulu, 1970-83; dean of students U. Mass. Med. Sch., Worcester, 1983-94; ret., 1994. Chmn. anatomy U. Hawaii, 1973-80. Contbr. articles to sci. jours. NIH rsch. grantee, 1966-75. Mem. Endocrine Soc., Soc. for Study of Reprodn., Am. Assn. Anatomists, Women in Endocrinology (sec. 1978-79, pres. 1987-88), Am. Coun. Edn. (bd. dirs., Mass. chpt., network identification program 1993-94), Phi Beta Kappa, Sigma Xi. Avocations: gardening, needlework, wood turning, reading. Home: 77618 Malone Cir Palm Desert CA 92211-0419

HOFFMANN, MELANE KINNEY, marketing and public relations executive, writer; b. Baton Rouge, Jan. 25, 1956; d. Kenneth Lee and Louise (Walker) Kinney; m. R. Thomas Hoffmann, Oct. 10, 1981; children: Robert James II, Halloran Kinney, Richard Walker. BA, Am. U., 1977. Gen. mgr. Dance Project, Inc., Washington, 1979-81; account exec. J. Walter Thompson Advt., Washington, 1981-84; v.p., account supr. Ketchum Advt., Washington, 1984-88, Demaine Vickers Advt., Alexandria, Va., 1988-89; sr. counsel Porter/Novelli Pub. Rels., Washington, 1989—. Dir. Resolve, Washington, 1992-93; bd. dirs. nat. capital area YWCA, Washington, 1980-82. Mem. Am. Mktg. Assn. (mem. program com. 1990-92, co-chair), Ad Club Washington (mem. membership com. 1985-90, Addy award 1987). Presbyterian. Avocations: owning and riding horses, gardening, literacy tutoring. Office: Poter/Novelli 1120 Connecticut Ave NW Washington DC 20036-3902

HOFFMANN, NANCY LARRAINE, state legislator; b. Needham, Mass., Sept. 22, 1947; d. Elmer and Juanita (Chauncey) Roth; children: Eva, Anna, Gustav. BA, Syracuse U., 1970; MS, U. Md., 1972. Prof. English and Journalism Onondaga C.C., Syracuse, 1974-76; mem. N.Y. State Senate, Albany, 1985—. Prodr. TV Sta. WIXT-TV, Syracuse, 1972-76; pub. rels. cons. Benson Media, Syracuse, 1986—. City councilor, Syracuse, 1980-84. Named Legislator of Yr. N.Y. State Rifle and Pistol Assn., 1994, Womens Press Club N.Y. State, 1992; recipient Pres. award Madison County Assn. Retarded Citizens, 1992, Circle of Friends award N.Y. State Farm Bur., 1990-95, Golden Trumpet award Firemens Assn. State of N.Y., 1995. Mem. LWV, NRA, Nat. Orgn. Women Legislators, Nat. Cattlemen's Beef Assn., Nat. Womens Polit. Caucus, N.Y. State Cattlemens Assn., N.Y. State Cattlewomens Assn., Women in Govt., Appalachian Mountain Club (dir.). Republican. Avocations: photography, canoeing, oxen. Office: 801 State Ofc Bldg 333 E Washington St Syracuse NY 13202-1422 Address: NY Senate 811 Legislative Ofc Bldg Albany NY 12247

HOFFMASTER, NANCY JO CLEMENT, social services professional, retired; b. Granite City, Ill., June 14, 1940; d. Cornelius Ellsworth and Ruth Virginia (Richardson) Townsend; m. David Eugene Clement, June 16, 1961 (div. Dec. 1984); children: Steve, Tom, Bret; m. B. H. Hoffmaster, Dec. 1, 1990. BS in Edn., U. Ill., 1962; student, Red Rocks Community Coll., Golden, Colo., 1979-88; postgrad., U. Colo., Denver, 1988. Cert. elem. tchr., Ill. Coord. homeless edn. program Jeffco Schs., 1998-2000, ret., 2001. Vol. Office of Jeffco Sch Dist., 1995-97. Pres. Jefferson County PTA, Golden, 1982-83; Jeffco chair Colo. Awards for Tchrs., Wheat Ridge, 1987-89, Jefferson Found., Golden, 1989-91, pres., 1989; chmn. enrichment program Jefferson County (Jeffco) Schs., Golden, 1982-91; chmn. Sch. Dist. Accountability, Jefferson County, 1983-85; bd. dirs. Interfaith Hosp. Network, 1996-2000; founder, chair Serving Kids, 1996—; hon. chair Jefferson Found. Crystal Ball, 1999. Named Citizen of Yr., Jefferson County Sch. Bd., 1984, Community Person of Yr. for Jefferson County, Phi Delta Kappa, 1990; recipient Kyffin award Jefferson County PTA, 1989, vol. award Nat. Assn. Ptnrs. in Edn., 1990, Good News Coalition award, 2000, Savvy award, 2000, Colo. Power of One, 2000. Home: 13902 E Marina Dr unit 307 Aurora CO 80014-3756

HOFFNER, MARILYN, university administrator; b. N.Y.C., Nov. 16, 1929; d. Daniel and Elsie (Schulz) H.; m. Albert Greenberg, May 29, 1949; children: Doren Roe, Peter Cooper. BFA, Cooper Union. Art dir. Printers' Ink mag., N.Y.C., 1953-63, Print Mag., N.Y.C., 1960-62; corp. art dir. Vision, Inc., L.Am., 1963-75, 92-95; dir. alumni rels. and devel. Cooper Union, 1974-96, exec. dir. instnl. advancement, 1996-99, cons., 1999-2001; pres. Alumni Assn., 1999-2001. Project dir. Nat. Graphic Design Archives, 1990-97; bd. dirs. Art Dirs. Club N.Y., 1973-75, 79-82, exec. sec., 1973-75, exec. treas., 1979-82. Contbg. editor Print mag., Art Direction, Graphis mag.; designer mags., advt., books and exhbns. Mem. Citizens Adv. Cultural Arts Com. Dutchess County, 1978-80. Recipient Gold medal Art Dirs. Club, 1979, N.Y. State Coun. of the Arts award, 1995; named Alumnus of the Yr., Cooper Union, 1968. Mem. Cooper Union Alumni Assn. (editor-in-chief 1971-74, 1st v.p. 1974-75), Coun. Advancement and Support of Edn., Type Dirs. Club (numerous awards), Nat. Arts Club (Exhbn. com.). Home: 51 5th Ave New York NY 10003-4320 E-mail: cu1948@aol.com.

HOFKIN, ANN GINSBURGH, photographer, poet; b. Holyoke, Mass., Dec. 20, 1943; d. Albert and Fruma (Winer) G.; m. Michael Gary Hofkin, June 30, 1966; children: Daniel, Benjamin. AB, Mt. Holyoke Coll., 1965; MSS, Bryn Mawr Coll., 1967. One-woman shows include Unicorn Galleries, Mpls., 1980, Warm Gallery, Mpls., 1982-85, 87-88, 90, 96, 98, St. Mary's Coll., Winona, Minn., 1986, U. Wis., Meml. Union, 1993, Bladin Found., 1990, Phipps Ctr. for the Arts, Wis., 1994, So. Light Gallery, Tex., 1994-95, MC Gallery, Mpls., 1986, 89, 91-92, 94, 97, Bethany Luth. Coll., Minn., 1999, Hoyt Inst. Fine Arts, 1999, Pietra di Luna Gallery, Fla., 2000, Coll. St. Benedict's, Minn., 2002, Bet Gabriel, Israel, 2003, Jerusalem Theatre, Israel, 2003, Alliance Francaise de Mpls./St.Paul, 2003, Mount Holyoke Coll, 2004; group shows include Gallery Triangle, Washington, 1996, Pindar Gallery, N.Y., 1987, Phinney Ctr., Seattle, 1987, Print Club, Phila., 1988, U. Minn., 1988, Plains Art Mus., 1988, U. Minn., 1989, Durango Arts Ctr., Colo., 1989, Northfield Arts Guild, Minn., 1982, 90, Mich. Friends of Photography, 1992, Jewish Cmty. Ctr., Houston, 1990, 92, Hennepin History Mus., 1992, LaGrange (Ga.) Coll., 1992, Chautauqua Art Assn., N.Y., 1992, Edn. Testing Svc., N.J., 1992, Slocumb Galleries, Tenn., 1993, Barrett House Galleries, N.Y., Erector Sq. Gallery, Conn., 1993, McPherson Coll., Ks., 1993, Middle (Tenn.) State U., 1993, Sioux City Art Ctr., Iowa, 1987, 89, 93, Mpls. Coll. Art and Design, 1987, 89, 94, Lubbock (Tex.) Fine Arts Ctr., 1995, Shoestring Gallery, N.Y., 1993, 94, 95, Phila. Art Alliance, 1995, Murray (Ky.) State U., 1996, Ctrl. Mo. State U., 1996, Stephen Austin State U. Tex., 1996, Houston Ctr. for Photography, 1995, 96, Perry House Galleries, Va., 1996, 97, U. S.D., Vermilion, 1994, 97, Nebr. Wesleyan U., 1997, U. No. Iowa, 1997, ekliktikos gallery, Washington, 1997, Chuck Levitan Gallery, N.Y., 1997-98; group exhibitions: Mpls. Inst. Arts, 85, 86, 2000, Minnesota State Fair, 1986-93, 95-97, 99-2000, U. Wisconsin, Green Bay, 1988, 94, 98, Coll. St. Catherine, MN, 1997, 99, Mpls., Jewish Community, Ctr., 1997, 99, Phipps Ctr. For the Arts, WI, 98, 99, Bausch & Lomb, Rochester, NY, 1998, Texas Nat., 1998, 2000, Savannah COll. of Art & Design, 1998, St. John's U., MN, 1999, Pentimenti Gallery, PA, 2000, Euro Galleries, MN, 2000, GOCAIA Gallery, AZ, 2000, San Diego Art Inst., CA, 2000, Wellington B Gray Gallery, NC, 2001, Rehab Inst. Chgo., 2003, Weisman Art Mus., U. Minn., 2003, Plains Art Mus., Fargo, 1988, 2001, 2003, Michael Lord Gallery, WI, 2003, FLATFILE, Chgo., 2001, 02, 03, Icebox Gallery, MN, 2004; represented in permanent collections Dana Farber Cancer Inst., Fidelity Investments, Mass. Gen. Hosp., Hennepin History Mus., Savannah Coll. Art & Design, Minn. Ctr. Environ. Advocacy, Valley Hosp. Finalist Jerome Foundation, Erector Square Gallery, Warm Land Mark Print Project, Northfield Arts Guild; recipient Qualex award, Wellington B. Gray Gallery; fellow Rimon Cultural Arts. Home: 1422 Tamarack Dr Long Lake MN 55356

HOFMANN, KAY JOYCE, sculptor, artist; b. Green Bay, Wis., Dec. 3, 1932; d. Walter and Marie (Vandersteen) H.; m. Carl E. Schwartz, June 18, 1955, (div. 1980); children: Dawn, Carilee. Grad., Art Inst. Chgo., 1955; postgrad, Acad. de Grande Chaumiere, Paris, 1955-56. Tchr. North Shore Art League, Winnetka, 1957-90, Suburban Fine Arts Ctr., Highland Park, Ill., 1965-92, Blackhawk Mountain Sch. of Arts, Colo., 1985-93. Recipient Ryersson fellowship Art Inst. Chgo., 1955, Nat. award Nat. Soc. Arts and Letters, Louisville, Ky., 1963; named Best of Show Artist Guild of Chgo., 1970. Democrat. Home: 3140 N 77th Ave Elmwood Park IL 60707-1111 Office Phone: 708-452-7048.

HOFMANN, POLLY A. physiologist, science educator; b. Dixon, Ill., July 8, 1960; married; 1 child. BS in Biology, U. Ill., 1982; PhD in Physiology, U. Pitts., 1987. Postdoctoral fellow dept. physiology U. Wis., Madison, Wis., 1987; asst. prof. dept. physiology and biophysics U. Tenn., Memphis, 1991—97, assoc. prof. dept. physiology, 1997—. Mem. prof. search com. Dept. Physiology and Biophysics, U. Tenn., 1991—92, grad. program tng. com., 1992—93, 1993—; student progress and promotions com. biomed. sci. Coll. of Medicine, U. Tenn., 1992—96; chmn. search com. Dept. Preventive Medicine, U. Tenn., 1993—94; Alma and Hal Reagan fellowship seletion com. Coll. Grad. Health Scis., U. Tenn., 1994—; mem. conflict resolution coun. of student mistreatment program Coll. of Medicine, U. Tenn., 1995—. Ad hoc reviewer Am. Jour. Physiology, Jour. Pharmacology and Exptl. Therapeutics; contbr. articles to profl. jours. Recipient Dave McClain Rsch. award, Am. Heart Assn., 1988, Established Investigator award, 1995; fellow predoctoral fellow, NIH, 1983—87, postdoctoral fellow, 1989—92, Am. Heart Assn., 1988—89; grantee, NIH, 1992—, Am. Heart Assn., 1992—93. Mem.: Internat. Soc. Heart Rsch. (Upjohn Young Investigator award 1990), Biophys. Soc., Am. Physiol. Soc. (career opportunities in physiology com. 1995—), Sigma Xi. Office: U Tenn 894 Union Ave Ste 426 Memphis TN 38163-0001

HOGABOOM, MAURINE HOLBERT, cultural organization administrator; b. Wichita Falls, Te., Feb. 3, 1912; d. Joseph Eggleston Holbert and Ada Viola Davis; m. Robert Edward Hogaboom, July 16, 1982 (dec. Nov. 1993). BA summa cum laude, Fordham U., 1976; MA, Goddard Coll., 1979; postgrad., U. of the South, 1992—95. Actor, dir., tchr., N.Y.C., 1955—57; founder Chrysalis Rsch. Ctr. for the Arts, N.Y.C., 1979—83; founder, co-dir. Synthesis Ctr. St. Mary's, 1990—. Founding mem., performer Arts Alliance, St. Mary's Coll., 1983—; active Trinity Episcopal Ch., St. Mary's City, Md., 2001—. Avocations: gardening, yoga.

HOGAN, BRIGID L. molecular biologist; b. England, Aug. 28, 1943; BA, U. Cambridge, 1964, PhD, 1968. NATO rsch. fellow dept. biology MIT, 1968-70; lectr. biochemistry U. Sussex, England, 1970-74; sci. staff Imperial Cancer Rsch. Fund, Mill Hill, England, 1974-84; head lab. molecular embryology Nat. Inst. Med. Rsch., Mill Hill, England, 1985-88; prof. cell biology Vanderbilt Med. Sch., Nashville, 1988—2002; chair, dept. cell biology Duke U. Med. Ctr., 2002—. Hortense B. Ingram chair molecular oncology Howard Hughes Med. Inst., 1993-2002; vice chair Basement Membrane Gordon Conf., 1994, chair, 1996; co-chair sci. human embryo rsch. panel NIH, 1994; Jenkinson meml. lectr. U. Oxford, 1995; Margaret Pittman lectr. NIH, 1996. Mem. Br. Soc. Cell Biology (com. 1982-86), Br. Soc. Devel. Biology (com. 1984-88), NAS Inst. Medicine, European Molecular Biology Orgn. Office: Duke U Med Ctr 388 Nanaline Duke Bldg, Box 3709 Durham NC 27710

HOGAN, DONNA HELEN, school librarian, educator; b. Dallas, Apr. 21, 1937; d. Donald William Ross and Lillian Ethel Andrews; m. Jerry Don Hogan, June 11, 1960 (div. Jan. 29, 1986); children: Laura, Leslie, Donald. BA, U. Tulsa, 1959; MLIS, U. Okla., Norman, 1990. Cert. secondary edn. tchg. Okla., 1965. Tchr. French, Eng. Midwest City Pub. Schs., Okla., 1965—67; tchr. French Lexington Pub. Sch., Okla., 1971—72; owner Hogan's Carpets, Purcell, Okla., 1976—86; staff asst. Bilingual Edn. Multifunctional Resource Ctr., U. Okla., Norman, 1987—90; libr. Met.

Libr. Sys., Oklahoma City, 1990—93, U. Ala. Librs., Tuscaloosa, 1993—98; asst. dean pub. svcs. U. Tex. at San Antonio Libr., 1998—. Guest spkr., libr. U. Ala., Tuscaloosa, 1994—97; 2d v.p Oklahoma Libr. Assn., Oklahoma City 1975—93; com. chair Ala. Libr. Assn., Birmingham, 1993—98. Contbr. articles to profl. jours. Treas. Norman Cmty. Choral Assn. Norman 1981—36; proof Tabvehood City. Choral Soc., 1993—96, trustee, chair Pioneer Multi-County Libr. Bd., Norman, 1975—83; pres. Friends of Librs. in Okla., Oklahoma City, 1980—82. Recipient Scholarship, Oklahoma Libr. Assn., 1988. Mem.: AAUW (Past Pres., Purcell Branch), ALA (com. chair New Mems. Roundtable 1990—2000, pres.'s program chair Reference and User Svcs. Assn. 1992—, chair mgrs. 1998—2000), Am. Soc. Engring. Edn. (mem. engring. libr. divsn.), Mortar Bd. Alumni Assn., San Antonio Choral Soc., Beta Phi Mu. Methodist. Avocations: travel, hiking, homemaking arts. Office: U Tex San Antonio Libr 6900 N Loop 1604 West San Antonio TX 78249 Office Phone: 210-458-4887. Business E-Mail: dhogan@utsa.edu.

HOGAN, ILONA MODLY, lawyer; b. Erlangen, Fed. Republic of Germany, Nov. 23, 1947; arrived in U.S., 1951, naturalized, 1960; d. Stephen Bela and Gunda Pauline (Gastiger) Modly; m. Lawrence J. Hogan, Mar. 16, 1974; children: Matthew Lawrence, Michael Alexander, Patrick Nicholas, Timothy Stefan. Student, Marymount Coll., 1965-67; AB in Internat. Affairs, George Washington U., 1969; JD, Georgetown U., 1974. Bar: D.C. 1975, Md. 1975. Intern and clk. AID, 1965-69; adminstrv. and legis. asst. to mem. Ho. of Reps., 1969-72; editor Legis. Digest, Ho. of Reps., Washington, 1972-73; asso. and law clk. firm Trammell, Rand, Nathan and Lincoln, Washington, 1972-74; mng. ptnr. firm Hogan and Hogan, Washington and Md., 1974-93; of counsel Venable, Baetjer, Howard & Civiletti, Washington, 1989-91; pres. Amcom Inc., 1978—; of counsel Salisbury & McLister, Frederick, Md., 1993-2001; global mgr. Bechtel Telecom., 2001—. Mem. Prince George's Bd. Libr. Trustees, Md., 1976—78, Prince George's County Econ. Devel. Adv. Com., 1979—82; v.p. St. John's Sch. Bd., 1987—88, pres., 1989; treas. U. Md. Bd. Regents, 1988—95; trustee St. James Sch., 1989—90; mem. Lawyers Steering com. for Reagan-Bush, 1980; nat. vice-chmn. Assn. Execs. for Reagan-Bush, 1984; mem. bus. and industry adv. com. 50th Am. Presdl. Inaugural, 1985; mem. Md. steering com. Bush for Pres., 1988; mem. Presdl. Personnel Adv. Com., 1989, Gov.'s Higher Edn. Transition Team, 1988; elected mem. County Commrs. Frederick County, 1994—2001; Frederick County co-chair Bush-Cheney Campaign, 2000; bd. advisors Frostburg State U., 2001—03; trustee Frederick Co. Found., 2001—03, Md. Higher Edn. Commn., 2003—. Mem.: ABA, D.C. Bar, Md. Bar Assn. Republican. Roman Catholic. Home: 5614 New Design Rd Frederick MD 21703-8306 Office: 5275 Westview Dr Frederick MD 21703-8306 E-mail: imhogan@bechtel.com.

HOGAN, MARY IRENE BERNADETTE, poet; b. Bonne Terre, Mo., Sept. 1, 1957; d. Robert Estol and Mathilda Carol Hogan. AAS, Purdue U., 1979. Staff writer Chronicle Sch. Newspaper, Gary, Ind., 1994, 1998, 1999. Guest poet Tolleston Br. Libr., Gary, 2002, Gary, 03. Author poetry. Active Friends Lake County Pub. Libr., Merrillville, Ind., 2003, Friends Hammond (Ind.) Pub. Libr., Mental Health Assn. Lake County, Highland, Ind., 2003; vol. St. Margaret Mercy Hosp., Dyer, Ind., 1988. Pvt. first class U.S. Army, 1979—80. Recipient Charles Nagy award, Mayor's Commn. on Disabilities, 1999; Undergrad. Rsch. grantee, Purdue U. Calument, 1998, 2001. Mem.: Ind. State Fedn. Poetry Clubs, Nat. Mus. Women in the Arts, Acad. Am. Poets (assoc.). Roman Catholic. Avocations: writing, reading, poetry. Home: 1592 Beverly St Hammond IN 46324-3359

HOGAN, ROXANNE ARNOLD, nursing consultant, risk management consultant, educator; b. Connellsville, Pa. d. Tyree Franklin Sr. and Reva Gayle (Thieler) A.; m. Patrick B. Hogan. AAS, Gloucester County Coll., 1983; BSN, Widener U., 1989. Lic. healthcare risk mgr. Fla.; RN Fla., cert. oper. rm. nurse. Staff devel. instr., nursing supr., cardiac care nurse Meth. Hosp., Phila., 1982-89; emergency nurse Underwood Meml. Hosp., Woodbury, NJ, 1988-89; critical care nurse Jupiter Hosp., Fla., 1989—92; emergency clin. nurse III Indian River Meml. Hosp., Vero Beach, Fla., 1990-92; EMT/paramedic instr. Indian River CC, Ft. Pierce, Fla., 1992-94; emergency asst. nurse mgr. Holmes Regional Med. Ctr., Melbourne, Fla., 1992-94; post anesthesia clin. nurse III Indian River Meml. Hosp., Vero Beach, Fla., 1994-98; surg. dir. Rosato Plastic Surgery Ctr., Vero Beach, Fla., 1998-99; nurse mgr. pre-admissions, IV team, ambulatory infusion, spl. procedures GI lab. Ambulatory Surgery Ctr., Indian River Meml. Hosp., Vero Beach, Fla., 1999—2001; pres. Treasure Coast Cons., Inc., 2001—02; risk mgmt. coord. HCA/St. Lucie Med. Ctr., Port St. Lucie, Fla., 2002—03; claims med. specialist S.E. Fla. Nationwide Ins., 2003—. Mem.: Am. Assn. Legal Nurse Cons. (South Fla. Chpt.), Assn. of Oper. Rm. Nurses (Platinum Coast Chpt.), Eta Beta Chpt., Sigma Theta Tau. Home: 5346 NW Rugby Dr Port Saint Lucie FL 34983-3384

HOGAN, RUTH DEWITT, artist; b. Colorado Springs, Colo., Nov. 5, 1943; d. Thomas Howland and Annie Carolyn (Pryor) DeWitt; m. Frank Holzer Hogan, Dec. 29, 1967. BS, U. Tex., 1965. Co-owner Orleans Art Gallery, Orleans, Mass., 1968—87; owner - artist Hogan Art Gallery, Orleans, 1995—. Curator Cape Mus. of Art, Dennis, 2000—02, mem. requisition com., 1996—. Prin. works include Mr. Bemis's Poppies (1st prize Creative Art Ctr., Chatham, Mass.), Airing the Quilts (Eugene and Ella Jackson award), exhibitions include The Danforth Mus., Framingham, Providence Art Club, Represented in permanent collections Cape Mus. Art, Provincetown Art Assn. and Mus., Meadowbrook Gallery Oakland U., in pastels and white - line woodblock prints. Mem. local boards, Orleans. Mem.: Cape Cod Print Makers, Pastel Painters Soc. of Am., Pastel Painters Soc. of Cape Cod. Avocation: gardening. Home: 9 Herringbrook Way Orleans MA 02653 Office: Hogan Art Gallery 39 Main St Orleans MA 02653 E-mail: frank.hogan@comcast.net.

HOGAN, SHEILA MAUREEN, biology educator, nurse; b. Lincoln, Ill., Mar. 20, 1958; d. Edward William and Cecilia Dolores (Shay) Krotz; children: Celia, Nicole. Cert., Practical Sch. of Nursing, 1979; AS, Richland Coll., 1983; BS, Millikin U., 1985, MS in Ednl. Adminstrn., 1998. Office nurse C.T. Johnson, Decatur, Ill., 1979-83; head nurse Community Ctr. for Developmentally Disabled, Decatur, 1981-84; lab. technician Millikin U., Decatur, 1983-85; tchr. biology Mt. Zion (Ill.) High Sch., 1985-96; pres., founder Positive Influences, Mem. Ill. Health Occupations, Ill. Vocat. Assn., Nat. Sci. Tchrs., Ill. Sci. Tchrs., Ill. Coordinating Coun. Vocat. Students (vice chmn. Springfield, Ill. chpt. 1987-96), Pi Lambda Theta. Roman Catholic. Avocations: reading, photography, needlework. Home: 1243 Seagreen Pl San Diego CA 92154-5805

HOGAN, SUSAN COX, association executive; b. Wheeling, W.Va., Dec. 9, 1949; d. Michael Cresap and Beatrice (Emblen) Cox; m. David Proctor Nelson, July 18, 1969 (div. 1973); 1 child, Michael David; m. William N. Hogan, Jr., Jan. 3, 1986; 6 stepchildren. Student, W.Va. U., 1967-69. Music dir. Bach Soc., Half Moon Bay, Calif., 1975-78; exec. dir. Wheeling Symphony Soc., W. Va., 1979-87; vol. U.S. Peace Corps, Benin, West Africa, 1987-91; exec. dir. YWCA of Wheeling, 1991—; exec. dir. Wheeling Symphony Orch Wheeling, W. Va. Bd. dirs. Homeless Coalition, 1991—, Soup Kitchen of Greater Wheeling 1991—, United Way Friends, 1993—, Victorian Wheeling Soc. 1993—; active Family Resource Network, Drug & Alcohol Coun. Mem. Returned Peace Corps Vols., Rotary. Democrat. Avocations: reading, art, music. Office: Wheeling Symphony Orch 1025 Main St Ste 811 Wheeling WV 26003-2724

HOGE, MEDORA DAVIDSON, dance educator; b. Merriam, Kans., July 2, 1930; d. John Archibald and Mabel Adelaide Davidson; m. Daniel Howe Hoge, Jr., Feb. 6, 1971 (div. June 14, 1984); m. Harry Lee Lydick, June 21, 1953 (div. Nov. 5, 1965); children: Harry Lee Lydick, Jr., Robin Louis

Lydick. Grad. h.s., Merriam, 1948. Instr. ballet, tap, jazz, gymnastics, ballroom dance, low-impact aerobics Davidson Dance Studio, Prairie Village, Kans., 1950—89; dance instr. N.A.D.A.A. city chpts., St. Paul, St. Louis, Omaha, Tulsa, Dallas, 1957—59, jazz dance instr. nat. faculty Nat. Assn. Dance and Affiliated Artists Inc., L.A. Dallas, Omaha, 1957—19; choreographer outdoor Mus. shows Johnson County (Kans.) Pks. and Recreation, 1971—73; choreographer Kansas City (Mo.) Royals Banquet shows, 1972—74; instr. ballet, tap, gymnastics Visitation Parochial Sch., Kansas City, Mo., 1989—91; former owner, instr. ballet, tap, jazz, gymnastics, low-impact aerobics Davidson Dance Studio, Ottawa, Kans., 1991—99; tchr. low-impact aerobics Albuquerque Sr. Ctrs., 1999—2000; tchr. modern dance and children's drama Carnegie Cultural Ctr., Ottawa, 2000—02, tchr. piano, 2002—04, instr. Kindermusik Internat., 2002—04, tchr. yoga, 2002—04. Dance therapist activity dept. Psychiat. Receiving Ctr., Western Mo. Mental Health Ctr., Kansas City, 1969—; taped 65 half-hour ballet class lessons for children Medora and Me, 1970—71; taped 65 half-hour interviews for women The Feminine Touch, 1970—71; dir. Picnic A.C.T. Ottawa!, Ottawa Cmty. Theatre, 1997; writer, dir. 3 plays Fine Arts Singles, Johnson County, Kans., 1990—91; dir. Show Boat Baldwin Cmty. Theater, Baldwin City, Kans., 1999; formed Crackerjack Children's Theatre, Ottawa, 2001; writer, dir. Coventown A.C.T. Ottawa!, Ottawa, 2001, dir. An Old Time Radio Show, 02, dir. Playboy of the Western World, 02; dir. Crackerjack Children's Theatre Christmas Reader's Theatre, 2001, Playboy of the Western World, Ottawa Cmty. Theatre, 2001, Nunsense 2003, Baldwin City Cmty. Theatre, 2003, Another Old Time Radio Show, Ottawa Cmty. Theatre, 2003, Bye, Bye, Bye Birdie, Baldwin City Cmty. Theatre, 2003, One Magical Christmas Eve, Ottawa Cmty. Theatre, 2003, Quilters, Ottawa Cmty. Theatre, 2004. Actor (plays) Gypsy, 1973, Lady Audley's Secret, 1976, The Farsighted Dragon and the Nearsighted Knight, 1985, Night of January 16th, 1994, Greater Tuna, 1996, The Tempest, 1998, Nunsense, 1999, 2003, Diamonds to Die For, 2000, Cabaret, A Black Tie Affair, 2001, Cabaret, For Ladies Only, 2003, Cabaret, Back & Better, 2004. Vol. dance therapist Johnson County Mental Health Ctr., Overland Park, Kans., 1967—69. Avocations: gardening, painting, sewing, reading. Home: 1103 S Main St Ottawa KS 66067-3523 E-mail: medorad@sbcglobal.net.

HOGENSEN, MARGARET HINER, librarian, consultant; b. Ottawa, Kans., Oct. 11, 1920; d. Hebron Henry and Nellie Evelyn (Godard) Hiner; widowed. BA, U. Wichita, 1942; BS in Library Sci., U. Denver, 1945. Circulation librarian Boise (Idaho) Pub. Library, 1945-49, Pomona (Calif.) Pub. Library, 1950-51; reference librarian WFIL-TV, Phila., 1963-69; rsch. dir. Concept Films, Washington, 1969-72; ind. researcher, cons. Greenbelt, Md., 1973-80. Bd. dirs. Greenbelt Homes, Inc., 1977-93, 98-2000, 2003—, pres., 1983-88, treas. 1998-2000; past mem. bd. dirs. Greenbelt Consumer Coop., Nat. Coop. Bus. Assn.; pres. Ea. Coop. Housing Orgn., 1992-95. Mem. Nat. Assn. Housing Coops (bd. dirs. 1986-87, 1990-94). Democrat. Christian Scientist. Avocation: travel. Home: PO Box 218 Greenbelt MD 20768-0218

HOGG, JUDITH E. neurologist, educator; b. Binghamton, N.Y. d. Edwin Charles and Virginia Anne (Pettinato) H. AB, MD, Boston U., 1970. Diplomate Am. Bd. Psychiatry and Neurology. Intern Lenox Hill Hosp., N.Y.C., 1970-71, resident in internal medicine, 1971-72; resident in neurology Mt. Sinai Hosp., N.Y.C., 1972-75; pvt. practice, 1975-77; neuro-epidemiology rschr. NIH, Bethesda, Md., 1977-79; asst. clin. prof. neurology George Washington U., Washington, 1979-88; staff neurologist Santa Clara Valley Med. Ctr., San Jose, Calif., 1988-91; assoc. prof. sch. medicine Tex. Tech. U., Lubbock, 1991-98; pvt. practice, 1998—. Mem. AMA, Greenville County Med. Soc., Am. Acad. Neurology, Am. Assn. Electrodiagnostic Medicine (assoc.), Phi Beta Kappa. Home: 26 Cypress Point St Greenville SC 29605-4014

HOGGARD, MINNIE COLTRAIN, gifted education educator, consultant; b. Williamston, N.C. d. Joshua Herbert and Nellie Mae (Wynne) Coltrain; m. Robert Lewis Hoggard; children: Robbin Lenora Hoggard Blake, Lewis Wynne Hoggard. BS, East Carolina U., 1975, MA in Ed., 1977, curriculum instrnl. specialist, 1988, EdS, 1991. Cert. reading specialist, instrnl. specialist, academically gifted tchr., supt., prin., N.C. Draftsman, bookkeeper East Coast Surveying Svc., Windsor, N.C., 1964-75; tchr. reading Washington County Schs., Washington, N.C., 1975; elem. tchr. Martin County Schs., Williamston, 1975-85, tchr. academically gifted, 1985-93, academically gifted specialist, coord., 1993-97, cons. academically gifted local plan, 1996-97, mentor coord., 1998—, asst. prin., 1997-98, 98-99. Supervising tchr. East Carolina U., Greenville, N.C., 1979-85; N.C. advisor Tar Heel Jr. Hist. Assn., Raleigh, 1986. Collaborating writer and tester elem. sch. curriculum in Can. for N.C. students; editor play Backwards into Time, 1986 (state award 1986). Pres. Windsor Jr. Woman's Club, 1969-71. Grantee Nat. Diffusion Network, 1986; recipient N.C. Advisor of Yr. award, 1986. Mem. Coun. for Exceptional Children, Nat. Assn. for Gifted Children. Democrat. Episcopalian. Avocations: recreational reading, walking, writing poetry, playing bridge, travel. Home: 302 Sutton Dr Windsor NC 27983-6737 Office: Martin County Schs 300 N Watts St Williamston NC 27892-2056

HOGGARTH, KAREN, lumber company executive; CFO, treas. Jeld-Wen, Inc., Klamath Falls, Oreg. Office: Jeld-Wen Inc 3303 Lakeport Blvd Klamath Falls OR 97601-1017 Fax: (541) 885-7425.

HOGLEN, JEWEL PAMELA, retired secondary school educator; b. Columbia, Miss., Sept. 22, 1919; d. Irvin Armstrong Blackburn and Inez Geraldine Dickens; m. Hubert J. Hoglen, Nov. 4, 1944; 1 child, Pamela J. BS, La. State Normal (now Northwestern State U. of La.), 1941; MA in Edn., Washington U., 1953. Cert. home economist, family & consumer scis. Home economist H.S., Kentwood, La., 1941—42; chmn. home economy Ward & Hanley Jr. H.S., U. City, Mo., 1947—69, Parkway N. H.S., Chesterfield, Mo., 1972—78; asst. prof. Meramec C.C., Kirkwood, Mo., 1972—75, ret., 1975. Vice chmn. profl. sect. Am. Home Econs. Assn., 1987—89; pres. Home Econs. Coun., St. Louis, 1964—65. Louis IX art mus. group Art Mus., St. Louis, 1978—. Recipient Disting. Svc. to the Profession award, Am. Home Econ. Assn., 1991—93, 50 Yrs. of Svc. award, Am. Home Econs. Assn., 1998. Mem.: AAUW, Mo. Home Econs. Assn. (pres. 1968—69, 1969—70, mem. home economists in homemaking section, Cert. for Outstanding Contbn. & Svc. to the Profession 1985, 50 Years Dedication & Svc. to Home Econs. Profession award 1998), Am. Assn. Home (history & archives com., svc. to leader in leadership mtg.), Coll. Club of St. Louis (chmn. Centennial birthday celebration 2000, pres. 2001—03). Republican. Protestant. Avocations: tailoring, reading, horse back riding, travel. Home: 1009 Dougherty Ferry Rd Kirkwood MO 63122

HOGUET, KAREN M. retail department store executive; m. David Hoguet; 2 children. Grad., Brown U.; MBA, Harvard U., 1980. With Boston Cons. Group, Chgo.; sr. cons. mktg. and long-range planning Federated Dept. Stores, Inc., Cin., 1982-85, dir. capital and bus. planning, 1985-87, operating v.p. planning and fin. analysis, 1987-88, corp. v.p., 1988-91, sr. v.p. planning, 1991—, treas., 1992—, CFO, 1997—, sr. v.p., CFO. Mem. Phi Beta Kappa. Office: Federated Dept Stores Inc 7 W 7th St Cincinnati OH 45202-2424 Fax: 513-579-7555.

HOHAUSER, MARILYN, artist; b. Bronxville, N.Y., May 7, 1934; d. Sterling Franklin Boos and Mildred Myntea Taylor; m. Sanford M. Hohauser, May 3, 1959; children: William Edward, Carol Miriam, Sanford Stephen. BA, Finch Coll., 1956. Pres. House Mart, N.Y.C., 1959-61, Hohauser Assocs., N.Y.C., 1959—, Rating The Svcs., Inc., N.Y.C.—. Author: Architectural & Interior Models, 1969, 86, Rating the Services, 1968, The Score Never Changes, 2000, Hill City Designs, 2000. Avocations: making models, collecting miniatures, military history, medical research. Home: 248 E 31st St Apt 1B New York NY 10016-9711

HOHENBERGER, PATRICIA JULIE, fine arts and antique appraiser, consultant; b. Holyoke, Mass. d. Ambrose Harrington and Irene Leo (Ducharme) Reynolds; m. John H. Hohenberger, June 27, 1953; children: Lisa Maria, Julie Suzanne, John Henry, James Reynolds, Patricia Antonia Hohenberger. Student U. Mass., Amherst, 1946—48, Winter Park Fine Art Studies, NYU, 1983. Cert. elem. edn. tchr., Mass. Tchr. Hadley (Mass.) Pub. Schs., 1950-52, Springfield (Mass.) Pub. Schs., 1952-54; owner, dir. The Brown House Nursery Sch., Williamstown, Mass., 1962-64; tchr. Coindra Hall, Huntington, N.Y., 1970-71, St. Edward the Confessor, Syosset, N.Y., 1971-81; pres. Patricia Reynolds Hohenberger Appraisals, Northport, N.Y., 1983—. Cons. O'Toole-Edward Art Assn., Inc., N.Y., 1984-91, Alexander-Benwood Co., Inc. Huntington, N.Y., 1991—; lectr. Symposium-Gen. Accident Ins., N.Y., 1994. Author: (monograph) Gentle Reminders of the Past, 1984. Recipient Recognition for Achievement award Alexander-Benwood Co., Inc., Huntington, N.Y., 1995. Mem. Nat. Trust for Historic Preservation, Nat. Mus. Women in the Arts (charter), New England Appraisers Assn. Roman Catholic. Avocations: collecting american decorative arts and antiques, photography. Home: 72 Burt Ave Northport NY 11768-2046

HOKANSON, CAROL, speech therapist, special education educator; b. Memphis, Oct. 21, 1954; d. William Thomas and Tommie Francis Sowell. BSE, Ark. State U., 1976, MSE, 1983. Speech and lang. pathologist. Speech therapist Evening Shade (Ark.) Sch., 1977-78; spl. edn. tchr. Sch. for Exceptional Children, Pocahontas, Ark., 1978-84, Eureka (Kans.) Pub. Schs., 1984-85; spl. edn. CBI tchr. Helena (Ark.) Pub. Sch., 1987-88; speech therapist Bearden (Ark.) Pub. Sch., 1988-91, Caddo Hills/Mt. Ida/Oden, Montgomery County schs., Norman, Ark., 1991—. Speech therapist Dawson Co-op, Arkadelphai, Ark., 1993—; psychol. examiner Psychol. Corps., Austin, Tex., 1991—. Participant chaperon Spl. Olympics, Pocahontas, Ark., 1978-84. Mem. NEA, Assn. Retarded Citizens. Presbyterian and Methodist. Home: PO Box 2112 Glenwood AR 71943-2112 Office: Caddo Hills Sch HC 65 Box 249 Norman AR 71957-9502

HOKE, SHEILA WILDER, retired librarian; b. Greensboro, N.C. d. Herbert Bruce Wilder and Virginia Dare (Caylor) Wilder-Dell; m. Robert Edward Hoke, Nov. 22, 1958 (dec.); children: Raymond Fellow, Philip Wilder. Student, Montclair Coll., 1948; BA in History, U. Kans., 1950, postgrad., 1951, BS in Edn., 1952; postgrad., JOhn Hopkins U., 1955; MLS, U. Wis., 1955; MS in Edn., Southwestern Okla. State U., 1977; postgrad., Johns Hopkins U., Montclair State Coll. Tchr. history Fredonia (Kans.) High Sch., 1952-54; student asst. U. Wis., Madison, 1954-55; children's libr. BR Enoch Pratt Libr., Balt., 1955-58; libr. dir. U.S. Army Spl. Svcs., Bavaria, Fed. Republic Germany, 1958-59; libr. U.S. Army Dependent Schs., Straubing, Fed. Republic Germany, 1959-60; cataloger Southwestern Okla. State U. Libr., Weatherford, 1963-69, libr. dir., 1969-93; ret., 1993. Mem. spl. projects com. Okla. Dept. Edn., 1974, adv. com. Okla. State Regents Libr., 1975-77. Mem. Okla. State Regents for Higher Edn. Libr. Networking, 1989-93; mem. sr. citizens choir 1st Bapt. Ch., Weatherford; vol. with children Agape Med. Clinic; reading tutor to 1st grade student Weatherford Pub. Schs.; vol. helper for home-bound; active sr. citizens groups. Mem. AAUW (pres., state bd. dirs. 1980, Weatherford br. 1981-83), Nat. Assn. Ret. Fed. Employees, Okla. Libr. Assn. (chmn. tech. svcs. divsn. 1969-70, chmn. coll. and univ. divsn. 1972-73, chmn. adminstrs. workshop 1973, chmn. libr. edn. divsn. 1975-76, chmn. recruitment com. 1978, archives com. 1980), Okla. Ret. Tchrs. Assn., Weatherford C. of C. (edn. com. 1974-75, cert. meritorious achievement from Gov. Nigh 1985), Custer County Hist. Soc., western Okla. Hist. Soc., Higher Edn. Alumni Coun. Okla., Delta Kappa Gamma (pres. Lambda chpt. 1980-82), Phi Alpha theta, Kappa Kappa Iota (pres. Lambda chpt. 1984-85). Republican. Baptist. E-mail: shoke@itlnet.net.

HOLBROOK, MEGHAN ZANOLLI, fundraiser, public relations specialist, political organization chairman; b. N.Y.C., Oct. 12, 1949; m. James R. Holbrook. BS in English and Edn., U. Tenn., 1971, postgrad., 1978-83. Dir. ancillary svcs. Ridgeview Psychiat. Hosp., Oak Ridge, Tenn., 1971-83; therapist The Children's Ctr., Salt Lake City, 1985-86; mgr. corp. contbns. Sundance Inst. and Film Festival, Salt Lake City, 1989-91; fund raising and pub. rels. cons. Salt Lake City, 1992—. Fundraiser congl. campaign Wayne Owens, 1986, bus. liaison, 1986-88; fin. dir. gubernatorial campaign Ted Wilson, 1988, mayoral campaign Deedee Corradini, 1991; campaign mgr. gubernatorial campaign Stewart Hanson, 1991-92; del. Dem. Nat. Conv., 1996; chair Utah State Dem. Party, 1996—; mem. bd. dirs. Sundance Inst., 1989—, Inst. at Deer Valley, 1995—; mem. Utah Air Travel Commn., 1996—; mem. pres.'s adv. com. on arts Kennedy Ctr., Washington, 1996—. Mem. Assn. State Dem. Chairs (exec. com. 1998—). Home: 775 Hilltop Rd Salt Lake City UT 84103-3311 Office: 455 S 300 E Ste 102 Salt Lake City UT 84111-3222

HOLBROW, GWENDOLYN JANE, artist, writer; b. NYC, Aug. 22, 1957; d. Charles Howard and Mary Ross Holbrow; m. Mark Joseph Kacvinsky; children: Hilary, Charles, Giles, Felicity. BA with honors, U. Wis., 1980; BA, Framingham State Coll., 2001. Cert. fluency in German as fgn. lang. Goethe Inst. Freelance writer, 1997—; instr. Danforth Mus. Schs., Framingham, Mass., 2001—. Freelance editor, graphic designer, desk-top pub., Frankfurt am Main, Germany, 1990—98; contbg. author Main City, Frankfurter Allgemeine Zeitung, Frankfurt am Main, 1997—98, Middlesex Beat, Groton, 2001—; lectr. Framingham State Coll., 2002—, AAUW, 2002; author, rev. artsMedia, Boston, 2002—. Mixed-media installation, The Throne Of The Queen Of The Universe and Her Handmaidens, 2000, mixed-media fountain with barbie doll, Keep It Clean, 2000 (First prize Concord Art Assn., 2000), acoustic copper sculpture, Gravity Chimes, 2001 (Juror's Choice award Cambridge Art Assn., 2001), poster, Universal Applicaton, 2002; author: (essay) Louse Bourgeois: Bridging the Chasm Between Self and Other, 2001 (Cheryl di Mento Art History Essay award Framingham State Coll., 2001). Town meeting mem. Town Meeting, Framingham, 2001—01. Named winner, Artists' Valentine Grant Competition, 2003; recipient Silver medal, Mass. Hort. Soc., 2002, Gold medal, 2004, Best of Show for Queen Kong sculpture, Cambridge Art Assn., 2004. Mem.: Soc. of Children's Book Writers and Illustrators, New Eng. Sculptors Assn., Concord Art Assn., Cambridge Art Assn., Internat. Sculpture Ctr., Framingham Artists' Guild. Unitarian Universalist. Avocation: singing in choirs and opera. Business E-Mail: holbrow@hotmail.com.

HOLCOMB, CARAMINE KELLAM, volunteer; b. Painter, Va., Jan. 23, 1941; d. Emerson Polk and Amine (Cosby) Kellam; m. Isaac Somers White, Nov. 25, 1961 (div. 1975); children: Kellam White Griffin, Caramine White, Virginia Somers White; m. Harry Sherman Holcomb III, May 12, 1979 (div. Mar. 2001). AA, St. Mary's Coll., Raleigh, 1960; Cert., Richmond Bus. Coll., 1961. Bd. dirs. Kellam Energy, Inc., Belle Haven, Va., 1980—, Auto Plus, Inc., Belle Haven, 1980-89, Shore Stop, Inc., Belle Haven, 1981-89. Contbr. articles to profl. jours. Trustee Northampton-Accomack Meml. Hosp., Nassawadox, Va., 1986-91, exec. com., pres., 1988-90, sec. bd. trustees, 1989-91, vice chmn., 1994-96; bd. dirs. Ea. Shore Hist. Soc., Onancock, Va., 1987-92, Shore Life Svcs., 1989—(pres. 2004-); bd. dirs. Eastern Shore C.C. Found., 1998—, v.p. Found. bd., 2001-03, pres., 2003—; bd. dirs. Med. Soc. Va. Alliance, Richmond, 1984-94, v.p., 1989-91, pres., 1992-93; sec. E. Polk Kellam Found., 1991—; mem. session Belle Haven Presbyn. Ch., 1999-2002, Shore Meml. Bd. Trustees, 2003—, sec. 2004—. Mem. AMA Alliance Bd. (ERF com. 1994, AMA-ERF com. 1994-95, field dir. 1995-98, bylaws chmn. 1999-2000), Med. Soc. Va. Trust, Garden Club Ea. Shore (pres. 1973-75, Garden Week chmn. 2001—02). Avocations: travel, reading, flower arranging. Home: PO Box 38 Franktown VA 23354-0038

HOLCOMB, CONSTANCE L. sales and marketing management executive; b. St. Paul, Oct. 28, 1942; d. John E. Holcomb and Lucille A. (Westerdahl) Hope; m. Walter D. Serwatka, May 1991. BS, U. Minn., 1965; MA in Intercultural Edn., U. of the Americas, Puebla, Mex., 1975. Rsch. analyst U.S. Dept. Def., Washington, 1965-66; br. gen. mgr. Berlitz Lang. Schs., Mexico City, 1966-68; pres., gen. mgr. Centro Lingüístico, Puebla, 1968-72; gen. mgr., prof. Lang. Ctr. Am. Sch. Found., Puebla, 1972-74; assoc. prof., dir. lang. programs U. of the Americas, Puebla, 1974-76; prof., dean faculty of langs. Nat. Autonomous U. Mex., Mexico City, 1976-78; dir. sales & mktg. Longman Pub. Co., N.Y.C., 1978-80, dir. internat. sales & mktg., 1980-84; mng. dir. ESL Pub. Div. McGraw-Hill Book Co., N.Y.C., 1984-85; dir. mktg. mgmt. McGraw-Hill Tng. Systems and Book Co., N.Y.C., 1985-86; dir. mktg. electronic bus. McGraw-Hill Book Co., N.Y.C., 1986-87; info. industry mgmt. cons., career mgmt. cons., ind. contractor, N.Y.C., 1987-91; mktg. cons. Sarasota, Fla., 1991—. V.p. MexTESOL, Mexico City, 1977-78. Editor: English Teaching in Mexico, 1975; pub.: Rubens to Rhubarb, The Ringling Museum of Art, 1995, Baroque, Basil and Thyme, The Ringling Museum of Art, 1997, Ringling, the Art Museum, The Ringling Museum of Art, 2002; contbr. articles to profl. jours. Bd. trustees, devel. com. mem. John and Mable Ringling Mus., 1993-99; bd. dirs. Safe Place and Rape Crisis Ctr., Sarasota, 1995-2002; bd. dirs. Friends of Selby Pub. Libr., 1997-99. Mem. Assn. Am. Pubs. (com. chmn. internat. div. 1980-84, exec. com. 1980-84), Info. Industry Assn., Nat. Assn. Women Cons., Am. Soc. Profl. and Exec. Women. Office: 340 S Palm Ave Sarasota FL 34236

HOLCOMB, MARY ANNE, councilwoman, municipal official; b. Detroit, July 8, 1951; d. Willard Oscar and Mary Elizabeth (Clark) Barnes; m. Winford Honzel Holcomb, Jr., July 12, 1969; children: Monica Leigh Holcomb Masters, Kenneth Curtis. BS in Edn., Jacksonville State U., 1969. Sr. adminstrv. sec. dept. pharmacology and toxicology U. Tex. Med. Br., Galveston; sec.-treas. Galveston (Tex.) County Health Dist., Bd. of Health, 2003—. Bd. mem., treas. Kemah (Tex.) Econ. Devel. Corp., 1994—96; bd. mem. Kemah Cmty. Devel. Corp., 1999—2001; councilwoman City of Kemah, 1996—; active Ctrl. Bapt. Ch., Hixson, Tenn., 1994—. Mem.: Order of the Ea. Star (past matron 1980—81). Republican. Avocations: politics, community activist, reading, baking. Home: 1710 Oak Meadow Dr Kemah TX 77565 Office: U Tex Med Br Dept Pharmacology and Toxicology 301 University Blvd Galveston TX 77555 1031 Office Phone: 409 772-9643.

HOLCOMB, RITA, landscaper; b. Bonham, Tex., Aug. 29, 1948; d. Guy M. and Marie (Moore) Ownby; m. Darrell Holcomb, July 29, 1972; 1 child, Stuart. A in Fine Arts, Grayson County Coll., Denison, Tex., 1974, A in Bus. Adminstrn., 1991. Owner Holcomb Miniatures, Sherman, Tex., 1980-90; sales Breathco/Mediserv, Sherman, 1990-94; owner Plants on the Move, Sherman, 1994—. Pres. bd. dirs. Red River Hist. Mus., Sherman, 1997, Sherman Cmty. Players Theater Guild, 1989; active Sherman City Coun., 1999—2000; co-chair Conv. and Visitors Coun., 2002; bd. dirs. Texoma Coun. Govts., 1999—2000, LWV Sherman/Grayson County, Tex., 2001—02, Grayson County Tri-County Nutrition, 1998—, Sherman Preservation League, 1995—97, 2000—01. Avocations: theater, miniatures, Tae Kwan Do, genealogy.

HOLDEN, BETSY D. food products company executive; b. Lubbock, Tex., 1956; BA, Duke U.; MA in edn., Northwestern U., MBA, 1982. Asst. product mgr. desserts Gen. Foods Corp., 1982—84; brand mgr., venture div. Kraft Foods Inc., 1984—85, brand mgr., Miracle Whip, 1985—87, group brand mgr., confections & snacks, 1987—90, v.p. new product devel. and strategy, 1990—91, v.p., mktg., dinners, & enhancers, 1991—93, pres. Tombstone Pizza, 1993—95, exec. v.p., gen. mgr. cheese divsn., 1995—97, pres. cheese divsn., 1997—98, exec. v.p., ops., procurement, research & devel., consumer insights and E-commerce, 1998—2000; pres., CEO Kraft Foods North America, 2000—01; co-CEO Kraft Foods Inc., 2001—03, pres., global mktg. & category devel., 2004—. Mem., bd. dirs. Kraft Foods, Tribune Co., Tupperware Corp. Pres. Chicago's Off the Street Club; mem., bd. Grocery Manufacturers of Amer., Evanston Northwestern Healthcare. Office: Kraft Foods Inc Three Lakes Dr Northfield IL 60093-2753*

HOLDEN, CAROL H. county official; b. Boston, Nov. 6, 1942; m. Donald B. Holden; 4 children. BA, Trinity Coll., 1964; MAT, Boston Coll., 1965. Intern U.S. Senate, 1963-64; mem. N.H. Ho. of Reps., 1984-97, vice chair children, youth and juvenile justice com.; mem. state-fed. rels. com.; asst. majority leader, 1996. Vice chair Hillsborough County Bd. Commrs., 1997—; mem. Amherst Ways and Means Commn., 1983-86; tchr., vol. coord. Del. N.H. Constl. Conv., 1984; pres. Amherst Women's Rep. Club, 1986-88; v.p. N.H. Fed. Rep. Women's Club, 1989-94, pres., 1994-95; mem. Amherst Sch. Dist. Mod., 1990—; dir. N.H. Ptnrs. in Edn., 1987—, sec., 1989—, vice chair, 1990—, chair, 1992—; mem. Gov.'s Steering Com. on Volunteerism, 1991-96; mem. N.H. Alliance for Effective Schs., 1991-96; v.p. N.H. Congress Parents and Tchrs., 1984-86, 90-92; trustee N.H. Childrens Trust Fund, 1997-98. Mem. Nat. Assn. of Counties (v.p.), Trinity Coll. Alumni Assn. (bd. dirs. 1980-87, sec. bd. dirs. 1994-97, 2d v.p. 1997-98), N.H. Assn. of Counties (1st v.p. 1999—2001, pres. elect, 2001-03, pres. 2003—), Nat. Assn. of Counties (steering com. labor and employment 1999—, bd. dirs. 2002—), Boston Coll. Club of N.H. (pres. 1999-2001), Vesta Roy Series (v.p. 2002—). Avocations: travel, sailing, tennis, skiing, reading. Home: PO Box 13 Amherst NH 03031-0013 Office: Bd Commrs 300 Chestnut St Manchester NH 03101-2412

HOLDEN, REBECCA LYNN, artist; b. Monterey, Calif., Nov. 29, 1952; d. Derrel Wayne and Zella Fay (Reed) Holden; m. Mark Stuart Bales, June 3, 1971 (div. Nov. 1983); children: Shelly Dawn Bales(dec.), Matthew Gregory Bales. BA, U. Ark., 1995. Potter/owner Rebecca Holden Studio, Searcy, Ark., 1984-94; artist/owner Rebecca Holden's Red Lick Mountain Studio, Clarksville, Ark., 1994-00; owner Old Carriage House Gallery and Studio, Jasper, Ark., 2000—. Established Old Carriage House Gallery and Studio, Jasper, Ark., 2000. Potter, sculptor, artist specializing in natural art forms. Recipient Art scholarship Susan Jones Rand Foun., 1992, 93. E-mail: carriage@jasper.yournet.com.

HOLDER, ANGELA RODDEY, lawyer, educator; b. Rock Hill, S.C., Mar. 13, 1938; d. John T. and Angela M. (Fisher) Roddey; 1 child, John Thomas Roddey Holder. Student, Radcliffe Coll., 1955-56; BA, Newcomb Coll., 1958; postgrad., Faculty of Law-King's Coll., London, 1957-58; JD, Tulane U., 1960; LLM, Yale U., 1975. Bar: La. 1961, S.C. 1960, Conn. 1981. Counsel Roddey, Sumwalt & Carpenter, Rock Hill, S.C., 1960-91; atty. criminal div. New Orleans Legal Aid Bur., 1961-62; counsel York County Family Ct., S.C., 1962-64; asst. prof. polit. sci. Winthrop Coll., Rock Hill, 1964-74; research assoc. Yale U. Law Sch., 1975-77, exec. dir. program in law, sci. and medicine, 1976-77; lectr. dept. pediatrics Yale U. Sch. Medicine, 1975-77, asst. clin. prof. pediatrics and law, 1977-79, assoc. clin. prof., 1979-83, clin. prof., 1983-2001; prof. practice of med. ethics Duke U. Med. Ctr., Durham, NC, 2001—, interim dir. Ctr. for Study of Med. Ethics and Humanities, 2004—. Trustee Am. Bd. Pediatrics, 2003—; mem. com. on pediat. palliative care Inst. of Medicine, 2001—02, mem. com. on clin. rsch. with children, 2002—04. Author: The Meaning of the Constitution, 1968, 2d edit., 1987, 3d edit., 1997, Medical Malpractice Law, 1975, 2d edit. 1978, Legal Issues in Pediatrics and Adolescent Medicine, 1977, 2d edit., 1985, 3d edit., 1997; contbg. editor: Prism mag.; contbg. editor., AMA; mem. editorial bd.: IRB, 1976=2000, Medicine and Health-Care, 1978-2000, Jour. Philosophy and Medicine; contbr. articles to profl. jours. Mem. Rock Hill Sch. Bd., 1967—68; chmn. bd. dirs. Family Planning Clinic, 1970—73; bd. trustees Ednl. Commn. for Fgn. Med. Grads., 1990—97, exec. com., 1997; bd. dirs. Conn. Planned Parenthood, 1993—99, exec. com., 1996—99; mem. lawyers' rev. group Health Care Task Force, The White House, 1993; bd. trustees Cushing/Whitney Med. Libr. at Yale U., 1996—2001; ethics com. Leeway AIDS Hospice, New Haven, 1996—2001; alumnae bd. visitors Nat. Cathedral Sch., Washington, 2000—; cons. Artificial Reproductive Techs. Com., Ct. Ho. of Reps. Mem. ABA, S.C. Bar Assn. (medico-legal com. 1973—), La. Bar Assn., New Haven County Bar Assn., Am. Soc. Law and Medicine (treas. 1981-83, sec. 1983-85, pres. 1986-88, bd. dirs. 1977-91). Democrat. Episcopalian. Home: 3408 Hope Valley Rd Durham NC 27707 Office: Ctr for Study of Med Ethics and Humanities Duke U Med Ctr Box 3040 108 Seeley G Mudd Bldg Durham NC 27710 Office Phone: 919-668-9010. E-mail: angela.holder@duke.edu.

HOLDER, ANNA MARIA, holding company executive; b. Key West, Fla., Feb. 22, 1966; d. James Paul Yaccarino, Sr. and Carol (Joskey) McInerny; m. Harold D. Holder, 1996; 1 child, Charlie Kadle. AA, St. Petersburg Jr. Coll., 1989; BS, Eckerd Coll., 1991; MA, U. South Fla., 1994, postgrad., 1995—. Adminstr. Chase Bank Fla., Pinellas Park, 1989-91; substance abuse adminstr. Centurion Hosp., Tampa, 1992; staff writer, asst. features editor The Oracle, Tampa, 1992-93; v.p. The Holder Group, Inc., Tampa, 1994—; pres. Sun-Suns Trading Co., Inc., Tampa, 1996—. Author: Relationships Among Six Business Variables in the Black Press, 1994. Bd. dirs. Hillsborough County HealthCare Adv. Bd., 1996—; co-founder Friends of Hillsborough HealthCare, Inc., 1998; mem. Healthy Start Hillsborough, 1997—. Mem. LWV (pres. Hillsborough County (Fla.) chpt. 1995-96). Republican. Avocations: reading, skiing, walking. Home: 900 Schellbourne St Reno NV 89511-7695

HOLDER, JANICE MARIE, state supreme court justice; b. Canonsburg, Pa., Aug. 29, 1949; d. Louis V. and Sylvia (Abraham) H.; m. George W. Loveland II, June 5, 1976 (div. Mar. 1987). Student, Allegheny Coll., 1967-68, Sorbonne, 1970; BS summa cum laude, U. Pitts., 1971; JD, Duquesne U., 1975. Bar: Pa. 1975, Tenn. 1979, D.C. 1988. Sr. law clk. to chief judge U.S. Dist. Ct. for Western Dist. Pa., Pitts., 1975-77; assoc. Catalano & Catalano, P.C., Pitts., 1977-79, Holt, Batchelor, Spicer & Ryan, Memphis, 1980-82; pvt. practice Memphis, 1983-87; assoc. James S. Cox & Assocs., Memphis, 1987-89; pvt. practice law Memphis, 1989-90; judge 30th Jud. Dist., Memphis, 1990-96; justice Tenn. Supreme Ct., 1996—. Solicitor Borough of McDonald (Pa.), 1978-79. Bd. dirs. Alliance for Blind and Visually Impaired, Memphis, 1985—94, Midtown Mental Health Ctr., 1995—97; trustee Memphis Bot. Garden Found., 1996—2002; mem. state coordinating coun. Tenn. Task Force Against Domestic Violence, 1994—96. Fellow: Tenn. Bar Found. (trustee 1995—99); mem.: ABA, Tenn. Trial Judges Assn. (exec. com. 1994—96), Tenn. Lawyers' Assn. for Women, Memphis Trial Lawyers Assn. (bd. dirs. 1988—90), Am. Inns Ct., Tenn. Jud. Conf. (treas. 1993—94, exec. com. 1993—96), Assn. for Women Attys. (treas. 1989, v.p. 1991, Marion Griffin-Frances Loring award 1999), Memphis Bar Assn. (bd. dirs. 1986—87, 1993—94, editor Memphis Bar Forum 1987—91, 1993—94, sec. 1993, treas. 1994, Sam A. Myar award 1990, Judge of Yr. divorce and family law sect. 1992, Chancellor Charles A. Rond award Outstanding Jurist 1992), Tenn. Bar Assn., Am. Bar Found. Office: Tenn Supreme Ct 119 S Main St Ste 310 Memphis TN 38103-3678

HOLDER, LINDA KAY, librarian; b. Fort Madison, Iowa, Sept. 3, 1946; d. Harold and Mildred Smith; children: Timothy, Christy, James, John Daniel. BS, U. of Tex. Pan Am., Edingburg, 1971. Cert. tchr. health, phys. edn., English Tex., 1971, libr. Tex., 1996. H.s. libr. Somerset Ind. Sch. Dist., Tex., 1997—. Author: (poetry) Who is This C.F. Child? (Editor's Choice Award, 1997). Svc. unit dir. Girl Scouts U.S., Lytle, Tex., 1985—90; den leader and cub master Boy Scouts of Am., Lytle, 1988—94. Mem.: Tex. Libr. Assn., Assn. of Tex. Profl. Educators. Community Of Christ. Home: PO Box 1808 Lytle TX 78052 Office: Somerset ISD PO Box 279 Somerset TX 78069

HOLDREN, JAMIE LYNN, music educator; b. Cin. d. Dallas E. Harper and Marlene Kirby; m. William P. Holdren; children: Nicholas J., James D. MusB in Edn., Georgetown (Ky.) Coll., 1982; MEd in adminstrn. and supervision, Xavier U., 1989. Gen. music tchr. Oak Hills Sch. Dist., Cin., 1982—83; choral and gen. music tchr. Princeton Jr. H.S., Cin., 1983—89, Robert E. Lucas Intermediate Sch., Cin., 1989—95; choral dir. Princeton H.S., Cin., 1993. Asst. dist. music coord. Princeton City Schs., Cin., 1995—2000. Dir.: A Prayer, 2000, 13th Annual Intermountain Choral Festival, 2003 (2nd Pl. award, 2003), I Know A Song; contbr. articles to profl. jours. Musician Mt. Carmel Bapt. Ch., Cin., 1978—2003. Mem.: Ohio Choral Dir.'s Assn., Ohio Music Educators Assn., Music Educators Nat. Conf. (Young Composer award 2000), Am. Choral Dir.'s Assn. (assoc.), Delta Kappa Gamma. Avocations: genealogy, reading, travel, gardening. Office: Princeton High School 11080 Chester Road Cincinnati OH 45246 E-mail: jholdren@princeton.k12.oh.us.

HOLDRIDGE, BARBARA, book publisher; b. N.Y.C., July 26, 1929; d. Herbert L. and Bertha (Gold) Cohen; m. Lawrence B. Holdridge, Oct. 9, 1959; 2 children. AB, Hunter Coll., 1950. Asst. editor Liveright Pub. Corp., N.Y.C., 1950-52; co-founder Caedmon Records, Inc., N.Y.C., 1952, ptnr., 1952-60, pres., 1960-62, treas., 1962-70, pres., 1970-75; co-founder Stemmer House Pubs. Inc., Owings Mills, Md., 1975, pres., 1975—2003; founder Stemmer House, Inc., Owings Mills, 2003, pres., 2003—. Co-founder, v.p. Shakespeare Rec. So., Inc., N.Y.C., 1960-70, Theatre Rec. Soc., Inc., N.Y.C., 1964-70, BEDE Prodns., 1984, History Rec. Soc., Inc., N.Y.C., 1964, pres., 1964-70; lectr. on Ammi Phillips, 1959—; lectr. on book pub., 1992—; adj. prof. writing media Loyola Coll., Balt., 1987-91. Author: Ammi Phillips, 1968, Aubrey Beardsley Designs from the Age of Chivalry, 1983, Chinese Cut-Out Designs of Costumes, 1989; articles on Am. paintings. Named to Hunter Coll. Hall of Fame, 1972, Nat. Women's Hall of Fame, 2001; recipient Am. Shakespeare Festival award, 1962, N.Y.C. cert. of appreciation, 1972, Lifetime Achievement award, Audio Pubs. Assn., 2001. Mem. 14 West Hamilton Street Club, Phi Beta Kappa Alumni Assn. of Greater Balt. (bd. dirs.). Office: 2627 Caves Rd Owings Mills MD 21117-2919 Office Phone: 410-363-3690. Personal E-mail: stemmerhouse@comcast.net. E-mail: stemmerhouse@comcast.net.

HOLDSCLAW, CHAMIQUE SHAUNTA, professional basketball player; b. Flushing, N.Y., Aug. 9, 1977; Grad., U. Tenn., 1999. Basketball player Washington Mystics, 1999—. Named Sports Illustrated and Sporting News Nat. Women's Player of Yr., 1999, Naismith finalist, AP Women's Basketball Player of Yr., 1997—98, 1998—99, N.Y.C. Player of Yr., Rawlings/WBCA Player of Yr., Player of Yr., Columbus, Ohio Touchdown Club, 1995, Rookie of the Yr., WNBA, 1999; named one of 12 female athletes selected as inspirational role models, Women's Sports and Fitness mag., 1998; named to Kodak 25th Anniversary Team, Women's Basketball Jour., Street & Smith All-Am., three-time, USA Today All-Am., WNBA All-Star Team, 1999, 2000, 2003, All-WNBA Team, 2000, 2001; recipient Sullivan award, Gold medal, 1998 World Championships, 1997 World Qualifying Tournament, 1995 Olympic Festival, USA Basketball Player of Yr. award, 1997, ESPY's for Female Athlete of Yr. award, second consecutive Women's Basketball Player of Yr. award, 1999, Naismith award, Atlanta's Tip-Off Club, 1995, Gold medal, U.S. Olympic Team, 2000. Office: Washington Mystics MCI Center 601 F St NW Washington DC 20004-1605

HOLDSWORTH, JANET NOTT, women's health nurse; b. Evanston, Ill., Dec. 25, 1941; d. William Alfred and Elizabeth Inez (Kelly) Nott; children: James William, Kelly Elizaveth, John David. BSN with high distinction, U. Iowa, 1963; M of Nursing, U. Wash., 1966. RN, Colo. Staff nurse U. Colo. Hosp., Denver, 1963-64, Presbyn. Hosp., Denver, 1964-65, Grand Canyon Hosp., Ariz., 1965; asst. prof. U. Colo. Sch. Nursing, Denver, 1966-71; counseling nurse Boulder PolyDrug Treatment Ctr., Boulder, 1971-77; pvt. duty nurse Nurses' Offcl. Registry, Denver, 1973-82; cons. nurse, tchr. parenting and child devel. Teenage Parent Program, Boulder Valley Schs., Boulder, 1980-88; bd. dirs., treas. Nott's Travel, Aurora, Colo., 1980—; nurse Rocky Mountain Surgery Ctr., 1996—. Instr., nursing coord. ARC, Boulder, 1979-90, instr., nursing tng. specialist, 1980-82. Mem. adv. bd. Boulder County Lamaze Inc., 1980-88; mem. adv. com. Child Find and Parent-Family, Boulder, 1981-89; del. Rep. County State Congl. Convs., 1972-96, sec. 17th Dist. Senatorial Com., Boulder, 1982-92; vol. Mile High ARC, 1980; vol. chmn. Mesa Sch. PTO, Boulder, 1982-92, bd. dirs., 1982-95, v.p., 1983-95; elder Presbyn. Ch. Mem. ANA, Colo. Nurses Assn. (bd. dirs. 1975-76, human rights com. 1981-83, dist. pres. 1974-76), Coun. Intracultural Nurses, Sigma Theta Tau, Alpha Lambda Delta. Republican. Home: 1550 Findlay Way Boulder CO 80305-6922 Office: Rocky Mountain Surgery Ctr 1630 30th St # 153 Boulder CO 80301-1014

HOLEC, ANITA KATHRYN VAN TASSEL, civic worker; b. Rahway, NJ, Nov. 11, 1947; d. Edward T. and Irene Eleanor (Barna) Van Tassel; m. Sidney W. Holec, Oct. 26, 1968. BS, U. Houston, 1969. Stockbroker Drexel Burnham Lambert, Inc., Miami, Fla., 1976-78, Merrill Lynch, Venice, Fla., 1979-80; fin. cons. Shearson Lehman Bros., Venice, 1981-87; owner, mgr. Closet Stretchers, Venice, 1987-89. Bd. dirs. Safe Place and Rape Crisis Ctr., Sarasota, 1987-99, Womens Resource Ctr., Sarasota, 1981-86, 90-94, Friends Venice Libr., 1992-94, New Coll. Libr., 1991-94, Planned Parenthood S.W. and Ctrl. Fla., 2001—; active Leadership Sarasota, 1991-95, Jr. League of Sarasota, 1982—, Argus Found., 1982— Mem.: Womens Resource Ctr. Sarasota County, Chautauqua Literary & Sci. Cir. Alumni Assn. (v.p. class of 2003), Chautauqua Women's Club. Avocations: reading, feminism. Mailing: PO Box 1049 Osprey FL 34229 E-mail: ansidco@aol.com.

HOLFORTY, PEARL MARTHA, accountant; b. Detroit, Oct. 31, 1928; d. Johannes and Martha Mary (Francoys) Kramer; m. Clifford W. Holforty, Mar. 27, 1948; children: Kathleen Diane, David Alan(dec.), Wendy Lauren, Michael Todd. Student, Mich. State U., 1945-47; BS, Wayne State U., 1970, MBA, 1973. Contr. Sta. WPON, Pontiac, Mich., 1958-60; bus. mgr. Holforty, Widrig & O'Neill Assocs., Inc., Troy, Mich., 1960-69; staff acct. Plante & Moran, CPAs, Southfield, Mich., 1970-77, ptnr., 1977-91; founder, chair, pres., CEO Liberty BIDCO Investment Corp., 1988—. Part-time faculty Wayne State U., 1974-77; mem. small bus. adv. coun. Fed. Res. Bank Chgo., 1985-87; del. White House Conf. on Small Bus., 1986. Past chair Met. Detroit YMCA; former mem. Gov.'s Entrepreneurial and Small Bus. Com.; former mem. employability skills task force State of Mich.; former trustee Mich. Accountancy Found.; former treas. Wayne County Intermediate Sch. Dist.-Found. for Excellence; past bd. dirs. United Way of S.E. Mich., United Am. Healthcare Corp.; bd. dirs. Auto Club Trust; past treas. Mich. Women's Found. Recipient Edward G. Erickson award, 1970, Elijah Watts Sells award, 1971, Headliners award Wayne State U., 1983, Corp. Leadership award Wayne State U., 1998; Phi Gamma Mu scholar, 1970; named Woman Advocate of Yr. SBA Mich., 1986. Mem. AICPA, Nat. Assn. Accts. (pres. chpt. 1979), Mich. Assn. CPAs, Nat. Assn. Women Bus. Owners (chpt. pres. 1986-87), Women's Econ. Club (pres. 1989-90), Beta Gamma, Presbyterian. Home and Office: # 316 41110 Fox Run Rd Novi MI 48377 E-mail: pholforty@lbico.com.

HOLGUIN, ROXANNA R. speech pathology/audiology services professional; b. Nogales, Ariz., Mar. 14, 1959; d. Hector Thomas and Annabelle G. Ramirez; m. Henry C. Holguin, Aug. 17, 1982; children: Henry J., Javi. BS in Commn. Disorders, Univ. New Mex., Albuquerque, New Mex., 1981, MS in Commn. Disorders, 1983. Cert. CCC-SLP Am. Speech-Lang. and Hearing Assn., 1984, AHCCCS State of Ariz., Dept. Health Svcs., K-12 Speech Therapy Ariz. Dept. of Edn., Divsn. Devel. Disabilities Ariz., lic. Speech Therapy Ariz. Speech pathologist Esperanza Para Nurtros Niños Spl. Preschool, Albuquerque, 1983—84, Conve Consolidated Sch. Dist., Bayard, N.Mex., 1984—86, Ednl. Assessment Svcs., Inc., Albuquerque, 1986—87, Tucson Unified Sch. Dist., Tucson, 1987—90; speech pathologist, parent educator Las Cruces Pub. Sch., Las Cruces, N.Mex., 1990—93; clin. supr., coll. instr. New Mex. State Univ., Speech and Hearing Clin., Las Cruces, N.Mex., 1993—96; speech pathologist Nogales Unified Sch. Dist., Nogales, N.Mex., 1996—97, Santa Cruz Valley Unified Sch. Dist., Rio Rico, Ariz., 1997—2002, Nogales Unified Sch. Dist., Nogales, Ariz., 2002—. Cons. speech therapy and evaluations Divsn. Devel. Disabilities, Nogales, Ariz., 2000—, Blake Found.-Birth to Three, Santa Cruz County, Ariz., 2000—. Prodr.(dir.): (early literacy videos) Early Book Stages (0-5 years), 1994, Spanish version, 1995. Team mother Local Boys Soccer Team, Nogales, Ariz., 1999; fundraising com. chmn. Am. Youth Soccer Orgn., Nogales, Ariz., 2000—01; treas. U-19 Boys Soccer Team, Nogales, Ariz., 2002. Recipient Tchr. of the Yr., Mesilla Elem., Las Cruces Pub. Sch., 1992, Feature Tchr., Rotary Club, 2001; grantee Mini-grant, Las Cruces Pub. Sch., 1991, 1992. Mem.: Am. Speech-Lang. Hearing Assn. Roman Cath. Avocation: reading.

HOLIDAY, EDITH ELIZABETH, former presidential adviser, cabinet secretary; b. Middletown, Ohio, Feb. 14, 1952; d. Harry Jr. and Kathlyn (Watson) H.; m. Terrence B. Adamson, June 8, 1985; children: Kathlyn Holiday Adamson, Elizabeth Holiday Adamson; 1 stepchild, Terrence Morgan Adamson. Student, Miami U., Oxford, Ohio, 1970-71; BS with honors, U. Fla., 1974, JD, 1977. Bar: Fla. 1977, D.C. 1978, Ga. 1984. Assoc. Read Smith Shaw & McClay, Washington, 1977-83, Dow Lohnes & Albertson, Atlanta, 1983-84; exec. dir. Commn. on Exec. Legis. and Jud. Salaries, Washington, 1984-85; spl. counsel polit. action com. Fund for Am. Future, Washington, 1985-87; dir. ops. George Bush for Pres., Inc., Washington, 1987-88; chief counsel, nat. fin. and ops. dir. Bush-Quayle 88, Washington, 1988; with legal svcs. staff George Bush for Pres. Compliance Com., Washington, 1988; asst. sec. for pub. affairs and pub. liaison, counselor to sec. Departmental Offices, U.S. Dept. Treasury, Washington, 1988; gen. counsel U.S. Dept. Treasury, Washington, 1989-90; asst. to U.S. pres., sec. of cabinet Washington, 1990-93. Legis. asst. to U.S. Sen. Nicholas F. Brady, Washington, 1982—83; bd. dirs. Amerada Hess Corp., H.J. Heinz Co., Beverly Enterprises, Inc., Franklin Templeton Group Funds, RTI Internat. Metals, Inc., Canadian Nat. Railway Co.; oper. trustee TWE Holdings I, II Trusts, 2002—. Recipient Alexander Hamilton award Sec. of Treasury, 1991, spl. citation John Marshall Bar Assn. Mem. Phi Delta Phi, Kappa Tau Alpha. Republican.

HOLIFIELD, PEARL KAM (KAM HOLIFIELD, MOMI KAM HOLIFIELD), poet; b. Honolulu, Dec. 13, 1916; d. Albert Tin Kam and Helen Wo Soon Lyau; m. Harold Desmond Holifield, 1947; children: Wallace Grant, Harry. BA, U. Hawaii, 1944; MA, U. Calif., Berkeley, 1945; postgrad., U. Wash., 1946—47. Univ. libr. U. Hawaii, Honolulu, 1945—46; children's libr. N.Y. Pub. Library, N.Y.C., 1948—80; haiku poet N.Y.C., 1978—. Author: Workshop Poems, 1989. Mem.: Spring St. Haiku Workshop, Haiku Soc. Am. Avocations: gardening, singing, hula.

HOLLADAY, WILHELMINA COLE, interior design and museum executive; b. Elmira, N.Y., Oct. 10, 1922; d. Chauncy E. and Claire Elizabeth (Strong) Cole; m. Wallace Fitzhugh Holladay, Sept. 27, 1946; children: Wallace Fitzhugh, Scott Cole. BA, Elmira Coll., 1944; postgrad. art history, U. Paris, 1953-54, U. Va., 1960-61; PhD (hon.), Moore Coll. Art, 1988, Mt. Vernon Coll., 1988, Elmira Coll., 1989. Exec. sec. Howard Ludington, Rochester, N.Y., 1944-45, Chinese Embassy, Washington, 1945-48; staff Nat. Gallery of Art, Washington, 1957-59; dir. interior design div. Holladay Corp., Washington, 1970-95. Dir. Adams Nat. Bank, 1978-86, chmn., 1978-86; founder, chmn., bd. dirs., creator art collection by women (Renaissance through contemp.), Nat. Mus. Women in Arts, 1982—. Founder archival libr. of periodicals, books, exhbn. catalogs on women's art for rsch. purposes; bd. dirs. Am. Field Svc., 1964-80, Internat. Student House, 1973—, Leeds Castle Found.; mem. coun. Friends of Folger Shakespeare Libr., 1978-82; mem. world svc. coun. YWCA; trustee

Corcoran Gallery of Art, 1980-90; mem. Mayor's Blue Ribbon Com. Decorated Order of Merit (Norway); named Woman of Achievement, Washington Ednl. TV Assn., 1984, Woman of Distinction, Coun. Ind. Colls., 1987, Birmingham So. Coll., 1991, Washingtonian of Yr., Washingtonian Mag., 1987, Hon. Citizen, State of Tex., laureate, Washington Bus. Hall of Fame, Hon. Alderman, Mayor of Athens, 2002; named to Nat. Women's Hall of Fame, 1996; recipient Horizon's Theatre award, 1987, Thomas Jefferson award, Am. Soc. Interior Designers, Disting. Woman's award, Northwood Inst., 1987, Disting. Achievement award, Nat. League Am. Pen Women, 1988, Women Achievers award, Internat. Alliance, 1991, Woman That Makes a Difference award, Internat. Women's Forum, 1991, Women First award, YWCA, 1993, Key to City of Kansas City, Fellow award for disting. svc. to arts, New Orleans Mus. Art, 1997, Disting. Washingtonian award in lit. and the arts, Univ. Club Washington, 1998, Gold medal honor award, Nat. Inst. Social Scis., 2000, honors, Women's Caucus for Art, 2001, Leadership award, Pine Manor Coll. Mem. Am. Assn. Mus., Am. Fedn. Art, Women's Caucus for Arts, Mus. Modern Art, Art Librs. N.Am., Archives Am. Art, Arttable, Smithson Soc., Internat. Women's Forum, Nat. Women's Econ. Alliance (bd. dirs. 1984—, Soaring Eagle award 1988). Episcopalian. Home: 3215 R St NW Washington DC 20007-2941 Office: Nat Mus Women Arts 1250 New York Ave NW Washington DC 20005

HOLLAND, ALLISON DENMAN, writing and film educator, film preservationist; b. Stuttgart, Ark., Oct. 21, 1946; d. Floyd Allison Denman and Vergie Alice McCollum; children: Allison Brooks Holland, Anne Denman Holland. BS in Edn., Ark. State U., 1968; MEd, La. State U., 1969, MA in English, 1972. Tchr. Stuttgart (Ark.) H.S., 1970-71, Pearl H.S., Nashville, 1972-75, Mt. St. Mary's Acad., Little Rock, 1975-78; with dept. rhetoric and writing U. Ark., Little Rock, 1984—, assoc. dir. writing ctr., 1993-98, dir. writing ctr., 1998—. Mem. dept. excellence rhetoric and writing U. Ark., 1998—. Columnist Ark. Women's Jour., 1993-96. With Jr. League Little Rock. Mem. Writing Program Adminstrs., Coll. Conf. on Composition and Comm., Nat. Coun. Tchrs. English, Internat. Writing Ctrs. Assn., South Ctrl. Writing Ctrs. Assn., Writing Ctr. Rsh. Project, Phi Kappa Phi, Alpha Epsilon Lambda, Delta Kappa Gamma. Avocations: reading, skiing, collecting historical movie related materials, creative writing, film preservation and research. Office: U Ark Little Rock Dept Rhetoric & Writing 2801 S University Ave Little Rock AR 72204-1000

HOLLAND, BETH, actress; b. N.Y.C. d. Samson and Florence (Liebman) Hollander; m. Louis L. Friedman, Aug. 28, 1953; children: Ellen Lynn, Cathy Jayne. Pvt. studies in acting, voice tng. Arts funding cons. N.Y. State Senate, 1974-89. Appeared in various roles on TV, film and theatre, also comedy video Your Favorite Jokes, 1988. Pres. Sonia Alden Found. Inc.; bd. dirs. Fla. Opera Soc., Symphony of Americas. Recipient Carbonell performance award Theatre League of South Fla., 1996. Mem. AFTRA (pres. N.Y. chpt. 1989-91, bd. dirs., trustee Health and Retirement Funds, past treas.), SAG, English Speaking Union, N.Y. TV Acad. (past bd. dirs.), Actors Equity Assn., Twelfth Night Club, Episcopal Actors Guild (mem. coun.), Players Club (libr. bd.), Lambs Club, Tower Club, Friars Club. Avocations: travel, politics, arts.

HOLLAND, CHRISTIE ANNA, biochemist, virologist; b. Newport News, Va., Aug. 25, 1950; d. Charles Everett and Helen (Bailey) Holland; 1 child, Helen. BS, U. Richmond, 1972; PhD, U. Tenn., 1977. Postdoctoral fellow Worcester Found. for Exptl. Biology, Shrewsbury, Mass., 1977-79, Ctr. for Cancer Rsch.-MIT, Cambridge, Mass., 1979-84; asst. prof. dept. radiation oncology U. Mass. Med. Ctr., Worcester, 1985-90, assoc. prof., 1990-91; dir. Ctr. for Virology, Immunology and Infectious Diseases Children's Nat. Med. Ctr., Washington, 1991—; assoc. prof. pediats., microbiology and biochemistry George Washington U. Med. Ctr., Washington, 1991-95, prof. pediats., assoc. prof. microbiology and biochemistry, 1995—. Mem.: AAAS, Am. Soc. Pediats., Am. Soc. Virology, Am. Soc. Cell Biology, Internat. Soc. Exptl. Hematology. Home: 9105 Goshen Valley Dr Gaithersburg MD 20882-1447 Office: Childrens Nat Med Ctr 111 Michigan Ave NW Washington DC 20010-2916 E-mail: chhollan@cnmc.org.

HOLLAND, ELLEN C. music educator; b. Washington, Nov. 6, 1960; d. Theodore R. and Frances W. Creel. BMus, East Carolina U., 1983; MMus, U. S.C., 1985. Music tchr. Virginia Beach (Va.) City Pub. Schs., 1986—, coord. dept., 2002—03. Music tchr. Holland Studio of Piano, 1986—95. Sec. Virginia Beach Chorale, 1988—92, audition com., 1988—98. Mem.: Va. Music Educators Assn. (co-chair dist. chorus II 1999—2000, chair dist. chorus II 2000—01), Smart Stockers Investment Club (founder/treas. 1990—).

HOLLAND, GENE GRIGSBY (SCOTTIE HOLLAND), artist; b. Hazard, Ky., June 30, 1928; d. Edward and Virginia Lee (Watson) Grigsby; m. George William Holland, Sept. 22, 1950; 3 children. BA, U. So. Fla., 1968; pupil of, Ruth Allison, Talequah, Okla., 1947-48, Ralph Smith, Washington, 1977, Clint Carter, Atlanta, 1977, R. Jordan, Winter Park, Fla., 1979, Cedric Baldwin Egeli Workshop, Charleston, S.C., 1984. Various clerical and secretarial positions, 1948-52; news reporter, photographer Bryan (Tex.) Daily News, 1952; clk. Fogarty Bros. Moving and Transfer, Tampa and Miami, Fla., 1954-57; tchr. elem. schs., Hillsborough County, Fla., 1968-72; salesperson, assoc. real estate, 1984-2000; owner, operator antique store, 1982-87. One-woman and group shows include Tampa Woman's Clubhouse, 1973, Cor Jesu, Tampa, 1973, Bank, Monks Corner, S.C., 1977, Summerville Artists Guild, 1977-78, Apopka (Fla.) Art and Foilage Festival, 1980, 81, 82, Fla. Fedn. Women's Clubs, 1980, 81, 82; numerous group shows, latest being Island Gifts, Tampa, 1980-82, Brandon (Fla.) Station, 1980-81, Holland Originals, Orlando, Fla.; represented in permanent and pvt. collections. Vol. ARC, Tampa, 1965-69, United Fund Campaign, 1975-76; pres. Mango (Fla.) Elem. Sch. PTA, 1966-67; pres. Tampa Civic Assn., 1974-75; vol. Easter Seal Fund Campaign, 1962-63; art chmn. Apopka Art & Foilage Festival, 1990; deaconness Ctrl. Christian Ch. Orlando, 1992-94, chmn. bible study, 1993-94; deaconness First Christian Ch. Tampa, 1996-99. Recipient numerous art awards, 1978-82. Mem. AARP (parlimentarian Apopka chpt.), Internat. Soc. Artists, Coun. Arts & Scis. for Cen. Fla., Fedn. Women's Clubs (pres. Tampa Civic 1974-75), Meth. Women's Soc. (sec. 1976-77), Nat. Trust Hist. PReservation, Nat. Hist. Soc., Fla. Geneal. and Hist. Soc., Am. Guild Flower Arrangers, The Nat. Grigsby Family Soc. (assoc. sec. 1991-92, corp. sect. 1992-96, dir. 1995-97, 99-2001, S.W. chpt. dir. 1997-2000), Internat. Inner Wheel Club (past chmn. dist. 696, pres. Tampa 1972-73), Friday Morning Musicale Club (1st v.p. bd. incorporators Tampa 1974-75, bd. dirs.), Gen. Fedn. of Fla. Clubs Apopka Woman's Club (pres. 1981-82, bd. dir. 1983-85, Woman of Yr. 1991-92), Apopka Tennis Over 50's Group Club (pres. 1988-90), Federated Garden Club Plant City Fla. (conservation chmn.), South Bay Geneal. Soc., Tampa PC User Group, Computer Club Inc. of Sun City Ctrs., Lexington Geneal. Assn. Home: 231 Mooring Ln Lexington SC 29072-9106

HOLLAND, GLORIA TEMPLE, psychotherapist; b. Tupelo, Miss., May 15, 1952; d. Eugene F. and Montez Parker Temple; m. G.L. Wilemon, Jr., May 6, 1972 (div. Oct. 1980); children: Ashley Wilemon, Emily Wilemon; m. Steve Holland, Dec. 31, 1982; 1 child, McKinley. BA in Social Work, Miss. State U., Starkville, 1973; MA in Cmty. Counseling, U. Miss., 1979. LCSW, lic. marriage and family therapist. Social worker Lee County Ext. Svcs., Tupelo, Miss., region III mental health therapist; therapist North Miss. Med. Ctr., Behavioral Unit, Tupelo, Miss. Social work adv. bd. Miss. State U., Starkville; mem. Regional Rehab. Bd., Tupelo. Mem.: Region III Mental Health Commn. (rec. sec. 2002—), MAMFT (bd. dirs. 2001—). Democrat. Meth. Office: North Miss Med Ctr Behavioral Unit 45795 Eason Blvd Tupelo MS 38801 E-mail: shollands@ebicom.net., gholland@nmhs.net.

HOLLAND, JOY, health care facility executive; b. N.Y.C., Oct. 24, 1946; d. Harry Walson and Edna May (Simmons) H.; m. Chesley Roderick Richardson, Sept.21, 1985; children: Carl Allen Fields, Craig Anthony Fields. AA in Nursing, Olive-Harvey Coll., 1972; BS, St. Joseph Coll., Bklyn., 1976; M in Health Adminstrn., C.W. Post Coll., 1978. Staff nurse U. Chgo. Hosp. and Clinics, Chgo., 1972; head nurse N.Y. Hosp., N.Y.C., 1972; clinic adminstr. Morrisania-Montefiore Hosp., Bronx, N.Y., 1973; head nurse, supr. Pilgrim Psychiat. Hosp., Brentwood, N.Y., 1974, assoc. dir. staff devel., 1974-76, dir. nursing, 1976-78; surveyor, cons Joint Commn. on Accrediation of Hosps., Chgo., 1978-82; dir. Ypsilanti (Mich.) Regional Psychiat. Hosp., 1986-90, Clinton Valley Ctr., Pontiac, Mich., 1990-93, Huron Valley Ctr., Ypsilanti, Mich., 1993-99, Southgate Ctr., Mich., 1999-2001; CEO St. Elizabeth's Hosp., 2001—. Dep. commr. dept. mental health State of Ohio, 1980-82; cons. Joint Commn. Accreditation of Hosps.; adj. lectr. Sch. Nursing, U. Mich.; cons. specialist, bd. dirs. Holland-Richardson Assocs., Detroit. Contbr. author (book) Guide to J.C.A.H. Nursing Standards, 1985, 86 edits. Bd. dirs. Women in Crisis, Inc., N.Y.C., 1979-85, Washtenaw County (Mich.) ARC; bd. dirs. psychiatry dept. Chelsea (Mich.) Hosp., 1989-91. Mem. N.Y. Acad. Sci. (life), Bus. and Profl. Women, Inc., Masons, Order Ea. Star, Alpha Kappa Alpha, Sigma Theta Tau. Republican. Avocations: chess, crochet, walking. Home: 425 8th St NW Apt 634 Washington DC 20004-2113 Office: St Elizabeths Hospital 2700 Martin Luther King Drive Washington DC 20004

HOLLAND, LESLIE ANN, special education educator; b. Oak Lawn, Ill., Sept. 26, 1969; d. Ronald Leo and Rosemary Seymour; m. Brian Michael Holland, Dec. 31, 1999. AA, Moraine Valley C.C., Palos Hills, Ill., 1991; BS in Edn., Ea. Ill. U., 1995. Day camp site dir. Southwest Spl. Recreation Assn., Alsip, Ill., 1996—2000, spl. edn. dept. chair Momence, Ill., 1996—; tchr., spl. edn. dept. Sylvan Learning Ctr., Tinley Park, Ill., 2001—; chair, spl. edn. dept. Momence H.S., 1996—. Home: 14600 W Aston Way Lockport IL 60441 Office: Momence Unit Sch Dist # 1 101 N Franklin Momence IL 60954

HOLLAND, NOY, writer, educator; b. Dayton, Ohio, Dec. 3, 1960; d. James Read and Elizabeth (Collings) Holland; m. Sam Michel, June 5, 1993. Student, U. Ala., Columbia U.; BA cum laude, Middlebury Coll., 1983; MFA, U. Fla., 1994. Instr. Hotchkiss Sch., Lakeville, Conn., 1983, N.Y. Assn. New Ams., N.Y.C., 1990, U. Fla., Gainesville, 1992-94; editl. asst. Esquire, N.Y.C., 1984-85; asst. to sr. editor Charles Scribner's Sons, N.Y.C., 1986-87; writer-in-residence Phillips Acad., Andover, Mass., 1994-96; assoc. prof. U. Mass., Amherst, 1997—, dir. MFA Program for Poets and Writers, 1999—2002. Author: (book) The Spectacle of the Body, 1994; contbr. articles to profl. jours. Fellow, Nat. Endowment Arts, 2004; Bread Loaf scholar, 1983, Porter fellow, U. Fla., 1992, Grinter fellow, 1992—94, John Gardner fellow, Bread Loaf Colony, 1994. Episcopalian. Home: PO Box 85 Heath MA 01346-0085 Office: U Mass Amherst MA 01003

HOLLAND, ROSEMARY SHERIDAN, program evaluation consultant; b. Detroit, Oct. 15, 1939; d. Geoffrey Francis and Mary Ann (Beirne) Sheridan; m. Neal Holland, Sept. 1961 (div. Apr. 1968); 1 child, Daniel Holland; m. Fred Fechheimer, Nov. 29, 1974; 1 child, Steve Fechheimer. PhB, U. Detroit, 1961; MSW, U. Mich., 1969, MA, PhD, U. Mich., 1984. Tchr. Prince Georges County Bd. Edn., Seat Pleasant, Md., 1961-63; adminstrv. asst. Neighborhood Svc. Orgn., Detroit, 1969-73; dir. mental health planning Cmty. Health Planning Coun. S.E. Mich., Detroit, 1971-73; coord. adult mental health svcs. Detroit/Wayne County Cmty. Mental Health Bd., 1973-76; asst. prof. U. Detroit, 1984-89. Mem. NASW, APHA, APA. Avocations: walking, travel, reading.

HOLLAND, RUBY MAE, social welfare administrator; BA in Sociology, Shaw Coll., 1976, MA in Comparative Lit., 1978; DD, Wayne Theol. Sem., 1992; D of Psychology, Western Mich. U., 1982. Adminstr. Terrell Day Care Ctr., 1980-83; instr. Reborn Acad., 1984-87; English instr. Ctrl. H.S., 1987-92; enabler Maplegrove children's program U. Mich., Dearborn, 1992—; adminstr., guidance counselor, tchr. Mothers Love, Oak Park, Mich., 1992—. Assoc. min. Unity Cathedral of Faith Ministries; mem. CEO Forums in Christ Ministries, Greater Haven of Rest.

HOLLANDER, ANNE, writer; b. Cleve., Oct. 16, 1930; d. Arthur and Jean Hill (Bassett) Loesser; m. John Hollander, June 15, 1953 (div. 1977); children: Martha, Elizabeth; m. Thomas Nagel, June 26, 1979. BA, Barnard Coll., 1952. Author: Seeing Through Clothes, 1978, Moving Pictures, 1989, Sex and Suits, 1994, Feeding the Eye, 1999, Fabric of Vision, 2002. Guggenheim fellow, 1975. Fellow N.Y. Inst. for the Humanities (interim dir. 1995-96); mem. Costume Soc. Am., College Art Assn., PEN Am. Ctr. (pres. 1995-96), Century Assn.

HOLLANDER, JEAN, literature educator, poet; m. Robert Hollander; children: Cornelia Variness, Robert B. Hollander III. MA in Lit., PhD, Columbia U. Staff Princeton U., Mercer Coll.; lectr. Princeton U.; asst. prof. Coll. N.J.; with Bklyn. Coll. Author: (poetry) Crushed into Honey, 1986 (Eileen W. Barnes award, 1986), Moondog, 1996, Daute's Comedia, 2000. Recipient Borestone Mt. Poetry award, 1974; grantee, N.J. State Coun. Arts, 1980, 1985, 1994. Mem.: Poetry Soc. Am. Avocation: hiking. Office: Coll NJ English Dept PO Box 7718 Ewing NJ 08628

HOLLANDSWORTH, PHYLLIS W. marriage and family therapist; b. Storm Lake, Iowa, Aug. 7, 1938; d. Lloyd Earl and Hildegarde Elaine (Uken) Williamson; m. James Richard Hollandsworth, Sept. 5, 1959; children: Michael, Mark. AA, Brewton-Parker Coll., 1984; BS, Valdosta State Coll., 1987; MS, Valdosta State U., 1988; cert. in marriage & family therapy, Voldosta State Coll., 1995; PhD in Human Sexuality, Miamionides U., 2004. Lic. marriage & family therapist Fla., 1996, cert. sex therapist Fla., 2002. Counselor Ga. Dept. Corrections, Albany, 1989—91; therapist, emergency screener North Fla. Mental Health, Lake City, Fla., 1992—96, ACT Corp., Daytona Beach, Fla., 1996—2000; intake coord., therapist Children's Home Soc., Daytona Beach, Fla., 2000—02; therapist Fla. Health Care Plans, Daytona Beach, Fla., 2002—; pvt. practice Daytona Beach, Fla., 2000. Mem.: Am. Acad. Clin. Sexologists (diplomate), Am. Psychotherapy Assn. (diplomate), Am. Assn. Marriage and Family Therapists. Office: 1635 S Ridgewood Ave Rm 216 South Daytona FL 32119 E-mail: hollyphyll@netzero.net.

HOLLEB, DORIS B. urban planner, economist; b. N.Y.C., Oct. 26, 1922; m. Marshall M. Holleb, Oct. 15, 1944; children: Alan, Gordon, Paul. BA magna cum laude, Hunter Coll., 1942; MA, Harvard U., 1947; postgrad., U. Chgo., 1959-60, 65-66. Economist Fed. Res. Bd., Washington, 1943—44; freelance journalist, 1945-63; econs. cons. Chgo. Dept. City Planning, 1963-64; rsch. assoc. Ctr. Urban Studies U. Chgo., 1966-78, sr. rsch. assoc., 1978-88; dir. Met. Inst., 1973-84, professorial lectr., 1979—. Chmn., Francis W. Parker Sch. Ednl. Coun., 1963-80; cons., 1980-92; bd. dirs. Adlai E. Stevenson Inst., 1972-79; mem. adv. coun. Ctr. for the Study Democratic Inst., 1975-79; bd. dirs. Inter. Am. Found., 1979-84, Pacific Basin Inst., 1981-98; mem. nat. adv. com. White House Conf. on Balanced Nat. Growth and Econ. Devel., 1978; mem. Northea. Ill. Planning Commn., 1973-77; mem. Chgo. Met. Area Transp. Coun., 1980-84; mem. adv. coun. to Nat. Ctr. Rsch. on Vocat. Edn., U.S. Dept. Edn., 1979-82, U.S. Dept. State adv. com. internat. investment, tech. and devel., 1979-81; commr. Chgo. Plan Commn., 1986—; bd. dirs. Internat. Ctr. for Rsch. on Women, 1985-91, Nat. Coun. on Humanities, 1998-2003. Author: Social and Economic Information for Urban Planning, 1968, Colleges and the Urban Poor, 1972; contbr. articles to profl. jours.; v.p. editl. bd. Ill. Issues, 1977-2001. Fellow: Phi Beta Kappa Soc. (bd. dirs.).

HOLLEMAN, SANDRA LEE, higher education administrator; d. Guy Lee and Gustine (Kirby-Sheets) Luna; m. Allen Craig Holleman. Cert., Eastfield Coll., 1979. With Annuity Bd. So. Bapt. Conv., Dallas, 1958—, mgr. personnel, 1983-85, dir. human resources, 1985-91, v.p. human resources, 1991-99; ret., 1999—. Mem.: Soc. Human Resource Mgmt., Dallas Soc. Human Resource Mgmt., Am. Mgmt. Soc. (dir. salary surveys local chpt. 1986—, v.p. chpt. svcs. 1987—), Am. Mus. Miniature Arts, Book End Rev. Club, Daus of Nile, Order of Ea. Star, Diversity Club Dallas (program chmn. 1976, v.p. 1977). Baptist. Avocations: needlepoint, genealogy, decorating, doll collecting.

HOLLENBECK, KAREN FERN, foundation consultant; b. Snover, Mich., Mar. 30, 1943; d. Glenn Lee and Ada Gertrude (Robinson) Roberts; m. Marvin Allan Hollenbeck, June 18, 1966. AA, Kellogg Community Coll., 1980; BSBA, Nazareth Coll., 1987. Dir. fellowships W.K. Kellogg Found., Battle Creek, Mich., 1979-85, asst. v.p. adminstrn., 1985-88, v.p. adminstrn., 1988—98; cons., 1999—. Bd. dirs. Cutting Edge Designs, Denver, 1993-96. Editor: Marco Messenger, 1999—. Bd. dirs. Arc Ministries, Allegan, Mich., 1982—, Vol. Bur., Battle Creek, 1984-86, ARC, Calhoun County, Mich., 1985-96, Emerging Young Leaders, 1996-2000; pres. com. Marco Presbyn. Ch., 2002—; trustee Ind. Wesleyan U., 2001—. Recipient Outstanding Young Women of Am. award. Mem. NAFE, Am. Mgmt. Assn., Soc. Human Resources Mgmt. Avocations: knitting, music, drama activities. Home and Office: 741 S Collier Blvd Apt 312 Marco Island FL 34145-6007

HOLLER, ANN K. music educator; b. Wytheville, Va., Sept. 22, 1946; d. Joseph C. and Alice (McKnight) Kelley; m. Peter D. Holler, Apr. 6, 1968; children: Elizabeth Ransom, Janet Bentley. BA in Math., King Coll., Bristol, Tenn., 1968; BA in Music, Va. Intermont Coll., Bristol, Va., 1983; MM in Music Theory, U. Tenn., 1993. Cert. tchr. music Tenn. Music Tchrs. Assn., 1992. Pvt. piano tchr. Holler Music Studio, Bristol, Tenn., 1973—2004; adj. instr. music King Coll., Bristol, Tenn., 2000—, East Tenn. State U., Johnson City, 1992—2002. Pres. Arts Alliance Mountain Empire, 2003—04. Chmn. editl. com. A! Magazine for the Arts and Antiques, 2001—. Mem.: Am. Composers Forum, Nat. Guild Piano Tchrs., Am. Matthay Assn., Music Tchrs. Nat. Assn. Home: 112 Evergreen Pl Bristol TN 37620

HOLLEY, KAY MOFFITT, nutrition instructor, dietitian; b. Davenport, Iowa, Nov. 29, 1943; d. Glen and Cora (Vogler) Moffitt; m. Robert Coulter Holley, Feb. 14, 1970; 1 child, Robert Coulter II. BS, Western Ill. U., 1965; MS, U. Ky., 1967; postgrad., Ariz. State U., summer 1968, Okla. State U., summer 1969. Cert. dietitian, Ky.; cert. lifetime tchr., Ky. Adminstrv. asst. Supt. Schs., Taylor Ridge, Ill., summers 1961-65; grad. asst. U. Ky., Lexington, 1965-66; tchr. home econs. Rockridge High Sch., Taylor Ridge, 1966-67; chair dept. home econs. Midway (Ky.) Coll., 1967-70; cons. dietitian Mallory-Taylor Hosp. and other nursing homes, LaGrange, Ky., 1970-75; asst. prof. Morehead (Ky.) State U., 1972-73; tchr. adult edn. Fayette Co., Lexington, 1976-78; dietitian, adminstrv. planning VA Hosp., Lexington, 1974-82; instr. food svc. acctg. U. Ky., 1986; community dietitian VA Med. Ctr., Lexington, 1978-94; adj. instr. UK Lex Community Coll., 1995—. Fgn. student advisor Midway Coll., 1969, dietetics rep. Employees' Assn., Lexington, 1990-94. Dietetic chmn. Leestown and Cooper Dr. divs. VA Combined Fed. Campaign, Lexington, 1976; dietetic chmn. Leestown div. VA Bond Dr., Lexington, 1988; mem. communion com. Meth. Ch., Lexington, 1989-91; mem. Vol. Svc. POW-MIA Nat. Recognition Day Com., 1989-94, Salute to Vets. Week Com., 1990-94; asst. Head-Start program, Midway, Ky. Recipient Good Citizen award Am. Legion, Reynolds, Ill., 1961; named Outstanding Young Woman Am., Western Ill. U., 1970. Mem. Am. Dietetics Assn., Kappa Delta Pi, Kappa Omicron Phi. Avocations: attending theatre performances, college volleyball, horseracing, traveling, collecting gourmet menus. Home: 2421 Wanda Way Lexington KY 40505-1919 Office: Lexington Community Coll Humanities and Bus Techs Academic Tech 101 Cooper Dr Lexington KY 40506-0001

HOLLEY, PAMELA SPENCER, retired librarian; b. Mpls., July 31, 1944; d. Boyd Edgar Gustafson, Jane Lenore Gustafson; m. Richard Howard Holley; m. Arthur Snow Spencer (dec. Oct. 24, 1996). BS Biology and Secondary Edn., Longwood Coll., 1965; MS, Coll. William and Mary, 1970; MLS, U. Md., 1973. Cert. libr. Va., 1973. Tchr. sci. Stephen Foster Intermediate/Fairfax County Pub. Schs., Alexandria, Va., 1965—72; libr. Lake Braddock Secondary Sch., Burke, 1973—75, Mount Vernon H.S., Alexandria, 1975—86; media specialist Area I Office, 1986—87; libr. Thomas Jefferson H.S. for Sci. and Tech., 1987—94; libr. program specialist Chapel Sq. Ctr., Annandale, 1994—96; coord. librs. FCPS, 1996—98; ret., 1998. Chair film series com. Virginia Beach Pub. Libr. Friends Bd., Va., 2000—, v.p., 2002—; mem. editl. adv. bd. Voice of Youth Advocates Mag., Lanham, 2000—; chair adv. com. Am. Econoclad Svcs., Topeka, 1988—95; host, co-host Cable 21 Ednl. Channel, Annandale, 1992—97; editl. adv. bd. Booklist Mag., Chgo., 1988—90; bd. dirs. Libr. Friends, v.p., 2002—03. Author: What Do Young Adults Read Next? (continuing series), 1993, (audiobooks) It Is!, 2002—, Column, VOYA, 2002—. Mem.: ALA (councilor 1995—99, bd. dirs. divsn. young adult libr. svcs. assn. 1990—93), Beta Phi Mu. Episcopalian. Avocations: kayaking, exercise, travel, reading, needlepoint. Home: PO Box 9 Assawoman VA 23302

HOLLEY, SHARON LAND, minister; b. Norfolk, Va., Sept. 7, 1953; d. James Edward and Margaret Butler Land. BA in Social Work, Norfolk State U., Va., 1974; MA in Mass Comm., Norfolk State U., 1978; MDiv, Va. Union U. Sch. of Theology, Richmond, 1994. Social worker Norfolk Divsn. of Social Svcs., Norfolk, Va., 1974—81; electronic graphic artist supr. Ft. Lee Army Base, Petersburg, Va., 1987—94; pastor Christian Temple United Ch. of Christ, Norfolk, Va., 1994—; prodr./dir./graphics artist Wvec Tv-13, Norfolk, Va., 1981—87. Comm. com. chairperson So. Conf. of the United Ch. of Christ, Norfolk, Va., 1998—2002; new ch. start com. mem. Ea. Va. Assn. of the United Ch. of Christ, Norfolk, Va., 2000—02. Mem.: NAACP. Avocations: travel, writing, aspiring musician. Office: Christian Temple United Church of Christ 300 West 33rd St Norfolk VA 23508 Personal E-mail: ctucc@visi.net.

HOLLIDAY, JENNIFER NEXSEN, elementary school educator, music educator; d. Junior Leland and Elizabeth Ann Nexsen; m. Jason Powell Holliday, Jan. 16, 1999; 1 child, Jason Leland. MusB in Music Edn. cum laude, Converse Coll., 1998; MEd in Curriculum Instruction, Lesley U., 2004. Tchr. music W. M. Anderson Primary, 1999—; interim min. music 1st Bapt. Ch., Kingstree, SC, 2000—00. State textbook adoption com. S.C. State Dept. Edn., Columbia, 2002, grant reader, rater, 2003—; video critique ETV, 2003. Grantee, Georgetwon Kraft Union, 2002—03, S.C. Dept. Edn., 2002—03. Mem.: Williamsburg County Tchr. Forum, Music Educators Nat. Conf., S.C. Music Educators Assn., Mortar Bd., Delta Omicron (pres. local chpt. 1997—98). Avocations: piano, reading, shopping. Office: W M Anderson Primary 500 Lexington Ave Kingstree SC 29556

HOLLIDAY, PATRICIA RUTH MCKENZIE, evangelist; b. Jacksonville, Fla., Nov. 17, 1935; d. Robert Irving and Leona Adele (Bell) McKenzie; m. Jan. 20, 1965; children: Connie, Katheryn, Alexander. Student, Massey Bus. Coll., 1969, Luther Rice Sem., 1976; DD, Southeastern Theol. Sem., 1986, ThD, 1989, PhD, 1992. Sec. Delta Drug Corp.,

Jacksonville, 1965—; pres. Microfilm Ctr., Jacksonville, 1974—, Miracle Outreach Ministry, Jacksonville, 1974—; pastor Miracle World Outreach, Jacksonville; prof. Southeastern Theol. Sem., Jacksonville, 1992—; with Internat. Evang. Miracle Outreach, 2000—. Author: Holliday for the King, 1978, Be Free, 1979, Only Believe, 1980, Born Anew, 1981, The Walking Dead, 1982, Anointing Power, 1982, Signs, Wonders and Reactions, 1984, Dealing with Heresies, 1986, Marriage Answers, 1992, Solitary Satanist, 1993, Entertaining Angels of Light, 1993, The Plan: Ascended Masters, 1994, The New World Aftershock, 1994, Can. Women Preach?, 1995, New Creations, 1995, From Curses to Blessings Vols. 1, 2 & 3, 1995, Angel Fire, 1995, Can Witches Be Saved, 1996, Spirit of Idolatry, 1996, Is Halloween Pagan?, 1996, Gods of the Stars, Astrology, 1997, Gifts of the Holy Spirit, 1997, Baptism of the Holy Spirit, 1997, Deliverance Manuals, Vols. 1, 2 & 3, 1997, Spiritual Welfare Army, 1997, Spiritual Warfare - Weapons, 1997, Healing & Miracles, 1998, The Spiritual Armor of God, 1998, Children of the New Age, 1998, Prayer Warriors, 1998, Battling Territorial Spirits, 1998, New Age Inner Healing, 1999, Demons Tremble, 1999, Transference of Spirits, 1999, Experiencing Jesus, 2001, Witch Doctor and the Man-Fourth Generational Witch Doctor Finds Christ, 2001, Satan's Romper Room, 2002, Never, Never Land, 2003, The Fallen Prince, 2003, others; columnist Christian Courier. Sec. Four Found., Inc.; Rep. candidate Fla. Ho. of Reps., 1972; mem. Fla. Rep. Com., 1976-80; lobbyist Fla. Legislature, 1978-80; hostess Pat Holliday TV Show, Jacksonville. Mem. Minutewomen of Fla. Club (founder) Univ. Women Club, Ponte Vedra Women's Club. Home: 9252 San Jose Blvd Apt 2804 Jacksonville FL 32257-9205 E-mail: mominK1@hotmail.com., holliday_pat@hotmail.com.

HOLLIDAY, POLLY DEAN, actress; b. Jasper, Ala., July 2, 1937; d. Ernest Sullivan and Velma Mabell (Cain) H. B. Music Edn., Ala. State Women's Coll. (now U. Montevallo), 1959; postgrad., Fla. State U., 1960; D.H.L. hon., Mt. St. Mary's Coll., 1982. Tchr. music Sarasota (Fla.) public schs., 1961. Appeared with Asolo Theatre Repertory Co., Sarasota, 1962-72; appeared in Off-Broadway, Wedding Band, 1972; Quarrel of Sparrows, 1993, The Time of the Cuckoo, 2000, Chaucer in Rome, 2001, A Few Stout Individuals, 2002, Broadway shows All Over Town, 1975, Arsenic and Old Lace, 1986-87, Cat on a Hot Tin Roof, 1990 (Tony nomination), Picnic, 1994; appeared in plays The Glass Menagerie, Tyrone Guthrie Theatre, Mpls., 1988; appeared as Flo on CBS TV series Alice, 1976-80 (4 Emmy nominations), Flo, 1981 (Emmy nomination); appeared in CBS-TV series The Client, 1995-96, Golden Girls, 1986, Amazing Stories, 1986, Home Improvement, 1993, 94; appeared in TV movies You Can't Take It With You, 1981, The Shadyhill Kidnapping, 1981, All the Way Home, 1981, Missing Children, 1982, A Gift of Love, 1983; PBS Wonderworks series Konrad, 1985, (TV movies) Triumph of the Heart, 1991, Surviving Love, 2003; appeared in feature films All The Pres.'s Men, 1975, The One and Only, 1977, Gremlins, 1984, Moon Over Parador, 1987, Mrs. Doubtfire, 1993, Mr. Wrong, 1996, The Parent Trap, 1998. Recipient Golden Globe award for best supporting actress on TV series, 1978, 79 Episcopalian.

HOLLIE, MARY H. social welfare administrator; b. Chgo., Dec. 26, 1957; d. Dean H. and Edith M. Henry; m. Larry J. Hollie, Sept. 7, 1985; 1 child, Breanna B. B of Social Work, Ill. State U., 1979; MSW, U. Ill., 1984. LCSW 1987. Dir. individualized treatment program Kaleidoscope Inc., Bloomington, Ill., 1980—85, clin. supr. Chgo., 1985—87; dir. adolescent family ctr. Rush-Presbyterian St. Luke's Med. Ctr., 1987—88; CEO Lawrence Hall Youth Services, 1988—. Mem. adv. bd. North Pk. U., Axelson Ctr. Nonprofit Mgmt., Chgo., 2000—, No. Ill. U., Ctr. Child Welfare and Edn., DeKalb, 2001—; chmn. Local Sch. Coun. Chgo. Pub. Schools, 1998—2002. Mem. Sauganash Cmty. Assn., Chgo., 2000—02. Mem.: Child Care Assn. Ill. (bd. dirs. 1999—, chmn. bd. dirs. 2001—03), Econ. Club Chgo. Office: Lawrence Hall Youth Svcs 4833 N Francisco Chicago IL 60625 Personal E-mail: mhollie@lawrencehall.org.

HOLLINBECK, ETHEL LINDELL, sculptor; b. Kewanee, Ill., Feb. 1, 1910; d. Gustav (Lindstrom) and Hilda Louise (Gustafson) Lindell; m. Richard Oftebro Hollinbeck, Mar. 27, 1928; children: Marilyn, David, Richard Jr. Grad., Mpls. Sch. of Arts, 1948. Exhibited in group shows at Met. Mus., N.Y.C., Walker, Mpls. on Com., Minn. First Outdoor Sculpture Show, Woman's Club of Mpls., Swedish Mus. of Art, St. Paul Gallery of Arts, Mpls. Inst. of Arts; works include many portraits. Recipient many awards. Mem. Soc. of Minn. Sculptors, Profl. Artists' Equity Assn. Home: PO Box C Norwood CO 81423-0693

HOLLINGER, PAULA COLODNY, state legislator; b. Washington, Dec. 30, 1940; d. Samuel and Ethel (Levy) Colodny; m. Paul Hollinger, Sept. 16, 1962; children: Ilene, Marcy, David. RN, Mt. Sinai Hosp. Sch. Nursing, N.Y.C., 1961. RN NY. Pub. health sch. nurse, resident camp nurse Balt. County Dept. Health; Myasthenia Gravis specialist Acute Stroke Unit U. Md. Hosp.; clin. instr. psychiat. nursing Tuskegee Inst.; head nurse surgery intensive care unit Mt. Sinai Hosp., N.Y., night charge nurse emergency rm.; Carter del., 1976; mem. Md. Ho. of Dels., Annapolis, 1978-86, Md. Senate, Annapolis, 1987—, majority whip, 2000—, vice chair senate edn, health and environ. affairs com., 1995—, senate chair joint com. on health care delivery and financing, 1995—, chair senate econ. and environ. affairs health sub-com., 1988—. Chmn. adminstrv., exec., legislative review com., health subcom., Md. Senate, Annapolis, 1987, chmn. 1991-95, chmn. joint. com. health care delivery and financing, 1995, chmn. joint com. fed. rels., 1987-90, vice-chair econ. and environ. affairs com.,1995, mem. exec. nominations com., 1995—; vice-chair health com. Nat. Conf. State Legis., 1990-91, chair health com., 1991-92, chair sci. and resources tech. com., 1984, com. long term care, 1985, chmn. women's network, 1993, vice chmn. 1992, 96, chmn., 1992, rep. assembly fed. issues; mem. joint oversight com. on health care cost containment, Medicaid joint com.; chmn. joint protocol com. Md. Gen. Assembly, 1998—; alt. mem. So. Legis. Conf. Coun. State Govts. Human Svcs. And Pub. Safety Com.; mem. Gov.'s Task Forces to Study: Nursing Crisis, Uses of Methlphenidate, 1997—, Class Size Reduction Programs in Md., 1998—, Alternative Methods of Coll. Financing, Joint Legis. Task Force on Organ and Tissue Donation, 1997-98, Task Forces on Violence and Extremism, Quality of Care in Nurisisng Facilities, 1999, AIDS; mem. Gov.'s adv. coun. on AIDS; mem. Gov.'s com. nursing issues in Md.; mem. Gov.'s commns. black and minority health, black males, chmn. health subcom.; mem. interagy. Coordinating coun. for infants and toddlers; mem. exec. com. Nat. Assn. Jewish Legislators, 1997—; mem. state adv. com. Office for Children, Youth and Families; mem. state adv. coun. organ and tissue donation awareness, 1998—; pres. Women Legislators of Md., 1986-88, v.p., 1985; lectr., spkr., guest panelist in field. Bd. dirs. Nat. Coun. Jewish Women, Safety First, 1990, Jewish Family Svcs., 1995—, Progress Unlimited, Inc., Juvenile Diabetes Assn. (hon.); adv. to bd. dirs. United Way Cmty. Partnership Balt.; adv. bd. Second Step, Inc., Md. Organ procurement Ctr., Inc.; bd. trustees Transplant Resource Ctr. Md., Inc., 1997—, Group for Independent Learning Disabled; grad. adv. coun. Notre Dame Coll.; mem. com. adolescent drug and alcohol abuse Md. Bar Assn., Environ. Matters Com.; faculty assoc. U. Md. Sch. Nursing, 1998—. Recipient Murry Guggenheim award, 1961, Bramson award Women's American ORT, 1981, Legis. award Mental Health Assn., 1983, Legislator of Yr. award Md. Nurse's Assn., 1984, Human Svc. award Constant Care Med. Ctr. 1984, Outstanding Contbns. to Edn. award Tchr.'s Assn. Balt. County, 1984, Outstanding Commitment and Dedication to Treatment of Alcoholic award Pilot House, 1984, Dedication and Commitment to Health and Environ. award Ctrl. Md. Health Sys. Agy., Edith Rosen Strauss award, 1987, Outstanding Svc. award Md. Psych. Assn., 1987, Pres.' award Md. Assn. Non-Profit Homes for Aging, 1987, Humanitarian award, Liberty Rd. Cmty. Coun., 1987, Leadership Laurel award Safety 1st Club Md., 1987, Outstanding Legis. Leadership award On Our Own Md., 1988, Outstanding Support and Devel. Rehab. Programs award Johns Hopkins Dept. Rehab., Md. Health Care Found., 1988, Legis. Honor Roll award Md. Assn. Psychosocial Svcs., 1988, Spl. award leadership Pikesville revitalization Pikesville Cmty. Growth Corp., 1988, Pres.' award Md. Assn. Home Care, 1988, Verda Welcome award for outstanding polit. achievements and pub. svc., 1989, Cmty. Svc. award Balt. Hebrew U., 1990, Physician's Asst. Appreciation award, 1991, Leadership and Commitment award Walbrook H.S. Primary Health Care Ctr., 1991, Betty Tyler Pub. Affairs award Planned Parenthood, 1992, 93, Excellence in Social Work Legislation award Md. Social Work Coalition, 1993, award Chesapeake Bay Found. Environ. Leadership, 1994, Policy Maker Leadership award Adv. for Youth, 1995, Ann. Leadership award Md. State Sch. Health Coun., 1996, Legis. award Legis. and Pub. Info. Com. Balt. County Commn. Disabilities, 1997, Legis. award Md. Retired Tchrs., 1997, award Md./D.C. Soc. Respiratory Care, 1997, Dedication and Support award Nat. Kidney Found. Md., 1998, Legis. award Md. Assn. Counseling and Devel., 1998, Sch. Health Advocacy award Sch. Nurse Inst., 2000, Outstanding Svc. award Md. Psychol. Assn., 2000, Pres.'s award Md. Nat. Capitol Home Care Assn., 2000, Presdl. award of Recognition Md. Occupl. Therapy Assn., 2001, Legis. of Yr. award, Mental Health Assn. Md., 2001, Pacesetter award Nat. Women Legis.'s Lobby, 2001, Distin. Leadership award Abilities Network and Epilepsy Found. of Chesapeake Region, 2002; named Woman of Yr., Women Realtors Anne Arundel County, 1988, Pikesville C. of C., 1989, Sen. of Yr., Md. Assn. Psychiat. Support Svcs., 1993, Oustanding Legislator, Md. Speech, Lang., Hearing Assn., 1993, Most Disting. Alumnus, Mt. Sinai Hosp. Sch. Nursing Alumnae Assn., 1998, Md.'s Top 100 Women, Daily Record, 1999, 2001, Legis. of Yr. AHA, 1999. Mem. Am. Assn. Marriage and Family Therapy (Mid Atlantic Divsn., hon. licensure), B'nai Brith Women, Hadassah, Na'Amat, Orgn. for Rehab. Tng. (Bramson award 1981), Chi Eta Phi (hon.). Office: Miller Senate Bldg Annapolis MD 21401-1991

HOLLINGSWORTH, DEBRA LYNN, elementary school educator; b. Wilmington, Del., July 8, 1969; d. Irvin John Hollingsworth, Jr. and Anne Marie Hickman. BS in Music Edn., West Chester (Pa.) U., 1991, MusM in Music Edn., 2001. Cert. tchr. level II Pa., 1999, tchr. level I Pa., 1991. Secondary music tchr. Christina Sch. Dist., Newark, Del., 1991—93; elem. music tchr. Owen J. Roberts Sch. Dist., Pottstown, Pa., 1993—. Music dept. chmn. Owen J. Roberts Sch. Dist., Pottstown, Pa., 2000—; HS musical music dir./prodr. Owen J. Roberts H.S., Pottstown, Pa., 2000—01, HS show choir dir., 2000—01. Actor(singer, dancer): (dinner theatre prodns.) including Nellie Forbush, in South Pacific, and Eliza in My Fair Lady, others, (cmty. theatre prodn.) Narrator, in Joseph and the Amazing Technicolor Dreamcoat, Cinderella, in Into the Woods, others, (regional theatre prodn.) Fiona MacLaren, in Brigadoon, Lili, in Carnival, others. Recipient State of Del. Rep. to the UN award, Odd Fellows and Rebekahs, 1985; Nat. Mushroom Queen Pageant winner, Nat. Mushroom Assn., 1989. Mem.: Pa, Music Educators' Assn., Music Educators' Nat. Conf., Roberts Edn. Assn., Pa. State Edn. Assn., NEA, Am. Orff-Schulwerk Assn., Pi Kappa Lambda, Sigma Alpha Iota. Republican. Avocations: travel, crafts, gardening, dance. Office: French Creek Elementary Sch 3590 Coventryville Rd Pottstown PA 19465 E-mail: dhollingsworth@ojrsd.com.

HOLLINGSWORTH, MARGARET CAMILLE, financial services administrator, consultant; b. Washington, Feb. 20, 1929; d. Harvey Alvin and Margaret Estelle (Head) Jacob; m. Robert Edgar Hollingsworth, July 14, 1960 (div. July 1980); children: William Lee, Robert Edgar Hollingsworth Jr., Barbara Camille, Bradford Damion; m. James Aldo Boland, Sept. 12, 1998 (dec. Aug. 1999). AA, Va. Intermont Coll., 1949. Bookkeeper Fred A. Smith Real Estate, Washington, 1949-53; adminstrv. mgr. Airtronic, Inc., Bethesda, Md., 1953-61; pers. adminstr. Sears Roebuck, Washington, 1973-74; adminstrv. mgr., communication mgr. Garvin GuyButler Corp., San Francisco, 1980-88, exec. sec., pers. mgr., 1989-95, adminstrv. cons., ret., 1996; adminstrv. cons., Concord, Calif. Assoc. Robert Hollingsworth Nuclear Cons., Walnut Creek, Calif., 1975-79. Bd. dirs. Civic Arts, Walnut Creek, 1975-2001. Recipient Spl. Recognition award AEC, 1974. Mem.: Rancho Bernardo Joslyn Ctr., San Diego Mus. Art, San Diego Natural Hist. Mus., Oaks North Country Club, Oaks North Travel Club, Beta Sigma Phi (pres. 1954). Democrat. Presbyterian. Avocations: travel, art appreciation, investments, hiking, reading. Home: 17758 Caminito Balata San Diego CA 92128 E-mail: mcb100501@aol.com.

HOLLINGSWORTH, MARTHA LYNETTE, secondary school educator; b. Waco, Tex., Oct. 9, 1951; d. Willie Frederick and Georgia Cuddell (Bryant); m. Roy David Hollingsworth, Dec. 31, 1971; children: Richard Avery, Justin Brian. AA, McLennan C.C., 1972; BBA, Baylor U., 1974, MS in Ednl. Adminstrn., 1992. Tchr. Connally Ind. Sch. Dist., Waco, 1974—. With Adult Edn. Night Sch., 1974—78; chair Area III leadership conf. Vocat. Office Careers Clubs Tex., Waco, 1985—. Active Lakeview Little League Booster Club, 1985—; mem. PTA. Mem.: Assn. Tex. Profl. Educators (v.p. local chpt. 1988—90), Vocat. Office Edn. Tchrs. Assn. Tex., Tex. Future Farmers Am. (hon.), Future Homemakers Am. Area VIII (hon.), Delta Kappa Gamma. Baptist. Office: Connally Vocat Dept 715 N Rita St Waco TX 76705-1140

HOLLINGSWORTH, REBECCA A. speech pathology/audiology services professional; AS, N.D. State U., Wahpeton, 1972; BS, Minot State U., 1974, MS in Speech Pathology, 1980. Cert. clin. competence speech lang. pathology, lic. speech lang. pathology N.D.; elem. edn. N.D. Speech lang. pathologist Oliver Morton Spl. Edn. Unit, Hazen, ND, 1974—80; speech lang. pathologist Morton Sioux spl. edn. unit Mandan (N.D.) Pub. Schs., 1980—. Mem. N.D. visitation team Dept. Pub. Instr. divsn. Spl. Edn., 1979; mem. com. Speech Lang. Eligibility, ND, 1989—90; mem. N.D. Spkrs. Bur., 2003. Mem.: Am. Speech Lang. Hearing Assn. Roman Catholic. Avocations: reading, walking. Office: Ft Lincoln Elem 2007 8th Ave SE Mandan ND 58554

HOLLINS, APRIL RIFE, music educator; b. Staunton, Va., Feb. 23, 1963; d. Janice Knick Good and Bobby Lee Rife; m. Gary Michael Hollins, Nov. 23, 1994; children: Morgan Nichole Brooking, Devon Michael. BA, Bridgewater Coll., Va., 1985. Cert. music tchr. N.C., 2000. Band dir. Madison County H.S. and Mid. Sch., Va., 1985—94; band/choir/asst. band dir. Rockbridge County HS and Maury River Mid. Sch., Lexington, Va., 1996—98; choir dir. Third Presbyn. Ch., Staunton, Va., 1996—2000; choral dir. Robert E. Lee H.S., Staunton, Va., 1998—2000; band dir. Manteo Mid. Sch., NC, 2000—03; band and choral dir. Manteo H.S., NC, 2000—. Mem.: Ea. N.C. Band Masters Assn. (assoc.), Music Educators Nat. Conf. (assoc.). Home: 166 Langley Ln Manteo NC 27954 Office: Manteo HS 616 Wingina Ave Manteo NC 27954 Personal E-mail: ghollins@coastalnet.com.

HOLLINSHEAD, ARIEL CAHILL, research oncologist, educator; b. Allentown, Pa., Aug. 24, 1929; d. Earl Darnell and Gertrude Loretta (Cahill) H.; m. Montgomery K. Hyun, June 12, 1957; children: William C., Christopher C. Student, Swarthmore Coll., 1947-48; AB, Ohio U., 1951, DSc (hon.), 1977; MA, George Washington U., 1955, PhD, 1957, MD, 1977. Asst. prof., fellow in virology Baylor U. Med. Ctr., 1958-59; asst. prof. pharmacology George Washington Med. Ctr., 1959-61, asst. prof. medicine, 1961-64, assoc. prof. medicine, head lab. virus and cancer rsch., 1964-73, prof., dir. lab. virus and cancer rsch., 1974-89; on sabbatical leave 1990, prof. medicine emeritus, 1991—; rschr. HI Virus and Cancer Rsch., 1991—. Clin. rschr. trials in oncology and virology; cons. to biotech. cos. and FDA panel; panelist FDA and NIH. Contbr. over 270 articles on active immunotherapy and immunochemotherapy of cancer and virus diseases to sci. jours. Bd. dirs. Nat. Women's Econ. Alliance, Ohio U., Med. Coll. Pa., 1980-2003, Women's Inst., 1995-97. Named Bicentennial Med. Woman of Yr., Joint Bd. Am. Med. Colls., 1976, one of Outstanding Woman of Am., 1987, Outstanding Alumnus of Yr., Ohio U., 1990; recipient Cert. Merit Med. Coll. Pa., 1975-76, Marion Spencer Fay Med. Woman of Year award Med. Coll. Pa.; decorated Star of Europe, 1980. Fellow AAAS (med. sci. com. 1993-96, 99—), Washington Acad. Sci. N.Y. Acad. Scis.; mem. Grad. Women in Sci. (nat. pres. 1985-86, bd. dirs. 1986-92, nat. liaison to Washington, 1992—), Internat. Soc. Preventive Oncology, Nat. Soc. Exptl. Biology and Medicine (Disting. Scientist award 1985, Disting. Scientist emeritus award for Outstanding Career in Tchg. and Rsch. in Medicine 1996, past pres. Greater Washington chpt.), Am. Soc. Microbiology, Am. Assn. Cancer Research, Am. Assn. Immunologists, Women in Cancer Rsch., Vet. Females Am., Clin. Immunology Soc., Internat. Soc. Antiviral Research, Am. Soc. Clin. Oncology, Internat. Assn. Study Lung Cancer, Internat. Union Against Cancer, Am. Med. Writers Assn., Soc. of the Emeriti, Kenwood Country Club, Blue Ridge Mountain Country Club, Burnt Store Country Club, Washington Forum (pres. 1987, 91), Phi Beta Kappa (alumnus 1990). Achievements include being first to purify, develop and test cancer gene products, including peptides and to study activities; first to invent field called proteomics; peptides were studied and identified for the ability to induce long-lasting cell-mediated immunity; developed proteomics technology and pioneered clinical testing and monitoring epitope activity during seventeen clinical trials; patentee in field. Home: 622 Rolls Landing 23465 Harborview Rd Port Charlotte FL 33980-2162

HOLLIS, JACQUELYN WILSON, music educator; b. Brunswick, Ga., July 7, 1962; d. Relious James and Eulalia Florine Wilson; m. Robert D. Hollis, Nov. 13, 1997. BA in Music Edn., Clark Coll., Atlanta, 1985. Min. of music Radcliffe Presbyn. Ch., Atlanta, 1980—87; choral dir. Russell H.S., East Point, Ga., 1985—87, Woodland Mid. Sch., East Point, Ga., 1987—88, Banneker H.S., College Park, Ga., 1988—93; accompanist Morris Brown Coll., Atlanta, 1986—87, Cascade United Meth. Ch., Atlanta, 1990—92; choral dir. Creekside H.S., Fairburn, Ga., 1993—2003; min. of music II Radcliffe Presbyn. Ch., Atlanta, 1997—2003. Pvt. piano instr., Fairburn, Ga., 1983—2003; freelance organist various chs., 1989—2003. Democrat. Presbyn. Avocations: reading, arts and crafts, horticulture, playing piano and organ.

HOLLIS, JANICE DENISE, publishing executive, minister; b. Hazelhurst, Ga., Dec. 13, 1964; d. Moses and Janie Hollis. DDiv(hon.), World Christianship Theol. Sem., 2002. Ordained minister. Pub. Hollis Pub. Network, Phila., 1996—; asst. pastor Olivet Bapt. Ch., Phila., 2001—. Author: Life is Positively Astounding, 2002, The Warrior Within, 2002, Personal Management: It Matters, 2003; singer: (music recording) You Stole My Heart, 1988. Founder Progressive Believers' Mins., 2003—; vol. Phila. Cares, 2001—02. Named to Sisters in Bus., Phila. Bus. News Jour., 1999. Mem.: NAACP, Women's Alliance Exclusive Assn. (pres. 1988—2002), Phila. Hist. Soc., Nat. Mus. Women in Arts. Baptist. Avocations: lecturing, sailing, rock climbing, singing, writing.

HOLLIS, KATHERINE MARY, information scientist, consultant; d. Albert George and Rosalyn Mary Duren; m. David Martin Hollis, Aug. 25, 1990; children: Kent David Miller, Jason Randolph Miller; children: Brittany Frances, David Christopher. MS in Nat. Security Strategy, Nat. War College, 1999; B in Polit. Sci., U. Minn., 1983. Dir. resource mgmt. installation support modules program Program Exec. Office - STD. Mgmt. Info. Sys., Ft. Belvoir, Va., 1989—93; program mgr. electronic commerce/electronic data interchange Def. Info. Sys. Agy., Falls Chruch, Va., 1993—96, spl. asst. to the dep., pub. key infrastructure program mgmt. office, 1999—2000; dep. dir. electronic processes initiatives coun. task force Office of the Deputy Sec. of Def., Rosslyn, Va., 1996—98; deputy dir. dept. def. Y2K office Office of the Sec. of Def., Crystal City, Va., 1998—99; dir. global info. assurance solutions Electronic Data Sys., Herndon, Va., 2000—. Adv. com. Fed. Electronic Commerce Coalition, Falls Church, Va., 1999—; chair smart card integrated process team Def. Info. Sys. Agy., 1999—2000; spkr. in field. Vol. educator Prince William County Schools, Manassas, Va., 2001. Recipient Commanders award, Dept. of the Army, Dept. of Def., 1989, Federal 100 award, Federal Computer News, 1998. Avocations: archaeology, Egyptology, travel, writing. Office: Electronic Data Sys 13600 EDS Dr (A2S-D49) Herndon VA 20171

HOLLIS, LOUCILLE, risk control administrator, educator; b. Ft. Myers, Fla., Feb. 16, 1949; d. Luke Sr. and Louise (Wilcox) Black; m. Benjamin L. Hollis, Jr., Sept. 26, 1985. BS, N.Y. Inst. Tech., 1982, MBA, 1984. Staff asst. Equitable, N.Y.C., 1977-79, budget analyst, 1979-81, fin. analyst, 1981-85, mgr. operational planning, 1985-87, mgr. expense control, 1987-88; project leader L.I. R.R. Co., Jamaica, N.Y., 1988-91, asst. risk mgr., 1991-97; specialist in risk coverage Met. Transp. Authority, N.Y.C., 1997—. Comml. arbitrator Am. Arbitration Assn. Bronx fundraiser Cancer Fund Am., Knoxville, Tenn., 1991, 92; mem. bd. placement project United Way Linkage; literacy vol. Recipient Psychology award N.Y. Inst. Tech., 1981, acad. scholarship Ft. Myers Bd. Edn., 1977; honoree LIRR Women's History Celebration. Mem. NAFE, Nat. Black MBA Assn., Risk and Ins. Mgmt. Soc., RR Ins. Mgmt. Assn., Conf. Minority Transp. Ofcls., Psi Nat. Honor Soc. Democrat. Avocations: reading, personal computers, phys. fitness. Home: 19 Craig Place Bloomfield NJ 07003 Office: Met Transp Authority 347 Madison Ave New York NY 10017-3706

HOLLIS, MARY FRANCES, aerospace educator; b. Indpls., Sept. 18, 1931; d. Lucian Albert and Clara Frances Coleman; divorced; 1 child, Booker Albert Hollis. BS, Butler U., 1952, MS, 1962; postgrad., Stanford U., 1975, San Francisco State U., 1980-81. Cert. elem. tchr., Ind., Calif. Kindergartern tchr. Lockerbie Nursery Sch., Indpls., 1952, Indpls. Pub. Schs., 1952-69; tchr. K-6 San Mateo (Calif.) City Sch. Dist., 1969-91; summer sch. prin. San Mateo City Sch. dist., Foster City, Calif., 1983-91; aerospace educator, 1982—. Bd. dirs. Coun. of Math./Sci. Educators of San Mateo County, Belmont, Calif.; resident mgr. Lesley Found., Park Twrs., 1999—. Editor: San Mateo County Math./Sci. Coun. quarterly newsletter, 1988-90. Bd. dirs. Arts Coun. of San Mateo County, 1986-91, Mid-Peninsula chpt. ACLU, San Mateo, 1990—, Unitarian-Universalist Ch. San Mateo, 1996-98; bd. dirs. Peninsula Funeral and Meml. Planning Soc., 1996-2000, co-pres., 1998-99; office mgr. Roger Winston Campaign for San Mateo Union H.S. Dist. Bd. Trustees, 1993; mem. adv. com. USAF-Pacific Liaison Region-CAP, 1988-94; sr. peer counselor San Mateo County Mental Health, 1996—. Recipient Life Down to Earth award NASA, Moffet Field, Mt. View, Calif., 1985-86, Earl Sams Tchr. of Yr. award Calif. Assn. Aerospace Educators, 1989, award of merit Am. Legion, San Bruno, Calif., 1989, citation Air Force Assn., Mountain View, Calif., 1991, Aviation Summer Sch. cert. of appreciation Am. Legion Dept. Calif. Aerospace Commn., 1994. Mem. NEA (life), AAUW (bd. dirs. San Carlos chpt. 1993-95), NAACP (life), Am. Bus. Women's Assn. (rec. sec. Foster City chpt. 1985), World Aerospace Edn. Orgn. Democrat. Unitarian-Universalist. Avocations: reading, travel, music-jazz, rhythm and blues, swimming, aerospace/aviation. Office: PO Box 625 Belmont CA 94002-0625 E-mail: mfrances@pacbell.net.

HOLLIS, SHEILA SLOCUM, lawyer; b. Denver, July 15, 1948; d. Theodore Doremus and Emily M. (Caplis) Slocum (dec.); m. John Hollis; 1 child, Windsong Emily Lanford. BS in Journalism with honors, BS in Gen. Studies cum laude, U. Colo., 1971; JD, U. Denver, 1973. Bar: Colo. 1974, D.C. 1975, U.S. Supreme Ct. 1980. Trial atty. Fed. Power Commn., Washington, 1974-75; assoc. firm Wilner & Scheiner, Washington, 1975-77; dir. office enforcement Fed. Energy Regulatory Commn., Washington, 1977-80; pvt. practice, 1980—; ptnr. Vinson & Elkins, Washington, 1987-92; sr. ptnr. Metzger, Hollis, Gordon & Alprin, Washington, 1992-97; mem. firm Duane Morris LLP, 2003—, mem. exec. com., 2004—, chair Washington office, mem. ptnrs. bd., 2004—. Professorial lectr. in energy law George Washington U., 1980—2000; bd. dirs. U.S. Energy Assn. Co-author: Energy Decision Making, 1983, Energy Law and Policy, 1989; mem. editl. bd. Oil and Gas Reporter, Pub. Utility Fortnightly; contbr. articles to profl. publs. Established and developed enforcement program Fed. Energy Regulatory Commn.; mem. adv. bd. Pub. Utility Ctr. N.Mex. State U., 1986—94; mem. adv. bd. N.Am. Energy Stds. Bd., 1998—; pres.

Women's Coun. Energy and Environment, 1997—2003; bd. dirs. Found. for Vets. Health Care., Wyo. State Soc., 2001—03, Am. Friends of Royal Soc. U. Denver scholar, 1972-73; named Woman of Yr. Women's Coun. Energy and Environment, 2003, One of 50 Key Women in Energy-Global, Commodities Now Mag., 2004. Fellow: ABA (chair coord. group energy law 1989—92, mem. ho. dels. 1992—2001, [illegible] group energy law 1995—97, chair standing com. environ. law 1997—2000, mem. bd. editors ABA Jour. 2000—, chair sect. environ., energy and resources 2001—02, standing com. on fed. judiciary 2002—); mem.: John Carroll Soc., Women's Bar Assn. D.C., D.C. Bar Assn., Colo. Bar Assn., Internat. Legal Edn. Ctr. (trustee), Oil and Gas Ednl. Inst., Energy Bar Assn. (pres. 1991—92), Am. Law Inst., Internat. Bar Assn., Comml. Bar of Eng. and Wales (hon.), Am. Friends Royal Soc., Thomas More Soc. (pres. 2003—), Cosmos Club, Nat. Press Club. Roman Catholic. Office: DuaneMorris LLP 1667 K St NW Ste 700 Washington DC 20006-1608 Office Phone: 202-776-7810. E-mail: sshollis@duanemorris.com.

HOLLIS, SUSAN TOWER, history educator; b. Boston, Mar. 17, 1939; d. James Wilson and Dorothy Parsons (Moore) Tower; m. Allen Hollis, Nov. 10, 1962 (div. Feb. 1975); children: Deborah Durfee, Harrison. AB, Smith Coll., 1962; PhD, Harvard U., 1982. Cert. C.C. instr. history and humanities. Asst. prof. Scripps Coll., Claremont, Calif., 1988-91; prof. Coll. of Undergrad. Studies The Union Inst., L.A., 1991-93; dean of the college and prof. humanities Sierra Nev. Coll.-Lake Tahoe, Incline Village, Nev., 1993-95; ind. scholar, cons. Reno, 1995-96; ctr. dir., assoc. dean Ctrl. N.Y. Ctr. Empire State Coll. of SUNY, Syracuse, 1996-99; assoc. prof. SUNY Empire State Coll., Rochester, N.Y., 1999—, coord. western region MA in Liberal Studies program, 2000—. Convener hist. studies Empire State Coll. of SUNY, 2000—03, co-chair acad. policies an learning programs com., 2003—. Author: The Ancient Egyptian "Tale of Two Brothers", 1990; editor: Hymns, Prayers and Songs: Anthology of Ancient Egyptian Lyrics & Poetry (by John L. Foster), 1996; co-editor: Feminist Theory and the Study of Folklore, 1993; contbr. articles to profl. jours, encys. Music vol. Open Readings, Belmont, Mass., 1982—88; vol. Sierra Club, 1988—; problem capt. Odyssey of the Mind, Nev., 1994—95, judge, 1997—98; crew chief Tahoe Rim trail, 1994—96; active Masterworks Chorale, NY, 1996—99. Mem.: N.Y. State Network for Women Leaders in Higher Edn. (bd. dirs. 1997—, assoc. coord. 1999—2000, coord. 2000—03), N.Y. Acad. Scis., Egyptological Soc. N.Y., Soc. Bibl. Lit. (co-chair Egyptology and Ancient Israel group 1995—96, chair Egyptology and Ancient Israel group 1996—, convenor Ancient Near East Consortium 1998—, Outstanding Svc. in Mentoring award 2003), Soc. for Study Egyptian Antiquities, Internat. Assn. Egyptologists, Am. Rsch. Ctr. Egypt, Am. Oriental Soc., Am. Folklore Soc., Am. Assn. Higher Edn., Am. Acad. Religion, Incline Village/Crystal Bay C. of C. (sec., bd. dirs. 1994—95), Ka-na-wa-ke Canoe Club (bd. dirs. 1998—2000), Adirondack Mountain Club, Appalachian Mountain Club (co-leader 1987—88). Democrat. Home: 7 New Wickham Dr Penfield NY 14526-2703 Office: Empire State Coll of SUNY 1475 Winton Rd N Rochester NY 14609-5803 E-mail: susan.hollis@esc.edu.

HOLLIS-ALLBRITTON, CHERYL DAWN, retail paper supply store executive; b. Elgin, Ill., Feb. 15, 1959; d. L.T. and Florence (Elder) Saylors; stepparent Bobby D. Hollis; m. Thomas Allbritton, Aug. 10, 1985. BS in Phys. Edn., Brigham Young U., 1981; cosmetologist, 1981. Retail sales clk. Bee Discount, North Riverside, Ill., 1981-82, retail store mgr., Downers Grove, Ill., 1982, Oaklawn, Ill., 1982-83, St. Louis, 1983; retail tng. mgr. Arvey Paper & Office Products (divsn. Internat. Paper), Chgo., 1984, retail store mgr., Columbus, Ohio, 1984—. Republican. Mem. LDS Ch. Avocations: writing, reading, travel. Office: Arvey Paper & Office Products 431 E Livingston Ave Columbus OH 43215-5586 Office Phone: 614-221-0153.

HOLLISTER, NANCY, state legislator; Lt. gov. State of Ohio, 1995-98, rep. Ho. of Reps., 1999—. Office: State House 77 S High St Columbus OH 43266-0001

HOLLISTER, PATRICIA HACKETT, psychotherapist, educator, marriage and family therapist; b. Wilmington, Del., May 9, 1940; d. Robert Sutliff and Jane Williamson Hackett; m. A. Phillip Simpson, Aug. 24, 1991; children: Kenneth David, Tracy Lynn. BA, Oberlin (Ohio) Coll., 1962; MEd, Duke U., 1967; MA, Azusa Pacific U., 1981. Lic. tchr. Ohio, 1962. Tchr. Lakewood (Ohio) City Schs., 1962—63, Durham (N.C.) City Schs., 1963—67; marriage and family therapist Torrance and Redondo Beach, Calif., 1985—93, HealthCare Ptnrs. Med. Group, Torrance, 1993—2000, Alamogordo (N.Mex.) Mental Health Svcs., Inc., 2000—. Instr. Parent Effectiveness Tng., Rancho Palos Verdes, Calif., 1973—75. V.p. bd. dirs. Cloudcroft (N.Mex.) Dance Theatre, 2001—02. Recipient First Pl. award, Sacramento (N.Mex.) Mountains Sports Assn., 2000, 2001, 2002, 2003. Mem.: Am. Assn. of Marriage and Family Therapists (assoc.; clin. mem. 1985—2003). Republican. Unitarian. Avocations: ballroom dancing, hiking, reading, movies, travel.

HOLLOMAN, MARILYN LEONA DAVIS, nursing non profit administrator, new product developer; b. Bklyn., Oct. 6, 1952; d. Leon Courbourne and Gwendolyn Omega (Crichlow) Davis; m. Theodore Albert Holloman, July 30, 1971 (div. Apr. 1975); children: Tedette Ann (dec.), Amina Omega Suedi. AAS in Nursing, Queensboro C.C., Bayside, N.Y., 1973; FNP, U. Miami, 1980. Founder, pres., CEO Women and Children 1st Inc., Miami, 1992—; v.p. Omega Health Network, inc., 2000—01. Allocations panel mem. United Way, Dade County, Fla., 1989-96; mem. at large Switchboard of Miami, 1992, treas., 1993-94, sec., 1994-95; fellow Common Ground Kellogg Found./U. Miami, 1993-95; primary cand. 1996 (Fla. House Rep., Dist 101). Author: Melody's of Life, 1982; editor Health Plan Baby Book, 1985; editor, pub. Legislative Update Women and Children 1st Inc., 1994—. Former pres. Dem. Black Caucus-Dade County chpt., 1991-92; Dem. candidate Fla. Ho. Reps., 1996; mem. Planned Giving Coun. of Dade County, 1994-95. Mem.: ANA (cert. specialist family nurse practitioner), Miami Parliamentary Law Unit (pres. 1993—95, v.p. 1995—97), Nat. Assn. Parliamentarians, Fla. Nurses Assn. (legis. dist. coord. 1984—99). Democrat. Achievements include patents pending for 9-11 Omega Buddysack/InjurEvac. Avocations: drama, reading, dance, travel. Home and Office: 114 SW Peacock Blvd #201 Port Saint Lucie FL 34986

HOLLOWAY, BARBARA R. health science association administrator; b. Bloomfield, N.J., Aug. 4, 1947; married; 2 children. BA in English and History, Siena Coll., 1969; MPH, Emory U., 1979. With La. Health Planning Coun., Baton Rouge, 1969-70; office mgr. Office of Resources Devel. Ga. Inst. Tech., Atlanta, 1970-72; tchr. Gwinnett County (Ga.) High Schs., 1973-75; edn. specialist, chief consultation and tng. sect., program svcs. br., tuberculosis control divsn. Ctr. Disease Control, Atlanta, 1975-79, pub. health advisor hosps. infections br., bacterial diseases divsn. Bur. Epidemiology, 1979-81, asst. dir. ops. divsn. surveillance and epidemiologic studies Epidemiology Program Office, 1981-86, asst. dir. program ops. Epidemiology Program Office, 1986-88, dep. dir. Epidemiology Program Office, 1988—. Home: 1517 Harts Mill Rd NE Atlanta GA 30319-1815 Office: HHS Ctrs Disease Control 1600 Clifton Rd NE Atlanta GA 30329-4018

HOLLOWAY, DIANE ELAINE, psychological consultant, psychotherapist, writer; b. Tulsa, Oct. 19, 1937; d. Lawrence Lynn and Helen May (Six) Hatcher; m. 1961; children: Brian, Kathleen; m. 2d, Bob Cheney, 1980. BS, Tex. Woman's U., 1972, MA, 1974, PhD, 1979. Lic. psychotherapist, Tex. Brit. rep. Study Abroad, Inc., London, 1957-59; psychologist Presbyn. Hosp., Dallas, 1970-75, dir. psychol. svcs., assoc. dir. continuing edn. psychiatry, 1976-78; mental health/mental retardation cons. Drug Rehab. and Law Enforcement Offices, Dallas County, 1975-77; psychotherapist in pvt. practice Dallas, 1978-89; assoc. Pain Therapy Assn., Dallas, 1979-81; pres. Security & Mgmt. Sys., Dallas, 1979-81, Mental Health Profl. Group, Dallas, 1980-89; drug coord. Dallas Office of Mayor, 1989-92; vis. prof. various univs., 1993—. Author: Before You Say I Quit, 1990, The Mind of Oswald, 2000, Dallas and the Jack Ruby Trial, 2001, Analyzing Leaders, Presidents and Terrorists, 2002; contbr. newsletter, articles to profl. jours.;, editor internet sites Hogg Found. [illegible], 1972-73. Mem. APA, Am. Med. Writers Assn., Internat. Assn. Chiefs of Police, Archaeol. Inst. Am., Soc. Police and Criminal Psychology, Mensa. Office: 20402 N 150th Dr Sun City West AZ 85375-5765

HOLLOWAY, JACQUELINE, county commissioner; b. Knoxville, Tenn., Mar. 16, 1935; d. Clyde Herbert and Ernestine Cooper; m. George Rudolph Holloway, July 21, 1951; children: Lynda, George Jr., Michelle, Cheryl, Ingrid. AA in Bus., Cooper Inst., Knoxville, 1961; cert., U. Tenn. Ctr. Govt. Tng., 1990. Cert. pub. adminstr. U. Tenn. Biol. technician Oak Ridge (Tenn.) Nat. Lab., 1963—96; county commr. Anderson County, Clinton, Tenn., 1990—2002. Chmn. Families First Coun., 1997—; vice chair Am.'s Promise, 1999—; bd. dirs. Anderson County Health Coun., 2000—, chmn., 2002, Quality Childcare Initiative, Tenn. Nutrition and Consumer Edn. Program; v.p. Coalition Oak Ridge Ret. Employees, 2000—03; v.p. cmty. problem solving United Way Anderson County; mem. Anderson County Headstart Policy Coun.; mem. exec. com. Anderson County Dems.; pres. Dem. Women, Tenn., 1996—98; v.p. Dem. Fedn., Tenn., 1996—2003; bd. dirs. Clinch River Home Health. Mem. Tenn. County Commn. Assn. (bd. dirs. 1991-2002), Tenn. County Svcs. Assn. Methodist. Home and Office: 102 Artesia Dr Oak Ridge TN 37830-7817 E-mail: G32284@aol.com.

HOLLOWAY, M(ARY) KATHARINE, research scientist, chemist; BS in Chemistry summa cum laude, U. Southern Miss., 1979; MA in Organic Chemistry, U. Tex., Austin, 1982, PhD in Organic Chemistry, 1985. Sr. rsch. chemist molecular sys. dept. Merck & Co., 1985-90, rsch. fellow molecular design and diversity, 1990-96, sr. rsch. fellow molecular design and diversity, 1996—. Recipient Inventor of Yr. award Intellectual Property Owners, 1997. Mem. ACS (sec. computers in chemistry divsn. 1992-95, co-editor newsletter 1992, mem. membership com. 1990-95, vice chair Quantitative Structure-Activity Relationships Gordon Conf. 1999, Award for Creative Invention 1999). Achievements include patents for HIV protease inhibitors useful in the treatment of AIDS, 1995, 97 (2), HIV protease inhibitors useful in the treatment of AIDS, and their preparation, 1996, treatment of Alzheimer's disease with 5-(tetradecyloxy)-2-furan carboxylic acid, 1997, method of finding transcription activators of the NER steroid hormone receptor, 1997. Home: 171 Forest Trail Dr Lansdale PA 19446-6416 E-mail: kate_holloway@merck.com.

HOLLOWAY, WANDA KAYE, psychotherapist, consultant; b. Mansfield, Mo., Sept. 10, 1960; d. Thomas McDonald and Patsy Jorene Smith; m. David Leigh Holloway, Sept. 7, 1996. BS, Coll. of the Ozarks, 1979—82; MEd, Univ. Ark., 1986—87; PsyD, Forest Inst. of Prof. Psychology, Springfield, Mo., 1995—2000. Vol. supr. of occupl. therapy Ozark Guidance Ctr., Springdale, Ark., 1983; outpatient counselor Decision Point, Springdale, Ark., 1983—88; therapist Charter Vista Hosp., Fayetteville, Ark., 1986—87; dir. substance abuse Burrell Behavioral Health, Springfield, Mo., 1988—99, intern, resident, 1999—2001, provisional lic. Psychologist, 2001—; therapist cons. Cox Med. Ctr., Springfield, Mo., 2003—. Mem.: Health Psychology Divsn., Am. Psychological Assn. Republican. Assembly Of God. Avocations: outdoor activities, bicycling, skeet shooting, target shooting, skiing, reading. Office: Burrell Behavioral Health 1300 Bradford Pky Springfield MO 65804

HOLLOWELL, DARIA MAE, social sciences educator; b. Atlanta, Jan. 21, 1949; d. Branton Alexander dePierre and Delia Irene Coppola; m. Christopher Wilson Hollowell, IV, Aug. 9, 1975; children: Elena Elizabeth, Justine Marie, Francis Andrew, Claire Adele. BA, U. Calif., LA, 1971; MA, Johns Hopkins Sch. of Advanced Internat. Studies, Wash., DC, 1973, U. San Diego, 1990. Various positions U.S. Fgn. Svc., 1973—2002; prof. polit. sci. U. Md. abroad, Naples, Italy, 1979—80, Southwestern CC, Chula Vista, Calif., 1989—90; dep. consul gen. Am. Embassy, London, 1994—2001; prin. officer Am. Consulate Gen., Florence, Italy, 2001—02; adj. prof. internat. rels. U. San Diego, 2002—; prog. dir. immigration Cath. charities Diocese/County of San Diego, 2004—. Mem.: Bilateral Safety Corridor Coalition (bd. dirs. 2002—), Timken Mus. Art (bd. trustees 2002—), Nat. Mus. Women in Arts (nat. adv. bd. 2002—). Democrat. Roman Catholic. Avocations: art, history, painting, drawing. Home: 1382 Valencia Loop Chula Vista CA 91910 E-mail: hollowelldd@hotmail.com.

HOLLY, ELLISTINE PERKINS, music educator; b. Grenada, Miss., Aug. 12, 1934; d. Addison Lampton and Anna Pearl (Powell) Perkins; m. Donald Beall, June 10, 1960 (div. June 1966); 1 child, Donna Camille; m. Kermit Wells Holly, Jr., Dec. 23, 1979. BA in Music and Piano, Fisk U., Nashville, 1955; M Music Edn., Ind. U., 1960; MusM, U. Mich., 1972, PhD, 1978. Tchr. Middleton Sr. High Sch., Tampa, 1955-58; instr. music Mary Holmes Jr. Coll., West Point, Miss., 1960-61; tchr. Jefferson Jr. High Sch., Pontiac, Mich., 1961-68; grad. asst. U. Mich., Ann Arbor, 1972-74; counselor Sch. Music, U. Mich., Ann Arbor, 1975-76; prof. music Jackson (Miss.) State U., 1976—. Vis. lectr. U. Paris, 1989, Institut du Monde Anglophone, Universite de Paris, 1989; reviewer travel grants Nat. Endowment for Humanities, 1986-87. Performing soloist Opera South Co., Jackson State U., 1983-85, U. Mich. Chamber Choir, U.S. Cultural Team to Russia, Germany, Spoleto, Italy, Opening Ceremonies Internat. Ballet Competition, Jackson, 1986, 90; editor, compiler: Biographies of Black Composers an Songwriters, 1989; contbr. articles to prof. jours.; creator, performer: (one woman show) Miss.'s African-Am. Divas. Mem. Jackson Arts Alliance, 1985—; bd. dirs. Miss. Musicians Hall of Fame, Miss. Inst. Arts and Letters, 1997-00, Miss. Opera Assn., 1998-00. Faculty rsch. scholar NEH, Harvard U., 1982, Chgo., 1985, Newberry Libr., Chgo., 1987, Ford Found., U. Miss., Oxford, 1987. Mem. Music Educators Nat. Conf., Nat. Assn. Tchrs. Singing (pres. Miss. chpt. 1984-87), Ctr. Black Music Rsch., Nat. Links, Inc., Miss. Hist. Soc., Sonneck Soc., Coll. Music Soc. (bd. dirs. so. region), Harmonica Music Club Inc. (pres. 1983-85), Delta Sigma Theta. Home: 261 Northgate Blvd Jackson MS 39206-2618

HOLM, CELESTE, actress; b. N.Y.C., Apr. 29, 1919; d. Theodor and Jean (Parke) H.; m. Wesley Addy, May 22, 1966; children: Theodor Holm Nelson, Daniel Schuyler Dunning. Ed., Univ. Sch. for Girls, Chgo., Lycee Victor Durui, Paris, Francis W. Parker Sch., Chgo., Adelphi Acad., Bklyn.; DHL (hon.), Centenary Coll., 1980, Northwood U., 1981; AA (hon.), Middle Ga. Coll., 1982; ArtsD (hon.), Ea. Mich. U., 1984; DHL (hon.), Kean Coll. of N.J., 1984, Felician Coll., 1985, Jersey City State Coll., 1986; DFA (hon.), Monmouth Coll., 1987; D Liberal Arts (hon.), Fairleigh Dickinson U., 1988; D Pub. Svc. (hon.), Ea. Ill. U., 1989; DFA (hon.), Seton Hall U., 1990. Appeared in Broadway shows Gloriana, 1938, The Time of Your Life, 1939, Another Sun, 1940, Return of the Vagabond, 1940, Eight O'Clock Tuesday, 1941, My Fair Ladies, 1941, Papa Is All, 1941-42, All the Comforts of Home, 1942, The Damask Cheek, 1942-43, Oklahoma!, 1943-44, 48, Bloomer Girl, 1944-45, She Stoops to Conquer, 1949, Affairs of State, 1950-51, Anna Christie, 1952, The King and I, 1952, His and Hers, 1954, Interlock, 1958, Third Best Sport, 1958, Invitation to a March, 1960-61, Mame, 1967, Candida, 1970, Habeas Corpus, 1975-76, The Utter Glory of Morrissey Hall, 1979, I Hate Hamlet, 1991; appeared in films Three Little Girls in Blue, 1946, Gentleman's Agreement, 1947 (Acad. Award for Best Supporting Actress), Carnival in Costa Rica, 1947, The Snake Pit, 1948, Road House, 1948, Chicken Every Sunday, 1948, Come to the Stable, 1949 (Acad. Award nomination for Best Supporting Actress), Everybody Does It, 1949, Champagne for Caesar, 1950, All About Eve, 1950 (Acad. Award nomination for Best Supporting Actress), The Tender Trap, 1955, High Society, 1956, Bachelor Flat, 1961, Doctor, You've Got to be Kidding, 1966, Tom Sawyer, 1972, Three Men and a Baby, 1987, Still Breathing, 1996; other stage appearances include (tours) Hamlet, 1937, The Women, 1937-38, Back to Methuselah, 1957, Finishing Touches, 1974, Light Up the Sky, 1975, (one-woman show) Paris Was Yesterday, 1978, (other prodns.) A Month in the Country, 1963, Madly in Love, [illegible], Night of the Iguana, 1964, Captain Brassbound's Conversion, 1966, Mame (nat. tour), 1967-68 (Sarah Siddons award), Hay Fever, 1979-83, Lady in the Dark (Eng.), 1981, The Trojan Women, 1985, The Road to Mecca, 1989, Love Letters, 1990, 94, The Cocktail Hour, 1990, 94, Allegro, 1994, 50th Anniversary of The Glass Menagerie, Chgo., 1994, Don Juan in Hell, Irish Rep., N.Y.C., 2000; numerous supper club appearances, N.Y.C., Chgo., San Francisco, Washington, L.A., 1943-59, (London cabaret debut) Pizza on the Park, 2003; U.S.O. entertainer, ETO, 1945; 21,000 mile tour of U.S. Army bases, 1949; TV appearances include (spls. & TV movies) Cinderella, 1965, The Shady Hill Kidnapping, 1979, Backstairs at the White House, 1979 (Emmy nomination), Nora's Christmas Gift, 1989, Polly, 1989, Polly, One Mo' Time, 1990; regular roles (series) Archie Bunker's Place, 1980-81, Falcon Crest, 1985, Loving, 1986 (Emmy nomination), 91-92, Christine Cromwell, 1989-90, Promised Land, CBS-TV, 1997-99, PBS Great Performances Talking With..., 1994; guest starring roles on Trapper John, M.D., The F.B.I., Disney's Wide World of Color, The Streets of San Francisco, Columbo, Medical Center, Captains and the Kings, Spencer For Hire, Magnum P.I., The Underground Man, Fantasy Island, The Love Boat, Whoopi, NBC-TV, 2004; radio interviewer People at the UN, 1963-65; toured with theatre-in-concert program Interplay, 1963-74; appeared in The Cole Porter 100th Birthday Celebration, Carnegie Hall, 1991. Past mem. gov. bd. U.S. Com. for UNICEF; mem. Nat. Mental Health Assn., 1965—, chmn., 1969-70; v.p. Arts and Bus. Coun.; mem. Nat. Arts Coun., 1982-88; chmn. bd. dirs. N.J. Film Commn., 1983—; bd. dirs. Mayor's Midtown Com., 1975—, Actor's Fund Am., 1988—; pres. bd. Creative Arts Rehab. Ctr., 1978—; mem. nat. vis. coun. for health scis. faculties Columbia U., N.Y.C., 1989—; mem. adv. bd. N.J. Sch. for the Arts, 1989—, adv. coun. UN Assn. of N.Y.C., 1992—; chmn. Stage South Supporting Players, S.C. State Theatre, 1977, Arts Horizons, 1995—. Decorated Dame King Olav of Norway; recipient Brotherhood award Nat. Conf. Christians & Jews, 1952, Disting. Svc. award United Jewish Appeal, 1953, Award of Merit, 1954, Achievement award Israel Bonds, 1958, Award of Appreciation March of Dimes, 1959, Hadassah, 1960, Nat. Assn. for Retarded Children award, 1961, Disting. Alumni award Francis W. Parker Sch., 1964, U.S. Com. for World Fedn. of Mental Health award, 1965, Performer of Yr. award Variety Clubs Am., 1966, Edward Strecker Meml. Medal for outstanding contbns. to mental health movement, rehab. of mentally disabled, 1971, Woman of Yr. award Anti-Defamation League, 1972, Golden Needle award Am. Home Sewing Coun., 1972, Woman of Yr. award N.Y. Variety Club, 1973, Woman of Yr. nomination Ladies Home Jour., 1975, Spirit of Am. award VFW, 1976, Woman of Yr. award Westchester Fedn. Women's Clubs, 1977, Woman of Yr. award Creative Arts Rehab. Ctr., 1977, Disting. Woman award Northwood Inst., 1977, Golden Scroll award Mayor's Midtown Citizens Com., 1979, Achievement in Arts award Northwood Inst./IASTA, 1979, Actor's Studio award, 1980, Mental Health Assn. Greater Chgo. award, 1982, Zonta Internat. Humanitarian award, 1984, Compostella award, 1984, Town Hall Friend of the Arts award, 1985, Humanitarian award Creative Arts Rehab. Ctr., 1988, Internat. Platform award, 1989, The Coalition of Arts Therapy Assn. Cert. Appreciation, 1990, Edwin Forrest award for Outstanding Contbn. to Theatre, Walnut St. Theatre, Phila., 1991, The Cardinal's Com of Laity Cardinal's award, 1991, The Ellis Island Medal of Honor, 1992, Gold medal Holland Soc. N.Y., 1994, Dorothea Dix award Mental Illness Found., 1995, Silver Circle award, 1999; named to The Theatre Hall of Fame, 1992, Grandparent of Yr., 1997, Utah Shakespeare Festivals Imperial Order, 2000; rsch. scholar in semiotics, Claremont Grad. Sch., Calif., 1988-89.

HOLM, JEANNE MARJORIE, writer, consultant, government official, former career officer; b. Portland, Oreg., June 23, 1921; d. John E. and Marjorie (Hammond) H. BA, Lewis and Clark Coll., 1956. Commd. 2d lt. U.S. Army, 1943; transferred to USAF, 1948, advanced through grades to maj. gen., 1973; chief manpower and mgmt. Hdqrs. Allied Air Forces So. Europe, Naples, Italy, 1957-61; congl. liaison officer, directorate manpower and orgn. Hdqrs USAF, Washington, 1961-65; dir. Women in the Air Force, 1965-73, Sec. Air Force Pers. Coun., Washington, 1973-75; ret., 1975; cons. Def. Manpower Commn., Washington, 1975, Undersec. Air Force, Washington, 1979-81. Spl. asst. to Pres., 1976-77; advisor United Svcs. Life Ins. Co., Washington; lectr. on manpower and women in mil., Presideo Press, Novato, Calif. Author: Women in the Military: An Unfinished Revolution, 1982, rev. edit., 1992; Editor, co-author: In Defense of a Nation: Servicewomen in World War II, 1997; contbr. Encyclopedia of the American Military, 1994; contbr. articles to profl. jours. Chair adv. com. women vets. VA, Washington, 1986-88; adv. com. USCG Acad., 1983-89; dir. U.S. com. for UN Fund for Women; trustee Air Force Aid Soc., 1988-96, Air Force Hist. Found.; mem. nat. adv. com. Women in Mil. Svc. Meml. Found.; mem. hon. coun. Vietnam Women's Meml. Project. Decorated DSM with oak leaf cluster, Legion of Merit, medal for Human Action (Berlin Airlift), Nat. Def. Svc. medal with bronze star; named Woman of Yr. in Govt. and Diplomacy, Ladies Home Jour., 1975; named to Nat. Women's Hall of Fame, Seneca Falls, N.Y., 2000; recipient Disting. Achievement award, Alumni Assn. Lewis and Clark Coll., Eugene Zuckert Leadership award, Arnold Air Soc., citation of honor, Air Force Assn., Living Legacy award, Women's Internat. Ctr., 1985, Sen. Margaret Chase Smith Leadership awrad, Women in Mil. Svc. Meml. Found., 1998, Internat. Hall of Fame award, Internat. Women's Forum, 1992. Mem.: Exec. Women in Govt. (founder, 1st chair), Ret. Officers Assn., Air Force Assn. (Lifetime Achievement award 2003). Home: 2707 Thyme Dr Edgewater MD 21037-1120

HOLM, JOY ALICE, psychology educator, goldsmith, artist, art educator; b. Chgo., May 21, 1929; d. Alvin Herbert and Willette Eugenia (Miller) Holm. BFA, U. Ill., 1952; MS in Art Edn. Inst. Design, Ill. Inst. Tech., 1956; PhD in Edn., U. Minn., 1967. Tchr. art, Eng. West Chgo. H.S., 1952-54; instr., tchr. art J.S. Morton H.S. & Jr. Coll., Cicero, Ill., 1954-65; asst. prof. art & design Mankato (Minn.) State U., 1965-66; asst. prof. art Ill. State U., Normal, 1966-69; assoc. prof. art & design So. Ill. U., Edwardsville, 1969-71; assoc. prof. art, art edn. Winona (Minn.) State U., 1971-75; assoc. prof., chmn. dept. art St. Mary's Coll. of Notre Dame, Ind., 1975-76; assoc. prof. art & design, secondary, continuing edn. U. Wis., Eau Claire, 1976-78; assoc. prof. art & design Sch. Art & Design Kent (Ohio) State U., 1978-80; lectr. Jungian studies C.G. Jung Inst., Chgo., 1980-82; adj. assoc. prof. art edn. Sch. Art and Design, Sch. Edn. U. Ill., Chgo., 1981-82; lectr. U. Calif. Ext., Santa Cruz, 1983—; adj. prof. art edn., design San Jose (Calif.) State U., 1983-84; owner bus. designer-goldsmith Oak Park, Ill., 1980-82, Carmel, Calif., 1982-87, Atelier XII, Winona, 1988—. Curriculum cons. North Ctrl. Assn. Accreditation Team State of Ill., Edwardsville, 1970; regional cons. Supt. Pub. Instrn., Springfield, Ill., 1970; juror exhbns.; panelist, spkr., presenter confs., meetings. Contbr., cons. Alternative Medicine: A Definitive Guide, 1994; contbg. author: Living Science, 2003; contbr. articles to profl. jours; one-woman shows: J. Sterling Morton H.S. & Jr. Coll., 1963, Russell Art Gallery, Bloomington, 1968, Owatonna (Minn.) Art Ctr., 1980, 86; exhbns. include La Grange (Ill.) Art League (Best of Show, 1st Place award prints), 1963, 64, Minn. Mus. Art, 1974, 75, Craft & Folk Art Mus., L.A., 1978, The Gallery Kent State U., 1978, 79, Saenger Nat. Small Sculpture and Jewelry Exhibit, 1978, Diamonds Internat., N.Y., 1978, Inst. Design Alumni, 1988, Internat. Biographical Ctr. Congress Exhbn., Edinburgh, Scotland, 1994, others. Fellow World Lit. Acad.; mem. AAUP, Nat. Art Edn. Assn. (rep. Wis. Women's Caucus Houston Conf. 1978, higher edn. divsn. 1961—), Am. Assn. Higher Edn., Coll. Art Assn., Soc. N.Am. Goldsmiths, Gemological Inst. Am., C.G. Jung Inst. (Chgo.), Hon. Soc. Illustrators (hon.), Internat. Soc. Study of Subtle Energies and Energy Medicine, Inst. Noetic Scis., Alpha Lambda Delta (hon.), Phi Kappa Phi (hon.). Methodist. Office: Atelier XII PO Box 183 Winona MN 55987-0183

HOLMAN, ILETTA MARCELLA, retired art educator; b. Wolseth, N.D., Jan. 12, 1904; d. George W. Holman and Julia Paulson. BS, U. Minn., 1939, postgrad., 1958; MS, Iowa State U., 1950. Instr. pub. sch., N.D., 1924-42, 1942-50, U. Moorhead, Minn., 1950-55; elem. art cons. Rochester, Minn., 1955-65; instr. Coll., Rochester, 1965-72; ret. Pres. Art Educators, Des Moines, 1947-49; asst., state dir. N.D. Ret. Tchrs., 1982-85. One-woman shows include Galerie internat. n.Y., 1970, Raymond Duncan Gallery, Paris, 1975, Washington, 1976, Chgo., 1978, Detroit, 1980, Boston, 1981. Vol. Commn. on Aging, Minot, N.D., 1980-87, Meals on Wheels, Minot, 1980-85. Mem. Nat. Mus. Women in Art (charter), Art Educators Minn. (com. chmn. 1994-97), Delta Kappa Gamma (com. chmn. 1995-97). Republican. Avocations: visual arts, painting. Home: 3434 Heritage Dr Apt 119 Edina MN 55435-2225

HOLMAN, MAUREEN, lawyer; b. Mpls., Jan. 30, 1952; BA, U. Nebr., 1973; JD, U. N.D., 1983. Bar: N.D. 1983, Minn. 1983. Atty. Serkland Law Firm, Fargo, ND. Mem.: ABA, Order of Coif, State Bar Assn. N.D. (bd. govs. 1995—97, joint task force on family law 1995—, disciplinary bd. Supreme Ct. 1997—), Cass County Bar Assn., Minn. State Bar Assn., Phi Delta Phi, Phi Beta Kappa. Office: Serkland Law Firm PO Box 6017 10 Roberts St Fargo ND 58108-6017

HOLMAN, ROSALIND DENISE, music educator; d. Robert Bruce and Mae Bess Wright; m. Marcel Holman, Dec. 18, 1976; children: Jennifer Leigh, Jessica Elaine. B, U. of Memphis, 1971—75. Band dir./ choral dir. Kirby Mid. Sch., Memphis, 1987—2001; band dir. Bearden Mid. Sch., Knoxville, Tenn., 2001—. Participant Sch. of Promise, Knoxville, Tenn., 2001—03. Mem.: Women Band Directors Internat. (assoc.). Home: 4637 Lonas Dr Knoxville TN 37909 Office: Bearden Middle School 1000 Francis Rd Knoxville TN 37909 Personal E-mail: holmanrosalind@hotmail.com.

HOLMAN-RAO, MARIE, retail executive; Grad., Rutgers U. Various design, fashion & merchandising positions Adrienne Vittadini, Perry Ellis, Macy's; sr. v.p., mgr. gen. merchandise Ann Taylor, 1992—93; v.p. product devel. Banana Republic, 1993—95, exec. v.p., 1995—97, pres., 1997, Limited Design Svcs., 1997—. Office: Limited Brands Inc Three Ltd Pkwy Columbus OH 43230*

HOLM-CIPOLLINI, LORI KATHERINE, gifted and talented educator; b. Belle Fourche, S.D., Sept. 21, 1964; d. Richard Hal Holm and Sand Jewett; m. Joseph George Cipollini, May 9, 1998; children: Scott, Holland, Sarah Jo. BS, Black Hills State U.; MS, Sonoma State U.; 6th year profl. diploma, U. Conn., 2002. Elem. sch. tchr. Venetia (Calif.) Pub. Schs.; talented and gifted tchr. Napa (Calif.) Pub. Schs.; tchr. Wallingford (Conn.) Program for the Artistically Talented; cons. gifted edn., differentiated curriculum, lit. circles; tchr. academically gifted program Cheshire (Conn.) Pub. Schs., Conn. Mailing: 30 Spring St Cheshire CT 06410 2717

HOLMES, ANN HITCHCOCK, journalist; b. El Paso, Apr. 25, 1922; d. Frederick E. and Joy (Crutchfield) H. Student, Whitworth Coll., 1940, So. Coll. Fine Arts, 1944. With Houston Chronicle, 1942—, fine arts editor, 1948-89, critic-at-large, 1989-98. Author: Presence, The Transco Tower, 1985, Joy Unconfined—Robert Joy in Houston: A Portrait of Fifty Years, 1986, Alley Theater: Four Decades in Three Stages, 1986. Mem. Houston Mcpl. Art Commn., 1965-74; mem. fine arts adv. coun. U. Tex., Austin, 1967—; bd. dirs. Rice Design Alliance, Houston, 1988-91, Alliance Francaise, Houston, 1989-93, Bus. Arts Fund, Houston, 1993-96. Recipient Ogden Reid Found. award for study of arts in Europe, 1953; Guggenheim fellow, 1960-61; recipient Ford Found. award, 1965, John G. Flowers award archtl. writing Tex. Soc. Architects, 1972, 74, 77, 80 Mem. Am. Theater Critics Assn. (exec. com. 1975—, co-chmn. 1987-88) Home and Office: 10807 Beinhorn Rd Houston TX 77024-3008 E-mail: annhholmes@aol.com.

HOLMES, ANNA-MARIE, ballerina, ballet mistress; b. Mission City, B.C., Can., Apr. 17, 1942; arrived in U.S., 1981; d. George Henry and Maxine Marie (Botterill) Ellerbeck; m. David Holmes; 1 child, Lian-Marie. Diploma, Royal Conservatory of Music. Lectr. in field. Dancer (ballets) Swan Lake, Cinderella, Romeo and Juliet, Sleeping Beauty, Bayadere, Laurencia, Paquita, Graduation Ball, Les Sylphides, Prince Igor, Giselle, Nutcracker, Firebird, Raymonda, Kirov Ballet, Leningrad, 1963, (films) Tour En L'Air, Ballet Adagio, Don Juan, Chinese Nightingale, numerous appearances on European N.Am. TV, Don Quixote, 1989—; co-dir.: (ballets) Massimo Opera Theatre, 1993; prodr.(film documentation): Kirov Vagonova Tchg. Sys.; choreographer Swan Lake, Tokyo, 1991, Norwegion Nat. Ballet, 1998, Sleeping Beauty Act III, Boston Ballet, 1991, Giselle, 1991, Sleeping Beauty, Boston Ballet, 1993, 1996, Tokyo, 1996, Le Corsaire, Boston Ballet, Am. Ballet Theatre, 1998, Great Performances, 1999, Met. Opera House, N.Y.C., 1999, Don Quixote, Boston Ballet, 2000; co-prodr.: Raymonda Finnish Nat. Ballet, 2003, Premier Am. Ball Theater, 2004; artistic dir. La Bayadere, Flanders-Antwerp Belgium, 2004. Recipient Emmy award, 2000. Office: Carnegie House 100 W 57th St Ste 11-O New York NY 10019 E-mail: Aellerbeck@aol.com.

HOLMES, BARBARAANN KRAJKOSKI, secondary school educator; b. Evansville, Ind., Mar. 21, 1946; d. Frank Joseph and Estella Marie (DeWeese) Krajkoski; m. David Leo Holmes, Aug. 21, 1971; 1 child, Susan Ann Sky. BS, Ind. State U., 1968, MS, 1969, specialist cert., 1976; postgrad., U. Nev., 1976-78. Acad. counselor Ind. State U., 1968-69, halls dir., 1969-73; dir. residence halls U. Utah, 1973-76; sales assoc. Fidelity Realty, Las Vegas, Nev., 1977-82; cert. analyst Nev. Dept. Edn., 1981-82; tchr. Clark County Sch. Dist., 1982-87, computer cons., adminstrv. specialist, instrnl. mgmt. sys., 1987-91, chair computer conf., 1990-92, adminstrv. specialist K-6, 1990-93; dean of student summer sch. site adminstr. Eldorado H.S., 1991-96; asst. prin. Garrett Mid. Sch., Boulder City, Nev., 1997-1999, So. Nev. Vocat. Tech. Ctr. Magnet H.S., 1999—. Mem. leadership design team Clark County Sch. Dist., 1996—98, 2001—. Named Outstanding Sr. Class Woman, Ind. State U., 1969; recipient Dir.'s award U. Utah Residence Halls, 1973, Outstanding Tchr. award, 1984, Dist. Excellence in Edn. award, 1984, 86, 87, 88. Mem. AAUW, Am. Assn. Women Deans, Adminstrs. and Counselors, Am. Pers. and Guidance Assn., Nat. Assn. Sch. Adminstrs. (Clark County sch. adminstrv. sec., 2002—), Clark County Assn. Secondary Sch. Prin. (sec. 2003—), Am. Coll. Pers. Assn., Alumnae Assn. Chi Omega (treas. Terre Haute chpt. 1971-73, pres., bd. officer Las Vegas 1977-81, state rush info. chair, 1997—), Clark County Panhellenic Alumnae Assn. (pres. 1978-79), Computer Using Educators So. Nev. (sec. 1983-86, pres.-elect 1986-87, pres. 1987-88, state chmn. 1988-89, conf. chmn. 1989-92, sec. 1994-96, Hall of Fame 1995), Job.'s Daus. Club (guardian sec. 1995-99, dir. music 1999-2001, Supreme Dep. 2001—), Order Eastern Star (worthy matron 2003—), Phi Delta Kappa (Action award 1990-96, newspaper editor 1992-93). Achievements include developing personal awareness program U. Utah, 1973-76. Home: 1227 Kover Ct Henderson NV 89015-9017 Office: So Nev Vocat Tech Magnet HS 5710 Mountain Vista St Las Vegas NV 89120-2310

HOLMES, CECILE SEARSON, religion editor; b. Columbia, S.C., Jan. 6, 1955; d. James Gadsden and Anne Keene (Searson) Holmes. BA in Journalism magna cum laude, U. S.C., 1977; fellow, U. N.C., 1982; MA in Liberal Studies, U. N.C., Greensboro, 1994. Religion writer Greensboro News and Record, 1984-87, Houston Chronicle, 1987-89, sect. religion editor, 1989-2000; clinical prof. Coll. Journ. and Mass. Commn. U. S.C., Columbia, 2000—. Mem. faculty summer journalism workshop Houston Chronicle, 1988-92; co-dir. minority journalism workshop News and Record, 1988. Author: Witnesses to the Horror: North Carolinians Remember the Holocaust, 1988; contbr. articles, book revs. to profl. jours. Mem. N.C. Episcopal Diocese Hunger Commn., 1980s; vol. Greensboro Urban Ministry, 1983-86; moderator NCCJ Forum, 1985, Ethics of Humane Care, Greensboro, 1986; mentor Edn. for Ministry, Houston, 1989—; advisor United Way Campaign for Homeless, Houston, 1991. Recipient award Piedmont Bapt. Assn., 1984, Community Journalism award N.C. A&T State U., 1984, Pub. Svc. award N.C. Press Assn., 1985, Wilbur award Religious Pub. Rels. Coun., 1986, others. Mem. Soc. Profl. Journalists (chpt. pres. and v.p., coord. registration nat. conv. 1989), Religion Newswriters Assn. (treas. 1990-92, 2d v.p. 1992-94, 1st v.p. 1994-96, pres. 1996—, 2d place award ann. contest 1989, 92, 1st place award religion sect. 1994), Houston Press Club, Beta Sigma Phi (past v.p. Greensboro chpt., Woman of Yr. award), Kappa Tau Alpha, Omicron Delta Kappa. Avocations: gardening, photography, reading, antiques. Office: U SC Coll Journalism & Mass Commn Columbia SC 29208 E-mail: cecile.holmes@usc.jour.sc.edu.

HOLMES, ERLINE MORRISON, retired educational administrator, consultant; b. Newark, Aug. 31, 1922; d. Samuel A. and Levada (Thurman) Morrison; m. William C. Holmes, Aug. 19, 1943 (dec. 1968); 1 child, William C. Jr. BS, Newark State Tchrs. Coll., 1943; MA, Seton Hall U., 1970. Cert. elem. and secondary social studies tchr., prin., sch. adminstr., N.J. Dir. employer women and working teens YWCA, Germantown, Pa., 1943-46; elem. tchr. Orange (N.J.) Bd. Edn., 1950-64; remedial and lang. arts tchr. South Orange (N.J.) Bd. Edn., 1965-66; secondary social studies tchr. Orange H.S., 1966-69, vice prin., 1969-72, prin., 1973-75; asst. supt. Orange Bd. Edn., 1975-90, interim supt., 1990; ret., 1990. Mem. N.J. Study Commn. on Adolescent Edn., 1976-77; cons. Nat. Inst. Edn., Washington, 1982, site evaluator, cons., Paterson and Newark, N.J. Dept. Edn., Trenton, 1990-96; site evaluator N.J. Coun. on Arts, 1993. Pres., bd. dirs. YWCA of Essex and West Hudson, Orange, 1978; pres. N.J. Alliance Black Sch. Educators, 1984-86; treas. Arts Coun. Essex Area, 1986-88; v.p. Family Svc. and Child Guidance Ctr., Orange, 1992-96; Orange Bd. Adjustment, 1986-97, chmn., 1997—. Cited for Outstanding Achievement in Edn., Negro Bus. and Profl. Women, 1979; recipient Cmty. Svc. award United Way of Essex, 1983-84, 84-85. Mem. Nat. Alliance Black Sch. Educators (life), Phi Delta Kappa. Presbyterian. Avocations: bowling, travel, reading, researching family history.

HOLMES, GENTA HAWKINS, former diplomat; b. Anadarko, Okla., Sept. 3, 1940; BA, U. So. Calif., 1962. Jr. officer U.S. Embassy, Abidjan, Ivory Coast, 1964-66; with office spl. assistance to Sec. of State for Refugee Affairs, 1966-68; spl. asst., youth officer U.S. Embassy, Paris, 1968-71; with N.Y. regional office OEO, 1972-73; with office devel. fin., econ. bur. U.S. Dept. State, 1973-74; chief econ. and commercial sect. U.S. Embassy, Bahamas, 1974-77; congl. fellow Am. Polit. Sci. Assn., 1977-78; with bur. congl. rels. U.S. Dept. State, 1978-79; asst. adminstr. legis. affairs AID, 1979-82; mem. 25th Exec. Seminar in Nat. and Internat. Affairs, 1982-83; mem. bd. examiners, 1983-84; dep. chief of mission U.S. Embassy, Lilongwe, Malawi, 1984-86, Port-au-Prince, Haiti, 1986-88, Pretoria, South Africa, 1988-90; U.S. amb. to Namibia, 1990-92; dir. gen. fgn. svc., dir. pers. U.S. Dept. State, Washington, 1992-95; diplomat in residence U. Calif., Davis, 1995-97; U.S. amb. to Australia, 1997—2000.

HOLMES, JEAN LOUISE, real estate investor, Holocaust scholar, educator; b. Butler, Mo., Dec. 9, 1943; d. Victor Julius and Helen Emilia (Knapheide) Witte; m. Eugene Philmore Carter Jr., Aug. 21, 1965 (div. Aug. 1992); children: Kristin, Lance; m. Reed M. Holmes, Jan. 26, 1993. AA, Graceland Coll., Lamoni, Iowa, 1963, BA, Iowa State U., 1965; postgrad., U. Paris, 1965, Tufts U., 1973; MA in Judaic Studies magna cum laude, Hebrew Coll., Brookline, Mass., 1989; postgrad., Ratisbonne Ctr. of Judaic Studies, Jerusalem, 1993-95, Hebrew U./Yad Vashem, 1992, 95, Yad Vashem/Poland, 1998. Lic. bldg. constrn. supr. Mass. Tchr. French, Iowa, Mass., 1966-69; tchg. English lang. and lit., 1966-67; real estate broker Carter Realty, Pepperell, Mass., 1975—; pres., mgr. Viewpax Mondiale, Independence, Mo., 1982—; pres. Keshet Hashalom, Jerusalem, 1989—. Propr., Holmes Mgmt., 1997—; clk. Ctrl. Middlesex Multiple Listing Svc., Concord, Mass., 1980-81, v.p., 1982, pres., 1983; lectr. Remembering for the Future II, Berlin, 1994, Internat. Holocaust Scholars Conf., Mpls., 1996; dir., adj. prof. student intercultural travel to Israel, Jordan, Egypt, Park U., Mo., Graceland U., 1982—. Co-author: The Forerunners, 2003. Adv. bd. Peace Ctr., Independence, 1989-91; interfaith rels. com. Cmty. of Christ, Independence, 2000—; dir. Maine Friendship House, 2003—; exec. com. Nat. Christian Leadership Conf. for Israel, 2001—. Recipient Friendship award Israel Ministry of Tourism, Jerusalem, 1992. Avocations: photography, archaeology, adventure travel, literature. Home: PO Box 680 Pepperell MA 01463-0680 Office: Holmes Mgmt 125 Littleton Rd Apt 9 Ayer MA 01432-1733 Personal E-mail: jeanreed@springmail.com.

HOLMES, JOAN, retired social welfare administrator; b. Jenkins Twp., Pa., Aug. 20, 1936; d. John and Eleanor Markowsky; m. Richard A. Holmes, June 14, 1958; children: Brian, Mark, Glenn, Colleen. BA, Montclair State U., 1958; gerontology cert., Rutgers U., 1994. Nursery sch. tchr. Christ Ch. Nursery Sch., Short Hills, NJ, 1971—78; tchr. Nature Discovery program Cora Hartshorn Arboretum, Short Hills, 1971—85, adult program dir., 1985—95; tchr. enrichment program Millburn-Short Hills Schs., Millburn Twp., 1980—85; asst. dir., Short Hills chpt. ARC, Millburn Twp., 1980—84; office mgr. Tanguay Assocs., Inc., Millburn, 1984—87; sr. citizen coord. Millburn Twp. Sr. Hotline Newsletter, 1988—95; dir. Sr. Ctr., Madison, NJ, 1995—2003; sr. citizen coord. Madison (N.J.) Borough, 1995—2003, ret. sr. ctr., 2003—. Editor: Sr. Prime Times, Madison Borough. Trustee New Eyes for the Needy, Short Hills, 1990-97; mem. adv. bd. Seton Hall U. Gerontology com., South Orange, N.J., 1988-95, St. Barnabas Hosp. Sr. Health, West Orange, 1988—, Essex County Coun. on Aging, East Orange, 1990-95; mem. gov.'s task force White House Conf. on Aging, Trenton, 1994; mem. Gov.'s Conf. on Aging, Trenton, 1994. Mem. Am. Soc. on Aging, Nat. Coun. on the Aging, Nat. Inst. of Sr. Ctrs., N.J. Assn. of Sr. Ctrs., N.J. Soc. on Aging. Republican. Roman Catholic. Avocations: book discussion, cooking, gardening, music.

HOLMES, KATHERINE NOELLE (KATIE HOLMES), actor; b. Toledo, Ohio, Dec. 18, 1978; d. Martin and Kathy Holmes. Actress, 1997—. Actor: (films) The Ice Storm, 1997, Disturbing Behavior, 1998, Go!, 1999, Teaching Mrs. Tingle, 1999, Wonder Boys, 2000, The Gift, 2000, Phone Booth, 2002, Abandon, 2002, The Singing Detective, 2003, Pieces of April, 2003; (TV series) Dawson's Creek, 1998—2003. Office: c/o BWR Pub Rels 9100 Wilshire Blvd West Tower 6th Fl Beverly Hills CA 90210

HOLMES, KATIE See HOLMES, KATHERINE

HOLMES, LOIS REHDER, composer, piano and voice educator; b. Canton, Ill., Jan. 8, 1927; d. John and Elizabeth Mary Grace (Staton) Kleinsteiber; div.; 1 child, Jessica Regina. BA in Sociology, Ill. Wesleyan U., 1949, MusB in Voice, Organ & Piano, 1950; MS in Reading, Western Ill. U., 1981. Cert. tchr., Ill. Libr. worker Withers Pub. Libr., Bloomington, Ill., 1950-51; music tchr. Toledo (Ill.) Schs., 1951-52; music and art librarian Hutchinson (Kans) Pub. Libr., 1952-53; pvt. practice piano & voice tchr. various cities, Ill., 1955—. Tchr. 1st & 2d grades South Fulton Sch., Havana, Ill., 1972-81. Composer: Musical Notions, 1991, Seascape, 1993, Divertimento, 1995, Bittersweet, 1996, Buglers at Sunrise, 1997, Dream Catcher, 1998, Fourteen New Christmas Carols for the 21st Century, 1999, The Abandoned Lighthouse, 2001, Do Daisies Dream, 2003, Petals On the Pond, 2003, Dragon Mist, 2003, Giselle, The Gypsy, 2003, others. Organist/choir dir. Ctrl. Christian Ch., Havana, 1974-79; vol. March of Dimes, Chgo., 1997—, Amnesty Internat. USA, Chgo., 1993—. Mem. Nat. Guild Piano Tchrs. (adjudicator internat. piano composition contest 1996—), Phi Kappa Phi. Home: 321 Mary Alice Rd Rantoul IL 61866-2832

HOLMES, MARY ANNE, geologist, research scientist; b. Atlanta, Ga., Mar. 12, 1954; d. Edward Gerald and Doris Dutel Holmes; m. David Kibler Watkins, Dec. 29, 1981. AA, Oxford Coll. of Emory Univ., Oxford, Ga., 1974; BS, Va. Polytechnic Inst. & State Univ., Blacksburg, Va., 1976, MS, 1978; PhD, Fla. State Univ., Tallahassee, Fla., 1989. Cert. Profl. geologist 2000. Rsch. asst. prof. Geosciences Dept., U. of Nebr.-Lincoln, Lincoln, Nebr., 1996—2002; rsch. assoc. prof. Geosciences Dept., U. of Neb.-Lincoln, Lincoln, Nebr., 2002—. Author: (manual) Phys. Geology Lab. Manual. Named Disting. Lectr., Joint Oceanog. Instn., 1995—96; recipient ADVANCE: Overcoming Barriers to Women Geoscientists' Success in Academia, Nat. Sci. Found., 2001—03. Mem.: Am. Assn. of Univ. Women (AAUW), Assn. for Women in Sci. (AWIS), Assn. for Women Geoscientists (pres. 2000—01). Office: Univ of Nebraska Lincoln 214 Bessey Hall Geosciences Dept Lincoln NE 68588-0340

HOLMES, MIRIAM H. publisher; b. Bavaria, Germany, June 2, 1951; came to U.S., 1952; d. Max J. and Mala (Rosenwasser) H.; m. Stephen H. Gelb, June 25, 1995. BA, Queens Coll., 1972; JD, Yeshiva U., 1987. Bar: N.Y. 1988. Pres. Holmes & Meier Pub., N.Y.C., 1990—. Mem. Assn. Jewish Book Coun. (exec. com.), Pubs. Mktg. Assn. Office: East Bldg 160 Broadway New York NY 10038-4201

HOLMES, NANCY ELIZABETH, pediatrician; b. St. Louis, Aug. 3, 1950; d. David Reed and Phyllis Anne (Hunger) Holmes; m. Arthur Erwin Kramer, May 15, 1976; children: Melanie Elizabeth Kramer, Carl Edward Kramer. BA in Psychology, U. Kans., 1972; MD, U. Mo., 1976. Diplomate Am. Acad. Pediatrics. Intern., resident in pediatrics St. Louis Children's Hosp., Washington U., St. Louis, 1976-81; pediatrician Ctrl. Pediatrics, St. Louis, 1981—. Sch. physician Sch. Dist. Clayton, Mo., 1985—92; assoc. prof. clin. pediats. Washington U., St. Louis, 1993—2000, assoc. prof., 2000—; cons. 1st Congregational Preschool, Clayton, 1984—86, Jewish Hosp. Daycare Ctr., St. Louis, 1993—97, Flynn Park EArly Edn. Ctr., University City, Mo., 1994—; cmty. outpatient experience Preceptor Hosp., St. Louis Children's Hosp., 1991—93, 1994—; mem. med. exec. com. St. Louis Children's Hosp., 1992—94. Vol. reading tutor Flynn Park Sch., University City, 1992—98, cub scout leader, 1993—98; mem. com. Troop 493 Boy Scouts Am., 2000—; elder Trinity Presbyn. Ch., University City, 1989—92, 1996—2001, bd. dirs. Children's Hosp Care Group. Fellow Am. Acad. Pediatrics; mem. AMA, Mo. State Med. Assn., St. Louis Metro. Med. Soc, St. Louis Pediatric Soc. Presbyterian. Avocations: reading, gardening, photography, travel. Office: Ctrl Pediatrics Inc 8888 Ladue Rd Ste 130 Saint Louis MO 63124-2056 Office Phone: 314-862-4002.

HOLMES, RACHEL ELLEN FLYNN, sculptor; b. Patomic River, Md., May 24, 1968; d. Richard E. Flynn and Diana Reynolds; m. Bryan K. Holmes, May 26, 1989. AA, Fla. Jr. Coll., 1996; postgrad., U. Fla., 1996—. Pres. Mastercrft Carpentry Contractors, Inc., 1999—; exec. officer, owner Holmes Constrn., LLC; gen. contractor. Exhibited in group shows Alexander Breast Gallery, Jacksonville, Fla., 1995, Beaches Fine Art Guild and Gallery, 1996, South Bank Gallery. Vol. adult studies Jacksonvile Literacy Coalition, Inc., 1996. Home: 2087 Cortez Rd Jacksonville FL 32246-0702

HOLMES, SANDRA, insurance underwriter; b. Boston, May 1, 1957; d. Edward and Ruth Ada (Hedman) H. Cert. ins. counselor Soc. Cert. Ins. Counselors, Profl. Ins. Woman. Workers comp. underwriter Indsl. Indemnity, Anchorage, 1976-77; acct. exec. asst. Alexander & Alexander, Anchorage, 1977-79; rating dept. supr. Providence Washington, Anchorage, 1979-81; acct. exec. asst. Erickson Ins., Anchorage, 1981-83; underwriting dept. supr. Alaska Nat. Ins., Anchorage, 1983-85; prodn. underwriter Cigna Ins. Co., Anchorage, 1985-92; sr. comml. underwriter Umialik Ins. Co., Anchorage, 1992—. Mem. Alaska Classification and Rating Com., Anchorage, 1994-96 Mem. edn. team Partnership Coun. on Safety, Anchorage, 1996-97; mem. Alaska Women's Resource Ctr., Amvets Aux., Anchorage; vol. Kids Voting, Anchorage, fire safety booth Alaska State Fair, 1997. Mem. Nat. Assn. Ins. Women (region IX Ins. Mem. of Yr. 1999, Communicate with Confidence 1st Runner Up 1999), Ins. Assn. Alaska, Soc. Cert. Ins. Counselors, Ins. Women Anchorage (Insurance Woman of Yr. 1998, past pres.). Avocations: advocate for women's rights, writing, reading, researching family history. Office: Umialik Insurance 1901 S Bragaw St #100 Anchorage AK 99508-3440

HOLMES, SHERIE BELL SHORTRIDGE, lawyer; b. Detroit, Mar. 27, 1956; d. Milton Harold and June Marie (Demarse) Bell; m. Wayne Hall Shortridge, Apr. 17, 1986 (div. 1992); 1 child, Kelly Campbell Shortridge; m. Barry T. Holmes, Mar. 27, 1992. BA, Emory U., 1976, JD, 1980. Bar: Ga. 1980, U.S. Dist. Ct. (no. dist.) Ga. 1981, U.S. Ct. Appeals (11th cir.) 1982. Assoc. Swift, Currie, McGhee & Hiers, Atlanta, 1980-83, Powell, Goldstein, Frazer & Murphy, Atlanta, 1984-1990, Jones, Day, Reavis & Pogue, Atlanta, 1994-96; of counsel Long, Aldridge & Norman LLP, Atlanta, 1996-98; ptnr. Holland & Knight LLP, Atlanta, 1998—. Mem. adj. faculty Nat. Ctr. Paralegal Tng., Atlanta, 1984. Bd. dirs. Southeastern Savoyards Light Opera Co., Atlanta, 1990-95, chmn. bd. dirs., 1993-94. Mem. ABA, Atlanta Bar Assn., Jr. League Atlanta, English Speaking Union, Consular Corps Women's Assn., Brit-Am. Bus. Group (bd. dirs., sec. to bd. dirs.). Presbyterian. Avocations: reading, charitable fundraising, music, piano, decorative arts. Home: 1707 W Wesley Rd NW Atlanta GA 30327-1909 Office: 2000 One Atlantic Ctr 1201 W Peachtree St NW Atlanta GA 30309-3449 E-mail: ssholmes@hklaw.com.

HOLMES, SUSAN G. music educator; b. Kansas City, Mo., Mar. 7, 1955; d. Burton E. and Gloria A. (Spencer) H. BA, U. Kans., Lawrence, 1980. Cert. music therapy, education. Tchr. Dade County Schs., Miami, Fla.; music therapist, tchr. ESOL Miami, Fla.; tchr., music therapist The Palace Retirement Cmty.; tchr. ESOL Miami-Palmetto (Fla.) Adult Edn. Ctr., Korean cmty., Miami, Fla.; instr. GED writing lab. Miami Dade C.C., Miami, Fla. Tchr. ESOL to newly-arrived immigrants. Recipient Honor for TV series CBS News. Mem. Nat. Orgn. for Exec. Women. Avocations: writing, music composition.

HOLMES, SUZANNE MCRAE, nursing supervisor; b. Birmingham, Ala., June 23, 1952; d. Paul Bickman and Mabel E. (Tyler) McRae; m. Bryan Thomas Holmes, Jan. 14, 1989; 1 child, Meredith Rae. ADN, Jefferson State Coll., Birmingham, 1988. RN, Ala.; cert. BCLS instr.; cert. asthma educator, Am. Lung Assn.; ACLS. Staff nurse burn unit The Children's Hosp., Birmingham, 1988-89; staff nurse dept. medicine The Kirklin Clinic at U. Ala.-Birmingham, 1989-90, head nurse gen. medicine clinic, 1990-91, head nurse allergy clinic, 1991—. Facilitator and spkr. on nursing at asthma workshops Aventis Pharms., Collegeville, Pa., 1994—; mem. faculty Genecom, N.Y.C., 1994—; operator 1-800 Allergy Info. Svc., 1991—92. Editor Allergy Update, 1991-92. Leader Girl Scouts Am. Mem. Am. Coll. Allergy and Immunology, Am. Acad. Allergy, Asthma and Immunology,mem. Am. Lung Assn. (cert. asthma educator), Asthma and Allergy Found. Am. (charter bd. dirs. Ala. chpt.), Assn. Asthma Educators. Methodist. Avocations: baking, sewing, gardening. Office: The Kirklin Clinic Allergy Clinic 4th Fl 2000 6th Ave S Birmingham AL 35233-2110

HOLMES, WILHELMINA KENT, community health nurse; b. Hamburg, N.J., Nov. 26, 1920; d. Harry Vanderhoof and Alison St. Clair (McDole) Kent; m. George Frederick Holmes Jr., Oct. 27, 1946 (dec. 1971); 1 child, Frederick Andrew. RN, Jersey City Med. Ctr., 1942; BSN, Seton Hall U., South Orange, N.J., 1953; cert., Bridgewater State Coll., 1961, Fitchburg State Coll., 1962; postgrad., Russell Sage Coll., Troy, N.Y., 1981-82. Sch. nurse, maternal child health nurse N.J. State Health Dept., Sussex County, N.J., 1947-53; acctg. asst. Bennington (Vt.) Coll., 1982-83; infirmary nurse Berkshire Farm Ctr. and Svcs. for Youth, Canaan, N.Y., 1982-86; emergency call nurse Blair Acad., Blairstown, N.J., 1989-94, clin. nurse, night nurse, 1994. Contbr. articles to profl. jours. Mem. Berkshire Farm Ctr. and Svcs. for Youth, Canaan. Mem. Jersey City Alumni Assn.

HOLMGREN, JANET L., college president; b. Chgo., Dec. 1, 1948; d. Kenneth William and Virginia Ann (Renshik) H.; m. Gordon A. McKay, Sept. 7, 1968 (div. 1990); children: Elizabeth Jane, Ellen Katherine. BA in English summa cum laude, Oakland U., Rochester, Mich., 1968; MA in Linguistics, Princeton U., 1971, PhD in Linguistics, 1974. Asst. prof. English studies Federal City Coll. (now U. D.C.), Washington, 1972-76; asst. prof. English U. Md., College Park, 1976-82, asst. to chancellor, 1982-88; assoc. provost Princeton (N.J.) U., 1988-90, vice-provost, 1990-91; pres. Mills Coll., Oakland, Calif., 1991—. Mem. external adv. bd. English dept. Princeton U. Bay Area Biosci. Ctr. Author: (with Spencer Cosmos) The Story of English: Study Guide and Reader, 1986, Narration and Discourse in American Realistic Fiction, 1982; contbr. articles to profl. jours. Faculty rsch. grantee U. Md., 1978; fellow NEH, 1978, Princeton U., 1968-69, 70-72, NSF, 1969-70; recipient summer study aid Linguistic Soc. Am., Ohio State U., 1970. Mem. Assn. Ind. Caif. Colls. and Univs. (exec. com.), Nat. Assn. Ind. Colls. and Univs., Am. Coun. on Education (chair office of women in higher edn.), Calif. Acad. Sci. (coun.). Democrat. Episcopal. Avocations: traveling, swimming, reading. Office: Mills Coll Office Pres 5000 Macarthur Blvd Oakland CA 94613-1301

HOLO, SELMA REUBEN, museum director, educator; b. Chgo., May 21, 1943; d. Samuel and Ghita (Hurwitz) Reuben; children from previous marriage: Robert, Joshua; m. Fred Croton, June 18, 1989. BA, Northwestern U., 1965; MA, Hunter Coll., 1972; PhD, U. Calif., Santa Barbara, 1980; postgrad., Mus. Mgmt. Inst., 1985. Lectr. Art Ctr. Coll. of Design, Pasadena, Calif., 1973-77; curator of acquisitions Norton Simon Mus., Pasadena, 1977-81; dir. Fisher Gallery and mus. MA art history/mus. studies program U. So. Calif., L.A., 1981—. Guest curator, cons. Getty Mus., Malibu, Calif., 1975-76, 81; guest curator Isetan Mus., Tokyo, 1982, cons. Nat. Mus. for Women in Arts, Washington, 1984; reviewer grants Inst. Mus. Svcs., Washington, 1986-87, Getty Grant Program, 1988-90; panel chmn. Internat. Com. on Exhbn. Exch., Washington, 1984; panelist NEA, Washington, 1985, 91-93, Idaho Commn. on the Arts; admission panel mem. Mus. Mgmt. Inst., 1990; hon. curator Tokyo Fuji Mus.; lectr. museology IVAM, Valencia, Spain, 1994, Complutense U. Masters in Museology, 1994, U. Castilla La Mancha in Museology, 1995; presenter Museo/Mus. Conf., Barcelona, Spain, 1996, Bilbao (Spain) Mus. Fine Arts Conf. on Mus. Edn., 1996; co-author survey com. mus. studies programs, 1986. Author: (catalogues) Goya: Los Disparates, 1976, Beyond the Prado: Musems & Identity in Democratic Sapin, 1999; co-author: La Tauromaquia: Goya, Picasso and the Bullfight, 1986; editor: Keepers of the Flame, The Unofficial Artists of Leningrad, 1990; guest editor New Observations, 1990; contbr. articles to profl. jours. and mag. Fellow La Napoule Art Found., 1988, Fulbright Found., 1994; Kress Found. grantee, N.Y., 1979, Internationes Fed. Republic of Germany grantee, 1985, 92; recipient Fuj Fine Art award, 1990, Sr. Rsch. Fulbright fellowship to Spain, 1994, award from program for cooperation between the program for the Ministry of Culture of Spain and N.Am. Univ. Mem. Am. Assn. Mus., Art Table. Office: U So Calif Fisher Gallery 823 Exposition Blvd Los Angeles CA 90089-0001

HOLONITCH, ROXANNE MICHELLE, art educator; b. Ravenna, Ohio, Dec. 12, 1974; d. Gary Eugene Paugh and Vickie Lynn paugh; m. Paul Joseph Holonitch, Mar. 30, 2002. BFA in illustration, Columbus Coll. Art and Design, 1997; MusM in edn. leadership, U. Dayton, 2001. Cert. tchg. Ohio Dominican U., 2000. Web designer Antique Networking, Columbus, Ohio, 1997—98; lib. asst. Columbus (Ohio) Metro. Lib., 1998—2000; art tchr. St. Joseph Montessori, Columbus, 2000—. Web site mgr., 2000. Recipient Nat. Collegiate Edn. award, 2000; scholar All-Am. award, 2000. Democrat. Meth. Avocation: acrylic painting. Office: St Joseph Montessori Sch 933 Hamlet St Columbus OH 43201 E-mail: rholonit@cdeducation.org.

HOLSAPPLE, LINDA HARRIS, retired editor; b. New Rochelle, N.Y., Nov. 20, 1948; d. Herbert Barney and Elizabeth (Curren) Harris; m. Earle Taylor Holsapple III; children: Elizabeth, John. BS in Intermediate Edn., Loyola Rome Ctr., Rome, 1970, Loyola U., 1971; MA in Higher Edn. Adminstrn., Cath. U., 1973; postgrad., U. Va., 1975; diploma di Merito in Italiano, 2000; postgrad., Scola Leonardo Da Vinci, Rome, 2002. Classroom tchr., admissions counselor various colls., 1971-78; mktg., comm. specialist, editor Rutgers Cmty. Health Plan, New Brunswick, NJ, 1978-85; dir. bus. devel. SciTech Devel., Detroit, 2002—; ret. Dir. bus. devel. SciTech, LLC, Detroit, 2002. Editor Rutgers Cmty. Health Plan Member News, 1979-85. Leader, cons. Warren (N.J.) Girl Scouts, 1987-96; leader Warren Cub Scouts, 1993-97. Leonardo DaVinci scholar, Rome, 2002. Mem. PTO (chair nomination com.). Avocations: nature hiking, italian. Home: 281 Kercheval Ave Grosse Pointe Farms MI 48236-3105

HOLSINGER, ADENA SEGUINE, music educator, community volunteer; b. Fostoria, Ohio, Aug. 8, 1926; d. Richard and Della Mable (Fry) Seguine; m. John Calvin Holsinger; 1 child, Coradella Elizabeth. BS in Edn., Ind. Wesleyan U., 1948. Cert. tchr., Ohio. Tchr. Canyonville (Oreg.) Christian Acad., 1948-50; music tchr. Ctrl. Bible Coll., Springfield, Mo., 1951—55, 1976—77; tchr. Bowling Green (Ohio) H.S., 1956-58; pvt. practice Costa Mesa, Calif., 1961—71, Springfield, Mo., 1971—. Pres., treas. Evangl. U. Aux., Springfield, 1984—. Mem.: DAR (vice regent 1994—96, regent 2001—02), Springfield Area Music Tchrs. Assn. (treas.), Springfield Piano Tchrs. Forum (pres. 1989, sec. 1999), Nat. Fedn. Music Clubs (dist. coord. 1989—91), Mo. Fedn. Music Clubs (state treas. 1980—87, state sec. 1987—89, regional v.p. 1991—99), Springfield Christian Women's Club (project advisor 1996—, treas.). Republican.

HOLST, RUTH MARY, medical librarian; b. Fond du Lac, Wis., Sept. 22, 1947; d. Delmar and Marie (Daun) H.; m. Robert Peter Thiel, May 7, 1977; 1 child, Alexandra. BS, U. Wis., 1970, MS, 1973. Med. libr. Columbia Hosp., Milw., 1970-82, dir. libr. svcs., 1983—2002; assoc. dir. nat. network libr. medicine U. Ill., Chgo., 2002—. Adj. asst. prof. U. Wis. Milw. Sch. Libr. and Info. Sci., 1981-90; dir. women's health Columbia Hosp., 1988-91, mgr. coordinated care, 1994-98; biomed. libr. rev. com. Nat. Libr. Medicine, Bethesda, Md., 1996-2000. Editor: Hospital Library Managament, 1983; mem. libr. adv. bd. New Eng. Jour. Medicine; contbr. articles to profl. jours. Bd. dirs. Friends of Golda Meir Libr., Milw., 1985-89. Grantee Nat. Libr. Medicine, 1990. Fellow Med. Libr. Assn. (bd. dirs. 2001—, sec., 2002—, editor The Med. Libr. Assn. Guide to Managing Health Care Librs. 2000); mem. Coun. Wis. Librs. (bd. dirs. 1993-97), Spl. Librs. Assn., Columbia History of Medicine Club (sec.), Acad. Health Info. Profls., Milw. Acad. Medicine. Avocations: reading, cooking, singing. Office: Univ Ill at Chgo Libr Health Scis 1750 W Polk St Chicago IL 60612

HOLT, BERTHA MERRILL, state legislator; b. Eufaula, Ala., Aug. 16, 1916; d. William Hoadley and Bertha Harden (Moore) Merrill; m. Winfield Clary Holt, Mar. 14, 1942; children: Harriet Wharton Holt Whitley, William Merrill, Winfield Jefferson. AB, Agnes Scott Coll., 1938; postgrad., U. N.C. Law Sch., 1939-40; LLB, U. Ala., 1941; grad., Sch. Creative Leadership, Greensboro, N.C., 1992. Bar: Ala. 1941. With Treasury Dept., Washington, 1941-42, Dept. Interior, Washington, 1942-43. Mem. N.C. Ho. of Reps. from 22d Dist., 1975-80, 25th Dist., 1980-94, chmn. select com. govtl. ethics, 1979-80, chmn. constl. amendments com., 1981, 83, mem. joint commn. govtl. ops., 1982-88, chmn. appropriation com. justice and pub. safety, 1985-88, co-chair House appropriation sub-com. transp., 1991-92, co-chair appropriation sub-com. Justice and Pub. Safety, 1993-94, Pres., Democratic Women of Alamance, 1962, chmn. hdqrs., 1964, 68; mem. N.C. Dem. Exec. Com., 1964-75, 95—; pres. Episcopal Ch. Women, 1968; mem. coun. N.C. Episcopal Diocese, 1972-74, 84-87, 95-98; chmn. budget com. 1987; chmn. fin. dept., 1973-75, parish grant com., 1973-80, mem. standing com., 1975-78; mem. Episcopal Diocese Ecclesiastical Ct., 1998—; chmn. Alamance County Social Svcs. Bd., 1970; mem. N.C. Bd. Sci. and Tech., 1979-83; chair Legis. Women's Caucus, 1991-94; past bd. dirs. Hospice N.C.; bd. dirs. State Coun. Social Legis., pres. SCSL 1996-97, State Conf. Social Work, N.C. Epilepsy Assn., N.C. Pub. Sch. Forum, 1989, U. N.C. Sch. Pub. Health Adv. Bd., Salvation Army Alamance County, N.C., Nursing Found., 1989, Epilepsy Found., 1989; bd. Alternatives for Status Offenders Burlington, N.C., Sch. Pub. Health Adv. Bd.; bd. dirs. N.C. ACLU, Partnership For Children (N.C.), 1993-98. Recipient Outstanding Alumna award Agnes Scott Coll., 1978, Legis. award for svc. to elderly Non-Profit Rest Home Assn., 1985, health, 1986, ARC, 1987, Faith Active in Pub. Affairs award N.C. Coun. of Chs., 1987, Ellen B. Winston award State Coun. For Social Legis., 1989, N.C. Disting. Women's award in gov., 1991, Disting. Svc. award Alamance County, 1992, Chi Omega award Women in Leadership, 1st ann. Hallie Ruth Allen Dem. Women award Alamance County, 1992, Disting. Svc. award Chi Omega, 1996, Svc. award Triennial Conv., Episcopal Ch. Women of U.S., 1997, Outstanding Alumna award U. N.C.-Chapel Hill, 1998, Gwyneth B. Davis award N.C. Assn. Women Attys., 1998, Outstanding Svc. award N.C. Assn. Women Attys., 1998, Disting. Alumna award U. N.C.-Chapel Hill, 1999, numerous others; named One of 5 Distinguished Women of N.C. (Govt.), 1991; award established Bertha B. Holt award, NC Bar Juvenile Justice Sect., first recepient, 2004; AAUW award for Edu. and Equity for Women and Girls, 2004. Mem. AAUW, NOW, N.C. Women's Forums, Law Alumni Assn. U. N.C. Chapel Hill (bd. dirs. 1978-81, 1994-99), N.C. Bar Assn. (bd. dirs. sr. lawyers sect., conditional rights sect. 1998-2004, juvenile justice and children's rights 1999-, chair 2002-03), English Speaking Union, N.C. Hist. Soc., Soc. Wine Educators, Les Amis du Vin, Pi Beta Phi, Phi Kappa Gamma, Delta Kappa Gamma, Phi Theta Kappa, Century Club. Address: PO Box 1111 Burlington NC 27216-1111 E-mail: bholt@netpath.net.

HOLT, FRIEDA M. nursing educator, former academic director; BSN with honors, U. Colo., Boulder, 1956; MS in Cmty. Health Nursing, Boston U., 1969, EdD, 1973. RN, Ariz., Calif., Colo., Mass., Md., Pa., Wash., Liberia, W. Africa. Instr., dir. of nursing Cuttington Coll., Liberia, Africa, 1964-67; teaching fellow sch. of nursing Boston U., 1969, asst. prof. sch. of nursing, 1969-74; assoc. prof., assoc. dean for grad. studies sch. of nursing U. Md., 1975-77, dean's dep. sch. of nursing, 1975-86, prof., assoc. dean for grad. studies sch. of nursing, 1977-86, acting dean sch. of nursing, 1978, acting asst. dean sch. of nursing, 1981-82, acting chmn. sch. of nursing, 1983-84, acting dean sch. of nursing, 1986-87, prof., assoc. dean for grad. studies, dean's dep. sch. of nursing, 1987-88, prof., exec. assoc. dean. sch of nursing, 1988-89, acting dean, prof. sch. of nursing, 1989-90, prof. sch. of nursing, 1990-91, dir. sch. of nursing, 1992-94, prof. sch. of nursing, 1994—. Project dir. Primary Care Adult Nurse Practitioner Leadership grant, 1976-82, Preparation for Tchrs. in Maternal Child Nursing, judge U. Md. grad. sch. rsch. awards, 1979-84; NLN vis. for Accreditation of Baccalaureate and Masters Nursing Program, SREB/SCCEN Task Force on Grad. Edn., presenter seminars, confs., workshop. Contbr. articles to profl. jours. Bd. dirs. Md. Nurses Found. (v.p., 1988—). Recipient VA Commendation award, 1990, Charter Trustee award Found. for Nursing of Md., 1990, Martin Luther King, Jr. Humanitarian award, 1990. Mem. ANA, ANA (coun. nurse rschrs.), APHA, AAUP, Nat. League for Nursing, Am. Edn. Rsch. Assn., Am. Edn. Rsch. Assn., Md. Assn. for Higher Edn., Soc. for Rsch. in Nursing Edn., Sigma Theta Tau. Home: 328-B Sellers Ln RD 1 Port Matilda PA 16870 Office: Pa State Univ 303A Health And Human Dev E University Park PA 16802-6509

HOLT, ISABEL RAE, radio program producer; b. Vineland, N.J., Oct. 5, 1946; d. Frederick Rae and Isabella A. (Foley) Steinborn; m. Robert Eugene Darby, Aug. 13, 1977 (div. 1999); children: Rachel Elisabeth Darby, Nora Odette Darby. BA in Primary Edn., Rowan U (formerly Glassboro State Coll.), 1968; postgrad., Pierce Coll., 1991-93. Dir., coord. Washington Area Free U., 1972-74; prodr. music program Sta. WGTB Georgetown U., Washington, 1972-74; prodr. music program Sta. WMGM, Atlantic City, N.J., 1974, Sta. KJAZ, Alameda, Calif., 1974-76, Sta. KPFA, Berkeley, Calif., 1974-76, Sta. KCRW, Santa Monica, Calif., 1977-88, Sta. KPCC, Pasadena, Calif., 1989-93. Concert prodr.; interviewer radio programs, 1980-95; prodr. tapes for dressage/equestrian free-style riders, 1994—, riding instr., trainer, 1999—; instr. Spl. Olympics, Boise, 1999. Mem. ACLU, Amnesty Internat., Childreach, Sierra Club. Democrat. Roman Catholic. Office: 1519 N 23rd St Boise ID 83702-0409

HOLT, KAREN ANITA YOUNG, English educator; b. Waltham, Mass., Oct. 23, 1949; d. Rexford Vernon and Linia Virginia (Duke) Young; m. Robert Jackson Holt, Dec. 30, 1974 (div. Sept. 1984). BA in English and French, Southwestern Okla. State U., 1971; MA in English, Okla. State U., 1973, postgrad., 1973-77, 86, Cen. State U., 1986. Cert. tchr., Okla. Instr. Okla. State U. Tech. Br., Oklahoma City, 1977-87; arts in edn. coord. Putnam City Schs., Oklahoma City, 1985-87; prof. Rose State Coll., Midwest City, Okla., 1987—. Dir. Righting Writing, Midwest City, 1989-91; coord. Poetry at Rose, Midwest City, 1988—, Students' Poetry, 1992—; chairperson long-range planning Cross Timbers Arts and Humanities Coun., Midwest City, 1990-91; cons. Excellence in the Arts project Kennedy Found. Sch. Bd., 1988, Okla. Writing Project, 1995. Editor: Chapbook, 1971; contbr. poetry to various publs.; poet An Evening with Oklahoma Poets, U. Okla., 1991, City Arts Conversations with the Book, 1997. Charter mem. Carpenter Sq. Theatre Vols., Oklahoma City, 1986—; mem. Rose State Coll. Speakers' Bur., Midwest City, 1990—, senator humanities divsn. faculty, 1991-94, faculty senate treas., 1993-94. Recipient honorable mention poetry award Red Dirt Press, 1988, Outstanding Prof. of Yr. award Phi Theta Kappa, 1993, keynote spkr., 1997; Adult Inst. for Arts scholar Okla. Arts Inst., 1990-92, Regents scholar, 1992-94; Project AIM grantee Nat. Endowment for Arts, 1986-87. Mem. Okla. Alliance for Arts Edn., Okla. Assn. Cmty. and Jr. Colls. (English chairperson 1989-90), Okla. Coun. Tchrs. of English, Rose State Coll. Faculty Assn., Rose State Coll. Founders Club, Okla. Arts Inst. Alumni Assn. Republican. Methodist. Avocations: reading, dance, film history, photography, flute. Home: 5800 NW 62nd St Oklahoma City OK 73122-7346 Office: Rose State Coll 6420 SE 15th St Oklahoma City OK 73110-2704

HOLT, LESLIE EDMONDS, librarian; b. Mpls. d. Peter Robert and Elizabeth Knox (Donovan) Edmonds; m. Glen Edward Holt, Jan. 29, 1994. BA, Cornell Coll., 1971; MA, U. Chgo., 1975; PhD, Loyola U., Chgo., 1984. Asst. children's libr. Indian Trails Libr. Dist., Wheeling, Ill., 1972-73; libr. Erikson Inst. for Early Edn., Chgo., 1973-75; youth svcs. libr. Rolling Meadows (Ill.) Libr., 1975-82; libr. multicultural head start resource ctr. Chgo. Pub. Libr., 1982-84; asst. prof. grad. sch. libr. and info. sci. U. Ill., Urbana, 1984-90, assoc. dean, 1988-89; dir. youth svcs. and family literacy St. Louis Pub. Libr., 1990—. Pre-sch. advisor Rolling Meadows (Ill.) Park Dist., 1978-85; cons. to reading program The Latin Sch., Chgo., 1980-82; vis. lectr. Loyola U. of Chgo., 1980-84, U. Ill. Extension, Belleville, 1992; product mgr. Mister Anderson's Co., McHenry, Ill., 1981-84; instr. Nat. Coll. Edn., Evanston, Ill., 1982-84, Webster U., Webster Groves, Mo., 1991; cons. for libr. devel. Ill. Math. and Sci. Acad., Aurora, Ill., 1986-90; peer reviewer, advisor U.S. Dept. Edn. Office Edn. Rsch. and Improvement, 1987-89; libr. cons. Reading Rainbow Resources Guide, Sta. WNET-TV, N.Y.C., 1987, 88; adj. instr. U. Mo., Columbia, 1991, 92, 93; literary advisor Grace Hill Neighborhood Svcs., 1991-95; cons. Paschen-Tishman-Jahn, 1988; presenter in field. Author: An Investigation of the Effectiveness of an On-Line Catalog in Providing Bibliographic Acccess to Children in a Public Library Setting, 1989, Family Literacy Programs in Public Libraries, 1990; contbr. articles to profl. jours. Mem. Success by Six Com., United Way of Met. St. Louis, 1993—. Grantee in field. Mem. ALA (mem. Carroll Preston Baber award jury 1992-94, World Book award 1986), Nat. Assn. Edn. Young Children, Internat. Reading Assn., Mo. Libr. Assn. (mem. summer reading program com. 1991, mem. Mark Twain award com. 1992), USA Toy Libr. Assn. (charter mem.), Assn. Libr. Svc. to Children (mem. toys, games and realia evaluation com. 1983-85, chair local arrangements 1984-85, chair rsch. com. 1985-88, mem. Randolph Caldecott com. 1987, mem. software evaluation 1988-89, mem. svc. to children with spl. needs 1989-91, chair Charlemae Rollins pres. program 1990-91, active, 1991, chair edn. com. 1991-93, 93—, bd. dirs. 1993-96, v.p., pres.-elect 1997-98, pres. 1998-99, past pres. 1999-2000), Children's Reading Round Table (mem. spl. award com. 1987-88). Office: St Louis Pub Lib 1301 Olive St Saint Louis MO 63103-2325

HOLT, MARJORIE JENSEN, artist; b. Salt Lake City, Nov. 3, 1919; d. Peter Joseph and Artimesia (Snow) Jensen; m. Robet Lewis Holt, Oct. 3, 1942; children: Karen Anne, Katherine, Robert, Elida, Peter. BS, U. Utah, 1941. Tchr. art Granite Sch. Dist., Salt Lake City, 1967-68, 68-69; tchr. graphic design Salt Lake CC, Salt Lake City, 1991—99. Exhibitions include Spraglie Libr., 1995—96. Mem.: Utah Water Color Soc. (pres. 1993—94). Republican. Mem. Lds Ch.

HOLT, MARJORIE SEWELL, lawyer, retired congresswoman; b. Birmingham, Ala., Sept. 17, 1920; d. Edward Rol and Juanita (Felts) Sewell; m. Duncan McKay Holt, Dec. 26, 1946; children: Rachel Holt Tschantre, Edward Sewell, Victoria. Grad., Jacksonville Jr. Coll., 1945; JD, U. Fla., 1949. Bar: Fla. 1949, Md. 1962. Pvt. practice, Annapolis, Md., 1962; clk. Anne Arundel County Circuit Ct., 1966-72; mem. 93d-99th Congresses from 4th Dist. of Md., 1973-86; armed svcs. com., vice-chair Office Tech. Assessment, 1977; chair Rep. Study com., 1975-76; of counsel Smith, Somerville & Case, Balt., 1986-90. Supr. elections Anne Arundel County, 1963-65; del. Rep. Nat. Conv., 1968, 76, 80, 84, 88; mem. Pres.'s Commn. on Arms Control and Disarmament, Gov.'s Commn. on Carefirst, 2003; mem. ind. commn. USAR; bd. dirs. Annapolis Fed. Savs. Bank; adv. bd. Crestar; co-chair George W. Bush Presdl. campaign, Md., 2000. Co-author: Case Against The Reckless Congress, 1976, Can You Afford This House, 1978. Bd. dirs. Md. Sch. for the Blind, Hist. Annapolis Found. Recipient Disting. Alumna award U. Fla., 1975, Trustees award U. Fla. Coll. Law, 1984, Alumnae Outstanding Achievement award, 1997. Mem. ABA, Md. Bar Assn., Anne Arundel Bar Assn., Phi Kappa Phi, Phi Delta Delta. Presbyterian (elder 1959).

HOLT, MILDRED FRANCES, educator; b. Lorain, Ohio, July 30, 1932; d. William Henry and Rachel (Pierce) Daniels; B.S., U. Md., 1962, M.Ed., 1967, Ph.D., 1977; m. Maurice Lee Holt, Sept. 11, 1949 (dec.); children—Claudia, Frances, William, Rudi. Tchr. spl. edn. St. Mary's (Md.) County Public Schs., 1962-64, coordinator Felix Johnson Spl. Edn. Center, 1964-66; demonstration tchr. spl. edn. U. Md., College Park, summer 1970, instr. spl. edn. dept. Coll. Edn., 1969-73; supr. spl. edn. Calvert and St. Mary's (Md.) Counties, 1968-69; asso. prof. spl. edn. W. Liberty (W.Va.) State Coll., 1973-75; asst. prof. Eastern Ill. U., Charleston, 1975-77; supr. spl. edn. Warren County Public Schs., Front Royal, Va., 1977-85; spl. edn. tchr. Dallas Ind. Sch. Dist., 1985— . Mem. NEA, Warren County Edn. Assn., Council Exceptional Children, Assn. for Gifted, Assn. Supervision and Curriculum Devel., Va. Edn. Assn., Va. Council Exceptional Children, Blue Ridge Orgn. Gifted and Talented, Assn. Children with Learning Disabilities, Nat. Assn. Gifted Children, Phi Theta Kappa, Kappa Delta Pi. Contbr. articles to profl. jours.; author: Reach Guidebook, 1979. Home: 2916 Sidney Dr Mesquite TX 75150-2253 E-mail: mholt@texas.net.

HOLT, THELMA, theatrical producer; Founder The Open Space Theatre, Eng.; dir. The Round House, Eng.; prodr. Royal Nat. Theatre, Eng., 1985-89; exec. prodr. The Peter Hall Co., Eng., 1989-90; founder, prin. Thelma Holt Ltd., Eng., 1990—. Prodr. plays Orpheus Descending, The Merchant of Venice, Three Sisters, Hamlet, Electra, The Clandestine Marriage, The Glass Menagerie. Recipient Laurence Olivier/Observer award for Outstanding Achievement. Mem. Arts Coun. of Eng., Drama Panel (chmn.). Office: Belasco Theatre 111 W 44th St New York NY 10036-4012

HOLTE, DEBRA LEAH, investment executive, financial analyst; b. Madison, Wis. d. Daniel Kennseth and Marian Anne Reitan. BA, Concordia Coll., Moorhead, Minn., 1973. Chartered Fin. Analyst, Cert. Divorce Planner. Capital markets specialist 1st Bank Mpls., 1981-83; v.p. Allison-Williams Co., Mpls., 1983-86; exec. v.p. Hamil & Holte Inc., Denver, 1986-93; pres. Holte & Assocs., Denver, Taos, N.Mex., 1993—. Active Denver Jr. League, Western Pension Com., 1986—; bd. dirs. Denver Children's Home, 1987—, treas., 1987-91, chmn. fin. com., 1987-91, v.p., 1990—, chmn. nominating com., 1991—, pres.-elect, 1994-95, bd. pres., 1995—; adv. bd. Luth. Social Svcs., 1987; co-chair U.S. Ski Team Fundraiser; bd. dirs. Minn. Vocat. Edn. Fin., Mpls., 1984-86; bd. dirs. Colo. Ballet, 1988-93, chair nominating com., 1991-93, v.p., 1992-93, chmn. bd., 1993; mem. Fin. Analyst Nat. Task Force in Bondholder Rights, 1988-90; bd. dirs. Ctrl. City Opera Guild, 1994-95, Western Chamber Ballet, 1994-96, Taos Humane Soc., 1997—; social co-chmn. The Arapahoe Fox Hunt, 1993-94; bd. dirs., mem. steering com. Denver Dumb Friends League, 2001—. Mem. Fin. Analysts Fedn., Denver Soc. Security Analysts (bd. dirs. 1990-97, chair ethics and bylaws com. 1987—, chair edn. com. 1988, chair membership com. 1989, rec. sec. 1990, sec. 1991, treas. 1992, program chair 1993, pres. 1994-95, dir. 1995-96).

HOLTER, PATRA JO, artist, art education consultant; b. Ashland, wis., Mar. 6, 1936; d. Cap and Sigrid (Gadda) H. BS, U. Wis., 1958; MA, U. Calif., Berkeley, 1962; student, Nat. Acad. Art and U. Oslo, 1963; cert. in adminstrn., Fairfield U., 1983; postgrad., New Sch. Social Rsch., UCLA, U. Colo., Pratt Inst. Cert. tchr., N.Y., Wis., adminstr., N.Y. Art tchr. Herricks Jr. H.S., New Hyde Park, N.Y., 1958-60; assoc. art U. Calif., Berkeley, 1961-62; adult art tchr. U. Calif. Alumni Camp, Pinecrest, summer 1961; elem. art tchr. Ctrl. Sch., Mamaroneck, N.Y., 1964, Edgewood Sch., Scarsdale, 1971-82; elem. and jr. H.S. art tchr. Quaker Ridge Sch., Scarsdale, N.Y., 1964-70; art tchr. Scarsdale Sr. H.S., 1982-84, chmn. art dept., 1984-93; dist. visual arts supr. Scarsdale Sch. Sys., 1989-93. Art tchr. workshops, curriculum developer, cons. in field, liaison Scarsdale; visual arts coord. Lincoln Ctr. Inst., N.Y.C., 1978-80; liaison art tchr. Westchester Coun. for Arts, Scarsdale, 1970's. Author, artist: Photography Without a Camera, 1972, reprinted 1980; contbr. articles, photographs to profl. publs.; group and solo exhbns. include Wis. Salon of Art, Madison, 1958, Worth Ryder Gallery, Berkeley, 1962, Am. Embassy, Oslo, 1963, Mount Mercy Coll. Gallery, Cedar Rapids, Iowa, 1988, Silvermine Galleries, 1994-2000, Waveny Carriage Barn, New Canaan, 1995-97, Washburn (Wis.) Hist. Mus. and Cultural Ctr., 1995-2000, Northland Coll., Ashland, 1996-99, Meridian Internat. Ctr., Washington, 1997, Tweed Mus. Art, Duluth, Minn., 1997-99, Ct. Graphic Arts Ctr., Norwalk, 1997-98, Wis. Arts Bd. Internat., Madison, 1999, Manhattan Borough Pres.'s Gallery, N.Y.C., 2001. Fulbright scholar, Norway, 1962-63, ext., summer 1963; recipient Exemplary Media award N.Y. Regents Adv. Coun., 1968; Scarsdale Sch. Sys. grantee, 1972. Mem., midwest rep. Fulbright Arts Task Force; mem. Fulbright Assn., Norwegian Fulbright Assn., Silvermine Guild of Art, N.Y. State United Tchrs. Assn., Am. Fedn. Tchrs., Nat. Mus. Women in Arts, N.Y. State Ret. Tchrs., Ashland Hist. Soc., Ashland Alliance for Sustainability, Chequamegon Bay Area Arts Coun., New Canaan Soc. for Arts, Wilton Garden Club, Nat. Coun. State Garden Clubs, Kappa Delta. Avocations: travel, horticulture, antiques. Home: 2140 Center St Stevens Point WI 54481-3836

HOLTHAUS, JOAN MARIE, elementary school educator; b. Wichita, Kans., June 3, 1964; d. Wilbur Ferdinand and Mary Teresa (Armstrong) Kruse; m. William Paul Holthaus, July 18, 1987; 1 child, Paul Thomas. BS in Edn., English, Kans. State U., 1986; Early Childhood Spl. Edn. Endorsement, Washburn U. 2nd grade and kindergarten tchr. Most Pure Heart Parochial Sch., Topeka, Kans., 1986—. Guardian Kans. Assn.

Protective Svcs., 1991-98; cons. Christ the King Daycare, 1995. Author: (resource guide) Guide for Students with Diabetes (Kans. State U.), 1985. Camp dir. Am. Diabetes Assn., Rock Springs, Kans., 1990-99, chmn. bd. dirs. Shawnee County chpt., 1995-96, mem. bd. dirs. Kans., 1993-98. Named Topeka's Favorite Kindergarten Tchr., Topeka Capital Jour. Poll, 1997. Mem. Am. Mothers (Kans. Mother of Yr. 1995-96), Topeka Area Parochial Kindergarten Tchrs. (founder), Alpha Delta Pi (mem. at large alumnae assn.). Roman Catholic. Avocations: cooking, gardening, sewing, skiing, painting.

HOLTHAUSEN, MARTHA ANNE, interior designer; b. Columbus, Ohio, Oct. 28, 1934; d. Clyde Aloysius and Olive Letitia (Marlowe) Gloeckner; m. Don Trudeau Allensworth, Aug. 14, 1960 (div. 1976); 1 child, Karen Ayn; m. Ernest Arthur Holthausen, Dec. 9, 1989. BFA cum laude, Ohio State U., 1956; postgrad., Baldwin-Wallace Coll., 1959, Mt. Vernon Coll., Washington, 1980, 81. Fashion illustrator The Marston Co., San Diego, 1956-57, The Higbee Co., Cleve., 1957-58; instr. art Lakewood (Ohio) Pub. Schs., 1958-60; tchr. Princes Georges County (Md.) Pub. Schs., 1960; account exec. Stansbury Design, Inc., Prince Georges County, Md., 1975-76; interior designer Berwin Interiors, Bethesda, Md., 1977-79, W. & J. Sloane, Inc., Washington, 1980-84; pres., interior designer Martha Allensworth Interior Design, Inc., Reston, Va., 1984—. Guest artist-in-residence Nat. Park Svc., Yosemite Nat. Park, Calif., summer 1988, 89, 91, 95. Watercolor and oil paintings in pvt. collections. Bd. dirs. C. of C. Herndon, Va., 1985-86; v.p. Montgomery County (Md.) Art Assn., 1962-63. Episcopalian. Avocations: gardening, bicycling, watercolor and oil painting. Office: Martha Allensworth Interior Design Inc Plaza America Dr No 732 Reston VA 20190-4700

HOLT-HUNTER, TRACY LYNN, language educator, artist; b. Greenwood, Miss., Sept. 30, 1968; d. James Lee Roscoe and Norma Ree Tolliver; m. Johnny Holt, Feb. 14, 1994 (div. Jan. 17, 2002); children: Erica Sandifer, Johnnay Holt; m. James Hunter, July 19, 2003. BA, Miss. Valley State U., 1992, MA in Tchg., 2002. Cert. tchr. Miss. Artist The John RIchard Collection, Greenwood, Miss., 1993; tchr. English Threadgill Jr. H.S., Greenwood, Miss., 1994, Greenwood H.S., Miss., 1994—2003. One-woman shows include Cottonlandia Mus., 2001, exhibitions include James John Audubon Mus., Henderson, Ky., 2002. Pres. Miss. Valley State U. Assn. of Grad. Students in Edn., 2001—02. Recipient Robert C. Woodell Meml. award for excellence in fine art, 1996, Fine Arts award, Alpha Kappa Alpha, 2003. Fellow: Miss. Tchr.'s Fellowship Program. Democrat. Ch. Of God. Avocations: painting, sculpting, jewelry making, writing.

HOLTKAMP, SUSAN CHARLOTTE, elementary school educator; b. Houston, Feb. 23, 1957; d. Clarence Jules and Karyl Irene (Roberts) H. BS in Early Childhood Edn., Brigham Young U., Provo, Utah, 1979, MEd, 1982. Cert. tchr. Utah, ESL endorsement U. Utah, 2002. 2d grade tchr. Nebo Sch. Dist., Spanish Fork, Utah, 1979-84, kindergarten tchr., 1984-85; tchr. 2d grade DODDS, Mannheim, Fed. Republic Germany, 1985-86; tchr. 3d grade Jordan Sch. Dist., Salt Lake City, 1987-92, tchr. 5th grade, 1992—2002, tchr. 6th grade, 2002—. Mem. NEA, JEA, Utah Edn. Assn., ASCD.

HOLTON, GRACE HOLLAND, accountant; b. Durham, N.C., Sept. 14, 1957; d. Samuel Melanchthon and B. Margaret (Umberger) Holton. BS in Math., Univ. N.C., Greensboro, 1978; MBA, Univ. N.C., Chapel Hill, 1984; M.Acctg. Sci., U. Ill., 1993. CPA N.C., cert. mgmt. acct. Indsl. engr. Burlington Industries, Inc., Mayodan, NC, 1978-79, plant indsl. engr. Stoneville, NC, 1979-80; methods indsl. engr. Blue Cross and Blue Shield of N.C., Durham, 1980-82; fin. analyst R.J. Reynolds, Inc., Winston-Salem, NC, 1984-85; accounting cons. Ryder Truck Rental, Inc., Miami, Fla., 1985-88; contr. Ryder Jacobs (divsn. Ryder Distbn. Resources), Jessup, Md., 1988-90; grad. asst. in acctg. U. Ill., Urbana, 1990-93; contr. Salem NationaLease, Winston-Salem, 1993-94; fin. officer Chapel Hill-Carrboro City Schs., 1994-99; mgr. benefits and payroll Ryder Pub. Transp. Svcs., Cin., 1999-2000; exec. dir. budget and evaluation Charlotte-Mecklenburg Schs., 2000—02; acctg. instr. Alamance C.C., Graham, NC, 2003—. Scholar KPMG-Peat Marwick scholar, 1991—92. Mem.: AICPA, N.C. Soc. CPA, Inst. Mgmt. Accts. Democrat. Methodist.

HOLT-STONE, C. YVONNE, judge; b. Washington, Feb. 26, 1950; m. William H., Jr. Stone. BA, Morgan State U., 1973; M of City Planning, U. Pa., 1973; JD, U. Md., 1979. Dist. planner Balt. City Planning Dept., 1973—75; specialist regional planning team Balt. City Pub. Schs., 1975—79, specialist Office Staff Rels., 1979—80; asst. state's atty. Howard County States Atty., 1980—81; master-in-chancery Circuit Ct. for Batl. City, 1981—91; judge Dist. Ct. Md., 1991—. Elected mem. Adminstrv. Judge Com. Dist. Ct. Md., 1999—. Sec. Black/Jewish Forum of Balt., 1989—91; pres. Harbor City Chpt. Links Inc., 1993—95; Elder Madison Ave. Presbyn. Ch., 1989—94, 1995—; bd. dirs. Leadership Greater Balt. Com., 1992—98. Recipient Profl. Achievement award, Balt. chpt. Coalition of 100 Black Woman, 1997, honoree, Bar Assn. Balt. City, 1995, Disting. Svc. award, Nat. Bar Assn., 1995, Monumental City Bar Assn., 1995. Mem.: U. Md. Black Law Students Assn. (mem. adv. bd. 1995—96), Md. State Bar Assn. and Md. Jud. Conf. (apptd. mem. select com. on gender equality 1998—), Nat. Assn. Woman Judges (bd. dirs. Md. chpt. 1991). Office: 5800 Wabash Ave Baltimore MD 21215

HOLTZ, DIANE, retail executive; Divsnl. v.p. Bloomingdale's; v.p. career merchandise and tops Ann Taylor, mgr. gen. merchandise, sr. v.p.; v.p. spl. projects design svcs. Limited Brands, Inc., 2000—02; pres. Limited Stores, Limited Brands Inc., 2002—. Office: Limited Stores Three Ltd Pkwy Columbus OH 43230*

HOLTZ, SARA, management consultant; b. L.A., Aug. 7, 1951; BA, Yale U., 1972; JD, Harvard U., 1975. Bar: D.C. 1975, Calif. 1982. Assoc. Brownstein, Zeidman & Schomer, Washington, 1975-77; dep. asst. dir. FTC, Washington, 1977-82; divsn. counsel Clorox Co., Oakland, Calif., 1982-90; v.p., dep. gen. counsel Nestle U.S.A., Inc., San Francisco, 1990-94; prin. Client Focus, 1996—. Mem. Am. Corp. Counsel Assn. (bd. dirs. 1986-95, chmn. 1994-95). Office: 5320 Olive Tree Ct Granite Bay CA 95746-9484

HOLTZ-BORDERS, KAREN LYNN, police officer; b. Glendale, Calif., Mar. 10, 1960; d. Denison Lee and Diane Arlyce (Shapiro) Baldwin; m. Steven Henry Holtz, June 1, 1985 (div. Jan. 1992); children: Ashley Holtz, Stacey Holtz. AS, Coll. of the Desert, 1985; BS, U. Redlands, 1992. Police officer Palm Springs (Calif.) Police Dept., 1982—, explorer advisor, 1985-89, detective, 1989-94, field tng. officer, 1994-96, domestic violence detective, 1996—2002, field tng. officer, 2002—. Co-host Time-Warner Crimewatch TV show; host Code 3 Desert Beat TV Show. Recipient Outstanding Cmty. Svc. award Domestic Violence Program, Palm Springs Police Dept., 1997, Medal of Valor, Am. Legion, 1989, Women Helping Women award, Soroptimists, 2001—02. Republican. Roman Catholic. Avocations: ice skating, reading, bicycling. Office: Palm Springs Police Dept 200 S Civic Dr Palm Springs CA 92262-7201 Office Phone: 760-778-8425. Personal E-mail: cobranodv@aol.com. Business E-Mail: karenb@ci.palm-springs.ca.us.

HOLTZCLAW, DIANE SMITH, elementary education educator; b. Buffalo, May 26, 1936; d. John Nelson and Beatrice M. (Salisbury) Smith; m. John Victor Holtzclaw, June 27, 1959; children: Kathryn Diane, John Bryan. BS in Edn. magna cum laude, SUNY, Brockport, 1957, MS with honors, 1961; postgrad., SUNY, Buffalo, 1960-65, Canisus Coll., 1979, Nazareth Coll., 1981-82. Tchr. Greece Cen. Sch., Rochester, N.Y., 1957-60; supr. SUNY, Brockport, 1960-64, assoc. prof. edn., 1960-64; dir. Early Childhood Ctr., Fairport, N.Y., 1968-80; tchr. Fairport Cen. Schs., 1971—; ednl. cons. in field; specialist child devel. Ch. music dir., Rochester, N.Y., 1983—; pres. bd. dirs. Downtown Day Care Ctr., Rochester, 1974-83; mem. exec. bd. Rochester Theatre Organ Soc., 1988—. Mem. Fairport Edn. Assn. (exec. bd. 1982-83, del. 1983), N.Y. State United Tchrs., AAUW (exec. bd. 1973-74, 77-79, 83-84, pres. Fairport br. 1971-73), Internat. Platform Assn., Kappa Delta Pi. Home: 1455 Ayrault Rd Fairport NY 14450-9301 Office: Fairport Cen Schs 38 W Church St Fairport NY 14450-2130

HOLTZMAN, ELIZABETH, lawyer; b. Bklyn., Aug. 11, 1941; d. Sidney and Filia Holtzman. AB magna cum laude, Radcliffe Coll., 1962; JD, Harvard U., 1965; L.D.S., Regis Coll., 1975, Skidmore Coll., 1980, Simmons Coll., 1981, Smith Coll., 1982. Bar: N.Y. 1966. Assoc. Wachtell, Lipton, Rosen, Katz & Kern, N.Y.C., 1965-67; asst. to mayor N.Y.C., 1968-69; assoc. Paul, Weiss, Rifkind, Wharton & Garrison, 1970-72; mem. 93d-96th Congresses from 16th dist., N.Y.; vis. prof. Law Sch. and Grad. Sch. Pub. Adminstrn. NYU, 1981; dist. atty. Kings County, Bklyn., 1982-89; comptr. City of N.Y., 1990-93. Mem. Am. Jewish Commn. on the Holocaust, Nazi and Japanese War Criminal Records Working Group, 1999—; Dem. nominee U.S. Senate, 1980; N.Y. State Dem. committee-woman, 1970—72; mem. Pres.'s Nat. Commn. on U.S. Observance Internat. Women's Yr., Helsinki Watch Com., 1981—88, Select Com. on Immigration Policy, 1979—80; bd. overseers Harvard U., 1976—82; bd. trustees Radcliffe Coll., Bklyn. Acad. Music Endowment Trust; mem. Lawyers Com. Internat. Human Right, 1981—88. Recipient Nat. Coun. Jewish Women's Faith and Humanity award, YWCA Elizabeth Cutter Morrow award, Maccabean award N.Y. Bd. Rabbis, Alumni recognition award Radcliffe Coll. Alumnae Assn., 1973, N.J. and L.A. ACLU awards for contbns. to def. of Constn. and preservation of civil liberties, 1981, Athena award N.Y.C. Commn. on Status of Women, 1985, Woman of Yr. award N.Y. League Bus. and Profl. Women, 1985, Jan Korzak award 5th Ann. Kent State Holocaust Conf., 1986, Outstanding and Meritorious Svc. award Jewish War Vets. of U.S., 1986, Award of Remembrance Warsaw Ghetto Resistance Orgn., 1987, Gates of Freedom award State of Israel Bonds, 1987; Award of Honor United Jewish Appeal, 1988, Deed of Tzedakah award, 1991. Fellow N.Y. Inst. Humanities; mem. Assn. of Bar of City of N.Y., Nat. Women's Polit. Caucus (Outstanding Svc. award 1987), Phi Beta Kappa. Office: Herrick Feinstein LLP 2 Park Ave New York NY 10016-9302 Office Phone: 212-592-1400.

HOLTZMAN, ELLEN A. foundation executive; b. N.Y.C., Mar. 5, 1952; d. Jerome and Corinne (Weinbaum) H.; m. Michael P. Bloom, June 18, 1978 (div. 1983); m. Robert S. Evans, Aug. 8, 1986. BA in Art History, George Washington U., 1973; MA in Art History, U. Calif., Santa Barbara, 1975. Cert. tchr., Calif. Asst. to dir. Bklyn. Mus., 1980-82, asst. mgr. pub. programs and media, 1983-85; asst. dir. Queens Mus., Flushing, N.Y., 1985-88; mng. dir. New Mus. Contemporary Art, N.Y.C., 1988-92; program dir. for arts Henry Luce Found., Inc., N.Y.C., 1992—. Adj. faculty Bank St. Coll. Edn., N.Y.C., 1990; participant exec. mgmt. workshop NYU, 1986. Exec. com. N.Y.C. Arts Coalition, 1988-92; mem. N.Y. Hist. Soc. Cmty. Adv. Bd., 1994. Mem. Am. Assn. Mus. (surveyor mus. assessment program 1990—), N.Y. Archival Soc., Art Table, Grantmakers in the Arts. Avocation: travel. Office: Henry Luce Found Inc 111 W 50th St New York NY 10020-1202

HOLTZMAN, JOAN KING, musician, composer; b. Aberdeen, S.D., Aug. 14, 1925; d. James Wilfred and Miriam Hughes (Evans) K.; m. Wayne Harold Holtzman, Aug. 23, 1947; children: Wayne Jr., James, Scott, Karl. B in Music Edn., Northwestern U., 1947; EdMA, Stanford U., 1948. Pres. Jojo's Prodns., Austin, Tex., 1991—. Author: (with Leslie Holtzman) The Fat Rat and This and That, 1997, (with Rosario Ahumada de Diaz) Happy Times with English, 1987; composer, pianist, singer children's cassettes Jo Jo's Songs for Growing Up, 1991, Beasts, Veggies and Sospetigious Things, 1993; composer melodies song book and cassette Symphony for Simple Simon, 1984 (award of excellence Am. Symphony Orch. League, 1984); composer numerous songs. Active Save Children Fedn., 1954—, pres. 1958; vol. Austin Cerebral Palsy Ctr., 1955-59; mem. Pan Am. Round Table, 1958—, sec. 1965-66; co-founder Internat. Hospitality Com. Austin, 1960—, chmn. host families, 1960-62; pres. PTA Austin H.S., 1972; mem. Austin Arts Commn., 1977-83; mem. nat. adv. coun. Nat. Sch. Vol. Program, Washington, 1976-91; mem. adv. com. Austin Ind. Sch. Dist., 1983-91, forming future com., 1982; mem. arts plan task force City of Austin, 1985; docent, gov. mansion, 1983—; nat. class rep. Northwestern U. Sch. Music, 1977-91; mus. vol. Austin State Hosp., 1967-83; sec., bd. dirs. Austin Symphony Orch. Soc., 1966—; state bd. dirs. Very Special Arts - Tex., 1987-91; bd. dirs., chmn. coms. Child and Family Svcs., Austin, 1965-82; bd. dirs. Austin Musical Theatre, 2000-. Named Outstanding Fundraiser Austin Symphony Devel. fund drive, 1981; Festival Favorite New Tex. Choral Music Festival, Austin, 1995, Yellow Rose Tex., Tex. Gov., 1995, Vol. of Yr., 1995. Mem. Women's Symphony League Austin (pres. 1958-59, charter mem., Woman of Yr. award 1991), Austin Jr. League (Vol. Extraordinaire award 1985), Mortar Bd. U. Tex. Austin (Citation award 1976), Playhouse Singers, Settlement Club, Austin Woman's Club, Univ. Ladies Club (pres. 1971-72), Sigma Alpha Iota (charter mem., pres. 1972-73, Rose of Honor award 1976). Office: Jojo's Prodns 3300 Foothill Dr Austin TX 78731-5823 E-mail: wayne.holtzman@mail.utexas.edu.

HOLTZMAN, MARY, engineering company executive; b. Sanford, Fla., Mar. 16, 1948; d. James Emory and Johnie Ruth (Hardy) McElhannon; m. Calvin Douglas Crenshaw, Sept. 1969 (div. July 1977); 1 child, Christa Ashlee Crenshaw; m. Dean Ward Hillegass, Sept. 1978 (div. July 1986); m. Joel Richard Holtzman, Jan. 12, 1990. BFA, U. Ga., 1972. Draftsman, designer Patterson & Dewar Engrs., Decatur, Ga., 1973-84; drafting supr. Mosler/Am. Standard, Norcross, Ga., 1984-86; GIS dept. mgr. Patterson & Dewar Engrs., Decatur, 1986—. Mem. DAR, Lake Jackson Homeowners Assn., Am. Assn. Ret. Persons, U. Ga. Alumni Assn., Peachtree Handspinners Guild, Red Hat Soc. Democrat. Avocations: photography, painting, internet design, reading, travel. Home: 3144 Caintal Ct Decatur GA 30033-1804 Office: Patterson & Dewar Engrs Inc 2685 Milscott Dr Decatur GA 30033-5906 Office Phone: 404-296-5990. Business E-Mail: mholtzman@pd-engineers.com. E-mail: maryholtzman@mindspring.com.

HOLTZMAN, ROBERTA LEE, French and Spanish language educator; b. Detroit, Nov. 24, 1938; d. Paul John and Sophia (Marcus) H. AB cum laude, Wayne State U., 1959, MA, 1973, U. Mich., 1961. Fgn. lang. tchr. Birmingham (Mich.) Sch. Dist., 1959-60, Cass Tech. H.S., Detroit, 1961-64; from instr. to prof. French and Spanish, Schoolcraft Coll., Livonia, Mich., 1964-84, chmn. French and Spanish depts., 1984—. Trustee Cranbrook Music Guild, Ednl. Community, Bloomfield Hills, Mich., 1976-78. Fulbright-Hays fellow, Brazil, 1964. Mem. AAUW, NEA, MLA, Nat. Mus. Women in Arts (co-founder 1992), Am. Assn. Tchrs. of Spanish and Portuguese, Am. Assn. Tchrs. of French, Mich. Edn. Assn. Avocations: swimming, book collecting, photography, travel. Office: Schoolcraft Coll 18600 Haggerty Rd Livonia MI 45152-2696 Business E-Mail: rholtzma@schoolcraft.edu.

HOLTZSCHER, DENISE ERIN, music educator; b. Decatur, Ill., Aug. 29, 1977; d. Anthony and Adeline Heckman; m. Andrew Jay Holtzscher, Aug. 12, 2000. MusB in Edn., Millikin U., 1999. Cert. K-12 music tchr. Ill., Mo. Asst. musical dir. Warrensburg (Ill.)-Latham HS, 1996—99; instrumental music dir. Our Lady of Lourdes Sch., Decatur, 1999—2002; pvt. instrumental tchr., 1998—; secondary music dir. Iberia (Mo.) R-V Sch. Dist., 2002—. Mem. sch. facility com., dance team coach Iberia R-V Sch. Dist., 2003—. Actor: Pulaski Fine Arts Assn. Mem. Decatur Mcpl. Band, 1995—2002; housing project facilitator First Site/Millikin U., Decatur, 1998. Mem.: Music Educators Nat. Conf. (assoc.), Pi Lambd Theta, Sigma Alpha Iota (life; pres. 1998—99, 2001—02, honor band festival coord. 1998—99, Provincial Leadership Award, Nat. Leadership Award Finalist 1999). Independent. Roman Catholic. Avocations: desktop publishing, ecclectic research, ballet, knitting.

HOLYER, ERNA MARIA, adult education educator, writer, artist; b. Weilheim, Bavaria, Germany, Mar. 15, 1925; d. Mathias and Anna Maria (Goldhofer) Schretter; m. Gene Wallace Holyer, Aug. 24, 1957 (dec. 1999). AA, San Jose Evening Coll., 1964; student, San Mateo Coll., 1965—67, San Jose State U., 1968—69, San Jose City Coll., 1980—81; DLitt, World U., 1984; DFA (hon.) (hon.), The London Inst. Applied Rsch, 1992. Freelance writer under pseudonym Ernie Holyer, 1960—; tchr. creative writing San Jose (Calif.) Met. Adult Edn., 1968—; artist, 1958—. Exhibited in group shows Crown Zellerbach Gallery, San Francisco, 1973, 74, 76, 77; I.B.C. Gallery, San Francisco, 1978 (medal of Congress, 1988, 89, 92, 94, Congress Challenge trophy, 1991), L.A., 1981, Cambridge, Eng., 1992, Cambridge, Mass., 1993, San Jose, Calif., 1993, Edinburgh, 1994, San Francisco, 1996. Author: Rescue at Sunrise, 1965, Steve's Night of Silence, 1966, A Cow for Hansel, 1967, At the Forest's Edge, 1969, Song of Courage, 1970, Lone Brown Gull, 1971, Shoes for Daniel, 1974, The Southern Sea Otter, 1975, Sigi's Fire Helmet, 1975, Reservoir Road Adventure, 1982, Wilderness Journey, Golden Journey, California Journey, 1997, Self-Help for Writers: Winners Show You How, 2002, Dangerous Secrets: A Young Girl's Travails Under the Nazis, 2003; contbr. articles to mags., newspapers and anthologies. Recipient Woman of Achievement Honor cert. San Jose Mercury-News, 1973, 74, 75, Lefoli award for excellence in adult edn. instr. Adult Edn. Senate, 1972, Women of Achievement awards League of Friends of Santa Clara County Commn., San Jose Mercury News, 1987, various art awards. Mem. N.L.A.P.W. Inc., World Univ Roundtable (doctoral). Home and Office: 1314 Rimrock Dr San Jose CA 95120-5611 E-mail: holyere@aol.com.

HOLZBAUR, ERIKA L. medical educator; BS in Chemistry and History with honors, Coll. William and Mary, 1982; PhD in Biochemistry, Pa. State U., 1987. Rsch. fellow, teaching asst. Dept. Molecular and Cell Biology, Pa. State U., 1982—87, postdoctoral scientist, 1987—88; postdoctoral fellow NIH, 1988—92; asst. prof. Dept. Animal Biology, Sch. Vet. Medicine, U. Pa., Phila., 1992—98; assoc. prof. biochemistry Dept. Animal Biology, Sch. of Vet. Medicine, U. Pa., Phila., 1998—; assoc. prof. physiology Univ. Pa. Sch. Med. Contbr. articles to profl. jours., chapters to books. Recipient Established Investigator award, Am. Heart Assn., 1996; fellow Grad. Sch., Pa. State U., 1984—85, 1985—86, Keith R. Porter Fellowship, 2000. Mem.: U. Pa. Cancer Inst., Pa. Muscle Inst., Am. Soc. Cell Biology, Phi Beta Kappa. Office: U Pa Dept physiology D400 Richards Bldg 3700 Hamilton Walk Philadelphia PA 19104-6085

HOLZER, JENNY, artist; b. Gallipolis, Ohio, July 29, 1950; d. Richard Vornholt and Virginia (Beasley) H.; m. Michael Andrew Glier, May 21, 1984, 1 child. Student, Duke U., 1968-70, U. Chgo., 1970-71; BFA, Ohio U., 1973, DA (hon.), 1994; MFA, R.I. Sch. Design, 1977; postgrad., Whitney Mus. Am. Art, 1977; PhD of Art (hon.), Williams Coll., 2000. One-woman shows include Rüdiger Schöttle Gall, Münich, 1980, Barbara Gladstone Gallery, NYC, 1983, 86, 94, Kunsthalle, Basel, Switzerland, 1984, Des Moines Art Ctr., 1986, MIT, Cambridge, 1986, Mus. Contemporary Art, Chgo., 1987, Inst. Contemporary Art, London, 1988, Bklyn. Mus., NYC, 1988, DIA Art Found., NYC, 1989, Guggenheim Mus., NYC, 1989, Am. Pavilion, 44th Biennale, Venice, Italy, 1990, La. Mus., Humlebaek, Denmark, 1991, Albright-Knox Art Gallery, Buffalo, 1991, Walker Art Gallery, Mpls., 1991, Ydessa Hendeles Art Found., Toronto, 1992, Dallas Mus. Art, 1993, Haus der Kunst, Munich, 1993, Bergen Mus. Art, Norway, 1994, Art Tower Mito, Japan, 1994, Williams Coll. Mus. Art, Williamstown, Mass., 1995, Kunstmus. des Kantons Thurgau, Kartouse Ittingen, Warth, Switzerland, 1996, Contemporary Art Mus., Houston, 1997, Cheim & Read, NY, 1997, Yvon Lambert Gallery, Paris, 1998, Inst. Cultural Itau, São Paulo, Brazil, 1998, Centro Cultural Banco do Brasil, Rio de Janeiro, 1999, BALTIC Ctr. Contemporary Art, Gateshead, 2000, Neue Nat. Galeri, Berlin, 2001, Mus. Contemporary Art, Bordeaux, France, 2001, Monterrey, Mex., 2001, Mönahehaus Mus., Goslar, Germany, 2002, Monika Spruth Philomerie Magers, 2002, others; exhibited in group shows at Documenta 7, Kassel, Germany, 1982, Contemporary Arts Ctr., Cin., 1984, Mus. Art Carnegie Inst., Pitts., 1985, Israel Mus., Jerusalem, 1986, Frankfurter Kunstverein, Frankfurt, Germany, 1986, Europa/Amerika Mus. Ludwig, Koln, 1986, Sonsbeck, Arnhem, The Netherlands, 1986, Whitney Mus. Am. Art, NYC, 1989, Mus. Contemporary Art, LA, 1989, Mus. Modern Art, NYC, 1988, 90, 96, Documenta 8, Kassel, 1987, Ctrl. Mus., Utrecht, The Netherlands, 1991, Kunsthalle, Basel, 1992, Guggenheim Mus., Soho, NYC, 1993, 96, Lenbachhaus, Munich, 1994, SITE Santa Fe, 1995, Pompidou Ctr., Paris, 1996, Biennale di Florence, Italy, 1996, Joseph Helman Gallery, NY, 1997, Kunsthalle Wien, Vienna, Austria, 1998, Nat. Gallery Australia, Canberra, 1998, Rhona Hofman Gallery, 1998, Oslo Mus. Contemporary Art, 2000; represented in permanent collections Ujazdowski Castle, Warsaw, Poland, Black Garden, Nordhorn, Germany, Erlauf (Austria) Peace Monument, Guggenheim Mus., Bilbao, Bundestag, Berlin, U. So. Calif., LA, Ludwig Mus., Aachen, Germany, Neue Nat. Galerie, Berlin, Toyota Mclpl. Mus. Art, Hamburg Kunstalie, US Fed. Courthouse, Sacramento, Allentown, Pa., Telenor Hdqr., Norway. Recipient Golden Lion award 44th Venice Biennale, 1990, Skowhegan medal for installation Skowhegen Sch. Painting and Sculpture, N.Y., 1994, Crystal award World Econ. Forum, Cologny-Geneva, Switzerland, 1996, BMW Art car, BMW, Munich, 1999, Kaiserring award City of Goslar, Germany, 2002. Fellow Am. Acad., Berlin, 2000. Avocation: reading. E-mail: studio@jennyholzer.com., gallery@cheimread.com.

HOLZMAN, ELIZABETH ESTHER, artist, director; d. George and sara Holzman; 1 child, Nathaniel Chapman. BA, Miles Coll., 1975; MFA, Calif. Inst. Arts, 1979. Freelance animator, LA, 1980—86; artist Disney Corp., LA, 1986—92; prodr. Warner Bros., LA, 1992—2002, dir., 1992—2002, writer, 1992—2002, artist, 1992—2002. Recipient Womens Image award, 2001. Mem.: Nat. Assn. TV Prodrs. Avocations: tree climbing, piano, poetry, ancient languages, sewing.

HOM, TRUDY A. music educator; b. Orlando, Fla., Mar. 14, 1956; d. Herbert Leroy and Virginia Mae Gardner; m. Nelson Edward Hom, Nov. 10, 1984. BA, U. Ctrl. Fla., 1980. Presch. tchr. The Learning Ctr., Orlando, 1980-85; ch. musician Ocoee United Meth. Ch., Fla., 1981-91; piano instr. pvt. studio, Orlando, 1978—; ch. musician Faith Luth. Ch., Winter Garden, 1998—. Mem. Fla. Federation Music Clubs (dist. pres. 1997—), Music Tchrs. Nat. Assn., Nat. Guild Piano Tchrs.; life mem. Sigma Alpha Iota (sword of honor 1980). Republican. United Meth. Avocation: antique shopping. Home: 230 Enka Ave Orlando FL 32835-1920

HOMAYSSI, RUBY LEE, small business owner; b. Jan. 14, 1945; d. Raymond and Elmira (Carter) K. BS in Food & Nutrition, So. U., Baton Rouge, 1967; MA, Pepperdine U., 1981; A.Hosp. Dietetics, Tuskegee Inst., Ala., 1969. Staff dietitian Nat. Naval Med. Ctr., Bethesda, Md., 1969-70; chief clin. nutrition and dietitian dept. Naval Hosp. Chelsea, Mass., 1970-74; chief dietitian, asst. food mgmt. officer Naval Submarine Med. Ctr., Groton, Conn., 1974-78; chief clin. nutrition Naval Hosp. Portsmouth, Va., 1978-83; chief clin. nutrition and dietetics Naval Hosp. Orlando, Fla., 1983-88; pres. Elmira's P.A.N.T.R.Y., Inc., Orlando, 1988—. Adv. bd. Fla. Hosp. Women; bd. dir. Bridgebuilders of Winter Pk.; cons. in field. Contbr. articles to profl. jours. Dir. Vol. Ctr. Seminole County, 1989-91; 3d v.p. Civic Theatre Bd. Ctrl. Fla., Orlando, 1989, 2d v.p., 1990—, pres., 1992-93; 1st v.p. Orlando Opera Co., 1987-88; bd. dirs. Maitland Arts Coun., New Hope For kids, gala chmn., 2002, 2003; pub. edn. chmn. Am. Cancer Soc., Orlando, 1987-90, bd. dirs.; prodn. chmn. March of Dimes, 1988—; bd. dirs. Hospice of Ctrl. Fla.; mem. cmty. advisors bd. TV-24; bd. dirs.

Seminole Chamber-Cmty. Rels., 1990-93, Citrus Coun. Girl Scouts; cmty. advisors bd. Symphony Orch. Assocs., 1991-92 Symphony Ball; bd. dir., chmn. Festival of Orchs., Inc., 2001-03; trainer Jr. Achievement, 1993—; chmn. Bridgebuilders, 2000-01; chmn. bd. dirs. Festival of Orchs., 2001-03; mem. Westside Winter Park Neighborhood Devel. Bd., 2000—; bd. dirs. Seminole County Arts Coun., 2003—. Named Woman of the Yr., Am. Bus. Women's Assn., 1987, Women of Achievement in Arts Downtown Exec. Women's Coun., 1989; recipient Angle award, 1989, Ruby Homayssi Day named in her honor City of Longwood, 199;; Paul Harris fellow Rotary, 2000. Mem. AAUW, NAFE, Am. Dietetic Assn., Fla. Dietetic Assn., Am. Bus. Women's Assn. (pres. 1987), Pvt. Industry Coun. of Seminole County (bd. dirs.), Girl Friends Club, Torch Club, Leadership Seminole, Delta Sigma Theta, Orlando Coun. of Christian Bus. Women, Subuuran Rep. Woman (bd.), Femmes de Coeur (pr chair & underwriting chair), Seminole County Rotary Club. Republican. Baptist. Avocations: reading, traveling, stock car racing, sewing. Home: 1409 Pylewood St Casselberry FL 32730-2450

HOMBORDY, HANNA LORE, artist; b. Rahway, N.J., Mar. 13, 1927; d. Fritz and Helen Galle; children: Ann Marie, Jane Louise. Cert. in Advt. Design with honors, Pratt Inst. Sch. Art and Design, 1947, BFA with honors, 1984. Asst. art dir. advt. agys., Newark, 1947—50, N.Y.C., 1947—50; indsl. designer, graphic designer GE, Schenectady, 1951—54; packaging and graphic designer Hobigant, Inc., N.Y.C., 1954—55; instr. recreation dept. mil bases, home studio, Del., 1959—84, 1959—84, 1959—84; freelance artist Ala., 1953—70, 1953—70, 1953—70, 1953—70, 1953—70; freelance author, photographer, artist, 1973—. Contbr. articles to profl. jours., photographs Handmade Tiles, 1994, photographs The Best of Pottery, 1996, photographs Resist & Masking Techniques, 1996, photographs Handbuilt Ceramics, 1997, photographs The Contemporary Potter, 2000, photographs Creative Ideas for Clay Artists, 2000, chapters to books. Fellow, City Ventura, Cultural Affairs Div., 2004. Mem.: Am. Ceramic Soc., Ventura County Potters' Guild (life).

HOMER, ELIZABETH ANN, curator; b. Flint, Mich., Jan. 17, 1943; d. John G. and Mary Ann Homer; m. John Mathew Giese, Aug. 22, 1964 (div. July 8, 1996); 1 child, Ann Margaret Giese. BA in Edn., U. Mich., 1964; MA in Occupl. Edn. Adminstrn., Ferris U., 1986. Elem. tchr., 1964—67; dir. Project on Equal Edn. Rights, NOWLDEF, Milford, Mich., 1978—84; cons. Mich. Dept. Labor, 1984—86; edn. dir., curator Mich. Women's Studies Assn., Mich. Women's Hall of Fame, Lansing, 1987—97; supr., curator Turner-Dodge House and Heritage Ctr., Lansing, 1997—. Chair NOW Edn. Task Force, Mich., 1989—; mem. Mich. Gender Equity Team, 1998—; bd. dirs. Mich. Cmty. Colls., 1993—99. Named Detroit Feminist of Yr., NOW, 2002; named to, Mich. Women's Hall of Fame, 1999; recipient Disting. Svc. award, Delta Kappa Gamma Soc., 1998. Mem.: Mich. Polit. History Soc. (bd. dirs.), Kiwanis. Democrat. Unitarian Universalist. Achievements include implementation of Title IX, development of Michigan Women's History. Home: 4149 Woodcreek Ln Lansing MI 48911 Office: Turner Dodge House 100 E North St Lansing MI 48906

HOMESTEAD, SUSAN E. (SUSAN FREEDLENDER), psychotherapist; b. Bklyn., Sept. 20, 1937; d. Cy Simon and Katherine (Haas) Eichelbaum; m. Robert Bruce Randall, 1956 (div. 1960); 1 child, Bruce David; m. George Gilbert Zanetti, Dec. 13, 1962 (div. 1972); m. Ronald Eric Homestead, Jan. 16, 1973 (div. 1980); m. Arthur Elliot Freedlender, Apr. 1, 1995. BA, U. Miami-Fla., 1960; MSW, Tulane U., 1967. Diplomate Am. Bd. Clin. Social Work; Acad. Cert. Social Workers, 1971, LCSW, Va., Calif. Psychotherapist, cons., Richmond, Va., 1971—, Los Altos, Calif.; pvt. practice Homestead Counseling, Richmond, Piedmont Psychiatric Ctr., P.C. (formerly Psychol. Evaluation Rehab. Cons., Inc.), Lynchburg, Va., 1994-97; cons. Family and Children's Svcs., Richmond, 1981—, Richmond Pain Clinic, 1983-84, Health Internat. Va., P.C., Lynchburg, 1984-86, Franklin St. Psychotherapy & Edn. Ctr., Santa Clara, Calif., 1988-90; pvt. practice, 1971—, Santa Clara County Children's Svc., 1973-75, 86-88. Co-dir. asthma program Va. Lung Assn., Richmond, 1975-79, Loma Prieta Regional Ctr.; chief clin. social worker Med. Coll. Va., Va. Commonwealth U., 1974-79; field supr. 1980 Census, 1981-87. Contbr. articles to profl. jours. Active Peninsula Children's Ctr., Morgan Ctr., Coun. Cmty. Action Planning, Cmty. Assn. for Retarded, Comprehensive Health Planning Assn. Santa Clara, Mental Health Commn., Children and Adolscent Target Group Calif., Women's Com. Richmond Symphony, Va. Mus. theatre; mem. adv. com. Va. Lung Assn.; mem. steering com. Am. Cancer Soc.(Va. divsn.), Epilepsy Found., Am. Heart Assn. (Va. divsn.), Ctrl. Va. Guild for Infant Survival; mem. fin. com. Robb for Gov. Mem. NASW, Va. Soc. Clin. Social Work, Inc. (charter mem., sec. 1975-78), Internat. Soc. Communicative Psychoanalysis & Psychotherapy, Am. Acad. Psychotherapists, Internat. Soc. for the Study of Dissociation, Am. Assn. Psychiatric Svcs. for Children. Address: 612 W Franklin St #10D Richmond VA 23220-4111 Fax: 804-740-3662. E-mail: SueEF@aol.com.

HOMMO, HARUMI, accountant; b. Kameda-machi, Niigata, Japan; came to U.S., 1990; BA, Tokyo U., 1980; MS in acct., Pace U., 1995. CPA. Sr. translator Goldman Sachs, Tokyo, 1985-86, Nat. West County Securities, Tokyo, 1986-89, Morgan Stanley, Tokyo, 1989-90, Daiwa Inst. Rsch., N.Y.C., 1990-97; acct. Ernst & Young, N.Y.C., 1998, Arthur Andersen LLP, N.Y.C., 1999; tax acct. Indsl. Bank Japan, N.Y.C., 2000—01; prin., owner HH Fin. Svcs., N.Y.C., 2002—. Mem. Am. Translators Assn. Avocations: readings, movies, travel, music, light sports. Home: 280 Park Ave S Apt 11D New York NY 10010-6130

HONAKER, STEVIE LEE, career counselor, consultant; b. Wewoka, Okla., Mar. 23, 1945; d. Joe Jack and Ruby Lee (Bowen) H.; 1 child, Charles Byron Howell. BA in Sociology, BA in Social Sci., Colo. State U., 1994, MEd, 1997, postgrad, 1997—. Lic. practicing counselor. Prin., owner Union Colony Shops, Greeley, Colo., 1970-79, Union Colony Interior Design, Greeley, Colo., 1980-83; career counselor Colo. State U. Career Ctr., Ft. Collins, Colo., 1996—. Trainer Colo. Sch. Counselors Assn., Denver, 1998; Myers-Briggs type indicato qualified, 1998; Strong interest inventory qualified, 1998; state rep. 1999. Co-author: Career Video Review, 1996-98. Active Commn. Status Women, Ft. Collins, 1993-95. Mem. Colo. Career Devel. Assn. (newsletter editor 1997-98, pres. 1998—, state rep. 1998), Alpha Kappa Delta. Avocations: scuba diving, mountain jeeping, gardening. Office: Colo State U Career Ctr 711 Oval Dr Fort Collins CO 80523-0001 Home: Apt 1308 5100 Old Birmingham Hwy Tuscaloosa AL 35404-4663 Fax: (970) 491-1134. E-mail: shonaker@lamar.colostate.edu.

HONANIE, JEANNETTE, special education educator; b. Tuba City, Arizona, Nov. 22, 1967; d. Silas and Florence Ponyah; m. Travis Honanie, Nov. 26, 1999; children: Daniel G., Loren S., Sunny L. M in spl. edn., Northern Ariz. U., Flagstaff. Tchr. aide Lake Havasu Sch. Dist., Lake Havasu City, Ariz., 1992—96; homebound tchr. Hopi Head Start, Tuba City, Ariz., 1997—99; tchr. Moencopi Day Sch., Tuba City, Ariz., 2000—. Mem.: Soc. for Advance of Chicanos and Native Americans in Sci., Coun. for Exceptional Children.

HONEA, JOYCE CLAYTON, critical care nurse; b. San Antoino, Oct. 4, 1952; d. Leslie James and Shirley Louis (Steinfeldt) Clayton; m. Bertrand N. Honea III, May 1, 1982; children: Matt Baker, Elissa Baker. BS in Nursing, Loretto Heights Coll., 1976; MS, Cen. Mich. U., 1990. Nursing faculty Front Range C.C., Ft. Collins, Colo., 1990—; family nurse practitioner U. No. Colo., 1999. Mem. ANA (sec. 1985-87).

HONEGGER, GITTA, language educator; PhD in Theater, U. Vienna, Austria. Prof. dramaturgy and dramatic criticism Yale Sch. Drama; stage dir. Yale Repertory Theatre; chair dept. drama Cath. U. Am., Washington; prof. theatre and English Ariz. State U., Tempe, Ariz. Author: Thomas Bernhard: The Making of an Austrian, 2001, Thomas Bernhard: Was ist das für ein Narr, 2002; contbg. editor Yale Theater Mag. Fellow, John Simon Guggenheim Meml. Found., 2003. Office: Ariz State U Dept English Tempe AZ 85287-0302

HONEYCUTT, JANICE LOUISE, nurse; b. Plainfield Twp., Pa., Feb. 8, 1943; d. Mortimer Singer and Mary Irene (Chase) Purdy; m. Billie B. Honeycutt, Aug. 8, 1987; 1 child, Jason G. ThB, Penns Creek (Pa.) Bible Sch., 1972; ADN, Westark C.C., 1985. Bd. cert. in gerontology and gen. nursing practice. Clinic dir. Highlands, Papua, New Guinea, 1973-76; case mgr. Kimberly Quality Care, Amarillo, Tex., 1988-95; asst. dir. of nursing Olsen Manor Nursing Home, 1995; case mgr. Casha Resource, 1996, quality assurance rep., 1997—; dir. profl. improvement VIP Home Care, Amarillo, 1998-2000; charge nurse Country Club Manor, Amarillo, Tex., 2000—01, Plum Creek Specialty Hosp., Amarillo, 2001—. Author: The Lighthouse, 1975; contbr. articles to profl. jours. Local st. campaign leader Arthritis Found., Amarillo, 1996. Mem. NGNA. Avocations: water color painting, crafts, sewing.

HONIG, ETHELYN, artist; b. N.Y.C., July 9, 1933; d. Samuel and Sophie (Brody) Blinder; m. Lester Jerome Honig, July 29, 1955 (dec. July 1992); children: Hillary Wynn Honig Ensminger, Deirdre Lynn Honig. Attended, Bennington Coll.; BA, Sarah Lawrence Coll., Bronxville, N.Y. Chair adv. bd. Sculpture Ctr. Battery Park Maritime Bldg., N.Y.C., 1987; curator art exhbn. for patients Manhattan Psychiatric Ctr., N.Y.C.; pub. Art Editions, Kenneth Noland Sol Lewitt, Chgo. 7 Portfolio. One person exhbns. include Benson Gallery, Bridgehampton, L.I., N.Y., 1968, 55 Mercer Gallery, N.Y.C., 1972, 74, 83, 84, 85, 86, 87, 89, 91, 94, 96, 2001, 03, Franklin Furnace Archive, N.Y.C., 1977, Mus. of Modern Art, 1974, 75, Rosa Esman Gallery, N.Y.C., 1975, South East Mus., Brewster, N.Y., 1978, Katonah (N.Y.) Gallery, 1981; group exhbns. include 55 Mercer Gallery, N.Y.C., 1975, 76, 78, 91, 93, U. Ariz. Mus., Tucson, 1980, So. Allegheny Mus. Art, 1981, Keene Coll. Art Gallery, Union, N.J. Foxworth Gallery, N.Y.C., 1985, Kenkelaba Gallery, N.Y.C., 1985, Somerstown Gallery, Somers, N.Y., 1985, Katonah (N.Y.) Gallery, 1987, Art Initiatives at Tribeca 148 Gallery, 1994, 95, Paula Cooper Gallery, N.Y.C., 1970, represented in permanent collections Mus. Modern Art, N.Y.C., Wadsworth Atheneum Mus., Patrick Lannon Found., Citi-Corps, Smith Coll. Mus., Northampton, Mass.; patentee in field. Founder and chairperson Clozapine Family Info. for the Alliance for the Mentally Ill, N.Y.S., 1990-96. Recipient Svc. awards Alliance for the Mentally Ill N.Y.S., Albany, 1990, Friends and Advocates for the Mentally Ill, 1990-91. Mem. Art Students League, 55 Mercer Artists (founding mem., pres. 1997-98). Avocations: amateur archaeology, swimming, cycling, photography. Home: 137 E 95th St New York NY 10128-1723

HONIGBERG, CAROL CROSSMAN, lawyer; b. Salina, Kansas, Sept. 23, 1955; d. Robert Denfield and Barbara Jane (Eckberg) Crossman; m. Paul Mark Honigberg, Aug. 18, 1979; children: Michael, Margaret Ann. BA, Duke U., 1977; JD, Vanderbilt U., 1980. Bar: Va., 1980. Assoc. Hazel and Thomas, P.C., Alexandria, Va., 1980—86; propr. Hazel and Thomas, P.C., Falls Ch., Va., 1986—99; ptnr. Reed Smith LLP (formerly Reed, Smith, Hazel, and Thomas, LLP), Falls Ch., 1999—, sec., 2001—. Columnist comml. investment real estate. Mem. ABA, CREW Network (pres. North Va. chpt. 1998-99, nat. del. 2000-01). Office: Reed Smith LLP 3110 Fairview Park Dr Ste 1400 Falls Church VA 22042-4503 Business E-Mail: chonigberg@reedsmith.com.

HONNER SUTHERLAND, B. JOAN, advertising executive; b. N.Y.C., Oct. 23, 1952; d. William John and Mary Patricia (Edwards) H.; m. Donald J. Sutherland, Oct. 3, 1987; children: Chelsea Lauren, Whitney Devon. Student, Endicott Coll., 1970-71. Art dir. Kerrigan Studio, Darien, Conn., 1971-73, Foote Cone and Belding, Phoenix, 1973-77, sr. art dir. Chgo., 1977-81; v.p., assoc. creative dir. J. Walter Thompson, Chgo., 1982-86; v.p., exec. art dir. BBDO Chgo., 1986-91; creative dir. Knautz & Co., Sarasota, Fla., 1992-93; co-owner X-L Advt., Sarasota, Fla., 1993-94; owner Beyond Design of Sarasota, Inc., 1994—; mktg. dir. Nelson Pub. Inc., Nokomis, Fla., 2001—. Cons. J. Walter Thompson, Toronto and San Francisco, 1983-84; owner Fla. Antiques, Geneva, Ill., 1986-90. Introduced Discover card, 1985. Tchr. elem. sch. art; mem. Southside Sch. PTA Bd., Sarasota, 1996-99; spl. projects Pine View Sch., Sarasota, 1999—. Recipient 1st pla. TV local campaign WGN, 6th dist. Addy, 1980, Kemp. Corp. Addy, 1990, Mktg. Flood awards FEMA/NFIP, 1997, 98, 99; Best Internat. TV campaign Pepsi Clio, 1985. Roman Catholic. Avocation: miniatures. Home: 4941 Commonwealth Dr Sarasota FL 34242-1421

HONNOLD, KATHRYN S. real estate agent; b. Pataskala, Ohio, Nov. 10, 1936; d. Harold S. and Stella E. (Slack) Williams; m. Robert I. Honnold, Aug. 18, 1956; children: Jayne, Robin. Student, Franklin U., N.Y. Sch. Modeling. Sales agt. USA-1Real Estate Corp., Pataskala, Ohio, 1978—; adminstrv. asst., office mgr., sec. Monsanto, Columbus, Ohio, 1983-87; coun. mem. Pataskala Village, 1987-98; adminstrv. asst. Bank One, 1988-99; asst. to exec. dir., asst. to pres. United Svcs. for Effective Parenting Ohio, Inc., 2002—. Pres. Pataskala Village Coun., 1990-92, 94, 96; mem. Pataskala Bd. Zoning Appeals Bd., 1997-2000; appointed mem. Licking County Sr. Citizen's Levy Adv. Bd., 1989-; adv. bd. Licking County Econ. Devel. Task Force, 1991-92; active Rep. Ctrl. Com. Licking County, 1998—; model for fashion shows. Named Sec. of Yr., 1987. Mem.: Nat., State and County Real Estate Assocs., Internat. Assn. Adminstrv. Pers. Home: 325 Laurel Ln Pataskala OH 43062-8547 E-mail: bkhonnold@msn.com.

HONOLD, LINDA KAYE, political organization executive, human resources development executive; b. Lansing, Mich., Aug. 16, 1956; d. Ervin Charles and Patricia Kathleen (Couzzins) Gaulke; m. Reynolds Keith Honold, dec. 5, 1987; 1 child, Samatha Kaye. BA in Polit. Sci., U. Wis., Eau Claire, 1980; MS in Indsl. Rels., U. Wis., Madison, 1987; PhD in Human and Orgnl. Sys., Fielding Grad. Inst., Santa Barbara, Calif., 1999. Editorial asst. Lake Pub. Co., Libertyville, Ill., 1980-81; econ. devel. rep. Projects With Industry, Menomonie, Wis., 1981-83; exec. dir. Am. Cancer Soc., Eau Claire, 1983-85; career counselor Hmong Assn., Sheboygan, Wis., 1985-87; mem. resource team personal devel. Johnsonville Foods, Sheboygan Falls, Wis., 1987—90; orgnl. devel. cons., 1990—. Author: Developing Employees Who Love to Learn, 2001; co-author: Organizational DNA, 2003; contbr. articles to profl. jours. Sec. Civil Svc. Commn., Sheboygan, 1986-95; del. Dem. Party, San Francisco, 1984, L.A., 2000; chair Wis. State Dem. Party, 2001—. Mem. Am. Soc. Personnel Adminstrs., Am. Soc. Tng. and Devel., Sheboygan County S. of C. (chmn. edn. coun.), Mortar Bd., Altrusa (sec. 1987-90), Sheboygan Svc. Club. Lutheran. Avocations: jogging, reading, sailing. Home: 1633 N Prospect Ave Unit 20B Milwaukee WI 53202-2482 Office: Democratic Party of Wisconsin 222 West Washington Madison WI 53703

HONOUR, LYNDA CHARMAINE, research scientist, educator, psychotherapist; b. Orange, NJ, Aug. 9, 1949; d. John Henry, Jr. and Evelyn Helena Roberta (Pietrowski) H. BA, Boston U., 1976; MA, Calif. State U., Fullerton, 1985, UCLA, 1989; PhD, U. So. Calif., 1997. Lic. marriage, family and child psychotherapist and psychologist, Calif. Prof. psychology Pepperdine U., Malibu, Calif., 1989-95; pvt. practice mind-body behavioral medicine, including clin. psychoneuroimmunology and psychoneuroendocrinology Santa Monica, Calif., 1991—. Clin. and vis. prof. throughout so. Calif., including Calif. Sch. Profl. Psychology, Calif. State U., Long Beach, Calif. State U., Northridge, 1989—; rsch. scientist in neuroendocrinology, neurochemistry and molecular biology in numerous labs including 3 Nobel Prize winning rsch. teams; condr. rsch. Neuropsychiat. Inst., Brain Rsch. Inst., Mental Retardation Rsch. Ctr., UCLA, Tulane U. Med. Sch., V.A. Med. Ctr., New Orleans, Salk Inst. Biol. Studies; rsch. cons. U. Calif. Med. Ctr., Irvine; cons. in rsch. or psychotherapy, 1976—; guest expert on safety issues regarding magnetic imaging Premiere Radio Network, 2001; rsch. scientist in neuroendocrinology and neurochemistry in numerous labs.; condr. rsch. Neuropsychiat. Inst., Brain Rsch. Inst., Mental Retardation Rsch. Ctr., UCLA, Tulane U. Med. Sch., V.A. Med. Ctr., New Orleans, Salk Inst. Biol. Studies; rsch. cons. U. Calif. Med. Ctr., Irvine, Salk Inst., others; cons. Thomson Internat. Pub.; hon. chmn., Bus. Adv. Coun. Nat. Rep. Congl. Com. Contbr. articles to profl. jours. including Hosp. Practice, Peptides, Physiology and Behavior, Pharmacology, Biochemistry and Behavior, others. Rsch. grantee Organon Internat. Rsch. Group, Netherlands, 1984-88. Mem. AAAS, APA, Soc. for Neurosci., Internat. Behavioral Neurosci. Soc., Internat. Brain Rsch. Orgn., Calif. Assn. Marriage and Family Psychotherapists, N.Y. Acad. Scis., Sons and Daus. of Pearl Harbor Survivors, Psi Chi. Roman Catholic. Achievements include identification of a peptide which facilitates and another peptide inhibits learning and memory task performance permanently in a developmental paradigm in mice; and facilitation peptide can permanently reverse induced learning/memory deficit, with implications for mental retardation and other learning/memory deficit treatment; mem. research team which isolated and characterized corticotropic hormone releasing factor; delineated various effects of peptides on behavior including bipolar disorders, endogenous depression, mania and others; research in risks associated with MRI exposure. Avocations: professional musician, artist, mind-related issues, time-space travel involving the unified field theories and others., metaphysics. Office: PO Box 369 Santa Monica CA 90406-0369

HONSA, VLASTA, retired librarian; b. Žilina, Czechoslovakia, Sept. 1, 1924; came to U.S., 1951; d. František Petr and Marie (Širkova) Petrova; m. Vladimir Honsa, June 26, 1948; children: Patricia, Eva Honsa-Hogg. BA, Charles U., Prague, 1947; MLS, Ind. U., 1968. Gifts libr. Ind. U. Libr., Bloomington, 1968-70; head reference dept. Clark County Libr., Las Vegas, Nev., 1970-80, asst. adminstr., 1980-94; ret., 1994. Coord. Found. Collection, part of the Found. Ctr.'s Cooperating Collections network, Clark County Libr., 1979-94. Author: Nevada Foundation Directory, 1984, 2d edit., 1989, 3rd edit., 1994. Bd. dirs. So. Nev. Musical Arts Soc., Las Vegas, 1989-92; organized and presented fundraising workshops for cmty. fund raisers sponsored by Las Vegas-Clark County Libr. Dist., 1979-94. Recipient Ind. U. grant-in-aid to conduct rsch. of publs. in cen. Am. univs. and nat. librs., 1970, Champion award Las Vegas-Clark County Libr. Dist., 1985. Mem. ALA, AAUW, Nev. Libr. Assn., Univ. Nevada Las Vegas Faculty Club. Roman Catholic. Avocations: reading, music, arts, travel. Home: 2680 Congress Ave Las Vegas NV 89121-1316 E-mail: honsa@worldnet.att.net.

HOOD, ANTOINETTE FOOTE, dermatologist; b. Honolulu, 1941; MD, Vanderbilt U., 1967. Cert. dermatology. Intern Vanderbilt Affiliated Hosps, 1967-68; fellow dermatology Harvard U., 1973-75, resident dermatology, 1975-76; resident dermatology-pathology Mass. Gen. Hosp., Boston, 1976-78; exec. dir. American Board of Dermatology, Detroit, 2001—. Office: Henry Ford Health System 1 Ford Place Detroit MI 48202

HOOD, DENISE PAGE, federal judge; b. 1952; BA, Yale Univ., 1974; JD, Columbia Sch. of Law, 1977. Asst. corp. counsel City of Detroit, Law Dept., 1977-82; judge 36th Dist. Ct., 1983-89, Recorder's Ct. for the City of Detroit, 1989-92, Wayne County Circuit Ct., 1993-94; district judge U.S. Dist. Ct. (Mich. ea. dist.), 6th circuit, 1994—. Recipient Judicial Service award Black Women Lawyers Assn., 1994. Mem. Am. Bar Assn., State Bar of Mich., Detroit Bar Assn. (Chmn. of Yr. award 1988), Assn. of Black Judges of Mich., Mich. Dist. Judges Assn., Am. Inns of Ct., Wolverine Bar Assn. (bd. of dirs.), Women Lawyers Assn. of Mich., Fed. Bar Assn., Nat. Assn. of Women Judges, Nat. Bar Assn. Judicial Coun., Mich. Judicial Inst. Office: US Courthouse 231 W Lafayette Blvd Rm 251 Detroit MI 48226-2789

HOOD, GLENDA E. state agency administrator; m. Charles M. Hood III; 3 children. BA, Rollins Coll.; postgrad., Harvard U., Ga. State U. Commr. City of Orlando, Fla., 1982-92, mayor, 1992—2002; sec. of state Florida, 2003—. Pres. Glenda E. Hood & Assocs., Inc. Vice chmn. mcpl. planning bd. City of Orlando, mem. nominating bd., chmn. task force bd. and commn. restructure; past chmn., founding mem. bd. dirs. Found. Orange County Pub. Schs.; co-chmn. Orlando Fights Back-Coalition for a Drug-Free Cmty.; bd. dirs. U. Ctrl. Fla. Found., Met. Orlando Urban League; past pres. exec. bd. Ctrl. Fla. Coun. of Boy Scouts; bd. overseers Rollins Coll. Crummer Grad. Sch. of Bus.; mem. adv. bd. Valencia C.C., Fla.- Costa Rica Inst.; past co-chmn. United Negro Coll. Fund; pres. Jr. League Orlando-Winter Park, Vol. Svc. Bur.; mem. Orange County Commn. on Children. Named Mcpl. Leader of Yr., Am. City and County Mag., 1992, one of Ten Outstanding Young Americans, U.S. Jaycees, one of Seven Outstanding Youth Floridians, Fla. Jaycees, Woman of Yr., Downtown Orlando Inc., one of Ten People to Watch, Fla. Trend, one of 100 Young Women of Promise, Good Housekeeping; recipient Willie J. Bruton award for cmty. svc. Met. Orlando Urban League, Summit award Women's Resource Ctr., Svc. to Mankind award Leukemia Soc. Am. Ctrl. Fla. chpt. Mem. Nat. League of Cities (past pres.), Fla. League of Cities (past pres.), Fla. C. of C. (past pres.), Greater Orlando C. of C. (past v.p.). Office: Florida Dept of State R A Gray Bldg 500 S Bronough Tallahassee FL 32399-0250

HOOD, LUANN SANDRA, special education educator; b. Bklyn., Jan. 10, 1955; d. Louie A. and Sylvia M. (Hall) Mayo; m. Stephen J. Hood. BA, St. Joseph's Coll., Bklyn., 1976; MS in Edn., Bklyn. Coll., 1979. Cert. tchr. N,K, 1-6, spl. edn., N.Y.C. lic. Edn. counselor adolescents Am. Indian Comty. House, Inc., N.Y.C., 1977-79; tchr. children with retarded mental devel. Pub. Sch. 273, Bklyn., 1979-83; tchr. early childhood Pub. Sch. 128, Bklyn., 1983-94; tchr. emotionally handicapped Pub. Sch.215, Bklyn., 1994-95; tchr. learning disabled Pub. Sch. 101, Bklyn., 1995-99, tchr. hard of hearing, 1999—. Mem. sch. leadership team, 1997—. Exec. sec. bd. trustees Am. Indian Cmty. House, Inc., N.Y.C., 1980-91. Regents scholar N.Y. State Edn. Dept., 1972; grantee Indian League of the Americas, Inc. 1972-75, Thunderbird Am. Indian Dancers, Inc., 1972-75, Internat. Order of King's Daughters and Sons, 1976. Mem. Coun. for Exceptional Children, N.Y. State Tchrs. of Handicapped. Democrat. Roman Catholic. Avocation: photography.

HOOD, OLLIE RUTH, health facilities executive; b. San Francisco, Nov. 26, 1947; d. Rodger Brown and Lucile Brooks (Reid); m. McKinley Hood, Aug. 27, 1969 (div. 1987); children: Antoinette Brown, Kirk Stewart, Seancy Hood. BA, San Francisco State U., 1971. Asst. sec., v.p. Weyerhauser Mortgage Co., L.A., 1971-80; asst. supr. Plaza Mortgage Co., L.A., 1980-84; data entry supr. Western Standard Truck, L.A., 1984-85; mgr. Kaiser Hosp., San Francisco, 1985-92; with Emory Clinic, Atlanta, 1995—. Patentee in field. Mem. Calif. Assn. Hosp. Admitting Mgrs., Nat. Assn. Hosp. Admitting Mgrs., NAFE, Kaiser Permanente Club (2d v.p. 1987), Nat. Assn. Women (v.p. 1989—). Home and Office: ORH Inc 10765 E Virginia Ave Unit F Aurora CO 80012-2058 Fax: 303-366-3797. E-mail: olliehood@attbi.com.

HOOD, PHYLLIS ILENE, special education educator; d. James H Brown and Viola Mae Riggle, Brown, Jones; m. James Richard Morris, May 27, 1954 (div. Mar. 6, 1986); m. Charles Gary Hood, Feb. 18, 1988 (div. Nov. 8, 1993); children: Stacy Lynn Gebhardt, James Richard Morris, Teresa Rene Thompson, Vilas Lester Morris, Ruth Ilene Owens, Richard Hayden Morris. BS in edn., NW Mo. State U., 1985—89, MS in edn., 1989—96. Elem. Edn. NW Mo. State U., 1989, Learning Disabled NW Mo. State U., 1989, Mentally Handicapped NW Mo. State U., 1991, Reading NW Mo. State U., 1996, Mild/Moderate Behavior Disorder U. of Ctrl. Ark., 2000. Spl. edn. and reading tchr. North Andrew R-VI Elem. Sch., Bolkow, Mo., 1989—90; spl. edn. tchr. Nodaway-Holt R-VII H.S., Graham, Mo.,

1990—92, Camdenton R-III Sch. Dist., Camdenton, Mo., 1992—98, Spl. Sch. Dist., Town and Country, Mo., 1998—. Cheerleader sponsor Nodaway-Holt R-VII Sch. Dist., Graham, Mo., 1991—92, Camdenton R-III Sch. Dist., Camdenton, Mo., 1992—94, Hazelwood Sch. Dist., St. Louis, 2000—01; sponsor Big Bros./Big Sisters, St. Louis, 2001—. Ladies aux. Mo. Army N.G., Maryville, Mo., 1989—96; club mem. Optimist Club of Camdenton, Mo., 1992—98, pres., 1997—98; club mem. Optimist Club of O'Fallon, O'Fallon, Mo., 1999—2003, pres., 2000—01. Recipient Disting. Pres., Optimist Internat.-West Mo. Dist., 1997—98, Honor Pres., Optimist Internat. -East Mo. Dist., 2000—01, Cert. of Appreciation, 2001—02. Mem.: Coun. for Exceptional Children (corr.). D-Liberal. Christian. Avocations: dance, travel, swimming, walking, gardening. Office: Hazelwood East High School 11300 Dunn Rd Saint Louis MO 63138

HOOD, SANDRA DALE, librarian; b. Edmond, Okla., Nov. 28, 1949; d. Rufus Gustav and Hope Louvica (Hutton) Farber; m. Frank D. Hood Jr., May 17, 1971; 1 child, Charles Richard. BA, U. Okla., 1971, MLS, 1972; MA in Bicultural Bilingual Studies, U. Tex., San Antonio, 1996. Libr. South Oklahoma City Jr. Coll., 1973, Daus. of Republic of Tex. Libr. at the Alamo, San Antonio, 1980—88; acad. outreach prof., automation and libr. sys. libr. Palo Alto Coll. Learning Resources Ctr., San Antonio, 1988—. Pres. faculty sen. Palo Alto Coll., 2001—02. Pres. tech. svcs. spl. interest group Coun. Rsch. and Acad. Librs., San Antonio, 1991-92, chmn. circulation and interlibr. loan spl. interest group, 1997—; sec., mem. exec. bd. Timberwood Park Property Owners Assn., San Antonio, 1991-94. Recipient NISOD award, 2003. Mem. ALA, Tex. Libr. Assn. (conf. planning com. 1992-93, 97-98, 2002-04), Tex. Accelerated Libr. Leader 1997, disaster relief com. 2002—), Bexar Libr. Assn. (exec. bd., dir. editor 1988-90), Tex. Cmty. Coll. Tchrs. Assn. Democrat. Lutheran. Avocations: travel, reading, computers. Home: 27030 Foggy Meadows St San Antonio TX 78260-1822 Office: Palo Alto Coll Learning Resources Ctr 1400 W Villaret Blvd San Antonio TX 78224-2417

HOOKER, ELAINE NORTON, news executive; b. Rockville Center, N.Y., Dec. 4, 1944; d. Henry Gaither and Ann Lou (Allen) Norton; m. Ronald Wayne Johnson (div.); m. Kenneth Ward Hooker Jr. (div.); children: Alisa, Miranda, Nora, Emily. Student, Wilson Coll., 1962-64, U. Hartford, 1965, Trinity Coll., 1974, Andover Newton Theol. Sch., 1988-89. Reporter, editor The Hartford (Conn.) Courant, 1969-74; newswoman AP, Hartford, 1974-75, Conn. news editor, 1975-79, western Mass. corr. Springfield, Mass., 1979-80, Mass. day news supr. Boston, 1981-84, Mass. news editor, 1984, Conn. bur. chief Hartford, 1984-88, dep. dir. corp. comm. N.Y.C., 1990, gen. exec. newspaper membership, 1991-97, Oreg. bur. chief Portland, 1997—. Spkr. in field. Active various coms. at chs. in Concord, Mass., Hartford, Briarcliff, N.Y., Greenwich, Conn., N.Y.C. Recipient Sigma Delta Chi award, 1974. Mem. Soc. Profl. Journalists (mem. Freedom Info. coun. 1984-87), New Eng. Soc. Newspaper Editors (rep. Soviet journalists conf. 1985), Open Oreg. Home: 1005 SW Park Ave Apt 406 Portland OR 97205-2416 Office: AP 121 SW Salmon St Ste 1450 Portland OR 97204-2924

HOOKER, MELINDA GRYDER, music educator; b. Honolulu, Mar. 16, 1973; d. Dennis Harold and Patricia James Gryder; m. James Lewis Hooker, July 17, 1999; 1 child, Tye Gryder. MusB in music edn., James Madison U., 1995. Tchr., band dir. Bath County Pub. Schs., Hot Springs, Va., 1995—. Named Outstanding Educator, Va. Govs. Sch. for Sci., Math and Tech., 2001. Mem.: Va. Band and Orch. Dirs. Assn., Music Educators Nat. Conf. Republican. Presbyterian. Home: Rt 2 Box 219 Hot Springs VA 24445 Office: Bath County HS Rt 1 Box 575 Hot Springs VA 24445 E-mail: melindah@bath.k12.va.us.

HOOLEY, DARLENE, congresswoman; b. Williston, N.D., Apr. 4, 1939; d. Clarence Alvin and Alyce (Rogers) Olsen; m. John Hooley (div.); children: Chad, Erin. BS in Edn., Oreg. State U., 1961, postgrad., 1963-65, Portland State U., 1966-67. Tchr. Woodburn (Oreg.) & Gervais Sch., 1962-65, David Douglas Sch. Dist., Portland, Oreg., 1965-67, St. Mary's Acad., Portland, 1967-69; mem. West Linn (Oreg.) City Coun., 1976-80; state rep. Oreg. State Ho. of Reps., 1980-87; county commr. Clackamas County (Oreg.) Bd., 1987-96; mem. U.S. Congress from 5th dist. Oreg., 1996—; mem. budget com., fin. svcs. com. Vice-chair Oreg. Tourism Alliance, Portland, 1991—. bd. dirs. Pub. Employees Ret. Bd., Portland, 1989—, Cmty. Corrections Bd., Oregon City, 1990—, Providence Med. Ctr., Portland, 1989—; acting chair Oreg. Trail Found. Bd., Oregon City, 1991—; mem. Urban Growth Policy Adv. Com., Portland, 1991—. Named Legislator of the Year Oreg. Libr. Assn., 1985-86, Oreg. Solar Energy Assn., 1985; recipient Spl. Svc. award Clackamas City Coun. for Child Abuse Prevention, 1989. Mem. LWV, Oreg. Women's Polit. Caucus (Women of the Yr. 1988). Democrat. Office: 2430 Rayburn Bldg Washington DC 20515-3705*

HOOPER, ANNE DODGE, pathologist, educator; b. Groton, Mass., July 16, 1926; d. Carroll William and Bertha Sanford (Wiener) Dodge; m. William Dale Hooper, June 17, 1952; children: Elizabeth Anne, Joan Elaine, Caroline Mae. AB, Washington U., St. Louis, 1947, MD, 1952. Diplomate in pathologic anatomy, clin. pathology and forensic pathology Am. Bd. Pathology. Rotating intern Virginia Mason Hosp., Seattle, 1952-53; resident in internal medicine St. Francis Hosp., Hartford, Conn., 1953-54; resident in pathologic anatomy and clin. pathology New Britain (Conn.) Gen. Hosp., 1954-57, Presbyn. Hosp., Phila., 1957-58; resident in forensic pathology Office Med. Examiner, Phila., 1958-60; from pathologist to acting chief lab svc. VA Hosp., Coatesville, Pa., 1960-66; dir. lab. St. Albans (Vt.) Hosp., 1966-69, Kerbs Hosp., St. Albans, 1966-71, Williamson Appalachian Regional Hosp., South Williamson, Ky., 1971-73, Beckley (W.Va.) Appalachian Regional Hosp., 1974-76; asst. prof. pathology W.Va. Sch. Osteo. Medicine, Lewisburg, 1977, assoc. prof. pathology, 1978-97, cons. in pathology, 1997—. Lab. accreditation insp. CAP, 1992—, Am. Osteo. Assn., 1986—99; assoc. med. examiner State of W.Va., 1999—; med. missionary Kijabe Hosp., Kenya, 1998; med. missionary, pathologist Pathologists Overseas at SALFA Lab., Madagascar, 2000; med. missionary with Glens Falls NY Med. Missionary Found., Nueva Santa Rosa, Guatemala, 2001. Contbr. articles to profl. jours. Pres. local elem. sch. PTA, St. Albans, 1967-68; pres. Greenbrier unit Am. Cancer Soc., Lewisburg, 1989-93, bd. dirs. W.Va. divsn., Charleston, 1987-94, profl. edn. com. W.Va. divsn., 1982-94; bd. dirs. ARC, Greenbrier County, W.Va., 2002—. Fellow Coll. Am. Pathologists, Am. Acad. Forensic Scis.; mem. AMA, W.Va. Med. Soc., Raleigh County Med. Soc., Am. Soc. Clin. Pathologists, Internat. Acad. Pathologists, Nat. Assn. Med. Examiners, Am. Osteo. Coll. Pathologists (assoc.). Avocation: playing violin and viola. Office: 63 Cedar Knoll Ronceverte WV 24970-9700

HOOPER, DENISE LYNN, technologist; b. Joliet, Ill., Mar. 24, 1955; d. Donald Patrick Schneider and Donna Rae Smith-Schneider; m. David Michael Hooper, June 24, 1983; children: Kevin, Kaitlin. BS in med. tech., biology, Lewis U., 1977. Cert. med. tech. 1977. Med. tech. Provena Med. Ctr., Joliet, Ill., 1981—84, Family Practice Cons., Joliet, 1988—; tchr. Joliet Cath. Acad., Joliet, 2003. Mem.: Am. Soc. of Clin. Pathologists. Avocations: gardening, exercise for health. Office: Joliet Cat Acad 1200 N Larkin Joliet IL 60435

HOOPER, EARLENE HILL, state legislator; b. Balt., Oct. 22; d. Otis Barnett Hooper and Thelma E. (Richardson) Young; 1 child, Charisse E. BA, Norfolk State U., 1996; MSW, Adelphi U., 1996; DHL, Five Towns Coll., 1997. Mgr. N.Y. State Dept. Social Svcs., N.Y.C.; mem. N.Y. State Assembly, 1988—. Mem. women's program, shop steward Pub. Employees Fedn., 1980-88, exec. bd. Exec. bd. Jack & Jill of Am., Inc., Nassau County, N.Y., 1985—; mem. Nat. Women's Polit. Caucus, N.Y.C., 1987—. Mem. Negro Bus. and Profl. Women (Cen. Nassau chpt.), Delta Sigma Theta. Democrat. Office: NY State Legislature State Capitol Albany NY 12224

HOORNBEEK, LYNDA RUTH COUCH, librarian, educator; b. Springfield, Ill., July 12, 1933; d. Willard Lee and Mabel Magdalene (Forberg) Couch; m. Louis Arthur Hoornbeek, Nov. 9, 1957; children— John Arthur, David William, Mark Benjamin. B.A. in Sociology, U. Ill., 1955; M.Ed., Cornell U., 1956; M.L.S., U. So. Calif., Los Angeles, 1973. Cert. tchr. Ill., N.Y. Tchr. elem. sch. North Haven (Conn.) Pub. Schs., 1956-57; library adminstr. Winfield (Ill.) Pub. Library, 1974-77; interim library adminstr. Bloomingdale (Ill.) Pub. Library, 1977-78; ref. librarian Franklin Park (Ill.) Pub. Library, 1978-83; state literacy dir. program Literacy Vols. of Ill., Chgo., 1983—84; research coordinator Ill. Literacy Council, Office of Sec. State, 1984—85; with office libr. outreach svcs. ALA, 1985-86; adult svcs. libr. Glen Ellyn (Ill.) Pub. Libr., 1986-94; ret., 1994. Bd. dirs. YWCA, Pitts., 1957—62; vol. archivist Glen Ellyn Hist. Soc., bd. dirs. 1994—. YWCA fellow 1954; Ford Found. fellow, 1955-56; U. Ill. scholar, 1951-55. Mem. Mortar Bd., Calif. Library Assn., Ill. Library Assn., ALA, AAUW, LWV, Beta Phi Mu, Pi Lambda Theta, Alpha Phi. Congregationalist. Home: 351 N Park Blvd Glen Ellyn IL 60137-5037

HOOSER, HELEN, artist; b. Mannsville, Okla., Oct. 11, 1921; d. Charlie Valentine Woolard and Lelia May Peterman; m. Ernest Hooser, Sept. 21, 1940; children: Patricia Ann Hooser Morgan, Carl Ernest. Student, Murray State Sch. Agr., Tishomingo, Okla., 1939-40, Okla. State U., 1940-41; grad., Famous Artist Corr. Sch., Westport, Conn., 1961. LPN; cert. med. technologist. Nurse, lab. technician Antlers (Okla.) Clinic, 1946-55, Engles Clinic, Durant, Okla., 1959-75; artist, 1975—. Exhibited in solo show at Kerr Mus., Poteau, Okla., 1969, Tex. Tech. Mus., Lubbock, 1970, Okla. Mus. Art, 1971, Peddler's Cart, Albuquerque, 1974, Omni Gallery, Dallas, 1995-99, Anderson Gallery, Oklahoma City, 1975, Gov.'s Gallery, Oklahoma City, 1980, Ariel Gallery, N.Y.C., 1989, Little Louvre Gallery, Denison, Tex., 1998, VanMeter Gallery, Durant, Okla., 1999, others; group shows include Lasting Impressions Gallery, Sherman, Tex., Art Works, Midway Mall, Sherman, Hooser Art Gallery, Durant, Madill (Okla.) Art Show, Soho Art competition, N.Y.C., Norman Wilkes Gallery, Oklahoma City, Ariel GAllery, N.Y.C.; featured in mag. articles. Mem. So. Watercolor Soc. (signature mem.), Okla. Watercolor Assn., Sherman Art League, Durant Creative Arts Guild, Epsilon Sigma Alpha (state pres. 1958-59). Baptist. Avocations: sewing, reading. Home: 1004 W University Blvd Durant OK 74701-3230

HOOVER, BETTY-BRUCE HOWARD, private school educator; b. Wake County, N.C., Mar. 20, 1939; d. Bruce Ruffin and Mary Elizabeth (Brown) Howard; m. Herbert Charles Marsh Hoover, Sept. 3, 1961; children: David Andrew, Howard Webster, Lorraine Hoover Clark. BA, Wake Forest U., 1961; MA, U. South Fla., 1978. Tchr. English Greensboro (N.C.) Sr. H.S., 1961-62, Lindley Jr. H.S., Greensboro, 1963, Berkeley Prep. Sch., Tampa, Fla., 1976—2002, chmn. English dept., 1977-85, dir., upper divsn., 1984-2000, chmn. curriculum com., 1982-86, historian, 1998—2002; ret., 2000. Author: Resources in Education, 1992, Berkeley Preparatory School: A Proud Legacy, 2002. Pres., Suncoast Midshipmen Parents Club, Tampa Bay Area, 1983-84. Mem. ASCD, Nat. Coun. Tchrs. English, Sociedad Honoraria Hispanica, The Nat. Coun. States, Wake Forest U. Alumni Assn., DAR, Hillsborough County Bar Aux., Cum Laude Soc. (sec. 1981-2000), Nat. Honor Soc., Phi Beta Kappa, Phi Sigma Iota, Sigma Tau Delta, Kappa Kappa Gamma. Mem.: Thespian Soc., Quill and Scroll, Mortarboard Alumni Assn., Berkeley Blazers, Beach Pk. Garden Club, Phi Betta Kappa Alumni Assn. (v.p. membership), Kappa Kappa Gamma Alumni Assn. Republican. Episcopalian. Avocations: sewing, gardening. Home: 11902 Wandsworth Dr Tampa FL 33626-2611

HOOVER, KATHERINE LACY, composer; b. Elkins, W.Va., Dec. 2, 1937; d. Samuel Randolph and Katherine F. (Lacy) Hoover; m. J. Christopher Schwab, July 14, 1964 (div. Aug. 1972); 1 child, Norman Daniel; m. Richard V. Goodwin, May 18, 1985. BMus Theory, perf. cert. in flute, Eastman Sch. of Music, Rochester, N.Y., 1959; MMus in Theory, Manhattan Sch. of Music, N.Y.C., 1974; student, Conductors Inst., Columbia, S.C., 1989-91. Tchr. of flute The Juilliard Sch. Prep., N.Y.C., 1962-69; tchr. of theory Manhattan Sch. of Music, N.Y.C., 1969-84; theory, composition lessons Tchrs. Coll., Columbia, N.Y., 1984-89; free-lance flutist Lincoln Ctr., Broadway, others, N.Y.C., 1962-85; composer, 1975—. Originator/dir. Festivals of Women's Music, I-IV, N.Y.C., 1978-81; ptnr. Papagena Press, N.Y.C., 1989—; guest lectr. in field. Composer numerous compositions, including: Night Skies, 1994, Quintet (Da Pacem), 1989, Eleni: A Greek Tragedy, 1986, Medieval Suite, 1984 (NFA award 1987), numerous chamber pieces including Trio, Op. 14, 1978, Lyric Trio, Op. 27, 1983, Sonata, Op. 44, 1991, String Quartet, Op. 58, 1999, others; numerous other orchestral compositions, including Two Sketches, Op. 42, 1989, Clarinet Concerto, Op. 38, 1987, Double Concerto, Op. 40, 1989, Summer Night, Op. 34, 1985, Stitch-Te Naku, 1996, others; composer solo instrumental music, including Kokopeli, 1990, Set for Clarinet, 1978, Stitch-Te Naku, 1996, Winter Spirits, 1997, piano pieces, 1977-82; composer choral music, including The Last Invocation, 1984, Songs of Celebration, 1983, Psalm 100, 1997, others; composer solo voice with instruments, including From the Testament of Francois Villon, 1982, Central American Songs, 1995, The Heart Speaks, 1997, Requiem 1865/2001, 2002, others. Recipient numerous awards including Acad. award in composition, Am. Acad. of Arts and Letters, N.Y., 1994, Composers Fellowship, Nat. Endowment for Arts, Washington, 1979, numerous ASCAP awards, 1979—; winner award for Newly Pub. Music, Nat. Flute Assn., 1987, 91, 93, 94; named Composer of the Yr., N.Y. Music Tchrs. Assn., 1989; grantee Alice M. Ditson Fund, 1984, Meet the Composer, 1976—; commd. N.Y. Flute Club, 1995, Ind. U., Pa., 1995, W. Dobbs and Marshall U., 1994, Vinland Ensemble, 1991, Duologue, 1991, N.J. Chamber Music Soc., others. Mem. ASCAP, Internat. Alliance Women in Music, Bohemians, Nat. Flute Assn. (bd. dirs. 2000-02), Conductors Guild, Am. Music Ctr., Bohemians. Avocations: reading, travel, gardening.

HOOVER, MARY LOU BALLENTINE, music educator; b. Kissimmee, Fla., Feb. 15, 1959; d. Joseph Charles and Katie Sawyer Ballentine; m. Jacob Charles Hoover, July 17, 1991 (div. Nov. 1998). MusB, Valdosta State U., Ga., 1982; ECE Cert., Valdosta State U., 1983, postgrad. With Valdosta State Admissions, 1982—86; tchr. music Lowndes County Bd. Edn., Valdosta, 1986—91; dir. choral music Waycross Mid. Sch., Ga., 1996—; monitor, asst. dir. Summer Feeding Program, Ware County, 1996—. Alto vocalist Satilla Area Cmty. Chorus, Waycross, 1998—; lead soprano Winona Park United Meth. Ch., Waycross, 1996—. Assoc. dir. children's activities Winona Park United Meth. Ch., Waycross, 1996—. Named Tchr. of the Yr., Pine Grove Elem. Sch., 1990—91; recipient Ga. Commendation medal, Ga. N.G., 1991. Mem.: Profl. Assn. of Ga. Educators, Ga. Music Educators Assn. Methodist. Avocations: gardening, home improvement/repair, animal rescue. Home: 2170 Lamar Ave Waycross GA 31501 Office: Waycross Middle Sch 700 Central Ave Waycross GA 31501

HOOVER, POLLY RUTH, humanities educator; b. Yokosuka, Japan, Aug. 28, 1956; came to U.S., 1957; d. Dwight Wesley and Nannie Elizabeth (Crosby) H.; m. Thomas Hoffer, July 12, 1986. BA in Classics, Beloit Coll., 1978; MA in Philosophy, U. Chgo., 1984; MA in Classics, U. Wis., 1990, PhD in Classics, 1995. Tchr. Keith Sch., Rockford, Ill., 1985-88; lectr. U. Wis., Madison, 1993-94; sr. lectr. Ohio State U., Columbus, 1995—97; lectr. humanities Wright Coll., 1999—2002, asst. prof. humanities, 2002—, chmn. humanities, art, fgn. langs., 2000—. Home: 5408 S University Ave Chicago IL 60615-5108 Office Phone: 773-481-8373.

HOPE, GERRI DANETTE, telecommunications management executive; b. Antelope, Calif., Feb. 28, 1956; d. Albert Gerald and Beulah H. AS, Sierra Coll., Calif., 1977; postgrad., Okla. State U., 1977-79. Instrnl. asst. II San Juan Sch. Dist., Carmichael, Calif., 1979-82; telecomm. supr. Delta Dental Svc. of Calif., San Francisco, 1982-85; telecomm. coord. Farmers Savs. Bank, Davis, Calif., 1987-95; telecomm. officer Sacramento Savs. Bank, 1987-95; telecomm. analyst II contractor dept. ins. State of Calif., Sacramento, 1995—. Owner GDH Enterprises, 1993-97; sr. telecomms. engr. Access Health, Inc., Rancho Cordova, Calif., 1996-97, Any Time Access, Sacramento, 1997-98, GDH Enterprises, North Highlands, 1993-97; employment devel. dept. staff, info. systems analyst specialist State of Calif., 1998—; founder Custom Label Designer, Sacramento, 1993-96; mem. telecomm. adv. panel Golden Gate U., Sacramento; lectr. in toll fraud prevention and voice network security. Ministry dir. dinner fellowship Calvary Chapel, Roseville Ch., 2000—. Mem. Telecomm. Assn. (v.p. membership com. Sacramento Valley chpt. 1992-94, v.p. dir. programs 1995-2003, corp. conf. com. programs bd. 1997-99, v.p. pub. rels. bd., dir. edn., webmaster 2002—), Am. Philatelic Soc., Sacramento Philatelic Assn., Errors, Freaks and Oddities Club, Philatelic Collectors. Republican. Avocations: writing, computers, stamp collecting/philately, animal behavior, participating in christian ministry. Home: 3025 U St Antelope CA 95843-2513 Office: State Calif EDD DPD Telecom 800 Capital Mall MIC 58-2S Sacramento CA 95814

HOPE, JAIME LYNN, foreign language educator; b. Seoul, Aug. 2, 1974; d. James Albert and Bonnie Jean (Barlow) H. BS, U. Md., College Park, 1996. Spanish tchr. U. Richmond, Va., 1993-94; mktg./advt. intern Phillips Bus. Info., Potomac, Md., 1995; mktg. intern Goodwill Industries Internat., Bethesda, Md., 1996; client rels. rep. Occupational Health & Rehab., Boston, 1996-97; asst. mgr. Macy's, Eatontown, N.J., 1997—. Mem. NAFE, Golden Key, Omicron Delta Kappa, Gamma Phi Beta (v.p. pub. rels. 1994-97), Alpha Kappa Psi. Democrat. Home: 309 Beach Front Manasquan NJ 08736-3907

HOPE, MARGARET LAUTEN, civic worker; b. NYC; 1 son, Frederick H., III. Privately educated. Ball com. various charity fund raising events. Mem. Jr. League NYC; Everglades Club, Palm Beach, Fla.; Women's Nat. Rep. Club (NYC); St. James Club (London). Address: PO Box 601 Palm Beach FL 33480-0601 Home: 236 Dunbar Rd Palm Beach FL 33480

HOPKINS, CATHERINE LEE, music educator; d. John James and Eleanor May (Hubert) Sanderson; m. Stephen Ernest Hopkins, June 26, 1965; children: Cheryl Lynne Hopkins Naquette, Scott Eric. MusB Edn., New Eng. Conservatory, 1961. Tchr. Nagautuck Schs., Conn., 1961—62, Attleboro Schs., Mass., 1962—68, Smithfield Schs., RI, 1982—. Parent coun. Boy Scouts Am., Smithfield, 1992—; advocate Special Olympics, Trudeau Center, 1995—, No. ARC, Woonsocket, RI, 1997—. Mem.: Am. Choral Dirs. Conf., Music Educators Nat. Conf. Home: 8 Appleseed Dr Greenville RI 02828

HOPKINS, DEBORAH C. diversified financial services company executive; b. Milw., Nov. 12, 1954. BS, Walsh Coll.; postgrad., U. Pa. With Ford Motor Co., Nat. Bank Detroit, Unisys Corp., v.p. corp. bus., 1991-93, v.p., corp. contr., chief acctg. officer, 1993-95, v.p., gen. mgr. worldwide info. svcs.; gen. auditor GM, 1995-97; v.p. fin., CFO GM Europe, Zürich, Switzerland; sr. v.p., CFO Boeing, Seattle, 1998—2000; CFO, exec. v.p. Lucent Tech., Murray Hill, NJ, 2000—01; sr. ptnr. Marakon Assocs.; chief ops. and tech. officer Citigroup, 2003—. Bd. dirs. E.I. DuPont De Nemours and Co. Bd. dirs. Seattle Symphony. Named one of 50 most powerful women in Am. bus. Fortune Mag., 1999, mgr. to watch in 2000 Bus. Week, 1999. Office: Citigroup 399 Park Ave New York NY 10043*

HOPKINS, JAN, journalist, newscaster; b. Warren, Ohio, May 22, 1947; d. Walter Charles and Lois Avelene (Botroff) Reed; m. Walter Hopkins, June 14, 1969 (div. Nov. 1981); m. Richard Trachtman, Nov. 8, 1986. Dir. news Sta. WTCL, Warren, Ohio, 1973-75; reporter, anchor Sta. WERE, Cleve., 1975-77; reporter Sta. WKBN-TV, Youngstown, Ohio, 1977-80; reporter, anchor Sta. WLWT-TV, Cin., 1980-82; assignment editor CBS News, N.Y.C., 1983; reporter, prodr. ABC News, N.Y.C., 1983-84; anchor bus. news CNN, N.Y.C., 1984—. Author: (chapter) Knight Bagehot Guide to Business Journalism, 1990, 2d edit., 2000. Trustee Hiram Coll., 1988—94; adv. bd. Knight Bagehot program journalism Columbia U., N.Y.C., 1994; mem. nat. bd. Girl Scouts USA, 2001—. Recipient Peabody award U. Ga., 1988, Front Page award Newswomen Club N.Y., 1988, Lifetime Achievement award Women's Econ. Roundtable, 2002; Knight Bagehot fellow Columbia U. Sch. Journalism, 1982-83; named to Hall of Excellence Ohio Found. Ind. Colls., 1993, Warren, Ohio, H.S. Disting. Alumni Hall of Fame, 1995. Mem. Econ. Club N.Y. Office: CNN Bus News 5 Penn Plz Fl 20 New York NY 10001-1810 E-mail: jan.hopkins@turner.com.

HOPKINS, JEANNETTE ETHEL, book publisher, editor; b. Camden, N.J., Dec. 7, 1922; d. Carleton Roper and Gladys Eugenia (Hull) H. BA, Vassar Coll., 1944; MS, Columbia Sch. Journalism, 1945. Asst. to Sunday editor New Haven Register, 1945-46; reporter Providence Evening Bull., 1946-50, Oklahoma City Times, 1950-51; sr. editor Beacon Press, Boston, 1951-56, Harcourt Brace, N.Y.C., 1956-64, Harper & Row, N.Y.C., 1964-73; v.p. Met. Applied Res. Ctr., N.Y.C., 1970-72, cons. editor, 1973-80, 89—; dir. Wesleyan Univ. Press, Middletown, Conn., 1980-89. Adj. prof. English Wesleyan U., 1987-89, U. N.H., 1989; propr. Portsmouth Athenaeum, 1991—. Author: Books That Will Not Burn, 1952, 14 Journeys to Unitarianism, 1951, (with K.B. Clark) Relevant War Against Poverty, 1968, Legacy: A History of the South Church Endowment, 1995, The Whole Thing: The Author, The Editor, and The Book, 2005. Mem. coun. Inst. Religion in an Age of Sci., 1968-72, 80-82, 88-91; mem. bd. Unitarian UN Office, 1977-80; mem. Commn. on Appraisal, Unitarian Universalist Assn., 1976-78; bd. dirs. ACLU, 1970-79, mem. nat. adv. coun., 1986—; bd. govs. Comty. Ch. N.Y., 1960-66, Unitarian-Universalist Ch., Portsmouth, 1990-93, lay min., 1991-95; trustee South Ch. Endowment Fund, 1996-99; v.p. Unitarian Fellowship for Social Justice, 1958-62. Louise Hart Van Loon fellow, Vassar Coll., 1944; recipient Disting. Alumni award Columbia Sch. Journalism, 1981. Democrat. Unitarian. Home and Office: 39 Pray St Portsmouth NH 03801-5226

HOPKINS, JUDITH, librarian; b. Wilkes-Barre, Pa., July 15, 1934; d. Charles and Anna (Pripstein) Hopkins. BA, Wilkes Coll., 1955; MLS, U. Ill., 1957, cert. advanced study, 1973. Cataloger Mt. Holyoke Coll., South Hadley, Mass., 1957—65; asst. head catalog dept. Yale Law Libr., New Haven, 1965—67; bibliographic editor OCLC Online Computer Libr. Ctr., Columbus, Ohio, 1970—72; head original cataloging sect., cataloging dept., ctrl. tech. svcs. U. Buffalo Librs., 1977—83, tech. svcs. rsch. and analysis officer, ctrl. tech. svcs., 1984—. Listowner of Autocat (internat. electronic discussion group on libr. cataloging), 1992—; cons. on implementation of Anglo-Am. Cataloguing Rules, 2d edit. Miami U., Oxford, Ohio, 1980; sec. faculty senate U. Buffalo, 1988—90, chair by-laws com., 1991—2004; spkr. confs. in field. Editor: (collection of original essays) Research Libraries and their Implementation of AACR2; author: Manual for OCLC Catalog Card Production; contbr. articles to profl. jours., chapters to books. Recipient Chancellor's award for Excellence in Librarianship, Chancellor of SUNY, 1985; Title IIB fellow, U.S. Office of Edn., 1969—70, 1970—72. Mem.: ALA (life; sec. tech. svcs. dirs. of large rsch. librs. discussion group of Assn. 1990—, various divsnl. and sect. offices), N.Y. Libr. Assn. (various com. offices and memberships 1979—89), Mensa (test proctor), Beta Phi Mu (internat. exec. com. 1991—93). Jewish. Avocations: reading, travel. Office: U Buffalo Librs 137 Lockwood Libr Bldg Buffalo NY 14260-2210 Office Phone: 716-645-2796. Business E-Mail: ulcjh@buffalo.edu.

HOPKINS, KAREN BROOKS, performing arts executive; b. 1951; d. Howard and Paula Brooks; divorced; 1 child, Matthew. BA in Theater Arts with honors, U. Md., 1973; MFA, George Washington U., 1980. Mem. group sales staff Am. Theater, Washington, 1973; cmty. rels. dir. Qwindo's Windo Dance Touring Co., Washington, [illegible] Players Touring Co., 1975-76, prodr., 1975-78; theater dir. Jewish Cmty. Ctr. of Greater Washington, 1976-78; devel. dir. The New Playwright's Theatre, Washington, 1978-79; devel. officer Bklyn. Acad. of Music, 1979-81, v.p. planning and devel., 1981-88, exec. v.p., 1988-98, COO and exec. v.p., 1998-99, pres., 1999—. Adj. prof. program for arts adminstrn. Bklyn. Coll., 1980-84. Author: Successful Fundraising for Arts and Cultural Organizations, 1989, 2d edit., 1997. Fundraising cons. art instns., 1979—; chair Performing Arts Ctrs. Consortium, 1994-96, Cultural Instns. Group, 2003; mem. adv. com. Salzburg Seminar-Alberto Vilar Project of Critical Issues for the Classical Performing Arts; ex-officio mem. N.Y.C. Cultural Affairs Adv. Commn., 2003.. Recipient King Olav medal Norwegian Nat. Ballet, 1982, Dramaten medal, 1995. Office: Brooklyn Acad Music 30 Lafayette Ave Brooklyn NY 11217-1430

HOPKINS, MARTHA ANN, sculptor; b. Meridian, Miss., Feb. 4, 1940; d. Hugh Wallace Markline and Martha Lou Morton; m. Harry L. Hopkins, Aug. 19, 1961; children: Peter Ashley, Caroline Baker. BA in Spanish, U. So. Miss., 1961; BA in Visual Art, U. Montevallo, 1982. Exec. sec., engr. asst. Humble Oil & Refining Co., New Orleans, 1961—65; modern lang. tchr. Meridian HS, 1967—71. Arts camp tchr. Birmingham (Ala.) Mus. Art, 1999, sculpture tchr. hs students, 2000. Prodr.: (films, demonstration video for Pub. TV) Found Object Sculpture, 2000; exhibitions include Celebrating Women Artists of Ala., 2001, Nat. Small Sculpture Exhbn., 2000, Three Rivers Arts Festival, Pitts., 1999, Gadsden (Ala.) Cultural Arts Ctr., 1998, Meridian Mus. Art, 1995, prin. works include Ala. Vets. Meml. sculpture, Red Tide sculpture, U. Ala., Birmingham, 1991, Wild Blue sculpture, Meridian Miss. Airport, 2003, (book) Carousels Around, 2003. Bd. dirs. Planned Parenthood Ala., Birmingham, 1998—2001. Mem.: Ala. Designer/Craftsmen (pres. 1978—2001), Birmingham Doll Club. Avocation: antique dolls. Home and Studio: 1800 Woodcrest Rd Birmingham AL 35209

HOPKINS, MARY BAZEMORE, landscape designer, consultant; b. Phila., Sept. 12, 1926; d. Earl Leroy and Mary Franklin Knott Bazemore; m. John Estaugh Hopkins; children: Elizabeth Haddon Blackstone, Caroline Kolb Shauger, John Estaugh. BA, Mt. Holyoke Coll., 1948; AD in Landscape Design, Temple U., 1971. Tchr. Episc. Acad., Merion, Pa., 1950—56; head pre-sch. Lower Merion-Radnor Schs., Ardmore, Pa., 1962—63; owner-dir. Landscape Design Cons. Svc., Wayne, Pa., 1968—78; instr. Barnes Found. Horticulture Sch., Merion, Pa., 1969—79; lectr. in landscape design, horticulture, 1972—2003. Founder, organizer seminars The Charleston Mus., Charleston, SC, 1999—. Home: Spring Valley Farm 616 Sones Hollow Rd Benton PA 17814

HOPKINS, NANCY H. biology educator; PhD, Harvard U., 1971. Prof. biology dept. MIT, Cambridge, 1972—; chmn. comm. on women faculty MIT, Sch. of Science; co-chmn. council on faculty diversity MIT. Recipient Laya Wiesner Community Award, 2001, Women's History Month Honoree of NY Academy of Sciences; fellow Amer. Academy of Arts and Sciences. Mem.: Institute of Med., 1999-. Office: MIT E17-341 77 Massachusetts Ave Cambridge MA 02139-4301 E-mail: nhopkins@mit.edu.

HOPKINS, SANDRA PARKER, power company administrator; b. Kenly, N.C., Feb. 17, 1952; d. Clinton Bunche and Catherine Parker Hicks; m. William Augustus Ganues, Aug. 29, 1970 (div. Dec. 1977); children: Dawn D. Ganues, Mari L. Ganues; m. Reginald B. Lee; children: Reginald H. Lee, Kathryn T. Lee; m. Wendell M. Hopkins. Student, LaSalle Correspondence Sch., Chgo., 1973, Halifax C.C., 1977, Old Dominion U., 2001. Display mgr. Montgomery Wards, Cheyenne, Wyo., 1974-77; draftsman N.C. Power, Roanoke Rapids, 1977-93; svc. coord. Va. Power, Chesapeake, 1996—2001; asst. sys. operator Dominion Va. Power, Richmond, Va., 2001—. Mem. adv. bd. Halifax C.C. Interior Design Program, Weldon, N.C., 1986-93. Co-founder Halifax County Cmty. Devel. Corp., Roanoke Rapids, 1992-96; assoc. dir. Ctr. for Adult and Adolescent Devel., Weldon, N.C., 1988-92; Dem. del. Halifax County, Littleton, N.C., 1990-97; pres. PTA, Halifax County Schs., Littleton, 1984-90. Recipient Disting. Svc. award Halifax County Cmty. Devel. Corp., 1996, Third Place award for oil painting Wilson Active Artist Competition, 1995. Baptist. Avocations: oil painting, weight lifting, photography, dance, sewing. Home: 9400 Evansway Ln Richmond VA 23235

HOPKINS, SUSAN SHIPLETT, music educator, director; b. Wilkes Barre, Pa., Aug. 30, 1949; d. Herman Wise and Joyce Rutter Shiplett; m. Kenneth Edward Hopkins, Aug. 23, 1975; children: Joshua Kenn, Sarah Elizabeth. Bachelor's Degree in Music Edn., Mansfield State U., Mansfield, PA, 1967—71; Master's Degree in Edn., Towson State U., Towson, MD, 1975—81. Cert. music educator State of Md., 1981. Band dir. Bel Air (Md.) Mid. Sch., 1971—77, Aberdeen (Md.) Mid. Sch., 1977—. Unified arts dept. chair Aberdeen (Md.) Mid. Sch., 1986—, sch. based decision making team; mem. music curriculum devel. com. Harford County, Bel Air. Dir.: State Band (Excellence in Performance award, 2003). Asst. girl scout leader GSA, 1995—; adult leader youth fellowship Havre de Grace United Meth. Ch., 1984—, mem. edn. com., 1984—. Mem.: Md. State Tchr.'s Assn., Music Educator's Nat. Conf. Republican. Meth. Avocations: reading, gardening, travel. Home: 913 Joyce Ct Aberdeen MD 21001 Office: Aberdeen Middle School 111 Mt Royal Ave Aberdeen MD 21001

HOPKINSON, SHIRLEY LOIS, library and information science educator; b. Boone, Iowa, Aug. 25, 1924; d. Arthur Perry and Zora (Smith) Hopkinson. Student, Coe Coll., 1942—43; AB cum laude, U. Colo., 1945; BLS, U. Calif., 1949; MA, Claremont Grad. Sch., 1951; EdM, U. Okla., 1952, EdD, 1957. Tchr. pub. sch., Stigler, Okla., 1946—47; tchr. Palo Verde HS., Jr. Coll., Blythe, Calif., 1947—48; asst. libr. Modesto (Calif.) Jr. Coll., 1949—51; tchr., libr. Fresno, Calif., 1951—52, La Mesa, Calif., 1953—55; asst. prof. librarianship, instrnl. materials dir. Chaffey Coll., Ontario, Calif., 1955—59; asst. prof. librarianship San Jose (Calif.) State Coll., 1959—64, assoc. prof., 1964—69, prof., 1969—. Bd. dirs. NDEA Inst. Sch. Librs., summer, 1966; mem. Santa Clara County Civil Svc. Bd. Examiners. Author: Descriptive Cataloging of Library Materials, Instructional Materials for Teaching the Use of the Library; editor: Calif. Sch. Libraries, 1963—64; asst. editor Sch. Libr. Assn. of Calif. Bull., 1961—63, book reviewer profl. jours.; contbr. articles to profl. jours. Honnold Honor scholar, Claremont Grad. Sch., 1945—46. Mem.: LWV (bd. dirs. 1950—51, publs. chmn.), AAUW (dir. 1957—58), NEA, ALA, AAUP, Kappa Delta Pi, Alpha Beta Alpha, Calif. Tchrs. Assn., San Diego County Sch. Librs. Assn. (sec. 1945—55), Sch. Librs. Assn. Calif. (com. mem., treas. No. sect. 1951—52), Audio-Visual Assn. Calif., Calif. Library Assn., Bus. Profl. Women's Club, Alpha Lambda Delta, Phi Beta Kappa (scholar 1944), Delta Kappa Gamma (sec. 1994—96, legis. liaison 1996—2002, corr. sec. 2002—), Phi Kappa Phi (disting. acad. achievement award 1981). Office: 1340 Pomeroy Ave Apt 408 Santa Clara CA 95051-3658

HOPP, TERRY A. computer company executive; BA in Bus. Adminstrn., Calif. State U., Fullerton. CPA, Calif. Audit ptnr. Earnst & Young LLP, 1981-98; v.p. fin. Western Digital Corp., Irvine, Calif., 1998, now sr. v.p., CFO. Mem. AICPA. Office: Western Digital Corp 20511 Lake Forest Dr Lake Forest CA 92630-7741

HOPPE, LAURA, air traffic controller; Instrumentation and communication officer flight contr. NASA Johnson Space Ctr., Houston. Avocations: volleyball, skiing, soccer, jogging, scuba diving. Office: NASA Johnson Space Ctr Phase 1 Mailcode TA Houston TX 77058

HOPPE, PHYLLIS DIANE, state representative; b. Sterling County, Colo., Dec. 14, 1947; 2 children. Grad., U. Colo., 1972. Cons., forest program coord.; state rep. dist. 65 Colo. Ho. of Reps., Denver, 1999—, chair agr. livestock and natural resources com., mem. appropriations and bus. affairs and labor coms. Recipient Disting. Legislature award, Colo. Assn. Conservation Dist., 2003, Spl. Legis. Recognition, Colo. Water and Power Devel. Authority, 2003, Legislator of Yr., Colo. Corn Growers Assn., 2003, Spl. Legis. Recognition, Colo. Timber Industry Assn., 2003, Legislator of Yr., Colo. Livestock Assn., 2000, 2002, Top Republican Rep. Mem. Friend of Farm Bureau award, Colo. Farm Bureau, 1999—2002, Leadership award, Colo. Petroleum Assn., 2002, Colo. Mining Assn., 2002, numerous others. Republican. Episcopalian. Avocations: hiking, fishing, travel. Office: State Capitol # 271 200 E Colfax Ave Denver CO 80203 Office Phone: 303-866-3706.

HOPPE, SHERRY LEE, academic administrator; b. Chickamauga, Ga. BS magna cum laude, U. Tenn., Chattanooga, 1969, MS, 1974; EdD, U. Tenn., Knoxville, 1981. Clk. new accounts Pioneer Bank, Chattanooga, 1965-66; asst. to dir. fin. aid, sec. U. Tenn., Chattanooga, 1966-69; counselor, tchr. Chattanooga Valley High Sch., 1969-77; from coord. vets. affairs to dean Chattanooga State Tech. Community Coll., 1977-87; interim pres. Nashville State Tech. Inst., 1987-88; pres. Roane State Community Coll., Harriman, Tenn., 1988—. Contbr. articles to jours. in field. Bd. dirs. Meth. Med. Ctr., Community Devel. Coun., Roane County, Oak Ridge Community Found., Chattanooga Area Am. Heart Assn., Multiple Sclerosis Soc., Sentenga chptr., Jr. Achievement, Chattanooga Venture, Met. Coun., Cherokee Area Coun. Boy Scouts Am., Am. Lung Assn. Southeastern Region, Sovran Bank, Henry Devel. Ctr.; account exec., sect. leader United Way, 1882-84, strategic action com., 1987; Mem. Pub. Rels. Task Force Vision 2000, 1984-85, planning adv. com. Chattanooga-Hamilton County Regional Planning Commn., 1985; chmn. Homecoming '86 Enterprise Com. Greater Chattanooga Area, Made in Chattanooga Exhbn., 1986; participator Leadership Chattanooga, Leadership Roane County. Mem. NEA, Tenn. Edn. Assn., C. of C. (pub. rels. task force 1983), Nat. Coun. Instructional Adminstrs., Am. Assn. Women in Community and Jr. Colls. (participated in Leaders of the '80s 1981), Chattanooga Indsl. Pers. Club, Chattanooga Area Pers. Assn., Rotary. Office: Roane State Community Coll Office of the President Harriman TN 37748

HOPPER, ANITA KLEIN, molecular genetics educator; b. Chgo., Sept. 24, 1945; d. Irving and Rose (Warshawsky) Klein; m. James Ernest Hopper, Jan. 3, 1971; 1 child, Julie Victoria. BS, U. Ill., Chgo., 1967; PhD, U. Ill., 1972. Postdoctoral researcher genetics U. Wash., Seattle, 1971-75; asst. prof. microbiology U. Mass. Med. Sch., Worcester, 1975-78, assoc. prof. microbiology, 1978-79; assoc. prof. biochemistry Hershey Med. Sch., Pa. State U., Hershey, 1979-87, prof. biochemistry, molecular biology, 1987—. Genetic biol panel NSF, Washington, 1981—85; mem genetic study sect NIH, Bethesda, Md., 1985—89, mem CDFI study sect, 1997—2000, chair CDFI study sect, 2001—; organizer RNA processing Cold Spring Harbor meetings, 1989, 90; co-chmn 5th Summer Symposium in Molecular Biol: The Nucleus Pa State Univ, 1986, co-chair YGM yr meeting, 2000—02, co-chair intercollege grad program genetic, 2001—. Editor: Molecular & Cellular Biology, 1989—2000; mem ed bd.: 1986—90, RNA, 1995—97. Fellow Postdoctoral, NIH, 1971—73; grantee NIH, 1979—, Univ Louisville Med Sch, 1989, NSF, 1988—91. Fellow: Am Acad Microbiology; mem.: AAAS, Am Asn Microbiology (chair Eli Lilly award comt 2000—), Am Asn Biochemists, Am Soc Microbiology (chair-elect genetics & molecular biol div 1987, chair genetics & molecular biol div 1988). Office: Pa State U Med Sch Dept Biochemistry & Molec Biol Hershey PA 17033

HOPPER, CAROL, meeting and incentive trip administrator; b. Montreal, Que., Can., Apr. 23, 1952; m. Cedric Heimrath; stepchildren: Natasha, Erik. Student, McGill U., 1972; cert., Canadian Inst. Orgnl. Mgmt., 1991. Asst. Ben Fuller Assocs., 1973-89; show dir. Nat. Ski Industries Assn., Montreal, 1989-91, exec. dir., 1991-96, dir. show svcs., 1997-98; project mgr. Chateau Travel, Carlson Mktg. Group, 1998—2002; project leader Vision 2000 Travel Group, 2002—. Mem. adv. com. sporting goods bus. program Sir Sandford Fleming Coll., 1994-98. Mem. Can. Assn. Exposition mgrs., Jr. League Montreal (bd. dirs., chmn. coms. 1987-92). Avocations: skiing, golf, reading, travel, sports. Home: 302 Perrault Rosemere QC Canada J7A 1B9

HOPPER, RUBY LOU, clergy member; b. Harrison, Ark., May 21, 1950; d. George C. and Ethel M. (Bethany) Eddings; m. Alfred Hopper, Aug. 1, 1970. Diploma, Berean Bible Coll., Springfield, Mo., 1989. Cert. technician class III, Nat. Assn. Radio and Telecomm. Engrs., 1986; ordained minister Evangelistic Messengers, 1986. Youth leader Sycamore Log Ch., Branson, Mo., 1984—; adult Sunday sch. tchr. Branson Ch. of God. Ins. office sec. Mo. Farm Bur., Hollister, 1990-93; sec. Foxen Comm., Hollister, 1993; prodn. dept. Applied Digital, Inc., Branson, 1996; freelance writer, Hollister, 1996. Vol. ARC, Branson, 1986-87; emergency coord. Amateur Radio Emergency Svc., Branson, 1988. Recipient Vol. Svc. award Pt. Lookout Health Care Ctr., 1991. Mem. Nat. Assn. Female Execs., Nat. Assn. Radio Telecomm. Engrs. (technician class III), Tri-Lakes Amateur Radio Club (v.p. 1984-88). Republican. Pentecostal. Avocations: sports, baseball cards, music, reading, travel. Home and Office: PO Box 332 Hollister MO 65673-0332 Office Phone: 417-335-6692.

HOPPER, SALLY HUNTER, former state legislator; b. Dayton, Ky., Sept. 26, 1934; widowed; children: Nancy, Joan, Caroline, Anne. BA, U. Wyo., 1956. Mem. Colo. Senate, Denver, 1987-99. Chair Senate Health, Environ., Welfare and Insts. com.; chair Criminal Justice Commn, mem. Judiciary com. Mem. nat. bd. Ptnrs. for Access to the Woods; mem., bd. dirs. Spalding Cmty. Found.; chair Colo. Intermountain Fixed Guideway Authority. Mem. Kappa Kappa Gamma. Republican. Episcopalian. Home: 21649 Cabrini Blvd Golden CO 80401-9487

HOPPER, TAMMY JANE, art educator; d. Francis Scott Key and Elizabeth Marion Coons; children: Jacob Jennings Hein, Ashlie Elizabeth Howell. B in elem. edn., U. of Wyo., 1980—88, MA in curriculum and instrn., MA in art edn., U. of Wyo., 1992—98. H.s. art tchr. Natrona County Sch. Dist. #1, Casper, Wyo., 1992—95, elem. art tchr., 1992—. Group facilatator High Plains DBAE Summer Art Inst., Laramie, Wyo., 2000—01; pres. Wyo. Art Edn. Assn., Casper, Wyo., 2001—03; art dept. chair Natrona County Sch. Dist. #1, Casper, Wyo., 2002—; art workshop facilatator Wyo. Art Alliance, Laramie, Wyo., 2003—. Mem.: Natrona County Edn. Assn., Wyo. Edn. Assn., Colo. ArtSource, Wyo. Art Edn. Assn. (pres. 1991—93), Phi Delta Capa. Avocations: snowshoeing, hiking, drawing, arts and crafts, writing.

HOPSON, ELAINE M. state representative; Grad., Purdue U.; M, Oreg. State U.; PhD, U. Oreg. From tchr. to supt. sch. dist., Detroit, Oreg.; with N.W. Women Ednl. Adminstrn.; owner grocery stores; dir. personnel, then supt., 1984—93; supt. Tillamook Sch. Dist., 1994—2000; mem. Oreg. Ho. of Reps., 1998—; ret., 2000. Chmn. adv. com. Tillamook County Health Dept.; mem. Edn. Commn. of States, Oreg. Commn. Children and Families. Mem.: Confederation Oreg. Sch. Adminstrs. (sch. funding coalition), Tillamook County C. of C. (bd. dirs.). Democrat. Office: 900 Court St NE H-376 Salem OR 97301

HORAK, TRISH, city government worker; b. Grand Saline, Tex., Aug. 24, 1946; d. Clinton Lee and Jewell Ruth Collier; m. Larry G. Horak, June 1972; children: Clinton Hammonds, John W., Marie. Grad. h.s. Cert. legal [illegible] 1973-81, sec. to city sec., 1981-82, sec. to city mgr., 1983-84, exec. asst. to mayor, 1984-88, exec. sec. human resources, 1989-91, exec. sec. City Mgrs. Office, 1992—. Asst. sec. Lone Star Park at Grand Prairie, Tex. Bd. dirs. YMCA, Grand Prairie, 1985-88; sec. bd. dirs. United Charities, Grand Prairie, 1983-88, 92-98; ann. campaign cord. United Way, Grand Prairie, 1997; sr. rep. Parent, Tchrs., Student Assn. Grand Prairie, 2000. Mem. Profl. Secs. Internat., Grand Prairie C. of C. (sec.-treas. women's divsn. 1982, Woman of Yr. 1993). Baptist. Avocations: gardening, crafts, crocheting, reading, writing. Home: 1637 Brent St Grand Prairie TX 75051-4321 Office: City Mgrs Office 317 College St Grand Prairie TX 75050-5636 E-mail: phorak@gptx.org.

HORAN, SHELLY, marketing professional; d. Jimmy Gaines and Lynn Rodriguez, Jack Rodriguez (Stepfather); m. Stacey Horan, Feb. 3, 1996; 1 child, Dylan. BBA magna cum laude, U. of St. Thomas, Houston, 1999. Cert. profl. cert. marketer Am. Mktg. Assn., 2001. Bus. devel. mgr. PrimeWay Fed. Credit Union, Houston, 2000—02, mktg. dir., 2002—. Mem.: Credit Union Nat. Assn. Mktg. Coun. (Diamond award for internal mktg. 2001, The Diamond award 2003), Tex. Credit Union League Mktg. Coun. (Lone Star award, award of merit in internal mktg. 2001, 2d pl. Lone Star award 2002, 1st pl. spl. events Lone Star award 2002), Am. Mktg. Assn. (collegiate rels. dir. 2002—), Delta Mu Delta (life). R-Liberal. Methodist. Avocations: reading, horseback riding, travel. Office: PrimeWay Federal Credit Union 3303 Main St Houston TX 77002

HORD, PAULINE JONES, primary school educator, educator; b. Memphis, Apr. 18, 1907; d. Samuel Anderson and Loretta (Hall) Jones; m. Andrew Frank Hord, Mar. 30, 1940 (div. Oct. 1946). BA, Southwestern Coll., Memphis, 1929; EdD (hon.), Crichton Coll., Memphis, 1991, Rhodes Coll., 1999. Tchr. Memphis City Sch. System, 1929-67; nat. cons. Phonovisual Products, Inc., Bethesda, Md., 1967-77; freelance cons., workshop dir. Memphis, 1978-87; dir. sing spell read and write model Memphis Sch. System, 1987-95. Dir. TV Lit. Program WKNO-TV, Memphis, 1955-60; acting dir. Primary Day Sch., Bethesda, Md., 1960-61; lit. TV Specialist with Peace Corps., Colombia, S. Am., 1963-64; dir. Heads Up Lit. Program, State Correctional Inst., Parchman, Miss., 1986-96. Author: Praying for the President, 2003, The Master Design, 2003. Lit. tchr. Heads Up Lit. Program, Parchman Penetentiary, 1987-92; bd. mem. Second Chance Prison Min., Tenn., Miss., 1988-92. Recipient Leadership Adult Edn. award Ford Found., 1958, Disting. Col. Christian Svc. award Miss. State Penetentiary, Parchman, 1987, Memphis Comml. Appeal award, 1989, 95th Daily Point of Light award, 1990, Person of Vision award Alliance for the Blind and Visually Impaired, 1993, Disting. Alumni award Rhodes Coll., 1998; named one of Outstanding Bus. Women of Yr., Women's Exec. Coun., Memphis, 1959, Sr. Citizen of Yr., Shelby County Coun. on Aging, 1988. Republican. Mem. United Meth. Avocations: reading, creating educational games, leading prayer groups. Home: 475 S Perkins Rd Apt 601 Memphis TN 38117-3926

HOREIN, KATHLEEN MARIE, music educator; d. Stephen Anthony and Florence Leona Krasienko; m. Timothy Dee Horein, Aug. 18, 1974; children: Michael Stephen, Kelly Marie. BS in Music Edn., Ball State U., 1974; MA in Music History and Lit., West Chester U., 1983. Instrnl. cert. II Pa. Music tchr. Ctrl. Dauphin Sch. Dist., Harrisburg, Pa., 1980—85, 1994—95, Sch. Dist. Lancaster, Pa., 1985—94, Lancaster Country Day Sch., 1996—. Oboist Lancaster Woodwind Quintet, 1980—2003, Lancaster Pops Orch., 1995—2003, Allegro Chamber Och., Lancaster, 2002—03, Lancaster Opera Co., 2000—03. Mem.: Pa. Music Educators Assn., Music Educators Nat. Conf., Kappa Delta Pi, Pi Kappa Lambda. Methodist. Home: Box 791 4 Hobson Ct Brownstown PA 17508 Office: Lancaster Country Day Sch 725 Hamilton Rd Lancaster PA 17603

HORI, KEIKO, English literature educator; b. Himeji, Hyogo, Japan, Jan. 18, 1954; d. Takeshi Nishiyama and Fumiko Hori; 1 child, Grace. BA summa cum laude, Osaka (Japan) U., 1976, MA, 1978; postgrad., U. N.H., 1979—80, Osaka (Japan) U., 1978—82. Instr. Osaka Kyoiku U., 1981-82, tenured asst. prof., 1982-87, assoc. prof., 1987-2000, prof., 2000—; instr. Osaka U., Toyonaka, Japan, 1988-90, 92-95. Vis. prof. U. Wyo., Laramie, 1986—87; vis. scholar UCLA, 2001—02. Co-author: Imeji to shite no Toshi: Gakusaiteki Toshi Bunkaron, 1996; annotator: (textbook) American Businessman: Lessons from Life, 1994; co-annotator: (textbook) American and English Ideals, 1991. Recipient Kusumoto award, 1976. Mem. Modern Lang. Assn., English Literary Soc. Japan, Japan Assn. English Romanticism, Japan Assn. Coll. English Tchrs. Home: 7-4-1-3 Umamikita Koryocho Kitakatsuragi-gun Nara 635-0831 Japan Office: Osaka Kyoiku U 4-698-1 Asahigaoka Kashiwara Osaka 582-8582 Japan

HORINKO, MARIANNE LAMANT, former federal agency administrator; BS, U. Md., 1982; JD, Georgetown U., 1986. Staff scientist Nat. Cancer Inst., Bethesda, Md.; atty. Morgan, Lewis, & Bockius, LLP, Washington; atty. advisor, solid wastes & emerg. response EPA, Washington, 1990—93; pres. Clay Assocs., Inc., 1993—2001; asst. adminstr. solid waste and emer. response EPA, 2001—03, acting adminstr., 2003. Office: EPA Ariel Rios Bldg 1200 Pennsylvania Ave NW Rm 3000 Washington DC 20460

HORLICK, RUTH, photographer; b. Frankfurt, Germany, July 17, 1921; came to U.S., 1937; d. Leo Don and Hanna Rosenstock; m. Max Horlick, 1942; children: Jeffrey, Jill, Robert. Student, Newark Sch. Fine & Indsl. Arts, U. Md., Latent Image Workshop; studied with, Lowell Anson Kenyon; student, Nikon Sch. Photography, Time Life Photography Workshop. Exhibited in one-woman shows: Prince George's County Arts Divsn Gallery, 1991, Hyattsville Mcpl. Bldg., 1996, Jewish Cmty. Ctr. of D.C., 1998, Colonial Theater, Annapolis, Md., 1999, U. Md. Sr. U., 1999; exhibited in group shows at Coun. of Greater Md. Camera Clubs, Md. Soc. Photo Pictorialists, Prince George C.C., Internat. Artist's Support Group, New Delhi, 2000, New Delhi and Beijing, 2001, Cooper St. Gallery, Memphis, 2000. Founding mem. Art Spin Gallery, West Hyattsville, Md. Recipient numerous awards Nikon Sch. Photography, Coun. Greater Washington Camera Clubs, Md. Soc. Photo Pictorialists, Prince George's C.C. Mem. Women in the Arts, Laurel Art Guild, Latent Image Workshop, Passageways Artists Studios, Wash. Project for the Arts Corcoran Art Gallery, Washington Ctr. for Photography, Hyattsville Cmty. Artists Alliance, Md.-Nat. Pk. and Planning Commn. Slide Bank, Rock Creek Gallery, Internat. Artist's Support Group. Avocations: foreign travel, symphonic music and opera, stamp collection, fine arts.

HORN, BARBARA B. state legislator; b. Mt. Pine, Ark., Oct. 11, 1936; Student, Texarkana Coll., 1955. Mem. Ark. State Senate, Little Rock, 2001—, mem. ins. and commerce com., pub. health, welfare and labor com. Active S.W. Ark. Planning and Devel. Dist., Com. of 100, Mountain View, Ark., S.W. Ark. Workforce Devel. Coun. Mem. Little River County C. of C., Foreman Kiwanis Club, Ashdown Rotary Club. Democrat. Baptist. Office: PO Box 64 Foreman AR 71836 also: State Capitol Rm 320 Little Rock AR 72201 Fax: 870-898-8124.

HORN, BRENDA SUE, lawyer; b. Beech Grove, Ind., Apr. 22, 1949; d. Donald Eugene Horn and Barbara Joyce (Waggoner) Christie. AB with distinction, Ind. U., 1971; MS, Purdue U., 1975; JD summa cum laude, Ind. U., 1981. Bar: Ind. 1981, U.S. Dist. Ct. (so. dist.) Ind. 1981. Assoc. Ice Miller, Indpls., 1981-87, ptnr., 1988—. Assoc. editor Ind. Law Rev., 1980-81. Bd. dirs. Ballet Internationale, 1995—, treas., 1996-2000; pres. Greenleaf Cmty. Ctr., 1992-93, 96-99, v.p., 1991, sec., 1990; bd. dirs., v.p.

Cmty. Alliance for the Far East Side, 1997-98, hon. dir. 1998-2003; bd. dirs. Big Sisters of Ctrl. Ind., 1995-98, hon. dir., 1998—2002; bd. dirs. Indiana Edn. Svcs. Authority, 1996—, Cmty. Orgns. Legal Assistance Project, 2000—, treas., 2001-2003, pres. 2003- Named among Influential Women in Indpls., Ind. Lawyer and Indpls. Bus. Jour., 1998; Disting. fellow Indpls. Bar Fond. Mem. ABA (com. on tax exempt fin.), Am. Coll. Bond Counsel (bd. dirs., v.p. 1995-98, pres. 1998-2001), Ind. Bar Assn., Indpls. Bar Assn. (bd. mgrs. 1992), Ind. Mcpl. Lawyers Assn., Nat. Assn. Bond Lawyers, Skyline Club (bd. dirs.), Phi Beta Kappa. Office: Ice Miller One American Sq Box 82001 Indianapolis IN 46282 E-mail: horn@icemiller.com.

HORN, FLORA LEOLA, retired administrative assistant; b. Putman, Tex., May 20, 1926; d. James Erasmos and Clara Maud (Davenport) Foller; m. Charles Edward Helm, Sr. (div.); children: Leola Florence Helm, Charles Edward, Jr. Helm, Barbara Ann Helm, Carol Elaine Helm, Beverly Sue Helm, Rodney Johnson Helm; m. Hoy Merie Duhon (dec.). Diploma in Writing, Long Ridge Writers Group, 2003. Contbr. poems in books. Active Bapt. Buckneer Home, Dallas. Named Silver leader, Comdrs. Club, 2001; recipient Golden award, World Poetry, 1986, award merit cert., 1987, cert. Appreciation, Marine Corps League, 1995, Good Work award, B.B.Q. Luncheon Fundraiser, 1997. Mem.: VFW Laides Aux. (life; chaplain 1991—2002, chmn. Nat. Children's Home 1999—2002, cert. Appreciation 1989—93), Nat. Children's Home (Rapid, Mich.) (life), Med. Ctr. Hosp. (Conroe, Tex.) (life), Women of the Moose (chaplain 1999—, Novice award 1977—99, Internat. Co-worker of Yr. award 2003). Avocations: writing, art, Bingo, shuffleboard, poetry. Home: PO Box 5436 1720 Thomas St Titusville FL 32780

HORN, JOAN KELLY, political research and consulting firm executive; b. St. Louis, Oct. 18, 1936; M. E. Terrence Jones; 6 children from previous marriage. BA, U. Mo., St. Louis, 1973, MA, 1975. Pre-sch., elem. sch. Montessori tchr.; founder pre-schs.; adj. faculty dept. polit. sci. U. Mo., St. Louis, 1982-86; with St. Louis County Office Community Devel., 1977-80, St. Louis Housing Authority, 1980-82; pres. Community Cons. Inc., 1975-90; elected to 102nd Congress from 2nd dist. Mo., 1990, mem., 1991-92; dir. community devel. agy. City of St. Louis. Author articles on pub. policy issues. Mem. Dem. State Com.; Dem. candidate for U.S. House, 1992, 96. Mem. U. Mo. Alumni Alliance, U. Mo.-St. Louis Alumni Assn. (bd. dirs.). Roman Catholic. Office: 1015 Locust Ste 1200pt 2 Saint Louis MO 63101

HORN, MARIAN BLANK, federal judge; b. N.Y.C., June 24, 1943; d. Werner P. and Mady R. Blank; m. Robert Jack Horn; 3 children. AB, Barnard Coll., 1962; student, Columbia U., 1965, NYU, 1965-66; JD, Fordham U., 1969. Bar: N.Y. 1970, D.C. 1973, U.S. Supreme Ct. 1973. Asst. dist. atty. Bronx County, N.Y., 1969-72; assoc. Arent, Fox, Kintner, Plotkin & Kahn, 1972-73; project mgr. Am. U. Law Sch. study on alts. to conventional criminal adjudication U.S. Dept. Justice, 1973-75; litigation atty. Fed. Energy Adminstrn., 1975-76; sr. atty. office gen. counsel strategic petroleum res. br. Dept. Energy, 1976-79, dep. asst. gen. counsel for procurement and fin. incentives, 1979-81; dep. assoc. solicitor div. surface mining Dept. Interior, 1981-83, assoc. solicitor div. gen. law, 1983-85, prin. dep. solicitor, acting solicitor, 1985-86; judge U.S. Ct. of Federal Claims, 1986—. Adj. prof. law Washington Coll. Law, Am. U., 1973-76, George Washington U. Sch. Law, 1992—. Office: US Ct Fed Claims 717 Madison Pl NW Washington DC 20439-0002*

HORN, SABRINA, public relations executive; b. Charleston, W.Va., Aug. 3, 1961; d. Dr. Christian Frederick and Christa (Winkler) H. BA, William Smith Coll., 1983; MS, Boston U., 1984. Sr. acct. exec. Edelman Pub. Rels., San Francisco, 1984—90; sr. acct. exec. Blanc & Otus; founder, pres. & CEO Horn Group, 1991—. Office: Horn Group 621 Howard St San Francisco CA 94105

HORN, SHARON K. government agency administrator; B in Bus. and Econs., U. Ga.; EdM, Tex. A&M U.; PhD in Higher Edn. and Curriculum, U. Tex. Legis. fellow labor and human resources com. U.S. Senate; secondary sch. tchr. of bus., econs. and polit. sci. Ga.; tchr. U. Tex., Tyler, S.W. Tex. STate U.; assoc. dir. Program on Ednl. Policy and Orgn. Nat. Inst. Edn., 1982; dir. info. svcs. Office Ednl. Rsch. and Improvement U.S. Dept. Edn., Washington, program officer, dir. Nat. Awards Program for Model Profl. Devel., dir. evaluation and dissemination Office Innovation and Improvement. Office: US Dept Edn FOB-6 Rm 4W332 400 Maryland Ave SW Washington DC 20202

HORN, SHIRLEY, vocalist, pianist; b. Washington; 1 dau., Rainy. Student, Howard U. Albums include Cat on a Hot Fiddle, 1959, Embers And Ashes, 1960, Live at the Village Vanguard, 1961, Loads of Love, 1963, Shirley Horn with Horns, 1963, Travelin' Light, 1965, For Love of Ivy, 1968, A Dandy in Aspic, 1968, Where Are You Going?, 1972, A Lazy Afternoon, 1979, All Night Long, 1987, Violets For Your Furs, 1983, The Sentimental Touch (titled Songbirds in U.S.), 1985, I Thought About You, 1987, Softly, 1988, Close Enough for Love, 1988, Tune in Tomorrow, 1990, You Won't Forget Me, 1991, Dedicated to You-Tribute to Sarah Vaughan with Carmen McRae, 1991, Here's to Life, 1992 (Grammy nomination, Best Jazz Vocal for "Light Out of Darkness", 1994), Violets for Furs, 1994, I Love You Paris, 1994, All Night Long, 1994, (with Charles Ables, Billy Hart) At Northsea, 1996, Jazz Round Midnight, 1998 (Grammy). Office: Verve Records 1755 Broadway Fl 3D New York NY 10019-3743

HORN, SUSAN DADAKIS, statistics educator; b. Cleve., Aug. 30, 1943; d. James Sophocles and Demeter (Zessis) Dadakis; m. Roger Alan Horn, July 24, 1965; children: Ceres, Corinne, Howard. BA, Cornell U., 1964; MS, Stanford U., 1966, PhD, 1968. Asst. prof. Johns Hopkins U., Balt., 1968-76, assoc. prof., 1976-86, prof. stats. and health svcs. rsch. methods, 1986-92; sr. scientist Intermountain Health Care, Salt Lake City, 1992-95; prof. dept. med. informatics Sch. Medicine U. Utah, Salt Lake City, 1992—; rsch. prof. U. Tex.-Houston Sch. Nursing, 1999—2001; vis. prof. Sch. Nursing, Vanderbilt U., 2004—. Sr. scientist Inst. for Clin. Outcomes Rsch., Salt Lake City; vis. prof. Vanderbilt U. Sch. Nursing, 2004—. Fellow Am. Statist. Assn., Assn. for Health Svcs. Rsch.; mem. APHA, Biometric Soc., Assn. for Health Svcs. Research, Sigma Xi, Phi Beta Kappa, Phi Kappa Phi. Presbyterian. Avocations: tennis, swimming. Home: 1793 Fort Douglas Cir Salt Lake City UT 84103-4451 Office: Inst Clin Outcomes 699 E South Temple Salt Lake City UT 84102-1282 E-mail: shorn@isisicor.com.

HORNAK, ANNA FRANCES, library administrator; b. College Station, Tex., June 3, 1922; d. Josef and Anna (Drozd) H. BA, U. Tex., Austin, 1944; B.L.S., U. Ill., Champaign-Urbana, 1945; Ed.M., U. Houston, 1956. Children's librarian Schenectady Pub. Library, N.Y., 1945-47; children's librarian Pasadena Pub. Library, Calif., 1947-49; supr. Juvenile Div. Houston Pub. Library, 1949-57, asst. dir., 1957-89, ret., 1989. Named Outstanding Woman, YWCA of Houston, 1977; Outstanding Houston Profl. Woman, Fed. Houston Profl. Women, 1982 Avocations: collecting miniature books; collecting Bohemian red glass; restoring antique furniture. Home: 2217 Woodhead St Houston TX 77019-6820

HORN-ALSBERGE, MICHELE MARYANN, school psychologist; b. Jersey City, Feb. 27, 1952; d. Charles Joseph Jr. and Beverly Theresa (Wackar) Horn; m. Edward John Rausch, Aug. 4, 1973 (div. June 1981); m. Gary Roy Alsberge, May 16, 1987; children: Kristen, Eric. AA, Harriman (N.Y.) Coll., 1971; BA, St. Peter's Coll., Jersey City, 1972; MA, Montclair (N.J.) State Coll., 1975; PhD, St. John's U., Jamaica, N.Y., 1999. Cert. sch. psychologist, N.J., social studies tchr., N.J. and N.Y., English tchr., N.J. Social studies tchr. Middletown (N.Y.) Bd. Edn., 1979-80, Monroe-Woodbury Bd. Edn., Central Valley, N.Y., 1980-82; English tchr. Vernon (N.J.) Twp. Bd. Edn., 1982-84; mktg. support rep. Computer Entry Systems, Fair Lawn, N.J., 1984-88; clin. specialist Ctr. for Mental Health, Newton (N.J.) Meml. Hosp., 1990-94; sch. psychologist North Warren Regional Bd. Edn., Blairstown, N.J., 1994—. Clin. specialist Prime Care, Newton, 1991—94; clinician St. John's U. Psychol. Svcs. Ctr., Jamaica, NY, 1986—90; clin. extern St. Clares/Riverside, Boonton, NJ, 1989—90; rsch. and clin. extern North Shore U. Hosp., Manhasset, NY, 1987—89; sec. Sussex-Warren Assn. Sch. Psychologists, 2000—. Com. mem. ctrl. planning commn. Pleasant Valley Sch. Dist., Brodheadsville, Pa., 1994—; mem. Girl Scouts USA. Named Outstanding Alumna Harriman (N.Y.) Coll., 1976. Mem. APA, N.J. Psychol. Assn., N.J. Edn. Assn. Roman Catholic. Avocations: reading, travel. Home: RR 3 Box 3231 Saylorsburg PA 18353-9680 Office: North Warren Regional HS PO Box 410 Blairstown NJ 07825-0410

HORNBAKER, ALICE JOY, writer; b. Cin., Feb. 3, 1927; children: Christopher Albert, Holly Jo, Joseph Bernard III. BA cum laude and honors in Journalism, U. Calif., San Jose, 1949. Asst. woman's editor San Jose Mercury-News, 1949-55; columnist Life After 50, Cin. Post newspaper, 1993—2002; freelance writer Cin.; writer, broadcaster The Alice Hornbaker Show Sta. 89.3 WMKVfm.org, 1996—; freelance feature writer www.grandparentworld.com. Owner, mgr. Frisch's Big Boy Restaurant, Cin., 1955-68; dir. pub. relations Children's Home Soc. Calif., Santa Clara, 1968-71; asst. dir. pub. relations United Fund Calif., Santa Clara, 1971—; editor Tristate Sunday Enquirer mag., 1986-89, columnist Generations Tristate mag.; editorial dir. Writers Digest Sch., Cin., 1971-75; columnist, critic, mag. writer, reporter, copy editor Tempo sec. Cin. Enquirer, 1975-93, also book editor and critic, columnist for Aging, feature writer Tempo sect.; reporter news segments on aging Sta. WKRC-TV; tchr. adult edn. Forest Hills Sch. Dist., Thomas More Coll., 1973—; reporter, specialist on aging for Cin. Enquirer, 1989-93, commentator on aging Sta. WMLX-AM, 1991-93; broadcaster, writer Sta. WMKV-FM, wmkvfm.org, 1995—. Author: (Book) Preventive Care: Easy Exercise Against Aging, 1974, columnist: internet 3 times weekly Life After 50; contbr. articles to various publs. including: People, Modern Maturity, St. Anthony Messenger, N.Y. Times Sun mag., Ohio Heitage mag.others., fiction to Enquirer mag. Recipient Bronze award in Am. health journalism Am. Chiropractic Assn., 1977, 78, Golden Image award Assn. Ohio Philanthropic Homes, 1989; 1st pl. for feature writing Cin. Editors Assn., 1983, 1st and 3rd pl. feature writing awards Ohio Profl. Writers, Inc., 1992, Journalist of Yr. award Ohio chpt. Am. Coll. Health Care Adminstrs., 1993, Journalism award Greater Cin. Joint Coun. on Geriat. Care, 1993. Mem. Blue Pencil of Ohio State U. (pres. 1981-82), Women in Comm., Ohio Newspaper Women's Assn. (v.p. 1981-83, 1st pl. human interest story 1977-85, 2d pl. column award 1979, Tops in Ohio award 1982, M.M. McMullen 2d pl. award, 1982, Recognition award 1985, 4th pl. on aging Nat. Legacies contest 1994), Soc. Profl. Journalists (treas. 1981-82), Ohio Press Women, Inc. (1st and 3d pl. awards for feature writing 1992). E-mail: ajhornbaker@yahoo.com.

HORNBECK, NITA LOU MCCLENNAN, university and secondary school educator; b. Macamey, Tex., Feb. 16, 1929; d. Major McKinley and Eupha Addie (Todd) McLennan; m. Carlton Wayne Hornbeck; children: Rebecca Diane Cudak, Susan Dawn Treese, Cynthia Jayne Chandler, Robert Carlton Hornbeck. BA, Southwestern U., Georgetown, Tex., 1950; MA, Tex. A&I U., 1973. Cert. tchr., supr. Tng. dir. Scarbrough's Dept. Store, Austin, 1950; sec. Sec. of State's Office, Austin, 1950-51; dental health educator, counselor State Health Dept., Austin, 1951; tchr. Alice (Tex.) H.S., 1964-80; instr. Bee County C.C., 1974-76, Tex. A&I U., Kingsville, 1977-79; tchr. Round Rock (Tex.) H.S., 1981-90, ret., 1990. Cons. Nat. Evaluation Sys., Austin, 1989—; presenter Using Computers in English Classrooms, 1989. Mem. AAUW (mentor for Austin 1990, outstanding woman of br. Austin 1991-92, 92-93, 95, newsletter editor Austin 1992-94, conv. dir. 1994, ctrl. Tex. dir., state bd. dirs. 1994—96, pub. policy chair Austin 1994-96, state program dir. 1996—, nat. conv. chmn., 2001, Austin chpt. pres., 2003—, outstanding women of Tex. award 1996, organizer, co-chair Voice of Reason 1995—, grant 1995, program v.p. Tex. 1996—98, grantee 1996, dir. voter's edn. campaign 1996), Assn. Pub. Policy (bd. dir. 2000-01), Tex. Retired Tchrs. Assn., (mem. pub. policy 1994—96, award of distinction 1995), Williamson County Retired Tchrs. (pres. 1992-94), Women's Legis. Days (bd. dirs. 1994-2003), Coalitions of Pub. Schools (exec. bd. 2003-04). Democrat. Methodist. Avocations: attending legislative hearings, state bd. edn. meetings, seminars. Office: Nat Evaluation Sys 2621 Ridgepoint Dr Austin TX 78754-5232 Home: 9400 W Parmer Ln Apt 1613 Austin TX 78717-4746

HORNBY-ANDERSON, SARA ANN, metallurgical engineer, marketing professional; b. Plymouth, Devon, Eng., Apr. 17, 1952; came to U.S., 1986; d. Foster John and Joanna May (Duncan) Hornby; m. John Victor Anderson, Sept. 2, 1978 (div. May 1987). BSc in Metallurgy with honors, Sheffield (Eng.) City Poly., 1973, PhD in Indsl. Metallurgy, 1980. Chartered engr. Metallurgist Joseph Lucas Rsch., Solihull, England, 1970, William Lee Malleable, Dronfield, 1972; tech. sales specialist Applied Rsch. Labs, Luton, 1973—74; quality assurance metallurgist Firth Brown Tools, Sheffield, 1974—75, rsch. metallurgist high speed steel, 1975; lectr. Sheffield City Poly., 1975—78; grad. metallurgist, strip devel. metallurgist British Steel Corp., Rotherham, 1978—80; program mgr. Can. Liquid Air, Montreal, Canada, 1980—85; group mktg. mgr. Liquid Air Corp., Countryside, Ill., 1986—90, tech. mgr. Walnut Creek, Calif., 1990—93; bus. devel. mgr.-metals and materials Can. Liquid Air, Toronto, 1993—97, N.Am. steel tech. mgr., 1995—97; dir. steelmaking tech. Goodfellow Techs. Inc., Mississauga, Canada, 1997, dir. ops., 1997—99; mgr. bus. devel. Stantec Global Techs. Ltd. (formerly Goodfellow Techs. Inc.), 1999; product mgr. steel making/ melting Midrex Techs., Inc., Charlotte, NC, 1999—2003; pres. Global Strategic Solutions, Inc., Charlotte, NC, 2003—. Bd. dirs., chmn. R & D com., mem. publs. com., chmn. promotions and mktg. com. Investment Casting Inst., Dallas; presenter to confs. in field. Contbr. articles to profl. jours.; patentee in field of metallurgy. Mem. AIME, Inst. Metals (young metallurgists com. 1974-80), Sheffield Metall. Soc. Inst. Metals (sec. 1978-80), Am. Foundry Soc., Iron and Steel Soc. (steering com. 1987-91, chmn. topics com. 1988-89, sec. 1992, vice chair 1993, chmn. process tech. divsn. 1994, bd. dirs., strategic planning com. 1995-98, internat. affairs com. 1998—, bd. dirs. ad hoc com. on internat. affairs 1998-99, univ. rels. com.). Avocations: scuba diving, horseback riding, swimming, siamese cats, gardening. Office Phone: 704-488-7969. Personal E-mail: felady@hotmail.com.

HORNE, MARILYN, mezzo-soprano; b. Bradford, Pa., Jan. 16, 1934; d. Bentz and Berneice Horne; m. Henry Lewis (div.); 1 child. Ed., U. So. Calif.; MusD (hon.), Rutgers U., 1970, Jersey City State Coll., 1973, Brown U., 1984, Juillard Sch. Music, 1994; DLitt (hon.), St. Peter's Coll.; LHD (hon.), Kean Coll., 1977. Singer: (Operas) (debut) as Hata in The Bartered Bride, 1954, (La Scala debut) Oepidus Rex, 1969, (Met. Opera debut) as Adalgisa in Norma, 1970, (other roles) Rosina in Barber of Seville, Cleonte in The Siege of Corinth, Isabella in L'Italiana in Algieri, Carmen at Met. Opera, 1972—73, Laura in Harvest, Chgo. Lyric Opera, Marie in Wozzeck, San Francisco Opera, (appeared in) Phigenie en Tauride, Semiramide, Samson et Dalila at Met. Opera, 1987, The Ghost of Versailles, 1991, Pelléas et Mélisande, 1995, Venice Festival by invitation of Igor Stravinsky, Am. Opera Soc., N.Y.C., for several seasons, Vancouver Opera, Philharm. Hall, N.Y.C., Paris, Dallas, Houston, Covent Garden, London, roles at La Scala, Italy, Rossini Opera Festival, Pesaro, Italy, Met. Opera, 1987, (recital debuts) Madrid, Dresden, East Berlin, 1987; performer: (at inauguration) of U.S. President Clinton, 1993, ann. recital at Carnegie Hall, European tour with husband for Dept. State, 1963; rec. artist London, Columbia, Deutsche Grammaphon and RCA records, recs. include soundtrack Carmen Jones. Founder Marilyn Horne Found. Named Musician of Yr. Musical Am., 1995; named to Harold C. Schonberg's N.Y. Times' list of 9 All-Time, All-Star Singers in Met. Opera's 100 Years, 1984; recipient Grammy awards, 1964, 1981, 1983, 1994, Handel medallion, 1980, Premio d'Oro, Italian Govt., 1982, Commendatore al merito della Repubblica Italiana, 1983, Gold Merit medal Nat. Soc. Arts and Letters, 1987, Fidelio Gold medal, 1988, George Peabody award, 1989, Silver medal Covent Garden Royal Opera House, 1989, Disting. Dau. of Pa. Silver medal San Francisco Opera, 1990, Nat. Arts medal, 1992. Achievements include Achievements includes having the leading exponent florid vocal style, music of Rossini, Handel, Vivaldi. Office: care Columbia Artists Mgmt Inc Wilford Divsn 165 W 57th St New York NY 10019-2201 also: care Met Opera Assoc Attention: Artistic Dept Lincoln Ctr New York NY 10023 also: BMG Classics/RCA 1540 Broadway New York NY 10036-4039

HORNE, RIKKI, school system administrator; b. NYC, Aug. 22, 1950; d. Arthur Douglas and Rose (Wagschal) Horne; m. Rudy Petersdorf, June 16, 1991; 1 child, Barbara Sofie Horne-Petersdorf. BA, SUNY, Albany, 1971, MLS, 1974; MBA, Northwestern U., 1980. Libr. U. Ill. Med. Sch., Chgo., 1974—76, Northwestern U. Med. Sch., Chgo., 1976—78; mktg. dir. Recycled Paper Products, Chgo., 1981—83; owner, pres. Med. Claims Mgmt., Newbury Park, Calif., 1983—2003; ret., 2003. Mem. bibliotherapy com. Am. Libr. Assn., Chgo., 1974—78; mem. certification exam com. Med. Libr. Assn., Chgo., 1976—78; mem. certification com. Nat. Assn. Claims Assistance Profls., Chgo., 1986—90. Vol. server Ojai Homeless Shelter, 1996—; mem. Ojai (Calif.) Unified Sch. Dist., 1994—, pres., 1998, 2001, 2004; active Ojai Valley Friends and Found., 2000—02; mem. adv. bd. Anti Defamation League, Ventura County, 2002—. Mem.: NOW, Nat. Women's Polit. Caucus (Ventura County chpt., treas. 1993—95). Democrat. Jewish. Avocations: reading, walking. Home: 930 N Signal St Ojai CA 93023-1823

HORNER, CONSTANCE JOAN, federal agency administrator; b. Summit, NJ, Feb. 24, 1942; d. David Earl and Cecelia (Murphy) McNeely; m. Charles Edward Horner, May 7, 1965; children: David Bayer, Jonathan Purcell. BA in English Lit., U. Pa., 1964; MA in English Lit., U. Chgo., 1967. Dep. asst. dir. policy planning and evaluation ACTION Agy., Washington, 1981-82, acting assoc. dir. domestic & anti-poverty ops., 1982-83, dep. assoc. dir. for VISTA & service-learning, 1982-83; assoc. dir. for econs. & govt. Office of Mgmt. and Budget, Washington, 1983-85; dir. Office of Pers. Mgmt., Washington, 1985-89; deputy sec. HHS, 1989-91; asst. to pres. and dir. presdl. pers. The White House, Washington, 1991-93; mem. U.S. Commn. on Civil Rights, Washington, 1993-98. Commr. The White House Fellows Commn., Washington, 1985-89; guest scholar The Brookings Inst., Washington, 1993—; vis. faculty Princeton (NJ) U., 1994; fellow, lectr. Johns Hopkins U., 1994-95; mem. adv. com. women in svcs. Dept. Def., 2003; bd. dirs. Pfizer, Inc., Prudential Fin., Inc., Ingersoll-Rand Co. Ltd. Bd. dirs. Annie E. Casey Found., Balt., 1994—. Fellow: Nat. Acad. Pub. Adminstrn.; mem.: Cosmos Club. Republican. Home: 3171 Porter St NW Washington DC 20008-3210

HORNER, DIANE L. dean; BSN, Ohio State U.; MSN in Burn Nursing, U. Cin.; EdD in Adult and Continuing Edn., No. Ill. U.; EdD in Adminstrn. in Higher Edn. Pub. health nurse Cleveland County (Okla.) County Health Dept., Norman, 1964-66; coord. maternal-child health program Dallas (Tex.) County Health Dept., 1966-67; staff nurse Washington Hosp., Fredricksburg, Va., 1968-70; staff nurse, supr. Crittenden Meml. Hosp., West Memphis, Ark., 1970-71, dir. staff devel., 1971-74; instr. U. Cin., 1976-77; asst. prof. Marycrest Coll., Davenport, Iowa, 1977-79; asst., then assoc. prof. Aurora (Ill.) U., 1979-83; dean St. Xavier U., Chgo., 1983-89, U. Miami, Coral Gables, Fla., 1990—. Mem. adv. com. Fla. Pub. Health Nursing, Geriatric Rsch. Edn. and Clin. Ctr., Nursing Spectrum, 1993-97; presenter workshops, confs. in field; mem. VA Deans com., 1990—, Wound Care Inst., 1990-93, U. Fla. acad. dean policy coun., 1990—, long range planning com., 1990—, med. sch. exec. com., 1990-92; bd. dirs. Good News Care Ctr. Contbr. articles to profl. jours. Bd. dirs. Cmty Ptnrship for the Homeless, mem. long range planning com. 1997. Recipient Hurricane Hero award Pts. of Light and Allstate Founds., 1993, Recognition award Transcultural Nursing Soc., 1992. Mem. ANA, Am. Assn. Colls. of Nursing, Am. Orgn. Nurse Execs., Chgo. Nurse Adminstrs. Conf. Group, Fla. Assn. Nurse Execs., Coun. on Grad. Edn. for Adminstrn. in Nursing., Fla. Nurses Assn., Ill. League for Nursing, Ill. Nurses Assn., Ill. Orgn. for Nurse Execs., Nat. League for Nursing (nominating com.), Nat. Orgn. Nurse Practitioner Faculties, Soc. for Rsch. in Nursing Edn. (founder), South Fla. Orgn. Nurse Execs., So. Coun. Collegiate Edn. for Nursing, U. Miami Iron Arrow, Golden Key Soc., Sigma Theta Tau, Kappa Delta Pi. Office: U Miami School of Nursing 5801 S Red Rd Coral Gables FL 33143-2343

HORNER, MATINA SOURETIS, retired academic administrator, corporate financial executive; b. Boston, July 28, 1939; d. Demetre John and Christine (Antonopoulos) Souretis; m. Joseph L. Horner, June 25, 1961; children: Tia Andrea, John, Christopher. AB cum laude, Bryn Mawr Coll., 1961; MS, U. Mich., 1963, PhD, 1968; LLD (hon.), Dickinson Coll., 1973; LLD, Mt. Holyoke Coll., 1973; LLD (hon.), U. Pa., 1975, Smith Coll., 1979, Wheaton Coll., 1979, U. Mich., 1989; LHD (hon.), U. Mass., 1973, Tufts U., 1976, U. Hartford, 1980, U. New Eng., 1987, Bentley Coll., 1989, New Eng. Coll., 1989, Pine Manor Coll., 1989, Am. Coll. Greece, 1990; DLitt (hon.), Claremont U. Ctr. and Grad Sch., 1988, Hellenic Coll., 1990; LHD (hon.), Colby Sawyer Coll., 1991. Teaching fellow U. Mich., Ann Arbor, 1962-66, lectr. motivation personality, 1968-69; lectr. social relations Harvard U., Cambridge, Mass., 1969-70, asst. prof. clin. psychology, 1970-72, assoc. prof. psychology, 1972-89, cons. univ. health svcs., 1971-89; pres. Radcliffe Coll., Cambridge, 1972-89, pres. emerita, 1989—; exec. v.p. TIAA-CREF, NYC, 1989—2003; ret., 2003. Bd. dirs. Neiman Marcus Group, Boston Edison Co.-NSTAR. Co-author: The Challenge of Change, 1983; contbr. psychol. articles on motivation to profl. jours. and chpts. to books. Mem. adv. coun. NSF, 1977-87, chair, 1980-86; bd. trustees Twentieth Century Fund, The Century Found., 1973—, Am. Coll. of Greece, 1983-90, Mass. Eye and Ear Infirmary, 1986-90, Com. for Econ. Devel., 1988—, vice-chmn., 1992-98; bd. trustees Mass. Gen. Hosp., Inst. Health Professions, 1988—, vice chmn., 1994, chair, 1995; bd. dirs. Coun. for Fin. Aid to Edn., 1985-89, Beth Israel Hosp., 1989-95; bd. dirs. Revson Found., 1986-92, chmn., 1992-97; bd. dirs. Women's Rsch. and Edn. Inst., 1979—, chair rsch. com., 1982—; mem. Coun. on Fgn. Rels., 1984—; exec. com. ACE Bus. Higher Edn. Forum, 1984-86; exec. com. New Eng. Colls. Fund, 1980—, 2d v.p., 1984-85, 1st v.p., 1985-88, pres., 1988-89; mem. nat. panel to study declining test scores Coll. Entrance Exam. Bd., 1976-77; exec. com., chair task force Pres.'s Commn. for Nat. Agenda for 1980s, 1979-80; adv. com. Women's Leadership Conf. on Nat. Security, 1982—; exec. com. Coun. on Competitiveness, 1986-89; chair task force on health care Challenge to Leadership Conf., 1987-89; bd. dirs. Greenwall Found., 1997, Fund for City of N.Y., chair, 1997. Recipient Roger Baldwin award Mass. Civil Liberties Union Found., 1982, citation of merit Northeast Region NCCJ, 1982, Career Contbn. award Mass. Psychol. Assn., 1987, Disting. Bostonian award, 1990, Ellis Island medal, 1990. Mem. NOW (nat. corp. adv. bd. of legal def. and edn. fund 1984—), Am. Laryngol. Voice Rsch. and Edn. Found. (pres.), Nat. Inst. Social Scis. (medal for outstanding svc. 1973), Phi Beta Kappa, Phi Delta Kappa, Phi Kappa Phi.

HORNER, MAXINE EDWYNA CISSEL, state legislator; b. Tulsa, Jan. 17, 1933; d. Earl Henry Sr. and Corrine (Burton) Cissel; m. Donald Montell Horner Sr., 1954; children: Shari, Donald Montell Jr. BS in Pers. Mgmt., Langston U., 1985. Personnel adminstr. Tulsa Job Corps Ctr., 1971-75; dir. minority women's employment U.S. Dept. Labor, 1975-81; staff asst. U.S Rep. James Jones, Tulsa, 1984-86; mem. Okla. State Senate, 1986—. Vice chmn. human resources com. 1987—; mem. bus. and labor, criminal jurisprudence, fin. coms., 1987—; chmn. govt. ops. & agy. oversight com., 1989—; mem. appropriations com., 1989—. Vol. VIP Read Aloud Program; v.p. North Tulsa Heritage Found., 1984—; pres. adv. bd. North Tulsa YMCA, 1985-86; active Corp. Membership Dr. Okla. Sickle Cell Anemia

Found., Gov.'s Task Force on Affirmative Action, Simon Estes Scholarship Found., Health and Human Svcs. Com. for Nat. Conf. State Legislators, Children, Families and Social Svcs. Com., Dem. Nat. Platform Com.; chair Okla. Legis. Black Caucus; co chair 1988 Nat. Black Caucus State Legislators Conf. Tulsa. Recipient spl. recognition Okla. Jay. Nu. Th. Woman, Oklahoma Writers' Acad.; academic scholarship Wiley Coll., Marshall, Tex., 1951; Outstanding Community Svc. awards Tulsa Urban League, North Tulsa Bus. and Profl. Women, Tulsa Job Corps, Sunray DX Oil Co., Omega Psi Phi, grant Harvard U., MPA Program, Mid-Career Profession. Mem. NAACP, LWV, Nat. Assn. Black Social Workers, Dem. Women Action Group, Delta Sigma Theta. Baptist. Avocations: reading, performing arts, movies. Home: 1010 W Queen Pl Tulsa OK 74127-2520 Office: State Capitol Senate House Oklahoma City OK 73105

HORNER, WINIFRED BRYAN, humanities educator, researcher, consultant, writer; b. St. Louis, Aug. 31, 1922; d. Walter Edwin and Winifred (Kinealy) Bryan; m. David Alan Horner, June 15, 1943; children: Winifred, Richard, Elizabeth, David. AB, Washington U., St. Louis, 1943; MA, U. Mo., 1961; PhD, U. Mich., 1975. Instr. English U. Mo., Columbia, 1966-75, asst. prof., 1975-80, chair lower divorce studies, dir. composition program, 1974-80, assoc. prof., 1980-83, prof., 1984-85, prof. emerita, 1985—; prof. English, Radford chair rhetoric and composition Tex. Christian U., Ft. Worth, 1985-93, Cecil and Ida Green disting. prof. emerita, 1993-97. Disting. Vis. Prof., Tex. Woman's U. Editor: Historical Rhetoric: An Annotated Bibliography of Selected Sources in English, 1980, The Present State of Scholarship in Historical Rhetoric, 1983, Composition and Literature: Bridging the Gap, 1983, Rhetoric and Pedagogy: Its History, Philosophy and Practice, 1995; author: Rhetoric in a Classical Mode, 1987, Nineteenth-Century Scottish Rhetoric: The American Connection, 1993, Life Writing, 1996; co-author Harbrace Coll. Hancbook, 11th edit., 1990, 12th edit., 1994, 14th edit., 1998. Named Disting. prof. Tex. Woman's U., 1999, Disting. Alumna, Washington U.; Inst. for the Humanities fellow U. Edinburgh, 1987; NEH grantee, 1976, 87. Mem. Internat. Soc. for History Rhetoric (exec. coun. 1986), Rhetoric Soc. Am. (bd. dirs. 1981, pres. 1987), Nat. Coun. Writing Program Administrs. (v.p. 1977-85, pres. 1985-87), Coll. Conf. on Composition and Communication (exec. com.), Modern Lang. Assn. (mem. del. assembly 1981). Home and Office: 1904 Tremont Ct Columbia MO 65203-5467 E-mail: hornerw@missouri.edu.

HORNICK, SUSAN FLORENCE STEGMULLER, secondary education educator, fine arts educator, curriculum specialist, artist; b. Aug. 29, 1947; d. August George and Florence Maybell (Meisinger) Stegmuller; m. Jesse Allan Hornick, July 20, 1974. BA, Queens Coll., 1969, MS in Art Edn., 1973; permanent N.Y. State reading cert., Hunter Coll., 1984, advanced cert. ednl. supervn./adminstrn. summa cum laude, 1996. Lic. tchr. fine arts, N.Y.C.; permanent cert. tchr. art, N.Y.; cert. in ednl. adminstrn. and supervision, N.Y.; permanent cert. sch. dist. adminstr. N.Y. Fine arts tchr. Hillcrest H.S., Jamaica, N.Y., 1973-74, Ea. Dist. H.S., Bklyn., 1974-75, Tottenville H.S., S.I., N.Y., 1975-76; fine arts tchr., title 1 reading tchr. Prospect Heights H.S., Bklyn., 1976-78; fine arts tchr. Grover Cleveland H.S., Ridgewood, NY, 1978—2003, dept. coord., 1986-98. Conceptual art tchr., conceptual facilitator, reading, writing and artistic skills with written and visual exemplification Grover Cleveland H.S., 1978—2003, yearbook advisor, 1979, tchr. reading. English and reading improvement through art, 1980—85, tchr. ecol. awareness, 1995—2003; cooperating tchr., trainer art tchrs. Queens Coll., Flushing, NY, 1991, 2000; tchr. "bridge" ESL and math. Newcomers Summer H.S., Long Island City, NY, 2000, ESL tchr., mem. Saturday lit. program, 2000—01. Exhbns. include U.S. Capitol, Washington, 1982, 86, 88, U.S. Capitol, Washington, Lever House Exhibit, 1984-97, City Hall, N.Y.C., 1984, Queensborough C.C. Art Gallery, Bayside, N.Y., 1984-94, N.Y.C. Transit Mus., 1987-99, Queens Borough Hall, Kew Gardens, N.Y., 1992, Sotheby's, N.Y., 1992, Internat. Arrivals bldg. JFK Kennedy Airport (award winning mural by Joanna Kadlubowska, 1992), Queens Theater in the Park, Flushing, N.Y., 1993, 97, Nat. Mus. Am. Indian, Smithsonian Inst., 1992, 93, Mus. of City of N.Y., 1998, Grover Cleveland H.S., Ridgewood, N.Y., 1998-2003, N.Y. Joint Bd. Unite, N.Y.C. 2000-01 Named Internat. Educator of Yr. award, Internat. Biographical Ctr. Cambridge, England, 2003; recipient Medal for Superior Performance, N.Y.C. Transit Authority, 1996, Cert. of Appreciation for Outstanding Performance as Art Educator in N.Y.C. Pub. Schs., N.Y.C. Bd. Edn., 1985, Cert. of Recognition for Accomplishments as Outstanding Tchr., Nat. Tchrs. Hall of Fame, 2000. Mem. ASCD, N.Y.C. Art Tchrs. Assn., Coalition for Ednl. Tchrs., Hunter Coll. Alumni Assn., Nat. Mus. Women in Arts (charter), Colonial Williamsburg Duke of Gloucester Soc., N.Am. Fishing Club (life), Downsville Women's Club. Home and Office: P O Box 482 Downsville NY 13755

HORNSBY, JUDITH ELIZABETH, special education educator; b. Xenia, Ohio, Aug. 26, 1942; d. Harry Algeo and Mary Elizabeth (Graves) Bennett; m. Orson Hornsby, Dec. 21, 1963; children: Jeffery William, Mary Katherine Hornsby. BS Ohio U., 1964; MA Special Ed., Ohio State U., 1966. Tchr., visually impaired Cincinnati Public Schs., 1964—70, 1975—80, Hamilton City Schs., 1980—; reading tchr. Cincinnati County Day Sch., 1972—75. Organist Northern Hills United Methodist Church, Cincinnati, 1991—; chair, div. 13 Assn. for the Ed. and Rehab. of the Blind & Visually Impared, Alexandria, Va., 1994—96; pres. Assn. for the Ed. and Rehab. of the Blind & Visually Impaired in Ohio, 2000—. Cons. for visually impaired Hamilton YMCA, Camp Campbell, Ohio, 1983—2001; co-chmn. High Vision Games, Cincinnati, 1997, 1999, 2001. Recipient Outstanding Lay Person, Hamilton YMCA, 1992, Educator of the Year, AERO, 1992, Golden Apple award, Ashland Oil, 1995. Mem.: Nat. Braille Assn., DAR, Eastern Star (Organist 1988—). Republican. Methodist. Avocations: reading, investment club, golf. Office: Hamilton City Schs 1165 Eaton Ave Hamilton OH 45013

HOROWITZ, CAROLE SPIEGEL, landscape contractor; b. Pitts., Mar. 24, 1940; d. Alvin Duane and Leah (Greinstein) Spiegel; m. Don Roy Horowitz, Jan. 31, 1960; children: Cindy H. Urback, Thomas Samuel. Student, Carnegie Mellon U., 1958-61. Cert. interior horticulturist, landscape profl. Owner Carole Horowitz Interior Design Plants, 1965-72; pres. Plantscape, Inc., Pitts., 1973—. Chmn. U. Pitts. Small Bus. Com., 1986-92; bd. dirs. United Way Allegheny County, Pitts., 1991-94, Jr. Achievment Allegheny County, Pitts., 1985-95, Vocat. Rehab. Ctr., Pitts., 1989-91. Recipient Nat. Landscape award White House and Am. Assn. Nurserymen, 1990, YWCA Entrepreneur Leadership award, 1990; named Entreprenuer of Yr. Ernst & Young & Inc. Mag., 1988, Pitts. Bus. Times Pa.'s Best 50 Women in Bus. award 1997. Mem. Interior Plantscape Assn. (sec., v.p. 1982-85), Associated Landscape Contractor of Am. (cert., chmn. Am. Bd. Govs. 1991-94), Internat. Facility Mgmt. Assn., Westmoreland Country Club, Longboat Key Club, Rotary (sec. Downtown Pitts. chpt.). Jewish. Avocations: travel, golf. Office: Plantscape Inc 3101 Liberty Ave Pittsburgh PA 15201-1400 E-mail: ch@plantscape.com

HOROWITZ, DIANA J., artist; b. N.Y.C., Sept. 26, 1958; d. Paul and Brenda (Stone) H.; m. Paul G. Conrad, May 21, 1989; 1 child, Julia. BFA, SUNY, Purchase, 1980; postgrad., Tyler Sch. Art/Temple Abroad, Rome, 1983-84; MFA, Bklyn. Coll., 1987. Adj. prof. Sch. of Art Inst. Chgo., 1987-89, Tyler Sch. Art, Rome, 1989-90. Bklyn. Coll., 1992-94. Grantee Ingram-Merrill Found., 1988, Pollock-Krasner Found., 1989, 93; recipient Rosenthal Found. award Am. Acad. Arts and Letters, 1996.

HOROWITZ, FRANCES DEGEN, academic administrator, psychology educator; b. Bronx, NY, May 5, 1932; d. Irving and Elaine (Moinester) Degen; m. Floyd Ross Horowitz, June 23, 1953; children: Jason Degen, Benjamin Meyer Levi. BA, Antioch Coll., 1954; EdM, Goucher Coll., 1954; PhD, U. Iowa, 1959. Tchr. elem. sch., Iowa City, 1954-56; grad. rsch. asst. Iowa Child Welfare Sta., U. Iowa, 1956-59; asst. prof. psychology U.

Oreg. Coll., Ashland, 1959-61; asst. prof. home econs. U. Kans., Lawrence, 1961-62, USHPS rsch. fellow, 1962-63, assoc. prof. dept. human devel. and family life, 1964-69, prof. dept. human devel. and family life, psychology, 1969—, chmn. dept., 1969-75, rsch. assoc, 1964-75, assoc. dean, 1975-79, 1978-91, dir. Infant Rsch. Lab., 1964-91; pres. Grad. Sch. and Univ. Ctr. CUNY, 1991—. Bd. dirs. Feminist Press; guest rsch. assoc. Bur. Child Rsch. U. Kans., and Parsons (Kans.) State Hosp. and Tng. Ctr., summer 1960; vis. prof. dept. psychology Tel Aviv U., 1973—74; guest rschr. dept. pediat. Kaplan Hosp., Rehovot, Israel, 1973—74; vis. lectr. dept. psychology Hebrew U., Jerusalem, 1976, cons. rsch. programs in early edn., 1980—; pres. Ctr. for Rsch., Inc., Lawrence, 1978—91; cons. OAS, 1971, U.S. Office Edn., 1969—73, NIMH, 1979; cons. to early infant stimulation program, Caracas, Venezuela, 76; lectr. infant devel., day care to local and regional cmty. groups, 1966—; adv. com. Carolina Inst. on Early Edn. of the Handicapped, 1978—83; reviewer NSF, 1978—91; mem. U. Kans. del. to Peoples Republic China, 1980; exch. scholar Chinese Acad. Scis., China, 1982; mem. Office Sci. Integrity Rev. Adv. Com. PHS, 1991—93; nominating com. Weizmann Women in Sci. award Am. Com. Weizmann Inst. Sci., 1994; mem. Nat. Task Force Grad. Edn., 1994—; workforce devel. subcom. N.Y.C. Partnership, 1994—; mem. U.S. Nat. Com. for the Internat. Union of Psychol. Sci., 1995—97; mem. overseers' com. to visit dept. psychology Harvard U.; mem. founding adv. bd. Sackler Inst. for Human Brain Devel., 1998—; bd. dirs. Nat. Coun. for Rsch. on Women; adv. coun. Nat. Inst. Child Health and Human Devel., 1999—2004; chair nat. adv. bd. Office Child Devel., U. Pitts.; lectr. in field. Editor Memoir Essay, 2002; co-editor science watch sect. Am. Psychologist, 1993—; mem. editl. bd. Jour. Devel. Psychology, 1969-75, Early Childhood Edn. Quar., 1974—, Devel. Rev., 1981—, Infant Behaviour and Devel., 1984—, Contemporary Psychology, 1986-1991; contbr. articles to profl. jours.; TV host Women to Women, 1994—. Trustee Antioch Coll., 1987-91, L.I. Univ., 1992—; bd. dirs. Cmty. Children's Ctr., 1965-68, Douglas County Vis. Nurse Assn., 1968-69; mem. workforce devel. subcom., N.Y.C. Partnership; mem. coun. advisors, Nat. Ctr. for Children in Poverty; mem. commn. on women in higher edn. Am. Coun. on Edn. Recipient Trustees award medal Cherry Lawn Sch., Conn., 1971, Outstanding Educator of Am. award, 1973, Disting. Psychologist in Mgmt. award Soc. for Psychologists in Mgmt., 1993, Rebecca Rice Alumni award Antioch Coll., 1996, Sue Rosenberg Zalk award The Feminist Press, 2003; named to Women's Hall of Fame U. Kans., 1974; Ford Found. fellow, 1954, Ctr. for Advanced Studies Behavioral Scis. fellow, Stanford U., 1983-84; Spl. Commendation NYC comptroller's office, 1997, NY Women's Agenda Star award, 2002. Fellow APA (pres. divsn. devel. psychology 1977-78, mem. publs. bd. 1985-91, chief sci. adviser 1989-93, pres. 1991-94, Centennial award 1992), AAAS, N.Y. Acad. Scis.; mem. Soc. Rsch. in Child Devel. (editor monographs 1976-83, pres. 1997-2002), Jewish Cmty. Rels. Coun. (mem. bd. 1999—), Hebrew Free Loan Soc. (mem. bd. 2000—), Am. Assn. on Mental Deficiency, North Ctrl. Accrediting Assn. (bd. commrs. 1977-80), Am. Psychol. Found. (pres. 1991-94), Coun. Rsch. Polic and Grad. Edn. (chair, mem. exec. com.), Assn. Grad. Schs. (mem. exec. com.), N.Y. Women's Forum (bd. dirs. 1995—), Nat. Assn. of State Univs. and Lnd-Grant Colls. (past chair commn. on human resources and social change, bd. dirs. 1999-2002), Sigma Xi, Phi Beta Kappa (hon.). Home: 145 Central Park W Apt 4A New York NY 10023-2404 Office: CUNY Grad Ctr 365 5th Ave New York NY 10016-4309 E-mail: pres@gc.cuny.edu.

HOROWITZ, MARY CURTIS See CURTIS, MARY

HOROWITZ, SARA, labor organizer; b. N.Y.C., Jan. 13, 1963; BS, Cornell U., 1984; MA, SUNY, Buffalo, 1992; MPA, Harvard U., 1995. Labor organizer Working Today. Grantee, fellow Stern Family Fund, Rockefeller Found., Echoing Green. Office: Working Today Inc 55 Washington St Ste557 Brooklyn NY 11201-1036

HOROWITZ, WINONA LAURA See RYDER, WINONA

HORRELL, KAREN HOLLEY, insurance company executive, lawyer; b. Augusta, Ga., July 10, 1952; d. Dudley Cornelius and Eleanor (Shouppe) Holley; m. Jack E. Horrell, Aug. 14, 1976. BS, Berry Coll., 1974; JD, Emory U., 1976. Bar: Ohio 1977. Corp. counsel Great Am. Ins. Co., Cin., 1977-80, v.p., gen. counsel, sec., 1981-85, sr. v.p., gen. counsel, sec., bd. dirs., 1985—; pres. corp. svcs. Great Am. Ins. Property & Casualty Group, 1999—; counsel Am. Fin. Corp., 1980-81; gen. counsel numerous subsidiaries Great Ins. Co.; sec., asst. sec. numerous other fin. and ins. cos. Bd. dirs. Tri-Health, Inc., Bethesda, Inc. Trustee Cmty. Chest, 1987—91, Seven Hills Sch., 1991—2000, v.p., 1995—99; mem. cabinet United Appeal, 1984; bd. dirs. YWCA, 1984—90, v.p. fin., 1986—89; mem. Hamilton County Blue Ribbon Task Force on Child Abuse and Neglect Svcs., 1989—91; trustee Ohio Ins. Inst., 1994—2000, chair, 1996—99, Bethesda Hosp. Inc.; chair Ohio Joint Underwriting Assn., 1992—97; trustee Berry Coll., 1999—; mem. Hamilton County Hosp. Commn., 1999—, vice chair, 2002—; bd. dirs. Children's Home, 2001—. Mem. ABA, Cin. Bar Assn. (admissions com. 1978-91, nominating com. 1987-90). Democrat. Home: 2355 Easthill Ave Cincinnati OH 45208-2608 Office: Great Am Ins Co 580 Walnut St Cincinnati OH 45202-3110

HORSLEY, GAIL PATRICIA, retired mental health nurse; b. Chgo., June 20, 1946; d. Raymond Hubert Petterson and Shirleen F. Staebell; m. Antonio Moses, Aug. 15, 1970 (div. Sept. 1987); 1 child, William Michael Moses. BSN, St. Olaf Coll., Northfield, Minn., 1968; MSN, UCLA, 1970; postgrad., Menninger Clinic, Topeka, Kans., 1988—90. RN Kans., cert. clinical nurse specialist, ANCC, advanced registered nurse practioner, Kans. Pub. health nurse State of Alaska, Nome, Seward, St. Lawrence Island, 1970—74; clin. nurse specialist Anch Cmty. MHC, Anchorage, 1976—78; role devel. instr. Alaska Meth. U., Anchorage, 1974—76; nurse mgr. Alaska Psychiat. Inst., Anchorage, 1978—80; nurse therapist pvt. practice, Anchorage, 1982—87; asst. prof. U. Alaska, Anchorage, 1980—87; clin. nurse specialist Colmery O'Neil VA Med. Ctr., Topeka, 1988—2003, ret., 2003. Mem. adv. bd. suicide prevention program VA, Wasington, 1999. Contbr. articles to profl. pubs., poetry to literary pubs. Vol., specialist Am. Red Cross, Topeka; vol. Kans. Internat. Mus. Recipient Heart of Healthcare award, U. Kans., 1987, Gold Pan award, Suicide Prevention Ctr., 1985. Mem.: Nurses' Orgn. VA Scholarship (chair 1995—97), Topeka Opera Soc., Sigma Theta Tau. Lutheran. Avocations: reading, travel, poetry, tai chi, opera. Home: 1413 SW MacVicar Ave Topeka KS 66604

HORSLEY, PAULA ROSALIE, accountant; b. Smithfield, Nebr., Sept. 7, 1924; Student, AIB Bus. Coll., Des Moines, 1942-44, YMCA Coll., Chgo., 1944-47, UCLA Extension, 1974. Acctg. mgr. Montgomery Ward & Co., Denver, 1959-62; acct. Harman & Co., CPAs, Arcadia, Calif., 1962-67; contr., officer G & H Transp., Montebello, Calif., 1967-78; comptroller Frederick Weisman Co., Century City, Calif., 1978-80; CFO, Luth. Shipping, Madang, Papua New Guinea, 1980-82; prin. village bookkeeper, acctg. cons. Moreno Valley, Calif., 1982-94; CFO, Insight Computer Products and Tech., Inc., San Gabriel, Calif., 1988—2003, Insight Video Net LLC, Rancho Cucamonga, Calif., 2003—. Vol. crisis counselor, supr. and instr. Melodyland Hotline, Anaheim, Calif., 1997-79. Home: 31130-100 S Gen Kearny Rd Temecula CA 92591 Office: Insight Video Net LLC 10134 6th St Ste M Rancho Cucamonga CA 91730

HORSMAN, LENORE LYNDE (ELEANORA LYNDE), soprano, educator, actress; b. Saginaw, Mich., Apr. 21, 1931; d. George Clark and Gwendolyn (Steele) McNabb; m. Reginald Horsman, Sept. 3, 1955; children: John, Janine, Mara. BS in Music and Piano, Ind. U., 1956, MA in Theatre-Opera, 1958. profl. certs. in voice, Villa Schifanoia, Florence, Accademia Musicale Chigiana, Siena, Accademia Di Virgiliana, Mantua, Mozarteum, Salzburg. Tchrs: Tito Gobbi, Ettore Campogalliani. Dir. Mt.

Clemens Studio of Music, Mich.; 1950: tchr. voice, piano and acting for singers Milw. Conservatory of Music, 1964-65; dir., tchr. pvt. voice studio, 1965; founder, dir., designer Milw. Opera Theater, 1966; vocal coach dept. opera U. Wis. Milwaukee, 1969. Dir. v. singers U.W.M. Opera Theatre, Milw., 1974, Opera for Two, Milw., 1975, Mu Phi Epsilon Sch. Music, Chgo., 1976-81; dir. tchr. pvt. voice studio, Chgo., 1976-92; voice coach Theatre X, Milw., 1977; tchr. of acting Northshore Theatre, Milw., 1978-80. More than 33 leading roles in opera, operetta, musicals and plays; performances and concerts in US and Italy. Pres. Wis. Women in the Arts, 1973-76; bd. dir. Internat. Women's Yr. Festival, Milw., 1975. Named Women of the Yr., Milw. Panhellenic Assn., 1975; recipient Career Achievement award, 1978, Singers medal of honor Amici della Lirica, Mantua, Italy, 1981, Palcoscenico Silver Stage award, 1981. Mem. AAUW (v.p. 1999-2000), Nat. Assn. Tchr. Singing, Nat. Opera Assn., Wis. Music Tchr. Assn., Writers' Forum, Mu Phi Epsilon, Theta Alpha Phi. Avocations: theater, opera, oil painting, writing poetry.

HORST, PAMELA SUE, medical educator, family physician; b. Hershey, Pa., Jan. 23, 1951; d. Ralph H. and Helen (Fry) H.; m. Thomas H. Dennison, Feb. 6, 1982; 1 child, Elizabeth Dennison. BS, Pa. State U., 1972; MD, Pa. State U., Hershey, 1976. Diplomate Am. Bd. Family Practice, Am. Bd. Hospice & Palliative Medicine (cert). Resident in family practice Shadyside Hosp., Pitts., 1979; family physician North Jefferson Health Svcs., Clayton, N.Y., 1979-82; physician emergency rm. Geisinger Med. Ctr., Philipsburg, Pa., 1982-84; asst. prof. family medicine Albany (N.Y.) Med. Coll., 1984-88; research fellow health sci. ctr. SUNY, Syracuse, 1988—. Med. dir. family practice ctr. St. Joseph's Hosp. Health Ctr., Syracuse, 1989—, assoc. residency dir. family practice residency, Syracuse, 1990—; physician Palliative Care Cons. Svc., 1999—, hospice physician, 2002—; chmn. St. Joseph's Health Alliance, 1995-97, SyraHealth, IPA, 1997-98. Author: (with others) Ambulatory Medicine, 1993, Manual of Family Practice, 1996. Mem. Am. Acad. Family Physicians, Soc. Tchrs. Family Medicine, Am. Assn. of Hospice and Palliative Medicine. Avocations: gardening, reading. Office: St Joseph's Health Ctr Family Practice Residency 301 Prospect Ave Syracuse NY 13203-1899

HORSTMAN, SUZANNE RUCKER, financial planner; b. Coral Gables, Fla., June 27, 1945; d. Thomas John Jr. and June Ethel Agusta (Stones) R.; m. James Winter Horstman, Dec. 28, 1989. BBA, Fla. Atlantic U., 1971, MBA, 1975. CFP; lic. real estate agt. Assoc. dir. Am. Soc. Cons. Pharmacists, 1971-73; assoc. dir. devel. Fairfax Hosp. Assn. Found., Springfield, Va., 1974-81; dir. devel. Arlington (Va.) Hosp. Found., 1982-86; prin. Suzanne June Rucker, CFP, Falls Church, Va., 1986-90; dir. devel. Phoenixville Healthcare Found., 1990-94, Tri-County TEC Found., 1994-96, philanthropy cons., 1996—; dir. devel. CARE, 1997—2002; exec. dir. Libr. Found. Martin County, 2002—. Instr. George Washington U., Washington; seminar spkr. in field. Mem. Treasure Coast Planned Giving Coun., Nat. Com. Planned Giving; bd. dirs. Ronald McDonald House, Wilmington, Washington, Salvation Army Aux., Washington, Rep. Working Women's Forum. Fellow: Assn. Health Care Philanthropy. Republican. Office Phone: 772-221-1409.

HORTON, JOANN, academic administrator; b. Lenoir, N.C., 1948; d. Jasper D. Horton and Laura Alice Patterson; m. Warren N. Moore (div.). BS in French, Appalachian State U., 1970, MA in French, 1971; PhD in Higher Edn. Adminstrn., Ohio State U., 1977. V.p. Olive Harvey Coll., City Coll. Chgo., 1982-86, provost, 1986-89; state adminstr. Iowa Divsn. C.C., Des Moines, 1989-93; pres. Tex. So. U., Houston, 1993-95; mid. cons., sc fellow Am. Coun. on Edn., 1996-98; pres. Kennedy-King Coll., 1998-99; dep. chancellor for strategic planning City Colls. Chgo., 1999-99; pres. Team Masters, Inc., 2000—. Cons. evaluator, commr. at large North Cen. Assn. Commn. on Insts. for Higher Edn., Chgo., 1984-93; bd. dirs. Appalachian State U. Grad. Schs., Boone, N.C., 1995-99; mid. cons., Chgo., 1996-98. Bd. dirs. Greater Houston Partnership, 1993-95, chair workforce devel. task force, 1994-95; chair urban scouting com. Boy Scouts Am., Houston, 1995; strategic planning facilitator 7th Congl. Edn. Com., Chgo., 1999. Recipient Disting. Alumni award Appalachian State U., Boone, 1994, commendation 74th Tex. Legis., 1995, Image, Svc. and Achievement award Kizzy Found., Chgo., 1999; inductee Tex. Black Women Hall of Fame, 1994; fellow Leadership Greater Chgo. Mem. Am. Assn. Higher Edn., Am. Assn. State Colls. and Univs., Am. Assn. Women in C.C., Nat. Assn. Women Bus. Owners, Third World Conf. Found. (vice chair 1993—, Svc. award 1999), Assn. Colls. of Ill. Orgnl. Devel. Network. Avocations: tennis, reading, music, travel.

HORTON, LYNN C. state legislator; b. Roscoe, N.Y., Apr. 12, 1920; m. Mary D. Horton; four children. Student, Bates Coll. Mem. N.H. Ho. of Reps., Concord, chmn. legis. adminstrn. com., mem. election land com. Chmn. Coos County Del., N.H., various yrs.; mem. N.H. State Rep. Com. Mem. White Mountain Region Soc. (treas.). Home: 149 E Side Dr Concord NH 03301-5465 Office: NH Ho of Reps State Capitol Lancaster NH 03584

HORTON, MADELINE MARY, financial planner, consultant; b. Chgo., Mar. 1, 1939; d. James P. and Priscilla Mary (Pendelepe) Fiduccia; m. Richard J. Dickman, July 7, 1962 (div. 1981); children: James Earl, Suzanne Dickman Noel; m. Larry B. Horton, June 30, 1984 (dec. 1993). BA in Math. cum laude, Rosary Coll. (now Dominican U.), River Forest, Ill., 1960; MS in Math., U. Miami, Coral Gables, Fla., 1962; postgrad., U. Va., 1974-78. Cert. fin. planner, Inst. Cert. Fin. Planners. Instr. in math. U. Miami, Coral Gables, 1962-63; prin. Dickman Deductions, Charlottesville, Va., 1964—65; instr. in math. Miami Dade C.C., 1964-65, St. Patrick's High Sch., 1968-69; instr. devel. math. Piedmont Community Coll., Charlottesville, Va., 1974-78; health affairs planner U. Va. Med. Ctr., Charlottesville, 1978-80; zone mgr. IDS, Inc., Charlottesville, 1980-83; fin. cons. Merrill Lynch, Charlottesville, 1983-86; mgr., fin. cons. Prudential-Bache Securities, Inc., Charlottesville, 1986-87; investment broker Wheat First Securities Inc., Charlottesville, 1987; prin., owner Horton Fin. Svcs. Inc., Charlottesville, 1987—2003; v.p. investments H&R Block Fin. Advisors, Charlottesville, 2003—. Humor columnist Charlottesville Daily Progress, 1971; featured in article Va. Bus. monthly mag., 1988. Mem. Internat. Mgmt. Coun. (sec. Charlottesville chpt. 1986-88, v.p. 1988-89), Kappa Gamma Pi. Roman Catholic. Avocations: art, music, public speaking. Home: 2276 Oak Ridge Ct Charlottesville VA 22911-2202 Office: The Horton Group H&R Block Financial Adv 1759 Worth Park Charlottesville VA 22911-7441

HORTON, PATRICIA MATHEWS, artist, violist and violinist; b. Bklyn., Mar. 6, 1932; d. Edward Joseph and Margaret (Briggs) Mathews; m. Ernest H. Horton Jr., Mar. 6, 1982; 1 stepchild, Carol Horton Tremblay. Student in viola, William Primrose Master Class, 1980; student, Glendale (Calif.) C.C., 1981—90, Glendale (Calif.) C.C., 1993, Glendale (Calif.) C.C., 1999—2002, Art Ctr. Coll. Design, Pasadena, Calif., 1988-93; student in painting composition, Peter Liashkov, L.A., 1993-97. Profl. musician on violin and viola, 1951-86; musician on tour, 1952-57. Played with New Orleans Philharm., 1959-61, U.S. Tour of San Francisco Ballet, 1965, L.A. Civic Light Opera, 1974-80; played L.A. engagements of Bolshoi Ballet Co., 1975, Am. Ballet Theatre, 1974-80, N.Y. Opera, 1974-80, Royal Ballet of London, 1978, Alicia Alonzo's Cuban Ballet, 1979, Harlem Ballet, 1984, Deutsche Oper Berlin, 1985, also motion picture and TV soundtrack recs.; one-woman shows include Claremont (Calif.) Sch. Theology, 1997, Pasadena First United Meth. Ch., 1997, 99, La Canada Flintridge Libr., 1999. Active Dem. Nat. Com., Women's Caucus for Art. Mem. Am. Fedn. Musicians (life). Avocations: hiking local mountains, desert and beaches, studying classical guitar.

HORTON, ROSALYN, underwriter; b. Nashville, July 13, 1946; d. W.D. and Irma Jean (Jackson) Donnell; m. Frederick Lee Horton, Aug. 6, 1965; children: Shane Scott, Sundai Horton Reeder, Shalako Lance. Broadcast

Diploma, Elkins Inst., Nashville, 1973. Cert. ins. counselor; cert. profl. ins. woman; cert. profl. ins. agt.; diversified advanced edn. designation. Office asst. Rich Printing Co., Nashville, 1973-76; office adminstr. Exhibit 4, Inc., Nashville, 1976-84; corp. sec. Horton Paper Svc., Nashville, 1984—; ocean/hull underwriter Fireman's Fund, Atlanta, 1992—. Mem. Mid. Tenn. Cath. Diocese Social Justice Conf., Nashville, 1997-2002; supporter Muscular Dystrophy Assn., Nashville, 1995—; strategy team leader Tying Nashville Together, 2000-02. Recipient T.J. Mims Achievement award, 1999, Achievement award Am. Assn. Mng. Gen. Agts., 1997, 2003; named Tenn. Coun. Ins. Woman of Yr., 2001 Mem.: Nat. Assn. Ins. Women (state dir. Tenn. coun. 1999—2000, co-chair nat. conv. 2003, region III Rookie of Yr. 1994, Tenn. State Ins. Woman of Yr. 2001), Nashville Ins. Profls. (pres. bd. dirs. 1995—99), Nashville Claims Assn. (parliamentarian 1998—2000, treas. 2000—01, asst. NAIW region III v.p. 2001—02). Democrat. Roman Catholic. Avocations: gardening, crafts, Harley Davidson motorcycle trips, reading. Office: Fireman's Fund McGee Marine 11605 Haynes Bridge Rd Ste 200 Alpharetta GA 30004 E-mail: rhorton@ffic.com.

HORTON, SHIRLEY A. state legislator, former mayor; BS in Acctg., San Diego State U. Pres. Grasser/Tate Real Estate Co., Calif.; planning commr. City of Chula Vista, Calif., 1985-91, councilwoman, 1991-94, mayor, 1994—2002; mem. Calif. Ho. of Reps., 2003—. Past govt. svc. positions include: bd. del. San Diego Assn. Govts.; Met. Transit Devel. Bd. alternate, mem. Otay Valley (Calif.) Regional Park Policy com., mem. San Diego Interagy. Water Quality panel, mem. South County Econ. Devel. Coun., mem. Interagy. Water Task Force, mgm. Gang Issues com., mem. Bayfront subcom., mem. Appropriate Techs. subcom. Mem. San Diego County Assessment Appeals bd., 1982-86, pres. South San Diego Bay Cities Bd. Realtors, 1987, mem. Scripps Meml. Hosp. Cmty. Adv. Bd., 1990-91, mem. South Bay YMCA Support Campaign com., 1990. Recipient San Diego Women Who Mean Bus. award, 1997. Mem. Calif. Assn. Realtors (regional v.p. 1989, dir. 1980-90), Chula Vista C. of C. (econ. devel. com. 1984-85). Office: PO Box 942849 Sacramento CA 94249

HORTON, SUSAN PITTMAN, bank executive; m. Stan Horton; 1 child, Alexandria Rose. BA in Bus. Adminstrn., Wash. State U., 1984. CPA. Ptnr. McFarland & Alton PS, 1989—99; pres., CEO, chmn. Wheatland Bank, Spokane, Wash., 1999—. Avocations: barrel racing, quarter horses. Office: Wheatland Bank 222 North Wall St Spokane WA 99201*

HORTON-WRIGHT, ALMA IRENE, retired elementary school educator; b. Austin, Tex., July 05; d. Ollon and Willie; m. Henry S. Wright, June 25; children: Sheila, Stanley, Gregory, Gerry. AA in Liberal Arts, San Bernardino Valley Coll., Calif., 1976; AA, Western Okla. State U., Altus, 1984; BA, Calif. State U., San Bernardino, 1979, postgrad.; MA in edn., Prairie View A&M U., 1993. Cert. tchr., Calif., life credential, Tex. Tchr. speed reading, edn. office Altus (Okla.) AFB; tchr. adult edn. Altus Sch. Dist.; elem. tchr. Rialto (Calif.) Unified Sch. Dist., Austin Ind. Sch. Dist. Mem. NEA, Tex. State Tchrs. Assn., Calif. State U. Almuni Assn., Edn. Austin, Phi Delta Kappa. Austin Ret. Tchrs. Assn., Tex. Ret. Tchrs. Assn. Avocations: travel, reading, art activities.

HORVATH, ANNETTE, home care administrator; b. Bronx, Mar. 12, 1963; d. Thomas and Roslyn DeGrazia; m. Leonard Horvath, Aug. 28, 1988; children: Jennifer, Rebecca. BSN, Lehman Coll., Bronx, 1996; MS in Adminstrv. Health Svc., Iona Coll., New Rochelle, N.Y., 1999. RN. Case mgr. Montifiore Hosp., Bronx, NY, 1993—98; project mgr. Jewish Home and Hosp., N.Y.C., 1998—99, dir. patient svcs. Bronx, 1999—2000; adminstr. Americare Inc., Bklyn., 2000—01, Village Care of N.Y., N.Y.C., 2001—. Mem.: NAFE, Cert. Home Health Agency, Women Health Mgmt., N.Y. State Health Care Providers, Women Arts Mus. Avocations: reading, cooking. Office: Village Care NY 154 Christopher St New York NY 10014 Office Phone: 212-337-5699.

HORVATH, FRANCES LOUISE, retired dean; b. Cleve., Mar. 1, 1940; d. Florian Al and Walburga Marie H. BS, Marygrove Coll., 1962; MD, St. Louis U., 1967. Intern St. Louis U. Hosp., 1967-68; resident in pediat. Cardinal Glennon Hosp., St. Louis, 1968-70; pediatrician City of St. Louis Dept. Health & Hosp., 1971-73; chmn. dept. physician asst. edn. St. Louis U. Sch. Allied Health Professions, 1973-80, prof., dean, 1980—2000. Commr. Commn. on Accreditation for Allied Health Edn1. Programs, Chgo., 1994—2000; cons. in field. Mem. editl. bd. Jour. Allied Health, 1983-91; contbr. articles to profl. jours. Chmn. com. on cmty. health and edn. ARC, St. Louis, 1989-90, emergency tng. com., 1982-89. St. Louis U. fellow, 1969-71; recipient Disting. Svc. award Assn. Physician Asst. Programs, 1988. Fellow Assn. Schs. Allied Health Professions; mem. AMA (chmn. com. on allied health edn. and accreditation 1990-92), Am. Acad. Physician Assts. (hon.). Office: # 3113 3437 Caroline St Saint Louis MO 63104-1111

HORVATH, POLLY, writer; b. Kalamazoo, Mich. married; 2 children. Co-author (with Gioia Fiammenghi): (book) An Occassional Cow, 1989; author: No More Cornflakes, 1990, The Happy Yellow Car, 1994, When the Circus Came to Town, 1996, The Trolls, 1999 (Nat. Book award finalist, 1999), Everything on a Waffle, 2001 (Newberry Honor Book), The Canning Season, 2003 (Nat. Book award, 2003). Office: Books for Young Readers Farrar, Straus & Giroux 19 Union Square West New York NY 10003

HORWITZ, BARBARA ANN, physiologist, educator, consultant; b. Chgo., Sept. 26, 1940; d. Martin Horwitz and Lillian Bloom; m. John M. Horowitz, Aug. 17, 1970. BS, U. Fla., 1961, MS, 1962; PhD, Emory U., 1966. Asst. rsch. physiologist U. Calif., Davis, 1968-72, asst. prof. physiology, 1972-75, assoc. prof., 1975-78, prof., 1978—, disting. prof., 2003—, chair animal physiology, 1991-93, chmn. neurobiology, physiology and behavior dept., 1993-98, vice provost acad. personnel, 2001—. Cons. Am. Inst. Behavioral Rsch., Palo Alto, Calif., 1980, Am. Inst. Rsch., Washington, 1993-99, NSF, Washington, 1981-84, NIH, Washington, 1995-99. Contbr. articles to profl. jours. Named Arthur C. Guyton Physiology Tchr. of the Yr., 1996, postdoctoral fellow, USPHS, 1966—68; recipient Disting. Tchg. award, 1982, U. Calif.-Davis prize for Tchg. and Scholarly Achievement, 1991, Pres.'s award for excellence in fostering undergrad. rsch., 1995. Fellow: AAAS; mem.: Phi Sigma (v.p. Davis chpt. 1983—, nat. v.p. 1989—), Phi Kappa Pi, Soc. Exptl. Biology and Medicine (exec. coun. 1990—94, pres.-elect 1999—2001, pres. 2001—03, past pres. 2003—04), N.Am. Assn. for Study of Obesity (exec. coun. 1988—92), N.Y. Acad. Scis., Am. Physiology Soc. (edn. and program coms. coun. 1993—96, pres.-elect 2001—02, pres. 2002—03, past pres. 2003—), Sigma Xi (pres. Davis chpt. 1980—81), Phi Beta Kappa (pres. Davis chpt. 1991—92, 2000—02). Office: U Calif Dept Neurobiology Phys Davis CA 95616 E-mail: bahorwitz@ucdavis.edu.

HORWITZ, ELEANOR CATHERINE, information and education official; b. N.Y.C., Dec. 21, 1941; d. Fritz and Hedwig E.F. (Kramer) Jahoda; m. Paul Horwitz, Aug. 15, 1964; children: Gregory Douglas, Catherine Helen, Laura Elizabeth. BA, Swarthmore Coll., 1962; MA, NYU, 1967; MS, Cornell U., 1969; postgrad., Oreg. State U., 1969-70. Sci. tchr. New Lincoln Sch., N.Y.C., 1962-67; coordinator outdoor edn. Lane County Int. Edn. Dist., Eugene, Oreg., 1969-70; staff writer Billerica (Mass.) Banner, 1971-72; instr., writer Mass. Audubon Soc., Lincoln, 1972-75; pub. use specialist U.S. Fish and Wildlife Service, Concord, Mass., 1975; staff writer Soc. Am. Foresters, Washington, 1975-76; mem. Mass. Gov.'s Forestry Rev. Bd., Boston, 1976-77; chief info. and edn. Mass. Div. Fisheries and Wildlife, Westborough, 1977—. Mem. steering com. Sec.'s Adv. Group on Environ. Edn. Exec. Office of Environ. Affairs, Commonwealth of Mass., 1990-2000, co-chair, 1992-97, chair, 1997-98; bd. dirs. Mass. Wildlife Fedn., 1986—, v.p., 1989-95, 97—, pres., 1995-97. Author: Clearcutting, A View from the Top, 1974; author, editor: Ways of Wildlife, 1977 (ACI Book award 1978); editor: (mag.) Massachusetts Wildlife, 1977—; contbr. articles to popular mags. Active Concord Natural Resources Commn., 1976-82, chmn. 1979-80; trustee Concord Land Conservation Trust, 1988—, trustee Holbrook Island Trust, 1995-2000; MBA rep. West Concord Union Ch., 1998-2003; deacon W. Concord Union Ch., 2003—, United Ch. of Christ, 2003-; instr. NRA, 2003. Recipient R.E. Dimmick award Oreg. Wildlife Soc., 1970, citation Worcester County League Sportsmen's Clubs, 1987, citation Minutemen chpt. Ducks Unltd., 1987, Conservation award Mahar Fish & Game Assn., 1991, Woman of Yr. award N.E. County Quabbin Anglers Assn., 1991, Sportsman of Yr. New England Outdoor Writers, 1998, Spl. award for Wildlife edn., Mass. Sportsmen's Coun., 2003, Disting. Svc. award Ducks Unltd., 2003. Mem. Outdoor Writers of Am., New Eng. Outdoor Writers Assn. (membership sec. 1987-90, bd. dirs. 1987—, sec. 1990-93, 2001-2003, v.p. 1993-94, 99-2000, pres. 1994-95), Am. Forestry Assn. (life), New Eng. Conservation Info. and Edn. Assn. (chmn. 1986-87, 90-91), Mass. Wildlife Fedn., Wildlife Soc. (profl. cert., chmn. edn. com. 1974-76, 84-87, nominating com. 1990-91, Leopold award com. 1996-98, cert. of recognition 1978), Nashoba Sportsmen's Club, Concord Rod and Gun Club, Maynard Rod and Gun Club (hon.). Mem. United Ch. of Christ. Office: Mass Divsn Fisheries and Wildlife Westborough MA 01581 E-mail: ellie.horwitz@state.wa.us.

HORWITZ, KATHRYN BLOCH, molecular biologist, educator, breast cancer researcher; b. Sosua, Dominican Republic, Feb. 20, 1941; came to U.S., 1952; d. Werner Meyerstein and Olga (Schlesinger) Bloch; m. Lawrence David Horwitz, June 14, 1964; children: Phillip Andrew, Carolyn Anita. BA, Barnard Coll., 1962; MS, NYU, 1966; PhD, U. Tex. Southwestern Med. Sch., Dallas, 1975; postdoctoral, U. Tex. Sch. Medicine, San Antonio, 1978. Instr. U. Tex. Sch. Medicine, San Antonio, 1978-79; asst. prof. U. Colo. Med. Sch., Denver, 1979-84, assoc. prof., 1984-89, prof. of medicine, pathology and molecular biology, 1989—. Cellular physiology panel NSF, 1985-88; biochem. endocrinology study sect. NIH, 1989-93; mem. Pres.'s Cancer Panel Spl. Commn. on Breast Cancer, 1992, Breast Cancer Task Force, NIH, 1981-84. Author over 150 breast cancer and steroid receptors research papers, books; assoc. editor, editl. bd. for several scientific jours. Chair, sci. adv. bd. Cancer League of Colo., 1987-91; organizer Keystone Symposia on Steroid Receptors, 1996, 98, 2000. Elected fellow AAAS, 2000; recipient Nat. Bd. award Med. Coll. Pa., 1986, Wilson Stone award M.D. Anderson Hosp. and Tumor Inst., 1976, Rsch. Career Devel. award Nat. Cancer Inst., 1981-86, MERIT award NIH, 1992, The U. Helsinki medal and Second Siltavouri lectr. Finland, 1993, William L. McGuire Meml. lectr., 1997, Bicentennial lectr. U. Louisville, 1998, Disting. Sci. award Clin. Ligand Assay Soc., 2000; grantee NSF, Am. Cancer Soc., Nat. Found. Cancer Rsch. Dept. of the Army, NIH. Fellow AAAS; mem. Endocrine Soc. (program com. 1989-91, nominating com. 1989-91, chair 1991, coun. 1992-95, pres.-elect 1997 98, pres. 1998-99, immediate past pres. 1999-2000, mem. devel. com. 2000—), Am. Fedn. Clin. Rsch., Am. Soc. Cell Biology, Am. Assn. Cancer Rsch. (program com. 1994-95, state legis. com. 1993—), Western Soc. Clin. Investigation, Am. Soc. Biochemistry and Molecular Biology, bd. dir. FASEB. Democrat. Jewish. Avocations: skiing, reading, gardening, traveling. Office: U Colo Dept Medicine PO Box B151 Denver CO 80201-0151

HORWITZ, SARI, reporter; b. Tucson; BA in Polit. Sci., Bryn Mawr Coll.; M in Politics, Philosophy and Econs., Oxford U. Writer, editor Congl. Quar., Washington; reporter Washington Post. Recipient Pulitzer prize gold medal, 1999, Selden Ring award, 1999, Grand prize, Washington-Balt. Newspaper Guild, Morton Mintz award. Office: Washington Post 1150 15th St NW Washington DC 20071

HOSCH, JULIE, state senator; b. Delaware County, Iowa, Dec. 7, 1939; Student, Kirkwood C.C., N.E. Iowa C.C. Mem. Iowa State Senate, DesMoines, 2003—, vice chair agr. com., mem. edn. com., human resources com., local govt. com. and ways and means com. Mem.: Iowa Cattlewomen's Assn., Am. Legion Aux. Republican. Office: State Capitol Bldg East 12th and Grand Des Moines IA 50319 Address: 22852 Butterfield Rd Cascade IA 50233

HO-SHING, LANA MAY, book seller; b. Falmouth, Jamaica; came to U.S., 1985; d. Cecil George and Lula M. (Lawful) H-S.; 1 child, Matthew Lee. RN, U. W.I., 1969, postgrad., 1973-74. RN, N.Y. Operating room nurse Nuttall Hosp., Kingston, Jamaica, 1969-70; sch. nurse Convent of Mercy Acad., Kingston, 1970-71; operating room nurse St. Barnabas Hosp., Bronx, N.Y., 1971-72; ICU nurse Univ. Hosp. W.I., Mona, Jamaica, 1973-76; nurse, mgr. staff day care Jamaica Devel. Bank, Kingston, 1976-80; mgr. indsl. clinic Broadway Industries, Kingston, 1981-82; owner, mgr. T. Squares Inc. Graphic Art and Printing, Kingston, 1976-85; dir., owner Briscoe Brown Books, Bronx, 1995—. Pres. Trade Wind Group of Cos., Bronx, 1995—. Sec. Baychester Mcht. Orgn., Bronx, 1995—; treas. Gerry Gallimore Found., 1994—. Democrat. Anglican. Avocations: collecting rare books, gardening, music. Office: Briscoe Brown Books 3642 Harper Ave Bronx NY 10466-5907

HOSIER, LINDA GRUBE, gifted and talented educator; b. Somerville, N.J., Mar. 15, 1948; d. Louis S. and Linda Julia (Braun) Grube; m. David Keith Short, Aug. 1, 1970 (div. Apr. 1986); children: Kristi Elizabeth, Andrew Alan; m. Robb R. Hosier, July 25, 1998; children: Robb R. Jr., Scott J., Timothy I., James E., Sherry H. BA, Pfeiffer Coll., 1970; MEd, U. N.C., 1973. Ordained min. of gospel Impact Worship Ctr., High Point, N.C., 1999, Internat. Fellowship New Testament Chs., Greensboro, N.C., 2002. Tchr. English Lexington (N.C.) City Schs., 1970-71; tchr. lang. arts, social studies Kannapolis (N.C.) City Schs., 1971-73; tchr. English, history Franklinton (N.C.) City Schs., 1973-74; tchr. English Bristol (Tenn.) City Schs., 1976-77; tchr. lang. arts, social studies High Point (N.C.) City Schs., 1983; tchr. acad. gifted lit., math. Stokes County Schs., Danbury, N.C., 1983-95; tchr. lang. arts and social studies Guilford County Schs., 1995-99, tchr. academically gifted, advanced learner curriculum specialist, 1999—. Coord. childrens ministries Cathedral of Praise Ch., Greensboro, NC, 1993—99; missionary to Haiti, The Sioux Indian Nation, Impact Worship Ctr., High Point, NC, 1999—2001; children's pastor, Sunday sch. supt. Emmanus Way Ch., Kernersville, NC, 2000—; missionettes coord. Emmaus Way Ch., Kernersville, NC, 2002—. Mem. NEA, N.C. Edn. Assn., N.C. Assn. of Gifted, N.C. Tchrs. of English. Avocations: reading, traveling, writing, gardening, singing. Home: 9027 Ambridge Ln Kernersville NC 27284-9267 E-mail: hosierl@guilford.k12.nc.us.

HOSKIE, LORRAINE, consumer products representative, poet; b. Nansemond County, Va., Aug. 26, 1953; m. Eddie Lewis Hoskie, July 7, 1972 (div. Oct. 1980); children: Jacqueline Marie, Quinton Lewis. BS, Va. Commonwealth U., 1977. Clk. Christian Children's Fund, Richmond, 1977—79, corr. rsch. clk., 1979—80; eligibility worker City of Richmond, 1982—83; substitute tchr. Sch. Bd., Richmond, 1983—86; telemarketer Energy Savs. Exterior, Richmond, 1995—96; CRT operator Snelling Pers. Svcs., Richmond, 1996; mail clk. Abacus, Richmond, 1997; office worker Kelly Svcs., Richmond, 1997; remittance processor Calipher, Inc., Richmond, 1997—2001; adminstrv. program specialist II VA Employment Commn., 2003—. Substitute tchr. Sch. Bd. of Franklin, Va., 1987; ch. sec. SDA-Ephesus, Richmond, 1981-82; vol. worker Bapt. Student Union Va. Commonwealth U., Richmond, 1971-72, math. tutor Spl. Svcs. Program, 1972. Sec. Ephesus Prison Ministry, 1996—; team sec. Ephesus Va. Dept. Correction, 1993-94. Named Golden Poet, World of Poetry, Sacramento, 1990, recipient award of merit cert., 1990; recipient Poet of Merit award Am. Poetry Assn., 1988, Appreciation award VA Dept. Corrections, 1994, Pres. award for literary excellence Nat. Authors Registry, 1994. Democrat. 7th Day Adventist. Avocations: crocheting, creative writing, music, poetry writing. Home: 3912 Chamberlayne Ave Apt D-17 Richmond VA 23227-4261 Office: VEC 703 E Main St Rm 123 Richmond VA 23218

HOSKINS, BARBARA R(UTH) WILLIAMS, elementary educator, elementary principal; b. Pineville, Ky., June 7, 1945; d. John and Patsy Ann (Buell) Williams; m. Teddy Michael Hoskins, Dec. 12, 1961; children: Susan Ann Hoskins Brown, Shelia Marie Hoskins Key. BS, Union Coll., 1977, MA, 1978, postgrad., 1980-89, U. Ky., 1990. Cert. elem. edn., elem./secondary principalship, elem./secondary supervision, dir. pupil pers., Ky. Tchr. Bell County Bd. Edn., Pineville, 1977—, prin., 1997—2000. Edn. instr. S.E. C.C., Middlesboro, Ky., 1987—; BLS instr. Am. Heart Assn., Corbin, Ky., 1990—. Co-author: History of Bell County, 1994. Active Bell County Hist. Soc., 1992—, Laubach Literary Action Agy., Bell County, 1991—, Nat. Arbor Day Found., Nebr., 1995. Mem. Bell County Edn. Assn., Bell Co. Agrl. bd., sec.,Upper Cumberland Edn. Assn., Ky. Edn. Assn., NEA, Nat. Alliance Tchrs. Math. and Sci., Bell County Extension Coun., Iota Sigma Nu. Republican. Baptist. Avocations: walking, jogging, science and math activities, local history research. Office: Bell Co Recovery Rte 1 Box 198E Pineville KY 40977-9712 Home: 69 Paula Dr Pineville KY 40977

HOSKINS, RHONDA SUE, real estate appraiser; b. Jefferson City, Mo., June 11, 1967; d. Ronald Eudean and Billie Sue Mahan; m. Dustin D. Hoskins, Oct. 6, 1990; children: C. Drake, Samuel Jacob, Maggie Paige. Attended, Ozark Christian Coll. Lic. real estate appraiser Mo. Closing off. Guaranty Land Title Inc., Jefferson City, Mo., 1991—95; appraiser Ctrl. Mo. Property Analyst, Jefferson City, 1995—97, Mo. Property Appraisals, Inc., Jefferson City, 1997—99; appraiser, ptnr. Appraisal Profls. Inc., Jefferson City, 1999—2002; appraiser, owner River city Appraisals LLC, Jefferson City, 2002—. Ambassador Jefferson City C. of C., 1999—. Recipient Outstanding Svc. award, Jefferson City Bd. of Realtors, 2001, Presdl. award of honor, Home Builders Assoc., 2000, 2001. Mem.: Jefferson City Bd. of Realtors, Home Builders Assoc., Appraisal Inst., Jefferson City C. of C., March of Dimes, Make a Wish, Planning and Zoning Comm. Republican. Home and Office: River City Appraisals LLC 1915 Seven Hills Rd Jefferson City MO 65101 E-mail: hlrhos@hotmail.com.

HOSKINSON, CAROL ROWE, middle school educator; b. Toledo, Mar. 10, 1947; d. Webster Russell and Alice Mae (Miller) Rowe; m. C. Richard Hoskinson, June 8, 1969; 1 child, Leah Nicole. BS in Edn., Ohio State U., 1968; MEd, Ga. State U., 1972. Tchr. Whitehall City Sch., Columbus, Ohio, 1968-69; tchr. DeKalb County Sch., Decatur, Ga., 1969-74, Mt. Olive Twp. Sch., NJ, 1974-75, DeKalb County Sch., Decatur, 1975-79, Fulton County Sch., Atlanta, 1991—. Substitute tchr. DeKalb County Schs., Decatur, 1980-91, Fulton County Sch., Atlanta, 1989-91. Pres. Esther Jackson PTA, Roswell, Ga., 1988-89; treas. Women of the Ch., Roswell, 1983-84; chairperson local sch. adv. Esther Jackson, Roswell, 1989-91; del. Women and Constn. Conv., Atlanta, 1988; mem. Supt.'s Adv. Com.; corr. sec. Chattahoochee HS PTSA, 1997-98; VIP dedicated hostess Olympic Games, Atlanta, 1996; treas. Chattahoochee Cotillion Club, 2000, 01; mem. leadership team Holcomb Bridge Mid. Sch., 1999-2004. Named Vol. of Yr. Fulton County Schs., 1988-89. Mem. AAUW (v.p. Atlanta chpt. 1970-89, edn. scholarship honoree 1984, 86), Atlanta Lawn Tennis Assn., Roswell Hist. Soc., Roswell Hist. Preservation Com., Nat. Mid. Sch. Assn., Zoo Atlanta, High Mus. Art, Ga. PTA, Ohio State Alumni Assn., Ga. State Alumni Assn., Profl. Assn. Ga. Educators. Democrat. Presbyterian. Avocations: tennis, reading, education-related activities. Home: 1670 Branch Valley Dr Roswell GA 30076-3007

HOSMAN, SHARON LEE, music educator; b. Bisbee, Ariz., Nov. 2, 1943; d. Roy Lee and Virginia Baldwin (Bandel) H. BA, Loretto Heights Coll., 1965; MA, U. No. Colo., 1979. Tchr. Livermore (Calif.) Sch. Dist., 1965-66, Jefferson County Pub. Schs., Golden, Colo., 1966-97. Faculty rep. North Area Citizens Adv. Com., Arvada, Colo., 1979-81, S.I.P.C., Arvada, 1982-83, North Area Sch. Improvement Process Com., Arvada, 1984-91, North Area Accountability com., 1991-92. Piano accompanist for sch. groups, 1965-97. Mem. NEA, DAR, Jefferson County Edn. Assn., Colo. Edn. Assn., Music Tchrs. Nat. Assn., Colo. State Music Tchrs. Assn., Denver Area Music Tchrs. Assn., Musicians' Soc. Denver, Am. Guild Organists, Hereditary Order of First Families of Mass., Smithsonian, Denver Rescue Mission, Denver Dumb Friends League, St. Luke's Hosp. Aux. (life). Republican. Episcopalian. Avocations: art, music, drama, reading, gardening.

HOSTER-BURANDT, NORMA J. musician, fundraiser; b. Phila., Sept. 29, 1956; d. Downey Delbert and Norma M. (Von Vital) H.; m. Timothy Lee Burandt; children: Jonathan Daniel Loudon, Jeremy Matthew Loudon. BMus Piano Performance summa cum laude, Temple U., 1978, MMus in Piano Pedagogy, 1980. Ordained deacon Presbyn. Ch. USA. Pvt. piano tchr., 1973—; devel. coord. Chesapeake (Va.) Gen. Hosp., 2001—. Piano tchr., accompanist Temple U. Music Prep., Phila., 1978-81; accompanist Choral Soc. Montgomery County, Blue Bell, Pa., 1991-93; founding accompanist Temple U. Children's Choir, Phila., 1992-99; organist Covenant Presbyn. Ch., Trenton, N.J., 1997-2001; accompanist Am. Choral Dirs. Assn. convs., 1996-98; accompanist in field; grants specialist Recording for the Blind & Dyslexic Nat. Headquarters, Princeton, N.J., 2000-01. Performances on local/nat. radio broadcasts, 1995, 97, 98; rec. artist Temple U. Children's Choir, 2001. Avocations: choral singing, needlecraft. Home: 202 North Hill Ln Chesapeake VA 23322-6604

HOSTETLER, ELSIE J. musician, music educator; b. Sugarcreek, Ohio, Apr. 8, 1942; d. Jonas B. and Lovina Hostetler. Student, Akron (Ohio) U., 1969-70. Cert. tchr. chord approach to piano, New Sch. Am. Music. Receptionist to office mgr. Milk, Inc., Akron, 1964-78; adminstr. Christian Tng. Ctr., St. Louis, 1987-88, music dir., 1989-91; music sec. Gospel Assembly Conv. Ctr., Louisville, 1992—; piano tchr. Red Bud, Ill., 1997—. Workshop leader EZ-Creative Piano, Red Bud, 1999—. Band dir., choir dir. Gospel Assembly Ch., Akron, 1959-78; asst. pianist, organist, instrumental tchr. Gospel Assembly Ch., St. Louis, 1981-91; music dir., pianist-organist Christian Assembly Ch., Millstadt, Ill., 1992—. Mem. Music Tchrs. Nat. Assn., Ill. State Music Tchrs. Assn. Home: 98 Jennys Way Smithton IL 62285-1656 E-mail: ezpiano98@aol.com.

HOSTETTER, MARGARET K. pediatrician, medical educator; MD, Baylor U. Diplomate Am. Bd. Pediatrics with subspecialty in pediat. infectious diseases. Resident Children's Hosp., Boston; fellow in pediat. infectious disease Harvard Med. Sch./Beth Israel Hosp., Boston; with U. Minn., Mpls.; prof. pediats., sect. chief pediat. immunology Yale U., New Haven, chmn. dept. pediatrs.; physician-in-chief Yale-New Haven Children's Hosp. Mem.: Inst. of Medicine of NAS. Office: Yale Univ Sch Medicine 333 Cedar St LMP 4085 PO Box 208064 New Haven CT 06520-8064

HOSTLER, SHARON LEE, pediatrics educator, rehabilitation center executive; b. Rutland, Vt., Oct. 24, 1939; d. John Gerald and Irene Adelaide (Whitney) H.; m. Alan Duane Dimock, Dec. 29, 1965 (dec. Sept. 1974); children: Kathleen Ann Dimock, Dylan Alan Dimock; stepchildren: Timothy Dimock, Gioia L. Dimock, Dorothy Dimock McNamara, Adam Dimock; m. Joseph Boardman, May 17, 1987. AB, Middlebury Coll., 1961; MD, U. Vt., 1965. Resident, fellow U. Va., Charlottesville, 1965-70, asst. prof. pediat., 1970-76, assoc. prof., 1976-87, prof., 1986, chief divsn. devel. pediat., 1978—, med. dir. Children and Youth Project, 1970-74, med. dir. Children's Rehab. Ctr., 1974—, chair Med. Sch. com. on women, 1989—, McLemore Birdsong chair Pediat., 1991—, assoc. chair dept. pediat., 1999—. Vis. prof. Hadassah Hosp. Ben Gurion U., Jerusalem, 1983-84; cons. Project Hope, Krakow, Poland, 1981-83; active Kluge/UCP Rsch. Project, Family Autonomy Project, MCH; mem. exec. com. U. Va. Health Svcs. Found. Contbr. articles to profl. jours. Bd. dirs. Ctrl. Va. Child Devel. Assn., Charlottesville, 1972-76; mem. Gov.'s Com. on Handicapped Child, Richmond, Va., 1972-78; founder Task Force on Ventilator Dependent

Children, Richmond, 1986-89; cons. pub. schs., 1972-78; mem. Children's Med. Ctr. Cmty. Bd.; chmn. bldg. com. Kluge Children's Rehab. Ctr.'s Outpatient Dept., chair com. on women Sch. Medicine; mem. task force on women U. Va., mem. permanent com. on women's concerns. Recipient Innovative Project award Am. Assn. Children's Health, 1986, Outstanding Alumni award U. Vt., 1993, Outstanding Women of Yr. award U. Va., Women's Profl. and Leadership Assn., 1993, Lectr. award Am. Assn. Children's Health, 1994, Leadership Devel. award Women in Medicine, 1995, Middlebury Coll. Alumni Achievement award, 1999; Gould Found. scholar, 1957-61. Fellow Am. Acad. Pediatrics (sect. adolescent medicine); mem. Am. Acad. Cerebral Palsy/Devel. Neurology, Soc. Adolescent Medicine, Am. Med. Women's Assn. (bd. dirs., chpt. pres. 1987, regional gov. 1988-90), Assn. Am. Med. Colls., Boars Head Sports Club, Alpha Omega Alpha. Home: 1340 Wendover Dr Charlottesville VA 22901-7713 Office: Kluge Childrens Rehab Ctr 2270 Ivy Rd Charlottesville VA 22903-4977

HOSTON, GERMAINE ANNETTE, political science educator; b. Trenton, NJ; d. Walter Lee and Veretta Louise H. AB in Politics summa cum laude, Princeton U., 1975; MA in Govt., Harvard U., 1978, PhD in Govt., 1981. Rsch. asst. Princeton U., NJ, 1973-75; tchg. asst. Harvard U., Cambridge, Mass., 1977-78; asst. prof. polit. sci. Johns Hopkins U., Balt., 1980-86, assoc. prof. polit. sci., 1986-92; prof. polit. sci. U. Calif., San Diego, 1992—, dir. Ctr. for Democratization and Econ. Devel., 1993-99; founder, pres. Inst. Trans Pacific Studies in Values, Culture and Politics, 1999—. Vis. prof. L'Ecole des Hautes Etudes en Sci. Sociales, Paris, 1986, Osaka City U., Japan, 1990, U. Tokyo, 1991; faculty advisor Chinese lang. program Johns Hopkins U., 1981-92, undergrad. ethics bd., 1980-83, pub. interest investment adv. com., 1982-85, undergrad. admissions com., 1983-84, 86-89, pres.'s human climate task force, 1987, dir. undergrad. program, 1987, 88-89, mem. com. undergrad. studies, 1987-91, organizer comparative politics colloquium, 1987-89, dept. colloquium, 1987-89, 91-92; Japanese studies program com. U. Calif., San Diego, 1992—, Chinese studies program, 1994—, field coord. comparative politics, 1994—95, dir. grad. studies comparative politics, 1997-98; bd. dir. Inst. East-West Security Studies, NYC, 1990-97; Am. adv. com. Japan Found., 1992—; edn. abroad program com. U. Calif., 1996—; adv. com. Calif. Ctr. Asia Soc.; mem. com. tech. comms. Inst. East West Security Studies, 1997—; participant numerous workshops and seminars; lectr. in field. Author: Marxism and the Crisis of Development in Prewar Japan: The Debate on Japanese Capitalism, 1986, The State, Identity, and the National Question in China and Japan, 1994, (with others) The Biographical Dictionary of Neo-Marxism, 1985, The Biographical Dictionary of Marxism, 1986, Culture and Identity: Japanese Intellectuals During the Interwar Years, 1990, The Routledge Dictionary of Twentieth-Century Political Thinkers, 1992; mem. editl. bd. Jour. Politics, 1997—2001; contbr. articles to profl. jours. Active Md. Food Com., 1983-92, program concepts subcom. CROSS ROADS Com., Diocese of Md., 1987-88, outreach com. St. David's Episcopal Ch., Balt., standing commn. human affairs Gen. Conv. of the Episcopal Ch., 1991-97; chair peace and justice commn. Episcopal Diocese Md., 1984-87, co-chair companion diocese com., 1987-92, chair CROSS ROADS program bd., 1988-92; exec. bd. dir. Balt. Clergy and Laity Concerned, 1985-86; alternate, regular lay del. 69th Gen. Conv. of The Episcopal Ch., Detroit, 1988; trustee Va. Theol. Sem., 1988-2000; lay del. 70th Gen. Conv. of The Episcopal Ch., Phoenix, Ariz., 1991; dep. Nat. Conv. Episcopal Ch., 1988-93. Am. Legion Aux. scholar, 1972, Am. Logistical Assn. scholar, 1972-76; fellow Harvard U., 1975-77, NSF, 1975-77; Lehman fellow Harvard U., 1978-79, Fgn. Lang. and Area Studies fellow, 1978-79; fellow Am. Assn. Univ. Women Ednl. Found., 1979-80; Fgn. Rsch. scholar U. Tokyo, 1979, 82, 84, 85, 86, 91; Travel grantee Assn. Asian Studies, Japan-U.S. Friendship Commn., 1981; Internat. fellow Internat. Fedn. Univ. Women, 1982, 83; Postdoctoral grantee Social Sci. Rsch. Coun., 1983; fellow NEH, 1983; Kenan Endowment grantee Johns Hopkins U., 1984-85; fellow Rockefeller Found. Internat. Rels., 1985-88; Travel grantee Assn. Asian Studies, 1991; grantee Japan-US Friendship Commn., 1997; rsch. grantee Acad. Senate Com. on Rsch., 1996. Mem. Asia Soc. (trustee 1994—2000), Am. Polit. Sci. Assn. (mem. coun. 1991-93, mem. com. on internat. polit. sci. 1997—2003, v.p. 1998—), Assn. Asian Studies (mem. N.E. Asia coun. 1992-95, vice-chair N.E. Asia coun. 1993—94, nominated editor Jour. Asian Studies 1994, mem. coun. on fgn. rels. 1990—), Internat. Platform Assn., Pacific Coun. on Internat. Policy, Women's Fgn. Policy Group. Democrat. Episcopalian. Avocations: reading, cooking, sailing, tennis, working out. Office: 9921 Carmel Mountain Rd Ste 323 San Diego CA 92129 E-mail: ghoston@myesa.com.

HOTCHKISS, HEATHER A. social worker, consultant; d. John L. and Patrecia W. Hotchkiss. MSW, U. Denver, 1996. Mental health clinician Colo. Mental Health Inst. at Ft. Logan, Denver, 1990—95; sr. cons. Colo. Dept. Edn., Denver, 1995—. Co-author: Making Standards Work: A Teachers Guide to Contextual Learning, 1999. Chair Colo. Sch. Social Work Com., Denver, 1998—2000. Named Colo. Sch. Psychologist Advocate of Yr., Colo. Soc. Sch. Psychologists, 2000—01; recipient Vision and Leadership award, Colo. Sch.-to-Career Partnership, 2001, All Means All School-to-Work award, 2000, Colo. Sch. Social Worker of Distinction award, Colo. Sch. Social Work Com., 2002. Mem.: NASW, Coun. for Exceptional Children (Donn Brolin award 2002). Office: Colo Dept Edn 201 E Colfax Ave Rm 300 Denver CO 80203

HOTCHKISS, JANET MCCANN, secondary school educator; b. White Plains, N.Y., July 11, 1950; d. Albino M. and and M. Catherine (Bodette) Grellet; m. Jonathan B. Hotchkiss, May 3, 1980; children: Craig, Kristina, Kevin, Marsha, Robert, Catherine. BS, Northeastern U., 1973; MS, Coll. New Rochelle, 1987. Cert. secondary English tchr., spl. edn. tchr., elem. tchr. Tchr. Greenburgh Eleven UFSD, Dobbs Ferry, NY, 1990—, White Plains (N.Y.) Pub. Schs., 1990—. Mem. Coun. Exceptional Children, 1995—, N.Y. State English Coun., 2003; mem. policy bd. Westchester Tchrs. Ctr., 1994—97; mem. N.Y. Adult and Continuing Cmty. Edn., 1995—. Co-author: Kosovo: Caught in the Middle, 2001. Named Tchr. of Yr. in N.Y. State, N.Y. Adult Continuing Cmty. Edn., 2001; grantee, Westchester Tchr.'s Ctr., 1996, 1999, 2002, Tech. and Literacy Challenge, 2000, The Living History Found., 2002. Mem.: Orton Guillingham Soc., White Plains (N.Y.) Coll. Club (scholarship com. 2003). Office: Greenburgh Eleven UFSD PO Box 501 Dobbs Ferry NY 10522

HOTCHNER, HOLLY, curator, museum director, conservator; BA in Art History and Studio Art, Trinity Coll., 1973; MA in Art History, diploma conservation, NYU, 1982. Exhbns. cataloguer, collections cataloguer Mus. Modern Art, N.Y.C., 1973-76; chief conservator N.Y. Hist. Soc., N.Y.C., 1984-88, dir. mus., 1984-95; dir. Am. Craft Mus. (now Museum of Arts and Design), N.Y.C., 1996—. Bd. dirs. Alliance for Contemporary Glass, Friends of Fiber Art; chmn. bd. 235 E. 73rd Owners Corp., 1994-2000; mem. edn. com. Whitney Mus. Am. Art, 1994—; mem. bd. trustees N.Y. Landmarks Conservancy, 1996—; mem. adv. bd. Friends of Contemporary Ceramics; lectr., panelist, juror in field. Mem. Am. Assn. Mus., Art Table, Phi Beta Kappa. Office: Museum of Arts and Design 40 W 53rd St New York NY 10019-6106*

HOTT, PEGGY A. mortgage banker; b. Flint, Mich., Dec. 15, 1952; d. Aaron Hilman and Alice E. (Fairs) Conger; m. Norman E. Baxter, Mar. 17, 1973 (div. 1986); children: Sarah, Stephanine, Alicia, Adam, Marcia; m. Virgil G. Hott Jr., Aug. 27, 1988. Student, Charles Stewart Mott Coll., Flint, Mich., 1973. Pub. rels. rep. and receptionist Turner Elec. Wks., Jacksonville, Fla., 1984-89; personal banking rep. and data entry operator Fla. Nat. Bank and First Union, Jacksonville, 1989; compliance/arbitration rep. First Union Nat. Bank, Jacksonville, 1989-90; customer svc. rep./reconciliation Am. Express Centurion Svcs. Corp., Jacksonville, 1990-96; credit mortgage-mortgage resource specialist Merrill Lynch Credit Corp. Cendant Mortgage, Jacksonville, 1995—. Clio Lions Club scholar, 1971. Mem. NAFE, Am. Soc. Notaries, Nat. Notary Assn., Toastmasters (charter mem. Am. Express chpt.). Republican. Home: 10252 Pine Breeze Rd W Jacksonville FL 32257-7585

HOTTOVY, SUSAN ELIZABETH, music educator; b. Lincoln, Nebr., July 23, 1961; d. Bernard Dean and Mary Ann Matthies; m. Thomas Ray Hottovy, June 17, 1984; children: Sara Elizabeth, Melissa Lee, Lindsay Ray. BA, St. Olaf Coll., 1983; MusM, U. Nebr., 1991. Tchr. Adams (Nebr.) Pub. Schs., 1983—94, Lincoln (Nebr.) Pub. Schs., 1994—. Clarinetist Lincoln (Nebr.) Mcpl. Band, 1995—2000. Mem.: Nebr. Music Educator's Assn. (chmn. mid. level affairs 1997—99), Nebr. State Bandmasters Assn. (awards chmn. 1994—97). Avocations: quilting, reading, camping, hiking. Home: 8849 E State Hwy 41 Adams NE 68301 Office: Irving Middle School 2745 So 22nd St Lincoln NE 68502

HOTZ, MARTHA PAULINE, artist; b. Looogootee, Ind., July 11, 1927; d. Francis Orval and Ethel Beatrice (Bradley) Summers; m. Donald Leo Hotz, Nov. 5, 1949; children: Donald Frederick, Daniel Richard, Anthony Francis, Timothy Lee, Jeffery Alan. Student, Art Instrns., Mpls., 1962-65, Art Acad., Ferdinand, Ind., 1965-67. Sec. Schwitzer-Cummins, Indpls., 1946-49; bookkeeper Reliance Mfg. Co., Loogootee, Ind., 1950-53; paste-up artist Loogootee Tribune, 1963-65, 71-86; v.p., buyer Hotz & Sons Corp., Loogootee, 1964-70; free lance artist, instr. Polly's Paintings, Loogootee, 1986—. Illustrator: (bookcover) Echoes from the Mountains, 1990, (book) Around the Clock in Rhyme and Time, 1991, (bookcover) When God Stepped In, 1992; 21 postcards, 1986-98. Pres. Tri County Art Guild, Loogootee, 1965-75, Daviess County Art League, Washington, Ind., 1991-92, adv. bd., 1992-98. Mem. VFW Aux., KC Aux., Legion of Mary. Roman Catholic. Avocations: poet, drawing, flowers and gardening, reading. Home: PO Box 244 Loogootee IN 47553-0244

HOUGEN, CARLENE LENORE, secondary school educator, department chairman; b. Chgo., Oct. 16, 1948; d. Charles and Lenore Audrey Doran; m. Gary Allen Hougen, Dec. 20, 1969; 1 child, Daniel Edward. BS, U. Ill., 1970; MS, U. Ill., Chgo., 1982; CAS, Nat. Louis U., 1991. Tchr. Forest View H.S., Arlington Heights, Ill., 1970—72, McHenry County Coll., Crystal Lake, Ill., 1979—80, Hoffman Estates (Ill.) H.S., 1982—86, Lake County Vocat. Ctr., Grayslake, Ill., 1986—90; tchr., dept. chair Willowbrook H.S., Villa Park, Ill., 1990—. Named to Those Who Excel-Adminstr. at Excellence Level, Ill. State Bd. Edn., 2003. Mem.: NSTA, ASCD, West Suburban Sci. Suprs. Achievements include research in magnesium protoporphyrin monoester destruction by extracts of etiola red kidney bean leaves. Avocations: gardening, reading, hiking. Office: Willowbrook HS 1250 S Ardmore Ave Villa Park IL 60181

HOUGGARD, SANTA CAROL HALL, family nurse practitioner; b. Ermine, Ky., Nov. 9, 1940; d. Russell L. and Ila (Amburgey) Hall; m. Byron L. Houggard, Apr. 30, 1965; children: Teresa Bramlet, Sutherland, Ronald L. Diploma, Sch. Profl. Nursing, Harlan, Ky., 1961; BSN cum laude, U. San Diego, 1981, MS in Nursing, 1983. Cert. family nurse practitioner. Staff nurse Whitesburg (Ky.) Meml. Hosp., 1961-62; nurse USN, 1962-65; pvt. duty nurse, 1965-77; nurse practitioner North County Health Svcs., San Marcos, Calif.; clin. adminstr., nurse practitioner Mountain Health Project, Campo, Calif., 1977-79; instr. U. San Diego, 1983-85; ind. contractor family nurse practitioner, Santee, Calif., 1985-88; family nurse practitioner NAVCARE, San Diego, 1988-89, Mountain Health Ctr., Campo, 1989-91, So. Indian Health Coun., 1991-95; prof. nursing Ariz. Western Coll., Yuma, Ariz., 1998—. Lt. (j.g.) USN, 1962-65. Mem.: Ariz. Nurses Assn. (pres. Rio Colo.-Yuma Chpt.), ANA, Sigma Theta Tau. Home: 12124 S Sandra Ave Yuma AZ 85367-6026 E-mail: carol.houggard@azwestern.edu.

HOUGH, JENNINE, artist; b. Charlotte, N.C., Mar. 17, 1948; d. Robert Harvey Hough and Josephine Ruth Frutchey; m. Joseph Vernon Myers, Sept. 19, 1987. BA, U. N.C., 1970; MFA, U. N.C., Greensboro, 1973; postgrad., Skowhegan (Maine) Sch. Painting and Sculpture, 1974. Instr. West Ga. Coll., Carrollton, 1973—75; instr. evening divsn. Emory U., Atlanta, 1979—85, Atlanta Coll. Art, 1986—87. Coord. exhbns. Aspen (Colo.) Chapel Gallery, 2002—03. One-woman shows include Columbus (Ga.) Mus. Art, 1977, Health Gallery, Atlanta, 1978, 1980, Monique Knowlton Gallery, N.Y.C., 1982, Marita Gilliam Gallery, Raleigh, N.C., 1991, Jane Haslem Gallery, Washington, 1993, The Mus. of Ghost Ranch, Abiquiu, N.Mex., 1994, The Fernbank Mus. of Natural History, Atlanta, 1994, The Royal Tyrrell Mus., Alta., Can., 1994—95, Contemporary S.W. Galleries, Santa Fe, 1998, Vectra, Aspen, 2001, exhibited in group shows at N.C. Mus., Raleigh, 1976, 1980, Southea. Watercolor Soc., Nashville, 1977, New Orleans Biennial, 1977, Pyramid Galleries, Washington, 1977, SECCA, Winston-Salem, N.C., 1977, 1979, 1981, 1982—83, 1987—88, LaGrange (Ga.) Nat., 1977, 1980, 1981, Miss. Mus. Art, Jackson, 1979—80, High Mus., Atlanta, 1980, Mint Mus., Charlotte, 1980, Monique Knowlton Gallery, N.Y.C., 1981, Mus. Gallery, White Plains, N.Y., 1982, Nexus, Atlanta, 1982, 1986, Wilhelm Gallery, Houston, 1984, Portfolio Gallery, Atlanta, 1987, Fla. Gulf Coast Arts Ctr., Belleaire, 1988, Galerie Simonne Stern, Atlanta, 1988, 1989, Mus. of the Hudson Highlands, Cornwall-on-Hudson, N.Y., 1989, Converse Coll., Spartanburg, S.C., 1989, Jane Haslem Gallery, Washington, 1991, Trinity Gallery, Columbus Coll., Atlanta, 1991, Greenville (N.C.) Mus. Art, 1991, Harmony Hall Regional Ctr., Ft. Washington, Md., 1992, Spruill Ctr. for the Arts, Dunwoody, Ga., 1994, Habitat for Humanity, Atlanta, 1994, Macon & Co. Fine Art, 1994, Marita Gilliam Gallery, Raleigh, 1996, The Spruill Ctr. Gallery, Dunwoody, 1997, Kennesaw State U., Atlanta, 1997, Aspen Mus. Art, 2001, 2003. Mem. adult edn. com. Christ Episcopal Ch., Aspen. Fellow, MacDowell Colony, Peterborough, N.H., 1976; grantee, NEA/SECCA, 1980—81. Mem.: AAUW, Nat. Assn. Univ. Women, Nat. Mus. Women in Arts, Nat. Assn. Women Artists, Women's Found. Colo. Avocations: piano, gardening, reading, hiking, skiing. Home: 421 W Hallam St Aspen CO 81611

HOUGHTALING, PAMELA ANN, technology marketing professional, writer; b. Catskill, N.Y., July 8, 1949; d. Stanley Kenneth and Mildred Edythe (Fyfe) H. BA, Princeton U., 1971; M in Internat. Affairs, Russian Inst., Columbia U., 1974, cert., 1976. Internat. rels. analyst Libr. of Congress, Washington, 1974-75, U.S. GAO, Washington, 1976-77; pub. affairs specialist IBM Corp., Washington, 1977-81; sr. external programs analyst IBM World Trade Americas/Far East Corp., North Tarrytown, N.Y., 1981-82; mgr. labor affairs/bus. practices U.S. Coun. Internat. Bus., N.Y.C., 1982-84; comms. specialist-advt. IBM Corp., Boca Raton, Fla., 1984-86, staff comms. specialist White Plains, N.Y., 1986-88, comms. cons., 1988-90; sr. mktg. specialist Wang Labs., Bethesda, Md., 1990-93; pub. rels. dir. STG Mktg. Comm., 1993-94; mgr. mktg. comm. Cable & Wireless, Inc., Vienna, Va., 1994-95; contractor to Applied Physics Lab. Johns Hopkins U., Laurel, Md., 1998-99, tech. comms. cons., 1995—98; mktg. program mgr. Info. Tech. Lab. Nat. Inst. Stds. and Tech., Gaithersburg, Md., 2000—03; fellow U.S. Dept. Commerce Sci. and Tech., 2003—. Mem. Am. Mktg. Assn., Armed Forces Comms. and Electronics Assn., Nat. Assn. Sci. Writers.

HOUGHTON, KATHARINE, actress; b. Hartford, Conn., Mar. 10, 1945; d. Ellsworth Strong and Marion Houghton (Hepburn) Grant. BA, Sarah Lawrence Coll., Bronxville, N.Y., 1965. Founding mem. Pilgrim Repertory Co. (Shakespeare touring co. sponsored by Ky. Arts Commn.), 1971-72, SC Arts Commn., 1972, Miss. Arts Commn., 1973, Conn. Arts Commn., St. Joseph Coll., 1974; lectr. in field. Debut on Broadway stage in A Very Rich Woman, 1965; appeared in stage plays Charley's Aunt, New Orleans Repertory, 1966, The Front Page, Broadway, 1968, Ten O'Clock Scholar, Royal Poinciana Playhouse, Fla., 1969, The Private Ear/The Public Eye, Sullivan, Ill., 1969, Sabrina Fair, Ivoryton Playhouse, 1968, The Miracle Worker, Sullivan, Ill., A Scent of Flowers (Theatre World award), Off Broadway, 1969, Misalliance, Hartford Stage Co., 1970, The Taming of the Shrew, Actors Theatre, Louisville, 1970, Poor Richard, Tartuffe, 1970, Ring Around the Moon, Hartford Stage Co., 1970, Major Barbara, The Glass Menagerie, Actors Theatre of Louisville, 1971, Play It Again Sam, Actors Theatre of Louisville, 1971, Suddenly Last Summer, Ivanhoe, Chgo., 1973, The Prodigal Daughter, Kennedy Center, Washington, 1973, Bell, Book and Candle, Pensacola, Fla., 1974, The Rainmaker, Ind. Repertory Co., 1975, Spiders Web, Atlanta, 1977, Hedda Gabler, Nashville, 1978, Dear Liar, Dayton, Ohio, 1978, 13 Rue de L'Amour, Ind. Repertory Co., 1978, Antigone, Nashville, 1979, Uncle Vanya, Acad. Festival Theatre, Lake Forest, 1979, Forty Carats, Radford U. Theatre, Va., 1979, A Doll's House, St. Edward's U. Theatre, Tex., 1979, The Sea Gull, Pitts. Public Theatre, 1979, The Glass Menagerie, Pa. Stage Co., 1980, Taming of the Shrew, Pa. State Festival, 1980, Terra Nova, Actors Theatre of Louisville, 1980, The Merchant of Venice, South Coast Repertory, Costa Mesa, Calif., 1981, A Touch of the Poet, Yale Repertory Theatre, 1983, To Heaven in a Swing, Am. Place Theatre, N.Y.C., tour various theaters, 1983-85, Sally's Gone She's Left Her Name, Am. Festival Theatre, NH, 1984-86, Vivat, Vivat Regina, Mad Woman of Chaillot, The Time of Your Life, Children of the Sun, Mirror Repertory Co., N.Y.C., 1985, A Bill of Divorcement, Westport Country Playhouse, Conn., 1985, One Slight Hitch, Charlotte Repertory Co., 1986, To Heaven in a Swing, Amherst Coll., Bowdoin Coll., 1986, and Bronson Alcott Centennial Celebration, 1988, The Hooded Eye, West Bank Downstairs Theatre Bar, 1987, Ivoryton Playhouse, 1987, Murder in the Cathedral, West Point Cadet Chapel, 1987, The Leaves of Vallombrosa, 1988, Our Town, Broadway, 1988-89, Love Letters, Ivoryton Playhouse, 1989, To Kill A Mockingbird, Paper Mill Playhouse, NJ, 1991, Best Kept Secret, Berkshire Theatre Festival, 2000, NJ Repertory Theatre, 2001, Sch. House Theatre, Croton Falls, NY, 2001, Lettice & Lovage, Ivoryton Playhouse, 2002; motion pictures include Guess Who's Coming to Dinner, 1967, The Gardener, 1972, Eyes of the Amaryllis, 1981, Mr. North, 1987, Billy Bathgate, 1990, Ethan Frome, 1992, The Night We Never Met, 1992, Kalamazoo, 1993, Let It Be You, 1994, The Pursuit of Happiness, 2003, Kinsey, 2003; TV series The Adams Chronicles, 1975; TV mini-series I'll Take Manhattan, 1986; appeared on TV in Legacy of Fear, 1974, The Color of Friendship, 1981, (day-time serials) One Life to Live, 1989, All My Children, 1992; toured in Sabrina Fair, 1975, The Mousetrap, Arms and the Man, Dear Liar, 1976, The Streets of New York, Westport, Conn., Guildford, NH, Dennis, Mass., Denver, 1980; appeared in To True to Be Good, Acad. Festival Theatre, Lake Forest, Ill., 1977, Spingold Theatre, Waltham, Mass., 1977, Annenberg Center, Phila., 1977; author: (plays) To Heaven in a Swing, 1982, Merlin, 1984, Buddha, On The Shady Side, The Right Number, 1986, (book) The Marry Month of May, 1988; (stage prodns.) Phone Play, 1988, Good Grief, 1988, Mortal Friends, 1988 (stage prodn. premiere 1988), The Lick Penny Lover, 1988, Only Angels, 1997, (screenplays) The Heart of the Matter, 1989, Journey to Glasnost, 1990, Good Grief, 1991, Motherman, 1993, Acting in Concert, 1994, Spot, 1996, (play) Best Kept Secret, A Dangerous Liaison in the Cold War, 1998; co-author: Two Beastly Tales, 1975; editor: MHG: A Biography, 1989; written, performed in lectr. engagements: The Secret Life of Louisa May Alcott, Small Press Ctr., NYC, 1998, Women of AchievementSeries, The Mount, Lenox, Mass., 2002, My Grandmother's House Near the River, Conn. River Mus., 1999, The Wadsworth Atheneum, Conn., 1999, The Hope Club, Providence, 2000, The Cosmopolitan Club, NYC, 2002, Katharine Times Three, Conn. Hist. Soc., 1999, Wadsworth Atheneum, 2000, Denver Town Hall, 2001, Met. Mus. Art., NYC, 2001, Conn. Women's Hall of Fame 10th Gala, 2003; appeared Larry King Live, 2003. Mem. Dramatists Guild.

HOULE, LOUANN, minister; b. Elma, Wash., May 24, 1954; d. Charles Gordies and Dora Alice (Rice) Sutten; m. Clement Andrew Houle, June 2, 1984; children: Philip Avery, Benjamin Andrew. AA, Grays Harbor Coll., 1974; BA in Music Edn., Western Wash. U., 1976; M in Religion, Waner Pacific Coll., 1983. Ordained Ch. of God, 1999. Libr. page Elma City Libr., 1968—72; maintenance supr. tech. Grays Harbor Coll., Aberdeen, Wash., 1972—74; with Grays Harbor Christian Sch., Aberdeen, 1976—79; music min. Alder Grove Ch. God, Aberdeen, 1976—79; music min., assoc. Alder Grove Ch. of God, Abderdeen, 1989—91; libr. tech. Warner Pacific Coll., Portland, Oreg., 1979—83; music min. Lents Gilbert Ch. of God, Portland, 1979—83; music min., assoc. Montesano (Wash.) Ch. of God, 1983—86; sr. pastor Elma Ch. of God, 1994—. Active Christian edn. state PNA of the Chs. of God, Wenatchee, Wash., active bd. ch. ext., with spiritual life WCG. Mem.: East County Ministerial Assn. Republican. Avocations: music, computers, sewing, reading. Home: PO Box 1019 Elma WA 98541-1019 Office: Elma Ch of God PO Box 684 Elma WA 98541-0684

HOULTON, LISE, performing company executive; m. Michael Gilliland; children: Kaitlyn, Raina. Tchr. Minn. Dance Theatre, Mpls.; dancer Am. Ballet Theatre, N.Y., Stuttgart Ballet, Germany, Minn. Dance Theatre. Office: Minn Dance Theatre 528 Hennepin Ave Sixth Fl Minneapolis MN 55403*

HOURANI, LAUREL LOCKWOOD, epidemiologist; b. Carmel, Calif., Sept. 10, 1950; d. Eugene Franklin and Katherine Ruth (Miller) Betz; m. Ghazi Fayez Hourani, Feb. 28, 1984; children: Nathan, Danna, Lisa. BA, Chico State U., 1977; MPH, Am. Univ. Beirut, 1983; PhD, U. Pitts., 1990. Prog. evaluator Community Hosp. Monterey Peninsula, Carmel, Calif., 1978-81; instr./researcher Am. Univ. Beirut, 1981-85; predoctoral fellow U. Pitts., 1985-89; researcher, cons. V.A. Med. Ctr., Pitts., 1988-90; dir., tumor registry Med. Ctr. U. Calif. Irvine, Orange, 1990-92; epidemiologist Naval Health Rsch. Ctr., San Diego, 1993-95, head divsn. health scis., 1995-2001; sr. epidemiologist Rsch. Triangle Inst., Research Triangle Park, N.C., 2001—. Cons. Nat. Devel. Commn. South Lebanon, 1981-83. Author: No Water, No Peace, 1985; contbr. articles to profl. jours. Bd. dirs. Am. for Justice in Middle East, Beirut, 1982-85, Nat. Devel. Com., South Lebanon, 1983-85. Recipient grant V.A., Pitts., 1989, rsch. grant U. Rsch. Bd., Beirut, 1985. Mem. Am. Psychol. Assn., Am. Pub. Health Assn., Soc. for Epidemiologic Rsch.

HOUSE, JANE E. director, writer, actress; b. Panama City, Panama, Oct. 23, 1945; arrived in U.S., 1958; d. Stephen Patrick and Ellen Myra Rachael House; m. Victor I. Wexner, Aug. 1967 (dissolved Aug. 1969). BA, Stanford U., 1967; PhD, CUNY, 1988. Actress CBS, As the World Turns, N.Y.C., 1968—72; asst. dir. Ctr. European Studies CUNY, N.Y.C., 1974—78, adj. tchr., 1986—95; theater project dir. Inst. on Western Europe, Columbia U., N.Y.C., 1984—90; assoc. dir. pub. affairs, The Grad. Ctr. CUNy, 2001—. Artistic dir. Jane House Prodns., NY, 2002—. Actor(Broadway): Lenny (originating role of Honey Bruce), Bedroom Farce, by Alan Ayckbourn, (nat. tour): An Inspector Calls, by J.B. Priestley, Bedroom Farce, (TV): Sophia, Edge of Night, Love is a Many Splendored Thing, (regional): Sweet Bird of Youth, Pygmalion, State of the Union, Tartuffe, Prometheus Bound, (Off Broadway): Storks, by Catherine Filloux-Mamilou, 1999, The Late Lamented, 1997, Harley Holmes, Noel Coward Festival, Hands Across the Sea, The Astonished Heart, The Big Knife, by Clifford Odets, The Tenor, by Wedekind-Helen, Folie-a-Deux, : various univ. theater prodns.; editor: 20th Century Italian Drama, 1995; contbr. articles to encys. and dictionaries; actor: (TV series) As The World Turns; italian translator. Mem.: SAG, AFTRA (women's com. 2000—01), Actors Equity Assn. (vested). Democrat. Avocations: cooking, walking, opera. Office: Office Pub Affairs & Publs CUNY Grad Ctr 365 Fifth Ave New York NY 10016 Office Phone: 212-817-7176. E-mail: janeehouse@juno.com.

HOUSE, KAREN ELLIOTT, company executive, former editor, reporter; b. Matador, Tex., Dec. 7, 1947; d. Ted and Bailey Elliott; m. Arthur House, Apr. 5, 1975 (div. Sept. 1983); m. Peter Kann, June 4, 1984; children: Hillary, Petra, Jason, Jade. BJ, U. Tex., 1970; postgrad. Inst. Politics, Harvard U. Edn. reporter Dallas Morning News, 1970-71, with Washington bur., 1971-74; regulatory corr. Wall Street Jour., Washington, 1974-75, energy and agr. corr., 1975-78, diplomatic corr., 1978-84, fgn. editor N.Y.C., 1984-89; v.p., Internat. Group Dow Jones & Co., 1989-95, pres. Internat. Group, 1995—; sr. v.p. Dow Jones Co pub. Wall St. Jour., 2002. Bd. dirs. Rand Corp.; mem. adv. bd. Ctr. Strategic Internat. Studies; dir. Coun. on Foriegn Rels. Trustee Boston U. Recipient Edward Weintal award for Diplomatic Reporting, Georgetown U., 1980-81, Edwin Hood award for Diplomatic Reporting Nat. Press Club, 1982, Disting. Achievement award U. So. Calif., 1984, Pulitzer prize for Internat. Reporting, 1984, Overseas Press Club Bob Considine award, 1984, 88; Harvard fellow, 1982. Fellow Nat. Acad. Arts and Scis. Office: Dow Jones & Co 200 Liberty St Fl 9 New York NY 10281-1003 E-mail: karen.house@dowjones.com.*

HOUSE, ROBIN CHRISTINE, real estate agent, art consultant; b. Orlando, Fla., Mar. 4, 1967; d. Roy Wilson and Joan Teresa (Leslie) H. BA in Art History, Coll. of Charleston, S.C.; AA in Art History, Ctrl. Piedmont C.C., Charlotte, N.C. Lic. N.C. Real Estate. Art cons. Charlotte Pipe and Foundry Co., Charlotte, N.C., 1996; real estate agt. Helen Adams Realty, Charlotte, N.C., 1997-2000; gallery dir. Ctr. of Earth Gallery, Charlotte, NC, 2000—01. Cons. Claudia Heath Fine Arts, Charlotte, N.C.; chair Dealer Hospitality Mint Mus. of Art Aux. Antiques Show, Charlotte, N.C.; loan exhibit chair Mint Mus. ARt Antiques Show, 2000; owner HouseFrog-.com, 2001. Author: (poem) Am I Like A Black Man?, 1994, The Art Collection of Charlotte Pipe and Foundry Company, 1997. Chair (CouSins) Christ Ch. Young Adult Group, Charlotte, N.C., 1997—; mem. Jr. League. Recipient Scholarship in Art History, 1993, Outstanding Student award, 1993, Coll. of Charleston; named Salesperson of Month, Helen Adams Realty, Charlotte, N.C., 1999. Independent. Episcopalian. Avocations: horseback riding, shotgunning. Address: 624 Dorothy Dr Charlotte NC 28203 E-mail: houser1234@hotmail., Robin@housefrog.com.

HOUSEL, NATALIE RAE NORMAN, physical therapist; b. Syracuse, N.Y., July 25, 1959; d. Rudolf Anthony and Pauline Mary (Proia) Norman; m. Thomas Hugh Housel, June 25, 1988; children: Heather, Tommy and Tiffany (twins). BS in Phys. Therapy, Ithaca Coll., 1981; MA in Applied Psychology, Fairfield U., 1986; EdD in Curriculum and Instrn., U. Ctrl. Fla., 2002. Cert. geriatric clin. specialist Am. Bd. Phys. Therapy Specialties, diplomate wound care specialist Am. Acad. Wound Mgmt. Staff phys. therapist, N.Y., 1981-85; sr. phys. therapist Rome (N.Y.) Devel. Ctr., 1987-89; asst. dir. phys. therapy Tioga (N.Y.) Gen. Hosp. and Nursing Home, 1989-91, Corning (N.Y.) Hosp., 1991-92; asst. dir. rehab. svcs. Arnot Ogden Med. Ctr., Elmira, N.Y., 1992-93; sch. phys. therapist Collier County Pub. Schs., Naples, Fla., 1993-94; pvt. practice phys. therapist Ft. Myers, Fla., 1995-96; dir. phys. therapy Beverly Enterprises, Ft. Myers, Fla., 1995-96; therapy supr. Lee Meml. Health Sys. Health Park Care Ctr., Ft. Myers, Fla., 1996-97; rehab. mgr. occupl., speech and phys. therapy Lee Meml. Home Health, Fort Myers, Fla., 1997-98. Instr phys. therapy assts. Broome C.C., 1989, wound care nutrition for Hosp. Food Adminstrs., 1997; oral examiner for phys. therapy licensees N.Y. State, Albany, 1988-90; adj. faculty S.W. Fla. Coll., Ft. Myers, 2003—, Edison C.C., 2003—. Adult group leader Family Faith Formation, St. Columbkill Ch., Ft. Myers, Fla., 1996-97. Mem.: APA, Am. Acad. Wound Mgmt. Avocations: flute, piano, swimming. Home: 1626 N Hermitage Rd Fort Myers FL 33919-6409

HOUSEMAN, ANN ELIZABETH LORD, educational administrator state official; b. New Orleans, Mar. 21, 1936; d. Noah Louis and Florence Marguerite (Coyle) Lord; m. Evan Kenny Houseman, June 25, 1960; children: Adrienne Ann, Jeannette Louise, Yvonne Elizabeth. BA, Barnard Coll., 1957; MA, Columbia U., 1962; PhD, U. Del., 1969. State supr. reading Dept. Pub. Instrn., Del., 1977-79; prin. M.L. King Jr. Elem. Sch., Wilmington, Del., 1979-80; adminstr., exec. dir. Del. State Arts Coun., Wilmington, 1980-84; acting dir. Divsn. Hist. and Cultural Affairs State of Del., Wilmington, 1983-84; prin. P.S. du Pont Intermediate Sch., Wilmington, 1984-91; dir. Mid.-Atlantic States Arts Consortium, Balt., 1980-84. Mem. adv. bd. Rockwood Mus., Wilmington, 1981-94; bd. dirs. Opera Del., Inc., Wilmington, 1984-97, pres., 1991-93, dir. devel., 1994-95, coord. adv. bd., 1996; bd. dirs. Del. Theatre Co., Wilmington, 1984-90; bd. dirs. Aux. of Alfred I. duPont Hosp. for Children, 1997—, pres., 2000-01. Mem. Phi Delta Kappa. Republican. Presbyterian. E-mail: houseman@udel.edu.

HOUSER, BARBARA J. lawyer; b. Scottsbluff, Nebr., Jan. 29, 1954; BS with honors, U. Nebr., 1975; JD, So. Meth. U., 1978. Bar: Tex. 1978, U.S. Dist. Ct. (no., so., ea., and we. dists.) Tex., U.S. Dist. Ct. (ea. dist.) Mich., U.S. Ct. Appeals (5th, 6th, and 11th cirs.), U.S. Supreme Ct. Shareholder Sheinfeld Maley & Kay, Houston. Lectr. nationally on insolvency, bankruptcy, and debtor/creditor relationships. Author: The Fifth Circuit in Review: A Retrospective of the First Decade Under the Bankruptcy Code, 1989; casenote and comment editor Southwestern Law Jour., 1977-78; contbg. author: Collier on Bankruptcy, 15th edit., Collier Bankruptcy Manual, 3d edit. Named One of Fifty Top Women Lawyers Nat. Law Jour., 1998. Fellow Am. Coll. Bankruptcy, Am. Bar Found., Tex. Bar Found.; mem. ABA, Nat. Bankruptcy Conf., Alpha Lambda Delta, Phi Delta Phi. Office: Sheinfeld Maley & Kay 1700 Pacific Ave Ste 4400 Dallas TX 75201-4678

HOUSER, CONSTANCE W. writer, artist; b. Goshen, N.Y., Aug. 16; d. Charles A. and Josephine E. Woodward; m. James C. Houser, Sept. 21, 1972; children: J. Jackson, Katrina J. AA, Palm Beach C.C., Fla., 1970; BFA, Fla. Atlantic U., 1971. News, editl., features Palm Beach Post-Times, Miami Herald, Fla., 1954—62; columnist, book reviewer Palm Beach Times, Lake Worth News, Fla., 1962—69; art reviewer Art Mags., N.Y.C., 1960—70; art features, art profiles Art Voices South, Fla., 1960—70; artist profiles Art News, 1970—89. Owner 4 Points Photo Ctr., West Palm Beach, Fla., 1958—69; art tchr. for srs., computer tutor, judge art and photo competitions. Over 10 one-woman shows, Exhibited in group shows at Gallery Camino, Real, Fla., Peter Rudolph Galleries, N.Y.; contbr. articles to profl. mags. and newspapers. Mem. Hobe Sound Art League, Fla., 1996—2000, Hobe Sound Women's Club, Fla., 1996—2000; v.p. Rep. Club, West Palm Beach, Fla., 1980. Recipient awards, Norton Gallery of Art, West Palm Beach, 1967, Soc. of the 4-Arts, 1970—74, Art Competition awards, Hortt Mus., 1974—79. Mem.: AAUW, Nat. Soc. Arts and Letters, Gallery Players (bd. dirs., pres., v.p.), 4-Points Photo Club (pres.). Republican. Episcopalian. Home: 8338 SE Coconut St Hobe Sound FL 33455

HOUSER, RUTH G. financial executive; b. Virginia Beach, Va., Feb. 25, 1953; BS in Acctg. cum laude, Wheeling Coll., 1975. CPA, Fla., Ga., W.Va. Sr. acct. Price Waterhouse, Pitts., 1975-79; mgr. Lockheed Space Opers. Co., Cape Canaveral, Fla., 1980-84; mgr. info. systems AT&T, Morristown, NJ, 1984—87, fin. dir. France and Italy Paris, 1987-89, mgr. acctg. policy Morristown, 1989-90, dir. billing svcs. Bridgewater, N.J., 1990-92, controller, Network Wireless Systems Morristown, N.J., 1992-93; fin. billing team dir. WorldPartners/WorldSource AT&T, Bridgewater, N.J., 1993-95; dist. mgr. Lucent Technologies Intellectual Property, Coral Gables, Fla., 1995-98; revenue assurance mgr. Data Networking Svcs., St. Petersburg, Fla., 1998-99; CFO, mergers and acquisitions mgr. Lucent Technologies, Tierra Verde, Fla., 1999—2001; contr. intellectual property Agere Sys., Orlando, Fla., 2001—. Vol. C. Dillon Libr., Bedminster, NJ, 1985, v.p. bd. trustees, 1988—92; sec., trustee Friends of C. Dillon Libr., 1992—95; committeewoman Bedminster Twp., 1995; trustee Ct. Against Spouse Abuse, St. Petersburg; treas. League to Aid Abused Children and Adults, St. Petersburg, 1999—2001, Cross of Lorraine Am. Lung Assn., 1999—2002, Disney 2002 Marathon, Orlando, Fla.; chmn. spring spectacular Ct. Against Spouse Abuse, St. Petersburg, 2001; mem. Heart of Fl. United Way Leadership Club, Fla., 2001; CFO Col. Potter Cairn Terrier Rescue, 2002—; committeewoman Somerset County Reps. Dist. 5, Bedminster, 1993—95. Recipient Cmty. Vol. award, Queen's Ct., Inc., 2001. Mem. AICPA, FICPA. Avocations: international travel, reading, sports, real estate investing. Home: 13524 Turtle Marsh Loop 611 Orlando FL 32837 Office: Agere Sys Rm 302W 2138 9333 John Young Pkwy Orlando FL 32819 Office Phone: 407-371-9700.

HOUSE-ROLLINS, SONYA, psychotherapist; b. Chgo. d. Oliver R. and Ann (Wilson) House; m. Calvin B. Rollins. BA in Polit. Sci., De Paul U., 1986; MA in Counseling, St. Mary's U., 1996; Paralegal Cert., Roosevelt U. Lic. profl. counselor, Tex., marriage and family therapist, Tex. Caseworker aide Crosspoint, Inc., San Antonio, 1995; marriage and family therapy intern St. Mary's U., San Antonio, 1995-96, U.S. Army, San Antonio, 1995-96; detention officer Bexar County Juv. Detention, San Antonio, 1995-96; psychotherapist Turning Pt. Ctr., Devine, Tex., 1996—. Rsch. asst. The Fielding Inst., Santa Barbara, Calif., 1997. Vol. Family Svcs. Assn., San Antonio, 1997; tutor Adult Literacy of Am., San Antonio, 1996; advocate Rape Crisis Ctr., San Antonio, 1995-96; mem. Interdenominational Youth Choir, Normal, Ill., 1983-84. Sgt. U.S. Army, 1988-96. Decorated Army Achievement medals. Mem. Am. Psycho. Assn., Am. Assn. of Marriage and Family Therapists, Chi Sigma Iota, Zeta Phi Beta. Avocations: performance dance, billiards, films, travel, exercise. Office: Turning Point Ctr 217 N Highway 132 Devine TX 78016-1822

HOUSHIAR, BOBBIE KAY, language arts educator; b. Fort Smith, Ark., Nov. 28; d. Ernest and Virgil Straham. BA, Saginaw Valley State U., 1973; MA in Elem. Edn. Adminstrn., Cen. Mich. U., 1975, Cert. Gen. Edn. Adminstrn., 1978. Elem. tchr. Saginaw (Mich.) Pub. Schs., 1973-74, jr. high tchr., 1975-76, tchr. middle sch., 1983—; learning ctr. coord. Saginaw Valley State U., University Center, Mich., 1974-75, instr. reading, 1974-75; tchr. ESL Refugee Ctr. of Saginaw, 1982-83. Instr. ind. study Cen. Mich. U., Saginaw, 1988-90; tutor bilingual students Delta Coll., Saginaw, 1987-96; supr./student tchrs. Saginaw Pub. Schs., 1988—; oratorical/writing instr. Saginaw Pub. Schs., 1983—. Editor: Young Writers in Michigan, 1989. Vol. Saginaw County chpt. ARC, 1996-99; mem./vol. League of Cath. Women, Saginaw, 1976—. Recipient Recognition award Saginaw Infant Mortality Coalition award, Saginaw Cooperative Hosp., 1998, Educator of Yr. award, Saginaw Coop. Hosp., 1999, Excellence in Tchg. English Writing Skills award, Saginaw Bd. Edn., 2002, Accent on Achievement award, Saginaw Pub. Sch. Bd. of Edn., 2002, others. Mem. NEA, Saginaw Edn. Assn., Mich. Edn. Assn., Nat. Coun. Tchrs. of English, ASCD, Mich. Mid. Sch. Assn., Delta Sigma Theta. Democrat. Roman Catholic. Avocations: reading, student mentor, tennis, swimming, horses. Office: South Middle Sch 224 N Elm St Saginaw MI 48602-2651 Personal E-mail: Siamak67@cs.com. Business E-Mail: BHoushiar@spsd.net.

HOUSKA-GREEN, KATHLEEN ANN, marketing professional, public relations executive; b. Hinsdale, Ill., May 15, 1974; d. Frank Stanley and Joan Margaret (McCarthy) Houska; m. Patrick E. Green, Aug. 22, 1998; 1 child, Ryan F. Green. BA in Orgnl./Corp. Comms. with honors, No. Ill. U., 1996. Intern Marcy Monyek and Assocs., Chgo., summer 1995, asst. mktg. assoc., 1996-97; pub. rels. coord. D.C. Systems, Oakbrook Terrace, Ill., 1997-99; mktg. comms. specialist Comark, Inc., Bloomingdale, Ill., 1999—2000; pres. Green Creative Svcs., Geneva, Ill., 2000—. Contbr. articles to profl. publs. Vol. Students with Disabilities, No. Ill. U., 1995-96. Mem.: Bus. Mktg. Assn. (mem. pub. rels. com.), Women in Comms., Inc. (v.p. programming 1994—95, pres. 1995—96). Avocations: Irish dancing, running, reading, writing, biking. Home: 39W372 W Mallory Dr Geneva IL 60134

HOUSTON, CONSTANCE T. state legislator; b. Vergennes, Vt., Feb. 10, 1949; m. William G. Houston; 1 child. Grad., Mary Fletch Sch. X-Ray Tech., 1968, Tri-State Real Estate Inst. State rep. dist. 14 Vt. Ho. of Reps., 1993—. With Manufactured Housing Sales and Self-Storage; mem. adv. bd. Bank of Vt., Vt. Fed. Bank. Trustee Addison County Econ. Devel. Mem. Addison C. of C. (former pres.), Addison County Bus. Roundtable, Nat. Fedn. Ind. Bus. Address: 3735 Basin Harbor Rd Vergennes VT 05491-9768

HOUSTON, GERRY ANN, oncologist; b. Baldwyn, Miss., July 16, 1953; d. Jeff Davis and Frances Holland (Agnew) Goodson; m. Terry L. Houston, Dec. 18, 1976 (dec. May 1987); 1 child, Claire Holland; m. Abe John Malouf, July 23, 1988. BA, U. Miss., 1974, MD, 1978. Diplomate Am. Bd. Internal Medicine, Am. Bd. Medical Oncology, Am. Bd. Hospice and Palliative Care. Intern U. Med. Ctr., Jackson, Miss., 1978-79; resident U. Med. Ctr., Jackson, Miss., 1979-81, fellow oncology, 1981-83; ptnr. Jackson (Miss.) Oncology Assocs., 1987—. Staff physician Miss. Bapt. Med. Ctr., Jackson, 1983—, Ctr. Miss. Med. Ctr., Jackson, 1983—, St. Dominic Hosp., Jackson, 1983—, River Oaks Hosp., Jackson, 1983—, Univ. Med. Ctr., Jackson, 1983—; med. dir. Hospice Ministries, Jackson, 1989—; mem. exec. com. Bapt. Med. Ctr., 1994, chief of staff, 2003—; med. dir. Bapt. Comprehensive Breast Ctr., 1997—. Contbr. articles to profl. jours. Chmn. exec. com. Miss. divsn. Am. Cancer Soc., 1993-95, pres., bd. dirs., 1989-93. Clin. rsch. fellow Am. Cancer Soc. Fellow ACP; mem. AMA, Nat. Hospice Orgn., Acad. Hospice Physicians, So. Assn. Oncology, Am. Soc. Clin. Oncology, Alpha Omega Alpha. Episcopalian. Avocations: jogging, reading, snow skiing. Office: Jackson Oncology Assocs 1227 N State St Ste 101 Jackson MS 39202-2413 Office Phone: 601-355-2485. E-mail: ghouston@mbmc.org.

HOUSTON, PENELOPE, singer, songwriter, recording artist; b. L.A., Dec. 17, 1957; d. David Brown Houston and Penelope Helen Vrachopoulos; m. Meletios Christos Peppas, May 17, 1983 (div. Apr., 1994); m. Patrick John Roques, June 9, 1995. Singer, songwriter Avengers, San Francisco, 1977-79; singer, songwriter, bandleader Penelope Houston and Her Band, San Francisco, 1994—. Video dir., San Francisco, 1986—. Singer, songwriter (recordings) Avengers, 1983, Birdboys, 1988, On Borrowed Time—Live in Frisco, 1991, The Whole World, 1993, Silk Purse, 1993, Karmal Apple, 1994, Crazy Baby, 1995, Cut You, 1996, Tongue, 1998, The Avengers Died for Your Sins, 1999, Once in a Blue Moon, 2000, Loners, Stoners and Prison Brides, 2001, Eighteen Stories Down, 2003, Snap Shot, 2003, Avengers Zero Hour, 2003, Avengers The American in Me, 2004, The Pale Green Girl, 2004. Named Best Folk Artist, San Francisco Weekly Music Awards, 1990, Best Singer Spex Mag., Hamburg, Germany, 1993, Outstanding Female Vocalist, Bay Area Music Awards, San Francisco, 1995. Avocations: graphic design, travel, women's issues. Office: PO Box 5001 Berkeley CA 94705-0001

HOUSTON, WHITNEY, vocalist, recording artist; b. East Orange, N.J., Aug. 9, 1963; d. John R. and Cissy Houston; m. Bobby Brown, July 18, 1992; 1 child, Bobbi Kristina Houston Brown. HHD (hon.), Grambling U. Mem. New Hope Bapt. Jr. Choir, 1974, background vocalist Chaka Khan, Lou Rawls, Cissy Houston, 1978, appeared in Cissy Houston night club act, fashion model Glamour Mag., Seventeen mag., 1981, record debut (duet with Teddy Pendergrass) Hold Me, 1984; singer: (albums) Whitney Houston, 1985 (Grammy Award Best Pop Vocal Performance, 1985), Whitney, 1986 (Grammy Award Best Pop Vocal Performance, 1987), I'm Your Baby Tonight, 1990; singer: (appears on) The Bodyguard soundtrack (song "I Will Always Love You"), 1992 (Grammy Awards: Record Of The Year, Album Of The Year, Best Pop Vocal Performance, 1993), Waiting to Exhale soundtrack, 1995, Prince of Egypt soundtrack (song "When You Believe" with Mariah Carey), 1998; singer: My Love Is Your Love, 1999 (Grammy Award Best Female R&B Vocal Performance, 1999), Just Whitney, 2002; appeared in HBO TV spl. Welcome Home, Heroes, With Whitney Houston, 1991; actor: (films) The Bodyguard, 1992, Waiting To Exhale, 1995, The Preacher's Wife, 1996 (Image award Outstanding Lead Actress in a motion picture, 1997), Scratch the Surface, 1997; prodr.: The Princess Diaries, 2001; actor, exec. prodr.: (TV films) Cinderella, 1997, The Cheetah Girls, 2003. Founder The Whitney Houston Found. for Children, Inc. Recipient BET Lifetime Achievement award, 2002.*

HOUSTOUN, FEATHER O'CONNOR, state official; b. Galveston, Tex., Aug. 24, 1946; d. Leroy A. and Bonny (Cross) Feather; m. Lawrence O. Houstoun Jr; children: Alexandra, Kate. B in Polit. Sci., U. Ariz., 1968; M in Polit. Sci., U. Tex., 1973. Rsch. dir. Rep. Party Tex., 1969-70; various positions, acting dep. asst. sec. policy devel. U.S. Dept. Housing and Urban Devel., Washington, 1971-82; exec. dir. N.J. Housing and Mortgage Fin. Agy., Trenton, 1982-86; treas. State of N.J., Trenton, 1986-90; chief fin. officer SEPTA, 1990-95; sec. Pa. Dept. Pub. Welfare, Harrisburg, 1995—. Bd. dirs. N.J. State Aquarium, Phila. Devel. Corp., Center City Dist., Center City Found. Recipient L.B. Johnson Fellowship in Pub. Affairs. Fellow Nat. Acad. Pub. Adminstrs., Phi Beta Kappa, Phi Kappa Phi. Office: Public Welfare Dept PO Box 2675 Harrisburg PA 17105-2675

HOUX, SHIRLEY ANN, personal and business services company executive, consultant, researcher; b. Claremore, Okla., Nov. 1, 1931; d. George Warren and Alta Zena (Starkweather) Pritchard; m. William Dean Munson, June 1, 1951 (div. June 1962); children— Debra Kay, Diana Sue, Donna Lynn; m. Leonard Houx, June 22, 1963 (div. Oct. 1989); 1 child, David Leonard. Student in bus. Okla. State U., 1949-50. Sec. Jack Gordon, P.A., Claremore, Okla., 1947-48; sec., personnel mgr. Gulf Oil Corp., Tulsa, 1950-51; exec. sec. to wing comdr. U.S. Air Force, Cocoa Beach, Fla., 1951-53; exec. sec. to gen. counsel Houston So., P.A., Stillwater, Okla., 1957-60; exec. sec. to exec. v.p. and sr. v.p. Williams Cos., Tulsa, 1962-64; owner, chief exec. officer Hallmark Exchange, Inc., Tulsa, 1981— ; cons. small bus., Tulsa, 1981— ; mem. small bus. adv. bd. Tulsa Jr. Coll., 1983—. Author: (drama) Wedding Rehearsal for the Bride of Christ, 1985. Contbg. editor The Chronicle, 1984. Co-creator, producer foot health program, 1967 (Am. Podiatry Assn. Outstanding award 1968); creator, advt. campaign for Cystic Fibrosis Found.: I'm One...Be One, 1978. Pres. women's aux. Okla. Podiatry Assn., Tulsa, 1966-82; sec.-treas. Okla. bd. examiners Okla. Podiatry Assn., 1969-76; nat. audio-visual chmn. women's aux. Am. Podiatry Assn., 1976; pres. Tulsa Cerebral Palsy Assn., 1977, Cystic Fibrosis Found. Aux., Tulsa, 1979. Named Miss Claremore, Claremore Bus. and Profl. Women, Okla., 1949; recipient Two-Star award Pure D'Lite Co., 1982. Mem. Nat. Assn. Female Execs. Democrat. Avocations: fashion design; the arts; writing.

HOVLAND, JODY, theater director; MA in English, U. N.Dak.; MFA in Acting, U. Iowa, 1981. Co-artistic dir. Riverside Theatre, Iowa City, 1981—. Artist-in-residence Dept. Theater and Comms. Studies Cornell U., 2004—. Named Best Actor, Iowa City (Iowa) News and Entertainment Weekly, 1997; recipient Svc. to Arts in Our Region award, Iowa City Area C. of C., 1999. Office: Riverside Theatre 213 N Gilbert St Iowa City IA 52245*

HOWARD, BARBARA BYERS, public policy consultant; b. Seattle, Mar. 9, 1930; d. Orva Oliver and Florence Viano (Soderback) Byers; m. Richard Wayne Howard, Aug. 15, 1959 (dec. Dec. 1970). BA, U. Wash., 1950; PhD, Ind. U., 1964. Reporter Bainbridge Rev., Winslow, Wash., 1950-51; publs. dir. Wash. State Assn. County Commrs., Olympia, 1951-56; rsch. cons. Inst. Pub. Adminstrn. Ind. U., Bloomington, 1956—59; instr., asst. prof. dept. govt. Ind. U., Bloomington, 1960-66; rsch. cons. bur. govtl. rsch. & svcs. U. Wash., Seattle, 1967-69; policy analyst Joint Com. on Higher Edn. Wash. State Legis., 1971-73; sr. policy analyst com. on govt. ops. Wash. State Senate, Olympia, 1973-93. Adv. bd. Munro seminar for tchrs., Western Washington U., 1998—; pub. mem. Warren Featherstone Reid award adv. com., Olympia, 1995—, cons. in field. Author: County Government in Washington State, 1957, Accounting Practices in County Road Departments in Illinois, 1957, Gaining Government Support for Your Arts Project: A Primer for Political Advocacy, 1995. Vol. Capitol Visitors Ctr., Lacey-Olympia centennial AMTRAK Sta. Mem. LWV, Am. Soc. Pub. Adminstrn., Women in Comm., Seattle Opera Assn., Seattle Art Mus. Avocations: photography, travel, cooking, visual & performance arts, paper crafting.

HOWARD, BARBARA VIVENTI, research foundation executive; b. East Orange, N.J., June 26, 1941; d. Louis and Angelina (DiBiase) Viventi; m. William James Howard, June 22, 1962; children: Laura, Sandra, Jeffrey. AB, Bryn Mawr Coll., 1963; PhD, U. Pa., 1968. Instr. U. N.C., Chapel Hill, 1968-70; asst. prof. George Washington U., Washington, 1970-73, Med. Coll. of Pa., Phila., 1973-76, assoc. prof. to vis. prof., 1976-91; scientist NIODIC-NIH, Phoenix, 1976-82; assoc. chief CONS-NIDDIC, NIH, Phoenix, 1982-88; dir. rsch. Medlantic Rsch. Found., Washington, 1988-90, pres., 1991—, Medstar Roach Inst. Chmn. Strong Heart Study Steering Com., Washington, 1988—; mem. nutrition study sect. NIH, Bethesda, Md., 1988-91. Editor: Insulin and the Cell Membrane, 1990, Lipoprotein Kinetics, 1982; assoc. editor:: Diabetes Care, 1990-91, Jour. Lipid Rsch., 1990—; contbr. over 100 articles to profl. jours. NIH grantee, 1988—, Corson Medal, Franklin Inst., 1994. Fellow Am. Soc. Biochemistry and Molecular Biology; mem. Am. Diabetes Assn., Am. Fedn. Clin. Rsch., Am. Soc. for Clin. Nutrition, Internat. Study Group for Inplantable Insulin Delivery, Am. Heart Assn. (exec. com.), Bryn Mawr Club. Republican. Episcopalian. Avocations: jogging, reading. Home: 2701 Church Creek Ln Edgewater MD 21037-1215 Office: Medstar Roach Inst Annex # 5 108 Irving St NW Washington DC 20010-2933

HOWARD, BETTIE JEAN, surgical nurse; b. Balt., Sept. 26, 1926; d. Milton James and Elizabeth Maria (Morgan) Knight; m. Stanley Lewis Howard; children: Amanda J. Scott, Sarah L. Howard, Mary McK. Strobel, Elizabeth M. Shaner, Roderick S. Diploma, Ch. Home and Hosp., Balt., 1947. RN, Md.; cert. bd. gastroenterology nurse. Head nurse med.-surg. unit Ch. Home & Hosp., Balt., 1947-48; surg. pediat. staff nurse Johns Hopkins Hosp., Balt., 1948-51, surg. pediat. acting head nurse, 1951-52, otolaryngology endoscopy head nurse, 1952-56; pediat. emergency rm. triage nurse U. Md. Hosp., Balt., 1966-68; head nurse surg. endoscopy nurse U. Md. Med. Ctr., Balt., 1968—2002, endofiberscope team coord. perioperative/trauma, 2002—. Adv. bd. Astra Merck for Patient Self Mgmt. Programs; spkr. Soc. Internat. Gastroent. Nurses and Endoscopy Assocs. VI Internat. Congress, Paris, 1996, VII Internat. Congress, Vienna, 1998. Contbr.: (book chpt. sect.) Policy and Politics for Nurses, 1993; contbr. articles to profl. jours. Chmn. Digestive Disease Nat. Coalition, Washington, 1993-95; coord. exec. panel Nat. Digestive Disease Info. Clearinghouse, NIH, Bethesda, Md., 1992-2002; adminstrv. bd. Grace United Meth. Ch., Balt., 1993-95. Mem. Soc. Gastroenterology Nurses and Assocs., Inc. (pres. 1988-89, Gabriele Schindler award 1991), Soc. Internat. Gastroenterol. Nurses and Endoscopy Assocs. (charter, spkr. 1998), Chesapeake Soc. Gastroenterology Nurses and Assocs. (charter, pres. 1981-83), Certifying Bd. Gastroenterology Nurses and Assocs. Inc. (pres. 1992-93). Republican. Avocations: reading, interior decorating, sewing, native-american collection. Home: 905 Saxon Hill Dr Cockeysville MD 21030-2905 Office: U Md Med Ctr 22 S Greene St Baltimore MD 21201-1544

HOWARD, CAROLE MARGARET MUNROE, retired public relations executive; b. Halifax, N.S., Can., Mar. 5, 1945; came to the U.S., 1965; d. Frederick Craig and Dorothy Margaret (Crimes) Munroe; m. Robert William Howard, May 15, 1965. BA, U. Calif., Berkeley, 1967; MS, Pace U., 1978. Reporter Vancouver (Can.) Sun, 1965; editl. assoc. Pacific N.W. Bell, Seattle, 1967-70, employee info. supr., 1970-72, advt. supr., 1972, project mgr. EEO, 1972-73, mktg. mgr., 1973, info. mgr., 1974-75; dist. mgr. media rels. AT&T, N.Y.C., 1975-77, dist. mgr. planning, 1977-78, dist. mgr. advt., 1978-80; media rels. mgr. Western Electric, N.Y.C., 1980-83; divsn. mgr. regional pub. rels. AT&T Info. Sys., Morristown, N.J., 1983-85; v.p., pub. rels. and comm. policy The Reader's Digest Assn., Inc., Pleasantville, N.Y., 1985-95; ret., 1995. Faculty profl. pub. course Stanford U., summer, 1993-95; bd. dirs. Andrew Corp. Author: On Deadline: Managing Media Relations, 1985, 2d edit., 1994, 3rd edit., 2000; contbg. author: Communicators' Guide to Marketing, 1987, Experts in Action: Inside Public Relations, 2d edit., 1988, Travel Industry Marketing, 1990,

The Business Speakers Almanac, 1994, Majoring in the Rest of your Life, 2000, Marketing Communications, 2002; newsletter editor Wash. State Rep. Ctrl. Com., 1973-74; contbg. editor Pub. Rels. Quar.; pres. The Reader's Digest Found.; adv. bd. Pub. Rels. News, Pub. Rels. Rev., Jour. Employee Comm. Mgmt., Ragan Pub. Rels. Jour. Corp. adv. bd. Caramoor Ctr. for Music and the Arts; bd. dirs. The Hundred Club of Westchester, Inc., The Lila Acheson Wallace Fund for Met. Mus. of Art, Madison Square Boy's and Girl's Club of N.Y.C. Mem. Women in Comm. (bd. dirs. Wash. state 1973), Internat. Assn. Bus. Communicators, Pub. Rels. Soc. Am., Nat. Press Women, Wash. Press Women (bd. dirs. 1972), Issues Mgmt. Assn., Pub. Rels. Seminar, Am. Cancer Soc., Arthur Page Soc., Wisemen, The Aspen Club, La Paloma Country Club, Gray Wolf Ski Club, San Juan Outdoor Club, Pagosa Springs Arts Coun., Pi Beta Phi. Anglican. Home and Office: PO Box 5499 Pagosa Springs CO 81147-5499

HOWARD, CAROLYN J. B. state legislator; b. Deland, Fla. married; 3 children. BS, Fla. A&M U.; MEd, Bowie State Coll. Supr. Chapt. I program Prince George's County; del. Dist. 24 Md. State Delegation, 1988-90, 91—, mem. ways and means com., mem. joint budget and audit com., vice chair county affairs com., chair transp. and telecomm. com., chair county affairs com., 1994-98; chair Ho. Dem. Caucus, 1999—, Md. Legis. Block Caucus, 1999—. Del. Dem. Nat. Conv., 1984, 92; dir. Dist. 3 Nat. Black Caucus of State Legislators. Named Disting. Alumni Nat. Assn. Equal Opportunity, 1983, 88; recipient Counselor's Adv. award PGMACD, 1988. Mem. NEA, ASCD, Md. State Tchrs. Assn., Prince George's County Educators Assn. (Outstanding Svc. in Politics award 1983), Nat. Coun. Negro Women (life), Bus. and Profl. Women's Club, Delta Sigma. Office: Md Ho of Reps Ste 204 State Capitol Annapolis MD 21401

HOWARD, CONSTANCE A. state representative; b. Chgo., Ill., Dec. 14, 1942; BS in Liberal Arts, MS in Corrections and Criminal Justice, Chgo. State U. Owner network mktg. bus.; mem. Ill. Ho. of Reps., 1994—. Alt. del. Dem. Nat. Conv., 1984, 1988; southside office coord. Braun for Senate, Chgo. Recipient LEAD award, Chgo. Tchrs. Union, Cert. of Appreciation, Ill. Coalition Against Domestic Violence, Twp. Officials Ill., Gapple Devel. Corp. Mem.: Nat. Polit. Congress Black Women, Ind. Voters Ill. (Best Freshman Voting Record Progressive Issues award), Cook County Dem. Women, Black Elected Officials Ill., Chgo. Urban League, Black Women's Network. Democrat. Office: 270-S Stratton Office Bldg Springfield IL 62706 Address: 8729 S State St Chicago IL 60619

HOWARD, CYNTHIA STOTTS, adult education educator; b. Mountain View, Calif., Mar. 25, 1964; d. Franklin Dee and Marjorie Opal (McCorkle) Stotts; m. John Avery Howard, Sept. 14, 1985; children: Amanda, Laurel, Gwen. BS, Stanford U., 1985, MS, 1987, PhD, 1993. Software engr. ASK Computer Sys., Los Altos, Calif., 1984-86; freelance tech. writer Palo Alto, Calif., 1996—98; parent educator Palo Alto (Calif.) Adult Sch., 1999—. Mem. Child Care Adv. Com., Palo Alto, 1994-97; leader LaLeche League, Menlo Park/Palo Alto, 1996—. Mem. Cap and Gown (alumnae bd. dirs.), Tau Beta Pi, Phi Beta Kappa.

HOWARD, GAIL VERITA, special education educator; b. Mobile, Ala., Aug. 31, 1954; d. Freddie Joseph and Doris Margaret Howard. AS, S.D. Bishop C.C., Mobile, 1982; Bachelor's, Ala. State U., 2001, postgrad. Cert. mortician Ala. Mortician Christian Benevolent, Mobile, 1982—87; forensic pathologist technician State of Ala., Montgomery, 1987—2001, tchr. spl. edn., 2001—. Mem. choir St. John African Meth. Episc. Ch., Montgomery, 2001—03, mem. layman orgn., 2002—03, class leader. Mem.: Coun. Exceptional Children. Avocations: gardening, travel. Office: Floyd Elem Sch 630 Augusta Ave Montgomery AL 36106

HOWARD, GRAZELL, risk management executive; JD. Founder, CEO The Libra Group, Ltd., Charlotte, 1991—. V.p. Nat. Coalition 100 Black Women. Mem.: Entrepreneurial Leadership Cir. Office: Libra Group Ltd 1101 S Boulevard Ste 202 Charlotte NC 28203*

HOWARD, JANET, elementary school educator; b. Marion, Ala. d. James H. and Marie (Russell) H.; divorced; children: Stratford Howard, Reginald Antoine. AA, Loop Jr. Coll., Chgo., 1975; BS, Chgo. State U., 1979; MA, Nat. Coll. Edn., 1982; postgrad., Roosevelt U., 1995—. Dental asst. Dental Ofice Dr. Max Newsome, Chgo., 1970-72, Michael Reese Hosp., Chgo., 1972-75; tchr. spl. edn., bd. mem. for spl. people students South Met. Assn., Dalton, Ill., 1979-84; tchr. Chgo. Bd. Edn., 1985—. Union del. Langston Hughes Sch., Chgo., 1996—. Author: A Leader's Guide To Developing a Coherent Curriculum, 1996. Democrat. Baptist. Home: 9616 S Leavitt St Chicago IL 60643-1637 Office: Langston Hughes Sch 224 W 104th St Chicago IL 60628-2510

HOWARD, JANET C. former state legislator; m. Allen Howard; children: Shirle, Raymond, George. Student, Ea. Ky. U., U. Cin. Councilwoman City of Forest Park, Ohio; senator Ohio State Senate, Columbus. Mem. Nat. Fedn. Rep. Women; bd. dirs. Hamilton County Rep. Women's Club; mem. Beechwood PTA, Forest Park Commn. Forum, adv. coun. Winton Woods Sch., adv. bd. Hamilton County Human Svcs., task force Forest Park Quality of Life. Mem. Greenhills-Forest Park Kiwanis.

HOWARD, JOAN ALICE, artist; b. N.Y.C., Apr. 28, 1929; d. John Volkman and Mary Alice Devlin; m. Robert Thornton Howard, June 26, 1949; children: Barbara Jo, Robert Thornton Jr., Gregory Lyon, Brian Devlin. Student, Hunter Coll., 1947-48, UCLA, 1967-68, Los Angeles Valley Coll., 1970-71. Dir., choreographer Acad. Dance, Floral Park and Forest Hills, N.Y., 1947-57; dir. dance. Cath. Parochial schs., N.Y.C., Bklyn., and Floral Park, N.Y., 1948-55; chair dept. dance Molloy Coll., 1958-67; artist sta. KNBC-TV, L.A., 1967-74, NBC, N.Y.C., 1974-78, sta. WNBC-TV, N.Y.C., 1978-79; artistic dir. Brookville (N.Y.) Sch., 1980-85; tchr. adult continuing edn. Lewisboro (N.Y.) Sch. Sys., 1995-98; instr. Art Works, Litchfield, SC, 1998—; instr. Sumi-e painting Coastal Carolina U., SC, 2002—03, instr., 2003—04. Dir. dance N.Y.C. YMCA, 1948; founder, dir. Queens-Nassau Regional Dance Theatre, 1950-55; choreographer Molloy Coll. Dance Theatre, 1959-67; cons. pre-natal exercise, L.I., N.Y., 1980—; judge art show Westbury (N.Y.) Mural Project, 1979; art cons. Chase Manhattan Bank, 1994-96, curator Chase Manhattan Bank, Cross River, N.Y., 1993-94, art cons. 1996-97; instr. continuing edn. Lewisboro Cross River, N.Y., 1996, 97, 98, Ridgefield, Conn., 1996, 97, 98; instr., speaker in field; instr. adult edn., Ridgefield and Lewisboro, N.Y., 1995-99; instr. all media Painted Fern Ct. Studio, 1998-2000, Brockgreen Gardens Murrells Inlet, S.C., 1999-2000; instr. painting Brookgreen Gardens and Art Works, Litchfield, S.C., 2001; instr. art Coastal Carolina U., Conway, S.C., 2002-03. One-woman shows include Dime Savs. Bank, Manhasset, N.Y., 1986-87, Ridgefield (Conn.) Guild Gallery, 1989-90, 91, 92, 93, Nardin Gallery Fine Arts, 1990, Chase Manhattan Bank, 1990-97, Manhasset Libr. Gallery, 1990-91, Hutchinson Gallery L.I. U., 1991, Rose Gallery, Kent, Conn., 1991, 92, 93, 94, Chelsea House, N.Y., 1991, Plandone Gallery, L.I., 1991, Sacco's, Ridgefield, 1991, Great Neck (N.Y.) Libr. Gallery, 1991, N.Y. Inst. Tech., Greenvale, N.Y., 1992, 93, Chase Manhattan Bank, Cross River, N.Y., 1992-93, 95-96, 96-97, Hicksville (N.Y.) Gallery, 1993, Chase Manhattan Bank, N.Y., 1995-97, Burroughs Chapin Mus., Myrtle Beach, S.C., 2002 & 2003,Aldrich Mus., 1995, 96, Ridgefield Libr., 1997, Adam Broderick Image Group, mural project Logans, S.C., Januven Gallery, S.C., 2001-02; exhibited in group shows at Valley Ctr. Arts Gallery, L.A., 1968-72, Home Savs. & Loan Art Exhibits, L.A., 1969-70, Westwood Art Gallery, L.A., 1972, Onion Gallery, L.A., 1972, North Ridge Women's Ctr. Gallery, L.A., 1972, Great Neck (N.Y.) Ctr. Gallery, 1976, A&S Gallery, Manhasset, 1976, Gloria Vanderbilt Designers Showcase, 1978, Ridgefield (Conn.) Guild Artists, 1983, Manhasset Libr. Gallery, 1985-89, Great Neck House Gallery, 1986-87, Hutchins Gallery C.W. Post Coll., L.I., 1986-90 (awards 1986, 87, 88, 89, 90), Dime Savs. Bank, Manhasset, N.Y., European Am. Bank, 1988, Nardin Fine Arts, Cross River, N.Y., 1989, Plandome Gallery, N.Y.C., 1990, Aldrich Mus., 1992 93, Hicksville (N.Y.) Gallery, 1993, Ridgefield (Conn.) Guild of Artists Gallery, 1993, Rose Gallery, Hicksville Gallery, 1993, Chase Manhattan Bank, N.Y.C., 1993-94, Tchr. Cont. Edn. Lernsboro Sch. Dist., N.Y., 1995-96, Adam Broderick Image Group, Ridgefield, Conn., 1995-96, Navden Gallery, N.Y., 1996, Masters Art Show, Litchfield, S.C., 2001, Sea Mist Resort, Myrtle Beach. S.C., 2003, Burroughs Chapin Mus., Myrtle Beach, S.C., Rice Mus., Georgetown, S.C. others; exhibited in juried shows Nassau County Mus. Fine Arts, Roslyn, N.Y., 1985, Plandome Gallery, 1987-88, Great Neck House Gallery, 1986-89 (hon. mention), East Meadow Libr. Gallery, 1988, Freeport Gallery, 1988, Shelter Rock Gallery, 1989, Ridgefield Gallery Portrait Show, 1989-90, Ridgefield Artists' Guild, 1989, 93, Nardin Gallery, 1989, Hutchins Gallery L.I. U., 1991, Rose Gallery, Kent, Conn., 1991, 92, 94, Chelsea House Mus. Cultural Commn., 1991, Manhasset Gallery, 1990-91, Sacco, Ridgefield, 1991, Great Neck Libr. Gallery, 1991, Chase Manhattan Bank, Cross River, N.Y., 1992-94, 95, Tchrs. Art Yorktown Artists Club, 1994, Aldrich Mus., 1993-94, Ridgefield (Conn.) Art Guild Gallery, 1993, 95, 96, 97, Hicksville (N.Y.) Art Gallery, 1993, Chase Manhattan Bank, N.Y., 1993, 94, 95, 96, 97, 98, HBO, N.Y.C., 1995, Ridgefield Libr. Gallery, 1997, instr. Brookgreen Gardens, Lichtfield, SC; exhibitor (exhbn.) Art Works Gallery, Litchfield, S.C., 2000, Janssen Gallery, Pawley's Island, S.C., 2000; murals, Logan's Roadhouse, SC, Adam Broderick Image grp., CT, Art Works Litchfield, S.C., 2000-02; choreographer contemporary ballet Crucifixion, 1960, Persephone, 1961, Cubes of Truth, 1962, Somewhere, 1965; appeared on radio show Coast to Coast on a Bus, 1939-47; Broadway prodn. Lady in the Dark, 1940-42; performed ballet in TV show Stars of Tomorrow, 1942, Sleeping Beauty, 1942; creator 7 murals Logam Road House, North Myrtle Beach, S.C., 4 paintings Eastport (N.Y.) Animal Hosp.; executor commd. work at color workshops All Media, 1998-2000, numerous others. Dem. committeewoman, Glen Cove, N.Y., 1954-58. Recipient Del Rey Perpetual Race championship trophy, 1974, Little Sabot Perpetual Race trophy, 1972-74, So. Calif. Women's Sailing Conf. sabot championship, 1972-74, 1st Woman trophy Olympic Regatta, 1973. Mem. Dance Educators Am., Manhasset Art Assn., Women's Sailing Com. of U.S. Yacht Racing Union (fund raiser 1980-81), Am. Women's C. of C. L.A., Tri-County Artists Ridgefield Art Guild, Waccemaw Art & Crafts Guild, Georgetown Watercolor Soc. Avocation: racing sail boats and rally cars. Home and Office: 4545 Painted Fern Ct Murrells Inlet SC 29576-6380

HOWARD, JOANNE FRANCES, marketing executive, researcher, funeral director; b. St. Louis, Feb. 5, 1953; d. Frank Henry and Evelyn Julia (Haeckel) Spellazza; m. Claude Lorrain Howard, May 20, 1978; children: Amy Julia, Laura Ann. BA, U. Mo., St. Louis, 1975; MS, Western Ill. U., 1976. Lic. funeral dir. Analyst Street Industries, Inc., St. Louis, 1977-78; rsch. analyst Gallup & Robinson Co., Princeton, N.J., 1978-80, Jack Eckerd Corp., Clearwater, Fla., 1980-82, sr. rsch. analyst, 1982-88; mktg. cons. Howard Assocs., 1986—; funeral dir., extended care coord. Pugh Funeral Home, Golden City, Mo., 1992—. Cons. Anson Lee Rector, Inc., Tarpon Springs, Fla., 1982—83, Med-Op Clinics, Tarpon Springs, 1983—88; analyst cons. H. L. Pugh Assocs. Consulting, Golden City, 1992—. Editor: (newsletter) The Dead Beat-A Caregiver's Soapbox. Active Pinebrook Homeowners Assn., Largo, Fla., 1983—84. Mem.: Mo. Inst. Funeral Profls., Mo. Funeral Dirs. Assn., Nat. Funeral Dirs. Assn., Am. Mktg. Assn. (past sec.-treas., newsletter editor Fla. W. Coast chpt. 1982—83). Democrat. Home and Office: 708 SE 70th Ln Golden City MO 64748-8152 E-mail: editor@thedead-beat.com.

HOWARD, JULIA C. state legislator; b. Salisbury, N.C., Aug. 20, 1944; d. Allen Leary and Ruth Elizabeth (Snider) Craven; m. Abe N. Howard Jr., 1962 (dec. Mar. 1994); children: Amedia Paige, Abe N. III. Grad., Davie H.S., 1962. Owner Davie Builders Inc., Howard Realty & Ins. Agy. Inc.; mem. N.C. Ho. of Reps., Raleigh, 1989—. Chmn. bd. trustees Davie County Hosp., 1978-85. Commr. Town of Mocksville, N.C., 1981-88; mem. youth coun. First United Meth. Ch., 1974-80, chmn. coun. of ministries, 1979-81. Mem. Realtors Assn. (pres. Davie County Bd. 1972, state dir. 1973-75), Sertoma Club. Home: 203 Magnolia Ave Mocksville NC 27028-2911 Office: NC Ho of Reps State Capitol Raleigh NC 27601-1096

HOWARD, KAREN, music educator, conductor; b. Bristol, Conn., Oct. 20, 1970; d. Lois and Peter Howard; m. Benjamin Thomas, June 26, 1999. MusM in Edn., U. Hartford, Conn., 1995. Cert. tchr. Conn., 1993. Vocal music tchr. East Hartford Pub. Schs., Conn., 1993—2002, West Hartford Pub. Schs., Conn., 2002—. Choral condr. Conn. Children's Chorus, West Hartford, 2002—. Musician. Choral resource cons. Conn. Music Educators Assn., Hartford, Conn., 2000—03. Named Elem. Music Educator of the Yr., Conn. Music Educators Assn., 2002-2003, Tchr. of the Yr., Wal-Mart of Rocky Hill, 2001-2002. Mem.: Music Educators Nat. Conf. (choral curricular resource 2000—03), Am. Choral Dirs. Assn., Am. Orff Schulwerk Assn. (Shields-Gillespie scholarship 1994). Office: Webster Hill Elem Sch 125 Webster Hill Blvd West Hartford CT 06107

HOWARD, KAREN S. retail executive; b. Little Rock, Feb. 21, 1965; d. James Neilly and Zeola Marie Howard; m. Frank Daniel Brown, Jan. 16, 1996 (div. Oct. 1998); 1 child, Frank Daniel II. BS, Western Carolina U., 1993. Store mgr. Lane Bryant, Atlanta, 1989-91; dist. mgr. One Price Clothing, Atlanta, 1991-93; area mgr. Mervyns Dept. Stores, Atlanta, 1993-95; regional visual merchandiser Pier 1 Imports, Atlanta, 1995-97, internat. visual tng. mgr. Ft. Worth, 1997-98, internat. merchandising mgr., 1997-2000, interactive merchandising mgr., 1999-2000; e-bus. mdse. dir. The Container Store, Dallas, 2000—. Home: 315 Ashford Pkwy Atlanta GA 30338-5530 E-mail: Karenhoward221@cs.com.

HOWARD, KATHLEEN, computer company executive; b. Norman, Okla., Nov. 3, 1947; d. Robert Adrian and Jane Elizabeth (Morgens) H.; m. Lawrence W. Osgood, Aug. 10, 1968 (div. Sept. 1970); m. Norman Edlo Gibat, Oct. 15, 1971. Student, U. Okla., 1966—68. Typesetter Selenby Press, Norman, 1968-72; owner, pres. Noguska Industries, Fostoria, Ohio, 1973—; co-founder Home Wine Mchts., Chgo., 1976; cons. Bechtel Corp., Ann Arbor, Mich., 1980—, Gaithersburg, Md., 1980—; chairperson Am. Software Project, 1985; ptnr. Popular Topics Pubs., 1993—; cons. Xerox Corp., Rochester, NY, 1998—. Author: All You Need to Know About MSDOS, 1993; co-author, illustrator: Lore of Still Building, 1972; co-author: Making Wine, Beer and Merry, 1973, Computer Comix Mag., 1986; pres. Popular Topics Press, Inc., also jours. and bus. mgmt. software. Trees. United Way of Fostoria, 1986-88, 2d v.p. 1988-90; bd. dirs. Pvt. Industry Coun., 1988-90. Recipient Founders award Home Wine and Beer Trade Assn. Chgo., 1976. Mem. BBB, Nat. Fedn. Ind. Bus., C. of C. (bd. dirs. 1986-92), Employer's Assn. Toledo, Altrusa Internat. Club (sec. Fostoria chpt. 1984-85, pres. 1986-88, editor dist. #5 1988-90, pres. 2001-03). Avocations: painting, printing, travel, reading. Office: Noguska Industries 741 N Countyline St Fostoria OH 44830-1586 Office Phone: 419-435-0404. E-mail: knoguska@yahoo.com.

HOWARD, LOU DEAN GRAHAM, elementary school educator; b. Conway, Ark., Aug. 11, 1935; d. Nathan Eldridge and Martha Regina (Sutherland) Graham; m. Robert Hunt Howard, June 4, 1961; 1 child, Kenneth Paul. BSE, U. Cen. Ark., 1957; MA, Vanderbilt U., 1960. Cert. sch. adminstr., prin./supr., curriculum specialist, mentor, grad. elem. Elem. tchr. Hughes (Ark.) Pub. Schs., 1957-59; supervisory tchr. Peabody Demonstration Sch., Nashville, 1959-61; elem. tchr. Orange County Pub. Schs., Orlando, Fla., 1965-68; elem. tchr., K-5 adminstr. Westchester Acad., High Point, N.C., 1968-77; tchr. alternative learning ctr.-mid. sch. Randolph County Pub. Schs., Archdale-Trinity, 1978; elem. tchr. Greensboro (N.C.) Pub. Schs., 1978-93, Guilford County Schs., High Point, N.C., 1993-97, ret., 1997. Contbr. articles to newspapers and AAUW Bull. Active Stephen Ministry, commnd. Stephen Leader, 2002; citizen ambassador program of People to People Internat. del. to U.S./China Joint Conf. on Women's Issues, Beijing, 1995, precinct chmn., county exec. com., state exec. com. of Dem. Party; mem. High Point (N.C.) Racial Justice Task Force. Mem.: AAUW (pres. N.C. state 1982—84, assn. nominating com. 1985—87, pres. High Point br. 1988—90, co-pres. 1998—2002, N.C. state parliamentarian 2002—04, Gift honoree Ednl. Found.), NEA (sch. rep., mem. instrnl. and profl. devel. com.), ASCD (archivist 2002), Clan Graham Soc. (sec. 1982—2002, soc. archivist 2003—, archivist 2002—, Disting. Svc. award), N.C. Coun. of Women's Orgns., Peabody Coll. Elem. Coun. (sec.), Ind. Schs. Assn., Assn. Childhood Edn. Internat. (past pres.), Order of The Golden Thistle (charter), Phi Delta Kappa, Delta Kappa Gamma (rsch. chair 1998—2000). Methodist. Home: 1228 Kensington Dr High Point NC 27262-7316

HOWARD, LYN JENNIFER, medical educator; b. Buxton, U.K., Jan. 19, 1938; came to U.S., 1965; naturalized, 1971; d. Peter and Bess (Donnelly) Marsh; m. Burtis Howard, Mar. 13, 1965 (div. 1988); children: Peter Howard, Thia Howard; m. Jack Alexander, Sept. 10, 1995. BA, Oxford U., 1960, MA, BM, BCh, 1964. Diplomate Am. Bd. Internal Medicine, diplomate Am. Bd. Nutrition. Intern London Hosp., 1964-65, Kans. City Med. Ctr., 1965-66, resident, 1966-70; fellow in clin. nutrition and gastroenterology Vanderbilt Hosp., 1971-73; dir. clin. nutrition program Albany (N.Y.) Med. Coll., 1973-80, asst. prof. medicine, pediat., 1973-76, assoc. prof. medicine, pediat., 1977-84, prof. medicine, 1984—, head divsn. clin. nutrition, 1986—. Asst. dir. Clin. Studies Ctr., Albany Med. Ctr., 1973-78; attending physician Albany Med. Ctr. Hosp., 1973—; attending physician, cons. clin. nutrition Albany VA Hosp., 1973—; cons. pediat. gastroenterology St. Peter's Hosp., Albany, 1974—; med. dir. Albany Home Health Resources, 1991-92; mem. working group Nat. Commn. Digestive Diseases, 1977; mem. NIH Consensus Devel. Conf., 1978, nutrition rsch. directions, 1979, spl. study sect. clin. nutrition rsch. units, 1980, nutrition study sect., 1989-93; cons. AMA Drug Evaluations, 1982, Medicare, Blue Cross/Blue Shield S.C., 1987—; keynote spkr. Australian Soc. Parenteral and Enteral Nutrition, Perth, 1993, 1st Clin. Nutrition Symposium, Kuala Lumpor, Malaysia, 1994. Contbg. editor Nutrition Reviews, 1981-87, 89; mem. editl. bd. Jour. Drug-Nutrient Interactions, 1984, Contemporary Issues in Clin. Nutrition, 1985, Jour. Am. Soc. Parenteral and Enteral Nutrition, 1987-90; contbr. articles, abstracts to profl. jours., chpts. to books. Exec. dir. Oley Found. for Home Parenteral and Enteral Nutrition, 1983-87, pres., 1987-91, med. dir., 1991; pres. Camphill Found., Pa., 1994. Recipient Clifton C. Thorne Cmty. Svc. award, 1990, Physician of Yr. award Albany chpt. Crohn's Colitis Found. Am., 1991; elected 1st woman mem. Great Lakes Interurban Club, 1990; Major County scholar, 1956; grantee Nutrition Found., 1973-79, U.S. Dept. Agriculture, 1978-81, William F. Donner Found., 1983, Oley Found. for Home Parenteral and Enteral Nutrition Patients, 1983—, Home Health Care of Am., 1983-88, Hosp. for Incurables Found., 1987-88, 91, Schaeffer Found. for Faculty Devel., 1988. Fellow Royal Coll. Physicians, Am. Coll. Physicians, Am. Coll. Nutrition (dir. 1985-88); mem. Am. Bd. Nutrition (dir. 1980, pres. 1982-84), Brit. Med. Assn., Am. Soc. Parenteral and Enteral Nutrition (abstract selection com. 1980, nutrition support standards com. 1984, future directions com. 1991, OASIS working group 1991-92, award 1992), Am. Soc. Clin. Nutrition (rsch. com. 1978, edn. com. 1979, councilor 1982-85, chair post grad. clin. nutrition tng. com. 1983-88, clin. practice in health and disease 1991), Am. Inst. Nutrition, Am. Gastroent. Assn. (co-organizer post grad. tng. course 1987, tng. and edn. com. 1988-91, abstract selection com. 1989), N.Am. Soc. Pediat. Gastroenterology, Am. Fedn. Clin. Rsch. (abstract selection com. 1986), Alpha Omega Alpha. Office: Albany Med Coll Albany NY 12208

HOWARD, MARILYN, school system administrator; BA in Edn., U. Idaho, 1960, MSc in Edn., 1965; EdD, Brigham Young U., 1986; postgrad., Idaho State U. adj. faculty Idaho State U., U. Idaho. Prin. Moscow West Park Elementary Sch., 1988—99; supervisor, devel. pre-school Moscow sch. dists., 1996—99; supt. pub. instrn. Idaho State Dept. Edn., Boise, Idaho, 1999—. Past state pres. Internat. Reading Assn., nat. rsch. and studies com; bd. dirs. State Bd. Edn., State Land Bd., Northwest Regional Edn. Lab. Office: Idaho State Dept Edn 650 W State St PO Box 83720 Boise ID 83720-0027 E-mail: mhoward@sde.state.id.us.

HOWARD, MILDRED, sculptor; b. San Francisco, 1945; AA, cert. in fashion arts, Coll. Alameda, 1977; MFA in Fiberworks, John F. Kennedy U., 1985. One-woman shows include Mill Valley (Calif.) Old Post Office, 1984, Dade County Libr., Miami, Fla., 1985, Calif. State U., Hayward, 1987, Headlands Ctr. for the Arts, Sausalito, Calif., 1991, San Francisco Art Inst., 1991, Gallery Paule Anglim, San Francisco, 1991, 93, INTAR, N.Y.C., 1992, U. Art Gallery, Sonoma State U., Rohnert Park, Calif., 1992, San Jose (Calif.) Mus. Art, 1994, Hammonds House Galleries, Atlanta, 1994, Capp St. Project, San Francisco, 1994; group exhbns. include Security Pacific Gallery, San Francisco, 1992, Lew Allen Gallery, Santa Fe, 1992, Shea & Bornstein Gallery, Santa Monica, 1992, Creative Time, N.Y.C., 1992, Berkeley Art Ctr., 1992, Nina Nielsen Gallery, Boston, 1993, New Mus. Contemporary Art, N.Y.C., 1993, Calif. Crafts Mus., San Francisco, 1994, U. Calif. Berkeley Mus. Art, Sci. and Culture, 1994, Laney Coll., Oakland, Calif., 1994, The Mus. at Blackhawk, Danville, Calif., 1994, Hampton (Va.) U. Mus., 1994, Gallery Resche, Paris, 1994, Yerba Buena Ctr. for the Arts, San Francisco, 1994, Installation Gallery, San Diego, 1994, Jewett Hall Gallery, U. Maine, Augusta, 1994, CCAC, Oakland, 1994, Oakland Mus., 1994, Louis Stern Fine Arts, L.A., 1995, Gallery Concord, 1995, others; represented in permanent collections Oakland Mus., Wadsworth Athaneum, Hartford, Conn., Rene and Veronica di Rosa Found., Napa, Calif., pvt. collections. Recipient Bank of Am. award, San Francisco, 1975, Small Projects award Inter Arts Marin, San Rafael, Calif., 1984, Adaline Kent award San Francisco Art Inst., 1991; fellow in mixed media Calif. Arts Coun., 1990, Lila A. Wallace/Reader's Digest Internat. Traveling fellow, 1992-93. Office: c/o Porter Troupe Gallery 301 Spruce St San Diego CA 92103-5626

HOWARD, MURIEL A. academic administrator; Grad., CUNY; MA in Edn., SUNY, Buffalo, 1973, D in Ednl. Orgn., Adminstrn., Policy, 1985. Asst. dir. Univ. Learning Ctr. SUNY, Buffalo, 1974-81, dir. University Learning Ctr., 1981-84, dir. Ednl. Opportunity Ctr., 1984-87, assoc. vice provost for spl. programs, 1987-90, asst. to pres., 1990-91, dep. to pres., 1991-92, v.p. pub. svc. and urban affairs, 1992-95; pres. Buffalo State Coll., N.Y., 1996—. Co-founder Buffalo Prep; co-chair adv. task force on gen. edn. SUNY Provost; bd. dirs. Merchants Mutual Ins. Co., Fleet Bank, Grace Manor Nursing Home, Greater Buffalo Devel. Found., Buffalo Mus. of Sci., Studio Area Theatre. Bd. dirs. United Way Buffalo and Erie County (campaign chair 1999); mem. Erie County Exec.'s transition team (chair subcom. Youth Svcs. and Edn.). Recipient Governor's State Divsn. of Women award, Am. Jewish Com. Inst. of Human Rels. award, Disting. Alumni award U. Buffalo, Disting. Alumna award Staten Island Coll., Educator of Yr. award Black Educators Assn. of Western N.Y., 1991, award for Community Svc. Minority Bar Assn. W. N.Y., Disting. Alumnus award Catholic Campus Ministry, Award of Excellence Project WIN's, 1993; charter inductee W. N.Y. Women's Hall of Fame. Mem. Am. Assn. State Colls. and Universities (bd. mem.); mem. pres.'s bd. Nat. Collegiate Athletics Assn. Office: Buffalo State Coll GC 517 1300 Elmwood Ave Buffalo NY 14222-1004

HOWARD, NANCY E. lawyer; b. Ft. Wayne, Ind., Aug. 13, 1951; BA, Stanford U., 1973, JD, 1977. Bar: Calif. 1977. Mem. Tuttle & Taylor, L.A., 1977—. Contbr. articles to profl. jours. Mem. Order of Coif., Phi Beta Kappa. Office: Tuttle & Taylor 355 S Grand Ave Fl 40 Los Angeles CA 90071-1560

HOWARD, SANDY, motion picture producer; b. N.Y.C., Aug. 1, 1927; d. George and Victoria (Ampolsk) Sokoloff. Student, Fla. So. Coll. Prin. Sandy Howard Prodns., Los Angeles, 1947—. Producer over 50 TV series and over 20 motion pictures including A Man Called Horse, 1970, Neptune Factor, 1973, Sky Riders, 1976, The Last Castle, 1976, Return of a Man Called Horse, 1976, The Island of Dr. Moreau, 1977, The Silent Flute, 1978, Jaguar Lives, 1979, Death Ship, 1980, Savage Harvest, 1981, Deadly Force, 1983, Triumph of a Man Called Horse, 1984, Perils of the Deep, One Step to Hell, Man in the Wilderness, The Battle, PrettyKill, 1987; co-producer Meteor, 1979, Circle of Iron, 1979, Vice Squad, 1982, Hambone and Millie, 1984, Avenging Angel, 1985, The Boys Next Door, 1985, Hollywood Vice Squad, 1986, KGB: The Secret War (Lethal), 1986. Recipient numerous TV awards Mem. Dirs. Guild Am., Writers Guild Am. Office: World Entertainment Bus Network 8755 Shoreham Dr Apt 403 Los Angeles CA 90069-2226

HOWARD, SUSAN J. small business owner; b. Albuquerque, May 6, 1963; d. John R. and Betty Finley Howard; m. Hugh L. Frazier Jr. (div. 1995). BA, Emory U., 1996; cert. in Graphic Arts, Atlanta Coll. Art, 2002. Dir. rsch. Woodruff Arts Ctr., Atlanta, 1997—99; corp. rels. mgr. ARC, Atlanta, 1999—2000; devel. mgr. Atlanta Coll. Art, 2000—02; owner Mission Accomplished, Inc., 2002—. Singer: (music rec.) The Right Tool for the Job, 2000; illustrator My New Best Friend, 2003, My New Furry Pal, 2003.

HOWARD-PEEBLES, PATRICIA N. clinical cytogeneticist; b. Lawton, Okla., Nov. 24, 1941; d. J. Marion and R. Leona (prestidge) Howard; m. Thomas M. Peebles, Aug. 16, 1975. BSEd, U. Ctrl. Okla., 1963; student, Randolph-Macon Coll. Women, 1964; PhD in Zoology (Genetics), U Tex. at Austin, 1969. Diplomate Am. Bd. Med. Genetics; cert. clin. cytogeneticist, med. geneticist. Sci. and history tchr. Piedmont (Okla.) Pub. Schs., 1963-64; biochem. technician biochemistry sect. biology divsn. Oak Ridge (Tenn.) Nat. Lab., 1964-66; instr. rsch. pediatrics dept. pediatrics, instr. cytotech. U. Okla. Health Scis. Ctr., Oklahoma City, 1971-72; asst. prof., dir. Cytogenetics Lab. U. So. Miss., Hattiesburg, 1973-77, assoc. prof., dir. Cytogenetics Lab., 1977-80; assoc. prof. dept. pub. health, staff Lab. Med. Genetics U. Ala., Birmingham, 1980-81; assoc. prof., dir. Cytogenetics Lab. dept. pathology U. Tex. Health Sci. Ctr., Dallas, 1981-85, prof., dir. Cytogenetics Lab., 1985-87; prof. dept. human genetics Med. Coll. Va., Richmond, 1987-2001; clin. cytogeneticist, dir. postnatal lab. Genetics & IVF Inst., Fairfax, Va., 1987-98, co-dir. cytogenetics lab., 1998-2000, genetic, cytogenetic cons., 2000—. Am. Cancer Soc. postdoctoral fellow dept. human genetics U. Mich. Med. Sch., Ann Arbor, 1969-70, dept. human genetics and devel. Coll. Physicians and Surgeons, Columbia U., N.Y.C., 1970-71; genetic cons. Ellisville (Miss.) State Sch., 1973-80; attending staff dept. pathology Parkland Meml. Hosp., Dallas County Hosp. Dist., 1981-87; mem. sci. adv. com. Fragile X Found., 1985-2002; mem. Internat. Standing Com. on Human Cytogenetic Nomenclature, 1991-96. Contbr. articles to profl. jours., chpts. to books; reviewer Am. Jour. Human Genetics, Am. Jour. Med. Genetics, Clin. Genetics, Human Genetics. Fellow Am. Coll. Med. Genetics (founding mem.); mem. AAAS, Am. Soc. Human Genetics, Assn. Genetic Technologists, Tex. Genetics Soc. (chmn. planning com. ann. meeting 1984), Delta Kappa Gamma, Sigma Xi. Baptist. Personal E-mail: phpeebles@yahoo.com.

HOWARD-WYNE, JOSIE, elementary school educator; b. Columbus, Miss., Nov. 6, 1947; d. Frank Earl Howard and Annie Lee Nelson-Howard; m. William James Wyne, Jr.; 1 child, Lisa Shennet Stinson. BS, Western Mich. U., Kalamazoo, 1972, Masters, 1976. Tchr./instructional specialist Kalamazoo Pub. Schs., 1972—. Mem.: NEA, Kairos Dwelling (bd. dirs. 1998—99), Chain Lake Dist. Assn. (treas. 2002—), Kalamazoo Ednl. Assn., Northside Assn. for Ednl. Advancement (sec. 1986—), Dulcet Club (program chmn. 1975—), Delta Sigma Theta (Golden Life mem. 1975—), Alpha Delta Kappa. Baptist. Avocations: singing, travel, sewing, crossword puzzles, mentoring. Home: 4202 Kingsbrook Dr Kalamazoo MI 49006 Office: Kalamazoo Pub Sch 1220 Howard St Kalamazoo MI 49006

HOWE, FLORENCE, English educator, writer; b. N.Y.C., Mar. 17, 1929; d. Samuel and Frances (Stilly) Rosenfeld AB, Hunter Coll., 1950; AM, Smith Coll., 1951; postgrad., U. Wis., 1951—54; DHL (hon.), New Eng. Coll., 1977, Skidmore Coll., 1979, DePauw U., 1987, SUNY Coll., Old Westbury, 1992, Pace U., 2000, Chatham Coll., 2000, U. Wis., 2004. Tchg. asst. U. Wis., Madison, 1951-54; instr. Hofstra Coll., 1954-57; lectr. English Queens Coll., CUNY, 1956-57; asst. prof. English Goucher Coll., 1960-71; prof. humanities and Am. studies SUNY, Old Westbury, 1971-85; prof. English City. Coll. and Grad. Sch., CUNY, 1985-95, Grad. Sch./CUNY, 1995—2001; pres., dir. The Feminist Press at CUNY, 1970—2000. Vis. prof. U. Utah, 1973, 75, U. Wash., 1974, John F. Kennedy Inst. Am. Studies Free U. Berlin, 1978, Oberlin Coll., 1978, Denison U., 1979, MLA Summer Inst. U. Ala., 1979, Coll. of Wooster, 1980; found. edit. Women's Studies Quarterly, 1972-82. Author: The Conspiracy of the Young, 1970, Seven Years Later: Women's Studies Programs in 1976, 1977, Myths of Coeducation: Selected Essays, 1964-1984, 1984; editor: (with Ellen Bass) No More Masks! An Anthology of Poems by Women, 1973, Women and the Power to Change, 1975; (with Nancy Hoffman) Women Working: An Anthology of Stories and Poems, 1979; (with Suzanne Howard, Mary Jo Boehm Strauss) Everywoman's Guide to Colleges and Universities, 1982; (with Marsha Saxton) With Wings: An Anthology of Literature by and About Disabled Women, 1987; (with John Mack Faragher) Women and Higher Education in American History, 1988, Tradition and the Talents of Women, 1991, No More Masks, An Anthology of 20th Century American Women Poets, 1993, The Politics of Women's Studies: Testimony from 30 Founding Mothers, 2000, (with Jean Casella) Almost Touching the Skies: Women's Coming of Age Stories, 2000; mem. editl. bd. Women's Studies: An Interdisciplinary Jour., 1971—, SIGNS: Women in Culture and Society, 1974-80, Jour. Edn., 1976—, The Correspondence of Lydia Marie Child, 1977-81, Research in the Humanities, 1977—; contbr. articles to profl. jours. Named NEH fellow, 1971—73, Ford Found. fellow, 1974—75, Fulbright fellow, India, 1977, Mellon fellow, Wellesley Coll., 1979, Rockefeller Found. fellow, T. Bellagio, 1997; recipient Mina Shaughnessy award, Fund for Improvement of Post-Secondary Edn., 1982—83, U.S. Dept. State grant, 1983, 1993, Team awards, Rockefeller Found., Bellagio, 2001—04. Office: The Feminist Press at CUNY 365 Fifth Ave New York NY 10016-4309 Office Phone: 212-817-7218. E-mail: fhowe@gc.cuny.edu.

HOWE, MARTHA MORGAN, microbiologist, educator; b. N.Y.C., Sept. 29, 1945; d. Charles Hermann and Miriam Hudson (Wagner) M.; m. Terrance Gary Cooper. AB, Bryn Mawr Coll., 1966; PhD, MIT, 1972. Postdoctoral fellow Cold Spring Harbor Lab, N.Y., 1972-74; asst. prof. bacteriology U. Wis., Madison, 1975-77, assoc. prof., 1977-81, prof., 1981-84, Vilas prof., 1984-86; Van Vleet prof. virology U. Tenn., Memphis, 1986—. Mem. genetic biology rev. panel NSF, 1980-82; mem. gen. rsch. support rev. com. NIH, Bethesda, 1982-86, mem. microbial physiology and genetics 2 study sec., 1997-2001; mem. sci. adv. com. instnl. rsch. grants Am. Cancer Soc., 1991-94. Assoc. editor Virology, 1983-92, Genetics, 1994; mem. editorial bd. Jour. Bacteriology, 1985-90; contbr. articles to profl. jours. and books. Recipient Rsch. Career Devel. award NIH, 1978; H.I. Romnes Faculty fellow U. Wis., 1981; Amoco Teaching award U. Wis., 1981. Fellow Am. Acad. Microbiology (bd. govs. 1991-99); mem. Am. Soc. Microbiology (chmn. divsn. H 1983, councillor divsn. H 1989-91, chmn. com. on awards 1990-96, pres.-elect 1999-2000, pres. 2000-2001, past pres. 2001-2002, Eli Lilly award 1985, ASM Founders Disting. Svc. award 1999), Am. Soc. Biochemistry and Molecular Biology, Genetics Soc. Am. (bd. dirs. 1989-91, program com. 1989-90). Office: U Tenn Dept Molecular Scis 858 Madison Ave Memphis TN 38163-0001 E-mail: mhowe@utmem.edu.

HOWE, SANDRA JO, library director; b. St. Louis, Sept. 30, 1960; d. Raymond Lee and Elizabeth Ann Griffin; m. Steven Howe, June 24, 1977 (div. Nov. 1978); children: Beth Marie Howe, Ricky A. Rudd. Student, Culver-Stockton Coll., 1997-99. Pharmacy technician Grand Leader Pharmacy, Canton, Mo., 1981-87; mgr., cons. Mo. Pizza Co., Canton, 1993-96; asst. libr. Canton Pub. Libr., 1996-97, dir., 1997—. Mem. ALA, ACLU, Mo. Libr. Assn. Avocations: reading, promoting literacy, nature walks, gardening. Office: Canton Pub Libr 409 Lewis St Canton MO 63435-1529 E-mail: sjhowe@yahoo.com.

HOWE, TINA, playwright; b. N.Y.C., Nov. 21, 1937; d. Quincy and Mary (Post) H.; m. Norman L. Levy, Aug. 31, 1961; children: Eben, Dara. BA, Sarah Lawrence Coll., Bronxville, N.Y., 1959; LittD (hon.), Bowdoin Coll., Brunswick, Maine, 1988, Whittier Coll., 1997. Adj. prof. playwriting NYU, 1983—; vis. prof. Hunter Coll., N.Y.C., 1990—. Author: (plays) The Nest, 1969, Museum, 1976, The Art of Dining, 1979, Appearances, 1982, Painting Churches, 1983, Coastal Disturbances, 1986 (Tony award nomination for best play 1987), Approaching Zanzibar, 1989, One Shoe Off, 1993, Pride's Crossing, 1997; Rembrandts Gift, 2002, publs. include Coastal Disturbances: Four Plays by Tina Howe, 1989, Approaching Zanzibar and other plays, 1995, Birth and After Birth, 1995, Prides Crossing, 1998. Nat. Endowment of Arts fellow, 1985, 95, Guggenheim fellow, 1990; Rockefeller grantee, 1984; recipient Obie award, 1983, Outer Critic's Circle award, 1983, Acad. award in Lit. Am. Acad. Arts and Letters, 1993, N.Y. Drama Critics Circle award, 1997-98, Sidney Kingsley award, 1998. Mem. Dramatists Guild (mem. coun. 1990—). Office: care Biff Liff William Morris Agy 1325 Ave of Americas New York NY 10019

HOWE, VIRGINIA HOFFMAN, nurse administrator; b. Buffalo, Apr. 14, 1940; d. George C. Jr. and Mabel (Parrish) Hoffman; m. Lawrence T. Howe, Apr. 11, 1970; children: Daniel George, Timothy Kelly. AAS, Trocaire, 1977; BS in Community Health Nursing, SUNY, Buffalo, 1986. RN, N.Y. Assoc. coord. oper. rm. Buffalo Gen. Hosp., head nurse oper. rm. gen. surgery, oper. rm. staff nurse, nurse clinician otolaryngology and ear, nose, throat dept., nurse clinician divsn. plastic and reconstructive surgery, nursing instr., educator, discharge planning nurse, cmty. health nurse, nurse paralegal, infection control nurse, supr., cons.; nurse legal cons. Cons. in field. Mem.: Nurse Paralegal Cons., Legal Nurse Cons., Assn. Operating Rm. Nurses.

HOWELL, BRADLEY SUE, librarian; b. McKinney, Tex., July 15, 1933; d. Jessie Leonard and Carrie Pearl (Nickerson) LaFon; m. Richard Dunn Howell, May 18, 1957; children: Mark Richard, Celeste Ella, Jane Elizabeth. BS in Edn., So. Meth. U., 1955; MS in Libr. Sci., East Tex. State U., 1968. Tchr. J.B. Hood Jr. High Sch., Dallas, 1955-56, Mineral Wells (Tex.) Jr. High Sch., 1957-58; libr. Ascher Silberstein Sch., Dallas, 1963, San Jacinto Sch., Dallas, 1960-62, 65-81, Woodrow Wilson High Sch., Dallas, 1981—. Pres. Tex. United Meth. Hist. Soc., 1980—84, v.p., 2000—; sec. South Ctr. Jurisdiction Archives and history of United Meth. Ch., 1980—88; v.p. local ch. sect. The United Meth. Hist. Soc., 1989—95, chmn., 1995—99; pres. PTA Woodrow Wilson H.S., 1983—84; leader Camp Fire, Inc., 1970—; v.p. South Ctrl. Jurisdiction, Archives and History The United Meth. Ch., 2000—04. Recipient Wakan award Camp Fire, Inc., 1976, Hilteni award, 1978, Sawnequas award, 1988, Gulick Vol. award, 1998, Terrific Tchr. award Tex. PTA, 1984, Jim Collins Outstanding award, 1986, Honor award Nat. Sch. Pub. Relation Assn., 1986, Dallas Positive Parents award, 1987, Golden Flame award, 1990; elected Woodrow Wilson H.S. Hall of Fame, 1999. Mem.: Am. Libr. Svcs. to Children (Newbery com. 1980), Tex. Libr. Assn. (chmn. archives and history roundtable 1990—92), Tex. Assn. Sch. Librs., Dallas Assn. Sch. Librs. (pres. 1975—76), Freedoms Found. and Valley Forge (pres. Dallas chpt. 1997—99, v.p. edn. 2003—), Pi Lambda Theta (Alpha Sigma chpt. pres. 1997—2002), Delta Psi Kappa, Phi Delta Kappa, Alpha Delta Pi, Delta Kappa Gamma (state achievement award 1988, Golden Gift Leadership mgmt. award 1985). Democrat. Home: 722 Ridgeway St Dallas TX 75214-4453 Office: Woodrow Wilson High Sch 100 S Glasgow Dr Dallas TX 75214-4598

HOWELL, CATHERINE JEANINE, retired secondary school educator; b. Benton, Ill, Apr. 15, 1935; d. Lloyd William Reed and Lena Pearl (Armstrong) Goodin; m. Charles Lindy Barnfield, Apr. 13, 1950 (div. Apr. 23, 1973); m. Charles E. Howell, June 28, 1975; children: Alan Reed, Robert, Timothy Michael Barnfield; stepchildren: Crystal Lea, Carla Sue. A in Technol., So. Ill. U., 1962, BA, 1968, MS in Edn., 1976, postgrad. specialist, 1986. Cert. educator and supr., Ill. Clk. Kroger, Benton, Ill., 1957-60; elem. tchr. Benton Elem. Sch. Dist. 47, 1968-70; secondary art tchr. Marion Cmty. Unit Sch. Dist. 2, Ill., 1970-94; ret., 1994. Instr. art John A. Logan C.C., Carterville, Ill., 1975-89, 97-98, instr. vocat. edn., 1992, part-time acad. instr. art, 1997-98, part time asst. literacy coord., 2001—; cons. in field. Prin. work includes Strings of Creation, 1988, Portrait Sketch of Brenda Edgar, 1991; currently, part time asst. Lit. Coord. @ John A. Logan CC, Carterville, Ill. Art judge DuQuoin (Ill.) State Fair, 1990-91; mem. Ill. State Bd. Edn. Leadership Canf., 1989-98; co-founder Downstate Art Educator's Assn. Recipient Award of Excellence Ill. State Bd. Edn., 1988, Sch. Bell award Williamson Co. ESR, 1988-89, Outstanding Art Educator award Ill. Alliance for Arts Edn., 1988, Ill. Art Educator award, 1989, Nat. Ill. Art Educator award, 1990, Senate Resolution Senator James Rea, 1989, Proclamation Gov. James Thompson, 1990; Ill. Art Ed. (IAEA) art Tchr. of the Yr., State of Ill., 1989. Mem. AAUW, Ill. Art Edn. Assn. (sec. dir. 1990), Little Egypt Arts Assn. on LEAA Bd. of Dir., Ill. Ret. Tchrs. Assn.,So. Ill. U. Alumni Life, Downstate Art Edn. (life), Elk Ladies, Delta Kappa Gamma, Phi Kappa Phi, Beta Sigma Phi. Avocations: graphic art, computer graphics. antique dealer, network marketing. Home: 114 N Chamberlain Dr Marion IL 62959-5503

HOWELL, DEBORAH, editor; b. San Antonio, Jan. 15, 1941; m. C. Peter Magrath; 8 stepchildren. Editor St. Paul Pioneer Press; chief Washington bur., editor Newhouse News Svc. Office: Newhouse News Svc 1101 Connecticut Ave NW Ste 300 Washington DC 20036-4395 E-mail: deborah.howell@newhouse.com.

HOWELL, DEBORAH S. career officer; b. Greenville, S.C. BA in Math., MPA; cert., Amphibious Warfare Sch., Naval War Coll., Federal Exec. Inst., Harvard U., Maxwell Sch.; &, MIT. From presidential mgmt. intern to budget program analyst, dep. branch head of manpower policy USMC, Arlington, Va., 1979-94, asst. dep. chief of staff manpower and reserve affairs, 1994—. Office: USMC/Manpower & Reserve Affairs Dept Arlington Annex Columbia Pike & Southgate Anx Washington DC 20370-0001

HOWELL, HELEN, state agency administrator; b. Seattle, Wash. BA, Vassar Coll.; diploma in legal studies, Oxford U.; JD, Columbia U. Law Sch. Counsel to Sen. Patty Murray; spl. asst. to Pres. Bill Clinton; dep. staff sec. at the White House; v.p. public policy Planned Parenthood Fedn. Am.; dir. intergovernmental affairs for Gov. Gary Locke, 1999; dep. chief of staff for Gov. Gary Locke, 1999—2002; dir. Wash. State Dept. of Fin. Insts., 2002—. Office: PO Box 41200 Olympia WA 98504-1200

HOWELL, JANET D. state legislator; b. Washington, May 7, 1944; d. Edward Fulton and Elsie (Lightbown) Denison; m. A. Hunt Howell; children: Eric, Brian. BA, Oberlin Coll., 1966; MA, U. Pa., 1968. Tchr. Phila. Pub. Schs., 1968-69; legis. asst. Gen. Assembly, Va., 1989-91; senator Va. State Senate, 1992—. Chair Fairfax County (Va.) Social Svcs. Bd., 1979-82, State Bd. Social Svcs., Va., 1986-91, Reston (Va.) Transp. Com., 1986-91; pres. Reston Community Assn., 1982-85, Citizen of Yr., 1990. Named Restonian of Yr., Reston Times, 1984, Virginian of Yr., Va. Assn. Social Workers, 1991, Senator of Yr., Fraternal Order of Police, 1998, Citizen of Yr., ARC, 1998. Democrat. Mem. Unitarian Ch.

HOWELL, JEANETTE HELEN, retired cultural organization administrator; b. Portsmouth, Hampshire, Eng., June 2, 1925; arrived in U.S., 1976; d. Henry Augustus and Mary Scott (Randall) Butler-Frere; m. Reginald Robert Howell, Aug. 14, 1948; children: Josephine Thalia Howell, Robert Henry Adam Howell, Matthew Charles Howell. Student, High Wycombe Coll. Art, 1967-71, Sutton Sch. Art. Dir./owner Bourne End (pre-sch.), Bucks, Eng., 1965-69; adminstr. Historic Denver, Denver, 1980-83; mgr. II Bur. Conservation, State of Maine, Thomaston, 1987-90; dir. Lincoln County Hist. Assn., Wiscasset, Maine, 1990-93; ret., 1993. Founder Decorative and Fine Arts N.J., pres., 1977; co-founder Decorative and Fine Arts Soc. U.K., 1966, Decorative and Fine Arts Soc. N.J. ednl. lectrs. and seminars (pres. 1977); bazaar chmn. St. John's Cathedral, Denver, 1981; pres. Damariscotta (Maine) Arts Coun., 1984-86; sr. warden St. Andrew's Ch., Newcastle, Maine, 1992-96; co-founder Friends of Colonial Pemaquid (Maine), 1993; trustee Maine Archives and Mus., 1999—; bd. dirs. Lincoln Home Assisted Living. Nurse emergency med. hosp., Weymouth, Dorset, Eng., 1942-48. Recipient Americans-By-Choice Outstanding Svc. award Citizenship Day com., Denver, 1983, Appreciation award Maine Vols. in Parks, 1997, Jefferson award enrichment of arts, 2004. Mem.: Maine Archives and Mus. (v.p. 2000, pres. 2002—04). Avocations: gardening, archaeology, history research, literature. Home: 534 Harrington Rd Pemaquid ME 04558-4214 E-mail: howell@lincoln.midcoast.com.

HOWELL, KAREN JANE, private school educator; b. Mpls., Apr. 24, 1946; d. John and Lorraine (Quale) Borgen; m. John Morris Howell; children: Laura, John. AS in Math. and Sci., Cottey Jr. Coll., Nevada, Mo., 1966; BS in Elem. Edn. Sci. and Math., U. No. Colo., Greeley, 1968; MS Science & Gifted Education, University Of Virginia, Alexandria, Va, 1980—83. Cert. 5/6th Grade Team Tchr. 1968, 6th Grade Gifted Tchr. 1971, K-6th Gifted Program Tchr. 1983. Team tchr. John Adams and Carver Elem. Schs., Colorado Springs, Colo., 1968—73; tchr. gifted 3-6th grade Math. and Sci. Washington Mill and Stratford Landing Elem. Schs., Alexandria, Va., 1973—83; tchr. gifted program Tokeneke Elem. Sch., Darien, Conn., 1983—85; 5-8th science, 1-8 art teacher Hillel Academy, Fairfield, Ct, 1985—. Art / science docent Smithsonian Instn. and Am. Mus. Nat. History, Washington, 1974—82; guide Discovery Mus., Bridgeport, Conn., 1985—. Author: (various workshops, teaching modules) Using Art Properties With Mus. Tours, 1980-1990, 1990, (teacher's guide) Motivational Techniques, Math Manipulatives, 1988,1992, 1994. Chairperson, bd. dirs. Fairfield (Conn.) Internat. Dance Co., 1990—2002; judge Conn. State Invention Conv., Hartford, 1983—87. Recipient Presdl. award for Excellence in Sci. Tchg., State of Conn., 1989, Presdl. award for Excellence in Math. Tchg., 1989, First Sci. Tchr. award, State Sci. Fair Conn., 1996, 1st Place, Middle Schs., Conn. State Sci. Fair, 1995, 1996, 1997, 1998, 1999. Mem.: NEA, Am. Chem. Soc., Nat. Math. Tchrs. Assn., Conn.. Earth Tchrs. Assn., Conn. Sci. Tchrs. Assn. (Conn. Sci. Tchr. of Yr. award 2002), Nat. Sci. Tchrs. Assn., Audubon Soc., Am. Mensa, Am. Ballet Theater (assoc.). Methodist. Avocations: ballet, jazz, dance. Office: Hillel Academy 1571 Stratfield Rd Fairfield CT 06432 Personal E-mail: j.howell@comsoc.org.

HOWELL, LAURA CLARK, biologist, educator, small business owner; d. Louie Earl Clark and Laura Elizabeth Stewart; m. Charles Samuel Howell. BS in Biology, Jacksonville State U., 1968; MS in Biology, Samford U., 1970; EdS, Jacksonville State U., 1984. Cert. profl. tchr. Ala., profl. guidance counselor Ala., registered psychometrist Ala., cert. profl. tchr. Ga. Microbiologist Ala. Dept. Pub. Health, Anniston, 1968; tchr. biology B.B. Comes Meml. Sch., Sylacanga, Ala., 1970—71; tchr. sci., anatomy, physiology, biology, chmn. sci. dept. Wellborn H.S., Anniston, 1971—94. Adj. instr. biology Jacksonville State U., Ala., 1975, supr. student tchrs., 96; adj. instr. biology, botany, zoology Gadsden State C.C., Anniston, 1983—91. Recipient Medal and Cert. Appreciation, SAR, 2003, Educator award, United Daus. Confederacy, 1980. Mem.: DAR, Nat. Assn. Biology Tchrs., The Jamestowne Soc., Colonial Dames XVII Century, U.S. Daus. War of 1812, Magna Charta Dames & Barons, Ala. Geneal. Soc., Anniston Mus. League, Ala.-Benton Geneal. Soc., Athena Study Club, Persephone Garden Club, Kappa Delta Pi, Alpha Delta Kappa, Delta Kappa Gamma. Methodist. Office: Anniston Coin and Jewelry 802 Quintard Ave Anniston AL 36201*

HOWELL, LYNNETTE, elementary school principal; b. Chgo., Mar. 8, 1950; d. Samuel and Betty Jane (Scherff) H. BS, Northeastern Ill. U., 1972; MS, Nat.-Louis U., 1987, MS, Cert. in Advanced Study, 1993. Tchr. jr. high St. Matthias Sch., Chgo., 1972-74; tchr., chair dept. jr. high math. Our Lady of Lourdes Sch., Chgo., 1974-95; prin. St. Pascal Sch., Chgo., 1995—. Grantwriter St. Pascal Sch., 1995—, Our Lady of Lourdes Sch., 1990-94, Archdiocese of Chgo., 1996—. Named Outstanding Tchr. St. Scholastica H.S., 1991, 93; nat. nominee Outstanding Tchr. Math., 1992. Mem. Nat. Assn. Secondary Sch. Prins., Nat. Cath. Educators Assn., Nat. Coun. Tchrs. Math., Ill. Coun. Tchrs. Math., Ill. Computer Educators, Internat. Soc. Tech. Educators, Nat. Mid. Sch. Assn. Avocations: travel, photography, reading, graphic arts, cycling. Office: St Pascal Sch 6143 W Irving Park Rd Chicago IL 60634-2598

HOWELL, MARY L. diversified company executive; b. Springfield, Mass., July 10, 1952; d. Walter Edward and Mary Patricia (Landers) Lynch; m. John N. Howell, Oct. 27, 1980; 1 child, Patrick. BA, U. Mass.; grad. advanced mgmt. program, Harvard U. Exec. v.p. Textron, Inc., Washington. Office: 1101 Pennsylvania Ave NW Washington DC 20004-2514

HOWELL, NELDA KAY, commissioner; b. Kinston, N.C., Apr. 30, 1938; d. John Franklin, Sr. and Reba Ellen (Davis) Howell. BS in Home Econs., East Carolina U., 1960; MEd in Adult and CC Edn., N.C. State U., 1970. Home agt. agrl. ext. svc. N.C. State U., Hyde County, 1959-62, home econs. ext. agt. Craven County, 1965-71; vocat. home econs. tchr. Richlands (N.C.) HS Onslow County Sch. Sys., 1962-65; assoc. dist. leader Piedmont Clemson (S.C.) U. Coop. Ext. Svc., 1971-84, dist. ext. chmn. Savannah Valley, 1984-87, dist. ext. dir. Savannah Valley, 1987-91; commr. Onslow County Hosp. Authority, 2001—; chair Onslow Ambulatory Svcs., 2003. Mem. land use and devel. com. Onslow County Comprehensive Plan, 2001—02; mem. policy com. Joint Land Use Study Onslow County, 2002—. Bd. dirs. Onslow Women's Ctr., 2000—, sec., 2003—; mem. staff com. 1st Bapt. Ch., Swansboro, NC, sec., 2000—01. Named Woman of the Yr., Swansboro Area C. of C., 1999; Kellogg fellow, Agrl. Policy Inst. N.C. State U., 1969. Mem.: AAUW (N.C. state membership v.p. 1996—98, parliamentarian 2001—02), N.C. Assn. Family and Consumer Scis. (southeastern region treas. 1996—97), Swansboro High Sch. Alumni (tres. 2003—), N.C. Women United (bd. dirs. 2003—), Onslow County Coun. Women (sec. 1994—95, co-chair 1999—2000), Swansboro Toastmasters (pres. 1997), Women's Forum N.C. (sec. 2001—02, treas. 2003—), E. Carolina U. Alumni Assn. (sec. Onslow County chpt. 1998), Gamma Sigma Delta. Democrat. Baptist. Avocations: volunteering, reading, travel, public policy. Home: 109 Howell Rd Hubert NC 28539-3911 E-mail: nhowell@ec.rr.com.

HOWELL, TERESA CHRISTINE WALLIN, elementary school educator; b. Corinth, Miss., Jan. 14, 1952; d. Reece and Agness (Winfield) W.; m. Bobby Braxton Howell, July 3, 1976 (div. Oct. 30, 1996); children: Chad Braxton Howell, Brad Braxton Howell. BS in Health, Phys. Edu., Miss. State Coll. for Women, 1975; MEd in Curriculum and Instr., U. Miss., 1990. With Gibson Discount Store, Corinth, Miss., 1975-76; factory worker ITT Telecom., Corinth, 1976-87; tchr. Alcorn County Sch. Sys., Corinth, 1977—, bus driver, 1987—. Brownie leader Girl Scouts U.S., Corinth, 1977-78; cub scout leader Boy Scouts Am., Corinth, 1990-93. Mem. Ea.

Star. Democrat. Baptist. Avocations: coin collecting, stamp collecting, antiques, pepsi memorabilia. Office: Alcorn County Sch System Corinth MS 38834

HOWELL, VICKY SUE, health [illegible]; b. [illegible], Okla., June 10, 1948; d. Alvin Henry and Alice Odessa (Redemer) H.; m. Ramiro Martinez, Aug. 20, 1971 (div. June 1977); 1 child, Micaela Martinez; m. Timothy Arthur Pierson, June 5, 1982 (div. July 1995). BA, U. Okla., 1971, MA, 1973, PhD, 1979. Lectr. U. Tex., El Paso, 1973-74, 77-78; tchg. asst. U. Okla., Norman, 1979; asst. prof. U. Miss., Oxford, 1980-81, Wichita (Kans.) State U., 1981-82; rsch. analyst II Mo. Dept. Health, Jefferson City, 1984-88, rsch. analyst III, 1988—99; epidemologist New Mex. Dept. Health, Santa Fe, 1999—2001, epidemologist, mgr. natality stats., 2001—03; epidemiologist N.Mex. Dept Health Office Performance Mgmt. and Budget, 2003—. Contbr. articles to profl. jours. Mem. Friends for Peace, Jefferson City, 1993-94; vol. House of Clara, Jefferson City, 1992-95. Democrat. Roman Catholic. Avocations: gardening, reading. Office: N Mex Dept Health 1190 S St Francis Dr PO Box 26110 Santa Fe NM 87502

HOWELLS, MURIEL GURDON SEABURY (MRS. WILLIAM WHITE HOWELLS), volunteer; b. White Plains, N.Y., May 3, 1910; d. William Marston and Katharine Emerson (Hovey) Seabury; m. William White Howells, June 15, 1929; children: Muriel Gurdon Howells Metz, William Dean. Founder Brit. War Relief Soc., Madison, Wis., 1941, pres., 1941-43; apptd. visitor dept. decorative arts and sculpture Boston Mus. Fine Arts, 1955-72, dept. Am. decorative arts, 1972-97. Mem. ladies com. Inst. Contemporary Art, Boston, 1955-68; co-founder, trustee Strawbery Banke Mus., Inc., Portsmouth, N.H., 1958-75, overseer, 1975-81, hon. overseer, 1981—; co-founder, steering com. Guild, 1959-91. Bd. dirs. Garden Club Am., 1959-62, nat. chmn. medal award com., 1962-65, judge flower arrangements; pres. Piscataqua Garden Club, 1952-54; mem. Harvard Solomon Islands Expdn., Malaita, 1968; 1st chmn. Boston chpt. Venice Com., Internat. Fund for Monuments (now Save Venice Inc.), 1970-71, vice chmn. Boston chmn., 1971-77, mem. exec. com., 1971-89, hon. chmn., 1989—; mem. ARC Motor Corps, 1941-43. Recipient King's medal for Svc. in the Cause of Freedom, 1946, Hist. Preservation award zone 1 Garden Club Am., 1976. Mem. Nat. Soc. Colonial Dames N.H., Soc. Preservation of New England Antiquities, Mayflower Soc., Women's Travel Club (pres. 1967-69), Chilton Club, Colony Club. Died July 1, 2002.

HOWER, JEANNE LOUISE, landscape designer; b. Mpls., Apr. 24, 1948; d. Archie Edward and Joyce Loucille (Cleve.) Hower; divorced; 1 child, Angela Marie. Student in landscape design, Olympic Coll., 1983-85; student in interior design, Life Time Career, Grand Rapids, Minn., 1975-77. Receptionist Bradfords, Inc., Anoka, Minn., 1966-67; inspector quality Pioneer Plating Co., Mpls., 1967-68, Honeywell County, Mpls., 1968-72; owner Jeanne's Profl. Finishing, Brementon, Wash., 1976-79; interior designer Office Interiors of Seattle, 1979-82; landscape designer, owner Horizon's Landscape Design, Bremerton, Wash., 1986-97. Art dir. fairgrounds, Bremerton, 1978-81; crafts artist Artist Club, Bremerton, 1981-88; profl. gardener Gardener's Club, 1988-97. Floral, landscape and interior design projects. Affil. mem. Epilepsy Assn., Seattle, 1987-97, Nature Conservaory, 1990-97, Save the Whales, 1985-90. Mem. Am. Soc. Landscape Designer (affill.). Avocations: reading, gardening, collecting, crafts, saving the earth. Home and Office: 1733 Winfield Ave Bremerton WA 98310-4438

HOWERTON, CHERYL ALLEY, secondary school educator; d. Kenneth William and Carol Mills Alley; m. David Keith Howerton, May 28, 1982; 1 child, Jeremy Andrew. BA, Marshall U., Huntington, W.Va., 1979, MA, 1985. Permanent tchg. cert. W.Va. State Edn. Dept., 1985. Art tchr. Logan County Bd. of Edn., Logan, W.Va., 1979—80, Wayne County Bd. of Edn., Wayne, W.Va., 1980—. Quilt trainer AEL, Charleston, W.Va., 1996—; presenter/trainer Wayne County Bd. of Edn., Wayne, W.Va., 1995—. High Schools That Work Brochure and Badge. Mem. C-K High Local Sch. Improvement Coun., Kenova, W.Va., 1995—96. Mem.: Am. Fedn. Teachers. Democrat. Avocations: drawing, photography, dog training & competition showing, travel, devoted sports mom. Home: 7 Mahood Trace Huntington WV 25705 Office: Spring Valley High Sch 1 Timber Wolf Drive Huntington WV 25704

HOWERTON, HELEN F. artist; b. Tulsa, Okla., Apr. 5, 1944; d. Leo Francis and Helen Nester Murray; m. Ronald G. Howerton, Aug. 27, 1966; children: Jeff A., Greg L. BFA, U. of Tulsa, Tulsa, OK, 1966. Comml. artist Okla. State U., Stillwater, Okla., 1966—67; advt. sales rep. Brazosport Daily Newspaper, Freeport, Tex., 1967—73; art instr. Tulsa Parks Dept., Tulsa, Okla., 1979; full-time wildlife artist Tulsa, Okla., 1980—; co-owner Color Connection Art Gallery, 2004—. Advt. dir. Women Artists of the West, International, 2000—; founding mem. Signature 16 Artists Soc., National, 1997—; founder Arts Ltd Gallery, Tulsa, Okla., 1991—95; canine artist registry Am. Kennel Club Mus. of the Dog, 1994—. Represented in permanent collections State of Okla., Fine Art Mus., Wichita Falls, TX, Tulsa (Okla.) Pub. Schs. Mem. Nature Conservancy, Okla., 1999—2002. Recipient Commn. / Design Artist, Haldor-Topsoe, Inc., 1992—97, 2001—04, Commn. Artist, Sutton Avian Ctr., 2000, Okla. Artist of the Yr., Ducks Unlimited Conservation, 1991. Mem.: Assn. Oil Painters Am., Nat. Oil and Acrylic Painters Soc., Signature 16 Artists Soc., Women Artists West, Nature Conservancy, Am. Women Artists, Oil Painters of Am. Conservative. Avocations: travel, hunting, motorcycle riding. Office: Howerton Studio 6304 S 69th E Place Tulsa OK 74133 E-mail: howerton@howertonart.com.

HOWES, GLORIA, state legislator; b. Gallup, N. Mex., 1931; BA, West Tex. U.; MA, U. N.Mex. County mgr. McKinley County, N.Mex., county comr.; mem. N. Mex. Senate, 4th dist., Santa Fe, 1988-. Democrat. Address: 1515 Monterey Dr Gallup NM 87301-5637 Office: NM State Senate State Capitol Rm 302 Santa Fe NM 87503

HOWES, LORRAINE DE WET, fashion designer, educator; b. Port Elizabeth, South Africa, Dec. 24, 1933; came to U.S., 1957; d. Jacobus Egnatius and Johanna Elizabeth (Lowenburg) de W. Student, Sch. Fashion Design, Boston, 1957-58. Apprentice Jonathan Logan & Adam Leslie, Johannesburg, South Africa, 1953-55; apprentice, wookroom asst., model Norman Hartnell, designer to the Queen, London, 1955-57; model Peter Lumley Agy., London, 1955-57; designer, dept. mgr. Design Rsch. Inc., Cambridge, Mass., 1957-59; model Hart Agy., Boston, 1957-76; designer, mgr. Estabrook & Newell, Boston, 1959-62; designer, owner Lorraine de Wet, Boston, 1962-79; mem. adj. faculty dept. apparel design RISD, Providence, 1972-76, asst. prof., assoc. prof., 1976-82, acting head dept., 1976-79, head dept., 1979-99, prof., 1988-2000, prof. emeritus, 2000—, interim dean arch. and design, 2000-2001. Designer, cons. apparel industry and theatre, 1979—2000; dir. Hamilton Cornell Mass., 1986-2000; design and tech. edn. cons. apparel and textiles Hangzhou Econ. Commn., China, 1986-88; mem. individual grants panel Nat. Endowment for Arts, 1994. Named Faculty Mem. of Yr., RISD Alumni Assn., 1984-85; recipient John R. Frazier Excellence in Tchg. award RISD, 1993, Hon. Alumna award RISD, 1995, Helen Rowe Metcalf award 2003; named champion R.I. Pub. Links, 1983, 84. Mem.: Costume Soc. Am., Fashion Inst. Tech. Design Lab., Fashion Group. Avocation: golf. Office: RISD Dept Apparel Design 2 College St Providence RI 02903-2784

HOWES, SOPHIA DUBOSE, writer; b. Balt., Apr. 20, 1954; d. John Carleton and Marie Josephine (Meeth) Jones; m. Edward Phillip Howes, Jan. 26, 1996; 1 child, Michael Laurence. BFA with honors, NYU, 1982, MFA, 1994; JD, Fordham U., 2002. Legal asst. Skadden, Arps, Slate, Meagher & Flom, N.Y.C., 1984-93; script reader Haft Nassiter Co., N.Y.C., 1994; editl. assoc. Matthew Bender & Co. Inc., N.Y.C., 1994-97. Extern Fordham U. Sch. Law, Surrogate's Ct., N.Y.C., 1999, rsch. asst. Securities Arbitration Clinic, Fordham Law Sch., 2000, Writing Rsch. [illegible] summer 2001. Author one act plays, including Better Dresses, Rosetta's Eyes, 1988, 1988, Adamov, 1992, two-act play The Poisoned Kiss, 1994; mem. staff Fordham Environ. Law Jour., 1999-2000, sr. notes and comments editor, 2000-01; dir. Who's Afraid of Virginia Woolf, 2004. Recipient Grad. award in playwriting, NYU-Tisch Sch. Arts, 1994, Seidman award for talent, 1982. Mem. Dramatists Guild. Avocation: mountain climbing. E-mail: edwardhowes@juno.com.

HOWL, JOANNE HEALEY, veterinarian, writer; b. Mariemont, Ohio, Mar. 16, 1957; d. Joseph Daniel and Claire Helen (Baillargeon) H.; m. Arthur Wesley Howl, May 12, 1990; children: Bryan Arthur, Martha Grace Claire DVM, U. Tenn., 1987. Sr. lab. animal technician Lab. Animal Facility, Knoxville, 1983-84; gnotobiology technician U. Tenn., Knoxville, 1984-86; assoc. vet. Mynatt Vet. Clinic, Knoxville, 1987-89; veterinary med. officer USDA Animal and Plant Health Inspection Svcs., Raleigh, N.C., 1989-90; owner Creature Comfort Vet. Relief Svc., Laurel, Md., 1991-95; assoc. veterinarian Muddy Creek Animal Hosp., West River, Md., 1996-97; freelance writer, West River, Md., 1995—. Author: Your Cat's Life, 1999; editor VMAT-2 News, 1996—; contbr. articles to profl. jours. Dep. team leader Vet. Med. Assistance Team-2. Mem. AVMA, Am. Animal Hosp. Assn., Am. Assn. Feline Practitioners, Md. Vet. Med. Assn. (chmn. pub. rels. com. 1995-98, sec./treas. 1998-2002, pres. 1999-2000), Am. Acad. Vet. Disaster Medicine (sec./treas. 1998-2002). Episcopalian. Avocations: hiking, gardening, house remodeling. Home and Office: 4304 Tenthouse Ct West River MD 20778-9797

HOWLAND, BETTE, writer; b. Chgo., Jan. 28, 1937; d. Sam and Jessie (Berger) Sotonoff; m. Howard C. Howland (div.); children— Frank, Jacob. BA, U. Chgo., 1955. Assoc. prof. com. social thought U. Chgo., 1993-97. Author: W-3, 1974, Blue in Chicago, 1978 (1st prize Friends of Am. Writers), Things to Come and Go, 1983, Trial, 1998, Calm Sea and Prosperous Voyage, 1999. Fellow Rockefeller Found., 1969, Marsden Found., 1971, Guggenheim Found., 1978, Nat. Endowment for the Arts, 1981, MacArthur Found., 1984. Jewish. Address: PO Box 405 Union Pier MI 49129-0405

HOWLAND, JOAN SIDNEY, law librarian, law educator; b. Eureka, Calif., Apr. 9, 1951; d. Robert Sidney and Ruth Mary Howland. BA, U. Calif., Davis, 1971; MA, U. Tex., 1973; MLS, Calif. State U., San Jose, 1975; JD, Santa Clara (Calif.) U., 1983; MBA, U. Minn., 1997. Assoc. librarian for pub. svcs. Stanford (Calif.) U. Law Library, 1975-83, Harvard U. Law Library, Cambridge, Mass., 1983-86; dep. dir. U. Calif. Law Library, Berkeley, 1986-92; dir. law libr., Roger F. Noreen prof. law U. Minn. Sch. of Law, 1992—, assoc. dean info. tech., 2001—. Questions and answers column editor Law Libr. Jour., 1986-91; memt. column editor Trends in Law Libr. Mgmt. & Tech., 1987-94. Mem. ALA, ABA (com. on accreditation 2001—), Am. Assn. Law Librs., Am. Assn. Law Schs., Am. Indian Libr. Assn. (treas. 1992—), Am. Law Inst. Office: U Minn Law Sch 229 19th Ave S Minneapolis MN 55455-0400

HOWLAND, NINA DAVIS, historian; b. Wichita, Kans., June 2, 1939; d. Earle Rosco Davis and Kathrine Keene Laurie; m. Kenneth Eugene Howland, Sept. 27, 1959; children: Douglas Earle, Christopher Keene, Karen Laurie, Rebecca Kathrine. BA with high honors, U. Md., London Center, Eng., 1970; PhD, U. Md., College Park, 1983; MA with distinction, U. London, 1972. Instr. U. Coll., U. Md., College Park, 1978-79, 82, Hood Coll., Frederick, Md., 1981; archivist Nat. Archives, Washington, 1984-85; historian Office of Historian U.S. Dept. of State, Washington, 1985—. Editor: Foreign Relations of the United States, 1961-63, vol. XXI, Africa, 1995, Foreign Relations of the United States, 1964-68, vol. XVI, Africa, 1999, Foreign Relations of the United States, 1964-68, vol. XXII, Iran, 1999, vol. XXI Near East Region, Arabian Peninsula, 2000; divsn. chief Middle East, South Asia & African divsn., 2002—. Rsch. grantee William Randolph Hearst Found., 1980. Mem. Soc. for Historians of Am. Fgn. Rels., Soc. for History in Fed. Govt., Peace History Soc., Phi Kappa Phi. Home: 9808 E Bexhill Dr Kensington MD 20895-3223 Office: Office of Historian US Dept of State 2401 E St NW Dept of State Washington DC 20522-0001 Fax: 202-663-1289. E-mail: ninakenhowland@juno.com.

HOWLETT, PHYLLIS LOU, retired athletics conference administrator; b. Indianola, Iowa, Oct. 23, 1932; d. James Clarence and Mabel L. (Fisher) Hickman; m. Jerry H. Howlett, Jan. 2, 1955 (dec. June 1972); children: Timothy A., Jane A. Field; m. Ronlin Royer, Dec. 30, 1977. BA, Simpson Coll., 1954. Tchr. phys. edn. Oskaloosa (Iowa) H.S., 1954-55; psychometrist Drake U., Des Moines, 1956-57, asst. to men's athletics dir., 1974-79; asst. dir. athletics U. Kans., Lawrence, 1979-82; asst. commr. Big Ten Conf., Inc., Park Ridge, Ill., 1982-97. Football TV com. NCAA, 1980-87, women's golf com., 1983-89, chmn. com. on women's athletics, 1987-94, spl. com. women's basketball TV, 1989-90, chair com. for women's corp. mktg., 1990-94, divsn. I championship com., 1990-95, first woman chair exec. com., 1990-97, chair task force on gender equity, 1992-94, exec. dir. search com., 1993, spl. com. divsn. I football playoff, adminstrv. com., 1995-97, joint policy bd., sec.-treas., 1995-97; NACDA Exec. com., 1986-90, NCAA Coun., 1995-97, NCAA Fin. com., chair, 1995-97, NCAA Found. bd., 1995-97. Editor yearbook Simpson Coll., 1953-54. Chair Iowa Commn. Status of Women, 1976-79; pres. Vol. Bus. of Greater Des Moines, 1969-70; chair Arts and Recreation Coun. of Greater Des Moines, 1975; pres. Iowa Children's and Family Svcs., 1973; nat. pres. Assn. Vol. Bus. Am., Inc., 1972-73. Named to, Simpson Coll. Hall of Fame, 1985, Indianola H.S. Hall of Fame, 1997, NACDA Hall of Fame, 2000; recipient Alumni Achievement award, Simpson Coll., 1988, Adminstrv. Achievement award, NACDA, 1995, Honda award of Merit, 1997, Spl. award, All-Am. Football Found., 1998, Lifetime Achievement award, Ind. Sports Corp., 1997, NACWAA, 2000, Svc. award, Assn. Vol. Mem. Nat. Assn. Coll. Women's Athletics Adminstrs., Pi Beta Phi (pres. Iowa Beta chpt. 1953-54). Home: PO Box 1117 Abiquiu NM 87510-1117

HOWLEY, TERESA MOOREHOUSE, artist; b. Canadiagua, N.Y., Aug. 22, 1944; d. William Joel Moorehouse and Ella Olive Haviland Knapp; m. John Leidenfrost, May 19, 1975 (dec. Sept. 1998); 1 child, Isadora Gabrielle Leidenfrost ; m. John Joseph Howley, July 1990. Grad., Penn Yan (N.Y.) Acad., 1962. Computer graphics illustrator Cornell U., Ithaca, NY, 1985—2002; sculptor, 1962—. Avocation: community service. Home: 99 Etna Rd Ithaca NY 14850 E-mail: tch3@cornell.edu.

HOWROYD, JANICE BRYANT, personnel placement executive; b. Tarboro, N.C. Pres., CEO, prin. ACT 1 Pers. Svcs., Torrance, Calif., 1978—. Lectr. in field. Mem. Minority Bus. Opportunity Day trade fair, LA, Jr. Achievement of Ctrl. Ariz. Inc., 1992-93, Project Life; bd. dirs. L.A. Urban League, St. Anne's Maternity Home, Internat. Visitors coun. for city of L.A., L.A. Urban League. Recipient Minority Enterprise Devel. Week Achievement award U.S. Dept. of Commerce, Ceert. of Achievement award No. Calif. Regional Purchasing coun., 1992, Entertainment and Bus. Cmty Achievement award NAACP Legal Def. Fund. 1992, Distinguished Svc. award Joint Conf., Inc., 1993, Nat. Minority Supplier of the Year award Nat. Minority Supplier Devel. coun., 1993, Black Women of Achievement AT & T Entrepreneur of the Year, 1994. Mem. Nat. Assn. of Women Bus. Owners; bd. dirs. Greater L.A. African Am. C. of C.; adv. bd. mem. Northrop-Rice Aviation Inst. of Technol. Office: ACT 1 Pers Svc 5334 Torrance Blvd Torrance CA 90503-4012

HOWSE, CATHY L. writer, researcher, entrepreneur; b. Murfreesboro, Tenn., Dec. 16, 1955; d. John Edd Sr. and Elmira Howse; children: Gregory Simpson Jr., Brandon J. BS, Met. State Coll., Denver, 1987. Author: Ultra Black Hair, 1990, 2000, Ultra Black Hair Growth II, [illegible]. Achievements include development of a method for hair growth and lengthening for black women. Office: UBH Publs Inc PO Box 22678 Denver CO 80222 E-mail: mail@ubhpublications.com.

HOWSE, JENNIFER LOUISE, foundation administrator; b. Glendale, Calif., Jan. 31, 1945; d. Benjamin McCausland and Patricia Louise (Naylor) H. BA, Fla. State U., 1966, MA, 1968, PhD in Child Lang. Devel., 1973; LHD (hon.), SUNY, Bklyn., 1990. Rsch. asst., instr. Inst. Human Devel. Coll. Edn., Fla. State U., Tallahassee, 1967-69; dir. planning and evaluation Wakulla County (Fla.) Sch. System, 1969-72; dir. NARC/HEW Liaison Project Nat. Assn. for Retarded Citizens, Govtl. Affairs Office, Washington, 1972-73; dir. Developmental Disabilities Bur., dir. Bur. Tech. Assistance and Regulation Fla. Dept. Health and Rehab. Svcs., Tallahassee, 1973-75; exec. dir. Willowbrook Rev. Panel, N.Y.C., 1975-78; assoc. commr. N.Y. State Office Mental Retardation and Developmental Disabilities, N.Y.C., 1978-80; state commr. for mental retardation Dept. Pub. Welfare, Harrisburg, Pa., 1980-85; exec. dir. Greater N.Y. chpt. March of Dimes Birth Defects Found., N.Y.C., 1985-89, pres. White Plains, NY, 1990—. Advisor Ctr. for Family Life in Sunset Park, Bklyn., 1992—. Bd. dirs. Salk Inst., La Jolla, Calif.; active Pew Environ. Health Commn. Office: March Dimes Birth Defects Found 1275 Mamaroneck Ave White Plains NY 10605-5298*

HOWSON, TAMAR D. pharmaceutical executive; Former sr. v.p., dir. bus. devel., mgr. SR One Ltd. venture capital fund SmithKline Beecham; sr. v.p. corp. devel. Bristol-Myers Squibb, 2001—. Former ind. bus. cons., corp. advisor. Office: Bristol-Myers Squibb Co 345 Park Ave New York NY 10154-0037

HOWZE, KRISTI CRENSHAW, music educator; d. Henry Terrell and Ann Chancey Crenshaw; m. Patrick Henry Howze III, Apr. 9, 1994; children: Patrick Henry Howze IV, Mary Elizabeth. MusB, Samford U., Birmingham, Ala., 1993. Cert. tchr. Ala., 1993. Fouth grade tchr. E.R. Dickson Elem., Mobile, Ala., 1994—97, elem. gen. music tchr., 1997—98, fifth grade sci. tchr., 1998—99, elem. gen. music tcgr, 1999—2000, elem. music/social studies/sci. tchr., 2000—02; choral dir. Murphy H.S., Mobile, Ala., 2002—. Bldg. leadership team mem. Murphy H.S., Mobile, 2002—; SACS planing team co-chair E.R. Dickson Elem., Mobile, 2000—02, bldg. leadership team - chair and scribe, 1997—2000; music textbook com. Mobile County Pub. Schools, Mobile, Ala., 1998—99. Dir.: (original opera) Two Families Forever. Hasbeen com. America's Jr. Miss; career bd. Gayfers/McRae's, Mobile, Ala., 1998—2000; coll. Sun. sch. leader First Bapt. Tillman's Corner, Mobile, Ala., 1998—2003, VBS musical dir., 1996—2003, children's choir dir., 1997—2003. Mem.: Music Educators Nat. Conf., Delta Omicron, Delta Kappa Gamma (music chair 2002—03). Southern Baptist. Avocations: singing, musical theatre, travel, arts and crafts. Home: 5514 Richmond Rd Mobile AL 36608 Office: Murphy High Sch 100 South Carlen St Mobile AL 36606

HOY, MARJORIE ANN, entomology educator; b. Kansas City, Kans., May 19, 1941; d. Dayton J. and Marjorie Jean (Acker) Wolf; m. James B. Hoy; 1 child, Benjamin Lee AB, U. Kans., 1963; MS, U. Calif., Berkeley, 1966, PhD, 1972. Asst. entomologist Conn. Agrl. Expt. Sta., New Haven, 1973-75; rsch. entomologist U.S. Forest Svc., Hamden, Conn., 1975-76; asst. prof. entomology U. Calif., Berkeley, 1976-80, assoc. prof. entomology, 1980-82, prof. entomology, 1982-92, prof. emeritus, 1992—; Fischer, Davies and Eckes prof., dept. entomology and nematology U. Fla., Gainesville, 1992—; chmn. Calif. Gypsy Moth Sci. Adv. Panel, 1982—; mem. genetics resources adv. com. USDA, 1992—, mem. adv. com. agrl. biotech., 2000—02; mem. com. on biol. threats to agrl. plants and animals NRC and NAS, 2001—02; F.E. Guyton disting. lectr. Auburn (Ala.) U., 1997. Chmn. Calif. Gypsy Moth Sci. Adv. Panel, 1982—; mem. genetics resources adv. com. USDA, 1992—, mem. adv. com. agrl. biotech., 2000—01; F.E. Guyton disting. lectr. Auburn (Ala.) U., 1997; mem. com. on biol. threats to agrl. plants and animals NRC and NAS, 2001—02; sci. cons. transgenic insects Pew Initiative Food and Biotech. Editor, co-editor: Genetics in Relation to Insect Managment, 1979, Recent Advances in Knowledge of the Phytoseiidae, 1982, Biological Control of Pests by Mites, 1983, Biological Control in Agricultural IPM Systems, 1985, Insect Molecular Genetics, 1994, 2d edit., 2003, The Phytoseiidae as Biological Control Agents of Pest Mites and Insects: A Bibliography, 1996, Managing the Citrus Leafminer, 1996; mem. editorial bd. Exptl. and Applied Acarology, Biol. Control, Biocontrol Sci. and Tech., Environ. Biosafety Rsch.; contbr. articles to profl. jours. Mem. Sec. Agrl.'s adv. com. agrl. biotechnology; cons. Pew Charitable Trust. Recipient citation for outstanding achievments in regulatory entomology Fla. Divsn. Plant Industry, 1995, USDA honor award Sec. of Agr., 1996, award for sci. Nat. Agri-Mktg. Assn., 1998, sr. faculty award U. Fla. chpt. Gamma Sigma Delta, 1998. Fellow AAAS, Royal Entomol. Soc. London, Entomol. Soc. Am. (mem. Pacific br. governing bd. 1985, Bussart award 1986, Founder's Memorial award 1992), Coun. Agr. Sci. and Tech. (Charles Black award 2004); mem. Nat. Acad. Scis. (com. on biol. threats to agr. plants and animals), NY Acad. Scis., Am. Genetic Assn., Internat. Orgn. Biol. Control (v.p. 1984-85), Am. Inst. Biol. Scis. (adv. coun. 1996-98, governing bd. 1999-2001), Acarological Soc. Am. (governing bd. 1980-84, pres. 1992), Soc. for Study of Evolution, Fla. Entomological Soc. (Team Rsch. award 1997, Outstanding Tchg. award 1999), Phi Beta Kappa, Sigma Xi (chpt. sec. 1979-81, Sr. Faculty Rsch. award 1996). Avocations: hiking, gardening, snorkeling. Home: 4320 SW 83rd Way Gainesville FL 32608-4131 Office: U Fla Dept Entomology and Nematology PO Box 110620 Gainesville FL 32611-0620 Office Phone: 352-392-1901. E-mail: mahoy@ifas.ufl.edu.

HOYE, MARIA PILAR, lawyer; BS, Calif. State U., Northridge, 1988; JD, UCLA, 1991. Bar: Calif. 1991. With Latham & Watkins, L.A., 1991—, ptnr., 1998—. Former adj. prof. environ. law U. So. Calif. Mem.: Orange County Bar Assn. (mem. exec. com. environ. law sect.), Calif. State Bar. Office: Latham and Watkins LLP 633 W Fifth St Ste 4000 Los Angeles CA 90071*

HOYT, CHARLEE VAN CLEVE, management executive; b. Bluefield, W.Va., May 21, 1936; d. Charles Ives Van Cleve and Kathryn Margarete (Harden) Perrow; m. Ronald Reiner Hoyt, 1959 (div. 1983); children: Dean Christopher, Jason Allen. BA in Edn., U. Fla., 1959, MEd, 1962, postgrad., 1963-64. Cert. spl. edn. tchr. Tchr. Amherst County Schs., Elon, Va., 1958; tchr. spl. edn. Marion County Schs., Ocala, Fla., 1959-61; counselor Univ. Counseling Ctr., Gainesville, Fla., 1962-63, Sunland Tng. Ctr., Gainesville, 1963; mem. community faculty Minn. Met. State Coll., Mpls., 1972-83; mem. council City of Mpls., 1975-86; ptnr. Van Cleve Assocs., 1980-87, 91—; pres. Van Cleve, Doran & Bruno, Inc. 1987-91; corp. officer BAM Leasing Co., Inc., 1987-97; dir. human resources Pascua Yagu Tribe, 1988-95; adj. faculty U. Phoenix, Tucson, 1995—2002; vis. tchr. Tucson Unified Sch. Dist., 1995—2002; pres. Van Cleve Assocs., 1991—; bus. mgr. An Actor's Studio, 1996-98; mem. faculty Govt. Tng. Service, St. Paul, 1978-86, Ariz. Govt. Tng. Services; pres. Minn. Women in City Govt., St. Paul, 1978-79; mem. Met. Land Use Adv. Bd., St. Paul, 1978-83; bd. dirs. Transp. Adv. Bd., St. Paul, 1979-81; mem. conf. faculty League of Minn. Cities, St. Paul, 1979-82; bd. dirs. Met. Council Criminal Justice Adv. Bd., St. Paul, 1979-82; pres. Women in Mcpl. Govt., Nat. League of Cities, Washington, 1980-81, founder minority caucus coalition, 1982, dir., 1982-84; curriculum cons. Nat. Women's Edn. Fund, Washington, trainer, 1982-86; officer JTPA Grantee Orgn. Region IX, 1994—; commr. Pima County/Tuscon Women's Commn. Presenter numerous workshops; contbr. articles to profl. jours. Mem. Women Helping Women YWCA, 1987—; various offices with Republican Party, Minn., 1970-86 ; pres. Burroughs

Elem. Sch. PTA, Mpls., 1973-74; panelist White House Conf., 1981; chmn. Senator Durenburger's Task Force on Women's Issues, Mpls., 1981-84; bd. dirs. Nat. Conf. Rep. Mayors and Council Mems., 1984-85; mem. Senator Durenburger's Intergovtl. Relations Adv. Com., Mpls., 1984-86; bd. dirs. Twin Cities Internat. Program, Mpls., 1983-86; participant Women's Dialogue US/USSR, Moscow, 1985; trustee Council Internat. Programs, Cleve., 1985-90; bd. dirs. At the Foot of the Mountain Theater, Mpls., 1985-86, Tucson Ctrs. for Women and Children, 1988-92; bd. dirs. GOP Feminists, Hamline U. Ctr. for Women in Govt.; mem. Nat. Women's Polit. Caucus, Hennepin County Women's Polit. Caucus; mem. Tucson Support for Success Team, 1986-92, Tucson YWCA Women Helping Women; bd. dirs. Tucson Ctrs. Women and Children. Mem. Am. Soc. Training and Devel., Minn. Women Elected Ofcls. (pres. 1983-85), Izaak Walton League, Tucson C. of C. Methodist. Club: Remington Investment (pres. 1968-70) (Mpls.). Avocations: lapidary, music, handwork, camping, science fiction. Home: 6932 E 2nd St Tucson AZ 85710-1222

HOYT, MARY G(ENEVIEVE), artist, educator; b. Oct. 7, 1929; d. Alvin Chase and Genevive Therese (Cahill) H.; children: John Frederick, Mary Elizabeth, Diane Marie, Jill Marie, Patricia Anne. BA in Art, Coll. St. Francis, 1950. Art instr. Malta Pub. High Sch., Dekalb, Ill., 1958; tchr. Lock Port (Ill.) Pub. Grade Sch., 1959; art tchr. Yauapai Coll., Prescott, Ariz., 1974-77, Allan Hancock Coll., Santa Maria, Calif., 1977-95. Lectr. in field; rschr., tchr. metaphysics and spirit, 1983-95. Author: the Spirit Masters' Guide Book to Enlightenment, 1995. Avocations: camping, fishing, reading, travel. Home: 228 Varner Ct Santa Maria CA 93458-9038 E-mail: spirit8A@yahoo.com.

HOYT, ROSEMARY ELLEN, trust advisor; b. Iowa City, Iowa, Apr. 12, 1949; d. Joseph Asa Hoyt and Mary Jane (Brobst) Vandermark; m. Louis O. Scott, Oct. 16, 1965 (div. Nov. 1968); children: Wayne L. Lawson, Jo Anna Jane Kollasch; m. David K. Duckworth, July 23, 1983 (div. Dec. 1994); 1 child, Mary Rose Duckworth. Cert. in applied banking/consumer credit, Am. Inst. Banking, 1988; BBA, So. Calif. U., 1992, MBA, 1997. Cert. in trust adminstrn; cert. trust ops. specialist; cert. in trust tax. Teller Community Bank of Fla., St. Petersburg, 1973-75; bookkeeper Chevron Svc. Sta., St. Petersburg, 1975-77, Landmark Bank, St. Petersburg, 1977-80; teller First Nat. Bank of Ely, Nev., 1981, Nev. Bank and Trust, Ely, 1982; asst. v.p. and trust officer First Nat. Bank Farmington, N.Mex., 1983-96; asst. v.p., trust officer Bank One, Dallas, 1997—. Pres., founder Day Camp Southside, St. Petersburg, 1976-77. Planning chmn. terr. 5 ann. meeting ARC, Farmington, 1990-91, babysitting instr., 1990-96, basic aid tng. instr., 1992, Project Read instr., 1994; coord. United Way, 1997. Recipient Appreciation award ARC, 1991. Mem. Fin. Women Internat. (by-laws com. 1990-91, treas. 1993-94), Nat. Assn. Trust Ops. Specialists (bd. dirs. 1992), Am. Bus. Women's Assn. (v.p. 1991, pres. 1992, Appreciation award 1989, Woman of Yr. 1995). Republican. Avocations: crocheting, cooking, gardening. Office: 1717 Main St 11th Fl Dallas TX 75243 E-mail: rehoyt@sbcglobal.net.

HOYT, SUSAN, retail stores executive; b. Phila., Mar. 12, 1944; d. Sidney and Elizabeth Knox (Collins) Silodor; m. H. Phillips Hoyt Jr., Sept. 10, 1966. BA, Randolph Macon Woman's Coll., Lynchburg, Va., 1965; MAT., Washington U., St. Louis, 1967. Tchr. University City (Mo.) Schs., 1967; tng. dir. Famous-Barr, St. Louis, 1969-75, dir. exec. devel., 1975-77; v.p., dir. pers. The Emporium div. Carter Hawley Hale, San Francisco, 1977-80, v.p. pers. Emporium-Capwell Co., San Francisco, from 1980, now exec. v.p. stores and visual merchandising; exec. v.p. store ops. Dayton Hudson Dept. Stores, Minneapolis, MN; exec. v.p. humna resources Staples, Inc., Westborough, MA. NDEA fellow, Washington U., 1967. Mem. Nat. Retail Mchts. Assn., Am. Mgmt. Assn., Am. Soc. Tng. and Devel., Phi Beta Kappa. Office: Staples Inc PO Box 9265 Framingham MA 01701-9265

HRENIUC, CARMEN LACRAMIOARA, food service executive; b. Suceava, Romania, Aug. 5, 1968; d. Vasile and Clemansa Carpiuc; m. Johnny Aurel Hreniuc, Aug. 5, 1994; children: Tommy Kevin, Nicole Laurel. Elec. Engring., Stefan cel Mare U., Suceava, 1986—94; BS in Internat. Bus., Western Internat. U., 2003. Restaurant asst. mgr. The Phoenician Resort and Spa, Scottsdale, Ariz., 1994—98; resort restaurant ops. mgr. The Ariz. Biltmore Resort and Spa, Phoenix, 1998—2000; dir. restaurants and lounges The Wigwam Resort & Golf Club, Litchfield Park, Ariz., 2000—03; dir. food and beverage outlets The Westin Kierland Resort & Spa, Scottsdale, 2003—. Named to Top 100 Bus. Women, Today's Ariz. Woman, 2001, 2003. Home: 6546 West Aster Dr Glendale AZ 85304 Office: The Westin Kierland Resort & Spa 6602 East Grewenway Pkwy Scottsdale AZ

HRICAK, HEDVIG, radiologist; came to U.S., 1972; MD, U. Zagreb, 1970; DMS, Karolinska Inst., 1992. Diplomate Am. Bd. Radiology 1978. Intern in radiology Hosp. M. Stojanovic, Zagreb, 1971-72; resident in radiology St. Joseph Mercy Hosp., Pontiac, Mich., 1974-77; fellow in diagnostic radiology Henry ford Hosp., Detroit, sr. staff diagnostic radiology, 1978-81; asst. clin. prof. diagnostic radiology U. Mich., Ann Arbor, 1979-81; from asst. prof. to assoc. prof. U. Calif., San Francisco, 1982-86, prof. radiology, urology, radiation oncology, ob-gyn., 1986-99; chmn. dept. radiology Meml. Sloan-Kettering Cancer Ctr., NY, 1999—; prof. radiology Weill Med. Coll. Cornell U., NY, 2000—. Author 19 books in field; assoc. editor, Jour. of Magnetic Resonance Imaging, 2001—, Radiology, 1998—, Jour. of Women's Imaging, 1996—, others; contbr. more than 250 articles to sci. and profl. jours. Recipient Marie Curie award, AAWR, 2002, Gold medal, ISMRM, 2003; grantee numerous grants in field, including NIH, Nat. Cancer Inst., Am. Cancer Soc., Dept. of Def.;, numerous hon. lectureships. Fellow Am. Coll. Radiology, Internat. Soc. Magnetic Resonance in Medicine, Soc. Uroradiology (corrs. mem., pres. 2001-03); mem. German Roentgen Soc., Acad. Radiology Rsch. (bd. dirs. 1997—), Radiol. Soc. N.Am. (chmn. pub. info. adv. bd. 1997-2002, bd. dirs. 2003—), Soc. for the Advancement of Women's Imaging (pres. 1997-99), Calif. Acad. Medicine (pres. 1999), Brit. Inst. Radiologists (hon.), Inst. of Medicine. E-mail: hricakh@mskcc.org.

HRICIK, LORRAINE E. bank executive; m. Nicholas DeGuercio; 2 children. B in Math. and Computer Sci., Ind. U., Pa., 1973; MBA, Columbia U., 1991. With Securities Industry Automation Corp.; exec. v.p. Chase Manhattan Bank (now J.P. Morgan); exec. v.p. and head J.P. Morgan Treasury Svcs. Mem. Chase Technology Governance Bd.; chair The Clearing House Interbank Payment Co. L.L.C. Adv. Bd.; mem Federal Reserve Bank of N.Y. Payments Risk Com., N.Y. Clearing House Steering Com.; bd. dirs. Internat. Ctr. N.Y. Inductee Academy of Women Achievers, YWCA, 1990. Office: Chase Manhattan Bank 270 Park Ave Fl 12 New York NY 10017-2089

HRINAK, DONNA JEAN, ambassador; b. Sewickley, Pa., Mar. 28, 1951; d. John and Mary (Pukach) H.; m. Gabino (Lou) Flores, July 15, 1977; 1 child, Wyatt A. Flores. BA, Mich. State U., 1972. State dept. officer Am. Embassy, Bogota, Colombia, 1979-81, former dep. prin. officer Warsaw, 1977-79, Mexico City, 1974-81, former min. counselor Teguciagalpa, Honduras, 1989-91; regional affairs officer for C.Am. Dept. State, Washington, 1982-84, dep. asst. sec. for inter-Am. affairs, 1991-93; dep. prin. officer U.S. Consultate Gen., Sao Paulo, Brazil, 1984-87; coord. Policy for Summit of Ams. 1994, 1993-94; amb. to Dominican Republic Santo Domingo, 1994-97; amb. to Bolivia-La Paz, 1197—2000; amb. to Venezuela, 2000—02; amb. to Brazil, 2002—. Named one of Ams. Ten Outstanding Young Working Women, Glamour mag., 1985. Mem. Am. Fgn. Svc. Assn., Exec. Women in Govt., Inter-Am. Dialogue Fgn. Policy Assn. Avocations: reading mysteries, playing tennis, watching baseball. Office: US Embassy SES Avenida das Nacaes 801 Lote 03 70403-900 Quadra Brazil

HRONIK, REBECCA JANE LEAKE, educator; b. Phila., Apr. 29, 1968; d. William Baker and Jane Whitcroft Leake; m. Richard Henry Hronik, Jr., Aug. 15, 1992; children: Richard Henry III, Caroline Jane. BA, Va. Tech, 1990; MEd, George Mason U., 1996. Tchr. Loudoun County Pub. Schs., Leesburg, Va., 1996—2001, Sylvan Learning Ctr., Purcellville, Va., 2001—. Co-coord. Mothers of Preschoolers, Leesburg, 2002—03. Mem.: Phi Delta Kappa. Home: 509 Valley View Ave SW Leesburg VA 20175

HRUBETZ, JOAN, dean, nursing educator; b. Collinsville, Ill., June 1, 1935; d. Frederick and Josephine (Nepute) H. RN, St. John's Hosp., St. Louis, 1956; BSN, St. Louis U., 1960, MA, 1970, PhD in Edn. and Counseling, 1975. Staff nurse St. John's Hosp., St. Louis, 1956-59; instr. med./surg. nursing St. Louis Mcpl. Sch. Nursing, 1960-63; asst. dir. nursing svc. Barnes Hosp., St. Louis, 1963-65, asst. dir. sch. nursing, 1965-68, ednl. cons., 1968-70, dir. sch. nursing, 1970-74; dir. undergrad. mprog. nursing St. Louis U., 1975-82, asst. to assoc. prof. nursing, 1975—, assoc. prof. pastoral health care, 1986—, dean Sch. Nursing, 1982—. Lectr. in field. Contbr. articles to profl. jours. Bd. dirs. Paraquad, Inc., Ctr. Independent Living, 1985-87, hon. mem., 1987—; bd. dirs. Kenrick-Glennon Seminar, 1988, sec. bd., 1989-90; mem. adv. com. project on Clin. Edn. in Care of Elderly, 1989. Group Health Found. grantee, 1987-88, 88-89, St. Louise U. Hosps. grantee, 1980-83, others. Mem. Mo. Assn. Adminstrs. of Baccalaureate and Higher Deg. Progs. in Nursing, St. Louis Assn. Deans and Dirs. of Schs. Nursing, Am. Assn. Colls. of Nursing (adv. com. to baccalaureate data project), Am. Nurses Assn., Mo. Nurses Assn., 3rd Dist. Mo. Nurses Assn., Nat. League Nursing, Mo. League for Nursing, St. Louis Reg. League for Nursing, Midwest Alliance in Nursing (governing bd. 1985-87, chair 1986-87, resolutions com. 1987-89), Conf. Jesuit Schs. Nursing, St. Louis Met. Hosp. Assn. Office: St Louis U Sch Nursing 3525 Caroline St Rm 222 Saint Louis MO 63104-1007

HSIA, SOPHIE S. language educator, researcher; b. Shanghai; came to U.S., 1973; d. Harvey J. and Helen (Tang) Hsia. MS, Georgetown U., 1976; EdD, Harvard U., 1989. Cert. in TESL. Lectr., rschr. Free U. Brussels, 1978-83; lectr., instr., tchg. fellow Tufts U., Lesley Coll., Northeastern U., Harvard U., 1986-90; assoc. prof. City U. Hong Kong, 1991-97; sr. fellow, assoc. prof. Nanyang Tech. U., Republic of Singapore, 2000—01; online faculty U. Phoenix Sch. Advanced Studies, 2002—, area chair rsch. EdD program, 2003—. Mem. acad. program coun. U. Phoenix, Ariz., 2002—. Rsch. grantee Hong Kong Govt., others. Home: 5555 N Sheridan Rd Apt 1816A Chicago IL 60640-1611 E-mail: shsia@email.uophx.edu.

HSU, CINDY KWANG-MEI, news correspondent, anchor; b. Honolulu, May 6, 1966; d. Kwang-Ping and Rosemary (Hu) H. BA, Va. Poly. Inst. and State U., 1988. Pub. rels. staff Alcoholic Beverage Control Bd., Richmond, Va., 1988-90; reporter WTOV-TV, Steubenville, Ohio, 1990-92; reporter/anchor WFRV-TV, Green Bay, Wis., 1992-93; corr. anchor WCBS-TV, N.Y.C., 1993—. Recipient Emmy award for best single hard news story Nat. Assn. TV Arts and Scis., 1994, Emmy award for best coverage anticipated breaking news, 1994. Mem. Asian Am. Journalists Assn. (v.p. 1994—), Newswatch Advisory Council. Office: WCBS-TV 524 W 57th St New York NY 10019-2924*

HSU, GLORIA, piano teacher; b. Taipei, Taiwan, Mar. 26, 1959; d. Robert and Anna Chiou (Lu) Hsu. Student, Juilliard Sch., 1970-75; BA, Hayward (Calif.) U., 1992. Cert. profl. music tchr. Profl. piano tchr. MTNA, Calif., 1992—. Fundraiser for Vietnamese refugees S.I. Orphanage, 1980. Appeared on World Jour. fundraiser for Vietnamese Refugees. Great Neck Symphony Soc. winner Tchrs. of Piano, 1972. Mem. Music Tchrs. Nat. Assn. Democrat. Christian. Avocations: listening to medieval music, reading culture and history books. Home: 3371 Isherwood Way Fremont CA 94536-3566

HSU, JUDY, newscaster; b. Taipei, Taiwan;, U.S. married; 1 child. BA in Broadcast Journalism, U. Ill., Champaign, 1992. With WPGU-FM, Champaign-Urbana, Ill., 1993—94, WCIA-TV, Champaign-Urbana, Ill., 1993—94; reporter KFMB-TV, San Diego, 1994—95, weekend anchor, 1995—96, anchor 4pm news, 1996—2001; anchor afternoon news updates KFMB-AM, San Diego, 1996—2001; co-anchor News This Morning and reporter WLS-TV, Chgo., 2001—, host All About Kids. Named one of San Diego Women Who Mean Bus., San Diego Bus. Jour.; recipient Best One-Hour Newscast Emmy, Outstanding Achievement Splty. Reporting Emmy, Best News Story, San Diego Press Club, Best Series, Best Show. Mem.: NATAS, Asian Am. Journalists Assn. Office: WLS-TV 190 N State St Chicago IL 60601

HSU, KYLIE, language educator, researcher, linguist; BA, U. Mich., 1980; MA, Calif. State U., Northridge, 1994; PhD, UCLA, 1996. Lang. and math. instr. U. Mich., Ann Arbor, 1976-80; asst. to pres. Am. GNC Corp., Chatsworth, Calif., 1980-86, exec. v.p., 1986-93; instr. in Chinese UCLA, 1994-95; dir. Lang. Inst. Pacific States U., L.A., 1996-97; asst. prof. Calif. State U., L.A., 1997—2002, assoc. prof., 2002—, assoc. chair dept. modern lang. and lit., 2003, assoc. dir. Chinese Studies Ctr., 1999—, assoc. chair dept. modern lang. lit., 2003. Conf. chair Eng. Lang. Tchg. Conf., L.A., 1996; editor-in-chief Pacific States U. Newsletter, 1997; judge Chinese Poetry Recital Contest, L.A., 1997; manual evaluator Edwin Mellen Press, Lewiston, NY, 1998—; com. chair Chinese Studies Scholarships, 1999—. Author: (book) Discourse Analysis, 1998, Selected Issues in Mandarin Chinese Word Structure Analysis, 2002; assoc. editor: Multimedia Ednl. Resource Learning and Online Tchg., 2000—; contbr. articles to profl. jours. Named one of 2000 Oustanding Scholars of 20th Century, 2000; recipient Hon. Sci. award, Bausch & Lomb, 1976; fellow, State of Calif., 1996—97; Olive M. Roosenraad Meml. scholar, 1976—80, Vieta Vogt Woodlock scholar, 1976—80, Lit., Sci. and Arts scholar, U. Mich., 1977—80, Alumnae Coun. scholar, 1976—80, Martin Luther King scholar, 1977—80, W. K. Kellog Found. scholar, 1977—78, James B. Angell scholar, 1979—80, Presdl. fellow/Rsch. grantee, U. Calif., Berkeley, 1996—97, Advanced Rsch. Lang. Acquisition grantee, U. Minn., Mpls., 2001, Regents-Alumni scholar, 1976—77. Mem.: IEEE (exhibits chair 1993), Assn. Linguistic Typology (scholar 1995), Am. Assn. Applied Linguistics (session chair 1995), Am. Coun. Tchg. Fgn. Langs. (panel chair 1997), Chinese Lang. Tchrs. Assn., Linguistic Assn. S.W. (organizer 31st ann. meeting), Phi Beta Kappa, Phi Kappa Phi. Office: Calif State U LA 5151 State University Dr Los Angeles CA 90032-8112 E-mail: kyliehsu@msn.com.

HU, EVELYN LYNN, electrical and computer engineering educator; b. N.Y.C., May 15, 1947; d. David Hosheng and Carolyn Jui-chen (Hsu) H. BA in Physics, Barnard Coll., 1969; MA in Physics, Columbia U., 1971, PhD in Physics, 1975. Mem. tech. staff AT&T Bell Labs., Holmdel, N.J., 1975-81, supr. Murray Hill, N.J., 1981-84; prof. elec. and computer engring. U. Calif., Santa Barbara, 1985—; assoc. dir. Ctr. Robotic Systems in Microelectronics, 1985—. Mem. MIT vis. com. EECS, 1983—; mem. program com. Nat. Research and Resource Facility for Submicron Structures; mem. steering com. Internat. Symposium on Electron, Ion and Photon Beams; chmn. Gordon Conf. on Chemistry and Physics of Microstructures, 1986. Contbr. articles to profl. jours.; patentee in field. Mem. IEEE, Am. Phys. Soc., Am. Vacuum Soc., Phi Beta Kappa, Sigma Xi. Office: U Calif Ctr Quantized Elec Structures Santa Barbara CA 93106

HU, GRACE M. economist; b. Taipei, Taiwan, Mar. 11, 1957; came to U.S., 1980; d. Jong-i and Shu-yun (Tai) Lee; m. Gilbert Hu, Mar. 5, 1986; children: Daniel, Jonathan. BA in econs., Nat. Taiwan U., 1979; MA in econs., U. Del., 1982; MS in stats. and rsch., Rensselaer Poly. Inst., 1985, PhD in econs., 1986. Lectr. Nat. Taiwan U., Taipei, 1979-81; rsch. asst. U. Del., 1981-82; lectr. Rensselaer Poly. Inst., Troy, N.Y., 1982-85, instr., 1985-86; statistician Maternal & Fetal Well-Being Inc., Carle Pl., N.Y., 1986-87; sr. econometrician Washington Cons. Group, 1987-90; sr. economist D.C. Pub. Svc. Commn., Washington, 1990-96, chief economist, 1996—. Spkr. Eastern Econ. Assn. meeting Pitts., 1985, Phila., 1986, Washington, 1987, Mid-Atlantic Conf. Regulatory Utilities Commrs., Phila., 1996, U.S. Energy Assn., Riga, Latvia, 1997, Fin. Investment Execs., Washington, 1997, Oressa Electricity Regulatory Commn., Bhubaneswar, India, 1998; mem. rsch. adv. com. Nat. Regulatory Rsch. Inst., Subcommittee Energy Efficiency of Energy Resources and the Environment Com., 1997—. Contbr. over 20 articles to profl. jours. Mem. Nat. Assn. Regulatory Utility Commrs. Avocations: reading, watching movies. Home: 1042 Ware St SW Vienna VA 22180-6476 Office: DC Public Service Commission 717 14th St NW Washington DC 20005-3200

HU, KELLY, actress; b. Honolulu, Feb. 13; Grad., Kamehameha Sch. Actor: (films) Friday the 13th Park VIII, 1989, The Doors, 1991, Harley Davidson and the Marlboro Man, 1991, Surf Ninjas, 1993, No Way Back, 1995, Strange Days, Scorpion King, 2002, Fakin' Da Funk, 1997, Martial Law: The Movie, 1998; (TV films) The Bold and the Beautiful, 1987; (TV series) Star Command, 1996, Nash Bridges, 1996, Sunset Beach, 1997, Hollywood Squares, 1998, Martial Law, 1998; (TV films) American Eyes, 1991, numerous TV guest appearances, 1987—. Named Miss Teen USA, 1985, Miss Hawaii, 1993. Office: c/o Gage Group 9255 Sunset Blvd # 515 Los Angeles CA 90069

HUANG, LINDA CHEN, plastic surgeon; b. Ithaca, N.Y., July 24, 1952; MD, Stanford U., 1979. Chmn. plastic surgery St. Joseph Hosp., Denver. Office: 1601 E 19th Ave Ste 3150 Denver CO 80218 Office Phone: 303-831-8400.

HUANG, PENG, statistician; d. WeiYou Huang and JinLian Luo. MS, Rochester Inst. Tech., 1995; MA, U. Rochester, 1996, PhD, 2000. Mathematician Fuzhou Agr. Bur., Fuzhou, China, 1989—93; rsch. and tchg. asst. U. Rochester, NY, 1995—2000; asst. prof. Med. U. S.C., Charleston, 2000—. Author: (optimal design) minimum aberration two-level split plot design, 1995 (Shewell award Am. Soc. Quality Control, 1997). Recipient Excellence prize, Chinese Nat. Intelligent Open Competition Com., 1987, Robust Design award, Quality Engring. by Design Symposium, Rochester Inst. Tech., 1994; fellow Dean's fellow, U. Rochester, 1997—98; grantee, NIH & NINDS, 2002—; scholar Richard A. Freund scholar, Am. Soc. Quality Control, 1994. Mem.: The Internat. Biometric Soc., Am. Soc. for Quality Control, Am. Statis. Assn., Math Assn. Am., Inst. Math. Stats., Internat. Chinese Statis. Assn. Home: 1645 N Woodmere Dr Apt F-25 Charleston SC 29407 Office: Med Univ SC 135 Cannon St Ste 303 Box 250835 Charleston SC 29425 Office Fax: 1-843-876-1126. E-mail: huangp@musc.edu.

HUBBARD, CHERYL A. director; b. North Hollywood, Calif., Sept. 18, 1960; d. Wayne Fredrick and Barbara Brooks Siegle; 1 child, Amanda Nicole. AA in Leadership Studies magna cum laude, William Penn U., 2003, student, 2002—. Gen. mdse. mgr. Drugtown Inc., Newton, Iowa, 1994—2000; supv. fine jewelry Kohl's, Clive, 2000—03; fin. aid counselor William Penn U., West Des Moines, 2000—02, fin. aid officer, 2003—. Food svcs. staff The Living Word Fellowship, Kalona, Iowa, 1996—2002; coord. assessment com. William Penn U., 2002—03, coord. curriculum rev. com., 2002, class rep., 2002—03; wellness ins. coord. Drugtown Inc., Newton, 1995—2000; team capt. Relay for Life Race for the Cure, 1998—99. R-Consevative. Christian. Avocations: travel, music. Office: William Penn U 4200 University Ave Suite 311 West Des Moines IA 50266 Home: 312A N Market St Oskaloosa IA 52577 Personal E-mail: cherriehubbard@hotmail.com. E-mail: hubbardc@wmpenn.edu.

HUBBARD, CONSTANCE E. language educator, piano teacher; b. Rapid City, S.D., Nov. 29, 1957; d. Charles Bruce and Helen Goodwin (Moorhouse) Crosswait; m. Todd Eugene Hubbard, June 1, 1991; children: Tobias Charles, Elizabeth Anne. BA in German, U. S.D., 1980; MA in German and English, U. Nebr., 1985. Tchr. German and English, Kimball (S.D.) H.S., 1980—81, Sundance (Wyo.) H.S., 1985—97; piano tchr. Hubbard Piano Studio, Sundance, 1990—2000; adj. instr. German and piano Black Hills State U., 2000—. Trustee Crook County (Wyo). Sch. Bd., 1998—2001; keyboardist Sundance Jazz Band, 1986—2001; accompanist h.s. choirs, 1985—; pianist, accompanist Spearfish UMC, 2001—; adj. German prof. Black Hills State U., 2000—; violinist Dakota Chamber Orch., 2001—. Actor: Sundance Cmty. Theater, 1987—97. Music dir., pianist United Meth. Ch., Sundance, 1988—2001. Mem. Am. Assn. Tchrs. German, Music Tchrs. Nat. Assn., Phi Beta Kappa, Alpha Lambda Delta. Democrat. Avocations: piano, reading, travel, music, violin. Home: 1407 Charles St Spearfish SD 57783

HUBBARD, ELIZABETH, actress; b. N.Y.C. d. Benjamin Alldritt and Elizabeth (Wright) H.; divorced; 1 son, Jeremy Danby Bennett. AB cum laude, Radcliffe Coll.; postgrad., Royal Acad. Dramatic Art, London. Leading role: CBS daytime TV serial As the World Turns, 1984— (9 Emmy nominations for Best Leading Actress), NBC daytime TV serial The Doctors (Best Leading Actress Emmy), First Ladies' Diary (Best Leading Actress Emmy); appeared on Broadway in Present Laughter, Joe Egg, Time for Singing, Look Back in Anger, I Remember Mama (musical), The Physicists (Clare Derwent awrad), others; appeared in off-Broadway prodn. Boys from Syracuse, Threepenny Opera (musicals); movie appearances include I Never Sang for My Father, The Bell Jar, Ordinary People, Center Stage; frequent guest TV talk shows. Former bd. dirs. Found. in Motion, Immigration and Refugee Svcs. of Am., U.S. Com. for Refugees, AFTRA Nat. Recipient Silver Medal, Royal Acad. Dramatic Art.

HUBBARD, ELIZABETH LOUISE, lawyer; b. Springfield, Ill., Mar. 10, 1949; d. Glenn Wellington and Elizabeth (Frederick) H.; m. A. Jeffrey Seidman, Oct. 27, 1974 (div. May 1982). BA, U. Ky., 1971; JD with honors, Ill. Inst. Tech.-Chgo. Kent Coll. Law, 1974. Bar: Ill. 1974, U.S. Dist. Ct. (no. dist.) Ill. 1974, U.S. Ct. Appeals (7th cir.) 1976, U.S. Supreme Ct. 1984. Atty. Wyatt Co., Chgo., 1974-75, Gertz & Giampietro, Chgo., 1975-81, Baum, Sigman, Gold, Chgo., 1981-98, Elizabeth Hubbard, Ltd., 1981-98, Hubbard & O'Connor, Ltd., Chgo., 1998—. Legal counsel NOW, Chgo., 1978-94, sec., 1977. Editor: Chgo. Kent Law Rev., 1970, Litigating Sexual Harassment and Sex Discrimination Cases, 1997—. Bd. dirs., mem. The Remains Theatre, 1985-94. Mem. Chgo. Bar Assn. (fed. civil procedure com.), Ill. State Bar Assn., Nat. Employment Lawyers Assn. (chair Ill. chpt. 1992-95, sec.-treas. 1997—). Home: 420 W Grand Ave Apt 4A Chicago IL 60610-4087 Office: Ste Six West 900 W Jackson Blvd Chicago IL 60607-3024 Fax: (312) 421-5310. E-mail: ehubbard@hubbardoconnor.com.

HUBBARD, JAYNE ELIZABETH, minister, marriage and family therapist; b. Phila., Dec. 14, 1952; d. Robert Forsyth and June Ann Hubbard. BA in History, BS in Secondary Edn., U. Minn., 1975; MA in Marriage and Family Therapy, Fuller Theol. Seminary, 1990; MDiv, Lancaster Theol. Seminary, 1997. Ordained clery United Ch. of Christ. Tchr./missionary mid. level Conservative Bapt. Mission Soc., Mombaya, Kenya, 1975—76; social worker recreation Mpls. Pk. and Recreation Dept., 1977—80; tchr. mid. level Randolph (Vt.) Union H.S., 1980—96; pastor Grace United Ch. of Christ, Lancaster, Pa., 1997—. Pvt. practice part-time therapist, Randolph, 1990—96; cons. stds. for social scis. Vt. Dept. Edn., Montpelier, Vt., 1990; cons. Youth at Risk Programs Vt., 1992—96. Jr. commr. Human Rights Commn. Hennipen County, Mound, Minn., 1970; bd. mem. Greenway Com., Randolph, 1984—86, Randolph Youth Ctr., Vt., 1991—96; chairperson Manheim Twp. Ministerium, 1997—. Mem.: Lancaster Sunrise Rotary Club (pres. 2000—01). Democrat. Avocations: chorale singing, guitar, travel, kayaking, watercolor. Office: Grace United Ch of Christ 1947 New Holland Pike Lancaster PA 17601

HUBBARD, MARGUERITE, elementary school educator; b. Elmhurst, Ill., Oct. 23, 1948; d. Edward C. and Mary Margaret Hinchley; m. Gary Lowell Hubbard, May 10, 1989; stepchildren: Audrey, Todd. BA, Elmhurst Coll., 1970; MS, U. Ill., 1975. Cert. tchr. music K-12 Ill., elem. tchr. Ill. Music tchr. Bellflower Sch. Dist., Ill., 1971—79, Belvidere Sch. Dist., Ill., 1979—. Singer Rockford Cmty. Chorale, Ill., 1980—89, 1998—2000. Mem.: NEA, Belvidere Edn. Assn. (bldg. rep. 1996—), Music Educator's Nat. Conf. Avocations: reading, swimming, crafts, walking. Office: Caledonia Sch 2311 Randolph Caledonia IL 61011

HUBBARD, RUTH, biology educator; b. Vienna, Mar. 3, 1924; came to U.S., 1938; d. Richard and Helene (Ehrlich) Hoffmann; m. Frank Twombly Hubbard, Dec. 26, 1942 (div. 1951); m. George Wald, June 11, 1958; children: Elijah, Deborah Hannah. AB, Radcliffe Coll., 1944, PhD, 1950; DSc, DSc, Clark U., 2003; LHD (hon.), So. Ill. U., Edwardsville, 1991. Lab. technician Tenn. Pub. Health Svc., Chattanooga, 1945-46; fellow U. Coll. Hosp. Med. Sch., London, 1948-49; Guggenheim fellow Carlsberg Lab., Copenhagen, 1952-53; rsch. fellow Harvard U., Cambridge, Mass., 1950-52, 54-58, rsch. assoc., lectr., 1958-74, prof., 1974-90, prof. emerita, 1990—. Vis. prof. MIT, Cambridge, 1972; cons. Boston Women's Health-book Collective 1982—; Regents lectr. U. Calif, Berkeley, 2002. Author: (with Margaret Randall) The Shape of Red: Insider/Outsider Reflections, 1988; author: The Politics of Women's Biology, 1990, (with Elijah Wald) Exploding the Gene Myth, 1993, 97, 99, Profitable Promises: Essays on Women, Science and Health, 1995; editor: Women Look at Biology Looking at Women, 1979, Genes and Gender II, 1979, Biological Woman--The Convenient Myth, 1982, Woman's Nature: Rationalizations of Inequality, 1983, Reinventing Biology: Respect for Life and the Creation of Knowledge, 1995; contbr. more than 250 articles on sci. and women's issues to profl. and lay books and jours. Adv. coun. mem. Nat. Women's Health Network, Washington, 1980-85; bd. dirs. Coun. Responsible Genetics, Boston, 1982-2002, Boston Women's Health Book Collective, 1998-99; mem. adv. bd. Boston Women's Fund, 1983-85, 2000-02; mem. adv. bd. Civil Liberties Union of Mass., 1990-91, 95—, bd. dirs., 1991-95. Recipient Paul Karrer medal Swiss Chem. Soc., 1967, Peace and Freedom award Women's Internat. League for Peace and Freedom, 1985, Feminist Marathoner award Boston chpt. NOW, 1991, Disting. Svc. award Am. Inst. Biol. Sci., 1992. Fellow AAAS; mem. Marine Biol. Lab. (trustee 1973-78, trustee emerita 1990—), Soc. Biol. Chemists, Nat. Women's Studies Assn., Phi Beta Kappa, Sigma Xi. Avocations: reading, music, yoga, swimming. Home: 21 Lake View Ave Cambridge MA 02138-3325

HUBBARD, SONIA Y. retail executive; Grad., U. Ark. CPA, Tex. Acct. with 2 acctg. firms, Texarkana, Tex., 1985-87; asst. contr. E-Z Mart, Texarkana, 1987, now CEO. Pres.-elect Texarkana Regional Arts and Humanities Coun.; trustee Wadley Hosp. Found. Mem. Four States Fair Assn. (past pres.). Office: E-Z Mart Stores 602 Falvey Ave Texarkana TX 75501-6677

HUBER, SISTER ALBERTA, college president; b. Rock Island, Ill., Feb. 12, 1917; d. Albert and Lydia (Hofer) H. BA, Coll. St. Catherine, St. Paul, 1939; MA, U. Minn., 1945; PhD, U. Notre Dame, 1954. Mem. faculty Coll. St. Catherine, 1940—, prof. English, 1953-97; prof. emerita, 1997; chmn. dept. Coll. St. Catherine, 1960-63, acad. dean, 1962-64, pres., 1964-79. Trustee Avila Coll., Kansas City, Mo., 1986-97, St. Joseph's Hosp., St. Paul, 1971-80; pres. UN Assn. Minn., 1980-81; bd. dirs. St. Paul YMCA, 1986-92. Decorated Chevalier, Ordre des Palmes Acad.; recipient Outstanding Achievement award U. Minn. Alumni Assn., 1981. Mem. Phi Beta Kappa, Pi Gamma Mu. Address: 1888 Ford Pky Saint Paul MN 55116-1916

HUBER, EVELYNE, political science educator; b. Zurich, Switzerland; Degree in social psychology, U. Zurich, 1972; MA in Polit. Sci., Yale U., 1973, PhD in Polit. Sci., 1977. Vis. asst. prof. polit. sci. U. R.I., 1976-77; lectr. polit. sci. U. Wis., Milw., 1978-79; asst. prof. polit. sci. Coll. of the Holy Cross, 1979-85; from asst. prof. to assoc. prof. polit. sci. U. Calif., Irvine, 1985-87; from assoc. prof. to prof. Northwestern U., Evanston, Ill., 1987-92; Morehead alumni disting. prof. polit. sci. U. N.C., Chapel Hill, 1992—. Dir. Inst. Latin Am. Studies, Duke U./U. N.C. programs, U. N.C.; mem. joint com. Latin Am. Social Sci. Rsch. Coun./ACLS, 1995-96, regional advice panel Latin Am., 1996-2001; editl. bd. Polit. Power and Social Theory, 1990—; mem. Inst. Advanced Study, Princeton, 1998-99. Author: The Politics of Workers' Participation: The Peruvian Approach in Comparative Perspective, 1980; co-author: Democratic Socialism in Jamaica: The Political Movement and Social Transformation in Dependent Capitalism, 1986, Capitalist Development and Democracy, 1992 (co-winner outstanding book award Am. Sociol. Assn. 1991-92), Development and Crisis of the Welfare State, 2001; co-editor: States Versus Markets in the World System, 1985. Grantee Fulbright Found. 1981, NSF, 1991-93, UN Rsch. Inst. for Social Devel.; fellow German Acad. Exch. Svc., 1991. Office: Inst of Latin Am Studies Univ NC Chapel Hill NC 27599-3205 also: U NC Dept Polit Sci Chapel Hill NC 27599-3265 E-mail: ehuber@unc.edu.

HUBER, JOAN ALTHAUS, sociology educator; b. Bluffton, Ohio, Oct. 17, 1925; d. Lawrence Lester and Hallie (Althaus) H.; ; m. William Form, Feb. 5, 1971; children: Nancy Rytina, Steven Rytina. BA, Pa. State U., 1945; MA, Western Mich. U., 1963; PhD, Mich. State U., 1967. Asst. prof. sociology U. Notre Dame, Ind., 1967-71; asst. prof. sociology U. Ill., Urbana-Champaign, 1971-73, assoc. prof., 1973-78, prof., 1978-83, head dept., 1979-83; dean Coll. Social and Behavioral Sci., Ohio State U., Columbus, 1984-92; coordinating dean Coll. Arts and Sciences, Ohio State University, Columbus, 1987-92, provost, 1992-93; sr. v.p., provost emeritus prof. Sociology emeritus, 1994. Author: (with William Form) Income and Ideology, 1973, (with Glenna Spitze) Sex Stratification, 1983. Editor: Changing Women in a Changing Society, 1973, (with Paul Chalfant) The Sociology of Poverty, 1974, Macro-Micro Linkages in Sociology, 1991. NSF research awardee, 1978-81 Mem. Am. Sociol. Assn. (v.p. 1981-83, pres. 1987-90), Midwest Sociol. Soc. (pres. 1979-80). Office: Ohio State U Dept Sociology 300 Bricker Hall 190 N Oval Mall Columbus OH 43210-1321 Home: 1812 Riverside Dr Apt 25 Columbus OH 43212-1829 Office Phone: 614-292-8872. E-mail: huber.3@osu.edu.

HUBER, MARIANNE JEANNE, art dealer, appraiser; b. Amboy, Ill., June 9, 1936; d. John Francis and Jeannette Marie (Wurth) Faivre; m. Robert L. Huber, Oct. 3, 1959; children: Michael Robert, Stephan Louis, Edward Francis. BA, Cardinal Stritch Coll., Milw., 1958. 6th grade tchr. St. Andrew's Sch., Rock Falls, Ill., 1958-59; jr. high tchr. Garside Sch., Mexico City, 1959-61; art dealer, cons. Huber Primitive Art, N.Y.C. and Dixon, Ill., 1963—; founder, pres. New World Art Svcs., N.Y.C. and Dixon, Ill., 1993—. Lectr., cons. Primitive Art Soc., Chgo., 1987, Freeport (Ill.) Art Mus., 1993, Indpls. Mus. Art, 1994, Nprstk Mus., Prague, Czech Republic, 1995; participant Maya Meetings, Austin, Tex., 1985—. Author: Echoes of a Distant Flute, 1984; co-prodr., author (documentary films) The Cuna, 1980, Nebaj, Cotzal and Chajul, 1987, 2003 Maya Calendar, 2004 Maya Calendar, collector, organizer traveling exhbns. The Cuna, 1980—. Election judge Ogle County, Ill., 1993—; committeewoman Dem. Precinct, 2002—. Mem.: LWV, AAUW, Ethnographic Art Soc., Am. Appraisers Assn., Am. Soc. Appraisers, Am. Assn. Dealers in Ancient Oriental and Primitive Art, Phidian Soc., Ill. Dem. Women, Indpls. Met. Mus. Art, Internat. Platform Assn. (gov. 1993—2001), Delta Epsilon Sigma. Democrat. Avocations: hiking, wilderness camping, painting, piano, travel. Home and Office: 1012 Timber Trail Dr Dixon IL 61021-8934 E-mail: tellapple@yahoo.com.

HUBER, MARY SUSAN, music educator; b. Buffalo, Feb. 14, 1946; d. Floyd M. Zaepfel and Thelma Zaeptel; m. David Conrad Huber, Dec. 27, 1971; children: David Conrad Jr., Kevin Michael. BS in Music, Daemen Coll., 1969; MEd in Music, State U. Buffalo, 1971; M in Ednl. Leadership U. North Fla., 1991. Elem. music tchr. Maryvale Sch. Sys., Buffalo, 1969—74, Lakeland Prep, Orlando, Fla., 1980—81, North Shore Elem., Jacksonville, Fla., 1981—85, Loretto Elem., Jacksonville, 1985—89, Mandarin Oaks Elem., Jacksonville, 1989—90; mid. sch. choral dir. Mandarin Mid. Sch., Jacksonville, 1990—. Contbr. articles to mags. and newsletters. Mem. citizens opinion rsch. forum County of Duval, Jacksonville, 1987; life mem. Duval County PTA, 1987—; mem. choir St. Joseph Cath. Ch., 1999—2002. Named Educator of Yr., Jaycee's, Jacksonville, 1987, Tchr. of Yr., Rotary, Mandarin, 1998. Mem.: Duval County Elem. Tchrs. Assn. (past elem. pres.). Republican. Roman Catholic. Home: 11068 Great Western Ln W Jacksonville FL 32257

HUBER, RITA NORMA, civic worker; b. Cin., July 16, 1931; d. Andrew Elwood and Mary Gertrude (Hille) Stewart; student Cin. Coll. Conservatory Music, 1949-50, Berlitz Sch., Cin., 1951-52; m. Justin G. Huber, July 17, 1954; children: Monica Ann, Sarah Marie, Rachel Miriam. Tchr. Russian lang. for officers' wives Ft. Sill, Okla., 1955-56; bd. dirs. United Community Svcs., Cedar Rapids, Iowa, 1969; founder, chairperson Linn County Consumers League, 1969-70; founder, pub. rels. dir. Cedar Rapids Rape Crisis Svcs., 1974—; owner/operator Huber Janitorial Svcs., 1982-84; chairperson Linn County Dem. Womens Club, 1966-67, Linn County Com., Eugene McCarthy for Pres., 1967-68; campaign mgr. Delores Cortez for Iowa Legislature, 1968, Jan V. Johnson for Iowa Legislature, 1970, Stanley Ginsberg for county supr. Linn County, 1974, E.L. Colton for Cedar Rapids pub. safety commr., 1977; chairperson Linn County Dem. Cen. Com., 1976-77, 88-90; state coord. Jerry Brown for Pres., 1976; chairperson Pat Kane for Linn County Recorder, 1982; chmn. Linn County Bd. Health, 1982-85; supr. Linn County, 1990-95; chairperson Linn County bd. Suprs., 1992; instr. parliamentary procedures Cedar Rapids Women's Community Leadership Inst., 1975-77; lectr. local colls. and svc. orgns.; tchr. conversational Russian, Pierce Elementary Sch., Cedar Rapids, 1976; instr. Russian, Community Edn. div. Kirkwood Community Coll.; mem. care rev. com. Pineview Care Ctr., Cedar Rapids, 1987-90. Named to Iowa Dem. Party DVP Hall of Fame, 1986, Linn County Dem. Party Hall of Fame, 2003; recipient Woman of Yr. award Women's Equality Day Cedar Rapids Iowa, 1993; Mem. Am. Inst. Parliamentarians. Roman Catholic (extraordinary minister of Eucharist). Composer: She is Risen, 1973. Home: 2050 Glass Rd NE Cedar Rapids IA 52402-3401

HUBER, VIRGINIA ROLLO, photojournalist, educator, artist; d. Earl Eugene Rollo and Pauline Celeste Ritter; children: John, Laurie Huber Sheffler, James A. BS in Journalism-English, U. Ill., 1941; MAT in Art-Journalism, Whitworth Coll., Spokane, Wash., 1968. File clk. U.S. Army, Marion, Ill., 1941—42; reporter Decatur (Ill.) Rev., 1941—42; writer Scott Field Air Base, Belville, Ill., 1942—43; asst. city editor Globe-Dem., St. Louis, 1943—45; co-owner, features, editls. York Daily News Times, York, 1947—55; contbr., art, writing Sacred Heart Hosp., Spokane, 1960—70; freelance feature writer Spokane Review-Chronicle, 1970—80; artist, instr. Rollo Fine Art, Port Orchard, Wash., 1999—; dir. art gallery U.S. Rte. 6 Tour Assn., Port Orchard, 2001—. Pianist, singer retirement cmtys., Silverdale, Port Orchard, Federal Way, Shelton, Wash., 1997—. Acrylic portrait, Innocence, BC Can. Regional Show, 1986 (Hon. Mention, 1994), prin. works include Pierce Gallery, Omaha, 2003; rewrite (Almanac); author: stories on banking industry, real estate devel. on Puget Sound South Kitsap Bus. Jour., 2001; prin. works include variuos local galleries. Writer Kitsap Ind., Port Orchard, Wash., 2000; reporter stories on banking industry, real estate devel. on Puget Sound South Kitsap Bus. Jour., Port Orchard, 2001. Mem.: South Kitsap Art Assn. (sec. 2002—), Peninsula Art League, Pi Beta Phi, Theta Sigma Phi. Avocations: swimming, walking, photography, piano, singing. Home: Bldg 1 Apt 202 1790 Sidney Ave Port Orchard WA 98366 Office: Rollo Fine Art Bldg 1 Apt 202 1790 Sidney Ave Port Orchard WA 98366

HUBERT, HELEN BETTY, epidemiologist; b. N.Y.C., Jan. 22, 1950; d. Leo and Ruth (Rosenbaum) H.; m. Carlos Barbaro Arostegui, Sept. 11, 1976 (div. May 1987); 1 child, Joshua Daniel Hubert. BA magna cum laude, Barnard Coll., 1970; MPH, Yale U., 1973, MPhil, 1976, PhD, 1978. Rsch. assoc. Yale U., New Haven, 1977-78; rsch. epidemiologist Nat. Heart, Lung and Blood Inst., Bethesda, Md., 1978-84; rsch. dir. Gen. Health, Inc., Washington, 1984-87; sr. rsch. scientist Stanford (Calif.) U., 1988—. Peer rev. Am. Jour. Epidemiology, Am. Jour. Pub. Health, Chest, Jour. AMA (JAMA), Archives Internal Medicine; contbr. articles to profl. jours., chpts. to books. NIH grantee, 1997—. Mem. Am. Coll. Epidemiology, Soc. Epidemiol. Rsch., Assn. Rheumatology Health Profls., Phi Beta Kappa, Sigma Xi (grant-in-aid for rsch. 1978). Office: Stanford Univ Med Ctr 701 Welch Rd Ste 3305 Palo Alto CA 94304-1701 Office Phone: 650-723-5639.

HUBLER, MARY, state legislator; b. Milw., July 31, 1952; BS, U. Wis., Superior, 1973; JD, U. Wis., Madison, 1980. Former tchr., coach; atty.; mem. from dist. 75 Wis. State Assembly, Madison, 1984—, vice chairwoman tourism, recreation and forest product coms., 1985-98, mem. joint fin. com., until 1996; rural affairs & forestry State of Wis. Mem. Wis. Bar Assn. Office: PO Box 544 Rice Lake WI 54868-0544 also: Wis State Assembly State Capitol Madison WI 53702-0001

HUBLEY, ELIZABETH, Canadian senator; b. Howlan, Prince Edward Island, Can., Sept. 8, 1942; m. Richard B. Hubley; children: Brendan, Susan, Allan, Amos, Jennifer, Florence. Student, Prince of Wales Coll., Charlottetown, Nova Scotia Coll. Art and Design, Halifax. Dance tchr.; owner, artistic dir., choreographer Stepping Out, 1980—; rep. old dist. of Fifth Prince Prince Edward Island Legis. Assembly, 1989—96; apptd. mem. Fed. Vets. Rev. and Appeal Bd., 1998—2001; senator The Senate of Can., Ottawa, 2001—. Mem. Prince Edward Island Coun. Arts; pres. Prince Edward Island Fiddlers Soc., Prince County Fiddlers; past pres. Kensington and Area Cultural Found.; founding mem. Kensington Step Dancing Festival. Liberal. Office: The Senate of Canada 351 East Block Ottawa Canada K1A 0A4

HUCK, LINDA A. music educator; d. Arnold and Betty Ann Basler; m. Keith M. Huck, June 10, 1983; children: Claire, Mallory. Bachelor of Music in Performance, Bachelor of Music in Edn., S.E. Mo. State U., 1982, Master's in Music Edn., 1986. Instr. music Farmington R-7 Schs., Mo., 1983—. Mem.: Music Tchrs. Nat. Assn., Mo. Music Educators Assn. (dist. pres. 2000—02, state band v.p. 2004—06, Outstanding Music Educator 2002—03). Office: Farmington Mid Sch 506 S Fleming Farmington MO 63640 Office Phone: 573-701-1330.

HUCKABEE, PHYLLIS, human resources specialist; b. Andrews, Tex., Aug. 11, 1963; d. Tommie Jack and Sylvia (Wingo) H. BBA in Fin., Tex. Tech U., 1984, MBA, 1986. Mgmt. trainee El Paso (Tex.) Nat. Gas Co., 1986-87, analyst rate dept., 1987-88, specialist Calif. affairs, 1988-91, rep. Calif. affairs, 1991-92; asst. dir. Cambridge Energy Rsch. Assocs., Oakland, Calif., 1992-93; regulatory rels. mgr. Pacific Enterprises, San Francisco, 1994-96, regional v.p. state regulatory rels., 1996-98; dir. fed. agy. rels. Sempra Energy, Washington, 1998—99, dir. corp. learning and rsch., 1999—2002, dir. human capital solutions, 2002—. Commr. Calif. Commn. in Improving Life Through Svc., 1997—98; mem. adj. faculty No. Calif. campus U. Phoenix, San Francisco, 1994—99; extension instr. U. Calif., San Diego, Calif., 2001—. Bd. dirs. El Paso Community Concert Assn., 1988, bd. dirs. Performing Arts Workshop, 1991-92, mem. adv. bd., 1992—94. Recipient Twin award, YWCA, 2002. Mem. Women Energy Assocs. (bd. dirs. 1990—), Leadership Calif. (Class of 1996), Leadership Am. Methodist. Democrat. Avocations: photography, bicycling, fine arts.

HUCKEBA, EMILY CAUSEY, retired elementary school educator; b. Carrollton, Ga., Aug. 26, 1941; d. Edward Clark and Audie Farmer Causey; m. Dale Malloy Huckeba, Aug. 27, 1961; 1 child, Catherine Nan. BS Elem. Edn., West Ga. Coll., 1962, M Edn., 1977. 2nd grade tchr. Whitesburg (Ga.) Elem. Sch., 1962—63; 1st grade tchr. Ctrl. Elem. Sch., Carrollton, Ga., 1963—68, Roopville (Ga.) Elem. Sch., 1968—96, music tchr., 1996—98, substitute tchr., 1998—2001. Mem. alumni coun. West Ga. Coll., Carrollton, 1991—93; pilot tchr. Whole Lang. Program Roopville (Ga.) Elem. Sch., 1993—95. Charter mem. Roopville Hist. Soc., 1984—; organist, pianist Roopville Bapt. Ch., 1960—. Mem.: NEA, Ga. Music Educators Assn., Carroll Heard Ret. Tchrs., Ga. Assn. Educators, Alpha Delta Kappa. Baptist. Home: 1135 S Hwy 27 Roopville GA 30170-2516

HUCLES, ANGELA KHALIA, professional soccer player; b. Va. Beach, Va., July 5, 1978; BA in anthropology, U. Va., 2000. Soccer player, midfielder U.S. Women's Nat. Team, 2001; mem. Boston Breakers, WUSA, 2001—03, San Diego Spirit, 2003—. Columnist women's sports Boston Metro, 2002. Named First Team All-ACC, 1996, 1997, 1998, 1999, Mid Atlantic All-Star, 1996, 1997, 1998, 1999. Office: US Soccer Fedn 1801 S Prairie Ave Chicago IL 60616*

HUDALLA, KAREN, court reporting educator, academic administrator; b. Chgo., June 11, 1951; d. Edward Mitchell Sr. and Stella Phyllis (Walenda) Kozak; m. Gregory A. Hudalla Sr., Dec. 23, 1972; children: Gregory A. II, Nicholas Mark. Cert. ct. reporter, Chgo. Coll. Commerce, 1980; cert. paralegal, Paralegal Inst., Phoenix, 1984; AS in Bus., Coll. DuPage, Glen Ellyn, Ill., 1994; BS, Ohio U., 1999. Cert. reporting instr. Tchr. Chgo. Coll. Commerce, 1980-82, South Suburban Coll., South Holland, Ill., 1999, Career Colls. Chgo./De Paul U., Chgo., acting dir. edn., acad. dean, 1980—; ofcl. ct. reporter Chgo., 1980—. Sec., owner K&G Svcs., Ltd., Downers Grove, 1975—. Cub scout leader Boy Scouts Am., Downers Grove, Ill., 1988-94; Resource Ctr. vol. Dist. 58, Downers Grove, 1988-92; tchr.'s aide vol. Burr Ridge (Ill.) Sch. Disst., 1986-88; bd. dirs. Burr Ridge Homeowners Assn., 1986-88, Near West Neighborhood Assn., Chgo., 1973-83. Mem. Nat. Shorthand Reporters Assn. (cert. ct. reporter). Avocations: reading, sewing, educational classes.

HUDDLESTON, VICKI JEAN, diplomat; b. San Diego, Dec. 13, 1942; d. Howard Stevens and Duane Louise (Dickinson) Latham; m. Robert Webb Huddleston, Jan. 31, 1970; children: Robert Stevens, Alexandra Duane. BA, U. Colo., 1964; MA, Johns Hopkins U., 1975. Chief econ. sect. Am. Embassy, Freetown, Sierra Leone, 1977-80, Bamako, Mali, 1983-86; internat. economist Dept. of State, Washington, 1980-82, econ. officer Office of Mexican Affairs, 1982-83, country officer for Bolivia, 1986-89, dep. dir. Office of Cuban Affairs, 1989-91, dir. Office of Cuban Affairs, 1991-93; charge d'affaires Am. Embassy, Port au Prince, Haiti, 1993, dep. chief of mission, 1993-95; amb. Rep. of Madagascar, 1995-97; dep. asst. secy. for Africa Dept. of State, Washington, 1997—99; prin. officer U.S. Interest Sect., Havana, Cuba, 1999—2002; U.S. amb. to Mali, 2002—. Dep. dir. Am. Inst. for Free Labor Devel., Rio de Janiero, Brazil, 1969-72, program officer, Lima, Peru, 1966-68. Vol. U.S. Peace Corps, 1964-66. Am. Polit. Sci. Congl. fellow, 1988-89; recipient Disting. Honor award, Presdl. Meritorious Svc. award, several Superior Honor awards. Mem. Am. Fgn. Svc. Assn., Alumni Johns Hopkins. Presbyterian. Avocations: skiing, scuba diving (master). Home: 14-16 rue Rainitouo Antsahauola Madagascar Office: American Embassy Bamako Rue Rochester NY*

HUDEL, CHESTELLA ALVIS, athletics educator; b. Temple, Okla., Jan. 13, 1931; d. James Chester and Jewel (McCain) Alvis; m. William August Hudel, June 14, 1952 (dec. June 1962); children: Mary Hudel Rinne, Nancy Hudel Parten, Joan Hudel Patrick. BS in Child Devel., Tex. Women's U., 1950. Tchr. Port Arthur (Tex.) Ind. Sch., 1950-53, Ridgewood Park Pre-Sch., Dallas, 1962-86; trainer Red Cross, Dallas, 1975—; adapted aquatics dir. YWCA, Dallas, 1975—. Trainer water safety instrs. Red Cross, Dallas, 1975-96; coach Spl. Olympics, 1993-98; educator Down's Syndrome Guild/Dallas Ind. Sch. Dist., 1994-96; counselor for breast cancer survivors Encore YWCA/Komen Found., Dallas, 1995-98. Elder Northridge Presbyn. Ch., Dallas, 1979-98; com. on adminstrn. YWCA, Dallas, 1980-86; active Northridge Learning Ctr. Bd., Northridge Presbyn. Ch., Dallas, 1987-97, active Bachman Recreation Ctr., Dallas, Park Cities YMCA, Dallas; swim program leader Light House for the Blind, 1986-90, Tom Landry Ctr. Baylor Hosp., 2003—; resource person Parent to Parent, 1993. Recipient Golden Rule award J.C. Penny, Dallas, 1983, Extra Step award Red Cross, Dallas, 1989, Spirit of Red Cross award, 1990, GM Vol. Spirit award GM, Dallas, 1992, George Washington medal of honor Freedom Found. Valley Forge, Dallas, 1997; named Vol. of the Yr., Helping Agys. Serving Richardson, Tex., 1990. Mem. Assn. for Retarded Citizens. Avocations: journal and scrapbook making, piano, bridge, bible study. Home: 6015 Sandhurst Ln Apt A Dallas TX 75206-4726

HUDELSON, JUDITH GIANTOMASS, elementary school educator; b. Phila., May 11, 1954; d. Thomas Peter and Viola D. Giantomass; m. Bradley A. Hudelson, Jan. 30, 1993; 1 child, Joshua Bradley. BE, Millersville U., Pa., 1976, ME, 1979; EdD in Edn. Adminstrn., Widener U., Pa. Tchr. grade 3 Rothsville Elem., Lititz, Pa., 1976—77; tchr. grade 3 and 5 Beck Elem., Lititz, 1977—94; tchr. grade 5 Bonfield Elem., Lititz, 1994—. Com. mem. Pa. Dept. Edn., Harrisburg, Pa., 1992—2003. Author: (book) Metacognition and Journaling in Process Reading: Their Relationships to Comprehension and Motivation to Read, 1997. Mem.: Warwick Edn. Assn., Pa. State Edn. Assn., Nat. Edn. Assn., Warwick Edn. Assn. for PACE (chairperson 2000—), Assn. for Supervision and Curriculum Devel., Phi Delta Kappa. Democrat. Roman Catholic. Avocations: swimming, golf, skiing, aerobics, reading. Home: 5739 Pine St East Petersburg PA 17520 Office: Warick Sch Dist 101 N Oak St Lititz PA 17543

HUDES, NANA BRENDA, marketing professional; b. N.Y.C., Nov. 25; d. Harry and Anita Lorraine (Seiken) Richter; m. Barton Hudes, Sept. 2, 1958 (div. Sept. 1972); children: Layne A., Michael F., Meredith A. Student, Skidmore Coll.; BA magna cum laude, Pace U., 1974; MS with honors, Coll. of New Rochelle, 1976. Dir. mail mktg. mgr. Pergamon Press, Elmsford, N.Y., 1979-80, spl. sales mgr., 1980-81; mktg. mgr. Knowledge Industry Publs., White Plains, N.Y., 1981-82, Grolier Electronic Pub., Danbury, Conn., 1982-84, dir. mktg., 1984-86; mktg. mgr. R.R. Bowker, New Providence, N.J., 1986-88, mktg. dir., 1988-91, sr. dir. mktg., 1991-99. Tchr. social studies Rye Neck (N.Y.) Mid. Sch., 1978-79; pres. NH Assocs., Mktg. Cons., 2000-01; dir. libr. mktg. Columbia U. Press, 2001—. Dist. leader, county committeeperson Dem. Party, Matawan Twp., N.J., 1964. Home: 233 E 69th St New York NY 10021-5414 E-mail: nhudes@mindspring.com.

HUDGENS, JEANNE ELLIS, advocate; b. Winston-Salem, Sept. 17, 1925; d. William J. and Cora N. Holland; m. Cornell Franklin Ellis, June 10, 1948 (dec. Oct. 1979); children: Cornell Jr. Ellis, Larry T. Ellis, Michael B. Ellis; m. Charles Edward Hudgens, July 18, 1981 (dec. Dec. 2000). BA, N.C. Ctrl. U., 1945; MA, Columbia U., 1969. Tchr. Mecklenburg County Pub. Schs., Charlotte, 1951—55, J.E. Wright H.S., Fredericksburg, Va., 1957—59; adminstr. Stamford (Conn.) Early Childhood, 1960—85; dir. Guilford County Head Star, Greensboro, NC, 1985—91; exec. dir. NAACP, Greensboro, 1991—. Mem. Child Care Study Commn., Norwalk, Conn., 1984—85. Recipient Edn. award, NAACP, 1996, Head Start award, Head Start, 1985, Presdl. Citation, Nat. Assn. for Equal Opportunity in Higher Edn., 1980, Letter of Recognition, Pres. Ronald Reagan, 1985, African-Am. Atelier Unsung Heroes award, 1995, State of Conn. Ofcl. citation, 1985; grantee No Puffing grantee, Moses Cone Long Cmty. Health Found., 2000. Mem.: Commn. on Status of Women (chair 1996—, Cert. 2000), Nat. Assn. Negro Bus. and Profl. Women (pres., Sojourner Truth award 1999), Lady Sertoma (pres., treas. 1987—, Sertoma of the Yr. 1990). Democrat. Baptist.

Avocations: writing, music, travel, reading. Home: 3 Bent Oak Ct Greensboro NC 27455-3007 Office: NAACP 1200 E Market St Greensboro NC 27401

HUDGENS, SANDRA LAWLER, retired state official; b. New Orleans, Feb. 15, 1944; d. Avril Lawler and Peggy V. (Crager) Kelly; m. Adolfo DiGennaro, Oct. 20, 1967 (div. 1970); 1 child, Daniel Darryn DiGennaro; m. Stanley Dalton Hudgens, Feb. 17, 1973; children: Stephanie Hudgens Cap, Richard Stanley, Michael Shane. Student, U. Nev., 1962-64, U. Grenoble, France, 1964-65, U. Aix-Marseille, Nice, France, 1965, U. Nev., Las Vegas, 1980-2000. Traffic ct. clk. III Clark County Juvenile Ct. Svcs., Las Vegas, 1965-71; planning commr. City of Las Vegas, 1988-92, chmn. planning commn., 1991-92; br. mgr. registration divsn. Dept. Motor Vehicles and Pub. Safety, State of Nev., Las Vegas, 1971-96. Rep. Weststar FCU, Las Vegas, 1988-96; advocate State of Nev. Employees Assn., Las Vegas, 1971-96; coord. State of Nev. team City of Las Vegas Corp. Challenge, 1987-90; dir. so. chpt. Am. Fedn. State, County and Mcpl. Employees/State Nev. Employees Assn. retirees AFL/CIO. Past treas., sec. Las Vegas Civic Ballet Assn., Las Vegas, 1987-93; treas. Women's Dem. Club Clark County, Las Vegas, 1996-97, pres., 1998; chmn., vice-chmn. United Blood Svcs. Adv. Coun., Las Vegas, 1993-96; chmn. 1st Ann. Flood Awareness Week, mem. adv. coun. Clark County Regional Flood Dist., Las Vegas, 1987-88; treas., sec., badge and advancement counselor Boy Scouts Am., Las Vegas, 1976-90; nat. living stones coord. Episcopal Diocese of Nev., 2002—. Mem.: Am. Bus. Women's Assn. (chmn. souvenir program Western Regional Conf. 1997), Commn. Ministries, Ret. Pub. Employees Nev. (v.p. 1999—2000, pres. 2000—01, 2002—). Democrat. Episcopalian. Avocations: hunting, knitting, photography, rving, biking. Home: PO Box 2103 Dayton NV 89403-2103

HUDKINS, CAROL L. state legislator; b. North Platte, Nebr., Feb. 21, 1945; m. Larry Hudkins; children: Janet, Kathy. Mem. Nebr. Legislature from 21st dist, Lincoln, 1992—; mem. agr. gen. affairs com.; mem. judiciary com. Mem. agr. gen. affairs com., judiciary com., rules com. (chair), natural resources com., transp. and comm. com, exec. bd., reference com. Mem. Saunders County Hist. Soc., Ned. Cattlemen, Saunders County Livestock Feeders; Neb. Cattlewomen. Republican. Methodist.

HUDSON, CAROLYN BRAUER, application developer, educator; b. Durham, NC, Dec. 17, 1945; d. Alfred Theodor and Hildegard Wolf Brauer; children: Paul Benjamin, Joel Stephen. BS in Math., U. N.C., 1967; MA in Forestry, Duke U., 1969; MS in Geology, U. S.C., 1979, PhD in Geology, 1995. Assoc. dir. office rsch. and evaluation, asst. prof. N.C. Ctrl. U., Durham, 1970—72; rsch. assoc. Nat. Lab. for Higher Edn., Durham, 1971—72; tchg. assoc. U. S.C., Columbia, 1973—74, tchg. asst., 1990—92, tchg. assoc., 1993—, programmer, 1999—; vis. scientist Geol. Survey of Can., Ottawa, 1979—82; statistician S.C. State Govt., Columbia, 1997—98. Mem. S.C. Gov's Nuclear Adv. Coun., Columbia, 2001—; tech. coord. profl. women on campus U. S.C., Columbia, 2000—. Contbr. articles to profl. jours. Vol. area pub. sch., 1978—93; Leader Boy Scouts of Am./Scouts Can., 1979—95; vol. Congaree Nat. Park, Hopkins, SC, 1999—. Recipient Dist. Merit award, Boy Scouts of Am., 1988, Silver Beaver award, 1991, Shofar award, 1993, Profl. Devel. award, Profl. Women on Campus, 2000. Mem.: U. N.C. Alumni Assn. (life), Friends of Congaree Swamp (edn. com. 1996—), Women of Reform Judaism (v.p. 1975—76), Audubon, Sierra Club (nuclear affairs subcom. 2001—, computer chair 2003—), Hadassah (life; bd. dirs. 1983—84), LWV. Jewish. Avocations: hiking, music, travel, reading. Business E-Mail: hudson-carolyn@sc.edu.

HUDSON, CHERYL L. communications executive; Pres. Intouch Comm. Group GlobalHue, Inc., Southfield, Mich. Recipient Outstanding Women in Mktg. and Comms. award, Ebony Mag., 2001. Office: GlobalHue Inc 26555 Evergreen Rd Ste 1700 Southfield MI 48076-4206*

HUDSON, DEBORAH M. public relations practitioner; b. Elk River, Minn., Oct. 28, 1955; d. Thomas R. and Rosella A. (Libor) H.; m. Rick Scott Pallansch, Dec. 3, 1994. BA, U. Minn., 1980. Reporter, columnist St. Cloud (Minn.) Daily Times, 1982-87; asst. dir. pub. rels. & publs. St. Cloud State U., 1987-93; dir. univ. comms. Ball State U., Muncie, Ind., 1993-96; comm. cons., 1996—98; asst. dean for external rels. Univ. Md. Coll. Edn., College Park, 1999—. Bd. dirs. Land of Lakes coun. Girl Scouts U.S., St. Cloud, 1989-93, chair nominating com., 1992; steering com. Muncie (Ind.) Children's Mus. Capital Campaign, 1995-96; bd. dirs. St. Cloud Area Arts Fund, 1987-92, Minn. Orch. at St. Benedict's, St. Cloud, 1989-93. Mem. Phi Kappa Phi. Mem. United Ch. of Christ. Avocations: fine arts, travel, gardening. Office: Univ Md 3119 Benjamin Bldg College Park MD 20742

HUDSON, JUDITH ANN, elementary school educator; b. Geneva, Ohio, Jan. 24, 1971; d. Gordon Hale Rudd, Jr. and Rachel Ellen Rudd; m. Dennis Alan Hudson, Aug. 9, 1997; 1 child, Charles Elmer Rudd. BS in Edn., Baldwin-Wallace Coll., 1994; MEd, Ashland U., 1998. Nat. bd. cert. tchr. mid. childhood generalist. Tchr. Rocky River City Schs., Ohio, 1994—. Mid. sch. cross country coach Rocky River City Schs., 1994—2002, mid. sch. track coach, 1997—2002; building math coord., 2000—. Grantee Australian Tchr. Exch. Program, Hands Across the Water, 2001. Mem.: Nat. Coun. for Tchg. Math., Kappa Delta Pi. Methodist. Avocations: travel, sports. Home: 20310 Marian Ln Rocky River OH 44116 Office: Kensington Intermediate School 20140 Lake Rd Rocky River OH 44116 Personal E-mail: judydenn@aol.com.

HUDSON, KAREN ANN SAMPSON, music educator; b. Greenville, Mich., Nov. 1, 1946; d. Elton J. Sampson and Freda Sampson Grunwald; m. James Gary Hudson, May 23, 1970; children: Alexander E., Annemarie M., Elaine K., Veronica L. BA, U. Mich., 1968. Piano tchr. Karen Hudson's Piano Studio, Reno, 1994—. Lay Carmelite Little Flower Lay Carmelites, Reno, 1997—. Mem.: Nat. Music Tchrs. Assn., Autism Soc. Am. Democrat. Home: 2055 Severn Dr Reno NV 89503

HUDSON, KATE, actress; b. L.A., Calif., Apr. 19, 1979; m. Chris Robinson, Dec. 31, 2000; 1 child. Actor: (films) Desert Blue, 1998, Ricochet River, 1998, 200 Cigarettes, 1999, About Adam, 2000, Gossip, 2000, Almost Famous, 2000 (Golden Globe award for Best Supporting Actress, 2001), Dr. T and the Women, 2000, The Cutting Room, 2001, The Four Feathers, 2002, How to Lose a Guy in 10 Days, 2003, Alex and Emma, 2003, Le Divorce, 2003; (TV series) Party of Five, 1996, EZ Streets, 1997.

HUDSON, KATHERINE MARY, manufacturing executive; b. Rochester, N.Y., Jan. 19, 1947; d. Edward Klock and Helen Mary (Rubacha) Nellis; m. Robert Orneal Hudson, Sept. 13, 1980; 1 child, Robert Klock. Student, Oberlin coll., 1964-66; BS in Mgmt., Ind. U., 1968; postgrad., Cornell U., 1968-69. Various postitions in fin., investor rels., communications, gen. mgr. instant photography Eastman Kodak Co., Rochester, 1970-87, chief info. officer, 1988-91, v.p., gen. mgr. printing and pub. imaging, 1991-93; pres., CEO Brady Corp., Milw., 1994—2003, chmn. bd., 2003. Bd. dirs. CNH Global N.V., Charming Shoppers, Inc. Mem. adv. coun. Ind. U. Sch. Bus., 1994—; trustee Alverno Coll., 1994—; bd. dirs. Med. Coll. Wis., 1995—. Recipient Chief of the Yr. award Info. Week Mag., 1990, Athena award Rochester C. of C., 1992, WESG Breaking Glass Ceiling award, 1993, Sacajewea award, 1995; Lehman fellow N.Y. State, 1968; named Wis. Bus. Leader of Yr., 1995. Republican. Avocations: golf, fishing, creative writing. Office: Brady Corp 6555 W Good Hope Rd PO Box 571 Milwaukee WI 53201-0571 E-mail: kathy_hudson@bradycorp.com.

HUDSON, LEE (ARLENE HUDSON), environmental activist; b. Oakland, Calif., Apr. 17, 1936; d. Clyde Edward and Helen Therese McIrvin; m. James Joseph Coté, Mar. 28, 1958 (div. 1963); 1 child, Steven Michael. BA in Psychology, Calif. State U., Sacramento, 1976, postgrad., 1977-78. Exec. field dir. Dem. State Cen. Com., Sacramento, 1967-68; mem. staff Calif. Legis., Sacramento, 1967-72; founder, chmn., editor newsletter The Group for Alternatives to Spreading Poisons, Nevada City, Calif., 1983—. Non-chem. advocate on adv. com. to Calif. Dept. Transp. Roadside Vegetation Mgmt. Com., 1993-97. Vol. various state, fed. and local campaigns or initiatives, 1967—; chmn. toxic subcom. Sierra Club, 1985-88; founding mem. Toxics Coordinating Project, San Francisco, 1985-90; co-founder Calif. Coalition for Alternatives to Pesticides, Arcata and Eureka, 1983—, pres., chmn. bd. dirs., 1989-2002; mem. Com. for Sustainable Agriculture, 1986—, mem. mktg.-order subcom., 1986-89; bd. dirs. NW Coalition for Alternatives to Pesticides, Eugene, 1987-93; mem., chmn. tech. writing com. Nevada County Adv. Com. on Air Pollution, 1988-93; mem. Hazardous Waste Transfer Facility Siting Com. for Nevada County, 1989-90; mem. Nevada County Hazardous Waste Task Force, 1987-95, chair tech. subcom., 1988-90; mem. Cen. Valley Hazardous Waste Minimization Com., 1990-91; mem. Nat. Coalition Against the Misuse of Pesticides, Nevada County Land Trust, Cmty. Alliance with Family Farmers, Activities Improvement Ctr., Californians for Pesticide Reform, Pesticide Watch, 1990—99, Sequoia Challenge, 1993-2002, Round Mountain Project, 1996-2002, Family Housing Coalition, 1998-2002, The Environtl. Health Network, Rural Quality Coalition, United Farmworkers, ACLU, So. Chrisian Leadership Conf., Coun. Responsible Genetics, Women's Forest Sanctuary, COOP Am., Sierra Nnev. Alliance, Humane Soc. Defenders Wildlife. Mem. Amnesty Internat. People's Med. Soc., Nat. Resources Def. Coun., Greenpeace, Planning and Conservation League, Nevada County Greens Alliance, North Columbia Schoolhouse Cultural Ctr., South Yuba River Citizen's League, Union of Concerned Scientists, Calif. Indian Basketweavers Assn., Nev. Placer Noxious Weed Mgmt. Group, Environ. Protection Info. Ctr., Yuba Watershed Inst., Planet Drum, San Juan Ridge Taxpayers Assn. Mem. Universal Life Ch. Office: PO Box 451 Nevada City CA 95959-0451

HUDSON, LINDA, health care executive; b. Tuscaloosa, Ala., Feb. 12, 1950; d. Elvin and Clara (Duke) Hudson; m. Charles Garrett Kimbrough, May 26, 1984. BS in Edn., U. Ala., 1971; MS in Psychology, U. So. Miss., 1984. Lic. profl. counselor. Recreational therapist West Ala. Rehab. Ctr., Tuscaloosa, 1971-72; flight attendant Delta Air Lines, Miami and New Orleans, 1972-80; pvt. practice psychotherapist Hattiesburg (Miss.) and Atlanta, 1984—. Program dir. Eating Disorders Adventist Health System/Wedst, Atlanta, 1985-88, regional dir./cons., 1986-87, exec. dir. mental health svcs., 1988-89; owner Hudson Cons. Assocs., 1989—, nat. cons., 1986—. Contbr. articles to profl. jours. Mem. Covington Jr. Svc. League, La., 1981-83; co-chmn. St. Tammany Rep. Polit. Action Com., 1980-81; coord. United Way of St. Tammany Parish, 1979-80. Mem. Am. Assn. Mental Health Counselors, Ga. Mental Health Counselors Assn., Nat. Coun. Sexual Addiction and Compulsivity (bd. dirs., pres.). Democrat. Avocations: interior design, antiques, swimming. Office: Bldg 29 Ste 300 1640 Powers Ferry Rd Marietta GA 30067

HUDSON, MELINDA B. foundation administrator; BA, Vanderbilt U., 1976; MBA, Columbia U., 1990. Staff asst. Office of Rep. G.V., 1977-78, Office of Senate Minority Dem. Leader, 1978-81; spl. asst. Office of Senate Sergeant at Arms and Doorkeeper, 1982-87; assoc. dir. White House Office of Pvt. Sector Initiatives, 1987-89; dir. comms. Comm. on Nat. and Cmty. Svc., 1991-93; dir. Office Pub. Liaison Corp. for Nat. Svc., Washington, 1993—. Office: Corp for Nat Svc Office Pub Liaison 1201 New York Ave NW Washington DC 20525-0001

HUDSON, PATRICIA ANN SIEGEL, association management specialist; b. Louisville, Mar. 29, 1955; d. Roy John and Theresa (Preate) Siegel. BS in human svc., Pa. State Univ., Scranton, 1977; M psychosocial sci., cert. cmty. psychologist, Pa. State U., Scranton, 1982. Field rep. Am. Cancer Soc., Bethlehem, Pa., 1978-80; teen dir. YWCA, Harrisburg, Pa., 1980-82; mgr. membership devel. AAUW, Washington, 1982-85; mgr. membership Boat Owners Assn., U.S. (BOAT/US), Alexandria, Va., 1985-88; asst. v.p. leadership and membership devel. Nat. Assn. Home Builders, Washington, 1988-95; prin. Siegel and Assoc. Internat., San Francisco, 1995—; founder and pres. Ctr. for Excellence in Assn. Leadership, San Francisco. Cons. to membership based assn., San Francisco, 1995—. Contbg. author: The National Chpt. Partnership, 1993; co-author: Thriving on Change: Discovering the Power of Your Assn. to Affect Soc. Change, 1999; Beyond Membership Mktg.: Developing on Innovative Plan that Guarantees Results, 1999; Get Them Active! Using Icebreakers, Energizers and Summarizers to Enhance Group Productivity, 1999. Recipient Award for Disting. Svc. in Cmty. Psychology, Pa. State U. Harrisburg Campus, 2000. Mem. Am. Soc. Assn. Exec.; cert. trainer, presenter conf. and meetings 1990-95; bd. dir. 1993-95; edn. com. 1995; charter chmn. chpt. rels. sect. 1993-95; award of membership excellence, 1992; cert. assn. exec. 1990. Avocations: reading, travel, walking. Office: 236 W Portal Ave # 782 San Francisco CA 94127-1423 Office Phone: 650-355-4094

HUDSON, SUNCERRAY ANN, analyst, research grants manager; b. San Francisco, Jan. 20, 1960; d. Charles Hudson and Nan Katherine (Coleman) Wagoner. BA, U. San Francisco, 1982; student, S.E. C.C., San Francisco, 1988; student in Orgl. Mgmt., U. Phoenix, San Jose, Calif., 2003—. Stock transfer clk. Bank Calif., San Francisco, 1983-85; prin. clk. U. Calif., San Francisco, 1985-87, adminstrv. asst. II, 1987-88, adminstrv. asst. III, 1988-95, adminstrv. analyst, 1995—; ind. dealer Nat. Safety Assocs., Inc., San Francisco, 1990-92. Art cons. Artistic Impressions, Inc., 1994—96; mem. Notary Pub. Commn., 1997—; shape rite distbr., 1997—99. Mem.: Nat. Coun. Negro Women, Acad. Bus. Officers' Group, Am. Soc. Notaries, Gamma Phi Delta. Avocations: donating to various orgns. and the homeless, rollerskating, reading. Office: U Calif Campus Box 0440 521 Parnassus Ave San Francisco CA 94122-2722

HUDSON, WENDY JOY, software manager; b. New Brunswick, N.J., May 27, 1955; d. Herbert Roy and Dorothy Louise (Kaepernik) Hansen; m. William Howard Hudson, June 12, 1982. BA in Computer Sci., Rutgers U., 1977, MS in Computer Sci., 1979. Computer cons. Bell Labs., Holmdel, N.J., 1977-79; sr. mem. tech. staff Concurrent Computer, Tinton Falls, N.J., 1979-81, mgr., 1981-83, sr. mgr., 1983-89, prin. mgr., 1989-91; mgr. Transarc, Pitts., 1991-92; group mgr. Ilex Sys., Shrewsbury, N.J., 1992-95; mgr. IBM, Dayton, N.J., 1995-97, Lucent Techs., Bell Labs., Holmdel, N.J., 1997—. Contbr. articles to profl. jours. Mem. Assn. Computing Machinery. Republican. Episcopalian. Avocations: genealogy, skiing, bicycling, traveling. Home: 619 High Bridge Rd Colts Neck NJ 07722-1320 Office: Lucent Techs Bell Labs Crawfords Corner Rd Holmdel NJ 07733-2611

HUDSON-ZONN, ELIZA, nurse, psychologist; b. Monrovia, Liberia, Dec. 12, 1956; arrived in U.S., 1978; d. Hartzell Gleh and Joan Eliza (Roberts) Killen; m. Henry Clay Hudson, July 28, 1979 (div. Apr. 1985); 1 child, Kimberly Clayde; m. Mawuli Sonny Zonn, July 31, 1988; 1 child, Jewel Lorraine. BA in Psychology, BSC in Nursing, U. So. Miss., 1984. RN, N.J., Tex. Pvt. duty nurse Maxim Healthcare, Inc., South Orange, NJ, 1990—; critical care nurse Midpoint Profl. Agy., East Orange, 1988; supervising nurse Interim Healthcare, Inc., Morristown, NJ, 1990—; staff nurse Montclair (N.J.) Gen. Hosp., 1989—91; pvt. nurse Beth-Israel Med. Ctr., Newark, 1988—92; staff nurse United Children's Hosp., Newark, 1989—92; critical care nurse Nat. Staffing Assn. Inc., East Orange, 1989—; DON Med. Day Care Ctr., New Cmty. Extended Care, Newark, 2003—. Charge nurse Cmty. Psychiat. Ctr., Houston, 1993. Rural health vol. Red Cross Liberia, Monrovia, 1973—74; women's refugees health adv. Union Sierra Leone for Liberia, 1990—95; human rights adv. Movement for Justice in Africa, 1975—; mem. Women Refugees Health Advocate Union Sierra Leone for Liberia, 1990—95; coord., health svcs. dir. Liberian Cmty. Assn. N.J., 2001; membership recruiter Student Unification Party, Monrovia, 1975—76; counselor Providence Bapt. Ch., 1975, St. Elmo Bapt. Ch., 1982. Recipient Pub. Svc. award East Miss. Bapt. Women Conv., 1972; So. Bapt. Conv. scholar, 1978-84, Nat. Bapt. Conv. scholar, 1972-84. Mem.: Nat. Staffing Assn. Skilled Home Care Nursing, Suehn Acad. Alumni Assn. (recruiter 1995, founding mem. 1995). Democrat. Avocations: reading, writing, athletics, decoration, antiques collecting. Home: 64 Hillyer St Orange NJ 07050 Office: Nat Staffing Assn Inc 134 Evergreen Pl East Orange NJ 07018

HUEFNER, DIXIE SNOW, special education educator; b. Washington, Dec. 7, 1936; m. Robert Paul Huefner, July 30, 1960; children: Steven Frederick, Eric William; m. Robert Paul Huefner. BA in Polit. Sci., Wellesley Coll., 1958; MS in Spl. Edn., U. Utah, 1977, JD, 1986. Clin. instr. dept. spl. edn. U. Utah, 1978-86; jud. clk. to hon. Stephen H. Anderson U.S. Ct. Appeals (10th cir.), 1986-90; clin. asst. prof. dept. spl. edn. U. Utah, Salt Lake City, 1986-89, vis. asst. prof. dept. spl. edn., 1989-90, asst. prof. dept. spl. edn., 1990—94, assoc. prof., 1994—99, prof., 1999—. Presenter in field. Contbr. articles prof. jours.; author: (book) Getting Comfortable with Spl. Edn.Law /Christopher-Gordon Pub., 2000; co-author: Edn. Law and the Pub. Sch./ Christopher-Gordon Pub., 1998. Apptd. to Utah State Bd. Edn. Adv. Com. on the Handicapped. Mem. ABA, Coun. for Exceptional Children, Learning Disability Assn., Learning Disability Assn. Utah, Nat. Assn. for Retarded Citizens, Women Lawyers Utah, bd. mem. Utah parent ctr., Edn. Law Assoc.. Office: U Utah Dept Spl Edn 1705 E Campus Ctr Dr Rm 221 Salt Lake City UT 84112-9253

HUEGEL, DONNA, historian, writer, artist, archivist; b. New Hampton, Iowa, Apr. 14, 1951; d. Herbert Henry and Marceile (Gilbert) Christoph; m. Leonard James Huegel, June 10, 1972; children: Eric Benjamin, Ryan Joseph. Student, Mount Mercy Coll., 1969—72, U. Iowa, 1974, Western Wis. Tech. Coll., LaCrosse, 1999. Writer Houston County News, LaCrescent, Minn., 1994—; mus. archivist, spkr. LaCrescent Area Hist. Soc., 1994—. Author: Many A Grove and Orchard--The Story of John S. Harris, 1994, (anthology) America's Heartland Remembers--Stories Before, During and After 9-11, 2001, 2002. Pres., chair PTA, Badger, Iowa, 1982—88; pres., chair art appreciation program Blanden Art Mus., Ft. Dodge, Iowa, 1982—88; sec., archivist LaCrescent Area Hist. Soc., Minn., 1992—2003. Named Edn. Vol. of Yr., Ft. Dodge Bd. Edn., 1988. Mem.: Writers' Group-LaCrosse, Wis. Roman Catholic. Avocations: dance-skating, dance, singing, guitar.

HUELSMAN, JOANNE B. state legislator; b. Mar. 21, 1938; married. JD, Marquette U., 1980. Attorney, realtor, businesswoman; former mem. Wis. Assembly from 31st dist.; mem. Wis. Senate from 11th dist., Madison, 1990—. Republican. Home: 235 W Broadway Ste 210 Waukesha WI 53186-4826 Office: Wis State Senate PO Box 7882 Madison WI 53707-7882

HUENERGARDT, MYRNA LOUISE, retired academic administrator, retired adult nurse practitioner; b. Medford, Oreg., Aug. 5, 1928; d. Henry and Matie Daisy (Vroman) H. BS, Columbia Union Coll., Takoma Park, Md., 1961; MA, Columbia U., 1963. RN, Calif.; cert. nurse practitioner. Charge nurse Glendale (Calif.) Adventist Hosp., 1954-57, 61-63; sch. nurse L.A. City Schs., 1957-60; instr. nursing Columbia Union Coll., Takoma Park, Md., 1964-68; dir. sch. nursing Branson Hosp. Sch. Nursing, Toronto, Ont., Can., 1968-71; chair paramed. dept. Southwestern C.C., Chula Vista, Calif., 1971-74; assoc. prof. nursing Loma Linda (Calif.) U., 1974-80; nurse rschr. U. So. Calif., L.A., 1981-83; nurse practitioner Community Health Projects, Covina, Calif., 1983-86; dir. student health svcs. Chaffey C.C., Rancho Cucamonga, Calif., 1986-94. Med. edn. cons. Merck, Sharp & Dohme, West Point, Pa., 1991-96; nurse practitioner New Horizon Care Corp., Loma Linda, 1987-95; nurse cons., med. claims reviewer Aetna Ins., Loma Linda, 1994-97. Bd. dirs. ARC, Inland Empire, Calif., 1986-91; cons. Master Plan Com., Substance Abuse, San Bernardino County, Calif., 1990-95. Recipient Sameas award Outstanding Educators of Am., 1972, Disting. Leadership award Am. Biog. Inst., 1989; Fed. Govt. traineeship awards, 1961, 63, 64. Mem. Assn. of Calif. C.C. Adminstrs., Calif. Coalition of Nurse Practitioners, C.C. Health Svcs. Assn. of Calif. (pres. 1992-93), Sigma Theta Tau, Kappa Delta Pi. Republican. Avocations: travel, biking, gardening, concerts, singing. Home: 10636 Amapolas St Redlands CA 92373-8401

HUERTA, DOLORES FERNANDEZ, labor union administrator; b. Dawson, N. Mex., Apr. 10, 1930; d. Juan and Alicia Fernandez; children: Celeste, Lori, Fidel, Emilio, Vincent, Alicia, Angela, Juanita, Maria, Elena, Ricky, Camilla. Co-founder, first v.p. United Farm Workers of Am., Keene, Calif., 1962—. Co-founder, first v.p., bd. mem. Fund for the Feminist Majority. Recipient Martin Luther King award NAACP, Roger Baldwin award ACLU, Labor award Eugene V. Debs Found., Trumpeters award Consumers Union, Women First award YWCA, 1993; inductee Nat. Women's Hall of Fame, 1993.

HUF, CAROL ELINOR, tax service company executive; b. Milw., Apr. 21, 1940; d. William Weiss and Florence H. (Melcher) Weiss Lange; m. Walter Franklin Huf, Sept. 9, 1961; children: Mardell Leslie, Walter Albert III. Student, Valparaiso U., 1958-60, Waukesha County Tech. Inst., 1968-69. Tax preparer H&R Block, Milw., 1967-84, instr. tax sch., 1969-83; job svc. interviewer State of Wis., Waukesha, 1984; pres. Personalized Tax Svc., Inc., West Allis, Wis., 1984—. Divsn. mgr. Primerica (formerly A.L. Williams), 1986. Vol. worker Girl Scouts US, Waukesha, 1970-80, Boy Scouts Am., Waukesha, 1975-92; swimming referee Wis. Interscholastic Athletic Assn., Milw., 1972-84. Recipient award Boy Scouts Am. Mem.: Wis. Assn. Accts., Nat. Assn. Tax Practitioners (Wis. bd. dirs. 1989—96), Nat. Soc. Pub. Accts., Met. Swimming Ofcls., U.S. Golf Assn. (regional affairs com. 1991—), Wis. Womens Pub. Links Golf Assn. (state tournament chairperson 1987, 2d v.p. 1988—, state tournament chairperson 1990, 1994, past pres.). Lutheran. Home: 5508 Bauers Dr West Bend WI 53095-8782 Office: Personalized Tax Service Inc 10533 W National Ave Milwaukee WI 53227-2041 E-mail: carol@pts.sterlingtech.net.

HUFF, EARLEEN, education educator; b. Amarillo, Tex., May 29, 1949; d. Earl Wayne and Velma Louise (Cawthon) Sutton; children: Kristen Louise, Nicol Leanne. BS, West Tex. State U., 1971, EdM, 1985. Kindergarten tchr. Hereford (Tex.) Ind. Sch. Dist., 1971—75; dir. West Tex. State U. Children's Ctr., Canyon, 1979—83; tchr. 5th grade Canyon Ind. Sch. Dist., 1983—87, prin. Lakeview Elem., 1987—2000; instr. Amarillo Coll., 2001—. Adj. instr. West Tex. State U., 1986—93. Bd. dirs. Potter-Randall County Child Protective Bd., Amarillo, 1983—99; mem. Friends of the Libr., Canyon, 1999; h.s. Sunday sch. tchr. 1st Meth. Ch., Canyon, 1991—94. Named TEPSAN of Yr., Prin. of Yr., Edn. Svc. Ctr. Region 16, Amarillo, 1993. Mem.: Panhandle Assn. for Edn. of Young Children, Delta Kappa Gamma (pres. Kappa Eta 1998—). Democrat. Avocations: reading, golf, gardening, sewing, cooking. Home: 17 Cottonwood Ln Canyon TX 79015 Office: Amarillo Coll Box 447 Amarillo TX 79178

HUFF, GAYLE COMPTON, advertising and marketing executive; b. Washington, Nov. 28, 1956; d. Walter Dale and Jeanne (Parker) C.; m. Lanny Ross Huff, May 22, 1982 (div. 2002). B in Gen. Studies, U. Mich., 1978. Mgr. br. merchandising CBS Records, Chgo., 1978, local promotion, mktg. mgr. Indpls., Boston, N.Y.C., 1978-81; spl. projects supr. Pickwick Internat. Musicland Group, Mpls., 1981-82; account exec. Campbell-Mithun Advt., Mpls., 1982-85; mktg. mgr., communications Universal Foods Corp., Milw., 1985-86; nat. advt. mgr. Thorobred Advt. Agy. (Jockey Internat., Inc.), Wis., 1986-88, dir. consumer and trade advt., 1988-89, v.p.

advt., 1990-92; dir. mktg./advt. Allen-Edmonds Shoe Co., Port Washington, Wis., 1993-95; v.p., dir. Fin. Mktg. Plus Direct Mktg. Group, Libertyville, Ill., 1995-97; dir. mktg. & merchandising AR Accessories Group Inc., Milw., 1997-98; v.p. creative svcs. Tucker-Knapp Integrated Mktg. Commns., Schaumburg, Ill., 1998-2000; [illegible] Fin. Svcs. (Morgan Stanley Dean Witter), Riverwoods, Ill., 2000—. V.p., sec. Java Masters, Inc., 1992—. Recipient Discover Leadership award, Discover Fin. Svcs. Inc., 2000, 2001. Mem. Traffic Audit Bur. for Media Measurement (bd. dirs. 1988-93), Assn. Nat. Advertisers (print adv. com., out of home advt. com. 1989-92). Avocations: dance, gymnastics, conga drumming. Office: Discover Fin Svcs 2500 Lake Cook Rd # 2W Deerfield IL 60015-3851 E-mail: gaylehuff@discoverfinancial.com.

HUFF, JANICE, newscaster, meteorologist; b. 1949; BS in meteorology, Fla. State U., Tallahassee. Weekend meteorologist WTVC-TV, Chattanooga, 1982—83; meteorologist/sci. reporter WRBL-TV, Columbus, Ga., 1983—87; meteorologist KSDK, St. Louis, 1987—91, KRON-TV, San Francisco, 1990—95; weekend meteorologist WNBC 4, NY, 1995—96; weekday meteorologist WNBC 4 News Channel 4 at 6pm and 11pm, NY, 1996—, WNBC 4 News Live at Five, 2000—. Recipient St. Louis Emmy award for best weathercaster, 1988. Mem.: Nat. Acad. TV Arts and Scis., Nat. Assn. Black Journalists, Am. Meteorological Soc. (Seal of Approval for TV Weathercasting 1985), Alpha Kappa Alpha. Office: 30 Rockefeller Plz New York NY 10112*

HUFF, JOAN, retired physicial education/dance educator; b. N.Y.C., May 10, 1929; d. Clarence R. and Marian W. (Waters) H. BS, Russell Sage Coll., 1950; MA, Mich. State U., 1958; EdD, U. Utah, 1967. Phys. edn., dance tchr. Hillsdale Dance Sch., Cin., 1950-52; phys. edn. tchr. Schoharie (N.Y.) Ctrl. Sch., 1952-57; prof. phys. edn., dance SUNY, Oswego, 1958-90. Bd. dirs. Oswego County Arts Coun., 1976-78; elder, trustee, bd. dirs., com. Presbyn. Ch./Faith United Ch., Oswego, 1971—. Grantee AAUW, 1994. Mem. AAUW (pres., v.p. program 1976—), Sacred Dance Guild (bd. dirs. 1974-77, dir. regions & chpts. 1988-96), Am. Dance Guild, Chi Rho Sacred Dancers (bd. dir.), Westminster Liturgical Dancers. Avocations: golf, tap dancing, travel. Home: 49 Baylis St Oswego NY 13126-1753

HUFF, MARILYN L. federal judge; b. 1951; BA, Calvin Coll., Grand Rapids, Mich., 1972; JD, U. Mich., 1976. Assoc. Gray, Cary, Ames & Frye, 1976-83, ptnr., 1983-91; judge U.S. Dist. Ct. (so. dist.) Calif., San Diego, 1991-98, chief judge, 1998—. Contbr. articles to profl. jours. Mem. adv. coun. Calif. LWV, 1987—, Am. Lung Assn.; bd. dirs. San Diego and Imperial Counties, 1989—; mem. LaJolla Presbyn. Ch. Named Legal Profl. of Yr. San Diego City Club and Jr. C. of C., 1990; recipient Superior Ct. Valuable Svc. award, 1982. Mem. ABA, San Diego Bar Found., San Diego Bar Assn. (bd. dirs. 1986-88, v.p. 1988, chmn. profl. edn. com. 1990, Svc. award to legal profession, 1989, Lawyer of Yr. 1990), Calif. State Bar Assn., Calif. Women Lawyers, Am. Bd. Trial Advs., Libel Def. Resource Ctr., Am. Inns of Ct. (master 1987—, exec. com. 1989—), Lawyers' Club San Diego (adv. bd. 1989-90, Belva Lockwood Svc. award 1987), Univ. Club, Aardvarks Lt. Office: US Dist Ct Courtroom 1 940 Front St San Diego CA 92101-8994

HUFF, MARSHA ELKINS, lawyer; b. Tulsa, Apr. 11, 1946; BA with honors, U. Tulsa, 1968, MA, 1970; JD cum laude, Loyola U. of Chgo., 1974. Bar: Wis. Ptnr. Foley & Lardner, Milw. Mem. editorial bd. Loyola U. Law Jour., 1973-74. Mem. ABA (mem. sect. taxation). Office: Foley & Lardner 777 E Wisconsin Ave Ste 3800 Milwaukee WI 53202-5367

HUFF, SARA DAVIS, nursing manager; b. Moundville, Ala., May 16, 1935; d. George W. and Maggie A. (Callahan) Davis; m. Eugene H. Huff, May 21, 1956 (div. June 1992); children: John Davis Huff, Timothy Eugene Huff. RN, Druid City Hosp. Sch. Nursing, Tuscaloosa, Ala., 1956; BS, Oglethorpe U., 1980. CNOR. RN, oper. rm. Druid City Hosp., Tuscaloosa, 1956-58; asst. head nurse, thoracic cardiovascular St. Joseph's Hosp., Atlanta, 1958-60; charge nurse/open heart thoracic Emory U. Hosp., Atlanta, 1960-64, edn. coord. oper. room, 1974-75; oper. rm. supr. H. Egleston Hosp. for Children, Atlanta, 1964-73; nurse cons. Cons. Surg. Svcs., Atlanta, 1986-92; dir. surg. svcs. Northside Hosp., Atlanta, 1975-86; staff nurse oper. rm. Northlake Hosp., Atlanta, 1990-92; dir. surg. svcs. Atlanta Hosp., 1989-90, Newton Gen. Hosp., Covington, Ga., 1992—98; clin. resource mgr. Emory Dunwoody Med. Ctr., Atlanta, 2002—. Spkr. in field. Mem. AORN (nat. bd. dirs. 1980-84, gen. AORN nat. congress 1980, other coms.), ANA, Assn. of Oper. Rm. Nurses of Atlanta (Nurse of Yr. 1975), Atlanta Area Oper. Rm. Suprs. (chmn. 1973-75). Home: 2534 Warwick Cir NE Atlanta GA 30345-1632 E-mail: graceD8669@aol.com.

HUFFINGTON, ANITA, sculptor; b. Balt., Dec. 25, 1934; d. Norris Jackson and Agnes (Hook) H.; m. Manuel Rubin Duque, Sept. 17, 1957 (div. Nov. 1964); 1 child, Lisa Huffington Duque; m. Henry Sutter, Dec. 4, 1964. BA, CCNY, 1973, MFA, 1975. Resident La Napoule (France) Art Found., 1996. One-woman exhbns. include U. Ark., Fayetteville, 1982, Valley House Gallery, Dallas, 1986, Benton Gallery, Southampton, NY, 1989, Ark. Art Ctr., Little Rock, 1990, O'Hara Gallery, NYC, 1994, 96, 99, 2001, 04, U. Ctrl. Ark., Conway, 1997, Triangle Gallery, San Francisco, 1998, Lisa Kurts Gallery, Memphis, 1999, 2003, Morris Mus., Augusta, Ga., 2004, Walton Art Ctr., Fayetteville, Ar., 2004; 2-person show Lisa Kurts Gallery, 1995; 3-person shows Louis Stern Gallery, West Hollywood, Calif., 1996, Triangle Gallery, San Francisco, 1996; group exhbn. include Internat. Women's Art Festival, NYC, 1976, U. Ark., Fayetteville, 1978, 92, Ark. Arts Ctr., Little Rock, 1979-81, Territorial Restoration Gallery, Little Rock, 1981, Harris Gallery, Houston, Tex., 1981-93, Sculptural Arts Mus., Altanta, 1982, Benton Gallery, Southampton, NY, 1988, Kornbluth Gallery, Fair Lawn, NJ, 1989, The Art Show, 7th Regiment Armory, NYC, 1989-2003, 04, Art of the 20th Century 7th Regiment Armory, N.Y.C., 2003, 04, Ft. Smith (Ark.) Art Ctr., 1990, Salon de Mars, Paris, 1992, U. Pa., Phila. US Artists Art Fair, Pa. Acad., 1992-2002, 2003, ARTexas, Dallas, 1993-94, Art Fair Seattle, 1995-97, Art Miami (Fla.), 1996, 98, Triangle Gallery, San Francisco, 1996, 99, 2000, Am. Acad. Arts and Letters, NYC, 1997, Columbus (Ga.) Mus. and Miss. Mus. Art, Jackson, 1997, Am. Acad. Arts and Letters, 1997, Two Sculptors, Inc., NYC, 1998, Valley House Gallery, Dallas, 1998, Art Palm Beach, 1998, 99, 2000, 01, Dallas Internat. Art and Antiques Fair, 2000-02, 50th Anniversary Show, Valley Ho. Gallery, Dallas, Hist. Ark. Mus., Little Rock, 2001; works in permanent collection of Met. Mus. of Art, N.Y.C., 2002, others; featured in various profl. publ., mag., newspapers, and videos. Recipient Jimmy Ernst award Am. Acad. Arts and Letters, 1997, others; Visual arts fellow Ark. Arts Coun.

HUFFMAN, CADY, actress; b. Santa Barbara, Calif., Feb. 2, 1965; d. Clifford Roy and Lorayne Dolores (Rote) H.; m. William Healy, 1994. Pvt. studies with, Nathan Lam, L.A., 1983-85, Maria Gobetti, 1984-85, Bill Reed, N.Y.C., 1987-90, Fred Kareman, 1988. Actress Broadway plays La Cage Aux Folles, 1983-84, Big Deal, 1985, The Will Rogers Follies, 1991-93, Steel Pier, 1997, The Producers, 2001-03 (Tony award best actress, 2001); (off Broadway) Gemini, 1990, Italian American Reconciliation, 1990, As You Like It, 1989, The Baker's Wife, 1982, They're Playing Our Song, 1983, Jekyll and Hyde, 1989, Dame Edna: The Royal Tour, 1999-2000, Short Talks on the Universe, 2002; TV shows The Guiding Light, 1986, Another World, 1987, Pig Sty, 1995, Mad About You, 1995, Law & Order: Criminal Intent, 2001, Curb Your Enthusiasm, 2004; films Hero, 1992, Space Marines, 1996, Sunday on the Rocks, 2004 (also prodr.); appeared in more than 30 TV commls., 1985-90. Vol. recreational therapist The Lighthouse, N.Y.C., 1986-87 Recipient 3d Place award Pacific Regional Ballet Assn., 1980. Avocations: piano, swimming, dance, singing.*

HUFFMAN, CAROL CICOLANI, music educator, consultant; b. Mansfield, Ohio, Apr. 12, 1950; d. John Joseph and Donna Mae Cicolani; m. Philip Dean Huffman, Aug. 29, 1970; 1 child, Nathan Curtiss. MusB in Edn., Ind. U., Bloomington, 1973; MA in Edn., Baldwin Wallace Coll., Berea, Oh, 1988, post grad., 2003—. Master of Orff Schulwerk Memphis State U. Dept. of Music/Tenn., 1981. Pres. greater Cleve. chapt. Am. Orff Schulwerk Assn., Cleve., 1980—81; regional rep. Am. Orff-Schulwerk Assn., 1983—85, nat. conf. chairperson, 1986—88, nat. interim treas., 1997—98, v.p., 1999—2001, pres., 2001—03, past pres., 2003—, chairperson of undergraduate music curriculum reform com., 2003—. Workshop clinician AOSA Local Chapters, 1973—; elem. music tchr. Parma (Ohio) City Schools, 1974—; adj. prof. Hofstra U., Hempstead, NY, 1990—; supr. of student teachers Baldwin-Wallace Coll., Berea, Ohio, 1998—; workshop cons. Kennedy Ctr. For the Performing Arts, Washington, 1999—; guest condr. Chorister's Guild. Composer: Share The Music (Supt. Commendation for Outstanding Tchg., 1997); prodr.(director): (multimedia presentation) Portrait of AOSA (Outstanding Tchr. of Dist., 1991); contbr. articles to Orff Echo, to profl. jors. Lay vol. Vol. Optometric Svcs. to Humanity, Ukraine, 1995. Recipient Martha Holden Jennings Found. Distinctive Tchg. award, 1997; grantee, Ohio, 1976.

HUFFMAN, JANET FAYE, secondary school educator; b. Liberal, Kans., Feb. 20, 1946; d. Kenneth D. and Ursula Idella Garten; divorced; children: Heidi Ann, Heather Sue. BA, U. Colo., 1968; MS, Ft. Hays (Kans.) State U., 1970. Cert. secondary English tchr., Mo. Tchr. Platte Community Coll., Columbus, Nebr., 1970-71, Arriba (Colo.) High Sch., 1980-82; English tchr. Limon (Colo.) High Sch., 1982—. Author: (poems) Inward Perspective, 1990. Mem. Limon Edn. Assn. (sec. 1990-91), Order of Eastern Star (worth matron 1989-90), First United Meth. Ch., Limon Heritage Soc. Avocations: reading, travel. Home: PO Box 846 Limon CO 80828 Office: Limon Sch PO Box 249 Limon CO 80828-0249

HUFFMAN, JOAN BREWER, history educator; b. Springfield, Ohio, Aug. 18, 1937; d. James Clarence and Berniece (Notter) Brewer; m. James Russell Huffman, Aug. 21, 1959; children: Jill Elizabeth, Jean Elaine. AB, Ohio U., 1959; MA, Ga. State U., 1968, PhD, 1980. Adj. prof. Wesleyan Coll., Macon, Ga., 1981-82; instr. history Macon State Coll., 1968-72, asst. prof., 1972-81, assoc. prof., 1981-86, prof., 1986-2000, prof. emerita, 2000—; owner The Printed Page, Macon, Ga., 1993-97, Picture Perfect, 1995—. Chmn. History adv. com. U. Sys. Ga., 1986—87. Contbr. articles to profl. jours. Mem., bd. dirs. Oklahatchee Pk., Perry, Ga., 1966-68, Macon State Coll. Found., 1985-90, Ga. Humanities Coun., Atlanta, 1983-87. Katharine C. Bleckley scholar English-Speaking Union, 1977; recipient Gov.'s award in the humanities, 1998. Mem. N.Am. Conf. on Brit. Studies, Am. Hist. Assn., Southern Hist. Assn. (membership com. 1988-89), Ga. Assn. Historians (pres. 1982-83), Phi Beta Kappa, Phi Alpha Theta (award 1978). Home: 135 Covington Pl Macon GA 31210-4445 E-mail: huffmanj@bellsouth.net.

HUFFMAN, LAURA CHRISTINE, computer programmer, educator; b. Celina, Ohio, Dec. 3, 1971; d. Richard Dean and Nancy Kay Huffman; 1 child, Kaitlan Danielle. BS in Bus. Adminstrn., Bowling Green State U., 1994. Computer instr. Lima (Ohio) Tech. Coll., 1996-98; programmer/analyst Ctrl. Mut. Ins., Van Wert, Ohio, 1997—. Mem. Nat. Assn. Ins. Women (cmty. svc. com.). Office: Ctrl Mut Ins 800 S Washington St Van Wert OH 45891-2357

HUFFMAN, LOUISE TOLLE, middle school educator; b. Tallahassee, Fla., July 24, 1951; d. Donald James and Mary Alice (McNeill) Tolle; m. Terry Lee Huffman, July 17, 1976; children: Cody McNeill, Hunter Tolle. BSEd in Spl. Edn./Elem. Edn., So. Ill. U., 1973; MSEd, No. Ill. U., 1979. Cert. elem. tchr., spl. edn. tchr. Ill. Title I reading tchr., Tonica, Ill., 1973-74; learning disabilities tchr. St. Charles, Ill., 1974-78; spl. edn. tchr. McWayne Elem. Sch., Batavia, Ill., 1978-80; tchr. grades 1, 3, 4, and 5 Steeple Run Elem. Sch., Naperville, Ill., 1980-98; tchr. Kennedy Jr. H.S., Naperville, 1998—. Com. to develop dual maj. in elem. edn. and sci. Benedictine U., Lisle, Ill., 1999—2000; curriculum developer Brookfield (Ill.) Zoo, 2001—02; facilitator of tchr. workshops Jurica Sci. Mus./ Benedictine U., Lisle, 1992—; facilitator sci. workshops Mus. Sci. and Industry, Chgo., 1991—96, Hamline U., St. Paul, 1990—93; Saturday Morning TV Sci. tchr. Dist. 203, Naperville, 1994; author Earth Rhythms Saturday Sch. program Benedictine U., 1996; tchr. summer sci. workshop Golden Apple Found., 1999—; mem. steering com. World Sch. Adventure Learning St. Thomas U., St. Paul, 1992—94; steering com. World Sch. Adventure Learning Hamline U., 1995, 2002. Co-author: Antarctica: A Living Classroom, 1991; contbg. author: Project Circles: The World School for Adventure Learning, 2002; contbr. articles to Cobblestone Mag., Good Apple Newspaper, Children's Digest; author of poetry. Co-covener, facilitator, NSF Polar Sci. Workshop, 2003; bd. dirs. Cmty. United Meth. Ch. Sojourners Sunday Sch., Naperville, 1995-2000; confirmation class tchr. Cmty. United Meth. Ch., 1999-2001. Recipient award of Excellence, Ill. Sci. Tchrs. Assn., 1992, 1996, Golden Apple award, 2002, tchr. rsch. assistantship in Antarctica, NSF, 2001—03; grantee, Naperville Edn. Found., 1994, 2002, Jeanine Nicarico Lit. grant, 1999. Methodist. Office: Kennedy Junior High Sch 2929 Green Trails Dr Lisle IL 60532-6262 E-mail: lhuffman@ncusd203.org.

HUFFMAN, MARY FRANCES, retired secondary school educator; b. Montgomery, Ala., Apr. 30, 1911; d. Mary Huffman; m. Alexander Lee, June 28, 1936 (div. Aug. 1938); 1 child, Patricia Day Smoke. BS, Ala. State U., 1951, MEd, 1961; postgrad., So. U., Baton Rouge, La., 1960, Beloit Coll., 1963, Talladega Coll., 1963—64. Cert. elem. and secondary tchr. Ala. Tchr. Elem. Schs., Troy, Ala., 1929-30, Prattville, Ala., 1930-32, Lowndes County, Ala., 1932-42, Union Springs, Ala., 1943-45, Montgomery, 1945-73, ret., 1973—. Sec. Nat. Caucus & Ctr. Black Aged, Congress Christian Edn., 1955—, Montgomery County Multi-Black Caucus; counselor Montgomery-Antioch Dist., Ala. State Women; me. program com. YMCA, 1969; treas. Alonzo Mitchell OES 636, Montgomery, 1980; Sunday sch. tchr. Holt St. Bapt. Ch., sec. matrons cir.; with Lilly Baptist Ch., 2002. Mem.: AARP, NEA, AAUW, Montgomery County Ret. Tchrs. Assn., Assn. Ret. Tchrs. Am., Twelve Tribes (rec. sec. Montgomery). Avocation: travel. Home: 955 Erskine St Montgomery AL 36108-3524

HUFFMAN, ROSEMARY ADAMS, lawyer, corporate executive; b. Orlando, Fla., Oct. 18, 1939; d. Elmer Victor and Esther (Weber) Adams; divorced; 1 child, Justin Adams Fruth. A.B. in Econs., Ind. U., 1959, J.D., 1962; LL.M., U. Chgo., 1967. Bar: Ind. 1962, Fla. 1963. Dep. prosecutor Marion County, Ind., 1963; ct. adminstr. Ind. Supreme Ct., 1967-68; pro-tem judge Marion County Mcpl. Ct., 1969-70; jud. coordinator Ind. Criminal Justice Planning Agy., 1969-70; dir. ctr. for Jud. Edn., Inc., 1970-73; pub. Jud. Xchange, 1972-73; instr. bus. law Purdue U., Indpls., 1962-63, Ind. U., Indpls., 1963-64; asst. Ind. Jud. Council, 1965; legis. intern Ford Found., 1965; sole practice, Indpls., 1962— ; pres., owner Abacus, Inc., Indpls., 1980—. Mem. Ind. Bar Assn., Fla. Bar Assn. Home and Office: 6630 E 56th St Indianapolis IN 46226-1781

HUFFMAN-MOSER, BARBARA S. criminal investigator; b. Gorman, Tex., Oct. 27, 1941; d. Joe Berkley and Betty Jean Huffman; m. John T. Moser. BBA, U. Tex., Austin, 1971. Sec. U.S. Dept. of HUD, Fort Worth, 1962—64, U.S. Dept. of State, Washington, 1964—65, U.S. Dept. of HUD, Fort Worth, 1965—69, Lt. Gov.'s Office, Austin, Tex., 1969—73; criminal investigator U.S. Dept of HUD, Dallas, 1973—78, U.S. Dept. of Edn., Washington, 1980—87, Dallas, 1980—87; supr. spl. agent U.S. Dept. of Vets. Affairs, Dallas, 1987—92; criminal investigator Resolution Trust Corp., FDIC, Dallas, 1992—95; ret., 1996. Mem.: Ladies Auxiliary of Am. Legion (sec. 1999—2000), Fedn. of Women's Clubs (dist. sec. 2002—04), 20th Century Club (pres. 2002—04), Methodist. Avocations: bridge, reading, cross stitching, traveling. Home: 988 Mockingbird Stephenville TX 76401

HUFNAGEL, LINDA ANN, biology educator, researcher; b. Teaneck, N.J., Nov. 7, 1939; d. Ernest Albert and Frances Marie (Hrbek) H.; m. Dov Jaron, 1969; children: Shulamit, Tamara; m. Robert Van Zackroff, June 1984. BA, U. Vt., 1961, MS, 1963; PhD, U. Pa., 1967. Lectr. U. Pa., Phila., summer 1967; NSF postdoctoral fellow Yale U., New Haven, 1967-69; rsch. assoc. Columbia U., N.Y.C., 1970; asst. prof. Oakland C.C., Farmington, Mich., 1970; rsch. assoc. Wayne State U., Detroit, 1971-73; lectr. biology U. R.I., Kingston, 1973-75, asst. prof., 1975-79, assoc. prof., 1979-86, prof., 1986—, dir. cen. electron microscope facility, 1973-96. NSF rsch. grantee U. R.I., 1975, Am. Heart Assn. rsch. grantee, 1979; Steps fellow Marine Biol. Lab., Woods Hole, Mass., 1978-79. Office: U RI Dept Cell Mol Biol Kingston RI 02881 Office Phone: 401-874-5914 2201. E-mail: lhufnagel@uri.edu.

HUFSTEDLER, SHIRLEY MOUNT (MRS. SETH M. HUFSTEDLER), lawyer, former federal judge; b. Denver, Aug. 24, 1925; d. Earl Stanley and Eva (Von Behren) Mount; m. Seth Martin Hufstedler, Aug. 16, 1949; 1 son, Steven Mark. BBA, U. N.Mex., 1945, LLD (hon.), 1972; LLB, Stanford U., 1949; LLD (hon.), U. Wyo., 1970, Gonzaga U., 1970, Occidental Coll., 1971, Tufts U., 1974, U. So. Calif., 1976, Georgetown U., 1976, U. Pa., 1976, Columbia U., 1977, U. Mich., 1979, Yale U., 1981, Rutgers U., 1981, Claremont U. Ctr., 1981, Smith Coll., 1982, Syracuse U., 1983, Mt. Holyoke Coll., 1985; PHH (hon.), Hood Coll., 1981, Hebrew Union Coll., 1986, Tulane U., 1988. Bar: Calif. 1950. Mem. firm Beardsley, Hufstedler & Kemble, L.A., 1951-61; practiced in L.A., 1961; judge Superior Ct., County L.A., 1961-66; justice Ct. Appeals 2d dist., 1966-68; circuit judge U.S. Ct. Appeals 9th cir., 1968-79; sec. U.S. Dept. Edn., 1979-81; ptnr. Hufstedler & Kaus, L.A., 1981-95; sr. of counsel Morrison & Foerster LLP, L.A., 1995—. Emeritus dir. Hewlett Packard Co., US West, Inc.; bd. dirs. Harman Internat. Industries. Mem. staff Stanford Law Rev, 1947-49; articles and book rev. editor, 1948-49. Trustee Calif. Inst. Tech., Occidental Coll., 1972-89, Aspen Inst., Colonial Williamsburg Found., 1976-93, Constl. Rights Found., 1978-80, Nat. Resources Def. Coun., 1983-85, Carnegie Endowment for Internat. Peace, 1983-94; bd. dirs. John T. and Catherine MacArthur Found., 1983—2002; chair U.S. Commn. on Immigration Reform, 1996-97. Named Woman of Yr. Ladies Home Jour., 1976; recipient UCLA medal, 1981. Fellow Am. Acad. Arts and Scis.; mem. ABA (medal 1995), L.A. Bar Assn., Town Hall, Am. Law Inst. (coun. 1974-84), Am. Bar Found., Women Lawyers Assn. (pres. 1957-58), Am. Judicature Soc., Assn. of the Bar of City of N.Y., Coun. on Fgn. Rels. (emeritus), Order of Coif. Office: Morrison & Foerster LLP 555 W 5th St Ste 3500 Los Angeles CA 90013-1024 Office Phone: 213-892-5804.

HUGENBERG, PATRICIA ELLEN PETRIE, product designer; b. N.Y.C., Oct. 17, 1934; d. Milton John Petrie and Miriam Lois Lampke-Rubenstein-Petrie; m. George John Hugenberg, Jan. 18, 1958; 1 child, Kurt John James. Student, Briarcliff Jr. Coll., 1954, U. Calif., Berkeley, 1966. Guidette NBC, N.Y.C., 1956; designer, resch. developer Designs for Prodn., Sausalito, Calif.; inventor games, toys, med. items, Sigi Design, San Francisco; pres. PPH Designs. Mem. pending bd. Milton & Carroll Petrie Found. for New Millenium, N.Y.C. Photographer: (book cover jacket) Baltimore; prin. works include plexiglass knitting needles, plexiglass embedded light space age stardust galaxy hammocks, space age crutch, new saddle design for mobile riding easels, kitchen veg-garnisher punch; patents pending in field. Mem. NRA. Avocations: music, oil painting, horseback riding, traveling, gardens. Home and Office: 10 Leeward Rd Belvedere CA 94920-2321

HUGG, ALICIA ESTHER, healthcare administrator; b. L.A., June 13, 1939; d. Alexander Page Schooler and Vivian Alicia Mingus Myles; m. Roger Dean Hugg, Aug. 6, 1982; children: Pamela, Julia, Michelle, Mia, Amber. ADN, San Joaquin Delta Coll., Stockton, Calif., 1971; BS in Orgnl. Behavior, U. San Francisco, 1992, MA in Human Resources and Orgnl. Devel., 1995. Asst. dir. nurses Crestwood Manor, Stockton, 1981-83; dir. nurses Palm Haven Convalescent Hosp., Manteca, Calif., 1983-84; supr. rev. Calif. Med. Rev. Inc., Stockton, 1984-90; mgr. utilization and quality Nat. Health Plan, Modesto, Calif., 1990-94; utilization rev. adminstr. Blue Shield of Calif., Lodi, 1994-97; dir. staff devel. Crestwood manor, Stockton, 1996-97; columnist, opinion page The Record, Stockton, 1991—; freelance writer nat. pubs., 2000—; instr. comms. Chapman U., Modesto, 1996—; regional mgr. health care svcs. Found. Health, Stockton, 1997-98, org. devel. cons., 1998—. Nursing cons. Crestwood Hosps., Stockton, 1996—. Mem. Libr. Literacy Bd., Stockton, 1997—; bd. dirs. Planned Parenthood Advocates, Stockton, 1996-97; mem. NAACP; mem. Stockton Unified Black Employees Assn., 1996-97. Mem. Stator: AAUW; mem.: Delta Sigma Theta, Chi Eta Phi. Avocations: reading, travel, camping, aerobics, art. Home: 742 Bronte Ave Watsonville CA 95076-3641

HUGG, GERALDINE BERTHA NOVOTNY, retired gerontology specialist, journalist; b. N.Y.C., Oct. 15, 1913; d. Jerry Joseph and Bertha Ann (Strnad) Novotny; m. Alan Eddy Hugg, Mar. 10, 1982 (dec. Feb. 1997). BA in Journalism, U. Wis., 1949; MS in Pub. Rels., Boston U., 1953. lic. profl. gerontology U. Mich., Drake U. Departmental sec. U. Conn., Storrs, 1933-41, departmental asst., 1941-43, asst. editor, publs. editor divsn. comm., 1950-60; specialist Inst. Gerontology, U. Conn., 1960-67; dir. Windham Area Sr. Ctr., Willimantic, Conn., 1967; cons. and field rep. Conn. State Dept. Aging, Hartford, 1967-76; ret., 1976. Advisor Conn. Coun. Sr. Citizens, 1960—; attended 9th Internat. Gerontol. Congress, Kiev, Russia, 1972. Contbg. editor Seniorage, 1976-2001; contbr. columns various newspapers. Vol. social action and edn. Conn. Soc. Gerontology, 1961-99, pres., 1981-83; participant Am. Exch. Corps, Caucuses, Russia, 1980, USSR People to People Program, China, 1994, South Africa, 1995, Russia and Estonia, 1996; active the Capitol Region Conf. Chs., 1996—; advcate for justice and peace Capitol Region Conf. of Chs., Hartford, Conn., 1997—; mem. Conn. Campaign to Abolish Nuclear Weapons, 1997; co-chmn. Conn. Coalition on Aging, Inc., Hartford, 1976-80; mem. United Srs. in Action, 1997—; mem. advocacy justice and peace Capitol Region Conf. Chs., Hartford, Conn., 1996— . Sgt. USMCR, 1943-45. Recipient David C. King award, Conn. Soc. Gerontology, Hartford, 1985—98, award 100 Years of Women, U. Conn., Storrs, 1993, ofcl. citation, Conn. State Gen. Assembly, 2000, Walter P. Reuther Disting. Svc. award, 2000. Mem. Nat. Coun. on Aging (life), Nat. Coun. Sr. Citizens (life, mem. com. to establish 1st set of stds. for sr. ctrs.), Conn. Coun. Sr. Citizens, (v.p.), Czechoslovak Am. Club (pres. 1939-60), Zonta Internat. Club of West Hartford (bd. dirs. 1970—), Womens Internat. League Peace and Freedom, Ch. Women United (Conn. chpt. adv. bd. 1984), Czechoslovak Culture Group, United Srs. in Action (vol. activist), UN Assn. (Greater Hartford, Conn.). Democrat. Unitarian Universalist. Avocations: swimming, oil painting, hiking. Home: PO Box 370040 West Hartford CT 06137-0040

HUGGINS, AMY BRANUM, music educator; b. Memphis, Dec. 20, 1954; d. Leon and Scharlene Oney Branum; m. R. David Huggins, May 8, 1976; children: Alexander, Stephanie. MusM in Edn. with Kodaly emphasis, Holy Names Coll., Oakland, Calif., 1985; MusB in Edn., Peabody Conservatory of Music, 1976. Pvt. piano instr., Balt., 1973—; early music tng. faculty prep. divsn. Peabody Conservatory of Music, Balt., 1976—83, music theory faculty prep. divsn., 1976—83, curriculum designer prep. divsn., 1976; condr., founder The Pine Grove Madrigals, Balt., 1976—; vocal music specialist Pine Grove Elem. Sch., Balt., 1976—; master tchr., supr. of student tchrs. Peabody Conservatory of Music, Shenandoah Conservatory of Music, Towson State U., U. of Md., Loyola Coll., Balt., 1978—; organizer, dir. choral festivals Balt. County Pub. Schs., Balt.,

1980—90; instr. Children's Chorus of Md., Balt., 1983—86; curriculum designer Balt. County Pub. Schs., 1991; pvt. voice instr. Balt., 1997—; cons. Children's Chorus of Md., Balt., 1998—99; dir., co-founder The Am. Kodaly Inst., Balt., 2000—; instr. grad. studies program Loyola Coll. in Md., Balt., 2001—. Kodaly clinician, cons. Orgn. of Am. Kodaly Educators, Moorhead, Minn., 1978—, Md. United Specialists in Kodaly, Balt., 1978—. Author: Elements: A Sight Singing and Rhythm Reading Book for Beginners, 1982, Kodaly, American Style, 2001, Folk Guitar for the Music Educator, 2002, 5-String Banjo for the Music Educator, 2003; columnist: The Kodaly Envoy, 2003—04; contbr. articles to profl. jours. Bd. dirs., sec. Children's Chorus of Md., 1981—83. Scholar, Mu Phi Epsilon Alumni Assn., 1975. Mem.: OAKE (overseer 1997—98, chair nat. conf. planning com. 1997—98, 1983—85, overseer tchr. tng. com. 1983—85, 1997—98), MENC, The VoiceCare Network, Soc. for Rsch. in Music Edn., Soc. for Music Tchr. Edn., Md. Music Educators Assn., Am. Choral Dirs. Assn., Orgn. of Am. Kodaly Educators (v.p. 1983—85, 1997—98), Md. United Specialists in Kodaly (pres. 1996—98, 1982—84, 1998—99, mem. at large 1995—96, sec. 1980—82), Mu Phi Epsilon. Home: 307 Southway Baltimore MD 21218 Office: Pine Grove Sch 2701 Summit Ave Baltimore MD 21234 Personal E-mail: amybhuggins@yahoo.com. E-mail: amybhuggins@hotmail.com.

HUGGINS, CHARLOTTE SUSAN HARRISON, secondary school educator, author, travel specialist; b. Rockford, Ill., May 13, 1933; d. Lyle Lux and Alta May (Bowers) Harrison; m. Rollin Charles Huggins Jr., Apr. 26, 1952; children: Cynthia Charlotte Peters, Shirley Ann Cooper, John Charles. Student, Knox Coll., 1951-52; AB magna cum laude, Harvard U., 1958; MA, Northwestern U., 1960, postgrad., 1971-73; cert. in conversation French, Berlitz Lang. Sch. Asst. editor Hollister Publs., Inc., Wilmette, Ill., 1959—65; tchr. advanced placement English New Trier H.S., Winnetka, Ill., 1965—, master tchr., 1979, leader tchr., 1988. With Task Force Commn. on Grading, 1973—74; Sabbatical project 1 yr. world travel History-Lit. Prospectus; cons. Asian Studies New Trier, 1987—88; mem. New Trier Supts. Commn. on Censorship, 1991; critic tchr. Northwestern U.; cons. McDougall-Littel's Young Writer's Manual, 1985—88; asst. sponsor Echoes, 1981—, Trevia, 1982, 83; sponsor New Trier News, 1988—; pres. Harrison Farms, Inc., Lovington, Ill., 1976—; spkr. North Suburban Geneal. Soc., 1990; presenter Asian lit. Ill. Humanities Coun., 1992, Nat. Scholastic Press Assn., No. Ill. Sch. Press Assn., 1992, 93, 94; instr., travel expert New Trier Adult Edn. Keys to the World's Last Mysteries, 1986—. Author: A Sequential Course in Composition Grades 9-12, 1979, A History of New Trier High School, 1982, Passage to Anaheim: An Historical Biography of Pioneer Families, 1984, Cambodia: A Place in Time, 1987; author: (video tapes) The Glory That was Greece, 1987; author: The World of Charles Dickens, 1987; editor: The Cornog Years, 2002. Women's bd. St. Leonard's House, Chgo., 1965—75; active Ctrl. Sch. PTA Bd., Wilmette, Ill., 1960—64; assocs. bd. Northwestern U. Settlement, Chgo., 1965—, pres., 1999—, fundraising com., 1997—, ctrl. bd. com., 2003—. Recipient Citizenship award, DAR, 1953, award, Phi Beta Kappa, 1957, Am. Legion, 1959, Cert. of Merit Graphic Arts Competition, Printing Industries of Am., 1983, 1st pl. award, Am. Scholastic Press Assn., 1990, Cert. of Merit, Am. Newspaper Pubs. Assn., 1990. Mem.: DAR (historian 1999—2000, regent 2000—02, parliamentarian 2002—), ASCD, MLA, NEA, Ill. Ret. Tchrs. Assn., IRTA, Ill. Journalism Edn. Assn. (sec. 1997—97, awards chmn., bd. dirs., Life Achievement award 2001), New Trier Edn. Assn. (sec. 1992, pres.-elect 1994, pres. 1995—96, parliamentarian 2000—), Ill. Assn. Tchrs. English, Ill. Edn. Assn., Nat. Scholastic Press Assn. (conv. del. 1991, spring conf. rep. 1991—92, 1992—93, 1993—94, presenter fall and spring conv. 1993—94, spring conf. rep. 1994—95, presenter fall and spring conv. 1994—95, 1994—95, spring conf. rep. 1995—96, presenter fall and spring conv. 1995—96, 1996—, newspaper judge, All-Am. Newspaper award 1990—91, Life Achievement award 2001), Nat. Coun. Tchrs. English, Alliance Français, Harvard U. Alumni Assn. (admissions candidate interviewer), Knox Coll. Alumni Assn., Terra Mus. Chgo. (charter), Chgo. Farmers, Women Comm., Inc., Nat. Huguenot Soc., Quill and Scroll (bd. dirs. 1992—93, George Gallup award 1990), Ill. Huguenot Soc., Columbia Scholastic Press Assn. (del. 1990, newspaper judge), Jr. Aux. U. Chgo. Cancer Rsch. Bd., Northwestern U. Alumni Assn., Mary Crane League, Art Inst. Chgo. (life), New Trier Ret. Tchrs. Assn. (newsletter editor), Lyric Opera (assoc.), Radcliffe Coll. Alunmae Assn., Univ. Club Chgo., Women's Club Willmette, Mich. Shores Club, Pi Beta Phi (North Shore Chgo. alumnae bd., publicity chair). Home: 700 Greenwood Ave Wilmette IL 60091-1748 Office: 385 Winnetka Ave Winnetka IL 60093-4238

HUGGINS, MARY LOUISE WHITE, English educator, small business owner; b. Big Wells, Tex., Jan. 7, 1933; d. Edwin Horatio and Cora Edith (English) White; m. Chester Huelon Huggins, Sept. 23, 1961; children: Mary Catherine, Clarice Nell, Lloyd Jefferson, Henry Nuelon, Chester Horatio. BA in English and Spanish, Tarleton State U., Stephenville, Tex., 1979, MA in Teaching, 1981. Cert. secondary tchr., Tex. Sec., bookkeeper Hico (Tex.) Pub. Sch., 1969-76; instr. English, Tarleton State U., 1983—, dir. summer program, 1987—. Clk. bookkeeper Blair's Hardware, Hico, 1972-83; owner, operator Mary's Garden, Stephenville, 1987—. Pres. Erath County Women's Polit. Caucus, Stephenville; speaker to garden clubs, 1986—. Named Erath County Woman of Yr., Erath County Com., 1989. Mem. Conf. Coll. Tchrs. English, Assn. Tchrs. Tech. Writing, South Cen. Women's Studies Assn., Tarleton State U. Faculty Women's Forum (treas. 1988-89), AAUW (pres. Stephenville br. 1987), Am. Iris Soc., Johnson County Iris and Daylily Soc. (pres. 1987-88, lst v.p. 1989-90). Avocations: writing, painting, gardening, home maintenance and remodeling. Home: 867 W Elm St Stephenville TX 76401-2415

HUGHES, A. N. psychotherapist; b. Ft. Meade, Md. d. G.M. and G.T. Nolen; m. E.L. Hughes, Oct. 21, 1961; 1 child, Andrew G. BS in Psychology, Rollins Coll., 1985, MA in Counseling, 1986; student in pub. speaking and human rels., Dale Carnegie Inst., 1981; student, Duke U., 1950-52. Lic. mental health counselor; nat. cert. counselor; nat. cert. gerontol. counselor. Supr. top secret control, audio/visual and small parts supply U.S. Army, Continental U.S. and Tokyo; adminstrv. sec. Sys. Devel. Corp., Rand Corp., Santa Monica, Calif.; adminstrv. asst., editor, exec. sec., adminstrv. sec. Aerospace Corp., El Segundo, Calif.; staff therapist Circles of Care, Melbourne, Fla. Developer program for leading divorce support groups for Brevard Women's Ctr. Various leadership positions PTA, Pittsford, NY, Brookfield, Wis., 1968—81; mem. Brevard Cmty. Chorus, 1991—, adv. bd., 1997; mem. Citizen's Emergency Response Team (CERT), 1999—2001; various vol. positions in several organizations in Brevard County, 1991—. Mem. DAR, Fla. Coun. on Aging, Space Coast PC Users Group, Geneal. Soc. South Brevard, Suntree Country Club, Suntree Master Homeowners Assn. (Twin Lakes rep. 1997—), Brevard County Alumnae Assn. of Kappa Kappa Gamma, Kappa Kappa Gamma. Avocations: photoimaging, fitness, genealogy, choral singing. Office: PO Box 410162 Melbourne FL 32941-0162

HUGHES, ANN HIGHTOWER, retired economist, international trade consultant; b. Birmingham, Ala., Nov. 24, 1938; d. Brady Alexander and Juanita (Pope) H. BA, George Washington U., 1963, MA, 1969. Asst. U.S. trade rep. Exec. Office of Pres., Washington, 1978-81; dep. asst. sec. trade agreements Dept. Commerce, Washington, 1981-82, dep. asst. sec. Western Hemisphere, 1982-95; dir. C & M Internat., Washington, 1995-97; ret. Recipient meritorious exec. award Pres. of U.S., 1982, 88, disting. exec. award, 1993.

HUGHES, BARBARA BRADFORD, manufacturing executive, real estate manager, community health nurse; b. Bragg City, Mo., Jan. 21, 1941; d. Lawrence Hurl Bradford and Opal Jewel (Prater) Puttin; m. Robert Howard Hughes, Dec. 9, 1961; children: Kimberly Ann Hayden, Robert Howard II. ASN, St. Louis Community Coll., 1978; student, Webster U., 1980. RN, Mo. Med. surg. nurse Alexian Bros. Hosp., St. Louis, 1979-80; staff nurse Midwest Allergy Cons., St. Louis, 1980; nurse high altitude Aviation Nurse, Ltd., St. Louis, 1980-81; cardiac telemetry staff nurse Jefferson Meml. Hosp., Crystal City, Mo., 1992-94; vol. nurse Med. Ministry Internat., Plano, Tex., 1998-2001; CEO Supreme Tool & Die, Fenton, Mo., 2001—. Chmn. bd. dirs., CEO, ptnr. Supreme Tool & Die Co., Fenton, Mo., 1988—; pvt. practice real estate mgmt., 1962—; mem. nursing adv. com. Jefferson Coll., Hillsboro, Mo., 1999, mem. adv. bd., 2000—01. Vol. Luth. Hosp., St. Louis, 1967—70; mem. Mo. Bot. Garden, St. Louis, 1976—, Mo. Hist. Soc., 1976, St. Louis Zoo Friends Assn., 1986—87, Nat. Trust for Hist. Preservation, 1990—, Channel 9-Ednl. TV, St. Louis; vol. health tchr. Spartan Aluminum Products, Sparta, Ill., 1984; mem. Rosie the Riveter women's pilot group project, readying a DC3 for FAA recert. through Wings of Hope, TWA and Remote Area Med. Knoxville, for use in med. relief in remote areas of U.S. and the world; mem. med. missions to nat. and internat. remote areas sponsored by Wings of Hope, 2000—; mem. field and med. support team Wings of Hope, St. Louis, vol. flight nurse in midwest, 2003; mem. field and med. support team Remote Area Medicad, Knoxville, Tenn. U. Mo. scholar, 1959. Mem.: AACN, Med. Ministries Internat., Nat. Tool and Machining Assn., U.S. Pilots Assn., Wings of Hope (St. Louis), Mo. Pilots Assn., Women in Aviation Internat. (charter), Tyospaye Club. Republican. Achievements include Giving direct med. treatment to patients in remote areas of the U.S.A. and Central and South Am. Avocations: flying, gardening, reading. Office: Supreme Tool & Die 1536 Fenpark Dr Fenton MO 63026

HUGHES, BRENDA BETHEA, state legislator; b. High Point, N.C. married. BS, N.C. Ctrl. State U.; postgrad., Ctrl. Mich. U. Me.m. Md. Ho. of Dels., Annapolis, 1993-98, mem. ways and means com., 1993-98; adminstr. The Port of Balt., 1998—. Mem. Prince Georges County Bd. Edn., 1988-93, Gov.'s Commn. on Disruptive Youth, 1993—. Mem. Delta Sigma Theta. Office: The Port of Balt E Pratt St World Trade Ctr/19th Flr Baltimore MD 21202

HUGHES, BRIGID, editor; d. Patrick and Patricia. BA in English, Northwestern U., 1994. Intern The Paris Rev., N.Y.C., 1995, editor, 1995—2000, mng. editor, 2000—04, exec. editor, 2004—. Office: The Paris Review 541 E 72nd St New York NY 10021

HUGHES, CATHERINE L. (CATHY HUGHES), radio personality, broadcast executive; b. Omaha, Apr. 27, 1947; 1 child. Student, Creighton U., U. Nebr. Lectr., asst. to dean comm. Howard U., Washington, 1971—73; gen. sales mgr. WHUR Radio, 1973—78; v.p., gen. mgr. WYCB Radio, 1978—80; owner, operator WOL-AM Radio, 1980—; now founder, chairperson Radio One. Trustee Lincoln U.; bd. mem. Balt. Devel. Corp.; small bus. adv. com. Fed. Res. Bank. Bd. mem. Piney Woods Sch., Balt. Mus. Art. Named Bus. Person of the Yr., Nat. Black C. of C., 1998, Prudential Media Black Woman on Wall St., 1999; recipient Mayor's Bus. award, 1995—99, Thomas A. Dorsey Leadership award, 1996, D.C. Cmty. Svc. award, 1995; scholar, Living Vision Scholarship Fund, 1995. Achievements include first to to be an African American woman to head a firm publicly traded on a stock exchange in the United States. Office: Radio One Inc 100 St Paul St Baltimore MD 21202*

HUGHES, CORRY HANKINSON, special education educator; d. William Joseph and Johanna Admiraal Hankinson; m. Roger Dale Hughes, Jan. 8, 1983; children: Shenandoah Sky, Season Elora. BS in Spl. Edn., Va. Commonwealth U., 1982; MS in Reading Specalist, Longwood Coll., 1993. Cert. spl. educator Va. Bd. Edn., reading specialist Va. Bd. Edn. Asst. buyer Thalhimers Dept. Stores, Richmond, Va., 1976—81; tchr. spl. edn. Amelia County Pub. Schs., Amelia, Va., 1983—. Mem. task force Improving Spl. Edn. Experiences, Va., 1996—2001; faculty liaison Spl. Edn. Local Adv. Com., Amelia, 1996—2002; mem. Collaborative Planning Team, Amelia, 1996—; presenter workshop/seminar Collaborative Classes: How to Make Them Successful, Longwood U., 2002. Coord., coach Spl. Olympics, Amelia, 1986—89, 1997—2001. Recipient long-term tech. assistance grant, Tng. Tech. Assistnace Ctr., Va. Commonwealth U., 1996—. Mem.: NEA, CEC, Epilepsy Found. Am., United Mitochondrial Disease Found., Internat. Rett Syndrome Assn., Dem. Nat. Com. Avocations: gardening, singing. Office: Amelia County Elem Sch 8533 N Five Forks Rd Amelia Court House VA 23002 Office Phone: 804-561-2433.

HUGHES, DEBORAH BRAY, special education educator; b. Dallas, May 29, 1953; d. Von M. Bray and Francis Barton Harris; m. David M. Park; children: Delain Barton, Devon Bray Miller. BS Magna cum laude in interdisciplinary studies, U. No. Tex., 2001. Cert. tchr. Tex., 2002. Tchg. asst. autistic group Garland (Tex.) Coop. Behavioral Ctr., 1977—79; tchr. Lake Highlands Christ. Child Enrichment Ctr., Dallas, 1983—84, Rockwall (Tex.) Pvt. Sch., 1987—88; tchr., dir. ops., v.p. mktg. Mem. Sch. of the Oaks, Houston, 1988—91; legal asst. Brown & Brown, Wetzel, Herron, & Drucker, LLP, Houston, 1991—94; behavioral therapist Pvt. Practice, The Woodlands, 1995—98, U. Houston, Tex. Young Autism Project, 1995—98; spl. edn. tchr. Denton Ind. Sch. Dist., 2002—. Adv. bd. Mem. Sch. Oaks Found., 1988—91. Author: (poem) World of Poetry Anthology, 1988 (Golden Poet award, 1988). Vol. So. Poverty Law Ctr., ACLU, March of Dimes, Habitat for Humanity, The Carter Ctr. Mem.: Families Early Autism Treatment, No. Tex., Nat. Assn. Edn. of Young Children, Golden Key Nat., Kappa Delta Pi, Internat. Honor Soc. in Edn. Avocations: reading, writing, art, music. Office: Denton Ind Sch Dist 3300 Evers Pkwy Denton TX 76201

HUGHES, DEBORAH ENOCH, circuit court clerk; b. Lynchburg, Va., Mar. 24, 1953; d. George Alexander Enoch and Inez (Hailey) Enoch Green; m. Frank Plunkett Hughes, Apr. 24, 1971; children: Frank P. II, Neal Thomas. Grad. in Data Processing, Ctrl. Va. C.C., 1974. Cert. circuit ct. clk., Va. Dep. real estate office Divsn. Commr. of Revenue, Rustburg, Va., 1971-75; data processing chief entry clk. Campbell County Sch. Bd., Rustburg, Va., 1975-79; dep. clk. Circuit Ct. Clk.'s Office, Campbell County, 1979-91, clk., 1992—. Mem. Va. Circuit Ct. Clk.'s Assn., Va. Assn. Elected Constnl. Officers (sec.). Office: Campbell County Circuit Ct Clks Office PO Box 7 Rustburg VA 24588-0007

HUGHES, DEBORAH L. minister, director; b. Albany, N.Y., Jan. 21, 1960; d. Richard Norman and Dorothea Jeanne Hughes. BS, U. Oreg., 1983; MDiv, Colgate Rochester Crozer, 1987. Ordained to Christian ministry Am. Bapt. Chs. Assoc. pastor First Bapt. Ch., Birmingham, Mich., 1987—94; retirement svcs. officer Mins. and Missionaries Benefit Bd., N.Y.C., 1994—2001; v.p. for devel. Colgate Rochester (N.Y.) Crozer, 2001—. Vol. Big Bros./Big Sisters, Rochester, 2002—; vol. pastoral counselor AIDS Interfaith Network, Detroit, 1988—91; trustee Lake Ave. Bapt. Ch., Rochester, 2003; bd. mem. Am. Bapt. Chs. Mich., East Lansing, 1989—94, Roger Williams Fellowship, Valley Forge, Pa., 1992—94, Riverside Ch., N.Y.C., 1996. Mem.: Assn. Welcoming and Affirming Bapts., Rochester Women's Network, Delta Delta Delta Alumnae. Office: Colgate Rochester Crozer Div Sch 1100 S Goodman St Rochester NY 14620

HUGHES, DEBRA, writer, educator; b. Alamogordo, N.Mex., Oct. 3, 1955; d. Clinton Don and JoEllyn Hughes; children: Austin Hughes-Blanks, Merritt Hughes-Blanks; m. Gary Paul Tyc. Diploma superior, U. Sorbonne, Paris, 1976; BA, U. Colo., 1977; MA, Ohio State U., 1986. Staff reporter The Albuquerque Tribune, 1978-80; freelance writer N.Mex. Mag., Bristol-Meyers-Squibb, USA Today, others, 1978—. Instr., creative writing workshop tchr. Ohio State U., Santa Fe C.C., Santa Fe Prep. Sch., Rio Grande Sch., 1983-96; v.p. bd. dirs. N.Mex. Lit. Arts, Santa Fe, 1995-97; lit. judge State Arts Couns. for Wyo., Colo., Utah, 1994-96. Author: (short stories) New Letters, 1995, Walking the Twilight, 1994, Tierra, 1989; contbr. articles to profl. jours. Vol. St. Elizabeth's Shelter, Santa Fe, 1996; vol. instr. Santa Fe Pub. Schs., 1994-99. Recipient Silver award, Internat. Regional Mag. Assn., 2001; fellow, Ohio State U., 1986; scholar, Bread Loaf Writer's Conf., 1992. Mem. PEN, PEN West, Assoc. Writing Programs.

HUGHES, ELLEN RONEY, historian, museum exhibition curator; b. Washington, Jan. 11, 1943; d. Joseph A. and Elizabeth Marshall (Chamblin) Roney; m. Gary Hughes, Jan. 25, 1974. BA in History, Salve Regina U., 1965; MA in Am. Studies, U. Md., 1991, PhD in Am. Studies, 2001. Museum specialist in postal history Nat. Mus. Am. History, Smithsonian Instn., Washington, 1972-74, cultural historian for sport, leisure and popular culture collections, 1977—, project mgr., curatorial asst. A Nation of Nations Exhbn., 1974-91, curator Smithsonian's Am. Exhbn., 1991-94. Exhbn. curator Sesame Street, 1969-1989, The First 20 Years, 1989, The Wizard of Oz and the Ruby Slippers, 1991, Jackie Robinson and the Integration of Major League Baseball, 1992, numerous others; lectr. on mus.; presenter and organizer symposia; mem. nominating com. for Women's Sports Hall of Fame, Women's Sports Found., 1975-85; v.p. Gary Hughes, Inc., Bethesda, Md., 1976—; adj. faculty Am. Studies Dept. U. Md., 1996—. Author: (with Bunch, Lubar and Brodie) Smithsonian's America: An Exhibition on American History and Culture, 1994, Machines For Better Bodies: The History of Exercise Machines, 1830-1950, 2001; contbr. articles to profl. publs., chpts. to books; prodr. films, video, TV and radio prodns. Mem. steering com. Smithsonian; chmn. Forum Material Culture, 1999—2001. Rsch. grantee Lemelson Ctr. for Study Invention and Innovation, 1996. Mem. Am. Studies Assn., Hist. Soc. Washington, N.Am. Soc. for Sport History, Soc. for History Tech. Democrat. Avocations: art, cooking. Office: Smithsonian Instn Nat Mus Am History Rm 4210A MRC 616 Washington DC 20560-0001

HUGHES, FRANCIS P. medical organization executive; PhD. Exec. v.p. Am. Bd. Anesthesiology, Raleigh, NC. Office: Am Bd Anesthesiology 4101 Lake Boone Trl Ste 510 Raleigh NC 27607 7506

HUGHES, GRACE-FLORES, business exeucitve; b. Taft, Tex., June 11, 1946; d. Adan Flores and Catalina San Miguel; m. Harley Arnold Hughes, May 25, 1980. BA, U. D.C., 1977; MPA, Harvard U., 1980. Sec. Dept. Air Force Kelly AFB, San Antonio, 1967-70, Pentagon-Office Sec. of Def., Washington, 1970 72; program asst., social sci. analyst HEW, Washington, 1972-78; social sci. analyst, acting dir. Office Hispanic Ams. HHS, Washington, 1978-81; vis. prof. Nebr. Wesleyan U., Lincoln, 1982-83, U. Nebr., Omaha, 1984; spl. asst. SBA, Washington, 1985-88, assoc. adminstr. for minority small bus., 1988; dir. community rels. Dept. Justice, Washington, 1988-92; pres. Grace, Inc., Alexandria, Va.; v.p. for intergovtl. affairs USTAK, LLCcs., Inc. Spl. asst. Reagan/Bush '84 Campaign, Nebr. and Washington, 1984, 50th Presdl. Inaugural, Washington, 1984-85, Office Pub. Liaison, The White House, 1985. Author: The Bureaucrat, Categorized Workforce, 1992; co-author: New Book of Knowledge, 1980; chair adv. bd. Harvard Jour. Hispanic Policy, 1989—; The Use and Abuse of Diversity Mag., 1994, Hispanic Mag., 1996. Adv. mem. U.S. Senate Rep. Task Force, Washington, 1988-91; alumni exec. bd. J.F. Kennedy Sch. Govt., Harvard U., Cambridge, Mass., 1989-93; mem. Rep. Hispanic Assembly, 1984—; apptd. by Gov. Allen of Va. to Bd. for Profl. and Occpl. Regulations, 1994—, Bd. for Agr. and Consumer Svcs., 1997—; bd. dirs. Hispanic Found. for Arts; apptd. by Pres. Bush Fed. Svc. Impasses Panel, 2000. Recipient Excellence award Nev. Econ. Devel. Corp., 1988, Leadership award Am. GI Forum, Omaha, 1989; named one of 100 Most Influential Hispanics in U.S. Hispanic Bus. Mag., 1988. Mem. Assn. Pub. Adminstrs. (Outstanding Pub. Svc. award 1990), Hispanic Bus. Roundtable, Coun. in Excellence in Govt. (prin.), Fedn. Rep. Women, Mex.-Am. Women's Nat. Assn., Univ. Club (Washington). Episcopalian. Avocations: tennis, jogging, aerobics, equestrian. Home and Office: 5208 Bedlington Ter Alexandria VA 22304-3551

HUGHES, JACQUELINE EMMA, information systems specialist; b. Baltimore, Md., Feb. 10, 1968; d. Hugh Price Hughes Jr. and Reta Theresa Hughes. BA in Psychology, Coll. Notre Dame Md., Balt., 1990; MBA, U. Phoenix, Columbia, Md., 2001. CPR, First Aid, and AED Instructor ARC, 2002. Armorer USMC Reserves, Savannah, Ga., 1988—99; counselor Mgmt. Tng. Corp., Washington, 1992—99; counseling mgr. Adams and Assocs., Laurel, Md., 1995—96; info. systems specialist TCU Manpower Tng. Dept., Rockville, Md., 1999—. Innovation com. mem. Mgmt. Tng. Corp., Randallstown, Md., 1993; cultural diversity coord. Adams and Assocs., Laure, Md., 1995—96. Author: (poetry) Look, 1999. Mem. Greater Arbutus (Md.) Cmty. Alliance, 2002—03; chair, Relay for Life Am. Cancer Soc., 2002—03. Mem.: NAFE. Avocations: travel, volunteer work. Personal E-mail: jackieehughes@earthlink.net.

HUGHES, JENNIFER, utilities executive, photographer; b. Chgo., June 28, 1963; d. Harold Henry and Mable (Lee) H. Student, U. Ill., 1982-83. Girls basketball coach, driver's edn. asst. Carver Area H.S., Chgo., 1981-83; drivers edn. tchr. Continental Driving Sch., Chgo., 1989-91; security guard Zayre Dept. Store, Chgo., 1985-89; utilities exec. Commonwealth Edison, Chgo., 1989-92, mem. maintenance crew, 1992-94, control ctr. operator, 1994—2001; utilities executive CPI, 1994—2001. Author: Inspired By It All, 2000, It's All About Her, 2000; author numerous poems. Cert. CPR instr., ARC. With USAR, 1983-89. Mem. Order Eastern Star. Avocations: creating abstract art, biking, tennis, movies, theater. Home: 7780 NW 78th Ave Apt 110 Tamarac FL 33321-4725

HUGHES, JUDITH ELAINE, not-for-profit developer, director; b. Boston, Sept. 28, 1951; d. Walter Lee and Eleanor (Ryan) Hughes; m. Michael Malyszko; 1 child, Maeve Malyszko. Cert., U. Paris, 1970; BA in History, U. Pa., 1972; MALD, Fletcher Sch., 1978. Paralegal Schnader Harrison, Phila., 1973—75; project adminstr. Fletcher Sch., Medford, Mass., 1977—78, program coord. Boston, 1978—; project adminstr. JFK Sch. Harvard U., Cambridge, Mass., 1980—81; ptnr. Malyszko Photography, Boston, 1981—2002; v.p. develop. Initiative Competitive Inner City, Boston, 2002—. Author (with Michael Malyszko): (book) Betty & Rita Go to Paris, 1999, Betty & Rita La Dolce Vita, 2001. Avocations: travel, cooking, horseback riding. Home: 90 South St Boston MA 02111-2835 Office: ICIC 727 Atlantic Ave Boston MA 02111 Business E-Mail: jhughes@icic.org.

HUGHES, JUDY LYNNE, political organization executive; b. San Antonio, Mar. 23, 1939; d. Timothy Endymion Gristy and Clovis Ruth (Mooring) Linville; m. Donald E. LaMora, Nov. 12, 1960 (div. Aug. 1980); children: Grant, Leigh, Eric; m. William J. Hughes, May 11, 1984 (div. 1990). Student, Tex. Tech. U., 1956-60. News reporter Colorado Springs (Colo.) Gazette Telegraph, 1960; vice chair pub. rels. Nat. Fedn. Rep. Women, Washington, 1974-76, mem.-at-large exec. com., 1976-78, 2d v.p., 1978-82, 1st v.p., 1982-86, pres., 1986-90; western rep. U.S. Dept. Interior, Golden, Colo., 1991-93; polit. edn. specialist Rep. Nat. Com., Washington, 1993-95, chief of staff to co-chmn., 1995-97, strategic and local coord., 1997; comms. specialist State of Tex. Dept. Econ. Devel., 1997-2000; adminstrn. technician Tex. Sec. of State, 2000—. Ofcl. del. U.S. State Dept., El Salvador, 1989; mem. Dept. Interior's Representation on Denver Interagy. Coun. on Homeless, 1990-93; mem. Denver Fed. Exec. Bd. Pub. Rels. Coun., 1990-93. Mem. RNC Com. Minority Participation, Washington, 1989, Hill Country Rep. Women Austin; bd. dirs. Colo. Coun. on Econ. Edn., 1991-93; pres. Colo. Fedn. Rep. Women, 1974-76. Named Rep. Woman of Yr., Shelby County Rep. Women's Club, 1988. Mem. Pikes Peak Rep. Women's Roundtable (Colorado Springs). Avocation: tennis. Home: 1000 Liberty Park Dr Apt 506 Austin TX 78746-6840 Office: Tex Sec of State 208 E 10th Austin TX 78701

HUGHES, KAREN PARFITT, former federal official; b. Paris, Dec. 1956; m. Jerry L. Hughes; 1 child, Robert. BA in English, BFA in journalism, So. Meth. U., 1977. Television reporter, 1977—84; Tex. media coord. Reagan/Bush Campaign, 1984; media cons. Rep. Party of Tex., 1985—91, exec. dir., 1991—94; dir. comm. to Gov. George Bush, 1994—2001; counselor to Pres. George Bush, 2001—02. Author: Ten Minutes From Normal, 2004.*

HUGHES, KAYLENE, historian, educator; b. Modesto, Calif., Aug. 4, 1952; BA, Miami-Dade (Fla.) Jr. Coll., 1972, Fla. Internat. U., 1976; MA, Fla. State U., 1977, PhD, 1985. Intern Fla. State Dept. Archives Records Mgmt., Tallahassee, 1977; Claims Control Supr. Sys. Devel. Corp., Tallahassee, 1978-81; editl. asst. Fla. Hotel and Motel Jour., Tallahassee, 1983-85; dir. edn., rsch. mgr. Fla. Hotel and Motel Assn., Tallahassee, 1985-87; historian U.S. Army Aviation & Missile Command, Redstone Arsenal, Ala., 1987—. Grad. asst. Fla. State U., Tallahassee, 1976-77, tchg. asst., 1981-83; adj. instr. history John C. Calhoun C.C., Huntsville, Ala., 1990—. Author: Florida's Lodging Industry: The First 75 Years, 1987, The Missile's Red Glare, 1992, Redstone Army Airfield: A Tradition of Aviation Support, 1992, Redstone Arsenal's Role in Operation Desert Shield/Desert Storm, 1992; contbr. articles to jours. and newspapers. Grantee Fla. State U., 1983. Mem. Phi Alpha Theta (sec. 1982-85), Phi Theta Kappa. Home: 342 Pawnee Trl SE Huntsville AL 35803-2280 E-mail: kaylene.hughes@redstone.army.mil.

HUGHES, LESLEY LYNNE, assistant principal; b. Norfolk, Va., Aug. 5, 1964; d. Clarence Allen Powell and Rebecca Turner Pallette; m. Charles Casey Hughes, June 27, 1987; children: Turner Ashby, Stuart Thayer. BA, Va. Wesleyan Coll., 1986; MA, George Washington U., 2000, postgrad. Cert. collegiate profl. Va. Tchr. Virginia Beach (Va.) City Pub. Schs., 1986—98, instrnl. specialist, 1998—2000, asst. prin., 2000—. Lifetime mem. PTA. Mem.: NAESP, ASCD, Phi Delta Kappa. Avocation: reading. Home: 2213 Childeric Rd Virginia Beach VA 23456 Office: Virginia Beach City Pub Schs 2828 Pleasant Acres Dr Virginia Beach VA 23453

HUGHES, LIBBY, writer; b. Pitts, Aug. 11, 1932; d. Lloyd Alfred and Vera Abby (Walker) Pockman; m. R. John Hughes, Aug. 20, 1955 (div. 1988); children: Wendy E., Mark E. BA, U. Ala., 1954; MFA, Boston U., 1955. Profl. actress, Kenya, S. Africa, 1955-59; drama critic and feature writer Cape Cod Newspapers, 1977-86, assoc. pubr., 1977-81, pubr., 1981-85. Pres. Desert Starfield Prodn., 1994; theatre critic www.capecodtoday. Author: Bali, 1969, Margaret Thatcher, 1989, Benazir Bhutto, 1990, Nelson Mandela, 1992, Good Manners for Children, 1992, H. Norman Schwarzkopf, 1992, West Point, 1992, Valley Forge, 1992, Colin Powell, 1996, School Manners Workbook, 1998, Christopher Reeve, 1997, Tiger Woods, 2000, Yitzhak Rabin, 2001, George W. Bush, 2003; editor: Ginger Rogers Autobiography, 1989, 91; playwright: Sin in the Attic (Chatham Drama Guild award 1999-2000), Pasta and Curry (New Opera and Musical Theatre Initiative award 2000), 26 others; theater reviewer www.capecodtoday.com Bd. dir. Wisdom Inst., 1984-86, Cape Cod Mus., 1984-86. Recipient Songwriting award, Eventide Arts Festival of Cape Cod, 2001. Mem. ASCAP, Dramatists Guild, Authors Guild, Ala. Wildlife Rescue Svc. (pres. 1988-89), Nat. Soc. Arts and Letters (chpt. pres. 1984-86, protocol officer 1984-86), Nat. League Am. Pen Women. Avocations: theatre, news, wildlife, breeding rhodesian ridgebacks. Home: June to August 23 Grove Lane Brewster MA 02631 also: September to May 988 Memorial Dr #81 Cambridge MA 02138 E-mail: libhughes@aol.com.

HUGHES, LINDA J. newspaper publisher; b. Princeton, B.C., Can., Sept. 27, 1950; d. Edward Rees and Madge Preston (Bryan) H.; m. George Fredrick Ward, Dec. 16, 1978; children: Sean Ward, Kate Ward. BA, U. Victoria (B.C.), 1972; LittD (hon.), Athabasca U., 1997; diploma in journalism (hon.), Grant MacEwan C.C., Edmonton, Alta., Can., 1999; LLD (hon.), U. Alberta, 2003. With Edmonton Jour., Alta., Can., 1976—, from reporter to asst. mng. editor, 1984-87, editor, 1987-92, pub., 1992—. Southam fellow U. Toronto, Ont., Can., 1977-78; recipient Disting. Citizen award Grant MacEwan C.C., 1999, Dist. Alumni award U. Victoria, 2000. Office: Edmonton Journal 10006 101st St PO Box 2421 Edmonton AB Canada T5J 2S6

HUGHES, MARIJA MATICH, law librarian; b. Belgrade, Yugoslavia; came to U.S., 1960, naturalized, 1971; d. Zarija and Antonija (Hudowsky) Matich. BA in Music, Mokranjac, Belgrade; BA in English, U. Belgrade and Calif. State U.; MLS, U. Md.; student, McGeorge Sch. Law; MHA in Health Care Adminstrn., George Washington U., 1985, M. in Adminstrv. Scis., 1989. Counselor, gen. mgr. Career Counseling Service, Sacramento, Calif., 1962-64; sec. to mgr. Sacramento State Coll., 1965-66; student librarian High John program U. Md., Fairmont Heights, 1967; reference librarian Calif. State Law Library, Sacramento, 1968; head reference library-faculty liasion librarian Hastings Coll. Law U. Calif., San Francisco, 1969-72; head law librarian AT&T, Washington, 1972-73; chief law librarian Nat. Clearinghouse Library, U.S. Commn. on Civil Rights, Washington, 1973-86; tech. info. specialist U.S. Dept. Labor, OSHA, Tech. Date Ctr., 1988—; owner, pub. Hughes Press. Author (compiler): The Sexual Barrier, Legal and Econ. Aspects of Employment, vols. 1 and 2, 1970—73, The Sexual Barriers: Legal, Medical, Economic and Social Aspects of Sex Discrimination, 1977, Computer Health Hazards, 1990, 1993, Computer Health Hazards, Eng. translation, 1996, Sick From Computers, 1994, Computers, Antennas, Cellular Telephones and Power Lines Health Hazards, 1996, Shadow at the Ball, 2001; contbr. articles to profl. jours. Mem. Cellular Phone Task Force. Mem. Am. Assn. Law Librs., Bioelectromagnetics Soc., Consumer Utilities Bd. Home: 2400 Virginia Ave NW Apt C501 Washington DC 20037-2644

HUGHES, MARVALENE, academic administrator; Student, Tuskegee U., NYU, Columbia U.; PhD in Counseling and Adminstrn., Fla. State U.; postgrad., Harvard U., U. Calif., San Diego. Dir. counseling and career devel. Eckerd Coll., Fla.; dir. counseling svcs. and placement, prof. and adminstr. San Diego State U.; assoc. v.p. student affairs Ariz. State U.; v.p. student affairs, prof. counseling and human svcs. U. Toledo; v.p. student affairs, vice provost, prof. ednl. psychology U. Minn.; pres. Calif. State U., Stanislaus, 1994—. Nat., internat. keynote spkr. Contbr. chpts. to books and articles to profl. jours. Keynoter Pres.-to-Pres. Address, Internat. Conf. Pres. and Chancellors, Puerto Rico, 1999; chmn. Women Pres. and Chancellors Am. Assn. State Colls. and Univs., 1999—, prof. devel. com.; adv. bd. 1st Nat. Women's Mus.; mem. divsn. II pres. coun. NCAA, mem. divsn. II budget and fin. com., liason pres. coun. divsn. II student athlete adv. com.; mem. evaluation com. Accrediting Commn. Sr. Colls. and Univs., We. Assn. Schs. and Colls.; mem. Lt. Gov.'s Commn One Calif., 1999. Mem. Leadership Calif. Office: 801 W Monte Vista Ave Turlock CA 95382-0256

HUGHES, MARY KATHERINE, lawyer; b. July 16, 1949; d. John Chamberlain and Marjorie (Anstey) H.; m. Andrew H. Eker, July 7, 1982. BBA cum laude, U. Alaska, 1971; JD, Willamette U., 1974; postgrad., Heriot-Watt U., Edinburgh, Scotland, 1971. Bar: Alaska 1975. Ptnr. Hughes, Thorsness, Gantz, Powell & Brundin, Anchorage, 1974-95; mcpl. atty. Municipality of Anchorage, 1995-2000; of counsel Hughes, Thorsness, Powell, Huddleston & Bauman, 2001—. Talkshow host KBYR 700 AM, 2002—. Host (talk show) KBYR 7:00 AM, 2002—. Trustee Willamette U., 1997—; bd. visitors WUCL, 1978—2001; bd. dirs. Alaska Repertory Theatre, 1986—88, pres., 1987—88; commr. Alaska Code Revision Commn., 1987—94; active U. Alaska Found., 1985—, trustee, 1990—; bd. visitors U. Alaska, Fairbanks, 1994—2002, bd. regents, 2002—; bd. dirs. Anchorage Econ. Devel. Corp., 1989—, chmn., 1994; mem. Providence Anchorage Adv. Coun., 1993—, Providence Alaska Found., 1998—, chair, 2002—; lawyer rep. 9th Cir. Jud. Conf., 1995—2000; pres., trustee Alaska Bar Found., 1984—98, trustee, 2001—, Athena Soc., 2003—. Fellow: Am. Bar Found.; mem.: Internat. Mcpl. Lawyers Assn. (state chair 1995—96, regional v.p. 1997—2000), Anchorage Assn. Women Lawyers (pres. 1976—77), Alaska Bar Assn. (bd. govs 1981—84, pres. 1983—84), Soroptimists (pres. 1986—87), Delta Theta Phi. Republican. Roman Catholic. Home: 1502 Coffey Ln Anchorage AK 99501-4977 E-mail: mkhughes@acsalaska.net.

HUGHES, MARY KATHERINE, nurse; b. Phila., Nov. 3, 1945; d. James Simon and Mary Katherine (MacLellan) Kiening; m. Robert William Hughes June 11, 1967; children: William, Jonathan, Sarah. BS, Tex. Woman's U., 1968, MS, 1988. Cert. grief therapist. Staff nurse Planned Parenthood, Houston, 1968-70, Staff Builder's, Houston, 1979-81, Meml. Southwest Hosp., Houston, 1981-90; nurse psychotherapist Woman's Christian Home, Houston, 1989-90; clin. nurse specialist U. Tex. MD Anderson Cancer Ctr., Houston, 1990—, clin. instr., 1995—. Mem. adj. faculty Tex. Woman's U., Houston, 1989-96; Mary Mazzwy lectr. Houston Oncology Nursing Soc., 1993. Facilitator Patient Group Am. Cancer Soc., 1993—, co-facilitator Grief Group, 1983—, Family Group, 1994—, bd. dirs., 1983-86, adv. bd., 1986-95. Recipient Sword of Hope award Am. Cancer Soc., 1986, Outstanding Nurse Oncologist Brown Found., 1993, Outstanding Vol. St. John's Presbyn. Ch., 1995; named 100 Gt. Nursing Alumni Tex. Woman's U., 2001. Presbyterian. Avocations: reading, music, opera, ballet, singing. Office: U Tex MD Anderson Cancer Ctr 1515 Holcombe Blvd # 431 Houston TX 77030-4009 E-mail: hughes@audumla.mdacc.tmc.edu.

HUGHES, MARY SORROWS, artist; b. Washington, Oct. 28, 1945; d. Howard Earl and Martha Jane (Summerville) Sorrows; m. Frank Broox Hughes, May 22, 1967; 1 child, Broox Bradley. BA in Art, Centenary Coll., 1967, BA in Edn., 1978. Draftsman for civil engring. dept. Texaco, New Orleans, 1967-70; owner, freelance artist Shreveport, La., 1979—. Illustrator Total Tales, 1984; included in The Best of Watercolor, 1995, Best of Watercolor: Painting Color, 1997, Floral Inspirations, 1998, Splash 7: The Qualities of LIght, 2002; represented in permanent collections Southwestern Electric Power Co., Shreveport, Burgess Corp. Collection, Calif.; featured artist Watercolor Mag., 2003, Phila. House Auction and Fund Raiser for AIDS, 2003. Bd. dirs. Child Care Svcs., Inc. of N.W. La., Shreveport, 1987-91, pres., 1991; Artport Airport Exhibit and Fundraiser for AIDS, Shreveport, 1991-2002; worker Habitat for Humanity, Shreveport, 1992, 94; trustee St. Luke's Meth. Ch., Shreveport, 1993-95, chair bldg. com., 1986; bd. dirs. Shreveport Art Guild, Friends of the Meadows Mus., 2000-03. Recipient Gary, Field, Landry & Bradford award La. Women Artists, Baton Rouge, 1994. Mem.: La. Watercolor Soc. (signature mem. 2004, chosen as one of 10 artists for Hwy. Haiku 2002), Hoover Watercolor Soc. (pres. 1986, treas., publicity chair, others, Jurors Choice award 2001, Transparent Watercolor award 2003), La. Artists (pres. 1994, 1998), Watercolor West (Yarka St. Petersberg Mdse. award 1995, Signature Mem. award 1996, W. Burgess Purchase prize 1998), Southwestern Watercolor Soc. (Signature Mem. award 1991, Edgar A. Whitney award 1992, Ansel Merchandise award 1999, Canson-Talons Inc. award 2000), Med. Aux. Wives Club. Democrat. Avocations: exercise, gardening, travel, reading, playing the flute. Home: 530 Atkins Ave Shreveport LA 71104-4448 Studio: 1700 Creswell Ave Shreveport LA 71101-4726 E-mail: maryhughes@marysorrowshughes.com.

HUGHES, MARY VIRGINIA, secondary school educator; b. Mobile, Ala., May 13, 1964; d. Grady Russell McLean and Susan Costa; m. Billy Joe Hughes, Dec. 19, 1989; 1 child, Lauren Virginia. BS in Music Edn., U. Ala., Tuscaloosa, 1987. Children/youth dir. Spring Hill Ave. United Meth. Ch., Mobile, Ala., 1987; choir dir., educator Hewitt-Trussville (Ala.) Jr. High, 1988—2000; choral dir. Gardendale (Ala.) H.S., 2000—. Dean music camp Fellowship United Meth. Musicians and Other Arts, Ala., 1994; coord. children's choir Gardendale Mt. Vernon United Meth. Ch., 1991—. Active Gardendale-Mt. Vernon United Meth. Ch., 1990—. Recipient Second Mile Tchr. award, Jefferson County Bd. Edn., 1998. Mem.: Ala. Fedn. Tchrs., Ala. Choral Dirs. Assn., Music Educator's Assn. Avocations: crafts, guitar. Home: 3024 Dogwood Ln Fultondale AL 35068 Office: Gardendale High Sch 850 Mt Olive Rd Gardendale AL 35071 Office Phone: 205-379-3600.

HUGHES, MICHAELA KELLY, actress; b. Morristown, N.J., Mar. 31; d. Joseph Francis and Mary Elizabeth (Coughlin) H. Scholarship student, Houston Ballet Acad., 1970-73; part-time scholarship student, Sch. Am. Ballet, 1971. Founder, owner Classic Stocking Co., 1992—. Child actress with Alley Theatre, Houston, 1969, 71, mem. Houston Ballet, 1974, Eliot Feld Ballet, N.Y.C., 1975—, prin. dancer, 1974-79, mem. Am. Ballet Theatre, 1979-81; Broadway appearances include On Your Toes, 1982, as Gloria Upson in Mame, 1983, Raggedy Ann, 1986, as Cassie in A Chorus Line, 1987, Anything Goes, 1988, (films) Hellfighters, A Chorus Line, Alice, The Human Quality; appeared as Fiona in Another World (serial), Loving, Saturday Night Live, Veronica's Closet (sitcom), numerous television commls. Mem. AFTRA, SAG, AEA, Am. Guild Mus. Artists.

HUGHES, MICHELLE D. minister, educator; b. Chgo., May 25, 1954; d. Thomas Alexander Hughes and Bobbie Jean Jones; children: Nia Brittany Randall-Wade, Joshua Thomas Wade. MDiv, Chgo. Theol. Sem., 1995. Ordained min. AME Ch., 2001. Adminstrv. asst., office of pres. Nat. Rainbow Coalition, Chgo., 1989; trainer Clergy & Laity Concerned, Chgo., 1994—2000; mem. faculty Queen of Peace H.S., Chgo., 1995—96; program dir. Protestants for the Common Ground, Chgo., 1997—2000; mem. faculty Sem. Consortium for Urban Pastoral Edn., Chgo., 2000—03, The Chgo. Semester; pastor New Wine Renewal Ministry, Chgo. Contbr. What Can Happen When We Pray, 2001; editor: Complete in God, 2002. Religious affairs chair Chgo. Southside NAACP; bd. pres. United Campus Ministry U. Ill. Chgo., 1998. Mem.: Nat. Soc. Exptl. Educators, Chgo. Met. Assn. United Ch. of Christ. Office: The Chgo Semester 407 S Dearborn # 1675 Chicago IL 60619 Business E-Mail: mhughes@chicagosemester.org.

HUGHES, NORAH ANN O'BRIEN, bank securities executive; b. Taftville, Conn., Aug. 17, 1948; d. William James and Mabel (Gouin) O'Brien; m. Gary Lee Hughes, Sept. 27, 1975. BA, Cushing Coll., Brookline, Mass., 1970; MA, NYU, 1972. V.p. instnl. sales trading Pitfield, Mackay & Co., Inc., N.Y.C., 1972-83; v.p. U.S. Treasury Bond trading Carroll, McEntee & McGinley, N.Y.C., 1983-84; v.p., mgr. U.S. Treasury trading Swiss Bank Corp. Internat. Securities, N.Y.C., 1984-89; 1st v.p., mgr. U.S. Treasury trading and sales Swiss Bank Corp. Govt. Securities Inc., N.Y.C., 1989-91; pres. Sumitomo Bank Securities, Inc., N.Y.C., 1991-97, chmn., 1997—. Mem. Women's Fin. Assn., Women's Econ. Round Table, Corp. Bond Club N.Y., Women's Bond Club N.Y. Avocations: skiing, golf. Home: 1 Hickory Tree Ln Far Hills NJ 07931-2300 Office: Sumitomo Bank Securities Inc 277 Park Ave New York NY 10172-0003

HUGHES, SARAH, figure skater; b. Great Neck, N.Y., May 2, 1985; Student, Yale U. Mem. U.S. Olympic Team, Salt Lake City, 2002. Competitive history includes: 1st place North Atlantic Novice, 1997, 1st place North Atlantic Novice, 1998, 1st place Eastern Jr., 1998, 1st place U.S. Championships Jr., 1998, 1998, 1st place World Jr. Team Selection Competition, 1st place Vienna Cup, 1999, 4th place Skate America, 1st place Keri Lotion vs. The World (Team USA-1st place), 1999, Gold Medal, Olympic Winter Games, 2002. recipient Sullivan award, 2002, ESPY award for best olympian; names USOC Sports Woman of the Yr., 2002, March of Dimes Sports Woman of the Yr., 2002 Avocations: reading, tennis, violin. Office: USFSA 20 1st St Colorado Springs CO 80906-3624*

HUGHES, SHARON MARY, trade association executive; b. Chgo., July 28, 1952; d. George Ingersoll and Rose Myrtle (Reed) H. BA in Polit. Sci. and Comm. cum laude, Am. U., 1980, MS in Bus., Govt. Rels., 1985. Freelance photographer, N.Y.C., 1972-76; advt. account exec. R.L. Newport and Co., N.Y.C., 1976-78; direct mail advt. mgr. John Wanamaker's, Phila., 1981-83; legis. intern U.S. Congressman James Florio, Washington, 1985; asst. dir. legis. affairs Nat. Food Processors Assn., Washington, 1985-87; mgr. govt. affairs Synthetic Organic Chem. Mfrs. Assn., Washington, 1987-89; exec. v.p. Nat. Coun. Agrl. Employers, Washington, 1989—. U.S. employer rep. Internat. Labour Orgn. High-Level Meeting on Achieving Equality in Employment for Migrant Workers, 2000; U.S. employer advisor 88th and 89th Session, Internat. Labor Conf, 2000, 01. Mem., sodalist Holy Rosary Ch. Sodality, Washington, 1989— (sec. 1997-99). Mem. Women in Govt. Rels. (bd. dirs. 1996-98, co-chmn. environ. task force 1988-89, mem. agrl. task force 1989-90, co-chmn. congl. rels. com. 1992-93), Am. League Lobbyists (bd. dirs. 2002—, sec. 2003—), Am. Soc. Assn. Execs. (cert. assn. exec.), Greater Wash. Soc. Assn. Execs., Boys and Girls Clubs of Greater Washington (bd. dir., 2001-03), Phi Kappa Phi. Roman Catholic. Avocations: photography, skiing, golf, history, travel. Office: Nat Coun Agrl Employers 1112 16th St NW Ste 920 Washington DC 20036-4825 Fax: 202-728-0303. E-mail: hughes@NCAEonline.org.

HUGHES, TERESA P. state legislator; b. N.Y.C., Oct. 3, 1932; m. Frank E. Staggers; children: Vincent, Deidre. BA, Hunter Coll.; MA, NYU; PhD, Claremont Grad. Sch. Prof. edn. Calif. State U., L.A.; social worker; mem. Calif. Assembly, 1975-92, Calif. State Senate, Sacramento, 1993—. Bd. trustees L.A. County H.S. for Arts and Edn. Coun. Music Ctr., Calif. Founder Aware Women. Mem. Nat. Coalition 100 Black Women, Calif. State Employees Assn., Calif. Tchrs. Assn., Coalition Labor Union Women. Democrat. Office: Calif Senate 5114 State Capitol Rm 5050 Sacramento CA 95814 also: 1 W Manchester Blvd Ste 600 Inglewood CA 90301-1750

HUGHEY, BRENDA JOYCE, supervisor; b. Linton, Ind., Jan. 23, 1951; d. William L. and Mary Margaret Pritchard; m. David Nelson Hughey, July 23, 1977; children: Allison, Brock. BS, Ind. State U., 1973, MS, 1977. Cert. administr. and supr. Middle Tenn. State U., 1994, career ladder III. Tchr. Switz City (Ind.) Elem. Sch., 1973—77, Franklin (Tenn.) Jr. High, 1978—84, Franklin (Tenn.) Mid. Sch., 1984—89; asst. prin. Liberty Elem. Sch., Franklin, Tenn., 1990—96; spl. edn. supr. Franklin (Tenn.) Spl. Sch. Dist., 1996—. Bd. dirs. Ct. Apptd. Spl. Adv., Franklin, Tenn., 2003—. Mem.: Tenn. Assn. Spl. Edn. Suprs., Assn. of Supervision and Curriculum Devel., Coun. for Exceptional Children. Baptist. Avocations: reading, gardening. Office: Franklin Spl Sch Dist 507 New Hwy 96W Franklin TN 37069 Home: 105 Bobby Dr Franklin TN 37069-6441 E-mail: Brenda@fssd.org.

HUGHS, MARY GERALDINE, accountant, social service specialist; b. Marshalltown, Iowa, Nov. 28, 1929; d. Don Harold Sr. and Alice Dorothy (Keister) Shaw; m. Charles G. Hughs, Jan. 31, 1949; children: Mark George, Deborah Kay, Juli Ann, Grant Wesley. AA, Highline C.C., 1970; BA, U. Wash., 1972. Asst. contr. Moduline Internat., Inc., Chehalis, Wash., 1972-73; contr. Data Recall Corp., El Segundo, Calif., 1973-74; fin. adminstr., acct. Saturn Mfg. Corp., Torrance, Calif., 1974-77; sr. acct., adminstrv. asst. Van Camp Ins., San Pedro, Calif., 1977-78; asst. adminstr. Harbor Regional Ctr., Torrance, Calif., 1979-87; active bookkeeping svc., 1978—. Instr. math. and acctg. South Bay Bus. Coll., 1976-77; treas., bd. dirs., Harbor Fed. Credit Union. Author: Iowa Auto Dealers Assn. Title System, 1955, Harbor Regional Center Affirmative Action Plan, 1980, Harbor Regional Ctr. Financial Format, 1978, Provider Audit System, 1978, Handling Client Funds, 1983. Sec. Pacific N.W. Mycol. Soc., 1966-67. Recipient award Am. Mgmt. Assn., 1979. Mem. Beta Alpha Psi. Republican. Mem. Ch. of Christ. Home and Office: 32724 Coastsite Dr Unit 107 Rancho Palos Verdes CA 90275 E-mail: mghughs@earthlink.net.

HUGILL, CHLOE, artist, office administrator; b. Fundao, Portugal, May 18, 1943; came to US, 1970; d. Herculano Rebordao and Guilhermina Carlota (Godinho) Ramos; m. John Varty Hugill, Jan. 14, 1967; children: John Rebordao Hugill, Claudia Rebordao Hugill. Grad., Pontifical U. Rio de Janeiro, 1961-62, 63-64, Montessori Coll., Rio de Janeiro, 1966. Cet. tchr. in Neo-Latin langs. and their lits. Tchr. Pontifical U. Rio de Janeiro, 1965-70; office mgr. John V. Hugill MD PA Plastic Surgery Office, Ft. Myers, Fla., 1970—. Judge art in pub. schs. Lee County (Fla.) Schs., 1999; spkr. in field. Fine artist working in watercolor, oils, acrylics. Hospital chmn. charity ball Lee County Med. Aux., Ft. Myers, 1979-81,; mem. fundaising coms., 1979-81; vol. Abuse Counseling and Treatment, 1981—. Recipient awards in oils and watercolor Charlotte County Visual Arts Ctr., 1995. Mem. Frizzel Artists Guild (pres. 1995, treas. 1996). Roman Catholic. Avocations: tennis, skiing, hiking, boating. Office: 8660 College Pkwy Ste 100 Fort Myers FL 33919-4873 Home: 250 Stable Gate Dr Campobello SC 29322-8037

HUGLEY, CAROLYN FLEMING, state legislator; m. Isaiah Hugley; children: Isaiah Jr., Kimberly. BA in Polit. Sci. summa cum laude, U. Ark., Pine Bluff, 1979; MPA, Miss. State U., 1980. Sr. analyst, joint com. on performance evaluation Miss. State Legis., mem. ins., edn., industry com., mem. legis. oversight com. for Ga. lottery, mem. Ga. legis. women's caucus, Ga. legis. Black caucus; planner Lower Chattahoochee Area Planning and Devel. Commn.; dir. planning and econ. devel. Lee County Coun. Govts.; ind. contractor, owner agt. State Farm Ins. Mem. choir and mission bd. dirs. Franchise Missionary Bapt. Ch.; mem. Gov.'s Task Force of Welfare Reform, 1992; chairperson Lower Chattahoochee Area Pvt. Industry Coun.; mem. Columbus Olympic Com., Columbus Conv. and Visitors Bur.; mem. local coord. coun. Peach Jobs Program. Mem. Columbus C. of C. (bd. dirs.) Alpha Kappa Alpha.

HUGO, MIRIAM JEANNE, counseling psychologist, educator; b. Pitts., Feb. 28, 1926; d. James Elmer and Gladys Marguerite (Bartlett) Hugo. BS, Miami U., Oxford, Ohio, 1948; MA, Ohio State U., 1953; PhD, Ohio U., 1969. Cert. counselor, Fla. Tchr. Lemon-Monroe Twp., Hamilton County, Ohio, 1948-49; head tchr. Ohio State Juvenile Diagnostic Ctr., Columbus, 1950-54, Columbus Children's Psychiat. Hosp., Columbus, 1954-59; tchr. Exptl. Class for Emotionally Disturbed Children, Miami, Fla., 1959-60; elem. sch. counselor Dade County (Fla.) Schs., Miami, 1960-66, sch. psychologist, 1969-70; counseling psychologist U. Wis., Eau Claire, 1970-76, assoc. dir. counseling svcs., 1976-84, assoc. dean of students, 1984-90, ret., 1990. Mem. adv. bd. County Coun. on Drug and Alcohol Abuse Prevention, Eau Claire, 1983, Planned Parenthood of Eau Claire, 1976-77. Mem. exec. bd. Friends of L.E. Phillips Meml. Pub. Libr., Eau Claire, 1993-96, v.p., 1993-94, pres., 1994-95. Mem. AAUW, Kiwanis Internat. (bd. dirs. Clear Water Club 1997-98), Phi Delta Kappa. Democrat. Episcopalian. Avocations: reading, travel, art and painting, volunteering. Home: 1450 Cummings Ave Eau Claire WI 54701-6569

HUHEEY, MARILYN JANE, ophthalmologist, educator; b. Cin., Aug. 31, 1935; d. George Mercer and Mary Jane (Weaver) H. BS in Math., Ohio U., Athens, 1958; MS in Physiology, U. Okla., 1966; MD, U. Ky., 1970. Diplomate Am. Bd. Ophthalmology. Tchr. math. James Ford Rhodes H.S., Cleve., 1956-58; biostatistician Nat. Jewish Hosp., Denver, 1958-60; life sci. engr. Stanley Aviation Corp., Denver, 1960-63, N.Am. Aviation Co., L.A., 1963-67; intern U. Ky. Hosp., 1970-71; emergency room physician Jewish Hosp., Mercy Hosp., Bethesda Hosp., Cin., 1971-72; ship's doctor, 1972; resident in ophthalmology Ohio State U. Hosp., Columbus, 1972-75; practice medicine specializing in ophthalmology Columbus, 1975—. Mem. staff Univ. Hosp., Grant Hosp., St. Anthony Hosp., 1975-79; clin. asst. prof. Ohio State U. Med. Sch., 1976—, dir. course ophthalmologic receptionist/aides, 1976; mem. Peer Rev. Sys. Bd., 1986-92, exec. com., 1988-92; mem. Ohio Optical Dispensers Bd., 1986-91; bd. dirs. Ctrl. Ohio

Radio Reading Svc., 1997—2003; mem. Ohio Bd. Cosmetology, 1999—. Dem. candidate for Ohio Senate, 1982; mem. Wicked Investment Club, 1998—, pres. 1999—. Fellow Am. Acad. Ophthalmology; mem. AAUP, Am. Assn. Ophthalmologists, Ohio Ophthalmol. Soc. (bd. govs. 1984-89, del. to Ohio State Med. Assn. 1984-88), Franklin County Acad. Medicine (profl. rels. com. 1979-82, legis. com. 1981-89, edn. and program com. 1981-88, chmn. 1982-85, chmn. cmty. rels. com. 1987-90, chmn. resolution com. 1987-92, mem. fin. com. 1988-92), Ohio Soc. Prevent Blindness (chmn. med. adv. bd. 1978-80), Ohio State Med. Assn. (dr.-nurse liaison com. 1983-87), Columbus EENT Soc., Am. Coun. of the Blind (bd. dirs. 1995-96), Life Care Alliance (pres. sustaining bd. 1987-88), United Way (planning com. 1992-93), LWV, Columbus Coun. World Affairs, Columbus Bus. and Profl. Women's Club, Columbus C. of C., Grandview Area Bus. Assn., Federated Dem. Women Ohio, Columbus Area Women's Polit. Caucus, Columbus Met. Club (forum com. 1982-85, fundraising com. 1983-84, chmn. 10th anniversary com. 1986), Mercedes Benz Club (dir. 1981-83), Zonta (program com. 1984-86, chmn. internat. com. 1983), Herb Soc., Phi Mu. Home: 2396 Northwest Blvd Columbus OH 43221-3829 Office: 1335 Dublin Rd Ste 25A Columbus OH 43215-1000 E-mail: huheey.1@osu.edu.

HUHTALA, MARIE THERESE, diplomat; b. L.A., Mar. 26, 1949; d. Joseph E. Sr. and Rosemary E. (Williamson) Mackey; m. Eino A. Huhtala Jr., July 10, 1971; children: Karen Rose, Jorma David. BA in French, Santa Clara U., 1971; diploma, Nat. War Coll., 1988; MA, Laval U., 1995. Joined Fgn. Svc., Dept. State, Washington, 1972; consular officer Am. Embassy, Paris, 1973-75; vice consul U.S. Consulate, Chiang Mai, Thailand, 1976-79; secretariat staff officer Fgn. Svc., Dept. State, Washington, 1979-80, congl. rels. officer, 1980-81, country officer for Chad, 1981-83, polit. officer U.S. Consulate Gen., 1985-87, chief East Asian assignments, bur. pers. divsn., 1988-90, dep. dir. Vietnam, Laos and Cambodia affairs, 1990-92, consul gen. U.S. Consulate Gen. Que., Canada, 1992—95; dep. chief mission U.S. Embassy, Bangkok, 1998—2001; U.S. amb. to Malaysia, 2001—. Bd. dirs. Orchestre Symphonique de Que., 1992—. Recipient Superior Honor award, Dept. of State, Meritorious Honor award. Mem. Am. Fgn. Svc. Assn., Acad. Polit. Sci., Nat. War Coll. Alumni Assn., Rotary Club of Que. (hon.). Roman Catholic. Achievements include speaks fluent French and Thai. Avocation: choral singing. Office: US Embassy Malaysia 376 Jalan Tun Razak Kuala Lumpur Malaysia*

HUIE, CAROL P. information systems educator; b. Kingston, Jamaica; AAS, Hostos C.C., N.Y.C., 1986; BSc, Lehman Coll., N.Y.C., 1988; MS, CCNY, 1994; postgrad., CUNY, 1994—99; doctoral student in computer info. sys., Nova Southeastern U., 2001—. Patient acct.coord. New Rochelle Med. Ctr., New Rochelle, NY, 1988-91; coll. lab tech. Hostos Community Coll., Bronx, NY, 1991-98, instr., 1994—2000, asst. professor, 2000—. Mem.: IEEE, Assn. Computing Machinery, Schomburg Ctr. Rsch. Black Culture, Consortium for Computing in Small Colls., CUNY Acad. for Humanities and Scis., Delta Pi Epsilon. E-mail: tennishuie@aol.com.

HULET, NICOLE, computer consultant, poet, artist; b. Sherman, Tex., May 10, 1963; d. Nadyne (Cavins) H. Cert. Computer Programming, Computer Learning Ctr., 1990; AS with highest honors, Irvine Valley Coll., 1996; postgrad., Ariz. State U., 1997—. Mgr. Pacific Theatres, L.A., 1979-84; acct. F.U.N., Inc., Garden Grove, Calif., 1984-88, Piping Products West, Anaheim, Calif., 1988-90; sr. sys. project specialist Automobile Club So. Calif., Costa Mesa, 1990-96; cons. CIBER, Inc., Phoenix, 1996—. Exhibited poetry and sculpture at DA Gallery, 1996; contbr. poetry to mags. Mem. NAFE, Phi Theta Kappa (comm. officer 1995, 96), Alpha Gamma Sigma. Avocations: writing, art, photography. Home: 1914 W Canyon Way Chandler AZ 85248-5467 Office: CIBER Inc 2020 N Central Ave Ste 1120 Phoenix AZ 85004-4508

HULIN, FRANCES C. retired prosecutor; AB, Northwestern U., 1957; JD, U. Ill., Urbana, 1971. Bar: Ill. 1973. Asst. states atty. Champaign County, IL, 1973-76, Macon County, Ill., 1977-78; prosecutor U.S. Attys. Office, Ctrl. Dist. Ill., 1978-93; U.S. atty. Dept. Justice, Springfield, Ill., 1993—2001.

HULKA, BARBARA SORENSON, epidemiologist, educator; b. Mpls., Mar. 1, 1931; d. Herbert Fritchof and Mable (Alquist) Sorenson; m. Jaroslav Fabian Hulka, Nov. 13, 1954; children: Carol Ann, Gregory Fabian, Bryan Herbert. BS, Radcliffe Coll., 1952; MS, Juilliard Sch. Music, 1954; MD, Columbia U., 1959, MPH, 1961. Diplomate Am. Bd. Preventive Medicine, lic. physician Pa., N.C. Research asst. prof. U. Pitts., 1966—67; asst. prof. U. N.C., Chapel Hill, 1967—71, assoc. prof., 1972—76, prof., 1977—, chmn. dept. epidemiology, 1983—93, Kenan prof., 1987—. Adj. prof. medicine Duke U. Med. Ctr., Durham, NC, 1982—; chair epidemiology and disease study sect., 1981—83, NIH, 1979—80; mem. Endpoint Rev. Safety Monitoring and Adv. Com. Breast Cancer Prevention Trial, Nat. Surg. Adjuvant Breast and Bowel Project, 1992—98; bd. sci. counselors Nat. Cancer Inst., 1980—94; mem. Inst. of Medicine com. toxic shock syndrome, NAS, 1981—82; mem. Sci. Rev. and Evaluation Bd. subcom. VA, 1983—85; mem. subcom. on long-term effects of short-term exposure to chem. agts. NAS, 1985; mem. preventive medicine and pub. health test com. Nat. Bd. Med. Examiners, 1985—88; mem. consensus conf. on smokeless tobacco Nat. Cancer Inst. Panel, 1986; mem. WHO Task Force on Safety and Efficacy of Fertility Regulating Methods, 1989—96; counsellor Internat. Soc. for Environ. Epidemiology, 1990—91; mem. Pres.' Cancer Panel Spl. Commn. on Breast Cancer, Nat. Cancer Inst., 1992—93; mem. bd. scientific counselors divsn. cancer etiology Nat. Cancer Inst., NIH, 1992—94; chair WHO steering com. of task force Epidemiologic rsch. in reproductive health, WHO, 1989—96; mem. steering com. for collaborative group on hormonal factors in breast cancer Oxford (Eng.) U., 1997—; mem. WHO Sci. and Tech. ADv. Group Human Reprodn. Program, Geneva, 1997—; mem. nat. sci. panel to the fed. jud. on silicone breast implants, 1996—99; mem. Nat. Adv. Environ. Health Scis. Coun. for Nat. Inst. Environ. Health Scis., 1998—2001. Mem. editl. bd.: Postgrad. Medicine, 1985—87, assoc. editor: Cancer Epidemiology, Biomarkers and Prevention, 1995—97; contbr. chapters to books, articles to profl. jours. Bd. dirs. Am. Cancer Soc., 1993—96. Recipient Disting. Achievement award, Am. Soc. Prevention Oncology, 1991; fellow travel study fellow, WHO, 1978; grantee, Health Resources Adminstrn., 1975—77, tng. grantee in cancer epidemiology, Nat. Cancer Inst., 1980—, prostate cancer grantee, 1983—85. Fellow: Royal Soc. Medicine; mem.: NAS (Inst. Medicine 1988, mem. com. crossroads nuc. test 1994—96, mem. commn. antiprogestins 1992—93, mem. com. passive smoking 1985—86, mem. Bd. on Environ. Studies and Toxicology/BEST 1997—, mem. commn. on life scis. nat. rsch. coun. 1998—2001), APHA (governing coun. 1976—78, chmn. epidemiol. sect. 1976—77), Am. Coll. Preventive Medicine (bd. regents 1986), N.C. Pub. Health Assn. (stats. and epidemiology sect. 1975, award for excellence), Am. Epidemiol. Soc., Soc. Epidemiol. Rsch. (pres. 1975—76, exec. com. 1973—77), Am. Coll. Epidemiology (Abraham Lilienfield award 1994), Delta Omega. Home: 2317 Honeysuckle Dr Chapel Hill NC 27514 Office: U NC Sch Pub Health Dept Epidemiol CB 7400 2104 E Mcgavran Chapel Hill NC 27599-0001

HULL, CATHY, artist, illustrator; b. N.Y.C., Nov. 4, 1946; d. Max H. and Magda M. (Stern) H.; m. Neil S. Janovic; 1 child, Julie. BA, Conn. Coll., 1968; cert., Sch. Visual Arts, N.Y.C., 1970. Instr. illustration and portfolio Sch. Visual Arts, N.Y.C., 1983-94, Parsons Sch. Design, N.Y.C., 1994—. Juror The 6th World Cartoon Gallery, Skopje, 1974, Soc. Pub. Designers, N.Y.C., 1982, Soc. Illustrators, N.Y.C., 1983, The Biennale of Humor, Fredrikstad, Norway, 1987, The 6th Internat. Simavi Cartoon Competition, Istanbul, Turkey, 1988; mem. exec. bd. Friends of H.S. of Art and Design. Contbr. to anthologies, books, mags. and newspapers including Time, Penthouse, Newsweek, Esquire, Playboy, MSNBC, Fortune, Wall Street Jour., Washington Post, Forbes, Chgo. Tribune, Ency. Brit., Disney, Sports Illustrated, N.Y. Times, Bus. Week, Travel and Leisure, Money, others; group shows include The 17th Nat. Print Exhbn., Bklyn., 1970, AIGA Show, N.Y.C., 1970-71, 74, Printing Industries Am., 1971, Soc. Illustrators, 1973, 80, 85, 94, 2001, World Cartoon Gallery, Skopje, 1972-75, Art Dir.'s Club, 1974, 82, Internat. Cartoon Exhbn., Istanbul, Turkey, 1974, Switzerland, 1974, 78, 80, 82, 90, Athens, Greece, 1975, Soc. Publ. Designers, 1974, 82, Musée de Beaubourg, Paris, 1977, Pacific Design Ctr., L.A., 1980, The Md. Inst., 1981, Scottsdale (Ariz.) Ctr. for Arts, 1981, Soc. Newspaper Design, 1984-85, Butler Inst. Am. Art, Youngstown, Ohio, 1983, Am. Peace Poster Exhibit, 1985, Quebec City Exhbn., Society of Illustrators, 2002; represented in permanent collections including Mus. Caricatures and Cartoons, Basel, Switzerland, Soc. Illustrators Advt. Ann. show, Smithtown Twp. Arts Coun.; designer playing cards sold at Cooper Hewitt Mus., N.Y., N.Y. Pub. Libr., L.A. County Mus. Art, St. Louis Art Mus., Chgo. Mus. Art, Nat. Mus. Scotland, Seibu, Japan, Contemporary Mus. of Honolulu, Contemporary Mus. San Diego, High Mus. Atlanta, Meml. Exhbn., Mus. Am. Illustration, 2002, Herbert F. Johnson Mus. of Art, 2002, Cornell U., Karikatur and Cartoon Mus., Basel, Switzerland, 2003, Mus. Am. Illustration, 2004, RSVP Portraits Show and N.Y. Times Show, Mus. Am. Illustration, 2004. Exec. bd. Friends of the H.S. Art and Design, 2002—. Office: 180 E 79th St New York NY 10021-0437

HULL, ELIZABETH ANNE, retired English language educator; b. Upper Darby, Pa., Jan. 10, 1937; d. Frederick Bossart and Elizabeth (Schmik) H.; m. Dean Carlyle Beery, Feb. 5, 1955 (div. 1962); children: Catherine Doria Beery Pizarro, Barbara Phyllis Beery Wintczak; m. Frederik Pohl, July 1984. Student, Ill. State U., 1954-55; AA, Wilbur Wright Jr. Coll., Chgo., 1965; B in Philosophy, Northwestern U., 1968; MA, Loyola U., Chgo., 1970, PhD, 1975. Teaching asst. Loyola U., Chgo., 1968-71; prof. English, coord. honors program William Rainey Harper Coll., Palatine, Ill., 1971-2001; ret., 2001; theater critic Lerner Newspapers, 2004—. Judge nat. writing competition Nat. Coun. Tchrs. of English, 1975-2002, John W. Campbell award, 1986—. Co-editor: (with F. Pohl) Tales from the Planet Earth; contbr. articles to profl. jours. Pres. Lexington Green Condominium Assn., Schaumburg, Ill., 1982-84; bd. dirs. Hunting Ridge Homeowner's Assn., Palatine, 1984-86; Dem. candidate for U.S. Ho. of Reps. for 8th Congl. Dist. Ill., 1996; bd. dirs. N.W. Cmty. Hosp. Aux., 2001-03; mem. steering com. Constituency on Vols. Ill. Hosp. Assn., 2001-03. Recipient Northwestern U. Alumni award for Merit, 1995, Thomas Clareson award Sci. Fictin Rsch. Assn., 1998, Excellence award Nat. Inst. for Staff and Orgnl. Devel., 1998. Mem. MLA, Midwest MLA, Popular Culture Assn., Sci. Fiction Rsch. Assn. (editor 1981-84, sec. 1987-88, pres. 1989-90), Ill. Coll. English Assn. (pres. 1975-77), World Sci. Fiction Assn. (N.Am. sec. 1978—, pres. Honors coun. Ill. region 1992-93), Palatine Area LWV (bd. dirs. 1991—, v.p. 1995-96, pres. 1998-2000), Am. Assn. for Women in C.C. (v.p. comm., bd. dirs. Harper Coll. chpt. 1993-96). Home: 855 Harvard Dr Palatine IL 60067-7026

HULL, FRANK MAYS, federal judge; b. Augusta, Ga., Dec. 9, 1948; d. James M. Hull Jr. and Frank (Mays) Pride; m. Antonin Aeck, Apr. 16, 1977; children: Richard Hull Aeck, Molly Hull Aeck. AB, Randolph-Macon Women's Coll., 1970; JD cum laude, Emory U., 1973. Bar: Ga. 1973, U.S. Ct. Appeals (5th cir.) 1973, U.S. Dist. Ct. (no. dist.) Ga. 1974, U.S. Ct. Appeals (11th cir.) 1982. Law clk. to Hon. Elbert P. Tuttle U.S. Ct. Appeals (5th cir.), Atlanta, 1973—74; assoc. Powell, Goldstein, Frazer & Murphy, Atlanta, 1974—80, ptnr., 1980—84; judge State Ct. Fulton County, Atlanta, 1984—90, Superior Ct. Fulton County, Atlanta, 1990—94, U.S. Dist. Ct., (no. dist.) Ga., 1994—97, U.S. Ct. Appeals (11th cir.), 1997—. Mem. commn. on family violence State of Ga., 1992—94, commn. on gender bias in jud. sys., 1988—90. Mem. Leadership Atlanta, 1986—, program co-chair criminal justice com., 1988—89; Sunday sch. tchr. Cathedral St. Phillip, Atlanta, 1983—88, children's com., 1981—82, outreach com., 1989—91; bd. dirs. Met. Atlanta Mediation Ctr., Inc., 1976—79, Atlanta Vol. Lawyers Assn., 1988—91. Fellow, AAUW, 1973—. Mem.: ABA (fin. sec. long range planning com. tort and ins. practice sect. 1979—82, chmn. contract documents divsn., forum com. on constrn. industry 1983—85, editl. staff jour. 1981—85, vice chmn. fidelity and surety law com. 1978—85), Nat. Assn. Women Judges, Ga. Assn. Women Lawyers, Atlanta Bar Assn., Am. Judicature Soc. (bd. dirs. 1990—96), Ga. Bar Assn., Order of Coif. Office: US Ct of Appeals 56 Forsyth St NW Rm 300 Atlanta GA 30303-2289*

HULL, GLYNDA, language educator; BA, Miss. U. for Women; PhD, U. Pitts. Co-editor (with Katherine Schultz): (book) School's Out! Bridging Out-of-School Literacies with Classroom Practice, 2002; author: Changing Work, Changing Workers: Critical Perspectives on Language, Literacy, and Skills, 1997; co-author (with J. Gee et al): The New Work Order: Behind the Language of the New Capitalism, 1996. Recipient Richard Braddock Meml. award for best article of yr. (2), Coll. Composition and Comm., award for best article reporting qualitative or quantitative rsch. related to tech. or sci. comm., Nat. Coun. Tchrs. English, 2001. Office: U Calif Berkeley Dept Edn 5629 Tolman Berkeley CA 94720-1670

HULL, GRETCHEN GAEBELEIN, lay worker, writer, lecturer; b. Bklyn., Feb. 5, 1930; d. Frank Ely and Dorothy Laura (Medd) Gaebelein; m. Philip Glasgow Hull, Oct. 24, 1952; children: Jeffrey R., Sanford D., Meredyth Hull Smith. BA magna cum laude, Bryn Mawr Coll., 1950; postgrad., Columbia U., 1950-52; DLitt (hon.), Houghton Coll., 1995. Major presenter Internat. Coun. on Bibl. Inerrancy, Chgo., 1986; guest lectr. London Inst. on Contemporary Christianity, 1988; lectr. at large Christians for Bibl. Equality, St. Paul, 1988-2000; major presenter Presbyn. Ch. (U.S.A.) Nat. Abortion Dialogue, Kansas City, Mo., 1989; disting. scholar lectr. Thomas F. Staley Found., Stony Brook, N.Y., 1991. Elder Presbyn. Ch. (U.S.A.); mem. Madison Ave. Presbyn. Ch., N.Y.C.; vis. prof. Regent Coll., Vancouver, B.C., 1992. Author: Equal to Serve, 1987; (with others) Women, Authority and the Bible, 1986, Applying the Scriptures, 1987, Study Bible for Women (New Testament), 1996, The Global God, 1998, The Gospel with Extra Salt, 2000, The IVP Women's Bible Commentary, 2002; editor Priscilla Papers, 1989-99; contbg. editor Perspectives, 1992—; mem. editl. bd. Prism, 1994—; contbr. articles to religious mags. Trustee Cold Spring Harbor Village Improvement Soc., 1966-69, Soc. of St. Johnland, Kings Park, N.Y., 1972-75. Mem. Woman's Union Missionary Soc. Am. (bd. dirs. 1954-71), Presbyns. United for Bibl. Concerns (bd. dirs. 1973-75), L.I. Presbytery (gen. coun. 1981-83), Christians for Bibl. Equality (bd. dirs. 1987-94), Latin Am. Mission (trustee 1989-95), Evangelicals for Social Action (bd. dirs. 1991-99, 2001—), Network Presbyn. Women in Leadership (steering com. 1994-98), Presbyns. for Renewal (bd. dirs. 1994-2000). Home and Office: 63 Meadow Lakes Hightstown NJ 08520

HULL, JANE DEE, former governor, former state legislator; b. Kansas City, Mo., Aug. 8, 1935; d. Justin D. and Mildred (Swenson) Bowersock; m. Terrance Ward Hull, Feb. 12, 1954; children: Jeannette Shipley, Robin Hillebrand, Jeff, Mike. BS in elem. edn., U. Kans., 1957; postgrad. in polit. sci., Ariz. State U., postgrad. in econs., 1972-78; grad., Josephson Sch. of Ethics, 1993. Spkr. pro tem Ariz. Ho. of Reps., Phoenix, 1993, chmn. ethics com., chmn. econ. devel., 1993, mem. legis. coun., 1993, mem. gov.'s internat. trade and tourism adv. bd., 1993, mem. gov.'s strategic partnership for econ. devel., 1993, mem. gov.'s office of employement implementation task force, 1993, spkr. of house, 1989—92, house majority whip, 1987-88; sec. of state State of Arizona, Phoenix, 1993—97; gov. State of Ariz., Phoenix, 1997—2003. Author (edited by Michael S. Josephson and Wes Hanson): The Power of Character; author: Character in Soc.: The Challenge of Pub. Svc.; contbr. opinion pieces to periodicals and newspapers. Mem. dean's coun. Ariz. State U., 1989—92; assoc. mem. Heard Mus. Guild; mem. Maricopa Med. Aux., Ariz. State Med. Aux., Valley Citizens League, Charter 100, Ariz. Women's Forum; hon. chmn. Race for the Cure; hon. bd. mem. Teach for Am.; assoc. mem. Cactus Wren Rep. Women; mem. Freedom Found., North Phoenix Rep. Women, 1970; Trunk 'N Tusk Legis. Liaison Ariz. Rep. Party, 1993; mem. Gov.'s Emergency Coun., Ariz. -Mex. Commn., Phoenix Commn. on Internat. Rels.; Ariz. chmn. George W. Bush for Pres., 2000; mem. Adv. Coun. Hist. Preservation; chmn. Western Gov.'s Assn., 2002, Border Gov.'s Assn., 2002; bd. dir. Morrison Inst. for Pub. Policy, Beatitudes D.O.A.R., 1992, Ariz. Town Hall, Ariz. Econs. Coun. Recipient Econ. Devel. award, Ariz. Innovation Network, 1993, Spl. Achievement award, Nat. Notary Assn., 1997, Appreciation award, No. Ariz. U. Sch. of Forestry students, 2000. Mem. Nat. Orgn. of Women Legislators, Am. Legis. Exch. Coun., Nat. Rep. Legislators Assn. (Nat. Legislator of Yr. award 1989), Soroptimists (hon.). Republican. Roman Catholic.

HULL, LEANNE VON NEUMEYER, public relations and communications executive, research consultant, writer; d. F. Louis and Greta Catherine (Clifford) von Neumeyer; children: Marc Lane, Kristin LeAnne, Michael Lane, Jamie Laird, Jeremy Leif, Breton Louis. Rschr., writer, owner Heritage Tree, Arcadia, Calif., 1970—; CEO von Neumeyer & Assocs., 1996—; project mgr., prodn. asst. One Light, KCM Prodns., 1999—; dir. comms. Vision Film Festival Vision in Arts Coun., 2001—. Internat. bd. advisors, dir. protocol, mem. scholarship grant rev. com. Neeley Scholarship Found., 1988-89; dir. pub. comm. Ch. of Jesus Christ of Latter-day Saints, Foothill and Glendale regions, Calif., 1975-92, dir. cmty. rels., 1984-92, asst. dir. area coun., 1984; adminstrv. asst. Calif. Pub. Affairs Dept., L.A., 1990—; seminar coord. R.E.D.I., Inc., L.A., 1982-91, corp. rels. dir., 1984-91; design cons. H.M.J. Fine Jewelers Time & Eternity Collection, L.A., 1985-95; mem. nat. adv. coun. motion picture studio Brigham Young U., Provo, Utah, 1986-89; adminstrv. dir. Pasadena Geneal. Libr., Calif., 1977-82; writer, co-prodr. KBIG, Sideband Div. Radio, L.A., 1979-80; exec. assoc. adminstr. Calif. Bicentennial Found. for the U.S. Constn., 1987; regional cons. Latter-Day Sentinel Newspaper, L.A., 1985-89, exec. dir., 1988-89; mem. Brigham Young U. Marriott Sch. Bus. Mgmt. Soc., L.A., 1990—; mem. com. on child pornography legis. chmn. pub. info. portfolio com., 1988-91, L.A. County Commn. on Obscenity & Pornography, 1988-91; internet moderator 21stRenaissance.com, 1999. Author: Honored Heritage, 1975, Woman's Place of Honor, 1976, Prologue and Tapestry, 1976, Moments with the Prophets, 1977, Southern California: The Earthquake Threat, 1981, Quake!: Preparing Home, Family and Community, 1982, DreamQuest: Along the Trail, 1982, The Peregrine Papers, 1986, Bridget 'Biddy' Smith Mason: Her Legacy Among the Mormons, 1996, Etherea, 1999, Preparing Home and Family, 1999, (novel and screenplay) The Dreamin' Jar, 2000, (screenplay) Snow Search, 2000; columnist Heritage Tree Foothill Intercity News, Knight-Ridder Pub., 1977-79; contbg. writer Women's Exponent Southern California edit., Sentinal: Journalism series, 1978-80; contbr. articles to profl. jours.; art exhibits include Wilshire Alma Exhibit, 1985, The Grand Artists Hall, 1986-88. Pres. Daus. Utah Pioneers-Los Angeles County, 1983-85; prodr. Calif. Gov.'s Gala, Philadelphia 1776; dir. protocol L.A. County Law Enforcement Conf., 1990; dir. recept. protocol State of Calif. Law Enforcement Conf. on Child Pornography, 1990; chmn. So. Calif. Task Force on Pornography, 1989-92; instr. earthquake preparedness and survival Arcadia chpt. ARC, L.A., 1983-85; mem. Cmty. Coordinating Coun., Arcadia, 1983-86; mem. exec. bd. Calif. Utah Women, L.A., 1977-79, 85-86, chmn. L.A. County Commn. Pub. Rels. Portfolio, 1988; exec. dir. Neeley Scholarship Found., 1989-91; coord. planning com. California '96: One Hundred Fifty Years LDS Sesquicentennial, 1994—; display coord. L.A. Temple Hill Visitors Ctr., 1994-96; lineage rsch. dir. von Neumeyer-Burches & Assocs., 1992-96; specialist Y2K Task Force on Family Preparedness, 1998—. Recipient Best of Exhibit award Sculptor's West Workshop, 1982, cert. of recognition L.A. County, 1989, cert. appreciation L.A. County, 1990. Mem. Nat. Assn. Female Execs., Found. for Ancient Rsch. and Mormon Studies, Mormon Hist. Assn., Assn. Latter-Day Media Artists (assoc. editor Voice of ALMA 1978-83, exec. bd. 1977-81, chmn. spl. events 1985-90, internat. bd. govs. fellow 1981-83), Am. Film Inst., Deseret Bus. and Profl. Assn., Marriott Bus. Mgmt. Soc. (L.A. chpt.), Assn. L.D.S. Pub. Rels. Profls., Pub. Rels. Soc. Am. (L.A. chpt.), Nat. Mus. Women in the Arts (charter), Arcadia Tournament of Roses Assn., Arcadia C. of C. (chmn. industry commn. of women's divsn. 1983-85, mem. exec. bd. 1985-86). Avocations: sculpting, oil painting. Office: 1591 E Temple Way Los Angeles CA 90024-5801 E-mail: mirialara@aol.com., PublicAffairsLA@aol.com.

HULL, LOUISE KNOX, retired elementary educator, administrator; b. May 24, 1912; d. William E. and Ruby Joe (Bradshaw) Knox; m. Berrien J. Hull, Jan. 1, 1953. BS in Edn., S.W. Mo. State U., 1933; postgrad., U. Colo., 1939, Northwestern U., 1945; MA in Edn., NYU, 1951. Cert. elem. and secondary tchr., Mo. Elem. tchr. R12 Sch. Dist., Springfield, 1936-70, supr. tchr., 1956-70, mem. adv. com. to supt., 1955-57; ret., 1970. Chmn. Christian edn. com. Westminster Presbyn. Ch., 1953-66, trustee, 1983-86, chmn. bd. trustees, 1986, circle chmn., 1986-89, mem. women's adv. bd., 1987-89, rep. witness and fin. com., 1990, pres. Women of Ch., 1970-73, 90-92, pres. bd. trustees, 1983-86, life mem. Wilson Creek Found., Springfield, 1954-67; sec. greene County Hist. Soc., Springfield, 1960-96, also life mem.; mem. Springfield Little Theater Guild, 1970—, Hist. Preservation Soc., Springfield, 1980—; docent Mus. of Ozarks, Springfield, 1976-85; chmn. dist. III, John Calvin Presbytery, 1974-76, sec., 1977-80; vol. St. John's Regional Med. Ctr., 1970-78. Mem. Springfield Ret. Tchr. Assn. (life), Mo. Ret. Tchr. Assn. (life), Ozarks Genealogy Soc. (sec. 1985-87, pub. info. rep. 1987-89), DAR, Mo. Fedn. Women's Clubs (chmn. home life com. 1986-89), Springfield City Fedn. Women's Club (pres. 1990-92), Brige Dept. of Sorosis, 1995-2003; Audubon Dept. of Sorosis; Sorosis Club (pres. Springfield 1980-82, chmn. hobby dept. 1986-88, 94-96, chmn. fine arts dept. 1988-90, mem. perpetual endowment com. 1992-96, chmn. 1994, parliamentarian 1998-2000, chmn. Audubon dept. 2000-02, sec. bridge dept. 1995—), Ch. Women United, Alpha Delta Pi (treas. house corp. 1932-60), Alpha Delta Kappa (sec. 1965-67, corr. sec. Psi chpt. 1990-92).

HULL, MARION HAYES, communications educator, researcher; b. Bronx, N.Y., Feb. 23, 1940; d. David Vernon and Jessie C. (Summerville) Hayes; m. Bernard Samuel Hull, Aug. 24, 1974; children: Karla Williams, Bernard S. II. BJ, L.I. U., 1961; MA in TV Writing, NYU, 1967; PhD in Polit. Sci., Am. U., 1996. Instr. Norfolk (Va.) State U., 1967-70; asst. prof. Shaw U., Raleigh, N.C., 1970-72; comm. specialist U.S. Dept. Justice, Washington, 1972-73; dir. telecom. programs Booker T. Washington Found., Washington, 1973-82; asst. prof. comm. Howard U., Washington, 1982—. Newscaster Sta. WAVY-TV, Portsmouth, Va., 1969-70; U.S. del. The World Adminstn. Radio Conf., (plan. com.) Washington, 1978-79; vis. scholar Rand Afrikaanse U., 1998. Author: (chpt.) Public-Cable Handbook, 1975-76; mem. editl. adv. bd. The Montgomery Times, 1990—; contbr. articles to profl. periodicals. Cmty. amb. City of Raleigh (N.C.), Sweden, 1971; exch. amb. Expt. Internat. Living, 1972—; com. Maryland Pub. Broadcasting Commn., 1998—; mem. The White House Conf. Minority Ownership, Washington, 1973; mem. cable comm. adv. com. Montgomery County (Md.) Govt., 1982-86, chmn. consumer adv. bd., 1989-95; chair clubs and orgns. United Negro Coll. Fund, Washington, 1989—; spkr. Montgomery County Pub. Schs., 1992—; bd. dirs., pres. Leadership Montgomery, 1996—. Recipient Excellence in Svc. award United Negro Coll. Fund, 1994, grad. Leadership Montgomery, 1995, Disting. Leadership award, Sprint and Nat. Assn. for cmty. leadership; Ford Found. grantee, 1968. Mem. Assn. Edn. Journalism and Mass Comm. (accreditation chair 1994—, vice chair commn. on status of minorities), Women's Inst. Freedom of the Press, Capital Press Club (pres., Leadership award 1977), Alpha Kappa Alpha (pres. local chpt. 1980-85, advisor to undergraduates 1990—, Leadership award 1984). Democrat. Baptist. Office: Howard U Sch Comm 525 Bryant St NW Washington DC 20059-0001

HULL, RITA PRIZLER, retired accounting educator; b. Lone Tree, Iowa, Mar. 29, 1936; d. Ernest Ralph and Mildred Lennis (Huskins) Prizler; m. J.W. Hull, May 29, 1954 (div. 1963); children: Mark, Marshall; m. John O. Everett, Sept. 1, 1976. BA in Acctg., Augustana Coll., Rock Island, Ill., 1967; MA in Acctg., Western Ill. U., 1973; PhD in Bus. Adminstrn., Okla. State U., 1978. CPA, Ill.; cert. internal auditor, Ill. Auditor Price Waterhouse & Co., Chgo., 1967-70; asst. prof. acctg. Bowling Green (Ohio) State U., 1976-78; assoc. prof. No. Ill. U., DeKalb, 1978-82; prof. Va. Commonwealth U., Richmond, 1982-2001. Contbr. articles, papers to profl. publs. Recipient Outstanding Women award Greater Richmond area, YWCA, 1995. Mem. AICPA, NOW (treas. Richmond chpt. 1987-88), Am. Soc. Women Accts. (treas. Richmond chpt. 1986-87, sec. 1987-88, pres. 1988-90, nat. bd. dirs. 1990-93, nat. sec. 1991-92, nat. v.p. 1992-93, Nat. Woman of Achievement award, 1994), Am. Acctg. Assn. (Trueblood seminars com. 1987-88, acctg. educator awards com. 1988-90, awards evaluation com. 1990-91, chmn.-elect gender issues in acctg. sect. 1991-92, chmn. 1992-93, coun. 1992-93), Inst. Internat. Auditors, Acad. Acctg. Historians. Democrat. Unitarian-Universalist. Avocations: travel, reading, gardening. Home: 810 Keats Rd Richmond VA 23229-6520 Office: Va Commonwealth U 1015 Floyd Ave Richmond VA 23284-9000 E-mail: ritahullcpa@verizon.net.

HULL, SUZANNE WHITE, writer, retired administrator; b. Orange, NJ, Aug. 24, 1921; d. Gordon Stowe and Lillian (Siegling) White; m. George I. Hull, Feb. 20, 1943 (dec. Mar. 1990); children: George Gordon, James Rutledge, Anne Elizabeth Hull Sheldon. BA with honors, Swarthmore Coll., 1943; MSLS, U. So. Calif., 1967. Mem. staff Huntington Libr., Art Gallery and Bot. Gardens, San Marino, Calif., 1969-86, dir. adminstrn. and pub. svcs., 1972-86, also prin. officer. Cons. Women Writers Project, Brown U., 1989-2001. Author: Chaste, Silent and Obedient, English Books for Women, 1475-1640, 1982, 88, Women According to Men: The World of Tudor-Stuart Women, 1996, Japanese edit., 2003; editor: State of the Art in Women's Studies, 1986. Charter pres. Portola Jr. HS PTA, LA, 1960-62; pres. Children's Svc. League, 1963-64, YWCA, LA, 1967-69; alumni coun. Swarthmore Coll., 1959-62, 83-86, mem.-at-large, 1986-89; adv. bd. Hagley Mus. and Libr., Wilmington, Del., 1983-86, Betty Friedan Think Tank, U. So. Calif., 1985-93, Early Modern Englishwoman: A Facsimile Libr. Essential Works, 1995-2001; hon. life mem. Calif. Congress Parents and Tchrs.; bd. dirs. Pasadena Planned Parenthood Assn., 1978-83, adv. com., 1983—; founder-chmn. Swarthmore-LA Connection, 1984-85, bd. dirs., 1985-92; founder Huntington Women's Studies Seminar, 1984, steering com., 1984-91, adv. bd., 1991-96; organizing com. Soc. for Study of Early Modern Women, 1993-94; mem. (hon.) Huntington Women's Com. Mem. Monumental Brass Soc. (U.K.), Renaissance Soc., Brit. Studies Conf., Western Assn. Women Historians, Soc. Study of Early Modern Women, Authors Guild, Beta Phi Mu (chpt. dir. 1981-84). Home: Apt 203 211 S Wilson Ave Pasadena CA 91106 Office: 1151 Oxford Rd San Marino CA 91108-1218

HULLETT, SANDRAL, hospital administrator, health facility administrator; BS in Biology, Ala. A&M U., 1967; MD, Med. Coll. of Pa., 1976; MPH, U. Ala., Birmingham, 1987, LHD (hon.), 1999. Lic. home nursing adminstr., Ala., 1988. Resident in family practice; physician, dir. Family HealthCare of Ala.; exec. dir. West Ala. Health Svcs., Inc., 1976—2001; interim dir. Cooper Green Hosp., Birmingham, 2001, CEO, med. dir., 2001—. Project dir., prin. investigator grants NCI, The Robert Wood Johnson Found., The Kellogg Found., Nat. Heart, Lung and Blood Inst., The Ford Found.; mem. practicing physicians adv. coun. U.S. Dept. HHS, Intercultural Cancer Coun.; mem. steering com. Ala. Partnership for Cancer Control in Underserved Populations; adv. com. Minority Med. Edn. Program. Contbr. articles to profl. jours. Active numerous civic orgns. including Ala. Women's Hall of Fame, Leadership Am., Family Practice Rural Health Bd.; bd. trustees U. Ala., 1982—2001; trustee U. Ala. System, 1995—2001; bd. dirs. UAB Health System. Named Rural Practitioner of the Yr., Nat. Rural Health Assn.; recipient Clin. Recognition award for edn. and tng., Nat. Assn. Cmty. Health Ctrs., 1993, Disting. Leadership award, Leadership Ala., 1996, Rural Leadership Image award, Nat. Black Chs. Family Coun., 1998. Mem.: Inst. of Medicine of NAS (com. on environ. justice, com. on changing mkt., managed care and the future viability of safety). Office: Cooper Green Hosp 1515 6th Ave S Birmingham AL 35462 : West Alabama Health Svcs PO Box 599 Eutaw AL 35462

HULS, GLENNA L. sociology educator, photographer; b. Clinton, Okla., Mar. 18, 1944; d. Maurice McLain and Ruby Lue (Rittel) Huls. BS in Psychology, Okla. State U., 1966; MA in Sociology, U. Okla., 1971. Tchr. Dumas (Tex.) H.S., 1967-68; tchg. asst. dept. sociology U. Okla., Norman, Okla., 1968-71; faculty sociology Camden C.C., Blackwood, N.J., 1971-98, assoc. prof. sociology, 1985—, chairperson dept. sociology, 1975-80; tchg. asst. sociology U. Pa., Phila., 1974-76, chair dept. sociology, 1978, 79, 85, 86, 87. Mem. gender equity taskforce Camden C.C., 1996, chair academic policies com. 1996-98; presenter Ann. Meeting Southwestern Social Sci. Assn., New Orleans, 2002, San Antonio, 2003, others; rschr. in field. Mem. Faculty Assn. Camden C.C. (pres. 1979-83, chair grievance com. 1996), N.J. Edn. Assn. (mem. higher edn. com. 1980-95), Ea. Sociol. Assn., So. Sociol. Assn., Southwestern Social Sci. Assn. Achievements include research of pioneer women. Avocations: photography, fiction writing. Office: Camden County C C PO Box 200 Blackwood NJ 08012-0200

HULTMAN, CAROL LINDA, elementary school educator; b. Janesville, Minn., Mar. 23, 1950; d. Henry Adolph and Margot (Kraft) Huelsnitz; m. John Kenneth Hultman, Aug. 3, 1974; children: Ann, Kristi, Lindsay. BS, U. Minn., 1972, MEd, 1984. Educator Ind. Sch. Dist. #624, White Bear Lake, Minn., 1972—. Coach Odyssey of the Mind. Recipient Golden Apple Achiever award Ashland (Ky.), Inc., 1996, 97; Tchr. Venture Fund grantee Edn. Ventures, Inc., 1992, 93. Fellow NEA, Nat. Sci. Tchrs. Assn., Minn. Edn. Assn.; mem. Gt. Explorations in Math. and Sci. (assoc.). Avocations: tennis, biking, skiing, coaching youth soccer, music. Office: Ctrl Middle Sch 4857 Bloom Ave Saint Paul MN 55110-2792

HUMBACH, MIRIAM JANE, publishing executive; b. N.Y.C., May 18, 1965; d. William Walter and Mildred (Wender) Humbach. BA in Bus.-Econs./Psychology, SUNY, Oneonta, 1986; MBA, Adelphi U., 1996; MS in Acctg., Pace U., 2002. Fin./acctg. staff N.Y. Times Co., N.Y.C., 1987-92, media svcs. rsch. asst., 1992-93, circulation/staff asst., 1993-95, mktg. cons., rsch. analyst, 1995—. Editor: Rethinking Equity Trading at Nasdaq, 1998, The Electronic Call Auction: Market Mechanism and Trading Building a Better Stock Market, 2001. Mem.: NAFE, Beta Alpha Psi (dir. cmty. svc.). Personal E-mail: mjhumbach@yahoo.com.

HUME, ELLEN HUNSBERGER, media analyst, journalist; b. Chevy Chase, Md., Apr. 24, 1947; d. Warren Seabury and Ruth (Pedersen) H.; m. John Shattuck, Feb. 14, 1991; 1 child, Susannah; stepchildren: Jessica, Rebecca, Peter. BA, Harvard U., 1968; PhD (hon.), Daniel Webster Coll., 1990, Kenyon Coll., 2001. Reporter Somerville (Mass.) Jour., 1968-69; feature writer Santa Barbara (Calif.) News Press, 1969-70; pub. service dir., copy writer KTMS Radio, Santa Barbara, 1970-72; edn. reporter Ypsilanti (Mich.) Press, 1972-73; bus. reporter Detroit Free Press, 1973-75; met. reporter L.A. Times, 1975-77, congl. reporter, 1977-83; White House corr., polit. writer Wall St. Jour., Washington, 1983-88; exec. dir. Shorenstein Ctr. on Press and Politics Harvard U., Cambridge, Mass., 1988-93; moderator The Editors TV program, Montreal, Que., 1990-93; adj. lectr. Kennedy Sch. Govt., 1991-93, Medill Sch. Journalism, 1993-94. Commentator Washington Week in Rev. PBS-TV, 1973—88, CNN, 1993—97; exec. dir. The Democracy Project PBS, 1996—98; cons. US-AID, 2002, Knight Found.; bd. dirs. Internews, U. Mass. Ctr. on Media and Soc., dir., 2004. Kennedy Inst. Politics fellow, Harvard U., 1981, Annenberg Washington Program fellow, 1993—95. Mem.: Nat. Press Club, Coun. of Fgn. Rels. Methodist. Address: 121 Hunnewell Ave Newton MA 02458 E-mail: ellen.hume@umb.edu.

HUME, SUSAN RACHEL, finance and economics educator; b. Englewood, N.J., Aug. 25, 1952; d. Philip and Anna Ann (Petrowski) Nachtigal; m. John Elliott Hume, Dec. 27, 1975; children: Philip John, Scot Elliott. BA, Douglass Coll., 1974; MBA, Rutgers U. Grad. Sch. Mgmt., 1976; PhD, CUNY, 2003. Bank analyst N.Y. Fed. Res. Bank, 1976-77, sr. credit analyst, 1977-79; sr. comml. loan officer 1st Pa. Bank, Phila., 1979-81; asst. v.p. Mfrs. Hanover Trust Co., N.Y.C., 1982-83, v.p., 1983-84, dept. head, hedge funding and asset liability mgmt., 1984-88; adj. assoc. prof. fin. and econs. Rider Coll., 1988-90; asst. adj. prof. Fairleigh Dickinson, Madison, N.J., 1991-93; adj. prof. dept. fin. and econs. Baruch Coll., N.Y.C., 1993—. Mem. Douglass Alumnae Endowment Fund Fin. Com., 1985—; pres. Douglass Coll. Class of 1974, 1990-; mem. internat. seminar interest rate risk mgmt. N.Y. Inst. Fin., N.Y.C., 1990-92. Mem. choir, Sunday Sch. tchr. Presbyn. Ch., Glendale; mem. investment com. Glendale Presbyn. Ch.; active Boy Scouts Am., PTO Cedar Hill and Ridge H.S.; former chairperson McGinn Elem. Sch. PTA Reading Program. Recipient Heller alumni award Rutgers U., 1976. Mem.: Beta Gamma Sigma.

HUMMEL, DANA D. MALLETT, librarian; BA in art history, Smith Coll., 1957; postgrad., Def. Lang. Inst., 1961, Instituto Mexicano-Norteameric, 1962; MA in libr. and info. sci., Denver U., 1968; postgrad., Cath. U. Am., 1974, Nat. War Coll., 1976, No. Va. Bus. Sch., 1978, Cath. U. Am., 1981; diploma, U. Italiana Stranieri, Perugia, Italy, 1997. Head libr., adminstrn. Howard AFB, Libr., Panama, 1969—70; asst. libr. Holmes Intermediate Sch., 1970-71; tchr. Spanish, substitute tchr. J.E.B. Stuart HS, 1972-77; sec., Office of Exec. Dir. Africa The World Bank, 1978-79; personal sec. rector Falls Church, Va., 1979—81; mgr. Info. Svcs. Ctr. BDM Internat., subs. Ford Aerospace Co. (now Northrop Grumman), McLean, Va., 1981-88. Mem. vestry Falls Church Epis. Ch., 1982; del. Rep. State Conv., 1981, 86; pres. Ravenwood Civic Assn., 1979-80, 80-81, 81-82; rep. Mason Dist., Fedn. Civic Assns.; mem. ann. plan rev. task force Mason Dist., 1981-82; gov. trustee Fairfax County Pub. Libr. Bd., 1982-88, chmn. bd. trustees; lead fund raiser Smith Coll., 1998-2002; active St. Boniface Epis. Ch. Named Outstanding Woman of Yr., Fairfax County Bd. Suprs. and Com. of Women, 1982. Mem. AAUP, ALA, Am. Soc. for Info. Sci., Spl. Libr. Assn., Va. Libr. Assn., DC Libr. Assn., Women in Def., Villa D'Este Assn. (bd. dirs. 1995-98, pres. 1997-98), Jr. League Sarasota, Fla., Tournament Players Club Prestancia, Fla., The Field Club, Marie Selby Botanical Gardens, The Smith Club of Sarasota. Home: 7355 Villa D Este Dr Sarasota FL 34238-5649

HUMMEL, MARGARET P. state representative; b. Binghamton, N.Y., Mar. 24, 1940; m. Manfred K. Hummel; four children. BA, Coll. New Rochelle, 1962; MA, Boston Coll., 1968, St. Michaels Coll., 1981. Mem. Vt. Ho. of Reps., 1996—. Mem. Underhill Selectboard, 1992—2001; chair Underhill Planning Commn.; mem. Burlington Sch. Gifted and Talented Task Force; trustee U. Vt., 1999—. Roman Catholic. Office: 38 Poker Hill Underhill VT 05489-9644

HUMMEL, MARIAN, retired art educator, photographer; b. Bethlehem, Pa., May 12, 1943; d. Donald Clare and Helen Florence (Harman) Conner; m. Gerard G. Hummel, June 29, 1998. BA in Fine Arts, Fairleigh Dickinson U., 1966; MA in Visual Arts, William Paterson Coll., Wayne, N.J., 1971, postgrad., 1991. Cert. art tchr., supr., prin., N.J. Tchr. art Hopatcong Sch. Sys., Lake Hopatcong, N.J., 1966-67; art instr. Am. Acad. for Girls, Istanbul, Turkey, 1967-68; art. instr. Boonton Twp. (N.J.) Sch. Sys., 1968-99, gifted/talented coord., 1989-99. Photographer for greeting cards; exhibited photographs in shows at Kemerer Mus., Bethlehem, Pa., 1974, Jockey Hollow Gallery, Morristown, N.J., 1979, Bergen Cmty. Mus., 1981; photos in permanent collection Lehigh U., Bethlehem. VOL. FOR ANIMAL SHELTERS. Recipient awards for tchg. and for photography. Mem ASCD, Art Educators N.J., Boonton Twp. Edn. Asn. (v.p. 1989-99, negotiations chair 1989-99). Republican. Presbyterian. Avocations: landscape and travel photography, reading, walking.

HUMMEL, MARILYN MAE, elementary school educator; b. Cleve., June 20, 1931; d. John Winfield and Meta E. (Timm) H. BS, Ohio U., 1953. Cert. elem. educator. Elem. tchr. Lakewood (Ohio) Bd. of Edn., 1953-83. Mem. Centennial Planning Com., Lakewood, Ohio 1989; vol. United Way, Lakewood Hosp. Jennings scholar, 1969-70; named Tchr. of the Yr., Franklin Sch., 1983. Mem.: Lakewood Hist. Soc., Kiwanis Club, Coll. Club West, Delta Kappa Gamma. Republican. Presbyterian.

HUMPHREY, DIANA YOUNG, fund raiser; b. Balt., Feb. 7, 1938; d. Edwin Parson and Elizabeth Miller (Hoskins) Young; m. David Henry Carls, July 27, 1963 (div. Dec. 17, 1997); children: Peter Van Patten Carls, Elizabeth Roy Carls, Susan Montanye Carls; m. George Lee Humphrey, May 22, 1999. AB, Smith Coll., Northampton, Mass., 1960. Lic. real estate broker, Mass., 1978. Fgn. rights sales Little, Brown & Co., Inc., Boston, 1960-63; speech writer DNA Rsch., N.Y.C., 1963-64; vol. fund raiser John V. Lindsay, N.Y.C., 1964-65, Smith Coll., Northampton, Mass., 1970-75, 90-95, Smith Coll. Club, Concord, Mass., 1976-89, Jr. League of Boston, 1967—; bd. mem. devel. Ctr. House, Inc., Boston, 1981-94; fund raiser events Boston Symphony Orch., 1975—; dir. edn. Hawthorne Ptnrs. Inc. Fund raising, events Mass. Soc. for Prevention of Cruelty to Children, Boston, 1997—. Editor: Huntington Hartford Gallery Modern Art, N.Y.C., 1963. Speechwriter, Nelson A. Rockefeller Presdl. campaign, N.Y.C., 1963-64; active John V. Lindsay for Mayor, N.Y.C., 1964-65; mem., chmn. Wayland (Mass.) Planning Bd., 1976-81, Wayland Housing Partnership, 1987—; mem. adv. com. REACH, Waltham, Mass.; mem. Patriots' Trail coun. Girl Scouts U.S. Mem. Jr. League of Boston, Weston Golf Club. Episcopalian. Avocations: golf, travel, gardening, singing, politics. Home: 42 Cutting Cross Way Wayland MA 01778-3845

HUMPHREY, ELIZABETH ANN, women's health nurse; b. Augusta, Maine, Aug. 6, 1940; d. Roy Sidney and Eda May (Messer) H. BSN, Keuka Coll., 1961; MSN, U. Md., 1965; EdD, U. So. Miss., 1977. Staff nurse Boston Lying-In Hosp., 1961-62; instr. U. Maine, Orono, 1962-64; asst. prof. La. State Med. Sch. Dept. Nursing, New Orleans, 1965-68, Tulane U. Sch. Pub. Health, New Orleans, 1968-75; prof., assoc. dean La. State U. Sch. Nursing, 1975—. Dir. nursing La. Family Planning Program; adj. prof. Tulane U. Sch. Pub. Health, 1984—; bd. dirs., v.p. La. State Bd. Nursing, New Orleans, 1992—; chair personnel com. La. Bd. Nursing Home Examiners, Baton Rouge, 1989—; bd. dirs. Maternal Child Health Coalition, Baton Rouge, 1989—; bd. dirs., vice chmn. adv. coun. on disability prevention, New Orleans, 1989—. Mem. Rural Health Care Authority, Baton Rouge, 1993—; mem. Vol. of Am. Adv. Coun. Mem. La. State Nurses Assn. (treas. 1983-87, pres. 1987-91), Sigma Theta Tau, Delta Omega. Avocations: handcrafts, china painting, reading. Office: LSU Med Ctr Sch Nursing 1900 Gravier St New Orleans LA 70112-2232

HUMPHREY, KAREN ANN, college director; d. Martin and Eleanor (Schwartau) Annexstad; m. Charles W. Humphrey; children: Karna, Kirk. BA in Am. Studies, U. Minn. Cmty. affairs editor KRBI Radio, St. Peter, Minn., 1976-77; assoc. editor Dassel Cokato Enterprise and Dispatch, Dassel, Minn., 1979-89; legis. asst. to U.S. Sen. Dave Durenberger, 1989-95; comms. cons. Karen Humphrey and Co., Watertown, Minn., 1995-98; cmty. rels. mgr. Barnes & Noble, Minnetonka, Minn.; pres. Minn. Hist. Soc., St. Paul, 1996-98; dir. planned giving Bethany Coll., Lindsborg, Kans., 1998—2002, coord. Disting. Professorship in Swedish Studies, 2000, v.p. instnl. advancement, 2002—. Mem. hon. com. for Vandringer Conf.: Norwegians in the Am. Mosaic, 2000. Active Bethany Luth. Ch., Bethany Coll. Symphonic Band, Lindsborg Cmty. Orch. Mem. Assn. Luth. Devel. Execs., U. Minn. Alumni Assn., Norwegian-Am. Hist. Assn. (bd. dirs.), Minn. Pub. Radio, Dassel Leikarring, Oral History Assn., Kans. State Hist. Soc. (bd. dirs.). Office: Bethany Coll 421 N 1st St Lindsborg KS 67456-1831 E-mail: khumphrey@ks-usa.net.

HUMPHREY, LOUISE IRELAND, civic worker, equestrienne; b. Morehead City, N.C., Nov. 1, 1918; d. R. Livingston and Margaret (Allen) Ireland; m. Gilbert W. Humphrey, Dec. 27, 1939; children: Margaret (Mrs. K. Bindhart), George M. II, Gilbert Watts. Educated pvt. schs. Nurse's aide ARC, 1944-64. Past. dir. Nat. City Bank, Cleve., Nat. City Corp., Cleve. 1981-86. Trustee Mus. Arts Assn.; hon. trustee, past pres. Vis. Nurse Assn.; hon. trustee Lake Erie Coll.; life trustee United Way Cleve.; trustee Archbold Med. Ctr. and Hosp., Thomasville, Ga.; hon. trustee Case Western Res. U., Bus. Coun. Internat. Understanding Inc.; bd. dirs. Monticello (Fla.) Opera Ho.; mem., former trustee, 2d v.p. Jr. League Cleve.; past pres., hon. chmn. bd. dirs. Met. Opera Assn., NY; bd. dirs. Lincoln Ctr., NY, Thomas County Entertainment Found.; past pres. No. Ohio Opera Assn.; mem. adv. bd. Coll. Vet. Medicine U. Fla., Gainesville; mem. Ohio Arts Coun., 1975—85; treas., trustee Wildlife Conservation Fund Am.; former master Foxhounds Chagrin Valley Hunt, Gates Mills, Ohio; past dir., zone v.p. U.S. Equestrian Team Inc., now hon. life dir.; mem. Garden Club Cleve.; bd. dirs., past pres. Nat. Homecaring Coun.; treas., bd. dirs. Wildlife Legis. Fund Am. Conservation Fund; past pres. bd. dirs. Thomasville Cultural Ctr.; bd. dirs. Cmty. Found. North Fla.; commr. Fla. Game & Fresh Water Fish, 1984—99. Home: Box 91102 Woodfield Springs Plantation Tallahassee FL 32309

HUMPHREY, MARY FRANCES, historian, writer, retired health care recruiter; b. Lowell, Mass., May 19, 1927; d. Frederick Vincent and Elizabeth Theresa Lynch; m. Keith Nelson Humphrey; children: Sharon Elizabeth Humphrey-Mason, Nancy Ellen Griffin, Janet Lynn Stephenson. Degree in Library Svcs., U. Maine, Presque Isle, 1977. Cert. librarian in charge. Payroll clerk Presque Isle AFB, 1944-46; sec. Maine Potato Growers, Inc., Presque Isle, 1946-52, U.S. Congressman Clifford G. McIntire, Washburn, 1954-58; librarian Washburn Meml. Library, 1970-73; librarian, sch. sec. Maine Sch. Adminstrn. Dist. # 45, Washburn, 1967-79; employment mgr.-recruiter The Aroostook Med. Ctr., Presque Isle, 1980-90; proofreader Echoes-No. Maine Jour., Caribou, 1992—; historian, author, 1990—. Trustee Washburn Meml. Libr., 1973—, Washburn Regional Health Ctr., 1978-88; sec. Aroostook County Sch. Libr. Assn., Presque, 1986-79. Vol. Well Baby Clinic, Washburn, 1954-60; leader Little Sisters 4-H Club, Washburn, 1960-65; mem. chair P.I. Cmty. Concert Assn., Presque Isle, 1952-64; mem. & officer Washburn PTA, 1965-73, Washburn Women's Ext., 1952-80; officer and fundraiser Dollars For Scholars, Washburn, 1969-75; mem. Pool Study Com., Washburn, 1995—, 911E Study Com., Washburn, 1995—. Recipient Hon. Alumni award Washburn Dist. H.S. Alumni, 1970, Plaque Washburn Regional Health Ctr. Bd., 1988. Mem. Salmon Brook Hist. Soc. (officer 1980), Friends of Aroostook County Hist. Ctr. Avocations: family and historical research, reading, quilting, attending elderhostel programs. Home: PO Box 68 7 Thompson St Washburn ME 04786

HUMPHREY-JEFFERSON, BEVERLY C. daycare administrator; b. Jamaica, West Indies; came to the U.S., 1974; d. Clifton Campbell and Linneth E. Ledgister; m. Edward Humphrey, July 19, 1972 (div. July 1982); children: Leonard, Lennox, FeAna; m. Michael L. Jefferson, Sept. 13, 1984. AS in Surg. Tech., Highland Park (Mich.) C.C., 1984; BS in Mental Health, Ga. State U., 1991; MA in Mgmt., Webster U., 1997. Lic. day care dir. Ednl. para-profl. Highland Park (Mich.) C.C., 1984-88; psychiat. unit clk. Mount Carmel Hosp., Detroit, 1988; supr., instr., outreach worker REACH, Atlanta, 1990-91, 94; group home supr. Edison Park Homes, Park Ridge, Ill., 1992; coord. Alzheimers program Parkside Sr. Svcs., Northfield, Ill., 1992-94; activities dir. Oakmont West Nursing Ctr., Greenville, S.C., 1995, Rolling Green Village, Greenville, S.C., 1996-98; sr. health svcs. technician Ga. Retardation Ctr.-State of Ga., Atlanta, 1998; owner, operator Granny B's Daycare, San Diego, 1999—. Vol. mem. adv. com. ARC, Greenville, S.C., 1996-99. Mem. Am. Counseling Assn., Nat. Cert. Coun. for Activities Profls., Webster U. Alumni Assn., Ga. State U. Alumni Assn., Golden Key Nat. Honor Soc. Home: 21114 Park Oak Ct Cypress TX 77433-4661 E-mail: beva51@hotmail.com.

HUMPHREYS, BETSY L. librarian; BA, Smith Coll., 1969; MLS, U. Md., 1972. Joined Nat. Libr. Medicine NIH, 1973, dep. asst. dir. libr. ops., 1984—99, asst. dir. health svcs. rsch. info, 1993—, assoc. dir. libr. ops., 1999—. Pub. and presenter in field including Eileen Roach Cunningham Lectr., Vanderbilt U., 1999, Priscilla Mayden Lectr., U. Utah, 1999, Janet Doe Lectr., Med Libr. Assn., 2001. Contbr. articles to profl. jours. Recipient Alumna of Year, Coll. Info. Studies Alumni Chpt., 2003. Fellow Am. Coll. Med. Informatics (1990-); mem. Inst. Medicine Nat. Acad. Sciences, Acad. Health Info. Profls. (disting. mem.), Am. Med. Informatics Assn., Med. Libr. Assn., Acad. Health Svcs. Rsch. and Health Policy. Office: Nat Libr Medicine NIH 8600 Rockville Pike Bldg 38 Bethesda MD 20894-0001*

HUMPHREYS, JOSEPHINE, novelist; b. Charleston, S.C., Feb. 2, 1945; d. William Wirt and Martha (Lynch) Humphreys. AB, Duke U., 1967; MA, Yale U., 1968. Author: Dreams of Sleep, 1984 (Ernest Hemingway Found. award 1985), Rich in Love, 1987, The Fireman's Fair, 1991, Nowhere Else on Earth, 2000 (So. Book award 2001). Recipient Lyndhurst Found. prize, 1985, Hillsdale prize, 1993; Guggenheim fellow, 1984; Woodrow Wilson Found. fellow, 1967, Danforth Found. fellow, 1967. Fellow So. Writers. Home and Office: care Harriet Wasserman Agy 137 E 36th St Ste 190 New York NY 10016-3528

HUMPHREYS, KATIE, health agency administrator; b. South Bend, Ind. BS, Western Mich. U.; MS, Ind. U., South Bend; MBA, U. Notre Dame. Dir. health care policy Gov. Evan Bayh's adminstrn.; interim gen. mgr. Ind. Toll Rd.; commr. Ind. State Dept. Adminstrn.; dep. dir. Ind. State Budget Agy.; city contr., dir. adminstrn. and fin. City of South Bend; dep. commr. Ind. State Dept. Health, 1997—. With St. Joseph's Med. Ctr. South Bend, No. Ind. Health Sys. Agy., Logan Ctr. South Bend, No. Ind. State Hosp.; tchr. South Bend Cmty. Schs. Office: Ind State Dept of Health 2 N Meridian St Indianapolis IN 46204-3003

HUMPHREYS, LOIS H. realtor; b. Abingdon, Va., Sept. 25, 1931; d. Howard Barnett Hagy and Deltia Sylvia Caudill; m. Paul Everett Humphreys, Apr. 15, 1951; children: Richard Everett, Jill Hagy Humphreys Dalton. Student, Am. Floral Arts, 1969. Cert. floral designer. Dental asst. Drs. Loving and Buchanan, Bristol, Abingdon, Va., 1949-54; sales staff Maxine's, Abingdon, 1955-65; sec. Gentrys Furniture, Abingdon, 1966-68; audio visual coord. Washington County Schs., Abingdon, 1968-70; retail merchant Humphreys Flowers and Gifts, Abingdon, 1969-87; realtor Va. Realtors Assn., Abingdon, 1976-93. Mem. Archtl. Rev. Bd., 1988—; chairperson Mount Rogers Planning Commn. Disabilities Bd., Marion, Va., 1988-98. Coun. mem. Town of Abingdon, 1988—, mayor, 1998—. Named Women of Yr., Abingdon Bus. and Profl. women, 1991-92. Mem.: DAR, C. of C., Abingdon United Meth. Women (pres. 1998—2002), Johnston Meml. Ladies Aux., Va. PTA (life). Avocations: doll collecting, traveling, family activities. Home: 790 Birdie Dr Abingdon VA 24211-3602 also: PO Box 789 Abingdon VA 24212-0789

HUMPHREYS, REBECCA, music educator, elementary school educator; d. Joseph Earnest and Dorris Ann McPherson; m. William Humphreys, III; 1 child, Heather. BSc in Edn., U. of Tenn., 1980, MusM in Vocal Performance, 1983. Cert. tchr. Tenn. Dept. of Edn., 1980. Voice tchr.

Johnson Bible Coll., Knoxville, Tenn., 1983—84; asst. choir dir. Fountain City United Meth. Ch., Knoxville, 1984—88; music and related arts tchr. New Market (Tenn.) Elem. Sch., 1995—. Singer: (plays) Camelot, 1982. Grantee Tech. Literacy grant, Tenn. Dept. of Edn., 1998, 1999, 21st Century Classroom grant, U.S. Govt., 1998; scholar, Ch. St. United Meth. Ch., 1977—80, Music Faculty Club scholarship, U. of Tenn., 1979—83, Fountain City United Meth. Ch., 1981—83, Vuola Bitzas scholarship, U. of Tenn., 1981—83. Mem.: NEA (assoc.), Tenn. Edn. Assn. (assoc.), Jefferson County Edn. Assn. (assoc.; assn. rep. 1999—2001), Music Educators Nat. Conf. (assoc.), Tenn. Music Educators Assn. (assoc.; workshop presenter 2003), East Tenn. Music Educators Assn. (assoc.; mem. elem. honors choir com. 2002—). Methodist. Achievements include development of On-line lesson plans for Track Star. Avocations: golf, travel, boating. Office: New Market Elementary School 1559 Old AJ Highway New Market TN 37820 E-mail: humphreysr@k12tn.net.

HUMPHREYS-HECKLER, MAUREEN KELLY, nursing home administrator; b. N.Y.C. d. Henry James and Eileen Frances (Kelly) Humphreys; m. Robert P. Heckler, Sept. 12, 1992. BA, Villanova U., 1983; M in Mgmt., Pa. State U., 1998. Lic. nursing home adminstr., cert. Asst. adminstr. Pennsburg (Pa.) Manor, 1983-84, adminstr., 1984-85, Roslyn (Pa.) Nursing and Rehab. Ctr., 1985-88; exec. adminstr. Gracecare, Inc., Blue Bell, Pa., 1988-92; adminstr. St. Mary Manor, Lansdale, Pa., 1992-98; dir. resident svcs. The Fairfax, Ft. Bervoir, Va., 1998—2000; gen. mgr. Marriott Brighton Gardens, Bethesda, Md., 2000—01; cadre gen. mgr. no. region Marriott Sr. Living Svcs., 2001, area dir. of ops., 2002—. Fellow: Am. Coll. Health Care Adminstrs.; mem.: Am. Assn. Sovereign Mil. Order of Knights of Malta (Dame), Villanova U. Alumni Assn. Republican. Roman Catholic. Avocations: golf, travel, reading, wine collecting. Home: 23 Brittany Ln Glenmoore PA 19343

HUMPHREYS TROY, PATRICIA, communications executive; b. Birmingham, June 3, 1946; m. Stephen Richard Troy; 1 child, David. BS in Edn., Auburn U., 1968, MEd, 1969; cert. advanced study in edn., Loyola Coll., 1989; cert., Inst. Orgn. Mgmt., U.S. Chamber at U. Del., 1999. Cert. assn. exec. Grad. tchg. asst. Auburn U., 1968—69; asst. libr. McKendree Coll., 1969—71; adj. instr. Chapman Coll., 1972—75; libr. Wroxeter-on-Severn, 1970—80; adminstrv. dir., media dir. Chesapeake Acad.1, 1980—89; pres., CEO Bay Media Inc., 1989—, Next Wave Group LLC, 2001—. Past vice-chair bd. trustees, chair strategic planning com. Anne Arundel Health Sys. and Anne Arundel Med. Ctr.; exec. dir. Assn. for Women in Comms. Unit pres. Am. Cancer Soc., 1986—92; pres. Panhellenic of Annapolis, 1976, Cultural Arts Found. Anne Arundel County, 1995—99, Greater Severna Park Coun., 1990—93; chair Small Area Plan for Severna Park, Anne Arundel County, 1997—2002, Anne Arundel County Cancer Control Task Force, 1994—96; bd. trustees, founding vice chair Chesapeake Acad., 1980—; grad. Leadership Anne Arundel; founding chair Assn. for Severna Park Improvement, Renewal and Enhancement, Inc., 1994—. Named One of Md.'s Top 100 Women, Daily Record, 1997, 1999, Bus. Leader of Yr., Anne Arundel Trade Coun., 1996, Women in Bus. Advocate, Md. Small Bus. Assn., Independence Day Parade Grand Marshal, Greater Severna Park Chamber, 1993; recipient Exec. citation for cmty. svc., Anne Arundel County, 1999, Disting. Alumni award, Leadership Anne Arundel, 1997, TWIN award, Anne Arundel County YWCA, 1996. Mem.: Am. Soc. Assn. Exec. (cert.), Anne Arundel Trade Coun./Annapolis and Anne Arundel County Chamber (edn. chmn. 1990—), Am. Bus. Women's Assn. (pres. Severn River/Md. Capital chpt. 1980—81, Woman of Yr. Severn River 1991, Bus. Assoc. of Yr., Severn River 1992, named among Top 10 Women in Bus. 2003), Women in Comms. (pres. Md. profl. chpt. 1991—92). Office: Ste S-28 780 Ritchie Hwy Severna Park MD 21146

HUMPHRIES, EDNA BEVAN, music educator, choir director; b. Cheyenne, Wyo., Sept. 21, 1922; d. Christopher Henry Droegemueller and Charlotte Adelheit Mueller; m. Elmer Wayne Bevan, Nov. 4, 1944 (div. Dec. 1988); children: David Wayne, Ronn Merrill, Paul Bevan (dec.), Philip Neal; m. John B. Humphries, Feb. 18, 1989. BS, U. Minn., 1943. Nat. and state cert. piano tchr. Freelance writer, Seattle, 1955—; piano tchr., 1955—; organist Luth. Ch., Seattle, 1950—80, choir dir., 1965—80; dir. bell choir John Knox Presbyn. Ch., Seattle, 1989—2002, Glendale Luth. Ch., Seattle, 1989—, Southminster Presbyn. Ch., Seattle, 2002—. Author: Christian Finger Plays and Games, 1955. Mem.: Wash. State Music Tchrs. Assn. (past treas., past pres. South King County chpt.). Avocation: square and folk dancing. Home: 830 SW Shoremont Ave Seattle WA 98166-3646

HUMPHRIES, JOAN ROPES, psychologist, educator; b. Bklyn., Oct. 17, 1928; d. Lawrence Gardner and Adele Lydia (Zimmermann) Ropes; m. Charles C. Humphries, Apr. 4, 1957; children: Peggy Ann, Charlene Adele. BA, U. Miami, 1950; MS, Fla. State U., 1955; PhD, La. State U., 1963; cert., W2RN Cable. Registered lobbyist State of Fla. Part-time instr. psychology dept. U. Miami, Coral Gables, Fla., 1964—66; prof. behavioral studies dept. Miami-Dade Coll., 1966—. Presenter, lectr. in field cruise ship Costa Romantica. Editl. staff, mag. author The Application of Scientific Behaviorism to Humanistic Phenomena, 1975, Rev. Edit., 1979, prodr. & host, Sigma Series video, cert.for TV Strategies in Global Modern Academia: Issues and Answers in Higher Education, 1993—94, Strategies in Global Modern Academia: Issues and Answers in Higher Education II, 1995; prodr.: (video series) Strategies in Global Modern Academia: Issues and Answers in Higher Education, III, 1996—97, Strategies in Global Modern Academia: Issues and Answers in Higher Education, IV, 2001—02, W2RN (cert.). Mem. Biofeedback Delegation, China, 1995; mem. Citizen Amb. Program Psychic Arts Delegation to Russia, 1997, Am. Mus. Natural History; life mem. Pastorius Home Assn., Inc., 2001; mem. Citizen Amb. Program Vizcayans Mus., Aldren Kindred of Am., Inc., Nat. Trust Hist. Preservation, The Charles F. Menninger Soc., People to People; mem. ladies aux. Fla. Soc. SAR; mem. Nat. Mus. Women in Arts; mem. women's history month com. Jr. Honor Women Recognition, women's leadership seminar. Recipient award in hon. of women recognition, Women's Hist. Month com. and Women's Leadership Seminar, 2003. Mem.: AAUP (past v.p. Fl. conf. 1986—88, mem. exec. bd. Fl. conf. 1989—90, pres. Miami-Dade Coll. chpt. 1986—, past v.p., sec.), AAAS, AAUW (life; former v.p. Tamiami br. 1983—88, Appreciation award 1977), APA (life), Dade-Monroe Psychol. Assn., Fla. Psychol. Assn., Biofeedback Soc. Fla. (pres. 1990—), Noetic Scis., N.Y. Acad. Scis. (life), Assn. Applied Psychophysiology and Biofeedback, Inst. Evaluation, Diagnosis and Treatment (past v.p. 1975—87, pres. 1987—, former bd. dirs.), Internat. Soc. for Study Subtle Energies and Energy Medicine (charter), Physicians for Social Responsibility, Am. Psychol. Soc. (charter), Biofeedback Soc. Am. (pres. 1989—), Am. Inst. Parliamentarians, Biltmore Hotel (Coral Gables), Pilgrim John Howland Soc., Hist. Homeowners Coral Gables, Soc. Mayflower Descs. (elder William Brewster colony), Colonial Dames 17th Century, Internat. Platform Assn. (bd. govs. 1979—, Silver Bowl award 1993), Mexico Beach C. of C. (bus. 1991—95), North Campus Spkrs. Bur. (Cmty. Lecture Series award), Regines in Miami, Heredity Order Descs. of Colonial Govs., Cellar Club, Coral Gables Country Club (life), Jockey Club (life), Phi Lambda Pi, Phi Lambda (Founder's Plaque 1976, Appreciation award 1987). Democrat. Achievements include research in biofeedback and human consciousness. Home: 1311 Alhambra Cir Coral Gables FL 33134-3521 Office: Miami Dade Coll North Campus 11380 NW 27th Ave Miami FL 33167-3418

HUMPHRIES BARKER, DEDRIA, humanities educator; b. Detroit, Dec. 19, 1952; d. Andrew John and Mary Jane Humphries; m. Michael D. Barker, June 28, 1980; children: Diallo Humphries, Terri N.H. Barker, David J. Barker. BA, Wayne State U., 1976, MA, 1989. Staff writer Gannett Co. Inc., Lansing, Mich., 1983—89, Danville, Ill., 1983—89; editor Coll. Human Medicine Mich. State U., E. Lansing, 1989—93, instr. Upward Bound, 2002; cons. WK Kellogg Found., Battle Creek, Mich., 1994—96; editor Blue Care Network Blue Cross Blue Shield Mich., E. Lansing, 1997—98; prof. Lansing C.C., 1999—; writer in residence Inside Out Arts Agy., Detroit, 2001—02. Adj. prof. Ctr. Ethics and Humanities in Life Scis. Mich. State U., 1997—. Author: One Good Job: Tradesman, 2001. Mem.: Mich. Edn. Assn. Avocations: cross country skiing, sewing.

HUNDERTMARK, JEAN L. state representative; b. Feb. 25, 1954; married; 2 children. Grad., Bryant and Stratton Coll., Milw., 1973. Restaurant owner; state assembly mem. Wis. State Assembly, Madison, 1998—, chair, labor and workforce devel. com., mem. aging and long-term care, edn., tax and spending limitations, and vets. adn mil. affairs coms. Office: State Capitol Rm 13W PO Box 8952 Madison WI 53708-8952

HUNDLEY, CRISTI MORAN, psychologist; d. Thomas Lee and Ann Grinton Moran; m. William Robert Hundley, Sept. 19, 1995; children: William Matthew, Elisabeth Ann. BA, U. Ky., 1994, MA, 1997, PhD, 1999. Lic. psychologist Ky. Psychologist pvt. practice, Lexington, Ky., 1999—2003; cons. Social Security, Frankfurt, 2001—03. Adj. prof. U. Ky., Lexington, 1997—2000, Lexington C.C., 1997—2001, Transylvania U., 1997—2001, Ea. Ky. U., Richmond, 1999—2001. Mem.: APA, Am. Psychologist Soc. Republican. Presbyterian. Avocations: horseback riding, scrapbooks, boating, fishing. Office: PO Box 22247 Lexington KY 40522-2247

HUNDLEY, ELAINE E. retired nursing education administrator; b. Mandan, N.D., Apr. 11, 1933; d. Valentine and Constantina Elisabeth (Braun) Helbling; m. James B. Hundley, Sept. 7, 1954; children: Mary Jo, Leslie, Jamie, John, Rachel. RN Diploma, Sisters of St. Joseph Sch. of Nursing of N.D., 1954; Coronary Care Cert., Parkland Coll., 1971; BA in Nursing, Sangamon State U., 1975; MA in Nursing Adminstrn./Edn., Columbia Pacific U., 1984. Cert. continuing edn. and staff devel., ANCC; cert. CNA instr. Clinic staff nurse Grand Forks (N.D.) Clinic, 1954-55; staff nurse med.-surg. units, house supr., nurse asst. instr. St. Michael's Hosp., Grand Forks, 1955-68; sch. nurse St. Michael's Sch., Grand Forks, 1960-64; coronary care staff nurse Burnham Hosp., Champaign, Ill., 1972-73; mem. ICU staff St. John's Hosp., Springfield, Ill., 1975; dir. staff devel. Springfield Humana Hosp., 1977-80, ICU staff nurse, staff nurse recovery rm., med.-surg. units, emergency rm., 1975-77; dir. continuing edn. nursing/allied health Lincoln Land C.C., Springfield, 1981-97, ret., 1997. Mem. profl. edn. bd. Am. Cancer Soc., Am. Heart Assn. Active planning bd. Sangamon County Health Dept., Ill. Mem. ANA, Ill. Nurses Assn. (pres., program chair, bd. dirs. 9th dist. 1975—, chair commn. continuing edn. 1993-97, Staff Devel./Continuing Edn. award 1999), State Nurses Active in Politics in Ill., Health Svcs. Area Region Ill. Coun. Continuing Edn. (pres., v.p., sec., treas. 1978—). Roman Catholic. Avocations: music, reading, gardening, quilting, photography. Home: RR 1 Rochester IL 62563-9801 Office: Lincoln Land CC Shepherd Rd Springfield IL 62794

HUNDLEY, JILL L. special education educator; b. Kansas City, Mo., Apr. 24, 1977; BS in Spl. Edn., Ind. U., 1999. Cert. Spl. edn. tchr. Kans., 1999. Spl. edn. tchr. 1-5 Clear Creek Elem., Shawnee, Kans., 2002—, Alcott Elem., Chanute, Kans., 1999—2001. Mem.: Coun. for Exceptional Children.

HUNEYCUTT, ALICE RUTH, lawyer; b. New Haven, Jan. 10, 1951; d. C. Jerome and Alberta (Piner) H.; m. Howard Mark Bernstein, Nov. 28, 1981; children: Ashley Laughton, Laura Whitney. BA in History, Duke U., 1972; JD, U. Miami (Fla.), 1979. Bar: Fla. 1980, U.S. Dist. Ct. (so. dist.) Fla. 1980, U.S. Ct. Appeals (5th cir.) 1980, U.S. Dist. Ct. (mid. dist.) Fla. 1982, U.S. Ct. Appeals (11th cir.) 1982. Corp. counsel Burger King Corp., Miami, 1980-82; assoc. Stearns Weaver Miller Weissler Alhadeff & Sitterson, P.A., Tampa, Fla., 1982-84, ptnr., 1984—. Bd. dirs. Am. Heart Assn., Tampa, 1986-91, chmn. elect, 1988-89, chmn. 1990-91. Mem. ABA (corp., banking and bus law sect.), Fla. Bar Assn. (pres.'s Pro Bono Svc. award 1987), Fla. Assn. Women Lawyers. Democrat. Methodist. Home: 1400 72nd Ave NE Saint Petersburg FL 33702-4610 Office: 401 E Jackson St Ste 2200 Tampa FL 33602-5251 E-mail: ahuneycutt@swmwas.com.

HUNGERFORD, CONSTANCE CAIN, art educator; b. Chgo., Apr. 26, 1948; d. Craig John and Jocelyn Enid (Mason) Cain. B.A., Wellesley Coll., 1970; M.A., U. Calif.-Berkeley, 1972, Ph.D., 1977. Instr. to prof. history of art Swarthmore (Pa.) Coll., 1975—, chmn. dept. art, 1981-86 . Exbitions include Ernest Meissonier Musee der Veaux Arts, Lyons, 1993; contbr. articles to profl. jours. Samuel H. Kress nat. fellow, 1973-75; Am. Council Learned Socs. grantee-in-aid, 1978; Am. Philos. Soc. grantee 1980. Mem. Coll. Art Assn. Am., AAUW (award 1983), Phi Beta Kappa. Office: Swarthmore Coll Dept Art 500 College Ave Swarthmore PA 19081-1306

HUNING, DEVON GRAY, actress, audiologist, dancer, photographer; b. Evanston, Ill., Aug. 23, 1950; d. Hans Karl Otto and Angenette Dudley (Willard) H.; divorced; 1 child, Bree Alyeska. BS with honors, No. Ill. U., 1981, MA, 1983; AAS in Vet. Tech. with honors, Colo. Mountain Coll., 2000. Actress, soloist, dancer, dir. various univ. and community theater depts., Bklyn., Chgo. and Cranbrook, B.C., Can., 1967—; audiologist, ednl. programming cons. East Kootenay Ministry of Health, Cranbrook, 1985-89; contractor, cons., trainer ednl., clin. and indsl. audiology BC, Wash., Oreg., 1989—97; ind. video prodn./photographer, 1979—; owner Maxaroma Espresso and Incredible Edibles, 1993-95; vet. technician specializing in exotics and avianix, writing and edn. rsch., 2000—; vol. NDMS/VMAT, 2001—. Master of ceremonies East Kootenay Talent Showcase, EXPO '86, Vancouver B.C., Can., 1986; creator, workshop leader: A Hearing Impaired Child in the Classroom, 1986. Producer, writer, dir., editor (video) Down With Decibels, 1992; author: Living Well With Hearing Loss: A Guide for the Hearing-Impaired and Their Families, 1992. Sec., treas. Women for Wildlife, Cranbrook, 1985-86; assoc. mem. adv. bd. Grand County Community Coll., Winter Park, Colo., 1975-77; assoc. mem. bd. dirs. Boys and Girls Club of Can., Cranbrook, 1985. Mem. Phi Theta Kappa. Avocations: snow and water skiing, scuba diving, dance, marine animals, studying animal behavior. Home and Office: PO Box 592 Harlowton MT 59036-0592 E-mail: d_huning@hotmail.com.

HUNSAKER, JILL ANN, public health administrator; b. Wheatridge, Colo., Oct. 28, 1968; d. William J. and Janet Lavon (Jeanneret) H. BA in Psychology & Sociology, U. Colo., 1991; MPH, U. No. Colo., 1998. Residentialtreatment counselor Alternative Homes for Youth, Lakewood, Colo., 1991-94, asst. dir. emacipation program, 1994-95; teen outreach specialist Jefferson County Dept. Pub. Health, Lakewood, Colo., 1995-97; adminstrv. program specialist Colo. Dept. Pub. Health & Environment, Denver, 1997-99, health planner, 1999—. Head gymnastic coach Jefferson County Pub. Schs., Golden, Colo., 1992—96. Mem. Nat. Fedn. Interscholastic Ocfls. Assn., Colo. Pub. Health Assn. (com. mem. 1997). Democrat. Avocations: jogging, piano, biking, waterskiing. Home: 1204 S Pennsylvania St Denver CO 80210-1533 Office: Colo Dept Pub Health & Environment 4300 Cherry Creek Dr S Denver CO 80246

HUNSBERGER, CHRISTINE LEE, accountant; b. Ocean, N.J., Mar. 21, 1976; d. Dennis John and Catherine Mary Hunsberger. BS, Millersville U., Pa., 1998. CPA N.Y. Pub. acct. Rotenberger Meril Solomon Bertiger & Gultilla, Woodbridge, NJ, 1998—2002, Anchin Block Anchin LLP, N.Y.C., 2002—. Mem.: AICPAs, N.J. Soc. CPAs. Avocations: reading, running, drawing, skiing.

HUNSPERGER, ELIZABETH JANE, art and design consultant, educator; b. Phila., Aug. 30, 1938; d. Francis Charles and Elizabeth Julia Thorpe; m. Robert George Hunsperger, Sept. 13, 1958; 1 child, Lisa Marie. AA in Design, Santa Monica Coll., 1974; student, UCLA, 1975-76; BA in Art History, U. Del., 1978; postgrad., Rutgers U., 1978-81; MA in Edn., Del. State Coll., 1993; postgrad. in ednl. technology, U. Del. Designer Huntingdon Mills, Phila., 1960-63, Rothschild's, Ithaca, N.Y., 1963-65, Cornell U., Ithaca, 1965-67; freelance designer Malibu, Calif., 1967-76; art and design cons., lectr. Art & Sci. Assocs., Newark, Del., 1980—2001, Galena, Md., 2001—. Art tchr. Cath. Diocese of Wilmington, 1988-95, Kent County High Sch., Md., 2002-; art and spl. edn. tchr. Red Clay Consolidated Sch. Dist. A.I. duPont H.S., Greenville, Del., 1995-97, Shorehaven Sch., Chesapeake City, Md., 1997-99, A.I. duPont Inst., Wilmington, Del., 1999—; with Leech Sch., 1994; cons. Arts and Sci. Assocs., Ednl. and Design Svcs., Newark, Del., 1995—; coord. Delmarva Edn. Action Learning Project; educator Kent County (Md.) Pub. Schs., 2002. Exhbns. include Malibu Art Assn. Show, 1973-74, Newark Art Show, 1987-88. Founding mem. bd. dirs., v.p. Newark Housing Ministry, Inc., 1983-94, pres., 1989-91; mem. social concerns com. and drug and alcohol task force Del.; active Coun. Exceptional Children. Recipient Outstanding Svc. award YWCA, Santa Monica, Calif., 1972, award of recognition Missionhurst, 1982, Gov.'s Vol. of the Yr. award State of Del., 1990. Mem. Nat. Art Edn. Assn., Am. Craft Coun., Art Educators of Del. (bd. dirs., pres.), Debutante Assemlby Club (N.Y.C.). Episcopal. Home: 14040 S Mill Rd Galena MD 21635 E-mail: elizabeth_hunsperger@usa.net.

HUNSTEIN, CAROL, state supreme court justice; b. Miami, Fla., Aug. 16, 1944; AA, Miami-Dade Jr. Coll., 1970; BS, Fla. Atlantic U., 1972; JD, Stetson U., 1976, LLD (hon.), 1993. Bar: Ga. 1976; U.S. Dist. Ct. 1978; U.S. Ct. Appeals 1978; U.S. Supreme Ct. 1989. Legal practice, Atlanta, 1976-84; judge Superior Ct. of Ga. (Stone Mt. cir.), 1984-92; justice Supreme Ct. of Ga., Atlanta, 1992—. Chair Ga. Commn. on Gender Bias in the Judicial System 1989—; pres. Coun. of Superior Ct. Judges of Ga., 1990-91; adj. prof. Sch. Law Emory U., 1991—. Bd. dirs. Ga. Campaign Adolescent Pregnancy Prevention, 1992—; chair Ga. Child Support Commn., 1993, 98, Supreme Ct. Equality Commn. Recipient Clint Green Trial Advocacy award 1976, Women Who Made A Difference award Dekalb Women's Network 1986, Outstanding Svc. commendation Ga. Legislature, 1993, Cmty. Svc. award Emory U. Legal Assn. for Women Students., 1993, Gender Justice award Ga. Commn. Family Violence, 1999, Margaret Burns award ABA, 1999; inducted to Fla. Atlantic U. Hall of Fame, 1993. Mem. Ga. Assn. of Women Lawyers, Nat. Assn. of Women Judges (dir. 1988-90), Bleckley Inn of Ct., State Bar Ga. Office: Supreme Ct Ga 244 Washington Street Atlanta GA 30334-9007 E-mail: hunsteic@supreme.courts.state.ga.us.*

HUNT, BONNIE, actress; m. John Murphy, 1988. Appeared in films Rain Man, 1988, Beethoven, 1992, Dave, 1993, Beethoven's 2nd, 1993, Only You, 1994, Now and Then, 1995, Jumanji, 1995 (Saturn award for best actress), Getting Away with Murder, 1996, Jerry Maguire, 1996, Kissing a Fool, 1998, A Bug's Life, 1998, Random Hearts, 1999, The Green Mile, 1999; TV series Davis Rules, 1992, The Building, 1993; prodr., star The Bonnie Hunt Show, 1995 (Founder's award Viewers for Quality TV awards 1996); dir., writer films Return to Me, 1998, Convenience, 1998. Office: Creative Artists Agy 9830 Wilshire Blvd Beverly Hills CA 90212-1825

HUNT, CAROLINE ROSE, hotel executive; 5 children. Student, Mary Baldwin Coll., U. Tex. Founder, hon. chmn., Rosewood Hotels and Resorts, including Mansion on Turtle Creek, Dallas, Hotel Crescent Ct., Dallas, Lanesborough Hotel, London, Badrutts Palace, St. Mauritz, Switzerland, La Samanna, Little Dix Bay, Caneel Bay and Martineau Bay, PR; owner Lady Primrose's Bathing Luxuries. Author: The Compleat Pumpkin Eater. Chmn. planning giving and endowment com. United Way of Dallas; bd. dirs. Nat. Mus. Women in the Arts, Mary Baldwin Coll. Named Grand Dame, Les Dames d'Escoffier; named one of 100 Most Influential Women in the U.S., Ladies Home Jour., 50 Most Powerful Women; recipient Alexis de Tocqueville award, United Way of Dallas. Mem.: Crescent Club (chmn.). Office: Rosewood Corp Office 500 Crescent Ct Ste 300 Dallas TX 75201

HUNT, COURTNEY LANEL, foundation administrator; b. Natchez, Miss., Apr. 3, 1972; d. LeRoy Lenel Hunt, Jr. and Brenda Carol Johnson-Hunt. BA, So. U. A&M Coll., 1994, MPA, 1996. Legis. asst. La. Ho. Reps., Baton Rouge, 1994—95; mgmt. intern Office for Citizen with Devel. Disabilities, Baton Rouge, 1995—97; exec. dir. Crusade to Save Our Children, Milw., 1998—2001; sr. fund devel. specialist YWCA of Greater Milw., 2001—02; exec. dir. Hillside Br. Boys and Girls Club of Greater Milw., 2002—. Bd. sec. Technology Learning Ctr., Milw., 1999—; bd. dirs. Milw. Urban League, YWCA Greater Milw., Northcott Neighborhood Ctr., Milw. Mem.: Milw. Urban League Young Profls. (pres. 2002), Delta Sigma Theta. Democrat. Baptist. Office: Hillside Boys and Girls Club 611 W Cherry St Milwaukee WI 53212*

HUNT, EFFIE NEVA, former college dean, former English language educator; b. Waverly, Ill., June 19, 1922; d. Abraham Luther and Fannie Ethel (Ritter) H. AB, MacMurray Coll. for Women, 1944; MA, U. Ill., 1945, PhD, 1950; postgrad., Columbia U., 1953, Univ. Coll., U. London, 1949-50. Key-punch operator U.S. Treasury, 1945; spl. librarian Harvard U., 1947, U. Pa., 1948; Instr. English U. Ill., 1950-51; librarian Library of Congress, Washington, 1951-52; asst. prof. English Mankato State Coll., 1952-59; prof. Radford Coll., 1959-63, chmn. dept. English, 1961-63; prof. Ind. State U., 1963-86; dean Ind. State U. (Coll. Arts and Scis.), 1974-86, dean and prof. emerita, 1987—. Author articles in field. Fulbright grantee, 1949-50 Mem. AAUP, MLA, Nat. Council Tchrs. English, Am. Assn. Higher Edn., Audubon Soc. Home: 3365 Wabash Ave Apt 4 Terre Haute IN 47803-1655 Office: Ind State U Root Hall Eng Dept Terre Haute IN 47809-0001

HUNT, HAZEL ANALUE STANFIELD, retired accountant; b. Butler, Mo., Apr. 4, 1921; d. Vernon Arthur and Myrrl Millicent (Henderson) Stanfield; m. Marvie Avanell Hunt, July 25, 1942; 1 child, Roger LeRoy. Grad., Sawyer Sch. Bus., L.A., 1939. Supr., bookkeeper, sec. Nethercutt Labs., Santa Monica, Calif., 1940-45; v.p., treas. Dwyer-Curlett, Inc., L.A., 1946-86. Pres. Nat. Assn. Accts., West Los Angeles, 1970-96, other offices. Mem. DAR, Beta Sigma Phi (pres. 1942, other offices). Presbyterian. Home: 1575 E Washington Blvd Apt 312 Pasadena CA 91104-2663 E-mail: hash@mailstation.com.

HUNT, HELEN, actress; b. L.A., June 15, 1963; d. Gordon and Jane Hunt. TV appearances include Amy Prentiss, The Swiss Family Robinson, The Fitzpatricks, It Takes Two, Having Babies, Land of Little Rain, Weekend, Mary Tyler Moore Show, Family, St. Elsewhere; TV movies include Pioneer Woman, All Together Now, Death Scream, The Spell, Transplant, Angel Dusted, Child Bride of Short Creek, The Miracle of Cathy Miller, Desperate Lives, Quarterback Princess, Bill: On His Own, Choices of the Heart, Sweet Revenge, Why Are You Here?, Murder In New Hampshire: The Pamela Smart Story, 1991, In the Comfort of Darkness, 1992; TV series Mad About You, 1992-99 (Emmy nomination, Lead Actress - Comedy, 1993, 94, Golden Globe award for Best Actress, musical or comedy, 1994, 95, Emmy award for Best Leading Actress in a Comedy series, 1996); films include Rollercoaster, 1977, Girls Just Want To Have Fun, 1985, Trancers, 1985, Empire, 1985, Peggy Sue Got Married, 1986, Project X, 1987, Miles From Home, 1988, Next Of Kin, 1989, The Waterdance, 1992, Only You, 1992, Bob Roberts, 1992, Mr. Saturday Night, 1992, Kiss of Death, 1995, Twister, 1996, As Good As It Gets, 1997 (Acad. award Best Actress in a Leading Role 1997), Twister: Ride It Out, 1998, Twelfth Night, 1998, Dr. T and the Women, 2000, Pay It Forward, 2000, Cast Away, 2000, What Women Want, 2000, Curse of the Jade Scorpion, 2001; plays include: Life (X)3, 2003 Address: Connie Tavel Mgmt 9171 Wilshire Blvd Beverly Hills CA 90210-5530

HUNT, HOLLY, small business owner; b. San Angelo, Tex., Nov. 19, 1942; d. Cagle O. and Zelma (Richardson) H.; m. Rowland Tackbary, Dec. 14, 1974 (div. 1987); children: Hunt Tackbary, Jett Tackberry, Trent Tackberry. BA in Eng. Lit., Tex. Tech., Lubbock, 1965. Buyer Foley's Dept. Store, Houston, 1965-68; designer Tempo, N.Y.C., 1969-73; owner, de- [illegible] Holly Hunt Inc., N.Y.C., 1973-83; owner, exec. v.p. Availco Equity Availco Syatems, Chgo.; owner, pres. Holly Hunt, Ltd., Chgo., 1983--, 1986. Mem., art collector, Mus. Contrary art Chgo., 1978--. Mem. ASN, ISID. Republican. Presbyterian. Avocations: tennis, skiing, reading, art. Office: Holly Hunt Ltd 1728 Merchandise Mart Chicago IL 60654

HUNT, JANE HELFRICH, volunteer; b. Buffalo, N.Y., Jan. 3, 1925; d. Henry Jacob Helfrich and Julia Christina Swanson; m. Charles Stuart Hunt, Dec. 27, 1946; children: Stephen, John(dec.), Peter, Kathleen. BS Nursing, Skidmore Coll., Saratoga Springs, N.Y., 1945. RN N.Y. State. RN Children's Hosp., Buffalo, 1946—48; lic. real estate agt. Hunt Real Estate Corp., Buffalo, 1963, lic. gen. ins. agt., 1966. Bd. dirs. Hunt Real Estate Corp., Buffalo, 1958—, H.R.E. Comml. Corp., Buffalo, 1991—; cons. Hunt Vanner Ins., Buffalo, 1991—. Mem. Ctrl. Pk. Meth. Ch., 1948—, choir; bd. dirs. Longview Niagara DayCare, Buffalo, Goodwill Industries, Buffalo. Recipient Dewitt Clinton Masonic award, Vol. Svc. to Cmty., 1998. Mem.: P.E.O. Sisterhood, Twentieth Century Club. Republican. Meth. Avocations: golf, singing, bridge, painting, gardening. Home: 187 Koster Row Buffalo NY 14226

HUNT, KATRINA WEISNER, marketing professional; b. Mooresville, N.C., Aug. 26, 1959; d. Rylan Campbell and Violet Ann (Jones) Weisner; 1 child, Samuel Clifton. BA, U. N.C., 1981. Libr. asst. Inst. Govt./U. N.C., Chapel Hill, 1981-83, mktg. and sales mgr., 1983—. Disc jockey Radio Sta. WXYC-FM, U. N.C., 1981-87. Office: Inst Govt U NC Cb 3330 Knapp Bldg Chapel Hill NC 27599-0001

HUNT, L. SUSAN, publishing executive; BA in Acctg., Stetson U., 1982; MBA, Rollins Coll., 1996. Auditor Peat Marwick Mitchell, Jacksonville, Fla., 1982—86, Price Waterhouse, Orlando, Fla.; asst. contr., ops. adminstrn. mgr., prodn. mgr. Orlando Sentinel, 1986—97; v.p. ops. South Fla. Sun-Sentinel, Ft. Lauderdale, 1997—99, v.p., gen. mgr., 1999—2001; pub., pres., CEO Morning Call, Allentown, Pa., 2001—. Office: Morning Call 101 N 6th St PO Box 1260 Allentown PA 18105*

HUNT, LORRAINE T. lieutenant governor; b. Niagara Falls, N.Y., Mar. 11, 1939; Student, Westlake Coll. Music. Former pres., CEO Perri Inc.; founder, also bd. dirs. Continental Nat. Bank; lt. gov. State of Nev., 1998—, pres. Senate, 1999—. Bd. dirs. First Security Bank Nev.; chmn. bd. trustees Las Vegas Convention and Visitors Authority; former commr. and vice chair Nev. Commn. on Tourism; dir. Nev. Hotel/Motel Assn.; vice chmn. Nev. Motion Picture Found., Nev. Motion Picture Commn. Commr. Clark county Commn., 1995-99; mem. cmty. bd. Wells Fargo Bank Named U.S. Small Bus. Adv. of the Yr., 1989, Nev. Restauranteur of Yr., 1992, Rep. Woman of Yr., 1996, Woman of Yr., Nev. Ballet Theater, 1998; recipient Govs. award for excellence in bus., 1987, Free Enterprise award, 1993, First Lifetime Achievement award, Govs. Conf. on Tourism, 1993. Republican. Office: 101 N Carson St Ste 2 Carson City NV 89701-4786 also: 555 E Washington Ave Ste 5500 Las Vegas NV 89101-1081*

HUNT, LUCILLE(LUCI) EDITH, real estate agent, real estate broker; b. Evansville, Ind., July 3, 1948; d. Edwin Vance Brady and Lucille Edith Schmidt; m. William Dawson Hunt, Sept. 25, 1948; children: Scott Michael, Jennifer Ann. Sales & Brokers License Ind., 1977. Real estate sales, broker assoc. FCTucker/ Emge, Evansville, Ind., 1977—. Mem.: Evansville Bd. of Realtors (assoc.). Office: FC Tucker/Emge Realtors 2040 Washington Evansville IN 47714 E-mail: lucihunt@insightbb.com.

HUNT, LYNNE, federal agency administrator; Grad., U. San Diego, 1977. Spl. agt. FBI, 1978, with legal counsel divsn., 1984—89, supr., 1989—91, 1991—95, chief health care fraud unit, 1995—96, asst. spl. agt. in charge Balt. divsn., 1996—98, sect. chief fin. crimes sect., 1998—2000, sgt. agt. in charge Balt. divsn., 2000—02, asst. dir. inspection divsn., 2002—. Office: FBI J Edgar Hoover FBI Bldg 935 Pennsylvania Ave NW Washington DC 20535

HUNT, MADELYN DORA, biologist, educator, director; d. George W. and B. Frances Davis; m. Travis Preston Hunt, June 10, 1972; 1 child, Kristyn E. BS, Lamar U., 1969; MPH, U. Tex., Houston, 1972, DPH, 1984. Cert. med. tech. Am. Soc. for Pathologists. Bacteriologist The Meth. Hosp., Houston, 1968—71; med. tech. Gume Solis, M.D., Port Arthur, Tex., 1972; biology prof. Lamar U., Beaumont, Tex., 1973—, exec. dir., 1998—, dir. McNair Scholars Program, 1999—. Lab. cons. Carotex Chem. Co., Port Arthur, 1991—92; clin. lab. cons. City of Beaumont Health Dept., 1992—; bd. mem. Park Place Med. Ctr., Port Arthur. Contbr. articles to profl. jours. Recipient Women of Excellence award, YWCA, 2000, Star award, Tex. Higher Edn. Coordinating Bd., 2002. Fellow: Am. Assn. State Colls. and Univs. (Millenium Leadership Inst.); mem.: Am. Soc. for Microbiologists. Avocations: reading, sewing, travel. Office: Lamar Univ PO Box 10883 Beaumont TX 77710

HUNT, MARTHA, sales executive, researcher; b. N.Y.C., May 17, 1924; d. Paul Andrew and Monika (Dobberstein) Pankau; children: Philip Brian Hunt, Susan Monica Hunt. Student, Syracuse U., 1943-47. Asst. controller Commonwealth Fund, N.Y.C., 1947-50; sales tech. Caldwell & Bloor, Mansfield, Ohio, 1958-64; sales promotion mgr. Vita Craft Corp., Shawnee, Kans., 1964-91, cons., 1964—. Mem. Meeting Planners Internat., Kans. City, 1982—. Author and editor: cookbooks, 1965-91. Pres. LWV, Akron, Ohio, 1951-53; gov. Soroptimists, 1978-80, bd. dirs., Phila., 1978-80, coord. 1980-84, pres., Kansas City, 1973-74; bd. dirs. Kansas City chpt. Shepherd's Ctr., 1972—; nat. bd. dirs. Shepher's Ctrs. Am., 1990—; bd. dirs. Rose Brooks Ctr., 1979-86, v.p., 1984-85; bd. dirs., founder Safehome, Inc., 1979—, hon. chmn. as founder for Celebration of Safehome 1980-2000, 200; pres. Metro Citizens Crusade Against Crime, Kansas City., 1983. Recipient Meritorious Svc. award, Kans. City Police Dept., 1975, Disting. Govs. award, Soroptimist Internat. Am., Phila., 1978-79, 79-80, Woman of Distinction award Santa Fe Trail Girl Scouts, 1993, Soroptimist Internat. Am., 1995, Milan Hulbert Humanitarian award Sales Profls. Internat., 1996, Mother of Our Movement award Kans. Coalition Against Sexual and Domestic Violence, 1999, Kansas City Chiefs/NFL Cmty. Quarterback award, 2002. Mem. Kappa Kappa Gamma (pres. 1948-49), Alumnae Assn. (N.Y.C.). Republican. Presbyterian. Avocations: traveling, volunteering. E-mail: mhunt5607@aol.com.

HUNT, MARY ALICE, library science educator; b. Lima, Ohio, Apr. 14, 1928; d. Blair T. and Grace (Henry) H. BA, Fla. State U., Tallahassee, 1950, MA, 1953; PhD, Ind. U., Bloomington, 1973. Instr., librarian Fla. State U., Tallahassee, 1955-61, asst. prof., 1961-74, assoc. prof., 1974-82, prof., 1982-95, assoc. dean, 1986-95, prof. emerita, 1995—. Author: Transitions: An Informal History of a School Celebrating its 50th Anniversary, 1997; co-author: (book) Multimedia Indexes, Lists, etc., 1975; editor: (book) Multimedia Approach To Children's Literature, 1983, (periodical) FSU/SLIS Alumni Newsletter, 1966-95, Florida Libraries, 1961-67; assoc. editor: (book) Folders of Ideas for Library Excellence, 1991. Mem. ALA (councilor at large 1986-94, 96-2000), Southeastern Library Assn., Fla. Assn. Media in Edn., Delta Kappa Gamma, Pi Lambda Theta (life), Pi Kappa Phi, Beta Phi Mu. Avocations: gardening, reading, photography, pastel drawing and watercolor painting. Home: 1603 Kolopakin Nene Tallahassee FL 32301-4733

HUNT, MARY ELIZABETH, religious studies educator; b. June 1, 1951; BA magna cum laude, Marquette U., Milw., 1972; M of Theol. Studies, Harvard Div. Sch., 1974; MDiv, Jesuit Sch. Theology, Berkeley, Calif., 1979; PhD, Grad. Theol. Union, Berkeley, 1980. Vis. prof. theology ISEDET, Fowler Internship in [illegible], 1980-82, co-dir., co-founder Women's Alliance for Theology, Ethics and Ritual, Silver Spring, Md., 1983—; vis. asst. prof. religion Colgate U., Hamilton, NY, 1986-87; rsch. fellow Ctr. for Study of Values in Pub. Life, Harvard Div. Sch., 2000—01. Lectr., condr. workshops in field; adj. assoc. prof. women's studies program Georgetown U., 1995-99; women's adv. com. Concilium. Author: Fierce Tenderness: A Feminist Theology of Friendship, 1990; mem. editl. bd. Jour. Feminist Studies in Religion, Jour. Religion and Abuse, Theology and Sexuality Jour.; editor: Good Sex: Feminist Perspectives from the World's Religions; contbr. articles to profl. jours. Recipient Isaac Hecker award Paulist Ctr., Boston, Prophetic Figure award Women's Ordination Conf., prize Crossroad Women's Studies, 1990. Mem. Am. Acad. Religion, Alpha Sigma Nu. Office: Women's Alliance Theology 8035 13th St Ste 5 Silver Spring MD 20910-4870 Fax: 301-589-3150. Office Phone: 301-589-2509. E-mail: mhunt@hers.com.

HUNT, MARY MELINDA, artist; b. Calgary, Alta., Can., May 16, 1958; d. Charles Warren and Patricia Gayford Hunt; children: Emily Hunt Olfson, Rachel Hunt Olfson. BA, Reed Coll., 1981; BFA, Mus. Art Sch., Portland, Oreg., 1981; MFA, Yale U., 1985. Author: (book) Hart Island; pub. art work, Circle of Hope, 1994, Letters to a Forest, 1995. Recipient Conn. Commn. on Arts award, 1987, Project award, N.Y. State Coun., 1995, Media award, 2000. Democrat. E-mail: huntolfson@earthlink.net.

HUNT, MARY REILLY, organization executive; b. N.Y.C., Apr. 17, 1921; d. Philip R. and Mary C. (Harten) Reilly; m. Robert R. Hunt, Apr. 10, 1943,; children: Marianne Schram, Philip R., Robert R., Elise Hannah. Student, CCNY, 1939. Tax investigator Ind. Dept. Revenue, 1970-80; pres. Ind. Right to Life, 1973-77; treas. Nat. Right to Life Com., Washington, 1974, 77, 78, mem. exec. com., 1974, 76-81, vice chmn., 1976, exec. dir., 1978, dir. devel., 1979-94, v.p. devel., 1994-97, hon. bd. mem., 1983—; v.p. devel. Nat. Life Ctr., Woodbury, 1997—; pres. Mary Reilly Hunt & Assoc., Inc., South Bend, Ind., 1985—. Bd. dirs., v.p. YWCA, 1968-73, bd. dirs. Mental Health Assn. St. Joseph Co., 1972-78; candidate for state legis., 1988; mem. St. Joseph County Rep. Women precinct com., South Bend, 1964-79, alt. del. to Nat. Rep. Conv., 1976, 84, 88, 92; mem. Souht Bend Symphony Women's Assn. Recipient St. Patrick's medal St. Patrick's Coll. and Sem. (Ireland), 1996. Mem. NAFE, Women Bus. Owners, Am. Soc. Sovereign Mil. Order of Malta. Republican. Roman Catholic. Avocations: gardening, antique collecting. Office: Nat Life Ctr 1102 N Lafayette Blvd South Bend IN 46617-1136

HUNT, PAMELA SUE, elementary school educator, music educator; d. Darwin and Nelvia Lowe Hunt. B in Music Edn., Ea. Ky. U., 1987. Level III Orff-Schulwerk music cert. Elem. music specialist McDowell County Schs., Welch, W.Va., 1989—93, 1994—98, Floyd County Schs., Prestonsburg, Ky., 1993—94, Mansfield (Ohio) City Schs., 1998—. Performer, prodr.: recording Mountain Flower, 2000. Active United Meth. Ch.; mem. Chancel Choir, Handbell Choir. Named Ky. Col., Gov. Ky., 1990. Mem.: Music Educators Nat. Conf., Kappa Delta Pi, Delta Omicron. Avocations: lap dulcimer, hammered dulcimer, autoharp, bowed psaltery. Office: 240 Euclid Ave Mansfield OH 44903

HUNT, SWANEE G. public policy educator, former ambassador; b. Dallas, May 1, 1950; m. Charles Alexander Ansbacher; 3 children. BA, Tex. Christian U., 1972; MA, Ball State U., 1976; MA in Religion, Iliff Sch. of Theology, 1977, PhD, 1986; PhD (hon.), Webster U., 1994. Pres. Hunt Alternatives Fund, 1981—; co-founder Karis Community, 1980-83; min. pastoral care Capital Heights Presbyn. Ch., 1983; vice chair Denver Community Mental Health Commn., 1983-87; with Gov. Policy Acad. on Families and Children at Risk, 1989-90; chair Colo. Coord. Coun. Housing and the Homeless, 1989-92; U.S. amb. to Austria, 1993-97; dir. Women and Pub. Policy Program, Kennedy Sch. Govt. Composer The Witness Cantata, 1985; author: This Was Not Our War, 2004; syndicated columnist Scripps Howard.. Bd. dirs., co-founder Women's Found. Colo.; chair Mayor's Human Capital Agenda Coun., 1992-93; co-chair Denver Initiative Children and Families; mem. UN High Commn. on Refugees; mem. Internat. Crisis Group, Internat. Alert. Recipient Martin Luther King Humanitarian award U. Colo., 1992, NCCJ, 1992, Denver Urban Ministries, 1991, United Meth. Ch., 1989, Internat. Women's Forum, 1989, Sta. KUSA-TV, 1989, Caring Connection, 1989, Nat. Mental Health Assn., 1985, Mental Health Assn. Colo., 1984, 94, Mile High award United Way, 1993, Am. Heritage award Anti-Defamation League, 1995, Cordon Bleu du Saint Esprit Peace award, 1996, Humanitarian Lifetime Svc. award Denver Holocaust Awareness, 1997, Together for Peace award, 1997, 3 decorations Austrian Govt., 1997, Amb. award The Conflict Ctr., 1997, Inst. for Internat. Edn. award, 1998. Office: 168 Brattle St Cambridge MA 02138-3309 also: Kennedy Sch Govt 79 Jfk St Rm T110A Cambridge MA 02138-5801

HUNT, VALERIE VIRGINIA, electrophysiologist, educator; b. Larwill, Ind., July 22, 1916; d. Homer Henry Hunt and Iva Velzora Ames. BS in Biology, Fla. State Coll., 1936; MA in Physiol. Psychology, Columbia U., 1941, EdD in Sci. Edn., 1946; DD, Phoenix Inst., San Diego, 1984. Sci. tchr. Anniston (Ala.) H.S., 1936-38; asst. anatomy nursing dept. Columbia U., N.Y.C., 1939-40; chmn. health edn. Boston YWCA, 1942-43; instr. Columbia U. Tchrs. Coll. and Coll. Physicians and Surgeons, N.Y.C., 1943-46; asst. prof. U. Iowa, Iowa City, 1946-47; assoc. prof., dir. divsn. phys. therapy UCLA, 1947-64, prof. physiology, dir. electromyographic lab., 1964-80, prof. emeritus, 1980—; dir. BioEnergy Fields Lab. BioEnergy Fields Found., Malibu, Calif., 1980—; CEO Malibu Pub. Co., 1995—. Cons. Nat. Bd. YWCA, 1943-46, Nat. Early Childhood Edn., 1948-50, UCLA Sch. Engring. Prosthetics Inst., 1949-51, Calif. Dept. Edn., 1950-60, Chrysler Motor Co. Space Divsn. Rsch., 1952, NASA Space Biology, 1958, Grand Kamalani Wellness Ctr., Maui, Hawaii; field reader U.S. Dept. HEW, 1958-65; reviewer sci. textbooks McMillan Pub., Prentice-Hall, McGraw-Hill, W.B. Saunders & Co., 1959-67; cons. Fetzer Found. Energy Field Rsch., 1989, Heart Math Found., 1992. Author: Recreation for the Handicapped, 1955, Corrective Physical Education, 1967, Movement Education for Preschool, 1972, Guidelines for Movement Behavior: Curricula for Early Childhood Education, 1974, Infinite Mind: Science of the Human Vibrations of Consciousness, 1996, Mind Mastery Meditations, 1997, Naibhu, 1998; contbr. articles to profl. jours. Pres. United Cerebral Palsy, L.A., 1947-51; mem. adv. com. Harlan Shoemaker Clinic for Neurol. Disabilities, 1948-53; bd. dirs. Found. for Jr. Blind, 1949-52, Crippled Children Soc., 1953-58, YWCA, L.A., 1955-65; adv. com., Internat. Congress for Exceptional Children, 1964-72, Rory Found., L.A., 1998—; vestry bd. mem. St. Matthew Episcopal Ch., L.A., 1965-69. Rsch. grantee USPHS, 1957-61, Adelphi Found., 1960-63, Rolf Found., 1965-71; recipient Heritage award Calif. Dance Educator Assn., 1987, N.B. Rudman award Found. Exceptional Leadership, 1995; Dame Order of St. John of the Ams., 1996. Mem. NSF, N.Y. Acad. Scis., Pi Lambda Theta, Kappa Delta Pi. Achievements include patents pending for Aurameter. Avocations: travel, gardening, music, art, lecturing. Office: BioEnergy Fields Found PO Box 6653 Malibu CA 90264-6653 E-mail: vhunt@bioenergyfields.org.

HUNT BROGDEN, CHRISTINE MICHELLE, music educator; b. Winston-Salem, N.C., Nov. 12, 1972; d. Ronald L. and Linda S. Hunt; m. James H. Brogden, Jr., July 12, 2003. MusB in Edn., La. State U., Baton Rouge, 1996. Cert. music edn. K-12 La., 1996, Ga., 1999. Dir. of bands and chorus Westdale Mid. Acad., Baton Rouge, 1997—99; dir. of bands Herschel Jones Mid. Sch., Dallas, Ga., 1999—2002; band and orch. dir. Woodstock (Ga.) Mid. Sch., 2002—. Alto saxophonist Baton Rouge Cmty. Band, 1998—99; tenor saxophonist Cobb Wind Symphony, Marietta, Ga., 1999—. Mem.: Ga. Music Educators Assocation, La. Music Educators Assocation, Sigma Alpha Iota (life; v.p. of membership 1993—95, sgt. at arms 1995—96, Sword of Honor Leadership award 1996). Home: 836 Windcroft Cir Acworth GA 30101 Office: Woodstock Mid Sch 2000 Towne Lake Hills S Dr Woodstock GA 30189 Personal E-mail: jimandchristi@yahoo.com.

HUNTE, BERYL ELEANOR, mathematics educator, consultant; b. N.Y.C. BA, CUNY-Hunter Coll., 1947; MA, Columbia U., 1948; PhD, NYU, 1965. Instr. math. So. U., Baton Rouge, 1948-51; tchr. math. Bloomfield (N.J.) H.S., 1951-57; tchr. maths. Friends Sem., N.Y.C., 1957-62; asst. prof. maths. Rockland C.C., Suffern, N.Y., 1962-63; instr. maths., supr. tchr. trainees NYU, N.Y.C., 1964; chmn. dept. math. Borough of Manhattan C.C., N.Y.C., 1964-67, 70-73, prof. maths., 1970-95, prof. maths. emerita, 1996, acting dean students, 1985-87, acting dean acad. affairs, 1987-88; dean for spl. projects CUNY, 1988-89. Assoc. U. Seminar on Higher Edn., Columbia U., N.Y.C., 1989-95. Author: (with others) (textbook) Mathematics Through Statistics, 1973. NSF fellow, summer 1960, 1963-64, Chancellor's Faculty fellow CUNY, 1980. Mem. N.Y. Acad. Scis., Am. Math. Soc., CUNY Acad. for Humanities and Scis. (bd. dirs. 1991—, first v.p. 1994—), UN Assn. N.Y.C. (bd. dirs., sec. 1980-86). Avocations: opera, concerts, ballet, bridge.

HUNTER, BARBARA WAY, public relations consultant; b. Westport, N.Y., July 14, 1927; d. Walter Denslow and Hilda (Greenawalt) Way; m. Austin F. Hunter, Jan. 24, 1953; children: Kimberley, Victoria. BA, Cornell U., 1949. Assoc. editor Topics Pub. Co., N.Y.C., 1949-51; publicist Nat. Dairy Product Corp., N.Y.C., 1951-53; account exec. Sally Dickson Assn., 1953-56; assoc. D-A-Y Pub. Relations (div. Ogilvy & Mather Co.), N.Y.C., 1964-70, exec. v.p., 1970-84, pres., 1984-89, Hunter & Assocs., Inc., 1989-97, chmn., 1997-2000. Bd. dirs. Mr. Steak Inc., Denver, Great River Arts Inst. Trustee Cornell U., Ithaca, N.Y., 1980-85; life mem. Cornell U. Coun.; bd. dirs. Point O'Woods Assn., Fire Island, N.Y., 1980-87, 2002—, pres., 2003—. Recipient Sparkplug award Internat. Foodservice Mfrs. Assn., 1970, Matrix award N.Y. Women in Communications Inc., 1980, Entreprenurial Woman award Women Bus. Owners, 1981, Nat. Headliner award Women in Communications Inc., 1984. Fellow Pub. Rels. Soc. Am. (pres. 1984, pres.-elect 1983, treas. 1982, pres. N.Y. chpt. 1980, Nat. Gold Anvil award 1993); mem. Found. Pub. Rels. Rsch. and Edn. (trustee 1982, 84), Walpole Hist. Soc. (bd. dirs. 2002-), Cornell Club of N.Y., The Club at Point O'Woods. also: 31 Wentworth Rd Walpole NH 03608

HUNTER, BRENDA ANN, writer, psychologist; b. Statesville, NC, Feb. 2, 1941; d. Ray Cameron and Florence Maureen (Smith) Morrison; m. David Lynn Larson, June 23, 1963; children: Holly Larson, Kristen Larson; m. Don R. Hunter, Feb. 23, 1975. BA in English, Wheaton Coll., 1963; MA in English, SUNY, Buffalo, 1967; PhD in Psychology, Georgetown U., 1990. Psychologist Minirth, Meier and Byrd Clinic, Arlington, Va., 1991—97; pvt. practice, 1980—. Instr. U. NC, Asheville, Georgetown U.; conf., presenter, spkr. in field. Author: Beyond Divorce, 1978, Where Have All the Mothers Gone?, 1984, Home by Choice, 1991, In the Company of Women, 1994, What Every Mother Needs to Know About Babies, 1994, A Wedding is a Family Affair, 1995, In the Company of Friends, 1996, The Power of Mother Love, 1997, My God, Do You Love Me?, 1998, Staying Alive: Life Changing Strategies for Surviving Cancer, 2004; contbr. articles to profl. jours. Home: 40 Ridgeview Dr Asheville NC 28804

HUNTER, CECILIA AROS, social studies educator, archivist, director; b. Tucson, Nov. 18, 1941; d. Jose Aviña and Josephine (Marchello) Aros; m. Louis Gerald Nuttycombe, Aug. 19, 1961 (dec. July 1965); children: Louis Garfield, Raquel Aviña; m. Leslie Gene Hunter, Aug. 15, 1969; children: Daniel Aros, Joseph Aros, Raquel Aviña. BA, U. Ariz., 1969, MLS, 1991; MA, Tex A&M U., Kingsville, 1976. Cert. social studies tchr., Ariz.; cert. social studies tchr., libr., computer literacy, mid-mgmt., Tex. Tchr. Kingsville (Tex.) Ind. Sch. Dist., 1975-80; prin. Epiphany Episcopal Sch., Kingsville, 1980-84; libr. and tech. coord. Santa Gertrudis Ind. Sch. Dist., Kingsville, 1984-90; archivist South Tex. Archives and preservation officer Jernigan Library Tex. A&M U., Kingsville, 1992—; preservation officer Jernigan Libr. Mem. adv. bd. Teacching and Computers Scholastic Publs., N.Y.C., 1987-90. Columnist on tech., The Social Studies Texan, 1989-91; co-author: (software) Spanish Missions of Texas, 1986, Historic Kingsville, Tex., vol. 1, 1994, vol. 2, 1997, Texas A&M, Kingsville, 2000. Mem. exec. com. Kleberg county Dem. Com., Kingsville, 1978—; election judge Kleberg County, 1980—; mem. Kleberg County Libr. Bd., 1980-83; vestrywoman Epiphany Episcopal Ch., 1985-88; preservation officer Kingsville Hist. Commn., 1992—. Recipient Friend of Computer Edn. award Tex. Computer Edn. Assn., 1986, award for using microcomputers Follett County, 1987; fellow NEH, Rutgers U., 1983, Columbia U., 1986, Fulbright-Hays fellow, China, 1984. Mem. ALA (Reforma scholar 1990), Am. Assn. Sch. Librs. (award for using microcomputers 1987), Soc. Am. Archivists, S.W. Soc. Archivists, Tex. Historic Commn. Bd. Rev., Tex. Hist. Records Adv. Bd., Phi Alpha Delta, Pi Sigma Alpha, Delta Kappa Gamma, Phi Delta Kappa. Avocation: computers. Home: 811 W Alice Ave Kingsville TX 78363-4262 Office: South Tex Archives and Spl Collections Tex A&M U Kingsville TX 78364-0197

HUNTER, EDWINA EARLE, elementary school educator; b. Caswell County, N.C., Dec. 29, 1943; d. Edgar Earl and Bessie C. (Brown) Palmer; m. James W. Hunter, July 2, 1966; children: James W. Jr., Anika Z., Isaac Earl. BA, Spelman Coll., 1964; MA in Teaching, Smith Coll., 1966. Tchr. vocal music El Paso (Tex.) Schs., 1975-77, Prince George's County Schs., Laurel, Md., 1977—. Instr. El Paso C.C., 1975-76; cons. Smithsonian Mus., Washington, 1978. Transcriber, performer rec. Children's Songs for Games from Africa, 1979. Named Outstanding Alumna, Nat. Assn. For Equal Opportunity in Higher Edn., 1989; grantee NEH, Vienna, Austria, 1990. Mem. Nat. Guild Piano Tchrs., Suzuki Assn. Am., Md. Music Educators, Nat. Alumnae Assn. Spelman Coll. (sec. Columbia chpt. 1985-87, pres. 1988-92, sec.-treas. N.E. region 1991-93, named Alumna of Yr. Columbia chpt., 2001). Democrat. Home: 10721 Graeloch Rd Laurel MD 20723-1122 Office: James H Harrison Elem Sch 13200 Larchdale Rd Laurel MD 20708-1744

HUNTER, FRANCES ELLEN CROFT, music educator; b. Greensboro, N.C., Jan. 25, 1941; d. John Wilkins Croft Sr. and Zara Louise Fisher Croft; m. C. Linwood Hunter, Jan. 25, 1964 (dec. Sept. 2, 1996); 1 child, Leticia Collette. BFA, Ohio U., 1962. Cert. tchr. music N.C., Ohio. Tchr. music Hoke County Schs., Raeford, NC, 1962—64, Harnett County Schs., Johnsonville, NC, 1964—65, Fayetteville City Schs., NC, 1965—70, Ft. Bragg Schs., NC, 1971—2001. Singer Cumberland Oratorio Singers, Fayetteville, 2003; singer and accompanist Ft. Bragg Stars and Stripes Singers, Fayetteville, 2003. Composer: Here's Looking At You Yr. 2000, 1987. Vol. Fayetteville Festival of Flight, 2003, Teen Involvement Projects, Inc. Recipient Svc. award, Music Educators Nat. Conf./N.C. Music Educators Assn., 1999, Cert. of Retirement, Dept. Def. Edn. Activity, 2001. Mem.: Nat. Assn. Ret. Fed. Employees, NC Ret. Govt. Employees' Assn., Music Educators Nat. Conf. Lutheran. Avocations: reading, dance.

HUNTER, GEORGIA L. clergywoman; b. Wiergate, Tex., June 14, 1938; d. George Clavert and Leria (Thomas) Spikes; m. LeRoy Hunter, Feb. 2, 1967; children— Balenda M. Spikes, Maria A. Spikes. Student Bible Moody Bible Inst; MDiv Universal Life Ch. Sch., Modesto, Calif.; A in Theology Grace Theol. Seminary, Atlanta, 1998. Ordained to ministry Christian Meth. Episcopal Ch., 1983; cert. tour guide. Counselor Ill. Dept. children and Family Services, Freeport, 1970-74; food service dir. Retirement Inc., Freeport, 1978—; pastor Christian Meth. Episcopal Ch., Madison, Wis., 1983-91; asst. pastor Miles Meml. Christian Meml. Episcopal Ch., Rockford, Ill., 1993; pastor Christ Mission Christian Meth. Episcopal

Ch., Milw., 1993; corr. Jour. Standard, Freeport, 1982-83; chairperson expansions and missions sect. Milw. dist. Christian Meth. Episcopal Ch.; mem. Com. Milw. Dist. Leadership Tng. Sch.; coord. Interdenominational Theol. Ctr. Ext. Program, Atlanta. V.p. Freeport Bd. Edn., 1977—; pres. Ch. Women United, Freeport, 1970-83; asst. dir. youth Rockford and Vicinity Dist. Assn., 1980-82; sec. Freeport Good Samaritan Refuge House; food pantry coord. Christian Meth. Episc. Ch., Milw.; supr. Rainbow Ridge Residential Home, 1996; mem. Freeport Mins. United For Change; site mgr. Ill. Linkchull House, Stephenson County, 1997. Recipient Human Relations award City Council Freeport, 1974, Spiritual Achievement award Martin Luther King Ctr., Freeport, 1983, Good Neighbor award Freeport Jour. Standard, 1983, Achievement award Ch. Women United, 1983. Mem. Fully Gospel Women Assn. (bd. dirs., coord.), Young Adult Christian Women (pres.). Democrat. Avocations: bowling; researcher; reading; sewing; writing poetry. Home: RRI Box 97 Wiergate TX 75977

HUNTER, GLORIA ELEANORE, secondary school educator; b. Chgo., May 24, 1927; d. David Waldren and Eleanore Dorothy (Kline) H.; m. Thomas Alexander Hunter III; children: Thomas A. IV, William Craig, Eleanore Tracey. BA, U. Mich., 1949; MS, U. Bridgeport, 1972. Tchr. Fenger H.S., Chgo., 1949-50, U. Mich. H.S., 1950-55; reporter, columnist Westport News, 1965-68; program writer Action for Bridgeport Cmty., 1968-70; tchr. Fairfield Jr. H.S., 1970-72; tchr., dir. reading Weston Schs., 1972-91. Cons. in field. Author cassette program READING/PLUS, Learning and Retention for Managers; columnist for local newspaper Minuteman, 1993—; contbr. articles to mags. and newspapers. Mem. Westport Bd. Edn., 1991-95; candidate Conn. Ho. of Reps., 1994. Mem. NEA (life), LWV. Democrat. Avocations: gardening, travel, knitting, entertaining, theatre. Home: 33 High Point Rd Westport CT 06880-3908

HUNTER, HELEN FRANCES, social worker; b. Somerville, N.J., July 26, 1958; d. Donald Joseph and Catherine Louise (Conner) Wells, m. Kevin Dore Hunter, Oct. 2, 1982; children: Brian Dore, Mary Kathryn. BA, Douglass Coll., 1980; MSW, Rutgers U., 1982. Lic. clin. social worker; cert. first aid, CPR. Ind. social svc. cons., Red Bank, N.J., 1985-86; staff social worker Vis. Nurse Assn. of Plainfield and North Plainfield (N.J.), 1985-86; social svc. cons. Med. Placement Svcs., Stratford, Conn., 1988-89, ind. social svc. cons. Stratford, 1986—; regional coord. Conn. Coaltion on Aging, 1989-90; cons. The Consultation Ctr., New Haven, Conn., 1990—. Workshop leader in field; case mgr. N.J. site of Channeling Long-Term Care Project, others. Mem. NASW, Nat. Coun. on Aging, Greater Bridgeport Elderly Svcs. Coun. (chmn.), Conn. Coalition on Aging (sec., bd. dirs.), Conn. Soc. Gerontology (bd. dirs.), Nat. Gerontol. Soc., also others.

HUNTER, HOLLY, actress, b. Conyers, Ga., Mar. 20, 1958; d. Charles Edwin and Opal Marguerite (Catledge) H; m. Janusz Kaminski, May 20, 1995 (div. 2001). BFA, Carnegie-Mellon U., 1980. Actress: (films) The Burning, 1981, Swing Shift, 1984, Broadcast News, 1987 (Acad. Award nomination for best actress, 1988), Raising Arizona, 1987, End of the Line, 1988, Always, 1989, Miss Firecracker, 1989, Animal Behavior, 1989, Once Around, 1991, The Piano, 1993 (Cannes Film Festival Award for best actress, 1993, Golden Globe for best actress, 1994, Acad. Award for best actress, 1994), The Firm, 1993 (Acad. Award nomination for best supporting actress, 1994), Home for the Holidays, 1995, Copycat, 1995, Crash, 1996, Hurly-burly, 1997, A Life Less Ordinary, 1997, Living Out Loud, 1998, Jesus' Son, 1999, Things You Can Tell Just By Looking at Her, 2000 (Emmy nomination for best supporting actress in a miniseries or movie, 2001), Woman Wanted, 2000, Timecode, 2000, O Brother, Where Art Thou, 2000, Moonlight Mile, 2002, Levity, 2003; (TV) Svengali, 1983, An Uncommon Love, 1983, With Intent to Kill, 1984, A Gathering of Old Men, 1987, Roe vs. Wade, 1989 (Emmy for best actress in a miniseries or special, 1989), Crazy in Love, 1992, The Positively True Adventures of the Alleged Texas Cheerleader-Murdering Mom, 1993 (Emmy for best actress in a miniseries or special, 1993, CableACE award for best actress in a movie or miniseries, 1994), Harlan County War, 2000 (Emmy nomination for best actress in a miniseries or movie, 2000), When Billie Beat Bobby, 2001 (Emmy nomination for best actress in a miniseries or movie, 2001); (Broadway stage prodns.) Crimes of the Heart, 1982, The Wake of Jamey Foster, 1982, Impossible Marriage, 1998; (regional stage prodns.) Buried Child, A Doll's House, Artichoke; (other stage prodns.) include A Lie of the Mind, L.A., Battery, N.Y.C., Miss Firecracker Contest, 1984, The Person I Once Was, N.Y.C.; Actress, exec. prodr.: (films) Thirteen, 2003 (Acad. Award nomination for best supporing actress, 2004, Golden Globe nomination for best supporting actress, 2004, Screen Actors Guild Award nomination for best supporting actress, 2004). Bd. dirs. Calif. Abortion Rights Action League.*

HUNTER, MATTIE, human services executive; b. Chgo., June 1, 1954; d. Lucious and Flabe (Davis) H. BA, Monmouth (Ill.) Coll., 1976; MA, Jackson (Miss.) State U., 1982. Summer counselor Chgo. Housing Authority, 1972-76; asst. mgr. Whitney's Fashions, Chgo., 1976; tng. specialist City Colls. of Chgo., 1977-81; youth service worker Dept. Human Services City of Chgo., 1977-81; program dir. Human Services Devel. Inst. Chgo., 1982-85, exec. asst. to pres., 1985—. Conf. planner, community liaison, and mktg. Bakeman & Assocs., Chgo., 1986—. Author: (newsletter) Nat. Elk Alcoholism Commn., 1982. Mem. Community Devel. Adv. Council City of Chgo., 1986; mem. steering com. Cook County Democratic Women, Chgo., 1985—; staff asst. Polit. Action Conf. of Ill., Chgo., 1984—; vol. Warren county Rep. Orgn., Monmouth, 1975; fundraiser Nat. Polit. Congress of Black Women, Chgo., 1985—; vol. coordinator Hands Across Am., Chgo., 1986, March of Dimes Telethon, Chgo., 1979-81, Muscular Distrophy, Chgo., 1980, 81, 85, local adv. council Chgo. Housing Authority, 1968-76; precinct coordinator congl. dist. race, Chgo., 1980, 1976, 3rd Ward Regular Democratic Orgn., Chgo., 1970-72; asst. ward coordinator Washington for Mayor City of Chgo., 1983; surveyor Joint Ctr. for Polit. Studies, Washington, 1973; ambassador of mercy United Way, Chgo.; vice chmn. adv. council Chgo. Intervention Network Dept. of Human Services, 1985—, convocations com. Monmouth Coll., 1973-74, cultural affairs com., 1975-76; bd. dirs. Black Leadership Roundtable of Ill., Chgo., 1986—. Named one of Outstanding Young Women Am., 1985; recipient award of Appreciation, Dept. Human Services City of Chgo., 1981, award of Gratitude, Human Resources Devel. Inst. Chgo., 1984. Mem. Notaries Assn. of Ill., Inc., Nat. Black Alcoholism Council (chmn. Orgn. Devel. Com., award of Appreciation), Nat. Forum Black Pub. Adminstrs., Nat. Assn. for Female Execs. Democrat. Baptist. Avocations: volleyball, softball, bowling. Home: 5604 S Prairie Ave Apt 3 Chicago IL 60637-5306

HUNTER, PATRICIA RAE (TRICIA HUNTER), state official; b. Appleton, Minn., June 15, 1952; d. Harlan Ottowa and Clara Elizabeth (Tryhus) H.; m. Clark Waldon Crabbe, May 28, 1978 (div. July 1994); 1 child, Samantha Marcantonio. AS in Nursing, Good Samaritan Hosp., Phoenix, 1974; BS in Nursing, U. San Diego, San Diego, 1981; M Nursing, UCLA, 1985. RN; cert. oper. rm. nurse. Surg. svcs. educator Stanford Hosp., 1983-85; oper. rm. supr. Alexian Bros., San Jose, Calif., 1985-86; dir. surg. svcs. Cmty. Hosp. Chula Vista, Calif., 1986-89; mem. Calif. State Assembly, San Diego, 1989-92; spl. asst. Gov. Wilson Office Statewide Health Planning and Devel., Sacramento, 1993-94; commr. Calif. Med. Assistance Commn., Sacramento, 1994-98, sr. v.p., mng. dir., 1998—, The Flannery Group, San Diego, 1997—2002; pvt. practice Hon. Tricia Hunter Legis. Advocated Cons., 2002—. Bd. mem. Premier Home & Health, Phoenix, 1994-95; cons. Summit Schs., Ontario, Calif., 1992-93, hosp., Monterey, Calif., 1984—; mem. adv. bd. Alheimers Assn., San Diego, 1990-92, Arthritis Found., 1990-92. Pres. Calif. Rep. League, 1995-97. Named Rockie Legislator of Yr., Calif. Psychol. Assn., 1990, Legislator of Yr. Calif. Nurse Practitioners Assn., 1992; recipient Alice Pauly award Nat. Women Polit. Caucus, San Diego, 1991. Mem. ANA (v.p. 1982-85), Assn. Oper. Rm. Nurses, NWPC, Bus. and Profl. Orgn., Rotary (bd. mem. 1993-94), San Diego Red Cross (bd. mem.), Sigma Theta Tau (leadership award 1991). Republican. Lutheran. Home: 3260 E Fox Run Way San Diego CA 92111-7723 Office: Hon Tricia Hunter 1121 L St Ste 409 Sacramento CA 95814 E-mail: thunter930@aol.com.

HUNTER BLAIR, PAULINE CLARKE, writer; b. Kirkby-in-Ashfield, Eng., May 19, 1921; d. Charles Leopold and Dorothy Kathleen (Milum) Clarke; m. Peter Hunter Blair, Feb., 1969. BA with honors, Somerville Coll., Oxford U., Eng., 1943. Free-lance writer, 1948—. Lectr. Author (writing as Pauline Clarke): (novels) The Pekinese Princess, 1948, The Great Can, 1952, The White Elephant, 1952, Smith's Hoard, 1955, The Boy with the Erpingham Hood, 1956, Sandy the Sailor, 1956, James, The Policeman, 1957, James and the Robbers, 1959, Torolv The Fatherless, 1959, 2d edit., 1973, The Lord of the Castle, 1960, The Robin Hooders, 1960, James and the Smugglers, 1961, Keep the Pot Boiling, 1961, The Twelve and the Genii, 1962 (Libr. Assn. Carnegie medal, 1962, Lewis Carrol Shelf award, 1963, Deutsche Jugend Buchpreis, 1968), Silver Bells and Cockle Shells, 1962, James and the Black Van, 1963, Crowds of Creatures, 1964, The Bonfire Party, 1966, The Two Faces of Silenus, 1972; author: (under pseudonym Helen Clare) Five Dolls in a House, 1953, Merlin's Magic, 1953, Bel The Giant and Other Stories, 1956, Five Dolls and the Monkey, 1956, Five Dolls in the Snow, 1957, Five Dolls and Their Friends, 1959, Seven White Pebbles, 1960, Five Dolls and the Duke, 1963, The Cat and the Fiddle and Other Stories from Bel, the Giant, 1968; author: (writing as Pauline Hunter Blair) The Nelson Boy, 1999, A Thorough Seaman, 2000, Warscape, 2001, Jacob's Ladder, 2003; book reviewer, contbr.: Times Lit. Supplement. Mem.: Brit. Soc. Authors. Home: Church Farm House Bottisham Cambridge CB5 9BA England Office: care Curtis Brown Ltd Haymarket House 28/29 Haymarket London SW1Y 4SP England also: care John Cushman Assocs Inc 24 E 38th St New York NY 10016-2502

HUNTER-STIEBEL, PENELOPE, art historian; b. Washington; d. Burton Leath and Beulah (Wooten) H.; m. Gerald G. Stiebel; 1 child, Hunter. BA, Barnard Coll., 1968; MA, NYU, 1971. With Met. Mus. of Art, N.Y.C., 1969-83, asst. curator, 1975-79, assoc. curator, 1979-83; curatorial cons. N.Y.C., 1983-86; prin. Rosenberg & Stiebel, Inc., N.Y.C., 1986-2000; consulting curator of European art Portland (Oreg.) Art Mus. Exhbn. curator Met. Mus. Art, Rochester (N.Y.) Meml. Art Gallery, Detroit Inst. Art, Philbrook Mus., Portland (Oreg.) Mus. Art. Editor: Stroganoff: The Palace and Collections of a Russian Noble Family, 2000, Stuff of Dreams from the Paris Musee des Arts Decoratifs, 2002, Triumph of French Painting: 17th Century Masterpieces, 2003. Office: 252 E 68th St New York NY 10021

HUNTLEY, DIANE E. dental hygiene educator; b. Concord, N.H., Oct. 1, 1946; d. George Williams and Esther A. (Gadwah) H. AS, Fones Sch. Dental Hygiene, Bridgeport, Conn., 1966; BA, U. Bridgeport, Conn., 1968; MA, SUNY, Buffalo, 1971; PhD, Kans. State U., 1985. Registered dental hygienist. Dental hygienist various gen. practice dentists, Conn., Colo., 1966-76; clin. instr. Fones Sch. Dental Hygiene, 1971-74; asst. prof. U. Colo. Dental Sch., Denver, 1974-76; asst. prof. dental hygiene Wichita (Kans.) State U., 1976-82, assoc. prof., 1982—. Vol. hygienist Good Samaritan Clinic, Wichita, 1989-90, 92—. Contbr. articles to profl. jours. Mem. dental adv. bd. United Meth. Urban Ministries, Wichita, 1990-92; mem. P.A.N.D.A. Coalition of Kans. Exec. Com., 1995—. Mem.: AAUP (Wichita State U. chpt. sec.treas. 1988—91), Am. Dental Hygienists Assn. (editl. dir. 1983—85, historian 1993—2001), Kans. Dental Hygienists assn. (del. 1989—93, treas. 1998—2000, parliamentarian 1998—2001, trustee 2000—03), Wichita Dental Hygienists Assn. (pres. 1982—83, treas. 1988—90, trustee 1990—91), Am. Dental Edn. Assn., Apha Eta, Phi Kappa Phi. Office: Wichita State U 1845 Fairmount St Wichita KS 67260-0144

HUNTLEY-WRIGHT, JOAN AUGUSTA (JOAN AUGUSTA HUNTLEY), musician; b. Tulsa, Aug. 17, 1934; d. John Augustus and Edna Ruby (Van Brunt) Murphy; m. Robert Walter Huntley, Sept. 6, 1955 (div. Feb. 14, 1981); children: Robert John, Gene Bush, Dawn Elise, Ben Patrick; m. Wilfred Cleveland Wright, Sept. 13, 1992 (dec. Apr. 2001). Student, New Eng. Conservatory, 1952-53, U. Tulsa, 1953-54, Boston U. & N.E. Conservatory, 1954-55, Roosevelt U., Chgo., 1970-72, Thronton C.C., 1970-72; B in Violin Performance, New Eng. Conservatory Music, 1981; M in Violin Performance, U. Mass., Lowell, 1990. Violinist Tulsa Philharm. Symphony, 1949-52, 53-54; first violinist Tassan Quartet, Chgo., 1962-64, Hucasa Trio, Chgo., 1964-72; concert mistress, leader of various orchestras and chamber ensembles, 1964—; artist in residence Thornton C.C., Harvey, Ill., 1968-72; first violinist Bowforte Ensemble, Boston, 1973-81; assoc. prof. Berklee Coll. of Music, Boston, 1985-91. Designed, tchr. pre-sch. instrumental and ear tng. classes Raygor Day Sch., Matteson, Ill, 1963-65, Humpty-Dumpty and YMCA Nursery Schs., Beverly, Mass., 1976-78; organizer benefit concerts for tornado victims, Ill., 1968. Creator, performer radio program Music Personalities KAKC, Tulsa, 1953; mgr., music dir., founder LaFemme/LaFemme Women Composers Ensemble, 1990-95; soloist Tulsa Philharm., 1952, Park Forest (Ill.) Symphony, 1958, 60, 62, Salem (Mass.) Philharm., 1981, 89; performer with Phila. Piano Quartet, 1997-99. Mem. Ill. Constitutional Com.; active in Boy Scouts Am. and Girl Scouts; active in PTA. Recipient Profl. Devel. award Mass. Assn. Women in Edn., 1995. Mem. AAUW, S.W. Fla. Symphony. Avocations: avid reader, walking, working out. Home: 9 Alderbrook Dr Topsfield MA 01983-2301 E-mail: wcompwill@cs.com.

HUNTOON, ABBY ELIZABETH, artist, teacher; b. Providence, R.I., Sept. 8, 1951; d. William Huntoon and Marjorie (Aldrich) Bradshaw; m. Phil Kaelin, Sept. 25, 1993. BS, Trinity Coll., 1973; MFA from program in Artisanry, Boston U., 1985. Instr. Boston U., 1983-84; co-owner, adminstr., tchr. Sawyer St. Studios, South Portland, Maine, 1989—. Project coord. Main Coll. of Art, 1988, mem. Maine Arts Commn., Visual Arts Panel, 1988-92; summer instr. Maine Coll. of Art, 1989, 90; workshop conductor Maine Coll. of Art, 1989, 95, U. Southern Maine, 1991. Artist: works exhibited at Makers 86, Bowdoin Mus. of Art, Brunswick, Maine, 1986, Ceramics Now, 27th Ceramic Nat. Exhibition (traveling U.S. for 2 years), 1987, Maine Coast Artists, Portland, Maine, 1988, 46th Ceramics Annual, Lang Art Gallery, Scripps Coll., Claremont, Calif., 1990; Northeastern Splendor (chosen ceramics rep. from Maine) Boston, 1991, Makers 93, Portland Mus. of Art, 1993; one person shows Architectural Ceramics, Frick Gallery, Belfast, Maine, 1990, 93; two person show Lakes Gallery, South Casco, Maine, 1995, Old York Hist. Soc., 1997, Round Top Ctr. for the Arts, 1997, Robert Clements Gallery, Portland, 1997; corp. collections include Putnam Hayes and Bartlett Inc., Cambridge, Mass., Standish Ayer and Wood, Boston, The Index Group Inc., Cambridge. Recipient Merit award Maine Crafts Assn., 1986; grantee: NEA, 1988. Avocations: sailing, skiing, political activities. Office: Sawyer Street Studios 131 Sawyer St South Portland ME 04106-2127

HUNZIKER, SUDHA, social worker; arrived in U.S., 1973; d. Chhabildas and Pushpaben Dalal; m. Jurg Hunziker, Apr. 15, 1976. BA in Psychology, U. Bombay, 1966; MA in Social Work, Tata Inst. Social Scis., Bombay, 1968; MSW, Smith Coll., 1974. Cert. social worker. Part-time social worker Samanvaya, Bombay, 1968—70, New Era Sch., Bombay, 1968—70; faculty asst. dept. family and child welfare Tata Inst. Social Scis., Bombay, 1970—73; psychiat. social worker N.Y.C., 1974—75; social worker foster care Brookwood Child Care, N.Y.C., 1975—77, supr. foster care unit, 1978—82, program dir. foster care, 1982—85, program dir. family svcs., 1986—88, cons., ind. reviewer, 1989—93; supr. foster care/adoption and AOBH Parsons Child and Family Ctr., Albany, NY, 1993—95, asst. exec. dir., 1996—2003, assoc. exec. dir., 2003—. Mem.: NASW, Family Support Am. Avocations: reading, travel. Office: Parsons Child and Family Ctr 60 Academy Rd Albany NY 12208

HUOT, RACHEL IRENE, biomedical educator, research scientist, physician; b. Manchester, N.H., Oct. 16, 1950; d. Omer Joseph and Irene Alice (Girard) Huot. BA in Biology cum laude, Rivier Coll., 1972; MS in Biology, Cath. U. Am., 1976, PhD in Biology, 1980; MD, La. State U. Health Sci. Ctr., Shreveport, 2000. Sr. technician Microbiol. Assocs., Bethesda, Md., 1974-77; chemist Uniformed Svcs. Univ. of Health Scis., Bethesda, 1977-79; biologist Nat. Cancer Inst., Bethesda, 1979-82; post-doctoral fellow S.W. Found. for Biomed. Rsch., San Antonio, 1982-85, asst. scientist, 1985-87, staff scientist, 1987-88; instr. U. Tex. Health Sci. Ctr., San Antonio, 1988-89; asst. prof., dir. basic urologic rsch. La. State U., New Orleans, 1990-96; resident in family practice Aultman Hosp., Canton, Ohio, 2001—02, U. Minn./Mayo Clinic, Waseca, 2002—. Judge sr. divsn. Alamo Regional Sci. Fair, San Antonio, 1989—90. Contbr. Vol. ARC, Christus Schumpert Hosp., Shreveport; patient educator vol. Martin Luther King Clinic, Shreveport, 1996—2000. Recipient Rsch. Svc. award, NIH, 1983—86, Searle Young Investigator award, 1994; grantee, NSF, 1972—74. Mem.: AMA, AAUW, LWV, AAAS, Minn. Acad. Family Practice, Am. Acad. Family Practice, Am. Soc. Experiment Biology, St. Vincent De Paul Soc., N.Y. Acad. Scis., Soc. In Vitro Biology, Fedn. Am. Scientists, Am. Soc. Cell Biology, Am. Assn. Cancer Rsch., Am. Soc. Microbiology, Sierra Club, Sigma Xi, Delta Epsilon Sigma, Iota Sigma Pi. Democrat. Roman Catholic. Avocation: Avocations: drawing, painting, roadracing, reading, Volksmarching. Home: 405 N 5th St Apt 416 Mankato MN 56001

HUPP, REBECCA, airport terminal executive; BS in Aviation Mgmt., MBA. Various positions Kansas City Internat. Airport; airport mgr. Aberdeen (S.D.) Regional Airport; asst. dir. Bangor (Maine) Internat. Airport, acting airport dir., airport dir. Office: Bangro Internat Airport 287 Godfry Blvd Bangor ME 04407

HURD, GALE ANNE, film producer; b. L.A., Oct. 25, 1955; d. Frank E. and Lolita (Espiau) H. Degree in econs. and communications, Stanford U., 1977. Dir. mktg. and publicity, co-producer New World Pictures, L.A., 1977-82; pres., producer Pacific Western Prodns., L.A., 1982—. Producer: (films) The Terminator, 1984 (Grand Prix Avoiriaz Film Festival award), Aliens 1986 (nominated for 7 Acad. awards, recipient Best Sound Effects Editing award, Best Visual Effects award Acad. Picture Arts & Scis.), Alien Nation (Saturn award for best sci. fiction film), The Abyss, 1989 (nominated for 4 Acad. awards, Best Visual Effects award), The Waterdance, 1991 (2 TFP Spirit awards, 2 Sundance Film Festival awards), Cast a Deadly Spell, 1991 (Emmy award), Raising Cain, 1992, No Escape, 1994, Safe Passage (Beatrice Wood award for Creative Achievement), 1994, The Ghost and the Darkness,(Acad. award) 1996, The Relic, 1996, Going West in America, 1996, Dante's Peak, 1997, Virus, 1997, Dead Man on Campus, 1997, Armageddon, 1998, Dick, 1999, Clockstoppers 2002, The Hulk, 2003 (TV series) Adventure, Inc., 2002, Terminator, 2003, Punisher, 2004, (TV pilot) Coven, 2004; exec. producer: (films) Switchback, 1997, Tremors, 1990, Downtown, 1990, Terminator 2, 1991 (winner 3 Acad. awards), Witch Hunt, 1994, Sugartime, 1995, Terminator 3, 2003, Punisher, 2004, (TV pilot) The Coven, 2004; creative cons. (TV program) Alien Nation, 1989-90. Juror Focus Student Film Awards, 1989, 90; chmn. Nicholl Fellowship Acad. Motion Picture Arts & Scis., 1989—; mem. Show Coalition, 1988—; mem. Hollywood (Calif.) Women's Polit. Com., 1987—; mem. U.S. Film Festival Juror; bd. dirs. IFP/West, Artists Rights Found.; trustee Am. Film Inst.; bd. dirs. L.A. Internat. Film Festival, Coral Reef Rsch. Found., Ams. for a Safe Future; mentor Peter Stark Motion Picture Producing Program, Sch. of Cinema-TV, U. of So. Calif., Women in Film Mentor Program. Recipient Spl. Merit award Nat. Assn. Theater Owners, 1986, Stanford-La Entrepreneur of Yr. award Bus. Sch. Alumni L.A., 1990, Fla. Film Festival award, 1994, Women in Film Crystal award, 1998, Ind. Vision award Temucula Film Festival, 2001, Nat. Bd. Rev. Prodr.'s award, 2004, Global Green Millennium award, 2004, Israel Film Festival Visionary award, 2004, Saturn awards, Donald Reed award, 2004; named Prodr. of Yr., Stunt Awards, 2003. Mem. AMPAS (prodr.'s br. exec. com. 1990—, festival grants com.), Am. Film Inst. (trustee 1989—), Americans for a Safe Future (bd. dirs. 1993—), Prodr.'s Guild Am. (bd. dirs.), Women in Film (bd. dirs. 1989-90,2000—), Inst. for Rsch. on Women and Gender (nat. adv. panel 1997—), Feminist Majority, The Ocean Consrvancy, Heal the Bay, Reef Check Internat. Seakeepers Soc., Mulholland Tomorrow, The Trusteeship, Phi Beta Kappa. Avocations: scuba diving, paso fino horses. Office: Valhalla Motion Pictures 8530 Wilshire Blvd Ste 400 Beverly Hills CA 90211

HURD, HEIDI M. law educator, humanities educator, dean; b. Laramie, Wyo., Oct. 19, 1960; d. Carroll Parsons and Jeanne Marie H.; m. Michael S. Moore, Aug. 8, 1987; children: Gillian K.J. and Aidan A. (twins). BA with honors, Queen's U., Kingston, Ont., Can., 1982; MA, Dalhousie U., Halifax, N.S., Can., 1984; JD, U. So. Calif., L.A., 1988, PhD, 1992. Asst. prof. U. Pa. Law Sch., Phila., 1989-94, prof. law and philosophy, 1994—2002, assoc. dean, 1994-96, co-dir. Inst. Law and Philosophy, 1998—2000; Herzog rsch. prof. law U. San Diego, 2000—02; dean, prof. philosophy, David Baum prof. law U. of Ill. Coll. Law, 2002—. Vis. asst. prof. dept. philosophy U. Iowa, Iowa City, 1991-92; vis. prof. law U. Va. Law Sch., Charlottesville, 1997-98. Author: Moral Combat, 1999; contbr. articles to profl. jours. Office: U Illinois College Law Dean Office 504 E Pennsylvania Ave Champaign IL 61820-6909

HURD, MARY K. civil engineer, writer; BSCE, Iowa State U., Ames; postgrad, U. Chgo., U. Mich., U. Ill. Assoc. editor spl. tech. publs. Am. Concrete Inst., 1966-67, staff engr., 1967-76; engr.-writer, cons., 1976-80, 90—; engring. editor Concrete Constrn. Mag., Addison, Ill., 1983-90, editor, 1981-83; pres. engr. publs. Farmington Hills, Mich. Past chmn. bd. dirs. Concrete Improvement Bd. Author: (book) Formwork for Concrete, 1963, 6th edit. 1995; contbr. numerous articles in field to profl. jours. including Constrn. Specifier, Concrete Internat., Jour. Am. Concrete Inst., Internat. Jour. of Ferrocement, Revista IMCYC Mexico, Pub. Works, Concrete Constrn., Concrete Prodr., PCI Jour.; presenter and organizer in field. Recipient Profl. Achievement in Engring. Citation award Iowa State U., 1982, Outstanding Achievement award Concrete Improvement Bd. Detroit, 1990; Named one of 125 Top People of Past 125 Years in Construction Industry. Mem. ASCE (life), Am. Concrete Inst. (hon. mem., past mem. bd. dirs., organizing chmn. com. 124 concrete aesthetics, com. 347 formwork for concrete, past pres. Mich. chpt., Constrn. Practice award 1982, 88, Delmar L. Bloem Disting. Svc. award 1990, Arthur Y. Moy award Mich. chpt. 1994, Henry C. Turner medal 1995); mem. Am. Soc. Concrete Contractors, Precast/Prestressed Concrete Inst. (profl.), The Concrete Soc. (U.K.), Constrn. Writers Assn., Tau Beta Pi, Phi Kappa Phi. Address: 33742 Lyncroft Rd Farmington Hills MI 48331-3647

HURD, RUTH, publishing executive; Publisher The Thomas Register of Am. Mfrs., N.Y.C., 1985—. Office: The Thomas Register 5 Penn Plz Fl 9 New York NY 10001-1810

HURD, VERONICA TEREZ, career officer; b. Lincoln Park, Mich., Aug. 11, 1962; d. James Julius Nelson and Julia Marie Shipp; m. Henry Hurd; children: Henry, Charles. AA, U. Md., 1989; BS, Upper Iowa U., 1995; MS, Ctrl. Mich. U., 1997; postgrad., The Union Inst., 1997—. Enlisted U.S. Army, 1980, advanced through grades to sgt. 1st class, 1983, equal opportunity advisor, 1993-97. Mem. AAUW, NAFE, Profl. Secs. Internat., Nat. Black MBA Assn., Am. Mgmt. Assn., OD Network. Avocations: quilting, sewing, cross stitching, cooking, reading.

HURET, MARILYNN JOYCE, editor; b. N.Y.C., Dec. 05; d. Hyman and Clara (Weinberg) Moskowitz; m. Barry Saul Huret, Feb. 11, 1961; children: Abbey Beth, Eric Alan. BA in Math., Adelphi U., 1961. Tchr. math. Dist. 281, Robbinsdale, Minn., 1974-77; puzzle constructor Marvel Comics,

N.Y.C., 1982-88, Great Puzzle Catalog, N.Y.C., 1982-83; editor, online sysop Crossword Am. LYRIQ Internat., 1995—; editor, Crossword America, puzzle mag. on-line LYRIQ Internat., Divsn. Enteractive, Inc., 1996-98; editor Crossroads Media Group, Inc., Newtown, Conn., 1998—, ptnr. GRM Enterprises; owner X-Word Co., 2003—. Mem. [illegible] County Courier Times, 1993—, editor, developer, constructor Crossroads Media Group, Inc.; computer sci. tchr., coord. Politz Acad., Phila., 1999; mgr. editl. content, editor Crossroads Media Group, Inc. divsn. Katerra, Inc.; editor, content coord. www.atthecrossroads.com.; editor www.garfieldgames.com; instr. computers Morrisville Sr. Svc. Ctr., 2000—; puzzle constructor Soft Disk Electronic Pub., N.Y. Times, Bucks County Courier, Yardley News; presenter in field. Co-author: Crosswords Diagramless Acrostics, Cryptograms for IDG Puzzle Series, Vols. I-V, Crowssword Puzzles for Dummies, IDG Series; contbr. articles to publs.; editor: Crosswrod Puzz.e Am.; mem. editl. bd. Bucks County Courier Times, 2004. Coop. weather observer Sta. WOR-TV, N.Y.C., 1965—71; severe weather spotter NOAA, 1972—77, 1977—79, Racine, Wis., 1980—, Phila., Mt. Holly, NJ; judge Delaware Valley Sci. Fairs, Phila., 1984—; adminstr. David Libr. Am. Revolution, Washington Crossing, Pa., 1988—95; dep. coord. emergency mgmt. Lower Makefield Twp., Pa., 1989—; bd. dirs. Delaware Valley Philharm. Orch., mem. season planning com.; guild mem. Newton (Pa.) Symphony; mem. MACA, 1997—; commr. pub. safety City of Golden Valley, Minn., 1972—77. Recipient Svc. award, Golden Valley City Coun., 1977. Mem.: AAUW (editor Makefield Area Connections 1993—96, organizer puzzle tournaments, Named Gift award 1994, Outstanding Woman of Yr. Makefield area 1995), LWV, Lower Bucks Computer Users Group, Bucks County Librs. Assn., Nat. Puzzlers League, Am. Women in Computing, Am. Cryptogram Assn., Spl. Libr. Assn. (assoc.), Spiffy's Gang, Toastmasters, Adelphi U. Alumni Assn. Home: 484 Kings Rd Yardley PA 19067-4652 Office: GRM Enterprises Box 544 Yardley PA 19067 Business E-Mail: puzzles@garfieldgames.com. E-mail: mhuret@mindspring.com.

HURFORD, CAROL, retired lawyer; b. Friedensburg, Pa., Sept. 30, 1940; d. Harvey Sydney and Ada Aldine (Lengle) Zerbe; m. John Boyce Hurford, Sept. 16, 1961 (div. 1975); m. Thomas W. McEnerney, Dec. 28, 1984. BA, UCLA, 1963; JD, Rutgers U., 1975. Bar: N.Y. 1976. Assoc. Breed, Abbott & Morgan, N.Y.C., 1975-78, Reavis & McGrath, N.Y.C., 1978-84; ptnr. Munves, Tannenhaus & Storch, N.Y.C., 1984-90. Editor Rutgers U. Law Rev. Pres. West Brooklyn Ind. Dems., 1970; bd. dirs. Ballet Tech. Found., Inc., N.Y.C., 1994—. Mem. LWV (chair voter svc. New Castle chpt. 1993-96, v.p. 1994-96, pres. 1996-98, bd. dirs. 1999—, bd. dirs. Chappaqua summer scholarship program 1991—). Democrat. Avocations: travel, reading, skiing, cycling. Home: 49 Marcourt Dr Chappaqua NY 10514-2506

HURLBURT, ANNE WEDEWER, municipal official; b. Dubuque, Iowa, June 17, 1956; d. Walter Francis and Mildred Theresa (Meyer) Wedewer; m. Steve Arthur Hurlburt, Aug. 20, 1977. BS in Urban Planning, Iowa State U., 1978. Planner City of Cottage Grove (Minn.), 1979-82, dir. planning, 1982-88; mgr. comprehensive planning and local assistance Met. Coun. of the Twin Cities, St. Paul, Minn., 1988-93; cmty. devel. dir. City of Plymouth (Minn.), 1993—. Bd. dirs. Sensible Land Use Coalition, Mpls., 1989-97, v.p., 1995-97. Treas. Cottage Grove Jaycees, 1986, 87. Mem. Am. Inst. Cert. Planners, Am. Planning Assn. Office: City of Plymouth 3400 Plymouth Blvd Plymouth MN 55447-1482

HURLBUT, GERALDINE, retired elementary education educator; b. Lima, Ohio, Apr. 3, 1933; d. Maurice and Sadye (Keeley) Owens; m. Willis Hurlbut, Sept. 17, 1955 (dec.); children: Bill, Mary, John (dec.). BA, Barat Coll, Lake Forest, Ill., 1955. Cert. elem. tchr., Ill. Tchr. 5th grade Nelson Sch., East Maine Sch. Dist. 63, Niles, Ill., 1971-87, tchr. 2d grade, 1987—, ret., 2001. Past team leader 5th grade Nelson Sch.

HURLEY, ALLISON RUTH, mentor coach specialist; b. Escanaba, Mich., Nov. 2, 1961; d. Paula Ann and Donald Faye Marvic(Stepfather). BS in Edn., Marian Coll. of Fond du Lac, Wis., 1986. Site dir. YMCA of Greater Sacramento, 1988—91; practicum/placement coord. Calif. Nanny Coll., Sacramento, 1991—92; resource and referral counselor Child Action, Inc., Sacramento, 1997; early head start program mgr. Calif. Human Devel. Corp. Head Start/Early Head Start for Yolo County, Woodland, 1999—2003; mentor coach specialist Devel. Assocs., Inc., Walnut Creek, Calif., 2003—; exec. dir. First Bapt. Head Start, Pittsburg, Calif., 2003—. Edn. specialist Calif. Human Devel. Corp. Head Start for Yolo County, Woodland, Calif., 1997—99. Mem.: NAFE, AAUW (treas. 1986—87), Calif. Head Start Assn., Infant Devel. Assn. (bd. dirs. 2001), Nat. Head Start (assoc.). Office: First Bapt Head Start 2240 Gladstone Dr Ste 5 Pittsburg CA 94565

HURLEY, CHERYL JOYCE, book publishing executive; b. Pitts., Oct. 30, 1947; d. John and Violet der Norsek; m. Kevin Hurley, July 27, 1974. Lang. and lit. cert., Université de Lyon, France, 1968; AB, Ohio U., 1969; MA, U. Mich., 1971. Research assoc. MLA, N.Y.C., 1972-74, dir. spl. programs, 1974-79; pub. The Library of America, N.Y.C., 1979—88, pres., 1988—. Cons. in field. Contbr. articles to profl. jours. Trustee French Inst./Alliance Francaise, 1992—, v.p., exec. com., 1994—, chmn. libr. com., 1996—; adv. com. N.Y. 100 Centennial, 1997-98; mem. humanities adv. coun. N.Y. Pub. Libr., 1996—; trustee Samuel H. Kress Found., 1999—; mem. dean's adv. bd. Rackham Grad. Sch. U. Mich., 2000-. Rackham fellow, 1969—70. Mem.: Assn. Internationale de Bibliophilie, Am. Antiquarian Soc. (councillor 1999—), Bridgehampton Club, Colony Club, Grolier Club, Century Assn., Phi Beta Kappa. Home: 1172 Park Ave New York NY 10128-1213 Office: Libr of Am 14 E 60th St New York NY 10022-1006

HURLEY, ELIZABETH, actress, model, film producer; b. Hampshire, Eng., June 10, 1965; m. Hugh Grant. Student, London Studio Ctr. Head devel. Simian Films, London and L.A., 1994—; model, cosmetic rep. Estee Lauder. Actress appearing in TV programs and movies including (films) Die Tote Stadt, 1987, Rowing with the Wind, 1988, Bloody Atlantic, 1991, The Orchid House, 1991, Passenger 57, 1992, El Largo Invierno, 1992, Beyond Bedlam, 1993, Goldeneye, 1995, Mad Dogs and Englishmen, Austin Powers: International Man of Mystery, 1997, (TV movies) The Shamrock Conspiracy, 1995, Samson and Delilah, 1996, Permanent Midnight, 1998, Edtv, 1999, My Favorite Martian, 1999, Austin Powers: The Spy Who Shagged Me, 1999, The Weight of Water, 2000, Bedazzled, 2000, Servicing Sarah, 2002, (TV series) Cristabel, 1989, Rumpole and the Barrow boy, 1989, Sharpe II, 1995; host (TV spl.) The World of James Bond, 1995; prodr. Mickey Blue Eyes, 1999. Office: Creative Artists Agy 9830 Wilshire Blvd Beverly Hills CA 90212-1804

HURLEY, JANET LEE, university health service administrator; b. Schenectady, N.Y., Sept. 8, 1948; m. Harry Spencer Turner; children: Scott Ashley, Jeffrey Douglas. BS, Miami U., Oxford, Ohio, 1970; MS, Kansas State U., 1980; PhD, U. Ky., 1993. Tchr. Lafayette Elem. Sch., Norfolk, Va., 1970-72, Roberts Pk. Elem. Sch., Norfolk, 1972-74, Westford (Vt.) Village Sch., 1974-76; coord. Univ. of Mid-Am. Kansas State U., Manhattan, 1978-80, coord. spl. projects, 1980-81, specialist continuing edn., 1981-85; assoc. dean continuing edn. U. Ky., Lexington, 1985-93, adminstr. univ. health svc., 1993—. Editor: History and Practice of College Health, 2002. Bd. dirs. YWCA, Lexington, 1995-98, Coll. of the Finger Lakes, Corning, N.Y., 1991-97, Tates Creek Band Boosters, Lexington, 1994, 95, 96. Fellow Am. Coll. Health Assn.; mem. Nat. Univ. Continuing Edn. Assn. (Program of Excellence award 1987, 92, Robertson Leadership award 1988, Advancing the Profession award 1992). Office: U Ky Univ Health Svc B-163 Ky Clinic Lexington KY 40536-0001 E-mail: jhurley@uky.edu.

HURST, DEBORAH, pediatric hematologist; b. Washington, May 9, 1946; d. Willard and Frances (Wilson) H.; m. Stephen Mershon Senter, June 14, 1970; children: Carlin, Daniel. BA, Harvard U., 1968; MD, Med. Coll. Pa., 1974. Diplomate Nat. Bd. Med. Examiners, Am. Bd. Pediatrics, Am. [illegible] N.Y.C., 1974-75, resident in pediatrics, 1975-76; ambulatory pediatric fellow Bellevue Hosp., N.Y.C., 1976-77; hematology, oncology fellow Bellevue Hosp., Columbia U., N.Y.C., 1977-80; assoc. hematologist Childrens Hosp. Oakland, Calif., 1980-92; asst. clin. prof. U. Calif. San Francisco Med. Ctr., 1992—; med. dir. Bayer Corp., Berkeley, Calif., 1992-98; sr. dir. clin. devel. Chiron Corp., Emeryville, Calif., 1998—. Hematology cons. Assn. Asian/Pacific Community Health Orgns., Oakland; dir. Satellite Hematology Clinic/Valley Childrens Hosp., Fresno, Calif., 1984-92; cons. state dept. epidemiology Calif. State Dept. Health, Berkeley, 1992; chelation cons. lead poisoning program Childrens Hosp., Oakland, 1986-92. Contbr. articles to profl. jours. Vol. cons. lead poisoning State Dept. Epidemiology and Toxicology, Berkeley, 1986-92. Fellow Am. Acad. Pediatrics; mem. Am. Soc. Hematology, Am. Soc. Gene Therapy, Am. Soc. Clin. Oncology, Am. Soc. Pediat. Hematology/Oncology, Nat. Hemophilia Found., Internat. Soc. Thrombosis and Hemostasis. Office: Chiron Corp 4560 Horton St MS120 Emeryville CA 94608-2900

HURST, LAURENDA LEE, library director, music educator; b. Muncie, Ind., Aug. 31, 1948; d. Martin Lewis Hurst, Retta Mae Hurst; m. Schuyler Townsend (div. Mar. 4, 1991); children: Schuyler Muench Townsend, Rebecca Lee Townsend McDole. BSc, Ball State U., 1992; MLS, Ind. U., 1996. Cert. tchr. Ind., 1992. Clk. Greentown Pub. Libr., Greentown, Ind., 1979—87, asst. dir., 1987—99, Tipton County Pub. Libr., Tipton, Ind., 1999—; pvt. music instr. Hurst Music Studio, Greentown, Ind., 1973—. Author: (plays) Greentown Once Upon a Time, 1998. Sec. Greentown Area Residents Assn., Greentown, 1999—2002; mem. Greentown Area Bus. Assn., Greentown, 1999—2002; pres. Ea. Parent Tchr. Orgn., Greentown, 1979—84; bd. dir. Ea.Howard Performing Arts Assn., Greentown, 2000—03. Grantee, Tipton Cmty. Found., 2000, 2002, Build Ind. grant, State of Ind., 2000, Am. Libr. Assn., 2001. Mem.: Ind. Libr.Fedn. (district II sec., treas. 1995—2003), Kokomo Morning Musicale (pres. 1985—87), Greentown Lion's Club, Tipton Rotary Club (cmty. resource chmn. 2001—02). Avocations: musical theater, live concerts, reading. Home: 802 East Hall Street Greentown IN 46936 Office: Tipton County Public Library 127 East Madison Street Tipton IN 46072 Business E-Mail: rhurst@tiptonpl.lib.in.us.

HURST, MARY JANE, English language educator; b. Hamilton, Ohio, Sept. 21, 1952; d. Nimrod and Leckie Gaines; m. Daniel L. Hurst, June 5, 1974; 1 child, Katherine Jane. BA summa cum laude, Miami U., 1974; MA, U. Md., 1980, PhD, 1986. Tchr. Groveport (Ohio) H.S., 1974-77; tchg. asst. U. Md., College Park, 1978-79, master tchr., 1979-82; asst. prof. English, Tex. Tech U., Lubbock, 1986-92, assoc. prof., 1992-99, prof., 1999—, assoc. dean Coll. Arts and Scis., 2000—. Vis. scholar Stanford U., summer 1987; steering com. Nat. Cowboy Symposium, Lubbock, 1988-89. Author: The Voice of the Child in American Literature, 1990; tech. editor: HTLV-I and the Nervous System, 1989; book rev. editor S.W. Jour. Linguistics, 1995-98; contbr. articles to profl. jours. Active Lubbock Cultural Affairs Coun., 1986-92, Lubbock Symphony Guild, 1992—; vol. Meals on Wheel, Lubbock, 1986-97, Habitat for Humanity, Lubbock, 1986-97, Interfaith Hospitality Network, 1998—. Mem.: MLA, AAUP (regional v.p. 1990—94), AAUW (alt. fellowships panel in linguistics 1988—90), South Ctrl. MLA, Coll. Tchrs. English Tex., Linguistic Assn. S.W. (pres. 1996—97, exec. dir. 1998—2001), Linguistic Soc. Am., Phi Beta Kappa, Alpha Lambda Delta, Sigma Tau Delta, Phi Kappa Phi. Avocations: geneaology, travel, west highland white terriers. Office: Tex Tech U Dept English Lubbock TX 79409

HURST, REBECCA MCNABB, language educator; b. Lynchburg, Va., July 17, 1951; d. Eugene Randolph and Lucy Margurite McNabb; m. Larry Lee Hurst, June 26, 1971; children: Monica Hurst Ferrebee, Meredith Hurst Mabe. MEd in Ednl. Adminstrn., William And Mary, Williamsburg, Va, 1988. Cert. post grad. profl. Va., 1988, nat. bd. cert. tchr., cert. in adolescent/young adult English/lang. arts. Tchr. Menchville HS, Newport News, Va., 1986—99; lead HS tchr. Enterprise Acad., 1999—. Devel. assets coord. Enterprise Acad., Newport News, Va., 2001—, sch. improvement team, 2000—, sch. newspaper founder and sponsor, 2000—. Founding mem. Nat. Campaign For Tolerance, Montgomery, Ala., 2000—03. Recipient Outstanding Youth Adv. award, Greater Peninsula Workplace Devel. Consortium, 2002. Mem.: NEA, Va. Assn. Teachers Of English, Nat. Coun. Tchrs. of English, Newport News Edn. Assn., Va. Edn. Assn., Assn. Supervision and Curriculum Devel. Office: Enterprise Acad Ste 110 813 Diligence Dr Newport News VA 23606 Office Phone: 757-591-4971. E-mail: becky.hurst@nn.k12.va.us.

HURST, SUSAN HENTHORN, music educator; d. Robert and Barbara Searle Henthorn; m. Foy Floyd Hurst, June 21, 1980; children: Rebecca, Katherine. MusB Edn., U. of Okla., Norman, Okla., 1973—77. Band dir. Picher-Cardin Pub. Schools, Picher, Okla., 1977—78; band and choral dir. Marlow Mid. Sch., Marlow, Okla., 1978—79; band dir. and music tchr. Temple Pub. Schools, Temple, Okla., 1979—88; lead teacher-pre-kindergarten First Christian Ch. Child Care Ctr., Edmond, Okla., 1988—90; musical dir. Okla. City Jr. Symphony, Okla. City, 1989—91; band and choral dir. Harding Mid. Sch., Okla. City, 1990—99; asst. band dir. John Marshall H.S., Oklahoma City, 1999—; band and orch. dir. Harding Mid. Sch., Oklahoma City, 2002—, band dir., 1999—2002. Dir., emerging spirits vocal ensemble First Christian Ch., Edmond, Okla., 1998—, dir., chancel ringers handbell choir, 2002—, dir., children's music ensembles, 1992—; dir. of children's activities Mt. Sequoyah Ecumenical Conf. on Missions, Fayetteville, Ark., 1993—. Arranger (concert music) We Three Kings; composer: (concert march) Procession of Eagles. Moderator First Christian Ch. Music Ministry Com., Edmond, Okla., 2001—02. Recipient All-State Orch., Okla. Music Educators Assn., 1973, Nat. Honor Soc. mem., Nat. Honor Soc., 1970—73, Okla. Honor Soc. mem., Okla. Honor Soc., 1970—73; scholar Music Scholarship, U. of Okla., 1976—77. Mem.: Am. Fedn. of Teachers, Ctrl. Okla. Directors Assn., Chorister's Guild, Ctrl. Okla. Ringers and Directors Handbell Orgn., Am. Guild of English Handbell Ringers, Okla. Music Educators Assn. D-Liberal. Christian Ch.-(Disciples Of Christ). Avocations: computers, music arranging and composing, reading, crocheting, knitting.

HURT, DAVINA THERESA, secondary school educator; b. Yonkers, N.Y., May 11, 1972; d. David Wallace and Sadie Theresa (Jeffries) H. Grad. in vocal music, School of the Arts, 1990; BS, Hampton U., 1995, postgrad.; cert. bus. edn., Nazareth Coll., 1997, MEd, 2001; MEd in Edn. Adminstrn., St. John Fisher Coll., 2003. Student intern IBM, Rochester, 1991; factory worker ITT, Rochester, 1994; contractor Man Power, Rochester, 1992-95; acctg. First Federal S&L, Rochester, N.Y., 1995-97; substitute tchr. Rochester City Sch. Dist., 1998—99; computer tchr. Josh Lofton H.S., Shape Alternative H.S., 2000—01, Edison Tech. Occupational and Ednl. Ctr., 2001—02; tchr. bus. Benjamin Franklin Career Academies, 2002—03. Bd. dirs. Ctr. for Youth Svcs., 1988-90; life mem. Ch. of God and Saints of Christ. Mem. AAUW. Home: 22 Dejonge St Rochester NY 14621-4606

HURWITZ, ELLEN STISKIN, college president, historian; b. Stamford, Conn., May 4, 1942; d. D.O. Bernard and Marjorie (Kanter) Stiskin; children: Jason, Sarah. BA, Smith Coll., 1964; MA, Columbia U., 1965, PhD, 1972. Vis. asst. prof. Wesleyan U., Middletown, Conn., 1972-73; asst. prof. Lafayette Coll., Easton, Pa., 1974-80, assoc. prof., assoc. dean, 1980-88; dean acad. affairs Ill. Wesleyan U., Bloomington, 1988-89, provost, dean of faculty, 1989-92; pres. Albright Coll., Reading, Pa., 1992—99. Cons. Nat. Faculty Arts and Scis., Inst. for Ednl. Mgmt., Harvard U., 1990. Author: Andrej Bogoljubskij: Man and Myth, 1972. NEH fellow, 1973-74. Mem. AAAS, Am. Assn. Higher Edn., Phi Beta Kappa. Avocations: tennis, art and book collecting, gardening. Office: Albright Coll PO Box 15234 Reading PA 19612 5234

HURWITZ, JOHANNA (JOHANNA FRANK), writer; b. N.Y.C., Oct. 9, 1937; d. Nelson and Tillie (Miller) Frank; m. Uri Hurwitz, Feb. 19, 1962; children: Nomi, Beni. BA, Queens Coll., 1958; MLS, Columbia U., 1959. Libr. children's sect. N.Y. Pub. Libr., 1959-64; lectr. in children's lit. Queen's Coll., N.Y.C., 1965-69; libr. Calhoun Sch., N.Y.C., 1968-75, New Hyde Park (N.Y.) Sch. Dist., 1975-77; libr. children's sect. Great Neck (N.Y.) Pub. Libr., 1978-92. Author: Busybody Nora, 1976, Nora and Mrs. Mind-Your-Own-Business, 1977, The Law of Gravity, 1978, Much Ado About Aldo, 1978, Aldo Applesauce, 1979, New Neighbours for Nora, 1979, Once I Was a Plum Tree, 1980, Superduper Teddy, 1980, Aldo Ice Cream, 1981, Baseball Fever, 1981, The Rabbi's Girls, 1982, Tough-Luck Karen, 1982, Rip-Roaring Russell, 1983, DeDe Takes Charge!, 1984, The Hot and Cold Summer, 1984, The Adventures of Ali Baba Bernstein, 1985, Russell Rides Again, 1985, Hurricane Elaine, 1986, Yellow Blue Jay, 1986, Class Clown, 1987, Russell Sprouts, 1987, The Cold and Hot Winter, 1988, Teacher's Pet, 1988, Anne Frank: Life in Hiding, 1988, Hurray for Ali Baba Bernstein, 1989, Russell and Elisa, 1989, Astrid Lindgren: Storyteller to the World, 1989, Class President, 1990, Aldo Peanut Butter, 1990, School's Out, 1991, E Is for Elisa, 1991, Roz and Ozzie, 1992, Ali Baba Bernstein, Lost and Found, 1992, The Up and Down Spring, 1993, Make Room for Elisa, 1993, Leonard Bernstein: A Passion for Music, 1993, New Shoes for Silvia, 1993, A Word to the Wise, 1994, School Spirit, 1994, A Llama in the Family, 1994, Ozzie on His Own, 1995, Birthday Surprises, 1995, Elisa in the Middle, 1995. Even Stephen, Down and Up Fall, 1996—, Spring Break, 1997, Ever-Clever Elisa, 1997, Helen Keller: Courage in the Dark, 1997, Faraway Summer, 1998, Starting School, 1998, A Dream Come True, 1998, Llama in the Library, 1999, Just Desserts Club, 1999, Summer with Elisa, 2000, Peewee's Tale, 2000, One Small Dog, 2000, Lexi's Tale, 2001, Russell's Secret, 2001, Oh No, Noah!, 2002, PeeWee & Plush, 2002, Dear Emma, 2002, Ethan, Out & About, 2002, Ethan at Home, 2003, Elisa Michaels, Bigger and Better, 2003, Fourth Grade Fuss, 2004. Recipient Bluebonnet award Tex. Libr. Assn., 1987, Wyoming Indian Paintbrush award 1987, W.Va. Children's Book award 1989, Sunshine State award Fla. Libr. Assn., 1990, Miss. Children's Book award Miss. Libr. Assn., 1990, S.C. Children's Book award, 1990, Garden State award N.J. Sch. Libr. Assn., 1991, 94, Weekly Reader Book Club award, 1993. Mem. PEN, Author's Guild, Soc. Children's Book Writers, Amnesty Internat. Address: 10 Spruce Pl Great Neck NY 11021-1904

HURWITZ, LINDA, music educator, musician; b. Washington, D.C., Sept. 24, 1960; d. Sol and Nina Hurwitz. BA, Colby Coll., 1982; MM, New Eng. Conservatory, 1985. Cert. tchr. Va. Violinist Portland (Maine) Symphony, 1981—86, Va. Symphony, Norfolk, Va., 1987—; dir. orch. Norfolk (Va.) City Pub. Schs., 1993—94, Va. Beach (Va.) City Pub. Schs., 1995—. Violinist New Orleans (La.) Symphony, 1989—90, Va. Opera, Norfolk, Va., 1987—96; guest condr. All City Orch., Va. Beach, 2002; violinist Grand Teton Music Festival, Jackson, Wyo., 1992—; instr. The Gov.'s Sch., Richmond, Va., 1993, 94. Musician: (albums) Live at Carnegie Hall, 1997, Seascapes, 1999, Shenandoah, 2003. Avocations: tennis, bicycling, skiing, hiking. Home: 545 Warren Crescent Apt 6 Norfolk VA 23507

HURWITZ, SAUNDRA HARRIET (SANDI HURWITZ), analyst, educator; b. Orange, N.J., May 19, 1937; d. Julius Meyer and Laura (Mann) H. BA, Calif. State U., 1958, MPA, 1972. Mgmt. specialist II City of L.A. Cmty. Devel. Dept., 1976-95; prin. devel. specialist County of L.A. Cmty. Devel. Commn., L.A., 1991-95; contract specialist L.A. Homeless Svcs. Authority, 1995-96; prof. Calif. State U., L.A., 1978—. Cons. SH & Assocs., 1997—. Chair Cmty. Devel. Commn., Monterey Park, Calif., 1985-94; bd. dirs. Plz. Cmty. Ctr., L.A., 1997—. Recipient Youth Achievement award Downtown Businessmen Assn., L.A., 1977, Outstanding Achievement Alumni appreciation Calif. State U. Alumni Assn., 1977. Mem. Am. Soc. Pub. Adminstrn. (bd. dirs.). Avocations: dance, painting, gardening, cooking, crafts, needlework. Home and Office: 3755 San Remo Dr Apt 158 Santa Barbara CA 93105

HURWOOD, REBECCA MAYRE, art association administrator; d. Ted and Bonnie Hurwood. BA in East Asian Studies, Lewis & Clark Coll., 2000. Rsch. asst. alumni rels. Lewis & Clark Coll., Portland, 1998—99, Chinese tutor Chinese dept., 1999—2000; kickboxing instr. One With Heart Martial Arts Inst., Portland, 1999—; tchrs. asst. Woodstock Elem. Chinese Immersion Program, Portland, 2000—00; membership dir., grantseeker Portland Classical Chinese Garden, 2000—. Kickboxing program and mktg. One With Heart Martial Arts Inst., Portland, 2002—03; crystal awards com. Willamette Valley Devel. Officers, Portland, 2003—03; newsletter com. Willamette Valley Devel. Officers, Portland, 2002—02. Mem.: Willamette Valley Devel. Officers, Poekoelan Tjimindie Tulen Assn. Personal E-mail: hurwood00@alumni.lclark.edu.

HUSBAND, JANET GRACE, library director, writer; b. Pitts., July 4, 1942; d. Edward Albert and Gertrude Alice (Keebler) Gray; m. Jonathan Fenton Husband, May 3, 1969; 1 child, Jessica Ann. BA, U. Pitts., 1966; MLS, Rutgers, 1967. Libr. Free Libr. Phila., 1967-70; acquisitions libr. Thomas Crane Pub. Libr., Quincy, Mass., 1973-85; libr. dir. Rockland (Mass.) Meml. Libr., 1985-98, Cohasset (Mass.) Free Libr., 1998—. Author: Sequels: A Guide to Novels in Series, 3d edit. 1997; contbr. articles to profl. jours. Recipient Libr. Trainee scholarship Pa. State Libr. Agy., Harrisburg, 1966. Mem. Am. Libr. Assn., Mass. Libr. Assn. Office: Cohasset Free Library Rockland Meml Library 106 S Main St Cohasset MA 02025-2097 Home: 67 Linnell Landing Rd Brewster MA 02631-1507

HUSEN, AINO MARIA, retired elementary school educator; b. Laurium, Mich., Nov. 15, 1929; d. Antti and Sigria Matilda (Hakola) Lepisto; m. Harold Lester Husen, June 15, 1952 (div. June 1965); children: Paavo Hans, Maria Elizabeth. BS, U. Minn., 1951, MA, 1968; cert., Boston U., 1968. Lic. elem. classroom tchr. Minn. Dept. Edn., cert. elem. remedial reading tchr. Minn. Dept. Edn., reading cons. K-12 Minn. Dept. Edn., ESL Hamline U., 1994. Tchr. 4 gr. Lakefield (Minn.) Pub. Sch., 1951—55; tchr. 4 & 5 gr. Windom (Minn.) Pub. Sch., 1955—56; remedial reading tchr. Minnetonka (Minn.) Pub. Sch., 1961—68, reading cons., 1968—93; ret., 1993. Eng. tchr. Evang. Luth. Ch., Ondangwa, Namibia, 1995—2001. Chair Jackson County Libr. Assn., Minn., 1958—59; co-facilitator WE CARE, Mpls., 1974—79. Mem.: Minn. Acad. Reading. (pres. 1974; 1984), Internat. Reading Assn., NEA, Minn. Reading Assn. (historian 1986—2003, Cert. for Svc. 1975, 2000). Democrat. Lutheran. Avocations: reading, gardening, hiking, travel, music. Home: 2625 Boone Ave S Saint Louis Park MN 55426

HUSER, GERI D. state official; b. Des Moines, Iowa, July 14, 1963; m. Dan Huser. BA, Briar Cliff Coll., 1985. Social worker Polk County Gen. Relief, 1986—90; program mgr. Polk County Family Enrichment Ctr., 1990—96; mem. Met. Planning Orgn., 1990—, Altoona City Coun., 1991—; planning specialist Polk County Social Svcs., 1996—; state rep. Iowa, 1997—. Mem. adminstrn. and rules com.; mem. local govt. com.; mem. transp. com.; mem. ways and means com. Mem. Child Abuse Prevention Coun., 1993—95, Altoona Family Home, 1990—, Greater Des Moines Housing Partnership, 1995—. Mem.: Pleasant Hill C. of C., East Polk Interagy. Assn., S.E. Polk Booster Club. Democrat. Office: State Capitol E 12th and Grand Des Moines IA 50319

HUSMAN, CATHERINE BIGOT, retired insurance company executive, actuary; b. Des Moines, Feb. 10, 1943; d. Edward George and Ruth Margaret (Cumming) Bigot; m. Charles Erwin Husman, Aug. 5, 1967; 1 child, Matthew Edward. BA with highest distinction, U. Iowa, 1965; MA, Ball State U., 1970. Actuarial asst. Am. United Life Ins. Co., Indpls., 1965—68, assoc. actuary, 1971—74, group actuary, 1974—84, v.p., corp. actuary, 1984—97, v.p., chief actuary, 1997—2002; cons., 2002—. Mem. group tech. com. Mut. Life Ins. Co., 1986-98; mem. profitability studies com. Life Office Mgmt. Assn. Inc., 1991-99. Mem. women's adv. com. United Way Cen. Ind., 1991-93; bd. dirs., mem. fin. com., St. Elizabeth's Home, 1991-99, sec., 1994, mem. exec. com., treas., 1995; bd. dirs., mem. adminstrv. svcs., mem. exec. com. Heritage Place, 1993-99, treas., 1995-99; mem. Exec. Svc. Corps, 2002—; docent Pres. Benjamin Harrison Home, 2002—. Fellow Soc. Actuaries; mem. Am. Acad. Actuaries, Actuaries Club Ind., Ky. and Ohio, Actuarial Club Indpls. (pres. 1979-80), Phi Beta Kappa. Republican. Roman Catholic. Avocations: reading, tennis. Home: 1411 N Claridge Way Carmel IN 46032-8333 E-mail: cbhusman@earthlink.net.

HUSS, BONNIE JEAN, intensive cardiac care nurse; b. Nashville, Kans., May 11, 1962; d. Eugene Edward and Betty Marie (Venard) Hauser; 1 child, Jamie Marie Huss; m. Harold Gene Huss, Jul. 3, 1989; 1 child, Skyler Matthew. LPN, Pratt Cmty. Coll., Pratt, Kans., 1983, AS, 1984, A of nursing, 1988; BSN, Newman U., Kans., 1998; MS in Nursing, Ft. Hays State U., 2000. Cert. ACLS. Charge nurse LPN Hilltop Manor, Cunningham, Kans., 1983-88; charge nurse medical surgy Medicine Lodge (Kans.) Meml. Hosp., 1988-91; charge nurse SCU Pratt Regional Medical Ctr., 1991-94. Instr. BLS Red Cross, Pratt, 1993—; ACLS cert. St. Joe, 1993. Mem. Am. Acad. Nurse Practitioners, Ft. Hays Grad. Nursing Assn., Kans. State Nurses Assn., Critical Care Nurses. Democrat. Roman Catholic. Avocations: reading, walking, family, religion. Home: 292 W Broadway Ave Nashville KS 67112-8302

HUSSUNG, ALLEEN MOSETTE, literary agent; b. Sheridan, Mont., July 19, 1934; d. Carl Stanley and Alleen (White) Aune; divorced; children: Carleen Simone, Bill Hussung. Diploma in Voice, Juilliard Sch. Music, 1955. Singer various tours, clubs, TV, film, radio and Broadway prodns., 1955-69; producer Windmill Dinner Theatres, Tex., 1969-70, Candlewood Theatre, New Fairfield, Conn., 1973; agent Samuel French, Inc., N.Y.C., 1974—, lit. agt., head profl. dept. Country Home, Swan Lake, NY, 1974—. Mem. Am. Theatre Actors (bd. dirs. 1977—). Avocations: gardening, boating on private lake, horseback riding. Home: 60 W 68th St New York NY 10023-6020

HUSTED, CHARLENE E. library media specialist, educator; b. Knowles, Okla., Sept. 10, 1930; d. Merle Lester and Bertha Mary Paasch Bond; m. Glenn Ray Husted, Oct. 5, 1947; children: Lester Glenn, Anita Faye Husted Whiteley. BA in Elem. Edn. summa cum laude, Okla. Panhandle State U., 1968; BS in Edn. summa cum laude, libr. media cert., Pittsburg (Kans.) State U., 1975; postgrad. with honors, Cen. State U., Edmond, Okla., 1989, U. Okla., 1989; postgrad., U. Guadalajara, Jalisco, Mex., 1989. Cert. in elem. edn.; cert. libr. media specialist; cert. in Spanish. Tchr. Washington Elem. Sch., Liberal, Kans., 1968-71; libr. media specialist Garrett Elem., Elmwood, Okla., 1971-77; tchr. Southlawn Elem. Sch., Liberal, 1977-80, Buffalo (Okla.) Jr./Sr. H.S., 1981-90; tchr. ESL and citizenship edn. Guymon, Okla., 1991-97; libr. media specialist, tchr. elem. Spanish Forgn (Okla.) H.S., 1995—. Workshop leader, Liberal schs., 1971, Ednl. Dist. Meeting, Woodward, Okla., 1988. Coord. local Heartland Share from Topeka; bd. dirs. Gate Mus. Libr., sec.-treas. Zelma Cemetery; pianist Nazarene Ch., Knowles; mem. Beaver County Nursing Home Aux. Mem. AAUW, NAFE, NEA (v.p., program chair Kans. chpt. 1970-71), Okla. Edn. Assn., Okla. Libr. Media Specialists (pres. 1981-90), Beaver County Edn. Assn., Panhandle State Assn., Knowles Alumni Assn. (com. mem.), Smithsonian Instn., Libr. of Congress Assocs., Nat. Mus. of Women in the Arts. Republican. Avocations: showing horses, reading, traveling. Home: RR 1 Box 165 Gate OK 73844-9617 Office: Forgan Pub Schs PO Box 406 Forgan OK 73938-0406

HUSTON, ANJELICA, actress; b. L.A., July 8, 1951; d. John and Enrica Huston; m. Robert Graham, 1992. Student, Loft Studio. Actress appearing in Hamlet, Roundhouse Theatre, London, Tamara, Il Vittorale Theatre, L.A.; appeared in films including A Walk with Love and Death, 1969, Hamlet, 1969, Sinful Davey, 1969, Swashbuckler, 1976, The Last Tycoon, 1976, The Postman Always Rings Twice, 1981, This is Spinal Tap, 1984, The Ice Pirates, 1984, Prizzi's Honor, 1985 (Academy award for best supporting actress 1985, N.Y.Film Critics award 1985, L.A. Film Critics award 1985), Captain Eo, 1986, Gardens of Stone, 1987, The Dead, 1987 (Best Actress award Ind. Filmakers 1987), Mr. North, 1988, A Handfull of Dust, 1988, Witches, 1989, Crimes and Misdemeanors, 1989, Enemies, A Love Story, 1989 (Acad. award nomination 1990), The Grifters, 1990 (Acad. award nomination 1991), The Addams Family, 1991, The Player, 1992, Addams Family Values, 1993, Manhattan Murder Mystery, 1993, The Crossing Guard, 1995, The Perez Family, 1995, Buffalo '66, 1997, Phoenix, 1998, Ever After, 1998, Breakers, 1999, Agnes Browne, 1999; TV films include the Cowboy and the Ballerina, 1984, Faerie Tale Theatre, A Rose for Miss Emily, Lonesome Dove, 1989, Family Pictures, 1993, And The Band Played On, 1993, Buffalo Girls, 1995; dir. Bastard Out of Carolina, 1996, Agnes Browne, 1999; TV guest appearances Laverne & Shirley, 1976, Inside the Actors Studio, 1994. Office: Internat Creative Mgmt c/o Toni Howard 8942 Wilshire Blvd Beverly Hills CA 90211-1934

HUSTON, DEVERILLE ANNE, lawyer; b. Great Falls, Mont., Mar. 2, 1947; d. Orion Joseph and Beverly Rosemary (Mower) H. BA, U. Minn., 1969; JD, William Mitchell Coll. Law, 1975. Bar: Minn. 1975, Ill. 1976, U.S. Dist. Ct. (no. dist.) Ill. 1976). Assoc. Sidley & Austin, Chgo., 1977-83, ptnr., 1983—. Fellow Am. Bar Found.; mem. ABA, Chgo. Bar Assn., Chgo. Fin. Exch., Law Club. Office: Sidley & Austin Bank One Plz 425 W Surf St Apt 605 Chicago IL 60657-6139

HUSTON, JOAN BONFIGLIO, psychotherapist; b. Jamestown, N.Y., Mar. 19, 1948; d. James Sebastian and Cora (Lombardo) Bonfiglio; m. Dale Edward Huston, Apr. 28, 1973; children: Tara Huston-Carlson, Lana. BA, SUNY, Fredonia, 1970, MA, 1974; PhD, Calif. Coast U., 1987. Cert. counselor Am. Counseling Assn., hypnotherapist Am. Bd. Hypnotherapy. Tchr. psychology Jamestown H.S., 1970—2003; pvt. practice psychotherapy, 1990—; ret. Jamestown H.S., 2003. Mem.: NEA, N.Am. Assn. Masters Psychology. Republican. Roman Catholic. Avocations: writing, playing piano, computers.

HUSTON, JOYCE A. web site design company executive; d. Loyce Pickens Huston and Herman Huston, Sr.; m. Z. Lipsky, July 21, 2001. BSBA, U. Redlands, 1988; postgrad., Rockhurst Coll. of Continuing Edn. Ctr., Nev., 2000—. Cert. DreamWeaver 3 The Learning Ctr., Nev., 2000, effective user support ZIFF Inst., Calif., 1993, Cost/Schedule Control Systems Criteria Humphreys & Assocs., Calif., 1991. Trumpeter/vocalist/arranger Albert King Blues Band, St. Louis, 1980—82; word processing specialist TRW, Los Angeles, Calif., 1986—88; pres. UniSun Prodns., Las Vegas, Nev., 1993—; website adminstr./systems analyst U.S. DOE (Bechtel SAIC, TRW, SAIC Contractors), Las Vegas, Nev., 1989—. Website adminstr. U.S. DOE/Bechtel SAIC LLC; Project Controls Systems, Las Vegas, Nev., 1989—; webmaster; nat. spokesperson Las Vegas Fibromyalgia/Chronic Fatigue Syndrome Support Group, Las Vegas, Nev.; music ministry (singer/songwriter/trumpeter) UniSun Prodns., Las Vegas, Nev., 1993—. Prodr.(composer/singer/trumpeter/synthesizers): (CD) Soul Stir Fry; composer: (popular songs) Songs Forever; (Catalog of Music Copyrights); author: (genealogical chronicles) The Black O'Kelleys in America; musician (trumpeter): (jazz album) Howard University Jazz Ensemble; entertainer : (Black History Presentations: Remembering the Freedoms) Clark County, Family Found., West Las Vegas Arts Ctr., others; (Black History Month performance accolades Las Vegas rev. jour., 2001, 2004); Shower of Stars, 2000; featured (pub.) Disting. Women So. Nev., 2002, (cover Gospel Gazette), St. Louis, 2003. Recruiter asst. Rainbow Coalition, Washington, D.C., DC, 1982—82; Census 2000 program asst. African Am. Cmty. Coalition of So. Nev., Las Vegas, Nev., 2000—00; mem. P.U.S.H Coalition, St. Louis, 1978—79. Mem.: Las Vegas Songwriters Assn. (assoc.), Las Vegas Fibromyalgia/Chronic Fatigue Syndrome Support Group (bd. mem., webmaster, nat. spokesperson 2000—), Nat. Spiritualist Assn. of Churches (assoc.). Democrat. Spiritualist. Achievements include research in Descendants of the slave Ellen-O'Kelley-Mathews-Fisher; Front Trumpeter in the Music Man with Tony Randall at the Municipal Opera House, St. Louis, 1978; Appeared on ABC, CBS, NBC (news), and Clark County, Las Vegas affiliate T.V. shows as performer, 2000 - 2003; Featured on cover of the Henderson Home News, 2001; Featured in Las Vegas Sun article, The Unseen Agony, 1997; Feature story in the Las Vegas What's On magazine, 2002; Performed on the Maintenance Shop Blues nationally syndicated T.V. show with Albert King, 1983; Performed at the Henderson Interfaith Coalition's Dr. M.L. King Jr. Observance, 2002, 2003; Performed in Las Vegas with Bill Pinkney and the Original Drifters, 1992; Debuted one-woman show at the Fitzgerald's Hotel & Casino, Las Vegas, 1997; Featured on Radio interviews on KLAV 1230AM, Las Vegas, 2004. Avocations: genealogy, computers, music, reading, swimming. Office: UniSun Productions 2375 E Tropicana Ave #353 Las Vegas NV 89119 Office Phone: 702-860-6006. Personal E-mail: thelady@msjoyce.com.

HUSTON, KATHLEEN MARIE, library administrator; b. Sparta, Wis., Jan. 7, 1944; BA, Edgewood Coll., 1966; MLS, U. Wis., Madison, 1969. Libr. Milw. Pub. Libr., 1969-90; city libr. Milw. Pub. Libr. System, 1991—. Office: Milwaukee Pub Libr 814 W Wisconsin Ave Milwaukee WI 53233-2309

HUSTON, MARGO, journalist; b. Waukesha, Wis., Feb. 12, 1943; d. James and Cecile (Timlin) Bremner; m. James Huston, Dec. 9, 1967 (div.); 1 son, Sean Patrick. AB in Journalism, Marquette U., 1965; Certificate in Muslim-Christian Dialogue, 2004. Editl. asst. Marquette U., Milw., 1965-66; feature editor, reporter Waukesha Freeman, 1966-67; feature reporter Milw. Jour., 1967-70, reporter Spectrum, women's and food sects., 1972-79, editl. writer, 1979-84, polit. reporter, 1984—, asst. picture editor, 1985-91, copy editor, 1992-95; reporter Milw. Jour Sentinel (merger Milw. Jour. and The Sentinel), 1995-99; mem. working bd. Cath. Herald, 2000—01; freelance journalist Milw., 2001—. Instr. mass comm. U. Wis., Milw. Recipient Penney-Mo. award for consumer abortion series, 1977, Pulitzer Prize for investigation into plight of elderly, 1977, Clarion award, 1977, Knight of Golden Quill award, Milw. Press club, 1977, Wis. AP writing award, 1977, Spl. award Milw. Soc. Profl. Journalists, 1977, Penney Mo. Paul Myhre award for excellence, 1978, By-Line award Marquette U. Coll. Journalism, 1980, Wis. UPI Best Editl. award, 1982, Wis. Women's Network award for journalist achievement for women's issues, 1983, Dick Goldensohn Fund award, 1991, 1st place award for investigative reporting Inland Press Assn., 1997, 98, 2d award Enterprise interpretive reporting Wis. Newspaper Assn., 1998; Wis. Arts Bd. Lit. Arts grantee, 1992. Mem. European Project for Interreligious Learning (cert. in Muslim-Christian Dialogue 2004), Milw. Press Club (Hall of Fame 2000). E-mail: mhuston@wi.rr.com.

HUSZAI, KRISTY RENEE, insurance agent; b. Pensacola, Fla., May 19, 1974; d. Stephen Edward and Mary Ellen Huszai. Grad. H.S., Gaithersburg, Md. Lic. ins. agt. Md. Sales asst. Paul Revere Ins., Rockville, Md., 1993—97; sec. CompDesign, Bethesda, Md., 1997—98; sr. account asst. Mut. Omaha, Washington, 1998—. Republican. Roman Catholic. Avocations: reading, travel, sports.

HUTCHENS, GAIL R. chemist; b. Bentonville, Ark., Aug. 22, 1938; d. Sidney Baxter and Mary Dena Maurine (Harral) Rakes; m. Charles Verlin Hutchens, Mar. 4, 1967 (dec. 2002); children: David Charles, Kimberly Gail. Student, Ark. State Tchrs. Coll., 1955—58; grad., U. Tenn., 1961. Exec. v.p. Galbraith Labs., Inc., Knoxville, Tenn., 1959—93; analytical svcs. supr. Materials Engring. & Testing, Oak Ridge, Tenn., 1993—96, Techmer PM, LLC, Clinton, Tenn., 1996—. Emergency first responder instr. Video editor Democrates, Knoxville, TN, 1998. Mem. ASTM, Assn. Offcl. Analytical Chemists, Soc. Plastic Engrs. (local sect. sec. 2002-2004), Am. Chem. Soc., Crestwood Hills Garden Club (pres. 1968-69), Small Chem. Bus. (sec. 1974-75), Beta Club Honor Soc., Alpha Chi. Avocation: diving instruction. Office: Techmer PM LLC 1 Quality Cir Clinton TN 37716-4017 Office Phone: 865-457-6700. Business E-Mail: ghutchens@Techmerpm.com.

HUTCHEON, BARBARA SILVER, lawyer; b. Elmer, N.J., Aug. 23, 1954; d. Milton Love and Barbara Hall Silver; m. Peter David Hutcheon, Feb. 14, 1986; 1 child, Peter Silver. BA, Rutgers U., 1976; JD, Widener U., 1980. Law clk. Superior Ct. N.J., Woodbury, 1980—81; assoc. Weber & Marcus, P.A., Woodbury, 1981—82; staff atty. N.J. State Bar Assn., Trenton, 1982—84; assoc. legis. counsel N.J. Office Legis. Svcs.-Judiciary Sect., Trenton, 1984—88; asst. counsel Office of Counsel to the Gov., Trenton, 1988—90; chief counsel N.J. Gen. Assembly, Trenton, 1992—98; asst. atty. gen., dir. policy and legis. affairs N.J. Dept. Law and Pub. Safety, Trenton, 2002—03, asst. atty. gen., counsel to the atty. gen., 2003; of counsel Wolff & Samson, P.C., West Orange, NJ, 2003—. Active Somerset County (N.J.) Mental Health Bd., Somerville, 1997—2002. Mem.: DAR (Camp Middlebrook Chpt.). Republican. Presbyterian. Avocations: cooking, reading, gardening. Office: Wolff & Samson PC One Boland Dr West Orange NJ 07052

HUTCHEON, LINDA ANN, English language educator; b. Toronto, Aug. 24, 1947; d. Vincent Roy and Elisa (Rossi) Bulfon Bortolotti; m. Michael Alexander Hutcheon, May 30, 1970. BA, U. Toronto, 1969, PhD, 1975; MA, Cornell U., 1971. Prof. McMaster U., Hamilton, Ont., Can., 1976-88, U. Toronto, 1988—95, 1995—. Vis. prof. U. Toronto, 1980-81, 81-82, 84-85, U. Wis., Madison, 1995, U. Ga., 1998, U. Queensland, Australia, 2001, U. Mich. Inst. for the Humanities, 2003. Author: Narcissic Narrative, 1980 (choice award, 1980), Formalism and the Freudian Aesthetic, 1984, A Theory of Parody, 1985, 2000, A Poetics of Postmodernism, 1988, The Canadian Postmodern, 1988, The Politics of Postmodernism, 1989, 2002, Splitting Images, 1991, Irony's Edge, 1995; author: (with M. Hutcheon) Opera: Desire, Disease, Death, 1996, Bodily Charm: Living Opera, 2000, Opera: The Art of Dying, 2004; assoc. editor: RS/SI, 1982—84, U. Toronto Quar., 1993—; mem. (editl. bd.) Texte, Toronto, 1983—, English Studies in Can., 1984—94, Italian Canadiana, 1984—, Textual Practice, 1987—2003, Can. Rev. Comparative Lit., 1987—, Can. Poetry, 1987—93, PMLA, 1990—92, Essays on Can. Writing, 1992—, Contemporary Lit., 1992—, Modern Fiction Studies, 1993—, CLIO, 1994—, Parallax (U.K.), 1994—. Woodrow Wilson Found. fellow, 1969, Social Scis. and Humanities Rsch. Coun. Can. fellow, 1983, 93-95, 96-99, 2000-2003, co-fellow maj. collaborative rsch. initiatives, 1996-2000; Can. Coun. fellow, 1972-75, Killam Found. fellow, 1978-80, 86-88, Connaught fellow, 1991-92, Guggenheim fellow, 1992-93. Fellow Am. Acad. Arts and Scis.; mem. MLA (del. assembly 1985-88, exec. coun. 1992-96, 2d v.p. 1998, 1st v.p. 1999, pres. 2000), AAAS (elected), Assn. Can. Coll. and Univ. Tchrs. English (exec. mem. 1978-81), Can. Comparative Lit. Assn. (sec.-treas. 1981-83), Internat. Comparative Lit. Assn. (coord. com. lit. history 1992-97).

HUTCHERSON, DONNA DEAN, retired music educator; b. Dallas, July 10, 1937; d. Lamar Shaffer and Lenora Fay (Newbern) Clark; m. George Henry Hutcherson, Jan. 31, 1959; children: Lamar, Michael, Mark Lee, Holly (dec.), Shela. B. Music Edn., Sam Houston State U., Huntsville, Tex., 1959; MA in Music, Stephen F. Austin State U., Nacogdoches, Tex., 1974; postgrad., Memphis State U., 1986-89. Cert. tchr. music K-12, Orff levels 1, 2, 3, Master, cert. computer literacy, Tex. Tchr. music 4th and 5th grades Carthage (Tex.) Ind. Sch. Dist., 1958-59; tchr. music grades 1-5 and H.S. choir Hallsville (Tex.) Ind. Sch. Dist., 1969-75, tchr. music K-4, 1975-78, tchr. music grades 3-4, 1978-86, tchr. music 4th grade, 1986-97; ret., 1997. Contbr. Jour. of Music Edn. Delegation to Vietnam Citizen Ambassador Program, 1993; chmn. Tex. Ann. Conf. United Meth. Ch. Commn. on Archives/History. Contbr. articles to profl. jours. Fellow United Meth. Musicians in Worship and Other Arts; mem. Music Educators Nat. Conf. (registered music educator), Tex. Music Educators Conf. (state Tri-M chmn. 1993-98), Tex. Music Educators Assn. (region IV chmn. 1975-93), Am. Orff Schulewerk Assn., Tri M Internat. Music Honor Soc. (local chpt. sponsor 1992—, hon. mem.). Methodist. Avocations: square dancing, sewing, travel, church work, summer mission trips. Home: 119 Mcpherson Rd Hallsville TX 75650-7707 E-mail: ddhutch@juno.com.

HUTCHERSON, RENE RIDENS, medical social services administrator; b. Memphis, Feb. 26, 1944; d. Samuel Haskins Sr. and Arahwana (Hendren) Ridens; 1 child, John Ridens. BA, Vanderbilt U., 1965; MSW, U. Tenn., 1967. Lic. social worker, Colo. Clin. social worker U. Colo. Med. Ctr., 1967-83; dir. med. social svc. dept. U. Colo. Health Scis. Ctr., 1983-90, clin. social worker, 1990—. Contbr. articles to profl. jours. Mem. NASW, Nat. Soc. Hosp. Social Work Dirs., Am. Assn. Continuity of Care, Acad. Cert. Social Workers (cert.), Colo. Soc. Clin. Social Worker (cert., diplomate).

HUTCHIN, NANCY LEE, corporate financial executive; b. Ft. Belvoir, Va., June 16, 1949; d. Walter James and Iyllis Elizabeth (Lee) H.; m. Stephen Lawrence Guiland Nov. 27, 1970 (div. 1983); children: Kai-Long Stephen Guiland, Petra Lee Guiland; m. John Edward Money, Jun. 7, 1986 (div. 1994). BA summa cum laude, U. Md., 1973, MA, 1976. Prin. sci. B-K Dynamics, Rockville, Md., 1978-86; sr. cons. James Martin Assoc., Reston, Va., 1986-88; cons. San Diego, 1989-95; cons. employee SAIC, San Diego, 1993-95, staff cons. Intergraph, Reston, 1995-99; practice mgr., bid and proposal mgr., program mgr. Keane Fed. Sys., Inc., Rockville, Md., 1999—2002; Capture/Alliance mgr. Gen. Dynamics Network Sys., Rockville, 2003—. Contbr. editor Enterprise Reengineering, 1994-96; assoc. pub. Black Riders, 1994-96; program com. Tools & Methods for Bus. Engring. Conf., 1995; mem. program com. Nat. Bus. Process Reengring. Conf., 1996, 98, SDPS Integrated Design and Process Tech. Conf., 1996, 98; bd. dirs. Strategic Info. Mgmt. & Tech. Solutions, Inc., Ogden, Utah, track chair changing human behavior Europe 98 Process and Knowledge Mgmt. Conf., London, 1998; program com. Women Execs. in State Govt. Leadership Conf. 2001, Lake Tahoe, Calif.; presenter in field. Contbr. articles to profl. jours. Pres. and bd. dirs. Exec. Women's Round Table. Mem. Women in Tech. DC chap., Soc. of Info. Mgmt., Soc. Design and Process Sci. Avocations: walking, travel, blues music. E-mail: nancy.hutchin@gd-ns.com.

HUTCHINS, CARLEEN MALEY, acoustical engineer, consultant; b. Springfield, Mass., May 24, 1911; d. Thomas W. and Grace (Fletcher) Maley; m. Morton A. Hutchins, June 6, 1943; children: William Aldrich, Caroline. AB, Cornell U., 1933; MA, NYU, 1942; DEng (hon.), Stevens Inst. Tech., 1977; DFA (hon.), Hamilton Coll., 1984; DSc (hon.), St. Andrews Presbyn. Coll., 1988; LLD (hon.), Concordia U., Montreal, Que., Can., 1992. Tchr. sci. Woodward Sch., Bklyn., 1934-38, Brearley Sch., N.Y.C., 1938-49; asst. dir., asst. prin. All Day Neighborhood Schs., N.Y.C., 1943-45. Sci. cons. Coward McCann, Inc., 1956-65, Girl Scouts Am., 1967-65, Nat. REcreation Assn., 1957-65; permanent sec. Catgut Acoustical Soc., Montclair, N.J., 1962-2000; exec. dir. New Violin Family Assn. Inc., 2000—; hon. cons. Catgut Acoustical Soc., Inc., 2000—; maker violins. Author: Life's Key, DNA, 1961, Moon Moth, 1965, Who Will Drown the Sound, 1972; author (with others). Science Through Recreation, 1964; contbr. violin acoustics sect. Grove's Dictionary of Music and Musicians, 1964, 96; editor: (2 vols.) Musical Acoustics, Part I, Violin Family Components, 1975, Musical Acoustics, Part II, Violin Family Functions, 1976, The Physics of Music, 1978, Research Papers in Violin Acoustics, 1973-94, 96; contbr. articles to profl. jours. in Sci. Am. Jour. of the Acoustical Soc. Am., Jour. Audio Engring. Soc., Physics Today, Am. Viola Soc., Catgut Acoustical Soc. Martha Baird Rockefeller Fund for Music grantee, 1966, 68, 74; Guggenheim fellow, 1959, 61; recipient several spl. citations in music, Carleen Maley Hutchins medal (1st recipient) Catgut Acoustical Soc., Hon. Fellowship award Acoustical Soc. Am., 1998; NSF grantee, 1971, 74. Fellow AAAS (electorate nominating com. 1974-76, Outstanding Performance in the Scis. award 1994), Audio Engring. Soc. (life), Acoustical Soc. Am. (emeritus, membership com. 1980-86, exec. coun. 1984-87, medal and awards com. 1987-89, nominating com. 1987-88, Silver Acoustics Medal 1981, tech. com. music acoustics 1964—, chmn. pres.'s ad hoc com. 1987-88, archives com. 1988—, mem. com. on women 1989-97); mem. So. Calif. Violin Makers Assn. (hon.), Viola da Gambda Soc. Am. (hon.), Scandinavian Violin Makers Assn. (hon.), N.Y. Viola Soc., Guild Am. Luthiers, Am. Viola Soc., Violoncello Soc., Amateur Chamber Music Players Assn., Am. Philos. Soc. (award violin acoustics 1968, 81), Mich. Violin Makers Assn., Materials Rsch. Soc., Three O'Clock Club, Dot and Circle, others, Sigma Xi, Pi Lambda Theta, Alpha Xi Delta. Home and Office: 42 Taylor Dr Wolfeboro NH 03894

HUTCHINS, DIANE ELIZABETH RIDER, librarian; b. Kearny, N.J., June 25, 1951; d. Thomas Lindsay and Dorothy Jane (Sommer) Rider; m. Clifford James Hutchins, Feb. 14, 2002. MusB magna cum laude, Westminster Choir Coll., 1973; MLS, Fla. State U., 1993. Intern preservation dept. U. Fla., Gainesville, 1993; intern free-net libr. Tallahassee (Fla.) Free-Net, 1993; reference libr. Broward County Main Libr., Ft. Lauderdale, Fla., 1994-95; libr., instr. Art Inst. Ft. Lauderdale, 1995-96, dir. Learning Resource Ctr., 1996-98; dean Nevin C. Meinhardt Meml. Libr., 1998-99; collection devel. coord. Washington State Libr., 1999—2002, program mgr. collection mgmt., 2002—. Vice chair, assoc. mem. com. S.E. Fla. Libr. Info. Network, 1996-97, chair assoc. mem. com., 1997-98, ex officio mem. bd. dirs. S.E. Fla. Libr. Info. Network, 1996-99; spl. librs. rep. Fla. Libr. Network Coun., 1998-99. Soloist St. Paul's Chapel, Columbia U., N.Y.C., 1973, Ch. of St. Mary the Virgin, N.Y.C., 1974. Recipient Outstanding Leadership award Wash. State Libr., 2000; Fla. State U. fellow, 1993-94, Coll. Tchg. fellow, 1992-93; Louis Shores scholar, 1992-93. Mem. Spl. Librs. Assn. (dir. Fla. and Caribbean chpt. 1997-99; Fla. rep., steering com. South Atlantic Regional conf. 1997-99), Geneal. Soc. Southwestern Pa., Sierra Club, Phi Kappa Phi, Beta Phi Mu. Avocations: vegetarian cooking, genealogy, the internet, reading. Office: The Wash State Libr PO Box 42460 Olympia WA 98504-2460 Office Phone: 360-704-7137. E-mail: dhutchins@secstate.wa.gov.

HUTCHINS, JOAN MORTHLAND, manufacturing executive, farmer; b. Pasadena, Calif., Aug. 8, 1940; d. Andrew and Constance Amelia (Gordon-Grant) Morthland; children: Andrew E. Bush, Georgia R. Bush, Alan S., Paul M. AB, Radcliffe Coll., 1961; hon. degree, Royal Coll. Music, London, 1979; AAS, SUNY, Farmingdale, 1985. Jr. mathematician Shell Devel. Co. (Shell Oil), Emeryville, Calif., 1961-63; mathematician Corp. for Econ. and Indsl. Rsch., London, England, 1964-65; mgmt. cons. McKinsey & Co., N.Y.C., 1965-67; v.p. devel. Compotite Corp., L.A., 1985-87, pres., 1987-89, pres., CEO, 1989—, MBH Farms, Inc., Elizaville, NY, 1986-2001, chmn., 2001—. Editor McKinsey & Co. Mgmt. Scis. News Bull., 1965-67; contbr. articles to profl. jours. Mem. bd. overseers Harvard U., Cambridge, Mass., 1994—2000, pres., 1999—2000, mem. overseers vis. com. Harvard athletic dept., 1986—91, mem. overseers vis. com. Arnold Arboretum, 1995—, chmn., 1997—2003, mem. overseers vis. com. Harvard Grad. Sch. Edn., 1995—, vice chmn., 2003—, mem. overseers vis. com. Harvard music dept., mem. nominating com. for overseers and HAA dirs., 2000—03; mem. adv. bd. Harvard U. Com. on Environment, 2001—; bd. dirs., v.p. Royal Music Found., N.Y.C., 1978—90; trustee Bowdoin Coll.

Summer Music Festival, Brunswick, Maine, 1978—88, L.I. Biol. Assn., Cold Spring Harbor, NY, 1986—88. Mem. Am. Nat. Stds. Inst. (nat. waterproofing stds. com. 1988—), Harvard Alumni Assn. (bd. dirs. 1990-93, nominating com. overseers and dirs., 2000-03), Harvard-Radcliffe Club L.I. (pres. 1988-90). Avocations: skiing, music, sports, ice hockey, travel. Home: 8 Soquonhoko Pl Oyster Bay NY 11771 1629 Office: Compodite Corp 355 Glendale Blvd Los Angeles CA 90026-5032

HUTCHINS, KAREN LESLIE, psychotherapist; b. Denver, Sept. 9, 1943; d. Kimball Frederick and Bonnie Illa (Small) H.; divorced; 1 child, Alec Klinghoffer. BA, U. Denver, 1965; MA, George Washington U., 1972. Lic. profl. counselor, chem. depencency counselor, registered sex offender treatment provider, Reiki master Shamanic healing, cert. Nat. Bd. Clin. Hypnotherapists. Tchr. Washington Schs., 1966-70; asst. housing adminstr. George Washington U., Washington, 1970-72; counselor/instr. No. Va. C.C., Annandale, 1972-77, Austin (Tex.) C.C., 1977-80; co-owner Hearts Day Care, Austin, 1980-81; supr./therapist MaryLee Resdl. Treatment, Austin, 1981-82; child protective svc. worker Dept. Human Resources, Austin, 1982-84; probation officer Adult Probation Travis County, Austin, 1984-90; lead therapist Cottonwood Treatment Ctrs., Bastrop, Tex., 1990-91; psychotherapist Austin, 1991—. Classes facilitator Shamanic Retreats. Presenter at confs. Vol. trainer Hotline, Austin, 1993—. Mem.: ACA, Tex. Counselors Assn., Tex. Assn. Addiction Profls., Internat. Soc. for Study of Dissociation, Internat. Soc. Trauma and Stress Studies. Democrat. Jewish. Avocations: sewing, bird watching, animal tending, making custom jewelry, facilitator for shamanic retreats and classes. Office: Cicada Recovery Svcs 3004 S 1st St Austin TX 78704-6388

HUTCHINSON, ANN, management consultant; b. East Stroudsburg, Pa., May 15, 1950; d. David Ellis and Susie (Ingalls) Hutchinson; m. Paul Harrison McAllister, Jan. 2, 1986. BS in Vocat. Edn., Fla. Internat. U., 1985; MBA, Pepperdine U., 1990. Cert. advanced vocat. tchr. Fla., cmty. coll. educator Ariz., pub. mgr., quality award examiner Ariz., 1997, Ariz. Tech. Integrity Coun., 2002. Motorcycle technician, Ft. Lauderdale, Fla., 1973-78; machinist, 1978-79; instr., motorcycle tech. Sheridan Vocat. Tech. Sch., Hollywood, Fla., 1979-85; adminstr., tng. program Am. Honda Motorcycle Divsn., Torrance, Calif., 1985-86, curriculum developer motorcycles svc. tech., 1986-90, coll. program coord., 1990-94; ednl. devel. dir. Clinton Tech. Inst., Phoenix, 1994-96; dep. mgr. tng. unit Ariz. State Dept. Econ. Security, Phoenix, 1996-99, mgmt. cons. office of total quality, 1999-2001; instrnl. sys. specialist Bur. Land Mgmt. Nat. Tng. Ctr., 2001—. Adj. faculty Ariz. State U., 2001—; chmn. high tech. acad. steering com. Pasadena (Calif.) United Sch. Dist., 1991—94; ednl. cons. Ctr. for Occupation R & D Sch.-to-Work Awards, 1994—97; mem. cert. pub. mgr. program adv. bd. Ariz. State U., 1998—2001. Examiner Gov.'s Award for Excellence, 1997—99; mem. Ams. With Disabilities Act com. Ariz. Dept. Econ. Security, 1995—2001; mem. Desert Hill Improvement Assn., 1996—, bd. dirs., editor, 1998—99, v.p., 1999—2001, pres., 2001—. Recipient State of Ky. Col. award, 1990. Mem.: ASTD, Am. Vocat. Assn., Vocat. Indsl. Clubs Am. (co-chmn. motorcycle tech. com. 1988—90, 1994—95, automotive nat. tech. com. 1990—94, adv. Hollywood, Fla. 1979—85), Cert. Pub. Mgr. Assn., Am. Motorcycle Assn., Toastmasters Internat. (Zenger Miller cert. 1996—). Avocation: Avocations: hiking, camping, st. motorcycle riding. Office: Bur Land Mgmt Nat Tng Ctr Office Total Quality 9828 N 31 Ave Phoenix AZ 85051 E-mail: behomes@attglobal.net.

HUTCHINSON, BRENDA IRENE, sound artist, sound designer, audio engineer; b. Trenton, N.J., June 15, 1954; d. William Garwood Dean Hutchinson, Sr. and Mary Ann (McElhoes) Byrnes. BFA in Music, Carnegie-Mellon U., 1976; MA in Music, U. Calif., San Diego, 1979. Audio engr. Harvestworks, Studio Pass, N.Y.C., 1980—; exhibit builder, video prodr., artist in schs., sound perception co-dir. The Exploratorium, San Francisco, 1982-92; sr. sound designer Convivial Design, Inc., San Francisco, 1995-97. Co-curator homemade instruments Lincoln Ctr., N.Y.C., summers 1995, 97, 99, 2003; affiliate artist Headlands Ctr. for Arts, Sausalito, Calif., 1991-95; guest instr. Calif. Coll. Arts and Crafts, Oakland, Calif., 1993-94, Mission Sci. Workshop, San Francisco, 1992—; guest lectr. Mills Coll., spring 1997-98; artist-in-residence Englehard Found., 1995; vis. assoc. prof. music Oberlin Conservatory Music, 2001, Bard Coll., 2002, 03. Composer (electro-acoustical works) A Grandmother's Song, 1979, (with Clive Smith) Liquid Sky, 1982, Apple Etudes, 1985, Interlude from Voices of Reason, 1985, Storytime, 1986, (with Gerald Lindahl) Slow Death on a Thorny Rose, 1986, Joy Chorus from Fly Away All, 1988, Sentences, 1989, EEEYAH!, 1988, Norris and American the Beautiful, 1990, Turaluralura Lament, 1990, Long Tube Solo, 1990, (with Constance De Jong) Vanishing Act, 1991, Voices of Reason, 1991, Delecate Lights, 1991, Long Tube Trio, 1993, Violet Flame, 1994, Another Long Tube, 1995, Every Dream Has Its Number, 1996, (with Laetitia Sonami and Beth Custer) Improvisation for Tube, Glove and Clarinets, 1996, Four for a Time, 1997, How Do You Get to Carnegie Hall, 1997-98, Vagabond Vaudeville, 2000; mem. improvisational group Vorticella, 1996—. Artist Ann Chamberlain Garden Project, San Francisco, 1995-96. Emergent Forms grantee N.Y. Found. for Arts, 1985, 91, Media Arts grantee Nat. Endowment for Arts, 1992, 94, grantee Calif. Arts Coun., 1995-96; commd. by Meet the Composer, 1996; recipient Gracie Allen award Am. Women Broadcast TV and Radio, 2003. Mem. The Lab (bd. dirs. 1993—). Avocations: reading, movies, camping, travelling. Office: Exploratorium 3601 Lyon St San Francisco CA 94123-1099

HUTCHINSON, EDNA M. home care nurse; b. Phoenix, Mar. 13, 1940; d. William Henry and Mary L. Hutchinson; children: Wendell, Antoinette, Lynette, Mary Maxine. Cert., San Diego CC, 1981, Grossmont CC, El Cajon, Calif., 1988. Cert. electrocardiographic technologist, Calif.; sec. sci. lab. Calif. Nurse asst., Phoenix, 1965—66, San Diego, 1966—69; med. asst. Med. Clinic, San Diego, 1980—85; electrocardiogram tech. Maricopa County Hosp., Phoenix, 1989—91; home care nurse Home Health Care, San Diego, 1991—. Songwriter Hill Top Records, Hollywood, Calif., 2000—. Author: (book) Inspiration Songs and Poems, 2000; songwriter In the Beginning, 2000, Jesus in the Inside, 2000; author: Etches in Time, 1997, (songs) God Creation, 2000; co-author: Best Poems and Poets, 2000, Poetry's Elite's Best Poets of 2001, 2001; contbr. over 400 poems to pubs. Daycare provider County of Riverside, Calif., 2001. Finalist Top Model, San Diego, Calif., 1976; named Ten Best Dressed, 1983; recipient Editor's Choice award for Outstanding Achievement in Poetry, State of Md., 1997, Poet of Merit award, Internat. Soc. Poets, 1997, Achievement award, Creative Writing Skills, 1999, Cert., Wall of Tolerance Nat. Campaign, 2001. Avocations: reading, music, songwriting. Home: 7422 W Superior Ave Phoenix AZ 85043-7243

HUTCHINSON, JANET LOIS, historical society administrator, writer, consultant; b. Washington, May 2, 1917; d. Lewis Orrin and Gertrude Elizabeth Hutchinson; divorced; 1 child, Jefferson Troy Siebert. Grad., So. Sem. and Jr. Coll., Buena Vista, Va., 1936; student, N.Y. Sch. Expression, 1923-30, Christine Dobbins Sch. Dance; studied with, Maude Adams, Clare Tree Major, 1934-35. Owner Broadlawn Inn Art Gallery, Camden, Maine, 1955-64; dir. Old Merchants House Mus., N.Y.C., 1962-63, Hist. Soc. Martin County, Stuart, Fla., 1965-91, dir. emeritus, 1991—; dir. Elliott Mus., Stuart, 1965-91, House of Refuge Mus., Stuart, 1965-91; pres., editl. cons. Hutchinson/Paige, Stuart, 1991—. Editl. cons. History of East Stuart, Fla. Author: Tiny Timid's Christmas Wish, 1953, The History of Martin County, 1975; editor: History of East Stuart Florida, 1999; host: (TV interview show) Chronicle. Active Nat. Hist. Preservation Soc., Nat. History Soc., Fla. History Soc.; bd. dirs. Pioneer Occupationa Ctr. for Handicapped, St. Michael's Pvt. Sch.; adv. bd. St. Joseph's Coll. and Fla. Inst. of Tech. Recipient Woman of Yr., AAUW, 1975, Martin County citation, Martin County Bicentennial award, Cmty. Leaders and noteworthy Am. award, Notable Am. of Bicentennial Era award. Fellow: Nat. Arts Club; mem.: DAR (Halpatiokee chpt.), Nat. Soc. Lit. and Arts, Nat. Pen Women (hon.), Smithsonian Instn., Antique Car Assn., Salmagundi Club. Home: 1023 NW Spruce Ridge Dr Stuart FL 34994-9513

HUTCHINSON, REBECCA, state representative; b. Iowa City, Iowa; m. Jonathan, two children. BS, U. N.D., 1974; MS, Antioch U., 1989. State rep. N.H. Ho. of Reps., 1996—. Chair Deerfield mcpl. budget com., 1994-97; mem. labor, indsl. and rehab. svc., N.H. Ho. Reps. Home: 30 Lang Rd Deerfield NH 03037-1411 Office: NH State Legis State House Concord NH 03301

HUTCHISON, BARBARA BAILEY, singer, songwriter; Recipient Grammy award for Best Musical Album for Children "Sleepy Time Lullabyes", 1996. Home: 7261 Kingston Rd Fairview TN 37062-8251 E-mail: barbara@bbhsings.com.

HUTCHISON, DORRIS JEANNETTE, retired microbiologist, educator; b. Carrsville, Ky., Oct. 31, 1918; d. John W. and Maud (Short) H. BS, Western Ky. State Coll., 1940; MS, U. Ky., 1943; PhD, Rutgers U., 1949. Instr. Russell Sage Coll., 1942-44, Vassar Coll., 1944-46; research asst. Rutgers U., 1946-48, research assoc., 1948-49; instr. Wellesley Coll., 1949-51; asst. Sloan-Kettering Inst., N.Y.C., 1951-56, assoc., 1956-60, assoc. mem., 1960-69, mem., 1969-90, mem. emeritus, 1990—, sect. head, 1956-90, acting chief div. exptl. chemotherapy, 1965-66, div. chief drug resistance, 1967-72, co-head lab. exptl. tumor therapy, 1973-74, lab. head drug resistance and cyto-regulation, 1973-84, coordinator field edn., 1975-81. Instr. Sloan-Kettering div. Cornell U. Grad. Sch. Med. Sci., N.Y.C., 1952-53, rsch. assoc., 1953-54, asst. prof., 1954-58, assoc. prof., 1958-70, prof. microbiology, 1970-90, prof. emeritus, 1990—, chmn. biology unit, 1968-74, assoc. dir., 1974-87; assoc. dean Cornell U. Grad. Sch. Med. Sci., 1978-87, asst. dean Cornell U., Ithaca, 1978-87; mem. Meml. Sloan-Kettering Cancer Ctr., 1984-90, mem. emeritus, 1990—; del. dir. Am. Cancer Soc., Inc., 1986-90. Bd. dirs. Westchester div. Am. Cancer Soc., 1976-90, exec. com., 1976-91; project chmn. Target 5, 1977-80, v.p., 1979-81, pres., 1981-83, sec., 1983-87, charter mem. So. Westchester Unit, 1984, pres., 1984-86. Named to Order of Ky. Cols., 1988; recipient Disting. Alumna, Western Ky. U., 2003; faculty fellow, Vassar Coll., 1946, USPHS fellow, 1951—53, Phillippe Found. fellow, Paris, 1959, Doris J. Hutchison fellowship established in her honor, 1999. Fellow N.Y. Acad. Sci., Am. Acad. Microbiology (charter), N.Y. Acad. Medicine (assoc.); mem. AAAS, Am. Assn. for Cancer Edn., Am. Assn. Cancer Research (emeritus), Harvey Soc., Genetics Soc. Am., Am. Inst. Nutrition, Am. Soc. for Microbiology (hon., councilor N.Y.C. br. 1954-58, pres. N.Y.C. br. 1958-60, nat. councilor 1961-63, chmn. nat. meeting 1967, mem. pres.'s fellowship com. 1973-76, chmn. 1975-76), Soc. for Cryobiology (hon. mem.), Am. Genetic Assn., Internat. Soc. Biochem. Pharmacology, N.Y. Soc. Ky. Women (pres. 1988—), N.Y. Found. Ky. Women (pres. 1990-2000), Bronxville Field Club, Elizabeth Hamilton Cullem Svc. Club, 2000—. Achievements include numerous publs. antibiotics and chems. effective in treatment of Tb and leukemia, reports on mechanisms explaining how leukemic cells become resistant to treatment; searches for more effective antileukemia drugs. Home: Southgate Bronxville NY 10708

HUTCHISON, EDNA RUTH, artist; b. Paoli, Ind., Mar. 7, 1920; d. Charles Floyd and Ora May (Agan) Wright; m. William Ira Hutchison, Mar. 24, 1940; 1 child, Carol Ann Hutchison Wyatt. Student, Ind. U., 1940—46, student, 1957—60. Exhibitions include Brown County Art Gallery, 1960—61, Indiana U., 1961, Morton West Coll., Chgo., 1965, Port St. Lucie Libr., Fla., 1994, others. Teddy Bear lady Treasure Coast Cmty. AIDS Network, Ft. Pierce, Fla., 1997, Christmas Kids St. Lucie County, Ft. Pierce, Fla., 1997—. Recipient 1st pl. oil painting, Nat. League/Am. Penwomen, 1990, 1992, 2nd pl. oil painting, 1991, 1994, 1995, 2nd pl. needlepoint classic, Scripps Aux., 1986. Mem.: Nat. League Am. Pen Women. Avocations: writing, jewelry making, travel, decorating, crafts.

HUTCHISON, JANE CAMPBELL, art history educator, researcher; b. Washington, July 20, 1932; d. James Paul and Leone Bailey (Warrick) H. BA in Fine Arts, Western Ma. Coll., 1954; MA in Art History, Oberlin Coll., 1958; PhD in Art History, U. Wis., 1964. Tech. illustrator Dept. Model Basin U.S. Navy, Washington, 1954-56; rsch libr. Toledo Mus. of Art, 1957-59; teaching asst. U. Wis., Madison, 1959-60,61-63; vis. asst. prof. Temple U., Phila., summer 1968; from instr. to assoc. prof. U. Wis., Madison, 1964—, prof., 1975—, dept. chmn., 1977-80, 92-93. Expert witness U.S. Dist. Ct. (so. dist.) N.Y., 2000; cons. in field. Author: Master of the Housebook, 1972, Early German Artists, vol. 8, 1980, vol. 9, 1981, vol. 9 part 2, 1991, vol. 8 part 6, 1996, Albrecht Dürer: A Biography, 1990 (German edit., 1994), Albrecht Durer: A Guide to Research, 2000; mem. editl. bd. Studies in Iconography, 1997—, Source, 2003, Sixteenth Century Jour., 2003. Pres. Madison chpt. AAUP, 1979-81, Midwest Art History Soc., 1983-85, treas., 2001-2004, sec., 2004—; sec.-treas. Historians of Netherlandish Art, 1995-99; pres. St. Andrew's Soc. Madison, 1995—; mem. spl. com. on arts funding Wis. State Legis. Coun., 2000-01. Grad. fellow Oberlin Coll., 1955-57, fellow U. Wis., 1959-60, 61-63, Fulbright fellow Rijksuniversiteit Utrecht, Netherlands, 1960-61, rsch. grantee NEH, Germany, 1982, German Acad. Exch. Svc., Germany, summer 1989; Grant in aid Am. Coun. Learned Soc., Amsterdam, 1984; recipient Alumni award Western Md. Coll. Trustees, 1987. Mem. AAUP (pres. Madison chpt. 1979-81), Internat. Coun. Mus., Am. Assn. Mus., Medieval Acad. Am., Coll. Art Assn., Univ. Club U. Wis. (bd. dirs. 1976-80, pres. 1980), Wis. Assn. Scholars (v.p. Madison chpt. 1990-95), Midwest Art History Soc. (pres. 1983-85, treas. 2001-03, sec. 2004—), Historians of Netherlandish Art (treas. 1995-99), Print Coun. Am., Wis. Acad. Scis., Arts and Letters, Minerva Soc. Home: 2261 Regent St Madison WI 53705-5321 Office: U Wis Dept Art History 800 University Ave Madison WI 53706-1414 E-mail: jchutchi@facstaff.wisc.edu.

HUTCHISON, KAY BAILEY, senator; b. Galveston, TX, July 22, 1943; d. Allan and Kathryn Bailey; m. Ray Hutchison. BA, U. Tex., 1992, LLB, 1967. Bar: Tex. 1967. TV news reporter, Houston, 1969-71; pvt. practice law, 1969-74; press sec. to Anne Armstrong Rep. Nat. Com., 1971; vice-chair Nat. Transp. Safety Bd., 1976-78; asst. prof. U. Tex., Dallas, 1978-79; sr. v.p., gen. counsel Republic Bank Corp., Dallas, 1979-81; pntr. Boyd-Levinson, Ltd., Houston and Dallas, 1981-91; mem. Tex. Ho. of Reps., 1972-76; elected treas. State of Tex., 1990; U.S. senator from Tex. Washington, 1993—; mem. appropriations com., commerce, sci. and transp. com., environment and pub. works com., rules and adminstrn. com. Mem., chmn. Military Constrn. Subcom., commerce, sci. and transp. com. (chmn. Aviation subcom.), environment and pub. works com., rules and adminstrn. com.; chmn., bd. visitors, US Military Acad. at West Point, US Delegate to Commn. on Security and Cooperation in Europe (The Helsinki Commn.); owner McCraw Candies; co-founder Fidelity Nat. Bank. Recipient Eagle award valued commitment to our nation's Hispanic Cmty., 1993; named Rep. Woman of Yr. Nat. Fedn. Rep. Women, 1995, Outstanding U. Tex. Alumnus, 1995, Texan of Yr. Tex. Legis. Conf., 1997; named to Tex. Women's Hall of Fame, 1997. Fellow, U. Tex. Law Alumni Assn. (pres. 1985-86). Republican.*

HUTCHISON, SANDRA LYNN, writer, educator; arrived in U.S., 1995; d. Harry Clinch Hutchison and Beryl Marie Schooley; m. Richard Vernon Hollinger, May 14, 1995; 1 child, Shira Anne Beatrice. BA in English Lit., U. Western Ont., London, Ont., Can., 1976, MA in English Lit., 1977; PhD in English Lit., U. Toronto, 1985; postgrad., Simon Fraser Ryerson U., 1988—89, Columbia U., 1995. Killam postdoctoral fellow U. B.C., Canada, 1986—88, lectr., 1995—96; fgn. expert Anhui U., Hefei, China, 1988—89; rschr. Baha'i World Ctr., Haifa, Israel, 1991—93; lectr. U. Hong Kong, 1996—99. Mem. faculty Wilmette (Ill.) Inst., 2002—03; lectr. Nat. Consortium About Tchg. Asia, Bangor, Maine, 2003; writer, lectr. Maine People's Alliance, 2000; sr. resident fellow Massey Coll., U. Toronto, 1994; del. 13th World Congress of Poets, Haifa, 1992; guest scholar, conf. vice-chairperson Sino-Am. Seminar on Women's Issues, Shanghai, 1992; cons., strand leader 1st Sino-Am. Women's Congress, Beijing, 1992; mem 1st Can. Women's Del. to visit Anhui Province, China, 1986. Author: (book) Chinese Brushstrokes: Stories of China, 1996 (Ont. Arts Coun. Works-in-Progress grant for best manuscript, 1994), (plays) A Prophet from the East, 1992; contbr. short stories, lit. criticisms, poetry, articles to profl. p. Bd. dirs. Orono Village Assn., 2002—03. Recipient Social Sci. and Humanities Internat. travel grant, 1990, Ont. Arts Coun. Writer's Reserve grant, 1989—90, Shastri Indo-Can. travel grant, 1987, Ont. grad. scholarship, 1982—83, U. Toronto Sch. Grad. Studies travel grant, 1981, U. Toronto Can. Studies Travel grant, 1980—81, U. Western Ont. Spl. Univ. scholarship, 1976—77, Ont. grad. scholarship, 1976—77. Mem.: Maine Poets and Writers' Alliance, Internat. Assn. Can. Studies (Washington), Internat. Assn. Can. Studies (Baroda, India). Avocations: fiddling, gardening. Address: 48 Mill St Orono ME 04473-4039

HUTSON, BETTY SWITZER, art educator, artist; b. Brunswick, Mo., Aug. 14, 1930; d. Henry William and Pearl Evelyn (Sayler) Switzer; m. Don L. Hutson, Sept. 7, 1952; children: Eric, Sheila Hutson, Robin Hutson-Montoya, Heather Hutson Daye. BFA, Ctrl. Meth. Coll., 1952; postgrad., U. Mo., 1953-54, Kansas City Art Inst., 1958-60, Avila Coll., 1981; MA in Art Edn., U. Mo., Kansas City, 1986. Cert. tchr. grades K-12, Mo. Elem. art cons. Md. Pub. Schs., Rockville, 1954-58; art instr. Ruskin High Sch., Hickman Mills, Mo., 1958-60, East High Sch., Kansas City, Mo., 1961-62, N.E. Sr. High Sch., Kansas City, 1964-65; dir. edn. All Souls Unitarian Ch., Kansas City, 1975-77; art instr. Westport Jr. High Sch., Kansas City, 1977-87; art instr., cons. De LaSalle Edn. Ctr., Kansas City, 1987-88; art instr. Nelson Mus. Art, Kansas City, 1987-88; visual arts resource tchr. Kansas City Middle Sch. Arts, 1988—99; ret., 1999. Art instr. U. Md., College Park, summer, 1956; resource cons. U. Mo., Kansas City, 1984-86; arts ptnrs. devel. Kansas City Sch. Dist. Learning Exch., 1985-86; curriculum author, task force mem. Kansas City Middle Sch. the Arts, 1988-90, Paseo Acad. Fine & Performing Arts, Kansas City, 1988-90; supervising tchr. student and practicum tchrs. Rockhurst Coll., Kansas City, 1976-92, Avila Coll., Kansas City, 1976-92, U. Mo., Kansas City, 1976-92, 94, Truman U., 1996-97, Park U., 1997-98. Author: Sampling the Basics, 1985; one-woman shows include Unitarian Gallery, 1987, 2001, Lebanon Gallery, 1988, Tchrs. Credit Union Gallery, 1989-90, Le Fou Frog, 2002-03; exhibited in group shows at Unitarian Gallery, Kansas City, 1985, 87, 89, 91, 93, 95, 97, 99, 2001, Nelson Mus. Art, Kansas City, 1989, Fed. Res. Bank, Kansas City, 1990, Kaw Valley Gallery, Kansas City, 1990, Blue Springs (Mo.) Art Exhbn., 1990, 91, Heartland Art Festival, St. Joseph, Mo., 1990-93, Allied Arts Coun., St. Joseph, 1990-93, Bruce Watkins Cultural Ctr., Kansas City, 1993, 94, 95, Muse Gallery, Kansas City, 1995, Kansas City Artists Coalition, 2000, Ashby-Hodge Art Gallery, 2001, Cultures w/o Borders Exhbn., 2001, Open Studios, 2001, 02, others; illus. Children's History of AME Church, 1997. Den mother, art leader Boy Scouts of Am., Raytown, Mo., 1967-69, Girl Scouts of Am., Raytown, 1969-75; vol. AIDSWalk 1998, 99, 2000, 01, 02, 03, Habitat for Humanity, 1992, 93, 94, 96, 2002, soup kitchen Ward Chapel AME, World Federalists, Kansas City, 1989—, Scholastic Arts Regional Com.; vol., fundraiser Peaceworks, Kansas City, 1986—; vol., leader, officer PTA, Kansas City, 1965-76; Jr. Great Books, Picture Lady, Headstart, Planned Parenthood, Friends of the Zoo; trustee All Souls Unitarian-Universalist, 1976-79, 96-99; vol. usher various orgns.; bd. dirs. Unitarian Gallery, 1989—, curator Elizabeth Layton exhibit, 1992. Recipient Disting. Svc. award All Souls Unitarian Ch., Kansas City, 1977, Outstanding Tchr. award Westport Jr. High Sch., Kansas City, 1987, Excellence in Tchtg. Art award, 1995. Mem. AAUW (v.p. 2002-04, art study chmn.), Nat. Art Edn. Assn., Art Edn. Connection (Svc. award 1991-92), Mo. Art Edn. Assn. (Outstanding Art Tchr. 1992), Friends of Art-Nelson Mus. Art, Demeters (pres. 1978-80, 90-91, v.p. 1965-68, 79, 89, co-pres. 2001-, Svc. award 1987), Kansas City Artists Coalition, Mo. Mid. Sch. Assn. Democrat. Unitarian Universalist. Avocations: travel, swimming, gardening, drawing, painting. Home: 7625 Baltimore Ave Kansas City MO 64114-1813

HUTSON, JACQUELYN COLLINS, pianist, educator; b. Gainesville, Ga., Sept. 5, 1938; d. Joseph Watson and Merta (Shuler) Collins; m. Billy Monroe Hutson, Jan. 1, 1959; children: Tamelyn Merta, Jonathan Monroe. AB, Young Harris Coll., 1957; BA in English, Tift coll., 1959; BA in Music, Mercer U., 1976. Tchr. pub. sch. Cobb County, Marietta, Ga., 1959-66; ind. piano tchr. Marietta, 1966—. Mem.: Cobb County Music Tchrs., Greater Marietta Music Tchrs. (v.p. chmn. solo festival 1997—99, pres. 2001—), Ga. Music Tchrs. Assn. (chmn. state conv. 1995, chmn. state piano auditions com. 1996—98), Ga. Music Educators Assn. (chmn. piano com.), Nat. Music Tchrs. Assn., Nat. Music Educators Assn. Republican. Baptist. Avocations: church choir, youth choir, accompanist. Home: 1827 Kimberly Dr SW Marietta GA 30008-4490

HUTSON, PATRICIA FAIN, artist, writer; b. Coalwood Road, W.Va., Sept. 2, 1940; d. Frank Albert and Callie Hull Fain; m. Penny Granville Hutson, Dec. 26, 1958; children: Lydia Gay, Honey Hutson Tawney, Christopher Patrick. Diploma, Washington Sch. of Art, 1965. Author: (novels) (poetry books) Gypsy Wings and Wild Roses, 1993, short stories, poems; contbr. articles to profl. jours. Recipient art and poetry awards., fiction award, HM Writer's Digest Writer's Competition, 1999, award, New River Community Coll. Winner's Booklet, 1989. Avocation: crafts, reading, flower gardening. Home: 1733 Blue Grass Trail Newport VA 24128

HUTSON, SHEILA, psychologist; b. Kansas City, Mo., Sept. 27, 1962; d. Donald Lee Hutson and Betty Jane Switzer Hutson; m. Jesse Stephen Bentley, May 23, 1981 (div. Aug. 1986); children: Justin Linn Bentley, Nikolai Ariel Hutson Montoya, Dominica Pilar Hutson-Montoya. MS in Clin. and Counseling Psychology, Ctrl. Mo. State U., 1994; D in Psychology, Forest Inst. Profl. Psychology, 1998. Co-owner, mgr. Resistal, Miami, Fla., 1988—90, Chiro Loco, Miami, 1988—90; mgr. Leslies Studio, Miami, 1988—89; grad. asst. Ctrl. Mo. State U., Warrensburg, 1992—93; intern Harlan & Assocs., Sedalia, Mo., 1994, Neuropsychol. Assocs., Springfield, Mo., 1997—98, resident, 1998—2000, psychologist, 2000—. Campaign vol. Hutson Campaign for Cir. Ct. Judge, Lebanon, Mo., 2002. Mem.: APA, Mo. Psychol. Assn. Avocations: travel, camping, horseback riding, reading. Office: Neuropsychological Assocs 3621 South Ave Springfield MO 65807

HUTT, EVELYN ANN, geriatrician, researcher; b. Tawngii, Burma, July 17, 1952; d. Martin Perry and Thelma Pearl Hutt; m. Norm Aaronson, June 14, 1998; children from previous marriage: Eliana Rosa Mastrangelo, Levi Noah Mastrangelo. BA, U. Chgo., 1974; MD, U. Colo., 1985. Diplomate Am. Bd. Internal Medicine, cert. of added qualification in geriatrics Am. Bd. Internal Medicine. Resident in internal medicine U. Minn., Mpls., 1985—88; fellow in geriatrics Stanford U., Palo Alto, Calif., 1988—90; dir. Sr. Plus, Denver Health Med. Ctr., 1990—95; physician Kaiser Permanente, Denver, 1995—98; asst. prof. U. Colo. Health Scis. Ctr., Denver, 1998—; dir. program for rsch. in long term care for veterans VAMC, Denver, 2000—. Mem. collaborative decision making com. Bromwell Elem. Sch., Denver, 1997—98; bd. dirs. Cmty. Talmud Torah, Denver, 1999—2000. Mem.: Physicians For Human Rights, Am. Geriat. Soc. (New Investigator award 2000). Liberal. Jewish. Avocation: triathlons.

HUTTER, TERESA ANN, art educator; b. Great Bend, Kans., Jan. 25, 1952; d. Harry and Wilma Witterstaetter; children: Trina, Troy. BA in Art Edn., U. Ctrl. Okla., 1987. Nat. bd. cert. tchr. Tchr. art Mustang Pub. Schs., Okla., 1988—; tchr. art camp So. Nazarene U., Bethany, Okla., 1996—2000; host Internat. Children's Art Exhbn., 1995, 2001; tchr. art Jr. Tng. Pks. Assn. Edn. program Okla. C.C., 1994—95. Okla. state judge state reflections program PTA, Oklahoma City, 1996—97. Mem.: NEA, Okla.

Edn. Assn., Okla. Art Edn. Assn. (sec. 1992—94, treas. 1994—98, chmn. young talent in Okla. 1998—2000, chmn. Okla. elem. div. 2000—02, chmn. we. region div. 1998—2000, Okla. Elem. Art Educator of Yr. 1995, Okla. Art Educator of Yr. 2000, Youth Arts Month Svc. award 1996, 2000), Delta Kappa Gamma (music chmn. 2000—01). Republican. Methodist. Avocations: reading, pottery, flute, hand bells. Office: Mustang Pub Schs 906 S Heights Dr Mustang OK 73064 Office Phone: 405-376-2409.

HUTTNER, CONSTANCE S. lawyer; b. Youngstown, Ohio, 1958; BSc with honors, Ohio State U., 1977; JD magna cum laude, Boston Coll., 1980. Bar: N.Y. 1981. Ptnr. Skadden, Arps, Slate, Meagher & Flom, N.Y.C. Mem. Phi Beta Kappa. Office: Skadden Arps Slate Meagher & Flom 4 Times Sq Fl 24 New York NY 10036-6595

HUTTON, CAROLE LEIGH, newspaper editor; b. Framingham, Mass., Aug. 23, 1956; d. James and Norma Inez (Vitali) Hamilton; m. Tom Huff. B Journalism, Mich. State U., 1978. Editor Natick (Mass.) Sun, 1978—79; reporter, city editor, mng. editor Hammond (Ind.) Times, 1979—87; dir. publs. CNA Ins. Cos., Chgo., 1987—88; day city editor, accent editor Detroit News, 1988—90; city editor Detroit Free Press, 1992—95, dep. mng. editor for news, 1995—96, mng. editor, 1996—2002, exec. editor, 2002—03, pub. and editor, 2004—. Tutor Detroit Pub. HS, 1994—94. Named one of 100 Most Influential Women in S.W. Mich., Crain's Detroit Bus.; recipient Local News Coverage award, Hoosier State Press Assn., 1982. Mem.: AP Mng. Editors, Mich. AP Editors Assn. (pres., bd. dirs. 2000—), Am. Soc. Newspaper Editors, IAP Mng. Editors. Office: Detroit Free Press 600 W Fort St Detroit MI 48226-2706

HUTTON, DEBORAH SPENCE, academic administrator; b. Winnipeg, Man., Can., Mar. 10, 1952; d. Frances Spence and Bette Margaret (Brown) H. BSc (hons.), Queen's U., 1975, BEd, 1977; MSEd, Northern Ill. U., 1981; EdS, Ind. U., 1998. Tchr. social studies Bishop's Coll. Sch., Lennoxville, Canada, 1977-80; from project asst. tchr. edn. project to co-instr. Ind. U., Bloomington, 1983-94, coord. outreach & spl. projects Ctr. Study Global Change, 1996—. Co-author: African Social Studies Program 1, 1991, African Social Studies Program 2, 1991; contbr. articles to profl. jours., chpts. to books. Cons. Russian Global Schs. Initiative, 1994-95; cons. com. Ctr. Canadian Studies Franklin (Ind.) Coll., 1993-94. Co-chair bldg. expansion steering com. Unitarian-Universalist Ch., Bloomington, 1995-98; pres. Georgetown Village Condominium Assn., Bloomington, 1991-94; mem. City Commn. on Status of Women, Bloomington, 1983-84. Mem. Nat. Coun. Social Studies, Ind. Coun. Social Studies, Global Edn. Network, Pi Lambda Theta. Avocations: gardening, bird watching, canoeing, reading. Office: Ind U Ctr Study Global Change 201 N Indiana Ave Bloomington IN 47408-4001

HUTTON, FIONA S. communications executive; Strategic planning coun. Gov. Pete Wilson, 1994-96; with Stoorza, Ziegaus and Metzger; v.p. corp. comm. Cadiz, Inc., Santa Monica, Calif. Mem. Pub. Rels. Soc. Am. Office: Cadiz Inc 100 Wilshire Blvd Ste 1600 Santa Monica CA 90401-1115

HUTTON, JENNY, music educator; b. Atlanta, July 14, 1976; d. D. Freeman and Sandra Pinschmidt Hutton. BA magna cum laude, Amherst Coll., 1998. Music tchr. Counterpane Sch., Fayetteville, Ga., 1998—. Recorder instr. Orff-Schulwerk levels I and II Gwinnett County Sch. Sys. Norcross, Ga., 2003. Composer: (electronic musical composition) Better Basketball videos and DVD's. Nat. Merit. scholar, Nat. Merit Scholarship Corp. Mem.: Am. Orff-Schulwerk Assn., Am. Choral Dirs. Assn., Music Educators Nat. Conf., Phi Beta Kappa. Avocation: reading. Home: 916 Greenwood Ave Atlanta GA 30306 Personal E-mail: huttonjc@bellsouth.net.

HUTTON, LAUREN (MARY LAURENCE HUTTON), model, actress; b. Charleston, S.C., 1944; d. Laurence Hutton. Student, U. Fla., Sophia Newcombe Coll. Fashion model, 1960—. Actress: (feature films) Paper Lion, 1968, Little Fauss and Big Halsey, 1970, Pieces of Dreams, 1970, The Gambler, 1974, Gator, 1976, Welcome to L.A., 1977, Viva Knieval!, 1977, A Wedding, 1978, American Gigolo, 1980, Zorro, the Gay Blade, 1981, Paternity, 1981, Lassiter, 1984, Once Bitten, 1985, A Certain Desire, 1986, Malone, 1987, Guilty As Charged, 1991, My Father, The Hero, 1994; (TV movies) Someone's Watching Me, 1978, Institute for Revenge, 1979, The Cradle Will Rock, 1983, Starflight: The Plane that Couldn't Land, 1983, Scandal Sheet, 1985, Timestalkers, 1987, Perfect People, 1988, Fear, 1990, 54, 1998; (TV series) The Rhinemann Exchange, 1977, Central Park West, 1995—, (stage prodn.) Extremities.

HUWILER, JOAN P. public relations executive, consultant; b. New Haven, Conn., June 15, 1963; d. Paul F. and Joan E. (Tickey) H. BA in Comm., Southern Conn. State Univ., 1985; MS in Journalism, Boston Univ., 1990. Account coord. Coates Pub. Rels. subs. Mason & Madison Advertising, Bethany, Conn., 1985-86; devel. fund raiser Atty. Gen. Joe Lieberman, Hartford, Conn., 1986; dep. press sec. Office Atty. Gen., State of Conn., Hartford, Conn., 1986-89; media dir. NOW Legal Def. and Edn. Fund, N.Y., 1990-92; cons., 1992-96; exec. dir. Schooner Inc., New Haven, Conn., 1992-93; comms. officer Cmty. Found. for Greater New Haven, New Haven, Conn., 1996-99; mktg. and comm. mgr. S. Ctrl. Regional Water Auth., New Haven, 1999—. Teaching asst. Boston Univ., 1989-90; pub. info. officer Hamden Bd. of Edn., 1984-85; writer, cons. Bank Mart, Bridgeport, Conn., 1985-86. Recipient Vanguard spl. merit award Women in Comm., 1991, Forty Under Forty award Bus. Times New Haven, 1999. Mem. Comm. Network in Philanthropy, Pub. Rels. Soc. Am. Democrat. Avocations: reading, cooking, gardening. Office: S Ctrl Conn Regional Water Auth 90 Sargent Dr New Haven CT 06511-5918

HUXTABLE, ADA LOUISE, architecture critic; b. N.Y.C. d. Michael Louis and Leah (Rosenthal) Landman; m. L. Garth Huxtable. AB magna cum laude, Hunter Coll.; postgrad., Inst. Fine Arts, NYU; hon. degrees, Harvard U., Yale U., NYU, Washington U., U. Mass., Oberlin Coll., Miami U., R.I. Sch. Design, U. Pa., Radcliffe Coll., Oberlin Coll., Smith Coll., Skidmore Coll., Md. Inst., Mt. Holyoke Coll., Trinity Coll., LaSalle U., Pace Coll., Pratt Inst., Colgate U., Hamilton U., Williams Coll., Rutgers U., Finch Coll., Emerson Coll., C.W. Post Coll. at L.I. U., Cleve. State U., Bard Coll., Fordham U., Parsons Sch. Design, Mass. Coll. Art, Nottingham U., England. Asst. curator architecture and design The Museum of Modern Art, N.Y.C., 1946-50; Fulbright fellow for advanced study in architecture and design Italy, 1950, 52; free-lance writer, contbg. editor to Progressive Architecture and Art in America, 1950-63; architecture critic N.Y. Times, N.Y.C., 1963-82, mem. editorial bd., 1973-82; Cook lectr. in am. instns. U. Mich., 1977; Hitchcock lect. U. Calif.-Berkeley, 1982. Corp. vis. com. Harvard U. Grad. Sch. Design, Sch. Visual and Environ. Arts; mem. adv. bd. Am. Trust Brit. Libr.; archtl. cons. Nat. Gallery, London, J. Paul Getty Trust, L.A., San Francisco Pub. Libr., Mus. Contemporary Art, Chgo., Kansas City Art Mus.; archtl. critic The Wall Street Jour., 1996—. Author: Pier Luigi Nervi, 1960, Classic New York, 1964, Will They Ever Finish Bruckner Boulevard?, 1970, Kicked a Building Lately?, 1976, The Tall Building Artistically Reconsidered: The Search for a Skyscraper Style, 1985, Goodbye History, Hello Hamburger 1986, Architecture Anyone? 1986, The Unreal America: Architecture and Illusion, 1997. Recipient 1st Pulitzer prize for disting. criticism, 1970, Spl. award Nat. Trust for Historic Preservation, 1971, Archtl. Criticism medal AIA, 1969, medal for lit. Nat. Arts Club, 1971, Diamond Jubilee medallion City N.Y., 1973, Mayor's Cultural award, 1984, Woman of Yr. award AAUW, 1974, Sec.'s award for conservation U.S. Dept. Interior, 1976, Thomas Jefferson medal U. Va., 1977, Archtl. Criticism medal Acad. d' Architecture Française, 1988; Guggenheim fellow for studies in Am. architecture, 1958, MacArthur fellow, 1981-86, fellow Ctr. for Scholars and Writers, N.Y. Pub. Libr., 1999-00; Henry Allen Moe prize Humanities Am. Philosophical Soc., 1992. Fellow Am. Acad. Arts and Scis., Royal Inst. Brit. Architects (hon.), AAAL; mem. AIA (hon.), Am. Acad. Arts and Letters, Soc. Archtl. Historians. Home: 969 Park Ave New York NY 10028-0322

HUYER, ADRIANA, oceanographer, educator; b. Giessendam, The Netherlands, May 19, 1945; arrived in Can., 1950; came to U.S., 1975; d. Jacob Catharinus and Sophia (Van Loon) H.; m. Robert Lloyd Smith. BS, U. Toronto, 1967; MS, Oreg. State U., 1971, PhD, 1974. Scientific officer Marine Scis. Branch, Ottawa, Can., 1967-73; rsch. scientist Marine Environ. Data Svc., Ottawa, Can., 1974-75; rsch. assoc. Oreg. State U., Corvallis, 1975-76, rsch. asst. prof., 1976-79, asst. prof., 1979-80, assoc. prof., 1980-85, prof., 1985—. Vis. scientist Csiro Marine Labs, Hobart, Australia, 1988. Contbr. articles to profl. jours. Mem. AAAS, Am. Meterol. Soc., Am. Geophys. Union, Can. Meterol. and Oceanographic Soc., Am. Soc. Limnology and Oceanography. Office: Oreg State U Coll Oceanic Atmospher Scis 104 Ocean Adminstrn Bldg Corvallis OR 97331

HUYSER, CYNTHIA GAYE, computer programmer, poet; d. Willis Cornelius and Gloria Nellie Huyser; life ptnr. Debra Lou Winegarten. BA in English, Tri State U., Angola, Ind., 1981; MS in Computer Sci., Southwest Tex. State U., San Marcos, 2002. Power plant operator City of Austin, Tex., 1991—96, power plant oper. supr., 1996—99; PC / lang. adminstr. Travis County, Austin, Tex., 1999—2000; rsch. engring. scientist asst. U. Tex., Austin, 0200—2002; engr. J3S, Inc., Austin, Tex., 2002—. Author: Layers, 1993; contbr. poems to Tex. Poetry Rev. Sec. Her Domain, Austin, Tex., 2002—. Mem.: IEEE, Tex. Writer's League.

HUYSMAN, ARLENE WEISS, psychologist, educator, writer; b. Phila., 1929; d. Max and Anna (Pearlene) Weiss; m. Pedro Camacho; children: Pamela Claire, James David. BA, Shaw U., 1973; MA, Goddard Coll., 1974; PhD, Union Inst. Grad., 1980. Diplomate Am. Bd. Psychol. Specialties, Med. Psychology, 1997. Actress, dir. Dramatic Workshop, N.Y.C., 1956—68; music and drama critic and columnist Orlando (Fla.) Sentinel Star, 1966—68; psychodramatist Volusia County Guidance Ctr., Daytona Beach, Fla., 1966—68; free-lance journalist, 1968—70; psychodramatist Psychiat. Inst. Jackson Meml. Hosp., Miami, 1972—77; dir. Adult Day Treatment Ctr., 1974—77, Lithium Clinic, 1976—77; psychodramatist South Fla. State Hosp., Hollywood, 1971—72; psychotherapy supr., Neurosci. program coord. Miami Heart Inst., 1984—; clin. dir. Family Workshop, 1985—, Adult Day Treatment Ctrs., 1987—; founder, dir. Geriatric Adult Day Treatment Ctrs. Adj. asst. prof. Med. Sch. U. Miami, 1976—; adj. prof. Union Inst., 1992—, Antioch U., 1995—; specialist in Bi Polar Disorders, U. Wis., 1980—. Author: A Mother's Tears, 1998, 2002, The Postpartum Effect: Deadly Depression in Mothers, 2003. Mem. adv. panel Fine Arts Coun. Fla., 1976—77. Recipient Best Dirs. award and Best Actress award, Fla. Theatre Festival, 1967. Mem.: APA, Fla. Assn. Practicing Psychologists (bd. dirs., pres.), World Fedn. Mental Health, Am. Assn. Group Psychotherapy and Psychodrama, Am. Soc. Aging, Internat. Assn. Group Psychotherapy, Mental Health Assn. Dade County, Dade County Psychol. Assn. (bd. dirs.), Fla. Psychol. Assn., Am. Coll. Forensic Examiners, Fedn. Partial Hospitalization Study Groups, Moreno Acad., Union Inst. Grad. Alumni Assn. (bd. dirs., southeastern rep., pres.-elect). Office: Ctr Psychol Growth 3050 Biscayne Blvd Miami FL 33137-4143 E-mail: drhuysman@yahoo.com .

HYAMS, HARRIET, artist; b. Jersey City, June 5, 1920; d. Maurice Krivit and Syd Ruth Baron; m. George Hyams, Oct. 20, 1951 (div. 1971); m. Charles Stimel, 1977; children: Irene Woodard, Andrew. BA, Rutgers U., Newark, 1950; MA, Columbia U., 1972. Instr. stained glass Columbia U., N.Y.C., 1972—74. Stained glass windows, West Point Jewish chapel, 1998, Dominican Chapel/Our Lady of the Rosary, 2001, etched folding doors, Trinity Luth. Ch., 2003, numerous exhbns., one person shows, commns.; contbr. articles to profl. jours. Recipient Bene awards, Ministry and Liturgy Mag., 2002, Arthur Wesley Dow Purchase award, Columbia U., 1972, Fulbright Design Selection Com. award, Inst. Internat. Edn., N.Y.C., 1993, 1996, 2000. Mem.: Union of Am. Hebrew Congregations, Stained Glass Assn. Am., Interfaith Forum on Religion, Art, Arch. Avocations: travel, reading, sailing, music. Home: PO Box 178 Palisades NY 10964-0178

HYATT, CAROLE S. author, speaker, coach; b. N.Y.C., Apr. 29, 1935; d. Arthur Edwin and Shirley (Unger) Schwartz; m. Gordon Hyatt, Oct. 25, 1966; 1 child, Ariel. BS in Theatre and Edn., Syracuse U., 1956; MA in Theatre Comm., U. Denver, 1959. Co-prodr., dir. Peppermint Players, N.Y.C. and elsewhere, 1960-66; prodr. CBS-TV, N.Y.C., 1961-66; instr., part-time faculty New Sch. for Social Rsch., N.Y.C., 1960-75; co-founder, CEO Child Rsch. Svc. Inc., N.Y.C., 1966-84; CEO, co-founder Hyatt/Esserman Assocs., Inc., N.Y.C., 1973-84. Adv. bd. NAFE, N.Y.C., 1980-91, Avon/Women of Enterprise, N.Y.C., 1986—; bd. dirs. Women in Need, N.Y.C., 1986-92, Berkshire Botanical Gardens, 1994—, Stockbridge, Mass., 1994—, Edith Wharton Restoration, Lenox, Mass., 1989-94. Author (keynote seminars): The Woman's Selling Game, 1977, Woman and Work, 1980, When Smart People Fail, 1987, updated edit. 1993, Shifting Gears, 1991; (videotape and book) Lifetime Employability, 1995; (book) The Woman's New Selling Game, 1998; keynote spkr. and presenter of workshops in U.S., Asia, S.Am., Ctrl. Am., Europe, Can., and South Africa visiting over 60 cities annually. Bd. dirs., v.p. global membership Internat. Women's Forum, 1997—; bd. dirs. J.F.K. Sch. Govt./Women's Global Leadership Initiative, 1995—; founder, The Carole Hyatt Leadership Forum. Mem. Internat. NOW (bd. dirs. Defense and Edn. Fund 1975-85), Women's Forum (program chair internat conv. 1995), N.Y. Women's Forum (bd. dirs. 1985-87, chair program com. 1987-90). Avocations: travel, gardening. Home and Office: 7 W 81st St New York NY 10024-6049

HYATT, MARY LOUISE, music educator, pianist; b. Harrisburg, Pa., Nov. 22, 1949; d. Leonard T. and Carolyn Gilchrist Willey; m. Robert Patrick Hyatt, Jan. 20, 1996; 1 child, Andrew L. Houk. MusB in Edn., U. Fla., Gainesville, 1971. Tchr. music Sch. Bd. of Alachua County, Gainesville, 1971—. Accompanist Gainesville Youth Chorus, 1999—; summer musical theatre dir. Gainesville HS, 1985—98; debate tournament judge Emory U., Atlanta, 1993—96, Atlanta, 1999; demonstration classroom tchr. U. Fla., Gainesville, 1991—. Contbr. articles to profl. jours. Recipient Tchr. of Yr., Idylwild Elem. Sch., 1994, Musician of Yr., Found. Promotion of Music, 2002. Mem.: Fla. Music Educators Assn., Music Educators Nat. Conf. Democrat. Presbyn. Office: Idylwild Elem Sch 4601 SW 20th Terr Gainesville FL 32608

HYDE, GERALDINE VEOLA, retired secondary school educator; b. Berkeley, Calif., Nov. 26, 1926; d. William Benjamin and Veola (Walker) H.; m. Paul Hyde Graves, Jr., Nov. 12, 1949 (div. Dec. 1960); children: Christine M. Graves Klykken, Catherine A. Graves Hackney, Geraldine J. Graves Hansen. BA in English, U. Wash., 1948; BA in Edn., Ea. Wash. U., 1960, MA in Edn., 1962. Cert. tchr. K-16, Wash.; life cert. specialist in secondary edn., Calif. English educator Sprague (Wash.) Consol. Schs., 1960-62, Bremerton (Wash.) Sch. Dist., 1962-63, Federal Way (Wash.) Sch. Dist., 1963-66; English, journalism and Polynesian humanities educator Hayward (Calif.) Unified Sch. Dist., 1966-86; ret., 1986. Charter mem. Hist. Hawaii Found., Honolulu, 1977-; founding mem. The Cousteau Soc., Inc., Norfolk, Va., 1973-; life mem. Hawaiian Hist. Soc., Honolulu, 1978-; mem. Molokai Mus. and Cultural Ctr., Kaunakakai, 1986-, Bishop Mus. Assn., Honolulu, 1973-, Mission House Mus., Honolulu, 1994, Bklyn. Hist. Assn., N.Y., 1994, Berkshire Family History Assn., Pittsfield, Mass., 1994-, Richville (N.Y.) Hist. Assn., 1994-, Swanton (Vt.) Hist. Soc., 1998-, N.Y. Geneal. and Biog. Soc., 1999-, New Eng. Hist. Genealogic Soc., 1998-, Gouverneur Hist. Assn., NY, 1998-, New Wing Luke Asian Mus., Seattle, 1994, Upham Family Soc., Inc., Melrose, Mass., 2001-, Calif. Ret. Tchrs Assoc. 2003. Mem. Libr. Congress Assocs. (charter), Nature Conservancy of Hawai'i, Smithsonian Inst. (contbg.), Nat. Geog. Soc., Nat. Trust Historic Preservation, Jr. League Spokane, U. Wash. Alumni Assn. (life), Ea. Wash. U. Alumni Assn. (life). Episcopalian. Avocations: historic and ecologic preservation, genealogy, shell collecting, needlework, crafts. Home: 5051 El Don Dr Apt 1301 Rocklin CA 95677-4470

HYDE, REBECCA MEDWIN, financial consultant; b. Frederick, Md., Aug. 30, 1947; d. William Herbert and Clella Evelyn Hyde. BA, Cath. U. Am., 1969; tchr. edn. cert., Towson State Coll., 1971; M Liberal Arts, Johns Hopkins U., 1973. Cert. fin. planner. Sr. jumbo underwriter, asst. v.p. Chase Home Mortgage Corp., Woodland Hills, Calif., 1988—95; fin. advisor Am. Express Fin. Advisors, Columbia, Md., 1995—. Guest lectr. U. Balt. Sch. Law, 2000—01. Mem.: Fin. Planning Assn. Home: 5764 Stevens Forest Rd # 421 Columbia MD 21045 Office: Am Express Fin Advisors Ste 501 5950 Symphony Woods Rd Columbia MD 21044 E-mail: rebeccamhyde@yahoo.com.

HYDE-SMITH, CINDY, state legislator; b. Brookhaven, Miss. m. Michael Hyde-Smith; 1 child, Anna-Michael. Student, Copiah-Lincoln C. C., U. So. Miss. Cons. congrl. affairs; mem. Miss. Senate from 39th dist., Jackson, 1999—. Vice chair wildlife and fisheries com., enrolled bills com. Mem. Am. Cancer Soc., Jr. Auxiliary, Hospice, Miss. Cattleman's Assn., Miss. Wildlife Fedn. Democrat. Baptist. Office: 339 Dunn Ratcliff Rd NW Brookhaven MS 39601 also: Miss Senate Rm 447-RB Jackson MS 39215-1018

HYLAND, BARBARA CLAIRE, state legislator; b. Sept. 17, 1943; m. George Hyland, 1966; children: Kevin, Dana. BA, Regis Coll., 1965. Svc. adv. N.J. Bell, Clifton, 1965-66, New England Telephone, Arlington, Mass., 1966-67; receptionist, adminstrv. asst. Maple Grove Manor Convalescent Home, Norwood, Mass., 1967-68; sec. Codex Corp., Mansfield, Mass., 1985-86; legal sec. John H. Michelmore & Robert E. Cutler, Jr., Foxboro, Mass., 1986-91; mem. Mass. Ho. of Reps., 1992—, mem. health care, housing, urban devel. coms., mem. house ways and means com., pers. and adminstrn. com. Mem. house ways & means com., pers. & adminstrn. com. Mass. Ho. of Reps. Pres. PTA, 1975-77; chmn. playing fields subcom., Foxboro, 1977-86, Foxboro Rep. Town Com., 1989—; mem. sch. com., Foxboro, 1977-86, chief negotiator, 1982-86; coord. WeLD/Celiucci Gubernatorial Campaign, Foxboro, 1989-90. Mem. Pi Gamma Mu. Office: State House Rm 541 Boston MA 02133

HYLAND, CHERYL C. health services administrator; b. Tulsa, Okla., Mar. 27, 1960; d. Clifford E. and Sue E. Foley; m. Thomas Patrick Hyland, June 1, 1985 (div. Sept. 1994); children: Kelli Sue, Sean Thomas. BS, Okla. State U., 1982; MEd, U. Okla., 1985. Lic. marriage and family therapist; cert. mediator. Primary clinician Heritage Treatment Ctr., Provo, UT, 1985-91, Shadow Mt. Hosp., Tulsa, Okla., 1991-92, dir. clin. outpatient svc. Bartlesville and Pawhuska, Okla., 1992-98; dir. therapeutic foster care Children's Med. Ctr., Tulsa, Okla., 1998—; asst. divsn. chair Tulsa Cmty. Coll., Okla., 1999—. Pres. Profl. Staff Orgn., Provo, Utah, 1987-88, instr., faculty liberal arts, Tulsa Cmty. Coll. Author: Essential Guide for Graduate Students, 1999. Mem. Habitat for Humanity, Tulsa, Okla., 1999. Recipient award of Appreciation for Crisis Intervention, Okla. City bombing, Gov. Okla. Clin. mem. Am. Assn. Marriage and Family Therapists. Methodist. Avocations: reading, collecting antiques. Office: Tulsa Comm Coll 3727 E Apache St Tulsa OK 74115-3150

HYLAND, SHARON ANN, adult nurse practitioner; b. Buffalo, N.Y., Nov. 29, 1946; d. Walter Praczkajlo and Jean Bak; 1 child, Michelle. BSc, SUNY, 1968; MSc, U. Rochester, 1982, student, 1991. Spl. project nurse U. Rochester, NY, 1974—82, clin. nurse specialist oncology, 1982—85; asst. prof. D'Youville Coll., Buffalo, 1985—86; advanced practice nurse Vets. Adminstrn., Buffalo, 1986—87; study coord. AIDS Clin. Trials UB Found., Buffalo, 1987—92; nurse practioner Roswell Pk. Cancer Inst., Buffalo, 1992—2003, JP Wilmot Cancer Ctr., Rochester, 2003—. Co-author: Genito Urinary Oncology, 1997, Instruments For Clinical Health Research, 2003. Mem.: Am. Soc. Clin. Oncology, C. Jung Analytical Soc., Sigma Theta Tau. Democrat. Avocations: golf, horseback riding, hiking. Home: 1946 Ontario St Honeoye Falls NY 14472 Office: JP Wilmot Cancer Ctr PO Box 704 601 Elmwood Ave Rochester NY 14642

HYLER, SHERYL ROOT, application developer; b. Hollywood, Calif. m. F.H. Hyler, June 9, 1990. BS, U. Calif., Santa Barbara, 1966; MBA, Stanford U., 1993. Programmer, mgr. compiler products Control Data Corp., Sunnyvale, Calif., 1966-75; v.p. internat. systems, v.p. systems Bank of Am., San Francisco, 1975-85; lab. mgr., dir. software engring. Hewlett Packard, Palo Alto, Calif., 1985—, dir. bus. strategy. Industry affil. Stanford U.; advisor Software Industry Coalition, Santa Clara, Calif., 1994—. Sponsor for L.E. Root Scholarship for Women in Engring., Stanford U. Bd. mem. Women in Tech. Internat., Stanford Bus. Sch.-Sloan, Teach for Am., Bay Area. Avocations: wines, opera, sailing.

HYLLA, LINDA KAY, sister, social worker; b. Granite City, Ill., Mar. 1, 1961; d. Leonard Albert and Loretta Ann Hylla. BA, Fontbonne U., 1987; MSW, Wash. U., St. Louis, 1992. Entrance into Sisters of Divine Providence, 1980; LCSW 1995. Coord. youth and human svc., Granite City, Ill., 1992—95; child care worker St. Elizabeth Med. Ctr., Granite City, 1986—95, outpatient therapist, 1995—2000; vocations dir. Sisters of Divine Providence, Bridgeton, Mo., 2000—. Clin. supr. pvt. practice, Madison, Ill., 1998—; founder Quest Ho., Madison, Ill. Contbr. poetry poetry.com. Bd. dirs. New Opportunities, Madison, 1989—91; chmn. bd. Rm. at the Inn Homeless Shelter, St. Louis County, 2002—. Named an Internat. Poet of Merit, Internat. Soc. of Poets, 2002; named to, Internat. Soc. Conf., 1999, TREND Hall of Fame, Nat. TREND Conf., St. Louis, 2000; Vocation grant, KC, 2003. Office: Sisters of Divine Providence 3415 Bridgeland Bridgeton MO 63044 E-mail: srlindahylla@hotmail.com.

HYLLAND, SUE, sports association executive; Team capt., edn. 1998 & 2000 Olympic games Can. Olympic Assn.; exec. dir. Can. Assn. for Advancement of Women & Sport & Phys. Activity, 2000—; pres., CEO Canada Games Coun., Ottawa, Canada, 2002—. Office: Can Assn Adv Women & Sport & Phys Activ N 202-801 King Edward Ave Ottawa ON K1N 6n5 Canada*

HYMAN, MARY BLOOM, science education programs coordinator; m. Sigmund M. Hyman, 1947 (dec.); children: Carol Hyman Piccinini, Nancy Louise. BA, Goucher Coll., 1971; MS, Johns Hopkins U., 1977. Asst. dir. Edn. Md. Sci. Ctr., Balt., 1976-81, dir. edn., 1981-90; coord. sci. edn. programs Loyola Coll., Balt., 1990—, coord. Inst. for Child Care Edn., 1992—. Trustee Goucher Coll., Franklin & Marchall Coll., Lancaster, Pa., 2003--; active Baltimore County Pub. Schs. Com. for Sch.-Based and Sch.-Linked Child Care; bd. dirs. Balt. Sch.-Age Child Care Alliance, Johns Hopkins U. Ctr. Talented Youth; mem. Gov.'s Task Force on Compensation of Child Care Providers, 1995-96. Recipient Disting. Women award Gov.'s Office, Annapolis, Md., 1981; Meritorious Svc. award Johns Hopkins U., 1983; Outstanding Svc. to Sci. Edn. award. Assn. Sci. Dept. Chairmen Balt. County Pub. Schs., 1989. Mem. Md. Assn. Sci. Tchrs. (bd. dirs.), Phi Beta Kappa, Phi Delta Kappa. Home: 10815 Longacre Ln Stevenson MD 21153-0665 E-mail: mhyman@loyola.edu.

HYMAN, MISTY DAWN, Olympic athlete; b. Mesa, Ariz., Mar. 23, 1979; d. Steve and Margaret Hyman. Student, Stanford U. Recipient Gold medal 200-meter butterfly Sydney Olympics, 2000, Bronze medal 200-meter butterfly, Gold medal 4 x 400-meter medley relay (team) World Championships, 1998; winner 3 individual NCAA titles, 1998, mem. 2 championship relay teams NCAA, 1998; named NCAA Swimmer of Yr., 1998. Office: USA Swimming 1 Olympic Plz Colorado Springs CO 80909-5746

HYMAN, PAULA E(LLEN), history educator; b. Boston; d. Sydney Max and Ida Frances (Tetelman) H.; m. Stanley Harvey Rosenbaum, June 7, 1969; children: Judith Hyman Rosenbaum, Adina Hyman Rosenbaum. BJED, Hebrew Coll., Brookline, Mass., 1966; BA, Radcliffe Coll., 1968; MA, Columbia U., 1970, PhD, 1975; degree (hon.), Jewish Theol. Sem., 2002. Asst. prof. Columbia U., N.Y.C., 1974-81; assoc. prof. history Jewish Theol. Sem., N.Y.C., 1981-86; dean. Sem., Coll. Jewish Studies, 1981-86; Lady Davis vis. assoc. prof. Hebrew U., Jerusalem, 1986; Lucy Moses prof. history Yale U., New Haven, 1986—. Author: From Dreyfus to Vichy, 1979, The Emancipation of the Jews of Alsace, 1991, Gender and Assimilation in Modern Jewish History, 1995, The Jews of Modern France, 1998; co-author: The Jewish Woman in America, 1976; co-editor: The Jewish Family: Myths and Reality, 1986, Jewish Women in America: An Historical Encyclopedia, 2 vols., 1997; editor: My Life as a Radical Jewish Woman, 2002; series editor Ind. U. Press, Bloomington, 1982—; contbg. editor Sh'ma Mag., N.Y.C., 1977—; contbr. articles to publs. Vice chmn. Zionist Acad. Coun., N.Y.C., 1982-83. NEH summer grantee, 1977; Am. Coun. Learned Socs. fellow, 1978; grantee N.Y. Coun. for Humanities, 1980; NEH fellow, 1986-87. Fellow Am. Acad. Jewish Rsch. (treas. 1995—, v.p. 1999-); mem. Am. Hist. Assn. (com. 1983), Assn. for Jewish Studies (bd. dirs. 1978-81, 83-85, 86—, v.p. for membership 1995-97), Nat. Found. Jewish Culture (chair acad. adv. com. 1996—), Leo Baeck Inst. (bd. dirs. 1979—), Yivo Inst. for Jewish Rsch., Phi Beta Kappa. Jewish. Office: Yale U Dept History New Haven CT 06520

HYMAN, TRINA SCHART, illustrator; b. Phila., Apr. 8, 1939; d. Albert Henry and Margaret Doris (Bruck) Schart; m. Harris Joel Hyman, May 29, 1959 (div. 1968); 1 child, Katrin. Student, Phila. Mus. Sch. Art, 1956—59, Boston Mus. Sch. Fine Arts, 1959—60, Konstfackskolan, Stockholm, 1960—61. Free-lance illustrator, 1961—; art dir. Cricket mag., LaSalle, Ill., 1971—79, staff artist, 1979—88. Greeting card artist, designer Pawprints, Inc., Jaffrey, NH, 1980—; free-lance figurine designer The Franklin Mint, Franklin Center, Pa., 1982—. Author, illustrator: How Six Found Christmas, 1969, Sleeping Beauty, 1977, A Little Alphabet, 1980, author, illustrator:: Self-Portrait, 1981, author, illustrator: Jakob Grimm and Wilhelm Grimm, 1983, The Enchanted Forest, 1984, illustrator: 132 books including Toffe and the Little Car, 1961, Curl Up Small, 1964, Billy Finds Out, 1966, The Five Trials of the Pansy Bed, 1967, Cinnamon Seed, 1967, The Half-Time Gypsy, 1968, All in Free but Janey, 1968, Dragon Stew, 1969, The Cabin on the Fjord, 1969, A Walk Out of the World, 1969, The Vi-Daylin Book of Minnie the Mump, 1970, The Walking Stones: A Story of Suspense, 1970, The Bigger They Come, 1971, A Room Made of Windows, 1971 (Boston Globe-Horn Book award, 1971), How I Went Shopping and What I Got, 1972, The Popular Girls Club, 1972, The Wanderers, 1973, King Stork, 1973 (Boston Globe-Horn Book award, 1973), Will You Sign Here, John Hancock?, 1976, Six Impossible Things before Breakfast, 1977, Ranger Rick's Holiday Book, 1980, The Man Who Loved Books, 1981, Ronia, the Robber's Daughter, 1983, St. George and the Dragon, 1984 (Caldecott medal, 1985), The Cat Walked through the Casserole: And Other Poems for Children, 1984, A Castle In The Attic, 1987 (Dorothy Canfield Fisher award, 1987); Sing a Song of Popcorn, 1988; illustrator: The Kitchen Knight: A Tale from King Arthur, 1990, Hershel and the Hanukkah Goblins, 1990, Ghost Eye, 1992, The Fortune Tellers, 1993 (Boston Globe-Horn Book award, 1993), Haunts: Five Hair-Raising Tales, 1996, The Serpent Slayer and Other Stories of Strong Women, 1998, A Child's Calendar, 2000 (Caldecott Honor Book, 2000), Children of the Dragon: Selected Tales from Vietnam, 2001, Sense Pass King: A Tale from Cameroon, 2002. Recipient Horn Book award for illustration, Boston Globe, 1973, 1984, Golden Kite award, 1984, Caldecott Honor Book award, ALA, 1983, 1989, 2000, Hope Dean award, 2002.*

HYMAN, URSULA H. lawyer; BA, Immaculate Heart Coll., 1973; MEd, Loyola Marymount Coll., 1977; JD, U. So. Calif., 1983. Bar: Calif. 1983. With Latham & Watkins, L.A., 1983—, ptnr., 1990—. Founding mem. ad hoc com. Chpt. 9 Reform. Mem.: ABA, L.A. Women's Lawyers Assns., Nat. Assn. Bond Lawyers, L.A. County Bar Assn., State Bar Calif. Office: Latham and Watkins LLP 633 W Fifth St Ste 4000 Los Angeles CA 90071*

HYNDE, CHRISSIE, musician; b. Akron, Ohio, Sept. 7, 1951; m. Jim Kerr, 1984 (div. 1990); 1 child, Yasmin Kerr ; m. Lucho Brieva, 1997. Student, Kent State U., 1970. Lead singer, songwriter, guitarist Pretenders, 1978. Recordings include The Pretenders, 1980 (Brass in Pocket top-selling single), Prentenders II, 1981, Learning to Crawl, 1984 (songwriter Middle of the Road, Show Me, Back in the Chain Gang), Get Close, 1986 (songwriter Don't Get Me Wrong), The Prentenders Live, 1988, Packed!, 1990, Last of the Independents, 1994 (songwriter I'll Stand By You), The Isle of View (live), 1995, Viva el Amor, 1999, Loose Screw, 2002; two songs featured in film G.I. Jane; song "Brass in Pocket" (I'm Special), featured in film Lost in Translation, 2003. Mem.: PETA (People Ethical Treatment Animals). Mailing: Artemis Records 130 5th Ave 7th Fl New York NY 10011*

HYNES, AEDHMAR, public relations executive; married; 3 children. Econs. degree, Univ. Coll., Galway, Ireland; postgrad. diploma in mktg. With London office Text 100, regional dir. N.Am. ops., 1997—. Office: Text 100 Corp San Francisco 2d Fl 30 Hotaling Pl Fl 2D San Francisco CA 94111-2201 Fax: (415) 836-5991. E-mail: ryand@text100.com.

HYNES, PATRICIA MARY, lawyer; b. N.Y.C., Jan. 26, 1942; BA, CUNY, 1963; LLB, Fordham U., 1966. Bar: N.Y. 1966, U.S. Dist. Ct. (so. and ea. dists.) N.Y. 1969, U.S. Ct. Appeals (2d cir.) 1982. Law clk. to Hon. Joseph C. Zavatt U.S. Dist. Ct. (ea. dist.) N.Y., 1966-67; mem. civil divsn. U.S. Dist. Ct. (so. dist.) N.Y., 1967-71, asst. U.S. atty., 1967-82, chief consumer fraud unit, 1971-78, chief ofcl. corruption and spl. pros. unit, 1978-80, exec. asst. U.S. atty., 1980-82; ptnr. Milberg Weiss Bershad Hynes & Lerach LLP, N.Y.C., 1983-99, of counsel, 2000—. Adj. prof. law Fordham U., 1978—83; lectr. trial advocacy Harvard U. Law Sch., 1983; lectr. Practising Law Inst.; mem. criminal justice act peer rev. panel U.S. Dist. Ct. (so. dist.) N.Y., 1982—83, mem. discovery com., 1982—84, mem. civil litig. com., 1983—84, chmn. merit selection panel for N.Y. magistrate judges, 2002—. Mem. Fordham Law Rev., 1964-66; mem. editl. bd. N.Y. Law Jour., 1994—. Mem. NYC Charter Revision Commn., 2002, Gov.'s Exec. Adv. Com. on Adminstrn. Criminal Justice, 1981—82, N.Y. Gov.'s Commn. on Govt. Integrity, 1987—90, Mayor's Adv. Com. on Jud., 1994—2001; chairperson N.Y. Regional Consumer Protection Coun., 1971—72. Named one of 50 Top Women Lawyers, Nat. Law Jour., 1998, 2001. Fellow: Am. Coll. Trial Lawyers; mem.: ABA (chair govt. litig. com. litig. sect. 1984—87, chair securities litig. com. 1987—89, coun. litig. sect. 1989—92, chair pre-trial practice and discovery com. 1992—94, standing com. on fed. jud. 1995—2000, chair 2000—01, criminal justice sect.), Legal Aid Soc. (bd. dirs. 1998—2003, chair 2004—), N.Y. Coun. Def. Lawyers, Fed. Bar Coun. (trustee 1983—91, treas. 1987—90, v.p. 1990, 1996—), N.Y. State Bar Assn. (consumer affairs com. 1974—78, criminal law com. 1980—84, police law and policy com. 1981—83, sec. 1982—84, ho. dels. 1983—84, exec. com. 1984—88, second century com. 1988—92, del. to ABA, ho. dels. 1990—94, chair fed. cts. com. 1992—95, del.), Assn. of the Bar of the City of N.Y., Am. Law Inst. (spl. advisor 1995—2001), Fordham Law Alumni Assn. Office: Milberg Weiss Bershad Hynes & Lerach LLP One Penn Plz New York NY 10119

HYNUS, ANITA EILEEN, music educator; b. Huntington, W.Va., Oct. 3, 1959; d. Richard Lee and MaryAnn Campbell; m. James R. Hynus, June 7, 1986; children: Cassandra Ann, Zachary Robert. BA in Music Edn., Marshall U., 1981, MA in Music Edn., 1983. Tchr. music K-12, gen. sci. 7-12 W.Va. Music tchr. Gallia County Local Schs., Gallipolis, Ohio, 1982—90; music edn. Robeson County Pub. Schs., Lumberton, NC, 1990—96; tchr. gen. music, orch. Orange County Schs., Hillsborough, NC, 1996—98; tchr. orch. Wake County Pub. Schs., Raleigh, NC, 1998—. Performer Huntington Pops Orch., 1985—90; elem. strings chmn. Wake County Pub. Schs., 2000—03. Leader Girl Scouts Am., Apex, NC, 2000—03, Cub Scouts Am., Apex, 2000—03. Scholar, Bd. Regents W.Va., 1978—91. Mem.: Profl. Educators N.C. (assoc.), Music Educators Nat. Conf. (assoc.), Delta Omicron (life). Republican. Lutheran. Avocation: travel. Home: 1114 Lexington Farm Rd Apex NC 27502 Office: Martin Mid Sch 1701 Ridge Rd Raleigh NC 27607 Personal E-mail: ahynus@aol.com.

HYTIER, ADRIENNE DORIS, French language educator; d. Jean and Katharine (Hytier) Matson. BA summa cum laude, Barnard Coll., 1952; MA, Columbia U., 1953, PhD, 1958. Instr. French Vassar Coll., 1959-61, asst. prof., 1961-66, assoc. prof., 1966-70, prof. French, 1970-96, Lichtenstein Dale prof. French, 1974-96. Vis. assoc. prof. Columbia U., 1966, U. Calif., 1968—69. Editor for French lit.: The 18th Century: A Current Bibliography Since 1970, 25 vols., Two Years of French Foreign Policy: Vichy 1940-42, 1958, 2d edit., 1974, Les Dépêches diplomatiques du Comte de Gobineau en Perse, 1959, La Guerre, 1975, 4th edit., 1991; contbr. articles to profl. jours. Decorated chevalier des Palmes Académiques; fellow Guggenheim Found., 1967-68. Mem. MLA, Am. Soc. 18th Century Studies, NE Soc. for 18th Century Studies, Internat. Soc. 18th Century Studies, Phi Beta Kappa. Home: 71 Raymond Ave Poughkeepsie NY 12603-0372 Office: Vassar Coll Box 372 Poughkeepsie NY 12604-0001

IADAROLA, ANTOINETTE, college president; BA cum laude, Saint Joseph Coll., West Hartford, Conn., 1962; MA, Georgetown U., 1968; student, Oxford U., England, 1970; Fulbright Scholar, London Sch. Econs., 1971-73; PhD, Georgetown U., 1975; postgrad., Yale U., 1976-77. Asst. to grad. dean Georgetown U., Washington, 1968-71; dir. grants, asst. prof. history Saint Joseph College, 1974-78, dir. grants, chair dept. history, 1978-80, spl. asst. to pres. planning and ednl. affairs, chair dept. history, 1981-83; administrv. intern to pres. and provost Hood College, Frederick, Md, 1980-81; provost, dean of faculty College of Mount Saint Joseph, Cin., 1983-86, Colby-Sawyer Coll., New London, N.H., 1986-92; pres. Cabrini Coll., Radnor, Pa., 1992—. Mem. exec. com. Mercy Higher Edn. Colloquium, 1977-81; cons. Am. Coun. Edn., Ctr. Leadership Devel. and Acad. Administrn., 1980-92; bd. dirs. Am. Conf. Acad. Deans, 1987-90; chair Strategic Planning Com., Coll. Mt. St. Joseph, 1983-86, Com. Chief Acad. Officers, Greater Cin. Consortium colls. and Univs., 1985-86, Teaching/Learning Com. Coeducation Transition, Colby-Sawyer Coll., 1989-92. Contrb. articles to profl. jours. Cons. YWCA, Waterbury, 1974-80, Farmington C. of C. Teenage Scholarship Program, 1976-79; bd. dirs. Ursuline Acad., Cin., 1983-86, Private Industry Coun., Cin., 1983-86, N.H. Humanities Coun., 1987-92, vice chair 1989-90; mem. adv. com. civic literacy, Women's City Club, Cin., 1984-86, devel. com. Shakers Village, Enfield, N.H., 1989-92; chair Town/Gown Community Forum, New London, N.H., 1986-92; coord. ecumenical adult edn. program, Our Lady of Fatima ch., New London, 1987-92; trustee Girard Coll., Phila., 1995, academic affairs and investement coms. Valley Forge Mil. Acad., Radnor, Pa., 1994—. Fellow Georgetown U., 1968-71, Yale U., 1976-77, Danforth Assoc., 1979-86, Am. Coun. Edn. Fellowship in Acad. Administrn., 1980-81; grantee Inst. Internat. Edn. to Oxford U., 1970, NEH, 1979; Fulbright Scholar, 1971-73; recipient Dist. Alumna award Saint Joseph college, 1982, Purple Aster award Order of Sons of Italy, 1994. Mem. AAUP, Am. Assn. Higher Edn., Am. Hist. Assn., League of Women Voters. Avocations: jogging, hiking, skiing (cross-training), golf, opera. Office: Cabrini Coll 610 King Of Prussia Rd Radnor PA 19087-3623

IADAVAIA, ELIZABETH ANN, marketing professional; b. N.Y.C., June 28, 1960; d. Vincent Anthony and Sally (D'Angelo) I. BA in Econs., Georgetown U., 1982; postgrad., CUNY, 1996; MS in Teaching, Pace U., 2000. Rsch. asst. Montefiore Hosp. Neurophysiology Labs., N.Y.C., 1979-80; in mktg. rsch. Sch. Bus. Adminstrn. Georgetown U., Washington, 1981-82; adminstrv. asst. Kolter Devel. Corp., N.Y.C., 1983-85; dir. ops. Merrill Lynch Realty, Stamford, Conn., 1985-88, Crown Group Real Estate Devel. & Fin., White Plains, N.Y., 1988-92; dir. mktg. Equitable, New Hyde Park, N.Y., 1992-94, N.Y.C., 1995-96, Ingrao, Inc., N.Y.C., 1996-99; with Pelham Pub. Schs., 1999-2000; 5th grade tchr. Pub. Sch. 95, N.Y.C., 2000—; teaching asst. Grad. Sch. Edn. Pace U., NY, 2001—02; mem. reading and writing project leadership program Tchr.'s Coll., 2001—03. Mem. St. Catherines Parish Coun., Bronxville. Winner 13th and 14th ann. Agy. Newsletter contest Life Ins. Mktg. and Rsch. Assn. Mem. N.Y. State MBA Assn., Sch. of the Holy Child Alumni Assn. (bd. dirs., chmn. Rye, N.Y. chpt. 1983—), Georgetown U. Alumni Assn. (class chmn. 1986—), Women in Sales Assn. (v.p. 1988-97), Nat. Second Mortgage Assn., VIP Young Adult Club (pres. 1985-87). Home: 17 Archer Dr Bronxville NY 10708-4601 Office: PS 95 3961 Hillman Ave Bronx NY 10463

IANNITELLI, SUSAN B. state legislator; b. Pawtucket, R.I., June 12, 1953; m. Ralph E. Iannitelli; 1 child, Ralph E. BA, Wheaton Coll., 1974; JD, Mercer U., 1977. Atty. Iannitelli Law Offices; rep. dist. 57 R.I. Ho. of Reps., Providence, 1998. Mem. judiciary com., joint com. on vet. affairs, R.I. Ho. of Reps. Mem. Rep. State Ctrl. Com., Rep. Town Com. Office: RI House of Reps State House Providence RI 02903

IASIELLO, DOROTHY BARBARA, clinical social worker, former brokerage company executive; b. Bklyn., Oct. 6, 1949; d. Albert William (dec.) and Josephine (Accardo) Rehorn; m. John Joseph Iasiello Jr., May 5, 1974. AAS in Mktg., N.Y.C. C.C., 1969; BS in Econs., Coll. Staten Island, 1978; MS in Social Work, Columbia U., 2000. With J.P. Morgan Securities, N.Y.C., 1978-81, asst. treas. sales, 1981-84, asst. v.p. sales, 1984-88, v.p. sales adminstrn. mgmt., 1988-91, v.p. sales, 1991-95; bus. cons., 1996—98; clin. social work practitioner, 2000—. Roman Catholic. Avocations: reading, foreign and domestic travel.

IBARRA, AVELINA C. music educator; b. Manila, Nov. 10, 1934; came to the U.S., 1963; d. Benjamin Jamias and Anita Quevedo Dela Cuesta; m. Rufino Paras Ibarra, Apr. 6, 1963; children: Pearl Marie C., Kenneth Joseph C., Gina Ann I. Coss, Alan Anthony C. A in Music, cert. tchr., Concordia Sch. Music, Manila, 1957; BS in Pharmacy, U. Santo Thomas, Manila, 1959. Music tchr. Am. Coll. Musicians, Austin, 1976—; adjudicator, faculty mem. Nat. Guild Piano Tchrs., Austin, 1990—. Mem. entertainment com. Filipino Womens Club Tidewater, Norfolk, Va., 1967-72, United Iloco Assn. Tidewater, Norfolk, 1972-77. Named to Hall of Fame, Piano Guild, 1985. Mem. Music Tchr. Nat. Assn. (profl. cert.), Nat. Fedn. Music Clubs (award of merit 1996, 97), Va. Music Tchrs. Assn. (profl., provisional and std. certs.), Tidewater Music Tchrs. Forum (historian 1995—), Scherzo Music Club (photographer 1998—, mem. hostess com. 1989—) Home: 4201 Gosnold Ave Norfolk VA 23508-2935

IBBOTSON, PATRICIA ANN, occupational health nurse, writer; b. Detroit, Nov. 17, 1940; d. Russell and Sophia (Nigbor) I. Diploma in nursing, Mercy Sch. Nursing, Detroit, 1961. RN, Mich. From staff nurse to clin. nursing supervisor Wayne County Gen. Hosp., Westland, Mich., 1961-84; corp. screening nurse Fairlane Health Sys., Birmingham, Mich., 1986-91; occupl. health nurse Ford Motor Co., Dearborn, Mich., 1990—99. Author: Eloise Poorhouse, Farm, Asylum and Hospital 1839-1984, 2002, Detroit's Hospitals, Healers, and Helpers, 2004. Avocations: genealogy, travel. Home: 22036 Nowlin St Dearborn MI 48124-2733

ICHINO, YOKO, ballet dancer; b. Los Angeles, Cali. Studied with Mia Slavenska, L.A. Mem. Joffrey II, N.Y.C., Joffrey Ballet, N.Y.C., Stuttgart Ballet, Fed. Republic Germany; tchr. ballet, 1976; soloist Am. Ballet Theatre, 1977-81, guest appearances, 1981-82; prin. Nat. Ballet Can., Toronto, Ont., 1982-90. Various guest appearances including World Ballet Festival, Tokyo, 1979, 85, Tokyo Ballet, 1980, with Alexander Godunov and Stars, summer, 1982, Sydney Ballet, Australia, N.Z. Ballet, summer 1984, Ballet de Marseille, 1985-87, Deutsche Opera Ballet Berlin, 1985-90, Munich Opera Ballet, 1987-90, Australian Ballet, 1987, 89, Staatsoper Berlin, 1989, 90, Komische Opera, Berlin, 1991-93, David Nixon's Dance Theater, Berlin, 1990, 91, Birmingham Royal Ballet, 1990-93, Deutsche Opera Ballet, Berlin, 1994-95; tchr. Australian Ballet, 1989, Birmingham Royal Ballet, 1991, 93, Nat. Ballet of Can., 1993, Cullberg Ballet, Sweden, 1994, Nat. Ballet Sch., 1994, 95, Ballet de Monte-Carlo, 1994, Geneva Ballet, 1995-98, Nederlands Dance Theater, 1995, Rambert Dance, 1995, Royal Winnipeg Ballet, 1999; tchr. numerous ballet workshops; dir. profl. program Ballet Met, 1995-2003; guest master tchr., coach No. Ballet Theatre, 2002--. First Am. women recipient medal Third Internat. Ballet Competition, Moscow, 1977. Office: No Ballet Theatre West Park Centre Spen Ln Leeds LS16 5BE England

IDDINGS, KATHLEEN, poet, editor, publisher, consultant; b. Ohio, June 25, 1945; d. Ralph Myers and Ruth Amelia Wolfe. BS in Edn., Miami U., Oxford, Ohio, 1968. Tchr. various Ohio schs., 1962-74; freelance photojournalist La Jolla, Calif., 1976-80; freelance pub. rels. mgr. San Diego, 1980-81; cons., 1981—; editor, pub. La Jolla Poet's Press, 1981—. Poetry cons. San Diego City Schs., 1990; resident Djerassi Artists' Colony, 1990. Author: (poetry) Sticks, Friction & Fire, 2001, 5 other books of poetry. Named Poet of Millenium, Internat. Poets Acad., 2000; fellow, NEA, 1989; grantee, PEN, 1988, 1990, Calif. Arts Coun., 1994, Carnegie Authors; scholar, Napa Poetry Conf. Mem.: PEN, San Diego Ind. Scholars, Associated Writers Program, Acad. Am. Poets, Univ. Club, Calif. San Diego Faculty Club (Chancellor's Assoc. 1999—2004). Democrat. Avocations: poetry readings, photography, college lectures, poetry contest judge. Office: La Jolla Poets Press PO Box 8638 La Jolla CA 92038-8638 E-mail: KathleenIddings@aol.com.

IDOL, ANNA CATHERINE, magazine editor; b. Chgo., July 8, 1941; d. Melvin Oliver and Louise Hildegard (Bullington) Lokensgard; m. William Ross Idol, Oct. 25, 1959 (div. Mar. 1962); 1 child, Laura Jeanne; m. Michael Wataru Sugano, Jan. 28, 1990. BS, Lake Forest (Ill.) Coll., 1980; MBA, Northwestern U., Evanston, Ill., 1982. treas. Chgo. Women in Pub., Chgo., 1970-71. Editor Rand McNally Co., Chgo., 1968-78, product mgr. adult reference, 1983-84; founder, pres. Bullington Laird, Inc., Chgo., 1986—; mng. editor Elks Mag., Chgo., 1997—. Pub.: Center Within, 1988 (award Heartsong Rev. 1989); writer, concept advt. alert, 1990 (Harvey Comm. award). Pres. Am. Buddhist Assn., 1985-93; mem. bd. Buddhist Temple Chgo., 1985-93; v.p. Buddhist Coun. Midwest, 1985-89. Democrat. Buddhist. Avocations: wilderness adventure, travel, reading. Office: Elks Mag 425 W Diversey Pkwy Chicago IL 60614-6196 E-mail: annai@elks.org.

IDOS, ROSALINA VEJERANO, secondary school educator; b. Ligao, Philippines, Mar. 18, 1944; arrived in U.S., 1987; m. Salvador Salcedo Idos, Dec. 21, 1969; children: Nathaniel, Rey, Lady Lou. BSc in Edn., U. of the East, Philippines, 1965; MSc in Edn., Nat. U., 2000. Cert. single subject tchg. in English, social studies, Filipino Calif., 1989. Tchr. Mayon H.S., Ligao City, Philippines, 1965—67; master tchr. in charge of student tchrs. U. of the East, Manila, Philippines, 1967—69, prof., 1969—87; tchr. San Diego Unified Sch. Dist. Morse H.S., San Diego, 1988—. Workshop presenter in field; curriculum writer Project Inclusion San Diego City Schs., San Diego, 1993—95. Recipient Outstanding Tchr. award, U. Calif., 1995—96, Educator of the Decade award, Filipino-Am. Educators Assn. San Diego, 1999, Svc. award, Fgn. Lang. Coun. San Diego, 1999, Recognition award, Filipino-Am. Educators of Calif., 2000. Fellow: Calif. Fgn. Lang. Project; mem.: San Diego Internat. Lang. Network (leadership team), Filipino-Am. Parents Assn. (adv. 1993—), Kaisahan Club (adv. 1990—). Roman Catholic. Avocations: reading, writing. Home: 6333 Viewpoint Ct San Diego CA 92139 Office: Morse High School 6905 Skyline Drive San Diego CA 92114

IENATSCH, GAYLEEN ELIZABETH, nursing educator; b. Mt. Horeb, Wis., May 20, 1940; d. Gerhard Palmer and Mayme Eileen (Grim) Steensrud; m. Grant Peter Ienatsch, June 3, 1962; children: Britt Christine Leach, Peter Jay, Perry Lee. Diploma in nursing, Madison (Wis.) Gen. Hosp. Sch. Nursing, 1961; BSN, Tex. Tech U., 1987, MSN, 1991. RN, Tex. Staff nurse CCU Midland (Tex.) Meml. Hosp., 1979-85; staff nurse ICU Med. Ctr. Hosp., Odessa, Tex., 1985-86; program dir., supr. cardiac rehab. for out-patients CardioCentral, Odessa, 1986-92; nursing instr. Tex. Tech. U. Health Sci. Ctr. Sch. Nursing, Odessa, 1992-94, acting regional dean, 1994-95, regional dean, 1995-98. Cons. CardioCentral, Odessa, 1992-98; mem. adv. com. Odessa Coll. Sch. Nursing, 1994-98; Midland Coll. Health Scis. divsn. chair, 1998—, bd. dirs. Am. Heart Assn., Ector Co., Tex., 1986—. Author chpt. to book; mem. editl. bd. Tex. Jour. Rural Health, 1994-98. Mem. cmty. adv. bd. Jr. League of Odessa, 1994-98. Recipient Disting. Svc. award Am. Heart Assn., 1990. Mem. APHA, ANA, Tex. Nurses Assn., Sigma Theta Tau. Presbyterian. Avocations: aerobic exercise, playing the organ. Home: 1524 Tanglewood Ln Odessa TX 79761-1824 Office: Midland Coll 3600 N Garfield St Midland TX 79705-6329 E-mail: gienatsch@midland.cc.tx.us.

IEZZONI, LISA I. medical educator, healthcare educator, researcher; MSc, Harvard U., 1978; MD, Harvard U., Boston, 1984. Sr. rschr. health care rsch. unit Boston U., 1984—85, asst. rsch. prof. dept. medicine, 1985—90, dir. health svcs. rsch. Health Policy Inst., 1988—90, asst. prof. health svcs., 1989—90; asst. prof. medicine Harvard Med. Sch., Boston, 1990—93, prof. medicine, 1993—; co-dir. rsch. divsn. gen. medicine and primary care Beth Israel Deaconess Med. Ctr., Boston. Mem. Nat. Com. on Vital and Health Stats.; bd. dirs. Nat. Forum for Health Care Quality Measurement and Reporting. Contbr. articles to profl. jours.; mem. editl. bds of maj. med. and health svcs. rsch. jours.; author (and editor): Risk Adjustment for Measuring Healthcare Outcomes. Recipient Investigator Award in Health Policy Rsch., The Robert Wood Johnson Found., 1996. Mem.: Inst. of Medicine of NAS. Avocations: gardening, painting, reading. Office: Beth Israel Deaconess Med Ctr Divsn Gen Medicine Libby 326 330 Brookline Ave Boston MA 02215

IGNAGNI, KAREN, healthcare association executive; Degree, Providence Coll.; MBA, Loyola U. Formerly with Com. for Nat. Health Ins., HHS; former profl. staff mem. U.S. Senate Labor and Human Resources Com.; dir. Dept. Employee Benefits AFL-CIO, 1990—93; pres., CEO Group Health Assn. Am., 1993—95, Am. Assn. Health Plans, 1995—. Office: Am Assn Health Plans 1129 20th St NW Ste 600 Washington DC 20036

IGNATIUS, NANCY WEISER, fundraising and administrative executive; b. Holyoke, Mass., Sept. 10, 1925; d. Richard Mather Weiser and Louise Gilbert Reynolds; m. Paul Robert Ignatius, Dec. 20, 1947; children: David, Sarah, Amy, Adi. BA, Wellesley Coll., 1947; MA, Am. Univ., 1969. With Dept. of Energy, Washington, 1977-79, cons., 1975-76, EPA, Washington, 1980-81. Contbr. articles to Cathedral Age mag. Trustee, bd. dirs. Washington Chorus, 1996—, chmn., 2000—; pres. Nat. Cathedral Assn., 1986-90, trustee, 1993—; pres. Com. for Nat. Security, 1998—; active chpt. Washington Nat. Cathedral. Mem. Chevy Chase Club, Sulgrave Club. E-mail: nanig3650@aol.com.

IKAWA-SMITH, FUMIKO, anthropologist, educator; b. Kobe, Japan, Sept. 10, 1930; arrived in Canada, 1960; d. Jokei and Sachi (Nakano) Ikawa; m. Takao Sofue, Jan. 1955 (div. 1958); m. Philip Edward Lake Smith, Nov. 1959; 1 child, Douglas Philip Edward. BA, Tsuda Coll., Tokyo, 1953; student Tokyo Met. U., 1954-55; AM in Anthropology, Radcliffe Coll., 1959; PhD in Anthropology, Harvard U., 1974. Asst. prof. McGill U., Montreal, 1968-74, assoc. prof., 1974-79, chmn. dept. anthropology, 1975-80, prof., 1997—2003, dir. Ctr. East Asian Studies, 1983-88, chmn. dept. East Asian langs. and lits., 1983-88, assoc. acad. vice prin., 1991-96. Vis. prof. Canadian studies Kwansei Gakuin U., Japan, 1996-97. Editor: Early Palaeolithic in South and East Asia, 1978, Proceedings of the First Meeting of The Social Sciences Association of Canada, 1989; mem. editl. bd. Anthrop. Sci., 1998—. Fellow Am. Anthrop. Assn. (exec. mem.-at-large archeology divsn. 1988-90), Current Anthropology (assoc.); mem. Pacific Sci. Assn. (life), Soc. Am. Archeology, Japan Studies Assn. Can. (acting pres. 1988-90, pres. elect 1998-99, pres. 1999-2000), Indo-Pacific Prehistory Assn. (exec. com. 1990-98), Can. Asian Studies Assn. (chair Japan com. 1991-94), Quebec-Japan Bus. Forum (bd. mem. 1998-2000). Avocations: horticulture, piano. Home: 3955 Ramezay Ave Montreal QC Canada H3Y 3K3 Office: McGill U Dept Anthropology 855 Sherbrooke St W Montreal QC Canada H3A 2T7 E-mail: fumiko.ikawa-smith@mcgill.ca.

ILCHMAN, ALICE STONE, foundation administrator, former college president, former government official; b. Cin., Apr. 18, 1935; d. Donald Crawford and Alice Kathryn (Biermann) Stone; m. Warren Frederick Ilchman, June 11, 1960; children: Frederick Andrew Crawford, Alice Sarah. BA, Mt. Holyoke Coll., 1957; MPA, Maxwell Sch. Citizenship, Syracuse U., 1958; PhD, London Sch. Econs., 1965; LHD, Mt. Holyoke Coll., 1982, Franklin and Marshall Coll., 1983. Asst. to pres., mem. faculty Berkshire C.C., 1961-64; lectr. Ctr. for South and S.E. Asia Studies U. Calif., Berkeley, 1965-73; prof. econs. and edn., dean Wellesley (Mass.) Coll., 1973-78; asst. sec. ednl. and cultural affairs Dept. State, 1978; assoc. dir. ednl. and cultural affairs Internat. Comm. Agy., 1978—81; advisor to sec. Smithsonian Instn., 1981; pres. Sarah Lawrence Coll., Bronxville, NY, 1981-98; chmn. bd. Rockefeller Found., N.Y.C., NY, 1995—2000. Dir. Jeannette K. Watson Fellowships, 1999—; intern, asst. to Sen. John F. Kennedy, 1957; dir. Peace Corps Tng. Program for India, 1965-66; chmn. com. on women's employment NAS; sr. advisor Thomas Watson Found., 1999—; bd. dirs. NYNEX, Seligman Group of Investment Cos. Author: The New Men of Knowledge and the New States, 1968, (with W.F. Ilchman) Education and Employment in India, The Policy Nexus, 1976, The Lucky Few and the Worhty Many: Selecting the World's Future Leaders, 2004. Trustee Mt. Holyoke Coll., 1970-80, Mass. Found. for Humanities and Pub. Policy, 1974-77, East-West Ctr., Honolulu, 1978-81, Expt. in Internat. Living, The Markle Found., The Rockefeller Found., chmn. bd. dirs., acting pres., 1998; trustee The U. of Cape Town, South Africa, Corp. Adv. Bd., Hotchkiss Sch.; mem. Smithsonian Coun., Yonkers Emergency Fin. Control Bd., 1982-88, Am. Ditchley Found. Program Com., Internat. Rsch. and Exch. Bd., Com. for Econ. Devel., The Masters Sch., Save The Children, Chamber Music Soc. Lincoln Ctr.; bd. dirs. Pub. Broadcasting Corp., 2000—. Hon. fellow Wadham Coll., Oxford U. Mem. NOW Legal Def. Edn. Fund, Coun. Fgn. Rels., Century Assn. (N.Y.C.), Bronxville Field Club. Home: 18 Highland Cir Bronxville NY 10708-5908 Office: Jeannette K Watson Fellowships 31st Fl 810 Seventh Ave New York NY 10019 E-mail: ailchman@jkwatson.org.

ILDSTAD, SUZANNE T. transplant surgeon, immunologist, educator; b. Mpls., May 20, 1952; m. David J. Tollerud, Dec. 19, 1971; children: David J. II, Suzanne K. BS in Biology summa cum laude, U. Minn., 1974; MD, Mayo Med. Sch., 1978. Diplomate Am. Bd. Surgery. Resident in gen. surgery Mass. Gen. Hosp., Boston, 1978 82, 85 86; immunology fellow transplantation biology sect. Nat. Cancer Inst., NIH, Bethesda, Md., 1982-85; clin. fellow pediatric surgery Children's Hosp. Med. Ctr., Cin., 1986-88; asst. prof. dept. surgery U. Pitts., 1988-93, assoc. prof., 1993-94; prof., chief dept. surgery Children's Hosp. Med. Ctr., Cin., 1994—; also dir. divsn. cellular therapeutics U. Pitts. Mem. Affirmative Action com., resident adv. com. dept. surgery U. Pitts., 1988-91; mem. instl. animal care and use com., 1991-94; mem. coord. com. rsch. integrity, 1992—; mem. lab. usage com., oncology com., GCRC adv. com., residency coord. dept. surgery Children's Hosp., Pitts., 1988-91; vis. prof. U. Minn., 1991, Children's Meml. Hosp., U. Chgo., 1992; mem. various coms. Children's Cancer Study Group; lectr., rschr. in field. Mem. editorial bd. Jour. Transplantation, 1992, Transplantation Sci., 1992, Jour. ACS; mem. adv. bd. Clin. Transplantation Procs., 1992; editor Chimerism and Tolerance; contbr. articles to profl. jours., also numerous abstracts, letters and presentations in field, chpts. to books. Recipient James A. Shannon Dirs.'s award, 1991; Instl. grantee Am. Cancer Soc., 1990-91; grantee U. Pitts., 1989-90, 91-92, Children's Hosp. Pitts. Rsch. Adv. Com., 1990-91, NIH - RO1, 1991-96, 92-95, U. Pitts. Med. Ctr., 1991-92, Juvenile Diabetes Found., 1991-92, Nat. Kidney Found., 1991-92, Am. Heart Assn., 1992-95, Am. Diabetes Assn., 1992-94. Fellow ACS (Pediatric Surg. Forum award 1990, Young Investigator award 1990-92, fellowship award 1990-92, sec. Pediatric Surgery Biology Club 1989-91); mem. AAAS, Am. Acad. Pediatrics, Am. Assn. Cancer Rsch., Am. Assn. Immunologists, Am. Fedn. Clin. Rsch., Am. Soc. Clin. Rsch., Am. Soc. Transplant Surgeons (program com. 1991-94), Assn. Acad. Surgeons, Mass. Med. Soc., Pediatric Transplant Study Group, Soc. Clin. Immunology, Soc. Head and Neck Surgeons (Resident/Fellow award 1983), Soc. Univ. Surgeons, Surg. Infection Soc. (travel grantee XII Internat. Congress, Sydney, Australia, 1988), Assn. Acad. Surgeons (program com. 1989-91), Cell Transplant Soc. (adv. bd. 1991, counselor-at-large 1992—). Office: Allegheny U of the Health Scis Broad and Vine Sts MS 490 Philadelphia PA 19102

ILES, EILEEN MARIE, bank executive; b. Highland Park, Ill., Sept. 29, 1965; d. Dennis Jay and Ida Sigrid (Calderelli) Connolly; m. Kenneth Robert Iles, Dec. 14, 1985; children: Kevin Andrew, Eric Robert. Student, U. Ill., Chgo., 1983—85; BBA in Acctg. and Mktg. Mgmt., U. N.Mex., 1988, M in Acctg., 1992. Acct. Charter Bank for Savs., Albuquerque, 1989-90, bank acctg. supr., 1990-91, asst. contr., 1991-2000, asst. v.p., 1992-2000; engagement mgr. Crowe Chizek & Co., LLC, Oak Brook, Ill., 2000, sr. engagement mgr., 2000—03, exec., 2003—. Instr. acctg. U. N.Mex., Albuquerque, 1994-99, Albuquerque Tech. Vocat. Inst., 2000; cons. in field. Mem.: Assn. Cert. Fraud Examiners, Inst. Internal Auditors, Inst. Mgmt. Accts. Office: One MidAm Plz PO Box 3697 Oak Brook IL 60522-3697 E-mail: eiles@crowechizek.com.

ILES, KAY C. state representative; b. Alexandria, La., July 15, 1942; d. George Shelton Sr. and Eloise (Holladay) Caillouet; m. Robert L. Iles, Jan. 28, 1961; children: Trey, Scott, Reneé, Michelle. Student, U. S.W. La., 1960. State rep. State of La. Mem. DeRidder Kiwanis (pres. 1994-95), DeRidder Days in the Park (founder, pres. 1987-95), Beauregard Parish Crimestoppers (co-founder), Boise Buddies (vol. 1991-95). Baptist. Avocations: reading, walking. Office: State Rep 163 Marvin Ave Deridder LA 70634-5756

ILEY, MARTHA STRAWN, music educator; b. Marshville, NC, June 1, 1925; d. Stephen Hasty and Lila Faircloth Strawn; m. Bryce Baxter Iley, Aug. 7, 1948; children: Deborah Iley Hodde, Sheila Iley McLean, Cheryl Iley Lindstrom, Stephanie Iley Salb. BA, East Carolina Tchrs. Coll., 1946; MA, Western Ky. State Coll., 1947; MusM, Winthrop Coll., 1973; EdM, U. NC, Charlotte, 1974; EdD, Nova U., 1979; M Theol. Studies, Gordon-Conwell Theol. Sem., 1998. Cert. Music Tchrs. Nat. Assn. Music tchr. Lincolnton City Sch., 1947—48, Alexander Graham Jr. HS, Charlotte, NC, 1948—52, Charlotte Country Day Sch., 1955—59; min. music Providence Bapt. Ch., Charlotte, 1954—57, Carmel Bapt. Ch., Charlotte, 1968—70, 1975—76; project dir. music edn. Ctrl. Piedmont C.C., Charlotte, 1974—83; founder, chmn. bd. dirs. Met. Music Ministries, Charlotte, 1984—. Editor: (newsletter) ARTY-FACTS, 1983. Bd. dirs., sec. Charlotte Cmty. Concert Assn., 1980—93; dir. recital series Shepherd Ctr., Charlotte, 1980—83; adjudicator piano and voice various orgns., NC, 1980—. Recipient Disting. Music Alumni award, East Carolina U., 2002. Mem.: Charlotte Piano Tchrs. Forum (bd. dirs., pres. 1979—81), Charlotte Clergy Assn., NC Music Tchrs. Assn. (cert. chmn., v.p. 1981—83), Charlotte Music Club (bd. dirs.). Republican. Baptist. Avocations: writing, painting. Home: 10151 Robinson Church Rd Harrisburg NC 28075-6607 Office: Met Music Ministries Inc 1311 Paddock Cir Charlotte NC 28209-2443

ILGEN, DOROTHY L. arts foundation executive; Asst. dir. Mo. Arts Coun.; exec. dir. Kans. Arts Commn., Ind. Arts Commn., Indpls., 1995—. Active numerous coms. and commns. various local, state, regional, and nat. orgns.; bd. dirs. Mid-Am. Arts Alliance, Arts Midwest, mem. program planning com.; bd. dirs., mem. planning and budget com., nominating com. Nat. Assembly of State Arts Agys.; panelist arts design panel NEA, Nat. Access Task Force. Office: Indiana Arts Commission 150 W Market St Ste 618 Indianapolis IN 46204

ILITCH, DENISE, food services executive; Pres. Bright Lites Inc., Detroit; vice chair Little Caesar Enterprises Inc., 1997—; pres. Olympia Devel. LLC, 1996—; exec. v.p. Ilitch Holdings, Detroit, 1999—. Bd. dirs. Detroit br. Fed. Res. Bank of Chgo. Office: Ilitch Holdings Inc 2211 Woodward Ave Detroit MI 48201-3467

ILITCH, MARIAN, professional hockey team executive, food service executive; m. Michael Ilitch; children: Denise Ilitch Lites, Ron, Mike Jr., Lisa Ilitch Murray, Atanas, Christopher, Carole. Co-owner, sec.-treas. Little Caesar Internat., 1959—, Detroit Red Wings, 1982—; sec.-treas. Olympia Arenas, Inc. (Olympia Entertainment Inc.), 1982—; co-owner, sec.-treas. Fox Theatre, 1987—, Detroit Tigers, 1992—, Little Foxes Fine Gifts, 1992—, The Second City, 1993—, Olympia Devel. LLC, 1996—, Hockeytown Cafe, 1999—, Blue Line Distributing, Uptown Entertainment, Champion Foods; co-founder, vice-chmn. Ilitch Holdings, Inc., 1999—. Recipient Pacesetter Award, Roundtable for Women in Foodservice, 1988, Nat. Preservation Honor Award, 1990. Office: Ilitch Holdings Inc Fox Office Ctr 2211 Woodward Ave Detroit MI 48201-3400*

ILLNER-CANIZARO, HANA, physician, oral surgeon, researcher; b. Prague, Czechoslovakia, Nov. 2, 1939; came to U.S., 1968; d. Evzen Pospisil and Emilie (Chrastna) Pospisilova; m. Pavel Illner, June 14, 1963 (div. 1981); children: Martin Illner, Anna Illner; m. Peter Corte Canizaro, Nov. 1, 1982. MD, Charles U., Prague, 1961. Diplomate Am. Bd. Oral Surgery. Resident in oral surgery Inst. of Health, Pribram, Czechoslovakia, 1961-63; attending physician Oral Surgery Clinic, Prague, 1963-68; rsch. assoc. dept. surgery U. Tex. Southwestern Med. Sch., Dallas, 1969-72, instr. surgery, 1972-74, U. Wash. Sch. Medicine, Seattle, 1974-77; asst. prof. surgery Cornell U. Med. Coll., N.Y.C., 1977-81, assoc. prof. surgery, 1981-83, Tex. Tech U. Health Scis. Ctr., Lubbock, 1984-88, prof. surgery, 1988—. Site visitor NIGMS Postdoctoral Tng. Grant, Bethesda, Md., 1987. Mem. editorial bd. Circulatory Shock, N.Y.C., 1981—; manuscript reviewer Surgery, Gynecology and Obstetrics, Chgo., 1985—; contbr. chpts. to books, articles to profl. jours. Grantee NIH, 1979-83, 87-92, Tex. Tech U. Health Scis. Ctr., 1985-86, U.S. dept. Army, 1988-90; Fogarty Sr. Internat. fellow, 1991-92. Mem. Shock Soc. Avocations: remodeling of historical homes, gardening, skiing, pottery. Home: 4622 8th St Lubbock TX 79416-4722 Office: Tex Tech U Health Scis Ctr 3601 4th St Lubbock TX 79430-0001 Office Phone: 806-743-2460 227.

ILLSTON, SUSAN Y. federal judge; b. 1948; BA, Duke U., 1970; JD, Stanford U., 1973. Ptnr. Cotchett, Illston & Pitre, San Francisco, 1973-95; judge U.S. Dist. Ct. (no. dist.) Calif., San Francisco, 1995—. Author: Insurance Coverage in a Toxic Tort Case, A Guide to Toxic Torts, 1987, California Complex Litigation Manual, 1990. Active Legal Aid Soc. San Mateo County, Svc. League San Mateo County. Recipient Appreciation for Vol. Svcs. cert. No. Dist. Calif. Fed. Practice Program, 1989, Svc. and Appreciation cert. 1992. Mem. ABA, ATLA, Assn. Bus. Trial Lawyers, San Mateo County Bar Assn. (Eleanor Falvey award 1994), State Bar Calif. (mem. jud. coun., mem. ethics com. 1975-79, mem. com. on women in law 1985-87, mem. jud. nominees evaluation commn. 1988, mem. exec. com. on litigation 1990-93), Calif. Women Lawyers, Calif. Trial Lawyers Assn., Trial Lawyers for Pub. Justice. Office: US Dist Ct No Dist Calif PO Box 36060 450 Golden Gate Ave San Francisco CA 94102-3661

ILSE-NEUMAN, URSULA, curator; d. Hermann Ilse and Charlotte Troeltsch; m. Lawrence Donald Neuman; 1 child, Andreas Neuman. BA, Hunter College (CUNY), 1977; MA, The New Sch., N.Y.C., 1992; postgrad., Bard Graduate Ctr. Studies Decorative Arts, N.Y.C., 1998—2002. Curator Mus. Arts and Design, N.Y.C., 1992—. Exhbn. juror various nat. and internat. orgns.; curator Corporal Identity - Body Lang., 2003, essayist, 03. Editor: (book) Made in Oakland: The Furniture of Garry Knox Bennett, 2001; author: (exhbn. catalog) None That Glitters: Perspectives on Jewelry in the Donna Schneier Collection, 2002, Radiant Geometries. Fifteen International Jewelers, 2001, Cabinets of Curiosities: Cabinets of Wonder and Delight, Corporal Identity-Body Language, 9th Triennial for Form and Content, USA and Germany, Operas, (Essay) Worthy of the Muses: The Furniture of John Eric Byers, 2001; contbr. essays and articles to publs. Fellow, Bard Grad. Ctr., 1999—2002, 20th Century Visual Arts fellow, Grad. Ctr., CUNY, 1992. Mem.: Glass Art Soc., Coll. Art Assn., Am. Mus.Assn., Internat. Curators Assn., Art Table, Furniture Soc. (mem. adv. bd. 1999—2002), Phi Beta Kappa. Office: Mus Arts and Design 40 W 53d St New York NY 10019 Personal E-mail: ursula.neuman@madmuseum.org. E-mail: uneuman@nyc.rr.com.

ILTIS, CAROLEE ELLEN, psychologist; b. Bklyn., Oct. 19, 1943; d. Charles Henry and Martha Iltis. Diplome d'Etudes de Civilisation Francaise, Sorbonne, Paris, 1964; BA, Allegheny Coll., Meadville, Pa., 1966; MA, New Sch. for Social Rsch., 1976; PsyD, Antioch U., 2002. Cert. lic. psychologist N.Y. Inventory control coord. and sec. Crowell, Collier & MacMillan, N.Y.C., 1970—71; sec./adminstrv. asst. Ford Found., N.Y.C., 1971—78, mgr., dissemination and adminstrn., 1978—98; pre-doctoral psychology intern Hudson River Psychiatric Ctr., Poughkeepsie, NY, 1998—99; emergency rm. cons.-crisis team Putnam County Crisis Team, Putnam Hosp. Ctr., Carmell, NY, 1998—; asst. psychologist Astor Home for Children-Early Childhood Programs, Poughkeepsie, 2000—03; psychologist Astor Home for Children-Family Ct. Evaluation Svc., Poughkeepsie, 2003—. UN NGO rep. Internat. Union Psychol. Sci., N.Y.C., 2001—; nom. com. for exec. officers NGO Com. on Mental Health, UN, N.Y.C. Contbr. articles to profl. jours. Mem.: APA (poster session 1997), Hudson Valley Psychol. Assn., N.Y. State Psychol. Assn. (sec., com. on multicultural concerns 1999—2002). Democrat. Avocations: travel, the arts, meeting people from other countries, ballroom dancing, animal welfare issues.

IMAN, (IMAN ABUDULMAJID), model; b. Somalia, July 25, 1955; m. Spencer Haywood (div. 1987); 1 child, Zulekha; m. David Bowie, Apr. 24, 1992. Student, U. Nairobi, Kenya. Joined Wilhelmina Model Inc., 1975; introduced to U.S. Iman's Kikois. Appearences include (films) The Human Factor, 1979, Out of Africa, 1985, Star Trek VI, 1986, No Way Out, 1987, Surrender, 1987, House Party II, 1991, Exit to Eden, 1994, The Deli, 1997, Omikron: The Nomad Soul, 1999, (TV) Heart of Darness, 1994; (TV series) Miami Vice, The Cosby Show, In the Heat of the Night.

IMBER, ANNABELLE CLINTON, state supreme court justice; b. Heber Springs, Ark., July 15, 1950; m. Ariel Barak Imber (dec. 2001); 1 child, William Pierce Clinton. BA magna cum laude, Smith Coll., 1971; postgrad., Inst. for Paralegal Tng., 1971, U. Houston, 1973-75; JD, U. Ark., 1977. Atty. Wright, Lindsey & Jennings Law Firm, Little Rock, Ark., 1977-88; apptd. cir. judge (5th divsn.) Pulaski and Perry Counties, Ark., 1984, elected chancery and probate judge (6th divsn.), 1989-96; elected assoc. justice Ark. Supreme Ct., 1997—. Bd. dirs. Ark. Advs. for Children and Families, 1985-90, pres. 1986-88; bd. dirs Pulsaki County Hist. Soc., 1992-95, Congregation B'Nai Israel, 1988-92, 2001-, Kiwanis Club 1995-98, YMCA of Greater Little Rock and Pulaski County, Our House-A Shelter for Homeless, 1992—, St. Vincent Devel. Found., 1989-93, UAMS Med. Ctr. Dept. Pastoral Care and Edn., 1996—. Mem. ABA, AAUW, Nat. Assn. Women Judges, Ark. Bar Assn., Ark. Women Exec., Assn. of Ark. Women Lawyers (pres. 1980-81, Judge of the Year award 1994), Pulaski County Bar Assn. (bd. dirs. 1982-84). Office: Ark Supreme Ct Justice Bldg 625 Marshall St Little Rock AR 72201-1054

IMBRIE, BARBARA MARIE, musician, music educator; b. Seattle, Aug. 1, 1943; d. Clarence Bardez and Iris Patricia Ramey; m. David Ernest André, June 27, 1965 (div. June 30, 1981); m. Robert Joe Imbrie, May 16, 1987; children: Kelly Denise, Candice Elaine. BA, U. Wash., 1965; MA, San Jose State U., 1971; postgrad., Victoria (BC) Cons. Music, 1974—79, U. Calif., Santa Cruz, 1972, Inst. Music and Art, Siena, Italy, 1993. Cert. music tchr. Gen. music tchr. pub. and pvt. schs.; opera singer Ariz. Opera, Phoenix, ret., 1999. Soprano Peninsula Chamber Singers, Port Angeles, Wash.; dir. Port Angeles Boys Choir. Performer: (Operas) Seattle Opera Chorus, U. Wash., Tchrs. Performance Inst., 1974, L.A. Chorale, 1980—88; soloist: Ariz. Masterworks Chorale. Scholar, Saratoga Potsdam Choral Inst., 1976, 1977, 1984, Aspen Choral Inst., 1985. Avocations: skiing, bicycling, hiking, walking. Office: 2405 SE Meadowlark Dr Hillsboro OR 97123-8342 E-mail: joemariebrie@cs.com.

IMBROGNO, CYNTHIA, magistrate judge; b. 1948; BA, Indiana U. Pa., 1970; JD cum laude, Gonzaga U., 1979. Law clk. to Hon. Justin L. Quackenbush U.S. Dist. Ct. (Wash. ea. dist.), 9th circuit, 1980-83; law clk. Wash. State Ct. of Appeals, 1984; civil rights staff atty. Ea. Dist. of Wash., 1984-85, complex litigation staff atty., 1986-88; with Preston, Thorgrimson, Shidler, Gates & Ellis, 1988-90, Perkins Coie, 1990-91; magistrate judge U.S. Dist. Ct. (Wash. ea. dist.), 9th circuit, Spokane, 1991—. Office: 740 US Courthouse 920 W Riverside Ave Spokane WA 99201-1010

IMBUS, SHARON HAUGHEY, neuroscience nurse; b. Norfolk, Va., Jan. 7, 1947; d., Everett Wayne and Bettie Louise Haughey; m. Charles Eugene Imbus, June 14, 1969; children: Edward Allen, Andrew Haughey. BSN, Ohio State U., 1969, MSN, 1971. RN, NP, Calif.; BLS instr. Charge nurse Children's Hosp., Columbus, Ohio, 1969-71; staff nurse L.A. County-U. So. Calif. Burn Ctr., 1971-72; biostatistician U. So. Calif., L.A., 1973-78; dir., spl. studies L.A. County-U. So. Calif. Burn Ctr., 1978-86; clin. specialist/nurse practitioner Imbus Fortanasce Neurology Ctr., Arcadia, Calif., 1989-2001; dir. neurol. rsch., clin. specialist/nurse practitioner Charles E. Imbus, MD, Inc., 1997—. Legal nursing cons., 1992; cert. ACE aerobis cinstr./rehab. staff Meth. Hosp., Arcadia, 1990; mem. ethics com. Meth. Hosp. of So. Calif., Arcadia, 1986—; speaker Internat. Ethics Conf., San Francisco, 1979. Contbr. articles to profl. jours. Mem.: Am. Assn. Neurosci. Nurses, Am. Burn Assn., Calif. Nurses Assn. Roman Catholic. Avocations: aerobic dancing, fitness, reading. Office: Charles E Imbus MD Inc 665 W Naomi Ave Ste 202 Arcadia CA 91007-7563

IMHOFF, PAMELA M. marketing educator; b. Lone Pine, Calif., Jan. 12, 1955; d. Buel Franklin Avery and Barbara Ann (Cohen) Wallace; m. Dennis Wayne Wallace,Mar. 28, 1972 (dec. Feb. 1973); 1 child, Jennifer Michelle; m. John Allen Imhoff, July 15, 1989; 1 child, Joshua Avery. AS, Tulsa Jr. Coll., 1975; BS, N.E. Okla. State U., 1978; MS, Okla. State U., 1981. Mktg. tchr., coord. Charles C. Mason H.S., Tulsa, Okla., 1978-79, Meml. H.S., Tulsa, Okla., 1979-80, Union H.S., Tulsa, Okla., 1980 91; mktg. tchr., coord. mktg. edn. Tulsa Tech. Ctr., Okla., 1991—. Salesmanship instr. Tulsa Jr. Coll., Okla., 1980; sales rep. Advertising Everything, Tulsa, Okla., 1984-86. Contbr. articles to profl. jours.; presenter in field. Mem. Gracemont Bapt. Ch., 1973—, Sunday sch. tchr., 1973-78; vol. Nat. Govs. Assn. Conf., Okla., 1993; mem. Tulsa Fire Fighter's Women's Aux., 1989—; coord., sponsor Turkey Challenge for Tulsa Area Schs., 1991—; vol., fundraiser United Way, 1982-90, Muscular Dystrophy Assn., 1980-90, Salvation Army, 1980-90; sponsor Sr. Citizen Day Target Stores, 1980-90. Recipient Tchr. of Yr. award AVA, 1995. Mem. NEA, Am. Vocat. Assn. (nat. conf. 1989, 90, 92, 93, mem. resolutions com. 1993—, nat. policy leadership seminar 1993, 94, chmn. Am. Vocat. Assn. conf. mktg. edn. divsn. 1993, tchr. of yr. Am. Vocat. Assn. regional IV 1994, nat. tchr. of yr. 1995), Nat. Bus. Edn. Assn., Okla. Edn. Assn., Okla. Vocat. Assn. (strategic planning com. 1994, chmn., mem. awards com. 1992—, mem. polit. action com. 1989—, rep. regional and nat. confs., 1988—, mem. awards banquet planning com. 1993, mem. adv. com. and exec. com. 1988-92, mem. membership svcs. com. 1991-92. tchr. of yr. 1993), Okla. Mktg. Edn. Tchrs. (chmn. awards com. 1992—, chmn. consititution com. 1984-92, pres. 1990-91, 1991-92, pres.-elect 1989-90, sec., treas. 1988-89, reporter 1987-88, mktg. tchr. of yr. 1993), Mktg. Edn. Assn., DECA (sec. state activities and awards com. 1982-86, mem. state exec. coun. 1982, 84, 85, 87, 93, 94, adv. state officers 1982, 84, 85, 87, 93, 94, adv., presenter, participant state fall leadership devel. conf., CSU mini-conf., OSU DECAthalon 1978—, event mgr. nat. conf. 1986, 90, 93, series dir. nat. conf. 1993, adult asst. nat. conf. 1980-92, 94, adv. nat. and state winners 1978—), Tulsa Area Vo-Tech Assn. Classroom Tchrs. Avocations: aerobics, reading. Office: Tulsa Community Coll 909 S Boston Ave Tulsa OK 74119

IMLAH, MARYPAT, sales, advertising and marketing executive; b. Bklyn., Oct. 25, 1957; d. Kenneth William Joseph and Ann Marie (Beckley) Olivarius; m. Craig Alexander Imlah, Sept. 18, 1982; children: Christopher Edward, Jamison Robert, Meghan Patricia. BS in Mktg. and Comm., Ramapo State Coll., N.J., 1979; MBA in Mktg. and Mgmt., Fairleigh Dickinson U., 1985. Rschr., pub. rels. MacNeil/Lehrer Report Sta. WNET-TV, N.Y.C., 1977; salesperson Terrace Realty, Montvale, N.J., 1977-79; direct mail advt. copywriter Prentice-Hall, Inc., Englewood Cliffs, N.J., 1979-81; editor, promotional designer Beauty & Barber Supply Inst., Englewood, N.J., 1981-83; nat. dir. advt. and pub. rels. Emerson Radio Corp., North Bergen, N.J., 1983—. Founder, pres. Imagery Print & Advt., Print Brokerage Design Agy., Promotional Items. E-mail: imagerypnt@aol.com.

IMMANUEL, LAURA AMELIA, dentist; b. Jakarta, Java, Indonesia, May 11, 1971; d. Gamaliel and Dewi Immanuel. BS, Union Coll., Schenectady, N.Y., 1993; postgrad., Columbia U., N.Y.C., 1993—94; DMD, Tufts U., 1999. Resident in AEGD program SUNY-Stony Brook Dental Sch., 1999—2000; assoc. dentist Total Dental Care, Middle Island, NY, 2000, Dr. Norman Rich, Wantagh, NY, 2000—02, Gentle Dental, Arlington, Mass., 2002—. Recipient award, Internat. Congress of Oral Implantologists, 1999. Mem.: ADA, Mass. Dental Soc., Sigma Xi. Presbyterian. Avocations: photography, painting, music, travel. Office: Gentle Dental 725 Massachusetts Ave Arlington MA 02476

IMPELLIZZERI, ANNE ELMENDORF, insurance company executive, non-profit executive; b. Chgo., Jan. 26, 1933; d. Armin and Laura (Gundlach) Elmendorf; m. Julius Simon Impellizzeri, Oct. 12, 1961 (dec.); children: Laura, Theodore (dec.). BA, Smith Coll., 1955; MA, Yale U., 1957. CLU; ChFC. With Met. Life Ins. Co., N.Y.C., 1959-88, asst. v.p., corp. social responsibility, 1978-80, v.p., 1980-85, v.p. group ins., 1985-88; v.p. N.Y.C. Partnership, 1988-90; pres., CEO Blanton-Peale Inst., N.Y.C., 1990-98; exec. dir. Russel Wright's Manitoga, Garrison, NY, 1998—2001. Bd. dirs. Women's City Club of N.Y., Bard Music Festival, Nuveen Funds, Scenic Hudson, treas., 1999—2002; trustee Smith Coll., 1991—96; mem. Bus. Urban Issues coun. The Conf. Bd., 1981—85, chair, 1983—85. Trustee Lakeland Bd. Edn., Westchester County, N.Y., 1967-71, pres., 1970-71; bd.

dirs. Nat. Safety Coun., 1974-80; pres. Am. Assn. Gifted Children, 1975-85, chair, 1985-90. Named to Acad. of Women Achievers, YWCA N.Y., 1978; Fulbright grantee, 1955-56. Mem. Yale Club of NYC, Yale Alumni Assn. (bd. govs. 1985-88), Phi Beta Kappa.

IMPERATO-MCGINLEY, JULIANNE LEONORE, endocrinologist, educator; b. N.Y.C., Sept. 22; d. Thomas and Marian (Crispinelli) Imperato; m. Patrick W. McGinley, Aug. 27, 1966; children: Alexandra Claire, Ian Patrick McGinley. BS in Chemistry cum laude, Coll. Mt. St. Vincent, 1961; MD with hons. in Pub. Health, SUNY, 1965. Intern in internal medicine St. Vincent's Hosp. and Med. Ctr., N.Y.C., 1965-66, resident in internal medicine, 1966-68; fellow in reproductive endocrinology NYU and Lenox Hill Hosps., N.Y.C., 1968-69; NIH fellow in endocrinology Cornell U. Med. Coll., N.Y.C., 1969-72; asst. physician The N.Y. Hosp., N.Y.C., 1969-72, physician to out-patient dept., 1972-75, asst. attending, 1975-81; from instr. in medicine to asst. prof. medicine Cornell U. Med. Ctr., N.Y.C., 1972-81; assoc. attending physician The N.Y. Hosp., N.Y.C., 1982—; assoc. prof. medicine Cornell U. Med. Coll., N.Y.C., 1982-93, assoc. dir. Gen. Clin. Rsch. Ctr., 1991-93, chief sect. androgen physiology divsn. endocrinology, 1992—, dir. Gen. Clin. Rsch. Ctr., 1993—, chief divsn. endocrinology, 1993—, prof. medicine, 1993-98, Rochelle Belfer prof. medicine, 1998—2001, Abby Rockefeller Mauzé disting. prof. endocrinology in med., 2001—. Cons. prof. Nat. U. Pedro Henriquez Urena, Santo Domingo, Dominican Republic, 1987, St. Vincent's Hosp. and Med. Ctr., N.Y.C., 1978—; mem. internat. adv. bd. 3rd Internat. Conf. on Geriat. Nephrology and Urology, 1991-92; expert ad hoc grant reviewer behavioral medicine study sect. NIH, 1984, ad hoc mem. biopsychology study sect., 1982, ad hoc mem. site visit team biophysiology study sect., 1981; organizing com. Serono Symposium on Sexual Differentiation, 1982; plenary lectr. Merck Med. Adv. Coun. Meeting, St. Andrews, Scotland, 1991, European Soc. for Pediat. Endocrinology, Vienna, Austria, 1990; mem. Gordon Rsch. Conf., Plymouth, N.H., 1986; Macomber lectr. in human sexuality Harvard Med. Sch., Dept. Ob-Gyn., Boston, 1980. Assoc. editor Jour. Clin. Endocrinology and Metabolism, 1993—; reviewer: Acta Endocrinologica, Archives of Internal Medicine, Clin. Endcrinology, Endocrine Revs., Endocrinology, Jour. Clin. Endocrinology and Metabolism, Jour. Urology, New England Jour. Medicine; contbr. over 100 articles to profl. jours. NIH fund rschr.; active fundraising and drug donations The Robert Reid Cabral Children's Hosp., Santo Domingo, 1988—. Recipient award for outstanding clin. rsch. Dominican Pediat. Endocrine Soc., 1988, Rsch. award 1st prize Am. Acad. Pediats., sect. urology, 1984, Nicholas Pichardo award and lectr. for outstanding rsch. contbns. to advancement of medicine in Dominican Republic, Santo Domingo, 1980, also numerous rsch. grants. Mem. AAAS, Am. Fedn. for Clin. Rsch., Endocrine Soc. (chair, lectr. symposium on steroid 5a-reductase ann. meeting San Antonio 1992, membership com. 1989-91, chair membership com. 1991-92, chair meetings 1984-88), N.Y. Acad. Scis., Soc. for Study of Reprodn., Harvey Soc., Women in Endocrinology, Kappa Gamma Pi. Roman Catholic. Achievements include Defined the condition of 5a-reductase deficiency in man. Office: NY Hosp-Cornell U/Weill Med Coll Divsn Endocrin/Gen Clin Rsc 525 E 68th St New York NY 10021-4870

IMRAN, AYESHA, internist; b. Karachi, Pakistan, Feb. 13, 1967; came to U.S., 1993; d. Muhammed Iqbal Ali Khan and Rasheed Fatima Iqbal; m. Muhammed Imran, Mar. 18, 1993; children: Sarah, Saba, Ahmed Ismail, Ishaq. BA, U. Karachi, 1986, MBBS, 1992. Cert. Am. Bd. Internal Medicine. House officer in surgery and medicine Dow Med. Coll. Civil Hosp., Karachi, 1992-93; rsch. asst. Rush Presbyn. St. Lukes Med. Ctr., Chgo., 1994—95; resident in internal medicine Chgo. Med. Sch., 1996—99; practice primary care internal medicine Chgo., 1999—2002; fellow in geriat. Loyola U., Maywood, Ill., 2002—. Social worker Patients Welfare Assn., Pakistan, 1985, Pediats. Dept., Pakistan, 1990. Mem. ACP. Avocations: current news, travel, cooking. Home: 2626 Wellington Ave Westchester IL 60154-4957 E-mail: geriatrics2@yahoo.com.

IMUS, DEIRDRE, health facility administrator; m. Don Imus; 1 child, Wyatt. BA in internat. rels., Villanova U. Founder, co-dir. with Don Imus The Imus Ranch; founder, dir. The Deirdre Imus Environ. Ctr. Pediat. Oncology, Hackensack U. Med. Ctr. Author: The Imus Ranch: Cooking for Kids and Cowboys, 2004. Named Women of Substance and Style, Organic Style mag. Achievements include completed several triathlons and ran the NYC marathon twice, in the time of 3 hours 31 minutes; instituting an environmentally sound award winning program called 'Greening the Cleaning' in The Deirdre Imus Environ. Ctr. Pediat. Oncology, Hackensack U. Med. Ctr. Office: Deirdre Imus Environ Ctr for Pediat Oncology David Jurist Rsch Bldg Rm 240 30 Prospect Ave Hackensack NJ 07601*

INA, KYOKO, professional figure skater; b. Tokyo, Oct. 11, 1972; Competitive history includes placing 1st, U.S. Championships, 1997-98, 2000-02; 3rd, World Championships, 2002; 4th, Winter Olympics, 1998; 5th, Winter Olympics, 2002; among others with ptnrs. Jason Dungjen, 1991-98, John Zimmerman, 1998-. Canadian Stars on Ice Tour, 2003; Stars on Ice Tour, 2004-. Avocations: jet skiing, horseback riding, Broadway shows, tennis. Office: c/o David Baden IMG 22 E 71st St New York NY 10021*

INCE, LAUREL T. music educator; b. Gonzales, Tex. m. Joe C. Ince; children: Joe C. Ince, Jr.(dec.), Mark A., Susan I. Burns, William C. BMus, Trinity U., 1950. Piano tchr. Ince Piano Studio, Gonzales, 1950—. Performer various internat. workshops, Austria, Can., Switzerland, Scotland, France; south ctrl. coord. music Link Found., 1990—. Contbr. articles to profl. jours. Advisor City Coun., Gonzales; accompanist First Bapt. Ch., Gonzales; pres. Sesame Club, Gonzales. Recipient Tchr. of Yr. award, Austin Music Tchrs. Assn., 1995, Pillar of the Point award, Inspiration Point Fine Arts Colony. Mem.: Nat. Guild Piano Tchrs., Tex. Music Tchrs. Assn. (state pres., Tchr. of Yr. award 1995), Nat. Fedn. Music Clubs (life; chmn. FAMA 1991, recording sec., lectr., performer), Tex. Fedn. Music Clubs (state pres., founder jr. state festival 1975), Sigma Alpha Iota (life). Avocations: entertaining, travel. Home: 723 St Francis Str Gonzales TX 78629 Home Fax: 830-672-5808. Personal E-mail: ljince@gvec.net.

INDICK, JANET, sculptor; b. Bklyn., Mar. 3, 1932; d. Charles and Sarah (Goldsmith) Suslak; m. Benjamin Philip Indick, Aug. 23, 1953; children: Michael Korie, Karen Leigh Indick Maizel. BS in Edn., Hunter Coll., 1953, postgrad., 1954, New Sch., 1961-62. Tchr. kindergarten pub. schs., Elizabeth, N.J., 1953-54; dir. nursery sch. Teaneck Jewish Ctr., N.J., 1964-92. Mem. Teaneck Arts Adv. Bd., 1982—88. Prin. works include Netzach Yisrael, Teaneck Jewish Ctr., 1974, Etz Chaim, 1981, Sanctuary Wall Menorah, 1983, Temple Beth Rishon, Wyckoff, N.J., 1981, 1983, Menorah, Franklin Lakes Pub. Sch., 1983, North Shore Synagogue, Syosset, N.Y., 1993, Temple Sharey Telfilo Israel, South Orange, N.J., 1993, one-woman shows include Discovery Art Gallery, Clifton, N.Y., 1976, Mari Art Gallery, Westchester, N.Y., 1983, Hebrew Tabernacle, N.Y.C., 1984, Chubb Corp., Basking Ridge, N.J., 1985, Edward Williams Gallery Fairleigh Dickinson U., Hackensack, N.J., 1986, Vineyard Gallery, N.Y.C., 1986, Maurice M. Pine Gallery Fairlawn (N.J.) Pub. Libr., 1990, Quietude Garden Gallery, East Brunswick, N.J., 1991—92, Vineyard Gallery, N.Y., N.Y., 1986, Bergen Mus. Art & Sci., Paramus, N.J., 1994, N.Y.C. Boathouse Cafe, 1998, Kerygma Gallery, Ridgewood, N.J., 1999, Interchurch Ctr., N.Y., 1999, Solo Outdoor Sculpture Exhibition Broadfoot Gallery, Boonton, N.J., 2000—01, Atrium Gallery J.C.C., Washington Twp., N.J., 2002, Johnson & Johnson Co., Skillman, N.J., 2003, Yeshiva U. Mus., N.Y.C., 2004, exhibitions include Morris Mus., N.J., 1979, 1984, Newark Mus., 1982, Jersey City Mus., 1983, Hebrew Tabernacle, N.Y.C., 1984, Parsons Gallery, 1984, Lillian Heidenberg Gallery, 1984—96, Schering-Plough Corp., Madison, N.J., 1987, Kerygma Gallery, Ridgewood, N.J., 1988—2000, Marabella Gallery, N.Y.C., 1989, So. Vt. Art Ctr., Manchester, 1990, Nat. Assn. Women Artists Traveling Exhbns., 1989—90, 1996, Traveling Exhbns., 1998—99, Fgn. Traveling Exhbns., India, 1989—90, Columbus (Ohio) Mus. Fine Art, 1989—90, Balt. Mus. Art, 1989—90, Marunouchi Gallery, N.Y.C., 1994, Waterside Gallery, West Stockbridge, Mass., 1995, L'Atelier Gallery, Piermont, N.Y., 1994—96, Polo Gallery, Edgewater, N.J., 1994—2000, Goethe Mus., Weimar, Germany, 2000—01, Staaliche Mus., Berlin, 2000—01, Grounds for Sculpture, Hamilton, N.J., 2001, Musedu Monnai, Paris, 2002, Mus. Wroclaw, Poland, 2002, Can. War Mus., Ottawa, 2002, Am. Numis. Mus., Colorado Springs, Colo., 2002, N.Y. Ind. Art Fair, N.Y.C., 2002, Represented in permanent collections Jane Voorhees Zimmerli Art Mus. Rutgers U., New Brunswick, N.J., Corp. Towers Perrin, N.Y.C., AMP Corp., Harrisburg, Pa., Myron Mfg. Corp., Maywood, N.J., Chiropractic Health Care, Bergenfield, N.J., Bergen Mus., Paramus, Weingroup Equities Corp., N.Y.C., Hubbards Cupboard Corp., Edison, N.J., Rosenthal Art Equities, N.Y.C., Franklin Lakes Pub. Schs., Temple Beth Rishon, Wykoff, North Shore Synagogue, Syosset, Temple Sharey Tefilo, South Orange, Teaneck Jewish Ctr., Broadfoot Collection, Boonton, Internat. Sculpture Ctr. Collection III, The Millenium Collection NAWA, New York, The Nat. Mus. of Women in the Arts, Washington, D.C. Recipient Charlotte Dunwiddie Meml. award, Medallic Art Pen & Brush, 2001, Medal of Honor, Nat. Arts Club, 2001, C.A. Brown award, Medallic Art Pen and Brush, 2000, Internat. award, Manhattan Arts, 1999, Merit award, IFFRA/AIA Forum on Religious Art/Architecture, 1984, Sculpture award, Nat. Assn. Painters and Sculptors, 1980, Nat. Assn. Painters, 1978, Art in the Park, Paterson, NJ, 1977; grantee Fellowship grant in Sculpture, N.J. State Council on the Arts, 1981. Mem.: Fedn. Internationale de la Medaille, Medallic Art Soc. of Can., Am. Medallic Sculpture assn., Sculpture Assn. of N.J., Am. Numis. Soc., Artists Equity, Catherine Lorillard Wolfe Art Club (bd. dirs. 1994—96, 2000—02, sculpture chair 2001—03, 1st Sculpture award 1999, Medal of Honor in Sculpture 2001, H.W. Frismuth Bronze Sculpture award 2000, Presidents award 1996, Corp. award Sculpture 1995, H.W. Frismuth Bronze Sculpture award 1992), N.Y. Soc. Women Artists (sculpture chair 1999—2000), Nat. Assn. Women Artists (pres. 1997—99, advisor 2000—, Aluminum Sculpture Merit award 2000, Gretchen Richardson Meml. sculpture award 2001, Merit award in Sculpture 2000, Jeffrey Childs Willis Meml. award 1997, Clara Shainess Meml. award Sculpture 1994, Pauline Law award 1974). Democrat. Jewish. Home: 428 Sagamore Ave Teaneck NJ 07666-2626 Personal E-mail: janetindick@aol.com.

INDINGARO, MARGARET ANN, supervisor; b. St. Louis, Mar. 25, 1946; d. Robert Allen and Margaret Amanda Utterback; m. Richart Cornelius Indingaro, Aug. 21, 1971; children: Jessica Lyn, Stephanie Joan, Katherine Ann. BA, Radcliffe Coll., Cambridge, Mass., 1968; MAT, Syracuse U., 1970. Cert. tchr. Tenn., adminstr. Tenn. Adminstrv. asst. Radcliffe Coll., Cambridge, 1968—69; tchr. 6-8th grade math Syracuse (N.Y.) Pub. Schs., 1970—71, Brookline (Mass.) Pub. Schs., 1971—77; tchr. 9-12th grade math Shelby County Schs., Memphis, 1985—93, instructional supr. 6-12th grade math, 1993—. Adj. instr. math. LeMoyne-Owen Coll., Shelby State CC, U. Memphis; writer Tenn. State Math. Curriculum Com., Nashville, 1997—99, 2003; mem. Tenn. Gateway Test Content Rev. Bd., Nashville, 2001, 03. Sch. com. interviewer Harvard Radcliffe Club Mid-South, Memphis, 1979—; mem. music com. Christ United Meth. Ch., Memphis, 2000—02; bd. dirs. Memphis Urban Math. Collaborative, 1994—. Grantee Gender Equity grant, NSF, 2001—. Mem.: AAUW (chmn. SHADES com. 1993—), Tenn. Coun. Suprs. and Leaders in Math. Edn. (pres. 2000—03), Memphis Area Coun. Tchrs. Math. (pres. 1999—), Nat. Coun. Suprs. of Math., Nat. Coun. Tchrs. Math. (mem. affiliated svcs. com. 2003—). Methodist. Avocations: choir, needlework. Office: Shelby County Schs 160 S Hollywood Memphis TN 38112 Home: 4666 Marcel Ave Memphis TN 38122

INES, AMY, elementary school educator; b. Wichita, Kans., Sept. 24, 1969; d. Stanley Daniel Baldwin and Karen Lee Swisher; m. David Teofilo Ines, June 26, 1993; children: Daved-Mychal, Jordan Daniel, Estevan Teofilo, Kaylie Hope. BEd, Wichita State U., 1993, M in Curriculum and Instrn., 1997. ESOL endorsement; cert. K-9 tchr. Tchr. grade 7 Pleasant Valley Middle Sch., Wichita, 1993-96, ESOL tchr., 1996—. Coord. Youth to Youth, Pleasant Valley; recycling coord., Pleasant Valley; sponsor student coun. qpa writing chair principal's leadership team. Democrat. Avocations: family activities, reading, walking. Office: Pleasant Valley Middle Sch 2220 W 29th St N Wichita KS 67204-4835

INEZ, DONNA LEE, hospital administrator; b. Flushing, N.Y. d. Walter and Ruth (Pringle) Jackowski; m. Virgil Inez, May 30, 1968. BS, So. Conn. State U., New Haven; EdM, Rutgers U., New Brunswick, N.J. RN, Conn.; cert. BLS instr. Asst. supr. med.-surg. Morristown (N.J.) Meml. Hosp., 1969-72; LPN instr. Morristown Sch. Practical Nursing, 1972-78, nursing edn. instr., 1973-90; nursing edn. instr., clin. info. system coord. Morristown Meml. Hosp., 1984-90; asst. dir., clinical coord. patient care sys. Gen. Hosp. Ctr. Passaic, N.J., 1990-99; ret., 1999. Mem. ANA, Am. Med. Informatics Assn., N.J. State Nurses Assn. (com.), Sigma Theta Tau. Home: 63 Grove Ave Morris Plains NJ 07950-2025

INFANTE-OGBAC, DAISY INOCENTES, sales executive, marketing executive, real estate broker; b. Marbel, The Philippines, Aug. 3, 1946; came to U.S., 1968; d. Jesus and Josefina (Inocentes) I.; children: Desiree Josephine, Dante Fernancio, Darrell Enerico; m. Rosben Reyes Ogbac, Jan. 30, 1987. AA with highest honors, Notre Dame of Marbel, Philippines, 1963; AB in English magna cum laude, U. Santo Tomas, Manila, 1965, BS in Psychology, 1966; MA in Comms., Fairfield U., 1971. Real estate broker, Fla. Columnist, writer Pinoy News mag., Chgo., 1975-76, Philippine News, Chgo., 1977-80; cons. EDP Cemco Systems, Inc., Oak Brook, Ill., 1980-81; pres. Daisener, Inc., Downers Grove, Ill., 1980-82; cons. EDP Robert J. Irmen Assocs., Hinsdale, Ill., 1981-82; pres. Data Info. Systems Corp., Downers Grove, Ill., 1982-84; broker, co. mgr. Gen. Devel. Corp., Chgo., 1984-86; columnist, writer Via Times, Chgo., 1984-86; owner, pres. Marbel Realty, Chgo., 1984-88; exec. v.p. Dior Enterprises, Inc., Chgo., 1986-88; real estate sales mgr. M.J. Cumber Co., Grand Cayman, Cayman Islands, 1988-89, Vet. Real Estate, Orlando, Fla., 1989-90; sales mgr. All Star Real Estate, Inc., Orlando, 1990-92; ruby network mktg. exec. Melaleuca, Inc., 1991—; pres. Dior Enterprises, Inc., Orlando, 1992—; prin., owner All Travel, Inc., 2002—. Bd. dirs. Network Mktg. Alliance, 1996—; team leader, sr. team leader The Winners Circle, 1998-99; mem. Orlando Distbn. Ctr. for Healthpower Internat. Inc., 2000—. Author: Songs of Love, Prayer, and Worship to the Lord, 1998, Poems of My Youth, 1982; (lyrics and music) My First Twenty Songs, 1981, The Lord is My Rock; song contbrn. CD Songs of Priase 2000; featured contbr. poems; American Poetry Anthology, vol. VIII, no. 4, Best New Poets of 1987, Journey of the Mind, 1995; composer lyrics and melody The Lord in My Rock, 2001; inventor fryer-steamer. Sec. Movement for a Free Philippines, 1984; active OO Pindy Orgn., 2003. Mem. NAFE, Am. Soc. Profl. Exec. Women, Philippine C. of C. (sec. Chgo. chpt. 1985), Bayanihan Internat. Ladies Assn., Lions (twister Fil-Am. club 1978-79). Roman Catholic. Avocations: bowling, swimming, racquetball, tennis. E-mail: iysiad@yahoo.com., diorentintl@yahoo.com.

INGALLS, JANE, university program director; BSN, Med. Coll. Va., 1966; MSN, Cath. U. Am., 1971; PhD in Nursing, George Mason U., 1996. Instr. nursing Fredericksburg (Va.) Ara Sch. Practical Nursing, 1966-69; staff nurs Mary Washington Hosp., Fredericksburg, 1980-84, 89-93; asst. prof. nursing Germanna (Va.) C.C., Locost Grove, 1984-91, assoc. prof. nursing, 1991-93, prof. nursing, 1994—, dir. nursing program, 1992—. Mem. Va. Coun. Assoc. Degree Nursing Educators, Coun. Program Heads; mem. adv. com. Stafford county Schs. Health Occupations; mem. health assembly MediCorp Health Sys. Contbr. articles to profl. jours. Mem. ANA,Nat. League for Nursing, Va. Nurses Assn., Va. League for Nursing (pres.-elect), Nat. Student Nurses Assn. (adv.), Sigma Theta Tau. Avocation: collectibles. Office: Germanna CC Sch Nursing 2130 Germanna Hwy PO Box 339 Locust Grove VA 22508-0339

INGALLS, MARIE CECELIE, former state legislator, retail executive; b. Faith, S.D., Mar. 31, 1936; d. Jens P. and Ida B. (Hegre) Jensen; m. Dale D. Ingalls, June 20, 1955; children: Duane (dec.), Delane. BS, Black Hills State Coll., 1973, MS, 1978. Elem. tchr. Meade County Schs., Sturgis, S.D., 1957-72, Faith Sch. Dist. 46-2, 1973-76; elem. prin. Meade Sch. Dist. 46-1, Sturgis, 1976-81; owner, operator Ingalls, Sturgis, 1978-99; mem., asst. majority whip S.D. House Reps., Pierre, 1986-92; lobbyist S.D. Legislature. Former sec. S.D. Rep. Orgn; Rep. nominee S.D. Commr. Sch. and Pub. Lands, 1998. Recipient Woman of Achievement award City of Sturgis, 1986, Retail Bus. of Yr. 1998. Mem. S.D. Cattlewomen, S.D. Stockgrowers (edn. chair), S.D. Farm Bur. (bd. dirs. dist. V 1993-2001, 03—, dist. dir. women's com. 2003—), Meade County Farm Bur., Faith C. of C. (pres. 1989), Sturgis C. of C. (past bd. dirs.), Key City Investment Club. Republican. Lutheran. Avocations: knitting, crocheting, piano, reading, golf. Home: 17054 Opal Rd Mud Butte SD 57758

INGALLS, SUDI-SUZANNE L. artist; b. Frankfurt, Germany; d. Robert Condit and Suzanne Little Ingalls. Student, William Jewell Coll., Liberty, Mo., William Woods Coll., Fulton, Mo., Ariz. State U., Tempe; Cert., Western Bus. Coll., Vancouver, Wash. With Ariz. State Hosp., Phoenix; phlebotomist Aberdeen Cmty. Hosp., Wash., Port Angeles Cmty. Hosp., Wash., Good Samaritan Hosp., Portland, Oreg.; pharmacy technician NCS Health Care, Vancouver, Wash.; with Septagon Graphics, Ariz. and Wash. Exhibitions include. Avocations: photography, wildlife, ghost towns, bird-watching. Home: 4112 NE 50th Ave Vancouver WA 98661

INGERSON, NANCY NINA MOORE, special education educator; b. Springfield, Ill., Sept. 10, 1940; d. Irvin Lysle and Dorothe Nina (Spencer) Moore; m. Paul Gates Ingerson, Aug. 13, 1966 (divorced); children: Paul G., Gregory M. BA in English Lit., U. Ill., 1963. Cert. secondary edn. educator, cert. spl. edn. educator. Sec., adminstrv. asst. Elec. Engring. Rsch. Lab. U. Ill., Urbana, 1958-66; adminstrv. asst. Hughes Aircraft Space and Comm., El Segundo, Calif., 1988-92; tchr. spl. edn. Narbonne H.S. L.A. Unified Sch. Dist., Harbor City, Calif., 1994—, social club chmn., 1996, 97, 99—, social club co-chmn., 2000—, mem. leadership coun., 1999—, chmn. dept. spl. edn., 2001—03. Independent. Lutheran. Avocations: porcelain doll making, tile painting, print making, drawing. Home: 3602 W Estates Ln Unit 103 Rolling Hills Estates CA 90274

INGLE, BEVERLY DAWN, elementary school educator; d. Elmer and Laura Mae Ingle. BS in Elem. Edn., U. Wis., 1978; MA in Diverse Learning, U. Phoenix, 1997. Tchr. Thompson R at J, Loveland, Colo., 1979—82, Cherry Creek Schs., Englewood, Colo., 1982—. Chmn. Front Range UniServ Unit, Aurora, Colo., 1988—94; del. Edn. Internat., 2001. Mem.: NEA (bd. dirs. 1999—), Colo. Edn. Assn. (Hazel Petrocco Women's Leadership award 1998), Cherry Creek Edn. Assn. (mem. exec. com. 1999—, pres. 1988—92).

INGLE, MARTI ANNETTE, protective services official, educator; b. Waynesville, N.C., Apr. 3, 1972; d. William Carroll Ingle, Shirley Grooms Ingle. Student, East Coast Bible Coll., 1987—89; EMT-paramedic cert., Haywood C.C., Clyde, NC, 1993, tech. rescue and fire fighting, 1996; degree culinary arts and scis., Alaska Vocat. Tech. Coll., Seward, AK, 2000—01. Cert. emergency rescue technician 1996; tech. rescue instr., swiftwater rescue technician II 1997, haz mat ops. 1994, sr. fire investigations 1999, emergency boat ops. 1999, personal watercraft rescue 1999, PALS 1991, ACLS 1992, advanced trauma life support 1991, pediat. emergencies for prehospital providers 2001, tchr. Alaska, 2001. EMT-paramedic Haywood County Emergency Med. Svcs., Waynesville, NC, 1991—2002; EMS/tech. rescue instr. Haywood C.C., Clyde, NC, 1994—2002; EMS evaluator State of N.C., Raleigh, 1994—2002; EMS/tech. rescue instr. Blue Ridge C.C., Hendersonville, NC, 1995—2002, Tri-County C.C., Murphy, NC, 1996—2002, Southwestern C.C., Sylva, NC, 1998—2002; EMS/fire/rescue instr. Alaska Vocat. Tech. Coll., Seward, Alaska, 2001—. Mem.: N.C. Assn. Paramedics, N.C. EMS and Rescue Assn., N.C. Assn. Fire Svc. Instrs., Haywood County Rescue Squad (life; 1st lt. and sgt. 1994—99). Avocations: travel, white-water rafting, cooking, reading, mountain biking. Home: 151 Children St Waynesville NC 28786 Office: 215 N Main St Waynesville NC 28786 Personal E-mail: rafty981@yahoo.com.

INGOLD, CATHERINE WHITE, academic administrator; b. Columbia, S.C., Mar. 15, 1949; d. Hiram Hutchison and Annelle (Stover) White; m. Wesley Thomas Ingold, June 13, 1970; 1 child, Thomas Bradford Hutchison. Student, U. Paris-Sorbonne, 1969; BS in French with honors, Hollins Coll., 1970; MA in Romance Langs., U. Va., 1972, PhD in French, 1979; DHum honoris causa, Francis Marion U., Florence, S.C., 1992. Assoc. prof. romance langs. Gallaudet U., Washington, 1973-88, dir. hons. program, 1980-85, dean arts and scis., 1985-86, provost, v.p. acad. affairs, 1986-88; pres. Am. U. of Paris, 1988-92, Curry Coll., Milton, Mass., 1992-96. Dep. dir. Nat. Fgn. Lang. Ctr. Johns Hopkins U., 1996—2000, U. Md., 2000—. Recipient Prix Morot-Sir de Langue et Littérature françaises (Hollins). Mem. MLA, Nat. Collegiate Honors Coun., Lychnos Soc. (U.Va.), Phi Beta Kappa. Episcopalian. Home: 2015 N Brandywine St Arlington VA 22207-2200 Office: Nat Fgn Lang Ctr 1029 Vermont Ave NW Washington DC 20005-3517 E-mail: cwingold@nflc.org.

INGOLFSSON-FASSBIND, URSULA G. music educator; b. Zurich, Switzerland, Dec. 22, 1943; arrived in U.S., 1980; d. Franz Bernardin Fassbind and Gertrud M. Schmucki; m. Ketill Ingolfsson; children: Katla Soffia, Judith, Mirjam, Bera Bjorg. Nat. tchrs. diploma, Conservatory Zurich, 1965, soloist diploma, 1968; postgrad., U. Ariz., 1969—70. Tchg. asst. Conservatory Zurich, 1966—68; with Reykjavik (Iceland) Music Coll., 1970—79, Settlement Music Sch., Phila., 1987—2000; founder, dir., tchr., performer Leopold Mozart Acad. and Franz Fassbind Found., Phila., 2001—. Founder, dir. The Leopold Mozart Chamber Music Concerts, 2002—. Grantee Excellency in Tchg. grant, Wilmington (Del.) Piano Co., 2003. Mem.: Am. Composers Guild, Music Tchr. Nat. Assn. Democrat. Avocations: painting, gardening. Home and Office: Leopold Mozart Acad 4833 Pulaski Ave Philadelphia PA 19144

INGRAHAM, LAURA, lawyer, political commentator; b. Glastonbury, Conn. BA in Russian and English lit., Dartmouth Coll.; JD, U. Va. Sch. of Law, 1991. Speechwriter White House and Dept. Edn. and Transp., 1986—88; law clerk to Supreme Ct. Justice Clarence Thomas and Ralph K. Winter, US Ct. Appeals Second Cir., 1992—93; criminal def. lawyer Skadden, Arps, Slate, Meagher & Flom, Wash., DC, 1993—96; host Watch It! with Laura Ingraham, MSNBC, 1996—2000, nat. syndicated radio program, The Laura Ingraham Show, 2001—. Co-founder The Dark Ages Weekend. Author: The Hillary Trap: Looking for Power in All the Wrong Places, 2000, Shut Up & Sing: How the Elites in Hollywood, Politics....and the UN are Subverting America, 2003; contbr. NY Times, Wash. Post, LA Times, San Francisco Chronicle. Office: Talk Radio Network PO Box 3755 Central Point OR 97502*

INGRAM, BARBARA AVERETT, minister; b. Decatur, Ga., May 8, 1960; d. Charles Cole and Avarilla Gleen (Caldwell) Averett; m. George Conley Ingram IV, Nov. 7, 1987; 1 child, Martha Elizabeth-Conley, Rebekah-Ann Elizabeth AS, Montreat-Anderson Coll., 1981; BA, Pfeiffer Coll., 1983; MDiv, Emory U., 1986; D of Ministry, Columbia Theol. Sem., 2003. Ordained to ministry United Meth. Ch. as deacon, 1986, as elder, 1988. Assoc. min. 1st United Meth. Ch., Lenoir, N.C., 1986-87, Cen. United

Meth. Ch., Mt. Airy, N.C., 1987-88; sr. min. Ogburn Meml. United Meth. Ch., Winston-Salem, NC, 1988—91, Ann St.-Bogers Chapel UMC, Concord, NC, 1991—, Shiloh UMC, Concord, 1997, Lebanon-Fairfield UMC, Denver, NC, 2000. Republican.

INGRAM, DIANA JOYCE, construction executive; b. Detroit, Feb. 21, 1947; d. John E. Bohr and Mildred Audrey (Day) Scott; m. Ronald S. Ingram, May 23, 1981; children: Brett MacMillan, Leslie Barrow, Lara McPherson. BA, Mich. State U. Instr. seminar Cattari, Calif., 1971-75; mgr. retail Lady J, Bay Area, Calif., 1975-79; counselor Roberts Employee Svc., San Jose, Calif., 1979-81; spl. edn. Agnew, Calif., 1980-81; tchr. drama San Jose City, 1987-89; broker Real Estate, Calif., 1989-93; owner, CEO Analytical & Constrn. Svc., Los Banos, Calif., 1991—. Corr. Los Banos Enterprise, 1996—. Author: (play) Time, 1976, numerous publications, 1978—. Bd. dirs. Am. Cancer Soc.; sec. LB Hosp. Guild; mem. adv. bd., sec. Salvation Army. Named Vol. of Yr./Citizen of Yr. C. of C., 1998. Mem. Am. Heart Assn. (bd. dirs.), Convali Hosp. Guild (pres.), Alzheimers Assn. (advocate 1991—), Soroptomist. Democrat. Presbyterian. Avocations: writing, reading, astronomy, animal advocacy.

INGRAM, HELEN MOYER, political science educator; b. Denver, July 12, 1937; d. Oliver Weldon and Hazel Margaret (Wickard) Hill; m. W. David Laird; children from by previous marriage: Mrill, Maia, Seth. BA, Oberlin Coll., 1959; PhD, Columbia U., 1967. Lectr., asst. prof. polit. sci. U. N.Mex., 1962-69; with Nat. Water Commn., Washington, 1969-72; assoc. prof. polit. sci. U. Ariz., Tucson, 1972-77, prof. polit. sci., 1979-96; dir. Udall Ctr. Studies Pub. Policy, 1988-96; Warmington chair Sch. Social Ecology U. Calif., Irvine, 1995—. Author: (with Dean Mann) Why Policies Succeed of Fail, 1980, (with Nancy Laney and John McCain) A Policy Approach to Representation: Lessons from the Four Corners States, 1980, (with Martin, Laney and Griffin) Saving Water in a Desert City, 1984, (with Brown) Water and Poverty in the Southwest, 1987, Water Politics: Continuity and Change, 1990, (with Nancy Laney and David Gillilan) Divided Waters: Divided Waters: Bridging the U.S.-Mexico Border, 1995, (with Ann Schneider) Policy Design for Democracy, 1997; editor: (with Rathgeb Smith) Public Policy for Democracy, 1993, (with Joachim Blatter) Reflections on Water, 2001; book rev. editor Am. Polit. Sci. Rev., 1987-92. Sr. fellow Resources for Future, Washington 1977-79. Mem. Policy Studies Orgn. (pres. 1985), Am. Polit. Sci. Assn. (coun., treas. 1985-87), Western Polit. Sci. Assn. (past pres., v.p.). Home: 4749 E San Francisco Blvd Tucson AZ 85712-1238 E-mail: hingram@uci.edu.

INGRAM, KATHARINE GOODRIDGE, language educator, writer; b. Mexico City, Mex., June 23, 1938; arrived in U.S., 1952; d. E. R. Goodridge and Helen; m. R. R. Ingram, Aug. 31, 1963 (dec. Apr. 12, 1982); 2 children. BA, Pomona U., 1959; TESL tchg. cert., U. Calif., Santa Barbara, 1993. Tchr. Hamlin Sch., San Francisco, 1959—61, Wesley Sch., Cape Coast, Ghana, 1963—65; gallery dir. Gallery Del Lago, Ajijic, Mexico, 1973—78; owner Mi Mexico Gallery, Ajijic, 1978—92, Gallery Bazar El Paseo, Santa Barbara, Calif., 1981—89; tchr. Ojai (Calif.) Valley Sch., 1992—94, Crane Sch., Santa Barbara, 1997—2002. Chmn. Spanish dept. Crane Sch., Santa Barbara, 1997—2002; tchr. Wesley Sch., Cape Coast, Ghana, 1963—65; dir., curator Gallery Del Lago, Ajijic, 1973—78; corr. Mexico City News, 1973—81. Contbr. poetry and stories to anthologies. Co-founder Santa Barbara Poetry Festival, 1990, Oak Hill Sch., Jalisco, Mexico, 1974. Scholar, Santa Barbara Writers Conf., 2002, 2003. Mem. Bill Downey's Meml. Writers' Group. Avocations: decorating, gardening, correspondence. Home: Box 90159 Santa Barbara CA 93190 E-mail: ki4488@aol.com.

INGRAM, MARTHA RIVERS, company executive; b. Charleston, SC, Aug. 20, 1935; m. E. Bronson Ingram (dec. 1995), Oct. 4, 1958; children: Orrin Henry III, John Rivers, David Bronson, Robin. BA in History, Vassar Coll., 1957. V.p., pub. affairs Ingram Industries Inc., Nashville, 1979—95, mem., bd. directors, 1981—, chmn. bd. dirs., 1995—. Bd. dirs. Baxter Internat., Weyerhaeuser Co., Ashley Hall, Vassar Coll., Harpeth Hall Sch., Ingram Micro Inc.; mem. adv. bd. Kennedy Ctr. for Performing Arts, Washington. Chmn. Tenn. Bicentennial Commn., 1996; bd. dirs. Tenn. Performing Arts Ctr., Nashville Ballet, Nashville Opera, Nashville Inst. for Arts, Nashville Symphony, Nashville Cmty. Found.; past chmn. United Way's Alexis de Tocqueville Soc.; founder, bd. dirs. Tenn. Repertory Theater; chmn. bd. trustees Vanderbilt U., 1999-. Mem. Nashville Area C. of C. Office: Ingram Industries Inc One Belle Mead Pl 4400 Harding Rd Nashville TN 37205-2244*

INGRAM, RENAY ELOISE, elementary school educator, school system administrator; b. New Haven, Feb. 26, 1951; d. James Brown Ingram and Mary Simmons; m. Dhafir Faheem, May 15, 1977; children: Hakim Johnson, Sabir Johnson, Dhafir Johnson, Mansour Johnson. BA in Am. History, Am. Internat. Coll., 1974, MA in Edn. with distinction, 1989, cert. advanced grad. studies in reading with distinction, 1991; postgrad., U. RI, 1985—86. Cert. reading specialist grades K-12. World cultures reading tchr. Chestnut Accelerated Mid. Sch., Springfield, Mass., 1990— Sch.-to-work instr. dept. CS Sq. program Springfield Sch., 1990—; founder, dir. Essentials Ednl. Svcs., 1976—87; mem. adv. bd. U. Mass. Ctr. for Internat. Edn., 1997—; presenter, cons. in field. Contbr. Bottom Line and Contact newspapers; author: (poetry) Moments Polished Supremely, Off the Heart and Into the Heat, Do You Love This Child, They Wear the Falsehoods, Tributes; travel writer: Mecca Travel Club, 1985—90. Co-founder Pan-African Hist. Mus., Springfield; cons., studio art leader, docent, exhibitor Springfield Libr. and Mus. Assn.; co-founder Pan-African Hist. Mus., 1999; mem. City-Wide Cmty. Cmty. Svc. Learning Adv. Bd., 1994—95; mem. study team Cohort Group on Violence in a Traumatic World, 1997—; prodr. African Percussion Drummers, 1994—. Recipient Tchr. Incentive award, Anti-Defamation League, 1998, Cmty. Svc. Learning Cert. of Excellence, 1994—97, Profl. Devel. Presenter Cert. of Recognition, 1994—97. Address: 108 Lakeside St Springfield MA 01109

INKSTER, JULI, professional golfer; b. Santa Cruz, Calif., June 24, 1960; m. Brian Inkster, July, 1980; 2 daughters. Student, San Jose State U. Professional golfer LPGA, 1983—. Mem. U.S. Solheim Cup teams, 1992, 98, 2000, 2002, 2003; mem. U.S. World Cup Team, 1980, 82. Named a Collegiate All-American, 1979, 1981—82. Achievements include winning 30 career LPGA victories including the Du Maurier Classic in 1984, and the Kraft Nabisco Championships in 1984 and 1989; winning the the McDonald's LPGA Championship in 1999 and 2000, and the U.S. Women's Open in 1999 and 2002; won U.S. Women's Amateur Title from 1980-1982. Office: care LPGA 100 International Golf Dr Daytona Beach FL 32124-1082

INMAN, JEAN A. political party official; Chmn. Mass. Rep. Party, Boston, 2002—. Office: Mass Republican Party 85 Merrimac St Boston MA 02114-4726

INMAN, MARIANNE ELIZABETH, college administrator; b. Berwyn, Ill., Jan. 9, 1943; d. Miles V. and Bessee M. (Hejtmanek), Plzak; m. David P. Inman; Aug 1, 1964. BA, Purdue U., 1964; AM, Ind. U., 1967; PhD, U. Tex., 1978. Dir. Comml. Div. World Instruction and Translation, Inc., Arlington, Va., 1969-71; program staff mem. Ctr. for Applied Linguistics, Arlington, 1972-73; lectr. in French No. Va. Community Coll., Bailey's Crossroads, 1973; faculty mem., linguistic researcher Tehran (Iran) U., 1973-75; intern mgmt. edn. rsch. & devel. S.W Ednl. Devel. Lab., Austin, Tex., 1977-78; asst. prof., program dir. Southwestern U., Georgetown, Tex., 1978; dir. English lang. inst. Alaska Pacific U., Anchorage, 1980-87, chairperson all-U. requirements, 1984-88, assoc. dean acad. affairs, 1988-90; v.p. dean of coll. Northland Coll., Ashland, Wis., 1990-95; pres. Ctrl. Meth. Coll., Fayette, Mo., 1995—. Contbr. Pres. Commn. Foreign Lang. and Internat. Studies, Washington, 1978-79; manuscript evaluator The Modern Lang. Jour., Columbus, Ohio, 1979-84; cons. Anchorage Sch. Dist., 1984-90; cons., evaluator N. Cen. Assn. Colls. and Schs., Chgo., 1990—; mem. dean's task force Coun. on Ind. Colls., 1993-95; pres. Ind. Colls. and Univs. Mo., 1996-2000. Co-author: English for Medical Students, 1976; co-author and editor: English for Science and Engineering Students, 1977; contbr. articles to profl. jours. Treas. Alaska Humanities Forum, Anchorage, 1982-87; mem. Anchorage Matanuska-Susitna Borough Pvt. Industry Coun., 1983-86; mem. Sister Cities Commn., Anchorage, 1984-90; mem. Multicultural Edn. Adv. Bd., Anchorage, 1987-90; with speakers bur. Wis. Humanities Com., 1992-95, Mcpl. Libr. Bd., 1993-95; active Mo. Humanities Coun., 1997-2003; bd. dirs. Mo. Colls. Fund, Ind. Colls. and Univs. of Mo.; mem. bd. Great Rivers Coun. Boy Scouts Am., 1996—. Named Fellow of Grad. Sch., U. Tex. Austin, 1977-78, Nat. Teaching Fellow, Alaska Pacific U., Anchorage, 1980-81; recipient Pub. Svc. award Sister Cities Commn., Anchorage, 1987, Kellogg Found. Nat. fellowship, Battle Creek, Mich., 1988-91. Mem. League of Women Voters, Nat. Assn. Women in Edn., Am. Assn. for Higher Edn., Am. Coun on Teaching of Foreign Langs., Tchrs. of English to Speakers of Other Langs., Nat. Coun. Tchrs. of English, Alpha Chi, Alpha Lambda Delta, Delta Rho Kappa, Gold Peppers, Kappa Delta Pi, Mortar Bd., Omicron Delta Kappa, Phi Kappa Phi, Pi Delta Phi, Pi Lambda Theta, Sigma Delta Pi, Sigma Epsilon Pi, Sigma Kappa. Avocations: community theater, hiking, camping, fishing. Office: Ctrl Meth Coll 411 CMC Sq Fayette MO 65248-1198 E-mail: minman@cmc.edu.

INNES, LAURA, actress; b. Pontiac, Mich., Aug. 16, 1959; BA in Theater, Northwestern U. Appeared in local and nat. plays, including A Streetcar Named Desire, Edmund, Two Shakespearean Actors, Our Town, Three Sisters; appeared in TV series, including Wings, My So-Called Life, Party of Five, Brooklyn Bridge, Louis, ER, 1995— (also dir. episodes); dir. episodes of The West Wing, Presidio Med; TV films include And the Band Played On, 1993, See Jane Run, 1995, Just Like Dad, 1995, The Price of a Broken Heart, 1999, Taking Back Our Town, 2001; appeared in feature film Deep Impact, 1998, Can't Stop Dancing, 1999. Office: Dan Buchwald & Assoc 9229 Sunset Blvd Ste 710 West Hollywood CA 90069

INNESA, LEVKOVA-LAMM, art critic, writer, curator; b. Moscow, Aug. 21, 1939; came to U.S., 1982; d. Efim Levkov and Irine Nikitina; m. Leonid Lamm, Jan. 9, 1969; 1 child, Olga. Degree in film engring., Leningrad Inst. Film Engrs., 1965; postgrad., Moscow Inst. Fgn. Langs., 1966-68. Freelance writer, art critic Lit. Rev., Moscow, 1967-82, Books' World, Literary Russia, Moscow, 1977-81, Novoe Russkoe Slovo, N.Y.C., 1983-95, Voice of Am., Liberty radio, N.Y.C., 1983-90, Panorama, L.A., 1984—, Contemporania Internat., Flash Art, N.Y. and Milan, 1988-90; chief curator Eduard Nakhamkin Fine Art, N.Y.C., 1989-91; freelance writer, art critic AP, N.Y.C., 1992—; pres. Imago Fine Art & Design Inc., 1999—. Ind. curator Baruch Coll. Gallery, N.Y.C., 1987, The Russian State Mus., Leningrad, 1990, The Artis House, Moscow, 1990, Berman Gallery, N.Y.C., 1991. Author: Back to Square One, 1991; co-author. Transit: Russian Art Between East and West, 1989, Kulturim Stalinism, 1994. Mem. Nat. Writers Union, Internat. Assn. Art Critics. Avocation: travel. Home and Office: 310 E 23rd St Apt 3A New York NY 10010-4735 E-mail: liki2108@aol.com.

INNES-BROWN, GEORGETTE MEYER, real estate broker, insurance broker; b. Wilmington, Del., Mar. 20, 1918; d. George and Flora Sue (Saunders) Meyer; m. Andrew T. Innes, Jr., Nov. 26, 1947 (dec.); m. Roy Glen Brown, Jr., Mar. 6, 1991. Grad. Real Estate Law, theory, Conveyancing and Practice, Phila. Bd. Realtors Sch., 1945; grad. Fire, Marine, Casualty Ins., North Phila. Realty Bd. Sch., 1946; cert. appraiser, Villanova Coll., 1974. Lic. realtor, Pa., ins. broker and appraiser, Phila. Ins. broker, realtor, Phila., 1945—; ins. broker, 1946—; also appraiser. Residential and single family home builder, Bucks County, Pa., Princeton, N.J., 1955-61. Mem., spkr. Juniata Pk. Civic Assn., Phila., 1984. Recipient Knights Legion award Italian-Am. Press, 1971. Mem. Nat. Assn. Realtors (sec.-treas. and v.p. chpt. 1975-80), Am. Bus. Women's Assn. (chpt. v.p. 1971, Business-woman of Yr. 1971), Phila. Women's Realty Assn. (pres. bd. govs. 1949-85, pres. 1949-51, Woman of Yr. 1972-73), Phila. Bd. Realtors (v.p. residential divsn. 1975), North Phila. Realty Bd. (v.p. 1975, 76, pres. 1977, Gustav A. Wick award 1979), Del. Coun. Realty Bds. (sec. 1974), Real Estate Multiple Listing Burs. (treas. 1972-76), Sigma Lambda Soc. (chpt. pres. 1948). Avocations: golf, dance, gardening, cooking, embroidery. Home: 1162 SW Walnut Ter Boca Raton FL 33486-5565

INNIS, PAULINE, writer, publishing company executive; b. Devon, England; came to U.S., 1954; m. Walter Deane Innis, Aug. 1, 1959. Attended, U. Manchester, U. London. Author: Hurricane Fighters, 1962, Ernestine or the Pig in the Potting Shed, 1963 (paperback 1992), The Wild Swans Fly, 1964, The Ice Bird, 1965, Wind of the Pampas, 1967, Fire from the Fountains, 1968, Astronumerology, 1971, Gold in the Blue Ridge, 1973, 2d edit., 1980, reprinted 1995, My Trails (transl. from French), 1975, Prayer and Power in the Capital, 1982, The Secret Gardens of Watergate, 1987, Attention: A Quick Guide to Armed Services, 1988, Desert Storm Dairy, 1991, The Nursing Home Companion, 1993, Bridge Across the Seas, 1995, The Gospel of Joseph, 1998, I've Smashed the Devil's Window, 1999; co-author: Protocol, 1977. Bd. dirs. Washington Goodwill Industries Guild, 1962-66; membership chmn. Welcome to Washington Club, 1961-64; co-chmn. Internat. Workshop Capital Spkr.'s Club, 1961-64; pres. Children's Book Guild, 1967-68; dir. Ednl. Commn., bd. dirs. Internat. Conf. Women Writers and Journalists, Nat. Arboretum, 1992-96; criminal justice com. D.C. Commn. on Status of Women; founder vol. program D.C. Women's Detention Ctr.; chmn. women's com. Washington Opera, 1977-79; mem. Liaison Com. Med. Edn., 1979-85; nat. trustee Med. Coll. Pa., 1980—; mem. Edn. Commn. for Fgn. Med. Grads., 1986-97. Named Hoosier Woman of Yr., 1966. Mem. Soc. Women Geographers, Authors League, Smithsonian Assocs. (women's bd.), English-Speaking Union, Spanish-Portuguese Group D.C. (pres. 1965-66), Br. Inst. U.S., Am. Newspaper Women's Club (pres. 1971-73), Internat. Soc. Poets (disting.), Sulgrave Club, Internat. Clubs (co-chair 1997), Venerable Order St. John Jerusalem (comdr.), Internat. Neighbors Club. Home: 2700 Virginia Ave NW Washington DC 20037-1908

INOS, RITA HOCOG, school system administrator; MA in Sch. Adminstrn. and Supervision, San Jose State U., 1983; EdD in Ednl. Planning, Policy and Adminstrn, USC, 1993. Commr. No. Mariana Islands Pub. Sch. System, Saipan, 2002—. Office: No Mariana Islands Pub Sch System 3rd Fl Retirement Fund Bldg Capitol Hill Saipan MP 96950

INOUYE, LORRAINE R. state legislator; b. Hilo, HI, June 22, 1940; m. Vernon Inouye; children: Ronald Jitchaku, Jay Kitchaku, Marcia Johansen. Mgr. Orchid Island Hotel, 1967-75; sales mgr. Hilo Hawaiian Hotel, Hilo and Kona Lagoon Hotels, 1975-86; pres. Aloha Blooms, Inc., 1998—; mem. Hawaii Senate, Dist. 1, Honolulu, 1998—; chair econ. devel. com. Hawaii Senate, Honolulu, mem. commerce and consumer protection com., mem. transp. and intergovtl. affairs com. Mayor County of Hawaii, 1990-92; mem. Hawaii County Coun., 1984-90, Hawaii County Planning Commn., 1974-79; dir. Girl Scout Coun. Hawaii, 1995X; charter mem. Ho'okumu, North Hawaii Cmty. Hosp., 1991X. Mem. Rotary Club of Hilo. Democrat. Office: State Capitol 415 S Beretania St Rm 201 Honolulu HI 96813-2407

INSALACO-DE NIGRIS, ANNA MARIA THERESA, middle school educator; b. N.Y.C., Oct. 18, 1947; d. Salvatore and Rosaria (Colletti) Insalaco; m. Michael Peter De Nigris, July 12, 1969; children: Jenniffer Ann, Tamara Alicia. BA in English and Langs., CCNY, 1969; MA in English Linguistics, George Mason U., 1988; postgrad., U. Va. Cert. endorsement in Adminstrn. and Supervision U. Va., 2002, English secondary tchr. Va. Tchr. Spanish and core subjects St. John's, Rubidoux, Calif., 1969-70; ESL specialist Sunset Hills Elem. Sch., San Diego, 1980; tchr. Sunrise Acres Elem. Sch., Las Vegas, Nev., 1984-85; tchr. 1st grade Talent House Pvt. Elem. Sch., Fairfax, Va., 1987-88; tchr. ESL Hammond Jr. High Sch., Alexandria, Va., 1988-90, Washington Irving Intermediate Sch., Springfield, Va., 1990-91; tchr. ESL 6th grade Ellen Glassgow Mid. Sch., Alexandria, 1991-92; tchr. ESL and English 7th grade Cooper Mid. Sch., McLean, Va., 1992-93; tchr. ESL Poe Mid. Sch., Annandale, Va., 1993-94; tchr. ESL and social studies Longfellow Mid. Sch., Falls Church, Va., 1994-95; tchr. ESL Herndon (Va.) Mid. Sch., 1995—; summer sch. asst. prin. Longfellow Mid. Sch., 2002. Tchr. adult ESL George Mason H.S., Falls Church, Va., 1988—89; chmn. for multicultural forum Coun. for Applied R&D George Mason U., 1990—94; mem. steering com., faculty adv. com. Herndon Mid. Sch., 1995—, program sponsor Reach for Tomorrow; coach for Krasnow Inst. George Mason U., 2000—; mem. sch. adoption com. Va. Dept. Transp., 1991, human rels. com., 1990—96, ESL Portfolio Assessment com., 1993—98; sch.-based mem. for minority achievement in prin.'s cabinet F.C. Hammond Jr. H.S., Alexandria, 1989—90; mem. Continuing Edn. Bd. Fairfax County, 1998—; co-chair WATESOL Secondary Interest Group, 1998—99, chair, 1999—2001; presenter in field. Vol. Family Svcs., Wright Patterson AFB, Ohio, 1971-72, ARC, Ohio and S.C., 1971-73; leader Girl Scouts U.S., 1980-87; Fairfax Edn. Assn. scholarship sponsor. Mem. Va. Edn. Assn. (del. 1990—), Nat. Assn. Bilingual Edn., ESL Multi-Cultural Conv. (presenter, facilitator 1989, socio-polit. concerns immigrant rights advocate 1995—), Tchrs. ESL, Washington Tchrs. ESL, Calif. Tchrs. ESL, Va. Assn. Tchrs. English, Fairfax Edn. Assn. (sch. rep., del. Va. Edn. Assn. and NEA), Italian-Am. Caucus (v.p. 1997-2000, pres. 2000—). Roman Catholic. Avocations: writing, reading, politics, helping others. Home: 9181 Big Springs Loop Bristow VA 20136-1290 E-mail: denigris@erols.com., annamaria.denigris@fcps.edu.

INSCHO, JEAN ANDERSON, retired social worker, landscape artist; b. Camden, NJ, Oct. 31, 1936; d. George Myrick and Alfrida Elizabeth (Anderson) Hewitt; m. James Ronald Inscho, June 4, 1955 (div. Mar. 1982); children: James Ronald Jr., Cynthia Ann, Michael Merrick. BA, Fla. Atlantic U., 1971; MA in Coll. Teaching, Auburn U., 1974, postgrad., 1998-99. Instr. So. Union State Jr. Coll., Wadley, Ala., 1973-75; social worker Jefferson County Dept. Human Resources, Birmingham, Ala., 1976-77, Shelby County Dept. Human Resources, Columbiana, Ala., 1977-78, Houston County Dept. Human Resources, Dothan, Ala., 1978-98. Adj. instr. Troy State U., Dothan, 1984-97. Bd. dir., v.p. Adolescent Resource Ctr., 1992-93, sec., 1993-95; mem. Alzheimer's Assn. EPDA fellow Auburn U., 1973, 74. Mem.: Am. Horticultural Therapy Assn. (Ga.-Ala. chpt.), Wiregrass Master Gardeners (pres. 1994—95), Ala. Master Gardeners Assn. (bd. dir., sec. 2003—, sec. 2003), Dist. 7 State Employees Assn. (polit. action com. rep. 1994—98), Ala. State Employees Assn. (bd. dir.), Am. Daffodil Soc. Episcopalian. Avocations: gardening, needlecrafts, church activities.

INSELMAN, LAURA SUE, pediatrician, educator; b. Bklyn., Nov. 2, 1944; d. Alexander M. and Rae (Bloom) Inselman. BA, Barnard Coll., 1966; MD, Med. Coll. Pa., 1970. Diplomate Am. Bd. Pediatrics, Am. Bd. Pediatric Pulmonology. Intern and resident St. Lukes Hosp. Ctr., N.Y.C., 1970-73; fellow in pediatric pulmonary disease Babies Hosp., N.Y.C., 1973-76; chief pediatric pulmonary divsn. Interfaith Med. Ctr., Bklyn., 1976-81, Newington Con. Children's Hosp., 1987-92; pulmunologist, med. dir. dept. respiratory care duPont Hosp. for Children, Wilmington, Del., 1992-99, med. dir. pulmonary function lab., 1992—. Asst. prof. pediatrics Cornell U. Med. Coll., N.Y.C., 1981-86, asst. clin. prof. pediatrics, Yale U. Sch. Medicine, New Haven, 1987-92; asst. prof. pediatrics, U. Conn. Health Ctr., Farmington, 1987-92; assoc. prof. pediatrics, Jefferson Med. Coll. Thomas Jefferson U. Hosp., Phila., 1992—; mem. staff Good Samaritan Hosp., West Islip, N.Y., 1982-87. Bd. dirs. Am. Lung Assn. Nassau-Suffolk, East Meadow, N.Y., 1983-86, Del., 1992—. Fellow Am. Acad. Pediatrics, Am. Coll. Chest Physicians; mem. Am. Thoracic Soc., Am. Fedn. Med. Rsch., N.Y. Acad. Medicine, Harvey Soc., Soc. Pediatric Rsch. Office: DuPont Hospital for Children 1600 Rockland Rd Wilmington DE 19803-3607 E-mail: linselm@nemours.org.

INSPRUCKER, NANCY RHOADES, career officer; b. Fort Campbell, Ky., June 16, 1959; d. Glen Lee and Mary Josephine (Lasell) Rhoades; m. John L. Inspruncker III, July 20, 1991. BS in Astro Engring., U.S. Air Force Acad., 1981; MS in Aero. and Astronaut. Engring., Stanford U., 1985. Commd. 2d lt. U.S. Air Force, 1981, advanced through grades to col., 1998; satellite test engr. space div. Los Angeles, 1981-84; instr. dept. astronautics USAF Acad., Colorado Springs, Colo., 1985-88; chief payload devel. and integration divsn. Office Sec. Air Force, L.A. AFB, 1988-90, chief mission processing divsn., 1990-92; chief sys. engr. Office Def. Landsat Pentagon, Washington, 1992-94; chief sys. engr. divsn. Office of Space Sys. Office Asst. Sec. Air Force, 1994-95, dir. advanced spacecraft acquisition Office Space & Tech., 1995-97; Gen. Moorman space chair Joint Mil. Intelligence Coll., 1997-99; program mgr. medium launch vehicles Space and Missile Ctr., L.A. AFB, Calif., 1999—2002, dep. dir. launch programs, 2002—. Recipient Medal of Merit, Nat. Air Force Assn., 1985; named Colorado Springs Mil. Woman of Yr., Gazette Telegraph newspaper, 1987. Mem. Air Force Assn., Am. Astronautical Soc., Soc. Women Engrs. Avocations: aerobics, long distance running, reading. Home: 2207B Voorhees Ave Redondo Beach CA 90278-2423 Office: SMC/CL 2420 Vela Way Ste 1467 El Segundo CA 90245-4659 E-mail: inspruck@earthlink.net.

INTILLI, SHARON MARIE, television director, small business owner; b. Amsterdam, N.Y., Aug. 11, 1950; d. Francisco Joseph Intilli and Virginia Eleanor (Tallman) Monaco. Cert., Paralegal Inst., 1973; BA in Psychology, Fordham U., 1995. Group assoc. editor Matthew Bender & Co., N.Y.C., 1974-77; prodn. sec. 20/20 program, ABC, N.Y.C., 1977-78, prodn. assoc., 1979-80, program prodn. asst., 1980-82; legal contract adminstr. ABC Sports, N.Y.C., 1978-79, dir., assoc. dir. for freelance projects, 1984-87; staff assoc. dir. ABC Television Network, N.Y.C., 1982-98; freelance assoc. dir., 1998—. Owner GreenBeing, Inc. Contbg. editor Bender's Forms of Discovery, Vols. 15 & 16, 1975. Active Bd. Health, Hillsdale, N.J., 1989-95. Recipient Outstanding Individual Achievement cert. Nat. Acad. TV Arts & Scis., 1980-81. Mem. Dirs. Guild of Am. Avocations: writing, photography, cooking, baking, singing. Office: 310 W 91st St # 3 New York NY 10024 E-mail: greenbe@worldnet.att.net.

INTRATER, CHERYL WATSON WAYLOR, career management consultant; b. Montreal, Que., Can., Sept. 8, 1943; naturalized, 1978; d. Alan Douglas and Jean Mary (Hughes) Watson; m. Donald L. Intrater, Nov. 11, 1990. BBA, Ga. State U., 1980. CPCU. Instr. ins. DeKalb Coll., Clarkston, Ga., 1978-79; mgr. divsn. Kemper Group, 1979-85; owner Ins. Support Svcs., Inc., Overland Park, Kans., 1986-91; v.p. Fortune and Co. Risk Mgrs., Inc., Overland Park, 1987—94. Owner Career Trend, Overland Park, 1994-97; v.p. orgnl. devel. and outplacement, ptnr., prin., career mgmt. cons. Alexander, Hoyt & Assocs., Overland Park, 1997-2001; owner Career Sys., Overland Park, Kans., 2001—; sr. cons. CSG Ptnrs. Inc., Overland Park, 2001-04; dir. Career Mgmt. Svcs., Jewish Vocat. Svc., Overland Park, Kans., 2002—; adv. coun. Johnson County C.C. Ins. Inst., Overland Park, 1990—; lectr. in field. Mem. Ctrl. Exch., 1998—, fin. resources com. Temple B'nai Jehudah, 2003-. Mem. Nat. Assn. Ins. Women (named Region V Ins. Profl. of Yr. 1992, cert. profl. ins. woman, Outstanding Mem. of Yr. 1992), Assn. of Career Profls. Internat. of Kansas City (charter mem. 2001, pres. 2002), CPCU Soc. (Kansas City chpt.). Republican. Avocations: fitness training, reading, traveling.

INTRILIGATOR, DEVRIE SHAPIRO, physicist; b. N.Y.C. d. Carl and Lillian Shapiro; m. Michael Intriligator; children: Kenneth, James, William, Robert. BS in Physics, MIT, 1962, MS, 1964; PhD in Planetary and Space Physics, UCLA, 1967. NRC-NASA rsch. assoc. NASA, Ames, Calif.,

1967-69; rsch. fellow in physics Calif. Inst. Tech., Pasadena, 1969-72, vis. assoc., 1972-73; asst. prof. U. So. Calif., 1972-80; mem. Space Scis. Ctr., 1978-83; sr. rsch. physicist Carmel Rsch. Ctr., Santa Monica, Calif., 1979—; dir. Space Plasma Lab., 1980—. Cons. NASA, NOAA, Jet Propulsion Lab.; chmn. NAS-NRC com. on solar-terrestrial rsch., 1983-86, exec. com. bd. atmospheric sci. and climate, 1983-86, geophysics study com., 1983-86; U.S. nat. rep. Sci. Com. on Solar-Terrestrial Physics, 1983-86; mem. adv. com. NSF Divsn. Atmospheric Sci. Co-editor: Exploration of the Outer Solar System, 1976; contbr. articles to profl. jours. Recipient 3 Achievement awards NASA, Calif. Resolution of Commendation, 1982. Mem. AAAS, Am. Phys. Soc., Am. Geophys. Union, Cosmos Club. Achievements include being a participant Pioneer 10/11 missions to outer planets; Pioneer Venus Orbiter, Pioneers 6, 7, 8 and 9 heliocentric missions. Home: 140 Foxtail Dr Santa Monica CA 90402-2048 Office: Carmel Rsch Ctr PO Box 1732 Santa Monica CA 90406-1732

INZANA, BARBARA ANN, professional musician, educator; b. Milw., Mar. 21, 1939; d. Joseph Lindsley and Marie Julia (Haerter) Raynor; m. John Thomas Inzana, June 19, 1965; children: Carolyn Marie, JoAnn Marian. BMus in Edn., Violin, Ind. U., 1961, MMus in Theory, 1969. Music tchr. Deerfield (Ill.) Pub. Schs., 1961—63; grad. teaching asst. theory dept. Ind. U. Music Sch., Bloomington, 1963—65; tchr. music St. James Elem. Sch., Falls Church, Va., 1975—82, St. Mary's Elem. Sch., Alexandria, Va., 1982—83; master tchr. music George Washington U., Washington, 1983—91; choir dir., soloist Nativity Ch., Burke, Va., 1986—91; music dir. Burke Presbyn. Ch., 1992—2002; substitute tchr. Fairfax County (Va.) Schs., 2002—. Pvt. instr. voice, violin, viola, piano, composition and theory, Falls Church, Va.; vocal cons. St. Phillips Ch., Falls Church, 1990—91; poster presenter Nat. Voice Found., 2001. Pub. Washerwoman's Holiday for intermediate string orch., 1997, He Is Born, the Holy One, soprano/alto, flute and piano. Mem. AFTRA, SAG, Am. Guild Mus. Artists, Am. String Tchrs. Assn., N.Am. Bluebird Assn., Ind. U. Alumni Assn. (life). Home: 403 W Rosemary Ln Falls Church VA 22046-3847

IONE, AMY, artist, researcher; b. Phila., Sept. 3, 1949; d. Martin Kessler and Barbara Angert. BA, Pa. State U., 1967; MA, John F. Kennedy U., Orinda, Calif., 1995. Instr. John F. Kennedy U., Orinda, Calif., 1995. Bd. dirs. Diatrope Inst.; presenter in field. Exhibited in group shows at U. Sch. Edn., Ann Arbor, Mich., 1974, ASUC Studio Gallery U. Calif., Berkeley, 1979, Haggin Mus., Stockton, Calif., 1985, Nat. Artists Equity Assn., Washington, 1986, Walnut Creek (Calif.) Civic Arts Gallery, 1985, 88; pvt. and permanent collections include Mills Coll. Art Gallery; creator for logo Visual Art Access, 1995; illustrator (with J. Bass) Tjokjok, 1989, 2d edit., 2002; (poster) San Francisco Arts Commn. Festival, 1986, Campanus Houses, 1976; author: Nature Exposed to our Method of Questioning, 2002. Home: PO Box 12748 Berkeley CA 94712-3748 E-mail: ione@diatrope.com.

IONE, CAROLE, psychotherapist, writer, playwright, director; b. Washington, D.C., May 28, 1937; d. Hylan Garnet Lewis and Leighla (Whipper) Ford; m. Salvatore Bovoso (div.); children: Alessandro, Santiago, Antonio. Student, Bennington (Vt.) Coll., 1959, NYU, New Sch. for Social Rsch.; practitioner, Helix Inst. for Psychotherapy and Healing, 1986-87, Chinese Healing Arts Ctr., 1995. Cert. qi gong therapist, hypnotherapist. Artistic dir. Renaissance House, N.Y.C., 1961, 62; founder, artistic dir., editor Letters (now Live Letters), N.Y.C., 1974—; editor of poetry choices Village Voice, N.Y.C., 1980-84; contbg. editor Essence, N.Y.C., 1981-83; co-artistic dir., v.p. Pauline Oliveros Found., Kingston, N.Y., 1985—; dir. Writers in Performance Manhattan Theatre Club, N.Y.C., 1985-86; psychotherapist Kingston and N.Y.C., 1986—; poetry curator Unison Lng. Ctr., New Paltz, N.Y., 1990-91. Past v.p., curator Deep Listening Space; bd. dirs. Ministry MAAT, Inc. Author: Pride of Family: Four Generations of American Women of Color, 1991, This is a dream!, 2000; playwright, dir. Njinga the Queen King, 1991—; dir. IO and Her, 2000, Deep Listening for Tunes A Lunar Opera, 2000. Mem. mayor's task force, Kingston, N.Y., 1996. Recipient S.C. Commn. for the Humanities award, 1983, Rockefeller Found. award, 1992, NEA award, 1992, N.Y. State Coun. for the Arts award, 1992, Charitable Trust award PEW, 1993, Dance Theater Workshop Suitcase Fund award, 1993. Fellow The Mac Dowell Colony, YADDO, Edward Albee Found., The Writer's Room; mem. Nat. Writers Union, Internat. Women's Writing Guild, The Author's Guild, Poets and Writers. Avocations: painting, visual arts, poetry. Office: Pauline Oliveros Found PO Box 1956 Kingston NY 12402-1956

IORIO, PAM, county official; b. Waterville, Maine, Apr. 27, 1959; d. John J. and Dorothy (Lockett) I.; m. Mark S. Woodard, May 30, 1987; children: Caitlin, Graham. BS in Polit. Sci., The Am. U., 1981; MA in History, U. South Fla., 2001. County commr. Hillsborough County, Tampa, Fla., 1985—92, supr. elections, 1993—2003; mayor Tampa, 2003—. Recipient Disting. Alumnus award, Leadership Fla., 2002. Mem.: Fla. State Assn. Suprs. Elections (pres. 2000). Office: City of Tampa Mayor's Office 306 East Jackson St Tampa FL 33602*

IQBAL, SYMA U. corporate financial executive; b. Karachi, Sind, Pakistan, Dec. 24, 1967; d. Hafeezuddin and Feroze Munshi; m. Umair Iqbal, Nov. 29, 1995; 1 child, Hamza. BComm, U. Karachi, Pakistan, 1989. Assoc. Chartered Acct., Inst. Chartered Accountants of Pakistan, 1995; cert. profl. Oracle U., 2001. Audit supr. Ernst & Young Pakistan, Karachi, Pakistan, 1989—93; Oracle applications functional cons. Softech Microsystems, Karachi, Pakistan, 1999—2000; mgr. accounts Security Leasing Corp. Ltd. - A Merrill Lynch, USA and CDC, UK Co., Karachi, Pakistan, 1994—99; Oracle financials cons. Amtex Systems Inc, N.Y.C., NY, 2001—. Bus. cons., ERP fin. applications Bi-State Devel. Agy. of St Louis, Mo., 2003; Oracle financials specialist Ingersoll Rand - Air Solutions Group, Davidson, NC, 2003, Ingersoll Rand - Constrn. and Mining Group, Annandale, NJ, 2002—03; Oracle financials cons. GE Power Systems, Milpitas, Calif., 2002; Oracle fin. applications - functional specialist Human Resource Adminstrn., N.Y.C., NY, 2001—02. Achievements include design of Business Process re-engineering architecture for financial applications at Ingersoll Rand - ASG; Business Process re-engineering architecture - NY City Human Resource Administration; Business process re-engineering documentation at GE Power Systems. Home: 228-B N Magnolia St Mooresville NC 28115 Office: Amtex Systems Inc 50 Broadway Suite 801 New York NY 10004 Personal E-mail: syma_iqbal@hotmail.com.

IRELAND, FAITH, state supreme court justice; b. Seattle, 1942; d. Carl and Janice Enyeart; m. Chuck Norem. BA, U. Wash.; JD, Willamette U., 1969; M in Taxation with honors, Golden Gate U. Past assoc. McCune, Godfrey and Emerick, Seattle; pvt. practice Pioneer Square, Wash., 1974; judge King County Superior Ct., 1984—98; justice Wash. Supreme Ct., 1998—. Past dean Washington Jud. Coll.; past mem. Bd. Ct. Edn. Served on numerous civic and charitable bds.; past pro-bono atty. Georgetown Dental Clin.; past bd. dirs. Puget Sound Big Sisters, Inc.; founding mem. Wing Luke Asian Mus., 1967—, past pres., past bd. dirs.; bd. dirs. Youth and Fitness Found., 1998. Named Judge of Yr., Washington State Trial Lawyer's Assn., Man of Yr. for efforts in founding Wing Luke Asian Mus.; recipient Disting. Svc. award, Nat. Leadership Inst. Jud. Edn., 1998. Mem.: Superior Ct. Judges Assn. (past bd. dirs., pres. 1996—97, vice chair bd. dirs. jud. adminstrn. 1996—98), Wash. State Trial Lawyer's Assn. (past chair bd. dirs.), Washington Women Lawyer's (founding mem., Pres.'s award, Vanguard award), Rotary (bd. dirs. Seattle No. 4 1998), Rainer Valley Hist. Soc. (life; founding mem.). Office: Washington Supreme Ct 415 12th St W PO Box 40929 Olympia WA 98504-0929

IRELAND, KATHY, actor, apparel designer; b. Glendale, Calif., 1962; d. John and Barbara Ireland; m. Greg Olsen, 1988; children: Erik, Lily. CEO, chief designer Kathy Ireland Worldwide. Appearances in Sports Illustrated's Ann. Swimsuit Issues, 25th Anniversary Show Swimsuit Edit., Kathy Ireland LPGA Championship, ESPN, 2001; films include: Alien from L.A., 1988, Necessary Roughness, 1991, Mom and Dad Save the World, 1992, National Lampoon's Loaded Weapon I, 1993, The Player, Mr. Destiny, Amore, Backfire; TV films include Beauty and the Bandit, 1994, Danger Island, 1994, Miami Hustle, 1995, Gridlock, 1996, Once Upon A Christmas, 2000, Twice Upon A Christmas, 2001; TV appearances include: Down the Shore, The Edge, Tales from the Crypt, Without a Clue, Grand, Charles in Charge, Perry Mason, Boy Meets World, Melrose Place, The Watcher, Deadly Games, Sabrina the Teenage Witch, Suddenly Susan, Gun, Cosby, Touched by an Angel, Pensacola, For Your Love, Strong Medicine. Office: Kathy Ireland Worldwide 10877 Wilshire Blvd #15 Los Angeles CA 90024-4341

IRELAND, PATRICIA, not-for-profit developer; b. Oak Park, Ill., Oct. 19, 1945; d. James Ireland and Joan Filipek; m. James Humble, 1968. BA, U. Tennessee, 1966; JD, U. Miami Law Sch., 1975. Flight attendant Pan Am. World Airlines, 1967-75; ptnr. Stearns, Weaver, Miller, Weissler, Alhadeff & Sitterson, Miami; nat. exec. v.p. NOW, 1987—91, pres., 1991—2001; initiator Global Feminist Conf.; rep. NOW; of counsel Katz, Kutter, Alderman, Bryant & Yon, 2001—03; CEO YWCA of the USA, Washington, 2003—. Author: What Women Want, 1996; contbr. law rev. Univ. Miami Law Sch. Office: YWCA 1015 18th St NW Washington DC 20036

IREY, CHARLOTTE YORK, dance educator; b. Oklahoma City, Apr. 29, 1918; d. Charles William and Annie Charlotte (Upsher) York; m. Eugene Floyd Irey, June 10, 1942; 1 child, Susan Gail. BS with honors., U. Wis., 1940. Instr. dance Stephens Coll., Columbia, Mo., 1940-43; prof. dance U. Colo., Boulder, 1945-88, chmn. dance divsn., dept. theatre and dance, 1973-88; sole practice Indpls., 1976—. Author: (with Frances Bascom) Costume Cues, 1952. Recipient Robert L. Steans award U. Colo., Boulder, 1973, Thomas Jefferson award, 1980; Charlotte York Irey Studio/Theatre at U. Colo., Boulder named in her honor, 1984. Mem. Nat. Dance Assn. (pres. 1975-76, Scholar of Yr. 1982-83, Heritage honoree 1990), AAHPERD, Am. Coll. Dance Festival, Coun. Dance Adminstrs., Congress Dance Rsch., Am. Dance Guild. Episcopalian.

IRISH, DIANA MARIA, wildlife rehabilitation agent; b. Grand Rapids, Mich., May 24, 1950; d. Robert Leroy and June Lorraine (Centilli) Newman; m. Harvey Alan Irish, Nov. 22, 1968; children: Timothy, Jamy, Corey, Windy, Robert, Wayne, Shellie. Grad. h.s., Grand Rapids, Mich. Author: My Talking Heart, 1992, Pictures of My Mind, 1994, Wings of Thought; recordings include A Rose for My Daddy and Forest Lane in (tape) Hilltop Country, 1998, Hight Country, Light of the World, Roll Gordon Roll, 1999, Freedom in the Meadow and Prayer of Our Ancesters in (CD) High Country, 1998, Rainbows End, Little Windy and Please Don't Worry in (CD) Light of the World, 1998. Bd. dirs. Coalition Rep. for Govt., Grand Rapids, 1997-99. Recipient Golden Poet award World of Poetry, 1988-99, Homer Honor Soc., 1990, Poet of Merit Internat. Soc. of Poets; named to Internat. Poets Hall of Fame, 1997-99. Mem. Weaving Ethnisity (sec. 1992-2002), C.R.G. (bd. dirs. 1998-2002), Grand Valley Am. Indian Lodge (bd. dirs., sec. 1992-2002), Inter Tribal (mem.-at-large). Avocations: writing, fishing, hunting, native american dancing, doll designer. Home: 5909 Ramsdell Dr NE Rockford MI 49341-9067

IRIZARRY, DEBRA EDITH, artist; b. N.Y.C., Mar. 26, 1964; d. Carlos Manuel Irizarry and Ramonita Mercado; m. Steven Andrew Hnizdo, Apr. 29, 1994; children: Gabriela Hnizdo, Alexander Hnizdo. AS, Fashion Inst. Technology, N.Y.C., 1986. Textile designer Phillips Van Heusen, N.Y.C., 1986—91; freelance CAD designer, 1991—93. Exhibitions include Pulcheriu Arte Exhib., Piacenza, Italy, 2001, exhibited in group shows at La Misma Sangre, San Juan, P.R., 2002. Recipient Best in Show, Arte Studio, Florence, Italy, 2001, exhbn. winner award, Pulcheria Arte, Florence, 2001. Home: #20 Patchogue Dr Rocky Point NY 11778

IRIZARRY, ESTELLE DIANE, foreign language educator, writer, editor; b. Paterson, N.J., Nov. 13, 1937; d. Morris Jerome and Ceil Pearl (Schwartz) Roses; m. Manuel Antonio, Dec. 14, 1963; children: Michael Carl, Steven Edward, Nelson Paul. BA, Montclair State U., 1959; MA, Rutgers U., 1963; PhD in Philosophy, The George Washington U., 1970. Tchr. Glen Rock (N.J.) H.S., 1958-60, Ramapo (N.J.) Regional H.S., 1960-63; instr. U. P.R., Rio Piedras, 1963-66, Howard U., Washington, 1966-68, George Washington U., Washington, 1968-70; prof. Georgetown U., Washington, 1970—. Editor Spanish sect. Humanities Computing Yearbook, Oxford, U.K., 1988, Hispania, 1993-2000. Author: Escritores-pintores españoles, 1990, Estudios Sobre Rafael Dieste, 1992, Informática y Literatura, 1997. Recipient Tomas Barros Essay prize, La Coruna, Spain, 1990, Spanish Cross of the Civil Order of Alphonse the Sage, 1998; grantee Quincentennial grant, P.R. Com. for the Quincentenary, 1989. Mem. Am. Assn. Tchrs. Spanish and Portuguese, N.Am. Acad. of the Spanish Lang., Royal Spanish Acad. (corr.), Sigma Delta Pi. Avocations: writing, painting, literary computing. Home: 1600 N Oak St Apt 1615 Arlington VA 22209-2758

IRLEN, HELEN, educational psychologist; b. Bklyn., Apr. 5, 1945; d. Moe and Katherine (Barnett) Lewis; m. Robert Irlen, July 16, 1967; children: David, Sandra. BS, Cornell U., 1967; MA, Calif. State U., Long Beach, 1969, credential, 1970. Sch. psychologist credential Calif. Career. Sch. assoc. Cornell U., Ithaca, NY, 1965—67; instr. Pepperdine U., 1970—71; sch. psychologist Newport-Mesa Unified Sch. Dist., Newport Beach, 1970—81; asst. prof., dir. adult learning disabilities Calif. State U., Long Beach, 1981—85; exec. dir. Irlen Inst., Long Beach, 1985—. Internat. lectr., dir. Irlen Clinics in Australia, New Zealand, Germany, Israel, Switzerland, Ireland, Hong Kong, Austria, Belgium, Can., Iceland, Spain, Malaysia, Jordan, Republic of Korea, South Africa, U.K., U.S., 1985—; interviews featured in London Times, 60 Minutes, BBC TV, Worldwide News with Peter Jennings, Australian Woman's Weekly mag., Brit. Reader's Digest. Book, Reading by the Colors; contbr. articles to rsch. publs. With Jr. League, Long Beach. Recipient awards, CARS, 1987. Office: Irlen Inst 5380 Village Rd Long Beach CA 90808

IRONS, ELLEN JANE, special education educator; b. Lewiston, Idaho; m. Ernest M. Irons Jr.; children: Jo Ann Ponder, Teresa Curtis, Elaine Irons, Dan Pavlica. BS in Edn., U. Fla., 1971; MEd, Trinity U., 1975; EdD, Northeastern U., 1984. Sch. psychologist Cecil County Ind. Sch. Dist., Rising Sun, Md., 1978-80; ednl. rschr. Behavior Rsch. Lab., Aberdeen Proving Ground, Md., 1978; edn. diagnostician Ft. Sam Houston Ind. Sch. dist., San Antonio, Tex., 1975-78; tchr. math. San Antonio Ind. Sch. Dist., 1971-74; lectr. math. Northeastern U., Boston, 1981-83; spl. edn. specialist Tex. Edn. Agy., Austin, 1984; dir. instrn. Am. Prep. Inst., Killeen, Tex., 1985; elem. prin. La Pryor (Tex.) Ind. Sch. Dist., 1986; ednl. program dir. Tex. Edn. Agy., Austin, 1987-90; dir. curriculum & instrn. Tex. Youth Commn., Austin, 1990-93; assoc. prof. spl. edn. Tex. Woman's U., Denton, 1993—. Contbr. articles to profl. jours. Mem.Tex. Coun. Adminstrs. Spl. Edn. (rsch. com. 1998—), Phi Delta Kappa, Kappa Delta Pi. Home: 109 Pennsylvania Dr Denton TX 76205-5465 Office: Tex Womans U PO Box 425769 Denton TX 76204-5769 E-mail: eirons@twu.edu.

IRONS, PAULETTE RILEY, state legislator, lawyer; b. New Orleans, May 19, 1953; d. Florida Wilson; m. Alvin L. Irons; children: Marseah Irons Delatte, Paul-Alvin. BBA, Loyola U., New Orleans, 1975; JD, Tulane U., 1991. Bar: La. 1991. Sr. cons. Small Bus. Devel. and Mgmt. Inst., New Orleans, 1992-93; mem. La. Ho. of Reps., Baton Rouge, 1992-94, La. Senate, Baton Rouge, 1994—. Vice-chmn. transp., hwys. and pub. works com., mem. health and welfare com., formr mem. fin. com., pres. women's caucus,1998, sgt.-at-arms legis. black caucus, 1993-95; sr. cons. Small Bus. Devel. and Mgmt. Inst., New Orleans, 1992-93; adj. prof. Tulane U. Law Clinic, New Orleans, fall 1995; atty. 1st City Ct., New Orleans, 1996-98; atty. Recorder of Mortgages Office, New Orleans, 1997—; adv. bd. women's network Nat. Conf. State Legislators, Denver, 1996—. Pres. bd. dirs. La. Initiative on Teen Pregnancy Prevention, 1995-2001, bd. dirs. New Orleans Area Literacy Coalition. Recipient Woman of Excellence award 2d Bapt. Ch., 1994, Outstanding African Am. Woman, Tulane Black Law Students, 1996, Good Housekeeping award, 2001; named Legislator of Yr., New Orleans Alliance for Good Govt., 1995. Fellow Japan Soc.; mem. LWV, AAUW, Nat. Order Women Legislators, Nat. Order Black Elected Legislators, Women for a Better La., Ind. Women's Orgn., La. League Good Govt. Democrat. Avocations: reading, travel. Office: La Senate 1010 Common St Ste 3040 New Orleans LA 70112-2417 Address: La Senate Ofc PO Box 94183 Baton Rouge LA 70804-9183

IRVINE, PHYLLIS ELEANOR, nursing educator, administrator; b. Germantown, Ohio, July 14, 1940; m. Richard James Irvine, Feb. 15, 1964; children: Mark, Rick. BSN, Ohio State U., 1962, MSN, 1979, PhD, 1981; MS, Miami U., Oxford, Ohio, 1966. Staff nurse VA Ctr., Dayton, Ohio, 1962-66; mem. nursing faculty Miami Valley Hosp. Sch. Nursing, Dayton, 1968-78; teaching asst., lectr. Ohio State U., Columbus, 1979-82; assoc. prof. Ohio U., Athens, 1982-83; prof., dir. N.E. La. U., Monroe, 1984-88; prof., dir. sch. nursing Ball State U., Muncie, Ind., 1988—. Reviewer Health Edn. Jour., Reston, Va., 1987; contbr. articles to profl. jours. Mem. Mayor's Commn. on Needs of Women, La., 1984-88; 1st v.p., bd. dirs. United Way of Ouachita, La., 1986-88. Mem. ANA, Ind. Nurses Assn., Ind. Coun. Deans and Dirs. of Nursing Edn. (pres. 1992-98), Internat. Coun. Women's Health Issues (bd. dirs. 1986-92, 98-2000), Assn. for the Advancement Health Edn., Sigma Theta Tau. Office: Ball State U Cn418 Nursing Muncie IN 47306-0001

IRVINE, ROSE LORETTA ABERNETHY, retired communications educator, consultant; b. Kingston, N.Y., Nov. 14, 1924; d. William Francis and Julia A.; m. Robert Tate Irvine Jr., Dec. 18, 1965 (dec. June 1968). BA, Coll. St. Rose, 1945; MA, Columbia U., 1946; PhD, Northwestern U., 1964. Tchr. English, Kingston H.S., 1946-47; tchr. English and speech Croton-Harmon H.S., Croton-on-Hudson, NY, 1947-49; instr. speech SUNY, New Paltz, 1949-53, asst. prof. New Paltz, 1953-57, assoc. prof., 1957-64, prof. speech communication, 1964-85, prof. emeritus, 1985—. Guest prof. Yon Sei U., Seoul, 1970; U.S. del. U.S. Bi-Nat. Conf., Manila, 1976; adv. bd. Rondout Nat. Bank Norstar (now Fleet Bank), 1973-85; U. Chancellor's adv. bd. SUNY Senate, Albany, 1974-80; guest prof. Celtic lore Princess Grace Libr., Monaco, 1987; mem. faculty sr. rsch. partnership program SUNY, Albany, 1999—; cons., rschr., writer, 1985—; presenter in field. Contbr. articles to Speech Tchr., Ednl. Forum, Readers Theatre, others; hist. rsch. "John Vanderlyn Letters from Paris", "A Tale of Three Lives: Aaron Burr, his Daughter Theodosia, and John Vanderlyn"; writer, performer hist. scripts. Active Nat. Jr. League, Kingston, 1958-90; dir. Puppet Theater for Srs., N.Y., 1982-83; bd. trustees Friends of the Senate House State Hist. Site, Kingston, 1996-99, pres. 1999; bd. Ulster County adv. coun. to Office for Aging, 1998—, v.p., 2000—, pres. 2001—; mem. Gov. Pataki's Adv. Coun. Aging Svcs., 2000—; allocations com. United Way, Ulster County, 1998-2000; mem. Cornell Coop. Extension Program Com., 2003--. Honor Tuition scholar Coll. St. Rose, Albany, N.Y., 1941; named Outstanding Educator of Am., 1971. Mem. AAUW (liaison SUNY New Paltz 1966-85), Speech Comm. Assn. (mem. legis assembly 1967-68, emeritus), N.Y. State Speech Assn. (emeritus), Zeta Phi Eta, Delta Kappa Gamma, Kappa Delta Pi, Pi Lambda Theta. Roman Catholic. Avocations: historic preservation, golf, swimming, travel, local history. Home: 105 Lounsbury Pl Kingston NY 12401-5231 Office: SUNY Communications Dept New Paltz NY 12561

IRVING, NANCY IRENE, volunteer; b. Creston, Iowa, July 11, 1948; d. Claire LeRoy and Hazel Irene Foltz; m. Patrick Gene Irving, June 23, 1968; children: Jeremy, Colby, Marissa. AA, C.E. Sch. Commerce, Omaha, 1968; student, Drake U., 1971—73. Exec. asst. Hublein Corp., Omaha, 1968—69, GM Acceptance Corp., Omaha and Des Moines, 1969—72, Physicians Assocs., PC, Mount Ayr, Iowa, 1974—78. Activities organizer PTA, Davenport, Iowa, 1979—85; food collector and promoter Cmty. Food Pantry, Davenport, Iowa, 1978—; multiple coms. and bds. Christ United Meth. Ch., Davenport, Iowa, 1978—; bd. dirs. Scott County Meals on Wheels, Davenport, Iowa, 1978—2000. Mem.: Crow Valley Golf Club, Carlton Club, Outing Club. Republican. Meth. Avocations: gardening, reading, collecting Peanuts comics, walking, skiing. Home: 4311 Kelling St Davenport IA 52806

IRVING, SUSAN JEAN, government executive; b. Washington, Apr. 25, 1949; d. Frederick and Dorothy Jean Irving; m. Joseph Alexander Rieser Jr., Feb. 28, 1976; 1 child, Alexander Hoon Irving Rieser. BA, Wellesley Coll., 1971; MAT, Harvard Grad. Sch. Edn., 1972; M in Pub. Policy, Harvard U., 1974, PhD, 1976. Cert. Govt. Fin. Mgr., Assn. Govt. Accts. Legis. asst. to U.S. Sen. Abe Ribicoff, Washington, 1976-79; staff dir. Exec. Office of the Pres. Pres.'s Coun. of Econ. Advisers, Washington, 1979-81; external rels. officer Internat. Monetary Fund, Washington, 1981-82; v.p. Com. for a Responsible Fed. Budget, Washington, 1982-84; sr. econ. advisor Mondale for Pres., 1984; legis. dir. for U.S. Sen. Max Baucus Washington, 1985; lectr. pub. policy John F. Kennedy Sch. Govt. Harvard U., Cambridge, Mass., 1986-89; faculty Tng. Inst. U.S. Gen. Acctg. Office, Washington, 1989—92, assoc. dir. for fed. budget issues, 1992-2000, dir. fed. budget analysis, 2000—; fellow Inst. Politics Harvard U., 1986. Bd. dirs. Am. Assn. Budget and Program Analysis. Co-pres. Stoddert PTA, Washington, 1997-98. Recipient Cert. of Appreciation Am. Assn. for Budget and Program Analysis, 1997, Outstanding Svc. award, 1993. Fellow Nat. Assn. for Pub. Adminstrn.; mem. Assn. Pub. Policy and Mgmt. Avocations: walking, needlepoint on plastic. Office: US Gen Acctg Office 441 G St NW Washington DC 20548-0001 Fax: (202) 512-4955. E-mail: irvings@gao.gov.

IRWIN, DENISE ANNE, human resources specialist; d. Frank T. and Rosemary A. Irwin. BSc in Pk. and Recreation Adminstrn., Ohio State U., 1991. Asst. cruise dir. Commodore/Cunard/Crown Cruise Line, Ft. Lauderdale, Fla., 1991—95; guest rels. hostess Walt Disney World, Orlando, Fla., 1995—97; human resources mgr. Disney Cruise Line, Orlando, 1997—2000; sr. tng. and devel. rep. Disneyland Resort, Anaheim, Calif., 2000—.

IRWIN, DONNA RICE, music educator; b. Union City, Tenn., Apr. 30, 1970; d. Fred L. and Linda F. Rice; m. David C. Tinnell Jr., June 5, 1993 (div. Dec. 15, 1997); children: Mitchell, Cory; m. Michael D. Irwin, May 27, 2000. MusB in Music Edn., Campbellsville Coll., 1992; MusM in Music Edn., Campbellsville U., 1999; postgrad., U. Ky., 2001—. Cert. tchr. Ky. Admissions asst. Campbellsville (Ky.) Coll., 1992; substitute tchr. Taylor County Mid. Sch., 1992—93; choral dir. Marion County Schs., Lebanon, Ky., 1993—2001; adj. prof. Sch. Music Campbellsville U., 2001—. Composer, arranger: choral works. Ch. pianist South Campbellsville Bapt. Ch., 1990—93; music dir. Asbury United Meth. Ch., 2003—. Recipient 1st place mixed choir, Festivals of Music, St. Louis, 2001. Mem.: 4th Dist. Choral Dirs.' Assn. (pres. 1999—2001), Ky. Music Educators Assn. (mem. state choral coun. 1999—2001, festival commn. 1999—2001, adjudictor 2001—). Avocations: reading, birdwatching, fishing, boating, camping. Home: 444 Dowell St Campbellsville KY 42718 Office: Campbellsville U 100 University Dr Campbellsville KY 42718

IRWIN, LINDA BELMORE, public relations/marketing consultant; b. Portland, Oreg., Apr. 29, 1950; d. Calvin C. and Dorothy B. (Belmore) Harper; m. Michael Hugh Irwin, June 24, 1989. Student, Portland State U., 1968—72. With Hyatt Regency, New Orleans, 1975-78; catering Hyatt Regency-Capitol Hill, Washington, 1978-80; dir. catering Hyatt, Anaheim,

Calif., 1978-80; mgr. Dockside Yacht Sales, Annapolis, Md., 1981-85; dir. sales and mktg. Loew's Hotel, 1985-86; dir. mktg. Annapolis Marriot, 1986-88; ind. mktg. cons. Washington, Dallas, Cin. and Loudoun County, Va., 1988—. Amb. State of Md., Annapolis, 1986-88; mktg. chair Tourism Coun. Annapolis and Anne Arundel County; curricula advisor Anne Arundel C.C.; mem. fund raising com. Ch. Circle Beautification Trust; chair of comm., 2002-, chair of fellowship, 2002-03; officer St. Peters Episc. Ch., 2002-, stewardship com., 2003-, mem. vestry bd., 2001-04; sec. Mt. Calvary Guild, 2003-; vol. Nat. Day Prayer, Loudoun Family Fest, Passion Play, Arts in the Alley, 2004-, VSA Arts for the Disabled; media/pub. rels. rep. Not Just Shakespeare, Inc.; media rep. Loudoun County; bd. dirs. Not Just Shakespeare Theatre, Round Hill Arts Ctr.; mem. steering com. Passion PLA. Mem. Nat. Banquet mgrs. Guild (founder L.A. chpt.), Nat. Assn. Female Execs. (area dir. 1985—), Annapolis C. of C. (ambassador 1985-88), Greater Washington Soc. of Assn. Execs., Anne Arundel Trade Coun., Md. Tourism Coun. (adv. bd.), Internat. Platform Assn. Republican. Episcopalian. Avocations: calligraphy, sailing, travel, literature, ballet. E-mail: LindaIrwin@megapipe.net.

IRWIN, MARY JANE, engineering educator; b. Cairo, Ill., July 14, 1949; BS in Math. magna cum laude, Memphis State U., 1971; MS in Computer Sci., U. Ill., 1975, PhD in Computer Sci., 1977; Doctorate (hon.), Chalmers U., Sweden, 1997. Grad. rsch. and grad. tchg. asst. computer sci. U. Ill., Champaign-Urbana, 1972—77; asst. prof. computer sci. Pa. State U., University Park, 1977—83; rsch. staff Supercomputing Rsch. Ctr. Inst. for Def. Analysis, Bowie, Md., 1986; assoc. prof. computer sci. Pa. State U., University Park, Pa., 1983—89, dept. head computer sci., 1991—93, prof. computer sci. and engring., 1989—99, disting. prof. computer sci. and engring., 1999—. Fellow: IEEE (Cert. of Appreciation 1993—95), Assn. Computing Machinery (Leadership award 1993); mem.: Nat. Acad. Engring. Office: Pa State Univ Dept Computer Sci and Engring 227 Pond Lab University Park PA 16802 Home: 108 Yost Dr Spring Mills PA 16875*

IRWIN, MIRIAM DIANNE OWEN, book publisher, writer; b. Columbus, Ohio, June 14, 1930; d. John Milton and Miriam Faith (Studebaker) Owen; m. Kenneth John Irwin, June 5, 1960; 1 child, Christopher Owen. BS in Home Econs., Ohio State U., 1952, postgrad. in bus. adminstrn., 1961-62. Editl. asst. Am. Home Mag., N.Y.C., 1953-56; salesman Owen Realty, Dayton, Ohio, 1957-58, Clevenger Realty, Phoenix, 1958-59; home economist Columbus and So. Ohio Electric Co., 1959-60; pub. Mosaic Press, Cin., 1977—. Owner Bibelot Bindery, 1987—. Author: Lute and Lyre, 1977, Forty is Fine, 1977, Miriam Mouse's Survival Manual, 1977, Miriam Mouse's Costume Collection, 1977, Miriam Mouse's Marrige Contract, 1977, Miriam Mouse, Rock Hound, 1977, Silver Bindings, 1983; editor: Tribute to the Arts, 1984, Chunging, 1996; contbg. author Publisher's Favorite, 1988; illustrator: Corals of Pennekamp, 1979. Daytime crew chief Wyoming Life Squad, Ohio, 1966-71. Recipient Norman Forgue award, 2000. Mem. Studebaker Family Nat. Assn. (archivist 2000—, bd. dirs. 2003-), Miniature Book Soc. (past bd. dirs., chair 1987 89, Glasgow Cup 2003). Presbyterian. Avocation: book collecting. Home and Office: 358 Oliver Rd Cincinnati OH 45215-2615 E-mail: mirwin@cinci.rr.com.

IRWIN-HENTSCHEL, NOËL, travel company executive; b. Fresno, Calif. m. Gordon Hentschel; 7 children. Co-founder, chmn., CEO Am. Tours Internat., L.A., 1977—. Bd. regents Loyola Marymount U.; rep. Gov.'s Crime Summit; speaker Gov.'s Conf. Women; bd. dirs. Travel Industry Assn., C. of C. Candidate Lt. Gov. Calif.; co-chair Nat. Policy Forum's Coun. Econ. Growth and Workplace Opportunities; active Gov. Pete Wilson's team. Recipient Entrepreneur of Yr. award Calif. Travel Industry, 1995, Woman Bus. Owner of Yr. award Nat. Assn. Women Bus. Owners, 1996; named Humanitarian of Yr. Calif. Mothers Assn., 1998, Top 100 Entrepreneurs Success Mag. Mem. L.A. World Affairs Coun., L.A. Libr. Found. Office: American Tours Internat LA Internat Airport 6053 W Century Blvd Los Angeles CA 90045-6430 Fax: 310-216-5807.

ISAAC, BINA SUSAN, data processing executive; b. Nainital, India, Jan. 9, 1958; came to U.S. 1980; d. Rajan Kurian and Susan (Thomas) George; m. Mathew Isaac, July 14, 1980; children: Sonya Susan, Shawn George. BA, Sarah Tucker Coll., Tirunelveli, India, 1978; MA, Madurai U., India, 1980; MEd, U. Toledo, 1981, MBA, 1984. Coord. computer svcs. and computer ctr. Lourdes Coll., Sylvania, Ohio, 1984-85, dir. computer svcs. and computer ctr., 1985-95, dir. info. tech. dept. svcs., 1995-97, part time instr. math. and phys. sci., 1985-97; from info. sys. dir. to chief tech. Coll. of the Desert, Palm Desert, Calif., 1997—2002, chief tech. officer, dean info. sys. and ednl. tech., 2002—. Instr. Continuing Edn. Dept., Sylvania, 1985-97. Mem. Assn. C.C. Adminstrs. Avocations: playing the piano, reading, outdoor activities. Office Phone: 760-776-0112. E-mail: BIsaac@collegeofthedesert.edu.

ISAAC, TERESA ANN, mayor, lawyer; b. Lynch, Ky., July 3, 1955; d. Samuel Thomas Sr. and Barbara Ann (Thomas) I.; children: Jacob, Alicyn. BA, Transylvania U., 1976; JD, U. Ky., 1979. Bar: Ky. 1979, U.S. Dist. Ct. (ea. dist.) Ky. 1979, U.S. Ct. Appeals (6th cir.) 1980, U.S. Supreme Ct. 1981, U.S. Ct. Appeals (D.C. cir.) 1984. Pvt. practice, Lexington, Ky., 1979—; vice mayor City of Lexington, 1993-99, mayor, 2002—. Asst. atty. Fayette County Prosecutors Office, Lexington, 1986-88; judge U. Ky. Trial Adv. Competition, Lexington, 1981; assoc. prof. dept. govt. and law Eastern Ky. U., 1983-88; acting dir. Eastern Ky. U. Paralegal Program, Richmond, 1985; legal counsel Ky. Women's Heritage Mus., Inc., 1986, v.p., 1987; selected as one of six Arab-Am. elected ofcls. to monitor the first Palestinian elections, 1996; econs. and govt. prof. Lexington C.C., 1996-97; mem. bldg. com. Fayette County Justice Ctr., 1997. Editor newsletter At Issue, Lexington Forum, 1983-85; pub. The Full Ct. Press, 1986—; author: Sex Equity in Sports Leadership: Implementing the Game Plan in Your Community, 1987. Mem. Lexington Human Resources Adv. Bd., 1982-85, Ky. Displaced Homemaker Adv. Bd., Lexington, 1982-84, NCAA Final Four Host Com., Lexington, 1985; chmn. Ky. Women's Suffrage Day Celebration, 1986—; project dir. Sports Equity Program-Model for South, Ky., 1986—; mem. Philmarm. Guild, 1986—; chmn. Ky. Nat. Women in Sports Day Celebration, 1988; mem.-at-large Lexington-Fayette Urban County Coun., 1990—; bd. dirs. Ky. World Trade Ctr., 1993-97, Housing Found., 1993-97; bd. control Ky. H.S. Athletic Assn., 1993-97; mem. adv. bd. LPGA Jr. Girls Golf Club, 1993-97; mem. Criminal Justice Commn., 1993-97; mem. nat. adv. bd. Dems. 2000, 1993-97; mem. Mil. Support Com., 1997; exec. dir. Lexington Fair Housing Coun., 1999—. Recipient Outstanding Svc. award Lexington Forum, 1985, Woman of Achievement award Miss Ky. Pageant, 1996, Pub. Advocacy award Nat. Assn. Women Bus. Owners, 1998, Sports Equity Leadership award, 1999; named Top 16 Women in Bus., 1995, Best Elected Ofcl. in the Bluegrass, 1994, 50 Most Powerful People in Sports, 1992. Mem. ABA (exec. com. delivery of legal svcs. to women, chair 1987-88, spl. com. on housing and urban devel. law, recipient Silver Key award 1979), AAUW (sec. 1986, state bd. dirs. 1987-88) Fed. Bar Assn., Ky. Bar Assn. (bd. of editors 1983-85, mem. Task Force on Gender Bias in Cts. 1987—), Ky. Acad. Trial Lawyers Assn., Am. Soc. for Pub. Adminstrn., Am. Assn. for Paralegal Edn., Nat. Assn. Women Lawyers (brief bank coord. 1985—), ACLU (chairperson legal panel 1983—), League of Women Voters (voter svc. com. 1985—), Ky. Women Advs. (treas. 1987—, v.p. 1988), Leadership Am., Ky. Women's Polit. Caucus (pres. 1992-93), Lexington C. of C., Phi Mi (legal advisor 1985—). Democrat. Roman Catholic. Avocation: running marathons. Office: Lexington-Fayette Govt Ctr 200 E Main St Lexington KY 40507

ISAAC, YVONNE RENEE, construction executive; b. Cleve., Apr. 13, 1948; d. Leon Warren and Vernice Leona (Hallom) I.; m. Harold E. Rhynie, Dec. 30, 1984. BA, Sarah Lawrence Coll., 1970; MS, Rensselaer Poly. Inst., 1973, Bklyn. Poly. Inst., 1976. Market rschr. GE Co., Phila., 1971-72; cons., planner SPA/Redco (subs. Perkins & Will), Chgo., 1972-75; sr. assoc. Perkins & Will, N.Y.C., 1975-76, project mgr., 1978-81; supply assoc. Mobil Oil Corp., N.Y.C., 1976-78; project mgr. Ehrenkrantz Group, P.C., N.Y.C., 1981-84; asst. dir. Met. Transp. Authority, N.Y.C., 1984-86; group dir. N.Y.C. Health & Hosps. Corp., N.Y.C., 1986-92; v.p. McDevitt Street Bovis, Atlanta, 1992-96; v.p., dir. profl. svcs. Bovis Constrn. Corp., Atlanta, 1996-98, sr. v.p., 1998—. Vis. assoc. prof. Pratt Inst., Bklyn., 1977; asst. prof. Columbia U. Grad. Sch. Architecture and Planning, N.Y.C., 1977-78. Mem. games adv. team Atlanta Paralympic Orgn. Com., 1995-96; bd. dirs. Girl Scout Coun. NW Ga., 1999—, exec. com., 2000—. Mem. Nat. Assn. for Equal Opportunity in Edn. (corp. advisory com.). Democrat. Home: 2333 Scarlett Walk Stone Mountain GA 30087-1106 Office: Bovis Lend Lease Ste 600 5909 Peachtree Dunwoody Rd NE 600 Atlanta GA 30328-8102

ISAAC-EMMONS, MERLYN HULDA, religious studies educator, academic administrator; b. Mt. St. George, Trinidad and Tobago, July 13, 1954; arrived in U.S., 1991, naturalized; d. Vonley and Carona Abigail Isaac; m. Kelvin Strickland Emmons, Nov. 24, 1994; children: Kezreel Emmons, Uzziel Emmons, Kemuel Emmons. AA, Caribbean Union Coll., Maracas, Trinidad, 1977; BS in Edn., Lang. Arts, Andrews Univ., Berrien Springs, Mich., 1989; MEd in Spl. Edn., Atlantic Union Coll., South Lancaster, Mass., 1996; PhD in Ednl. Adminstrn. and Supervision, Trinity Internat. Univ., Springfield, Mo., 1999. Cert. reading U. West Indies, Trinidad, 1984. Clk. I Ministry for Tobago Affairs, Tobago, Trinidad and Tobago, 1972—73; tchr. South Caribbean Conf. Seventh Day Adventists, Trinidad, Trinidad and Tobago, 1973—84, prin., 1984—91; tchr. Northeastern Conf. Seventh Day Adventist, Jamaica, NY, 1993—; instr. Medgar Evers Coll., Bklyn., 2001—; v.p., prof. Jehova Jireh Non-Denominational Biblical Inst. Trinity Internat. U., Bklyn., 2002—. Instr. GED CUNY, 2003—. Author: Brighten Your Corner: Stories Are Fun, 2001, He Will Not Depart from It, 2003; contbr. articles. Foster parent Jewish Childcare Agy., Miracle Makers Agy., 1996—. Democrat. Seventh Day Adventist. Avocations: reading, travel, writing children's stories, soap operas, storytelling. Home: 573 Van Siclen Ave Brooklyn NY 11207 Office: Northeastern Conf Seventh Day Adventist 115-50 Merrick Blvd Jamaica NY 11434

ISAACMAN, CARRIE EDEL, actor, educator; d. Max David Isaacman and Joyce Glick(Stepmother), Joanne Isaacman; m. Roger Dale Stude, Mar. 7, 2004. BA, San Francisco State U., 1993; MA, Antioch U., Yellow Springs, Ohio, 2000. Cert. substitute tchr. N.Y. Bd. Edn., 1999. Substitute tchr. N.Y. Bd. Edn., N.Y.C., 1999—2001; contract fin. adminstr. Bear Sterns, N.Y.C., 2001—. Tchg. artist Black Moon Theatre Co., Bklyn., San Francisco Shakespeare Festival, 1996—97; artist-in-residence Rockport (Maine) Coll. Actor: (plays) The Tempest by Shakespeare; prodr.(actor): (evening of women's one act plays) Weaving the Words. Recipient Critic's Choice award for Pericles by Shakespeare, Off-Off Broadway Reveiw, 2000. Mem.: SAG, Twelve Miles West Theatre Co., Workshop Theatre Co., NJ. Repertory Co. Home: 2 Adrian Avenue #6A Bronx NY 10463 Office Phone: 917-202-1135. Personal E-mail: carrieedel@earthlink.net.

ISAAC NASH, EVA MAE, secondary school educator; b. Natchitoches Parish, La., July 24, 1936; d. Earfus Will Nash and Dollie Mae (Edward) Johnson; m. Will Isaac Jr., July 1, 1961 (dec. May 1970). BA, San Francisco State U., 1974, MS in Edn., MS in Counseling, San Francisco State U., 1979; PhD, Walden U., 1985; diploma (hon.), St. Labre Indian Sch., 1990. Nurse's aide Protestant Episcopal Home, San Francisco, 1957-61; desk clk. Fort Ord (Calif.) Post Exchange, 1961-63; practical nurse Monterey (Calif.) Hosp., 1963-64; tchr. San Francisco Unified Schs., 1974; counselor, instr. City Coll. San Francisco, 1978-79; tchr. Oakland (Calif.) Unified Sch. Dist., 1974—. Pres. sch. adv. coun., Oakland, 1977-78, faculty adv. coun., 1992-93; advt. writer City Coll., San Francisco, 1978; instr. vocat. skill tng., Garfield Sch., Oakland, 1980-81; pub. speaker various ednl. insts. and chs., Oakland, San Francisco, 1982—; lectr. San Jose State U., 1993; creator Language Arts-Step By Step program E. Morris Cox Elem. Sch., Oakland, 1995, 96; author, presenter material in field. Author video tape Hunger: An Assassin in the Classroom, 1993-94. Recipient Community Svc. award Black Caucus of Calif. Assn. Counseling and Devel., 1988, Cert. of Recognition, 1990; named Citizen of the Day, Sta. KABL, 1988. Mem. ASCD, Internat. Reading Assn., Nat. Assn. Female Execs., Am. Personnel and Guidance Assn., Calif. Personnel and Guidance Assn., Internat. Platform Assn. (Hall Fame 1989, Profl. Speaking cert. 1993), Phi Delta Kappa. Democrat. Avocations: travel, hiking, tennis, music, dance. Office: Oakland Unified Sch Dist 1025 2nd Ave Oakland CA 94606-2296

ISAACS, AMY FAY, political organization executive; b. Phoenix, Nov. 11, 1946; d. Richard and Bessie (Wagner) Hamburger; m. John David Isaacs, Oct. 6, 1974; children: Rachel Elizabeth, Stanley Richard. Student, U. Cologne, Germany, 1967-68; BA, Am. U., 1969; MA, Sch. for Internat. Tng., Brattleboro, Vt., 1970. With AID, Washington, 1965-66; tchr. English, Turkish Am. Univs. Assn., Istanbul, 1969; direct mail and fundraising cons., Washington, 1986-87; sr. coord. communications Planned Parenthood Fedn. Am., Washington, 1987-89; various positions Ams. for Dem. Action, Washington, 1969-86, nat. dir., 1989—. Observer del. Liberal Internat., Stockholm, 1984; del. Am. Coun. on Germany, Berlin, Dallas, 1985-87; mem. fin. com. Dukasis for Pres., Washington, 1987-88; mem. quality of care com. Group Health Assn., Washington, 1987-93. Democrat. Jewish. Home: 2018 Pierce Mill Rd NW Washington DC 20010-1023 Office: Ams for Dem Action 1625 K St NW Ste 210 Washington DC 20006-1611

ISAACS, BARBARA SHIVITZ, painter; b. N.Y.C. d. David I. and Helen Plumer Shivitz. Student, Bennington (Vt.) Coll., 1955; BFA, Parsons Sch. Design, N.Y.C., 1990. One-person shows include Angeleski Gallery, N.Y.C., 1960, 61, exhibited in group shows at 11th Ann. New Eng. Exhbn., The Silvermine Guild of Artists, New Canaan, Conn., 1960, Parsons Sch. of Design, N.Y.C., 1989, 90; represented in permanent collections at Loeb Collection, NYU, Albright-Knox Gallery, Buffalo, Brewran Corp., Roslyn (N.Y.), Champion Internat. Corp., Stamford, Conn.; also pvt. collections; paintings exhibited at Edward Thorp Gallery, N.Y.C., 1996; writer, director, cinematographer Marie & Henry, The Knowledge Box, School of Design, 1964-67, Fifteen Women, 1968, Negative Earth, Revolution for Two, 1980-83, Town With the Jitters, 1985; contbr. articles to profl. jours. Recipient scholarship Parsons Sch. Design, 1987, Young Film Maker's grant USIA, Washington, 1968, fellowships Va. Ctr. for Creative Arts, Sweet Briar, 1994, 95. Home: 33 E 43rd St New York NY 10017-4831

ISAACS, DIANE SCHARFELD, English educator; b. Washington, Nov. 11, 1939; d. Arthur William Sharfeld and Lucille Speer Smith; m. Stephen D. Isaacs, June 8, 1963 (dissolved 2000); children: Deborah, David, Sharon; m. Jay L. Halio, May 26, 2002. BA with honors, Smith Coll., 1961; MA, Stanford U., 1972; EdD, Columbia U., 1982. Cert. tchr. English K-12, Social Studies, 7-12, prin., N.Y., N.J. Tchr. English, George Mason H.S., Falls Church, Va., 1963-65, Woodrow Wilson H.S., Washington, 1966-71; tchr. English and social studies Fieldston Sch., Riverdale, N.Y., 1971-74; tchr. English, Sidwell Friends Sch., Washington, 1974-78; asst. prof. Afro-Am. studies U. Minn., Mpls., 1978-83; vice prin. humanities Tenafly Bd. Edn., Tenafly, N.J., 1985-87; assoc. prof. Fordham U., Bronx, 1983-99; chmn. English dept. Nyack (N.Y.) Pub. Schs., 1987-93; coord. English grades 6-12 Manhasset (N.Y.) Pub. Schs., 1993-95; English dept. chair Wayne Hills, N.J., 1997-99; ret. Reader A.P. lit. U. Del., 2002; tchr. English U. Md., G.W.U., Am. U., 2000—. Sec., treas. adminstrv. unit dist. dept. chairs, 1998—, class meml. chair Smith Coll., 1991-2001; class sec. Nat. Cathedral Sch., 1957—; mem. Westchester Holocaust Commn. Recipient Yavner award N.Y. State Bd. of Regents, 1991. Mem. MLA, ASCD, Nat. Coun Tchrs. English (exec. com.), Conf on English Leadership, Am. Studies Assn. Avocations: theatre, black memorabilia, travel, folk art. Home: 8 Country Hills Dr Newark DE 19711 E-mail: dsipst@aol.com.

ISAACS, SUSAN, novelist, screenwriter; b. Bklyn., Dec. 7, 1943; d. Morton and Helen (Asher) I.; m. Elkan Abramowitz, Aug. 11, 1968; children: Andrew, Elizabeth. Student, Queens Coll., 1965, DHL (hon.), 1996; LittD (hon.), Dowling Coll., 1988. From editorial asst. to sr. editor Seventeen mag., N.Y.C., 1965-70; freelance writer, 1970-76. Author: Compromising Positions, 1978, Close Relations, 1980, Almost Paradise, 1984, Shining Through, 1988, Magic Hour, 1991, After All These Years, 1993, Lily White, 1996, Red, White and Blue, 1998, Brave Dames and Wimpettes: What Women Are Really Doing on Page and Screen, 1999, Long Time No See, 2001, Any Place I Hang My Hat, 2004; screenwriter Compromising Positions, 1985; screenwriter, co-producer Hello Again, 1987. Trustee Queens Coll. Found.; bd. dirs. North Shore Child and Family Guidance Assn; adv. bd. Nassau County Coalition Against Domestic Violence; bd. trustees Walt Whitman Birthplace Assn. Recipient Writers for Writers award Poets and Writers, 1996, The John Steinbeck award, 1999. Mem. PEN, Mystery Writers Am. (pres. 2001-02), Nat. Book Critic Circle, Poets and Writers (bd. dirs. 1994—, chmn. 1998—), Authors Guild, Internat. Assn. Crime Writers, Feminists for Free Expression, Creative Coalition, Am. Soc. Journalists and Authors. Jewish.

ISAACSON, ARLINE LEVINE, food association administrator; b. Jan. 28, 1946; d. Harry and Sally (Fogelman) Levine; m. Leslie Robert Isaacson, Oct. 31, 1964 (div. July 1970); 1 child, Eric Michael. AAS in Hotel and Restaurant Mgmt., N.Y.C. Tech. Coll., 1983. Mgr. restaurant and lounge Holiday Inn, N.Y.C., 1982-83; mgr. Astors St. Regis Hotel, N.Y.C., 1983-84; mgr. banquet and conf. Mariner 15 Conf. Ctr., N.Y.C., 1984-85; dir. banquets, confs. and sales Sardi's Restaurant Corp., N.Y.C., 1985-87; dir. catering sales Days Inn Hotel, N.Y.C., 1987-91; mgr. catering sales St. Moritz on the Park Hotel, N.Y.C., 1991-92; dir. catering Roosevelt Hotel, N.Y.C., 1992-93; mgr. catering sales Sheraton Park Ave., N.Y.C., 1993-94; exec. dir. Wharton Bus. Sch. Alumni Assn., N.Y.C., 1997—. Dem. vol. Koch Re-election Campaign, N.Y.C., 1985. Mem. Food and Beverage Mgrs. Assn. (sec. 1984-88, 91, exec. dir. 1995—), Roundtable for Women in Food Svc. (treas. 1986-87), Meeting Planners Internat., Soc. Incentive Travel, Hotel Sales and Mktg. Assn., Internat. Food Svc. Execs., N.Y.C. Tech. Coll. Alumni Assn. (bd. dirs., v.p. 1986-87). Jewish. Avocations: dance, travel, theatre, gourmet cooking. Home: 1836 E 18th St Brooklyn NY 11229-2965 Office: Wharton Club of NY PO Box 297-006 Brooklyn NY 11229-7006

ISAACSON, ELAINE MARIE, sales and training agent; b. Jersey City, N.J., Aug. 16, 1963; d. George Agamemnon and Pauline (Skokos) Poulo; Student, Rutgers U., 1981—82, George Mason U., 1992, No. Va. C.C., Sterling, 1992—93. Legal sec. various law firms, Jersey City and Washington, 1979—91; exec. sec. Ritz-Carlton, Tysons Corner, Va., 1992; internal help desk Am. Online, Tysons Corner, Va., 1994; regional sales mgr. Pulsecom, Herndon, Va., 1995—2002; enroller NASE, 2002—; UGA ins. agt. Mega Life and Health Ins., 2003—. Pres., owner Isaac's Pearl poetry and short stories, Herndon and Germantown, Md., 1992—. Author (book of poetry): I Wander Lonely as a Cloud, 1991, The Dark Side of Yesterday A Brighter Tomorrow, 1995, One Sun One Moon and a Star, 2000. Chorus leader Pulsecom, Herndon, 1996—99; commencement spkr. St. Basil Acad., 2001; mem. missions team Reston (Va.) Presbyn. Ch., 1995; steward St. George Greek Orthodox Ch., 1998—. Greek Orthodox. Avocations: writing poetry, reading, power walking, weightlifting, volunteer work. Home: 12114 Flag Harbor Dr Germantown MD 20875 Office: PO Box 1905 Germantown MD 20875-1905 E-mail: elaine1@nase.org.

ISAACSON, MARJORIE JEAN, retired elementary school educator; b. Kirksville, Mo., Feb. 20, 1929; d. Floyd Nicholas and Mertie Eathel Myers; m. Leroy Vernon Isaacson, Dec. 12, 1952 (dec. June 1981); m. Roger Thomas Vole, Aug. 7, 1982; 1 child, Pamela Jean Harrison. BA, Wis. State U., Stevens Point, 1951, MA, 1967. Tchr. Appleton Elem. Sch., Wis., 1951—53, Elem. Sch., Rosholt, Wis., 1954—59, Stevens Point, Wis., 1959—87, ret., 1987—. Republican. Avocations: reading, swimming, gardening. Home: 2716 Clark St Stevens Point WI 54481-4011

ISABELLE, BEATRICE MARGARET, artist; b. Phila., Dec. 8, 1930; d. Renaud Joseph Isabelle, Carmela Didio; m. Sven Fritz Carstens, Jan. 1953 (div. Jan. 1977); children: Jana C. Young, Kai Bruce Carstens, Dane Fritz Carstens; m. Robert Dean Graves, Sept. 6, 1984. AA L.A. City Coll., 1973; BA, Calif. State U., L.A., 1975, MA, 1979. Cert. tchr. K-9 Calif., bilingual/cross cultural specialist pre-K-12, adult, cmty. coll. ethnic studies. Tchr. Hobart St. Elem. Sch., L.A., 1971—73, McDonnell Ave. Sch., L.A., 1973—76, Albion St. Elem. Sch., L.A., Calif., 1976—85, Dolores St. Elem. Sch., L.A., Calif., 1985—91; ret., 1991. Exhibitions include Huntington Beach Art Ctr., 1995, 1999, 2000, 2001, 2001, 2002, Golden West Coll. Art Gallery, 1997, 1998, 1999, 2000, 2001, 2002, Guggenheim Gallery, Chapman U., 2001. Vol. mental health svcs., Amigas Program L.A. Unified Sch. Dist., 1967—69; vol. Chicano field work EPIC, 1978; vol. youth facility MacLaren Hall, 1978. Recipient Award for Marine Edn. Program, Sch. Edn., U. So. Calif., 1981, award for theatre, Herald Examiner, 1982, Children's Theatre, 1983, Sculpture award, Orange County Artists, 2000, Orange Art Assn., 2001; scholar Scholarship award, Orange County Fine Arts, 2001. Mem.: Kappa Delta Pi, Psi Chi. Avocations: travel, reading, painting, sculpting, flying. Home: 6941 Cumberland Dr Huntington Beach CA 92647

ISAKI, LUCY POWER SLYNGSTAD, lawyer; b. Jersey City, Oct. 21, 1945; d. Charles Edward and Ann Mary (Power) Slyngstad; m. Paul S. Isaki, Aug. 26, 1967. BA summa cum laude, Seattle U., 1973; JD cum laude, U. Puget Sound, 1977. Bar: Wash. 1977. Case worker San Joaquin County Welfare, Stockton, Calif., 1968-70, Alameda County Welfare, Oakland, Calif., 1971-73; legal intern King County Prosecutor's Office, 1976-77; law clk. to hon. Justice Hamilton Wash. Supreme Ct., 1977-78; ptnr. Bogle & Gates, Seattle, 1978-99, mem. exec. com., 1990-94; sr. asst. atty. gen. State of Wash., 1999—. Cons. Region X, HHS, 1975; chair Atty. Gen. Gregoire's Task Force on Alternative Dispute Resolution, 1993-94. Bd. dirs. King County Family Svcs., Seattle, 1982-84, Wash. State Coun. Crime and Delinquency, 1981, Northwest Kidney Ctr., 2001—, vice chair 2003—; vice chair bd. trustees N.W. Kidny Ctr., 2003-; treas. Mother's Against Violence in Am., 1994; trustee emeritus U. Puget Sound, 1985—, Seattle Youth Symphony, 1995, Ea. Wash. U., 1998-99; chmn. law sch. bd. visitors Seattle U., 1984-96; trustee Legal Found., Wash., 1992-95, sec. bd. dirs. 1993, v.p. bd. dirs. 1994, pres. 1995; pres. Kinnear Vistas Homeowners' Assn., 2003-. Dean's scholar U. Puget Sound, 1976-77; recipient Disting. Law Grad. award U. Puget Sound, 1984, Majis award Seattle U., 1997. Mem. Wash. Women Lawyers (pres. Seattle-King County chpt. 1982, v.p. 1984), ABA (del. Ho. of Dels., 1995-97), Wash. State Bar Assn. (bd. govs. 2000-03), King County Bar Assn. (sec. 1986-87, trustee 1987-90, treas. 1995-97, 1st v.p. 1998, pres. 1999-2000), U. Puget Sound Law Alumni Soc. (pres. 1979). Democrat. Office: Atty Gens Office 900 4th Ave Ste 2000 Seattle WA 98164-1076 Office Phone: 206-389-2598. E-mail: lucyi@atg.wa.gov.

ISAY, JANE FRANZBLAU, publisher; b. Cin., Aug. 24, 1939; d. Abraham Norman and Rose (Nadler) Franzblau; children: David Avram, Joshua Daniel. AB, Bryn Mawr Coll., 1961. First reader Harcourt, Brace Co., 1963; asst. editor, then assoc. editor Yale U. Press, 1964-66, editor, then exec. editor, 1966-79; assoc. publisher Basic Books Inc., N.Y.C., 1979, co-pub., exec. v.p., 1979-83; v.p., dir. electronic and tech. pub. Harper & Row, 1983-84; v.p., pub. Touchstone Books, Simon & Schuster, N.Y.C., 1985-87; editorial dir. trade books Addison-Wesley Pub. Co., 1987-91, v.p., 1990-91; pub. Grosset Books G.P. Putnam's, N.Y.C., 1991-97; exec. editor nonfiction Harcourt Brace & Co., N.Y.C., 1997-98, editor-in-chief, 1998—. Bd. advisers pub. program NYU; mem. adv. bd. Wesleyan U. Press; bd. dirs. The New Press, 1994-99, Rutgers U. Press, 1998—. Bd. dirs. Ezra Acad.,

New Haven, 1964-79, Yale U. Friends of Hillel, 1965-68, Bd. Women's Media Group, 1994—, Partnership for Caring, 1998—; mem. vis. com. Harvard Grad. Sch. Edn. Fellow Timothy Dwight Coll., Yale U., 1969— Mem. Assn. Am. Pubs. (chair freedom to read com. 1990-94), Jewish Publ Soc. (bd. dirs. 1990-94). Office: Harcourt Brace & Co 15 E 26th St Fl 15 New York NY 10010-1595

ISBELL, RITA ANETTE, special education educator; d. Bill Newton and Eva Pearl (White) Smith; m. Robert James Isbell; 1 child, James Robert. BA, Wayland Bapt. U., 1973; MEd, Midwestern State U., 1995. Cert. profl. recognized spl. educator Coun. for Exceptional Children, profl. ednl. diagnostician Tex. Tchr. Alvord (Tex.) Ind. Sch. Dist., 1985—88; spl. edn. tchr. Lakeworth Ind. Sch. Dist., Ft. Worth, 1990—94, Goldburg Ind. Sch. Dist., Stoneburg, Tex., 1994—96; ednl. diagnostician Matagorda County Spl. Edn., Bay City, Tex., 1996—98, Castleberry Ind. Sch. Dist., Ft. Worth, 1998—2000, Wise County Spl. Edn., Bridgeport, Tex., 2000—02; tchr. English Internat. Sch. Que., Queretaro, Mexico, 2002. Contbr. articles to spl. edn. jours. Mem.: Tex. Profl. Ednl. Diagnosticians, Tex. Ednl. Diagnostician Assn., Coun. for Exceptional Children, Delta Kappa Gamma.

ISBIN, SHARON, classical guitarist, guitar educator; b. Mpls., Aug. 7, 1956; d. Herbert Stanford and Katherine (Brudnoy) I. BA, Yale U., 1978, MusM, 1979. Prof. of guitar Manhattan Sch. Music, N.Y.C., 1979-89, Mannes Coll. Music, N.Y.C., 1984-89; prof., dept. head The Juilliard Sch. Music, N.Y.C., 1989—. Artistic dir. Guitarstream Internat. Festival Carnegie Hall, N.Y.C., 1985, Guitarfest Ordway Music Theatre, St. Paul, 1985-87, Guitarjam series Am. Pub. Radio, 1988-89. Recordings include Dances for Guitar, 1984, 3 Guitars 3, 1985, Brazil with Love, 1987, Rhapsody in Blue/West Side Story, 1988, J.S. Bach: Complete Lute Suites, 1988 (named Critic's Choice Recording of Yr. Gramaphone mag. 1989, Editor's Choice Best Recording CD Rev. 1989), Road to the Sun: Latin Romances, 1989 (named Favorite Selection CD Rev. 1990), Rodrigo & Vivaldi Concerti, 1991, Lullabies & Love Songs, 1991. NEA solo recitalist grantee; recipient 1st Prize Toronto Internat. Guitar Competition, 1975, Top Prize Munich Internat. Competition, 1976, 2nd Prize Queen Sofia Internat. Competition, 1979. Avocations: cross country skiing, hiking, backpacking, languages. Office: The Juilliard Sch 60 Lincoln Center Plz New York NY 10023-6588

ISBISTER, JENEFIR DIANE WILKINSON, microbiologist, researcher, educator, consultant; b. Rahway, N.J., June 4, 1936; d. Edwin Guy and Alvira Marie (Andrews) Wilkinson; m. James David Isbister, July 23, 1960; children: Wendy Jill Isbister Kalavritinos, Kirstin Ann Isbister Hammond. BS, Newberry (S.C.) Coll., 1957; MS in Med. Tech., Jefferson Med. Sch., Phila., 1958; PhD in Microbiology, U. Md., 1977. Med. technologist Princeton (N.J.) Hosp., 1958-60; instr. med. tech. sch. George Washington U., Washington, 1960-62, rsch. asst., 1976-77; rsch. microbiologist Environ. Biospherics, Inc., Rockville, 1978-80; group leader environ. microbiology dept. Atlantic Rsch. Corp., Alexandria, Va., 1980-89; pvt. practice cons. microbiologist Potomac, Md., 1989—; sr. tech. advisor ARCTECH, Inc., Chantilly, Va., 1989-92. Adj. prof. George Mason U., 1988-92, rsch. prof., 1992—; cons. Orkand Corp., Silver Spring, Md., 1979-80, U.S. DOE, Pitts., 1988-89, Advancis Pharm., Gaithersburg, Md., 2001—. Contbr. to book, articles to profl. jours. Sci. fair judge Montgomery and Fairfax County Schs., Md. and Va., 1975—; bd. dirs. Bedford (Pa.) Springs Music Festival, 1984-89. Va.-Carolina Chem. Corp. scholar, 1953; recipient Congl. High Tech. award Congl. Caucus for Sci. and Tech., 1985. Mem. ASTM (vice chair 1983-92, 99-2002), Am. Soc. for Microbiology, Am. Soc. for Clin. Pathologists, Cosmos Club, Phi Kappa Phi, Phi Sigma, Chi Beta Phi. Episcopalian. Avocations: reading, music, tennis, restoring old houses and furniture. Home: 9521 Accord Dr Rockville MD 20854-4302 Office: George Mason U Rm 303E Prince William II 10900 University Blvd Manassas VA 20110 E-mail: jisbiste@gmu.edu.

ISBURGH, ANNE MARIE, engineering manager; b. Ft. Dix, N.J., July 29, 1957; d. Ernest Francis and Virginia Marion Condina; m. Robert Karl Isburgh, Oct. 17, 1981; 1 child, Dane Karl. BSME, Rensselaer Poly. Inst., 1979, MSME, 1980. Registered profl. engr., Ohio. Engr. Buckeye Cellulose, Memphis and Perry, Tenn./Fla., 1980-84; engr. turbine aero & cooling design GE Aircraft Engines, Cin., 1984-88, lead engr. turbine aero & cooling design, 1988-94, staff engr. Turbine Airfoils Ctr. of Excellence, 1994-97, engring. black belt, 1997-99, subsect. mgr. Turbine Airfoils Ctr. of Excellence, 1999—. Patentee in field. Recipient Clarence E. Davies award ASME, 1980. Mem. Elfuns. Home: 11637 Windy Hill Ct Loveland OH 45140-1969 Office: GE Aircraft Engines MD A406 1 Neumann Way Cincinnati OH 45215-1915 Fax: 513-243-3621. E-mail: anne.isburgh@ae.ge.com.

ISDALE, MARGARET HOLLY, lawyer; married. BA cum laude, Cornell U., 1986; JD, Boston U., 1990. Bar: N.Y. 1990, Mass. 1990, Conn. 1990, D.C. 1990. Atty. Fried Frank Harris Shriver & Jacobson, N.Y.C., 1990—94; v.p. J. P. Morgan, N.Y.C., 1994—99; mng. dir. Goldman Sachs, Phila., 1999—. Mem.: N.Y. State Bar Assn., 85 Broads, Inc., 100 Women in Hedge Funds. Office: Goldman Sachs & Co 1735 Market St 26th Floor Philadelphia PA 19103

ISENHOUR, KATHLEEN CHANEY, special education educator, consultant; b. Lexington, Ky., Aug. 26, 1960; d. John Kenneth and Tommye Joe Chaney; m. Mark S. Isenhour, June 21, 1996; children: Drew, John-Richard, Sammy. BA, U. Ky., 1983. Cert. tchr., spl. edn. Tchr. Fayette County Pub. Schs., Lexington, 1991—; cons. Academic & Behavioral Cons., Lexington, 2002—. Coord. Children and Adults with Attention Deficit Disorder, Lexington, 2001—03; area coord. Behavior Disorder Divsn. Coun. Exceptional Child, Lexington, 2002—03; presenter in field. Pres. women's group Tates Creek Ch., Lexington, 1988—2003. Mem.: Ctrl. Ky. Edn. Assn. Avocations: scrapbooks, stamping. Home: 3036 Old Field Way Lexington KY 40513

ISENOR, LINDA DARLENE, grocery retailer, marketing professional; b. Calgary, Alta., Can., Oct. 3, 1955; d. Frank Carl and Mavis Ella (Jarnett) Kachmarski; m. Larry Douglas Isenor, Oct. 13, 1973. Diploma in mktg., So. Alta. Inst. Tech., Calgary, 1988. Cert. travel cons. Calgary Bd. Edn. Cashier to asst. mgr. G&S Restaurants Balmoral Ltd., Calgary, 1972-74; cashier, supr. Calgary Coop. Assn. Ltd., 1974-75, supr., 1975-78, head cashier, 1978-80, asst. grocery merchandiser, 1980-81, grocery merchandising specialist, 1981-82, grocery procurement specialist, 1982-83, grocery mktg. supr. for pricing and costing, 1983-93, grocery mktg. mgr., 1993-95, grocery & liquor mktg. mgr., 1996-98; ret., 1998; retail mktg. cons. Crowfoot Cruise Ship Ctr., Calgary. Avocations: cooking, traveling, hiking, reading. Fax: 403-208-3017. E-mail: isenor@attglobal.net.

ISENSTEIN, LAURA, library director; b. Toledo; BA in History, U. Mich., 1971, MA in Libr. Sci., 1972. Libr. Baltimore County Pub. Libr., 1972-81, area branch mgr., 1981-85, coord. info. svcs., 1985-94; founder, prin. LIA Assocs., Tng. Consultancy, 1988-95; dir. Pub. Libr. Des Moines, 1995-00. Mem. OCLC Adv. Coun. for Pub. Librs.; spkr. in field. Mem. editl. bd. Jewish Press; contbr. articles to profl. jours. Mem. cmty. edn. advt. coun. Des Moines Pub. Schs.; mem. Mayors' Select Com. Shared Svcs. Focus Group. Mem. ALA, Pub. Libr. Assn. (chmn., mem. various coms.), Urban Librs. Couns., Iowa Libr. Assn., Rotary Internat., Greater Des Moines Leadership Inst. Avocations: gourmet cooking, travel, reading mysteries. Office: Pub Libr Des Moines 100 Locust St Des Moines IA 50309-1767

ISHIKAWA-FULLMER, JANET SATOMI, psychologist, educator; b. Hilo, Hawaii, Oct. 17, 1925; d. Shinichi and Onao (Kurisu) Saito; m. Calvin Y. Ishikawa, Aug. 15, 1950; 1 child, James A.; m. Daniel W. Fullmer, June 11, 1980. B of Edn., U. Hawaii, 1950, MEd, 1967, MEd, 1969, PhD, 1976; postgrad., Queen's Med. Ctr., 1980—82. Diplomate Am. Acad. Pain Mgmt. Postdoctoral trainee Queen's Med. Ctr., intern pain diagnosis tng., biofeedback/self hypnosis tng.; prof. Honolulu Bus. Coll., 1953-59; prof., counselor Kapiolani Community Coll., Honolulu, 1959-73; prof., dir. counseling Honolulu Community Coll., 1973-74, dean of students, 1974-77; psychologist, pres., treas. Human Resources Devel. Ctr., Inc., Honolulu, 1977—. Cons. United Specialties Co., Tokyo, 1979, Grambling (La.) State U., 1980, 81, Filipino Immigrants in Kalihi, Honolulu, 1979-84, Legis. Ref. Bur., Honolulu, 1984-85, Honolulu Police Dept., 1985; co-founder Waianae (Hawaii) Child and Family Ctr., 1979-92. Co-author: Family Therapy Dictionary, 1991, Manabu: The Diagnosis and Treatment of a Japanese Boy with a Visual Anomaly, 1991; contbr. articles to profl. jours. Commr. Bd. Psychology, Honolulu, 1979-85; co-founder Kilohana United Meth. Ch. and Family Ctr., 1993—. Recipient Outstanding Educator award, 1977, Pres.'s award, Grambling State U., 1984. Mem. APA, ACA, Hawaii Psychol. Assn., Pi Lambda Theta (sec. 1967-68, v.p. 1968-69, pres. 1969-70, 96-98), Delta Kappa Gamma (sec., v.p. scholarship 1975, Outstanding Educator award 1975, Thomas Jefferson award 1993, Francis E. Clark award 1993). Avocations: jogging, tennis, dance. Home: 154 Maono Pl Honolulu HI 96821-2529 Office: Human Resources Devel Ctr 1750 Kalakaua Ave Apt 809 Honolulu HI 96826-3725

ISKANDER, SYLVIA WIESE, English literature educator; b. Boston, June 27, 1940; d. Herbert Edward and Mary Elizabeth (Cavin) Wiese; m. William H. Patterson Jr., June 2, 1962 (div. Apr. 1977); 1 child, Deborah Ann; m. Awad A. Iskander, May 22, 1982; 1 child, Alexandra Lucia. BS, La. State U., 1961; MA, U. Southwestern La., 1965; PhD, Fla. State U., 1969. From asst. prof. to prof. emeritus U. La., Lafayette, La., 1969—2001, prof. emeritus, 2001—. Lectr. English, U. Houston, 1965-66. Author: Rousseau's Emile and Early Children's Literature, 1971; contbr. articles to profl. jours.; editor (book) The Image of the Child, 1991. Founder Lafayette Greenbelt, 1975. Grantee AAUW, 1975. Mem. MLA, Children's Lit. Assn. (treas. 1994-97, v.p./pres.-elect 1997-98, pres. 1998-99), Internat. Rsch. Soc. Children's Lit., Nat. Coun. Tchrs. English, Phi Kappa Phi. Avocations: reading, traveling, gardening.

ISLAMBOULY, HAGAR ABDEL-HAMID, consul general; b. Cairo, Jan. 5, 1947; d. Abdel Hamid and Souad (ElSherif) I.; m. Mohamed Adel Ezzat, Jan. 22, 1970. Diploma, Am. Coll. Girls, Cairo, 1964; BSc in Polit. Sci., Cairo U., 1969. With state info. svc. Ministry Information, Cario, 1970-74; with the cabinet of the ofcl. spokesman Ministry Fgn. Affairs Diplomatic Inst., Cairo, 1974; mem. internat. orgn. dept. Ministry Fgn. Affairs, Cairo, 1975-76; second sec. Embassy of Egypt, Madrid, 1976-80; with cabinet of the asst. minister of fgn. affairs for legal internat. orgns. affairs Ministry Fgn. Affairs, Cairo, 1980-81, mem. cabinet of the head of Egyptian mechanism for negotiation with Israel, 1981-84; counselor Egyptian Embassy, Bonn, Germany, 1984-88; dep. dir. Israeli affairs dept. Ministry Fgn. Affairs, Cairo, 1988-90, dep. dir. internat. orgns. dept., 1990-91, dir. environ. affairs dept., 1991-93, dir. internat. environ. affairs dept., 1991-95, dir. internat. economic affairs dept., 1993-95; consul gen., chief of mission Egyptian Consulate, San Francisco, 1995—. Attended UN Conf. for Environ. and Devel., Rio De Janeiro, 1992, Middle East/North Africa Economic Summit, UN Gen. Assembly, UN Agencies and UN Environ. Programs, UN Conf. Trade and Devel., UN Conf. on Population and Devel., 1991-95; attended Morocco Conf. Internat. Trade for Gen. Agreements of Tarrifs and Trade, Uruguay, 1994; mem. Egyptian Gen. Com. assigned to prepare for the Peace Conf. in the Middle East, Ministry Fgn. Affairs, 1990-95; head of the Egyptian delegation to the working group of environ.-multi lateral track of the Peace Conf. in the Middle East, Ministry Fgn. Affairs, 1991-95. Contbr. articles to profl. jours. Active environ. groups in Egypt; mem. regional organization and related com., summits Islamic Conf. Orgn., Arab League, Orgn. African Unity, 1993-95. Recipient The Order of Civil Merit, King of Spain, 1980, Order of Civil Merit, Pres. Germany, 1988. Mem. World State Forum (coord. Middle East affairs 1996—), World Trade Club, UN, San Francisco Consular Corps., World Affairs Coun., San Francisco Ladies of Consular Corps, Commonwealth Club. Islamic. Avocations: reading, classical music, jogging. Office: Egyptian Consulate 3001 Pacific Ave San Francisco CA 94115-1099 Fax: 415-346-9480.

ISLER, ERIKA LISBETH, journalist; b. N. Tarrytown, N.Y., Apr. 8, 1967; d. Robert Klaus and Sally Layne (von Holzhausen) Isler. BS in Mag. Journalism, Syracuse U., 1989. Asst. editor N.Y. Daily News, N.Y.C., 1988; staff writer Syracuse Herald Jour., 1989; assoc. editor Magazineweek, N.Y.C., 1989-90, sr. editor, 1990-91, west coast editor, 1991-92, Cowles Business Media's Folio: First Day, Folio: Magazine, 1992—95; editor State Coll. Mag., 1992—. Mem. Women in Communications, Western Publs. Assn. Avocations: skiing, photography, writing. Home: 932 Ishler St Boalsburg PA 16827-1226

ISRAEL, LESLEY LOWE, retired political scientist, consultant; b. Phila., July 21, 1938; d. Herman Albert and Florence (Segal) Lowe; m. Fred Israel, Dec. 18, 1960; children: Herman Allen, Sanford Lawrence. BA, Smith Coll., 1959. Dir. media advance Humphrey for Pres., Washington, 1967-68, dir. polit. intelligence, 1972; dir. scheduling Bayh for Pres., Washington, 1971; spl. asst. Jackson for Pres., Washington, 1975-76; coord. nat. labor Kennedy for Pres., Washington, 1979-80; sr. v.p. Kamber Group, Washington, 1981-87; pres., CEO Politics, Inc., Washington, 1987-95. Mem. nat. commn. ADL, 1991—94, mem. nat. exec. commn., 1994—; v.p. Nat. Conf. Soviet Jewry, 1990—; dir. Internat. Found. Election Sys., 1997—; pres. Jewish Cmty. Ctr. Greater Washington, Rockeville, Md., 1981—83, internat. election monitor and coord., 1995—; chmn. Washington regional bd. ADL, 1991—94; sr. election officer Orgn. Security and Coop. Europe, Bosnia-Herzegovina, 1996; internat. election monitor U.S. Dept. State, 1997—; mem. Dem. Charter Commn., 1982—83, Dem. Del. Selection Commn., 1983—84, Dem. Site Selection Com., 1989—90, 1990—; bd. mgrs. Adas Israel Synagogue, 1981—83; former chmn. Washington bd. Friends Tel Aviv U. Named one of 100 Most Powerful Women, Washington mag., 1990; recipient Spl. Svc. award, Jewish Cmty. Ctr., 1984. Jewish. Home: PO Box 69 Royal Oak MD 21662-0069

ISRAEL, MARGIE OLANOFF, psychotherapist; b. Atlantic City, Apr. 30, 1927; d. Herman and Mary (Salter) Olanoff; m. Allan Edward Israel, Sept. 20, 1953; 1 child, Janet. Student U. Miami, 1945-46, 50, Am. Acad. Dramatic Arts, 1946-47; BA in Psychology cum laude, Hunter Coll., 1970; MSW with honors in fieldwork, Hunter Sch. Social Work, 1972; psychoanalytic tng. N.Y. Soc. Freudian Psychologists, 1965-70, Manhattan Ctr. for Advanced Psychoanalytic Studies, 1972-74, 76. Bd. cert. diplomate in clin. social work Am. Bd. Examiners of Clin. Social Workers. Celebrity interviewer Lunchin' with Marge radio show Sta. WFPG, Atlantic City, 1947-48; co-host Steel Pier Midnight radio show, 1949; publicity writer Hy Gardner Astor Hotel, N.Y.C., 1948; writer theatrical interviews Miami (Fla.) Daily News, 1950-51; sec. to exec. dir. Hebrew Old Age Ctr., Atlantic City, 1951-55; sec. to dir. TV-films and radio Nat. Office, Am. Cancer Soc., N.Y.C., 1959-66, asst. to dir. TV-films and radio,1966-70; social worker Bellevue Hosp., N.Y.C., 1972-76; field instr. socialworkN.Y. U., 1975-76; pvt. practice psychotherapy, N.Y.C., 1973—, Providence, 1991—, Wilmington, N.C., 1996—. Mental health disaster vol. Cape Fear N.C. chpt. Red Cross, 1997—. Fellow N.Y. State Soc. Clin. Social Work, Am. Orthopsychiat. Assn.; mem. NASW (diplomate), Nat. Fedn. Socs. Clin. Social Work (com. on psychoanalysis), Acad. Cert. Social Workers, N.Y. Acad. Scis. AAAS, Psi Chi. Home and Office: 5711 Andover Rd Wilmington NC 28403-3409

ISRAELOV, RHODA, financial planner, writer, entrepreneur; b. Pitts., May 20, 1940; d. Joseph and Fannie (Friedman) Kreinen; divorced; children: Jerome, Arthur, Russ. BS in Hebrew Edn., Herzlia Hebrew Tchrs. Coll., N.Y.C., 1961; BA in English Lang. and Lit., U. Mo., Kansas City, 1965; MS, Coll. Fin. Planning, 1991. CFP, CLU. Hebrew tchr. various schs., 1961-79; ins. agt. Conn. Mut. Life, Indpls., 1979-81; fin. planner, 1st v.p. investments Smith Barney, Inc., Indpls., 1981—. Instr. for mut. fund licensing exams. Pathfinder Securities Sch., Indpls., 1983-87; cons. channel 6 News, 1984-85. Contbr. columns in newspapers Indpls. Bus. Jour., 1982, Jewish Post & Opinion, 1982—86, Beacon, 1985, Indianapolis Star; regular guest (Radio show) WTUX Radio, 1990—94. Recipient Gold Medal award Personal Selling Power, 1987; named Bus. Woman of Yr., Network of Women in Bus., 1986. Mem. Fin. Planning Assn., Nat. Assn. Life Underwriters, Women's Life Underwriters Conf. (founder), Soc. Fin. Svc. Profls., Nat. Coun. Jewish Women, Nat. Assn. Profl. Saleswomen, Nat. Spkrs. Assn. (pres. Ind. chpt. 1986-87, treas. 1984), Registry Fin. Planning Practitioners, Toastmasters (chpt. ednl. v.p. 1985-86), Soroptimists (bd. dirs.), Ctrl. Ind. Mensa. Avocations: piano, folk, square, folk and ballroom dancing, theatre. Office: Smith Barney Bank One Center Tower 111 Monument Cir Ste 3100 Indianapolis IN 46204-5193 E-mail: israelov@yahoo.com., rhoda.israelov@rssmb.com.

ISTOMIN, MARTA CASALS, performing arts administrator, former educator; b. P.R., Nov. 2, 1936; d. Aquiles and Angelica M. (Martinez) Montanez; m. Pablo Casals, Aug. 3, 1957 (dec. 1973); m. Eugene Istomin, Feb. 15, 1975. Student, Mannes Coll. Music, N.Y.C., 1950-54; Mus.D. (hon.), World U., P.R., 1972; L.H.D. (hon.), Marymount Coll., 1975; Doctorate (hon.), U. P.R., 1984, Dickinson Coll., Carlisle, Pa., 1986; D (hon.), Shenandoah Coll., 1986, Interam. U., P.R., 1989. Prof. cello Conservatory Music, San Juan, P.R., 1961-64; vis. prof. cello Curtis Inst., Phila., 1974-75; co-chmn. bd., music dir. Casals Festival, 1974-77; artistic dir. John F. Kennedy Center for Performing Arts, Washington, 1980-90; dir. Evian Music Festival, France, 1990—; pres. Manhattan Sch. Music, N.Y.C., 1992—. Mem. Nat. Coun. on Arts, 1990; cons. Latin Am. ednl. projects. Trustee Marlboro Sch. Music and Festival; trustee Marymount Sch., N.Y.C., World U. Recipient Puerto Rican Fedn. Women's Clubs award, 1967; award for cultural achievements City of San Juan, 1975; Nat. Conf. Puerto Rican Women award, 1975; Casita Maria medal for outstanding contbns. to culture N.Y.C., 1978; Outstanding Contbns. Performing Arts in Nation's Capitol award, 1983; Family Place Outstanding Community Service award, 1986; Mayor's Excellence in Service Arts award, Washington, 1986; Nat. Fedn. Music Clubs citation, 1987; named Outstanding Woman of Yr. P.R., 1975; Woman of Achievement Sta. WETA-TV, Washington, 1981; Order of Isabella the Cath. govt. Spain, 1986; Officer, Order Arts and Letters govt. France, 1986; Officer's Cross Order Merit govt. Fed. Republic Germany, 1987. Mem. Nat. Coun. on the Arts. Roman Catholic. Office: Manhattan School Music 120 Claremont Ave New York NY 10027-4698

ITNYRE, JACQUELINE HARRIET, systems analyst; b. Camden, N.J., May 13, 1941; d. John Harold and Harriet Geraldine (Rankine) Bruynell; m. Thomas James Itnyre, Oct. 13, 1968 (dec. 1978); children: Beth Thierry, John. AS in Engring., Mercer County Coll., 1961; BA in Liberal Studies, San Jose State U., 1980, MLS, 1981. Media ctr. mgr. Milpitas (Calif.) Unified Sch. Dist., 1975-81; tech. libr. Lockheed Missiles and Space Co., Sunnyvale, Calif., 1981, programmer, 1982-83, with ground support Challenger-Space Lab 2 Palo Alto, Calif., 1984-85; systems mgr. gen. clin. rsch. ctr. Stanford (Calif.) U. Med. Sch., 1985-87, computing systems specialist divsn. epidemiology, 1988-96, local network adminstr. cancer biology rsch. labs., 1996-99; ind. contractor sys. and networking cons., web page designer, microarray data analyst, 1999—. Edna B. Anthony scholar San Jose State U., 1981. Mem. Assn. for Computing Machinery, ALA, Sierra Club. Avocations: cycling, travel, sewing, drawing, genealogy. Home: 1775 Southwood Dr San Luis Obispo CA 93401-6031 Personal E-mail: jitnyre@charter.net.

ITTELSON, MARY ELIZABETH, museum director; b. Dayton, Ohio; d. Richard W. and Lois (Koblitz) I.; m. Richard Carl Tuttle. BA, NYU, 1979; MBA, Stanford U., 1985. Dir., choreographer Premiers Dance Theatre, N.Y.C., 1976-78; exec. dir. Crossroads Inc., N.Y.C., 1978-79; asst. prof. dance Northwestern U., Evanston, 1979-83; assoc. McKinsey & Co., Inc., Chgo., 1985-88; acting dir. Mus. Contemporary Art, Chgo., 1988-89, assoc. dir., 1989-95; pres. Ittelson Consulting, 1996. Chair performance com. Mus. of Contemporary Art, Chgo., bd. trustees. Choreographer: (dance) In Three Places, 1977, Garland Epitaphium, 1981, Sir Gawain and the Green Knight, 1982, Little Children Lost, 1983. Am. Dance Festival fellow, 1980.

ITURBIDE, GRACIELA, photographer; b. Mexico City, May 16; married, 1962; children: Manuel, Claudia, Mauricio. Student, U. Nat. Autanoma Mexico, 1969—72. Asst. Manuel Breva. Exhibitions include Galeria José Clemence Orosco, Mexico City, 1975, Midtown Y Gallery, N.Y.C., 1976, Centre Georges Pompldeu, Paris, 1982. Recipient prize, UN Internat. Labor Orgn., 1986, W. Eugene Smith award, 1987; Consejo Mexicano de Fotografia grantee, 1983, Guggenheim Found. grantee, 1987. Mem.: Mexican Coun. Photography (founding mem.). Home: c/o Cityscape Assocs 32 E Colorado Blvd Pasadena CA 91105

IULIANELLO, CARMELA, tax specialist; b. Rochester, N.Y., Aug. 26, 1933; d. James Vincenzo Lamuraglia and Mary Leone; m. Cesidio Iulianello, Oct. 10, 1953; children: Vincent F., Anthony V., Patrick J. Realtor Bay Mar Realty, Webster, NY, 1976—96; tax preparer C. Iulianello, 1956—2003. Roman Catholic. Home: 410 Thomar Dr Webster NY 14580 E-mail: ciuliane@rochester.rr.com.

IVANICK, CAROL W. TRENCHER, lawyer; b. Springfield, Mass., Mar. 6, 1939; d. Joseph George and Daisy Wolf; m. Michael Ira Trencher, July 30, 1960 (div. Feb. 1984); children: Christopher, Daniel, Deborah; m. Peter Alan Ivanick (div. 1998). BA, Wellesley Coll., 1959; JD, Yale U., 1962. Bar: N.Y. 1963. Assoc. Cleary, Gottlieb et al, N.Y.C., 1962-67; ptnr. Dewey, Ballantine LLP, N.Y.C., 1976—. Chmn. adv. com. Pension Benefit Guaranty Corp., Washington, 1978-80; visiting lectr. Yale Law Sch., New Haven, Conn., 1978-79, 82-83. Avocations: ceramics, bowling, tennis. Home: 110 Riverside Dr New York NY 10024-3715 Office: Dewey Ballantine 1301 Avenue Of The Americas New York NY 10019-6022

IVENS, MARY SUE, microbiologist, mycologist; b. Maryville, Tenn., Aug. 23, 1929; d. McPherson Joseph and Sarah Lillie (Hensley) Ivens. BS, East Tenn. State U., 1949; MS NIH rsch. trainee, Tulane U. Sch. Medicine, 1963; PhD, La. State U. Sch. Medicine, 1966; postgrad., Emory U. Sch. Medicine, 1960. Diplomate Am. Bd. Microbiology. Dir. microbiol. and mycol. labs. Lewis-Gate Hosp., Roanoke, Va., 1953—56; rsch. mycologist Ctrs. Disease Control, Atlanta, 1957—60; rsch. assoc. La. State U. Sch. Medicine, New Orleans, 1963—66; instr. medicine La. State U., 1966—72, instr. microbiology, 1966—72, clin. prof., 1972—. Dir. micology lab. La. State U. Sch. Medicine, 1963—72, lectr. sch. dentistry, 1968—70; assoc. prof. natural scis. Dillard U., New Orleans, 1972—; assoc. Marine Biol. Lab., Woods Hole, Mass., 1978—; cons. in field. Contbr. articles to profl. jours. Commr. conf. on ctr. Mycotic sera WHO, 1969; mem. La. assn. def. counsel expert witness bank, 1985—; bd. dirs. La. coun. Girl Scouts US, Cmty Relationships Greater New Orleans, Zoning Bd. River Ridge, La.; mem. exec. bd. River Ridge Civic Assn., 1982—98, sec., 1982—84; chmn. pers. bd. Riverside Bapt. Ch., River Ridge; dir. outreach First Bapt. Ch., New Orleans, 1989—97; chmn. gold medal award com. Sigma Xi, 1978. Recipient Rosicrucian Humanitarian award, 1981; fellow Macy, MBL, 1978—79; grantee NSF, NIH. Mem.: Nat. Inst. Sci., AAAS, Am. Soc.

Microbiology (Nat. com. on membership 1983—87), Med. Mycological Soc. Am., Internat. Soc. Human and Animal Mycology, Sigma Xi. Office: Dillard U Div Natural Sci New Orleans LA 70122 Home: 809 Prestwick Dr Maryville TN 37803-6757

IVERSON, CARLENE V. principal; children: Christine S., Kathleen E. MS in Ednl. Adminstrn., U. of So. Maine, Gorham, 1993. Cert. ednl. adminstr. Maine, 1993. Elem. prin. Peaks Island Sch., Maine, 1996—99, Marion T. Morse Elem. Sch., Lisbon Falls, Maine, 1999—2004, Lisbon Cmty. Sch., 2004—. Bd. dirs. Androscoggin County Head Start, Lewiston, Maine, 2000—03. Scholar Living Meml. scholar, Alpha Delta Kappa, 1998. Mem.: Alpha Delta Kappa (exec. bd. mem. 2001—03). Avocations: travel, gardening, reading. Home: 180 Forest St Westbrook ME 04092 Office: Lisbon Cmty Sch 33 Mill St Lisbon ME 04250 E-mail: civerson@union30.org.

IVERSON, CAROL JEAN, retired library media specialist; b. Villisca, Iowa, July 2, 1937; d. Paul Gerald and Garnet Blanche (Dunn) Smith; m. Merlin Gerald Iverson, June 11, 1961; children: Robert Mark, Jean Marie Iverson Howe. BA, U. No. Iowa, 1960. Elem. tchr. Manning (Iowa) Community Schs., 1957-58, Mason City (Iowa) Sch. Dist., 1960-61, Manson (Iowa) Community Schs., 1961-63, Blooming Prairie (Minn.) Community Schs., 1963-64, 65-66; elem. tchr., K-12 librarian Rockwell (Iowa) Swaledale Community Schs., 1973-80; libr. media specialist Mason City Sch. Dist., 1980-96. County co-chair Cerro Gordo County Reps., Howard Baker campaign, 1979; campaign worker Dukakis for Pres., 1987. Mem. AAUW (v.p. 1989-91, pres. 1993-95), NEA (del. rep. assembly), Iowa State Edn. Assn. (del., resolutions com. 1975-78), Iowa Ednl. Media Assn. (legis. chair 1987-89), Delta Kappa Gamma Soc. Internat. (pres. chpt. 1986-88, Upsilon state pres. 1999-2001), U.S. Forum (N.W. rep.), Iowa Ednl. Equity Coun., Phi Delta Kappa. Democrat. Lutheran. Avocations: travel, gardening, reading, children's literature. Home: 1505 Limestone Ct Mason City IA 50401-6976

IVERSON, KRISTINE ANN, federal agency administrator; b. Elgin, Ill, Aug. 15, 1953; d. Theodore Clarence and Vivian (Schumaker) I. BA, DePauw U., Greencastle, Ind., 1975; MA, George Mason U., 1985; postgrad., Va. Poly. Inst. and State U., 1970. Legis. aide Rep. John B. Conlan, Washington, 1975-76; legis. asst. Sen. Orrin G. Hatch, Washington, 1977-81, sr. policy advisor, 1993-94, legis. dir., 1995—; employment policy dir. Senate Labor and Human Resources Com., Washington, 1981-88, minority staff dir., 1988-92; asst. sec. Congl. intergov. affairs US Dept. Labor, Washington, 2001—. Cons. Reagan-Bush Transition, 1980 Pres. The Ron Freeman Chorale, Arlington, Va., 1987-2000; steering com. George Mason U. Tech. Forum, 1983; del. 11th Dist. Rep. Conv., Fairfax, Va., 1992; mem. DePauw U. Alumni Bd., Greencastle, Ind., 1993-99; mem. Bd. of Visitors 2000-03. Recipient Young Alumni award DePauw U., Greencastle, 1993, John C. Stennis Congrl. fellow, 1999-2000. Mem. Alpha Omicron Pi;mem. The Falls Ch. (Episcopal). Republican. Avocations: music, sports. Office: US Dept Labor Congressional Intergovt Affairs 200 Constitution Ave NW Washington DC 20210

IVES, COLTA FELLER, museum curator, educator; b. San Diego, Apr. 5, 1943; m. E. Garrison Ives, June 14, 1966; 1 child, Lucy Barrett. BA, Mills Coll., 1964; MA, Columbia U., 1966. Staff Met. Mus. Art, N.Y.C., 1966—, curator in charge prints and photographs, 1975-93, curator dept. drawings and prints, 1993—; guest scholar J. Paul Getty Mus., 2002. Adj. prof. Columbia U., 1970-87. Author: The Great Wave, 1974, Art Libraries Assn. award, 1975, The Flight Into Egypt, 1972, R. Rauschenberg Photos In and Out City Limits. New York, 1981, French Prints in the Era of Impressionism and Symbolism, 1988, Toulouse-Lautrec in the Metropolitan Museum of Art, 1996; co-author: The Painterly Print, 1980, Pierre Bonnard: The Graphic Art, 1989, Daumier Drawings, 1992, Goya in the Metropolitan Museum of Art, 1995, The Private Collection of Edgar Degas, 1997 (Best Show of 1997-98 N.Y.C. Mus. Internat. Assn. Art Critics), Romanticism and the School of Nature, 2000, The Lure of the Exotic: Gauguin in New York Collections, 2002. Chmn. grants com. Met. Mus. Art, 1986-87; bd. dirs. Bidwell House, Mass. Mem. Print Coun. Am. (exec. bd. 1975-77, 84-87, v.p. 1989-93), Assn. Art Mus. Curators (exec. bd. 2002-04). Office: Met Mus Art Fifth Ave New York NY 10028-0198

IVEY, ANDI, special education educator; d. Costas and Antoinette Zacharoudis; m. R. Mike Ivey, Sept. 29, 1973; children: Tonya Michelle, Brett Jason. BS in Elem. and Spl. Edn., No. Ariz. U., 1973. Ednl. profl. developer. cons. Ivey League, Kailua, Hawaii, 1996—; spl. educator Scottsdale Unified Schs., Ariz., 1983—99. Acad. dean, dept. chairperson Desert Mountain H.S., Scottsdale, 1995—99; dist. profl. developer Scottsdale Unified Schs., 1996—99; team leader, spl. edn. rep. Mohave Mid. Sch., Scottsdale, 1990—95; trainer of trainers - Project Adapt Dept. Edn. State of Ariz., Phoenix, 1994—98, mem. creating equity and access com. Dept. Edn., 1995—95. Named Tchr. of the Yr., Phi Delta Kappa Scottsdale Chpt., 1997, Tchr. of the Yr. - State of Ariz., Learning Disabilities Assn. of Ariz., 1993. Mem.: ASCD, Coun. for Exceptional Children, Phi Delta Kappa (Scottsdale Chpt. Tchr. of the Yr. 1997). Avocations: scuba diving, walking on the beach, swimming, golf, travel. Home and Office: 41 Palione Pl Kailua HI 96734 Personal E-mail: iveyleague@hawaii.rr.com.

IVEY, DENISE H. publishing executive; b. 1950; Asst. contr. Gainesville (Ga.) Times Gannett, Pensacola, Fla., 1983-84, contr., 1984, pres., pub., 1986, 1989; v.p., pub. Pensacola New Jour. Gannett East Regional Group, 1991-94, pres., pub. Pensacola New Jour., 1994—. Office: Pensacola News Jour PO Box 12710 Pensacola FL 32574-2710

IVEY, ELIZABETH S. retired physicist, educator; b. Schenectady, N.Y., Apr. 21, 1935; married, 1957 (div.), remarried, 1982; 5 children. BS in Physics, Simmons Coll., 1957; MA in Teaching, Harvard U., 1959; PhD in Mech. Engring. Acoustics, U. Mass., 1976. Prof. physics Simmons Coll., 1958-59, Bucknell U., 1960-63, Colo. State U., Ft. Collins, 1964-68, assoc. dean faculty, 1982-85, Louise Wolff Kahn prof., from 1985; prof. physics Smith Coll., 1969-90, chmn. dept. physics, 1983-90; provost Macalester Coll., St. Paul, 1990-95, U. Hartford, West Hartford, Conn., 1995-2000, provost emerita, 2000—. Vis. prof. Yale U., 1982. Bd. dirs. Minn. Inst. Talented Youth, 1990-95, World Press Inst., 1990-93, St. Paul Area United Way, 1990-95, Assn. Women Sci., 2001—; bd. trustees Hartford Coll. Women, 1995—, Mitchell Coll. 2003-; corporator Simmons Coll., 2000—. Recipient Woman Engr. award Soc. Women Engrs., 1988. Fellow AAAS; mem. Acoustical Soc. Am., Am. Assn. Physics Tchrs., Assn. Women in Sci. (pres.-elect 2003-04, pres. 2004—). Home: 25 High Wood Rd Bloomfield CT 06002 E-mail: ivey@hartford.edu.

IVEY, KAY ELLEN, state official; b. Repton, Ala., Oct. 15, 1944; d. Boardman Nettles and Barbara Elizabeth Ivey. BS, Auburn U., 1967; cert. in mktg., U. Colo., 1975; cert. in banking, U. South Ala.; cert. in Strategic Leadership for State Execs., Duke U., 1989. Tchr., coach forensics Rio Linda (Calif.) High Sch., 1968-69; asst. v.p. Mchts. Nat. Bank, Mobile, Ala., 1970-79; cabinet officer Office of the Gov., State of Ala., Montgomery, 1979-81; reading clk. Ala. Ho. Reps., 1981-82; exec. v.p. St. Margaret's Hosp. Found., 1982-85; dir. govt. affairs Ala. Commn. Higher Edn., 1985—88; treas. State of Ala., 2003—. Owner, cons. Ivey Enterprises, Montgomery, 1982—; speaker in field. Editor (audio-visual presentation) What Price Freedom (award of Excellence), 1976, St. Margaret's Hosp. Heart tabloid, 1983. Mem. adv. bd. Sch. Bus. Auburn U., 1980-83; candidate Ala. State Auditor, 1982; sec. Ala. div. Am. Cancer Soc., 1985—; bd. dirs. Ala. Girl's State Sch., 1983-85, Stetson Hoedown Rodeo Queen's Pageant, Montgomery, 1986—; bd. trustees Sheriff's Boys and Girls Ranches. Mem. Indsl. Developers Ala., Young Men's Bus. Orgn., Pub. Relations Council Ala. (bd. dirs. 1976-82), DAR (state chmn. 1985-86), Alpha Gamma Delta (disting. citizen award 1986). Republican. Presbyterian. Avocations: horseback riding, public speaking. Office: State Treasurers Office Rm S-106 State Capitol Bldg Montgomery AL 36130

IVEY, SUSAN, tobacco company executive; With Brown & Williamson Tobacco Corp., 1981—, dir. mktg. Far East, head internat. brands U.K., sr. v.p. mktg., 1998—2000, pres., CEO, 2001—. Office: Brown & Williamson Tobacco Corp 200 Brown and Williamson Tower 401 S Fourth Ave Louisville KY 40202*

IVIE, CHRISTINE MARIE, principal; b. St. Cloud, Minn., Aug. 4, 1968; d. David A. and Mary C. Hegg; m. Aaron O. Ivie, Apr. 23, 2003. BA, Coll. St. Catherine, 1992; MEd, Northwest Nazarene U., 1997. Cert. sch. adminstr. Idaho, pupil pers. svcs. and std. secondary tchg. Idaho. Dir., tchr. Cornerstone Pre-Sch., Boise, Idaho, 1994—96; counselor, tchr. Camos County Schs., Fairfield, Idaho, 1996—98; counselor Meridian H.S., Idaho, 1998—2001; prin. Ctrl. Elem. Sch., Nampa, Idaho, 2001—02; dir. Northwest Children's Home/Treasure Valley Edn. Centos, Nampa, Payette, Idaho, 2002—. Mem.: ASCD, Coun. Exceptional Children, Am. Counselor Assn. (chair Idaho membership com. 1999—2000). Avocations: music, camping, backpacking, water sports. Home: 1423 Spruce Creek Loop Nampa ID 53684 Office: Northwest Childrens Home 504 E Florida Nampa ID 83651*

IVINS, MARCIA S. astronaut; b. Balt., Apr. 15, 1951; d. Joseph L. Ivins. BS in Aerospace Engring., U. Colo., 1973. Lic. pilot. Engr. NASA Johnson Space Ctr., Houston, 1974—80; flight engr. Shuttle Tng.. Aircraft, Aircraft Ops., Houston, 1980—; co-pilot NASA Adminstrv. Aircraft, Houston, 1980—. Mem. Exptl. Aircraft Assn., 99's, Internat. Aerobatic Club. Achievements include over 6000 flight hours in civilian and NASA aaircraft, 5 space missions, 1, 318 hours in space. Avocations: flying, reading, baking. Office: Astronauts Office NASA Johnson Space Ctr Houston TX 77058

IVINS, MOLLY, columnist, writer; b. Texas, 1944; d. Jim and Margo I. BA, Smith Coll., 1966; postgrad., Inst. Polit. Sci., 1966; MA in Journalism, Columbia U., Paris, 1967. Former reporter The Houston Chronicle, The Mpls. Star Tribune, 1964-1976; reporter The Texas Observer, Austin, 1970-76, The New York Times, 1976-82, Rocky Mountain bur. chief, 1976-82; former columnist The Dallas Times Herald, 1982-91; columnist Fort Worth Star-Telegram, 1992—2001; syndicated columnist Creators Syndicate, LA, 2001—. Author: Molly Ivins Can't Say That, Can She?, 1991, Nothin' But Good Times Ahead, 1993; contbr. to periodicals including The Nation, N.Y. Times Book Rev., Mother Jones, Ms., Progressive, others. Office: Creators Syndicate 5777 W Century Blvd Los Angeles CA 90045

IVORY, GOLDIE LEE, retired social worker, educator; b. Apr. 19, 1926; d. Percey Carr and Edna M. (Scott) Carr Williams; m. Sam Ivory, Aug. 7, 1947; children: Kenneth L., Kevin D. BS, Ind. U., 1949; MA, U. Notre Dame, 1956; MSW, Ind. U.-Purdue U., Indpls., 1977. Registered cert. clin. social worker, Ind. Juvenile probation officer St. Joseph County Juvenile Probation Dept., South Bend, Ind., 1949-56, intake supr., 1956-59; chief probation officer South Bend City Ct., 1959; psychiat. social worker Beatty Meml. Hosp., Westville, Ind., 1960; instr. sociology Ind. U., South Bend, 1960-67; relocation rep. Urban Redevel. Commn., South Bend, 1960-62; social worker Elkhart (Ind.) Cmty. Schs., 1962-66, supr. social svcs., 1966-69, dir. human rels., 1970-87; mem. faculty Goshen (Ind.) Coll., 1971—, asst. prof. social work, 1981-91, assoc. prof. social work emerita, 1993—. Pvt. practice social work Ivory Caring Corner, 1981-87; family therapist Family Learning Ctr., South Bend, 1987-94, clinician emerita, 1994—; workshop cons. human social svcs.; instr. sociology and social work St. Mary's Coll., 1967-69, dir. Upward Bound program, 1970; guest lectr. dept. sociology U. Swaziland, South Africa, 1983. Author articles in field. Recipient Human Svc. award Acad. Human Svcs., 1974-75, Merit award Indpls. Pub. Schs. Dept. Social Work, 1977, Designation BCD award Am. Bd. Examiners in Clin. Soc., 1985, plaque for cmty. svcs. Mayor of Elkhart, 1981, Black Achiever award in edn. Ind. Black Expo, 1983; state chpt. Delta Kappa Gamma scholar, 1969-70. Mem. NASW, AAUW, Nat. Black Child Devel. Inst., Nat. Assn. Black Social Workers, Acad. Cert. Social Workers, The Links, Delta Kappa Gamma, Delta Sigma Theta, Alpha Delta Mu. Mem. Church of God in Christ. Home: 1309 Bissell St South Bend IN 46617-2108

IVY, MARILYN ATKINSON, artist, educator, art director; m. Larry Don Ivy; children: Lauren Ivy Chiong, Travis Wade. BFA, Tex. Christian U., 1970; M, Tex. Woman's U., 2000. Cert. tchr. Tex., Nat. Bd. Prof. Tchg. Stds. Artist Smith Stained Glass Studios, Ft. Worth, 1968—74, Ft. Worth, 1970—; art tchr. Hurst-Euless-Bedford Ind. Sch. Dist., Tex., 1980—; coord. art edn. Tex. Christian U., Ft. Worth, 2003—. Liaison, cons. State Farm Ptnrs. in Learning Cmty./Nat. Bd. Profl. Tchg. Stds., Dallas, 1998—, El Paso, Tex.; mem. of renewal devel. team Nat. Bd. for Profl. Tchg. Standards, Edn. Testing Svc., Philadelphia, Pa.; presenter Nat. Bd. Profl. Tchg. Stds., Washington, 1998—. Exhibited in group shows at 500X Gallery Open Show, 20th Ann. Nat. Juried Exhbn., Navarro County, Tex., 2003 (3d pl., 2003). Grantee, Fulbright Meml. Fund. Mem.: Tex. Art Edn. Assn. (assoc.), Nat. Art Edn. Assn. (assoc.), Tex. State Tchr. Assn. (assoc.). Mem. Disciples Of Christ. Avocations: reading, remodeling houses, travel. Home: 2608 S University Dr Fort Worth TX 76109 Office: L D Bell HS 1601 Brown Trl Hurst TX 76054 Personal E-mail: marilynivy@yahoo.com.

IWUANYANWU, EUCHARIA CHIEGE, physician assistant; b. Portharcourt, Nigeria, June 6, 1959; came to U.S., 1987; d. Semion Ogueruand Maryrose (Uwaezuoke) Uzomah; m. Christian Iheanyichukwu Iwuanyanwu, Feb. 2, 1988; children: Iyke, Kelechi, Chinyere. BSc in Food Sci. and Tech., U. Nigeria, 1983; BSc, Physician Asst., U. Tex., Galveston, 1996. Lic. physician asst., Tex. Quality control officer Standard Flour Mills, Lagos, Nigeria, 1983-87; pharmacy asst. Ag. White Pharmacy, Houston, 1988-93; physician asst. Tex. Children's Hosp., Houston, 1996-97; physician extender U. Tex. Med. Br., Galveston, 1997—. Fellow Am. Acad. Physician Assts., Tex. Acad. Physician Assts., Alpha Eta. Roman Catholic. Avocations: reading, volunteering, movies.

IZAWA, CHIZUKO, psychologist, researcher; b. Tokushima, Japan; came to U.S., 1961; m. Robert G. Hayden, July 15, 1973; 1 child, Althea J.E.K. Izawa-Hayden. BA in Psychology, U. Tokyo, 1960; MA in Psychology, Stanford U., 1962, PhD in Psychology, 1965. Asst. prof. psychology San Diego State U., Calif., 1965-67; postdoctoral fellow Inst. Human Learning U. Calif., Berkeley, 1967-68; asst. prof. psychology SUNY, Buffalo, 1968-72; assoc. prof. psychology Tulane U., 1972-80, prof. psychology, 1980—. Cons., question constructor Am. Assn. State Psychology Bds.; examiner, interviewer selection com. JET program Consulate Gen. Japan, 1983—; invited vis. fgn. scientist U. Tsukuba, Japan, 2001; co-organizer, chair 4th Tsukuba Internat. Conf. on Memory, 2003-; visiting scholar, Univ. Tsukuba, 2001. Author: Current Issues in Cognitive Processes, 1989, Cognitive Psychology Applied, 1993, On Human Memory, 1999; reviewer numerous jours. including Am. Psychologist, Am. Jour. Psychology, Jour. Exptl. Psychology: Gen. Jour. Exptl. Psychology: Learning, Memory, and Cognition, Memory & Cognition, Jour. Math. Psychology, Jour. Appl. Psychology, Japanese Jour. Psychonomic Sci., Cognitive Psychology, others; cons. reviewer NSF, NIMH, Oxford U. Press, Cambridge U. Press, Stanford U. Press, Harcourt, Sage, others; review panelist Directorate Sci. Edn., Div. Sci. Manpower Improvement, NSF; contbr. numerous articles to profl. jours.; presenter in field. NIMH grantee; Flowerree Found. grantee; Japanese Edn. Rsch. Publ. grantee; Japanese Edn. Min. grantee; Aron Found. grantee; Japanese Monbusho, educ. ministory grantee. Fellow APA, WPA, Am. Psychol. Soc. (charter), WPA; mem. AAUP, Asian Am. Psychol. Assn., Japanese Psychol. Assn., Southeastern Psychol. Assn. (co-chair annual meeting local arrangements subcom. 1972-73, co-chair commn. for status women student rsch. awards 1975-78, chair com. on equality profl. opportunity rsch. awards 1978-80, various program coms. 1975-90, program com. learning, memory, cognition 1995—, chair com. equality profl. opportunity minority interest group 1996-98, exec. com. mem.-at-large 1998-2001, chair spl. grad. rsch. awards 1998-2000), Regional Psychol. Assn., Psychonomic Soc., Psychometric Soc., Soc. Math. Psychology, Soc. Cross-Cultural Psychology, Soc. Cross-Cultural Rsch., Internat. Coun. Psychologists (co-chair annual meeting local arrangements 1973-74), Southeastern Workers in Memory (chmn. 1974-75), Japan Prize World-Wide Nomination Com., Sigma Xi. Office: 411 Pine St New Orleans LA 70118-3715

IZZO, LUCILLE ANNE, sales representative; b. Rochester, N.Y., Apr. 1, 1954; d. Peter George and Dorothy June Izzo. B of Gen. Studies, U. Conn., 1995. Regional sales mgr. T.R. Miller Co., Inc., New Milford, Conn., 1986-87; program mgr. Jr. Achievement SW Conn., Stamford, 1987-88, adviser, cons., 1986-93; sec. Eastman Kodak Co., Rochester, 1972-84, consumer products sales rep. Oklahoma City, 1984-86, copy products sales rep. Stamford, 1988-91, office imaging sales rep. Hartford, Conn., 1992-94, major account rep., 1994-96; acct. exec. Lexis-Nexis, Danbury, Conn., 1996-98; maj. account mgr. Gartner Group, Stamford, Conn., 1998—2002; major acct. exec. Ikon Office Solutions, Milford, Conn., 2003—04; relationship exec. Tower Group, 2004—. Grad. asst. Dale Carnegie Human Rels. Course, 1987, 88, 96. Bus. cons. Region One Jr. Achievement Conf., 1988, 90; guest speaker West Conn. Jr. Achievement Conf., 1990; adviser, recruiter Greater Rochester Jr. Achievement, 1980-83, Small Bus. Owner, Accessorize, 1994—. Mem. NAFE, Am. Mgmt. Assn. Avocations: travel, reading, music. Home: 2006 Eaton Ct Danbury CT 06811

JABER, LILA A. state official; BA in Polit. Sci., Stetson U., DeLand, Fla.; JD, Stetson U., St. Petersburg, Fla. Bar: Fla., ct. cert. mediator:. Apptd. commr. Fla. Pub. Svc. Commn., 2000, chmn. Mem. com. on telecomm. and com. on consumer affairs Nat. Assn. Regulatory Utility Commrs.; chair Fed.-State Jt. Conf. on Advanced Svcs. (FCC); apptd. Fed.-State Jt. Bd. on Universal Svc., 2001—; past co-chair e-infrastructure subcom. Info. Svc. Tech. Devel. Task Force; mem. Fla. Rsch. Consortium. Office: 2540 Shumard Oak Blvd Tallahassee FL 32399-0850

JABLONSKI, VALERIE, librarian; b. Kingston, N.Y. Master's degree, SUNY, Albany, 2000. Libr. N.Y. Tax coord. asst. Cleary, Gottlieb, Steen, & Hamilton, N.Y.C., 2001; dir. of info. svcs. Globe Inst. of Tech., N.Y.C., 2002—03. With USAF, 1984—86.

JABLOW, BERNICE R. architectural designer and space consultant; b. N.Y.C., June 1, 1914; d. Maurice and Dorothy (Fineberg) Rentner; m. Arthur Jablow, Apr. 12, 1937 (dec. July, 1996); children: Michael L., John G., Peter A. Student, Columbia Coll., 1933-34, Berlitz Sch. Lang., 1935. Cons. to numerous interior designers, architects and builders, N.Y., N.J., Conn. Home: 2412 Euclid Heights Blvd Apt 402 Cleveland Heights OH 44106-2748

JACK, DANA CROWLEY, psychologist, educator; b. Houston, Mar. 19, 1945; d. John Thomas Crowley and Dorothy Jane (Mohr) Beach; m. Rand File Jack, Mar. 16, 1968; children: Darby, Kelsey. BA summa cum laude, Mt. Holyoke Coll., 1967; MSW, U. Wash., 1972; EdD, Harvard U., 1984. Counselor, therapist Western Wash. U., Bellingham, 1972-79, prof. Fairhaven Coll., 1986—. Author: Moral Vision and Professional Decisions, 1989, Silencing the Self: Women and Depression, 1991, Behind the Mask: Destruction & Creativity in Women's Aggression, 1999; contbr. articles to profl. jours., chpts. to books. Recipient Depression Rsch. grant Stone Ctr., Wellesley Coll., 1986, Rsch. grant Western Wash. U., 1993, 95. Mem. APA, Phi Beta Kappa. Office: Western Wash Univ Fairhaven Coll Bellingham WA 98225

JACK, DIXIE LYNN, software consultant, social worker; b. Orlando, Fla., Apr. 7, 1943; d. Alex and Dorothy Ellen (Dixon) J. BA, U. Wash., 1965; AA, Highline C.C., Des Moines, 1971. Tchr. Archdioces, Burien, Wash., 1968-70, Tukwila (Wash.) Sch. Dist., 1970-75; fin. svcs. technician Dept. Welfare, Seattle, 1982-84; social worker, supr. Dept. Children and Family Svcs., Everett, Wash., 1984-94; user support/tng. mgr. Lockheed Martin, Hartford, Conn., 1995-97; computer based tng. mgr. Am. Mgmt. Sys., Manchester, Conn., 1997; implementation, bus. process cons. Ctr. for Support of Families, Chevy Chase, Md., 1998; documentation specialist Amber Systems Inc., Bloomfield Hills, Mich., 1999—2002; implementation site coord. RCM Techs., 2002—. Cons. Juvenile Justice, Supreme Ct., Seattle, 1988-95. Mem. Assn. Univ. Women, Scarab Club, Birmingham-Bloomfield Arts Assn. Home: 836 Golf Dr Apt 302 Pontiac MI 48341

JACK, JANIS GRAHAM, judge; b. 1946; RN, St. Thomas Sch. Nursing, 1969; BA, U. Balt., 1974; JD summa cum laude, South Tex. Coll., 1981. Pvt. practice, Corpus Christi, Tex., 1981-94; judge U.S. Dist. Ct. (so. dist.) Tex., Corpus Christi, 1994—. Jud. mem. The Maritime Law Assn. U.S. Mem. ABA, Fed. Judges Assn., Fifth Cir. Dist. Judges Assn., Nat. Assn. Women Judges (jud. conf. com. info. tech.), Tex. Bar Found., State Bar Tex., The Philos. Soc. Tex., Order of Lytae, Phi Alpha Delta. Office: US Dist Ct 1133 N Shoreline Blvd Corpus Christi TX 78401

JACK, MORGANN TAYLLOR, writer, artist; d. William H. and Emma Lee (Williams) Blanks; m. Charles D. Jack, July 21, 1957 (dec. Sept. 20, 1979). AA in Fine Arts, Allan Hancock Coll., 1975. Editl. asst. The Cycler Champlin Oil Co. house organ, Ft. Worth, 1957; columnist, reporter, corr. Santa Barbara News-Press, Lompoc, Calif., 1961—64; freelance journalist AP, Springfield (Mass.) Rep., 1966—68; staff reporter features, 1st editor weekend entertainment supplement, Lompoc Record, 1968—71; feature writer Lompoc Valley News, 1980—84; feature writer, cover artist Cen. Coast Mag., Santa Maria, Calif., 1989—90. Guest artist Binnenheide Art Exhbn., Kevelaer, Germany, 1994. Space 'N Lace, 1961—63, monthly mag., Space 'n Lace, 1961—63; creator, editor, artist : (weekly newsletter) Reeflector, 1964—65; weekly newsletter, Recife, Brazil, A Word About Birds in Rhyme Time, 1984, commd. garden sculpture, for Lompoc Mayor (reception benefitting Lompoc Mus.), 1978, exhibitions include Office Idaho State Treas., 1988—93. Mem. Santa Barbara County Commn. for Women, 1999—2000. Recipient regional awards, juried art shows and competitions, 1951—86, Plaque in Appreciation of Outstanding Cmty. Svcs., City of Lompoc, 1968—71. Mem.: Santa Barbara Mus. Art, Nat. Mus. Women in the Arts (charter mem.). Avocations: travel, adventure, reading, paleosciences.

JACK, NANCY RAYFORD, supplemental resource company executive, consultant; b. Hughes Springs, Tex., June 23, 1939; d. Vernon Lacy and Virginia Ernestine (Turner) Rayford; m. Kermit E. Hundley, Dec. 19, 1979; 1 child by previous marriage, James Bradford Jack, III. Cert. in bus. adminstrn., Keller Grad. Sch. Mgmt., 1980; cert. in acctg., Harper Coll., 1972, cert. in corp. law and tax law, paralegal, 1973. Sr. sec. Gould, Inc., Rolling Meadows, Ill., 1971-73, staff asst., 1973-74, asst. sec., 1974-77, corp. sec., 1977-89, v.p., 1985-89; pres. The Corp. Ofcl. Sec., Wheaton, Ill., 1989-92, Corp. Minutes and More, Wheaton, 1992-99; assoc. dir. The Bus. Owners' Trustee, The Woodlands, Tex., 1999—. Recipient cert. of leadership YWCA Met. Chgo., 1975 Mem.: Kingwood Country Club, Beta Sigma Phi. Home and Office: 162 Linton Downs Pl The Woodlands TX 77382-1692

JACKER, CORINNE LITVIN, playwright, writer; b. Chgo., June 29, 1933; d. Thomas Henry and Theresa (Bellak) Litvin. Student, Stanford U., 1950-52; BS, Northwestern U., 1954, MA, 1955, postgrad., 1955-56. Editor Liberal Arts Press, 1959-60, Macmillan Co., 1960-63, Scribner's, 1963-65; story editor Sta. WNET-TV, N.Y.C., 1969-71, CBS-TV, N.Y.C., 1972-74; instr. playwriting NYU, 1976-79, [illegible] playwriting Yale U., 1979-81. Adj. prof. Princeton U., 1986, 88, Columbia U., 1988-99, Breadloaf Sch. of English, 1988, NYU, 1990-91, U. Ga., 1995—; sci. cons. Benton Project for Broadcasting, U. Chgo., 1988-90. Exec. story editor, head writer (TV series) Best of Families, PBS, N.Y.C., 1975-77; head writer (TV series) Another World, 1981-82; author: Man, Memory, and Machines, 1964 (N.Y. Pub. Library 50 Best Books of Yr. 1964), Window on the Unknown, 1966 (AAAS 50 Best Books of Yr. 1966), A Little History of Cocoa, 1966, The Black Flag of Anarchy, 1968 (Pubs. Weekly 25 Best Books of Yr. 1968), The Biological Revolution, 1971, The Chocolate Bar Bust, 1994; playwright: The Scientific Method, 1970, Seditious Acts, 1970, Travellers, 1973, Breakfast, Lunch, & Dinner, 1975, Bits and Pieces, 1975 (Obie award 1975), Harry Outside, 1975 (Obie award 1975), Night Thoughts & Terminal, 1976, Other People's Tables, 1976, My Life, 1977, After the Season, 1978, Later, 1979, Domestic Issues, 1981, In Place, 1982, Songs from Distant Lands, 1985, (adaptation) Hedda Gabbler, 1989, The Island, 1991, (adaptation) Three Sisters, 1992, In the Dark, 1993, Light, 1993, Getting Home, 1994, A New Life, 1995, The Promised Land, 1995, The Machine Age, 1996, Parties, 2000; TV writer, including: 3 episodes Actors' Choice, NET, 1970 (Emmy citation 1970), Virginia Woolf: The Moment Whole, NET, 1972 (CINE Golden Eagle award 1972); story editor: 4 episode series Benjamin Franklin, CBS, 1974 (Emmy citation 1974); The Adams Chronicles, 1975 (Peabody award 1975); Bicentennial Minutes, 1975, Loose Change, 1978, 3 episode series, NBC, 1978, 3 episodes of Best of Families, NET, 1978, The Jilting of Granny Weatherall, NET, 1980, Night Thoughts and Terminal BBC, 1978, Overdrawn at the Memory Bank, NET, 1983 (Rotterdam Film Festival, Am. Film Inst. Video Feature Film Festival). Rockefeller Found. grantee, 1979-80; residency Villa Serbelloni, Bellagio, Italy, 1987. Mem. Dramatists Guild, Writers Guild Am. East, PEN Home and Office: 110 W 86th St New York NY 10024-4049 Office Phone: 212-496-9698. E-mail: jacaranda@verizon.net.

JACKLE, KAREN DEE, real estate company executive; b. Santa Ana, Calif., June 26, 1945; d. Franklin Suits and Dorothy (Miller) Todd; m. Paul Herman Jackle, Oct. 12, 1968; children: Lara Irene, Julie Maureen. BA in History, Calif. State U., Long Beach, 1967. Elem. tchr. L.A. City Schs., 1967—68; social worker Los Angeles Dept. Pub. Social Svcs., 1968—70; with Seablue Pools, Harare, 1970; co-owner, property mgr., appraiser Paul Jackle & Assocs., Inc., Huntington Beach, Calif., 1971—; property mgr., appraiser Paul Jackle & Assocs., Huntington Beach, Calif., 1973—86, property developer, mgr., 1986—; pres. June Coast Corp., 1993—, chmn., 2003—04. Vice chmn. Huntington Beach Human Rels. Task Force, 1997—2002, chmn. events, 1997, chmn., 2003—; block rep. H. Seacliff Homeowners Assn.; mem. Huntington Beach Intrastructure Com., 1998—. Recipient Achievement award, Orange County Human Rels. Task Force, 1998. Mem.: AAUW (mentoring program 1990—94, chmn. edn. found. 1991—92, chmn. membership com. 1992—94, pres. 1995—97, pub. policy 1997—, program v.p. 2000—01, state program com. 2001—03, pres. 2002—03, state comm. com. 2003—, Huntington Beach chpt., Nat. Assn. Businesswomen Remarkable Women award 2001). Avocations: aerobics, walking, theater, reading, travel. Office: 18652 Florida St Ste 300 Huntington Beach CA 92648-6069 E-mail: karen@pjackle.com.

JACKMAN DABB, HOLLY PIEPER, publisher; b. Scottsbluff, Nebr., Jan. 12, 1965; d. John Matthew and Mardell B. Pieper; m. Lynn Richard Jackman, Dec. 28, 1985 (div. Nov. 17, 1993); children: Matthew, Jace, Lance; m. Randy Dabb, Sept. 27, 2003. AS, Western Wyo. Cmty. Coll., Rock Springs, 1985; BS, U. Wyo., 1986. Reporter Rock Springs Newspaper, Wyo., 1987-90; bus. mngr. Jackman Construction, Rock Springs, 1990-93; special editions editor Rock Springs Newspaper, 1993-98, publisher, 1998—. Squadron comdr. CAP, Wyo., 1991-1995; mem. Local Emergency Planning Commn.; Wyo. rep. USWest Policy Bd. for squaredance policy, 2003—. Brewer award Civil Air Patrol, 1993, Bus. and Professioal Woman of the Year award BPW, 1993, 98. Mem. C. of C. (bd.dirs., 2001-02), Sashay Pardners (v.p. 1999, treas. 1997, pres. 1999-2001), Kiwanis, Rock Springs (Wyo.) Soccer Assn. (bd. mem. 1999-2002, chmn. econ. environ. com.), Wyo. Press Assn. (bd. dir. 2003—). Democrat. Avocations: reading, gardening, water sports, square dancing, flying, skiing, moutain climbing. Home: 3 Wardell Ct Rock Springs WY 82901-7248 Office: Rock Springs Newspaper 215 D St Rock Springs WY 82901-6234

JACK-MOORE, PHYLLIS, strategist, educational consultant; b. Charlotte, N.C., Aug. 23, 1934; d. William Thomas and Connie LaVerne (Childers) Harris; children: Michael Harris, Julie Dawn Jack Rodgers. BA, U. N.C., 1965, MEd, 1969; postgrad., North Tex. State U., 1982-83. Cert. tchr., N.C., Tex. Elem. tchr. Chapel Hill (N.C.) Pub. Schs., 1965-68; staff devel. coordinator Learning Inst. N.C., Durham, 1969-72; child devel. specialist Tex. Dept. Human Resources, Ft. Worth, 1975-77; child care tng. coordinator North Tex. State Univ., Denton, 1978-81; dir., owner Resources for Children, Inc., Ft. Worth, 1984-88; pvt. practice work family strategy, ednl. cons. Ft. Worth, 1988—. Instr. Tarrant County Jr. Coll., Ft. Worth, North Tex. State U., 1982—; frequent guest speaker; appearances on TV; coord. for tng. in establishment of pub. sch. kindergarten program in State of N.C., 1972-73; cons. for family support svcs. State Dept. Pub. Instrn., Raleigh. Contbg. author: Room to Grow; mem. editorial rev. bd. Child Care Quar., Austin, 1984—. Trustee Tarrant County Youth Collaboration, 1982—86; mem. adv. bd. Ft. Worth's A Better Childhood Com., 1990—, Office of Early Childhood Coordination of Tex., 2002—, Healthy Child Care Tex., 2002—; coord. Tex. State Parent Action, 1989—; mem. gov.'s task force Head Start Collaboration, 1991—; bd. dirs. Tarrant County Med. Aus., 1983—84, City of Austin Fund for Child Care Excellence, 2000—; state bd. dirs. Mental Health Assn. in Tex., 2001—. Recipient Brous Outstanding Advocate award, 1984, All State Good Hands award, 1996, Excellence in Child Abuse Prevention award, 2001, Jeannette Watson ADvocacy award, Austin, 2002. Mem. Nat. Assn. for the Edn. of Young Children (gov. bd. nominee 1988—, nat. field rep. 1983—), Tex. Assn. for the Edn. of Young Children (state pres. 1982-83, Adminstr. of the Yr. award 1993), Ft. Worth Assn. for the Edn. of Young Children (pres. 1976-78), So. Assn. for Children Under Six (com. chair 1978-80, conf. co-chair 1987), Rotary, Phi Beta Kappa, Phi Delta Kappa. Clubs: Ft. Worth Woman's (v.p. and auditor 1983-86). Lodges: Rotary. E-mail: pjmoore@flash.net.

JACKOBOICE, SANDRA KAY, artist; b. Detroit, July 22, 1936; d. Virgil Ellsworth and Lucille Elizabeth LeSeur; m. Edward James Jackoboice, Jan. 11, 1958; children: E. Michael, Timothy Jon. BA, Aquinas Coll., Grand Rapids, Mich., 1989. Co-owner Fashion Plate, Grand Rapids, 1975-79; wardrobe cons. Steketees, Grand Rapids, 1980-82; owner Color Plus, Grand Rapids, 1983—. One-woman shows include FMB, Lowell, 1993, 1995, City Hall, Bielsko-Biala, Poland, 1995, Terryberry Gallery, Grand Rapids, 1997, Frederick Meijer Gardens, 1998, exhibited in group shows at Bot. Images Exhbn., Lansing, Mich., Artist Alliance Group Shows, represented by, Grand Gallery, Grand Rapids, Art Encounter Galleries, Las Vegas, Tamarack Gallery, Naples, Fla.; featured in Artists' Photo Reference Book, Pastel Artist Internat. mag., others. Mem. Jr. League, Grand Rapids, 1962—96, Downtown Mgmt. Bd., Grand Rapids, 1993—96, Grand Rapids Parking Commn., 1993—96; bd. dirs. Arts Coun. Greater Grand Rapids, 1997—2000. Recipient awards for art work. Mem.: S.W. Fla. Pastel Soc. (founder, advisor to bd. dirs. 2002—), Internat. Assn. Pastel Socs. (publicity chair 2001—, bd. dirs. 2003), Pastel Soc. Am., Am. Soc. Bot. Artists, Grand Valley Artists, Artists Alliance, Great Lakes Pastel Soc. (pres. 1997—2001, advisor to bd. dirs. 2002—, co-founder). Republican. Avocations: travel, art, tennis, golf. Office: Color Plus PO Box 6775 Grand Rapids MI 49516-6775

JACKSON, ALFREDA MURRAYE, adult education educator; b. McComb, Miss., Sept. 20, 1958; d. Fletcher Benjamin and Mildred Marie Williams. BS, Jackson State U., 1983. Tchr. Pearl River Valley Opportunity, McComb, 1992—2001. Supr. Girlie Higgins Youth Club, McComb, 2000—; youth choir dir. Christ T[illegible] Ch. [illegible] McComb, 2000—; supr. Recreation Mini Park, McComb. Mem.: Ga. Westbrook Federated Club (reporter). Avocation: reading. Home: 217 Denwiddie Ave Mccomb MS 39648

JACKSON, ANNE (ANNE JACKSON WALLACH), actress; b. Allegheny, Pa., Sept. 3, 1926; d. John Ivan and Stella Germaine (Murray) J.; m. Eli Wallach, Mar. 5, 1948; children: Peter, Roberta, Katherine. studied with Sanford Meisner and Herbert Berghof at Neighborhood Playhouse, with Lee Strassberg at Actor's Studio. Tchr. Herbert Berghoff Sch. Profl. debut: Cherry Orchard; mem. Am. Repertory Co.; Broadway plays include: Summer and Smoke, Oh, Men! Oh, Women!, Middle of the Night, Major Barbara, Rhinoceros, Luv, Waltz of the Toreadors, Diary of Anne Frank, 1978, Twice Around the Park, 1982-83, Nest of the Woodgrouse, 1984, Café Crown, 1989, Love Letters, 1991-92, Lost in Yonkers, 1992, In Person, 1993, The Flowering Peach, 1994, off-Broadway plays: Tennessee Williams Remembered, 1999, Mr. Peter's Connection, 1998, Down the Garden Path; London stage performances of The Typists, The Tiger, 1966; film appearances include: So Young, So Bad, 1950, Secret Life of an American Wife, 1968, Dirty Dingus McGee, 1970, Lovers and Other Strangers, 1970, The Shining, 1980, Sam's Son, 1985, Funny About Love, 1992, Folks, 1992, Johnnie Twennies, 1998, Something Sweet, 2000; TV appearances include: 84 Charing Cross Road, Private Battle, Everything's Relative, 1987, Law & Order, 1997, Education of Max Bickford, 2002; TV films: Family Man, Golda I and II, Out on a Limb, Baby M, 1988, The Rescuers: The Lady on the Bicycle, 1997; author: (autobiography) Early Stages, 1979. Recipient Obie award. Mem.: Actor's Studio (life). Office: care Paradigm 200 W 57th St Ste 900 New York NY 10019-3211 Office Phone: 212-874-2267.

JACKSON, BARBARA ANN, systems engineer; b. San Francisco, Feb. 15, 1955; d. Thomas John and Bertha Belle (Seeley) J. BS in Metall. Engring., Calif. Poly. State U., San Luis Obispo, 1979; MA in Marriage/Family/Child Counseling, Azusa Pacific U., 1985; MS in Sys. Mgmt., U. Denver, 1992; postgrad., Saybrook Grad. Sch., 2003. Registered counselor, Wash.; lic. massage therapist, Wash. Chief metallurgist Grove Valve and Regulator Co., Oakland, Calif., 1979; metallurgist, software sys. engr. Lockheed Missiles & Space Co., Sunnyvale, Calif., 1979-85; prin. engr. Lockheed Martin Hanford, Richland, Wash., 1996-97; software test engr., project mgmt. engr. Hewlett Packard, Cupertino, Calif., 1985-87; aircraft safety engr. sys. integration Boeing Co., Seattle, 1987-93; sys. engr. Westinghouse Hanford Co., Richland, 1994-96; sr. gen. sys. engr. MITRE Corp., Bedford, Mass., 1997—99; prin. software engr., prin. sys. engr. Raytheon Sys. Co., Tucson, 1999—2002; contract engr., info. security sys. engr. Gen. Dynamics Decision Sys., Scottsdale, Ariz., 2002—; pres. Fully Alive, Inc., 2002—. Pvt. practice family-centered massage Fully Alive Therapy, 1992—; career counselor Take Your Dau. to Work Day, MITRE Corp., 1998. Appeared in spotlight on infant massage KEPR-TV, 1995. Increasing human affectiveness instr. Nat. Mgmt. Assn., Sunnyvale, 1983, awards chair capital's Working Women's Seminar, 1984; elder Centerville Presbyn. Ch., Fremont, Calif., 1980, missionary to ch. in Tuxtepec, Mex., 1979, sr. high group leader, 1979; navigator, discipleship leader Fremont Neighborhood Ch., 1982-84; bone marrow transplant family vol. Fred Hutchinson Cancer Ctr., Seattle, 1987-88; crisis counselor Tri Cities Contact Helpline, Richland, 1994-98; facilitator for survivors of sexual abuse group Eastside Foursquare Ch., Kirkland, Wash., 1993-94; vol. hosp. chaplain U. Med. Ctr., Tucson, 2002—. Food Machinery Corp. scholar, 1978. Mem. Am. Assn. Marital and Family Therapy (assoc.), Am. Massage Therapy Assn., Internat. Coun. on Sys. Engring. Avocations: cross-country skiing, martial arts, opera, symphony, travel. Home: 4915 E Thomas Rd #113 Phoenix AZ 85018

JACKSON, BETTY EILEEN, music and elementary school educator; b. Denver, Oct. 9, 1925; d. James Bowen and Fannie (Shelton) J. MusB, U. Colo., 1948, MusM, 1949, MusB in Edn., 1963; postgrad., Ind. U., 1952-55, Hochschule fur Musik, Munich, 1955-56. Cert. educator Colo., Calif. Tchr., accompanist, tchr. H.L. Davis Vocal Studios, Denver, 1949-52; tchg. assoc. Ind. U., Bloomington, 1952-53, U. Colo., Boulder, 1961-63, vis. lectr., summers 1963-69; tchr. Fontana (Calif.) Unified Sch. Dist., 1963—2002; pvt. studio, 1966—. Lectr. in music Calif. State U., San Bernardino, 1967-76; performer, accompanist, music dir. numerous musical cos. including performer, music dir. Fontana Mummers, 1980—, Riverside Cmty. Players, Calif., 1984—; performer Rialto Cmty. Theatre, Calif., 1983—; head visual and performing arts com. Cypress Elem. Sch., 1988-92. Performances include numerous operas, musical comedies and oratorios, Cen. City Opera, Denver Grand Opera, Univ. Colo., Ind. Univ. Opera Theater (leading mezzo), 3 tours of Fed. Rep. Germany, 1956-58; oratorio soloist in Ind., Ky., Colo., and Calif., West End Opera (lead roles), Riverside Opera (lead roles). Judge Inland Theatre League, Riverside, 1983-92; mem. San Bernardino Cultural Task Force, 1981-83; bd. dirs. Riverside-San Bernardino Counties Met. Auditions, 1988—; mem. adv. bd. Riverside Concert Opera, 1990-95. Fulbright grantee, Munich, 1955-56; named outstanding performer Inland Theatre League, 1982-84; recipient Outstanding Reading Tchr. award, 1990, Tchr. of Yr. nominations, 1990, 91, hon. svc. award, 1992. Mem. AAUW (bd. dirs., cultural chair 1983-86), NEA, Nat. Assn. Tchrs. Singing (exec. bd. 1985-89), Internat. Reading Assn., Music Educators Nat. Conf., Calif. Tchrs. Assn., Calif. Elem. Educators Assn., Fontana Tchrs. Assn., Music Tchrs. Assn., Arrowhead Reading Coun., San Bernardino Valley Concert Assn. (bd. dirs. 1977-83), Internat. Platform Assn., Nat. Assn. Preservation and Perpetuation of Storytelling, Order Eastern Star, Kappa Kappa Iota (v.p. 1982-83), Sigma Alpha Iota (life), Chi Omega. Avocations: community theater and opera, travel, collecting hummels and plates. Home: PO Box 885 Rialto CA 92377-0885

JACKSON, BETTY L. DEASON, real estate developer; b. Wichita, Kans., Mar. 31, 1927; d. Orville John and Ida Mabel (Wolfe) Deason; m. James L. Jackson, July 2, 1966 (dec. Feb. 1983); children: Rebecca Lou, Jennifer Mae. AA, SW Baptist U., Bolivar, Mo., 1946; BA, Cen. Mo. State U., 1963; MA, U. Mo., 1964. Lic. realtor, Kans. Salesperson Sears, Kansas City, Mo., 1943-44; bookkeeping clk. Hallmark Cards, Kansas City, Mo., 1945-46; civil service Camp Pendleton, Oceanside, Calif., 1947; sec. Ford Motor Co., Kansas City, Mo., Jim Taylor Olds Co., Independence, Mo., 1952-54; tchr. Consol. Sch. Dist. #2, Mo., 1954-55, tchr. adminstr., 1963-78; owner mgr. B.J.'s Florist Car Wash Laundramat, Stockton, Mo., 1979-82; owner, ptnr. J and S Realty, Stockton, Mo., 1983—. Officer J-S Corp., Stockton, 1986-94. Mem. Nat. Assn. Realtors, Mo. C. of C., AARP, Greater Ozark Bd. Realtors. Democrat. Baptist. Avocations: play organ, piano, church clubs. Office: Coldwell Banker J-S Realty PO Box 159 Stockton MO 65785-0159 Home: 1600 Garfield St Apt 10 Enumclaw WA 98022-2278

JACKSON, CAROL, state legislator; m. Glen Jackson (dec.); 2 children. Grad. magna cum laude, Truett McConnell Coll.; degree in bus. adminstrn., North Ga. Coll. Owner trucking co., Cleveland, Ga.; clk. Superior Ct. White County, Ga., 1984-98; mem. 50th dist. Ga. State Senate, 1998—, sec. agr. com., vice-chmn. corrections, correctional instns./properties com. Mem. Cleveland C. of C., Rotary Club. Democrat. Office: 18 Capitol Sq SW Atlanta GA 30334-9003 also: PO Box 2246 Cleveland GA 30528-0040

JACKSON, CAROL E. federal judge; BA, Wellesley Coll., 1973; JD, U. Mich., 1976. With Thompson & Mitchell, St. Louis, 1976-83; counsel Mallinckrodt, Inc., St. Louis, 1983-85; magistrate U.S. Dist. Ct., Ea. Dist. Mo., 1986-92, dist. judge, 1992—. Adj. prof. law Washington U., St. Louis, 1989-92. Trustee St. Louis Art Mus., 1987-91; dir. bi-state chpt. ARC, 1989-91, Mo. Bot. Garden. Mem. Nat. Assn. Women Judges, Fed. Magistrate Judges Assn., Mo. Bar, St. Louis County Bar Assn., Bar Assn. Metro. St. Louis, Mound City Bar Assn., Lawyers Assn. St. Louis. Office: US Courthouse [illegible] Saint Louis MO 63101-2034

JACKSON, CHERYL ANN, music educator, director; b. Appleton City, Mo., Mar. 3, 1947; d. Woodrow Clifton and Orpha Mae Bray. BA in Music Edn., Ctrl. Mo. State U., Warrensburg, Mo., 1984, MA in Music Edn., 1989; PhD Music Edn., Mich. State U., East Lansing, 1996. Cert. instrumental and vocal music (K-12) Mo., music composite (K-12) S.D. Dir. music Deepwater (Mo.) Sch. Dist., 1970; dir. music Davis R-12 Sch. Dist., Clinton, Mo., 1979—81, Miami R-1 Sch. Dist., Amoret, Mo., 1984—87, Smithton R-6 Sch. Dist., Smithton, Mo., 1989—90; dir. bands Avon Sch. Dist4-1, Avon, SD, 1990—93; assoc. prof. music edn. Ea. Ky. U., Richmond, Ky., 1996—. Asst. music dir. First United Meth. Ch., Richmond, Ky., 1997—; private music instr., Richmond, 1963—. Contbr. articles to profl. jours. Member Ctrl. Ky. Concert Band, Lexington, 1998—. Grantee Collaborative Rsch. Grant, Ky. Music Educators Assn., 2000—01. Mem.: Coll. Music Soc., Music Educators Nat. Conf., Phi Delta Kappa Internat. (Ea. Ky. U. chpt.) (rep. Ednl. Found. 2000—02). Methodist. Avocations: sewing, travel. Office: Eastern Kentucky Univ 521 Lancaster Ave Richmond KY 40475

JACKSON, CLORA ELLIS, counselor, psychologist, educator; d. Scott and Ethel J. (Peeler) Ellis; m. Harold Coyage Jackson, Jr.; children: Sheriel, Lauren (dec.), Adrienne, Duaine. AA in Secretarial Sci., L.A. S.W. Coll., L.A., 1971; BS in Psychology, U. So. Calif., 1975, MS in Higher Edn., 1977; MS in Counseling, Calif. State U., Long Beach, 1979. Cert. psychologist 1981. Bus. edn. instr. Orange Coast Coll., Costa Mesa, Calif., 1979-80; tchr., counselor L.A. Unified Sch. Dist., 1977-81, sch. psychologist, 1981-83; tchr. bus. edn./math. Long Beach Unified Sch. Dist., 1983-90, counselor, 1990—99. Vol. Habitat for Humanity, 1990—. Mem. AAUW, Women in Arts, Pi Lambda Theta. Mem. Baha'i Faith.

JACKSON, CYNTHIA L. lawyer; b. Houston, May 6, 1954; BA, Stanford U., 1976; JD, U. Tex., 1979. Bar: Tex. 1979, Calif. 1980. Mem. Heller, Ehrman, White & McAuliffe, Palo Alto, Calif., 1983—99, Baker & McKenzie, Palo Alto, 1999—. Mem. ABA. Office: Baker & McKenzie 660 Hansen Way Palo Alto CA 94304-1044 Office Phone: 650-856-5572.

JACKSON, DONNA ANN, musician, piano instructor; b. Houston, Sept. 25, 1951; d. Gerald Averitt and Mary Patricia (Helton) Brewer. Student, Baylor U., 1969-71, U. Tex., 1971-72; MusB, Mont. State U., 1978; M Liberal Arts, Houston Bapt. U., 1990. Pianist, vocal coach Intermountain Opera Co., Bozeman, Mont., 1978-79; staff pianist Mont. State U., Bozeman, 1977-79; owner, operator Starnote Music, Brenham & Houston, 1981—; instr. piano Blinn Coll., Brenham, Tex., 1987-90; adminstr. devel. dept. Houston Grand Opera, Houston, 1991-93; organist Reid Meml. Meth. Ch., 1993-95. Creator, producer radio program Radio Central Artsguide, weekly, 1981-88. Organist, Brenham Presbyn. Ch., 1984-87; bd. dirs. Brenham Fine Arts League, 1984-87, Arts Coun. Washington County, Brenham, 1984-89; entertainment dir. Brenham Downtown Assn., 1987-88. Recipient Bronze medal Internat. Piano Recording Competition, 1985; Arts Achievement award Arts Coun. Washington County, 1989. Mem. Music Tchrs. Nat. Assn., Tex. Music Tchrs. Assn., Brenham Area Music Tchrs. Assn. (bd. dirs. 1984-90), Mensa. Democrat. Presbyterian. Avocations: baseball, opera, musical theater. Mailing: 1143 Peachford Ln Houston TX 77062 Office Phone: 281-486-7827.

JACKSON, DONNA E. legal secretary, administrative assistant; b. Washington, June 18, 1958; Cert. in secretarial scis., 1978. Mem. legal/adminstrv. support staff law firm, Washington, 1988—. Author: (cmty. newsletter) A Royal Priesthood A Chosen Generation, 1997. Vol. Nat. Coun. Negro Women, Washington, 2000. African Methodist Episcopalian/Baptist. Avocations: poetry, reading, sewing, mentoring. Personal E-mail: Essenceofroyalty@yahoo.com.

JACKSON, FELICIA DENISE, elementary school educator; d. Archie Jackson, Jr. and Necie Josephine (Anthony) Jackson; m. Mitchell Davis, July 11, 1992 (div. June 1997); m. Dwight E. Jones, Mar. 25, 2000; children: Krystal, Emanuel Jones. BA in Spanish, U. Houston, 1991; MA in Edn., Stephen F. Austin U., 1994. Cert. gifted/talented tchr., bilingual cert. Cheerleading coach Hambrick Mid. Sch., Houston, 2000—01. V.p. Dwight Jones Found., Spring, 2003; Bible sch. tchr. Champion Forest Bapt., Spring, Tex., 2001. Mem.: ATPE, Tex. Assn. Fgn. Lang. Tchrs., Suburban Houston Area Bilingual Educators (Tchr. of Yr. nominee 2002—03). Avocations: cooking, reading, bicycling, tutoring. Home: 17122 Silverthorne Ln Spring TX 77379 Office: Aldine Ind Sch Dist 160 Millstream Rd Houston TX 77060

JACKSON, FELICITY ANNE, performing arts organization administrator; b. Hitchin, Hertfordshire, Eng., Apr. 16, 1949; d. Brian John and Jacqueline Anne (Barnes) J. BA with honors, Cambridge U., Eng., 1970; B Philosophy, Exeter U., Eng., 1972. Planning coord. Glyndebourne Festival, Sussex, Eng., 1979-82; head artistic planning Nat. Opera, Brussels, 1982-84; casting mgr. Glyndebourne Festival, Sussex, Eng., 1988-90; casting cons. Leipzig Opera, Germany, 1990-92, Netherlands Opera, Amsterdam, Holland, 1990-92; artistic adminstr. Can. Opera Co., Toronto, Can., 1992-94; dir. artistic adminstrn. Glimmerglass Opera, N.Y., 1994-97; gen. mgr. European Union Opera, London, 1997-98. Casting cons. Fla. Grand Opera, 2000-01, dir. young artist studio, casting mgr., 2001—; artistic cons. Chgo. Opera Theater, 2000-01. Dir. Fla. Grand Opera Young Artist Studio. Avocations: canoeing, travel. E-mail: fjackson@fgo.org.

JACKSON, GERALDINE, entrepreneur; b. Barnesville, Ga., Oct. 30, 1934; d. Charles Brown and Christine (Maddox) J.; 1 child, Prentiss Andrew. Nurses aide Grady Hosp., Atlanta, 1953—54; mail handler U.S. Post Office, Cicero, Ill., 1966-70; sec., tour guide Walgreens Lab., Chgo., 1970-74; credit clk. Sterling Jewelers, Atlanta, 1974-2000; sec. Willie A. Watkins Funeral Home, Atlanta, 2000—. Mem. Nat. Law Enforcement Officer Meml. Fund; assoc. mem. presdl. task force Rep. Nat. Com.; active Sacred Heart League. Mem. AARP, DAV, NAACP, Nat. Assn. Police Orgn., Internat. Assn. Chief Police, Ga. Sheriff's Assn., Nat. Right to Life. Democrat. Home: 1890 Myrtle Dr SW Apt 422 Atlanta GA 30311-4954 Office Phone: 404-758-1731.

JACKSON, GLORIA LEIGH, genealogist, retired archivist; b. Milw., Aug. 24, 1929; d. Thurman Ralph Bailey and Beth Alice Goddard; m. Robert Morton Jackson, Apr. 14, 1951 (dec. Sept. 1993); children: Ann Elizabeth, Carol Jean, David Robert, Daniel Edwin, Douglas Scott. BA, U. Wis., LaCrosse, 1973. Profl. watercolorist, LaCrosse, 1965—80; libr. asst. U. Wis., LaCrosse, 1980—83; collections mgr., archivist LaCrosse Hist. Soc., 1983—93; cert. genealogist Chaseburg, Wis., 1997—. Author: John Goddard of Northeastern Wisconsin/Ancestors & Descendents, 1999 (State Hist. Soc. Wis. Gen. Book award, 2000), Descendants of Charles Bailey and Lydia Benton, 2002. Treas. bd. dirs. LaCrosse County Hist. Soc., 1994—96; treas. Eastbank Artists Assn., LaCrosse, 1978—80. Mem.: DAR (registrar and regent LaCrosse chpt. 1986—87), Soc. Mayflower Descendents (Wis. chpt.). Home: S2272 County Hwy K Chaseburg WI 54621

JACKSON, GUIDA MYRL, writer, magazine editor, book editor, publisher; b. Clarendon, Tex., Aug. 30; d. James Hurley and Ina (Benson) Miller; m. Prentice Lamar Jackson (div. Jan. 1986); children: Jeffrey Allen, William Andrew, James Tucker, Annabeth Broomall Davis; m. William Hervey Laufer, Feb. 14, 1986. BA, Tex. Tech U.; MA, Calif. State U., 1986; PhD, Greenwich U., 1990. Tchr. secondary sch. English, Houston Ind. Sch.

Dist., 1951-53, Ft. Worth Ind. Sch. Dist., 1953-54; pvt. tchr. music, freelance writer, Houston, 1956-71; editor newsletter Tex. Soc. Anesthesiologists, Austin, 1972-80; editor-in-chief Tex. Country mag., Houston, 1976-78; mng. editor Touchstone, lit. mag., Houston, 1976—. Contbg. editor Houston Town and Country mag., 1975—76; book editor Arte Publico, 1987—88; editor, pub. Panther Creek Press, 1999—; lectr. English U. Houston, 1986—95; instr. Montgomery Coll., 1996—; freelance writer, Houston, The Woodlands, Tex., 1978—. Author: (novels) Passing Through, 1979, A Common Valor, 1980, (play) The Lamentable Affair of the Vicar's Wife, 1989, (biog. reference) Women Who Ruled, 1990 (best reference lists award Libr. Jour. and Sch. Libr. Jour. 1990), (nonfiction) Virginia Diaspora, 1992, Virginia Diaspora CD-ROM, 2001, (lit. reference) Encyclopedia of Traditional Epic, 1994 (best reference list award ALA), (lit. reference) Traditional Epics: A Literary Companion, 1995, Encyclopedia of Literary Epics, 1996, (play) Showdown at Nosegay Cottage, 1997, (play) The Man From Tegucigalpa, 1998, (reference) Women Rulers Throughout the Ages, 1999, (play) Julia is Peculiar; editor: (anthologies) Heart to Hearth, 1989, African Women Write, 1990, Fall From Innocence, Memoirs of the Great Depression, 1998, (nonfiction) Legacy of the Texas Plains, 1994, Through the Cumberland Gap, 1995. Mem.: Houston Writers Consortium, Writers' Forum, Montgomery Lit. Arts Coun., Dramatists Guild, Woodland Writers Guild, Houston Writers Guild, PEN Ctr. West, Women in Comm. Avocations: music, gardening, poetry. Office: Panther Creek Press PO Box 130233 Spring TX 77393-0233 E-mail: panthercreek3@hotmail.com.

JACKSON, HANNAH BETH, state legislator; BA, Scripps Coll.; JD, Boston U. Atty. Santa Barbara (Calif.) County Dist. Atty. Office; pvt. practice; assembly mem. Calif. State, Santa Barbara. Chair State Commn. Status of Women; appointee Blue Ribbon Commn. Child Support Devel. and Enforcement; task force Family Equity, State Senate. Office: Calif State Assembly 101 W Anapamu St Ste A Santa Barbara CA 93101-3140 Fax: 805-564-1651. E-mail: assemblymember.Jackson@assembly.ca.gov.

JACKSON, HEATHER, secondary school educator; b. Kingston, Jamaica, Jan. 21, 1972; d. Balfoe and Beryl Jackson. BA, William Paterson U., 1991, MEd, 1998; EdD, Seton Hall U., 2003. Cert. secondary English tchr., student pers. svc., supr., prin., sch. adminstr. NJ. Subs. tchr. Paterson Bd. Edn., 1996—97, tchr., 1997—2000; kindergarten tchr. East Orange Little Phil. Sch., 1997—99; adminstr. Seton Hall U., South Orange, 1999—2000. Adj. prof. William Paterson U., Wayne, NJ, 1998—99. Mem.: Paterson Edn. Assn., N.J. Edn. Assn., Kappa Delta Pi. Avocations: writing, physical fitness, reading.

JACKSON, JACQUELYN C. federal agency administrator; BA, Howard U.; M in edn., Doctorate in edn., George Washington U. Dir. student achievement sch. accountability programs US Dept. Edn., Wash., 2002—; staff US Dept. Edn., Off. Spec. Edn. and Rehab. Svcs., Wash.; tchr., adminstr. Pub. Schs., DC; adj. prof. George Washington U., Wash.; tchr. Trinity Coll., U. DC, Wash., DC. Office: US Dep Edn Student Achievement Sch Accountability 400 Maryland Ave FOB-6 Rm 3W230 Washington DC 20202

JACKSON, JANE W. interior designer; b. Asheville, N.C., Aug. 5, 1944; d. James and Willie Mae (Stoner) Harris; m. Bruce G. Jackson; children: Yvette, Scott. Student, Boston U., 1964; BA, Leslie Coll., 1967; postgrad., Artisan Sch. Interior Design, 1980-82. Tchr. Montessori, Brookline, Mass., 1969-72; interior designer, owner Nettle Creek Shop, Honolulu, 1980 88; owner Wellesley Interiors, Honolulu, 1988—. Active Mayor's Com. for Small Bus., Honolulu, 1984. Mem. Honolulu Club. Democrat. Office: Wellesley Interiors PO Box 1622 Kaneohe HI 96744-1622 Office Phone: 808-261-6667.

JACKSON, JANET DAMITA JO, vocalist, dancer; b. Gary, Ind., June 16, 1966; d. Joseph and Katherine J.; m. James DeBarge, 1984 (div. 1985), m. René Elizondo, 1991 (div. 2000). Albums include Janet Jackson, 1982, Dream Street, 1984, Control, 1986, Rhythm Nation 1814, 1991, janet, 1993, Design of a Decade: 1986-1996, 1995, The Velvet Rope, 1997, All For You, 2001 (Grammy award, Best Dance Recording, 2002), Damita Jo, 2004; actress (TV series) Good Times, 1977-1979, A New Kind of Family, 1979, Diff'rent Strokes, 1981-1982, 1984, Fame, 1984-1985; (films) Poetic Justice, 1993 (Academy award nomination Best Original Song 1993), Nutty Professor II: The Klumps, 2000. Recipient 6 Am. Music awards, 1987, 1988, 1991, 5 Grammy nominations, MTV Video Vanguard award, 1990, Grammy award, Best R&B song 1994 for "That's the Way Love Goes" with Terry Lewis and James Harris III; MTV Best Female Video for "If". Office: Creative Artists Agency 9830 Wilshire Blvd Beverly Hills CA 90212-1825*

JACKSON, JANET ELIZABETH, city attorney, association executive; b. Randolph, Va. d. Robert and Joan (Morton) J.; 1 child, Harrison Michael Sewell. BA, Wittenberg U., 1975; JD, George Washington U., 1978. Bar: Ohio 1978, U.S. Dist. Ct. (so. dist.) Ohio 1979, U.S. Dist. Ct. (no. dist.) Ohio 1983. Asst. atty. gen. Office Ohio Atty. Gen., Columbus, 1978-80, chief crime victims compensation sect., 1980-82, chief workers compensation and civil rights sects., 1983-87; with Sindell, Sindell & Rubenstein, Cleve., 1982-83; judge Franklin County Mcpl. Ct., Columbus, 1987-97; city atty. City of Columbus, 1997—. Atty. gen.'s ethics and profl. responsibility adv. coun.; joint task force gender bias Ohio Supreme Ct. and Ohio State Bar Assn.; mem. com. to study impact of substance abuse on cts., Supreme Ct., 1989-90. Chair bd. trustees YWCA, 1988-95; vice-chair bd. trustees, mem. exec. com. United Way Franklin County; chair Right from the Start Community Forum; bd. dirs. Met. Women's Ctr., 1980-86, S.E. Community Mental Health Ctr., 1987, Columbus Urban League, 1987-90, Maryhaven, 1987-89, Riverside Meth. Hosp.; trustee Wittenberg U.; chair task force child care City of Columbus; vol. Columbus Pub. Schs.; past mem., chairperson Minority Task force on AIDS; mem. AIDS community adv. coalition, 1987-90, task force domestic violence, 1988; mem. svc. team Explorer Divsn. Boy Scouts Am.; trustee Franklin U. Recipient Sharon Wilkin award Met. Women's Ctr., Dr. Martin Luther King Jr. Humanitarian award Love Acad., 1987, Polit. Leadership award 29th Dist. Citizens' Caucus, 1987, Citizenship award Omega Psi Phi, 1987, Outstanding Accomplishments award Franklin County Dem. Women, 1988, Community Svc. award Met. Dem. Women's Club, 1989, Warren Jennings award Franklin County Mental Health Bd., 1989, Martin Luther King Jr. Humanitarian award Columbus Edn. Assn., 1991, Women of Achievement award YWCA, 1992, Citizen's award Columbus Assn. Edn. Young Children, 1993, Citations award Pi Lambda Theta, 1993, Blue Chip award Social Svcs., 1994, Peacemaker award Choices, David D. White award Black Alumni Assn. Capitol Law Sch., Cmty. Svc. award Columbus-Franklin County AFL-CIO. Mem. Internat. Mcpl. Lawyers Assn. (state chmn., mem. steering com. legislation and pub. policy and mgmt.), Nat. Conf. Black Lawyers (Disting. Barrister award 1988, John Mercer Langston award 1994), Ohio State Bar Assn. (coun. dels. 1993—, commn. racial and ethnic fairness, bd. govs. women in the profession sect.), Columbus Bar Assn., Women Lawyers Franklin County, The Links, Inc. (pres. Twin Rivers chpt. 1992-94), Columbus Mortar Bd. Alumni Club, Golden Key Nat. Honor Soc. (hon.). Office: Columbus City Atty City Hall 90 W Broad St Rm 200 Columbus OH 43215-9013

JACKSON, JEANNE PELLEGREN, apparel executive; b. Denver, Aug. 10, 1951; d. John James and Barbara (Grove) Pellegren; m. Douglas Emmett Jackson, Nov. 23, 1984; children: Lindsay, Craig. BS in Fin., U. Colo., 1974; MBA, Harvard Bus. Sch., 1978. Buyer, mgr. Bullocks Dept. Stores, L.A., 1978-85; sr. v.p. merchandise mgr. to sr. v.p. direct mail pvt. brands Saks Fifth Ave., N.Y.C., 1985-89; sr. v.p. merchandising Walt Disney Attractions, Orlando, 1989-92; exec. v.p. merchandising Victoria's Secret, Columbus, Ohio, 1992-95; CEO Banana Republic, 1996-2000, Wal-Mart.com, 2000—. Instr. mktg. U. So. Calif., L.A., 1979-81; adv. bd. Navy Exch., Norfolk, Va., 1991—. Bd. dirs. Orlando Mus. Art, 1990-92. Republican. Avocations: skiing, tennis. Office: Walmartcom 135 Constitution Dr Menlo Park CA 94025

JACKSON, JEWEL, retired state agency administrator; b. June 3, 1942; d. Willie Burghardt and Bernice Jewel (Mayberry) Norton; children: Steven, June Kelly, Michael, Anthony. With Calif. Youth Authority, 1965-91, group supr., 1965-67, youth counselor Ventura, 1967-78, sr. youth counselor Stockton, 1978-81, parole agt., 1986, treatment team supr., program mgr. Whittier & Ione, 1981-91; ret., 1991. Pres. Valley Paralegal Svc., Stockton. Past bd. dirs. Samuel Hancock Christian Sch.; past pres. San Joaquin Valley Girls Horsewomen's Assn. Mem. Internat. Egg Art Guild. Avocations: reading, horseback riding, decorative egg art, decoupage. Home and Office: PO Box 8267 Stockton CA 95208-0267 Office Phone: 209-712-9744. E-mail: juul@jps.net.

JACKSON, KATE, actress; b. Birmingham, Ala., Oct. 29, 1949; d. Hogan and Ruth Jackson; m. Andrew Stevens, Aug. 23, 1978 (div. 1981); m. David Greenwald, 1982 (div. 1984). Student, U. Miss.; student, Birmingham U.; grad., Am. Acad. Dramatic Arts, 1971. Worked as model. Appeared in TV series Dark Shadows, 1966-71, The Rookies, 1972-76, Charlie's Angels, 1976-79, The Scarecrow and Mrs. King, 1983-87, Baby Boom, 1988-89; TV appearances include Movin' On, The Jimmy Stewart Show; TV movies include: Satan's School for Girls, 1973, Death Cruise, 1974, Killer Bees, 1974, Death Scream, 1975, Charlie's Angels, 1976, Death at Love House, 1976, James at 15, 1977, Topper, 1979, Inmates: A Love Story, 1981, Thin Ice, 1981, Listen to Your Heart, 1983, The Stranger Within, 1990, Quiet Killer, 1992, Homewrecker, 1992, Adrift, 1993, Empty Cradle, 1993, The Shrine of Lorna Love, 1993, Arly Hanks, 1993, Armed and Innocent, 1994, Justice in a Small Town, 1994, The Silence of Adultery, 1995, The Cold Heart of a Killer, 1996, A Kidnapping in a Family, 1996, New Passages, 1996, Panic In the Skies, 1996, What Happened to Bobby Earl, 1997, Sweet Deceptions, 1998, Satan's School for Girls, 2000, A Mother's Testimony, 2001, Miracle Dogs, 2003; motion picture appearances include: Dirty Tricks, 1981, Making Love, 1982, Loverboy, 1989, Error in Judgement, 1998, Larceny, 2004; dir. numerous episodes The Scarecrow and Mrs. King. Recipient 3 Emmy award nominations Nat. Acad. TV Arts and Scis. Mem. AFTRA, Screen Actors Guild, Actors Equity Assn., Dirs. Guild Am. Office: care Triad Artists Inc 10100 Santa Monica Blvd 16th Fl Los Angeles CA 90067*

JACKSON, KATHY MERLOCK, communications educator; b. Pitts., Aug. 27, 1955; d. Anthony Jacob and Irvia Josephine (Fasano) Merlock; m. Joe William Jackson Jr., Aug. 6, 1983; 1 child, Nicholas. BA, W.Va. U., 1977; MA, Ohio State U., 1979; PhD, Bowling Green State U., 1984. Tchg. assoc. dept. English Ohio State U., Columbus, 1977—79; employment counselor QPA Pers. Cons., Boston, 1979; rschr., writer Office R&D Tufts U., Medford, Mass., 1979—81; rschr. Smithsonian Instn., Divsn. Transp., Nat. Mus. Am. History, Washington, 1982; tchg. fellow depts. speech comm. and English Bowling Green (Ohio) State U., 1981—83, rsch. cons. Office of Devel., Mileti Alumni Ctr., 1982—83; prof. and coord. comm. Va. Wesleyan Coll., Norfolk, 1984—. Rsch. cons. Rsch. Comm., Ltd., Boston, 1986—89. Author: Image of Children in American Film, 1986, Walt Disney: A Bio-Bibliography, 1993; contbg. writer, columnist: Portfolio Mag., 2000—; editor: Jour. Am. Culture; contbr. articles to profl. jours. Active PTA, Virginia Beach, Va., 1995—2003. Grantee, Mednick Found. Va., 1986, 2000. Mem.: Am. Culture Assn. (bd. mem. 1991—95, recorder 1995—99, v.p. 1999—2001, pres. 2001—03). Democrat. Roman Catholic. Avocations: cooking, traveling. Home: 3948 Shady Oaks Dr Virginia Beach VA 23455 Office: Va Wesleyan Coll 1584 Wesleyan Dr Norfolk VA 23502

JACKSON, LAUREN, professional basketball player; b. Australia, May 11, 1981; Profl. basketball player Seattle Storm, 2001—. Mem. Gems team Jr. World Championships, 1997; mem. WNBL Championship team, 2000. Named 3d internat. player selected 1st overall 5 yr. history, WNBA, 1 of 3 Australian players chosen in 1st round, All-Star Five Selection, WNBL, 2000, League's Most Valuable Player, WNBA, 2000, res. Western Conf. team, WNBA All-Star Game, Orlando, 2001, All-Star Five Selection, WNBL, 2001, First Round Draft Pick, WNBA, 2001, res. All-Star Team, 2001; recipient Olympics Silver medalist, 2000. Office: Seattle Sonics and Storm 351 Elliott Ave W Ste 500 Seattle WA 98119 E-mail: StormFans@sonics-storm.com.

JACKSON, LINDA B. social worker; b. N.Y.C., Feb. 16, 1956; d. Willie Chelsea Jackson, Fannie Mae Jackson; children: Athena Johnson, Alethea, Althea, Walter. BSW, Mercy Coll., 1986; FDC tng., Cornell U., 2002. Social worker Peekskill City Sch. Dist., Peekskill, NY, 1987—. Author: Poetry From the Soul; author: (poetry) Titanic, 2001 (Pres.'s award). Recipient Famous Poets award, 2002, Shakespeare trophy of excellence, Poet of Yr. medallion, 2002. Mem.: Poetry Soc. Am. Avocation: writing. Home: 218 N James St Peekskill NY 10566-2848

JACKSON, LOLA HIRDLER, art educator; b. Faribault, Minn., Mar. 2, 1942; d. Earl Arthur and Marian Barbara (Pavek) Hirdler; children: Carilyn, Cherilyn, Marc. BS in Art Edn., Mankato State U., 1972, MA, 1975. Cert. tchr.; nat. bd. cert. tchr. Instr. art YWCA, Mankato, 1968-70; art instr. Mankato Area Vocat. Tech. Inst., 1971-72; pres., tchr., art dir. Jackson Studios, Mankato, 1969-78; art tchr. New Richland (Minn.) High Sch., Mankato (Minn.) State U., 1973-74; pres. Lola Ltd. Lt'ee Art Distbn., N.C., 1976—; tchr. art Lincoln Sch. Math. and Sci. Tech., Greensboro, NC, 1988—90, chmn. dept., 1988, 89-90; tchr., chmn. art dept. Shallotte Mid. Sch., 1990—; instr. art Brunswick C.C., Supply, N.C., 1990-92; co-owner, pres. Jackson Carpenter Galleries, Ltd., Little River, S.C., 1997-99. Staff artist The Reporter, 1970-73; pres., bd. dirs. Fine Arts Inc., Gallery 500, Mankato, 1972-75. Bd. mem. Mankato Area Found., 1976-83. Recipient award Busch Found. Minn. Arts Coun., Nat. Endowment Arts, 1974. Mem. Profl. Pictures Framers Assn., N.C. Assn. of Edn. Republican. Roman Catholic. Avocations: stamp collecting, botany, birdwatching, biking, ballroom dancing.

JACKSON, MARY L. health services executive; b. Phila., June 25, 1938; d. John Francis and Helen Catherine (Peranteau) Martin; m. Howard Clark Jackson III, Dec. 17, 1954; children: Michael, Mark, Brian, Bert. Student, Bucks County C.C., 1977-83. Asst. mgr. retail divsn. Sears Roebuck & Co., Bensalem, Pa., 1972-77; educator, adminstr., dir. Trevos Behavior Modification Program, Pa., 1975—, leadership tng. workshops, 1979—. Participant rsch. studies in field; salesman Makefield Real Estate, Morrisville, Pa., 1977-78; mortgage fin. cons. Tom Dunphy Real Estate, Feasterville, Pa., 1978-81; weight loss cons., Hulmeville, Pa., 1984—, also TV and radio appearances on behavior modification for weight loss and maintenance. Co-author: The Official Calorie Book; pub., columnist monthly newsletter The Modifier, 1977—; pub. several studies in weight loss field; pub. co-author multi-studies in field. Recipient Chapel of Four Chaplain award, 1977. Mem. Assn. Advancement Behavior Therapy, Bucks County Bd. Realtors, Hulmeville Hist. Soc. (founder, charter mem.). Democrat. Presbyterian. Avocations: reading, classical music, speed walking, knitting, fishing. Home: 218 Main St Hulmeville PA 19047-5635

JACKSON, MILLIE, vocalist, songwriter, playwright, producer; b. Thomson, Ga., July 15, 1944; div.; children: Keisha, Jerroll. Sec., 1971-82; represented by Spring Records. Performer Harlem's Crystal Ballroom, 1964; founder Keishval Enterprises, Inc., Atlanta; singer evenings and weekends, 1964-72; prodr., mgr. Recordings include Millie, 1973, Caught Up, 1974, Still Caught Up, 1975, Free and In Love, 1976, Lovingly Yours, 1976, Get It Out'cha System, 1978, A Moment's Pleasure, 1979, Royal Rappin', 1979, Live and Uncensored, 1979, I Had to Say It, 1980, For Men Only, 1980, Just a Little Bit Country, 1981, Live and Outrageous, 1982, Hard Times, 1982, ESP, 1984, An Imitation of Love, 1987, Back to the S--t, 1989, Young Man, Older Woman, 1992, The Very Best! of Millie Jackson, 1994, Rock N' Soul, 1994. Named Best Female Rhythm and Blues Vocalist, Cash Box, 1973. Office: Keishval Enterprises Inc 133 Cedar Ln Teaneck NJ 07666-4416 also: Ichiban Records Ste 712 1791 Blount Rd Pompano Beach FL 33069-5133

JACKSON, NANCY MORRISON, architect; b. Pitts., Aug. 15, 1922; d. Robert Kirk and Marcella Genevieve (Pfendler) Morrison; m. George Clark Jackson, Aug. 25, 1945; children: Ellen Jackson Rudy, Robert Clark, Mary Jackson Porter. BArch, Carnegie Mellon U., 1946. Arch. Prack & Prack, Pitts., 1942, Kaiser, Neal & Reid, Pitts., 1943—44, Marks & Simboli, Pitts., 1947, Edward C. Roock, Syracuse, NY, 1958, Austin-Mead, Hartford, Conn., 1967—70, Kane Farrel White, 1970—72; pvt. practice Farmington, Conn., 1972—78; gen. svcs. adminstrn. Washington, 1978—. Mem. Nat. Archtl. Accrediting Bd.; citations U.S. State Dept. Mem. admissions coun. Carnegie Mellon U.; mem. Cath. Family Svcs., Commn. for Ecumenical Affairs, Conn. Mem.: AIA (Masterspec rev. com.), Am. Arbitration Assn. (constrn. industry arbitrator), Conn. Soc. Arch. Bd., Arts Club of Washington, Kappa Alpha Theta. Roman Catholic. Home: 1307-3 E Abingdon Dr Alexandria VA 22314

JACKSON, NICOLE RENÉE, mechanical engineer, educator; b. Cleve., July 15; d. Eddie and Juliette Jackson. BS in Mech. Engring., N.C. State U., Raleigh, 1988, M in Materials Sci. and Engring., 1998. engr. in tng., N.C. Follow up svcs. engr. Underwriters Labs., Research Triangle Park, N.C., 1989-90; sr. mfg. engr., Advanced Mfg. Tech., Delphi Chassis, Dayton, Ohio, 1996-97, Sandusky, Ohio, 1998-99; sr. brake systems engr. Delphi Chassis-Energy, Brighton, Mich., 1999—; advanced tech. platform mgr. Robert Bosch, 2003. Instr. N.C. State U., 1997. Contbr. articles to profl. jours. Mem. membership com. Nat. Bus. League, Dayton, 1992-93; tutor Edn. Partnership with Patterson H.S., Dayton, 1993-95; vol. Jr. Achievement, 1998; co-dir. GM-Wright Steep program for mentoring young engrs., 1991-92. Gem fellow, 1996. Mem. SAE, Am. Soc. Metals, NOW, Internat. Platform Assn., Sierra Club. Avocations: reading, travel, business ventures, public speaking, writing.

JACKSON, NONA ARMOUR, writer, illustrator; b. Denison, Tex., Sept. 22, 1939; d. Thomas Jefferson and Novella Mae (Binion) A.; m. R.L. Jackson, Jr., Apr. 16, 1966. Supr., illustrator Diaper Jeans, Inc., Denison, 1959-62; clothing pattern maker, designer Srader's Sportswear, Denison, 1963-65; receptionist Glad Tidings Ch., Sherman, Tex., 1981-84, pastor elderly ministry, 1984-87; author Pottsboro, Tex., 1987—. Spkr. in field. Author, illustrator, photographer: The Cotton Mill! Can Anything Good Come from There? Vol. I-IX, 1995, Industries 1873-1981, Vol. I, 1995, Churches 1906-1991, vol. II 1995, Schools 1890-1964, vol. III, 1995, Golden Rule Independent School Extra-Curricular Activities, vol. IV, 1995, Cotton Mill Community, vol. V, 1995, The People: A Biography in Three Volumes, Vols. VI-VIII, 1995, Associates, Vol. IX, Index, Vols. VI-IX, 1995, Vol. X, 2001, Addenda, 1998-2001; author, illustrator: Pioneers of North West Grayson County, Texas Mid to Late 19th Century and Early 20th Century: Delaware Bend, Red Branch/Prairie Valley, Rock Creek with Some Dexter, Texas Data, 1996, Pioneers of Central Grayson County, Texas Mid to Late 19th Century and Early 20th Century: Cherrymound and Ambrose, 1996, Pioneers of Central Grayson County, Texas Mid to Late 19th Century and Early 20th Century: Cedar Community, 1996, Pioneers of South East Grayson County, Texas Mid to Late, 19th Century and Early 20th Century: Pilot Grove, 1996, Series 1 (4000 B.C.-A.D. 1607) The Overseas Connection, Big Oaks from Little Trees Grow, vols. I-III, 2000, Series 2 (A.D. 1607-A.D. 1837) Immigrant & Colonial Ancestors, vols. IV-VIII, 2000, Series 3 (A.D. 1937-A.D. 1987) A Grayson County, Texas Epic-One Hundred and Fifty Years, vols. IX-XV, 2000, Series 4 (A.D. 1855-A.D. 1991), Twentieth Century-Big Oaks-Precious Memories, vols. XVI-XVII, 2000, Series 5-10 The Collective Works of Nona Jackson vols. XVIII-XXXIX, 2000, Series 11, Jesus or Die!, Father, Son & Holy Ghost, Obedience, and Walking With God, vols. XL-XLII, 2000, Yummy, Yummy, Sweets for the Tummy, 2002, Pass the Taters Please, 2002, Me, Myself & I, 2002, My Split Apart, vol. 59, 2002, The Final Chapter-Part I, The Cotton Mill! Can Anything Good Come From There?, 2002, Addenda-Part II, Nona's Family Update: The Last Report, vol. 60, 2002; contbr. articles and photographs to pubs. Sec., treas., young people's supt. Sunnyside Bapt. Ch., Denison, 1963-65; Sunday sch. tchr. Glad Tidings Ch., Sherman, 1978-83; tour guide, hostess Grayson County Frontier Village, Inc., Denison, 1978-97; active Adopt a Nursing Home, Tex. Dept. Human Resources, 1999— Mem. Grayson County Humane Soc., Nat. Audubon Soc., Nat. Trust Hist. Preservation, Libr. Congress Assoc. (charter). Republican. Avocations: guitar, art, nature, theology, genealogy. Home: Unit 1 109 Houston Ave Pottsboro TX 75076-3031

JACKSON, REBECCA R. lawyer; b. Ark., 1942; BA magna cum laude, St. Louis U., 1975, JD, 1978. Bar: Mo. 1978, Ill. 1979. Ptnr. Bryan Cave, St. Louis. Mem. ABA. Office: Bryan Cave One Met Sq 211 N Broadway Saint Louis MO 63102-2733

JACKSON, RENÉE BERNADETTE, English language educator; b. York, Pa., July 20, 1954; d. William Brice and Helen Elizabeth (Webb) J.; 1 child, Karla Janine. BA in Comm., Pa. State Harrisburg, Middletown, 1995, MA in Humanities, 1997; postgrad., Temple U., 1997—. Newsroom intern, journalist Harrisburg Patriot News, 1995; newsroom intern, corr. York (Pa.) Daily Record, 1995-96; rsch. asst. for coord. Master's Humanities Program Pa. State Harrisburg, Middletown, 1995-97; adj. prof. Harrisburg Area C.C., 1997; tchg. asst. African-Am. studies Temple U., Phila., 1997, rsch. asst. broadcasting, telecom. and mass media dept., 1998; adj. English prof. C.C. of Phila., 1999—; GMAT essay evaluator Educl. Testing Svc., Princeton, N.J., 1998—. Mem. AAUW, Assn. for Edn. in Journalism and Mass Comm., Am. Journalism Historians Assn., Nat. Assn. Black Journalists, Assn. for the Study of Afro-Am. Life and History, Assn. Black Women Historians, Soc. Profl. Journalists, Middle-Atlantic Popular Culture Conf. (exec. bd. mem., mem. planning com.). Avocations: historical writing projects, composing piano music, travel. Home: 107 Shelbourne Dr York PA 17403-3821

JACKSON, RHONDA, telecommunications professional, poet; b. NYC; d. William Aaron and Emmeline Jackson; m. Ronald Anthony Nurse. AAS, Berkeley Coll., 1995; BA, NYU, 1998. Telecom. tech. assoc. Bell Atlantic, N.Y.C., 1980—; pres. Poetress Music, Fresh Meadows, N.Y., 1997—. Exec. dir. Excelsior Multicultural Inst., St. Albans, N.Y., 1997—; amb. People to People, Spokane, Wash., 2000—. Author: The Best Poems of 1997, 1997 (Editors Choice award 1997), Daybreak on the Land, 1997 (Editors Choice award 1997), The Line, 1998, Quiet Moments, 1999. Big sister Big Bros., Big Sisters, NYC, 1997; bd. dirs. Internat. Ambs., Raleigh, N., 1999; events coord. City Harvest, NYC, 1999; tutor English and math. Literacy Ptnrs., NYC, 2000; sec.-gen. United Cultural Conv., 2001; pres. Ophelia DeVore Alumni Performing Co., 2001; del. Nat. Writers Assn., 2001; senator World Nations Congress, 2003. Recipient Outstanding Achievement in Poetry, Famous Poets Soc., Ashland, Oreg., 1999, Pres. award for lit. excellence Nat. Authors Registry, Ohio, 2000, Diamond Homer trophy, 1999, Internat. Peace prize United Cultural Conv., 2002; named Poet of Yr., Famous Poets Soc., Ashland, 2000; inductee Internat. Poetry Hall of Fame, Internat. Soc. Poets, Owings Mills, Md., 1998, Profl. Bus. Women's Hall of Fame, 2003, Internat. Honor Soc., others; honored as one of 500 Living Legends in the World, 2002. Mem. NARAS, Nat. Writers Union, Assn. for Telecom. Execs., Songwriters Guild Am., Nat. Acad. Am. Poets, Assn. Women in Radio and TV. Home: PO Box 650136 Fresh Meadows NY 11365 E-mail: contactus@witww.org.

JACKSON, ROBBI JO, agricultural products executive, lawyer; b. Nampa, Idaho, Apr. 12, 1959; d. William R. Jackson and Marilyn K. Samp Jackson Nunez. BS in Fin., U. Colo., Boulder and Denver, 1981; JD, U. Denver, 1987, LLM in Taxation, 1990. Bar: Colo. 1988. Asst. office mgr. Jerome Karsh & Co., Denver, 1982; office mgr. Almirall & Assocs., [illegible] 1988-89; assoc. Moye, Giles, O'Keefe, Vermeire & Gorrell, Denver, 1989-90, Holme Roberts & Owen, Denver, 1990-92; in-house gen. counsel Cmty. Corrections Svcs., Denver, 1992-96; CEO Enviro Cons. Svc., LLC, Lakewood, Colo., 1996—. Mem. staff Adminstrv. Law Rev., Denver, 1985, editor, 1985, mng. editor, 1986-87; co-author course of study materials; presenter in field. Mem. fin. com. Mile-High chpt. ARC, Denver, 1990-92; food delivery person Vols. of Am., Meals-on-Wheels, Denver, 1990-92. Recipient scholarships. Mem.: ABA, Colo. Bar Assn. (chmn. ethics com. 2003—04). Republican. Avocations: running marathons and other races, biking, hiking, swimming, piano and organ playing. Office Phone: 303-238-4637.

JACKSON, ROSA M. retired elementary school educator; b. Columbia, S.C., Dec. 8, 1943; d. Alvin Jr. and Rosa Lee (Reese) Oree; m. Olin D. Jackson, June 14, 1969; children: Zandra Lalita, Delin Jawaski. BA, Benedict Coll., 1966; MEd, S.C. State U., Orangeburg, 1981. Cert. tchr. Tchr. 1st grade Richmond County Bd. Edn., Augusta, Ga.; tchr. 2nd grade McDuffie County Bd. Edn., Thomson, Ga.; tchr. 5th grade Lancaster County Bd. Edn., Kershaw; tchr. 2nd grade Richmond County Bd. Edn., Augusta, Ga. Mem. Richmond County Schs. Leadership Team. Sci. tchr. in residence. Mem. GAE, RCAE, NEA, Nat. Sci. Tchrs Assn., Ga. Sci. Tchrs. Assn., Ga. Staff Devel. Coun., Assn. for Multicultural Sci. Edn. Home: 3003 Bramble Wood Trl Augusta GA 30909-4105

JACKSON, RUTH MOORE, academic administrator; b. Potecasi, N.C., Sept. 27, 1938; d. Jesse Thomas and Ruth Estelle (Futrell) Moore; m. Roderick Earle Jackson, Aug. 14, 1965; 1 child, Eric Roderick. BS in Bus., Hampton Inst., 1960; MSLS, Atlanta U., 1965; PhD, Ind. U., 1976. Asst. edn. libr. Va. State U., Petersburg, Va., 1965-66, head reference dept., 1966-67, asst. prof., 1976-77, assoc. prof., program coord., 1977-84, interim dept. chair, 1978-79; teaching fellow Ind. U., Bloomington, Ind., 1968, vis. lectr., 1971-72; asst. dir. librs. U. N. Fla., Jacksonville, 1984-88; dean univ. librs. W.Va. U., Morgantown, W.Va., 1988—, asst. to provost libr. outreach programs. Pers. cons. Va. State U., 1980; archival cons. N.C. Ctrl. U., Durham, N.C., 1984-85; automation cons. W.Va. Acad. Libr. Consortium, 1991—; co-prin. investigator State-Wide Electronic Libr. Network (Project Infomine), 1994-98. Editor: W.Va. U. Press, 1990—; contbr. to books. Active Big Brother/Big Sister of Am., Jacksonville, Fla., 1985-88; den leader Boy Scouts of Am., Petersburg, Va., 1976-78. U.S. Office Edn. fellow, 1968-71, Rsch. fellow So. Fellowships Found., 1973-74; recipient Outstanding Alumni award Hampton Inst., 1980, Non-Italian Woman of Yr. award, 1992, Disting. West Virginian award Gov. W.Va., 1992. Mem. NAFE, ALA, Southeastern Libr. Assn. (mem. standing com.), Assn. Coll. and Rsch. Librs. (mem. standing com., mem. Fla. chpt.), W.Va. Libr. Assn., Libr. Info. Tech. Assn., Coalition for Networked Info., Coun. of State Univ. Librs. (founding mem.), Addison-Wesley Higher Edn. Tech. Bd., Alpha Kappa Alpha. Democrat. Roman Catholic. Avocations: walking, sightseeing, collecting rare coins and artifacts. Office: WVa Univ Main Libr PO Box 6069 Morgantown WV 26506-6069 Home: Apt 301 2931 N Governeour St Wichita KS 67226-1782

JACKSON, SANDRA WILLETT, marketing professional; d. William and Margaret Willett; m. Neal Andrews Jackson. BA, Wesley Coll, 1976; MPA, Harvard U. JFK Sch. Govt., Cambridge, 1976; cert. (hon.), Inst. des Scis. Politiques, 1964, Meyers Briggs, 1995. Dir. consumer edn. U.S. Office Consumer Affairs, Washington, 1971—76; exec. dir. Nat. Consumers League, 1976—83; v.p. consumer affairs John Hancock Life Ins., Boston, 1983—92; country dir. U.S. Peace Corps, Budapest, Hungary, 1992—95; spl. rep. comml. bus. affairs U.S. Dept. State, Washington, 1998—2001; co-founder, pres. Strategies Structures Internat., 2001—; pres. Vital Voices Global Partnership, 2003—. Exec. dir. Copley Square Centennial Com., 1985—92; bd. dir. Planned Parenthood League, Boston, 1988—91, Dumbarton Concerts, Inner City Inner Child, 1997—; bd. pres., founder Hope Children Vietnam, Washington, 2001—. Named U.S. Minimum Wage Study Commr., Washington, 1978—81; recipient Malcom Baldrige Quality award, Examiner, 1988—90. Avocations: pottery, sailing, gardening, photography, hiking. Home: 3408 Reservoir RD NW Washington DC 20007

JACKSON, SHIRLEY ANN, academic administrator, physicist; b. Wash., D.C., Aug. 5, 1946; d. George Hiter and Beatrice (Cosby) Jackson; m. Morris A. Washington; 1 child, Alan. BS in Physics, MIT, 1968, PhD, 1973; DSc (hon.), Bloomfield Coll., 1991, Fairleigh Dickinson U., 1993; LLD (hon.), Villanove, 1996. Rsch. assoc. Fermi Nat. Accelerator Lab, Batavia, Ill., 1973—76; mem. tech. staff AT&T Bell Labs, Murray Hill, NJ, 1976—91; prof. physics Rutgers U., Piscataway, NJ, 1991—95; chairperson Nuclear Reg. Commn., 1995—99; U.S. Rep. to Gen. Conf. Internat. Atomic Energy, 1995—99; pres. Rensselaer Poly. Tech., 1999—. Vis. scientist European Orgn. Nuclear Rsch., Geneva, 1974—75; visitor Stanford Linear Accelerator Ctr., 1976, Aspen Ctr. Physics, 1976—77; mem. com. edn. and employment women in sci. and engring. Nat. Rsch. Coun., 1980—95, cons., 1977—91, NSF, 1977; mem. ednl. coun. MIT, 1976—80, Internat. Nuclear Regulators Assn., 1997—99; bd. trustees Lincoln U., Pa., 1980—, exec. com., 1985—92; bd. trustees Rutgers U., 1986—, bd. gov., mem. ednl. planning and policy com., 1990; bd. trustees Associated U., Inc., 1993, Brookings Instn., 2000; trustee Georgetown U., Rockefeller U., Emma Willard Sch., Troy, NY; mem. bd. dirs. NY Stock Exchange, 2003—; mem. Coun. Fgn. Rels.; mem. exec. com. Coun. Competitiveness; coun. mem. Govt.-U.-Industry Rsch. Roundtable; dir. NJ. Resources Group, Pub. Svc. Enterprise Group, PSE&G, FedEx Corp., AT&T Corp., Marathon Oil Corp., Medtronic, Inc.; life mem. bd. trustees MIT Corp.; mem. Nat. Adv. Coun. Biomedical Imaging and Bioengineering, Nat. Inst. Health (NIH); US Comptroller-Gen. adv. com. Govt. Acctg. Office (GAO). Editl. adv. bd. (jour.) Jour. Sci. Tech. and Human Values, 1982; contbr. articles to physics jours. Mem. NJ Commn. Sci. and Tech., Com. Status Women in Physics, 1986—88. Named one of Top 50 Women in Sci., Discover mag., 2002, 50 Most Inspiring African Am., pub. book, ESSENCE, 2002, 50 R&D Stars to Watch, Industry Week mag., 2002; named to Nat. Women's Hall Fame, 1998, Women Tech. Internat. Found. Hall Fame (WITI), 2000; recipient Candace award, Nat. Coalition 100 Black Women, Salute to Policy Makers award, Exec. Women NJ, 1986, Black Achievers in Industry award, Harlem YMCA, 1986, NJ Gov.'s award, 1993, 100 Women Excellence award, Albany-Colonie Regional C. of C. and Women's Bus. Coun., 2000, eLeadership award, Ctrl. NY Tech. Devel. Orgn. and CASE Ctr., Syracuse U., 2000, Golden Torch award for Lifetime Acheivement in Academia, Nat. Soc. Black Engrs., 2000, Richtmyer Meml. Lecture award, Am. Assn. Physics Tchrs., 2001, Immortal award, 15th Annual Black History Makers award, Associated Black Charities, 2001, Black Engr. Yr. award, US Black Engr. and Info. Tech. mag., 2001; fellow, Ford Found., 1971—73; grantee, 1974—75; trainee, NSF, 1968—71. Fellow: Am. Acad. Arts and Scis., Am. Phys. Soc. (mem. com. status of women in physics 1986); mem.: AAAS Am. Assn. Advancement Sci. (com. sci., freedom and responsibility, pres. 2004), Nat. Acad. Engring., Nat. Soc. Black Physicists (pres. 1980—82), Nat. Inst. Sci., NY Acad. Scis., MIT Alumni Assn. (v.p. 1986), Delta Sigma Theta, Sigma Xi. Office: Rensselaer Polytechnic, Pres Office 3031 Troy Bldg, 3rd Fl 110 8th St Troy NY 12180-3590*

JACKSON, SUSANNE LEORA, retired creative placement firm executive; b. Rochester, N.Y., June 9, 1934; d. Daniel T. and Gertrude (Grantham) Sheriff; m. David K. Jackson, Mar. 12, 1954; children: Jonnie Sheehan, Jaynette Kettler. Student, Santa Fe Sch. Art, 1952-53, Midwestern U., 1953-55. Supr. ANR Prodn. Co., Houston, 1976-83; v.p. Robinhawk Drafting & Design, Houston, 1983-85; pres., CEO, chmn. bd. Houston Creative Connections, 1985-99; ret., 2000. Advt. & mktg. dir. Geotech Assn., Houston, 1989-90; past pres. Am. Inst. Design & Drafting, 1984-86; CEO NMASS Comm., 1998, Full Svc. Advt. Agy., 1996-99, Houston Tech. Connections, 1996-99, Outsource and Tech. Placement, 1996-99, Houston Creative Svcs., [illegible]; bd. dirs. HyperDynamics. Design cons.: (mag.) Urbane, 1989-94. Mem. Mus. Fine Arts, Houston, 1988—2002, Greater Houston Partnership, 1989—98; mem. com. for advt. U. Houston-Math and Sci. Dept., 1999—; mem. nat. steering com. Women's Input Com., Houston Women Bus. Coun., 1999; bd. dirs. Literacy Advance, 1993—, pres. bd., 1999; bd. dirs. Women's Input Com., Houston Women Bus. Coun. Recipient Nat. Multimedia award Am. Advt. Fedn., 1999, also regional award. Mem. NAFE, Houston Advt. Fedn. (Silver and Merit awards 1989, Merit award 1990, Bronze award 1991, 2 Bronze awards 1992, 2 Gold and 4 Merit awards 1992, Gold and Bronze awards 1995, 3 Addys for Interactive 1999, 3 Gold Addys for Multimedia, Nat. Addy award 1999, Houston's Top Women Bus. Owners award 1995, 96, 97, 98, Top Tex. Bus. Women Owner award 1997), Greater Heights C. of C. (bd. dirs. 1994—, vice-chmn. 1996), Galleria C. of C., Rotary (treas. 1992, pres.-elect 1993, pres. 1994), U.S. C. of C. (Blue Chip Enterprise award 1993), Heights C. of C. (chairwoman Women in Action 1997); finalist Ernst & Young Entrepreneur of the Yr., 1998. Republican. Episcopalian. Avocations: oil painting, fishing, cooking. Studio: Las Animas Studio 4501 Brookwoods Houston TX 77092

JACKSON, VALERIE LYNNETTE, social worker; b. Vicksburg, Miss., June 7, 1959; d. Eugene and Joyce (Flood) J. BS in Social Work, Jackson State U., 1980; MSW, U. So. Miss., 1983. Lic. social worker. Social work teaching asst. Miss. Adoption Tng. Project, Jackson, 1979; collection correspondent Sears Dept. Store, Jackson, 1977-81; resident mgr. Univ. So. Miss., Hattiesburg, 1981-82; relief program specialist Cath. Charities, Jackson, 1983-85; sr. med. social worker Miss. Meth. Rehab. Ctr., Jackson, 1983—. Chmn. housing com. Handicapped Svc. Coalition, Jackson, 1985; chmn. nominations Living Independence for Everyone, Jackson, 1986; chmn. ctrl. Miss. chpt. Nat. Spinal Injury Assn., 1995-98. Named Outstanding Young Women Am., 1988. Mem. NASW (chmn. merit award com. 1984-88, chmn. hospitality com. 1995—), Support Group for Families Individuals with Disabilities, Am. Assn. Spinal Cord Injury Psychologists and Social Workers, State Wide Edn. Enforcement Prevention System. Baptist. Avocations: travel, shopping. Office: Miss Meth Rehab Ctr 1350 E Woodrow Jackson MS 39216

JACKSON, VALERIE PASCUZZI, radiologist, educator; b. Oakland, Calif., Aug. 25, 1952; d. Chris A. Pascuzzi and Janice (Mayne) Pacuzzi; 1 child, Price Arthur III. AB, Ind. U., 1974, MD, 1978. Diplomate Am. Bd. Radiology. Intern, resident in diagnostic radiology Ind. U. Med. Ctr., 1978-82; from asst. prof. radiology to prof. radiology Ind. U. Sch. Medicine, Indpls., 1982-94, John A. Campbell prof. radiology, 1994—. Dir. residency program in radiology Ind. U. Sch. Medicine, 1994—2003, interim chair dept. radiology, 2003—; trustee Am. Bd. Radiology. Contbr. over 50 articles to profl. jours., chpts. to books. Fellow: Soc. Breast Imaging (pres. 1990—92), Am. Coll. Radiology (bd. chancellors, chair 3 coms., pres. 2002—03); mem.: AMA, Radiol. Soc. N.Am., Am. Roentgen Ray Soc., Am. Inst. Ultrasound in Medicine, Alpha Omega Alpha. Office: Indiana U Sch Med Dept Rad 550 N Univ Blvd Rm 0663 Indianapolis IN 46202-2859

JACKSON, VELMA LOUISE, lawyer; b. Sewickley, Pa., Aug. 2, 1945; d. Matthew Edward and Sarah Frances (Carter) J. BS, Duquesne U., 1968; MEd, U. Pitts., 1977; JD, U. Cin., 1982. Bar: W.Va. 1985, Pa. 1986. Chemist Calgon Corp., Pitts., 1969-70; mgr. lab. svcs. Polytech Inc., Cleve., 1970-76; engr. Procter & Gamble Co., Cin., 1976-79; v.p. F.U.T.U.R.E. Assocs., Sewickley, 1982—; law clk., jud. asst. Orphans Ct. div. Ct. Common Pleas, Pitts., 1985-89; pvt. practice Pitts., 1989—. Environ. cons. Creative Mgmt. Systems, Detroit, 1979-81; tech. writer O.H. Materials Inc., Findlay, Ohio, 1980-81; instr. bus. law Carlow Coll., Pitts., 1986-91; bd. dirs. Sentinel Fin. Svcs. Inc. Writer poetry; contbr. articles to profl. jours.; developed cut plant preservative, 1975. Bd. dirs. Sewickley Community Ctr., 1983-89, 91—, Group Against Smog and Pollution, Pitts., 1987—; treas. Quaker Valley Dist. Dems., 1984-92, commr. Police Civil Svcs. Commn., Sewickley, 1986—; invitee Citizen Amb. Project to India, Republic of China and USSR Internat. Amb. Programs Inc., Spokane, Wash., 1987-88; trustee Sewickley Valley Hosp., 1996-99, Pitts. Tech. Inst., 1997—, Meade Educultural Cons., 1997—. Mem. ABA, AAUW, Nat. Assn. Colored Women's Club (local pres. 1985-87, state 1st v.p. 1988-92), Nat. Assn. Negro Bus. and Profl. Women, Pa. Bar Assn., W.Va. Bar Assn., African Ams. for Self-Determination (co-founder), Am. Biographical Inst. Rsch. Assn. (mem. adv. coun.), Internat. Biographical Ctr., Delta Sigma Theta. Baptist. Avocation: fiction and poetry writing. Home: 339 Little St Sewickley PA 15143-1468

JACKSON, VICTORIA LYNN, actress, comedienne; b. Miami, Fla., Aug. 2, 1959; d. James McCaslin and Marlene Esther (Blackstad) J.; m. Nisan Mark Eventoff, Aug. 5, 1984; 1 child, Scarlet Elizabeth. Student, Fla. Bible Coll., 1976-77, Furman U., 1977-79, Auburn U., 1979-80. Actress Summerfest/Town & Gown, Birmingham, Ala., 1980; stand-up comedienne Variety Arts Ctr., L.A., 1982-83, Tonight Show with Jonny Carson, NBC, L.A., 1983—; actress-comedienne The Half Hour Comedy Hour, Dick Clark, L.A., 1983; comedienne Bizarre/John Beiner, Toronto, Can., 1983; actress commls. L.A., 1983—; comedienne Bob Munkhouse Show, London, 1983; actress-comedienne Saturday Night Live, NBC, N.Y.C., 1986—. Actress series Half Nelson, NBC, L.A., pilot Walter Fox, L.A. Actress (films) Stoogemania, Double Exposure, The Pick Up Artist, 1986, Baby Boom, 1987, Couch Trip, 1987, Dream a Lil Dream, 1988, Casual Sex, 1988, UHF with Weird Al, 1989, Family Business, 1990, I Love You to Death, 1990. Mem. ASCAP, SAF, AFTRA. Baptist. Avocations: motherhood, photography, gymnastics.

JACKSON, WENDY S. LEWIS, social worker; b. Grand Rapids, Mich., May 9, 1965; d. Thomas James and Karen Susan (Kinard) L. BA, U. Mich., 1987, MSW, 1989. Investigator def. D.C. Pub. Defender Officer, Washington, 1985; program asst. Detroit Urban League, 1989; coord. housing Ann Arbor (Mich.) Housing Commn., 1989-90; sr. assoc. United Way, Grand Rapids, 1990-93; program coord. The Grand Rapids Found., 1993-94, program dir., 1994—. Mgr. database Kent County Emergency Needs Task Force, Grand Rapids, 1990—, editor, 1990—; sec. Kent County Emergency Food Subcom., Grand Rapids, 1990—; mem. Kent County Domestic Violence Coordinating Com., Grand Rapids, 1990—; mem. pub. affairs com. Mich. League for Human Svcs., Lansing, 1990—; adj. prof. Grand Valley State U. Sch. of Social Work, 1994—. Contbr. articles to profl. jours. Vol. Blodgett Meml. Med. Ctr., Grand Rapids, 1982—; mem. task force Citizens League, Grand Rapids, 1990—; mem. pub. affairs task force United Way, Lansing, 1990—. Recipient Leadership award Kiwanis Club, 1983; Old Kent Bank and Trust scholar, 1983-87; Am. Marshall Meml. fellow, German Marshall Fund of U.S., 2001. Mem. NASW, Nat. Assn. Black Social Workers, U. Mich. Social Work Govs. (bd. mem. 1991—), U. Mich. Alumni Assn., Women's Leadership Coun., Urban League. Democrat. Episcopalian. Avocations: tennis, racquetball, photography, travel. Home: 16534 Huntington Rd Detroit MI 48219-4072 Office: The Grand Rapids Found 209-C Waters Bldg 161 Ottawa Ave NW Ste 209C Grand Rapids MI 49503-2757

JACKSON, WYNELLE REDDING, children's services educational administrator, tax preparer; b. Atlanta, Sept. 3, 1947; d. Edwin Turner and Eva Josephine (Davis) Redding; m. Ronald Van Watson, Aug. 10, 1974 (div. Aug. 1978); m. Toney Jackson, Sept. 16, 1995. BA in Elem. Edn., CUNY, 1968; MEd in Supervision and Adminstrn., U. N.H., 1982. Lic. notary pub., N.Y. Tchr. Pub. Sch. 129 N.Y.C. Bd. Edn., Bklyn., 1969-74, coord. career edn. dist. 16, 1974-75, tchr. Pub. Sch. 243, 1975-80, tchr. Pub. Sch. 85 Queens, 1980-82; dir. ednl. svcs. The Salvation Army Social Svcs. for Children, N.Y.C., 1982—. Treas. Black Am. Heritage Found., Jamaica, N.Y., 1982—; mem. Women's [illegible] Queens Village, N.Y., 1994—. Recipient Josephine H. Pettie Humanitarian award Black Am. Heritage Found., 1993. Mem. ASCD, Nat. Notary Assn., N.Y. State Assn. Supervision and Curriculum Devel., Phi Delta Kappa, The Nat. Sorority of Phi Delta Kappa, Inc. (fin. sec. Beta Omicron chpt. 1980-81, treas., 1983-87, fin. sec. eastern region 1991-95). Episcopalian. Avocation: bowling. Home: 99-10 211th St Queens Village NY 11429 Office: The Salvation Army Social Svcs for Children 132 W 14th St New York NY 10011-7389

JACKSON, YVONNE, pharmaceutical executive; BA, Spelmen Coll.; MA, Harvard U. Various mgmt. positions Sears, Roebuck & Co., Torrance, Calif., N.Y.C.; sr. human resources positions Avon Products, Inc., 1980—93; sr. v.p. worldwide human resources Burger King Corp., 1993—99; sr. v.p. human resources Compaq Computer Corp., Houston, 1999—2002, Pfizer, Inc., 2003—. Chmn. bd. trustees Spelman Coll.; bd. dirs. Inst. Women's Policy Rsch.; mem. adv. bd. Catalyst. Office: Pfizer Inc 235 E 42d St New York NY 10017

JACKSON-CALLANDRET, SHIRLEY LORRAINE, music educator; b. New York city, NY, Aug. 4, 1964; d. Grover and Bert Jackson; m. Shirley Lorraine Jackson, Feb. 24, 1990. BA, Bennett Coll., 1982—86; MA, Fla. Atlantic U., 2000—02. Music tchr. Roward County Pub. Schools, Fort Lauderdale, Fla., 1988—. Adjudicator Broward County NAACP ACTSO Talent Competition, Ft. Lauderdale, Fla., 1991—93; treas. Broward County Music Educator Conf., Ft. Lauderdale, Fla., 1994—95; coord. Broward County Area Music In Our Schools Month, Ft. Lauderdale, Fla., 1995; adjudicator Omega Psi Pfi Frat. Talent Hunt, Ft. Lauderdale, Fla., 1995—2000; coord. Broward County Elem. Honor Choir, Ft. Lauderdale, Fla., 1995, Broward County North Area Music In our Sch. Month Concert, Ft. Lauderdale, Fla., 1995—96; adjudicator South Fla. Regional Showtime At The Apollo Auditions, Ft. Lauderdale, 1995; membership Music Educators Nat. Conf., Ft. Lauderdale, Fla., 1988—; grade chairperson N. Andrews Gardens Elem. Sch. Performing Arts Dept., Ft. Lauderdale, Fla., 2000—01, magnet coord., 2001—. Music director: performance Fla. Citrus Bowl, Disney Magic Music Days; music teacher (performance) Miami Heat Halftime Show, Music Usa Festival (first pl. in elem. show choir category, 2000), Annie Jr; Fiddler On The Roof, Jr; Oklahoma; Into The Woods, Jr. Music dir. Rising Stars Summer Theatre Camp, Ft. Lauderdale, Fla., 1999—2001. Mem.: Nat. Aspiring Educators Sch. Pers., Fed. Educators Assn., Broward County Teachers Union, Fla. Music Educator Assn. (corr.), Nat. Dance Alliance (assoc.). Avocations: singing, dance, travel. Home: 11440 NW 41 St Sunrise FL 33323 Office: Broward County Schools/ North Andrews Ga 345 NE 56 St Fort Lauderdale FL 33334 E-mail: shirlnotes@aol.com.

JACKSON-HOLMES, FLORA MARIE, lawyer, educator; b. Miami, Fla., June 1, 1957; d. Andrew and Elizabeth (Oliver) Jackson; m. Myron William Holmes, Apr. 16, 1988. BS, Fla. Meml. Coll., 1978; JD, Howard U., 1982. Bar: Fla. 1984, U.S. Dist. Ct. (so. dist. Fla.). Staff atty. James E. Scott Cmty. Assn., Miami, 1985-87, sr. atty., 1987-89; pvt. practice Miami, 1990—. Code enforcement hearing officer Dade County; adj. prof. law, Fla. Meml. Coll., Miami, 1989—; legal advisor Delta Sigma Theta Alumnae of Dade County, 1997. Recipient Pro Bono award Domestic Violence Legal Aid of Greater Miami, 1996, Cert. Appreciation Charles R. Drew Elem. Sch., 1997, Miami Golden Glades Optimists, 1996. Mem. Nat. Black Lawyers (treas. 1986-87), Fla. Bar Assn. (women lawyer's divsn.), NBAWLD (sec. 1996), Delta Sigma Theta. Democrat. Baptist. Avocations: reading, working with youth, travel. Home: 15728 NW 7th Ave Miami FL 33169-6255 Office: 10735 NW 7th Ave Miami FL 33168-2103

JACKSON LEE, SHEILA, congresswoman; b. Queens, N.Y., Jan. 12, 1950; d. Erica Shelwyn and Jason Cornelius Bennett; m. Elwyn C. Lee; 2 children. BA, Yale U., 1972; JD, U. Va., 1975. Sr. counsel select com. on assassinations U.S. Ho. of Reps., 1977; trial atty. Fulbright and Jaworski, 1978-80; sr. atty. United Energy Resources, Inc., 1980; assoc. judge Houston Mcpl. Ct., 1987-89; mem. Houston City Coun., 1990-94, U.S. Congress from 18th Tex. dist., 1995—; mem. judiciary com., sci. com.; ranking dem. subcom. immigration and claims, mem. crime subcom. Mem. Select Com. Homeland Security; 1st vice chmn. Congl. Black Caucus; founder bipartisan Congl. Children's Caucus. Mem.: Tex. State Bar, Tex. Mcpl. Judges Assn., State Bar Assn. Justice Com. Democrat. Office: US House Reps 2435 Rayburn Ho Office Bldg Washington DC 20515-4318*

JACKSON MCCABE, JEWELL, not-for-profit developer; b. Wash., DC, Aug. 2, 1945; d. Hal Jackson; m. Frederick Ward (div.); m. Eugene L. McCabe, Jr. (div.). Attended, Bard Coll., 1963—66; doctorates (hon.), Iona, Tugaloo Coll. Dir. pub. affairs NY Urban Coalition, 1970—73; pub. rels. officer Special Svc. Children NYC, 1973—75; assoc. dir. pub. info. Women's Divsn. Office Gov., NY State, 1975—77; dir. gov. comm. affairs WNET-TV/Thirteen, 1977—82; pres. Nat. Coalition 100 Black Women, 1977—91, chair, 1981—; pres. Jewell Jackson McCabe Assoc. Bd. mem. Reliance Group Holdings, Inc., Alight.com, NYC Investment Fund, Wharton Sch. Bus., Bard Coll., Nat. Alliance Bus., NYC Partnership, Rsch. Am., NYC Commn. Status Women, Children's Advocacy Ctr. Manhattan; chair NY State Job Training Partnership Coun. Mem. US Holocaust Meml. Coun., NY State Coun. on Fiscal and Econ. Priorities. Recipient Guild award, Urban League, 1979, Civic award, Seagrams, 1980, 1980, Cmty. Leadership award, Malcolm/King Coll., 1980. Office: Nat Coalition 100 Black Women Inc 38 W 32nd St Ste 1610 New York NY 10001-3816 Office Phone: 212-947-2196.*

JACKSON-TKAC, STEPHANIE ANN, nurse; b. Thomasville, N.C., Jan. 2, 1960; d. Ellis Wade and Nancy (Myers) J. BSN, East Carolina U., 1982. RN, cert. case mgr., infusion nurse. Staff nurse Pitt County Meml. Hosp., Greenville, N.C., 1981-83, N.C. Bapt. Hosp., Winston-Salem, N.C., 1983-87, Duke U. Med. Ctr., Durham, N.C., 1987-91, Rex Hosp., Raleigh, 1991—92; nurse clinician Health Infusion, Morrisville, 1992—95, Coram Health Care (formerly Health Infusion), Morrisville, 1992—94, infusion care mgr. Goldsboro and Kinston brs., 1995-96; with Chartwell S.E., 1996-97; per diem mgr. Columbia Home Care, Raleigh, N.C.; home health per diem clin. nurse U. N.C., Chapel Hill; collections spec. Am. Red Cross; case mgr. Killette and Assocs., Inc., 1999—. Mem.: Infusion Nurses Soc., Case Mgr. Soc. Am. Republican.

JACOB, CHRISTINA MARIE, social worker; b. Evansville, Ind., July 9, 1976; d. Kenneth Ray and Carolyn Sue Beeler; m. Jeremy Michael Jacob, May 25, 2002. B of Social Work, U. So. Ind., 1998, MSW, 2000. LSW, qualified prevention profl. Case mgr. The Salvation Army, Evansville, Ind., 1998—99; social worker Evansville-Vanderburgh Sch. Corp., 1999—2003. Facilitator Youth First Found., Evansville. Mem.: NASW, Ind. Assn. Prevention Profls. Avocations: reading, exercise, outdoor activities. Office Phone: 812-435-8223.

JACOB, DEIRDRE ANN BRADBURY, manufacturing executive, business educator, consultant; b. Providence, Mar. 7, 1952; d. John Joseph and Marion Damon (Shute) Bradbury; m. Thomas Keenan, Nov. 15, 1975 (div. Dec. 1980); 1 child: Victoria Irene; m. Robert A. Jacob, June 22, 1996; 1 child, Meggin Rosemary. BA in Govt. and Law, Lafayette Coll., 1973. Supr. Procter & Gamble Mfg. Co., S.I., N.Y., 1973-76, mgr. warehouse dept., 1976-79, mgr. shortening and oils, 1979-81, fin. mgr. food plant, 1981-82, mgr. personnel, 1982-86, mgr. total quality and pub. affairs, 1986-91; ptnr. Avraham Y. Goldratt Inst., New Haven, Conn., 1991—. Cons. Procter & Gamble, S.I., 1987—89, Cin., 1989—91. Trustee Lafayette Coll., 1985-90.

Mem. Lafayette Coll. Alumni Assn. (pres. 1992-94, Clifton P. Mayfield award), Maroon Club (Easton, Pa., pres. 1987-89). Roman Catholic. Avocation: singing. Office: Avraham Y Goldratt Inst 442 Orange St New Haven CT 06511-6201

JACOB, DIANNE, county official; m. Paul, 1961; 1 son, Tom. Tchr. East County; mem. Jamul/Dulzura Sch. Bd.; supr. dist. 2 San Diego County Bd. Suprs., 1992—. Co-chmn. Criminal Justice Coun.; mem. San Diego (Calif.) Planning Commn., chmn.; pres. Calif. State Sch. Bds.; adv. bd. Mothers Against Drunk Driving; bd. dir. East County Econ. Devel. Coun. Recipient Alumna of Yr. award San Diego State U. Coll. Edn., 1993, Women Who Mean Bus. award San Diego Bus. Jour., 1995, Legislator of Yr. award Indsl. Environ. Assn., 1995, Most Accessible Politician award Forum Publs., award of excellence Endangered Habitats League, 1999, Legislator of Yr. award Calif. Narcotics Assn., 1998, Legislator of Yr. award Border Solution Task Force, 1998, Legislator of Yr. award San Diego Mchts. Assn., 2000, Ofcl. of Yr., San Diego Domestic Violence Coun., 2000, Legis. of Yr. award Indsl. Environ. Assn., 2000, Legis. of Yr. award Bldg. Owners and Mgrs. Assn., 2001, Headliner of Yr. award San Diego Press Club, 2002. Avocation: golfing. Office: Office County Supr County Adminstrn Ctr 1600 Pacific Hwy Ste 335 San Diego CA 92101-2470

JACOB, ROSAMOND TRYON, librarian; b. Mpls., May 20, 1928; d. Philip Dorn and Rachel Chase (Denison) Tryon; m. Bernard Michel Jacob, Feb. 17, 1951; children: Clara, Paul. BA summa cum laude, Smith Coll., 1949; MA in Libr. Sci., U. Minn., 1974. Sec. Thames & Hudson Pubs., N.Y.C., 1950-51, Columbia Law Sch., N.Y.C., 1952-54, U. Minn., Mpls., 1955-59; libr. St. Paul Pub. Libr., 1976—98, ret. Coun. mem. Depository Libr. Coun. to Pub. Printer, Washington, 1985-88. Co-author: Minnesota State Documents: A Guide for Depository Libraries, 1984; author: (newsletter) Documents/Classified, 1980-96; editor: (newsletter) DOCSOUP, 1980-90. Mem. St. Paul LWV, 1965—. Mem. ALA (Bernadine Abbott Hoduski Founder award govt. documents roundtable divsn. 1994), Minn. Libr. Assn. (Disting. Achievement award 1990).

JACOB, SUSAN MARIE, nurse; b. New Brunswick, N.J., Dec. 30, 1961; BSN, U. Del., 1984; M in Nursing Adminstrn., La. State U. Health Sci. Ctr., 2001. RN, La.; cert. coding specialist, cert. procedural coder. Staff/charge nurse Tex. Children's Hosp., Houston, 1984-90; patient care coord. Lakeview Home Health, Covington, La., 1994-96; dir. nursing Trinity Home Health, New Orleans, 1996-98; coder Children's Hosp., New Orleans, 1998-99; auditor Ochsner Clinic, New Orleans, 1999—. Mem. Am. Acad. Profl. Coders. Home: 854 Cross Gates Blvd Slidell LA 70461-4104

JACOBI, KERRY LEE, information systems specialist; b. Smithtown, N.Y., Jan. 19, 1970; d. Patrick R. and Karen A. (Koch) J. BS in Acctg., Marymount Coll., 1991; MPA, Marist Coll., 1993; student, SUNY, New Paltz, 1998; student in biodynamic massage therapy, instr. Arthur Giacolone, Walnut Creek, Calif., 1999—. Cert. in Reiki II. Asst. adminstr. Dutchess Radiology Assoc. P.C., Poughkeepsie, N.Y., 1992-94; planning, mktg. exec. Vassar Bros. Hosp., Poughkeepsie, N.Y., 1994-97; billing ops. mgr. Dutchess Radiology Assocs., Poughkeepsie, N.Y., 1997-98; dir. mktg. DRA Imaging, Poughkeepsie, 1998-99, info. tech. specialist, 1999—. Mem. Marist Coll. MPA Adv. Coun., Marist Coll. Mentoring Program; campaign fin. mgr. Citizens to Elect Judy Green, 96th Assembly Dist., N.Y. State Assembly, City of Poughkeepsie mayoral race, 1999. Mem. NOW (past pres. mid Hudson chpt. 1995-97). Democrat. Avocations: competitive weight lifting, fencing, scuba diving. Office: DRA Imaging PC Westage Med Office Bldg Reade Pl Poughkeepsie NY 12601-1749 E-mail: KLJACOBIZ@aol.com.

JACOBOWITZ, ELLEN SUE, museum curator, museum and temple administrator; b. Detroit, Feb. 21, 1948; d. Theodore Mark and Lois Clairesse (Levy) Jacobowitz. BA, U. Mich., 1969, MA, 1970; postgrad. in art history, Bryn Mawr Coll., 1976-83; postgrad., Wharton Sch., 1997. Curator Phila. Mus. Art, 1972-90; adminstr. Cranbrook Inst. Sci., Bloomfield Hills, Mich., 1991-94; adminstr. Temple Emanu-El, Oak Park, Mich., 1995-96. Cons. ArtServe Mich., 1997; primary caregiver, 1998—. Author: The Prints of Lucas Van Leyden, 1983, American Graphics, 1860-1940, 1982. Treas. Sat. Luncheon Club, 1995—96, pres., 1999—2000; active Leadership Oakland, Detroit Inst. Arts; bd. dirs. Nat. Coun. Jewish Women, Detroit, 1990—91, Print Coun. Am., Balt., Netherlands Am. Amity Trust, Washington, 1982—84, Mich. Mus. Assn., 1993—94. Mem.: Detroit Inst. of Arts, U. Mich. Alumni Assn., Am. Jud. Com. Avocations: cooking, gardening, reading, the arts, sports.

JACOBS, ALEXIS A. automobile company executive; With Columbus (Ohio) Fair Auto Auction, now owner, CEO, pres. Amb. Charity Newsies; mem. athletic dept. steering com. Ohio State U., Columbus;, also sponsor 3 athletic scholarships; bd. dirs. Salesian Boys and Girls Club, also former chmn. fundraising com.; formerly active Recreation Unltd., Dave Thomas Adoption Found. Three-Tour Challenge. Mem. Nat. Auto Auction Assn. (pres.). Office: Columbus Fair Auto Auction 4700 Groveport Rd Columbus OH 43207-5217 Fax: 614-497-1132.

JACOBS, ALICIA MELVINA, account executive; b. Newark, June 24, 1955; d. Alvin and Melvina (McKinney) J. BA, Oberlin Coll., 1977. Caseworker Essex County Welfare Bd., Newark, 1977-78; sr. audit analyst N.J. Blue Cross, Newark, 1978-80; fin. analyst N.Y. State Office of the Spl. Cont., N.Y.C., 1980-81; account exec. Fortune Temporary Personnel, N.Y.C., 1981-84; sales mgr. Wall St. Temporary, N.Y.C., 1984-85; account exec. Prentice Hall, N.Y.C., 1985-90, Rsch. Inst. Am., Newark, 1990-91, Westfield, 1992-93, Century City, Calif., 1993-96; regional acct. mgr. Interactive Search, Calif., 1997-98, Gia Info. Group, Calif., 1998-99, v.p., dir. bus. devel., 1999—; v.p. client svcs. Right Mgmt. Cons., 2001—. Fund-raising chmn. The Africa Project, N.Y.C., 1989-91; sec. We Are Family, Newark, 1989—; mentor, tutor Welcome Bapt. Ch., Newark, 1991—; vol. Scott-Krueger Cultural Ctr., Newark, 1991—; vol. mentor Jr. Achievement, Sisters Having Our Say, SOS Group, Faithful Central Employment Vol., The Restaurant Club, Women Who Cook 1994; chairperson Oberlin Coll. AA Cluster Reunion, Ohio, 1997; mem. alumni com. to select bd. trustee mems. Oberlin Coll., 2001-02; bd. dirs. People Coordinated Svcs., 2002. Recipient Heroine award Montclair (N.J.) High Sch., 1990, Participant award Madison Ave. Sch., Newark. Mem. NAACP, N.J. Law Librs. Assn., Coalition of 100 Black Women. Avocations: teaching children, aerobics, reading. Home: 6922 Knowlton Pl Apt 305 Los Angeles CA 90045-2099

JACOBS, ANNETTE M. music educator; MusB in Music Edn., BA in History, Miami U., Oxford, Ohio, 1999. Orch. dir. Troy (Ohio) City Schs., 1999—2000; band dir. Lynchburg-Clay Local Schs., 2000—01; elem. music tchr. Twin Valley Cmty. Local Schs., West Alexandria, 2001—. Mem., asst. band dir. Oxford Cmty. Band, Ohio, 2001—; mem. Fayette County Cmty. Band, 2000—01. Mem.: NEA, Ohio Edn. Assn., Ohio Music Edn. Assn., Music Educators Nat. Conf. (vol. book reviewer, Music Educators Jour. 2003—), Nat. Flute Assn., Girl Scouts of Am. (life). Avocations: historical research, quilting, flute, computer.

JACOBS, CHARLOTTE DE CROES, medical educator, oncologist; b. Oak Ridge, Tenn., Jan. 27, 1946; BA, U. Rochester, 1968; MD, Washington U., St. Louis, 1972. Diplomate Am. Bd. Internat. Medicine, Am. Bd. Med. Oncology, Nat. Bd. Med. Examiners. Acting asst. prof. oncology Stanford (Calif.) U. Med. Sch., 1977-80, asst. prof. medicine and oncology, 1980-86, assoc. prof. clin. medicine, 1986-92, assoc. prof. medicine and oncology, 1992-96, prof., 1996—, sr. assoc. dean. edn. and student affairs, 1990-97, acting dir. Clin. Cancer Ctr., 1994-97; dir. Oncology Day Care Ctr. Stanford Med. Ctr., 1977-90, dir. Clin. Cancer Ctr., 1997—. Bd. dirs. Nat. Comprehensive Cancer Network, Rockledge, Pa., 1994—. Recipient presdl. citation Am. Soc. for Head and Neck Surgery, 1990, Aphrodite Hofsomner award Washington U., 1993. Mem. AMA, Am. Soc. Clin. Oncology (bd. dirs. 1992-95), Am. Assn. for Cancer Rsch. Office: Clin Cancer Ctr 300 Pasteur Dr H-3249 Stanford CA 94305-5225

JACOBS, DEBORAH L. librarian; b. L.A., Feb. 28, 1952; d. Morton Daniel and Adrienne (Rimmel) J.; m. Brian Brogan, Mar. 29, 1982 (div. 1985); 1 child, Jacob Brogan. BA in Govt., Mills Coll., 1974; MLS, U. Oreg., 1975. Children's libr. Deschutes Libr., Bend, Oreg., 1976-77; extension svcs. libr. Sacramento (Calif.) City Libr., 1977-78; libr., libr. dir. Corvallis (Oreg.)-Benton Pub. Libr., 1978-97; city libr. Seattle Pub. Libr., 1997—. Treas. Freedom to Read Found., Chicago, 1994-98. Bd. dirs. Northwest Sch., Seattle, Boys & Girls Club, Corvallis, 1993-97; chair Commn. Children & Families, Corvallis, 1992-97; sec., bd. dirs. da Vinci Days, Corvallis, 1993-97. Named libr. of yr. Libr. Jour., 1995, pub. employee of yr. Mcpl. League King Couny, Seattle, 1999, leader of yr. City of Seattle Mgmt. Assn., 1999, Governing Mag.Pub., Ofcl. of the Year, 2001. Mem. Am. Libr. Assn. (co-chair presdl. initiative 1997-99, v.p. Leroy-Merritt F und. 1998—, intellectual freedom champion 1995), Oreg. Libr. Assn. (pres. 1992-93), Wash. State Women's Forum, Wash. Libr. Assn., Bertelsmann Founds. Internat. Network Pub. Librs., Rotary. Democrat. Jewish. Avocations: baking, gardening, running, pottery. Office: Seattle Pub Libr 1000 4th Ave Seattle WA 98101-3922

JACOBS, ELEANOR, art consultant, retired art administrator; b. N.Y.C., July 25, 1929; d. Samuel and Mary (Praw) Cohen; m. Raymond Jacobs, Dec. 29, 1955; children: Susan, Laura. BA, NYU, 1979. Co-founder, v.p. The Earth Shoe Co., N.Y.C., 1969-79; art adminstr. Print Dept., Sotheby's, N.Y.C., 1980-81; exec. asst. Care, N.Y.C., 1982-84; exec. adminstr. Hirschl & Adler Galleries, N.Y.C., 1984-93. Art cons. Recipient Founders Day award NYU, N.Y.C., 1978; Artists fellow, 1985—. Mem. Nat. Arts Club (gov. 1989-97, exhbns. com. 1984—, curatorial com. 1990—, founder, editor exhibiting artists newsletter 1987—, admissions com. 1995—), Nat. Trust for Hist. Preservation, Artists Fellowship, 1985, Dutch Treat Club. Avocations: tennis, travel.

JACOBS, ELEANOR R. retired volunteer; b. N.Y.C., Nov. 19, 1912; d. Leo and Florence May (Schiff) Rosenberger; m. Saul Jacobs, Nov. 29, 1935 (dec. Sept. 1966); 1 child, Diane M. Grad. high sch. Sec. to pres. Kelly Springfield Tire Co., N.Y.C., 1930-34; program dir. USO, Panama Canal Zone, 1953-54; asst. mission chief C.A.R.E., Panama City, Republic of Panama, 1954-56; mil. air transport coord. USAF, Albrook AFB, Panama Canal Zone, 1956; pers. analyst U.S. Army, Ft. Amador, Panama Canal Zone, 1957-58; info. officer U.S. Tropic test Ctr., Ft. Clayton, Panama Canal Zone, 1958-66; info./pub. rels. adminstr. L.Am. reg. office Credit Union Nat. Assn., Panama City, 1966-72, asst. mng. dir. advt. and pub. rels. Madison, Wis., 1972-76. Dir. Nat. Assn. Ret. Credit Union People, 1978-86. Mem. Am. Assn. Ret. Persons, Friend of AAUW, LWV, Common Cause, Amnesty Internat. Christian Scientist. Avocations: weaving, writing, teaching english as a second lang. Home: 8301 Old Sauk Rd Apt 188 Middleton WI 53562-4392

JACOBS, GRACE GAINES, retired gerontologist, adult education educator; b. Mpls., Aug. 29, 1919; d. Abe S. and Ruth (Justman) Gaines; m. Michael M. Jacobs, Mar. 30, 1943; children: Laurence Bruce, Tami Arlene, Robert Marc. AA, Santa Monica City Coll., 1969; BA in Anthropology, Calif. State U., Northridge, 1971, MA in Ednl. Psychology, 1973. Owner, editor, pub. Publicraft Assocs., Detroit, 1948-50; instr. adult edn. L.A. City Schs., 1974-80. Writer: (handbook) Teaching Older Adults, 1978. Nat. program chair Gray Panthers, Phila. and Washington, 1982-84, mem. nat steering com., 1978-86; host Speaking of Seniors radio program KPFK-Pacifica, L.A., 1976-85; mem. Consumer Action Bd., San Francisco, 1988-93; mem. Pacific Bell Intelligent Network Task Force, San Francisco, 1984-87; mem. housing adv. com. City of Santa Cruz, Calif., 1984-90; obtained funding and site for startup SeniorNet Computer Ctr., Santa Cruz, 1989. Mem. Am. Soc. Aging, AAUW, LWV (chair 2 yr. study on nat health Santa Cruz, Calif., 1993-95), Geneal. Soc., Lifelong Learners Univ. Santa Cruz (pres. 1993-94). Democrat. Avocations: writing, family history.

JACOBS, GRETCHEN HUNTLEY, psychiatrist; b. N.Y.C., July 20, 1941; d. L. Gordon and Gertrude Mary (Eberz) La Pointe; m. Michael Edward Jacobs, Dec. 26, 1965 (div.); children: Dylan Huntley, Danielle La Pointe. BS, Fordham U., N.Y.C., 1963; MD, SUNY, Bklyn., 1968. Diplomate Am. Bd. Psychiatry and Neurology, Am. Bd. Child and Adolescent Psychiatry. Pediatric intern St. Luke's Hosp., N.Y.C., 1968—69; psychiatry resident George Washington U. Hosp., Washington, 1969—71; child psychiatry resident Beth Israel Hosp., Boston, 1972—73, McLean Hosp. Children's Ctr., Waltham, 1973—74; coord. health and human devel. Martha's Vineyard Sch. Sys., 1974—80; pvt. practice adult and adolescent/child psychiatry, 1974—; asst. clin. prof. child psychiatry Tufts U. Med. Sch., Boston, 1974—. Contbr. articles to profl. jours. Cons. Mass. Dept. Pub. Health Svcs. to Multi-Handicapped Children, 1974-75; bd. dirs. Mass. Dept. Social Svcs., 1979-83; founding mem., clin. dir. Vineyard Child Assault Prevention Project, 1986, Com. on Rural Child Psychiatry, 1988-92; mem. Hospice of Martha's Vineyard, Coun. for Young Children. Mem. AMA, NAACP, LWV, Am. Psychiat. Assn., New England Coun. Child and Adolescent Psychiatry, Am. Acad. Child and Adolescent Psychiatry, Mass. Med. Soc., Rotary Internat. Avocations: music, dance, travel, sailing, theater, basketball. Home and Office: Tashmoo Farm RR 1 Box 600 Vineyard Haven MA 02568-9733

JACOBS, JANE L. artist, state agency administrator; b. Birmingham, Ala., Sept. 27, 1942; d. Ellis Dice Lineberry and Catherine Cleary; m. Louis Ray Jacobs, June 30, 1998; children: Dana Mitchell, Tim; m. James D. II Faulkner, Aug. 6, 1965 (dec. May 1990). BA in Art Edn., Troy (Ala.) State Coll., 1964; M in Art Edn., U. Ala., 1986; diploma, TSUM, Ala., 1987. Tchr. Hawkins Jr. High, Hattiesburg, Miss., 1966—68; caseworker Heard County, Ga., 1972—74; photo studio artist Leon Loard Studios, Montgomery, Ala., 1974—76; libr. Troup County, Ga., 1975—77; studio artist, craftsman Studio One, Montgomery, Ala., 1980—; tchr. Macon and Bullock Counties, Ala., 1989—91; adminstrv. asst. State Dept. Rehab., Montgomery, Ala., 1999—. Asst. to Anne Mae Turner Bullock County Devel. Authority, 1984; sec. Bullock County C. of C. Mem.: Southeast Watercolor Soc., Ala. Watercolor Soc., Montgomery Art Guild. Baptist. Avocations: collecting dolls, antique hats, gloves and fans, making beaded jewelry. Home: 1352 Devonshire Dr Montgomery AL 36116-2887 E-mail: janellou@juno.com.

JACOBS, JUDITH, county legislator; b. N.Y.C., Jan. 13, 1939; d. George and Dorothy Bodkin; m. Sidney N. Jacobs, June 7, 1959; children: Jacqueline, Leonard, Linda. BA, Hunter Coll., 1960. Cert. in early childhood edn., N.Y. Mem. Nassau County Legislature, Mineola, N.Y., 1996—, minority leader, 1999—, presiding officer, majority leader, 2000—. Committeeperson, zone leader, asst. dist. leader, Town of Oyster Bay leader Dem. Party Nassau County, 1970—. Democrat. Jewish. Avocation: reading.

JACOBS, KAREN LOUISE, medical technologist; b. Kingston, N.Y., May 7, 1943; d. William Charles and Vera Elizabeth (Kelly) J. BS in Applied Tech., Empire State Coll., 1976; MS in Pub. Svc. Adminstrn., Russell Sage Coll., 1982. Sr. lab. tech., hosp. lab. supr. City of Kingston Labs., 1962-68; sr. rsch. asst. Dudley Obs., Albany, N.Y., 1972-75; lab. adminstr. Albany Med. Coll., 1976-99, faculty, 1982-97; tchr. environ. edn. Five Rivers Environ. Edn. Ctr., Delmar, NY, 1999—; tchr. natural sci. Heldeberg Workshop. Guest lectr. Sage Coll.; coord. complex labs. JCAHO regulations, 1997; infection control com. and subcoms. on AIDS mgmt. and human immunodeficiency virus universal precautions Albany Med. Ctr. Infection Control, 1987-97, accreditation regulatory oversight com.; pvt. piano tchr. Albany Acad. for Boys, 1999—; accompanist Siena Coll./Cmty. Chorale; accompanist Colonie Sr. Citizens, 2002-03. Bd. dirs. chpt. Leukemia Soc. Am., 1983-87; judge sci. and tech. summer issue on excellence in Am. U.S. News and World Report; vol. asst. naturalist Five Rivers Environ. Ctr. Mem. Clin. Lab. Mgmt. Assn. (del. citizen amb. program to China 1989), Am. Soc. Clin. Pathologists, Earthwatch, Nat. Speleological Soc., Hudsonia (bd. dirs. 1995), Adirondack Mountain Club. Home: 50 Meadowbrook Dr Apt 149 Slingerlands NY 12159-2146

JACOBS, LIBBY SWANSON, state official; b. Lincoln, Nebr., Oct. 1, 1956; m. Steven G. Jacobs. BA, U. Nebr.; MPA, Drake U. Dir. pub. rels. Am. Lung Assn., 1983—86; dir. comms. IA Bankers Assn., 1986—88; mgr., ops. mgr. disability income svcs. Prin. Fin. Group, 1989—96, asst dir., 1996—2002, dir. cmty. rels., 2002—; state rep. Iowa, 1994—. Mem. adminstrn. and rules com.; mem. appropriations com.; mem. commerce and regulation com.; mem. state govt. com. Bd. mem. Drake Univ., Blank Children's Hosp.; co-chair Downtown Cmty. Alliance; chair Midwestern Legis. Conf. Mem.: PEO, LWV, Jr. League Des Moines, Variety Club Iowa. Republican. Office: State Capitol E 12th and Grand Des Moines IA 50319

JACOBS, LILLIAN LAURA, secondary school educator; b. Hollywood, Calif., Feb. 25, 1966; d. John Sherman and Naomi Ruth Lathrop; m. William Cole Jacobs, Dec. 20, 1997; children: Lillian Laura, Lorelei Lorene. BA in Psychology, U. Calif., San Diego, 1989; tchg. credential, Calif. State U., L.A., 1997. English tchr. Montebello (Calif.) H.S., 1991—92, math tchr., 1992—93; sci. tchr. Vail H.S., Montebello, 1992—2001, govt./econs. tchr., 2001—, sci. chair, 1993—2001. Waterpolo and swimming coach Montebello H.S., 1990—99; union rep. Vail H.S., Montebello, 1993—2001, tupe coord., 2001—02. Mem.: North Hollywood Rep. Women Federated. Republican. Avocations: reading, writing, water polo, politics. Home: 5667 Eunice St Simi Valley CA 93065 Office: Vail HS 1230 S Vail Ave Montebello CA 90640-6391

JACOBS, LOIS ELIZABETH, art educator; d. Ralph Herman and Mildred Larue (Fink) Keibler; m. Irwin Clay Jacobs, Jan. 30, 1971; children: Josephine, Margaret. BS in Art, Towson U., 1972; student, Drexel U., 1968—71; cert. in Art, Rockhurst Coll., 1975; MAT, Webster U., 1997. Cert. K-12 art Mo., gifted Mo. Tchr. art De La Salle Acad., Kansas City, Mo., 1977—79, Metro Christian Sch., Sunset Hills, Mo., 1989—91, Life Christian Sch., Sunset Hills, 1992—93; art specialist K-5 and gifted art Webster Groves Sch. Dist., Mo., 1993—98; art specialist K-5 Valley Pk. Sch. Dist., Mo., 1998—. Program dir. and theater dir. Eureka Arts Coun., Mo., 1992—2002. One-woman shows include Eureka Arts Coun., 1996, Mo. Art Educators Assn., 2003 (Hon. Mention), exhibited in group shows at Florissant (Mo.) Invitational Show, 1996, juried show, St. Louis Artist's Guild, 1998, Women's Caucus for Art, St. Louis, 1999, 2002, Mid-Am. Elem. and Secondary Art Tchrs., N.W. Mo. State U., 2000, Tchr. as Artist Show, 2002. Mem. Luths. for Life, Eureka, 1986—91; bd. dirs. St. Marks Luth. Sch., Eureka, 2002—03, Tri-County Birthright, Eureka, 1992—98. Grantee, St. Louis County Cable TV, 2003. Mem.: Mo. Art Educators Assn., St. Louis Women's Caucus for Art, St. Louis Artists Guild. Avocations: travel, gardening, music, reading.

JACOBS, MARIAN, advertising agency owner; b. Stockton, Calif., Sept. 11, 1927; d. Paul and Rose (Sallah) J. AA, Stockton Coll. With Bottarini Advt., Stockton, 1948-50; pvt. practice Stockton, 1950-64; with Olympius Advt., Stockton, 1964-78; pvt. practice Stockton, 1978—. Pres. Stockton Advt. Club, 1954, Venture Club, Stockton, 1955; founder Stockton Advt. and Mktg. Club, 1981. Founder Stockton Arts Comms., 1976; co-founder Sunflower Entertainment for Institutionalized, 1976, Women Execs., Stockton, 1978; founding dir. Pixie Woods, Stockton; bd. dir. Goodwill Industries, St. Mary's Dining Room, Alan Short Gallery; mem. Calif. Coun. for the Humanities, 1994-95. Paul Harris fellow Rotary Club, 1994; recipient Woman of Achievement award San Joaquin County Women's Coun., Stockton, 1976, Achievement award San Joaquin Delta Coll., Stockton, 1978, Friend of Edn. award Calif. Tchrs. Assn., Stockton, 1988, Stanley McCaffrey Disting. Svc. award, U. of the Pacific, Stockton, 1988, Athena award for Businesswoman of Yr. Greater Stockton C. of C., 1989, Role Model award Tierra del Oro Girl Scouts U.S., 1989, Heart of Gold award Dameron Hosp. Found., 2000; named Stocktonian of the Yr. Stockton Bd. of Realtors, 1978, Outstanding Citizen Calif. State Senate & Assembly, 1978, Woman of Yr. State of Calif. Assembly, 2002, Woman of Achievement Kaiser-Permanente Womens Wellness Conf., 2002, Disting. Alumni Vol., Univ. of the Pacific, 2003; the Marian Jacobs Literary Forum was established in her honor. Republican. Roman Catholic. Avocations: art, photography. Home and Office: 4350 Mallard Creek Cir Stockton CA 95207-5205

JACOBS, MARILYN ARLENE POTOKER, gifted education educator, consultant, author; b. N.Y.C., Oct. 22, 1940; m. David Jacobs, Dec. 10, 1960. BA in Psychology, Hunter Coll. CUNY, 1961, MS in Edn., 1963; cert. in gifted edn., U. South Fla., 1977. Cert. elem. edn., gifted and early childhood edn., Fla. Tchr. Yonkers (N.Y.) Pub. Schs., 1961-63; dir., tchr. Creative Corners Pre-Sch., Pomona, N.Y., 1971-74; tchr. of gifted, tchr. trainer Pinellas County Schs., Clearwater, Fla., 1975—. Pvt. practice computer edn. cons., 1987—; freelance grant writer, 1976—, freelance curriculum writer, 1993—. Contbr. articles to profl. jours. Recipient numerous county, state and nat. Econs. Edn. Curriculum awards, 1982—. Mem. NEA, ASCD, Coun. for Exceptional Children (Educator of the Yr. 1985), Assn. for Gifted, Fla. Assn. Computer Educators, Phi Delta Kappa, Phi Beta Kappa, Kappa Delta Pi, Psi Chi. Office: Eisenhower Elem Sch 2800 Drew St Clearwater FL 33759-3010

JACOBS, MARY LEE, lawyer; b. Pitts., June 29, 1950; d. George and Mary Jane (Swinderman) Jacobs. BA in History, Wellesley Coll., 1972; JD, Boston U., 1974. BAr: Mass. 1975, U.S. Dist. Ct. Mass. 1976, U.S. Ct. Appeals (1st cir.) 1978, U.S. Supreme Ct. 1981. Gen. counsel Tufts U., Medford, Mass., 1984—. Mem. ABA, Boston Bar Assn., Nat. Assn. Coll. and Univ. Attys. Office: Tufts Univ Ballou Hall 3d Fl Medford MA 02155

JACOBS, NANCY, state legislator; Mem. Md. Ho. of Dels., Annapolis, 1995-99, Md. Senate Dist. 34, Annapolis, 1999—. Republican. Office: 29 West Courtland St Bel Air MD 21014

JACOBS, NANCY CAROLYN BAKER, writer; b. Milw., Dec. 9, 1944; d. Alvin Donald and Wilma Carolyn (Robertson) Moll; m. James Ross Baker, Aug. 28, 1965 (div. 1979); 1 child, Bradley; m. Jerome Martin Jacobs, June 20, 1981. BA, U. Minn., 1965, MA, 1973; MFA, U. So. Calif., 1977. Reporter St. Paul Dispatch, 1965-66; pub. rels. writer U. Minn., Mpls., 1966-67, Northwest Airlines, St. Paul, 1967-69; TV scriptwriter Control Data Corp., Mpls., 1971-73; dir. news and pub. Met. State U., St. Paul, 1973-75; author, free lance journalist, 1975—; pvt. investigator Spl. Reports, L.A., 1986-90; journalism lectr. Calif. State U., Northridge, 1977-92. Author: Deadly Companion, 1986, The Turquoise Tattoo, 1991, A Slash of Scarlet, 1992, See Mommy Run, 1992, The Silver Scalpel, 1993, Cradle and All, 1995, Daddy's Gone A-Hunting, 1995, Rocking the Cradle, 1996, Double or Nothing, 2001 Star Struck, 2002, Flash Point, 2002, Ricochet, 2003 (nominated Mary Higgins Clark award Mystery Writers Am.), Desperate Journeys, 2004; (as Nancy C. Baker) Babyselling: The Scandal of Black Market Adoption, 1978, Act II: The Mid-Career Job Change and How to Make It, 1980, New Lives for Former Wives: Displaced Homemakers, 1980, Cashing in on Cooking, 1982, The Beauty Trap: Exploring Woman's Greatest Obsession, 1984, Relative Risk: Living with a Family History of Breast Cancer, 1991 (Am. Med. Writers Assn. Rose Kushner award). Mem. Mystery Writers Am., Pvt. Eye Writers Am., Authors Guild, Sisters in Crime. Personal E-mail: Nancy@NancyBakerJacobs.com.

JACOBS, [illegible] [illegible] b. Chgo., Dec. 24, 1941; d. Clarence Joseph and Frances Irene Hayden; m. E. Lowell Jacobs, Aug. 21, 1941; children: Andrew, Thomas, John. BS, Loyola U., Chgo., 1963; MSW, U. Ill., 1972. Day care licensing rep. Ill. Dept. Children and Family Svcs., Champaign, 1963-64, instn. and pvt. agy. licensing rep. Springfield, 1968-70; child welfare supr. Cecil County Social Svcs., Elkton, Md., 1978-79; social worker Children's Bur. of Del., Wilmington, 1980-85; program dir. CHILD, Inc., Newark, Del., 1985-2001, ret., 2001. Contbr. articles to profl. jours. Election judge Bd. of Elections, New Castle County, Del., 1995—; bd. dirs. S.O.A.R., Inc., Wilmington, 1998-2000; vol. capt. Riverfront Art Ctr., Wilmington, 1998-99; mem. planning com. Charity and Justice Conf., Wilmington, 1997-99. Mem. NASW, Foster Family Based Treatment Assn. (editl. com. 1986—). Democrat. Roman Catholic. Avocations: crafts, beach home vacations.

JACOBS, RHODA S. state legislator; b. Bklyn. m. Jerry Jacobs; 3 children. BA, Bklyn. Coll. Co-founder, formerly co-dir. Bklyn. Coll. Day Care Ctr.; mem. N.Y. State Assembly, 1978—, co-chair task force on homeless, task force New Americans, chair majority program com. Mem. banks com., corps., authorities and commns. com. ins. com., health com., legis. women's caucus. Mem. Bklyn. Women's Polit. Caucus, Nat. Assn. Jewish Legislators (sec., treas.). Office: NY State Assembly Lob Rm 733 Albany NY 12248-0001

JACOBS, RUTH HARRIET, poet, playwright, sociologist, gerontologist; b. Boston, Nov. 15, 1924; d. Samuel J. Miller and Jane G. (Miller); m. Neal Jacobs, Aug. 1948 (div.); children: Eli, Edith. BS, Boston U, 1964; Ph.D, Brandeis U., 1969. Reporter, feature writer Herald-Traveler, Boston, 1943-49; tchr. Mass. Bay Community Coll., Northeastern U., 1961-69; prof. sociology Boston U., 1969-82; prof., chmn. dept. sociology Clark U., Worcester, Mass., 1982-87; rsch. scholar Ctr. for Rsch. on Women Wellesley Coll., Mass., 1985—; prof. human svcs. Springfield Coll., Manchester, N.H., 1988—; lectr. Regis Coll., Weston, Mass., 1989—2002. Vis. prof. Coll. William and Mary, 1990; vis. rsch. scholar Five Colls. Women's Rsch. Ctr., Mount Holyoke Coll., 1992; spkr. in field. Author: Life After Youth: Female, Forty, What Next, 1979, Button, Button, Who Has the Button, 1983, rev. edit., 1996, (manual) Older Women Surviving and Thriving, 1987, Out of Their Mouths, 1988, Be an Outrageous Older Woman: A.R.A.S.P., 1991, rev. edit., 1993, 2d rev. edit., 1997, We Speak for Peace: An Anthology, 1993, Women Who Touched My Life: A Memoir, 1996, The ABC's of Aging: Mother Ruth Rhymes for Ageing, Sageing and Rageing, 2000; co-author: Re-Engagement in Late Life: Re-Employment and Re-Marriage, 1979, (Play) Coming Into Eighty, 2003; contbr. articles to profl. jours., chpts. to books, poetry to anthologies and mags. NIMH grantee, 1972-75; Faculty fellow NSF, 1977-78; recipient Dewing Peace award, Pendle Hill, Walingford, Pa., 1993 Mem.: New Eng. Sociol. Assn. (v.p. 1976, Pioneer award 1993, Athena award for mentoring 1998). Mem. Soc. Of Friends. Home and Office: 75 High Ledge Ave Wellesley MA 02482-1042

JACOBS, SUSAN S. ambassador; b. Detroit, Jan. 1945; m. Barry Jacobs; 3 children. BA in Polit. Sci., U. Mich.; postgrad., George Washington Univ. Various former positions in Caracas, Tel Aviv, New Delhi and San Salvador U.S. Dept. of State; former dep. asst. sec. for global affairs Bur. of Legis. Affairs, Washington; U.S. amb. to Papua New Guinea, 2000—. Office: DOS Amb 4240 Port Moresby Pl Washington DC 20521

JACOBS, SUZANNE, state legislator; b. Chgo., July 6, 1936; d. Saul Wolff and Ruth (Margolis) J.; m. Gerald William Saperstein, Dec. 20, 1959 (div. 1974); children: Natalle Saperstein Eisner, Hilary Saperstein Shenfeld; m. Earl Stewart Hamburger, Aug. 27, 1976; stepchildren: David Hamburger, Steven Hamburger, Joel Hamburger. BA, U. Calif., 1958; MS in Edn., Nat. Louis U., Evanston, Ill., 1972; postgrad., Vanderbilt U., 1981-84. Tchr. 4th, 6th, and 8th grade Pub. and Pvt. Sch. Systems, Chgo., 1960-70; dir. The Tchr. Ctr., Arlington Heights Sch. Dist., Ill., 1972-76; mgr. coop. edn. Oakton C.C., Des Plaines, Ill., 1977-83; legis. asst. Florida Legis., 1985-90; mem. Fla. Ho. Reps., Tallahassee, 1992, 94—, vice chair, higher edn. oversight com., mem., fin. and taxation com., chair, aging and human svcs. com., mem., corrections com. Featured in 60 Minutes TV Show, 1994. Bd. dirs. Anti Defamation League of Palm Beach County, 1993—, The Homeless Coalition of Palm Beach County, Inc., 1990-93, Caldwell Theatre Co., 1993—, Jewish Federation Task Force on Social Justice, 1990-93; pres. Cmty. Counseling Svcs of Boca, Inc., 1991—, NOW, 1991-92; founding bd. dir. Aid to Victims of Domestic Assault Shelter, Inc., 1986; legis. com. chair Palm Beach County Dem. Exec. Com., 1988-90, program chair, 1990-92; del. Dem. Nat. Convention, 1988; coord. South Palm Beach County Dem. Predsl. Campaign, 1988. Recipient Outstanding Legislator Consumers Rights award Acad. Fla. Trial Lawyers, 1994; named Freshman Friend of Edn. by Fla. Teaching Profession and United Faculty of Fla., 1994. Democrat. Jewish. Office: Fla Ho Reps 302 House Office Bldg Tallahassee FL 32399 also: 990 S Congress Ave Ste 5 Delray Beach FL 33445-4681

JACOBS, WENDY, editor, writer, translator; b. Conn. d. Gerald and Eileen Jacobs. BA, U. Conn., 1974; postgrad., Norwich U. (now Vt. Coll.), 1974, Ind. U., 1975, U. Toronto, 1979. Mem. editl. dept. Plenum Pub., N.Y.C., 1974-77; editor Macmillan Pub., Toronto, Ont., Can., 1978-79; cons., writer, editor Bus., Govt., Pub., Toronto, 1980-91, Bus., Acad., Pub., New Orleans, 1991—. Office: 5645 Lakeview Mews Dr Boynton Beach FL 33437

JACOBSEN, DIANE DEMELL, business executive and foreign policy specialist; b. N.Y.C., Sept. 21, 1944; d. A. Leonard and Lizette DeMell; m. Thomas H. Jacobsen, June 15, 1985 (dec. July 20, 2002). Bachelors Degree, CUNY, 1965; M in Liberal Arts, Washington U., 1995, M in Internat. Affairs, 2000, PhD in Internat. Affairs, 2003. Sr. exec. Internat. Bus. Machine, Armonk, N.Y., 1965-86; sr. v.p. Bapt. Health Inc., Jacksonville, Fla., 1987-88; pres., CEO Dependable Ins. Group, Jacksonville, 1988-91; pres. DeMell Group, Ponte Vedra Beach, Fla., 1991—. Conflict resolution specialist Ctr. for Internat. Understanding, St. Louis, 1995-2003; adv. dir. internat. leadership program Washington U., St. Louis, 1998-2003; mem. adv. group, Coun. Fgn. Rels., 2002-. Commr. St. Louis Art Mus., 1992-2003; trustee Children's Hosp., St. Louis, 1992-94, Repertory Theater, Webster Grove, Mo., 1992-95. Mem. Women's Fgn. Policy Group. Avocations: woodworking, swimming, cycling.

JACOBSEN, MAGDALENA GRETCHEN, former mediator, former federal agency executive; b. N.Y.C., July 26, 1940; d. Carl J. and Helen Jacobsen; m. Bruce Donald Henricus, Dec. 20, 1986. Cert. labor studies, AFL-CIO, 1971; cert. labor studies, bargaining and arbitration, Harvard U., 1973; cert. indsl. rels., U. Calif., San Francisco, 1975; BS, U. San Francisco, 1987; MS, Golden Gate U., 1989. Sec. CBS TV, Hollywood, Calif., 1962-65; flight attendant Continental Airlines, L.A., 1965-69, mgr. labor rels., 1972-76; local union official, sec.-treas. steward and stewardess divsn. ALPA, Washington, 1966-72; commr. Fed. Mediation and Conciliation Svcs., San Francisco, 1976-89, Portland, Oreg., 1992-93; dir. employee rels. City and County of San Francisco, 1989-92; bd. Nat. Mediation Bd., Washington, 1993—2002; active past pres. Industrial Relations Research Assn., Champagne, Ill., 2002—. Mem. Indsl. Rels. Rsch. Assn. (mem. exec. bd. 1980—, pres. San Francisco chpt. 1985-87, Portland chpt. 1992, D.C. chpt. 1997-98, nat. pres.-elect, 2000, pres. 2001); bd. dirs., US Airways Group, Inc., 2003- Avocations: golf, swimming, poetry, short-story writing.*

JACOBSEN, SALLY, communications executive; b. Colo. BA, Iowa State U.; MA, Cornell U. Reporter AP, Balt., 1976-85, corr. Mexico City, 1985-88, corr. European Union and NATO Brussels, 1988-95, asst. editor N.Y.C., 1995-99, dep. internat. editor, 1999—. Office: Assoc Press 50 Rockefeller Plz Fl 6 New York NY 10020-1666

JACOBSEN-THEEL, HAZEL M. retired historian; b. Becker County, Minn., June 1, 1909; d. Julius and Helma Clara (Klug) Mielke; m. Albert Arthur Jacobsen, June 2, 1933 (dec. June 1984); children: Harry James, Karen Bel; m. Bruce Theel, Jan. 7, 1989 (dec. Dec. 1992). Student, U. Minn., 1926-27; BA in Science and Edn., U. N.D., 1930; postgrad., U. Minn., summers 32-33. Cert. tchr. N.D. and Minn. Dining room mgr. Lake Side Hotel, Detroit, 1922-30; tchr. N St. Paul (Minn.) Pub. Sch. system, 1930-33; with Gt. Northern Railway at Glacier Park Entrance Hotel, summer 1932; tchr. Dept. Interior Bur. Ind. Affairs, N.D., 1933-42; mem. aircraft assembly line Higgins Air Craft, La., 1942-45; science tchr. St. Johns (N.D.) Pub. Sch. system, 1945-46; hardware mcht. Jacobsen Hardware Inc., Minn., 1946-73. Contbr. articles to profl. jours. Vol. tour guide of historic places, 1961; life mem., past officer Dakota County Hist. Soc.; charter mem. Dakota County Pioneer Village; tour leader Hastings Area, 1960-89; founder Hastings Vol. Group, 1976-77; established Albert A. and Hazel M. Jacobsen Meml. Fund U. N.D., 1988, Archtl. Treasure Hunt, 1994; supporter Turtle Mountain Indian Mus., Belcourt, N.D., life mem., 1994—; charter mem. gov. apptd. Dakota County Bicentennial Commn., 1976. First woman to be selected Grand Marshall River Town Days and Minn. Aquatennial Miss. River Flotilla, 1992; established Bruce Theel High Sch. Vocat. scholarship meml. for Mt. Pleasant Pub. Sch. Dist. Found., Rolla, N.D. Mem. AAUW, Women's Orgn. Minn. Hist. Soc. (charter mem., officer), Hastings Preservation Commn. (charter mem.), Minn. Territorial Pioneers (Outstanding award 1987), U. N.D. Alumni Assn. (Sioux award 1987), U. Minn. Alumni Assn. (life), Am. Legion Aux. (life), Dakota County Hist. Soc. (rsch. assoc.), Fedn. Women N.D., OES (grand officer N.D.), 1006 Summit Ave. Soc. (life, charter). Avocations: avid bridge player, marathon winner dancing, reading, cooking, foreign travel. Address: 313 Ramsey St Hastings MN 55033-1222

JACOBS GIBSON, ROSE, city councilwoman, non-profit company executive; b. Fisher, La., Mar. 18, 1947; d. Henry Lee and Clara Lee (Williams) Jacobs; 1 child, Andre Lynard Gibson. Student, San Francisco City Coll., 1965-66, Canada Coll., Redwood City, Calif., 1987, Foothil Coll., 1988-91. Lic. ins. agt., Calif. Ops. officer Bank of Am., Palo Alto, Calif., 1969-72; pers. asst. SRI Internat., Menlo Park, Calif., 1972-75; ins. saleswoman John Hancock Mut. Life, San Jose, Calif., 1975-77; banking office mgr. Security Pacific Bank, San Carlos, Calif., 1978-87; office mgr. YMCA, Palo Alto, 1988-90; founder, pres., CEO Hagar Svcs. Coalition, Inc., East Palo Alto, Calif., 1994—. Co-founder Cmty. Network, E. Palo Alto, 1993—; pres. Reign Women's Orgn., E. Palo Alto, 1989-91, E. Bayshore divsn. Am. Heart Assn., E. Palo Alto, 1993-95; mem. Internat. Bible Study Fellowship, Los Altos, 1987-94, Svc. League of San Mateo County, Redwood City, 1993-98; bd. dirs. Am. Heart Assn., Silicon Valley Civic Action; pers. commr. City of E. Palo Alto, 1990-92, city coun. mem., 1992-99, mayor, 1995, 96; mem. San Mateo County Success Adv. Com., Redwood City, 1995—; appointed San Mateo County Bd. Supervisors for the 4th dist. (Redwood City, Menlo Park, E. Palo Alto, N. Fair Oaks), 1999—. Recipient Govt. Svc. award Santa Clara County Mcpl. African Am. Employees Assn., San Jose, 1996, Golden Mic award Frederick Gilbert Assn., Inc., Redwood City, 1996. Mem. Nat. League of Cities, League of Calif. Cities, Calif. Elected Women Assn. Edn. Rsch. Democrat. Baptist. Avocations: creative crafts (gift baskets), bookstore ministry, walking, event planning. Office: Hagar Women's Ctr 1836A Bay Rd East Palo Alto CA 94303-1311

JACOBSON, ANNA SUE, finance company executive; b. Ft. Smith, Ark., Aug. 13, 1940; d. Ray Bradely and Joy Anna (Person) McAlister; m. Lyle Norman Jacobson, Nov. 23, 1958; children: Lyle Michael, Daniel Ray, Julie Ann, Eric Joseph. Cert., Coll. Fin. Planning, 1985. Cert. fin. planner, coll. fin. planning 1985, registered paraplanner. Office mgr. Twin Cities Lithographic Inst., St. Paul, Minn., 1963-66, sec., 1971-78; asst. to pres., office mgr. Planners Fin. Svcs., Mpls., 1978-85, asst. corp. treas., 1987-88; fin. paraplanner McAlmont Investment Co., Mpls., 1985-96, office mgr., 1988-96; registered rep. USR Fin. Svc. Inc., 1996-98; nat. retail mktg. coord. Carlson Leisure Group, Minnetonka, Minn., 1998—, nat. retail op. coord. Mpls., 1996-200; v.p., CFO J&J Splty. Co., 1993—; sr. v.p. AdPro Internat., Inc., Wayzata, Minn., 1996—; acctg. coord. Carlson Wagonlit Travel, 2000—. Ind. fin. cons.; co-creator Paraplanning Profession Advisor; bd. dirs. Planners Fin. Svcs.; mem. bd. advisors Coll. Fin. Planning, Denver, 1982—; mem. Fin. Alternatives Mpls., Wayzata, 1996—, Mpls., 1985—; v.p. J & J Splty. Co., St. Paul, 1995—; spkr. in field. Del. Dem. Farmer Labor Com., St. Paul, 1980, campaign chmn. mayoral election, Roseville, Minn., 1983, county commr. city coun. election Roseville, 1980, 84; local chmn. passage of ERA Minn., mem. Am. Lung Assn., St. Paul, Ramsey Found. Minn., Como Cons. Hist. Soc.; past pres. PTA, Minn.; mem. exec. coun. Boy Scouts An., 1977-81; mem. adv. bd. Dist. 623, Roseville, 1978-81; fund raising com. mem. Twin Cities Pub. TV. Sta., 1975—; mem. ch. coun. deacons St. Michael's Luth. Ch., St. Paul, 1996—, pres. congregation and coun., Roseville, 1998-99. Recipient volunteerism award State Minn., 1981, Cert. Appreciation Minn. Bicentennial Com., 1976; named 1st Fin. Paraplanner in History of Industry. Mem. Internat. Assn. Fin. Planning, Twin Cities Assn. Fin. Planners, Internat. Assn. Bus. and Profl. Women (bd. dirs. 1977-86, pres. 1980-82, Woman Yr. 1982), Minn. Women's Consortium Como Conservatory Hist. Soc., Concordia Acad. Booster Club, Beta Sigma Phi (Nu Phi Mu chpt.). Lutheran. Avocations: tennis, riding, reading, piano, harp. Home: 2171 Dellwood Ave Saint Paul MN 55113-4329 Office: Carlson Leisure Group 701 Lakeshore Pkwy Minnetonka MN 55305-5240 E-mail: lnsjacob@aol.com.

JACOBSON, BONNIE BROWN, writer, energy executive, statistician, researcher; b. Annapolis, Md., Feb. 15, 1952; d. Albert Robert and Ruth Marie (Puhak) Brown. BS cum laude, LaRoche Coll., Pitts., 1974; MS, U. Pitts., 1976. Rsch. assoc. Squibb Inst. Med. Rsch., Princeton, NJ, 1976-78; assoc. statistician N.E. Utilities Svc. Co., Hartford, Conn., 1978-80, statistician, 1980-82, sr. statistician, 1982-83, mgr. consumer rsch., 1983-87, corp. statistician, 1987-89; project mgr. energy div. ICF Kaiser Engrs., Fairfax, Va., 1989-91, v.p., 1991-92, AUS Conss., Phila., 1992-94; owner/cons. Energy Access, Maple Glen, Pa., 1995—. Cons. stats., Hartford, 1976—89; adviser Electric Power Rsch. Inst., Palo Alto, Calif., 1978—89; rsch. plan developer Conn. Energy Assistance Study Project, Hartford, 1983—84; evaluation prin. investigator Conn. Low Income Weatherization Conservation Program, 1988—92; microgravity rschr. KC-135 Mission 89-2 NASA, 1989; chmn. Space Access, Inc., 1989—90. Rsch. scholar, U. Pitts., 1974—76. Mem.: Electric Utility Market Rsch. coun., Am. Mktg. Assn., Am. Statis. Assn., Amelia Earhart Soc. Avocations: golf, skiing, tennis, racquetball, reading. Home and Office: Energy Access 1804 Hood Ln Maple Glen PA 19002-6104 E-mail: energybbj@aol.com., energyaccweb@aol.com.

JACOBSON, DOROTHY TROUP, English and education educator; b. Providence, Dec. 21, 1930; d. Charles Leon and Celia (Shulman) Troup; children: Deborah, Donald, Ezra. BA, Boston U., 1952; MA, SUNY, Albany, 1962. Cert. permanent secondary edn. educator. Tchr. Enlarged City Sch. Dist., Troy, N.Y., 1965-95; tchr. trainer Am. Fedn. Tchrs.-Ind. Capital Dist., N.Y., 1980-96; adj. prof. SUNY, Albany, 1995—. Mem. exec. bd. N.Y. State United Tchrs.-Troy Tchrs. Assn., 1980-90; local site coord. Am. Fedn. Tchrs.-Ednl. Rsch. and Dissemination, Troy, 1990-92; chair edn. Berith Sholom, Troy, 1995—; adj. prof. SUNY, Albany, 1996—. Human rights commr., 1987-95; dir. GIVE-Learn and Serve Am., Troy, 1990-96; pres. [illegible] 1991; bd. mem., Jewish Family Svcs. Policy, Jewish Feratio Capital Dist. Named Tchr. of Yr., Coalition of Tchr. Educators, 1987, Woman of Yr., Congregation Berith Sholom, Troy, N.Y., 1999, Vol. of Yr., Jewish Family Svcs. of the Capitol Dist., 1999; recipient cert. of Merit, State Humanities Assn., N.Y., 1985, Eddy N.E. Health award, 2002. Mem. N.Y. State Ret. Tchrs. Assn. Jewish. Avocations: reading, gardening, art museums, community service. Home: 82 Troy Rd East Greenbush NY 12061-1306

JACOBSON, FRANCES M. history educator; b. Norfolk, Va., June 23, 1942; d. Joseph Alexander Morris Jr. and Ann Beatrice Ball; m. John Albin Jacobson, June 13, 1967 (deceased); 1 child. BA in Polit. Sci., Old Dominion U., 1983, MA in History, 1990. Figure skating instr. Haygood Skating Ctr., Virginia Beach, Va., 1983-90; adj. prof. history Tidewater C.C., Virginia Beach, 1990-97, asst. prof., 1997—. Adj. prof. history Old Dominion U., Norfolk, Va., 1990-99; dir. internat. studies honors program Tidewater C.C., Virginia Beach, 1998—. Editor: The American Story as Told by Participants, 1999. Historiographer Episcopal Diocese So. Va.; former vestry mem. St. Andrew's Ch. Mem. AAUW, C.G. Jung Soc. Avocations: tai chi, skating. Office: Tidewater CC 1700 College Cres Virginia Beach VA 23456-1918 E-mail: fjacobson@tcc.vccs.edu.

JACOBSON, HELEN GUGENHEIM (MRS. DAVID JACOBSON), civic worker; b. San Antonio; d. Jac Elton and Rosetta (Dreyfus) Gugenheim; m. David Jacobson, Nov. 6, 1938; children: Liz Helenchild, Dottie J. Miller. BA, Hollins U. With news and spl. events staff NBC, N.Y.C., 1933-38; 1st v.p. San Antonio Bexar County coun. Girl Scouts U.S.A., 1957-63; Tex. state rep. UNICEF, 1964-69; bd. dirs. U.S. com. UNICEF, 1970-80, hon. bd. dirs., 1980—. Bd. dirs. Nat. Fedn. Temple Sisterhoods, 1973-77, Temple Beth-El Sisterhood, Youth Alternatives, Inc., Child Guidance Ctr., chmn. bd., 1960-63; bd. dirs. Sunshine Cottage Sch. for Deaf Children, chmn. bd. 1952-54; pres. Cmty. Welfare Coun., 1968-70; pres. bd. trustees San Antonio Pub. Libr., 1957-61; trustee Nat. Coun. Crime and Delinquency, 1964-70, San Antonio Mus. Assn., 1964-73; bd. dirs. Cancer Therapy and Rsch. Ctr. South Tex., 1974—, sec. 1977-83; pres. S.W. region Tex. Coalition for Juvenile Justice, 1977-79; chmn. Mayor's Commn. on Status of Women, 1972-74; del. White House Conf. on Children, 1970; mem. Commn. on Social Action of Reform Judaism, 1973-77; chmn. Foster Grandparent project Bexar County Hosp. Dist., 1968-69; sec. Nat. Assembly for Social Policy and Devel., 1969-74; pres. women's com. Ecumenical Ctr. for Religion and Health, 1975-77; chmn. criminal justice planning com. Alamo Area Coun. of Govts., 1975-77, 1987-88; mem. Tex. Internat. Women's Yr. Coordinating Com., 1977; co-chmn. San Antonio chpt. NCCJ, 1980-84; chmn. United Negro Coll. Fund Campaign, 1983, 84; sec. nat. bd. Avance, Inc., 1991-93; trustee Target 90/Goals for San Antonio, 1986-90; hon. mem. bd. dirs. Witte Mus., 1994—. Recipient Headliner award for civic work San Antonio chpt. Women in Comms., 1958, Nat. Humanitarian award B'nai B'rith, 1975, City of Peace award, 1991; named Vol. Woman of Yr. Express-News, 1959, Spl. Svc. award Tex. Soc. Psychiat. Physicians, 1994; honoree San Antonio chpt. NCCJ, 1970, Nat. Jewish Hosp., 1978; inductee San Antonio Women's Hall of Fame, 1986, others. Mem. Nat. Coun. Jewish Women (Hannah G. Solomon award 1979), Internat. Women's Forum, San Antonio 100, Argyle Club. Home: 207 Beechwood Ln San Antonio TX 78216-7345

JACOBSON, JEANNE MCKEE, humanities educator, writer; b. New Brunswick, NJ, Oct. 26, 1931; d. Edward Price and Jean Sheppard McKee; m. John H. Jacobson; children: John E., Jean K. Pokrzywka, Jennie, James G. BA, Swarthmore Coll., 1953; MS, SUNY, Brockport, 1973; PhD, SUNY, Albany, 1981. Gen. studies prin. Hebrew Acad. Capital Dist., Albany, N.Y., 1980-87; adj. faculty SUNY-Albany, Coll. St. Rose, 1983-87; from asst. to assoc. prof. Western Mich. U., Kalamazoo, 1987-95, interim dept. chair, 1993-95; adj. prof. Hope Coll., Holland, Mich., 1995-99; rsch. fellow A.C. Van Raalte Inst., Holland, 1995—2003, rsch. fellow emeritus, 2003—. Author (with others): Albertus C. Van Raalte: Dutch Leader & American Patriot, 1996, A Dream Fulfilled, 1997; author: (textbook) Content Area Reading: Integration with the Language Arts, 1998, Detecta-Crostics: Puzzles of Mystery, 2003; editor: Reading Horizons, 1988—95; assoc. editor: Drood Rev. of Mystery, 1989—. Active majority coun. EMILY's List. Democrat. Presbyterian. Avocations: reading, creating puzzles. Home and Office: 1521 S Lakeshore Dr Sarasota FL 34231-3405 E-mail: jacobsonj@hope.edu.

JACOBSON, JOAN LEIMAN, writer; b. N.Y.C., Apr. 17, 1928; d. Jacob and Sally Grossman Leiman; m. Wilbur Arnold Cowett (div.); children: Frederick D. Cowett, Anne F. Cowett; m. Julius H. Jacobson II, Nov. 2, 1973. BA, Smith Coll., 1947. Editor bull. Parents League NY, 1965—68; pres. YM-YWHA of NY, N.Y.C., 1978—83, also bd. dirs. Mem. planning and allocations cabinet United Jewish Appeal/Fedn. Jewish Philanthropies, N.Y.C., 1983—; mem. adv. coun. Harvard Sch. Pub. Health, Boston, 1997—; conservator NY Pub. Libr., N.Y.C., 1995—; bd. dirs. Hudson Rev., N.Y.C., 1999—. Bd. overseers Ctr. for Jewish History, 2004—. Mem.: Smith Coll. Club NY (bd. dirs. 1965—68), Poetry Soc. Am. (bd. govs. 1999—), Cosmo. Club.

JACOBSON, KATHERINE LOUISE, musician, music educator; b. Mpls., Feb. 16, 1948; d. Donald Robert Jacobson and Clarice Adeline Graff; m. Leon Fleisher, Oct. 6, 1982. MusB, St. Olaf Coll., 1970; MusM, Cleve. Inst. Music, 1974. Piano instr. Cleve. Inst. Music, 1970—76, Peabody Inst. Preparatory, Balt., 1976—86; asst. prof. Goucher Coll., Towson, Md., 1980—. Piano ensemble coach Peabody Conservatory Music, Balt., 2000—; performer NPR Performance Today, Aspen Summer Music Festival, 2001, 02, 03. Musician: Chgo. Symphony, Balt. Symphony, Balt. Chamber Symphony, Gulbenkian Orch. Portugal, Royal Conservatory Orch. Pres. Fleisher-Jacobson Internat. Children's Edn. Found., Balt., 1990—2001; bd. mem. Young Audiences Md., Balt., 1988—90. Recipient 1st prize, Nat. Piano Ensemble Competition, 1977; grantee, Mayor's Adv. Com. on Art and Culture, Balt., 1990. Mem.: Daus. of Norway. Democrat. Avocations: ballet, yoga, swimming. Office: Peabody Conservatory Music I E Mt Vernon Pl Baltimore MD 21202 Office Phone: 410-659-8100 1135.

JACOBSON, LESLIE SARI, biologist, educator; b. N.Y.C., May 22, 1933; d. William and Gussie (Mintz) Goldberg; m. Homer Jacobson, Aug. 18, 1957 (div. Dec. 1995); children: Guy Joseph, Ethan Samuel. BS, Bklyn. Coll., 1954, MA, 1955; postgrad., Columbia U., 1956; postgrad. (NIH fellow), Calif. Inst. Tech., 1960; PhD, NYU, 1962. Instr. dept. biology Bklyn. Coll., 1954-57; prof. biology L.I. Coll. Nursing, Bklyn., 1963-74, dean Grad. Sch., 1973-74; asst. prof. biology Long Island U., Bklyn., 1963; fellow dept. chemistry Bklyn. Coll., 1961-63, prof. health sci., 1974—, dean Sch. Gen. Studies and Continuing Higher Edn., 1974-80, dean Grad. Studies and Continuing Higher Edn., 1980-82, dean Grad. Studies, 1980-88, dean Grad. Studies and Rsch., 1988-89, prof. dept. health and nutritions scis., 1989—, chair dept. health and nutrition sci., 2003—, exec. dir. Applied Scis. Inst., 1994-95, Koppelman prof., 1995-97; acting v.p. Rsch. Found. CUNY, N.Y.C., 1998—2000. Chair Brooklyn Coll. Dept. Health And Nutrition Sci., 2003-2006; nat. program chmn. Assn. Continuing Higher Edn., 1978, nat. bd. dirs., 1978-81, pres.-elect, 1980-81, pres., 1981-82; bd. dirs. Center for Labor and Mgmt., N.Y.; dir. N.Y. Regional Cabinet Adult Continuing Edn., 1982—; mem. adv. com. on minorities Coun. Grad. Schs., 1987-90, svcs. com. Grad. Record Exam. Bd., 1990-93, chmn. Acad. policy com. all-univ. senate CUNY, 1992-98; exec. com. univ. com. rsch. awards, CUNY, 1994, vice chmn. com. rsch. awards, 1995-97, co-chair univ. com. rsch. awards, 1996-97; bd. dirs. Hyperion Capital Mgt.;

invited spkr. at nat. meetings Issues in Higher Edn.; founder Inst. Ret. Profls. and Execs., Bklyn. Coll., 1976. V.p. Alpha Sigma Lambda Found., 1983-88; v.p. Mapleton Midwood Cmty. Health Bd. Inc., 1990—; v.p. B'nai B'rith Hillel JACY Assn., 1986-93; exec. mem. Hillel of N.Y., 1986-97; bd. dirs. Meth. Hosp., 1989—; v.p. Am. Lung Assn. of Bklyn.; mem. exec. com. Am. Lung Assn., 1996; pres.-elect Am. Lung Assn. City of N.Y., 2002; mem. Nat. Coun. Am. Lung Assn., 2001-. Recipient Founders Day award NYU, 1961, N.Y. Outstanding Adult Educator award, N.Y.C., 1978, Nat. Merit award, Assn. Continuing Higher Edn., 1984, Leadership award, 1986, Citation for svc. to cmty. N.Y.C. Coun., 1987, Citation for excellence in edn. Bklyn. Boro Pres., 1987, Citation for outstanding svc. to cmty. N.Y. State Assembly, 1987, N.Y. State Senate, 1987, Disting. Preventive Health Leadership award Am. Lung Assn. Bklyn., 1999. Mem. Sigma Xi, Alpha Sigma Lambda (nat. pres. 1978-80) Achievements include rsch. and publs. in bacterial virology and endocrine physiology, and on issues in higher edn. Office: Bklyn Coll CUNY Dept Health Nutritional Sci Bedford Ave & Ave H Brooklyn NY 11210 E-mail: jacobson@brooklyn.cuny.edu.

JACOBSON, MARIAN SLUTZ, lawyer; b. Cin., Nov. 10, 1945; d. Leonard Doering and Emily Dana (Wells) Slutz; m. Fruman Jacobson, Sept. 21, 1975; 1 child, Lisa Wells. BA cum laude, Ohio Wesleyan U., 1967; JD, U. Chgo., 1972. Bar: Ill. 1972, U.S. Dist. Ct. (no. dist.) Ill. 1972, U.S. Ct. Appeals (7th cir.) 1973. Assoc. Sonnenschein Nath & Rosenthal, Chgo., 1972-79, ptnr., 1979—. Vis. com. U. Chgo. Law Sch., 1992-94. Mem. ABA, Chgo. Coun. Lawyers, Met. Club Chgo. (bd. govs. 1998—), Hyde Park Neighborhood Club (bd. dirs. 1993—). Office: Sonnenschein Nath & Rosenthal 233 S Wacker Dr Ste 8000 Chicago IL 60606-6491 E-mail: mjacobson@sonnenschein.com.

JACOBSON, NINA, film company executive; Doc. rschr. Arnold Shapiro Prodns.; story analyst Disney Sunday Movie, 1987; dir. develop. Silver Pictures; head develop. McDonald/Parkes Prodn.; sr. v.p. prodn. Universal Pictures, 1994—95; sr. film exec. DreamWorks SKG, 1995—98; exec. v.p. prodn. Walt Disney Pictures/Hollywood Pictures, 1998; co-pres. Buena Vista Motion Pictures Group, Burbank, Calif., 1999—2000, pres., 2000—. Office: Buena Vista Motion Pictures Group 500 S Buena Vista St Burbank CA 91521-9722

JACOBSON, SANDRA ANN, music educator; b. L.A., Sept. 20, 1954; d. Arthur and Bernice Annette Jacobson; m. Howard Richard Malis, Nov. 15, 1952. AA cum laude, L.A. Valley Coll., 1975; BA in Music with high honors, Calif. State U., L.A., 1978, MA in Music, 1983. Tchg. credential lifetime single subject music Calif., tchg. credential supplementary English Calif., cert. Orff-Schulwerk level II music Calif., Orff-Schulwerk level III music Calif. Violin tchr. Saturday Conservatory of Music Calif. State U., L.A., 1978—83; pvt. violin tchr. L.A., 1979—94; music educator East Whittier City Sch. Dist., Whittier, Calif., 1980—. Violin clinician L.A. City Sch. Music Assn., 1998. Mem.: Am. Recorder Soc. (assoc.), Am. Orff Schulwerk Assn. (assoc.), Music Educators Nat. Conf. (assoc.), So. Calif. Sch. Band Orch. Assn. (assoc.), Am. String Tchr. Assn. (assoc.), Kappa Delta Pi (assoc.), Phi Kappa Phi (assoc.). Office: East Whittier City School District 14535 E Whittier Blvd Whittier CA 90605 Personal E-mail: sajmusic@aol.com. Business E-Mail: ewcsd@k12.ca.us.

JACOBSON, SANDRA W., lawyer; b. Bklyn., Feb. 1, 1930; d. Elias and Anna (Goldstein) Weinstein; m. Irving Jacobson, July 31, 1953; 1 child, Bonnie Nancy. BA, Vassar Coll., 1951; LLB, Yale U., 1954. Bar: N.Y. 1955, U.S. Supreme Ct. 1960, U.S. Dist. Ct. (so., ea. dists.) N.Y. 1972, U.S. Ct. Appeals (2nd cir.) 1975. Ptnr. Mulligan, Jacobson & Langenus, N.Y.C., 1964-88, Hall, McNicol, Hamilton & Clark, N.Y.C., 1988-92; sole practitioner N.Y.C., 1992—2003; atty. NY Sisters Place Legal Counsel Ctr., 2003—. Lectr. in family law. Contbr. articles to profl. jours. and chpts. to books. Mem.: ABA (family law sect.), Internat. Acad. Matrimonial Lawyers, Westchester Women's Bar Assn., Ind. Jud. Screening Panel, Com. to Improve Availability of Legal Svcs., Am. Acad. Matrimonial Lawyers (bd. mgrs. N.Y. chpt. 1987—89, 1991—93, chair lawyer specialization com. 1999—2000, bd. mgrs. N.Y. chpt., 1995-98, 2000-2002, v.p., 1998-2000, 2002-), Westchester County Bar Assn., Assn. of Bar of City of N.Y. (com. women in the cts. 1986—96, sec. 1987—90, state cts. of superior juridiction 1987—90, women in the profession 1989—92, chair 1990—93, chmn. 1990—93, judiciary 1995—99, family law 1999—2000, com. matrimonial law, 1984-87, 2001-, chmn. 1990-98), Women's Bar Assn. of State of N.Y. (chair cts. com. 1987—88, CLE com. 1998—99, by-laws 1999—2001, co-chair amicus com. 2002—, matrimonial com., co-chmn. 1987-89, co-chair task force on ct. reogrn.), N.Y. Women's Bar Assn. (matrimonial and family law com. 1984—2000, chmn. 1986—88, jud. screening com. 1987—88, pres. 1989—90, ethics commn. 1990—), N.Y. State Bar Assn. (co-chair lawyer specialization 1999—, family law sect., legis. and exec. com.), Phi Beta Kappa. Office: NY Sisters Place 2 Lyon Pl Ste 300 White Plains NY 10601

JACOBSON, SUSAN BOGEN, psychotherapist; b. Far Rockaway, N.Y., June 19, 1957; d. Paul and Blanche (Itzkowitz) Bogen; m. Adam Hartley Jacobson. BS in Bus. Adminstrn., SUNY, Albany, 1977; MS in Mental Health Counseling, Nova U., Ft. Lauderdale, Fla., 1992. Nat. cert. counselor; lic. mental health counselor, Fla. Pvt. pactice psychotherapist, Boca Raton, Fla., 1992—; instr. CCM Partnerships, Inc., Delray Beach, Fla., 1995—. Officer Coun. for Marriage Preservation and Divorce Resolution, Boca Raton, 1995; mem. 15th Judicial Cir. Ctl Arbitration Com. for Fla. Bar, 1999-2000. Bd. dirs. Aid for Victims of Domestic Assault, 1998. Mem.: ACA. Avocations: golf, boating, gourmet cooking. Office: 1498 W Palmetto Park Rd Ste 498 Boca Raton FL 33486

JACOBSON, TRACEY ANN, ambassador; m. Lars Anders Johansson; 1 stepchild, Emmelie Johansson. BA, MA, John Hopkins U. Dep. exec. sec. Nat. Security Coun. for the White House; dep. chief of mission U.S. Embassy, Riga, Latvia, 2000—03, amb., 2003—. Fgn. svc., Seoul, Republic of Korea, Nassau, The Bahamas, Moscow; with Bur. of Intelligence and Rsch., Bur. of Western Hemisphere Affairs, Under Sec. for Mgmt. Office: Am Embassy 9 1984 St 744000 Ashgabat Turkmenistan*

JACOBUS, ELIZABETH LOOMIS, volunteer; b. Chgo., Apr. 18, 1922; d. Eustis Holcomb and Elsie Violet (Cole) Loomis; student public schs., Bothell, Wash.; m. Elbert Ross Jacobus, July 3, 1995, div. Samuel Walker Griffin,; children: James Loomis Ferguson, Thomas Eustis Wells. Bookkeeper, Bekins Moving Co., 1940-42, Keener's Meat Market, 1957-67. Mem. Northshore Bicentennial Com., Bothell, 1974-76; vol. Northshore Senior Ctr.; pres. Colonial Dames XVII Century, 1974-76; dist. pres. Vets. World War I Aux., 1977-78; state regent DAR, Wash., 1978-80. Recipient Americanism award VFW, 1978; medal of appreciation SAR, 1978. Mem. New Eng. Women, Am. Legion Aux., Daus. Brit. Empire, Bothell Hist. Soc., Wash. Gens., Freedom Found., Daus. Am. Colonists. Republican. Baptist. Clubs: Navy Mother's, Rebekahs. Home: 23632 N Lake Cir Bothell WA 98021-8574

JACOBY, BEVERLY SCHREIBER, art consultant; b. Cin., Mar. 25, 1950; d. Ben and Sylvia Schreiber; m. John Eric Jacoby, Aug. 3, 1975; children: Elizabeth, Charles. BA magna cum laude, Barnard Coll., 1972; PhD in Fine Arts, Harvard U., 1983. Expert dept. old master drawings Sotheby's, N.Y.C., 1979-82; fine art cons. Nordstern Ins. Co. Am., N.Y.C., 1985-87; from head dept. old master drawings to sr. tech. expert Christie's, N.Y.C., 1989-92; founder and pres. Beverly Schreiber Jacoby Fine Arts & Appraisal Svcs., Ltd., N.Y.C., 1992—. Art adv. Weininger Found., Inc., 1999-; cons. Naval War Coll. Ctr. Naval Wargaming Studies (CNWS), Newport, R.I., 2000-01; adj. faculty N.Y.U., Programs in Art Adminstrn., Sch. Continuing and Profl. Studies, 2002-; conf. co-dir., Art in an Age of Uncertainty, 2002; lectr. in field. Contbg. author, N.Y. Law Jour.; contbr. articles to profl. jours. Chair arts & culture adv. com. 14th Congl. Dist., N.Y.C., 1992—; active Sec. Navy's Adv. Subcom. on Naval History, Washington, 1995-2004; juror 14th Congl. Dist. N.Y. Congl. Arts Caucus Art Competition, 2003-. Guest scholar J. Paul Getty Art Mus., Malibu, 1986; Smithsonian fellow, 1978-79, Agnes Mongan Travelling fellow Harvard U., 1977. Fellow The Pierpont Morgan Libr.; mem. Am. Assn. Mus., Appraisers Assn. Am., N.Y. Hist. Soc. (collections com. 1994-2003, juror scholastic art & writing awards 1995), Soc. History Art Francais, Harvard Club N.Y.; mem. ArtTable, Inc.

JACOBY, TERESA MICHELLE, animal behaviorist, business owner, entrepreneur; b. El Dorado, Ark., Feb. 12, 1956; d. Ray Ralph and Billie Jean (Burns) Phillips; m. Robert Gregory Oshel Jr., June 23, 1973 (div. Sept. 1975); m. Max Mason Jacoby, Aug. 30, 1976; children: Misty Marie, Melany Michelle. BS in Animal Psychology, Pa. State U., 1980. Nat. spokesperson, show judge Am. Dog Breeders Assn., Salt Lake City, 1984—; owner Rocking J Ranch, Emory, Tex.; First Choice Contractors; co-owner Totalease Concepts Corp. Owner MDM Interior Painting and Design. Author: Innervisions. Mem. S.W. Pit Bull Assn. (charter, founding, past pres.), Lone Star State Pit Bull Club (past sec.), Endangered Breed Assn. (nat. rep.), Responsible Dog Owners of Tex. (founding), North Tex. Pit Bull Club, Am. Quarter Horse Assn., World Wildlife Fedn., Greenpeace. Baptist.

JACOFF, RACHEL, Italian language and literature educator; b. N.Y.C., Apr. 5, 1938; d. Richard and Natalie (Wiener) J. BA, Cornell U., 1959; MA, Harvard U., 1960, MPhil, 1963; PhD, Yale U., 1977. Acting asst. prof. U. Va., Charlottesville, 1974-78; asst. prof. Italian, Wellesley (Mass.) U., 1978-83, assoc. prof., 1983-85, prof., 1985—, Carlson prof. comparative lit., 2001—. Vis. prof. Cornell U., Ithaca, N.Y., 1984; vis. prof. Stanford (Calif.) U., 1989, dir. NEH Stanford Dante Inst., 1988. Co-author: Inferno II: Lectura Dantis Americana, 1989; editor: (essays) Dante: The Poetics of Conversion, 1986 (hon. mention Marraro prize 1987), The Poetry of Allusion, 1991, The Cambridge Companion to Dante, 1993, The Poets' Dante, 2001. Fellow NEH, 1981-82, 91-92, Bunting Inst., 1981, Villa I Tatti, 1982, Stanford Humanities Ctr., 1986-87, Rockefeller Found. Bellagio, 1993, 99, Bogliasco Found., 1999. Mem. MLA, Dante Soc. Am. (coun. 1989-92), Medieval Acad. (asst. editor Speculum 1986-99), Save Venice Charter. Office: Wellesley Coll Dept Italian 106 Central St Wellesley MA 02481-8268

JACOX, ADA KATHRYN, nurse, educator; b. Centreville, Mich. d. Leo H. and Lilian (Gilbert) Jacox. BS in Nursing Edn., Columbia U., 1959; MS in Child Psychiat. Nursing, Wayne State U., 1965; PhD in Sociology, Case Western Res. U., 1969. RN. Dir. nursing Children's Hosp.-Northville State Hosp., Mich., 1961—63; assoc. prof., then prof. Coll. Nursing Univ. Iowa, Iowa City, 1969—76; prof., assoc. dean Sch. Nursing U. Colo., Denver, 1976—80; prof., dir. rsch. ctr. sch. nursing U. Md., Balt., 1980—90, dir. ctr. for health policy rsch., 1988—90; prof. sch. nursing, Independence Found. chair health policy Johns Hopkins U., Balt., 1990—95; prof., assoc. dean for rsch. Coll. Nursing Wayne State, Detroit, 1996. Co-chmn. panels to develop clin. guidelines for pain mgmt. U.S. Agy. for Health Care Policy and Rsch., 1990—94; chair AIDS study sect. NIH, 1990—92. Co-author: Organizing for Independent Nursing Practice, 1977 (named Book of Yr., Am. Jour. Nursing), A Process Measure for Primary Care: The Nurse Practitioner Rating Form, 1981 (named Book of Yr., Am. Jour. Nursing); editor: Pain: A Sourcebook for Nurses, 1977 (named Book of Yr., Am. Jour. Nursing). Recipient Disting. Achievement in Nursing Rsch. and Scholarship, Alumni Assn., Columbia U. Tchrs. Coll., 1975, Disting. award for spl. achievement, Nat. Coalition for Cancer Survivorship, 1994, Cameo award for rsch. excellence, Sigma Theta Tau, 1996, Rozella Schlotfeldt Leadership award, MAIN, 1997; fellow Carver fellow, U. Iowa, 1972. Fellow: Am. Acad. Nursing; mem.: Wayne State U. Alumni Assn. (Disting. Alumni award 1994), Inst. of Medicine, NAS (com. on nat. needs for biomed. and rsch. pers. 1984—87), Am. Acad. Nursing, Am. Health Quality Assn. (bd. dirs. 1998—2001), Am. Pain Soc. (chair clin. practice guidelines com. 1995—2000, bd. dirs. 1999—2001), Am. Nurses Found. (pres. 1982—85), AMA (mem. health policy agenda work group 1983—86), ANA (dir. 1978—82, 1st v.p. 1982—84). Office: Wayne State U Coll Nursing 5557 Cass Ave Detroit MI 48202-3615

JACOX, MARILYN ESTHER, chemist; b. Utica, NY, Apr. 26, 1929; d. Grant Burlingame and Mary Elizabeth (Dunn) J. BA, Syracuse U., 1951; PhD, Cornell U., 1956; ScD (hon.), Syracuse U., 1993. Postdoctoral rsch. assoc. U. NC, Chapel Hill, NC, 1956-58; fellow in fundamental rsch. Mellon Inst., Pitts., 1958-62; rsch. chemist Nat. Bur. Std., Washington, 1962—; fellow Nat. Bur. Std. (now Nat. Inst. Std. and Tech.), Gaithersburg, Md., 1986-95, sci. emeritus, 1996—. Mem. editorial bd. Revs. Chem. Intermediates, 1984-89, Jour. Chem. Physics, 1989-91; contbr. numerous articles to profl. jours. Recipient gold medal U.S. Dept. Commerce, 1970, Fed. Women's award, 1973, Lippincott award, 1989, Hillebrand prize Chem. Soc. Washington, 1990, WISE lifetime achievement award, 1991, E. Bright Wilson award in Spectroscopy, Am. Chem. Soc., 2003. Fellow AAAS, Am. Phys. Soc., Washington Acad. Scis. (Phys. Sci. award 1968); mem. Am. Chem. Soc., Exec. Women in Govt. (sec. 1981, vice-chmn. 1982), Inter-Am. Photochemical Soc. (exec. com. 1978-79), Sigma Xi (pres. elect NBS chpt. 1987-88, pres. 1988-89). Office: Nat Inst Standards & Tech Optical Technology Division Gaithersburg MD 20899-8441 E-mail: marilyn.jacox@nist.gov.

JACQUES, CHERYL ANN, state legislator; b. Millis, Mass. BS, Boston Coll., 1984; JD, Suffolk U. Law Sch., 1987. Asst. dist. atty., Middlesex County; asst. atty. gen.; mem. Mass. Senate, Boston, 1993—; chmn. joint com. on judiciary; mem. criminal justice, elec. laws and ethics coms. Past instr. paralegal prog. Katherine Gibbs Sch., trustee. Home: 41 Hancock Rd Needham MA 02492-1831 Office: State House Rm 312B Boston MA 02133

JACQUETTE, YVONNE HELENE, artist; b. Pitts., Dec. 15, 1934; Student, R.I. Sch. Design, 1952-56; studies with John Frazier, Robert Hamilton, Herman Cherry, Robert Roche. Instr. Moore Coll. Art, Phila., 1972; instr. painting, vis. artist U. Pa., 1972-76, 79-82, instr. Grad. Sch. Fine Arts, 1979-84; instr. Parsons Sch. Design, 1975-78; instr. painting Pa. Acad. Fine Arts Grad. Sch., 1991—. Vis. artist Nova Scotia Coll. Art, 1974; artist in residence Harvard U., 1995; represented by DC Moore Gallery, N.Y.C., Mary Ryan Gallery (Prints) N.Y.C.; instr. in field. One-woman shows include St. Louis Art Mus., 1983-84, Berggruen Gallery, San Francisco, 1984, Yuracho Seibu-Takanawa Art, Tokyo, 1985, Brooke Alexander Inc., 10 shows 1974-88, 90, 92, 95, N.Y. Mus. Art, Bowdoin Coll. Mus. Art, Maine, 1986, D.C. Moore Gallery, 1997, 2000, 2003, Mary Ryan Gallery, 1997, Huntington (W.Va.) Mus., 1997, Mention: Retrospective, Cantor Arts Ctr., Stanford (Calif.) U., 2002, Colby Coll. Mus., Waterville, Maine, 2002, Utah Mus., Salt Lake City, 2002, Hudson River Mus., Yonkers, NY, 2003; 2-person show Mary Ryan Gallery, 1997; exhibited at Rutgers U. Art Gallery, 1972, Whitney Mus. Art, 1972, N.Y. Cultural Ctr. and U.S. Travelling Show, 1972-73, Internat. Biennial, Tokyo, 1974, Art Inst. Chgo., 1975, Mus. Modern Art, N.Y., 1981-82, Weatherspoon Gallery, N.C., Met. Mus. Art, Mus. Modern Art, Whitney Mus. Am. Art, N.Y., Colby Coll. Mus., Library Congress, Washington, Staatliche Mus., Berlin, Carnegie Inst. Mus. Art, Pitts., Am. Acad. Inst. Arts and Letters, N.Y.; prin. works include painting in oil N. Cen. Bronx Hosp., 1973, five color lithograph Horace Mann Sch., Riverdale, N.Y., 1974, mural for Fed. Bldg. and Post Office, Bangor Maine, 1979-82; prints commissioned by Provincetown Fine Arts Workcenter, 1992, Zimmerli Mus. Rutgers, 1993, Bus. Com. for the Arts, 1994; illustrator Country Rush, Adventures in Poetry, 1982, Aerial, Eyelight Press, 1981, Fast Lanes, 1984; film (with Rudy Burckhardt) Night Fantasies, 1992; set designer Sch. Hardknocks, Dance Theatre Workshop, N.Y.C. and nat. tour, 1989; print commd. by Cleve. Print Club, 1999. Recipient Nat. Acad. Painters award, 1998; Guggenheim Meml. Found. grantee, 1997-98. Mem.: Am. Acad. Arts and Letters (Painting award 1990), Artists Equity Assn., Nat. Acad. (Painting award 1998, Print award 1999). Office: 50 W 29th St New York NY 10001-4227 E-mail: yvonnejb@mymailstation.com.

JAEGER, ELLEN LOUISE, small business owner; b. Spokane, Wash., Nov. 11, 1949; d. L. Walter and Patricia E. (Kelly) Matson; m. Jerald J. Jaeger, Mar. 24, 1948; children: Jennifer Ann, Jason Joseph. BS in Bus. Mgmt., Lewis-Clark State Coll., 1993; MA in Counseling and Human Svcs., U. Idaho, 1993, M specialist degree in sch. psychology, 1999, doctoral student in counseling and human svcs., 1999—. Lic. profl. counselor, Idaho. Owner, operator, buyer Reflections Gift Shop, Coeur d'Alene, Idaho, 1986-96; cons. Eagle Springs Gift Shop, Bonners Ferry, Idaho, 1987-90; sch. counselor Sovensen Elem. Sch., 1996—2001; intern in psychology, 2001—. Appointee N.W. Retail Adv. Bd., Seattle, 1991-95. Vol. office support staff Coeur d'Alene H.S., 1985—86; fundraiser United Way Kootenai County, 1988; mem. Gov.'s Task Force on Immunization and Sch. Safety Panel, 1999—2000, Gov.'s Transition Team, 1999, Gov.'s Task Force on Child Care, 1999; bd. dirs., fundraiser Cancer Cmty. Charities, 1971—91, hon. bd. dirs., 1991—; bd. dirs. PTA-Lakes Jr. H.S., 1980—84, rpes. bd. dirs., 1983—85; bd. dirs., sec. bd. dirs. Kootenai Med. Ctr. Found.; bd. dirs. Coeur d'Alene Pub. Libr. Found. Mem. Rotary Internat. (chmn. group study exch. com. 1992-95, bd. dirs.), Coeur d'Alene C. of C. (bd. mem.). Home: 700 S 15th St Coeur D Alene ID 83814-3800

JAEGER, PATSY ELAINE, retired secondary education educator, artist; b. Douglas, Ariz., Mar. 18, 1936; d. Thomas Conrad and Cora Maxine Forbes; m. John Walter Jaeger, Aug. 26, 1956 (div. Feb. 1984); children: Sherilee Jaeger Zigan, John Everett. BA in Fine Arts, Chapman U., 1961; MA in Art History, Calif. State U., L.A., 1970; MA in Edn. Adminstrn., San Francisco State U., 1988. Life gen. secondary credential life gen. jr. h.s. spl. secondry credential, spl. secondary art credential, preliminary adminstrv. credential, Calif. Tchr. adult edn. oil painting Novato Unified Sch. Dis., 1973—78; tchr. art, chmn. fine arts dept. Torrance (Calif.) H.S., 1962-71; tchr. art and math., chmn. art dept. San Jose Jr. H.S., Novato, Calif., 1974—79; tchr. art and English, chmn. site coun. Hill Jr. H.S., Novato, 1979-83; tchr. English, San Marin H.S., Novato, 1983-95, leadership tchr., 1995-96, tchr. art, 1996-98; semi-ret., 1998; specialist tobacco use edn. Marin County Office Edn., 2000—03. Chmn. site rev. team Novato Unified Sch. Dist., 1981; specialist tobacco use edn. Marin County Office Edn., 2000-03. Set designer Cavalleria Rusticana, 1981; cover designer Dimensions III, 1987, also contbr. articles. Coord. cmty. vol. program Hill Jr. H.S., 1981-83; mem. Lydia Circle, United Meth. Women, 1999—. Recipient pub. svc. award U.S. Postal Svc., Torrance, 1968, Tchr. of Yr. award Parent-Tchr.-Student Assn. Hill Jr. H.S., 1983, Extra Step award Marin Spl. Edn. Adv. Com., 1996. Mem. Nat. Mus. Women in Arts (charter), Fine Arts Mus. San Francisco. Republican. Avocations: book illustration, painting, gardening, singing. Home: 40 Brown Dr Novato CA 94947-7404

JAFFE, ELAINE JUNE, creative fiberwork designer; b. Cleve., June 9, 1924; d. Benjamin and Beatrice (Rapkin) Michael; m. Leonard Jaffe, Oct. 23, 1949; children: Barbara (dec.), Ronald Howard, Norman David. Student, Ohio State U., 1945-48. Tchr. fibre-work for adults and children, 1975—. Originator (banner project) Threads of Jewish Life, 1980, (wall hangings) Jerusalem 3000, 1996; exhibited fibre work in galleries, 1975—. Mem. nat., Hadassah, Na Amat and prime time couples bds. Pomengranate Guild of Judaic Needlework, originator, designer matzoh covers, 1998; bd. dirs. Nat. Coun. Jewish Women; originator Prime Time Couples of Jewish Cmty. Ctr. of Greater Washington. Democrat. Jewish. Home: 418 Sisson Ct Silver Spring MD 20902-3151

JAFFE, GWEN DANER, museum educator; b. NYC, July 8, 1937; d. Izzy and Selma (Hess) Daner; m. Anthony R. Jaffe; children: Thomas, Elizabeth. BA in Art History, Skidmore Coll., 1957; cert. in elem. tchg., Hofstra U., 1960; postgrad., N.Y. Sch. Interior Design, 1964, Columbia U., 1973. Spl. edn. tchr. Payne Whitney Hosp., 1958-65, Bd. Coop. Ednl. Svcs., Westchester, N.Y., 1958-65; designer Jaffe-Halperin Design Firm, N.Y.C., 1965-86; tour guide Walker Art Ctr., Mpls., 1987-89; tchr. Art Express Sch. mus. program Carnegie Mus. of Art, Pitts., 1989—; mem. staff Peace Arts Exch. program Pitts. Children's Mus., 1992-93; interior designer pvt. practice, 1998—. Designer briefcases and handbags Gwynne Collection, 1993-95, fabric design, 2003. Mem. Fiber Arts Guild. Home: 1056 Lyndhurst Dr Pittsburgh PA 15206

JAFFE, KATHARINE WEISMAN, retired librarian; b. Cambridge, Mass., Apr. 27, 1927; d. Maurice and Esther (Feinberg) W.; m. Myron I. Jaffe, Dec. 18, 1949; children: Stephen Philip, Jane Elizabeth J. Martin, Samuel Morris. AB in Am. Civilization, Colby Coll., 1948; MS in Libr. Sci., Simmons Coll., 1952. Asst. children's libr. Boston Pub. Libr., 1948-51; libr. Mishkan Tefila Synagogue, Newton, Mass., 1955-58, Temple Emmanuel, Newton, 1958-59; reserve libr. Brandeis U., Waltham, Mass., 1960-62; reference libr., archives libr., rare books libr. Boston Coll., 1963-75; vol. libr. and archives libr. Berkshire Hist. Soc., Pittsfield, Mass., 1994-96; chairperson Friends of Libr., New Marlborough, Mass., 1978-94. Libr. rep. to design referenc and Atrium New Libr. Boston Coll., 1973-75; founding chair bookstore Brandeis Women's Com., Noami Lodge, 1950-75; book group leader, organizer, 1955-75; voter edn. chair South and Ctrl. Berkshire chpt. LWV, 1994-96, 97-2001, pres. 1996-97, mem. governing bd.; docent Edith Wharton Home, Mount Lenox, 1988-92; class sec. Colby '48, 1993-98, class agt., 2000—; assoc. editor New Marlborough Hist. Soc. Pictorial Hist. New Marlborough, 2001, sec. New Marlborough Hist. Soc., 2002—; co-v.p., 2002—; founder Knowledgable Voter Participation acad. rsch/comms. voter enhancement project, 2003—. Jewish. Avocations: reading mysteries and U.S. and international politics, travel. Home: PO Box 113 Mill River MA 01244

JAFFE, LOUISE, English language educator, creative writer; b. Bronx, NY, May 17, 1936; d. Joseph and Anna (Movitz) Neuwirth; m. Steven Jaffe, Aug. 26, 1962 (div. 1975); 1 child, Aaron Lawrence; m. Leo Gerber, 1993. BA, Queens Coll., 1956; MA, Hunter Coll., 1959; PhD, U. Nebr., 1965; MFA, Bklyn. Coll., 1991. From instr. to prof. English Kingsborough C.C., Bklyn., 1965-95, prof. emerita, 1995—. Author: Hyacinths and Biscuits, 1985, Wisdom Revisited, 1987, Light Breaks, 1995, The Great Horned Owl's Proclamation and Other Hoots, 1997; author numerous poems and fiction stories; mem. editl. bd. Cmty. Review CUNY, 1984—. Recipient First prize N.Y. Poetry Forum, 1980, First honorable mention Shelley Soc. N.Y., 1983-84, others. Mem.: Am. Mensa. Democrat. Jewish. Avocations: creative writing, scrabble, crossword puzzles., people watching, poetry. Home: 2411 E 3rd St Brooklyn NY 11223-5357 Office: Kingsborough Cmty Coll Oriental Blvd Brooklyn NY 11235-4906 E-mail: athena9x@aol.com.

JAFFE, MARCIA WEISSMAN, elementary school educator; b. Bklyn., June 23, 1934; d. Adolph and Marigold (Bush) Weissman; m. Stanley Jaffe, Nov. 23, 1957; children: David, Andrew, Steven. BA, Bklyn. Coll., 1956; MA, John Carroll U., 1977. Tchr. 3d grade E. Meadow (N.Y.) Sch. Dist.; 6th grade tchr., race rels. advisor Shaker Heights (Ohio) Bd. Edn. Founder, adviser student group race rels. S.G.O.R.R, 1983—. Recipient Gov.'s award, Nat. Sch. Bd., Martin Luther King award City of Shaker Heights. Address: 2729 Rochester Rd Cleveland OH 44122-2166 Office Phone: 216-295-4271.

JAFFE, SUSAN, ballerina; b. Washington; Student, Md. Sch. Ballet; student, Sch. Am. Ballet, Am. Ballet Theatre Sch. With Am. Ballet Theatre II, 1978-80; with Am. Ballet Theatre, 1980—, soloist, 1981-83, prin., 1983—2002, tchr., advisor. Repertoire includes: Le Corsaire, The Merry Widow (by Ronald Hynd), Apollo, Eugene Onegin (by John Cranko), La Bayadere, Bourree Fantastique, Carmen, Cinderella, Concerto, Duets, Giselle, The Guards of Amager, Push Comes to Shove, Symphonie Concertante, Ballet Imperial, Coppelia, Etudes, Giselle, Jardin auxLilas, Romeo and Juliet, The Sleeping Beauty, Other Dances, Theme and Variations, Swan Lake, La Sylphide, Undertow, Voluntaries, Dim Lustre, Manon, Gala Performance, Don Quioxte, Cruel World, Sextet, The Snow Maiden, Fall River Legend, Grande Pas Classic, Stepping Stones, Without Words (by Nacho Duato), Anastasia, others; created role Lynne Taylor-Corbett's Great Galloping Gottschalk, Bruch Violin Concerto No. 1, Serious Pleasures; appeared Spoleto in An Evening of Jerome Robbins Ballets, 1982, Known by Heart (Twyla Tharp); appeared with Kirov Ballet, 1988; guest appearances with The Royal Swedish Ballet, The Royal Danish Ballet, The English Nat. Ballet, La Scala Ballet, Milan, 1997, 98, The Royal Ballet, 1998, 2000, Stuttgart Ballet, 1998, 2000, The Munich Opera Ballet, The Vienna State Opera Ballet; dir. (movie) Angie, by Martha Koolidge. Recipient N.Y. Woman-Lancome Paris Woman of Yr. award, 1989, Dance Mag. award, 2003 Office: Am Ballet Theatre 890 Broadway 3d Fl New York NY 10003-1211

JAFFER, MOBINA S.B. Canadian senator; b. Uganda, Aug. 20, 1949; 2 children. LLB, London U.; exec. devel. program, Simon Fraser U. Counsel Dohm, Jaffer and Jeraj, Canada, 1978—; senator The Senate of Can., Ottawa, 2001—. Bd. dirs. YWCA of Can., pres., 1999—2001; mem. Beijing Organizing com., 1995—96; bd. dirs. Lions gate Hosp., North Vancouver, 1995—96; mem. Can. panel Violence Against Women, 1992—94; bd. dirs. New Door transition Home, 1991—92; mem. Hastings Inst., 1990—94; rep. Duke of Edinburgh Award for North Vancouver, 1987—99; founding pres. Immigrant and Visible Minority Women of BC and Yukon, 1987—90; bd. dirs. Big Sisters Orgn., 1978—80, Liberal Internat.; v.p. Liberal Party of Can., 1994—98. Recipient Influential Women in Bus. award, Women Entrepreneurs of Can., 2001, Women of Distinction award, YWCA, 1993, Justice Achievement award, Law Cts. Edn. Soc. BC, 1993, Dr. William Black award, Vancouver Multicultural Soc., 1991. Mem.: ATLA (vice-chair Can. membership 1997—), Nat. Women's Liberal Commn., Law Soc. BC (Multicultural com. 1992—96), Can. Bar Assn. (Multicultural com. 1994—95, Peoples Law Sch. com. 1995—99), Trial Lawyers of BC (bd. govs. 1993—, Immigration and Refugee bd. 1994—, Outstanding Svc. to Legal Profession 1993), Internat. Network of Liberal Women. Liberal. Office: The Senate of Canada 900 Victoria Bldg Ottawa ON Canada K1A 0A4

JAGACINSKI, CAROLYN MARY, psychology educator; b. Orange, N.J., Apr. 12, 1949; d. Theodore Edward and Eleanor Constance (Thys) Jagacinski; m. Richard Justus Schweickert, Dec. 27, 1980; children: Patrick, Kenneth. AB with honors in psychology, Bucknell U., 1971; MA in Psychology, U. Mich., 1975, PhD in Psychology and Edn., 1978. Rsch. assoc. U. Mich., Ann Arbor, 1978-79, Purdue U., West Lafayette, Ind., 1979-80, vis. asst. prof., 1980-83, rsch. psychologist, 1983-86, vis. lectr., 1986-88, asst. dean, 1988-89, asst. prof. psychology, 1988-94, assoc. prof., 1994—. Contbr. articles to profl. jours. U. Mich. predoctoral fellow, 1977-78, dissertation grantee, 1977-78; Exxon Edn. Found. grantee, 1983-84. Mem. APA, Midwestern Psychol. Assn., Soc. for Judgment and Decision Making, Am. Ednl. Rsch. Assn., Psychonomic Soc., Sigma Xi, Psi Chi. Avocations: tennis, reading. Office: Purdue Univ Dept Psychol Scis West Lafayette IN 47907

JAGGER, JANINE, epidemiologist; BA, Moravian Coll., 1972; MPH, U. Pitts., 1974; PhD in Epidemiology, U. Va., 1987. Rsch. assoc. Yale U., 1978; faculty medicine U. Va., 1979—; founder Internat. Healthcare Worker Safety Ctr., 1994—. Cons. in field. Founder, editor-in-chief: Advances Exposure Prevention. Named MedTech Hero, Advanced Med. Tech. Assn., 2001; recipient Disting. Inventor award, Intellectual Property Owners Inc., 1988; fellow MacArthur Found. fellow, 2002. Achievements include development of IPINet surveillance system; patents in field. Office: Internat Health Care Worker Safety Ctr PO Box 800764 Charlottesville VA 22908-0764

JAGGERS, VELMA MARY LEE, foundation administrator, educator; b. McAlester, Okla., Dec. 12, 1919; d. John Jaggers; m. O. Lee Jaggers, June, 1957; 1 child, Robin. Student, U. of World Ch., 1965; MA, Nat. Eccles U., London, 1970; PhD, DLitt. Ordained to ministry. Pres. Arch Elder's Commn. Internat., Inc., L.A., Miss Velma's Found., Inc., L.A.; univ. tchr. L.A. Contbr. articles to profl. publs. Recipient citation Pres. of U.S., V.P. of U.S., various govs., mayors, fgn. potentates. Address: Apt 2301 800 W 1st St Los Angeles CA 90012-2431

JAHN, CHERI E. state representative; children: Kendrick, Kelli, Michael. State rep., dist. 24 Colo. House Rep., Denver, 2000—. Mem. Finance Com., House Svcs. Com., Judiciary Com. Vol. Victim Outreach Info. Democrat. Avocations: hiking, horseback riding, gardening. Office: State Capitol #307 200 E Colfax Ave Denver CO 80203

JAITE, GAIL ANN, music educator; b. Painesville, Ohio, Mar. 11, 1953; d. Gail Clarence King and Barbara Mary Safick; m. Charles E. Jaite, Jr., Mar. 22, 2003. BA, Hiram Coll., 1975. Music tchr. Jordak Elem. Sch., Middlefield, Ohio, 1975—; prin., owner Tall Pines Dog Tng., 2002—. Instr. dog agility Kenston Cmty. Edn., Auburn, Ohio, 2000—; dir. tri-sch. honors band Cardinal Schs., Middlefield, 1984—. Active in cmty. theatre; soloist Geauga County hunger task force. Mem.: Music Educators Nat. Conf., Northeastern Ohio Edn. Assn. (leader workshops), Ohio Music Edn. Assn., LELRC Dog Club, Northeastern Ohio Dog Club (pres.), Buckeye Retriever Club, Delta Kappa Gamma. Home: 13769 Old State Rd Middlefield OH 44062

JAKAB, IRENE, psychiatrist; b. Oradea, Rumania; came to U.S., 1961, naturalized, 1966; d. Odon and Rosa A. (Riedl) J. MD, Ferencz József U., Kolozsvar, Hungary, 1944; lic. in psychology, pedagogy, philosophy cum laude, Hungarian U., Cluj, Rumania, 1947; PhD summa cum laude, Pazmany Peter U., Budapest, 1948; Dr honoris causa, U. Besançon, France, 1982, U. Pécs, Hungary, 1999. Diplomate Am. Bd. Psychiatry, Am. Bd. Pediatric Neuropsychology. Rotating intern Ferencz József U., 1943-44; resident in psychiatry Univ. Hosp., Kolozsvar, 1944-47, resident in neurology, 1947-50; resident internal medicine Univ. Hosp. for Internal Medicine, Pécs, Hungary, 1950-51; chief physician Univ. Hosp. for Neurology and Psychiatry, Pécs, 1951-59; staff neuropathol. rsch. lab. Neurol. Univ. Clinic, Zurich, 1959-61; sect. chief Kans. Neurol. Inst., Topeka, 1961-63; dir. rsch. and edn., 1966; resident psychiatry Topeka State Hosp., 1963-66; asst. psychiatrist McLean Hosp., Belmont, Mass., 1966-67, assoc. psychiatrist, 1967-74; prof. psychiatry U. Pitts. Med. Sch., 1974-89, prof. emerita, 1989—, co-dir. med. student edn. in psychiatry, 1981-89. Dir. John Merck Program, 1974-81; mem. faculty dept. psychiatry Med. Sch., Pecs, 1951-59; asst. Univ. Hosp. Neurology, Zurich, 1959-61; assoc. psychiatry Harvard U., Boston, 1966-69, asst. prof. psychiatry, 1969-74, program dir. grad course mental retardation, 1970-87; lectr. psychiatry, 1974—; mem. Am. Bd. Pediatric Neuropsychiatry, editor in chief newsletter. Author: Dessins et Peintures des Aliénés, 1956, Zeichnungen und Gemälde der Geisteskranken, 1956, Pictorial Expression in Psychiatry, 1998; editor: Psychiatry and Art, 1968, Art Interpretation and Art Therapy, 1969, Conscious and Unconscious Expressive Art, 1971, Transcultural Aspects of Psychiatric Art, 1975; co-editor: Dynamische Psychiatrie, 1974; mem. editl. bd. Confinia Psychiatrica, 1975-99; contbr. articles to profl. jours. Recipient 1st prize Benjamin Rush Gold medal award for sci. exhibit, 1980, Bronze Chris plaque Columbus Film Festival, 1980, Leadership award Am. Assn. on Mental Deficiency, 1980; Menninger Sch. Psychiatry fellow, Topeka, 1963-66. Mem. AMA, Am. Psychol. Assn., Am. Psychiat. Assn., Société Medico Psychologique de Paris, Internat. Rorschach Soc., N.Y. Acad. Scis., Internat. Soc. Psychopathology of Expression (v.p. 1959—), Am. Soc. Psychopathology of Expression (chmn. 1965—, Ernst Kris Gold Medal award 1988), Royal Soc. of Medicine (overseas fellow), Internat. Soc. Child Psychiatry and Allied Professions, Internat. Assn. Knowledge Engrs. (v.p. for medicine 1988-95), Deutschsprachige Gesellschaft für Psychopathologie des Ausdruckes (hon. Prinzhorn prize 1967), Hungarian Psychiat. Assn. (hon. 1992), World Psychiat. Assn. (co-chmn. sect. on mass and media and mental health, co-chmn. sect. on psychopathology of expression). Home and Office: 74 Lawton St Brookline MA 02446-5801

JAKACKI, DIANE KATHERINE, multimedia entertainment company executive; b. Englewood, N.J., July 27, 1964; d. Bernard and Barbara (Logie) J. BA, Lafayette Coll., 1986. From asst. to mktg. mgr. to website v.p. Home Box Office, N.Y.C., 1987—2001; co-founder, ptnr. Headgear Prodns., New Canaan, Conn., 2001—. Author: (plays) Beowulf: A 20th Century Evening in a 10th Century Mead Hall, 1992, Blocked, 1994, Rubbing Brass, 1996. Youth group leader Congl. Ch., New Canaan, Conn., 1994-96. Avocations: theatre, computers, british history, golf, cycling. Office: Headgear Prodns 30 Crystal St New Canaan CT 06840 Home: 49 Danforth Dr New Canaan CT 06840-2412

JAKOBSSON, NAOMI D. state representative; b. Somerville, NJ, Sept. 28, 1941; m. Eric Jakobsson. BA, Univ. of Ill., 1977, MA, 1979. State Rep. House of Rep., Dist. 103, Ill., 2002—; instr. Univ. of Ill., 1980—84; recorder of deeds Champaign County, 1984—. Candidate Ill. State House of Rep., dist. 103, Ill., 2002. Mem.: Gov. Accountability & Streamlining, Elections & Campaign Reform, Habitat for Humanity of Champaign County (bd. mem.), Internat. Assoc. of Clerks, Recorders, Election Officials & Treas., Ill. Assoc. of County Clerks & Recorders, Univ. YWCA (exec. dir., Champaign), State Gov. Admin., Higher Ed., Develop. Disabilities - Mental II, appropriations - Higher Ed., Appropriations Comm.- Elem. & Secondary Ed. Democrat. Office: Capitol 284-S Stratton Office Bldg Springfield IL 62706 also: District 206 N Randolph Suite 120 Champaign IL 61820

JAKUB, KATHLEEN ANN, medical/surgical nurse; b. Pitts., June 9, 1947; d. Michael E. and Mary Ellen (Kirchner) J. Diploma, St. Francis Med. Ctr., 1968; BA in Sociology, BA Adminstrn. Justice, U. Pitts., 1979, BSN, 1992; MS in Profl. Leadership, Carlow Coll., 1996. Cert. intermediate care nurse, trauma nurse, otorhinolarnygology and head-neck nurse. Staff nurse phys. rehab. St. Francis Med. Ctr., Pitts., 1968—70; staff nurse-orthopedics-plastics U. Pitts. Med. Ctr., 1970-75; staff nurse head/neck and ophthalmology, 1975—88; patient care mgr. med. and surg. unit U. Pitts. Med. Ctr., 1988—96, case mgr. neurosurgery dept., 1996—99, case mgr. performance improvement dept., 1999—2001; mgr. quality improvement U. Pitts. Cancer Ctrs., 2001—03; triage nurse, outpatient dept. Hillman Cancer Ctr., 2003—. Nursing rep. radiation safety com. U. Pitts. Med. Ctr. Mem. Soc. Head and Neck Nurses, Am. Trauma Soc. Home: 4372 Winterburn Ave Pittsburgh PA 15207-1185 E-mail: jakubk@msx.upmc.edu.

JALALI, BEHNAZ, psychiatrist, educator; b. Mashad, Iran, Jan. 26, 1944; came to U.S., 1968; d. Badiolah and Bahieh (Shahidi) Samimy; m. Mehrdad Jalali, Sept. 18, 1968. MD, Tehran (Iran) U., 1968. Rotating intern Burlington County Meml. Hosp., Mt. Holly, N.J., 1968-69; resident in psychiatry U. Md. Hosp., Balt., 1970-73; asst. prof. psychiatry dept. psychiatry Sch. Medicine Rutgers U., Piscataway, N.J., 1973-76, Yale U., New Haven, Conn., 1976-81, assoc. clin. prof. psychiatry, 1981-85; assoc. clin. prof. psychiatry dept. psychiatry UCLA, 1985-94, clin. prof. psychiatry dept. psychiatry Sch. Medicine, 1994—. Dir. psychotherapy Sch. Medicine Rutgers U., Piscataway, 1973-76; dir. family therapy unit dept. psychiatry Yale U., New Haven, 1976-85; chief clin. med. svcs. Mental Health Clinic, 1987-96; coord. med. student edn. in psychiatry West L.A. VA Hosp., 1985—2000; dir. family therapy clinic W.Va. VA Hosp., 1991—, co-leader Schozophrenia Clinic, Mental Health Clinic, West Los Angeles VA Med. Ctr., 1996—. Author: (with others) Ethnicity and Family Therapy, 1982, Clinical Guidlines in Cross-Cultural Mental Health, 1988; contbr. articles to profl. jours. Fellow Am. Psychiatric Assn., Am. Orthopsychiatry Assn., Am. Assn. Social Psychiatry; mem. Am. Family Therapy Assn., So. Calif. Psychiatric Assn. (chair com. for women 1992), World Fedn. Mental Health. Avocations: photography, hiking, cinema, painting. Home: 1203 Roberto Ln Los Angeles CA 90077-2304 Office: UCLA Dept Psychiatry West LA VA Med Ctr B116aa Los Angeles CA 90073-1003 Office Phone: 310-268-4651.

JALENAK, PEGGY EICHENBAUM, volunteer; b. Little Rock, Oct. 14, 1935; d. E. Charles and Helen Lockwood Eichenbaum; m. Leo Richard Jalenak, Jr., Aug. 28, 1955; children: Laurie J. Williamson, Terri J. Mendelson, Jan J. Ordway, E. Charles. Commr., vice chair Tenn. Art Commn., Nashville, 1975—80; bd. dirs., exec. com. Tennesseans for the Arts, Nashville, 1981—85; bd. dirs. Tenn. State Mus. Found., Nashville, 1994—2003. Bd. dirs. Nat. Found. Jewish Culture, N.Y.C., 1999—; former bd. dirs. Ballet Memphis, Theatre Memphis, Memphis Arts Coun.; former bd. dirs., sec., treas. Opera Memphis; bd. dirs. Memphis Jewish Fedn., 1997—; bd. dirs., past pres., sec. Memphis Jewish Hist. Soc. Memphis & Mid-South, 1998—; bd. dirs. Temple Israel Mus., 2001—, Bornblum Solomon Schechter Sch., 2002—; adv. bd. Judaic studies program U. Memphis, 2000—. Named Tenn. Arts Amb., Tenn. Arts Commn., 1985. Home: 6025 River Oaks Rd Memphis TN 38120

JALLEPALLI, RAJI, food service executive; Chef, owner Restaurant Raji, Memphis; owner The East India Company, Memphis, 1989. Author: (cookbook) Raji Cuisine: Indian Flavors, French Passions. Office: Restaurant Raji 712 Brook Haven Cir Memphis TN 38117

JALLINGS, JESSICA, reporter, newscaster; b. Wis. BA in Journalism, U. Wis. With WISC-TV, Madison, Wis.; reporter WGBA-TV, Green Bay, Wis., WGLV-TV, Jacksonville, Fla.; reporter, anchor WISN, Milw., 2001—. Office: WISN PO Box 402 Milwaukee WI 53201-0402

JAMES, BARBARA FRANCES, school nurse, special education educator; b. Elizabeth, N.J., June 29, 1941; d. Edward Joseph and Frances Veronica (Szypula) Turkiewicz; 1 child, John Wayne James. Certificate in group tchg., Kean Coll., 1981; diploma, Elizabeth Gen. Sch. Nursing, 1962; BS magna cum laude, Jersey City State Coll., 1994. Cert. tchr. health edn., cert. sch. nurse, cert. infant specialist, cert. family svc. provider trainer, N.J.; RN, N.J. Oper. room nurse Alexian Bros. Hosp., Elizabeth, 1962-63; obstetrical nurse Rahway (N.J.) Hosp., 1964-65; pvt. duty nurse Alexian Bros., St. Elizabeth and Elizabeth Gen. Hosps., 1964-65; office nurse Stephan S. Halabis, MD, Linden, N.J., 1965-71; tchr. developmentally disabled Assn. for Retarded Citizens, Winfield, N.J., 1971-76; early intervention tchr., home trainer The Arc of Union County/Kohler Child Devel. Ctr., Winfield, 1976—; sch. nurse Kohler Child Dev. Ctr., Winfield, N.J., 1976—. Guest lectr. developmental disabilities Kean Coll., Middlesex County Coll., Rutgers U., Jersey City State Coll., Fla. Atlantic U., Union Coll., 1980-92; mem. pres. com. on mental retardation U.S. Dept. Health and Human Svcs., N.J. State Nurses Assn., Elizabeth Pub. Schs. One-woman shows include Elizabeth Gen. Med. Ctr., Woodbridge, N.J., 1984; exhibited in group shows at N.J. State Mus., Trenton, 1959, Elizabeth Gen. Med. Ctr., 1960-62, Found. Arts and Scis., Long Beach Island, 1981, Kean Coll., Union, N.J., 1981, Woodbridge (N.J.) Mall, 1981; author, illustrator (booklet) Recognizing Childhood Illness, 1973. Mem. legis. com. Union County Protection Coun., Elizabeth, 1975; mem. supervisory com. Winfield Fed. Credit Union, 1977; active Dem. com. Twp. of Winfield, 1978, mem. drug alliance coun., 1990; active local, county and state health fairs. Recipient Health Fair Pub. Svc. award State of N.J., Rutgers U., 1986; Garwood (N.J.) Women's Club scholar, 1959; named Teacher of the Year ARC of Union County, 1981. Mem. Coun. for Exceptional Children, League for Ednl. Advancement of Nurses. Avocation: fine arts painting. Home: 66B Wavecrest Ave Winfield Park NJ 07036-6633 Office: Arc Kohler Sch 1137 Globe Ave Mountainside NJ 07092

JAMES, CHERYL, vocalist; Student, Queensborough C.C. Customer svc. rep. Sears Roebuck and Co.; vocalist Salt-N-Pepa, 1985—. Albums include Hot, Cool & Vicious (Platinum 1988), 1986, A Salt with a Deadly Pepa (Gold 1988), 1989, Blacks' Magic, 1990, A Blitz of Salt-N-Pepa, 1991, Juice, 1992, Very Necessary, 1993, Brand New, 1998; single releases include Push It (Gold 1988), Tramp; contbr. soundrack Colors. Contbr. For the Children: The Concert, 1993. Nominee Grammy award Nat. Acad. Recording Arts and Scis., 1989. Office: Polygram Records/Island World Wide Plz 825 8th Ave Fl 23 New York NY 10019-7416

JAMES, CLARITY (CAROLYNE FAYE JAMES), mezzo-soprano; b. Wheatland, Wyo., Apr. 27, 1945; d. Ralph Everett and Gladys Charlotte (Johnson) J. Mus.B., U. Wyo., 1964; Mus.M., Ind. U., 1967. Cert. instr. Radiance Technique. Prof. voice Radford (Va.) U., 1990—. Asst. prof. voice U. Iowa, Iowa City, 1968-72 Debut in opera as Madame Flora in: The Medium, St. Paul Opera, 1971; also sang role with Houston Grand Opera, 1972, Opera Theatre St. Louis, 1976, Augusta (Ga.) Opera Co., 1976; N.Y.C. Opera debut as Baroness in: The Young Lord, 1973; N.Y.C. Opera debut as Widow Begbick in Mahogonny, Opera Co. of Boston, 1973; created role Mother Rainey in: The Sweet Bye and Bye, 1973; Mrs. G. in: Captain Jinks, 1976; Mrs. Cratchit in A Christmas Carol (Musgrave), 1979; created Mrs. Doc in world premiere of A Quiet Place (Leonard Bernstein), Houston, 1983; debut Chgo. Lyric Opera, 1983, Vienna Staatsoper, 1986, National Symphony, 1986, Phila. Orch., 1986; numerous appearances with opera cos. throughout U.S. and fgn. countries including, Dallas Civic Opera, Cin. Opera Co., Netherlands Opera, Amsterdam, Florentine Opera. Rec. artist. Martha Baird Rockefeller grantee, Corbett Found. grantee, 1968; Met. Opera Assn. grantee; recipient Lillian Garabedian award Santa Fe Opera, 1967, Exemplary Alumni award U. Wyo., 1994; named Young Artist Nat. Fedn. Music Clubs, 1972. Office: Radford U Dept Music Radford VA 24142 E-mail: cjames@radford.edu.

JAMES, DONNA A. diversified financial services company executive; m. Larry James; children: Christopher, Justin. B in Acctg., NC Agrl. & Tech. State U. CPA. Auditor Coopers and Lybrand; with Nationwide Mutual Ins. Co., 1981—, v.p., asst. to chmn. and CEO, 1996, v.p. human resources, 1996—97, sr. v.p. human resources, 1997—99, sr. v.p., chief human resources officer, 1999—2000, exec. v.p., chief adminstrv. officer, 2000—03, dir. life ins. and life and annuity ins., 2001—02, pres. strategic investments, 2003—. Bd. dirs. Ltd. Brands, Inc. Bd. govs. United Way; bd. advisors sch. bus. NC Agrl. Tech. Sate U.; trusususutee Bennett Coll. Recipient Spirit of Advocacy award, 2001, Outstanding African-Am. Woman in Fin. Svcs. award, Mark D. Philmore Urban Bankers, Ohio Women of Courage award. Office: Nationwide Mutual Ins Co One Nationwide Plaza Columbus OH 43215-2220*

JAMES, DONZELLA, state legislator; b. Atlanta; m. Elmo James; children: Brian, Kerry (dec.). Student, Morris Brown Coll.; HHD (hon.), Emmanuel Bible Coll., Macon, Ga. Mem. Nat. Alliance Postal and Fed. Employees; tchr. cmty. schs. program Atlanta Pub. Schs.; senator 35th dist. Ga. State Legislature, 1994—. Former polit. cons.; vice chair state and local govt. ops. com., sec. youth, aging and human ecology com., sec. consumer affairs com., mem. ethics and agr. coms., mem. policy com. of senate Dem. caucus, former chair senate study com. on solid waste reduction, chair senate recycling and econ. devel. study com., 1996, mem. senate young drivers study com., 1996, Ga. State Senate. Del. 2 nat. Dem. convs.; mem. South Fulton (Ga.) 2002, Vision 2000, Atlanta Women's Polit. Caucus, Nat. Polit. Congress of Black Women, Nat. Assn. Negro Bus. and Profl. Women; chair edn. com. Tri-Cities cluster Atlanta Project; co-founder, chair Task Force for Good Govt.; mem. adv. coun. Benjamin E. Mays H.S.; bd. dirs. adv. com. Atlanta Job Corp.; mem. pastoral coun. Blessed Sacrament Cath. Ch., Atlanta. Recipient Legis. Svc. award Ga. Mcpl. Assn., Assn. County Commrs. of Ga., award Nat. Alliance Postal and Fed. Employees, Ga. Hwy. Safety Mgmt. Sys. Office: Legis Office Bldg 18 Capitol Sq SW Rm 320 Atlanta GA 30334-9003 also: 3800 Pittman Rd College Park GA 30349-1435

JAMES, DOROTHY LOUISE KING, special education educator; b. Columbus, Miss., Jan. 1, 1952; d. T.B. and Dorothy (Lee) King; m. Willie Earl James, July 7, 1979, children: Ebun, Shantana, Leah, Trinita, Caleb. BS magna cum laude, Harris Stowe Coll., 1979; M in Spl. Edn., U. Mo., 1988; EdD in Guidance Counseling, Lael Coll. and Grad. Sch., 1998. Itinerant resource instr. Northwest High Sch., St. Louis, 1978-80; instr. learning disabilities Cleveland High Sch., St. Louis, 1980-84, Clinton Mid. Sch., St. Louis, 1984-91; resource tchr., unit leader A-team for alternative edn. Stevens Mid. Sch., St. Louis, 1992—2002; resource tchr. Vashon H.S., 2003—. Team leader, resource tchr., The New Vashon HS, 2003—; "A" team unit leader alternative edn. Stevens Mid. Sch. 1988-2000, Drug Free Schs. and Communities Program, 1993; counselor King-James Enterprises, St. Louis, 1988—; team leader, resource tchr., founder Student Response Team, St. Louis, 1988—. Editor (speech) Internat. Yr. of the Child, 1979 (Bravo award Youth Adv. Comsn. St. Louis County Youth Programs), Clinton Middle School Student Handbook, 1989, team leader Drug Free Schools Community Program. Youth adv. mem. Conflict Mediation, 1992-96; mem. support coun. Stevens Mid. Sch., 1992-96; active New Ebenezer Bapt. Ch. Recipient Excellence in Drug Prevention award U.S. Dept. Edn., 1994, cert. of commendatio, 1994; granteee Power X, The Positive Peer Coalition; winner KPLR-TV Promoting Pers. and Comty Health, 1997. Mem. Coun. for Exceptional Children, Alpha Kappa Alpha. Avocations: reading, walking, stamp collecting, cooking. Home and Office: 2431 Strawberry Fields Ct Florissant MO 63033-1765

JAMES, ELIZABETH JOAN PLOGSTED, pediatrician, educator; b. Jefferson City, Mo., Jan. 15, 1939; d. Joseph Matthew Plogsted and Maxie Pearl (Manford) Plogsted Acuff; m. Ronald Carney James, Aug. 25, 1962; children: Susan Elizabeth, Jason Michael. BS in Chemistry, Lincoln U., 1960; MD, U. Mo., 1965. Diplomate Am. Bd. Pediat., Am. Bd. Neonatal-Perinatal Medicine. Resident in pediat. U. Mo. Hosps. & Clinics, Columbia, 1965-68, fellow in neonatology, 1968-69, dir. neonatal-perinatal medicine Children's Hosp., 1971—; fellow in neonatal-perinatal medicine U. Colo. Hosps., Denver, 1969-71; from asst. to assoc. prof. pediatrics and obstetrics sch. medicine U. Mo., 1971-83, prof. child health and obstetrics, 1983—. Dir. pediatric edn. program dept. child health sch. medicine U. Mo., Columbia, 1989-98. Mem. editl. bd. Mo. Medicine, 1983—; contbr. chpts. to books and articles to profl. jours. Fellow Am. Acad. Pediat. (sect. neonatal-perinatal medicine); mem. Mo. State Med. Assn., Boone County Med. Soc., Alpha Omega Alpha. Roman Catholic. Avocations: classical music, bicycling, herb gardening. Office: U Mo Hosps & Clinics Childrens Hosp 1 Hospital Dr Columbia MO 65201-5276 E-mail: jamese@health.missouri.edu.

JAMES, ELIZABETH R. bank executive; b. Columbus, Ga., June 11, 1961; m. David M. (Sandy) James Jr.; children: David, Parker. BA in polit. sci., Auburn U., 1983; grad., Cannon Fin. Inst. Trust Sch., 1988; grad, Duke U. Exec. Edn., 1990. Mem. staff Trust Dept. Columbus Bank and Trust Co. Synovus Fin. Corp., Columbus, Ga., 1986—89, dir. training TSYS, 1989—90, v.p., human resources dir. TSYS, 1990—94, sr. v.p., human resources dir. TSYS, 1994—95, sr. v.p., human resources divsn. officer

Synovus Svc. Corp., 1995—96, pres. Synovus Svc. Corp., 1996—2000, chief people officer, 1996—2003, vice chmn., chief info. officer, 2000—, dir., 2001—. Mem. tech. secretariat adv. group Banking Industry. Chmn. staff parish St. Paul United Meth. Ch., mem. adminstrv. bd.; chmn. The Alexis de Tocqueville Soc. of United Way; bd. dir. Columbus (Ga.) Symphony, Ronald McDonald House; mem. YMCA Task Force Com.; chmn. Leadership Devel. Task Force Gov.'s Comm. for a New Ga. Named Woman of Yr. in Tech., Tech. Assn. of Ga.; named one of The 25 Most Powerful Women in Banking, US Banker mag., 2003. Office: Synovus Financial Corp PO Box 120 Columbus GA 31902*

JAMES, ESTELLE, economist, educator; b. Bronx, NY, Dec. 1, 1935; d. Abraham and Lee (Zeichner) Dinerstein; m. Ralph James (div. 1971); children: Deborah, David; m. Harry Lazer, June 27, 1971 (dec. 1994). BS, Cornell U., 1956; PhD, MIT, 1961. Lectr., econs. dept. U. Calif., Berkeley, 1964-65; acting asst. prof. Stanford U., 1965-67; assoc. prof. SUNY, Stony Brook, 1967-72, prof., 1972-94, provost, div. Social and Behavioral Sci., 1975-79, chmn. dept., 1982-86. Vis. scholar Yale U., Australian Nat. U., Tel Aviv U., Brookings Inst., others; cons. World Bank, Washington, 1986—91, sr. economist, 1991—94, lead economist, 1994—2000, cons., 2000—; vis. fellow Urban Inst., Washington, 2002—04. Author: (book) Hoffa and the Teamsters, 1964, The Nonprofit Sector in Market Economies, 1986, Pub. Policy and Pvt. Ed. in Japan, 1988, The Nonprofit Sector in Internat. Perspective, 1989, Averting the Old Age Crisis, 1994, The Gender Impact of Pension Reform, 2005; contbr. articles to profl. jour. Fellow, Woodrow Wilsont Internat. Ctr., Washington, 1981—82, Netherlands Inst. Advanced Study, 1986—87, US Dept. Edn., 1988, Sec. of Navy, 1990, AAUW, Soc. Sci. Rsch. Coun.; grantee, Spencer Found., USAID, NEH, Exxon Edn. Found., Mich. Retirement Rsch. Consortium, Smith Richardson Found.; Fulbright awardee, 1979. Mem.: Am. Econs. Assn. Office Phone: 202-338-1451. E-mail: ejames@estellejames.com.

JAMES, ETTA, recording artist; b. L.A., Jan. 25, 1938; d. Dorothy Leatherwood Hawkins; m. Artis Dee Mills, May 20, 1969; children: Donto, Sametto. Blues singer Johnny Otis, L.A., 1954, Bihari Bros. Record Co., L.A., 1954, Leonard Chess Record Co., L.A., 1960, Warner Bros., L.A., 1978, Fantasy Record, L.A., 1985, Island Record, L.A., 1988. Record Albums include Respect Yourself, 1997, Love's Been Rough on Me, 1997, Come A Little Closer. The Essential Etta, 1993, Etta James Rocks the House, Etta, Red Hot'n Live, Her Greatest Sides, Vol. 1, Live, 1994, Mystery Lady: Songs of Billie Holliday, 1994 (Grammy award 1994), R&B Dynamite, 1987, reissue, 1991, The Right Time, 1992, Rocks the House, 1992, The Second Time Around, 1989, Seven Year Itch, 1988, Sticking to My Guns, 1990, The Sweetest Peaches, 1989, The Sweetest Peaches: Part One, 1989, The Sweetest Peaches: Part Two, 1989, Tell Mama, 1988, These Foolish Things: The Classic Balladry of Etta James, 1995, Time After Time, (with Eddie Cleanhead Vinson) Blues in the Night, Lane Supper Club, 1986, Blues in the Night, Vol. 2, 1987, Twelve Songs of X-mas, 1988, Life, Love & the Blues, 1988, Heart of a Woman, 1999, 20th Century Master: The Best of Etta James, 1999, Platinum Series, 2000, The Chess Box, 2000. Recipient Lifetime Achievement award Rigby & Blues Assn., 1989, Living Legends award KJLH, 1989, Image award NAACP, 1990 W.C. Handy award, 1989, Blue Soc. Hall of Fame award, 1991; 5th Handy Blues award, 1993, 94, Soul of Am. Music award, 1992; 8 Grammy nominations, Beyond War award, Best Song, 1984; inducted into Rock & Roll Hall of Fame, 1993, sang opening ceremony of 1984 Olympics. Office: Etta James Enterprises 16409 Sally Ln Riverside CA 92504-5629

JAMES, FRANCES CREWS, retired zoology educator; b. Phila., Sept. 29, 1930; divorced; children: Sigrid Bonner, Helen Olson, Avis James. AB in Zoology, Mount Holyoke Coll., 1952; MS in Zoology, Louisiana State U., 1956; PhD in Zoology, U. Ark., 1970. Summer rsch. asst. Am. Mus. Natural History, NYC, 1950; grad. teaching asst. Louisiana State U., 1952-54; part time instr., botany, zoology, and physical edn. U. Ark., 1960-70; rsch. assoc. U. Ark. Mus., 1971-73; asst. program dir. ecology NSF, Washington, 1973-76, assoc. program dir., 1976; assoc. prof. and curator of birds and mammals Fla. State U., 1977-84, prof. and curator of birds and mammals, 1984—; prof. biol. sci. Pasquale Graziadei, 2000—, ret., 2003—. Instr. summer faculty U. Minn., 1978-81; vis. prof. fall semester Cornell U., Ithaca, N.Y., 1988; rsch. assoc. spring semester Smithsonian Inst., 1989, summer faculty Mtn. Lake Biol. Sta., 1992; adv. coun. Systematic and Environ. Biology, Smithsonian Fgn. Currency Program, 1983-87; mem. nongame wildlife adv. program Fla. Game and Fresh Water Fish Commn., 1985-86; bd. dirs. World Wildlife Fund/Conservation Found., Cornell Lab. Ornithology, Am. Inst. Biol. Scis.; ctrl. com. mem. Internat. Ornithol. Congress; com. mem. Nat. Rsch. Coun. Editorial Bd.: American Birds, 1978-88, Ecology and Ecological Monographs, 1989-91, Ecological Applications, 1999-, Annual Review of Ecology and Systematics, 1986-90; assoc. editor 1991-2000; Current Ornithology, assoc. editor, 1982-87, American Midland Naturalist, 1978-84. Contbr. numerous articles to profl. jours. NSF grantee 1979, 80, 83, 92-94, 96-2002, U.S. Fish and Wildlife Svc. grantee, 1980 (2), FSU Found. grantee, 1982, 91, Nat. Geographic Soc. grantee 1983 (2), 1984, 85, 86, 87, 88, Fla. Game and Fresh Water Fish Comm. grantee, 1986-87, Cayahoga Trust grantee, 1986—, Nat. Fish and Wildlife Found. grantee, 1990-92, R. G. Crews Fund grantee 1990-2000, Conservation and Rsch. Found grantee, 1991. Fellow AAAS, Sigma Xi, Soc. Systematic Zoology; mem. Am. Ornithologist Union (pres. 1984-86, fellow 1976, permanent mem. coun., 1984—, Eliot Coues award 1992), Wilson Ornithological Soc. (M.M. Nice medal 1999), Ecological Soc. Am. (Eminent Ecologist award 1998), Fla. Ornithological Soc. (pres. 2003-), Am. Inst. Biol. Scis. (pres. 1997), Cooper Ornithological Soc. Achievements include research on habitat relationships and size variation in birds, population dynamics of the Red-cockaded Woodpecker, and analyses of population trends in North American landbirds based on data from the Breeding Bird Survey. Home: 2113 Gibbs Dr Tallahassee FL 32303-4765 Office: Florida State Univ Dept Biological Scienc Tallahassee FL 32306-2043

JAMES, HELEN ANN, plastic surgeon; b. Palmerston North, New Zealand, May 5, 1940; came to U.S., 1977; d. George Headley and Mary Beatrice (McDonald) J.; married (dec. Apr. 1993). MB, ChB, U. Otago, Dunedin, New Zealand, 1964; Fellow, Royal Coll. Surgeons, London, England, 1972. Diplomate Am. Bd. Plastic Surgery. Internship Palmerston North Hosp., New Zealand, 1965-66; residency plastic surgery Brdg Earn Hosp., Perthshire, England, 1973-74, St. Lukes Hosp., Bradford, England, 1975-77; fellow plastic surgery Mount Sinai Med. Ctr., Miami Beach, 1977-79; residency plastic surgery N.C. Meml. Med. Ctr., Chapel Hill, 1979-81; St. Joseph Hosp., Bellingham, Wash.; pvt. practice Bellingham, Wash. Mem. AMA, Am. Soc. Plastic and Reconstructive Surgeons, Am. Soc. Aesthetic Plastic Surgeons, Wash. State Med. Assn. Avocations: tennis, birding, cycling. Office: 3001 Squalicum Pkwy Ste 5 Bellingham WA 98225-1950

JAMES, JEANNETTE ADELINE, state legislator, accountant; b. Maquoketa, Iowa, Nov. 19, 1929; d. Forest Claude and Winona Adeline (Meyers) Nims; m. James Arthur James, Feb. 16, 1948; children: James Arthur Jr., Jeannette, Alice Marie. Student, Merritt Davis Sch. Commerce, Salem, Oreg., 1956-57. Payroll supr. Gen. Foods Corp., Woodburn, Oreg., 1956-66; cost acctg., inventory control clk. Pacific Fence & Wire Co., Portland, Oreg., 1966-67, office mgr., 1968-69; substitute rural carrier U.S. Post Office, Woodburn, 1967-68; owner, mgr., acct. and tax preparer James Bus. Svc., Goldendale, Wash., 1969-75, Anchorage, 1975-77, Fairbanks, Alaska, 1977—; co-owner, mgr. Lolly Acres Motel, North Pole, Alaska, 1987—; mem. Alaska Ho. of Reps., Juneau, 1993—2003; chmn. House State Affairs, 1995-2000, jud. coms. 1998—2002; vice chmn. Rules Coun., 1995-96; chmn. joint com. Adminstrv. Regulation Rev., 1997-98, ho. majority leader, 2001—02. Cert. workshop and seminar leader, 1989-91;

instr. workshop Comm. Dynamics, 1988; railroad advisor to Gov. Morkowski, 2003-. Vice chmn. Klickitat County Dems., Goldendale, 1970-74; bd. dirs. Mus. and Art Inst., Anchorage, 1976-80; pres. Anchorage Internat. Art Inst., 1976-78; chmn. platting bd. Fairbanks North Star Borough, 1980-84, mem. Planning Commn., 1984-87; treas., vice chmn. 18th Dist. Reps., North Pole, Alaska, 1984-92; mem. City of North Pole Econ. Devel. Com., 1992-93. Named Legislator of Yr., Alaska Farm Bur., 1994, Alaska Outdoor Coun., 2000, Juneau Empire, 2002, Guardian of Small Bus., Nat. Fedn. Ind. Bus., 1998, Friend of Psycology, 2001; recipient Defender of Freedom award, NRA, 1994, Friend of Municipalities award, Alaska Mcpl. League, 1996, Courage in Preserving Equal Access award, Alaska chpt. Safari Club Internat., 2000, Cmty. Svc. award, Arctic Alliance for People, 2001. Mem. Internat. Tgn. in Comm. (Alaska State winner speech contest 1981, 86), North Pole C. of C., Emblem Club, Rotary (treas. North Pole 1990), Eagles, Women of Moose. Presbyterian. Avocations: bowling, dolls, children. Home: 3068 Badger Rd North Pole AK 99705-6117 E-mail: jamesjeannette@gci.net.

JAMES, JEFFERSON ANN, performing company executive, choreographer; b. July 12, 1943; d. Robert Mitchell and Dorothea Jefferson (Lewis) Miller; m. Martin Edward James, June 16, 1964; 1 child, Rachel Eleanor. Student, Juilliard Sch. Music, N.Y.C., 1961—63; BFA, Coll. Conservatory Music, U. Cin., 1970. Vis. prof. Western Coll., Oxford, Ohio, 1970—72; artistic dir. Dance '70, Cin., 1970, Contemporary Dance Theater, Cin., 1972—. Bd. dirs. Cin. Commn. on Arts, 1981—87, OhioDance Assn., Cleve., 1984—92, Cleve., 2000—. Choreographer Corbett Awards Finalist, 1975, artist category, 1995; dir.: Corbett Awards (Arts Orgn. 1982, finalist 1990, 95). Mem. presenting/touring panel Ohio Arts Coun., 1993—96; active Cin. Arts Allocation Com., 1994—2000, chmn., 1996—97; cmty. arts coord. for grand opening celebration Aronoff Ctr. for Arts, 1995; mem. steering com. Regional Cultural Planning Com. (Ohio, Ky., Ind.), 1996—98. Recipient Ohio Gov.'s award for the Arts, 1998, Ohio Dance award for contbns. to field, 1999. Office: Contemporary Dance Theater Inc 1805 Larch Ave Cincinnati OH 45224-2928 Office Phone: 513-591-2557. E-mail: Jfrsonj@aol.com.

JAMES, KAREN DAWN, performing arts educator; d. Everett Rodney and Frieda May Ryden; m. Rodney Wayne James, Jan. 24, 1976; children: Aaron, Nathan, Noah. BFA cum laude, Southwestern U., 1995 Cert. tchr Tex. Peace officer U. Tex. P.D., Austin, 1975—77; owner and operator KJ Svcs., Austin, 1981—94; tchr. Jameson Sch., Austin, 1985—88, Georgetown Ind. Sch. Dist., Tex., 1996—. Dir. and cons. drama team First Bapt. Ch., Georgetown, 1994—; dir. Georgetown Ctr. Performing Arts, 1999—. Tech. dir.: various plays and musicals, musical dir.: Once Upon a Mattress, 2003. Mem.: Tex. Classroom Tchrs. Assn., Tex. Ednl. Theatre Assn., Alpha Psi Omega, Alpha Chi. Baptist. Avocations: theater, singing, gardening. Office: Georgetown Ctr Performing Arts 2209 N Austin Ave Georgetown TX 78626 E-mail: stagetex@juno.com.

JAMES, KATHRYN A. secondary school educator; b. Springfield, Mo., Aug. 1, 1925; d. Joseph Fred and Sybil Mae (Rogers) Giboncy; m. Charles Elwyn James, Jan. 24, 1948 (wid. May 1999); children: Kathryne Janette, Jacquelyn Annette, Charles Roger. BSEd, S.W. Mo. State Tchrs. Coll., Springfield, 1945, MA, U. Mo., 1955; postgrad., U. Va., 1968. Life-term tchg. cert. in art, design, and home econs.; tchg. certs. in 6 states. Art supr. Mountain Grove (Mo.) Pub. Schs., 1945-47; art instr. Moberly (Mo.) Jr. Coll., 1947-49, Expt. Sch., Springfield, Mo., 1949-54, art and home econs. instr. Ashland (Ky.) Pub. Schs., 1954-59; itinerant art tchr. Boyd County (Ky.) Pub. Schs., 1960-63; tchr. U. Ky., Lexington, 1963-65; art inst. Fairfax Pub. Schs., Va., 1965-68; art tchr. Terre Haute (Ind.) Pub. Schs., 1968-73, Springfield (Mo.) Pub. Schs., 1973-87. Judge sewing contests Singer Sewing Machine Co., Ashland, 1957-59; tchr. sewing classes pub. schs., adult evening and pub. sch. art classes, Ashland, 1956-58, Springfield, 1982-83. Author curriculum/art dept. Ashland and Terre Haute schs., 1955, 67-68; designer/banner constructor: Richard Ghephardt, Springfield, 1987. Campaigner Mo. State Legislators, Springfield, 1980-81, others. Recipient Gov.'s award Hon. Order of Ky. Cols., Lexington, 1965. Mem. Ky. Cols., Nat. DAR (flag chmn. 1991—, art awards 1995-97). Methodist. Avocations: china painting, interior decorating, freelance art work. Home: 1019 Joanne Dr Webb City MO 64870-1778 E-mail: jameswood@joplin.com.

JAMES, KAY COLES, federal agency administrator; b. Portsmouth, Va., June 1, 1949; d. Susie Armistead Coles; m. Charles Everett James; children: Charles Jr., Elizabeth, Robert III. BS, Hampton (Va.) Inst., 1971. Traffic svc. advisor C&P Telephone, Roanoke, Va., 1971-72, group supr., 1973, force mgr., 1974; conf. coord. devel. disabilities project State of Va., Richmond, 1978-79; asst. to housing coord. Housing Opportunities Made Equal, Richmond, 1980-81, dir. community edn. and devel., 1981-83; personnel dir. Cir. City Stores, Beltsville, Md., 1983-85; dir. pub. affairs Nat. Right to Life Com., Washington, 1985-88; asst. sec. pub. affairs Dept. Health and Human Svcs., Washington, 1989—90; assoc. dir. Office of Nat. Drug Control Policy, 1991—93; sr. v.p. Family Rsch. Coun., 1993—94; sec. Health and Human Resources Dept. Richmond, Va., 1994—96; dean Sch. of Govt. Regent U., 1996—99; sr. fellow of the Citizenship Project Heritage Found., 1999—2001; dir. O.P.M., Washington, 2001—. Pres. Black Ams. for Life, Washington, D.C., 1985-88; asst. sec. pub. affairs HHS Office of the Sec., Washington, D.C., 1989—; mem. White House Com. on Children, Washington, D.C., 1988, White House Task Force on Blacks, Washington, D.C., 1988, Nat. Coalition on Pro-Family Issues, Washington, D.C., 1988; co-founder Nat. Family Inst., Washington, D.C., 1987; chair, Nat. Gambling Impact Study Com., 1999-2001. Contbr. numerous articles to jours. and newspapers. Republican. Presbyterian. Avocations: reading, walking, cooking. Office: OPM Off of Dir Theodore Roosevelt Bldg 1900 E St NW Washington DC 20415-1000*

JAMES, KAY LOUISE, management consultant, healthcare executive; b. Little Rock, Feb. 13, 1948; d. Charles Robert and Mary Virginia (Morgan) J. BA, Vanderbilt U., 1970; MBA, U. Chgo., 1986. Diplomate Am. Coll. Healthcare Execs.; CPA, Ill., Mo. Mgr. Wallace Community Mental Health Ctr., Nashville, 1978-79; sr. cons. Ernst & Whinney, Washington, 1978-79, Chgo., 1979-81, mgr., 1981-84; dir. Am. Hosp. Supply Corp., Evanston, Ill., 1984-85; mgr. Am. Hosp. Supply Fin. Corp., Evanston, 1985-86; sr. mgr. KPMG Peat Marwick, Kansas City, Mo., 1986-89, ptnr., 1989-92, Katz, James & Assocs., Inc., Plymouth Meeting, Pa., 1992-93; pres. James Mgmt. Assocs., Inc., Nashville, 1994—2003; CEO U.S. Med. Minds, 2000—02; pres. TAB Nashville, 2001—. Spkr. mgmt. and entrepreneurial topics various grad. programs and profl. assns. Mem. AICPA. Democrat. Avocation: tennis. Office: TAB Nashville 3200 West End Ave Ste 500 Nashville TN 37203-1322

JAMES, LOMA GAYLE, construction executive, realtor; b. Silverton, Tex., July 17, 1939; d. Charlie Alexander and Ida Irene (Oliver) Holt; m. Robert Richard James, Jan. 11, 1959; 1 child, Charles Monk II; 1 child, Rhonda Renee DesChamp. Grad., Ahrens Real Estate Sch., Art Alley. Sales Goettee Builders, Spring, Tex., 1973—75; realtor Century 21, Houston, 1975—80; ind. broker Spring, 1980—93; home builder Cornerstone Homes. Mem.: Houston Bd. Realtors, Houston Home Builders Assn. Avocations: painting, decorating, travel, boating. Home: 323 Springwoods Spring TX 77386 Office: Cornerstone Homes 5910 FM 1488 Magnolia TX 77354 E-mail: gjames@cornercustomhomes.com.

JAMES, MARIA-ELENA, federal judge; b. 1953; BA, U. Calif., Irvine, 1975; JD, U. San Francisco, 1978. Dir. consumer fraud unit Office of Dist. Atty., San Francisco, 1978-80; dep. pub. defender San Francisco, 1980-84; dep. city atty., 1984-88; commr. Calif. Superior Ct., 1988-94; apptd. magistrate judge no. dist. U.S. Dist. Ct. Calif., 1994. Office: 450 Golden Gate Ave San Francisco CA 94102-3661 Fax: 415-522-2140.

JAMES, MARIE MOODY, clergywoman, musician, vocal music educator; b. Chgo., Jan. 23, 1928; d. Frank and Mary (Portis) Moody; m. Johnnie James, May 25, 1968. B Music Edn., Chgo. Music Coll., 1949; postgrad., U. Ill., Champaign-Urbana, 1952, 72, Moody Bible Inst., Chgo., 1963-64; MusM, Roosevelt U., 1969, MA, 1976; DD, Internat. Bible Inst. and Sem., Plymouth, Fla., 1985; postgrad., Trinity Evang. Div. Sch., Deerfield, Ill., 1995; DRE, Logos Grad. Sch., 1995. Key punch operator Dept. Treasury, Chgo., 1950-52; tchr. Posen-Robbins Bd. Edn., Robbins, Ill., 1952-59; tchr. vocal music Englewood High Sch., Chgo., 1964-84; music counselor Head Start, Chgo., 1965-66. Exec. dir. House of Love DayCare, 1983, 88, Mary P. Moody Christian Acad., 1989, supt., 1989; dir. Handbell Choir for Srs. Maple Park United Meth. Ch., 1988-92; bd. dirs. Van Moody Sch. Music, Chgo. Composer, arranger choral music: Hide Me, 1963, Christmas Time, 1980, Come With Us, Our God Will Do Thee Good, 1986, The Indian House, 1987, Behold, I Will Do a New Thing, 1989, Mary P. Moody Christian Academy School Song 1989, Glory and Honor, 1992. Organist Allen Temple A.M.E. Ch., 1941-45; asst. organist Choppin A.M.E. Ch., 1945-49; organist-dir. Progressive Ch. of God in Christ, Maywood, Ill. 1950-60; missionary Child Evangelism Fellowship, Chgo., 1955-63; unit leader YWCA, New Buffalo, Mich., 1956-58; min. of music God's House of All Nations, Chgo., 1960-80; pastor God's House of Love, Prayer and Deliverance, Robbins, 1982—; chmn. Frank and Mary Moody Scholarship Com., 1984—; dir. music Christian Women's Outreach Ministry, 1984-88; mem. Robbins Community Coun., 1987-88; camp counselor Abraham Lincoln Ctr., 1951-53. Coppin A.M.E. Ch. scholar, 1946; recipient Humanitarian award God's House of Love, Prayer and Deliverance, 1992, Disting. Leadership award God First Ministries, 2002. Mem. Music Educators Nat. Conf., Good News Club (tchr. 1987-90, Robbins, Ill.). Home: 8154 S Indiana Ave Chicago IL 60619-4712

JAMES, MARION E. retired humanities educator; b. Durham, N.H. d. Charles and Marion Elizabeth (Templeton) James. BA, U. N.H., 1940; MA, Harvard U., 1949, PhD, 1955. Tchr. Walpole (N.H.) H.S., 1941—43; instr. Lasell Jr. Coll., Auburndale, Mass., 1943—48, Wheaton Coll., Norton, Mass., 1952—54; from instr. to prof. U. N.H., Durham, 1955—87. Chair univ. senate U. N.H., 1982—83; faculty observer U. N.H. Bd. Trustees, 1983—84. Chair Historic Dist. Commn., Durham, 1995—97; trustee U. N.H., 1990—94; pres. Durham Historic Assn., 1997—2000, Univ. Historian, 2002—; founder, pres. U.N.H. Ret. Fac. Assn., 1990—; pres. bd. adv. The Art Gallery of U. N.H., 2002—. Mem.: Ret. Faculty Assn. (pres. 2001—02), Colonial Dames of Am. Avocation: painting. Home: 4 Wood Rd Durham NH 03824

JAMES, MURIEL MARSHALL, writer, lecturer, psychotherapist; b. Berkeley, Calif., Feb. 14, 1917; d. John Albert and Hazel (Knowles) Marshall; m. Paul Wesley James (div.); children: Ann, Duncan, John. BA with honors, U. Calif., Berkeley, 1956; MDiv, DDiv, Ch. Divinity Sch. Pacific, 1957, 2000; EdD, U. Calif., 1964. Lic. family psycho therapist, Calif. Instr., coord. ARC, San Francisco, 1941-43; safety inspector Kaiser Shipyards, Richmond, Calif., 1943-44; tchr. Oakland (Calif.) Pub. Schs., 1948-52; min. Orinda (Calif.) Cmty. Ch., 1957-59; dean Laymen's Sch. Religion, Berkeley, Calif., 1959-68; instr. U. Calif. Ext., Berkeley, 1966-69; dir., therapist Oasis Edn. & Treatment Ctr., Lafayette, Calif., 1968-73; psychotherapist pvt. practice, Lafayette, Calif., 1969—. Lectr. James Inst., Lafayette, 1969—. Author, co-author: Born to Win: Transactional Analysis with Gestalt Experiments, 1971, Winning with People: Group Exercises in Transactional Analysis, 1973, Born to Love: Transactional Analysis in the Church, 1973, Transactional Analysis for Moms and Dads: What Do You Do With Them Now That You've Got Them?, 1974, The Power at the Bottom of the Well, 1974, The OK Boss, 1975, The People Book: Transactional Analysis for Students, 1975, The Heart of Friendship, 1976, Techniques for Psychotherapists and Counselors, 1977, A New Self. Self Therapy with Transactional Analysis, 1977, Marriage is for Loving, 1979, Breaking Free: Self-Reparenting for a New Self, 1981, Winning Ways in Health Care, 1981, It's Never Too Late to Be Happy, 1985, expanded edit. 2002, The Better Boss in Multicultural Organizations, 1991, Hearts on Fire: Romance and Achievement in the Lives of Great Women, 1991, Passion for Life: Psychology and the Human Spirit, 1991, Religious Liberty on Trial: Hansard Knollys, Early Baptist Hero, 1997, Perspectives in Transactional Analysis, 1998; contbr. chpts. to books, articles to profl. jours. Named to Internat. Educators Hall of Fame, 2000. Mem. Interat. Transactional Analysis Assn. (pres. 1980-82). Avocations: friends, family, travel, teaching, creating new books. Address: PO Box 356 Lafayette CA 94549-0356

JAMES, NANCY ELLEN, art educator; b. East St. Louis, Ill., Dec. 11, 1947; d. Homer Jean and Eva Lee Harris; m. Michael James James, June 15, 1970; children: Peter James, Eva Catherine. BA, S.W. Baptist U., 1970; MA, U. SC, 1990. Cert. tchg. Nat. Bd. Profl. Tchg., 2002, Mo., 1970, NJ, 1971, SC. Tchr. 2nd grade Jacobstown Elem. Sch., NJ, 1970—71; tchr. art Calvary Christian Sch., Florissant, Mo., 1977—78, Grace Christian Sch., Owatonna, Minn., 1979—80, tchr. kindergarten, 1980—81; tchr. art Calvary Christian Sch., Waterboro, Wis., 1985—86; tchr. 1st grade Grace Christian Sch., West Columbia, SC, 1986—87; tchr. art Richland One Sch. Dist., Columbia, 1988—. Tchr. coaching Columbia Coll., SC, 1999—, U. SC, 2002. Editor: (children's book) Bad Little John, 1996, Rocky and Bandit, 1997; Represented in permanent collections. Organizer, artist Hyatt Pk. PTO Fundraiser, Columbia, SC, 2002—03. Mem.: NEA, SC Arts Advocacy, Nat. Art. Edn. Assn. Republican. Baptist. Avocations: sculpting, painting, writing. Home: 159 North Shore Dr Chapin SC 29036 Office: Hyatt Pk Elem Sch Main St Columbia SC 29201 E-mail: 88doc@bellsouth.net., njames@richlandone.com.

JAMES, PHYLLIS A. lawyer; b. L.I., N.Y., Mar. 23, 1952; BA, Harvard U., 1974, JD, 1977. Bar: Calif. 1978. Mem. Pillsbury Madison & Sutro, San Francisco; corp. counsel City of Detroit Law Dept. Office: City of Detroit Law Dept 1650 First National Building 660 Woodward Ave Detroit MI 48226-3516

JAMES, P(HYLLIS) D(OROTHY) (BARONESS JAMES OF HOLLAND PARK OF SOUTHWOLD IN COUNTY OF SUFFOLK), author; b. Oxford, Eng., Aug. 3, 1920; d. Sidney Victor and Dorothy May Amelia (Hone) J.; m. Connor Bantry White, 1941 (dec. 1964); children: Clare Bantry, Jane Bantry. Student Brit. schs.; LittD (hons.), U. Buckingham (Eng.), 1992, U. Hertfordshire (Eng.), 1994, U. Glasgow (Scotland), 1995, Durham U., 1998, Portsmouth U., 1999; DLitt, U. London, 1993; D, U. Essex, Eng., 1996. Adminstr. Nat. Health Service, 1949-68; apptd. prin. Civil Svc. Home Office, 1968; prin. Police Dept., 1968-72, Criminal Policy Dept., 1972-79. Author: Cover Her Face, 1962, A Mind to Murder, 1963, Unnatural Causes, 1967, Shroud for a Nightingale, 1971; (with T.A. Critchley) The Maul and the Pear Tree, 1971; An Unsuitable Job for a Woman, 1972, The Black Tower, 1975, Death of an Expert Witness, 1977, Innocent Blood, 1980, The Skull Beneath the Skin, 1982, (play) A Private Treason, 1985, A Taste for Death, 1986, Devices and Desires, 1989, The Children of Men, 1992, Original Sin, 1994, A Certain Justice, 1997, Time to be in Earnest, 1999, Death in Holy Orders, 2001, The Murder Room, 2003. Gov. BBC, 1988-93; bd. dirs. Brit. Coun., 1988-93; bd. dirs., chair lit. adv. panel Arts Coun. Gt. Britain, 1988-92. Decorated Order Brit. Empire, 1983; created life peer (Baroness) of U.K., 1991; assoc. fellow Downing Coll., Cambridge, 1986, hon. fellow, 2000; hon. fellow St. Hilda's Coll., Oxford, 1996, Girton Coll., Cambridge, 2000; recipient Grandmaster award Mystery Writers of Am., 1999. Fellow Royal Soc. Lit., Royal Soc. Arts; mem. Soc. of Authors (chmn. Pres. 1997—), Detection Club. Office: Greene & Heaton Ltd 37 Goldhawk Rd London W12 8QQ England

JAMES, ROSE VICTORIA, sculptor, poet; b. East Amherst, N.Y., Feb. 11, 1922; d. Joseph and Mary (Plewniak) Glichowska; m. Clarence William James, Aug. 28, 1943 (dec. Dec. 1995); children: Robert, Sandra Lee,

David, Mary, Kevin. Attended, Atlanta Coll. Art, 1960-64; B in Visual Arts in Sculpture, Ga. State U., 1973, postgrad., 1977-78. Legal sec. Law Office, Buffalo, 1941-42; sec. to comdr. Air Stas. Navy Dept., Washington, 1942-43; with pers. dept. Naval Air Station, Alameda, Calif., 1943-44; radio programmer, announcer ARC, Vets. Hosp., Buffalo, 1950-54. Atlanta 1950-62, tchr., owner Studio 7 North Art Gallery, Roswell, Ga., 1974-76. Freelance artist, studio art instr. regional adult programs, 1960-72; competitive exhibiting artist, 1976-2003; chairperson 1st profl. women artist show Cushman Corp. Colony Sq., Atlanta, 1976; chairperson Atlanta Women in Arts Coop. Gallery, 1979-83; spkr. in field. Exhibited in group shows including Galleria Complex, Marietta, Ga., Colony Sq., Atlanta, Atlanta Hilton Ctr., Peachtree Ctr. Complex, Atlanta, Peachtree Summit, Atlanta, Atlanta Coll. Art Gallery, Woodruff Art Ctr., Atlanta, Bklyn. Coll. Student Ctr., N.Y.C., Alt. Space, N.Y.C., La Grange Coll., Ga., Ga. State U., Atlanta, Southeastern Colls. and Univs. 1-Yr. Traveling Exhibit, Auburn U., Ga. Inst. of Tech., Atlanta, DeKalb Coll., Atlanta, Hanson Gallery, New Orleans, AWIA Gallery, Atlanta, M. Baird Gallery, Atlanta, Handshake Gallery, Atlanta, Marietta Fine Arts Ctr., Ga., High Mus. of Art Regional Juried Art Shows, others. Visual arts panel Fulton County Commrs., Atlanta, 1980-81; panel moderator Ga. State U. So. Scholars on Women, 1981, Atlanta-Fulton County Libr., 1984. Grantee Bur. Cultural Affairs and Atlanta Arts Festival, 1978, Corp. Funding, 1980-81; recipient Mortar Bd. Honor Soc. Outstanding Leadership award, 1973. Mem. Internat. Sculpture Ctr. Republican. Roman Catholic. Avocations: golf, travel, reading, poetry, photography. Home: 6240 Weatherly Dr NW Atlanta GA 30328-3630

JAMES, RUBY MAY, retired librarian; b. Tucson, Ariz., Nov. 13, 1924; d. Theophil Frederic and Etelka Eva (Blumberg) Buehrer; m. Hubert R. James, Apr. 7, 1945; 1 child, Judith M. Victor. BA, U. Ariz., 1946, MEd, 1976; student, U. Iowa. Cert. elem. libr. Tchr. Tucson Unified Sch. Dist., 1947-48, elem. libr., 1974-89; ret. Recipient YMCA Svc. to Children award; Edn. Enrichment grantee. Mem. Pi Lambda Theta, Alpha Delta Kappa, Delta Kappa Gamma. Home: 1550 E River Rd #314 Tucson AZ 85718-5897

JAMES, SHERYL TERESA, journalist; b. Detroit, Oct. 7, 1951; d. Reese Louis and Dava Helen (Bryant) J.; m. Eric Torgeir Vigmostad, June 15, 1974; children: Teresa, Kelsey. BS in English, Ea. Mich. U., 1973. Staff writer, editor Lansing (Mich.) Mag., 1979-82; staff writer Greensboro (N.C.) News & Record, 1982-86, St. Petersburg (Fla.) Times, 1986-91, Detroit Free Press, 1991—. Cons. Poynter Inst., St. Petersburg, 1989—; cons. to high sch. newspapers, St. Petersburg, 1989—. Recipient Penney Missouri Awd. U. Missouri/J.C. Penney, 1985, 1st Pl. Feature Writing Awd. Fla. Soc. Newspaper Editors, 1991, Pulitzer Prize, Feature Writing, 1991, finalist, 1992, Alumna Achievement Awd. Eastern Michigan U., 1992. Democrat. Roman Catholic. Office: Detroit Free Press 600 W Fort St Detroit MI 48226-2706

JAMES, VANESSA, theater educator, department chairman; arrived in U.S., 1968; d. Alfred Victor and Pauline James; m. Donald Thomas Sanders, Aug. 30, 1968; 1 child, Valentine James Sanders. Diploma in art and design, Wimbledon Sch. Art, London, 1966; cert. in drama, U. Bristol, Eng., 1967. Freelance designer Joseph Papp Pub. Theatre, N.Y.C., 1968—80; freelance art dir. CBS, NBC, PBS, N.Y.C.; prof., chair dept. theatre arts Mount Holyoke Coll., South Hadley, Mass., 1991—. Guest artist, lectr. Princeton U., Pa., 1990, Princeton Coll., Columbia U., N.Y.C., 1991; cons. Mass. Internat. Festival of the Arts, 1993—. Author: Vanessa James, Paper and Plastic, 2002, The Genealogy of Greek Mythology, 2003. Recipient Emmy citation; grantee, Nat. Endowment for the Arts; Faculty grantee, Mount Holyoke Coll., 2003. Mem.: United Scenic Artists Local 829. Avocations: Greek mythology, travel. Office: Mount Holyoke Coll South Hadley MA

JAMES, VERLA ALICE, academic administrator, educator; b. Lexington, Ky., Aug. 24, 1949; d. John Robert and Anna Mildred James; m. Terry Lee Cain, Apr. 22, 1989; children: Erika Cassel, Jaimie Cain, Lori Cain-Dossey. BS in Home Econs., Ea. Ky. U., 1971; MS in Adult Edn., Kans. State U., 1993. Regional edn. adminstr. Fed. Bur. Prisons, Kansas City, Kans., 1994—99, coord. Kans. City, 1999—2001, supr. edn. U.S. Penitentiary Leavenworth, Kans. Dir. OutFront Adult Edn. Ctr. U. St. Mary. Mem.: AAUW (pres. Leavenworth br. 2001), Ret. Fed. Bur. Prisons Employees, Correctional Edn. Assn., Human Svcs. Coun. Leavenworth County (pres. 2001). Home: 1319 Revolutionary Ct Leavenworth KS 66048 Office: U St Mary OutFront 111 A-2 Delaware St Leavenworth KS 66048

JAMES, VIRGINIA LYNN, contracts executive; b. March AFB, Calif., Feb. 6, 1952; d. John Edward and Azella Virginia (Morrill) Anderson; children: Raymond Edward, Jerry Glenn James Jr. Student, Sinclair C.C., 1981-83, U. Tex., San Antonio, 1980, Redlands U., 1986, San Diego State U., 1994. With specialized contracting USAF, Wright-Patterson AFB, Ohio, 1973-77, with logistics contracting Kelly AFB, Tex., 1977-81, contract specialist Wright-Patterson AFB, Ohio, 1981-84; spl. asst. Peace Log, Tehran, Iran, 1977; acting chief of contracts cruise missile program Gen. Dynamics/Convair, San Diego, 1984-86; contracts mgr. VERAC, Inc., San Diego, 1986-90, Gen. Dynamics, San Diego, 1990-92; mgr. contracts Scientific-Atlanta, San Diego, 1992-93; dir. contracts GreyStone, San Diego, 1993-95; dist. constn. mgr. OHM, San Diego, 1995-98; v.p. contract and procurement MWH Ams., Inc., Louisville, 1998—. Cons. Gen. Dynamics, San Diego, 1985, Efratrom, 1986. Mem.: NAFE, Nat. Contract Mgmt. Assn., Nat. Mgmt. Assn. Republican. Office: Montgomery Watson Ste 101 9401 Williamsburg Plz Louisville KY 40222 E-mail: ginger.james@mw.com.

JAMESON, PATRICIA MARIAN, government agency administrator; b. Pitts., Mar. 17, 1945; d. Vernon L. and Dorothy Leam (Wilson) J. BA, Northwestern U., 1967; MA, Ohio State U., 1969. With HUD, 1970-2000, project mgr., 1976-77, acting dir. housing mgmt., 1978, dep. area mgr. Milw. Area Office, 1978-85, acting area mgr., 1979-80, 82, regional dir. adminstrn. Chgo. Regional Office, 1985-95, dir. adminstrv. svc. ctr., 1995-2000, ret., 2000. Vol. ARC, Sierra Club; active Denver World Affairs Coun., Internat. Inst. for Edn.; vol. Habitat for Humanity; vol. tax aide program AARP. Recipient Quality Performance award HUD, 1973, 75, 80, Outstanding Performance award, 1980, 85, 87, 88, 90, 91, 92, 94, 96, 97, 98, 99, 2000, Disting. Svc. award 1992, 2000, Secs. award for Supervisory Excellence, 1998. Mem. NAFE, Fed. Execs. Inst. Alumni Assn., Phi Beta Kappa, Pi Sigma Alpha.

JAMESON, PAULA ANN, lawyer; b. New Orleans, Feb. 19, 1945; d. Paul Henry and Virginia Lee (Powell) Bailey; children: Paul Andrew, Peter Carver. BA, La. State U., 1966; JD, U. Tex., 1969. Bar: Tex. 1969, D.C. 1970, U.S. Dist. Ct. D.C. 1970, U.S. Ct. Appeals (D.C. cir.) 1972, Va. 1973, U.S. Supreme Ct. 1973, U.S. Dist. Ct. (ea. dist.) Va. 1976, U.S. Ct. Appeals (4th cir.) 1976, N.Y. 1978, U.S. Ct. Appeals (5th cir.) 1978, U.S. Ct. Appeals (2d cir.) 1985. Asst. corp. counsel D.C. Corp. Counsel's Office, 1970-73; sr. asst. county atty. Fairfax County Atty.'s Office, Fairfax, Va., 1973-77; atty. Dow Jones & Co., Inc., N.Y.C., 1977-79, ho. counsel, 1979-81, asst. to chmn. bd., 1981-83, ho. counsel, dir. legal dept., 1983-86; sr. v.p., gen. counsel, corp. sec. PBS, Alexandria, Va., 1986-98; ptnr. Arter & Hadden, Washington, 1998-2000; v.p., gen. counsel Gibson Guitar Corp., Nashville, 2000-01; pres. Jameson Legal & Cons. Svcs., McLean, Va., 2000—03; exec. v.p., COO Children's Def. Fund., Washington, 2003—04. Mem.: D.C. Bar Assn., Fed. Comms. Bar Assn. Democrat. Roman Catholic. E-mail: paulajameson@att.net.

JAMGOCHIAN, VICTORIA, interior designer; b. Richmond, Va., Apr. 18, 1922; d. John A. and Azniv (Marsevonian) Jamgochian. BS in Psychology, Coll. William and Mary, 1946; cert. interior design and architecture, Parsons Sch. Design, N.Y.C., France, Italy, 1955. Cert. comml., residential and office interior designer. Asst. interior designer McMillen, Inc., N.Y.C., 1955-56, Lord and Taylor, N.Y.C., 1956-57; interior designer J. Frank Jones Interiors, Richmond, 1957-61, Miller & Rhoads, Richmond, 1961-67, Thalhimer's Indsl. Design, Richmond, 1967-74; exec. dir. design [illegible] Interiors, Richmond, 1975—2001. Projects pub. in Hospitality Mag., 1967, Interiors Mag., 1968, 69, Va. Record, 1971. Interior designer (prin. works) Country Club of Va., The Woman's Club, Richmond, Va., Busch Gardens Hospitality Ctr., Williamsburg, Va., Pres.'s House, U. Richmond, Richmond Meml. Hosp., Va. Bapt. Hosp., Lynchburg, Engineer's Club, Richmond, Rotunda Club, Hilton Hotel, Wilmington, NC, Wachovia, Richmond, Chemtreat, Inc., Cascades Restaurant and Meeting Ctr., Woodlands, Colonial Williamsburg, Inc. Mem.: William and Mary Alumni Soc., Kappa Delta. Avocations: tennis, travel, horseback riding, piano. Home: 211 Sleepy Hollow Rd Richmond VA 23229-7153

JAMIESON, KATHLEEN HALL, dean, communications educator; b. Mpls., Nov. 24, 1946; d. Wayne and Katherine Hall; m. Robert D. Jamieson; children: Robert, Patrick. BA, Marquette U., 1967; MA, U. Wis., 1968, PhD, 1972. From asst. prof. to prof. U. Md., College Park, 1971-86; G.B. Dealey Regents prof. of comm., chair speech comm. dept. U. Tex., Austin, 1986-89; prof. of comm. U. Pa., Phila., 1989—, dean Annenberg Sch. Comm., 1989—, Walter Annenberg deanship, 1993—. Polit. commentator Nat. Pub. Radio, 1980-82; dir. comm. House Com. on Aging, U.S. Congress, 1977-78; Presdl. apptd. White House Conf. on Aging, 1980; mem task force NIH Health Message Testing, 1978-80; cons. Nat. Cancer Inst., 1980-84; bd. dirs. Ctr. for Pub. Integrity, 1990—; invited lectr. Mt. Vernon Coll., 1975, U. Calif., Davis, 1976, SUNY, Albany, 1979, The Brent Soc. Lecture, Alexandria, Va., 1980, Harvard U., Cambridge, Mass., 1981, U. Mass., Amherst, 1982, Am. Film Inst. Lecture, 1983, Columbia U., N.Y.C., 1984, AAWU of Hawaii, Honolulu, 1985, Mt. Holyoke, Mass., 1986, Twentieth Century Fund's Theodore White Seminar on Presdl. Debate, Harvard U., 1986, U. Tex., 1987, Clemson U., 1987, The Kenneth Murray Lecture on First Amendment, U. Mich., 1989, William and Mary Coll., 1989, Pa. LWV, 1991, Duke U., Durham, N.C., 1992, Children's Def. Fund, 1992, NEA, Balt., 1992, Smithsonian Inst., Washington, 1992, The Freedom Forum, Columbia U., N.Y.C., 1992, Coll. St. Catherine, St. Paul, 1993, Nat. Conf. Editl. Writers, Phila., 1993, U. Pitts. Inst. Politics, 1993, Eagleton Inst. Politics, Rutgers U., New Brunswick, N.J., 1994, Congl. Clearinghouse on the Future, Washington, 1994, The Penn Club, N.Y.C., 1994, Internat. Women's Media Found., Washington, 1994, and many others. Author: A Critical Anthology of Public Speeches, 1978, Packaging the Presidency: A History and Criticism of Presidential Advertising, 1984 (Golden Anniversary Book award Speech Comm. Assn. 1984), 3rd edit., 1996, Eloquence in an Electronic Age, 1988 (Winans-Wichelns Book award Speech Comm. Assn. 1989), Dirty Politics: Deception, Distraction and Democracy, 1992, Beyond the Double Bind: Women and Leadership, 1995; co-author: Debating Crime Control, 1967, The Interplay of Influence: Media and Their Publics in News, Advertising and Politics, 1983, 3d edit., 1991, Presidential Debates: The Challence of Creating an Informed Electorate, 1988, Deeds Done in Words: Presidential Rhetoric and The Genres of Governance, 1990, Spiral of Cynicism: The Press and the Public Good, 1997; editor: Age Stereotyping and Television, 1978, Televised Advertising and the Elderly, 1978; co-editor: Form and Genre: Shaping Rhetorical Action, 1978, Communication Research, 1994; assoc. editor QJS, 1975, also book rev. editor, 1975-77, Encoder, 1973-75, Comm. Quar., 1976-78, Comm. Monographs, 1978-80, 89-91, Comm. Edn., 1979-81, Quar. Jour. Speech, 1981-83; regional editor EXETASIS, 1976-80; guest editor The So. States Speech Comm. Jour., 1986, Comm. Edn., 1987; contbr. numerous articles to profl. jours. Knapp fellow, 1967-68, Ford fellow, 1969-71 Fulbright fellow, 1982, East-West Ctr. fellow, 1985, 88; Eli Lily Found. grantee, 1976, Andrew Mellon Found. grantee, 1980, NEH grantee, 1987-88, Woodrow Wilson grantee, 1989, MacArthur grantee, 1992, 93, Markle grantee, 1992, Schuman grantee, 1992, Robert Wood Johnson grantee, 1993-94, Ford Found. Grantee, 1995-96, Carnegie Found. grantee, 1995-96, PEW Charitable Trust grantee, 1996-97; recipient Zeta Phi Eta award, 1979, Past Pres. award for outstanding scholarly achievement Ea. Comm. Assn., 1984, Alumni Merit award Marquette U., 1984, Douglas Ehninger award, 1990, JFK Joan Shorenstein Barone Ctr. Goldsmith award, 1992, Disting. Career in Scholarship award Speech Comm. Assn., 1992, Sara award Phila. chpt. Women in Comm., 1993-94, Murray Edelman Disting. Career award for lifetime contbn. to study of polit. comm. Am. Polit. Sch. Assn. Polit. Comm. Divsn., 1995. Mem. Am. Philosoph. Soc. Office: U Pa Annenberg Sch for Comm 3620 Walnut St Philadelphia PA 19104-6220

JAMIESON, MARY JEANETTE, state legislator; m. William Jamieson; 3 children. Acct. Jamieson Acctg. Tax Svc.; mem. Ga. Ho. of Reps., Atlanta, 1985—; vice chmn. ways and means com.; mem. natural resources and environ., spl. rules coms.; also state planning and cmty. affairs com. Pres. Ga. Resource, Conservation and Devel. Coun. Recipient Pres. Environ. Conservation award, Mamie K. Taylor Legis. award Bus. Profl. Women Ga.; named Legis. of Yr., Ga. Pharm. Assn., Citizen of Yr., North Ga. Realtors Assn., Woman of Yr., Ga. Assn. Conservation Dist. Supr. Mem. Nat. Resource, Conservation and Devel. Assn. (1st v.p.). Democrat. Baptist. Office: Rm 401 State Capitol Atlanta GA 30334

JAMISON, ELIZABETH ALEASE, drafting and design business owner; b. Rockwood, Tenn., July 8, 1954; d. Ross Leslie and Alice Elizabeth (Collier) J. Student, Roane State C.C., Harriman, Tenn., 1974-75, Tenn. Tech. U., 1980-83. Cert. Autocad Level I. Drafter ETE Consulting Engrs., Inc., Oak Ridge, Tenn., 1983-84, Edge Group, Nashville, 1984-88; sr. drafter Woodard & Curran, Inc., Portland, Maine, 1988-91; owner Casco Bay Drafting & Design, Portland, Maine, 1991—; tech. program coord. Portland Adult Edn., 1994—. Adj. faculty mem. So. Maine Tech. Coll., South Portland, 1990—; instr. Women Unltd., Augusta, Maine, 1993—; archtl. drafting & design instr. Portland Arts & Tech. H.S., 1997-2003. Featured in film Women Working, 1994. Bd. officer Portland YWCA, 1992-94; exec. bd. mem. Coalition Women in Trades & Tech., 1996—; mem. Maine Fire Svc. Tech. Women's Task Force, 1998—. Mem. NOW (1st v.p. Tenn. chpt. 1986-88, Tenn. state pres. 1988). Avocations: cooking, traveling, reading, motivational speaking. Home and Office: Casco Bay Drafting & Design 59 Marlborough Rd Portland ME 04103-4313 Office Phone: 207-878-0093. E-mail: ejamison@maine.rr.com.

JAMISON, JAYNE, publishing executive; Grad., Penn. St. U., 1978. Advertising dir. American Health, pub.; group pub., parenthood group Gruner & Jahr USA Pub., N.Y.C., 1994—97; pub. v.p. Redbook, 1997—2003; pub., v.p. Seventeen, 2003—. Office: Seventeen Mag 1440 Broadway 13th Fl New York NY 10018

JAMISON, JUDITH, dancer; b. Phila., May 10, 1943; d. John Jamison. Student, Fisk U., Phila., Phila. Dance Acad. (now U. of Arts); studied with, Anthony Tudor, John Hines, Delores Brown, John Jones, Joan Kerr, Madame Swaboda. Dancer Alvin Ailey's Am. Dance Theatre, N.Y.C., 1965-80; artistic dir. Alvin Ailey's Am. Dance Theatre, N.Y.C., 1990—; dancer, choreographer touring U.S., Europe, Asia, S.Am., Africa, 1980—; formerly with Maurice Hines Dance Sch., N.Y.C.; founder Jamison Project, 1988-91. Vis. disting. prof. U. Arts; guest assoc. artistic dir. 30th ann. tour Alvin Ailey's Am. Dance Theatre, 1990—; guest appearances Harkness Ballet, Am. Ballet Theatre, San Francisco Ballet, Dallas Ballet. Dancer debut Agnes DeMille's The Four Marys, 1965, (Broadway plays) Joseph's Legend, Vienna Opera, Le Spectre de la Rose, Brussels, Paris, N.Y.C., Maskela Language, 1969, Cry, 1971, Choral Dance, 1971, Mary Lou's Mass, 1971, The Lark Ascending, 1972, The Mooche, 1975, Passage, 1978, (Broadway plays) Sophisticated Ladies, 1980, choreographer Divining Hymn for Alvin Ailey Am. Dance Theatre, works for Maurice Bejart, Dancers Unltd., Dallas, Washington Ballet, Jennifer Muller/The Works, Alvin Ailey Repertory Ensemble, Ballet Nuevo Mundo de Caracas, Riverside for Alvin Ailey Am. Dance Theatre, (Operas) Boito's Mefistofele, Opera Co. Phila.; author: Dancing Spirit, 1993. Recipient Dance Mag. award, 1972, Key to City, N.Y.C., 1976, Spirit of Achievement award Nat. Women's Divsn., Yeshiva U. Albert Einstein Coll. Medicine, 1992, Golden Plate award, Am. Acad. Achievement, 1993. Address: Alvin Ailey Am Dance Theater 211 W 61st St Fl 3 New York NY 10023-7832*

JAMISON, KAY, psychologist; BA, MA, UCLA, 1971, CPhil, 1973, PhD, 1975. Asst. UCLA, 1974—87, assoc. prof. of psychiatry, 1974—87; prof. psychiatry Sch. Medicine Johns Hopkins U., Balt., 1987—. Hon. prof. English U. St. Andrews, Scotland. Author: (book) Touched With Fire: Manic-Depressive Illness and the Artistic Temperament, 1993 (Most Outstanding Book in biomed. sci. Am. Assn. Pubs., 1990), An Unquiet Mind, 1995 (NY Times Bestseller), Night Falls Fast: Understanding Suicide, 1999; contbr. articles to profl. jours. Named Hero of Medicine, Time mag.; named one of Best Drs. in U.S., five chosen for pub. TV series Great Minds of Medicine; recipient William Styron award, Nat. Mental Health Assn., 1995, Rsch. award, Am. Suicide Found., 1996, Leadership award, Cmty. Mental Health, 1999; fellow MacArthur fellow, 2001. Office: Johns Hopkins Hosp Dept Psychiatry Meyer 3-181 Psychiatry 600 North Wolfe St Baltimore MD 21287

JAMISON, SHEILA ANN ENGLISH, stockbroker, retirement planning specialist; b. Hattiesburg, Miss., July 19, 1950; d. Stanley Gear and Vivian (Gillis) English; m. Troy James Creel, Dec. 21, 1968 (div. 1980); m. Richard Allen Jamison, Oct. 24, 1981. BS in Mgmt. magna cum laude, Fairleigh Dickinson U., 1986; postgrad., U. Pa. Purchasing asst. Dept. Hosps. State La., Independence, 1973-77; sales rep. Fisher Sci., Houston, 1977-79; account v.p. Paine Webber, Clifton, N.J., 1981-87; sr. v.p. investments Morgan Stanley Dean Witter, N.Y.C., 1987—. Spkr. The Cons. Firm, Saddle Brook, N.J., 1987; sec. Dean Witters Womens Bus. Exch., 1994-96, mem. steering com. Dir. Gene Michael Scholarship Fund, Bergenfield, N.J., 1986; mem. fund raising com. Tomorrow's Children Fund, Hackensack, N.J., 1987; mem. Group Against Smoking Pollution, 1987—; co-chair communications com. Friends of the Inst. of Noetic Scis. Mem. Am. Soc. Women Accts., Advt. Women N.Y., Direct Investment Adv. Bd., Barron's High Tech. Round Table, Internat. Platform Assn., Morgan Stanley Dean Witter's Dirs. Club, Pres. Club, Phi Zeta Kappa, Delta Mu Delta, Phi Omega Epsilon. Baptist. Avocations: photography, cooking, reading, hiking, snorkeling. Office: Dean Witter 330 Madison Ave Fl 8 New York NY 10017-5001

JAMISON, SUZANNE, management consultant; b. Oelwein, Iowa, Aug. 17, 1946; d. Harold Hacking Jamison and Mary Gene Masters; children: Judith Zulfiqar, Jamye Fé Michele, Harold Llwyn, John Theodore Shan-Ts'ai Connell, Sujata Marie Inez Lung-Nu Connell. BA in Mass Comms., N.Mex. State U., 1969; cert. in elem. edn., Coll. Santa Fe, 1972. Rschr., writer periodicals, N.Mex., 1966—80; mgr. Theater Arts Corp. playwriting, 1974—76; office mgr. La Fabrica Azteca, Guadalajara, Mexico, 1972—73; mgmt. collective Armory for the Arts, Santa Fe, 1975—78; cofounder, program dir. Santa Fe Coun. for Arts, 1978—80, exec. dir., 1980—85; sole owner Jamison Mgmt. and Devel., N.Mex., 1983—. Treas., bd. dirs. Lore of the Land, 2004—. Asst. editor: ornithol. jour. The Condor, 1966—69. Recipient numerous grants in field. Mem.: ACLU, AAUW, Virtual Activism Network, Women's Internat. League for Peace and Freedom, Upper Gila Watershed Assn., Spanish Colonial Arts Soc., So. Povery Law Ctr., Navajo Sheep Project, Animal Protection of N.Mex., Am. Livestock Breeds Conservancy. Avocations: native plant gardening, cultures and history, theology, theater, films. E-mail: sznjmsn@gilanet.com.

JAN, CHWU-CHING HWANG, environmental chemistry consultant; b. Taipei, Taiwan, July 10, 1956; d. Chau-Ching and Hsiu-Mei (Lin) Huang; m. Deng-Yang Jan; 1 child, Avery. BS, Nat. Cheng-Kung U., 1978; MBA, U. Chgo., 1995; PhD, Ohio State U., 1986. Rsch. asst. Nat. Sci. Found., Taipei, Taiwan, 1978-79; lab. mgr. Nat. Tsing Hua U., Hsinchu, Taiwan, 1979-81; sr. rsch. chemist UOP, Des Plaines, Ill., 1986-92; cons. IRIS DC Inc., Elk Grove Village, Ill., pres., 1993—. Advisor tech. CASDAY Co., Ltd., Hsinchu, Taiwan, 1993—. Contbr. articles to profl. jours. including Jour. Electro.-analytical Chem., Interfacial Electrochem., Analytical Chemistry. Mem.: Am. Chem. Soc. (Internat. Student grant 1985). Achievements include patents for hydrotreating processes for organic and halogenerated organic feedsocks containing undesirable olefinic and/or halogen components and/or organic materials, process for decomposing peroxide impurities in a tertiary butyl alcohol feedstock. Office: IRIS DC Inc 1644 Von Braun Trl Elk Grove Village IL 60007-3100 E-mail: dyccjan@aol.com.

JANAK, CAROLYN ANN, special education educator; b. Yoakum, Tex., Mar. 15, 1972; d. William Joseph Janak, Jr. and Sandra Lee (Casal) Janak. BS, U. Houston, Victoria, 1996; MEd, Southwest Tex. State U., 2002. Cert. non-violent crisis intervention Crisis Prevention Inst. Inc. Spl. edn. tchr. Luling (Tex.) Ind. Sch. Dist., 2002. Mem. Region 13 Tchr. Edn. Svc. Ctr., Austin, Tex., mem. Region 20, San Antonio. Mem.: Tex. Classroom Tchrs. Assn., Assn. Childhood Edn. Internat., Coun. Exceptional Children. Roman Catholic. Avocations: travel, visual and theatre arts, fishing, wildlife. Home: 107 Elenora Yoakum TX 77995 Office: 118 W Bowie St Luling TX 78648-2908

JANDA, KIM D. chemist, educator; b. Cleve., Aug. 23, 1958; married; children: Nikole, Christopher. BS, U. Southern Fla., 1980; MS, U. Ariz., 1983, PhD, 1984. Adj. asst. mem. dept. molecular biology Rsch. Inst. Scripps Clinic, La Jolla, Calif., 1987-88, asst. prof. dept. molecular biology, 1989-90, assoc. prof. dept. molecular biology and chem., 1991-92, assoc. prof., 1993—. Cons. Procter and Gamble, Unilever Rsch., Inc.; sci. adv. bd. mem. Catalytic Antibodies, Inc., Found. CombiChem.; lectr. in field. Contbr. numerous articles to profl. jours. Named Scholar Athlete of Yr. U. South Fla., 1979-80; recipient Alfred P. Sloan fellowship, 1993-95, NIH First award, 1990-95, Carl S. Marvel fellowship U. Ariz., 1984; numerous other grants. Fellow Am. Inst. Chemists; mem. Am. Chem. Soc. (Arhtur C. Cope Scholar Award, 1999), Themis Honor Soc., Sigma Phi Epsilon. Office: The Scripps Rsch Inst 10550 N Torrey Pines Rd La Jolla CA 92037-1000

JANECEK, LENORE ELAINE, insurance specialist, consultant; b. May 2, 1944; d. Morris and Florence (Bear) Picker; m. John Janecek, Sept. 12, 1964; children: Frank, Michael. MAJ in Speech Comms., Northeastern Ill. U., 1972; postgrad., U. Notre Dame, 1979-80; MBA, Columbia Pacific U., 1982; cert. in C. of C. mgmt., U. Colo., 1982. Adminstrv. asst., exec. dir. Ill. Mcpl. Regirement Fund, Chgo.; pres., owner Secretarial Office Svcs., Chgo., 1976-78; founder, pres. Lincolnwood (Ill.) C. of C. and Industry, 1978-85; pres. Lenore E. Janecek & Assocs., Lincolnwood, 1985—. Rep. 10th dist. U.S. C. of C., 1978—; appointee Health Care Reform Task Force, 1992—; apptd. by Pres. Bill Clinton Selective Svc. Bd., 1993—; apptd. by Gov. Jim Edgar Ill. Health Care Cost Containment Coun., 1994—; mem. adv. bd. Women Healthcare Execs. Network, Chgo. Artists Coalition, Ill. Lincoln Scholars Series Program, Leadership Ill. Author: Health Insurance: A Guide for Artists, Consultants, Entrepreneurs and Other Self-Employed, 1993. Mem. mktg. bd. Niles Twp. Sheltered Workshop; pres. Lincolnwood Sch. Dist. 74 Sch. Bd. Caucus; bd. dirs., officer, founder Ill. Fraternal Order Police Aux.; bd. dirs., officer Lincolnwood Girl's Softball League, PTA; bd. dirs. United Way, 1982-83; mem. sch. curriculum com. Lincolnwood Bd. Edn.; apptd. by Pres. Reagan to Selective Svc. Bd., 1983; pres. United Way Skokie Valley, Ill., 1989; pres., founder Leadership Ill., 1992—, Twp. Coord. and Health Care advisor, Gov. Jim Edgar, Ill., 1990—; founder, pres. Save the Patient, 2001. Talent scholar Northeastern Ill. U., 1972; Ill. Assn. C. of C. Execs. scholar, 1979-80; named Disting. Grad. of Yr. Nat. Honor Soc., 1985; chosen one of Top 100 Women Leaders in Am., 1988; recipient

Outstanding Women in Healthcare Mgmt. award Women Health Exec. Network, 1994. Mem. Hadassah. Office: 980 N Michigan Ave # 1400 Chicago IL 60611-7500 E-mail: ljanecek@aol.com., ljainsurance@aol.com.

JANEWAY, BARBARA, public relations executive; Coord. pub. rels. Ralph's Grocery, Compton, Calif., 1987—. Office: Ralphs Grocery 1100 W Artesia Blvd Compton CA 90220-5186

JANI, SUSHMA NIRANJAN, pediatric psychiatrist; b. Gwalior, Madhya, Pradesh, India, Sept. 26, 1959; came to U.S., 1983; d. Kirty Ambalal and Purnima Kirty (Bhatt) Dave; m. Niranjan Natwerial Jani, Mar. 30, 1983; children: Suni Jani, Raja Jani, Roma Jani. Intern Sci., Mithibai Coll., Bombay, India; MB, BS, B.J. Med. Coll., Ahmedabad, India; MD in Adult Psychiatry, Ind. U., 1984; MD in Child Psychiatry, Johns Hopkins U., 1987. Diplomate Am. Bd. Psychiatry and Neurology, sub-bd. Child Psychiatry, Am. Bd. Pediat., Am. Bd. Forensic Examiners. Pediat. emergency physician Mercey Hosp., Balt., 1997—99; child psychiatrist Johns Hopkins Univ. Hosp., Balt.; asst. clin. prof., mem. faculty dept. pediats. and psychiatry Georgetown U. Med. Ctr., Balt., assoc. prof. pediat. and psychiatry; assoc. prof. psychiatry Georgetown U.; med. dir. Chesapeake network Devereux Found., Md., Va., W.Va., Washington and Del., 1998-99; med. dir. Riverside Hosp., Washington, 1999—; pediat. emergency physician Howard County Hosp., 1999—. Chief cons. psychiatrist Balt. Detention Ctr., 1988-89, cons. psychiatrist Vets. Hosp., Indpls., 1986-87. Vol. Radha-Krishna Leprosy Camp, Bombay, 1981-83. Mem. AMA, Am. Acad. Child & Adolescent Psychiatry, Am. Psychiatry Assn., Md. Psychiat. Soc., Columbia Assn., India Assn., Am. Acad. Podiatrics. Hindu. Avocations: reading, knitting, sewing, letter-writing. Home: 10485 Owen Brown Rd Columbia MD 21044-3835 Office: Riverside Hosp 4460 Macarthur Blvd NW Washington DC 20007-2516 Office Phone: 410-997-5500. E-mail: sjani@jhu.edu.

JANIGA, MARY ANN, art educator; b. Lackawanna, N.Y., June 14, 1950; d. Jacob and Julia (Zatlukal) Mazurchuk; m. William B. Janiga, Nov. 23, 1972; children: Nicholas, Matthew. BS, State U. Coll., Buffalo, 1972, MS, 1974, cert. advanced study, 1995. Cert. in sch. adminstrn. and supervision. Tchr. art Buffalo Pub. Schs., 1972—. Art facilitator Olmsted Sch., Buffalo, 1985—, World Connect Multi-cultural Program, 2003, 04; supervising tchr. State Univ. Coll., Buffalo; liaison Albright-Knox Art Gallery, 1994—, art presenter fed. pre-kindergarten program, 1998; wrote art curriculum Buffalo Pub. Sch., 2002. Carnegie Hall, N.Y.C., 2002; co-ordinated with Fisher-Price Designers, Buffalo Pub. Sch. Art Program, 2003. Exhibited in group shows at Cheektowaga (N.Y.) Art Guild, 1979, Erie County Parks Art Festival, 1979, Lockport Art Festival, 1980, Allentown Art Exhibit, Kennan Ctr. Recipient various awards for art; grantee Buffalo Tchr. Ctr., 1986-90, Olmstead Home Sch. Assn., 1991-97, Allentown Village Soc., 1994; grantee Fisher Price, 2003. Mem. NEA, PAT (life), Olmsted Home Sch. Assn., SUNY-Buffalo Alumni Assn., Buffalo Tchrs. Fedn., Buffalo Fine Arts Acad., Buffalo Soc. Natural Scis., Zool. Soc. of Buffalo, Lancaster H.S. Home Sch. Assn. (rec. sec. 1998-99, co-pres. 1999-01). Avocations: reading, concerts, theater, art exhibits. Office: Olmsted Sch 64 874 Amherst St Buffalo NY 14216-3502

JANIS, ELINOR RAIDEN, artist, educator; b. N.Y.C., Dec. 8, 1934; d. Edward and Lea Raiden; m. Leon Janis, July 14, 1957 (div. Jan. 5, 1970); children: Madeline, Richard, Cheryl. BA in Elem. Edn., UCLA, 1957; MFA, Instituto Allende, San Miguel De Allende, Mex., 1973. Instr. elem. schs., 1957—66, Woman's Workshop, Granada Hills, Calif., 1971—73; painting instr. Instituto Allende, 1974, 1976—77, Santa Monica (Calif.) Pks. and Recreation, 1977; instr. L.A. City Schs., 1978—86; profl. artist, 1986—. One-woman shows include Galeria Conde, San Miguel de Allende, Mex., 1974, Beyond Baroque Gallery, Venice, Calif., 1977, Canyon Cafe, Glendale, Calif., 2000—01, exhibited in group shows at Barnsdall Pk., L.A., 1972, Emerson Gallery, 1972, Brentwood (Calif.) Art Ctr., 1973, Geleria Pintora de Jovenes, Mexico City, 1974, McCaffery Galleries, L.A., 1973, Ryder Gallery, 1973, Galeria Pintora de Jovenes, Mexico City, 1974, Powerhouse Gallery, Montreal, Can., 1975, Woman's Bldg., L.A., 1975, Women's Ctr., Ridgefield, Con., 1975, Assn. Humanist Artists, San Francisco, 1975, Museo de Arte Contemporaneo, San Miguel de Allende, 1977, others. Mem. Amnesty Internat., L.A., 1995—2001, NOW, 1985—2001, Handgun Control, 1990—2001. Recipient scholarship, Instituto Allende, 1974, 2d prize, Burbank Creative Arts Ctr. Show, 2001. Mem.: Valley Artists Guild, L.A. County Mus. Art. Democrat. Jewish. Avocations: pottery, stone carving, etching. Office: Elinor Janis Studio 14417 Chase St # 298 Panorama City CA 91402

JANKO, MAY, graphic artist; b. N.Y.C., Feb. 27, 1926; d. Jacob and Clara (Schupler) J. BA, Hunter Coll., 1946, MA, 1952; student, Art Students League, 1949-53. Tchr. art N.Y.C. Pub. Schs., 1953-58; textile designer DNE Walter & Co., N.Y.C., 1958-63, Old Deerfield, N.Y.C., 1963-68, M. Lowenstein Corp., N.Y.C., 1968-84. Exhibited in group shows: Libr. of Congress, Washington, 1956, 63, American Prints Today, 1959, Whitney Mus. Am. Art, N.Y.C., 1959, Pa. Acad., Phila., 1959, Bklyn. Mus., 1960, Taipei (Taiwan) Nat. Mus., 1984, 90, 92, Bronx Mus. Arts, 1989, Krasdale Satellite Gallery of Bronx Mus. Arts, 1989, Salmugundi: 13th Ann. Exhbn., 1990; represented in permanent collections: Met. Mus. Art, N.Y.C., Rockefeller Collection, N.Y.C., Cin. Mus. Art, Nat. Gallery, Washington. Recipient Achievement award Hunter Coll., 1959, Arts award Louis Comfort Tiffany Found., 1959, Leo Meissner award NAD, N.Y.C., 1984, I.B. Markell award in graphics Audubon Artists, N.Y.C., 1961, Daniel Serra y Navas Meml. award, 1994, Art Students League N.Y. Graphics award, 1995. Mem. Soc. Am. Graphic Artists (life; mem. coun. 1977, Henry B. Shope award 1954, Graphic Chem. award 1985), Boston Printmakers, Am. Color Print Soc., Art Students League (life).

JANNEY, ALLISON, actress; b. Dayton, Ohio, Nov. 19, 1960; BA, Kenyon Coll.; pvt. studies in acting, Neighborhood Playhouse, N.Y.C. Appeared in feature films: Big Night, 1996, Private Parts, 1997, Primary Colors, 1998, Six Days, Seven Nights, 1998, The Ice Storm, 1997, Celebrity, 1998, 10 Things I Hate About You, 1999, Drop Dead Gorgeous, 1999, Nurse Betty, 2000, American Beauty, 1999, Leaving Drew, 2000, Finding Nemo (voiceover), 2003, How to Deal, 2003; plays (on Broadway) A View From The Bridge (Tony award nominee 1998, Outer Critics Circle award,Drama Desk award); appearances on TV: The West Wing (role C.J. Gregg), 1999—, A Girl Thing (TV min), 2000 Recipient Outstanding Featured Actress in a Play for "A View From the Bridge", Drama Desk Award, 1998, Outstanding Supporting Actress in a Drama Series for "The West Wing", Emmy Award, 1999, 2000, Best Actress in a Television Series Drama for "The West Wing", Golden Satellite, 2000, Best Ensemble Cast Performance for "The West Wing", 2000, Outstanding Female Actor in a Drama Series for "The West Wing", The Actor Awards, 2000, Outstanding Ensemble in a Drama Series for "The West Wing", 2000, Outstanding Supporting Actress in a Drama Series for "The West Wing", Emmy Awards, 2001, Outstanding Female Actor in a Drama Series for "The West Wing", The Actor Awards, 2001, Outstanding Ensemble in a Drama Series for "The West Wing", 2001, Outstanding Female Actress in a Drama Series for "The West Wing", Emmy Awards, 2002. Office: John Wells Prodns Warner Bros TV Rm 204 4000 Warner Blvd Bldg 133 Burbank CA 91522-0001

JANOW, LYDIA FRANCES, meeting planner; b. N.Y.C., Dec. 2, 1957; d. John and Angie (Bizzios) J. BA cum laude, CCNY, 1978; grad., CBS Div. Publ., 1984. Cert. meeting planner. Exec. sec. Family Weekly Mag., N.Y.C., 1978-81, asst. mdse. mgr., 1981-83; spl. events mgr. Family Weekly/USA Weekend, N.Y.C., 1983-86; mgr. meetings & events Mag. Pubs. Assn., N.Y.C., 1986-88; conv. svcs. mgr., sales & catering mgr. Sheraton Heights Hotel, Hasbrouck Heights, N.J., 1989-91; conf. mgr. Aviation Week Group McGraw Hill Inc., N.Y.C., 1991-93, dir. tradeshows and confs., 1993—. Editor: Newsletter Heights Hotel, 1991; contbr. articles to profl. jours. Camp counselor, Hellenic-Am. Neighborhood Action Com., N.Y.C., 1974-78; tchr., Sunday sch., St. Spyridon Ch., N.Y.C., 1974-80. Mem. Internat. Assn. Exhibit Mgrs., Meeting Planners Internat., Assn. Trade Show Exhibitors, Internation Assn. for Exposition Mgmt., Exhibit Mgrs. and Conf. Organizers. Greek Orthodox. Avocations: photography, sports, reading. Home: 29 Levitt Ave Bergenfield NJ 07621-1904 Office Phone: 212-904-3225. Personal E-mail: ljanow@aviationnow.com.

JANSEN, ANGELA BING, artist, educator; b. N.Y.C., Aug. 17, 1929; d. Lester and Jean Bing; m. Gunther Jansen, Mar. 8, 1956; children—Edmund, Douglas. BA, Bklyn. Coll., 1951; MA, NYU, 1953; student, Bklyn. Mus. Art Sch., 1947-50, Atelier 17, N.Y.C., 1950-52. Tchr. art, public schs., N.Y.C., 1954-60. One-man shows: Madison (Wis.) Art Center, 1977, Gimpel & Weitzenhoffer, N.Y.C., 1974, 78, group shows: Bklyn. Mus., 1950, 70, 76, Library of Congress, Washington, 1969, 71, Ljubljana Internat. Print Biennale, Yugoslavia, 1971, 73, 75, 77, Venice Biennale, 1972, Internat. Exhbn. Drawing, Rejeka, Yugoslavia, 1972 (award), Internat. Print Biennale, Cracow, Poland, 1978; represented in permanent collections: Mus. Modern Art, N.Y.C., Met. Mus. Art, N.Y.C., N.Y. Pub. Library, Art Inst. Chgo., Tate Gallery, London, Victoria and Abert Mus., London, Bibliotheque Nationale, Paris, Bklyn. Mus., Phila. Mus. Art, Fonds d'Art Contemporain, Centre de Recherche et d'Etude de la Sculpture Contemporaine, Mauberge, France, Musée du Petit Format, Couvin, Belgium, Bklyn. Mus., Francine Tyler Art Forum, summer, 1979. Nat. Endowment for Arts grantee, 1974-75

JANSON, BARBARA JEAN, publisher; b. Mason City, Iowa, Mar. 7, 1942; d. Harley Arnold and Helen Victoria (Henrickson) J.; m. W. John Shallenberger, Feb. 24, 1963 (div. Sept. 1980); children: Mona, Ann; m. John Batty Henderson, Sept. 8, 1984 (div. 1990); m. Arthur R. Hilsinger, Aug. 31, 1997. BS in Math., Iowa State U., 1965; MS in Math., Trinity Coll., 1970; MBA, U. R.I., 1982. Cert. math. tchr., Iowa, N.Y., Conn. Math. tchr. Pub. High Schs., Avon, Farmington, Bloomfield, Conn., 1966-68, Ulster Acad., Kingston, N.Y., 1971-73; math. instr. Ulster County Community Coll., Kingston, 1973; math. editor Houghton Mifflin Co., Boston, 1974-77; math. instr. Bristol County Community Coll., Fall River, Mass., 1977-78; asst. dir. editorial Am. Math. Soc., Providence, 1978-81, dir. of publ., 1982-85; founder, pres. Janson Publs., Inc. (purchased by Tribune Edn. Group), Providence and Dedham, Mass., 1985-96; pres. Janson Publs., Inc., Dedham, 1996-98; pub. cons. Everyday Learning/Tribune Edn. Group, 1996-98; pres. Janson Assocs., Dedham, 1996—; overseer Boston Ballet, 2003—. Mem. expert panel materials devel. ref. NSF, 1996-99; rep. sci. publ. com. Am. Heart Assn., 1986-90; mem. R.I. State Adv. Commn. on Librs.; mem. R.I. Legis. Commn. for Math. and Sci. Edn., 1991; mem. adv. com. R.I. State Systemic Initiative in Math. and Sci., 1993-94; Mass. state adv. bd. Math. & Sci. Edn., 2000—. Editor: Scholarly Publishing: Managing Today, Planning for Tomorrow, 1986. Bd. dirs. Planned Parenthood of R.I., Providence, 1986-87, First Parish Unitarian Ch., Beverly, Mass., 1975-76; mem. steering com. Am. Math. Project, Berkeley, Calif., 1986-92; mem. oversight com. Resources Math. Reform Edn. Devel. Ctr., Newton, Mass.; adv. mem. R.I. State Coun. on Librs. Recipient Mortar Bd. award Iowa State U., 1965. Mem. AAAS, LWV, Soc. for Scholarly Publishing (bd. dirs. 1986-90, chair ann. meeting 1985), N.Y. Acad. Sci., Am. Math. Soc., Math. Assn. Am., Nat. Coun. Tchrs. Math., Assn. Am. Publishers (jours. com. 1982-85), Nat. Assn. Women Bus. Owners. Unitarian Universalist. Home and Office: 8 Jackson Pond Rd Dedham MA 02026-3324

JANSON, JULIA S. utilities executive; m. Chip Janson; children: Jennifer, Rachel. BA in Am. Studies, Georgetown Coll.; JD, U. Cin., 1988. Bar: Ohio 1988. Law clk. Adams, Brooking, Stepner, Wolterman & Dusing, Covington, Ky., Cin. Gas & Electric Co., 1987—88, supr. securities processing, transfer agt. common and preferred stock, 1988—93; corp. atty., key mem. legal team responsible for completing merger of Cin. Gas & Electric Co. and PSI Energy Cinergy Corp., 1993—94, mgr. investor rels., 1995—96, counsel, 1996—98, sr. counsel, 1998—, corp. sec., sr. counsel, 2000—. Bd. dirs. Lighthouse Youth Svcs., 2000—01. Office: Cinergy Corp 139 E 4th St Cincinnati OH 45202

JANSSEN, ANNE L. music educator; b. Santa Fe, July 13, 1957; d. Julian H. and Louise M. Burttram; m. David C. Janssen, May 21, 1983; children: Daniel C., Timothy J., Andrew M., Michael J. MusB, Baylor U., 1979; MEd, Idaho State U., 2000. Cert. tchr. Utah. Music tchr., Sandy, Utah, 1986—2000.

JANSSEN, MARYBETH, airframe and power plant mechanic; b. Tulsa, May 1, 1956; d. Henry Floyd and Bessie Viola (Barr) Kinyon; m. Lawrence Eric Janssen, Dec. 23, 1977 (div. Oct. 1987). Grad. H.S., Los Gatos, Calif. Cert. airframe and powerplant mechanic, FAA. Jet engine mechanic USAF, 1976-84; flight engr. USAFR McChord AFB, Tacoma, 1984-86; flight attendant Trans World Airlines, St. Louis, 1986-89, airframe and powerplant mechanic, 1989-90, Am. Airlines, Inc., Tulsa, 1990-92, tech. crew chief instr. Ft. Worth, 1992-94, airframe and powerplant mechanic, 1994—. Jet engine technician Mo. Air N.G., St. Louis, 1987-90, Okla. Air N.G., Tulsa, 1990-92, non-commd. officer-in-charge maintenance tng., 1992-94; jet engine mechanic USAF/NAS, Ft. Worth, 1995. With USAF, 1976-84. Decorated Air Force Achievement medal and Meritorious Svc. medal USAF, Robins AFB, Ga., 1983, Meritorious Svc. medals Mo. Air Nat. Guard, St. Louis, 1990, Okla. Air Nat. Guard, Tulsa, 1993. Mem. Transport Workers Union, Aircraft Mechanics Fraternal Assn., Am. Legion. Avocations: gardening, decorating, cooking, travel, fly fishing. Home: RR 1 Box 48 Murfreesboro AR 71958-9719

JANSSEN-PELLATZ, EUNICE CHARLENE, healthcare facility administrator; b. Urania, La., Mar. 23, 1948; d. Luther Clarence and Eunice Bobby (Pendarvis) Smith. BS in Nursing, Humboldt State U., 1970; MS in Nursing, Calif. State U., Fresno, 1980. Dir. nurses, asst. adminstr., coord. patient care svcs. Mad River Community Hosp., Arcata, Calif.; nursing supr. Fresno (Calif.) Community Hosp.; emergency response coord. Humboldt County Pub. Health Dept. Mem. Am. Soc. Healthcare Risk Mgmt. Home: 824 Diamond Dr Arcata CA 95521-8212 Office Phone: 707-268-2133. E-mail: pellatz@humboldt1.com.

JANZ, GAIL DIANE, media director; b. Kankakee, Ill., Nov. 30, 1956; d. Warren Arthur and Betty (Brown) Kent; m. Jon Henry Janz, July 12, 1975; children: Nathan, Brittany. AA, Ill. V. C.C., 1975; BS, Ill. State U., Normal, 1979; MLIS, U. Ill., 2002. Media asst. Tonica (Ill.) Schs., 1976-78; media dir. Mid-County Dist. 4 Sch., Varna, Ill., 1980—98, Morris Cmty. H.S., 1998—. Mem. adv. bd. Starved Rock Libr. Systems, Ottawa, Ill., Region 9 computer Consortium, Ottawa; bd. dirs. Heritage Trail Libr. Sys., 2000, 2003. Mem. Empty Arms (co-founder local chpt.). Avocations: golf, technology, flower gardening, reading. Home: RR 1 Box 45B Tonica IL 61370-9766 Office: Morris Cmty HS 1000 Union St Morris IL 60450

JANZEN, NORINE MADELYN QUINLAN, medical technologist; b. Fond du Lac, Wis., Feb. 9, 1943; d. Joseph Wesley and Norma Edith (Gustin) Quinlan; m. Douglas Mac Arthur Janzen, July 18, 1970; 1 son, Justin James. BS, Marian Coll., 1965; med. technologist, St. Agnes Sch. Med. Tech., Fond du Lac, 1966; MA, Ctrl. Mich. U., 1980. Med. technologist Mayfair Med. Lab., Wauwatosa, Wis., 1966-69; supr. med. technologist Dr.'s Mason, Chamberlain, Franke, Klink & Kamper, Milw., 1969-76, Hartford-Parkview Clinic, Ltd., 1976-94; patient svc. ctrs. supr. Med. Sci. Labs., Wauwatosa, Wis., 1994-97, Poole Med. Tech. Med. Sci. Labs, 1997-98; clin. mgr. Planned Parenthood Wis., 1997-99; coord. health in bus. Hartford Parkview Clin., 1990-91, drug program coord., 1991-94; outreach coord. Cmty. Meml. Hosp., Menomonee Falls, Wis., 2000—. Co-chair joint mtg. Clin. Lab. Mgrs. Assn. and Wis. Assn. for Clin. Lab. Scientists, 1993-94. Coord. Warhawk Band Booster Uniform Project, 1997—99; mem. Dem. Nat. Com., 1973—; substitute poll worker Fond du Lac Dem. Com., 1964—65; post card ministry coord. Meth. Ch., 1996—2001, cmty. league youth col., recognition coord.; focus team leader Coll. Youth Ministries, Meth. Ch., 2000—; mem. Post Card Ministry Bd., 1998—2001; lay leader to ann. conf. United Meth. Ch., Menomonee Falls; bd. dirs. Menomonee Falls Teen Ctr., 2000—. Mem.: AAUW (corr. sec. 1994—96, rec. sec. 1996—98, pub. policy chair 1998—2001, chair Evening of Literary Excellence 2001—02, pres. 2001—03, treas. 2003—, state, dist. 2 coord. 2003—), Southeastern Suprs. Group (co-chmn. 1976—77), Milw. Soc. Clin. Lab. Scientists (pres. 1971—72, bd. dirs. 1972—73, exec. sec. 1999—), Clin. Lab. Mgmt. Assn. (co-chair joint meeting 1993—94), Wis. Assn. Clin. Lab. Scientists (chmn. awards com. 1976—77, treas. 1977—81, dir. 1977—84, pres.-elect 1981—82, pres. 1982—83, chmn. awards com. 1984—85, dir. 1985—87, chmn. awards com. 1986—87, chair ann. meeting 1987—88, exec. sec. 1991—, Mem. of Yr. award 1982, 1995, numerous svc. awards), Nat. Soc. Clin. Lab. Scientists (awards com. chair 1984—87, 1988—91, nominations com. 1989—92), Am. Soc. Clin. Lab. Scientists (people to people clin. lab. scientist del. to People's Rep. China 1989, Mem. of Yr. award 1997), Warhawk Band Boosters (uniform fundraiser chair 1996—98, chair Tryst-ing Place tent party fundraiser 1997—2000), Comms. of Wis. (chmn. 1977—79, originator), LWV, Cmty. League, Alpha Mu Tau, Alpha Delta Theta (nat. dist. chmn. 1967—69, nat. alumnae dir. 1969—71). Methodist. Home: N 98 W 17298 Dotty Way Germantown WI 53022-4618 Office: Cmty Meml Hosp W180 N 8085 Town Hall Rd Menomonee Falls WI 53051 Office Phone: 262-257-3453. E-mail: nmjanzen@aol.com.

JAQUES, KATHRYN MISBACH, tax consultant; b. Kansas City, Mo., June 23, 1936; d. Lorenz Edwin and Henrietta Louise (Satterlee) Misbach; m. Vernon P. Jaques, June 7, 1960; children: Barbara Louise, Valerie Kathryn. BA in Sociology magna cum laude, Oberlin Coll., 1959. Tax auditor Calif. Franchise Tax Bd., San Diego, 1975-82; tax mgr. Coopers and Lybrand LLP, San Diego, 1982-87, Arthur Andersen LLP, San Diego, 1987-92, tax prin., 1993—2001. Cons. in field, San Diego, 1993, 2001—; adj. instr. San Diego State U., 1981—; mem. adv. bd. U. Calif.-Davis State and Local Tax Inst., Davis, 1992—; spkr., conf. chair Calif. CPA Edn. Found., Redwood City, Calif., 1982—. Mem. editl. bd. Jour. Multistate Taxation, 1993—. Mem. fin. com. San Diego Automotive Mus., 1995-96. Tribute to Women in Industry honoree San Diego YWCA, 1986. Avocation: sports car road racing official.

JAQUET, WENDY S. state representative; b. Seattle, Wash., Sept. 16, 1943; m. Jim Jaquet; children: Michael, Brian. BA, U. Wash., 1965, MA, 1967. Staff San Francisco Redevel. Agy., U.S. HUD, 1968—70; bus.mgr. North Taylor Stonington, 1980—83; exec. dir. Sun Valley Ketchum C. of C., 1983—96, Regional Econ. Action Project, 1986—; state rep. dist. 25A Idaho Ho. of Reps., Boise, 1994—, mem. state affairs com. 1st Security Boulder Mountain Tour, 1990—95; coord. Ketchum Wagon Days, 1980—; bd. dirs. Job Tng. Partnersihp com., 1990—93; commr. Idaho Arts Commn., 1983—89; bd. dirs. Cmty. Libr., 1979—81; v.p. Blaine County Dem. Com. Democrat. Episcopalian. Office: State Capitol PO Box 83720 Boise ID 83720-0038

JARAMILLO, JUANA SEGARRA, chancellor; b. San Sebastian, P.R., Mar. 24, 1937; d. Joaquin M. and Carmen M. (Gerena) Segarra; m. Edgar J. Jaramillo, Apr. 13, 1957; children: Jeanette, Yila, Yvonne, Melissa, Edgar Jr. BA, Poly. Inst. P.R., San German, 1956; postgrad., U. Fla., 1956-57; MS, La. State U., 1963. Libr. dir. Inter-Am. U., Aguadilla (P.R.) Regional Coll., 1975-76, cons. libr. and accreditation, 1983—; libr. U.P.R.-Aguadilla Regional Coll., 1976-77, libr. dir., 1983-86, libr., 1986-89, chair steering com. for accreditation, mem. directive coun. honors program, 1989—, dir. instl. planning and rsch., 1989-90, libr. dir., 1990-94, acting assoc. acad. dean, 1994—, dean, dir., 1994-99; libr. dir. EDP Coll. P.R., San Sebastian, 1979-83; acting assoc. acad. dean U. P.R., Aguadilla, 1994, dean, dir., 1994—; chancellor U. P.R. at Aguadilla, 1999—. Mem. steering com. nat. edn. program Am. Coun. Edn., P.R., 1982-86, adv. bd. Coun. Higher Edn., P.R., 1982—; external evaluator Middle States Assn. Colls. and Schs., 1997—. Author: Manual bibliografico Electronica, 1987; co-author: El Desarrollo del Pensamiento Critico en Futuros Maestros, 1989; contbr. articles to profl. jours. Mem. Club Civico de Damas, Aguadilla, 1989—. With U.S. Army, 1963-66. Mem. ALA, Am. Assn. Higher Edn., Assn. Caribbean Univs., Rsch. and Instl. Librs., Sociedad de Bibliotecarios de P.R. (pres. continuing edn. 1984-90), Mid. States Assn. Colls. and Schs. (evaluating team mem. 1998—), Rotary-Anns (pres. 1974), Internat. Altrusan, Alpha Delta Kappa. Avocations: cooking, water sports, traveling. Office: UPR Aguadilla PO Box 160 Ramey Aguadilla PR 00604-0160 E-mail: losjara@prtc.net., j_segarra@cora.upr.du.edu.

JARAMILLO, MARI-LUCI, retired federal agency administrator; b. Las Vegas, N.Mex., June 19, 1928; BA magna cum laude, N.Mex. Highland U., 1955, MA with honors, 1959; PhD, U. N.Mex., 1970. Tchr., Albuquerque and Las Vegas, N.Mex., 1955-65, asst. prof. U. N.Mex., 1965-72, assoc. prof., chmn. dept. elem. edn., 1972-75, assoc. prof. edn., 1976-77, prof., 1977, spl. asst. to pres., 1981-82, assoc. dean Coll. Edn., 1982-85, v.p. for student affairs, 1985-87; amb. to Republic of Honduras U.S. Dept. State, 1977-80, dep. asst. sec. for Inter-Am. affairs, 1980-81; asst. v.p., dir. Ednl. Testing Service, Emeryville, Calif., 1987-93; dep. asst. sec. for Inter-Am. affairs Dept. Def., Washington, 1993-95. Bd. trustees Tomas Rivera Nat. Policy Ctr., Claremont (Calif.) Coll. Grad. Sch., 1985-93; minority recruiter Dept. State, Washington, 1990-2000; commr. Calif. Commn. of Post-Secondary Edn., Sacramento, 1990-93; active Coun. Am. Ambs., Washington, 1983-; bd. dirs. Latin Am. Scholarship Program for Am. Univs., Boston, Children's TV Workshop, N.Y.C.; cons. for curriculum, tchr. tng. and sch. reform, 1960-; vice chair, bd. regents, N.Mex. Highlands U. Author: Madame Ambassador; The Shoe Maker's Daughter, 2002; contbr. articles to jours., chpts. to books. Bd. dirs. Internat. House, U. Calif., Berkeley, 1989-93; scholar panelist Nat. Latino Comm. Ctr., L.A., 1990—; active Bay area Network L.Am. Women, San Francisco, 1987-93; reget N.Mex. Highlands U., 2003—. Decorated Order Francisco Morazan (Honduras), Order of Great Silver Cross (Honduras); recipient Cubberly award Stanford U., 1975, N.Mex. Disting. Svc. award, 1977, Anne Roe award Harvard U. Grad. Sch. Edn., 1986, PRIMERA award Mex. Am. Women's Nat. Assn., 1990; named Outstanding Chicana, 1975, Hon. Honduran Citizen, Govt. of Honduras, 1980, Disting. Woman of Yr., U. N.Mex. Alumni Assn., 1985, Disting. Hispanic lectr. Calif. State U. at Fullerton, 1988, Outstanding Hispanic Educator, 1988, Outstanding Leader in Edn. to Hispanic Cmty., 1991. Mem. Nat. Assn. Bilingual Edn., Latin Am. Assn., Am. Assn. Colls. for Tchr. Edn., Nat. Council La Raza. Home: 4829 Mesa Prieta Ct NW Albuquerque NM 87120-4620

JARAMILLO, SANDRA JULIER, nutritionist, researcher; b. Queens, N.Y., Jan. 20, 1970; Cert. chiropractic asst., Parker Coll., Dallas, 1992; AA, AS, Houston (Tex.) C.C., 1998, BS, 2001. Massage therapist Homeopathic Massage The Natural Approach, Houston, 1995—2001; rsch. coord. Children's Nutrition Rsch. Ctr., 2001—. Avocations: arts, sports, reading. Home and Office: 7802 Vernwood St Houston TX 77040-2714

JARANILLA, SARAH J. critical care nurse, consultant; arrived in U.S., 1976; d. Angelo C. and Leonor J. Jaranilla; children: Christine Joy Reynoso, Jerome Jay Laguilles, Sarah Joy Laguilles. BSN, Philippine Union Coll., Manila, 1973. RN Tex. Head nurse med./surg. unit Bacolod (The Philippines) Sanitarium & Hosp., 1973—75; charge nurse med./surg. unit Hansford Hosp., Spearman, Tex., 1976—77; critical care RN Monterey Park (Calif.) Hosp., 1978—80; DON, owner Sarnel Nurse Registry, West Covina, Calif., 1980—85; DON CJS Nursing Svcs., West Covina,

1985—93; adminstr., dir. patient svcs. Alpha Omega Home Health Svcs., Inc., Glendora, Calif., 1994—96; adminstr., owner Alternative Staffing, Inc., Torrance, Calif., 1997—2002; adminstr., dir. patient svcs. Gen. Home Health Care, Glendale, Calif., 2003—. Recipient Virgo Nurse of the Yr. award, Virgo Prodn., 2000. Mem.: Philippine Nurses Assn. So. Calif

JARCHO, JUDITH LYNN, artist; b. Mpls., Mar. 24, 1944; d. Paul and Lillian (Garetz) Brazman; m. Michael Jarcho, Nov. 24, 1968; children: Jason M., Johanna Molly. BFA, Mpls. Coll. of Art & Design, 1968; tchg. credential elem. and art edn., Coll. St. Rose, Albany, N.Y., 1975. Grades K-6 art tchr. Albany Sch. Dist., 1971-74; art tchr. Portrait Soc., La Jolla, Calif., 1996, San Digeto Art Assn., Del Mar, Calif., 1996, El Cajon (Calif.) Art Assn., 1997. Juror Del Mar Art Fair/Art Exhbn., 1995, El Cajon Art Assn. Annual Exhbn., 1996, San Diego Art Inst., 1998. Works exhibited San Diego Mus. Art, 1994, Rose-Hulman Inst. Tech., Terre Haute, Ind., 1994, Nat. Arts Club, N.Y.C., 1994, Poudre Valley Artist League, Denver, 1995, Tijuana (Mexico) Cultural Ctr., 1995, Hampton Classic, Bridgehampton, N.Y., 1995, Perry House Galleries, Old Town Alexandria, Va., 1995, Linda Joslin Gallery, La Jolla, Calif., 1995, Mpls. Found., 1996, Robert Mondavi Food & Wine Ctr., Orange County, Calif., 1996, The Parrish Art Mus., South Hampton, N.Y., 1996, San Diego Mus. Art, 1995-99, Univ. Club, San Diego, 1998. Philantropist Helen Woodward Animal Ctr., Rancho Santa Fe, Calif., 1996-98; past pres. San Diego Mus. of Art Artist Guild. Named Entrepreneur of Yr., Vishe Corp., San Diego, 1998, Best Canine Artist, Manhattan Guest mag., 2001, Overall Gold award ann. report competition League Am. Comm. Profls., 2001. Office Phone: 888-518-2424. E-mail: jjarcho@msn.com.

JARED, MARGARET ELLEN, music educator; b. Altus, Okla., Dec. 16, 1957; d. Wabern Carroll Davidson and Evelyn Joan DeVore Connell; m. Robert Joseph Jared, July 1, 1978; children: Emily Carol, Stephen Steven. BS, Trevecca Nazarene U., Nashville, 1979; MME, Belmont U., Nashville, 1992; postgrad., Cumberland U., Lebanon, Tenn., 1997. Cert. tchr. K-12 vocal/instrumental music Tenn. Tchr. Met. Nashville Bd. Edn., Nashville, 1979—80; tchr. music Englewood Acad., Independence, Mo., 1980—83; libr. asst. So. Bapt. Theol. Sem., Louisville, 1983—84; tchr. Victory Acad., Louisville, 1984—85, Met. Nashville Bd. Edn., 1995—. Cons. BeautiControl, Dallas, 1996—; chair Faculty Adv. Bd., Hermitage, Tenn., 2000—04, mem., 1998—2004. Composer: (songs) Coming Home for Christmas, 1996, I Will Be Your Instrument, 2002, Come & See, 2003. Mem.: NEA, Music Tchrs. Edn. Assn. Ch. Of The Nazarene. Home: 1895 Keyes Rd Greenbrier TN 37073 Office: Tulip Grove Elem Sch 441 Tyler Dr Hermitage TN 37076

JARLES, RUTH SEWELL, education educator; d. Nashville Clyde Sewell and Zetta Marie Hurt; m. Terry Waters Milligan, June 16, 1990; m. Marion Evert Jarles, Dec. 19, 1957 (div. Mar. 1980); children: Leslie Marie Murphy, Eva Colleen Wakeley, Brian Keith. AA, Western Okla. State Coll., 1976; BA magna cum laude, U. Colo., Colorado Springs, 1982; MDiv, U. Denver, 1985, PhD, 1993. Dir. Christian edn. Patrick Henry Village Army Chapel, Heidelberg, Germany, 1973—74; dir. curriculum Grace Child Devel. Ctr., Altus, Okla., 1976—77; dir. Christian edn. First Congl. Ch., Colorado Springs, Colo., 1980—84; asst. to the dir. joint PhD program U. Denver, Iliff Sch. Theology, 1991—92; adj. faculty, tchg. or rsch. asst. U. Denver, Iliff Sch. Theology, Front Range and Auraria C.C., 1983—98; asst. materials sci. br. Nat. Renewable Energy Lab., Golden, Colo., 1994—95; exec. dir. Colo. Libr. Assn., Denver, 1995—98; gen. edn. faculty Art Inst. Colo., Denver, 1998—. Seminar leader Gender Differences in Comm. in the Workplace; session convenor, panel mem. Women in Religion. Contbr. articles to profl. jours. Student senate Iliff Sch. Theology, Denver, 1984—86; mentor students cmty. svc. projects Art Inst. Colo., Denver, 1997—; chair/mem. South Africa task force, race and religion com., women's com. Iliff Sch.Theology, Denver, 1984—92; mem. publs. com. Colo. Women's Agenda, Denver, 1993—95; chair/mem. edn., fin., adminstrv. bd., music and fine arts, peace with justice coms. Trinity United Meth. Ch., Denver, 1984—92; mem. exec. com. Nat. Renewable Energy Lab. Women's Network, Golden, 1994—95; active Art Inst. Colo. Christmas project Denver Safe Ho., 2001—. Recipient E. Craig Brandenburg award, United Meth. Ch.; scholar Ea. Star Tng. awards for Religious Leadership, The Grand Chpt. Colo., Order Ea. Star, 1984—86; Oliver Read Whitley scholar, Iliff Sch. Theology, Seminarian scholar, Ctr. for Biblic Studies, Jerusalem, Israel, Ga. Harkness scholar, United Meth. Ch. Mem.: AAUW, Denver Art Mus., Nat. Women's History Mus., Nat. Mus. for Women in the Arts. Office: Art Inst Colo 1200 Lincoln St Denver CO 80203 Home: 6240 W 24th Ave Edgewater CO 80214-1034 Office Phone: 303-824-2151.

JAROSH, COLLEEN MARIE, nursing educator, consultant; b. Cresco, Iowa, July 4, 1951; d. Raymond James and Marjorie Ester (Burr) McGee; m. Kenneth Charles Jarosh, July 21, 1979; children: Michael, Rebecca. ADN, N.E. Iowa Tech. Inst., Calmar, 1974; BSN, Upper Iowa U., Fayette, 1980; MAE in Edn., U. No. Iowa, Cedar Falls, 1984. RN, Iowa. Nurse Schoitz Meml. Hosp., Waterloo, Iowa, 1974-76, USPHS, Tuba City, Ariz., 1976-77, Phoenix Indian Med. Ctr., 1977-78, Palmar Meml. Hosp., West Union, Iowa, 1978-79; instr. N.E. Iowa Tech. Inst., 1979; sch. nurse Upper Iowa U., 1979, adj. instr., 1979-83; writer, co-editor newsletter Dept. Human Svcs., Waterloo, 1994-98; emtl. cons. Janesville, Iowa, 1980—. Mediator Child Welfare, 1998—. Vol. St. Mary's ch., Waverly, Iowa, 1994—; support group leader Luth. Social Svcs., Waterloo, 1994. Mem. Rosary Soc., Iowa Foster Adoptive Parents Assn (bd. dirs.), Acad. Family Mediators. Avocations: special needs adoption, prairie restoration, tree planting, reading. Office: Colleen Jarosh Ednl Cons 9405 Taylor Rd Janesville IA 50647-1124

JARRELL, IRIS BONDS, elementary school educator, business executive; b. Winston-Salem, N.C., May 25, 1942; d. Ira and Annie Gertrude (Vandiver) Bonds; m. Tommy Dorsey Martin, Feb. 13, 1965; 1 child, Carlos Miguel; m. 2d, Clyde Rickey Jarrell, June 25, 1983; stepchildren: Tamara, Cris, Kimberly. Student, U. N.C., Greensboro, 1960-61, 68-69, student, 1974-75, Salem Coll., 1976; BS in Edn., Winston-Salem State U., 1983; M in Elem. Edn., Gardner-Webb Coll., 1992. Cert. tchr. N.C. Tchr. Rutledge Coll., Winston-Salem, 1982-84; owner, mgr. Rainbow's End Consignment Shop, Winston-Salem, 1983-85; tchr. elem. edn. Winston-Salem/Forsyth County Sch. Svcs., 1985-96; dir. Knollwood Bapt. Pre-Sch., 1996-97; tchr. gifted/talented students Winston-Salem/Forsyth County Schs., 1998; tchr. Clemmons Elem. Sch., 1998—. Contbr. poetry to mags. Mem. Assn. of Couples for Marriage Enrichment, Winston-Salem, 1985-86; mem. Winston-Salem Symphony Chorale; mem. Planned Parenthood. Mem. NOW, Internat. Reading Assn., N.C. Assn. Adult Edn., Forsyth Assn. Classroom Tchrs., World Wildlife Fund, Greenpeace, KlanWatch. Democrat. Baptist. Avocations: singing, writing, sewing, gardening, reading. Home: 101 Cheswyck Ln Winston Salem NC 27104-2905 E-mail: ijarrell@bellsouth.net.

JARRELL, LEEANN, investment company executive; CFO, human resources officer Capital Group Cos., L.A. Office: Capital Group Companies 333 S Hope St Los Angeles CA 90071 Office Fax: (213) 486-9217.

JARRETT, ALEXIS, insurance agent, lawyer; b. Independence, Kans., July 2, 1948; d. Robert Patterson and Betty June (Johnson) Jarrett. BS, U. Minn., Duluth, 1970; postgrad., U. Mo., 1974—77; JD, John Marshall Law Sch., 2001. Lic. property and casualty ins., life and health ins. Ind., cert. Life Underwriting Tng. Coun.; coach Minn. Tchr. Esko (Minn.) Pub. Schs., 1970-74; asst. dir. athletics, head coach basketball, softball, track U. Mo., Columbia, 1974-77; pvt. practice Schererville, Ind., 1984—; pres., CEO INFINITE Sports and Entertainment, Inc., 2002—. Women's basketball and softball color analyst Regional Radio Sports, N.W. Ind., 1992—94; with Moot Ct. Coun., 1999; jud. extern Cir. Ct. Cook County, Chgo., 1999;

coord. Women's Sports Info. Dept., U. Mo., 1974—77; v.p. legal affairs Nat. Assn. State Farm Agts., Inc., 1997—2000; contract advisor NFL Players Assn., 2002—, Women's Nat. Basketball Players Assn., 2002—, CFL Players Assn., 2003. Contbr. articles on sports to newspapers. Sponsor Lake County (Ind.) HS Girls Basketball Dinner, 1989—99, Jr. u.s. Jamaiian Counseling Ctr. N.W. Ind., pres., 1994; bd. dirs. VNA Found., sec.-treas., 1994; celebrity Am. Heart Assn. Celebrity Dinner; v.p. S.W. Lake divsn. Am. Heart Assn., 1992—94; mem. bd. advisors Basketball Hall of Fame, 1999—; bd. dirs. Boys and Girls Club N.W. Ind.; mem. adv. bd. indsl. rsch. liaison program Ind. U., Bloomington, 1990—96. Recipient Individual with Vision award, Ind. HS Athletic Assn., 1996. Mem.: ABA (entertainment and sports law forum, labor and law com., ins. law com., sports law subcom.), Sports Lawyers Assn., Chgo. Bar Assn. (labor and employment law com., ins. law com., immigration law com., health law com.), Ind. State Med. Assn. Alliance (chair media rels. 1990—91, treas. 1992—93, chair media rels. 1993—94), Am. Bus. Women's Assn. (pres. New Image chpt. 1983, Woman of the Yr. 1983), Lake County Med. Soc. Alliance (pres. 1992—94), Nat. Life Underwriters (bd. dirs. N.W. Ind. chpt. 1995, 1996, 1997). Address: 2330 Wicker Blvd Schererville IN 46375-2810 Office Phone: 219-322-4447.

JARRETT, JINGER ELAINE, freelance/self-employed writer; b. Toccoa, Ga., June 21, 1963; d. Jimmie Jarrett Brown and John Henry Jarrett, Hughlon Doyle Brown (Stepfather); children: Ashley Nicole Timon, Danielle Kristen Timon, Alexandra Kay Timon. BAA in Journalism and English, Ctrl. Mich. U., Mt. Pleasant, 1994. Mil. journalist Mil. Tng. Command, Camp Grayling, Mich., 1991—98; freelance writer/owner SmallBusinessHowTo.com, Anderson, SC, 2000—. Fixed ciphony repair/adminstrn. U.S. Army, Grafenwoehr, Germany, 1982—86. Webmaster Anderson County Taxpayers Assn., SC, 2002—03. With U.S. Army, 1982—86. Mem.: Am. Legion (assoc.; publicity chmn. 2002—03), Golden Key Nat. Honor Soc. (life). Libertarian. Baptist. Avocations: reading, travel, veterans' causes, computers, helping others. Home and Office: SmallBusinessHowTocom 1502 Mitchell St Anderson SC 29624 Personal E-mail: beloved_warrior_7@yahoo.com. E-mail: jingerjarrett@smallbusinesshowto.com.

JARROW, GAIL, literature educator, writer; b. Dallas, Nov. 29, 1952; d. Paul and Joan Goundry; m. Robert Jarrow, May 14, 1974; children: Kyle, Tate, Heather. BA magna cum laude, Duke U., 1974; MA, Dartmouth Coll., 1980. Tchr. 4th-8th grades pub. and pvt. schs., Hanover, NH, 1974—76, 1978—79, Cambridge, Mass., 1976—78; writing instr. Inst. Children's Lit., Redding Ridge, Conn., 1991—. Bd. dirs. Family Reading Partnership, Ithaca, NY, 2000—. Author: (book) Beyond the Magic Sphere, 1994, Naked Mole-Rats, 1996, Animal Baby Sitters, 2001, Parasites: Hookworms, 2004, Parasites: Chiggers, 2004, Animals Attack: Rhinos, 2003, Animals Attack: Bears, 2003. Recipient Outstanding Sci. Trade Book for Children, Nat. Sci. Tchr. Assn., 1996, Outstanding Secondary Sci. Book, Soc. of Sch. Librs. Internat., 1997, Top Title New Adult Readers, Pub. Libr. Assn., 1997. Mem.: Authors Guild, Soc. Children's Book Writers and Illustrators.

JARVEY, PAULETTE SUE, publishing executive; b. Camp LeJuene, N.C., Aug. 10, 1945; d. Charles O. and Reva Wanda (Shirley) McCord; m. John M. Jarvey, Aug. 22, 1964; children: Shawn M., J. Adam. Student, Portland Community Coll., Oreg., 1973. Teller new accounts Bank of Am., Anaheim, Calif., 1964-68; owner The Mouth Nut, Canby, Oreg., 1971-85, P.J. Promotions, Canby, 1972-85; pres. Hot Off the Press, Inc., Canby, 1980—. Founder N.W. Assn. Book Pubs., Portland, 1983. Author: You Can Dough It, 1980, Let's Dough It Again, 1982, Dough Art Lumpies, 1983, Dough It For Christmas, 1983, Decorative Dough, 1984. Mem. Soc. Craft Designers. Democrat. Avocations: white water rafting, reading. Office: Hot Off Press Inc 1250 NW 3rd Ave Canby OR 97013-3499

JARVIK, GAIL PAIRITZ, medical geneticist; b. Evanston, Ill., Feb. 8, 1959; d. Lawrence Alan and Lenore Mae P.; m. Jeffrey Gil Jarvik, Aug. 22, 1992. PhD in Human Genetics, U. Mich., 1986; MD, U. Iowa, 1987. Sr. rsch. fellow U. Wash., Seattle, 1992-95, asst. prof. medicine, divsn. med. genetics, 1995-2000, assoc. prof., 2000—. Affiliate mem. Fred Hutchinson Cancer Rsch. Ctr., Seattle, 1994—. Contbr. to profl. jours. Howard Hughes Rsch. fellow, 1992-95; Pew scholar, 1997—. Mem. Am. Soc. Human Genetics, Internat. Genetic Epidemiology Soc.

JARVIS, CHARLENE DREW, university administrator, former scientist; b. Washington, July 31, 1941; two children. BA, Oberlin (Ohio) Coll., 1962; MS in Psychology, Howard U., 1964; PhD in Neuropsychology, U. Md., 1971; DSc (hon.), Amherst Coll., 1994, George Washington U., 2001. Supr. statis. lab. Howard U., 1965-66, prof. psychol., 1970-71; rsch. psychologist NIMH, 1971-78; coun. mem. Coun. of the D.C., 1979-2000; chair com. on housing and econ. devel. coun. of the D.C., 1981-2000; chair pro temp Coun. of the D.C., 1994-2000. Chair bd. dirs. Met. Washington Coun. of Govts.; bd. dirs. Pa. Ave. Devel. Corp., Nat. Health Mus., Fed. City Coun.; BB&T Regional Bank, Washington office; mem. steering com. Greater Washington Mktg. Partnership of the Greater Washington Bd. of Trade, 1993—; mem. coms. NIMH, adv. coun., 1993—; mem. breast cancer task force, 1993—; mem. Ronald Reagan Ctr. for Emergency Medicine, George Washington U. Hosp., 1993—. Bd. dirs. Girl Scouts Am., Pvt. Industry Coun., 1986—; mem. Leadership Washington, 1991-92; chair transp. subcom. D.C. chpt. ARC; del. Nat. Dem. Conv., 1980, 84, 88, 92; nat. co-chair Mondale for Pres., 1984, Clinton/Gore campaign, 1992; candidate for mayor, D.C., 1982, 90; chair pro tempore Coun. D.C., 1997—; pres. Southeastern U., 1996—; chair cmty. bus. partnership com. Greater Washington Bd. of Trade; chair, bd. dirs. Washington D.C. Conv. and Tourism Corp., 2001—. Recipient Howard U. Alumni award, 1993, over 100 others; Named one of 50 Most Powerful Women in the Washington Area Washington Bus. Jour., 1985, 100 Most Powerful Women in the Washington Area, Washingtonian Mag., 1989, 94, Washingtonian of Yr. Washingtonian Mag., 1999. Mem. Nat. Assn. Ind. Colls. and Univs. (bd. dirs.), D.C. C. of C. (pres.-elect). Home: 1789 Sycamore St NW Washington DC 20012-1030 also: Southeastern Univ 501 I St SW Washington DC 20024-2715 E-mail: president@admin.seu.edu.

JARVIS, DEBRA JEAN, fire chief, consultant; b. Indpls., June 1, 1953; d. George and Phyllis Joyce (DeHart) Bretzlaff; m. Greg A. Jarvis, Nov. 19, 1994. AS in Fire Sci., Ind. U., Kokomo, 1982; BS in Mgmt., Ind. Wesleyan U., 1988; Exec. Fire Officer, Nat. Fire Acad., 1996; MA in Leadership Studies, Lewis U., 2000. Firefighter, EMT Pike Twp. Fire Dept., Indpls., 1978-81, station officer, 1981-84, battalion chief, 1984-90; divsn. chief Lawrence Twp. Fire Dept., Indpls., 1990-95; fire chief Homewood (Ill.) Fire Dept., 1995-97, Oakbrook (Ill.) Fire Dept., 1997—. Trustee Women in the Fire Svc., 1989-92; coms., spkr., 1981—; contractor Inst. Pub. Safety Personnel, Inc., Indpls., 1994—. Leadership in action field. Precinct inspector, Ind. Election Bd., Indpls., 1990-95; small gp. leader Living Springs Cmty. Ch., Homewood, Ill., 1996—; firefighter-training dir. Worth Twp. Vol. Fire Dept., Whitestown, Ind., 1986-90. Named Firefighter of Yr., Homewood (Ill.) C. of C., 1996, Forum Series honoree Girls, Inc., Indpls., 1992. Mem. Dupage County Chiefs Assn., Internat. Assn. Fire Chiefs, Internat. Soc. Fire Svc. Instrs., Ill. Fire Chiefs. Avocations: photography, flower arranging. Home: 1530 190th St Homewood IL 60430-4007

JASINSKI-CALDWELL, MARY L. company executive; b. Chester, Pa., May 8, 1959; d. A. Robert and Helen M. Jasinski; m. William A. Caldwell, Aug. 4, 1990; children: Helaina M., Anna L. Student, Loyola Coll., Balt., 1980; AS, Goldey Beacom Coll., Wilmington, Del., 1982, BS, 1983. Registered orthotic fitter; cert. sr. pharmacy technician. Gen. mgr. pension plan City Pharmacy of Elkton (Md.) Inc., 1975-96, treas., 1987-96, jr. ptnr., 1994, v.p., 1996—; founder, pres. City Home Health Care, Inc., Elkton, 1997—. Disc jockey, promoter Garfield's Restaurant, Elkton; editl. writer

local newspapers; pro-life columnist KC newsletter; nat. bd. advisors McKesson Drug Co., 2001—. Creator ednl. program PARTICIP.A.A.T.E. For Life. Advisor Cecil County Pregnancy Ctr., Cecil County Rd. Edn. Textbook Aduption Policy Com., 1995; pro-life educator City of Elkton, Ind. chpt., 2000—01; bd. dirs. Mission Am., Inc., Md. Right to Life, 1993—94, co-chair Cecil County chpt., 1993—94. Alpha Chi scholar, Linback scholar; recipient J.W. Miller award, Outstanding Achievement in Excellence award K.C., 1994, Ralph and Eleanor Hicks Outstanding Vol. svc. award ARC, Cecil County, Md., 1999-2000; named Family of Yr., 1995; named to Honor Roll of Best 250 Independents in U.S., Drug Topics, 1992. Mem. NAFE, NRA, Am. Pharmacists Assn. (assoc.), Am. Mgmt. Assn., Nat. Fedn. Ind. Bus., Bd. Orthotic Cert., Am. Assn. Pharm. Technicians, Nat. Right to Life Com., Am. Life League, Internat. Platform Assn., Pro-Life Md., Christian Coalition, Cath. Alliance, Cecil County C. of C., Stopp Internat., Human Life Internat., Concerned Women for Am., Pharmacists for Life, Goldey Beacom Coll. Alumni Assn., Movement for a Better Am., Cath. League, Liberty Alliance, Epic Pharmacies, Inc., Susan B. Anthony List, Alpha Chi. Republican. Roman Catholic. Avocations: home improvement, gardening, social concerns, pro-life education, reading. Office: City Pharmacy Inc 723 N Bridge St Elkton MD 21921-5398 Personal E-mail: williamandmary.1@juno.com

JASON, J. JULIE, portfolio manager, writer, lawyer; b. Owensboro, Ky. d. Richard and Grazina Pauliukonis; m. Marius J. Jason; Dec. 19, 1970; children: Ilona, Leila. BA, Baldwin-Wallace Coll., 1971; JD, Cleve. State U., 1974; LLM, Columbia U., 1975. Bar: Ohio 1974, N.Y. 1976, U.S. Dist Ct. (so. dist.) N.Y. 1976, U.S. Ct. Appeals (2d cir.) 1976, U.S. Supreme Ct. 1978. Pvt. practice, N.Y.C., 1974-78; asst. gen. counsel Paine Webber, N.Y.C., 1978-83; pres. P.W. Trust and Paine Webber Futures Mgmt. Co., N.Y.C., 1983-88; sr. fin. svcs. atty. Donovan, Leisure, Newton & Irvine, N.Y.C., 1988-89; co-founder, mng. dir. Jackson, Grant & Co., Stamford, Conn., 1989—. Arbitrator NYSE; mediator U.S. Bankruptcy Ct., 1997. Author: You and Your 401(K), 1996, The 401(K) Plan Handbook, 1997, Strategic Investing, 2001; columnist: 401-OK. Mem. ABA, AAUW (chair scholarship com. 1992-93), Nat. Assn. Securities Dealers (cert. arbitrator, cert. mediator), Am. Soc. Journalists & Authors, Investment Co. Inst. (sec. regulation com. 1978-83), The Corp. Bar, Columbia U. Alumni Club of Fairfield County (pres. 1993-94, chair pres.'s coun. 1994-96). Office: Jackson Grant & Co 1177 High Ridge Rd Stamford CT 06905-1203

JASON, KATHRINE, language educator, writer; b. Bklyn., Feb. 9, 1953; d. Leon and Lucille Lee Jason; m. Peter Rondinone, Apr. 23, 1983 (dec. Nov. 2002). BA, Bard Coll., 1975; MFA, Columbia U., 1978. Instr. English, Hunter Coll., N.Y.C., 1981—93; prof. English, Nassau C.C., Garden City, NY, 1993—. Editor, translator: Words in Commotion & Other Stories, 1985, Name and Tears: 40 Years of Italian Fiction, 1991; author: Exploring American Culture, 1994; contbr. articles to profl. jours. Fulbright grantee, Rome, 1978—79, Lit. grantee, NEA, 1985. Mem.: Pen Am. Avocation: travel. Home: 680 Washington St New York NY 10014 Office: Nassau CC 1 Education Pl Garden City NY 11530 Office Phone: 516-572-7798. E-mail: jasonk@ncc.edu.

JASSO, GUILLERMINA, sociologist, educator; b. Laredo, Tex., July 22, 1942; d. José Jasso-Rodríguez and Guillermina de los Santos-Lozano. BA, Our Lady of the Lake Coll., 1962; MA, U. Notre Dame, 1970; PhD, Johns Hopkins U., 1974. Asst. prof. Barnard Coll. and Columbia U., N.Y.C., 1974-77; spl. asst. to commr. U.S. Immigration and Naturalization Svc., Washington, 1977-79; dir. rsch. U.S. Select Commn. on Immigration and Refugee Policy, Washington, 1979-80; asst. prof. U. Mich., Ann Arbor, 1980-82; assoc. prof. U. Minn., Mpls., 1982-86, prof., 1986-87; prof., dir. theory workshop U. Iowa, Iowa City, 1987-91; prof. NYU, N.Y.C., 1991—, dir. methods workshop, 1991-97. Mem. study sect. on social sci. and population NIH, 1991-95; mem. U.S. Com. for Internat. Inst. for Applied Sys. Analysis, 1993—; mem. various programs NSF 1987-96, 98-99; panel on demographic and econ. impacts of immigration NAS, 1995-97; population rsch. subcom. Nat. Inst. Child Health and Human Devel., NIH, 1998-2002, adv. com. SBE Directorate, NSF, 2003—; vis. prof. Zentrum Umfragen, Methoden, und Analysen, Mannheim, Germany, 1995, U. Leipzig, Germany, 1996; core rsch. team bination study on migration between Mex. and US, U. Commn. on Immigration Reform, 1995-97; disting. alumni lectr. U. Notre Dame, 1987; pub. lectr. Our Lady of Lake U., 1989; disting. lectr. NSF, 2003. Author: The New Chosen People, 1990; mem. editl. bd. Social Justice Rsch., 1985—, Jour. Math. Sociology, 1985—, Rationality and Society, 1999—, European Sociological Review, 2001-, Internat. Jour. Computer Sociology, 2001-; dep. editor Am. Sociol. Rev., 1996-99; contbr. articles to profl. jours. Grantee Russell Sage Found., 1983-85, Rockefeller Found., 1985-86, NSF, 1994-97, 2000-2002, NIH, 1995-99, 2000-, PEW, 2001-; fellow Ctr. for Advanced Study in Behavioral Scis., Stanford, Calif., 1999-2000. Fellow Johns Hopkins Soc. Scholars; mem. Am. Sociol. Assn. (chair internat. migration sect. 1996-99, chair theory sect. 1996-99, chair rat. choice sect. 2000—, chair soc. psychol. sect. 2002-), Sociol. Rsch. Assn. Office: NYU Dept Sociology 269 Mercer St 4th Fl New York NY 10003-6633 E-mail: gj1@nyu.edu.

JASSO, NANCY, dermatologist; b. 1960: BS in Human Biology, Stanford U., 1983; PhD in Dermatology, Harvard Med. Sch., 1988. Resident UCLA Med. Ctr., 1988—91; chief, dermatology Kaiser Permanente, Calif., 1994—. Named one of 10 Incredible Women Making History, KNBC-TV, Los Angeles, 1999. Achievements include discovery of a laser tattoo-removal project for the San Fernando Valley Violence Prevention Coalition. Office: 13652 Cantara St Panorama City CA 91402*

JAUDON, VALERIE, artist; b. Greenville, Miss., Aug. 6, 1945; d. Baize R. and Gladys E. (Hill) J.; m. Richard Kalina, Oct. 23, 1979. Student, Miss. State Coll. for Women, 1963-65, Memphis Acad. Art, 1965, U. of Americas, Mexico, 1966-67, St. Martins Sch. Art, London, 1968-69. One-woman shows of paintings include, Holly Solomon Gallery, N.Y.C., 1977-79, 81, Pa. Acad. Fine Arts, Phila., 1977, Galerie Bishofberger, Zurich, Switzerland, 1979, Galerie Hans Strelow, Dusseldorf, Fed. Republic Germany, 1980, Corcoran Gallery, Los Angeles, 1981, Sidney Janis Gallery, N.Y.C. 1983, 85, 86, 88, 90, 93, 96, Quadrat Mus., Bottrop, Fed. Republic Germany, 1983, Amerika Haus, Berlin, 1983, Dart Gallery, Chgo., 1983, Fay Gold Gallery, Atlanta, 1985, Macintosh/Drysdale Gallery, Washington, 1985, Barbara Scott Gallery, Bay Harbor Islands, Fla., 1994, Miss. Mus. Art, Jackson, 1996, Betsy Senior Gallery, N.Y.C., 1998, Stadel Mus., Frankfurt, Germany, 1999-2000, Von Lintel Gallery, N.Y.C., 2003; numerous group shows including, Mayor Gallery, London, 1979, Galerie Habermann, Cologne, Germany, 1979, Galerie Hans Strelow, Dusseldorf, 1979, Galerie Modern Art, Vienna, Austria, 1980, Mus. Modern Art, Oxford, Eng., 1980, Greenberg, Gallery, St. Louis, 1980, Sidney Janis Gallery, N.Y.C., 1980, San Francisco Art Inst., 1980, Mus. Modern Art, N.Y.C., 1980, Leo Castelli Gallery, N.Y.C., 1980, Thomas Segal Gallery, Boston, 1980, Venice (Italy) Biennale, 1980, Nat. Gallery of Art, Washington, 1980, Chgo. Art Inst., 1981, Mus. Fine Arts, Boston, 1982, Neuberger Mus., Purchase, N.Y., 1982, Hudson River Mus., Yonkers, N.Y., 1983, Berkshire Mus., Pittsfield, Mass., 1983, La Jolla Mus., Calif., 1983, Margo Leavin Gallery, Los Angeles, 1984, Bronx Mus., 1985, Am. Fine Arts, Chgo., 1986, Dayton Art Inst., 1987, Cin. Art Mus., 1989, Tel Aviv Mus. Art, 1992, Robert McClain Gallery, Houston, 1996, Turner/Runyon Gallery, Dallas, 1997, Kunsthallen Brandts Kaledefabrik, Odense, Denmark, 2001, Angel Row Gallery, Nottingham, England, 2001, Porin Taidemuseo, Eleränta, Finland, 2002, Von Lintel Gallery, N.Y.C., 2002; executed ceramic mural Equitable Bldg., N.Y.C., 1988, brick and granite plaza Police Plaza, N.Y.C., 1989; Blue Pools Courtyard Birmingham (Ala.) Mus. Art, 1993; mosaic floor Washington Nat. Airport, 1997; represented in permanent collections including Hirshhorn Mus., Washington, Mus. Modern Art, N.Y.C., Albright-Knox Art

Gallery, Buffalo, N.Y., Fogg Art Mus., Cambridge, Mass.,Sammlung-Lugwig Mus., Aachen, Fed. Republic Germany, Dayton (Ohio) Art Inst., Nat. Museum of Women in the Arts, Washington, St. Louis Art Mus., Ludwig Mus., Budapest, Hungary, Miss. Mus. Art, Jackson. Recipient 1st prize award So. Contemporary Arts Festival, 1967, Art award Miss. Inst. Arts and Letters, 1981, 97, Excellence in Design award N.Y.C. Art Commn., 1988, civic Spirit award Women's City Club of N.Y., Merit award Am. Soc. Landscape Architects Ala. chpt., 1994; named Honored Artist from State of Miss. Nat. Mus. Women in Arts, Washington; N.Y. State CAPS grantee for graphics, 1980; Visual Arts Fellowship grant Nat. Endowment Arts, 1988; N.Y. Found. for Arts grantee in painting, 1992. Address: 795A Accabonac Rd East Hampton NY 11937-1807 E-mail: vjaudon@earthlink.net.

JAUQUET-KALINOSKI, BARBARA, library director; b. Crystal Falls, Mich., Mar. 12, 1948; d. Herbert Francis and Lenore Mary (Roell) Jauquet; m. Gregory Clem Kalinoski, Nov. 12, 1983; children: Stacia Amee, Sara Amee, Michael Thomas and Thomas Michael (twins.). BS, No. Mich. U., 1970; MLS, Western Mich. U., 1974. Adminstrv. asst. Mid-Peninsula Libr. System, Iron Mountain, Mich., 1970-74, asst. dir., 1975-79; periodical libr. U. Wis., Superior, 1980; dir. N.W. Regional Libr., Thief River Falls, Minn., 1981—. Chmn. planning, evaluation and reporting curriculum com. for sch. dist., also mem. other sch. dist. coms. Named Woman of Honor, AAUW, 1990. Mem. ALA, Minn. Libr. Assn. (past pres., mem. continuing edn. com.), Thief River Falls C. of C., Rotary (past pres.). Roman Catholic. Avocations: children's activities, community issues, architecture and interior decoration, travel, sports. Office: NW Regional Libr 101 1st St E Thief River Falls MN 56701-2041

JAUREGUI, CONNIE LEE, internist; b. Cin., Apr. 3, 1962; d. James Harold and Joan Lee (Marston) S.; Luis Jauregui, Sept. 16, 2000. BS in Biology cum laude, U. Cin., 1984; MD with honors in Psychiatry, Med. Coll. Ohio, 1991. Histocompatibility technologist Hoxworth Blood Ctr., Cin., 1985-87; intern in internal medicine Pa. State U. Hershey Med. Ctr., 1991-92; resident in internal medicine Med. Coll. Ohio, Toledo, 1992-94; pvt. practice, Toledo, 1994—. Contbg. author: Diagnois and Management of Bone Infections, 1995. Mem. AMA, Ohio Med. Assn., Toledo Acad. Medicine. Lutheran. Avocations: swimming, travel to exotic locations. Office: 7055 W Central Ave Toledo OH 43617

JAVENS, KATHLEEN ELIZABETH, artist; b. Kennett, Mo., Dec. 1, 1959; d. Jack Ransom and Lee Creato Javens; m. Wade Schuman, July 16, 2002. Cert. of Fine Art, Pa. Acad. Fine Arts, Phila., 1985. Represented in permanent collections Phila. Mus. Art, Pa. Acad. Fine Arts, Palmer Mus. Art. Recipient Disciplinary Winner in Painting award, P.E.W., 1995; grantee Pa. Coun. on the Arts Painting fellowship, Mid Atlantic Coun. on the Arts, 1998; MacDowell fellow, MacDowell Colony, 1996, 1998, 2000, Spl. Opportunity stipend, Pa. Coun. on the Arts, 2001. Mem.: Elizabeth Found. for the Arts, (studio award 2003-2005). Avocations: bicycling, running. Studio: Elizabeth Found Arts Studio 313 323 West 39th St New York NY 10018

JAVIER-DEJNEKA, AMELIA LUISA, accountant; arrived in U.S., 1964; d. Ladislao Walter Dejneka and Elena Angelica Gomba; m. Washington Javier, July 14, 1973 (dec. June 1985); children: Walter Daniel, Maria Elena. BBA, Fla. Internat. U., 1976; degree in Computer Programming, Miami Tech. Coll., 1986. Investor Atlantic Acct. & Investment, Miami, Fla., 1984—; acct., owner A&M Acct. & Mgmt., Miami, 1999—; designer, owner A&M Designer Gallery, Miami, 1999—; prin., owner A&M Profl. Svc., Miami, 2002—. Recipient Blue Ribbon award, Argentina Consulate & Com., 1995. Avocations: swimming, dance, walking, travel. Home: 9449 Byron Ave Miami FL 33154

JAWIN, ANN JULIANO, human resource specialist; b. Barnesboro, Pa. d. Santo and Benedetta (Vanchiere) Giuliano; m. Edward Henry Jawin; children: Ronald, Paul. BA, Hunter Coll., 1943; PhD, St. John's U., 1976. Asst. personnel dir. Davis & Geck, N.Y.C., 1945-52; guidance counselor h.s. divsn. N.Y.C. Bd. Edn., 1962-86; dir. guidance Bramson Tech. Coll., N.Y.C., 1986-89; pres., founder Ann J. Jawin Assocs., N.Y.C., 1990—; founder, chair bd. dirs. Ctr. Women N.Y., N.Y.C., 1987—. Author: A Women's Guide to career Preparation, 1979, Report on Sex Bias in N.Y. Public Schools, 1977, Where's the Money for College?, 1985. Founder, chair bd. dirs. Dougbay Manor Civic Assn., Douglaston, N.Y., 1966—; pres. Bay Terrace Cmty. Coun., Bayside, Queens, N.Y., 1955-66; N.Y. State Committeewoman N.Y. State Dem. Party. Recipient Susan B. Anthony award NOW, 1985, Ralph Bunche award UN Assn., 1996, vol. svc. award Mayor Rudolph Giuliani, N.Y.C., 1997, Citation of Merit Fernando Ferrer Bronx Borough Pres., 1998, Hall of Fame award Hunter Coll., 1993, Ralph Burche award, 1996; named Humanitarian of Yr. Dems. for New Politics, 1995, Hunter Coll. Hall of Fame, 1993. Mem. AAUW (Leadership award 2001), N.Y. State Guidance Assn., Ams. of Italian Heritage (founder, chair bd. dirs. 1987—, Woman of Yr. 1998, Disting. Leadership award 2002). Avocations: walking, reading, swimming, gardening. Office: Queen's Women's Ctr 12055 Queens Blvd Rm 325 Jamaica NY 11424-1015 E-mail: Qwomenstr@aol.com.

JAWORSKA, TAMARA, painter, tapestry maker; b. Archangel, Russia; arrived in Can., 1969; d. Antonio Jankowski; m. Tadeusz Jaworski, 1957; children: Ewa, Piotr. BFA in Painting, State Acad. Fine Arts, Lodz, Poland, 1950, MFA in Design and Weaving Art, 1952; M of Painting (hon.), Accademia Italia, 1982. From asst. prof. to sr. asst. prof., lectr. State Acad. Fine Arts, Poland, 1952-58. One-woman shows include State Gallery of Textiles, Lodz, 1965, State Gallery of Fine Arts,Warsaw, 1965, Pushkin Nat. Mus., Moscow, 1966, Fine Arts Mus., Plymouth, U.K., 1968, Scottish Woolen Gallery, Galashields, 1968, Richard Demarco Gallery, Edinburgh, Scotland, 1968, Rothman's Art Gallery, Stratford, 1970, Merton Gallery, Toronto, 1970, London Art Gallery, 1971, Glendon Art Gallery, Toronto, 1972, Nienkamper Art Gallery, Toronto, 1979, Art Gallery of Hamilton, 1980, Nat. Museums and Art Galleries in Spain, 1980-81, Can. Cultural Ctr., Paris, 1981, Galerie Inard, Paris, 1981, Munich Art Gallery, Germany, 1982, Galerie Inard, Toulouse, France, 1982, 91, Galerie Inard, Paris, 1984, 91, Leo Kamen Gallery, Toronto, 1987, 89, John B. Aird State Gallery, Toronto, 1992, Peak Gallery, Toronto, 1997, Solo Gallery, Toronto, 2003, also exhibits in France, Germany, Belgium, Switzerland, Luxembourg, U.K., Spain, Austria, Poland, Russia, Hungary, U.S., Mex., Can., Paris, Eng., Scotland, Holland, Austria, Spain, Moscow, Poland, Hungary, Can., U.S., others; group exhbns. include Warsaw and Lodz art galleries, Pushkin Mus., European Art Gallery, Moscow, Richard Demarco Gallery, Edinburgh, Fine Art Mus., Plymouth, Eng., Merton Gallery, Toronto, Hermitage Leningrad Mus., USSR, Nat. Art Gallery, Teheran, Mus. Modern Art, Mexico City, Art Gallery of Ont., RCA-Art 2000, Toronto and Stratford, 2000; exhibited tapestries at New Coll., Galerie Inard, Ctr. Nat. de la Tapisserie d'Abusson, Paris, later in Madrid, Barcelona, Valencia, San Sebastian, Paris, Munich, Zurich, others; works in permanent collections of Pushkin Nat. Mus., European Art Gallery, Moskau, Russia, Nat. Mus., Warsaw, Nat. Mus. of Textile Arts, Lodz, Poland, Nat. Mus. of Home Army, King City, Krakow, Poland, Galashields Art Inst., Scotland, Bank of Montreal, Toronto, Bell Can., Ottawa, Molson Canadian, Toronto, Mut. Ins. of Can., Toronto, First Can. Pl. Main Lobby, Gulf Can. Sq. Main Lobby, and many corp. and pvt. collections in Europe, Am., Mid. East, Centre Nat. de la Tapisserie D'Aubusson Galerie Inard, Paris; subject of articles in art books and mags. Apptd. to Order of Can. for outstanding achievements in creative arts, 1994; recipient Gold medal-Triennial di Milano, Interior Design and Architecture, Milan, 1957, award for excellence Wool Gathering, Montreal, 1974, Gold medal Academia Italia delle Arti, 1980, Gold Centaur, Academia Italia delle Arti, 1982, Gold medal and 1st prize Internat. Art Competition, N.Y.C., 1985, Commemorative medal Gov. Gen. Can., 1993, Highest Civilian Recognition for Achievements in Field of Creative Visual Arts, Order of Can., 1994, Golden Jubilee medal Her Majesty Elizabeth II, 2002. Fellow York Univ.; mem. Royal Can. Acad. Arts, Academia Italia delle Arti, Ontario Soc. Artists. Home: 49 Don River Blvd Toronto ON Canada M2N2M8 E-mail: tamtad@ica.net., qts@gallery.solo.com.

JAY, NORMA JOYCE, artist; b. Wichita, Kans., Nov. 11, 1925; d. Albert Hugh and Thelma Ree (Boyd) Braly; m. Laurence Eugene Jay, Sept. 2, 1949; children: Dana Denise, Allison Eden. Student, Wichita State U., 1946-49, Art Inst. Chgo., 1955-56, Calif. State Coll., 1963. Illustrator Boeing Aircraft, Wichita, 1949-51; co-owner Back Door Gallery, Laguna Beach, Calif., 1973-88. Guest artist Coos Art Mus., 2003. One-woman shows include Milcir Gallery, Tiburon, Calif., 1978, Newport Beach City Gallery, 1981, exhibited in group shows at Am. Soc. Marine Artists ann. exhbns., 1978—2001, Peabody Mus., Salem, Mass., 1981, Mystic Seaport Mus. Gallery, Conn., 1992—95, Grand Ctrl. Gallery, N.Y., 1979—84, The Back Door Gallery, Laguna Beach, 1973—88, Mariners' Mus., Newport News, Va., 1985—86, Nat. Heritage Gallery of Fine Art, Beverly Hills, Calif., 1988—, Md. Hist. Mus., 1989, Kirsten Gallery, Seattle, 1991—97, R.J. Schaefer Gallery Mystic (Conn.) Seaport Mus., 1992, Vallejo Gallery, Newport Beach, 1992, Caswell Gallery, Troutdale, Oreg., 1994—95, Columbia River Maritime Mus., Astoria, Oreg., 1994, Arnold Art Gallery, Newport, Conn., 1994, Mystic Internat. Exhbn., 1995, Lu Martin Galleries, Laguna Beach, 1996—, Frye Art Mus., Seattle, 1997, Cummer Mus. Art & Gardens, Jacksonville, Fla., 1997—98, Cape Mus. Fine Arts Inc., Dennis, Mass., 2001, Coos Art Mus., Coos Bay, Oreg., 2003, Newport (R.I.) Art Mus., 2003, Maine Maritime Mus., Bath, 2003, Connecticut River Mus., Essex, 2004, Represented in permanent collections James Irvine Found., Newport Beach, Niguel Art Assn., Laguna Niguel, Calif., Deloitte, Haskins & Sells, Costa Mesa, Calif., M.J. Brock & Sons Inc., North Hollywood, Calif., others. Recipient Best of Show award Ford Nat. Competition, 1961, First Pl. award Traditional Artists Exhbn., San Bernadino County Mus., 1976, artist award Chriswood Gallery Invitational Exhbn., Rancho California, Calif., 1973, Dirs. Choice award, People's Choice award Coos Art Mus. Marine Exhbn., 1996, featured guest artist, 1998, Coos Art Mus., 2003, 1st Pl. award Maritime Art Exhibit, Newport Harbor Nautical Mus., Newport Beach, 1998-99. Fellow Am. Soc. Marine Artists (charter); mem. Niguel Art Assn. (first pres. 1968, hon. life mem. 1978), Artists Equity, Am. Artists Profl. League. Democrat.

JAYE, KAREN A. human resources specialist; b. New Hyde Park, N.Y., May 15, 1964; d. Rubin and Moira Chernow; m. Douglas P. Jaye, Jan. 14, 1989; 1 child, Amanda Lee. Assocs. Degree, SUNY, Farmingdale, 1984; BS in Fin., SUNY, Old Westbury, 1989. Cert. internal auditor, govt. fin. mgr. From internal auditor to sr. internal auditor internal audit dept. Lee County Clk. Cts., Ft. Myers, Fla., 1991—2002, human resources dir., 2002—. Mem.: Assn. Govt. Accts., Inst. Internal Auditors (bd. govs., pres. 1996—97, Gold award Chpt. Achievement Program 1997). Avocations: rollerblading, photography. Office: Lee County Clk Cts 2115 Second St Fort Myers FL 33902

JAYNE, ARLENE MAE, artist; b. Gilroy, Calif., Nov. 6, 1939; d. Theryon Rowe and Annie Kaleta; m. Gary Grant Jayne, July 31, 1959; children: Gary Daniel, Joy Elaine, Faith Renee. Student, Bapt. Bible Coll., Springfield, Mo., 1958—59, El Reno (Okla.) Jr. Coll., 1983—85, Morgan Art Sch., Issaquah, Wash., 1980—82. Sales clk. Kohl's Pharmacy, Ness City, Kans., 1956—58; sec. Evangel Coll., Springfield, 1960—61; sec., bookkeeper Knollwood Bapt. Sch., Topeka, 1970—78; art instr. Hobby Lobby, Oklahoma City, 1984—85; sec., bookkeeper Berean Bapt. Ch., Puyallup, Wash., 1986—2003; artist, instr. ArtRageous Talent, Puyallup, 2000—03; artist Puyallup, 1979—; sec., music dept. Fine Arts Baptist Bible Coll., Springfield, Md., 2004. Tchr. home econs. Knollwood Bapt. Sch., Topeka, 1972—78; counselor Berean Bapt. Ch., Puyallup, 1986—2003; dir. Ladies Enrichment and Fellowship Retreat, Puyallup, 1989—99; tchr. women's seminars and retreats, 1976—2000. Author: (book) A's of a Christian Woman, 1976; editor: (newsletter) Bapt. Bible Fellowship Talent Talks; exhibitions include Talent Talks, Vancouver, BC, 1999—2002, Rainier Art League, 2001—03, ArtRageous Talent, 2002—03; hostess (exhibitions) Wash. State Sewing Expo, 2000—03, photographer (Internat. Libr. of Photography), 2002. Recipient State Scholastic award in home econs., 1956—57, Blue Ribbon 1st pl. award, Rainier Art League, 2002. Republican. Baptist. Avocations: sewing, scrapbooks, camping, travel. Home: 621 W Talmage St Springfield MO 65803

JAYNE, CYNTHIA ELIZABETH, psychologist; b. Pensacola, Fla., June 5, 1953; d. Gordon Howland and Joan (Rockwood) J. AB, Vassar Coll., 1974; MA, SUNY, Buffalo, 1978, PhD, 1983. Lic. psychologist, Pa. Instr. dept. psychiatry Temple U. Sch. Medicine, Phila., 1982-84, asst. prof., 1984-85, asst. dir. outpatient svcs., asst. dir. residency tng., 1982-85, clin. asst. prof., 1985—2003; pvt. practice psychology Phila., 1985—. Adj. prof. Chestnut Hill Coll., 1994-98. Contbr. articles to profl. jours. Soc. for Sci. Study Sex scholar, 1981; Sigma Xi grantee, 1981, Kinsey Inst. Dissertation award, 1983. Mem. Pa. Psychol. Assn., N.Am. Soc. Psychosocial Obstetrics Gynecology, Soc. for Sci. Study Sex (bd. dirs. 1984-86).

JAYNES, JOYCE WHITFIELD, real estate company executive; b. Magnolia, Miss., Dec. 29, 1925; d. Joseph Judson and Lucile (Goodrum) Mayfield; m. W.E. Whitfield, May 31, 1946 (dec. Jan. 1970); children: Cynthia Whitfield Bell, Elizabeth Whitfield Cleveland, Camille Whitfield Vincent; m. Robert L. Jaynes, Dec. 7, 1974 (dec. Aug. 1990). BS in Elem. Edn. with honors, N.Mex. State U., 1945; cert., U. Pa., 1985. Pres., CEO, Whitfield Enterprises, Inc., El Paso, Tex., 1980—. Former mem. bd. dirs. Newark Meth. Maternity Hosp., El Paso Symphony Assn., Planned Parenthood; mem. mem. bd. Rio Grande Hist. Collections, N.Mex. State U., Las Cruces, now mem. bus. coun.; former mem. adv. bd. El Paso Cmty. Found.; former mem. bd. dirs. and investment com. N.Mex. State U. Found.; former trustee Lydia Patterson Inst.; trustee, hon. mem. Nat. YWCA; trustee Meth. Found., El Paso YWCA Found.; pres. adv. panel, hon. mem. El Paso YWCA; former mem. adminstrv. bd. and trustee Trinity 1st United Meth. Ch. Mem. Pan Am. Roundtable, PEO, El Paso Symphony, El Paso Mus. Art, Pro Musica, Chi Omega. Avocations: reading, travel. Office: Whitfield Enterprises Inc 6420 Escondido Dr # 5 El Paso TX 79912-2972

JAYSON, MELINDA GAYLE, lawyer; b. Dallas, Sept. 29, 1956; d. Robert and Louise Adelle (Jacobs) J. BA, U. Tex., 1977, JD, 1980. Bar: Tex. 1980, U.S. Dist. Ct. (no. dist.) Tex. 1980, U.S. Ct. Appeals (5th and 11th cirs.) 1981, U.S. Dist. Ct. (so. dist.) Tex. 1989, U.S. Ct. Appeals (8th cir.) 1990, U.S. Supreme Ct. 1991. Assoc. Akin, Gump, Strauss, Hauer & Feld, Dallas, 1980-86, ptnr., 1987-96, Melinda G. Jayson, P.C., 1996—; gen. counsel Hall Fin. Group, Dallas, 1999—. Comml. arbitrator, mem. regional adv. coun. Am. Arbitration Assn.; arbitrator, mediator N.Y. Stock Exch., NASD Regulation, Inc.; mediator U.S. EEO Commn., 1999-2000; arbitrator Nat. Arbitration Forum, 2000—. Named one of Outstanding Young Women Am., 1983. Mem. Tex. Bar Assn., Dallas Bar Assn., State Bar of Tex. (mem. dist. 6A grievance com. 1997-99, mem. professionalism enhancement com. 1997-99). Office: Ste 2015 5445 Caruth Haven Ln Dallas TX 75225-8166 E-mail: mjayson@hallfinancial.com.

JEAN, CLAUDETTE R. retired elementary school educator; b. Nashua, N.H., Sept. 26, 1930; d. Thomas Noel and Elise Marie (Archambault) J. BA, Rivier Coll., 1952; MA, Fitchburg (Mass.) Coll., 1956. Cert. tchr. Elem. tchr. Donald St. Sch., Beford, N.H., 1952-53, Arlington St. Sch., Nashua, N.H., 1953-56, J.B. Crowley Sch., Nashua, N.H., 1956-65, Sunset Heights Sch., Nashua, N.H., 1965-91, Nashua; ret. Rep. N.H. Gen. Ctr., Concord, 1992—. Negotiating team Nashua Tchrs. Union, 1969—; state Dem. com. N.H. Dems., Concord, 1992; Hillsborough County com. County Delegation, Manchester, N.H., 1992. Recipient Toland award AFL-CIO, 1991. Mem. Nashua Tchrs. Union (cons. 1991-94), Sr. Citizens Club, Retired Tchrs. Assn., Nashau Coll. Club. Roman Catholic. Avocations: golf, travel, reading.

JEAN-BAPTISTE, TRICIA, public relations executive; married; 1 child, Nicholas. Pub. rels. positions Le Parker Meridien Hotel, NY, Doral Hotels and Resorts; mgr. corp. comm. Days Inn Am., Parsippany, NJ, 1998; founder Tricia Jean-Baptiste Comm., 1998—. Recipient Golden Bell Bronze award, Hotel Sales and Mktg. Assn. Mem.: NY Women in Comm. (past bd. mem.). Office: Tricia Jean-Baptiste Comm 375 Greenwich St Ste 804 New York NY 10013 Office Phone: 212-941-3988. Office Fax: 212-941-3989. Business E-Mail: trica@tricapr.com.*

JEANNOTTE, MARY ELIZABETH, psychologist, educator; b. Whitman, Mass., May 30, 1952; d. Robert Francis and Margaret Mary Jeannotte. PhD, U. Buffalo, 1993. Clin. psychologist Hutchings Psychiat. Ctr., Syracuse, NY, 1993—; pvt. practice Fayetteville, NY, 1997—. Adj. asst. prof. Syracuse U., 1995—; mem. tng. com. psychology internship program Hutchings Psychiat. Ctr., Syracuse, 2000—. Mack Diamond Rsch. grantee, U. Buffalo, 1992—93. Fellow: APA, Ctrl. N.Y. Psychol. Assn. Avocations: tennis, hiking, kickboxing. Office: Hutchings Psychiat Ctr 205 Oneida St Syracuse NY 13202 Business E-Mail: hucymej@gw.omh.state.ny.us.

JECKLIN, LOIS UNDERWOOD, art corporation executive, consultant; b. Manning, Iowa, Oct. 5, 1934; d. J.R. and Ruth O. (Austin) Underwood; m. Dirk C. Jecklin, June 24, 1955; children: Jennifer Anne, Ivan Peter. BA, State U. Iowa, 1992. Residency coord. Quad City Arts Coun., Rock Island, Ill., 1973-78; field rep. Affiliate Artists Inc., N.Y.C., 1975-77; mgr., artist in residence Deere & Co., Moline, Ill., 1977-80; dir. Vis. Artist Series, Davenport, Iowa, 1978-81; pres. Vis. Artists Inc., Davenport, 1981-88; pres., owner Jecklin Assocs., Davenport, 1988—2004. Asst. to exec. dir. Walter W. Naumburg Found., N.Y.C., 1990-2004; cons. writer's program St. Ambrose Coll., Davenport, 1981, 83, 85; mem. com. Iowa Arts Coun., Des Moines, 1983-84; panelist Chamber Music Am., N.Y.C., 1984, Pub. Art Conf., Cedar Rapids, Iowa, 1984; panelist, mem. com. Lt. Gov.'s Conf. on Iowa's Future, Des Moines, 1984. Trustee Davenport Mus. Art, 1975-98, hon. trustee, 1998-2003; emeritus regional bd. Nat. Adv. Coun., Figge Ctr. for the Arts, Davenport, 2004-; trustee Nature Conservancy Iowa, 1987-88; steering com. Iowa Citizens for Arts, Des Moines, 1970-71; bd. dirs. Tri-City Symphony Orch. Assn., Davenport, 1968-83; founding mem. Urban Design Coun., HOME, City of Davenport Beautification Com., 1970-72; bd. govs. Mus. Arts and Design, NYC, 1995—; devel. coun. U. Iowa Mus. Art, 1996-2002. Recipient numerous awards Izaak Walton League, Davenport Art Gallery, Assn. for Retarded Citizens, Am. Heart Assn., Ill. Bur. corrections, many others; LaVernes Noyes scholar, 1953-55. Mem. Am. Symphony Orch. League, Crow Valley Golf Club, Outing Club. Republican. Episcopalian. Home and Office: 2717 Nichols Ln Davenport IA 52803-3620 E-mail: jecklin@webtv.net.

JECKO, LAURA ANN (LAURA ENGEL, LAURA WALLACE), music educator; b. Elmhurst, Ill., Apr. 20, 1964; d. Timothy John Wallace and Janet Sue Engstrom; m. Bryan Hays Engel-Wallace, Nov. 26, 2002. MusB in Edn., U. of Wis., Eau Claire, 1986; MusM, U. of Wis., Milw., 1995. Orch. dir. Superior Wis.) Pub. Schools, 1987—88; elem. orch. tchr. New Berlin Pub. Schools, Wis., 1988—2001; orch. dir. Eisenhower HS, New Berlin, 1995—2001; adj. cello prof. Palm Beach Atlantic U., West Palm Beach, Fla., 2001—; music tchr. Indian Pines Elem. Sch., 2001—02, Belvedere Elem., 2002—03; orch. dir. St. Ann Sch., 2003—. Prin. cellist U. Wis. - Eau Claire Symphony Orch., Milw. Catholic Symphony Orch., Palm Beach Atlantic U. Symphony Orch.; master judge Wis. Sch. Music Assns. Festival. Mem.: Fla. Assn. of Music Tchrs. Home: 222 South Palmway Lake Worth FL 33460 Office: Palm Beach Atlantic U 901 South Flagler Drive PO Box 24708 West Palm Beach FL 33416-4708 Personal E-mail: lakeworthcello@msn.com. E-mail: lakeworthcello@msn.com.

JEEVARAJAN, JUDITH A. chemist; b. Madras, India, June 6, 1964; arrived in U.S., 1988; d. Susei Kulandai and Mary Jaya Raja; m. Antony Susiah Jeevarajan, May 18, 1988; children: Jessie, Jerome, John. BS, Stella Maris Coll., 1984; MS, Loyola Coll., Madras, 1986, U. Notre Dame, 1991; PhD, U. Ala., 1996. Scientist Lynntech, Inc., College Station, Tex., 1996-97; postdoctoral rschr. Tex. A&M U., College Station, 1997; scientist Lockheed Martin Space Ops., Houston, 1998—2003, NASA-Johnson Space Ctr., Houston, 2003—. Contbr. articles to profl. jours. Recipient award, Dept. Def., USAF. Mem.: Electrochem. Soc. Roman Catholic. Avocations: reading, gardening, travel. Home: 15407 Pinenut Bay Ct Houston TX 77059 Office: NASA-JSC MSEP5 2101 NASA Pky Houston TX 77058

JEFFERS, EVE JIHAN See EVE

JEFFERS, LYNETTE A. anesthetist; b. Cleve., Oct. 21, 1952; m. Jerry L. Jeffers, Oct. 1, 1950; children: Mark, Michael, Matthew. BA, BSN, Ursuline Coll., 1990; MSN, Case Western Reserve U., 1992, postgrad. RN; cert. registered nurse anesthetist. Anesthetist Mt. Sinai Med. Ctr., Cleve., 1985—, Medina (Ohio) Cmty. Hosp., 1993—; clin. instr. Sch. Nurse Anesthesia, Case Western Reserve U., Cleve., 1996—; pres. Sports Trauma Network, Medina, 1996—. Contbr. articles to profl. jours. Fellow Am. Acad. Pain Mgmt. (bd. cert.); mem Am. Assn. Nurse Anesthetists, Internat. Trauma Anesthesia and Critical Care Soc. Home: 4744 Sleepy Hollow Rd Medina OH 44256-8336

JEFFERS, TRELLIE LEE JAMES, language educator, dean; b. Eatonton, Ga., Dec. 12, 1933; d. Charlie and Florence (Paschal) James; m. Lance F. Jeffers, May 26, 1959 (dec. July 1985); children: Valjeanne Jeffers Thompson, Sidonie Jeffers Jones, Honorée F. BA, Spelman Coll., 1955; MA, Calif. State U., 1970; DA, Atlanta U., 1986. Cert. adminstrn. and supervision. Tchr. high schs., Ga., Ill., N.C., Fla., 1955-66; asst. prof. Calif. State U., Long Beach, 1969-71; freelance writer Carolina Times, Durham, N.C., 1979-82; coord. Learning Resource Ctr., chmn. Resource Ctr. Clark Coll., Atlanta, 1983-85; prof. English Talladega (Ala.) Coll., 1985—, dean divsn. humananities and fine arts, 1998—. Vis. lectr. N.C. Ctrl. U., Durham, 1975-81, chair English component acad. skills, 1977-78. Author: poems; contbr. article to book. Fellow NEH, 1988, 93. Mem. Libr. Congress, Coll. Lang. Assn., So. Conf. on African Am. Studies (mem. adv. bd. 1992, 99), Ala. League Advancement Edn., George Moses Horton Soc., Pi Lamda Theta, Kappa Delta Pi. Democrat. Roman Catholic. Avocations: sewing, creative writing, cooking, singing, gardening. Home: 219 Edgewood Ave Talladega AL 35160-3021 Office: Talladega Coll 627 Battle St W Talladega AL 35160-2354 E-mail: tjeffers@talladega.edu.

JEFFERSON, DENISE, dance school director; b. Chgo. Studied ballet with, Edna L. McRae; BA, Wheaton Coll.; MA, NYU; Ph.D. (hon.), Wheaton College, 2000. Co-founder, co-dir. Chgo. Dance Ctr.; tchr. dance U. Ill., Chgo.; with Pearl Lang Dance Co.; mem. dance faculty Sch. Arts NYU, Alvin Ailey Dance Ctr., 1975—80; dir. Alvin Ailey Am. Dance Ctr. Scholarship program, 1980-84, Alvin Ailey Dance Sch., 1984—; v.p. Nat. Assoc. of Schools of Dance. Remedial writing tchr. Seek program Hunter Coll.; developed modern dance program Benedict Coll.; guest tchr. U.S., internat.; mem. internat. team dance profls. Dutch govt. to evaluate Dance acads. in Holland, 1990; adjudicator Arts Recognition, Talent Search Confederation Nat. de Danse, Fedn. Interprofl. de la danse, 1992. Mem. adv. bd. Profl. Children's Sch.; mem. adv. com. dance dept. U. Okla.; trustee Elisa Monte Dance Co. Grantee Nat. Endowment Arts and Humanities; scholar Martha Graham Sch. Contemporary Dance. Mem. Nat. Assn. Schs.

Dance (bd. dirs. 1989-91, program evaluator, mem. commn. accredation), N.Y. State Coun. Arts (dance panel, appeal panel). Office: Alvin Ailey Am Dance Ctr 211 W 61st St Fl 3 New York NY 10023-7832*

JEFFERSON, KATHLEEN HENDERSON, retired secondary school educator; b. Pine Bluff, Ark., Sept. 20, 1928; d. Horace and Fannie Henderson; children: Ellen, Regina. BS in Chemistry, U. Ark., 1951; MEd in Maths. Edn., Tuskegee (Ala.) Inst., 1973. Cert. tchr., D.C., Ark. Tchr. Ark. Pub. Schs., Pine Bluff, 1952-78, U. Ark., Monticello, 1978-79, D.C. Pub. Schs., Washington, 1979—; chairperson maths. dept., tchr. Dunbar Sr. High Sch., Washington, 1982-96; ret., 1996. Adj. prof. U. D.C., 1997—. Mem. LWV, Pine Bluff, 1973-77, St. Francis De Sales Ch., Washington; vol. mathematics tutor, St. Francis De Sales Sch., 2000—. NSF fellow, 1960, Internat. Paper Co. fellow, 1970-73. Mem. ASCD, D.C. Coun. Tchrs. of Maths., D.C. Tchrs. Union Local, Delta Sigma Theta. Roman Catholic. Avocations: reading, swimming, chess.

JEFFERSON, MARGO L. journalist; b. Chgo., Oct. 17, 1947; BA in English and Am. Lit. cum laude, Brandeis U., 1968; MS, Columbia U., 1971. Editor Newsweek, 1973—78; asst. prof. dept. journalism NYU, 1979—83, 1989—91; contbg. editor Vogue, 1984—89, 7 Days, 1984—89; lectr. Am. Lit., performing arts & criticism Columbia U., N.Y.C., 1991—93; critic culture desk The New York Times, 1993—95, Sunday theater critic, 1995—97, cultural corr., 1997—. Recipient Pulitzer Prize for criticism, 1995. Office: The New York Times 229 W 43rd St New York NY 10036-3959

JEFFERSON, MYRA LAVERNE TULL, sales executive; b. Chester, Pa. d. Clarence Ernest and Mary Marie (Gaines) Tull; m. Bernard Carr Jefferson III, Mar. 11, 1983. BS in Computer Sci., Roosevelt U., 1987; postgrad., Chaminade U., 1986-87. Computer programmer Integrated Computer Techs., Phila., 1979-83; cons. Honolulu, 1983-88; data base mgr. E.S.R.D. Network Coordinating Council, Honolulu, 1984-88; comptr. Static Control Products, Phoenix, 1989-93; pres. Lion-S Sales & Svc., Mesa, Ariz., 1991—. Cons. NCC #1 Med. Rev. Bd., Honolulu, 1985, Thrifty Constrn. Co., Honolulu, 1986-87, Computer Support, 1985. Apptd. by mayor to the city of Mesa Economic Devel. adv. bd.; apptd. to Industrial Devel. Authority Commn. of Maricopa County; apptd. by gov. Econ. Security Adv. Bd.; treas. bd. Mesa Cmty. Action Network, 1992-95, 2d vice chair, 1995-96; bd. dirs. WOW Project; alumnae Mesa Leadership Tng. Program, Valley Leadership Program, black bd. dirs. project; bd. dirs., co-chair Black Women's Task Force, 1994-95, bd. dirs. the Family Svc. Agy.; treas. Pol. Dist. 29. Recipient award for Outstanding Contbns. to Data Processing, Am. Inst., 1987, Profl. and Scholastic Achievement award Am. Inst., 1986, Outstanding Achievement in Data Processing Profession, Am. Inst., 1986; fellow Ariz. Edn. Policy Fellowship Program. Mem. AAUW, Math. Assn. Am., Am. Math. Soc., Women in Computing, Am. Assn. Ind. Investors, Am. Express Com. Diversity Bd., Coalition for Tomorrow, U.S. Congressman Matt Salmon's Small Bus. Adv. Group, captain Precinct 54 Committeemen. Avocations: reading, crosswords, chess, computers. Home and Office: PO Box 3149 Tempe AZ 85280-3149

JEFFERSON, SANDRA TRAYLOR, choreographer; b. Tarboro, N.C., Feb. 28, 1942; d. Charles Labon and Doris Vivian (Parker) Traylor; m. Milton Franklin Jefferson, July 2, 1960; children: Mark Franklin, Todd Christopher. Student, Parks Sch. Dance, Petersburg, Va., 1947-58, Sch. of the Richmond (Va.) Ballet, 1958-60; diploma, Julia Mildred Harper Sch. Dance, Richmond, 1960; studied with Robert David Brown, Sterling, Va., 1978-80. Soloist Ballet Impromptu, Richmond, 1958-60; freelance dance instr. Chantilly, Va., 1968-70; ballet coach Artistic Skating Club of Sterling, 1980; founder, dir. Ballet for Skaters, Manassas, Va., 1980-89; artistic dir., cons. in choreography No. Va. Artistic Skating Club, Manassas, 1986-89. Artistic dir. Skating Club of Manassas, 1989; founder, dir. Ballet for Skaters, Seabrook, Md., 1989-94; choreographer, ballet coach Nat. Capitol Dance and Figure Club, Seabrook and Washington, 1989-94; founder, dir. Ballet for Figure Skaters, Sterling, Va., 1993-94; students include nat. medalists in the U.S. and Can. and mems. Can. World Team, U.S. Olympic Sports Festival Team; freelance choreographer, ballet coach, Sterling, 1993—. Developer: Brosano Technique Vocabulary of Movement, 1986, Free Form Ballet, 1993; co-developer (artistic skating technique) Brosano Technique, 1981. Social dir. Jaycee-ettes, Winchester, Va., 1963—67. Recipient Achievement award Jaycee-ettes, 1963, 64, 65, 66, 67, U.S. S.E. Soc. Roller Skating Tchrs. Am. award, 1988, World Decoration of Excellence award Am. Biog. Inst., 1989. Mem.: Profl. Dance Tchrs. Assn. Methodist. Avocations: art, music. Home and Office: 507 S Maple Ct Sterling VA 20164-2710

JEFFERSON, ZANOBIA BRACY, art educator, artist; b. Chgo., Sept. 3, 1926; d. Francis Wright and Hattie Ocie (Robinson) Bracy; m. Robert L. Jefferson, June 4, 1950 (dec. Dec. 23, 1983); children: Heidi V. Long, Robyn F. Sims, Ionis M. Swoope, Robert L. Jr., Gisele Z. Mestre. BA, Fisk Univ., Nashville, Tenn., 1948; MEd, Nova Univ., Ft. Lauderdale, Fla., 1987. Tchr. Fla. A & M Univ., Tallahassee, 1948—50; adult educator Ft. Pierce, Fla. Sch., Ft. Pierce, Fla., 1950—70; art tchr. St. Lucie Co. Pub. Sch., Ft. Pierce, Fla., 1960—93; tchr. art edn. Nova Univ., Ft. Pierce, Fla., 1980. Sculpture, 3-4ft. children, St. Anatasia Cath. Ch., 1988, Felix Elem. Sch., 1986. Bd. dirs. Backus Art Gallery; manpower com. Gov. Graham, Tallahassee; bd. Sunrise Theater, St. Pierce, Fla. Mem.: Opera Soc., African Am. Exo. for the Arts, Ret. Educators of Fla., Links Inc., Alpha Kappa Alpha. Christian. Achievements include mentor to highwaymen artists group, tchr. of original group, Afred Hair, James Gibson, Rodney Demps, etc. Avocations: art, crafts, travel, gardening, coin collecting. Home: 2300 Valencia Ave Fort Pierce FL 34946

JEFFRESS, LYNN, writer, education educator; d. Jessie Kathleen Macklin and Joseph Peter Bird; 1 child, Nicholas Joseph. PhD in romance lang. and lit., U. of Oreg., 1981, MFA in creative writing, 1987—89. Tchg. fellowship U. Ore., 1974—81; am./french prof. exch. U. of Oreg., Poitiers, France, 1977—78; esl instr. Am. Ctr. in Paris, 1981—83; prof. Am. Coll. in Paris, 1986—87; english instr. Portland C.C., Oreg., 1989—; french prof. Linfield Coll., McMinnville, Oreg., 1985—86; rsch. writing instr. U. of Oreg., 1999—. Fiction editor NW Rev., Eugene, Oreg., 1988—90; dir. -Yachats Arts Festival Oreg. Coast C.C., 1989—92. Author: (short stories) I Want to Go Home with the Armadillo; contbr. articles in Z Magazine, Oregon Quarterly, The Bayfront, Ink Fish, News Times; author: The Novels of Michel Tournier; author: (with Ken Kesey) (novels) Caverns; editor: (anthology) Moon Fish; author: (play) A Life in the Night of Andy Warhol (original scripts winner, 1994), (poetry) Oregon Poets Against the War; editor: (memoir) Writing Under the Influence: A Year with Ken Kesey. Grant for devel. of online French course, State of Oreg., 1998. Personal E-mail: lcjeffress@charter.net.

JEFFREY-SMITH, LILLI ANN, biofeedback specialist, educator, administrator; b. Bedford, Ind., 1944; d. Charles Constantine and Adelai (Malon) Jeffrey-Smith. Grad., Ind. Bus. Coll., 1963; BS, Ind. U., 1973; grad., psychosomatic Med. Clinic, Berkeley, Calif.; PhD in Behavioral Sci., Kennedy-Western U., 1988. Diplomate Am. Bd. Disability Analysis; cert. biofeedback specialist. Project assoc., stress mgmt. clinician City of Indpls., 1973-79; pres., dir. Biofeedback Tng. and Treatment Ctr., Edina, Minn., 1979—; dir. biofeedback dept. Sister Kenney Inst., Mpls., 1979-81; outreach coord. Abbot-Northwestern Hosp., Mpls., 1981; dir. biofeedback dept. Noran Clinic, Mpls., 1981-83. Mem. faculty U. Minn., Mpls., 2000—; cons. in field. Author, narrator health and wellness tape series. Mem. Rep. Presdl. Task Force, 1984—, NCS, 1985; co-chmn. Mayor's Handicapped Task Force, Indpls., 1975; founder, pres. Miss Wheel Chair Ind., Inc. Named Hon. Lt. Gov., State of Ind., 1978; given Key to the City of Indpls., 1973, Flag of the City if Indpls., 1975. Mem. ABDA, NAFE, AAUW, AAAS, Am. Inst. Stress, N.Y. Acad. Sci., Edina C. of C., Minn. Women's Network, Biofeedback Soc. Am., Biofeedback Soc. Minn., Am. Assn. Control Tension, Am. Assn. Behavioral Therapists, Am. Assn. Biofeedback Clinicians, Nat. Assn. Bus. Owners, Soc. Open Focus and Tng. Rsch., Assn. Trainers Clin. Hypnosis, Internat. Stress and Tension Control Assn., Minn. Assn. Rehab. Providers, Internat. Platform Assn, Nat. Women's Health Resource Ctr. (bd. mem., 2000). Avocations: music, stamp collecting, shooting, poetry. Office: Biofeedback Tng & Treatment Ctr 7300 France Ave S Ste 200 Minneapolis MN 55435-4542

JEFFRIES, KIM, radio personality; b. Tex. m. Bruce Jeffries; 4 children. In Theater and Speech, Northwestern U.; grad. Broadcasting, Brown Inst. Host Sta. WJON-Radio, St. Cloud; host Sta. KS95; reporter Sta. WCCO-TV, Mpls.; host Morning Show Sta. WCCO Radio, Mpls., 1998, radio host midday live. Contbr. articles to profl. jours. Vol. Charis prison ministry, numerous other orgns. Avocations: church activities, sports, travel. Office: WCCO 625 2nd Ave S Minneapolis MN 55402

JEFFRIES, MARY, public relations executive; Contr. Shandwick Internat., Mpls., 1988—, CFO, COO Shandwick U.S., 1993—, mng. dir. Shandwick U.S., 1996—. Office: Shadwick US Ste 500 8400 Normandale Lake Blvd Bloomington MN 55437-3889

JEFFRIES, PAMELA DEPPERMAN, advertising executive, entrepreneur; b. Omaha, Aug. 1, 1965; d. Robert Edwin and Ruth Arlyn (Bock) Depperman; m. Cordell Ray Jeffries, Feb. 29, 1992. BS in Journalism, U. Mo., 1987. Asst. acct. exec. TBWA Chiat Day, St. Louis, 1988-90; acct. exec. Louis London, Inc., St. Louis, 1991-93, Randazzo & Blavins, Inc., San Francisco, 1993-95; acct. supr. Hodskins Simone & Searls, Inc., Palo Alto, Calif., 1995-97; mktg. comms. mgr. PeopleSoft, Inc., Pleasanton, Calif., 1997—2000, dir. corp. advt., 2000—02. Project Bus. cons. Jr. Achievement, San Francisco, 1995; reading tutor/editor Literacy Coun., St. Louis, 1990-93; vol. Nat. Abortion Rights Action League, St. Louis, 1992-93. Mem. Omicron Delta Kappa. Avocations: biking, hiking, tennis, reading. Home and Office: 770 Prospect Ave Oakland CA 94610-3843 E-mail: pdjeffries@hotmail.com.

JEFFRIES, ROBIN, computer engineer; BA in Math. summa cum laude, U. Iowa, 1969; MA in Quantitative Psychology, U. Colo., 1977, PhD in Quantitative Psychology, 1978. Rsch. assoc. U. Colo., Boulder, Carnegie-Mellon U., 1983-93; mem. tech. staff Hewlett Packard Labs.; disting. engr. Sun Microsystems, Palo Alto, Calif., 1993—. Office: Sun Microsystems 17 Network Cir MPK 17-114 Menlo Park CA 94025

JEFFUS, MARGARET M. (MAGGIE JEFFUS), state representative, retired elementary school educator; b. Va., Oct. 22, 1934; m. Charles Oliver Jeffus (dec. Jul. 1983); children: Edward Dane, Holly Jeffus Thomas; m. Ted J. Thompson, Dec. 29, 1991. BA, Guilford Coll., 1965; MEd, UNC, 1970. Retired tchr., 1997; state rep. N.C. 89th Dist., 1991-92, 93-94, 1997-98, 99—. Mem. Dem. State exec. com., 1983—; del. to Dem. Nat. Conv., San Francisco, 1984; alt. del. to Dem. Nat. Conv., 1992; precinct chair, 1980-90; mem. Starmount Presby. Ch.; mem. N.C. 2000 Com., chair edn. sect. Guilford Coun., 1981-82; capt. United Way, 1983, 84, mem. Greensboro Task Force Bond Com., 1985, mem. Greensboro Visions Edn. Com., 1987-88; vol. Cancer Soc., 1990; bd. dirs. Summit House, 1992-95; bd. dirs N.C. Sch. for the Deaf Found., 1996-97, 98—; appropriations human resources, 1991-92, gen. govt. 1993-94, 97—, legis. rsch. commn.; appt. mem. Southern Legis. Conf.; bd. dirs. U. N.C. Musical Arts Guild, 1995-99. Named Greensboro Tchr. of Yr., 1972-73. Mem. N.C. Assn. Educators (pres. dist. 7 1982-83, 85-86, local unit. pres. 1979-80, 86-87, 87-88), Phi Delta Kappa. Home: 1801 Rolling Rd Greensboro NC 27403-1723

JEGEN, SISTER CAROL FRANCES, religion educator; b. Chgo., Oct. 11, 1925; d. Julian Aloysius and Evelyn W. (Bostelmann) J. BS in History, St. Louis U., 1951; MA in Theology, Marquette U., 1958, PhD in Religious Studies, 1968; hon. degree, St. Mary of the Woods, Terra Haute, Ind., 1977. Elem. tchr. St. Francis Xavier Sch., St. Louis, 1947-51; secondary tchr. Holy Angels Sch., Milw., 1951-57; coll. tchr. Mundelein Coll., Chgo., 1957-91; prof. pastoral studies Loyola U., Chgo., 1991—. Adv. coun. U.S. Cath. Bishops, Washington, 1969-74; trustees Cath. Theol. Union, Chgo., 1974-84. Author: Jesus the Peace Maker, 1986, Restoring Our Friendship with God, 1989; co-author: (with Byron Sherwin) Thank God, 1989; editor: Mary According to Women, 1985. Participant Nat. Farm Worker Ministry, Fresno, Calif., 1977—; mem. Pax Christi, U.S.A., 1979—, Jane Addams Conf., Chgo., 1989. Recipient Loyola Civic award Loyola U., Chgo., 1981, Chgo. medallion for Excellence in Catechesis, 1996, Sor Juana award Hispanic Ministry, 2000; named one of 100 Women to Watch Today's Chgo. Woman, 1989. Mem. Cath. Theol. Soc. Am., Coll. Theology Soc., Cath.-Jewish Scholars Dialog, Liturgical Conf. Democrat. Roman Catholic. Avocations: music, gardening. Home: Wright Hall 6364 N Sheridan Rd Chicago IL 60660-1700 Office: Loyola U Inst Pastoral Studies 6525 N Sheridan Rd Chicago IL 60626-5385

JEHLEN, PATRICIA D. state legislator; b. Austin, Tex., Oct. 14, 1943; d. Paul Kindred Jr. and Ruth Miller (Zumbrunnen) Deats; m. Alain Peter Jehlen, Aug. 29, 1969; children: Nicholas, Wendy, Peter. BA, Swarthmore Coll., 1965; MA in Teaching, Harvard U., 1969. Rschr. Harvard Sch. Edn., Cambridge, Mass., 1966-67; tchr. history Brookline (Mass.) H.S., 1968-71; mem. Somerville (Mass.) Sch. Com., 1976-91, Mass. Ho. of Reps., Somerville, 1991—. VISTA vol. Cook County Migrant Coun., Chicago Heights, Ill., 1965-66. Democrat. Home: 67 Dane St Somerville MA 02143-3730 Office: Mass Ho of Reps Rm 275 Boston MA 02133

JELINEK, VERA, university director; b. Kosice, Czechoslovakia, Dec. 16, 1935; came to U.S., 1947; d. Joseph and Margit (Lefkovits) Schnitzer; m. Josef E. Jelinek, June 19, 1960; children: David, Paul. BA in History, CUNY, 1956; MA, Johns Hopkins U., 1958; PhD in Modern European History, NYU, 1977; diploma, Sch. Advanced Internat. Study, Bologna, Italy. Translator Rockefeller Bros. Fund, N.Y.C., 1958-59; exec. dir. U.S. Youth Coun., N.Y.C., 1959-63; dir. internat. programs, social and natural scis. NYU, N.Y.C., 1985—, dir. Lillian Vernon Ctr. for Internat. Affairs, 2000—, dir. The Energy Forum, 2000—. Mem. adv. com. N.Y.C.-Budapest Sister City Program, 1991-94; prin. dir. pilot tng. program for new UN diplomats NYU, 1996-97. Author audio cassette: Before You Go-Italy, 1985. Mem. edn. com. Mus. Am. Folk Art, N.Y.C.; edn. co-chair The Am. Antiques Show, 2002—03. Recipient fellowship Ford Found., 1960, grant NYU Curriculum Challenge Fund, 1989, 90, 99, Phillip E. Frandson award Nat. Univ. Continuing Edn. Assn., 1991. Mem. Am. Folk Art Soc., Carnegie Coun. on Ethics and Internat. Affairs, Women's Fgn. Policy Group, Phi Beta Kappa. Democrat. Avocations: tennis, jogging, folk art, cooking, travel. Office: Lillian Vernon Ctr Internat Affairs 58 W 10th St New York NY 10011

JELKS, MARY LARSON, retired pediatrician; b. Galva, Ill., 1929; MD, U. Nebr., 1955. Diplomate Am. Bd. Pediats., Am. Bd. Allergy and Immunology. Intern Johns Hopkins Hosp., Balt., 1955-56, resident, 1956-57, 58-60, Grace-New Haven Hosp., 1957; fellow U. Fla. Tchg. Hosp., 1960-61; clin. asst. prof. U. South Fla.; ret.; active aerobiology, 1985—. Fellow Am. Acad. Allery and Immunology, Am. Acad. Pediats.; mem. AMA. Achievements include active research in aerobiology. Home: 1930 Clematis St Sarasota FL 34239-3813 E-mail: mjelks99@cs.com.

JELLISON, KATHERINE KAY, historian, educator; b. Garden City, Kans., Jan. 5, 1960; d. Billy Dean and Margaret Ruth (Brown) Jellison; m. David John Winkelmann, Aug. 10, 1985. BA, Ft. Hays (Kans.) State U., 1982; MA, U. Nebr., 1984; PhD, U. Iowa, 1991. Asst. prof. Memphis State U., 1991-93, Ohio U., Athens, 1993-96, assoc. prof. history, 1996—. Author: Entitled to Power: Farm Women and Technology, 1913-1963, 1993. Named Outstanding Young Alumni Ft. Hays State U., 1994; recipient Excellence in Feminist Pedagogy award Ohio U., 1994; Smithsonian Instn. fellow, 1989. Mem. NOW, Am. Hist. Assn., Orgn. Am. Historians, Berkshire Conf. on History of Women, Social Sci. History Assn., Ohio Acad. History. Democrat. Methodist. Avocations: hiking, watching old movies. Office: Ohio University Dept History Bentley Annex Athens OH 45701 E-mail: jellison@ohio.edu.

JELSMA, ELIZABETH BARBARA, music educator; b. Newark, Aug. 24, 1934; d. Joseph Augsdorfer and Clara Stiehl; m. Lawrence Franklin Jelsma, June 15, 1967 (div. Sept. 30, 1976); children: Deborah Lynn, Lawrence Frank, Elizabeth Louise, Mark Andrew. Degree in music edn., Northwestern U., 1959, MusM, 1961. Tchr. 1st grade Jenner Sch., Chgo.; tchr. music grades K-8, Yavapai Sch., Scottsdale, Ariz., 1969—95; pvt. piano tchr. NJ. Judge piano Ariz. State U., Tempe, 1962—63; accompanist Bach Madrigal Soc., Phoenix, 1964—66. Singer (soloist): Northwestern Symphony Orch., 1960. Recipient various awards for solo performances. Mem.: Sigma Alpha Iota. Republican. Roman Catholic. Avocations: reading, travel, swimming.

JELUS, SUSAN CRUM, writer, editor; b. Cin., Sept. 14, 1952; d. Robert Malcolm and Jean Moses Crum; m. Raymond Jelus, Aug. 1, 1975 (div. Dec. 1989). BA, Miami U., Oxford, Ohio, 1974. Continuity mgr. Sta. WLWT TV, Cin., 1975-77; traffic mgr. Sta. WCKY-WWEZ, Cin., 1977-79; advt. coord. Cintas Corp., Cin., 1979-80; audio-visual writer-prodr. Dayton, 1981-84; tech. writer Sinclair C.C., Dayton, 1984-86; sr. instrnl. developer The Reynolds & Reynolds Co., Dayton, 1986-95; publs./on-line help author Rsch. Computer Svcs., Dayton, 1995—; editor, pub. New Song Press, Dayton, 1995—2003. Editor: (lit. jour.) A New Song, 1996-2003; contbr. poetry to anthologies and lit. mags. Bd. dirs. Hist. Dist. Archtl. Rev. Bd., Germantown, Ohio, 1990-93; campaign tng. chairperson United Way, Dayton, 1987; dir. Jr. Handbell Choir, South Park United Meth. Ch., Dayton, 1995; dir. youth choir Centerville (Ohio) United Meth. Ch., 2000-01; dir. handchime choir Huffman Pl., 2002—. Recipient Commendation award for poetry Chester H. Jones Found., 1995, Award of Merit, Soc. for Tech. Comm., 1989. Mem. AAUW, Nat. Mus. for Women in the Arts, Soc. Tech. Comm. Democrat. Avocations: painting, acoustic guitar. Home: 4 Dellwood Ave Dayton OH 45419-3104

JEMISON, MAE CAROL, physician, engineer, entrepreneur, philanthropist, educator, former astronaut; b. Decatur, Ala., Oct. 17, 1956; d. Charlie and Dorothy (Green) J. BS in ChemE, BA in African-Am. Studies, Stanford U., 1977; MD, Cornell U., 1981. Physician Peace Corps, Sierra Leone, Western Africa, 1983—85; pvt. practice L.A.; mission specialist NASA, Houston, 1987—93, astronaut on space shuttle Endeavor, 1992; prof. Dartmouth Coll., 1995—2002; mem, bd. dirs. Scholastic Inc.; national sci. literary advocate Bayer Corp., 1995—. Founder, pres. BioSentient Corp., The Jemison Group, Inc., 1993—, The Earth We Share Internat. Sci. Camp; A.D. White prof.-at-large Cornell U.; founder, pres. The Dorothy Jemison Foundation for Excellence, 1994—; mem., bd. dirs. Scholastic, Inc.; national sci. literary advocate Bayer Corp., 1995—; bd. dirs. Valspar Corp., Kimberly-Clark Corp. Author: Find Where The Wind Goes, 2001; TV host Discovery Channel, World of Wonder, 1994—95. Mem.: NAS Inst. Medicine. Achievements include being first woman of color to fly in space. Office: Jemison Group Inc PO Box 591455 Houston TX 77259

JEMMOTT, LORETTA SWEET, nursing educator; BSN, Hampton Inst., 1978; MSN in Mental Health Nursing, U. Pa., 1982, PhD in Human Sexuality Edn., 1987. Asst. prof. nursing Rutgers U. Coll. of Nursing, Newark, 1987-93, assoc. prof. nursing, 1993-94; dir. Ctr. for AIDS Rsch. Columbia U. Sch. Nursing, N.Y.C., 1994-95; assoc. HIV Ctr. for Clin. & Behaviors Studies Columbia U. and N.Y. State Psychiatric Inst., N.Y.C., 1994—; vis. rsch. scholar dept. psychology Princeton U., NJ, 1995—; rsch. assoc. Population Studies Ctr. U. Pa., Phila., 1995—, assoc. prof. grad. sch. edn., 1995—, assoc. prof. nursing Ctr. for Urban Health Rsch., 1995—, dir. Ctr. for Urban Health Rsch. Sch. Nursing, 1996—. Contbr. articles to profl. pubs. Fellow Am. Acad. Nursing, 1992; recipient Outstanding Nursing Achievement and Rsch. award Concerned Black Nurses, 1989, Outstanding Service award, Rutgers Coll. Nursing, 1990, Gov. of N.J. Nurse Merit award in Advanced Nursing Practice, 1992, Outstanding Rsch. award Northern N.J. Black Nurses Assn., 1992, Congressional Merit award, 1995. Mem.: Inst. of Medicine, 1999-. Office: U Pa Ctr for Urban Health Rsch Philadelphia PA 19104 also: U Penn Sch Nursing 420 Gaurdian Dr Rm 345 NEB Philadelphia PA 19104-6096 E-mail: jemmott@pobox.upenn.edu.

JENIK, ADRIENE, artist, educator; d. Carol Anne and Richard Michael Jenik. BA, Douglas Coll., Rutgers U., New Brunswick, NJ, 1982—86; MFA, Rensselaer Poly. Inst., Troy, NY, 1993—96. Assoc. engr. Disney Online, North Hollywood, Calif., 1996—97; assoc. prof., computer & media arts UC, San Diego, La Jolla, Calif., 1997—. Exec. com. Lyn Blumenthal Meml. Fund for Ind. Media, Chgo., 2000—. Interactive cinema, MAUVE DESERT: A CD-ROM Transl.; dir.: (interactive television) El Naftazteca (Best exptl. work, Austin cinefest, 1995); internet street theater, Desktop Theater (with Lisa Brenneis) (Future of the Present, Franklin Furnace, 2001), video art, What's the Difference Between an Yam & a Sweet Potato? (Whiney Biennale Those Fluttering objects of Desire, 1993); dir.: (mobile computing event) Active Campus Exploration. Founding mem. San Diego Ind. Media Ctr., San Diego, Calif., 2000—03. Fellow Grad. fellowship, Jacob Javits, 1994, 1995, 1996, New Media Fellowship, Rockefeller Found., 1997, Hellman Fellowship, UC San Diego, Hellman Fellowship Com., 1999; grantee Desktop Theater workshop, LA Cultural Ctr./REACH LA, 2001. Mem.: Desert Survivors. Progressive. Achievements include first to in interactive TV, cinema and internet street theatre. Avocations: reading, making music, hiking, dreaming, travel. Office: UC San Diego Visual Arts Dept 9500 Gilman Dr La Jolla CA 92093-0084

JEN-JACOBSON, LINDA, biochemist, educator; b. Kunming, China, Oct. 29, 1941; PhD, U. Ill., 1967. Assoc. prof. U. Pitts., 1993—98, prof., 1998—. Rschr. U. Pitts., 1967—. Fellow: AAAS; mem.: Am. Soc. Biochemistry and Molecular Biology, Protein Soc., Biophys. Soc. Office: U Pitts Dept Biol Scis Pittsburgh PA 15217-1308 E-mail: ljen@pitt.edu.

JENKINS, ALICE MARIE, secondary school educator; b. Adair, Iowa, June 7, 1922; d. Charles Erwin Hall and Elizabeth Catherine Clarke Hall; m. Doyce Gwendon Pitts, June 27, 1943 (dec. Mar. 27, 1977); 1 child, Beverly Lou ; m. Richard Jenkins, June 24, 1978. BA, Drake U., 1963. Tchr. rural and county schs., 1940—54, Linden (Iowa) Pub. Sch., 1954—55, Woodward (Iowa) State, 1955—60, 1971—93, Boone (Iowa) Pub. Sch., 1960—71, Woodward Cmty., 1993—. Mem.: VFW, Am. Legion Aux. (past pres.), Alpha Delta Kappa (past pres.). Democrat. Methodist. Avocations: cooking, reading, music. Office: Woodward-Granger HS 306 W 3rd St Woodward IA 50276-1033

JENKINS, ALYCE MITCHEM, writer; b. Harvard, Ill., Nov. 3, 1935; d. John Foster and Queenie Black Mitchem; m. Reese Valmer Jenkins, Dec. 27, 1962; children: David William, Elizabeth Ann Jenkins Manfredi. BA, U. Colo., 1957; MS, U. Wis., 1961. Cert. tchr. Ill., Wis., Ohio, N.J. English tchr. Crystal Lake (Ill.) H.S., 1957—60; demonstration tchr. No. Ill. U., DeKalb, 1961—62; English, social studies tchr. H. Schenk Jr. H.S., Madison, Wis., 1962—66; homebound tchr. Cleve. Pub. Schs., 1971—76, 1977—78; tchr. social studies Laurel Sch., Shaker Heights, Ohio, 1977—78; English instr. Kean U., Union, NJ, 1980; social studies, English tchr. Middlesex (N.J.) H.S., 1980—85, 1993—94; freelance writer, 1985—.

Founder, leader Rainbow Writers, Bridgewater, 1992—95. Author: Lost in a Blizzard, 2001; co-author: College Board Achievement: English Composition, 1988; contbr. over 100 articles to adult and juvenile periodicals. Founder, leader Connected Hearts Adoption Triad Support, North Plainfield, NJ, 1997—; instr., mentor Sisters Aftercare, Bridgewater, NJ, 2001—; mem. adv. bd. N.J. Adoption Resource Clearing House, 2003—; mem. Presbyn. Women, 1997—. Fellow Knapp Grad., U. Wis., 1960—61. Mem.: Bound Brook Writers, Soc. Children's Book Writers and Illustrators (award com., Mag. Merit awards 1999, Mag. Merit award 1996), Pi Lambda Theta, Kappa Delta Pi, Phi Beta Kappa. Democrat. Presbyterian. Avocations: genealogy, reading, gardening, correspondence, grandchildren. Home: 11 Clifton Ave New Brunswick NJ 08901 Personal E-mail: alycemj@aol.com.

JENKINS, BARBARA ALEXANDER, pastor and overseer; b. Ft. Bragg, N.C., Oct. 13, 1942; d. Archie Herman Alexander and Hattie Elizabeth (Thigpen) Truitt; m. Warren Keith Jenkins, Aug. 22, 1964 (div. Sept. 1980); children: Pamela, Eric, Jason. BS, Ea. Mich. U., 1964, postgrad., 1964-66, Duke U., 1978; DD (hon.), Ch. of Christ Bible Coll., Madras, India, 1988. Ordained to ministry, World Faith Clinic Inc., 1983, A.M.E. Zion Ch., 1982. Min. World Faith Clinic Inc., Fayetteville, N.C., 1981-83, A.M.E. Zion Ch., Fayetteville, 1982-84; pastor Noah's Ark Ministry, Fayetteville, 1985-86; founder, pastor Rainbow Tabernacle of Faith Ministries, Inc., Winston-Salem, N.C., 1984—; founder Rainbow Raleigh (N.C.) Outreach Ministries, 1986—, Rainbow Tabernacle of Faith, Charlotte, N.C., 1987—. Dir. Spotlight on Truth Internat. Radio Ministries, Winston-Salem, 1985—, overseer hdqrs. Ogun State, Nigeria, 1992, others; founder Rainbow Internat. Crusade Ministry, Winston-Salem, 1986—; pres. Rainbow Bible Coll., Winston-Salem; dean Rainbow Inst. Commensurate Studies, Winston-Salem, 1985—; mem. Internat. Conv. Faith Ministries, Tulsa, 1989—. Author: Guidelines for Ministers, 1994; contbr. articles to religious jours. Concert vocalist N.C. Black Repertory Co., Winston-Salem, 1987, 88, youth coord. Jerry Lewis Muscular Dystrophy Telethon, Raleigh, 1987, 88; guest speaker Wake Forest U., Winston-Salem, 1991. Recipient Outstanding Svc. award Rainbow Tabernacle Faith, Inc., 1987; scholar March of Dimes-Easter Seals, 1960-64. Mem. NAFE, N.C. Women in Ministry (bd. dirs.), Am. Assn. Christian Counselors, Nat. Assn. Religious Profls., Delta Theta (project coord. 1979-80). Democrat. Office: Rainbow Tabernacle Faith Ministries Inc 4091 New Walkertown Rd Winston Salem NC 27105-9734 also: 1119 Cypress Cir Winston Salem NC 27106-3307

JENKINS, BILLIE BEASLEY, film company executive; b. Topeka, June 27, 1943; d. Arthur and Etta Mae Capelton; m. Rudolph Alan Jenkins, Nov. 1, 1935; 1 child, Tina Caprice. Student, Santa Monica City Coll., 1965-69. Exec. sec. to v.p. prodn. Screen Gems, L.A., 1969-72; exec. asst. Spelling/Goldberg Prodns., 1972-82; dir. adminstrn. The Leonard Co./Mandy Films, 1982-85, v.p., 1985-87; exec. asst. to pres. and chief oper. officer 20th Century Fox Film Corp., L.A., 1986-87, dir. adminstrn., 1987-90, dir. prodn. svcs. & resources Fox Motion Pictures div., 1990-92. Program coord. Am. Film Inst. Gary Hendler Minority Filmmakers Program, 1990-93; pres., CEO Masala Prodns., Inc., 1991—. Asst. to exec. producer: (films) War Games, 1984, Spacecamp, 1986; (movies for TV) Something about Amelia, 1984, Alex, The Life of a Child, 1985; (series) Paper Dolls, 1985, Cavanaughs, 1987, Charlie's Angels, Rookies, others; exec. prodn. cons. (documentary) The Good, The Bad, The Beautiful, 1995-96. Commr. L.A. City Cultural Heritage Commn., 1992-93. Named 1991 Woman of Excellence, Boy Scouts Am.; honored First African-Am. Women Pioneers of So. Calif. Top Ladies of Distinction City of Angels chpt. L.A., 1999. Mem.: Motivating Our Students Through Experience (mem. exec. bd.), Ind. FeatureProdns./West, Am. Film Inst., Black Women's Network, Women in Film Assn. (pres. 1991, 1992, advisor to exec. bd. 1993—95), Top Ladies of Distinctions. Avocations: photography, gardening, writing. E-mail: masalainc@aol.com.

JENKINS, BRENDA GWENETTA, early childhood and special education specialist; b. Durham, N.C., Aug. 11, 1949; d. Brinton Alfred and Ophelia Arden (Eaton) Jenkins. BS, Howard U., 1971, MEd, 1972; postgrad., Trinity Coll., Am. U., U. D.C., Marymount Coll., 1976—. Cert. tchr., Washington; cert. Advanced Grad. Studies Spl. Edn., aerobics instr., Nat. Dance Exercise Instr.'s Tng. Assn. Cheerleading coach Howard U., Washington, 1971-86; aerobics instr. D.C. Pub. Schs., Washington, 1982-97, tchr.; v.p. Nerdlihc Corp., Washington, 1985—; co-owner Fantasia Early Learning Acad., Washington, 1985-98; ptnr. Jenkins, Trapp-Dukes and Yates Partnership., Washington, 1984; instr. aerobics Washington Dept. Recreation, Washington, 1988-93; instr. You Fit, Inc. Nat. Children's Ctr. Washington, 1991-93, Anthony Bowen YMCA, Washington, 1992-93; instr. health, nutrition support Rockville, Md., 1992; instr., coach Maryvale PomPom/cheerleaders, Montgomery County, Md., 1992-94, asst. chmn. tchr. collabrative program, 1992-94, co-chair program com. tchr. collaborative, 1995-96; fitness instr. Oxedine Performing Arts Acad., Prince George's County, 1995-96; Goals 2000 English, lang. arts, history writer D.C. Pub. Schs., 1995-96. Aerobic instr. handicapped Coun. Exceptional Children, Washington, 1982, recreation svcs., City of Rockville, 1986—; developer My Spl. Friend program, 1984, BJ's Thinking Cap, 1991, Learning Creations, 1994, Girlfriends; bldg. rep. Washington Tchrs. Union AFT, AFL-CIO, 1987-89, 91-94, 1996, 97—, asst. bldg. rep., 1990-91, 94-95; supr. foster grandparent program Sharpe Health Sch., 1988—; trainer AIDS in Workplace, 1990, Early Childhood Substance Abuse Project Tng., 1992-93, Substance Abuse Prevention Edn., 1995, Metro Foster Grandparent Program, Washington, 1992-93; mem. preschool adv. bd. D.C. Pub. Schs., 1992-93, coordinating curriculum coun., 1994-96; master tchr. Coop. Tchr. Corp., 1993; curriculum writer, 1993; v.p. spl. edn. Washington Tchrs. Union Local 6, 1994—; stds. specialist, 1997—; del. 75th convention Am. Fed. Tchrs., 1998; mem. adv. bd. Supt.'s Tchr. Affairs, 1999; mem. Spl. Edn. State Adv. Panel, Washington, 1998-2000, D.C. Parent Tng. and Info. Ctr., ARC, Inc. Adv. Panel; exec. bd. dirs. Assembly of Petworth, 1998—; D.C. Pub. Schs. recruiter Nat. Alliance Black Sch. Educators, Nashville, 1999, resident mentor tchr., 1999-2004; mem. Disting. Educators Roundtable, 1998; mem. supt. search com. D.C. Pub. Schs., 2004; presenter in field; spkr. in field. Singer: 2000 Voices Lincoln Meml., 2000. Active D.C. Spl. Edn. State Adv., 1998, presenter AFT Civil, Human, Women's Rights Conf., 1998; Internat. Space Camp, Huntsville, Ala., 1998. Recipient Outstanding Svc. award Kappa Delta Pi, 1978, 79, 81, 82, 84, citation Washington Tchr. Union, 1985, State winner Elem. Level Nat. Citizenship Edn. Tchr.'s award Ladies Aux. VFW, Washington, 2002-03.; named DC Tchr. of Yr. Coun. Chief State Sch. Officers, 1998; grantee spl. edn. DC Pub. Sch. state office, 1993, Citibank, 1994; named to Hall of Fame Bison Found. Inc., Howard U., 1995; recipient Washington Post grants in the arts, 1999-2000, 2000-01, 01-02, Masonic Scottish Rite Educator excellence award, 2001, recipient Elem. Level Nat. Citizenship Edn. Tchr. award VFW, 2002-2003. Mem.: ASCD, Am. Fedn. Tchrs. (presiding officer WTU Spl. Educator and Svc. Provider Forums 1998—, tchr. speaker on Capitol Hill 1999, 2000, sch. to careers tchr. extern 2001, tchr. speaker on Capitol Hill 2001, DCPS new tchr. orientation trainer 2001, new tchr. coord. 2001—, DCPS new tchr. orientation trainer 2002, 2003, mem. 2000 voices at Lincoln Meml., Washington, D.C., tchr. speaker on Capitol Hill "No Child Left Behind" Legis. 2003, Nat. State Tchrs. of Yr.), Coun. Exceptional Children, Howard Alumni Cheerleaders Assn. (co-founder 1977, pres. 1990—94, v.p. 1998—, Outstanding Recognition award 1984, Recognition award named Brenda G. Jenkins Outstanding Cheerleader award 1987), D.C. Parents and Friends of Children with Special Needs (mem. critical ptnrs. group/supts. task force 2003, bd. dirs.), Kappa Delta Pi (convocation presenter, Balt. 1999, exec. com. Theta Alpha chpt.). Democrat. Avocations: alumni cheerleading, fashion design, cooking, dance, poetry writing.

JENKINS, DAWN, special education educator, dancer; b. Harrisburg, Pa., Sept. 12, 1955; d. Reese Walls and Catherine Verbos Jenkins; m. Richard Jay Uchitel, June 25, 1980 (div. 1990). EdB magna cum laude, U. Miami, Fla., 1977, EdM, 1978. Cert. profl. educator Fla., cert. assoc. master tchr. Fla. Tchr. of mentally challenged Holmes Elem. Sch., Miami, 1978—79; tchr. of hearing impaired Auburndale Elem. Sch., Miami, 1979—80; tchr. elem. deaf and hard of hearing Arcola Lake Elem., Miami, 1980—93; tchr. of deaf and hard of hearing Palm Springs Mid. Sch., Hialeah, Fla., 1993—. Choreographer and tchr. South Fla. Theatre of the Deaf, Miami, 1990—96; presenter very spl. arts movement workshop, incorporating dance into curriculum Mid. Sch. Conv., Ft. Lauderdale, Fla., 1991; choreographer, dance tchr. for deaf students Very Spl. Arts Project; adj. prof. Interpreters Deaf program Miami Dade Cmty. Coll., 1998—2000. Mem. Homeowners' Assn., Miami Lakes, Fla., 1995—98; founding mem. local club for the deaf Optimist Internat., Miami Lakes, 1996—97; fund raising sponsor Am. Cancer Soc., Miami, 1995—2003. Grantee, Impact II Com. of Miami Dade Schs., 2000; scholar, U. Miami Marching Band, 1973—77. Mem.: Fla. Registry Interpreters, Nat. Dance Edn. Orgn., Nat. Assn. of the Deaf, Coun. Exceptional Children, Conv. Am. Instrs. Deaf. Presbyterian. Avocations: dance, exercise, travel, reading. Office: Palm Springs Mid Sch 1025 W 56th St Hialeah FL 33012

JENKINS, ELIZABETH ANN, federal judge; b. 1949; BA, Vanderbilt U., 1971; JD, U. of Fla. Coll. of Law, 1976. Bars: Fla. 1977, D.C. 1978. Atty. advisor U.S. Dept. of Justice, 1976-78; asst. U.S. atty. Middle Dist. of Fla., Orlando, FLa., 1978-82, Southern Dist. of Fla., West Palm Beach, Fla., 1983-85; magistrate judge U.S. Dist. Ct. (mid. dist.) Fla., 1985—. Office: US Courthouse 801 N Florida Ave Ste U32 Tampa FL 33602-3849

JENKINS, JANET S. minister; b. Charleston, W.Va., Apr. 22, 1946; m. Douglas A. Jenkins, July 24, 1977. BA in Theology and Sociology Franciscan U., Steubenville, Ohio, 1987; MDiv, San Francisco Theol. Sem., San Anselmo, Calif., 1990. Ordained minister Presbyterian Ch., 1991. Chaplain intern Berkeley Chaplaincy to Homeless, Berkeley, Calif., 1989—90; co-pastor North Shenango Presbyn. Ch., Hartstown, Pa., 1991—95; pastor Watson Run Presbyn. Ch., Meadville, Pa., 1995—97; co-pastor Lucaya Presbyn. Ch. of Scotland, Freeport, Bahamas, 1997—2001; pastor Sarah Hearn Presbyn. Ch., Erie, Pa., 2001—. Supply chaplain Pa. Women's Security Prison, Cambridge Springs, Pa., 1994—97; mission ministries Ch. of Scotland, Freeport, Bahamas, 1997—2001; mem. com. on ministry Lake Erie Presbytery, Erie, Pa. Sec. Am. Women's Club, Freeport, Bahamas. Office: Sarah Hearn Presbyn Ch 947 W 9th St Erie PA 16502 E-mail: grandmarev@hotmail.com.

JENKINS, JONI LYNN, state legislator; b. Louisville, Dec. 6, 1958; d. James Paul and Alice Marie (Feig) J. BA in Journalism, U. Ky., 1980. Fund raiser Cystic Fibrosis Found., Louisville, 1980-81; tchr. Jefferson County Pub. Schs., Louisville, 1981-82; office mgr. Jefferson County Atty., Louisville, 1982-86; spl. projects coord. Jefferson County Govt., Louisville, 1986-87, speechwriter, 1987-90, pers. analyst, 1990-92, trainer, 1992-94; rep. Ky. Ho. of Reps., Frankfort. Democrat. Office: House of Representatives State Capitol 700 Capitol Ave Frankfort KY 40601-3410

JENKINS, KATHLEEN MARIA, web site design company executive; b. Evansville, Ind., Oct. 1, 1965; d. Ronald W. and Elizabeth (Gibbs) Butler; 1 child, James Ford J. AA, Henderson C.C., 1985; BA, Western Ky. U., 1987. Anchor, reporter Sta. WVJS/WSTO-Channel 2, Owensboro, Ky., 1989-90; mktg. cons. Space Design Internat., Cin., 1990-92; product mgr. Cincom Systems Inc., Cin., 1992-96; dir. internet development College View, 1996—2001; dir. e-business Aurora Casket Co., 2001—03; founder, pres. Fordhaven Cons., 2003—. Cons. in field. Avocations: writing, collecting quotes, designing web sites, church activities, cooking. Office: 1505 Huntcrest Dr Cincinnati OH 45255 Home: 1505 Huntcrest Dr Cincinnati OH 45255-3035

JENKINS, LOUISE SHERMAN, nursing researcher, educator; b. Normal, Ill., Jan. 19, 1943; d. Fred and Zylpha Louise (Garrett) Sherman; m. Gary L. Jenkins, Oct. 30, 1965 (div. July 1976). Diploma, Evanston Hosp. Sch. Nursing, 1963; BS, No. Ill. U., 1979; MS, U. Md., Balt., 1982, PhD, 1985. Asst. head nurse intensive care Cmty. Meml. Hosp., LaGrange, Ill., 1963-65; head nurse coronary care Luth. Gen. Hosp., Park Ridge, Ill., 1965-69; nurse clinician hemodialysis unit Evanston (Ill.) Hosp., 1969-74; head nurse Skokie (Ill.) Valley Cmty. Hosp., 1974-75; faculty dept. continuing edn. N.W. Cmty. Hosp., Arlington Heights, Ill., 1975-80; Walter Schoeder chair nursing rsch. U. Wis. Milw. Sch. Nursing and St. Luke's Med. Ctr., Milw., 1987-96; faculty Sch. Nursing U. Md., Balt., 1996—, acting dir. grad. studies, 1997-98, dir. grad. studies, 1998—2003. Mem. editl. bd. Jour. Cardiopulmonary Rehab., mem. rev. panel Am. Jour. Health Behavior, Nursing Rsch., Heart & Lung. Bd. dirs. Am. Heart Assn., Milw., 1988—95, exec. bd. dirs. Wis. affiliate, 1995—96, fellow, 2001; chair Coun. Cardiovasc. Nursing, Dallas, 1995—97, fellow. Fellow, Am. Heart Assn., 2001; fellow, Clin. Nurse scholar, Robert Wood Johnson Found., U. Calif., San Francisco, 1985—87. Mem.: N.Am. Soc. Pacing and Electrophysiology, Coun. Nursing Rsch., Midwest Nursing Rsch. Soc. (gov. bd. 1993—95), Wis. Nurses Assn. (bd. dirs. 1988—90, Excellence in Nursing Rsch. award 1995), Am. Assn. Cardiovasc. and Pulmonary Rehab. (bd. dirs.-at-large 1993—95), Sigma Xi, Sigma Theta Tau. Office: Sch Nursing U Md 655 W Lombard St Baltimore MD 21201-1512 E-mail: jenkins@son.umaryland.edu.

JENKINS, LYNN M. state official, former state legislator; b. Topeka, June 10, 1963; m. Scott M. Jenkins; children: Hayley, Hayden. AA, Kans. State U., 1984; BS, Weber State Coll., 1985. CPA, CPA, 1985—; rep. Kans. State Ho. Reps., 1998—2000; mem. Kans. State Senate, 2000—03, mem. gen. govt. budget com., ins. com., post audit com., govt. orgn. and elections com., taxation com.; treas. State of Kans., 2003—. Mem. adv. bd. Ct. Apptd. Spl. Advocate; bd. dirs. YMCA Metro, Family Svc. and Guidance Ctr.; treas., bd. dirs. Prince of Peace Presch.; active Jay Snideler PTO, Susanna Wesley United Meth. Ch. Mem. Kans. Soc. CPAs. Republican. Methodist. Office: 900 SW Jackson St Ste 201 Topeka KS 66612-1235*

JENKINS, MARGARET LUDMILLA, choreographer, dancer; b. Berkeley, Calif., Dec. 1, 1942; d. Hyman David and Edith Arnstein J.; m. Albert J. Wax, Apr. 2, 1972; 1 dau., Leslie Marissa. Student, Juilliard Sch. Music, 1960-61, UCLA, 1961-63. Dancer Jack Moore Dance Co., N.Y.C., 1960, Al Huang Dance Co., 1961, Gus Solomons Jr. Dance Co., 1963-65; tchr. Merce Cunningham Sch., N.Y.C., 1965-70; asst. to Merce Cunningham, N.Y.C., Boston, Stockholm, La Rochelle, France, 1965-74; dancer Twyla Tharp Dance Co., 1965-67, Viola Farber Dance Co., 1967-70; tchr. Paris, London, Stockholm, 1967; artistic dir. Margaret Jenkins Dance Co., San Francisco, 1972—; panelist NEA, Nat. Endowment for Arts, 1977-80; vice-chmn. DANCE/USA, also bd. dirs. Mem. challenge ct. panel and final rev. panel NEA, 1986, Rockefeller Choreography Project, 1986, Sundance Inst., 1986. Choreographer: Videosongs, 1976, Copy, 1977, About The Space In Between, 1977, Into Three, 1978, Red Yellow Blue, 1978, No One But Whittington, 1978, Straight Words, 1979, Invisible Frames, 1979, Duets, 1980, Versions By Turns, 1980, Harp, 1981, Cortland Set, 1982, In the Round I, 1982, In the Round II, 1982, First Figure, 1984, Max's Dream, 1984, Inside Outside (Stages of Light), 1985, Pedal Steal, 1985, Home Pt. 1, 1986, Home Pt. 2, 1986, Shelf Life, 1987, Georgia Stone, 1987, Shorebirds Atlantic, 1988, And So They, 1988, Rollback, 1988, Light Fall, Miss Jacobi Weeps, 1989, Woman Window Square, 1990, Age of Unrest, 1991, Sightings, 1991, Strange Attractors, 1992, The Gates (Far Away Near), 1993, Liquid Interior, 1995, Fault, 1996. Active Andrew W. Mellon Found., 1995, Nat. Dance Project, 1996, Nat. Dance Residency Program, 1996. Guggenheim fellow, 1980; Nat. Endowment for Arts fellow, 1978-79, 80, 81; recipient San Francisco award of Honor in Dance, 1984. Mem. San Francisco Bay Area Dance Coalition., Am. Arts Alliance (trustee) Office: Margaret Jenkins Dance Co 3973 25th St # A San Francisco CA 94114-3812

JENKINS, NANCY A. research scientist; PhD in Molecular and Cellular Biology, Ind. U. Postdoctoral rschr. Dana-Farber Cancer Ctr., Harvard Med. Sch.; assoc. staff scientist Jackson Lab.; assoc. prof. microbiology and molecular genetics U. Cin. Coll. Medicine; head molecular genetics of devel. sect. ABL-Basic Rsch. Program, 1985; prin. investigator Nat. Cancer Inst., Ctr. for Cancer Rsch., 1999—. Chair animal care and use com. FCRDC, 1988. Editor-in-chief: Genomics, 1997. Office: Nat Cancer Inst Bldg 539 Rm 229 Frederick MD 21702-1201

JENKINS, PATTY, film director, scriptwriter; Student in Painting, Cooper Union; degree in Dir.'s Program, Am. Film Inst. Dir.: (films) Just Drive, 2001; author: (films) Just Drive, 2001; dir.: (films) Velocity Rules, 2001 (Short Film award Telluride Indiefest, 2001); author: (films) Velocity Rules, 2001; dir.: (films) Monster, 2003 (nominated Golden Bear award Berlin Internat. Film Fest, 2004, nominated Ind. Spirit award, 2004); author: (films) Monster, 2003. Office: Creative Artists Agency 9830 Wilshire Blvd Beverly Hills CA 90212-1825*

JENKINS, PEGGY ANN, counselor; b. Utah, Aug. 16, 1946; d. George Woodrow and Mary Louise (O'Brien) McKellar; m. Charles John Jenkins, Feb. 6, 1965; children: Raymond Charles, Jannie Lynn, Jennifer Ann, Johnathan David. BS in Psychology with honors, U. Houston, 1984, MEd in Ednl. and Counseling Psychology, 1989. Lic. profl. counselor; cert. tchr.; cert. cognitive behavioral therapist. Presdl. asst. H.M.R. Cons., Houston, 1984-85; tchr. Houston Ind. Sch. Dist., 1985-89; inern Diagnostic Learning Ctr., U. Houston, 1988-89, Montrose Counseling Ctr., 1989; treatment psychologist adult forensic unit Mental Health and Mental Retardation Authority Harris County, Houston, 1989-92; psychol. evaluator Robbie Burnett and Assocs., Houston, 1993; pvt. practice Jenkins & Assocs., Houston and Clearlake, Tex., 1993-98; quality assurance case mgr. Interface Employee Assistance Program, 1997-98; sch. psychology intern Hitchcock (Tex.) Ind. Sch. Dist., 1998—. Adj. prof. Houston C.C., 1992—. Recipient McCarey Endowment scholarship U. Houston, 1984, Student rsch. grant U. Houston, 1984, Shell Oil grant Houston Ind. Sch. Dist., 1986, Impact II grant Houston Ind. Sch. Dist. 1988. Mem. Nat. Assn. Cognitive Behavioral Therapists, Assn. for Spiritual, Ethical and Religious Values in Counseling, Assn. Promotion of Profl. Women, Am. Assn. Counseling and Devel., Tex. Counseling Assn., Mortar Bd. Roman Catholic. Avocation: sailing. Office: 16455 Parksley Dr Houston TX 77059-4718

JENKINS, RENEE R. medical educator, pediatrician; b. Phila., Jan. 16, 1947; MD, Wayne State U. Diplomate Am. Bd. Pediatrics. Intern Jacobi/Albert Einstein Hosp., Bronx, 1971—72, resident in pediats., 1972—74; fellow in adolescent medicine Montefiore Hosp. Ctr., Bronx, 1974—75; prof., chmn. dept. pediats. Howard U., Washington; staff pediatrician Howard U. Hosp., Washington. Mem.: SAM, NMA, APS, Am. Acad. Pediats., Inst. Medicine of NAS. Office: Howard Univ Hosp 2041 Georgia Ave NW Washington DC 20060

JENKINS, SEBETHA, college president; one child, Jennifer. BA in English, Jackson State U.; MA in English, Delta State U.; EdD in Adminstrn., Miss. State U., 1978. Various adminstrv. positions Coahoma Jr. Coll., Miss. State U., 1960-86; asst. to the pres., dir. minority affairs U. Akron, Ohio, 1986-90; pres. Jarvis Christian Coll., Hawkins, Tex., 1991—. Apptd. to Pres.'s Bd. of Advisors on Historically Black Colls. and Univs., 1994; spkr. and educator in field. Vol. United Way, Boy Scouts Am., NAACP, YWCA; bd. dirs., pres. Big Bros./Big Sisters; bd. dirs. Arthritis Found., Akron Cmty. Svc. Ctr., Urban League, Summit County Human Svcs. Adv. Bd., Air Univ. Bd. of Vis. at Maxwell AFB, Consortium of Black Doctors, Ind. Colls. and Univs. of Tex., others; participant in Leadership Akron, Leadership Starkville. Recipient Most Outstanding Woman in Higher Edn., Miss., 1980; named Most Outstanding Profl. Woman, Miss. State U., 1985; recipient Hawkins C. of C. Outstanding Achievement award in Higher Edn., 1991, others; inducted into Black Women of Tex. Hall of Fame, 1996. Mem. Delta Sigma Theta.

JENKINS, TWYLAH LA'TRIECE, pharmaceutical sales representative; b. Okinawa, Japan, Mar. 12, 1977; d. Leonard and Marzette Bryant Jenkins. BA, U. NC, 1999. Account mgr. Warner-Lambert Co., Dallas, 1999—2001; pharmaceutical sales rep. Odyssey Pharmaceuticals, Inc., East Hanover, NJ. Baptist. Avocations: fitness, cooking, horseback riding, reading, travel. Office: Odyssey Pharmaceuticals Inc 72 Eagle Rock Ave East Hanover NJ 07936 Personal E-mail: twylah_jenkins@sbcglobal.net.

JENKINS, ZERETHA LENORE, publishing executive; b. Monroe, La., Jan. 10, 1959; d. Woodrow and Rosa Lee Jenkins. BA in Psychology, U. La., 1981; MFA in Dramatic Writing, NYU, 1990. CICM N.Y., ICM N.Y. Pres., CEO E.F.S. Enterprises, Inc., N.Y.C., 1994—; pres. E.F.S. Prodns., N.Y.C., 1998—; pres., CEO Rosewood Internat. Prodns., Pub., Publicity, NYC, 2003—. Bd. dirs. Washington Heights Home Health Care Program, N.Y.C., 1994—. Author: Walking by Faith: An Afro American Trilogy, 1999; screenwriter: screenplays The Rape of Leila Meshki, 1998, author poetry, short stories. Named winner script category, Writer's Digest Ann. Writing Competition, 1990. Mem.: The Drama League, Am. Screenwriters Assn. Avocations: tennis, video games, piano, ice skating, jazz. Office: EFS/Rosewood Internat Enterprises Ste 6E 2844 Eighth Ave New York NY 10039

JENKINS-ANDERSON, BARBARA JEANNE, pathologist, educator; b. Chgo. d. Carlyle Fielding and Alyce Louise (Walker) Stewart; m. Sidney Bernard Jenkins, Sept. 22, 1951 (div. June 1970); children: Kevin Jenkins, Judy Kelly, Sharolyn Sanders, Marc Jenkins, Kayla French; m. Arthur Eugene Anderson, Sept. 30, 1972. BS, U. Mich., 1950; MD, Wayne State U., 1957. Diplomate Am. Bd. Pathology. Intern Providence Hosp., Detroit, 1958-59, resident in psychiatry, 1959-60; resident in pathology Henry Ford Hosp., 1961-62, U. Mich. Affiliated Program, 1962-65; staff pathologist Wayne County Hosp., 1966-70, Detroit Receiving Hosp., 1970-72; asst. prof. pathology Wayne State U. Med. Sch., Detroit, 1970—72, assoc. prof. pathology, 1973—; adminstrv. med. dir. Detroit Med. Ctr. Univ. Labs., Detroit, 1988—; chief pathology Detroit Receiving Hosp./Univ. Health Clinic, Detroit, 1990—. Instr. U. Mich., 1966-70. Recipient Leonard Sain award U. Mich., 1980. Mem. Alpha Omega Alpha. Avocations: golf, interior design. Office: DMC Univ Labs 4201 Saint Antoine St Detroit MI 48201-2153

JENKINS-BRADY, TERRI LYNN, publishing executive, journalist; b. Albuquerque, Sept. 19, 1952; d. Hubert Arnold Jenkins and Helen Hope Zumwalt; m. Timothy Daniel Brady, July 4, 2000; stepchildren: Cori Danielle Brady, Colt Mitchell Brady. Student, U. Albuquerque, 1971—75, U. N.Mex., 1976. Pub. rels./fund-raiser March of Dimes; asst. to editor Prime Time, Albuquerque, 1995—2000, columnist, 2000—02; editor Al Bowl Querque Times, Albuquerque, 2000; editor in chief, ptnr. Write Up The Road Pub., Kenton, Tenn., 2002—; retail sales rep., freelance writer, 1974—79. Co-author: Romancing the Road, 2002; author, editor: newsletter Billy Beaver's Traveler, 2001—04; editor: Driven 4 Profits Fin. Newsletter, 2003, Oh, Pegasus: A Work of Love Thoughts, 2003. Mem. adv. bd. Hiland Sr. Ctr., Albuquerque, 1996—97; co-founder Further Up the Road scholarship Rotary Club, Union City, Tenn., 2002. Recipient Bronze and Silver medals, Imperial Soc. Tchrs. Ballroom Dance, 1981. Mem.: Small Pubs. Assn. N.Am., Writer's Ink. Avocations: travel, writing, designing wearable art, astrology, ballroom dancing. Office: Write Up The Road Pub PO Box 69 Kenton TN 38233-0069 Office Phone: 731-749-8567. E-mail: info@writeuptheroad.com.

JENKS, ROSEMARY ELIZABETH, lawyer; d. Walter F. and Madeleine M. Jenks. BA magna cum laude, Colo. Coll., Colorado Springs, 1990; JD magna cum laude, Harvard U., 2001. Bar: Va. 2001. Analyst/editor Ctr. for Immigration Studies, Washington, 1991—92, sr. analyst/editor, 1992—96, dir. of policy analysis/editor, 1996—97; immigration cons. Washington, [illegible] Va. State Bar, Pi Sigma Alpha, Pi Gamma Mu, Phi Beta Kappa. Office: NumbersUSA 310 6th St SE Washington DC 20003 Personal E-mail: rjenks@post.harvard.edu.

JENKS-DAVIES, KATHRYN RYBURN, retired daycare provider and owner, civic worker; b. Lynchburg, Va., Oct. 9, 1916; d. Charles Arthur and Jessie Katherine (Moorman) Ryburn; m. Thomas Edgar Jenks Jr., Sept. 9, 1941 (dec. June 1975); children: Thomas Edgar III, Jessika, Timothy; m. Robert E. Davies, Dec. 27, 1986 (dec. Mar. 1996). BS, State Tchr. Coll., 1938; postgrad., Mary Washington Coll., 1947-48, U. Va., 1957-58, William and Mary Coll., 1967-68, Va. Commonwealth U., 1969-70. Elem. tchr. various schs., Grundy, Va., 1939-41; phys. therapist U.S. Army, Ft. Bragg, N.C., 1942, operator motor pool Ft. Still, Okla., 1943-44, occupational therapist Augusta, Ga., 1944-45; instr. phys. edn. King George (Va.) High Sch., 1947-48, Stafford (Va.) High Sch., 1949-50, substitute tchr., 1950-53; owner, dir. Kay's Kindergarten, Fredericksburg, Va., 1959-83; ret., 1983. Featured in Fredericksburg Times mag., The Free Lance-Star and Richmond Newspapers. Counselor Girl Scouts U.S.A., Grundy, Va., 1939-41; life mem. Kenmore Assn., 1949—; mem. Hist. Fredericksburg Found., Inc., 1953—, vol. Garden Week and Christams Open House; mem. Mental Health Bd., 1978-84; founder Ford Franklin Found., 1968-78; mem. Fredericksburg Clean Cmty. Commn., 1987—; rep. United Way, Fredericksburg; instr. art ceramics Cmty. Ctr. Fredericksburg, 1950-80; bd. dirs. Miss Fredericksburg Fair Pageant, 1965-88; participant cmty. parades; coord. Fredericksburg Agrl. Fair 18th Century Craft People and Artisans, 1988-93, also others; bd. dirs. Antique Farm Implements, Gas and Steam Engines, 1989-93, Fredericksburg Fair, 1994-96; active State Fair of Va., 1981-95, Am. Heritage Showcase Endl. Reenactment Pioneer Farmstead, 1981-96. Recipient Virginia Ellison Vol. Svc. award Fredericksburg Clean Community Commn., 1976-87, Recognition of Svc. award, 1983-84, 1st, 2nd. and 3rd pl. trophies cmty. parades, awards radio Stas. WFLS and WFVA, 1949-89; honored by Kiwanians for travelogue for fund raiser, 1995—, vol. award, 1997. Mem. AAUW (advt. chmn. travelogue 1971-89, Donor Honoree award 1983, 98, bd. dirs. 1971-79), Lioness Club (bd. dir. 1968-87, Lioness Tamer 1984—, bd. dirs. 1996-97, Tongue Wagger 1985, 96—), Soroptimist Internat. Fredericksburg (life mem., sec. 1971-73, pres. 1973-75, bd. dirs. 1971-78, co-chmn. Soroptimist Travelogue 1991-93, First Class Pub. Recognition Trophy 1986, Women Helping Women award 1982, named 1 of 5 who have made a difference in cmty. 1994), Order of Eastern Star (hostess 1995, 96, 97, 98), Nat. League of Fredericksburg (bd. dir., Svc. Recognition Trophies 1963, 69, 80), Izaac Walton League (bd. dir. Dog Mart parade 1965-72). Republican. Episcopalian. Avocations: ceramics, drama, dance, travel, golf. Home: 8 Blair Rd Fredericksburg VA 22405-3025

JENNEMANN, KAREN SUE, judge; b. Louisville, Dec. 6, 1955; d. Noel and Meta Sue (Scales) Lemons; m. Thomas Joseph Jennemann, Aug. 3, 1974 (div. Sept. 1988); 1 child, Thomas William Noel. BS in Edn. with honors., No. Ariz. U., 1977; postgrad., U. Louisville, 1978-79; JD, Coll. William and Mary, 1983; postgrad., Coll. of William and Mary, 1980-83, postgrad. Bar: Va. 1983, U.S. Dist. Ct. (ea. dist.) Va. 1983, U.S. Dist. Ct. (mid. dist.) Fla. 1984, U.S. Ct. Appeals (4th cir.) 1983, U.S. Dist. Ct. (no. dist.) Fla. 1987, U.S. Ct. Appeals (11th cir.) 1988. Law clk. to Presiding Justice Hon. Robert G. Doumar, U.S. Dist. Ct., Norfolk, Va., 1983-84; assoc. atty. Smith & Hulsey, 1984-88; ptnr. Mahoney, Adams & Criser, Jacksonville, Fla., 1988-93; bankruptcy judge U.S. Bankruptcy Ct. (Fla. mid. dist.), 11th circuit, Orlando, 1993—. Atty., guardian Guardian Ad Litem Program, Jacksonville, 1985—. Asst. editor: Dickens Studies Newsletter. Bd. dirs. Jacksonville Legal Aid Soc., 1984-86. Named Outstanding Senior, Highest Ranking Scholar; recipient Frier Found. scholarship. Mem. ABA, Jacksonville Bar Assn. (chmn. Bankruptcy Law Sec. 1988-90), Fla. Bar Assn. Legal Needs Children, Fla. Bar Assn. (publ. chairperson, exec. coun. of bus. law sect.), Kappa Delta Pi, Phi Kappa Phi. Methodist. Office: US Courthouse 135 W Central Blvd Fl 9 Orlando FL 32801-2430

JENNESS, REBECCA ESTELLA, artist, educator; b. L.A., Aug. 16, 1946; d. Russell Albert and Estella Virginia (Guzman) J. Student, Cape Sch. Art, Provincetown, Mass., 1971; diploma, Vesper George Sch. of Art, 1972; BFA, Southeastern Mass. U., 1981. Mem. panel R.I. State Coun. on the Arts, 1989-93; mem. adv. bd. Warwick Art Mus., R.I., 1990-94, New Eng. Found. on the Arts, Boston, 1990-94, Sarah Doyle Gallery, Brown U., 1991-95; mem. multicultural art literacy coun. State Coun. on the Arts, R.I., 1991-94. Exhibited in group shows at Soviet Hall of Art, Moscow, 1988, U. N.H., 1989, Fitchburg Art Mus., 1990, R.I. Sch. Design Mus. of Art, 1992-93, Lyman Allen Mus., Conn., 1994, Artists for Shelter, Providence, 1995, Mus. of Art, 1995, 97. Art advocate New England Artists Trust, 1990-95, Perishable Theater, Providence, 1993, New Eng. Conf., Providence, 1993-94, Studio and Living Spaces for Artists, Providence, 1995-96; artists for food Amos House, Providence, 1993. Democrat. Avocations: american indian and mexican indian art and design studies, poetry, gardening. Home: PO Box 41395 Providence RI 02940-1395 Studio: 220 Weybosset St Ste 4 Providence RI 02903-3707

JENNETT, SHIRLEY SHIMMICK, health facility administrator; b. Jennings, Kans., May 1, 1937; d. William and Mabel C. (Mowry) Shimmick; m. Nelson K. Jennett, Aug. 20, 1960 (div. 1972); children: Jon W., Cheryl L.; m. Albert J. Kukral, Apr. 16, 1977 (div. 1990) Diploma, Rsch. Hosp. Sch. Nursing, Kansas City, Mo., 1958. RN, Mo., Colo., Tex., Ill. Staff nurse, head nurse Rsch. Hosp., 1958-60; head nurse Penrose Hosp., Colorado Springs, Colo., 1960-62, Hotel Dieu Hosp., El Paso, Tex., 1962-63; staff nurse Oak Park (Ill.) Hosp., 1963-64, NcNeal Hosp., Berwyn, Ill., 1964-65, St. Anthony Hosp., Denver, 1968-69; staff nurse, head nurse, nurse recruiter Luth. Hosp., Wheat Ridge, Colo., 1969-79; owner, mgr. Med. Placement Svcs., Lakewood, Colo., 1980-84; vol., primary care nurse, admissions coord., team mgr. Hospice of Metro Denver, 1984-88, dir. patient and family svcs., 1988, exec. dir., 1988-94; pres., profl. geriatric care mgr. Care Mgmt. & Resources, Inc., Denver, 1996—. Mem. NAFE, Nat. Women Bus. Owners Assn., Nat. Hospice Orgn. (bd. dirs. 1992-95, coun. former bd. mems. 1995—), Nat. Orgn. Profl. Geriatric Care Mgrs., Denver Bus. Women's Network. Mem. Ch. of Religious Sci. Avocations: reading, walking, golf. Office: Care Mgmt & Resources Inc 2055 S Oneida St Ste 150 Denver CO 80224-2435 Office Phone: 303-639-5455. E-mail: sjennett@earthnet.net.

JENNICHES, F. SUZANNE, engineering executive; BS in Biology, Clarion State Coll., 1970; MS in Environ. Engrng., Johns Hopkins U., 1978. Postgrad. with def. decision making internat. affairs Cath. U. Am.; v.p., gen. mgr. Govt. Sys. Divsn. Northrop Grumman Corp., L.A. Bd. dirs. Tech. Coun. Greater Balt. Com., 1990-2002, army sci., 2002-; active Nat. Acad. Engrng. Task Force on Celebration of Women in Engrng., 1997—. Fellow Soc. Women Engrs. (life, pres. Balt. Washington sect. 1978-80, rep. Balt. Washington sect. 1981-83, Disting. New Engr. award 1983, co-chair internat. conf. on women in engrng. and sci. 1984, regional dir. mid-atlantic area 1984-85, nat. v.p. student svcs. 1985-86, nat. sec. 1986-87, nat. pres.-elect 1987-88, nat. pres. 1988-89); mem. Am. Assn. Engrng. Socs. (bd. govs. 1988-89). Office: Northrop Grumman ES PO Box 17320 MS B-500 Baltimore MD 21203-7320 E-mail: suzanne.jenniches@ngc.com.

JENNINGS, CAROL, marketing executive; b. Marion, Ohio, Oct. 2, 1945; d. Richard P. and Mary (LeMaster) J.; m. John Putnam Merrill Jr., Jan. 3, 1981. BA, Miami U., Oxford, Ohio, 1967. News editor Penton Pub. Inc., Cleve., 1967-69; pub. rels. exec. Cen. Nat. Bank, Cleve., 1969-71; dir. pub. rels. New Eng. Conservatory of Music, Boston, 1971-74, Bklyn. Acad. Music, N.Y.C., 1974-75; account exec., supr. Hill and Knowlton, N.Y.C., 1975-81, from v.p. to mng. dir., 1981 87; sr. v.p., gen. mgr. Hill, Holliday, Connors, Cosmopolus, Boston, 1987, Hill and Knowlton, [illegible] dir. corp. communications Bain and Co., Boston, 1991-93; dir. mktg. Heidrick and Stiuggles, Inc., Atlanta, 1995-97; mktg. and pub. rels. cons. Palm Beach, Fla., 1997—.

JENNINGS, ELIZABETH FORREST, music educator; d. Thomas Ward and Diane Williams Forrest; m. Michael Douglas Jennings, Aug. 1, 1992; children: Peyton Thomas, Allyson Denise. MusB, Carson Newman Coll., 1992; MS in Edn., Old Dominion U., 1998. Profl. lic. Va., 2003. Trust asst. Commonwealth Wealth Mgmt. Svcs., Louisville, 1992—94, Old Point Trust Divsn., Newport News, Va., 1995—97; music tchr. Hampton (Va.) City Schs., 1997—2000; music specialist Chesterfield County Pub. Schs., Moseley, Va., 2000—. Dir. music Hampton Bapt. Ch., 1999—2000. Mem.: Nat. Assn.Music Educators (assoc.), Delta Omicron (life; dir., alumni-at-large 2002), Phi Kappa Phi (assoc.). Home: 5301 Chestnut Bluff Pl Midlothian VA 23112

JENNINGS, GABRIELLE, artist; b. San Francisco, Dec. 23, 1966; Student, U. Paris, 1988; BFA, U. Calif.-San Diego, La Jolla, 1990; MFA, Art Ctr. Coll. Design, Pasadena, Calif., 1994. Artist-in-residence 200 Gertrude Street, Melbourne, Australia, 1996, Künstlerhaus Bethanien, Berlin, 1997-98. Solo exhbns. include Künstlerhaus Bethanien, 200 Gertrude Street, Art Ctr. Coll. Design, Pasadena, Guardshack, Bergamot Sta., Santa Monica; exhibited in group shows Rutgers U., New Brunswick, N.J., MFA Gallery, Art Ctr. Coll. Design, 1991, 94, Guggenheim Gallery, Chapman U., Orange, Calif., 1994, L.A. Ctr. for Photog. Studies, Hollywood, Calif., 1994, 95, Calif. State U., L.A., 1994, Mark Moore Gallery, Santa Monica, Calif., 1994, Bergamot Sta., Santa Monica, 1995, David Zwirner Gallery, N.Y.C., 1996, U. Chgo., 1996, Post, L.A., 1997, W139, Amsterdam, 1997, La. Mus. Art, Humlebaek, 1997, OSMOS, Berlin, 1998, West Space, Melbourne, 1998, Para/Site, Hong Kong, Castello di Rivoli, Turin, Sunshine and Noir Art, L.A., 1960-97, Artists Space, N.Y., 2000, Kunst-Und Kunstgewebereviern, Pforzheim, 2001, Mus. New Art, Detroit, 2002, others; videography includes She Disappeared First, 1993, Agapanthus Lapsus, 1994, To Whom It May Concern, 1994, Momentary Suspension, 1995, The Kiss, 1996, (prelude) Eight Minutes, 1995, The Kiss, 1996, A Small Fortune, 1996, Here and There, 1998, Triptych, 1999, Motion Studies, 2000, Rainbow, 2001, Circus Series, 2002-2003, others. Fellow Art Matters Inc., 1996. Avocations: fiction, video, painting, installation art. E-mail: tv3d@sbcglobal.net.

JENNINGS, JACKIE, construction executive, contractor; Pres. Johnson & Jennings Gen. Contracing, San Diego, 1979—. Chair San Diego Regional Econ. Task Force. Bd. mem. St. Vincent de Paul, San Diego. Recipient Woman-Owned Small Bus. Yr. award, 1998. Office: Johnson & Jennings 6165 Greenwich Dr Ste 180 San Diego CA 92122-5910 Fax: 619-612-1108. E-mail: info@johnsonandjennings.com.

JENNINGS, JULIANNE, cultural organization administrator; b. Providence, Mar. 13, 1961; d. James Jennings; m. Francis J. O'Brien Jr., Feb. 2, 1995 (div. 2002); children: Brian Coelho, Julia Coelho, Lily-Rae O'Brien. Student in Nursing, C.C. R.I., Warwick. Cons. R.I. Indian Coun., Providence. Cons. R.I. State Coun. Arts, R.I. Com. Humanities. Co-author: Understanding Algonquian Indian Words, 1996, A Massachusett Language Book, Vol. 1, 1998, Bringing Back Our Lost Language, 1999; author: Succotash, 1998; creator (audio cassette tape) Nokas-I Come From Her, 2000. Grantee R.I. Com. Humanities, 1996, R.I. Found., 1997, R.I. State Coun. Arts, 1998. Avocations: native american basket making, native american beading, native american singing, native american painting. Home and Office: 40 Union Ave Warwick RI 02889-8529

JENNINGS, MARCELLA GRADY, rancher, investor; b. Springfield, Ill., Mar. 4, 1920; d. William Francis and Magdalene Mary (Spies) Grady; student pub. schs.; m. Leo J. Jennings, Dec. 16, 1950 (dec.). Pub. relations Econolite Corp., Los Angeles, 1958-61; v.p., asst. mgr. LJ Quarter Circle Ranch, Inc., Polson, Mont., 1961-73, pres., gen. mgr., owner, 1973— ; dir. Giselle's Travel Inc., Sacramento; fin. advisor to Allentown, Inc., Charlo, Mont.; sales cons. to Amie's Jumpin' Jacks and Jills, Garland, Tex. Investor. Mem. Internat. Charolais Assn., Los Angeles County Apt. Assn. Republican. Roman Catholic. Home and Office: 509 Mount Holyoke Ave Pacific Palisades CA 90272-4328

JENNINGS, MARIANNE MOODY, lawyer, educator; b. Sept. 11, 1953; d. James L. and Jennie (Ure) Moody; m. Terry H. Jennings, Nov. 5, 1976; children: Sarah Anne, Claire Elizabeth. BS in Fin., Brigham Young U., 1974, JD, 1977. Bar: Ariz. 1977, U.S. Dist. Ct. Ariz. 1977. Law clk. Fed. Pub. Defender, Las Vegas, 1975; U.S. atty. Las Vegas, 1976, Udall, Shumway, Bentley, Allen & Lyons, Mesa, Ariz., 1976; from asst. prof. bus. law to assoc. prof. Ariz. State U., Tempe, 1977-83, prof., 1983—, assoc. dean, 1986-88. Columnist Tribune newspapers. Author: Business Strategy for the Political Arena, 1984, Real Estate Law, 6th edit., 2000, Business: Its Legal, Ethical and Global Environment, 5th edit., 2000, Avoiding and Surviving Lawsuits: An Executive Guide to Legal Strategy, 1988, N.Y. Times MBA Pocket Scenes: Corporate Boards, 2000. Bd. dirs. Ariz. Pub. Svc., Inc., 1987-2000. Named Outstanding Undergrad. Bus. Prof., Ariz. State U., 1980, 85, 2000; recipient Burlington No. Found. Tchg. Excellence award, 1986; Dean's Coun. of 100 scholar, 1996—. Mem. Ariz. Bar Assn., Am. Bus. Law Assn., Pacific S.W. Bus. Law Assn. Mem. Lds Ch. Office: Ariz State U c/o M Jennings Coll Bus Tempe AZ 85287 E-mail: marianne.jennings@asu.edu.

JENNINGS, SUSAN JANE, lawyer; b. Providence, June 23, 1952; d. John Edward and Betty Jean (Frost) Stedman; m. James Albert Jennings, Jan. 2, 1982; children: Olivia Arden, Caroline Alexis, Susan Alexandra. BA, Ind. U., 1973; JD, Tex. Tech U., 1978; LLM in Taxation, So. Meth. U., 1985. Bar: Tex. 1978, U.S. Dist. Ct. (no. dist.) Tex. 1979, U.S. Tax Ct. 1986. Advanced mktg. cons. Southwestern Life Ins., Dallas, 1978-81; asst. gen. counsel Res. Life Ins., Dallas, 1981-85; gen. counsel, corp. sec., v.p. Life Ins. Co. SW, Dallas, 1986—. Of counsel Erhard, Ruebel and Jennings, Dallas, 1981—; bd. dirs. Tex. Legal Res. Ofcls. Assn., 1994-95. Contbr. articles to profl. jours. Mem. ABA (editor Tort and Ins. Law Jour. 1996-99, TIPS professionalism standing com. 1999—), Dallas Bar Assn. (chmn. corp. counsel sect. 1996-97, ho. com. 1998—, history com. 1998—), Kappa Delta (pres. Dallas alumnae 1983-84), Phi Delta Phi. Republican. Presbyterian. Avocations: swimming, cycling, cooking, music. Home: 4001 Miramar Ave Dallas TX 75205-3129 Office: Life Ins Co SW 1300 W Mockingbird PO Box 47421 Dallas TX 75247

JENNINGS, TONI, lieutenant governor; b. Orlando, Fla., May 17, 1949; d. Jack C. and Margaret (Murphy) J. BA, Wesleyan Coll., Macon, Ga., 1971; postgrad., Rollins Coll., 1972-73. Pres. Jack Jennings and Sons, Inc., Gen. Contractors, Orlando, 1973—; mem. Fla. Ho. of Reps., 1976-80, Fla. Senate, 1980—2000, pres., 1996—2000; lt. gov. Florida, 2003—. Republican leader pro tempore, 1982-83, 85, 86, Rep. leader, 1984, 86-88. legis. del. Orange County, 1980-82, 86-88. Bd. dirs. Salvation Army; active Rep. Women's Federated Club of Winter Park, Orlando Women's Rep. Club Federated. Recipient Spl. Commendation award Fla. Restaurant Assn., 1979, Meritorious Svc. award Fla. Fedn. Humane Socs., 1979, Disting. Alumni awrd Wesleyan Coll., 1981, Freedom award Women for Responsible Legislation, 1982, Support of Law Enforcement award Fla. Sheriffs Assn., Outstanding Efforts award Tampa Missing Children Help Ctr., 1983, Outstanding Svc. award Grocers' Assn. Fla., 1983, Legis. award Fla., 1983, Legis. award Fla. Chiropractic Assn., 1983, 86, Appreciation award Fla. Med. Assn. and Physicians of Fla., 1983, 2d Ann. Frank J. Fahrenkopf, Jr. Outstanding State Minority Leader award, 1988, Ann. Legis. award for Leadership in Econ. Devel. Legislation award Fla. C. of C., 1987; named [illegible] Orlando Area Bd. Realtors (Friend of Realtors award 1989), Builders and Contractors, Ctrl. Fla. Builders Exch., Delta Kappa Gamma, Phi Kappa Phi, Kappa Delta Epsilon. Office: Lt Gov The Capitol PL-05 Tallahassee FL 32399-0001

JENNINGS, SISTER VIVIEN, English language educator; b. Jersey City; d. Eugene O. and Alice (Smith) J. BA, Caldwell Coll.; MA in English, Cath. U. Am.; MS in Telecommunications, Syracuse U.; PhD in English, Fordham U.; postgrad., Oxford (Eng.) U., 1994; EdD (hon.), Providence Coll.; LittD (hon.), Caldwell Coll.; DHL (hon.), St. Peter's Coll. Prof. English Caldwell Coll., 1960-69; major supr. Dominican Sisters-Caldwell, 1969-79; instr. broadcasting writing Syracuse U., 1979-80; with community affairs dept. Sta. WIXT TV, Syracuse, N.Y., 1980; dir. telecommunications Barry U., 1982-83; dir. pub. affairs Cath. Telecommunications Network Am., 1983-84; pres. Caldwell Coll., 1984-94, prof. English, 1995-99; prin. St. Dominic Acad., Jersey City, 1999—. Originator, designer campus TV studios Caldwell Coll., Barry U.; curriculum planner, coord. new grad.-level curriculum in telecommunications Barry U.; lectr. on edn1. and media issues. Producer: Centenary Journey, 1981, Advent Vesper Chorale, 1981, American Immigrant Church, 1982, Las Casas: Ministry of Presence, 1987; co-producer: The Boat People, 1980. Founder, dir. Children's TV Experience; founder Project Link Ednl. Ctr., Newark. Recipient Gov.'s Pride N.J. Albert Einstein award for edn., 1989. Office: St Dominic Acad 2572 Kennedy Blvd Jersey City NJ 07304-2107

JENNINGS, WANDA T. state legislator; b. Feb. 9, 1946; m. Terry Lee Jennings. Student, Memphis State U. State legislator Miss. Ho. of Reps., Jackson, 1996—. Mem. judiciary B., juvenile justice, municipalities, and oil and gas coms. Miss. Ho. of Reps. Sec. DeSoto County Rep. Party; dir. Olive Br. Cmty. Theatre; mem. Southaven Rep. Mcpl. Exec. Com., DeSoto Area Rep. Women. Mem. Southaven C. of C., DeSoto Rep. Club (bd. dirs.). Republican. Home: 1535 Sherwood Ln Southaven MS 38671-8818 Office: State Capitol Bldg PO Box 1018 Jackson MS 39215-1018

JENSEN, BAIBA, principal; Prin. Hawkins Elem. Sch., Brighton, Mich. Recipient Elem. Sch. Recognition awards U.S. Dept. Edn., 1989-90. Office: Hawkins Elem Sch 8900 Lee Rd Brighton MI 48116-2000

JENSEN, BARBARA WOOD, interior design business owner; b. Salt Lake City, Apr. 30, 1927; d. John Howard and Loretta (Sparks) Wood; m. Lowell N. Jensen, June 26, 1947 (dec. Aug. 2000); children: Brent Lowell, Robyn Lynn, Todd Wood; m. Thomas A. Mackey, Feb. 24, 2001. Interior decorator paint and wall paper co., 1947-49; cons., interior designer, 1950-60; pres., treas. Barbara Jensen Interiors, Inc., Salt Lake City, 1960-79; interior designer, 1979—; owner Barbara Jensen Designs, St. George, Utah and Las Vegas; lectr. in field. Lectr. in field; dir. 1st Women's Bancorp, Utah. Chmn. Utah Legis. Rep. Ball, 1970, Utah Symphony Ball, 1979. Fellow Inst. Profl. Designers (London); mem. Assistance League, Com. Fgn. Affairs, Interior Design Soc. (assoc.), Ft. Douglas Country Club, Knife and Fork Club, Hi-Steppers Dance Club, Ladies Lit. Club, Pres.'s Club of Utah, Bloomington Country Club, Elks. Mem. Lds Ch. Home: 2575 Kuhio # 1504 Honolulu HI 96815

JENSEN, EVA MARIE, medical/surgical nurse; b. Santa Maria, Calif., Sept. 2, 1956; d. Paul Cabello and Dolores Margaret Gutierrez; m. Royal George Jensen, Mar. 22, 1986 (div. Mar. 15, 1993). AA, Cuesta Coll., 1977; lic. vocation nurse, Hartnell Coll., 1980. RN Calif., 1982, cert. psychiat. and mental health nurse, Calif., 1995. Nurse Atascadero (Calif.) State Hosp., Atascadero, 1986—2003, Twin Cities Hosp., Templeton, 1982—86, 2003—. Participant nurses' health study Harvard Med. Sch., Boston, 1992—. Democrat. Roman Catholic. Avocation: adopting and rescuing abandoned animals.

JENSEN, GLORIA VERONICA, adult nurse practitioner; b. Montreal, Que., Can., Aug. 29, 1931; arrived in U.S., 1955; d. William Russell Boyd and Veronica Elizabeth Clarke; m. Joseph Edgar Jensen Jr., May 26, 1955 (div. June 11, 1989); children: William, Joanne, Neil, Christina, Karen. RN Calif.; lic. real estate agt. Calif. Nurse emer. rm. Royal Victoria Hosp., Montreal, 1953—55; postpartum nurse Good Samaritan Hosp., L.A., 1955—56; pvt. duty nurse Laguna Hills, Calif., 1988—91; relief work nurse Allergy and Asthma Assn., Mission Viego, Calif., 1992—99; nurse Saddleback Med. Group, Laguna Hills, 1998—. Vol. ARC, Subic Bay, Philippines, 1965—67, chmn. vols., 1965—67; mem. Valiant Women Mission Hosp., Mission Viejo, Calif. Mem.: Kiwanis. Republican. Roman Catholic. Avocations: opera, sewing, music, sailing. Home: 30922 Lucia Ln Laguna Beach CA 92677

JENSEN, HANNE MARGRETE, pathology educator; b. Copenhagen, Dec. 9, 1935; came to U.S., 1957; d. Niels Peter Evald and Else Signe Agnete (Rasmussen) Damgaard; m. July 21, 1957 (div. Apr. 1987); children: Peter Albert, Dorte Marie, Gordon Kristian, Sabrina Elisabeth. Student, U. Copenhagen, 1954—57; MD, U. Wash., 1961. Resident and fellow in pathology U. Wash., Seattle, 1963-68; asst. prof. dept. pathology U. Calif. Sch. Medicine, Davis, 1969-79, assoc. prof., 1979—2001, dir. transfusion svc., 1973—, prof., 2001—. McFarlane prof. exptl. medicine U. Glasgow, Scotland, 1983. Mem. No. Calif. Soc. for Electron Microscopy, U.S. and Can. Acad. of Pathology, Am. Cancer Soc., Am. Soc. Clin. Pathologists, AAAS, Am. Assn. of Blood Banks, Calif. Blood Bank Sys., People to People Internat., Internat. Platform Assn; fellow Pacific Coast Obstetrician and Gynecol. Soc., Coll. of Am. Pathologists. Office: U Calif Sch Medicine Dept Pathology Davis CA 95616 Office Phone: 530-752-7229. E-mail: hmjensen@ucdavis.edu.

JENSEN, KATHRYN PATRICIA (KIT), public radio and television station executive; b. Fairbanks, Alaska, June 20, 1950; d. Edward Leroy and Doris Patricia (Fee) Bigelow; 1 child, Alexander Morgan. BA, U. Alaska, 1974. Sta. mgr., program dir. Sta. KUAC-FM, U. Alaska, Fairbanks, 1976-82; gen. mgr. Sta. KUAC-FM-TV, U. Alaska, Fairbanks, 1982-87; pres., gen. mgr. Sta. WCPN-FM, Cleve. Pub. Radio, 1987-2001; COO, WVIZ/PBS and 90.3 WCPN, 2001—. Founding mem. Alaska Pub. Radio Network, 1978-85; bd. dirs. Nat. Pub. Radio, 1983-89, Pub. Radio Internat., 1998—. Recipient Elaine B. Mitchell award Alaska Pub. Radio Network, 1988, Oebie award, 1992, 95, William H. Kling Innovation and Entrepreneurship award Pub. Radio Internat., 1995, Leadership in Non-profit Mgmt. award Case We. Res. U., Mandel Ctr. Non-Profit Orgns., 1999; named Pub. Radio Gen. Mgr. of Yr., DEI/PRADO, 1999. Episcopalian. Avocations: reading, gardening. Office: WVIZ/PBS & 90-3 WCPN 3100 Chester Ave Ste 300 Cleveland OH 44114-4604

JENSEN, MARGARET, real estate broker; b. Payson, Utah, Aug. 12, 1948; d. Basil D. Broadbent and V. Merlene Ellsworth; m. Don E. Jensen, Sept. 27, 1997; children: Chad, Troy, Kristin, Dean, Debbie, Sean, Julie. AS, Casper Coll., 1968; BS with distinction, Colo. State U., 1989, postgrad., 1990. Grad. Realtor Inst., CRB, CRS, EMT. Clk. Colo. 8th Jud. Dept., Loveland; owner, CEO Lil Rascals, Ft. Collins, 1980-96; real estate salesperson Hometown Advantage, Loveland, 1996, Century 21, Ft. Collins, 1996; pres. Home Sweet Home Realty, Inc., Ft. Collins, 1997—; owner Home Sweet Home Bakery, Inc., Home Sweet Home Knitted Creations, Inc. Rental cons. Ft. Collins, 1985-99; tax cons., Ft. Collins, 1975-90; family cons. Ft. Collins, 1990-97. Participant Miss Am. Pageant, 1968; instr. ARC, Ft. Collins, 1975-85; tax preparer for VITA IRS, Ft. Collins,

1975-90; supr. trip to Russia People to People, 1990. Mem. Lions Club Internat., Mortar Bd., Golden Key Nat. Honor Soc., Colo. Assn. of Realtors, Nat. Assn. of Realtors, Omicron Nu, Alpha Gamma Delta, Phi Kappa Phi. Avocations: knitting hats for oncology patients and newborns, piano. Home and Office: 2205 Stonecrest Dr Fort Collins CO 80521-1318 Office Phone: 970-482-2320. E-mail: buycolorado@aol.com.

JENSEN, MARION PAULINE, singer; b. Glendale, Calif., June 29, 1931; d. Paul Morton and Marion (Grus) Bellows; m. Maynard I. Jensen, Aug. 15, 1959; children: Clare, Steven, Jeannetta, Lauretta, Paul, Tony, Phil. Studied voice with, Barbara Burk Prosper, San Francisco Opera, Christina Carlson, Edward Schick, Robert Kyber, Gibner King, David Jimerson; currently studies voice with, Christine Meadows. Pvt. tchr. music. Profl. performer of stage, concert, radio and TV; piano bar entertainer; author: So You Want To Sing, 1983; opera/stage roles include mother in Amahl and the Night Visitors, Kate in Brigadoon, Olga Navakovich in Merry Widow, Tuptim in The King and I, Mable in Pirates of Penzance, Bride in trial by Jury, Josephine in H.M.S. Pinafore, Sherry in Paint Your Wagon, Dolly in Rio Rita, others; opera cos. performed with include Oregon Light Opera, Pacific Theatre Arts, Oreg. Opera Ensemble, Vancouver Civic Theatre, Portland Opera; numerous concerts and recitals in L.A., San Francisco, various cities in Wash., Oreg.; strolling entertainer Nendels Inn, Sylvia's Downtown Restaurant; singer/hostess Frontier Room; singer Portland Hilton, others. Tchr. English Laubach (Oreg.) Literacy, 1972—. Mem. Internat. Assn. Musicians, Nat. Assn. Tchrs. Singing, Music Tchrs. Nat. Assn., Oreg. Music Tchrs. Assn., Nat. Fedn. Music Clubs of Am. (state chmn. student auditions). Democrat. Roman Catholic. Avocations: raising birds, designing and sewing, writing and illustrating children's books. Home: 10230 N Tyler Ave Portland OR 97203-1251

JENSEN, SANDE KELSEY, technologist, church administrator; b. Park Ridge, Ill., Nov. 9, 1943; d. Dennis Clark and Iris (Heinze) Kelsey; m. Larry L. Jensen, Feb. 9, 1977 (dec. Dec. 1998); children: Kimberly Marie, Anthony Kelsey. BSMT, Alverno Coll., 1965; MDiv, St. Francis Sem., 1998. Registered med. technologist ASCP, cert. immunology specialist SI. Supr. immunology/chemistry Kenosha Meml. Hosp., Wis., 1978—88; min. Christian Formation St. Mary, 1989—95; pastoral assoc. St. Therese, 1995—2001; dir. parish St. John Nepomuk Ch., Racine, Wis., 2001—. Adj. faculty Marian Coll., Fondulac, Wis., 1998—. Roman Catholic. Avocations: reading, birdwatching, writing, painting, travel. Office: St John Nepomuk Ch 700 English St Racine WI 53402*

JENSEN, SUSAN, instructional designer, multimedia producer; b. Salt Lake City, Dec. 13, 1961; d. Ronald Ray and Carolyn Jensen. BA in Comms., Brigham Young U., 1985. Intern Pt. Authority of N.Y. and N.J., N.Y.C., 1985; designer, prodr. The Ch. of Jesus Christ of LDS, Salt Lake City, 1985-87, Help-U-Sell, Inc., Salt Lake City, 1987-88; tech. writer, editor Unysis Inc., Salt Lake City, 1989-90; designer, prodr. Allen Comm., Salt Lake City, 1990-95; multimedia dir. Infobases Inc., Provo, Utah, 1995, v.p. of devel., 1995-96; pres., cons. The Ditigal Ranch, Salt Lake City, 1996—. Cons. in multimedia, Salt Lake City, 1985—. Designer, prodr.: (children's multimedia) The Adventures of Andrea and Alexander "Sunday...That One Day," 1995. Tchr. children's orgn., Bountiful, Utah, 1993-95, teenager's orgn., 1995-98, Sunday sch., Salt Lake City, 1990-92; pres. Young Women's Orgn., Bountiful, 1998-99, sec. regional presidency, 1999—. Mem. Acad. Interactive Arts and Scis. (bd. govs. 1994-96). Avocations: travel, theater, film, skiing, tennis. Office: The Digital Ranch 1354 E 3300 S Ste 300 Salt Lake City UT 84106-3082

JENSEN-RUOPP, HELGA SPITKO, school program administrator, consultant; b. Kosterchan, May 24, 1946; came to US, 1954. d. George and Greta Maria Spitko; m. John Martin Jensen, June 9, 1968 (div. May 1984); children: John-Karl, Caroline, Michael, Heidi; m. James Martin Ruopp, Apr. 9, 1988. BA, Adelphi U., 1968, MA, 1970, We. Conn. State U., 1992; EdD, Columbia U., 1992, 2000. Biology tchr. Danbury (Conn.) High Sch., 1986-98; coord. K-12 sci. Danbury Pub. Schs., 1998—. Tchr. German German Lang. Sch. Danbury; adj. instr. Western Conn. State U., Danbury, 1993—, cons., 1998-2000; instr. Coop. Program for Superior High Sch. Students, 1993; scientist, tchr. drug metabolism Boehringer Ingelheim Pharm., 1989-90; ecologist Key Issues Inst.: Keystone Sci., 1997; mem. Goals 2000 Grant Implementation; presenter in field. Mem. Candlewood Lake Authority, Danbury, 1993. Fellow Conn. Sci. Tchrs. Assn., N.Y. Acad. Scis., Phi Delta Kappa, Kappa Delta Pi; mem. AAUW, Conn. Sci. Suprs. Assn., Assn. Supervision and Curriculum Devel. Lutheran. Avocations: excercising, walking, mountain biking, painting, sculpting. Office: Danbury Bd Edn Beaver Brook Rd Danbury CT 06810

JENSON, PAULINE ALVINO, retired speech and hearing educator; b. Orange, N.J. m. Bernard A. Jenson; 1 child, Mark J. BS, Trenton State Coll., 1948; MA, Columbia U., 1950, PhD, 1969. Tchr. English and history Bordentown (N.J.) H.S., 1948-49; tchr. Lexington Sch. for Deaf, N.Y.C., 1950-51, with rsch. dept., 1969-70; tchr. N.J. Sch. for Deaf, West Trenton, 1951-56, 58-61, St. Mary's Sch. for Deaf, Buffalo, 1956-58; speech pathologist Hunterdon Med. Ctr., Flemington, N.J., 1959-60, dir. speech and hearing, 1960-62; asst. prof. Trenton (N.J.) State Coll., 1962-65; instr., lectr. Teacher's Coll., Columbia U., N.Y.C., 1966-69; prof. dept. speech pathology and audiology Trenton (N.J.) State Coll., 1970-95; Yrbk Dedica, 1978; prof. dept. lang. and comm. sci. Coll. N.J. (formerly Trenton State Coll.), 1995-98, chmn. dept., 1991-94, prof. emerita, 1998. Cons. Universal Films & Visual Arts, N.Y.C., 1968-70, State Agys. and Schs. for Handicapped, N.J., N.Y., 1976-98; evaluator Coun. on Edn. of Deaf, Washington, 1979-83. Author: (with others) Speech for the Deaf Child, 1971; inventor cueing system for deaf speakers, 1976; editor: (info. booklets) Topics, Princeton, N.J., 1980-86 Help line vol. N.J. Assn. for Children with Hearing Impairments, Princeton, 1973-95; co-author, cons. Senate Bills on Deafness, Trenton, 1979-98; commr. Legislative Commn. to Study Svcs. for Hearing Impaired Children, Trenton, 1988-90. Post Master's scholar U.S. Office Edn., Tchrs. Coll., Columbia U., 1965-66; grantee N.J. Dept. Edn., 1973, N.J. Dept. Human Svcs., 1992-96. Mem. N.J. Assn. for Children with Hearing Impairment (founder, exec. dir. 1973-95, Pauline Jenson award at The Coll. of N.J. named in her honor, 1996), N.J. Speech, Lang. and Hearing Assn. (life, Disting. Svc. award 1985, disting. clin. svc. award 1998), Am. Speech, Lang. and Hearing Assn. (cert., life). Avocation: bibliophily. Office: PO Box 1336 Princeton NJ 08542-1336

JERDEE, SYLVIA ANN, minister; b. Alpine, Tex., Apr. 18, 1941; d. Rolf Walter and Marjorie O. Kaasa; m. Joseph C. Jerdee, June 15, 1963; children: Jonathan, Peter, Theodore. BA, Luther Coll., 1963; EdM, Boston U., 1978; MDiv, Luther Seminary, 1995. Ordained min. Evang. Luth. Ch. Am., 1995. Tchr. Washington H.S., Sioux Falls, SD, 1963—64, Army Edn. Ctr., Dept. Def., Germany, 1974—78, Frankfurt (Germany) Am. H.S., 1978—85, guidance counselor, 1985—91; pastor Calvary LUth. Ch., Orr, Minn., 1995—99, Faith Little Norway Luth. Parish, Mentor, Minn., 1999—. Avocations: travel, reading. Office: Faith Little Norway Luth Parish Box 186 Mentor MN 56736

JERGENS, MARIBETH JOIE, school counselor; b. Cleve., May 3, 1945; d. Raymond Wenceslaus and Elsie Koryta J.; children: Annemarie Gurchik, Keith Robert Gurchik. Student, St. Joseph Acad., Cleve., 1959—63, U. Vienna, Austria, 1965; BS in Elem. Edn., Coll. Mt. St. Joseph on-the-Ohio, 1967; MEd in Ednl. Counseling, Cleve. State U., 1984; cert. in Ednl. Adminstrn., Akron U., 1988; postgrad. in edn. and clin. psychology, Kent State U., 1989—. Cert. elem., spl. edn. and adult edn. tchr., counselor. Coord. info. svcs. Halle Bros., Cleve., 1961—67; tchr. North Olmstead (Ohio) City Schs., 1967-75; tchr. adult basic edn. Polaris Vocat. Sch., Berea, Ohio, 1977-78; tchr. adult edn., ESL Lakewood (Ohio) City Schs., 1978-79; tchr. 2d grade St. Rose Sch., Lakewood, 1979-80; tchr. learning disabled students, tutor Cleve. Pub. Schs. Watterson-Lake Elem. Sch., 1980-85; tutor handicapped Cleve. Christian Home, 1982-84; elem. sch. counselor, tchr. learning disabilites Cleve. Pub. Schs., A.B. Hart Mid. Sch., 1995-97; tchr. human devel. and learning Kent (Ohio) State U., 1997-98; sch. psychologist asst. PSI Assocs., Inc., 1998-99; tchr. Wade Park Sch. Cleve. Mcpl. Sch. Dist., 1999-2000; pvt. practice Rocky River Psychol. Svcs., Ohio, 1999—2003; intervention specialist Dike Montessori Magnet Sch., 2000-01. Counselor West Side Cmty. Mental Health Ctr., Cleve., 1983-84; sales mgr. Field Enterprises Inc., Cleve., 1975-77; fund raising spkr., vol. Cerebral Palsy Camp Rosemary Home for Children United Torch, Cleve., 1961-65; coordinated vol. svcs. area colls. Allen Halfway Ho., Cin., 1965-67; rschr. interventions children with guns and violence in Am. schs., 1998-99; elem. counselor Cleve. Pub. Schs. Adams-Rhodes Cluster, 1985-94; spkr. in field. Contbr. articles to newspapers. Vol. Fairview Gen. Hosp., Cleve., 1959-63, Cerebral Palsy Camp, 1959-63, Allen Halfway House for Children, Cin., 1963-67; co-founder Westshore Separated, Div. and Remarried Caths., Cleve., 1975-85; chair North Olmsted Jr. Women's Club; parish coun. St. Brendan Ch., North Olmstead, 1975-87, founder cath. separated and div. ministry, 1976-85, counselor; mem. com. Cleve. Symphony, Cleve. Art Mus.; summer civil rights activist to implement Fed. Ct. Order Desegregation, Ctrl. H.S., Little Rock, 1957, New Orleans, 1958, Mobile, Ala., 1959; active Am. Aeobics and Fitness Assn., Audobon Soc., Cleve. Natural History Mus., Cleve. Mus. Art, Dem. Party, Edgewater Yacht Club (NCSS), English-Speaking Union, Holden Arboretum, St. Malachi Cath. Ch., Cath. Ch. Spl. Commn. on Priests Sexual Abuse, 2002-03; mem. rev. bd. Cleve. Cath. Diocese, 2003--. Recipient Speaker's United Torch award United Way, Cleve., 1st Pl. prize in clothing design Stretch & Sew, 1975, 1st Pl. prize in needlepoint Framemakers Art, 1983, 1st Pl. in three interstate art contests, musical recording, singing with the Cleve. Symphony Orch., NCSS regatta. Mem. Am. Assn. Counseling and Devel., AAUW, Am. Assn. Marriage and Family Therapists, Am. Psychol. Assn., Assn. for Curriculum and Supervision, Am. Sch. Counselor Assn., N.E. Ohio Counselors Assn., Ohio Counselors Assn., Ohio Assn. Counseling and Devel., Coun. for Exceptional Children, Am. Sch. Counselor Assn., ASCD, Gestalt Inst., Audubon Soc., Cleve. Psychol. Assn., Cleve. Mus. Art, Cleve. Natural History Mus., Cleve. Tchrs. Union, Gestalt Inst., Am. Aerobics and Fitness Assn., Edgewater Yacht Club, English Speaking Union, Holden Arboretum, Pi Lambda Theta. Democrat. Avocations: aerobics, art, cycling, dance, gardening. Home: 727 Tollis Pkwy Broadview Heights OH 44147

JERNIGAN, TAMARA E. astronaut; b. Chattanooga, Tenn., May 7, 1959; d. Terry L. and Mary P. J. BS in Physics with honors, Stanford U., 1981, MS in Engineering Science, 1983; MS in Astronomy, U. Calif., Berkeley, 1985; PhD in Space Physics and Astronomy, Rice, 1988. Rsch. scientist Theoretical Studies Branch NASA, 1981-85, astronaut candidate, 1985, astronaut, 1986—, mission specialist Space Shuttle Columbia, 1992; administrator sci. experiments Space Shuttle Endeavor, 1995. Recipient NASA Space Flight Medal, 1991, 1992, 1995, 1996, Exceptional Svc. Medal, 1993, Outstanding Leadership Medal, 1996, Disting. Svc. Medal, 1997. Mem. Am. Astron. Assn., Am. Physical Soc., U.S. Volleyball Assn. Avocations: volleyball, racquetball, tennis, softball, flying. Office: NASA Johnson Space Ctr Astronaut Office Houston TX 77058

JERNIGAN, VICKI LOUISE MACKECHNEY, clinical nurse specialist; b. Joliet, Ill., Aug. 2, 1953; d. Arthur Frank and Edna Eloise (Baker) Mackechney; m. George Norman Jernigan, Dec. 11, 1981 (div.); children: Nicole Dyan, Lani Michelle, Lindsay Lauryn. Diploma, Galveston County Meml. Hosp., LaMarque, Tex., 1976; RN assoc. degree, Galveston Coll., 1986; BS in nursing, MS in nursing, U. Conn., 2000. RN. Staff ward clerk, LUN & RN Galveston Memorial Hosp. (med. surg., ICU, CCU, ER, constant care units, skilled nursing units, post partum, nursery, surg., out patient, home health, La Marque, TX; indsl. nurse Gulf Coast Marine Works, Galveston, TX; nurse Staff Relief Inc., Houston; same day surg. recovery room nurse Surgi-Med. Inc., Dickinson, TX. Recruited as a Nurse Warrant Ofcr., Desert Storm/Desert Shield, United States Nurse Corps., 1991, A/D Lt., Nurse Corps., USN. Recipient, Navy Achievement Medal, 2 Navy Meritorious Unit Commendation Medals, Nat. Defense Svc. Medal, Outstanding Vol. Svc. Medal, Navy & Marine Corps Svc. Ribbon (3. yrs.), expert Pistol Merkmenship Ribbon. Home: PO Box 498 Santa Fe TX 77510-0498 also: 2511 Fairfax Dr Albany GA 31707-3028

JEROME, NORGE WINIFRED, nutritionist, anthropologist; b. Grenada, Nov. 3, 1930; arrived in U.S.A., 1956, naturalized, 1973; d. McManus Israel and Evelyn Mary (Grant) Jerome. BS magna cum laude(hon.), Howard U., 1960; MS, U. Wis., 1962, PhD, 1967. Cert. nutrition splty.; fellow Am. Coll. Nutrition. Asst. prof. U. Kans. Med. Sch., Kans. City, 1967—72, assoc. prof., 1972—78, prof., 1978—95, dir. cmty. nutrition divsn., 1981—95; dir. Office of Nutrition, AID, Washington, 1988—91; sr. rsch. fellow Univ. Ctr., AID, Washington, 1991—92; interim assoc. dean minority affairs U. Kans. Med. Sch., Kans. City, 1996—98, prof. emerita, 1996—. Tech. adv. group The Nat. Ctr. for Minority Health; dir. ednl. resource centers U. Kans. Med. Center, 1974-77, head cmty. nutrition lab., 1978-95; cons. Children's TV Workshop, 1974-77; chair adv. bd. Teenage Parents Ctr., 1971-75; planning and budget coun., children and family svc. United Cmty. Svc., 1971-80; panel on nutrition edn. White House Conf. on Food, Nutrition and Health, 1969; bd. dir., health care com. Prime Health, 1976-79; bd. dir. Coun. on Children, Media and Merchandising; consumer edn. task force Mid Am. Health Systems Agy., 1977-79; commr. N. Am. working group Commn. Anthropology Food and Food Habits, Internat. Union Anthrop. and Ethnol. Sci., 1979-80; chmn. com. nutritional anthropology Internat. Union Nutritional Sci., 1979-80; lipid metabolism adv. com. NIH, 1978-80; nat. adv. panel multi-media campaign to improve children's diet U.S. Dept. Agrl., 1979-81; bd. advisers Am. Coun. on Sci. and Health, 1985-88; cons. in field. Sr. author: Nutritional Anthropology, 1980; asso. editor: Jour. Nutrition Edn., 1971-77; adv. council, 1977-80; editor: Nutritional Anthropology Communicator, 1974-77; mem. editl. bd.: Med. Anthropology: Cross Cultural Studies in Health and Illness, 1976-88, Internat. Jour. Nutrition Planning, 1977-88, Nutrition and Cancer: An Internat. Jour, 1978-2000, Jour. Nutrition and Behavior, 1981-86; contbr. articles to profl. journals. Mem. com. man food sys. NRC, 1980-83; bd. dir. Kans. City Urban League, 1969-77, Crittenton Ctr., Kans. City, Mo., 1979-80; mem. awards com. in nutrition edn. Met. Life Found., 1983-85; pres. Assn. for Women in Devel., 1991-93; trustee U. Bridgeport, Conn., 1992—; trustee Child Health Found., 1992-2000, chmn. bd. dir., 1996-98; v.p., bd. trustees U. Bridgeport, Conn., 1997—; bd. dir. Black Health Care Coalition of Kans. City, 1993-2002, Johnson County, Kans. Found. on Aging, 2001-; bd. dir. Solar Cookers Internat., 1992-2000, pres., 1998-99; mem. Commn. on Aging, Johnson County, Kans., 1997—, vice chair Cmty. Adv. Com., Kans. City Health Care Found., 2004-. Decorated Dau. Brit. Empire.; recipient First Higuchi Irvin Youngberg Rsch. Achievement Award, U. Kans., 1982, Excellence in Academia Award Inst. Caribbean Studies, 2002. Fellow Am. Soc. for Nutritional Sci., Am. Anthrop. Assn. (chair com. nutritional anthropology 1974-77, founder com. nutritional anthropology 1974), Soc. Applied Anthropology, Am. Coll. Nutrition, Soc. Med. Anthropology, Am. Soc. Nutritional Sci., 1998; mem. Am. Public Health Assn. (food and nutrition coun. 1975-78, governing coun. 1982-85), Am. Inst. Nutrition (program com. 1983-86), Am. Soc. Clin. Nutrition, Am. Men and Women of Sci., Nat. Acad. Sci. (world food and nutrition study panel), N.Y. Acad. Sci., Inst. Food Technologists, Am. Dietetic Assn., Assn. for Women in Devel. (pres. 1991-93), Soc. Behavioral Medicine, Club of Rome (U.S. assoc.) Office: U Kans Med Ctr 3901 Rainbow Blvd Mail Stop 1008 Kansas City KS 66160-7313 Office Phone: 913-588-2770. E-mail: njerome@kumc.edu.

JEROSE, TERESE M.J. librarian; b. Jacksonville, N.C., Aug. 25, 1959; d. Robert Lee Jones and Joyce R. Coventry; m. David Arthur Jerose, June 18, 1983. BA in French, East Carolina U.; MLS, U. N.C., Greensboro. Serials libr. Queens Coll., 1990—91, head acquisitions, 1991—95; head pub. svcs. and ref. Southeastern Bapt. Theol. Sem., Wake Forest, NC, 1996—. Rsch. and libr. cons. Mem.: NASIG, Am. Theol. Libr. Assn. ATLA, Kiwanis Club Wake Forest. Office: Libr Southeastern Bapt Theol Sem 114 N Wingate St Wake Forest NC 27587

JERVIS, JANE LISE, college official, science historian; b. Newark, N.J., June 14, 1938; d. Ernest Robert and Helen Jenny (Roland) J.; m. Kenneth Albert Pruett, June 20, 1959 (div. 1974); children: Holly Jane Pruett, Cynthia Lorraine Pruett; m. Norman Joseph Chonacky, Dec. 26, 1981; children: Philip Joseph Chonacky, Joseph Norman Chonacky. AB, Radcliffe Coll., 1959; MA, Yale U., 1974, MPhil, 1975, PhD in History of Sci., 1978. Freelance sci. editor and writer, 1962-72; lectr. in history Rensselaer Poly. Inst., 1977-78; dean Davenport Coll., lectr. in history of sci. Yale U., 1978-82; dean students., assoc. prof. history Hamilton Coll., 1982-87; dean coll., lectr. in history Bowdoin Coll., 1988-92; pres. Evergreen State Coll., Olympia, Wash., 1992-2000. Cons. in field. Author: Cometary Theory in 15th Century Europe; contbr. articles to profl. jours.; book reviewer; presenter in field. Trustee Maine Hist. Assn., 1991-92, Stonehill Coll., 1996-02, Providence St. Peter's Hosp., 1997-2000; chair Maine selection com. Rhodes Scholarship Trust, 1990-92, chair N.W. selection com., 1992-93; commr. N.W. Assn. Schs. and Colls. Commn. on Colls., 1994-99. E-mail: jjervis99@comcast.net.

JERVIS-HERBERT, GWENDOLYN THERESA, mental health services professional; b. N.Y.C., July 15, 1950; d. Nehemiah (Stepfather) and Margaret Rose Campbell; m. Samuel A. Herbert, Sept. 13, 1970 (div. May 1984). BS in Edn., SUNY, Buffalo, 1976, MS, 1989. Coord. case mgr., counselor Geneva B. Scruggs HEalth Care Ctr., Buffalo, 1983—87; counselor mental health Kaleida Health, 1987—2001, med. social worker, 2001—02, sr. counselor, 2002—. Clin. liaison Women Human Rights & Dignity, Buffalo, 1993—2001, clins. cons., conf. planner Mental Health Assn., 1997. Multi-cultural diversity com. Kalieda Health, Buffalo, 1995—99; cons., presenter Strive for Women, Inc., 2002. Scholar, Neighborhood Youth Corp., Bronx, 1968. Democrat. Avocations: reading, jazz, travel, mentoring. Home: 347 Florida St Buffalo NY 14208 Office Phone: 716-859-2886.

JESCHKE, CAROL T. arts/theater consultant, real estate investor; b. Cazenovia, N.Y., May 22, 1938; d. Howard Edward Trivelpiece and Pearl Ada Chapman Trivelpiece-Duva; m. Edmund H. Jeschke, Feb. 11, 1961 (dec. July 1990); children: Edaina E., Eric B. Student, Vt. Coll. for Women, 1956; BA in English, Syracuse U., 1960, postgrad., 1966, Purdue U., 1973, Harvard U., 1976. Cert. womens bus. enterprise; cert. facility exec. Acting exec. dir., dep. dir., dir. programming & pub. rels. Cultural Resources Coun., John H. Mulroy Civic Ctr., Syracuse, N.Y., 1966-91; exec. dir. Stone Quarry Hill Art Park, Cazenovia, 1991 94; pres. CME Real Estate Assocs., Ltd., 1996 ; arts/theater cons. Carol T. Jeschke & Assocs. Founder Nat. Showcase of Performing Arts for Young People, 1979; U.S. rep. to Conf. on Arts and Culture, Austria, 1983, Arts Dialogue/Australia, 1987; founding trustee Assn. Internat. Performing Arts Festivals for Children, 1990-92. Editor: On the Dotted Line: The Anatomy of a Contract, 1979, Help! A Guide to Selecting and Surviving an Arts Consultant, 1983. Mem. Internat. Assn. Auditorium Mgrs. (hon., founding trustee, Mid Grood Perry award for creativity 1981). Avocations: art, writing. Home and Office: 433 West Lake Rd De Ruyter NY 13052

JESKEWITZ, SUZANNE E. state representative; b. Galesville, Wis., Feb. 21, 1942; m. James Jeskewitz; 2 children. BA, U. Wis., LaCrosse, 1964. Tchr., 1964—69; program dir. YMCA, 1978—87; assoc. dlr. Menomonee Falls C. of C., 1987—91; pub. rels. rep.; cmty. banking coord.; real estate broker, 1990—95; state assembly mem. Wis. State Assembly, Madison, 1996—, chair, ways and means com., mem. children and families, colls. and univs., and criminal justice coms. Mem. planning comm., Menomonee Falls, Wis., 1992—96; mem. chamber amb. com., scholarshp bd., bd. leadership; bd. mgrs. YMCA. Republican. Office: State Capitol Rm 314 N PO Box 8952 Madison WI 53708-8952

JESSEN, JOEL ANNE, not-for-profit executive, art educator; b. Seattle, Sept. 7, 1940; d. John Paagard and Anne Vilma Jessen. BA, U. Wash., 1962, MFA, 1964. Instr. Cornish Coll. Arts, Seattle, 1965—76; pres., CEO Kappeler Inst., Inc., Seattle, 1975—. Instr. U. Wash., Seattle, 1970—71, Highline Coll., Seattle, 1970—71. Author: The Imperative Step, 1972, The Physical, The Mental, and The Spiritual, 1978. Mem.: U. Wash. Alumni. Avocation: art. Office: Kappeler Inst Inc PO Box 99735 Seattle WA 98139-0735 E-mail: kplrins@mindspring.com.

JESSUP, CONSTANCE M. music educator; b. Niagara Falls, N.Y., Nov. 22, 1925; BM, Oberlin Conservatory, 1948; postgrad., Tanglewood Inst., Mass., 1965, Westminster Choir Coll., Princeton, N.J., N.Y. State U. Pvt. studio for piano and voice, Poughkeepsie, N.Y., 1952-82; music educator adult edn., Poughkeepsie, 1955-57, Regina Coeli Sch., Hyde Park, N.Y., 1960-63; choir dir. Holy Trinity Ch., Poughkeepsie, N.Y.; pvt. studio Royal Palm Beach, Fla., 1982-98, Raleigh, 1998-99. Asst. condr., soloist Cmty. Mixed Chorus, Poughkeepsie, 1955-65; soloist, bd. dirs. Hudson Valley Opera, Poughkeepsie, 1962-70; workshop clinician Fla. State Music Tchrs. Conv., 1988. Historian, editor: Reserch Music Transformations, 1983; performer compositions of Charles Gilbert Spross. Mem. Music Tchrs. Nat. Assn. (cert.), Nat. Assn. Tchrs. Singing (founder, pres. Intracoastal chpt. 1996-98, mem. N.C. chpt.), Sonneck Soc. Am. Music, Raleigh Piano Tchrs. Assn.

JESSUP, JAN AMIS, arts volunteer, writer; b. Chgo., Aug. 10, 1927; d. Herman Harvey and Anita (Lincoln) Sinako; m. Everett Orme Amis, Dec. 20, 1970 (dec. Nov. 1981); m. Joe Lee Jessup, Apr. 16, 1989. BA, U. Minn., 1948; postgrad., Rutgers U., 1969-70. Bd. dirs., mem. exec. com. Broward Ctr. Performing Arts Pacers, Ft. Lauderdale, Fla., 1985—88, pres., 1987—88; spkr. U. Internat. Bus., Beijing, 1985. Active not-for-profit orgns. including Girl Scouts U.S., Boy Scouts Am., Presbyn. Ch.; active beautification com., Lighthouse Point, Fla., 1978—89, sec., 1988—91; rep. to Fla. Art Orgns., 1987—88; bd. dirs. Archways, Ft. Lauderdale, 1987—91, Fla. Grand Opera, 1993—; trustee Miami City Ballet, 1991—94; adv. bd. Guild of the Palm Beaches, 1994—95; bd. govs. Fla. Philharm. Orch., 1981—98, v.p. representing all affiliates, 1985—87, 1992, 1994—96, exec. com., 1989—93, v.p. individual giving, 1991—92, Boca Raton bd. dirs., 1994—2002, chmn. affiliate com., 1994—95; mem. program com. Boca Raton Ctr. for Arts, 2002—; trustee Harid Conservatory, 1997—; founding pres. Harid Guild, 1997—99; pres. symphony soc. Symphony of the Ams., 2004—. Mem.: Symphony of Am. Soc. (pres. 2004—), Royal Dames Cancer Rsch. (trustee 1995—97), Gold Coast Jazz Soc. (bd. dirs. 1992—98, v.p. 1994—98), Ft. Lauderdale Philharm. Soc. (bd. dirs. 1986—), The Opus Soc. (chmn. 1981—85, bd. dirs., mem. exec. com. 1981—96, pres. 1989—93), Opera Soc. (sec. 1986—87, bd. dirs. 1986—, v.p. pub. rels. 1987—88), Royal Palm Dinner Theatre (bd. dirs. 1998—2000), Am. Symphony Orch. League Vol. Coun. (sec. 1986—87, bd. dirs. 1986—92), Nat. Soc. Arts and Letters, Internat. Game Fish Assn. (adv. coun. 2001—), Am. Symphony Orch. League (v.p. 1987—88, vice chmn. 1989—90, pres. 1989—90, advisor 1990—91), assoc. Resource Devel. Inst. 1996—98, bd. dirs. 1998—, liaison and com. mem. Nat. Youth Orch. Festival 2000 Com. 2000—), Centre For The Arts (program com. 2002—), Harid Conservatory of Music, Inc., Ocean Reef Club, Sea Grape Garden Club (past pres.), Royal Palm Yacht and Country Club Women's Club, Boca Raton Resort and Club. Republican. Avocations: music listening, boating, fishing, writing, bridge. Home: 133 Coconut Palm Rd Boca Raton FL 33432-7975 E-mail: janjessup@aol.com., amisj@bellsouth.net.

JESSUP, SARAH H. anthropologist, educator; b. Thessaloniki, Greece, Aug. 21, 1964; d. John Knox Jessup and Anne Mathews Hamilton. BA, Vassar Coll., 1987; MA, U. Wis., 1994; PhD, U. Mich., 2000. Eng. tchr. Fudan U., Shanghai, 1987—88; program asst. Com. Econ. Ednl. Rsch. in China, Washington, 1989; rsch. asst. Internat. Ctr. Rsch. on Women, ▓▓▓▓▓▓▓▓▓▓ ▓▓▓▓ ▓▓▓, ▓▓▓▓▓▓▓ A▓▓▓▓▓▓▓ ▓▓▓ ▓▓▓▓▓▓▓▓ ▓▓ ▓▓▓▓ Kong, 1991; instr. women's studies U. Mich., Ann Arbor, Mich., 1996—97; vis. student Rsch. Inst. Traditional Chinese Operas & Their Relics Shanxi Tchrs. U., Shanxi, China, 1997—99; student U. Mich., 1997—. Vis. lectr. Harry S. Truman Peace Ctr. Hebrew U., Jerusalem, 2003. Translator: An Historical Guide to Vietnam, 1991; co-author: An Historical Guide to the Silk Road, 1992; reporter Third World View WORT Radio, Madison, Wis., 1993—94. Nominations com. mem. Nat. Assn. Student Anthropologists, Washington, 1993—95; student rep. Graduate Orgn. Ethnology Students Dept. Anthropology U. Mich., Ann Arbor, 1996—97; organizer Orphan Found., Washington, 1989. Fellow, Fulbright-Hays, 1997—98, Social Sci. Rsch. Coun., 1999, Ctr. for the Edn. of Women, 1998, Ctr. for Chinese Studies, 1998—99. Mem.: Am. Anthrop. Assn. Avocations: running, travel, opera. Home: 105 Walden St West Hartford CT 06107

JETT, JOAN (JOAN LARKIN), musician; b. Phila., Sept. 22, 1960; Guitarist, vocalist The Runaways, 1975—79, Joan Jett & the Blackhearts, 1981—; signed with Mercury Records, 1981. Musician (with The Runaways): (albums) The Runaways, 1976, Queens of Noise, 1977, Live in Japan, 1977, Waitin' For The Night, 1977, Little Lost Girls, 1981, I Love Playing With Fire, 1982, And Now...The Runaways, 1978, Flaming Schoolgirls, 1980, Best Of The Runaways, 1987, Born To Be Bad, 1993, Neon Angels, 1991, The Runaways featuring Joan Jett and Lita Ford, 1998; musician: Joan Jett, 1981, Bad Reputation, 1981, I Love Rock 'n' Roll, 1981, Album, 1983, Glorious Results Of A Misspent Youth, 1984, I Need Someone, 1984, Good Music, 1986, Up Your Alley, 1988, Hit List, 1990, Notorious, 1991, Flashback, 1993, Do You Wanna Touch Me, 1993, Pure & Simple, 1994, Fit To Be Tied: Great Hits, 1997, Fetish, 1999, Naked, 2004; prodr.(by The Germs): (album) G.I.; co-author: (songs) House of Fire performed by Alice Cooper on album Trash, 1989; actor: (films) Light of Day, 1987, Talking About the Weather, 1994, Boogie Boy, 1997, By Crook or By Hook, 2001, The Sweet Life, 2003, (guest appearances): (TV series) Highlander, 1992, Walker, Texas Ranger, 2000, : (Broadway plays) The Rocky Horror Picture Show, 2001. Nominee Grammy award for best rock performance by a group for single I Hate Myself for Loving You, 1989. Office: Blackheart Records 636 Broadway New York NY 10012*

JEWEL, (JEWEL KILCHER), folk singer, songwriter; b. Payson, Utah, May 23, 1974; d. Lenedra Carroll and Atz Kilcher. Grad., Interlochen Arts Acad., Mich., 1992. Co-founder/owner Magic Lantern Entertainment, 2002—. Musician: (albums) Pieces of You, 1995, Spirit, 1998, Joy: A Holiday Collection, 1999, This Way, 2001, 0304, 2003, (singles) Woman to Woman, 1994, For the Last Time, 1995, Who Will Save Your Soul, 1996, (performs on soundtracks) I Shot Andy Warhol, 1996, The Craft, 1996, Phenomenon, 1996, Wizard of Oz in Concert: Dreams Come True, 1996, Batman & Robin, 1997, Ride with the Devil, 1999, Life or Something Like It, 2002, Sweet Home Alabama, 2002; actor: (films) Ride With the Devil, 1999; author: (book of poetry) A Night Without Armor, 1998, (memoir) Chasing Down the Dawn, 2000. Co-founder Higher Ground for Humanity, 1998—. Recipient Am. Music Award for Favorite Pop/Rock New Artist, 1997. Office: care Atlantic Records 75 Rockefeller Plz New York NY 10019-6908*

JEWELER, ROBIN, lawyer; b. Washington, Sept. 11, 1951; d. David Baer and Jeanne Carolyn (Weiss) J.; m. Laurence Donald Wiseman, May 29, 1978; children: Justin Jeweler, David Baer. BA with honors, U. Md., 1973; JD, George Washington U., 1976. Bar: Md., Washington. Jud. clk. Supreme Ct. Appeals, Charleston, W.Va., 1977-78; atty. Matthew Bender, Inc., N.Y.C., 1978-79; legis. atty. Congrl. Rsch. Svc., Libr. Congress, Washington, 1980—. Contbr. articles to profl. jours. Bd. dirs. Jewish Hist. Soc., Washington, 1996-2001, sec., 1999, asst. treas., 2000; pres. Bells Mill PTA, 1993. Mem. ABA, Fed. Bar Assn., Am. Bankruptcy Inst. Home: 10621 Democracy Ln Potomac MD 20854-4016 Office: Libr Congress 101 Independence Ave SE Washington DC 20540-0002 Fax: 202-707-8595. E-mail: rjeweler@crs.loc.gov.

JEWELL, DEBORAH LYNN, minister, educator; b. Salem, N.J., Mar. 8, 1958; d. Wesley Thomas Foster, Jr. and Mary Estella Foster; children: Tameca Chari, Stephany Sheri, Steve Winston III. B in Counseling, Renewal of the Spirit Inst., 2001. Min. Whole Man Word Assembly, Wilmington, Del., 1994—; youth leader Holy Temple Nursing Home Ministry, Penns Grove, NJ, 2000—01, missionary, 2000—01, overseer youth girls Praise Dance team; counselor family and youth Renewal of Spirit, Newark, Del., 2001—; chaplain Christiana Med. Ctr., Newark, 2001—; prayer warrior Guidepost, N.Y.C., 2001—; dir., tchr. Whole Man Word Assembly, Wilmington, 2003—. Mentor, counselor Baylor Women's Correctional Facility, 2000—, Grace Cottage Girls Correctional Facility, 2000—01. Parents adv. bd. Boys and Girls Club Del., Newark, 2000—01, vol., tutor, mentor girls youth group, 1999—2000, coach girls step team, 1995, coach 12-14 yr. old boys basketball team (Nat. championship winner), 1997; leader Assemblies of God, 1997; vacation Bible Sch. tchr., Girl Scout mother, Sunday Sch. tchr. Schofield Barracks, Hawaii, 1982—85; bd. dirs. Boys and Girls Club Del., Newark, 1995—2000. Recipient Cert. of Achievement, Early Care and Edn., Del. Early Childhood Ctr. Mem.: NCCCP, NAACP. Democrat. Avocations: swimming, basketball, sewing, crafts, softball. E-mail: burden4souls44@webtv.net., burden4souls45@yahoo.com.

JEWELL-SHERMAN, DEBORAH, school system administrator; m. Cornelius Sherman; 2 stepchildren. BA, NYU, 1976; EdM, Kean U., 1981, Harvard U., 1992, EdD, 1995. Former tchr. N.Y.C., Newark, Fairfax County, Va., former guidance counselor, asst. prin., prin.; prin. Hampton, Va., 1989—92; asst. supt. Virginia Beach, Va., 1992—95; assoc. supt. Richmond, Va., 1995—2002; supt., 2002—. Office: Richmond Pub Schs 301 N 9th St Richmond VA 23219

JEWETT, MARY (BETSY) ELIZABETH, artist, conservationist; b. Spokane, Wash., Aug. 13, 1954; d. George Frederick and Lucille Winifred (McIntyre) Jewett; m. David Kemp Coombs, Dec. 8, 1984 (div. Mar. 2003); children: Sarah Elizabeth, David Frederick. AB in Biology, Dartmouth Coll., 1976; MES, MPPM, Yale U., 1982; postgrad., Corcoran Sch. Art, 1982-83. Devel. field coord. Nature Conservancy, Arlington, Va., 1977-79; intern U.S. Nat. Pk. Svc., Rocky Mountain Nat. Pk., 1980; bus. analyst Weyerhauser Co., Tacoma, 1981; program dir. Am. Farmland Trust, Washington, 1982-83; cons. Calif. Acad. Scis., San Francisco, 1984; project coord. EPA, San Francisco, 1985-86; bd. v.p. Coombs Mfg. Co., 1996—2003. Bd. dirs. World Wildlife Fund, Washington, 1983-89, No. Lights Inst., Missoula, Mont., 1983-93; bd. dirs. Inland N.W. Sci. Tech. Ctr., 2003—, chmn. design com.; treas., bd. dirs. Inland Northwest Land Trust, Spokane, 1991-97, chmn. land protection com., 1998—; mem. steering com. Conservation Futures, Spokane, 1995-96. Mem. Spokane Club. Avocations: gardening, photography, skiing, hiking.

JEYNES, MARY KAY, college dean; b. Miami, Fla., Oct. 31, 1941; d. Nasrallah and Martha (Jabaly) Demetry; m. Paul Jeynes, Sept. 30, 1978. BS, Fla. State U., 1963. Program dir. Orange County YMCA, Orlando, Fla., 1964-69, Ea. Queens YMCA, Belrose, N.Y., 1970-73; regional coord. N.Y. State Park and Recreation Commn., N.Y.C., 1974-77; dir. health, fitness and recreation YWCA of N.Y.C., 1978-79; dean continuing edn. and adult programs Marymount Manhattan Coll., N.Y.C., 1980—. Mem.: Manhattan (N.Y.) C. of C. (hon.; pres. 1996—97, chmn. bd. dirs. 1998—2002). Office: Marymount Manhattan Coll 221 E 71st St New York NY 10021-4532

JHABVALA, RUTH PRAWER, writer; b. Cologne, Germany, May 7, 1927; lived in India, 1951-75; came to U.S., 1975; d. Marcus and Eleonora (Cohn) Prawer; m. Cyrus S. H. Jhabvala, 1951; 3 children. MA, London U., 1951, DLitt (hon.), 1986, LHD (hon.), 1995, D Arts (hon.), 1996. Author: (novels) To Whom She Will, 1955, The Nature of Passion, 1956, Esmond In India, 1957, The Householder, 1960, Get Ready for Battle, 1962, A Backward Place, 1965, A New Dominion, 1972, Heat and Dust, 1975 (Booker award for fiction Nat. Book League 1975), In Search of Love and Beauty, 1983, Three Continents, 1987, Poet and Dancer, 1993, Shards of Memory, 1995; (short story collections) Like Birds, Like Fishes and Other Stories, 1964, A Stronger Climate: Nine Stories, 1968, An Experience of India, 1971, How I Became a Holy Mother and Other Stories, 1976, Out of India: Selected Stories, 1986, East Into Upper East, 1998; (film scripts) The Householder, 1963 (with James Ivory), Shakespeare Wallah, 1965 (with Ivory), The Guru, 1968, Bombay Talkie, 1970, Autobiography of a Princess, 1975, Roseland, 1977, Hullabaloo over Georgie and Bonnie's Pictures, 1978, The Europeans, 1979, Jane Austen in Manhattan, 1980, Quartet, 1981, Heat and Dust, 1983, The Bostonians, 1984, A Room With a View, 1986 (Writers Guild of Am. award for best adapted screeplay 1986, Acad. award for best adapted screenplay 1986), (with John Schlesinger) Madame Sousatzka, 1988, Mr. and Mrs. Bridge, 1990, Howards End, 1992 (Acad. award for best adapted screenplay 1992), Remains of the Day, 1993 (Acad. award nomination for best adapted screenplay 1993), Jefferson in Paris, 1995, Surviving Picasso, 1996, (with James Ivory) A Soldier's Daughter Never Cries, 1998, The Golden Bowl, 2000. Decorated comdr. Brit. Empire; Guggenheim fellow, 1976; Neil Gunn. Internat. fellow, 1979; MacArthur Found. fellow, 1984-89. Home: 400 E 52d St New York NY 10022-6404

JHINGRAN, ANUJA, oncologist, educator; b. India, Nov. 15, 1962; arrived in U.S., 1980; BA. Smith Coll., 1984; MD, Tex. Tech. U., 1988. Intern Baylor Coll. Medicine, Houston, resident in radiation oncology, 1993; radiation oncologist John Sealy Hosp., Galveston, Tex., 1993-95, Rosewood Med. Ctr., Houston, 1995-96, Columbia Spring Br. Hosp., Houston, 1995-96, Brazosport Hosp., Lake Jackson, Tex., 1995—, Columbia West Houston Hosp., 1996. Asst. prof., clin. dir. U. Tex. Med. Br., Galveston, 1993-95; asst. prof. U. Tex. MD Anderson Cancer Ctr., Houston, 1996—. Contbr. articles to profl. jours. Mem. AMA, Am. Radiol. Soc., Am. Assn. Women Radiologists, Am. Radium Soc., Am. Soc. Therapeutic Radiation Oncology, Tex. Med. Assn., Tex. Radiol. Soc. Office: UT MD Anderson Cancer Ctr Box 97 1515 Holcombe Blvd Houston TX 77030

JIANG, WEI, chemist; b. Shenyang, Liaoning, China, Nov. 17, 1964; arrived in U.S., 2001; d. Shigi Jiang and Lixin Zhang; m. Cunli Xiang, July 14, 1989; children: Jenny, Harold. BS, Dalian U. Tech., Dalian, Lianong, China, 1986; MS, Dalian U. Tech., 1989; PhD, Monash U., Victoria, Australia, 2001. Lectr. Dalian U., China, 1989—96; rsch. fellow Monash U., Melbourne, Australia, 2000—01; rsch. assoc. Wayne State U., Detroit, 2001—03; rsch. fellow Henry Ford Hosp., Detroit, 2003—. Author: (Book) Downstream of Biotechnology, 1992; contbr. articles to profl. jours. Recipient Citation for tchg. and rsch. excellence, Dalian U. Tech., 1992, scholaship, Monash U., Victoria, Australia, 1997. Mem.: Am. Chem. Soc. Achievements include patents for peptide purification by means of metal-ion affinity chromatography; notable finding: modification of structure of Cibaeron Blue for more efficient purification of human serum albumin from waste plasma; characterized a series of signals inside oligodenrocytes that are related to neurodegenerative diseases such as Alzheimers, Parkinsons and Huntingtons. Avocations: reading, swimming, travel. Office: Henry Ford Hosp Detroit MI 48202

JIBBEN, LAURA ANN, state agency administrator; b. Peoria, Ill., Oct. 1, 1949; d. Charles Otto and Dorothy Lee (Skaggs) Becker; m. Michael Eugene Hagan, July 7, 1967 (div. Apr. 1972); m. Louis C. Jibben, July 14, 1972. BA in Criminal Justice, Sangamon State U., 1984; MBA, Northwestern U., 1990. Asst. to chief of adminstrn. Ill. Dept. Corrections, Springfield, 1974-77, exec. asst. to dir., 1977-80, dep. dir., 1980-81; mgr. toll services Ill. Tollway Dept., Oak Brook, 1981-86; chief adminstrv. officer Regional Transp. Authority, Chgo., 1986-90, fund mgr. loss financing plan, 1987-90, also, chmn. pension trust, exec. dir., 1990-96; v.p., gen. mgr. MTA, Inc., Chgo., 1996-99; ptnr. Hanson Engrs., Inc., Oak Brook, Ill., 1999-2000; sr. project mgr., cons. mgmt. Alfred Benesch & Co., 2000—02, v.p., 2002—. Cons. labor studies Sangamon State U., Springfield, 1981; bd. dirs. Chgo. Found. for Women. Mem. surface transps. adv. group U. Ill., 1997—2000; apptd. mem. transp. adv. bd. City of Naperville, 1988—90; bd. dirs. Family Shelter Svcs., 1990—91; bd. dirs., chair devel. com. Govt. Assistance Program, 1997—2000, sec. bd., 1999; mem. nat. adv. bd. Women's Transp. Seminar, 1996—2000; mem. Peoria Women's Fund Grants Com., 2003; mem. traffic seminar Bradley U., 2002—; acting pres. Ctrl. Ill. chpt. WTS, 2004. Recipient Appreciation award VFW, Chgo., 1983, award Ill. State Toll Hwy. Authority, 1986; named Woman of Yr., Nat. Women's Transp. Seminar, 1991, AAUW, 1991. Mem. NAFE, Women's Transp. Seminar (Woman of Yr. award Chgo. chpt. 1991, Nat. Woman of Yr. 1991), Beta Sigma Phi (treas., v.p., corr. sec. Naperville and Easton, Ill. chpts.), Lambda Alpha. Avocations: reading, jogging, gardening, golf. Office: Alfred Benesch & Co 401 Main St Ste 1110 Peoria IL 61602-1241 E-mail: ljibben@benesch.com.

JILCOTT, REBECCA ANN, music educator; b. Ahoskie, N.C., Feb. 20, 1965; d. Lanny Edward and Rebecca Sue Jilcott. B in Music Edn., James Madison U., 1988. Cert. instrumental and vocal instr. Dir. orch. Chester Mid. Sch. Chesterfield (Va.) Pub. Schs., 1988—91, dir. orch. L.C. Bird H.S., 1988—97, head music dept., dir. orch. Carver Mid. Sch., 1991—. Violist Petersburg Symphony, 1996; dir. summer strings program Va. Music Camp staff, 1995, 96. Mem.: NEA, Va. Edn. Assn., Chesterfield Educators Assn. (mem. bd. dirs. 2000—04), Music Educators Nat. Conf., Thespian Soc., Chesterfield Womens Soccer Assn. (registrar 1998—2000), Sigma Alpha Iota (life). Baptist. Avocations: soccer, reading, gardening, travel, guest conductor. Office: Carver Mid Sch 3800 Cougar Trail Chester VA 23831 Personal E-mail: BJilcott@aol.com.

JILES, KENDRA D'ANTOINETTE, special education educator; b. Georgetown, S.C., Sept. 8, 1973; d. James and Louise Jiles. BS in Learning Disabilities, S.C. State U., 1995; MEd in Behavioral/Emotional Disabilities, Elon Coll., 1999. Cert. learning disabilities tchr., behaviorally/emotionally disabilities tchr., nat. bd. cert. tchr. Asst. One-on-One Continuum of Care, Columbia, SC, 1996; resource tchr. Broadview Mid. Sch., Burlington, NC, 1996—98; resource/inclusion tchr. Neal Mid. Sch., Durham, NC, 1998—2000; tchr. Maryville Elem. Sch., Georgetown, SC, 2000—. Asst. mgr. After Sch. Neal Mid. Sch., Durham, 1999—2000; mem. steering com. Spl. Olympics, Georgetown, 2001—. Mem.: NEA, S.C. Alliance Black Sch. Educators, Coun. Exceptional Children (editor Georgetown chpt. newsletter 2001—03), Delta Sigma Theta (asst. rec. sec. 2003—). Democrat. Episcopalian.*

JIMENEZ, KATHRYN FISHER, nurse, patient educator; b. Indiana, Pa., Nov. 23, 1948; d. Homer Leonard Fisher and Ruth Maxine (Foltz) Barclay; m. Adalberto Beltran Jimenez, Apr. 24, 1971; 1 child, Adalberto Jr. AAS in Nursing, Borough Manhattan C.C., 1982. RN, N.Y.; cert. BCLS Am. Heart Assn. Dietary cons. Indiana Hosp., 1966-68; LPN Brookdale Hosp. Med. Ctr., Bklyn., 1970-79, staff nurse, 1982—, asst. head nurse diabetes edn., 1990—. Presenter workshops on diabetes mgmt.; presenter at profl. confs. Mem. Am. Assn. Diabetes Educators (cert.), Am. Diabetes Assn. Office: Brookdale Hosp Med Ctr 1 Brookdale Plz Brooklyn NY 11212-3139

JIMENEZ, MERCY, corporate financial executive; BA, Northwestern U.; MBA, Harvard Grad. Sch. Bus. Mgr. fin. product lines Citigroup-Global Payments Products; v.p. corp. devel. Chase Manhattan Mortgage Corp.,

Tampa, Fla., 1994—96; joined Fannie Mae, 1996, v.p. corp. devel., 1996, v.p. sr. products, 1998, v.p. mktg. Southwestern region Dallas, 2000, sr. v.p. Southwestern region, 2000—02, sr. v.p. bus. and product devel., 2002—. Bd. dirs. Nat. Assn. Hispanic Real Estate Profl., Tex. Mortgage Bankers Assn., Atlantic Coun. Office: Two Galleria Tower 13455 Noel Rd Ste 600 Dallas TX 75240-5003 Office Phone: 972-773-7444.*

JIN, DEBORAH, physicist, educator; AB, Princeton U., 1990; PhD, U. of Chgo., 1995. Rsch. assoc. Nat. Inst. of Standards and Tech., 1995—97, physicist, 1997—; fellow, and asst. prof. adjoint U. of Colo., Boulder, 1997. Recipient Pres. Early Career for Sci. and Engr., 2000, Maria Goeppert-Meyer prize, Am. Phys. Soc., 2002, Nat. Acad. of Sci. award for initiatives in rsch., 2002; fellow MacArthur Found., 2003. Office: Univ of Colo JILA 440 UCB Boulder CO 80309

JINDRA, CHRISTINE, editor; b. Cleve., Sept. 18, 1947; d. Lad Joseph and Ann Frances (Makar) J.; m. Peter J. Junkin, Aug. 1, 1970 (div. Dec. 1987); children: William Patrick, Michael Lad. BS in Journalism, Ohio State U., 1969. City reporter Buffalo News, 1969-70; metro reporter Plain Dealer, Cleve., 1970-82, assignment editor. nat. reporter, 1982-84, state editor, 1984-86, metro editor, 1986-88, feature editor, 1988-92, asst. mng. editor, 1992-2001, Sunday editor, 2001—. Mem. Women's Cmty. Found., Women's City Club. Avocations: skiing, gardening, traveling, cooking. Office: Plain Dealer 1801 Superior Ave E Cleveland OH 44114-2198 E-mail: cjindra@plaind.com.

JIROVEC, MARY ANN, music educator; b. Milw., Sept. 6, 1952; d. John Frank and Irene Doris (Spychalski) J. BFA, U. Wis., Milw., 1974, MS in Mus. Edn., 1978. Music tchr. grades 5-12 Harlem (Mont.) Pub. Schs., 1974-76; music tchr. grades 5-9 West Allis (Wis.) Sch. Dist., 1976-89, 91-93; O.M. summer ministry team Ukraine and Poland, 1992; music tchr. West Allis (Wis.) Sch. Dist., 1995—; overseas refugee worker Operation Mobilisation, Austria, Poland, Romania, Czech Republic, 1989-90; secondary English tchr. Szczecinek (Poland) Schs., 1994-95. Participant tchr. exch., Novosibirsk, Russia, 1996, Wales/Poland cultural exch. program, 1998. Music and drama teams, English workshops, Int. Messengers, Operation Mobilization local Polish chs., Ukraine, Czech Republic, 1989—, Poland summer campaign coord., 1990; spl. ministry team leader, Yucatan, Mex., 1999, 2001; vacation bible sch. leader, 2001-03; coord., praise leader Milw. March for Jesus, 1992-94, 1996-2001; Eng. tchr. ELIC, China, 2004 U. Wis. Grad. Music grantee, 1976-77. Mem.: Wis. Contemporary Music Forum (sec. 1977), Knighwind Ensemble, Delta Omicron (Wis. pres. 1973—74), Phi Kappa Phi. Avocations: international travel, cultural events, reading. Home: 6183 W Howard Ave #14 Greenfield WI 53220

JOACHIM, BRIGITTA GOLDEN, writer, advertising agency executive, media consultant; b. Berlin; d. Carl and Gisele (Zeisel) Golden; children: Nancy, Lynne, James. Student, Manhattan Sch. Mus., NYU, 1947-49; cert. TV workshop, Hofstra U., 1972, BA cum laude, 1973, MA with honors, 1976; postgrad., Columbia U., 1973-74. Cert. speech pathologist, N.Y. Election interviewer CBS News, N.Y.C., 1970; comm. specialist South Nassau Communities Hosp., Nassau County, N.Y., 1970-74, Assn. for Help Retarded Children, Brookville, N.Y., 1970-74, Beth Israel Hosp., N.Y.C., 1970-74; talent and rsch. coord. Am. Alive NBC-TV, N.Y.C., 1978-79; creative dir., writer Jim Sant Andrea Shows Producers, N.Y.C., 1979-82; pres., creative dir. Media for the XX's, N.Y.C., 1982—. Tchr. Hendrix St. Day Nursery; prof. media and comm. Touro Coll., N.Y.C., 1987—; media cons. Researcher Investigative News Group, N.Y.C., 1987—; judge radio and TV Internat. Clio awards, 1981—; media writer Writers Conf. to China, 1984; finalists judge Am. Film Festival, 1986-87; judge Internat. Film and Video Awards, 1987—, Cable Ace awards; blue ribbon panel Emmy awards, 1987—, Internat. Emmy awards, 1999. Editor ednl. film Mother and Child, 1976; scriptwriter The Chase is On, A Breed Apart, Women of Louisiana, Model of Tommorrow, Sexually Speaking, Stress, 1981-88, The New You (Physicians Med. Pub.), 1988; dir. Fitness Fables I, II & III with Tony Randall. Past pres. Westbury PTA, Old Westbury, N.Y.; active Lincoln Ctr. Theatre, Mus. Modern Art; host, sponsor fgn. students AFS; dir. Children's Video Project, 1990-91, Children's Media Project, 2000—. Mem. Brit. Acad. Film and TV Arts, Nat. Acad. TV Arts and Scis. (forum producer N.Y. chpt. 1978, mem. nominating com. bd. govs.), N.Y. Alumni Assn. (mem. Hofstra U. exec. bd.), N.Y. Women in Film and TV (bd. dirs. 1997-2000), Fgn. Press Assns., Cinema Club, Sigma Pi, Nat. Honor Soc. Jewish. Avocations: walking, music, theater, films, travel. Office: Media for the XXs 60 W 66th St Ste 20E New York NY 10023-6214 E-mail: BJMEDIAXX@aol.com.

JOB, LYNN RENEE, composer, poet; b. Huron, S.D., May 27, 1959; d. Frederick Delano and Barbara Ann (King) Job. MusB, Calif. State U., Fullerton, 1982; MusM, U. North Tex., Denton, 1988; D of Mus. Arts, U. North Tex., 1998. Lead logistics engr. Tex. Instruments/Raytheon, McKinney, 1988—98; sole proprietor Buckthorn Studios, Denton, 1998—; mng. editor, owner Buckthorn Music Press, Denton, 1999—; lead sound engr., owner Buckthorn Records, Denton, 1999—; founding writer, owner Buckthorn Books, Denton, 1999—. Player, prodn. staff Denton Cmty. Theatre, 2000—01; concert office mgr. Coll. of Music, U. North Tex., Denton, 2000—; team mem. Judean Desert Exploration and Excavation Project, Qumran, Israel, 1989; adj. instr. music and culture of China Arts, Panchiao, Taiwan, 2001; website editor buckthornstudios.com; lectr. in field. Composer over 100 musical scores; author: Windhoven: A Journal of Christian Literature, 2000; contbr. numerous articles to profl. jours. Sponsor World Vision, 1980—; mem. Greater Denton Arts Coun. Decorated Nat. Def. Medal; named Honored Composer, U. Ctrl. Okla., 2003; recipient Std. Award in Composition, ASCAP, 2001—, Composer Assistance award, Am. Music Ctr., 2001, Poet's Residency, Salmon Pub., 1999, Summer Mus. Theatre Composing grantee, Meadow's Sch. of the Arts, So. Meth. U., Dallas, 1999. Mem.: ASCAP, Soc. of Electro-Acoustic Music in the U.S., Internat. Computer Music Assn., Soc. for Music Theory, Nat. Assn. of Composers USA, Internat. Alliance for Women in Music, Electronic Music Found., Denton Lit. Soc., Christian Fellowship of Art Song Composers, Am. Music Ctr., Coll. Music Soc. (bd. dirs. South Ctrl. chpt. 2001—), Pi Kappa Lambda (officer Alpha Alpha chpt. 2002—). Republican. Messianic. Avocations: Biblical archaeology, photography. Office: Buckthorn Studios 516 W Oak St #22 Denton TX 76201-9070

JOB, RAE LYNN, state legislator; b. Rock Springs, Wyo., May 2, 1948; BA, MS in Speech Lang. Pathology, U. Wyo. Dir. Office Tchg. and Learning Sweetwater Sch. Dist #1; mem. Wyo. Senate, Dist. 12, Cheyenne, 1996—; mem. appropriations com. Wyo. Senate, Cheyenne, mem. revenue com., mem. transp. and selected water com. Mem. Western Interstate Compact on Higher Edn., mem. Am. Cancer Soc. Mem. Wyo. Edn. Assn., Sweetwater Edn. Assn., Phi Delta Kappa. Democrat. Office: 1344 Moran St Rock Springs WY 82901-7319 also: Wyo Senate State Capitol Cheyenne WY 82002-0001 Business E-Mail: rjob@senate.wyoming.com.

JOBE, ANN CONNOR, dean, educator; B Biology, Secondary Edn., Middlebury Coll.; RN, Col. St. Catherine, 1976; MSN Med.-Surg. Nursing/Edn., U. Minn., 1978; MD, U. Nevada, 1986. Asst. prof. dept. family medicine, asst. dean student affairs Sch. Medicine, assoc. dean student affairs, 1992—94, assoc. prof., 1993—97, assoc. dean student affairs, acad. programs, 1994—95, sr. assoc. dean, 2001—, prof., 1997—, asst. vice chancellor health scis., 1998—2001; instr. dept. family medicine East Carolina U.'s Brody Sch. Medicine, 1989; resident in family practice Fla. Hosp., Orlando; instr. nursing U. Nevada, Las Vegas, Nev.; nurse in neurosurgery U. Hosps., Minneapolis; interim vice chancellor health scis. East Carolina U., Greenville, NC, adj. clin. prof. Sch. Nursing, 1994—; dean Mercer U.-Sch. Medicine, 2001—. Spkr. in field. Contbr.

articles to nat. jours. including Am. Jour. Clin. Nutrition, multimedia edn. projects, Family Medicine, Jour. Nutrition Edn., Acad. Medicine, Archives Family Medicine, Family Community Health. Founding bd. chmn. non-profit orgn. Common Ground Solutions. Grantee Nat. Cancer Inst., W.K. Kellogg Found., U.S. Dept. Health and Human Svs., Am. Acad. Family Physicians Found. Office: 1550 College St Macon GA 31207

JOBE, MURIEL IDA, medical technologist, educator; b. St. Louis, Apr. 17, 1931; d. Ernest William and Mable Mary (Hefflinger) Meissner; m. James Joseph Jobe, Sr., May 17, 1952 (dec. 1984); children: James J. Jr., Timothy D. (dec. 1976), Jonathan J., Daniel D. BS, Wash. U., St. Louis, 1971; med. technologist tng., Mo. Bapt. Hosp., St. Louis, 1973-74; postgrad., Webster U., St. Louis, 1981-83. Cytogenetic tech. St. Luke's Hosp., St. Louis, 1963-65; med. technologist Mo. Bapt. Hosp., St. Louis, 1974-76, 82-84, sr. instr., 1976-82, lead technologist, 1985; mgr., clin. instr. St. Louis U. Hosp., 1985-96; retired, 1996. Mem. student selection com. Mo. Bapt. Hosp. Med. Technologists, St. Louis, 1975-78; observer Nat. Com. Clin. Lab. Stds., Villanova, Pa., 1989-90, advisor, 1991-92, 93-95. Co-author: Clinical Hematology: Principles, Procedures, Correlations, 1991, 2d edit., 1997, 8th Revision PER Handbook, A Review Manual for Clinical Laboratory Exams., 1992. Counselor La Leche League; participant Ecology Day; community rels. chmn. The Life Seekers, St. Louis. Mem. Am. Soc. Clin. Pathologists (staff asst. 1984, 86, 88, 89, 94, 95, dir. workshops 1990, 91, bd. dirs. 1990-92, state advisor 1992-96, chmn. regional adv. com., adminstrv. bd. assoc. mem. sect., Regional Assoc. Mem. award 1994, Assoc. Mem. Sect. Disting. Svc. award 1997), Am. Assn. Clin. Chemists, Am. Soc. Med. Tech. (dir. workshop 1984), Mo. Soc. Med. Tech. (pres. 1985-86), Clin. Lab. Mgrs. Assn. (chmn. devel. St. Louis chpt.). Mem. United Ch. of Christ. Avocations: travel, cooking, gardening, dance.

JOCHUM, PAM, state representative; b. Dubuque, Iowa, Sept. 26, 1954; AA, BA, Loras Coll. Residence hall dir., pub. info. and mktg. dir. Loras Coll.; mem. Iowa Ho. Reps., Des Moines, 1993—, mem. various coms. including judiciary, ranking mem. state govt. ways and means com. Chair Alzheimer Memory Walk, CROP Walk; del. Dem. Nat. Conv., 1980, floor whip, 1984; chair Dubuque County Dem. Ctrl. Com., 1982; statewide co-chair U.S. Senator Tom Harkin's Re-Election Com.; former bd. mem. Dubuque County Assn. for Retarded Citizens, Dubuque County Compensation Bd., Loras Coll. Arts and Lectr. Series, Nat. Cath. Basketball Tournament, Sacred Heart Cath. Ch., Women's Recreation Assn. Democrat. Office: State Capitol East 12th and Grand Des Moines IA 50319 also: 2368 Jackson St Dubuque IA 52001

JOCHUM, VERONICA, pianist; b. Berlin; d. Eugen and Maria (Montz) J.; m. Wilhelm V. von Moltke, Nov. 15, 1961. MusM, Staatliche Musikhochschule, Munich, 1955, Concert Diploma, 1957; pvt. study with, Edwin Fischer, Josef Benvenuti, 1958-59, Rudolf Serkin, Phila., 1959-61. Faculty Settlement Sch. Music, Phila., 1959-61, New Eng. Conservatory Music, Boston, 1965—, Berkshire Music Center, Tanglewood, 1974, Radcliffe Inst., Cambridge, Mass. Recs. with Laurel, Deutsche Grammophon, Philips, Golden Crest, Pro Arte, GM Recs., CRJ, Tahra recs., Tudor; Numerous tours, throughout N. and S. Am., Asia, Europe and, Africa; as soloist with world renowned orchs., including Boston Symphony, Balt. Symphony, London Philharmonic, Los Angeles Chamber Orch., London Symphony, Mpls. Symphony, Berlin, Hamburg and Munich Philharmonics, Bavarian and Bamberg Symphonies, Munich Chamber Orch., radio orchs. of Hamburg, Munich, and Frankfurt, Orch. Maggio Musicale, Florence, La Fenice Orch., Venice, RAI-Orch., Naples, Mozarteum Orch., Salzburg, Concertgebouw Orch., Amsterdam, The Hague Philharmonic, Venezuelan Symphony, Caracas, Jerusalem Symphony, others; appearances on radio and TV, recitals in more than 50 countries on 4 continents; participant, Marlboro Music Festival, Montreux Festival, Bregenz Festival, Mecklenburg Festival, Festival de Vallonie (Belgium), Tanglewood, N.W. Bach Festival, Spokane, Ea. Music Festival, Chambermusic East. Bd. mem. Berkshire Inst. Theology and the Arts. Recipient cross Order of Merit (Germany); Bunting fellow Harvard U., 1996-97. Office: New Eng Conservatory Music 290 Huntington Ave Boston MA 02115-5018

JOERSZ, FRAN WOODMANSEE, secondary school educator; b. Bismarck, N.D., Apr. 29, 1954; d. Joe G. and Winnie (McGillic) Woodmansee; m. Jon D. Joersz; children: Brett, Ben, Courtney. Student, Bismarck State Coll., 1972; BA in Edn., U. Wyo., 1975. Tchr. 3rd grade Deer Trail (Colo.) Pub. Sch., 1975-76; tchr. 8th grade remedial reading Mandan (N.D.) Jr. High Sch., 1976-78; tchr. title I reading Saxvik St. Mary's Grade Sch., Bismarck, 1979; tchr. 8th grade devel. reading Wachter Jr. High Sch., Bismarck, 1979-81; tchr. 7th grade devel. reading written and oral communications Hughes Jr. High Sch., Bismarck, 1981—. Bd. dirs. Rape Victim Adv. Program; founding bd. dirs. Our Kids Need to Know; state bd. dirs. Make A Wish Found. Recipient Milken award, 1994; named Edn. alumna of Yr., U. Wyo., 2003. Mem. PEO, N.D. Edn. Assn. (Tchr. of Yr. 1991, Profl. Courage award 1994), Internat. Reading Assn., Nat. Assn. Student Activity Advisers. Avocations: walking, reading, volleyball, writing, traveling. Home: 520 N Mandan St Bismarck ND 58501-3748 Office: Horizon Mid Sch 500 Ash Coulee Dr Bismarck ND 58503

JOFFE, BARBARA LYNNE, computer management professional, computer artist; b. Bklyn., Apr. 12, 1951; d. Lester L. and Julia (Schuelke) J.; 1 child, Nichole. BA, U. Oreg., 1975; MFA, U. Mont., 1982. Cert. project mgr. IBM; cert. project mgmt. profl. Project Mgmt. Inst. Applications engr., software developer So. Pacific Transp., San Francisco, 1986-93; computer fine artist Barbara Joffe Assocs., San Francisco, Englewood, Colo., 1988—; instr. computer graphics Ohlone Coll., Fremont, Calif., 1990-91; adv. programmer, project mgr.-client/server Integrated Sys. Solutions Corp./IBM Global Svcs. So. Pacific/Union Pacific Railroads, Denver, 1994-97; applications sys. mgr. IBM Global Svcs./CoBank, Greenwood Village, Colo., 1997-99; exec. project mgr. IBM/GM Web Hosting, 2000—01, IBM/Cendant, 2001—. Artwork included in exhibits at Calif. Crafts XIII, Crocker Art Mus., Sacramento, 1983, Rara Avis Gallery, Sacramento, 1984, Redding (Calif.) Mus. and Art Ctr., 1985, Euphrat Gallery, Cupertino, Calif., 1988, Computer Mus., Boston, 1989, Siggraph Traveling Art Shown, Europe and Australia, 1990, 91, 4th and 7th Nat. Computer Art Invitational, Cheney, Wash., 1991, 94, Visual Arts Mus., N.Y.C., 1994, 96, IBM Golden Circle, 1996. Recipient IBM Project Mgmt. Excellence award, 1998. Mem. Project Mgmt. Inst. (cert.), Assn. Computing Machinery. Avocations: art, gardening, hiking.

JOHANANOFF, PAMELA, jewelry designer, manufacturer, gemologist; b. Edinburg, Scotland, Oct. 17, 1964; came to the U.S., 1965; d. Samuel Cohen and Ann Merriman Johananoff. BA in Internat. Rels., Emory U., 1986; grad. gemologist, Gemol. Inst. am., 1993; MFA, Royal Soc. Art, Paris, 1997. Broker Shearson Lehman Hutton, Paris, 1986-89; market developer Comptoir Africain du Batiment, Paris, Tunis, Tunisia, 1989-92; ptnr. Ann Cline Art Objects, Little Rock, 1993-97; jewelry dir. Christie's Edn., Paris, 1997; owner PMJ Designs, Little Rock, Paris, 1997—. Mem. adv. bd. Piranese, N.Y.C., 1994—, French Friends Israeli Mus., Paris, 1998—. Bd. dirs. Jr. Guild, Paris, 1994—, G&P Found., N.Y.C., 1997—, Reps. Abroad, Paris, 1997—. Fellow Aspen Inst.; mem. Delta Delta Delta. Episcopalian. Avocations: art, tennis, horses, travel, gardening. Office: 4817 Country Club Blvd Little Rock AR 72207-4719

JOHANNES, KAY L. insurance company executive; b. Milw., July 3, 1952; d. James Ben and Evelyn (Horne) J.; m. Thomas A. Rozek, June 13, 1972 (div. Oct. 1975); m. Alexander David Bub, Jan. 5, 1982; 1 child, David A. AAS in Visual Comm., Milw. Area Tech. Coll., 1972; BS in Instrnl. Tech., Rochester Inst. Tech., 1977. Audio visual tech. Nicolet H.S., Glendale, Wisc., 1972-75; visual designer, animator Pohlman Studios, Milw., 1977-79; designer multimedia AV Centrum AB, Stockholm, 1979-80; owner, prodr. Johannes, Milw., 1980-82; audio visual prodr. Photography Unltd., Milw., 1982-87; sr. salestrack specialist Northwe. Mut. Life Ins. Co., Milw., 1987—. Chair visual comm. adv. bd. Milw. Area Tech. Coll., 1990—. Vol. Big Brothers/Big Sisters, Ozaukee County, Wisc., 1978-91. Mem. order of Amaranth (royal matron), White Shrine Jerusalem (worthy high priestess). Methodist. Avocations: motorcycles, computer web design. Home: W4802 Knuth Rd Random Lake WI 53075 Office: Northwestern Mut Fin Network 720 E Wisconsin Ave Milwaukee WI 53202 E-mail: kayj@myexcel.com.

JOHANSEN, JUDITH A. lawyer; b. Colo. Springs, Colo., June 17, 1958; d. John Carlo and Joan Elizabeth (Bischof) B.; m. Kirk Johansen, May 16, 1992. BA in Polit. Sci., Colo. State U., 1980; JD, Lewis & Clark Law Sch., 1983. Bar: Oreg. 1983, Washington 1986, U.S. Dist. Ct. Oreg. 1989, U.S. Ct. Appeals (9th cir. 1983). Staff counsel Pub. Power Coun., Portland, Oreg., 1983-86; assoc. Gordon, Thames, Honeywell, Tacoma, Wash., 1986-89, ptnr. Seattle, Wash., 1989-91; sr. policy advisor U.S. Dept. Energy, Bonneville Power Admin., Portland, Oreg., 1992-93, dir. fish and wildlife, 1993-94, v.p. generation supply, 1994-96; v.p. bus. devel. Avista Energy, WA Water Power, 1996-98; adminstr. and CEO Bonneville Power Adminstr., Dept. of Energy, Portland, OR, 1998—. Mem. editorial bd. Nat. Resource & Environ. Mag., 1992—. Contbr. articles to profl. jours. Mem. ABA, (vice chair 1989-91, chair 1992—). Democrat. Avocations: skiing, gardening, cooking, traveling, fishing. Office: Bonneville Power Adminstrn Dept Energy PO Box 3621 Portland OR 97208-3621

JOHANSEN, KAREN LEE, retired sales executive; b. Sheldon, Iowa, Dec. 5, 1945; d. Alvin Anthony and Marjory Gertrude (Kuiper) Eich; m. Pete Brunsting, May 15, 1964 (div. Dec. 1983); children: Jeffrey Brunsting, Keri Wallenstein; m. Alan Brockberg, Oct. 30, 1988 (div. Apr. 1991); m. Alan Johansen, Aug. 21, 1993. Student, Sioux Valley Hosp. Sch. Nsg., 1963-65; grad., S.D. Police Acad., 1978; postgrad., Phoenix Paralegal Inst., 1981-82. Owner Redwood Steak House and Lounge, White, S.D., 1975-76; dep. sheriff Brookings (S.D.) County Sheriff's Office, 1978-79; clk. of ct. City of Gillette, Wyo., 1980-82; child support enforcement officer Campbell County, Gillette, 1982-84; jud. asst. Wyo. Dist. Ct., Sheridan, 1984-85; office mgr. Felt & Martin Law Firm, Billings, Mont., 1985-87; owner paralegal svcs. office, Pipestone, Minn., 1987-89; dist. agt. Prudential Ins. Co. Am., Pipestone, 1989-91, sales mgr. Austin, Minn., 1991-93, mgr. S.W. Minn. Prudential Ins. Co., Worthington, Minn., 1993-94; cons. Aanenson Agy., Inc., Fulda, Slayton, Minn., 1994-95; estate planner, agt. Farm Bur. Ins. Co., Slayton, Minn., 1994-96, Prudential Ins., Slayton, Minn., 1996-97; ret. Asst. Campaign to Re-Elect Andy Steensma, Pipestone, 1990; mem. Ihlen (Minn.) City Coun., 1990; chair Brookings Summer Art Festival, 1976-79, chair, 1977-79, chair entertainment, 1976. Mem. Nat. Assn. Life Underwriters, Nat. Assn. Security Dealers. Democrat. Avocations: reading, travel, animals.

JOHANSON, PATRICIA MAUREEN, artist, architect, park designer; b. N.Y.C., Sept. 8, 1940; d. Alvar Einar and Elizabeth (Deane) J.; m. E.C. Goossen (dec.); children: Alvar Deane, Gerrit Hull, Nathaniel James. Student, Bklyn. Mus. Art Sch., 1958, Art Students League, 1961; AB, Bennington Coll., 1962; MA, Hunter Coll., 1964; BS, BArch, City Coll. Sch. Architecture, 1977; DFA (hon.), Mass. Coll. of Art, 1995. Vis. prof. art SUNY-Albany, 1969; vis. artist MIT, 1974, Oberlin (Ohio) Coll., 1974, Alfred (N.Y.) U., 1974, West Tex. State U., 1988, Yale U., 1989, Mass. Coll. Art, Boston, 1994, Calif. State U., Monterey Bay, 1997, 99; Southworth lectr. Colby Coll., Waterville, Maine, 1981; cons. Mitchell-Giurgola Assocs., architects, N.Y.C., Phila., 1972—, Oikos, Seoul, South Korea, 1996, Yukong Ltd., Ulsan, South Korea, 1996, Seoul Devel. Inst., Seoul, 1999, Millenium Park, Seoul, 1999, Nat. Endowment for Arts, Washington, 1988, City of Petaluma, Calif., 1999, Carollo Engrs., 2001, The Murie Ctr., Moose, Wyo., 2001—; artist-in-residence N.Y. Found. for Arts, 1987—; del. Survival and the Arts, Sundance Inst., Utah, 1991; del. Global Forum Gen. Assembly, Kyoto, Japan, 1993, Art & Environ., Ankara, 1997, Year 2000 Symposium, Dumbarton Oaks, Washington, keynote spkr. Internat. Fedn. of Landscape Architects, Belem, Brazil, 2002, Wuhan U., China, 2004, Art in Embassies program U.S. Dept. State; mem. grants selection com. NEA, 2000. Solo shows Tibor de Nagy Gallery, N.Y.C., 1967, SUNY at Albany, 1969, Montclair (N.J.) State Coll., 1974, Rosa Esman Gallery, N.Y.C., 1978, 79, 81, 83, Dallas Mus. Art, 1982, Philippe Bonnafont Gallery, San Francisco, 1984, New Arts Program, Kutztown, Pa., 1987, Albany Acad., 1987, Painted Bride Art Ctr., Phila., 1991; National Museum of Kenya, Nairobi, 1996—, Salina Art Ctr., Kans., 2001; retrospectives, Bennington Coll., 1973, 91, Twining Gallery, N.Y.C., 1987, Berkshire Mus., Pittsfield, Mass, 1987; group shows, Hudson River Mus., Yonkers, N.Y., 1964, Bennington Coll., 1964, 84, Stable Gallery, N.Y.C., 1966, Tibor de Nagy Gallery, N.Y.C., 1966, 68, Larry Aldrich Mus., Ridgefield, Conn., 1968, Mus. Modern Art, N.Y.C., 1968, Grand Palais, Paris, 1968, Kunsthaus Zurich, 1969, Tate Gallery, London, 1969, Vassar Coll., 1969, Finch Coll. Mus., 1971, Everson Mus., Syracuse, N.Y., 1971, Detroit Inst. Arts, 1973, MIT, 1974, 83, Casa Thomas Jefferson, Brasilia, Brazil, 1975, Pa. Acad. Fine Arts, Phila., 1975, Greenwich (Conn.) Library Art Gallery, 1977, Bklyn. Mus., 1977, 80, New Gallery Contemporary Art, Cleve., 1977, Cleve. State U., 1977, Cooper-Hewitt Mus., N.Y.C., 1978, Mus. Modern Art, N.Y.C., 1979, Berkshire Mus., Pittsfield, Mass., Newark Mus., 1979, Graham Gallery, N.Y.C., 1980, U. Mass., Amherst, 1980, Mus. Contemporary Art, Chgo., 1981, Sotheby-Parke Bernet, N.Y.C., 1980, Centro de Documentación de Arte Actual, Barcelona, Spain, 1980, 81, Galeria O'Patacón la Coruña, Spain, 1981, SUNY, Old Westbury, 1981, Rosa Esman Gallery, 1981, 82, 83, Miami U., 1981, Met. Mus. Art, N.Y.C., 1982, 83, Berkshire Mus., 1982, 86, Laumeier Sculpture Park, St. Louis, 1982, 93, 94, Teatro Contadino, Naples, 1982, Dallas Mus. Natural History, 1982, 93, Suzanne Gross Gallery, Phila., 1984, Harvard U., 1984, Stamford Mus., Conn., 1985, 89, Md. Inst. Art, 1985, Bard Coll., N.Y., 1985, 90, U. Calif., La Jolla, 1985, Ark. Art Ctr., Little Rock, 1985, Warwick Mus., R.I., 1985, Marisa Del Re Gallery, N.Y.C., 1986, Am. Acad. Arts and Letters, N.Y.C., 1986, Hunter Coll. Art Gallery, 1986, 91, 93, Stamford Mus., Ct., 1989, Albany Inst. History and Art, 1988, Kouros Gallery, N.Y., 1988, L.I. U., 1989, Blum-Helman Gallery, N.Y., 1989, Murray State U., Ky., 1989, N.Y. State Mus., 1989, Burchfield Art Ctr., Buffalo, 1990, Grand Rapids (Mich.) Art Mus., 1990, U. North Tex., Denton, 1990, Hofstra U. Art Mus., 1990, Salina (Kans.) Art Ctr., 1991, U. Houston, 1991, Crocker Art Mus., Sacramento, 1991, Laguna (Calif.) Art Mus., 1991, 94, Centro Insular de Cultura, Spain, 1991, San Jose State U., 1991, Nat. Theater, Brasilia, Brazil, 1992, Queens (N.Y.) Mus. of Art, 1992, Whatcom Mus., Bellingham, Washington, 1993, Calif. Crafts Mus., San Francisco, 1993, 94, Nat. Mus. of Fine Arts, Rio De Janeiro, 1993, La Defense, Paris, 1993, San Jose Mus. of Art, Calif., 1993, U. Pa., 1993, Salt Lake Art Ctr., Utah, 1993, Madison (Wis.) Art Ctr., 1993, La Virreina, Barcelona, Spain, 1994, Longwood Art Ctr., Va., 1994, De Cordova Mus., Mass., 1994, Ctr. for the Arts, Miami, 1994, Dahl Fine Arts Ctr., S.D., 1994, Gallery Nikko, Tokyo, 1994, 96, Soho 20 Gallery, N.Y.C., 1994, Internat. Sculpture Ctr., Washington, 1994, Pratt Manhattan Gallery, N.Y.C., 1994, Skidmore Coll., 1996, Brickbottom Gallery, Somerville, Mass., 1996, 2003, Michael Fuchs Gallery, Berlin, 1997, City Coll. N.Y., 1997, Gallery Route One, Point Reyes, Calif., 1999, The Presidio, San Francisco, 1999, Villa Medici, Rome, 2000, Mass. Coll. Art, 2000, French Cultural Svcs. Gallery, N.Y.C., 2000, Institut Francais D' Architecture, Paris, 2000, Contemporary Arts Ctr., Cin., 2002, Mus. of Contemporary Art, L.A., 2004; represented in permanent collections, Detroit Inst. Arts, Dallas Mus. Art, Mus. Modern Art, Met. Mus. Art, N.Y.C., Nat. Mus. Women in Arts, Washington, Herbert F. Johnson Mus., Cornell U., Berkshire Mus., N.Y. State Council on Arts Film Collection, Syracuse, Storm King Art Ctr., Mountainville, N.Y., Crawford and Chester Sts. Park, Cleve., Oberlin Coll., Bennington Coll., Brandeis U., U. Mass., Amherst, also pvt. collections; films The Art of the Real, USIA, 1968, Stephen Long, CBS-TV, 1968, Patricia Johanson: Cyrus Field, 1974, The City Project: Cleveland, 1977, A Conversation with Patricia Johanson, Heritage Cablevision, 1985, Patricia Johanson, Berks (Pa.) Community TV, 1990, Patricia Johanson: The Leonhardt Lagoon, 1992, Patricia Johanson: A Sense of Place, 1992, Patricia Johanson: Multilevel Designs, Aesthetic, Ecological, Functional, Cedar Arts Forum, Iowa, 1994, Q&A with Patricia Johanson, PBS, 1998, Chicken Scratch with Patricia Johanson, Petaluma, California Cmty. TV, 1999, Johanson interview The Environment Show Nat. Pub. Radio, 2000; author: Art and Survival: Creative Solutions to Environmental Problems, 1992; works include park design, sculpture, ecol. landscapes, street furniture, pavement designs, site planning for Consol. Edison Co., Yale U., Columbus East H.S., Ind., House and Garden mag., Internat. Yr. of Child Commn., Fair Park Lagoon, Dallas, Corning Preserve, Albany, Cathedral Sq., Sacramento, Pelham Bay Pk., N.Y.C., Candlestick Pt. State Park, San Francisco, Omame Project, Brasilia, Brazil, Park for a Rainforest, Amazonas, Brazil, Nairobi River Park, Kenya, Ulsan Dragon Park, Ulsan, Korea, The Rocky Marciano Trail, Brockton, Mass., Millenium Park, Seoul, French Cultural Svcs. Garden, N.Y., South Ninth St. Corridor, Salina, Kans., Lakeville Water Recycling Facility and Tidal Wetlands Park, Petaluma, Calif., Pub. Art Master Plan, Rockland County, N.Y., 1990, Ecol. Master Plan Greater Boston Met. Region, 1994—, Sugarhouse Pedestrian Crossing, Salt Lake City, Living Water Garden, Duluth, Minn. Bd. dirs. New Arts Program, Pa., 1988—; bd. advisors Artists Representing Environ. Arts, Inc., N.Y.C., 1991—. Guggenheim fellow, 1970, 80, NEA fellow, 1975, Olesen fellow Bennington Coll., 1991; Adolph & Esther Gottlieb Found. grantee, 1998; recipient 1st prize Environ. Design Competition, Montclair State Coll., 1974, Internat. Womens Yr. award, 1976, Gold medal Acad. Italia delle Arti, Parma, 1979, Townsend Harris medal CCNY, 1994, Arts and Healing Network award, 2003; named to Hunter Coll. Hall of Fame, 1987; named to Mepham H.S. Hall of Fame, 1998, Arts and Healing Network award, 2003. Mem. Global Forum Arts Group. Home: 179 Nickmush Rd Buskirk NY 12028-3202 E-mail: johansonsite@aol.com.

JOHANSSON, ALICIA BARBARA, musician; b. Warsaw, May 21, 1941; d. Boleslaw Bielik and Halina Helena Napiorkowska; m. Evert Johansson, May 13, 1972 (div. 1978); m. Kjell Johansson, Jan. 2, 1980 (div. 1986); 1 child, Sandra ; m. James McClung, Nov. 29, 1986 (div. 1995). BA in Piano Solo, Conservatory of Warsaw, 1961, MA in Musical Sci., 1968; cert. organist, U. Stockholm, 1984. Radio anchor Polish Radio and TV, Warsaw, 1959—63; piano accompanist Royal Opera, Stockholm, 1973—78, Cramer and Cullberg Ballet, Stockholm, 1974—80, Opera Ballet Sch., Stockholm, 1973—86, various concerts, Stockholm, 1978—86, Cleve. Ballet, 1986—90, Colo. Ballet, Denver, 1990—2000; organist various chs., Cleve. and Denver, 1987—; pvt. accompanist; tchr. piano and organ Denver, 1990—; organist, choir dir. Jefferson Ave. United Meth. Ch., Denver, 2003—. Performer: numerous organ and piano concerts; composer ch. music, 1973—. Organizer Royal Opera and Ballet Club, Stockholm, 1975—86. Mem.: Music Tchrs. Assn., Am. Guild Organists, Musicians Union. Democrat. Avocations: investing, hiking, travel, nature. Home and Studio: 7165 S Gaylord St E-6 Littleton CO 80122

JOHANSSON, SCARLETT, actress; b. N.Y.C., Nov. 22, 1984; Student, The Lee Strasberg Theatre Inst., N.Y.C. Actor: North, 1994, Just Cause, 1995, If Lucy Fell, 1996, Manny & Lo, 1996, Fall, 1997, Home Alone 3, 1997, The Horse Whisperer, 1998, My Brother the Pig, 1999, Ghost World, 2000 (award for best actress Toronto Film Critics Assn., 2001), The Man Who Wasn't There, 2001, An American Rhapsody, 2001, Eight Legged Freaks, 2002, Lost in Translation, 2003 (award for best actress Boston Soc. Film Critics, 2003, Upstream prize for best actress Venice Film Festival, 2003), Girl with a Pearl Earring, 2003, The Perfect Score, 2004. Office: Artists Mgmt Group 9465 Wilshire Blvd #519 Beverly Hills CA 90212-2604*

JOHN, DOLORES, architect, consultant; b. Morgantown, W.Va., June 20, 1959; d. Thomas and Anna (Marrara) John; m. Joseph Ambrusico; children: Gabriella Ambrusico, Thomas Ambrusico. MArch, Cath. U. Am., 1986; BS, W.Va. U., 1981. Registered arch., N.Y., N.J. Assoc. SBLM Archs., N.Y.C., 1986—93; archtl. constrn. mgr. Pathmark Stores, Inc., Woodbridge, NJ, 1993—96; pres. Dolores John Arch., P.C., Blairstown, NJ, 1996—2003; dir. archtl. svcs. Pathmark Stores, Inc., Carteret, NJ, 2003—. Big Sister Catholic Big Sisters, New York, NY, 1991—2001; Member H.O.P.E. Historic Preservation, Hope, NJ, 2001—01. Roman Catholic. Avocations: gardening, cooking. Office: Pathmark Stores Inc 200 Milik St Carteret NJ 07008

JOHN, SELENA LATRICIA, systems analyst; b. Savannah, Ga., Feb. 18, 1972; d. Gloria W. John. B in Social Work, Savannah State Coll., 1995; MPA, Savannah State U., 1999. Med. social svcs. profl. Meml. Health U., Savannah, 1997-98; adolescent counselor Tidelands Cmty. Svc. Bd., Savannah, 1999; grad. intern. Chatham County Fin. Dept., Savannah, 1999; logistics acct. analyst Diamond Crystal Brands, Savannah, 1999—. Intern, vol. Boys and Girls Clubs of Am., Savannah, 1993-95; vol. ARC, 1998-99, campaign com. Mayor, Savannah, 1997; coord., organizer Voter Registration, Savannah, 1998-99; vol. Buckle-up Am., St. Joseph's Candler Hosp., Habitat for Humanity. Grad. Students scholar Ga. Regents Bd. Acad. Scholarship, 1998-99. Mem. NASW, Coalition Minority Pub. Adminstrs., Am. Soc. Pub. Adminstrs., Sigma Gamma Rho. Home: 1123 Darwin St Savannah GA 31415 Office: 3000 Tremont Rd Savannah GA 31405-1500 E-mail: slj1922@hotmail.com.

JOHN, SUSAN V. state representative; b. Nov. 20, 1957; BA, George Washington U.; JD, Syracuse U. Bar: N.Y. Assoc. Phillips, Lytle, Hitchcock, Huber and Blaine, 1983—; mem. N.Y. State Assembly, mem. jud. com., edn. com., also mem. energy com., librs. and edn. tech. com., chair labor com. Chair Legis. Commn. on Solid Waste Mgmt., 1995—97, Alcholism and Drug Abuse Com., 1997—99, Govtl. Ops. Com., 1999—2000; served on First Legis. Joint Budget Conf. Com. on Mental Health, 1998, Joint Budget Conf. Com. on Edn., 1999—2000. Chair Majority Steering Com.; serves on Judiciary, Edn., Energy, Libraries and Tech. and Social Svcs. Coms.; chair subcom. Pub. Sch. Violence. Mem. Greater Rochester Assn. Women Attys. Office: 840 University Ave Rochester NY 14607 also: NY State Assembly LOB Rm 522 Albany NY 12248-0001 E-mail: johns@assembly.state.ny.us.

JOHNS, BEVERLEY ANNE HOLDEN, special education administrator; b. New Albany, Ind., Nov. 6, 1946; d. James Edward and Martha Edna (Scharf) Holden; m. Lonnie J. Johns, July 28, 1973. BS, Catherine Spalding Coll., 1968; MS, So. Ill. U., 1970; postgrad., Western Ill. U., 1973-74, 79-80, postgrad., 82, U. Ill., 1984-85. Cert. adminstr., tchr. Ill. Demonstration tchr. So. Ill. U., Carbondale, 1970-72; instr. MacMurray Coll., Jacksonville, Ill., 1977—79, 1990—93, 2002—; intern Ill. State Bd. Edn., Springfield, 1981; program supr. Four Rivers Spl. Edn. Dist., Jacksonville, 1972—2003; learning and behavior cons., 2003—. Chair Ill. Spl. Edn.; conf. coord. Ill. Alliance, Champaign, 1982-94; lectr., cons. in field. Author: Report on Behavior Analysis in Education, 1972; author: (with V. Carr) Techniques for Managing Verbally and Physically Aggressive Students, 2002; author: (with V. Carr and C. Hoots) Reduction of School Violence: Alternatives to Suspension, 1997; author: (with B. Johns, E. Crowley & E. Guetzloe) Effective Curriculum for Students with Behavioral Disorders, 2002; author: (with J. Keenan) Techniques for Managing a Safe School, 1997; author: (with E. Crowley) Students with Disabilities & General Education: A Desktop Reference for School Personnel, 2003; editor: Position Papers of Ill. Council for Exceptional Children, 1981; contbr. articles to profl. jours.; author (with E. Paula Crowley): (book) Students with Disabilities and General Education: A Desktop Reference for School Personnel. Bd. dirs. Jacksonville Area Assn. Retarded Citizens, v.p., 1993-94, sec. 1996-99; govt. rels. chair Internat. Coun. Exceptional Children, 1984-87; fed. liason Ill. Adminstrs. Spl. Edn., 1985-86. So. Ill. U. fellow, 1968; resolution honoring Beverly H. Johns Internat. Coun. for

Exceptional Children Conv., 1982; recipient Recognition cert. Ill. Atty. Gen., 1985, Outstanding Leadership award Internat. Coun. Exceptional Children, 2000; named Jacksonville Woman of Yr., Bus. and Profl. Women, 1988, Unsung Hero Jacksonville Jour.-courier, 1993. Mem. ASCD, Assn. Retarded Citizens (com. 1982-85), Ill. Coun. for Children with Behavioral Disorders (founder, past pres., pres. Ill. divsn. for learning disabilities 1991-92, Presdl. award 1985), Ill. Alliance for Exceptional Children (v.p. 1982-94), Learning Disabilities Assn. (bd. dirs., pres. 2000-03), Ill. Coun. Exceptional Children (past pres., chair govt. rels. com. 1982-95, 97-98, 2002—, governing bd. 1984-95, Presdl. award 1983, Lifetime Achievement award 1989, First Lady 1993), Internat. Coun. for Children with Behavioral Disorders (pres. 1997), West Cen. Assn. for Citizens with Learning Disabilities (founder, com. chair 1997), Internat. Pioneer Press (editor CEC pioneer divsn., pres. internat. pioneers divsn.), Internat. Divsn. Learning Disabilities (exec. bd.), Delta Kappa Gamma (chpt. pres. 1988-90, state exec. bd. 1991—), Phi Delta Kappa. Roman Catholic. Avocation: world travel. Home: PO Box 340 Jacksonville IL 62651-0340 Office Phone: 217-245-5781. Personal E-mail: bevjohns@juno.com.

JOHNS, DIANA, secondary school educator; BS, Mich. State U.; MS, U. Mich. Jr. high school tchr. Crestwood Dist. Schools, Dearborn Heights, Mich., sr. high sch. tchr., sci. dept. chair. Outstanding Earth-Sci. Tchr. award, 1992, Tchr. of the Year award Crestwood Sch. Dist., Scholarship award Crestwood High Sch. Chpt. NHS. Mem. Nat. Assn. Geology Tchrs., Mich. Earth Sci. Tchrs. Assn. Office: Crestwood Sr High Sch 1501 N Beech Daly Rd Dearborn Heights MI 48127-3403

JOHNS, JANET SUSAN, physician; b. Chgo., July 18, 1941; d. Nicholas C. and Doris Ann (Douglas) J.; m. Harlan R. Bullard; children: George, Sam. AB, Ind. U., 1963, MD, 1966. Diplomate Am. Acad. Family Practice. Intern Meml. Hosp., South Bend, Ind. Office: Purdue U Student Health 1826 Push West Lafayette IN 47905 Home: 22526 N Gernisukki /dr Sun City West AZ 85375-3045

JOHNS, MARIE C. telecommunications industry executive; m. Wendell Johns; 1 child. BS, Indiana U.; MPA, JFK Sch.Gov't., Harvard U.; LHD (hon.), Trinity Coll., 1999. Pres. Verizon Communications, Washington; chairperson Wash. DC Tech. Coun., 2001—. Dir. DC C. of C. Trustee Howard U.; mem. Fed. City Coun.; mem. sr. bd. stewards Met. African M. E. Ch. Mem.: Wash. Performing Arts Soc., Economic Club Wash. Office: 1710 H St NW Washington DC 20006*

JOHNS, SUSAN D. state senator; b. Oct. 7, 1954; BA, MA, Georgetown Coll. Mem. Ky. State Senate from 36th Dist., 1991-94; rep. Ky. State Legislature, 1997—. Chmn. senate econ. devel., tourism, and energy com. Ky. State Senate, chmn. legis. program rev., investigations com., former vice chmn. senate health and welfare com.; v.p. Republic Bank & Trust Co. Former tchr., ofcl. Ky. Dept. Edn., corp. mgr. Presbyn. Ch. USA. Recipient Outstanding Legislator award Ky. Assn. for the Edn. of Young Children, Ky. Victims Coalition, Voice of Children award Community Coordinated Child Care; named One of 10 Best Legislators in Ky., Lexington Herald-Leader. Mem. NEA, Ky. Edn. Assn., Louisville Women's Polit. Caucus, St. Matthews Bus. & Profl. Women's Assn. Democrat. Baptist. Home: 3120 Runnymede Rd Louisville KY 40222-6144 Office: Ky State Senate State Capitol Frankfort KY 40601

JOHNSEN, BARBARA PARRISH, writer, educator; b. Fort Madison, Iowa, Feb. 21, 1933; d. Lloyd Lynn and Genevieve Agnes (Peter) P.; m. James Cotten Johnsen (dec.); 1 child, Holly Ann. BA, Fla. So. Coll., 1959; MEd, Boston U., 1964. Cert. tchr., Calif. Account exec. Ledger Pub. Co., Lakeland, Fla., 1954-62; tchr., counselor Long Beach (Calif.) Unified Sch. Dist., 1965-74; owner Ednl. Counseling and Cons., Cazenovia, N.Y., 1990-2000. Mem. Madison County Coun. on Alcohol and Substance Abuse, 1986-92. Chair Madison County Cmty. Svcs. Bd., 1987-95; v.p. LWV N.Y. State, Albany, 1993-97. Avocations: writing, poetry, travel.

JOHNSEN, KAREN KENNEDY, marketing professional; b. Easton, Pa., June 28, 1939; d. Charles Edward and Gladys Swensen Kennedy; m. Henry Lehmann Johnsen, May 26, 1962; children: Erik Lehmann, Elisa Beth Johnsen Peters. BS in Bus. cum laude, Russell Sage Coll., Troy, N.Y., 1961; MS in Bus. Edn., SUNY, Albany, 1970. Cert. bus. tchr. N.Y., 1970. Sec., account svc. divsn. McCann-Erickson, Inc., N.Y.C., 1961—62; exec. asst. pub. relations Johnson & Johnson, New Brunswick, NJ, 1962—65; sec., staff writer investment divsn. Glens Falls Ins. Co., NY, 1965—66; exec. sec. to pres., sec.-treas. Glens Falls Portland Cement Co., 1966—69; fund raising, pub. relations, audience developer Lake George Opera Festival, Glens Falls, 1970—73; publicity dir. fund raising campaign Glens Falls YMCA; freelance writer, adminstrn./media/mktg. cons., 1974—; exec. asst., media dir., staff writer Kimberly Comm., Inc., Chatham, NJ, 1974—82; sales mgr. Lifelines Gifts & Cards, N.Y.C., 1982—84; entrepreneur mktg., sales and mgmt. KJ Assocs., 1985—. Charter sec. pub. relations Scotch Plains Assn. Concerning Environment, 1999—; former bd. dirs. Plainfield Symphony Soc.; sec. Lake George Opera Guild, 1970—73, Edvard Grieg Soc., 1996—2000; chair sec. adv. bd. Project 2000, Norwegian Immigration Assn., 1996—. Mem.: NAFE, AAUW (chpt. treas. 1972, comm. chmn. 1998—), Vesterheim Norwegian-Am. Mus., Am. Scandinavian Found., Scandinavian Am. Heritage Soc., Russell Sage Coll. Alumnae Assn. (class agt., alumnae admissions liaison 1995—, class reunion chair 2001, 2006), Vasa Order of Am. (past dist. sec., cultural leader, supr. children's clubs, N.J. dist., past sec., past chmn., cultural leader, supr. children's clubs local lodge), Order Ea. Star, Delta Pi Epsilon. Presbyterian. Avocations: skiing, singing, writing, folk-art painting. Home and Office: 109 Glenside Ave Scotch Plains NJ 07076

JOHNSEN, MAY ANN, artist, sculptor; b. Port Chester, N.Y., May 12; d. Michael Colangelo and Mary Agnes (Visconti) Visconti; m. David Stanley May Johnsen, Nov. 6, 1940; 1 child, David Mark. Artist Silver Point Gallery, Brainard, N.Y. Exhibited national and internationally including: Hamilton Miniature Nat. Exhibit, Ohio (miniature marine award), World Miniature Art Exhbn., Tasmania, Australia, Silvermine Guild Artists Nat. Exhibition of New Canaan, Conn. (marine award), Nat. Marine Painter Internat. show Breverd Mus. Florid, Internat. Soc. Marine Painters show Heritage Plantation Mus., Sandwich, Mass., Miniature Soc. Painter Sculptors Internat. show, Fla., Miniature Soc. Painters Sculptors Gravers Internat. show, Ga., Miniature Soc. Painter Graders Scuptor N.C. Internat. show, Miniature Internat. show Painters Gravers Sculptors Ark., Harness Racing Art Exhibit, Lexington, Ky., Allegheny Internat. Miniature Painters show, Bluefield, W.Va., Nat. Miniature Show, South Port, N.C., Albany Inst. History and Art, Albuquerque Nat. exhibit, Bertrand Russel Peace Found., Gold Medal Competition for Distinguished Marine Art, Franklin Mint Gallery, Pa., Internat. Exhibit, Smithsonian Inst., Washington, Drawings Internat., Barcelona, Spain, Nat. Exhibit, Catherine Lorillard Wolf, N.Y.C., Mural Exhibit, Schuyler Sch., Albany, N.Y., others. Recipient Spl. Mariner award, Nassau, N.Y., two first prizes Columbia County Fair, Chatham, N.Y. Recipient 1st and 2d Pl. Watercolor awards, 2nd Pl. Graphic Silver Point award, Calvatone, Italy. Mem. Am. Soc. Miniature Painters of N.J., Soc. Marine Painters, Marine Painters Am., Miniature Painters, Sculptors and Gravers of Washington, D.C. (assoc.), N.J. Soc. Miniature, Graver, Sculptors, Painters, Washington D.C. Miniature Soc., Ohio Miniature Soc., Soc. Internat. Marine Painters, Wofld Fedn. Miniaturists. Roman Catholic. Home: Silver Point Gallery Box 5 Route 20 Brainard NY 12024 Office: Silver Point Gallery Rt 20 Box 5 Brainard NY 12024

JOHNSON, ABIGAIL, investment company executive; BA in Art History, Hobart and William Smith Coll., 1984; MBA, Harvard U., 1988. Rsch. assoc. Booz, Allen and Hamilton; portfolio mgr. Fidelity Investments, Boston, 1988—, assoc. dir., 1994—, sr. v.p., 1998—, pres., 2001—. Bd. dirs. FMR Corp. Office: Fidelity Investments 82 Devonshire St Boston MA 02109-3003

JOHNSON, ADDIE COLLINS, secondary education educator, former dietitian; b. Evansville, Ind., Feb. 28; d. Stewart and Willa (Shamell) Collins; m. John Q. Johnson, Sept. 6, 1958 (dec. Aug. 1991); 1 child, Parker. BS, Howard U., 1956; MEd, Framingham State Coll., Mass., 1967. Registered dietitian, Mass. Dietitian Boston Lying-In Hosp., 1957-61; dietitian Diet Heart Study, Harvard U. Sch. Pub. Health, Boston, 1962-63; tchr. Foxboro (Mass.) Pub. Sch., 1968-2000; dietitian Sch. Medicine Boston U., 1975-77, Westinghouse Health Systems, Boston; faculty Dept. Nursing Boston State Coll., 1979-82; real estate sales assoc. Century 21, Sharon, Mass., 2001—. Nutrition cons. Head Start program Westinghouse Sch., Boston, 1979-82; instr. dept. nursing U. Mass., 1981-89, Bridgewater (Mass.) State Coll., 1982-97; mem. state adv. coun. Dept. Edn Bur. Nutrition Edn., 1981-83; participant NSF Project Seed, 1992; chmn. edn. com., bd. dirs. Consumer Credit Counseling Svcs. of Mass., Inc., 1996-99. Bd. dirs. Norfolk-Bristol County Home Health Assn., Walpole, Mass., 1975-78; presenter Nat. Social Studies Assn., Boston, 1984-85; instr./trainer health svcs. edn. ARC, 1987-90. Nominated for Mass. Tchr. of Yr., 1999. Mem.: AAUW, NAACP (life), Consumer Credit Counseling Svc. (bd. chair edn. com. 1998—99), Mass. State Dept. Edn. (adv. bd. 1995—98), Soc. Nutrition Edn., Mass. Tchrs. Assn. (higher edn. com. 1984—87), Ea. Mass. Home Econs. Assn. (bd. dirs. 1978), Am. Home Econs. Assn., Am. Dietitic Assn., Delta Kappa Gamma (journalist Iota chpt. 1986—88, membership com. 1988—92, v.p. 1994, pres. Iota chpt. 1996—98, state world fellowship chairperson, Internat. Area Achievement award 2001). Avocations: travel, bicycling. Home: 92 Morse St Sharon MA 02067-2719

JOHNSON, ADELE CUNNINGHAM, marina executive; b. Vineland, N.J., May 14, 1934; d. Charles and Lorraine (Durand) Cunningham; m. Carl H. Johnson Jr., May 14, 1955; children: C. Howard III, Lorraine Johnson Bonifield, Charles Victor. BS, Syracuse U., 1955. Owner, mgr. Avalon (N.J.) Anchorage Marina, 1984—. Mem. U.S. Power Squadron, 1968—; capt. lic., USCG, 1985; adv. bd. Bank of N.J., Vineland, 1970-75. Organizer, dir. Millville (N.J.) Youth Week, 1956; organizer Millville Hosp. Vol. Svcs., 1966, dir., 1966-70; bd. dirs. United Way Millville, Millville YMCA Swim Team, 1969-77; v.p. Millville YMCA, 1970-75; mem. Newcomb Hosp. Found., Vineland, 1981-88; pres. Cumberland County Coll. Found., Vineland, 1986—. Mem. N.J. Marine Trades Assn., Millville Womens Club, State Fedn. Womens Clubs (2d dist. v.p. 1982-84), Avalon C. of C., Cape May County C. of C., Zonta. Republican. Methodist. Home: 403 20th St Avalon NJ 08202-2103 Office: Avalon Anchorage Marina 885 21st St Avalon NJ 08202-2116

JOHNSON, ADRIA ELAINE, financial analyst, accountant; b. Louisville, Ky., Apr. 13, 1971; d. William Phillip and Brenda Carole Swafford; children: Brenlie Elaine Rhodes, Kenneth Lafranzo Rhodes; m. John Edward Johnson, June 29, 2002. BS, Ball State U., 1994. Accountant Humana, Louisville, 1994—97, LG&E Energy Corp., Louisville, 1997—99; fin./mktg. analyst Brown & Williamson Tobacco Corp., Louisville, 1999—. Contbr. poems to various publs. Pres. Sanctuary Choir-5th Street Baptist Ch., Louisville, 1999—2001. Mem.: Nat. Black MBA Assn. Democrat. Baptist. Home: 12511 Bridgetown Pl Louisville KY 40245 Office: Brown and Williamson Tobacco Corp 401 South 4th St Ste 200 Louisville KY 40202

JOHNSON, ALICE M. state legislator; b. Apr. 1, 1941; four children. AA, Mpls. Cmty. Coll., 1986; BA, Concordia Coll., St. Paul, 1993. Dist. 48B rep. Minn. Ho. of Reps., St. Paul, 1986—. Chair K-13 education fin. divsn.; mem. labor mgmt. rels., Internat. Trade Com. Minn. Ho. Reps. Home: 801 Ballantyne Ln NE Minneapolis MN 55432-2054 Office: Minn Ho of Reps State Capital Bldg Saint Paul MN 55155-0001

JOHNSON, ALLISON, corporate communications specialist; b. Pa. B.J, U. Fla. With Chem. Banking Corp., Wells Fargo Bank, Apple Computer Co.; dir. corp. comm. Netscape, IBM; v.p. global brand and comm. Hewlett-Packard Co., Palo Alto, Calif., sr. v.p. global brand and comm., 2001—. Office: Hewlett-Packard Co 300 Hanover St Palo Alto CA 94304*

JOHNSON, AMANDA A. computer scientist; b. Ogden, Utah, May 4, 1978; d. Shane J Johnson and Barbara A Brown, Richard W Brown (Stepfather). Student, Weber State U., Ogden, Utah, 1996—. Barista Grounds for Coffee, Clearfield, Utah, 1996—97; computer software technician Am. Online Inc., Ogden, Utah, 1997—.

JOHNSON, ANNE ELISABETH, medical assistant; b. Springfield, Mass., Nov. 3, 1955; d. Michael Francis Xavier and Miriam Rose (Coombs) Gigliotti. Grad., NSCC, Beverly, Mass., 1976. Cert. med. transcriptionist; cert. med. asst.; Nat. Marine Fisheries permit as operator of all comml. vessels and fishing vessels, state and fed. waters; lic. capt. USCG 100GT. Home health aide Sr. Home Care Svcs., Gloucester, Mass., 1974-76; lab technician, EKG technician, phlebotomist Addison Gilbert Hosp., Gloucester, Mass., 1976—81; exec. asst. MGA Inc., Gloucester, Mass., 1980—99; med. asst. Cape Ann Med. Ctr., Gloucester, 1983—98; med. transcriptionist, med. sec., orthopedic asst. Orthopedic Assocs. of Cape Ann, P.C., Gloucester, 1995-97. Dance instr., 1973-85. Sec. Am. Cancer Soc., Gloucester, 1978-79; polit. asst. Dem. Party, Gloucester, 1974-85; active People for the Ethical Treatment of Animals. Mem. NAFE, Mass. Soc. for Prevention of Cruelty to Animals, Doris Day Animal League, Surfrider Found. Roman Catholic. Avocations: ballet, jazz, tap, modern dance. Home: 127 Eastern Ave PMB # 135 Gloucester MA 01930 Office: Anne Elisas Profl Svcs Gloucester MA 01930

JOHNSON, ANNE HALE, educational association administrator, director; b. Rochester, N.Y., Oct. 12, 1923; d. Ezra Andrews and Josephine (Booth) Hale; m. Arthur William Johnson, July 20, 1957; children: Joy Sanborn, Randall, Christiane Brooks (dec.). BA, Smith Coll., 1945; MA, Columbia U., 1952; MDiv, Union Theol. Sem., N.Y.C., 1956. Exec. dir. Rochester Assn. for the UN, 1946-49; asst. to dir. World Fedn. UN Assns./Internat. Student Movement for UN, Paris, 1950-51; exec. dir. Citizens for Ike, Rochester, 1951-52; midwest field rep. U.S. Com. for UNICEF, Chgo., 1953; dir. Christian edn. Swarthmore (Pa.) Presbyn. Ch., 1956-57; tchr. and coord. adult edn. issues Georgetown Presbyn. Ch., Washington, 1957-72, 85—; tchr. Old and New Testament courses Madeira Sch., McLean, Va., 1961-62. Spkr. in fields of fgn. policy, religious activities, women's issues. Contbr. articles to newspapers. Mem. bd. Union Theol. Sem., 1990—, chair, 1996—; mem. bd. Madeira Sch., 1993-97, Faith and Politics Inst., Washington, 1992—, Presbyn. Women, Washington, 1992-96; v.p. bd. The Living Pulpit, Bronx, N.Y., 1991—; sec.-treas. Safe Travel Am., Potomac, Md., 1987—; founding bd. mem. Rep. Coalition for Choice, Washington, 1989—, bd., 2002—; mem. Montgomery County Rep. Ctr. Com., 1994-2002; mem. steering com. Covenant Network of Presbyns., 1998, mem. adv. com., 2002; mem. Planned Parenthood Found., 1998—. Republican. Presbyterian. Home: 10600 Red Barn Ln Potomac MD 20854-1953

JOHNSON, ANNE STUCKLY, retired lawyer; b. Axtell, Tex., Jan. 8, 1921; d. Arnold Joseph and Angeline (Morris) Stuckly; m. Edward James Johnson, Oct. 9, 1943 (dec. 1967); children: Edward M., Ronald J., Dennis L., Shawn T., Rozlynn Jan, Anne J'lynn, Kevin J, Karal Ian, Donna Lynn. BA, Baylor U., 1940; MA in Econs., St. Mary's U., 1974, JD, 1980. Bar: Tex. 1980. Claims clk. Social Security Adminstrn., Amarillo, Tex., 1940-42; asst. chief divsn. pers. Pantex Ordnance Plant, Amarillo, Tex., 1942-43; chief divsn. pers. Cactus Ordnance Works, Dumas, Tex., 1943-44; citations unit supr. Gen. Hdqrs. Far East Command, Tokyo, 1950-51; v.p., treas. Drive-Safe Corp., San Antonio, 1967-69; counseling psychologist ARC, San Antonio, 1969-69; [illegible] Ft. Sam Houston, 1969, pers. mgmt. specialist, 1969-77; pvt. practice Oliver B. Chamberlin Offices, San Antonio, 1981-86, San Antonio, 1987-93; ret., 1994. Active Am. Heart Assn., 1983—. Mem. ABA, San Antonio Bar Assn., Tex. Bar Assn., Am. Trial Lawyers Assn., Assn. Social Econs., Tex. Trial Lawyers Assn., Phi Alpha Delta, Pi Gamma Mu, Omicron Delta Epsilon. Home: 3714 Hunters Point San Antonio TX 78230

JOHNSON, ANNIE COOPER, music educator; b. Panama City, Fla., Dec. 1, 1948; d. Andrew Johnson and Jewel Duncan Cooper; m. Arthur Walter Johnson, Jr., May 17, 1969; children: Amy, Abby, Ashley. BA, U. West Fla., 1970. Music therapist Archangel Acres, New Iberia, 1983—87; music tchr. Alachua County Sch. Bd., Gainesville, Fla., 1988—. Music dir. St. Michael's Eipscopal Ch., Gainesville; accompanist Gainesville Youth Chorus. Mem.: Fla. Music Educators Assn., Music Educators Nat. Conf. Avocations: sewing, calligraphy, embroidery, bowling, interior decorating. Home: 1524 NW 117th Terrace Gainesville FL 32606

JOHNSON, ANTONIA AXSON, corporate executive; b. Sept. 6, 1943; d. Axel Axson and Antonia Johnson; m. P. Göran Ennerfelt; children: Alexandra Mörner, Caroline Mörner, Axel Mörner, Sophie Mörner. Student, Radcliffe Coll., 1963-64; MA in Psychology and Econs., U. Stockholm, 1971. With Nordstjernan AB, 1971-79, Axel Johnson AB, Stockholm, 1979—, chmn., 1982—. Chmn. bd. Axel Johnson Inc., Stamford, Conn., City Mission of Stockholm; bd. dirs. The Axel and Margaret Axson Johnson's Found.; bd.dirs. NCC Nordic Constrn. Co.; bd. dirs. World Childhood Found.; mem. IVA-Royal Swedish Acad. of Engring. Scis., Xerox Corp.; bd. dirs. Axfood AB, Nordstjernan AB, Axel Johnson Internat., Sweden. Named Profl. Woman of Yr., 1987, Fin. Woman of Yr., 1988; named # 1 of Am.'s Top 25 Women Bus. Owners, Nat. Found. for Women Bus. Owners and Working Woman, 1992, named # 4 of Am.'s Top 50 Women Bus. Owners, 1993. Office: Axel Johnson AB Villagatan 6 PO Box 26008 S-100 41 Stockholm Sweden also: Axel Johnson Inc 300 Atlantic St Stamford CT 06901-3522

JOHNSON, B. JEAN, music educator, musician; d. Kem Charles and Edith Belle Pickard; m. Walter Lyle Johnson, Sept. 25, 1965 (div. Sept. 15, 1981); children: Laurie Ann Logan, Corydon Kem, Barton Edward. B of Music Edn., Simpson Coll., Indianola, Iowa, 1961; MusM, Andrews U., Berrien Springs, Mich., 1972. Cert. permanent tchg. cert. N.Y. State. Mgr. Mfrs. and Traders Bank, Rochester; owner Jean's Music Ctr., Penfield, NY, 1977—84; vocal music tchr. Rochester City Sch. Dist., 1984—89; gen. mgr. Kurt Saphir Pianos, Wilmette, Ill., 1989—91; pub. sch. music tchr. City Sch. Dist., Rochester, NY, 1996—; sales mgr., caterer Woolard Gallery, Rochester, 1997—2001. Soprano soloist Mu Phi Epsilon, Rochester, 1987—. Singer concert soloist. Choir dir. Fairplain Presbyn. Ch., Benton Harbor, Mich., 1969—71; sub-deacon Christ Episcopal Ch., Rochester, 1994—97, every mem. canvas dir., 1997—98, choir soloist, 1998—99; com. mem. Rochester Philharm. Orch., Rochester, 2003—. Grantee, Eastman Sch. of Music, 2000. Mem.: Epsilon Sigma, Mu Phi Epsilon (life; pres. 1999—2002). Democrat. Episcopalian. Avocations: caterer, gardening. Home: 61 Netherton Rd Rochester NY 14609-4837 Office: George Mather Forbes Sch #4 198 Dr Samuel McCree Way Rochester NY 14611

JOHNSON, BADRI NAHVI, sociology educator, real estate company officer; b. Tehran, Iran, Dec. 1, 1934; came to U.S., 1957; d. Ali Akbar and Monir Khazraii Nahvi; m. Floyd Milton Johnson, July 2, 1960; children: Rebecca, Nancy, Robert. BS, U. Minn., 1967, MA, 1969, PhD, 2001. Stenographer Curtis 1000, Inc., St. Paul, 1958-62; lab. instr. U. Minn., Mpls., 1966-69, teaching asst., 1969-72; chief exec. officer Real Estate Investment and Mgmt. Enterprise, St. Paul, 1969—; prof. emeritus sociology Anoka-Ramsey C.C., Coon Rapids, Minn., 1973—2003. Pub. speaker, bd. dirs., sponsor pub. radio KFAI, Mpls., 1989-93; established an endowed scholarship for women Anoka Ramsey C.C., 1991. Radio talk show host KCW, Brookline Parks, Minn., 1993. Organizer Iranian earthquake disaster relief, 1990; bd. dirs. dist. 7 Cmty. Coun., 1996-98. Recipient Earthquake Relief Orgn. citation Iranian Royal Household, 1968, Islamic Republic of Iran citation for organizing earthquake disaster relief, 1990. Mem.: NEA, Sociologists of Minn., Minn. Edn. Assn., Women's Leadership Forum, Nat. Social Scis. Assn., U. Minn. Alumni Assn. Avocations: world travel, classical and historical novels, exotic food, gardening. Home: 1726 Iowa Ave E Saint Paul MN 55106-1334 Office: Anoka-Ramsey Cmty Coll 11200 Mississippi Blvd NW Minneapolis MN 55433-3470 E-mail: john1800@tc.umn.edu.

JOHNSON, BARBARA E. adult education educator; b. Butte, Mont., Jan. 27, 1924; d. Warner Alexander and Ellen Onerva (Hermanson) Newman; m. Harold Arvid Johnson, Dec. 13, 1941; children: Carol Johnson Evans, Beth Johnson Egner, Adele Johnson Osborne, Divra Johnson Perkins, Eden. Adult edn. credential, Yuba Coll., 1980; clear life credential, Sacramento State Coll. Nurse's asst. Kaiser Hosp., Walnut Creek, Calif., 1970-75; dental nurse U.S. Army, Camp Abbot, Oreg., 1940-42; dental nurse, San Francisco, 1940-41; tchr. adult edn. Marysville (Calif.) Sch. Dist., 1975-79; instr. adult edn. Umpqua C.C., Roseburg, Oreg., 1996—. Bd. dirs. Yuba County Resource Conservation Dist., Yuba City, Calif., 1976-80. Mem. Epsilon Sigma Alpha (pres. 1974). Democrat. Lutheran. Avocations: gardening, painting, sculpting, dance. Home: 180 Emerald St Sutherlin OR 97479-7604

JOHNSON, BARBARA ELIZABETH, lawyer; b. Des Moines, Aug. 2, 1957; d. William Frederick and Dorothy Jane (Colvin) Spotz; m. Richard Gordon Johnson, Mar. 4, 1984. BS, Grove City (Pa.) Coll., 1979; JD, Coll. of William and Mary, 1984. Bar: Pa. 1984, U.S. Dist. Ct. (we. dist.) Pa. 1984, U.S. Ct. Appeals (3d and Fed. cirs.) 1984. Patent agt. NASA-Langley Rsch. Ctr., Hampton, Va., 1982-84; assoc. atty. The Webb Law Firm, Pitts., 1984-92, shareholder, dir., 1992—. Mng. dir. The Webb Law Firm, 2001-2004; chmn. Obershenk Medallion Trust, Aspen Quality Care, Inc.; bd. dirs. Precision Staffing Svcs., Inc., Metro Family Practice. Mem.: Pitts. Intellectual Property Law Assn. (pres. 2000—01), Am. Chem. Soc. (chmn. Pitts. sect. 1995), Pitts. Chemists Club. Republican. Avocations: piano, writing, figure skating, auto repair. Office: The Webb Law Firm 436 7th Ave Ste 700 Pittsburgh PA 15219-1827 E-mail: bjohnson@webblaw.com.

JOHNSON, BARBARA ELLA JACKSON, city official; b. Lexington, Ky., Aug. 4, 1934; d. William Atress and Nancy Lee (Thomas) Jackson; widowed; children: Elizabeth Y., William C., Antojean. Food activities mgr. Army and Air Force Exch., Ft. Campbell, Ky., 1973-90; vol. various orgns., Clarksville, Tenn., 1990—; mem. City Coun., Clarksville, 1999—. Mem. adv. bd. Tenn. Vocat. Tng. Ctr., Clarksville, 1999—; mem. bus. adv. coun. Goldwill Industries, Clarksville, 1999—. Mem. Montgomery County Millennium, 1999—; mem. Leadership Clarksville, 1999—. Mem. NAACP (prs. 1997—), Clarksville C. of C., Tenn. Mcpl. League Women in Govt., Internat. Tng. in Comm. (prs. 1982-90), Order Eastern Star. Democrat. Baptist. Avocations: working with people with disabilities, voter registration, teaching Sunday school. Home: 2218 Robin Dr Clarksville TN 37042-5696

JOHNSON, BARBARA JEAN, retired judge, lawyer; b. Detroit, Apr. 9, 1932; d. Clifford Clarence and Orma Cecile (Boring) Barnhouse; m. Ronald Mayo Johnson, June 24, 1965; 1 child, Belinda Etezad. BS, U. So. Calif., 1953, JD, 1970. Bar: Calif. 1971. Ptnr. Angela, Burford, Johnson & Tookay, Pasadena, Calif., 1970-77; judge L.A. Mcpl. Ct., 1977-81, L.A. Superior

Ct., 1981-97; ret., 1997. Lectr. U. So. Calif. Law Sch. profl. program; adj. prof. Southwestern U. Law Sch. Recipient Ernestine Stahlhut award, 1981. Mem. Calif. Judges Assn., 1977-98, Nat. Assn. Women Judges, 1980-98, Calif. Women Lawyers Assn. (pres. 1976-77), Women Lawyers Assn. LA (pres. 1975-76), Christian Legal Soc. Home: 1000 Prospect Blvd Pasadena CA 91103-2810

JOHNSON, BARBARA L. retired municipal official; b. Birmingham, Ala., Nov. 20, 1927; d. Robert F. Nichols and Lula Henderson; m. Sam Johnson Jr., Apr. 9, 1949; children: William Mark, Karen Ann, Pamela Denise. Inventory acct. Birmingham Bd. Edn., 1970—94. 4 time pres., mem. com. PTA, Birmingham, 1960—70; vol. Birmingham Mus. Art, 2001; mem. Blount County Edn. Found.; host, 8 foreign students; active in mission work Smoke Rise Bapt. Ch. Recipient Citizen of Yr. award, Blount County, 2000. Mem.: Smoke Rise Homeowners Assn. (past pres.), Smithsonian Instn., Smoke Rise Garden Club, Blount County C. of C. Home: 1556 Grandview Trl Warrior AL 35180

JOHNSON, BARBARA PIASECKA, philanthropist, art historian and collector, business investor; b. Staniewicze, Poland; d. Pelagia and Wojciech Piasecki; m. J. Seward Johnson 1971 (dec.1983). Grad., U. Wroclaw. Chair., dir. trustee Barbara Piasecka Johnson Found., 1974—. Owner extensive art collection, Barbara Piasecka Johnson Collection; mem. bd. mgrs. Wistar Inst., Phila., 1989-91; mem. chmn.'s coun. Met. Mus. Art, N.Y.C., 1986; mem. adv. com. Nat. Gallery Art, Washington, 1980-91; bd. dirs. Inst. for Polish-Jewish Studies, Oxford, Eng.; mem. fine arts com. U.S. Dept. State, 1978-85; mem. strategic adv. com. dept. molecular genetics and microbiology Robert Wood Johhson Med. Sch., U. Medicine and Dentistry N.J. Trustee, bd. dirs. Atlantic Found., 1972-85, Harbor Br. Found., 1972-85; trustee, chair Paderewski Ctr.; mem. coun. Found. for U. Wroclaw, 1991-92. Recipient Heritage award Polish Am. Congress, 1989, Nat. Citizen of Yr. award Am-Pol Eagle, 1989, Disting. Svc. award Am. Coun. for Polish Culture, 1990, Award St. Brother Albert Chmielowski, 1990, Hon. Citizen award State of Calif., 1990, Appreciation diploma Min. Fgn. Affairs Republic Poland, 1991, Gold medal U. Wroclaw, 1991, Sci. Devel. award Acad. Agriculture Wroclaw, 1991, Crystal Heart award Found. for Devel. Cardiac Surgery Zabrze, 1992, Merit cert. Pres. Coun. N.Y.C., 1993, Champion of Democracy award Coll. Democracy Washington, 1993, Waclaw Nizynski medal Polish Artists Agy, 1994, Living Legacy award Women's Internat. Ctr., 1994, The Order of Saint Charles Officer decoration conferred by H.S.H. Prince Rainier III in recognition of svcs. rendered to the Principality of Monaco, 1995. Mem. Am. Assn. for Polish-Jewish Studies (hon. chmn.), Rotary Internat. (Paul Harris fellow 1988). Office: BPJ Holding Corp 4519 Province Line Rd Princeton NJ 08540-2211*

JOHNSON, BERIT BAILEY, psychologist, consultant; b. Houston, Nov. 1, 1974; d. Weldon D. and Paula McIlvain Bailey; m. Jeffrey Shane Johnson, Apr. 13, 2002. BA with honors, U. Texas, Austin, 1993—97; PhD, U. of Tex. Southwestern Med. Ctr., Dallas, 2001. Licensed Psychologist Tex. State Bd. Examiners of Psychologists, 2003. Tchg. asst. U. of Tex. Southwestern Med. Ctr., Dallas, 1998—2001, clin. intern and rschr., 1998—2001; psychology resident Tex. Pain Medicine Clinic, Dallas, 2001—03; pvt. practice clin. psychologist Dallas Mind/Body Medicine, Dallas, 2003—; psychologist Baylor U. Med. Ctr., 2004—. Psychotherapy supr. U. of Tex. Southwestern Med. Ctr., Dallas, 2003—, blind evaluator depression rsch., 2003—. Contbr. articles to profl. jours. Recipient Phi Beta Kappa, Alpha Chpt. of Tex., 1997; scholar Undergraduate Rsch. Scholarship, U. of Tex. at Austin, 1997. Mem.: APA, Tex. Psychol. Assn., Phi Beta Kappa. Achievements include research in effects of physical and sexual abuse on treatment outcomes of chronic pain patients. Avocations: theology, yoga, walking, travel, art. Office: Berit Johnson PhD PC Ste 106 3100 Carlisle St Dallas TX 75204 E-mail: beritjohnsonphd@flash.net.

JOHNSON, BERNETTE J. state supreme court justice; b. Ascension Parish, La. d. Frank Joshua Jr. and Olivia W. Johnson. BA, Spelman Coll., Atlanta, 1964; JD, La. State U., 1969. Bar: La. Law intern Civil Rights divsn. U.S. Dept. Justice; judge La. Civil Dist. Ct., 1984-94, chief judge, 1994; assoc. justice La. Supreme Ct., New Orleans, 1994—. Legal svc. atty. New Orleans Legal Asst. Corp. Bd. dirs. YMCA, New Orleans; chmn. bd. Learning Ctr., Great St. Stephen Full Gospel Bapt. Ch. Named Woman of Yr., LaBelle chpt. Am. Bus. Women's Assn., 1994. Office: Supreme Ct Bldg 301 Loyola Ave New Orleans LA 70112-1814*

JOHNSON, BETH MICHAEL, school administrator; b. New Orleans, Dec. 7, 1938; d. Carney Leon and Amy Juanita (Monju) J. BA, St. Mary's Dominican, 1963; MEd, U. New Orleans, 1978. Cert. elem. tchr., prin., sch. supt., supr. student teaching, parish supr. of instruction, La. Tchr. Holy Rosary, New Orleans, 1959-68, Cath. High, New Roads, La., 1968-69; prin. St. Ignatius, Grand Coteau, La., 1969-71; asst. prin. Lourdes Community, New Orleans, 1972-74, prin., 1974-77; asst. prin., guidance counselor Our Lady of Prompt Succor, Westwego, La., 1977-78; prin. Our Lady of Perpetual Help, Belle Chasse, La., 1978-85; asst. prin. Archbishop Chapelle H.S., Metairie, La., 1985-89, prin., 1989-97, pres., 1997—. Author: (workbook) A Study Guide of Europe, 1983. Recipient Exemplary Sch. award U.S. Dept. Edn., 1986, 91. Mem. ASCD, Nat. Cath. Edn. Assn. Secondary Prin. Assn. (exec. bd. 1991—, pres. 1993—), Nat. Assn. Secondary Sch. Prins. (pres. 1993), Elem. Prins. Assn. (exec. bd. 1974-80, pres. 1976-80). Democrat. Roman Catholic. Avocation: travel. Office: Archbishop Chapelle High Sch 8800 Veterans Memorial Blvd Metairie LA 70003-5235

JOHNSON, BETSEY LEE, fashion designer; b. Hartford, Conn., Aug. 10, 1942; d. John Herman and Lena Virginia J.; m. John Cale, Apr. 4, 1966; 1 child, Lulu; m. Jeffrey Olivier, Feb. 7, 1981. Student, Pratt Inst., N.Y.C., 1960-61; BA, U. Syracuse, 1964. Editorial asst. Mademoiselle mag., 1964-65; prin. designer Paraphernalia (owned by Puritan Fashions, Inc.), 1965—69; ptnr., co-owner Betsey, Bunky & Nini, N.Y.C., 1969; designer Alvin Duskin Co., San Francisco, 1970; head designer Alley Cat by Betsey Johnson (div. LeDamor, Inc.), 1970—74; freelance designer jr. women's div. Butterick Pattern Co., 1971—75; designer Betsey Johnson's Kids Children Wear, Shutterbug, Inc., 1974—77, Jeanette Maternities, Inc., 1974-75, 1974—75; designer first line womens clothing Gant Shirtmakers, Inc., 1974—75; designer Tric-Trac by Betsey Johnson, Womens Knitwear, 1974—76; head designer jr. sportswear Star Ferry by Betsey Johnson and Michael Milea, 1975—77; owner, head designer B.J., Inc., N.Y.C., 1978—; owner retail stores N.Y.C, L.A., San Francisco, Coconut Grove, Fla., Venice, Calif., Boston, Chgo., Seattle, London, Eng., Vancouver, B.C. Hon. chair. Fashion Targets Breast Cancer initiative, CFDA, 2004. Named to Fashion Walk of Fame, 2002; recipient Coty award, 1972, Timeless Talent award, CFDA, 1999. Mem. Coun. Fashion Designers Am., Women's Forum. Office: Betsey Johnson Co 251 E 60th St New York NY 10022*

JOHNSON, BETTY LOU, secondary school educator; b. Stockwell, Ind., Apr. 4, 1927; d. Paul Stanley Jones and Ethel Leona (Royer) J.; m. Kenneth Odell Johnson, Aug. 5, 1950; children: Cynthia Jo (Mrs. James P. Greaton), Gregory Alan. BS in Home Econs., Purdue U., 1948; postgrad., Northwood Inst. Culinary Arts, 1981, 83. Cert. home economist. Tchr. LaCrosse (Ind.) Jr.-Sr. High Sch., 1948-49, Wendell L. Willkie High Sch., Elwood, Ind., 1949-51, Thomas Carr Howe High Sch., Indpls., 1951-57; substitute tchr. Gt. Oaks Joint Vocat. Sch. Dist., Cin. Mem. AAUW, Am. Home Econs. Assn. (life), Ohio Home Econs. Assn. (life), John Purdue Club, Purdue Pres.'s Coun., Purdue U. Alumni Assn. (life), Gamma Sigma Delta. Home: Cincinnati, Ohio. Deceased.

JOHNSON, BEVERLY J. lawyer, congressman; b. Alameda, Calif., Oct. 2, 1958; d. Robert Harold and Jean Ann Follrath; m. Michael Francis Johnson, Feb. 21, 1982; children: Geoffrey Michael, Katherine Ann. MusB, Calif. State U., Hayward, 1980; JD, U. Pacific, 1986. Bar: Calif. 1986, U.S. Dist., 1986, U.S. Cir. Ct. (9th Cir.), 1986, U.S. Supreme Ct., 1996. Law clerk U.S. Atty.'s Office, Sacramento, Calif., 1984-85; atty. Law Offices of Wilance Russum, Alameda, 1986-93, Dist. Atty.'s Office, Alameda, 1994-95; prin. Law Offices Beverly J. Johnson, Alameda, 1997—; mem. city coun. City of Alameda, 1999—. Commr. Alameda Reuse and Redevel. Authority, 1998—, Alameda Housing Authority, 1998—. Trustee Alameda Hosp. Found., 1991—, Children's Learning Ctr., Alameda, 1993—; trustee, bd. dirs. Alameda Edn. Found., 1999—; bd. dirs. Alameda Planning Bd., 1995-98. Mem. U.S. Supreme Ct. Hist. Soc., State Bar Calif., Kiwanis Club Alameda. Avocations: sports, music, art. Office: City of Alameda 2263 Santa Clara Ave Alameda CA 94501-4400 also: 512 Westline Dr Ste 300 Alameda CA 94501-5870 Fax: 510-865-1882. E-mail: Bkillybegs@aol.com.

JOHNSON, BONNIE SUE, piano educator; b. Macon, Ga., Aug. 17, 1958; d. Herbert Franklin and Betty Jean (Gattis) Green; m. Michael Marwood Johnson, July 10, 1982; children: Pamela Elaine, Phillip Michael. B of Music Edn., Wesleyan Coll., 1980. Ch. pianist Lynmore Meth. Ch., Macon, 1985-86, Cross Keys Bapt. Ch., Macon, 1986-87, Park Meml. Meth. Ch., Macon, 1987-97, Bass United Meth. Ch., Macon, 1997-98; tchr.'s aide Northminister Presbyn. Pre-Sch., 2001—. Composer (tape) Unspoken Melodies, 1996, S & S Cafeteria comml., 1996, (song) Macon's Cherry Blossom, 1996. Accompanist grand chorus 1st Bapt. Ch., 1997—; ch. pianist Tattnall Sq. Presbyn. Ch., 1999—. Fellow Macon Music Tchrs. Assn. (v.p. membership 1996-98, v.p. publicity. 1999); mem. Music Tchrs. Nat. Assn., Morning Music Club. Avocations: walking, swimming, reading. Home: 4731 Leo Pl Macon GA 31210-3001

JOHNSON, BRENDA ANN, special education educator; b. Buffalo, N.Y., Jan. 15, 1963; d. William Seaborn and Mary Ellen Hudson; m. Kenneth Dewayne Johnson, Mar. 17, 1990; children: Chaz Dewayne, Jandia Ellen. BS in Criminal Justice, Brockport State U., 1985; M in Emotional Behavior Disorders, West Ga. U., 2000. Cert. tchr. specific learnings disability. Lead spl. edn. Cass HS Bartow County Bd. Edn., Cartersville, Ga., 1995—, head dept., 1995—. Head girls track coach Cass HS, 1996—2003; coord. Reality Through Reading Grant, 2000. Coord. Baby Think It Over, Cartersville, 1999—; ednl. adv. Afro Social Civic Assn., Cartersville, 1989—. Capt. U.S. Army, 1985—99. Named Disability Tchr. of Yr., Bartow Cartersville, 2000; recipient Honor Tchrs. award, Atlanta (Ga.) Jour. Constn., 1999. Mem.: Ga. Assn. Educators, Ethnic Club (founder 1990—). Baptist.

JOHNSON, BROOKE BAILEY, consultant, former television executive; b. L.A., May 12, 1951; d. Edwin Beauvais and Jeanne (Foote) Bailey; m. Peter Michael Johnson, Sept. 18, 1982; children: Bailey Peter, Lee Keating. BA, Northwestern U., 1973, MS in Journalism, 1974. Promotion dir. Sta. KGUN-TV, Tucson, 1975-77; asst. programming dir. Sta. WLS-TV, Chgo., 1977-82; dir. programming Sta. WABC-TV, N.Y.C., 1982-89; became v.p. programming Arts & Entertainment Network, N.Y.C., 1989, sr. v.p. programming and production, 1989—2000; cons. A&E; sr. v.p. and gen. mgr. The Food Network, N.Y.C., 2003—. Mem. NOW. Mem. Nat. Cable Acad., Cable TV Assn., NATAS, Nat. Assn. TV Program Execs. (Iris award), Kappa Alpha Theta. Office: The Food Network 1180 Avenue of the Americas New York NY 10036

JOHNSON, CAMILLE, media executive; BA in Journalism, U. Oreg. With Chiat/Day Advt., San Francisco, 1980-90; sr. v.p., media dir. GMO/Hill Holliday, San Francisco, 1990—. Office: GMO/Hill Holliday 600 Battery St San Francisco CA 94111-1802

JOHNSON, CANDICE ELAINE BROWN, pediatrics educator; b. Cin., Mar. 21, 1946; d. Paul Preston and Naomi Elizabeth Brown; m. Thomas Raymond Johnson, June 30, 1973; children: Andrea Eleanor, Erik Albert. BS, U. Mich., 1968; PhD Microbiology, Case Western Reserve U., 1973, MD, 1976. Diplomate Am. Bd. Pediat., 1981. Intern, resident in pediat. Rainbow Babies and Children's Hosp./Met. Gen. Hosp., Cleve., 1976-78; fellow in ambulatory pediatrics Met. Gen. Hosp., 1978-79; asst. prof. pediat. Case Western Res. U., Cleve., 1980-90, assoc. prof., 1990-97; prof. pediat. U. Colo., Denver, 1997—; pediatrician Children's Hosp., Denver, 1997—. Mem. rev. panel NIH, Washington, 1993; faculty sen. Case Western Res. U., 1988-91. Contbr. articles profl. jours. Mem. Am. Acad. Pediat., Pediat. Infectious Disease Soc., Soc. for Pediatric Rsch., So. Utah Wilderness Alliance, Sierra Club. Home: 2290 Locust St Denver CO 80207-3943 Office: Child Health Clinic B032 1056 E 19th Ave Denver CO 80218-1007 E-mail: johnson.candice@tchden.org.

JOHNSON, CAROL ANN, editor; b. Seattle, Aug. 19, 1941; d. Jack Rutherford and Marian Frances (Cole) Schisler; m. Gary L. Johnson, Sept. 8, 1962; children: Deborah Carol Johnson Erickson, Barbara Ann Johnson Lilland. Grad., Bethany Coll. of Missions, Mpls., 1962. Typesetter Bethany Printing Div., Mpls., 1960-69; librarian Bethany Coll. of Missions, Mpls., 1969-79; editl. dir. Bethany House Pubs., Mpls., 1980-98, v.p. editl., 1998—. Avocations: reading, sewing, tennis, bicycling, cooking, hiking. E-mail: carol.johnson@bethanyhouse.com.

JOHNSON, CAROL R. school system administrator; BA in Elem. Edn., Fisk U., 1969; MA in Curriculum and Instrn., U. Minn., 1980, D in Edn. Policy and Adminstrn., 1997. Elem. tchr. Washington Pub. Schs., 1969; elem. tchr., coord. career opportunities Mpls. Pub. Schs., 1970-76; coord. R&D, project dir. tng. urban educators U. Minn., Mpls., 1976-86; prin., asst. prin. elem. schs. Mpls. Pub. Schs., 1986-89, asst. to assoc. supt. elem. edn., assoc. supt., 1989-95; supt. St. Louis Park (Minn.) Schs., 1995-97, Mpls. Pub. Schs., 1997—. Spkr. in field. Bd. dirs. The Found., Health Sys. Minn., Boy Scouts Am. Viking Coun., adv. com. Learning for Life; commn. mem. Golden Valley Police, Civil Svc., 1990—, chair, 1994-95, U. Minn. Alumni Assn., comm. and fin. com. Bush Leadership fellow, 1993-94; recipient Apple for Teacher award Iota Phi Lambda, 1992-93, Leadership award Omega Psi Phi, 1996. Mem. ASCD (Minn. chpt.), NAS/Nat. Rsch. Coun. (strategic edn. rsch. program feasibility study 1996—), Am. Assn. Sch. Adminstrs., Minn. Assn. Sch. Adminstrs. (edn. policy com. 1996-97), LWV Golden Valley, Mpls. Links, Inc. (St. Paul chpt.), Jack and Jill, Inc. (Mpls. chpt.), Children First Exec. Com. and Vision Team St. Louis Park, Delta Sigma Theta. Home: 416 Turnpike Rd Golden Valley MN 55416-1155 Office: Mpls Pub Schs 807 Broadway St NE Minneapolis MN 55413-2332 Fax: 612-627-2005; 612-541-0080.

JOHNSON, CAROLE JEAN, investment company executive; b. Temple, Tex., June 5, 1959; d. Lloyd Melvin Johnson and Shirley Faye (Bruss) Druley; 1 child, James Adam. AA, NE Wis. Tech. Coll., 1988. Bookkeeper, sec. White House Music, Waukesha, Wis., 1976-77; acct. Lamplight Farms, Brookfield, Wis., 1979; prodn. clk. W.A. Krueger, Brookfield, Wis., 1979-80; data processing asst. Video Images, West Allis, Wis., 1980-85; adminstrn. asst. Jones Intercable, Brookfield, 1985; computer programmer Anamax Corp., Green Bay, Wis., 1988-89; quality assurance analyst Nielsen Mktg. Rsch., Green Bay, Wis., 1989; applications programmer N.E. Wis. Tech. Coll., Green Bay, 1990—95; programmer/analyst Fabry Glove & Mitten Co., Green Bay, 1995-96; tech. svcs. mgr. Technology Cons. Corp., Green Bay, 1996—2001; pres. Strategic Property Investments, Thornton, Colo., 2001—. Roman Catholic. Office: 4011 E 129th Way Thornton CO 80241

JOHNSON, CAROLE A. writer, artist; b. L.A., Calif., Nov. 19, 1952; d. Wilson Henry and Beverly Boswell Albertson; m. Alan Norman O'Kain, Apr. 1976 (div. Aug. 1984); m. Geary Francis Johnson, May 14, 1985. Student, San Diego State U., 1972; BA, UCLA, 1974; student, L.A. Sch. for Bus., 1974—76. Receptionist/sec. Kaufman & Broad Home Sys., L.A., 1974—76; mgr. for prodn. and sales Melles Griot Indsl. Lenses, New Port Beach, Calif., 1976—82; leasing sec. Santa Anita Devel. Corp, Newport Beach, Calif., 1982—84; law sec. Geary F. Johnson, Esq., Pacific Palisades, Calif., 1986—88; sec./receptionist MacGuard Security, Pacific Palisades, Calif., 1990—94. Author: (poetry in 22 anthologies) in Nat. Libr. Poetry (Best Elite Poets, 2000, 2001, 2002), (short stories) Tickled By Thunder (Yr.'s Best Fiction, 1997), of numerous editls., novels; writer: of numerous songs. Recipient Bronze medallion, Internat. Libr. of Poetry, Pres.'s award for Lit. Excellence, Iliad Press, Twelve Editor's Choice, Internat. Libr. of Poetry, Best Outstanding Poets, Amherst Soc., 1999, Outstanding Achievement in Poetry Silver award Cup. Mem.: Am. Screenwriters Assn., Songwriters Am., Internat. Soc. Poets, Newport Beach Jr. League Calif., UCLA Alumnus, Nat. Authors Registry, Nat. Charity League, Assistance League Calif., Nat. Home Gardening Club. Avocations: photography, needlework. Home: 6413 Firebrand St Los Angeles CA 90045-1208

JOHNSON, CAROLINE JANICE, insurance company executive; b. Chgo., Jan. 6, 1941; d. LeRoy Paine and Johnetta Louise (Brock) Collins; m. Charles Robert Rice (divorced); 1 child, Robert Michael; m. James Arthur Lunningham (divorced); 1 child, Mark LeRoy; m. George Bolds (div. 1970); 1 child, Troy Andrew; m. Howard Edward Johnson Sr., May 4, 1985 (separated 1997). Sec. Roosevelt U., Chgo., 1959-60; police steno Chgo. Police Dept., Chgo., 1960-62; sec., dental asst. Dr. Lucien Holman, Joliet, Ill., 1962-64; sec. Amoco Chems., Joliet, Ill., 1964-68; ins. sales Allstate, Joliet, Ill., 1978-85; dept. mgr., ins. sales Beneficial Ins. Co., Chgo., 1985-86; agy. mgr. Heritage Agy. Inc., Chgo., 1987-88; owner Ins. Coun., Inc., Chgo., 1988—. Mem. Chgo. Assn. Ins. Women (bd. dirs. communication Chgo. chpt. 1989—), Internat. Horsemen's League (Chgo. pres. 1987-88, 97—, bus. mgr. 1988-97, pres. 1997—). Democrat. Avocation: riding and showing horses. Home: 18100 Lawndale Ave Homewood IL 60430-2616 Office: 2010 S Wabash Ave Ste 2R Chicago IL 60616-1779

JOHNSON, CAROLYN M. librarian, writer; b. Bklyn., Apr. 3, 1949; AA in Liberal Arts, Queensborough C.C., Bayside, N.Y., 1970, BA in English and Am. Lit., Hunter Coll., 1973; M Libr. and Info. Sci., St. John's U., Jamaica, NY, 1975, MA in English and Am. Lit., 1980. Cataloging libr. Pace U. Libr., N.Y.C., 1978—79, N.Y. Bot. Garden Libr., Bronx Park, NY, 1979—81; libr., web rschr., writer Greenwood Press, Westport, Conn., 1980—2002, Librs. Unltd. divsn. Greenwood Pub. Group, Westport, 2002—. Online libr., ednl. writer THE BOOK BAG on Am. Online, N.Y.C., 1996—2001; web site rschr., evaluator, site summary writer studyweb.com, San Diego, 1999—2000; web site evaluator Ctr. for Montessori Tchr. Edn., White Plains, NY, 1997—99. Author: Discovering Nature with Young People: An Annotated Bibliography and Selection Guide, 1987, Using Internet Primary Sources to Teach Critical Thinking Skills in the Sciences, 2003; contbr. articles to profl. jours., articles to lit. mags. Mem.: Soc. Children's Book Writers and Illustrators. Avocations: photography, reading, genealogy, classical music. E-mail: WriterLibr@aol.com.

JOHNSON, CARYN ELAINE See GOLDBERG, WHOOPI

JOHNSON, CATHERINE GRAHAM, religious organization administrator; b. Athens, Greece, Aug. 15, 1965; d. Henry L. Graham Jr. and Patricia Q. Graham; m. Paul C. Johnson, Aug. 17, 1991. BS in Biology, U. Scranton, 1987; MA in Religious Studies, Villanova U., 1991. Dir. ministry Merion Mercy Acad., Merion Station, Pa., 1991—; exec. co-dir. Heartful Ministries, Inc., Aston, Pa., 2002—. Mem. adv. bd. Cabrini Mission Corps, Radnor, Pa., 2003—. Author: Give Your Gifts: 40 More Prayer Services for Young People. Named Apostle to Youth, Archdiocese Phila., Office Youth and Young Adults, 1999—2000; named to Wall Fame, U. Scranton Athletic Dept., 1999. Mem.: Nat. Assn. Pastoral Musicians. Home: 315 Brookmead Dr Cherry Hill NJ 08034 Office Phone: 610-358-4210. Personal E-mail: cathj315@aol.com.

JOHNSON, CHARLENE ELIZABETH, adult education educator, language arts consultant, educator; b. Aurora, Ill., June 7, 1933; d. Floyd Clark and Marion Priscilla Smith; m. Bennett F. Johnson, July 25, 1955 (div. 1961); children: Roderick Julian, Marshall Floyd. BSE, Butler U., 1960, MSE, 1968, EdS, 1982; EdD in Leadership Early & Mid Childhood, Nova U., 1992. Classroom tchr. Indpls. Pub. Schs., 1960-68, reading tchr., 1968-71, lang. arts cons., 1972-82, reading tchr., 1982-90. Condr. parent workshops in reading Flanner House, 1980, 4 parent workshops, N.E. orgns., 1988; conducted workshops for Even Start Parents, 1990-92; adult edn. tchr. Even Start Family Literacy Program, 1990-99, ret., 1999. Author: Parent Primer, 1979. Instrumentalist Butler U. Orch., 1971-92, Christian Ch. String Ensemble, Indpls. Philharm. Orch., bd. dirs. 1995; trainer reading tutors Pub. Housing Authority; vol. Ptnrs. in Edn., Harshman Jr. H.S. Mem. NEA, NAACP, Nat. Assn. Edn. Young Children, Internat. Reading Assn., Indpls. Reading Assn., Ind. Reading Assn., Nat. Coun. Negro Women, Indpls. Edn. Assn., Ind. State Tchrs. Assn., Indian Assn. for Edn. Young Children, Midwest Assn. Edn. of Young Children, Nat. Assn. for Edn. of Young Children, Delta Sigma Theta, Sigma Alpha Iota, Phi Delta Kappa.

JOHNSON, CHERI MARIE, writer, humanities educator; b. Salida, Colo., Oct. 9, 1976; d. Robert Oliver Johnson and Carolyn Johson. BA in English, Augsburg Coll., 1999; MA English, Creative Writing, Hollin U., 2001. Libr. asst. Blake Sch., Mpls., 1999—2000; pvt. tutor Austin, Tex., 2001—02; instr. English Univ. Minn., Mpls., 2002—. Author poetry to profl. publ., (short stories) Touchstone, 2003, Clare, 2003. Recipient Gertude Claytor Prize for Poetry, Hollins Univ., 2001, Andrew James Purdy Short Fiction Prize, 2001, Gesell award for fiction, Univ. Minn., 2003. Green Party. Avocations: reading, baking, walking. Office: Univ Minn 207 Ch St Lind Hall Minneapolis MN 55414

JOHNSON, CHERYL L. labor association administrator, activist; b. Toledo, July 23, 1946; d. James L. and Isabelle M. (Lorenz) Byers; m. Glen N. cook, Apr. 15, 1965 (div. July 1970); m. Larry W. Johnson, Sept. 9, 1979. Grad. high sch., Toledo. Switchboard operator Rumpf Answering Svc., Toledo, 1962-64; bank teller, loan officer United Savs. and Loan, Toledo, 1964-66; bookkeeper, receptionist Main Line Distbrs., Toledo, 1966-69; clk., office mgr. Toledo Teamsters Fed. Credit Union, 1969-74, treas., 1974-85; polit. action coord., state coord. Teamsters local union, Toledo, 1980—; pres. Internat. Teamsters Women's Caucus, U.S. and Can., 1995—; trustee Teamsters Local 20, Toledo, 1997-99; dir. human rights com. Internat. Brotherhood of Teamsters, 1999—. Del. to Dem. Nat. Conv., Chgo., 1996. Mem. United Way pvt. industry coun., mental health bd., hypertension bd.; mem. City of Toledo Planning Commn., Toledo Northwest Ohio Food Bank, Mayor's Coun. on Drugs, Boy Scouts Am., Lucas County Children Svcs. Bd., Vets. Cmty. Found. Democrat. Lutheran. Avocations: reading, travel, entertaining. Office: Teamsters Local #20 435 S Hawley St Toledo OH 43609-2398

JOHNSON, CHERYL L. nursing administrator; 1 child, Nikki. BSN, U. Mich., 1972. Critical care nurse U. Mich. Health Systems, Ann Arbor; pres., chair United Am. Nurses, 1999—. Mem. AFL-CIO Exec. Coun. Named one of 100 Most Powerful People in Health CAre, Modern Healthcare mag., 2003. Mem.: U. Mich. Profl. Nurse Coun. (chair, vice-chair), Mich. Nurses Assn. (pres. 2003—, former v.p., pres. Washtenaw-Livingston-Monroe chpt.). Office: United Am Nurses 600 Maryland Ave NW Ste 100W Washington DC 20024 Business E-Mail: UANinfo@uannurse.org.

JOHNSON, CLAUDIA ANDERSON, psychologist, Jungian analyst, educator; b. Duluth, Minn., June 15, 1940; d. Carl Engwald and Irma Rose (Seymour) Anderson; m. Giles C. Upshur Jr.; children: Jean Marie, Julie Ann. BA summa cum laude, U. Minn., 1968; MA, U. Utah, 1971, PhD, 1974. Surveyor Joint Commn. on Accreditation of Hosps. Orgn., Chgo., 1978—80; pvt. practice Roanoke, Va., 1981—91, Richmond, 1991—97, Woodbridge, 1997—2003, Franktown, 2003—. Quality assurance coord. VA Med. Ctr., Salem, Va., 1980-85; asst. prof. Med. Coll. Va., 1991-96; instr. Eastern Shore C.C., 2004—. Mem. Inter Regional Soc. Jungian Analysts (candidate rep. 1996-97). Avocations: reading, gardening, writing, fishing. Home: 8470 Creek St Franktown VA 23354

JOHNSON, CONSTANCE GREEN, health facility administrator; b. Laurel, Del., Aug. 20, 1941; d. Emerson and Rosalie Dricella (Brooks) Green; (div. 1966; div. 1979); m. Charles Bassett Johnson, Aug. 2, 1986; children: Hope Vaughn Brown, Patricia Ann Moody. MS, Wilmington Coll., 1996. Cert. nuclear med. technologist. Nuclear med. technologist Wilmington (Del.) Med. Ctr., 1968-73; chief technologist Wilmington Vets. Med. Ctr., 1974-97; health administrator Prison Health Svcs., Wilmington, 1997—. Fundraising chairperson Coalition of 100 Black Women, Wilmington, 1995—, Alpha Kappa Alpha, Wilmington, 1996—; bd. dirs. Layton Home, Wilmington, 1996—, Sister in Session, Wilmington, 1996—. Mem. AAUW, Am. Assn. Clin. Pathology. Democrat. Home: 530 Ruxton Dr Wilmington DE 19809-2830

JOHNSON, CORNELIA, city sheriff, gift shop owner; b. Charlottesville, Va., Sept. 14, 1943; d. Murry McKinley and Ellen Marie (Williams) Dowell; m. Willie Davis Johnson, Nov. 22, 1970 (div. June 1984); 1 chlid, Carmelita Annette Johnson Fields; m. James Parham Robinson III, Dec. 10, 1985. Cert., Blue Ridge Coll., Wyers Cave, Va., 1976, Jefferson Nat. Bank Sch., Charlottesville, 1995. Law enforcement officer Charlottesville Police Dept., 1976-98; mgr., owner Dynasty Gift Shop, Charlottesville, 1985-99; sheriff Charlottesville City Sheriffs Office, 1998—. Bd. dirs. Charlottesville Hist. Soc., 1994—, Oratorio Soc., Charlottesville, 1995—, PVCC C.C., Charlottesville, 1993—; mem. Regional Jail Bd., 1998—; pres. Charlottesville Minority Bus., 1993-95. Recipient Women First award City of Charlottesville, 1999. Mem. Exch. Club, Bus. and Profl. Women. Democrat. Baptist. Avocations: tennis, entertaining, travel, visiting historical sites. Home: 1100 Hilltop Rd Charlottesville VA 22903-1221 Office: Charlottesville Sheriff Office 315 E High St Charlottesville VA 22902-5118

JOHNSON, CRYSTAL DUANE, psychologist; b. Houston, Mar. 2, 1954; d. Alton Floyd and Duane (Mullican) J.; m. Donald Beecher Hart, Mar. 21, 1989. BA, U. Tex., 1983, MS, 1985. Lic. profl. counselor, psychol. assoc., marriage and family therapist, specialist in sch. psychology, cert. chem. dependency specialist. Student devel. specialist U. Tex., Tyler, 1985-86, intake counselor, 1986-88; staff psychologist Sabine Valley Ctr., Longview, Tex., 1987-88, Mental Health/Mental Retardation Ctr. of East Tex., Tyler, 1988-89; pvt. practice psychologist Tyler, 1989—. Counselor Juvenile and Adult Probation Depts., 1988—, ICF/MR Resdl. Homes, 1991—, Children's Advocacy Ctr., 2000—; spl. edn. counselor, 1990—. Mem. Smith County Humane Soc., Tyler, 1985—, Humane Soc. of the U.S., Washington, 1987—, Am. Soc. Prevention Cruelty to Animals, 1987—, Nat. Wildlife Fedn., 1986—, World Wildlife Fedn., 1986—. Avocations: horticulture, oil and watercolor painting, traveling.

JOHNSON, CYNDA ANN, physician, educator; b. Girard, Kans., July 16, 1951; BA in Biology and German with honors, Stanford U., 1973; MD, UCLA, 1977; MBA, U. Mo., Kansas City, 1999. Diplomate Am. Bd. Family Medicine (bd. dirs., pres. 1999-2000). Tchg. fellow U. N.C., Chapel Hill, 1980-81; intern U. Kans. Med. Ctr., Kansas City, 1977-78, 1978-80, prof., acting chair dept. family medicine, 1998—99; prof., head dept. family medicine U. Iowa Coll. Medicine, Iowa City, 1999—2003; dean Brody Sch. Medicine East Carolina U., Greenville, NC, 2003—. Mem. Am. Acad. Family Physicians, Soc. Tchrs. Family Medicine, N.C. Acad. of Family Physicians, N.C. Med. Soc., Iowa Med. Soc. Office: E Carolina U Brody Sch Medicine Brody AD52 600 Moye Blvd Greenville NC 27834 E-mail: johnsoncyn@mail.ecu.edu.

JOHNSON, D'ELAINE ANN HERARD, artist, consultant; b. Puyallup, Wash., Mar. 19, 1932; d. Thomas Napoleon and Rosella Edna (Berry) Herard; m. John Lafayette Johnson, Dec. 22, 1956. BA in Art Edn., Ctrl. Wash. U., 1954; MFA in Painting, U. Wash., 1958, postgrad., 1975, U. London, 1975. Instr. art Seattle Pub. Schs., WA, 1954-78; instr. Mus. History and Industry, Seattle, 1954-56; art dir., instr. Martha Washington Sch. for Girls, Seattle, 1955-58; instr. art workshops Seattle Pub. Schs., WA, 1960-70; dir. Mt. Olympus Estate, Edmonds, WA, 1971. Cons. art groups, Wash. State, 1954—; lectr. Ctrl. Wash. State U. Seattle PTA, Creative Arts Assn., Everett, Everett C.C., Women's Caucus for Art, Seattle, Llubs Art Gallery d'Elaine, Edmonds, Wash., 1957-62, numerous others; pvt. art instr. Seattle, 1960-68; served as art juror for numerous shows; TV art instr., TV-9 U. Wash., 1968; lectr. in field. Exhibited in group shows: Seligman Gallery, Seattle, 1956, Woessner Gallery, Seattle, 1957, 58, Henry Art Gallery, Seattle, 1958, 62, 64, 65, 69, 72, 73, Seattle Art Mus., 1959, 65, 75, Mus. History and Industry, Seattle, 1959, 60, 63, 64, Wash. State Art Exhbns., Wenatchee, 1959, 60, 62, 67, Pacific N.W. Arts and Crafts Fair, Bellevue, 1959, 60, 72-78, Nova Scotia Art Mus., Halifax, 1960, 71, Seattle U., 1965, Nat. Art Gallery, Seattle, 1966—, Art Gallery Hawaii, Oahu, The Gallery, Maui, 1966-68, Park's Gallery, San Jose, Calif., 1967, 68, Park's Galleries, San Jose, San Francisco, Santa Barbara, Carmel, Newport Beach, Calif., 1967, 68, State Capitol Mus., Olympia, Wash., 1968-70, 74, 80, Diamond Head Gallery, Honolulu, 1968, 69, The Gallery Lahaina, Hawaii, 1969, Centennial Art Gallery, Halifax, N.S., 1970, Dartmouth Heritage Mus., Halifax, 1970, 71, Mt. St. Vincent U. Art Gallery, Halifax, 1970, Zwicker's Gallery, Halifax, 1970-73, Gallery 1667, Halifax, 1970-71, Avelles' Gallery, Creative Fine Arts Gallery, Vancouver, The Creative Eye Gallery, Friday Harbor, Wash., 1970, 134th St. Gallery, Halifax, 1971, Panaca Gallery, Bellevue, 1971, 73, Anacortes Arts and Crafts Fair, Wash., 1972, 76-78, Seattle Art Mus. Pavillion Sales Gallery, 1973-75, Meml. U., St. John's Nfld., 1974, Whatcom Mus. Bellingham, Wash., 1974, 75, 80, 82, Grand Gallery, Seattle, 1975, Mus. No. B.C., Maritime Mus., Vancouver, Frye Art Mus., Seattle, 1975, 76, 88, 89, 91, 92, Shoreline Mus. History, Wash., 1976-80,Wash. State Cousteau Soc., Seattle, 1980, U. Oreg., 1981, Edmonds Art Mus., Wash. 1984, 94, Missoula Art Mus., Mont., 1984, Gallery II, Phoenix, 1985, Newport Mus., Oreg., 1986, New Space Gallery, Seattle, 1987, The Viking Gallery, The Chrysalis Gallery, Bellingham, Wash., Art 54 Gallery, N.Y., Emory U., Atlanta, 1988,Prince George Art Gallery, B.C., 1989, Nordic Heritage Mus., Seattle, Rosicrucian Egyptian Mus., San Jose, 1990, King County Arts Commn. Gallery, St. Mark's Cathedral, Seattle, 1991, Kinsey Gallery, Seattle, 1992, Karshner Mus., Puyallup, Wash., 1994, 95, Ilwaco Heritage Mus., Wash., 1994, Northlight Gallery, Everett, Wash., Newmark Gallery, Seattle, 1995, Columbia River Maritime Mus., Astoria, Oreg., 1997, Bon Marché Gallery, Seattle, 1998. Founder Mt. Olympus Preserve for Arts, Edmonds, Wash., 1971, sponsor art events, 1971—; active Wash. Coalition Citizens with Disabilities. Elected to Wash. State Art Commn. Registry, Olympia, 1982; recipient numerous awards. Mem. Nat. Artist Equity, Internat. Soc. Artists, The Cousteau Soc., Creative Arts Assn., Am. Coun. for Arts, Nat. Women's Studies Assn., Nat. Mus. Women in Arts, Women's Caucus for Art, Assn. Am. Culture, Internat. Platform Assn., Nat. Pen Women., Retired Tchrs.' Assn., Kappa Delta Pi, Kappa Pi. Avocations: scuba diving, camping, travel, violin, writing. Home and Office: 16122 72nd Ave W Edmonds WA 98026-4517

JOHNSON, DEBORAH VALERIE GERMAINE, parish administrator; b. Bakersfield, Ca., Jan. 16, 1957; d. Joseph Harvey and Fern (Stoker) J.; m. Robert Arthur Richmond, Jr., Oct. 2, 1982; children: Abelard, Neville, Bane. BA, U. Calif., Davis, 1979; MA, Sch. for Internat. Tng., Brattleboro, Vt., 1981; PhD, Loyola U., L.A., 1988. Life cert. Master Catechist, Calif. Conf. Cath. Bishops; life credential Adult Edn. Philos. and Theology, Calif. Legis. analyst 94th Congress, Washington, 1976-78; adult edn. analyst Orgn. Am. States, Washington, 1979-80; adult edn. dir. Diocese of Fresno, Bakersfield, Calif., 1988-91; lit. and philos. prof. Cerro Coso Coll., Kern Valley, Calif., 1989-90, philos. prof. Porterville (Calif.) Coll., 1997-98, parish adminstr. St. Joseph's Ch., Bakersfield, Calif., 1997—; master prof. U. Phoenix, Bakersfield, Calif., 1996—. Reconnaissance adv. Buziman Acad., Bakersfield, Calif., 1992—; fibonacci forcaster Furman, Jameson & Rumpole, Dover, 1993—; devel. analyst Naylor and Naylor, Mt. Eldora, Calif., 1997—; sr. assoc. Tigrone Excursions, Bakersfield, Calif., 1998—. Author: Volcan, 1989, Freirean Andragogy, 1991, Wittgenstein, 1993, General Systems Theory, 1994. Mem. Audubon Soc., Bakersfield, Calif., 1994—, Sequoia Forest Alliance, Kernville, Calif., 1994—, Internat. Human Rights Campaign, N.Y.C., 1995—; lay assoc. Sisters of Mercy, Burlingame, Calif., 1988—. Named Tchr. of Yr. Cerro Coso Coll., Kern Valley, Calif., 1990, Kern C.C., Bakersfield, Calif., 1992; recipient Prof. Achievement award Hoyden Found. Mt. Eldora, Calif., 1995, Innovation in Andragogy award Synesthetic Soc., Bakersfield, Calif., 1998. Mem. AAUP, APA, Asakawa Assn. Calif., Johnson Garry Partnership Ltd., Internat. Herge Ecolier, Mt. Eldora Decartes Excursions. Roman Catholic. Avocations: cricket, arboreal architectonics, fractal synergy, hagiography, gastronomy. Office: 2225 Eldora Pl Bakersfield CA 93306-3329

JOHNSON, DENISE EVA, director, researcher; b. Chicago, Ill., Feb. 13, 1951; d. Charles Sumner and Eva Patricia Jackson; m. Howard Cornelius Johnson, Sept. 3, 1977; children: Howard Cornelius, Charles Dennis. BS, Ill. State U., 1968—72; M, Chgo. State U., 1973—75; CAS, Syracuse U., 1982—85, PhD, 1986—99. School District Administrator Elem. & K-12 Spl. Edn., NY State, 1977. Tchr. Chgo. Pub. Schools, 1972—77, Syracuse City Sch. Dist., NY, 1977—81, spl. edn. liaison, 1981—85, vice prin., 1985—88, dir. of gifted program, 1988—91, asst. dir. of pupil services, 1991—2000, dir. of pupil services/student behavior, 2000—. Chairperson, design & compliance com. Lymestone Hill Assn., Exec. Bd. Neighborhood, Fayetteville, NY, 2000—03; cmty. wide mem. Mental Health Steering Com., Syracuse, 1998—2003; co-chair - county wide Violence Prevention Network, Syracuse, 2002—03; bd. dirs., mem. city-wide Contact Cmty. Services, Syracuse, 1998—2003. Recipient Acad. of Diversity Achievers award, YWCA, 2002. Mem.: Syracuse Assn. Sch. Administrators (assoc.), Phi Delta Kappa (assoc.), Assn. for Supervisory & Curriculum Devel. (assoc.), NY State Assn., Sch. Administrators (assoc.). Office: Syracuse City School District 725 Harrison St Syracuse NY 13210

JOHNSON, DENISE HORTON, speech pathology/audiology services professional; d. James McKendree and Lillian Frances (O'Kelley) Horton; m. Burl Eugene Johnson, Feb. 9, 1955; children: James Michael, David McKendree, Anna Elizabeth, Daniel Hunter. AA, East Ctrl. Jr. Coll., Decatur, Miss., 1974; BS, Miss. State U., 1976; MS, Miss. U. for Women, 1977. Speech pathology cert. Miss. Dept. Health, cert. tchr. Miss. Dept. Edn. Speech pathologist Calhoun County Pub. Sch., Calhoun City, Miss., 1978—79, Tenn-Tombigbee Home Health Assn., Corinth, Miss., 1979—81, Corinth (Miss.) City Sch., 1979—81, Newton County Health Dept., Decatur, Miss., 1981—89, Newton County Schs., Decatur, 1981—89, Laird Hosp./Home Health Assn., Union, 1989—, Union Pub. Sch., 1989—. Mem.: Miss. Speech Lang. Hearing Assn., Am. Speech-Lang.-Hearing ASsn. (cert. clin. competence), Union Home and Garden Club (officer), Kappa Kappa Iota. Methodist. Avocations: gardening, reading. Office: Union Pub Schs 101 Forest St Union MS 39365

JOHNSON, DENISE REINKA, state supreme court justice; b. Wyandotte, Mich., July 13, 1947; Student, Mich. State U., 1965-67; BA, Wayne State U., 1969; postgrad., Cath. U. of Am., 1971-72; JD with honors, U. Conn., 1974; LLM, U. Va., 1995. Bar: Conn. 1974, U.S. Dist. Ct. Conn. 1974, Vt. 1980, U.S. Ct. Appeals (2d cir.) 1983, U.S. Dist. Ct. Vt. 1986. Atty. New Haven (Conn.) Legal Assistance Assn., 1974-78; instr. legal writing Vt. Law Sch., South Royalton, 1978-79; clerk Blodgett & McCarren, Burlington, Vt., 1979-80; chief civil rights divsn. Atty. Gen.'s Office, State of Vt., 1980-82; chief pub. protection divsn. Atty. Gen.'s Office, Montpelier, Vt., 1982-88; pvt. practice Shrewsbury, Vt., 1988-90; assoc. justice Vt. Supreme Ct., Montpelier, 1990—. Chair Vt. Human Rights Commn., 1988-90. Mem. Am. Law Inst., Am. Judicature Soc. Office: Vt Supreme Ct 109 State St Montpelier VT 05609-0001*

JOHNSON, DIANA ATWOOD, business owner, innkeeper; b. Rochester, N.Y., Nov. 3, 1946; d. Edwin Havens and Barbara (Field) A.; m. Kenneth Durant Milne, June 10, 1967 (div. Apr. 1982); m. Howard Samuel Tooker, May 5, 1985 (div. Aug. 1994); m. John Samuel Johnson, June 2, 1996. BA, Skidmore Coll., 1968. Owner, innkeeper Old Lyme (Conn.) Inn, 1976-2001. Vice-chmn., bd. dirs. Maritime Bank & Trust, Essex, Conn., 1995-99; adv. bd. Webster Bank, 1999-2001; incorporator Lawrence Meml. Hosp., New London, Conn., 1990-95. Trustee Conn. River Mus., Essex, 1976-98, pres., 1989-94, chmn., 1994-96; trustee Lyme Hist. Soc., Old Lyme, 1985-87, Lyme Acad. Fine Arts, Old Lyme, 1980—, chmn. 1996—2003, treas., 1992-96; trustee Mystic Coast Travel and Leisure Coun., 1992—, chmn. 1994-96; bd. dirs. Conn. chpt. Nature Conservancy, 1994—, sec., 2001, chair govt. rels. com. 2001—; chmn. Town of Old Lyme Open Space Com., 1998-2000, mem., 1998—; mem. State of Conn. Natural Heritage, Open Space and Watershed Land Acquisition Rev. Bd., 1998—; mem. adv. bd. Norwich Navigators, 1995-99, Tidewater Inst., 2004-; dir. Southeastern Conn. Enterprise Region, 1995-2001; del. Rep. Nat. Conv., San Diego, 1996; chmn. Rep. Town Com., 2000-02, vice chmn., 1998-99; mem. Conn. Rep. Fin. Com., 1997-2003; state ctrl. committeewoman 20th Dist. Conn. Republican Party, 2001-03. Recipient Disting. Adv. for the Arts award Conn. Commn. on the Arts, 1999. Mem. Nat. Restaurant Assn., Conn. Restaurant Assn. (bd. dirs. 1991-93, 99-2001), Prof. Assn. Innkeepers, Gray Gables Croquet Club (founder), U.S. Croquet Assn. Republican. Presbyterian. Avocations: american antiques, antique house restoration, croquet. Home: 12 Tantummaheag Rd Old Lyme CT 06371-1137 Office: 75 Crystal Ave New London CT 06320 also: PO Box 787 Old Lyme CT 06371 E-mail: dianaajohnson@aol.com.

JOHNSON, DOLORES DEBOWER, consultant; b. Schuyler, Nebr., Nov. 8, 1932; d. Ernest Edward and Edna Cecelia (Stone) DeBower; m. Richard Allan Johnson, Sept. 3, 1952 (dec. 1983); children: Erik, Kristi, Kurt. BA summa cum laude, U. Minn., 1972; cert., Harvard U., 1975. Mgr. St. Paul Chamber Orchestra, 1973-77, Houston Symphony, 1977-80; gen. mgr. Minn. Opera, St. Paul, 1980-81; dir. devel. Walker Art Ctr., Mpls., 1981-84; mng. dir. Houston Grand Opera, 1984-96. Adj. lectr. Goucher Coll., Balt., 1998—. Bd. dirs. Cultural Arts Coun. Houston, 1986-90, Bus. Vol. in Arts, 1991-96. Bush Found. fellow, 1975. Mem. Minn. Composers Forum (pres. 1982-84). Office: PO Box 162 Schuyler NE 68661-0162 Home: PO Box 162 Schuyler NE 68661-0162 Fax: 402-352-2598.

JOHNSON, DOLORES ESTELLE, retired small business owner; b. Phila., Dec. 2, 1932; d. William Johnson Bellamy and Sadie Louise (Waddell) Messado; m. Edward Harding Johnson Jr., Aug. 29, 1953 (dec. Feb. 1981); children: Louise P., Edward A., Marie E., Michael G. Parking enforcement officer City of Phila. Police Dept., 1957—59; jeweler, owner LuBelle Jewelers, Phila., 1963—83; originator, owner, baker Pizzarama, Phila., 1965—67; armed guard Globe Security Corp., Phila., 1977—79; artist, jeweler, owner Piercing Eyes Indian Crafts, Phila., 1982—97; ret., 1997. Recipient Outstanding Cmty. Svc. award, Pepsi Cola Co., 1966, award, Chapel of the Four Chaplains for humanitarian works. Mem. United Am. Indians of Delaware Valley, Amerindian Soc. (v.p.), Atlantic City's Garden Ctr. Mus. Art (life). Episcopalian. Avocations: poetry, art, music, camping.

JOHNSON, DOROTHY CURFMAN, elementary school educator; b. Smithsburg, Md., Nov. 21, 1930; d. Paul Frank and Rhoda Pearl (Witmer) Curfman; m. Robert Nelson Johnson, Jan. 24, 1953 (div. Dec. 1965); children: Gregory Nelson, Eric Paul. Student, Gettysburg Coll., 1948-50, Waynesboro Bus. Coll., 1950, Broward C.C., Ft. Lauderdale, Fla., 1967, BS in Edn., Fla. Atlantic U., 1969, postgrad., 1975-76. Cert. tchr., Fla. Sec. to prodn. mgr. Westinghouse Elec. Corp., Sunbury, Pa., 1951-53; sec. to v.p., sales Metal Carbides Corp., Youngstown, Ohio, 1966; tchr. Sch. Bd. of Broward County, Ft. Lauderdale, Ohio, 1969-93, curriculum specialist, 1993-96. Masters in Edn. Prog., 1973-74, team coord. Sanders Park Elem., Pompano Beach, Fla., 1985-96; mem. North Area Adv. Bd., Pompano Beach, 1990-96; sec. Sanders Park PTA, Pompano Beach, 1994-96. Sec.-treas. Georgen Arms Bd. of Dirs., Pompano Beach, 1997—; dir. Georgen Arms Condo, Inc., Pompano Beach, 1974—; active Jr. League, Youngstown. Recipient Master Tchr. award State of Fla., 1981-82. Mem. Alpha Xi Delta. Lutheran. Home: 280 S Cypress Rd Apt 5 Pompano Beach FL 33060-7038

JOHNSON, DOROTHY PHYLLIS, retired counselor, art therapist; b. Kansas City, Mo., Sept. 13, 1925; d. Chris C. and Mabel T. (Gillum) Green; BA in Art, Ft. Hays. State U., 1975, MS in Guidance and Counseling, 1976, MA in Art, 1979; m. Herbert E. Johnson, May 11, 1945; children: Michael E., Gregory K. Art therapist High Plains Comprehensive Mental Health Assn., Hays, Kans., 1975-75; art therapist, mental health counselor Sunflower Mental Health Assn., Concordia, Kans., 1976-78, Pawnee Mental Health Svcs., 1978-91, co-dir. Project Togetherness, 1976-77, coord. partial hospitalization, 1978-82, out-patient therapist, 1982-91; pvt. practice, 1991-97, ret., 1997; dir. Swedish Am. State Bank, Courtland, Kans., 1960—, sec., 1973-77. Mem. Kans., Am. art therapy assns., Am. Mental Health Counselors Assn., Am. Counseling Assn., Kans. Counseling Assn., Assn. for Humanistic Psychologists, Assn. Transpersonal Psychologists, Assn. Specialists in Group Work, Phi Delta Kappa, Phi Kappa Phi. Contbr. articles to profl. jours. Home: PO Box 200 Courtland KS 66939-0200

JOHNSON, EDDIE BERNICE, congresswoman; b. Waco, Tex., Dec. 3, 1935; d. Lee Edward and Lillie Mae (White) J.; m. Lacy Kirk Johnson, July 5, 1956 (div. Oct. 1970); 1 child, Dawrence Kirk. Diploma in Nursing, St. Mary's Coll. of South Bend, 1955; BS in Nursing, Tex. Christian U., 1967; MPA, So. Meth. U., 1976; LLD (hon.), Bishop Coll., 1979, Jarvis Coll., 1979, Tex. Coll., 1989, Houston-Tillotson Coll., 1993, Paul Quinn Coll., 1993. Chief psychiat. nurse psychotherapist Vets. Hosp., Dallas, 1956-72; state rep. Tex. Ho. Reps. Dist. 33-0, Dallas, 1972-77; regional dir. HEW, Dallas, 1977-79, exec. asst. to adminstr. for primary health care policy Washington, 1979-81; v.p. Vis. Nurse Assn. of Tex., Dallas, 1981-87; mem. Tex. State Senate, dist. 23, 1986-93, U.S. Congress from 30th Tex. dist., Washington, 1993—, mem. sci., transp. and infrastructure coms.; chair Black caucus 107th U.S. Congress. Cons. div. urban affairs Zales Corp., Dallas, 1976-77; exec. asst. personnel div. Neiman-Marcus, Dallas, 1972-75; pres. Eddie Bernice Johnson & Assocs., Inc., Metroplex News, Dallas-Ft. Worth Airport. Bd. dirs. ARC. Recipient Citizenship award Nat. Conf. Christians and Jews, 1985; named an Outstanding Alumnus St. Mary's Coll. of Nursing, 1986. Mem. Alpha Kappa Alpha. Democrat. Office: US Ho of Reps 1511 Longworth HOB Washington DC 20515-4330

JOHNSON, EDNA RUTH, editor; b. Sturgeon Bay, Wis., Dec. 23, 1918; d. Charles Frederick and Georgina (Knutson) Johnson; m. Al Larson, 1955. BA, U. So. Fla., 1971. With The Churchman, 1950-89; editor The Human Quest (formerly The Churchman), St. Petersburg, Fla., 1958—98. Tchr. ballroom dancing to Eckerd Coll. Students, St. Petersburg, Fla., 1995-96. Co-author (with Antoni Gronowicz): Sergei Rachmaninoff, 1946; editor: Friendship News (USA-USSR), 1975—88; mem. editl. bd. The Humanist, Amherst, N.Y., 1980—. Bd. dirs. ACLU, Nat. Emergency Civil Liberties Com., N.Y.C. Named Fla. Humanist of Yr. Am. Humanist Assn. Fla., 1975, Pres. Soc. of Fine Art Arts, Pinellas Park, Fla., 1970-90. Mem. Acad. Sr. Profls. at Eckerd Coll. Avocations: ballroom dancing, ballet, painting. Home and Office: 830 N Shore Dr NE Saint Petersburg FL 33701-2028

JOHNSON, EILEEN, curator, educator, commissioner; Commr., chmn. antiquities adv. bd. Tex. Hist. Commn., Austin, 1997—; curator Lubbock (Tex.) Lake Landmark; curator anthropology, prof. mus. sci. Tex. Tech U., Lubbock. Office: PO Box 12276 Austin TX 78711-2276

JOHNSON, ELEANOR MAE, education educator; b. St. Paul, Mar. 22, 1925; d. Emil H. and Leona W. (Warner) Busse; m. Edward Charles Johnson, May 13, 1950; 1 child, Mary Jo Johnson Tuckwell. BS, U. Wis., Stout, 1946, MS, 1959, edn. specialist, 1981. Cert. home economist, tchr., Wis. Instr. home econs. various pub. schs., Wis., 1946-48, 56-64; home economist U. Wis. Extension, various locations, 1948-51, 52-56; tchr. educator U. Wis.-Stout, Menomonie, 1965-87; ret., 1987. Summer session guest prof. U. Man., Winnipeg, Can., 1970, 71, S.D. State U., Brookings, 1978; dir. Native Am. curriculum for home econs. Fed. Vocat. Project, U. Wis.-Stout, 1978-80; cons. vocat. evaluation team U. Wis.-Stout, 1982-90; presenter at profl. confs.; team mem. interdisciplinary consumer edn. teaching materials Joint Coun. Econ. Edn., 1980-82. Editor teaching materials for Native Ams., 1978-80. Sr. statesman Wis. Coalition on Aging, 1990-2004; adv., vol. Office of Aging, 1992-2004. Mem. Am. Home Econs. Assn. (del. nat. and internat. confs., Inner City fellow 1970), Life mem. with - Am. Vocat. Assn., Wis. Edn. Assn., U. Wis.-Stout Alumni, Assn. Tchr. Educators and Am. Assn. Ret. Persons. Avocations: national and international travel, collecting historical canning jars, stamps, antique dolls, genealogy. Home: 623 Elm Ave Barron WI 54812-1712

JOHNSON, ELISSA SARAH, speech pathology/audiology services professional, writer; b. Bklyn., Nov. 3, 1932; d. Frank Wilford and Doris Antonia (Licorish) Ward; m. Edward Paul Johnson, Dec. 31, 1957 (div. July 1962); 1 child, Paul. BA in Edn. Speech, Bklyn. Coll., 1954, MA in Speech Pathology, 1955; postgrad, Howard U., 1968-70. Speech tchr. therapist N.Y.C. Sch. Sys., Bklyn., 1954-67; speech pathologist Bklyn. Coll. Speech Clinic, 1955-57; instr. speech dept. Howard U., Washington, 1968-70; cons. Health Edn. Welfare, Washington, 1969-70; diagnostician speech pathology Tucson Unifed Sch. Dist., 1977-79, speech clinician spl. edn., 1979-86; writer poet Columbia, Md., 1970-77; freelance writer Tucson, 1986—. Mem. Harlem Writer's Guild, Bklyn., 1962-68. Author: (book of poetry) Soul of Wit, 1978; contbr. poetry and articles to profl. publs. and mags. Pres. Bunche House, Bklyn. Coll., 1954; mem. steering com. Dem. Nat. Com., 1995—. Recipient Fire Prevention Theme medal Mayor's Office, 1942; scholar Bklyn. Coll., 1950-54. Mem. AAUW, NOW, NEA. Avocations: playing organ, movies, plays, painting. Home: 500 S Placita Quince Tucson AZ 85748-6834

JOHNSON, ERMA JEAN, human services administrator; b. Little Rock, Dec. 20, 1951; d. Odessa Johnson; m. Willie R. Johnson, June 19, 1977 (div. Apr. 6, 1985); 1 child, Preya D. AA, Lamar (Colo.) Coll., 1970; BA, Chgo. State U., 1973; MS, Almeda Coll. and Univ., Boise, Idaho, 2002. Social worker, coord. East Ctr. Cmty. Mental Health, Toledo, 1977—78; social worker Toledo Mental Health Ctr., 1979—80, social program coord., 1980—84, mental health administr., 1984—85; supt. Ohio Dept. Youth Svcs., Warrensville, 1985—87, regional adminstr. Toledo, 1987—2002; pres., CEO New Hope Recovery Ctr., Holland, Ohio, 2002—. Mem. adv. bd. Children and Family First, Toledo, 1985—2002, Lourde Coll., Sylvania, Ohio, 1999—2001; v.p. Am. Bus. Women Am., Toledo, 1995—97. Recipient Humanitarian award, Youth Svc. Cmty. Svcs., 1999, recognition for vol. counseling ex-offenders, Lucas County Adult Probation Dept., Toledo, Operation DARE, Chgo.; grantee, Target Stores, 1999—2000. Mem.: NAFE. Baptist. Avocations: walking, bowling, flower arranging, creating community programs. Office Phone: 419-356-3320.

JOHNSON, EVELYN, minister, educator; b. Jefferson County, Ala., Jan. 18, 1945; d. Johnie Sr. and Virginia Sherrer Johnson; div.; children: Thaddeus R., Ralph D. II. BA in Philosophy and Religion, Kean U., 2000. Cert. radiol. technologist, N.J.; ordained Mount Zion AME Ch., 1997. Radiology technologist Hosp., N.J., 1968-87; sch. crossing guard Union Twp. Police Dept., N.J., 1990-99; cafeteria aide Bd. Edn., Union, N.J., 1993-99, sub. tchr. Union County, N.J., 1999—; min. St. Luke AME Ch., Newark, 1990—. Author: From The Mortar to The Glue, 1998. Dir. St. Luke Cmty. Multi-purpose OutReach Ctr., Newark; pres. Union County Women Polit. Caucus, 1984, Recreation Adv. Com., Union, 1987-88; v.p. Union Twp. Betterment Com., Twp. of Union, 1987; coord. Hands Across Am., Twp. of Union, 1987. With U.S. Army, 1966-68. Named Woman of Yr., Calvary Bapt. Ch., Vauxhall, N.J., 1984; resolution Union Twp. Governing Body, 1988. Avocations: singing, walking, writing. Home: 1000 Valley St Vauxhall NJ 07088-1035 Office: St Luke AME Ch 146 Clinton Ave Newark NJ 07114-1958 Fax: 973-623-4030. E-mail: Jhnsone@Hotmail.com.

JOHNSON, EVELYN BRYAN, airport terminal executive; b. Corbin, Ky., Nov. 4, 1909; d. Edward William and Myme Estelle (Fox) Stone; m. Wyatt J. Bryan, Mar. 21, 1931 (dec. 1963); m. Morgan N. Johnson, Feb. 25, 1965 (dec. Mar. 1977). Grad., Tenn Wesleyan Jr. Coll., 1929; student, U. Tenn., 1930-32. With Morristown (Tenn.) Flying Svc., Inc., 1947-97, designated pilot examiner, 1952—, sec.-treas., 1949-62, pres., 1962-82; mgr. Moore Murrell Airport, 1962—. Gov.'s appointee Tenn. Aero. Commn., 1983—2001, vice-chmn., 1987—89, chmn., 1989—91, 1994—96. Recipient Carnegie Hero medal, 1958, Svc. to Mankind award Morristown Sertoma Club, 1981, Kitty Hawk award, FAA, 1991, Friends of Aviation award Tenn. Aviation Assn., 1992, Stewart G. Potter Aviation Edn. award Aviation Distbrs. and Mfrs. Assn., 1992, Elder Statesman of Aviation award Nat. Aeronautics Assn., 1993, Katherine Wright Meml. award Nat. Aeronautics Assn. and the Nenety Nines, 2002; named Flight Instr. of Yr., Nashville Dist. 1973, 79, So. region 1979, Nat., 1979 (all FAA), Outstanding Alumnus Tenn. Wesleyan Coll., 1981, Inductee Women in Aviation Pioneers Hall of Fame, 1994, Hamblen Women Hall of Fame, 1997, Flight Instr. Hall of Fame, EAA Air Venture Mus., Oshkosh, 1997, Ky. Aviation Hall of Fame, 2000, Tenn. Aviation Hall of Fame, 2002, Kathryn Wright Meml. award Nat. Aeronautics Assn., 2002; holder of record most flying time for women pilots, 1995, Guiness Book of Records 1995—. Mem. CAP, Morristown Area C. of C., Nat. Assn. Flight Instrs. (bd. dirs., treas 1987-88, award 1992), Ninety-Nines, Whirly Girls (plaque 1992), Aircraft Owners and Pilots Assn., Silver Wings (bd. dirs. 1987-2002, Woman of Yr. 1981, Carl Fromhagen award 1992, Ninety Nines award of merit 1994), United Flying Octogenarians. Republican. Baptist. Home: 775 Commanche Dr Jefferson City TN 37760 Office: PO Box 1013 Morristown TN 37816-1013

JOHNSON, EVELYN PORTERFIELD, journalist, educator; b. Kansas City, Mo., Jan. 7, 1937; d. Roy LaVerne and Lorraine (Lardie) Porterfield; m. Robert Luck Johnson, June 30, 1962 (div. 1972); children: Jennifer, Lara, Tracey, Virginia. BA, Ea. Bapt. Coll., St. Davids, Pa., 1958. Tchr. Lower Merion Sch. Dist., Ardmore, Pa., 1958—60, Prince Georges County, Md., 1961—62, Loudoun County Sch., Leesburg, Va., 1977—92; freelance journalist local newspapers and mags. Chmn. Regional English Tchrs. Conf., Leesburg, 1991. Author: book, 2003. Founder Bluemont (Va.) Fair, 1970—, Friends of Bluemont, 2002—; mem. Keep Loudoun Beautiful; mem. Blue Ridge Dist. Loudoun's Women Commn.; Blue Ridge rep. Loudoun County Archtl. Rev. Com., 1992. Mem.: Preservation Soc. Loudoun County (founder, pres. 1974—). Democrat. Baptist. Avocations: reading, collecting local history, antiques, old house tours. Home: PO Box 247 Bluemont VA 20135*

JOHNSON, FREDA S. public finance consultant; b. N.Y.C., Mar. 17, 1947; m. J. Chester Johnson, May 7, 1989. BA in Polit. Sci., CUNY, 1968; grad. Advanced Mgmt. Program, Harvard U., 1986. Analyst mcpl. div. Dun & Bradstreet Corp., N.Y.C., 1968-71; sr. analyst Moody's Investor Svc., Inc. (subs. Dun & Bradstreet), N.Y.C., 1972, v.p., assoc. dir. mcpl. dept., 1973-79, sr. v.p., dir. mcpl. dept., 1979-81, exec. v.p., 1981-90; pres. Govt. Fin. Assocs., Inc. pub. fin. adv. co., 1992—. Mem. Anthony Commn. for Pub. Fin.; former sr. credit advisor Ecolink, joint Soviet-Am. pub. fin. project; Congl. testifier U.S. Senate Com. on Banking, Housing and Urban Affairs, subcom. fiscal affairs and health U.S. Ho. of Reps., U.S. Senate Com. Govtl. Affairs, Joing Econ. Com. Congress; bd. dirs. MBIA Inc., Nat. Assn. Ind. Pub. Fin. Advisors, 1993-95, Queens Coll. Corp. Adv. Bd., 1994-99; bd. govs. Coun. Mcpl. Performance, 1984-86; instr. New Sch. for Social Rsch., 1982-83; mem. adv. bd. City Almanac, 1982-84; trustee Citizens Budget Com.; spkr. numerous profl. orgns., univs.; adj. prof. Grad. Sch. Bus. Adminstrn. Columbia U., spring 1991. Avocations: theater, museums, basketball fan. E-mail: freda.gfa@prodigy.net.

JOHNSON, GERALDINE ESCH, language specialist; b. Steger, Ill., Jan. 5, 1921; d. William John Rutkowski and Estella Anna (Mannel) Pietz; m. Richard William Esch, Oct. 12, 1940 (dec. 1971); children: Janet L. Sohngen, Daryl R., Gary Michael; m. Henry Bernard Johnson, Aug. 23, 1978 (dec. 1988). BSBA, U. Denver, 1955, MA in Edn., 1958, MA in Speech Pathology, 1963; vocat. credential, U. No. Colo., 1978, postgrad., Metropolitan State Coll., U. Colo., Colo. State U., Colo. Sch. of Mines, U. Hawaii. Cert. speech therapist, Colo.; cert. tchr., class A counselor, tchr. educationally handicapped, Colo. Tchr. music Judith St. John Sch. Music, Denver, 1946-52; tchr. West High Sch., Denver, 1955-61, chmn. bus. edn. dept., 1958-61, reading specialist, 1977-78; speech therapist, founder South Denver Speech Clinic, 1965-71; tchr. Educationally Handicapped Resource Rm., Denver, 1971-74, Diagnostic Ctr., The Belmont Sch., Denver, 1974-77; speech-lang. specialist elem. and jr. high schs., Denver, 1978-86; itinerant speech-lang. specialist various elem. and jr. high schs., Denver, 1978—; ret. Denver Pub. Sch. System, 1986. Home lang tchr. Early Childhood Edn., Denver, 1975; mem. Ednl. TV Adv. com., Colo.; sec. Cen. Bus. Edn. Com., Colo; tchr. letter writing clinics, local bus., Denver, 1960—. Former judge Colo. State Speech Festivals; demonstrator, lectr. Speech-Lang. and Learning Disabilities area Colo. Edn. Assn., 1971-73; vol. communications and prereading skills tchr. YMCA (cert. recognition for 10 yrs. svc. 2001), Denver Pub. Schs. Ret. Employees Assn. (cert. of recognition for 10 yrs. cmty. svc.). Recipient Spl. Edn. award Denver Pub. Schs., 1986. Mem. Speech-Lang.-Hearing Assn. (cert.), U. Denver Sch. Bus. Alumni Bd., Beta Gamma Sigma, Kappa Delta Pi, Delta Pi Epsilon. Home: 2020 S Monroe St 612 Denver CO 80210-1263

JOHNSON, GLORIA, labor union administrator; m. David Johnson; children: Toni, David. Bookkeeper Internat. Union Electronic, Elec., Salaried, Machine and Furniture Workers, 1954, chmn. Women's Coun.; coord. women's activities Internat. Union Electronic, Elec., Salaried, Machine and Furniture Workers-CWA; v.p. AFL-CIO, 1993; treas., founding mem. Coalition Labor Union Women, pres., 1993—. Rschr., spkr. in field. Named Pres.'s Commn. Celebration Women in Am. History, Pres. Bill Clinton, 1998; recipient Op. PUSH award Outstanding Women in Labor Movement, Econ. Equity award, Women's Equity Action League, 1981, award, So. Christian Leadership Conf., 1985, Achievement award, A. Philip Randolph Inst., 1994, Wise Women award, Ctr. Women Policy Studies, 1995, Ann. Pathway to Excellence award, NAACP, 1995, Eugene V. Debbs Labor award, 1999, Nat. Black Caucus State Legis. Labor Leader award, 2000, Nat. Com. Pay Equity's Winn Newman award, 2000. Office: 1925 K St NW Ste 402 Washington DC 20006

JOHNSON, JACQUELINE, psychologist, researcher; b. N.Y.C., Aug. 10, 1966; d. John Gerald Johnson and Maria Lopez de Rivera; 1 child, Matthew Isaiah Rivera. BS in Psychology, summa cum laude, SUNY, Albany, 1993, MS in Edn. Psychology and Stats., Cert. of Advanced Study, SUNY, Albany, 1996, D in Psychology, 2000. Cert. sch. psychology NY State Dept. of Edn., 1996, psychologist NY State Dept. of Edn., 2003. Cmty. mental health specialist St. Mary's Hosp., Amsterdam, NY, 1998—2000; sch. psychologist Chatham Ctrl. Sch. Dist., Chatham, NY, 2000—01; asst. dir. child and adolescent svcs. rsch. N.Y. State Office Mental Health, Albany, NY, 2001—. Cons. Inst. Cmty. Rsch., Hartford, Conn., 1996—97, VanGuard Comm., 2003—; rsch. cons. SUNY, Buffalo, 1994—96; behavioral health cons. Multiple Sch. Dists. in Urban and Rural Counties, Multiple, NY; presenter in field. Contbr. articles to profl. jours., chapters to books. Adv. and adv. mem. Coalition of Latino Svc. Providers, Amsterdam, NY, 1998—2000; youth mentor Third Ref. Ch. of Am., Albany, NY, 1996—2000; presenter Am. Ednl. Rsch. Assn., San Francisco, 1995; adv. mem. Coordinated Children's Svcs. Intitiative, Amsterdam, NY, 1998—2000. Post-Doctoral Rsch. fellow, Ctr. for Info. Tech. and Evaluation Rsch., 2002—03, State Planning grantee, NIMH, 2003—, Challenge grantee, NY State Divsn. Criminal Justice, 2001—02. Mem.: Nat. Assn. Sch. Psychologists (assoc.), Soc. Rsch. in Child Devel. (assoc.), APA (assoc.), Golden Key, Phi Beta Kappa. Avocations: travel, gardening, dancing and music, theater, reading and writing. Office: NY State Office of Mental Health 44 Holland Ave Floor 6 Albany NY 12229

JOHNSON, JANA E. pathologist; d. Janet S. and Ray J. Renz; m. Jason P. Johnson, Aug. 13, 1994. BS in Speech Pathology, Kans. State U., 1994, MS in Comm. Disorders, 1996. Cert. clin. competence. Speech pathologist Twin Lakes Ednl. Coop., Clay Center, Kans., 1996—97; traveling speech pathologist Therapists Unltd., Woburn, Mass., 1997—98; speech pathologist Wellesley Pub. Sch. Sys., 1998—2000, Wolf Sch.-Pvt. Sch., Providence, 2000—. Mem.: Am. Speech and Hearing Assn.

JOHNSON, JANE ANN BOCKWOLDT, music educator, small business owner; b. Davenport, Iowa, Feb. 10, 1952; d. Robert Frederick Nicholas and Delorus Mae Brandt Bockwoldt; m. Gary Dean Johnson, June 10, 1978; children: Eric Michael, Travis Robert, Kyle Christopher. MusB, Iowa State U., 1974; MEd, Viterbo Coll., 2001. Cert. tchr. Iowa. Audition educator Tanglewood, Mass., 1974; tchr. Davenport (Iowa) Pub. Schs., 1974—75; music tchr. Cardinal Cmty. Schs., Eldan, Iowa, 1975—2000, Newton (Iowa) Cmty. Schs., 2000—. Festival host ICDA, Iowa, 2003—; presenter in field. Pres. TTT, Iowa, 1979, 2003. Mem.: Gordan Inst. Music Learning, Nat. Choral Dirs., Music Educators Nat. Conf. Independent. Luth. Home: 706 W 9th St South Newton IA 50208 Office: Newton Comm School Berg Elem 1900 N 5th Ave E Newton IA 50208

JOHNSON, JANE ELAINE, medical educator; BS in Chemistry magna cum laude, U. Wash., 1983, PhD in Biochemistry, 1988. Postdoctoral fellow Calif. Inst. Tech., 1988-92; asst. prof. dept. cell biology and neurosci. U. Tex. Southwestern Med. Sch., Dallas, 1993—. Contbr. articles to profl. jours. Devel. Biology Predoctoral Tng. grantee NIH, 1984-88; Postdoctoral fellow Muscular Dystrophy Assn., 1989-91; recipient Young Investigator award Neurofibromatosis Found., 1993, Established Investigator award Am. Heart Assn., 1995. Office: U Tex SW Med SchDept Cell Biology 5323 Harry Hines Blvd Dallas TX 75390-0001

JOHNSON, JANE PENELOPE, freelance/self-employed writer; b. Danville, Ky., July 1, 1940; d. Buford Lee Carr and Emma Irene (Coldiron) Sebastian; m. William Evan Johnson, July 15, 1958; children: William Evan Jr., Robert Anthony. Grad., Famous Writer's Sch. Fiction, Westport, Conn., 1967; grad. writer's div., Newspaper Inst. Am., N.Y.C., 1969; grad., Am. Assn. Chrisitan Counselors, 2001; LittD (hon.), The London Inst. Applied Rsch., 1993. Lay counselor Caring for People God's Way. Author numerous poems; author song lyrics: Everlasting Freedom, Answered Prayer, Glory Bound, Americans Standing Tall; recs. include America, 1997-98, The Light of the World, 1998-99; contbr. Hilltop Gospel Songbook. Patron Menninger. Ennobled by Prince John, The Duke of Avram, Tasmania, Australia; semifinalist Internat. Libr. Poetry, N.Am. Poetry Open; recipient 28 Editor's Choice awards for poetry Nat. Libr. of Poetry, 1994, Editor's Choice award Internat. Libr. Poetry, 2000, Coat of Arms, Coll. of Heraldry; named to Internat. Poetry Hall of Fame, 1996, Pres. award, 2002; named World Laureate, Internat. Writer of Yr. Cambridge Gold Medal, Poet of Merit trophy Internat. Soc. Poets. Fellow The World Lit. Acad. Eng.; mem. NAFE, Smithsonian Assocs., Peale Ctr. for Christian Living, Sweet Adelines, Internat. Soc. Poets (life, advisor), Internat. Platform Assn., Charles Menniger Soc. (life), Internat. Order of Merit, Nat. Writer's Club, Nat. Authors' Registry, Poetry Guild N.Y., Norman Vincent Peale Fellowship (founder). Republican. Avocations: swimming, skating, dance, piano. Office: Gardenside Br PO Box 8013 Lexington KY 40504-8013

JOHNSON, JANET HELEN, Egyptology educator; b. Everett, Wash., Dec. 24, 1944; d. Robert A. and Jane N. (Osborn) J.; m. Donald S. Whitcomb, Sept. 2, 1978; children: J.J., Felicia. BA, U. Chgo., 1967, PhD, 1972. Instr. Egyptology U. Chgo., 1971-72, asst. prof., 1972-79, assoc. prof., 1979-81, prof., 1981—; dir. Oriental Inst., 1983-89; research assoc. dept. anthropology Field Mus. of Natural History, 1980-84, 94-99, 2003—; Morton D. Hull disting. svc. prof. U. Chgo., 2003—. Author: Demotic Verbal System, 1977, Thus Wrote Onchsheshonqy, 1986, 3d revised edit., 2000, (with Donald Whitcomb) Quseir al-Qadim, 1978, 80; editor: (with E.F. Wente) Studies in Honor of G.R. Hughes, 1977, Life in a Multi-Cultural Society, 1992. Smithsonian Instn. grantee, 1977-83; NEH grantee, 1978-81, 81-85; Nat. Geog. Soc. grantee, 1978, 80, 82 Mem. Am. Rsch. Ctr. in Egypt (bd. govs. 1979—, exec. com. 1984-87, 90-96, v.p. 1990-93, pres. 1993-96). Office: U Chgo Oriental Inst 1155 E 58th St Chicago IL 60637-1540 E-mail: j-johnson@uchicago.edu.

JOHNSON, JANET LOU, real estate company executive, writer; b. Boston, Aug. 22, 1939; d. Donald Murdoch and Helen Margaret (Slauenwhite) Campbell; m. Walter R. Johnson, Mar. 31, 1962; children: Meryl Ann, Leah Kathryn, Christa Helen. Student, Gordon Coll., Hamilton, Mass., 1962-64. Adminstr., account exec. Fuller/Smith & Ross, Boston, 1958-63; adminstr. Walter R. Johnson, P.E., Gloucester, Mass., 1970-76; broker Realty World, Gloucester, 1976-77, Hunneman & Co., Gloucester, 1977-79; pres., owner Janet L. Johnson Real Estate, Gloucester, 1979—. Author, illustrator, pub: The Ritz Carlton Cat, 1999. Mem. Nat. Assn. Realtors, Mass. Assn. Realtors (bd. dirs. 1985-87), Cape Ann C. of C., Cape Ann Bd. Realtors (pres. 1984-85, state dir. 1985-86), North Shore Assn. Bd. Realtors. Office: Janet L Johnson Real Estate 160 Main St Rockport MA 01966 Home: 160 Main St Rockport MA 01966-2017 Business E-Mail: jjrealest@aol.com.

JOHNSON, J(ANET) SUSAN, psychologist; b. Ramey AFB, P.R., Mar. 24, 1948; d. Wesley Roger and Marie Dolores (Stecher) J. BA in Psychology, San Diego State U., 1970, Ma in Psychology, 1974. Nat. exec. lab. coord. Navy Nat. Elec. Lab., San Diego, 1970-72; assoc. dir. clin. decisions Navy Health Rsch. Ctr., San Diego, 1972-78; exec. dir. The Edwards Assocs., San Diego, 1978—; clin. intern in clin. psychology TRI Cmty. Svcs. Outpatient Clinic, San Diego, 1978-80; exec. dir., v.p. Strategic Vision, San Diego, 1983—. Cons. in field; co-founder Ctr. for Value Centered Life, 1999; key spkr., program coord. for nat. presidencies, prime mins., Fortune 100 CEO's, 1978—; pvt. practice on theoretical devel. of value centered psychology, 1972—; rschr. in U.S., U.K., France, Germany, Hungry, Bulgaria, Japan, Brazil, Italy, Greece, Russia and numerous other countries.. Contbr. articles to profl. publs. Avocations: skiing, boating, scuba diving, gardening. E-mail: susan@vision-inc.com.

JOHNSON, JANIS G. Canadian senator; b. Winnipeg, MB, Can., Apr. 27, 1946; 1 child, Stefan. BA in Polit. Sci., U. Manitoba, 1968. Senator The Senate of Can., Ottawa, 1990—. Progressive. Avocation: Avocations: jogging, flyfishing, golf, theatre, literature. Office: 335 East Block The Senate of Canada Ottawa ON Canada K1A 0A4

JOHNSON, JEAN ELAINE, nursing educator; b. Wilsey, Kans., Mar. 11, 1925; d. William H. and Rosa L. (Welty) Irwin. BS, Kans. State U., 1948; MS in Nursing, Yale U., 1965; MS, U. Wis., 1969, PhD, 1971; DS (hon.), Univ. Wis., 1998. Instr. nursing, Iowa, 1948—58; staff nurse Swedish Hosp., Englewood, Colo., 1958—60; in-svc. edn. coord. Gen. Rose Hosp., Denver, 1960—63; rsch. asst. Yale U., New Haven, 1965—67; assoc. prof. nursing Wayne State U., Detroit, 1971—74, prof., 1974—79; dir. Ctr. for Health Rsch., 1974—79; assoc. dir. oncology nursing Cancer Ctr. U. Rochester, NY, 1979—93, prof. nursing, 1979—95, prof. emerita, 1995—. Rosenstadt prof. health rsch. Faculty Nursing, U. Toronto, 1985; vis. prof. U. Utah Coll. Nursing, 1996—97, U. Wis., Madison, 1998. Author: Self-Regulation Theory: Applying Theory to Your Practice, 1997; contbg. author Handbook of Psychology and Health, vol. 5, 1984; contbr. articles to profl. jours. Recipient Bd. Govs. Faculty Recognition award, Wayne State U., 1975, award for disting. contbn. to nursing sci., Am. Nurses Found. and ANA Coun. for Nurse Rschrs., 1983, Grad. Tchg. award, U. Rochester, 1991, Disting. Rschr. award, Oncology Nursing Soc., 1992, Outstanding Contbns. to Nursing and Psychology award, divsn. of health psychology APA, 1993; grantee, NIH, 1972—95. Fellow: Am. Psychol. Soc., Acad. for Behavioral Medicine Rsch., AAAS; mem.: Inst. Medicine of NAS (com. on patient injury compensation 1976—77, membership com. 1981—86, gov. coun. 1987—89), ANA (chmn. coun. for nurse rschrs. 1976—78, commn. for rsch. 1978—82), Phi Kappa Phi, Omicron Nu, Sigma Xi. Home: 4924 Whitecomb Dr Apt 15 Madison WI 53711-2661

JOHNSON, JENNIE, chaplain, social worker; b. Houston, Sept. 18, 1952; d. James L.C. and Marilyn Mildred (Frazier) J.; children: Alan, David. BS in Social Work, Tex. Woman's U., 1976; postgrad., Bishop's Sch. of Theology, Denver, 1979-80, Samaritan Theol. Sem., L.A., 1982-84, Episcopal Theol. Sem., Austin, Tex., 1986-87, postgrad., 2004—. Cert. social worker, Tex.; oblate Order of St. Benedict, 1998; mem. Daus. of the King, 2003—. Comdr. 94th Ord. Det. USAR, Ft. Carson, Colo., 1978-80, evaluator 1st maneuver tng. command Denver, 1980-81; prodn. control planner Elmo Semiconducter, L.A., 1981-83; quality control planner TRW Def. and Space Guidance, L.A., 1983-84; dir. chpt. svcs. Greater Amarillo (Tex.) Red Cross, 1985-86; chaplain Austin State Hosp., 1987-88, Brackenridge Hosp., Austin, 1988-91, Hospice Austin, 1992-95; asst. dir. Centex Chpt. ARC, Austin, Tex., 1995-96; chaplain Seaton Medical Ctr., Austin, 1998—. Conveener Integrity Austin, 1989-90, 92-94, 96-97; conf. presenter Nat. Episcopal AIDS Coalition, Cin., 1990, mem., 1990—. Founding bd. dirs. Out Youth Austin/YWCA, 1990-92; mem. Tex. AIDS Network, Austin, 1992-2001; foster parent Casey Family Program, Austin, 1992-94; diocesan del. St. Michael's Episcopal Ch., Austin, 1988—, jr. warden, 1993-95, mem. vestry, 1993-97, mem. divsn. for spiritual devel. of diocese Mentor Edn. for Ministry; mem.-at-large Women for Social Witness Network, Nat. Episcopal Ch., 1992-96; mem. Episcopal Womens Caucus, 1993—, Nat. Hospice Orgn., 1993—, Tex. Hospice Orgn., 1992—, presenter state conf., 1995, Order of St. Luke the Physician, 1984—. 1st lt. U.S. Army, 1975-80. Democrat. Avocations: paleontology, needlework, reading, fishing, camping. E-mail: jkhaslund2@aol.com.

JOHNSON, JENNIFER TOBY, military officer; b. Syracuse, N.Y., May 23, 1976; d. Norman Edward and Barbara Catherine Johnson. BS, U.S. Military Acad., 1998; attended, U.S. Army Flight School, 1998—2000, U.S. Army Captains Career course, 2003—04. Commd. 2d lt. U.S. Army 1st Battalion (Attack), 3rd Aviation Regiment, 3rd Infantry Div. (Mechanized), Ft. Hood, Tex., 2000—01, advanced through grades to capt., 2001—, served at Hunter Army Airfield, Ga., 2000—03, served in Iraq, 2003—, served in Kuwait, 2003—. Decorated Presdl. Unit Citation Pres. George W. Bush. Republican. Lutheran. Avocations: golf, skiing, violin. Home: 6004 Bay Hill Cir Jamesville NY 13078 Office: 21st Cavalry Brigade Air Combat III Corps Fort Hood TX 76544

JOHNSON, JOAN BRAY, insurance company consultant; b. Kennett, Mo., Nov. 19, 1926; d. Ples Green and Mary Scott (Williams) Bray; m. Frank Johnson Jr., Nov. 6, 1955; 1 child, Victor Kent. Student, Drury Coll., 1949-51, Cen. Bible Inst. and Coll., 1946-49. Staff writer Gospel Pub. Co., Springfield, Mo., 1949-51; sec. Kennett Sch. Dist. Bd. Edn., 1951-58; spl. features corr. Memphis Press-Scimitar, 1959-60; sec. to v.p. Cotton Exchange Bank, Kennett, Mo., 1959-60; proposal analyst Aetna Life Ins. Co., El Paso, Tex., 1960-64, pension adminstr., 1964-71, office mgr. Brokerage div. Denver, 1971-78, office adminstr. Life Consol. div. Oakland, Calif., 1979-82, office adminstr. PFSD div. Walnut Creek, Calif., 1983-86, office adminstr. PFSD-Health Mktg. div. Sacramento, 1986-89, regional adminstr. Hartford, Conn., 1989-91, cons. Santa Ana, Calif., 1991—, Met-Life Ins. Co., Dallas, 1998—, Transamerica Life, LA, 1999—, Reliar Star Ins., 1999—. Officer local PTA, 1964-71; pres. Wesley Svc. Guild, 1968-71; den mother Boy Scouts Am.; fin. sec. Green Valley United Meth. Ch., 1992—. Recipient Tex. Life Svc. award PTA, 1970. Fellow Life Office Mgmt. Assn. (instr. classes); mem. DAR (regent Silver State Nev. chpt. 1994-96, Nev. state treas. 1998—01, bd. dirs. Nev. 1996—), Assn. Bus. and Profl. Women, Life Underwriters Assn., Clark County Heritage Mus., Last Monday Club, Opti-Mrs., Allied Arts Club. Democrat. Home: 2415 La Estrella St Henderson NV 89014-3608

JOHNSON, JOAN (JAN) HOPE VOSS, communications executive, photojournalist, public relations executive; b. Exira, Iowa, Nov. 18, 1922; d. George Carl Alfred Voss and Evelyn Hope Rendleman; m. Conrad Loren Johnson, Jan. 5, 1955 (div. Mar. 29, 1982); children: Scott Conrad, Dawn Ann Bissell, Lisa Ann Lewis; m. James Francis Voss, Nov. 23, 1941 (div. Nov. 15, 1952). Traffic/continuity dir., broadcaster KJAN Radio, Atlantic, Iowa, 1952—53; dir. of women's programming KVTV-TV, Sioux City, Iowa, 1953—57; prodr., dir., broadcaster, women's programming tv WMT-TV/WMT Radio, Cedar Rapids, Iowa, 1957—70; consumer cons. a.k.a. Bette Schaper, 1st lady of games industry Schaper Mfg. Co., Minneapolis, Minn., 1966—67; dir. publ. and cmty. rels. Grant Wood Area Edn. Agy., Cedar Rapids, Iowa, 1970—76; mktg./ins. coord. Perpetual Savs. and Loan, Cedar Rapids, Iowa, 1977—82; audio-visual cons., dir. of fund raising Muree Christian Sch., Jhika Gali, Pakistan, 1982—84; dir. pub. rels./devel. McKean Leprosy Inst., Chiang Mai, Thailand, 1984—85; dir. of devel./ Murree Christian Sch., Jhika Gali, Pakistan, 1986—88; profl. spkr. Jan Voss Johnson Enterprises, Atlantic, Iowa, 1988—. Nat. v.p. Am. Women in Radio and TV, Cedar Rapids, Iowa, 1966—67. Contbr. articles; author: (family history, paternal) Quo Fata Vocant; editor: (illustrated poetic anthology) Poems My Mother Taught Me. Dem. candidate for pub. office Iowa State Legislature, Cedar Rapids, Iowa, 1969—70. Seaman, second class S 2/C WAVES USN, 1942—43, N.Y. Mem.: Iowana Coun. (exec. bd.), Camp Fire Girls (bd. mem. 1966—67). D-Liberal. United Ch.Of Christ. Avocations: family, photography, cooking, travel, history of eastern cultures. Home: 108 East 22nd St #5 Atlantic IA 50022-2875

JOHNSON, JOANN K. management consultant; b. Rockville, Conn., June 4, 1946; d. Joseph Stanley Klatka and Veronica Agnes Wasilefsky; m. William Moran Johnson, Apr. 12, 1969. BS, Univ. Conn., Storrs, Conn., 1968; MBA, Univ. Tampa, Fla., 1976. Cert. evening layman Tampa Bay Bible Coll., 1981, GTE advanced mgmt. cert. GTE Mgmt. Devel. Ctr. Programmer analyst United Aircraft Corp., E. Hartford, Conn., 1968—71; systems analyst Hartford Ins. Co., Conn., 1971—73; systems analyst, supr., mgr. GTE Data Svc., Tampa, Fla., 1973—86; IM dir.-systems GTE N.W., Everett, Wash., 1987—88; dir. product engr. GTE Info. Svc., Tampa, Fla., 1989—94, dir.-U.K.B.S. ops., 1991—94; pres., founder JKJ Cons. Inc., Ponte Verda Beach, Fla., 1994—. Mission work Global Missions, Eastern Europe, 1993; humanitarian aid internat. E. W. Ministries, Dallas, 1993—97; mem., election polling Young Rep., Coventry Conn., 1971—72. Recipient Honors Convocation, Univ. Tampa, 1976; Hav-A-Tampa Fellowship, Hav-A-Tampa Cigar, Fla., 1975. Mem.: Project Mgmt. Inst., Nat. Assn. Female Exec. Republican. Non-Demon.

JOHNSON, JOANN MARDELLE, federal agency administrator; b. Massena, Iowa, Feb. 24, 1949; BA in Edn., U. No. Iowa, 1971. Former tchr.; grain and livestock prodr.; mem. Iowa Senate from 39th dist., Des Moines, 1994—2000; mem. appropriations com., mem. commerce com.; chair ways and means com.; chair commerce com.; mem. Nat. Credit Union Admin. Alexandria, Va. 2007—; vice chair, mem. various cmty. orgns.; campaign mgr. Rep. Dwight Dinkla, 1992, Congressman Jim Lightfoot, 1990, orgn. dir., 1986-88. Mem. Am. Legis. Exch. Coun., Farm Bur., Cattleman's Assn. Republican. Office: Nat Credit Union Admin Off of the Bd 1775 Duke St Alexandria VA 22314-3428 E-mail: boardmember.johnson@ncua.gov.

JOHNSON, JOY ANN, diagnostic radiologist; b. New Richmond, Wis., Aug. 16, 1952; d. Howard James and Shirley Maxine (Eidem) J.que BA in Chemistry summa cum laude, U. No. Colo., 1974; D of Medicine, U. Colo., 1978. Diplomate Am. Bd. Radiology, Nat. Bd. Med. Examiners; cert. added qualification pediatric radiology. Resident in radiology U. Colo., 1978-81, fellow in pediat. radiology, 1981-82; asst. prof. diagnostic radiology and pediatrics, chief sect. pediatric radiology Clin. Radiology Found. U. Kans. Med. Ctr., Kansas City, 1982-87; radiologist Radiology Assocs. Ltd., Kansas City, Mo., 1987-92; mem. staff Bapt. Med. Ctr., Kansas City, Mo., 1987-92; radiologist Children's Mercy Hosp., Kansas City, 1987-92, Leavenworth-Kansas City Imaging, 1996—; assoc. prof. U. Mo., Kansas City, 1992—; chief of staff Cushing Mem. Hosp., 2002—04. Speaker Radiol. Soc. Republic of China, 1985, RSNA 2000 panel mem. Contbr. articles to med. jours. Nat. Cancer Inst. fellow, 1982. Mem. AMA, Am. Coll. Radiology, Radiol. Soc. N.Am., Am. Inst. Ultrasound in Medicine (mem. program com. Kansas City 1984), Soc. Pediatric Radiology (mem. com. for cmty. bsed pediat. radiologists 1998-2003), Am. Assn. Women in Radiology, Lambda Sigma Tau. Avocations: horseback riding, physical fitness, sports, reading. Office: Leavenworth-Kansas City Imaging 9201 Parallel Pkwy Kansas City KS 66112-1528

JOHNSON, JOY K. biofeedback consultant, educator; b. Elizabeth, NJ, Oct. 4, 1932; d. Edward I. Kalt and Rose Orkin Oser; m. Ronald A. Jakelis, Oct. 16, 2002; children: Mark Solloway, Ken Solloway, Greg Solloway, Hilary. AA, Hillsborough CC, 1973; MA, U. So. Fla., 1975; PhD, Internat. Coll., 1977. Cert. biofeed tech. Florida, 2002, Canada, 2003. Owner, operator Quantum Balance, Tampa, Fla., 1973—2003. Mem.: Healing Arts Alliance (co-dir., dir.). Avocations: teaching ballet, yoga, travel. Home: 3301 Bayshore Blvd #1502 Tampa FL 33629

JOHNSON, JOYCE, retired military officer; m. Jim Calderwood; 1 child, James. DO, Mich. State U., 1980; DSc (hon.), Des Moines U., 2002. Commd. into US Pub. Health Svc.; various positions US Food and Drug Adminstrn., Nat. Inst. Mental Health, Substance Abuse and Mental Health Svcs. Adminstrn.; chief med. officer, surgeon gen. US Coast Guard, 1997—2003, dir. health and safety, 1997—2003; ret., 2003. Bd. trustees US Coast Guard Acad. Named Physician Exec. Yr.; recipient Dr. Nathan Davis award for outstanding govt. svc., Am. Med. Assn. Achievements include among the first to do AIDS rsch. with Ctr. Disease Control, Atlanta; first female flag officer; first woman to serve on bd. trustees Coast Guard Acad. Avocations: cooking, travel.*

JOHNSON, JOYCE MARIE, psychiatrist, epidemiologist, public health officer; b. Baton Rouge, Jan. 30, 1952; d. Gene Addison and Helen Marie (Kalcik) J.; m. James Albert Calderwood, Mar. 28, 1987; 1 child, James. BA, Luther Coll., Decorah, Iowa, 1972; MA, U. Iowa, 1974; DO, Mich. State U., 1980; DFA (hon.), NY Inst. Tech., 2001. Cert. in psychiatry, pub. health and preventive medicine, and clin. pharmacology. Cooking instr. Kirkwood C.C., Iowa City, Iowa, 1974-76; health planner Iowa Regional Med. Program, Iowa City, 1974-76; commd. USPHS, advanced through grades to rear adm./asst. surgeon gen.; intern USPHS Hosp., Balt., 1980-81; med. epidemiologist Hepatitis Labs., Ctrs. Disease Control, Phoenix, 1981-83, AIDS, Ctrs. Disease Control, Atlanta, 1983-84; resident in psychiatry NIMH, 1984-87, staff psychiatrist, 1987-88; epidemiologist, divsn. dir. FDA, 1995—2003; dir. divsn. nat. treatment demonstrations, Substance Abuse and Mental Health Svcs. Adminstrn., 1993-97; chief med. officer USCG, 1997-2003; v.p health scis. Battelle Meml. Inst., 2004—. Med. Perspectives fellow, New Guinea and Thailand, 1978-79; mem. clin. faculty Mich. State U., 1983-93, Georgetown U. Med. Ctr., 1988—; Uniformed Svcs. U. of the Health Scis. Recipient Dr. Nathan Davis award for Outstanding Work in Govt. Svc., 2001. Mem. Explorers Club, Mensa, Cosmos Club. Address: 5518 Western Ave Bethesda MD 20815-7122

JOHNSON, JOYCE THEDFORD, state agency administrator; b. Hazelhurst, Miss., June 27, 1956; m. Leo Kleb Johnson; 1 child, Harmony Saige. Student, Hinds Jr. Coll.; BA, U. Miss., 1979. Lic. social worker. Divsn. sec. Temple Industries, Port Gibson, Miss., 1975; coord. programs North Miss. Retardation Ctr., Oxford, 1976-77; sec. dept. edn. U. Miss., 1977-78, office mgr. mineral rsch. inst., 1978-80; from analyst to rsch. asst. to legis. asst. Miss. State Senate, Jackson, 1980-93; dir. divsn. family and children svcs. Miss. Dept. Human Svcs., 1993-94; ops. cons. Sta-Home Home Health Agy., 1995-96, Medshares Mgmt. Svcs., Inc., 1996—. Coord. Ho. and Senate Joint Indigent Care Study Com., Joint Resdl. Child Care Study Com.; Senate Interim Study Coms. Rural Health and Sunset; mem. staff reorgn. com., steering com. Kellogg Initiative, children's advisory coun., disabilities prevention coun.; chairperson infant mortality task force, Pres. Nat. Adv. com. Rural Health; mem. Robert Wood Johnson Adv. Com.; facilitator various nat. assns. and fed. govt. meetings. Vol. Mother's March, Spl. Olympics; sponsor Luth. Youth Group; cheerleader sponsor Exchange Club; room mother Rankin County Schs.; bd. dirs. Rankin County PTO; active Nativity Luth. Ch., Brandon, Miss. Recipient Outstanding Young Women of Am., 1980, Outstanding Career Women in Miss., 1991. Mem. U. Miss. Alumni Assn., Alpha Omicron Pi. Office: Medshares Home Care of North MS 8705B Northwest Dr Ste 11 Southaven MS 38671-2432

JOHNSON, JUDITH A. educational administrator; b. Bklyn., July 17, 1939; d. Charles Washington and Gwendolyn (Allen) Johnson; divorced; children: Pamela Johnson, Paul Johnson. BA, Bklyn. Coll., 1961; MA, NYU, 1966; 6th yr. cert., SUNY, New Paltz, 1981; postgrad., Columbia U., 1984—. Tchr. N.Y.C. Pub. Schs., 1960-62, asst. prin., guidance counselor, 1964-66, coord. guidance, 1971-73; prin. Mamaroneck (N.Y.) Pub. Schs., 1974-79; dir. instrnl. svcs. So. Westchester Bd. Coop. Ednl. Svcs., Portchester, N.Y., 1979-85; dir. curriculum K-12 Nyack (N.Y.) Pub. Schs., 1985-90; asst. supt. for curriculum and instrn. White Plains (N.Y.) Pub. Schs., 1990-97; dep. asst. secy Office of Elementary and Secondary Edn., Washington, DC, 1997—, Co-author curriculum guides. Recipient cert. of appreciation Phi Delta Kappa, 1982, Founder's award Westchester Prins. Ctr., 1988, One of 100 Exec. Educator's N.Am. award Nat. Sch. Bd. Assn., 1990, achievement award Nyack Bd. Edn., 1990; also numerous grants and awards in field. Mem. Assn. for Supervision and Curriculum Devel. (nat. bd. dirs. 1986-88), N.Y. State Assn. for Supervision and Curriculum Devel. (sec., bd. dirs. 1986—), Am. Ednl. Rsch. Assn., NAACP. Avocations: theatre, concerts, walking, tennis. Home: 48 Fessler Dr Spring Valley NY 10977-2004 Office: OESE 400 Maryland Ave SW Washington DC 20202-0001

JOHNSON, JULIA A. writer; b. Des Plaines, Ill., Sept. 8, 1961; d. John J. and Margaret J. Roarty; m. Quinten R. Johnson; 1 child, Raymond. BA English, Mount St. Mary's Coll., Emmitsburg, Md., 1983. Office svcs. pers. First Boston Corp, N.Y.C., 1984—86; fixed income trader Kidder Peabody, Inc., N.Y.C., 1986—88; mergers & acquisitions staff Scott-Macon, Ltd., N.Y.C., 1991—92; brokerage asst. Paine Webber, Hackensack, NJ, 1997—98; pub. rels. writer In House, Inc., Vienna, Va., 2000—01; freelance writer, pub. rels. cons. Julie Johnson, Leesburg, Va., 1993—. Writer, cons. Issue Action Publs., Leesburg, Va., 1999—2000. Author: (novels) Loudoun County: Blending Tradition with Innovation, 2000; contbr. articles to profl.

jours. Mem.: Loudoun C. of C., Loudoun County C. of C. Democrat. Roman Catholic. Avocations: running, travel, hiking, biking, reading. Office: PO Box 285 Leesburg VA 20178-0285

JOHNSON, JULIA F. bank executive; Sr. v.p., Banc One Corp, Columbus, since 1995; with Bank One, Columbus, 1983—99, dir., office of info. and policy, 1999—2003. Office: Banc One Corp Dept OH-0152 100 E Broad St Dept Oh-152 Columbus OH 43215-3607

JOHNSON, JULIE MARIE, lawyer, lobbyist, judge; b. Aberdeen, S.D., Aug. 7, 1953; d. Howard B. and Jerauldine (Dilly) J.; m. Bryan L. Hisel. BA in Govt., Comm., U. S.D., 1974, MA in Polit. Sci., JD, U.S.D., 1976. Bar: S.D. 1977, U.S. Dist. Ct. S.D. 1977. Assoc. Siegel, Barnett Law Firm, Aberdeen, 1977; law clk. Fifth Judicial Circuit Ct., Aberdeen, 1977-78; ptnr. Maloney, Kolker, Fritz, Hogan & Johnson, Aberdeen, 1978-84; dep. sec. S.D. Dept. Labor, Aberdeen, Pierre, 1983-84, sec. Gov.'s Cabinet, 1985-87; pres. Industry and Commerce Assn. of S.D., Pierre, 1987-95; sec., Gov.'s Cabinet S.D. Dept. Revenue, Pierre, 1995; exec. dir. S.D. Rural Devel. Coun., Pierre, 1995—2003; acting exec. dir. S.D. Math., Sci. and Tech. Coun., 2002—03; adminstrv. law judge, 2003—. Treas. S.D. Cmty. Found., Pierre, 1987-95; mem. Pvt. Industry Coun., 1985-87, S.D. Coun. on Vocat. Edn., 1985-87; bd. dirs. Mo. Shores Women's Resource Ctr., Pierre, 1988-89; chmn. S.D. Main St. Adv. Coun., 1987-91; bd. dirs. United Way, 1988-96, chmn., 1991; mem. Shortgrass Arts Coun., 1987—, South Dakotans for the Arts, 1981—, Solid Waste Mgmt. Plan Task Force, 1990, S.D. Citizens Adv. Coun. on Hazardous Waste, 1991-92, gov.'s adv. coun. on health care reform, 1992-93, gov.'s Homestate Underground Lab adv. coun., 2002—; bd. dirs. Hist. S.D. Found., 1996-99; founding mem., legal counsel Outdoor Women of S.D., Inc., 1995—; bd. trustees USD Found., 1992—; trustee, mem. bus. affairs com., 1996—, com. on trustees, Kelley Ctr. for Entrepreneurship adv. bd., presdl. search com. Dakota Wesleyan U., 1999-2000; founding mem., treas. S.D. Discovery Ctr. and Aquarium, Inc., bd. dirs., 1988-92; mem. S.D. Water Congress, 1990—97, bd. dirs., 1987-95; bd. dirs. Nyoda Girl Scout Coun., 1997-99; mem. adv. bd. W.O. Farber Ctr. for Excellence in Civic Leadership, 1998—; bd. dirs. Farber Fund, 1987—; founding mem. S.D. Chambers and Econ. Devel. Coun., 1989—; mem. Network Mgmt. Team Nat. Rural Devel. Partnership, 1998—2001; mem. Children's Care Hosp. and Sch. Found. Bd., 1997—, investment com., 1999—, mem. devel.com., 2004—; mem. Nat. Rural Devel. Partnership Presdl. Transition Team, 2000-01, Agr. and Econ. Devel. Task Force, 2001, S.D. Habitat for Humanity Bd., 2001—; bd. dir. Historic S.Dak. Found., 1995-98, Genesis of Innovation, 2000—; acting exec. dir. S.D. Math., Sci. and Tech. Coun., 2000-03; vol. chmn. S.D. WWII Meml. Dedication, 2001; vol. chair Korean War Meml. Dedication Com., 2003-04; bd. dirs. S.D. Habitat for Humanity, 2001—; founder, treas. Friends of Discovery Ctr., S.D.; trustee, mem. coms. Dakota Wesleyan U., Children's Care Hosp. Found., U.S.D. Found. Bd. RJR Nabisco fellow Women Execs. in State Govt., Harvard, 1986; named Outstanding Young Citizen Jaycees, Aberdeen, 1982, S.D. Jaycees, 1983. Mem. S.D. Bar Assn. (chmn. adminstrv. law com. 2001-, mem. CLE com., Worker's compensation com.), Industry and Commerce Assn. S.D. (bd. dirs. 1985-87), U.S.D. Alumni Assn. (exec. com. 1987-96, pres. 1990-92), AAUW, Bus. and Profl. Women U.S.A. (nat. legis. chmn. 1987-88, 92-94, nat. chmn. issues mgmt. 1991-93, pres. S.D. 1984-85, Woman of Yr. award Aberdeen chpt. 1982), Women Execs. in State Govt. (bd. didrs. 1985-87), Coun. State Mfrs. Assn., S.D. Mining Assn. (bd. dirs. 1991-95, Gold PAC, 1995-), Nat. Indsl. Coun., Coun. State C.'s of C., Ducks Unltd., Rotary, Zonta, ABC Investment Club, Women's Investment Group, Rocky Mountain Elk Found. Republican. Lutheran. Address: 1100 E Church St Apt 352 Pierre SD 57501-2354 Office: 210 E 4th St Pierre SD 57501 Home: 1414 Sharpstone Dr Mitchell SD 57301-6250 E-mail: juliem.johnson@state.sd.us.

JOHNSON, JUNE MARILYN, music educator; b. Humbolt, S.D., June 2, 1937; d. Herman William and Mildred Ida (Carls) Meves; m. Alfred James Johnson, Feb. 19, 1955; children: Kathleen, Kenneth, Kevin. Pvt. music tchr., Humboldt, SD, 1955—; sec. & bookkeeper West Ctrl. Sch., Hartford, SD, 1975—80; computer data entry Sen. Larry Pressler, Sioux Falls, SD, 1981—86; tchr. aide Montrose Sch., Montrose, SD, 1988—2001. Treas. Parent Tchr. Assn., Humboldt, 1965—66; leader Brownie Scouts, Humboldt, 1968—69. Recipient Cmty. Fine Arts award, West Ctrl. Sch., 1991. Republican. Lutheran. Avocations: travel, piano playing. Home: 108 North Ford Street Humboldt SD 57035

JOHNSON, KAREN, professional society administrator; b. Jersey City, N.J. BS, Loretto Heights Coll., 1977; MS, Yale U., 1984. Cert. mental health clin. nurse specialist. Commd. nurse officer USAF, advanced through grades to lt. col., ret., 1992; from mem. staff to v.p. NOW, Washington, 1975—90, co-chair, nat. com. on racial diversity, 1990—93, v.p., 1993—2001, exec. v.p., 2001—. Mem., nat. bd. dirs, NOW, 1986-90; adv. bd. Cornell U. Peace Studies Program's Women in the Military Project. Contbr. articles to mags. Vol. soup kitchens, New Haven, Conn., Dayton, Ohio, San Antonio Free Clin., San Antonio Battered Women's Shelter; sr. ptnr. Partners Program, Denver; bd. mem. Am. Cancer Soc., Greene County, Ohio. Recipient Keeper of the Flame award State of Ohio, 1990; decorated Air Force Commendation medal 1992. Mem. Kappa Gamma Pi, Sigma Theta Tau. Office: NOW 733 15th St NW 2nd Fl Washington DC 20005*

JOHNSON, KAREN, legislation and congressional affairs secretary; BA comm., Appalachian State Univ., NC. Asst. Conv. Mgr. for Pub. Liaison Rep. Nat. Conv., 2000; instr. of Polit. comm. and Pub. Rels. Internat. Rep. Inst.; asst. sec. of edn. for legis. and congl. affairs U.S. Dept. Edn., Washington, 2003—; v.p. of Soc. Mark. and Pub. Affairs Porter Novelli. Fellow: Univ. of Pa. Annenberg Sch. for Comm. She also traveled to China and Hong Kong to serve as a delegate for the Am. Coun. of Young Polit. Leaders. Office: Dept of Ed 400 Maryland Ave SW Rm 7E307 Washington DC 20202

JOHNSON, KAREN ELAINE, secondary school educator, tax preparer; b. San Diego, Feb. 7, 1957; d. Alan Jerome and Clarex Irene Johnson. AA, Mesa Coll., San Diego, 1978; BA, San Diego State U., 1981; MA, Calif. State U, San Bernardino, 1985; MS, Nat. U., Vista, Calif., 1993. Cert. tchr., reading specialist in adminstrv. svcs. Calif. Tchr. William S. Hart Union H.S. Dist., Newhall, Calif., 1982, San Jacinto (Calif.) Unified Sch. Dist., 1982—85, Grossmont Union H.S. Dist., La Mesa, Calif., 1985—86, Oceanside Unified Sch. Dist., 1986—; tax preparer H & R Block, Encinitas, Calif., 1996—2001. Mem. Oceanside Unified Sch. Dist. Strategic Plan Com., 1996—; chair-8th grade lang. arts/social studies Oceanside Unified Sch. Dist., 1989—99. Mem.: AAUW (Carlsbad bd. dirs. 1992—2001, legal advocacy v.p. 2000—04, Carlsbad bd. dirs. 2002—, named Gift Honoree 1993, 1996, 1999), Delta Kappa Gamma (Carlsbad chpt. rec. sec. 1993—95, 1997—99, corr. sec. 2000—04, chpt. pres. 2004—). Avocations: crocheting, knitting, music, reading. Home: 2651 Regent Rd Carlsbad CA 92008-6413 Office: Oceanside Unified Sch Dist 2111 Mission Ave Oceanside CA 92054 Personal E-mail: bigbodaciousbabe@yahoo.com

JOHNSON, KARISA ANN, political activist; b. Stevens Point, Wis., Aug. 31, 1971; d. Fred H. Johnson and Lynn A. (Bierman) Gilles; m. Kenneth R. Strasma, Dec. 3, 1997. BA in Polit. Sci., U. Wis., Madison, 1993. Various positions Wis. Sane/Freeze, Madison, 1990-92; asst. field dir. Clarenbach for Congress, Madison, 1992; finance asst. Feingold for U.S. Senate, Madison, 1992; legis. asst. State Sen. Alice Clausing, Madison, 1993; campaign coord. U.S. Sen. Russ Feingold, Middleton, Wis., 1993-94; legis. asst. State Sen. Chuck Chvala, Madison, 1994-95; state polit. dir. Dem. Ctrl. Com. Wis., Madison, 1995-96; campaign mgr. Julie Johnson for Congress, Green Bay, Wis., 1996; chief of staff U.S. Rep. Jay Johnson, Washington, 1997—99; with Naral Pro-Choice Am., Washington, 1999—2003; cons. in field Washington, 2003—. Mem. faculty Dem. Leadership Devel. Inst.,

Stevens Point, 1995-96. Vice chair elections, nominating chair Dem. Ctrl. Com. Dane County, Madison, 1992-94; orgnl. v.p. Young Dems. Wis., Madison, 1991-92. Home: 13 Coachlamp Ct Silver Spring MD 20906-5837

JOHNSON, KARI LADD, veterinarian; b. Haxtun, Colo., July 27, 1957; d. Henry Edward and Twila Faun (Jacobson) Kohler; m. Arthur Que Johnson, Sept. 22, 1977; children: Russell, Kohler Scott, Marc. Cattle rancher, Kanab, Utah, 1981—. Bd. dirs. S.W. Utah Dept. Health, St. George; bd. dirs., pres. Kanab C. of C.; charter mem. Nat. Coun. Women's Adv. to Congress, Washington; ambassador Mountain Am. Credit Union, St. George; sec. County Rep. Party, Kanab, Utah; pres. PTA, Kanab. Mem. Internat. Assn. Clks., Recorders, Election Ofcls., Treas., Friendship and Cultural Exch. Soc., Coalition of Resources and Economies, Utah Assn. Counties (bd. dirs.).

JOHNSON, KATHERINE HOLTHAUS, health care marketing professional; b. Denver, Mar. 19, 1961; d. William Philip and Barbara Kristine (Nielsen) Holthaus; m. Robert Scott Johnson; children: Katie Maree, Brian David, Kiersten Rose. B in Applied Math. Engring., U. Colo., 1983; MBA, U. Denver, 1992. Acctg. intern Cooper, Haugen & Co., CPAs, Englewood, Colo., 1982-84; market analyst mktg. dept. Porter Meml. Hosp., Denver, 1985-88; account exec. Tallant LaPointe & Ptnrs., Inc., Englewood, 1988-92; advt. mgr. Micromedex, Inc., Denver, 1992-93; mktg. cons. Highlands Ranch, Colo., 1993-96; product mgr. Micromedex, Inc., Englewood, Colo., 1996-98; mktg. cons. Highlands Ranch, Colo., 1999—. Judge, vol. 4-H Clubs, Denver, 1979—; supt. Sunday sch. Ascension Luth. Ch., Littleton, Colo., 1985—87, 2001—. Mem. Soc. for Healthcare Planning and Mktg., Am. Hosp. Assn., Acad. for Health Svcs. Mktg., Am. Mktg. Assn., Alpha Chi Omega. Republican. Avocations: bicycling, swimming, aerobics, reading, baking.

JOHNSON, KATHY VIRGINIA LOCKHART, art educator; b. Aberdeen, Miss., May 5, 1951; d. Clovis Clinton and Marium Kathleen (Bowen) Lockhart; m. Gary Wayne Johnson, Aug. 5, 1973; 1 child, Daniel Clinton. BFA, Miss. U. Women, 1973; postgrad., U. Ala., 1973—92. Cert. tchr. Ala. Inventory clk. Johnson Showroom, Columbus, Miss., 1970—73; student tchr. Armory Mid. Sch., Amory, 1973; tchr. art Huntsville Art League, Huntsville, 1974, 1983—84, Evangel Schs., 1974—75, 1st Christian Early Childhood, 1984—88, Huntsville Mus. Art, 1990, Huntsville City Schs., 1989—. One-woman shows include, 1974, Tchr. Show Youth Art Month, 1994, Ann. NASA Picnic, 1998. Mem.: Huntsville Edn. Assn., Ala. Edn. Assn., Nat. Art Edn. Assn., Alpha Delta Kappa (bd. dirs. 1999—, pres. 1996—, sec. 1999—2002). Mem. Christian Ch. (Disciples Of Christ). Avocations: painting, gardening, football. Home: 122 Regent Ctr Madison AL 35758

JOHNSON, KAY DURBAHN, real estate manager, consultant; b. Crookston, Minn., Apr. 4, 1937; d. Wilbert John and Frieda (Johnson) Durbahn; m. Ray Arvin Johnson, May 14, 1960; children: Sherry Kay Johnson Johnston, Diane Rosalind Johnson Peterson, Laura Faye Johnson. BA, U. Minn., 1959. Reference analyst Indsl. Rels. Ctr. U. Minn., Mpls., 1959-61; real estate mgr. Minnetonka, Minn., 1976—; ptnr. Broadmoor Plantation Investors, Fargo, N.D., 1976—; v.p. D&T Property, Inc., Minnetonka, 1990—, also bd. dirs.; v.p. Comreco, LLC, 2002—, bd. dirs. Tax reduction cons. R.A. Johnson & Assocs., Minnetonka, 1985—; bd. dirs. Empire Aggregate, Inc., 2001—. City of Minnetonka Planning Commn., 1972-74, vice chair, 1973-74; mem. Land Use Task Force, 1972-74; liaison Ridgedale Devel.; mem. choir, various coun. positions Minnetonka Luth. Ch. Mem. Mpls. Inst. Arts. Republican. Avocations: art, music, travel.

JOHNSON, KRISTEN MARIE, art director; b. Thorton, Colo., June 17, 1969; d. William and Cheryl (Mathews) Avery; m. Christian John Johnson, May 26, 1996. Degree in visual comm., Colo. Inst. of Art, Denver, 1989; graphic design degree, Calif. Coll. Arts and Crafts, 1992. Jr. deisgner Steve Rank, Inc., San Francisco, 1990-92; editl. illustrator Contra Costa Times, Walnut Creek, Calif., 1992; imaging technician Miller Freeman, San Francisco, San Mateo, Calif., 1992-95; sr. designer Fawcette Tech. Publs., Palo Alto, Calif., 1995-97; pres., owner Johnson Design & Illustration, Pasadena, Calif., 1995—. Freelance graphic design Johnson Design and Illustration, Pasadena, 2000—. Graphic design adv. coun. Diablo Valley Coll., Pleasant Hill, Calif., 1994-95. Republican. Avocations: rollerblading, hiking, camping, mountain biking. Office: Johnson Design 621 Deodara Dr Altadena CA 91001-2307

JOHNSON, KRISTINA M. technology director; BSEE, MSEE, PhD in Elec. Engring., Stanford U. Rschr. IBM, Trinity Coll., Ireland; mem. faculty U. Colo. 1985; prof. elec. engring. U. Colo.; dir. emeritus Optoelectronics Computing Sys. Ctr. U. Colo, 1994—; dean Edmund T. Pratt, Jr. Sch. Engring. Duke U., 1999—. Bd. dirs. Minerals Techs. Inc.; co-founder Colo. Advanced Tech. Inst. Ctr. for Excellence in Optoelectronics, ColorLink Inc., KAJ LLC. Recipient Emmy award nomination, 1991. Achievements include patents in field. Office: Duke U Pratt Sch Engring 305 Teer Bldg Box 90271 Durham NC 27708

JOHNSON, KYSA NICOLE, artist; b. Evanston, Ill., Dec. 24, 1974; d. Craig Daniel and Karyne Lee Johnson; life ptnr. BFA, Glasgow Sch. of Art, Glasgow, Scotland, 1994—97. Artist. Installation empire state building, Blow Up Project, solo exhibition nas, body of work/drawing, (NYFA fellowship, 2003). Recipient Emmy Sachs Prize, Glasgow Sch. of Art, New Am. Paintings #44, New Am. Paintings/ Charlotta Kotick, 2003. Fellow: NYFA. D-Liberal.

JOHNSON, LADY BIRD (MRS. CLAUDIA ALTA TAYLOR), former First Lady of the United States; b. Karnack, Tex., Dec. 22, 1912; d. Thomas Jefferson Taylor; B.A., U. Tex., 1933, B.Journalism, 1934, D.Letters, 1964; LL.D., Tex. Woman's U., 1964; D.Letters, Middlebury Coll., 1967; L.H.D., Williams Coll., 1967, U. Ala., 1975; H.H.D., Southwestern U., 1967; m. Lyndon Baines Johnson (36th Pres. U.S.), Nov. 17, 1934 (died Jan. 22, 1973); children: Lynda Bird Johnson Robb, Luci Baines. Mgr. husband's congl. office, Washington, 1941-42; owner, operator radio-TV sta. KTBC, Austin, Tex., 1942-63, cattle ranches, Tex., 1943—, First Lady of the U.S., 1963-68. Hon. chmn. Nat. Headstart Program, 1963-68, Town Lake Beautification Project; also cotton and timberlands, Ala. Mem. Advisory council Nat. Parks, Historic Sites, Bldgs. and Monuments; bd. regents U. Tex., 1971-77, mem. internat. conf. steering com., 1969; trustee Jackson Hole Preserve, Am. Conservation Assn., trustee emeritus Nat. Geog. Soc.; founder Nat. Wildflower Research Ctr., Austin, 1982. Recipient Togetherness award Marge Champion, 1958; Humanitarian award B'nai B'rith, 1961; Businesswoman's award Bus. and Profl. Women's Club, 1961; Theta Sigma Phi citation, 1962; Disting. Achievement award Washington Heart Assn., 1962; Industry citation Am. Women in Radio and Television, 1963; Humanitarian citation Vols. of Am., 1963; Peabody award for White House TV visit, 1966; Eleanor Roosevelt Golden Candlestick award Women's Nat. Press Club; Damon Woods Meml. award Indsl. Designers Soc. Am., 1972; Conservation Service award Dept. Interior, 1974; Disting. award Am. Legion, 1975; Woman of Year award Ladies Home Jour., 1975; Medal of Freedom, 1977; Nat. Achievement award Am. Hort. Soc., 1984. Life mem. U. Tex. Ex-Students Assn. Episcopalian. Author: A White House Diary, 1970. Address: LBJ Libr and Mus 2313 Red River St Austin TX 78705-5702

JOHNSON, LAURA STARK, secondary school educator, administrator; b. Unityville, S.D., Jan. 9, 1913; d. Fred Hartman and Catherine (Culver) Stark; m. Falk Simmons Johnson, June 11, 1940; children: Mark, Bruce, Martha, Craig (dec.). BA, Dakota Wesleyan U. 1937; MA, Northwestern U., 1966; MS in Edn., No. Ill. U., 1982. Tchr. pub. schs., Unityville,

1932-36, McIntosh (S.D.) H.S., 1937-38, Washington Sch., Wauwatosa, Wis., 1938-40, Mark Twain Sch., Des Plaines, Ill., 1964-65, Maine S. H.S., 1965-69, Evanston (Ill.) H.S., 1969-96. Tchr., reading cons., 1969-76; tchr. Adult Continuing Edn., 1972-85; adult edn. dept. coord. ABE/GED/Literacy, 1985-96; adj. faculty mem. Northeastern Ill., 1974-76, Loyola U., Chgo., 1974-75, Oakton C.C., 1977-79, Triton C.C., 1981-86; spkr. World Congress Reading, Singapore, 1976, Gold Coast, Australia, 1988, Stockholm, 1990; literacy Oakton C.C., 1998-2000. Chost writer Ency. Britannica Films, Sci. Rsch. Assn., 1958-60; author, cons. Coronet Instrnl. Media, 1974-79; editor Reading and Adult Learner, 1980, Internat. Reading Assn., Alaska Jour. Collection, 1981, Curriculum Guide for ABE Language Arts, 1988, Curriculum Pub. Clearing House, Reading in the Content Areas, New Readers Press, 1990-92; cons. Barron's Ednl. Series, 1994—; mem. adv. bd. Jour. Reading, 1972-76; contbr. articles to profl. jours. Mem. Internat. Reading Assn. (pub. com. 1976-79), Internat. Reading Assn., Ill. Reading Assn. (officer 1969-72), Suburban Reading League, Ill. Adult Continuing Edn. Assn. Home: 7624 Maple St Morton Grove IL 60053-1641

JOHNSON, LINDA ARLENE, transportation executive; b. Sparta, Wis., Mar. 6, 1946; d. Clarence Julius and Arlene Mae (Yahnke) Jessie; children: Darrick, Larissa. With Union Nat. Bank & Trust Co., Sparta, 1964-69, Hill, Christensen & Co., CPA's, Tomah, Wis., 1969-75; owner Johnson of Wis. Oil Co., Inc., Tomah, 1969-95; with Larry's Express, Inc., Tomah, 1975-78; owner Johnson Rentals, 1979—, Johnson of Wis. Transport Co., Inc., Tomah, 1982—. Mem. Forward Tomah Devel., Inc., 1999—; active St. Paul's Luth Ch., Tomah. Mem.: Petroleum Marketers Assn. Wis., Am. Trucking Assn., Petroleum Marketers Assn. Am., Tomah Area Credit Union (bd. dirs. 1993—, sec. 1993—94), Tomah Area C. of C., Rotary (bd. dirs. 1997—99), Beta Sigma Phi (Larueate Phi chpt.). Home and Office: 24011 Flatter Ave Tomah WI 54660-4424

JOHNSON, LINDA SUE, academic administrator, state agency administrator, retired state legislator; b. Ft. Worth, Dec. 4, 1950; d. William Jr. and Helen Adelene (Loya) McCormick; m. Jerry Eugene Johnson, May 24, 1974 (div. 1984); children: Jeremy Scott, Nicholas Adam, Jennifer Leigh. BA in Biology, U. Tex., 1972; ADN, Shoreline C.C., Seattle, 1986; M in Healthcare Adminstrn., U. Wash., 1988. RN, Washington. Physician's asst. Children's Med. Ctr., Austin, Tex., 1973; collections corr. Sears Roebuck & Co., Seattle, 1973-77; nurse Northwest Hosp., Seattle, 1985-88; intern Univ. Hosp., Seattle, 1987-88; clin. mgr. ops. Evergreen Urgent Care Ctr., Woodinville, Wash., 1988-90; dir. med. staff Evergreen Hosp. Med. Ctr., Kirkland, Wash., 1990-94; mem. Wash. Ho. Reps., Olympia, 1993-95; immunization program mgr. Wash. Dept. Health, Olympia, 1995—98; dir. prof. svs. Ctrl. Oreg. Dist. Hosp., 1998—2000; assoc. provost Cascades campus Oreg. State U., 2000—03. Trustee, pres. Trustees Assn. Tech. and Community Colls., Olympia, 1990-92; trustee Shoreline C.C., 1987-92; active PTA. Mem. Am. Coll. Healthcare Execs., Wash. State Nurses Assn. (legis. com. 1991-93). Democrat.

JOHNSON, LIZABETH LETTIE, small business owner, insurance agent; b. Dallas, Aug. 24, 1957; d. Winfred Herschel Johnson and Mary Francis (Flowers) Goff; children: Brandi, Elissa. Student, Georgetown (Ky.) Coll., 1975-76, U. Ky., 1976-78. Staff analyst Met. Ins. Co., Lexington, 1979-81, ins. agt., 1981-82; sr. account agt. Allstate Ins. Co., Lexington, 1982—2003; owner Fanfare Jewelry, LLC, 2002—. Vol. Big Bros./Big Sisters, 1979-84, Life Adventure Camp, 1989-92; hotline counselor Lexington Rape Crisis Ctr., 1984-92, bd. dirs., 1988-91; vol. Christians in Comty. Svc., 1986-93, Hope Ctr., 1998—; mem. Bluegrass Adoptive Parent Support Group, 1985-92. Fellow Life Underwriting Tng. Council; mem. NAACP, Nat. Assn. Life Underwriters. Democrat. Episcopalian. Avocations: aerobics, walking, racquetball, needlework, reading, breeding himalayan cats and standard poodles. Office: Fanfare Jewelry LLC PO Box 12813 Lexington KY 40583 Office Phone: 859-281-9422. E-mail: ljohnson82@aol.com.

JOHNSON, LOLA NORINE, retired advertising and public relations executive, educator; b. Austin, Minn., Dec. 28, 1942; d. Alton E. and Evelyn M. (Quast) Milbrath; m. Dennis D. Johnson, June 15, 1963 (div. July 1973); children: Brenda J., Erik B. Attended, Coll. of St. Thomas. Pub. rels. account rep. Kerker & Assocs. Advt. and Pub. Rels., Bloomington, Minn., 1973-78; comm. mgr. Norwest Bank Mpls., 1978-83; dir. media rels., account supr. Edwin Neuger & Assocs. Pub. Rels., Mpls., 1983-85; v.p., mng. dir. The Richards Group, Mpls., 1985-86; owner, pres. PR Plus, Edina, Minn., 1986-2000; ret., 2000. Mem. cmty. faculty, instr., counselor Met. State U., Mpls., St. Paul, 1980-93. Cons. comm. United Way, Mpls., 1982. Recipient Gold award United Way Mpls., 1982. Home: 7151 York Ave S Apt 807 Minneapolis MN 55435-4435

JOHNSON, LORNA, state representative; b. Laramie, Wyo., Dec. 23, 1943; children: Shawna Wendland, Heather, Brian, Gavin. Student, U. Wyo. State rep. dist. 45 Wyo. State Legis., Cheyenne, 1999—. Democrat. Jewish. Home: 615 E Clark St Laramie WY 82072 Office: Capitol Bldg Wyo State Legis Cheyenne WY 82002

JOHNSON, LUAN, disaster management consultant; b. Provo, Utah, Apr. 27, 1956; d. Jack R. and Colleen (Kesler) J. BA, Brigham Young U., 1981, MA, 1984; PhD, U. Wash., 1994. Dir. Tchg. Resource Ctr., Provo, 1980-84; tchg. asst. comms. dept. Brigham Young U., Provo, 1982-83; counselor Master Acad., Salt Lake City, 1985; ednl. designer, program mgr. City of Sunnyvale, 1986-90; tchg. asst., rsch. asst., speech comm. dept. U. Wash., Seattle, 1991-93; program mgr. City of Seattle, 1993—. Recipient Best Ednl. Campaign award Internat. Assn. Emergency Mgrs., 1998, Nat. Coord. Coun. of Emergency Mgmt. Best Newsletter award, 1996, 98, 2002, 1st pl.-best ednl. campaign Internat. Assn. Emergency Mgrs., 1998, Outstanding Pub. Svc. award Seattle Police Dept., 1999, 1st pl.-best ednl. video Internat. Assn. Emergency Mgrs., 1999. Mem.: Phi Kappa Phi. Mem. Lds Ch. Avocation: collecting and flying kites. Home: 6609 224th St SW Mountlake Terrace WA 98043-2324

JOHNSON, MARGARET ANN (PEGGY), library administrator; b. Atlanta, Aug. 11, 1948; d. Odell H. and Virginia (Mathiasen) J.; m. Lee J. English, Mar. 4, 1978; children: Carson J., Amelia J. BA, St. Olaf Coll., 1970; MA, U. Chgo., 1972; MBA, Met. State U., 1990. Music cataloger U. Iowa Librs., Iowa City, 1972-73; analyst Control Data Corp., Bloomington, Minn., 1973-75; br. libr. St. Paul Pub. Librs., 1975-77; head tech. svcs. St. Paul Campus Librs., U. Minn., 1977-86; collection devel. officer Univ. Librs., U. Minn., Mpls., 1987-90; asst. dir. St. Paul Campus Librs., U. Minn., 1987-95; planning officer U. Librs. U. Minn., Mpls., 1993-97, asst. univ. libr., 1997—2003, interim univ. libr., 2002, assoc. univ. libr., 2003—. Libr. cons. Mekerere U., Kampala, Uganda, 1990, U. Nat. Rwanda, 1990, Inst. Agr. and Vet. Hassan II, Rabat, Morocco, 1992—, Ecole Nat. Agr., Meknes, Morocco, 2000, China Agrl. U., Beijing, 2001—. Author: Automation and Organizational Change in Libraries, 1991, The Searchable Internet, 1996, Fundamentals of Collection Development and Management, 2004; editor: New Directions in Technical Services, 1997; editor Technicalities Jour., 2000—, Libr. Resources and Tech. Svcs., 2003—; editor Guide to Tech. Svcs. Resources, 1994, Recruiting, Educating and Tng. Librarians for Collection Devel., 1994, Collection Mgmt. and Devel., 1994, Virtually Yours, 1998; contbr. articles to profl. jours. Recipient Samuel Lazerow Rsch. fellowship Assn. Coll. and Rsch. Librs., Inst. for Sci. Info., 1987. Mem. ALA, Minn. Libr. Assn., Internat. Assn. Agrl. Librs. and Documentatists, U.S. Agrl. Info. Network, Assn. for Libr. Collections and Tech. Svcs. (pres. 1999-2000). Office: U of Minn Librs 499 Wilson Libr 309 19th Ave S Minneapolis MN 55455-0438 E-mail: m-john@umn.edu.

JOHNSON, MARGARET BROWN, music educator; b. Dallas, June 11, 1963; d. Jerry R. and Johnnie Faye Brown; children: Samantha Lee, Jennifer Suzanne. B in Music Edn., Tex. Wesleyan U., 1985; MusM, Tex. Tech U., 1992. Cert. tchr. Tex., 1986. Orch. dir. Grand Prairie (Tex.) Ind. Sch. Dist., 1986—88, Tyler (Tex.) Ind. Sch. Dist., 1988—89, Lubbock (Tex.) Ind. Sch. Dist., 1989—. Violinist Lubbock Symphony Orch., 1995—; condr. Lubbock Youth Symphony, 2001—; master tchr. Tex. Tech String Project, Lubbock, 2001—. Musician: Caprock Strings. Pres. Pilot Club Lubbock, 1994—98; musician First Bapt. Ch., Bacon Heights Bapt. Ch., Lubbock, 1989—98, Tate Springs Bapt. Ch., Arlington, Tex., 1986—88. Mem.: Music Educator's Nat. Conf., Am. String Tchrs. Assn. (treas. 2002—), Tex. Orch. Dirs. Assn., Tex. Music Educator's Assn. (region 16 orch. chair, region 16 sec. 1990—2002), Tex. Music Adjudicator's Assn., Mu Omicron, Sigma Alpha Iota (sec., pres. 1982—84, Coll. Chpt. Achievement award 1982). Avocations: travel, cake decorating, scrapbooks. Home: 5734 Dartmouth Dr Lubbock TX 79416-1333 Office: Irons Junior High School 5214 79th Lubbock TX 79424 Personal E-mail: mbjviolin@aol.com. E-mail: margaretjohnson@lubbockisd.org.

JOHNSON, MARGARET HILL, retired educational administrator, consultant; b. Dundee, Scotland, June 26, 1923; came to U.S., 1946, naturalized, 1957; d. John Barnet and Isabella Rae (Watson) Hill; children: Anne Hill Doughty, James Appleton Doughty (dec.), Joanna Elizabeth Doughty Going. Student, Inverness Royal Acad., Scotland, 1940, Edinburgh Royal Coll. Art, 1940-43; EdD, U. Mass., 1985. Latin and remedial English tutor Harvey Sch., N.Y.C., 1947-52; tchr. athletics Pingree Sch. for Girls, Hamilton, Mass., 1959-61, Shore County Day Sch., Beverly, Mass., 1952-60; assoc. dir. Theodore S. Jones & Co., design mgmt. cons., Milton, Mass., 1960-94; dir. career plannig and placement, Fulbright advisor Mass. Coll. Art, 1974-94, cons., 1997—; freelance art cons., grant writer, 1998—. Spkr. Lesley Coll., 1977, Cambridge (Mass.) Cmty. Schs., 1977—, MIT, Harvard U., R.I. Sch. Design, Hofstra U.; artist cons., grant writer for artists and designers. Served with Brit. Women's Royal Naval Svc., 1943-46. Mem. North River Art Assn. Home: PO Box 75 Marshfield Hills MA 02051-0075

JOHNSON, MARGARET KATHLEEN, business educator; b. Baylor County, Tex., Oct. 30, 1920; d. George W. and Julia Rivers (Turner) Higgins; m. Herman Clyde Johnson, Jr., July 27, 1949 (dec.); 1 child, Carolyn Kay. BS, Hardin-Simmons U., 1940; M in Bus. Edn., North Tex. State U., 1957, EdD, 1962. Clk. Farmers Nat. Bank, Seymour, Tex., 1940-41; adminstrv. sec. U.S. Navy, Corpus Christi, Tex., 1941-46; adminstrv. asst. Hdqrs. 8th Army, Yokohama, Japan, 1946-49; instr. Coll. Bus. Adminstrn., U. Ark., 1957-60; teaching fellow Sch. Bus. Adminstrn., North Tex. State U., 1960-62, instr., 1962-63; asst. prof. bus., tchr. edn. and secondary edn. Tchrs. Coll., U. Nebr., Lincoln, 1963-65, asso. prof., 1966-70, prof., 1970—. Guest lectr. U. N.Mex., 1967, Curriculum Devel. in Bus. Edn., N.S. Dept. Edn., 1969, North Tex. State U., 1970, East Tex. State U., 1972; in Policies Commn. for Bus. and Econ. Edn., 1979-83, mem. bd. devel. Hardin-Simmons U., 1994-97. Author: Standardized Production Typewriting Tests series, 1964-65, National Structure for Research in Vocational Education, 1966; co-author: Introduction to Word Processing, 1980, 2d edit., 1985, Introduction to Business Communication, 1981, 2d edit., 1988, Business Communication Principles and Applications, 1996; editor: Nat. Bus. Edn. Assn. Yearbook, 1980. Recipient United Bus. Edn. Assn. award as outstanding grad. student in bus. edn. North Tex. State U., 1957; award for outstanding service Nebr. Future Bus. Leaders Am., 1968; Mountain-Plains Bus. Edn. Leadership award, 1977; merit award Nebr. Bus. Assn., 1979 Mem. Nat. Bus. Edn. Assn. (exec. bd. 1975, 76-78), Mountain-Plains Bus. Edn. Assn. (exec. sec. 1970-73, pres. 1975), Nebr. Bus. Edn. Assn. (pres. 1966-67), Nebr. Council on Occupational Tchr. Edn., Delta Pi Epsilon. E-mail: margaretklhj@aol.com.

JOHNSON, MARGUERITE See ANGELOU, MAYA

JOHNSON, MARIAN ILENE, education educator; b. Hawarden, Iowa, Oct. 3, 1929; d. Henry Richard and Wilhelmina Anna (Schmidt) Stoltenberg; m. Paul Irving Jones, June 14, 1958 (dec. Feb. 1985); m. William Andrew Johnson, Oct. 3, 1991. BA, U. La Verne, 1959; MA, Claremont Grad. Sch., 1962; PhD, Ariz. State U., 1971. Cert. tchr., Iowa, Calif. Elem. tchr. Cherokee (Iowa) Sch. Dist., 1949-52, Sioux City (Iowa) Sch. Dist., 1952-56, Ontario (Calif.) Pub. Schs., 1956-61, Reed Union Sch. Dist., Belvedere-Tiburon, Calif., 1962-65, Columbia (Calif.) Union Sch. Dist., 1965-68; prof. edn. Calif. State U., Chico, 1972-91. Avocation: travel. Home: 26437 S Lakewood Dr Sun Lakes AZ 85248-7246

JOHNSON, MARIE-LOUISE TULLY, dermatologist, educator; b. N.Y.C., July 26, 1927; d. James Henry and Mary Frances (Dobbins) Tully; m. Kenneth Gerald Johnson, June 10, 1950. AB, Manhattanville Coll., 1948; PhD, Yale U., 1954, MD, 1956. Intern, then resident Yale-New Haven Med. Ctr., 1956-59; asst. prof. medicine, dermatology Yale U., 1961-67, clin. prof. dermatology, 1980—; chief dermatologist med. svc. Atomic Bomb Casualty Commn., Hiroshima, Japan, 1964-67; assoc. prof. dermatology NYU, 1967-70, 74-76, prof. dermatology, 1976-80; assoc. prof. dermatology, coord. continuing med. edn. Dartmouth Coll., Hanover, NH, 1971-74; chief dermatology Bellevue Hosp., N.Y.C., 1974-80; dir. med. edn. Benedictine Hosp., Kingston, NY, 1980-93. Cons. Health and Nutrition Exam. Survey I, II, Health Stats., Washington, 1967-84. Contbg. author: Cecil's Textbook of Medicine, 15th edit., 1979, 16th edit., 1982, 17th edit., 1985, Dermatology in General Medicine, 2d edit., 1979. Mem. Cardinal Cooke Pro-Life Commn., Albany, N.Y., 1986-87; bd. dirs. Maternity and Early Childhood Found., Albany, 1984-2001, pres., 1987-2001; bd. dirs. Sulzberger Inst. for Dermatologic Edn., 1986-93; pres. Mid-Hudson Consortium for the Advancement of Edn. for Health Professions, 1989-92; bd. govs. Yale U. Alumni Assn., 1991-94; v.p. Assn. Yale U. Alumni in Medicine, 1991-93, pres., 1993-95. Named Disting. Alumna, Manhattanville Coll., 1977, Rose Hirschler award Women's Dermatologic Soc., 1993, Papal Cross Pro Ecclesia et Pontifice Pope John Paul II, 1994, Clark W. Finnerud award Dermatology Found., 1997. Fellow Am. Acad. Dermatology (master, bd. dirs. 1976-80, Presdl. citation 1999); mem. Am. Dermatol. Assn. (bd. dirs. 1986-92, v.p. 1991-92, pres. 2000-01), Inst. Medicine of NAS, Internat. Physicians for Prevention of Nuc. War (del. 1982, 83, 87, 88, 89). Roman Catholic. Home: 15 Strawberry Bank Rd High Falls NY 12440-5128 Office: Kingston Hosp Med Arts Bldg Ste 202 368 Broadway Kingston NY 12401-5159 Office Phone: 845-338-7472.

JOHNSON, MARILYN, retired obstetrician, gynecologist; b. Houston, May 7, 1925; d. William Walton and Marilyn (Henderson) J. BA, Rice Inst., 1945; MD, Baylor U., 1950. Intern New Eng. Hosp. Women and Children, Boston, 1950-51; resident Meth. Hosp., Houston, 1951-53; fellow in gynecol. pathology Harvard Med. Sch., 1952-53; resident in gynecology M.D. Anderson Tumor Inst., Houston, 1954, fellow, 1955; practice medicine specializing in ob-gyn. Houston, 1954-81, Fredericksburg, Tex., 1981-97; ret., 1997. Mem. staffs St. Joseph's, Meml., Meth., Park Plaza, Hill Country Meml. Rosewood, South Austin Cmty., Comfort (Tex.) Cmty. hosps.; clin. instr. ob-gyn Coll. Medicine, Baylor U., 1954—, Postgrad. Sch. Medicine, U. Tex., 1954—; gynecologist De Pelchin Faith Home, Houston, 1954—, also Rice U., Richmond State Sch.; med. dirs. Birthright, Inc., Houston, 1973—; chief med. staff Hill Country Meml. Hosp., Fredericksburg, Tex., 1990-92; cons. Tex. bd. Blue Cross Blue Shield; pro-life public spkr. Bd. dirs. Right to Life, Houston, Found. for Life. Grantee Sandoz Labs., 1973, 75, Delbay Pharm. Co., 1977. Fellow Am. Coll. Obstetricians and Gynecologists; mem. AMA, Am. Soc. Colposcopic Pathologists, Tex. Med. Assn., Am. Med. Women's Assn., Internat. Infertility Assn., Harris County Med. Soc., Postgrad. Med. Assembly South Tex., Houston Ob-Gyn. Soc., Tex. Folklore Soc., Zonta, Fredericksburg Rockhounds. Republican. Baptist. Home: 2301 Lakeside Ct Rockport TX 78382-3519

JOHNSON, MARLENE M. nonprofit executive; b. Braham, Minn., Jan. 11, 1946; d. Beauford and Helen (Nelson) J.; m. Peter Frankel. BA, Macalester Coll., 1968. Founder, pres. Split Infinitive, Inc., St. Paul, 1970-82; pres., bd. dirs. Face to Face Health and Counseling Clinic, 1977-78; with Working Opportunities for Women, 1977-82; lt. gov. State of Minn., St. Paul, 1983-91; sr. fellow Family Support Project, Ctr. for Policy Alternative, 1991-93; assoc. adminstr. for adminstrn. GSA, Washington, 1994-95; v.p. for people and strategy Rowe Furniture Corp., McLean, Va., 1995-97; CEO NAFSE: Assn. Internat. Educators, 1998—. Founder, past chmn. Nat. Leadership Conf. Women Execs. in State Govt.; mem. exec. com., midwestern chair Nat. Conf. Lt. Govs.; bd. dirs. AFS-USA, Inc., 1992-98, Nat. Capitol Region coun. Girl Scouts U.S., 1997-2004, bd. trustees AFS Internat. programs, 1998-2002; mem. adv. bd. Comm. Consortium Media Ctr., 2000-, Ctr. for Children in Poverty, Columbia U., 2002. Chmn. Minn. Women's Polit. Caucus, 1973-76, Dem.-Farmer-Labor Small Bus. Task Force, 1978, Child Care Task Force, 1987; dir. membership sect. Nat. Women's Polit. Caucus, 1975-77; vice chmn. Minn. Del. to White House Conf. on Small Bus., 1980; co-founder Minn. Women's Campaign Fund, 1982; bd. dirs. Nat. Child Care Action Campaign; chair Children's 2000 Commn., 1990; candidate for Mayor St. Paul, 1993. Recipient Outstanding Achievement award St. Paul YWCA, 1980, Disting. Svc. award St. Paul Jaycees, 1980, Disting. Citizen citation Macalester Coll., 1982, Disting. Contbns. to Families award Minn. Coun. on Family Rels., 1986, Minn. Sportfishing Congress award, 1986, Royal Order of Polar Star Govt. Sweden, 1988, Children's Champion award Def. Fund, 1989, Jane Preston award Minn. State Coun. on Vocat. Tech. Edn., 1989, Legis. Leadership award Am. Fedn. Tchrs., 1991; named One of Ten Outstanding Young Minnesotans, Minn. Jaycees, 1980; Swedish Bicentennial Commn. grantee, 1987. Mem. Nat. Assn. Women Bus. Owners (past pres.). Office Phone: 202-737-3699. E-mail: marlenej@nafsa.org.

JOHNSON, MARLYS MARLENE, elementary school educator; b. Omak, Wash., Mar. 13, 1946; d. Beverly Wayne and Mary Etta (Greene) McGrath; m. Gary Vaughn Johnson, Aug. 13, 1967 (div. June 3, 2001); children: Chad, Shane, Aubrey. BS in Edn., Wash. State U., 1967, MEd, 1991. Cert. profl. educator Wash., tchr. Va. Substitute tchr. Pullman (Wash.) Sch. Dist., 1970—80, home hosp. tutor, 1973—77, tchr. 2d grade, 1980—2001; tchr. 5th grade Alexandria (Va.) City Pub. Schs., 2001—02, tchr. 1st grade, 2002—03, tchr. 3d grade, 2003—. Pres. Profl. Edn. Adv. Bd. Office Supt. Pub. Instrn. and Wash. State U., Olympia and Pullman, 2000; tchr. leader Curriculum Instrn. Leadership Coun., Pullman, 1996—2001; presenter in field. Contbr. articles to profl. jours. Host family chair Wash. State Jr. Miss, Pullman, 1998—2001; awards chairperson Pullman Swim Club; mother advisor Rainbow for Girls; mem. scholarship com. 4-H. Recipient Christa McAuliffe Excellence in Edn. award, State of Wash./OSPI, 1990; grantee Contextual Tchg. grantee, U.S. Dept. Edn., 1999—2001, Rsch. Tech. grantee, RMC Rsch. Corp., Pullman, 1999—2000. Mem.: Wash. Edn. Assn. (rep. assembly del.), Pullman Edn. Assn. (exec. sec.), Phi Kappa Phi. Methodist. Home: 1501 N Highview Ln #110 Alexandria VA 22311

JOHNSON, MARY ALICE, magazine editor; b. Rochester, Ind., Apr. 16, 1942; d. Nolan Lee and Alice Lavida (Ruede) Lewis; m. Manford Warren Johnson, May 28, 1960 (dec. Oct. 1998); children: Nola (dec.), John Jay, June Jeannette. Grad. high sch., Hillsboro, Oreg., 1960. Owner, baker, decorator Mary's Custom Cakes and Cake Parts, St. Helens, Oreg., 1980-87; creator Sweet Tooth Confections Candy, 1981—; founder, mng. editor Sugar Art Sharing Confectionary Ideas mag., 1986-88; chmn. Sugar Art Ltd. Partnership, McMinnville, Oreg., 1986-93; owner Double Rainbow Enterprises (now Double Rainbow Ministries), Redmond, 1993—. Tchr. cake decorating, candy and gingerbread houses, 1981-99; owner Peace Acres Bible Retreat, 2003—. Author: ABC Bible, 1967, I See God In Everything, 1975, The Wedding Book, 1983, Friends Feasts & Fellowship, 1992, God and Money, 1992, Looseleaf Pattern Library, 1992, Mary's Cook Book, 1993, It's Time to Oil the Lamps, 1994, (videotape) Gingerbread Mansions, 1996. Leader, Country Kids and Friends 4-H, St. Helens, 1979-85; organizer rural fire dept., Rainier, Oreg.; Sunday sch. tchr. Luth. Ch., 1956-74, officer women's groups, 1960-77; sec. Tualitan Valley Rabbit Breeders Assn., 1964-67, fair dinner booth chmn., 1965-66; ballot clk. Columbia County Election Bd., 1972-80; decorated cake supt. Columbia County Fair, 1983-85; decorations chmn. Christian Women's Club, McMinnville, 1989-90; founder youth hobby club Pettis Fours Club, 1989. Winner awards for entries in numerous county and state fairs, cake shows. Mem. Internat. Cake Exploration Soc. Republican. Lutheran. Avocations: crafts, oil painting, reading. Office: Double Rainbow Ministries 58486 Carrico Rd PO Box 196 Christmas Valley OR 97641 Office Phone: 541-480-5158.

JOHNSON, MARY ANN, vocational school owner; b. Chgo., June 26, 1956; d. Truly and Pearlie Mae (Bell) J.; children: Pamela Ann, Russell Alan Jr. AA, Joliet (Ill.) Jr. Coll., 1990; student mgmt. info. systems, Governor State U. Student intern Argonne (Ill.) Nat. Lab., 1972-79; owner, pres. Tech. Soft Svcs., Chgo., 1991—. Lectr., condr. seminars on running small bus. Author: Running a Small Business, 1996. Avocations: self defense, computer and software edn. Office: Tech Soft Svcs 160 E Illinois St Ste 603 Chicago IL 60611-3859 Office Phone: 312-527-1200. Personal E-mail: tssch60610@aol.com.

JOHNSON, MARY ELIZABETH, retired elementary education educator; b. St. Louis, Sept. 17, 1943; d. Richard William Blayney and Alice Bonjean (Taylor) Blayney Needham; m. Clyde Robert Johnson, Aug. 31, 1963; children: Brian (dec. 1991), Elizabeth Johnson Meyer, David. BS cum laude, U. Ill., 1966; MA, Maryville U., 1990; postgrad., So. Ill. U., 1990. Cert. elem. tchr., Ill., Mo. Tchr. Hazelwood Sch. Dist., Florissant, Mo., 1971-93, positive intervention tchr., 1989-91. Author play: Say No to Drugs, 1991. Author: Secret Study Skills for Third Graders, 1990. Mem. Hazelwood Schs. Music Boosters, 1980-88; mem. coms. Townsend PTA, Florissant, 1976—; contbr. Schlarship Run-Walk, 1982—; mem. Children's United Rsch. Effort in Cancer, 1986—; vol. Spl. Love, Inc., camp for children with cancer, 1986—; active The Children's Inn, Bethesda, Md., 1990—, Bailey Scholarship Fund, U. Ill., 1994—; mem. scholarship com. Clark County Sch. Dist., Las Vegas, Nev., 2001-04. Fred S. Bailey scholar, 1962-66, Edmund J. James scholar, 1964-65; named Townsend Tchr. of Yr., 1989-90. Mem. NEA, Internat. Platform Assn., Kappa Delta Pi, Alpha Lambda Delta, Phi Kappa Phi. Baptist. Avocations: travel, reading, crafts, writing, music. Home: 2016 Bay Tree Sun City Las Vegas NV 89134-5235

JOHNSON, MARY KATHERINE (KATIE JOHNSON), elementary school educator; b. Prescott, Wis., June 12, 1945; d. Walter Frank and Mary Jane (Larson) Johnson; m. William F. Hilton, June 23, 1968 (div. 1985); children: Bradley Eric, Karin Louise. BA, Mich. State U., 1967, MA, 1970; postgrad., U. Calif., Berkeley, 1970—. Cert. elem. tchr., Calif. Tchr. East Lansing (Mich.) Pub. Schs., 1967-68, Hall's Crossroads Sch., Aberdeen, Md., 1968-69, Oakland (Calif.) Pub. Schs., 1970-82; tchr., cons. Bay Area Writing Project, Berkeley, 1978—, Bay Area Math. Project, Berkeley, 1994—, Bay Area Calif. Arts Project, Berkeley, 1997—; cons. Child Devel. Project, San Ramon, Calif., 1985; tchr. Berkeley Unified Sch. Dist., 1986—, support provider, beginning tchr. support and assessment program, 2000—, tchr math leader, 2003—; coord. pub. programs, math. edn. program Lawrence Hall of Sci., U. Calif., Berkeley, 1996-98; curriculum developer, writer U. Calif. Bot. Gardens, 2001—, tchr. trainer. Mem. MATHTEQ U. Calif, Berkeley, 1987—90; mem. com. of credentials Commn. for Tchr. Preparation and Licensing, Sacramento, 1974—76; spkr. Asilomar Math. Conf., 1991—, mem. program com., 1995—2000; spkr. Assn. for Persons with Severe Handicaps (Calif. chpt.) Conf., 1992, 94, 97, 98, 2000, 01, 03, bd. dir., 1997—; spkr. Assn. for Persons with Severe Handicaps Internat. Conf., 1993, 2001, 02, 04, Supported Life Conf., 1992; rep. No. Regional

Spl. Edn. Local Plan Area Com., 1994—98, Region III Full Inclusion Task Force for State of Calif., 1994—98; participant Calif. Rsch. Inst., 1992; mem. adv. task force on tchr. preparation in mainstreaming Calif. Commn. on Tchr. Credentialling, 1996; adv. bd. Profl. Internship Program., U. Calif., Berkeley; tchr. leader Profl. Insvc. for New and Experienced Tchrs., 1997—; mem. tchr. leader Profl. Instrn. for New and [illegible] 1998—2002; pres. Alameda/Contra Costa County Math Educators, 2000—, bd. dirs.; math tchr. leader Berkeley Unified Sch. Dist., 2003—, mem. spl. edn. task force, 2004—. Contbg. author: Portfolio Assessment in Mathematics, 1990, Teacher Handbook on Homework, C.M.C. Communicator, 1993. Coord. children's coun. Epworth Meth. Ch., Berkeley, 1985-88, 96-98, Youth Coun., 1993-95; cert. lay spkr. Bay View dist. Calif.-Nev. United Meth. Ch., Berkeley, 1989—, trustee, 1994-96, 98-2002; pres. bd. trustees Maya's Music Therapy Fund, 1994—; mentor tchr. Berkeley Unified Sch. Dist., 1996, 99; mem. adv. bd. Calif. Urban Partnership program U. Calif., Berkeley, 1999—. Recipient Outstanding Alumni K-12 Tchr. award Mich. State U. Coll. Edn. Alumni Assn., 2002; named Math. Tchr. of Yr. Alameda/Contra Costa Counties Math. Educators, 1996; Berkeley Pub. Edn. Found. grantee, 1988, 89, 90, 92, 94, 95, 98, 2000-03, 2004, In Dulce Jullibo Inc. grantee, 1989, 90, 92, 94, 95, 99, 2003, BAMP grantee, 1995, Calif. Math. Coun. grantee, 1995; fellow Bay Area Math. Project, 1994, Oakland-Bay Area Writing Project, 1977, Bay Area Writing Project, 1978, 98, Bay Area Calif. Arts Project, 1997. Mem. Nat. Coun. Tchrs. English, Nat. Coun. Tchrs. Math., Calif. English Coun., Calif. Math. Coun., P.E.O., Profl. Instr. for New and Established Teacher; bd. dirs. CA Chpt. Assn. Persons with Severe Handicaps, 1997—, Alameda-Contra Costa County Math. Educators (pres. 2000—). Democrat. Avocations: singing, jogging, swimming, gourmet cooking, sewing. Home: 1016 Keeler Ave Berkeley CA 94708-1404 Office: Oxford Sch 1130 Oxford St Berkeley CA 94707-2624

JOHNSON, MARY KATHRYN, legal assistant; b. Oak Park, Ill., Sept. 5, 1942; d. Herbert Gold and Vera Lillian (Engel) Oldham; m. James Arnold Johnson, Feb. 17, 1968 (div. 1970); 1 child, Stephanie Louise. BA in German, U. Ill., 1966. Cert. legal assistantship; cert. tchg. ESL; lic. tax preparer, Calif. Editl. asst. U. Chgo., 1968; legal asst. Harry W. Brelsford, Atty., Santa Barbara, Calif., 1974-83; pvt. legal asst. Santa Barbara, 1984—. Instr. H&R Block, Santa Barbara, 1992, Santa Barbara City Coll., 1992-93; tax preparer, Santa Barbara, 1992—. Mem. Legal Assts. Assn. Santa Barbara (life, pres. 1987-89). Home and Office: PO Box 2280 Santa Barbara CA 93120-2280

JOHNSON, MARY LOU, lay worker, educator; b. Moline, Ill., July 15, 1923; d. Percy and Hope (Aulgur) Sipes; m. Blaine Eugene Johnson, May 30, 1941 (dec.); children: Vivian Johnson Sweedy Maday, Michael D. (dec.), Amelia Johnson Harms Thomas, James Michael (dec.). Grad. high sch., Moline. From chmn. Christian edn. to dir. 1st Christian Ch., Moline, 1971—88, dir. Christian edn., 1988—93, ret., 1993, chmn. Christian edn., 2001—03. Sunday sch. tchr. 1st Christian Ch., Moline, 1958-84; cluster del. Christian Chs. Ill. and Wisc., Moline, 1988-89; bd. dir. Wee Care Day Care Ctr. Author: (poem) What Is A Mother?, 1965. Officer various positions PTA, Moline, 1972-75, hon. life mem. State of Ill., 1972; leader, dist. chair Girl Scouts U.S., Moline, 1955-65; skywatcher USAF Ground Observer Corps, Moline, 1955-57; vol. telethon coord. Muscular Dystrophy Assn., Moline, 1971-94; del. lt. gov.'s Commn. on Aging, Springfield, Ill., 1990; historian 1st Christian Ch., Moline, 1996—, libr., 2000—; vol. C.A.R.E. Ministry, 1999—, Ring for Care, 1999-2002, We. Ill. Area Agy. on Aging, 1998-2003; bd. dirs. Wee Care Day Care Ctr. Recipient Appreciation award Muscular Dystrophy Assn., 1964-94. Republican. Home: 2014 9th St Moline IL 61265-4779 Personal E-mail: grmalou624@aol.com.

JOHNSON, MARY MARGARET DICKENS, researcher, consultant; b. Ottumwa, Iowa, July 10, 1955; d. Donald Milton and Maxine Margaret Dickens; m. Donald Hampton Johnson, July 30, 1944; children: Laurie Anne Davidson, Donald, Jr. Hampton. M, U. Hawaii, 1979; B, Iowa State U., 1976; M, Johns Hopkins Sch. Advanced Internat. Studies, 1986; Cert. of Completion, U. Va., 1988—92; candidate in pub. affairs, Fla .Atlantic U., 2003—. Cert. purchasing mgr. Rsch. asst. Iowa State U., Dept. of Sociology & Anthropology, Ames, Iowa, 1974—76; rsch. grantee East West Ctr., Honolulu, 1976—78; fgn. affairs specialist U.S. Dept. of State/Agy. for Internat. Devel., Washington, 1980—81; fed. summer intern U.S. Dept. of Commerce/Nat. Telecom. and Info. Adminstrn., Washington, 1980—80; export adminstrn. specialist U.S. Dept. of Commerce, Washington, 1982—85; English lang. tchr. INTERAC, Tokyo, 1985; tchr., pub. rels. officer Overseas Devel. Co., Kowloon, Hong Kong, 1986—87; English lang. tchr. Phillips Lang. Learning Systems, Tokyo, 1986; sr. contracts mgr. Systems Flow, Inc., Rockville, Md., 1997—98; contract specialist U.S. GSA, Washington, 1987—94, Wash. Suburban San. Commn., Laurel, Md., 1996—97. Workshop/seminar leader Nat. Contract Mgmt. Assn., Long Beach, Calif., 2002—02; third v.p. Alpha Chi Omega Sorority, Ames, Iowa, 1975—76; outstanding scholar U.S. GSA, Washington, 1987—94; workshop leader Nat. Contract Mgmt. Assn. World Congress, Long Beach, Calif., 2002—02; author Nat. Def. Coll. Symposium, Rockville, Md., 1998—98; field study grant for ind. rsch. East West Ctr. Communication Inst., Honolulu, 1977—77; student project for amity among nations rschr. in nigeria Iowa State U., Ames, Iowa, 1974—74; workshop/seminar leader Nat. Contract Mgmt. Assn., Idaho Falls, Idaho, 2002—02, West Palm Beach, Fla., 2000—00, Nat. Assn. of Purchasing Managers, Boca Raton, Fla., 2002—02; pres. Nat. Contract Mgmt. Assn., South Fla. Chpt., Boca Raton, Fla., 2003—; author Nat. Contract Mgmt. Assn., Contract Mgmt. Mag., McLean, Va., 1996—; fellow Nat. Contract Mgmt. Assn., McLean, Va., 2003—; mem. Mortar Bd., Iowa State U., Ames, Iowa, 1976—2003; pres. Alpha Lamda Delta, Ames, Iowa, 1973—74; rsch. asst. Pub. Procurement Rsch. Ctr., 2003—. Author: (article contract mgmt. mag.) Planning for Y2K: What the Government Did Right, (jour. article) Minority Preferences at a Cross Roads for State and Local Governments, Understanding the EAR: Federal Export Regulations, Government Contract Terminations: A Primer, How the Government of the District of Columbia Outsourced Procurement, The United Nations CISG. Mem. Chapel St. Andrew, Boca Raton, Fla., 1998—2003. Fellow: Nat. Contract Mgmt. Assn. (cert. profl. contracts mgr. 2002, cert. assoc. contracts mgr. 2002, pres. 2003, grant to participate in World Congress 2002); mem.: Nat. Assn. Purchasing Mgmt. (workshop leader 2002, Monetary award presentation 2002). Avocations: bicycling, walking, needlepoint, cooking, gardening. Home: 1926 NE 2nd St Deerfield Beach FL 33441 Office: Florida Atlantic U 111 East Las Olas Blvd Fort Lauderdale FL 33301 Personal E-mail: conchcontracts@aol.com.

JOHNSON, MARY MURPHY, social worker, writer; b. N.Y.C., Mar. 5, 1940; d. Richard and Nora (Greene) Murphy; m. Noel James Johnson, Oct. 8, 1961 (dec.); children: Valerie Johnson Powell, Donna Homan, Noreen Marie Pettitt, Richard. BA in English/History magna cum laude, BS in Sociology magna cum laude, Jacksonville State U., 1983, MA in History, 1984, B in Social Work magna cum laude, 1988. Cert. gerontology specialist. Asst. activities dir. Jacksonville (Ala.) Nursing Home, 1985-86; social services dir. Beckwood Manor, Anniston, Ala., 1987—. Cons. in field. Editor: Vladivostak Diary, 1987. Mem. AAUW, Nat. Assn. for Family and Cmty. Edn., Ala. Archaeol. Soc., Coosa Valley Archaeol. Soc. (sec. 1982-87), Soc. Ala. Archivists, Human Svcs. Coun., Treasure Forest Assn., Vietnam Vets. Am., Soc. for Creative Anachronism (Reeve, Canton of the Peregrine), Phi Eta Sigma, Phi Alpha Theta, Sigma Tau Delta, Omicron Delta Kappa. Russian Orthodox. Avocations: collecting antiques and depression glass, hiking, reading, archaeology. Home: 4040 Brookside Ln Oxford AL 36203-9233

JOHNSON, MARY P. freelance writer; b. Balt., Sept. 23, 1927; d. Frederick and Marie Rosina (Walter) Manke; m. Alvin H. Walker, June 21, 1947 (div. Mar. 1955); m. Maurice P. Johnson, July 1, 1955; 1 child, Carol Joy. Student, Johns Hopkins U., 1959-63. Assoc. dir. Centennial planning and programs Johns Hopkins U., Balt., 1973-77; arts reviewer Balt. Sun-Arundel, 1997—; reviewer concerts and theater, reporter Severna Park (Md.) Voice, 1998—. Mem. Journalism and Women Symposium, 2002. Bd. dirs. Performing Arts Assn., Linthicum, Md., 1995—. Mem.: AAUW, Am. [illegible] Women in Comms., Friends of Annapolis Opera, Friends of Annapolis Chorale, Friends of Annapolis Orch., Balt. Symphony, Balt. Opera, Met. Opera Guild. Democrat. Lutheran. Personal E-mail: marybud@toad.net.

JOHNSON, MARY PAULINE (POLLY JOHNSON), nursing executive; b. Ohio, May 23, 1940; BSN summa cum laude, Ohio State U., 1962; MSN, Duke U., 1980. RN, N.C. Staff nurse psychiatry unit Univ. Hosps., Ohio, 1963-64; pediatric office nurse Gaithersburg, Md., 1971-73; clin. nurse coord. N.C. Meml. Hosp., Chapel Hill, 1973-86; grant coord. N.C. Assn. Home Care, 1988; practice cons. N.C. Bd. Nursing, Raleigh, 1988-96, assoc. dir. practice, 1996-97, exec. dir., 1997—. Adv. com. PREP Project Citizens Advocacy Ctr. Mem. ANA, Nat. Coun. State Bds. Nursing (bd. dirs., rep. N.C. chpt.), N.C. Nurses Assn., N.C. Orgn. Nurse Leaders. Office: NC Bd of Nursing 3724 National Dr Raleigh NC 27612-4070 E-mail: polly@ncbon.com.

JOHNSON, MARYFRAN, editor; married; 2 children. BA in French Lit., SUNY, Albany; B in Journalism, U. Fla.; M in Journalism, Ohio State U. Reporter The Gainesville (Fla.) Sun, Framingham, Mass., The Tri-City Herald, Wash., The Cin. Enquirer; tech. reporter Computer World, Framingham, Mass., 1989, founding editor Client/Server Jour., 1993, news editor, 1994, exec. editor, 1996, editor-in-chief, 1999—. Spkr. in field. Office: Computer World PO Box 9171 Framingham MA 01701-9171

JOHNSON, MARYL RAE, cardiologist; b. Fort Dodge, Iowa, Apr. 15, 1951; d. Marvin George and Beryl Evelyn (White) Johnson. BS, Iowa State U., 1973; MD, U. Iowa, 1977. Diplomate Am. Bd. Internal Medicine, Am. Bd. Cardiovasc. Diseases. Intern U. Iowa Hosps., Iowa City, 1977-78, resident, 1978-81, fellow, 1979-82; assoc. in cardiology U. Iowa Hosps. and Clins., Iowa City, 1982-86, asst. prof. medicine cardiovasc. divsn., 1986-88; asst. prof. medicine Med. Ctr. Loyola U., 1988-92, assoc. prof., 1992-94, Rush. U., 1994-97, Northwestern U. Med. Sch., 1998—2002; prof. medicine U. Wis. Med. Sch., Madison, 2002—. Med. dir. cardiac transplantation U. Iowa Hosp., 1986—88; assoc. med. dir. cardiac transplantation Loyola U., 1988—94, assoc. med. dir. Rush Heart Failure and Cardiac Transplant Program, 1994—97; dir. heart failure cardiac transplant program Northwestern U. Med. Sch., 1998—2001, dir. heart failure program, 2001—02; med. dir. heart failure and transplantation U. Wis. Hosp. and Clinics, 2002—. Editor (assoc. editor): Jour. Heart and Lung Transplantation, 1995—99; mem. editl. bd.:, 2000—. Mem. Nat. Heart Lung and Blood Adv. Coun., Bethesda, Md., 1979—83; mem. biomed. rsch. tech. rev. com. NIH, 1990—93, chairperson, 1992—93, chair biomed. rsch. tech. spl. emphasis panel, 1999—. Recipient Jane Leinfelder Meml. award, U. Iowa Coll. Medicine, 1977, Clin. Investigator award, NIH, 1981, New Investigator Rsch. award, 1981, 1986; Barry Freeman scholar, 1974. Mem.: ACP, AAAS, AMA, Am. Soc. Transplantation (chair membership com. 2003—), Am. Coll. Cardiology (heart failure and cardiac transplant com. 2002—, chair 2004—), Am. Heart Assn., Ctrl. Soc. Clin. Rsch., Internat. Soc. Heart and Lung Transplantation, Order of Rose, Alpha Omega Alpha, Iota Sigma Pi, Phi Kappa Phi, Alpha Lambda Delta. Office: U Wis Madison E5/582D CSC 5710 600 Highland Ave Madison WI 53792 Office Phone: 608-263-0080. E-mail: mrj@medicine.wisc.edu.

JOHNSON, MATTIEDNA, medical/surgical nurse; b. Amite County, Miss., Apr. 7, 1918; d. Isaac and Minnie (Ramsey) J.; m. Robert William Kelley, Oct. 19, 1943 (div. May 1980); children: Bobby Lou, Robert William Jr., Patricia Elaine, Frances Minette. RN, Terrell Meml. Hosp.; postgrad., Homer G. Phillips Hosp.; MA, Ashland Theol. Sem. RN, Tenn., Mont., Minn.; diaconal min. United Meth. Ch. Head nurse Jane Terrell Hosp., Memphis; staff nurse Homer G. Phillips Hosp., St. Louis; lab. tech. U.S. Army U. Minn., Mpls.; pvt. duty nurse Mpls. Dist. Minn. State, Mpls.; medical missionary Gbarnga (Liberia) Meth. Mission; pvt. duty night nurse Mo., Tenn., Ohio. Author: Tots Goes to Gbarnga, 1994, Johnson's Instructors Guide, 1949, Johnson's Manual-Church Nursing, 1994. Created ch. nursing Am. Red Cross., 1949—, vol. instr. Recipient Last Living Natural Scientist of 2000 Millennium award. Mem. ANA, Nat. Black Nurses Assn. (sec. 1970—). Achievements include crystallization of penicillin mold for gun shot wounds; tests of staphlococcus germs and terriable mice mold against streptococcus hymolyticus germ of scarlet fever; developed R13 Mold penicillin crystals for the injectable IV-Intra Muscular. Home: 13606 Abell Ave Cleveland OH 44120-3954

JOHNSON, MELISSA CAROL, poet, educator; b. Lancaster, SC, Feb. 4, 1968; d. Kelly Luther and Carol Cody Johnson; m. Joseph H. Schaub, Nov. 6, 1999; m. Kristian M. Niemi, Feb. 3, 1990 (div. 1996). BA, Coll. of Charleston, SC, 1986—89; MFA, U. S.C., Columbia, 1993—96, Grad. Cert. in Women's Studies, 1996—2001, PhD, 1996—2002. Asst. prof. Newberry Coll., SC, 2003—. Editor: (literary journal) Yemassee, 1996—99; co-author (with Robert Newman and Jean Bohner): (textbook) Uncommon Threads: Reading and Writing About Contemporary America, 2003; author: (published poems) The Connecticut Rev., New Rev., Borderlands, Farmer's Market, West Wind Rev. Reed Smith Meml. fellow, U. S.C., 1993—94, Bates fellow, 1997, 1998, 2000. Mem.: AAUW, Newberry County Hist. Soc., Phi Kappa Phi, Sigma Tau Delta (assoc.). Liberal. Avocations: reading, travel, jogging. Office: Newberry College 2100 College St Newberry SC 29108 E-mail: melissa.johnson@newberry.edu.

JOHNSON, MELODY, school system administrator; BS in Sociology, Phillips U.; PhD in Ednl. Adminstrn., U. Tex., Austin. Tchr., Okla., Dallas, Selma, San Antonio, 1975—82; asst. prin. Meridith Magnet Sch., Tex., 1983—85; prin. Travis Mid. Sch., Tex., 1985—89; state sr. dir. Mid. Sch. Edn. for Tex., 1992—95; dist. area supt. for San Antonio, 1995—97; assoc. supt. for curriculum, instrn. and student support San Antonio Ind. Sch. Dist., 1997—2000; dep. supt. Providence Schs., 2000—. Pres. Coop. Superintendency Exec. Leadership Program, U. Tex. Fellow Broad Found. Nat. Supt.'s Acad., 2002, Coop. Superintency, 1989. Achievements include commended by State Comptr. of Tex. for excellent curriculum frameworks and stds. documents; acknowledged by Carnegie Corp. N.Y. for having served as one of 15 state dirs. of nat. mid. sch. initiative. Office: Providence Pub Schs 797 Westminster St Providence RI 02903-4045*

JOHNSON, MILDRED GRACE MASH, investment company executive; b. Castle Rock, Wash., Mar. 3, 1922; d. Percival and Hilda C. (Nyberg) M.; widowed, 1988; children: John, Joy, Judy, Chris, Steven. Student, U. Wash. Pres. Johnson Investment Co., Seattle, 1988—. Deacon U. Presbyn. Ch., Seattle, 1981—. Mem. Am. Bus. Women's Assn. (v.p. 1979-89, Woman of Yr. 1981), Apt. Opt. Assn. (hon. 25 Yr. Mem.), Master Builders, Daus. Nile, Order of Ea. Star. Republican. Avocations: entertaining, skiing, writing, reading, traveling. Home: 3812 E Mcgilvra St Seattle WA 98112-2427

JOHNSON, MITZI, state representative; b. Clifton Park, N.Y., Nov. 18, 1970; BS, U. Vt., 1993. Mgr. vegetable prodn. and apple harvest Allenholm Farm, South Hero; state rep. State of Vt., 2003—. Cons. Freedom to Marry Task Force; pvt. piano tchr.; substitute tchr. Capt., EMS South Hero Rescue; founding mem., bd. dirs. South Hero Land Trust; mem. Route Two Radio Troupe. Democrat. Office: PO Box 144 South Hero VT 05486

JOHNSON, MYRTLE ALICE HARRIS, elementary and secondary school educator; b. Phila., Aug. 10, 1947; d. James and Margaret (Robinson) Harris; m. Ronald Walter Johnson, May 24, 1975; 1 child, Craig Noel. BS in Edn., Temple U., 1977; MDiv, New Brunswick Theological Seminary, 2000. Cert. tchr., Pa., N.J. Tchr. Pine Hill (N.J.) Bd. Edn., 1977—84; language tchr. Passaic (N.J.) Bd. Edn., 1987—88. Creative bible instr. preachers kids Internat. Assn. of Min. Wives and Min. Widows, Inc., 1986—92; chair preachers kids Internat. Assn. of Min. Wives and Min. Widows, Inc., 1993—2002. Sunday sch. tchr. Union Bapt. Ch., Passaic, N.J., organizer, dir., tchr. Vacation Bible Sch.; dir., tchr. Vacation Bible Sch. Jones Meml. Bapt. Ch., Phila. Recipient Outstanding Leadership award Vacation Bible Sch., Jones Meml. Bapt. Ch., Phila., Muriel Lemon Johnson Internat. award, 2001; crowned Queen Women's Convention, Nat. Bapt. Convention, 2002-03. Mem. Internat. Interdenominational Min.'s Wives and Min.'s Widows, Inc., N. Jersey Bapt. Assn., Missionary Bapt. Assn., Inc. (1st v.p. women's aux. N. Jersey dist. 2001—). Home: 219 Myrtle Ave Passaic NJ 07055-3212

JOHNSON, NANCY LEE, congresswoman; b. Chgo., Jan. 5, 1935; d. Noble Wishard and Gertrude Reid (Smith) Lee; m. Theodore H. Johnson, June 27, 1932; children— Lindsey Lee, Althea Anne, Caroline Reid BA, Radcliffe Coll., 1957; postgrad., U. London, 1957-58. Vice chmn. Charter Commn. New Britain, Conn., 1976-77; mem. Conn. Senate from 6th dist., 1977-82, 98th-108th Congresses from 6th and 5th Conn. dist., Washington, 1983—; mem. ways and means com., chmn. health subcom. 101st-108th Congresses from 6th and 5th Conn. Dist., Washington. Pres. Friends of Libr., New Britain Pub. Libr., 1973-76, Radcliffe Club Northern Conn., 1973-75; bd. dirs., pres. Sheldon Cmty. Guidance Clinic, 1974-75; dir. religious edn. Unitarian Universalist Soc. New Britain, 1967-72; bd. dirs. United Way New Britain, 1976.79. Recipient Outstanding Vol. award United Way, 1976; English Speaking Union grantee, 1958-59 Republican. Home: 141 S Mountain St New Britain CT 06052-1511 Office: Ho of Reps 2113 Rayburn Bldg Washington DC 20515-0705

JOHNSON, PAM, former newspaper editor, communications educator; Mng. editor Phoenix Gazette, 1989—93, Ariz. Republic, Phoenix, 1993-96, sr. v.p. news, exec. editor, 1996—2001; educator, Poynter Inst., St. Petersburg, Fla., 2001—. Office: The Poynter Institute 801 3rd St S Saint Petersburg FL 33701 E-mail: pjohnson@poynter.org.*

JOHNSON, PATRICIA B, medical, surgical nurse, mental health nurse; b. Memphis, Feb. 27, 1934; d. Walter Jones and Georgia Taylor; m. Clarence Johnson, July 23, 1961; 1 child, Pamela Suzanne Johnson Taylor. Diploma, Homer G. Phillips Sch. Nurses, St. Louis; diploma in nursing, L.A. City Coll.; diploma sec. bus. admin., Oakwood Coll.; postgrad., San Antonio Coll. CPR instr., BLS. Staff RN Homer G. Phillips Hosp., St. Louis, Barnes Hosp., St. Louis, Milw. City Hosp.; ret. RN Brooke Army Med. Ctr./Fort Sam Houston, San Antonio; ret., 2000. Contbr. to videos on nursing, skill books in field. Mem. Iota Phi Lamba. Avocations: professional modeling, designing clothes, cake decorating, real estate investment.

JOHNSON, PATRICIA DIANE, nurse anesthetist; b. Bklyn., Mar. 27, 1956; d. Evelyn Smith Walker; m. Gregory Leroy Johnson, Sept. 17, 1983; children: Ebony, Aisha, Clinton, Garrett, Gerald. BS in Biology, St. John's U., Queens, N.Y., 1977; BS in Nursing, Downstate Med. Sch. Nursin, Bklyn., 1979; anesthesia cert., Kings County Sch. Anesthesia, Bklyn., 1985; M Cmty. Health, Bklyn. Coll., 1994. Cert. anesthesia for nurses. Nurse cardiac ICU, neurology, oncology Mt. Sinai Hosp., N.Y.C., 1979-83; nurse anesthetist, instr. Kings County Hosp., Bklyn., 1985-88; nurse anesthetist Queens (N.Y.) Hosp. Ctr., 1988. Pres. First Jerusalem Bapt. Ch. Ednl. Club, Bklyn., 1994-95, pres. pastor's aide, 1994-99, Sunday Sch. tchr., 1993-99, choir mem., 1994—; v.p. PTA-St. Mark Day Sch., Bklyn., 1994—. Mem. Am. Assn. Nurse Anesthetists. Avocations: reading, volleyball, singing, computers, children's programs. Home: 109 Hampton Ridge Rd Macon GA 31220-4008

JOHNSON, PATRICIA LUCILLE, editor, writer; b. Des Moines, Dec. 29, 1949; d. Kenneth Lyle Parker and Phyllis Arlene Horton; m. Andrew Johnson, Jr., Dec. 21, 1999; children: John Kenneth, Jeffrey Robert, Kathryn Linn. BFA, cert. in Art Tchg., U. Iowa, 1972; student in Personnel and Counseling, Drake U., 1988—90. Cert. tchr. U. Iowa. Tchr. Parker Sch. of Art, Des Moines, 1978—80, U. N.Mex., Roswell, N.Mex., 1980—81, Roswell (N.Mex.) Mus. and Art Ctr., 1981—82; editor Heartland Area Edn. Agy., Johnston, Iowa, 1988—99, Writeview, Slidell, La., 1999—. Adminstr. Internet Writing Workshop, 2002—03. Editor: The Book of Remembrance, 2002—, The Green Tricycle, 2003—; author: Purple Hammered Gold, 2003—. Fellow: Poetry Soc. Am. Avocations: art, poetry, writing. Office: Writeview 315 Queen Anne Drive Slidell LA 70460-8437

JOHNSON, PATSY, nursing association administrator; Exec. administr. Kans. State Bd. Nursing, Topeka. Office: Kans State Bd of Nursing Landon State Office Bldg 900 SW Jackson St Rm 551 Topeka KS 66612-1225

JOHNSON, PENNY SUE, auditor; b. Washington Court House, Ohio, Jan. 20, 1951; d. Virgil Wayman and Nellie Louise (Lower) Hardman; m. Marvin E. Matthews, Sept. 4, 1976 (div. July 1980); m. Glen O. Johnson, Sept. 8, 1984. Student, Ohio U., 1969-71, So. State C.C., Wilmington, Ohio, 1985-86. Acctg. clk. Fayette Landmark Inc., Washington Court House, 1971-85; billing clk. Mead Container Corp., Washington Court House, 1985-86; dep. auditor Fayette County Auditor's Office, Washington Court House, 1986-95; auditor, chief fiscal officer Fayette County, Washington Court House, 1995—. V.p. Fayette County Rep. Women, Washington Court House, 1981, pres., 1982-83, 88-89; assoc. mem. Fayette County Commn. on Aging, 1994—. Mem. Bus. Profl. Women's Club (rec. sec. 1994-95, 2d v.p. 1995-96, 1st v.p. 1996-97, sec. region 8 1997-98, named Woman of Yr. 1996-97), Fayette County C. of C. (amb. 1995—), Ohio Treasurers and Clks. Assn., S.W. Dist. Auditors Assn. (22 county dist. sec./treas. 1996, v.p. 1997, pres. 1998), Ohio Fedn. Rep. Women (South Dist. pres. 2000), Fayette County Hist. Soc., Order Ea. Star. Republican. Methodist. Avocations: church pianist, choir director, horses, bowling. Home: 4652 Miami Trace Rd SW Washington Court House OH 43160-8764 Office: 110 E Court St Washington Court House OH 43160-1355

JOHNSON, PHYLLIS ELAINE, chemist, researcher; b. Grafton, N.D., Feb. 19, 1949; d. Donald Gordon and Evelyn Lorraine (Svaren) Lanes; m. Robert S.T. Johnson (dec. Mar. 2001), Sept. 12, 1969; children: Erik, Sara. BS, U. N.D., 1971; PhD, 1976. Instr. chemistry Mary Coll., Bismarck, N.D., 1971-72; postdoctoral rsch. fellow U. N.D., Grand Forks, 1975-79, chemist, 1977-79; rsch. chemist USDA Human Nutrition Rsch. Ctr., 1979-87, rsch. leader for nutrition, biochemistry and metabolism, 1987-91; assoc. dir. Pacific West Area USDA-ARS, 1996-97; dir. Beltsville Area USDA, ARS, 1997—; Disting. Chemistry Alumni lectr. U. N.D., 1998. Editor: Stable Isotopes in Nutrition, 1984; mem. editl. bd. Jour. Micronutrient Analysis, 1988-91, Jour. Nutrition, 1998—; contbr. articles to profl. jours. Chmn. Parents of Gifted and Talented, 1984—86. Recipient Arthur S. Flemming award Outstanding Sci. Achievement, 1989, Women in Sci. and Engring. award, 1993, Sioux award N.D. Alumni Found., 1998, Fed. Energy and Water Mgmt. award, 1998, Presdl. Rank award of Meritorious Exec., Pres. of U.S., 1999, White House Closing the Circle award for Environ. Mgmt. from Pres. Bush, 2002, for Biobased Products Program, 2003. Mem. Am. Soc. Clin. Nutrition, Am. Chem. Soc., Am. Inst. Nutrition, Internat. Soc. Trace Element Rsch. in Humans (sec. 1992-98), Exec. Women in Govt., Sr. Exec. Assn., Soc. Exptl. Biology Medicine, Rotary, Sons of Norway (dist. v.p. 1984-86, dist. pres. 1986-88, internat. bd. dirs. 1988-92), Phi Beta Kappa, Sigma Xi, Gamma Sigma Delta. Lutheran. Avocations: cooking, skiing, needlework, camping. Home: 7868 Manet Way Severn MD 21144-1649 Office: USDA Bldg 003 Rm 223 10300 Baltimore Ave Beltsville MD 20705-2350 E-mail: johnsonp@ba.ars.usda.gov.

JOHNSON, RAMEY KAYES, community health nurse; b. Chgo., Oct. 11, 1946; d. Henry Vincent and Louise (Waskom) Kayes; m. Walter E. Johnson, Aug. 6, 1967; children: Gretchen, Roger, Aniela. Diploma, Presbyn. Hosp., Denver, 1968; BSN, Metro State Coll., Denver, 1989; MSN, U. Colo., 1993. CCNP. Staff nurse, CCU Luth. Med. Ctr., Wheatridge, Colo., homecare/hospice nurse; home care discharge planner Columbia Health Care System; surveyor Colo. Dept. Pub. Health & Environment, 2001—02; mem. Colo. State Ho. of Reps., 2002—. Mem. Health Edn. Environment Com., Agriculture, Livestock, & Natural Resources Com., Health Care Task Force. Scholar, Friends of Nursing. Home: 675 Estes St Lakewood CO 80215-5412

JOHNSON, RAYMONDA THEODORA GREENE, humanities educator; b. Chgo., Jan. 12, 1939; d. Theodore T. and Eileen (Atherley) Greene; m. Hulon Johnson, June 27, 1964; children: David Atherley, Theodore Cassell, Alexander Ward. BA in English, DePaul U., 1960; MA in English, Loyola U., Chgo., 1965. Cert. high sch. English tchr., Ill. Tchr. high sch. English, Chgo. Pub. Schs., 1960-65; instr. English, Harold Washington Coll. (formerly Loop Coll.), City Coll., Chgo., 1965-66, asst. prof., 1966-91, assoc. prof., 1991-96, faculty advisor coll. newspaper, 1989-92, 96-98, pres. faculty coun., 1990-92, mem. faculty coun., 1990-94, chairperson English and Speech Dept., 1992—, coord. coll. assessment plan com., 1995-99, prof., 1996—. Mem. Brit. Partnership Articulation team, 1997—. Middle sch. v.p. parents coun. Latin Sch., Chgo., 1974-76, trustee, 1987-93; mem. adv. bd. high jump program Latin Sch. Chgo., 1989-98; cubmaster, leader cub scouts Boys Scouts Am., Chgo., 1974-81; mem. black creativity adv. com. Mus. Sci. and Industry, Chgo., 1984-96; mem. steering com. St. Thomas the Apostle Anti-Racism Ethnic Sensitivity, 1999—; chmn. St. Thomas the Apostle Parish Diversity Dinners, 1999—; cohort U. Ill. Urhbana-Champaign C.C. Exec. Leadership Program, 2003. Recipient svc. award religious edn. program St. Thomas the Apostle Ch., Chgo., 1984. Mem. Twigs Mothers Club (pres. 1982-84), Alpha Kappa Alpha. Democrat. Roman Catholic. Avocations: reading, sewing, modern dance, theater, music. Home: 6747 S Bennett Ave Chicago IL 60649-1031 Office: Harold Washington Coll 30 E Lake St Rm 602A Chicago IL 60601-2403 E-mail: rajohnson@ccc.edu.

JOHNSON, REBECCA J. literature educator; b. Wichita, Kans., Mar. 8, 1952; d. George Frederick and Mary Catherine (Kennedy) Johnson. BA in English and Lit., Vt. Coll., 1999; MFA in Writing and Lit., Bennington Coll., 2002. Mgr. mktg. com. CompuServe/Collier Jackson, Tampa, Fla., 1983—94; v.p. mktg. LGE Sport Sci., Orlando, Fla., 1995—98; prof. English Valencia C.C., Orlando, 2002—. Cons. Brain Res., N.Y.C., 1999, Susan Mitchell, PhD, Orlando, 1999—2003. Contbr. articles to profl. jours. Mem.: Fla. Coun. Tchrs. English. Home: 4330A Lake Underhill Rd Orlando FL 32803

JOHNSON, ROSALIND B. psychologist, researcher; b. Long Branch, NJ, Oct. 4, 1969; d. Albert L. and Mary L. Johnson; m. David C. Wilson, Aug. 3, 1996. BA, Rutgers U., 1992; MS, New Sch. U., 1994; PhD, Mich. State U., 1999. Project dir. Georgetown U., Washington, 1998—99; sr. rsch. assoc. USPS Commn., Washington, 1999—2000; program officer Packard Found., Bethesda, Md., 2000—02; rsch. assoc. Child Trends, Washington, 2002—. Cons. NYC Dept. Fin., 1994, Kellogg Found., Battle Creek, Mich., 1996—97. Co-editor: Infancy and Culture, 1999; author: (chpt.) Infancy Research in Africa, 1999, Research on Infants of Africa, 1999. Co-chair Christmas in Apr., Ingham County, Mich., 1996; citizens adv. coun. Montgomery County, Md., 2002—. NIH grantee, 2003. Mem.: Am. Psychol. Soc., Am. Psychol. Assn., Soc. Rsch. Child Devel., Psi Chi, Golden Key. Avocations: gardening, walking, bicycling, crafts, puzzles.

JOHNSON, ROSEMARY WRUCKE, personnel management specialist; b. Leith, N.D., Sept. 21, 1924; d. Rudolph Aaron and Metta Tomina (Andersen) Wrucke; m. Robert Johnson Jr., Sept. 28, 1945 (div. 1964). Student, George Washington U., 1944-45, 47, Nat. Art Sch., Washington, 1943-45. Supr. Displaced Persons Commn., Frankfurt, Germany, 1950-52, FBI, Washington, 1952-81; cons. position mgmt. orgn. design Arlington, Va., 1981—. Mem. NAFE, Classification and Compensation Soc., Soc. FBI Alumni (membership chmn. 1985-91), Internat. Platform Assn. Lutheran. Avocations: painting, sketching. Home and Office: 3710 Lee Hwy Arlington VA 22207-3721

JOHNSON, RUBY LAVERNE, retail executive; b. Ada, Okla., Oct. 31, 1917; d. James Lee and Minta Estelle (Speights) Eppler; m. Albert Howard Johnson, Dec. 22, 1938; children: Phyllis, Richard, Jim, Bruce. With So. Bell Telephone, Ada, 1936-38; founder, owner, buyer Johnson's Furniture, Bossier City, La., 1963—. Mem. La. Home Furniture Assn., Bossier City C. of C., Univ. Club Shreveport. Avocations: gardening, shopping, travel, camping. Home: 3376 Jon Rd Shreveport LA 71119-2236 Office: Johnsons Furniture 921 Westgate Ln Bossier City LA 71112-3595

JOHNSON, RUTH CRUMLEY, economics educator; b. Bristol, Tenn., Feb. 13, 1936; d. Glenn Pine and Marian Grace (Thomas) Crumley; m. Robert William Johnson, June 10, 1971 (dec. May 1995); m. Edwin Douglas Smiley, Aug. 2, 1998. BS, U. Tenn., 1970, MS, 1971, PhD, 1981. Grad. rsch. asst. U. Tenn., Knoxville, 1978-79; rsch. assoc. Oak Ridge (Tenn.) Nat. Lab., 1979-80, Oak Ridge Associated Univs., 1980-82; pres., co-founder Econ. Sys. Analysis, Inc., Oak Ridge, 1983-85; economist Sci. & Tech., Inc., Oak Ridge, 1986-88; mem. adj. faculty Pellissippi State Tech. C.C., Knoxville, 1988—. Mem. People to People Internat. del. of economists to USSR, 1989. Contbr. articles to profl. jours. Chairperson Anderson County Youth Workers Coun., Oak Ridge, 1977; bd. dirs. Anderson County Health Coun., Oak Ridge, 1975-77, Anderson County Cmty. Action Commn., Clinton, Tenn., 1972-74; chairperson bd. dirs. United Ch., Oak Ridge, 1997. Mem. AAUW, Am. Econ. Assn., Phi Kappa Phi, Gamma Sigma Delta, Omicron Nu. Avocations: gardening, hiking, travel, genealogy. Home: 105 Adelphi Rd Oak Ridge TN 37830-7807

JOHNSON, RUTH FLOYD, educational consultant; b. Plateau, Ala., Apr. 19, 1935; d. Nathan Daniel and Ora Anna (Ellis) Floyd; children: Anthony, Walter, Camille, Quinitta, Annette. Student, Tuskegee Inst., 1951-53; BS in History, Bowie (Md.) State U., 1970; MEd in Counseling, U. Md., 1977; PhD in Human Svcs. Adminstrn., Univ. for Humanistic Studies, San Diego, 1982. Cert. tchr., counselor. Radio personality Sta. WMOZ, 1953-56; owner, dir. Azalea Sch. Dance, 1954-56; numerous posts for fed. govt., 1957-69; tchr., adminstr. Pub. Schs. of Prince George's County, Md., 1970-78; tchr.-counselor Dunbar S.T.A.Y. Sch., Washington, 1974-75; instr. child and youth study divsn. U. Md., 1977-78; CEO Diametron Corp., 1979-81; tchr. L.A. Unified Sch. Dist., 1980-82, Pasadena (Calif.) Unified Sch. Dist., 1982-83, Rialto (Calif.) Unified Sch. Dist., 1984—; profl. devel. coord. Calif. State Polytech. U., 1995—. Author: Remediating Mass Poverty: Development of a Model Program, 1982, Pep Squad handbook, 1991, (with others: Government/Contemporary Issues: A Curriculum Guide, 1976. Active PTAs; mem. organizing com. Peppermill Village Civic Assn., 1966; vol. Boy Scouts Am., 1968-72, Sr. Citizens of Prince George's County, 1974-76; bd. dirs.Mill Point Improvement Assn., 1975-78, Combined Communities in Action, 1976-78; mem. Prince George's County Hosp. Commn., 1978; mem. Altadena Town Coun., 1983; founder Rialto Freedom and Cultural Soc., 1988; mem. Calif. 36th Dist. Bicentennial Adv. Com., 1989; mem. exec. com. Rialto Police/Community Rels. Team, 1993. Recipient Outstanding Svc. to Children and Yourh award Md. Congress PTA, 1969, Services to Boy Scouts Am. award, 1969, Svcs. to Sr. Citizens award, 1975, Community Svc. award Rialto Freedom and Cultural Soc., 1993, others. Mem. NEA, NAACP, Nat. Assn. Univ. Women, Nat. Coun. Negro Women, Zeta Phi Beta, Gamma Phi Delta. Avocations: world travel, theatre, tennis, spectator sports, outdoor activities. Home: PO Box 1946 Rialto CA 92377-1946 Fax: 909-820-6001.

JOHNSON, SAKINAH, paralegal; b. Passaic, N.J., Nov. 10, 1971; d. Hosea P. Sr. and Claudette E. Johnson. B in Polit. Sci. magna cum laude, Norfolk State U., 1993. Paralegal Law Offices of Sellinger & Sellinger P.A., Clifton, N.J., 1993-98, Law Offices of Rosemarie Arnold, Ft. Lee, N.J., 1998—. Active Mt. Pilgrim Missionary Bapt. Ch., 1991—. Mem. NAACP, Norfolk State U. Alumni (N.J. chpt.), Spartan Alpha Tau. Avocations: exercise, reading, dance, traveling, time with family and friends. Home: 164 Sherman St Passaic NJ 07055-8408

JOHNSON, SALLY A. nurse, educator; b. Rockford, Ill., Apr. 24, 1923; d. Herbert A. and Aileen (Peyton) Johnson; children: Ann Elizabeth Scannell, Stacey Aileen Lerager. RN Good Samaritan Hosp., 1945; nurse obstetrics delivery Women's Hosp., N.Y.C., 1947-49, St. Francis Hosp., Evanston, Ill., 1953; charge, head nurse Broward Gen. Hosp., Ft. Lauderdale, Fla., 1968; night supr. Ashbrook Convalescent and Nursing Hosp., Scotch Plains, N.J., 1968—. Owner Thomas A. Edison Brick Co., Sally Johnson Enterprises. Coun. chmn. Betty Merit Tchrs. Scholarship, 1962; area nat. organizer Girl Scouts U.S.A., 1962-65; Westfield (N.J.) Round-Up and Health chmn., 1962-63; pres. Tamaques Sch., 1965, adviser Parent Tchr. Orgn., 1966, fgn. relationship chmn., 1967-68; exec. bd. chmn. Westfield HS PTA Newsletter, 1968-70; chmn. Nat. Space Edn., Westfield, 1964; Westfield chmn. fgn. nurses Overlook Hosp., Summit, N.J., 1964-69. Recipient scholarship to Harvard U. Coll. Bus. Mem. Nat. Assn. Investors Corp., Nat. Dist. Nurses Assn., NOW (N.J. coord. 1967-68), Am. Contract Bridge League, Bridge Tchrs. Assn., Naples Investment Club (sec. 1995-96). Republican. Achievements include patent for marking devices. Office: 50 Quiche Ct Fort Myers FL 33912 Home: 8415 Excalibur Cr B-3 Naples FL 34108 E-mail: sallyjohnson@comcast.net.

JOHNSON, SAMIRA EL-CHEHABI, marketing professional; b. Niagara Falls, N.Y., Mar. 2, 1958; d. Munzir and Ismat (Zakaria) El-Chehabi; m. Kenneth M. Johnson, Sept. 21, 1991; 1 child, Davis B. BS in Med. Tech. magna cum laude, SUNY, Buffalo, 1980. Component lab. supr. ARC, Detroit, 1982-85; sr. med. technologist Rush Presbyn. St. Lukes Med. Ctr., Chgo., 1985-86; tech. cons. Baxter Internat., Deerfield, Ill., 1986-88, ednl. svcs. mgr., 1988-89, market mgr., 1989-93, sr. market mgr., 1993-99; dir. mktg. Cerus Corp., Concord, Calif., 1999—2003; freelance cons., 2003—. Assoc. editor Continuous Flow, 1988-90, Component Therapy Digest, 1988-90; patentee in field. Mem. Nat. Blood Data Resource Ctr., 1996—. Mem. ANA (program adminstr. 1988-98), Am. Soc. Clin. Pathologists, Am. Soc. Med. Technologists (program adminstr. 1988-98), Am. Assn. Blood Banks, Internat. Soc. Blood Transfusion. Avocations: sailing, scuba diving, theater, horseback riding, rollerblading. Home and Office: 859 Sanctuary Dr Apt 305B Lake Villa IL 60046-7982 E-mail: samira_johnson@direcway.com.

JOHNSON, SAMMYE LARUE, communications educator; b. Dallas, Oct. 8, 1946; BS in Journalism with distinction, Northwestern U., 1968, MS in Journalism with highest distinction, 1969. Asst. editor Where Mag., Chgo., 1969; feature writer Chicago Today newspaper, Chgo., 1969-71, editor Sunday mag., 1971-73; pub. rels. mgr. U.S. Armed Forces Pub. Libr. Sys., Nurnberg, Germany, 1974—75; editor San Antonio Mag., 1976-79; comms. dir. VIA Met. Transit Sys., San Antonio, 1979; asst. prof. journalism William Allen White Sch. Journalism U. Kans., Lawrence, 1979-80; asst. prof. journalism Trinity U., San Antonio, 1980-85, assoc. prof. comm., 1985—91, prof. comm., 1991—, Carlos Augustus de Lozano chair journalism, 1998—. Cons. pub. rels. Community Guidance Ctr., San Antonio, 1985-88, Funding Info. Ctr., San Antonio, 1983—, Bexar County Women's Ctr., San Antonio, 1984—. Author: The Magazine from Cover to Cover, 1999, Magazine Publishing, 2000; contbr. articles to profl. jours., consumer and trade mags., newspapers. Named Today's Woman of Achievement San Antonio Light Newspaper, 1981, Pub. Rels. Educator of Yr. Tex. Pub. Rels. Assn., 1984-85. Mem. Women in Comms. (dir. 1978-80, pres. chpt. 1983-84, Proliner award 1981, 82, 83, 86, 87, 88, 90, 93, 96, 97, Comms. Headliner of Yr. 1984), Internat. Assn. Bus. Communicators (bd. dirs. 1979, Gold Quill award 1979, named Communicator of Yr. 1981, numerous other awards 1976-96), Assn. for Edn. in Journalism and Mass Comms. (sec., vice chair, chair mag. divs. 1985-89, Mag. Educator of Yr. 1997), Kappa Tau Alpha. Home: 7523 Bridgewater Dr San Antonio TX 78209-3113 Office: Trinity U Dept Communication 1 Trinity Pl San Antonio TX 78212-7200 E-mail: sjohnson@trinity.edu.

JOHNSON, SANDRA ANN, counselor, educator; b. Houston, Apr. 27, 1958; d. Johnnie and Area (Bradford) Johnson. AA, Houston C.C., 1991; BBA, Tex. So. U., 1994; MA, Prairie View A&M U., 1998; PhD, Tex. So. U., 2000; PhD in Psychology, Berne U. Lic. profl. counselor. Tchr. computers Houston Sch. Dist., 1981—. Instr. North Harris Coll., Houston, 1996—, Houston C.C.; counselor Houston C.C. Sys.; rsch. resident, Saint Kitts and Nevis. Vol. Herman Hosp., Houston, 1987—88, U. Tex. Health Sci. Ctr.; intern, vol. DePelchin Children Ctr., 1997—98; counselor Vision of Hope Women, Houston, 1996—97, Cmty. Devel. Corp.; contact person Houston Mayor's Camp, 1997; pres., bd. dirs. Vision of Hope; pres. CAP Cmty. Devel.; pro bono counselor Black Ams. in low income areas; summer resident St. Kitts, West Indies. Named Disting. Role Model of Houston, North Main Ch. of God in Christ, 1998; recipient Outstanding Counselor, Houston C.C. Sys. Mem. Chi Sigma Iota. Democrat. Baptist. Avocations: tennis, golf, jogging, reading, racquetball. Office: Houston Cmty Coll System Southeast Campus Houston TX 77088-7102 E-mail: sondra_johnson@yahoo.co.uk.

JOHNSON, SANDRA BARTLETT, city official; b. Phoenix; d. Hartley Williams and Alice C. (Johnson) Bartlett; divorced, 1994; 1 child, Nicole Elizabeth. Student, Fla. State U., 1958-61, Ga. State U., 1970-72. Chem. lab. tech. Agrl. Ext. Sta., U. Fla., Bradenton, 1963-65, The Coca-Cola Co., Atlanta, 1965-72, lab. supr., 1972-79, purchasing agt., tech. divsn., 1979-84; mem. city council City of Alpharetta, Ga., 1960—. Mgr. constitutent svcs. Fulton County Commn. Dist. # 2, Atlanta, 1995; bd. dirs. YMCA, Alpha Convention and Visitors Bd. Sr. Svcs. No. Fulton, Ga. Mcpl. Assn., vice chmn. Alpharetta Planning Bd., 1958-60, sec., treas., v.p., state pres., Ga. Assn. Zoning Adminstrs., 1976—. Named for Resolution of Commendation Ga. House Rep., 1997; recipient Diamond Clover 4H award St. Kitts, W.I., 1993, Achievement certs. U. Ga., 1996, 2000. Mem. AAUW (cmty. leader Roswell 1997), Nat. Assn. Purchasing Mgmt. (local and dist. mem. chmn.), Purchasing Mgmt. Ga., Ga. Mcpl. Assn., Am. Planning Assn., North Fulton Coun. Local Govts., Lions Club (bd. dirs., program chair 1994—), Alpharetta Rotary Club (various coms, 1991—, Paul Harris fellow 1996). Republican. Episcopalian. Home: 240 Pebble Trl Alpharetta GA 30004-1227 Office: City of Alpharetta 2 S Main St Alpharetta GA 30004-1936 E-mail: sandrajohnson@juno.com.

JOHNSON, SANDRA G. engineering company executive; m. Doug Johnson; children. BS in Maths., La. Tech U.; MBA in Bus. Mgmt., U. Houston. Engr. Barrios Tech., Houston, various other positions, pres. Cmty. vol. United Way, chair Bay Area Fundraising Campaign, 1995, 96; treas. exec. bd. dirs. Clear Lake Area Econ. Devel. Found.; active Aerospace Adv. Coun., Membership Devel. Coun.; chair elect devel. and adv. coun. U. Houston, Clear Lake. Recipient Disting. Alumnus award U. Houston, Clear Lake, 1996, Mgr. of Yr. awrd Gulf Coast Coun. Nat. Mgmt. Assn., 1997, Vocat. Excellence award Space Ctr. Rotary, Outstanding Bus. Person Rotary Dist. 5890, JSC Small Contractor of Yr. award Govt. Procurement Connection, 1998; named one of the Top 10 Women on the Move Tex. Exec. Women, 1998. Mem. Spaceweek Internat. Assn. (bd. dirs.), Internat. Coun. Sys. Engring. (Houston chpt.). Office: Barrios Tech Inc 2525 Bay Area Blvd Ste 300 Houston TX 77058-1556 Fax: 281-280-1901.

JOHNSON, SANDRA K. journalist; Grad., S.D. State U. Reporter AP, Bismarck, N.D., 1978-81, corr., dir. news coverage Sioux Falls, S.D., 1981-83, editor, reporter, writer Washington, 1983-96, dep. bur. chief, 1996-98, bur. chief, 1998—. Office: Assoc Press 2021 K St NW Fl 6 Washington DC 20006-1082

JOHNSON, SHANNON, professional basketball player; b. Aug. 18, 1974; Grad., U.S.C., 1996. Mem. 2 ABL Champion Columbus Quest; profl. basketball player Valencia, Spain, Orlando Miracle (now Conn. Sun), 1999—2002, Conn. Sun, 2003, San Antonio Silver Stars, 2004—. Named All-WNBA 2nd Team, 1999, 2000, Inaugural WNBA All-Star Team, 1999, WNBA All-Star Team, 2000, 2002, 2003. Office: c/o San Antonio Silver Stars 1 SBC Center San Antonio TX 78219*

JOHNSON, SHANNON JOY, children's advocate; b. Gretna, La., Sept. 16, 1967; d. Wayne Thomas Sr. and Suzanne Margaret (Vinyard) J. BA, Loyola U., New Orleans, 1990. Rsch. asst. Inst. Human Rels., New Orleans, 1989-90; outreach/ops. coord. Agenda For Children, New Orleans, 1990-93; cons. State of La., Baton Rouge, 1996—; kids count coord. Agenda For Children, New Orleans, 1993—. Co-convenor Child Watch Coalition, New Orleans, 1995; mem. bd. dirs. Women's Resource Ctr., New Orleans, 1993—, La. Health Care Campaign, Baton Rouge, 1996—. Co-author, editor (data book) Kids Count Data Book on La. Children, 1993—. Vol. Project SHIELD/Agenda For Children, New Orleans, 1989-90, Women Elect 2000, New Orleans, 1992; gala vol. La. State U. Eye Ctr., New Orleans, 1991-96. Democrat. Avocations: boxing, historic preservation, pursuing graduate degree. Home: 1707 2nd St New Orleans LA 70113-1654 Office: Agenda For Children 1720 St Charles Ave New Orleans LA 70130

JOHNSON, SHARON BRABSON, music educator; b. Balt., Mar. 25, 1954; d. Oscar Raymond and Frances Spears Brabson; m. William Percell Johnson, Jr., Dec. 19; 1 child, April Camille. BS in Music Edn., Va. State U., 1976. Tchr., band dir. Matoaca H.S., Petersburg, Va., 1976—77, Bedford County Pub. Schs., Bedford, Va., 1979—84, Roanoke (Va.) City Pub. Schs., 1986—. Mem.: Va. Music Educators Assn., Roanoke Edn. Assn., Delta Sigma Theta. Democrat. Baptist. Avocations: reading, gardening. Office: Patrick Henry High Sch Band 2102 Grandin Rd SW Roanoke VA 24015

JOHNSON, SHARON ELAINE, elementary school educator; b. Grant County, Wis., Dec. 31, 1936; d. Ralph Philip and E. Blanche (Fry) Long; m. Edward Dean Johnson, Apr. 15, 1961; 1 child, Perry Edward; 1 stepchild, David Dwight. B Music Edn., Coe Coll., Cedar Rapids, Iowa, 1959; M Elem. Edn., Murray (Ky.) State U., 1965; M Spl. Edn., U. Mo., Kansas City, 1980. Cert. elem. and music tchr., Kans., Iowa, Ky.; cert. elem., music and spl. edn. tchr., Mo. Elem. tchr. Kans. City (Kans.) Bd. Edn., 1959-63, 65-66; tchr. vocal music Marshall County Bd. Edn., Benton, Ky., 1963-65; elem. tchr. Consol. Sch. Dist. 1, Hickman Mills Bd. Edn., Kansas City, Mo., 1966-79, tchr. kindergarten, 1980—93; sub. tchr. Sunshine Ctr. for Handicapped Pre-Sch., 1993—2003. Mem. NEA, ASCD, Internat. Reading Assn. (historian 1985-86), Mo. Edn. Assn. (bldg. rep. 1976—). Avocations: needlepoint, reading education journals, word puzzles, helping children learn, spectator sports. Home: 1022 S Park Ave Independence MO 64050-4225

JOHNSON, STEPHANIE KAY, school counselor; b. Water Vliet, Mich., Oct. 18, 1951; d. Dexter F. and Shirley L. (Fogelsanger) Beary; m. Loyd Edwin Johnson; 1 child, James Edwin. BA, Southwestern Adventist Coll., 1973; MA, Rollins Coll., 1991. Choir dir. Jefferson (Tex.) Acad., 1973-74; piano tchr., choir dir. Houston Jr. Acad., 1974-77; from English tchr., music tchr. to chaplain Mt. Pisqah Acad., Candler, N.C., 1977-88; sch. counselor Forest Lake Acad., Apopka, Fla., 1988-98, Campion Acad., 1998—. Student esteem program dir., trainer Walker Meml. Jr. Acad., Mt. Pisqh Acad., Forest Lake Acad., 1990-98, Ga.-Cumberland Acad. Mem. Am. Assn. Christian Counselors. Adventist. Avocations: snow skiing, camping, travel. Home: 300 42nd St SW # 11 Loveland CO 80537-7520

JOHNSON, STEPHANIE L. B. small business owner, office manager; b. Colorado Springs, Colo., Sept. 29, 1945; d. George Edgar and Anne Eastwood Bates; m. Johnny B. Johnson, Dec. 26, 1964; 1 child, Jennifer L. B. Johnson-Bahr. A, Blair Coll., 1964. Office mgr., girl Friday W. E. Nash, Arch., Bryan, Tex., 1965—69; owner, mgr. Bates Enterprises, Colorado Springs, Colo., 1991—; office mgr. Becker-Johnson, Inc., 1991—. Chair Platte Ave. Improvement Dist. Maintenance Adv. Bd., Colorado Springs, 2000—; chairperson The RIDER Com. [] NSA Oversight Com., 2002—. Editor (creator): (newsletter) The Gold Std. (Sertoma Dist. Newsletter of the Yr., 2003), Knob Hill Neighbor. Pres. Platte Ave. Bus. & Neighborhood Assn., Colorado Springs, 1999—2003; v.p. Police Adv. Com., 2002—03. Mem.: History Day Scholars, Inc. (assoc.; sec.-treas. 1985—2003), Cheyenne Mountain Sertoma Club (assoc.; bd. mem. 1999—2003, Ben Franklin award 1996, Sertoman of Yr. award 2002), Rocky Mountain Youth Leadership Found., Inc. (assoc.; pres. 1989—99, Stephanie L. B. Johnson award 1995), Mil. Order of World Wars (life; treas. 1997—99, Patrick Henry Silver medal 1990). Conservative. Methodist. Avocations: historical preservation, travel, antique toy collecting, old english sheepdogs, classic & special interest cars. Home: 116 E Columbia St Colorado Springs CO 80907 Office: Becker-Johnson Inc 2601 Platte Pl Colorado Springs CO 80909 Office Phone: 719-473-5653. E-mail: oneblonde1@prodigy.net.

JOHNSON, SUSAN ANN, writer; b. Huntsville, Ala., July 8, 1950; d. Samuel Felix Morgan and Mildred Anthony Johnson. BA in English Lit., Ga. State U., 1982, MA in English Lit., 1988. Consultant editor, writer Lockheed-Martin Pacific Rim, Seoul, Republic of Korea, 1993—94; lectr., writer Langgram Publ., Seoul, 1992—95; lectr. English lit. and lang. Calhoun Coll., 1996—2000; editor English lang. tng. Internat. Thomson/Heinle, Boston, 1998—2000, Cambridge U. Press, NYC, 2001—02, McGraw-Hill, NYC, 2002—. Cons., lectr. in field. Author: All of a Piece, 2000; mem. editl. bd. Words in Focus, 1999, ReadSmart, 2002—, World Class Readings, 2002—, Send Me a Message, 2003, others; author: (book) Dali, Chagall, Picasso, Gauguin, Van Gogh for young adults, others., 1995. Vol. instr. English reading program Sisters of Charity, Seoul, 1994. Mem.: Tenn. Writers Alliance, Internat. Womens Writing Guild. Avocations: painting, poetry, art, reading. Office Phone: 256-509-3012.

JOHNSON, SUSAN L. B. human resource administrator; b. Granite City, Ill. d. Richard C. and Helen N. (Newhart) Buenger; m. Brian K. Johnson, Apr. 25, 1987. BS, So. Ill. U., 1986; MS, Nat. Coll. of Edn., 1990. Office mgr. Soccer for Fun, Granite City, Ill., 1981-85; adminstrn. St. Louis U. Hosp., 1985-91, Barnes Hosp., St. Louis, Mo., 1991—. Office: Barnes-Jewish Hosp One Barnes-Jewish Plz Saint Louis MO 63110

JOHNSON, SYLVIA SUE, university administrator, educator; b. Abiline, Tex., Aug. 10, 1940; d. SE Boyd and Margaret MacGillivray (Withington) Smith; m. William Ruel Johnson; children: Margaret Ruth, Laura Jane, Catherine Withington. BA, U. Calif., Riverside, 1962; postgrad., U. Hawaii, 1963. Elem. edn. credential, 1962. Chmn. bd. regents U. Calif., 2000—. Mem. bd. regents U. Calif.; mem. steering com. Citizens Univ. Com., chmn., 1978-79; bd. dirs., charter mem. U. Calif.-Riverside Found., chmn. nominating com., 1983—; pres., bd. dirs. Friends of the Mission Inn, 1969-72, 73-76, Mission Inn Found., 1977—, Calif. Bapt. Coll. Citizens Com., 1980—; bd. dirs. Riverside Cmty. Hosp., 1980—, Riverside Jr. League, 1976-77, Nat. Charity League, 1984-85; mem. chancellors blue ribbon com., devel. com. Calif. Mus. Photography; state bd. dirs. C. of C., 2003. Named Woman of Yr., State of Calif. Legislature, 1989, 91, Citizen of Yr., C. of C., 1989; recipient Golden Key award Soroptimist Internat.,

2000, Chancellor's medal U. Calif. Riverside, 2002; recipient Silver Raincross medal, Jr. League Riverside, 1993. Mem. U. Calif.-Riverside Alumni Assn. (bd. dirs. 1966-68, v.p. 1968-70), Calif. C. of C. (bd. dirs. 2003—).

JOHNSON, URSULA ANNE, artist; b. St. Louis, Oct. 11, [illegible]; d. Lorenzo Bates and Ursula Agnes Lea; m. Herbert Crittenden Johnson, June 10, 1951; children: Amelia Anne Bosque, Raymond Brian. Studied, Ohio State U., 1951, Denison U., 1948. Artist The Columbus Citizen, Ohio, 1951—52; fashion illustrator F & R Lazarus and Co., Columbus, Ohio, 1952—55. Artist's adv. coun. Marin Soc. of Artists, Ross, Calif., 1965—67, v.p., 1970—71, bd. dirs., 1970—72. Printmaking, Lost Words Found, 1980, Twice-told Tales, 1980, The Waiting Game, 1980, Aeon's Ago, 1980, Omen, 1980, CORROSION, 1981, Primitif, 1981, Symbol, 1981, Forgotten Imaye, 1981, Kenoe, 1983, Represented in permanent collections Bank of Am. Corp., Bank of San Francisco. Mem. Art Coun. of Placer Counnty, Auburn, Calif., 1992—2003. Avocations: garden design, swimming, hiking, travel. Business E-Mail: ursulaj4@aol.com.

JOHNSON, VERDIA E. marketing professional; B in Mktg., Howard U.; MBA in Mktg., NYU. With Colgate Palmolive Co., Standard Brands, Nabisco Brands; dir. advt. Black Enterprise Mag.; v.p. bus. devel. and sales Gannett Outdoor; v.p., gen. mgr. Stedman Graham & Ptnrs.; pres., founding ptnr. Footsteps, LLC, NYU, NY, 2000—. Named 25 Most Black Influential Women in Bus., Network Mag.; recipient Outstanding Women in Mktg. and Comm. award, Ebony Mag., 2001, Urban Wheels award, 2002. Office: Footsteps LLC 200 Varick St Rm 610 New York NY 10014-7487*

JOHNSON, VICKIE, professional basketball player; b. Apr. 15, 1972; B of Sociology & Psychology, La. Tech. Inst., 1996. Guard-forward Tarbes, France, 1996—97, WMBA - N.Y. Liberty, N.Y.C., 1997—. Named NCAA Tournament All-Final Four, 1994, Sun Belt Conf. Player of Yr., MVP, Kodak All-Am., 1995, Street & Smith All-Am., 1996; recipient La. Player of Yr., 1996. Avocations: movies, shopping, friends, tennis. Office: NY Liberty 2 Penn Plz New York NY 10121-0101

JOHNSON, WENDY S. women's healthcare company executive; BS in Microbiology, U. Md.; MS in Clin. Microbiology, Hahnemann Med. Sch.; MBA, Loyola U., Balt. Asst. dir. Ctr. for Devices and Radiol. Health, FDA, 1976-86; internat. affairs adminstr. Coralab Rsch., 1986-88; mgr. bus. devel. Synbiotics Corp., 1988-90; v.p. bus. devel. and regulatory affairs Cytel Corp., 1990-94; v.p. corp. devel. and ops. Prizm Pharms. (now Selective Genetics Inc.), 1994-98; v.p. bus. devel. Women First HealthCare, Inc., San Diego, 1998—. Office: Women First HealthCare Inc 12220 El Camino Real Ste 400 San Diego CA 92130-2091 Fax: 619-509-1353.

JOHNSON-BROWN, LINDA LEE, music educator; b. Anchorage, Alaska, Dec. 19, 1952; d. Charles Arthur Johnson and Marion Lorraine Bancroft-Johnson; m. Raymond Lee Brown, July 5, 1980; children: Michelle, Lorri, Joshua, Jennifer, Jacqui, Daniel; m. Robert Michael Arnold, Dec. 22, 1976 (div. Jan. 15, 1979); 1 child, Lorraine Marie. MusB, Ill. State U., 1976; MEd, Marygrove Coll., 2000. Tchr. Joliet (Ill.) Pub. Schs., 1976—79, Herscher (Ill.) Cmty. Schs., 1979—80, Watseka (Ill.) Cmty. Schs., 1980—81, St. Anne (Ill.) Pub. Schs., 1981—82, Donovan (Ill.) Cmty. Schs., 1985—90, Shelby County Pub. Schs., Memphis, 1990—94; tchr. Dillon Elem. Carman-Ainsworth Cmty. Schs., Flint, Mich., 1994—. Mem. curriculum devel. fine arts com. State of Ill., Watseka, 1989; mem. task force Gov. Jennifer Grandhilms, Flint, 2003. Pres. Kid's for Am. America's Fund Afghan Orphans, Flint, 2001—02; min. music Assemblies of God, 1995—2003. Mem.: DAR, Music Educators Nat. Conf., Music Educators Assn. Republican. Avocations: reading, history, writing, music, singing. Home: 13490 Lakebrook Drive Fenton MI 48430 Office: Carman Ainsworth Community Schs Dillon Elem 1197 E Schumacher Ave Burton MI 48529

JOHNSON-CHAMP, DEBRA SUE, lawyer, educator, writer, artist; b. Emporia, Kans., Nov. 8, 1955; d. Bert John and S. Christine (Brigman) Johnson; m. Michael W. Champ, Nov. 23, 1979; children: Natalie, John. BA, U. Denver, 1977; JD, Pepperdine U., 1980; postgrad., U. So. Calif., 1983-84. Bar: Calif. 1981. Pvt. practice, Long Beach, Calif., 1981-82, L.A., 1981-87, Woodland Hills, Calif., 1993-99; of counsel Greenbaum & Champ, 1999—. Legal reference librarian, instr. Southwestern U. Sch. Law, L.A., 1982-88; adj. prof. law, 1987-88; atty. Contos & Bunch, Woodland Hills, 1988-93; free lance writer/artist; owner The Purple Iguana, 1997—; of counsel Greenbaum & Champ LLP, 1999—. Editor-in chief: Southern Calif. Assn. Law Libraries Newsletter, 1984-85; mem. law rev. Pepperdine U., 1978-80; contbr. articles to profl. jours. Trustee United Meth. Ch., Tujunga, Calif., 1986-88. West Pub. Co. scholar, 1983; recipient H. Wayne Gillis Moot Ct. award, 1980, Vincent S. Dalsimer Best Brief award 1979. Mem. ABA, So. Calif. Assn. Law Libr., Am. Assn. Law Libr., Calif. Bar Assn., Southwestern Affiliates, Friends of the Libr. L.A. Democrat. Home and Office: 5740 Valerie Ave Woodland Hills CA 91367-3967 Office Phone: 818-888-7900. E-mail: legaldebi2@prodigy.net.

JOHNSON HIRT, JACQUELINE MARIE, elementary school educator; b. Phila., Jan. 22, 1968; d. Barry Carlton and Delores Johnson; m. David Jonathan Hirt, Nov. 24, 2000. BS, Brooks Inst. Photography, 1992; BA, Prescott Coll., 1996; MA in Curriculum Instrn., U. Phoenix, 2000. Cert. tchr. with gifted edn. and middle sch.endorsements Ariz. State Bd. Edn. Sr. ednl. cons. Ariz. State U., Tempe, 1995—2000; gifted edn. coord. Scottsdale (Ariz.) Sch. Dist., 1997—99; lang. arts tchr. Deer Valley Sch. Dist., Phoenix, 1999—. Gifted edn. cons. JH Consulting, Phoenix, 1994—. Recipient award, Phoenix Reading West Coun., 2000, Internat. Reading Assn., 2000. Avocations: photography, hiking, writing, singing.

JOHNSON-LEESON, CHARLEEN ANN, former elementary school educator, insurance agent, insurance consultant, regional executive assistant; b. Battle Creek, Mich., June 10, 1949; d. Kenneth Andrews Leeson and Ila Mae (Weed/Lesson) McCutcheon; m. Lynn Boyd Johnson, Aug. 8, 1970; children: Eric Andrew, Andrea Johnson McGrath. BA, Spring Arbor Coll., 1971; MS, Reading Specialist, Western Ill. U., 1990. Cert. elem. and secondary tchr., Mich., elem. tchr., Ill., reading K-9, Ill. Tchr. Hanover (Mich.) Horton Schs., 1972-73, Virden (Ill.) Elem. Sch., 1984-90; ins. agt. State Farm Ins., Virden, Ill., 1991-95, cons. Springfield, Ill., 1995-97, regional exec. asst. Bloomington, Ill., 1997-99, agt. Myrtle Beach, S.C., 1999—. Collegiate and jr. high sch. cheerleading advisor in field; course leader Agt. Schs. 1, 2, and 3. Music dir., pianist Zion Luth. Ch., Farmersville, Ill., 1979-88, organist, pianist Olive St. Friends, Battle Creek, 1961-67. Recipient Honor the Educator award World Book, 1988, 89, Soaring Eagle award Millionair/Amb. Club, 1991-98, Amb. Club, 2001-02; Wilson Stone scholar, 1990, Mich. State scholar, 1967. Mem. AUA, Internat. Reading Assn., S.C. Assn. Life Underwriters, Nat. Assn. Ins. and Fin. Advisors, Gideon Aux. (pres. 2004), Alpha Upsilon Alpha. Avocations: music (piano and organ), writing. Home: 9621 Chestnut Ridge Dr Myrtle Beach SC 29572 Office: 119 Waccamaw Med Park Conway SC 29526-8902 E-mail: charleen.johnson.cyxd@statefarm.com.

JOHNSON-LEIPOLD, HELEN P. outdoor marine recreation company executive; b. 1957; V.p. consumer mktg. svcs. worldwide SCJ, 1992-95, exec. v.p. N.Am. businesses, 1995-97, v.p. personal and home care products, 1997-98, v.p. worldwide consumer products-mktg., 1998-99; chmn., CEO Johnson Outdoors (formerly Johnson Worldwide Assocs. Inc.), Miami Beach, Fla., 1999—. Office: 1326 Willow Rd Sturtevant WI 53177-0901 Office Fax: 262-884-1600.

JOHNSON-LIBKIND, JEAN SUE See **LIBKIND, JEAN SUE JOHNSON**

JOHNSON-MILLER, CHARLEEN V. teacher coordinator; b. Cleve., Ohio, Jan. 17, 1948; d. Leroy and Alice Vivian Carter; m. [illegible] Miller, [illegible], 1 child, Patrice. BS in Edn., Ctrl. State U., 1970; MS in Edn., Cleve. State U., 1979; postgrad., Clevel. State U., 1985, John Carrol U., 1983. Permanent tchg. cert. Ohio, 1985. Cleve. Tchrs. Union rep. Cleve. Pub. Schs., 1982—86, cons. tchr., mentor, 1988—93, guidance/drug liaison, 1992—95; lead tchr. Cleve. Mcpl. Schs., 1995—99, grade level chairperson, 1996—2000, safety patrol dir., 1998—, Helping One Student to Succeed/tutor vol. coord., 1999—. Cons. tchr., facilitator human devel. Kent (Ohio) State U., 1983—90; program developer, curriculum planner guidance program Cleve. Pub. Schs., 1985—91, dist. prof. developer, 1993—99. Mem. Present Day Bapt. Ch. Scholar Martha Holden Jenning scholar, Martha Holden Jennings Found., Cleve., 1990. Mem.: Cabinettes, Scrabblers (past pres., v.p., sec.), Alpha Kappa Alpha, Phi Delta Kappa, Inc. (life). Avocations: tennis, bowling, aerobics, kickboxing, line dancing.

JOHNSON-RICHT, CHERYL LYNN, performing artist; b. McHenry, Ill., June 28, 1963; d. Richard William and Gail Lynn Johnson; m. Jürgen A. Richt, Dec. 29, 1992; children: Elisabeth, Alexander, Christopher. MusB, U. Ill., 1985, MusM, 1986; Grad. Performance Cert., Peabody Conservatory Music, 1991. Pvt. music instr. Frankfurt Internat. Sch., Oberursel, Germany, 1991—2000; freelance performing artist Frankfurt, 1991—2000, Ames, Iowa, 2001—. Sec. German-Am. Club, Wetzlar, Germany, 1996—99, Des Moines Metro Opera Guild. Mem.: Iowa Music Tchrs. Assn., Nat. Assn. Tchrs. Singing, Music Educators Nat. Conf., Des Moines (Iowa) Metro Opera Guild (Ames chpt. bd. dir.). Avocations: sports, travel. Home: 1501 Reagan Dr Ames IA 50010

JOHNSON-SIEBOLD, JUDITH ELOISE, minister; b. Worcester, Mass., Nov. 16, 1947; d. G. Louis and Vera Eloise Johnson; m. E. Allen Siebold, Aug. 17, 1968; children: Jennifer, Rebeccah, Amanda, Dashanna. BA, Syracuse U., 1968; MDiv, Garrett Theol. Sem., Evanston, Ill., 1971; PhD, Syracuse U., 1991. Ordained elder United Meth. Ch., 1971. Min. United Meth. Ch., 1971—. Mem. Wyo. Conf. Bd. Ministry United Meth. Ch., N.Y. and Pa., 2000—01, mem. Wyo. Conf. Leadership Table, N.Y. and Pa., 2000—01, mem. Wyo. Conf. Witness and Discipleship Table, N.Y. and Pa., 2000—01. Author: (newspaper column) Education Conversations, 1999—; editor: (book) Personal Narratives About the History of Christian Education, 1999—. Mem.: Assn. Profs. and Rschrs. in Religious Edn., United Meth. Assn. Scholars in Christian Edn., Pi Lambda Theta. United Methodist. Avocation: writing. Home: 22 Church St Greenwich NY 12834 Office: Centenary United Meth Ch 18 Ch St Greenwich NY 12834

JOHNSON VELAZCO, NANCY RUTH, marketing professional; b. Phila., Feb. 4, 1948; d. Samuel Blaine and Ruth Dorothy (Carpenter) Johnson; m. Julio Horacio Velazco, Dec. 6, 1982 (div. Oct. 1984); 1 child, Cristine. BA in Spanish, Ursinus Coll., Collegeville, Pa., 1970; MA in Spanish, Villanova U., 1974; MBA, The Wharton Sch. U. Pa., 1978. Secondary tchr. Spanish, William Penn Sch. Dist., Lansdowne, Pa., 1970-76; indsl. rsch. analyst indsl. rsch. unit Wharton Sch., U. Pa., Phila., 1976-78; sales rep. pharma. Eli Lilly & Co., Providence, 1978-79, market rsch. analyst Indpls., 1979-80, mktg. mgr. Buenos Aires, 1980-82; Intron product mgr., bus. devel. mgr. Schering Plough Corp., Miami, Fla., 1983-84, regional mktg. dir. for L.Am., 1984-89, dir. respiratory, dermatology and antifungals Kenilworth, N.J., 1989-90, sr. mktg. dir. global mktg., 1991—2003; sr. dir. Global Profl. Svcs., 2003—. Author: The Political, Economic and Labor Climates in Mexico, 1977, The Political, Economic and Labor Climates in Peru, 1978; patentee # 6, 297, 227 B1. Chmn. party events Children's Specialized Hosp., Mountainside, N.J., 1994—; mem. bd. trustees Meadowland Hosp., Secaucus, N.J. Mem. Nat. Soc. DAR (treas. Westfield chpt. 1995-2002). Republican. Office: Schering-Plough Corp 2000 Galloping Hill Rd Kenilworth NJ 07033-1328 Home: 6469 Indigo Bunting Pl Bradenton FL 34202 E-mail: nancy.johnson@spcorp.com.

JOHNSON-WATSON, REVA MAE, non-commissioned officer, consultant; d. John H. Jr. and Georgia L. Johnson; 1 child, Charles Christopher Watson. BS, Fla. A & M U., 1973. Sgt. Edgerton Grier & Germanhousan, Kennedy Space Ctr., Fla., 1983—89, lt., 1989—98, Space Gateway Support, 1998—2002, 1st lt., 2002—. Ind. bus. cons. Am. Communication, Rocklegde, Fla., 2001—. Staff sgt. U.S. Army, 1978—. Mem.: Fla. A&M U. Nat. Alumni Assn. (life; membership chairperson 1993—2003), Alpha Kappa Alpha. Democrat. Mem. Ch. Of Christ. Avocations: lawn and grounds maintenance, community service, fundraising for scholarships, coordinating community health fairs.

JOHNSTON, CAROLYN JUDITH, construction engineer; b. Atlanta, Nov. 24, 1961; d. Lynn H. and Doris S. (Lacy) J.; m. Paul William Miller, July 20, 1996; 1 child, Savannah Lee. BS in Constrn. Mgmt., So. Tech. U., 1990; MS in Constrn. Mgmt., Clemson U., 1997. Cert. profl. constructor. Journeyman plumber Quality Mech., Norfolk, Va., 1984-86; asst. supt. R.G.Moore Bldg., Virginia Beach, Va., 1986-87; asst. field engr. Holder Constrn., Atlanta, 1987-89; clk. of works Sharondale Constrn., Atlanta, 1989-90; constrn. engr. Bechtel, Aiken, S.C., 1990-95; project engr. R.W. Allen & Assocs., Augusta, Ga., 1995-97; project mgr. York Internat., Aiken, S.C., 1997-99; sr. project mgr. ACTS, Inc., New Ellenton, S.C., 2000; Bell Co. project engr. U.S. Dept. Energy Project/Tritium Extraction Facility, Aiken, S.C., 2001—. Nat. Assn. Women Constrn. scholar, Atlanta, 1990. Mem. Am. Inst. Constructors, Profl. Constrn. Estimators (sec. 1996-98, newsletter editor 1996-98), Nat. Mgmt. Assn., Constrn. Specification Inst. Office: Bell Techs Tritium Extraction Facility Bldg 264-4H Savannah River Site Aiken SC 29808 E-mail: tritium@thebellcompany.com.

JOHNSTON, DIANE MILLER, librarian; b. Attleboro, Mass., Nov. 30, 1947; d. Gordon William and Rena Mae (Miller) J. BA, Wheaton Coll., 1969; MA in Classics, NYU, 1970; MLS, Columbia U., 1981. Libr. N.Y. Pub. Libr., N.Y.C., 1970—2002; libr. Robert F. Wagner Archives Tamiment Inst. Libr. NYU, N.Y.C., 2003—. Selection officer for classics, women's studies, Romanian and Albanian, N.Y. Pub. Libr., N.Y.C., 1981—. Office: Tamiment Wagner Archives New York U 70 Washington Square South New York NY 10012-1091 E-mail: dmj5@nyu.edu.

JOHNSTON, GLADYS STYLES, university official; b. St. Petersburg, Fla., Dec. 23, 1942; d. John Edward and Rosa (Moses) Styles; m. Hubert Seward Johnston, July 30, 1966. BS in Social Sci., Cheney U., 1963; MEd in Ednl. Adminstrn., Temple U., 1969; PhD in Ednl. Adminstrn.-Orgnl. Theory, Cornell U., 1974. Tchr. Chester (Pa.) Sch. Dist., 1963-66, West Chester (Pa.) Sch. Dist., 1966-67, asst. prin., elem. prin., dir. Summer Sch., 1968-71; dir. Head Start Chester County Bd. Edn., West Chester, 1967-69; teaching asst., rsch. asst. Cornell U., Ithaca, N.Y., 1971-74; asst. prof. ednl. adminstr. and supervision Rutgers U., New Brunswick, N.J., 1974-79, assoc. prof., chmn. dept. Grad. Sch. Edn., 1979-83, chmn. dept. mgmt. Sch. Bus., 1983-85; dean, prof. Coll. Edn., Ariz. State U., Tempe, 1985-91; provost, v.p. for acad. affairs DePaul U., Chgo., 1991-93, chancellor, 1993—. Disting. Commonwealth vis. prof. Coll. William and Mary Sch. Edn., Williamsburg, Va., 1982-83; manuscript reviewer Jour. Higher Edn., Jour. Ednl. Leadership, Prentice Hall Pub. Co., Englewood Cliffs, N.J.; speaker and conf. presenter in field; cons. AT&T, Ednl. Testing Svc., Prentice-Hall Pub. Co.; cons. to coordinating bd. Tex. Coll. and Univ. System. Author: Research and Thought in Administration Theory, 1986; mem. editorial bd. Ednl. Evaluation and Policy Analysis, Ednl. Adminstrn. Quar., Ednl. and Psychol. Rsch. Jour.; contbr. articles and book revs. to profl. jours., chpts. to books. Bd. dirs. Edn. Law Ctr., 1979-86, Sta. KAET-TV, Phoenix, 1987—, Found. for Sr. Living, 1990-91; mem. adv. coun. to bd. trustees Cornell U., 1981-86; trustee Middlesex Gen. Univ. Hosp., 1983-86. Recipient Outstanding Alumni award Temple U.; Andrew D. White fellow Cornell U. Mem. ASCD, Am. Assn. Colls. for Tchr. Edn., Nat. Conf. Profs. Ednl. Adminstrn., [illegible] (proposal reviewer 1979—, chmn. task force for participation and membership 1981—, chmn. E.F. Linquist award com. 1985, mem. govt. rels. com. 1986—, publ. com. 1986—), Phi Kappa Phi, Phi Delta Kappa, Alpha Phi Sigma. Office: U of Nebraska at Kearney Office of Chancellor 905 W 25th St Kearney NE 68845-4238

JOHNSTON, GWINAVERE ADAMS, public relations consultant; b. Casper, Wyo., Jan. 6, 1943; d. Donald Milton Adams and Gwinavere Marie (Newell) Quillen; m. H.R. Johnston, Sept. 26, 1963 (div. 1973); children: Gwinavere G., Gabrielle Suzanne; m. Donald Charles Cannalte, Apr. 4, 1981. BS in Journalism, U. Wyo., 1966; postgrad., Denver U., 1968-69. Editor, reporter Laramie (Wyo.) Daily Boomerang, 1965-66; account exec. William Kostka Assocs., Denver, 1966-71, v.p., 1969-71; exec. v.p. Slottow, McKinlay & Johnston, Denver, 1971-74; pres. The Johnston Group, Denver, 1974-92; chair, CEO JohnstonWells Pub. Rels., Denver, 1992—. Adj. faculty U. Colo. Sch. Journalism, 1988-90. Bd. dirs. Leadership Denver Assn., 1975-77, 83-86, Mile High United Way, 1989-95, Denver's 2% Club, chair, 1996—; bd. dirs. Spring Inst., 1997—, Lower Downtown Denver, Inc.; bd. dirs. Colo. Jud. Inst., 1991—, Inst. for Internat. Edn., 1998-99, U. Wyo. Found., 2000—. Recipient Athena award Colo. C. of C., 1999. Fellow Am. Pub. Rels. Soc. (pres. Colo. chpt. 1978-79, bd. dirs. 1975-80, 83-86, nat. exec. com. Counselor's Acad. 1988-93, sec.-treas. 1994, pres.-elect 1995, pres. 1996, profl. award Disting. Svc. award 1992); mem. Colo. Women's Forum, Rocky Mountain Pub. Rels. Group (founder), Denver Athletic Club, Denver Press Club. Republican. Home: 717 Monaco Pky Denver CO 80220-6040 Office: JohnstonWells Pub Rels 1512 Larimer St Ste 720 Denver CO 80202-1610

JOHNSTON, JOANNE SPITZNAGEL, lawyer, writing consultant; b. Peoria, Ill., Mar. 11, 1930; d. Elmer Florian and Anna E. (Kolb) Spitznagel; m. Charles Helm Bennett, June 12, 1951 (div. 1978); children: Mary Jaquelin Bennett Graub, Ariana Holliday Bennett, Caroline Helm Bennett Ammerman, Joanne Mary Bennett Jeffers; m. Donald Robert Johnston, Nov. 25, 1981. A.B., Vassar Coll., 1951; MA, Ind. U., 1970, PhD, 1974; JD, Ind. U.-Indpls., 1980. Bar: Ind. 1980, Minn. 1985. Lectr. Ind. U., Indpls., 1968-81, U.-Indpls., 1970-76; writing cons. U. Minn., Mpls., 1982-91; sole practice Indpls., 1980-86, Mpls., 1986-91. Mem.: Garden Club Am. (Indpls. chpt.), Indpls. Womans, Dramatic. Methodist. Home: 1066 Winterthur Indianapolis IN 46260-2232 also: 1469 Landings Circle Sarasota FL 34231

JOHNSTON, JOSEPHINE ROSE, chemist; b. Cranston, R.I., Aug. 9, 1926; d. Robert and Rose (Varca) Forte; m. Howard Robert Johnston, Mar. 7, 1949 (dec.); 1 child, Kevin Howard. Student, Carnegie Inst., 1945-47; BS, Mich. State U., 1972, MA, 1973; postgrad., MIT, 1973—. Med. technologist South Nassau Community Hosp., Rockville Centre, N.Y., 1947-50, Mich. State U., East Lansing, 1950-53, faculty specialist, 1966-76; dept. pathology Albany (N.Y.) Med. Ctr., 1953-54; med. lab. supr. Bulova Watch Co., Jackson Heights, N.Y., 1954-57; sr. chemistry technologist Mid Island Hosp., Bethpage, N.Y., 1958-66; sr. rsch. assoc. Uniformed Svcs. Univ., Bethesda, Md., 1976-78, asst. to chmn. dept. physiology, 1978-82, assoc. to chmn., 1982-96; sr. scientist NASA-Spaceline/Archive, Bethesda, 1997-99; owner, operator Slipstream II, 1997—. Author: Patriarch: The Life of T.J. Haddy, 1994; contbr. articles to profl. jours. With Danzinger Found., Lauderdale, Fla., 1990-91; vol. tech. com. fundraising Twinridge Elem. Sch., 1997-98. Mem. Analytical Chem. Soc., Data and Electronic Soc., Internat. Platform Assn., Kiwanis (bd. dirs.). Lutheran. Office: Slipstream II 6813 Woodville Rd Mount Airy MD 21771-7611 Office Phone: 301-829-7805. E-mail: slipstreamII@msn.com.

JOHNSTON, KRISTEN, television personality; b. Washington, D.C., Sept. 20, 1967; BFA, N.Y. Univ. Mem. Atlantic Theatre Co., Chelsea, N.Y.; actress CBS Television, L.A. Appeared in numerous stage productions; guest appearances on television include Chicago Hope, Heart's Afire, The Five Mrs. Buchanans; TV series Third Rock from the Sun; movies include Austin Powers: The Spy Who Shagged Me, 1999. Office: 3rd Rock from the Sun c/o Carsey Werner Prods 4024 Radford Ave Bldg 3 Studio City CA 91604-2101

JOHNSTON, KRISTEN ELIZABETH, psychologist, researcher; b. Houston, Nov. 7, 1972; d. Thomas William and Joan Elizabeth Johnston; m. Silvano R. Saretto, Nov. 17, 1972. BA with high honors, U. Tex., 1994; MS, Pa. State U., PhD in Devel. Psychology, 2000. Vis. asst. prof. psychology Gettysburg (Pa.) Coll., 2000—01; postdoctoral scholar, project coord. Pa. State U., University Park, 2001—03, family rsch. consortium III postdoctoral fellow Ctr. for Human Devel. and Family Rsch. in Diverse Contexts, 2002—. Ad hoc reviewer for profl. journals. Grantee, Soc. for the Psychol. Study of Social Issues, 1999; Family Rsch. Consortium III Postdoctoral fellow, NIMH, 2002—03. Mem.: APA Soc. for the Psychol. Study of Social Issues, APA Soc. for the Psychol. Study of Ethnic Minority Issues, Soc. for Rsch. in Child Devel., Phi Beta Kappa. Achievements include research in children's stereotype acquisition and experiences with discrimination.

JOHNSTON, LINDA TIDWELL, municipal official; BA in Psychology, U. Fla., 1969. Tchr. English, speech and drama Cocoa H.S., Rockledge, Fla., 1969-70; exec. trainee Burdines Dept. Store, West Palm Beach, Fla., 1970-72; adminstrv. asst., counselor Fortune Personnel, Cocoa Beach, 1972-73; social worker State of Fla., Cocoa, 1973-74; dir. ret. sr. vol. program City of Raleigh, 1974-79, dir. citizen involvement divsn., 1979-91, dir. neighborhood svc. divsn. cmty. svcs. dept., 1996—, divsn. dir. cmty. svcs. dept, 1991—96. Mem. N.C. Assn. Vol. Adminstrs., Woman's Club Raleigh. Office: Cmty Svcs Dept 310 W Martin St # 201 Raleigh NC 27601-1326

JOHNSTON, LYNN BEVERLEY, animator; b. Collingwood, Ont., Can., May 28, 1947; d. Mervyn and Ursula (Bainbridge) Ridgway; m. Rod Johnston; children: Aaron, Katherine. Student, Vancouver Sch. Art, 1964-67. Med. illustrator McMaster U. Cartoonist, For Better or For Worse, 1979—; author: David We're Pregnant 1974, Hi, Mom, Hi, Dad, 1975, Do They Ever Grow Up?, 1977, Growing Like a Weed, 1997; 18 collections of comic strips including Middle Age Spread, 1998. Recipient Reuben award Nat. Cartoonist's Soc., 1985; named to disting. Order of Can., 1992; nominated Pulitzer prize for editl. cartooning, 1994. Mem. Nat. Cartoonists Soc. (pres. 1988). Office: United Feature Syndicate Newspaper Enterprise Assn 200 Madison Ave Fl 4 New York NY 10016-3911

JOHNSTON, MARGUERITE, journalist, author; b. Birmingham, Ala., Aug. 7, 1917; d. Robert C. and Marguerite (Spradling) J.; m. Charles Wynn Barnes, Aug. 31, 1946; children: Susan, Patricia, Steven, Polly. AB, Birmingham-So. Coll., 1938. Reporter Birmingham News, 1939-44; Washington corr. Birmingham News, Birmingham Age-Herald, London Daily Mirror, 1945-46; columnist Houston Post, 1947-69, fgn. news editor, mem. editorial bd., 1969-85, assoc. editor editorial page, 1972-77, asst. editor editorial page, 1977-85. Lectr. in field, 1947— ; instr. creative writing U. Houston, 1946-47, lectr. feature writing, 1965-66; lectr. Baker Coll., Rice U., 1977-78; del. Asian Am. Women Journalists Conf., Honolulu, 1965, 1st World Conf. Women Journalists, Mexico City, 1969 Author: Public Manners, 1957, A Happy Worldly Abode, 1964, Houston: The Unknown City, 1836-1946, (Winedale Historical Ctr. Ima Hogg award, Otis Lock award East Tex. Historical Assn.), 1991. Bd. dirs. Tex. Bill of Rights Found., 1962-64; bd. dirs. Planned Parenthood, 1953-55, Population Inst., 1985-91; mem. Mcpl. Art Commn., 1971-76, Houston Com. Fgn. Relations. Recipient Theta Sigma Phi Headliner award, 1954, 1st ann. award of merit Houston Com. Alcoholism, 1956, cert. of merit Gulf Coast chpt. Am. Soc. Safety Engrs., 1960, Agnese Carter Nelms award Planned Parenthood, 1968, Sch. Bell award Tex. State Tchrs. Assn., 1974, 75, Gold Key award Nat. Council Alcoholism, 1975, Global award Population Inst., 1981. Mem. Tex. Soc. Architects (hon.), Philos. Soc. Tex., Phi Beta Kappa, Pi Beta Phi Home: 2929 Buffalo Speedway Houston TX 77098

JOHNSTON, MARILYN FRANCES-MEYERS, physician, medical educator; b. Buffalo, Mar. 30, 1937; BS, Dameon Coll., 1966; PhD, St. Louis U., 1970, MD, 1975. Diplomate Am. Bd. Pathology, Diplomate Nat. Bd. Med. Examiners. Fellow in immunology Washington U., St. Louis, 1970-72; resident in pathology Washington U. Hosp., St. Louis, 1975-77, St. John's Mercy Med. Ctr., St. Louis, 1977-79; research fellow hematology St. Louis U. Sch. Medicine, 1979-80; instr. biochemistry St. Louis U., 1972-75, asst. prof. pathology, 1980-87, assoc. prof., 1987-92, prof., 1992-99, prof. emeritus, 1999—, dir. transfusion svcs., 1980-99; staff pathologist Christian Hosp. Barnes Jewish Christian Hosps., St. Louis, 1999—. Med. dir. Mo./Ill. Regional Red Cross, 1983-88; area chmn. for inspection and accreditation Am. Assn. Blood Banks, Arlington, Va., 1984; med. dir. transfusion svc. Christian Hosps., Barnes-Jewish-Christian Hosp. Sys., St. Louis, 1999—. Author: Transfusion Therapy, 1985. Named Goldberger fellow, AMA, 1979; recipient Transfusion Medicine Acad. award, Nat. Heart, Blood and Lung Inst., 1984—. Mem. Am. Assn. Blood Banks, Am. Assn. Immunologists, Internat. Soc. Blood Transfusion, Am. Soc. Clin. Pathologists, Sigma Xi. Office: Christian Hosp NE 11133 Dunn Rd Saint Louis MO 63136 Office Phone: 314-653-4065.

JOHNSTON, YNEZ, artist, educator; b. Berkeley, Calif., May 12, 1920; BFA, U. Calif., Berkeley, 1941, MFA, 1946. Lectr. art U. Calif., Berkeley, 1950-51, Colorado Springs Fine Arts Center, 1954, 55, Chouinard Art Inst., 1956, Calif. State U., Los Angeles, 1966, 67, U. Judaism Sch. Fine Arts, Los Angeles, 1967, Otis Art Inst., Los Angeles, 1978-81; artist-in-residence Fullerton Coll. (Calif.), 1982 One-man exhbns. include: San Francisco Mus. Art, 1943, Redlands U., 1947, Santa Barbara (Calif.) Mus. Art, 1952, 57, Pasadena (Calif.) Mus. Art, 1955, 62, Colorado Springs (Colo.) Fine Arts Center, 1955, Calif. Palace Legion of Honor, 1956, The O'Hana Gallery, London, 1958, Paul Kantor Gallery, Los Angeles, 1952, 53, 55, 57, 58, 61-62, 63, Beloit (Wis.) Coll., 1961, Barbara Cecil Gallery, New Orleans, 1963, Mex., 1959, Occidental Coll., L.A., 1955, Esther Bear Gallery, 1967, Ball State U., 1967, Stewart-Verde Galleries, San Francisco, 1966, San Francisco Mus. Art, 1967, Mekler Gallery, L.A., 1970-82, 84, 89, Tokyo Shoten Gallery, N.Y.C., 1976, Mitsukoshi Gallery, Tokyo, 1977, Wiener Gallery, N.Y.C., 1977, Worthington Gallery, Chgo., 1982, 85, 88, Mekler Gallery, 1987, 89, Tomlyn Gallery, Fla., 1990-99, 2003, Fresno Mus. Art, 1992, Tortue Gallery, Santa Monica, 1994-96, Tobey Moss Gallery, L.A., 1994, 2003, Kennedy Museum, Athens, Ohio, 1997, Lyman Allyn Mus, New London, Conn., 1998, Schmidt-Bingham Gallery, N.Y.C., 1998, 99, 2001, Santa Cruz Mus., Calif. 1998, Norton Simon Mus., Pasadena, Calif., 2004; also exhibited numerous group shows including: Whitney Mus. Am. Art, 1953-56, Mus. Modern Art, 1952, 54, Carnegie Inst., 1951, 55, I.F.A. Gallery, Washington, 1963, 100 Prints of the Year, N.Y.C., 1963, Bklyn. Mus., 1966, Vancouver (B.C., Can.) Print Internat., World Print Competition, San Francisco, 1977, Met. Mus., 1978, L.A. County Mus., 1980-81, Drawings from Their Collection, Nat. Gallery Smithsonian, Washington, Wight Gallery UCLA, 1988, Nat. Gallery Modern Art, New Delhi, 1988, Memory Gallery, Nagoya, Japan, 1990, Gallery IV, L.A., 1990, Worcester Art Mus., 1991, Amon Carter Mus., 1991, Women's Art Mus., Washington, 1994, Met. Mus. Fresno, Calif., 1994, Brigitie Haasner Gallery, Wiesbaden, Germany, Norton-Simon Mus., 1999, Traveling Show in China, Macao, Municipal Gallery, Rio Honda Coll., L.A., Taiwan, 2001, others; represented in permanent collections numerous museums including, Santa Barbara Mus. Art, Mus. Modern Art, Philbrook Art Center, Los Angeles County Mus., City Art Mus. St. Louis, Whitney Mus. Am. Art, Phila. Mus. Art, San Diego Mus. Art, U. Ill., Met. Mus. Art, Hirshhorn Collection, Herbert F. Johnson Collection (Cornell U.), San Francisco Mus. Art, Otis Art Inst., Milw. Art Center, Worcester Art Mus. (travelling print exhbn. to Terra Mus., Chgo., Amon Carter Mus., Ft. Worth, 1990), Santa Fe Mus. of Fine Art, The Nat. Mus. Israel, Jerusalem, Gift Gardens Bot./Sculpture Pk., Fla., Norton-Simon Mus., numerous schs. and colls., other museums, also pvt. collections. Recipient San Francisco Mus. Art award oil painting, 1946; awards Calif. State Fair, 1951, 61, 62; award etching Los Angeles County Mus., 1950; exhbn. first award Met. Mus. Art, 1952; purchase award Exhbn. Fgn. Artists, Rome, Italy, 1952; purchase award Otis Art Inst., 1963; purchase award Los Angeles Municipal Art Dept., 1967; also commns.; John Simon Guggenheim Found. grantee, 1952; Louis Comfort Tiffany grantee, 1955, 56; Huntington Hartford grantee, 1957; James Phelan grantee, 1958; MacDowell Colony grantee, 1959; Tamarind workshop fellow, 1966; Nat. Endowment Arts painting grantee, 1976, 85 Home and Studio: 579 Crane Blvd Los Angeles CA 90065-5019

JOHNSTONE, JOYCE VISINTINE, education educator; b. Columbus, Ohio, Nov. 12, 1943; d. James Joseph and Virginia (Vogel) Visintine; m. James S. Luckett, Nov. 27, 1965 (dec. May 1969); children: Anne, Robert; m. William E. Kuhn, Sept. 1, 1995. BA, Cath. U. Am., 1965; MA, Butler U., 1974; PhD, Ind. U., 1994. Tchr. Columbus Pub. Schs., 1965-68, Hawaii Pub. Schs., Wahiawa, 1968-69, Montgomery County (Md.), Wheaton, 1969-70; chair edn. dept. Marian Coll., Indpls., 1975-98; Ryan dir. ednl. Outreach U. Notre Dame, South Bend, 1998—, fellow Inst. for Ednl Initiative, 1998—. Dir. Ind. Cath. Prins. Inst., 1989-94. Cath. Prins. Inst. grantee Lilly Endowment, Indpls., 1990, Project Enhance grantee Ind. Bell, Indpls., 1991, 95; Parent Partnership grant Danforth Found., 1995-97. Mem. ASCD, Assn. Tchr. Educators (pres. 1990-91, Turkey Run Outstanding Educator 1990), Ind. Assn. Colls. for Tchr. Edn. (pres., 1990-92, Outstanding Svc. award 1995). Roman Catholic. Office: Inst Ednl Initiative Univ Notre Dame Notre Dame IN 46556

JOHNSTONE, MARVA JEAN (JEANIE JOHNSTONE), insurance agency executive; b. Macon, Ga., Aug. 20, 1957; d. Preston Lester and Mable Marie Greenlee; m. Neil Scott Johnstone, June 17, 1978; children: Jeremy S., Aimee M. Grad. high sch., Rutledge, Tenn. Customer svc. rep. Fred S. James Ins., Wichita, Kans., 1979-80; comml. lines rep. Mannings Ins., Wichita, Kans., 1980-84; customer svc. rep. Marsh & McLennan, Wichita, Kans., 1984-85; small bus. mgr. Dorth Coombs Ins., Wichita, Kans., 1985-87; v.p. Fin. Guardian, Wichita, Kans., 1987-90; CEO Asset Builders Ins., El Dorado, Kans., 1990-91; mktg. mgr. Dulaney, Johnston & Priest, Wichita, 1991-2001; sr. mktg. specialist IMA of KS, Inc., Wichita, 2001—. Mem. Ins. Women Wichita (legis. officer 1987-89). Avocation: scuba diving. Home: 239 Frontier Dr Mulvane KS 67110-1106 Office: IMA of KS Inc 250 W Water Wichita KS 67201 E-mail: scubajeanie@hotmail.com., jeanie.johnstone@imacorp.com.

JOLES, CANDACE RAE, special education educator; b. Lawrenceville, Ill., Oct. 27, 1966; d. Joseph Franklin Joles Jr. and Linda Sue Joles; m. Brian Joseph Schuh, June 11, 2001. BS in Elem. Edn., Eastern Ill. U., 1988; MA in Spl. Edn., Ball State U., Muncie, Ind., 1999; MAE in Ednl. Adminstrn., postgrad., Ball State U., 2002—. Lic. tchr. elem. edn. Ill., 1984, cert. behavioral specialist Ill., 2002. Step instr., options coord., cope tutor Vincennes U., Ind., 1994—98, supr. learningplus, 1998—2001; doctoral asst. to Meek's Disting. prof. Ball State U., Muncie, 2001—. Student liason for north ctrl. accreditation Ball State U., Muncie, Ind., 2001—. Contbr. articles to profl. jours. Mem. Cmty. Food Pantry, Parker City, Ind., 2002—; vol. and fundraiser Bridgeport Sr. Citizens Ctr., Ill., 1998—2002; festival fundraiser coord. Parker City United Meth. Ch., Parker City, Ind., 2003—; bd. trustees Lawrence Twp. Libr., Lawrenceville, Ill., 1998—2001. Grantee Eli Lilly Coll. Prep. grantee, Eli Lilly, 1998—2001, Ill. Libr. Constrn. grantee, State of Ill., 1999; scholar Lyle Bussell scholar, Ball State U., 2002. Mem.: ASCD, Ind. Assn. for Devel. Edn. (treas. 2000—01), Bus. and Profl. Women (sec. 1999—2001), Ind. Coun. for Children with Behavioral Disorders (sec. and membership 2003—), Ind. Coun. for Exceptional Children (pres. elect 2003—), Phi Delta Kappa, Lawrenceville Rod N Gun Club, VFW Aux., Pi Lamdba Theta. Avocations: target shooting, quilting, gardening, cooking, reading. Home: 287 North Franklin St Parker City IN 47368 Office: Ball State Uni Dept Spl Edn Muncie IN E-mail: crjoles@bsu.edu.

JOLIE, ANGELINA, actress; b. L.A., June 4, 1975; d. Jon Voight and Marcheline Bertrand; m. Jonny Lee Miller, 1995, (div. Feb. 1999), Billy Bob Thonton, 2000, (div. 2003). 1 child: Maddox (adopted). Student, Strasberg Theatre Inst.; Grad. in Film, NYU. Actress. Former profl. model, London, N.Y., L.A, goodwill ambassador for the United Nations High Commissioner for Refugees, Geneva, Switzerland, 2001-. Actress: (films) Lookin' to Get Out, 1982, Cyborg 2, 1993, Angela & Viril, 1993, Hackers, 1995, Without Evidence, 1995, Foxfire, 1996, Mojave Moon, 1996, Love Is All There Is, 1996, True Women, 1997, George Wallace, 1997, Playing God, 1997, Gia, 1998, Hell's Kitchen, 1998, Playing by Heart, 1998, Pushing Tin, 1999, The Bone Collector, 1999, Girl, Interrupted, 1999, Dancing in the Dark, 2000, Gone in Sixty Seconds, 2000, Original Sin, 2001, Life or Something Like It, 2002, Lara Croft Tomb Raider: The Cradle of Life, 2003, Beyond Borders, 2003, Taking Lives, 2004; (music videos) Meat Loaf, Lenny Kravitz, Antonello Venditti, The Lemonheads; actress five student films for U. So. Calif. Sch. of Cinema. Recipient BFCA award Best Supporting Actress: Girl, Interrupted, 2000; Oscar award for Girl, Interrupted, 1999, nominated Emmy award Outstanding Supporting Actress: George Wallace, 1998; recipient Golden Globe awards Best Performance Actress in a Supporting Role: Girl, Interrupted, 2000, Best Peformance Actress in a Mini-Series: Gia, 1999, George Wallace, 1998, L.A. Outfest award for Outstanding Actress: Gia, 1998, Nat. Bd. of Rev. award for Playing by Heart, 1998, Screen Actors Guild award, Gia, 1999. Avocations: collecting knives, mortuary sci. Office: William Morris Agency 151 El Camino Dr Beverly Hills CA 90212-3635*

JOLIVETTE, CAROLA KATE, assistant principal; b. Rayne, La., June 6, 1954; d. Benton Anthony and Rose Rita Jolivette; m. Michael John Papillion (div. Nov. 6, 1996); children: Kimberly Sherrell, Michael Ian Papillion. B in Vocat. Edn., U. La., 1977; MEd, McNeese State U., 2000, M in Adminstrn., 2001, specialist in supervision, 2002. Cert. prin. La. Elem. sch. tchr Ross Elem. Sch., Crowley, La., 1979—80; pub. h.s. tchr. Church Point (La.) H.S., 1980—2003; asst. prin. Church Point Mid. Sch., 2003—. 1st responder Acadian Ambulance, Lafayette, La., 2001—. Mem.: Nat. Assn. Univ. Women (rec. sec. 2000—01, 2d v.p. 2001—03). Avocations: sewing, cooking, balloon arrangements, mentoring.

JOLLES, JANET K. PILLING, lawyer; b. Akron, Ohio, Sept. 5, 1951; d. Paul and Marjorie (Logue) Kavanaugh; m. Martin Jolles, Mar. 6, 1987; children: Madeleine Sloan Langdon Jolles, Jameson Samuel Rhys Jolles. BA, Ohio Wesleyan U., 1973; JD, U. Mo., 1976; LLM, Villanova U., 1985. Bar: Pa. 1976, U.S. Tax Ct. 1976, U.S. Dist. Ct. (ea. dist.) Pa. 1976, Ohio 1996. Atty. Schnader, Harrison, Segal & Lewis, Phila., 1976-83; gen. counsel Kistler-Tiffany Cos., Wayne, Pa., 1983-95; lawyer Janet Kavanaugh Pilling Jolles & Assocs., Berea, Ohio, 1996-99; v.p. First Union Trust Co., Wilmington, Del., 1999—2002, Wachovia Trust Co., Wilmington, 2002—. Mem. Estate Planning Coun. Del., Wilmington Tax Group, Phila. Estate Planning Coun., Estate Planning Coun. Cleve., Estate Planning Coun. Del. Mem.: ABA, Wilmington Women in Bus., Pa. Bar Assn., Phila. Bar Assn. (probate sect., tax sect.), Cuyahoga County Bar Assn., Cleve. Bar Assn., Ohio State Bar Assn., Berea Women's League, Phi Beta Kappa, Phi Delta Phi. Office: 3 Beaver Valley 4th Fl Wilmington DE 19803 Office Phone: 302-477-7651. E-mail: janet.jolles@wachovia.com., jjolleslaw@aol.com.

JOLLEY, CATHY JENNA, music educator; b. Santa Monica, Calif., Jan. 6, 1949; m. Douglas Orin Jolley, Mar. 9, 1991; 1 child, Cole Douglas. MusB, Brigham Young U., 1989. Tchr. Music Utah, 1989. Choral music tchr. American Fork Jr. H.S., American Fork, Utah, 1989—94, Mountain Ridge Jr. H.S., Highland, Utah, 1994—. Chmn. of state jr. high honor choir Utah Music Educators Assn., Utah, 1995—2003. Mem.: Music Educators Nat. Conf. R-Consevative. Lds Ch. Avocations: travel, reading, crocheting, scrapbooks, cooking. Home: 6040 West 9740 N Highland UT 84003 Office: Mountain Ridge Jr High 5525 West 10400 N Highland UT 84003 Personal E-mail: orinj116@msn.com.

JONAITIS, ALDONA CLAIRE, museum administrator, art historian; b. N.Y.C., Nov. 27, 1948; d. Thomas and Demie (Genaitis) J. BA, SUNY, Stony Brook, 1969; MA, Columbia U., 1972, PhD, 1977. Chair art dept. SUNY, Stony Brook, 1983-85, assoc. provost, 1985-86, vice provost undergrad. studies, 1986-89; v.p. for pub. programs Am. Mus. Natural History, N.Y.C., 1989-93; dir. U. Alaska Mus., Fairbanks, 1993—. Author: From the Land of the Totem Poles, 1988; editor, author: Chiefly Feasts: The Enduring Kwakiutl Potlatch, 1991; editor: A Wealth of Thought: Franz Boas on Native American Art History, 1995, Looking North: Art from the University of Alaska Museum, 1998, The Yuquot Whaler's Shrine, 1999. Mem. Am. Assn. Mus. (bd. dirs. 1999-2002), Am. Assn. Mus./ICOM (bd. dirs. 2000-2003), Native Am. Art Studies Assn. (bd. dirs. 1985-95). Office: U Alaska Mus 907 Yukon Dr Fairbanks AK 99775 E-mail: ffaj@naf.edu.

JONAS, RUTH HABER, psychologist; b. Tel Aviv, Aug. 24, 1935; d. Fred S. and Dorothy Judith (Bernstein) Haber; m. Saran Jonas, Sept. 16, 1956; children: Elizabeth, Frederick. AB, Barnard Coll., 1957; MA, New Sch. for Social Rsch., 1977, PhD, 1987; grad. psychotherapy and psychoanalysis, NYU, 1996. Lic. psychologist, N.Y. 1st and 2d yr. intern clin. psychology NYU Med. Ctr.-Bellevue Hosp., N.Y.C., 1985-87; postdoctoral rsch. fellow NYU Med. Ctr., N.Y.C., 1987-88; clin. instr. psychiatry NYU Sch. Medicine, N.Y.C., 1987, clin. asst. prof. psychiatry, 1991; sr. psychologist forensic svc. Bellevue Hosp., N.Y.C., 1988—; pvt. practice psychology N.Y.C., 1988—. Fellow Am. Orthopsychiat. Assn.; mem. APA, N.Y. State Psychol. Soc., Manhattan Psychol. Assn., Am. Heart Assn. (fellow stroke coun.). Office: 200 E 33d St Ste 2J New York NY 10016-4827 Office Phone: 212-684-2721.

JONAS, TRUDY ANN, principal; d. George Joseph Jonas and Dorothy Marie Culp; m. Christopher J. Petrovic, July 12, 1986; children: Mary Agnes Petrovic, Christopher John Petrovic Jr. BA, Rockhurst Coll., 1983; MA, Rockhurst U., 1999; M in Edn. Adminstrn., Benedictine Coll., Atchison, Kans., 2003. Lifetime tchg. cert. Mo., cert. prin. Kans. Tchr. St. Ann's Sch., Independence, Mo., 1993—97; devel. dir. St. Mary's H.S., Independence, 1997—2000, prin., 2000—. Mentor tchr. coord. Kansas City (Mo.) Diocese, 2002—. Trustee Kansas City Pub. Libr., 2001—; mem. TIF commn. City of Sugar Creek, Mo., 2001—. Roman Catholic. Avocations: reading, crossword puzzles.

JONASSON, OLGA, surgeon, educator; b. Peoria, Ill., Aug. 12, 1934; d. Olav and Swea C. (Johnson) J. MD, U Ill., Chgo., 1958; DSc, Newberry (S.C.) Coll., 1982. Diplomate Am. Bd. Surgery (bd. dirs. 1988-94). Intern and resident U. Ill. Rsch. & Ednl. Hosps., 1959-64; prof. surgery U. Ill., 1975-87; chief of surgery Cook County Hosp., Chgo., 1977-86; chmn., prof. dept. surgery Ohio State U., Columbus, 1987-93; mem. staff U. Ill. Hosps., Chgo., 1993—, dir. edn. and surg. dept., 1993—. Markle scholar John & Mary Markle Found., 1969. Fellow ACS; mem. Am. Surg. Assn. Office: Am Coll Surgeons Surg Svcs Dept 633 N Saint Clair St Chicago IL 60611-3234

JONDAHL, TERRI ELISE, importing and distribution company executive; b. Ukiah, Calif., May 6, 1959; d. Thomas William and Rebecca (Stewart) J. AA in Bus. Adminstrn., Mendocino Coll., 1981; BA in Adminstrn. and Mgmt., Columbia Pacific U., 1993. Office systems analyst County of Mendocino, Ukiah, 1980-83; micro systems analyst Computerland of Annapolis, Md., 1983-84; controller Continental Mfg. Inc., Nacogdoches, Tex., 1984-87, mktg. mgr., 1987-89, dir. sales and mktg., 1989-95; exec. v.p., chief oper. officer CAB Inc., Oakwood, Ga., 1995—2002; CEO Cab Inc., 2002—. Co-author: National Federation of Business & Professional Women Local Organization Revitalization Plan, 1989. Mem. Hall Co. C. of C. Mem.: NAFE, Am. Bus. Women's Assn., Ukiah Bus. and Profl. Women (pres. 1981—82), Nacogdoches Bus. and Profl. Women (pres. 1987—88), Tex. Fedn. Bus. and Profl. Women (state pres. 1994—95), Gwinnett County C. of C. (CEO exec. roundtable), Nacogdoches County C. of C. (small bus. adv. com. 1990). Home: 6344 Green Oak Rdg Flowery Branch GA 30542-6630 Office: CAB Inc 4161 Chamblee Rd Oakwood GA 30566-3518 E-mail: tjondahl@cabinc.com.

JONES, A. ELIZABETH, federal agency administrator; married; 2 children. BA in history, Swarthmore Coll., 1970; studied Arabic, in Beirut, Tunis and Cairo, 1975—77; in Internat. Rels., Boston U., 1986. Joined Fgn. Svc., 1970; fgn. svc. post Kabul, Afghanistan, 1971—72; pub. affairs officer Near East and South Asia Bur., 1972—73; polit. officer, 1973—75, Amman, Jordan, 1977—79; dep. prin. officer U.S. Interests Sect., Baghdad, Iraq, 1979—80; dep. chief mission Islamabad, Pakistan, 1988—92; Lebanon desk officer, 1981—83; dep. dir. for Lebanon, Jordan, Syria, and Iraq, 1983—84; head econ./comml. sect. U.S. Mission, West Berlin, 1985—88; dep. chief mission Bonn, Germany, 1992—93; exec. asst. Sec. of State, 1993—94; amb. Rep. of Kazakhstan, 1995—98; prin. dep. asst. sec. bus. Near Eastern Affairs U.S. State Dept., 1998—2000; sr. advisor Caspian Basin Energy Diplomacy, 2000—01; asst. sec. for European and Eurasian affairs U.S. Dept. of State, Washington, 2001—. Office: US Dept of State European and Eurasian Affairs 2201 C St NW Washington DC 20520

JONES, ANGELA DIANE, music educator; d. Leo Jones Jr. and Minnie Lee Pritchett; children: Christopher Andre' Reed, Alys LeAnna Reed. MusB in Edn., Nicholls State U., 1991. Cert. tchr. La. Gen. music tchr. St. Charles Parish Sch. Sys., Luling, La., 1992; choral dir. Lafourche Parish Sch. Sys., Thibodaux, La., 1992—94, Terrebonne Parish Sch. Sys., Houma, La., 1995—; pvt. piano and vocal instr. South La. Ctr. for the Arts, Houma, La., 2001—. Mid. sch. honor choir guest clinician St. Charles Parish Pub. Schs., Hahnville, La., 1997. Actor: (plays) Joseph and the Amazing Technicolor Dreamcoat (Best Actress award, 1987); singer: (plays) Le Nozze di Figaro, Cosi Fan Tutti; actor: (Operas) Nunsense. Mem.: La. Music Educators Assn. (elem. honor choir clinician 2002, State Choral Festival Sweepstakes 2001, 2002, 2003), Music Educators Nat. Conf. Office: H L Bourgeois High School 1 Reservation Ct Gray LA 70359 Personal E-mail: sing2angie@aol.com.

JONES, ANITA KATHERINE, computer scientist, educator; b. Ft. Worth, Mar. 10, 1942; d. Park Joel and Helene Louise (Voigt) J.; m. William A. Wulf, July 1, 1977; children: Karin, Ellen. AB in Math., Rice U., 1964; MA in English, U. Tex., 1966; PhD in Computer Sci., Carnegie Mellon U., 1973, PhD in Sci. and Tech. (hon.), 2000. Programmer IBM, Boston, Washington, 1966-69; assoc. prof. computer sci. Carnegie-Mellon U., Pitts., 1973-81; founder, v.p. Tartan Labs. Inc., Pitts., 1981-87; free-lance cons. Pitts., 1987-88; prof., head computer sci. dept. U. Va., Charlottesville, 1988-93, prof., 1997—, univ. prof., 1998—, Lawrence A. Quarles prof. engring. and applied sci., 1999; dir. def. rsch. and engring. Dept. Def., Washington, 1993-97. Mem. Def. Sci. Bd., Dept. Def., 1985-93, 98—; mem. sci. adv. bd. USAF, 1980-85; governing bd. Nat. Sci. Found.; vice-chair governing bd. NSF, 1998-2000; bd. dirs. Sci. Applications Internat. Corp., InQTel; trustee Mitre Corp., 1989-93, chair Va. Rsch. and Technology Adv. Commn., 1999-2002, Commonwealth of Va. Advs. Commn.; mem. corp. Charles Stark Draper Labs., 1999—. Editor: Perspectives on Computer Science, 1977, Foundations of Secure Computation, 1971. Recipient Air Force Meritorious Civilian Svc. award, 1985, Medal for Disting. Pub. Svc. Dept. of Def., 1996, Disting. Svc. award Computing Rsch. Assn., 1997. Fellow IEEE, AAAS, Assn. Computing Machinery (editor-in-chief Transactions on Computer Sys. 1983-91), Am. Acad. Arts and Scis.; mem. Nat. Acad. Engring., Sci. Found. of Ireland (bd. dirs. 2000-2003), Sigma Xi. Avocation: gardening. Office Phone: 434-982-2224. Business E-Mail: jones@virginia.edu.

JONES, APRIL LYNN, music educator; b. Toledo, May 6, 1971; d. Terry Richard and Harriet Kay Cooper; m. Chad Aaron Jones, Jan. 7, 1994; 1 child, Morgan Lynnae. BS in Music Edn., Ky. Christian Coll., 1993; postgrad., U. Toledo, 1989—90; MA in Edn., Morehead State U., 1999. Tchr. Carter County Bd. Edn., Grayson, Ky., 1995—. Curriculum com. Carter County, Ky., 2002. Named Best Tchr. in Carter County, Grayson Jour., 2000. Mem.: Music Educators Nat. Conf. Republican. Mem. First Ch. Of Christ. Avocations: piano, antiques. Home: 4646 S St Hwy 7 Grayson KY 41143 Office: Carter County Bd Edn 228 S Carol Malone Blvd Grayson KY 41143

JONES, AUDREY BEYER, dietician; b. Madison, Wis., Feb. 1, 1921; d. Adelbert John and Hazel Mae (Crocker) Beyer; m. Frank C. Jones, July 11, 1954 (dec. Jan. 23, 2003); children: Philip Lynn(dec.), Paul Douglas, David Scott. BS, Milw.-Downer Coll., 1941; BA, U. Wis., 1947; Tchg. Cert., U. Corpus Christi, Tex., 1962. Lic. dietitian, Tex. Dietitian Charity Hosp., New Orleans, 1942-43, 12th Evac Hosp./U.S. Army, 1943-44, VA Hosp., Wood, Wis., 1948-51; clinic dietitian VA Reg. Office, Milw., 1951-53; chief dietitian Kuakini Hosp., Honolulu, 1954-55; nutrition cons. various hosps. Corpus Christi, 1964—. Docent Art Mus. So. Tex., Corpus Christi, 1990-93. 1st lt. U.S. Army, 1943-44; ETO. Recipient Cmty. Bldr. award Masonic Grand Lodge of Tex., 2000. Mem. AAUW (pres. Corpus Christi br. 1994-96), Am. Dietetic Assn. (registered dietitian), Tex. Dietetic Assn., Corpus Christi Dietetic Assn. (pres. 1972). Republican. Lutheran. Avocations: travel, birding, reading, crossword puzzles, bridge. Home: 4621 Monette Dr Corpus Christi TX 78412-2344

JONES, BARBARA CHRISTINE, linguist, creative arts designer, educator; came to U.S., 1964, naturalized, 1971; d. Martin and Margarete (Roth-Rommel) Schulz von Hammer-Parstein; m. Robert Dickey, 1967 (div. 1980); m. Raymond Lee Jones, 1981. Student, U. Munich, 1961, Philomatique de Bordeaux, France, 1962; BA in German, French, and Speech, Calif. State U., Chico, 1969, MA in Comparative Internat. Edn., 1974. Cert. secondary tchr., C.C. instr., Calif. Fgn. lang. tchr. Gridley Union H.S., Calif., 1970-80, home econs., decorative arts instr., cons., 1970-80, English study skills instr., 1974-80, ESL coord., instr. Punjabi, Mex. Ams., 1970-72, curriculum com. chmn., 1970-80; program devel. adv. Program Devel. Ctr. Supt. Schs., Butte County, Oroville, Calif., 1975-77; opportunity tchr. Esperanza H.S., Gridley, Calif., 1980-81, Liberty H.S., Lodi, Calif., 1981-82, resource specialist coord., 1981-82; Title I coord. Bear Creek Ranch Sch., Lodi, Calif., 1981-82, instr., counselor, 1982-83; sub. tchr. Elk Grove (Calif.) Unified, 1982-84. Freelance decorative arts and textiles designer, 1982-95; internat. heritage and foods adv. AAUW, Chico, Calif, 1973-75; lectr. German, Schreiner Coll., Kerrville, Tex., 1993; workshop dir. Creative Arts Ctr., Chico, 1972-73; workshop dir., adv. Bus. Profl. Women's Club of Gridley, 1972-74; mem. Cowboy Artists Mus., Kerrville, 1996-99; v.p. Golden State Mobile Home League, Sacramento, 1980-82; mem. publicity Habitat for Humanity, Kerrville br., 1992-94. Weavings-wall hangings (1st pl. 10 categories, Silver Dollar Fair, Chico, Calif., 1970). Vol. Ariz. Superior Ct., Foster Care Review Bd., 2003. Mem.: AAUW (publicity dir. cultural activities Kerrville br. 1991—92), Am. Assn. German Tchrs., German Texan Heritage Soc., USAR Non-Commd. Officer's Assn. (ednl. adv. 1984—86), Turtle Creek Social Cir. (pioneer 1992—99), Am. Cancer Soc. (publicity 1992—95), Kingmen Social Club (membership chair 2001—, removal vol. Supreme Ct., Foster Care 2003—), Kerrville Garden

Club (publicity 1993—97), United European Am. Club, Kappa Delta Pi. Avocations: textile design, swimming, travel, real estate, mosaics. Home: 3350 Pasadena Ave Kingman AZ 86401-5046

JONES, BARBARA ELLEN, neuroscientist, educator; b. Phila., Dec. 19, 1944; d. Charles and Ella (Yeager) J.; m. John Gordon Galaty, Aug. 12, 1972; 1 child, James Gordon. BA, U. Del., 1966, MA, 1969, PhD, 1971. Rsch. assoc., asst. prof. U. Chgo., 1972-77; asst. prof. dept. neurology and neurosurgery McGill U., Montreal, 1977-82, assoc. prof., 1982-88, prof., 1989—. Vis. lectr. U. Nairobi, Kenya, 1974-75; vis. scientist Oxford U., Eng., 1984-85; vis. prof. U. Geneva, 1991-92, 98-99. Contbr. articles to profl. jours. Postdoctoral fellow Coll. de France, Paris, 1970-72. Mem. Am. Neurosci. Soc., Sleep Rsch. Soc. Avocations: horseback riding, skiing. Home: 97 Arlington Ave Westmount QC Canada H3Y 2W5 Office: McGill Univ 3801 Univ St Montréal QC Canada H3A 2B4

JONES, BEVERLY ANN MILLER, nursing administrator, retired patient services administrator; b. Bklyn, July 14, 1927; d. Hayman Edward and Eleanor Virginia (Doyle) Miller; m. Kenneth Lonzo Jones, Sept. 5, 1953 (dec.); children: Steven Kenneth, Lonnie Cord. BSN, Adelphi U., 1949. Chief nurse regional blood program ARC, NYC, 1951-54; asst. dir., acting DON M.D. Anderson Hosp. and Tumor Inst., Houston, 1954-55; asst. DON Sibley Meml. Hosp., Washington, 1959-61; assoc. dir. nursing svc. Anne Arundel Gen. Hosp., Annapolis, Md., 1966-70; asst. adminstr. nursing Alexandria Hosp., Va., 1972-73; v.p. patient care svc. Longmont United Hosp., Colo., 1977-93; pvt. cons., 1993-99; ret. Instr. ARC, 1953-57, chmn. nurse enrollment com. D.C. chpt., 1959-61; mem. adv. bd. Boulder Valley Vo.-Tech. Health Occupations Program, 1977-80; del. nursing adminstrs. good will trip to Poland, Hungary, Sweden and Eng., 1980. Contbr. articles to profl. jours. Mem.-at-large exec. com. nursing svc. adminstrs. sect. Md. Nurses' Assn., 1966-69; bd. dir. Meals on Wheels, Longmont, 1978-80, Longmont Coalition for Women in Crisis, Applewood Living Ctr., Longmont; mem. utilization com. Boulder (Colo.) Hospice, 1979-83; mem. task force on nat. commn. on nursing Colo. Hosp. Assn., 1982, mem. coun. labor rels., 1982-87; mem. U. Colo. Task Force on Nursing, 1990; vol. Champs program St. Vrain Valley Sch. Dist., Prestige Plus program Longmont United Hosp., 1999—. Named Outstanding Vol. of Yr., St. Vrain Valley Sch. Dist., 2002. Mem. Am. Orgn. Nurse Exec. (chmn. com. membership svc. and promotions, nominee recognition of excellence in nursing adminstrn.), Colo. Soc. Nurse Exec. (dir. 1978-80, 84-86, pres. 1980-81, mem. com. on nominations 1985-86, Outstanding Vol. of Yr. 2002). Home: 853 Wade Rd Longmont CO 80503-7017

JONES, BLANCHE, nursing administrator; b. Edgecombe, N.C., Nov. 11, 1935; d. Cosevelt Ewuell and Evelyn (Jones) Harrison. Diploma, CUNY Hunter Coll., 1971; AAS, CUNY Medgar Evers Coll., 1986; BS in Cmty. Health, Gerontology and Med. Surg. Sci., St. Joseph's Coll., 1990. RN, N.Y.; RN in med.-surg., ANCC. From nurse aide to head nurse Bellevue Hosp., N.Y.C., 1958-77; head nurse Coney Island Hosp., Bklyn., 1978-90, clin. supr., 1990—. Contbr. articles to profl. jours. Bd. dirs. Baisley Park Neighbors Inc., Jamaica, N.Y., 1968—. Mem. Orthopaedic Nurses Assn., N.Y. Nurses Assn. (del. 1972), Bowling League, Fishing Club, Target Pistol Club. Democrat. Baptist. Office: Coney Island Hosp 2601 Ocean Pkwy Brooklyn NY 11235-7791 Home: 1741 Oakville Pl Lady Lake FL 32162-7681

JONES, BONNIE QUANTRELL, automobile dealer; b. Detroit, Apr. 13, 1944; d. Arthur Everett and Eleanor Marie (Zander) Quantrell; m. Billy Gatton Jones. BA, U. Minn., 1966. Writer, producer Pillsbury Co., Mpls., 1966-68; writer, prodn. mgr. Creative Ctr., Inc., Mpls., 1968-71; freelance writer, producer Mpls., 1971-75; owner, pres. Cameron & Co., Mpls., 1975-79; sales mgr. Quantrell Cadillac, Lexington, Ky., 1979-81; pres., owner Quantrell Cadillac and Quantrell Porsche-Audi, Lexington, 1982—. Adv. bd. Cen. Bank, Lexington, 1987—. Pres. Jr. Achievement Bluegrass, Lexington, 1986-87, Better Bus. Bur. Lexington, 1987; mem. Lexington Philharm. Guild, 1986—. Mem. Nat. Automobile Dealers Assn., Ky. Automobile Dealers Assn., Internat. Automobile Dealers Assn., Cadillac Nat. Dealer Council (nat. rep. 1986-87), Volvo Nat. Dealer Council (nat. rep. 1985—, parts chmn. 1987-88), Phi Beta Kappa. Clubs: Lexington, Lexington Country. Avocation: tennis. Office: Quantrell Cadillac Inc 1490 E New Circle Rd Lexington KY 40509-1098

JONES, BRENDA GAIL, school district administrator; b. Winnipeg, Man., Can., Nov. 5, 1949; d. Glen Allen and Joyce Catherine (Peckham) McGregor. BA, San Francisco State U., 1972; MA, U. San Francisco, 1983. Cert. tchr., sch. adminstr., Calif. Tchr. Lakeport (Calif.) Unified Sch. Dist., 1973-82, asst. prin., 1982-88, dir. ednl. svcs. and spl. projects, 1988-2000; dir. pupil personnel svcs. Redwood City (Calif.) Sch. Dist., 2000—. Instr. English Mendocino Coll., Ukiah, Calif., 1977-82. Mem. Assn. Calif. Sch. Adminstrs. (past pres. 1987, Lake County charter), Order Ea. Star (past matron Clear Lake chpt. 1995, dep. grand matron 1999). Democrat. Episcopalian. Avocations: health, fitness, walking, reading, gardening. Home: 1315 20th St Lakeport CA 95453-3051 Office: Redwood City sch Dist 750 Bradford St Redwood City CA 94063

JONES, CAROLE MOODY-ANDERSON, retired outreach representative; b. Terre Haute, Ind., Sept. 19, 1929; d. Willard and Constance (Hathecock) Moody; m. Orville Merle Anderson, Mar. 27, 1948 (div. 1963); children: Larry Joe (dec.), Orville M., Dorian Trent, Younte Pierre, Peter Shawn; m. Pleasant Thomas Jones, June 13, 1969 (dec. 1986); 1 child, H. Mina. Student, Ind. State U., 1948, 63, 79. Nurse asst. St. Anthony H.S., Terre Haute, Ind., 1950-61; file clk. customer svc. Columbia Record, Terre Haute, Ind., 1961-67; long distant operator Gen. Tel., Terre Haute, Ind., 1967-68; clk. J.C. Penney, Terre Haute, Ind., 1971—72; libr. and tchr. asst. Clay Cmty. Schs., Brazil, Ind., 1972—79; field agt. Purdue Co-op Ext., Brazil, Ind., 1980—87; outreach rep. Health Care Excel, Terre Haute, Ind., 1989—96; ret., 1996. Part-time beneficiary svc. rep., 1999—. Active with props, makeup and costumes, actress Terre Haute Cmty. Theater, 1963-67; PTA mem., v.p. PTO, Brazil, 1969-79; pres. Ind. State U.-Adv. Bd. Upward Bound., 1976-79; asst. Girl Scouts Am., Brazil, 1977-80; bd. mem. Rose Southside Day Care, Terre Haute, 1988-96; presenter ch. workshops, 1942—. Recipient Nat. Beneficiary Svcs. Merit award Health Care Fin. Adminstrn., Balt., 1995, Lifetime Achievement award Ky. Consol. Health Sys., Louisville, 1995, Nat. Mature Media Program award Mature Market Resource, Am. Custom Pub. Co., 1995. Mem. NAACP, Order Ea. Star, Am. Assn. of Ret. Persons, United Sr. Action Fund, Pioneer Post 340 Aux., Alpha Pi Chi (Alpha Beta chpt.). Avocations: reading, walking, writing speeches, research. Home: 210 S Lambert St Brazil IN 47834-3210

JONES, CAROLYN, insurance company executive; b. 1956; Grad., Coll. William and Mary. CPA. With Ernst & Young LLP, Richmond, Va., 1977-89; joined Hilb, Rogal and Hamilton Co., Glen Allen, Va., 1989, v.p., contr., 1991—, sr. v.p., CFO, treas., 1997—. Mem. AICPA. Office: PO Box 1220 Glen Allen VA 23060-1220 also: 4235 Innslake Dr Glen Allen VA 23060 Office Fax: 804-747-6046.

JONES, CAROLYN EVANS, writer, speaker; b. Middleboro, Mass., Sept. 5, 1931; d. King Israel and Kleo Estelle (Hodges) Evans; m. John Homer Jones, Sept. 9, 1966 (dec. July 1986); 1 child, David Everett. BA in English, Tift Coll., 1952; M Religious Edn., Carver Sch. Missions and Social Work, 1958; BA in Art, Mercer U., 1982. Cert. secondary tchr., Ga. Tchr. McDuffie County Bd. Edn., Thomson, Ga., 1952-53, Colquitt County Bd. Edn., Norman Park, Ga., 1953-55; missionary Home Mission Bd. SBC, New Orleans and Macon, 1958-66; spl. edn. tchr. Bibb County Bd. Edn., Macon, 1968-70, 75-79; owner, operator Laney Co. Imprinted Specialties, Macon, 1986-97; writer, 1998—. Contbr. numerous articles and poems to profl. jours. Bible tchr. YWCA, Macon, 1980-85; deacon 1st Bapt. Ch., Macon. Mem.: Inst. Noetic Scis., Ga. Bapt. Women in Ministry, Southeastern Writers Assn., Ga. Writers Inc. Democrat. Avocations: reading, travel, attending conferences

JONES, CHERRY, actress; b. Paris, TN, Nov. 21, 1956; Founder Amer. Rep. Theatre, Cambridge, Mass., 1980—; guest artist Arena Stage, Washington, D.C., 1983-84. Stage appearances include: (with Amer. Rep. Theatre) King Lear, Twelfth Night, Major Barbara, Caucasian Chalk Circle, The Serpent Woman, Platonov, Life Is a Dream, The School for Scandal, The Three Sisters, As You Like It, Baby with the Bathwater, A Midsummer Night's Dream, Journey of the Fifth Horse, (Off Broadway) Desdemona, Goodnight Desdemona, Baltimore Waltz (Obie award), And Baby Makes Seven, Light Shining in Buckinghamshire, Big Time, Ballad of Soapy Smith, I Am a Camera, The Philanthropist, The Importance of Being Earnest, (Broadway) Angels in America, Our Country's Good, Macbeth, Stepping Out, The Heiress (Tony award Best Actress 1995), The Night of the Iguana, 1996; television appearances include: (movies) Alex: The Life of a Child, 1986; film appearances include: The Big Town, 1987, Light of Day, 1987, Housesitter, 1992, The Tears of Julian Po, 1997, (voice) Out of the Past, 1998, The Horse Whisperer, 1998, Murder in a Small Town, 1999, Cradle Will Rock, 1999,, The Perfect Storm, 2000, Erin Brockovich, 2000, Signs, 2002. Office: The William Morris Agy 151 S El Camino Dr Beverly Hills CA 90212-2775

JONES, CHRISTINE MASSEY, retired furniture company executive; b. Columbus, Ga., Nov. 7, 1929; d. Louis Everett and Donia (Spivey) Massey; divorced; children— James Raymond, Jr., James David. Student, Ga. Southwestern Coll., 1947-48. With Muscogee Mfg. Co., Columbus, Ga., 1948-56, sec. to pres., 1956; sec. to pres. and treas., corp. sec. Haverty Furniture Cos., Inc., Atlanta, 1956-59, sec. to pres. and treas., 1959-63, sec. to pres., 1963-72, sec. to pres., adminstrv. asst., 1972-74, sec. to pres., adminstrv. asst., asst. corp. sec., 1974-78, corp. sec., 1978-86, corp. sec., asst. v.p., 1986-93; v.p. stockholder rels., sec. Haverty Furniture Cos., Atlanta, 1993-97, ret., 1997. Mem. Am. Soc. Corp. Secs. (securities industry com.)

JONES, CLAUDIA FENTRESS, minister, artist; b. Norfolk, Va., June 8, 1943; d. Claude Hillary Fentres, Jr. and Beatrice (Brockwell) Fentress; m. Charles Nelson Eskey, Jr., Sept. 15, 1962 (div. Aug. 1981); children: Tammy Lee Eskey Lindauer, Charles N. Eskey III; m. Bobby Lee Jones, Sr., Apr. 21, 1982. Cert., Word of Life Internat. Bible Sch., 1982, art courses, 1983—89. Ordained min. Word of Life Faith Ctr. Internat., 1982. Missionary to Trinidad Word of Life Faith Ctr., Internat., 1987—2003, missionary to Surinam and Guyana, 1989—2003; adminstr. Ivory Coast Word of Life Faith Internat. Bible Inst., 2002—03; artist, 1980—2003. V.p. Word of Life Faith Ctr. Internat., Dry Fork, Va., 1983—2003; home furnishings cons. Haynes Furniture, Virginia Beach, 1977—81; owner Earthen Vessels Inc., Nags Head, 1981. Mem.: Am. Ctr. for Law and Justice. Avocations: painting, pottery, boating, flying, interior decorating. Home: 1685 Whitnell School Rd Dry Fork VA 24549 Office: Word of Life Faith Ctr Internat 79 Yeatts Rd Martinsville VA 24112 E-mail: wordoflifefaithcenter@msn.com.

JONES, CORI, education educator, writer; d. Harriman Jones and Elizabeth Bacon Pike; life ptnr. Neil Warrener. MFA, Cornell U., 1972—74. Author: (short fiction) F-Stops, Priests, Fish, Sugar River (CLMP/Gen. Electric award for Younger Writers, 1989), New Car, Starring, Time Zones, The Man with the Truck, Little Deaths, Night Ride. Recipient Artistic Merit award, NJ State Coun. on the Arts, 1985; fellow Disting. Artist award, 1988. Avocations: fitness activities, drawing/painting, travel, photography. Office: Raritan Valley Community College Rte 28 and Lamington Rd North Branch NJ 08876 Personal E-mail: wick1860@aol.com.

JONES, CYNTHIA TERESA CLARKE, artist; b. Bklyn., Aug. 12, 1938; d. Arthur Ottio and Emma (Gibbs) Clarke; m. Robert H. Jones. Apr. 21, 1968 (div. Sept. 1977); 1 child, Kim Marie. Student, Bklyn. Mus., 1954-57, Art Career Sch., 1958, Hunter Coll., N.Y.C., 1963-65. One woman shows include Queens Borough Pub. Libr., Jamaica, N.Y., 1986, Baruch Coll., 1972; exhibited in group shows Queens Coun. on Arts Exhibit at Gertz Dept. Store, 1972, Queens Coll. Arts Festival, 1972, Dist. Coun. 37, First Art Exhbn., 1972, Artist Equity Group Shows Union Carbide, 1975, 77, Queensborough Community Coll. Invitational Show at Holocaust Resource Ctr., 1985, Pen and Brush, 1990, AQA Gallery, 1990, AQA at Chung Cheng Gallery at St. Johns U., 1987-90, Lowenstein Libr. Gallery Fordham U., 1989, Arlington Arts Ctr., 1991, Pursuit of Peace Ceres Gallery, 1991; designer cover Rsch. Papers Stats. Dept. Bernard M. Baruch Coll., 1973; works reprinted in Locally Speaking Local 384 newsletter. Donator work to MUSE Gallery, 1990, to Hale House Ctr., Inc.; active Women's Caucus for Art. Recipient Joseph Grumbacher Co. award, 1958, Scholastic Art award and key, 1957, Fine Arts award Queensboro Soc., 1973, Outstanding Painting award, 1973, France Lieber Meml. award Nat. Assn. Women Artists, Inc., 1992, two certs. of merit Latham Found., 1956-58; scholar Latham Found., 1958. Mem. Artists Equity Assn., Inc. N.Y., Alliance of Queens Artists, Coll. Art Assn., Queens Coun. on Arts, Ind. Arts Assn., Arlington Arts Ctr. Va., Queensboro Coll. Art Gallery (assoc.), Nat. Assn. Women Artists (The Kreindler Meml. award 1995), Print Club, Guild Am. Papercutters. Office: 11332 Mayville St Jamaica NY 11412-2410

JONES, DIANA WYNNE, writer; b. London, Aug. 16, 1934; d. Richard Aneurin Jones and Marjorie (Jackson) Hughes; m. John Anthony Burrow, Dec. 22, 1956; children: Richard, Michael, Colin. BA, St. Anne's Coll. U. Oxford, Eng., 1956. Free-lance writer part-time, Essex, Oxford, Eng., 1944-70; full-time writer Oxford, Bristol, Eng., 1970—. Panel judge Guardian Award for Children's Books, London, 1979-83, Whitbread Prize for Lit., Children's Sect., London, 1988; judge World Fantasy Awards, 2001. Author: (children's and young adults' books) Wilkins' Tooth (in U.S. Witch's Business), 1973, The Ogre Downstairs, 1974, Eight Days of Luke, 1975, Cart and Cwidder, 1975, Dogsbody, 1975, Power the Three, 1976, Drowned Ammet, 1977, Charmed Life, 1977 (Guardian award 1978), Who Got Rid of Angus Flint, 1978, The Spellcoats, 1979, The Magicians of Caprona, 1980, The Homeward Bounders, 1981, The Time of the Ghost, 1981, Witch Week, 1982, Warlock at the Wheel, 1984, Archer's Goon, 1984 (Boston Globe/Horn Book award), Fire and Hemlock, 1985, Howl's Moving Castle, 1986 (Boston Globe/Horn Book award), A Tale of Time City, 1987, The Lives of Christopher Chant, 1988, Chair Person, 1989, Wild Robert, 1989, Hidden Turnings, 1989, Castle in the Air, 1990, Black Maria, 1991, A Sudden Wild Magic, 1992, The Crown of Dalemark, 1993, Stopping for a Spell, 1993, Hexwood, 1993, Fantasy Stories, 1994, Everard's Ride, 1995, The Tough Guide to Fantasyland, 1996, Minor Arcana, 1996, Deep Secret, 1997, Dark Lord of Derkholm, 1998, (retelling of) Puss n' Boots, 1999, Mixed Magics, Year of the Griffin, 2000, The Merlin Conspiracy, 2003, Unexpected Magic, 2004, Changeover, 2004. Recipient, Mythopoeic Soc. award, 1995, 99, Joseph Wagner award Brit. Fantasy Soc., 1999. Mem. Soc. of Authors, Brit. Fantasy Soc. Avocations: cooking, hiking, owning a cat. Home: 9 The Polygon Bristol BS8 4PW England Office: care Greenwillow Books 105 Madison Ave New York NY 10016-7418

JONES, DONNA MARILYN, state agency administrator, former legislator; b. Brush, Colo., Jan. 14, 1939; d. Virgil Dale and Margaret Elizabeth (McDaniel) Wolfe; m. Donald Eugene Jones, June 9, 1956; children: Dawn Richter, Lisa Shira, Stuart. Student, Treasure Valley Community Coll., 1981-82; grad., Realtors Inst. Cert. residential specialist. Co-owner Parts, Inc., Payette, Idaho, 1967-79; dept. mgr., buyer Lloyd's Dept. Store, Payette, Idaho, 1979-80; sales assoc. Idaho-Oreg. Realty, Payette, Idaho, 1981-82; mem. dist. 13 Idaho Ho. of Reps., Boise, 1987-90, mem. dist. 10, 1990-94, mem. dist. 9, 1995-98; assoc. broker Classic Properties Inc., Payette, 1983-91; owner, broker ERA Preferred Properities Inc., 1991-98; mem. dist. 9 Idaho Ho. of Reps., 1992-98. Co-chmn. Apple Blossom Parade, 1982; mem. Payette Civic League, 1968-84, pres. 1972; mem. Payette County Planning and Zoning Commn., 1985-88, vice-chmn. 1987; field coordinator Idaho Rep. Party Second Congl. Dist., 1986; mem. Payette County Rep. Cen. Com. 1978—; precinct II com. person, 1978-79, state committeewoman, 1980-84, chmn. 1984-87; outstanding county chmn. region III Idaho Rep. Party Regional Hall of Fame, 1985-86; mem. Payette County Rep. Women's Fedn., 1988—, bd. dirs., 1990-92; mem. Idaho Hispanic Commn., 1989-92, Idaho State Permanent Bldg. Adv. Coun., 1990-98; bd. dirs. Payette Edn. Found., 1993-96, Western Treasure Valley Cultural Ctr., 1993-96; nat. bd. dirs. Am. Legis. Exchange Coun., 1993-98; mem. legis. adv. coun. Idaho Housing Agy., 1992-97; committeeperson Payette County Cen.; chmn. Ways and Means Idaho House of Reps., 1993-97, House Revenue & Taxation Com., 1997-98; mem. Multi-State Tax Compact, 1997-98; Idaho chmn. Am. Legis. Exchange Coun., 1991-95; exec. dir. Idaho Real Estate Commn., 1998—. Recipient White Rose award Idaho March of Dimes, 1988; named Payette/Washington County Realtor of Yr., 1987. Mem. Idaho Assn. Realtors (legis. com. 1984-87, chmn. 1986, realtors active in politics com. 1982-98, polit. action com. 1986, polit. affairs com. 1986-88, chmn. 1987, bd. dirs. 1984-88), Payette/Washington County Bd. Realtors (v.p. 1981, state dir. 1984-88, bd. dirs 1983-88, sec. 1983), Bus. and Profl. Women (Woman of Progress award 1988, 90, treas. 1988), Payette C. of C., Fruitland C. of C., Wiesr C. of C.. Republican. Avocations: reading, interior decoration. Home: 1911 1st Ave S Payette ID 83661-3003 Office: Idaho Real Estate Commn 633 N 4th St Boise ID 83720-0001

JONES, DORIS (ANNA DORIS VOGEL), apparel buyer; b. Woodstock, Mich., Oct. 31, 1917; d. Lowren Orville and Lela Irene (Gallatin) Vogel; m. Verl Richard Huntley, April 13, 1946 (dec. 1966); 1 child, Karyl Lynn Huntley; m. Donald R. Jones, April 28, 1957 (dec. 1989). BA in Psychology, U. Mich., 1939. Salesperson J.L. Hudson Dept. Store, Detroit, 1939-40, Bullocks, L.A., 1940; asst. store mgr. Elaine Shop, Jackson, Mich., 1940-48; store mgr. Joseph Magnin, Sacramento, 1949-52; women's sportswear buyer Steinfelds Dept Store, Tucson, 1952-57; pvt. practice spiritual counselor Tucson, 1977-82; religious sci. practitioner, tchr. Golden Gate Ch. of Religious Sci., Corde Madero, Calif., 1982—, Santa Rosa (Calif.) Ch. of Religious Sci., 1992—98. Adv. bd. United Ch. of Religious Sci., L.A., 1994-98, practitioner emeritus religious sci., 1997. Recipient Meritorious Practitioner award United Ch. of Religious Sci., 1997. Home and Office: 284 Mockingbird Cir Santa Rosa CA 95409-6240 Personal E-mail: djones1917@aol.com.

JONES, DOROTHY F. judge; b. Sept. 3, 1946; d. Birl Floyd Madden and Aszie (Brown) Madden Simpson; m. Raymond Wilkerson (div. Jan. 1972); 1 child, Vicky; m. Allen J. Jones, Aug. 15, 1987 (dec. Aug. 1997); 1 stepchild, Felicia. BA, DePaul U., 1974, JD, 1979. Bar: Ill. 1979, U.S. Dist. Ct. (no. dist.) Ill. 1980, U.S. Supreme Ct. 1983. Acct. Allied Radio, Chgo., 1962-68, Atlantic Richfield, Chgo., 1968-72; tchr. Chgo. Pub. Schs., 1974-80; asst. pub. defender Cook County Pub. Defender's Office, Chgo., 1980-92; elected cir. judge Daley Ctr. Cir. Ct. Cook County, Chgo., 1992—, retained, 1998. Legal adviser 28th Ward alderman, Chgo., 1982-83. Chmn. prin.'s com. Suder Sch., Chgo., 1978, rec. sec. cmty. coun., 1979; adviser Westside People for Progress, Chgo., 1982; bd. dirs. Chgo. Youth Ctrs.; founder Concerned Citizens, Mother's House. Recipient certs. merit Clemente H.S. Bilingual Dept., Chgo., 1979, Kinsey Elem. Sch., Chgo., 1980, Kennedy H.S., Chgo., 1980. Mem. ABA, Ill. State Bar Assn., Chgo. Bar Assn., Cook County Bar Assn. (bd. dirs. 1982-84, rec. sec. young lawyers sect. 1982-83, Merit award 1982, cert. of appreciation 1998), Am. Arbitration Assn., Nat. Assn. Criminal Def. Attys., Ill. Judges Assn., Ill. Jud. Coun., Austin Cmty. Club, Mix Bowling League. Democrat. Methodist. Home: 133 S Waller Ave Chicago IL 60644-3948 Office: Richard J Daley Ctr Cir Ct Cook County 50 W Washington St Chicago IL 60602-1305

JONES, EDITH HOLLAN, federal judge; b. Phila., Apr. 7, 1949; BA Cornell U., 1971; JD with honors, U. Tex., 1974. Bar: Tex. 1974, U.S. Supreme Ct. 1979, U.S. Ct. Appeals (5th and 11th cirs.), U.S. Dist. . (so. and no. dists.) Tex. Assoc. Andrews & Kurth, Houston, 1974—82, ptnr., 1982—85; judge U.S. Ct. Appeals (5th cir.), Houston, 1985—. Gen. counsel Rep. Party of Tex., 1981—83. Master: ABA; mem.: State Bar Tex. Presbyterian. Office: 12505 US Courthouse 515 Rusk Ave Houston TX 77002-2655*

JONES, EDITH IRBY, physician; b. Conway, Ark., Dec. 23, 1927; d. Robert and Mattie (Buice) Irby; m. James Beauregard Jones, Apr. 16, 1960 (dec. Oct. 1989); children: Gary Ivan, Myra Vonceil Jones Romain, Keith Irby. BS, Knoxville Coll., 1948; MD, U. Ark., 1952. Intern Univ. Hosp., Little Rock, 1952-53; gen. practice medicine Hot Springs, Ark., 1953-59; resident in internal medicine Baylor Coll. Medicine, Houston, 1959-62; practice medicine specializing in internal medicine Houston, 1962—; mem. staff Meth. Hosp., Houston, Hermann Hosp., Houston, Riverside Gen. Hosp., Houston, St. Elizabeth Hosp., Houston, St. Anthony Ctr., Houston, St. Joseph Hosp., Houston, Thomas Care Ctr., Houston, Town Park, Houston, chief of staff. Clin. asst. prof. medicine Baylor Coll. Medicine, U. Tex. Sch. Medicine, Houston; dir. Prospect Med. Lab.; bd. dirs., sec. Mercy Hosp. Comprehensive Health Care Group; ptnr. Jones, Coleman and Whitfield; grand med. examiner Ct. Calanthe Jurisdiction, Tex.; cons. Social Security Agy., Tex. Pub. Welfare Dept., Vocat. Rehab. Assn., Tex. Rehab. Commn.; bd. dirs. Std. Savs. Assn., Houston; others. Contbr. articles to profl. jours. Bd. dirs. Houston Internat. U., Drug Addiction Rehab. Enterprise, March of Dimes, Houston, Odessey House, Houston; adv. bd. Houston Coun. on Alcoholism; com. for revising justice code, Harris County, Tex.; chmn. bd. trustees Knoxville Coll.; impartial hearing officer Houston Ind. Sch. Dist.; trustee Mut. Assn. for Profl. Svc.; mem. Cmty. Welfare Planning Assn., Friends of Youth, Human Svcs. Adv. Coun., Houston; bd. visitors U. Houston; others. Dr. Edith Irby Jones Day proclaimed by State of Ark., 1985, City of Little Rock, 1985, City of N.Y.C., 1986; named one of 30 Most Influential Black Women Houston, 1984; named to Tex. Black Women's Hall of Fame, 1986; commended by Calif. Senate, 1969; proclamation by city coun., Houston, 1985, Mayor of Houston, 1986; recipient cert. of citation Ho. of Reps. State of Tex., 1986, Volunteerism and Cmty. Svc. award Tex. Acad. Internal Medicine, 2000, Scroll of Merit award Nat. Med. Assn., 2001; portrait placed in entrance hall U. Ark. for Med. Scis., 1985; others; named one of 100 Leading Black Physicians Black Enterprise mag., 2001. Fellow Am. Coll. Medicine, Am. Soc. Internal Medicine (Oscar E. Edward award 2001); mem. AMA, Am. Med. Women`s Assn. (v.p. Houston chpt.), Nat. Med. Assn. (past pres., Scroll of Merit 2001), Lone Star Med. Assn., Harris County Med. Assn., Houston Med. Forum, Tex. Assn. Disability Examiners, Bus. and Profl. Women, Nat. Coun. Negro Women, Inc. (v.p. Dorothy Height chpt.), NAACP, PTA, YMCA, Alpha Kappa Mu, Delta Sigma Theta, Eta Phi Beta. Clubs: Links, Inc., Top Ladies of Distinction, Girl Friends, Inc., Women of Achievement, Inc. (Hall of Fame 1985). Lodges: Order Eastern Star. Democrat. Avocations: travel, walking, swimming. Home: 3402 S Parkwood Houston TX 77021 Office: 2601 Prospect St Houston TX 77004-7737 Office Phone: 713-529-3145. E-mail: eijones@advmed.com.

JONES, ELAINE HANCOCK, humanities educator; b. Niagara Falls, N.Y., Feb. 17, 1946; d. Roy Elmer and June Edna (Clark) Hancock; m. Ralph Jones III, Oct. 9, 1971 (div. June 1981). AAS in Comml. Design, U. Buffalo, 1962; BFA, SUNY, Buffalo, 1971, MFA in Painting, 1975; postgrad., Fla. State U., 1993—. Med. illustrator Roswell Park Meml. Inst., Buffalo, 1967-70; designer, animator Acad. McLarty Film Prodns., Buffalo, 1970-73; publs. designer Buffalo/Erie County Hist. Soc., 1974-78; dir. publs. Daemen Coll., Amherst, N.Y., 1978-80; owner, art dir. Plop Art Prodns., Melbourne, Fla., 1981-86; instr. humanities Brevard C.C., Melbourne, 1986—; prof. humanities Brevard campus Rollins Coll., Melbourne, 1995—. One-woman shows include SUNY, Buffalo, 1974, Upton Gallery, N.Y., 1975, Gallery Wilde, Buffalo, 1978; exhibited in group shows at Fredonia Coll., N.Y., 1975, Upton Gallery, 1975, Brevard Art Mus., Melbourne, Fla., 1987. Mem. docent program Art Mus./Sci. Ctr., Melbourne, 1983-84, mem. edn. com., 1995—; officer Platinum Coast chpt. Sweet Adelines Internat., 1984-90. Nat. Merit scholar, 1971-75; recipient cert. of merit Curtis Paper Co., 1977; N.Y. State Coun. on Arts grantee, 1975. Republican. Home: 2240 Sea Ave Indialantic FL 32903-2524 Office: Brevard CC Liberal Arts Dept 3865 N Wickham Rd Melbourne FL 32935-2310

JONES, ELAINE R. civil rights advocate; b. Norfolk, Va., Mar. 2, 1944; AB, Howard U., 1965; LLB, U. Va., 1970. Pres., dir.-counsel, atty. NAACP Legal Def. and Ednl. Fund, Washington, 1993—2004. Mem. panel arbitration Am. Stock Exch. Recipient Recognition award Black Am. Law Student Assn, 1974, Spl. Achievement award Nat. Assn. Black Women Attys., 1975. Mem. Nat. Bar Assn., Internat. Fedn. Women Lawyers, Old Dominion Bar Assn., Va. trial Lawyers Assn., Delta Sigma Theta.

JONES, ELIZABETH ORTON, artist, author; b. Highland Park, Ill., June 25, 1910; d. George Roberts and Jessie Orton Jones. Student, The Art Inst., Chgo., 1931-32; PhB, U. Chgo., 1932; Diploma, Ecole des Beaux Arts, Fontainebleau, France, 1932; MA (hon.), Wheaton Coll., 1946; postgrad., The DeCordova Mus., Lincoln, Mass., 1955-56. Artist. Author/illustrator: How Far Is It To Bethlehem?, 1955, Twig, 1944, Maminka's Children, 1940, Ragman of Paris, 1937; author/editor: History of Mason, N.H., 1968; illustrator/editor: David, 1937; co-author/illustrator: Minnie the Mermaid, 1939; illustrator numerous books including Deep River, 1955, This Is the Way, 1951, Little Red Riding Hood, 1947, A Little Child, 1946, Secrets, 1945, A Prayer for Little Things, 1945, Prayer For a Child, 1944 Caldecott medal ALA), What Miranda Knew, 1944, Small Rain, 1943, Big Susan, 1947, others; murals Crotched Mountain Rehab. Ctr., Greenfield, N.H., 1953. Recipient Charles Muller prize, Chgo. Soc. Etchers, 1939. Mem. Chgo. Children's Reading Round Table (hon.), N.H. Art Assn., New Eng. Hist. Geneal. Soc., Mason Hist. Soc., Soc. of Mayflower Descendants, Highland Park Hist. Soc., Delta Kappa Gamma. Avocations: hist. rsch. and genealogy, teaching. Home: 849 Valley Rd Mason NH 03048-4613

JONES, ELIZABETH WINIFRED, biology educator; b. Seattle, Mar. 8, 1939; d. Kenneth Clifford Harris and Dorothea (Dowty) J. BS, U. Wash., 1960, PhD, 1964. Postdoctoral fellow MIT, Cambridge, 1964-67, instr. in biology, 1967-69; asst. prof. Case Western Res. U., Cleve., 1969-74; assoc. prof. Carnegie Mellon U., Pitts., 1974-82, prof., 1982—, dept. head, 2000—, Frederick A. Schwertz Disting. Prof. of Life Scis., 2000—. Vis. scientist Sch. Medicine Wash. U., 1981-82; adj. prof. in psychiatry U. Pitts., 1985—; mem. genetics tng. com. NIH, Bethesda, Md., 1972-73, mem. genetics study sect., 1976-80, 84-86, chair, 1990-93. Co author: (with D.L. Hartl) Genetics. Principles and Analysis, 1998, (with D.L. Hartl) Essential Genetics, 1999, Genetics: An Analysis of Genes and Genomes, 2000; editor: Molecular Biology of the Yeast Saccaromyces, 2 vols., 1981, 82, Molecular and Cellular Biology of the Yeast Saccaromyces, 3 vols., 1991, 92, 97; assoc. editor Genetics, 1980-96, editor-in-chief 1997—; assoc. editor Yeast, 1984—, Ann. Rev. of Genetics, 1990—; mem. editl. bd. Molecular Biology of the Cell, 1992-2000. Recipient Rsch. Career Devel. award NIH, 1971-74, 75-77. Fellow AAAS; mem. Am. Soc. Microbiology, Am. Acad. of Microbiology, Am. Soc. Cell Biology (coun. 1992-93), Genetics Soc. Am. (pres. 1987), Am. Soc. Human Genetics. Office: Carnegie Mellon U 4400 5th Ave Pittsburgh PA 15213-2617

JONES, ERIN MARGUERITE, music educator, b. Newark, Ohio, July 27, 1971; d. John Joseph Jones, Jr. and Arlene Matilda Jones. B in Music Edn., Baldwin-Wallace Coll., 1993; M in Music Edn., VanderCook Coll. Music, 2001. Cert. music tchr. grades K-12 Ohio Dept. Edn., 1993. Pvt. flute tchr. Baldwin-Wallace Coll., Berea, Ohio, 1990—93, The Broadway Sch. Music, Cleve., 1992—93; music tchr. (5th band, 4th strings, h.s. orch.) Berea City Sch. Dist., 1993—, music tchr. (5th grade all-city band dir.), 1994—. Music articulation team Berea City Sch. Dist., 1994—, music curriculum writing team, 1994—, curriculum coun., 1994—95, mem. profl. devel. com., 2000—; currliculum leader Midpark H.S., Middleburg Heights, Ohio, 2000—01. Mem.: Nat. Music Educators Conf., Ohio Music Educators Assn., Mu Phi Epsilon (treas. 1991—93). Roman Catholic. Avocations: flutist, reading, softball. Office: Berea City School District 390 Fair St Berea OH 44017 Personal E-mail: ejones@berea.k12.oh.us.

JONES, EVELYN GLORIA, medical technologist, educator; b. Roanoke, Va., Aug. 13, 1940; d. William Darnell and Elizabeth (Harris) Powell; m. Theodore Joseph Jones, Aug. 21, 1965. BS in Biology, Tenn. State U., 1973; cert. in med. tech., Vanderbilt U., 1974; MEd in Adminstrn. and Supervision, Tenn. State U., 1993. Cert. clin. lab. scientist Nat. Cert. Agy. Med. Lab Pers. Med. technologist Metro Gen. Hosp., Nashville, 1974-78, Vanderbilt Med. Ctr., Nashville, 1978-97; microbiologist Tenn. Dept. Health Lab. Svcs., Nashville, 1997—. Tech. cons. Vanderbilt Point of Care Program, 1993-96; lectr. St. Thomas Program Med. Tech., Nashville, 1991-94; mem. adv. bd. Tenn. State U./Meharry Med. Tech. Program, Nashville; instr. tchg. faculty Pub. Health Lab. Svcs., State Tenn., Nashville. Nashville bd. dirs. Tenn. Valley Region ARC Blood Svcs., 1996-2002; asst. sec. Henderville area chpt. The Links, Inc., 1997-2002; docent Frist Mus.; info. guide Fisk U. Mem.: AAAS, So. Assn. Clin. Microbiology, Am. Soc. Clin. Pathologist (assoc.; cert. med. technologist), Alpha Kappa Alpha, Phi Delta Kappa. Roman Catholic. Home: 1003 Cross Bow Dr Hendersonville TN 37075-9403 Office: Tenn Dept Health Lab Svcs Dept Microbiology Nashville TN 37202 E-mail: EvelynJones@mail.state.tn.us.

JONES, FELICIA M. director; b. N.Y.C., June 20, 1961; d. Michael W. Toreno, Myrna L. Toreno. BS, Butler U., 1984; MS in Edn., Old Dominion U., 1997, student. Registered diagnostic med. sonographer, vascular technologist, diagnostic cardiac sonographer Am. Registry Diagnostic Med. Sonographers. Instr. Hillsborough C.C., Tampa, Fla., 1988—90; sect. leader sonography Mary Washington Hosp., Fredericksburg, Va., 1990—92; program dir. Tidewater C.C., Virginia Beach, Va., 1992—; chief sonographer Preferred Diagnostic Svcs., Inc., Largo, Fla., 1985—88. Coord. distance learning Tidewater C.C., Virginia Beach, 1998—2000; site visitor Joint Rev. Com. on Edn. in Diagnostic Med. Sonography, Bedford, 2000—. Co-author: Ultrasonography: An Introduction to Normal Structure and Function, 1995, Ultrasound Scanning: Principles and Protocols, 1999, Ultrasonography, 2004. Grantee, Va. C.C. Sys. Profl. Devel. Com., 1997, Tidewater C.C., 1998. Mem.: N.C. Ultrasound Soc., Am. Inst. Ultrasound in Medicine, Soc. Diagnostic Med. Sonographers. Office: Tidewater CC 1700 College Crescent Virginia Beach VA 23453 Office Phone: 757.822.7271. Home Fax: 757.427.1338; Office Fax: 757.427.1338. Business E-Mail: fjones@tcc.edu.

JONES, FLORENCE M. music educator; b. West Columbia, Tex., Apr. 11, 1939; d. Isaiah and Lu Ethel (Baldridge) McNeil; m. Waldo D. Jones, May 29, 1965; children: Ricky, Wanda, Erna. BS, Prairie View A&M U., 1961, MEd, 1968; postgrad., Rice U., 1988, U. Houston, 1980. Cert. tchr. elem. edn., math. Tchr. English and typing Lincoln High Sch., Port Arthur, Tex., 1961-62; tchr. grades three and four Houston Ind. Sch. Dist., 1963-90, tchr. gifted and talented, 1990-94; tchr. piano Windsor Village Liberal Arts Acad., Houston, 1994—. Dist. tchr. trainer Houston Ind. Sch. Dist., 1985-90; shared decision mem. Sch. decision Making Team, 1993-94; coord. gifted/talented program, Petersen Elem. Sch., Houston, 1990-94; participant piano Recital Hartzog Studio, 1985-88; film previewer Houston Media Ctr. Curriculum writer Modules to Improve Science Teaching, 1985; author sci. pop-up book, 1980, gifted/talented program, 1994; contbr. poems to lit. jours. Youth camp counselor numerous non-denominational ch. camps, U.S., 1961-89; active restoration of Statue of Liberty, Ellis Island Found., N.Y.C., 1983-85; lay minister Ch. of God, 1961-94; charter founder The Am. Family History Immigration Ctr., Ellis Island, N.Y.C. Recipient Letter of Recognition for Outstanding Progress in Edn., Pres. Bill Clinton, 1994, Congresswoman Sheilia Jackson Lee, Tex. Gov. George Bush, State Rep. Harold V. Sutton Jr., Houston Mayor Bob Lanier, Tex. Gov. Ann Richards; Gold Cup/Highest Music award Hartzog Music Studio, 1987, Diamond Key award Nat. Women of Achievement, 1995, Editors Choice award Nat. Library Poetry, 1995, cert. recognition Quaker Oats Co. and NCNW Inc., 1999, Youth Advisors trophy and New Millennium Leader plaque Nat. Women Achievement, 2001, others; inductee The Internat. Poetry Hall of Fame. Mem. NEA, Houston Assn. Childhood Edn. (v.p. 1985-88), Assn. for Childhood Edn. (bd. dirs. 1979-91), Houston Zool. Soc., World Wildlife Fund, Nat. Storytelling Assn., Tejas Storytelling Assn. (life), Soc. Children's Book Writers and Illustrators, Nat. Audubon Soc., Am. Mus. Natural History, Tex. Ret. Tchrs. Assn. (life), Internat. Soc. Poets (disting. life mem., Silver Cup Award for outstanding poetry achievement, 2003), others. Democrat. Avocations: writing, reading, storytelling, collecting sea shells, arts and crafts. Home: 3310 Dalmatian Dr Houston TX 77045-6520

JONES, GEORGIA ANN, publisher; b. Ogden, Utah, July 6, 1946; d. Sam Oliveto and Edythe June Murphy; m. Lowell David Jones; children: Lowell Scott, Curtis Todd. Sculptor, 1964-78; journalist, 1968-80; appraiser real property Profl. Real Estate Appraisal, San Carlos, Calif., 1980-95; online columnist, 1995-97; owner, pub. Ladybug Press, Sonora, 1996—. Leader workshops for writers, 1994—; founder, prodr. internat radio stas. Ladybughive, 1998—, Teen Talk Network, 1999—, Moose Meals, 2001—; owner IA Connections Network, 2001—. Author: A Garden of Weedin', 1997, Write What You Know: A Writer's Adventure, 1998, In Line at the Lost and Found, 2000, The Real Dirt on the American Dream: Home Ownership and Democracy, 2000; patentee Scruples-tag, 1980; editor, pub. Women on a Wire, 1996, vol. 2, 2001; author, playwright, A Stitch in Time, 1995, The Usual Suspects, 1995. Spkr. Jubillenium Interfaith Conf. for World Peace, 1999. Mem. Internat. Forum of Lit. and Culture (bd. dirs., U.S. chpt., Pave Peace keynote spkr. internat. congress 1999). Avocations: drawing, designing and building homes, landscape gardening. Office: 16964 Columbia River Dr Sonora CA 95370 Business E-Mail: georgia@ladybugbooks.com.

JONES, GRETCHEN KUYKENDALL, computer specialist, statistician; b. Seattle, Feb. 11, 1939; d. Jerome Kenneth and Jane Madeline (Brehm) K.; m. Stanley Edmund Jones, June 5, 1965 (div. Aug. 1969). BA, Dickinson Coll., Carlisle, Pa., 1961; MA in Math., U. Del., 1964; MA in Statistics, Am. U., 1986. Computer systems analyst Nat. Ctr. for Health Stats., Dept. HHS, Washington, Rockville, Md., Hyattsville, Md., 1969—. Co-author: Atlas of United States Mortality, 1997; contbr. articles to ency. and jours. Sec. bd. dirs. Waterford Condominium, Kensington, Md., 1994—. Recipient Honor award in stats. and data processing CDC, 1989, Best. Paper in Stats., SAS Users Group Internat. Conf., 1988. Democrat. Unitarian-Universalist. Avocations: playing piano, singing, creative writing, artistic design, water aerobics. Home: 3333 University Blvd W Apt 404 Kensington MD 20895 1833 Office: NCHS 6525 Belcrest Rd Hyattsville MD 20782-2003

JONES, GWENYTH ELLEN, publishing information systems/technology executive; b. Omaha, Sept. 21, 1952; d. Robert Lester and Mary Ellen (Ouren) J.; m. William F. Knoff Jr.. BA, U. Va., 1974, MA in English, 1982. Mktg. dir. John Wiley & Sons, N.Y.C., 1986-89, pub., 1989-90, dir. info. systems and tech., 1990-97, exec. dir. pub. info. systems and techs., 1997—2001; v.p. Pub. INfo. Sys. and Techs., 2001—. Mem. Assn. Am. Pubs. Avocations: dance, tennis. Office Phone: 201-748-6109.

JONES, HENDREE EVELYN, research scientist, psychologist; b. Richmond, Mar. 11, 1972; d. Clinton Edward Jones and Hendree Fitzgerald Mason; m. Erik Matthew Lensch, June 28, 1997; 1 child, Ashley Carter Lensch. BA, Randolph-Macon Coll., 1992; MA, U. Richmond, 1994; PhD, Va. Commonwealth U., 1997. Postdoctoral fellow Johns Hopkins U., Behavioral Pharm. Rsch. Unit, Balt., 1997—98; instr. Johns Hopkins U., Behavioral Biology, Dept. Psychiat., 1998—99; rsch. dir. Johns Hopkins U., Ctr. for Addiction and Pregnancy, 1998—; asst. prof. Johns Hopkins U., Behavioral Biology, Dept. Psychiat., 1999—; program dir. cornerstone Johns Hopkins U., 2000—. Rsch. panel mem. Ctr. for Substance Abuse Treatment, Chevy Chase, Va., 2000; grant reviewer Nat. Inst. Drug Abuse, Washington, 2002; reviewer Nat. Registry for Effective Treatment Programs, Washington, 2003—. Contbr. articles various profl. jours. Vol. Hopkins House, Alexandria, Va., 2000—. Recipient Young Psychopharmacologist award, 1999. Fellow: Md. Psycho. Assn.; mem.: Coll. on the Problems of Drug Dependence, Am. Psycho. Assoc., Phi Beta Kappa. Achievements include development of animal model of abused inhalants during pregnancy; behavioral therapy for treating drug abusing partners of pregnant drug dependent women; research in pharmacotherapies for pregnant women. Avocations: reading, scuba diving, exercising, scrapbooks. Home: 310 Wendover Rd Baltimore MD 21218 Office: Johns Hopkins Bayview Med Ctr 4940 Eastern Ave D 3 E Baltimore MD 21224 Office Phone: 410-550-7684. Business E-Mail: jejones@jhmi.edu.

JONES, HETTIE COHEN, writer, educator; b. Bklyn. d. Oscar and Lottie (Lewis) Cohen; m. LeRoi Jones, Oct. 13, 1958 (div. 1965). BA in Drama cum laude, U. Va., 1955; postgrad., Columbia U., 1956. Freelance editl. svcs., N.Y.C., 1965—. Adj. prof. Parsons Sch. Liberal Studies, 1992-2004, grad. writing program New Sch. U., 2003—; faculty writing 92nd St Y, N.Y.C., 1992—, New Sch., 1991, SUNY Purchase, NYU, CUNY, Mercy Coll., U. Wyo, 1993-94, Pa. State U., 1997; asst. to the editors Partisan Rev., 1957-61; staff writer Mobilization for Youth, 1966-68; editl. cons. Curriculum Concepts, Inc., 1984, Visual Edn. Corp., 1983; lectr. in field. Contbr. numerous articles to profl. jours.; contbr. poetry and fiction to publs.; author: All Told, 2003, How I Became Hettie Jones, 1990, paperbacks, 1991, 97, Drive, 1998 (Norma Farber award Poetry Soc. Am., 1999), The Trees Stand Shining, 1971, 2d edit. 1993, Big Star Fallin' Mama, 1974, 2d edit. 1995 (selected as one of 20 best new books for young adults N.Y. Pub. Libr.); co-author: (with Rita Marley) No Woman No Cry, 2004; co-editor: Yugen mag., 1958-61. Chmn. bd. dirs. Ch. of All Nations, 1972-76; cons. Grace Ch. Opportunity Project, Day Care Coun. of Greater N.Y., 1968-72, 85; co-chair PEN Prison Writing Com.; condr. writing workshop N.Y. State Correctional Facility for Women, Bedford Hills, 1989—; grant recommender Lower Manhattan Cultural Coun., 1994—; mem. lit. panel N.Y. State Coun. on the Arts, 1994-97.

JONES, HILDA HOBBS, minister; b. Lena, Miss., Mar. 27, 1948; d. Jessie A. and Ida Nichols Hobbs; m. Raymond L. Jones, Feb. 1, 2000; children: Raymond L. Jr., Terrise Brown, Laforisse Whitaker, Angelo James, Toni Hill. Student, Alcorn A&M Coll., 1968; corr. cert., Moody Bible Sch., 1974; cert., Cram C.C., New Bern, N.C., 1983, cert., 1994. Ordained elder AME Luth. Ch., 1981. Advisor Hempstead Parent Camp, New London, Conn., 1973—76; chairperson Head Start Regional Policy Coun., Southeastern, Conn., 1973—76; treas. New London County Opportunities Indsl. Commn., 1975—77; dir. evangelism New Bern (N.C.) Dist. African Meth. Episc. Zion Ch., 1989—98; pastor Cedar Grove African Meth. Episc. Zion Ch., Aurora, NC, 1998—2003, St. Mark African Meth. Episc. Zion Ch., Morehead City, NC, 2003—. Adminstr., presiding elder New Bern Dist., Havelock, NC, 1985—98; sec. budget and fin. com. N.C. Conf., New Bern, 1991—98; dean Beaufort Dist. Preachers Inst., New Bern, 2000—. Author plays. Active Craven County Schs., 1987—97, Dem. Women, Dem. Party, New Bern, 1982—87; campaign com. Craven Dem. Party, New Bern, 1994—2000; com. to elect Quinn Craven County Cmty., New Bern, 1999. Mem.: Ladies of Craven Civitan Club (pres. 1982—86, Civitan award 1984). Avocations: writing, travel, teaching, bicycling, reading. Home: 1011 Massey Dr Kinston NC 28504 Office: St Mark AME Zion Church 5106 Hwy 70W Morehead City NC 28557

JONES, INGRID SAUNDERS, food products executive; b. Detroit; EdB, Mich. State U.; EdM, Ea. Mich. U., 1973; HHD (hon.), Mich. State U., Atlanta Coll. Art, Morris Brown Coll. Tchr. pub. sch. sys., Detroit, Atlanta; exec. dir. Detroit/Wayne County Child Care Coordinating Coun.; legis. analyst to the pres. Atlanta City Coun.; exec. asst. to Mayor Maynard Jackson; asst. to v.p. for urban and govtl. affairs The Coca-Cola Co., 1982—86, mgr. urban projects, 1986—87, dir. urban affairs, 1987—88, asst. v.p., 1988—91, v.p., mgr. corp. external affairs, 1991, sr. v.p. corp. external affairs, 2000—. Chair The Coca-Cola Found.; bd. dirs. Girls, Inc., Mich. State U. Found., Andrew Young Sch. Policy Studies, Ga. State U., Desmond Tutu Peace Found., Coca-Cola Scholars Found., Cmty. Found. Greater Atlanta, 1994—, Nat. Black Arts Festival, Coun. on Founds., Woodruff Arts Ctr., United Way Met. Atlanta, chair. Named to Hall of Fame, Ga. State U. Sch. Bus., 1998; recipient Pres. award, Morehouse Coll., 1988, Nat. Equal Justice award, NAACP Legal and Edn. Fund, 1997, Jondelle Johnson Legacy award, NAACP-Atlanta Chpt., 1998, Woman of Achievement award, YWCA Greater Atlanta, 1998, John B. Gerlach Devel. award, Ohio State U. Found., 1998, Nat. Action Networker's Keepers of the Dream award, 2001. Mem.: Soc. Internat. Bus. Fellows, Atlanta Rotary Club. Office: The Coca-Cola Co PO Box 1734 Atlanta GA 30301*

JONES, JACQUELINE, historian; b. 1948; m. Jeffrey B. Abramson, May 18, 1980; children: Sarah, Anna. BA in Am. Studies, U. Del., 1970; MA in History, U. Wis., 1972, PhD in History, 1976. Asst. prof. Wellesley Coll., 1976-82, assoc. prof., from 1982, prof.; now prof. Am. civilization, chair dept. history Brandeis U., Waltham, Mass. Author: Soldiers of Light and Love: Northern Teachers and Georgia Blacks, 1865-1873, 1980, Labor of Love, Labor of Sorrow: Black Women, Work and the Family from Slavery to the Present, 1985 (Philip Taft Labor History award, 1985), The Dispossessed: America's Underclasses from the Civil War to the Present, 1992, American Work: Four Centuries of Black and White LAbor, 1998, A Social History of the Laboring Classes: From Colonial Times to the Present, 1999. Recipient grant-in-aid Am. Council of Learned Socs., 1977, research fellowship, 1979-80; Mellon Research fellowship, 1979-80, NEH research fellowship, 1979-80, Bancroft prize, 1986; MacArthur fellow John D. and Catherine T. MacArthur Found., 1999. Mem. Orgn. of Am. Historians, So. Assn. for Women Historians, Nat. Women's Studies Assn. Office: Brandeis U Dept History Olin Sang 215 Mail Stop 036 PO Box 9110 Waltham MA 02454-9110

JONES, JACQUELINE LEE, health facility administrator; d. Vern Franklin and Mildred Naoma (Mohney) Moore; m. Richard Theodore Sawicky, July 10, 1982. BS in Psychology and Sociology, LaRoche Coll., Pitts., 1978; MSW, U. of Pitts., 1980. LCSW OH, 1988. Social work supr. Bethesda Youth Svcs., Meadville, Pa., 1980—81; group home coord. Three Rivers Youth Inc, Pitts., 1981—85; protective supr./intake dept head/adminstr. Summit County Children Svcs., Akron, Ohio, 1985—2002; clin. supr. mental health/dd AssistedCare, Wilmington, NC, 2003—; part time mental health screener Cmty. Support Svcs., Akron, Ohio, 1986—91; part time counselor Cmty. Drug Bd., Akron, 1991—93; part time prof. U. of Akron, Akron, Ohio, 1993—98. Mem.: NASW (corr.). Home: 1010 Tallgrass Ln Leland NC 28451

JONES, JAN LAVERTY, mayor; B degree, Stanford U. Dir. human resources S.M.C. Restaurants, Menlo Park, Calif., 1972-74; dir. R & D Thriftmart Corp., 1976-85; CEO Jan-Mar Corp., 1985-89, mayor City of Las Vegas, 1991-99. Former pres. Fletcher Jones Mgmt. Group; bd. dirs. Bank of Am., Nev., Desert Springs Hosp., Pub. Edn. Found. Founder, chair Mayor's Com. for a Better Cmty.; adv. bd. U. Nev. Las Vegas Law Sch., Nathan Adelson Hospice, Lied Discovery Mus., Shade Tree Shelter for Homeless Women and Children. E-mail: mayor-jjjones@ci.las-vegas.nv.us.

JONES, JANET DULIN, writer, film producer; b. Hollywood, Calif., Sept. 6, 1957; d. John Dulin and Helen Mae (Weaver) J. BA, Calif. State U., Long Beach, 1980. Developer mini-series and TV series Embassy Comm., L.A., 1981-84; assoc. to producer Hotel Aaron Spelling Prodns., L.A., 1984-85; writing intern Sundance Film Inst., L.A., 1985; freelance screenplay and play writer, L.A. and N.Y.C., 1986—. Author: (screenplays) Fad Away, 1986, Alone in the Crowd, 1987, Story of the Century, 1988, The Long Way Home, 1989, Cousin Judy, 1989, The Set-up, 1990, Roommates, 1991, Local Girl, 1991, Dickens and Crime, 1992, Little Bear Books, Vols. 1-5,[;] actor: A Weighty, Waity Matter-My Adventures with India, 1992; author: (screenplays) Coming and Going, 1993, Watching the Detectives, 1994, The Ambassadors, 1994, Words of Love, 1995, Map of the World, 1995, Katherine, 1996, Vanity Fair, 1996, Sarah's Mark, 1998; dir.: Words of Love, 1998, Custom of the Country, 1999, Nevermore, 2002, The Romantics, 2001; author: (non-fiction) Cook & Tell, 2002, (plays) The Dickens Project, 2003, What If God Were The Sun, 2001. Bd. dirs. Starling Cir. of Aviva Ctr. for Girls, 1990; bd. dirs., rec. sec., steering com. The Creative Coalition, 1991-92; mem. Canine Hosp. Vols., Santa Monica Hosp., Bd. dirs. Young Filmmakers Acad., 2004 Mem. ACLU, Women in Film, Earth Communication Office (TV and film coms.), Writers Guild Am., Ind. Feature Project, Am. Film Inst., Sundance Film Inst. (pre-selection com. 1985-87), The Antaeus Theatre Co., People for Am. Way, Habitat for Humanity, Amnesty Internat., Delta Gamma. Address: 1518 Franklin St # 4 Santa Monica CA 90404

JONES, JANICE, newscaster; b. St. Croix; m. Donald Jones. Grad. in Meteorology, Miss. State U.; grad. in Journalism, Fla. State U. Cert. scuba diver. Chief meteorologist WOFL, Orlando, Fla.; meteorologist NBC 17, Raleigh, NC. Avocations: fly fishing, hiking, camping, cooking. Office: NBC 17 Studios 1205 Front St Raleigh NC 27609

JONES, JANICE COX, elementary school educator, writer; b. Jackson, Miss., Nov. 4, 1937; d. Eugene Debs and Thelma Corelli (Beard) Cox; m. June 20, 1959 (div. June 1985); children: Allison Jones Griffiths, Tamara Jones McKee. BS with highest distinction, Miss. Coll., 1959; MEd magna cum laude, U. Miami, 1968. Cert. elem. edn. Tchr. Jackson Pub. Sch., 1959-60, Arlington (Tex.) Pub. Schs., 1960-63, Houston Pub. Schs., 1963-64, Miami-Dade County Pub. Schs., 1967-1980, 1988—97; pres. Palm Tree Prodns., Ltd., 1980-88. Tchr. English ESOL Say Sch., Tokyo, 1985; tutor, child welfare worker CBS, Twentieth Century Fox, N.Y.C., Miami, 1981-; pvt. tutor, owner Think, Ink!, Miami, 1983-; piano tchr. MDCPS Cmty. Sch., Miami, 1991-; participant Miss. Gov.'s Edn./Econ. Task Force, 1990-91; workshop presenter Children's Cultural Coalition & Arts for Learning; speaker/poet in field; usher Coconut Grove Playhouse, Actor's Playhouse, Gablestage, Biltmore. Author several books of poetry, Geography Fun Facts: A Trip Across the U.S.A. in Poetry, Numbered & Named: A Preventive for Math Anxiety in Children and Adults. Dist. exec. adv. com. to sch. bd. for gifted edn. Miami-Dade County Pub. Schs., 1987-91; adv. bd. Metro-Dade Rapid Transit, 1974-77; parent sponsor Olympics of the Mind Team, 1984; parent sponsor Queen's Ct., Jr. Orange Bowl, Coral Gables, Fla., 1983; vol. pianist, organist, music dir. Village Green Baptist Mission, Miami, 1973; vol. Habitat for Humanity, 1991-. Recipient nat. poetry award, Byline Mag., 2002, ann. conf. scholarship, World Future Soc.; grantee, NEA, 1973. Mem. Am. Fedn. Tchrs., Dade Heritage Trust (edn. com., writer), Miami Writer's Club, Fla. Freelance Writers Assn., Nat. Writers Assn. South Fla. chapt. (bd., exec. sec. 1997-, nat. writing contest chair, 1998-2001), United Tchrs. Dade (bldg. steward 1976-78), Tropical Audubon Soc., Coun. for Internat. Visitors, Internat. Platform Assn. (red carpet com.), Soc. Children's Book Writers and

Illustrators, Miami Arts Exch., Nature Conservancy, Sierra Club. Avocations: Broadway plays and musicals, museums, fishing, photography, travel, accordion, accordion. Home: 6301 SW 93rd Ct Miami FL 33173-2317

JONES, JEAN CORREY, organization administrator; b. Denver, Jan. 12, 1942; d. Robert Magnie and Elizabeth Marie (Harpel) Evans; m. Stewart Hoyt Jones, Aug. 3, 1963; children: Andrew and Correy. BS in History, Social Studies and Secondary Edn., Northwestern U., 1963. Cert. non-profit mgr. History tchr. Glenbrook South H.S., Glenview, Ill., 1963-65; advocacy rsch. dir. Episc. Diocese of Denver, 1977-80; pub. affairs adminstr. United Bank of Denver, 1980-82; pres., CEO Mile Hi coun. Girl Scouts U.S., Denver, 1982—. Substitute tchr. Denver Pub. Schs., 1965-80. Active Minoru Yasui Cmty. Vol. Award com., 1979-201, Women's Forum of Colo., 1989-2002, Leadership Denver (Member of Yr., 1988), 1988—; pres. Jr. League, Denver, 1979-80, Rotary, Denver, 1995—, pres., 1995-96, commr., chair Colo. Civil Rights commn., Denver, 1987-96, vice chair Health One, Denver, 1996; bd. dirs. Hist. Denver, Inc., 1994—, Samaritan Inst., Denver, 1999; chair, trustee Colo. Trust, 2002; pres. Women's Forum of Colo. Inc., 1999—; trustee Rotary Found., Am. Humane Assoc., 2002—, Colo. Health Inst., 2003—; v.p. Univ. Club, 2002—. Named Profl. Woman of Achievement Colo. Women's Leadership Coalition and Colo. Easter Seal Soc., 1995, Martin Luther King Social Responsibility award. Mem. Denver Metro C. of C., Univ. Club. Republican. Episcopalian. Avocations: swimming, tennis, reading. Office: Girl Scouts Mile High Coun PO Box 9407 Denver CO 80209-0407

JONES, JEANNE PITTS, pre-school administrator; b. Richmond, Va., Oct. 19, 1938; d. Howard Taliaferro and Anne Elizabeth (Warburton) Pitts; m. Jack Hunter Jones, Nov. 17, 1962; children: Jack Hunter, Jr., Judith Anne, James Howard, Jon Martain. BA, Marshall U., 1961, postgrad., 1962, Presbyn. Sch. Christian Edn., Richmond, 1974, 94, Va. Commonwealth U., 1987-88, MEd in Early Childhood Edn., 2000. Cert. tchr. Va. Tchr. Richmond Pub. Schs., 1961-65; founder Bon View Sch. Early Childhood Edn., Richmond, 1971, tchr., 1971-91, dir., 1971—. Validator Nat. Assn. for Edn. of Young Children, 1993—, mentor, 1994-98; acad. affairs chmn. Good Shepherd Episcopal Sch. Bd., Richmond, 1985-88; mentor Ecumenical Child Care Network Nat. Coun. Chs., Washington, 1990-92. Chmn. room parents Crestwood Sch. PTA Bd., Richmond, 1974-80; publicity chmn. Va. Swimming, Richmond, 1978-88, children's coord. Bon Air United Meth. Ch., Richmond, 1985-93, v.p. Bon Air United Meth. Women, 1991-94; dir. Camp Friendship, Bon Air UMC, Richmond, 1992—; Va. Children's Action Network, Va. Conf. of United Meth. Ch., rep., 1993-95; Va. Conf. United Meth. Ch., weekday com. 1992-94. Recipient Spl. Mission recognition Bon Air United Meth. Women, Richmond, 1987. Mem.: Va. Assn. for Early Childhood Edn. (bd. dirs. 2002—, mentor "Success by Six" 2002), Chesterfield Coalition Early Childhood Educators (bd. dirs. 1993—97), Presch. Assn. Ch. Ednl. Dirs. (pres. 1993—95), Richmond Early Childhood Assn. (mem.-at-large 1994—96, rec. sec. 1996—98, 1998—2000, v.p. membership 2000—02, pres.-elect 2001—02, pres. 2002—, Richmond Early Childhood Adv. of the Yr. 2002). Republican. Avocations: aerobics, reading. Home: 9103 Whitaker Cir Richmond VA 23235-4053 Office: Bon View Sch Early Childhood Edn 1645 Buford Rd Richmond VA 23235-4274 Office Phone: 804-320-7043.

JONES, JEWEL, social services administrator; b. Oklahoma City, Okla., Dec. 7, 1941; d. Joseph Samuel and Jewell (Hathyel) Fisher; m. Maurice Jones, July 17, 1976; children: Anthony, Carmen. BA in Sociology, Langston (Okla.) U., 1962; MA in Pub. Adminstrn., U. Alaska, Anchorage, 1974. Tchr. Seidman Sch., L.A., 1962; correctional oifcer State of Calif. Dept. Corrections, Corona, 1963-65; probation officer County of San Bernardino, Calif., 1965-67; dep. exec. dir. Cmty. Action Agy., Anchorage, 1967-70; social svcs. dir. City of Anchorage, 1970-87; social svcs. mgr. Municipality of Anchorage, 1987-2000, dir. health & human svcs., 2000—. Chmn. bd. Alaska Housing Fin. Corp., Anchorage, 1995—; pres. Anchorage KidsPlace Project, 1994-95; chair Alaskan of the Yr. Scholarship Com., 1985—; chmn. bd. Janet Helen Tolan Gamble and Toby Gamble Ednl. Trust, 1998—. Mem. adv. bd. Salvation Army, Anchorage, 1982-87, Alaska R.R., Anchorage, 1990—; trustee United Way of Anchorage, 1990-97; bd. dirs Alaska Ctr. for Performing Arts, 1987-97. Recipient Pres.'s award Alaska Black Caucus, 1984, Employment of Handicapped award Mayor of Anchorage, 1979, Execs. in Profile award Region X Blacks in Govt. award, 1998. Mem. NAACP (Harambe award 1973), Alaska Black Leadership Conf. (Cmty. Svc. award 1979-80), Links Inc., Quota Club Intenrat., Valli Vue Homeowners Assn. (v.p.), Zeta Phi Beta. Democrat. Avocations: cooking, reading, gardening. Office: Municipality Anchorage PO Box 196650 Anchorage AK 99519-6650

JONES, JOAN MEGAN, anthropologist; b. Laramie, Wyo., Sept. 7, 1933; d. Thomas Owen and Lucille Lenoir (Magill) J. BA, U. Wash., 1956, MA, 1968, PhD, 1976. Mus. educator Burke Mus. U. Wash., Seattle, 1969-72; anthropologist Quinault Indian Nation, Taholah, Wash., 1976-77; researcher, corp. officer Profl. Anthropology Consulting Team/Social Analysts, Seattle, 1977-79; research assoc. dept. anthropology U. Wash., Seattle, 1982-91. Research investigator Dept. Social and Health Services State of Wash., Seattle, 1977; vis. lectr. Dept. Anthropology U. B.C., Vancouver, 1978; research specialist Artsplan Arts Alliance Wash. State, Seattle, 1978; vis. instr. Dept. Anthropology Western Wash. U., Bellingham, 1981; rsch. and archives dir. Samish Indian Nation, Anacontes, Wash., 2001—; cons. in field. Author: Northwest Coast Basketry and Culture Change, 1968, Basketry of Quinault, 1977, Native Basketry of Western North America, 1978, Art and Style of Western Indian Basketry, 1982, Northwest Coast Indian Basketry Styles. Wenner-Gren Found. Anthrop. Research fellow, 1967-68; Ford Found. fellow, 1972-73; Nat. Mus.'s. Can. grantee, 1973-74. Fellow Am. Anthrop. Assn., Soc. Applied Anthropology; mem. Nat. Assn. Practicing Anthropologists, Assn. Women in Sci., Skagit Valley Weavers Guild (v.p. Skagit County chpt. 1985-86, 89-90, corr. sec. 1988-89), Whidbey Weavers. Avocations: handweaving, hand spinning, knitting.

JONES, JUDITH MILLER, director; Spl. asst. Office Dep. Asst. Sec. Legis. Dept. Health, Edn. and Welfare, Washington; dir. Nat. Health Policy Forum The George Washington U., Washington, 1972—. Mem. Nat. Com. Vital and Health Stats., 1988—91, chmn., 1991—96; lectr. The George Washington U. Office: National Health Policy Forum 2131 K Street NW Ste 500 Washington DC 20037

JONES, KERRI-ANN, director scientific organization; AB, Barnard Coll., 1975; MA in Molecular Biophysics and Biochem., Yale U., 1981, PhD in Molecular Biophysics and Biochem., 1985. Fellow AAAS, 1985-96; indep. cons., 1986-89; program officer NIH Fogarty Internat. Ctr. Internat. Health, 1989-92; staff NSF Tchr. Enhancement program, 1982-89; from science officer to chief coordn. U.S. AID, 1989-95; dep. to assoc. dir. Nat. Sec. and Internat. Affairs, 1995-96; assoc. dir. Internat. Sec. and Internat. Affairs, 1996-98, acting dir., 1998; analyst White House Off. Science and Tech. Pol., 1995—. Contbr. articles to profl. jours.; presenter in field. Vol. My Sister's Place, 1989-92 (bd. dirs. 1991-92). Mem. AAAS, Coun. For. Rels. Office: PO Box 5 Castine ME 04421-0005

JONES, KRISTEN GAE, chemistry educator; b. Lemmon, S.D., May 13, 1959; d. Jack Martin and Barbara Harriet (Olson) Wanstedt; m. Bruce G. Henry, May 22, 1982 (div. Aug. 1995); children: Karissa, Kelli; m. Samuel J. Jones, June 14, 1997; 1 child, Samuel. BS, S.D. State U., 1980; MS, Tex. A&M U., 1982. Chemistry tchr. A&M Consol. H.S., College Station, Tex., 1985—. Cons. in advanced placement chemistry, 1992—. Contbr. articles to profl. jours. Recipient S.W. Regional award in H.S. Chemistry Tchg., Am. Chem. Soc., 1993, AP award S.W. Region Coll. Bd., 1995. Mem. Sci. Tchr.'s Assn. of Tex., Assn. Chemistry Tchrs. of Tex. Lutheran. Avocations: reading, science, children. Home: 2905 Colton Pl College Station TX 77845-7719 Office: A&M Consol HS 1801 Harvey Mitchell Pkwy S College Station TX 77840-5146

JONES, LAURETTA MARIE, artist, designer, computer science researcher; b. Cleve., Mar. 13, 1953; d. Richard Llewellyn and Loretta (Jares) J. BFA, Cleve. Inst. Art, 1975; postgrad., N.Y. Inst. Tech., 1981, 87. Instr. Sch. Visual Arts, N.Y.C., 1984-94, dir. undergrad. computer studies, 1988-90. Adj. prof. art Manhattanville Coll., Purchase, NY, 1985—86; instr. N.Y. Bot. Gardens, 2000—, Western Conn. State U., 2001—; cons. Trintex/Prodigy, White Plains, NY, 1986—87, IBM Gallery Sci. and Art, N.Y.C., 1987—88; cons. graphic design IBM T.J. Watson Rsch Ctr., Yorktown Heights, NY, 1988—90, adv. graphic designer, 1990—95, devel. engr., 1995—; rsch. staff mem. Network Transaction Systems, 1997—99, mgr., 1997—99; mgr. Cognitive Human-Computer Interaction, 1999—2000, Next Web HCI Components, 2001—. Exhibited paintings, drawings in shows worldwide, 1983—; represented in permanent collection Franklin Inst., Phila., Mus. Sci. and Industry, Chgo. Mem. ACLU, Assn. for Computing Machinery-Spl. Interest Group on Computer Human Interactions, Nat. Computer Graphics Assn. (speaker 1987), Guild of Nat. Sci. Illustrators (rec. sec. N.Y. chpt.), Am. Soc. of Bot. Artists (edn. adv. com.), Small Computers Arts Network (speaker 1984-89), Computer Arts Discipline Graphic Artists Guild (founding, steering com. 1984-88), ACM-SIGGRAPH (N.Y.C. chpt. editor newsletter, bd. dirs. 1986-92, speaker 1991, nat. courses com. 1991-92, design show jury 1993), Am. Inst. Graphic Arts, Amnesty Internat., NOW, Nature Conservancy, Nat. Resources Def. Coun. Avocations: tandem biking, hiking, ballroom dancing, gardening, botanical art. Office: IBM TJ Watson Rsch Ctr PO Box 704 Yorktown Heights NY 10598-0704

JONES, LAURIE LYNN, magazine editor; b. Kerrville, Tex., Sept. 2, 1947; d. Charles Clinton and Jean Laurie (Davidson) J.; m. C. Frederick Childs, June 26, 1976; children: Charles Newell (Clancy), Cyrus Trevor; 1 stepchild, Ariel Childs. BA, U. Tex., 1969. Asst. to dir. coll. admissions Columbia U., N.Y.C., 1969-70; asst. to dir. Office Alumni-Columbia U., N.Y.C., 1970-71; asst. advt. mgr. Book World, 1971-72, Washington Post-Chgo. Tribune, 1971-72; editl. asst. N.Y. Mag., N.Y.C., 1972-74, asst. editor, 1974, sr. editor, 1974-76, mng. editor, 1976-92, Vogue Mag., N.Y.C., 1992—. Mem. Am. Soc. Mag. Editors, Women in Coummunication, Advt. Women N.Y. Republican. Methodist. Home: 40 Great Jones St New York NY 10012-1109 Also: 62 Giles Hill Rd Redding Ridge CT 06876 Office: Vogue Magazine 4 Times Sq New York NY 10036-6561 Office Phone: 212-286-6910. E-mail: LaurieJones@vogue.com.

JONES, LEONADE DIANE, media publishing company executive; b. Bethesda, Md., Nov. 27, 1947; d. Leon Adger and Landonia Randolph Jones. BA with distinction, Simmons Coll., 1969; JD, MBA, Stanford U., 1973. Bar: Calif. 1973, D.C. 1979. Summer assoc. Davis Polk & Wardwell, N.Y.C., summer 1972; securities analyst Capital Rsch. Co., L.A., 1973-75; asst. treas. Washington Post Co., 1975-79, 86-87, treas., 1987-96; dir. fin. services Post-Newsweek Stas., Inc., Washington, 1979-84, v.p. bus. affairs, 1984-86; ind. mgmt. cons., pvt. equity investor, 1997-99, 2001—; CFO, sec. VentureThink, LLC, 1999-2001; exec. v.p., CFO Versura, Inc., 2000-01. Bd. dirs. Am. Balanced Fund, Inc., Income Fund Am., Inc., Fundamental Investors, Growth Fund Am., Inc., The New Economy Fund, Smallcap World Fund, Inc.; mem. investment mgmt. subcom. of benefit plans com. Am. Stores Co., 1992—99; mem. investment adv. com. N.Y. State Tchrs. Retirement Sys., 1999—; mem. investment mgmt. subcom. Albertson's Inc., 1999—. Bd. dirs. The Women's Found. Named D.C. Women's Hall of Fame, 1992; recipient Candace award for bus., 1992, Serwa award, 1993. Mem.: D.C. Bar Assn., Calif. Bar Assn., Nat. Bar Assn., Stanford U. Bus. Sch. Alumni Assn. (bd. dirs. 1986—88, pres. Washington-Balt. chpts. 1984—85). Address: 4105 Illinois Ave NW Washington DC 20011-5949 E-mail: leonade@att.net.

JONES, LINDA, communications educator; BA in English, U. Mich., 1972; MS in Journalism with distinction, Northwestern U., 1985. Reporter The Chelsea (Mich.) Standard, 1973-75; county govt., police reporter The Marshall (Mich.) Evening Chronicle, 1975-77; edn. reporter The Bay City (Mich.) Times, 1977—79, asst. met. editor, 1979-81, met. editor, 1981-86; vis. asst. prof. dept. journalism Roosevelt U., 1986-88; asst. prof. Medill Sch. Journalism Northwestern U., 1988-92, dir. tchg. newspaper program, 1992—; assoc. prof. journalism Roosevelt U., Chgo., 1992—, dir. Sch. Comm., 1995—. Acting dir. Multicultural Journalism Ctr., Urban Journalism Ctr.; tchr. workshop sessions Journalism Edn. Assn./Nat. Scholastic Press Assn. convs., 1992-96, chair Multicultural Scholarship Com., 1996. Contbr. articles to profl. jours.; judge and lectr. in field. Office: Roosevelt Univ 505 E Ctr for Profl Advancement 430 S Michigan Ave Chicago IL 60605-1394

JONES, LINDA MAY, tour guide, writer; b El Dorado, Kans., Nov. 9, 1937; d. Forrest Edward and Edith May Carlson; m. William Stanley Conard, Sept. 1, 1957 (div. Nov. 1970); children: Chris Dale Conard, Carin Dene Conard, Curtis Dean Conard; m. Verl Ray Jones, Nov. 6, 1982. Student, U. Kans., 1955-57, U. Colo., 1970-71. Tour guide Queen City Tours, Denver, 1976-84, tour guide coord., 1977-84, Am. Travel Brokers, Denver, 1977-84; owner Columbine Tours, Denver, 1984-92; tour dir. Backyard Tours, Englewood, Colo., 1993—2002, Mountains and More Tour Co., Golden, Colo., 1993—, JPS Enterprises, 1998—, Great Times Tours, 2002—. Mem. tourism adv. com. Metro Denver Conv. and Visitors Bur., 1990; seminar presenter; staff writer Colo. Gambler, 1994—. Co-author: Mile High Denver, A Guide to the Queen City, 1981; contbr. hist. articles to mags. V.p. Rep. Ctrl. Com., Gilpin County, Colo., 1983-93; v.p. Gilpin County Hist. Soc., Central City, Colo., v.p. 1988-90, pres., 1990—. Mem. Mt. Lookout DAR, Rotary, Alphi Phi. Methodist. Avocations: hiking, horseback riding. Home: PO Box 615 Black Hawk CO 80422 E-mail: linda@fairburnmountain.com.

JONES, LINDA R. WOLF, company executive; b. Jersey City, Sept. 4, 1943; d. Eugene Leon and Lottie (Pinkowitz) Rubin; m. Frank Paul Jones, Oct. 21, 1973 (div. Nov. 1987); 1 child, Elisabeth Noel. AB, Bryn Mawr Coll., 1964; MA, Yale U., 1968; DSW, Yeshiva U., N.Y.C., 1985. Dir. planning and tng. N.Y.C. Dept. Employment, 1971-77; dir. legislation N.Y.C. Community Devel. Agy., 1977-78; supervisory legis. analyst N.Y.C. Human Resources Adminstrn., 1978; sr. policy analyst Community Svc. Soc. N.Y., 1978-85; dir. pub. policy YMCA Greater N.Y., 1985-89; dir. spl. projects Phoenix House, N.Y.C., 1990-92; dir. income security policy Community Svc. Soc., N.Y.C., 1992-94; exec. dir. Therapeutic Communities Am., Washington, 1994—2002; dir. internat. ops. Conwal divsn. Axiom Resource Mgmt., Falls Church, Va., 2002—. Mem. adj. extension faculty Cornell U./N.Y. State Sch. Indsl. and Labor Rels., N.Y.C., 1975-80; dir. Nonprofit Coordinating Com. N.Y., N.Y.C., 1986-94, Govt. Affairs Profls., N.Y.C., 1989-94. Author (book) Eveline M. Burns and the American Social Security System 1935-60, 1991; mem. editorial bd. New Eng. Jour. Human Svcs., 1981—; contbr. articles to profl. jours. Mem. Civic Affairs Forum, N.Y.C., 1985-94; mem. legis. task force N.Y. State Gov.'s Office Vol. Svc., N.Y.C., 1987-90. Mem. Women in Govt. Rels., Am. Pub. Welfare Assn. (dir. 1982), Bryn Mawr Club Westchester (bd. dirs., past pres. 1974-94), Bryn Mawr Club Washington. Home: 6621 7th Pl NW Washington DC 20012 Office: Conwal Divsn Axiom Resource Mgmt Inc Ste 300 5203 Leesburg Pike Falls Church VA 22041

JONES, LINDA W. federal agency administrator; B in bus. admin., U. DC, 1973; M in pub. admin., U. Maryland, 1976. Dir. fund for improvement of Edn. US Dept. Edn., Innovation and Improvement, Wash., 2002—. Office: US Dept Edn Innovation and Improvement 555 NJ Ave NW Rm 308C Capitol Pl Washington DC 20208-5645 Office Phone: 202-219-2153.

JONES, LOUISE CONLEY, drama and literature educator, academic administrator; b. Buffalo, Dec. 17, 1945; d. Donald Lee and Pauline Hoelle Conley; m. William O. Jones, May 28, 1966 (div. Nov. 1984); children: Jeffery, Joy. BA, St. Francis Coll., 1968, MS, 1972; PhD, Ball State U., 1991. Various English, speech and drama positions various high schs., 1968-83; with Ball State U., 1983-86, 90, U. Ctrl. Fla., 1986-88, Ind. U., Ft. Wayne, 1991, St. Francis Coll., 1992-94; asst. prof. William Penn Coll., 1991-93; vis. prof. Ind. U./Purdue U., Ft. Wayne, 1993; liberal arts modules Concordia U., Ft. Wayne, 1994-96; interpersonal comm. IVY tech. Coll., 1996—; tchr. drama Ft. Wayne Magnet Schs., 1996—; dir. Concordia U., Ft. Wayne, 1997—. Presenter in field. Author: Stage Action as Metaphor, 1996 (plays) The Ladies Room: Women as Artists, A Fine Madness: The Death of Christopher Marlowe; contbr.: Oxford Companion to Crime and Mystery Writing; contbr. articles to profl. jours.; dir numerous plays at local theatres. Mem. Ft. Wayne Police Merit Commn.; bd. dirs. Gra-light Theatre, Muncie, Ind.; co-founder Women in Theatre, Ft. Wayne; vol. CASA. Mem.: MLA, AAUW, Jane Austen Soc., Marlowe Soc. Avocations: antiques, gardening, travel, detective fiction. Office: Concordia U 6600 N Clinton St Fort Wayne IN 46825-4916

JONES, LOVANA S. state legislator; b. Mansfield, Ohio, Mar. 28, 1935; 2 chilren. BA, Ohio State U. Mem. from 5th dist. Ill. Ho. of Reps., formerly asst. majority leader. Mem. children and family law com., edn. fin. elections com., pub. safety and infrastructure appropriationcoms., chmn. reapportionment com., mem. state govt. com. Supr. anti-gang program Chgo. Intervention Network. Office: Ill State Senate State Capitol 109 State House Springfield IL 62706-0001

JONES, MALLORY See DANAHER, MALLORY

JONES, MARCELINE YVONNE, secondary school educator; b. Detroit, Mich., May 25, 1949; d. Simon Dewel and Martha Lou Wood; children: Calli Elisha, Charles Edward Jones, Jr. MEd, Wayne State U., Detroit, 1985. Cert. Math.Edn. Mich., 1985. Tchr. Detroit Bd. Of Edn., Detroit, Mich., 1976—. Tutoring/counseling Detroit Bd. Of Edn., Mich., 1981—2003. Nasa participant (workshop-newest) Math./ Sci. (Honors Tchr. award for Math./Sci., 1989). Recipient Booker T. Washington Bus. Award, Detroit Bd. Of Edn. Home: 23155 Sutton Dr Southfield MI 48034 Personal E-mail: novaa525@aol.com.

JONES, MARION, track and field athlete; b. L.A., Oct. 12, 1975; m. C.J. Hunter, 1998 (div. 2001); 1 child, Timothy Montgomery. Graduate, U. NC. Named Women's Athlete of the Yr., Track and Field News, 1997, 1998, 2000, Athlete of the Year, ESPN, Reuters, and the IAAF, 2000; recipient AP and USOC Female Athlete of the Yr., 2000, Jesse Owens award winner, 1997—98, 2002. Achievements include won 100m gold, World Championships, 1997; ranked #1 in the world at 100m & 200m by T&FN, 1997-2002; won 100m, 200m, World Cup, 1998; USA Outdoor 200m champ US title in the event, 1998-2001, 100m and long jump, 1997; undefeated in every competition until her last one of the year, 35 of 36 total, 1998; won Goodwill Games 100m, 1998, 2001, 200m, 1998; ran anchor on 4x200m USA team that set the world record (1:27.46) at USA vs. THE WORLD at the Penn Relays, 2000; ran anchor in gold medal winning 4x100m relay at Worlds, 2001; World 200m champion, 2001; 100m, 200m champion, USA, 2002; won World Cup 100m, which completed the first undefeated season of her career, 2002; won 3 gold medals for 100, 200, 4x100, Sydney Games, 2000. Office: c/o USA Track & Field 1 Rca Dome Ste 140 Indianapolis IN 46225-1023*

JONES, MARLENE ANN, retired education supervisor; b. Bluffton, Ohio, Nov. 22, 1936; d. Waldo J. and Blanche M. (Criblez) Wilkins; m. Marvin O. Jones, July 3, 1965; children: John O., Dianne M. BS, Bowling Green State U., 1958, EdS, 1978; MA, Ohio State U., 1962. Cert. family and consumer scis. Vocat. home econs. tchr. 7-12 Liberty Ctr. (Ohio) Bd. Edn., 1958-61; asst. state supr. Ohio Dept. Edn., Columbus, 1962-65; chair home econs. techs. Owens C.C. (formerly Penta Tech. Coll.), Toledo, 1965-71; supr. Penta County Vocat. Sch., Perrysburg, Ohio, 1965—2001. Pres. United Meth. Women, Colton, Ohio, 1967—. Named 1 of 10 Outstanding Women in Toledo Jaycees, 1971-72; recipient Disting. Centennial Svc. award Ohio Agrl. and Home Econs. Rsch. and Devel. Ctr., 1982, Home Econs. Grad. fellowship award Am. Vocat. Assn., 1990; named Alum of Yr. Coll. of Edn., Bowling Green State U., 1990. Mem. ASCD, Am. Ohio Vocat. Assn., Am. Family and Consumer Svcs. Assn. (past state pres.), Ohio Vocat. Family and Consumer Svcs. Suprs. Assn. (treas.), N.W. Ohio FHA/HERO Alumni Assn. (sec.), Phi Delta Kappa, Phi Upsilon Omicron (past pres. Alumni chpt. 1965—). Methodist. Home: 5-212 US Hwy 24 Liberty Center OH 43532 E-mail: mo.majones@bright.net.

JONES, MARY D. court clerk; b. Danbury, Wis., Aug. 12, 1951; d. Eugene F. and Darlene M. Burlingame; m. Larry James Truitt, Nov. 5, 1966 (div. June 1971); children: Jeanne Lynn Truitt Justice, Colleen Regina Truitt Elder; m. Cecil L. Jones, Mar. 5, 1972; children: James A., Andy D.; stepchildren: Gary Wayne Jones, Terri A. Jones. Cert., Muscatine (Iowa) Jr. Coll. With Plastic Factory, Muscatine, 1969-71; sec. Dr. Shoemaker, Kahoka, Mo., 1972-73; rschr. Clark County Abstract, Kahoka, 1973-74; dep. clk., recorder Clark County Cir. Clk. and Recorder's Office, Kahoka, 1974-94; elected officio Cir. Clk. and Recorder, Kahoka, 1995—. Mem. Clark County Dem. Com., Kahoka, 1988, State Dem. Com., Mo., 1995—, Clark County Crime Victim Program, Kahoka, 1997—; mem., past pres. Blackhawk PTO, Kahoka, 1995—; mem., past leader Boy Scouts Am., Kahoka, 1973—. Mem. Mo. Recorder's Assn., Mo. Cir. Clk.'s Assn., Kahoka Hist. Soc. Baptist. Avocations: reading, fishing, listening to radio. Home: 475 N Lincoln St Kahoka MO 63445-1234

JONES, MARY GARDINER, lawyer, educator, consumer interest organization executive; b. N.Y.C., Dec. 10, 1920; d. Charles Herbert and Anna Livingston (Short) Jones; B.A., Wellesley Coll., 1943; J.D., Yale U., 1948. Intern tchr. George Sch., Newtown, Pa., 1943-44; research analyst, research and analysis br. Internat. Law sect. OSS, Washington, 1944-46; admitted to N.Y. bar, 1949; asso. firms Donovan, Leisure, Newtown and Irvine, 1948-53, Webster, Sheffield, Fleischmann, Hitchcock & Chrystie, 1961-64 (both N.Y.C.); trial atty. antitrust div. Dept. Justice, N.Y.C., 1953-61; commr. FTC, Washington, 1974; prof. Coll. Commerce and Bus. Adminstrn. and Coll. Law, U. Ill., Urbana, 1973-75; v.p. for consumer affairs Western Union Telegraph Co., Washington, 1975-82; pres. Consumer Interest Research Inst., Washington, 1983— ; mem. Consumer Research Found. dir. MCA, Inc., Universal City, Calif., Safeway Stores, Oakland, Calif. Mem. com. on sci. and tech. Fed. Council Sci. and Tech.; non-trustee mem. research and policy com.; chmn. bd. Council Econ. Priorities, 1976-84, Inst. Future, 1977— ; dir. Council Better Bus. Burs., 1982— ; mem. Pres.' Panel on Antitrust Laws, 1977-78. Trustee Wellesley Coll., 1971— ; nat. adv. council Hampshire Coll.; Mem. Fed. Bar Assn. Internat. Law Assn., Assn. Bar City N.Y., Am. Arbitration Assn., Yale Law Sch. Assn. (v.p. D.C. 1969-70, exec. com. 1971-76), AAUW (2d v.p. Washington br. 1968-69, adv. council). Bd. editors Jour. Consumer Affairs; editorial rev. bd. Jour. Consumer Interest; contbr. articles law jours. Office: Suite 800 1819 H St NW Ste 800 Washington DC 20006-3631

JONES, MARY LAURA, developer, fundraiser; b. Mpls., 1946; d. William Ray and Emily Mary H. Jones; children: Donald Aaron, Justin David, Mark Joseph Bushman. BA in English, U. S.C., 1968; M in Liberal Studies, Northwestern U., 2004. Vol. U.S. Peace Corps, 1968—71; assoc. dir. Funding & Devel., Chgo., 1971-75, The Inst. of Cultural Affairs, Chgo.; dir. Cleve. Region, 1975-79, Pacific, Oceania Region, Apia, Western Samoa, 1979-83. Co-creator Human Devel. Tng. Curriculum, 1984-85. Dir. pilot project for Uptown Cmty. Resource Ctr. Inst. of Cult. Affairs, Chgo.,

1986-2004. Mem. Uptown C. of C. (pres.), Internat. Women Entrepreneurs. Lutheran. Home and Office: Inst Cultural Affairs 4750 N Sheridan Rd Chicago IL 60640-5042 E-mail: mbushman@ica-usa.org.

JONES, MARY LOU, real estate broker, real estate company executive; b. Palermo, W.Va., Sept. 3, 1932; d. Robert R. and Elwa F. Lovejoy; m. Jerald E. Jones, Dec. 22, 1954; children: Jeffrey Todd, Perry Brooks, Suzanne Paige. Student, Marshall U., 1954. Sec. W.Va. U., Morgantown, 1956-59; real estate agt. Kaufman Real Estate, Bridgeport, W.Va., 1988-93; real estate broker/owner Homefinders Plus Real Estate, Inc., Bridgeport, 1993—. Pres. Friends of the W.Va. State Bar, 1997. Mem. Nat. Assn. Realtors, W.Va. Assn. Realtors, Harrison County Assn. Realtors, Clarksburg, W.Va., 1998-99. Republican. Avocations: reading, bridge, painting, poetry. Home: 133 Vista Dr Bridgeport WV 26330-1043 Office: Homefinders Plus Real Estate 104 State St Bridgeport WV 26330-1376

JONES, MARY M. landscape architect; Student, U. Tex., Austin, 1974—75; Bachelor of Landscape Arch. magna cum laude, Tex. A&M, 1979. Registered landscape arch., Mass., Calif., Tex., Ohio, Ariz., Mich., Minn. Arch. Johnson Johnson & Roy, Inc., Ann Arbor, Mich.; prin. Hargreave Assocs., 1983—. Mem. Mayor's Inst. on City Design, 2002, 03; mem. Sch. Arch. found. adv. coun. U. Tex., Austin, 2002; mem. dean's external adv. coun. Sch. Arch. Tex. A&M, 2001—02; co-chair Landscape Arch. CEO Roundtable, 2000—01; mem. landscape adv. coun. dept. landscape arch. and environ. planning U. Calif., Berkeley; mem. adv. bd. and publ. com. Designed Landscape Forum; mem. design rev. bd. Bay Conservation Devel. Commn.; lectr. in field; vis. critic landscape arch. Harvard Design Sch. Contbr. articles to profl. jours. and mags.; prin. works include Sydney Olympics Master Concept Design, U. Cin. Master Plan, Guadalupe River Pk., Byxbee Pk., Crissy Field, San Francisco. Mem.: Am. Soc. Landscape Artists (Honor award for excellence in the study of landscape arch. 1979), San Francisco Planning and Urban Rsch. Assn., Am. Acad. Rome (Prince Charitable Trusts fellow 1997—98). Office: Hargreaves Assocs 118 Magazine St Cambridge MA 02139 also: Hargreaves Associates 398 Kansas Street San Francisco CA 94103

JONES, MAXINE, vocalist; b. Paterson, N.J., 1966; Vocalist En Vogue, Atco/Eastwest Records, N.Y.C., 1988—. Albums include Born to Sing (Platinum 1990), Funky Divas, Remis to Sing, Runaway Love, The Best of En Vogue, 1999. Recipient Soul Train Music award, 1991; nominated Grammy award, 1990. Office: care En Vogue Atco/Eastwest Records 75 Rockefeller Plz New York NY 10019-6908

JONES, MELBA KATHRYN, elementary school educator, librarian; b. Marshall, Ark., Mar. 13, 1924; d. Willie Claud and Bessie Kathryn (Mason) Holder; m. Rex Gene Jones, Aug. 9, 1947; children: Mickey Gene, Terry John, Cathryn Jayne. BA, Coll. Ozarks, 1972. Tchr. Everton (Ark.) Pub. Schs., 1942-47; libr. Valley Springs (Ark.) Pub. Schs., 1966-85. Mayor City of Everton, 1979-87, council woman, 1988-91; bd. govs. North Ark. Regional Med. Ctr., 1993—; mem. bd. Ark. Cattlemen's Assn., 1993; mem. city coun., Everton, Ark., 1996—; dir. Cmty. Ctr., 2004; chmn. adminstrn. bd. Meth. Ch., 1980-2003. Grantee, Ark. Indsl. Devel. Commn., 1985, ADEC, 1999, 2000, 2003. Democrat. Methodist. Avocations: oil painting, reading, sewing, crafts, cooking. Home: PO Box 12 Everton AR 72633-0012

JONES, NORAH, vocalist, musician; b. N.Y.C., Mar. 30, 1979; d. Ravi Shankar and Sue Jones. Student, U. North Tex. With Blue Note Records, 2001—. Musician: (albums) First Sessions, 2001, Come Away With Me, 2002 (Grammy awards: Album of Yr., 2002, Record of the Yr., 2002, Best New Artist, 2002, Best Female Pop Vocal Performance, 2002, Best Pop Vocal Album, 2002), Feels Like Home, 2004, (recording) A Very Special Acoustic Christmas, Where We Live: Stand For What You Stand On, Remembering Patsy Cline, Just Because I'm a Woman (tribute to Dolly Parton), (soundtrack for film) Love Actually, 2003. Named Best Young Female Singer, VH1, 2002. Office: Macklam Feldman Mgmt Ste 200 1505 W 2d Ave Vancouver V6H 3Y4 Canada*

JONES, PAMELA S. real estate development executive; Sr. v.p. fin., CFO, bd. dirs. Schuler Homes Inc., Honolulu, 1996—. Office: Schuler Homes Inc 828 4th St Mall Fl 4 Honolulu HI 96813-4321

JONES, PATRICIA BENGTSON, sculptor; b. Janesville, Wis., Aug. 5, 1932; d. Clarence Edward and Phyllis Ann (Eau Clair) Bengtson; m. Robert S. Jones, July 3, 1953 (div. Aug. 1986); children: Pamela Ann Eau Clair, Diane Marie. AA, DeAnza Jr. Coll., Cupertino, Calif., 1974; BA in Painting, San Jose State U., 1977, MA in Sculpture, 1983. Cmty. colls. instr. credential, Calif. Exhibit curator Yucca Gallery, Albuquerque, 1964-67. Curator N.Mex. Art League, Albuquerque, 1966-67, Peninsula Art Assn., San Mateo, Calif., 1969; co chmn. fine arts San Mateo Fair, 1969; chmn. fine arts San Mateo County Fair, 1970; asst. installor De Young Mus., San Francisco, 1976; restorer Santa Clara Artist's Foundry, 1981-84; marble cons. Leitch & Co., San Francisco,, 1984-86; instr. Studio Carlos Nicoli, Carrara, Italy, 1995; cutlery cons. R.H. Macy's, San Leandro, Calif., 1986-97; restoration cons., subcontractor, workshops; sculpture, 1985—; mentor John F. Kennedy U., Berkeley, Calif., 1989—. Group exhbns. at New Leaf Garden Gallery, Calif., 1992-2003, The Art Foundry Gallery, 1999, Heritage Mus., Seattle, 1998, Claudia Chapline Gallery, Stinton Beach, Calif., 1998—, Contract Design Ctr., San Francisco, 1996-2003, Triton Mus. of Art, Santa Clara, Calif., 1967-94; group exhbns. include N.Mex. Art Mus., Santa Fe, 1965-66, Frye Art Mus., Seattle, 1987, Bedford Gall., Walnut Creek, CA, 1991, Spectrum Gallery, San Francisco, 1991, Downey (Calif.) Mus. Art, 1990-92, Sho-en Sculpture and Gallery, Ramona, 1992-94, Contract Design Ctr. for San Francisco, 1993, N.Am., The Foothill Art Ctr., Colden, Colo., 1985-91-94, One Bush Gallery, San Francisco, 1994, Oakland (Calif.) Mus., 1994. Bd. dirs. YWCA, Beloit, Wis., 1956-60; various positions Gen. Fedn. Women's Clubs, Wis., 1956-60; vol. fund drives Mental Health Drive Wis., Beloit, 1956-60; room mother Campfire Girls, Albuquerque, 1961-62. Recipient John Cavanaugh Meml. award N.Am. Sculpture Exhbn., Golden, Colo., 1985. Mem. Internat. Sculptors Assn., Pacific Rim Sculptors Group (founder), Nordic Fine Arts Group (chmn. & curator, 2003), Fine Arts Mus. San Francisco, Sculptors Guild San Jose, World Affairs Coun., San Francisco Mus. Modern Art, Sierra Club, Commonwealth Club Calif. Democrat. Studio: 2019 2d St Berkeley CA 94710

JONES, PATRICIA LOUISE, elementary counselor; b. Moorhead, Minn., Aug. 20, 1942; d. Harry Wilfred and Myrtle Louise Rosenfeldt; m. Edward L. Marks (div.); m. Curtis C. Jones, July 16, 1973; children: Michon, Andrea, Nathan, Kirsten, Leah. BS, Moorhead State U., 1965; MS, Mankato State U., 1990. Cert. K-12 sch. counselor, Minn. Tchr. Anoka (Minn.) Hennepin Schs., 1966-68; pvt. practice Youth Ctr., Truman, Minn., 1969-72; bookkeeper Fairmont (Minn.) Glass & Sign, 1973, Truman Farmers Elevator, 1973-87; libr. Martin County Libr., Truman, 1988-89; sch. counselor St. James (Minn.) Schs., 1989—. Coord. Internat. Fun Fest, St. James, 1992, 96; originator, advisor Armstrong After Sch. Hispanic Club, St. James, 1991-2001. Coord. Truman Days Parade, 1991, 92, 94-2000; mem. adv. bd. Watonwan County Big Buddy Program, 1993—; mem. Watonwan County Corrections Adv. Bd., 1998-2002; foster parent, 1999. Mem. ACA, Am. Sch. Counselors Assn., Minn. Sch. Counselors Assn. (bd. dirs. 1997-99), S.W. Minn. Counselors Assn. (Elem. Counselor of Yr. 1993, pres. 1997-99). Avocations: genealogy, walking, photography. Office: Saint James Sch Dist 500 8th Ave S Saint James MN 56081 Home: PO Box 215 Truman MN 56088-0215 E-mail: pjones@stjames.k12.mn.us.

JONES, PAULINE REID, speech pathology/audiology services professional; b. San Rafael, Calif., Nov. 28, 1950; d. Eldon S. Reid and Elayne Warnock; m. Donald Fredrick Jones, Nov. 17, 1990; children: Aaron J., Andrew G., Adam C. Merrill, Alanson G., Nicole D. Merrill. Bachelors Degree, Brigham Young U., 1972; Masters Degree, Towson State U., 1983. Speech-lang. instr. Salisbury (Md.)State Coll., Salisbury, Md., 1981—82; speech-lang. pathologist Anne Arundel County Pub. Schs., Annapolis, Md., 1984—97, Papillion (Nebr.)-LaVista Schs., 1998—. Alternative-augmentative comm. cons. Papillion-LaVista Schs., 1998—; as clin. fellowship yr. supr. Am. Speech-Lang. Assn., Papillion, 1998—99. Mem.: Am. Speech-Lang.-Hearing Assn. (assoc.; cert. clin. competence 1984). Democrat. The Church Of Jesus Christ Of Latter-Day Saints. Avocations: quilting, counted cross stitch.

JONES, PEGGY W. poet; b. Marshall, Tex., Dec. 14, 1953; d. Herbert and Lottie Mae (Wilson) J. AAS in Pattern Design, El Centro Jr. Coll., 1981. Employee U.S. Postal Svc. Author: (poem) Tomorrow's Dream, 1996. Mem., vol. coord. Jr. Black Acad., Dallas, 1988-94; docent African Mus., Dallas, 1992-94; active St. Luke Cmty. United Meth. Ch. Mem. Afro Am. Postal League, First Class Toastmaster (v.p. 1986, v.p. edl., v.p., pres. 1986). Avocations: sewing, designing crafts, walking, reading. Home: 6415 Rhapsody Ln Dallas TX 75241-2639

JONES, PHYLLIS EDITH, nursing educator; b. Barrie, Ont., Can., Sept. 16, 1924; d. Colston Graham and Edith Luella (Shand) J. BScN, U. Toronto, 1950, MSc, 1969; DNSc (hon.), U. Turku, Finland, 1993. With Victorian Order Nurses, Toronto, 1950-53, asst. dir., 1959-63; supr. Vancouver Dept. Health, 1953-58; prof. nursing U. Toronto, 1963-89, dean Faculty Nursing, 1979-88, prof. emeritus, 1989—. Cons. WHO, 1985, 86 Contbr. articles to profl. jours. Can. Nurses Found. fellow, 1967-69; recipient grants Nat. Health Research and Devel.; recipient grants Ont. Ministry Health. Fellow Am. Public Health Assn.; mem. Coll. Nurses Ont., Registered Nurses Assn. Ont., Can. Public Health Assn., Can. Soc. Study Higher Edn., N.Am. Nursing Diagnosis Assn. (charter), ProNursing Finland (hon.). Home: RR 2 Owen Sound ON Canada N4K 5N4

JONES, PHYLLIS GENE, judge; b. Fargo, N.D., May 29, 1923; d. Joseph C. and Rosina Belle (Pinkham) Bambusch; m. Dwight Bangs Jones, May 29, 1945 (dec.); children: Stephanie Martineau, Jacqueline Ridge, Kent Carroll; m. David D. Norman, Oct. 9, 1970 (dec.). BA, Macalester Coll., 1944; JD, William Mitchell Coll. Law, 1960. Bar: Minn. 1960. Wirephoto operator AP, St. Paul, 1943-45; reporter St. Paul Pioneer Press, 1945-46; asst. county atty. Ramsey County, St. Paul, 1960-71; gen. counsel Minn. Urban County Attys. Bd./Minn. County Attys. Coun., St. Paul, 1971-75; pvt. practice St. Paul, Cottage Grove, Minn., 1975-84; judge Minn. Dist Ct. 10th Jud. Dist., Anoka, 1984-93. Mem. Minn. Adv. Coun. to State Investment Bd., 1983-84; mem. Washington County Pers. Com., Stillwater, Minn., 1982-84. Supr., Grey Cloud Town Bd., Minn., 1971-75. Mem. ABA, Minn. State Bar Assn. (chmn. victimless crimes com. 1974-75, co-chair sr. lawyers com. 1997-99), Ramsey County Bar Assn. (exec. com. 1982-83), Washington County Hist. Soc. (dir. 2000—). Achievements include distinction of being the first full-time female prosecutor in Minnesota.

JONES, RENEE KAUERAUF, health care administrator; b. Duncan, Okla., Nov. 3, 1949; d. Delbert Owen and Betty Jean (Marsh) Kauerauf; m. Don Elkins Jones, Aug. 3, 1972. BS, Okla. State U., 1972, MS, 1975; PhD, Okla. U., 1989. Diplomate Am. Bd. Sleep Medicine. Statis. analyst Okla. State Dept. Mental Health, Okla. City, 1978-80, divisional chief, 1980-83, adminstr., 1983-84; assoc. dir. HCA Presbyn. Hosp., Oklahoma City, 1984-2000; mng. ptnr. Sleep Assocs., LLC, Oklahoma City, 2000—, Sleep REMedies, LLC, Okalhoma City, 2003—. Adj. instr. Okla. U. Health Sci. Ctr., 1979—; assoc. staff scientist Okla. Ctr. for Alcohol and Drug-Related Studies, Okla. City, 1979—; cons. in field. Assoc. editor Alcohol Tech. Reports jour., 1979-84; contbr. articles to profl. jours. Mem. assoc. bd. Hist. Preservation, Inc., treas. 1994. Mem. APHA, NAFE, Assn. Health Svcs. Rsch., Alcohol and Drug Problems Assn. N.Am., Am. Sleep Disorders Assn., N.Y. Acad. Scis., So. Sleep Soc. (sec.-treas. 1989-91), Phi Kappa Phi. Democrat. Methodist. Avocations: skiing, scuba diving, racewalking, bicycling, painting. Home: 810 NW 15th St Oklahoma City OK 73106 Office: The Sleep Clinic 5530 N Francis Ave Oklahoma City OK 73118 Office Phone: 405-767-6970. Personal E-mail: sleepdr1@cox.net.

JONES, ROSE, professional golfer; b. Santa Ana, Calif., Nov. 13, 1959; Grad., Ohio State U., 1981. Joined LPGA, 1982; winner Rail Charity Golf Classic, 1987, USX Golf Classic, 1988, Nestle World Championship, 1988, Santa Barbara Open, 1988, Rochester Internat., 1991, 1998, Pinewild Women's Championship, 1995, LPGA Corning Classic, 1996, 1997, Kathy Ireland Championship, 2001, JAL Big Apple Classic, 2001, Asahi Ryokuken Internat. Championship at Mt. Vintage, 2003. Mem. Solheim Cup Team, 1990, 96, 98, 2000, 00, 02, 03. Recipient Move of Month award, Century 21 Fine Homes & Estates, 2001. Mem.: Exec. Women's Golf Assn. (hon. chair mem.-get-a-mem. campaign 2004). Avocations: fishing, dance, woodworking, gardening, arts & crafts. Office: Ladies Profl Golf Assn 100 Internat Golf Dr Daytona Beach FL 32124-1092*

JONES, SALLY DAVIESS PICKRELL, writer; b. St. Louis, June 4, 1923; d. Claude Dildine and Marie Daviess (Pittman) Pickrell; m. Charles William Jones, Sept. 2, 1943 (dec.); 1 child, Matthew Charles (dec.). Student, Mills Coll., Oakland, Calif., 1941-43, U. Calif.-Berkeley, 1945, Columbia U., 1955-58. Author: (novel) The Lights Burn Blue, 1947. Mem. Met. Mus. Art, Nat. Coun. Women, Asia Soc., Fgn. Policy Assn., UN Assn. Episcopalian. Address: 1525 Pelican Point Dr Apt H101 Sarasota FL 34231-6774

JONES, SANDRA LEE, dean; b. Chgo., May 21, 1950; d. Clifford Robert and Dorothy Lucille (Rutzen) Harry; m. Martin Dexter Jones, Sept. 5, 1970; 1 child, Matthew Shawn Jones. BA in English, Columbus Coll., 1972, MEd in English Edn., 1977; EdD in Vocat. and Adult Edn., Auburn U., 1991. Classroom English tchr. Don C. Faith Jr. H.S., Ft. Benning, Ga., 1972-73, McIntosh Jr. H.S., Albany, Ga., 1977-80; lang. arts supr. Dougherty County Schs., Albany, 1980-82; classroom English tchr. Carroll H.S., Ozark, Ala., 1982-83; adj. instr. English Troy State U. at Dothan, Ala., 1983-84, instr. of English, 1984-93, asst. prof. edn., 1993—98, assoc. prof. edn., 1998—2002, dir. profl. internship program, 1994—99, certification officer, 1994—2001, prof. edn., 2002—. Profl. edn. pers. evaluation trainer of evaluators Ala. State Dept. Edn., 1997—; advisor Troy State U. chpt. Student Ala. Edn. Assn., 1995-2000, state advisor, 1998-2000. Mem. Nat. Coun. Tchrs. of English, Internat. Soc. for Tech. in Edn., Women in the Acad. Deanship, Ala. Assn. for Colls. of Tchr. Edn., Am. Assn. for Colls. of Tchr. Edn., Mensa, Sigma Tau Delta (advisor 1996-2002), Kappa Delta Pi, Delta Kappa Gamma. Avocations: reading, antique collecting, music, travel. Office: Troy State U at Dothan 501 University Dr Dothan AL 36303-1568 Office Phone: 334-983-6556 x1360.

JONES, SARA SUE FISHER, librarian; b. Rupert, Idaho, May 2, 1962; d. Richard Sherman and Dana Louise Fisher; m. Martin R. Jones, Jan. 7, 1984; children: Russel, Elaine. BA in Comms., Boise State U., 1983; MLS, Syracuse U., 1999. Libr. dir. Stanley (Idaho) Cmty. Libr., 1984-86; English tchr. Minidoka County Schs., Rupert, Idaho, 1986-88; children's librarian Elko (Nev.) County Libr., 1988-95, libr. dir., 1995-2000; state libr., divsn. adminstr. Nev. State Libr. and Archives, 2000—. Commr. State Nev. Commn. on Ednl. Tech. Elko County Libr. Bd. scholar, 1997-99. Mem. Nev. Libr. Assn. (pres. 2000—, pub. trustee, chair, Dorothy McAlindin award 1995, scholar 1997-98), Nev. Libr. Orgn. (chair N.E. dist.), Philanthropic Edn. Orgn., Soroptimist Internat. (pres. 1995-96). Avocations: reading, camping, golf. Office: 100 N Stewart St Carson City NV 89701

JONES, SARAH ASHLEY, realtor, consultant; b. Jackson, Miss., Feb. 27, 1951; d. James Robert and Mary Berry Ashley; m. Lloyd Michael Jones, July 10, 1976; 1 child, Michael Ryan. BA, U. Miss., 1973; MA, U. So. Miss., 1980. Lic. realtor Miss., 1992. Tchr. Rankin County Schs., Brandon, Miss., 1973—76, Simpson County Schs., Mendenhall, Miss., 1976—85; realtor Underwood Homes, Brandon, 1991—96, RE/MAX, Jackson, 1996—. Mem.: Jr. Auxilliary Rankin County. Avocations: interior decorating, gardening, travel, reading. Home: 1012 Northwind Lane Brandon MS 39047 Office: REMAX Real Estate Group 369 Towne Centre Blvd Ridgeland MS 39157

JONES, SARAH LUCILLE, supervisor, consultant; b. Pinewood, S.C., Aug. 12, 1947; d. Aaron Mack and Sarah Jane Green; m. Flynn Raymond Jones, June 5, 1976; 1 child, Flynn Raymond Jones Jr. BS, S.C. State U., 1970; MS, Drexel U., 1974; Cert. in Supervision and Adminstrn., Georgian Ct. Coll., 1993. Cert. tchr. N.J., N.Y., Pa., Ind., S.C. Head tchr. Head Start, Phila., 1970—76; tchr. Rochester (N.Y.) City Schs., 1977—79; dir. ACEOC Head Start, Ft. Wayne, Ind., 1979—82; tchr. Freehold Regional H.S., Englishtown, NJ, 1982—2000; edn. specialist Brookdale C.C., Lincroft, NJ, 1989—95; dept. supr. Manalapan (N.J.) H.S., 2000—. Nutrition cons. MCEOC Head Start, New Brunswick, NJ, 1985—; state trainer AHEA/NJHEA, NJ, 1987—88; daycare cons. Espic Diosese, Keyport, NJ, 1987—88; mem. numerous curriculum coms., faculty rep., faculty advisor Freehold Regional H.S. Dist. Mem.: N.J. Assn. Family and Cons. Sci. (treas. 1992—93, corr. sec. 1993—94), Mon-Ocean Assn. Family and Cons. Sci. (pres. 1989—90, councilor 1994—, v.p. program 1999—2002). Avocations: reading, gardening. Office: Freehold Regional HS Dist 11 Pine St Englishtown NJ 07726 Office Phone: 732-792-7200.

JONES, SHIRLEY, actress, singer; b. Smithton, Pa., July 31, 1934; d. Paul and Marjorie (Williams) J.; m. Jack Cassidy, Aug. 5, 1956 (div. 1975); children: Shaun, Patrick, Ryan; m. Marty Ingels, 1977. Grad. high sch., 1952; student, Pitts. Playhouse. Appeared with chorus South Pacific, 1953, in Broadway prodn. Me and Juliet, 1954; other state appearences include The Beggar's Opera, 1957, The Red Mill, 1958, Maggie Flynn, 1968, On a Clear Day, 1975, Show Boat, 1976, Bitter Suite, 1983; films include role of Laurey in Oklahoma, 1954, later stage tour Paris and Rome, sponsorship U.S. Dept. State, Carousel, 1956, April Love, 1957, Never Steal Anything Small, 1959, Bobbikins, 1959, Elmer Gantry, 1960 (Acad. Best Supporting Actress award 1961), Pepe, 1960, The Two Rode Together, 1961, The Music Man, 1962, The Courtship of Eddie's Father, 1963, A Ticklish Affair, 1963, Bedtime Story, 1964, The Secret of My Success, 1965, Fluffy, 1965, The Happy Ending, 1969, The Cheyenne Social Club, 1970, Beyond the Poseidon Adventure, 1979, Tank, 1984, There Were Times, Dear, 1985; night club tour with husband, 1958, later TV and summer stock; star TV series The Partridge Family, 1970-74, Shirley, 1979; guest star: TV series McMillan, 1976; TV films include: Silent Night, Lonely Night, 1969, But I Don't Want To Get Married!, 1970, The Girls of Huntington House, 1973, The Family Nobody Wanted, 1975, The Lives of Jenny Dolan, 1975, Winner Take All, 1975, Yesterday's Child, 1977, Evening in Byzantium, 1978, Who'll Save Our Children, 1978, A Last Cry for Help, 1979, The Children Of An Lac, 1980, Inmates: A Love Story, 1981, There Were Times Dear, 1987; one-woman concert: TV series Shirley Jones' America 1981; author: Shirley and Marty: An Unlikely Love Story, 1990. Nat. chairwoman Leukemia Found. Named Mother of Yr. by Women's Found., 1978. Office Phone: 818-278-0123. E-mail: suiteone@earthlink.net.

JONES, SHIRLEY CAROL, music educator; d. Orville Preston and Katie Butler Pollitt; m. Lloyd Arthur Jones II, Sept. 20, 1969; children: Craig Anthony, Chad Arthur. Bachelor of Music, Morehead State U., 1970; Master of Music Edn., U. S.C., 1975. Tchr. music grades 7 and 8 Butler H.S., Louisville, 1970—73; tchr. music grades 1-5 Meadowfield and Atlas Rd. Elem. Schs., Columbia, SC, 1974—79; choral dir. grades 7-12 Stuart Pepper Mid. Sch., Brandenburg, Ky., 1981—, Meade County H.S., Brandenburg, 1981—. Mem.: Delta Kappa Gamma (music dir. 1982—), Tri-M Music Honor Soc. Baptist. Avocations: singing, piano, music.

JONES, SHIRLEY JOYCE, small business owner, fashion designer; b. Chgo., Aug. 13; d. Roman C. Carpen and Mary A. Mleczko; m. William T. Jones, May 2, 1959; children: Debra Ann, Lisa Courtney. Student, Wright Coll., 1955-56, Triton Coll., 1963-64; grad., Ippolito Beauty Sch., 1973. Lic. cosmetologist, Ill. Pres. St. Vincent Ferrer, River Forest, Ill., 1973-74; owner Shirley Jones Beauty Studio, Chgo., 1979-93, Flare Schaumburg, 1983-87, Surprise Boutique, Oakbrook, Ill., 1988-96, Shirley Jones Boutique, Chgo., 1993-96; founder, chmn. gala cancer charity September Surprise, Oak Brook, Burr Ridge, Ill., 1990—. V.p. Oak Brook Republican Womens Club, 1999; active Dupage Fedn. Republican Women, Nat. Fedn. Republican Women, Ill. Fed. Repub. Women (chief of protocol, vice chmn., chaplain). Grantee Ippolito Beauty Sch., 1973. Mem. Fashion Group Internat., Chgo. Fashion Group, Nat. Arts and Letters Soc., Oakbrook, Ill. Roman Catholic. Avocations: golf, dance, travel, antiques, gourmet cooking. Home and Office: 6812 Fieldstone Dr Burr Ridge IL 60527-6967

JONES, SHIRLEY M. state legislator; b. Chgo., Nov. 9, 1939; 2 children. Ed., George Williams Coll. Mem. from Dist. 6, Ill. Ho. of Reps., 1987—, vice chmn. aging com. Also mem. higher edn., housing, human svc. appropriations, pub. utilities, revenue and state adminstrn. coms. Home: 541 W Roosevelt Rd Ste 2306 Chicago IL 60607-4915 Office: Ill State Senate State Capitol Springfield IL 62706-0001 Also: 47 W Polk St Ste M6 Chicago IL 60605-2088

JONES, SONIA JOSEPHINE, advertising agency executive; b. Belize, Brit., Honduras, Nov. 9, 1945; came to U.S., 1962; naturalized, 1986; d. Frederick Francis and Elsie Adelia (Gomez) Alcoser; m. John Marvin Jones, Mar. 21, 1970; children: Christopher William Edward, Joshua Joseph Paul. Student, Lamar U., 1964-66. With Foley's Federated Dept. Store, Houston, 1965-67; media buyer Vance Advt., Houston, 1967-68; media buyer, planner O'Neill & Assocs., Houston, 1968-75; media supr. Ketchum Houston, 1975-76; v.p., media dir. Rives Smith Bladwin Carlberg/Y&R, Houston, 1976-86; sr. v.p. media dir. Black Gillock & Landberg, Houston, 1986-89; pres. JMM Group, Inc., Houston, 1989—. Lectr. U. Houston, 1983—. Vol. Women in Yellow, Houston, 1966; mem. Tom's Moms, St. Thomas H.S., 1992—, mem. sch. bd. spl. projects, fundraising vol. women's club, 1992—; vol. translator St. Cecilia Clinic, 1993—; mem. sch. bd. spl. projects St. Cecilia Cath. Sch.; head sacristan St. Cecilia Cath. Ch., 1995—. Mem. Houston Advt. Fedn., Santana Doston Found. (bd. dirs. 1998—). Republican. Office: JMM Group Inc 2500 City West Blvd Ste 300 Houston TX 77042

JONES, STAR (STARLET MARIE JONES), television host; b. Badin, NC, Mar. 24, 1962; BA, Am. U.; JD, U. Houston. Bar: N.Y. Sr. asst. dist. atty. Bklyn. Dist. Atty.'s Office, 1991; studio commentator Court TV, 1991; legal corrs. NBC's Today, Nightly News; host syndicated tv show Jones and Jury, 1994; co-host ABC Daytime's The View, 1997—; lawyer; former sr. corr., chief legal analyst Inside Edition. Office: 320 W 66th St New York NY 10023-6304*

JONES, STEPHANIE J. federal agency administrator; BA in English Lit. & Afro-Am. Studies, Smith Coll.; JD, U. Cin. Bar: Ohio 1986, U.S. Dist. Ct. Appeals (6th cir.) 1989, U.S. Dist. Ct. (so. dist.) Ohio 1987. Assoc. Graydon, Head & Ritchey, Cin., 1986-90; law prof. Salmon P. Chase Coll. Law Northern Ky. U.; chief edn. rep., spokesperson Dept. Edn. Region V, 1994—. Adj. prof. law Northwestern U. Sch. Law, Chgo.; lectr. in field; investigative, gen. news, feature reporter Cin. Post, 1982-83; exec. asst.

Lionel Richie and the Commodores. Mem. Ohio Atty. Gen.'s Coun. on Ethics and Profl. Responsibility, 6th Cir. Jud. Conf. (life). Office: 111 N Canal St Ste 1094 Chicago IL 60606-7204

JONES, STEPHANIE TUBBS, congresswoman, lawyer; b. Cleve., Sept. [illegible] 1971, JD, 1974 [illegible] Dist. Ct. (no. dist.) Ohio 1975, U.S. Ct. Appeals (6th cir.) 1981, U.S. Supreme Ct. 1981. Asst. gen. counsel, EEO adminstr. N.E. Ohio Regional Sewer Dist., 1974-76; asst. prosecutor Cuyahoga County Prosecutor's Office, 1976-79; trial atty. Cleve. dist. office EEO, 1979-81; judge Cleve. Mcpl. Ct., 1982-83, Cuyahoga County Ct. of Common Pleas, 1983-91; prosecutor Cuyahoga County, Cleve., 1991-98; mem. U.S. Congress from 11th Ohio dist., 1999—; mem. banking and fin. svcs. com., 1999—2002; mem. com. on small bus., 1999—2002; mem. ways and means com., 2003—. Mem. Stds. Ofcl. Conduct, 1999-; vis. com. bd. overseers Franklin Thomas Backus Sch. Law, Case Western Res. U. Bd. trustees Comty. Re-entry Program; bd. trustees class of 1984 Leadership Cleve. Alumnae; mem. Task Force on Violent Crime, Substance Abuse Initiative; trustee Cleve. Police Hist. Soc.; bd. trustees Bethany Bapt. Ch. Recipient Outstanding Vol. Svcs. in Law and Justice award Urban League Greater Cleve., 1986, Women of Yr. award Cleve. chpt. Nat. Assn. Negro Bus. and Profl. Women's Clubs, Inc., 1987, award in recognition of outstanding svc. to judiciary and black comty. Midwest region Nat. Black Am. Law Student Assn., 1988, Career Women of Achievement award YWCA, 1991, Disting. Svc. award Cleve. chpt. NAACP, 1997; named Black Profl. of Yr., Black Profl. Assn. Cleve., 1995, 1994 Ohio Dem. of Yr., Ohio Dem. Party, 1995; inductee Collinwood H.S. Hall of Fame, 1994, Soc. Benchers of Case Western Res. U. Sch. of Law, 1996. Mem. ABA, Nat. Black Prosecutor's Assn., Nat. Dist. Atty.'s Assn. (met. prosecutor's com.), Nat. Coun. Negro Women, Nat. Coll. Dist. Attys. (bd. regents), Ohio State Bar Assn. (Nettie Cronise Lutes award 1997), Ohio Prosecuting Attys. Assn. (exec. com.), Cleve. Bar Assn. (trustee), Norman S. Miner Bar Assn. (past treas.), Cuyahoga Women's Polit. Caucus, Delta Sigma Theta (Greater Cleve. Alumnae chpt., Althea Simmons award 1993). Democrat. Office: Ho of Reps 1009 Longworth Hob Washington DC 20515-3511 also: Dist Office 3645 Warrensville Ctr Rd Ste 204 Shaker Heights OH 44122

JONES, SUSAN CHAFIN, management consultant; b. Bryan, Tex., July 14, 1951; d. Othel Viron and Norma Beatrice (Bartley) Chafin; m. Robert Lewis Jones, Apr. 9, 1973 (dec.); 1 child, Kelli Sanness. BS in Edn., Stephen F. Austin State U., 1973; MA, U. Tex., Austin, 1976. Cert. rehab. counselor; lic. marriage and family therapist. Tng. coord. Behavioral Systems Scis. Assoc., Austin, 1973-76; pres., CEO Jones Counseling & Cons., Inc. (formerly Jones, Bright Internat.), The Woodlands, Tex., 1976—; CEO Jones, Ragain Internat., Inc., The Woodlands, 1997-99; team leader Guatemala Med. Mission, 1999-2000; interim exec. dir. Interfaith of the Woodlands, Tex., 1999—2001. Author: Feelings Beneath Words and Messages in Action, 1974, Supervisor's Notes: Guidelines on Employee Counseling, 1977, Youth Ministry: A Manual for Youth Counselors, Leaders and Workers, 1991, 360o Intermetrics, Assessment for Individuals and Organizations, 1993, Therapeutic Approaches to Women's Health: A Program of Exercise and Education, 1995. Active McCullough High Sch. PTA, The Woodlands, 1992-95; v.p. McCullough Highsteppers Parent Club, 1993-95; dir. Stephen Ministry The Woodlands United Meth. Ch., 1992-96, mem. adminstrv. bd., 1993-96; bd. mem. Montgomery County Young Life, 1991-92. Mem. Montgomery County C. of C., Am. Assn. Marriage and Family Therapy (clin.), Am. Assn. Christian Counselors (profl., charter), Christian Counselors Tex., Rotary Internat., Women's Energy Network. Republican. Avocations: playing piano, skiing, writing. Office: Jones Counseling & Cons Inc 10655 Six Pines Dr #160 The Woodlands TX 77380-0655 Office Phone: 281-367-2579.

JONES, SUSAN DORFMAN, real estate broker, writer; b. N.Y.C., Oct. 4, 1939; d. Joseph and Sarah (Sorrin) Dorfman; m. William Harry Jones, Sept. 18, 1960; children: Jeffrey Scott, Eric David, Timothy Mark BA, Syracuse U., 1961. Pres., owner Antiques Corp. Am., 1972-77; pres., owner Susan & Sons Antiques, 1977—; communications officer Riggs Bank, Washington, 1978-81; mgr. publs. Potomac Electric Power Co., Washington, 1981-82; sr. mgr. corp. communications MCI Corp., Washington, 1982-83; dir. corp. communications Sears World Trade, Washington, 1983-85; dir. corp. communications and govt. rels. Oxford Devel. Corp., Bethesda, Md., 1985-87; communications expert pub. health svc./health and human svcs. U.S. Alcohol, Drug Abuse, Mental Health Adminstrn., Rockville, Md., 1989-91; real estate broker Weichert Realtors, Washington, 1991—. Vol. staff Cleve. Clinics, Cleve. H.S. of Arts, 2003—; free-lance writer, cons., Washington, 1975-92; radio personality Sta. 4KQ, Brisbane, Australia, 1962; adj. prof. comms. Am. U., Washington, 1978-82. Author, editor, project mgr. corp. ann. reports. Recipient 1st pl. award for columns N.Y. Press Assn., 1961, Gold Quill award Internat. Assn. Bus. Communicators, 1980. Mem.: Greater Capital Area Assn. Realtors, Nat. Assn. Realtors, Pub. Rels. Soc. Am., Women in Telecommunications, Nat. Assn. Bank Women, Internat. Assn. Bus. Communicators, Nat. Press Club. Democrat. Jewish. Home and Office: 30650 Jackson Rd Orange Village OH 44022-1731 Office: 5035 Wisconsin Ave NW Washington DC 20016-4113 Office Phone: 202-326-1300. E-mail: suebillj@yahoo.com.

JONES, SUSAN EMILY, fashion educator, administrator, educator emeritus; b. N.Y.C., Sept. 9, 1948; d. David and Emily Helen (Welke) J.; m. Henry J. Titone, Jr., Oct. 21, 1974 (div. 1980); m. Douglas S. Robbins, Aug. 21, 1985 B.F.A., Pratt Inst., Bklyn., 1970. Designer Sue Brett, N.Y.C., 1970-74, St. Tropez, 1975; prof. fashion Pratt Inst., Bklyn., 1972-2000, chairperson fashion dept., 1981-2000, chairperson merchandising and design programs fashion dept., 1983-2000; computer software cons., 1988-89; owner, designer Sej Wearable Artworks, 1992—. Internat. observer Jeunes Createurs de Mode, Paris, 1987, judge, 1988; U.S. rep. SAGA Internat. Design Ctr., Copenhagen, 1992, serdesigns, Hawaii, 2001—. Tech. book reviewer, 1994—. Recipient Young Am. Designer award Internat. Ladies Garment Workers Union, 1970, Ptnr. in Edn. award N.Y.C. Pub. Sch. System Chancellor, 1992-93. Mem. Fashion Group (regional com. 1983-87, mem. com. 1990-93, ednl. com. 1995-96, co-chair ednl. com. 1996-98), Nat. Retail Fedn., Under Fashion Assn. Home: 79-7199 Mamalahoa Hwy 351 F Holualoa HI 96725 Office: Pratt Inst Dept of Fashion Design 200 Willoughby Ave Brooklyn NY 11205-3899 E-mail: sejpratt@aol.com., sjones@pratt.edu.

JONES, SUSIE, radio personality; Grad. Speech Comms., U. Minn. With Sta. KSTP, Sta. KARE, Sta. WCCO-TV, Mpls.; radio host afternoon drive Sta. KCCO-AM, Mpls., 1996—, Saturday radio host. Office: WCCO 625 2nd Ave S Minneapolis MN 55402

JONES, SUZANNE P. public relations executive; b. Niagara Falls, N.Y., Sept. 4, 1946; d. Morris G. and Betty (Connolly) J. BA in English, Niagara U., 1969; MA in Theater, U. Conn., 1971. Editor Niagara Observer, Niagara Falls, 1971-74, Niagara Free Press, Niagara Falls, 1974-75; pub. info. dir. City of Niagara Falls, 1975-76; advt. dir. Orion Enterprises, Lewiston, N.Y., 1976-79; v.p. Bozell and Jacobs Pub. Rels., N.Y.C., 1980-86, Porter/Novelli, N.Y.C., 1987-90, Geltzer & Co., 1991-93; dir. in-house pub. rels. Black & Decker Household Products, Shelton, Conn., 1993—. Mem. Theatre Hist. Soc., Larchmont Manor Soc., Larchmont Hist. Soc., Friends Niagara U. Theatre, Niagara U. Coun. Democrat. Roman Catholic. Home: 2221 Willow Ave Niagara Falls NY 14305-3051

JONES, VIRGINIA MCCLURKIN, retired social worker; b. Anniston, Ala., Mar. 13, 1935; d. Louie Walter and Virginia Keith (Beaver) McClurkin; m. Charles Miller Jones, Jr., Mar. 16, 1957; children: Charles Miller III, V. Grace. BA, Agnes Scott Coll., 1957; MA, U. Tenn., 1965, MSSW, 1979. English instr. U. Tenn., Knoxville, 1967-71; religious edn. dir. Oak Ridge Unitarian Ch., 1972-73, 76-78; co-owner, mgr. The Bookstore, 1973-76; English instr. Roane State C.C., 1975-80; pvt. practice clin. social work Oak Ridge, 1980-98. Cons. Mountain Cmty. Health Ctr., Coalfield, Tenn., 1980-83, Valley Ridge Hospice, 1987-89. Contbr. articles to newspapers. Mem.: NASW, Concord Yacht Club, Rotary. Democrat. Episcopalian. [illegible] Oak Ridge Turnpike Oak Ridge TN 37830-0334

JONES, WINONA NIGELS, retired library media specialist; b. Feb. 24, 1928; d. Eugene Arthur and Bertha Lillian (Dixon) Nigels; m. Charles Albert Jones, Nov. 26, 1994; children: Charles Eugene, Sharon Ann Jones Allworth, Caroline Winona Jones Pandorf. AA, St. Petersburg Jr. Coll., 1965; BS, U. So. Fla., 1967, MS, 1968; advanced MS, Fla. State U., 1980. Libr. media specialist Dunedine (Fla.) Comprehensive H.S., 1967-76; libr. media specialist, chmn. dept. Fitzgerald Mid. Sch., Largo, Fla., 1976-87; dir. media svcs. East Lake H.S., Tarpon Springs, Fla., 1987-93; ret., 1993. Dir., vol. North Pinellas Hist. Mus.; active Palm Harbor Hist. Soc., Pinellas County Hist. Soc.; del. White Ho. Conf. Libr. and Info. Svcs. Named Educator Yr. Pinellas County Sch. Bd. and Suncoast C. of C., 1983, 88, Palm Harbor Woman Yr. Palm Harbor Jr. Women's club, 1989, Palm Harbor Citizen Yr., Palm Harbor C. of C., 2002. Mem. ALA (coun. 1988-92), NEA, AAUW, ASCD, Assn. Ednl. Comm. and Tech. (divsn. sch. media specialist, coms.), Am. Assn. Sch. Librs. (com., pres.-elect 1989, pres. 1990-91, mem. exec. bd. 1991-92), Southeastern Libr. Assn., Fla. Libr. Assn., Fla. Assn. Media Edn. (pres.), U. So. Fla. Alumni Assn., Fla. State Libr. Sci. Alumni Assn., U. So. Fla. Libr. Sci. Alumni Assn. (pres. 1991-92, 92-93), Phi Theta Kappa, Phi Rho Pi, Beta Phi Mu, Kappa Delta Pi, Delta Kappa Gamma (parliamentarian 1989-90, legis. chmn. 1990, sec. 1994-96), Inner Wheel Club, Pilot Club, Civic Club, Order Ea. Star (Palm Harbor, past worthy matron). Democrat. Home: 911 Manning Rd Palm Harbor FL 34683-6344 Office Phone: 727-724-3054.

JONES-ATKINS, DEBORAH KAYE, state official; b. Bradenton, Fla, July 2, 1958; d. Ralph and Jewelle Vanessa (Gayle) Jones; 1 child, Omari Gayle Jones-Atkins. AS with distinction, cert. in human svcs., Monroe C.C., Rochester, N.Y., 1986; BIS, Va. State U., Petersburg, 1995; postgrad., SUNY, Brockport, 1998. Credit investigator Sears Roebuck & Co., Rochester, NY, 1980; customer svc. rep. B. Forman Co., Rochester, NY, 1980-81; youth counselor Brighton Youth Agy., Rochester, NY, 1976-81; staff asst. Makro Inc., Capitol Heights, Md., 1981-82; customer svc. rep. MetroVision Inc., Capitol Hts., 1983-84; teen parent counselor Urban League of Rochester, 1985, program coord., 1988; job developer YWCA of Rochester, 1985-87; prog. support technician, sr. Dept. Med. Assistance Svc., Commonwealth of Va., Richmond, 1989-96; alt. health care supr. Commonwealth of Va. Med. Assist. Svc., 1989-96; subs. tchr. Rochester City Sch. Dist., 1996-2000; SOL tudor, subs. tchr. Henrico County Pub. Sch., 2000; social worker County of Henrico Dept. Social Svc. Mem. Women's Resource Ctr., Richmond, 1989—; heir link The Links Inc., Rochester, 1982—; vol. United Negro Coll. Fund Telethon, Rochester, 1988, N.Y. State Dept. Labor Career Edn. Expo, 1989, WXXI Auction 21, Rochester, 1989, YMCA Greater Rochester, 1989, Arts Coun., Richmond, Richmond Children's Festival, 1989, Sci. Mus. Va., Richmond, 1989, Arts Coun. Richmond 15th Ann. June Jubilee, 1990, Children's Book Festival, 1990, Maymont Found. Flower Garden Show, 1990, 91, Va. Spl. Olympics, 1990—, Jr. League Richmond 45th Book and Author Dinner, 1990, dinner asst. ticket chairperson 46th Book and Author Dinner, 1991, hostee 45th Dinner, Children's Book Festival Arts Coun. Richmond; mem. agy. svc. com. Friends Assn. for Children, 1990—; mem. student adv. com. Va. Commonwealth U. Health Svcs., 1991, Friends of Art Richmond Mus. Fine Arts, 1991; mem. membership com., audience devel. com. Richmond Profl. Women's Network; placement counselor placement com. Jr. League Richmond, 1991, mem. tng. com., 1991; mem. adv. com. Children's Mus. Richmond; mem. exec. bd. YWCA of Richmond, 1992-95, mem. fin. com., 1996—; mem. policy bd. Jr. League Richmond, 1992-93; bd. dirs. Urban League of Richmond, 1996-2001; 3rd v.p. vols. PTA Echo Lake Elem. Sch.; mem. Echo Lake Elem. PTA County Coun, 2001; mem. architect com. 2001 Springcreek Assn. Named one of Outstanding Young Women of Am., 1988. Mem. NAFE, Nat. Coun. Negro Women, Jr. League of Rochester, Nat. Trust Hist. Preservation, Richmond Profl. Women's Network (rec. sec., exec. bd. 1992—), Richmond Jaycees. Democrat. Avocations: jogging, aerobics, tennis, racquetball, the arts, reading, travel. Home: PO Box 6582 Glen Allen VA 23058 Office: 8600 Dixon Powers Rd Richmond VA 23228

JONES-BUTLER, JACQUELINE, painter, poet; b. Jacksonville, Fla., Dec. 9, 1931; d. James Lester and Ruby Elizabeth (Jones) Butler; children: David Lester Glasgow, Ralph Clayton Glasgow, Kathryn Gail Glasgow. Student, U. Fla., Gainesville, U. Wash., Seattle, U. Alaska, Fairbanks. Interior decorator, designer display windows, owner Images North, Lynnwood, Wash., 1965—70; owner antique shop Paraphernalia West, Lynnwood, 1965—70; needlepoint designer, owner Images North, Fairbanks, Alaska, 1973—79; owner, artist, photographer Smiling Bear Studio, Two Rivers, Alaska, 1975—. Reporter Tundra Times, Fairbanks, 1971—73; exhibit designer U. Alaska, Geophys. Inst., Fairbanks, 1975; muralist Downtown Assn., Fairbanks, 1979; artist, photographer, owner. art tchr. Smiling Bear Studio, Two Rivers, Alaska, 1975—. Avocations: gardening, ski-joring with Alaskan Huskies.. Home and Office: 184 Kaufman Ln Fairbanks AK 99712

JONES DAME, GWYNETH, soprano; b. Pontnewynydd, Wales, Nov. 7, 1936; d. Edward George and Violet (Webster) J. Student, Royal Coll. Music, London, Accademia Chigiana, Siena, Italy, Internat. Opera Ctr., Zurich, Switzerland; Dr. h.c. musica, U. Wales and Glamorgan. Mem. Royal Opera, Covent Garden, Eng., 1963—, Vienna (Austria) State Opera, 1966—, Deutsche Opera Berlin, 1966, Munich Bavarian State Opera, 1967—. Guest performances in numerous opera houses including Hamburg, Bayreuth, Dresden, Paris, Zurich, Rome, Chgo., San Francisco, Los Angeles, Tokyo, Buenos Aires, Munich, La Scala, Milan, Met. Opera, N.Y.C., Bayreuth Festival, Salzburg Festival, Verona; appeared in 50 leading roles including Tosca, Minnie, Turandot, Leonora in Il Trovatore, Desdemona in Otello, Lady MacBeth, Fidelio, Aida, Senta, Sieglinde, Marschallin, Isolde, Ortrud, Salome, Brunnhilde, Medea, Kundry, Madame Butterfly, Elizabeth/Venus in Tannhauser, Ariadne, Farberin, Elektra, Helena in Aegyptische Helena, Poppea, Santuzza, Donna Anna in Don Giovanni, Begbick in Mahagonny, Hannah Glawari, Erwartung, La Voix Humaine; court singer, Bavaria, Austria; rec. artist for Decca, Deutsche Grammophon, Philips, EMI, CBS; prodr.: Der Fliegende Hollander, Weimar Nat. Theatre, 2003; films, TV and concert appearances. Decorated dame comdr. Order Brit. Empire, 1986, Commandeur Des Arts Et Lettres, 1992, Verdienst-Krenz I. Klasse, Austria Bundes Ver, 1998, others; recipient Shakespeare prize Hamburg, 1987, Verdienst Kreuz I Klasse Fed. Republic Germany, 1988, Golden Medal Honour, Vienna, 1991, Premio Pucci award Torre Del Lago, 2003. Fellow Royal Coll. Music. Address: Box 2000 CH-8700 Küsnacht Switzerland

JONES-KOCH, FRANCENA, school counselor, educator; b. Bunnell, Fla., Dec. 3, 1948; d. Roosevelt Jones and Naomi Stafford; m. William H. Koch, July 1976 (div. Aug. 1980); 1 child, Ahmad Yussef Shaw. BS, Fla. Meml. Coll., 1972; M in Elem. Edn., Nova Southeastern U., 1984, specialist degree, 1994. Intermediate tchr. Miami (Fla.) Dade County Pub. Schs., 1973—88, guidance counselor, 1988—. Adj. prof. Fla. Meml. Coll., Miami, 1984—87; juvenile GED instr. Women's Detention Ctr., Miami, 1994—96; planner summer 2000 Inmate to Inmate Tutoring Program Dept. Corrections, Miami, 2000; mem. region 5 steering com. Dade County Pub. Schs., Miami, mem. dist.'s student svcs. adv. coun., 2002—; amb. United Way-Dade County Pub. Schs., Miami; pres. Dade Counseling Assn., Miami, 2002—; dir. comms. Herstory Inc., 1975—2000. Vol. United Way Dade County, Miami, 1999—. Mem.: Am. Sch. Counselor Assn., AAUW (Miami br. chair Gwen Cherry awards 2000—, designer 21st Century Women's Wisdom Project 2001, prodr. 21st Century Women's Wisdom Project 2001), Fla. Counseling Assn., United Tchrs. Dade County, United Way of Dade County, Zeta Phi Beta Sorority, Inc. (pres. Beta Zeta chpt. 1997—99). Avocations: reading, community service, creative writing, travel, visiting book stores. Home: 10850 SW 164th St Miami FL 33157

JONES-LUKACS, ELIZABETH LUCILLE, physician; b. Norfolk, Va. d. Oliver C. and Gertrude (Layden) Jones; m. Michel J. Lukacs (dec.); children: Amanda, Laurel, Angelique, Klara. BS, Oglethorpe U., 1955. Diplomate, fellow Am. Bd. Family Practice. Intern Beth Israel Hosp., N.Y.C., 1964-65; family practice medicine Goshen, N.Y., 1965-73, Buckingham, Va., 1973-78; commd. maj. U.S. Air Force, 1978; flight surgeon Andrews AFB, Md., 1978-85, chief exec. med. program, 1991-2000; med. dir. Armed Forces Benefit Assn., Alexandria, Va., 2000—. Unit charge physician Student Health Ctr., U. Md., College Park, 1985—91; bd. dirs. Falcon's Landing Mil. Officers Retirement Home. Author: The Curies Radium & Radioactivity, 1962, The Golden Stamp Book of Flying Animals, 1963. Col. USAFR, commd. 459th USAF Clinic. Mem. Am. Med. Womens Assn. (pres. Br. I), Md. Thoroughbred Breeders. Episc. Home: 15430 Mount Calvert Rd Upper Marlboro MD 20772-9616 Office: 909 N Washington St Alexandria VA 22314

JONES-MORTON, PAMELA, human resources specialist; b. Balt., Aug. 21, 1947; d. Robert Alfred and Lois Enola (Skilliter) Jones; m. Wayne Daniel Morton, Sept. 7, 1968 (div. Aug. 1990). BS, Frostburg State U., 1970; MA, Mich. State U., 1976; PhD, Ohio State U., 1989. Tchr. Alleghaney High Sch., Cumberland, Md., 1970-72, Am. Sch. in Japan, Tokyo, 1972-74, dept. head, 1974-77; tchr. The Tatnall Sch., Wilmington, Del., 1977-78; dept. head, athletic dir. Internat. Sch. Dusseldorf, West Germany, 1979-82; athletic dir. Escola Americana De Rio de Janeiro, 1982-85, Am. Cmty. Sch., London, 1985-86; grad. asst. Ohio State U., Columbus, 1986-89; univ. prof. W.Va. U., Morgantown, 1989-91; mgr. human and bus. devel. Honda of Am. Mfg., Inc., Columbus, 1991-95, asst. mgr. expatriate adminstrn. dept., 1995—98, mgr. orgnl. devel. expatriate adminstrn., 1998-99, mgr. strategic sect., orgnl. devel., 1999—2002, mgr. expatriate adminstrn. dept., 2002—03; global human resource devel. cons. PJM Cons., Dublin, Ohio, 2003—. Pres. Kanto Plains Athletic Assn., Tokyo, 1973-77; mem accreditation team European Coun., London, 1982; spkr., trustee I Know I Can, Columbus, Ohio; mem. TARGET, The Ohio State U. and Columbus Japanese/Am. Bus. Cmty. Author: (chpt.) Transferring Learning to the Work Place, 1997; contbr. articles to profl. jours. Active Dolphin Rsch. Ctr., Marathon Shores, Fla., 1992; docent Columbus Zoo and Acquarium, 1999—. Mem. AAUW, Am. Soc. Tng. and Devel. (benchmarking forum 1991-95, spkr. 1993, 94, 95), Soc. Human Resource Mgmt., Inst. Internat. Human Resources, Phi Delta Kappa. Democrat. Avocations: gardening, scuba diving, traveling, photography, puzzles. Office: Honda of Am Mfg Inc 24000 Honda Pkwy Marysville OH 43040-9251

JONES - OLIVER, MARILYN A. special education educator; b. Hughes, Ark., Jan. 12, 1962; m. Jessie J. Oliver, June 18, 1978; children: Jesse Oliver, Mario Oliver, Je'Ana Oliver, Mia Oliver, Maxwell Oliver. BBA, St. Mary's U., San Antonio, 1997, MA, 2001; postgrad., Our Lady of the Lake U., San Antonio, 2002—, U. Tex., 2003. Cert. tchr. Tex. Tchr. spl. edn. Harlandale Ind. Sch. Dist., San Antonio, 1999—2003; missionary Natalia (Tex.) Ind. Sch. Dist., 2003—. Counselor Ctr. of Hope Ministries, San Antonio, 2000—; doctoral program cohort leader Our Lady of the Lake U., San Antonio, 2002—; spkr., mentor for disadvantaged women. Founder Diamond Readers Book Club, 2002—; mem. Ch. of God in Christ. Mem.: Assn. for Supervision and Curriculum Devel., Assn. Tex. Profl. Educators, Coun. Exceptional Children, Bus. and Profl. Women (Bowden cpt.). Avocations: jogging, reading, sewing, writing, singing. Home: 10470 Pine Glade San Antonio TX 78245 Office: Natalia Ind Sch Dist PO Box 548 8th & Pearson Natalia TX 78059 Business E-Mail: golivm@lake.ollusa.edu.

JONES-THURMAN, ROSANNA M. psychologist; d. Paul E. and Rosemary H. Jones; m. Daniel W. Thurman, Dec. 29, 1995; children: Johnathan A. Thurman, Derek P. Thurman, Nichollis W. Thurman. PhD, CSPP, 1990—95. Clin. psychologist Prairie Rose Mental Health Ctr., Harlan, Iowa, 1995—2000, Psychol. Svcs., Omaha, 2000—. Cons. Prairie Rose Mental Health Ctr., Harlan, Iowa, 2000—. Mem.: APA (Jeffrey Tanaka hon. mention award 1996), Psi Chi. Office: Psychological Services 10506 Burt Circle Omaha NE 68114 E-mail: drthurman@psychserv.net.

JONES-WILLS, EUNICE STEPHANIE, mental health nurse, researcher; b. Guyana, Nov. 14, 1955; came to the U.S., 1967; d. Esther (Fredericks) Elder; m. Bernard Jones, June 3, 1974 (div. Sept. 1989); m. Aloysius Ignatius Wills, May 25, 1991; children: Dwayne, Anton, Denise, Brandon, Andrew. AAS, N.Y.C. Tech. Coll., Bklyn., 1987; BS, U. Md., 1994, MS, 1996. RNC; RN, Md., D.C., Va; clin. specialist of psychiat. and mental health. Med.-surg. nurse Providence Hosp., Washington, 1987-88; charge nurse Crownsville (Md.) Hosp. Ctr., 1988-92; team leader Dept. Mental Health Svcs., Washington, 1992-96; psychiat. rsch. nurse NIH, Bethesda, Md., 1996-98; clin. nurse Bureau of Prisons Fed. Dentention Ctr., Miami, Fla., 1998—. CPR instr. Dept. Health and Human Svcs., Washington, 1993-96; head judge sci. fair regionals Pub. Health Svc., Rockville, Md., 1997, 98, presenter pub. schs. health week, 1997, 98. Lt. comdr. USPHS, 1996—. Mem. ANA (psychiat. and mental health cert.), Res. Officer Assn., Commd. Officer Assn., Sigma Theta Tau, Phi Theta Kappa. Democrat. Roman Catholic. Avocations: reading, traveling, shopping, biking. Home: 4010 NW 73rd Ave Coral Springs FL 33065-2142 Office: Federal Dentention Ctr 33 NE 4th St Miami FL 33132-2111

JONES-WILSON, FAUSTINE CLARISSE, retired education educator; b. Little Rock, Dec. 3, 1927; d. James Edward and Perrine Marie (Childress) Thomas; m. James T. Jones, June 20, 1948 (div. 1977); children: Yvonne Dianne, Brian Vincent; m. Edwin L. Wilson, July 10, 1981. AB, Ark. A.M.&N. Coll., 1948; AM, U. Ill., 1951, EdD, 1967; LLD, U. Ark., Pine Bluff, 2003. Tchr., sch. libr. Gary (Ind.) Pub. Schs., 1955-62, 1964-67; asst. prof. Coll. Edn., U. Ill., Chgo., 1967-69; assoc. prof. adult edn. Fed. City Coll., Washington, 1970-71; prof. edn., grad. prof. Howard U., Washington, 1969-70, 71-93, acting dean Sch. Edn., 1991-92, prof. emeritus, 1993—. Author: The Changing Mood in America; Eroding Commitment, 1977, A Traditional Model of Educational Excellence: Dunbar High School of Little Rock, Arkansas, 1981; co-author: Paul Laurence Dunbar High School of Little Rock, Arkansas: Take From Our Lips a Song, Dunbar to Thee, 2003; editor Jour. Negro Edn., 1978-91, 92-93; co-editor: Encyclopedia of African-American Education, 1996; assoc. editor Jour. of Edn. for Students Placed at Risk, 1996-2000. Chmn. East Coast steering com. Nat. Coun. on Educating Black Children, 1986—88, 1990—92, 3d v.p., 1992—94, bd. dirs., 1994—98. Recipient Frederick Douglass award Nat. Assn. Black Journalists, 1979, Disting. Scholar-Tchr. award Howard U., 1985, Exemplary Leadership award Am. Assn. Higher Edn. Black Caucus, 1988, Gertrude E. Rush award Nat. Bar Assn., 1990, Disting. Career award V.P. for Acad. Affairs, Howard U., 1993, Disting. Alumni award Coll. Edn. U. Ill., 1997; Phelps Stokes Fund sr. fellow, 1993-2000. Mem. Am. Ednl. Studies Assn. (pres. 1984-85), John Dewey Soc., Soc. Profs. of Edn. (Mary Anne Raywid award 2002), Phi Delta Kappa (pres. Howard U. chpt. 1986-87, Svc. key 1990). Democrat. Methodist. Home: 6605 Allview Dr Columbia MD 21046-1005

JONG, ERICA MANN, writer; b. N.Y.C., Mar. 26, 1942; d. Seymour and Eda (Mirsky) Mann; m. Michael Werthman, 1963 (div. 1965); m. Allan Jong (div. Sept. 1975); m. Jonathan Fast, Dec. 1977 (div. Jan. 1983); 1 child, Molly; m. Kenneth David Burrows, Aug. 5, 1989. BA, Barnard Coll., 1963; MA, Columbia U., 1965. Faculty, English dept. CUNY, 1964-65, 69-70, overseas div. U. Md., 1967-69; mem. lit. panel N.Y. State Council on Arts, 1972-74; faculty Breadloaf Writers Conf. Middlebury, Vt., 1982;

mem. faculty Saltzburg Seminar, Saltzburg, Austria, 1993, 98. Author: (poems) Fruits and Vegetables, 1971, reissued edit., 1997, Half Lives, 1973, Loveroot, 1975, At the Edge of the Body, 1979, Ordinary Miracles, 1983, Becoming Light: Poems New and Selected, 1992; (novels) Fear of Flying, 1973, How to Save Your Own Life, 1977, Fanny: Being the True History of the Adventures of Fanny Hackabout-Jones, 1980, Parachutes and Kisses, 1984, Serenissima, 1987 (reissued as Shylock's Daughter, 1995), Any Woman's Blues, 1990, Inventing Memory, 1998, Sappho's Leap, 2003, (poetry and non-fiction) Witches, 1981, reissued edit., 1997, (juvenile) Megan's Book of Divorce, 1984 (reissued as Megan's Two Houses, 1995), (memoir) The Devil at Large, 1993, What Do Women Want?, 1998, (autobiography) Fear of Fifty, 1994, (non-fiction) What Do Women Want?, 2001; composer lyrics: Zipless: Songs of Abandon from the Erotic Poetry of Erica Jong, 1995, (fiction) Inventing Memory, 1997. Recipient Bess Hokin prize Poetry mag., 1971, Prix Literaire, Deauville Film Festival, 1997; named Mother of Yr., 1982; Woodrow Wilson fellow; Nat. Endowment Arts grantee, 1973. Mem. PEN, Authors Guild U.S.A. (coun. 1975—, pres. 1991-93), Poets and Writers Bd., Writers Guild Am.-West, Poetry Soc. Am. (Alice Faye di Castagnola award 1972), Phi Beta Kappa. Office: Erica Jong Prodns c/o Kenneth David Burrows 451 Park Ave S Fl 8 New York NY 10016-7390

JONKOUSKI, JILL ELLEN, materials scientist, ceramic engineer, educator; b. Chgo. d. Joseph and Ruth Jonkouski. BS in Ceramic Engring., MS in Ceramic Engring., U. Ill. Former rschr. Battelle Meml. Inst., Columbus, Ohio; former ceramic engr. Austenal Dental, Inc., Chgo.; former rsch. scientist BIRL Indsl. Rsch. Lab. Northwestern U., Evanston, Ill.; ceramics mfg. engr., fed. project dir. Office of Sci., Office of Programs and Project Mgmt. divsn. U.S. Dept. Energy, Argonne, Ill., 1991—. Past adj. faculty Triton Coll., River Grove, Ill.; chair Internat. Gas Turbine Inst., ASME Turbo Expo, 2002, 2003, chair Ann. Conf. on Composites, Materials and Structures, 1997-2004, presenter in field. Mem. Am. Ceramic Soc. (spkr., tech. presenter 1983, 84, 95, 96, chair Chgo.-Milw. sect. 1993-94), U.S. Figure Skating Assn., U. Ill. Alumni Assn. Avocations: ice skating, hiking, flying, tennis. Office: US Dept Energy Office Programs and Project Mgmt 9800 S Cass Ave Argonne IL 60439-4899 E-mail: jill.jonkouski@ch.doe.gov.

JONQUIÈRES, LYNNE, travel agent; b. Albany, N.Y., Dec. 12, 1946; d. Edward Livingston Trudeau and Margaret Wing Gray; m. Jean-Louis Jonguieres, July 20, 1969 (dec. Apr. 1974); 1 child, Alexandra Jonquieres Oakley. Owner, photographer Image 2, Albany, 1975-82; registered rep. Prudential, Albany, 1983—2002; travel agt., owner Lineage Travel, Albany, 1999—. Bd. dirs. Downtown Day Care Ctr., Albany, 1989-2002. Mem. Schyler Meadows Club. Republican. Episcopalian. Home: The Cottage Princess Green Loudonville NY 12211

JORCZAK, NANCY, history educator; b. Trenton, N.J., May 4, 1948; d. Joseph Stanley and Phyllis (Grotkowski) J. BA, Colby Coll., Waterville, Maine, 1970; MA in Teaching, Trenton (N.J.) State Coll., 1973. Cert. secondary tchr., Pa., N.J. Tchr. Okayama (Japan) Cultural Ctr., 1971-72, Coun. Rock H.S., Newtown, Pa., 1973—. Fulbright scholar, 1981. Mem. Am. History Assn., World History Assn., Huntingdon Valley Kennel Club (pres. 1995), Pharaoh Hound Club Am. (pres. 1995-96). Republican. Avocations: coursing and showing hounds, needle work. Home: PO Box 745 Wshngtn Crsng PA 18977-0745 Office: Coun Rock H S 62 Swamp Rd Newtown PA 18940-1578

JORDAHL, PATRICIA ANN, music educator, theater director; b. Clarkfield, Minn., June 1, 1951; d. Robert Stanley and Norma Burnette Shefveland; m. Owen Warren Jordahl, June 11, 1977; children: Melody Ann, Matthew Owen. BA, Luther Coll., Decorah, Iowa, 1969—73; MA, Western N.Mex U., Silver City, N. Mex, 1987—90. Cert. Cmty. Coll. Lifetime Tchr. Ariz., 1993. K-12 music tchr. Hubbard Cmty. Schools, Hubbard, Iowa, 1973—77; pvt. music tchr. Self-employed, Iowa Falls, Iowa, 1977—85; k-12 music tchr. Thatcher Cmty. Schools, Thatcher, Ariz., 1986—93; music/music theatre prof. Ea. Ariz. Coll., Thatcher, Ariz., 1993—. Music tech. chair/bd. of directors Ariz. Music Educator's Assn., Phoenix, 1995—99; music dept. chair Ea. Ariz. Coll., Thatcher, Ariz., 2001—. Recipient O.M. Hartsell Excellence in Tchg. award, Ariz. Music Educator Assn., 1998. Mem.: Am. Choral Dir. Assn. (assoc.), Music Educator Nat. Conf. (assoc.), Ariz. Music Educator Assn. (assoc.; sec. 1999—2001). Conservative. Meth. Avocations: travel, music, swimming, reading, theater. Office: Eastern Arizona Coll 615 North Stadium Ave Thatcher AZ 85552

JORDAHL, SUSAN MARIE, music educator; b. Sebeka, Minn., Apr. 29, 1958; d. Charles Albert and Esther Ljungren; m. Delroy Alan Jordahl; children: Jessica, Jason. MEd, N.D. State U., 1980. Tchr. West Fargo (N.D.) Schs., 1985—. Trollwood Performing Arts Sch., Fargo, ND, 1995—. Bd. dirs. F-M Area Youth Symphony, Fargo, ND, 1996—98. Chmn. (program) Orchestra, 1998 (American String Teacher Recognition, 1999). Recipient Tchr. of Month award, West Fargo C. of C., 1999. Mem.: Sigma Alpha Iota (life; Variety over the years, Rose of Honor, Sword of Honor). Lutheran. Avocations: playing piano, gardening, cake decorating. Home: 1714 27th Ave S Moorhead MN 56560 Office: West Fargo HS 801 9th St E West Fargo ND 58078

JORDAN, BERNICE BELL, retired elementary school educator; b. Calvert, Tex. d. Ocie Wade and Nannie B. (Westbrook) Bell; m. William B. Jordan, Sept. 28, 1956; children: Beverly, Terrence, Keith. Student, Prairie View A&M, Tex. Western Coll.; BA, San Jose State Coll., 1959, MA, 1985. Cert. elem. edn., fine arts, multi-cultural tchr., specially designed acad. instrn. English. Writer curriculum guide, fine arts Alum Rock Union Elem. Sch. Dist., San Jose, Calif., elem. tchr., 1959—99; writer sch. plan Goss Elem.; ret., 1999. Mem. adv. com., tchr.-cons. writing project San Jose U., 1992—. Mem.: NEA, ASCD, Calif. Ret. Tchrs. Assn., Santa Clara County Reading Coun., Calif. Elem. Edn. Assn., Calif. Reading Assn., Calif. Tchrs. Assn., Alum Rock Edn. Assn., Nat. Coun. Negro Women, Delta Kappa Gamma, Alpha Delta Kappa. Home: 3282 Fronda Dr San Jose CA 95148-2015

JORDAN, BRENDA MOORE, artist; b. Roanoke Rapids, NC, Feb. 4, 1946; d. John Leroy and Sarah (Williams) Moore; m. John Richard Jordan, Jr., June 26, 1982; m. James Edwin Harlow, Nov. 27, 1966 (div.); 1 child, Edwin Scott Harlow. BS cum laude in Art Edn. and Painting, Barton Coll., Wilson, NC, 1980; student, U. NC, Greensboro. One-woman shows include Chowan College, Murfreesboro, N.C., 2001, Wake County Mcpl. Bldg., Raleigh, N.C., 2001, Wilson (N.C.) Art Coun. Bldg., 2001, Barton Coll., Wilson, N.C., Alumni Art Exhbn. Barton Coll., 1991, 2001. Bd. dirs. (3 gubernatorial appointments) Murfreesboro Hist. Commn.; bd. dirs. U. N.C. Thurston Arthritis Rsch. Ctr., Chapel Hill, 1998—99, N.C. divsn. Am. Cancer Soc., Raleigh, 1982—92, N.C. Tri-Agy. Health Bd., Raleigh, 1990—92, Sch. Pub. Health, Chapel Hill, NC, N.C. Lit. and Hist. Assn., Raleigh, Wake County Hist. Assn., Raleigh, 1984—88, Friends Libr. D.H. Hill Libr. NC State U., 1992—98. Democrat. Baptist. Home: 809 Westwood Dr Raleigh NC 27607

JORDAN, CAROLE JEAN, political organization administrator; married; 1 child. Sec. exec. com. Nat. Fedn. Rep. Women, 1995-97, mem. at large, dir. region 3, 1997—. Pres. Fla. Rep. Women, 1992-97, bd. dirs.; regent, co-chair Orlando 87 conv. Nat. Fedn. Rep. Women; pres. Rep. Women Indian River; mem. exec. com. Fla. Rep. Com.; nat. committeewoman, Fla., 1996-, rep. rules com. Rep. Nat. Com.; del.-at-large Rep. Nat. Conv., San Diego; del., at-large alternative Rep. Nat. Conv., Houston, 1992, del. to pres. I, II, II; co-chmn. RPOF Election 1996 com.; joint owner Jordan Irrigation and Well Drilling, Inc. Active George bus. for Pres.; active statewide steering com. Jeb Bush for Gov.; candidate for U.S. Congress, 1994; sec., vice chmn. Rep. Exec. Com. Indian river County; vol. Indian River County Mental Health Soc., Indian River Meml. Hosp. Woman's Bur., Indian River Hist. Soc., Environ. Learning Ctr., Jr. League, Vera Beach Ctr. for Arts; past pres. St. Edward's Sports Assn. Mem. Nat. Small Bus. Assn., Nat. Fedn. Ind. Businesses, Vero Beach/Indian River C. of C., Coast Builders Assn. (treas.). Office: Nat Fedn Rep Women 124 N Alfred St Alexandria VA 22314-3011 Fax: 703-548-9836.

JORDAN, CYNTHIA, counselor, educator; d. Lucius Donald and Marlene Drury Jordan. BS, Baylor U., 1980; MS, U. Memphis, 1981, EdD, 1990. Lic. profl. counselor Tenn., National Board Cert. Counselor, lic. sr. psychol. examiner Tenn., bd. cert. ednl. therapist Assn. Ednl. Therapists, cert. spl. tchr. reading Tenn. Asst. prof. U. of Mo., St. Louis, 1990—91; dir. student acad. support svcs. U. of Tenn. Ctr. Health Scis., Memphis, 1991—2000, asst. vice chancellor student svcs., 1999—2000, assoc. prof., 1991—; dir. learning ctr. Hutchison Sch., Memphis, 2000—02; dir. counseling Presbyn. Day Sch., Memphis, 2002—. Cons. Dartmouth Coll., Coll. Bd., 1995—2000, Ednl. Testing Svc., Princeton, NJ; cons. on grad. and profl. students with disabilities various univs. Co-author: Documentation Guidelines for Learning Disabillities, Documentation Guidelines for Attention Deficit Disorder, Documentation Guidelines for Psychiatric Disabilties; educator, teaching (educator); contbr. articles to refereed profl. jours. Team mgr. Destination Imagination, Memphis, 1999—2003; Sunday sch. tchr. Second Presbyn. Ch., Memphis. Mem.: ACA, NASP, Learning Disabilities Assn., Assn. on Higher Edn. and Disabilities (pres. 1997—98), Am. Sch. Counseling Assn., Assn. Ednl. Therapists. Republican. Avocations: play therapy, working with children, reading. Office: Presbyterian Day Sch 4025 Poplar Memphis TN 38111

JORDAN, ELKE, molecular biologist, government medical research institute executive; b. Gottingen, Germany, Apr. 8, 1937; came to U.S., 1953, naturalized, 1961; d. Peter Friederich and Elisabeth A.K. (Lehmann) J.; m. Thomas H. Edelson, Aug. 21, 1972 (div. 1991). BA, Goucher Coll., 1957; Ph.D, Johns Hopkins U., 1962. In various rsch. positions Harvard U., 1962-64, U. Cologne, Fed. Republic Germany, 1964-68, U. Wis., Madison, 1968-69, U. Calif., Berkeley, 1969-72; grants assoc. NIH, Bethesda, Md., 1972-73; coord. for collaborative rsch. Nat. Cancer Inst., NIH, Bethesda, Md., 1973-76; health scientist adminstr. Nat. Inst. Gen. Med. Scis., NIH, Bethesda, 1976-82, assoc. dir., 1982-88; dir. Office of Human Genome Rsch., NIH, Bethesda, 1988-89; dep. dir. Nat. Human Genome Rsch. Inst., NIH, Bethesda, 1989—2002; with Found. for NIH, Bethesda, 2002—. Contbr. articles on molecular biology of E. coli and bacteriophage lambda to profl. jours. NIH fellow, 1959-65; Helen Hay Whitney Found. fellow, 1965-68. Fellow AAAS; mem. Am. Soc. for Human Genetics. Office: Found for NIH 1 Cloister Ct Ste 152 Bethesda MD 20814-1460

JORDAN, JUDITH VICTORIA, clinical psychologist, educator; b. Milw., July 28, 1943; d. Claus and Charlotte (Backus) J.; m. William M. Redpath, Aug. 11, 1973. AB, Brown U., 1965; MA, Harvard U., 1968, PhD, 1973; DHL (hon.) (hon.), New Eng. Coll., 2001. Diplomate Am. Bd. Profl. Psychology. Psychologist Human Relations Service, Wellesley, Mass., 1971-73; assoc. psychologist McLean Hosp., Belmont, Mass., 1978-93, psychologist, 1993—, dir. women's studies program, 1988—, dir. tng. in psychology, 1991, dir. Women's Treatment Network, 1992—. Vis. scholar Stone Ctr. Wellesley Coll., 1985—; asst. prof. psychiatry Harvard Med. Sch., 1988—; co-dir. Jean Baker Miller Tng. Inst., Wellesley Coll. 1998; adv. bd Fox TV Network, Women First healthcare., 1998; disting. prof. Menninger Clinic, 1999. Author: Empathy and Self Boundries, 1984, Women's Growth in Connection, 1991, (with others) The Self in Relation, 1986; editor, author: Relational Self in Women; editor: Women's Growth in Diversity, 1997; editor: The Complexity of Connection, 2004. Recipient Outstanding Contbn. award, Feminist Therapy Inst., 2002. Fellow Am. Psychol. Assn.; mem. Mass. Psychol. Assn. (bd. dirs. 1983-85, Career Achievement award for outstanding contbns. to advancement of psychology as a sci. and a profession), Phi Beta Kappa. Office: McLean Hosp 114 Waltham St Lexington MA 02421-5415

JORDAN, KAREN, newscaster; b. Nashville, Tenn. d. Robert Jordan; m. Christian Farr. BA in English, Spelman Coll., Atlanta, 1994; MA in Broadcast Journalism, Medill Sch. of Journalism, Evanston, Ill., 1995. Medill News Svc. reporter WMAQ-AM, Chgo., 1995; reporter WIFR-TV, Rockford, Ill., 1995—97; weekend anchor and reporter WKEF-TV, Dayton, Ohio, 1997—99; main anchor and reporter WRGT-TV, Dayton, Ohio, 1999—2000; anchor weekend news and reporter WPHL-TV, Phila., 2000—03; co-anchor weekend news WLS-TV, Chgo., 2003—. Office: WLS-TV 190 N State St Chicago IL 60601

JORDAN, KARLA SALGE, early childhood education educator; b. Berlin, July 4, 1943; came to U.S. 1965; d. Hubert Ernst Richard and Irmgard Klara Salge; m. William Jackson Jordan, May 28, 1963 (div. 1980); 1 child, Michael Bond. BA, Berlin Tchrs. Coll., 1964, Meth. Coll., Fayetteville, N.C., 1974; MA, Fayetteville State U., 1986. Cert. tchr., N.C., ednl. supr., 1995, cert. early childhood generalist Nat. Bd. Edn., 2000. Tchr. Eastover Elem. Sch., Fayetteville, 1974-75, Montclair Elem. Sch., Fayetteville, 1975—. Workshop presenter Cumberland County Sch., Fayetteville, spring 1983, 92-95; mem. bldg. leadership team Montclair Elem. Sch., 1992-93, chair, 1994-95, grade chair, 1980-90, 1999-2001, 2002-2003, 2003-2004, sch. improvement team chair, 1995-98, 2001-03. Treas. Montclair PTA, 1987-88, sec., 1988-90, pres. 1985, 86; youth choir dir. Eureka Bapt. Ch., Fayetteville, 1990—, min. of music, 1995—; mem., bible study leader for German fellowship Walstone Bapt. Ch., Fayetteville, German fellowship coord., 1999—. Fayetteville Jr. League mini grantee, 1991; named Tchr. of the Yr. Montclair Elem. Sch., 1987-88; recipient Fayetteville Tchr. of the Week Jr. League and the Huntington Learning Ctr., 1997. Mem. ASCD, Cross Creek Reading Coun. (rec. sec. 1990), Fayetteville Assn. for Edn. of Young Children, N.C. Assn. of Edn. (bldg. rep. 1981-83), Pi Lambda Theta. Republican. Avocations: sewing, crafts, gardening, travel, reading. Home: 845 Mary Jordan Ln Fayetteville NC 28311-7075 Office: Montclair Elem Sch 555 Glensford Dr Fayetteville NC 28314-2326 Office Phone: 910-868-5124. E-mail: karla-sjs@msn.com., karlajordan@ccs.k12.nc.us.

JORDAN, KATIE L. minister; d. Lewis and Eva Still; m. Andrew Jordan, Apr. 28, 1961; children: Kathy Keyes, Stephanie Warner, Patrick, Sonja, Andrew Jordan, III. Diploma, Greenville (S.C.) Tech. Coll. Ordained pastor Enoree River Bapt. Assn., S.C., 1993. Min. prison ministries Queen St. Bapt. Ch., Greenville, 1980, min. of music, 1975—90, pastor, 1990—. Advisor Outreach Ministry, Greenville, 1993—, Food & Clothing Bank, Greenville, 1993—; com. mem. Hope 6 Devel. Project, Greenville, 2002—. Pastor (community service) Community Involvement and Helps Ministry; singer: Savoy Record Label, 1983. Pastor Cmty. Involvement and Helps Ministry. Recipient Human Svc. award, Community Involvement and Helps Ministry, 2002. Mem.: Enoree River Bapt. Assn., Nat. Women Ministers, Inc., The Golden Women Min. Fellowship (pres. 1992—94), We. Carolina Music Assn. (1st v.p. 1995—). Democrat. Baptist. Avocations: sewing, reading, music, sports, working with youth. Home: 6 Baywood Ave Greenville SC 29607 Office: Queen Street Baptist Ch 6 Baywood Ave Greenville SC 29607 E-mail: mwilliams@queenstbc.org.

JORDAN, LINDA DIANE, music educator; b. Joliet, Ill., July 29, 1957; d. Arthur Michael Rechkemer and Norma Jean Gimpel; m. Charles Campbell Jordan, June 8, 2002; m. Lawrence Arthur Roelandts (div. June 1, 1990); children: Matthew Kane Roelandts, Kara Beth Roelandts. MusB, Palm Beach Atlantic Coll., 2000. Cert. Music (Grades K-12) Fla., 2000. Tchr. chorus, handbell Western Pines Mid. Sch., West Palm Beach, Fla., 2001—; tchr. music Golden Grove Elem. Wellington Elem. Schools, 2000—01. Dir. ch. music camp Oceanview United Meth. Ch., Juno Beach, Fla., 1991—; bd. mem. Spotlight Young Musicians, West Palm Beach, Fla., 2003—; dir. of ch. music camp Trinity United Meth. Ch., Palm Beach Gardens, Fla., 1989—94. Dir.: (handbell performance) Kravis Ctr. (Condr. Mid. Sch. H.S. Honors Handbell Choir, 2003). Assoc. music Oceanview United Meth. Ch., Juno Beach, Fla., 1998—2003. Mem.: Fla. Vocal Assn., Fla. Music Educator's Assn. Office: Western Pines Mid Sch 5949 140th Ave North West Palm Beach FL 33411

JORDAN, LOIS WENGER, foundation official; b. Madison, Wis., Dec. 28, 1943; d. Alfred and Phyllis Mae (Shaffer) Wenger; m. William Malcolm Jordan, Dec. 28, 1963; children: William Andre, Christopher Allan Wenger. BS, Millersville (Pa.) U., 1969. Tchr. Hempfield Sch. Dist., Lancaster, Pa., 1969-70, Lancaster Sch. Dist., 1975-80; dir. Upward Bound, Millersville U., 1980-82; dir. devel. St. Joseph Hosp., Lancaster, 1982-87; assoc. dir. devel. Pa. State U. Coll. Medicine, Hershey, 1987-97; dir. devel. Pa. State U., Capital Coll., 1997-2000; nat. dir. revenue devel. Am. Coll. Physicians/Am. Soc. Internal Medicine, 2000—02; pres. Jordan Assocs., Lancaster, Pa., 2002—. Author: (children's book) What's a Hospital Like?, 1972. Mem. Lancaster Jr. League, 1975—; trustee St. Joseph Hosp., 1979—82, James Buchanan Found., Lancaster, 1982—94; bd. trustees Penn Manor Found., 1998—2000; trustee Highland Presbyn. Ch., Lancaster, 1982—85. Recipient Cheston M. Berlin Svc. award Pa. State U. Alumni Assn., 1995, Outstanding Cmty. Svc. award Jr. League Assn., 1995. Mem. Assn. Healthcare Philanthropy (bd. dirs. 1990-92). Republican. Avocations: travel, hiking, international cooking. Home: 1734 Colonial Manor Dr Lancaster PA 17603-6034 E-mail: loisjordan@blazenet.net.

JORDAN, LOUISE HERRON, art educator; b. Shanghai, Dec. 25, 1938; d. Edwin Warren Herron and Marie Standley; m. Michael Dean Salmon, June 21, 1958 (div. Jan. 21, 1976); m. John Patrick Jordan, June 24, 1995; children: Catherine Louise Boggess, Michael Dean Salmon, Richard Dean Salmon, Marianne Gabriel Fisher. Student, Smith Coll., 1956—58. Parish sec. St. Lawrence Cath. Ch., Alexandria, Va., 1977—80; dir. meetings and mem. Am. Inst. Biological Sci., Wash., DC, 1985—93; exec. asst. to pres. Lawrence Tech. U., Southfield, Mich., 1993—95; tchr. art Jewish Cmty. Ctr., New Orleans, 2002—. One-woman shows include The Long Gallery, Oschner Hosp., New Orleans, La., 2000, 2002, St. Tammany Art Assn., Holiday Inn, Covington, La., 2001, The Upstairs Gallery, 2001, Café Degas, New Orleans, La., 2002, exhibited in group shows at Masur Mus. Juried Show, 1997, Fest for All, Baton Rouge, La., 1997, New Orleans Art Assn. Nat. Exhibit, 1997, River Road Juried Exhibit, Baton Rouge, La., 2002, Dominican Inst. Arts Group Show, Sparkill, NY, 2003. Bd. dirs. Bancroft Pk. Civic Assn., New Orleans, 1997—; professed lay mem. Dominican Order, New Orleans, 1997—; mem. Dominican Inst. of the Arts, Adrian, Mich., 2001—. Mem.: St. Tammany Art Assn. (assoc.), New Orleans Art Assn. (assoc.), La. Watercolor Soc. (life; pres. 1998—2000, signature mem., pres. 1998—2000, chmn. internat. exhbn. 1997—99, workshop dir. 1999—), Xavier U. Alumni Assn. (hon.), Smith Coll. Alumni Assn. (assoc.) Roman Catholic. Home: 4644 Bancroft Dr New Orleans LA 70122 Office: St Anthony Studio 6218 St Anthony St New Orleans LA 70122 Personal E-mail: bayoulou222@aol.com.

JORDAN, MARTHA B. lawyer; m. David Lee Jordan; children: Stacy, Kristen. BS, Pa. State U., 1976; MBA, U. Chi., 1978, JD, U. Calif., Berkeley, 1983. Bar: Calif. 1983. With Latham & Watkins, L.A., 1986—90, ptnr., 1990—98, mng. ptnr., 1998—. Named one of Calif.'s Top 100 Most Influential Lawyers, Calif. Law Bus., 1999. Office: Latham and Watkins LLC 633 W Fifth St Ste 4000 Los Angeles CA 90071*

JORDAN, MARY, editor-in-chief, reporter; m. Kevin Sullivan; 2 children. Grad., Georgetown U., 1983; student, Trinity Coll., Dublin; M in Journalism, Columbia U., 1984; postgrad., Georgetown U., 1994—95, Stanford U., 1999—2000. Nat. edn. reporter Washington Post, mem. met. and nat. staffs, 1984, co-bur. chief N.E. Asia bur., 1995—99, co-bur. chief Mexico City bur., 2000—. Recipient Nieman fellowship, Harvard U., 1989—90, Pulitzer prize for internat. reporting, 2003. Office: Washington Post 1150 15th St NW Washington DC 20071

JORDAN, MARY ANN, secondary school educator, director; d. Clyde Elton and Odessa Peeples Manning; children: James Landon, Tasya Elizabeth. BA, Baylor U., 1970; MS, mid. mgmt. cert., Tex. A&M U., 1994; supt. cert., Tex. Women's U., 2000; postgrad., U. North Tex., 1999—. Cert. secondary English and math. tchr. Tex. State Bd. Edn. Cert. Tchr. Troy (Tex.) Ind. Sch. Dist., 1970—71, San Antonio Ind. Sch. Dist., 1971—72, Northside Ind. Sch. Dist., San Antonio, 1972—79; v.p. Jordan Propeller, Inc., San Antonio, 1979—90; tchr. Boerne (Tex.) Ind. Sch. Dist., 1990—94; adminstr. Eastland (Tex.) Ind. Sch. Dist., 1994—. Dir. King's Ranch, Bandera, Tex., 1973—74; spkr. Eastland Ind. Sch. Dist., 1999—2003, Tex. Woman's U., Denton, 2001; cons. Edn. Svc. Ctr., Abilene, Tex., 1999—2001. Vice chair bd. Bapt. Children's Home, San Antonio, 1982—91; chairperson Baylor U., Waco, Tex., 1988; sec. Tex. Elem. Prins. Region 14, 2002. Recipient Disting. Adminstr. award, Migrant Conf., Abilene, Tex., 2002. Mem.: Edn. Svc. Ctr. 14 (prin. leadership com. 1996—2003), Baylor Alumni Assn., Phi Delta Kappa, Delta Kappa Gamma (com. chair 2000—03). Avocations: harp, attending musicals and sporting events, reading, singing, gardening. Home: 1011 S Seaman Eastland TX 76448

JORDAN, MARY LUCILLE, commissioner; m. Ben C. Elliott, Aug. 23, 1980; children: Elizabeth Elliott, Armando Elliott, C. Daniel Elliott. Student, Hull U., 1969-70; BA cum laude, Bonaventure U., 1971; JD, Antioch Law Sch., 1976. Bar: N.Y., 1977, D.C., 1978. Atty. Office of Fed. Register Nat. Archives & Records Adminstrn., Washington, 1976-77; sr. staff atty. United Mine Workers Am., Washington, 1977-94; chmn. Fed. Mine Safety and Health Rev. Commn., Washington, 1994—. Office: Fed Mine Safety Health Rev Commn 1730 K St NW Fl 6 Washington DC 20006-3868

JORDAN, MICHELLE DENISE, lawyer; b. Chgo., Oct. 29, 1954; d. John A. and Margaret (O'Dood) J. BA in Polit. Sci., Loyola U, Chgo., 1974; JD, U. Mich., 1977. Bar. Ill. 1977, U.S. Dist. Ct. (no. dist.) Ill. 1978. Asst. state's atty. State's Attys. Office, Chgo., 1977-82; pvt. practice Chgo., 1983-84; with Ill. Atty. Gen.'s Office, Chgo., 1984-90, chief environ. control div., 1988-90; ptnr. Hopkins & Sutter, Chgo., 1991-93; apptd. dep. regional adminstr. region 5 U.S. EPA, Chgo., 1994—. Active Operation Push, Chgo., 1971—. Recipient Kizzy Image Achievement and Svc. award, 1990, Suzanne E. Olive Nat. EEO award 1996; named in Am.'s Top 100 Bus. and Profl. Women, Dollars and SenseMag., Chgo., 1988. Mem. Ill. Bar Assn., Chgo. Bar Assn. (bd. mgrs., chmn. criminal law com. 1987-88, mem. hearing divsn., jud. evaluation com. 1987-88, exec. coun. 1987-88), Cook County Bar Assn., Nat. Bar Assn., Alpha Sigma Nu. Democrat. Baptist.

JORDAN, RAYLENE O. insurance agent; b. Avon Lake, Ohio, Aug. 7, 1948; d. Chester Barr and Grace Lucille McCurdy Barr Current, Paul Coleman Current (Stepfather); m. Thomas Michael Jordan, Oct. 12, 2001; children: Kelley Anne Doyle Mayes, John Allan Doyle, Jeffery Thomas Doyle, James Robert Doyle. Student, Redlands Coll., El Reno, Okla., 1986—87; B in Computer Sci., Okla. State U., 1995; cert. in med. terminology, Austin CC, 1997. Group I ins. lic. Tex.; notary pub. Tex. Bus. owner BB Inc., Cedar Park, Tex., 1995—98; case mgr. Hammerman & Gainer, T.P.A., Austin, 1998—99; examiner J.S. List & Assocs., Austin,

1999—2000, Amil Internat. Ins. Co., Austin, 2000—01. Mem.: NAFE (hon.), Internat. Assn. Female Execs. Roman Catholic. Avocations: travel, cooking, horses, black labrador retrievers, fitness. Home: 16503 Tejas Trail Cypress TX 77429

JORDAN, RUTH ANN, physician; b. Oct. 17, [illegible] d. Willard and [illegible] (Fouts) J.; children: Diane J., Linda J. AB, Ind. U., 1950; MD, Columbia U., 1957. Intern St. Luke's Hosp., N.Y.C., 1957—58, asst. resident, 1958—59; physician Met. Life Ins. Co., N.Y.C., 1960—62, Standard Oil Co. of N.J., N.Y.C., 1962, MIT, Cambridge, Mass., 1963—71, New Eng. Mut. Life Ins. Co., Boston, 1963—66, asst. med. dir., 1971—74; fellow internal medicine Mass. Gen. Hosp., Boston, 1974—75; physician Simmons Coll., Boston, 1975—78, Northeastern U., Boston, 1976—78; assoc. med. dir. New Eng. Telephone Co., Boston, 1978, med. dir. clin. svcs., 1978—86; dir. occupl. medicine Gen. Med. Assn., Boston, 1986—91; assoc. med. dir. Allmerica, Worcester, Mass., 1991—97; plant med. dir. GM, Westwood, Mass., 1995—; physician Health Resource, Woburn, Mass., 1996—. Therapeutic dietitian Meth. Hosp., Indpls., 1951-53, Presbyn. Hosp., N.Y.C., part-time 1954-57; nat. coord. com. on cholesterol, 1986—, Mass. Adv. Coun. for Workers Compensation, 1986-89. Fellow: Am. Coll. Occupl. and Environ. Medicine (health edn. com. 1984—, membership com. 1985—88, bd. dirs. 1986—92); mem.: PEO, DAR, AMA, Mass. Med. Soc. (mem. ho. of dels. 1984—, chmn. environ. and occupl. health com. 1985—88, mem. interspecialty com. 1985—88, mem. nutrition com. 2001—, mem. bylaws com. 2001—, bd. trustees 2003—), Norfolk Dist. Med. Soc. (v.p. 1998—99, mem. edn. com. 1998—, mem. exec. com. 1998—, pres. 1999—2001, rep. to Mass. Med. Soc. nominating com. 2000—02, rep. to renovating com. 2003—, nominating com. 2003—), New Eng. Occupl. Med. Assn. (bd. dirs. 1980—89, pres. 1981—84), The Country Club, Columbia U. Club of New Eng. (v.p. 1981—84, bd. dirs. 1981—91, pres. 1989—91), Alpha Chi Omega. Home: 105 Rockwood St Brookline MA 02445-7408

JORDAN, SANDRA, public relations professional; b. Pasadena, Tex., Oct. 10, 1952; d. Royal Wilson and Kathryn Ann (Speck) J.; m. William Anderson Mintz, Aug. 10, 1974 (div. 1980). B of Journalism, U. Tex., 1974. Reporter Austin (Tex.) American Statesman, 1974-76; news dir. KTAE Radio, Taylor, Tex., 1974-76; dir. of news and info. Inst. of Texan Cultures, San Antonio, 1976-82; pub. rels. dir. San Antonio Mus. Assn., 1982-83; dir. news/info. Univ. Tex., San Antonio, 1983-86; sr. publicist Rogers & Cowan, Inc., Washington, 1986-87; communications dir. NARAL, Washington, 1987-88; assoc. Parker, Vogelsingers & Assocs., Washington, 1988-90; pub. rels. and mktg. dir. Girl Scout Coun., Washington, 1990-99; mgr. media rels. Planned Parenthood Fedn. Am., Washington, 1999-2000; fellow Population Leadership Program, Washington, 2000—; dir. comms. and outreach USAID, Washington, 2000—. Pub. rels. cons. YWCA, Washington; judge, ad contest, Women in Comm., Iowa, 1993; workshop organizer Washington Ind. Writers, 1990; publicity com. CASE Conf., San Antonio, 1986, Smithsonian Nat. Assoc. Prog., San Antonio, 1980; panelist Women in Comms. Roundtable, 1996, Global Health Coun., Washington, 2003; presenter in field. Contbg. author: Folk Art in Texas, 1985. Prog. cons. KLRN-TV (pub.) San Antonio, 1981, 82; del. Dem. Nat. Conv., Taylor, 1976; docent Kennedy Ctr., Washington, 1989. Recipient Apex award, 1991-93, 95, 97-98, Comm. Concepts, 1991, Design honors, Tex. Assn. of Mus., 1993, IABC Silver Inkwell award, 1995, Silver Anvil award, 1996. Mem. Women in Comm. (D.C. chpt., literacy project 1992, mentoring program com., v.p. for programs 1998—), Women in Advt. and Mktg., Am. Soc. Assn. Execs., The Writers Ctr., Pub. Rels. Soc. Am. Avocations: fiction writing, quilt making. Home: 6305 E Halbert Rd Bethesda MD 20817-5409 Office: USAID G/PHN/POP The Ronald Reagan Bldg 1300 Pennsylvania Ave Washington DC 20523 E-mail: sjordan@usaid.gov.

JORDAN, TAMECIA MICHELLE, computer engineer; d. Darryl Wiggins and Sharon S. Jordan; m. David S. Alford, May 24, 2003. B in Computer Engring., Ga. Tech., 1997; postgrad., Duke U. Tech. support co-op IBM, Atlanta, 1992—93; software engr. co-op IBM/Lotus, Atlanta, 1994—96; intern AT&T, Atlanta, 1996; system integration and test engr. Hewlett Packard, Cupertino, Calif., 1997—99, hardware design engr., 1999—2001, project mgr. III-engring., 2001—03. Recipient Martin Luther King Svc. to Mankind award, Lambda Delta Rho, 1997; Ga. Hope scholar, State of Ga., 1997. Mem.: Nat. Soc. Black Engrs.-Alumni Ext. (Hero award 2000, Leadership award 2000), Nat. Black MBA Assn., Inc., Alpha Kappa Alpha (SA Region Outstanding Undergraduate 1996). Baptist. Achievements include being 1st African American female to earn Bachelor of Computer Engineering degree from Georgia Tech. Avocations: tennis, arts and crafts. Personal E-mail: tamecia_jordan@yahoo.com.

JORDAN, THERESA JOAN, psychologist, educator; b. Irvington, N.J., Sept. 17, 1949; d. Ernest Anthony and Helen Joan (Debski) Balazs; 1 child, Theresa-Helena. BA, NYU, 1971, MA, 1972, PhD, 1979. Lic. psychologist, N.Y., N.J.; diplomate Am. Bd. Forensic Medicine, Am. Bd. Forensic Examiners, Am. Bd. Forensic Psychologists. Grad. fellow Nat. Inst. Occupational Safety and Health, N.Y.C., 1971-74; rsch. asst., rsch. coord. Project City Sci. NYU, 1974-79, assoc. dir. for rsch. Ctr. for Devel. Studies, 1979-82; asst. prof. medicine N.J. Med. Sch., Newark, 1982-92; assoc. prof. applied psychology NYU, 1992—. Dir. Ctr. for Med. Info. N.J. Med. Sch., Newark, 1989—; cons. Ctrs. for Disease Control, Atlanta, 1990; spkr. Am. Lung Assn., N.Y., 1990-96, Am. Thoracic Soc., N.Y., 1998-99; spkr. Asia-Pacific Congress on Lung Diseases, Bangkok, Thailand, Bali, Indonesia. Author: Overcoming the Fear of Riding, 1996, Understanding Medical Information, 1999; contbr. articles to profl. jours. Mem. U.S. Icelandic Demonstration Team. Mem. APA, Assn. for the Advancement Ednl. Rsch. (pres.-elect 1998—), Soc. for Med. Decision-Making, Eastern Ednl. Rsch. Assn. (2d v.p. 1985-87), Mem. Internat. Union Against Tuberculosis & Lung Disease. Avocation: rider and trainer of icelandic horses. Office: NYU Dept Applied Psychology 239 Greene St New York NY 10003-6674

JORDEN, ELEANOR HARZ, linguist, educator; b. N.Y.C. d. William George and Eleanor (Funk) Harz; m. William J. Jorden, Mar. 3, 1944 (div.); children: William Temple, Eleanor Harz, Marion Telva. AB, Bryn Mawr Coll., 1942; MA, Yale U., 1943, PhD, 1950; D.Litt. (hon.), Williams Coll., 1982; D.H.L. (hon.), Knox Coll., 1985; D. Langs. (hon.), Middlebury Coll., 1991; D. Univ. (hon.), U. Stirling, Scotland, 1993. Instr. Japanese Yale U., 1943-46, 47-48; dir. Japanese lang. program and Fgn. Service Inst. Lang. Sch., Am. Embassy, Tokyo, 1950-55; sci. linguist Fgn. Service Inst., Dept. State, Washington, 1959-69; acting head Far East langs., 1961-64; chmn., 1964-67, 69; chmn. Vietnamese lang. div., 1967-69; vis. prof. linguistics Cornell U., 1969-70, prof., 1970-87, Mary Donlon Alger prof. linguistics, 1974-87, prof. emeritus, 1987—. Bernhard disting. vis. prof. Williams Coll., 1985—86, vis. prof., 1986—87, adj. prof., 1987—92; dir. Japanese FALCON program, 1972—87; Univ. prof., Disting. fellow Nat. Fgn. Lang. Ctr. Sch. Advanced Internat. Studies Johns Hopkins U., 1987—91; acad. dir. Exchange: Japan's Tchr. Tng. Inst., 1988—; sr. cons. prep. framework Japanese lang. curriculum and Japanese coll. bd. exam, 1991—93; sr. cons. Japanese multi-media project U. Md., 1995—97, cons. Part 2, Ohio State U., 2002—03; dir. SPENG Program, 1980—; co-dir. Survey on Japanese Lang. Study, 1988—92; guest scholar Wilson Ctr. Smithsonian Instn., 1982; cons., permanent disting. dir. Nat. Assn. Self-Instrnl. Lang. Programs, pres., 1977—78, 1984—85; mem. Fulbright-Hays Com. on Internat. Exch. Scholars, 1972—75; mem. area adv. com. for East Asia, 1972—76; chmn. Social Sci. Rsch. Coun. Task Force on Japanese Lang. Tng., 1976—78; mem. adv. com. Japan Found., 1979—81; mem. Lang. Attrition Project, 1981—87; advisor Ctr. for Japanese Studies, Stirling U., Scotland, 1988—92; mem. Yale U. Coun. Com. Langs. and Lit., 1990—98. Author: (with Bernard Bloch) Spoken Japanese, 1945, Syntax of Modern Colloquial Japanese, 1955, Gateway to Russian, 1961, Beginning Japanese, Part 1, 1962, Part 2, 1963, (with Sheehan, Quang and others) Basic Vietnamese, vols. I, II, 1965, (with Quang) Vietnamese Familiarization Course, 1969, (with Hamako Chaplin) Reading Japanese, 1976, (with Mari Noda) Japanese: The Spoken Language, part 1, 1987, part 2, 1988, part 3, 1990, (with Richard Lambert) Japanese Language Instruction in the U.S.: Resources, Practice and Investment Strategic, 1992. Decorated Order of Precious [illegible] Emperor of Japan, 1995, [illegible] Superior Svc. award Dept. State, 1965, Japan Found. and Social Sci. Rsch. Coun. sr. fellow, 1976, Toyota award Twentieth Anniversary Fund grantee, 1978; Japan Found. award, 1985, Papalia award for Excellence Tchr. Tng., 1993, N.E. Conf. award Disting. Svc. and Leadership in Profession, 1994; honoree Eleanor Harz Jorden Festival, Portland State U., 1995. Mem. Assn. Asian Studies (v.p. 1979-80, pres. 1980-81), Linguistic Soc. Am., Am. Coun. Tchrs. Fgn. Langs., Nat. Assn. Self-Instrnl. Lang. Programs (pres. 1978, 85, permanent disting. dir. 1991—), Assn. Tchrs. Japanese (exec. com., pres. 1978-84), Japan Soc. N.Y. (bd. dirs. 1982-88), Exchange: Japan (bd. dirs., v.p., sec. 1998—). Office: 3300 Darby Rd Apt 1302 Haverford PA 19041-1067 Fax: 610-658-2563. Office Phone: 610-649-2409. E-mail: ejorden@brynmawr.edu.

JORDEN, YON YOON, health services company executive; B in Acctg., Calif. State U. V.p., controller FHP Internat. Corp.; sr. v.p., CFO, WellPoint Health Networks, Inc., Blue Cross Calif., Aera Energy LLC; exec. v.p., CFO Oxford Health Plans Inc., Norwalk, Conn., 1998—. Office: AdvancePCS 750 W John Carpenter Fwy, Ste 1200 Irving TX 75039

JORGENSEN, JUDITH ANN, psychiatrist, educator; b. Parris Island, S.C. d. George Emil and Margaret Georgia Jorgensen; m. Ronald Francis Crown, July 11, 1970 (dec. Oct. 1996). BA, Stanford U., 1963; MD, U. Calif., 1968. Intern Meml. Hosp., Long Beach, Calif., 1969-70; resident County Mental Health Svcs., San Diego, 1970-73; staff psychiatrist Children and Adolescent Svcs., San Diego, 1973-78; practice medicine specializing in psychiatry La Jolla, Calif., 1973—. Staff psychiatrist County Mental Health Svcs. San Diego, 1973—78, San Diego State U. Health Svcs., 1985—87; psychiat. cons. San Diego City Coll., 1973—78, 1985—86; asst. prof. dept. psychiatry U. Calif., 1978—91, assoc. prof., 1991—96; chmn. med. quality rev. com. Dist. XIV, State of Calif., 1982—83. Fellow: Am. Psychiat. Assn.; mem.: Sex Therapy and Edn., Soc. Sci. Study of Sex, San Diego Soc. Adolescent Psychiatry (pres. 1981—82), Am. Soc. Adolescent Psychiatry, San Diego Psychiat. Soc. (chmn. membership com. 1976—78, v.p. 1978—80, fed. legis. rep. 1985—87, fellowship com. 1989—), Rowing Club. Office: 470 Nautilus St Ste 211 La Jolla CA 92037-5981 Fax: (858) 551-0964. Office Phone: 858-459-1140.

JORGENSEN, VIRGINIA DYER, antique dealer, museum consultant; b. Arlington, Va., Sept. 18, 1955; d. Gordon Wade and Maureen Glesner Dyer; m. Bruce Kenneth Hopkins, Feb. 21, 1987 (div. Jan. 1992); children: Lauren Gardner, Brett Gardner, Lacy Marie Hopkins, Dustin Kenneth Hopkins; m. William Dennis Jorgensen, Sept. 30, 1994. AA, Kellogg C.C., Battle Creek, Mich., 1977; BA magna cum laude, We. Mich. U., 1998. Pub. rels., tour guide Kellogg Co., Battle Creek, 1975—80; supply publs. writer U.S. Dept. Def., Battle Creek, 1984—88; sales team leader I.I. Stanley Automotive Lighting, Battle Creek, 1990—94; devel. coord. Mich. Maritime Mus., South Haven, 1998; antique dealer Crossroads Antique Mall, Seymour, Ind., 2000—, Exit 76 Antique Mall, Columbus, Ind., 2000—03. Trustee Kentwood (Mich.) Pub. Sch. Edn. Found., 1997—99; bd. mem. Preservation Action Alliance, Battle Creek, 1994—96; mem. design consulting bd. Housing Partnership Inc., Columbus, Ind., 2000. Recipient Edith Mange award for disting. scholarship, Western Mich.U., 1998. Mem.: Colonial Williamsburg Found., Nat. Trust for Historic Preservation, Golden Key Nat. Honor Soc., Phi Alpha Theta. Presbyterian. Avocations: breeding pugs, buying and restoring old buildings. Home and Office: 1069 Redwing Dr Columbus IN 47203 Office Phone: 812-350-0171. E-mail: wdandvl@rnetinc.net.

JORGENSON, MARY ANN, lawyer; b. Gallipolis, Ohio, 1941; BA, Agnes Scott Coll., 1963; MA, Harvard U., 1964; JD, Case Western Res. U., 1975. Bar: Ohio 1975, N.Y. 1982. Ptnr., chair firm's corp. practice Squire, Sanders & Dempsey, 1990—. Office: Squire Sanders & Dempsey LLP 127 Public Sq Ste 4900 Cleveland OH 44114-1284 E-mail: mjorgenson@ssd.com.

JORSTAD, TAMARA J. information technology manager; d. Leslie Lee Parrott and Nancy Lee Olski; m. Van B. Jorstad. BA in Mgmt., Nat.-Louis U., Wheaton, Ill., 1993; MS in Mgmt., Nat.-Louis U., McLean, Va., 1996. Info. tech. network mgr. Digital Equipment Corp., Colorado Springs, Colo., 1981—90, ctrl. states program mgr. Chgo., 1990—93; info. tech. network cons. and account mgr. Fannie Mae, Washington, 1993—95, cmty. rels. mgr., 1996—96; br. chief, info. tech. strategic planning Exec. Office of the Pres., Office of Adminstrn., Washington, 2000—01; dir. of info. tech. Am. Institutes for Rsch., Washington, 2001—. Chairperson, charity & devel. Internat. Women's Club of Moscow, Moscow, Russia, 1998—2000. Independent. Office: Am Insts Rsch 1000 Thomas Jefferson St NW Washington DC 20007 E-mail: tjorstad@air.org.

JOSEFF, JOAN CASTLE, manufacturing executive; b. Alta., Can., Aug. 12, 1922; naturalized U.S. citizen, 1945; d. Edgar W. and Lottie (Coates) Castle; BA in Psychology, UCLA; widowed; 1 son, Jeffrey Rene. With Joseff-Hollywood, jewelry manufacture and rental and aircraft components and missiles, Burbank, Calif., 1939—, chmn. bd., pres., sec.-treas. Numerous TV appearances including CBS This Morning, Australia This Morning, Am. Movie Channel. Mem. Burbank Salary Task Force, 1979—, L.A. County Earthquake Fact-Finding Commn., 1981— ; bd. dirs. San Fernando Valley area chpt. Am. Cancer Soc., treas., Genesis Energy Systems, Inc., 1993—; mem. Rep. Cen. Com.; del. Rep. Nat. Conv., 1980, 84, 88, 92, 96, 2000; voting mem. Calif. Rep. Party; chmn. Women Legis.; active Beautiful People Award Com. Honoring John Wayne Cancer Clinic; appointed by Gov. Wilson to Barber and Cosmotology Bd; appointed br Pres. Clinton to Selective Svc. System. Recipient Women in Achievement award Soroptomist Internat., 1988. Mem. Women of Motion Picture Industry (hon. life), Nat. Fedn. Rep. Women (bd. dir., Caring for Am. award 1986), Calif. Rep. Women (bd. dir., treas. 1986-90), North Hollywood Rep. Women (pres. 1981-82, parliamentarian), Nat. Fedn. of Rep (voting mem., program chair, 1994—, bylaws chair 1998—), Calif. Fedn. of Rep. Women (chaplain, Americanism chmn. so. div., regent chmn. Women of Achievement award 1988), L.A. County Fedn. of Rep. Women (scholarship chmn.). Home: 10060 Toluca Lake Ave Toluca Lake CA 91602-2924 Office: 129 E Providencia Ave Burbank CA 91502-1922

JOSELL, JESSICA (JESSICA WECHSLER), public relations executive; b. Balt., June 17, 1943; d. Maury J. and Rose E. (Lodin) Snyder; m. Neil B. Josell, Apr. 30, 1965 (dec. Nov. 1967); m. Steven James Wechsler, Jan. 12, 1980. BA, U. Fla., 1965. V.p., gen. mgr. Morton Dennis Wax & Assocs., N.Y.C., 1976-81; v.p. The Raleigh Group, Ltd., N.Y.C., 1981-87; pres. Josell Communications, Inc., N.Y.C., 1981—. Exec. officer, bd. dirs. The Bridge, Inc., N.Y.C. Mem.: N.Y. Women in Film and TV. Home and Office: Josell Communications Inc 185 W End Ave Ste 22C New York NY 10023-5549

JOSEPH, EDITH HOFFMAN, retired editor; b. Syracuse, N.Y., Jan. 4, 1928; d. Max and Ida (Hodis) Finkelstein; m. Irving Hoffman, Sept. 4, 1949 (dec. Dec. 1965); children: Kenneth R., Maxine E. Neuhauser; m. William Jacob Joseph, May 19, 1968; stepchildren: David E., Harlan L., Saul J., Gail C. (dec. Nov. 1999). BS in Journalism/Bus. Adminstrn., Rider Coll., 1949. Copywriter advt. Swern's-Lit Bros., Trenton, N.J., 1949-51; pub. info. asst. N.J. Div. Pensions, Trenton, 1967-69; pub. rels. asst. N.J. Dept. Labor & Industry, Trenton, 1969-70; mng. editor newsletter N.J. Dept. Environ. Protection, Trenton, 1971-74; environ. news editor N.J. Dept. Environ. Protection-N.J. Outdoors Mag., 1974-84; editor newsletter N.J. Dept. Environ. Protection-Environ. News, 1985-90; editor environ. news sect. N.J. Dept. Environ. Protection N.J. Outdoors Mag., 1991. Contbr. articles to profl. jours. Avocations: travel, reading, walking, [illegible] Home: 1 Highgate Dr Apt 113 Trenton NJ 08618-2001

JOSEPH, ELEANOR ANN, health science association administrator, consultant; b. Cleve., Mar. 6, 1944; d. Emil and Eleanor (Leelais) Dienes; m. Abraham Albert Joseph, Oct. 28, 1984. BS in Math. cum laude, Cleve. State U., 1978, MPA in Health Care Adminstrn., 1991. Cert. profl. healthcare quality, coding specialist, accredited records technician, registered record adminstr., health info. adminstr., cert. in healthcare privacy. Asst. dir. med. records Suburban Hosp., Warrensville Heights, Ohio, 1963-77; coder Shaker Med. Ctr., Shaker Heights, Ohio, 1965, Huron Rd. Hosp., Cleve., 1965; instr. Cuyahoga C.C., Cleve., 1970-72; dir. med. records Hillcrest Hosp., Mayfield Heights, Ohio, 1977-84; med. records technician Vis. Nurse Assn., Cleve., 1985; coord. med. record svcs. Ctr. for Health Affairs Greater Cleve. Hosp. Assn., 1985-88, dir. coding svcs. Ctr. Health Affairs, 1988-89, dir. health record svcs. Ctr. Health Affairs, 1989-98; v.p. health info. mgmt. svcs. Greater Cleve. Healthcare Assn., 1999—2004, privacy officer Ctr. Health Affairs, 2001—, v.p. revenue cycle mgmt. Ctr. Health Affairs, 2004—. Coding instr. cmty. edn. dept. Cleve. State U., 1998—; instr. cmty. edn. Lakeland CC, mem. adv. task force cert. program med. office mgmt., 1992—96, coding tchr., 1999; spkrs. bur. Hillcrest Hosp., Mayfield Heights, 1978—84; adv. com. Cuyahoga CC, 1973—80, 1994—, faculty, 1999—2003; coord. seminars in field; cons. in field. Co-author: (manual) Quality Assurance Program for Medical Records Deparment, 1981, Dollars and Sense: A Reference Guide to Coding and Prospective Payment System Reimbursement Issues, 1988; co-editor: Care and Management of Health Care Records, 1988, 1992. Active Holden Arboretum, Kirtland, Ohio, 1975—, Ohio Hist. Soc., Columbus, 1975—. Recipient Outstanding Svc. award, Ctr. Health Affairs/Greater Cleve. Healthcare Assn., 1997. Mem.: N.E. Ohio Health Info. Mgmt. Assn. (chmn. coding roundtable 1993—), Ohio Health Info. Mgmt. Assn. (project leader alliances 1992—94, data quality reimbursement coun. 1992—, liaison to ambulatory sect. 1994—96, project leader developing coding seminars 1996—97, co-chmn. data quality and reimbursement coun. 1996—98, pres.-elect 1998—99, pres. 1999—2000, dir. and del. coord. 2000—01, del. to Am. Health Info. Mgmt. Assn. 2002—03, Disting. Mem. award 1997, Profl. Achievement award 2003), Ohio Assn. Healthcare Quality, Ohio Med. Record Assn. (alt. del. 1982, med. record coun. 1985—92, del. for state assn. mem. at nat. ann. mtg. 1989, legis. com. 1989—90, del. for state assn. mem. at nat. ann. mtg. 1990), N.E. Ohio Med. Record Assn. (treas. 1979, v.p. 1980, pres. 1982—83, counselor 1983, ednl. com. 1984, chmn. nominating com, 1986, ednl. com. 1987, cons. com. 1987—91, audit com., membership com., bylaws com., pub. rels. com.), East Ohio Med. Record Assn., Nat. Assn. Healthcare Quality, Am. Guild Patient Accts. Mgrs., Am. Health Info. Mgmt. Assn. (quality assurance and long term care sects., ambulatory records sec. 1992—2001, del. 1997—2000, item writing panel for cert. coding exams 1997—2003, accredited record tech. practitioner 2000—02, co-chmn. coun. cert. 2001, chair coun. on cert. 2002, nominating com. 2002—03), Am. Med. Record Assn. (cons. roster 1976, charter mem. assembly on edn. 1989), Am. Acad. Profl. Coders (treas. local chpt. 1994, endorsed as tchr. for profl. med. coder curriculum, cert.), Holden Arboretum, Northeastern Ohio Assn. for Healthcare Quality, Cleve. City Club. Lutheran. Avocations: cultural events, nature walks, golf, music. Office: Greater Cleve Healthcare Assn Ctr for Health Affairs 1226 Huron Rd E Cleveland OH 44115-1702 E-mail: eleanor.joseph@chanet.org.

JOSEPH, ELLEN R. lawyer; BA, Barnard Coll., 1960; JD, Columbia U., 1976. Bar: N.Y. 1977. Ptnr. Kaye Scholer LLP, N.Y.C. Mem. ABA (mem. real property law sect.), N.Y. State Bar Assn. (mem. real property law sect.), Assn. Bar City N.Y., Phi Beta Kappa. Stone Scholar. Office: Kaye Scholer LLP 425 Park Ave New York NY 10022-3506

JOSEPH, GERI MACK (GERALDINE JOSEPH), former ambassador, educator, journalist; b. St. Paul, June 19, 1923; BS, U. Minn., 1946; LLD, Bates Coll., 1982; DHL (hon.), Macalester Coll., 1997; LLD, Carleton Coll., 1998; DHL (hon.). Staff writer Mpls. Tribune, 1946-53, contbg. editor, 1972-78; amb. to The Netherlands, Am. Embassy, The Hague, 1978-81; sr. fellow internat. programs U. Minn. Hubert H. Humphrey Inst. Pub. Affairs, Mpls., 1984-94, chmn. adv. bd., 1997—; dir. Mondale Policy Forum, 1990-94. Bd. dirs. Nat. Dem. Inst. for Internat. Affairs, George A. Hormel Co.; mem. U.S. President's Commn. on Mental Health, Minn. Supreme Ct. Commn. on Mentally Disabled and the Cts., mem. Coun. on Fgn. Rels., 1985—; mem. com. on Mid. East, Brookings Instn., 1987. Vice chmn. Gov.'s Commn. on Taxation, 1983-84; trustee Carleton Coll., 1975-94; mem. Democratic Nat. Com., 1960-72, vice chmn., 1968-72; pres. Nat. Mental Health Assn., 1970-72, co-chairperson Minn. Women's Campaign Fund, 1982-84; co-chmn. Atty. Gen.'s Com. on Child Abuse within the Family, 1986. Democrat. E-mail: gerimj@cs.com.

JOSEPH, MARILYN SUSAN, gynecologist; b. Aug. 18, 1946; BA, Smith Coll., 1968; MD cum laude, SUNY Downstate Med. Ctr., Bklyn., 1972. Diplomate Am. Bd. Ob-Gyn, Nat. Bd. Med. Examiners. Intern U. Minn. Hosps., 1972-73, resident in ob-gyn, 1972-76; med. fellow specialist U. Minn., 1972-76, asst. prof. ob-gyn, 1976—, dir. women's clinic, 1984—. Med. dir. Boynton Health Svc., 1993—. Author: Differential Diagnosis Obstetrics, 1978. Fellow Am. Coll. Ob-Gyn (best paper dist. VI meeting 1981); mem. Hennepin County Med. Soc., Minn. State Med. Assn., Mpls. Coun. Ob-Gyn, Minn. State Ob-Gyn Soc. Avocations: cooking, bird watching, travel. Office: Boynton Health Svc 410 Church St SE Minneapolis MN 55455-0346

JOSEPH, ROSALINE RESNICK, hematologist and oncologist; b. N.Y.C., Aug. 21, 1929; d. Joseph and Malca (Rosenbeg) Resnick; m. Robert J. Joseph, Jan. 2, 1954; children: Joy S., Nina B. AB, Cornell U., 1949; MD, Women's Med. Coll. Pa., Phila., 1953; MS, Temple U., 1958. Intern Kings County Hosp., Bklyn., 1953-54; resident Phila. Gen. Hosp., 1954-55, Temple U. Hosp., 1955-57; instr. dept. medicine Temple U. Med. Ctr., Phila., 1957-60, assoc. in medicine, 1960-63, asst. prof. medicine, 1963-69, assoc. prof. medicine, 1969-77; course co-coordinator Sys. Oncology Interdisciplinary Course, 1968-73; prof. medicine, dir. Med. Coll. Pa., Phila., 1977, prof. emeritus, 1999, course coordinator, 1978, prof. emeritus, 1999. Pres. med. staff Med. Coll. Pa., 1990-91. Contbr. articles to profl. jours. Del. dir. Am. Cancer Soc., 1989—. Recipient Lindback award for disting. teaching, Christian & Mary Lindback Found., 1982, Am. Cancer Soc. Div. Disting. Svc. award, 1987. Fellow ACP; mem. Am. Soc. Hematology, Am. Soc. Clin. Oncology, Alumni Assn. Med. Coll. Pa. (pres. 1988-90). Office: Med Coll Pa Hosp 3300 Henry Ave Philadelphia PA 19129-1191

JOSEPH, SHIRLEY TROYAN, retired executive; b. Buffalo, N.Y., Dec. 13, 1925; d. Louis and Betty (Eisman) Troyan; m. Norman Clifford Joseph, Oct. 20, 1946; children: Todd Michael, Marc Dana, Jonathan L. BA in Polit. Sci., U. Mich., 1947; postgrad., Vanderbilt U., 1973. Instr. SUNY, Buffalo, 1977; area rep. Am. Jewish Com., Buffalo, 1980-82; pub. policy coord. Jewish Fedn., Buffalo, 1984-87; first exec. dir. Erie County Commn. on Status of Women, 1988-92, ex-officio mem., 1997—. Accredited non-govtl. rep. UN World Confs. on Women, Copenhagen, Nairobi, Beijing, 1980, 85, 95; mem. Hilary Clinton's Beijing Conf. Circle; co-chair status of women Internat. Coun. Jewish Women, 1999-2002; mem. steering com. Food for All, Buffalo Area Met. ministries, 1984-88; cmty. adv. bd. Sch. Health Demonstration Project, Buffalo, 1989-92; cmty. advisor Jr. League, Buffalo, 1989-99; founding pres. Women's Taking Action in Politics Fund, Western N.Y. State, 1992—; chair 10 Year Status of Women in Erie County Update.

Vice chair U.S. Nat. Commn. for UNESCO, 1973-77, Nat. Jewish Cmty. Rels. Adv. Coun., 1989-93; v.p. Jewish Fedn. Greater Buffalo, 1975-80; del. U.S. Nat. Women's Conf., Houston, 1977; bd. Erie County Mental Health Svcs.-Corp. 2, 1979-80; pres. Jewish Fedn. Housing, Buffalo, 1980-82. Recipient Women Helping Women award, Buffalo and Erie County chpt. NOW, 1992, award of excellence, Everywoman Opportunity Ctr., 2003. Mem. Nat. Coun. Jewish Women (nat. v.p. 1975-83, hon. nat. v.p. 1985—, Buffalo sect. Hannah Solomon Woman of Yr. award 1978), Nat. Women's Conf. Com. (various chairs 1979—, sec. 1997-98). Democrat.

JOSEPH, WENDY EVANS, architect; B in Design of Environ. (summa cum laude), U. Pa., 1977; MArch (with hons.), Harvard U., 1981. With Archl. Resources Cambridge, Inc., Boston, 1978, Pei Cobb Freed, 1985—93; pvt. practice NYC, 1994—. Mem. archl. team US Holocaust Meml. Mus., Washington. Chair alumni coun. Harvard U. Recipient Rome prize, 1983. Mem.: Archl. League (v.p. architecture), AIA (chair nat. com. design). Office: 500 Park Ave New York NY 10022

JOSEPHER, SUSAN ANN, art educator, consultant; b. N.Y.C., Feb. 20, 1940; d. Harry David and Frances Deborah Behrman; m. Herbert Josepher, June 19, 1960 (div. 1976). BA, Bklyn. Coll., 1961; MA, U. Colo., 1975, PhD, 1986. Elem. tchr. N.Y.C. Pub. Schs., 1961—64; bus. mgr. Colo. Philharm., Evergreen, 1975—77; devel. dir. Colo. State Ballet, Denver, 1977—79; prof., chair Art Dept. Met. State Coll. of Denver, 1980—2000, prof. emeritus art, 2001—; cons. arts edn. Santa Monica, Calif., 2001—. Chair Stds. Devel. Task Force Colo. Dept. Edn., Denver, 1994—97; cons. for documenting exemplar CalArts Theater Program, Valencia, Calif., 2001; cons. for arts assessment L.A. Unified Sch. Dist., 2001—02; dir. summer arts inst. Met. State Coll. of Denver, 1982—86; dir. Coll. to Cmty. Visual Arts Outreach Program Strasburg Schs., Colo., 1998. (Curator) Mizel Mus. Judaica Exhbn., Denver, Colo., 2000; actor: (films) Regnital. Chair Denver Pub. Schs. Arts Resource Coun., 1991—93; chair edn. com. Mizel Mus., Denver, 1995—99; pres. Colo. Art Edn. Assn., 1989—94; docent prorgram coord. Skirball Cult. Ctr., L.A. Named Higher Edn. Art Educator of Yr., Colo. Art Edn. Assn., 1989, Colo. Art Educator of Yr., 1994. Mem.: Calif. Arts Assessment Network, Nat. Art Edn. Assn. Office: 1122 18th St #108 Santa Monica CA 90403 Personal E-mail: sajosepher@earthlink.net.

JOSEPHIAN, JENNY ADELE, acupuncturist, artist; b. Berkeley, Calif., Mar. 5, 1959; d. Roger Eslie Josephian and Carolyn Marie Wrasse. BA, Antioch U. West, San Francisco, 1986; diploma of competence, Traditional Acupuncture Inst., Columbia, Md., 1988, M Acupuncture, 1990. Lic. acupuncturist, Calif. Mem. office staff, acupressure practitioner Acupressure Inst., Berkeley, 1981-85; pvt. practice acupressure, Berkeley, 1981-88; pvt. practice acupuncture, 1988—. Exhibited works in show at Nexus Gallery, Berkeley, Calif., 2000. Avocations: travel, gardening, dance, writing. Office: 1502 Walnut St Ste A Berkeley CA 94709-1563

JOSEPHS, BABETTE, legislator; b. N.Y.C., Aug. 4, 1940; d. Eugene and Myra A. Josephs; children: Lee Aaron Newberg, Elizabeth Master. BA, Queens Coll., 1962; JD, Rutgers U., 1976. Sole practice, Phila., 1976-78; exec. dir. Nat. Abortion Rights Action League of Pa., Phila., 1978-80, Citizens Coalition for Energy Efficiency, Phila., 1980-81; pvt. practice cons., fundraiser Phila., 1981-84; mem. Pa. Ho. of Reps., Phila., 1984—. Bd. dirs. ACLU. Mem. Phila. Bar Assn. Democrat. Jewish. Office: 1528 Walnut St Philadelphia PA 19102-3004

JOSEPHSON, DIANA HAYWARD, not-for-profit company executive; b. London, Oct. 17, 1936; came to U.S., 1959; d. Robert Hayward and Barbara Bailey. BA with honors, Oxford U., Eng., 1958, MA, 1962; M in Comparative Law, George Washington U., 1962. Bar: Eng. and Wales 1959, D.C. 1963. Assoc. Covington & Burling, Washington, 1959-68; asst. dir. Office of the Mayor, Washington, 1968-74; exec. dir. Nat. Capital Area ACLU, Washington, 1975-78; dep. asst. adminstr. policy and planning, satellites NOAA, U.S. Dept. Commerce, Washington, 1978-82; pres. Am. Sci. and Tech. Corp., Bethesda, Md., 1982-83, Space Am., Bethesda, Md., 1983-85; v.p. mktg. Arianespace, Inc., Washington, 1985-87; v.p. Martin Marietta Comml. Titan Inc., Washington, 1987-89; dir. bus. devel. Martin Marietta Advanced Launch Systems, Denver, 1989-90, Martin Marietta Civil Space and Communications Co., Denver, 1990-93; dep. under sec. commerce oceans and atmosphere, NOAA U.S. Dept. Commerce, Washington, 1993-97; prin. dep. asst. sec. for installations and environ. Dept. Navy, Washington, 1997-2000; sr. v.p. Environ. Def., N.Y.C., 2000—. Mem. adv. coun. Nat. Ctr. for Atmospheric Rsch., 2003—; mem. Space Applications Bd., NRC, 1988-89, Comml. Space Transp. Adv. Commn., U.S. Dept. Transp., Washington, 1984-85; mem. adv. bd. Washington Space Bus. Roundtable, 1985-87. Mem. D.C. Law Revision Commn., Washington, 1975-78, D.C. Internat. Women's Yr. State Coordinating Com., 1977. Mem. Am. Astronautical Soc. (bd. dirs. 1985-88), Nat. Space Club (bd. govs.), Women in Aerospace, Washington Space Bus. Roundtable (adv. bd. 1985-87). Avocations: sailing, reading. Office: Environ Def 257 Park Ave S 17th Fl New York NY 10010

JOSEPHSON, NANCY, talent agent; d. Marvin J.; m. David Stern; 3 children. Grad., Brown U., 1980, Harvard Law Sch., 1982. Atty., 1982-86, Internat. Creative Mgmt., Beverly Hills, 1986, head N.Y. TV dept.; various positions as an agent, 1979-87; head TV lit. dept. Internat. Creative Mgmt., Beverly Hills, 1987-95, exec. v.p. of TV, 1995—, co-pres., 1998—. Developer (TV shows) Friends, Nash Bridges, Caroline in the City, The Simpsons. Named one of top twenty-five most important women in entertainment Hollywood's Reporter. Office: Internat Creative Mgmt 8942 Wilshire Blvd Ste 219 Beverly Hills CA 90211-1934

JOSHI, PRATIBHA C. immunologist, researcher; b. Bombay, Dec. 30, 1955; came to U.S., 1980; d. Shankar R. and Mrunalini S. Gokhale; m. Chandrashekhar V. Joshi, Mar. 23, 1980; children: Neil, Nina. BSc, Bombay U., 1976, MSc, 1978; PhD, Miss. State U., 1988. Postdoctoral fellow NIH, Jackson, 1989-90, 92-93; from rsch. assoc. to sr. rsch. assoc. U. Miss. Med. Ctr., Jackson, 1993-96, assoc. prof. surgery, rschr., 1996—. Contbr. articles to profl. jours. Mem. AAAS, Am. Assn. Immunologists, N.Y. Acad. Scis. Avocations: travel, reading, painting.

JOSLIN, JANINE ELIZABETH, preservation consultant; b. Kansas City, Mo., Mar. 16, 1948; d. James Bryce and Isabel Quezon (Carr) Traner; m. Jack Leslie Joslin, Dec. 4, 1971; children: Jaclyn, Aaron, Amanda. BA in History, U. Mo., Kansas City, 1971; MA in Heritage Presevation, Ga. State U., 1992. Pvt. practice cons., Rome, Ga., 1989—92; dir. Chieftains Mus., Rome, 1992—94; pres. Gaia Walkers Inc., Leawood, Kans., 1996—99; pvt. practice cons. Leawood, 1999—. Bd. mem. Women Vision Internat., Overland Park, Kans., 1996—; pres. bd. Donnelly Internat., Kansas City, Kans., 1997—98; team leader Sci. City Mus., Kansas City, Mo., 1998—99. Contbr. articles to mags. Commr. Leawood Hist. Commn., 1998—; bd. mem. Kans. Preservation Alliance, Topeka, 2001—. Grantee, IMS, 1994, Ga. Heritage 2000, 1995, Kans. Why 150, 1999. Avocations: rowing, hiking, rafting. Home: 12508 Catalina Leawood KS 66209

JOY, CARLA MARIE, history educator; b. Denver, Sept. 5, 1945; d. Carl P. and Theresa M. (Lotito) J. AB cum laude, Loretto Heights Coll., 1967; MA, U. Denver, 1969, postgrad., 1984-87. Instr. history Cmty. Coll., Denver; prof. history Red Rocks C.C., Lakewood, Colo., 1970—. Cons. for innovative ednl. programs; reviewer fed. grants, 1983-89; mem. adv. panel Colo. Endowment for Humanities, 1985-89. Contbr. articles to profl. publs. Instr. vocat. edn. Mile High United Way, Jefferson County, 1975; participant Jefferson County Sch. Sys. R-1 Dist., 1983-88; active Red Rocks C.C. Spkrs. Bur., 1972-89, strategic planning com., 1992-97; chair history discipline Colo. Gen. Edn. Core Transfer Consortium, 1986-96, faculty transfer curriculum coun., 1997—; mem. Colo. C.C. curriculum com., 1999—; mem. history, geography, civics stds. and geography frameworks adv. com. Colo. Dept. Edn., 1995-96; steering com. Ctr. Tchg. Excellence, 1991-92, 96-97; with North Ctrl. Self-Study Process, 1972-73, 80-81, 86-88, 96-98; with K-16 Linkages Colo. Commn. for Higher Edn., 1997-98; mem. evaluation team for Colo. Awards, edn. and civic achievement for Widefield Sch. Dist. #3, 1989; mem. Red Rocks C.C.-Clear Creek Sch. Sys. Articulation Team, 1990-91; mem. Statue of Liberty-Ellis Island Found. Inc., 1987—. Ford Found. fellow, 1969; recipient Cert. of Appreciation Kiwanis Club, 1981, Telecomm. Coop. for Colo.'s Cmty. Colls., 1990-92, Master Tchr. award U. Tex.-Austin, 1982. Mem. NEA, Am. Hist. Assn., Am. Assn. Higher Edn., Nat. Coun. Social Studies, Nat. Geog. Soc., Omohundro Inst. Early Am. History and Culture, Colo. Edn. Assn., Colo. Coun. Social Studies, World Hist. Assn., Orgn. Am. Historians, The Colo. Hist. Soc., Colo. Geog. Alliance, Soc. Hist. Edn., Phi Alpha Theta. Home: 1849 S Lee St Apt D Lakewood CO 80232-6252 Office: Red Rocks C C 13300 W 6th Ave Lakewood CO 80228-1213

JOYCE, ANNE RAINE, editor, director of publications; b. South Bend, Ind., Oct. 2, 1942; d. James Agee and Marjorie Elizabeth (Gilstrap) Raine; m. Glenn Russell Joyce, Aug. 19, 1962; 1 child, Adam Russell. AB, Cen. Meth. Coll., 1962; MA in French, U. Mo., 1966; MA in Linguistics, U. Iowa, 1979. Cert. tchr., Mo. Tchr. Centralia (Mo.) High Sch., 1962-64; instr. Coe Coll., Cedar Rapids, Iowa, 1978-79, Georgetown U., Washington, 1980-83; asst. editor Am.-Arab Affairs, Washington, 1983-84; editor, dir. publs. Mid. East Policy, Washington, 1984—; gen. sec. Mid. East Policy Coun., Washington, 1991—, v.p., 1993—. Mem. edn. com. Fairfax County (Va.) PTA Bd., 1986-88. U.S. Dept. Def. fellow, 1964-66; recipient Recognition award Am.-Arab Affairs Coun., 1988, Disting. Alumni award. Cen. Meth. Coll., 1990. Mem. Middle East Studies Assn., LWV (fin. chair Fairfax county chpt. 1981—). Home: 6916 Tulsa Ct Alexandria VA 22307-1730 Office: Middle East Policy Coun 1730 M St NW Ste 512 Washington DC 20036-4516

JOYCE, BERNITA ANNE, former federal government agency administrator; d. Albert A. and Margaret C. Joyce; m. Kenneth B. Lucas, Aug. 2, 1975. BA, Duchesne Coll.; MBA, U. Santa Clara, PhD, 1974. With Wolfe & Co. CPAs, Washington, 1971-72; fin. dir. Nat. Forest Products Assn., Washington, 1972-74; budget and fiscal officer ICC, Washington, 1974-77, Office Mgmt. and Budget, 1977-80; asst. dir. mgmt. svcs. Bur. Mines, Dept. Interior, 1980-85; asst. dir. Office Policy Analysis, Dept. Interior, 1985-96, asst. spl. trustee Am. Indians, 1996—99; asst. adminstr. S.J. Cmty. Georgetown U., 2000—. Author: Financial Viability of Private Elementary Schools. Mem. AICPA, Sr. Execs. Assn., Assn. Govt. Accts., Cosmos Club, Beta Gamma Sigma. Home: 6001 Bradley Blvd Bethesda MD 20817-3807

JOYCE, DIANA, psychologist, education educator; d. Donald Ray and Caroline Ann Joyce. PhD, U. Fla., Gainesville, FL, 2000. Cert. Nat. Sch. Psychologist NASP, 2001; Fla. Clin. Educator Dept. of Edn., Fla., 2002, lic. School Psychologist 2003, Psychologist 2004. Media ctr. coord. U. Fla., Tech. Transfer, Gainesville, Fla., 1995—99; outside examiner Psychol. Corp., Orlando, Fla., 2001 03; adj. instr. U. of Fla., Ednl. Psychology, Gainesville, Fla., 2002—02; sch. psychologist Hillsborough County Schools, Tampa, 2000—03; faculty U. Fla. Ednl. Psychology, Gainesville, Fla., 2003—. Mem.: NASP, NCSP, APA, Fla. Assn. of Sch. Psychologists Meth. Achievements include research in temperament-based learning style preferences of students with oppositional defiant disorder and conduct disorder in psychiatric hospital and adjudicated youth programs; in temperament differences between gifted and nongifted children; in sex differential in self-handicapping behaviors of male and female undergraduate students. Avocations: travel, hiking, camping, theater, art. E-mail: djoyce@coe.ufl.edu.

JOYCE, JANET S. psychologist; b. Dayton, Ohio, Mar. 9, 1957; d. Jerome S. and Jane R. Sallo; m. Matthew Clark Joyce, Oct. 27, 1991; children: Rachel Leah, Sarah Anne. BA in Am. Studies, U. Calif., Santa Cruz, 1988; MS in Clin. Psychology, Pacific Grad. Sch. Psychology, 1992, PhD in Clin. Psychology, 1994. Lic. psychologist, Calif., Colo. Early childhood educator U. Calif., Santa Cruz, 1984-87; asst. editor CTB-McGraw Hill Pub. Corp., Monterey, Calif., 1987-88; predoctoral intern Alcohol and Drug Treatment Ctr. Stanford (Calif.) U. Med. Ctr., 1992-93; rsch. health scientist VA Hosp., Palo Alto, 1994—; mental health cons. U.S. Dept. Labor Job Corps Ctr., San Jose, Calif., 1993-2000; pvt. practice Los Gatos, Calif., 1994-2000, Boulder, Colo., 2000—. Mem. APA, Calif. Psychol. Assn., Colo. Psychol. Assn., U. Calif. Alumni Assn. Office: 767 Pearl St Ste 220 Boulder CO 80302 E-mail: janetsjoyce@earthlink.net.

JOYCE, MARIE CALDWELL, medical, surgical, and mental health nurse; b. Buffalo, June 29, 1927; d. Vernon Gordon and Dorothy Fleming (Sullivan) Caldwell; m. Howard C. Joyce, June 10, 1950; children: Kathleen, Kristine, Kandice, Kendall. Diploma, U. Rochester, 1949; student, Loyola U., New Orleans, Our Lady of Holy Cross, William Carey Sch. Nursing. Cert. psychiat./mental health nurse. Nurse Dade Dental Hosp., Buffalo, 1963-65; staff nurse Our Lady of Victory Hosp., Lackawanna, N.Y., 1965-67, VA Med. Ctr., Buffalo, 1968-73; med.-surg. nurse Dept. Vets. Affairs, New Orleans, 1973-84, nurse in substance abuse treatment, 1985-95; ret. Mem. ANA, Nurses Orgn. Vets. Affairs (pres. New Orleans chpt. 1990-92), Am. Psychiat. Nurses Assn., Nat. Nurses Soc. on Addictions. Home: 3601 Behrman Pl Apt 222 New Orleans LA 70114

JOYCE, MARY ANN, principal; b. Bklyn., May 29, 1935; d. Alfred and Antoinette (Polito) Lo Sasso; m. Michael J. Joyce, Jr., Mar. 2, 1957 (dec. 1982); children: Michael, Debra Grammer, Patricia Sommers. BA in Elem. Edn., Social Scis., Mount St. Mary Coll., 1972; MS in Elem. Edn., Reading, SUNY, New Paltz, 1975, CAS in Ednl. Adminstrn., 1983. Cert. tchr. N-6, N.Y., reading tchr., K-12, N.Y., sch. dist. administr., N.Y., sch. administr./supr., N.Y. Tchr. grades 3 and 4 Temple Hill Sch., Newburgh, N.Y., 1972-74, tchr. reading, 1974-83, tchr. gifted and talented, 1976-83, asst. prin., 1983-85; prin. Horizons-on-the-Hudson Magnet Sch., Newburgh, 1985-98; exec. dir. curriculum and instrn. Newburgh Enlarged City Schs., 1998—. Tchr. summer sch. Newburgh (N.Y.) Free Acad., 1976-81; adj. prof. SUNY, New Paltz, 1989-91; nat. review panelist Blue Ribbon Sch. Competition, 1991, 92, FIRST family-sch. partnership program, 1992; speaker numerous confs., seminars. Recipient Elem. Sch. Recognition award U.S. Dept. Edn., 1989-90, 93-94, Excellence in Adminstrn. award Mid-Hudson Sch. Study Coun., 1993, award for Outstanding Leadership, Achievements and Contributions Toward Making the Edn. of our Nation's Youth a Safe and Productive Experience, 1991. Mem. ASCD, Am. Assn. Female Execs., Nat. Assn. Elem. Sch. Prins. (Excellence in Edn. award 1990, 94), State Adminstrs. Assn. N.Y. State (Elem. Schs. Excellence award 1990, 94), Newburgh Suprs. and Adminstrs. Assn., United Univ. Profs., Delta Kappa Gamma. Avocations: reading, sewing, needlework. Office: Newburgh Enlarged City Schs 124 Grand St Newburgh NY 12550-4615

JOYCE, MARY HOLT, retired social worker; b. Denver, July 10, 1915; d. Robert Vail and Mary Sayre (Stearns) Barkalow; m. Marmaduka Burrell Holt, Jr., Oct. 3, 1942 (wid. Oct. 1976); children: John S., Peter B., Katherine B.; stepchildren: Marmaduke B. III, Robert W., Alan M.; m. Robert Henry Joyce, May 1, 1981 (wid. Jan. 1985); 1 stepchild, Nancy J. Woodward. BA, Colo. Coll., 1938; Grad., U. Denver, 1941. Social worker Big Sister Agy., Denver, 1939-40; probation officer Denver Juv. Ct., 1940-42. Bd. dirs. Florence Crittendom Home, Denver, 1945-48; bd. trustees Graland Country Day Sch. 1940; pres. Women Vestry, St. John's Cathedral/Episcopal, 1960-61, founder Referral Svc. for Srs., 1987, cochair search com. for dean, 1990-91. Mem. Colonial Dames, Monday Literary Club, Denver Art Mus., Colo. Symphony, Univ. Club. Episcopalian. Avocations: reading, music, travel, family. Home: Emerson St Apt 325 111 Park Ave W Denver CO 80205-3209

JOYCE, PHYLLIS NORMA, educational administrator; b. Bronx, N.Y., June 8, 1955; d. Philip Emmanuel and Dolores (Pizzolanella) Malizio; m. Thomas Patrick Joyce, June 11, 1983; 1 child, Diana. BA, CUNY, 1978; MA, Nova U., 1995. Tchr. St. Raymond's Sch., Bronx, 1980-83; tchr., head English dept. St. Anne Sch., Las Vegas, Nev., 1983-94, prin., 1994—, coord. jr. high Sch., 1988-94. Spl. Olympics vol. KC, Las Vegas, 1983-90; vol. Sons of Erin, Las Vegas, 1990—; pastoral coun. St. Anne Parish, 1996—. Democrat. Roman Catholic. Avocations: tennis, working out, family recreational activities. Office: St Anne Sch 1813 S Maryland Pky Las Vegas NV 89104-3104

JOYCE, ROSEMARY ALEXANDRIA, anthropology educator; b. Lackawanna, N.Y., Apr. 7, 1956; d. Thomas Robert and Joanne Hannah (Poth) J.; m. Russell Nicholas Sheptak, Jan. 7, 1984. BA, Cornell U., 1978; PhD, U. Ill., 1985. Instr. Jackson (Mich.) Community Coll., 1983; lectr. U. Ill., Urbana, 1984-85; asst. curator Peabody Mus., Harvard U., Cambridge, Mass., 1985-86, asst. dir., 1986-89; asst. prof. anthropology Harvard U., Cambridge, Mass., 1989-91, assoc. prof. anthropology, 1991-94, U. Calif., Berkeley, 1994—2001, prof., 2001—. Author: Cerro Palenque, 1991, Encounters with the Americas, 1995, Gender and Power in Prehispanic Mesoamerica, 2001, The Languages of Archeology, 2002, Embodied Lives, 2003; editor: Maya History, 1993, Women in Prehistory, 1997, Social Patterns in Preclassic Mesoamerica, 1999, Beyond Kinship, 2000, Mesoamerican Archeology, 2003; contbr. articles to profl. jours. NEH grantee, 1985, 86, NSF grantee, 1989, 98, 2001, Famsi grantee, 1996, Heinz Found., Wenner-Gren Found. grantee, 1997; Fulbright fellow, 1981-82. Mem. Soc. for Am. Archaeology, Am. Anthropol. Assn. Office: U Calif Anthropology Dept 232 Kroeber Hall # 3710 Berkeley CA 94720-3710 E-mail: rajoyce@berkeley.edu.

JOYNER, ELIZABETH, curator; m. Raymond Joyner; 1 child, Travis Ray. BA in Comms., Miss. State U., 1982. Seasonal employee Nat. Park Svc., Vicksburg, Miss., 1980-82, in charge of info. desk main vis. ctr., Cairo Mus., 1982-90, curator, supr. Cairo site, 1990—. Mem. S.E. Registrar's Assn. Office: Cairo Mus 1 Cairo Cir Vicksburg MS 39183

JOYNER, LORINZO LITTLE, commissioner; b. Wadesboro, N.C., May 8, 1948; BS in English Edn., N.C. A&T State U., 1969; JD, U. N.C., 1981. Tchr. English, Greensboro/Durham (NC) pub. high schs.; mem. N.C. Utilities Commn., 2001—; lawyer Office of Atty. Gen. Democrat. Office: 4325 Mail Svc Ctr Raleigh NC 27699-4325 Business E-Mail: ljoyner@ncuc.net.

JOYNER, MARGUERITE AUSTIN, secondary school educator; b. Memphis, Apr 14; d. Cathey Monroe and Marguerite Victoria (Davis) Austin; m. Guy Eugene Joyner, Jr. (div. Aug. 1980); children: Marguerite Parker, Guy E. III; m. Philip O'Neil Nicar, Apr. 18, 1986. AA, William Woods Coll.; BA, So. Meth. U.; postgrad., U. Memphis, Rhodes Coll., 2003. Lic. profl. tchr. Tenn., real estate Tenn. Counselor Memphis/Shelby County Juvenile Ct., 1979—81; tchr. Briarcrest Christian Schs., Memphis, 1972—75; counselor Southaven H.S., Memphis, 1981—83; dir. recruiting ERA Sterling Realtors, Memphis, 1984—86; asst. recruiter Fed. Express/Manpower, Memphis, 1990—97; tchr. Shelby County Alt. Sch., Memphis, 2001—. Mem. Tchrs. Credit Union, Memphis; bus. cons. Melody Lane Atrium Cafe, Memphis. Active Les Passees Memphis, Memphis Symphony League; trustee St. Mary's Episcopal Sch., Memphis; cofounder St. Mary's Episcopal Sch. Alumnae Assn.; asst. chmn. Rep. Precinct 44-2, Memphis. Mem.: Jr. League of Memphis (chmn. day care project). Avocations: cooking, calligraphy, collecting first edition books, designing houses. Office: Shelby County Alt Sch 2911 Brunswick Rd Memphis TN 38122

JOYNER KERSEE, JACQUELINE, former track and field athlete; b. East St. Louis, Ill., Mar. 3, 1962; d. Alfred and Mary Joyner; m. Bob Kersee, Jan. 11, 1986. BA in History, UCLA, 1985; LLD (hon.), Washington U., St. Louis, 1992, Iona Coll., 1994; DHL (hon.), Harris-Stowe State Coll., 1993, Fontbonne Coll., St. Louis, 1998, Spelman Coll., 1998, Howard U., 1999, George Washington U., St. Louis, 1999. Winner 4 consecutive Nat. Jr. Pentathlon Championships; winner heptathlon Goodwill Games, Moscow, 1986, U.S. Olympic Festival, 1986; winner USA/Mobil Outdoor Track and Field Championship, 1987; winner, long jump and heptathlon World Track and Field Championships, 1987; winner Grand Prix Indoor Championships, winner indoor world record 55m hurdlers 7:37 seconds, 1989; winner heptathlon Goodwill Games, St. Petersburg, Russia, 1994; ret., 2001. Pres., founder JJK & Assocs., Inc. Author: (autobiography) A Kind of Grace: the Autobiography of the World's Greatest Female Athlete, 1997; co-author: A Woman's Place Is Everywhere, 1994. Founder JJK Cmty. Found. (name now JJK Found.); chmn. St. Louis Sports Commn., 1996-2000, chmn. emeritus, 2001—; Barbie Amb. of Dreams. Recipient Silver medal for heptathlon L.A. Summer Olympic Games, 1984, Sullivan award, 1986, Jesse Owens award, 1986, 87, Am. Black Achievement award Ebony mag., 1987, Gold medal for long jump at 24 ft. 3 1/2 in. and heptathlon Seoul Summer Olympic Games, 1988, 1st Female Athlete of Yr. award Sporting News, 1988, Gold medal for heptathlon Barcelona Summer Olympic Games, 1992, Bronze medal for long jump Barcelona Summer Olympic Games, 1992, Gold medal for heptathlon World Track and Field Championships, 1993, Bronze medal in long jump in Atlanta, 1996, Jim Thorpe award, 1993, Jackie Robinson "Robie" award, 1994, Grand Prix Outdoor Champion, 1994, Parenting Leader award Parenting mag., Jesse Owens Humanitarian award, 1999, Humanitarian award Women Sports and Fitness, Pres.'s award Nat. Conf. Black Mayors; named Athlete of Yr., Track & Field News, 1986, Female Athlete of Yr., AP, 1987, Female of Yr. IAAF, 1994, St. Louis Ambassadors Sportswoman of Yr., Hon. Harlem Globetrotter, Goodwill Game heptathlon champion, 1986, 90, 94, 98, Woman Athlete of Century, Sports Illustrated, 1999; inductee Nat. Boys and Girls Club Hall of Fame Achievements include setting world record of 7161 points at U.S. Olympic Festival, 1986; set world record of 7291 points at Seoul Summer Olympic Games for heptathlon, 1988; holder Am. record in long jump, 1994, 50 meter hurdles, 60 meter hurdles. Office: Elite Internat Sports Mktg and Mgmt 1034 S Brentwood Blvd Ste 1530 Saint Louis MO 63117-1215

JOYNES, BARBARA COLE, marketing executive; b. Rahway, N.J., Sept. 4, 1960; d. Clayton Eugene and Margaret (Fitzgerald) Cole; m. Matthew Thomas Thornhill, Oct. 15, 1983 (div. 1996); children: Allison, Clark; m. Stanley Knight Joynes III, June 24, 2000. BBA in Mktg., Coll. of William and Mary, 1982. Asst. account exec. March Direct/McCann Direct, N.Y.C., 1983-84, account exec., 1984-86, account supr., 1986-87; dir. comml. client divsn. Huntsinger & Jeffer Direct, Richmond, Va., 1987-89; v.p., account supr. The Stenrich Group, Richmond, 1989-90, sr. v.p., dir. account mgmt., 1990-92, exec. v.p., dir. account mgmt., bd. dirs., 1992-95; exec. v.p. for integrated mktg. comm., mem. exec. com. The Martin Agy., Richmond, 1995-96, exec. v.p., chief adminstrv. officer, 1996—. Mem. profit sharing com. The Martin Agy., Richmond, 1993—2003, chair mgmt. com., 1999—2002. Exec. com. bd. trustees Richmond Children's Mus., 1992-99, dir. bd. trustees, 1991-92; area coord. William and Mary Alum Admissions Network, Richmond, 1988-98; co-chair William and Mary Class of 82 Reunion com., 1997; mem. Leadership Metro Richmond Class of 1997; book fair chair Maybeury Elem. Sch., 1997—2000; cookie chair Brownie Troop #292, Girl Scouts U.S., 1996-98, bd. dirs. Commonwealth coun., 1999-2002; bd. dirs. Arts Coun. Richmond, 1998—2002; bd. dirs. Leadership Metro Richmond, 1998—2004, mem. exec. com., 1999—2004, also chair devel. com., chair mem. programs com., awareness/pub. rels. com., recruitment com.; bd. dirs., v.p. YWCA of Richmond, 2001—. Recipient

Silver Echo award Direct Mktg. Assn., 1991, 94, Gold Echo award, 2003, Richmond Area Marketer of Yr. award Am. Mktg. Assn., 1992, 93, 94, Gold Effie award, 1992, Silver Effie award, 2000, YWCA Outstanding Woman award, 1999. Mem. Greater Richmond C. of C. (mem. exec. com. 2002—, bd. dirs. 2000—), Willow Oaks Country Club, Farmington Country Club. Avocations: travel, family, reading, golf. Office: The Martin Agy One Shockoe Plz Richmond VA 23219-4132

JUBINSKA, PATRICIA ANN, ballet instructor, choreographer, artist, anthropologist, archaeologist; b. Norfolk, Va. d. Joseph John and Lucy (Babey) Topping; children: Vanessa Meredith, Courtney Hilary. Student, Md. State Ballet Sch., Sch. Am. Ballet, N.Y.C.; BA, R.I. Coll.; MA, Wesleyan U.; PhD, Union Inst., 1999. Mem. N.Y.C. Ballet; freelance artist Chamber Ballet of L.A., San Antonio Ballet, Md. State Ballet; artistic dir. Blackstone Valley Ballet, Harrisville, RI, 1983-84, Am. Ballet, Pascoag, RI, 1984-92; asst. artistic dir. Odessa Ukrainian Dancers, Woonsocket, RI, 1991-92; freelance guest artist, 1992—; mem. Mandrivka Dancers of Boston, 1993—; mem. faculty Fine Arts West Warwick Sch., 1995—; mem. faculty Roger Williams U., 2000—. Avocation: equestrian. Home: 110 Gold Mine Rd Chepachet RI 02814

JUDD, ASHLEY, actress; b. Granada Hills, Calif., Apr. 19, 1968; d. Michael Ciminella and Naomi Judd; m. Dario Franchitti, Dec. 12, 2001. BA in French, U. Ky., 1990. Actor: (films) Kuffs, 1992, Ruby in Paradise, 1993, Smoke, 1995, Heat, 1995, The Passion of Darkly Noon, 1996, A Time To Kill, 1996, Normal Life, 1996, The Locusts, 1997, Kiss the Girls, 1997, Simon Birch, 1998, Eye of the Beholder, 1999, Double Jeopardy, 1999, Where the Heart Is, 2000, Someone Like You, 2001, High Crimes, 2002, Divine Secrets of the Ya-Ya Sisterhood, 2002, Frida, 2002, Twisted, 2004; (TV films) Till Death Us Do Part, 1992, Norma Jean & Marilyn, 1996, The Ryan Interview, 2000; (TV series) Sisters, 1991—93, Star Trek: The Next Generation, 1991. Named One of the 50 Most Beautiful People In The World, People Magazine, 1996. Mem.: Phi Beta Kappa. Office: William Morris Agy 1 William Morris Pl Beverly Hills CA 90212-2775*

JUDD, BARBARA ANN EASTWOOD, financial management professional, union activist; b. Moline, Ill., 1950; d. Albert Floyd and Ruth Eleanor (Smith) Eastwood; m. Blue Klemenz Branley, May 1978 (div. June 1982); 1 child, Chaya Eastwood; m. Marvin E. Judd, Nov. 1987. BS in Geology and Botany, U. Wash., 1992; MBA, Western Wash. U., 1996. Cert. fin. mgmt., 1998, mgmt. acct., 1998. Personal property tax auditor King County Dept. Assessments, Seattle, 1975-78; program adminstr. Edmonds C.C., Lynnwood, Wash., 1981-85; fixed assets acct. Stimson Lane Wine & Spirits, Woodinville, Wash., 1987-90, fin. analyst, 1990-96; tax analyst, developer SCS/Compute, Bellevue, Wash., 1996-97; sr. fin. analyst NEXTEL, Kirkland, Wash., 1997; tax analyst, developer Microsoft, Redmond, Wash., 1998-2000, enrolled agent, 2002—, fin. cons., 2000—, Eastwood Fin. Svcs., Tax Preparation; self-employed. Active Nat. Dem. Party. Recipient Student Achievement award Wall St. Jour., 1996, Cert. Disting. Performance CFM, 1998, Washtech/CWA leadership award, 2000. Mem. NOW, Inst. Mgmt. Accts., Nat. Assn. Enrolled Agents, NARAL, Beta Gamma Sigma. E-mail: barb_judd@earthlink.net.

JUDD, JACQUELINE DEE (JACKIE JUDD), journalist, reporter; b. Johnstown, Pa., Nov. 29, 1952; 2 children. BA in Journalism and Polit. Sci., Am. U., 1973. Reporter WKXL Radio, Concord, N.H., 1974-75, WBAL Radio, Balt., 1975-76; reporter, anchor All Things Considered, Morning Edit., Nat. Pub. Radio, Washington, 1976-82; news anchor, reporter, anchor CBS Radio, N.Y.C., 1982-87; reporter ABC TV, Washington, 1987—. Recipient Overseas Press Club citation Overseas Press Club, N.Y.C., 1989, Emmy award Am. Acad. Arts and Scis., N.Y.C., 1990, 96, Lodestar award Am. U., 1993, Dupont award, 1994, Joan Barone award, 1999, Headliner award, 1999, Murrow award, 1999, Clarion award, 1999. Mem. Radio TV Corr. Assocs. of Capital Hill (exec. com. 1993-96), Am. Fedn. Radio and TV Artists. Office: ABC News Washington Bur 1717 Desales St NW Washington DC 20036-4407

JUDD, NAOMI, country music entertainer, singer, songwriter, writer; b. Ashland, Ky., Jan. 11, 1946; m. Larry Strickland; children: Wynonna, Ashley. Mem. country mus. duo The Judds; songs include: Had a Dream, 1983, Mama He's Crazy, (Grammy award), 1984, Why Not Me, (Single of Yr. Country Music Assn.), 1984, Girls Night Out, 1985, Rockin' with the Rhythmn of the Rain, 1986; albums include: Why Not Me?, The Judds, Rockin' with the Rhythm, Heartland, Christmas Time With The Judds, River of Time, 1989, 96, Love Can Build a Bridge, Greatest Hits Vols. I (sold over 15 million albums), Greatest Hits Vols. II, In Concert, 1995, The Judds Reunion: Live, 2000, Number One Hits, 2000; author: Love Can Build a Bridge, 1993 (N.Y. Times Best Seller); NBC mini-series Naomi and Wynonna: Love Can Build a Bridge, 1995; appeared in films More American Graffiti, 1979, Family Tree, 2000, TV films Living Proof: The Hank Williams Jr. Story, 1983, Rio Diablo, 1993, A Holiday Romance, 1999. Recipient 7 Grammy awards, Acad. Country Music award 1984, 85, 86, 87, 88, 89, 90, 91, Vocal Duo award (with Wynonna Judd), Country Music Assn. award, 1984, 85, 86, 87, 88, 89, 90, 91. Office: RCA 30 Music Sq W Nashville TN 37203-3235 Address: 1700 Hayes St Nashville TN 37203-3014

JUDE, CASSANDRA JOY, music educator; d. Bradley Kincaid and Nancy Iness Kiser; m. Lowell Edward Jude, Dec. 13, 1975; 1 child, Joshua Caleb. B of Music Edn., Morehead State U., 1976, Eastern Ky. U. Tchr. elem music Clark County Bd. Edn., Winchester, Ky., 1976—2004. Dir. plays Sch. Ch., Winchester, Ky., 1976—2003; dir. children's choir Ctrl. Bapt. Ch., 1982—92; tchr. music Clark County Bd. Edn., 1991—96; tchr. advisory bd. Macmillan McGraw Hill, 1992; dir. choir Ctrl. Bapt. Ch., Winchester, Ky., 1998—2001. Dir. vacation bible sch. Ivory Hill Bapt. Ch., Irvine, Ky., 1976—79; tchr. Sunday sch. Ctrl. Bapt. Ch., Winchester, 1986—88. Grant, Clark County Edn. Found. Mem.: NEA, Ky. Orff Schulerk Assn. (Orff Schulwerk Level I cert.), Am. Orff Schulwerk Assn., Music Edn. Nat. Conf. Baptist. Avocations: reading, antiques, decorating, travel, movies. Home: 419 Skylark Dr Winchester KY 40391 Office: Providence Elem 7076 Old Boonesboro Rd Winchester KY 40391

JUDELSOHN, JENNIFER, artist, psychotherapist; BA, SUNY, Buffalo, 1985, JD, 1988; MSW, U. Md., Balt., 1996. Bar: N.Y. 1989; lic. clin. social worker Va., LCSW Md. Artist, Merrifield, Va., 1993—; social worker Arlington, Va., 1997—2000; psychotherapist Merrifield, 2001—; prin. Neshama Soulworks Studio, Merrifield, 2002—. Author, illustrator (book) Songs of Creation: Meditations on the Sacred Hebrew Alphabet, 2002; one-woman shows include Ein Sof: Without Ending, Bunis Family Gallery, Buffalo, Soulworks, Dupont Pilgrims Gallery, Washington, Possibility, Silk Road Cafe, Balt., exhibited in group shows at Her Voice From Within, Bodzin Gallery, Fairfax, Va., The Big Show: Collaborations:96, Creative Alliance, Balt., Creative Hands, Bodzin Gallery, Fairfax, Va. Mem.: NASW, Soc. Spirituality and Social Work, Forum Integrating Mental Health, Spirituality, and Cmty., Women's Caucus Art Greater Washington. Avocations: swimming, feng shui, sea kayaking, travel. Office: Neshama Soulworks Studio PO Box 2716 Merrifield VA 22116-2716 E-mail: mandalas@hotmail.com.

JUDGE, DOLORES BARBARA, real estate broker; b. Plymouth, Pa. m. Richard James Judge; children: Susan, Nancy, Richard Jr. Student, North Harris County Coll., 1984-85, U. Tex., 1985, Houston Community Coll., 1988-89. Real estate agt. comml. real estate cos. in area, 1981-84; owner D-J Investment Properties, Conroe, Tex., 1984—; pres., ptnr. J&M Mgmt. Co., 1996-97; pres. Judge Mgmt. Co., 1997—. Mem. first adv. bd. First Nat. Title Co., Conroe, 1989-90. Chmn. North Houston Econ. Devel. Showcase, 1990; bd. dirs. Montgomery County Crime Stoppers, Inc., 1993-2003. Mem. Conroe C. of C., Comml. Real Estate Assn. Montgomery County (pres. 1986-87, bd. dirs. 1988), Conroe Art League (exec. bd. 2003-) Avocations: golf, travel, computers, reading. Office: D-J Investment Properties 306 Tara Park Conroe TX 77302-3756

JUDGE, JEAN FRANCES, management consultant; b. N.J., Aug. 25, 1922; d. Frank Theodore and Frances Marie (O'Brien) J. BS, Coll. St. Elizabeth, 1944. Asst. dietitian Hoffman LaRoche, Inc., 1944-45; dir. sch. lunch program for handicapped children Jersey City Sch. System, 1945-51; dir. field home econs. United Fruit Co., 1951-55; extension prof. consumer food mktg. Rutgers U., New Brunswick, N.J., 1955-70; dir. consumer affairs Grand Union Co., Elmwood Park, N.J., 1970-74; owner, pres. Jean Judge Assocs., Inc., Hackensack, N.J., 1974-93. Trustee Coll. St. Elizabeth, 1987-96, mem. mktg. com., capital fund campaign, mem. planned giving com. Recipient Mother Xavier award Coll. St. Elizabeth, 1973. Mem. Soc. Consumer Affairs Profls. in Bus. (charter bd. dirs. 1974-75, Outstanding Svc. award 1975, Individual Achievement award 1985), SOCAP Found. (bd. trustees 1986-96).

JUDGE, NANCY ELIZABETH, obstetrician, gynecologist; b. Holyoke, Mass., May 21, 1951; d. Martin P. and Barbara Judge; m. David B. Wood, Oct. 30, 1982; children: David, William, Elizabeth, Meredith. AB, Smith Coll., 1973; MD, U. Mass., 1977. Intern Case Western Res. U./MetroHealth Med. Ctr., Cleve., 1977-78, resident, 1978-81; staff physician MetroHealth Med. Ctr. Case Western Res. U. Hosps., Cleve., 1981-90; dir. reproductive imaging ctr. Case Western Res. U. Hosps., 1990—, maternal-fetal medicine cons., 1990—. Asst. prof. reproductive biology Case Western Res. U., 1981—. Contbr. articles to profl. jours. Active Cleve. Art Mus., Playhouse Sq. Assn., Cleve. Garden Ctr. Fellow ACOG; mem. Cleve. Ob.-Gyn. Soc. (pres.).

JUDGE, RAJINDER, psychiatrist; b. Jullundur, India, Mar. 22, 1961; arrived in Eng., 1964,arrived in U.S., 1996; d. Sadhu and Parkash Judge. MD, U. Birmingham, Eng., 1984. Intern Wordsley Hosp. and Russells Hall Hosp., Dudley, England, 1984—85; sr. house officer psychiatry Midland Nerve Hosp., Birmingham, 1985—86; physician Riyadh, Saudi Arabia, 1986—87; psychiatry registrar North Worcester, England, 1987—89; assoc. med. dir. Smith Kline Beecham, England, 1991—96; dir., global physician for Prozac, Lilly & Co., Indpls., 1997—2000; psychiatrist Nat. Health Svc., 1991—94; registrar, sr. registrar London Charing Cross Rotation, 1989—91; v.p. neuroscience Novartis, East Hanover, NJ, 2000—03; pharm. cons., 2003—. Forensic med. examiner London Met. Police Force, 1991—. Contbr. articles to profl. jours. Mem.: ENCP, Royal Coll. Psychiatrists. Avocations: automobiles, movies, travel.

JUE, SUSAN LYNNE, interior designer; b. Berkeley, Calif., July 7, 1956; d. Howard Lynn and Rosie (Fong) J. AA with honors, Cabrillo Coll., 1977; BA, Calif. Coll. Arts and Crafts, 1979. Interior designer Lucasfilm Ltd., San Anselmo, Calif., 1980-81, Whisler-Patri Architects and Planners, San Francisco, 1982, Barry Reischmann Design Studio, San Francisco, 1983, Kaplan, McLaughlin, Diaz Architects and Planners, San Francisco, 1984-85; Gensler & Assocs., Architects San Francisco, 1985, Hirano Assocs., San Francisco, 1987-88, Clocktower Design, San Ramon, Calif., 1988-89, Reel/Grobman & Assocs., San Francisco, 1989-90; interior designer Primo Angeli Inc., San Francisco, 1990-92, Guillermo Rossello, Architect, Berkeley, Calif., 1992-94, Jean Coblentz & Assocs., San Francisco, 1995, Safeway, Pleasanton, 1996—. Chmn. Children's Discovery Mus. of San Jose, 1996. Recipient No. Calif. Home & Garden Design Achievement award 1992. Mem. Internat. Interior Design Assn. (newsletter editor No. Calif. chpt. 1987-88, resource index com. 1987-88, chmn. graphic com. 1987-88, Ronald McDonald House com. 1988-89, chmn. Salvation Army project com. 1990-91, chmn. Bread and Roses project com. 1991, chmn. Ctr. for AIDS, 1991-92, chmn. Maitri AIDS Hospice, 1995-97, chmn. ARIS, 1995-96, guide dogs for blind 1997-98, bd. dirs. 1991—, Cert. of Appreciation 1989, 91, 92, 97, 98, 99, Cmty. Svc. Program award 1993, 97, 98, pres. No. Calif. chpt. 1999—). Avocations: travel, graphic design. Home: 3339 Montevideo Dr San Ramon CA 94583-2606

JUENEMANN, SISTER JEAN, hospital executive; b. St. Cloud, Minn., Nov. 19, 1936; d. Leo A. and Teresa M. (Oster) J. Diploma, St. Cloud Sch. Nursing, 1957; student, Coll. St. Benedict, 1957-59; BSN cum laude, Seattle U., 1967; MHA, U. Minn., 1977. Dir. nursing svc. Queen of Peace Hosp., New Prague, Minn., 1963-65, 67-77, asst. adminstr., 1967-77, CEO, 1977—. Mem. bd. Bush Med. Fellows Program; spkr. at confs. Chmn. Cmty. Com. Prevention Chem. Abuse, New Prague, 1975-80; bd. dirs. St. Cloud (Minn.) Hosp., St. Benedict's Coll., St. Joseph, Minn. Recipient Disting. Svc. award Minn. Hosp. & Health Assn., 1996; Bush Found. Summer fellow Cornell U., U. Calif., Berkeley, 1982. Fellow Am. Coll. Healthcare Execs.; mem. AAUW (past pres. New Prague chpt.), Am. Hosp. Assn. (CEO of Yr. 1989), Soc. Health Care Planning & Mktg., Cath. Hosp. Assn., Women's Health Leadership Trust, New Prague Opportunities, Rotary (pres. New Prague chpt. 1994-95, asst. gov. dist. 1998-99), Sigma Theta Tau. Fax: (612) 758-5009. E-mail: Sjean@qofp.org.

JUFFER, KRISTIN ANN, research analyst; b. Omaha, Mar. 2, 1947; d. Theodore Arnold and Adeline (Brinks) J.; m. Gregory Paul Awbrey, Jan. 26, 1985 (div.); 1 child, Michael John. BA, U. Nebr., 1969; MA, U. Iowa, 1979, PhD, 1983. Cert. tchr., supt., Iowa. Tchr., acting curriculum coordinator Cedar Rapids (Iowa) Pub. Schs., 1970-80; asst. prof. then assoc. prof. edn. Western Ill. U., Macomb, 1979-86, asst. dir. bilingual edn., 1979-84, adminstrv. asst. to v.p., 1983-84, researcher, 1984-86; program officer, acad. specialist USIA, Washington, 1985-86, research analyst Voice of Am., 1986-88, dir. audience research, 1988-97; dir. U.S. radio rsch. The Arbitron Co., 1998-99; cons. HealthEducation.com; social sci. rsch. analyst Health Care Fin. Adminstrn., 2000—01; sr. study dir. Temple U., 2001—. Coordinator European Bus. Seminars, Tempe, Ariz., 1980-84; researcher, test devel. Iowa Testing Program, Iowa City, 1982-83; researcher, cons. U. Nebr., Lincoln, 1984-86; v.p. Am. Fedn. Tchrs., Cedar Rapids, 1973. Co-convenor Cedar Rapids Women's Caucus, 1970, Iowa Women's Polit. Caucus, 1972; pres. Iowa Dem. Women's Caucus, 1971. Mem. Soc. Intercultural Tng. Edn. and Research, Soc. Internat. Devel., Nat. Assn. Fgn. Student Affairs, Am. Assn. Pub. Opinion Research, Phi Delta Kappa.

JUHL ZELLE, DOROTHY HELEN, retired social worker; b. Cedar Falls, Iowa, May 3, 1928; d. Karl Henry and Leona Margaret (Wedeking) Brandhorst; m. Eugene Edward Juhl, Feb. 19, 1955; children: Jane Marie, John Karl, Edward Eugene; m. Herbert E. Zelle, July 12, 2003. BA, Capital U., 1949; MSW, Washington U., St. Louis, 1952. Cert. social worker Acad. Cert. Social Work, Nat. Assn. Social Work; lic. ind. social worker, Iowa. Counselor Luth. Children's Home, Waverly, Iowa, 1949-55; dir. Grundy County Dept. Human Svcs., Grundy Center, Iowa, 1968-70; psychiat. social worker Dr. W.G. Stone, Waterloo, Iowa, 1970-76; psychiat. social worker, family and individual therapist Luth. Social Svcs. Iowa, Waterloo, 1976-97; retired, 1997. Cons. Bremer-Butler Hospice, Waverly, 1996—. Sec., chair Bremwood Auxiliary, Waverly, 1955-68, Black Hawk-Grundy Mental Health Ctr., Waterloo, 1962-68, 72-77; officer Dike (Iowa) Sch. PTA, 1962-80; bd. dirs., sec. Cedar Falls Luth. Home, 1977-82; bd. dirs., chair Grundy County Farm Bur., Grundy Center, 1982-90; juvenile justice adv. People to People, China, Japan, Taiwan, Hong Kong, 1984; bd. dirs. Luth. Rural Econ. Empowerment Com., Des Moines, 1993-98, Christian Crusaders Radio Ministry, Waterloo, 1994-98, N.E. Iowa Synod Women of Evangel. Luth. Ch. in Am., Waverly, 1995-99; mental health counselor Self-Help Internat., Ghana, West Africa, 1997—; mem. various bds. and coms. St. Paul's Luth. Ch., Waverly; mem. Amvet Auxiliary, Waverly Cmty. Hosp. Aux., sec., 1999-2003; mental health counselor Self-Help Internat., Ghana, 1997. Recipient Svc. award Luth. Social Svc. Iowa, 1996. Mem. AAUW (pres.), NASW, ACSW. Republican. Avocations: gardening, reading, baking, antiques. Home: 818 6th St NW Waverly IA 50677-1501

JULANDER, PAULA FOIL, health care and political consultant, state senator; b. Charlotte, N.C., Jan. 21, 1939; d. Paul Baxter and Esther Irene (Earnhardt) Foil; m. Roydon Odell Julander, Dec. 21, 1985; 1 child, Julie McMahan Shipman. Diploma, Presbyn. Sch. Nursing, Charlotte, N.C., 1960; BS magna cum laude, U. Utah, 1984; MS in Nursing Adminstrn., Brigham Young U., 1990. RN, Utah. Nurse various positions, Fla. and S.C., 1960-66; co-founder Am. Laser Corp., 1970-79; tchg. asst. U. Utah, Salt Lake City; mem. Utah Ho. of Reps., Salt Lake City, 1989-92; Dem. nominee lt. gov. State of Utah, 1992; minority whip Utah State Senate, Dist. 1, Salt Lake City, 1998—2000; health care/polit. cons. Salt Lake City, 1998—2000. Mem. adj. faculty Brigham Young U. Coll. Nursing, 1987—95; bd. dirs. Block Fin. Svcs.; mem. Utah state exec. bd U.S. West Comm., 1993—96; bd. regents Calif. Luth. U., 1994—97; trustee KUED TV, 2000—, Intermountain Health Care Hosps., 2000—. Med. cons. ("Health Tracks, A Practical Guide to Mng. Your Health"), 2000; co-author (cookbook): Utah State Fare, 1995. Pres. Utah Nurses Found., 1986—88; mem. Nat. Conf. of State Legis. Com. on Families and Children, 1999—, The Coun. of State Govt. Com. on Health and Aging, 1999—, Women's Polit.Caucus, Statewide Abortion Task Force, 1990; bd. dirs. Cmty. Nursing Svc. Home Health Plus, 1992—94; mem. Planned Parenthood Assn. Utah, 1994—, Utahns for Choice, 1995—; trustee Westminster Coll., 1994—, HCA-St. Mark's Hosp., 1994—95; elected sen. State of Utah, 1998—. Recipient Utah pub. health hero award, 2000. Mem.: Nat Orgn. Women Legislators, Utah Nurses Assn. (legis. rep. 1987—88, Lifetime Achievement award), ANA, Phi Kappa Phi (Susan Young Gates award 1991), Sigma Theta Tau. Home: 476 B St Salt Lake City UT 84103-2544

JULIA, MARIA, social worker, educator, consultant; b. San Juan, P.R., Dec. 04; d. Juan and Josefa Julia; m. James Billups, Oct. 11, 1979. BA in Sociology, U. P.R., 1968, MSW, 1969; PhD in Social Work, Ohio State U., 1981. Lic. social worker, Ohio. Social worker Dept. Health, San Juan, P.R., 1970-78; cons. Ohio State Health Dept., Columbus, 1984-89; from asst. prof. to prof. social work Ohio State U., Columbus, 1988—. Presenter numerous meetings., confs., symposiums; guest reviewer Jour. Free Inquiry in Creative Sociology, 1998—, Rsch. on Social Work Practice, 1993-94; rsch. cons. GRUPEL Rsch. Network, U. Zambia, 1999—; mem. grant proposals evaluation com. Dept. Edn., Officer Higher Edn., Washington, 1999; mem. comms. com. and program devel. com. Ohio Commn. on Minority Health, Columbus, 1998—; grant proposals reviewer DHHS, Adminstrn. for Children, Youth, and Families, Washington, 1994—, NIMH, Pub. Health Svcs., Washington, 1994, Ohio Commn. on Minority Health, Columbus, 1988—; bd. examiners doctoral program Bharathidasan U., Tamil Nadu, India, 1994—; mem. task force on depression after delivery Ohio Dept. Mental Health, Columbus, 1990-95; trustee Columbus Internat. Program, 1991-95; mem. adv. bd. World Congress on the Family, Columbus, 1990-92; mem. rsch. and edn. com. Ohio Adv. Coun. on Newborn Screening for Hemoglobinopathies, Columbus, 1990-92. Mem. editl. bd. Jour. Social Devel. Issues, 1997—; contbr. articles to profl. jours. including Social Devel. Issues, Devel. in Practice, Internat. Social Work, Jour. Tchg. in Social Work, Jour. Global Awareness, Social Work, Adoption and Fostering, among others. Mem. internat. com. ARC, Columbus, 1989-92; mem. health and edn. com. Ohio Commn. on Spanish Speaking Affairs, Columbus, 1989-91; mem. post-partum adv. coun. Office of Gov., Columbus, 1989-90; mem. rev. com., interprofl. grant proposals Ohio Dept. Health, Columbus, 1989, mem. black infant mortality task force, 1985-89. Mem. NASW, Assn. Faculty and Profl. Women, Assn. for Rsch. on Nonprofit Orgns. and Vol. Action, Colegio de Trabajadores Sociales de P.R., Columbus Internat. Program, Coun. on Social Work Edn., Global Awareness Soc. Internat. (bd. dirs. 1991-94), Internat. Assn. Schs. Social Work, Internat. Coun. on Social Welfare, Inter-Univ. Consortium for Internat. Social Devel., Ohio State U. Alumni Soc. (Disting. Alumna of Yr. 1991), Soc. for Transcultural Family Rels., Women and Children Health Coop., Women in Internat. Devel., Phi Beta Delta, Phi Kappa Phi. Office: Ohio State U Coll Social Work 1947 N College Rd Columbus OH 43210-1123

JULIAN, FRANCES BLOCH, volunteer; b. Indpls., July 11, 1923; d. Joseph Meyer Bloch, Roslyn Sommers (Liepold) Bloch; m. Jacob William Julian; children: William II, Jonathan, Anne Lennon. BA, Sarah Lawrence Coll., 1945. Founder, bd. mem. Ind. Repertory Theatre, 1970; bd. dirs. Indpls. Symphony Orch., 1979—82; chmn. bd. dirs. Children's Mus., Indpls., 1979—81, hon. life trustee, 1985—2001; bd. dirs. WFYI Channel 20 Pub. TV, Indpls., 1990—97; mem. fin. com. Inpls. Found., 1995—2001; bd. dirs. Athenaeum Found., Indpls., 1997—2001. Jewish. Avocations: travel, bicycling.

JULIAN, LINDA S. music educator, director; b. Chgo., Jan. 13, 1955; d. Reginald Victor and Evelyn May Lord; m. Alfred J. Julian, Aug. 9, 1980; children: Adam T., Bryan A. BA in Gen./Vocal Music, Carthage Coll., Kenosha, Wis., 1977; MEd, Nat.-Louis U., Evanston, Ill., 2003. Cert. music instr. Ill. Music specialist Kenosha Unified Sch. Dist., 1977—84; childrens choral dir. Grace Luth. Ch., Loves Park, Ill., 1992—99; gen. and vocal music dir. Prairie Hill Consol. Sch. Dist. 133, South Beloit, Ill., 1998—. Dir.: (musical) Guys and Dolls, 2000, The Music Man, 2002, Once on This Island, 2004. Leader, counselor Boy Scouts Am., Roscoe, Ill., 1990—2003. Mem.: Nat. Assn. for Music Edn. (assoc.), Ill. Music Edn. Assn. (assoc.). Office: Prairie Hill Consol Sch 133 14714 Willowbrook Rd South Beloit IL 61080 Business E-mail: julianl@prairiehill.org.

JULIAN, ROSE RICH, music educator, director; b. Asheboro, N.C., Sept. 9, 1937; d. Herbert C. and Esther Dennis Rich; m. Cecil Perry Julian, May 30, 1959 (div. Apr. 1977); children: Alan Perry, Keri Dawn Julian Sorensen, Derrick Kyle. AA in Voice, Mars Hill Coll., 1957; BS in Music, East Carolina U., 1959; postgrad., U N.C., 1971—79, Western Carolina U., 1995. Cert. music tchr. N.C. Dir. music USAF Chapel Choir, 1960—71; tchr. Rowan/Salisbury (N.C.) Schs., 1972—79, 1988—; dir. music Thyatira Pres Ch., Salisbury, 1982—88, Coburn U. N.C., Salisbury, 1991—97. Conductor Salisbury Choral Soc., 1993; pianist 1st Bapt. Ch., Salisbury, 1999—; judge Protestant Chapels of Europe, Frankfurt, Germany, 1970. Mem.: AOSA, NAE, Nat. Assn. Tchrs. Singing, Music Educators Assn., Piano Guild. Baptist. Home: 36 Old Farm Rd Salisbury NC 28147

JULIBER, LOIS D. manufacturing executive; b. 1949; m. John Adams. BA, Wellesley Coll.; MBA, Harvard U. Former v.p. Gen. Foods Corp.; from gen. mgr. to pres. Far East/Can. divsn. Colgate-Palmolive Co., N.Y.C., 1988-92, chief tech. officer, 1992-94, pres. Colgate—N.Am. divsn., 1994—97, exec. v.p., chief ops. developed markets, 1997—2000, COO internat. ops., 2000—02, COO L. Am. and growth functions, 2002—. Bd. dirs. DuPont Corp., 1995- Bd. trustees Brookdale Found., Wellesley Coll., Girls Inc. Recipient Luminary Award, Corp. Innovator Category, Com. 200, 2002. Mem. Harvard Bus. Sch. Club N.Y. (bd. dirs.) Avocations: tennis, gardening, cooking. Office: Colgate Palmolive Co 300 Park Ave Fl 8 New York NY 10022-7499*

JULIEN, CATHERINE, history educator; BA in Anthropology, U. Calif., Berkeley, 1971, MA in Anthropology, 1975, PhD in Philosophy, 1978. Dir. mus. programs Courthouse Mus., Merced, Calif.; lectr. and internat. study tour leader Smithsonian's Am. Mus. Natural History and Calif. Alumni Assn.; instr. Calif. State U., U. Bonn (Germany), U. Calif., Berkeley; assoc. prof. history We. Mich. U., Kalamazoo, 1996—. Author: Reading Inca History (Erminie Wheeler-Voegelin prize, 2000, Katherine Singer Kovacs prize MLA). Fellow, John Simon Guggenheim Meml. Found., 2003. Office: We Mich U Office Univ Rels 1903 W Michigan Ave Kalamazoo MI 49008-5433

JULIEN, GAIL LESLIE, model, public relations professional; b. L.I., N.Y., Apr. 13, 1940; d. David William Syme and Virginia Martha (Burth) Miller; m. Michael Louis Woodman, Sept. 12, 1958 (div.); children: Jho'meyr Renei, Sabrina Michelle; m. Francis Dana Julien, Dec. 24, 1977. Diploma in modeling, Coronet of Calif., 1960; grad., Am. Beauty Finishing Sch., 1961. Playboy bunny Playboy Club, Kansas City, Mo., 1970-72; Gremlin girl AMC, Kansas City, 1972; Dodge girl Dodge, Kansas City, 1972-73; owner, pres. Gail Woodman Enterprises Inc., Overland Park, Kans., 1972-76; sales rep. Kansas City Brit. Motors, Lenexa, Kans., 1976-78; dir. pub. rels., mktg. Downtown Air Ctr., Kansas City, 1978-80; dir. pub. rels., media rels. Bretney Corp., Kansas City, 1980-82; v.p. Nuwalters Co., Overland Park, 1983-84; regional mgr. aviation Multi Svc. Corp., Overland Park, 1984—. Rep. Nat. Bus. Aircraft Assn., 1984—, Can. Bus. Aircraft Assn., 1984—, Nat. Aircraft Transp. Assn., 1984—, Abbotsford Internat. Airshow, 1991, 93, 95, 98, Schedulars & Dispatchers Conv., 1994-2003, Internat. Operators Conf., 1998, 2002, Women in Aviation, 1997-2003, Helicopter Assn. Internat., 1994-2003; internat. v.p. Women in Corp. Aviation, 2003—, Schedulers and Dispatchers Support Com., 1999-2000. Author: Physician's Nutritional Guide, 1984; former editor WCA Newsletter; author numerous poems, self improvement and modeling course. Vol. Live On Stage '88 (AIDS), Santa Ana, Calif., 1988, St. Joseph Hosp., Kansas City, 1986-88; v.p. Young Dems., Midland, Mich., 1960; active Northshore Animal League, Christian Children's Fund, L.A. Mission, former bd. of dir., City of Hope, L.A., 1991; bd. dirs., fundraiser Make A Wish of Tri Counties. Recipient Outstanding Sales Achievement award Brit. Leyland, 1976-77. Mem. Am. Bus. Women's Assn. Avocations: art, writing, swimming, acting. Home: 28129 Peacock Ridge Dr Apt 312 Palos Verdes Peninsula CA 90275-7121 Office: Multi Svc Corp 8650 College Blvd Shawnee Mission KS 66210-1886

JULIFS, SANDRA JEAN, community action agency executive; b. Jersey City, July 12, 1939; d. Roy Howard and Irma Margrete (Barkhausen) Walters; m. Harold William Julifs, July 22, 1961; children: David Howard, Steven William. BA, U. Va., 1961; postgrad., U. Minn., 1962-63, Mankato State Coll., 1963. Cert. comty. action profl. Tchr. St. James (Minn.) Pub. Schs., 1961-62; substitute tchr. Sleepy Eye (Minn.) Pub. Schs., 1963-67, home bound tutor, 1967; lay reader, rater U. Wis., Stevens Point, 1968; co-founder Family Planning Service Portage County, Stevens Point, 1970-72; family planning dir. Tri-County Opportunities Coun., Rock Falls, Ill., 1971-77, energy programs coord., 1977-78, planner, EEO officer, 1978-83, pres., chief exec. officer, 1983—. Sec. Ill. Ventures for Comty. Action Springfield, 1983-91, bd. dirs. 1991-94, 96—. Mem. Nat. Cmty. Action Found., Washington, 1987—; bd. dirs. Twin Cities Homeless Coalition, 1989-96; mem. adv. coun. Sauk Valley Coll. Human Svcs., 1990-99; mem. Sauk Valley Coll. Workforce Devel. Coun., 1999—; mem. Whiteside County Overall Econ. Devel. Coun., 1990-99; mem. adv. coun. Inst. for Social and Econ. Devel., 1992-95; cons. com. No. Ill. Synod, Evang. Luth. Ch. Am., 1993-99, churchwide assembly del., 1995; mem. Statewide Rural Poverty Conf. Com., 1996-97; mem. Ill. State Microenterprise Initiative; mem. cmty. svcs. adv. com. Ill. Dept. Commerce and Cmty., 1998—, chair, 2003-. Recipient Appreciation award Western Ill. Agy. on Aging, 1980, 81, Spl. Recognition award Ill. Head Start and Day Care Assn., Recognition award Ill. Community Action Fund, 1984, Recognition award Ill. Ventures for Cmty. Action, 1996. Mem. AAUW, NAFE, Whiteside County Welfare Assn., Lee County Welfare Assn. (sec.-treas. 1983-84), Nat. Cmty. Action Assn., Cmty. Action Partnership, Ill. Cmty. Action Assn. (com. chair 1985-88, dir. exec. com. 1986-93, treas. 1988, 89, sec. 1989, 90, v.p. 1991-93, pres. 1993-97, dir. 2000-03, Recognition award 1985-95, 2000-03). Lutheran. Avocations: travel, reading. E-mails. Office: Tri-County Opportunities Coun PO Box 610 Rock Falls IL 61071-0610 E-mail: sjulifs@wmccinc.com., hwjulifs@essex1.com.

JULMY, CAMILLE P. real estate company executive; Degree in Bus. Adminstrn., Coll. St. Michel, Fribourg, Switzerland; Degree in Econs., U. Fribourg. With Fidinam, Lugano, Switzerland, 1973—74, sr. analyst Toronto, Canada, 1974—77, v.p. Chgo., 1977—78; vice chmn., co-founder US Equities REalty, Chgo., 1978—. Mem. exec. bd. UNICEF; bd. dirs. Roosevelt U., Pomerleau Constrn. Co., Montreal, Canada. Mem.: Swiss-Am. C. of C., Ctrl. Mich. Ave. Assn. (sec., mem. exec. bd.), Greater North Mich. Ave. Assn. (sec., mem. exec. bd.), Execs. Club Chgo. Office: US Equities Realty Ste 400 20 N Michigan Ave Chicago IL 60602

JUMONVILLE, FLORENCE M. librarian, historian; b. New Orleans; d. Warren P. and Florence E. (Seither) J. BA, U. New Orleans, 1971, MEd, 1976, MA, 1988, PhD, 1997; MS, La. State U., 1972. Libr. Hist. New Orleans Collection, 1972-74, 78-82, head libr., 1982-96; libr. Belle Chasse (La.) State Sch., 1974-78; head La. and spl. collections Earl K. Long Libr., U. New Orleans, 1997—. Adj. instr. libr. sci. La. State U., Baton Rouge, 1994, 96. Author: Bibliography of New Orleans Imprints, 1764-1864, 1989, Louisiana History: An Annotated Bibliography, 2002; editor: LLA Bull., 1990—95; co-editor: A History of the Louisiana Library Association, 1925-2000, 2003; contbr. articles to profl. jours. Adv. bd. Ethel and Herman L. Midlo Ctr. for N.O. Studies, La. Hist. Records; bd. dirs. Theatre Libr. Assn. Recipient Lucy B. Foote award La. Libr. Assn., 1985, Fannie Simon award Spl. Librs. Assn. Mus., Arts and Humanities Divsn., 1997. Mem. ALA, Am. Antiquarian Soc., Am. Hist. Assn., Am. Printing History Assn., Assn. Moving Image Archivists, Bibliog. Soc. Am., Soc. for the History of Authorship, Reading and Pub., La. Hist. Assn., La. Libr. Assn., Beta Phi Mu, Phi Delta Kappa, Kappa Delta Pi. Avocations: needlework, classic movies, reading. Office: Earl K Long Libr Univ New Orleans Lakefront New Orleans LA 70148-0001 E-mail: fjumonvi@uno.edu.

JUNG, ANDREA, cosmetics executive; Grad. magna cum laude, Princeton U. Sr. v.p. gen. mdse. I. Magnin; exec. v.p. Neman Marcus; sr. v.p. Avon Products, Inc., N.Y.C., 1994-97, pres., 1998-2000; CEO, 2001—. Bd. dirs. Fragrance Found., Cosmetic Exec. Women. Sale Corp., Donna Karan Internat. Office: Avon Products Inc 1345 Avenue Of The Americas New York NY 10105-0302*

JUNG, BETTY CHIN, epidemiologist, research analyst, educator, medical/surgical nurse; b. Bklyn., Nov. 28, 1948; d. Han You and Bo Ngan (Moy) C.; m. Lee Jung, Oct. 1, 1972; children: Daniel, Stephanie. AA, King's Coll., 1968; BS, Columbia U., 1971; MPH, So. Conn. State U., 1993. RN, Conn., Miss., N.Y.; cert. health edn. specialist. Adminstrv. asst. Columbia U., N.Y.C., 1968-69; practical nurse Babies Hosp., N.Y.C., 1969-70, charge nurse, 1974-76; staff nurse Columbia-Presbyn. Hosp., N.Y.C., 1971-73; sch. nurse Nassau County Sch. System, Long Island, N.Y., 1984-85; grad. asst. So. Conn. State U., New Haven, 1991-92; coop. edn. intern Conn. Dept. Health Svcs., Hartford, 1991-92; intern North Ctrl. Dist. Health Dept., Enfield, Conn., 1992; epidemiologist Conn. Dept. Pub. Health, Hartford, Conn., 1992-98, health program assoc., 1998-2001, cardiovascular health epidemiologist, 2003—; staff nurse Quinnipiac Coll. Student Health Svcs., 1998; mem. multicultural adv. coun. Conn. Dept. Children and Families, assoc. rsch. analyst, 2001—03. Health promotion cons. dept. pub. health So. Conn. State U., New Haven, 1991, mem. adv. coun. dept. pub. health, 1999—, lectr., adj. faculty, 1998—, tchg. asst., 1992, curriculum developer, 92, vol. rsch. analyst, 93, founder grad. alumni mentor program, 1993—94, webmaster E-comm. web site, 2000, univ. asst. webmaster, 2001—; instr. Albertus Magnus Coll., 1995—96; computer cons., course dir. contg. edn. program dept. pub. health So. Conn. State U., 1998—; health columnist Baldwin Newcomers Club, NY, 1977—78; coord. Dept. Pub. Health and Svcs./Conn. EPI Info. Network, Hartford, 1994—2001; mem. Nat. Lead Info. Ctr. Spkrs. Bur., 1997—98; vol. scientist Sci.-By-Mail, 1997—98; mem. Nat. Safety Coun. Environ. Health Ctr. Spkrs. Referral Bur., 1998—2001; apptd. mem. Conn. Dept. Pub. Health's Affirmative Action Employee Adv. Com., 1998—2001; mem. Permanent Commn. Status of Women Talent Network, 1996—, chair news subcom., editor affirmative action newsletter, 2001; apptd. mem. multicultural adv. coun. Conn. Dept. Children and Families, 2002—03; med. policy cons. Anthem, 2003; supercourse lectr. U. Pitts., 1999—; pilot reviewer CDC Pub. Health Tng. Network, 2002—. Mem. editl. bd.: Data Quality, 1994—98, mem. manuscript rev. bd.: Jour. Clin. Outcomes Mgmt., 1995—, Pub. Health Reports, 1997—98; contbg. editor: Episource, A Guide to Resources in Epidemiology, 1998—99; editor/web pub.: SCSU Pub. Health E-News Bull., 2000—01, Public Health E-news, 2001—, Public Health Jobs Electronic Newsletter, 2000—, book proposal reviewer: Jossey Bass Pubs., 2003—; contbr. articles to profl. jours. Vol. nurse health educator, coord. Chinatown's First Ann. Health Fair, 1971-72; treas. Tenant Assn., Bronx, N.Y., 1976-77; pre-confirmation tchr. Bethlehem Luth. Ch., Baldwin, N.Y., 1981-85. Recipient cardiovascular health grant, CDC, 2003—; grantee, USPHS, 1992—98, Fed. HUD, 1995—98, U.S. Preventive Health and Health Svcs., 1998, block grant, Maternal Child Health, 1998—2001; scholar Merit, Kings Coll., 1968, Columbia U., 1968—69, Women's Florist Assn., 1968, Bessie Lee Gambrill scholar, So. Alumni Assn., 1992. Fellow: Soc. for Pub. Health Edn.; mem.: Pub. Health Expertise Network of Mentors (program dir. 2002—), Internat. Assn. Webmasters and Designers, Boston Mus. Sci., Nat. Acad. Sci. (mentor career planning ctr. beginning scientists & engrs. 1997—98), Columbia U. Sch. Nursing Alumni Assn. (survey cons. 1994—95), So. Conn. State U. Alumni Assn. (founder pub. health cht. 1994, interim pres, then pres. 1994—98, founder, coord. pub. health alumni mentor program 1994—2002, chair coms. 1994—, numerous other positions 1994—, editor MPH Alumni Record 1995—, founder, dir., coord. pub. health alumni spkrs. bur. 1997—, founder, program dir. pub. health expertise network of mentors 2002—, Alumni Appreciation award 1998), Internat. Assn. IT Trainers (assoc.), Conn. Pub. Health Assn., Nat. Lead Info. Ctr. Spkrs. Bur., Conn. State and Territorial Epidemiologists (alternate cons. 1996—, co-leader Healthy People 2010 1999—2001, lead diabetes 2002—, lead cardiovasc. disease 2002—), Am. Statis. Assn. (OSPA media experts list 1997—), APHA (health care reform activist network, peer assistance the model stds. project). Avocations: reading, writing, research, web development and design, bicycling. Home: 25 Driftwood Ln Guilford CT 06437-1929 Office: Conn Dept Pub Health 410 Capitol Ave Hartford CT 06106 Office Phone: 860-509-7711.

JUNG, CHARLENE, city treasurer; b. Maoui, Hawaii; BA, Univ. S.C., 1977; postgrad., Calif. State Univ. City treas., Anaheim, Calif., 1992—. Office: City Hall 200 S Anaheim Blvd Anaheim CA 92805-3820

JUNG, DORIS, dramatic soprano; b. Centralia, Ill., Jan. 5, 1924; d. John Jay and May (Middleton) Crittenden; m. Felix Popper, Nov. 3, 1951; 1 son, Richard Dorian. Ed., U. Ill., Mannes Coll. Music, Vienna Acad. Performing Arts; student of, Julius Cohen, Emma Zador, Luise Helletsgruber, Winifred Cecil. Debut as Vitellia in: Clemenza di Tito, Zurich (Switzerland) Opera, 1955, other appearances with, Hamburg State Opera, Munich State Opera, Vienna State Opera, Royal Opera Copenhagen, Royal Opera Stockholm, Marseille and Strasbourg, France, Naples (Italy) Opera Co., Catania (Italy) Opera Co., N.Y.C. Opera, Met. Opera, also in Mpls., Portland, Oreg., Washington and Aspen, Colo.; soloist: Wagner concert conducted by Leopold Stokowski, 1971; with, Syracuse (N.Y.) Symphony, 1981, voice tchr., N.Y.C., 1970— . Home: 40 W 84th St New York NY 10024-4749

JUNGBLUTH, CONNIE CARLSON, wealth strategist; b. Cheyenne, Wyo., June 20, 1955; d. Charles Marion and Janice Yvonne (Keldsen) Carlson; m. Kirk E. Jungbluth, Feb. 5, 1977; children: Tyler Ryan. BS, Colo. State U., 1976. CPA, Colo., Ariz. Sr. acct. Rhode Scripter & Assocs., Boulder, Colo., 1977-81; mng. acct. Arthur Young, Denver, 1981-85; asst. v.p. Dain Bosworth, Denver, 1985-87; v.p. George K. Baum & Co., Denver, 1987-91; acct. Ariz. Luth. Acad., 1994-95; sr. tax acct. Ernst & Young, LLP, Phoenix, 1995-96; nat. tax mgr. personal wealth mgmt. RSM McGladrey, Inc., Phoenix, 1996-2000; mgr. pvt. client svcs. Arthur Andersen, Phoenix, 2000—01; sr. v.p., wealth strategist Bank of Am. Pvt. Bank, Phoenix, 2002—. Mem. profl. adv. bd. Ariz. Cmty. Found., 2002—, Jewish Cmty. Found., 2002—. Active Denver Estate Planning Coun., 1981-85, Ctrl. Ariz. Estate Planning Coun., 1997-98, S. Nev. Estate Planning Coun., 2003—; organizer Little People Am., Rocky Mountain Med. Clinic and Symposium, Denver, 1986; adv. bd. Children's Home Health, Denver, 1986-89; fin. adv. bd. Gail Shoettler for State Treas., Denver, 1986; campaign chmn. Kathi Williams for Colo. State Legislature, 1986; mem. Sch. dist. 12 Colo. Edn. Found. Bd., 1991, Napa Sch. Dist. Elem. Site com., 1992-94; apptd. Ariz. Gov.'s Coun. Developmental Disabilities, 1998-99, chmn. planning com., 1998-99; mem. profl. adv. bd., editor Charitable Giving Guide, Ariz. Cmty. Found., 2002—. Named one of 50 to watch, Denver mag., 1988. Mem. AICPA, Fin. Planning Assn., Colo. Soc. CPAs (strategic planning com. 1987-89, instr. bank 1983, trustee 1984-87, pres. bd. trustees 1986-87, bd. dirs. 1987-89, chmn. career edn. com. 1982-83, pub. svc. award 1985-87), Little People of Am., Colo. Mcpl. Bond Dealers, Ariz. Herb Assn., Metro North C. of C. (bd. dirs. 1987-90), Denver City Club (bd. dirs. 1987-88), Phi Beta Phi. Avocations: faith, family, horticulture, philanthropy, gourmet cooking. Office: Bank of America Pvt Bank 201 E Washington Ste 2300 Phoenix AZ 85004

JUNGER, PATRICIA CAROL, nurse; b. Buffalo, Mar. 16, 1943; d. James John and Rose (Menno) Colello; m. Edward Michael Junger, Sept. 19, 1964 (div. 1990); children: Kevin, Steven and Paul (twins). AAS, Erie C.C., 1976. RN, N.Y. Staff nurse med. tchg. fl. Buffalo Gen. Hosp., 1977—. Mem. unit practice coun. Buffalo (N.Y.) Gen. Hosp., 2003—. Religious edn. tchr. St. Barnabas Roman Cath. Ch. Recipient Peer Recognition award from co-workers, 1997. Mem. Comm. Workers of Am. Democrat. Roman Catholic. Avocations: playing organ and piano, gardening, reading, crafts, playing music for the blind and elderly.

JUNZ, HELEN B. economist; d. Samson and Dobra Bachner. BA, PhD, U. Amsterdam; MA, New Sch. Social Rsch. Acting chief consumer price sect. Nat. Indsl. Conf. Bd., N.Y.C., 1953-58; research officer Nat. Inst. Econ. and Social Research, London, 1958-60; economist Bur. Econ. Analysis, Dept. Commerce, Washington, 1960-62; adviser div. internat. fin. bd. govs. Fed. Res. System, Washington, 1962-77; dep. asst. sec. Office of Asst. Sec. for Internat. Affairs, Dept. Treasury, Washington, 1977-79; v.p., sr. advisor 1st Nat. Bank Chgo., 1979-80; v.p. Townsend Greenspan & Co., Inc., N.Y.C., 1980-82; sr. advisor European dept. IMF, 1982-87, dep. dir. exch. and trade rels. dept., 1987-89, spl. trade rep., dir. Geneva office, 1989-94; dir. gold econs. svc. World Gold Coun., Geneva, Switzerland, 1994-96; pres. HBJ Internat., London, 1996—. Adviser OECD, Paris, 1967-69; sr. internat. economist Council of Econ. Advisers, The White House, Washington, 1975-77. Author: Where did all the money go?, 2002; contbr. articles to profl. jours. Mem. Am. Econ. Assn., Coun. Fgn. Rels., Cosmos Club, Reform Club. Office: HBJ Intnat 39 Chalcot Sq London NW1 8YP England E-mail: hbjunz@planet.nl.

JUODVALKIS, EGLE (EGLÉ JUODVALKÉ), writer; b. East Chicago, Ind., Jan. 28, 1950; d. Antanas and Ona (Norkuté) J.; m. Henryk Skwarczynski, Sept. 2, 1989. BA, U. Chgo., 1973. Sr. editor Radio Free Europe/Radio Liberty, Inc., Munich, 1976-95. Author: (poetry) If You Touch Me, 1972, Who Has the Ring?, 1983, The Necklace of Mnemosine, 1996, (prose) Sugar Mountain or The Adventures of a Lithuanian Diabetic in America and Other Exotic Places, 2000, (bilingual poetry and CD of author's reading) Veidrodis ir tuštuma/The Mirror and the Void, 2002. Mem. Santara-Šviesa, Korp! Neo-Lithuania. Avocation: touring Greece. Home: 8608 Sayre Ave Burbank IL 60459-2260

JURAN, SYLVIA LOUISE, editor; b. Chgo. d. Joseph Moses and Sadie (Shapiro) J. BA, U. Minn.; MA, Columbia U., 1960; PhD, Harvard U., 1975. Project editor Macmillan Pub. Co., N.Y.C., 1981-91; editor Ralph Appelbaum Assocs. Inc., N.Y.C., 1991—. Faculty The New Sch., N.Y.C., 1980-82. Project editor: Ency. of the Holocaust, 1990 (Dartmouth medal ALA, 1990), Ency. of the Third Reich, 1991; editor scripts for mus. exhbns.; contbr. articles to profl. jours. Nat. Def. fgn. lang. fellow, 1960-61, 62-63. Mem. Harvard Club of N.Y.C., Harvard Grad. Sch. Alumni Assn. (N.Y. exec. com. 1984—), James Beard Found. Office: Ralph Appelbaum Assocs Inc 88 Pine St New York NY 10005-1801

JURGENSEN, KAREN, former newspaper editor; BA in Eng., U. N.C., 1971. Editorial and feature writer, columnist, editorial page layout editor Charlotte (N.C.) News, 1972-75; writer, editor Sea Grant Coll. Program U. N.C., Raleigh, 1976-79; from asst. lifestyle editor to lifestyle editor Miami News, 1979-82, asst. city editor, 1982; topics editor, life dept. USA Today, McLean, Va., 1982, spl. projects editor, life dept., 1983-85, dep. mng. editor, life dept., 1985-86, mng. editor, cover stories dept., 1986-87, sr. editor, days/spl. projects, 1987-91, editor of editorial page, 1991-99, editor of newspaper, 1999—2004. Participant Penney-Mo. Workshop, Columbia, Mo., 1981, Am. Press Inst. Workshops, 1981, 84, newspaper execs. mktg. sem. Am. Newspaper Pubs. Assn., 1986. Bd. vis. Chapel Hill Sch. Journalism and Mass Comm., U. N.C., chair, 1996-99. Recipient Matrix award Women in Comm. D.C. chpt., 2000, Women's Leadership Nat. Lifetime Legacy award D.C. Chamber of Commerce, 2002; named to U. N.C. Sch. Journalism Hall of Fame, 2001; named one of 100 Most Powerful Women in Washington, Washington Mag., 2001; Exchange scholar U. P.R., 1969-70. Mem. Am. Soc. Newspaper Editors (chair/vice chair press bar com. 1993-95, convention com. 1991-94, vice chair convention com. 1995-96, vice chair, chair literacy com. 1989-91, future of newspapers com. 1988-90, 91, writing awards bd. 1989-91).

JURGUTIS, DANGUOLE, artist; b. Lithuania, Jan. 16, 1935; came to U.S., 1949; d. Jonas and Ona Seputa; m. George Jurgutis; children: Asta, Paulius, Darius (dec.). BS, Wayne State U., 1956; student, Oakland C.C., 1972-73, U. London, 1976. Exhibited in shows at Detroit Art Inst., 1997, Port Huron Art Mus., Lincoln Ctr., N.Y.C., Mich. State Fine Arts, Ellen Sharp Mus., Jackson, Miss., Chgo., Toronto, 1998; artist-in-residence Farmington Hills, City of Farmington, Mich., others; pvt. collections in U.S., Can., Lithuania, Eng., Japan. Mem. Farmington Artists Club (v.p. 1995-97, program chair 1993-95), Mich. Watercolor Soc.

JURKA, EDITH MILA, psychiatrist, researcher; b. N.Y.C., Dec. 4, 1915; d. Charles Anton and Edith Dorothy (Schevcik) J. BA, Smith Coll., 1936; postgrad., Charles U., Prague, Czechoslovakia, 1936-38; MD, Yale U., 1944. Diplomate Am. Bd. Psychiatry and Neurology. Intern in children's med. svc. Bellevue Hosp., N.Y.C., 1944-45, asst. alienist, 1947-49; rotating intern Gallinger Hosp., Washington, 1945-46; intern N.Y. State Psychiat. Inst., N.Y.C., 1946-47; asst. psychiatrist Mt. Sinai Hosp., N.Y.C., 1949-51; pvt. practice N.Y.C., 1949—; asst. psychiatrist Roosevelt Hosp., N.Y.C., 1954-57; chief psychiatrist Pleasantville (N.Y.) Cottage Sch., 1961-74. Bd. dirs. intuition network Inst. Noetic Scis.; dir. Wind Song Inst. Sec. Jane Coffin Childs Fund, 1938-41. Fellow Am. Orthopsychiat. Assn.; mem. Am. Psychiat. Assn., N.Y. Coun. Child and Adolescent Psychiatry, N.Y. County Med. Soc., N.Y. State Med. Soc. (psychiat. medicine com.), Westchester Psychiat. Soc. Avocations: architecture, parapsychology, travel, gardening, theater. Home: 16 Apple Bee Farm Ln Croton On Hudson NY 10520-3612 Office: 116 E 66th St New York NY 10021-6547 Office Phone: 212-737-0591.

JURKIEWICZ, MARGARET JOY GOMMEL, secondary school educator; b. Indpls., Sept. 5, 1920; d. Dewey Ezra and Joy Agnes (Edie) Gommel; m. Walter Stephen Jurkiewicz, Jan. 1, 1942; children: Mary Margaret, Dewey John, Walter Stephen Jr., Hugh Louis. BS, Ind. U., 1941; postgrad., U. Minn., 1942-43, Butler U., 1950-51, U. Cin., 1958-60, Ind. U., 1971-72, Ball State U., 1974-75. Cert. secondary tchr., Ind., Ohio. Tchr. home econ. Plymouth HS, Ind., 1941-42, Indpls. Pub. Sch., Ind., 1949-57, Mt. Confort-Hancock Co. Sch., Mt. Comfort, Ind., 1957-58, Cin. Pub. sch., 1958-61; tchr. 6th grade Plymouth Sch. corp., Ind., 1961-63; tchr. home econ. and art Argos Cmty. Sch., Ind., 1963-67; tchr. home econ. Penn-Harris-Madison Sch., Mishawaka, Ind., 1967-83; tchr. chpt. I South Bend Sch. Corp., Ind., 1983-85; vol. tchr. art various sch., Ind., 1985—, various sch., Mich., 1985—96, various sch., Ill., 1985-96. Author newsletter and booklet Polish Cultural Soc., 1979—. Bd. dir. Area Agy. on Aging Coun., Plymouth, Ind., 1987-94, Garden Cts. Sr. Housing, Plymouth, 1989—; mem. legis. com. Five County Area Agy. on Aging, 1994--; vol. tchr. sch., libr., children's mus. and sr. ctr., 1985—. Mem.: AARP (editor newsletter Marshall County chpt. 1993—), AAUW (pres., chair various coms.), Plymouth Pub. Libr. Friends (pres., chair various coms.), Marshall County Ret. Tchr. (pres. 1993—95), Ind. Assn. Family and Consumer Sci., Am. Assn. Family and Consumer Sci., PEO, Tippecanoe Audubon Soc., Ind. Polish Cultural Soc. (v.p., chair various coms.). Methodist. Avocations: gardening, camping, travel, football games, sewing. Home: 11570 9th A Rd Plymouth IN 46563-9581 E-mail: mjjurkiewicz@yahoo.com.

JURKIEWICZ, MARY LOUISE, elementary school educator; b. Wadsworth, Ohio, May 30, 1947; d. William Nicholas and Margaret Rose (Cattin) Lieberth; m. Eugene John Jurkiewicz, Apr. 10, 1971; children: William Nicholas, Emily Johanna. BA, Marygrove Coll., 1969; MAT in Reading, Oakland U., 1972. Cert. permanent tchg. cert. Mich. Tchr. primary edn. Kensington Acad., Bloomfield Hills, Mich., 1969—74; tchr. 1st grade Detroit Country Day Sch., Bloomfield Hills, 1981—. Master tchr., team leader 1st grade Detroit Country Day Sch., Bloomfield, 1986—2003. Sec. St. Owen Parish Coun., Bloomfield Hills, 1978—79; tchr. religious edn. St. Owen Ch., Bloomfield Hills, 1979—81. Recipient Longevity award, Mich. Coun. Tchrs. Math., 1995, Mich. Top Tchr. award, Met. Woman Mag., 1997. Mem.: Ind. Sch. Assn. of Cen. States (sch. rep. 1982—94), Assn. Ind. Mich. Schs. (sch. rep. 1982—94, pres. 1990—92). Roman Catholic. Avocations: gardening, travel, reading. Home: 6489 Wing Lake Rd Bloomfield Hills MI 48301 Office: Detroit Country Day Sch 3003 W Maple Rd Bloomfield Hills MI 48301

JUROWICZ, KIMBERLY DEBORAH, special education educator, elementary school educator; b. Phila., July 25, 1975; d. Albert Frank Jurowicz, Sr. and Joan (Palermo) Jurowicz. BA in Elem. Edn. cum laude, Holy Family U., 1998. Cert. tchr. instrnl. I Pa. Camp counselor Bensalem (Pa.) Twp. Pks. and Recreation Dept., 1991; tutoring instr. Holy Family U., Phila., 1998; camp counselor St. Jerome's Summercamp, Phila., 1998—99; elem. and mid. sch. tchr. Sch. Dist. Phila., 1998—2003; autistic tchr. Woods Svcs., Langhorne, Pa., 2003—. Elem. tchr. West Phila. Charter Sch.; athletic coord. Sheridan Elem. Sch., Phila., 1999, Phila., 2000; fundraising coord., participant Sch. Dist. Phila., 1999—2002; co-owner, pres., mgr. Home Sweet Home Enterprises, 2000—02. Vol. ARC, Levittown, Pa., 1997—99; fundraiser, gift donor St. Vincent's Orphanage, Phila., 1999—2003; soccer and basketball coach St. Charles Borromeo Ch., Bensalem, Pa., 1987—91; ch. canter various chs., Bensalem, Phila., 1992—99. Xavier grant/scholar, U. Scranton, 1993—94. Fellow: Phila. Fedn. Tchrs., Diversified Investors' Group. Republican. Avocations: singing, writing, sports, photography, reading. Home and Office: 1620 Lavender Rd Bensalem PA 19020

JUST, GEMMA RIVOLI, retired advertising executive; b. N.Y.C., Nov. 29, 1921; d. Philip and Brigida (Consolo) Rivoli; m. Victor Just, Jan. 29, 1955. BA, Hunter Coll., N.Y.C., 1943. Copy group head McCann Erickson, N.Y.C., 1958-62; copy supr. Morse Internat., N.Y.C., 1962-67; v.p., dir. creative svcs. Deltakos divsn. J. Walter Thompson, N.Y.C., 1967-75; v.p., copy dir. Sudler & Hennessey divsn. Young & Rubicam, N.Y.C., 1980-87, sr. v.p., assoc. creative dir. copy, 1987-88, ret., 1989. Mem. Episcopal Ch. Women of Ch. of Incarnation, N.Y.C., also ch. altar guild pres. and acolyte. Recipient Aesculapius awards Modern Medicine mag., 1980-88; named

Best Writer, Art Dirs. Club N.Y., 1979, Best Writer Young & Rubicam, 1981. Mem. Coun. Comms. Soc., Pharm. Advt. Coun., Am. Med. Writers Assn. (exec. com. 1973). Home: 155 E 38th St Apt 5D New York NY 10016 2663

JUST, JENNIFER RAMSAY, television and video producer, writer; b. Lake Forest, Ill., Dec. 30, 1958; d. Ward Swift Just and Jean Claudia (Ramsay) Bower; m. F. Corey Darling, Sept. 10, 1988; children: Cameron, Evan. BA in Psycholinguistics, Brown U., 198l. Editorial asst. The Writer, Inc. and Plays, Inc., Boston, 1981-82, asst. editor, 1982-83, assoc. editor, 1983-84; prodn. asst. Sta. WGBY-TV, pub. TV, Springfield, Mass., 1984-86, assoc. producer, 1986-88, producer, 1988-90; freelance writer, video producer Easthampton, Mass., 1990-95; freelance writer Southington, Woodbridge, Conn., 1990—; columnist On the Homefront. Mem. Easthampton Conservation Commn., 1990—94, Southington Parent-Tchr. Coun., 1998—2000, Southington Arts Coun., 1999—2000, Beecher Road Sch. PTO, 2000—, Woodbridge Cable Adv. Coun., 2001—; bd. mem. C.B. Ramsay Found., F. Ward Just Scholarship Fund, 2001—. Recipient 1st place award Advt. Club. Western Mass., 1987, ACE award, 1990, Excellence in Cable Programming awards, 1991-96, Emmy award nomination, 1996, ACE award nomination, 1996. Mem.: Internat. Women Writers Guild, Sisters in Crime, Mystery Writers Am. Inc. Democrat. Avocations: gardening, geneology, reading, travel. Home: 157 Center Rd Woodbridge CT 06525-1840 E-mail: jenniferjust@yahoo.com.

JUSTICE, SARAH C. social worker, volunteer; b. Hampton, Tenn., Feb. 1, 1902; d. Richard Campbell and Lillie Elizabeth (Smith) J. BA, Tusculum Coll., 1927; MA, Vanderbilt U., 1951; postgrad., Dept. Health, Edn., Welfare, Washington, 1961. Lic. clin. social worker, Tenn. Tchr. high sch., Hawkins County, Tenn., 1927-29, Hancock County, Tenn., 1929-31; mgr. Tusculum Coll. Bookstore, Greenville, Tenn., 1931-32; social worker Pub. Welfare Dept. State Tenn., 1932-69; vol. social work agys., Green county, 1969—. Co-worker cmty. svc. com. Takoma Adventist Hosp.; bd. dirs. U.S. Foster Grandparents Program. Mem. Tusculum Coll. Aluni Soc. (Pioneer plaque), Greenville Breakfast Exch. Club (booster), Tenn. State Employees Assn. (chair com., Plaque 1996), Order of Ea. Star (sec. Christian scholarship com., Mosheim chpt., Grand chpt. Tenn.), The Humane Soc. (parliamentarian), Interagy. Coun. (chmn. by-laws com.), Greenville/Green County Dem. Woman's Club (parliamentarian, mem. exec. bd.), Commanders Club (contbr., Coolidge award 1997). Democrat. Presbyterian. Avocations: reading, writing, history of church. Home: 29 Justice Ln Greeneville TN 37745-0943

JUVVADI, ANITA REDDY, pediatrician; arrived in U.S., 1991; d. Ram Reddy Guntku and Sujana Reddy; m. Sridhar Juvvadi, Dec. 20, 1990; children: Mihir, Vishesh. MBBS, Gandhi Med. Coll., 1990; MD, U. Calif., 1998. Diplomate Am. Bd. Pediats., 00. Pediatrician Palo Alto (Calif.) Med. Found., 1998—2000, Hosp. Dr. Pediats., Mountain View, Calif., 2000—. Facilitator Support Group for Children with Life Threatening Illnesses, San Francisco, 1997—99. Facilitator various breast feeding support groups, Palo Alto, 1998—2000. Mem.: Am. Acad. Pediats. Avocations: reading science fiction, hiking, travel. Office: Pediatric Office 2500 Hospital Dr Bldg 12 Mountain View CA 94040

KAABAR, JOANNE FLORENCE, special education educator, poet; b. L.A., Dec. 15, 1946; d. Nathan Noah and Rosalind J. Perlman; 1 child, Rudy Legarda. BA, Calif. State U., L.A., 1982. Substitute tchr. Alhambra (Calif.) Unified Sch. Dist., 1993—96; para educator for developmentally disabled studies Long Beach (Calif.) Unified Sch. Dist., 1999—. Author poetry. Mem.: NOW.

KABRICH, JEANINE RENEE, broadcaster, educator; b. Concord, Calif., May 29, 1963; d. Robert Nicolas and Judith Lynn (Johnson) Kabrich; m. Douglas Michael Curry, June 15, 1985 (div. Sept. 1987). BS in Mass Comm/Broadcast Journalism, Emerson Coll., Boston, 1989. Cert. broadcast specialist Def. Info. Sch. News reporter, writer, part-time anchor KDOC-TV Channel 56, Anaheim, Calif., 1990; creator, prodr., host, reporter, editor The Coachella Valley news mag. Palmer Cablevision, Palm Desert, Calif., 1992; news and airborne traffic reporter KFMB AM/FM/TV, San Diego, 1992-93; comm. and journalism instr. Palomar Coll. and Grossmont Coll., San Diego, 1993-96; helicopter traffic reporter KTTV-TV Fox 11, L.A., 1997-98; news anchor, news reproter KABC-AM 790, KNX AM 1070, L.A., 1996-98; So. Calif. media rep., media specialist team leader U.S. Census Bur. Census 2000 campaign, L.A., 1999—. Part-time actress, spokeswoman Burkett Talent Agy., L.A. Weekend co-host Ask the Builder, KSDO-AM, San Diego; prodr. radio comml. Served with U.S. Army, 1982-88. Mem. Radio and TV News Dirs. Assn., Soc. Profl. Journalists, Broadcast Edn. Assn. Republican. Roman Catholic. Avocations: cooking, exercise, reading, teaching.

KACHMAN, FRANCES GUIDUCCI, artist; b. Peckville, Pa., May 9, 1949; d. Joesph Guiducci and Eva Piccholi Born; m. James P. Kachman; children: Darren, Dean. Student, Coll. of Art, Detriot, 1959, student, 1962; study with, Edgar Yeager, 1973—80, John Sanden, N.Y., Russer Ketter, Ctr. for Creative Studies, Joseph Maniscalco, Janice Tremp, Marie Larson. Exhibitions include Std. Fed. Bank, Scarab Club, Detroit Athletic Club, Detroit Med. Ctr., Represented in permanent collections Palms (Mich.) Mus., Dr. Larry Lloyd, Dr. Michael Busuittio, Olhand Lake Sem., Orchard Lake, Bon Secours Hosp., Mich., Fla., Hawaii, Jamaica, Bermuda, Mex., Eng., France, exhibited in group shows at Grosse Pointe Art Exhibit. Recipient numerous art awards. Mem.: Lakeside Pallet Club (past bd. dir.), Scarab Club (past bd. dir.). Home: 22901 Lakeshore Saint Clair Shores MI 48080

KACHUR, BETTY RAE, elementary school educator; b. Lorain, Ohio, June 12, 1930; d. John and Elizabeth (Stanko) Kachur. BS in Edn., Kent State U., 1963; MEd, U. Ariz., 1971. Cert. tchr., in reading. Tchr. Lorain City Schs., 1961-94. Bd. dirs. Habitat for Humanity Lorain County, 1997—2001, Lorain Pub. Libr., Ohio Friends LIbrs.; treas. Lorain Downtown Ministerial Assn.; profl. storyteller Northeastern Ohio Western Res. Assn. for Preservation and Perpetuation of Storytellers. Mem.: AAUW (social com., scholarship com. 1999), Daniel T. Gardner Reading Assn. (pres. 1978—79, treas. 1988—94), Internat. Reading Assn. (by-laws com. Ohio Coun.). Mem. United Ch. Of Christ. Avocations: reading, writing, quilting, travel.

KACIR, BARBARA BRATTIN, lawyer; b. Buffalo, Ohio, July 19, 1941; d. William James and Jean (Harrington) Brattin; m. Charles Stephen Kacir, June 3, 1973 (div. Aug. 1977). BA, Wellesley Coll., 1963; JD, U. Mich., 1967. Bar: Ohio 1967, D.C. 1980. Assoc. Arter & Hadden, Cleve., 1967-74, ptnr., 1974-79; ptnr. Jones, Day, Reavis & Pogue, Washington, 1980-83, Cleve., 1983-95; dep. gen. counsel-litigation Textron Inc., Providence, 1995—; instr. trial tactics Case-Western Res. U., Cleve., 1976-79. Mem. nat. com. visitors, nat. fund raising com. U. Mich. Mem. ABA, Ohio Bar Assn., D.C. Bar Assn., Cleve. Bar Assn. (trustee 1973-76, treas. 1978-79), Am. Law Inst., Def. Rsch. Inst. Republican. Office: Textron Inc 40 Westminster St Ste 2 Providence RI 02903-2525

KACZANOWSKA, LAURIE HYSON SMITH, lawyer; b. Palmerton, Pa., July 7, 1953; d. James Donaldson and Mary Ann (Hyson) Smith; m. Donald James Gerber, Aug. 1976 (div. May 1981); m. Witold Kaczanowska, Dec. 11, 1993 (div. Feb. 2002); 1 child, Wit Thomas Kaczanowski. BS, Pa. State U., 1975; MSW, U. Denver, 1981; JD, Northeastern U., 1989. Adminstrv. staff, resource coord., vol. coord., counselor Women in Crisis, Lakewood, Colo., 1977-79; program adminstr. Big Sis. of Colo., Life Choices Program, Denver, 1979-80; legis. coord., lobbyist Common Cause, Denver, 1980-81; social work advocate Denver Legal Aid Soc., 1982-86; legis. analyst Nat. Conf. State Legis., Denver, 1987; mediator, intake coord. Harvard Law Sch., Cambridge, Mass., 1988; law clk. Supreme Jud. Ct. State Mass., Boston, 1988-89; legis. staff Rep. Patricia Schroeder, U.S. [illegible] Denver, 1990—91; asst. city atty., sr. atty., founder alternative resolution program, dir. cmty. justice program Denver City Attys. Office, Denver, 1991—. Mem.: Denver Bar Assn., Colo. Bar Assn., Colo. Women's Bar Assn. Presbyterian. Home: 3216 E 6th Ave Denver CO 80206-4407 Office: Denver City Attys Office 303 W Colfax Ave Ste 500 Denver CO 80204-2623 E-mail: lauriesmithk@msn.com.

KACZMAREK, JANE, actress; b. Dec. 21, 1955; d. Edward and Evelyn Kaczmarek; m. Bradley Whitford; 3 children. BFA in Theatre, U. Wis.; MFA, Yale Sch. Drama, 1982. Actor: (TV series) Malcolm in the Middle (nominated for 3 Golden Globe awards for best performance actress tv series, nominated for 4 Emmy awards for outstanding lead actress comedy series, Am. Comedy award, Family Friendly award, 2 Individual Achievement in a Comedy awards, TV Critics Assn., nominated best actress quality comedy, Viewers for Quality TV), St. Elsewhere, Felicity, American Playhouse, The Paper Chase-The Second Year (ACE nomination), Hometown, Equal Justice, Big Wave Dave's, Party of Five, Frasier, The Practice, Cybill, (guest appearances) Touched by an Angel, Picket Fences, L.A. Law, Hollywood Division, : (TV films) All's Fair, 1989, Apollo 11, 1996, Educating Mom, 1996, Jenifer, 2001, The Deception, Boys Will Be Boys, I'll Take Manhattan, Something About Amelia, The Christmas Story, The Three Kings; (films) The Chamber, 1996, The Spittin' Image, 1997, Pleasantville, 1998, Wildly Available, 1999, Vice Versa, Uncommon Valor, D.O.A., The Heavenly Kid, Falling in Love; (plays, Broadway) Lost in Yonkers; (plays) Kindertransport, Raised in Captivity, Wasp, Escape from Happiness, Eve's Diary, Pride and Prejudice, The Legends of Oedipus, Loose Ends, Ice Cream/Hot Fudge, Better Living, Hands of Its Enemy. Office: Innovative Artists 1999 Ave of the Stars Los Angeles CA 90067*

KADAR, KARIN PATRICIA, librarian; b. Oil City, Pa., May 30, 1951; d. Michael Joseph and Bette Lee (Painter) Kadar; divorced; 1 child, Michael L. BS, Clarion U., 1973; MLS, U. Pitts., 1975; postgrad., U. S.C. Lic. instrnl. II in libr. sci. and elem. edn., pub. libr. lic. Substitute tchr. McKeesport (Pa.) Area Schs., 1973, elem. sch. libr., 1973-75, 3d grade tchr., 1975-78, elem. sch. libr., 1978-81; adj. prof. Pa. State U., McKeesport, 1988; periodicals libr. Seton Hill Coll., Greensburg, Pa., 1986-89; dir. Penn Twp. Pub. Libr., Level Green, Pa., 1989-90; grade sch. libr. substitute St. Agnes Sch., North Huntington, Pa., 1992; mid. sch. libr. substitute Belle Vernon (Pa.) Area Sch. Dist., 1993-95; dir. West Newton (Pa.) Pub. Libr., 1993-95, Highland Cmty. Libr., Richland, Pa., 1996; libr. Ridgeland (S.C.) Elem. Sch., 1996-98; spl. orders coord. Barnes and Noble, Hilton Head Island, SC, 1998-99; mgr. Bluffton (S.C.) Cmty. Libr., 1998-99; media specialist Jasper (S.C.) County H.S., 1999—2001, dist. libr./ media specialist coord., 1999—; sch. tech. coord. West Hardeeville Sch., 2001—, media specialist, 2002—. Mem. consumer appeals bd. Ford Motor Co., 1989-92, coord. Sch. Dist. Libr. Media Svcs., 2000—; staff writer Current Diversions. Author: (booklet) Sammy the Smokeless Dragon, 1976. Panelist Scan Trak Shoppers, 1984—, Nat. Family Opinion, 1984—; vol. Am. Cancer Soc., 1969-94, pub. edn. chmn., 1974-80, cancer prevention study II chmn., 1982-88, pub. affairs chmn., 1984-86, residential area crusade chmn., 1984-85. Named Vol. of Yr. Am. Cancer Soc. Mon Youch Unit, 1983-84; recipient Crusade award Am. Cancer Soc., Mon Yough unit, 1985-86. Mem. ALA, Pa. Libr. Assn., Parent-Tchr. Guild, Pa. State Edn. Assn., Low Country Reading Assn. (pres-elect), S.C. Assn. Sch. Librs. (regional rep. Jasper County, writer and mem. editl. bd. Messenger), Westmoreland County Hist. Soc., McKeesport Coll. Club, Heritage Hist. Assn. (Hilton Head, S.C.). Avocations: freelance writing, collecting books, genealogical research. Office: West Hardeeville Sch Hwy 46 Hardeeville SC 29927 Office Phone: 843-717-1251.

KADDEN, JUDITH, author, educator, journalist; b. N.Y.C., Nov. 5, 1949; d. Albert and Greta Kay Kadden. BS, U. Cin., 1971; MA, Boston U., 1983. Rschr. The Washington Post, Washington; pres. Children's Wear Showroom, Chgo.; instr. Boston U., Harvard U., Bentley Coll., Fla. Atlantic U. Radio host WNN. Author: Traveling Through Idioms, Traveling the World Through Idioms. Mem. TESOL, Women in Comms. Home: 241 Perkins St Apt C303 Jamaica Plain MA 02130-4010

KADEN, ELLEN ORAN, lawyer, consumer products company executive; b. N.Y.C., Oct. 1, 1951; m. Lewis Kaden; 2 children. AB, Cornell U., 1972; MA, U. Chgo., 1973; JD, Columbia U., 1977. Bar: N.Y., 1978. Law clerk U.S. Dist. Ct. (so. dist.) N.Y., 1977-78; asst. prof. Columbia U. Sch. Law, 1978-82, assoc. prof., 1982-84; exec. v.p., gen. counsel, sec. CBS Inc., N.Y.C., 1991-98; sr. v.p. law and govt. affairs Campbell Soup Co., Camden, N.J., 1998—. Reporter jud. coun. 2nd Cir. Adv. Comm. on Planning for Dist. Cts., 1979-81; assoc. Cravath, Swaine & Moore, 1981-86. Trustee Columbia U. Mem. Nat. Legal Aid and Defender Assn. (corp. adv. com.), Inst. Jud. Adminstrn. (trustee), Lawyers' Com. for Civil Rights (internat. rule of law coun.). Office: Campbell Soup Co One Campbell Pl Camden NJ 08103*

KADING, LAURA J, special education educator; b. Appleton, Wis., July 26, 1972; d. John C. and Margaret A. Kading. BS - Spl. Edn., U. of Wis. Eau Claire, Eau Claire, WI, 1990—95; ME - Ednl. Computing, Cardinal Stritch U., Milwaukee, WI, 2002—03. Learning Disabilities and Cognitive Disabilites Teacher Wis. DPI, WI, 1995. Tchr. Kimberly H.S., Kimberly WI, Wis., 1999—, Wautoma H.S., Wautoma, Wis., 1995—99. Publicity chair person Waushara County Habitat for Humanity, Wautoma, Wis., 1996—98. Mem.: Wis. Edn. Assn., NEA, Coun. for Exceptional Children (assoc.). Catholic. Avocations: reading, computing, golf, singing. Office: Kimberly High School W2662 Kennedy Ave Kimberly WI 54136 Personal E-mail: lkading@new.vv.com. E-mail: lkading@kimberly.k12.wi.us.

KADUSHIN, KAREN DONNA, law school dean; b. L.A., Sept. 3, 1943; BA, UCLA, 1964; JD, Golden Gate U., 1977. Bar: Calif. 1977, U.S. Dist. Ct. (no. dist.) Calif. 1977. Mem. adj. faculty law Golden Gate U. and U. San Francisco, 1977-84; assoc. Law Offices Diana Richmond, San Francisco, 1978-80; ptnr. Richmond & Kadushin, San Francisco, 1981-83; prin. Kadushin Law Offices, San Francisco, 1983-88; ptnr. Kadushin-Fancher-Wickland, San Francisco, 1989-94; dean Monterey (Calif.) Coll. Law, Monterey, Calif., 1995—. Judge pro tem settlement confs. dept. domestic rels. San Francisco Superior Ct., 1985-95; bd. dirs. Lawyers Mut. Ins. Co. Author: California Practice Guide: Law Practice Management, 1992—. Bd. dirs. Legal Assistance for Elderly, San Francisco, 1983, San Francisco Neighborhood Legal Assistance Found., 1984. Mem. Calif. Women Lawyers, Bar Assn. San Francisco (bd. dirs. 1985-86, pres. 1993, Merit award 1980, 90), Barristers Club (pres. 1982), Monterey County Women Lawyers (treas. 1999-2000, pres. 2001). Office: Monterey Coll Law 404 W Franklin St Monterey CA 93940-2303 Fax: 831-373-0143. E-mail: kdkdean@montereylaw.edu.

KAEHELE, BETTIE LOUISE, accountant; b. Sherwood, Tenn., Oct. 29, 1950; d. James Henry and Ruby Katherine (Clark) Shetters; divorced; children: Josiah Dean, Dana Marie. AAS, Albuquerque Tech. Vocat. Inst., 1980; BSBA, Nat. Coll., Albuquerque, 1991. Acctg. clk. Am. Auto Assn., Albuquerque, 1980-81, Ryder Truck Rental, Inc., Albuquerque, 1981-82; bookkeeper, sec. Grants Steel Sash & Hardware, Albuquerque, 1986-87; owner Sherwood Svcs., 1982-86; acctg. specialist Burton & Co., Albuquerque, 1987, Neff & Co., Albuquerque, 1987-91; acctg. tech. U. N.Mex. Found., Albuquerque, 1991-92, acct., 1992—2002, sr. acct., 2002—; acct. biology dept., acct. II U. N.Mex., Albuquerque, 1997—2002, sr. acct., 2002—. Bible study Bernalillo County Detention Ctr. Republican. Avocations: reading, dance, theatre, poetry, writing. Home: 7408 Desert Canyon Pl SW Albuquerque NM 87121-6424

KAEN, NAIDA, state representative; [illegible] 1940; m. Fred R. Naida; two children. BEd, U. Mich., 1968; MBA, U. N.H., 1977. Coll. instr. acctg.; state rep. N.H. Ho. of Reps., 1995—. Mem. sci., tech. and energy com. N.H. Ho. Reps. Mem. Audobon Soc., Wamprey River Watershed Assn. Office: NH State Legis State House Concord NH 03301 Address: 22 Toon Ln Lee NH 03824-6507

KAFKA, BARBARA POSES, writer; b. N.Y.C., Aug. 6, 1933; d. Jack and Lillian (Shapiro) Poses; m. Ernest Kafka, June 19, 1959; children: Nicole, Michael. AB cum laude, Radcliffe Coll., 1954. Cons. in field. Author: American Food California Wine, 1981, 94, (Tastemaker award), Microwave Gourmet, 1987 (N.Y. Times Best Seller), Food for Friends, 1987, 93, Microwave Gourmet Healthstyle Cookbook, 1989, (Tastemaker award), Party Food, 1992, Roasting A Simple Art, 1995 (Julia Child Cookbook award), Soup, A Way of Life, 1998; compiler, editor pro bono: The James Beard Celebration Cookbook, 1990; editor: The Four Seasons, 1980, The Cook's Catalogue, (mags.) Cooking, The Pleasures of Cooking; contbg. editor Vogue, 1981-89, Gourmet, 1988-96; contbg. columnist N.Y. Times, 1987—; contbr. articles to profl. jours. Mem. Internat. Assn. Culinary Profls., Am. Inst. Wine and Food, Culinary Historians Boston, James Beard. Home and Office: 23 E 92nd St New York NY 10128-0607

KAFOURY, DEBORAH, state representative; b. Walla Walla, Wash., Aug. 19, 1967; m. Nic Blosser; 1 child, Alexander. BA in English, Whitman Coll., 1989. Aide Oreg. Congressman Les AuCoin, Washington; mem. Oreg. Ho. of Reps., 1998—; ho. Dem. whip, 2001; ho. Dem. leader. Founder, former chair X-PAC; mem. adv. bd. I Have A Dream Found.; vice chair. Transition Projects; coord. city coun. campaign Erik Sten; bd. dirs. Citizens Sensible Transp. Democrat. Office: 900 Court St North East H-395 Salem OR 97301

KAGAN, CHERYL C. state legislator; b. Washington, July 2, 1961; AB, Vassar Coll., 1983; postgrad., U. Md., 1991—. Polit. cons.; lobbyist Handgun Control Inc., 1991, 93; chief of staff U.S. Congress, 1991-92; exec. dir. Ind. Action, 1989-91; dir. devel. Nat. Women's Polit. Caucus, 1986-87; state legislator Md. House of Dels., Annapolis, 1995—2003, vice chair House Dem. Rsch. Group. Mem. charter rev. commn. Montgomery County, 2003—; bd. adv. U. Md., Shady Grove, 1995—2003; mem. Md. State Arts Coun., 1995—2003. Mem. Arts and Humanities Coun. of Montgomery County, 2003—; chair., exec. session chm. Leadership Montgomery Class of 2002; vice chair House Joint Audit Committee; Bd. American Jewish Committee (D.C. Chpt.); bd. dir. Ams. Dem. Action, 1981—; exec. dir. Carl M. Freeman Found., 2003—. Named one of Md.'s Top 100 Women, Daily Record, 2003; recipient Named one of Top 10 Rising Stars Balt. Sun, 1996; Flemming fellow Ctr. for Policy Alts., 1996—97. Democrat. Home and Office: 1048 Wintergreen Ter Rockville MD 20850-1005

KAGAN, CONSTANCE HENDERSON, philosopher, educator, consultant; b. Houston, Sept. 16, 1940; d. Bessie Earle (Henderson) Davis; m. Morris Kagan, May 27, 1967. BA, Baylor U., 1962; MSSW, U. Tex. Austin, 1966; PhD, U. Okla., 1979. Dir. Acacia Pk. Ctr. for Continuing Edn., Great Falls, Va., 1996—. Congl. fellow, 1981-82. Mem. Am. Philos. Assn. Office: PO Box 1290 Great Falls VA 22066-1290 Business E-Mail: ckagan@continuingedu.org.

KAGAN, ELENA, law educator; b. 1960; BA summa cum laude, Princeton, 1981; MPhil, Worchester Coll., Oxford, 1983; JD magna cum laude, Harvard Law School, 1986. Law clk. US Ct. of Appeals for Judge Abner Mikva of the US Supreme Ct. for the DC Circuit, 1986—87, US Ct. of Appeals for Justice Thurgood Marshall of the US Supreme Ct., 1987—88; assoc. Williams & Connolly, Wash., DC, 1989—91; faculty mem. Univ. of Chgo. Law Sch., Chgo., 1991—99; nominated to serve as judge US Supreme Ct. of Appeals, Wash., DC, 1999; asst. prof. Univ. of Chgo. Law Sch., 1991, prof. of law tenure, 1995; assoc. counsel to the Pres. White House, Wash., DC, 1995—96, dep. asst. to the Pres. for Domestic Policy, 1997—99, dep. dir. of the Domestic Policy Coun., 1997—99; vis. prof. Harvard Law Sch., Cambridge, Mass., 1999, prof., 2001—, dean, 2003—, Charles Hamilton Houston prof. of law, 2003—. Author: (article) Harvard Law Rev. Article, "Pres. Admin.", 2001 (honored as the year's top scholarly article by the Am. Bar Assoc. Section on Admin. Law and Reg. Pract., 2001). Kagan has also written on a range of First Amendment issues, including the role of governmental motive in different facets of First Amendment doctrine, and the interplay of libel law and the First Amendment. Mem.: Harvard Law Sch. faculty appt. comm., Harvard Law Sch. Locational options comm. (chair 2001—02). Kagan is a prof. of law at Harvard fLaw Sch. where she teaches admin. law, constitutional law, and civil procedure. Her recent sholarship focuses primarily on the role of the Pres. of the US in formulating and influencing fed. admin. and regulatory law. Office: Harvard Law Sch Griswold 200 1563 Mass Ave Cambridge MA 02138

KAGAN, JULIA LEE, magazine editor; b. Nurnberg, Fed. Republic Germany, Nov. 25, 1948; d. Saul and Elizabeth J. Kagan. AB, Bryn Mawr Coll., 1970. Rschr. Look Mag., N.Y.C., 1970-71; editl. asst., asst. editor McCall's mag., N.Y.C., 1971-74, assoc. editor, 1974-78, sr. editor, 1978-79; articles editor Working Woman mag., N.Y.C., 1979-85, exec. editor, 1985-88; editor Psychology Today, 1988-90; sr. editor McCalls, 1990-91; contbg. editor Working Woman, 1991-93; editor-in-chief Lamaze Parents' Mag., 1992-93, Lamaze Baby Mag., 1993; spl. projects dir. Child Mag., 1993-94; sr. v.p. EDK Assocs., N.Y.C., 1994; psychology/health dir. Fitness Mag., N.Y.C., 1995-96; dep. editor Consumer Reports Mag., Yonkers, NY, 1996, editor, 1996-2000; v.p. and editl. dir. Consumers Union, 2000—. Vis. J. Stewart Riley prof. journalism Ind. U., 1991-93. Co-author: Manworks: A Guide to Style, 1980; contbg. author: The Working Woman Success Book, 1981, The Working Woman Report, 1984. Pres. Appleby Found., N.Y.C., 1982-84; trustee Bryn Mawr Coll., 2000—. Recipient 2d Ann. Advt. Journalism award Compton Advt., 1983 Mem. Am. Soc. Mag. Editors, Womens Media Group (bd. dirs.), Journalism and Women Symposium (treas. 1993-94, pres. 1995-96). Clubs: Princeton (N.Y.C.). Office: Consumer Reports 101 Truman Ave Yonkers NY 10703-1044*

KAGAN, MARILYN D. retired architect; b. Providence, Nov. 13, 1930; d. Jacob L. and Emma Kenner Kagan. BS in Arch., Drexel U., 1972. Cartographer U.S. Army Map Svc., Providence, 1952-53, Redevel. Authority, Phila., 1958-68; arch. George Ewing Inc., Phila., 1969-70, City of Phila. Water Dept., 1971-91; ret., 1991. Designer jewelry. Bd. dirs. Philly Walks-Pedestrian Safety Coalition, 1996-98; chair Soviet Jewry Com. of Society Hill Synagogue, Phila., 1980-90. Recipient Cert. of Appreciation, Jewish Family Svc., 1993-96. Mem.: Na'Amat/Pioneer Women (pres. R.I. chpt. 2002—). Democrat. Jewish. Avocations: jewelry design, painting, photography, gardening, travel. Home: 311 Rochambeau Ave Providence RI 02906-3507

KAGAN, SARAH HOPE, geriatrics services professional, educator; AB, U. of Chgo, 1984; BS, Rush U., 1989; PhD., U. Calif., San Francisco, 1994. Fellow, assoc. prof. of gerontol. nursing, gerontol. specialist Inst. on Aging at the U. of Penn, 1995—; secondary appointment Dept. of Otorhinolaryngology, 1995—. Author: (book) Older Adults Coping with Cancer: Intergrating Cancer into a life Mostly Lived, 1997. Recipient John and Mary Lindback award for Dist. tchg., 1998; fellow Macarthur Found., 2003. Office: Univ of Penn Sch of Nursing Rm 365 NEB 420 Guardian Dr Philadelphia PA 19104

KAGGEN, LOIS SHEILA, non-profit organization executive; b. N.Y.C., Jan. 2, 1944; d. Elias and Sylvia (Muntner) K.; m. Harold Jay Burns, June 29, 1969 (dec. June 1975); 1 child, David Henry (dec.); m. Michael Francis McCann, Sept. 26, 1984. BS in Fine Arts, Skidmore Coll., 1964; postgrad., Cooper Union, 1967-70; MA in Art Edn., CCNY, 1973; PhD in Art Edn., NYU, 1997. Tchr. fine arts grades 7-9 Jr. H.S. 149, Bronx, N.Y., 1967-74; founder, pres. Resources for Artists With Disabilities, N.Y.C., 1987—. Traumatic Brain Injury Consumer Adv., 1977—; mem. adv. bd. com. Art in Edn. Project, N.Y. State Coun. on the Arts, Ctr. for Safety in the Arts, N.Y.C., 1987; cons. Ea. Paralyzed Vets. Assn., Guggenheim Mus. Art, N.Y.C., 1990; mem. bd. advisors Ind. Arts Gallery, Queens Ind. Living Ctr., Jamaica, N.Y., 1987-97, 98; mem. steering com. Ann. Disability Independence Day March, 1992-93, mem. Media Outreach, 1992; provider written and oral testimony in field to orgns.; bd. dirs. Ctr. for Independence of the Disabled of N.Y., Inc., N.Y.C., 1996—, Gov.'s appt. to Traumatic Brain Injury Svcs. Coordinating Coun., Albany, 1997-2001, others; presenter NIH Consensus Devel. Conf. on Rehab. of Persons with Traumatic Brain Injury, Bethesda, Md., 1998, 5th Ann. Conf., Traumatic Brain Injury Program, N.Y. State Dept. Health, Albany, 1998, Info. and Comm. Com. TBISEC (TBI Coun.) NYS-DOH, Delmar, N.Y., 2001, N.Y. State Assembly task force on people with disabilites: pub. hearing City U. N.Y. Grad. Ctr., N.Y., 2001; originator, conf. com. co-organizer, consumer panelist NYU Moses Ctr. for Students with Disabilities and Ctr. for Independence of Disabled of N.Y., Loeb Student Ctr., NYU, N.Y.C., 1998; panel organizer, moderator, presenter Inst. for Rsch. on Women's 16th Ann. Celebration of Our Work Conf., Douglass Coll., Rutgers U., New Brunswick, N.J., 1998; mem. search com. Whitney Mus., N.Y., 2004, The Tang Tchg. Mus. and Art Gallery, Skidmore Coll., Saratoga Springs, N.Y., 2004; gave testimony Taxi and Limousine Commn., 2004; art presenter in field. Photography exhbns. include 80 Washington Sq. East Galleries, N.Y.C., 1977, Soho Photo Gallery, N.Y.C., 1978, 4th St. Photo Gallery, N.Y.C., 1979, Womanart Gallery, N.Y.C., 1979, Leslie-Lohman Gallery, N.Y.C., 1980, 81, Window Gallery, Met. Savs. Bank, N.Y.C., 1980, Cathedral St. John-the-Devine Gallery, N.Y.C., 1980, Donnell Libr. Gallery, 1981; originator, organizer various exhbns. African-Am. Artists with Disabilities, Artists with Phys. Disabilities; contbr. articles, photographs to profl. jours. Mem. Nat. Inst. Disability and Rehab. Rsch.; mem. Office Spl. Edn. and Rehab. Svcs. U.S. Dept. Edn., Washington, mem. per rev. registry, 1995—; active Disabled in Action of Greater N.Y., 1989—, Manhattan Borough Pres. Disability Adv. Coun., 1988—98, 1999—; access subcom. 504 Dem. Club for Persons with Disabilities, 2000—; mem. Mayor's Adv. Com. on People with Disabilities, N.Y.C., 1991—93, Citywide Coalition on Disability, N.Y.C., 1994—95; active in assistive signage needs Planning Meeting NYC Coun./Dept. Disabled, 2000; mem. info. subcom. NYC Coun. Planning Com. Dept. Disabled, 2000—; mem. Disabilities Network of NYC, 2000—; mem. search com. for dir. The Tang Tchg. Mus. and Art Gallery, Skidmore Coll., 2004; mem. disability rights steering com. 504 Dem. Club for Persons with Disabilities, 1987—88, mem. exec. com., 1990—2002; mem. N.Y. County Dem. Com. 102ED, 1995—; mem. at-large exec. bd. Village Ind. Dems., 2003—04. Grantee Whitney Mus. Am. Art and the Smithsonian Instn., summer 1967, summer film inst. Stanford U., 1968; Cooper Union scholar, 1967-70; recipient Appreciation cert. Manhattan Borough Pres., 1991, Dean's Disting. Alumni Achievement award NYU, N.Y.C., 1998. Mem. Coll. Art Assn. (com. mems. with disabilities for accessible programs and places 1990—), N.Y.C. Coun. dept. for disabled. Office: Resources for Artists with Disabilities 77 7th Ave Ste PH-H New York NY 10011-0043

KAHAN, MARLENE, professional association executive; b. Bronx, N.Y., June 10, 1952; d. Meyer and Ruth (Baroth) Schmulewitz. BA in Psychology, CUNY, 1973. Tchr. elem. sch., Bronx, 1974-75; asst. to pres. Mag. Pubs. Am., N.Y.C., 1976-83; asst. dir. Am. Soc. Mag. Editors, N.Y.C., 1983-90, exec. dir., 1990—. Recipient Gold Key award PR News, 1991. Mem. Am. Soc. Assn. Execs., N.Y. Soc. Assn. Execs. (bd. dirs. 2000—03), Women in Comms. (program com. N.Y.C. 1991-93, bd. dirs. 1993-95, v.p. programs 1993-95). Avocations: ballet, jazz dance and music. Office: Am Soc Mag Editors 810 7th Ave New York NY 10019 E-mail: mkahan@magazine.org.

KAHANA, EVA FROST, sociology educator; b. Budapest, Hungary, Mar. 21, 1941; came to U.S., 1957; d. Jacob and Sari Frost; m. Boaz Kahana, Apr. 15, 1962; children: Jeffrey, Michael. BA, Stern Coll., Yeshiva U., 1962; MA, CCNY, CUNY, 1965; PhD, U. Chgo., 1968; HLD (hon.), Yeshiva U., 1991. Nat. Inst. on Aging predoctoral fellow U. Chgo. Com. on Human Devel., 1963-66; postdoctoral fellow Midwest Council Social Research, 1968; with dept. sociology Washington U., St. Louis, 1967-71, successively research asst., research assoc., asst. prof.; with dept. sociology Wayne State U., Detroit, 1971-84, from assoc. prof. to prof., dir. Elderly Care Research Ctr., 1971-84; prof. Case Western Res. U., Cleve., 1984—, Armington Prof., 1989-90, chmn. dept. sociology, 1985—, dir. Elderly Care Research Ctr., 1984—, Pierce and Elizabeth Robson prof. humanities, 1990—. Cons. Nat. Inst. on Aging, Washington, 1976-80, NIMH, Washington, 1971-75. Author: (with E. Midlarsky) Altruism in Later Life, 1994; editor: (with others) Family Caregiving Across the Lifespan, 1994; mem. editl. bd. Gerontologist, 1975-79, Psychology of Aging, 1984-90, Jour. Gerontology, 1990-94, Applied Behavioral Sci. Rev., 1992—; contbr. articles to profl. jours., chpts. to books (recipient Pub.'s prize 1969). Bd. dirs. com. on aging Jewish Community Fedn., Cleve.; vol. cons. Alzheimer's Disease and Related Disorders Assn., Cleve. NIMH Career Devel. grantee, 1974-79, Nat. Inst. Aging Merit award grantee, 1989—; Mary E. Switzer Disting. fellow Nat. Inst. Rehab., 1992-93; recipient Arnold Heller award excellence in geriatrics and gerontology Menorah Park Ctr. for Aged, 1992, Diekhoff awrd for disting. grad. tchg., 2002; named Disting. Geontological Rschr. in Ohio, 1993. Fellow Gerontol. Soc. Am. (chair behavioral social sci. com. 1984-85, chair 2000—, Disting. Mentorship award 1987, Polisher award 1997); mem. Am. Sociol. Assn. (coun. sect. on aging 1985-87, Disting. Scholar award sect. on aging and life course 1997, chair sect. on aging and life course, 2000-2001), Am. Psychol. Assn., Soc. for Traumatic Stress, Wayne State U. Acad. Scholars (life), Sigma Xi. Avocations: reading, antiques, travel.

KAHL, MARY L(OUISE), communication educator; b. Cheboygan, Mich., Apr. 17, 1954; d. Harris Allan and Mollie Grace (Riordan) K. BA with honors, U. Mich., 1976; MA, Ind. U., 1979, PhD, 1994. Lectr. U. Calif., Davis, 1982-86; asst. prof. Stonehill Coll., North Easton, Mass., 1986-90; assoc. prof. SUNY, New Paltz, 1990—. Contbr. articles to profl. jours. Vol. Dukakis Presdl. Campaign, Boston, 1988; mem. local Dem. com., Newburgh, N.Y., 1992—. Rsch. grantee Ind. U., Bloomington, 1980; recipient Term Faculty Devel. award United Univ. Professions, SUNY, New Paltz, 1994. Mem. Nat. Comm. Assn. (pub. divsn. chair 1998-1999), Ea. Comm. Assn. (rhetoric divsn. chair 1988-89, exec. coun. 1989-92, polit. comm. divsn. chair 1995-96. pres. 2003-2004). Office: SUNY New Paltz 75 S Manheim Blvd New Paltz NY 12561-2499

KAHLER, NANCY J. music educator, director; d. Frederick Charles and Grace Miriam (Moyer) Krerr; children: Denise Marie, Timothy Charles, Debra Joan Bucklin, Allan Curtis, Donald James. B in Music Edn., Esther Boyer Coll. Music, Phila., 1983. Music tchr. Camden Bd. Edn., NJ, 1984—. Organist, choir dir. Karmel UCC, Phila., 1982—2000; organist St. Hedwig's, Phila., 1983; dir. music Temple Lutheran, Pennsauken, NJ, 2000—; elections' chair Camden Edn. Assn., NJ, 2000. Contbr. articles to profl. jours. Mem.: Music Tchrs. Nat. Assn., Music Educators Nat. Convention, Am. Guild Organists, Delta Mu. Avocations: baking, gardening, composing. Home: 7703 West Chester Pike Upper Darby PA 19082-1418 E-mail: studiok@snip.net.

KAHLOW, BARBARA FENVESSY, statistician; b. Chgo., June 26, 1946; d. Stanley John and Doris (Goodman) Fenvessy; m. Lloyd Fitch Reese, Dec. 6, 1969 (div. 1977); m. Allan Howard Young, Mar. 31, 1979 (div. 1982); m. Ronald Arthur Kahlow, Sept. 28, 1985 (div. 1990). BA, Vassar Coll., 1968. Statistician U.S. Govt./Dept. HEW, Nat. Ctr. Health Stats., 1968-70, Nat. Ctr. for Ednl. Stats., 1970-72, Exec. Office of Pres. Office Mgmt. and Budget, Washington, 1972-98. Staff dir. subcom. on energy policy, natural resources and regulatory affairs House Govt. Reform Com., 1998—. Author: Motor Vehicle Accident Deaths in the U.S.: 1950-69, 1970; contbr. articles to profl. jours. N.Y. State Regents scholar, 1964-68. Mem. Am. Statis. Assn., Foggy Bottom Assn., League of Rep. Women of D.C., Friends of the Kennedy Ctr., Friends of the Corcoran, Smithsonian Assocs., Washington Vassar Club. Republican. Episcopalian. Home: Apt #404 2555 Pennsylvania Ave NW Washington DC 20037-1640 Office: House Govt Reform Com # B-377 Rayburn House Office Bldg Washington DC 20515-0001 Business E-Mail: barbara.kahlaw@mail.house.gov.

KAHN, EIKO TANIGUCHI, artist; b. Fukuoka, Kyushu, Japan, Jan. 24, 1929; came to U.S., 1955, naturalized, 1958; d. Tosuke Yamashita and Masano Taniguchi; m. Frederick Joseph Kahn, Sept. 28, 1954; children: Karen, Miho Kahn Wiedis. Gen., Sumiyoshi Women's Sch., Osaka, Japan, 1944. Solo exhbns. include Gregg Gallery, N.Y.C., 1982, Nat. Arts Club, Celadon Gallery, N.Y.C., 1988, The Korby Gallery, Cedar Grove, N.J., 1995, AWS Salmagundi Club, N.Y.C., 1995, The Koh Gallery, Union City, N.J., 1996, AT&T Bell Lab. Gallery, Hopewell, N.J., 1996, Ocean County Artists Guild Gallery, N.J., 1996, Gratella Gallery, Princeton, N.J., 1997, Ellarslie Trenton City Mus., 2000. Recipient Pres.'s award Nat. Arts Club, 1981, Ablert Baldwin prize Nat. Acad. Design, 1983, Award for Excellence Middlesex County Mus., 1985. Mem. N.J. Water Color Soc. (award 1990), Audubon Artists (Medal of Honor 1981), Artists Fellowship. Avocations: golf, gardening. Address: 217 Cleveland Ln RD 4 Princeton NJ 08540-9517

KAHN, FAITH-HOPE, nurse, administrator, writer; b. N.Y.C., Apr. 25, 1921; d. Leon and Hazel (Cook) Green; RN, Beth Israel Med. Center, N.Y.C., 1942; student N.Y. U., 1943; m. Edward Kahn, May 29, 1942; children: Ellen Leora, Faith Hope II, Paula Amy. First scrub nurse operating room Beth Israel Hosp., N.Y.C., 1942; supr. operating room Hunts Point Gen. Hosp., 1942; gynecol. reconstrn. procedures researcher Phoenixville (Pa.) Gen. Hosp., 1943, Sydenham Hosp., N.Y.C., 1945; supr. ARC Disaster Field Hosp., Queens, N.Y., 1950-51; adminstr., mgr. team coordinator Dr. Edward Kahn, FACOG, Queens Village, N.Y., 1945—. Inventor, publicity chmn. Girl Scouts U.S.A., 1953; exec. dir. publicity Woodhull Schs., 1956-60, pres., 1961-62; exec. dir. publicity N.Y. Dept. Parks Figure Skating, 1956-70; exec. dir. publicity and applied arts St. John's Hosp., Smithtown, N.Y., 1965-66; state advisor N.Y., U.S. Congressional Adv. Bd., Washington, 1981—; nat. adv. bd. Am. Security Council, 1978—; founder Am. Security Found.; bd. trustees, Am. Police Hall of Fame and Mus., 1983—; mem. Republican Presdl. Task Force, 1986, Statue of Liberty and Ellis Island Centennial Commn., N.Y., 1986—. Recipient citation ARC, 1951, Am. Law Enforcement Officers Assn., Bronze medal Am. Security Council Ednl. Found., 1978, spl. recognition award Center Internat. Security Studies, 1979, Meml. Plate, Patriots of Am. Bicentennial, 1976, Great Seal of U.S.A. Plate, cert. Am. Sons Liberty, 1987, Good Smaritan award, 1987, Justice award Cross of Knights, 1987 Knights of Justice award, 1987; named Knight Chevalier Venerable Order of Michael the Archangel, 1987. Fellow, World Lit. Acad. (life), Acad. Nat. Law Enforcement (hon.); mem. Am. Acad. Ambulatory Nursing Adminstrn., Nurses Assn., Nat. League Nursing, Am. Coll. Obstetricians and Gynecologists, Nat. Assn. Physicians' Nurses, Nat. Critical Care Inst., Assn. Operating Room Nurses, AAAS, Nat. Assn. Female Execs., N.Y. Acad. Scis., Am. Police Acad. (cert. appreciation 1979, 83), Am. Fedn. Police, The Retired Officers Assn., Internat. Platform Assn., Security and Intelligence Found. (cert. appreciation 1986), Internat. Intelligence and Orgnd. Crime Investigators Assn., Smithtown Hist. Soc., Nat. Audubon Soc., NRA. Clubs: Tiyospaye, Paul Revere, Sterlingshire Woman's. Author, editor: The Easy Driving Way for Automatic and the Standard Shift, 1954; (with Edward Kahn) The Pelvic Examination, Outline and Guide for Residents, Internes and Students, 1954; (with Edward Kahn) Traction Hysterosalpingography for Uterine Lesions, 1949; contbr. articles profl. and lay jours. Home and Office: 21316 85th Ave Jamaica NY 11427-1324

KAHN, HERTA HESS (MRS. HOWARD KAHN), retired securities trader; b. Wuerzburg, Germany;, naturalized, U.S. d. Ferdinand and Lilly (Suesser) Hess; m. Herbert Levy (dec.); 1 child, Linda Levy ; m. Howard Kahn (dec.). Student, Northwestern U. Sch. Commerce. Joined Paine, Webber, Jackson & Curtis, Inc., Chgo., 1941; registered rep. Paine, Webber Inc., acct. v.p., v.p. investments; ret., 1994; mktg. cons., 1995—. Author: (book) What Every Woman Should Know About Investing Her Money, 1968. Hon. life mem. nat. commn., hon. life. mem. Chgo. exec. com. Anti-Defamation League B;nai B'rith; bd. dirs. Found. Hearing and Speech Rehab., Chgo. Mem.: Chgo. Crime Commn., Chgo. Fin. Exch., Assn. Investment Mgmt. and Rsch., Investment Analysts Soc. Chgo., N.Y. Soc. Security Analysts, Tamarisk Country Club (Rancho Mirage, Calif.), Execs. Club (Chgo.), Econ. Club, Std. Club, Northmoor Country Club (Highland Park, Ill.). Address: The accad 970 Aurora Ave F 305 Boulder CO 80302

KAHN, LESLY JANE, performing arts educator; d. Richard Louis and Patricia Ann (O'Donnell) Kahn. MFA, Yale U., 1987. Actor, Hollywood, Calif., 1984—94; owner Lesly Kahn & Co., L.A., 1994—. Personal E-mail: lesly@leslykahn.com. E-mail: lesly@leslykahn.com.

KAHN, LINDA MCCLURE, actuary, consultant; b. Jacksonville, Fla. d. George Calvin and Myrtice Louise (Boggs) McClure; m. Paul Markham Kahn, May 20, 1968. BS with highest honors, U. Fla.; MS, U. Mich., 1964. Actuarial trainee N.Y. Life Ins. Co., N.Y.C., 1964-66, actuarial asst., 1966-69, asst. actuary, 1969-71; v.p., actuary U.S. Life Ins., Pasadena, Calif., 1972-74; mgr. Coopers & Lybrand, L.A., 1974-76; sr. cons. San Francisco, 1976-82; dir. program mgmt. Pacific Maritime Assn., San Francisco, 1982-97; pres., CEO P.M. Kahn & Assocs., 1997—; chmn., CEO Paul and Linda Kahn Found., 1998—. Bd. dirs. San Francisco Nat. Maritime Mus. Libr., 1998—; trustee ILWU-PMA Welfare Plan, 1982—97, SIU-PD-PMA Pension and Supplemental Benefits Plans, 1982—90, Seafarers Med. Ctr., 1982—90; chmn. Quarter Century Plan Devel. Com., 2003; bd. dirs. Pacific Heights Residents Assn., 1978—93, sec.-treas. bd. dirs., 1981; bd. dirs. Friends of St. Frances Childcare Ctr., 2002—, CFO, treas., 2003—. Fellow Soc. Actuaries (chmn. com. on minority recruiting 1988-91, chmn. actuary of future sect. 1993-95), Conf. Cons. Actuaries; mem. Internat. Actuarial Assn., Internat. Assn. Con. Actuaries, Actuarial Studies Non-Life Ins., Am. Acad. Actuaries (enrolled actuary), Western Pension and Benefits Conf. (newsletter editor 1983-85, sec. 1985-88, treas. 1989-90), Actuarial Club Pacific States, San Francisco Actuarial Club (pres. 1981), Met. Club, Commonwealth Club, Soroptimists (v.p. 1973-74), Concordia-Argonaut Club, Pacific Club (Honolulu), Book Club Calif., Colophon Club. Home and Office: 2430 Pacific Ave San Francisco CA 94115-1238

KAHN, NANCY VALERIE, publishing and entertainment executive, consultant; b. N.Y.C., Dec. 15, 1952; d. Alfred Joseph and Miriam (Kadin) K. BA magna cum laude, Princeton U., 1974. Dir. prodn. and devel. Bus. Rsch. Publs., Inc.-MacRAE's Directories, N.Y.C., 1984-86; assoc. pub., exec. editor Leadership Directories Inc., N.Y.C., 1987-88; dir. new product devel. Gale Rsch. Inc., N.Y.C., 1988-89; pub., editorial dir. directories and info. devel. Adweek, N.Y.C., 1989—93; v.p. Everlink Corp., N.Y.C., 1993—94; prin. NVK Comm., N.Y.C., 1994—. Univ. scholar Princeton U., 1974. Mem. Directory and Database Pubs. Forum & Network, Manhattan Assn. Cabarets. Avocations: arts, musical theatre, cabaret, foreign travel, walking. Office: NVK Comm PO Box 826 New York NY 10021

KAHN, PHYLLIS, state legislator; b. Mar. 23, 1937; m. Don Kahn; two children. BA, Cornell U., 1957; PhD in Biophysics, Yale U., 1962; MPA, Harvard U., 1986. Dist. 59B rep. Minn. Ho. of Reps., St. Paul, 1972—. Former chmn. state dept. divsn. appropriations com., Minn. Ho. of Reps., former mem. econ. devel., agr., environ. and natural resources coms.; chmn. govt. op. com., state govt. fin. divsn. and edn.-higher edn. fin. divsn. coms. Home: 367 State Office Bldg Saint Paul MN 55155-0001 Office: Minn State Senate State Capitol Building Saint Paul MN 55155-0001

KAHN, SANDRA S. psychotherapist; b. Chgo., June 24, 1942; d. Chester and Ruth Sutker; m. Jack Murry Kahn, June 1, 1965; children: Erick, Jennifer. BA, U. Miami, 1964; MA, Roosevelt U., 1976. Tchr. Chgo. Pub. Schs., 1965-67; pvt. practice psychotherapy, Northbrook, Ill., 1976—. Host Shared Feelings, Sta. WEEF-AM, Highland Park, Ill., 1983—; author: The Kahn Report on Sexual Preferences, 1981, The Ex Wife Syndrome Cutting The Cord and Breaking Free After The Marriage Is Over, 1990; columnist Single Again mag. Mem. Ill. Psychol. Assn., Chgo. Psychol. Assn. (past pres. 1990). Jewish. Office: 801 Skokie Blvd Northbrook IL 60062-4039 Office Phone: 847-272-2228.

KAHN, SUSAN, artist; b. N.Y.C., Aug. 26, 1924; d. Jesse B. and Jenny Carol (Peshkin) Cohen; m. Joseph Kahn, Sept. 15, 1946 (dec.); m. Richard Rosenkranz, Feb. 1, 1981. Grad., Parsons Sch. Design, 1945; student, Moses Soyer, 1950-57. Subject of: book Susan Kahn, with an essay by Lincoln Rothschild, 1980; One-woman shows include Sagittarius Gallery, 1960, A.C.A., Galleries, 1964, 68, 71, 76, 80, Charles B. Goddard Art Center, Ardmore, Okla., 1973, Albrecht Gallery Mus. Art, St. Joseph, Mo., 1974, N.Y. Cultural Center, N.Y.C., 1974, St. Peter's Coll., Jersey City, 1978, Heidi Neuhoff Gallery, N.Y.C., 1989, Sindin Galleries, 1996; exhibited in group shows Audubon Artists, N.Y.C., Nat. Acad., N.Y.C., Springfield (Mass.) Mus., City Center, N.Y.C., A.C.A., Galleries, N.Y.C., Nat. Arts Club, N.Y.C., Butler Inst., Youngstown, Ohio, Islip Art Mus., East Islip. N.Y., 1989, Fine Arts Mus. of S., Mobile, Ala., 1989, Chatanooga Regional History Mus, 1989, Longview (Tex.) Mus. Art, 1990; represented in permanent collections, Tyler (Tex.) Mus., St. Lawrence U. Mus., Canton, N.Y., Fairleigh Dickinson U. Mus., Rutherford, N.J., Syracuse U. Mus., Sheldon Swope Gallery, Terre Haute, Ind., Montclair (N.J.) Mus. Fine Arts, Butler Inst. Am. Art, Youngstown, Ohio, Reading (Pa.) Mus., Albrecht Gallery Mus. Art, St. Joseph(Mo.), Cedar Rapids (Iowa) Art Center, N.Y. Cultural Center, N.Y.C., Edwin A. Ulrich Mus., Wichita, Kans., Wichita State U., Johns Hopkins Sch. Advanced Internat. Studies, Washington, Joslyn Mus., Omaha, U. Wyo., Laramie. Recipient Knickerbocker prize for best religious painting, 1956; Edith Lehman award Nat. Assn. Women Artists, 1958; Simmons award, 1961; Knickerbocker Artists award, 1961; Nat. Arts Club award, 1967, Knickerbocker Medal of Honor, 1964; Famous Artists Sch. award, 1967 Mem. Nat. Assn. Women Artists (Anne Barnett Meml. prize 1981, Solveig Stromsoe Palmer Meml. award 1987, Dorothy Schweitzer award 1990), Artists Equity, Met. Mus., Mus. Modern Art, Nat. Assn. Women Artists (meml. award 1987).

KAHN, VICTORIA ELAINE HOPKINS, special education educator; b. Grand Junction, Colo., Dec. 11, 1953; d. William Stanley Hopkins, Jr. and Bernice Irene (Porter) Hopkins; m. James Michael Humphrey, Sept. 17, 1982 (div. June 1986); m. Jerome Isidor Kahn, May 1, 1988. AA in Theatre Arts, Santa Ana Coll., 1974; BA with distinction in psychology, San Diego State U., 1985. Cert. edn. specialist Calif. State U., 2001. Owner, freelance photographer Victoria Vincent Photography, San Diego and Vista, Calif., 1984—94, Glendale, Ariz., 1993—94; enrichment instr. Felicita Found. for the Arts, Escondido, Calif., 1990—91; photographer, artist Vista (Calif.) Initiative for the Visual Arts, 1990—93; sub. tchr. and aide spl. edn. grades K-14 Orange County Dept. Edn., Costa Mesa, Calif., 1996—98; sub. tchr. spl. edn. grades K-6 Garden Grove (Calif.) Unified Sch. Dist., 1997—2002; resource specialist tchr. grades 1-5 Long Beach (Calif.) Unified Sch. Dist., 2002—03; sub. spl. edn. tchr. grades K-6 Encinitas (Calif.) Union Sch. Dist., 2003—; owner, designer Curriculum Creations, San Diego, 2003—. Charter mem., artist Gallery Vista (Calif.) Artists' Assn., 1989—91; artist, photographer Holman Gallery, Scottsdale, Ariz., 1993—94. Editor: (book of poetry) Autumn Meditations, 1994, The Complete Poems of James L.O. Porter, 2002, (novella) The Chance, 2002. Vol. genealogy rsch. rm. Nat. Archives and Records Adminstrn., Laguna Niguel, Calif., 1998—2001. Recipient Achievement award, Nat. Archives and Records Adminstrn., 2000, 2001. Mem.: Dubois Family Assn., Tchrs. Assn. Long Beach, Coun. for Exceptional Children, Nat. Soc. DAR (Los Cerritos chpt., conservation com. chmn. 2002—), Phi Kappa Phi, Pi Lambda Theta. Achievements include patents pending for a scenario method of teaching multiplication and division concepts (Cowboy Tim); a multi-sensory method of motivating students to read and write (The Reading Drum). Avocations: historial and geneaological research, writing, art, educational manipulatives and methods design, bird and nature watching. E-mail: kahnv@msn.com.

KAIDA, TAMARRA, art and photography educator; b. Lienz, Austria, July 6, 1946; came to U.S., 1950; d. Ivan and Matrona (Bratasuk) K.; m. Paul S. Knapp; 1 child, Krister. BA, Goddard Coll., 1974; MFA, SUNY, Buffalo, 1979. Tutor photography Empire State Coll., 1977-79; asst. dir. dept. edn. Internat. Mus. Photography, George Eastman House, 1976-79; vis. lectr. Ariz. State U., Tempe, 1979-80, asst. prof., 1980-85, assoc. prof., 1985-92, prof., 1992—; represented by Etherton Gallery, Tucson, Califia Books, San Francisco. Mem. faculty Internat. Sommerakademie fur Bildende Kunst, Salzburg, Austria, 1985, Friends of Photography Summer Workshop, Carmel, Calif., 1989, vis. photographers program R.I. Sch. Design, 1989, guest artist lecture and lazer print transfer demonstration Photography Studies in France, Paris, 1991; panelist NEA S.W. Regional Photography Task Force, 1980; juror nat. photography competition Calif. Inst. Arts, Valencia, 1981; curator, lectr., cons. in field. Author: (with Rita Dove) The Other Side of the House, 1988; Tremors from the Faultline, 1989; contbr. articles to profl. jours.; author short stories; many one-woman shows including Scottsdale (Ariz.) Ctr. Arts, 1987, Fine Arts Gallery RISD, 1989, OPSIS Found. Gallery, N.Y.C., 1990, Fyerweather Gallery U. Va., Charlottesville, 1991, Photography Gallery, Fine Art Ctr., U. R.I., Kingston, R.I., 1992, Kharkov (Ukraine) Regional Mus. Art, 1993, Sky Harbor Airport, Phoenix, Ariz., 1994; numerous nat. and internat. group shows including Coconino Ctr. Arts, Flagstaff, Ariz., 1985, Frankfurt Art Soc., Germany, 1985, Mus. Art and Trade, Hamburg, Germany, 1985, Boulder (Colo.) Ctr. Visual Arts, 1985, Art Inst. Chgo., Mpls. Coll. Art & Design, 1986, Hood Mus. Art Dartmouth Coll., Hanover, N.H., 1987, Lawrence (Kans.) Art Ctr., 1987, Miller's Studio, Zurich, Switzerland, 1987, Palazzo Braschi, Rome, 1987, Sante Fe Ctr. Photography, 1987, Dinnerware Gallery, Tucson, 1987, Sante Fe Ctr. Arts (purchase award), 1987, Rockwell Mus., Corning, N.Y., 1987, Grand Canyon Coll., Phoenix, 1987, Tucson Mus. Art, 1988, Halsey Gallery Coll. of Charleston, S.C., 1988, Long Beach (Calif.) Coll. Fine Arts, 1988, Atrium Gallery U. Conn. Storrs, 1988, Gallery of Kans. City (Mo.) Artists Coalition (1st prize, fellowship award) 1989, Lieberman and Saul Gallery, N.Y.C., 1989, Downey (Calif.) Mus. Art, 1989, Anderson Ranch Arts Ctr., Aspen, Colo., 1989, San Francisco Camerawork, 1990, Phoenix Mus. Art, 1990, Ctr. for Photography, Cin., 1991, Mus. Art U. Okla., 1991, Rockford (Ill.) Coll., 1991, Ctr. for Creative Photography, Tucson, 1991-92; Huntington Gallery, Mass. Coll. Art, Boston, 1992, Ariz. State Capital, Phoenix, 1992, Barbara Zusman Art and Antiques Gallery, Santa Fe, N.Mex., 1992; internat. traveling exhbns.; represented in permanent collections Union Russian Art Photography, Moscow, U. Calif. Santa Cruz, Kennedy Ctr. Performing Arts, Washington, L.A. County Mus. Art, Internat. Mus. Photography George Eastman House, Rochester, N.Y., N.Y. Pub. Libr., SUNY Buffalo, Libr. Congress, Polaroid

Corp., Cambridge, Mass., Sante Fe Mus. Fine Arts, Scottsdale Ctr. Art, Snell and Wilmer, Phoenix, Valley Nat. Bank, Phoenix, others; photographs featured various works. Judge spring art show Scottsdale C.C., 1980; organizer Artist Against Hunger money and food drive Ariz. State U. Sch. Art, 1984; juror New Times Newspaper, 1985, Tempe Fine Arts Ctr., 1989, Yavapai Coll., Prescott, Ariz., 1989. Recipient Faculty Grant-in-Aid, 1982, 85, 93, Current Works 1989 Excellence award Soc. Contemporary Photography, Visual Arts fellowship grant Nat. Endowment for Arts, 1986, rsch. grant Coll. Fine Arts, 1987, 93, grant Arts/Social Svcs./Humanities, 1989, Sch. Art Assistance to Faculty, 1990, Visual Arts fellowship grant Ariz. Commn. Arts, 1989-90, Inst. for Studies in Arts, 1992, materials grant Polaroid Corp., 1992, Gov.'s Arts award, 1992, Women's Studies Summer Rsch. award., 1992. Mem. Coll. Arts Assn., Soc. Photographic Edn. (co-chair, organizer West/S.W. Regional Conf. 1983), Friends of Photography (Ferguson award 1983). Democrat. Russian Orthodox. Home: 534 N Orange Mesa AZ 85201-5609

KAIGE, ALICE TUBB, retired librarian; b. Obion, Tenn., Jan. 27, 1922; d. George Easley and Lucile (Merryman) Tubb; m. Richard H. Kaige, Aug. 1952; children: Robert H., Richard C. (dec.), John S. (dec.) BA, Vanderbilt U., 1944; BS in Libr. Sci., Geo. Peabody Coll., 1947. Libr. Martin (Tenn.) High Sch., 1946-47, Demonstration Sch. Geo. Peabody Coll. Joint U. Librs., Nashville, Tenn., 1947-52; acquisitions libr. Lincoln Libr., Springfield, Ill., 1967-70; office coord. Springfield (Ill.) Chpt. ACLU, 1974; staff rep. Am. Fed. State, County & Mcpl. Employees, Springfield, 1975; libr. Ill. Dept. of Commerce and Community Affairs, Springfield, 1976-89. Vice chmn. Women's Internat. League for Peace and Freedom, 1969-70, various coms., 1970—; treas. Cen. Ill. Women's Lobby, 1971-72; com. on local govt. League of Women Voters, 1973-76; career day com. Urban League Guild, 1970-71; co-founder West Side Neighborhood Assn., Springfield, 1977. Recipient Elizabeth Cady Stanton award, Springfield Women's Political Caucus, 1982. Mem. Sangamon County Hist. Soc., Women's Internat. League for Peace and Freedom, War Resisters League. Avocations: reading, walking. Home: 1912 Turnberry Ct Springfield IL 62704-6211

KAIMANN, DIANE S. writer, educator; b. NYC, May 14, 1939; d. Arthur R. and Martha Riss Schwartz; m. Richard Kaimann, 1987 (dec. 1999); children: Bruce A. Falbaum, Margery L. Krueger; m. William E. Forman, 2001. BA, Duke U., Durham, N.C., 1956—60. English tchr. N.C. Pub. Schs., 1960—64; owner, operator Evelyn Wood Reading Dynamics, Milw., 1978—90; freelance creative writing instr. Milw., 2002—. Mktg., mgmt., sales cons., Milw., 1990—2000. Author: Common Threads: Nine Widows' Journeys through Love, Loss, and Healing, 2002. Mem.: Phi Beta Kappa.

KAISER, ANN CHRISTINE, magazine editor; b. Milw., Apr. 7, 1947; d. Herbert Walter and Annette G. (Werych) Gohlke; m. Louis Dan Kaiser; children: Richard L., Michael D. BS in Journalism, Northwestern U., 1969. Reporter Waco (Tex.) Tribune-Herald, 1969-71; editor Country Woman, Greendale, Wis., 1971—; mng. editor Taste of Home, Greendale, 1993—. Named among People of the Yr., Milw. Mag., 1998. Lutheran. Avocations: sailing, tennis, golf, travel. Office: Reiman Publs 5400 S 60th St Greendale WI 53129-1404

KAISER, CARLENE PEARL, counseling administrator, media specialist; b. Jacksonville, Fla., Sept. 21, 1946; d. Carl Leslie Young and Marguerite Pearl Marr-Young; m. John Franklin Kaiser; children: Raymond John, Scott Leslie. BS, Kans. State U., 1987, MS, postgrad. in EdD Leadership, Kans. State U., 1996—. Cert. counselor Kans., Mo., Ark., Okla. Media specialist, counselor St. Francis Xavier, Junction City, Kans., 1990—95; instr. Barton C.C., Ft. Riley, Kans., 1988—90, Kans. State U., 1993—95; counselor Sabetha (Kans.) Union Sch. Dist. 441, 1998—2000, North Ctrl. H.S., Morrowville, Kans., 2000—. Counseling adv. bd. North Ctrl. H.S.; freelance photographer, 1978—; co-owner Contrast Devel. Photography. Mem. Rep. com., Manhattan, Kans., 1998. Recipient Smoky Hill Vocat. Edn. award, Salina, Kans., 2000. Mem.: Kans. Sch. Librs., Kans. Counseling Assn., Phi Delta Kappa, Golden Key. Democrat. Avocations: Christian counseling, photography, interior design, journalism.

KAISER, DOROTHY CAROLYN, social worker; b. Springfield, Mo., Mar. 6, 1935; d. Jeanne Elizabeth Fugitt-Fort and Otto Emerson Fort; m. Jack Allen Charles Kaiser, Oct. 5, 1991; m. Samuel Bentley Darnes, July 5, 1953 (div. June 8, 1987); children: Linda Sue Darnes-Hubert, Jack Emerson Darnes, Donald William Darnes, Victoria Jean Darnes-Brooke. MSW, U. Md. Sch. of Social Work, 1985; BS, U. Md., 1981—81. LCSW State of Md., 1988. Med. sec. Dept. of HEW, Washington, 1962—86; social worker Child Protective Svcs. Investigative Unit P.G. Dept. of Social Svcs., 1986—94; foster care worker P.G. County Dept. of Social Svcs., Hyattsville, Md., 1994—98; social worker Lakeland Regional Hosp., Springfield, 1999—2001; pvt. practice Allied Health Profls., Springfield, Mo., 2001—. Vol. Coun. of Churches, Springfield, 2000—; outreach com. mem. St James Episc. Ch., Springfield, 1999—; vol. tutor Springfield Pub. Schools, 1998—2001. Mem.: NASW. Independent. Episcopalian. Avocations: square dancing, gardening, church activities. Home and Office: 3026 E Glenwood St Springfield MO 65804

KAISER, KAREN SUE, elementary school educator; d. Reuben and Dorothy Ruth Miller; m. Richard Eugene Kaiser, Dec. 11, 1971; 1 child, Bryan Patrick. AA, Northeastern Jr. Coll., Sterling, Colo., 1969; EdB, U. No. Colo., 1972. K-2 tchr. Atwood (Colo.) Elem., 1972—73; kindergarten tchr. Sexson and Padroni Elems., Sterling, Colo., 1974—75, Sexson Elem., Sterling, 1976—84, Campbell Elem., Sterling, 1985—89, 4th grade tchr., 1990—. Art instr. Colo. Christian U., Denver, 2003; mem. achievement coun. RE-1 Valley Sch. Dist., Sterling, 1990—. Mem.: Colo. Edn. Assn., Alpha Delta Kappa (Silver Sister award 2002).

KAISER, LINDA SUSAN, lawyer; b. Alexandria, Va., Apr. 7, 1956; d. Thomas Raymond Kaiser and Joanne May (Wilber) Raynolds. BA, Pa. State U., 1978; JD, U. Pitts., 1981. Asst. counsel Pa. Ins. Dept., Harrisburg, 1981-85; sr. counsel Cigna Corp., Phila., 1985-92; asst. gen. counsel Reliance Ins. Co., Phila., 1992-95; ins. commr. Commonwealth of Pa., Harrisburg, 1995-97; sr. v.p., gen. counsel and sec. Reliance Ins. Co., Phila., 1997-2000; ptnr. Saul Ewing, LLP, 2000—03, Cozen O'Connor Attys., 2003—. Property casualty steering com. Ins. Fedn. Pa., Phila., 1992-95; alternate Pa. Workers Compensation Gov. Bd., 1993-95; bd. dirs. Nat. Assn. Ind. Insurers, 1997-2000, vice-chair membership com., 1999-2000; bd. dirs. Ins. Fedn. Pa., 1998-2000; vice chair Issues Com., 2003—, Com. Seventy, 2003-. Pres. Huntington's Disease Soc. Am., Delaware Valley, Phila., 1993-96, v.p., 1996-2002; bd. dirs. Phila. Theatre Co., 2002— Mem. ABA, Soc. CPCU, Soc. Nat. Assn. Ins. Commrs. (vice chair N.E. zone 1997), Order of Coif, Barristers, Com. of Seventy. Office: 1900 Market St Philadelphia PA 19103 E-mail: lkaiser@cozen.com.

KAISER, NINA IRENE, health care consultant; b. San Diego, Nov. 29, 1953; d. Louis Frederick and Mary Elizabeth (Wright) K.; children: Kellen Anne Kaiser, Ethan Andrew Kaiser-Klimist. BSN, BA in Women Studies, San Francisco State U., 1980; MBA, U. Phoenix, 2001. RN, Calif. RN Calif. Pacific Med. Ctr., San Francisco, 1980-81, Ralph K. Davies Med. Ctr., San Francisco, 1982-85, Planned Parenthood, San Francisco, 1985-86, Visiting Nurses and Hospice, San Francisco, 1986-88; RN supr. St. Mary's Home Care, San Francisco, 1991-93; RN dir. St. Vincent's Homecare and Hospice, Fremont, Calif., 1993-94, Home Health Link, San Leandro, Calif., 1994-99; mgmt. cons. Kaiser Home Health, Oakland, Calif., 1999—2002, mgr., 2003—. Regional coun. chair San Francisco Bay Area, 1999. Pres. Daus. of Bilitis, San Francisco, 1977-78; founding mem. Buena Vista Lesbian and Gay Parents Assn., San Francisco, 1985; treas., bd. dirs. Holladay Ave. Homeowners Assn., San Francisco, 1984-96; bd. dirs. Midrasha High Sch., Berkeley, Calif., 1996. With USN, 1971-74. E-mail: missnynak@aol.com

KAISER-BOTSAI, SHARON KAY, retired early childhood educator; b. Waterloo, Iowa, Aug. 9, 1941; d. Peter A. Ley and Lorraine (Worthington) Burton; m. Hugh W. Kaiser, Aug. 28, 1968 (div. 1981); 1 child, Kiana; m. Elmer E. Botsai, Dec. 5, 1981; children: Kiana, Don, Kurt. BSBA, U. Ariz., 1963; MEd, U. Hawaii, Honolulu, 1970; postgrad., U. Hawaii, 1972-88. Cert. elem. edn. tchr., Hawaii. Sec. Donald M. Drake, San Francisco, 1964-66; tchr. St. Mark's Kindergarten, Honolulu, 1966-73; head tchr. Cen. Union Preschool, Honolulu, 1967-77; tchr. Waiokeola Preschool, Honolulu, 1974-76, 77-88; tchr. staff instruction Honolulu Dist. Dept. of Edn., 1989-90; tchr. students of ltd. English proficiency Kaahumanu Sch., Honolulu, 1990-94; tchr. kindergarten Palolo Sch., Honolulu, 1991-97, Waialae Chartered Sch., 1997—2003. Pvt. instr. in Hawaiian dance, 1977-79; workshop leader marine sea crafts Sea Grant Inst. for Marine Educators, 1977, HAEYC Conf., 1979, 82, 84, 85, 86, chair workshops in music and creative drama, 1977, drama workshop, 1994, Drama Nat. Conf. workshop leader, 1982, multiple intelligences workshop leader, 1998; speaker Celebration of Life Sta. KHON-TV, 1979; workshop leader MECAP Conf., 1985; mem. com. Improvement Symphony Performance for Preschoolers, 1977; art advisor, coord. Sunday sch. program Waiokeola Ch., 1973, speaker creative communication, 1984; validator accreditation program Nat. Acad. for Edn. of Young Children, 1986—; asst. to co-chair conf. Hawaii Assn. for Edn. Young Children, 1987-88; Hawaii State Tchrs. Assn. rep. Palolo Sch., 1993; lectr. in field. Author: Creative Dramatics, 1990; co-author: Preschool Activities, 1990. Actress Presido Playhouse, San Francisco, 1962, Little Theatre, Honolulu Zoo, 1976; instr. spl. edn. students Kaneohe YWCA, 1967; troop co-leader Girl Scouts U.S.A., 1981-84; bd. dirs. Zoo Hui, 1984-86; trustee, stewardship chmn. Waiokeola Ch., 1986-88. Mem. Hawaii Assn. for Edn. of Young Children (First recipient Phyllis Loveless Excellence in Teaching award 1979), Delta Delta Delta. Lutheran. Avocations: tennis, water and snow skiing, creative drama, traveling, scuba diving. Home: 321 Wailupe Cir Honolulu HI 96821-1524

KAISERLIAN, PENELOPE JANE, publishing company executive; b. Paisley, Scotland, Oct. 19, 1943; came to U.S., 1956; d. W. Norman and Magdalene Jeanette (Houlder) Hewson; m. Arthur Kaiserlian, June 29, 1968; 1 child, Christian. BA, U. Exeter, Eng., 1965. Copywriter, sales rep. Pergamon Press, Elmsford, N.Y., 1965-68; exhibits mgr. Plenum Pub., N.Y.C., 1968-69; asst. mktg. mgr. U. Chgo. Press, 1969-76, mktg. mgr., 1976-83, assoc. dir., 1983-2001; dir. U. Va. Press, 2001—. Mem. Soc. for Scholarly Pub., Assn. for Documentary Editing, Am. Geog. Assn., Colonnade Club. Office: Univ Va Press PO Box 400318 Charlottesville VA 22904-4318

KAISH, LUISE CLAYBORN, sculptor, former educator; b. Atlanta, Sept. 8, 1925; d. Harry and Elsa (Brown) Meyers; m. Morton Kaish, Aug. 15, 1948; 1 child, Melissa. BFA magna cum laude, Syracuse U., 1946, MFA, 1951; student, Escuela de Pintura y Escultura, Escuela de las Artes del Libro, Taller Grafico, Mexico, 1946-47. Artist-in-residence Dartmouth Coll., 1974; prof. sculpture and painting, 1980-93, chmn. div. painting and sculpture Columbia U., 1980-86, prof. emerita, 1993; vis. artist U. Wash., Seattle, Battelle seminars and study program, Seattle, 1979; artist-in-residence U. Haifa, Israel, 1985. One-man shows Meml. Art Gallery, Rochester, N.Y., 1954, Sculpture Ctr., N.Y.C., 1955, 58, Staempfli Gallery, N.Y.C., 1968, 81, 84, 87, 88, Minn. Mus. Art, St. Paul, 1969, Jewish Mus., N.Y.C., 1973, U. Ark., 1990, The Century Assn., 1998; exhibited (with Morton Kaish), Rochester Meml. Art Gallery, 1958, USIS, Rome, 1973, Dartmouth Coll., 1974, Oxford Gallery, Rochester, 1988; represented in permanent collections Whitney Mus. Am. Art, N.Y.C., Met. Mus. Art, N.Y.C., Jewish Mus., N.Y.C., Export Khleb, Moscow, Minn. Mus. Art, Gen. Mills Corp., Minn., Rochester Meml. Art Gallery, Smithsonian Instn., Nat. Mus. Am. Art, Washington, also numerous pvt. collections, commns., Syracuse U., Temple B'rith Kodesh, Rochester, Temple Israel, Westport, Conn., Holy Trinity Mission Sem., Silver Springs, Md., Temple Beth Shalom, Wilmington, Del., Beth-El Synagogue Ctr., New Rochelle, N.Y., Temple B'nai Abraham, Essex City, N.J., Continental Grain Co., N.Y. Trustee Am. Acad. in Rome, 1973-81, mem. exec. com., 1975-81, trustee emerita, 1994; trustee St. Gaudens Found., 1978-90, mem. exec. com., 1980-90. Recipient awards Everson Mus., Syracuse, 1947, awards Rochester Meml. Art Gallery, 1951, awards Ball State U., 1963, awards Ch. World Service, 1960, awards Council for Arts in Westchester, 1974, Emily Lowe award, 1956, Audubon Artists gold medal, 1963, Honor award AIA, 1975, Arents Pioneer medal, Syracuse U., 1989; Louis Comfort Tiffany grantee, 1951; Guggenheim fellow, 1959; Rome prize fellow Am. Acad. in Rome, 1970-72 Mem. Nat. Acad. Design, The Century Assn., Eta Pi Upsilon. Home and Office: 610 W End Ave # 9-a New York NY 10024-1605

KAJI, HIDEKO, pharmacology educator; b. Tokyo, Jan. 1, 1932; came to U.S., 1954; d. Sakae and Tsuneko (Matsuda) Katayama; m. Akira Kaji, Aug. 23, 1958; children: Kenneth, Eugene, Naomi, Amy. BS, Tokyo U. Pharm. Scis., 1954; MS, U. Nebr., 1956; PhD, Purdue U., 1958. Vis. scientist Oak Ridge (Tenn.) Nat. Lab., 1962-63; assoc. U. Pa., Phila., 1963-64; rsch. assoc. The Inst. Cancer Rsch., Phila., 1965-66, asst. mem., 1966-76; vis. mem. Max Planck Inst. Molek. Gen., Berlin, 1972-73, Nat. Inst. Med. Rsch., London, 1973; assoc. prof. Jefferson Med. Coll., Phila., 1976-82; vis. prof. Wistar Inst., Phila., 1984-85; prof. biochemistry and molecular pharmacology Jefferson Med. Coll., Phila., 1983—. Cons. Nippon Paint Co., Ltd., Tokyo, 1990—, Coatesville (Pa.) VA Hosp., 1982-84. Contbr. articles to profl. jours. Fellow NIH (bd. dirs. 1986-89); mem. Am. Soc. Biochemistry and Molecular Biology, Am. Soc. Pharmacol. and Exptl. Therapeutics, Am. Soc. Microbiology, Sigma Xi. Home: 334 Fillmore St Jenkintown PA 19046-4328 Office: Jefferson Med Coll 1020 Locust St Philadelphia PA 19107-6731 Business E-Mail: hideko.kaji@jefferson.edu.

KAKUTANI, MICHIKO, critic; Chief book critic N.Y. Times, N.Y.C. Recipient Pulitzer prize for criticism, 1998. Office: c/o NY Times Culture New 229 W 43d St New York NY 10036

KALABZA-BALSAMO, DEBRA ALYCE, music educator; b. Astoria, N.Y., Apr. 26, 1963; d. John Francis Kalabza and Frances Adele Gualtieri-Kalabza; m. Edward Richard Balsamo, Aug. 11, 1996. AS music performance, Suffolk County C.C., Selden, N.Y., 1983; BS in Edn. and performance, Hofstra U., 1985; MS in Edn. and Performance, L.I. U., Greenvale, N.Y., 1989, profl. diploma in Ednl. Admin., 1996; postgrad., St. John's U., 2004—. Choral and band substitute tchr. Half Hollow Hills Ctrl. Sch. Dist., Melville, NY, 1986; elem. band and orch. substitute dir. Sachem (N.Y.) Ctrl. Sch. Dist., 1986; h.s. and elem. band dir. Island Trees Ctrl .Sch. Dist., Levittown, NY, 1987—88; elem. band dir. Smithtown (N.Y.) Ctrl. Sch. Dist., 1988—91; elem. band dir. and gen. music tchr. Harborfields Ctrl. Sch. Dist., Greenlawn, NY, 1991—93; mid. sch. band dir., lead tchr. Smithtown Ctrl. Sch. Dist., 1993—2001, h.s. band dir., 2001—. Mem.: Nat. Flute Assn., L.I. Flute Club, N.Y. Flute Club, N.Y. State Coun. Adminstrs. for Music Educators, Suffolk County Music Edn. Assn., Music Educators Nat. Conf., Phi Delta Kappa. Avocations: music, golf, basketball, softball, travel. Home: 6 Angela Ct Saint James NY 11780 Office: Smithtown High Sch 100 Central Rd Smithtown NY 11787

KALAJIAN-LAGANI, DONNA, publishing executive; b. Mountainside, N.J., Feb. 8, 1955; d. Jack and Analid Kalajian; m. Ron Galotti, Oct. 14, 1981. BS, Penn State U., 1975. Internat. credit analyst Irving Trust Co., N.Y.C., 1976—77; ad sales rep. BMT Pub., N.Y.C., 1977—79, Woman's Day Mag., N.Y.C., 1979—81, cosmetics mgr., 1981—83, ea. mgr., 1984—87; v.p., advt. dir. Ladies' Home Jour., N.Y.C., 1987—89, v.p., pub., 1989—95; pub./sr. v.p. Cosmopolitan Mag., 1996—99; publ. dir. Cosmopolitan Group, N.Y.C., 1999—, sr. v.p., 1999—. Home: 100 Park Ave New York NY 10017-5516 Office: Cosmopolitan Hearst Magazines 224 W 57th St New York NY 10019-3299

KALATA, MARY ANN CATHERINE, architect; b. Passaic, N.J., Sept. 7, 1962; d. John Joseph Kalata and Filomena Katherine Kurnat. BS Archl. Technology, N.Y. Inst. Technology, 1984. Model builder, field coord. Perkins & Will, Russo & Sonder Architects, N.Y.C., 1984—94; archl. designer Andrew G. Antoniades Architects, N.Y.C., 1994—97; archl. coord. MIchael J. Romanik Architects, Paterson, NJ, 1997—. Mem. Rep. Nat. Com., Washington. Recipient gold medal in archl. technology, N.Y. Inst. Technology, 1984. Mem.: ASC/AIA, U.S. Navy League. Republican. Roman Catholic. Avocations: photography, travel, model building, audio technology. Home: 8 Baker Ct Clifton NJ 07011

KALAYJIAN, ANIE, psychotherapist, nurse, educator, consultant; b. Aleppa, Syria; came to U.S., 1971; d. Kevork and Zabelle (Mardikian) Kalayjian; m. Shahé Navasart Sanentz, Dec. 16, 1984 (div. 1999). BS, L.I. U., 1979, DSc (hon.), 2001; MEd, Columbia U., 1981, profl. nursing tng. course, 1984, EdD, 1985; cert. photography, Pratt Inst., 1979. RN, N.Y., N.J., Conn.; cert. psychiat. mental health specialist; Dutch diplomate in logotherapy; advanced cert. in Eye Movement Desensitization and Reprocessing, advanced cert. in disaster mgmt. ARC; bd. cert. expert in traumatic stress; cert. expert in crisis mgmt. Psychiat. nurse Met. Hosp., N.Y.C., 1979-84; staff psychiat. mental health nurse Project Renewal, N.Y.C., 1978-2000; instr. Hunter Coll., N.Y.C., 1980-82; prof. Bloomfield (NJ) Coll., 1984-85; lectr. Jersey City (NJ) Coll., 1985; prof. Seton Hall U., South Orange, NJ, 1985-87; assoc. prof. grad. program St. Joseph Coll., 1987-91; prof. John Jay Coll. Criminal Justice, 1991-92, Fairleigh Dickinson U., 1991—92; vis. prof. Pace U., N.Y.C., 1994-95. Adj. prof. Coll. Mt. St. Vincent, Riverdale, NY, 1995—97, Fordham U., 1998—, Coll. New Rochelle, 1998—99; disting. lectr. Columbia U., N.Y.C., 1995; spkr. in field; keynote spkr. Mid Am. Logotherapy Inst., 1995, Coll. Mt. St. Vincent, 1995, Hollins Coll., Va., 1995, UN; NGO exec. com. vice-chair, 2000—; chair DPI/NGO annual conf.; lectr., Argentina, Toronto, Ireland, U.N., 2003; program chairperson Divsn. 52 APA, Hawaii, 2004. Author: Disaster and Mass Trauma: Global Perspectives on Post Disaster Mental Health Management, 1995; contbr. articles to profl. jours., chapters to books; reviewer: Readings: A Journal of Reviews and Commentary in Mental Health, 1990—; TV appearances ABC, CNN, NY1, Tokyo TV, —, radio appearances WSOU, WFUV, WBAI, Voice of America, —. Active com. for presdl. task force on nursing curriculum Soc. for Traumatic Stress Studies; co-founder, East coast coord. Mental Health Outreach to Earthquake Survivors in Armenia; program dir. Mental Health Outreach to Earthquake Survivors in Turkey, 1999; dir. Julia Richman-Pace U.-N.Y. State Bd. Edn.-Vis. Nurse Svc.-Partnership program, 1991-92; UN rep. World Fedn. for Mental Health, mem. mental health/human rights com., 1996—. Recipient Clark Found. scholarship award, 1985, Outstanding Rsch. award Columbia U., 1993, ABSA Outstanding Achievement award APA, 1995; rsch. grantee Pace U., 1992; Endowed Nursing Edn. Columbia U., scholar, 1984; Armenian Relief Soc. scholar, 1976-77, Armenian Students Assn. Am. scholar, 1976-78; recipient Columbia U. Tchrs. Coll. Outstanding Rsch. award, 1993. Fellow APA (chair Hawaii program, 2004, treas. divsn. 52 Internat. Psychology, 2004-), Am. Orthopsychiat. Assn., N.Y. State Nursing Assn. (planning com. nursing edn.), APA (program chmn. divsn. 52, Hawaii, 2004, outstanding achievement award 1995); mem. Coun. on Continuing Edn., Psychiat. and Mental Health Nursing, Am. Psychol. Soc., Am. Psychiat. Nurses Assn., Am. Acad. Experts in Traumatic Stress, Internat. Coun. Psychologists, Internat. Trauma Counselors, Inst. for Psychodynamics and Origins of Mind, Armenian Students Assn. (treas. 1980-81, pres. 1981-83, scholarship chairperson 1983-85, v.p. ctrl. exec. com. 1987-88, pres. 1988-89, nat. pres. 1988-90), Armenian Info. Profls. (corr. sec. 1992—), Armenian-Am. Soc. for Studies on Stress and Genocide (founder, pres. 1988—), N.Y. RN's Assn. (chair edn. com. 1989-99), World Fedn. for Mental Health (UN rep. 1994—, treas., sec., UN com. on human rights 1994—, chair human rights com. 1996—), Univ. for Peace (corr. sec. UN com.), Internat. Soc. Traumatic Stress Studies (v.p. N.Y. chpt. 1993-95, pres. 1995—), Global Soc. for Nursing and Health (pres., co-founder), N.Y. Counties RN Assn. (Jane Delano Disting. Svc. award 1994), Kappa Delta Pi (advisor 1989-90), Sigma Theta Tau. Avocations: aerobics, photography, acting, hiking. Office: 130 W 79th St New York NY 10024-6477 E-mail: kalayjiana@aol.com.

KALBACH, AUDREY A. family practice nurse practitioner, psychiatric nurse practitioner; d. Earl E. and Irene Lutz; m. Larry L. Kalbach, Sept. 8, 1959; children: Jeffrey, Bruce. BSN, U. Tex., Arlington, 1978, MSN, 1981; FNP, U. Tenn., Memphis, 1994. RN Tenn., cert. Clin. Specialist, Tenn. RN, gastroenterology Lewisville (Tex.) Hosp., 1977—82; CNS evaluation coord. Psychiat. Inst., Ft. Worth, 1982—87; educator, CNS Meth. Hosp., Memphis, 1987—89; educator, FNP, CNS U. Tenn., Memphis, 1990—98; primary care nurse VA Med. Ctr., Dallas, 1994—2000. Founder primary care clin. VA Med. Ctr. Sys. of Memphis. V.p., bd. mem. Woodchase Homeowners Assn., Cordova, Tenn., 1989—93. Mem.: ANA, Advanced Practice Assn. Greater Memphis, W. Tenn. Psychiat. Advanced Practice, Sigma Theta Tau. Unitarian Universalist. Avocations: reading, golf, bridge, cooking, hiking. Home: 1967 Woodchase Cove Cordova TN 38016

KALIKOW, THEODORA JUNE, university president; b. Lynn, Mass., June 6, 1941; d. Irving and Rose Kalikow AB, Wellesley Coll., 1962; ScM, MIT, 1970; PhD, Boston U., 1974. From instr. to prof. Southeastern Mass. U., North Dartmouth, 1968-84; dean Coll. Arts and Scis., U. No. Colo., Greeley, 1984-87; dean of the coll. Plymouth (N.H.) State Coll., 1987-94, interim pres., 1992-93; pres. U. Maine, Farmington, 1994—. Contbr. articles to profl. jours., 1975— Chair steering com. Maine ACE/NIP, 1995—; chair Coun. Pub. Liberal Arts Colls., 1997-99. Named to, Maine Women's Hall of Fame, 2002; recipient Am. Coun. on Edn. fellow, Brown U., Providence, 1983—84, Mary Ann Hartman award, 2000; grantee, NSF, 1978. Mem.: Assn. Am. Colls. and Univs. (bd. dirs. 2000—03), Western Mountains Alliance (chmn. 2000—03), Am. Coun. on Edn. (commn. on women 1994—97, 2000—03), Soc. Values in Higher Edn. (bd. dirs. 1991—94). Office: U Maine at Farmington Office of the Pres 224 Main St Farmington ME 04938-1911 Office Phone: 207-778-7256.

KALIN, D(OROTHY) JEAN, artist, educator; b. Kansas City, Mo., Feb. 11, 1932; d. William Warner and Esther Dorothy (Peterson) Johnson; m. John Baptist Kalin, Jr., Jan. 5, 1952; children: Jean Loraine, Debra Ann, Diana Yvonne. AA, St. Joseph (Mo.) Jr. Coll., 1951. Artist Hallmark Cards, Inc., Kansas City, Mo., 1952-53, 73-93; freelance artist Kansas City, 1953-72; owner Portraits of Life, Kansas City, 1986—, art tchr., 1988—. Illustrator article for Directory of Am. Portrait Artists, 1985; featured in Rockport Pubs. Best of Watercolor 2 and Painting Light and Shadow, 1997, Am. Artist Mag., 1998, 2000, Splash 5, 1998, Best of Collected Watercolor, 2002, Midwest Art, 2003, The Artists' Mag., 2003. Kansas City Art Inst. scholar, 1951-52. Mem. Nat. Oil and Acrylic Painters Soc. (signature mem.), Nat. Acrylic Painters Assn. (signature mem.), Kans. Watercolor Soc. (signature mem.), Women Artists of the West (signature mem.), Am. Watercolor Soc. (assoc.), Nat. Watercolor Soc. (assoc.), Midwest Watercolor Soc. (assoc.), Nat. Mus. Women in the Arts (charter mem.), Mo. Watercolor Soc. (signature mem., bd. dirs. 1999—), Western Colo. Watercolor Soc. (signature mem.), Internat. Platform Assn. Avocations: gardening, traveling. Address: 20650 State Rt 371 Platte City MO 64079-9344 Office Phone: 816-992-3744.

KALIN, KARIN BEA, retired secondary school educator, consultant; b. N.Y.C., June 22, 1943; d. Lawrence Leon and Celia (Siskind) Elkind; children: Laura, Howard. BS, SUNY, Oswego, 1965; MS, CUNY, 1967.

Cert. social studies tchr., N.Y. Tchr. Benjamin Franklin H.S., N.Y.C., 1965-66, Grover Cleveland H.S., Ridgewood, N.Y., 1967-73, Aviation H.S., L.I. City, N.Y., 1979-99, sex equity coord., 1982-90, local equal opportunity coord., 1983-91, sch. recruiter, 1985-91; with N.Y.C. H.S. Transfer Ctr., 2000—. Curriculum developer OEO N.Y.C. Bd. Edn., fall, 1985; global studies curriculum writing, 1997—98; panelist Aerospace Edn. Workshop for Elem. Tchrs., Career Exploration Seminar, Aerospace Edn. Conf., 1990; placement counselor East Meadow (N.Y.) Sch. Dist., 1989—; cons. Coll. Aerospace, NY, 1986, Profl. and Clerical Employees of Internat. Ladies Garment Workers Union, N.Y.C., 1989; with L.I. Coun. for Equal Edn. and Employment, 1990; placement counselor N.Y.C. H.S., 2000—; with N.Y.C. H.S. Transfer Ctr., 2000—. Mem. Women on the Job, Port Washington, NY, 1986—91, L.I. Coun. Equal Edn. and Employment, 1990—, Coalition to Advocate for Women of Color in Edn.; vol. Goodwill Games, 1998, Empire State Games, 1999, Hamlet Cup, 1999—, Friends of the Arts, 1999—, L.I. Fair at Old Bethpage Restoration, 1999, L.I. Studies Inst., 2000, Divsn. 1 NCAA Women's Swimming & Diving Championship, 2001, Big East, 2002; mem. com. Nassau Dem. Com., Westbury, NY, 1988—. William Robertson Coe fellow, 1992; grantee Columbia U., 1967, 69, N.Y.C. Bd. Edn., 1983, Nat. Coun. for Humanities, 1985, Project Voice/Move, 1984-85; named to Nat. Women's Hall of Fame. Mem.: AFL-CIO, LWV, NAFE, AAUW (roundtable on gender equity in classroom 1992, co-chair social justice 2000—, Nassau County chair Sister to Sister 2001), NOW (chair conciousness raising com. 1982, chair women and employment com. 1987—90, chair social justice), Nat. Women's Hall of Fame, Nat. Women's History Mus., Assn. Tchrs. of Social Studies, United Fedn. Tchrs., Nat. Women's Hall of Fame, Nat. Women's Polit. Caucus (chair polit. action com. 1990—96, bd. dirs.), N.Y. State Alliance for Women and Girls in Tech., Bachelor and Bachelorettes for Square Dancing (pres. L.I. chpt. 1994—96, founder). Jewish. Avocations: swimming, reading, visiting museums, square dancing, round dancing, bridge. Home: 700 Barkley Ave East Meadow NY 11554-4501 E-mail: karin622@att.net.

KALISCH, BEATRICE JEAN, nursing educator, consultant; b. Tellahoma, Tenn., Oct. 15, 1943; d. Peter and Margaret Ruth Petersen; children— Philip P., Melanie J. BS, U. Nebr., 1965; MS, U. Md., 1967, PhD, 1970. Pediatric staff nurse Centre County Hosp., Bellefonte, Pa., 1965-66; instr. nursing Philipsburg (Pa.) Gen. Hosp. Sch. Nursing, 1966, pediatric staff nurse Greater Balt. Med. Center, Towson, Md., 1967; asst. prof. maternal-child nursing Am. U., 1967-68; clin. nurse specialist N.W. Tex. Hosp., Amarillo, 1970; assoc. prof. maternal-child nursing, curriculum coordinator nursing Amarillo Coll., 1970-71; chmn. baccalaureate nursing program, asso. prof. nursing U. So. Miss., 1971-74; prof. nursing, chmn. dept. parent-child nursing U. Mich. Sch. Nursing, Ann Arbor, 1974-86, Shirley C. Titus Disting. prof., 1977—, Titus Disting. prof. nursing mgmt., 1989—, dir. nursing bus. and health sys. program, 2000—; prin., dir. nursing consultation svcs. Ernst & Young, Detroit, 1986-89. Prin. investigator USPH grant to study image of nurses in mass media and the informational quality nursing news, U. Mich., 1977-86, prin. investigator to study intrahosp. transport of critically ill patients, 1991—; prin. investigator to study use of HIA nurse in N.Y.C. labor market, U. Mich.; prin. investigator to study the impact of managed care on critical care, U. Mich.; vis. Disting. prof. U. Ala., 1979, U. Tex., 1981, Tex. Christian U., 1983. Author: Child Abuse and Neglect: An Annotated Bibliography, 1978; co-author: Nursing Involvement in Health Planning, 1978, Politics of Nursing, 1982, Images of Nurses on Television, 1983, The Advance of American Nursing, 1986, revised, 1994, The Changing Image of the Nurse, 1987; co-editor: Studies in Nursing Mgmt.; contbr. articles to profl. jours. Recipient Joseph L. Andrews Bibliog. award Am. Assn. Law Libraries, 1979; Book of Yr. award Am. Jour. Nursing, 1978, 83, 86, 87, Outstanding Achievement award U. Md., 1987, Distinguished Alumni award U. Nebr., 1985, Shaw medal Boston Coll., 1986; USPHS fellow. Fellow Am. Acad. Nursing; mem. Am. Coll. Healthcare Execs., ANA, APHA, Am. Orgn. Nurse Execs., Sigma Theta Tau, Phi Kappa Phi. Presbyterian. Home: 27675 Chatsworth St Farmington MI 48334-1821 Office: U Mich Sch Nursing 400 N Ingalls St Ann Arbor MI 48109-0482 E-mail: bkalisch@umich.edu.

KALISKI, MARY, psychologist; b. Bratislava, Czechoslovakia, Dec. 9, 1938; came to U.S., 1950; d. Frank and Margaret (Fleischman) Reichenthal; m. Thomas Kaliski, Sept. 21, 1957; children: Karen, Kenneth. BS summa cum laude, C.W. Post Coll., 1978; MS, profl. diploma, St. John's U., 1980, PhD, 1987. Psychologist North Shore Schs., L.I., 1977-79, Herricks Schs., L.I., 1979—. Speaker in field. Chief psychologist Stepfamily Found. L.I., 1987-92; bd. dirs. Nassau Psychol. Svcs. Inst., 1989—. Mem. Am. Psychol. Assn., Nassau County Psychol. Assn.

KALLIR, JANE KATHERINE, art gallery director, author; b. NYC; d. John Otto and Joyce (Ruben) Kallir. BA, Brown U., 1976. Asst. to dir. Lefebre Gallery, NYC, 1977, Galerie St. Etienne, NYC, 1977-78, co-dir., 1979—. Guest lectr. NYU, 1987—85, Mus. Am. Folk Art, NYC, 1982—85; guest curator NY State Mus., Albany, 1983, Internat. Exhbn. Found., Washington, 1984—85, Mus. of City of Vienna, 1986, Austrian Nat. Gallery, 1990, Nat. Gallery Art, Washington, 1994, Indpls. Mus. Art, 1994, San Diego Mus. Art, 1994; guest lectr. Nat. Gallery Art, 1994, Ft. Lauderdale Mus. Art, 1996, guest curator, Fla., 96; guest lectr. Mus. Modern Art, 1997, Internat. Found. for Art Rsch., 1998, Wexner Ctr., Columbus, Ohio, 1999, NYU, 1999, San Diego Mus., 2001; guest curator Nat. Mus. of Women in the Arts, 2001, Orlando Mus. of Art, Fla., 2001, Museo del Vittoriano, Rome, 2001, San Diego Mus. Art, 2001; guest lectr. Columbus Mus. of Art, 2002, Clark Art Inst., 2002. Author: Gustav Klimt-Egon Schiele, 1980, Austria's Expressionism, 1981, The Folk Art Tradition, 1981, Grandma Moses, The Artist Behind the Myth, 1982, Arnold Schoenberg's Vienna, 1984, Viennese Design and the Wiener Werkstaette, 1986, Gustav Klimt: 25 Masterworks, 1989, Egon Schiele: The Complete Works, 1990, rev., 1998, Richard Gerstl/Oskar Kokoschka, 1992, Egon Schiele, 1994, Egon Schiele: 27 Masterworks, 1996, Grandma Moses, 25 Masterworks, 1997, Grandma Moses in the 21st Century, 2001, The Essential Grandma Moses, 2001, Egon Schiele, Watercolors and Drawings, 2003. Mem.: Art Dealers Assn. Am. (bd. dir. 1994—97, chmn. pub. rels. com. 2001—, v.p. 2003—). Democrat. Office: Galerie St Etienne 24 W 57th St New York NY 10019-3918 Office Phone: 212-245-6734. E-mail: gallery@gse.art.com.

KALLMAN, KATHLEEN BARBARA, marketing and business development professional; b. Aurora, Ill., Mar. 23, 1952; d. Kenneth Wesley and Germaine Barbara (May) Eby. Legal sec. Sidley & Austin, Chgo., 1973-76, Winston & Strawn, Chgo., 1976-78; exec. sec. Beatrice Cos., Inc., Chgo., 1978-81, adminstrv. asst., 1981-83, asst. v.p., chmn. bd. dirs., 1983—84, v.p., 1984-85; pres., mng. dir. Stratxx Ltd., Charlotte, N.C., 1985—. Mem. Chgo. Coun. on Fgn. Rels., 1986—. Mem. Am. Soc. Profl. and Exec. Women, Nat. Assn. Women Bus. Owners, Charlotte Women Bus. Owners Assn., Charlotte Assn. Profl. Saleswomen, Chgo. Assn. Profl. Saleswomen, Internat. Assn. Bus. Communicators. Avocation: photography.

KALLOSH, RENATA, physics educator; BS, Moscow State U., 1966; PhD, Lebedev Physical Inst., Moscow, 1968. Prof. Lebedev Physical Inst., Moscow, 1981-89; sci. assoc. CERN, Switzerland, 1989-90; prof. physics Stanford U., Calif., 1990—. Avocations: gardening, biking, hiking, swimming, travelling. Achievements include research in unified theories of fundamental interactions including gravity, different aspects of supersymmetry, supergravity, and superstring theory, gen. theory of quantization, manifestly supersymmetric quantization of superparticle and superstring theory, quantum theory of black holes and gravitational waves in supersymmetric theories. Office: Stanford U Varian 342 Stanford CA 94305 Fax: 650-725-6544. E-mail: kallosh@physics.stanford.edu.

KALNAY, EUGENIA, university administrator, meteorologist; b. Buenos Aires, Oct. 1, 1942; came to U.S., 1971; d. Jorge and Susana (Zwicky) K.; m. Alberto Mario Rivas, July 24, 1965 (div. 1981); 1 child, Jorge Rodrigo; m. Malise Cooper Dick, July 13, 1981. Lic. in meteorology, U. Buenos Aires, 1965; PhD in Meteorology, MIT, 1971. Asst. prof. U. Uruguay, Montevideo, 1971-73; rsch. assoc. MIT, Cambridge, 1973-75, asst. prof. meteorology, 1975-76, assoc. prof., 1977-78; sect. head NASA Goddard Space Flight Ctr., Greenbelt, Md., 1979-82, br. head, 1983-86; chief devel. div. Nat. Weather Svc., NOAA Nat. Meteorology Ctr., Washington, 1987-99; prof., chair dept. meteorology U. Md., 1999—. Mem. several coms. NRC, NAS, Washington; prin. investigator NASA, 1973—; adj. prof. meteorology U. Md., 1980-83. Editor several jours.; contbr. over 100 articles to sci. jours. Recipient gold medal for exceptional sci. achievement NASA, 1981, silver medal Dept. Commerce, 1990, Gold medal Dept. Commerce, 1993, 97. Mem. NAE, Am. Meteorl. Soc. (Charney award 1995). Home: 56 Lakeside Dr Greenbelt MD 20770-1904

KALONJI, GRETCHEN, engineering educator; Degree in Engring., MIT, 1980, PhD, 1982. Asst. to assoc. prof. MIT, 1982—90; prof. dept. materials sci. & engring. U. Wash., 1990—. Dir. Engring. Coalition Schs. Excellence Edn. and Leadership U. Wash; lectr. Symposium Japanese Soc. Engring. Edn. Tokyo; with Tech. Edn. Resource Ctr.; vis. scholar Max Planck Inst., Stutgart, U. Paris. Recipient Young Investigator award 1984, George Westinghouse award ASEE, 1994. Fellow: AAAS. Office: U Wash Box 352120 Seattle WA 98195-2120

KALSNER-SILVER, LYDIA, psychologist; b. Winnipeg, Can., May 26, 1964; d. Stanley and Jenny Kalsner; m. Jay Silver, Aug. 20, 1994; children: Dylan, Chloe. BS in Psychology, U. Toronto, 1987; MA, EdM, Columbia U., 1992; EdD in Counseling Psychology, Rutgers U., 2000. Dir. clin. assessment dept. psychiatry SUNY, Bklyn., 1992—97; psychology resident Jackson Meml. Hosp., Miami, 1997—98, post-doctoral fellow Juvenile Gun Offender Program, 2000—01; sch. psychologist Temple Beth Am Day Sch., Miami, 2001—02; psychologist Divsn. Alternative Outreach Miami (Fla.) Dade Country Pub. Schs., 2002—; pvt. practice psychotherapist Miami, 2002—. Grant reviewer crime prevention com. Miami (Fla.) Dade Criminal Justice Counsel, Miami, 1997; adj. faculty U. Miami, 1997—98; rsch. writer Higher Edn. Ext. Svc. Columbia U., N.Y., 1991—92; instr. Rutgers U., New Brunswick, NJ. Contbr. articles to profl. jours. Scholar, Tchrs. Coll. Columbia U., 1990. Mem.: APA, Soc. Personal Assessment, Fla. Psychol. Assn. Avocations: cooking, travel. Home: 5151 Collins Ave Miami Beach FL 33140 Office: 975 Arthur Godfrey Rd Ste 302 Miami Beach FL 33140

KALSOW-BERNHARD, KATHRYN MARIE, choir director; b. Chgo., Jan. 5, 1948; d. William H. and Frances C. Perkins; m. Leroy F. Bernhard, June 9, 2001; m. Stephen Allan Kalsow, Aug. 31, 1968 (div. Nov. 12, 1997); children: Sandra Kristen Moore, Jeffrey Stephen Kalsow, Julie Anne Kalsow. AA, Lyons Twp. Jr. Coll., LaGrange, Ill., 1967; BMus, Millikin U., Decatur, Ill., 1970; MA in Curriculum and Instrn., Concordia Coll., River Forest, Ill., 1988. Elem. music tchr. Ontarioville and Laurel Hill elem. schools, Ontarioville, Bartlett, Ill., 1970—72; music tchr. and choir dir. Eastview Jr. High, Bartlett, Ill., 1972—81, Canton Mid. Sch., Streamwood, Ill., 1981—97; condr. Elgin Children's Chorus-Treble Choir, Elgin, Ill., 1995—2002; choir dir. Elgin (Ill.) H.S., 1997—; guest condr. Sch. Dist. 300 Choral Festival, Dundee, Ill., 2001—01, Sch. Dist. U-46 Mid. Sch. Choral Festival, Elgin, Ill., 2002—02. Dir. kinderchoir First Congl. Ch., Elgin, 1986—89; instr. music for elem. tchrs. Elgin C.C., 1989—96; instr. music methods Judson Coll., 1997—98. Mem. Elgin Choral Union & Arts Chorale, Elgin, Ill., 1994—99; mem., soloist 1st Congl. Ch. Choir; choir chair Fox Valley Music Festival, Ill., 1998—2000. Mem.: Ill. Music Educators Assn. (chair Dist. IX 1999—2002), Am. Choral Dirs. Assn. (life), Music Educators Nat. Conf. (life). Office: Elgin High School 1200 Maroon Drive Elgin IL 60177 Personal E-mail: kmbernhard@aol.com. E-mail: kalsow_k/me@dns.u46.k12.il.us.

KALUZA, SHERYLE SIEGFRIED, music educator, vocalist, composer; b. Mpls., Jan. 4, 1950; d. Ervin Vern and Dorothy Lorraine Siegfried; m. Charles Leo Kaluza, Apr. 14, 1972; children: Karl Nicholas, Ruth Alayne. BA, Augsburg Coll., Mpls., 1972. Cert. tchr., Mo. Tchr. vocal music Memphis (Mo.) Sch. Dist., 1972, Immaculate Mary Cath. Sch., Kirksville, Mo., 1973-76; asst. choir dir. St. Edmund's Cath. Ch., Warren, Mich., 1977-81; choir dir. Ch. of Redemption, Bartlett, Tenn., 1981-84, Emmanuel Presbyn. Ch., West Linn, Oreg., 1984-85, Ch. of Resurrection, West Linn, 1987-94, music coord., 1993-95; instr. voice Marylhurst (Oreg.) Coll., 1994-96, Heartsong Studio, West Linn, 1985—; voice cons. Eastmoreland Ear, Nose and Throat Clinic, Portland, Oreg. Instr. Liturgical Arts Resource Ctr., 1989; participant Nat. Assn. Tchrs. Singing, Superior, Wis., 1987; participant vocal master class Linfield Coll., McMinnville, Oreg., 1989, 90, Nat. Pastoral Musicians Composers Forum, St. Paul, 1992. Composer: (song cycle) The Lark Songs, 1991; singer, arranger rec. Real Lullabies, 1989. Ch. cantor Ch. of Resurrection, 1985—, also mem. choir; pres. Portland Aux. Osteo. Physicians and Surgeons Oreg., 1986-87; asst. dir. Ah! Chantez, Marylhurst, 1988-89. Mem. Music Tchrs. Nat. Assn. (soloist for song cycle Summer Fragments composer competition 1992), Oreg. Music Tchrs. Assn. Avocations: watercolor, glass painting, decorating, walking, fishing. Office: Eastmoreland Ear Nose & Throat Clinic 2816 SE Steele St Portland OR 97202-4525

KALVEN, JANET, education educator, writer, consultant; b. Chgo., May 21, 1913; BS, U. Chgo., 1934; MEd, Boston U., 1971. Instr. Great Books program U. Chgo., 1937-42; lectr., adminstr. ednl. program for women U.S. Grail Movement, Libertyville, Ill., 1942-43, Loveland, Ohio, 1944-64; coord. internat. meetings Internat. Grail Movement, Paris, 1964-67; coord. academic program Grailville Conf. Ctr., Loveland, Ohio, 1967-78, conf. coord., lectr., 1978—2002; assoc. dir. self directed learning program U. Dayton (Ohio), 1972-86. Founder, trainer Women Into Tomorrow, Cin., 1971-76. Co-author, editor: Your Daughters Shall Prophesy, 1980, Value Development, 1982, Women's Spirit Bonding, 1984, With Both Eyes Open, 1988, Women Breaking Boundaries, 1999; contbr. article to profl. jour. Mem. nat. commn. Ch. Women United, N.Y., 1970-71; bd. dirs. Women Ch. Convergence, Balt., 1984—, Metro. Area Religious Coalition, Cin., 1969-72, Cin. Indsl. Mission, 1971-74; founder, bd. dirs. Womens Inst. for Religion and Soc., Cin., 1985-93; co-founder, bd. dirs. Womens Rsch. Devel. Ctr., Cin., 1988—. Elected to Ohio Women's Hall of Fame, 1990. Mem. NOW, Nat. Women's Studies Assn., Women's Ordination Conf. (program com.), Phi Beta Kappa. Home: 1615 Chase Ave # 3D Cincinnati OH 45223 Office Phone: 513-541-4009.

KALVER, GAIL ELLEN, dance company executive, musician; b. Chgo., Nov. 25, 1948; d. Nathan Eli and Alice Martha (Jaffe) K. BS in Music Edn., U. Ill., 1970; MA in Clarinet Chgo. Musical Coll., Roosevelt U., 1974. Profl. musician, Chgo., 1970-77; assoc. mgr. Ravinia Festival, Highland Park, Ill., 1977-83; exec. dir. Hubbard Street Dance Chgo., 1984—. Bd. dirs. Chicago Dancers United, Ill. Arts Alliance; mem. dance panel Ill. Arts Council, Chgo., 1983-85; mem. grants panels Chgo. Office Fine Arts, 1985. Editor: Music Explorer (for music edn.), 1983-86. Mem. grants panels NEA, 1992-94; cons. music Nat. Radio Theatre, Chgo., 1983—; mem. adv. coun. Dance Initiative Chgo. Cmty. Trust, Dancers Responding to AIDS; mem. exec. com. Dance for Life, 2003. Office: Hubbard St Dance Chgo 1147 W Jackson Blvd Chicago IL 60607-2905

KALVIN-STIEFEL, JUDY, public relations executive; b. Valley Stream, Long Island; m. Lewis Stiefel; 1 child, Amy. BA in lit. and journalism, SUNY, Oneonta. Writer, editor Corp. Design mag., 1985—87; account supr. Howard J. Rubenstein Assoc.; dir. pub. rels. Gerstman+Meyers, 1989—93; v.p. pub. rels. Gerstman+Meyers (now Interbrand), 1993—97, Addison, NYC, 1997—99; v.p., dir. comm. Sterling Group, NYC, 1999—2001; founder, pres. Kalvin Pub. Rels., Forest Hills, NY, 2001. Author: Defining Woman: Natural Workout for Body and Mind, 1993. Recipient Women Achievement Pacesetter award, NYC Coun., 2002, NEAL award bus. writing, championship title, World Natural Bodybuilding Fedn., 1990. Mem.: NY Women in Comm. Avocation: bodybuilding. Office Phone: 718-520-1660. Business E-Mail: jkalvin@kalvinpr.com.*

KAMADA-COLE, MIKA M. allergist, immunologist, medical educator; b. Denver, Dec. 9, 1957; m. Joe Lyn Cole, Dec. 7, 1991. BA in Biology, BA in Chemistry, U. Mo., 1980, MD, 1982. Diplomate: Am. Bd. Allergy and Immunology, Am. Bd. Internal Medicine, Nat. Bd. Med. Examiners. Intern in medicine Barnes Hosp., St. Louis, 1982-83, jr. resident in medicine, 1983-84; rsch./clin. fellow in allergy and immunology Dept. of Rheumatology and Immunology Brigham and Women's Hosp., Boston, 1985-88; assoc. in medicine Washington U., 1982-85; rsch. fellow in medicine Harvard Med. Sch., 1985-88, instr. in pediatrics, 1988-90; instr. Southwestern Med. Sch., 1991-92, U. Tex. Health Sci., 1992—; staff Santa Rosa Healthcare, San Antonio, 1992—, Southwest Gen. Hosp., San Antonio, 1992—, Methodist Hosp., San Antonio, 1992—. Contbr. munerous articles to med. jours. Recipient Vice Chancellor for Student Affairs Honor, 1982, Honor Grad. award Am. Med. Women's Assn., Schering Rsch. award. Fellow Am. Coll. Allergy; mem. Am. Acad. Allergy and Immunology (mem. com. asthma mortality 1987—), Tex. Med. Assn., Bexar County Med. Soc. Office: 5323 Broadway St San Antonio TX 78209-5713 E-mail: mkcole@dnamail.com.

KAMALI, NORMA, fashion designer; b. N.Y.C., June 27, 1945; d. Sam and Estelle (Mariategui) Arraez. Grad., Fashion Inst. of Tech., 1965. Established Kamali Ltd., N.Y.C., 1967-78; owner, designer On My Own Norma Kamali, N.Y.C., 1978—. Designer costumes for Emerald City in The Wiz, 1978; for Twyla Tharp dance In the Upper Room, 1986; Parachute Designs displayed Met. Mus. of Art, N.Y.C., 1977; prodr., dir. (video) Fall Fantasy, dir. (video) Fashion Aid, 1985. Recipient CFDA award, 1982, 1985, Coty award, 1981, 82, 83, Ernie awards Earnshaw Rev., 1983, Fashion Inst. Design and Merchandising award, 1983, Annual Interiors award Interiors Mag., 1985, Salute to Women award N.Y. Fashion Group, 1986, Disting. Arch. award N.Y. chpt. AIA, 1986, Outstanding Grad. award Pub. Edn. Assn. N.Y., 1988, Award of Merit, Internat. Video Culture Competition, 1988, Am. Success award Fashion Inst. Tech., 1989, Youth Friends award Sch. Art League, 1997, Pencil award, 1999, Willow award Lower East Side Girls Club, 1999, Fashion Outreach Style award, 1999, Bus. Outreach award Manhattan C. of C., 2002-, Entrepreneur award Fashion Group, 2002-, Women's History Month award N.Y.C. Controllers Office, 2002-; featured exhibit Met. Mus. Exhibit, 2001-; inducted into Fashion Walk of Fame Fashion Ctr. Bus. Improvement Dist. Office: 11 W 56th St New York NY 10019-3902

KAMATOY, LOURDES AGUAS, artist; b. San Fernando, Pampanga, Philippines, June 29, 1945; came to U.S., 1966; d. Juan Gutierrez and Segunda Mercado (De La Cruz) Aguas; m. Ernesto Gabriel Kamatoy, Apr. 28, 1973; 1 child, Lisette Marie. BA in English, U. Santo Tomas, Manila, Philippines, 1964; MA in Ednl. Theatre, NYU, 1972; overseas cert. theatre, Rose Bruford Coll. Speech, Kent, Eng., 1966. Supr. Arthur Andersen & Co., N.Y.C., 1966-73; instr. theatre U. So. Ind., Evansville, 1973-75; pres. Bodega, Evansville, 1975-79; artist rep. Lulu Represents, Chgo., 1986-92; ptnr. MK Videostar, Chgo., 1989-92; account exec. Kamatoy Creative, Encino, Calif., 1992—2001; exec. dir. Valley Women's Ctr., Canoga Park, Calif., 2001—. Pres. Evansville Arts and Edn. Coun., 1983; v.p. U. Evansville Theatre Soc., 1984; panelist Ind. Arts Commn., Indpls., 1985; bd. dirs. Arts Insight, Indpls., 1985, USI Soc. Arts and Humanities, Evansville, 1988, Valley Cultural Ctr., Woodland Hills, Calif., 1996, v.p., 1997—2000. Mem. Rotary Club (officer Warner Ctr. chpt.). Roman Catholic. Avocations: going to theatre, eating at fine restaurants. Office: 21515 Vanowen St Ste 114 Canoga Park CA 91303 Office Phone: 818-713-8700.

KAMBOUR, ANNALIESE SPOFFORD, lawyer; b. Schenectady, N.Y., Nov. 19, 1961; d. Roger Peabody and Virginia Louise (Dyer) K. BA, Harvard U., 1983, JD, 1986. Bar: Mass. 1986, N.Y. 1987, U.S. Tax Ct. 1987. Assoc. Paul, Weiss, Rifkind, Wharton & Garrison, N.Y.C., 1986—. Mem. NOW, N.Y. State Bar Assn. Office: Paul Weiss Rifkind Wharton & Garrison Ste 4A 1285 Avenue Of The Americas Fl 21 New York NY 10019-6028

KAMERMAN, SHEILA BRODY, social worker, educator; b. Jan. 7, 1928; d. S. Lawrence and Helen (Golding) Brody; m. Morton Kamerman, Sept. 11, 1947; children: Nathan Brody, Elliot Herbert, Laura Kamerman-Katz. BA, NYU, 1946; MSW, Hunter Coll., 1966; D in Social Welfare, Columbia U., 1973; PhD (hon.), York U., Eng., 1998. Social worker N.Y.C. Dept. Social Svcs., 1966-68; social work supr. Bellevue Psychiat. Hosp., 1968-69; assoc. prof. social work Hunter Coll., 1977-79; from rsch. assoc. to sr. rsch. assoc. Columbia U. Sch. Social Work, 1971-79, assoc. prof. social policy and planning, 1979-81; prof. Sch. Social Work Columbia U., 1981—, Compton Found. Centennial prof., 1996—, interim dean Sch. Social Work, 2001—02. Dir. Columbia U. Inst. for Child and Family Policy, 1998—; chair NAS-NRC panel on work, family and community, 1980-82; mem. Com. Child Devel. Rsch. and Pub. Policy, 1983-88; mem. com. on prenatal care Inst. Medicine, 1986-88; cons. in field; mem. numerous social welfare coms. and adv. bds.; mem. Gov. Cuomo's Task Force on Poverty and Welfare Reform, 1986-87, adv. com. on Work and Family, 1987-88, UN Expert groups on social welfare and family policies; mem. Inst. Medicine/Nat. Rsch. Coun. bd. on children and families, 1998—. Author: (with Alfred J. Kahn) Not for the Poor Alone, 1975, Social Services in the United States, 1976, Social Services in International Perspective, 1977, Family Policy: Government and Families in Fourteen Countries, 1978, Child Care, Family Benefits and Working Parents, 1981, Parenting in an Unresponsive Society, 1980, Maternity and Parental Benefits and Leaves, 1980, Helping America's Families, 1982, Maternity Policies and Working Women, 1983, Income Transfers for Families with Children, 1983, Child Care: Facing the Hard Choices, 1987, The Responsive Work Place, 1987, Child Support: From Debt Collection to Social Policy, 1988, Mothers Alone: Strategies for a Time of Change, 1988, Privatization and the Welfare State, 1989, Social Services for Children, Youth and Families in the United States, 1990, Child Care, Parental Leave, and the Under 3's, 1991, A Welcome for Every Child, 1994, Starting Right: How America Neglects Its Youngest Children and What We Can Do About It, 1995, Children in big Cities, 1996, Confronting the New Politics of Child and Family Policies, (series of 6 reports), 1997, Family Change and Family Policies in Britain, Canada, New Zealand and the United States, 1998, Big Cities in the Welfare Transition, 1998, Contracting for Child and Family Services, 2000; editor: Early Childhood Education and Care, 2001; co-editor: (with Ronald A. Feldman) The Columbia University School of Social Work, 2001, (with Alfred J. Kahn) Beyond Child Poverty, the Social Exclusion of Children, 2002; contbr. over 200 articles to profl. jours. Recipient Hexter award Hunter Coll. Sch. Social Work, 1977, Nat. Leadership award in Social Policy, Heller Sch. Brandeis U., 1989, Social Welfare Policy & Practice Lifetime Achievement award, 2002; named to Hunt Coll. Hall of Fame, 1981; fellow Ctr. Advanced Study in Behavioral Scis., 1983-84, named to Columbia U Sch. of Social Work Hall of Fame, 2003. Mem. NASW, Am. Pub. Human Svcs. Assn., Assn. Policy Analysis and Mgmt., Phi Beta Kappa. Home: 1125 Park Ave New York NY 10128-1243 Office: Columbia U Sch Social Work 622 W 113th St #1D New York NY 10025-7982 E-mail: sbk2@columbia.edu.

KAMIL, ELAINE SCHEINER, pediatric nephrologist, educator; b. Cleve., Jan. 26, 1947; d. James Frank and Maud Lily (Severn) Scheiner; m. Ivan Jeffery Kamil, Aug. 29, 1970; children: Jeremy, Adam, Megan. BS magna cum laude, U. Pitts., 1969, MD, 1973. Diplomate Am. Bd. Pediats., Am. Bd. Pediat. Nephrology. Intern in pediats. Children's Hosp. Pitts., 1973-74, resident in pediats., 1974-76; clin. fellow in pediat. nephrology Sch. Medicine, UCLA, 1976-79, acting asst. prof. pediats., 1979-80, rsch. fellow in nephrology Harbor UCLA Med. Ctr., Torrance, Calif., 1980-82; med. dir. The Children's Clinic of Long Beach, Calif., 1984-87; med. dir. pediat. nurse practitioner program Calif. State U., Long Beach, 1984-87; asst. clin. prof. pediats. Sch. Medicine, UCLA, 1988-91, assoc. clin. prof. pediats., 1991-97, clin. prof. pediats., 1997—; assoc. dir. pediat. nephrology and transplant immunology Cedars-Sinai Med. Ctr., L.A., 1990—2001, clin. dir. pediatric nephrology, 2001—. Adj. asst. prof. pediats. Harbor-UCLA, Torrance, Calif., 1983-87, UCLA, 1987-88; cons. in pediat. nephrology Hawthorne (Calif.) Cmty. Med. Group, 1981-2000. Author chpts. to books; contbr. articles to profl. jours. Pres.-elect med. adv. bd. Nat. Kidney Found. So. Calif., 2000-2002, pres. exec. com., 2002-04. Recipient Vol. Svc. award Nat. Kidney Found., 1998. Mem. AAUW, Am. Soc. Nephrology, Am. Soc. Pediat. Nephrology, Am. Fedn. Clin. Rsch., Internat. Soc. Nephrology, Internat. Soc. Pediat. Nephrology, Internat. Soc. Peritoneal Dialysis, Renal Pathology Soc., So. Calif. Pediat. Nephrology Assn. (chair steering com. 1998—), Nat. Kidney Found. So. Calif. (med. adv. bd. 1987-96, rsch. com. 1987-90, chmn. pub. info. med. adv. bd. 1988-92, handbook com. 1988, co-chair med. adv. bd. cmty. svcs. com. 1992-93, chair-elect patient svcs. and cmty. edn. com. 1993-94, chair patients svcs. and cmty. edn. com. 1994-95, kidney camp summer vol. physician 1988-91, 93, 94, 97, 99-2003, Arthur Gordon award 1991, Exceptional Svc. award 1992, Exceptional Leadership and Support award 1995, bd. dirs. 1995-96, 2002—), Alpha Omega Alpha, Phi Beta Kappa. Office: Cedars Sinai Med Ctr 1165 WT 8700 Beverly Blvd Los Angeles CA 90048-1865 Office Phone: 310-423-4747.

KAMINSKI, PATRICIA JOYCE, lab administrator; d. Lucile Anne Roberts and Tadeusz Kaminski; children: Grant Matthew, Joshua Alan. Cert. dental tech., So. Calif. Coll. Med. and Dental Careers, 1975. Cert. advanced dental implant lab. Germany, spl. jaw reconstruction Calif., prosthetic tng. ITI Straumann, Mass. Implant specialist Haupt Dental Lab., Brea, Calif., 1992—2002; tech. services mgr. Dentsply Friadent Ceramed, Lakewood, Colo., 2002—03; implant dept. mgr. Dynotech Dental Lab., Corona, Calif., 2003—04; owner Kaminski Dental Lab., Orange, Calif., 2004—. Tech. cons. Home Bus., Orange, 2000—. Avocations: travel, boating, 10K races, yoga, gardening.

KAMINSKY, ALICE RICHKIN, English language educator; b. N.Y.C. d. Morris and Ida (Spivak) Richkin; m. Jack Kaminsky (dec.); 1 son, Eric (dec.). BA, NYU, 1946, MA, 1947, PhD, 1952. Mem. faculty dept. English NYU, 1947-49, Hunter Coll., 1952-53, Cornell U., 1954-57, Broome Community Coll., 1958-59, Cornell U., 1959-63, SUNY, Cortland, 1963—, prof., 1968-91, prof. emerita, 1991—, faculty exchange scholar. Author: George Henry Lewes as Critic, 1968, Logic: A Philosophical Introduction, 1974; editor: Literary Criticism of George Henry Lewes, 1964, Chaucer's Troilus and Criseyde and the Critics, 1980, The Victim's Song, 1985; contbr. more than 75 articles and revs. to numerous jours. Mem. MLA, Chaucer Soc.

KAMM, BARBARA B. bank executive; BA in Comm., Stanford U.; M of Internat. Mgmt., Am. Grad. Sch. Internat. Mgmt. Exec. v.p., group mgr. So. Calif. Tech. and Life Scis. teams and Entertainment; chief adminstrv. officer Silicon Valley Bank, Santa Clara, Calif., 1996-98, exec. v.p., strategic products & svcs., 1998—. Chmn. adv. bd. UCI ACCELERATE Tech. SBDC. Bd. dirs. So. Calif. Entrepreneurship Acad., Orange County United Way. Office: Silicon Valley Bank Corp Hdqrs 3003 Tasman Dr Santa Clara CA 95054-1191

KAMM, LINDA HELLER, lawyer; b. N.Y.C., Aug. 25, 1939; d. Seymour A. and Mary Heller; children: Lisa, Oliver. BA in History, Brandeis U., 1961; LLB, Boston Coll., 1967. Bar: Mass. 1967, D.C. 1978, U.S. Supreme Ct. 1985. Counsel Dem. Study Group, Washington, 1968-71; counsel select com. on coms. U.S. Ho. of Reps., Washington, 1973-75, gen. counsel budget com., 1975-77; gen. counsel U.S. Dept. Transp., Washington, 1977-80; ptnr. Foley and Lardner, Washington, 1980-84, of counsel, 1984-95; pvt. practice, 1995—; of counsel Boies, Schiller & Flexner, 2001—. Address: 188 E 70th St Apt 24C New York NY 10021-5170

KAMMERER, ANN MARIE, geotechnical engineer; b. Sacramento, Calif., May 24, 1968; d. Rodney Dean and Karen Christine (Hvolboll) K.; m. Brian Louis Faudoa. AS, City Coll. of San Francisco, 1994; BS, U. Calif Berkeley, 1996, MS, 1998, PhD, 2002. Cert. engr. Engr. Olivia Chen Cons., San Francisco, 1995-96, GEI Cons., San Francisco, 1996-97; grad. rschr. U. Calif. Berkeley, 1997—2002, lectr., 2002, postdoc. rschr., 2003—; sr. geotech. engr. Arup USA, San Francisco, 2002—. Contbr. articles to profl. jour. Chair City Coll. San Francisco Women's Resource Ctr., 1993—94; chair student leadership coun. Pacific Earthquake Engring. Ctr., 1999—2000; student trustee San Francisco C.C. Dist., 1994. Recipient Calif. Alumni Assn. Leadership scholarship, 1994, Howard D. Eberhart Meml. scholarship, 1996, Nat. Sci. Found. grad. fellowship, 1997-2000; Earthquake Engring. Rsch. Inst./Fed. Emergency Mgmt. Agy. Nat. Earthquake Hazards Reduction Program grad. fellow, 2001. Mem. ASCE, Earthquake Engring. Rsch. Inst., Pacific Earthquake Engring. Rsch. Ctr., Golden Key Nat. Honor Soc., Tau Beta Pi (pres. 1995). Democrat. Avocations: scuba diving, skiing, rock hunting. Office: Arup 901 Market St Ste 260 San Francisco CA 94103-0001 E-mail: annie.brian@mindspring.com., Annie.Kammerer@Arup.com.

KAMMERZELL, SUSAN JANE, elementary school educator, music educator; b. Greeley, Colo., Mar. 4, 1953; d. Carl Warren and Charlotte Josephine Strandberg; m. Arnold Henry Kammerzell, Sept. 11, 1976; 1 child, Jeffrey Scott. BA in Elem. Edn., U. No. Colo., 1975. Elem. tchr. grade 1 Ft. Morgan (Colo.) Sch. Dist., 1975—76; presch. dir., tchr. Wiggins (Colo.) Presch., 1987—89; elem. tchr. grade 1 Wiggins Sch. Dist., 1989—91, elem. tchr. kindergarten, 1991—96, elem. tchr. gen. music, 1996—. Sunday sch. tchr. grades 4 and 5 Wiggins Cmty. Ch., 1996—. Mem.: Nat. Assn. for Music Edn. Republican. Mem. United Church Of Christ. Avocations: travel, reading, music. Home: 5446 Road O Wiggins CO 80654 Office: Wiggins Sch Dist RE-50J Wiggins Elem 320 Chapman Wiggins CO 80654

KAMMEYER, SONIA MARGARETHA, real estate agent; b. Stockholm, June 21, 1942; came to U.S., 1964; d. Bengt Henrik and Margot Elsa M. (Hodin) Sjoberg; m. Whitman Ridgway, June 13, 1964 (div. 1978); children: Sean, Siobhan; m. Kenneth C.W. Kammeyer, Dec. 28, 1982. Student, Fleisher's Art Meml. Sch., Phila., 1966-69. With Ben Bell Real Estate, Lanham, Md., 1972-73, Robert L. Gruen Real Estate, Silver Spring, Md., 1973-81, Panarama Real Estate, Silver Spring, 1981-82, Long & Foster Real Estate, Inc., Silver Spring, 1982—. Named to Montgomery County Bd. Realtors Hall of Fame, 1994; recipient Nat. Sales Award, Realty Alliance, 1997. Mem. Montgomery County Bd. Realtors (life), Howard County Bd. Realtors, Swedish Profl. Women. Avocations: sculpture, painting, jewelry making, gardening, guitar playing. Home: 14600 Triadelphia Mill Rd Dayton MD 21036-1217 Office: Long & Foster Real Estate 3901 National Dr Burtonsville MD 20866-1141 Office Phone: 301-476-8656.

KAMPFE, DORIS ELAINE, storyteller, folk artist, poet; b. Monona, Iowa, Feb. 2, 1926; d. Frederick Conrad and Alvina Ulrika (Hass) Daugs; m. LaVern Arthur Kampfe, June 1, 1945; children: Lanny, Elisa Kay. Student, U. No. Iowa, 1965-68. Sec. Singer Sewing Machine Co., Denver, 1943, Interstate Power Co., Dubuque, Iowa, 1944, Ill. Supreme Ct., Chgo., 1979; tchr., mem. adv. bd. Headstart, Waterloo, Iowa, 1965-68; sec., tutor Japan Trade Ctr., Chgo., 1979—; feature writer Shopping News, Cedar Falls, Iowa, 1981-85, writer column Personalities and Wandering Around Waverly, 1981; folk artist Iowa Arts Coun., Des Moines, 1986—; storyteller Very Spl. Arts Iowa, Des Moines, 1992—. Cruise storyteller Delta Steam-[illegible] libs., chs., schs., colls., retirement ctrs., Spl. Olympics, theatre, Old Opera House, Chgo. (Ill.) Hist. Lincoln Soc., Brucemore Mansion Ragtime, restaurants, nature ctrs. and parks, banquets and confs., reunions, parties, county homes and country clubs, civic ctrs., Brucemore Mansion, Hawkeye Coll., Chgo. Hist. Soc., Rockford, Ill. Author: (play) Caramella, The Curious Camel, 1982; contbr. poetry to various publs., anthologies. Advisor N.W. opportunity bd. Headstart, Hoffman Estates, Ill., 1979; mem. social concerns bd. St. Paul's Luth. Ch., Waverly, Iowa, 1981, mem. cable TV cmty. bd., 1990; dinner vol. Waverly Dem. Com., 1995. Recipient award for poetry Pen Women, Inc., 1995, 96, 98; grantee Iowa Arts Coun., 1992, 95, 97, 98, 2000. Mem. AAUW, Nat. League Am. Pen Women, Nat. Assn. Storytellers, Iowa Poetry Assn., Northlands Storytellers, Haiku Club, Women in Arts, Friends of Ctr., Print Club. Avocations: watercolor, gourmet cooking, reading, gardening. Home: 2384 Arnold Ave Rockford IL 61108-8167 E-mail: doriskampfe@aol.com.

KAN, DIANA ARTEMIS MANN SHU, painter, art educator, writer; b. Hong Kong, Mar. 3, 1926; came to U.S., 1949, naturalized, 1964; d. Kam Shek and Sing-Ying (Hong) K.; m. Paul Schwartz, May 24, 1952; 1 son, Kan Martin Meyer Sing-Si. Student, Art Students League, 1949-51, Beaux Arts, Paris, 1951-52, Grande Chaumiere, 1951-52, Ecole Beau Arts, 1952—54. Instr. watercolor Phila. Mus. Art, 1972, Sumi-e Soc., 1974—2003, Art Students League of NY, 1985, The Nat. Acad. Design, 2001, The Smithsonian Inst., Wash., DC. Fgn. corr., city editor Cosmorama Pictorial Mag., Hong Kong, 1968; art reviewer Villager, N.Y.C., 1960-69; lectr. Birmingham So. U., N.Y. U., Mills Coll., St. Joseph's Coll., Phila. Mus., Smithsonian Instn; keynote spkr. Wellsley's Coll. Asia Week, MA, 1993. Author: White Cloud, 1938, The How and Why of Chinese Painting, 1974, Am. Artist Magazine, 1974, 86; One-man shows, London, 1949, 63, 64, Paris, 1949, Hong Kong, 1937, 39, 41, 47, 48, 52, Shanghai, 1935, 37, 39, Nanking, 1936, 38, Macao, 1947, 48, Bankok, 1947, Casablanca, 1951, 52, San Francisco, 1950, 67, N.Y.C., 1950, 54, 59, 67, 71, 72, 74, 78, Naples, 1971, Elliot Mus., Stuart, Fla., 1967, 73, Bruce Mus., Greenwich, Conn., 1969, Nat. Hist. Mus., Taipei, Taiwan, 1971, N.Y. Cultural Center Mus., 1972, Galerie Barbarella, Palm Beach, Fla., 1972, Hobe Sound (Fla.) Galleries, 1976, 81, Nat. Arts Club, 1979, Dyansen Galleries, 1987-Shenchen Mus., China, 1996, Hong Kong Art Ctr., 1996, 90 others; exhibited in group shows Allied Artists of Am., 1957-90, Royal Acad. Fine Arts, London, 1963-64, Royal Soc. Painters, London, 1964, Nat. Arts Club, N.Y.C., 1964-90, Am. Water Color Soc., N.Y.C., 1966-90, Nat. Acad. Design, N.Y.C., 1967-2003, Charles and Emma Frye Mus., Seattle, 1968, Willamette U., Salem, Oreg., 1968, Columbia (S.C.) Mus. Art, 1969, Audubon Artist, 1974-90, Evansville (Ind.) Mus., 1991, Dyansen Gallery, Boston, 1991; represented permanent collections, Met. Mus. Art, Phila. Mus. Art, Nelson Gallery, Elliot Mus., Fla., Bruce Mus., Dalhousie U., Atkin Mus., Kansas City, Nat. Hist. Mus., Taipei, The Government House, Vancouver, BC, Can., Midtown Payson Galleries, China 2000 Fine Art Gallery; subject of film Eastern Spirit, Western World—A Profile of Diana Kan; paintings were published by UNICEF (christmas cards): Four Children Going Fishing, 1996, Lantern Festival, 1999, Flower Drum Song, 2002, Snow Mountain, 2002. Recipient Summer Festival award N.Y.C., 1959, 1st Prize Nat. Art Club, 1982; named most Outstanding Profl. Woman of the Yr., Washington Sq. chpt. N.Y. League Bus. and Profl. Women's Club, 1971, 79, Gold medal of honor Knickerbocker Artists, 1990, Gold medal of honor Audubon Artists, 1991, 2000, Salmagundi Club, Pres. Gold medal of honor, 1998, Audobon Artists Gold Medal of Honor; Diana Kan Appreciation Day proclaimed by Mayor of Boston, 1991, Diana Kan Appreciation Day proclaimed by Mayor of NY, 2000; offl. citation proclaimed by Pres. Senate of Mass., 1991. Fellow Royal Soc. Arts; mem. Pen and Brush Club (dir. 1968, Brush Fund award 1968, Alice S. Buell Meml. award 1969, Margaret Sussman award 1991), Nat. Acad. Design (assoc., John Pike Meml. award 1987, cert. of merit 1991), Am. Watercolor Soc. (traveling award 1968, Marthe T. McKinnon award 1978, dir. 1975-77), Art Students League, Nat. League Pen Women, Audubon Artists (v.p. 1983), Allied Artists Am. (Barbara Vassilieff Meml. award 1969, Ralph Fabri Meml. award 1975, corr. sec. 1975-78), Catharine Lorillard Wolf Art Club (Anna Hyatt Huntington bronze medal 1970, 74, Gold medal of honor 1982), NYC Cultural Affairs Adv. Commn., 1999. Clubs: Overseas Press Am., Lotos, The Nat. Arts (NYC), The Salamagundi. Mailing: The Nat Arts Club 15 Gramercy Park S New York NY 10003-1705 E-mail: dianakan@dianakan.com.

KAN, SUSAN, publishing executive, editor; b. Chevy Chase, Md., Sept. 28, 1962; BA in Econs. and English, Bucknell U., 1984; MFA in Creative Writing, Warren Wilson Coll., 1996. Founding dir. Perugia Press, Florence, Mass., 1997—. Freelance copy editor, 1985—. Editor: Red, 2002, Seamless, 2003, others. Recipient Greenwall Fund award, Acad. Am. Poets, 2003. Mem.: Coun. for Literary Mags. and Presses, Poetry Soc. Am., Assn. Writing Programs. Office: Perugia Press PO Box 60364 Florence MA 01062

KANDARIAN, SUSAN CHRISTINE, medical educator; b. Apr. 10, 1959; BS in Biology cum laude, Albion (Mich.) Coll., 1981; MS in Edn., U. Mich., 1983, PhD in Kinesiology, 1988. Asst. prof. health scis. Boston U., 1988-94, postdoctoral, 1989-91, rsch. asst. prof. physiology, 1991-96, rsch. asst. prof. neuromuscular rsch. ctr., 1993-96, assoc. prof. health scis., 1994—, rsch. assoc. prof. neuromuscular rsch. ctr., 1996-97. Reviewer profl. jours.; contbr. numerous articles to profl. jours. Grantee Boston U., 1989-92, Am. Coll. Sports Medicine Found., 1989-90, Am. Heart Assn. 1992—, NIH, 1992—, Nat. Aero. and Space Adminstrn., 1995-96. Fellow Am. Coll. Sports Medicine; mem. AAAS, Am. Physiol. Soc. Office: Boston U SAR Dept Health Scis 635 Commonwealth Ave Boston MA 02215-1605

KANDOIAN, JANET ADRIENNE, elementary school educator; b. NYC, Sept. 22, 1947; d. Armig Ghevont and Jane Arax Erganian Kandoian. AB, Simmons Coll., 1969; MA in Edn., Washington U., St. Louis, 1971. Lic. classroom tchr. K-8 Maine. Elem. sch. tchr. South Portland (Maine) Pub. Schs., 1971—. Home: 181 Pine St Portland ME 04102 Office: South Portland Pub Schs 130 Wescott Rd South Portland ME 04106 Business E-Mail: kandoija@spsd.org.

KANE, AGNES BREZAK, pathologist, educator; b. Danbury, Conn., Nov. 3, 1946; d. John Edward and Mary Elizabeth (Hatfield) Brezak; m. David E. Kane, June 22, 1970. BA, Swarthmore Coll., 1968; MD, Temple U., 1974, PhD, 1976. Diplomate Am. Bd. Pathology. Resident Temple U. Hosp., Phila., 1975-76, 77-78; postdoctoral fellow Karolinska Inst., Stockholm, 1976-77; asst. prof. Temple U. Sch. Medicine, Phila., 1977-82, Brown U., Providence, 1982-87, assoc. prof. pathology, 1987-95, prof. pathology, 1995-96, chair dept. pathology and lab. medicine, 1996—. Mem. merit rev. bd. for basic scis. VA, Washington, 1984-86; cons. R.I. Commn. for Safety and Occupational Health, Providence, 1986—; commr. Commn. to Identify Occupational Diseases, Providence, 1987-88; mem. rev. com. Nat. Inst. Environ. Health Scis., Research Triangle Park, N.C., 1988—. Assoc. editor Am. Jour. of Pathology, 1992—; contbr. articles on exptl. pathology to sci. publs. Lucretia Mott fellow Swarthmore Coll., 1969-71; recipient Rsch. Career Devel. award NIH, 1981-86. Mem. Am. Assn. Pathologists (women's com. 1987—, program com. 1990—), Assn. Women Med. Faculty Brown U. (founder, coord.), Women in Medicine (faculty advisor Brown U. chpt.; Mary Putnam Jacobi award 1986), Phi Kappa, Sigma Xi. Avocation: gardening. Office: Brown Univ Box G Providence RI 02912

KANE, ALICE THERESA, lawyer; b. N.Y.C., Jan. 16, 1948; AB, Manhattanville Coll., 1969; JD, NYU, 1972; grad., Harvard U. Sch. Bus. Program Mgmt. Devel., 1986. Bar: N.Y. 1973, U.S. Dist. Ct. (so. dist.) N.Y. 1974. Atty. N.Y. Life Ins. Co., N.Y.C., 1972-83, v.p., assoc. gen. counsel, [illegible] gen. counsel, 1986-89, corp. sec., 1989-94, exec. v.p., gen. counsel, sec., 1992-95, exec. v.p. asset mgmt., 1995-98; exec. v.p. Am. Gen. Investment Mgmt. Corp., N.Y.C., 1998—. Mem. ABA (chmn. employee benefits com., tort and ins. practice sect. 1984-85, mem. corp., banking and bus. law sects., tort and ins. practice sects.), NASD, Assn. Life Ins. Counsel (deps. solvency com.). Office: Am Gen Investment Mgmt Corp 390 Park Ave 6th Fl New York NY 10022 E-mail: alice_kane@agfg.com.

KANE, ANNETTE PIESLAK, religious organization executive; b. Trenton, N.J., May 2, 1933; d. Theodore P. and Stella (Mackiewicz) Pieslak; m. Joseph P. Kane, Sept. 6, 1958; children: Paula M., Stephen J., Brian P., Christine A. BA, Trinity Coll., Washington, 1954; MA, U. Pa., 1956. Asst. prof. Rosemont (Pa.) Coll., 1955-58, Trinity Coll., Washington, 1958-61, editor alumni jour., 1973-79; program dir. Nat. Coun. Cath. Women, Washington, 1979-86, exec. dir., 1986—. Bd. dirs. Nat. Coun. Aging, Washington, 1985-87, CARA-Ctr. for Applied Rsch. in Apostolate, Washington, 1989—, Nat. Relig. Partnership for Environ., 1993—. Roman Catholic. Office: Nat Coun Cath Women 1275 K St NW Ste 975 Washington DC 20005-4006 E-mail: akane1@winstar.mail.com.

KANE, CECELIA DRAPEAU, state legislator, registered nurse; b. Concord, N.H., Oct. 12, 1915; d. Esdras and Marguerite Elizabeth (Carter) Drapeau; m. Thomas J. Kane, Jan. 23, 1986 (dec.); children: Maureen, Cheryl, Charlene, Thomas D. (dec.). Diploma, Sch. Nursing, 1938; postgrad., 1939. Legislature N.H. House of Reps., Portsmouth, N.H., 1988—. Mem. Cath. Daughters Am., Portsmouth, 1987, Dem. State Com., 1942—, N.H. OWLS, 1990—; bd. registrars Supr. of Checklist, Portsmouth, 1987—; bd. dirs. Betty's Dream, Portsmouth, 1990—. Democrat. Roman Catholic. Avocations: knitting, crocheting. Home: 391 Colonial Dr Portsmouth NH 03801-4706 Office: NH State House State Capitol Concord NH 03301

KANE, KAREN MARIE, public affairs consultant; b. Colorado Springs, Colo., Mar. 7, 1947; d. Bernard Francis and Adeline Marie (Logan) K. Student, Mills Coll., Oakland, Calif., 1965-66; BA, U. Wash., 1970, MA, 1973, PhC, 1977, postgrad. Pub. affairs cons., housing subcom. Seattle Ret. Tchrs. Assn., 1981-84; pub. affairs cons. 1st U.S. Women's Olympic Marathon Trials, 1982-83, Seattle, 1985—. Contbr. articles to newsletters and mags. Chmn. hist. preservation LWV, Seattle, 1989—, co-chmn. land use com., 2000—; trustee Allied Arts of Seattle, 1987—96, past chmn. hist. preservation com., sec. bd. trustees, mem. exec. com., 1987—96; trustee Allied Arts Found., 1999—, mem. sponsorship application approval com., 2002—; mem. Mayor's Landmark Theatre Adv. Group, 1991—93, Pike Place Market Hist. Commn., Seattle, 1992—98, chmn., 1997—98; mem. Pike Place Market Com. to Rev. the Hildt Agreement, 1998—99, The Market Constituency, 1999—, Friends of the Market, 1999—; vol. various polit. campaigns, Seattle; bd. dirs. Showboat Theatre Found./Bravo (formerly Showboat Theatre Found.), 1984—2002. Recipient Award of Honor Wash. Trust for Hist. Preservation, 1990, Recognition award Found. for Hist. Preservation and Adaptive Reuse, Seattle, 1991; Am. Found. grantee, 1989, 91. Mem. AAUW, Internat. Platform Assn., Mills Coll. Alumnae Assn., U. Wash. Alumni Assn., Nat. Trust for Hist. Preservation, Hist. Hawai'i Found., Found. for San Francisco's Archtl. Heritage, Wash. Trust for Hist. Preservation, Hist. Seattle Preservation and Devel. Authority.

KANE, LORIE, professional golfer; b. Prince Edward Island, Can., Dec. 19, 1964; d. Jack Kane. Student, Acadia U. Mem. Can. Internat. Team, 1989-92, Can. World Amateur Team, 1992; golfer LPGA, 1993—; du Maurier Ltd. Series champion, 1994, 95; series event winner, 1993-95; 2d place Toray Japan Queens Cup, 1997. Recipient Heather Farr Player Award, 1998, William and Mousie Powell Award, 2000. 1 LPGA career hole-in-one. Office: c/o LPGA 100 International Golf Dr Daytona Beach FL 32124-1082

KANE, MARGARET BRASSLER, sculptor; b. East Orange, N.J., May 25, 1909; d. Hans and Mathilde (Trumpler) Brassler; m. Arthur Ferris Kane, June 11, 1930; children: Jay Brassler, Gregory Ferris. Student, Packer Collegiate Inst., 1920-26, Syracuse U., 1927, Art Students League, 1927-29, N.Y. Coll. Music, 1928-29, John Hovannes Studio, 1932-34; PhD (hon.), Colo. State Christian Coll., 1973. Head craftsman sculpture, arts and skills unit ARC, Halloran Gen. Hosp., NY, 1942—43; jury mem. Bklyn. Mus., 1948, Am. Machine & Foundry Co., 1957; com. mem. An Am. Group, Inc. Exhibitions include, Phila. Mus., Chgo. Art Inst., Am. Fedn. Arts, N.Y. Bot. Garden, 1981, 60th Anniversary Exhbn. Lever House, 1987—98, Sculptors Guild 50th Anniversary Exhbn., Lever House, 1987—96, 1st Bi-Coastal exhibits San Francisco, Collection Donald Trump, 1988, Collection Rene Anselmo, 1991, Shidoni Galleries, Santa Fe, N.Mex., 1989, Am. Sculpture, Hofstra Mus., 1990, exhibitions include nat. tour Am. sculpture by EducArt Projects Inc., 1992, exhibitions include, Stamford Mus. and Nature Ctr., 1996, Zimmerli Art Mus. Historical Exhibit, 1999—2000, Smithsonian Mus. Tour, 2000—02, numerous others, Represented in permanent collections, Zimmerli Art Mus., Rutgers U., N.J., 1992, Nat. Mus. Am. Art, Smithsonian Instn., Washington, 1993, 2000, Bruce Mus., Greenwich, Conn., 1996, Packer Collegiate Inst., Bklyn., 2003, one-woman shows include sculpture, Friends Greenwich (Conn.) Library, 1962, prin. works include 18 foot carving in limewood, 2002, prin. works include six oot carving Reaching the Galaxies, 2002—, prin. works include sculpture Packer Collegiate Inst., Bklyn., 2003, prin. works include plaque Burro Monument, Fair Play, Colo.; reprodns. Contemporary Stone Sculpture, 1970, Contemporary Am. Sculptures, Am. References, Chgo.; CD-ROM, Smithsonian Nat. Mus. Am. Art, Washington, 1995; contbr. articles to mags. Recipient Hyatt Huntington award, 1942, Am. Artist Profl. League and Monclair Art Assn. awards, 1943, 1st Henry O. Avery prize, 1944, Sculpture prize, Bklyn. Soc. Artists, Bklyn. Mus., 1946, John Rogers award, 1951, Lawrence Hyder prize, 1952, 1954, David H. Zell Meml. award, 1954, 1963, Hon. Mention, U.S. Maritime Commn., 1941, A.C.A. Gallery Competition, 1944, medal of Honor for Sculpture, Nat. Acad. Galleries, N.Y., prize for carved sculpture, 1955, prize for animal sculpture, 1956, 1st award for sculpture, Ann. New Eng. Exhbns., Silvermine, Conn. Fellow: Internat. Inst. Arts and Letters (life); mem.: Nat. Trust Hist. Preservation, silvermine Guild Artists, Internat. Soc. Artists (charter), Internat. Sculpture Ctr., Greenwich Soc. Artists (mem. coun.), Bklyn. Soc. Artists, Artists Coun. U.S.A., Pen and Brush (emeritus 1992), Nat. League Am. Pen Women, Inc. (OWL award for the Arts 1991), Nat. Assn. Women Artists (2d v.p. 1943—44), Sculptors Guild, Inc. (life; sec. to exec. bd. 1942—45, chmn. exhbn. com. 1942, 1944). Home and Studio: 30 Strickland Rd Cos Cob CT 06807-2729

KANE, MARILYN, real estate company executive; m. Jeffrey Nichols (div.); children: Joshua, Julie, Joseph; m. David Kane, 1990. Co-pres. Butler Kane, Inc., N.Y.C. Founder N.Y. chpt. Nat. Coalition for Family Justice. Office: Butler Kane Inc 171 Madison Ave #1000 New York NY 10016*

KANE, MARILYN A. occupational therapist, educator; b. Scranton, Pa., May 23, 1943; d. James William and Pauline Margaret (Buckavecky) K. BA, Marywood U., Scranton, 1967; MA, NYU, 1972. Cert. occupl. therapist; lic. occupl. therapist, N.Y. Chief ACT therapy, program dir. Hutchings Psychiat. Ctr., Syracuse, N.Y., 1972-80; team leader, chief occupl. therapy Willard (N.Y.) Psychiat. Ctr., 1980-95; pvt. practice occupl. thearpy, Trumansburg, N.Y., 1992-97; asst. prof., field work coord. Keuka Coll., Penn Yan, N.Y., 1992-97; asst. prof. occupl. therapy Ithaca (N.Y.)

Coll., 1997—. Contbg. author: (manual) Functional Need Assessment for CHR Psychiatric Patients, 1990; co-author: (manual) FNA Treatment Guide, 1996. Mem. AAUP, AAUW, Am. Occupl. Therapy Assn., N.Y. State Occupl. Therapy Assn., Assn. for Driver Rehab. Specialists. Home: 109 Indian Creek Rd Ithaca NY 14850-1309

KANE, MARY KAY, dean; b. Detroit, Nov. 14, 1946; d. John Francis and Frances (Roberts) K.; m. Ronan Eugene Degnan, Feb. 3, 1987 (dec. Oct. 1987). BA cum laude, U. Mich., 1968, JD cum laude, 1971. Bar: Mich. 1971, N.Y., Calif. Rsch. assoc., co-dir. NSF project on privacy, confidentiality and social sci. rsch. data sch. law U. Mich., 1971-72, Harvard U., 1972-74; asst. prof. law SUNY, Buffalo, 1974-77; mem. faculty Hastings Coll. Law U. Calif., San Francisco, 1977—, prof. law, 1979—, assoc. acad. dean, 1981-83, acting acad. dean, 1987-88, acad. dean., 1990-93, dean, 1993—; chancellor U. Calif., San Francisco, 2001—. Vis. prof. law U. Mich., 1981, U. Utah, 1983, U. Calif., Berkeley, 1983-84, sch. law U. Tex., 1989; cons. Mead Data Control, Inc., 1971, 74, Inst. on Consumer Justice, U. Mich. Sch. Law, 1972, U.S. Privacy Protection Study Commn., 1975-76; lectr. pretrial mgmt. devices U.S. magistrates for 6th and 11th cirs. Fed. Jud. Ctr., 1983; Siebenthaler lectr. Samuel P. Chase Coll. Law, U. North Ky., 1987; reporter ad hoc com. on asbestos litigation U.S. Jud. Conf., 1990-91, mem. standing com. on practice and procedure, 2001—; mem. 9th Cir. Adv. Com. on Rules Practice and Internal Oper. Procedures, 1993-96; spkr. in field. Author: Civil Procedure in a Nutshell, 1979, 5th edit., 2003, Sum and Substance on Remedies, 1981; co-author: (with C. Wright and A. Miller) Pocket Supplements to Federal Practice and Procedure, 1975—, Federal Practice and Procedure, vols. vol. 7, 3d edit., 2001, 10, 10A and 10B, 3d edit., 1998, vols. 7-7C, 2d edit., 1986, vols. 6-6A, 2d edit., 1990, vols. 11-11A, 2d edit., 1995, (with J. Friedenthal and A. Miller) Hornbook on Civil Procedure, 3d edit., 1999, (with C. Wright) Hornbook on the Law of Federal Courts, 2002, Federal Practice Deskbook, 2002; mem. law sch. divsn. West. Adv. Edtl. Bd., 1986—; contbr. articles to profl. jours. Mem. standing com. on rules of practice and procedure U.S. Jud. Conf., 2000—. Mem. ABA (mem. bar admissions com. 1995-2000), Assn. Am. Law Schs. (com. on prelegal edn. statement 1982, chair sect. remedies 1982, panelist sect. on prelegal edn. 1983, exec. com. sect. on civil procedure 1983, 86, panelist sect. on tchg. methods 1984, spkr. new tchrs. conf. 1986, 89, 90, chair sect. on civil procedure 1987, spkr. sects. civil procedure and conflicts 1987, 91, chair planning com. for 1988 Tchg. Conf. in Civil Procedure 1987-88, nominating com. 1988, profl. devel. com. 1988-91, planning com. for workshop in conflicts 1988, planning com. for 1990 Conf. on Clin. Legal Edn. 1989, chair profl. devel. com. 1989-91, exec. com. 1991-93, 2000-02, pres.-elect 2000, pres. 2001), Am. Law Inst. (co-reporter complex litigation project 1988-93, coun. 1998—), ABA/Assn. Am. Law Schs. Commn. on Financing Legal Edn., State Bar Mich. Home: 8 Admiral Dr Ste 421 Emeryville CA 94608-1567 Office: U Calif Hastings Coll Law 200 Mcallister St San Francisco CA 94102-4707

KANE, PATRICIA LANEGRAN, language professional, educator; b. St. Paul, June 23, 1926; d. Walter B. and Lita E. (Wilson) Lanegran; m. Donald Patrick Kane, Apr. 1, 1947; children: Laura Kane Gustafson, Maura L. Kane Hackenmueller. BA cum laude, Macalester Coll., St. Paul, 1947; MA, U. Minn., 1950, PhD, 1961. Mem. faculty Macalester Coll., 1950-91, prof. English, 1971-91, DeWitt Wallace prof., 1978-91, prof. emeritus, 1992—, chmn. dept. 1977-86, faculty assoc. office of v.p. acad. affairs, 1979-83; mem. Minn. planning com. nat. identification project advancement women in acad. adminstrn. Nat. Council Edn., 1979-81. Co-author: A St. Paul Omnibus, 1979; Contbr. articles to profl. jours. Recipient Jefferson prize for teaching excellence, 1980, Disting. Alumni citation Macalester Coll., 1992; Danforth grantee, 1957-58. Mem. MLA, Soc. Study So. Lit.

KANE, STEPHANIE C. social anthropologist, educator; b. N.Y.C., Jan. 24, 1951; d. Bernard David and Gerry Kane. BA in Biology, Cornell U., 1972; MA in Zoology, U. Tex., 1981, PhD in Social Anthropology, 1986. Tchg. asst. Biology and Physiology Labs, Dept. Zoology, U. Tex., Austin, 1981, Dept. Anthropology, U. Tex., Austin, 1985-86; resident faculty Sch. for Field Studies, Virgin Islands, 1987; adj. asst. prof. Dept. Anthropology, Ind. U., 1992—; asst. prof. Dept. Criminal Justice, Ind. U., 1992-99, assoc. prof., 1999—. Author: The Phantom Gringo Boat, 1994, AIDS Alibis: Sex, Drugs and Crime in the Americas, 1998; co-editor: Crime's Power: Anthropologists & the Study of Crime, 2003; contbr. to profl. papers and jours. Recipient rsch. grant Inst. Latin Am. Studies U. Tex., Austin, 1979-80, 84-85, Fulbright rsch. grant Coun. for Internat. Exch. of Scholars, 1989-90, rsch. grant Rural Ctr. for Study and Promotion of HIV/STD Prevention, Ind., 1995, rsch. grant Wenner-Gren Found. for Anthropol. Rsch., 1995-96, 99-2000, rsch. and travel grantee IND. U., 2001, 02; scholarship U. Tex., Austin, 1979-83; Lang. and Area Studies fellowship Inst. Latin Am. Studies, U. Tex., Austin, 1982-83, Tng. fellowship Orgn. Am. States, 1984-85, Rockefeller Humanities fellowship rsch. grant SUNY, Buffalo, 1991-92, Coll. Arts and Scis. Summer Faculty fellowship Ind. U., Bloomington, 1994. Mem. NOW, Am. Anthropol. Assn. (mem. task force on AIDS, 1991-93), Am. Soc. Criminology, Law and Soc. Assn., Amnesty Internat. Avocations: art, gardening, travel. Office: U Ind Dept Criminal Justice and Gender Studies 302 Sycamore Hall Bloomington IN 47405

KANE, YVETTE, lawyer, judge; b. Donaldsonville, La., Oct. 11, 1953; d. Thomas R. Pregeant and Julia Tucker; children: Kathleen, Madeline. BA, Nicholls State U., Thibodeaux, La., 1973; JD, Tulane U., 1976. Bar: Pa. Trial atty. U.S. Equal Employment Opportunity Commn., 1977-78; asst. atty. gen. Colo. Atty. Gen.'s Office, 1978-80; dep. dist. atty. Denver Dist. Atty.'s Office, 1980-86; dep. atty. gen. rev. and advice sect. Pa. Office Atty. Gen., 1986-91; chief counsel Pa. Ind. Regulatory Rev. Commn., 1991-92; sr. assoc. Wolf, Block, Schorr & Solis-Cohen, Harrisburg, Pa., 1993-95; sec. state Commonwealth of Pa., 1995-98; U.S. dist. judge U.S. Dist. Ct. (mid. dist.) Pa., Harrisburg, 1998—. Office: US Dist Ct Box 11817 228 Walnut St 8th Fl Harrisburg PA 17108

KANE HITTNER, MARCIA SUSAN, bank executive; b. N.Y.C. d. Howard Eugene and Sydell (Friedman) Kane; m. Ellis Hittner. cert. fin. planning, BA in Comm., NYU. Cert. Nat. Ret. Plans Tng. Ctr., software capability maturity model cert. interim profile adminstr. Carnegie Mellon U. Pension specialist Union Dime Savs. Bank, N.Y.C., 1978—81; money market specialist Goldome (formerly Union Dime Savs. Bank), N.Y.C., 1981—82; mgr. customer svc. Citibank, N.A., N.Y.C., 1982—85, mgr. mktg. product, 1986—87, mgr. shareholder comm., 1988—89, asst. v.p., tax shelter conversions, 1990—93, asst. v.p. tech. client interface, 1993—95, asst. v.p. U.S., Europe consumer bank, 1995—99; with product design and devel. Software Engring. Process Group, 1995—99; v.p. mktg. strategy EAB subs. ABN-AMRO, 1999—2001, cons. bus. and mktg. strategy, 2001—. Author: (with others) Critical Reading-Level G, 1980. Bd. dirs. Forest Hills Owners Corp., N.Y.C., 1991-92, 99—.

KANEKO-ADAMS, NAOKO, business executive; b. Kobe, Hyogo, Japan, Aug. 2, 1943; d. Mikiya and Kazuko Kaneko; m. Albert Adams, Nov. 28, 1976. Cert. in ESL, St. Michael's Sch., Cambridge, Eng., 1962; AA, Lehigh County C.C., Schnecksville, Pa., 1980; BS, Cedar Crest Coll., 1985. Coord. Blue Cross and Blue Shield, Balt., 1977-78, Air Products and Chems., Allentown, Pa., 1980-86; adminstr. Odani Rsch. Co., Inc., Larchmont, N.Y., 1986-87; sr. rsch. analyst, rsch. mgr. Sunstar Inc., N.Y.C., 1987—2003; info. broker Kaneko-Adams Joho Ctr., Mamaroneck, N.Y., 1995—. Interpreter area TV program, Toronto, Ont., Can., 1975. Mem. Am. Mktg. Assn., Soc. Competitive Intelligence Profls., Cosmetic Exec. Women. Avocations: opera, film study. Home: 490 Bleeker Ave Mamaroneck NY 10543-4537 Office: Kaneko-Adams 490 Bleeker Ave Mamaroneck NY 10543-4537

KANE-VANNI, PATRICIA RUTH, lawyer, paleontology educator; b. Phila, Pa, Jan. 12, 1954; d. Joseph James and Ruth Marina (Ramirez) Kane; m. Francis William Vanni, Feb. 14, 1981; 1 child, Christian Michael. AB, Chestnut Hill Coll., 1975; JD, Temple U., 1985; postgrad., U. Pa. Bar: Pa. 1985, US Ct. Appeals (3d cir.) 1988. Freelance art illustrator, Phila., 1972-80; secondary edn. instr. Archdiocese of Phila., Pa., 1980-83; contract analyst CIGNA Corp., Phila., 1983-84; jud. aide Phila. Ct. of Common Pleas, Pa., 1984; assoc. atty. Anderson and Dougherty, Wayne, Pa., 1985-86; atty. cons. Bell Tele. Co. of Pa., Pa., 1986-87; sr. assoc. corp. counsel Independence Blue Cross, Phila., 1987-96; pvt. practice law, 1996-97; dinosaur educator Acad. Natural Scis., Phila., 1997—. Atty. cons., 1996-2003; counsel Reliance Ins. Co., Phila., 1998-2000, contract atty., 2000-2003; counsel Westmont Law Assoc., 2002; atty. Westmont Assoc., Haddonfield, NJ, 2002; legal counsel, Ho. Authority, Phila., Pa., 2003-; cons. Coll. Consortium on Drug and Alcohol Abuse, Chester, Pa., 1986-89; paleo-sci. educator Pa. Acad. Natural Sci., 1997—; paleontology field expdns. include Mont., 1999. 2000, Isle of Wight, Eng., 1999, Bahariya Oasis, Egypt, 2000; spkr. in field. Contbr. articles and illustrations to profl. mag.; performer: Phila. Revels. Judge Del. Valley Sci. Fairs, Phila., 1986, 87, 98, 99; Dem. committeewomen, Lower Merion, Pa., 1983-87; ch. cantor, soloist, mem. choir Roman Cath. Ch.; bd. dir. Phila. Assn. Ch. Musicians. Recipient Legion of Honor award Chapel of the Four Chaplins, 1983. Mem. ABA, Pa. Bar Assn., Phila. Bar Assn. (Theatre Wing), Phila. Assn. Def. Counsel, Phila. Vol. Lawyers for Arts (bd. dir.), Nat. Health Lawyers Assn. (spkr. 1994 ann. conv.), Hispanic Bar Assn., Soc. Vertebrate Paleontology, Pa. Acad. Nat. Sci. (vol.), Delaware Valley Paleontol. Soc. (v.p. 1998—). Democrat. Avocations: choral and solo vocal music, portrait painting and illustrating, paleontology. Home: 119 Bryn Mawr Ave Bala Cynwyd PA 19004-3012 E-mail: pkv1@erols.com., Paleopatti@hotmail.com.

KANG, BANN C. immunologist; b. Kyungnam, Korea, Mar. 4, 1939; d. Daeryong and Buni (Chung) K.; came to U.S., 1964, naturalized, 1976; A.B., Kyungpook Nat. U., 1959, M.D., 1963; m. U. Yun Ryo, Mar. 30, 1963. Intern, L.I. Jewish Hosp.-Queens Hosp. Center, Jamaica, N.Y., 1964-65, resident in medicine, 1965-67; teaching assoc. Kyungpook U. Hosp., Taegu, Korea, 1967-70; fellow in allergy and chest Creighton U., Omaha, 1970-71; fellow in allergy Henry Ford Hosp., Detroit, 1971-72; clin. instr. medicine U. Mich. Hosp., Ann Arbor, 1972-73; asst. prof. Chgo. Med. Sch., 1973-74; chief allergy-immunology Mt. Sinai Hosp., Chgo., 1975—; asst. prof. Rush Med. Sch., Chgo. 1975-84, assoc. prof., 1984-86; assoc. prof. U. Ky. Coll. Medicine, 1987-92, prof., 1992-2002, prof. emeritus, 2003—; cons., 1976—, Nat. Heart, Lung, Blood Inst., 1979—; mem. Exptl. Transplantation Adv. Bd., Ill., 1985-86, Diagnostic and Therapeutic Tech. Assessment (AMA), 1987—, Gen. Clin. Rsch. Com. (NIH), 1989-93; adv. com. Ctr. for Biologics and Rsch., FDA, 1993-96; counselor Chgo. Med. Soc., 1984-86, mem. policy com., adv. com. to health dept. Chgo. and Cook County, 1984-86. Recipient NIH award U. Mich., 1972-73. Diplomate Am. Bd. Internal Medicine, Am. Bd. Allergy-Immunology. Fellow ACP, Am. Acad. Allergy; mem. Am. Fedn. Clin. Research, AMA, Inter-Asthma Assn. Contbr. over 50 articles to profl. jours. Home: 2716 Martinique Ln Lexington KY 40509-9509 Office: U Ky Coll Medicine K528 Albert B Chandler Med Ctr 800 Rose St Lexington KY 40536-0001 E-mail: BCKang0@uky.edu.

KANICK, VIRGINIA, retired radiologist; b. Coaldale, Pa., Nov. 10, 1925; d. Martin and Anna (Pisklak) K. BA, Barnard Coll., 1947; MD, Columbia U., 1951. Diplomate Am. Bd. Radiology. Intern Western Reserve U. Hosps., Cleve., 1951-52; resident in radiology St. Luke's Hosp., N.Y.C., 1952-55, attending radiologist, 1955-74; acting dir. radiology St. Luke's Roosevelt Hosp., N.Y.C., 1981-84, dep. dir. of radiology, 1984-89; ptnr. West Side Radiology, N.Y.C., 1989—2003; ret., 2003. Clin. prof. radiology Coll. Physicians and Surgeons Columbia U., N.Y.C., 1975—; pres. Med. Bd. St. Luke's Roosevelt Hosp., 1980-82. Contbr. articles to profl. jours. Bd. dirs. Health System Agy. of N.Y.C., 1978-81. Fellow Am. Cancer Soc., 1955. Fellow Am. Coll. Radiology; mem. Am. Roentgen Ray Soc., Radiol. Soc. N.Am., N.Y. County Med. Soc. (sec., dir. 1978—), N.Y. State Radiol. Soc. (bd. dirs. 1975—). Independent. Avocations: skiing, travel, archeology. Home: 560 Riverside Dr Apt 17B New York NY 10027-3215

KANIM, LINDA ELIE ALIEA, medical researcher; b. L.A. d. Elie Sab and Margaret Lucille K. Student, U. Calif., Santa Barbara, 1975, UCLA, 1975; BA, Calif. State U., L.A., 1975; MA, Am. U. Beirut, Lebanon, 1983; postgrad., U. Mich., 1986. Rsch. asst. dept. behavioral scis. Am. U. Beirut, 1977-79; rsch. asst. coronary care unit Am. U. Beirut Hosp., 1978-80, rsch. asst. dept. anesthesiology, 1978-82; rsch. assoc. Sch. Pub. Health UCLA, 1982-84, rsch. assoc. Jonsson Comprehensive Cancer Ctr., 1982-84, rsch. assoc. dept. orthopedic surgery Sch. Medicine, 1986-91; rsch. assoc. UCLA Comprehensive Spine Ctr. and West Coast Spine Inst., 1991-93, UCLA Comprehensive Spine Ctr. and Univ. Spine Assocs., 1993—2000, Spine Inst., St. John's Health Ctr., Santa Monica, Calif., 2000—. Rsch. cons. in design and statistics Am. U. Beirut Hosp., 1978-83; statis. programmer Sch. Pub. Health UCLA, 1996-97. Contbr. articles to profl. jours., chpts. to books; artist book cover. Recipient award Internat. Soc. Study of the Lumbar Spine, 1999; co-recipient Russell Hibbs award Scoliosis Rsch. Soc., 1999. Avocations: swimming, gymnastics, skiing, white water rafting, scuba diving. Office: Spine Inst at St Johns Hlth Ctr UCLA Comprehen Spine Ctr 1301 20th St Ste 400 Santa Monica CA 90404-6990 E-mail: lkanim@espineinstitute.com.

KANIN, DORIS MAY, political scientist, consultant; b. Somerville, Mass., Mar. 28, 1928; d. Sidney J. and Ida Gail (Gelbsman) Small; m. Irving L. Kanin, June 11, 1944; children: Dennis, Erik, Lisa Hochheiser. BA in Govt., Boston U., 1966; MA in Govt., 1970; postgrad., Boston U., 1970-74. Dir. cultural activities Staff of George McGovern, 1972; legis. dir. to congressman Joe Moakley, 1972-74; nat. polit. dir. Frank Church for Pres., 1975-76; spl. asst. Paul Tsongas U.S. Senate campaign, Boston, 1977-78; dir. Human Svcs. Dept. Fed. State Rels., Mass., 1979-81; nat. dir. pub. affairs Physicians for Social Responsibility, 1981-82; exec. of Pub. Rels. and Comms. Lynwood Labs. Inc., 1982—; polit. advisor Paul Tsongas for Pres. campaign, Mass., 1991—92. Inventor, creator: Spray-n-Starch aerosol, 1968; editor: Quincy Mass. Cmty. Ctr. Newsletter, 1956-58, Mass. Liberal Citizens of Mass. Bulletin; journalist Boston Daily Record, 1944; reporter Boston Daily Record-Am. Pres. LWV, Norwood, Mass., 1956—59, Mass. Citizens for Participation in Politics, Boston, 1973—74; chair, bd. dirs., mem., state bd. Mass. Civil Liberties Union, Boston, 1976—81; mem. steering com. women's caucus Capitol Hill Women's Polit. Caucus; elected del. to all Nat. Nominating Convs., 1972—92; del. Dem. Nat. Conv., 1972, 1976, 1980, 1982, 1986, 1992, Fla. Dem. Party Conf., 2002; dir. Mass. Cultural Affairs for Pres. Campaign, George McGovern; mem. Dem. Nat. Com., 1972—76, mem. women's caucus, 1972—76, mem. edn. and tng. coun., 1976—80; bd. dirs. Mass. Ams. for Dem. Action, 1978—80, Mass. Pax; del. Mass. Dem. Party Conv., 2002, Fla. Dem. State Party Conf., 2002, Mass. Dem. Party Conv., 2003. Named: Woodrow Wilson Semi-Finalist, 1972-76, Mass. Spelling Bee Champion, Boston Herald Traveler, 1939. Mem. Internat. Aerosol Congress. Democrat. Avocations: travel, painting, poetry writing, opera, ballet. Home (Summer): 511 Boylston St Brookline MA 02445-5701 Home (Winter): 1289 Breakers West Blvd West Palm Beach FL 33411-1881

KANIN, FAY, screenwriter; b. N.Y.C. d. David and Bessie Mitchell; m. Michael Kanin (dec.); children: Joel (dec.), Josh. Student, Elmira Coll., LHD (hon.), 1981; BA, U. So. Calif. Mem. Western regional exec. bd., judge Am. Coll. Theatre Festival, 1975-76. Writer: (with Michael Kanin) screenplays including The Opposite Sex, Teacher's Pet; Broadway plays including Goodbye My Fancy, His and Hers, Rashomon, Grind (Tony nomination 1985); writer, co-prodr. TV spls. including Friendly Fire, ABC-TV (Emmy award for best TV film, San Francisco Film Festival award, Peabody award), Hustling (Writers Guild award for best original drama), Tell Me Where It Hurts (Emmy award, Christopher award); Heartsounds (Peabody award). Recipient Humanitas prize prestigious Kieser award, 2003. Mem. Writers guild Am. West (pres. screen br. 1971-73, Val Davies award 1975, Morgan Cox award 1976), Am. Film Inst. (trustee), Acad. Motion Picture Arts and Scis. (pres. 1979-82), Nat. Ctr. Film and Video Preservation (co-chmn.), Am. Film Preservation Bd. (chmn.).

KANNENSTINE, MARGARET LAMPE, artist; b. St. Louis, Apr. 1, 1938; d. John Avery and Elizabeth (Phillips) Lampe; m. Louis Fabian Kannenstine, Oct. 3, 1959; children: David Edward, Emily Ann. BFA, Washington U. St. Louis, 1959; postgrad., Art Students League, N.Y.C., 1959-61. Trustee Pentangle Coun. Arts, 1982—88, 1993—96, chair, 1984—87, 1994, 95, hon. bd., 1997—; trustee Vt. Studio Ctr., 1989—94, chair, 1990—93; trustee Vt. Coun. Arts, 1994—2001, chair, 1994—98; trustee Nat. Assembly Arts Agencies, 2001—, sec., 2004. One-woman shows include Vt. Artisans, Strafford, 1976, Gallery Two, Woodstock, Vt., 1974, 1977, 1985, Red Mill Gallery, Johnson, Vt., 1990, Green Mountain Power Corp., South Burlington, Vt., 1991, 1991, Vt. Coun. on Arts, Montpelier, Vt., 1991, Woodstock Gallery Art, 1991, 1994, Beside Myself Gallery, Arlington, Vt., 1992, Taylor Gallery, Meriden, N.H., 1993, Kimball Union Acad., Dartmouth Coll., Hanover, N.H., 1993, 1999, Kent (Conn.) Sch., 1993, Chittenden Bank, Burlington, Vt., 1994, Windy Bush Gallery, New Hope, Pa., 1995, N.H. Coll., Manchester, 1996, Flynn Theater Gallery, Burlington, 1996, 1998, Nat. Wildlife Fedn. Gallery, Vienna, Va., 1996, McGowan Fine Art, Concord, N.H., 1997, Grayson Gallery, Woodstock, 1997, 1999, Spheris Gallery, Walpole, N.H., 1997, The Gallery at Johnny D's, Somerville, Mass., 1997, AVA Gallery, Hanover, Lebanon, 1998, Main Street Mus. Art, Hartford, Vt., 1999, Collis Ctr., Dartmouth Coll., 1999, Gallery of Graphic Arts, N.Y.C., 1999, Lyndon State Coll., Lyndonville, Vt., 1999, 2002, Supreme Ct., Montpelier, 1999, Cushing Acad. Gallery, Ashburnham, Mass., 2001, Prince St. Gallery, N.Y.C., 2003, Woodstock Town Hall, Vt., 2002, one-man shows include Vt. Gov.'s Office Gallery, 2003, exhibited in group shows at Gallery Two, 1973—88, Carl Battaglia Gallery, N.Y.C., 1979—80, The Gallery, Williamstown, Mass., 1981—84, Vt. Coun. Arts, 1988, 1996, AVA Gallery, Hanover, 1989—98, Woodstock Gallery Art, 1989, Beside Myself Gallery, 1990, Fleming Mus., U. Vt., Burlington, 1991, Bennington Coll., 1992, Windy Bush Gallery, 1994, VCA, Woodstock, 1994, Riverfest, White River Junction, Vt., 1995, Firehouse Gallery, Burlington, 1995, McGowan Fine Art, Concord, N.H., 1995, Chaffee Gallery, Rutland, Vt., 1997, Helen Day Art Ctr., Stowe, Vt., 1997, Champion Internat., Stamford, Conn., 1997, New Art New England, Newport, N.H., 1997, Gallery Graphic Art, N.Y.C., 1998—2000, Grayson Gallery, Woodstock, Vt., 2000, Ute Stebich Gallery, Lenox, Mass., 1999—2001, Elsa Mott Ives Gallery, N.Y.C., 2000, Arts Alive Gallery, Burlington, 2001, G. Wilson Gallery, Stonington, Maine, 2001, Patricia Carega Gallery, Sandwich, N.H., 2002, 2003, Woodstock (Vt.) Folk Art and Prints, 2003, Represented in permanent collections The Hood Mus., Hanover, Robert Hull Fleming Mus., Burlington, Vt. Employees Credit Union, Montpelier, Champion Internat. Corp., Stamford, Conn., Union Mut. Ins. Co., Montpelier, Vt. Law Sch., South Royalton, Fletcher Allen Hosp., Burlington, Vt. Hist. Soc., Montpelier, Cushing Acad., Ashburnham, Mass., Springfield (Mo.) Art Museum. Apptd. by Sen. Leahy to Millenium Commn. of Friends of Art and Preservation in Embassies, 1999-2000; trustee New Eng. Found. for Arts, 1996-2001; incorporator Upper Valley Cmty. Found., 1996-2000, trustee, 1999, founding dir. Woodstock Cty. Trust, v.p. 1998, 99, pres., 2000, 01; charter mem. Creative Economy Coun. of New Eng. Coun., Vt. Creative Economy Policy Coun., 2003—, Vt. Coun. Culture Innovation, 2003. Recipient Citation for achievement in arts, Vt. Arts Coun., 2002; scholar Washington U. scholar, 1955. Mem. Cosmopolitan Club. Avocations: music, gardening, hiking. E-mail: mlkannen@aol.com.

KANNER, BERNICE, columnist; b. N.Y.C. d. Al and Lillian Kanner; m. David B. Cuming, Oct. 10, 1982; children: Elisabeth, Andrew. BA, Harpur Coll., Binghamton, N.Y., 1969; MA in English Lit., SUNY, Binghamton, 1972. Account exec. J. Walter Thompson, N.Y.C., 1974-77; sr. editor, reporter Advt. Age Mag., N.Y.C., 1977-81; columnist Daily News, N.Y.C., 1980-81; sr. editor, columnist N.Y. Mag., 1981-94; columnist Bloomberg Bus. News, N.Y.C., 1994—, ScreamingMedia, N.Y.C., 2000; editor-in-chief WomensBiz.US, N.Y.C., 2002—. Author: Are You Normal?, 1995, Lies My Parents Told Me, 1996, The 100 Best TV Commercials And Why They Worked, 1999, Are You Normal About Money, 2001, The Super Bowl of Advertising: How the Commercials Won the Game, 2003, Are You Normal About Sex, Love and Relationships, 2004, Pocketbook Power: Marketing to Women in the 21st Century, 2004. Mem.: exec. com., Women's Bus. Coun. for Peace. Office: WomensBiz US 155 E 55th St Ste 6H New York NY 10022

KANOFF, MARY ELLEN, lawyer; m. Chris Kanoff. BA in Econs., U. Calif., Berkeley, 1978, JD, 1984. Large systems mktg. rep. IBM, 1978—81; with Latham & Watkins, L.A., 1984—, ptnr., 1991—. Bd. trustees St. Matthews Sch., Pacific Palisades, Calif., St. John's Hosps., Santa Monica, Calif.; bd. dirs. Chrysalis. Named one of Top 25 Lawyers in Calif. under 45, Calif. Law Bus., 1993, Up and Coming Bus. Persons in So. Calif., L.A. Bus. Jour., 1997; recipient Founders Spirit of Chrysalis award. Mem.: ABA (bus. law and entertainment law sects.), L.A. County Bar Assn., Calif. Bar Assn. Office: Latham and Watkins LLP 633 W Fifth St Ste 4000 Los Angeles CA 90071*

KANT, GLORIA JEAN, retired neuroscientist, researcher; b. Chgo., June 6, 1944; d. Hans Georg and Jo Sefa Kant; m. Philip Herbert Balcom, July 1, 1967 (div. 1976). BS in Chemistry, Mich. State U., 1965; PhD in Physiol. Chemistry, U. Wis., 1969. Chemist dept. psychiatry Walter Reed Army Inst. Rsch., Washington, 1970-71, neurochemist dept. microwave rsch., 1971-77, neurochemist dept. med. neuroscis., 1977-87, chief dept. med. neuroscis., 1987-95, dir. divsn. neuroscis., 1995—2001; ret. Mem. editl. bd. Pharmacology, Biochemistry and Behavior, 1991—; contbr. over 80 articles to sci. jours. Mem. AAAS, Soc. for Neurosci., Internat. Behavioral Neurosci. Soc., Women in Neurosci. Avocation: golf. Home: 1124 Dennis Ave Silver Spring MD 20901-2171

KANTER, JENNIFER LYNNE, curator; b. Lakeland, Fla., Dec. 21, 1974; d. Karen Myers and Fred Mac Kanter, Anne Magers Kanter (Stepmother). A, U. Fla., 1998. Arts specialist AmeriCorps Arts USF, Tampa, Fla., 1999—2000; edn. program coord. Tampa Mus. Art, 2000—01, asst. curator edn., 2001—. Com. chair children's activities Gasparilla Festival of Arts, Tampa, 2001—; steering com. Am. Music Festival, Tampa, 2001—; pre-jury juror Tarpon Springs (Fla.) Art Festival, 2001; exhbn. curator 11th Congl. Dist. Art Competition Com., Tampa, 2002—. Curator (exhibition) Self-Adornment/Self Esteem, Tampa Mus. Art, 2001, Young at Art, 2002—04, Next Generation, 2002—03, Birds of a Feather, 2002. Mem. adv. com. Mayor's Youth Coun., 2003—. Fla. Academic scholar, State of Fla. Dept Edn., 1992. Mem.: Nat. Art Edn. Assn., Fla. Art Edn. Assn., Fla. Assn. Mus., Soc. Creative Anachronism (trimarian coll. scribes libr. 2001—, OWS - Local Chpt. Svc. Award, AOA - Regional Chpt. Svc. Award 2002), Eta Sigma Phi (life). Avocations: medeival history and culture, middle eastern dance, travel, calligraphy, theater costume and set construction. Home: 7515-B Pitch Pine Cir Tampa FL 33617 Office: Tampa Mus Art 600 N Ashley Dr Tampa FL 33617

KANTER, ROSABETH MOSS, management educator, consultant, writer; b. Cleve., Mar. 15, 1943; d. Nelson Nathan and Helen (Smolen) Moss; m. Stuart Alan Kanter, June 20, 1963 (dec. Mar. 1969); m. Barry Alan Stein, July 2, 1972; 1 child, Matthew Moss Kanter Stein. BA in Sociology magna cum laude, Bryn Mawr Coll., 1964; MA, U. Mich., 1965, PhD, 1967; postgrad., Harvard U. Law Sh., 1975-76; MA (hon.), Yale U., 1978, Harvard U., 1986; DSc (hon.), Bucknell U., 1980, Babson Coll., 1984, Bryant Coll., 1986, Bentley Coll., 1990, U. Mass., Boston, 1996; LHD (hon.), Antioch U., Westminster Coll., 1984, Suffolk U., N. Adams State Coll., 1987, Colby-Sawyer Coll., 1988, U. New Haven, 1989; DCL (hon.), Union Coll., 1987; LLD (hon.), Regis Coll., 1987; DSS (hon.), Fla. Internat. U., 1990; DHL (hon.), SUNY Inst. Tech., 1991, Dowling Coll., 1991, Claremont Coll., 1992, Monmouth Coll., 1994, U. Mass., Boston, 1996; DBA (hon.), 2001. Vis. prof. mgmt. Harvard U., 1973-74, MIT, 1979-80; from assoc. to asst. prof. Brandeis U., 1967-77; prof. Yale U., 1977-86; Class of 1960 prof. bus. adminstrn. Harvard U. Bus. Sch., 1986-2000, Ernest L. Arbuckle prof. bus. adminstrn., 2000—. Chmn. bd. Goodmeasure, Inc., 1977—; trustee Coll. Retirement Equities Fund, N.Y., 1985-89, Am. Leadership Forum, Houston, 1982-86; mem. work group on entrepreneurship Pres.'s Commn. Indsl. Competitiveness, 1984; Govs.'s innovation adv. com. Commonwealth of Mass, chair subcom., 1986; mem. Spl. Commn. on Employee Involvement and Ownership, Mass., 1986-87; mem. Gov.'s Commn. Rev. Anti-Takeover Laws, Mass. 1988; mem. Gov.'s Counc. Econ. Growth, Mass., 1994—, co-chair internat. trade task force, 1995—; Katz-Newcomb lectr. in social psychology U. Mich., 1986; Disting. speaker Orgn., Theory, Careers and Women in Mgmt. divs. Nat. Acad. Mgmt., 1987, Eastern Acad. Mgmt., 1993; Centenniel lectr. APA, 1992; Lilly Found. Disting. lectr. Nat. Assn. Community Leadership Orgns., 1985; Leavey Disting. lectr. U. Santa Clara, 1984; vis. scholar Newberry Libr. Program in Humanities, Chgo., 1973, Norwegian Rsch. Coun. on Sci., and Humanities, Oslo, 1980; Kellogg Found. 50th Anniv. lectr. Am. Assn. Higher Edn., 1979, Blazer lectr. U. Ky., 1974, Davidson lectr. U. N.H., 1975; Sigma Chi scholar-in-residence Miami U., Oxford, Ohio, 1978; bd. dirs. Am. Productivity and Quality Ctr., Houston; mem. bd. advisors RVC VEnture Capital, London, 2001—, Legal Seafoods, 1999—. Author: Work and Family in the U.S., 1977, Men and Women of the Corporation, 1977 (C. Wright Mills award 1977), 93, The Change Masters, 1983, (with M.S. Dukakis) Creating The Future: The Massachusetts Comeback and Its Promise for America, 1988, When Giants Learn to Dance, 1989 (Johnson Smith Knisely Exec. Leadership award 1990), (with B.A. Stein and T.F. Jick) The Challenge of Organizational Change: How Companies Experience It and Leaders Guide It, 1992, World Class: Thriving Locally in the Global Economy, 1995, Rosabeth Moss Kanter on the Frontiers of Management, 1997, Evolve!: Succeeding in the Digital Culture of Tomorrow, 2001; 6 other books, also monographs; mem. editorial bd. Human Resource Mgmt. jour., 1982-89, Orgn. Dynamics jour., 1983-85, 89, Jour. Bus. Venturing, 1985-89, Jour. Contemporary Bus., 2987-89, others; adv. bd. Society jour., 1987-89; editor Harvard Bus. Rev., 1989-92; contbr. over 150 articles to profl. jours., books, mags. (articles Harvard Bus. Rev. McKinsey award). Bd. dirs. Alliance for the Commonwealth, 1995—, City Yr., 1995—, NOW Legal Def. and Edn. Fund, N.Y.C., 1979-86, 93-95, Ctr. New Democracy, Washington, 1985-88, Am. Prodn. and Quality Ctr., Houston, 1989—, Econ. Policy Inst., 1994-2000; incorporator Babson Coll., 1984-87, Boston Children's Mus., 1984—, Mt. Auburn Hosp., 1991—; bd. overseers Malcolm Baldridge Nat. Quality Award U.S. Dept. Commerce, 1994—. Guggenheim fellow; numerous rsch. grants; named Woman of Yr. New Eng. Women's Bus. Owners, 1981, Internat. Assn. Personnel Women, 1981, MS Mag., 1985; named to Cleve. Heights H.S. Hall of Fame, 1986, Working Woman Hall of Fame AT&T/Working Women Mag., 1986, Ohio Women's Hall of Fame, 1990; recipient Athena award Intercollegiate Assn. Women Students, 1980, Gold medal award Big Sister Assn. Greater Boston, 1985, Women Who Make a Difference award Internat. Women's Forum, 1988, Richard M. Cyert award Profl. Excellence Carnegie-Mellon U. Grad. Sch. Indsl. Adminstrn., 1989, Project Equality award, 1990, Crohn's and Colitis Found. award, 1993, 1994, McFeely award YMCA, 1995, Leadership award New Eng. Coun., 1995, New Eng. Women's Leadership award, 1999, Acad. Women Achievers award YWCA, 1998, Disting. Career award Acad. Mgmt., 2001. Fellow Acad. Mgmt. (Disting. speaker mgmt. cons. divsn. 1985, women in mgmt. divsn. 1987, orgn. mgmt. theory divsn. 1994, Disting. Scholar award OMT divsn. 1994), Am. Soc. Quality & Participation, World Productivity Cong. (Ams. divsn.), World Econ. Forum; mem. Am. Sociol. Assn. (exec. coun. 1982-85), Eastern Sociol. Soc. (exec. com. 1975-78, Gellman award 1978), Soc. for Advancement of Socio-Econs., Com. of 200 (founder), Internat. Women's Forum, Coun. on Fgn. Rels. Avocations: tennis, swimming. Office: Harvard Bus Sch Grad Sch Bus Adminstrn Soldiers Field Rd Boston MA 02163

KANTER, STACY J. lawyer; b. N.Y.C., 1958; BS magna cum laude, SUNY, Albany, 1979; JD, Bklyn. Law Sch., 1984. Bar: N.Y. 1985. Ptnr. Skadden, Arps, Slate, Meagher & Flom LLP, N.Y.C. Mng. editor Bklyn. Law Rev., 1983-84. Named among N.Y.'s rising stars in bus. Crain's mag., 1997. Office: Skadden Arps Slate Meagher & Flom LLP 4 Times Sq Fl 24 New York NY 10036-6595

KANTROWITZ, JEAN, health products executive; b. Passaic, N.J., May 27, 1922; d. Nathan and Yetta (Applebaum) Rosensaft; m. Adrian Kantrowitz, Nov. 25, 1948; children: Niki, Lisa, Allen. BS, Rider Coll., 1942; MS, U. N.C., 1945; MPH, U. Mich., 1975. Adminstrv. asst. Maimonides Med. Ctr., Bklyn., 1961-70, Sinai Hosp., Detroit, 1970-78, '80-83; program coord., sr. clin. instr. child psyciatry divsn. Case Western Res. U. Sch. Medicine, Cleve., 1978-80; v.p. adminstrn. and bus. devel. L.VAD Tech., Inc., Detroit, 1983—. Mgmt. cons. NIH, Washington, 1974— Mem. Am. Soc. Artificial Internal Organs (co-chairperson project bionics, history work group). Home: 70 Gallogly Rd Auburn Hills MI 48326-1227 Office: LVAD Tech Inc 300 River Place Dr Ste 6850 Detroit MI 48207-5095

KANTROWITZ, SUSAN LEE, lawyer; b. Queens, N.Y., Jan. 15, 1955; d. Theodore and Dinah (Kotick) Kantrowitz; m. Mark R. Halperin; 1 child, Jacob Joseph Kantrowitz-Sirotkin. BS summa cum laude, Boston U., 1977; JD, Boston Coll., 1980. Bar: Mass. 1982. Assoc. producer Sta. KOCE-TV, Huntington Beach, Calif., 1980-81; acct. exec. Bozell & Jacobs, Newport Beach, Calif., 1981; atty. WGBH Ednl. Found., Boston, 1981-84, dir. legal affairs, 1984-86, gen. counsel, dir. legal affairs, 1986—, v.p., gen. counsel, 1993. Co-author: Legal and Business Aspects of the Entertainment, Publishing and Sports Industries, 1984. Mem. ABA, Mass. Bar Assn., Boston Bar Assn.

KANUK, LESLIE LAZAR, management consultant, educator; b. NYC; d. Charles and Sylvia Lazar; m. Jack Lawrence Kanuk; children: Randi Kanuk Dauler, Alan Robert. MBA, Baruch Coll., 1964; PhD, CUNY, 1974; PhD (hon.), Mass. Maritime Acad., 1981, Maine Maritime Acad., 1988. Pres. Leslie Kanuk Assocs., NYC, 1965—78, 1981—; Lippert Disting. chair Baruch Coll., N.Y.C., 1981-84; prof. CUNY, 1981—99, prof. emeritus, 1999—. Bd. dirs. Cleve. Cliffs Inc.; mem. maritime transp. research bd. Nat. Acad. Scis., 1975-78; commr., vice chmn., chmn. Fed. Maritime Commn., 1978-81; chmn., pres., dir. Containerization and Intermodal Inst., 1981-93; panelist NRC-NAS, 1975-78, 91; vis. prof. grad. studies program Maine Maritime Acad., 1984-93. Author: Mail Questionnaire Response Behavior, 1974, Toward an Expanding U.S.M.M., 1976, Consumer Behavior, 1978, rev. edits., 1983, 87, 89, 94, 97, 2000, 04; mem. editl. bd. Intermodal Forum, 1984-92. Trustee United Seamen's Svc., 1988—; bd. visitors Maine Maritime Acad., 1989-97. Recipient Connie award Containerization and Intermodal Inst., 1980, Diamond Superwoman award Harpers Bazaar mag., 1980, Person of Yr. award N.Y. Fgn. Freight Forwarders and Brokers Assn., 1981, Person of Yr. award Baruch Fgn. Trade Soc., 1981, Disting. Alumnus award CCNY, 1984, Disting. PhD Alumni award CUNY, 1988, Townsend Harris medal, 1986. Mem. Beta Gamma Sigma.

KANWISHER, NANCY G. neuroscientist; SB in Biology, MIT, 1980, PhD in Cognitive Psychology, 1986. Asst. rsch. psychologist U. Calif., Berkeley, 1988-90; asst. and assoc. prof. UCLA, 1990-94, Harvard U., 1994-97; assoc. prof. dept. brain and cognitive scis. MIT, Cambridge, Mass., 1997—. Recipient Troland Rsch. award NAS, 1999. Achievements include research in visual cognition and cognitive processing; discovered repetition blindness in which people fail to perceive the second ocurrence of a repeated item; characterized two new regions of the brain. those involved in the perception of faces and places. Office: MIT Dept Brain & Cognitive Sci 77 Massachusetts Ave Cambridge MA 02139-4307 E-mail: ngk@psyche.mit.edu.

KANY, JUDY C(ASPERSON), health policy analyst, former state senator; b. June 29, 1937; d. Helmer C. and Florence P. Casperson; m. Robert Kany, Aug. 16, 1958; children: Kristin, Geoffrey, Daniel. BBA, U. Mich., 1959; MPA, U. Maine, Orono, 1976. Mem. Maine Ho. of Reps., 1975-82, Maine Senate, 1982-92; project dir. for health professions regulation Med. Care Devel., Augusta, Maine, 1993—; mem. task force on health workforce regulation Pew Health Professions Commn., 1994-97; mayor Waterville, Maine, 1988-89; mem. issues and policy adv. com. Citizens Advocacy Ctr., Washington, 1994—2000; cmty. liaison Amity Found., Tucson, 2003—. Chmn. Maine's Adv. Commn. on Radioactive Waste, 1981-87, Joint Standing Com. Legal Affairs, 1987-88, Joint Standing Com. on State Govt., 1979-82, Joint Standing Com. Energy and Natural Resources, 1983-84, 89-90, Joint Standing Com. Banking and Ins., 1991-92, com. Maine Lakes, 1990-92, adv. com. on accountability to the Maine Health Care Reform Commn., 1994-95; mem. Commn. on Maine's Future, 1976, 87-89. Democrat. Home: 36832 S Stoney Flower Dr Tucson AZ 85739 E-mail: jkany@aol.com.

KANYO, DEBORAH SUE, elementary school educator, music educator; b. Springfield, Mo., Nov. 5, 1951; d. Perry Gene and Peggy Colleen Jordan; m. Roger Dale Davault, June 26, 1982 (div. Apr. 1996); children: Dustin, Derrick; m. James Peter Kanyo, Aug. 9, 1997; children: Jeremy, Courtney. B in Music Edn., S.E. Mo. State U., 1974. Cert. tchr. Mo., 1974, Ill., 1986, Colo., 1994. Vocal music tchr. grades K-6 Gasconade City R-II, Owensville, Mo., 1974—78, vocal music tchr. grades K-8, 1980—86; vocal music tchr. grades K-6 St. James (Mo.) Schs., 1978—80; vocal music tchr. grades 2-5 Alton (Ill.) Sch. Dist., 1986—94, vocal music tchr. grades 3-5, 1995—; vocal music tchr. grades 6-8 Adams County Schs., Denver, 1994—95. Music dir. Main St. United Meth., Alton, 1986—. Dir. Encounter Main St. United Meth. Ch., Alton, 1990—. Named Woman of Yr., Main Street United Meth. Ch., 1994. Mem.: Music Educators Nat. Conf., Am. Choral Dirs. Assn. Republican. Avocations: stamping, scrapbooks.

KANYUK, JOYCE STERN, secondary art educator; b. Irvington, N.J., June 29, 1951; d. Paul Stern and Jean Hannah (Oberdofer) Dubin; m. Peter Kanyuk, June 10, 1973; 1 child, Paul. BFA in Art Edn., Syracuse (N.Y.) U., 1973; MA, Coll. of New Rochelle, 1977. Art tchr. Felix Festa Mid. Sch., West Nyack, 1973—. Exhibited in group shows at Orangeburg Town Hall, 1991, Nanuet Libr., 1992, 93, 94, 95, 97, Suffern Libr., 1992, 93, Allendale Borough Hall, 1992, N.E. Watercolor Soc., 1991, 94, 97, Audubon Artists Ann. Exhbn., 1994-97, Cmty. Arts Assn. Tri-State Open Juried Show, 1990, 91, 92, 96, South Nyack Fine Arts Festival, 1989-95, Ringwood Manor Assn. of the Arts Open Juried Show, 1990, 92, 1992 Morris County ARt Assn. Tri-State Juried Exhbn., Mari Galleries Nat. Fine Arts Exhbn., 1992, 93, 94, Exhibit of Mixed Media, Nabisco Gallery, 1993. Recipient Best of Show award Milburn-Short Hills Art Fair, 1994, Second Pl. award Mari Galleries, 1994, Honorable Mention Morris Count Art Assn., 1992, South Shore Watercolor Artists award East Islip Arts Coun., 1994, 95. Mem. Arts Coun. of Rockland, Cmty. Arts Assn. (membership chmn.), Ringwood Manor Art Assn., Audubon Artists, North East Watercolor Soc., N.Y. State Art Tchrs. Assn., Piermont Fine Arts Gallery. Avocations: figure skating, bicycling, cross country skiing. Home: 29 John St New City NY 10956-3650 Office: Felix Festa Mid Sch 30 Parrot Rd West Nyack NY 10994-1028

KAO, YASUKO WATANABE, retired library administrator; b. Tokyo, Mar. 30, 1930; came to U.S., 1957; d. Kichiji and Sato (Tanaka) Watanabe; m. Shih-Kung Kao, Apr. 1, 1959; children: John Sterling, Stephanie Margaret. BA, Tsuda Coll., 1950; BA in Lit., Waseda U., 1955; MSLS, U. So. Calif., 1960. Instr., Takinogawa High Sch., Tokyo, 1950-57; catalog librarian U. Utah Library, 1960-67, Marriott Library, 1975-77, head catalog div., 1978-90; dir. libr. Teikyo Loretto Heights U., 1991-95. Contbr. articles to profl. jours. Vol., Utah Chinese Am. Community Sch., 1974-80, Asian Assn. Utah, 1981-90. Waseda U. fellow, 1958-59. Mem. ALA, Asian Pacific Librs. Assn., Assn. Coll. and Rsch. Librs., Beta Phi Mu. Home: 2625 Yuba Ave El Cerrito CA 94530-1443

KAPELMAN, BARBARA ANN, internist, gastroenterologist, educator; b. N.Y.C., Apr. 30, 1949; d. Leonard A. and Helen (Hass) K.; m. Lawrence William Koblenz, Mar. 24, 1979; 1 child, Adam. BA, Barnard Coll., 1970; MS in Microbiology, Yale U., 1972; MD, Albert Einstein Coll. Medicine, 1975. Diplomate Am. Bd. Internal Medicine, Am. Bd. Gastroenterology. Clin. asst. prof. hepatology and gastroenterology Mt. Sinai Sch. Medicine Mt. Sinai Hosp., 1981—82; intern Roosevelt Hosp.-Columbia U., N.Y.C., 1975-76, resident, 1976-78, fellow gastroenterology, 1978-80; fellow liver diseases Mt. Sinai Sch. Medicine-CUNY, N.Y.C., 1980-81; asst. attending physician in gastroenterology Beth Israel Hosp., N.Y.C., 1982-88, assoc. attending physician in medicine and gastroenterology, 1988-96, attending physician in medicine and gastroenterology, 1996—; clin. instr. in medicine Mt. Sinai Sch. of Medicine, N.Y.C., 1981-87, asst. clin. prof. medicine, 1987-94; bd. dirs. Beth Israel Med. Ctr., N.Y.C., 1984—, trustee, med. liaison, 1996-97; asst. clin. prof. medicine Albert Einstein Coll. Medicine, N.Y.C., 1994—. Trustee Med. Bd. Liaison, 1996-97; attending physician Beth Israel North, Beth Israel Med. Ctr., N.Y.C., 1982—, Hosp. for Joint Diseases-Orthopedic Inst., N.Y.C., 1982—; vis. clin. fellow Columbia U. Coll. Physicians and Surgeons, N.Y.C., 1975-80; cons. gastroenterology and liver disease. Co-author: Gastroenterology for the House Officer, 1989; contbr. articles to profl. jours. Fellow ACP, Am. Coll. Gastroenterology; mem. Am. Women's Med. Assn., Women's Med. Assn. N.Y.C. (officer), Am. Gastroent. Assn., Am. Assn. for Study of Liver Diseases, Am. Soc. for Gastrointestinal Endoscopy, Am. Med. Informatics Assn., N.Y. Acad. Gastroenterology, N.Y. Soc. for Gastrointestinal Endoscopy. Avocations: computers, culinary arts, medical informatics, educational activities. Office: Ste 210A 133 E 73rd St New York NY 10021-3556 Office Phone: 212-628-8000.

KAPIKIAN, CATHERINE ANDREWS, artist; b. Cleve., Oct. 18, 1939; d. John Robert and Anne Alva (Cosgrove) Andrews; m. Albert Zaven Kapikian, Feb. 27, 1960; children: Albert, Thomas, Gregory. Student, Carnegie Mellon U., 1957—59; BA, U. Md., 1963; MTS summa cum laude, Wesley Theol. Sem., Washington, 1979. Gen. illustrator NIH, Bethesda, Md., 1959-61; artist-in-residence Wesley Theol. Sem., 1979—, mem. faculty, dir. Henry Luce III Ctr. for the Arts and Religion, 2001—. Designer, fabricator liturgical tapestries, banners, paraments and vestments; mem. commn. on worship and the arts Nat. Coun. Chs., 1991-97. Works exhibited in group shows including Interfaith Forum on Religion, Art and Architecture, Phoenix, 1979, Chgo., 1981, Phila., 1987, Houston, 1989, Boston, 1990, St. Thomas More Newman Ctr. Liturg. Arts Exhibit, Bowling Green (Ohio) U., 1981, Archdiocese of Chgo., 1984, Biennial Exhbns. Liturgical Art Guild of Ohio, Columbus, 1985, 91, 93, 95, 97, 2001; author: Through the Christian Year: An Illustrated Guide, 1983; contbr. forward to (book) Full Circle, 1988; contbr. articles and images to profl. jours. Bd. dirs. Episcopal Ch. Visual Arts, 2002—. Mem. Arts and Religion Forum of Washington Theol. Consortium (founder, mem. steering com.), Interfaith Forum on Religion, Art and Architecture (bd. dirs. 1983-85, 87-90), Schuyler Inst. Worship and the Arts (bd. dirs. 1987-90). Democrat. Avocations: opera, remote control airplanes. Office: Wesley Theol Seminary Henry Luce III Ctr for Arts and Religion 4500 Massachusetts Ave NW Washington DC 20016-5632 Office Phone: 202-885-8617. E-mail: ckapiklan@wesleysem.edu.

KAPLAN, ALICE, humanities educator, writer; b. Mpls., June 22, 1954; d. Leonore Yaeger and Sidney Joseph Kaplan. BA, U. Calif., Berkeley, 1975; PhD, Yale U., 1981. Asst. prof. N.C. State U., Raleigh, 1981—83, Columbia U., N.Y.C., 1983—86; assoc. prof. Romance studies Duke U., Durham, NC, 1986—94, prof. Romance studies and lit., 1994—, Lehrman prof. Romance studies, 2003—; founding dir. Duke Ctr. French and Francophone Studies, 1999—2002. Author: The Collaborator: The Trial and Execution of Robert Brasillach, 2000 (Book prize in history L.A. Times, finalist Nat. Book award, finalist Nat. Book Critics Cir. award, 2001), French Lessons: A Memoir, 1993 (finalist Nat. Book Critics Cir. award in autobiography/biography, 1993), Sources et citations dans "Bagatelles pour un massacre", 1988, Reproductions of Banality: Fascism, Literature and French Intellectual Life, 1986; translator: (novels) Le Pierrot Noir , 1998, Partita , 2001, OK Joe, 2003. Named Officier dans l'Ordre des Palmes Academiques, French Ministry of Edn., 2001; fellow, Nat. Humanities Ctr., 1989—90, Guggenheim Found., 1994, Stanford Humanities Ctr., 1994—95. Mem.: PEN, MLA, Am. Lit. Translators Assn., Assn. Pour l'Autobiographie et le Patrimoine Autobiographique. Office: Duke U Lit Program 109 Art Mus Durham NC 27708

KAPLAN, BARBARA JANE, retired city planner; b. N.Y.C., Sept. 8, 1943; d. Richard S. and Fannie I. (Schutz) Benson; m. Jerry Martin Kaplan, May 29, 1966. BA, Barnard Coll., 1965; MS, U. Southern Calif., 1969. Asst. planner L.A. Regional Planning Commn., 1968-69; from asst. planner to assoc. planner San Diego Comprehensive Planning Orgn., 1969-71; asst. dir. of regional planning North Ctrl. Tex. Coun. of Govts., Arlington, 1971-73; dir. Pennsport Civic Assn., Phila., 1974; city planner III Phila. City Planning Commn., 1974-76, city planner V, 1976-80, dep. exec. dir., 1980-83, exec. dir., 1983-2000, ret., 2000. Trustee U. of the Arts, Phila., 1987—2001; pres. Ctr. for Literacy, Phila., 1991—96, bd. dirs., 1984—, Neighborhood Gardens Assn., Phila., 1987—. Mem.: Pa. Hort. Soc. (bd. dirs. 1993—, v.p. 2000—01, mem. coun.), Nat. Trust for Hist. Preservation, Am. Planning Assn. Avocations: reading, tennis. Home: 2421 Fairmount Ave Philadelphia PA 19130-2517 E-mail: barbarajkaplan@msn.com.

KAPLAN, BETSY HESS, school board member; b. Bridgeton, N.J., Aug. 12, 1926; d. Alfred N. and Betsy (Bolton) Hess; m. Robert Leon Kaplan, June 11, 1953; children: Bruce Alfred, James Edward, Joan Ann. AB, Wesleyan Coll., 1947; BFA, Wesleyan Conservatory, 1948. Cert. tchr., Fla. Tchr. 4th grade Miami (Fla.)-Dade County Pub. Schs., 1950-53; edn. and cultural arts adv., 1961—88; instr. Miami Dade Cmty. Coll., 1979-81; admintrv. asst. to Ethel K. Beckham Miami-Dade County Sch. Bd., 1980-82, mem. sch. bd., 1988—, chair, 1993-95. Chair fed. rels. network Fla. Sch. Bds., Tallahassee, 1996-98; bd. dirs. New World Sch. of Arts, Miami, 1996—; mem. Performing Arts Ctr. Trust, Miami, 1993—, student mentor. Mem. Emily's List, Washington, 1990—, Women's Emergency Network, Miami, 1990—, Women's Polit. Caucus, 1988—; cultural amb. Heart of the City cultural series Miami-Dade Park and Recreation Dept., 2002. Named Woman Worth Knowing, Miami Beach Commn. on Status of Women, 1994, Woman of Yr., King of Clubs, 2000; recipient Alumnae Disting. Achievement award, Wesleyan Coll., 1987, French Acad. Palms award, French Min. of Edn. of Youth and Sports, 1991, Co. of Women, Pioneer award, Miami-Dade County Pks. Dept., 1997, Ruth Wolkowsky Greenfield award, Am. Jewish Congress, 1993, Woman of Impact award, Cmty. Coalition for Women's History, 1995, Red Cross Spectrum award, Women in Edn., 1997, Trailblazer award, Women's Com. of 100, 1993, Lifetime Svc. to Music Edn. in Fla. and U.S., Fla. Music Educators Assn., 2000, Branches of Learning award, Women's Divsn. Greater Miami State of Israel Bonds Orgn., 2001. Mem.: AAUW (Phoenix award 1999), LWV, Alliance for Aging (mem. adv. bd. 1996—), Fla. Sch. Bds. Assn. (bd. dirs. 1990—99, Pres.'s award 2001), Phi Kappa Phi, Delta Kappa Gamma, Phi Delta Kappa. Democrat. Jewish. Avocations: studying art history, reading and interpreting poetry, studying and practicing French language, cooking. Home: 6790 SW 122d Dr Miami FL 33156-5459 Office: Miami Dade County Sch Bd 1450 NE 2d Ave Ste 700 Miami FL 33132 E-mail: bakaplan60@aol.com., bhkaplan@dadeschools.net.

KAPLAN, CLAUDETTE S. (CLAUDIA KAPLAN), volunteer; b. Chgo., June 4, 1931; d. Jacob and Celia (Lopaty) Mirotsnic; m. Saul M. Kaplan, Nov. 28, 1953 (dic. Mar. 1980); children: Allan, Laurie K., David. Grad., Chgo. City Coll., 1951; student, Coll. Jewish Studies, 1951-53. Pres. Hadassah, Memphis, 1970-72, So. region, 1978-81, nat. svc. com., 1981-83, mem. nat. pres.'s coun., 1984—, founder major and big gifts event, 1974, area founders chair nat. major gifts dept. Nat. Israel Edn. Svcs. Com., chpt. cons., 1999; bd. dirs. NCCJ, Memphis Jewish Cmty. Rels. Coun., Memphis Jewish Fedn./Unite Jewish Appeal, 1972-80; mem. So. Poverty Law Ctr. Recipient 25th Anniversary award State of Israel Bonds, 1973, Guardian of the Dream Founder award Hadassah, 1995. Mem. Am. Israel Pub. Affairs Com. (exec. com. Memphis coun.), Nat. Coun. Jewish Women, World Jewish Congress, Am. Soc. for Yad Vashem Simon Wiesenthal Ctr., Hadassah Women's Zionist Orgn. of Am. (life), City Hope (life), Memphis and Mid-South Jewish Hist. Soc., B'nai B'rith. Home: 408 River Oaks Pl Memphis TN 38120-2538

KAPLAN, DAILE, photographer; d. Edward Kenneth and Irma Hannah (Rosen) K. BA, Harpur Coll., 1971, SUNY, 1973. Dir., hist. photo collection The United Meth. Ch., New York, NY, 1980—82; ind. curator Libr. of Congress, Washington, 1984—86, Islip Art Mus., Islip, NY, 1988—89, Alice Austen Ho., Staten Island, NY, Musee de la Croix-Rouge, Geneva, 1988—89; adjunt prof. of history NY U., New York, NY, 1990—91; v.p. and dir., photographs Swann Auction Galleries, New York, NY, 1990—; ind. curator Art Gallery Ontario, Toronto, Canada, 2003. Adj. prof. NYU Grad. Sch., 1990; cons. and lectr. in field. Author: Lewis Hine in Europe, The Lost Photographs, 1988, Photo Story, Letters and Photographs of Lewis W. Hine, 1992. Tutor Ctrs. Reading and Writing, N.Y.C., 1988; bd. dirs. Fifty Crows Found.; bd. advisors Palm Beach Photographic Ctr. Grantee Smithsonian Inst., 2000, Ludwig Vogelstein Found., 1981, 84, Kaltenborn Found., 1984, 91, Globus Fund, 1985, Met. Life Found., 1985, N.Y. Coun. Humanities, 1988. Mem. Soc. for Photographic Edn., Am. Photographic Hist. Soc. (bd. dirs. 1989-90, fellow 1988), Daguerreian Soc. Achievements include coined the term pop photographica to describe the convergence of photography and popular culture; discovery of a cache of Lewis Hine's lost European photographs in the Library of Congress. Avocations: tennis, yoga, antiques, travel. Office: Swann Auction Galleries 104 East 25 St New York NY 10010 Personal E-mail: daile@popphotographica.com. E-mail: dkaplan@swanngalleries.com.

KAPLAN, DEBORAH RENEE, artist; b. Livingston, N.J., Dec. 26, 1965; d. Barbara Esther and William Kaplan. BA, Hampshire Coll., 1990; MFA, Yale U., 2002. Cert. in painting NY Studio Sch. Drawing, Painting & Sculpture, 1999. Tchr. Hampshire Coll., Amherst, Mass., 1989; tchg. asst. Henry St. Settlement, New York, 2000, Yale U., New Haven, 2001. Editl. intern Art on Paper, New York, 2003. One-woman shows include Light, The Dark Room. Senatorial rep.,Yale U. Sch. Art Grad.-Profl. Student Senate, New Haven, 2000—02; student rep. Student Adv. Bd., New Haven, 2000—02; admissions assoc. Hampshire Admissions Assocs. Program, Amherst, Mass., 2002—03. Nominee Skowhegan, N.Y. Studio Sch., 1999; recipient Excellence in Painting and Sculpture Merit award, 1999, Chautauqua Summer Scholarship award, 1998, Hallmark Honor Prize, Scholastic, 1984, Cert. of Merit, Congl. Art Competition, 1984, Susan H. Whedon award, Yale U. Sch. Art, 2002; Residency grantee, Vt. Studio Ctr., 2000. Achievements include design of Yale University School of Art scarves. Home and Office: 114 East 62nd St Apt 4R New York NY 10021 Personal E-mail: bubalashane@yahoo.com.

KAPLAN, ELAINE D. lawyer; b. Bklyn., Dec. 18, 1955; BA, SUNY, Binghamton, 1976; JD, Georgetown U., 1979. Atty. Office of the Solicitor U.S. Dept. Labor, 1979-83; atty. State and Local Legal Ctr., Washington, 1983-84; asst. dir. litigation, asst. counsel Nat. Treas. Employees Union, 1984—88, dep. gen. counsel, 1988-97; spl. counsel Office of Spl. Counsel, Washington, 1998—2003; of counsel Bernabei & Katz PLLC, Washington, 2003—. Mem., editorial bd. Journal of Pub. Inquiry, 2000—02. Office: Bernabei & Katz PLLC 1773 T St NW Washington DC 20009-7139*

KAPLAN, ERICA LYNN, typing and word processing service company executive, pianist, educator; b. Aug. 6, 1955; d. George William and Raylia (Eagle) Kaplan; m. James Laurence Kellermann, Feb. 26, 1982. B in Mus., Manhattan Sch. Music, N.Y.C., 1976, M in Mus., 1979. Pres. Erica Kaplan Typing/Word Processing/Music Svcs., N.Y.C., 1980—; from accompanist to tchr. Stuyvesant Adult Ctr., N.Y.C., 1988—97, tchr. performance singing, 1997—. Accompanist Literally Alive/Victory Theatrical, 2000—, mus. dir., 2001—. Transl., annotator with additional mus. examples: L'Anacrouse dans la Musique Moderne, 1978; composer: (songs) Four by Feiffer, 1978, Hey Boys, 1984, Unborn Child, 1988, Neighbor, 1991, Watch the Closing Doors, 2001; arranger Postcards from the Apple, 1993, Isn't It Romantic, 1996. Mem. Common Cause, Washington, 1983—, SANE/FREEZE, 1988—. Mem.: Am. Fedn. Musicians, Mensa. Democrat. Jewish. E-mail: ELKK@aol.com.

KAPLAN, GABRIELA DIANA, radiologist; b. Quito, Ecuador, Apr. 28, 1947; arrived in U.S., 1963; d. Isidor and Rosa Ortiz Kaplan. MD, U. Autonoma Guadalajara, 1972; BA, Whittier Coll. Diplomate Am. Bd. Radiology. Fellow in body imaging Johns Hopkins U., Balt., 1980, fellow in neuroradiology, 1982; fellow in whole body magnetic resonance U. Mich., Ann Arbor, 1989, asst. prof. radiology Med. Ctr., 1988—89; asst. prof. Columbia U./Presbyn. Hosp., N.Y.C., 1979; lectr. diagnostic radiology Johns Hopkins Hosp., Balt., 1980—82; pres. Lifewatch Group, Cleve. Author: (book) Wealth, Hunger and Peace, 1989, (web page) www.arrowweb.com/life. Decorated Legion of Merit; recipient Ptnrs. in Conservation award, World Wildlife Fund, 1999, Internat. award of Merit, Internat. Soc. Poetry, 2001. Mem.: Am. Coll. Radiology, P.I.B. Yacht Club (fleet surgeon). Republican. Roman Catholic. Achievements include invention of device to aid women in family planning. Avocations: environmental concerns, poetry, gardening.

KAPLAN, GRISEL ARIAS, bank executive; b. Feb. 1954; BA, State U. NY, New Paltz; JD, Temple U. Sch. Law, Phila. Compliance officer Heritage Bank, N.A.; dir. compliance First Fidelity Bancorporation, 1989—98; mgr. info. sys. tech. compliance Citibank/Citigroup, 1998—2001; sr. v.p., chief compliance officer Providian Fin. Corp., 2001—03, Union Bank of Calif., 2003—. Served on The Fin. Svcs. Roundtable, NJ Banker's Assn. Compliance Com. Named Top Hispanic Woman in Corp. Am., Hispanic mag., 1998; named an Elite Woman for 2004, Hispanic Bus. mag.*

KAPLAN, HELENE LOIS, lawyer; b. N.Y.C., June 19, 1933; d. Jack and Shirley (Jacobs) Finkelstein; m. Mark N. Kaplan, Sept. 7, 1952; children: Marjorie Ellen, Sue Anne. AB cum laude, Barnard Coll., 1953; JD, NYU, 1967; LLD (hon.), Columbia U., 1990. Bar: N.Y. 1967. Pvt. practice, N.Y.C., 1967-78; ptnr. Webster & Sheffield, N.Y.C., 1978-86, counsel, 1986-90; of counsel Skadden, Arps, Slate, Meagher & Flom, N.Y.C., 1990—. Bd. dirs. The May Dept. Stores Co., Met. Life Inc. and Met. Life Ins. Co., JP Morgan Chase & Co., Exxon Mobil Corp. Trustee N.Y. Coun. for Humanities, 1976-82, chmn., 1978-82; trustee Barnard Coll., 1973-99, chair bd. trustees, 1984-94, trustee and chair emerita, 1999—; trustee Columbia U. Press, 1977-80, MITRE Corp., 1978-95, N.Y. Found., 1976-86, John Simon Guggenheim Meml. Found., 1981-98, NYU Law Ctr. Found., 1985-87, Neuroscis. Rsch. Found., 1986-92, Am. Mus. Natural History, 1989—, vice chair, 1993—; trustee Am. Trust for Brit. Libr., 1991-93, Com. for Econ. Devel., 1993-96, Commonwealth Fund, 1990-2003, vice chair, 1996-2003; trustee and chair emerita Inst. for Advanced Study, 1986-2002, trustee emerita, 2002—; trustee J. Paul Getty Trust, 1992—, vice chair 1997—; trustee Olive Free Libr.; trustee Carnegie Corp. N.Y., 1979—, vice-chair bd. trustees, 1981-84, 98-2002, chair, 1984-91, 2002—; chair, trustee Mt. Sinai Sch. Medicine, 1999-01, Mt. Sinai NYU Health, 1998-2001, vice-chair bd. trustees, 1993-99; trustee N.Y.C. Pub. Devel. Corp., 1978-83, vice-chair bd. trustees, 1978-82; mem. Adv. Com. on South Africa, U.S. Sec. of State, 1986-88; mem. N.Y. State Gov.'s Task Force on Life and the Law, 1985-90, Women's Forum, Inc., 1982—, Rockefeller U. Coun., 1984-94, Bretton Woods Com., 1985-96, Carnegie Coun. on Adolescent Devel., 1986-96; chair task force on sci. and tech. and jud. decision making Carnegie Commn. on Sci., Tech. and Govt., 1988-93; ptnr. N.Y.C. Partnership, 1987-92; bd. dirs. Am. Arbitration Assn., 1978-82. Mem.: N.Y.C. Bar Assn. (treas. 1991—93, mem. com. on philanthropic orgns. 1975—81, mem. com. on recruitment of lawyers 1978—82, mem. com. on profl. responsibility 1980—83), Am. Philos. Soc., Am. Acad. Arts and Scis., Century Assn., Cosmopolitan Club.

KAPLAN, HUETTE MYRA, business educator, training consultant; b. Chgo., July 11, 1933; d. Max and Jeannette (Smith) Lazan; m. Jerrold M. Kaplan, Feb. 14, 1954 (dec.); children: Lawrence, Jeffrey. BS in Bus. Edn., DePaul U., 1971. Instr. Pub. Svc. Careers Program State of Ill., Chgo., 1971-72; instr., dir. Patricia Stevens Bus. Sch., Chgo., 1972; relocation mgr., tng. specialist, dir. tng. and devel. Zurich-Am. Ins. Cos., Chgo. and Schaumburg, Ill., 1972-80; pres., tng. cons. H.K. & Assocs., Lansing, Ill., 1980—. Tng. dir. Calumet Area Lit. Coun., Hammond, Ind., 1985—; trainer Chgo. Literacy Coordinating Ctr., 1988-93; instr. Purdue U.-Calumet, Hammond, 1976—; substitute tchr. Sch. Dist. 171, Lansing, 1995-2002. Mem. task force Chgo. Coalition for Edn. and Tng. for Employment, 1984—86; literacy vol. tutor; candidate Dist. 215 Sch Bd., 1999; docent Chgo. Architecture Found., 2001—; bd. dirs. Temple Beth El, Hammond, 1986—88, Calumet Area Literacy Coun., 1990—92, 1994—95, pres., 1995—2002, 2003—. Jewish. Avocations: reading, pet therapy programs, travel. Home and Office: HK & Assocs 2843 192nd St Lansing IL 60438-3717 E-mail: huettek1@aol.com.

KAPLAN, JANET ANN, art historian, educator; b. Chgo., May 14, 1945; d. Morris and Dorothy (Weiss) K.; m. Warren O. Angle, June 17, 1984; 1 child, Dana Kaplan-Angle. BA, Brandeis U., 1966; PhD, Columbia U., 1982. Arts faculty U. Wis., River Falls, 1975-76; arts faculty chair Franconia (N.H.) Coll., 1976-78; arts faculty U. N.H., Plymouth, 1978-79; prof., chair liberal arts Moore Coll. Art and Design, Phila., 1980—; grad. faculty Vt. Coll., Montpelier, 1991—; exec. editor Art Jour., N.Y.C., 1996—2002. Adv. bd. Voices of Dissent Conf., Phila., 1987-89, Phila. (Pa.) Redevel Authority, 2001—; cons. U.S. Holocaust Meml. Mus., Washington, 1990-92, Rosenbach Mus. and Libr., Phila., Pa., 2000—; reviewer NEH, Washington, 1990; co-orgn. of alternative sites exhbns. Internat. Sculpture Conf., Phila., 1992; juror Mid-Atlantic-New Painting, Fredericksburg, Va., 1997; vis. faculty Inst. Fine Arts NYU, 2000. Author: Unexpected Journeys: the Art and Life of Remedios Varo, 1988, 94, in Spanish 1988, 94, in Japanese, 1992; editor: A Woman's Thesaurus, 1988; contbr. articles to profl. jours. Organizer Art Squad-Polit. Activists, Phila., 1980-83. Summer Inst. fellow NEH, Stanford, Calif., 1979, Geneva, N.Y., 1987, fellow NEH, 1984-85, Program for Cultural Cooperation Between Spain's Ministry of Culture and U.S. Univs., 1990, fellow Pa. Coun. Humanities, 2002; scholar-in-residence Rockefeller Found., Bellagio, Italy, 1985. Mem. Coll. Art Assn., Assn. Internat. des Critiques D'Art. Home: 250 Grape St Philadelphia PA 19128-4927 Office: Moore Coll Art & Design 20th and The Pkwy Philadelphia PA 19103

KAPLAN, JEAN GAITHER (NORMA KAPLAN), reading specialist, retired educator; b. Cumberland, Md., Dec. 14, 1927; d. Frank Preston and Elizabeth (Mcneil) Gaither; m. Robert Lewis Kaplan, Dec. 4, 1959; 1 child, Benjamin Leigh. AB in Edn., Madison Coll., Harrisonburg, Va., 1950; MA in Edn., U. Va., 1956; postgrad., U. Va., William and Mary, 1958-61; reading specialist degree, U. Va., 1976. Tchr. Frederick County Sch. System, Winchester, Va., 1950-51, Washington County Sch. System, Hagerstown, Md., 1951-55, Charlottesville (Va.) Sch. System, 1955-60, York County (Va.) Sch. System, 1962, Newport News Sch. System, Denbigh, Va., 1963, Internat. Sch. Bangkok, 1965-67; tutor Reston Reading Ctr., Fairfax County, Va., 1972-74; tutor homebound, substitute tchr. Fairfax County Sch. Systems, 1974-78; pvt. practice pvt. tutor McLean/Middleburg, Va., 1978-89. Pres. Tutorial Svcs., Inc., McLean, 1985-87; sec. The Rumson Corp., Middleburg, 1981—. Active No. Va. Conservation Coun., Fairfax County, 1976-81, Piedmont Environ. Coun.; bd. dirs. Nat. Environ. Leadership Coun. Mem. AAUW, LWV, Bangkok Am. Wives Assn., Tuesday Afternoon Club (pres. 1974-75, treas. 1995-96), Ayr Hill Garden Club, Soc. John Gaither Descs. Inc., Bluestone Soc., Goose Creek Assn., Kappa Delta Pi, Alpha Sigma Tau. Avocations: reading, theater, concerts, travel. Home and Office: PO Box 1943 Middleburg VA 20118-1943 Office Phone: 540-687-3308., 540-687-3309. Personal E-mail: jk96ook@juno.com.

KAPLAN, MADELINE, legal administrator; b. N.Y.C., June 20, 1944; d. Leo and Ethel (Finkelstein) Kahn; m. Theodore Norman Kaplan, Nov. 14, 1982. AS, Fashion Inst. Tech., N.Y.C., 1964; BA in English Lit. summa cum laude, CUNY, 1982; MBA, Baruch Coll., 1990. Free-lance fashion illustrator, N.Y.C., 1965-73; legal asst. Krause Hirsch & Gross, Esquires, N.Y.C., 1973-80; mgr. communications Stroock & Stroock & Lavan Esquires, N.Y.C., 1980-86; dir. adminstrn. Cooper Cohen Singer & Ecker Esquires, N.Y.C., 1986-87, Donovan Leisure Newton & Irvine Esquires, N.Y.C., 1987-93, Proskauer Rose Goetz & Mendelsohn, N.Y.C., 1993-95, Kaye Scholer LLP, N.Y.C., 1995—. Mem. adv. bd. Grad. Sch. Human Resources Mgmt. Mercy Coll., 1997—; bd. dirs. Suitability. Contbr. articles to profl. jours. Founder, pres. Knolls chpt. of Women's Am. Orgn. Rehab. Through Tng., Riverdale, N.Y., 1979-82, v.p. edn., Manhattan region, 1982-83; adv. bd. Suitability; vol. Starlight Found. Mem. ASTD, Assn. Legal Adminstrs. (program com.), MBA Alumni Assn. (bd. dirs.), Sigma Iota Epsilon (life). Office: 425 Park Ave New York NY 10022-3506

KAPLAN, MARJORIE, broadcast executive; married; 2 children. B in Semiotics, Brown U. Dir. advt. Kraft Gen. Foods; v.p. Ogilvy & Mather; exec. v.p. Lancit Media Entertainment; sr. v.p. children's programming and products Discovery Networks, U.S., 1997—. Cons. Warner Amex Satellite Entertainment; developer Discovery Kids. Office: Discovery Comm 7700 Wisconsin Ave Bethesda MD 20814*

KAPLAN, MARJORIE ANN PASHKOW, school district administrator; b. Bronx, N.Y., Apr. 10, 1940; d. William B. and Laura (Libov) Pashkow; m. Marvin R. Kaplan, Aug. 16, 1962 (dec. 1980); children: Eliot, Mara; m. Timothy Sweeney, 1985 (div. 1986). BA, Smith Coll., 1962; MA, Ariz. State U., 1974, PhD, 1979. Presch. dir., tchr. Temple Beth Israel, Phoenix, 1967-72; tchr. Washington Sch. Dist., Phoenix, 1972-74, coord., 1974-75, prin., 1975-81; asst. supt. Paradise Valley Unified Sch. Dist., Phoenix, 1981-83, supt., 1984-92, Shawnee Mission Unified Sch. Dist., Overland Park, Kans., 1992—. Named Ariz. Supt. of Yr., 1992, Ariz. Sch. Bd. Assn. Supt. of Yr., 1987-88; named to Top 100 Educators, Exec. Educator mag., 1986. Mem. Am. Assn. Sch. Adminstrs. Office: Shawnee Mission Unified Sch Dist 512 7235 Antioch Rd Shawnee Mission KS 66204-1758

KAPLAN, NADIA, writer; b. Chgo., Feb. 28, 1921; d. Peter and Aniela (Buchynska) Charydchak; m. Norman Kaplan, July 25, 1942 (dec. July 1989); children: Fawn Marie Stom, Norma Jean Martinez. BEd, Pestalozzi Froebel Tchrs. Coll, Chgo., 1948; postgrad., UCLA, 1947, L.A. City Coll., U. Hawaii, Pepperdine U., 1970, Santa Monica Coll., 1981-87. Cert. tchr., Calif. Photographer, mgr. Great Lakes (Ill.) Naval Tng. Sta., 1942-45; primary/kindergarten tchr. L.A. Unified Sch. Dist., 1946-81. Contbr. articles to profl. jours.; creator puzzles various mags. Vol. recreational tchr. Found. for Jr. Blind, L.A., 1956-75, vol. camp counselor Camp Bloomfield, Calif., camp dir., 1956-61, leader cross-country study tour for blind teenagers, 1962; mem. dem. Nat. Com., 1985—. Pestalozzi Froebel Tchrs. Coll. scholar, 1938-41; recipient Norman Kaplan Life Achievement award, 2003. UK Blind, 2003. Mem. AAUW, Women Writers West (membership chair 1982-84), United Tchrs. L.A., Calif. Ret. Tchrs. Assn., Assn. Ret. Tchrs. Ukrainian Orthodox. Avocations: writing, bonsai cultivation, doll collecting, travel, golf. Home: 1827 Fanning St Los Angeles CA 90026-1439

KAPLAN, PHYLLIS, artist, composer; b. Bklyn. d. Abraham and Ida (Heller) Kaplan. BFA, Cooper Union, 1972; postgrad., Domus Acad., Milan, 1985. Curator art exhibit Orgn. Ind. Artists, NYC, 1995—96, Westside Arts Coalition, 1997; artist in residence Hungarian Multicultural Ctr., Lake Balaton, Hungary, 2002, F. J. Music Sch., Balatonfured, 2002. Lectr., presenter in field. Exhibitions include Lever House, NYC, 1969, Berkshire Mus., Pittsfield, Mass., 1970, LI U., NYC, 1975, Internat. Female Artists Biennial, Stockholm, 1994, Nat. Mus. Women in the Arts, Beijing, 1995, Three Rivers Arts Festival, Carnegie Mus., Pitts., 1995—96, 2001, Fine Arts Mus. L.I., Hempstead, 1996—97, Cork Gallery, Lincoln Ctr., NYC, 1997, Blue Mountain Gallery Invitationals, 1996—98, Trevi Flash Art Mus., Italy, 1998, World Artists for Tibet at Blue Mountain, 1998, Halpert Biennial, Boone, NC, 1999, Blue Mountain Gallery Invitationals, NYC, 2000, 2001, Montgomery Coll. Gallery of Art, Rockville, Md., 2002, Canajoharie Libr. and Art Gallery Invitational, 2002 (Honorable Mention, 2002), City Hall, Balatonfured, 2002, Canajoharie Libr. and Art Gallery Invitational, 2003; contbr. paintings to various publs. including Kings Courier, 1974, The Villager N.Y.C., 1994, Vizivarosi Gallery, Budapest, 2004, ann. calendar Orgn. Ind. Artists; exhibitions include Biola U., La Miranda, Calif. Recipient award for patriotism, US Savs. Bond Dr., 1987, hon. mention award, Sharjah Art Mus., United Arab Emirates, 2000, Open Space Gallery, 2000, Mayfair, Allentown, Pa., 2000, Art Environ. Advocacy U. Oreg., Eugene, 2000, Virtue Coll. Visual Arts Gallery, St. Paul, Minn., 2000, Snapshot Contemporary Mus., Balt., 2000, 35th Internat. Exhbn., San Bernardino County Mus., Redlands, Calif., 2000—01, U. South Fla. Coll. Marine Sci., St. Petersburg, 2001, Sharjah Internat. Arts Biennial, United Arab Emirates, 2001, Univ. Place Gallery, Cambridge Art Assn. Nat. Prize Show, Mass., 2001, pub. project, bear sculpture painting project for Black Bear Film Festival, Milford, Pa., 2001, Artists Studio Tour, Hoboken, NJ, 2001; grantee Artists Space, Ind. Project, 1999. Mem.: Greene County Coun. Arts, Monroe County Arts Coun. (instr. 2001). Avocations: travel, classical music. E-mail: phylliskaplan@mymailstation.com.

KAPLAN, ROSALIND PERLOW, ophthalmologist; b. Bklyn., Oct. 23, 1939; d. Jack and Sylvie (Novick) Perlow; m. Barry Kaplan, June 24, 1962; children: Andrew, Scott. BS magna cum laude, CUNY, 1960; postgrad., Albert Einstein Coll. Medicine, 1960-62; MD, U. Md., Balt., 1964. Diplomate Am. Bd. Ophthalmology. Intern Washington Hosp. Ctr., 1964-65; resident in ophthalmology Bronx (N.Y.) Eye Infirmary, 1965-69; pvt. practice, N.Y.C., 1969-91; fellow in neuro-ophtholmology Columbia-Presbyn. Hosp., N.Y.C., 1992-93, assoc. attending in neuro-ophthalmology, 1993-95. Fellow Am. Acad. Ophthalmology; mem. Am. Med. Women's Assn. (exec. bd. Westchester br., past chpt. pres.), New York County Med. Soc., Phi Beta Kappa. Avocations: tennis, cosmology, fitness, art, painting. Home: 190 E 72d St # 15D New York NY 10021

KAPLAN, RUTH JEAN, mental health services professional, social worker; b. L.A., June 3, 1952; M of Social Welfare, U. Calif., Berkeley, 1980. LCSW. Dir. adolescent svcs. Gladman Meml. Hosp., Oakland, Calif., 1980—88; dir. cmty. svcs. Telecare Corp., Alameda, Calif., 1988—91; dir. intake ops. U.S. Behavioral Health, Emeryville, Calif., 1991—93, v.p. employer divsn. San Francisco, 1995—98; sr. v.p. pub. sector divsn. United Behavioral Health, San Francisco, 1998—, sr. v.p. strategic initiatives, 2002—. Sec. NASW, 1991—93. Sec.-treas. NASW, Berkeley, 1988—91, sec., 1991—93. Recipient Nat. award, Eli Lilly and Nat. Mental Health Congress, 2000. Office: United Behavioral Health 425 Market St 27th Fl San Francisco CA 94105 Business E-Mail: ruth_j_kaplan@uhc.com.

KAPLAN, SANDRA LEE, artist; b. Cin., May 23, 1943; d. Howard and Helen (Katz) K.; m. Stanley Joseph Dragul, 1964 (div. 1974); 1 child, Sacha; m. Robert Lawrence Denerstein, 1986. Student, Art Acad. Cin., 1960-61; BFA with honors, Pratt Inst., Bklyn., 1965; student, CUNY, 1968-70. Illustrator Christian Sci. Monitor, Boston, 1991—94; drawing instr. Denver C.C., 1991—92; antique dealer Wazee Deco, Denver, 1992—2002; painting instr. Art Students League of Denver, 2001—. Com. mem. Arvada Ctr. for the Arts, 1994-96. Sole exhibits in various galleries including Dubins Gallery, L.A., 1988, Ventana Gallery, Santa Fe, 1985-90, Land-Escapes in Arvada Ctr. for the Arts, Arvada, Colo., 1991, Human and or Nature in Nicolaysen Mus., Casper, Wyo., 1992, Rule Modern & Contemporary, Denver, 1993, 96, Land-Escape in Wave Hill, Riverdale, N.Y., 1995, Great Am. Artists, Cin., Ohio, 1996-2003, Boulder (Colo.) Mus. Contemporary Art, 1997, Indigo Gallery, Boca Raton, Fla., 1997, Laura Paul Gallery, Cin., Ohio, 1998, Cline Fine Art, Santa Fe, N.Mex., 1999, 2000, William Havu Gallery, Denver, 2003, "Eden" Mingel Ctr. for the Arts, Denver, 2003; commd. works Hong Kong Marriott Hotel, 1988, Gt. West Life Assurance Co., 1991, Arvada City Hall, 1993, Sch. Pharmacy U. Colo., 1994. Trustee Mus. Contemporary Art, Denver, 2002—, sec., 2003—. Yaddo Corp. fellow, 1985; Ludwig Vogelstein grantee, 1986, Covisions grantee Colo. Coun. of Arts, 1992. Democrat. Jewish. Avocations: exercise, reading, movies. Studio: St Francis Sch 235 S Sherman St Denver CO 80209-1620

KAPLAN, SHARON BARBARA BERNSTEIN, music educator; b. Detroit, Dec. 1, 1939; d. David and Lillian Cecelia (Schwartz) Bernstein; m. Eli Kaplan, Nov. 22, 1970; children: Ari Moshe, Adina Chai, Julie Rachel MacTaggart. BA in Music, U. Minn., 1977; postgrad., Wayne State U., 1978—81. Ind. music tchr., Detroit and Mpls., 1962—. Performer; mem. KOLOT performing group, 1994—98. Creator, illustrator 8 music activity books, composer (2 piano books). Vol. local schs., 1970s through 1980s. Mem.: Nat. Guild of Piano Tchrs. (pres. Oak Park, Mich. chpt. 1966—68), Nat. Fedn. Music Clubs (pres. local chpt. 2001—), Minn. Music Tchrs. Assn. (sec. exec. bd. 1992—96, adminstr. sight playing program 1995—98, v.p. for convs. 1998—2002, chair piano exam devel. com. 2001—, tech. chair 1993—95, nat. cert. tchr. music, 5-time winner piano duet competition, named Vol. of Yr. 2003). Avocations: on-line jigsaw puzzles, reading, dancing. E-mail: sharonkaplan@sihope.com.

KAPLAN, SHEILA, academic administrator; b. Bklyn. BA in History, Hunter Coll.; MA, The Johns Hopkins U.; PhD in History, CUNY. Instr. history CUNY System; dir. spl. baccalaureate program CUNY; v.p. acad. affairs Winona (Minn.) State U.; vice-chancellor for acad. affairs Minn. State U. System; chancellor U. Wis.-Parkside, Kenosha, 1986-93; pres. Met State Coll., Denver, 1993—. Bd. dirs. Kenosha Area Devel. Corp., Racine County Econ. Devel. Corp.; chmn. bd. Council for Adult and Experiential Learning. Office: Metropolitan State Coll Office of President PO Box 173362 Denver CO 80217-3362

KAPLAN, SYDNEY JANET, English educator; b. L.A., Dec. 28, 1939; d. Leo and Frieda (Kaufman) Zendell; divorced; 1 child, Frederick Nathan Kaplan. BA, UCLA, 1961, MA, 1966, PhD, 1971. Tchr. Manual Arts High Sch., L.A., 1963-64; asst. prof. U. Wash., Seattle, 1971-77, assoc. prof., 1978-91, dir. women's studies, 1982-92, prof., 1992—. Author: Feminine Consciousness in the Modern British Novel, 1975, Katherine Mansfield and the Origins of Modernist Fiction, 1991; contbr. articles to profl. jours; assoc. editor Signs: Jour. of Women in Culture and Soc., 1995-2000; mem. editorial bd. Tulsa Studies in Women's Literature, 1981. Travel grantee U. Wash., 1978, 1998, Royalty Rsch. Fund scholar, 1998; NEH fellow, 2000-01. Mem. Modern Lang. Assn., Virginia Woolf Soc., Wash. Trails Assn., Sierra Club. Democrat. Avocation: hiking. Office: U Wash Dept English PO Box 354330 Seattle WA 98195-4330

KAPLE, DEBORAH A. writer; d. John D. and Esther L. Kaple; m. Miguel A. Centeno, June 27, 1992; children: Alexander Kaple Centeno, Maya Kaple Centeno. BA, Ohio State U., 1979; MA, George Washington, 1982; PhD, Princeton U., 1991. Writer John W. Wright Lit. Agy., New York, NY, 1992—2003; assoc. dir. Sandra Starr Found., Princeton, NJ, 1999—2002. Tchr. Princeton U., Princeton, NJ, 1997—2000. Author: Dream of a Red Factory. Assoc. dir. Sandra Starr Found., Princeton, NJ, 1999—2002. Recipient First place fiction award, Coll. N.J., 2003. Democrat. Avocations: reading, travel, creating art. Home: 115 Prospect Ave Princeton NJ 08540

KAPLOWITZ, KAREN (JILL), lawyer, business consultant; b. New Haven, Nov. 27, 1946; d. Charles Cohen and Estelle (Gerber) K.; m. Alan George Cohen, Aug. 17, 1980; children: Benjamin, Elizabeth. BA cum laude, Barnard Coll., 1968; JD, U. Chgo., 1971. Bar: Calif. 1971, U.S. Dist. Ct. (Cen. Dist.) Calif. 1971. Assoc. O'Melveny & Myers, L.A., 1971-74; ptnr. Bardeen, Bersch & Kaplowitz, L.A., 1974-80, Alschuler, Grossman & Pines, L.A., 1980-96, of counsel, 1997—. Contbr. articles to profl. jours. Mem. vis. com. U. Chgo. Law Sch., 1990-93. Mem. ABA (chmn. employer-employee rels. com. of tors and ins. practice sect.), Assn. Bus. Trial Lawyers (pres.), Calif. Women Lawyers (Fay Stender award 1982), Women Lawyers Assn. L.A. Home: 1 Woodside Ln New Hope PA 18938-9281 Office: 1620 26th St Fourth Fl N Tower Santa Monica CA 90404-4060 E-mail: kkaplowitz@newellis.com.

KAPLUN BRAUN, JEANNETTE, announcer, communications consultant; b. El Paso, Tex., Mar. 19, 1973; d. Robert M. and Doris Zeldis Kaplun; m. Joseph M. Braun, Dec. 26, 1998. B in Social Scis., U. Gabriela Mistral, Santiago, 1991; B in Mass Comm., Pontificia U. Católica de Chile, Santiago, 1995; postgrad., U. Miami, 1997—. Reporter Editl. Sipimex, Santiago, 1994; news reporter, prodr. Channel 13, Santiago, 1994—96; tchg. asst. Journalism Sch. Pontificia U. Catolica de Chile, Santiago, 1994—97; account exec. Fleishman-Hillard, Inc., Coral Gables, Fla., 1997—98; host of vida@linea@ Discovery Channel Latin Am./Iberia, Miami, Fla., 1998—2001; v.p. content and comm. TodoBebe.com, Inc., Aventura, Fla., 1999—. Radio talk show host TodoBebe Radio, 2002—. Recipient award, Hispanic Media 100, 2002; scholar Acad. Merit scholar, U. Gabriela Mistral, 1991. Mem.: Soc. of Profl. Journalists, Nat. Assn. of Hispanic Journalists. Avocations: travel, technology, photography. Personal E-mail: jkaplun@todobebe.com.

KAPNER, LORI, marketing professional; d. Joseph and Marion Kapner; m. Walter David Hosp, Oct. 7, 2001. BA in journalism, U. Md. Asst. editor Am. Machinist mag.; assoc. mng. editor Success mag., 1984; mgr. bus. devel. Lippincott & Marguiles Inc., NYC, v.p., 1992; sr. v.p. Addison, NYC, 1995—98, prin., 1998—99; founder, pres. Kapner Consulting Inc., NYC, 1999—. Adv. bd. Make-a-Wish Found. Mem.: NY Women in Comm. Office: Kapner Consulting 1 Penn Plaza New York NY 10119 E-mail: lkapner@kapnerconsulting.com.*

KAPPAN, SANDRA JEAN, elementary school educator; b. Buffalo, N.Y., Sept. 25, 1961; d. Joseph Albert Sr. and Margaret Alice (Krupa) Savash; 1 child, Jason T. Cert. in dental assisting, Bd. of Coop. Ednl. Svcs., 1979; AAS in Secretarial Sci., Erie C.C., 1982; BS, Daemen Coll., 1997; MS in Edn. and Reading, St. Bonaventure U., 1998. Cert. spl. edn., pre-kindergarten, kindergarten, grades 1-6. Acctg. clk. Children's Hosp. of Buffalo, 1984-87; legal sec., receptionist Lofton, Savage, & Cain, Esqs., Charleston, S.C., 1987-88; sec., transciptionist Trident Regional Med. Ctr., Charleston, S.C., 1988-90; adminstrv. asst. Children's Hosp. of Buffalo, 1990-93; substitute tchr. Erie 1 Bd. Coop. Ednl. Svcs., Erie County, N.Y., 1996-97; resource room tchr. Lancaster (N.Y.) Ctrl. Sch. Dist., 1997; spl. edn. tchr. Erie I Bd. Ednl. Ednl. Svcs., Erie County, N.Y., 1997-98; elem. tchr. St. James Sch., Depew, N.Y., 1998-99, Amherst Ctrl. Sch. Dist., 1999-2000; spl. edn. tchr. Ctrl. Sch. Dist., West Seneca, N.Y., 2000—. Spl. edn. tchr. Erie I BOCES, summer 1999; presenter in field. Vol. PTA, Lancaster Ctrl. Sch. Dist., 1994—, Boy Scouts Am.; vol. after-sch. reading/math. program West Seneca Sch. Dist.; vol. Americare Kids Reading Program, 2000—; vol., mem. St. John's Luth. Ch., Sunday Sch. and Choir, Lancaster, 1993—. Scholarship Lancaster Assn. of Svc. Pers., 1996. Mem.: Daemen Coll. Alumni Assn., Phi Delta Kappa. Democrat. Lutheran. Home: 479 Lake Ave Lancaster NY 14086-9666

KAPPENBERG, MARILYN KASCIUS, library director; b. Hicksville, N.Y., July 19, 1948; d. Adolf A. and Mary T. Kascius; m. Richard L. Kappenberg, Apr. 5, 1975; children: Neal, Glenn. BA, Molloy Coll., 1970; MLS, L.I. U., 1972. Children's libr. Hicksville (N.Y.) Pub. Libr., 1972-90; head ref. Hicksville Pub. Libr., 1990-95, asst. libr. dir., 1992-95; libr. dir. Wantagh (N.Y.) Pub. Libr., 1992—, Plainedge Pub. Libr., Massapequa, NY, 2001—. Sec. Hicksville Lions Club, 1990-95. Mem. ALA, Nassau County Libr. Assn., Wantagh C. of C. (mem.-at-large 1995—). Avocations: writing, volunteering. Home: 2873 Janet Ave North Bellmore NY 11710-2026 Office: Plainedge Pub Libr 1060 Hicksville Rd Massapequa NY 11758

KAPPLER, ANN M. lawyer, finance company executive; b. New Brunswick, N.J., Dec. 24, 1957; AB magna cum laude, Darmouth Coll., 1979; JD, NYU, 1986. Bar: N.Y. 1988, DC 1989. Law clk. to Hon. Abner J. Mikva U.S. Ct. Appeals (DC cir.), Washington, 1986—87; law clk. to Hon. Harry Blackmun U.S. Supreme Ct., 1987—88; assoc. Jenner & Block, 1989—93, ptnr., 1994—98; sr. v.p., gen. counsel Fannie Mae, Washington, 1998—. Editor-in-chief: NYU Law Rev., 1985—86. Mem.: ABA, Order of Coif, DC Bar Assn., Internat. Human Rights Law Group (bd. dirs. 1999—2001), Coun. Ct. Excellence (bd. dirs. 1999—2001), Wash. Lawyers Com. Civil Rights and Urban Affairs (bd. dirs. 1999—2001). Office: Fannie Mae Legal Dept 3900 Wisconsin Ave NW Washington DC 20016

KAPPNER, AUGUSTA SOUZA, academic administrator; b. Bronx, June 25, 1944; d. Augusto and Monica Thomasina (Fraser) Souza; m. Thomas Kappner, Aug. 14, 1965; children: Tania, Diana. AB, Barnard Coll., 1966; MSW, Hunter Coll., N.Y.C., 1968; DSW, Columbia U., 1984. Cert. social worker, N.Y. Lectr., community affairs specialist Dept. Urban Affairs, Grad. Div., Hunter Coll., 1968-70; adj. instr., field supr. N.Y.C. C.C., 1970-71; instr., coord. urban leadership unit Columbia U. Sch. Social Wk., 1970-72; asst. prof., dir. admissions and student svcs. SUNY, Stony Brook, 1973-74; assoc. prof., chmn. human svcs. divsn. LaGuardia C.C., 1974-78, prof., dean continuing edn., 1978-84; dean acad. affairs Adult & Continuing Edn., CUNY, 1984, dean acad. affairs, instructional rsch., adult learning, 1984-86; pres. Borough of Manhattan C.C./CUNY, 1986-92; asst. sec. of vocat. and adult edn. Dept. of Edn., Washington, 1993-95; pres. Bank Street Coll., N.Y.C., 1995—. Cons. in field; lectr. in field; Adult Literacy Media Alliance; mem. adv. panel Nat. Ctr. for Innovation in Governing Am. Edn., Nat. Writing Project; mem. N.Y.C. Bd. Edn. Adv. Bd. for Universal Pre-Kindergarten; former mem. Commn. for Nation of Lifelong Learners; commr., Commn. Higher Edn., Middle States Assn.; former mem. adv. bd. Fund for the Improvement of Post Secondary Edn., U.S. Dept. of Edn. Trustees Marymount Manhattan Coll.; mem. N.Y. State Edn. Commr.'s Task Force for the Edn. of Children and Youth at Risk, N.Y. State Gov.'s Coun. on Literacy, N.Y.C. Bd. Edn. Chancellor's U./Schs. Collaborative steering com.; appointed by Mayor of City of N.Y. to Joint Commn. on Integrity in Pub. Schs.; bd. dirs. N.Y. Urban Coalition; mem. N.Y.C. Coun. on Econ. Edn. Whitney M. Young Jr. fellow, 1982, USPHS awardee, 1981, Ford Found. fellow, 1973, Silverman Fund awardee, 1968, NIMH fellow, 1967, others; recipient Harlem Sch. Arts Humanitarian award, 1990, Am. Assn. Women in Community and Jr. Colls. Presdl. award, 1989, Asian Ams. for Equality Community Svc. award, 1989, Columbia U. Medal of Excellence, 1988, Barnard Coll. medal of distinction, 1988, Found. for Child Devel. Centennial award, 1999, Morris T. Keeton award Coun. for Adult and Exptl. Learning, others. Mem. Am. Coun. on Edn.

KAPRIELIAN, RACHEL, state legislator; Mem. Mass. Ho. of Reps., Boston, 1991—. Home: 320 Mt Auburn St Watertown MA 02472-1965 Office: Mass Ho of Reps State House Rm 33 Boston MA 02133

KAPRIELIAN, VICTORIA SUSAN, medical educator; b. The Bronx, N.Y., June 30, 1959; d. Walter and Julia (Hachigian) K. BA, Brown U., 1981; MD, UCLA, 1985. Diplomate Am. Bd. Family Practice. Resident Duke-Watts Family Practice, Durham, N.C., 1985-88; fellow UCLA Family Medicine, L.A., 1988-89; asst. clin. prof. Duke U. Med. Ctr., Durham, N.C., 1989-98; chief, divsn. predoctoral edn. and faculty devel., dept cmty and family medicine Duke U., Durham, N.C., 1994-96; assoc. clin. prof. Duke U. Med. Ctr., Durham, NC, 1998—2003, clin. prof., 2003—; fellowship dir., dept. cmty. and family medicine Duke U., Durham, N.C., 1994-99, 2000—, dir. predoctoral edn. and faculty devel., 1996-99. Dir. inpatient svc. divsn. cmty. medicine Duke U., 1989-90, dir. sports medicine, 1989-94, dir. arts medicine, 1989-95, dir. predoctoral edn., 1990-2000; dir. quality improvement and continuing med. edn. dept. cmty. and family medicine, 1996—; dir. faculty devel. dept. cmty. and family medicine, Duke U., 2000—. Fellow Am. Acad. Family Physicians (pub. com. 1985, mental health com. 1986-88); mem. N.C. Acad. Family Physicians (bd. dirs. 1998-02, edn. com. 1989-90, med. sch. affairs 1990—2001, chair of com. 1991-97), Soc. Tchrs. Family Medicine (steering com., predoc. dir. working group 1995-98, chair 1998). Avocations: physical fitness, singing, science fiction, ethnic cooking. Office: Duke U Div Family Medicine PO Box 3886 Durham NC 27710-0001

KAPSNER, CAROL RONNING, state supreme court justice; b. Bismarck, N.D. m. John Kapsner; children: Mical, Caithlin. BA in English lit., Coll. of St. Catherine; postgrad., Oxford U.; MA in English lit., Ind. U.; JD, U. Colo., 1977. Pvt. practice, Bismarck, 1977-98; justice N.D. Supreme Ct., 1998—. Mem. N.D. Bar Assn. (past bd. govs.), N.D. Trial Lawyers Assn. (past bd. govs.), Big Muddy Bar Assn. (past pres.). Office: Supreme Ct State Capitol 600 E Boulevard Ave Dept 180 Bismarck ND 58505-0530 Fax: 701-328-4480. E-mail: ckapsner@ndcourts.com.

KAPSNER, MARY, state representative; b. Anchorage, Alaska, Aug. 31, 1973; 1 child, Conrad. Grad., U. No. Colo., 1994, U. Alaska, Fairbanks, 1995, U. Alaska, Anchorage, 1998. Coord. bethel Coastal Village Seafoods; fisheries technician Alaska Dept. Fish and Game; coml. fisherman; ptnr. Harvest Moon Seafoods, Inc.; legis. intern, 1996; mem. Alaska Ho. of Reps., 1998—. Legis. corr. ARCS Midday News. Youth rep. Nat. Congress Am. Indians, 1995—96; youth con. Inuit Circumpolar Conf., 1998—; mem. bd. dirs. Lower Kuskokwim Econ. Devel., 1998—, Gov. Coun. Safe Water and Sanitation, 1998—; mem. bd. dirs. statewide expansion Boys and Girls Clubs, Anchorage, 1999—; rural outreach coord. Girls and Boys Clubs Am. Democrat. Avocations: fishing, travel. Office: State Capitol Rm 424 Juneau AK 99801-1182

KAPTUR, MARCIA CAROLYN, congresswoman; b. Toledo, Ohio, June 17, 1946; BA, U. Wis., 1968; M. Urban Planning, U. Mich., 1974; postgrad., U. Manchester, (Eng.), 1974, MIT; LLD (hon.), U. Toledo. Urban planner; asst. dir. urban affairs domestic policy staff White House, 1977-79; mem. U.S. Congress from 9th Ohio dist., Washington, 1983—; mem. appropriations com., Agr. subcom., D.C. subcom., VA, HUD, and indep. agys. subcom. Bd. dirs. Nat. Ctr. Urban Ethnic Affairs; adv. com. Gund Found.; exec. com. Lucas County Democratic Com.; mem. Dem. Women's Campaign Assn. Mem. Am. Planning Assn., Am. Inst. Cert. Planners, NAACP, Urban League, Polish Mus., U. Mich. Urban Planning Alumni Assn. (bd. dirs.), Polish Am. Hist. Assn. Clubs: Lucas County Dem. Bus. and Profl. Women's, Fulton County Dem. Women's. Democrat. Roman Catholic. Office: US House of Reps 2366 Rayburn Washington DC 20515-0001 also: One Maritime Pla 6th Fl Toledo OH 43604*

KARABATSOS, ELIZABETH ANN, career counseling services executive; b. Geneva, Nebr., Oct. 25, 1932; d. Karl Christian and Margaret Maurine (Emrich) Brinkman; m. Kimon Tom Karabatsos, Apr. 21, 1957 (div. Feb. 1981); children: Tom Kimon, Maurine Elizabeth, Karl Kimon. BS, U. Nebr., 1954; postgrad., Ariz. State U., 1980; Cert. contemporary exec. devel., George Washington U., 1985; M Orgnl. Mgmt., U. Phoenix, 1994; student, Scottsdale (Ariz.) C.C., 1999. Cert. tchr. Ariz. Instr. bus. Fairbury (Nebr.) H.S., 1954—55; staff asst. U.S. Congress, Washington, 1955—60; with Karabatsos & Co. Pub. Rels., Washington, 1960—73; conf. asst. to asst. adminstr. and dep. adminstr. Gen. Services Adminstrn., Washington, 1973—76; dir. corr. Office Pres.-Elect, Washington, 1980; assoc. dir. adminstrv. svcs. Pres. Pers.-White House, Washington, 1981; dept. asst. to Sec. and Dep. Sec. Def., Washington, 1981—86, asst. to, 1987—89; dir. govt. and civic affairs McDonnell Douglas Helicopter Co., Mesa, Ariz., 1989—90, gen. mgr. gen. svcs., 1990—92, co. ombudsman, community rels. exec., 1992—95; exec. asst. to dir. adminstrn. State of Ariz., 1995—96; prin., owner Karabatsos & Assocs., bus. consulting and mediation svcs., Scottsdale, 1995—. Bur. chief Office Prevention and Health Promotion Ariz. Dept. Health Svcs., 1997-98; adj. prof. Met. Coll. Phoenix, 2004. Mem. Nat. Mus. Women in Art, Washington; bd. dirs. U.S. C. of C. Com. on Labor & Tng.; mem. Gov.'s Sci. and Tech. Com.; mem. Ariz. Com. Employer Support the Guard and Res., 1991; active Gov. Com. for Ariz. Clean and Beautiful, World Affairs Coun. Ariz. Mem.: ASTD, AAUW, Ariz. Dispute Resolution Assn. (bd. dirs.), Assn. Conflict Resolution, Am. Arbitration Assn., Women in Def., U. Nebr. Cather Group, Internat. Friends Transformative Art, Order Ea. Star, Pi Beta Phi, Pi Omega Pi. Episcopalian. Home and Office: 4446 E Camelback Rd # 110 Phoenix AZ 85018 Office Phone: 602-956-3317. Office Fax: 602-954-0225. Personal E-mail: ebkarabats@aol.com.

KARAER, ARMA JANE, ambassador; b. St. Paul, Apr. 17, 1941; m. Yasar Mehmet Karaer; 2 children. BA, U. Minn., 1962; postgrad., Osmania U., Hyderabad, India. With Fgn. Svc., 1967—, consular officer, 1967-69, consular bur. Dept. State, 1969-71, 1972, comml. officer Kinshasa, Zaire, 1976-80, comml. attache Ankara, Turkey, 1980-84, desk officer for Turkey Dept. State, 1984-86, dep. prin. officer, 1986-88, dep. chief mission Mbabane, Swaziland, 1988-91, chief coordination divsn. Bur. Intelligence & Rsch. Dept. State, 1991-93, dep. chief mission, 1993-96, U.S. amb. to Papua, New Guinea, Solomon Islands and Vanuatu, 1996—. Office: Dept State Washington DC 20520-0001

KARAIM, BETTY JUNE, retired librarian; b. Devils Lake, N.D., May 27, 1936; d. Erick Henry and Anna Caroline (Steen) Keck; m. William James Karaim, Dec. 7, 1955 (dec. 1983); children: Reed, Lisa, Ryan, Lynn, Rachel, Lee, Lara. BS in Edn., Mayville (N.D.) State U., 1958; postgrad., U. N.D., summer 1961; MLS, U. Okla., 1972; postgrad., No. Mont. Coll., 1979, 81. Libr. Cando (N.D.) High Sch., 1960-62; asst. libr., tchr. Mayville State Coll., 1962-79; libr. Havre (Mont.) Pub. Schs., 1979-82; libr. dir. Mayville State U., 1982-99, ret., prof. emerita, 1999. Bd. dirs. Mayville (N.D.) Pub. Libr., 1991-97, 2000—, pres., 1994-97, v.p., 2002—; bd. dirs. Goose River Heritage Ctr., Mayville, 2000—, pres., 2002—; bd. dirs. M300 Assn. (arm of Mayville State U. Found.), 2000—, sec., 2002—. Recipient Orville Johnson Meritorious Svc. award, 1992, Disting. Alumni award Mayville State U. Alumni Found., 1997. Democrat. Avocations: reading, travel. Home: 320 1st St NW Mayville ND 58257-1107 E-mail: bjkaraim@polarcomm.com.

KARAKEY, SHERRY JOANNE, real estate company executive, interior designer; b. Wendell, Idaho, Apr. 16, 1942; d. John Donald and Vera Ella (Frost) Kingery; children: Artist Roxanne, Buddy (George II), Kami JoAnne, Launi JoElla. Student, Ariz. State U., 1960. Corp. sec., treas. Karbel Metals Co., Phoenix, 1963-67; sec. to pub. Scottsdale (Ariz.) Daily Progress, 1969-72; with D-Velco Mfg. of Ariz., Phoenix, 1959-62, dir., exec. v.p., sec., treas., 1972-87; mng. ptnr., financial and real estate investment Karitage, Ltd., Scottsdale, 1987—. E-mail: footnotes@cox.net.

KARALEKAS, ANNE, business executive; b. Boston, Nov. 6, 1946; d. Christus and Helen (Vogiantzis) K. AB, Wheaton Coll., Norton, Mass., 1968; AM, Harvard U., 1969, PhD, 1974. Chief project mgr. def. and arms control project Commn. on Orgn. of Govt. for Conduct of Fgn. Policy, Washington, 1974-75; sr. staff mem. Senate Select Com. on Intelligence, Washington, 1975-78; sr. assoc. McKinsey & Co., Washington, 1978-85; mktg. mgr. The Washington Post, 1985-87, dir. mktg., 1987-89; pub. Washington Post Mag., 1989-96, dir. specialty products group, 1993-96; gen. mgr. Washington Sidewalk, Microsoft Corp., Washington, 1996-99; bd. dirs. Digital Globe, Longmont, 1999—. Author: History of the CIA, 1976; contbr. articles and book revs. to profl. jours. Advisor fgn. policy Mondale-Ferraro Presdl. Campaign, Washington, 1984; trustee Wheaton Coll., Norton, 1985-88. Mem. Council on Fgn. Relations, Phi Beta Kappa. Greek Orthodox. Avocation: twentieth century art and lit.

KARAMAS, JOYCE EFTHEMIA, art educator, consultant, artist; b. Chgo., July 27, 1926; d. Nicholas Ernest Karamesoutis and Anastasia Asemake Vaselopoulos. BA in Art Edn., Sch. Art Inst., Chgo., 1951; MLS, Chgo. State U., 1961. Cert. art tchr. K-12 Ill., sch. libr. Ill. Tchr. Chgo. Pub. Schs., 1951—62, art supr., 1962—72, tchr., libr., 1972—80, art. coord. curriculum dept., 1980—85; artist Douglas, Mich., 1986—. Coord. sch. art at local mus., Chgo., 1962—72, Chgo., 1980—84; coord. organized children's exhibits at pub. places, Chgo., 1980—84. Exhibited in group shows at Mus. Contemporary Crafts, N.Y.C., 1966, Ill. State Traveling Exhbn., 1968, one-woman shows include Chgo. Pub. Libr., 1972. Recipient Merit award, Am. Craftsmen Coun., 1966, Invitational award, Ill. Craftsmen coun., 1968. Avocations: photography, travel. Home: PO Box 174 3057 Peach St Douglas MI 49406-0174

KARAN, DONNA (DONNA FASKE), fashion designer; b. Forest Hills, N.Y., Oct. 2, 1948; m. Mark Karan, 1971 (div.); 1 child, Gabrielle; m. Stephan Weiss, 1983 (dec. June 2001) BFA, Parsons Sch. Design, 1987. Intern Liz Claiborne; With Addenda Co., to 1968; with Anne Klein & Co., N.Y.C., 1968-84, co-designer, 1971-74, designer, 1974-84; owner, designer, ptnr. Donna Karan Co., N.Y.C., 1984-96, created DKNY clothing line, 1988, chmn. bd., chief designer, 1996—2001; (Donna Karan merges with LVMH, 2001); chief designer Donna Karan Co., N.Y.C., 2001—. Showed first complete collection for Anne Klein & Co. in 1974; collaborator on Anne Klein collections with Louis dell'Olio; author: DKNY: NYC, 1994. Bd. dirs. Design Industries Found. for AIDS; co-chair Kids for Kids, 1993, Ovarian Cancer Rsch. Super Saturday, East Hampton, N.Y, summers 1998, 99. Recipient Coty award, 1977, Awards Coun. of Fashion Designers of Am., 1985, 86, 92, Frontrunner award Sara Lee Corp., 1992; co-recipient (with Louis dell'Olio) Coty Return award, 1981, Coty Hall of Fame citation, 1982, Coty award, 1984; named Menswear Designer of Yr. Coun. Fashion Designers Am., 1992. Mem. Fashion Designers Am. (bd. dirs.) Office: Donna Karan Co 550 Seventh Ave New York NY 10018*

KARANT-NUNN, SUSAN CATHERINE, history educator; b. Evanston, Ill. d. Max and Catherine (Cass) Karant; m. Frederick M. Nunn. BA, Cornell Coll., Mt. Vernon, Iowa, 1963; MA, Ind. U., 1967, PhD, 1971. Asst. prof. Portland (Oreg.) State U., 1970-76, assoc. prof., 1976-83, prof., 1983—. Author: Luther's Pastors, 1979, Zwickau in Transition, 1987; co-editor: Germania Illustrata, 1992; contbr. articles to profl. jours. Recipient Kathryn McHale fellowship Ind. AAUW, 1968, grad. fellowship Ind. U., 1969, Travel grant to German Dem. Republic Am. Coun. Learned Socs., 1975, Exchange fellowships Internat. Res. and Exchanges Bd. to German Dem. Republic, 1977, 86, Travel grant to Germany Am. Philosophical Soc., 1979. Mem. Soc. for Reformation Rsch. (coun. mem. 1992—), Sixteenth Century Studies Conf. (pres. 1991-92). Office: Portland State Univ PO Box 751 Portland OR 97207-0751

KARASEK, MARY HAPAC, city treasurer, community volunteer; b. Cicero, Ill., Jan. 11, 1924; d. Martin Emil and Eva (Capak) Hapac; m. Edward Anton Karasek, Apr. 20, 1952; 1 child, Edward Anton Jr. Degree in liberal arts, Morton Coll., 1944. Libr. Pub. Libr., Cicero, Ill., 1947-53; treas. City of Berwyn, Ill., 1985—. Mem. Morton H.S. Bd. Edn., Cicero, 1968—76; trustee Morton Coll., Cicero, 1976—2001; mem. Berwyn PTA, 1959—; precinct capt. Berwyn Dem. Orgn., 1985—. Named Berwyn Citizen of the Yr. for Millennium Yr., 2000; recipient Alumnus award, Ill. C.C., 1991, Women in History award, Morton Twp., 1993, Sr. Citizen of Yr. award, Congressman Lipinski, 1992, Those Who Excel award, Ill. State Bd. Edn., 1982, Robert W. Teeter award, Berwyn Cicero YMCA, 1982, Disting. Pub. Svc. award, Berwyn Homeowners, 1996. Mem. Delta Kappa Gamma. Avocations: reading, walking, basketball, baseball. Home: 7015 29th Pl Berwyn IL 60402-2941

KARCH, JACQUELINE, artist; b. Newark, Jan. 17, 1946; d. Samuel Arthur and Miriam Francis K.; m. William Clinton Keach, June 27, 1991. Student, Art Students League, 1962—66; BFA, Syracuse U., 1968; MAT, R.I. Sch. of Design, 1971. Art tchr. Providence (R.I.) Pub. Schs., 1972-2000; artist, ceramic tile Ceramic Tiles, Providence, 1983-2000, LeLand, N.C., 2000—. One-woman shows include Gallery 401, Providence, RI, 1980, 1987, WHQR Gallery, Wilmington, N.C., 2003, exhibited in group shows at San Regret Gallery, Boston, 1980, Am. Soc. on Aging, San Diego, 1988, Gallery 401, Providence, 1986, Bell St. Gallery, 1991—92, visual documentary, Trinity Square Repertory Theatre Productions, 1983—85, Jewish Home for the Aged, 1988; costume designer : (plays) The Charlatans, 1972; The Red Hat; author: Recipes Remembered, 1996. Mem. The Arts Students League (life). Avocations: animal rescue, calligraphy, costume design, cooking, gardening. Office: Ceramic Tiles-Jacqueline Karch 904 Woodridge Ct SE Leland NC 28451 Office Phone: 910-383-6108.

KARCH, KAREN BROOKE, principal; b. Greensburg, Pa., Feb. 17, 1944; d. John Daniel and Louise Fluke (Reinfried) Karle; m. Robert Charles Karch, Apr. 2, 1966; children: Kara Brooke, Krista Kimberly. BA, Ohio Wesleyan U., 1965; MEd, Am. U., 1973, EdD, 1981. Tchr. Prince George County schs., Md., 1965-70; instr. English Montgomery Coll., Rockville, Md., 1976-79, No. Va. C.C., Alexandria, 1977-79; reading specialist Frederick (Md.) County Bd. Edn., 1979-81, media specialist, 1981-82, vice-prin., 1982-83; prin. Mid. sch., Walkersville, Md., 1983-88, Gaithersburg (Md.) Elem. Sch., 1988-94, Potomac (Md.) Elem Sch., 1994—. Instr. Bowie State U.; presenter in field. Leader Capital coun. Girl Scouts U.S.A., 1977-80. Mem. ASCD, Md. Mid. Sch. Assn., Nat. Mid. Sch. Assn., Nat. Assn. Secondary Sch. Prin., Montgomery County Elem. Sch. Adminstrs. Assn. (pres. 1989-90), Phi Kappa Phi, Phi Delta Kappa, Delta Kappa Gamma. Republican. Methodist. Avocations: running, skiing, sailing, tennis. Home: 13001 Glen Rd North Potomac MD 20878-8851 Office: Potomac Elem Sch 10311 River Rd Potomac MD 20854-4971

KARCHER, ELLEN M. state senator; b. Feb. 28, 1964; d. Alan J. Karcher; m. John L. Hochberg; children: Beth Hochberg, Avie Hochberg, Lael Hochberg. BA in English, MA in Polit. Sci. and Pub. Policy, Rutgers U. Mem. Marlboro (N.J.) Twp. Coun., 2001—, v.p., 2002, pres., 2003—; mem. N.J. State Senate, 2004—. Campaign mgr. N.J.'s Jobs, Edn. and Competitiveness Bond Issue, 1988. Mem.: Am. Polit. Sci. Assn., Mid Jersey Mothers Multiples, Phi Beta Kappa. Democrat. Mailing: 41 Center St Freehold NJ 07728

KARCHER, SUSAN MARIE, speech pathology/audiology services professional; b. Miami, Aug. 15, 1956; d. Walter Charles Hmielewski and Mary Ellen Kennedy; m. Guy Andrew Karcher, Oct. 19, 1996; children: Aaron, Sean, Sarah, Kaitlyn; m. Ernest Victor Collins IV, Apr. 15, 1981 (div. May 10, 1990); children: Melissa, Ernest. BS in Edn., We. Carolina U., 1978, MA in Edn., 1979. Cert. tchr. N.C., 1979, lic. speech pathologist N.C., 1980, cert. of clin. competence Am. Speech Hearing Assn., 1980. Speech pathologist Mountain Projects, Waynesville, NC, 1979—81, Cherokee (N.C.) Reservation Schs., 1981—86, Jackson County Schs., Sylva, NC, 1986—. Supr. student tchrs. Jackson County Pub. Schs., 1986—. Cheerleading coach We.Carolina U., Sylva, 1994—2001, Fairview Sch., Sylva, 1994—2001; chmn. parish coun. St. Mary's Cath. Ch., Sylva, 2001—02. Mem.: Am. Speech Hearing Assn., Couple to Couple League (instr. natural family planning 2001—). Republican. Roman Cath. Office: Fairview School Big Orange Way Sylva NC 28779

KARDON, JANET, museum director, curator, educator; b. Phila. d. Robert and Shirley (Drasin) Stolker; m. Robert Kardon, Nov. 19, 1955; children: Ross, Nina, Roy. BS in Edn., Temple U.; MA in Art History, U. Pa. Lectr. Phila. Coll. Art, 1968-75, dir. exhbns., 1975-78; dir. Inst. Contemporary Art, Phila., 1978-89, Am. Craft Mus., N.Y.C., 1989-95; ind. curator, 1996—. Adj. prof. Fashion Inst. of Tech., N.Y.C., Pratt Inst., Bklyn., Cooper Hewit; cons., panel mem. Nat. Endowment for Arts, 1975—; mus. panel mem. Pa. Coun. on Arts, Phila., 1988—; U.S. commr. Venice Biennale, Venice, 1980. Exhibitions include Labyrinths, Time, Artists SEts and Costumes, Laurie Anderson, Robert Mapplethorpe, David Salle, Gertrude and Otto Natzler; editor: Twentieth Century American Craft: A Centenary Project, The Ideal Home, 1900-1920, Revivals/Diverse Traditions, 1920-1945, Craft in the Machine Age, 1920-1945. Grantee Nat. Endowment for Arts, 1978. Home and Office: 150 E 69th St Apt 21J New York NY 10021-5704 E-mail: jakardon@aol.com.

KAREN, LINDA TRICARICO, interior designer; b. Bklyn., June 8, 1961; d. John William and Phyllis Jean (D'Addario) T. Student, Bucks County Community Coll., 1978-79; AAS, Fashion Inst. Tech., 1982. Retail mgr. Canadians, Brooks, Casual Corner, 1980—83; coord. sales and design Sure Snap Corp., NYC, 1983—84; asst. designer E.S. Sutton Inc., NYC, 1984—86; designer Good 'N Plenty Inc., NYC, 1986—90; sr. designer, merchandiser Leonard A. Feinberg, Inc., NYC, 1991—98; freelance designer, ind. contractor, 1998—; mem. retail sales staff Oilily, 1999—; children's interior design cons. BOCES N.Y. Interior Decorating, 2000—, Sheffield Sch. Interior Design, 2001—; sales and design cons. Furniture Options, Goshen, NY, 2001—; interior designer Suffern (N.Y.) Furniture, 2002—; decorating cons. Gervic Paint & Decorating Ctr., Monroe, NY. Free-lance illustrator, designer; children's designer, party planner, 1999—; seminar spkr. in field. Contbr. fashion trend reports, Milan, Italy, 1984, Rome, 1985, Milan and Florence, Italy, 1986, London and Paris, 1987, Montreal, 1988, 94, 95, L.A., 1993, 95, 96. Mem. Fashion Soc., Women of the Monroe Area, Orange County C. of C., Warsick Valley C. of C. Republican. Roman Catholic. Avocations: fashion design, illustration, travel. Home: 124 Dug Rd Chester NY 10918-2620

KARENTTE, BETTY, state legislator; b. Paducah, Ky., Sept. 13, 1931; m. Richard; 1 child, Mary. BA, MA, Calif. State U., Long Beach. Tchr. L.A. Unified Sch. Dist., 1961-92, cons., substitute tchr., 1994-96; mem. Calif. State Senate, Sacramento, 1996—. Office: 3711 Long Beach Blvd Ste 81 Long Beach CA 90807 Fax: 562-997-0799. E-mail: senator.karnette@sen.ca.gov.

KARESH, JANICE LEHRER, special education consultant; b. N.Y.C., May 22, 1924; d. Maxwell and lillian (Cohen) Lehrer; m. Irwin Karesh, June 15, 1947 (dec. 1959); children: Sara, Hyman, Ann, Charles. BS in Pre-Medicine, Rutgers U., 1945; MA in Psychol. Counseling, NYU, 1946. Tchr. algebra Chicora H.S., Charleston, S.C., 1946-47; tchr. math. Charleston H.S., 1963; tchr. gifted Addleston Hebrew Acad., Charleston, 1963-64; tchr. physics, biology Rivers H.S., Charleston, 1964-65; cons. spl. edn. S.C Dept. Mental Retardation, Charleston, 1966-69; dir. spl. svcs. Beaufort (S.C.) Sch. Dist., 1969-89; ind. cons. spl. edn. Charleston, 1989—. Vol. advocate guardian at litem, Family Ct., S.C., 1990—; mem. exec. com. Charleston Democratic Party, 1994—. Mem. LWV (past bd. dirs.), Nat. Coun. Jewish Women (pres. 1951, past bd. dirs.), Coun. for Exceptional Children, Poetry Soc. of S.C., Douglass Alumnae Assn. (v.p. 1995—). Democrat. Jewish. Avocations: needlepoint, writing poetry and essays, child advocacy issues. Home: 150 Wappoo Creek Dr Apt 9 Charleston SC 29412-2140 E-mail: j.karesh@bellsouth.net.

KARG, THELMA AILEEN, writer, retired educator; b. Crawfordsville, Ind., June 30, 1918; d. Fred and Orpha Fern (Stewart) Crow; m. Henry Herbert Karg, Aug. 18, 1944 (dec. June 1982); children: Susan Marie Trissell, Karen Ann Weiss. MS, Ind. State U., 1937; BS, Taylor U., 1952. Sec. Harry N. Fine Atty. at Law, Crawfordsville, Ind., 1937—42; office control clerk R.R. Donnellys & Sons Co., 1942—43, Allisons GM, Indpls., 1943—46; accts. receivable Mid States Steel and Wire Co., 1943-46; tchr. Ind. State Tchrs. Assn.-Nat. Edn. Assn., Milw., Oreg., 1952-55, ISTA-NEA, Crawfordsville, Ind., 1955-62, Evang. United Brethren Ch., Terre Haute, Ind., 1962-65, Harrison, Ohio, 1968-70, Perrysville Highland Elem. Sch., Perrysville, Ind., 1970-74, various schs., Danville, Ill., 1975-76, Shelbyville, Ind., 1976-82, Waldron, Ind., 1983-95. Contbr. article to profl. jours. and newspapers. Mem. Nat. Rep. Congrl. Com., 1993—, senatorial com.; spkr. ladies groups United Meth.; nurse's aid ARC WWII. Recipient Editor's Choice award Nat. Soc. Poets, 1992-95. Mem. Christian Writers' (leader 1983-95), Ind. State Tchrs. United Methodist. Avocations: symphonies, plays, reading, entertaining, flowers. Home: 1004 Cottage Ave Crawfordsville IN 47933-1506

KARKUT, BONNIE LEE, retired dental office manager; b. Muskegon, Mich., Feb. 7, 1934; d. Fay Henry Hohenstein and Doris Catherine (Nelson) Collins; m. Joseph Paul Karkut, Dec. 29, 1956; children: Deborah, Joseph, Bradley, Elizabeth. BA in Speech Pathology, Mich. State U., 1955; postgrad. studies, U. Hawaii, 1956, U. Mich., Saginaw, 1959. Cert. speech pathologist. Speech pathologist Pub. Schs., Muskegon, Mich., 1955-56, Saginaw, Mich., 1956-59; office mgr. Dental Office, Naples, Fla., 1984-95; retired. Pres. Saginaw (Mich.) County Dental Aux., 1978-79; vol. North Bay Civic Assn. Bd., 1999-2003. Mem. AAUW, Fla. Dental Assn. (dental asst. and aux. sect.), Delta Zeta (program chmn. 1988-89), Panhellenic Soc. Republican. Roman Catholic. Avocations: skiing, boating, swimming, reading. Home: Tarpon Cove Villages #202 945 Carrick Bend Cir Naples FL 34110-3635 Office: Dental Office 850 Central Ave Ste 103 Naples FL 34102-6036 E-mail: BonJo1960@cs.com.

KARL, HELEN WEIST, pediatric anesthesia and pain management educator, researcher; b. NYC, Oct. 28, 1948; d. Edward C. and Louise (Stursberg) Weist; m. Stephen R. Karl, June 1, 1974 (div. 1990); children: Katherine L., Thomas R., John W. BA in Philosophy, Smith Coll., 1970; MD, U. Va., 1976. Diplomate Am. Bd. Anesthesiology, Nat. Bd. Med. Examiners. Intern Hartford (Conn.) Hosp., 1976-77, resident in anesthesia, 1977-79; fellow pediat. anesthesiology Children's Hosp. of Phila., 1979-81; staff anesthesiologist St. Christopher's Hosp. for Children, Phila., 1981; asst. prof. anesthesiology and pediatrics Pa. State U., Hershey, 1981-90; asst. prof. anesthesiology U. Washington, 1990-97, assoc. prof. anesthesiology, 1997—; Parker B. Francis fellow in pulmonary rsch. Pa. State U., Hershey, 1986-88; dir. pain mgmt. Children's Hosp., Seattle, 1994-99. Adj. assoc. prof. dental pub. health scis., U. Wash., 1997-2000. Contbr. articles to profl. jours. Mem.: AAUW, Wash. Soc. Anesthesiologists, Am. Med. Women's Assn., Am. Soc. Anesthesiologists. Avocations: swimming, trumpet. Office: Children's Hosp & Med Ctr 4800 Sand Point Way NE Seattle WA 98105-3901 E-mail: helen.karl@seattlechildrens.org.

KARLE, ISABELLA L. chemist; b. Detroit, Dec. 2, 1921; d. Zygmunt Apolonaris and Elizabeth (Graczyk) Lugoski; m. Jerome Karle, June 4, 1942; children: Louise Hanson, Jean Marianne, Madeleine Tawney. BS in Chemistry, U. Mich., 1941, MS in Chemistry, 1942, PhD, 1944, DSc (hon.), 1976; DSc (hon.), Wayne State U., 1979, U. Md., 1986, Athens (Greece) U., 1997, U. Pa., 1999; LHD (hon.), Georgetown U., 1984; DSc (hon.), Harvard U., 2001; Doctor honoris causa, Jagiellonian U., Cracow, Poland, 2002. Assoc. chemist U. Chgo., 1944; instr. chemistry U. Mich., Ann Arbor, 1944—46; physicist Naval Rsch. Lab., Washington, 1946—. Paul Ehrlich lectr. NIH, 1991; exec. com. Am. Peptide Symposium, 1975—81; adv. bd. Chem. and Engring. News, 1986—89. Mem. editl. bd.: Biopolymers Jour., 1975—, Internat. Jour. Peptide Rsch., 1981—; contbr. articles to profl. jours. Named to Mich. Women's Hall of Fame, 1989; recipient Superior Civilian Svc. award, USN, 1965, Fed. Women's award, U.S. Govt., 1973, Annual Achievement award, Soc. Women Engrs., 1968, U. Mich., 1987, Dexter Conrad award, Office Naval Rsch., 1980, WISE Lifetime Achievement award, Women in Sci. and Engring., 1986, award for disting. achievement in sci., Sec. of Navy, 1987, Gregori Aminoff prize, Swedish Royal Acad. Scis., 1988, Adm. Parsons award, Navy League U.S., 1988, Ann. Achievement award, CCNY, 1989, Bijvoet medal, U. Utrecht, The Netherlands, 1990, Vincent du Vigneaud award, Gordon Conf. (Peptides), 1992, Bower Sci. award, Franklin Inst., 1993, Nat. medal of sci., Pres. of the U.S., 1995. Fellow: Am. Inst. Chemists (Chem. Pioneer award 1984), Am. Acad. Arts Scis.; mem.: NAS (Chem. Scis. award 1995), Biophys. Soc., Am. Philos. Soc., Am. Phys. Soc., Am. Chem. Soc. (Garvan award 1976, Hillebrand award 1970, Ralph Hirschmann award in peptide chemistry 1998), Am. Crystallographic Assn. (pres. 1976). Home: 6304 Lakeview Dr Falls Church VA 22041-1309 Office: Naval Rsch Lab Code 6030 Washington DC 20375-5341 Office Phone: 202-767-2624. E-mail: williams@harker.nrl.navy.mil.

KARLE-SWAILS, JEANINE, neuroscience clinical nurse specialist; b. Cin., Mar. 19, 1970; d. Gerald Michel and Judith Marianne Karle. m. Christopher Swails, June 1, 2001. BSN, U. Cin., 1992; MSN, Med. U. S.C., 1996. RN; cert. neurosci. nurse. Staff nurse Med. U. S.C., Charleston, 1992-96; neurosci. clin. nurse specialist Roper Hosp., Charleston, 1996—2001; staff nurse U. Hosp. Neuroscience ICU, 2001—; vis. clin. faculty U. Cin. Coll. of Nursing, 2002—. Parish nurse St. John the Beloved Cath. Ch., Summerville, S.C., 1996-98. Recipient Outstanding Achievement award Trident Area Cmty. Excellence, 1998; grantee Nat. Stroke Assn., 1999. Mem. Am. Assn. Neurosci. Nurses (pres. S.C. chpt. 1998-99), Nat. Stroke Assn. (bd. dirs. S.C. Lowcountry chpt. 1998-2001), Sigma Theta Tau. Roman Catholic. Avocations: exercise, travel, pets. Office: U Cin Coll of Nursing PO Box 210038 Cincinnati OH 45221-0038 Home: 3654 Ridgewood Ave Cincinnati OH 45211

KARLIN, LISA MARIE, academic administrator; b. Hays, Kans., June 21, 1968; d. Gary Paul and Mary Louise (Weigel) Dinkel; m. Craig Eugene Karlin. BBA, Ft. Hays State U., 1990. Bank examiner Fed. Deposit Ins. Corp., Hays, Kans., 1990-92; asst. alumni dir. Ft. Hays State U. Alumni Assn., 1992-97; asst. to pres. Ft. Hays State U., 1997—. Sponsor Student Alumni Assn., Ft. Hays State U., 1992-97; sponsor VIP Student Ambassadors, 1997—. Mem. Coun. Advancement & Support Edn., Mortar Bd. Sr. Honor Soc., Alpha Kappa Psi (bus. fraternity sec. 1989-90). Independent. Roman Catholic. Avocations: walking, cooking, reading, bicycling. Office: Ft Hays State U Office of Pres 600 Park St Hays KS 67601-4099

KARLIN, SUSAN, design company executive; 1 adopted child, Mia Baixue. BA in comm., MA in spl. edn. Various positions including ptnr. AKM Assoc., 1985—92; founder, pres. Suka Design Inc, NYC, 1992—. Mem.: Fin. Women's Assn., Internat. Assn. Bus. Communicators, Am. Inst. Graphic Arts, NY Advt. and Comm. Network, NY Women in Comm. Achievements include conceived and her firm designed the World Trade Ctr. tribute poster, Americans Side By Side, after 9/11. Office: Suka Design Inc 560 Broadway Ste 107 New York NY 10012 Office Phone: 212-219-0082.*

KARLINS, MIRIAM, mental health and volunteer services consultant; b. Cleve., Aug. 23, 1918; widow; children: Annette Weinberg, Sandra, Marvin. Dir. vol. svcs. Minn. Dept. Pub. Welfare, St. Paul, 1951-74, dir. edn. and tng. mental health divsn., 1960-74; mental health cons., 1974—. Cons. NIMH, Washington, 1974-80, Minn. Gov.'s Coun. on Devel. Disabilities, 1986-94; former guest lectr., cons. on devel. and expansion vol. svcs. to hosps., London; former mem. adj. faculty dept. hosp. adminstrn. U. Minn., Mpls.; lectr., condr. tng. sessions for numerous pvt. and pub. agys.; condr. tng. for surveyors mental facilities Health Care Fin. Adminstrn., Social Security Adminstrn. Contbr. articles to rofl. publs.; prodr. films, TV and radio prodns., including For Whose Good?, Dehumanization and Total Institution, World of the Right Size, How Are You? Life hon. mem. bd. dirs., advisor Opportunity Workshop. Recipient numerous awards Nental Health Assn., Assn. for Retarded Citizens, Minn. Dept. Human Svcs.; Miriam Karlins scholarship named in her honor Minn. Assn. Vol. Adminstrn.; Karlins Ctr. named in her honor Opportunity Workshop, 1996. Fellow Assn. Vol. Adminstrs. (hon. life, organizer, 1st pres., awards). Home: 6450 York Ave S Minneapolis MN 55435-2345

KARLL, JO ANN, retired judge, lawyer; b. St. Louis, Nov. 16, 1948; d. Joseph H. and Dorothy Olga (Pyle) K.; m. William Austin Hernlund, Sept. 9, 1990. BS magna cum laude, Maryville U.; JD, St. Louis U. Bar: Mo. 1993. Ins. claims adjuster, 1967-88; mem. Mo. Gen. Assembly dists. 104 and 105, 1991-93; dir. Mo. State Divsn. Workers' Compensation, Jefferson City, 1993-2000, adminstrv. law judge, 2000—03; pvt. practice High Ridge, Mo., 2003—. Founder, 1st pres. scholarship fund Mo. Kids' Chance, Inc., 1995-96, bd. dirs., 1995—. Internat. Assn. of Indsl. Accident Bds. and Commns. (past pres.). Office: Karll Law Ctr LLC 1682 Old Gravois Rd High Ridge MO 63049 Office Phone: 636-677-7000.

KARLUK, LORI JEAN, craft designer, copy editor; b. Scranton, Pa., Aug. 29, 1958; d. Edward Julius and Josephine Anne (Cuozzo) K. Grad., high sch., 1976. Consignor, designer various shops, Pa., 1982-85; owner mail order bus. Loveables, 1983-85; staff designer Tradition Today, Roselle, Ill., 1985-86; designer All Occasion Crafts, Sparks, Nev., 1986-88; copy editor McCalls, N.Y.C., 1987-90; copy editor, product designer Herrschners, Inc., Schaumburg, Ill., 1988-92; designer Banar Designs, Fallbrook, Calif., 1991-92, Yarn Kits, Inc., N.Y.C., 1992-94; freelance designer, 1984-99; prin., owner Josie's Inspiration Studio, 1999—. Author: Safari Friends, 1987, Bear-E-Tale Bears, 1991. Sec. MADD, Lackawanna County, 1991. Recipient numerous spl. awards for designs. Mem. NOW, Soc. Craft Designers, People for the Ethical Treatment of Animals, United Friends of the Children, Internat. Soc. for Animal Rights, Teddy Bear Artists Assn., Good Bears of the World. Avocations: travel, reading, art. Home and Office: PO Box 68 Jessup PA 18434-0068 E-mail: ljkbears@aol.com.

KARMEL, ROBERTA SEGAL, lawyer, educator; b. Chgo., May 4, 1937; d. J. Herzl and Eva E. (Elin) Segal; m. Paul R. Karmel, June 9, 1957 (dec. Aug. 1994); children: Philip, Solomon, Jonathan, Miriam; m. S. David Harrison, Oct. 29, 1995. BA, Radcliffe Coll.; LLB, NYU, 1962; HHD (hon.), King's Coll., 1998. Bar: N.Y. 1962, U.S. Dist. Ct. (so. and ea. dists.) N.Y. 1964, U.S. Ct. Appeals (2d cir.) 1968, U.S. Supreme Ct. 1968, U.S. Ct. Appeals (3d cir.) 1987. Asst. regional adminstr. SEC, Washington, 1962-69, commr., 1977-80; assoc. Willkie Farr & Gallagher, N.Y.C., 1969-72; ptnr. Rogers & Wells, N.Y.C., 1972-77, of counsel, 1980-85; ptnr. Kelley Drye & Warren, N.Y.C., 1987-94, of counsel, 1995—2002. Adj. prof. law Bklyn. Law Sch., 1973-77, 82-85, prof., 1985—, co-dir. Ctr. for Study of Internat. Bus. Law; bd. dirs. Kemper Ins Cos.; trustee Practicing Law Inst. Author: Regulation by Prosecution, 1982; contbr. articles to profl. jours. Fellow Am. Bar Found.; mem. ABA, Assn. Bar City N.Y., Am. Law Inst., Fin. Women's Assn. Home: 66 Summit Dr Hastings On Hudson NY 10706-1215 Office: Bklyn Law Sch 250 Joralemon St Brooklyn NY 11201-3700 E-mail: roberta.karmel@brooklaw.edu.

KARNES, LUCIA ROONEY, psychologist; b. Moncton, N.B., Can., Mar. 9, 1921; d. Charles William and Jean Waring (Robson) Rooney; m. Thomas Campbell Karnes, June 7, 1946; children: Eleanore, Campbell, Timothy, Charles. BS, Ga. State Coll., 1942; MA, Emory U., 1946; PhD, U. N.C., 1967. Tchr. Decatur Girls High, Decatur, Ga., 1942-46; tchr. Summit Sch., Winston-Salem, N.C., 1947; prof. Salem Coll., Winston-Salem, 1949-54, 60-77; lang. therapist Bowman Grey Sch. Medicine, Winston-Salem, 1950-57, Orton Reading Ctr., Winston-Salem, 1957-72; dir. Ctr. for Spl. Edn., Salem Coll., Winston-Salem, 1972-77; pvt. practice psychology Winston-Salem, 1977—. Dyslexic cons. Jefferson Acad., Winston-Salem, 1980—, Greenfield Sch., Wilson, 1986—, Wingate (N.C.) U., 1988—. Creator Using Computers in Psychology courses, 1972; author (video) Teaching Dyslexics, 1975. Founder, pres. state bd. LWV, Winston-Salem, 1953; pres. state bd. AAUW, Winston-Salem, 1950-54; bd. dirs. YWCA, Winston-Salem, 1950-54; v.p. bd. dirs. Arts Coun., Winston-Salem, 1954-60. Named Outstanding Reading Tchr., Reading Assn., Winston-Salem, 1982; fellow Orton-Gillingham Acad. Mem. APA, Orton Dyslexia Soc. (v.p. bd. dirs. 1960-77), N.C. Psychol. Assn., Assn. for Children with Learning Disabilities (v.p. bd. dirs. 1972—, Orton-Gillingham Acad. fellow), Sorosis Club, Delta Kappa Gamma. Democrat. Presbyterian. Avocation: travel. Home: 131 Lamplighter Cir Winston Salem NC 27104-3419 Office Phone: 336-768-8323.

KARNETTE, BETTY, state senator; b. Paduch, Ky., Sept. 13, 1931; m. Richard Karnette; 1 child, Mary. BA, MA, Calif. State U. Sec, office mgr. Terminal Island; tchr. L.A. Unified Sch. Dist., 1961—92; mem. Calif. State Assembly, 1992—94, dist. 27, Calif. State Senate, 1996—. Cons. edn., 1994—96; subs. tchr., 1994—96; mem. Banking, Commerce and Internat. Trade, Edn. Com., Govt. Orgn. Com., Pub. Employment and Retirement Com., Rules Com., Transp. Com. Mem. Long Beach Meml. Hosp. Children's Clinic; mem. assoc. bd. Sage House in San Pedro; bd. dirs. Young Horizon. Democrat. Mailing: State Capitol Rm 5066 Sacramento CA 95814 Office: 3711 Long Beach Blvd Ste 801 Long Beach CA 90807

KARNOFSKY, MOLLYNE, artist, educator, poet; b. New Orleans, July 19, 1932; d. Samuel and Lena (Gaethe) Finegold; m. Dave E. Winston, Sept. 17, 1952 (div. Sept. 1975); children: Craig T. Winston, Janelle R. Winston Lewis. BBS in Bus. Adminstrn., Tulane U., New Orleans, 1966; student in Art Studio Courses, Tulane, Newcomb Coll., New Orleans, 1966-70; MAT in Painting and Teaching, Tulane U., New Orleans, 1972. Lic. teaching La., 1972, N.Y.C. Bd. Edn., 1986. Dir., owner La. Lic. Art Sch., New Orleans, 1972-77; art tchr., art workshops N.Y.C., 1977—. Mem. univ. course and policy study com. Tulane U., 1952; panelist Artists Talk on Art, N.Y.C., 1993, 94; guide to internat. artists, Mid. Am. Arts Alliance, N.Y.C., 1994. One-woman shows include Vincent Mann Gallery, New Orleans, 1974, Spirit of New Orleans, 1976, Viridian Gallery, N.Y.C., 1977, 79, Spring St. Performance Painting for Artists' Day, N.Y.C., 1977, PS1 Inst. Art and Urban Resources, Long Island City, N.Y., 1978, Contemporary Art Ctr., New Orleans, 1978, Galerie Forum, Stockholm, 1980, Satellite gallery Bronx Mus. Art, N.Y., 1980, Galerie Leger, Malmö, Sweden, 1980, Ave. B Gallery, 1985, Asphalt Green Cmty. Ctr., N.Y.C., 1988, N.Y. Pub. Libr., 1988, Leonard Stern Bldg. NYU, 1994, Galerie Lafitte, New Orleans, La., 2001, (Site Specific: Found Spaces and Other Places) Eclectic Properties, 1979, Rudolph Bass Power Tool Co., N.Y.C., 1982, Galeriex, Istanbul, Turkey, 2003; exhibited in group shows at Judson Poets Theater, N.Y.C., 1977, World Trade Ctr., N.Y.C., 1979, Ear Inn, N.Y.C., 1979, Artists' Day Art Parade, 1979, 83, Bklyn., Atlantic Ave. Galleries, Bklyn., 1979, Bklyn. Arts Cultural Assn., 1981, Emily Harvey Gallery, N.Y.C., 1983, WPA Gallery, Washington, 1983, Jack Tilton Gallery, N.Y.C., 1983, Jon Leon Gallery, N.Y.C., 1984, Franklin Furnace, N.Y.C., 1984, Minor Injury Gallery, Williamsburg, Bklyn., 1989, World Congress Arts and Medicine, N.Y.C., 1992, Tribeca 148, N.Y.C., 1993, 94, Printmaking Workshop, N.Y.C., 1997, Chuck Levitan Gallery, N.Y.C., 1998, Broome St. Gallery, N.Y.C., 2000, Lyman-Eyer Gallery, Newton, Mass., 2001, 2002, Gallery X, N.Y.C., 2002, Lyman Eyer Gallery, Provincetown, Mass., 2001-02, Ch. of All Sts., 2002, Extreme Exteriors, 2002, Lyman Eyer Gallery, Newton and Provincetown, Mass., 2001-02, Ch. of All Souls, N.Y.C., 2002; permanent collections include Cigna, Insurance Co. of N.Am., Mollyne Karnofsky Papers, NYU Library, Anthology Film Archives, N.Y.C., 1996, Chuck Levitan Gallery, N.Y.C, 1998; subject of art Coll. Art Assn., N.Y.C., 1980; documentary video of art exhbn. Vesteras Mus., Sweden, 1981; documentary video of art ehbn. and interview Fuji Network, Japan, 1981; contbr. articles to profl. jours. Pres. Tulane Commerce Women's Club, New Orleans, 1951; publicity dir. Chevra Thilim Sisterhood, New Orleans, 1960-63; com. mem. Coun. of Jewish Women, New Orleans, 1965-70; tour dir. Spring Fiesta Assn., New Orleans, 1965. Grantee for performance poetry, Poets and Writers, N.Y.C., 1982, 92, 98; named Artist in Residence Avenue B. Gallery, N.Y.C., 1985, honorarium, spl. project, Coal Bin PSI Inst. for Arts and Urban Resources, Queens, N.Y., 1978, Contemporary Art Ctr., New Orleans, 1978. Mem. Tulane Alumni Assn. (bd. dirs. 1970-71, editor bus. review 1971), Artists Equity, Mcpl. Art Soc. Avocations: writing, music, urban archaeology. E-mail: MKarnArt@aol.com.

KARNS, CYNTHIA DENISE, art educator; d. J. Roland and Patricia Ruth Lafferty; m. John Robert Karns, Aug. 12, 1978; children: Christopher John, Heather Lyn. BA, Thiel Coll., 1975; M in Edn., Edinboro (Pa.) U., 1981. Tchr. Crawford Ctrl. Sch. Dist., Meadville, 1978—. Instr. photography, pottery, enameling, Meadville, 1980—. Leader Pa. Lakes Girl Scout Coun., Meadville, 1994—2002. Mem.: Nat. Edn. Assn., Nat. Art Edn. Assn., Crawford Ctrl. Edn. Assn. Republican. Methodist. Avocations: camping, hiking. Office: West End Elem Sch 12068 Brooks Rd Meadville PA 16335

KARNS, PHYLLIS J. SPEAR, dean, BSN, Baylor U., 1960; MSN in Parent-Child Nursing, U. Colo., 1977; PhD in Psychol. Founds. Edn., U. Wyo., 1985. From instr. to asst. prof. U. Wyo., Laramie, 1977-87; dean Sch. Nursing, prof. Baylor U., Dallas-Waco, 1987—. Cons. U. Tulsa, 1993. Contbr. articles to profl. jours. Recipient Baylor U. Rsch. award, 1990; Grantee Wyo. Coun. Humanities, 1986, 80, 86. Mem. ANA, Am. Assn. Colls. Nursing., Christian Nurse Educators (chair 1992—), Nat. League Nursing (cons. 1990—), So. Collegiate Coun. Edn. Nursing (Tex. rep. 1989-90, mem. nominating com. 1988, 89), Tex. Nurses Assn. (bd. dirs. dist. 4 1991-93, mem. sch. adv. com. 1991-92), Sigma Theta Tau. Office: Baylor U Sch Nursing 3700 Worth St Dallas TX 75246-2091

KAROL, MERYL HELENE, medical educator, researcher, health facility administrator, science educator; b. N.Y.C., Aug. 10, 1940; m. Paul Jason; children: Darcie, Deverin, Meredith. BS, Cornell U., 1961; PhD, Columbia U., 1967. Rsch. asst. SUNY, Stony Brook, 1976-79, assoc. prof., 1979-85, prof. environ. and indsl. health, 1985—, assoc. dept. chair, 1993-2000; prof. environ. and indsl. health U. Pitts., 1985—, assoc. dean rsch., 2002, assoc. dean acad. affairs, 2002—. Sec.-gen. Internat. Union Toxicologists, 1998—; advisor numerous govt. health adv. bds., agys.; lectr. in field; advisor to sec. U.S. Dept. HHS; mem. adv. panel FDA, CDC, 2003; chair sci. adv. panel Mickey Leland Ctr., 2001—03; mem. sci. adv. bd. U.S. EPA. Assoc. editor: Toxicology Sci., mem. editl. bd.: Inhalation Toxicology, Environ. Health, Toxicology and Ecotoxicology News, Biomed. and Environ. Scis.; contbr. articles to profl. jours. Recipient Women in Sci. award, U. Mich., 1986, Rachel Carson award, 1993, Outstanding Contbns. to Pub. Health, 1999; fellow NIH, SUNY, 1967—68. Mem.: AAAS, Soc. Toxicology (v.p. 1993, pres. 1994, Frank R. Blood award), Internat. Union Toxicologists (sec.-gen. 1998—2001), N.Y. Acad. Scis., Am. Conf. Govt. Indsl. Hygienists, Am. Assn. Immunologists, Am. Thoracic Soc., Am. Chem. Soc. Avocations: sports, design, travel, biotechnology. Office: U Pitts Dept Environ & Occupl Health 130 DeSoto St Pittsburgh PA 15261 Office Phone: 412-624-3097. E-mail: mhk@pitt.edu.

KARP, HARVEY LAWRENCE, metal products manufacturing executive; b. N.Y.C., Nov. 26, 1927; BSS CCNY; LLB, Yale U. Pres., founder Monogram Industries Inc., L.A., 1960—83; chmn. bd. Mueller Industries, Memhis, 1991—. Office: Mueller Industries 8285 Tournament Dr Ste 150 Memphis TN 38125

KARP, NAOMI KATHERINE, United States government administrator; b. Tucson, Mar. 6, 1942; d. James Jacob and Rose (Sosnowsky) Silver; m. Eugene Robert Karp, Oct. 23, 1965; children: Gail, Kevin. Student, Mills Coll., 1960-62; BA in Psychology, U. Ariz., 1964, M in Edn., 1965. Spl. edn. tchr. Tucson Pub. Schs., 1965-77, Fairfax (Va.) County Schs., 1978-80; program specialist U.S. Dept. Edn. OSERS, Washington, 1980-90; cons. Family & Integration Resources, Arlington, Va., 1990-92; pvt. practice Arlington, Va., 1992-93; spl. advisor to asst. sec. & acting dir. of early childhood learning U.S. Dept. Edn. Office Ednl. Rsch. and Improvement, Washington, 1993-95; dir., Nat. Inst. of Early Childhood Devel. and Edn. Dept. of Edn., Washington, 1995—. Cons. to universities, advocacy orgns. and profl. groups, 1990-93. Author: Advocacy for Families, 1991; author, editor: Inclusion: A Right not a Privilege, 1994. Mem. Am. Assn. on Mental Retardation (nat. bd. 1991-92); mem., co-founder Fed. of Families for Children's Mental Health (nat. sec., nat. bd. 1989-92, achievement award 1992). Office: Dept of Edn Early Child Devel & Edn 555 New Jersey Ave NW Ste 522 Washington DC 20001-2029

KARP, ROBERTA S. wholesale apparel and accessories executive; married; 2 children. BA, SUNY, Binghampton; JD, Hofstra U. Atty. Kramer, Levin et al., N.Y.C.; from legal counsel to v.p. corp. affairs and gen. coun. Liz Claiborne, Inc., N.Y.C., 1986-2000, sr. v.p. corp. affairs, gen. coun., 2000—. Office: Liz Claiborne Inc 1 Claibourne Ave North Bergen NJ 07047-6499

KARP, ROSANNE, oncology and women's health nurse; b. Lynn, Mass., Oct. 8, 1946; d. Max and Dorothy (Cohen) Sidman; children: Stacy, Matthew. ADN, Northeastern U., 1967; postgrad., Lesley Coll., 1990—2002. RN, Mass. Staff nurse Holy Family Hosp., Methuen, Mass., 1969-90; staff nurse Mass. Gen. Hosp., Boston, 1990-96, case mgr. gynecology/oncology svc., 1996—. Chair, prof. edn. Greater Lawrence unit Am. Cancer Soc., bd. dirs. Mass. div., 1990-92. Recipient Excellence in Med./Surg. Nursing award Merrimack Valley Area Health Edn. Ctr., 1988, Award for Disting. Vol. Leadership Greater Lawrence unit ACS, 1995, nat. leadership award Hadassah, 1997, Ptnrs. award Ptnrs. Healthcare Sys., Inc., 1999.

KARPAN, KATHLEEN MARIE, former state official, lawyer, journalist; b. Rock Springs, Wyo., Sept. 1, 1942; d. Thomas Michael and Pauline Ann (Taucher) K. BS in Journalism, U. Wyo., 1964, MA in Am. Studies, 1975; JD, U. Oreg., 1978. Bar: Wyo. 1983, U.S. Dist. Ct. Wyo., U.S. Ct. Appeals (D.C. and 10th cirs.). Editor Cody Enterprise, Wyo., 1964; press sec. to U.S. Congressman Teno Roncalio, U.S. Ho. of Reps., Washington, 1965-67, 71-72, adminstrv. asst., 1973-75; asst. news editor Wyo. Eagle, Cheyenne, 1967; free-lance writer, 1968; tchg. asst. dept. history U. Wyo., 1969-70; desk editor Canberra Times, Australia, 1970; dep. dir. Office Congl. Relations, Econ. Devel. Adminstrn. U.S. Dept. Commerce, Washington, 1978-80, atty. advisor Office of Chief Counsel, Econ. Devel. Adminstrn., 1980-81; campaign mgr. Rodger McDaniel for U.S. Senator, Wyo., 1981-82; asst. atty. gen. State of Wyo., Cheyenne, 1983-84, dir. Dept. Health and Social Services, 1984-86, sec. of state, 1987-95; dir. surface mining reclamation Dept. of the Interior, 1997-2000, prin. dep. asst. sec. lands and minerals mgmt., 2000—. Del. Dem. Nat. Conv., San Francisco, 1984, Atlanta, 1988, N.Y.C., 1992, 2000; mem. bd. govs. Nat. Dem. Leadership Coun., drafting com. Dem. Nat. Platform, Santa Fe, 1992. W.R. Coe fellow, 1969 Mem. Wyo. Bar Assn., Bus. and Profl. Women. Roman Catholic. Office: Dept of the Interior 1951 Constn Ave NW Washington DC 20240-0001 Home: 410 W 2nd Ave Cheyenne WY 82001-1211

KARPATKIN, RHODA HENDRICK, consumer information organization executive, lawyer; b. N.Y.C., June 7, 1930; d. Charles and Augusta (Arkin) Hendrick; m. Marvin Karpatkin, June 16, 1951 (dec.); children: Deborah Hendrick, Herbert Isaac, Jeremy Charles. BA, Bklyn. Coll., 1951; LLB, Yale U., 1953. Bar: N.Y. 1954. Pvt. practice law, 1954-74; ptnr. Karpatkin & Karpatkin, 1958-61, Karpatkin, Ohrenstein & Karpatkin, N.Y.C., 1961-74; pres. Consumers Union of U.S. Inc., Yonkers, N.Y., 1974—, Internat. Orgn. Consumers Unions (name changed to Consumers Internat.), 1984-91, v.p., 1994-97; pres. Consumers Union U.S., Inc., 1994—; hon. sec. Consumers Internat., 1997—, also bd. dirs. Spl. counsel for decentralization N.Y.C. Bd. Edn., 1969-70; adj. prof. dept. urban studies Queens Coll., 1972-74; commr. Nat. Commn. on New Tech. Uses of Copyrighted Works, 1975-78; mem. Pres.'s Com. Trade Policy and Negotiation, 1993—; mem. Pres.'s Trade and Environ. Policy Adv. Com., 1995—. Contbg. author: Current School Problems, 1971, Consumer Education in the Human Services; contbr. articles to profl. publs. Mem. Local Sch. Bd. 5, N.Y.C., 1966-70, chmn., 1967-69; mem. Community Sch. Bd. 3, N.Y.C., 1970-71; mem. com. acad. freedom ACLU, 1973-84; mem. Pres.'s Commn. for Nat. Agenda for the Eighties., 1979-80; trustee Pub. Edn. Assn., 1972-85. Mem. ABA (commn. on law and the economy 1976-79, commn. to reduce costs and delay 1978-84, commn. access to justice 2000 1993—), Assn. of Bar of City of N.Y. (com. consumer affairs 1969-80, chmn. 1974-79, com. on internat. human rights 1987-90, audit com. 1982-83, com. Ea. European affairs), Nat. Inst. for Dispute Resolution (bd. dirs. 1982-89), Helsinki Watch (mem. adv. bd.), Assn. Yale Alumni (rep.-at-large 1982-85). Office: Consumers Union of US Inc 101 Truman Ave Yonkers NY 10703-1057

KARPEN, MARIAN JOAN, financial executive; b. June 16, 1944; d. Cass John and Mary (Jagiello) Karpen. BA, Vassar Coll.; postgrad., Sorbonne, Paris, NYU, 1974—77. New England corr. Women's Wear Daily, 1966—68; Paris fashion editor Capital Cities Network, 1966—69; syndicated newspaper columnist, photojournalist Queen Features Syndicate, N.Y.C., 1971—73; acct. exec. Blyth Eastman Dillon (merged into Paine Webber), 1973—75, Oppenheimer, N.Y.C., 1975—76; v.p. mcpl. bond coord. Faulkner Dawkins & Sullivan (merged into Shearson Hayden Stone Smith Barney et al), 1976—77; mgr. retail mcpl. bond dept., nat. fin. lectr. Warburg Paribas Becker-A.G. Becker (merged into Merrill LYnch), sr. v.p., prin., 1977—84; sr. v.p., ltg. ptnr. Bear Stearns & Co., 1984—87, assoc. dir., 1987—90; pres., prin., CEO EuroEast® Group, Inc., N.Y.C., 1990—92; writer, creator newsletter Ea. European News; founder, pres., CEO Work Talk, The Forum Work Talk, Inc., N.Y.C., 1992—; creator, writer newsletter The WorkTalk Times website; pres., founder, CEO Career Renewal Ctr.®, Inc. Writer, lectr., seminar organizer and leader; former mem. Bus. Adv. Coun. U.S. Senate. Contbr.: articles, photographs to newspapers and mags.; author: Career Crossroads: Ideas and Inspiration for Your Work/Life Journey. Mem. benefit com. March of Dimes, 1983; mem. Torchlight Ball com. Internat. Games for Disabled, 1984; vol. Whitney Mus. Am. Art. Named New Yorker of Week, Channel One, 1996. Mem.: Vassar Club NY (bd. dirs., exec. com., ex-officio chmn. corp. devel. com., chmn. benefit holiday open house 1989, chmn. major scholarship benefit 1991, chmn. scholarship fundraising raffle benefit 1992). Office: WorkTalk® 180 E 76th St at Lexington Ave New York NY 10021 Home: 233 E 69th St New York NY 10021-5414 Office Phone: 212-949-9300. E-mail: mjkarpen@aol.com.

KARPIAK, TANYA, lawyer, educator; d. John Karpiak and Helen Macosta; children: Tara, Ena. BS, Calif. U., 1963; JD, Boston Coll., 1975. Reporter Sta. WNAC-TV, Boston, 1974—83; asst. editor Ladies Home Jour., N.Y.C., 1968—70; pvt. practice Braintree, Mass., 1983—88; asst. dist. atty. Norfolk County, Canton, Mass., 1988—. Adminstrn. Niscupp exch. Boston U. Law and Tomsk State U., Tomsk, Russia, 2002—; adj. prof. Boston U. Law Sch., 2002—; mem. Russian Am. Rule of Law Consortium, Burlington, Vt., 2001—; cons. Internat. Fed. Electoral Sys., U.S. Dept. Justice, others, Washington. Exhibitions include Bunting Inst., Radcliff, others. Mem.: ABA (legal specialist), Ukrainian-ABA (bd. dirs. 2000—01). Home: 35 Kelveden Rd Waban MA 02468 Office: 45 Shawmut Rd Canton MA E-mail: tanyakarpiak@yahoo.com.

KARPIEL, DORIS CATHERINE, state legislator; b. Chgo., Sept. 21, 1935; d. Nicholas and Mary (McStravick) Feinen; m. Harvey Karpiel, 1955 (div.); children: Sharon, Lynn, Laura, Barry. AA, Morton Jr. Coll., 1955; BA, No. Ill. U., 1976. Real estate sales assoc. Bundy-Morgan BHG; coordinator Bloomingdale Twp. Republican Presdl. Hdqrs., Ill., 1960, 64, 68; former pres. Bloomingdale Twp. Rep. Orgn.; mem. Twp. Ofcls. of Ill.; trustee Bloomingdale Twp., 1974-75, supr., 1975-80; precinct committeewoman Bloomingdale Twp. Rep. Central Com., 1972, chmn., 1978-80; mem. Ill. Ho. of Reps., 1979-82, Ill. State Senate from 25th Dist., 1984—. Mem. Am. Legislators Exchange Council, Rep. Orgn. Schaumberg Twp.; former sec. DuPage County Suprs. Assn.; former sec. DuPage County Twp. Ofcls.; mem. DuPage County Women's Rep. Orgn., Meml. Hosp. Guild, Am. Cancer Soc. Mem. LWV, DuPage Bd. Realtors, Pi Sigma Alpha. Clubs: Bloomingdale Roselle and Streamwood Country, University Women's, St. Walters Women's. Office: Ill State Senate 123 Capitol Bldg Springfield IL 62706-0001 Address: 400 Lake St Ste 220 Roselle IL 60172-3572

KARPINSKI, HUBERTA ELAINE, library trustee; b. Cato, N.Y., Jan. 4, 1925; d. Alfred Raymond and Lena Margaret (Fuller) Tuxill; m. Edward Karpinski, Nov. 17, 1956; children: Susan Tanielian, Rebecca Hitch, Amy Jaward. Student, U. Mich., 1943-45, Wayne U., 1949-50; grad., N.Y. Art Acad. Design, 1972. Operator to svc. observer supr. Mich. Bell Telephone Co., Detroit, 1946-57; tchr. art Birmingham (Mich.) Pub. Sch., 1977-87; libr. trustee Redford (Mich.) Twp. Dist. Libr., 1971—. Chmn. Lola Valley Civic Assn., Redford, 1960-70; vice chmn. Redford Twp. Coun. Civic Assn., 1967-71; bd. dirs. 17th Dist. Mich. Dem. Party, Redford, 1968-71. Mem. Nat. Mus. Women in arts (charter), Mich. Porcelain Artists, Internat. Porcelain Art Tchrs. Avocations: portrait painting in colored pencil, pastel, oil or on porcelain. Home: 17418 Macarthur Redford MI 48240-2241

KARR, BEVERLY ANN, counselor; b. Birmingham, Ala., Jan. 24, 1967; d. Ollis Graham and Betty Lou (Simmons) Karr; m. Judson Barber. BS in English/Spanish/Secondary Edn., U. Ala., Birmingham, 1990, MA in Agy. Counseling, 1993, MA in Sch. Counseling, 1994, Edn. Specialist in Sch. Counseling, 1999. Cert. secondary edn. tchr., sch. counselor. Tchr. Birmingham Bd. Edn., 1990-91; acad. counselor Bradford Adolescent, Pelham, Ala., 1991-93; counselor Jefferson County Bd. Edn., 1994—. Mem. ACA, U. Ala. Birmingham Alumni Assn. (bd. dirs.), Sigma Delta Pi, Chi Sigma Iota, Kappa Delta Pi, Delta Kappa Gamma. Democrat. Office: 225 16th St S Irondale AL 35210-1647 Home: 4455 Preserve Dr Hoover AL 35226-4160

KARR, KATHLEEN, writer; b. Allentown, Pa., Apr. 21, 1946; d. Stephen and Elizabeth (Szoka) Csele; m. Lawrence F. Karr, July 13, 1968; children: Suzanne, Daniel. BA, Cath. U. of Am., 1968; MA, Providence Coll., 1971; postgrad, Corcoran Sch. Art, 1972. Tchr. English and speech Barrington (R.I.) H.S., 1968-69; curator R.I. Hist. Soc. Film Archives, 1970-71; archives asst. Am. Film Inst., Washington, 1971-72, mem. catalog staff, 1972; gen. mgr. Washington Circle Theatre Corp., Washington, 1973-78; advt. dir. Circle/Showcase Theatres, Washington, 1979-83, dir. pub. rels., 1984-88; mem. pub. rels. staff Circle Mgmt. Co./Circle Releasing, Washington, 1988-93. Asst. prof. George Washington U., 1979, 80-81; lectr., instr. in film and comms. at various instns.; lectr. at film and writing confs.; juror Am. Film Fest., 1971, Rosebud Awards, 1991; mem. adv. bd. Children's Literature, 1994—. Author: It Ain't Always Easy, 1990 ("100 Books for Reading and Sharing" citation N.Y. Public Libr., 1990), Oh, Those Harper Girls!; or, Young and Dangerous, 1992 (Parents' Choice Story Book citation, 1992), Gideon and the Mummy Professor, 1993, The Cave, 1994, In the Kaiser's Clutch, 1995, Light of My Heart, 1984, From This Day Forward, 1985 (Golden Medallion award for best inspirational novel Romance Writers of Am., 1986), Chessie's King, 1986, Destiny's Dreamers Book I: Gone West, 1993, Destiny's Dreamers Book II: The Promised Land, 1993, Go West, Young Women!, 1996, Phoebe's Folly, 1996, Spy in the Sky, 1997, The Great Turkey Walk, 1998, The Lighthouse Mermaid, 1998, Oregon, Sweet Oregon, 1998, Gold-Rush Phoebe, 1998, Man of the Family, 1999 (notable book for 2000 award ALA), Skullduggery, 2000, The Boxer, 2000 (Best Books for Young Adults award ALA, The Golden Kite award 2000), It Happened in the White House, 2000, Playing with Fire, 2001, Bone Dry, 2002, Gilbert and Sullivan Set Me Free, 2003, The 7th Knot, 2002, Exiled: Memoirs of a Camel, 2004; editor: The American Film Heritage: Views from the American Film Insitute Collection, 1972; author of various short films; contbr. to numerous jours. Mem. Washington Romance Writers (bd. dirs. 1985-86, pres. 1986-87), Children's Book Guild (pres. 2000-01). Office: McIntosh & Otis 353 Lexington Ave Rm 1500 New York NY 10016-0900

KARRAS NEBOYSKEY, ANGELA ROSE, lawyer; b. Oak Park, Ill., Feb. 10, 1975; d. Ernest Christ and Marion Rose Karras; m. David A.P. Neboyskey, Dec. 30, 2001. BS in Journalism, Northwestern U., 1997; JD, Ind. U., 2000. Bar: Ill. 2000, Ind. 2001. Atty. Swanson, Martin & Bell, Chgo., 2000—. Notes editor: Fed. Comm. Law Jour., 1999—2000. Mem.: ABA (young lawyer liaison 2000—), Hellenic Bar Assn., Ill. State Bar Assn., Ind. State Bar Assn. Avocations: piano, creative writing, travel, philanthropic work. Office: Swanson Martin & Bell One IBM Plz Ste 3300 330 N Wabash Chicago IL 60611

KARRER, CAROL CONVERSE, nursing educator, consultant; b. Columbus, Ohio, Dec. 10, 1940; d. Edward Beck and Elma Louise (McClain) Converse; m. George Henry Karrer, Aug. 26, 1961; children: Andrew (dec.), Matthew, James. Dipl. Nursing, Grant Hosp. sch. Nursing, Columbus, 1961; BSN, Ohio State U., 1963, MSN, 1964, PhD in Family Rels. and Human Devel., 1984. RN, Ohio. Nurse Grant Hosp., Columbus, 1961-63; instr., rsch. assoc. Ohio State U. Sch. Nursing, Columbus, 1964-67; organist and presch. music tchr. St. Andrew Presbyn. Ch., Columbus, 1967-71; instr. nursing Grant Hosp. Sch. Nursing, Columbus, 1971-72; nursing coord. Ohio State U. Sch. Nursing, Columbus, 1973-75; asst. prof. nursing Ohio Wesleyan U., Delaware, 1976-80; prof. nursing Franklin U., Columbus, 1981—2001; adj. prof. Capital U., 2001—. Cons. evaluator North Cen. Assn. Colls. and Schs., Commn. on Instns. of Higher Edn., Chgo., 1991-2002. Contbr. articles to profl. jours., chpt. to book. Mem. Union County Bd. of Health, 2001—. Ohio State U. Home Econs. Alumni Assn. rsch. grantee, 1978. Mem. Mid-Ohio Nurses Assn. (pres. 1986-90), Ohio Bd. Nursing (chmn. ednl. adv. com. 1989-90). Home: 13887 Robinson Rd Plain City OH 43064-9028

KARRIEM, FATIMA, real estate broker; b. Houston, Tex., Feb. 12, 1955; d. Hara Lee Washington and Eudora Robbie Hannah; m. Timothy Carlsbeth Moon, July 5, 1972 (div. Aug. 2, 1987); children: Taurus Cornelius Moon, Onica Monique Moon, Tamathy Cee Moon. Degree in Acctg., Upper Iowa U., Fayette, 1991. Lic. Real Estate Broker Tex. Real Estate Commn., 1995, Mortgage Broker Tex. Savs. and Loan, 2003. Cable splicing techician Southwestern Bell Tel. Co., Houston, 1977—92, installation techician Dallas, 1992—95; acctg. rep. We Wholesale, Dallas, 1991—95; reservationist SW Airline, Dallas, 1995—98; real estate agt. Henry S Miller Realtors, Duncanville, Tex., 1993—97, Century 21 Galloway-Herron, Dallas, 1997—2000; real estate agt. / broker ORG Realty, Dallas, 2000—01; broker Meirrak Realty / URA / Mortgage, Desoto, Tex., 2001—. Techician tng. Southwestern Bell Tel. Co., Houston, 1990—92; broker, adminstrn., tng. Meirrak Realty / URA, Desoto, Tex., 2001—. Vol. Paint the Town of Oak Cliff, 1995—2002; adminstr. Dallas Islamic Mosque, Dallas. Recipient Appreciation, Dallas Islamic Acad., 1997—2000, Volunteerism award, Greater Dallas Assn. Realtors, 1996—2002, Relocation Specialists award, Henry S Miller, Realtors, 1997. Mem.: Women's Coun. of Realtors (assoc.), Tex. Assn. Real Estate Brokers (assoc.), Nat. Assn. Real Estate Brokers (assoc.), Greater Dallas Assn. Realtors (assoc.; mem affiliate team, Volunteerism award 1996—2002), Grievance and Profl. Std. Com. (assoc.; com. mem., bd. dirs. 2001—03), Dallas Assn. Real Estate Brokers (assoc.), Paint the Town Oak Cliff (assoc.), Oak Cliff C. of C. (assoc.), Cedar Hill C. of C. (assoc.). Independent. Moslem. Avocations: martial arts, bicycling, body building, golf, creative advertising. Office: Meirrak Realty / URA P O Box 0931 Desoto TX 75123 Office Phone: 214-734-1125. E-mail: fkarriem@sbcglobal.net.

KARSEN, SONJA PETRA, retired American-Hispanic literature educator; b. Berlin, Apr. 11, 1919; came to U.S., 1938, naturalized, 1945; d. Fritz and Erna (Heidermann) K. Titulo de Bachiller, 1937; BA, Carleton Coll., 1939; MA (scholar in French), Bryn Mawr Coll., 1941; PhD, Columbia U., 1950. Instr. Spanish Lake Erie Coll., Painesville, Ohio, 1943-45; instr. modern langs. U. P.R., 1945-46; instr. Spanish Syracuse U., 1947-50, Bklyn. Coll., 1950-51; asst. to dep. dir. gen. UNESCO, 1951-52, Latin Am. Desk, tech. assistance dept., 1952-53, mem. tech. assistance mission Costa Rica, 1954; asst. prof. Spanish Sweet Briar Coll., Va., 1955-57; assoc. prof., chmn. dept. Romance langs. Skidmore Coll., Saratoga Springs, N.Y., 1957-61, chmn. dept. modern langs. and lits., 1961-79, prof. Spanish, 1961-87, prof. emerita, 1987; cons. Hudson-Mohawk Assn. Colls. and Univs., 1990. Faculty rsch. lectr. Skidmore Coll., 1963; mem. adv. and nominating com. Books Abroad, 1965-67; Fulbright lectr. Free U. Berlin, 1968; lectr. U. Gesamthochschule, Paderborn, Germany, 1995, 99. Author: Guillermo Valencia, Colombian Poet, 1951, Educational Development in Costa Rica with UNESCO's Technical Assistance, 1951-54, 1954, Jaime Torres Bodet: A Poet in a Changing World, 1963, Selected Poems of Jaime Torres Bodet, 1964, Versos y prosas de Jaime Torres Bodet, 1966, Jaime Torres Bodet, 1971, Ensayos de Literatura E Historia Iberoamericana/Essays on Iberoamerican Literature and History, 1988, Papers on Foreign Languages, Literature and Culture, 1982-87, 88, Bericht Über Den Vater: Fritz Karsen 1885-1951, 1993; translator: The Role of the Americas in History (Leopoldo Zea), 1992; editor Lang. Assn. Bull., 1980-83; mem. edit. adv. bd. Modern Lang. Studies, 1977-93; contbr. articles to profl. jours. Decorated Chevalier dans l'Ordre des Palmes Académiques, 1964; recipient Leadership award N.Y. State Assn. Fgn. Lang. Tchrs., 1973, 76, 78, Nat. Disting. Leadership award, 1979, Disting. Service award, 1983, 86, Capital Dist. Fgn. Language Disting. Service award, 1987; recipient Spanish Heritage award, 1981, Alumni Achievement award Carleton Coll., 1982; exchange student auspices Inst. Internat. Ednl. at Carleton Coll., 1938-39; Buenos Aires Conv. grantee for research in Colombia, 1946-47; faculty research grantee Skidmore Coll., summer 1959, 61, 63, 64, 67, 69, 70, 73, ad hoc faculty grantee, 71, 78, 85. Mem. Am. Assn. Tchrs. Spanish and Portuguese (emeritus), Nat. Assn. Self-Instructional Lang. Programs (v.p. 1981-82,pres. 1982-83), AAUW (life), AAUP (life), MLA (del. assembly 1976-78, Mildenberger medal selection com. 1984-86), El Ateneo Doctor Jaime Torres Bodet (founding mem.), Nat. Geog. Soc., Asociación Internacional de Hispanistas, UN Assn. U.S.A., Am. Soc. French Acad. Palms, Fulbright Alumni, Phi Sigma Iota, Sigma Delta Pi. Home: 1755 York Ave Apt 37A New York NY 10128-6875

KARSON, CATHERINE JUNE, database administrator; b. Salt Lake City, Jan. 26, 1956; d. Gary George and Sylvia June (Naylor) Anderson; m. Mitchell Reed Karson, June 14, 1987; 1 child, Rhonda. A in Gen. Studies, Pima C.C., Tucson, 1989, AAS in Computer Sci., 1990. Night supr. F.G. Ferre & Son, Inc., Salt Lake City, 1973-76, exec. sec., 1977-79; operating room technician Cottonwood Hosp., Salt Lake City, 1976-77; customer svc. rep., System One rep. Ea. Airlines, Inc., Salt Lake City and Tucson, 1979-88; edn. specialist Radio Shack Computer Ctr., Tucson, 1988-89; programmer/analyst Pinal County DPIS, Florence, Ariz., 1989-90; systems analyst Carondelet Health Svcs., Tucson, 1990; programmer/analyst Misys Healthcare Sys., Tucson, 1990-94, sr. tech. proposal specialist, 1994-95, software developer, 1995-97, sr. sys. software specialist/dba, 1997—99; cons. Tucson Hebrew Acad., 2002—03. Cons. Pinal County Pub. Fiduciary, Florence, 1990, UBET, Barbados, W.I., 1990-96, numerous clients, Tucson, 1990-93. Mem. bus. adv. coun. Portable Practical Ednl. Preparation, Inc., Tucson, 1990-91. Mem. Nat. Sys. Programmer Assn. Republican. Jewish. Avocations: reading, painting, music, light opera performance, dance classes. Home: 5413 N Ventana Vista Rd Tucson AZ 85750-7203

KARU, GILDA M(ALL), lawyer, federal agency administrator; b. Oceanport, NJ, Dec. 1, 1951; d. Harold and Ilvy (Meriloo) Karu; m. Frederick F. Foy, May 23, 1981. AB, Vassar Coll., 1974; JD, Ill. Inst. Tech., 1987. Bar: Ill. 1987, U.S. Dist. Ct. (no. dist.) Ill. 1987. Quality control reviewer Food and Nutrition Svc. USDA, Robbinsville, NJ, 1974-77, team leader, 1977-78, supr., 1978-81, sect. chief Food and Nutrition Svc. Chgo., 1991-2000, acting dir. field ops., 1998, acting dir. food stamp program, 1999, regional dir. civil rights/EEO for midwest region Food and Nutrition Svc., 2000—. Employer adviser Ctr. Rehab. and Tng. Disable Persons, Chgo., 1986—93; chief mgmt. negotiator collective bargaining agreement Nat. Treasury Employees Union, 1990; acting regional dir. Food Stamp program, 1999, 2000; chair. diversity adv. com. Chgo. Fed. Exec. Bd., 2001—, co-mediator shared neutrals ADR program, 2003—. Mem. Chgo. Vol. Legal Svcs., Friends Arlington Heights Meml. Libr.; vol. dep. voter registration officer Cook County, Ill.; v.p. 1st Estonian Evang. Luth. Ch., Chgo., treas., 1994—2003; bd. dirs., legal counsel, regional dir. N. Ctrl. Estonian Am. Nat. Coun., N.Y.C. Recipient cert. of recognition, William A. Jump Meml. Found., 1987, Arthur S. Flemming award, Washington Downtown Jaycees, 1987, Ill. Dem. Ethnic Heritage award, 1989, cert. of appreciation, Assn. Persons with Disabilities Agr., 1992. Mem.: LWV (bd. dirs. 1992—, v.p. chpt. 2000—, newsletter editor), AAUW, ABA, United Coun. Welfare Fraud, Baltic Bar Assn., Chgo. Bar Assn., Ill. Bar Assn., Mensa, Chgo. Area Seven Sisters Coll. Consortium (sec. 1995—), Vassar Club (chpt. treas. 1988—90, v.p. 1990—91, coord. pub. rels. 1991—2000). Avocations: photography, reading, travel, crafts. Office: USDA Food and Nutrition Svc 77 W Jackson Blvd Fl 20 Chicago IL 60604-3591

KASAKOVE, SUSAN, interior designer; b. Newark, N.J., Nov. 11, 1938; BFA, U. Buffalo, 1958, Hunter Coll., 1960; postgrad., N.Y. Sch. of Interior Design, 1960-64, New Sch. for Social Rsch., 1967-68, Pratt Inst., 1968-69. Asst. interior designer Rodgers Assocs., N.Y.C., 1964-66; interior designer Walter Dorwin Teague Assocs., N.Y.C., 1966-70; sr. interior designer N.Y. State Facilities Devel. Corp., N.Y.C., 1970-95; Dormitory Authority for the State of N.Y., 1995—. Reading tutor Vols. for Children's Svcs., N.Y.C., 1976-82; chair Friends of White Plains (N.Y.) Symphony, 1981-83, Met. Mus. Art; vol. dept. Asian Dept. Work Endod, 1995, vol. guide edn. dept., 1978—; Rep. treas. 11th Ward, Yonkers, N.Y., 1979-81. Recipient Outstanding Svc. to Sch. award Rockland County (N.Y.) Lions Club, 1955. Mem. Environ. Design Rsch. Assn. Avocations: photography, history of art and architecture, golf, swimming. Home: 793 Palmer Rd Apt 3F Bronxville NY 10708-3337 Office: 1 Penn Plz Fl 52 New York NY 10119-5299

KASCHUB, MICHELE ELLEN, music educator, researcher; b. East Millinocket, Maine, Dec. 16, 1967; d. David James and Juanita Ruth Pressley; m. Alan Robert Kaschub, Aug. 12, 1995; children: David, Kathryn, Daniel. BS in Music Edn., U. So. Maine, 1990; MM in Choral Conducting, U. Maine, Orono, 1994; PhD in Music Edn., Northwestern U., 1999. Cert. profl. level music tchr. Maine. Tchr. gen. music, Camden, Maine, 1990—94, Glencoe, Ill., 1994—95; instr. Northwestern U., Evanston, Ill., 1995—97; asst. prof. U. So. Maine, Gorham, 1997—. Contbr. articles to profl. jours. Mem.: Am. Choral Dirs. Assn. (state chair 1986—), Music Educators Nat. Conf. (state chair 1986—). Office: U So Maine Sch Music 37 College Ave Gorham ME 04038 Business E-Mail: kaschub@usm.maine.edu.

KASDORF, JULIA MAE, language educator, poet; b. Lewistown, Pa., Dec. 6, 1962; d. John Lee Spicher and Virginia Joy Peachey; m. David Mark Kasdorf, July 27, 1986; 1 child, Amelia Clare. BA in English, NYU, 1985, MA in English and Creative Writing, 1989, PhD in English Edn., 1997. Asst. prof. Messiah Coll., Grantram, Pa., 1996—2000; assoc. prof. Pa. State U., 2000—. Author: (poems) Sleeping Preacher, 1992 (Starrett prize, 1991), Eve's Striptease, 1998, (essays) The Body and the Book, 2000 (CCL Book of the Yr., 2001), Fixing Tradition: Joseph W. Yoder, Amish American, 2002. Recipient Pushcart prize, 2003. Home: 230 W Linn St Bellefonte PA 16823-1520 Office: Pa State U 116 Burrowes Bldg University Park PA 16802

KASHDIN, GLADYS SHAFRAN, painter, educator; b. Dec. 15, 1921; d. Edward M. and Miriam P. Shafran; m. Manville E. Kashdin, Oct. 11, 1942 (dec.). BA magna cum laude, U. Miami, 1960; MA, Fla. State U., 1962, PhD, 1965. Photographer, N.Y.C. and Fla., 1938-60; tchr. art Fla. and Ga., 1956-63; from asst. prof. to prof. humanities U. South Fla., Tampa, 1965-87, prof. emerita, 1987—. Lectr., adv. bd. Hillsborough County Mus., 1975—84. Exhibitions include 68 one-woman shows, 55 group exhbns., The Everglades, 1972—75, Aspects of the River, 1975—80, Processes of Time, 1981—91, Retrospective, 1941—96, Tampa Mus. Art, 1996, Appleton Mus. Art, Ocala, 1999, 2001—02, Mus. Sci. and Industry, Tampa, 2003, Represented in permanent collections, Taiwan, China, Columbus Mus. Arts, LeMoyne Art Found., Tampa Internat. Airport, Tampa Mus. Art, Appleton Mus. Art, Ocala, Mus. Sci. and Industry, Tampa, Miss. Mus. Art, Jackson, Jan Kaminis Platt Libr., Tampa, U. So. Fla. Spl. Collections Libr. Mem. U.S. Fla. Status of Women Com., 1971-76, chmn., 1975-76; mem. nat. bd., Mus. Sci. and Industry, Tampa, 2003—. Recipient Women Helping Women in Art award Soroptimist Internat., 1979, Citizens Hon. award Hillsborough Bd. County Commrs., 1984, Mortar Bd. award for tchg. excellence, 1986, Recognition award for lifetime achievement in arts and scis. So. Acad. Letters, Arts and Scis., 2002. Mem. AAUW (1st v.p. Tampa br. 1971-72), Phi Kappa Phi (chpt.-pres. 1981-83, artist/scholar award 1987). Home: 441 Biltmore Ave Temple Terrace FL 33617-7207

KASI, LEELA PESHKAR, pharmaceutical chemist; b. Bombay, July 15, 1939; came to U.S., 1971; d. Subbaraman and Lakshmi (Shastri) Peshkar; m. Kalli R. Kasi, June 10, 1971. BS, U. Bombay, India, 1958; PhD, U. Marburg, W. Germany, 1968. Jr. chemist Khandelwal Labs., Bombay, India, 1958-59; trainee Farbwerke Hoechst, Frankfurt, W. Germany, 1960; teaching asst. U. of Marburg, W. Germany, 1967-68; sr. chemist Boehringer-Knoll Ltd., Bombay, India, 1969-71; mgr. quality control Health Care Ind., Michigan City, Ind., 1972-77, U. Tex.-M.D. Anderson Cancer Ctr., Houston, 1979-95, assoc. prof. nuclear medicine, faculty mem., 1990-95, dir. Exptl. Nuclear Medicine Lab., 1979-95; cons. Radiopharms. Devel., Houston, 1995—. Mem. grad. faculty U. Tex., 1984-90. Asst. editor Jour. Nuclear Medicine, 1984-89. Mem. AAAS, Am. Assn. Cancer Rsch., Soc. of Nuclear Medicine. Home and Office: 4710 Mcdermed Dr Houston TX 77035-3706 E-mail: lkasi@hal-pc.org.

KASKINEN, BARBARA KAY, author, composer, songwriter, musician, music educator; d. Norman Ferdinand and Martha Agnes (Harju) Kaskinen. AA, Broward C.C., Coconut Creek, Fla., 1978; BA with honors, Fla. Atlantic U., 1981, MA, 1995; postgrad., U. Miami, 2000—. Instr. adult piano Atlantic H.S., Delray Beach, Fla., 1981-82; organist, combo dir. Affirmation Luth. Ch., Boca Raton, Fla., 1981-86; studio musician, composer/arranger Electric Rize Prodns., Margate, Fla., 1982-94; ind. instr. piano, electronic keyboard and guitar, Margate, 1979-91. Co-founder Oasis Coffee House, Boca Raton, Fla., 1990—92; co-owner Electric Rize Publ, 1991; asst dir TOPS Piano Camp, 1994—96; mem. adj faculty Fla. Atlantic Univ., 1995—, Broward C.C., Coconut Creek, 1996—, Miami Dade Coll., 2003; staff accompanist Palm Beach Atlantic Univ., West Palm Beach, Fla., 2003. Musician (bass, keyboard player): Electric Rize Band, 1982—91; composer: Hansen House, 1987—88; author: Adult Electronic Keyboard Course Book I, 1988, Adult Electronic Keyboard Course Books II and III, 1989. Mem.: ASCAP, Nat. Piano Found., Music Guild Boca Raton, Broward County Music Tchr's Asn (treas), Fla State Music Tchr's Asn, Nat Guild Piano Tchrs, Fla Atlantic Univ Alumni Asn. Home: 6601 NW 22nd St Pompano Beach FL 33063-2117 Address: 6601 NW 22 St Margate FL 33063 E-mail: neniksa@aol.com.

KASLOW, FLORENCE WHITEMAN, psychologist, educator, family business consultant; b. Phila., Jan. 06; d. Irving and Rose (Tarin) Whiteman; m. Solis Kaslow; children: Nadine Joy, Howard Ian. AB in Sociology with distinction, Temple U., 1952; MA, Ohio State U., 1954; PhD, Bryn Mawr Coll., 1969. Lic. psychologist, marriage and family therapist, Fla., cert. psychologist Am. Bd. Clin. Psychology, Am. Bd. Forensic Psychology, Am. Bd. Family Psychology. Pvt. practice, Palm Beach Gardens, Fla., 1964—; dir. Fla. Couples and Family Inst., 1982—; adj. prof. med. psychology Duke U. Med. Ctr., Durham, N.C., 1982—; vis. prof. psychology Fla. Inst. Tech., Melbourne, 1985—; disting. vis. prof. Calif. Grad. Sch. Family Psychology, 1989-92. Cons. USN Dept. Psychiatry Residency Tng. Programs, San Diego, Portsmouth, Va., Phila., 1976-88, Palm Beach Inst., 1983-90, weekly radio guest Voice of Am., Focus on Families, 1993-2003; pres. Am. Bd. Forensic Psychology, 1977-80, Am. Bd. Family Psychology, 1996-2000. Editor: Voices in Family Psychology, 1990; author: (with L.L. Schwartz) Dynamics of Divorce: A Life Cycle Perspective, 1987, The Military Family in Peace and War, 1993, Handbook of Relational Diagnoses and Dysfunctional Family Patterns, 1996, Painful Partings: Divorce and Its Aftermath, 1997, Handbook of Couple and Family Forensics, 1999, Comprehensive Handbook of Psychotherapy, 4 vols., 2002, (with L.L. Schwartz) Welcome Home: an International and Non Traditional Adoption Reader, 2004; contbr. articles to profl. jours., chpts. to books; mem. editl. bd. Jour. Marital and Family Therapy, 1976—, Marriage and Family Rev., 1977-92, Jour. Sex and Marital Therapy, 1984—, Jour. Clin. Child Psychology, 1986—, Jour. Psychotherapy, 1988—. Recipient Disting. Psychology Contbn. award Am. Bd. Profl. Psychology, 1994, Outstanding Family Therapy Contbn. award Am. Assn. Marriage and Family Therapy, 1991, NIMH trainee, 1969. Mem. APA (divsn. family psychology pres. 1987, sec. 1983-85, com. mem. 1987—, pres. divsn. media psychology 1993. Disting. Contbn. to Internat. Psychology award 2000, 05), Am. Assn. Marital and Family Therapy, Am. Family Therapy Acad., Coalition Family Diagnosis (chmn. 1989-93), Am. Assn. Sex Educators, Counselors and Therapists, Internat. Family Therapy Assn. (founding pres. 1987-90), Acad. Family Mediators (bd. dirs. 1982-88, treas. 1985 87). Office Phone: 561-625-0288. E-mail: kaslowfs@worldnet.att.net.

KASPROW, BARBARA ANNE, biomedical scientist, writer; b. Hartford, Conn., Apr. 23, 1936; d. Stephen G. and Anna M. Kasprow. AB cum laude, Albertus Magnus Coll., 1958; postgrad., Laval U., 1958, Yale U., 1958-61; PhD, Loyola U., Chgo., 1969. Staff microbiology dept. Conn. State Dept. Health, 1957; lab. asst. dept. microbiology Yale U., New Haven, 1958—59; tng. scholar USPHS, 1959—60; asst. rsch. and editl. dept. anatomy Yale U., New Haven, 1961; rsch. assoc. N.Y. Med. Coll., 1961—62; rsch. assoc. to sr. rsch. assoc. and adminstrv. assoc. Inst. for Study Human Reprodn. St. Ann Ob-Gyn. Hosp., Cleve., 1962—67, asst. to dir. grad. med. edn., asst. dir. adminstrn. grad. rsch. endocrinology, Inst. for Study Human Reprodn., 1962—67; sr. rsch. assoc. dept. anatomy Stritch Sch. Medicine, Chgo., Hines, Ill., 1967—69; asst. prof. anatomy Loyola U., Chgo., 1969—75; asst. to v.p. University Rsch. Sys., 1975-79; v.p. med. topics Univ. Rsch. Sys., 1979—; asst. to pres. Internat. Basic and Biol.-Biomed. Curricula, Lombard, Ill., 1979—. Lectr. in field; invited U.S. del. on reprodn. to Vatican, 1964; round table leader Brazil-Israel Congress on Fertility and Sterility, Brazil Soc. Human Reprodn., São Paulo, 1972. Editl. asst. vol. VIII/3 Handbuch der Histochemie, Gustav Fischer Verlag, 1963; prodn. aide ednl. med. film The Soft Anvil, 1965-66; co-editor: Biology of Reproduction, Basic and Clinical Studies, 1973; contbr. articles to profl. jours. Recipient Certificate of Outstanding Achievement and Scholarship award Am. Assn. German Tchrs. and New Britain German Assn., 1954; named Honorary Citizen São Paulo, 1972. Mem. AAAS (life), Am. Assn. Anatomists, Am. Soc. Zoologists-The Soc. Integrative and Comparative Biology, Pan Am. Assn. Anatomy (co-organizer symposium on reproduction New Orleans 1972), Midwest Anatomists Assn. (program officer ann. meeting Chgo. 1974), Sigma Xi (life). Roman Catholic. Achievements include biological elucidation of growth horizons in uterine development, growth, and maturity; perfection of a hormonal model-system in highly controlled (surgerized) animals to ascertain quantitative relationships of purified estradiol-17beta and progesterone required for promotion of and duplication of these uterine growth horizons; development of experimental paradigms for the biomorphological elucidation of hormonally stimulated growth responses in endocrine target organs, and cyto- and histochemical elucidation of growth stimulants. Office: 607 E Wilson Ave Lombard IL 60148-4062

KASS, EMILY, art museum administrator; Director Tampa (Fla.) Mus. of Art, 1996—. Office: Tampa Mus Art 600 N Ashley Dr Tampa FL 33602-4305

KASSEBAUM, NANCY See BAKER, NANCY KASSEBAUM

KASSEL, CATHERINE M. community, maternal, and women's health nurse, consultant; b. Bklyn., Dec. 18, 1953; d. Christopher Frank and Ana Rosa (Sousa) Pannone; m. David L. Kassel, Dec. 27, 1979. Diploma in nursing, Kings County Hosp., Bklyn., 1974; BA in Cmty. Health, CUNY, 1979; BSN with honors, Columbia U., 1989. RN, N.Y. V.p. Kassel Mgmt. Co., N.Y.C., 1985—; pres. Kassel & Co., LLC, N.Y.C. Bd. dirs., co-chair legis. com. N.Y. Counties of RNs, Dist. 13, trustee, treas. polit. action com.; past bd. dirs. Nat. Abortion Rights Action League; bd. dirs., treas., chmn. fundraising, nominating com., adv. coun., Global Kids Inc.; mem. Women's Leadership Forum of Dem. Nat. Com. Mem. ANA (polit. action com.), ANA Found. (founding mem.), N.Y. State Nurses Assn., PAC. Home: 145 W 67th St Apt 7H New York NY 10023

KASSEL, VIRGINIA WELTMER, television producer, writer; b. Omaha; d. Tyler and Inez (Willard) Weltmer. BA, Bryn Mawr Coll. Producer Sta. WGBH-TV, Boston; producer NET, N.Y.C., coordinator nat. programs; mgr. spl. projects, exec. prodr. humanities programs WNET, N.Y.C.; sr. producer CBS Cable, N.Y.C., 1981-83; dir. devel. and prodn. East Coast Primetime Entertainment, Inc., 1983-87; v.p. East Coast Primetime Entertainment, Inc., 1987-89; assoc. dir. performance programs, prodn. exec. Great Performances Sta. WNET-TV, N.Y.C., 1989-91; producer, dir., writer Potter Prodns., 1991-92; dir. devel. Internat. Cultural Programming, 1992-94. Creator, prodr.: The Adams Chronicles, Sta. WNET, N.Y.C.; prodr.: The Soong Connection, 1995; contbr. articles to profl. publs. Recipient George Foster Peabody award, 1977, 2 Ohio State awards, 1977, Spl. Achievement award Nat. Assn. Ednl. Broadcasters, 1977, Triangle award, 1986, NEH, Mellon Found. grants. Mem.: NATAS, N.Y. Women in TV and Film, Brit. acad. Film and TV Arts, Brit. Acad. Film and TV Arts (N.Y. and London, mem. U.S./China rels. com.), Am. Acad. TV Arts and Scis., Writers Guild Am. East, Women's City Club N.Y. (bd. dirs.), Princeton Club (N.Y.). Home: 4 E 89th St New York NY 10128-0636

KASSELL, PAULA SALLY, editor, publisher; b. N.Y.C., Dec. 5, 1917; d. Daniel Herman and Bertha Blanche (Jaret) K.; m. Gerson Gustav Friedman, Aug. 16, 1941 (dec.); children: Daniel Kassell, Claire Florence Friedman. BA, Barnard Coll., 1939. Tech. editor Bell Labs., Whippany, N.J., 1955-65, methods analyst Murray Hill, N.J., 1965-70; founder, editor, pub. New Directions for Women, Dover, N.J., 1971-77, assoc. editor Englewood, N.J., 1977-87, sr. editor, 1987-93, index editor Dover, 1993-98. V.p., UN rep. Women's Inst. for Freedom of Press, Washington, 1990—; convenor, mem. media task force Com. on Status of Women, UN, 1990-98. Contrubutor chapters to books: "Planning an International Communications System for Women" in Communications at the Crossroads: The Gender Gap Connection (Ablex Publishing Corporation, 1989). "The Birth, Success, Death and Lasting Influence of a Feminist Periodical: New Directions for Women (1972-1993-?)" in Women Transforming Communications: Global Intersections (Sage Publications, 1996). "New Directions for Women" in Women's Periodicals in the United States: Social and Political Issues (Greenwood Press, 1996). Co-convenor Lakeland chpt. NOW, Dover, 1970; v.p. Dover (N.J.) Child Care Ctr., 1979-91; bd. dirs. Nat. Woman's Party, Washington, 1991-98; mem. media com. Forum 95, UN, N.Y.C., 1994-95; mem. adv. bd. Vet. Feminists Am., Lafayette, La., 1995—; mem. TV task force Morris County NOW, Morristown, N.J., 1995—; trustee Women's Media Initiative, 1997. Recipient First Feminist Action award NOW NJ, 1985, Women Making Herstory award, 1995, Elizabeth Cady Stanton award Women's Rights Info. Ctr., 1993, Woman of Achievement award Douglass Coll., 1994, Medal of Honor, Vet. Feminists Am., 1998, Millicent Carey McIntosh Feminism Award Barnard Coll., 2004. Featured in exhibit on NJ feminists by Morris County (NJ) Hist. Soc., September 17, 2000 to March 18, 2001, Journalist of Month, on women's e-news, www.womensenews.org, 2002. Mem. Am. Journalism Historians Assn., Internat. Women's Media Found., Journalism & Women Symposium. Avocations: attending opera, concerts, ballet performances, visiting museums, travelling. Home: 25 W Fairview Ave Dover NJ 07801-3417

KASSOY, HORTENSE (HONEY KASSOY), artist, sculptor, painter, printmaker; b. N.Y.C., Feb. 14, 1917; d. Adolph and Mary (Apfel) Blumenkranz; m. Bernard Kassoy, June 30, 1946; children: Meredith, Sheila. Diploma, Pratt Inst., 1936; BS, Columbia U., 1938, MA, 1939; student, Parsons Sch. Design, Paris, U. Colo., 1966, NYU, 1966-67; studied sculpture with Sahl Swarz, Chaim Gross & Oronzio Maldarelli. Solo exhbns. include Caravan House Gallery, 1974, Women in the Arts Gallery, 1978, Ward-Nasse Gallery, 1986, Pioneer Gallery, Cooperstown, N.Y., 1987, 91, 97, 80th Birthday Retrospective Solo of Wood Sculpture Prints and Watercolors, Vladeck Hall Gallery, N.Y., 1997, 2002, Pioneer Gallery, Cooperstown, 1997, 2002; group exhbns. include Bronx (N.Y.) Mus., 1971, 75, 85-86, Toledo Mus. Art, Toronto Mus. Art, Hudson River Mus., Bklyn. Mus., New Age Gallery, Lever House, Bklyn. Coll., Fordham U., Lehman Coll., Cork Gallery, Nat. Acad. Design; permanent collections include Slater Meml. Mus. Co-chair visual arts Bronx (N.Y.) Coun. on Arts, 1973 76. Fellow Va. Ctr. for Creative Arts, 1986, 88, 89, 92, 95, 97; recipient 1st prize in watercolor Painters Day at N.Y. World's Fair, 1940, Walker prize for sculpture, Oneonta, NY, 2002. Mem. Am. Soc. Contemporary Artists (v.p. 1989-94, 99-2003, awards in sculpture 1979, 80, 83, 90, 92, 96, 2000, 02), N.Y. Artists Equity Assn. (v.p., bd. dirs. 1971-83), Internation Assn. Art (corr. sec. 1979-93), del. to 10th Congress 1983), Contemporary Arts Guild (rec. sec. 1981-89), Fedn. Modern Painters and Sculptors. Home: 130 Gale Pl Apt 6B Bronx NY 10463-2853 also: Butternut Hill Studio 1577 County Route 16 Burlington Flats NY 13315-3211

KASTE, SUE CREVISTON, pediatric radiologist, researcher; b. Lakewood, Ohio, Feb. 25, 1952; d. Donald P. and Marion S. Creviston; m. Ronald H. Kaste, Apr. 28, 1984; children: Rebecca, Steven, Matthew. BA, Lake Erie Coll., 1974; AAS Physicians Asst., Cuyahoga C.C. and Cleve. Clin., 1977; DO, Chgo. Coll. Osteo. Medicine, 1981. Diplomate Am. Bd. Radiology cert. added qualifications pediat. radiology; cert. osteopath Osteo. Nat. Bd. Med. Examiners. Intern Chgo. Coll. Osteo. Medicine, Ill., 1981-82; diagnostic radiology U. Hosps. Cleve., 1982-86, fellow pediat. radiology, 1986-87; officer in charge pediat. radiology KTTCMC, Keesler AFB, Biloxi, Miss., 1987-90, chief diagnostic radiology, 1990-91; cons. dept. radiology LeBonheur Children's Med. Ctr., Memphis, 1991—2003; prof. dept. radiology U. Tenn. Coll. Medicine, Memphis, 1991—2003, prof., 2003—; full mem. dept. diagnostic imaging St. Jude Children's Rsch. Hosp., Memphis, 2002—. Reviewer Am. Jour. Roentgenology, 1994—, Pediat. Radiology, 1997—, Cancer, 1997—; contbr. articles to profl. jours. Leader/asst. leader Girl Scouts Am., Cordova, Tenn., 1992-99; youth club asst. Advent Presbyn. Ch., Cordova, 1993-98, mem. ch. orch. Maj. USAF Med. Corps, 1977-91. Grantee, Soc. Pediat. Radiology, 1998. Mem. Children's Oncology Group, Am. Coll. Radiology, Radiologic Soc. N.Am., Midwest Soc. Pediat. Radiology. Avocations: flute, painting, drawing, swimming. Office: St Jude Childrens Rsch Hosp Dept Diagnostic Imaging 332 N Lauderdale St Memphis TN 38105-2729 Fax: 901-495-3962. E-mail: sue.kaste@stjude.org.

KASTEN, MARY ALICE C. state legislator; b. Matthews, Mo., June 6, 1928; d. Clarence Alvin and Ruth (Hill) Critchlow; m. Melvin C. Kasten, 1949; children: Mark, Michael, Margaret. BS, Southeast Mo. State U., 1949; postgrad., U. Pitts. State rep. Mo. State Congress. Del. Nat. Conf. Edn. and Citizenship; mem. Cape Girardeau Sch. Bd., Nat. Joint Com. Representing Sch. Bd. Assn., Mo. State Bd. Edn., State Adv. Com. on Vocat. Edn. Bd. Regents mem. Southeast Mo. State U. Mem. Nat. Sch. Bd. Assn., Mo. Sch. Bd. Assn. Office: Mo Ho of Reps State Capitol Building Jefferson City MO 65101-1556

KASTER, LAURA A. lawyer; b. N.Y.C., May 24, 1948; BA, Tufts U., 1970; JD magna cum laude, Boston U., 1973. Bar: Mass. 1973, Ill. 1975. Law clk. to Hon. Frank M. Coffin, U.S. Ct. Appeals for 1st circuit, Boston, 1973-75; assoc. Jenner & Block, Chgo., 1975-81, ptnr., 1981-97; gen. atty. law and govt. affairs AT&T Corp., Bedminster, NJ, 1997—. Co-author: Sanctions in Federal Litigation, 1991; co-editor: The Attorneys' Guide to the Seventh Circuit Court of Appeals, 1987; note editor Law Rev. Boston U., 1973-72; contbr. chpt. to book and articles to profl. jours. Fellow Am. Bar Found. (life); mem. ABA, Ill. Bar Assn., 7th Circuit Bar Assn., Fed. Cir. Bar Assn. Personal E-mail: lkaster@att.com.

KASTON, LISA MARSHA, social services administrator; b. N.Y.C., Apr. 1, 1955; d. Seymour Albert Kaston and Susan Zuckerman Kaston; children: Adam Louis Garcia, Emily Beth Garcia. MPS, New Sch. U., N.Y.C., 1987. Mgr. grants and cmty. initiatives Devereux Fla., Orlando, 1995—2002; dir. program devel. and contract mgmt. Hope and Help Ctr. of Ctrl. Fla., Winter Park, 2002—. Mem. steering com. coun. agy. execs. Heart of Fla. United Way, Orlando, 1998—2002; mem. Leadership Orlando, 1999—2000; mem. funding rev. panel Victims of Crime Assistance Program, 18th Jud. Cir., Brevard and Seminole Counties, Fla., 1999—2001. Mem.: Grant Profls. Network Ctrl. Fla. (pres. 2000—01, Excellence in Grant Professionalism and Advocacy Award 2000). Avocations: travel, reading, arts. Office: Hope and Help Ctr of Ctrl Fla 1935 Woodcrest Dr Winter Park FL 32792 Personal E-mail: joliadem@aol.com. E-mail: lkaston@hopeandhelp.org.

KATA, MARIE L. securities dealer, brokerage house executive; b. Redwood Falls, Minn. m. M. T. Kata, 1984; children: Namue, Karwehn. BS in Bus., U. Minn., 1979. Lic. Series 24, cert. Series 65, Series 7. Stockbroker R.J. Steichen, 1992, Montano Securities, 1993—95, Res. Fin., 1996—97, Eisner Securities, 1997—2001, br. mgr., 1997—2001; stockbroker LaSalle St. Securities, Edina, Minn., 2001—, br. mgr., 2001—. Recipient Hon. Advisor award, Fidelity Investments, 2001. Avocations: skiing, reading, spirituality. Office: LaSalle St Securities LLC 7701 France Ave S #200 Edina MN 55435

KATEN, KAREN L. pharmaceutical executive; BA polit. sci. and economics, U. Chgo., 1970, MBA mktg. and fin., 1974. Mktg. assoc. pharms. Pfizer, 1974, various positions Roerig divsn. product mgmt. group, 1975—78, group product mgr. Pfizer Labs., 1980, dir. product mgr. Pfizer Labs., v.p. mktg. Roerig divsn., 1983—86, v.p., dir. ops. Roerig divsn., 1986—91, v.p., gen. mgr. Roerig divsn., 1991—93, exec. v.p. Pfizer US Pharms. Group, 1993—95, pres. Pfizer U.S. Pharms. Group, 1995—2002, v.p., 1992—99; exec. v.p. Pfizer Global Pharmaceuticals (formerly Pfizer Pharmaceuticals Group), 1997—2001; sr. v.p. Pfizer, 1999—2001; pres. Pfizer Global Pharmaceuticals, 2001—; exec. v.p. Pfizer, Inc., 2001—. Bd. dirs. GM, Harris Corp., Catalyst, Nat. Alliance Hispanic Health; mem. internat. coun. J.P. Morgan Chase & Co.; mem. coun. U.S. and Italy, U. Chgo. Grad. Sch. Bus.; trustee U. Chgo.; nat. bd. trustees Am. Cancer Soc. Rsch. Found.; health bd. advisors RAND Corp.; bd. corp. advisors Am. Diabetes Assn. Recipient Salute to Women Achievers award, YMCA, Women Yr. award, Boy Scout Am. Greater N.Y. Coun., N.Y. Women's Agenda Star award, Bus. Leadership award, Burden Ctr. Aging, Iphigene Ochs Sulzburger award, Barnard Coll., Am. Fedn. Aging Rsch. Distinction award, Woman of Yr. award, N.Y.C. Police Athletic League, 2001. Mem.: Am. Diabetes Assn. (mem. bd. corp. advisors, Women of Valor award), Am. Cancer Soc. Rsch. Found. (mem. nat. bd. trustees), Nat. Alliance Hispanic Health, European Fedn. Pharm. Industry Assns. (bd. mem.), Health Leadership Coun., Pharm. Rsch. and Mfrs. Assn. Am. Office: Pfizer Inc 235 E 42nd St New York NY 10017-5755*

KATES, CHERYL L. legal nursing consultant; b. Rochester, N.Y., July 4, 1970; d. John Edward Leavy and Jean Ellen (Boyle) Leavy-Ellis; 1 child, Markas J. LPN, SUNY, Brockport, 1991; AA, Monroe C.C., Rochester, 1998; BA, St. John Fisher Coll. Cert. EMT; LPN. LPN Unique Staffing, Rochester, 1991—94. Tutor Literacy Vols., Rochester, 1996—; co-dir. Edge of Justice; bd. dirs. legal com. NYCLU, Rochester. Avocations: ceramics, African American studies. Home: 6072 E Lake Rd Honeoye NY 14471-9747

KATHAN, JOYCE C. social worker, administrator; b. Middletown, Conn., Oct. 28, 1931; d. Herbert G. and Mabel Elizabeth (Lee) Clark; m. Boardman W. Kathan, Aug. 17, 1952; children: Nancy Lee, David Wardell, Robert Boardman. BSW magna cum laude, So. Conn. State U., 1976. Dist. dir. Coun. Greater Boston Camp Fire Girls, 1969-73; dir. sr. citizen programs Town of Woodbury, Conn., 1976-97; info. officer Conn. Coalition of Aging, 1998—. Participant Global Assembly of Women and Environ., 1991; adv. bd. VNA health Care, 1985-95. Co-author: Youth Where the Action Is, 1970, (with others) Management of Hazardous Agents, Vol. 2: Social and Political Aspects, 1992. Bd. dirs. E. Irene Boardman Found., 1996—, Waterbury YWCA, 1977—83, rec. sec.; mem. Prospect (Conn.) Commn. on Aging, 1979—89, chair, 1979—87; apptd. mem. Congl. Dist. 5 adv. coun. Conn. Permanent Commn. on Status of Women, 1996—; bd. dirs. Western Conn. Area Agy. on Aging, 1986—92, pres., 1990—92, adv. coun., 1994—2003; bd. dirs. Robin Ridge Elderly Housing, 2001—03; pres. Greater Waterbury AAUUD, 2001—05. Recipient Outstanding Conn. Women award, 1987, Vol. of Yr. award Conn. Coalition on Aging, 1999. Mem.: LWV (pres. Cheshire chpt. 1989—93), AAUW (pub. policy chmn. Conn. chpt. 1996—2000, Assn. Pub. Policy Com. 1985—89, local and state coms. 1978—, pres. Greater Waterbury chpt. 2000—, Named Gift award Conn. chpt. 1981, 1985, 1997, Outstanding Cmty. Svc. award Conn. chpt. 1994), NASW, Conn. Assn. Sr. Ctr. Pers. (charter mem., rec. sec. 1995—97, Svc. award 1986), Women's Environ. and Devel. Orgn., Conn. LWV (pub. policy com. 1988—). E-mail: jckccoa@aol.com.

KATO, TERRI EMI, elementary school and gifted and talented educator; b. Gardena, Calif., Sept. 1, 1953; d. Shunji James and Ruby Miyo (Sumi) K. BA, Calif. State U., Long Beach, 1976; MA, U.S. Internat. U., 1987. Cert. tchr. multiple subjects, learning handicapped, severely handicapped, resource specialist, lang. devel. specialist, c.c.'s, Calif. Learning disabled group specialist Montebello (Calif.) Unified Sch. Dist., 1979-81; resource specialist ABC Unified Sch. Dist., Cerritos, Calif., 1981-82; spl. day class tchr. Santa Ana (Calif.) Unified Sch. Dist., 1982—; math. resource tchr., 1990-98; 1st and 2nd grade tchr. Santa Ana (Calif.) Unified Sch. Dist., 1996-98, kindergarten tchr., 1999—. Mem. NEA, Calif. Tchrs. Assn., Santa Ana Educators Assn. (mem. spl. edn. task force rules and election com., bldg. rep. 1992—, mem. supt.'s cabinet 1995—), Coun. for Exceptional Children, Orange County Math. Coun. Avocations: travel, reading, hiking, dog grooming, golf. Office: James Monroe Elem 417 E Central Ave Santa Ana CA 92707-3501

KATSAKIORES, PHYLLIS MAY, small business owner, city councilor; b. Saugus, Mass., Sept. 22, 1934; d. Robert D. and Eva M. (Clemonts) Harrie; m. Charles Hemeon, Sept. 11, 1954 (div. 1976); children: Debbie, Charles, Laurie; m. George N. Katsakiores, Oct. 9, 1983. Grad. high sch., Saugus. City councilor Town of Derre, N.H., 1985; rep. from Rockingham dist. 13 State of N.H., 1985; rep., chair Rockingham County, Derry, 1985-92; employee Shaws Supermarkets, Derry, 1982—. Bd. dirs. Nat. Foun. Women Legislators; task force health and human svc. Nat. Coun. State Legislators. Hostess : (TV series) Capitol Chat. Chmn. Rockingham Rep. Party, 1978-86. Mem. Am. Legis. Exch. Coun., Orgn. Women Legislators. Home: 1 Bradford St Derry NH 03038-4258 Office: NH Ho of Reps State House Concord NH 03301

KATSEKAS, BETTE SUSAN, counseling education educator; b. Goffstown, N.H., May 8, 1951; d. Charles J. and Angelina (Chagrasuis) K. BA, U. N.H., 1973, MEd, 1976, CAGS, 1979; EdD, U. Maine, 1979. Lic. clin. profl. counselor, Maine. Counselor, cons. Human Devel. Cons., Portland, Maine, 1979—; assoc. prof. of counselor edn. U. So. Maine, Portland, 1992—. Mental health adv. bd. U. So. Maine, Gorham, 1993-95, coord., counseling edn. program, 1993-95, trained mediator, 1994-95. Author: Love, Happiness and Emotional Prosperity, 2003. Mem. Maine Clin. Counselors Assn. (chair profl. devel. com. 1992-94). Office: Univ of So Maine 400 Bailey Hall Gorham ME 04038

KATSER, DONNA DURHAM, critical care nurse, educator; b. Detroit, Aug. 19, 1952; d. Harry Richard and Mary Lou (Purcell) Durham; m. Arthur Normon Katser, Sept. 10, 1978. Nursing diploma, Grace Hosp. Sch. Nursing, 1973; BS in Nursing, Wayne State U., 1980, MS in Nursing, 1994. ACLS provider, instr., BLS instr. trainer; RN. Staff nurse Grace Hosp., Detroit, 1973-74; staff nurse intensive care William Beaumont Hosp., Royal Oak, Mich., 1974-76, staff nurse hemodialysis, 1976-77; staff nurse intensive care Hutzel Hosp., Detroit, 1977-79, critical care educator, 1979-82, staff nurse, 1983-85; critical care educator, asst. dir. nursing Detroit Osteopathic Hosp., 1985-87; critical care educator Harper Hosp., Detroit, 1987—2002, nurse in cardiology, 2002—. Cons. Radius Nursing Svc., Southfield, Mich., 1982-83; presenter in field. Mem. Am. Assn. Critical Care Nurses, Am. Heart Assn., Nat. Staff Devel. Orgn., Mich.

Abortion Rights Action League, NARAL Southeast Mich. Assn. Critical Care Nurses (program planning com. 1995-96, pres.-elect 1981-82, pres. 1982-83, Outstanding Mem. 1981), Southeast Mich. Staff Devel. Orgn., Detroit Zool. Soc., Sigma Theta Tau (dia founders). Avocations: photography, yoga, travel. Home: 26066 York Rd Huntington Woods MI 48070-1311

KATTENHORN, LISA ANN, music educator; b. Santa Clara, Calif., Feb. 18, 1975; d. Glen Allen and Donna Sievers Kattenhorn. MusB in edn., Mont. State U., 1992—97. Vocal music dir. Clarksville Cmty. Sch., Iowa, 2000—; vocal music/theatre arts tchr. South Umpqua Sch. Dist., Myrtle Creek, Oreg., 1998—2000. State pres. Collegiate Music Educators Nat. Conf., Bozeman, Mont., 1995—96. Music director (musicals including) The Music Man and No! No! Nanette; singer: (concert tour) MSU Chorale Tour 1996. Mem.: Am. Choral Directors Assn., Music Educators Nat. Conf. Avocations: travel, singing, dance, cooking, reading. Office: Clarksville Community School PO Box 689 Clarksville IA 50619 E-mail: lkattenhorn@clarksville.k12.ia.us.

KATZ, BARBARA S. special education educator; b. Springfield, Mass., July 22, 1933; d. Harry and Pearl (Black) Stein; m. Charles Murry Katz, July 14, 1957; children: Helen Lee, Robert Alan. BS, Am. Internat. Coll., Springfield, 1956, MA in Ednl. Psychology in Learning Disabilities, 1979. Cert. in elem. edn., moderate spl. needs, Mass. Elem. tchr. Springfield Pub. Schs., 1956-60; Jr. Great Books discussion leader, 1968-69; Gillingham remedial tchr. Pub. Schs., Longmeadow, Mass., 1975-78, spl. edn. tchr. Chicopee, Mass., 1978-98, reader, 1998—, Pioneer Valley Collaborative, East Longmeadow, Mass., 1998—2003; ret., 2003. Pres. Kodimoh Synagogue Women's Group, Springfield, 1972-74; troop leader Girl Scouts U.S., Longmeadow, 1967-70. Horace Mann grantee, 1988. Mem. NEA, Mass. Tchrs. Assn. Avocations: painting, reading, walking, swimming. Home: 407 Bliss Rd Longmeadow MA 01106-1538

KATZ, COLLEEN, publisher; b. Newark; BA in Math., Montclair (N.J.) Coll.; cert., Ctr. Linguistique Etrangers, Tours, France. Assoc. editor Fawcett Publs., N.Y.C., 1972-73, editor, 1973-76; editorial dir. Butterick Fashion Mktg. Co., N.Y.C., 1976-77; editor Ency. of Textiles, N.Y.C., 1979; editor in chief N.J. Monthly, Morristown, 1982-85; dir. publs. Ins. Info. Inst., N.Y.C., 1985-88; pub., editor-in-chief Journal of Accountancy, N.Y.C., 1988—. Adj. prof. Audrey Cohen Coll., 2000. Editor Ins. Rev., 1985-88; pub. mags. and newsletters AICPA, 1997—; editor Huguenot Heritage, 1999. Vol. tchr. Elizabeth (N.J.) Sch. System; vol. editor Nat. Council Jewish Women, NJ, 1967—71; vol. pub. relations worker Essex County Mental Health Assn., NJ, 1980—81. Named Woman of Yr., Cen. N.J. March of Dimes, 1984, Outstanding Alumnus, Montclair Coll., 1984; recipient Gold Cir. award Am. Soc. Assn. Execs., 1989, award for pub. excellence Comm. Concepts, 1990, Pub. Excellence award Mag. Week, 1990, Gen. Excellence award Soc. Nat. Assn. Publs., 1991, Golden Page award, 2000-01. Mem.: Conf. des Vins du Cahors, Soc. Nat. Assn. Publs. (Silver medal for gen. excellence 1997), Am. Soc. Mag. Editors, Soc. Profl. Journalists, Nat. Arts Club. Avocation: foreign languages. Office: Jour of Accountancy Harborside III Jersey City NJ 07311

KATZ, DEBORAH A. lawyer; b. Phila., Apr. 5, 1952; BA in Japanese Studies magna cum laude, Yale U., 1974; JD with honors, U. Mich., 1977. Bar: D.C. 1977. Counsel to bd. dirs. Nat. Labor Rels. Bd., 1977-85, sr. counsel, expert, 1984-85, asst. chief counsel to bd. dirs., 1985-94; legal counsel and spl. advisor to chair Occupl. Safety and Health Rev. Commn., Washington, 1994—. Mem. ABA, Soc. for Profls. in Dispute Resolution, Washington Area Lawyers for the Arts, D.C. Bar Assn. Office: Occupl Safety and Health Rev Commn 1120 20th St NW Rm 924 Washington DC 20036-3406

KATZ, JANE, swimming educator; b. Sharon, Pa., Apr. 16, 1943; d. Leon and Dorthea (Oberkewitz) Katz BS in Edn., CCNY, 1963; MA, NYU, 1966; MEd, Columbia Tchrs. Coll., 1972, EdD, 1978. Faculty Bronx C.C., CUNY, 1964—, prof. phys. edn., 1972—. Mem. U.S. Round-the-World Synchronized Swim Team, 1964; synchronized swimming solo tour of Eng., 1969; founding co-organizer, coach 1st Internat. Israeli Youth Festival Games, 1970; mem. winning U.S. Maccabiah Swim Team, 1957; vice-chair U.S. Masters All-Am. Swim Team, 1974—; mem. Nat. Masters All-Am. Swim Team, 1974—, synchronized swimming solo champion, 1975; spkr. judge in field. Author: Swimming for Total Fitness, A Progressive Aerobic Program, 1981, rev. ed. 1993, Swimming Through Your Pregnancy, 1983, W.E.T. Workouts: Water Exercises and Techniques to Help You and Tone Up Aerobically, 1985, Fitness Works: Blueprint for Lifelong Fitness, 1988, Swim 30 Laps in 30 Days, 1991, The Workstation Workout, 1994, Aquatic Handbook for Lifetime Fitness, 1996; author: (video) The New W.E.T. Workout, 1994, The All-American Aquatic Handbook: Your Passport to Lifetime Fitness, 1996, The W.E.T. Workout, 1996; contbr. Encyclopedia Britannica Med. and Health Ann., 1997, Swim Basics Video, 2001, Tri Synchro Video, 2003, Your Water Workout, 2003; papers in field. Trainee Fed. Adminstrn. Aging, 1971-72; mem. Internat. Hall of Fame, Ft. Lauderdale. Named Healthy Am. Fitness Leader U.S. Jaycees and the Pres.'s Coun. on Phys. Fitness, 1987, Outstanding Masters Synchronized Swimming, 1987; recipient CCNY Towsend Harris Acad. medal, 1989, Outstanding Lifetime Leadership award Fedn. Internat. Nat. Amateur, 1999, cert. of merit Fedn. Internat. de Natation Amateur (FINA), Sydney, Australia, 2000, Lifetime Contbrn. to Swimming award Internat. Olympic Com., 2000. Mem.: AAHPER, Internat. Aquatics (Hall of Fame Paragon award), U.S. Com. Sports for Israel (co-chmn. women's swimming com. 1970—, dir.), Internat. Swimming Hall of Fame (bd. of dir. 2002—). Address: 400 2nd Ave Apt 23B New York NY 10010-4052 Office Phone: 212-237-8394. E-mail: jkatz@jjay.cuny.edu.

KATZ, JANYCE C(HARLENE), lawyer; b. Cin., Aug. 19, 1949; d. Louis and Ida (Schreiber) K.; m. Mark Glazman. BA, Boston U., 1971; MA in History, U. Cin., 1974, ABD, 1976, JD, 1989. Teaching asst., instr. history dept. U. Cin., 1973-76; prodr., writer, announcer Sta. WGUC-FM, Cin., 1976-78, part-time prodr., announcer, sub. tchr., 1985—89; prodr., writer, announcer Sta. WCET-Pub. TV, Cin., 1978; pub. rels. dir. Nat. Women's Polit. Caucus, Washington, 1979-82; mktg. and pub. rels. mgr. AAUW, Washington, 1982-83; pres. Janyce Katz Prodns., Washington, L.A. and Cin., 1983-89; asst. atty. gen. taxation sect. Ohio Atty. Gen. Office, Columbus, 1989—. 24 arguments before Ohio Supreme Ct.; cons. in field; organizer tax seminar for new Ams.; speaker at profl. confs. Writer, producer radio documentaries: Oil in America, 1977 (award), 100 Yrs. of Music Hall, 1977 (award), Employment at Will, 1988 (1st prize), others; contbr. many articles and TV programs. Dem. precinct exec., Cin., 1986-89; bd. dirs. Cin. Am. Jewish Com., 1986-92, Columbus Women's Polit. Caucus, 1992—, PAC treas., 1992-1996; New Am. Assn., 1992—, founding mem. bd.; PAC treas., 1992-94; mem. bd. Columbus Women's Pol Caucus, 1992-96; state pres. edn. fund Nat. Abortion Rights Action League, 1991-94, Champion of Choice award, 1999; founding mem. bd. Franklin County Consortium Good Govt., chmn. bd., 1991-; v.p. Columbus Coun. Jewish Women; nat. v.p., capitol com. Nat. Coun. Jewish Women, chmn. 1981-87, pres. DC sect. 1982-84, co-pres. VP Columbus sect. 1993, vice chair Ohio pub. affairs com., 1999-2000, co-chair state PAC, 1999; mem. bd. League Women Voters, 2001-; Columbus rep. State Jewish Community Rels. Coun.; chmn. Noontime Showtime Art at Lunch, 1998-2000. Recipient Best Pub. Rels. Effort award Pub. Rels. Soc. Am., 1983, Nat. Women's Polit. Caucus, 1981. Mem. Women in Govt. (steering com. 2004-), Ohio Bar Assn. (mem. media com. 1990—, chmn. pub. understanding law com. 1995-97, mem. editl. bd.), Columbus Bar Assn. (co-chairperson media com. 1991-92, community svcs., mem. editl. bd. Columbus Bar Briefs 2002-, mem. bd., bylaws chmn. Franklin County Women Lawyers 1992-95), Law Women of U. Cin. Law Sch. (pres. 1989), Women's Equality Celebration (founder, chair 1991-99), Phi Delta Phi. Avocations: reading, writing, painting, guitar, horseback riding. Office: Ohio Atty Gen Taxation Sect 30 E Broad St Columbus OH 43215 Office Phone: 614-466-5967.

KATZ, JOETTE, state supreme court justice; b. Bklyn., Feb. 3, 1953; BA, Brandeis U., 1974; JD, U. Conn., 1977. Bar: Conn. 1977. Pvt. practice, 1977-78; asst. pub. defender Office Chief Pub. Defender, 1978-83; chief legal svcs. Pub. Defender Svcs., 1983-89; judge Superior Ct., 1989-92; assoc. justice Conn. Supreme Ct., Hartford, 1992—; adminstrv. judge Appellate Sys., Hartford, 1994-2000. Instr. U. Conn. Sch. Law, 1981-84; instr. ethics and criminal law Quinnipiac Coll. Sch. Law, 1999—. Mem. Justice Edn. Ctr. Mem. Am. Law Inst.; Chair Evidence Code Drafting Com., Chair Adv. Com. for Appellate Rules; Am. Inns Ct. (past pres. Fairfield County br.), Assn. Reproductive Tech. (mem. com.). Office: Conn Supreme Ct Drawer N Sta A 231 Capital Ave Hartford CT 06106-1548

KATZ, LINDA M. social worker; b. Jersey City, Dec. 17, 1944; d. David A. and Florence (Friedlander) Moritz; m. Robert Lawrence Katz, June 19, 1965; children: Peter Moritz, Douglas Andrew. AA, Briarcliff Coll., Briarcliff Manor, N.Y., 1965; BS in Edn., Wheelock Coll., Boston, 1967; MSSA, Case Western Res. U., 1990. Lic. ind. social worker. Social worker, Cleveland Heights, Ohio, 1990—; case cons. Office on Aging, Cleveland Heights, 1990—. Trustee Schnurmann House for Sr. Adult Living, Mayfield Heights, Ohio, 1997—. Mem. women's coun. Cleve. Mus. Art, 1994—; group leader Cleveland Heights Sr. Activity Ctr., 1990—. Mem. NASW. Avocation: musical talent/singing. Home: 22099 Parnell Rd Shaker Heights OH 44122

KATZ, LOIS ANNE, internist, nephrologist; b. Rockville Centre, N.Y., Dec. 1, 1941; d. Irvin Martin and Frances (Berenstein) Fradkin; m. Arthur A. Katz, Aug. 18, 1962; children: David, Brian. BA, Wellesley Coll., 1962; MD, NYU, 1966. Diplomate Am. Bd. Internal Medicine, Am. Bd. Nephrology. Intern medicine Bellevue Hosp., NYU, N.Y.C., 1966-67, resident medicine, 1967-68; sr. resident medicine N.Y. Hosp., N.Y.C., 1968-69; from chief resident medicine to assoc. chief staff N.Y. VA Med. Ctr., N.Y.C., 1969—2000, assoc. chief of staff spl. emphasis programs and quality mgmt., 2000—; asst. prof. clin. medicine NYU Sch. Medicine, N.Y.C., 1974-79, assoc. prof., 1979-94, prof. clin. medicine, 1994—. Fellow: ACP; mem.: Am. Soc. Hypertension, Women in Nephrology (treas. 1985—89), Soc. Gen. Internal Medicine, Am. Med. Women's Assn., Am. Soc. Nephrology, Wellesley Coll. Alumnae Assn. (region 2 admission rep. 1997—2001), Sigma Xi, Alpha Omega Alpha. Jewish. Avocations: reading, swimming, cooking, music. Office: Dept Vets Affairs NY Harbor Healthcare System 423 E 23rd St New York NY 10010-5013 Office Phone: 212-951-6875.

KATZ, MARCIA, public relations company executive; b. N.Y.C., Mar. 20, 1950; d. Alexander and Dorothy Harriet (Frank) K.; m. R. Glenn Brode, Oct. 3, 1982; 1 child, Richard Gregory. BS magna cum laude, CUNY, 1972, MS, 1975. Tchr. N.Y.C. Bd. Edn., 1972-76; exec. v.p. worldwide Burson-Marsteller, N.Y.C., 1976-91; exec. v.p. U.S.A. Hill and Knowlton, N.Y.C., 1991-92; pres., CEO InterScience, N.Y.C., 1993—. Cons. Nat. Coun. on Patient Inf. and Edn., Washington, 1985—, Am. Health Found., N.Y.C., 1991—. Editor: Perspectives on Aging Worldwide, 1989; contbr. articles to profl. jours. Cons. Nat. Neurofibromatosis Soc., 1988-90; mktg. counselor Nat. Multiple Sclerosis Soc., 1990—. Named to Acad. Women Achievers, YWCA, N.Y.C., 1985. Mem. Healthcare Bus. Women's Assn., Healthcare Comms. Council (pub. rels. chair 1985), Phi Beta Kappa. Office: InterScience 1675 Broadway New York NY 10019-5820

KATZ, MARTHA LESSMAN, lawyer; b. Chgo., Oct. 28, 1952; d. Julius Abraham and Ida (Oiring) Lessman; m. Richard M. Katz, June 27, 1976; children: Julia Erin, Meredith Evin. AB, Washington U., St. Louis, 1974; JD, Loyola U., Chgo., 1977. Bar: Ill. 1977, U.S. Dist. Ct. (no. dist.) Ill. 1977, Calif. 1981, U.S. Dist. Ct. (so. dist.) Calif. 1981, U.S. Dist. Ct. (no. dist.) Calif. 1982, Md. 1993, U.S. Supreme Ct. 1993, D.C. 1994. Assoc. Fein & Hanfling, Chgo., 1977-80, Rudick, Platt & Victor, San Diego, 1981-82, 84-91; asst. sec., counsel Itel Corp., San Francisco, 1982-84; ptnr. Katz & Mann, Attys. at Law, 1991-95; with legal dept. U.S. Fidelity and Guaranty Co., 1995-99; prin. intellectual property and tech. practice group Miles & Stockbridge PC, Balt., 1999—. Mem. Greater Balt. com. Tech. Coun.; mem. High Tech. Coun. and Ops. Com. Md. Mem. Calif. State Bar Assn., Md. Bar Assn. (spl. com. on tech.), Ill. State Bar Assn., Bar Assn. Balt. City (tech. com.), Bar Assn. D.C., Phi Beta Kappa. Jewish. Office: 10 Light St Baltimore MD 21202-1435 Fax: 410-385-3700. E-mail: mkatz@milesstockbridge.com.

KATZ, MARYA RUTH, music educator; b. Rochester, NY, Nov. 12, 1953; d. Elmer Eugene and Marjorie Lucile Foote. BA, Alderson-Broaddus Coll., Philippi, WV, 1971—75; MA, Marshall U., Huntington, WV, 1977—81. Cert. National Board Certified Teacher Nat. Bd. for Tchg. Standards, 2002. Music tchr. Maine Sch. Adminstrv. Dist. #56, Searsport, Maine, 1975—76, Mercer County Pub. Schs., Princeton, W.Va., 1977—79, Montgomery County Pub. Schs., Christiansburg, Va., 1979—. Choir dir. North Side Presbyn. Ch., Blacksburg, Va., 1981—; performer Simple Gifts of the Blue Ridge, Blacksburg, Va., 1991—; dulcimer tchr./workshop leader Winston-Salem Dulcimer Festival, Winston-Salem, NC, 1999—2001; dulcimer tchr. Swannanoa Gathering, Asheville, NC, 2001—; workshop leader Cranberry Gathering, Binghamton, NY, 2003—. Composer: (book) Dulcimations I, 1998, Dulcimations II, 2002; composer: (contributor) (dulcimer tune) Dulcimer Players News pub. Ebony and Leather. Logos asst. Northside Presbyn. Ch., Blacksburg, Va., 2002—. Recipient $1000 for Am. Music Contest, Am. Music Edn. Initiative, 2002; grantee Chinese Music/Art Collaboration, Va. Commn. for the Arts, 2002. Mem.: Music Educators Nat. Conf. D-Liberal. Presbyterian. Avocations: gardening, woodworking, cross-country skiing, hiking, travel. Office: Kipps Elementary School 2801 Price's Fork Road Blacksburg VA 24060

KATZ, SAFRA, computer company executive; Various banking positions, 1986—94; sr. v.p. Donaldson, Lufkin & Jenrette, 1994—97, mng. dir., 1997—99; sr. v.p. Oracle Corp., Redwood City, Calif., 1999, exec. v.p., 1999—2004, co-pres., 2004—, also bd. dirs. Office: Oracle Corp 500 Oracle Pkwy Redwood City CA 94065

KATZ, SHERI LYNN, learning disabilities specialist, tutor; b. Balt., June 10, 1953; d. Irving and Sybil (Breskin) K.; m. Asher Samuel Kahn; children: Zachary Aaron, Alexandra Katz. BA, New Coll. USF, 1976; MS, Bank St. Coll. of Edn., 1978. Cert. early childhood and spl. edn. Tchr., therapist Infant Care Ctr. of JBFCS, N.Y.C., 1978-81; reading specialist, lang. arts coord. Fieldston Lower Sch., Riverdale, N.Y., 1982—. Pvt. tutor, Riverdale, N.Y., 1979—, East Hampton, N.Y., 1991—. Contbr. articles to profl. jours. Recipient grants Ethical Culture/Fieldston Schs., 1988-95. Mem. NOW, Planned Parenthood, Orton Dyslexia Soc., Wave Hill, Wildlife Conservation Soc., Am. Mus. Natural History. Democrat. Jewish. Avocations: travel, trail walking, sunset beach picnics, reading, writing. Home: 4525 Henry Hudson Pkwy Bronx NY 10471-3808 Office: Fieldston Lower Sch Fieldston Rd Riverdale NY 10471

KATZ, SUSAN ARONS, language arts specialist, author, poet; b. N.Y.C., Dec. 3, 1939; d. Edward Maurice and Selma (Stark) Arons; m. Donald Ira Katz, June 20, 1961; children: David Lawrence, Elizabeth Cheryl. BFA, Ohio U., 1961. Poet-in-residence N.Y. State Poets in Pub. Svc., N.Y.C., 1975-96; book rev. editor Bitterroot Internat. Lit. Mag., 1985-91. Workshop dir. Lang. Arts Nat.-Internat. Workshops, U.S. and Can., 1995—; mem. reading panel Poets in Pub. Svc.; workshop coord. sr. citizen and intergenerational workshops Finklestein Meml. Libr., Spring Valley, NY, 1989; cons. Disney Interactive, 1996; invited guest poet Donnell Libr. Ctr., N.Y. Pub. Libr., 1980—90; presenter in field. Author: Teaching Creatively by Working the Word, 2d edit., 1996, The Word in Play, 2004, (poetry books) The Separate Sides of Need, 1984, Two Halves of the Same Silence, 1985, An Eye for Resemblances, 1991. Recipient Henry V. Larom prize Rockland C.C., 1978, Blue Ribbon award So. Poetry Assn., 1988; nominee Pushcart prize, 1976. Mem. Poetry Soc. Am., Conservatory of Am. Letters, Ga. Poetry Soc., Ariz. State Poetry Soc. (judge). Avocations: skiing, hiking, bike and horseback riding, sailing, gardening. Office Phone: 203-241-1836. E-mail: poetlady@earthlink.net.

KATZ, TONNIE, newspaper editor; BA, Barnard Coll., 1966; MSc, Columbia U., 1967. Editor, reporter newspapers including The Quincy Patriot Ledger, Boston Herald Am., Boston Globe; Sunday/projects editor Newsday; mng. editor Balt. News Am., 1983-86, The Sun, San Bernardino, Calif., 1986-88; asst. mng. editor for news The Orange County Register, Santa Ana, Calif., 1988-89, mng. editor, 1989-92, editor, v.p., 1992-98, editor, sr. v.p., 1998—. Office: Orange County Register 625 N Grand Ave Santa Ana CA 92701-4347

KATZ, VERA, mayor, former college administrator, state legislator; b. Dusseldorf, Germany, Aug. 3, 1933; came to U.S., 1940; d. Lazar Pistrak and Raissa Goodman; m. Mel Katz (div. 1985); 1 child, Jesse. BA, Bklyn. Coll., 1955, postgrad., 1955-57; PhD (hon.), Lewis & Clark Coll., Portland (Oreg.) State U. Market research analyst TIMEX, B.T. Babbitt, N.Y.C., 1957-62; mem. Oreg. Ho. of Reps., Salem, 1985—91; former dir. devel. Portland Community Coll.; mayor City of Portland, Oreg., 1992—. Mem. Gov.'s Council on Alcohol and Drug Abuse Programs, Oreg. Legis., Salem, 1985—; mem. adv. com. Gov.'s Council on Health, Fitness and Sports, Oreg. Legis., 1985—; mem. Gov.'s Commn. on Sch. Funding Reform; mem. Carnegie task Force on Teaching as Profession, Washington, 1985-87; vice-chair assembly Nat. Conf. State Legis., Denver, 1986—2003. Recipient Abigail Scott Duniway award Women in Communications, Inc., Portland, 1985, Jeanette Rankin First Woman award Oreg. Women's Polit. Caucus, Portland, 1985, Leadership award The Neighborhood newspaper Portland, 1985, Woman of Achievement award Commn. for Women, 1985, Outstanding Legis. Advocacy award Oreg. Primary Care Assn., 1985, Service to Portland Pub. Sch. Children award Portland Pub. Schs., 1985, Visionary Leadership award, 1998, Legal Citizen of Yr. award, 2002. Fellow Am. Leadership Forum (founder Oreg. chpt.); mem. Dem. Legis. Leaders Assn., Nat. Bd. for Profl. Teaching Standards. Democrat. Jewish. Avocations: camping, jogging, dance. Office: Office of the Mayor City Hall 1221 SW 4th Ave Rm 340 Portland OR 97204-1995*

KATZEN, MOLLIE, writer; b. Rochester, N.Y., Oct. 13, 1950; d. Leon and Betty (Heller) K.; m. Jeffrey David Black, June 26, 1983 (div. Oct. 1985); 1 child, Samuel Katzen Black; m. Carl Shames, Dec. 12, 1986. BFA, San Francisco Art Inst., 1972. Author, illustrator: Mossewood Cookbook, 1977, Enchanted Broccoli Forest, 1982, Still Life with Menu, 1988, Molly Katzen's Still Life Sampler, 1993, Pretend Soup & Other Real Recipes: A Cookbook for Preschoolers & Up, 1994, Enchanted Broccoli Forest, 1995, Moosewood Cookbook Classics: Miniature Edition, 1996. Recipient Graphic Arts award Arnot Art Gallery, 1976, Cert. of Commendation, Calif. State Assembly, 1989. Jewish. Avocations: classical pianist, painter. Office: care Ten Speed Press PO Box 7123 Berkeley CA 94707-0123

KATZEN, SALLY, lawyer, educator; b. Pitts., Nov. 22, 1942; d. Nathan and Hilda (Schwartz) K.; m. Timothy B. Dyk, Oct. 31, 1981; 1 child, Abraham Benjamin. BA magna cum laude, Smith Coll., 1964; JD magna cum laude, U. Mich., 1967. Bar: D.C. 1968, U.S. Supreme Ct. 1971. Congl. intern Senate Subcom. on Constl. Rights, Washington, 1963; legal rsch. asst. civil rights divsn. Dept. Justice, Washington, 1965; law clk. to Judge J. Skelly Wright U.S. Ct. Appeals (D.C. cir.), 1967-68; assoc. Wilmer, Cutler & Pickering, Washington, 1968-75, ptnr., 1975-79, 81-93; gen. counsel Coun. on Wage and Price Stability, 1979-80, dep. dir. for policy, 1980-81; adminstr. Office of Info. and Regulatory Affairs Office of Mgmt. and Budget, Washington, 1993-98, counselor to the dir., 1999-2000, dep. dir. mgmt., 2000-2001; dep. dir. Nat. Econ. Coun., The White House, Washington, 1998-99. Adj. prof. Georgetown U. Law Ctr., 1988, 1990—92, U. Pa. Law Sch., 2003; resident scholar and lectr. Smith Coll., 2001—; vis. lectr., fellow Johns Hopkins U., 2002—03; vis. prof. U. Mich. Law Sch., 2004; pub. mem. Adminstrv. Conf. U.S., 1988, govt. mem. and vice chair, 1993—95; mem. exec. com. Prettyman-Leventhal Inn of Ct., 1988—90, counselor, 1990—91; mem. Jud. Conf. for D.C. Cir., 1972—91. Editor-in-chief U. Mich. Law Rev., 1966-67. Mem. com. visitors U. Mich. Law Sch., 1972—; cons., sr. policy advisor Joe Lieberman for Pres., 2003-04. Fellow ABA (ho. of dels. 1978-80, 89-91, coun. adminstrv. law sect. 1979-82, chmn. adminstrv. law and regulatory practice sect. 1988-89, governing com. forum com. comm. law 1979-82, chmn. standing com. Nat. Conf. Groups 1989-92); mem. D.C. Bar Assn., Women's Bar Assn., FCC Bar Assn. (exec. com. 1984-87, pres. 1990-91), Women's Legal Def. Fund (pres. 1977, v.p. 1978), Order of Coif. Home: 4638 30th St NW Washington DC 20008-2127 E-mail: dykatzen@earthlink.net.

KATZEN-GUTHRIE, JOY, performance artist, engineering services executive; b. Memphis, Nov. 11, 1958; d. Eli and Bess (Bloomfield) Katzen; m. Mark C. Guthrie, Aug. 7, 1983. BFA in Music cum laude, BA in Comms. magna cum laude, Stephens Coll., Columbia, Mo., 1980. Traffic dir. WPLP News/Talk Radio, Pinellas Park, Fla., 1981-83, ops. mgr., 1982-83; traffic reporter WUSA-FM and WDAE-AM, Tampa, Fla., 1985-86; announcer, programmer, pub. rels. mgr. WXCR-FM Classics 92, Safety Harbor, Fla., 1983-87; v.p., dir. Katzen and Guthrie Assocs., Inc., Palm Harbor, Fla., 1987—; pres. Tune-of-the-Century Music, 1989—. Creator, designer, owner website www.JoyfulNoise.net, 1998—. Co-author, composer musical comedy Once Around Manhattan, 1985; author: (one-act play) A Murder in Pine County, 1987; composer, lyricist some 600 songs; performance artist CD/Cassette albums Seasons of Joy, 1989, Heart of Ancient Promise, 1993, New State of Mind, 1993, How Good and Pleasant, 1996, Passages, 1998; studio vocalist Jeff Arthur Prodns., St. Petersburg, Fla., 1985, 86, Studio C. Prodns., Tampa, 1991-92; studio vocalist, jingle writer West End Rec., Tampa, 1989, 90; session musician Hurricane Pass Studios, Clearwater, Fla., 1993—. Music dir. religious sch. Temple B'nai Israel, Clearwater, 1988-89; music dir. Perry-Mansfield Performing Arts Camp, Steamboat Springs, Colo., 1987; cantorial soloist B'nai B'rith Hillel Found., Tampa, 1990-93, Temple Shir Shalom, Gainesville, 1994-99, Congregation B'nai Emmunah, Tarpon Springs, 1996-99, Congregation Aliyah, Clearwater, 1999-2000, Temple B'nai Israel, Clearwater, 2000—. Recipient 1st and 3d place awards Memphis Songwriters Assn. Competition, 1988, others; Pinellas County Arts Coun. grantee, 1997. Mem. AAUW (dir. pub. rels. 1985-97), ASCAP, Songwriters Guild Am., Dramatists Guild, Nat. Acad. Songwriters, Nashville Songwriters Assn. Internat., Guild of Temple Musicians, Fla. Music Assn., Women's Musicians' Alliance (bd. dirs. 1998—), Hadassah (life). Democrat. Jewish. Avocations: photography, travel, music, theatre, film, books. Home and Office: 2487 Indian Trl E Palm Harbor FL 34683-2806 Office Phone: 727-785-4568. E-mail: joyfulnoise@earthlink.net.

KATZIN, CAROLYN FERNANDA, nutritionist, consultant; b. London, July 21, 1946; came to U.S., 1983; naturalized US citizen, 1992. d. John Mourier and Shelagh B. A. (Tighe) Lade; m. Anthony Arthur Speelman, Mar. 18, 1968 (div. Dec. 1984); 1 child, Zara Jane; m. David Brandeis Katzin (div. Mar. 1999). BS with honors, U. London, 1983; MS in Pub. Health, UCLA, 1988. Nutritionist, L.A., 1985—. Chair dean's adv. bd. UCLA Sch. Pub. Health, 1997—; mem. profl. adv. bd. The Wellness Cmty., L.A., 1998—; pres. Am. Cancer Soc., L.A., Coastal Cities U., 1999-2002. Author: The Advanced Energy Guide, 1994, The Good Eating Guide and

Cookbook, 1996, The Cancer Nutrition Ctr. Handbook, 2001, 2d edit., 2003. Democrat. Jewish. Office: 12011 San Vicente Blvd Ste 402 Los Angeles CA 90049-4946 E-mail: cfk@aol.com.

KATZOWITZ SHENFIELD, LAUREN, philanthropic consultant, foundation executive; m. Marc Shenfield. BS in Comparative Lit. with honors, Brandeis U., 1970; MS with honors, Columbia U., 1971. With Newsweek mag.; then with Phila. Bull.; freelance writer, editor, cons., until 1975; cons. Ford Found., 1972-75; mgr. PBS programs Exxon Corp., 1978-81; mgr. Exxon Rsch. and Engring. Co., 1981-84; regional liaison for Europe and Africa, Exxon Corp., 1984-86; exec. dir. Found. Svc., 1986—2003, Philanthropy Advisors of UJA-Fedn. of N.Y., 2004—; pres. Lauren Katzowitz Cons., Croton on Hudson, N.Y., 1986—. Mem. profl. adv. coun. Met. Mus. of Art, 2000—, Central Park Conservancy, 2001—; bd. dirs. N.Y. Regional Assn. of Grantmakers, 2000—, Women and Philanthropy, 2003—. Named one of 12 Women to Watch in the Eighties, Ladies' Home Jour., 1979. Office: Lauren Katzowitz Consulting 4 Hamilton Ave Croton On Hudson NY 10520-2521

KAUFER, CONNIE TENORIO, retired reading specialist; b. Saipan, No. Mariana Islands, June 12, 1945; d. Lino Pangelinan and Magdalena Faosto (Arriola) Tenorio; m. Leonard James Kaufer, Jan. 20, 1974; 1 child, Lucile Tenorio. AA in Elem. Edn., Chaffey Coll., 1968; BS in Lang. Arts, Calif. State Poly. U., 1971; MA in Edn., San Jose State U., 1983. Cert. tchr., Calif., Mariana Islands. Elem. tchr. Marianas Dept. Edn., Chalan Kanoa, Saipan, Mariana Islands, 1964-66, 74-76, 80-84, elem. and h.s. tchr., 1970-71, elem. sch. supr. Lower Base, Saipan, 1971-74, elem. sch. prin. Tanapag Village, Saipan, 1979-80; comprehensive lang. arts skills project dir. Pub. Sch. Sys., Lower Base, Saipan, 1984-87, reading specialist, 1984-94, trainer Marianas instrument for obs. of tchr. activities, 1986—94, trainer onward to excellence, 1988—94; ret., 1994. Part-time instr. U. Guam Ext., No. Marianas Coll., Saipan, 1993 ; sec. Diocesan Bd. Edn. Saipan, 1985-90; trainer pacific region pacific effective schs. Pacific Region Edn. Lab., Honolulu and Saipan, 1991-93; presenter in field. Mem. Mariana Islands rep. Trust Ter. Curriculum Coun., Saipan, 1970-72; coord. cross cultural Peace Corps, Saipan, 1973, coord. Chamorro lang., 1975; pres. Chalan Kanoa Sch. Saipan Tchrs. Assn., 1981-83. Scholar Marianas Edn. Found., 1966-70, Bilingual Edn. scholar Trust Ter. Dept. Edn., 1975. Mem. ASCD, AAUW, Internat. Reading Assn. (Saipan chpt. pres. 1975-76), Pacific Islands Bilingual/Bicultural Assn., Phi Delta Kappa. Roman Catholic. Avocations: raising orchids, cooking, baking. Home: PO Box 7611 Saipan MP 96950

KAUFER, KAREN EVANS, academic administrator; b. Easton, Pa., Apr. 24, 1954; d. George Richard Evans and Rose Ann Luntz; m. Richard Elliot Kaufer, Oct. 14, 1983; 1 child, Zachary. BA in Art, Wilkes U.; MA in Art History, Bloomsburg (Pa.) U. Caseworker Luzerne/Wyoming County Mental Health Ctr., Wilkes-Barre, Pa., 1977—84; dir. devel. rsch. Wyoming Sem., Kingston, Pa., 1992—97, bus. mgr. Kingston (Pa.) Vet. Clinic, 1997—2000; interim dir. Sordoni Art Gallery Wilkes U., Wilkes-Barre, 2000—01, assoc. dir. Sordoni Art Gallery, 2001—. V.p. programming Wilkes-Barre (Pa.) Chpt.Hadassah, 1987—89; bd. dirs. Fine Arts Fiesta, 1999—, v.p. bd. dirs., 2003—; bd. dirs. Wyoming Valley Montessori Sch., 1992—98, Luzerne County Hist. Soc., 1990—2000. Mem.: Pa. Fedn. Mus. and Hist. Orgs., Nat. Mus. Women in Arts, Am. Assn. Mus. Avocations: gardening, reading, travel. Office: Sordoni Art Gallery Wilkes Univ 150 S River St Wilkes Barre PA 18766

KAUFER, SHIRLEY HELEN, artist, painter; b. Bklyn., Oct. 3, 1920; m. Bernard Goldberg, Apr. 18, 1943; children: Alice, Marjorie. Art dir. Advt. Agys., N.Y.C., 1938-63; art cons. N.Y.C., 1964-73; sculptor Vero Beach, Fla., 1973-77; graphic designer Jewish Fedn. Coun., L.A., 1977-82. With Haystack Mt. Art Colony, Deer Isle, Maine, summers 1959-73; instr. advt., design, illustration Pels Art Sch., N.Y.C., 1968-71; instr. painting Indian River C.C., Vero Beach, 1973-77. Represented in permanent art collection pf UCLA Med. Ctr., L.A.; exhibited in numerous nat. and internat. galleries; 2 films produced on her life and works. Home: 1029 Via De La Paz Pacific Palisades CA 90272-3534 Office Phone: 310-454-4636.

KAUFER, VIRGINIA GROSS, family therapist, mental health program manager, chemical dependency researcher, therapist; b. Middletown, N.Y., Apr. 8, 1937; d. Bernard and Estelle (Singer) Gross; divorced; children: Michael, Jill, Jonathan, Wendy, Elizabeth, Amy, Abigail. BS with honors, Carnegie Inst. Tech., 1959; MA summa cum laude, U. Pitts., 1982, postgrad., 1980-85. Case worker Allegheny County Children and Youth, Pitts., 1988-89, 92-93; therapist chem. dependency St. Francis Med. Ctr., Pitts., 1989-91; mental health case mgr. Charters Mental Health/Mental Retardation, Pitts., 1991-92; therapist chem. dependency Ligonier Outpatient, Pitts., 1992-93; family therapist Alternative Program Assn., Pitts., 1993-97; mgr., family therapist Auberle, residential treatment facility, McKeesport, Pa., 1997-99; chem. dependency therapist Zoar New Day Treatment, 1999—. Bd. dirs. Recovery Ctr., Pitts.; rschr. in field. Mem. Integrated Allegheny County Permanency Planning Task Force. Mem. Integrated Delivery Network. Republican. Jewish. Avocations: dogs and cats, design ing, making and creating needlepoint canvases, acrylic painting, fashion design. Office: Zoar New Day Treatment 801 Union Ave Pittsburgh PA 15212-5523 Home: 1669 Edgebrook Ave Pittsburgh PA 15226-1411

KAUFFMAN, AMY, political organization worker; b. Ardmore, Pa., Sept. 14, 1963; d. William J. Kauffman, Joanne Solomon Kauffman; m. Kenneth R. Weinstein; children: Eden Weinstein children: Raina Weinstein, Harrison Weinstein. BA, U.Pa., 1985; MBA, Georgetown U., 1996. Political cons. Senators John Heinz, Arlen Specter, Dick Thornburgh, Mike Dewine, various, DC, 1986—94; dir. Campaign for Am., Washington, 1996—99; dir. campaign & election law project Hudson Inst., Washington, 1999—. Office: Hudson Institute 1015 18th Street NW; Suite 300 Washington DC 20036-5200

KAUFFMAN, B. SUZANNE, investment company professional; b. Macomb, Ill., June 14, 1930; d. Kenneth Dill and Louise (Zimmerli) Murrell; m. Thomas Lindenfelser (div. 1953); children: Charles Thomas II, Donald Mark. BA, U. Fla., 1982. Field archaeologist Yorktown (Va.) Hist. Ctr., 1985-86; sr. assoc. First Investors Corp., N.Y.C., 1986—2001; ret., 2001. Oral historian Ky. History Ctr. Mem. Nature Conservancy, Libr. Congress (charter assoc.), Nat. Wildlife Assn., Whale Adoption/Friends of the Forest, Ky. Hist. Soc., Ky. Geneol. Soc., McDonough County Gene Soc. Avocations: herb gardening, yoga, painting.

KAUFFMAN, KAETHE COVENTON, artist, writer, art educator; b. Washington, Aug. 12, 1948; d. Richard G. and Kathleen B. (Coventon) K.; m. James William Hite, Oct. 23, 1983; children: James Haydn, Kauffman Hite. BA, U. Wash., 1970, U. Nev., 1975; MFA, U. Calif., Irvine, 1978; PhD, Union Inst. Cin., 1989. Art dept. faculty U. Nev., Las Vegas, Mount St. Mary's Coll., L.A.; chmn. art dept. Sierra Nevada Coll., Incline Village, 1989-91, assoc. prof., 1991-2001, Chaminade U., Honolulu, 2001—, adj. faculty, 2001—. Faculty dept. art U. Calif., Irvine; bd. dirs. Buddhist Studies Ctr. Press. Author: Sex and the Avant-Garde: A Gender Revolution in the Visual Arts 1830-1993, Female Forms of Originality and the New, Women Artists in the Avant-Garde, How Art Professors Teach Avant-Garde Values, Women Artists Deconstruct the Male Avant-Garde, A Modern Renaissance of the Arts; columnist: Lake Tahoe World newspapers; art exhibited at Utrecht, Holland, 1977, Inst. Modern Art, Brisbane, Australia, 1978, George Patton Gallery U. Melbourne, Australia, 1979, Newport Harbor Art Mus., Calif., 1980, Fiberworks Gallery, Berkeley, Calif., 1981, Galerie Triangle, Washington, 1982, Nev. Mus., Reno, 1983, Schoharie Nat., Cobleskill, N.Y., 1984, Pinnacle Gallery, N.Y., 1986, Space Gallery, Las Vegas, Nev., 1988, Manville Gallery, U. Nev., Reno, 1989, Galerie Art-Jeunesse, Montreal, Que., 1990, Kleinert Gallery, N.Y., 1991, West Gallery, Claremont Grad. Sch., 1992, Sierra Nev. Coll. Art Gallery, Lake Tahoe, Nev., 1995, Exhbn. Hall U. Prague, Czech Republic, CERES Gallery, N.Y., Women's UN Conf., Beijing, Nat. Mus. Women in Arts, Washington, Gallery of the Pali, Honolulu, Czech Mus. Fine Arts, Prague; represented in permanent collections Women's Studio Workshop, N.Y.C., Calif. Mus. Photography, L.A., Fluor Corp., L.A., Harris Found., Las Vegas, Nev., Computer Scis. Corp., L.A., Sheraton Plaza Inn, L.A., Glendale Fed. Bank, L.A.; mem. editl. bd. Collegiate Press. Juror 3d biennial Nev. Craft Show. Recipient Max H. Block award for Humanism, Juror's award Am. Pen Women Biennale, Dr. Wu and Elsie Ject-Key meml. award for photography Nat. Assn. Women Artists, N.Y.; Laguna Beach Festival of the Arts fellow; TOSCO Corp. grantee; Artists grantee Sierra Arts Found. Mem. Nat. Mus. Women in Arts, Women's Caucus for Art, Nat. Assn. for Women Artists (medal of honor for works on paper, Elizabeth Morse Genius Found. award), Ceres Gallery, Am. Pen Women (3 awards for non-fiction writing nat. competition), Arts and Letters, Natl. Assn. for Women Artists.

KAUFFMAN, MARTA, producer; m. Michael Skloff. With Bright-Kauffman-Crane Prodns., Burbank, Calif. Creator, prodr. Dream On, 1990-96; creator, exec. prodr. Friends, 1994-2004 (Emmy nominee 1995, 96), Veronica's Closet, 1997-2000, Jesse, 1998-2000; lyricist Friends theme I'll Be There for You. Office: Bright Kauffman Crane Prodns 3400 W Riverside Dr Ste 750 Burbank CA 91505-4654*

KAUFFMAN, SANDRA DALEY, state legislator; b. Osceola, Nebr., Jan. 26, 1933; d. James Richard and Erma Grace (Heald) Daley; m. Larry Allen Kauffman, Sept. 4, 1955; children: Claudia Kauffman Boosman, Matthew Allen. BA, U. Nebr., 1954; postgrad., U. Kansas City, summer 1957. Tchr. Falls City (Nebr.) High Sch., 1954-55, Westport High Sch., Kansas City, Mo., 1955-59; sales rep. Manson Industries, Topeka, Kans., 1974-75; dir. pub. affairs Bishop Hogan High Sch., Kansas City, 1985-86; mem. Mo. Ho. of Reps., Jefferson City, 1987-98. Mem. Kansas City Citizens Assn., 1981—, Kansas City Consensus, 1985—; mem. women's coun. U. Mo., Kansas City, 1986—; mem. rsch. mental health bd., bd. govs. Carondelet Aging Svcs., 1992—. Recipient Friend of Edn. award Ctr. Edn. Assn., 1986, Disting. Legislator award Mo. C.C. Assn.; named Mem. of Yr., Mo. Congress Parents and Tchrs., 1979. Mem. Am. Legis. Exch. Coun., Nat. Conf. State Legislatures, Network Bd., Nat. PTA (hon. life), Nat. Order Women Legislators, Mo. PTA (hon. life), South Kansas City C. of C., Grandview C. of C., Women C. of C., Mo. Women's Coun., Women Legislators Mo. (pres.). Republican. Methodist. Home: 620 E 90th Ter Kansas City MO 64131-2918 Office: Mo Ho of Reps State Capitol Building Jefferson City MO 65101-1556

KAUFFMAN, TERRY, broadcast and creative arts communication educator, artist; b. San Francisco, Aug. 24, 1951; d. Raymond Roger and Patricia Virginia Kauffman. BA in Journalism with honors, U. Calif., Berkeley, 1974; MA in Comm. summa cum laude, U. Tex., 1980; PhD in Psychology, Comm., and Creative Expression with distinction, Union Inst., 1996. With Alta. Ednl. TV, 1976; sr. writer, prodr. and dir. Ampex Corp., Calif., 1980; writer, news prodr., reporter, anchor ABC, Tex., 1974-75; mem. faculty dept. radio, TV and motion pictures U. N.C., Chapel Hill, 1985; mem. faculty dept. comm. N.C. State U., Raleigh, 1986—2001; founder, artist Cozy Cards, Cards by Terry, 2000—. Adj. prof. music, theatre and comm. dept. Meredith Coll., Raleigh, 1990—; adv. bd., chmn. publicity Raleigh Conservatory Music; v.p. Wake Visual Arts Assn. and Gallery; tchr. art Meredith Coll., 1995—; founder, owner Creative Spaces; founder Cozy Cards by Terry Kauffman, 2003; expressive art therapist at psychiat. hosps. and pvt., 1994—. Author: I'm Clueless, Confessions of a College Teacher, The Script as Blueprint, 1994, 8 vol. set poetry including Psalms of Teresa, Secret Place, Just Visiting, others; author numerous poems; composer, prodr., dir. When the Wind Blows, The Rainbow, The Seasons of Change, PBS, Women Today, Profiles in Leadership, Little Miss Puppet Talks to the Angels, I'm One Person or Another, One; commd. and exhibited in solo shows (1st place painting), San Francisco, Raleigh; artist for documentary series, rschr., writer, Alta., Can., 1976; prodr., dir., writer, composer I'm One Person...Or The Other, Thanksgiving (PBS), 1980—; writer, prodr. Consumer Hotline, PBS, Customs Operations at the Border; main character, vocalist, composer Little Miss Puppet Talks to the Angels; pub. music book: Songs by Terry Kauffman; prodr., dir. Coming Home. (1st place, creativity in directing); contbr. articles to prof. jours. Singer/composer for chs. and retirement homes; past bd. dirs. Tex. Consumer Assn., Wake visual Arts. Named Outstanding Lectr. of Yr., Coll. of Humanities and Social Scis., N.C. State U., 1996; recipient Emmy nomination for documentary Otters from Oiled Waters, 1991, more than 15 1st place nat. awards in TV, including writing, producing, directing, music composition, acting, art and photography, vrious art and music shows. Mem. APA, NATAS, Internat. TV Assn. (judge nat. contests), Nat. Broadcasting Soc. (8 1st place nat. awards 1973—, named Outstanding Mem., 1993-94, Profl. Mem. of Yr. 1994), Internat. Expressive Art Therapists Assn., Calif. Scholastic Fedn. (life), Calif. Scholastic Assn., Berkeley Honor Soc., Am. Psychol. Assn., Phi Kappa Phi. Home: 407 Furches St Raleigh NC 27607-4017

KAUFFOLD, RUTH ELIZABETH, clinical psychologist; b. Decatur, Ill., Sept. 5, 1946; d. James Henry and Elizabeth Opal Kauffold; m. Paul Dwight Entner, Aug. 23, 1968; 1 child, James Paul. BA, Cedarville (Ohio) Coll., 1968; MEd, Wright State U., 1972; MS, U. Dayton, 1986; Ph.D, The Union Inst., 1997. Tchr. Springfield (Ohio) Pub. Schs., 1968-72, Pomona (Calif.) Unified Sch. Dist., 1973-76, Bethel Sch. Dist., New Carlisle, Ohio, 1977-81; practicum Sycamore Hosp., Miamisburg, Ohio, 1994; intern, resident clin. psychology Agape Counseling Ctr., Centerville, 1995-2000. Co-hostess radio talk show WHIO Radio Sta., Dayton, 1998; lectr. nat. and internat. profl. convs.; spkr. AACC World Conf., 2001. Lectr., missionary Project Ptnr., Lima, Peru, 1986; lectr., tchr. For Hills Bapt. Ch., Dayton, Ohio, 1997; lectr., tchr. Fair Haven Ch., 2000. Jennings scholar Martha Holden Jennings Found., 1972. Mem. APA, Dayton Area Psychol. Assn. Avocations: interior design, architecture, gardening, reading, walking. Office: Agape Counseling Ctr 175 S Main St Centerville OH 45458-2372

KAUFMAN, ANNE MULL, education educator; d. William Louis Mull and Dorothy Carolyn Jensen; m. Ronald Lee Kaufman, June 30, 2001; children: Catherine Nelson, Matthew Fleener. BS, U. Minn., 1969, MA, 1976, PhD, 1994. Social studies tchr. Henry Sibley H.S., West St. Paul, Minn., 1969—73; instr. U. of Minn., 1976—87; assoc. prof. Augsburg Coll., Mpls., 1987—. Sch. bd., dir. Minnetonka Pub. Schools, Minn., 1986—89; Minn. bd. of tchg., mem. Minn. Dept. of Edn., 1991—99; dir. of paideia program Augsburg Coll., Mpls., 1999—. Dir., vice-chair Minn. Bd. of Tchg., 1991—99; dir., sec. Minnetonka Pub. Schools, Minnetonka, Minn., 1986—89. Recipient Skipper award for volunteerism, Minnetonka Pub. Schools, 1990, Tchr. Induction Model, Minn. Assn. of Curriculum Devel. (MASCD), 1999; Improving Tchr. Quality grant, Minn. Higher Edn. Svc. Office and No Child Left Behind Act, 2003—, Asset Bldg., Assn. and Supervision of Curriculum Devel. (ASCD), 1998—99. Mem.: Paideia Group Inc., Minn. Coun. for the Social Studies. Avocations: aerobics, reading, travel. Office: Augsburg Coll 2211 Riverside Ave Minneapolis MN 55454 Office Phone: 612-330-1188. E-mail: kaufman@augsburg.edu.

KAUFMAN, ANTOINETTE D. business services company executive; b. Phila., Mar. 10, 1939; d. Joseph and Maria Falcone; m. John R. Kaufman, Apr. 30, 1988. Ed., St. Joseph's U., 1968. With N.W. Ayer & Son, Inc., N.Y.C., 1956-81; adminstrv. asst. N.W. Ayer ABH Internat., 1960, asst. corp. sec., 1977, corp. sec., 1978-79, stock transfer agt., 1969-79, info. specialist, 1979-81; exec. v.p., sec., creative dir., chief oper. officer Help Bus. Svcs., Inc., Swarthmore, Pa., 1981—. Avocations: ballroom dancing, cooking, violin, piano, gardening. Office: Help Bus Svcs Inc 110 Park Ave HBS Bldg Swarthmore PA 19081

KAUFMAN, BEL, author, educator; b. Berlin; d. Michael J. and Lala (Rabinowitz) K.; divorced; children: Jonathan Goldstine, Thea Goldstine. BA magna cum laude, Hunter Coll., 1934; DHL, Hunter Coll, 2001; MA with highest honors, Columbia U., 1936; LLD honors, Nasson Coll., Maine, 1965. Adj. prof. English CUNY; lectr. throughout country, also appearances on TV and radio. Mem. Commn. Performing Arts. Editorial bd., Phi Delta Kappan.; Author: Up the Down Staircase, 1965, Love, etc, 1979; also short stories, articles, TV play, translations from Russian, lyrics for musicals. Bd. dirs. Shalom Aleichem Found.; adv. council Town Hall Found. Recipient plaque Anti-Defamation League, award and plaque United Jewish Appeal, Paperback of Year award, Ky. Col. award, Bell Movie award, Nat. Treasure awrd Seasoned Citizens Theatre, 2001; also ednl. journalism awards; named to Hall of Fame Hunter Coll., winner short story contest sponsored by NEA and PEN, 1983. Mem. Author's Guild, Dramatists Guild, P.E.N., English Grad. Union, Phi Beta Kappa. Address: 1020 Park Ave New York NY 10028-0913 E-mail: belkau@aol.com.

KAUFMAN, BEVERLY, political organization administrator; married; 1 child. County clk. Harris County, Tex., 1994—; mem. at large, 4th v.p., regent Nat. Fedn. Rep. Women, 3rd v.p., dir. region 7. Liaison to various area c. of c.; active Internat. Rep. Inst., Bangkok; presdl. elector, del. at large, vice chmn. of the host com. Rep. Nat. Conv., Houston, 1992. Mem. Houston Profl. Rep. Women's Club (charter), Tex. Fedn. Rep. Women. Office: Nat Fedn Rep Women 124 N Alfred St Alexandria VA 22314-3011 Fax: 703-548-9836. E-mail: bkredding@aol.com.

KAUFMAN, CHARLOTTE KING, artist; b. Balt., Dec. 5, 1920; d. Ben and Belle (Turow) King; m. Albert Kaufman, July 22, 1945; children: Matthew King, Ezra King. AB, Goucher Coll., 1969; MPH, Johns Hopkins U., 1972, MEd, 1976. Dir. pub. rels. Balt. Jewish Cmty. Ctr., 1962-67; rschr., editor Johns Hopkins U. Sch. Hygiene and Pub. Health, Balt., 1969-72, admissions officer, 1972-74, dir. admissions and registrar, 1974-86, dir. study cons. program for undergrads., 1985-89, pub. health acad. adviser, 1989-95; studio artist, Palm Desert, Calif., 1996—. Mem. APHA, Am. Assn. for Higher Edn., Am. Assn. Collegiate Registrars and Admissions Officers, Artists Equity Assn. (v.p. Md. chpt. 1988-90), Md. Printmakers (exec. bd. 1989-94), Palm Springs Desert Mus. Artists Coun. (exec. bd. 1997-2002), Delta Omega. Democrat. Jewish. Home: Monterey Country Club 159 Las Lomas Palm Desert CA 92260-2153 Studio: Studio 21 68-895 Perez Rd Ste 21 Cathedral City CA 92234 E-mail: kaufmanchar@dc.rr.

KAUFMAN, CHARLOTTE S. communications executive; b. Bridgeport, Conn., Mar. 8, 1918; d. Samuel N. and S. Elizabeth (Cohen) Schnee; m. William Kaufman, May 9, 1940. BA, U. Mich., 1938. Med. office assoc., 1941-63; dir. pub. rels. Parents and Friends of Retarded Children, Bridgeport, 1965-66; founder, exec. dir. Family Life Film Ctr. of Conn., Fairfield, Conn., 1967-74; exec. producer Topic '69/WNHC-TV, New Haven, Conn., 1969; project dir. pilot project with Social/Rehab. Svc. U.S. Dept. HEW, 1969-70; pub. rels. chmn. Friendship Fair of Aux./Bridgeport Regional Ctr. Retarded, 1979. Founder CAT-TV, pub. access channel, Winston-Salem and Forsyth County, 1991; coord. five annual Film Day Workshops, Fairfield U., 1967 71; coord. coms. of jurors for Am. Film Festival, N.Y.C., 1968-74; chmn./mem. planning and adv. bd. Bridgeport Regional Ctr. for the Retarded; exec. bd. Bd. of Assocs., U. Bridgeport, others; film use cons. to many local and state orgns. Author: Film Discussion: A Technique to Communicate Information About Rehabilitation, 1970; exec. producer: A Day in the Life of P.T. Barnum, 1971; author publs. in field. Vol. patient advocate for nursing homes, Southwestern Conn. Area Agy. on Aging, 1976-78; v.p. Oronoque Village Improvement Assn., 1986-88. Mem.: Kappa Tau Alpha, Theta Sigma Phi. Home: 3180 Grady St Winston Salem NC 27104-4008 E-mail: wkaufman@pol.net.

KAUFMAN, JANICE HORNER, foreign language educator, women's and gender studies educator; b. Mattoon, Ill., Apr. 30, 1949; d. Daniel Ogden and Julia Betty (McDermid) Horner; m. Richard Boucher Kaufman, June 24, 1972 (div. Mar. 27, 2002); children: Julia Ogden, Richard Pearse. AB, Duke U., 1971; MA in Liberal Studies, Hollins Coll., 1979; postgrad., NYU, 1986; PhD in French, U. Va., Charlottesville, 1997. Tchr. in French Roanoke (Va.) City Pub. Schs., 1971-72, North Cross Sch., Roanoke, Va., 1974-82; instr. French Va. Poly. Inst. and State U., Blacksburg, 1984-86, 88, 90, 94, 98, asst. dir. fgn. lang. camps, 1984-85, administrv. dir., 1986; French, English interpreter, translator Coll. Architecture and Urban Studies, Blacksburg, 1988; instr. ESL U. Cmty. Internat. Coun., Cranwell Internat. Ctr., Blacksburg, 1987-89; instr. French Hollins Coll., Roanoke, Va., 1989-90, Radford (Va.) U., 1989-90; grad. tchg. asst. U. Va., Charlottesville, 1992; adj. assoc. prof. French No. Va. C.C., Woodbridge and Alexandria, 1997-99; asst. prof. French and women's and gender studies SUNY-Oneonta, 2000—. Student counselor Am. Inst. Fgn. Study, Greenwich, Conn., 1977; session leader Russell County Pub. Schs., Lebanon, Va., 1985, Va. Assn. Ind. Schs., Richmond, 1986; asst. tchr. Am. Coun. for Internat. Studies "Toujours en France," 1995; faculty cons. advanced placement exam in French, Ednl. Testing Svc., Trenton State Coll., 1991-95, 97-98; adj. prof. French, George Mason U., Fairfax, Va., 1999-2000; acad. dir. study abroad in Strasbourg, France, George Mason U. Ctr. for Global Edn., summer 2000; presenter in field. Contbr. articles to profl. jours. Mem. MLA, Am. Assn. Tchrs. French, African Lit. Assn., Women in French, Pi Delta Phi, Phi Sigma Iota. Avocations: reading, travel, hiking. Home: 6 Walnut St Oneonta NY 13820-1824 E-mail: kaufmajh@oneonta.edu.

KAUFMAN, MONICA, newscaster; m. Clinton Deveaux, 1978 (div. 1983); 1 adopted child, Claire Deveaux 1 child ; m. Clarence Lott, 1988 (div.); m. Jerry Kaufman (div.). Grad., U. Louisville. Pub. rels. staff Brown-Forman Distillers; reporter, anchor STa. WHAS-TV, Louisville; anchor Sta. WSB-TV, Atlanta, 1975—. Named Citizen-Broadcaster of Yr., Ga. Broadcasters Assn., 1993, Broadcaster of Yr., U. Ga., 2001; named to U. Ky. Journalism Hall of Fame, 2001; recipient Women's Sports Journalism award, Women's Sports Found. and Miller Lite, 1992, Commendation award, Nat. Am. Women in Radio and TV, Emmy award. Mem.: Atlanta Assn. Black Journalists, Nat. Assn. Black Journalists, Soc. Profl. Journalists, Atlanta Jr. League, Sigma Delta Chi. Office: Sta WSB-TV 1601 W Peachtree St NE Atlanta GA 30309

KAUFMAN, RAYLENE DYANE, secondary school educator; b. Oakland, Calif., Feb. 13, 1972; d. Harold A. Kaufman, Jr. and Joyce L. Kaufman. BA, Knox Coll., 2000. Rehab. aide Assn. Mentally Handicapped, Springfield, Mo., St. Mary's Square, Galesburg, Ill.; tchr. M.S. Palmer HS, Marks, Miss., 2000—. Advisor Teach for Am., Houston, 2002; tutor 21st Century Tutoring Program, 2001—. Co-founder The Playground Fund, Marks, 2002—03. Nominee Nat. Tchg. Recognition award, Teach for Am., 2002; fellow, U. Miss., 2003. Office: MSPHS Hwy 3 South Marks MS 38646

KAUFMANN, RACHEL NORSWORTHY, social sciences educator; b. Los Angeles, Feb. 12, 1964; d. Ralph Henry and Audely (Gutierrez) N.; m. Karl Alexander Kaufmann, May 28, 1988. BA, Scripps Coll., 1988; MA, Webster U., 1997. Pharmacy tech. Torrance (Calif.) Meml. Hosp., 1982-88, St. Mary Med. Ctr., Long Beach, Calif., 1987-88; asst. area mgr. AutoFuel Co., Abilene, Tex., 1989-90; adminstrv. asst. McMurry U., Abilene, 1990-92; 911 tech. asst. West Cen. Tex. Coun. of Govts., Abilene, 1992-94; adminstrv. asst. Piedmont Natural Gas, Greenville, S.C., 1995-97; gen.

psychology and devel. psychology tchr. Sandhills C.C., Pinehurst, NC, 1998—2001; marriage and family counselor pvt. practice, 1999—2002; dir. counseling svcs. St. Andrews Presbyn. Coll., 2001—. Auction com. Am. Cancer Soc., Abilene, 1994; bd. dirs. West Tex. Girl Scout Coun., Abilene, 1992-94. Mem. AAUW (bd. dirs. 1989-94). Presbyterian. Avocations: sewing, cooking, travel, music. Home: 565 S Bethesda Rd Southern Pines NC 28387-6401

KAUGER, YVONNE, state supreme court justice; b. Cordell, Okla., Aug. 3, 1937; d. John and Alice (Bottom) K.; 1 child, Jonna Kauger Kirschner. BS magna cum laude, Southwestern State U., Weatherford, Okla., 1958; cert. med. technologist, St. Anthony's Hosp., 1959; JD, Oklahoma City U., 1969, LLD (hon.), 1992. Med. technologist Med. Arts Lab., 1959-68; assoc. Rogers, Travis & Jordan, 1970-72; jud. asst. Okla. Supreme Ct., Oklahoma City, 1972-84, justice, 1984-94, vice chief justice, 1994-96, chief justice, 1997-98, justice, 1998—. Mem. appellate div. Ct. on Judiciary; mem. State Capitol Preservation Commn., 1983-84; mem. dean's adv. com. Oklahoma City U. Sch. Law; lectr. William O. Douglas Lecture Series Gonzaga U., 1990. Founder Gallery of Plains Indian, Colony, Okla., Red Earth (Down Towner award 1990), 1987; active Jud. Day, Girl's State, 1976-80; keynote speaker Girl's State Hall of Fame Banquet, 1984; bd. dirs. Lyric Theatre, Inc., 1966—, pres. bd. dirs., 1981; past mem. bd. dirs. Civic Music Soc., Okla. Theatre Ctr., Canterbury Choral Soc.; mem. First Lady of Okla.'s Artisans' Alliance Com. Named Panhellenic Woman of Yr., 1990, Woman of Yr. Red Lands Coun. Girl Scouts, 1990, Washita County Hall of Fame, 1992. Mem. ABA (law sch. accreditation com.), Okla. Bar Assn. (law schs. com. 1977—), Washita County Bar Assn., Washita County Hist. Soc. (life), St. Paul's Music Soc., Iota Tau Tau, Delta Zeta (Disting. Alumna award 1988, State Delta Zeta of Yr. 1987, Nat. Woman of Yr. 1988). Episcopalian.

KAVADAS-PAPPAS, IPHIGENIA KATHERINE, preschool administrator, educator, consultant; b. Manchester, N.H., Oct. 24, 1958; d. Demetrios Stefanos and Rodothea (Palaiologou) K.; m. Constantine George Pappas, July 29, 1979; children: George Demetrios, Rodothea Constance. BA magna cum laude, U. Detroit, 1980; MAT summa cum laude, Oakland U., 1985. Cert. tchr., Mich. Pre-sch. tchr. Assumption Nursery Sch., St. Clair Shores, Mich., 1977-80, interim dir., 1984, bd. dirs., 1980—; Sunday sch. tchr. Assumption Greek Orthodox Ch., St. Clair Shores, 1985—; chairperson pre-sch. curriculum com. Greek Orthodox Archdiocese Dept. Religious Edn., Brookline, Mass., 1987—. Cons. Assumption Nursery Sch., 1985—; validator preschs. program for cert. Co-author: Pre-school Curriculum Manual for Greek Orthodox Archdiocese, 1990, Pre-School Curriculum for National Use, 1991. Mem. Assumption Greek Orthodox Ch. Philoptochos Soc., 1978-87; trustee Assumption Nursery Sch., 1979—, Sunday sch. presch. tchr., 1985—; spl. events coord. Assumption Sunday Sch., 1999—; vol. svcs. Bemis Elem. Sch., Boulan Park Mid. Sch., 1991-96; mem. Nat. Ctr. for the Early Childhood Work Force; vol. Troy H.S., 1996—, Rainbow Connection Orgn. Recipient Vol. Svc. award Angus Elem. Sch., 1989. Mem. AAUW, Nat. Assn. for the Edn. Young Children (validator presch. programs for accreditation), Nat. Multiple Sclerosis (adv. bd. 2000). Office: Assumption Greek Orthodox 21800 Marter Rd Saint Clair Shores MI 48080-2464

KAVALER-ADLER, SUSAN, clinical psychologist, psychoanalyst; b. N.Y.C., Jan. 31, 1950; d. Solomon and Alice (Zelikow) Weiss; m. Thomas Kavaler, July 12, 1970 (div. 1975); m. Saul Michael Adler, Aug. 14, 1983. PhD in Clin. Psychology, Adelphi U., 1974. Cert. in psychotherapy, psychoanalysis; diplomate in psychoanalysis, 2003. Psychologist Beth Israel Hosp., N.Y.C., 1974-76, Manhattan Psychiat. Children's Ctr., N.Y.C., 1977-80; pvt. practice psychotherapy-psychoanalysis N.Y.C., 1976—; founder, exec. dir. Object Rels. Inst. Psychotherapy and Psychoanalysis, 1991. Condr. writing and mourning groups; founding dir., supr. faculty, tng. analyst Object Rels. Inst. for Psychotherapy and Psychoanalysis, 1991—; mem. faculty Postgrad. Ctr. Mental Health, N.Y.C., 1984-86, 90; mem. faculty, supr. Nat. Inst. Psychotherapies, N.Y.C., 1985-91; bd. dirs., supr. Bklyn. Inst. Psychotherapy and Psychoanalysis; adj. prof. Fordham U.; founding exec. dir. Object Rels. Inst. Psychotherapy and Psychoanalysis, 1991--; spkr pvt. seminars, writing groups. Author: (books) The Compulsion to Create, 1993, 2d edit., 2000, Women Writers and Their Demon Lovers, 1993, rev. edit., 2000, The Creative Mystique: From Red Shoes Frenzy to Love and Creativity, 1996, International Forum of Psychoanalysis, 1999, The Divine, the Deviant and the Diabolical: A Female Artist's Developmental Journey from Self Fragmentation to Self Integration in a Creative Process Group, 2000; contbr. over 43 articles to profl. jours. and books; editor: book chpts. Recipient 6 writing awards, Postgrad. Ctr. for Mental Health. Office: 115 E 9th St Apt 12P New York NY 10003-5420 also: 41 Central Park West New York NY 10023 E-mail: suska674@aol.com.

KAVANAGH, CORNELIA KUBLER, sculptor; b. New Haven, Apr. 8, 1940; d. George Alexander and Elizabeth Bushnell Kubler; m. James Penniston Kavanagh, Feb. 6, 1971; children: Alexander, Elena. BA, Barnard Coll., 1962; MA, Columbia U., 1970-71. Solo shows include: Cornelia Kubler Kavanagh "The Shape of Time", Kirshenbaum, Bond, N.Y., 2002-03. Cornelia Kubler Karanagh "bronze, Plaster, Stone", Tucker Robbins, N.Y. 2001. Qualita Fine Art, Las Vegas, Nev., 1999-2000, Artspace, New Haven, 1997, Conn. Art Competition Stamford Mus. and Nature Ctr., 1992, Art Asia, Hong Kong, 1992, The Discovery Mus., Bridgeport, Conn., 1997, Parish-Hadley Assocs., N.Y., 1996, Silvermine Guild Arts Ctr., New Canaan, Conn., 2000, Openasia, Venice, 2004; commd. works include Long Wharf Theater, Lancaster Winery, Sonoma, Calif.; represented in corp. collections at Kirshenbaum, Bond and Ptnrs., N.Y.C., Parish-Hadley Assocs., Inc., N.Y.C., So. Wine and Spirits, Miami, Sunbelt Beverage Corp., N.Y.C.; represented by Blue Mountain Gallery, N.Y., artformedia.com, PMW Gallery, Stamford, CT; subject of articles. Sec. bd. dirs. New Canaan (Conn.) Country Sch., 1984-88; sec. Rowayton (Conn.) Civic Assn., 1984-88; vol. Mid Fairfield Hospice, Conn., 1984-99; mem. parents exec. com. Colby coll., 1990-98.; mem. cmty. outreach bd. Ctr. for Hope, Darien, Conn., 1996—. Recipient Best Sculpture award Discovery Mus. and Nature Ctr., Bridgeport, Conn., 1997, 1st Pl. award for stone sculpture Art of the Northeast Silvermine Sch. Art, Ct., 2000, Amidar Meml. award for stone sculpture, 2000. Mem. Nat. Sculpture Soc., Conn. Women Artists.

KAVANAGH, EILEEN J. librarian; BA, Ladycliff Coll.; MS in Libr. Sci., Columbia U., 1969; MA in Liberal Studies, SUNY, Stonybrook, 1980. Reference libr. Farmingdale (N.Y.) Pub. Libr., 1969-70; from reference libr. to libr. dir. Bay Shore-Brightwaters (N.Y.) Pub. Libr., 1970—. Office: Bay Shore-Brightwaters Pub Libr 1 S Country Rd Brightwaters NY 11718-1513 Office Phone: 631-665-4350. Business E-Mail: ekavanag@suffolk.lib.ny.us.

KAVANAUGH, BONNIE B. corporate communications executive; b. Dayton, Ohio, July 22, 1948; d. Joseph Edward and Phyllis Jean (Shook) Smith. BS in Journalism, Ohio U., 1970. Accredited bus. communicator. Reporter Piqua (Ohio) Daily Call, 1970—71; asst. dir. pub. rels. Bethesda Hosps., Cin., 1971—76; dir. comm. St. Joseph's Hosp., Ft. Wayne, Ind., 1976—81; publs. editor E. Ohio Gas Co., Cleve., 1981—88; coord. customer comm. East Ohio Gas Co., Cleve., 1988—90; mgr. employee comm. Picker Internat., Inc., Highland Heights, Ohio, 1990—96; mgr. internal comm. Prudential HealthCare, Roseland, NJ, 1996—97; comm. mgr. human resources Prudential Ins., Newark, 1997—99, dir. human resources comm., 1999—2002; mgr. employee comm. Chiquita Brands Internat., Cin., 2003—. Speaker, seminar leader various hosps., bus. and profl. orgns., 1975—. Outreach vol. Cleve. Children's Mus., 1986-88, co-chmn. outreach program, mem. speaker's bur., 1988-89, mem. pub. rels. task force, 1989-92. Recipient numerous awards Ohio Hosp. Assn., Ohio Press Women, Acad. Hosp. Pub. Rels., Cin. Editors Assn., also others. Mem. Internat. Assn. Bus. Communicators (dir. mem. svcs. internal communications coun. 1985-88, chmn. directory mktg. coun. 1988-90, dir. examiners accreditation bd. 1986-88, pres. Greater Cin. chpt., 2003—), numerous awards 1975—). Avocations: needlepoint, reading, gardening. Office Phone: 513-784-8951. E-mail: bkavanaugh@cinci.rr.com.

KAVANDI, JANET LYNN, aerospace power engineer, chemist; b. Springfield, Mo., July 17, 1959; d. William Winfred and Wanda Ruth (Garner) Sellers; m. Farhad John Kavandi, June 5, 1982. BS magna cum laude, Mo. So. State Coll., 1980; MS, U. Mo., Rolla, 1982; PhD, U. Wash., 1990. Project engr. Eagle-Picher Industries, Joplin, Mo., 1982-84; prin. engr. power systems tech. Boeing Def. and Space Group, Seattle, 1984—; Astronaut NASA, Houston, 1995—. Mem. AIAA, Am. Chem. Soc. Avocations: snow skiing, horseback riding, windsurfing, sailing, camping. Home: 696 Pineloch Dr Webster TX 77598-1828 Office: Astronauts Program Lyndon B Johnson Space Center Houston TX 77058

KAVESH, EDEN, fraud investigator, financial consultant; BA in Musicology with honors, UCLA, 1998. Mktg. asst. Corp. Profiles, Encino, Calif., 1998—99; fraud investigator Moorpark, Calif., 1999—. Regents scholar, U. Calif., 1996. Mem.: Calif. Fin. Crimes Investigators Assn., Internat. Assn. of Fin. Crimes Investigators, Nat. Mus. of Women in the Arts, Golden Key Nat. Honor Soc. (life). Progressive. Avocations: art, writing, music. Home: 160 Conifer Circle Oak Park CA 91377

KAVNER, JULIE, actress; b. L.A., Sept. 7, 1951; Grad., San Diego U., 1971. Actress: (TV series) Rhoda, 1974-78 (Emmy award 1978), Petrocelli, 1975, Lou Grant, 1977, Taxi, 1980, The Tracey Ullman Show, 1987-90, The Simpsons, (voice of Marge Simpson and others) 1990—, Sibs, 1991, Birdland, 1994, Tracey Takes On, 1996, (TV movies) Katherine, 1975, The Girl Who Couldn't Lose, 1975, No Other Love, 1979, Revenge of the Stepford Wives, 1980, Don't Drink the Water, 1994, Jake's Women, 1996, (feature films) National Lampoon Goes to the Movies, 1981, Bad Medicine, 1985, Hannah and her Sisters, 1985, Radio Days, 1987, Surrender, 1987, New York Stories, 1989, Awakenings, 1990, Alice, 1990, This Is My Life, 1992, Shadows and Fog, 1992, I'll Do Anything, 1994, Forget Paris, 1995, Deconstructing Harry, 1997, Doctor Dolittle (voice), 1998, A Walk on the Moon, 1999, Judy Berlin, 1999, Story of a Bad Boy, 1999, Someone Like You (voice), Barn Red, 2003, The Lion King 1 1/2, 2004.*

KAVOVIT, BARBARA, entrepreneur; b. Bronx; 1 child, Zachary. Degree in fin., SUNY, Oswego, 1987. Asst. commodities trader; former founder, chief exec. Anchor Constrn. Inc., N.Y.C.; founder Barbara K Enterprises, 2002—. Mem. pres.'s adv. bd. New Rochelle Coll. Named one of Superstar Entrepreneurs of Small and Large Bus.; recipient N.Y. State Dept. Econ. Devel. award, Gov. Mario Cuomo. Mem.: Profl. Women in Constrn. Office: Anchor Constrn Inc 25 W 45th St 2nd Fl New York NY 10036*

KAWAKAMI, BERTHA C. state representative; b. Honolulu, July 28, 1931; children: Wendall, Lyndall. BA in Edn., U. Hawaii, 1953; MA in Edn., NYU, 1962. Elem., resource tchr. Eleele, Pearl Harbor Intermediate Sch., Nanaikapono, 1954—61; mem. lang. arts dist. team, 1962—65; prin., elem. intermediate Eleele and Kekaha Schs., 1965—79; ednl. specialist Kauai Dist. Office, 1980—87, dep. dist. supr. dept. edn., 1987; asst. majority fl. leader, 1987—. Trustee Blood Bank of Hawaii, 1992—; mem. adv. com. Cmty. Health Nursing Divsn., 1991—; mem. quality assurance com. Kauai Vets. Meml. Hosp., 1991—; bd. dirs., v.p. Comml. Properties Inc., 1988—; mem. Waimea United Chs. of Christ, 1989—. Mem.: Japanese Am. Nat. Mus. (hon. chairperson), Hawaii State Found. on Culture and Arts, Delta Kappa Gamma Soc. Internat. Democrat. Office: State Capitol Rm 434 415 S Beretania St Honolulu HI 96813 E-mail: repkawakami@capitol.hawaii.gov.

KAWAMURA, GEORGINA K. finance company executive; b. Lanai City, Hawaii, Sept. 19, 1952; m. Gary Kawamura, 1973; children: Bryan, Jon. AA in Acctg., Maui CC. Clk. to office mgr., budget dir. Maui (Hawaii) County Mayor's Office, 1987—88; planner Castle and Cooke Resorts, Lanai, Hawaii, 1998—2002; dir. fin. Dept. Budget and Fin., Hawaii, 2002—. Avocations: hula, reading. Office: Dept Budget and Fin PO Box 150 Honolulu HI 96810*

KAWAZOE, ROBIN INADA, federal official; b. Wilkinsburg, Pa., Jan. 13, 1959; d. George and Hanako (Nishio) Inada; children: Amy, Steven. BA, U. Md., 1982. Program analyst Alcohol, Drug Abuse & Mental Health Adminstrn., Rockville, Md., 1981-85, 85-87, com. mgmt. officer, 1985—86, extramural programs officer, 1987-88; spl. asst. Nat. Inst. on Drug Abuse, Rockville, 1988-90, dep. dir. Office Sci. Policy and Comm., 1990-96; dir. Office of Sci. Policy and Planning, 1997—. Recipient Recognition award, Pub. Health Svc., 1992, Dir.'s award, NIH, 1994, Dir.'s Group award, 2000. Office: NIH Office of Sci Policy & Planning 9000 Rockville Pike Bldg 1, rm 218 Bethesda MD 20892-0003

KAWCZYNSKI, DIANE MARIE, elementary and middle school educator, composer; b. Milw., Jan. 22, 1959; d. Adalbert Lawrence and Joan (Zernia) K. BMus, Lawrence U., 1981; MMus, U. Wis., 1985. Cert. music tchr. Va., adminstrn. and supervision pre-K-12 Va. Suzuki violin instr., string methods instr. Brandon (Manitoba, Can.) Univ. Sch. Music, 1982-83; violin/viola instr., univ. prep program U. Wis. Sch. of Music, Madison, 1983-85; elem. and middle sch. string instr. Albuquerque Pub. Schs., 1985-86; middle sch. string and chorus instr. Ft. Morgan (Colo.) Pub. Schs., 1986-87; elem. string instr., middle sch. orchestra instr. Norfolk Pub. Schs., 1987—. Mem. NEA, Am. String Tchr. Assn., Music Educators Nat. Conf. Avocations: knitting, walking, crafts. Home: 860 Gaslight Ln Virginia Beach VA 23462-1232 E-mail: dkawcz@nps.k12.va.us.

KAWECKI, JEAN MARY, sculptor; b. June 24, 1926; came to U.S., 1951; d. Donald McRae and Doris (Hankey) Cameron; m. Wladyslaw Kawecki, May 16, 1951; 1 child, Tim Stefan. Student, Lowther Coll., North Wales, 1937-41, Liverpool (Eng.) Coll. Art, 1941-44. Freelance artist, London, 1946-51, N.Y.C. and N.J., 1951-68; sculptor, 1970—; founder, dir. Doubletree Gallery Fine Art, Montclair, N.J., 1975-85; co-founder Studio Montclair Assn. Profl. Visual Artists, 1997—. Prin. works include wall sculpture First Montclair Housing Corp., 1982, Acquisitional Frenzy (Audubon Artists award 1978), Three Robed Figures in Motion (Carrier Found. award 1993), series of 8 sculptures for Ctr. for Women Policy Studies. Work included in time capsule Ency. of Women Artists, 1995. Mem. Women Artists Montclair, Montclair Art Mus., World Wildlife Fund. Avocations: travel, dance, world wildlife. Home: 28 Mountainside Park Ter Montclair NJ 07043-1209

KAWESKI, SUSAN, plastic surgeon, naval officer; b. Oil City, Pa., Jan. 27, 1955; d. Richard Francis and Lottie Ann (Malek) K.; m. Henry Nicholas Ernecoff, Aug. 7, 1983. BA, Washington and Jefferson Coll., 1976; MA, SUNY, Buffalo, 1979; MD, Pa. State U., 1983. Diplomate Am. Bd. Surgery, Am. Bd. Plastic Surgery. Commd. lt. USN, 1983, advanced through grades to capt., 1993; intern Naval Hosp., San Diego, 1983-84; head med. dept. USN, 1984-85; resident in gen. surgery Naval Hosp., San Diego, 1985-89; resident in plastic surgery Pa. State U., Hershey, 1989-91; staff plastic surgeon Naval Med. Ctr., San Diego, 1991-95; head divsn. plastic surgery, surgeon gen. advisor USN, 1994-95; craniofacial fellow Dr. Ian T. Jackson, Mich., 1995-96; head cleft palate/craniofacial team Naval Med. Ctr., 1996-98; resigned, 1998; pvt. practice, 1998—. Chmn. Cleft Palate/Craniofacial Bd., San Diego; plastic surgery advisor to surgeon gen. USN, 1994-95; presenter in field. Author chpt. to book. Recipient Ernest Witebsky Meml. award for proficiency in microbiology SUNY at Buffalo, 1978. Fellow ACS (assoc., 1st Place Rsch. award 1991); mem. Am. Assn. Plastic and Reconstructive Surgeons, Am. Cleft Palate Assn., Am. Assn. Women Surgeons, Am. Med. Women's Assn., Assn. Mil. Surgeons U.S., Univ. Club. Republican. Roman Catholic. Avocations: skiing, tennis, swimming, oil painting, playing piano. Home: 1158 Barcelona Dr San Diego CA 92107-4151 Office: Craniofacial Reconstructive 3444 Kearny Villa Rd Ste 401 San Diego CA 92123-1964 E-mail: skaweski@pacbell.net.

KAWEWE, SALIWE MOYO, social work educator, researcher; children: Neo Jomo, Rujeko. BSW, University Of Zambia, Lusaka, Zambia, 1970—74; MSW, Washington U., St. Louis, Mo., 1977—79; PhD, St. Louis U., 1981—85. Cert. edn. accreditation reaffirmation Coun. on Social Work, 2001. Adminstrv. asst. University of Zambia, Lusaka, Zambia, 1974—77; social svcs. officer, probation officer Dept. Social Svcs., Bulawayo, Zimbabwe, 1979—81; instr. Bd. Edn. St. Louis Public Schools, Saint Louis, Mo., 1981—83; social service worker II Mo. Div. of Family Services, St. Louis, 1984—85; asst. prof. Southeastern La. U., Hammond, La., 1985—88, Central State U., Wilberforce, Ohio, 1989, James Madison U., Harrisonburg, Va., 1989—91, Wichita State U., Wichita, Kans., 1991—96; assoc. prof. Southern Ill. U., Carbondale, Ill., 1996—2001, grad. program dir., 1996—98, prof., 2002—. Chair Coun. on Social Work Edn. Internat. Commn.'s Internat.l Issues Symposium, Alexandria, 1999—; contract bargaining team mem. Southern Ill. U. Faculty Assn., IEA-NEA, Carbondale, 1998—2003, dept. rep., 1998—99. Contbr. chapters to books Social Welfare with Indigenous Peoples, 1995, Black Women in the Academy: Promises and Perils, 1997, Zimbabwe Education System World Education Encyclopedia, 2001, World Press Encyclopedia, 2003, Encyclopedia African History; editl. bd. mem.: Social Devel. Issues, 1998—, guest editl. bd. mem.: Nat. Women Studies Jour., 1997—98; contbr. articles and conf. proceedings to profl. jours. and publs. Mem. Nat. Assn. Social Workers, Bulawayo, Zimbabwe, 1980—82; Africa regional rep. Inter-Univ. Consortium for Internat. Social Devel., Wichita, 1992—94; mem. Tangipohoa Parish Mayor's commn. on Needs of Women, Hammond, La., 1985—88, Inter-Univ. Consortium for Internat. Social Devel., Carbondale, 1995—, Ill. Hunger Coalition, Chgo., 1998—; sec. Kans. Coun. on Social Work Edn., Topeka, 1992—93; mem. Com. to Enhance Minority, Human and Civil Rights, Springfield, 2000—. Recipient Outstanding Scholastic Achievement award, George Warren Brown Sch. of Social Work, Wash. U., 1979, Superior Acad. Achievement award, St. Louis U. Internat. Student Assn., 1984, Appreciation for Continuing Svc. as a Faculty Advisor, Nat. Assn. Black Social Workers, 2001, Appreciation as Faculty Advisor, 2000, certificate of Dedication, African Student Coun. So. Ill. U. at Carbondale, 2001, Internat. Student Coun So. Ill. U. at Carbondale, 2001, Award of Appreciation of Svc., Nat. Assn. Black Social Workers, 2000, Recognition of Dedicated Svc., African Student Coun. So. Ill. U. at Carbondale, 1998, Dedication of Svc., African Student Coun., So. Ill. U. at Carbondale, 1997, Outstanding Leadership and Guidance, Student Orgn. of Social Work, Wichita State U., 1996, Outstanding Multilateral Study Del. award, World Congress on the Family, 1992; grantee Summer Rsch. Travel Grant, Wichita State U., 1994. Mem.: NASW (asst. dist. chair 1997—99), Internat. Coun. on Social Welfare, Internat. Assn. for Schs. of Social Work, Soc. for Study of Social Problems, Peace and Social Justice Ctr. of So. Ctrl. Kans., Inter-U. Consortium for Internat. Social Devel., Coun. on Social Work Edn., Coun. on Social Work Edn. Internat. Commn., Internat. Assn. Feminist Econs., So. Ill. U. Women's Caucus, Nat. Women Studies Assn., So. Ill. HIV Care Consortium (bd. mem. 1997—2001), Internat. Fedn. Social Workers (life), Beta Delta of Phi Alpha (hon.). Office: So Ill U Sch Of Social Work Mailcode 4329 Carbondale IL 62901 Office Phone: 618-453-3359. Business E-Mail: smkawewe@siu.edu.

KAY, BONNIE KATHRYN, management consultant; b. Indpls., Nov. 15, 1942; d. Carl Gaines Wiltshire and Evelyn Phyllis Davison; m. David Lee Kay, June 29, 1963 (div. 1970); 1 child, Pamela Jean. BA, Calif. State U., Sacto., 1985; MA, U. Ariz., 1987; PhD, Temple U., 1993. Adj. prof. U. Pa., Wharton Sch. Bus., Phila., 1988-91; asst. prof. W.Va. U., Morgantown, 1991-93; adj. prof. Calif. State U., Sacramento, 1995-99; cons., pres. Orgnl. Solutions, Sacramento, Calif., 1993—. Author: Organizational Consulting, 1992; contbr. articles to profl. jours. Bd. dirs. Huntington Beach (Calif.) Playhouse, 1991-94, Seacliff, 1992-94; vol. KVIE Auction, Sacto., 1975-85, Am. Ballet Theatre, N.Y.C., 1987-91, Huntington Beach Playhouse, 1991-94. Mem. Project Mgmt. Inst. Republican. Avocations: golf, crafts.

KAY, CAROL MCGINNIS, literature educator; b. Gadsden, Ala., Jan. 14, 1941; d. Gaston G. and Ruth (Owen) McGinnis; 1 child, David McGinnis Kay. BA, U. Ala., 1962, MA, 1963; PhD, U. Tenn., 1967. Scholar-tchr. U. Ala., 1967-78, chair dept. English, 1978-81, spl. asst. to pres., 1981-82; dean of coll. Randolph-Macon Woman's Coll., 1982-86; dean coll. humanities and social scis. U. S.C., Columbia, 1986-93, prof. English, 1993—. Co-author: "G" Is for Grafton, 1997 (Edgar award for critical work of 1997); co-editor: Shakespeare's Romances Reconsidered, 1978; contbr. articles to profl. jours. Trustee Folger Shakespeare Theatre, Washington, 1986-93, Heathwood Hall Episcopal Sch.; bd. dirs. Coun. Colls. Arts and Scis. Fellow Am. Coun. on Edn., 1981-82; recipient Mortar Bd. Tchg. award, 1994. Mem. Southeastern Renaissance Conf. (past pres.), South Caroliniana Soc. Episcopalian. Avocations: collecting antiques, mystery novels, travel. Home: 359 S Stonehedge Dr Columbia SC 29210-4225 Office: U SC Dept English Welsh Humanities Bldg Columbia SC 29208-0001

KAY, ELIZABETH ALISON, zoology educator; b. Kauai, Hawaii, Sept. 27, 1928; d. Robert Buttercase and Jessie Dowie (McConnachie) K. BA, Mills Coll., 1950, Cambridge U., Eng., 1952, MA, 1956; PhD, U. Hawaii, 1957. From asst. prof. to prof. zoology U. Hawaii, Honolulu, 1957-62, assoc. prof., 1962-67, prof., 1967-98, prof. emeritus, 1998—. Research assoc. Bishop Mus., Honolulu, 1968—. Author: Hawaiian Marine Mollusks, 1979, Shells of Hawaii, 1991; editor: A Natural History of the Hawaiian Islands, 1972, 94. Chmn. Animal Species Adv. Commn., Honolulu, 1983-87; v.p. Save Diamond Head Assn., Honolulu, 1968-87, pres., 1987—; trustee B.P. Bishop Mus., Honolulu, 1983-88. Fellow Linnean Soc., AAAS; mem. Marine Biol. Assn. (Eng.), Australian Malacol. Soc. Episcopalian. Office: U Hawaii Manoa Dept Zoology 2538 The Mall Honolulu HI 96822-2200

KAY, HAZEL T. local commissioner; b. Muskegon, Mich., Sept. 21, 1924; d. Alonzo Stansell and Laura Estelle Gasaway; m. Heinz Theodore Kay, Nov. 21, 1951 (widowed, Dec. 3, 1992); children: Joanne, Carolyn, Cezane, Ben. BS, Mich. State U., 1945; postgrad, UCLA, 1949, U. So. Calif., 1949. Lab. tech. Vets. Administrn, L.A., 1946-48; mgr. hosp. lab, x-ray Trans-Arabian Pipeline, Ras El Mishab, Saudia Arabia, 1948-50; chief technologist Bio-Science Lab., L.A., 1950-54; manufacturing chemist Cyclo-Chemical Co., L.A., 1954-58; petroleum chemist Petroleum Techology, Inc., Montebello, Calif., 1958-60; chief tech., lab. tech. Santa Paula Meml. Hosp., Calif., 1968-90; commr. Housing Authority, Santa Paula, 1992—. Woman's activity coun. Interface Children Svc., Santa Paula, 1997—, dir. Interface-Ventura County, Camarillo, Calif., 1998—; pres. Woman's Adv. Coun. Mem. Kiwanis Internat., Santa Paula, 1988-91; officer (all posiitons) Assn. Retarded, Ventura, Calif., 1966—; pres., v.p., treas. Tri-Counties Regional Ctr., Santa Barbara, Calif., 1998—; trustee Unitarian Universalist Ch., Santa Paula, 1986-88. Recipient Lifetime Achievement award Girl Scouts of Am., 1965, Bus. Woman of Yr. award Soroptimists Internat., 1972, Woman of Dist. award, 1980-90, Cmty. Svc. award C. of C., Santa Paula, 1994, Calif. State Vol. of Yr. award ARC-Calif., 2000. Mem. C. of C. Santa Paula, Assn. Retarded Citizens of Calif., Assn. Retarded Citrizens of Ventura County, Soroptimist Internat., Interface Children and Family, Ventura County Greenline Parents, Found. for the Retarded of the Desert, Sacramento Assn. for the Retarded. Democrat. Universalist Unitarian. Avocations: duplicate bridge, coin collector, swimming, stamp collecting/philately, photography, traveling, reading, community service. Home: 514 Anacapa Ter Santa Paula CA 93060-1902

KAY, HERMA HILL, education educator; b. Orangeburg, S.C., Aug. 18, 1934; d. Charles Esdorn and Herma Lee (Crawford) Hill. BA, So. Meth. U., 1956; JD, U. Chgo., 1959. Bar: Calif. 1960, U.S. Supreme Ct. 1978. Law clk. to Hon. Roger Traynor Calif. Supreme Ct., 1959-60; from asst. prof. to assoc. prof. law U. Calif., Berkeley, 1960-62, prof., 1963, dir. family law project, 1964-67, Jennings prof., 1987-96, dean, 1992-2000, Armstrong prof., 1996—; co-reporter uniform marriage and div. act Nat. Conf. Commrs. on Uniform State Laws, 1968-70. Vis. prof. U. Manchester, England, 1972, Harvard U., 1976; mem. Gov.'s Commn. Family, 1966. Author (with Martha S. West): (book) Text Cases and Materials on Sex-Based Discrimination, 5th edit., 2002; author: (with D. Currie and L. Kramer) Conflict of Laws: Cases, Comments, Questions, 6th edit., 2001; contbr. articles to profl. jours. Trustee Russell Sage Found., NY, 1972—87, chmn. bd. trustees, 1980—84; trustee, bd. dirs. Equal Rights Advs., Calif., 1987—88, chmn., 1976—83; pres. bd. dirs. Rosenberg Found., Calif., 1987—88, bd. dirs., 1978—. Recipient Rsch. award, Am. Bar Found., 1990, Margaret Brent award, ABA Commn. Women in Profession, 1992, Marshall-Wythe medal, 1995; fellow, Ctr. Advanced Study Behavioral Sci., Palo Alto, Calif., 1963. Mem.: ABA (sect. legal edn. and admissions to bar coun. 1992—99, sec. 1999—2001), Order of Coif (nat. pres. 1983—85), Am. Philos. Soc., Am. Acad. Arts and Scis., Assn. Am. Law Schs. (exec. com. 1986—87, pres.-elect 1988, pres. 1989, past pres. 1990), Am. Law Inst. (mem. coun. 1985—), Calif. Women Lawyers (bd. govs. 1975—77), Bar U.S. Supreme Ct., Calif. Bar Assn. Democrat. Office: U Calif Law Sch Boalt Hall Berkeley CA 94720-7200 E-mail: kayh@law.berkeley.edu.

KAY, PEG (MARJORIE A. KAY), information technology executive; b. Chgo. d. Eli and Lillian Eva Nimz; m. Irvin W. Kay; children: Lilyan, Eli. BA, U. Mich., 1953; MPA, Am. U., 1976. Spl. asst. to exec. v.p. acad. affairs Wayne State U., Detroit, 1976; rsch. asst. then assoc. Urban Inst., Washington, 1973—77; asst. program mgr. NSF, Washington, 1976; acting chief planning Inst. Computer Scis. Nat. Bur. Stds. Social Sci., 1981—85; pres. and CEO Vertech Inc., Washington, 1986—. Co-author: Government Operations and Evaluability Assessment, 1982; co-inventor Cablemote. Fellow, U.S. Dept. Commerce Sci. and Tech., 1984—85. Fellow: Washington Acad. Scis. (v.p. affiliated socs. 1997—2001, pres. elect 2003); mem.: Assn. Info. Tech. Profls. (exec. v.p. NOVA chpt. 1999—2000). Avocations: photography, webmaster. Office: Vertech Inc 6111 Wooten Dr Falls Church VA 22044

KAYAFAS, STEPHANIE ANN, special education educator, consultant, supervisor, actress; b. Pitts., Oct. 18, 1957; d. Nicholas and Helen Kayafas. BS, Rutgers U., 1979; MA, Georgian Ct. Coll., Lakewood, N.J., 1996. Cert. tchr. handicapped, elem. tchr., supr., prin., sch. bus. adminstr. N.J. N.J. spl. edn. tchr. Old Farmers Rd. Elem. Sch., Long Valley, NJ, 1979—82; spl. edn. tchr. Tinton Falls (N.J.) Mid. Sch., 1982-83, Rugby Sch., Wall, NJ, 1982—83; owner, operator Charlie's Auto Body Facility, Asbury Park, NJ, 1983—86; computer trainer Dendrite Internat. Inc., Morristown, N.J., 1998-99; actress Actor's Reps, N.Y.C., 1998—; real estate referral cons. Ind. Referral Cons., Woodstown, N.J., 1999—; spl. edn. tchr. Marlboro (NJ) HS, 1987—2000, supr. spl. edn., 2002—. Mem. People to People Internat., 2001—; del. People's Republic of China Amb. Program, 2001. Mem.: ASCD, Am. Coun. Exercise, Rutgers Alumni Assn. Avocations: reading, writing poetry, weight training. Home: Riverview Twrs 28 Riverside Ave Unit 10G Red Bank NJ 07701 Office: Marlboro HS 95 N Main St Marlboro NJ 07746 E-mail: stephanieknj@aol.com.

KAYE, CAROLE, museum director and curator; b. Somerville, N.J., Apr. 24, 1933; d. Harry and Grace (Schwartz) Golison; m. Paul Littman, June 29, 1952 (dec. Apr. 1960); children: Fern, Alan; m. Barry Kaye; children: Howard. Student, Syracuse U., 1951. With Barry Kaye Assocs., L.A.; owner, curator Carole and Barry Kaye Mus. Miniatures, L.A.; v.p. Barry Kaye Assocs. Mus., 1994—. Past pres. Hadassah, Beverly Hills, Calif.; founder Music Ctr., Cedars-Sinai Hosp., L.A.; mem. Jewish Fedn. Mem. Friends of Ben Gurion U. Office: Ste 440 5100 Town Center Cir Boca Raton FL 33486-1008

KAYE, CELIA ILENE, pediatrics educator; b. July 12, 1943; m. Tod B. Sloan. BS, Wayne State U., 1965, MS, 1968, MD, 1969; PhD, Northwestern U., 1975. Diplomate Am. Bd. Pediatrics, Am. Bd. Med. Genetics; lic. physician, Mich., Ill., Tex. Resident in pediat. Bronx (N.Y.) Mcpl. Hosp. Ctr., 1969-71, U. Ill. Hosp., Chgo., 1971-72; fellow in biochem. genetics Children's Meml. Hosp., Chgo., 1972-75; instr. pediat. Northwestern U. Coll. Medicine, Chgo., 1974-75; from asst. prof. to assoc. prof. pediat. U. Ill. Coll. Medicine, Chgo., 1975-89; chmn. divsn. genetics dept. pediat. Cook County Hosp., Chgo., 1975-80, attending physician divsn. genetics dept. pediat., 1980-89; dir. sect. genetics and genetics lab. divsn. pediat. Luth. Gen. Hosp., Park Ridge, Ill., 1980-89, co-med. dir. perinatal ctr., 1986-89; dep. chmn. Santa Rosa Children's Hosp. Activities, co-dir. clin. cytogenics lab. U. Tex. Health Sci. Ctr., San Antonio, 1990-97, prof. depts. pediat. and cellular and structural biology, 1990—, chief sect. metabolism, 1990—99, vice-chmn. dept. pediat., 1993-97, chmn. dept. pediat., 1997—2002, vice dean med. sch., 2001—, co-dir. cytogenetics lab., 1990—98. Mem. quality assurance com. cytogenetics lab. dept. cellular and structural biology U. Tex. Health Sci. Ctr., 1991-97, chair clin. faculty promotions com. dept. pediats., 1991-97, chair com. for devel. plan for selection, evaluation and promotion of clin. faculty dept. pediats., 1990-91, med. perinatal mktg. com. dept. pediats., 1990-91, mem. residency adv. com. dept. pediats., 1990-2002, mem. faculty tenure and promotions com., 1995-97, mem. search com., chmn. dept. pathology, 1995-96, mem. dual degree program com., 1995-98, vice-chmn. bd. dirs. Univ. Physicians Group, 1995-97, 2001—, chmn. fin. com., 2000—, exec. com. mem, 2000—, mem. contract rev. com. 1995-97, bd. dirs.; mem. clin. coord. com., 1990-92, 2000, ad hoc clin. care com., 1990—, MSRDP adv. bd., 1991-93, 97—, search com. chmn. dept. medicine, 1992-93; chmn. program comm. sect. on genetics and birth defects Am. Acad. Pediat., 1995-99; dir. sect. genetics, Ctr. Craniofacial Anomalies, U. Ill. Coll. Medicine, Chgo., 1975-85; mem. med. adv. bd. Santa Rosa Children's Hosp., 1990-91, mem. exec. com. sect. on genetics and birth defects, Am. Acad. Pediat., 1995-2001, dir. med. edn., 1991-97, exec. com., 1992-2002, medicine policy com., 1992-97, chair med. edn. com., 1992-94; assoc. med. dir. cytogenetics lab. Santa Rosa Med. Ctr., San Antonio, 1991-98; vis. assoc. prof. pediats. Rush-Presbyn.-St. Luke's Med. Ctr., Chgo., 1979-89; mem. Genetics Task Force Ill., 1981-89, sec., 1981-83, pres., 1983-85; mem. genetics svc. com. Tex. Genetics Network, 1989-94, chmn. steering com., 1992-2000, mem. data com., 1995-2002; chmn. sci. adv. com. on birth defects Tex. Dept. Health, 1995-97; del. Nat. Coun. Regional Genetics Networks, 1992-99, mem. exec. com., 1993-97, bd. dirs., 1997-99; mem. Ill. Genetic and Metabolic Diseases Adv. Bd., 1984-89, chmn. lab. subcom., 1985-89; mem. sci. adv. com. Tex. Dept. Health, 1992-2000; sr. advisor Nat. Newborn Screening and Genetics Resource Ctr., 1998—; chmn. exec. com. Pub. Health Spl. Interest Group Am. Coll. Med. Genetics, 2002—; mem. steering com. Children's Regional Health Care Network, San Antonio, 1993-94; mem. mgmt. com. Children's Regional Health Care Sys., San Antonio, 1993-94; mem. instl. rev. bd. Cook County Hosp., Chgo., 1975-80, Luth. Gen. Health Care Sys., Park Ridge, Ill., 1988-89; chmn. pediat. edn. com. Luth. Gen. Hosp., Park Ridge, 1981-86, chmn. pediat. bioethics com., mem. faculty adv. com., 1986-89; mem. faculty com. tenure and promotion com., 1995, mem. search com. chmn. dept. pathology, 1995-96, mem. cons. Med. Ctr. Hosp. Ward and Nursery, Bapt. Hosp. Sys., Santa Rosa Children's Hosp., Meth. Hosp., Humana Women's Hosp.; mem. by laws com. Santa Rosa Healthcare, San Antonio, 1995-97. Mem. adv. bd. Am. Jour. Med. Genetics; reviewer Am. Jour. Human Genetics, Pediatric Dermatology; contbr. articles to profl. jours., chpts. to books. Mem. program planning com. March of Dimes Defects Found., Chgo., 1985-89; mem. health profl. adv. com., 1983-89, chmn., 1981-83; mem. health profl. adv. com. South Ctrl. Tex. chpt., 1989-90; bd. dirs., mem. exec. com. Harkness House for Children, Winnetka, Ill., 1988-89; mem. Ill. Spina Bifida Assn., 1983-89; mem. exec. bd. El Valor Corp. for Handicapped Children, Chgo., 1980-81; mem. med. adv. com. Tex. Sickle Cell Assn., 1990-91. Fellow Am. Coll. Med. Genetics (founding, edn. com. 1993-97, pub. health com., moderator pub. health and delivery of svcs. sect. ann. meeting 1994); mem. AMA, Am. Soc. Human Genetics (info. and edn. com. 1990-94), Am. Acad. Pediats. (genetics sect., com. on genetics, liaison to bone and joint decade 2002, judge sci. awards uniformed svcs. sect. 1992-93, chair program com. sect. on genetics and birth defects 1995—, mem. exec. com. sect. on genetics and birth defects 1995—), Soc. for Pediat. Rsch., Soc. for Inherited Metabolic Diseases, So. Soc. for Pediat. Rsch. (moderator genetics sect. ann. meeting 1993), Tex. Med. Soc., Tex. Genetics Soc., Tex. Pediat. Soc., Bexar County Med. Soc., San Antonio Pediat. Soc. Office: U Tex Health Sci Ctr Med Dean's OFfice 7703 Floyd Curl Dr San Antonio TX 78229-3900

KAYE, JANET MIRIAM, psychologist, educator; b. New Haven, Mar. 2, 1937; d. Al and Rose (Marcus) Sovitsky; m. Donald Kaye, June 26, 1955; children: Kenneth, Karen, Kendra, Keith. BS, NYU, 1958, MA, 1960; PhD, Med. Coll. of Pa., 1980. Clin. instr. Med Coll. Pa., Phila., 1980-82, asst. prof., 1982-86, assoc. prof., 1986-94, Med. Coll. Pa. Hahnemann Sch. Medicine, Phila., 1994-96, prof., 1996—2002; prof. coll. medicine Drexel U., Phila., 2002—. Contbr. articles to profl. jours. Mem. APA, Am. Assn. Cancer Edn., Am. Soc. Clin. Hypnosis, Soc. Health and Human Values, Gerontol. Soc. Am., Am. Soc. Psychiat. Oncology, Coll. Physicians Pa., Internat. Soc. Exptl. Hypnosis. Avocations: jogging, working out, swimming, reading.

KAYE, JUDITH SMITH, state appeals court chief judge; b. Monticello, N.Y., Aug. 4, 1938; d. Benjamin and Lena (Cohen) Smith; m. Stephen Rackow Kaye, Feb. 11, 1964; children: Luisa Marian, Jonathan Mackey, Gordon Bernard BA, Barnard Coll., 1958; LLB cum laude, NYU, 1962; LLD (hon.), St. Lawrence U., 1985, Union U., 1985, Pace U., 1985, Syracuse U., 1988, L.I. U., 1989. Assoc. Sullivan & Cromwell, N.Y.C., 1962-64; staff atty. IBM, Armonk, N.Y., 1964-65; asst. to dean Sch. Law NYU, 1965-68; ptnr. Connelly Chase O'Donnell & Weyher, N.Y.C., 1969-83; assoc. judge N.Y. State Ct. Appeals, N.Y.C., 1983-93, chief justice, 1993—. Bd. dir. Sterling Nat. Bank. Contbr. articles to profl. jours. Former bd. dirs. Legal Aid Soc. Recipient Vanderbilt medal NYU Sch. of Law, 1983, Medal of Distinction, Barnard Coll, 1987. Fellow Am. Bar Found.; mem. Am. Law Inst., Am. Coll. Trial Lawyers, Am. Judicature Soc. (bd. dirs. 1980-83). Democrat. Office: NY Court of Appeals Court of Appeals Hall 20 Eagle St Albany NY 12207-1009 also: NY Court of Appeals 230 Park Ave Ste 826 New York NY 10169-0007*

KAYE, RUTH LINCOLN, historical researcher; b. Buffalo, N.Y., Dec. 3, 1918; d. C. Arthur Lincoln and Ethel Elizabeth Green; m. B. Franklin Boan, Oct. 25, 1941 (div. 1949); m. Merwin Whitcomb Kaye, Sept. 4, 1953 (dec. 1987); children: Merrie L., Arthur Lincoln, Larisa Elizabeth. BA, Randolph Macon Women's Coll., 1939. Author: (book) Thomas Lincoln Taunton Mass., 1972, Legends & Folk Tales of Old Alexandria, 1976—, (book) 215 histories Alexandria Va. homes, 1980—, History of St. Paul's Episcopal Church, 1984—. Mem.: Alexandria Hist. Soc., Alexandria Libr. Co., Soc. Mayflower Descendants, Alexandria Assn. & Nat. Trust Hist. Preservation, Nat. Geneal. Soc., Historic Alexandria Found. Republican. Home: 708 Braxton Pl Alexandria VA 22301

KAYE/KANTROWITZ, MELANIE, writer, educator; b. Bklyn., Sept. 9, 1945; d. Milton E. Kantrowitz and Violette E. (Wolfgang) Kaye. BA, CCNY, 1966; MA, U. Calif., Berkeley, 1968, PhD, 1975. Instr. comparative lit. U. Calif., Berkeley, 1971-72; asst. prof. Univ. Scholars Portland (Oreg.) State U., 1972-76, instr. women's studies, 1977-79; counsellor Rape Relief Hotline, Portland, 1977-78; adj. faculty Goddard Coll., Plainfield, Vt., 1978-81, Vt. Coll., Montpelier, 1981-85, asst. then assoc. prof., 1985-92; exec. dir. Jews for Racial and Econ. Justice, N.Y.C., 1992-95; Jane Watson Irwin prof. Hamilton Coll., Clinton, NY, 1995—97; prof. Bklyn. (N.Y.) Coll., 1997—98; dir. Queens Coll. Worker Edn. Extension Ctr. CUNY, 1999—. Co-editor: The Tribe of Dina, 1986; editor, pub. (jour.) Sinister Wisdom, 1983-87; author: (poetry) We Speak in Code, 1980, (fiction) My Jewish Face, 1990, (essays) The Issue is Power, 1992. Mem. Phi Beta Kappa. Jewish. Home: Stony Clove Ln Chichester NY 12416

KAYE-HUNTINGTON, SUSAN B. psychologist; b. Albany, N.Y., May 13, 1946; BA, NYU, 1969; MCAT, Hahnemann U., Phila., 1977; PsyD, Immaculata (Pa.) Coll., 2001. Lic. psychologist Pa., registered and certified art therapist. Pvt. practice art therapist, Phila., 1983—2002; staff clinician Hall-Mercer Mental Health Ctr. Pa. Hosp., Phila., 1990—2001; pvt. practice psychologist Phila., 2002—. Adj. asst. prof. Hahnemann U., Phila., 1977—, U. Arts, Phila., 2000—; cons. Hall Mercer Mental Health Ctr. Pa. Hosp., Phila., 2001—03, Sch. Dist. Phila., 1998—2001. Mem.: APA, Phila. Soc. Clin. Psychologists, Am. Art Therapy Assn. Avocations: hiking, travel, reading, tennis, pottery. Office: 1315 Walnut St Ste 1700 Philadelphia PA 19107

KAYS, SANDRA ELIZABETH, research chemist;, naturalized, USA, 1985; d. Mark and Lily Wood; m. Stanley John Kays, Mar. 19, 1968; children: Adrian Leigh, Asha Renée. BS, Univ. Coll. North Wales, Bangor, 1967; MS, Mich. State U., 1969; PhD, U. Ga., 1991. Grad. asst. U. Ga., Athens, 1988—91, postdoctoral fellow, 1991—94; postdoctoral assoc. USDA, Athens, 1994—97, rsch. chemist, 1997—. Adj. asst. prof. U. Ga., Athens, 2000—. Contbr. articles to profl. jours., chpts. to books. Coord. blood dr. ARC, Russell Rsch. Ctr., Athens, 1999—2003. Recipient postdoctoral rsch. fellowship, Nat. Kidney Found. Ga., 1992—94; fellow, Japan Internat. Sci. and Tech., 1999. Mem.: AOAC Internat., Internat. Coun. for Near Infrared Spectroscopy (treas. 2001—05), Inst. Food Technologists, Am. Chem. Soc. Achievements include patents for prediction of total dietary fiber in cereal products using near-infrared reflectance spectroscopy. Avocations: hiking, reading. Office: USDA Agrl Rsch Svc 950 College Station Rd Athens GA 30605

KAYSE, KATHLEEN, publishing executive; b. Chgo, Ill, 1959; Grad., Univ. of Ill. Media planning Wells, Rich, Greene and J. Walter Thompson, Chgo., 1980—83; sales trainee Time, 1983; midwest advt. mgr. Time Mag., 1987; nat. advt. dir. Time for Kids; pub. Fortune Small Bus. (FSB), Time Mag., NYC, 1998—2001, Money mag., 2001—02, People mag., 2002—. Named Most powerful women in the US, Fortune. Mem.: Fin. Comm. Soc., Advertising Women of NY. Achievements include She is the only woman in the position of publisher within AOL/Time/Warner. Office: People Mag 1271 Ave of the Americas New York NY 10020-1393

KAZMAREK, LINDA ADAMS, secondary school educator; b. Crisfield, Md., Jan. 18, 1945; d. Gordon I. Sr. and Annie Ruby (Sommers) Adams; m. Stephen Kazmarek, Jr., Aug. 2, 1981. B of Music Edn., Peabody Conservatory of Music, 1967; postgrad., Morgan U., Towson U. Cert. advanced profl. tchr., K-12, Md.; nat. cert. tchr. Mayron Cole piano method. Organist, choir dir. Halethorpe United Meth. Ch., Balt., min. music, 1978-92, 93-99; organist, choir dir. Olive Branch United Meth. Ch., 1973-77, 1978-83, 93—; piano tchr. Modal Cities Program, Balt., Balt. Community Schs; tchr. vocal music Balt. City Schs., 1967-99; min. music Halethorpe Meth. Ch., 1978-92, 93-99, St. John's Episcopal Parish Day Sch., 1999-2001; music specialist. Piano accompanist Witness Sing, 2000, Christian Choir, 2000-01; pianist Chestnut Ridge Bapt. Ch., 2001; pianist and performer Joppa Gospel Tabernacle, 2002-; pvt. tchr. piano and organ, concert artist. Composer, arranger: A Family of Care (award, 1991, Praise Song, 1992, Thy Way, Lord, 1993, Peace and Rest, 1994, Sing Praise to Jesus, 1994, Trilogy for piano solo, 1994, Shine Your Light, 1994, Resurrection, 1995, 1-800-Heaven, 1995, God Has A Plan for You, 1995, Christmas Joy, 1998, His Name is Jesus, 1998, Only Love, 1999, Be Still and Listen, 1999, Awesome Love, 2001, The Gifts of the Vine, 2002, (piano arrangements) The First Noel, Angels We Have Heard on High, O Come All Ye Faithful, All Through the Night/Lullaby, I Heard the Bells on Christmas Day/Silent Night Christmas Medley, I Saw Three Ships; rec. Christmas CD His Name is Jesus, 2000, Gifts of the Vine, 2002; guest performer S.W. Emergency Svcs., 1999, Joppa Gospel Tabernacle; CD Praise, Peace and Promise, 2002; rec. America the Beautiful/America, Jesus Loves Me, The Promise, Blessings, His Eye Is on the Sparrow, I Bowed on My Knees and Cried Holy, Praising My Saviour, 2002. Concert perfomer for Halethorpe Meth. Ch., 1994, Meth. Bd. Child Care, 1989, Balt. S.W. Emergency Svcs., 1991; guest performer Balt. City Tchrs. Appreciation Banquet, 1991, S.W.E.S. 18th Yr. Celebration, 1999; concert artist and performer, 2001—. Recipient vol. award for music enrichment summer program, 1973, award for voluntarism Fund. for Ednl. Excellence, 1985; Fund for Ednl. Excellence grantee, 1988. Mem. NEA, Md. State Tchrs. Assn., Balt. City Tchrs. Assn., Md. Music Educators Assn. (award for 30 yrs. of svc. in music and music edn. 1997), Music Educators Nat. Conf., Md. State Music Tchrs. Assn., Nat. Music Tchrs. Assn., Gospel Music Assn., Peabody Alumni Assn. E-mail: Kazmarekl@comcast.net.

KEANE, MARIE JEANETTE (MARIA KEANE), art educator, artist; b. N.Y.C., Mar. 31, 1931; d. Nicholas Joseph and Mary Christine (Passaretti) Santora; m. Thomas Roger Keane; children: Roger, Kathleen, Elisabeth, Mary, Julia. BA, Hunter Coll., N.Y.C., 1953; MA, U. Del., 1994. Cert. tchr., N.Y. Tchr. Niagara Falls (N.Y.) Pub. Sch. Sys., 1953-56; instr. watercolor DuPont Country Club, Wilmington, Del., 1975-78; tchr. Mt. Pleasant Sch. Dist., Wilmington, 1975-78; artist in residence Archmere Acad., Claymont, Del., 1979-83; sr. docent Del. Art Mus., Wilmington, 1987-88; artist in residence Del. Divsn. of Arts, Wilmington, 1983-93; asst. prof. fine arts and art history Wilmington Coll., 1986—. Lectr. U. Del., Wilmington, 1981—; docent Historic Howard Pyle Studio, Wilmington, 1990—; lectr. arts in edn. Del. Divsn. Arts, 1982—; participant master workshop in art L.I. U., 1991; participant master workshop in monoprint Bennington (Vt.) Coll., 1993; printmaker Benning Coll., 1992, 95; juror Internat. Art Exhibit, Hercules; vol. Classes for Christian Formation of Spl. Populations, 1970-80; art chair Christ in Christmas Com., 1979-88; exec. bd. for physically challenged Cath. Diocese of Wilmington, 1980-87; exec. bd., com. Very Spl. Arts Festival, 1984-90; docent Del. Art Mus., 1987-88; juror Del. Camera Club Regional Exhbn., 1992; exhbn. chair Christ in Christmas Retrospect, 1992; juror Reflections Del. Scholastic State-wide Exhbn., 1993-94, Dover Art League (members exhbn), 2004; lectr. excellence in rsch., art history U. Del., 1993; scholarship chair Studio Group, Inc., 1992—; docent Smithsonian Tour, Howard Pyle Studio, Wilmington, pres., 1980-82; lectr. various colls., orgns. and confs. Illustrator: Touch of Spring, 1976; author, illustrator: Watercolor Wings, 1976; author: Heroines and Housewives, 1994; one-person shows at Luther Towers Gallery, Wilmington, Friends Sch., Wilmington, Du Pont Country Club, Wilmington, Wilmington Drama League, 1995, 909 Gallery, Wilmington, Immaculata Coll., Exton-Paoli, Pa., Del. State Arts Coun., 1989, Goldey Beacom Coll., 1992, Wilmington Drama League, 1995, Grass Gallery, 2003; exhibited in group shows at Atrium Gallery, Wilmington, 1988, Wilmington Coll., 1988, 89, 90, 94, 96, 2003, Del. Nature Soc., 1990, Del. Mus. Natural History, 1990, L.I. U., 1991, U. Del., 1992, 93, Howard Pyle Studio, 1993, 2001, Chester County Art Assn., 1993-2004, Wilmington Coll., 1994, Gov. of Del., 1995, Revsia Gallery, Phila., 2000, others; represented in permanent collections Wilmington Coll., Newcastle, Del., U. Del., Newark, Zimmerli Mus., Rutgers State U., New Brunswick, Archmere Acad., Claymont, Del., Wilmington Divsn. Librs., So. Va. Coll. for Women, Buena Vista, Va., Del. Divsn. Arts, Wilmington, Mary Mother of Hope House, Wilmington, Del. Art Mus. Circulating Gallery, Studio Group Inc. Barnes Found. scholar, Merion, Pa., 1978-80; recipient Jill Jones Nauta award Chester County Art Assn., 1988, J. Lanier Jordan Meml. award, 1989, awards Chester County Art Assn., 1992, 93, 95, award Ctr. for Creative Arts, 1992, 94, award Howard Pyle Studio Regional Exhbn., 1994, Mary Derrickson McCurdy award Rehoboth Art League, 1994, awards Rehoboth Art League, 1995, profl. fellowship Del. Divsn. Arts and Nat. Endowment Arts, 1996-97, Grumbacher Gold medal award Phila. Sketch Club, 1997. Mem. Coun. Del. Artists (publicity and exhbn. curator, Svc. award), Studio Group, Inc., Nat. League Am. Pen Women (prizes 1985, 87, 89, 91, 93, 95, 97, 99, 2001, nat. exbhn. Tampa 1998, two literary awards in poetry nat. conv. 1998), Chester County Art Assn., Nat. Assn. Women Artists, Nat. Collage Soc. (merit award, 2003), Am. Watercolor Soc. (assoc.), Phila. Watercolor (assoc.), Phi Kappa Phi. Democrat. Roman Catholic. Avocations: photography, crafts, travel. Home: 332 Spalding Rd Wilmington DE 19803-2422 Office: Wilmington Coll 320 N Dupont Hwy New Castle DE 19720-6434

KEANS, SANDRA B. state legislator; b. Rochester, N.H., Apr. 9, 1942; m. F. Roland Keans (dec.); 1 child. BA, U. N.H., 1965. Mem. dist. 181 N.H. Ho. of Reps., Manchester. Mem. family law, judiciary, and pub. works coms., N.H. Ho. of Reps. Former vice chmn. Rep. City Com., Rochester (N.H.), mem. planning bd., 1982-85, City Coun., 1986—; bd. dirs. Heritage Trust, 1976-79; sec.-treas. Chamberlain St. PTO, 1985-86. Mem. Vis. Nurses Assn. (bd. dirs. 1985—), Rochester Bus. and Profl. Women's Club (legis. chmn., former treas.), Am. Legion Aux. (treas. unit 7 1981-84). Home: 1 Sweetbriar Ln Rochester NH 03867-3735 Office: NH State Senate State Capital Concord NH 03301

KEARNEY, ANNE, chef; Sous chef Emeril's, New Orleans; chef, now co-proprietor, exec. chef Peristyle, New Orleans. Office: Peristyle 1041 Dumaine St New Orleans LA 70112

KEARNEY, IRENE SPRUILL, elementary school educator; b. Warrenton, N.C., May 17, 1937; d. Hughley and Janet (Alston) Spruill; m. Raymond Kearney, Sr.; children: Alfreda, Raymond Jr. BS, Elizabeth City State U., 1959; MEd, N.C. Cen. U., 1976; EdD, Nova U., 1987; PhD, Am. Theol. Sem., 1988. Cert. early childhood edn., supervision, adminstrn., middle sch., pastoral counseling. Camp dir. N.C. Cen. U. PTA, Durham; pvt. prac. Warrenton, N.C.; cons., tchr. Warren County Schs., Warrenton. Author: Sparking Divergent Thinking, 1985. Mem. NEA, Warren County Assn. Educators (pres.) Franklinton Assn. Univ. Women (V.p.), Alpha Kappa Alpha, Phi Delta Kappa. Home: 195 Big Woods Rd Warrenton NC 27589-9706

KEARNEY-NUNNERY, ROSE, nursing administrator, educator, consultant; b. Glen Falls, NY, July 8, 1951; d. James J. and Helen F. (Oprandy) K.; m. Jimmie E. Nunnery. BS(hon.), Keuka Coll., 1973; M of nursing, U. Fla., 1976, PhD, 1987. Asst. prof. La. State U. Med. Ctr., New Orleans, 1976-87; project coord., indigent health care U. Fla., Gainesville, 1984-85; asst. prof. U. of South Fla., Tampa, Fla., 1987-88; dir. nursing programs State Univ. of N.Y., New Paltz, NY, 1988-94; project dir. MS in gerontol. nursing advanced nursing edn. grant U.S. Health Resources and Svc. Adminstrn. Div. Nursing, 1992-94; head nursing dept. Tech. Coll. of the Low Country, Beaufort, SC, 1995-97, v.p. acad. affairs, 1997—. Author: Advancing Your Profession Concepts for Profl. Nursing, 1997, Advancing Your Profession: Concepts for Profl. Nursing, 2001. Bd. dirs. Beaufort Co. First Steps, 2000-01; Ulster County unit Am. Cancer Soc., 1991-94; nursing edn. com., 1990-92; bd. dir. Mid-Hudson Consortium for Advancement Edn. for Health Profl., 1988-94; nursing edn. com., 1988-92; scholarship com., 1989-93; com. chmn., 1990-93, treas., 1992-94; prof. devel. program SUNY, Albany, 1989-92; adv. coun. Ulster CC, 1989-94; adv. regional planning group for early intervention svc. United Cerebral Palsy Ulster County Inc., Children's Rehab. Ctr., 1989-91; mem. Ulster County adv. com. Office for Aging, 1991-94; state del. S.C. Conf. on Aging, 1995; bd. dir. Beaufort County Coun. on Aging, 1995; cmty. adv. bd. Hilton Head Med. Ctr. and Clinics, 1996-2000; mem. SC Bd. Nursing, 2000—, pres. 2000-03; accreditation evaluator So. Assn. Coll. and Sch. Commn. on Coll.

Mem. ANA, S.C. Nurses Assn. (editl. bd. 1994-99, chair 1996-99); Nat. Coun. of State Bd. of Nursing (mem. practice, regulation, and edn. com. 2001—); Sigma Theta Tau. Roman Catholic. Home: 80 Peninsula Dr Hilton Head Island SC 29926-1119

KEARNS, [illegible] ELIZABETH BANKERT, chemist; b. Geneva, N.Y., June 3, 1970; d. Robert Lee and Janet Frye Bankert; m. Douglas Gene Kearns, Aug. 12, 1995; children: Elizabeth Lorraine, Benjamin Wade, Nicholas James. BS, William Smith Coll., 1992; PhD, Ohio U., 1997. Molecular spectroscopist Xerox Analytical Svcs., 1997—2000; product devel. engr. Xerox Media Tech. Ctr., Webster, NY, 2000—01, mgr. new product devel. & color hardware engagement, 2001—02, mgr. continuing engring. & market support, 2002—03, mgr. product devel. & quality, 2003—. Mem.: NAFE, Women's Alliance. Conservative. Roman Catholic. Avocations: gardening, travel, hiking.

KEARNS, COLLEEN, physical therapist; b. Scranton, Pa., Nov. 13, 1977; d. Paul Joseph and Mary Ann Kearns. BS in Health Scis., MS in Phys. Therapy, Coll. Misericordia, 2000. Phys. therapist Moses Taylor Hosp., Scranton, Pa., 2000—03, Mid Valley Hosp., Peckville, Pa., 2002—03, CMC Hosp., Scranton, 2003, Viewmont Med. Svcs., Dickson City, Pa., 2003—. Phys. therapist Ace Program, Scranton, 2000—02; clin. instr., lectr. diabetes edn. Mem.: Am. Phys. Therapists' Assn. Home: 118 Swartz St Dunmore PA 18512 Office: Viewmont Med Svcs Dickson City PA 18508

KEARNS, MERLE GRACE, state representative; b. Bellefonte, Pa., May 19, 1938; d. Robert John and Mary Katharine (Fitzgerald) Grace; m. Thomas Raymond Kearns, June 27, 1959; children: Thomas, Michael, Timothy, Matthew. BS, Ohio State U., 1960. Tchr. St. Raphael Elem. Sch., Springfield, Ohio, 1960-62; substitute tchr. Mad River Green Dist., Springfield, 1972-78; instr. Clark Tech. Coll., Springfield, 1978-80; commr. Clark County, Ohio, 1981-91; mem. Ohio Senate, Columbus, 1991-2000, Ohio Ho. of Reps., Columbus, 2001—. Mem. fin. and appropriations, edn. com. Ohio Ho. of Reps., chair human svcs. subcom. of fin & app, mem. health com., mem. jt. com. agy. rule rev.; pres. bd. county commrs., 1982, 83, 86, 87, 90; v.p., 85, 88, 89. Sec. County Commrs. Assn. Ohio, 1988, 2d v.p., 1989—90, 1st v.p., 1990; mem. exec. com. Springfield Reps., 1984—2001; chair Ohio Children's Trust Fund, 1995—2000, Legis. Office of Edn. Oversight; mem. NCSL Welfare Reform Task Force, 2001—; vice-chair Policy Consensus Initiative Bd., 2002—; chair Head Start Plus Study Coun.; bd. dirs. Springfield Symphony, 1980—86, Arts Coun., 1980—85; bd. dirs., mem. exec. bd. Nat. Conf. State Legislatures, 2000—03. Named Woman of the Yr., Springfield Pilot Club, 1981, Wittenburg Woman of Accomplishment, 1991, Watchdog of Treasury, 1991, 1996, 2000, Legislator of the Yr., Assn. Mental Health and Drug Addition Svcs. Bds., 1996, Pub. Childrens Svcs. Agys. Ohio, 1999, Ohio Cmty. Colls., 1997, Ohio Disting. Nurses, 2000, Advance Practice Nurse Assn., 2002, Legis. Co-Person of the Yr., Assn. Joint Vocat. Sch. Supts., 1996, Mental Health Adv. of the Yr., 2002, Outstanding Head Start Legislator of the Yr., Miami Valley, 2002, Legislator of Yr., Ohio Fedn. Tchrs., 2003, Advocate of Yr., Ohio Coun. Alzheimer Assn., 2004, Alzheimer Legis. Advocate of Yr., 2004; recipient Pub. Policy Leadership award, 1997, Disting. Svc. Pub. Ofcls. award, Assn. Ohio Philanthropic Homes, 1999, 1st Ann. Jane Swart Disting. Svcs. to Nursing, 2000, Citizenship award, Ohio State U. Coll. Human Ecology, 2000, Legislator of Yr., Behavioral Health Authorities Assn., 2003, Ohio Better World award, Ohio Mediation Assn., 2004;, Ohio State U. scholar, 1957—59. Mem.: LWV (bd. dirs. 1964—78, pres. 1975—78), Ohio Nurses Assn. (Legislator of the Yr. 1995, 1999), Rotary, Omicron Nu. Roman Catholic. Avocation: reading. Office: Ohio Ho of Reps 72d Dist 77 S High St Columbus OH 43215 E-mail: district75@ohrstate.oh.us.

KEARSE, AMALYA LYLE, federal judge; b. Vauxhall, N.J., June 11, 1937; d. Robert Freeman and Myra Lyle (Smith) K.. BA, Wellesley Coll., 1959; JD cum laude, U. Mich., 1962. Bar: N.Y. 1963, U.S. Supreme Ct. 1967. Assoc. Hughes, Hubbard & Reed, N.Y.C., 1962—69, ptnr., 1969—79; judge U.S. Ct. Appeals (2d cir.), 1979—. Lectr. evidence NYU Law Sch., 1968—69. Author: Bridge Conventions Complete, 1975, Bridge Conventions Complete, 3d edit., 1990, Bridge at Your Fingertips, 1980; transl., editor: Bridge Analysis, 1979; editor: Ofcl. Ency. of Bridge, 3d edit., 1976; mem. editl. bd.: Charles Goren, 1974—. Trustee N.Y.C. YWCA, 1976—79, Am. Contract Bridge League Nat. Laws Commn., 1975—; mem. Pres.'s Com. on Selection of Fed. Jud. Officers, 1977—78; Bd. dirs. NAACP Legal Def. and Endl. Fund, 1977—79, Nat. Urban League, 1978—79. Named Women's Pairs Bridge Champion Nat. div., 1971, 1972, World div., 1986, Nat. Women's Teams Bridge Champion, 1987, 1990, 1991. Mem.: ABA, Lawyers Com. for Civil Rights Under Law (mem. exec. com. 1970—79), Am. Law Inst., Assn. of Bar of City of N.Y. Office: US Ct Appeals US Courthouse 40 Foley SqRm 2001 New York NY 10007*

KEATING, ISABEL, actress; Actor: (regional stage shows) Dinner With Friends, The Rise and Fall of Little Voice, Three Sisters, One Foot on the Floor, Chilean Holiday, Indian Ink, 2000 (Helen Hayes award best actress, 2000); (Broadway plays) Enchanted April, 2003, The Boy From Oz, 2003 (nominated Outer Critics Cir. best actress, 2004, Tony nom. best featured actress in a play, 2004), (off Broadway shows) Bonnie, Once in a Lifetime, Waiting at the Waters Edge, The Museum of Dreams. Office: c/o Blue Ridge Entertainment 41 Union Sq W New York NY 10003*

KEATING, LAURA LEE M. historian, records management professional; b. N.Y.C., Dec. 13, 1952; d. Matthew Joseph and Florence Patricia Salamone; m. Craig L. Keating, May 3, 1975. Student, Coll. of White Plains, N.Y.; cert. in records mgmt., Westchester C.C. Records mgmt. and property mgmt. AT&T, White Plains, 1970—2001; mcpl. historian Town of Cortlandt, Cortlandt Manor, NY, 2001—. V.p. Inst. of History, Arch., and Edn., Inc., 2003—. Trustee Cortlandt Hist. Soc., 1991—; pres. Bear Mtn. Bridge Toll House Vis. Ctr. Found., 2002—. Mem.: Westchester Civil War Round Table (pres. 2000—). Avocations: crafts, collecting reproductions of 18th and 19th century clothing, collecting antique books, living history interpretation. Home: 12 Cross Ln Cortlandt Manor NY 10567-5108

KEATING, REGINA G. computer analyst consultant; b. Bryn Mawr, Pa., Mar. 20, 1940; d. Francis Stanislaus and Frances Mulligan Gear; m. Frank J. Keating, Mar. 4, 1972 (div. Dec. 1978); 1 child, Frank. BBA, Temple U., 1981, MBA, 1982. Sr. staff local govt. com. Pa. Constnl. Conv., 1967-68; adminstr. Blank Rome Comisky & McCauley, Phila., 1968-72; computer programmer Lee Tire & Rubber Co., Valley Forge, Pa., 1984-86; programmer, analyst Amerigas Corp., Valley Forge, 1986-88, Am. Electronic Labs., Lansdale, Pa., 1988-93; cons. computer analyst Polin Assocs., Richboro, Pa., 1993—. Instr., adj. lectr. Temple U., Phila., 1981, 85. Sec., registration chmn. Dem. Com., Haverford Twp., Pa., 1964-71, com. woman, Abington Twp., 1978—. Mem. NAACP, NOW, NAFE, ACLU, World Affairs Coun.-Phila., So. Poverty Law Ctr., Pub. Citizen.

KEATING, SUSAN C. credit foundation executive; b. L.A., Oct. 21, 1950; m. John Keating; 1 child, Caroline. Student, Northwestern U., 1972, Rutgers U., 1985. Sr. v.p. consumer banking 1st Bank Sys., 1987—88; sr. v.p. Balt. consumer banking Md. Nat. Bank, 1988—90; fin. exec., v.p. cmty. banking MNC, 1990—92; pres., sr. banking exec. NationsBank, 1993—95; pres., CEO Allfirst Fin. Inc., 1996—2002; pres. Nat. Found. for Credit Counseling, 2004—. Mem. Balt. Women's Forum, Com. 100 Northwestern U., Fin. Svcs. Roundtable. Co-chairperson Kennedy Krieger Inst. Festival of Trees, 1996; Bd. dirs. Empower Balt. Mgmt. Corp., St. Paul's Sch. for Girls; Balt. Life Cos.; bd. dirs. Shock Trauma, Balt. Mus. Art, Balt. Children's Mus. Named Northwestern Univ. Coun. 100, one of Top 100 Profl. Women in Md., one of Pa.'s 50 Best Women; recipient Magnificent Seven award, Bus. and Profl. Women USA, 1994. Office: National Foundation for Credit Counseling 801 Roeder Road Suite 900 Silver Spring MD 20910

KEATON, DIANE, actress; b. Santa Ana, Calif., Jan. 5, 1946; Student, Neighborhood Playhouse, N.Y.C., 1968. Appeared on N.Y. stage in Hair, 1968, Play It Again Sam, 1969, The Primary English Class, 1976; appeared in numerous films including Lovers and Other Strangers, 1970, Play It Again Sam, 1972, The Godfather, 1972, Sleeper, 1973, The Godfather Part II, 1974, Love and Death, 1975, I Will, I Will...For Now, 1975, Harry and Walter Go To New York, 1976, Annie Hall, 1977 (Best Actress Acad. award 1978, Brit. Acad. Best Actress award 1978, N.Y. Film Critics Circle award 1978, Nat. Soc. Film Critics award 1978), Looking for Mr. Goodbar, 1977, Interiors, 1978, Manhattan, 1979, Reds, 1981 (Acad. award nominee), Shoot the Moon, 1982, Little Drummer Girl, 1984, Mrs. Soffel, 1984, Crimes of the Heart, 1986, Radio Days, 1987, Baby Boom, 1987, The Good Mother, 1988, The Lemon Sisters, 1990, The Godfather Part III, 1990, Father of the Bride, 1991, Manhattan Murder Mystery, 1993, Look Who's Talking Now, 1993 (voice), Father of the Bride 2, 1995, Marvin's Room, 1996, First Wives Club, 1996, The Only Thrill, 1997, The Other Sister, 1999, Hanging Up, 2000, Town and Country, 2001, Plan B, 2001, Something's Gotta Give, 2003 (Golden Globe for best actress in a musical or comedy, 2004, Acad. Award nomination for best actress, 2004, Screen Actors Guild Award nomination for best actress, 2004); (TV movie) Running Mates, 1992, Amelia Earhart, 1994, Sister Mary Explains It All, 2001, Crossed Over, 2002, On Thin Ice, 2003; dir. film: Heaven, 1987, Wildflower, 1991, Unstrung Heroes, 1995; accomplished artist and singer; author book of photographs: Reservations, 1980; editor: (with Marvin Heiferman) Still Life, 1983, Mr. Salesman, 1994; prodr.: The Lemon Sisters, 1990; exec. prodr.: Northern Lights (TV), 1997. Recipient Golden Globe award, 1978 Office: John Burnham William Morris Agy 151 S El Camino Dr Beverly Hills CA 90212-2704

KEATON, FRANCES MARLENE, insurance sales representative; b. Redfield, Ark., July 1, 1944; d. John Thomas and Pauline (Hilliard) Wells; m. Larry Ronald Keaton, Sept. 17, 1946. Cert. in acctg., Draughon's Sch. Bus., 1972. Lic. ins. agt. Acctg. supr. Home Ins. Co., Little Rock, 1962-70; auditor St. Paul Ins. Co., Little Rock, 1970-74; spl. agt. Continental Ins. Co., Little Rock, 1974—. Vol. Ark. Sch. for the Blind, Little Rock, 1968. Mem. Little Rock Field Club, Casualty Roundtable, Auditor's Assn., Ins. Women, Underwriters Roundtable, The Executive Female, Ind. Ins. Agts. Assn., Profl. Ins. Assn. Democrat. Methodist. Avocations: golf, tennis, racquetball, travel. Home and Office: 111 Red River Rd Sherwood AR 72120-5851

KEATOR, CAROL LYNNE, library director; b. Annapolis, Md., Aug. 9, 1945; d. Lyle H. and Juanita F (Waits) K. BA, Syracuse U., 1967; MS, Simmons Coll., 1968. Librarian Bristol (Conn.) Pub. Sch.s, 1968-69, MIT, Cambridge, 1969-72, Santa Barbara (Calif.) Pub. Library, 1972-77, br. supr., 1977-81, prin. librarian, 1981-88, library dir., 1988—. Mem. ALA, Calif. Libr. Assn., Pub. Libr. Assn. Unitarian Universalist. Office: Santa Barbara Pub Libr 40 E Anapamu St Santa Barbara CA 93101-2722

KEATOR, MARGARET WHITLEY, legislative aide; b. Suffolk, Va., Oct. 27, 1945; d. Jacob Jordan and Margaret Mitchell Whitley; m. Philip John Keator, Sept. 2, 1967; 1 child, Jennifer. AB in Govt., Coll. William and Mary, 1968. Tchr. Newport News (Va.) Pub. Sch., 1968-69, 72-84; rsch. asst. Marine Corps. Ops. Analysis Group, Arlington, Va., 1969-72; v.p. Keator Signs, Inc., Newport News, 1990-93; sr. legis. asst. Congressman Bobby Scott, Newport News, 1993—. Polit. cons., Newport News, 1990-93. Mem. Newport News City Coun., 1982-90, Peninsula planning dist. com., 1982-90, Newport News planning com., 1982-87; exec. bd. Va. Peninsula Econ. Devel. Com., Newport News, 1986-90; vice chmn. environ. quality policy com. Va. Mcpl. League, 1988-90; bd. trustees Peninsula Marine Inst., 1992—; citizen adv. bd. Newport News Healthy Families Initiative, 1997—. Mem. AAUW (Newport News br.), Soroptimist Club (pres. 1996-98), Kiwanis, Monitor Club (pres.), Visionaries (rec. sec. 1997—), Church Women United (chair citizen action 1994—). Democrat. Methodist. Office: Congressman Bobby Scott 2600 Washington Ave Ste 1010 Newport News VA 23607-4333 E-mail: maggiekeator@netscape.net.

KEDDERIS, PAMELA JEAN, academic administrator; b. Waterbury, Conn., May 15, 1956; d. Leo George and Evelyn Helen (Fenske) K. Student, U. Nice, 1976-77; BA, Assumption Coll., 1978; MBA, U. New Haven, 1981. Cert. fin. mgr. Credit analyst Citytrust Bank, Bridgeport, Conn., 1980-81, sr. credit analyst, 1981-82, fin. analyst, 1982-83, seminar instr., 1981-83; planning analyst Continental Ins. Co., N.Y.C., 1983-84, sr. planning analyst, 1984-85, dir. planning, 1985-87, asst. v.p., 1987-92, v.p., 1992-95; v.p., controller Marine Office of Am., Cranbury, N.J., 1995-97; exec. officer for fin. Conn. State Univ. Sys., Hartford, 1997-98, CFO, 1998—2003, cert. mgmt. acct., 2004—. Mem. State of Conn. Ins. and Risk Mgmt. Bd., 2002—. Mem.: Conn. Coun. Chief Fiscal Officers, Inst. Mgmt. Accts., New Eng. Resource Ctr. for Higher Edn. CFO Think Tank. Democrat. Lutheran. Avocations: music, travel. Office: Conn State Univ Sys 39 Woodland St Hartford CT 06105-2337 Business E-Mail: kedderisp@so.ct.edu.

KEEBLER, LOIS MARIE, elementary school educator; b. Jasper, Ala., Nov. 24, 1955; d. Roosevelt T. and Marie (Smiley) K. Student, Cen. State U., Wilberforce, Ohio; cert., North Ala. Regional Hosps., 1981. Cert. tchr., Ala. Tchr. Mamani Vallied Children Devel. Ctr., Dayton, Ohio. Vol. pub. schs. Democrat. Baptist. Avocation: bowling.

KEECH, ANN MARIE, training design and multimedia consultant; b. Salt Lake City, July 25, 1951; d. Stanley Michael and Rose Elma (Migliore) Bachmurski; m. Michael Ross Keech, July 21, 1972 (div. 1983); 1 child, Jason Michael. BA in English, Christopher Newport Coll., 1976. Mgr. publs. Newport News (Va.) Shipbuilding, 1981-84; office mgr. Computer Scis. Corp., Newport News, 1984-86; mgr. Comsell, Atlanta, 1986-87, Crawford Comms., Inc., Atlanta, 1988-91; cons. Coastal Video Comms., Inc., Virginia Beach, 1991-93; project mgr. Star Mountain, Inc., Alexandria, Va., 1991-96; v.p. D&A World Wide, Inc., Atlanta, 1996-97; owner, cons. AMK, Newport News, 1997—. Writer, developer: (tng. materials) BTOS FSA Programming Guide, 1988 (Soc. for Tech. Comm. Cert. of Achievement 1989); developer: (multimedia tng. program) Confined Space Entry, 1993; mgr., editor, developer: (internat. tng. materials) International Technical Training for Telecommunications, 1996-97; developer, editor: (tng. program) Family Violence Prevention Program, 1997; developer Web-based Training Style Guide, 2000. Vol. Newport News Police, Cmty. Svc. Dept.; aux. mem. 106th Infantry Divsn. Assn., 76th Infantry Divsn. Assn., 2d Divsn. Assn. 13th Airborne Divsn. Assn., 18th Airborn Corps Assn., 1st Infantry Divsn. Assn., 3d Infantry Divsn. Assn. Mem. Am. Soc. for Law Enforcement (trainer). Avocations: music, horseback riding, pleasure reading. Office: AMK 824 Cascade Dr Newport News VA 23608-3223 Fax: (757) 988-0448. E-mail: amkeech@mindspring.com.

KEECH, ELOWYN ANN, interior designer; b. Berrien County, Mich., Oct. 5, 1937; d. Earl Docker and Elizabeth Hall (Paullin) Stephenson; 1 child, Robert Earl Stephenson. Contract and residential interior designer. Print designer, 1957-75; freelance interior designer, photoset and video set designer, 1975—; owner Fog Horn Records & Tapes. Trustee Mich. Maritime Mus., 1994—97; bd. dirs., mem. steering and long-range planning coms. United Way Mich., 1980—87; bd. dirs. Blossomland United Way, 1981—86. Mem.: Internat, Interior Design Assn., Fort Miami Heritage Soc., New Territory Arts Alliance, Econ. Club S.W. Mich., Am. Rottweiler Club, Rotary Club.

KEEFAUVER, NANCY ANN, pre-school educator; b. Dunkirk, N.Y., May 7, 1940; d. Earl Lester and Olive Adelaide Zimmer; m. Norman James Peters, Feb. 29, 1964 (dec. Oct. 1998); children: Patricia Ann Peters McClennan, Elaine Suzanne Peters Medley; m. Donald Leon Keefauver, June 10, 2000. BS, SUNY, 1962. Tchr. Rochester Bd. Edn., NY, 1962—64, Madison Bd. Edn., Minn., 1966, Penfield Bd. Edn., NY, 1976—77; tutor Blue Star Camps, Hendersonville, NC, 1994—99, pvt. practice, 1984—94; tchr. pre-sch. Trinity Presbyn. Ch., 1986—88, dir. pre-sch., 1988—2000; ret. Contbr. articles to mags. Mem. Hendersonville Cmty. Bd., social chair, 1991—2003; family mentor Interfaith Assistance Ministry, Hendersonville, 2001—03; neighborhood chair Unitarian Universalist Fellowship. Scholar, Highlights for Children, Chautauqua, N.Y., 1997. Avocations: swimming, golf, reading, music. Home: 5 Old Applewood Ln Hendersonville NC 28739 E-mail: dnkeefau@brinet.com.

KEEFE, CAROLYN JOAN, tax accountant; b. Huntington Park, Oct. 11, 1926; d. Paul Dewey and Mary Jane (Parmater) K. AA, Pasadena (Calif.) City Coll., 1947; BA, U. So. Calif., 1950. Tax acct. Shell Oil Co., L.A., 1950-71, Houston, 1971-91, ret., 1991. Advisor Midwest Mus. of Am. Art, 1993—; vol. Houston Mus. of Fine Arts, 1991—; vol. docent Houston Mus. of Natural Sci., 1991—, Theatre Under the Stars, 1991—, Houston Pub. TV Channel 8, Houston, 1989—; donor 2 ann. coll. scholarships in memory of Paul Dewey and Mary Jane Keefe. Mem. LWV, Inst. Mgmt. Accts. (emeritus life mem.), Desk and Derrick Club (bd. dirs. 1994-95), Houston Alumni Club of Alpha Gamma Delta, USC Houston Alumni Club. Christian Scientist. Avocation: travel. Home: 1814 Auburn Trl Sugar Land TX 77479-6333

KEEFE, DIANE MARIE, portfolio manager; b. Milton, Mass., Sept. 10, 1958; d. John Edwin and Louise Marie Keefe; m. John David Levin, Aug. 25, 1991; children: Eliza Hope Levin, Abraham Rosco Levin. BA in Polit. Economy, Wellesley Coll., 1978; MBA in Fin., Columbia U., 1984. CFA. Assoc. mcpl. investment banking Paine Webber, Inc., N.Y.C., 1984—85; v.p. mortgage backed securities dept. Oppenheimer Govt. Securities, N.Y.C., 1986; sr. v.p. fixed income Dillon, Read & Co., N.Y.C., 1987—97; dir. high yield bond dept. UBS Warburg, Stamford, Conn., 1998; portfolio mgr. Pax World Mgmt. Corp., N.Y.C., 1999—. Chairperson, bd. dirs. Co-op Am., Washington, 1995—; mem. investment com. Anthem Found., Conn., 2002; trustee investment com. yearly meeting Religious Soc. Friends, N.Y.C., 2001—02. Author: (book chpt.) Social Investment Almanac, 1994. Mem. majority coun. Emily's List, Washington, 2000—. Mem.: AIMR, N.Y. Soc. Securities Analysts. Democrat. Mem. Soc. Of Friends. Office: Pax World Funds c/o HG Wellington 17th Fl 14 Wall St New York NY 10005 E-mail: dkeefe@paxfund.com.*

KEEFE, MARY, architectural firm executive; BA, Newton Coll., 1975; MBA, U. of Pa., 1981. Assoc. MGA Ptnrs., Phila., 1991—. Bd. mem. Ctrl. Phila. Devel. Corp., 1997—, exec. com., 2001—02; founding mem. The Salon, 2001—. Mem.: Wharton Alumni Club (bd. mem. 1997—, chair liaison com. 1997—2002). Office: MGA Ptnrs Architects 234 Market St Philadelphia PA 19106 E-mail: mkeefe@mgapartners.com.

KEEFE, MAUREEN RUTH, dean; b. Madison, Wis., Oct. 30, 1947; m. Michael Gaviglio; children: Erin, Ryan. BSN, U. Mich., 1970; MS, U. Colo., 1974, PhD, 1984, postgrad., 1985. Cert. PNP. pub. health nurse Washtenaw County Health Dept., Ann Arbor, 1971-73; PNP Denver (Colo.) Health and Hosps., 1974-75, Univ. Hosp., Denver, 1978-85; instr. dept. psychology Univ. Colo., Denver, 1985-86; v.p. nursing The Children's Hosp., Denver, 1985—; assoc. dir. Kempe Rsch. Ctr., Denver, 1985—; asst. prof. Univ. Colo., Sch. Nursing, Denver, 1985-90, assoc. prof., 1990—; dean Coll. Nursing Med. U. S.C., Charleston, U. Utah, Salt Lake City. Cons. Emergent Tech. Corp., Boca Raton, Fla., 1985; vis. prof. Children's Hosp., Columbus, Ohio, 1990; mem. Nat. Adv. Bd. for Clin. Trials of the Preterm; mem. adv. bd. Johnson & Johnson Pediat. Inst. Co-author: A Primary Care Process Measure: The Nurse Practitioner Rating Form, 1981. Troop leader Brownies, Denver, 1983-84; bd. mem. Step Families Assn. Denver, 1984-85, pres., 1985. Recipient Book of Yr. award Am. Jour. Nursing, 1981, First award NIH/NCNR, 1987; named People to Watch, Denver Mag., 1988. Mem.: Western Inst. Nursing (exec. com. 1992—), Nat. Assn. Pediatric Nurse Assocs. and Practitioners (co-chair Internat. Yr. of the Child 1979), Sigma Theta Tau (perinatal grant selection com./Mead Johnson 1991, internat. rsch. com. 1992—, Alpha Kappa chpt. rsch. com. 1984—85, 1991—92, v.p. 1985—87, pres. 1988—90, bd. dirs. 2000—, Rsch. Excellence award 1988). Office: U Utah Coll Nursing Deans Office 10 S 2800 E Front Salt Lake City UT 84112-5880

KEEFER, JUDITH E. elementary school educator; b. Conneaut, Ohio, Dec. 19, 1950; d. Donald Boyd and Ruth Almeda Hazen; m. Dayle Frederick Keefer, June 8, 1973; children: Jamie, Kevin, Brian, Emily. BS in Edn., Edinboro (Pa.) U., 1972; MEd, Fredonia (N.Y.) State U., 1989. Kindergarten tchr. Northwestern Sch. Dist., Albion, Pa., 1973—74; Kindergarten, 1st grade tchr. Bemus Point (N.Y.) Sch. Dist., 1987—. Mem., NY, 1987. Cheerleading advisor Midget Cheerleaders and Wrestling, Bemus Point, 1990—92, 1995; music dir. Fluvanna Cmty. Ch., Jamestown, 1981—, choir dir., playwright, 1977—, organist, 1976—, tchr. Sunday sch., 1981—. Mem.: Concerned Women for Am., Eagle Forum. Republican. Avocations: piano, reading, walking, spending time with grandchildren. Home: 3368 Fluvanna Ave Ext Jamestown NY 14701

KEEFER, SUSAN, voice educator; b. North Manchester, Ind., June 22, 1951; d. Harlan and Bernice Hornaday; m. Philip Keefer; children: Megan, Jennifer, Christopher. BS, Manchester Coll., 1973, MS in Secondary Edn., 1978. Cert. choral/gen. music tchr. grades K-12. Choral music dir. Wabash (Ind.) Mid. and HS, 1973—. Wabash County honors choir coord. Wabash Valley Music Assn., sponsor, 1992—. Recipient Tchr. of the Yr., Wabash City Sch., 2003. Mem.: Indpls. Symphony Women's Soc., Am. Choral Dirs. Assn., Ind. Choral Dirs. Assn., Music Educators Nat. Conf., Ind. Music Educators Assn. (Cir. the State area coord. 1994—).

KEEGAN, JANE ANN, insurance executive, consultant; b. Watertown, N.Y., Sept. 1, 1950; d. Richard Isidor and Kathleen (McKinley) K. BA cum laude, SUNY, Potsdam, 1972; MBA in Risk Mgmt., Golden State U., 1986. CPCU. Comml. lines mgr. Lithgow & Rayhill, San Francisco, 1977-80; risk mgmt. account coord. Dinner Levison Co., San Francisco, 1980-83; ins. cons. San Francisco, 1983-84; account mgr. Rollins Burdick Hunter, San Francisco, 1984-85; account exec. Jardine Ins. Brokers, San Francisco, 1985-86; ins. cons. San Francisco, 1986-87; ins. adminstr. Port of Oakland, 1987—, risk mgr., 1989—, mgr. accts. payable, 1996—. Vol. San Francisco Ballet vol. orgn., 1981-96, Bay Area Bus., Govt. ARC disaster conf. steering com., 1987-88, 89, 90, 91-92; mem. Nob Hill Neighbors Assn., 1982—, City of Oakland Emergency Mgmt. Bd., 1990—. Mem. Safety Mgmt. Soc., CPCU Soc. (spl. events chairperson 1982-84, continuing profl. devel. program award 1985, 88, chair loss prevention), Calif. Assn. of Port Authorities (ins. chair 1998—), Risk and Ins. Mgr. Soc. (dep.-sec. 1990—, dir. legis. 1993, dir. conf.). Democrat. Roman Catholic. Home: 17 Calafia Ct San Rafael CA 94903-2464 Office Phone: 510-627-1535. E-mail: jkeegan@portoakland.com.

KEEGAN, LISA GRAHAM, state agency administrator; m. John Keegan; 5 children. BS in Linguistics, Stanford U.; MS in Comm. Disorders, Ariz. State U., 1983. Mem. Ariz. Ho. of Reps., 1991-95, chair edn. com., joint legis. budget com., 1993-94; state supt. of pub. instrn. Dept. of Edn., State of Ariz., Phoenix, 1994—2001; CEO Edn. Leaders Coun., Washington, 2001—. Office: 1225 19th St NW Ste 400 Washington DC 20036

KEELEY, IRENE PATRICIA MURPHY, federal judge; b. 1944; BA, Coll. Notre Dame, 1965; MA, W.Va. U., 1977, JD, 1980. Bar: W. Va., 1980. Atty. Steptoe & Johnson, Clarksburg, W.Va., 1980-92; dist. judge U.S. Dist. Ct. (no. dist.), W. Va., 1992—. Adj. prof. law W.Va. U., 1990-91; bd. dirs. W.Va. U. Alumni Assn., 1995—, 1st v.p., 1997-98; mem. bd. advisors W.Va. U. Vis. com. W.Va. U. Coll. Law, 1987-91, 94-98; chmn. adv. bd. W.Va. U., 1997-98. Mem. ABA, Nat. Conf. Fed. Trial Judges (exec. com. 1996—.), W.Va. State Bar, W.Va. Bar Assn., Harrison County Bar Assn., Clarksburg Country Club, Oral Lake Fishing Club, Immaculate Conception Roman Cath. Ch. Office: US Courthouse PO Box 2808 500 W Pike St Rm 202 Clarksburg WV 26302-2808

KEENAN, BARBARA MILANO, judge; b. Vienna, 1950; BA, Cornell U., 1971; JD, George Wash. U., 1974; LLM, U. Va., 1992. Asst. commonwealth atty., Fairfax County, Va., 1974—76; pvt. law practice, 1976—80; judge Gen. Dist. Ct., Fairfax County, 1980-82, Circuit Ct., Fairfax County, 1982-85, Ct. Appeals, Va., 1985-91; assoc. justice Supreme Court Va., Richmond, 1991—. Recipient Am. Jurisprudence award, Fairfax Bar Assn., 1995. Office: Ste 425 200 Golden Oak Ct Virginia Beach VA 23452-8509

KEENAN, KATHLEEN, state legislator; b. Burlington, Vt., May 7, 1940; d. Roland and Madelyn M. (Cahill) K.; 8 children. Dipl., Jeanne Mance Sch. Nursing, 1961; postgrad., U. Vt., 1976. Nurse; mem. Vt. Ho. of Reps., Montpelier, 1989—, former chair commerce com. Mem. Hinesburg Dem. Com., 1954-68, chair, 1965-68; mem. St. Albans Dem. Com., 1968—; mem. Vt. Econ. Progress Coun., 1994-98; bd. dirs. Efficiency Vt., Vt. Electric Power Prodrs., State Human Resources Investment Coun. Mem. St. Albans Skating Assn. (charter), Emergency Nurses Assn., Nat. Conf. Ins. Legislators (mem. exec. com., chair health ins. com.), Bus. and Profl. Women (exec. com. Franklin County. Address: 8 Thorpe Ave Saint Albans VT 05478-1834

KEENAN, MARY JOSEPHINE, communications executive; b. Grand Island, Neb., Mar. 14, 1954; d. Joseph Lyle and Mary Elizabeth (Brand) K. Attended, Spoon River Coll., 1984. Bookkeeper, receptionist Rush Motor Co., Boulder, Colo., 1972-74, Royal Pontiac Buick GMC, Macomb, Ill., 1974-80; acctg. clk. III We. Ill. U., Macomb, Ill., 1980-83; office mgr. Kelly Pontiac/Kelly Equipment, Macomb, Ill., 1981-87; bookkeeper, acct., sec. bd. Pro-Class Gym Sys., Macomb, Ill., 1987—; office mgr. Intercontinental Mktg. LTD, Macomb, Ill., 1987-88; stenographer McDonough County Rehab. Ctr., Macomb, Ill., 1988-89; officer mgr. Lamberson Chrysler-Plymouth-Dodge, Macomb, Ill., 1989-91; exec. asst. to pres. Kelly Co. World Group, Inc., Carthage, Ill., 1991—2000; v.p. ops. FutureComGlobal, Scottsdale, Ariz., 2000—. Fundraiser Radio Info. Svcs., Macomb, Ill., 1981. Mem. Bushnell (Ill.) Presbyn. Bell Choir, 1987—. Mem. Philanthropic Edn. Orgn. (guard), Nat. Notary Assn. Republican. Roman Catholic. Avocations: travel, cooking, listening to music, bowling, reading. Office: FutureComGlobal 15690 83rd Way Scottsdale AZ 85260

KEENAN, NANCY A. state agency administrator; BA in Elem. and Spl. Edn., Mont. Coll., 1974. Tchr. Yellowstone Boys' Ranch, 1974-75; tchr. spl. edn. Anaconda, Mont., 1975-88; mem. Mont. Ho. of Reps., 1982-88; supt. of pub. instrn. State of Mont., 1988—. Mem. taxation, edn., local govt. and revenue oversight coms., 1982-84; chmn. ho. human svcs. and aging com.; asst. Dem. whip. Active Anaconda Local Devel. Corp.; past pres. A.W.A.R.E.; bd. dirs. Deer Lodge County Hospice; mem. Mont. Coun. for Exceptional Children. Recipient Pub. Svc. award Mont. Coun. for Exceptional Children, 1981. Mem. AAUW. Office: Public Instruction Office State Capitol Rm 106 PO Box 20251 Helena MT 59620

KEENAN, RETHA ELLEN VORNHOLT, retired nursing educator; b. Solon, Iowa, Aug. 15, 1934; d. Charles Elias and Helen Maurine (Konicek) Vornholt; m. David James Iverson, June 17, 1956; children: Scott, Craig; m. Roy Vincent Keenan, Jan. 5, 1980. BSN, State U. Iowa, 1955; MSN, Calif. State U., Long Beach, 1978. Cert. nurse practitioner adult and mental health. Pub. health nurse City of Long Beach, 1970-73, 94-96, cons., 1998, 99, 2000, coord. continuing edn., 1999, 2000. Pub. health nurse Hosp. Home Care, Torrance, Calif., 1973-75; patient care coord. Hillhaven, L.A., 1975-76; mental health cons. InterCity Home Health, L.A., 1978-79; instr. C.C. Dist., L.A., 1979-87; instr. nursing El Camino Coll., Torrance, 1981-86; instr. nursing Chapman Coll., Orange, Calif., 1982, Mt. St. Mary's Coll., 1986-87; cons., pvt. practice, Rancho Palos Verdes, Calif., 1987-89, 98, 99. Contbg. author: American Journal of Nursing Question and Answer Book for Nursing Boards Review, 1984, Nursing Care Planning Guides for Psychiatric and Mental Health Care, 1987-88, Nursing Care Planning Guides for Children, 1987, Nursing Care Planning Guides for Adults, 1988, Nursing Care Planning Guides for Critically Ill Adults, 1988. Mem. Assistance League of Temecula Valley, Calif. NIMH grantee, 1977-78. Mem. Sigma Theta Tau, Phi Kappa Phi, Delta Zeta. Republican. Lutheran. Avocations: traveling, writing, reading. Home: PO Box 205 Temecula CA 92593-0205

KEENAN, TERRY, anchor, correspondent; Degree in math., Johns Hopkins U. Anchor bus. news programs CNBC; from segment prodr. to on-air corr. CNN Fin. News, N.Y.C., co-anchor Street Sweep, sr. corr. The Moneyline News Hour with Lou Dobbs. Writer, prodr. Wall St. Week with Louis Rukeyser; editor fin. newsletter Going Pub. Recipient Cable Ace award. Office: CNN 5 Penn Plz Fl 20 New York NY 10001-1810

KEENAN-ABILAY, GEORGIA ANN, service representative; b. Denver, Oct. 3, 1936; d. Lawrence Edward and Helen Kathleen (Gray) K.; m. Charles Henry Dupree, May 31, 1958 (div. Nov. 1977); children: Phoenix, Therese, Mark, John; m. Joseph D. Abilay, Nov. 26, 1988. BA, Regis Coll., 1968; MA, St. Thomas U., 1978. With reservations United Airlines, Denver, 1956-57; stewardess Trans World Airlines, Chgo., 1957-58; in elem. edn. Notre Dame Sch., Denver, 1969-72; dir. religious edn. Notre Dame Parish, Denver, 1972-77, Archdiocese Denver, 1977-80; v.p., treas. Kilfinane and Cook, Denver, 1980-82; dir. human resources Cosmopolitan Hotel, Denver, 1982-83, Kaanapali Beach Hotel, Lahaina, Hawaii, 1983-85, Royal Lahaina Resort, Hawaii, 1985-90; corp. dir. human resources Hawaiian Hotels and Resorts, Lahaina, 1988; dir. human resources Rock Resorts Lanai Resorts Ptnrs., Island of Lanai, 1990-94; ptnr. Blue Ginger Cafe, Lanai, 1995—. Trainer Amfac Hotels and Resorts, Hawaii, 1984-86; vice chmn. Maui Hotel Assn., 1987; bd. dirs. Project 714, Lahaina, 1987. Bd. dirs. Archdiocesan Women's Bd., Denver, 1981-83, Passages, Denver, 1980-83, Maui Econ. Devel. Bd., Kahalui, 1984; chairperson Charity Walk, 1984-86. Named Handicapped Employer of Yr., State of Hawaii, 1987. Mem. Council Hawaii Hotels, Am. Soc. Personnel Assn. Clubs: Distributive Edn. of Am. (Hawaii) (bd. dirs. 1984—). Avocations: fishing, boating. Home: PO Box 721 Lanai City HI 96763-0721 Office: Blue Ginger Cafe PO Box 1090 Lanai City HI 96763-1090

KEENE-BURGESS, RUTH FRANCES, military official; b. South Bend, Ind., Oct. 7, 1948; d. Seymour and Sally (Morris) K.; m. Leslie U. Burgess, Jr., Oct. 1, 1983; children: Michael Leslie, David William, Elizabeth Sue, Rachael Lee. BS, Ariz. State U., 1970; MS, Fairleigh Dickinson U., 1978; grad., U.S. Army Command and Gen. Staff Coll., 1986. Inventory mgmt. specialist U.S. Army Electronics Command, Phila., 1970-74, U.S. Army Communications-Electronics Material Readiness Command, Fort Monmouth, N.J., 1974-79; chief inventory mgmt. div. Crane (Ind.) Army Ammunition Activity, 1979-80; supply systems analyst Hdqrs. 60th Ordnance Group, Zweibruecken, Fed. Republic Germany, 1980-83; chief inventory mgmt. div. Crane (Ind.) Army Ammunition Activity, 1983-85, chief control div., 1985; inventory mgmt. specialist 200th Theater Army Material Mgmt. Ctr., Zweibruecken, 1985-88; analyst supply systems U.S. Armament, Munitions and Chem. Command, Rock Island, Ill., 1988-89; specialist logistics mgt. U.S. Army Signal Command, Ft. Huachuca, Ariz., 1989—. Troop leader Girl Scouts Am. Mem. Federally Employed Women (chpt. pres. 1979-80), NAFE, Soc. Logistics Engrs., Assn. Computing Machinery, Am. Soc. Public Adminstrn., Soc. Profl. and Exec. Women, AAAS. Democrat.

KEENEY, KAREN ELAINE, photographer, educator, anthropologist; b. Long Beach, Calif., Nov. 4, 1945; BA with distinction, U. Colo., 1996, MA, 1999. Cert. tchr. Colo. Dept. Higher Edn. Freelance photographer, 1980—; instr. Art Inst. Colo., Denver, 2000—. Mem. White Ho. News Photographers, Washington, 1982—85. Vol. World Cup Ski Race, Aspen, Colo., 1988—89. Grantee Rsch., U. Colo., 1996. Mem.: AAUW, Assn. Soc. Anthropology Oceania, Phi Theta Kappa, Golden Key, Phi Beta Kappa. Democrat. Lutheran. Achievements include first to study the culture of the remaining Anglo-Tahitian descendants of the 1789 Mutiny on the Bounty on the island of Pitcairn in the South Pacific. Avocations: skiing, hiking, backpacking, horseback riding. Home: PO Box 1985 Carbondale CO 81623-4985 Personal E-mail: karenkeeney@earthlink.net.

KEEP, JUDITH N. federal judge; b. Omaha, Mar. 24, 1944; BA, Scripps Coll., 1966; JD, U. San Diego, 1970. Bar: Calif. 1971. Atty. Defenders Inc., San Diego, 1971-73; pvt. practice law, 1973-76; asst. U.S. atty. U.S. Dept. Justice, 1976; judge Mcpl. Ct., San Diego, 1976-80, U.S. Dist. Ct. (so. dist.) Calif., San Diego, 1980—, chief judge, 1991-98; judge U.S. Office: US Dist Ct Ct Rm 16 940 Front St Ste 5190 San Diego CA 92101-8917

KEESEE, PATRICIA HARTFORD, volunteer; b. Nashville, Apr. 29, 1928; d. William Donald and Mary Carolyn (Gwyn) Hartford; m. Thomas Woodfin Keesee Jr., June 26, 1953 (dec. Jan. 2000); children: Thomas Woodfin III, Anne Hartford Keesee Niemann; 1 stepson: Allen P.K. Keesee. BA in English, Radcliff Coll., 1950; BA in Environ. Scis., SUNY, Purchase, 1977. Lab. asst. Rockefeller U. (formerly Rockefeller Inst. Med. Rsch.), N.Y.C., 1951-54. Chmn. Byram com. Nature Conservancy, Bedford, N.Y., 1970-81, mem. Conservation Bd. Town of Bedford, 1978-88, Westchester County Environ. Mgmt. Commn., 1979-88, Coun. of N.Y. Bot. Garden, Bronx, N.Y., 1982—, Wetlands Commn., Bedford, 1988-97; trustee Lower Hudson chpt. Nature Conservancy, Katonah, N.Y., 1980-90, 91-99, chmn., 1983-86, vice chmn., 1995-99; pres. Fed. Conservationists of Westchester County, Purchase, 1985-87; trustee N.Y. State Bd. Nature Conservancy, Albany, 1983-91, vice-chmn., 1986-88; bd. dirs. Lady Bird Johnson Wildflower Ctr., 2000—. Mem. N.Y. Acad. Scis., Garden Club Am. (conservation com. 1983-85, 95-97, vice chmn. conservation com. 1985-87, bd. dirs. 1989-91, vice chmn. scholarship com. 1991-94). Episcopalian. Avocations: gardening, hiking, tennis, birding, botanizing. Home: 140 Sarles Rd RD 3 Mount Kisco NY 10549-4733

KEESHEN, KATHLEEN KEARNEY, public relations consultant; b. N.Y.C., Dec. 4, 1937; d. James William and Hannah Pauline (Mansfield) Kearney, 1 child (by previous marriage), John Christopher Day; m. Walt Keeshen Jr.; stepchildren: Michael Patrick, Walt John III, Kathleen Marie, William Thomas, Ralph Timothy. BA in English, U. Md., 1959, MA in Journalism, 1973, PhD in Am. Studies, 1983; MLA, Stanford U., 1995. Cert. profl. sec. Congl., legal, med., acad., corp. sec. various orgns., East and Midwest, 1954-63; staff and mgmt. positions IBM, Washington, Md., 1963-73, lab. comm. mgr. Systems Comm. Div. Manassas, Va., 1974-76, comm. staff corp. hdqrs. Armonk, N.Y., 1977-83, comm. and community rels. mgr. Almaden Rsch. Ctr. San Jose, Calif., 1983-92; prin. Keeshen Comm., Coyote (Calif.) Press., 1992—. Lectr. in field. Contbr. articles to profl. jours. Mem. adv. bd. Friends of San Jose Pub. Libr., 1987—, Silicon Valley Info. Ctr., 1986-92, Media Report to Women; mem. corp. task force Stanford U. Inst. for Rsch. on Women and Gender, 1990—, affiliated scholar, 1992-94, assocs. bd., 1994-96; affiliated scholar Beatrice M. Bain Rsch. Group on Gender, U. Calif., Berkeley, 1994-95; libr. commr. City of Morgan Hill, Calif., 1999-2003, commr. chair, 2001-2002 Mem. Am. Journalism Historians Assn., Assn. for Edn. in Journalism and Mass Comm., Women in Comm., San Jose Rotary Club, San. Jose Profl. Womens Literary Assn., Calif. Writers Club, Alpha Xi Delta, Calif. Libr. Assn., Calif. Assn. of Libr. Trustees and Commrs., Santa Clara Art Assn., Los Gatos Art Assn. Office: Keeshen Comm Coyote Press PO Box 13154 Coyote CA 95013-3154

KEESLER, DEBORAH ELIZABETH, civil engineer; b. Mt. Kisco, N.Y., Dec. 18, 1966; d. Dennis James and Deborah Ann Malanchuk; m. John A. Thomas, Oct. 9, 1993; m. James W. Keesler, May 18, 2002. BE in Civil Engring., The Cooper Union for Advancement of Sci. & Art, 1988. Registered Profl. Engr., N.Y., lic. profl. Engr., 1997. From mem. staff to assoc. city planner II N.Y.C. Dept. Environ. Protection, 1988—94, assoc. city planner II, 1994—. Mem.: N.Y. State Soc. Profl. Engrs. (chpt. treas. 2001—, Young Engr. of Yr. award 2001), Soc. Women Engrs. (life), Girl Scouts of Westchester Putnam (life). Office: NYC DEP 465 Columbus Ave Valhalla NY 10595

KEESLING, RUTH MORRIS, foundation administrator; b. New Brunswick, N.J., Apr. 4, 1930; d. Mark Loren and Louise Weber Morris; m. Thomas Marion Keesling, June 30, 1956; children: Thomas Mark, James H., Frank M. BS in Journalism, U. Colo., 1953. Advt. dept. Burlingame (Calif.) Advance, 1953—54; news dept. Oakland (Calif.) Tribune, 1954; pub. rels. Mark Morris Assoc., Inc., Topeka, 1955; co-owner Pub. Rels., Inc., Denver, 1955—64; pres. Digit Fund, Denver, 1986—88; founder, sponsor Mountain Gorilla Vet. Project, Denver, 1986—2001; founder, pres. Mountain Gorilla Conservation Fund, Denver, 2001—. Founder Morris Animal Found., Denver, 1955—; pres. Dian Fossey Gorilla Fund, Denver, 1988—91, pres. internat., 1991—93; bd. trustees Dian Fossey Gorilla Fund Europe, London, 1989—; trustee Denver Zool. Found., Denver, 1969—; lectr. mountain gorillas; sponsor, founder Mt. Gorillas in Africa, 1987—; founder Wildlife Animal Medicine Dept. Makerene U., Uganda, 1994; head task force Rwandan Govt., 2000. Author: (brochures) Small Animal Clinical Nutrition, 1959; designer (exhibitions) Mus. Display Diane Fossey items, 1992—94. Recipient Outstanding Alumni award, U. Colo., 1976, award for animal welfare, Collier County Humane Soc., 2002, Lifetime Achievement award, Brit. Airways, 2002, award, Collier County Humane Soc., 2002. Mem.: Port Royal Club, Naples Yacht Club, Denver Country Club, Pi Beta Phi (chmn. adv. bd. 1957—60, mem. house bd. 1958—61, Carolyn Lichtenberg Crest award 2000). Home: 3220 Cherryridge Rd Englewood CO 80110 Office: Mountain Gorilla Conservation Fund PO Box 2211 Englewood CO 80150-2211 E-mail: RuthKee@aol.com.

KEETS, ELIZABETH, activist, educator; b. Peoria County, Ill. d. Jack and Billie June Russell; m. Nov. 23, 1972 (div. Sept. 1989); children: John Charles (dec. 1994), Matthew Calvin. Cert. AIDS educator ARC. Dressmaker local bus., Canton, Ill., 1973-83; dental asst. Dr. John Lefebvre, Canton, 1983-98; AIDS educator John Keets Found., 1991—. Named woman of yr. YWCA, Canton, 1996, person of week WHOI-TV, Peoria, 1996, weekly hero WEEK-TV, Peoria, 1997, person of week, 1998, 99. Avocations: reading, walking, working with youth, mentoring school programs.

KEFALAS, JESSIE AE, visual merchandiser, artist; b. Bklyn., Nov. 3, 1972; d. John Kostas and Anita Kay K. A of Fine Arts, Fashion Inst Tech., 1993; BFA, U. Del., 1997. Merchandiser GAP, Inc., N.Y.C., 1996—. Greek Orthodox. Avocation: painting. Home: 9 Laura Ln East Setauket NY 11733-1821

KEFFER, MARIA JEAN, environmental auditor; b. Sacramento, Dec. 10, 1951; d. George Edwin and Genevieve Nellie (Babuska) Scott; m. Gerry Craig Keffer, Nov. 6, 1971; children: Annemarie, Gregory, Margaret. AA in Liberal Arts, San Bernardino Valley Coll., Calif., 1973; BS in Natural Scis., U. Alaska, 1988, MS in Environ. Quality, 1995. Cert. environ. auditor Nat. Registry of Environ. Profls., prin. environ. auditor/EARA - U.K.; registered environ. health specialist, Nat. Environ. Health Assn. and State of Calif. Rsch. lab. assoc. VA/Loma Linda (Calif.) Hosp., 1988-90; environ. health specialist San Bernardino County, Calif., 1990-91, S&S Engring., Eagle River, Alaska, 1991-92; regulatory specialist ENSR Consulting and Engring., Anchorage, 1992-94; quality assurance environ. specialist Alyeska Pipeline Svc. Co., Anchorage, 1994-98; ISO 14001 project mgr. Hoefler Consulting Group, Anchorage, 1998—. Mem. Environ. Auditing Roundtable Office: Hoefler Consulting Group 701 Sesame St Ste 200 Anchorage AK 99503-6641 E-mail: mkeffer@gci.net.

KEGLEY, JACQUELYN ANN, philosophy educator; b. Conneaut, Ohio, July 18, 1938; d. Steven Paul and Gertrude Evelyn (Frank) Kovacevic; m. Charles William Kegley, June 12, 1964; children: Jacquelyn Ann, Stephen Lincoln Luther. BA cum laude, Allegheny Coll., 1960; MA summa cum laude, Rice U., 1964; PhD, Columbia U., 1971. Asst. prof. philosophy Calif. State U., Bakersfield, 1973-77, assoc. prof., 1977-81, prof., 1981—. Vis. prof. U. Philippines, Quezon City, 1966-68; grant project dir. Calif. Coun. Humanities, 1977, project dir. 1980, 82; mem. work group on ethics Am. Colls. of Nursing, Washington, 1984-86; mem. Am. Bd. Forensic Examiners; chair acad. senate Calif. State U., 2000-03. Author: Introduction to Logic, 1978, Genuine Individuals and Genuine Communities, 1997; editor: Humanistic Delivery of Services to Families, 1982, Education for the Handicapped, 1982, Genetic Knowledge, 1998; mem. editl. bd. Jour. Philosophy in Lit., 1979-84; contbr. articles to profl. jours. Chair CSU Acad. Senate, 1999—; Bd. dirs. Bakersfield Mental Health Assn., 1982—84, Citizens for Betterment of Community. Recipinet Golden Roadrunner award Bakersfield Cmty., 1991, Wang Family Excellence award, 2000. Mem. Philosophy of Sci. Assn., Soc. Advancement Am. Philos. Soc. (chmn. Pacific divsn. 1979-83, nat. exec. com. 1974-79, 2003-), Philosophy Soc., Soc. Interdisciplinary Study of Mind, Am. Philos. Assn. (bd. mem. 1999-2003, chair com. on tchg.), Dorian Soc., Phi Beta Kappa. Democrat. Lutheran. Avocations: music, tennis. Home: 7312 Kroll Way Bakersfield CA 93309-2336 Office: Calif State U Dept Philosophy Bakersfield CA 93311 Office Phone: 805-664-2249. Business E-Mail: jkegley@csub.edu.

KEHOE, CHRISTINE T. state official; b. Troy, N.Y., Oct. 3, 1950; BA, SUNY, Albany, 1972. Editor San Diego Enyzette, 1984—86; coord. San Diego AIDS Assistance Fund, 1987—88; exec. dir. Hillcrest Bus. Assn., 1988—89; aide San Diego City Coun., 1989—92; cmty. devel. specialist San Diego, 1992—93; mem. San Diego City Coun., 1993—2000; mem. city mgr.'s office Econ. Devel., 1993; candidate Calif. Dist. 49 U.S. Congress, 1998; state assembly mem. Dist. 76 Calif. State Assembly, 2000—. Mem. arts, entertainment, sports, tourism and Internet media com.; mem. housing and cmty. devel. com.; mem. pub. employees, retirement and social security com.; mem. transp. com.; mem. water, parks, and wildlife com.; mem. VA com.; chair select com. on park and river restoration, 2001—; chair pub. safety and neighborhood svcs. com., 1995—96; legis. aide State of Calif., 1992; coun. rep. City of San Diego, 1989—92; campaign coord. San Diegans for Neil Good, 1987, San Diego Says No on 64, 1986. Mem.: NOW, San Diego Assn. Govt., San Diego Small Bus. Adv. Bd., San Diego Cen. Dem. Com. (mem. San Diego City Coun. 1993—2000, chair subcom. on econ. prosperity 1998), Calif. Women in Edn., Sierra Club, San Diego Dem. Club. Democrat. Mailing: Rm 3152 PO Box 942849 Sacramento CA 95814 Office: Ste C-207 1010 University Ave San Diego CA 92130

KEHOE, JENNIFER SPUNGIN, English language educator, writer; b. Princeton, N.J., Apr. 21, 1969; d. Gardner Mawney and Susan Jay Spungin; m. Christopher Michael Kehoe, May 24, 1995 (div. Jan. 1, 2003); children: Kelsey Jane, Conley Jay. BA, Skidmore Coll., 1991; MA, SUNY, Albany, 1993; PhD, SUNY, Buffalo, 2000. Cert. permanent 7-12 English tchr. N.Y. Tchr. English Nazareth Acad., Rochester, NY, 1992—94; lectr. English SUNY, Geneseo, NY, 1994—96; prof. English St. John Fisher Coll., Rochester, 1996—. Adj. prof. Daemen Coll., Amherst, NY, 1994—96; presenter in field. Author: (book of poetry) Gallop, 1984, (book) Teacher's Handbook for Susan B. Anthony and Justice for All, 1995; contbr. poetry to anthologies. Recipient Millard Fillmore Coll. tchg. grants (2), 1995—97, SUNY-Buffalo tchg. fellowships (4), 1995—97, Elizabeth Luce Moore award in poetry, 1989. Democrat. Avocation: dressage and combined equine training. Home: 36 Town Pump Spencerport NY 14559 Office: St John Fisher Coll 3690 East Ave Rochester NY 14618

KEHRET, PEG, writer; b. LaCrosse, Wis., Nov. 11, 1936; d. Arthur Robert and Elizabeth (Showers) Schulze; m. Carl Edward Kehret, July 2, 1955; children: Bob. C., Anne M. Kehret Konen. Student, U. Minn., 1954—55. Trustee Pacific Northwest Writers Conf., Seattle, 1983-86. Author: Vows of Love and Marriage, 1979, Refinishing and Restoring Your Piano, 1985, Winning Monologs for Young Actors, 1986, Deadly Stranger, 1987 (Children's Choice award, 1988), The Winner, 1988, ENCORE!-More Winning Monologs for Young Actors, 1988, Nightmare Mountain, 1989 (Young Hoosier Book award, 1992, Golden Sower award Nebr. Libr. Assn., 1993, Iowa Children's Choice award, 1994, Maud Hart Lovelace award, 1995), Wedding Vows, 1989, Sisters, Long Ago, 1990, Cages, 1991 (Maud Hart Lovelace award, 1996), Acting Natural, 1992, Terror at the Zoo, 1992 (Pacific N.W. Young Reader's Choice award, 1995, N.Mex. Land of Enchantment award, 1995, Iowa Children's Choice award, 1996), Horror at the Haunted House, 1992 (Sequoyah Children's Book award, 1995, Young Hoosier award, 1995), Night of Fear, 1994, Richest Kids in Town, 1994, Cat Burglar on the Prowl, 1995, Danger at the Fair, 1995, Bone Breath and the Vandals, 1995, Don't Go Near Mrs. Tallie, 1995, Desert Danger, 1995, The Ghost Followed Us Home, 1996, Earthquake Terror, 1996 (W.Va. Children's Book award, 1998, Children's Crown award Nat. Christian Sch. Assn., 1998, Utah Children's Book award, 1999, Va. Young Readers award, 1999), Race to Disaster, 1996, Screaming Eagles, 1996, Backstage Fright, 1996, Small Steps: The Year I Got Polio, 1996 (Soc. Children's Book Writers and Illustrators Golden Kite award nonfiction, 1997, PEN Ctr. USA West award, 1997, Dorothy Canfield Fisher award, 1998, Mark Twain award, 1999, Young Hoosier award, 2001), Searching for Candlestick Park, 1997, The Volcano Disaster, 1998 (Fla. Sunshine award, 2000), The Blizzard Disaster, 1998, The Flood Disaster, 1999, Shelter Dogs, 1999, I'm Not Who You Think I Am, 1999, The Secret Journey, 1999, My Brother Made Me Do It, 2000, Don't Tell Anyone, 2000, The Hideout, 2001, Saving Lilly, 2001 (Henry Bergh award ASPCA, 2001), The Stranger Next Door, 2002, Five Pages a Day: A Writer's Journey, 2002, Spy Cat, 2003, Escaping the Giant Wave, 2003, (plays) Cemeteries are a Grave Matter, 1977, Let Him Sleep 'Till It's Time for His Funeral, 1978, Spirit!, 1979 (Forest Roberts Playwriting award No. Mich. U., 1979, Best New Play award Pioneer Drama Svc., 1980), Dracula, Darling, 1980, Charming Billy, 1981, (musical) Bicycles Built for Two, 1985; contbr. articles to mags., short stories to mags. Vol. Humane Soc., SPCA, Bellevue, Wash., 1975—. Recipient Achievement award Pacific N.W. Writers, Celebrate Lit. award N.W. Reading Coun. of Internat. Reading Assn., 1993, Lamplighter award Nat. Christian Sch. Assn., 2003; named Artist of Yr., Redmond Arts Commn., 1998. Mem. Author's Guild, Soc. Children's Book Writers. Office: Curtis Brown Ltd Ten Astor Pl New York NY 10003

KEIFER, JULIA A. retired dental hygienist; b. Springfield, Ohio, Apr. 19, 1933; d. Cleo Christopher and Mary Louise (Soper) Hangen; m. William White Keifer, Sept. 1, 1956; children: Elizabeth, Martha, Daniel, Joseph, Theodore. Cert. in dental hygiene, Ohio State U., 1952. Dental hygienist at various dental offices, Ohio and Conn., 1953—93; ret., 1993. Author:

family genealogies; contbr. newspaper columns to Hartford Courant and Hartford Times. Mem. recreation commn. Wethersfield Town Bd., 1961—70. Recipient Hon. Mention, Soc. Profl. Journalists, 1976, 1978. Home: 15 South St Litchfield CT 06759

KEIM, BETTY LOU, actress, literary consulant; b. Malden, Mass., Sept. 27, 1938; d. Buster and Dorothy Clair (Tracy) Keim; m. Warren Berlinger, Feb. 18, 1960; children: Lisa, David, Edward, Elizabeth. Grad., Lodge Acad., N.Y.c., 1956. Appeared in films These Wilder Years, 1956, Teenage Rebel, 1956, Wayward Bus, 1957, Some Came Running, 1958; appeared on Broadway in Strange Fruit, Rip Van Winkle, Crime and Punishment, Texas Lil Darlin, The Remarkable Mr. Pennypacker, Roomful of Roses; appeared on TV in Omnibus, Playhouse 90, Alcoa Hour, Philco PlayHouse; appeared in TV series My Son Jeep, The Deputy. Assoc. Aid Project L.A., 1984-97; life mem., vol. Actors Fund of Am. Recipinet Motion Picture award Calif. Women's Club, 1956, Filmdoms Famous Five award Film Daily Critics, 1956, Laurel award, 1956.

KEIPER, MARILYN MORRISON, elementary school educator; b. South Gate, Calif., June 12, 1930; d. David Cline and Matilda Ruth (Pearce) M.; m. Edward E. Keiper, June 18, 1962; children: Becky S. Swickard, Edward M. BA, Calif. State U., L.A., 1954; postgrad., UCLA, 1968. Elem. tchr. Rosemead (Calif.) Sch. Dist., 1954—. Recreation leader L.A. County, 1951-62, 2d reader 1st Ch. Christ Scientist, Arcadia, Calif., 1991-94; mem. cons. Janson Adv. Group, Rosemead, 1985-95; bd. dirs. Janson PTA, Rosemead, 1985-99; participant Sta. KNBC Spirit of Edn., 1990-92; leadership team Jason Sch.; mem. M.B. Janson Leadership team. Named Tchr. of the Yr., L.A. County, 1983-84; recipient Recognition award for outstanding service to children, Theta Kappa Chpt. Delta Kappa Gamma, 1996; featured in articles in Pasadena Star News, Rosemead C. of C., 2000; Janson Sch. auditorium named Keiper Auditorium in her honor for outstanding svc. to sch., 2001. Fellow Rosemead Tchrs. Assn., Delta Kappa Gamma.

KEISER, MARY ANN MYERS, special education educator; b. Phila., Feb. 13, 1932; d. Edgar Miller and Mary (Bickley) Myers; m. John F. Keiser, Jr., Dec. 25, 1963 (wid. Sept. 1977); children: Jill, Kimberly, Beth (tiwns), Mary Ann, Meg (twins). BA, Dickinson Coll., 1954; MS, Temple U., 1957; MEd, Pa. State U., 1979. Tchr. sci. Media (Pa.) H.S., 1954-56; elem. tchr. Phoenixville (Pa.) Sch. Dist., 1956-57, Springfield (Pa.) Sch. Dist., 1957-64, Neshaminey Sch. Dist., Langhorne, Pa., 1964-65; reading tchr., cons. Main Line Day Sch., Haverford, Pa., 1971-79; spl. edn. tchr. West Chester (Pa.) Sch. Dist., 1979-97. Vol. R.S.V.P. and West Chester Sch. Dist. Ford Found. grantee Temple U., Phila., 1954-57. Mem. NEA, Pa. Edn. Assn. (life), Chester County Hist. Soc., PSEA-R, DAR (past sr. state pres. Pa.), Children Am. Revolution (past sr. state pres. Pa.), Needlework Guild Assn. (past pres. Paole, Malvern br.). Methodist. Avocations: doll collector, tutor for care children, travel, reading. Home: 423 Gateswood Dr West Chester PA 19380-6324

KEISER, NANETTE MARIE, research associate, project administrator; b. Flint, Mich., May 22, 1957; d. Charles Kenneth Jr. and Suzanne Mary (Sayan) Stevens; m. W. Jack Keiser, May 29, 1993; stepchildren: Christopher, Elizabeth, Laura. BS, Western Mich. U., 1980, MA, 1996, EdD, 2000. Edn. dir. Tandy Computer Ctr., Kalamazoo, 1980-85; dir. fin., adminstrn. Deming, Hughey et al, Kalamazoo, 1985-91; chief fin. and adminstrv. officer Kalamazoo Found., 1991-95; computer project dir. Coun. Mich. Founds., 1995-97; cons. W.K. Kellogg Found., 1997—2000; evaluator We. Mich. U., Kalamazoo, 1996—. Presenter in field. Bd. dirs., pres. YWCA. Mem.: AAUW, Am. Evaluation Assn. (bd. dirs., treas.), Mich. Assn. for Evaluation (bd. dirs., treas.), Phi Kappa Phi, Phi Delta Kappa. Avocations: sailing, reading, music, biking, computers.

KEISLING, MARY WEST, volunteer; b. Sparta, Tenn. d. Herbert Jones West and Dannie Young; m. John Kermit Keisling, Dec. 9, 1939 (dec. 1986); children: John H., Robert West. AB, George Washington U., 1938. State pres. Tenn. Fedn. Women's Clubs, 1968-70; vice chmn. Tenn. Arts Commn., 1977-82; mem. nat. bd. Med. Coll. Pa., 1977-91; county commr. Tenn. County Ct., 1978-85; pres. Plateau Mental Health Ctr., 1980-84; state historian DAR, 1987-90; nat. pres. U.S. Daughters 1812, 1988-91. Home: 427 Gaines St Sparta TN 38583-2124

KEISTER, LISA A. social studies educator; b. Erie, Pa., Jan. 30, 1968; d. James and Barbara Vargo; m. James Wilson Moody, Aug. 21, 1999. PhD, Cornell U., 1997. Asst. prof. U. N.C., Chapel Hill, 1997—99, Ohio State U., Columbus, 1999—2000, assoc. prof., 2000—. Author: Wealth in America, 2000, Chinese Business Groups, 2000. Home: 1066 Neil Ave Columbus OH 43201 Office: 300 Bricker Hall 190 N Oval Mall Columbus OH 43210 E-mail: keister7@osu.edu.

KEISTLER, BETTY LOU, accountant, tax consultant; b. St. Louis, Jan. 2, 1935; d. John William and Gertrude Marie (Lewis) Chancellor; m. George E. Keistler, Aug. 3, 1957 (div. Mar. 1981); children: Kathryn M., Deborah Emnett(dec.). AS, St. Louis U., 1956; BBA, U. Mo., 1986. Asst. treas. A.G. Edwards & Sons, St. Louis, 1956-57; owner, mgr. B.L. Keistler & Assoc., St. Louis, 1969-82; contr. Family Resource Ctr., Inc., St. Louis, 1982-87; registered rep. Equitable Fin. Svcs., Mo., 1987-88; bus. mgr. Mo. Bapt. Coll., St. Louis, 1987-88, Barnes Hosp. Sch. of Nursing, St. Louis, 1989-91, U. South Fla., St. Petersburg, 1991—. Cons. in field, 1982-91; cert. two star sales assoc. Youngevity, Inc., 1995, area assoc. trainer; registered rep. Equitable Fin. Svcs., 1987-88; adminstrv. and profl. coun. mem. U. South Fla., 1994. Treas. Pkwy. Townhouses at Village Green, Chesterfield, Mo., 1985—87; exec. core United Way Greater St. Louis, 1984—91; mem. Gulfport Hist. Soc., 1996—; mem. bldg. and grounds com. Pasadena Bapt. Ch., Sunday sch. gen. sec., 1994—95, chair trustee com., 1996—97; sec. Sunday sch. Friendship Bapt. Ch., 2001—02, mem. stewardship com., 2001—02. Scholar Phillip Morris Corp., St. Louis, 1982-84. Mem. Am. Bus. Womens Assn. (v.p. 1978-79, pres. Lewis and Clark chpt. 1979-80, treas. nat. conv. 1981, pres. ADITI chpt. 1988-90, Sand and Sea chpt. 1992—, edn. chmn. Sunshine City chpt., v.p., 2002-03, Woman of Yr. 1980, 95), U. South Fla. Women's Club, Am. Soc. Women Accts., Ind. Accts. Mo. (sec. 1978-79, v.p. 1980-81, state sec. 1978-79), St. Louis Women's Commerce Assn., 1904 World's Fair Soc., Internat. Platform Assn., Gulfport Hist. Soc., Am. Biog. Inst. (hon. advisor, rsch. bd. advisors nat. divsn. 1991), NAFE, Gulfort Hist. Soc., Alpha Sigma Lambda (life). Republican. Avocations: travel, public speaking, entertaining, reading. Office: U South Fla 140 7th Ave S Terr 410 Saint Petersburg FL 33701-5016 E-mail: bkeistle@stpt.usf.edu.

KEITH, CAROLYN AUSTIN, secondary school counselor; b. Mobile, Ala., July 15, 1949; d. Lloyd James Jr. and Aletia Delores (Taylor) Austin; m. Carlos Lamar Keith Sr., Aug. 14, 1971; children: Carlos Lamar Jr., Carolyn Bernadette Austin Keith. BA in English and History, Mercer U., 1971; Cert. in Gifted Edn., Valdosta State Coll., 1979, MEd in Counseling, 1982, postgrad., 1987, Nova Southeastern U., 1997—. Tchr. English Crisp County High Sch., Cordele, Ga., 1971-77; tchr. gifted Tift County Jr. High Sch., Tifton, Ga., 1977-81, Dooly County Sch. System, Vienna, Ga., 1981-82; counselor Worth County High Sch., Sylvester, Ga., 1982-86, Monroe Comprehensive High Sch., Albany, Ga., 1986-91, Dougherty County Alternative Sch., Albany, 1991-98, Dougherty County Mid. Sch., Albany, 1998—. Cons. Ga. State U., Atlanta, 1986-89, Dept. Family and Children Svcs., Albany, 1993, 94; presenter Nat. Dropout Prevention Fall conf., 1997. Mem. West Point Parent's Club, U.S. Mil. Acad., 1992-96, Dougherty County Commn. on Children/Youth, Albany, 1991—; mem. adv. bd. Southwest Ga. Prevention Resource Ctr., Teen Plus Clinic, 1998, S.W. Ga. Area Health Edn. Ctr., 1996—; mem. Nat. Family Life Inst., U. N.C., Charlotte, 1997; presenter Nat. Dropout Prevention Fall Conf., 1997. Named Vol. of Yr., Dougherty County Coun. on Child Abuse, 1993, Student Assistance Program Counselor of Yr. for State of Ga., 1994. Mem. Am. Counseling Assn., Ga. Sch. Counselors Assn. (sec. 2d dist. 1985-91, Counselor of Yr. 1993), Am. Sch. Counselors Assn., Nat. Bd. Cert. Counselors (cert. family life instr.), Ga. Lic. Profl. Counselors, South Ga. Regional Assn. Lic. Profl. Counselors, Delta Sigma Theta. Democrat. Roman Catholic. Avocations: reading, classical music. Office: PO Box 50261 Albany GA 31703-0261

KEITH, JENNIE, anthropology educator and administrator, writer; b. Carmel, Calif., Nov. 15, 1942; d. Paul K. and Romayne Louise (Fuller) Hill; m. Marc Howard Ross, Aug. 25, 1968 (div. 1978); 1 child, Aaron Elliot Keith Ross; m. Roy Gerald Fitzgerald, June 21, 1980; 1 child, Kate Romayne Keith-Fitzgerald. BA, Pomona Coll., 1964; MA, Northwestern U., 1966, PhD, 1968; Dr.Letters (hon.), Pomona Coll., 2002. NIMH fellow, Paris, 1968-70; asst. prof. anthropology Swarthmore Coll., 1970-76, assoc. prof., 1976-82, prof., 1982—, Centennial prof. anthropology, 1990—, chmn. sociology and anthropology, 1987-92, provost, 1992-2001; exec. dir. Eugene M. Lang Ctr. for Civic and Social Responsibility, 2002—. Mem. rsch. edn. rev. com. NIMH, Washington, 1979-82; co-dir. workshop on age and anthropology Nat. Inst. Aging, Washington, 1980-81, task group leader nat. rsch. plan on aging, 1981; mem. human devel. rev. bd. NIH, 1985-89; mem. adv. coun. Brookdale Found., 1990-93. Author: Old People, New Lives, 1977, 2d paperback edit., 1982 (Am. Jour. Nursing Book of Yr. 1978), Old People as People, 1982; co-author: The Aging Experience, 1994 (Richard Kalish award Gerontol. Soc. Am. 1994); co-editor: New Methods for Old-Age Research, 1980, 2d edit., 1986, Age in Anthropological Theory, 1984; mem. editorial bd. Gerontologist, 1981-89, Jour. Gerontology, 1987-91, Jour. Aging Studies, 1989-98; assoc. editor Rsch. on Aging, 1981-88. Bd. dirs. Cmty. Svcs., Folsom, Pa., 1980-82, Inst. Outdoor Awareness, Swarthmore, 1980—; bd. dirs. Kendal-Crosslands, 1987-92, chmn., 1989-92, Kendal Corp., 1992-95. Conf. grantee Nat. Inst. Aging, 1980, rsch. grantee, 1982-90. Fellow Am. Anthrop. Assn., Gerontol. Soc. Am. (exec. bd. behavioral and social scis. sect. 1985-87, program chmn. 1989, chair 1989-90, publs. com. 1993-95); mem. Assn. Anthropology and Gerontology (founder, sec. 1980-81). Office: Swarthmore Coll Lang Ctr for Civic and Social Responsibi Swarthmore PA 19081 E-mail: jkeith1@swarthmore.edu.

KEITH, PAULINE MARY, artist, illustrator, writer; b. Fairfield, Nebr, July 21, 1924; d. Siebelt Ralph and Pauline Alethia (Garrison) Goldenstein; m. Everett B. Keith, Feb. l4, l957; l child, Nathan Ralph. Student, George Fox Coll., l947-48, Oreg. State U., l955. Illustrator Merlin Press, San Jose, Calif., l980-8l; artist, illustrator, watercolorist Corvallis, Oreg., 1980-94. Author 6 chapbooks including Christmas Thoughts, Retelling the Story, 1985, Poems, 1999; editor: Four Generations of Verse, 1979; author numerous poems; contbr. articles to profl. jour; one-woman shows include Roger's Meml. Libr., Forest Grove, Oreg., 1959, Corvallis Art Ctr., 1960, 98-99, Human Resources Bldg., Corvallis, 1959-61, Corvallis Pastoral Counseling Ctr., 1992-94, 96, Hall Gallery, Sr. Ctr., 1993-2003, Consumer Power, Philomath, Oreg., 1994, 2002, Art, Etc., Newburg, Oreg., 1995-2002; exhibited in group shows at Hewlett-Packard Co., 1984-85, Corvallis Art Ctr., 1992, Chintimini Sr. Ctr., 1992, 1994, 2001-04. Co-elder First Christian Ch. (Disciples of Christ), Corvallis, 1988-89, co-deacon, 1980-83, elder, 1991-93; sec. Hostess Club of Chintimini Sr. Ctr., Corvallis, 1987, pres., 1988-89, v.p., 1992-94; mem. Luth. Ch. Coun., 1998, 99-2000. Recipient Watercolor 1st price Benton County Fair, 1982, 83, 88, 89, 91, 2d prize, 1987, 91, 3d prize, 1984, 90, 92. Mem. Oreg. Assn. Christian Writers, Internat. Assn. Women Mins., Am. Legion Aux. (elected poet post II Covallis chpt. 1989-90, elected sec. 1991-92), ArtVine (Pres.'s Choice, 1999-2002). Republican. Avocations: nature walks, singing in church choir. Office: 304 S College St Newberg OR 97132-3114

KEITH, PENNY SUE, mayor, educator; b. Louisville, Sept. 15, 1949; d. John G. Jr. and Edna Lee (Butler) K. AS, U. Ky., 1974; BS, U. Louisville, 1978, MEd in Spl. Edn., 1982, MEd in Curriculum Studies, 1984. Cert. tchr., Ky. Adv. tchr. St. Stephan Martyr Sch., Louisville, 1978-80; tchr. learning disabled students South Oldham Mid. Sch., Crestwood, Ky., 1980-87; dir., prodr. WSOM News, 1988—; pub. rels. liason South Oldham Mid. Sch., 1987-90; mayor City of Parkway Village, Ky., 1990—. Prodr./dir. WSOM News, South Oldham Middle Sch., 1988—, WSOH News, South Oldham High Sch., 1994—. Editor: Through the Eyes of 6th Graders, 1978, Interview with Famous People in the Louisville Times, 1987, An Interview with Diane Sawyer, Louisville Mag.. Nov. 1992. Commr. City of Parkway Village, Louisville, 1982-85, 88-89; treas., 1986; mem. Regional Airport Authority, Louisville, 1992-93; mem. Community Adv. Com., Louisville, 1992. Mem. NEA, Ky. Mcpl. League, Ky. Cols., Oldham County Edn. Assn., Atwood Sr. Citizens (pres. 1985-90). Democrat. Methodist. Home: 850 Melford Ave Louisville KY 40217-2006 Office: Chenoweth Elem Sch 3622 Brownsboro Rd Louisville KY 40207

KEITH, SUSAN JAYNE, music educator; d. Floyd Edward and Carolyn Theresa Thompson; m. Mike Warren Keith, July 24, 1993; 1 child, Shannon Elyse. MusB, Kans. State U., 1990, MusM, 2000. Instr. elem. music Ellsworth Elem. Sch., Kans., 1990—. Choir dir., organist St. Bernard's Cath. Ch., Ellsworth, Kans., 1990—; accompanist Ellsworth Kanopolis Schs., 1994—; guest organist, Kans., 1995—. Pres. St. Bernard's Parish Coun., Ellsworth, Kans., 1995—96. Mem.: Kans. Coaches Assn., Music Educators Nat. Conf. (life), Kans. State U. Alumni Assn. (life), Kappa Alpha Theta, Pi Kappa Lambda (hon.), Mu Phi Epsilon (assoc.). Roman Catholic. Avocations: volleyball, traveling, snorkeling, reading. Office: Ellsworth Elementary Sch 110 East Third St Ellsworth KS 67439

KEITH, SUSAN S. lawyer, business executive; V.p., sec. and corp. counsel Halliburton Co., Dallas, 1990—. Office: Halliburton Co 3600 Lincoln Plaza 500 N Akard St Dallas TX 75201-3391 E-mail: susan.keith@halliburton.com.

KEITH, SUZANNE GREGORY, legal association administrator; b. Grand Rapids, Mich., Sept. 20, 1946; d. Joseph Eldridge and Yvonne LeBone (Belmont) Gregory; m. Thomas Alexander Harvey, May 31, 1964 (div. 1968); 1 child, William Alexander; m. W. Steven Keith, May 31, 1969 (div. Dec. 1996); children: Martin Gregory, Nathan Edan. Student, Murray State U., 1964-66; MusB, Western Ky. U., 1969; JD, Nashville Sch. of Law, 1981. Bar: Tenn. 1983; cert. tchr. Tenn., Ky. Music band and vocal tchr. Fayette County Schs., Lexington, Ky., 1969-73; pub.'s asst. Freeman-Harr Pub. Co., Nashville, 1974-75; customer svc. rep. Baird Ward Printing Co., Nashville, 1977-80; asst. to pres. W.F. Holt Constrn. Co., Brentwood, Tenn., 1981-83; cheif jud. planner Tenn. Supreme Ct.- Adminstrn. Office, Nashville, 1984-92, dep. state ct. adminstr., 1992—2000; exec. dir. Tenn. Trial Lawyers Assn., Nashville, 2000—. Jud. edn. consortium mem. State Justice Inst., Washington, 1990-93. Author: Presiding Judge Handbook; editor: Court Clerk Manual. Vol. St. Patrick's Shelter for the Homeless, Nashville, 1984-94, St. Thomas Hosp., Nashville, 1995—. Mem. Nat. Assn. Ct. Mgmt., Nat. Assn. State Jud. Educators (jud. edn. and ct. mgmt. cons. 1990—, chair nominating com. 1992-94, 95—). Presbyterian. Avocations: music, dance, handwork, remodeling. Home: 4006 Corbin Sneed Rd Springfield TN 37172-6700 Office: Tenn Trial Lawyers Assn 1963 Division St Nashville TN 37203-0609

KEIZER, SUSAN JANE, artist; b. Montreal, Que., Can., Sept. 26, 1940; d. Roy Laver and Eulalia Frances (Shively) Swank; m. Joel Edward Keizer, Dec. 8, 1964; children: Sidney Jacob, Sarah Rebecca. BA, Reed Coll., 1964; postgrad., U. Calif. Davis, 1973-77, Md. Inst., 1978-79; MA, Calif. State U. Sacramento, 1981. Sci. illustrator Oreg. Health Scis. U., Portland, 1964, Santa Cruz, Davis, Calif., 1967—72; instr. drawing Davis Art Ctr., 1976-78; artist Davis, 1976—. Guest artist San Jose (Calif.) Mus. Sch., 1986; coord. West Coast Women's Conf., Heceta Head, Oreg., 1983; assoc. dir. Lester Gallery, Inverness, Calif., 1981-82; adj. faculty art Am. River Coll., Sacramento, 1997; guest instr. art Calif. State U., Sacramento, 1983, vis. lectr. U. Calif. Davis, 1989, 2000-02; mem. faculty summer Haysack [illegible] Exhibited in numerous one-woman and group shows, 1976—; represented in numerous corp. and pvt. collections. Mem. exec. bd. Nelson ARTfriends U. Calif., Davis, 1992-96, chair benefit exhbn. Nelson Gallery, 1994-2001. MacDowell Colony fellow, Peterborough, N.H., 1986. Mem.: AAUW. Home and Office: 2513 Madrid Ct Davis CA 95616-0141 Office Phone: 530-758-0613. E-mail: skeizer@cal.net.

KELEHEAR, CAROLE MARCHBANKS SPANN, legal administrator; b. Morehead City, N.C., Oct. 2, 1945; d. William Blythe and Gladys Ophelia (Wilson) Marchbanks; m. Henry M. Spann, June 5, 1966 (div. 1978); children: Lisa Carole, Elaine Mabry; m. Zachariah Lockwood Kelehear, Sept. 15, 1985. Student, Winthrop Coll., 1963-64; grad., Draughon's Bus. Coll., 1965; cert. in med. terminology, Greenville Tech. Edn. Coll., 1972; grad., Millie Lewis Modeling Sch. Office mgr. S.C. Appalachian Adv. Commn., Greenville, 1965-68, Wood-Bergheer & Co., Newport Beach and Palm Springs, Calif., 1970-72; asst. to Dr. J. Ernest Lathem Lathem & McCoy, P.A., Greenville, 1972-75; asst. to Gov. Robert E. McNair, McNair, Konduros, Corley, Singletary and Dibble Law Firm, Columbia, S.C., 1975-77; office mgr. Dr. James B. Knowles, Greenville, 1977-78, Constangy, Brooks & Smith, Columbia, 1978-83; legal asst. to sr. ptnr. William L. Bethea Jr., Bethea, Jordan & Griffin, P.A., Hilton Head Island, 1983—88; legal asst. Rajko D. Medenica, MD, PhD, 1988—95; adminstr. Dibble Law Offices, Columbia, 1995-96; admin. asst. Haynsworth Sinkler Boyd, P.A., Columbia, 1997—. Notary pub.; vol. Ladies aux. Greenville Gen. Hosp., 1966-72, South Coast Hosp., Laguna Beach, Calif., 1973, St. Francis Hosp, Greenville, 1974-76, Hilton Head Hosp., 1983-92. Mem. Hilton Head Hosp. Aux., Profl. Women's Assn. Hilton Head Island, Am. Bus. Women's Assn., Nat. Assn. Female Execs., Am. Soc. Notaries, Beta Sigma Phi.

KELER, MARIANNE MARTHA, lawyer; b. Budapest, Hungary, Oct. 2, 1954; d. Tibor and Margaret (Feja) K.; m. Michael Richmond Kershow, Aug. 21, 1981; children: Stefan, Madeleine. BS, Georgetown U., 1976, JD, 1980. Bar: D.C. 1980. Law clk. to Assoc. Judge U.S. Ct. Appeals (D.C. cir.), Washington, 1980-81; staff atty. Office of Gen. Counsel, SEC, Washington, 1981-83; counsel to chmn. Office of Gen. Counsel, IRS, Washington, 1983-84; sr. atty. Student Loan Mktg. Assn., Washington, 1985-86, asst. gen. counsel, 1986-88, sr. asst. gen. counsel, 1988-90, v.p., assoc. gen. counsel, 1990-97, sr. v.p., gen. counsel, 1997—. Mem. ABA (corp. and securities div.), Am. Corporate Counsel Assn. Office: SLM Holding Corp 11600 Sallie Mae Dr Reston VA 20193-0001

KELLAIGH, KATHLEEN, conservatory artistic director; b. N.Y.C., June 28, 1955; d. Joseph Anderson and Alice Rendell (French) Kelly; m. Joel Wayne Robertson, Oct. 1, 1988; children: Christopher, Sarah. BFA summa cum laude, U. Ill., 1976. Performer United Stage, Mich., 1977-78, Hartman Stage, Conn., 1978-79, Guiding Light-CBS TV, N.Y.C., 1979-81; dir. Center Stage Bravo, 1981-82; performer Nassau Rep., N.Y., 1983-84, Sail-Away Prodns., World Cruises, 1983-86; producer (transferred from City of London Festival) Narnia, Adonai Arts Found., N.Y.C., 1986; performer All My Children, N.Y.C., 1987, America's Most Wanted, Fox TV, N.Y.C., 1988; producer, assoc. producer Adonai Arts Found., N.Y.C., 1988-90; founder, artistic dir. Action Theatre Conservatory, Clifton, N.J., 1990—; dir. Waldwick, N.Y.C., 1992, An Evening of Ed Dixon One-Acts, N.Y.C., 1994, The Fourth Chair, N.Y.C., 1995, A Christmas Carol, NJ, 2000, 2001, Our Town, NJ, 2002, Narnia, 2003, Full Moon Cafe (benefit for Cystic Fibrosis Found.), 2003, Full Moon Cafe (benefit for Arts & Spirituality Initiative, Montclair, NJ), 2004. Prodr. Rumors, 2000, Social Security, 2000, The Miracle Worker, 2001, Witness for the Prosecution, 2001, The Conservatory Players, NJ, The Good Doctor, 2002, Twelve Angry Men, 2002, Comedy Tonight: Durang Style, 2003; make-up artist Sarah Caldwell's bicentennial prodn., Be Glad Then America, Pa., 1976; make-up artist, instr. Nat. Acad. Dance, 1974—77; playwright-in-residence Little Theatre/Genesius Guild, Ill., 1971—72, Ill., 1981—90, 1971—72, NY, 1981—90; artistic dir. Art for God's Sake, Montclair, NJ, 1992, Montclair, 94; evaluator Rising Star Awards, 1998—; liturgist, N.Y.C., Montclair, 1982—90, N.Y.C., Montclair, 1999—; prodr. Midsummer Night's Dream, 2004, Diary of Anne Frank, 2004, Midsommer Night's Dreame, 2004. Author: (plays) The Separate World, 1971, Chapter 33, 1981, Alternatives, 1993, Bridges, 1993, The Music's Not So Beautiful Anymore, 1994, Hijinks, 1996; lyricist, book writer for musical Beauty's Rose, 1989; playwright, lyricist A Mall and the Night Shifters, 2003; Musical Journey, 2004. Chmn. Episcopal Peace Fellowship, N.Y.C., 1982-86; mem. Diocesan Task Force on World Peace, N.Y., 1982-88. Phi Kappa Phi Acad. scholar, 1975-76. Mem. Am. Fedn. TV and Radio Artists, Screen Actors Guild, Actors Equity Assn., Actors Fund, Episcopal Actors Guild, Genesius Guild (sec. 1987-88), Phi Kappa Phi. Office Phone: 973-772-6998. E-mail: atcstudios@aol.com.

KELLAR, CHARLOTTE AVRUTIS, writer; b. N.Y.C., Nov. 15; d. Aaron and Fannie (Kantor) Avrutis; m. Harold Kellar, Feb. 14, 1947 (dec. Mar. 1980); 1 child, Jeffrey Hamilton. BA, NYU, 1951; student, Harrison Lewis Dramatic Sch. Editor Futurific Mag.; contbr. stories and articles to jours. and newspapers; appeared in films and music videos. Recipient 3d Prize Fiction Contest, West Side Spirit, 1988, First Prize Essay Contest, 1989, 4th Prize, W.O.R. Radio, 1988, 2d pl. award N.Y. Daily News, 1989, 3d prize Woman's Day, 1984. Mem. Pen and Brush Club (3d prize poetry 1982, 2d prize fiction 1985, 87, 1st prize poetry 1984, 4th prize prose 1989), West Side Arts Coalition (grantee 1987), Screen Actors Guild. Avocations: theatre, music. Home: 645 W End Ave New York NY 10025-7322

KELLER, ARMOR, artist, arts advocate; b. Montgomery, Ala., June 16, 1937; d. Alton Mason and Margaret Elizabeth (Bell) ARmor; m. Ronald Thomas Keller, Nov. 28, 1958; 1 child, Kimberlin Marie. Student, Huntingdon Coll., 1955-56, U. Guam, 1972-74; BA, U. Ala., 1982. Mem. planning bd. Nat. Book Makers Conf., Tuscaloosa, Ala., 1995; panelist grant rev. Ala. State Coun. on Arts, Montgomery, 1995, 96, 98; judge high sch. art exhibn. 6th Congl. Dist. Arts Caucus, Birmingham, Ala., 1995, 96; cons. Birmingham Mus. Art, 1996. Shows include Meridian (Miss.) Mus. Art, 1986, Vanderbilt U., Nashville, 1987, Birmingham Mus. Art, 1989, Birmingham So. Coll., 1990, Kennedy-Douglas Ctr. for the Arts, Florence, Ala., 1992, Wiregrass Mus. Art, Dothan, Ala., 1993, Ctr. Cultural Arts, Gadsden, Ala., 1994, Kentuck Mus., Northport, Ala., 1994, Ch. of the Nativity, Huntsville, Ala., 1996, Huntsville Mus. Art, 1999, Heritage Hall Mus., Talladega, Ala., 2000, Masur Mus. Art, Monroe, La., 2001, Mercedes-Benz Internat., Mus. and Visitor Ctr., Tuscaloosa, Ala., 2003; featured in (film, book, calendar) Wild Wheels, 1992, 93, Smithsonian, Japan Esquire, Spiegel; illustrator: Haiku: The Travelers of Eternity, 2001. Artist del. Sister City Commn., Japan, 1994; mem. Sister City Japan Com., Birmingham, 2002—; mem. Birmingham Sister City Commn., 2003—. Fellow Escape to Create Seaside (Fla.) Inst., 1993, 94. Mem. Nat. League Am. Pen Women, Watercolor Soc. Ala. (pres. 1988-89), Birmingham Art Assn. (pres. 1982-83), Montgomery Art Guild (pres. 1976-78), Space One Eleven (pres. 1991-93), Bluff Park Art Assn. (project dir. 1997), Japan Am. Soc. of Ala. (bd. dirs. 2002-2003). Avocations: tai chi, ikebana, travel, music. Home: 204 Vestavia Cir Birmingham AL 35216-1328

KELLER, DEBORAH DUCOTE, civil engineer; b. New Orleans, Dec. 7, 1957; d. Andrew Raymond and Marilyn V. Ducote; m. Brian Steven Keller, June 23, 1979; 1 child, Stephanie Christine. BS, Tulane U., 1979; MS, U. New Orleans, 2001. Registered profl. engr., La. Dir. of engring. Burk & Assocs., Inc., New Orleans, 1979—88; chief engr. Port of New Orleans,

1988—97, dir. port devel., 1997—, v.p. engr., 1997—98, sr. mgr. opers., 1998—2003. Commr. planning commn., St. Bernard, La., 1996—, Econ. Devel. Commn., St. Bernard, 1998—; bd. dirs. Hannan H.S., Meraux, La., 1999—, Nunez Comm. Coll., Chalmette, La., 2003—. Named St. Bernard Parish Woman of the Yr., St. Bernard Bus. & Profl. Women's Club, 2001, City Bus. Woman of the Yr., New Orleans Pub. Group, 2001. Mem.: ASCE (pres.-elect 2003—, bd. dirs. 2001—, Outstanding Civil Engr. in Govt. 1997), La. Fedn. Bus. & Profl. Women (Leadership award 1998), Fedn. Bus. & Profl. Women USA (dist. dir. 2001—02). Avocations: golf, genealogy. Office: Port of New Orleans 1350 Port of New Orleans Pl New Orleans LA 70130

KELLER, DEBORAH KIM, former soccer player; b. Winfield, Ill., Mar. 24, 1975; Student in phys. edn., U. N.C. Mem. U.S. Nat. Women's Soccer Team, 1995—. Named Soccer Am. Player of Yr., 1996, Offensive Most Valuable Player, NCAA Tournament, 1996, U. N.C. Athlete of Yr., 1997. Achievements include 3d-place 1995 FIFA Women's World Cup, Sweden; mem. U-20 Nat. Team, Nordic Cup, Germany, 1994; mem. gold-medal North team, 1995 U.S. Olympic Festival, Denver; led U. N.C. to NCAA Championship, 1996. Office: US Soccer Fedn 1801-1811 S Prairie Ave Chicago IL 60616

KELLER, JANICE N. lawyer, councilwoman; b. L.A., Nov. 29, 1947; d. Max B. and Ruth (Dobris) Musicer. BA, U. Calif., Santa Barbara, 1969; JD, U. Pacific, 1984. Bar: Calif. 1986; cert. C.C. tchg. Campaign cons. various candidates, Santa Barbara, 1978—88; mng. atty. Legal Aid Found., Lompoc, 1988—91; dep. pub. defender Santa Barbara County, Santa Maria, Calif., 1991—; councilwoman City of Lompoc, Calif., 1998—. Instr. Allan Hancock C.C., Lompoc, 1989—98. Environ. rev. commr. City of Santa Barbara, 1985—88; human svcs. commr. City of Lompoc, 1991—92, planning commr., 1992—98. Recipient Cmty. Svc. award, Citizens Planning Found., 2001, Sadie West Pub. Servant award, No. Santa Barbara County Women's Polit. Com., 2001, Cert. Congl. Recognition, U.S. Congress, 2001. Mem.: No. Santa Barbara County Bar Assn. Avocations: photography, travel. Home: PO Box 504 Lompoc CA 93438

KELLER, MARY BETH, consumer research consultant; b. N.Y.C., Dec. 18, 1960; d. Thomas Francis and Cynthia Ann E. BA in Psychology, U. Rochester, 1982. With Mfrs. Hanover Trust Co., N.Y.C., 1982-88, mgmt. trainee, 1982-85, quality circle facilitator human resources area, 1982-83, fin. planner, 1983-84, account analysis supr. cen. bookkeeping, 1984, communication officer, Communications & Mktg. Ops. div., 1984-86, dir. course adminstrn. corp. profl. devel., 1986-87, tng. analyst, 1987-95; creative rsch. assoc. Saatchi & Saatchi Worldwide Advt., N.Y.C., 1988-95; owner, prin. cons., consumer rsch., new product devel. Creative Waves. Innovations in Qualitative Rsch., Pleasantville, N.Y., 1995—. Editor employee publ., 1985-86, employee devel. course catalog, 1986. Mem. U. Rochester Admissions Network, 1982—. Recipient Productivity awards Ops. div. Mfrs. Hanover Trust, 1983, 84, 85. Mem. Nat. Assn. Bank Women (chmn. edn. and tng. 1987-88, trainer 1987-88, scholarship award 1987), Am. Bus. Women's Assn., Rsch. Cons. Assn., U. Rochester Alumni Assn. (editor newsletter 1983-86, founder, pres. N.Y. chpt. 1982-88), Qualitative Rsch. Cons. Assn. Clubs: Rochester Alumni (pres. 1982-86). Roman Catholic. Avocations: family, church, creative writing, crafts. Home and Office: 20 Wilton Rd Pleasantville NY 10570-2022

KELLER, MARYANNE, state senator; b. Buffalo, Feb. 19, 1949; m. Steve Keller; children: Tim, Amy. BS in Speech and Lang. Therapy, Buffalo State Coll., 1971; MS in Edn. and Hearing Handicapped, Canisius Coll., 1972. Tchr.; state rep. Colo. Ho. of Reps., Denver, 1992—2000; state sen. dist. 20 Colo. State Senate, Denver, 2002—, mem. appropriations, local govt., and state vets. and mil. affairs coms. City councilwoman Wheat Ridge (Colo.) City Coun., 1983—89; bd. dirs. Nat. Alliance Mentally Ill, Jefferson Ctr. Mental Health Found., Deveroix-Cleo Wallace Ctr. Children. Democrat. Roman Catholic. Office: State Capitol 200 E Colfax Ave Denver CO 80203

KELLER, MICHELLE R. science educator, secondary education educator; b. Rolla, N.D., Aug. 15, 1951; d. Raymond Charles Halone and Yvonne M. (Klier) Edwards; m. Fred F. Keller, June 30, 1973; 1 child, Brent F. BS in Foods and Nutrition, N.D. State U., 1973; cert. sci. edn., Minot State U., 1977; MEd in Secondary Sci. Edn., N.Dak. State U., 2001. Instr. sci. Bisbee (N.D.)-Egeland H.S., 1975—. Judge Seiko Youth Challenge, 1993, 94; mem. N.Dak. State Sci. Stds. com., N.Dak. Stds. Awareness facilitator. Access Excellence fellow Genentech/NSF, 1994; recipient Presdl. award for excellence in sci. tchg., 1993, Edn.'s Unsung Hero award 1998; named Hon. Mention Tchr., Radio Shack/Tandy scholars program, 1998, 99. Mem. Am. Assn. Physics Tchrs. (pres. N.D. sect. 2001—), Nat. Sci. Tchrs. Assn., N.D. Sci. Tchrs. Assn., N.D. Orienteering Alliance, Nat. Edn. Assn., N.D. Edn. Assn. Democrat. Roman Catholic. Avocations: walking, reading, gardening. Home: PO Box 265 201 3rd Ave W Bisbee ND 58317-0265 Office: Bisbee-Egeland H S P O Box 217 204 3rd Ave W Bisbee ND 58317 Office Phone: 701-656-3536. E-mail: mkeller@alum.ndsu.nodak.edu.

KELLER, NANCY ANNE, special education educator; b. Washington, Iowa, Mar. 26, 1952; d. Paul Laverne and Mary Kathleen (Clarahan) Adam; m. David Keith Keller; children: Jeremy, Sarah. BEd, U. Northern Iowa, Cedar Falls, 1974. Cert. Elementary Education- Special Ed Iowa, 1974, teacher of the Severe-Profound Iowa, 1987, teacher of the Mildly Handicapped Iowa, 1994. Tchr.- Severe-Profound North H.S., Davenport, Iowa, 1992—. Recipient Outstanding Tchr. award, Davenport (Iowa) Masons, 1997. Mem.: Alpha Delta Kappa (exec. bd. 1998—2002). Roman Catholic. Avocations: reading, travel. Home: 5520 Hillside Court Davenport IA 52806

KELLER, NATASHA MATRINA LEONIDOW, nursing administrator; b. Nyack, N.Y., June 12, 1958; d. Paul and Matrina (Butich) L.; children: Alexandra, Mary, John. AAS, Rockland C.C., 1979; BS in Nursing cum laude, SUNY Coll. Technology, Utica, 1982; MS in Nursing magna cum laude, Syracuse U., 1985. RN, N.Y.; cert. nurse adminstr. Staff nurse Englewood Hosp., N.J., 1979-80; chare nurse Mary Imogene Bassett Hosp., Cooperstown, N.Y., 1980-82, nursing svc. coord., 1983-86, asst. dir. sys. devel., 1986-87; assoc. nursing practice coord. Strong Meml. Hosp.-U. Rochester, N.Y., 1987-88; asst. dir. nursing Bayfront Med. Ctr., St. Petersburg, Fla., 1988—, adminstr. on duty, 1998. Translator: Excellence in Russian Language, 1976 (Otrada award). Served as 1st lt. USAFR, 1990-91, Persian Gulf War, Saudi Arabia. Mem. Fla. Orgn. Nurse Execs., Tampa Bay Orgn. Nurse Execs., Sigma Theta Tau. Office: Bayfront Med Ctr 701 6th St S Saint Petersburg FL 33701-4814 Fax: 727-893-6859. E-mail: nkeller-612@msn.com.

KELLER, PATRICIA HUGGINS, music educator; b. Bowling Green, Ky., Nov. 18, 1943; d. Farrell John Huggins and Dimple Huggins Zaya; children: Kimberly Anne, Katharine Anne Keadle, Kevin David. MusB, Western Ky. U., Bowling Green, 1965; MEd, Georgetown (Ky.) Coll., 1981. Cert. tchr. Ky., 1965. Elem. music tchr. Bowling Green (Ky.) Ind. Schs., 1988—; adj. music instr. Western Ky. U., Bowling Green, 1993—94. Mem.: Ky. Music Educators Assn. (Ky. Elem. Music Tchr. of the Yr. 2003), Alpha Delta Kappa (pres. 1996—98, Cleo Dawson award 1998). Avocations: bridge, piano, cross stitch, grandchildren. Home: 2744 Cheyenne Dr Bowling Green KY 42104 Personal E-mail: petunia213@aol.com.

KELLER, SHARON FAYE, judge; Presiding judge Tex. Ct. Criminal Appeals. Office: Tex Ct Criminal Appeals PO Box 12308 Austin TX 78711-2308

KELLER, SHARON PILLSBURY, speech pathologist; b. L.A., Sept. 28, 1935; d. Edward Gardner and Iris Noriene (Hager) Pillsbury; m. Clarence Stanley Keller (dec. 1982); children: Jann Kathleen, Jennifer Beth, Lauren Elaine. AA, Chaffey Community Coll., Alta Loma, Calif., 1971; BA, U. La Verne, 1978, MS in Communicative Disorders, 1983. Lic. speech pathologist, sch. audiometrist, calif.; life svc. credential clin. and rehabilitative, Calif. Lang. speech and hearing specialist Chino (Calif.) Unified Schs., 1978-86, Rim of the World Sch. Dist., Lake Arrowhead, Calif., 1986—; speech and lang. pathologist Lake Arrowhead Elem. Sch., 1986-89, Mary P. Henk Mid. Sch., 1986-89, Valley of Enchantment Elem. Sch., Lake Arrowhead, Calif., 1989—. Cons. Assn. Speech and Hearing Svcs., Chino, 1984; former cons. infant lang. devel., teenage parent program Buena Vista Continuation H.S., Boys' Republic H.S., Chino; trainer pre-sch. and parent/child interaction Headstart, Chino; active Home program Mountain Cmtys., San Bernardino County Pre-Sch., 1988-89. Anchor Mountain Cmtys. News, Falcon Cable TV. Mem. bd. deacons, moderator Presbyn. Ch., 1991-94, 94—, mem. English handbell choir, 1988-92, children's storyteller, 1994—, pastor nominating com., 1994-95, elder, 1994-97. Mem. AAUW (rec. sec.), Am. Speech-Lang. Hearing Assn. (cert. clin. competence speech-lang. pathologist), Calif. Speech and Hearing Assn., Calif. Tchrs. Assn., Delta Kappa Gamma. Republican. Avocation: interior design. Home: PO Box 1745 Crestline CA 92325-1745 Office: Valley Enchantment Elem Sch PO Box 430 Lake Arrowhead CA 92352-0430

KELLER, SUZANNE, sociologist, psychotherapist; arrived in U.S., 1942; d. Joseph and Martha Infield; m. Charles M. Haar, July 5, 1975. PhD, Columbia U., N.Y.C., 1955; HHD (hon.), Hunter Coll., N.Y.C., 1990. Rsch. assoc. ctr. internat. studies MIT, Cambridge, Mass., 1955—58; asst. prof. of sociology Brandeis U., Waltham, Mass., 1959—62, Vassar Coll., Poughkeepsie, NY, 1963—64; fulbright scholar Athens Ctr. of Ekistics, Greece, 1964—68; prof. of sociology Princeton U., NJ, 1967. Author: (books) Beyond the Ruling Class, 1963, Community: Pursuing the Dream, Living the Reality, 2003; editor: Bldg. for Women. Pres. Ea. Sociol. Soc., 1986, Queenston Common Homeowners Assn., 1992. Recipient Hon. Fellow, AIA, 1974. Mem.: AIA (life hon.), Am. Sociol. Assn. (life; v.p. 1984), World Soc. for Ekistics (life; pres. 1991), Phi Beta Kappa. Achievements include first woman granted tenure in the 226 year history of Princeton University. Avocations: reading, opera, travel, philanthropy, writing. Office: Princeton U Dept of Sociology 107 Wallace Hall Princeton NJ 08544 E-mail: skeller@princeton.edu.

KELLERMAN, LYDIA SUZANNE (SUE), librarian; b. Bellefonte, Pa., Nov. 28, 1957; d. Paul Eugene and Janet Kathryn (Albright) K. BA, Pa. State U., 1979; MLS, U. Pitts., 1982. Asst. reference libr. U. Ky., Ashland C.C., 1982-84; Pa. newspaper project catalog libr. Pa. State U., University Park, 1985-88, serials record/binding libr., 1988-90, acting head, acquisitions receiving, 1990-91, preservation libr., 1992-98, head preservation dept., 1998—. Mem. adv. com. Pa. Preservation Consortium, Phila., 1997—; reviewer Inst. Mus. & Libr. Svcs., Washington, 1998, 99; cons. in field. Co-author: Advances in Preservation and Access, 1995. NEH grantee, 1991, 94, 96, 98, 99. Mem. ALA, Mid-Atlantic Regional Libr. Assn., Pa. Libr. Assn. Republican. Avocations: collecting newspapers, rare books and pottery, miniature furniture. Home: 118 Apollo Dr Boalsburg PA 16827-1126 Office: Pa State U Pattee Libr University Park PA 16802

KELLERMAN, SALLY CLAIRE, actress; b. Long Beach, Calif., June 2, 1937; d. John Helm and Edith Baine (Vaughn) K.; m. Richard Edelstein, Dec. 19, 1970; 4 step daughters; m. Jonathan Krane, 1980. Student, Los Angeles City Coll., Actor's Studio, N.Y.C. Stage appearances include Singular Man, N.Y.C., Breakfast at Tiffany's; films include Reform School Girl, 1959, The Third Day, 1965, The Boston Strangler, 1968, The April Fools, 1969, M*A*S*H, 1970 (Acad. award nominee 1970, Golden Globe award 1970), Brewster McCloud, 1970, Last of the Red-Hot Lovers, 1972, Slither, 1973, Reflection of Fear, 1973, Lost Horizon, 1973, Rafferty and the Gold Dust Twins, 1975, The Big Bus, 1976, Welcome to L.A., 1977, The Mouse and His Child, 1977 (voice), Magee and the Lady, 1978, It Rained All Night The Day I Left, 1978, A Little Romance, 1979, Foxes, 1980, Loving Couples, 1980, Serial, 1980, Head On, 1980, September Gun, 1983, Moving Violations, 1985, Lethal, 1985, Back to School, 1986, That's Life, 1986, Meatballs III, 1987, Three for the Road, 1987, Someone to Love, 1987, Paramedics (voice), 1988, You Can't Hurry Love, 1988, All's Fair, 1989, Limit Up, 1989, The Secret of the Ice Cave, 1990, Happily Ever After, 1990 (voice), The Player, 1992, Younger and Younger, 1993, Mirror, Mirror 2: Raven Dance, 1994, Ready to Wear (Prêt-à-Porter), 1994, It's my Party, 1995, She's So Lovely, 1997, The Maze, 1997, The Lay of the Land, 1997, Live Virgin, 1998, Bar Hopping, 1999; also TV roles Chrysler Theatre, Mannix, It Takes a Thief, Columbo: Ashes to Ashes; TV films Verna: USO Girl, 1978, For Lovers Only, 1982, Dempsey, 1983, Secret Weapons, 1985, Elena, 1985, Boris and Natasha, 1992; miniseries Centennial, 1978-79. Recipient nominations Acad. and Golden Globe awards for MASH. Mem. Actor's Equity, AFTRA. Office: Innovative Artists 1999 Ave Of Stars Ste 2850 Los Angeles CA 90067-4612 also: 7944 Woodro Wilson Dr Los Angeles CA 90046

KELLERMAN, SHIRLEY ROSE, artist; b. Comyn, Tex., Jan. 9, 1928; d. William Ellis and Rose Bessie (Touchtone) Pulley; m. Robert Eugene Kellerman, Sept. 3, 1949; children: Scott, Shellie. B in Journalism, U. Tex., 1949; postgrad., Tex. Christian U., Ft. Worth, 1965—. Represented by Evelyn Siegel Gallery, Ft. Worth, 1994—, McMahon Fine Arts, Ruidoso, N.Mex., 2000—. One person shows include Dallas Gallery, Ruidoso, N.Mex., 1991, Trinity Arts Guild, Bedford, Tex., 1993, Gallery 10, Ft. Worth, 1994, Fenton's Art Gallery, Ruidoso, 1994, 97, Evelyn Siegel Gallery, Ft. Worth, 1996, 2001, McMahon Fine Arts, Ruidoso, N.Mex., 2000—; exhibited in group shows at Mus. of the Horse, Ruidoso, 1994-2002, Evelyn Siegel Gallery, 1994-97. Mem. Nat. Mus. Women in Arts (charter). Avocations: piano, poetry, golf, mountain home. Studio: 4833 Lafayette Ave Fort Worth TX 76107-3725 also: 103 Spring Canyon Rd Ruidoso NM 88345-7221

KELLEY, BARBARA BANNIN, physical education educator; b. Far Rockaway, N.Y., Feb. 29, 1952; d. Robert Joseph and Regina (Auspitzer) Bannin; m. Edward L. Kelley, Feb. 14, 1976; children: Ryan Patrick, Timothy Bannin. BS, Longwood Coll., 1974; MEd, U. Maine, 1976. Cert. tchr., Maine. Phys. edn. tchr. Mecklenburg County Schs., South Hill, Va., 1974-75, Bangor (Maine) Sch. Dept., 1975—. Mem. Nat. Bd. Profl. Teaching Standards, Washington, 1992—. Named Coach of Yr., Maine High Sch. Coaches Assn., 1981, Tchr. of Yr., Maine Assn. Health, Phys. Edn., Recreation and Dance. Mem. NEA (bd. dirs. 1991—), Maine Tchrs. Assn. (bd. dirs. 1986—), Bangor Edn. Assn. (chief negotiator 1985-92). Democrat. Avocation: tennis. Office: Vine St Sch Bangor ME 04401 Home: 1105 Ivy Ln Raleigh NC 27609-4733

KELLEY, COLLEEN M. labor union administrator; b. Pitts., 1944; B Acctg., Drexel U.; MBA, U. Pitts. CPA. Agt. revenue IRS; dir. membership and benefits programs Nat. Treasury Employees Union; pres., chief steward, v.p. chpt. 34 Nat. Treasury Employees Union, Pitts., nat. exec. v.p.; exec. v.p. Nat. Treasury Employees Union; pres. Nat. Treasury Employees Union, 1999—. Avocation: skiing. Office: Nat Treasury Employees Union 901 E St NW Ste 600 Washington DC 20004

KELLEY, DELORES GOODWIN, state legislator; b. Norfolk, Va., May 1, 1936; d. Stephen Cornelius and Helen Elizabeth (Jefferson) Goodwin; m. Russell Victor Kelley, Jr., Dec. 26, 1956; children: Norma Kelley Johnson, Russell III, Brian. BA, Va. State Coll., 1956; MA, NYU, 1958, Purdue U., 1972; PhD, U. Md., 1977. Dir. religious edn. N.Y.C. Protestant Coun., Bronx, 1959-60; tchr. N.Y.C. Pub. Schs., Bklyn., 1962-64, Ctrl. Sch. Dist., Plainview, N.Y., 1965-66; asst. prof. Morgan State U., Balt., 1966-70; prof. speech comms. and English Coppin State Coll., Balt., 1973—; mem. Md. Ho. of Dels., Annapolis, 1991—94; former chmn. Joint Com. on Fed. Rels./Md. Senate; vice-chmn. exec. nomination com. Md. Senate, 1995—. Joint com. legis. policy, joint com. legis. ethics, co-chair joint com. on fair practices Md. State Senate, 1999—, joint com. on health care delivery and fin., 2000—, fin. com.; senate chair Joint Com. on Adminstrv., Exec. and Legis. Rev., 2001—02; vice-chair sen. com. exec. nomination; vice-chair Balt. County Senate Delegation, 2003—; panelist, reviewer NEH, Washington, 1978—82, Nat. Inst. Justice, 1998—; dean Coppin State Coll., Balt., 1979—82; fellow Am. Coun. on Edn., Washington, 1982—83; vice-chair bd. dirs. Harbor Bank Md., 1982—; mem. Gov.'s Commn. on Adoption, 1995, Atty. Gen's. and Lt. Gov's. task force on family violence, 1996—, Md. Commn. on Criminal Sentencing Policy, 1996—, Md. Commn. on Infant Mortality, 1999—2002; mem. strategic planning com. Balt. County Schs., 1999—2000; adv. com. Md. Medicaid, 1998—. Editor (monograph) Concepts of Race, 1981; moderator (TV series) Teaching Writing: Process Approach, 1982. Sec. Md. Dem. Party, Annapolis, 1986-90; bd. dirs. Balt. Urban League, 1986-89; pres. Black Jewish Forum, Balt., 1990-92; commr. Md. Commn. on Values, Annapolis, 1980-85; bd. dirs. Balt. Mental Health Systems, 1991-95; host Internat. Visitors Ctr., 1976—; commn. mem. Md. Commn. Hereditary and Congenital Disorders, Balt., 1992-95; del. White House conf. on Aging, 1995. Fellow Purdue U., 1970-72; grantee Md. Com. for Humanities, Balt., 1977-78, NEH, Washington, 1988-89; recipient Racial Justice award YWCA of Met. Balt., 1995; named to Md. Top 100 Women, Warfields Bus. Record, 1995, 97, 2004. Mem. Nat. Inst. Justice (panelist, rev. 1997). Inst. for Govtl. Svcs. (bd. dirs. 1993-94), Nat. Polit. Congress Black Women (bd. dirs., Balt. chair 1993-95), Women Legislators Md. (1st v.p. 1995-96, pres. 1998-99), 10th Dist. Dem. Club Md. (founder, pres. 1995—). Baptist. Avocations: travel, public speaking, reading. Office: 302 James Senate Office Bldg Annapolis MD 21401-1991 E-mail: delores_kelley@senate.state.md.us.

KELLEY, SISTER HELEN, health facility executive; b. Niagara Falls, N.Y., July 25, 1922; d. Robert Vincent Jr. and Helen Gertrude (O'Neil) K. BSN, Cath. U., 1953; MHA, St. Louis U., 1957; postgrad., Cath. U., Seton Hall, Wayne U., St. Louis U. RN, D.C., N.Y., Mass., Mo. Tchr. elem. and jr. high sch., Endicott, NY, 1942-50; faculty divsn. nursing St. Joseph Coll., Emmitsburg, Md., 1953-55; adminstr., pres. bd. dirs. St. Agnes Hosp., Balt., 1958-62; asst. adminstr. Sisters of Charity Hosp., Buffalo, 1962-64; adminstr., pres. bd. dirs. Carney Hosp., Boston, 1964-69; provincial councilor Daus. of Charity, N.E. Province, 1969-71; internat. work with Vincentian priests Mex., Panama, Paris, 1971-73; adminstr., pres. Our Lady of Lourdes Hosp., Binghamton, NY, 1973-76; pres. Nat. Cath. Health Assn., St. Louis, 1976-78; exec. dir. Laboure Ctr., Boston, 1979-82; adminstr. St. Louise House, Albany, NY, 1982-83; dir. mktg., planning Carney Hosp., 1983-85; assoc. dir. Intercounty Home Health Care Agy. Diocese of Albany, 1985-86; dir., coord. health and social svcs. Cath. Worker of Niagara Falls, 1986-88; dir./coord. clin. svcs. Cath. Charities' Programs Adult Developmentally Disabled, Bklyn. and Queens, 1988-91, v.p. mission svcs. Sisters of Charity Hosp., Buffalo, 1991—; dir. activities St. Louise Retirement Residence and Infirmary, Albany, 1996; docent St. Joseph Provincial House, Emmitsburg, Md., 1997. Mem. bd. Filmore Leroy Residents Assn., FLARE, Inc., Buffalo; bd. dirs. St. Mary's Hosp., Rochester; trustee Good Samaritan Hosp., Pottsville, Pa.; participant internat. Commns. Daus. of Charity, 1968; pres. bd. trustees Carney Hosp., Our Lady of Lourdes Hosp., St. Agnes Hosp.; chair, participant profl. religous cmty. studies; cons., spkr. Mercy Hosp., Pitts., St. Mary's Hosp., Amsterdam, N.Y.; mem. couns., coms. nursing, pers., profl. practice, other groups. Docent Nat. Shrine of Elizabeth Ann Seton, Emmitsburg, Md., 1996-97. Recipient Community Svc. award Cedar Grove Civic Assn., Boston, Ladies of Charity, Binghamton, CHA Pres., St. Louis. Fellow Am. Coll. Healthcare Execs.; mem. Am. Acad. Cath. Leadership. Home: 27 Webster St Malone NY 12953-1717 Office: DePaul Provincial House c/o St Louise House 96 Menands Rd Albany NY 12204 also: Pastoral Assoc St John Bosco Parish 57 Rennie St Malone NY 12953-1138

KELLEY, LINDA ROSE, human resources specialist; b. Memphis, Apr. 4, 1948; d. Simon Nmi and Elma Rose Leigh; children: Marvin Antone, Cheryl Monique Khouri. Student, U. of Memphis, 1966—78. Cert. mediator Tenn., 2003. Paralegal specialist EEOC, Memphis, 1979—81; EEO specialist Def. Depot Memphis, 1984—86, program analyst, 1986—87, EEO specialist, 1987—88, equal employment mgr.; mgmt. analyst Def. Indsl. Plant Equipment Ctr., Memphis, 1989—92; EEO specialist Def. Logistics Agy., Memphis, 1992—95; sr. EEO specialist Def. Distbn. Depot, Warner Robins, Ga., 1995—99; human resource specialist Navy Pers. Command, Millington, Tenn., 2000—03; EEO Ter. mgr. EEO and Diversity Office, Memphis IRS Ctr., 2003—; lead EEO counselor Robins AFB, Warner Robins, Ga. Pres. Blacks In Govt., Memphis, 2003—. Mem. Operation PUSH, Macon Jazz Assn., Ga., Black Cultural Awarenss Com., Millington; mem. cultural diversity awareness com. City of Millington; minister of music New Jackson Ave. Ch., Memphis. Mem.: Federally Employed Women, Inc., Fed. Exec. Assn. Democrat-Npl. Baptist. Avocations: travel, pianist, reading, music. Home: 2177 Heard Ave Memphis TN 38108 Office: Memphis IRS Ctr EEO & Diversity Office PO Box 30309 AMF Stop 19 Memphis TN 38130

KELLEY, LUCILLE MARIE KINDELY, dean, psychosocial nurse; m. Robert Kelley; children: Ryan Patrick, Megan Maura. Diploma, St. Vincent Hosp., Bridgeport, 1965; BSN, U. Conn., 1969; MNursing, U. Wash., 1973, PhD, 1990. Assoc. prof., RNB program dir. Seattle Pacific U., 1985-99, dean Sch. Health Sci., 1998—. Sr. cons. healthcare The Effectiveness Inst., Redmond, Wash., 1984-99. Pres. Nat. Coun. Cmty. Mental Health Ctrs., 1983-84. Recipient Disting. Svc. award Eastside Mental Health, 1987, Tchg. award Burlington No., 1993. Mem. Sigma Theta Tau. Office: Seattle Pacific U Sch Health Sci Marston Hall 3307 3rd Ave W Seattle WA 98119-1940

KELLEY, LYDIA, animal trainer; b. Albany, N.Y., May 27, 1947; d. Frederick Williams and Aubrey (McKowan) Kelley. BA in History, Western Coll. for Women, 1969. Tng. dir. Handi-Dogs, Tucson, 1981—86; co-founder, tng. dir. Top Dog, Tucson, 1986—. Instr. Old Pueblo Dog Tng. Club, Tucson, 1981—, Palo Verde Golden Retriever Club, Tucson, 1985—99. Author: Teamwork, 1997, Teamwork II, 1998, How to Start a Service Dog Training Program, 1998, Communities Like You, 2002; editor (newsletter): Paw Prints. Lectr. AZ Sonora Desert Mus., Tucson, 1976—79. Recipient Gaines medal, Handi-Dogs, 1981. Mem.: Internat. Cmty. Submitters, Inter-religious Coun. Southern Ariz. (pres. 1997—98), Ariz. Sonora Desert Mus., Old Pueblo Dog Training Club (chief steward 1995—2002). Avocations: travel, photography, walking. Office: Top Dog 800 N Swan Ste 126 Tucson AZ 85711

KELLEY, MARGARET MARY, music educator, musician; b. Milw., Oct. 16, 1952; d. Thomas Crawford and Josephine (Kenney) K. BM, U. Iowa, 1975; MM, U. Idaho, 1978, MEd, 1979. Pianist, Pullman, Wash., 1980—; mem. piano faculty Lewis-Clark State Coll., Lewiston, Idaho, 1984-87, U. Idaho, 2001—03. Performed as soloist, chamber, accompanist, 1971—; author: In Good Time: College, 2000, Getting There, 2001. Spay/neuter chair Humane Soc., Moscow, Idaho, 1996—, bd. dirs. 2000—, pres. bd. dir. 2001-04. Mem. ACLU (bd. dirs. Music Pullman), Music Tchrs. Nat. Assn., Pullman Music Tchrs. (pres. 1982-83, 87-88, v.p. 1983-85, treas. 1990—), Amnesty Internat. Avocations: writing, running, swimming, reading. Home: 860 SW Alcora Dr Pullman WA 99163-2053

KELLEY, MARY ELIZABETH (MARY LAGRONE), information technology executive; b. Temple, Tex., Feb. 12, 1947; d. Harry John and Mary Erma (Windham) LaGrone; m. Roy Earl Kelley, May 10, 1968; children: Roy John, James Lewis, Joanna Marylu. BS, U. Mary Hardin-

Baylor, 1968. Cert. tchr., Tex. Math tchr. Killeen HS, Tex., 1977-78; clk. typist Readiness Region VIII, Aurora, Colo., 1979; statis. clk. Fitzsimons Army Med. Ctr., 1980-81, mgmt. asst., 1981-83; clk. typist Corpus Christi Army Depot, Tex., 1984; mgmt. asst. Health Care Studies and Clin. Investigation Act, Fort Sam Houston, 1984-85; computer programmer, analyst Health Care Systems Support Act, 1985-88, computer systems analyst, 1988-92, computer specialist, 1992-94, data base adminstr., 1994-96, Lotus Notes sys. adminstr., 1996-98; process integrator, asst. comdr. force integration US Army Med. Dept. Ctr. and Sch., 1998-99, computer specialist, 1999—2002, info. tech. specialist, 2002—. Tchr. Fitzsimons Army Med. Ctr., 1978-79, cons., 1978-79. Author: (databases) Health Care Management System, 1988-94. Vol. Parents Encouraging Parents, Denver, 1979-83, Friends of Safe House, Denver, 1980-83, Heidi Search Ctr., San Antonio, 1990, Family Assistance Crisis Team, San Antonio Police Dept., 1997-99, Vols. in Policing, San Antonio Police Dept., 1998-99; founder Top of the HIll Residents' Alliance, San Antonio, 1997. Recipient achievement medal for civilian svc., Dept. Army, 1991. Mem. DAR, Daus. of Republic of Tex., United Daus. of Confederacy, Tex. Soc. of Mayflower Descs., Alpha Chi, Delta Psi Theta, Sigma Tau Delta, Alpha Phi. Roman Cath. Avocations: reading, needlework, genealogy, Special Olympics, writing poetry.

KELLEY, MARYELLEN R. economist, management consultant; b. Boston, Apr. 26, 1951; d. Albert Francis and Agnes Mary (Athy) K.; m. Bennett Harrison, Jan. 25, 1981, (dec. Jan. 17, 1999). BA, Brandeis U., 1971; M in City Planning, Harvard U., 1976; PhD in Mgmt., MIT, 1984. Harman fellow Harvard U., Cambridge, 1982-83; asst. prof. mgmt. U. Mass., Boston, 1984-88; vis. asst. prof. mgmt. and pub. policy Carnegie Mellon U., Pitts., 1988-89, asst. prof. mgmt. and pub. policy, 1989-91, assoc. prof. mgmt. and pub. policy, 1991-97; sr. economist Nat. Inst. Standards and Tech., 1997—2000; prin. Pamet Hill Assocs., 2001—. Vis. scholar MIT Indsl. Performance Ctr., Cambridge, 1994—96; vis. assoc. prof. tech. policy dept. polit. sci. MIT, Cambridge, 1994—95. Contbr. articles to Scientific, Economic and Mgmt. jours. Dissertation fellow AAUW, 1981. Mem. AAAS, Acad. of Mgmt. Office: Pamet Hill Assocs PO Box 636 Truro MA 02666-0636 E-mail: Maryellen.Kelley@direcway.com.

KELLEY, MICHAELANN, art educator; BA in Graphic Design, Coll. Mount St. Joseph, Cin., 1985, M of Art in Edn., 1992; postgrad., U. Houston. Cert. art tchr. Ohio, Tex. Advtg. coord. A.C.G.I.H., Inc., Cin., 1984-92; tchr. ceramics/art Eisenhower H.S., Houston, 1992—. Mem. tchr. of the yr. com. Eisenhower H.S., Houston, 1992-94, mem. tchr's. adv. com., 1993-95. Presenter numerous confs. in field. Sunday sch. tchr. All Saints Ch., Houston, 1994. Recipient Outstanding Alumna award Coll. Mount St. Joseph, 1995. Mem. Nat. Art Edn. Assn., Am. Craft Coun., Tex. Art Edn. Assn., Tex. Fedn. of Tchrs., Houston Art Edn. Assn., Mus. Fine Arts Houston. Roman Catholic. Avocations: pottery, reading, travelling, writing, football games. Office: Eisenhower HS 7922 Antoine Dr Houston TX 77088-4312

KELLEY, PATRICIA HAGELIN, geology educator; b. Cleve., Dec. 8, 1953; d. Daniel Warn and Virginia Louise (Morgan) Hagelin; m. Jonathan Robert Kelley, June 18, 1977; children: Timothy Daniel, Katherine Louise. BA, Coll. of Wooster, 1975; AM, Harvard U., 1977, PhD, 1979. Instr. New Eng. Coll., Henniker, N.H., 1979; asst. prof. U. Miss., University, 1979-85, assoc. prof., 1985-89, acting assoc. vice chancellor acad. affairs, 1988, prof., 1989-92, assoc. dean, 1989-90; program dir. NSF, Washington, 1990-92; prof., chmn. dept. geology U. N.D., Grand Forks, 1992-97; prof. U. NC, Wilmington, 1997—, chmn. dept. earth scis., 1997—2003. Contbr. articles to profl. jours. Deacon Bethel Presbyn. Ch., Olive Branch, Miss., 1985-90. Rsch. grantee NSF, 1986-89, 90-99, 2000-03; NSF fellow, 1976-79. Fellow Geol. Soc. Am.; mem. AAAS, Paleontol. Soc. (coun. 1984-85, 95-96, 98—, chair S.E. sect. 1984-85, chair N.C. sect. 1995-96, pres.-elect 1998-2000, pres. 2000-2002, past pres. 2002—), Assn. Women Geosci. (Outstanding Educator award 2003), (Paleontol. Rsch. Inst. (trustee 2003-), Soc. Econ. Paleontologists and Mineralogists, Sigma Xi, Phi Beta Kappa. Presbyterian. Avocations: family, ch. work, writing, music, travel. Office: Dept Earth Scis Univ NC Wilmington NC 28403 Office Phone: 910-962-7406. Business E-Mail: kelleyp@uncw.edu.

KELLEY, SHEILA SEYMOUR, public relations consultant; b. Bronxville, N.Y. d. William Joseph and Jane (Seymour) K.; m. Robert Max Kaufman, 1959. BA magna cum laude, Syracuse U., 1949. Reporter Yonkers Herald Statesman, N.Y.C., 1950; reporter, editor Close Up column Herald Tribune, N.Y.C., 1950-53; writer, producer Sta. WNBC-TV, N.Y.C., 1953-54; media cons. to Senator Jacobs K. Javits, N.Y.C., 1956-74, press sec. Washington, 1958-61; account supr., v.p. Harshe Rotman Druck, N.Y.C., 1961-76; founder, pres. VOTES, Inc., N.Y.C., 1973-75; v.p. Doremus Pub. Rels., N.Y.C., 1976-86, sr. v.p., 1987-90, exec. v.p., 1990, Gavin Anderson & Co., N.Y.C., 1990-96, sr. counselor, 1996-97; prin. The Dilenschneider Group, N.Y.C., 1997—. Mem.: Women Execs. in Pub. Rels. (pres. 1987—88, dir. found. 1999—, bd. dirs. 2003), Pub. Rels. Soc. Am. (accredited), Hon. Order Ky. Cols., Phi Beta Kappa. Republican. Avocations: skiing, golf, gardening. E-mail: sbskk@aol.com.

KELLEY, VIRGINIA WIARD (JUDY KELLEY), dance educator; b. Washington, Nov. 17, 1937; d. David Kyle and Mary Margaret (Barber) Wiard; m. Leo Gilbert Kelley, July 2, 1960; children: Cheryl, Raymond, John, Brenda. Degree in bus. adminstrn., Miller-Motte Bus. Coll., 1958; dance edn. degree, Kent State U., 1986. Grad. Dance Masters of Am. Performer Tony Grant Stars of Tomorrow, Atlantic City, N.J., 1951-53; performer Cressetts Betty Cress Dance Studio, tour of East Coast, 1958, Jacksonville, N.C., 1958-59; instr., performer, choreographer Cuppett's Performing Arts Ctr., Vienna, Va., 1981-99, Vienna Comty. Ctr., 1982-99. Actress Wilmington (N.C.) Theatrical Soc., 1957; performer Miss Wilmington Pageant, 1958. Helper Dem. Party, Vienna, 1992. Named Ms. Senior N.C., 2000. Mem. Dance Masters of Am. (dance educator 1981—), Cameo Club. Democrat. Roman Catholic. Avocations: tap dancing, weight lifting, line dancing, swimming. Home: 1207 Brougham Dr Wilmington NC 28412-7203 E-mail: traintap@aol.com.

KELLEY, WENDY THUE, fine art advisor, independent curator; b. Santa Monica, Calif., July 4, 1941; d. Horace Wendel and Marjory (Simmons) Thue; children: David Byron Jr., Christopher S., Jennifer M. AA, Stephens Coll., 1960; BA, Phillips U., 1963; postgrad., NYU, 1996, Instituto Allende, San Miguel de Allende, 1993—. Cert. tchr., Conn. Founder, dir. Artworks Fine Art Advisors, Old Greenwich, 1985. Curator exhbns. Home Box Office/Time Warner, N.Y.C., Hines, Inc.; cons. curator Discovery Mus., Bridgeport, Conn.; cons. Aetna, Cornell Med. Ctr., Time-Warner, Apple Computer, Marriott Corp. Bd. dirs. YMCA, 1987-93, Greenwich Art Coun. Mem. N.E. Appraisers Assn., Kappa Alpha Theta. Avocations: printmaking, photography, travel, books. Office: Artworks Fine Art Advisors 15 Potter Dr Old Greenwich CT 06870-1507 Home: #LOWR 207 Ocean Ave Ext Santa Monica CA 90402-1213 E-mail: wtko@mindspring.com.

KELLIE, DIANE, special education educator; b. Maine; m. Andrew Kellie; children: Shawn, Scott, Brandon. BA, U. Maine, 1970; MA, Murray State U. Professionally Recognized Special Educator Coun. for Exceptional Children, cert. Profl. in spl. edn. Commonwealth of Ky., Profl. Exceptional Children Commonwealth of Ky. Edn. tchr. Stetson Elem. Sch., Maine, 1970—72; elem. tchr. Tremont Elem. Sch., Maine, 1972—77; spl. edn. tchr. Marshall County Schs., Benton, Ky. Mentor Ky. Dept. Edn. Grantee Calvert City Cmty. Devel. Grant, Calvert City Com., Learning and Serving Grant, Ky. Edn. Dept., Svc. Learning, Am. Humanics. Mem.: NEA, Coun. for Exceptional Children. Office: Benton Elementary School 208 West 11th Street Benton KY 42025 E-mail: dkellie@marshall.k12.ky.us.

KELLIHER, JUSTINE OREN, retired nurse, educator; b. Boston, Oct. 22, 1920; d. Ralph Sidney and Margaret Elizabeth (Smith) Woollett; m. Giles Clement Kelliher, Apr. 10, 1948; children: Giles Jr., Ralph, Margaret Anne, Justina, Julia, David. BA, Manhattanville Coll., 1942; MA, Brown U., 1943; MN, Yale U., 1946; MS, Boston U., 1970. Staff nurse Boston Lying-in Hosp., 1946-47, Boston Vis. Nurse Assn., 1947-48; instr. childbirth educator Boston Assn. Childbirth Edn., 1953-78; parent educator St. Elizabeth's Hosp., Boston, 1967; staff nurse Beth Israel Hosp., Boston, 1968, Newton-Wellesley Hosp., Newton, Mass., 1970-71, Chetwynde Nursing Home, Newton, 1972-77, Bapt. Nursing Home, Newton, 1980-82, ret., 1982. Mem. Boston Assn. Childbirth Edn. (founder, instr., cons. 1953-96). Avocations: active energy and environmental groups, travel, swimming, boating, gardening. Home: 25 Chestnut Ter Newton MA 02459-1659

KELLISON, DONNA LOUISE GEORGE, accountant, educator; b. Hugoton, Kans., Oct. 16, 1950; d. Donald Richard and Zepha Louise (Lowry) George. BA in Elem. Edn. with honors, Anderson (Ind.) U., 1972; MS in Elem. Edn., Ind. U., 1981. CPA, Ind.; lic. tchr., Ind.; lic. in ins., Ind.; cert. gen. securities rep.; cert. investment advisor. Tchr. elem. Maconaquah Sch. Corp., Bunker Hill, Ind., 1972-73; office mgr. Eskew & Gresham, CPA's, Louisville, Ky., 1973-78; para-profl. Blue & Co., Indpls., 1979-83, tax compliance specialist, 1983-84, tax sr., 1984-86, tax supr., 1986-87, tax mgr., 1987-90, tax prin., 1990-92, tax sr. mgr., 1992-94, tax dir., 1995—; pres. Blue Benefits Cons., Inc., 1998—, Olympic Fin. Svcs. LLC, 1999—. Vol. Children's Clinic, Indpls., 1985-92; chairperson Most Wanted campaign Am. Cancer Soc., 1995; bd. dirs. Indpls. Estate Planning Coun., 1995—, sec., 1995-96, vice-chair, 1998, chair 1998-99, charter mem. Bus. Women Connect, 2003-. Mem. AICPA, Ind. CPA Soc. (tax inst. com. 1989-93, govt. rels. com. 1994-95), Ind. Tax Inst. (chair 1993). Presbyterian. Home: 382 Pintail Ct Carmel IN 46032-9125 Office: 12800 N Meridian St Ste 400 Carmel IN 46032

KELLOGG, ANN MARIE, retired publishing executive, consultant; b. Pitts., Oct. 2, 1939; m. Eugene Krasnoff (div.); children: Peter Lawrence, Stephanie Ann; m. Jack L. Kellogg, Nov. 10, 1979. BS, U. Wis., 1961. Prodn. and bus. mgr. Collective Advt., Inc., Princeton, N.J., 1973-83; dir. publs. Community Pride, Inc., Princeton, 1983-87, Exclusive Publs., Ltd./Relocation Guides, Boca Raton, Fla., 1987-94. Chair Abortion Law Reform Com. of N.J., Princeton, 1967-71. Mem. Soroptimist Internat. (pres. Pompano Beach chpt. 1991-92). Home: 4 Clarendon Ct Williamsburg VA 23188-1514

KELLOGG, HILDE, state representative; b. Scottsbluff, Nebr., Oct. 17, 1918; Grad., Grand Island Sr. H.S., 1935. Owner Western Wear/Gifts, 1952—81, Beauty Salons, Post Falls, Idaho, 1972—, home constrn. co.; state rep. dist. 2 Idaho Ho. of Reps., Boise, 1983—91, 1993, state rep. dist. 5A, 1982—, vice chair revenue and taxation com., mem. assessment, bus., edn., and transp. and def. coms., and joint legis. econ. outlook and revenue assessment com. Pres. Coeur d'Alene Conv. and Visitors Bur., 1987—96; sec.-treas. Panhandle Area Coun., 1976—80; councilwoman Post Falls City Coun., 1976—80; chair Post Falls Planning and Coming Commn., 1974—80; adv. coun. Area Agy. on Aging, 1992—98; mem. Indian Gaming Tribal Coun., 2001—; bd. dirs. Idaho Spl. Olympics, Jobs Plus, Coeur d'Alene, 1987—, North Idaho Coll. Found.; adv. bd. State Hosp. North; past bd. dirs. United Way. Mem.: Post Falls C. of C., Kootenai YMCA. Roman Catholic. Office: State Capitol PO Box 83720 Boise ID 83720-0038

KELLOGG, JOAN BARRETT, grief therapist, counseling astrologer, educator, author; b. Evanston, Ill., Aug. 3, 1947; d. Arthur Merritt Jr. and Ruth Eleanor Barrett; children: Christine Elizabeth, Caroline Elizabeth. AA in Bus. Real Estate, AS in Engring. and Math., William R. Harper Coll., 1982; BA in Psychology with honors, Roosevelt U., 1985, MA in Thanatology, 1988; postgrad., Ill. Sch. Profl. Psychology, 1995—. Cert. transpersonal therapist, profl. cert. in astrology. Hotel/real estate mgr. Ambassador Hotels, Chgo., 1974-76, Deer Path Inn, Lake Forest, Ill., 1976-77, Am. Invsco, Chgo., 1977-78; ptnr. The Concord Group, Barrington, Ill., 1979-88; pvt. practice as counseling astrologer Barrington, Ill., 1979—; pvt. practice as grief therapist, 1988—; adj. prof. Dept. of Psychology, W. R. Harper Coll., Palatine, Ill., 2003—. Coord. Cmty. Bereavement Support Groups Hospice Northeastern Ill., Barrington, 1987-89, Rainbows for all Children, Barrington, 1988-90; founder The Goddess Network, 1990—; cons. Compassionate friends, Arlington Heights, Ill., 1995, 96; co-founder Barrington Gifted Mentor Program, 2002—, adj. faculty Dept. Psychology, Harper Coll., Palatire, Ill., 2003—. Author: The Yod: It's Esoteric Meaning, 1989; contbr. articles to profl. jours. Mem. Ct. Appointed Spl. Advocate (CASA), 1995-97, Lake County, Ill., chmn. Friends of CASA, 1995-96; forum dir. Sacred Psychology, Microsoft New Age Network, 1996-97. Mem. APA, ACA, Nat. Assn. Grief Therapists, Nat. Coun. for Geocosmic Rsch., Am. Fedn. Astrologers, Inc. (dir. 1992-94), Profl. Astrologers, Inc. (honors in lectures 1992), Internat. Soc. for Astrol. Rsch., Northwest Suburban Counselors Assn., Lake County Counselors Assn. (pres. 1996-97), Northwest Suboban Counselers Assn. (pres. 2003-04), Barrington Breakfast Rotary, Psi Chi. Episcopalian. Avocations: needlepoint, walking. Office: Ste 210 202 S Cook St Barrington IL 60010-4351 Office Phone: 847-382-2286.

KELLOGG FAIN, KAREN, retired history and geography educator; b. Pueblo, Colo., Oct. 10, 1940; d. Howard Davis and Mary Lucille (Cole) Kellogg; m. Sept. 1, 1961; divorced; 1 child, Kristopher. Student, U. Ariz., 1958-61; BA, U. So. Colo., 1967; MA, U. No. Colo., 1977; postgrad., U. Denver, 1968, 72-93, Colo. State U., 1975, 91, Chadron State Coll., 1975, U. No. Ill., 1977, 83, Ft. Hayes State Coll., 1979, U. Colo., 1979, 86-87, 92, Ind. U., 1988. Cert. secondary tchr. Colo., 1967. Tchr. history and geography Denver Pub. Schs., 1967-96; tchr. West H.S., Denver, 1992-96. Area adminstr., tchr. coord. Close Up program, Washington, 1982-84; reviewer, cons. for book Geography, Our Changing World, 1990. Vol., chmn. young profls. Inst. Internat. Edn. and World Affairs Coun., Denver, 1980—; mem. state selection com. U.S. Senate and Japan Scholarship Com., Denver, 1981-89, Youth for Understanding, Denver; mem. Denver Art Mus., 1970—; vol. Denver Mus. Natural History, 1989—, Am. Cancer Soc. "Jail and Bail", 1996, "Climb the Mountain", 1996, Denver Conv. Bur., 1997; bd. overseas Dept. Def. Dependents Sch., Guantanamo Bay, Cuba, 1990-91; screening panelist Tchr. to Japan Program Rocky Mtn. Regional Fulbright Meml. Fund, 1997; vol. tour guide Colo. State Capitol, 1997-2001. Fulbright scholar Chadron State Coll., Pakistan, 1975; Geog. Soc. grantee U. Colo., 1986; recipient award for Project Prince, Colo. U./Denver Pub. Schs./Denver Police Dept., 1992. Mem.: AAUW, Colo. Coun. on Internat. Orgns. (mem. bd. 1999—), Colo. Geographic Alliance (steering com. 1986), Rocky Mountain Regional World History Assn. (steering com. 1984—87), Am. Forum for Global Edn., Fulbright Assn. (bd. dirs. and regional liaison Colo. chpt. 2001—), World History Assn., Nat. Coun. Social Studies (del. 1984), Colo. Coun. Social Studies (sec. 1984—86), Denver Bot. Gardens, Kappa Kappa Iota, Gamma Phi Beta. Episcopalian. Avocations: traveling, hosting international visitors, swimming, reading. Home: 12643 E Bates Cir Aurora CO 80014-3315 E-mail: karenfain@hotmail.com.

KELLS, KARI JOY, indexer, librarian; b. Columbus, Ohio, May 25, 1970; d. Paul Kerry and Myrnella Joy (Barney) McDowell; m. Raymond Lee Bero, Nov. 9, 1992 (div. 1998). BA, U. Ill., 1993, MS, 1994. Owner, indexer Index West (formerly Bero-West Indexing Svcs.), Olympia, Wash., 1994—; libr. U. Wash., Seattle, 1994-95; libr. faculty, internet trainer Pierce Coll., Lakewood, Wash., 1995-97; libr. faculty Highline C.C., Des Moines, Wash., 1997-99, Pierce Coll., Puyallup, Wash., 1999—. Contbr. articles to profl. jours. Mem. Am. Soc. Indexers (Web Site com. 1995-98, Webmaster 1995-97, vice chmn. Pacific N.W. chpt. 1997-98, chmn. Pacific N.W. chpt. 1998-99, Webmaster Pacific N.W. chpt. 1996—), Indexing & Abstracting Soc. of Can., 2003-. Office: PO Box 615 Olympia WA 98507 E-mail: info@indexw.com.

KELL-SMITH, CARLA SUE, federal agency administrator; b. Highland Park, Mich., Sept. 15, 1952; d. Carl William and Margie May (Cannon) Bodner; m. Joseph Mark Kell, Oct. 10, 1971 (div. Dec. 1980); m. Richard Charles Smith, Jan. 28, 1989; Student, Anderson Coll., 1970-71, Glendale Coll., 1976-77, Ariz. State U., 1978-79, Mesa Coll., 1979-80. Private tutor English, Fed. Republic of Germany, 1971-74; office mgr. Bell & Schore, Rochester, Mich., 1974-75, COL Press, Phoenix, 1978-80; publicity mgr. O'Sullivan Woodside & Col, Phoenix, 1980-81, gen. mgr., 1982-84; pub. relations/promotion cons. GPI Publs., Cupertino, Calif., 1985; pub. cons., 1985-88; project adminstr. FAA, 1986—; account coord. Bernard Hodes Advt., Tempe, Ariz., 1981; cons. freelance mktg., Phoenix, 1983. Vol., Fiesta Bowl Parade Com., Phoenix, 1983, FAA Airport Improvement Project. Office: 1200 Bayhill Dr Ste 224 San Bruno CA 94066-3006

KELLY, ANASTASIA DONOVAN, lawyer; b. Boston, Oct. 9, 1949; d. Charles A. and Louise V. Donovan; m. Thomas C. Kelly, Aug. 23, 1980; children: Michael, Brian. BA cum laude, Trinity Coll, 1971; JD magna cum laude, George Washington U., 1981. Bar: D.C. 1982, Tex. 1982. Analyst Air Line Pilots Assn., 1971-74; dir. employee benefits Martin Marietta Corp., Bethesda, Md., 1974-81; assoc. Carrington, Coleman, Sloman & Blumenthal, Dallas, 1981-85, Wilmer, Cutler & Pickering, Washington, 1985-90, ptnr., 1990-95; sr. v.p., gen. counsel, sec. Fannie Mae, Washington, 1995-99, Sears, Roebuck & Co., 1999—2003, exec. v.p., gen. counsel, 2003—. Bd. dirs. Owens-Ill., Toledo. Trustee Trinity Coll., Washington, 2003—; mem. adv. coun. Woodrow Wilson Ctr. for Internat. Scholars, 2001—; bd. dirs. Equal Justice Works, 1999—. Named one of Outstanding Young Women of Am., 1980; recipient Aiing High award Nat. Laegue Def. Fund, 2002, Myra Blackwell award Chgo. Women's Bar, 2002. Mem. Am. Bar Found., Am. Corp. Counsel Assn. (bd. dirs. 2001-), Order of Coif. Republican. Roman Catholic.

KELLY, ANGELA MARY, photographer, educator; b. Belfast, No. Ireland, Oct. 25, 1950; arrived in U.S., 1980; d. Patrick Joseph and Mary Frances (Somerville) K.; m. Bernard Joseph Hasken, Sept. 25, 1982; 1 child, Emma. Diploma in edn., Mary Ward Coll., Nottingham, Eng., 1972; diploma in photography, Trent Poly., Nottingham, 1975; MA, Columbia Coll., Chgo., 1989. Lectr. I Nelson (Eng.) & Colne Coll., 1975-78; lectr. II Manchester (Eng.) Met. U., 1978-80; vis. artist Sch. Art Inst. Chgo., 1980-94, assoc. prof., 1992-94; instr. Columbia Coll., Chgo., 1985-89; assoc. prof., coord. MFA program Rochester (N.Y.) Inst. Tech., 1994—99, assoc. prof., 1994—2003. Co-chair Randolph St. Gallery exhibns., Chgo., 1990-94; coord. women's caucus program Soc. Photographic Edn., 1993-94, MFA photo program Rochester Inst. Tech., 1995—; juror nat. grad. seminar NYU, 1995. Participant, exhibitor: Spaces for the Self: The Symbolic Imagery of Place, 1995, Visions of Hope and Despair, 1995; participant: (photo history book) A History of Women Photographers, 1995; curator, exhibn. organizer: (multi-media art exhibit) When Push Comes To Shove, 1993. Vol. photographer Rainbow House Shelter, Chgo., 1993-94. NEA Artists fellow, 1987, Ill. Arts Coun. Artists fellow, 1989; recipient Focus Infinity Fund commn., 1992. Fellow Inst. of Incorporated Photographers, Nat. Soc. Photographic Edn. (bd. dirs., mem. womens caucus conf. program coord. 1993). Avocations: garden design, walking, reading, cooking, bicycling. Office: Rochester Inst Tech 70 Lomb Memorial Dr Rochester NY 14623-5604

KELLY, BARBARA JEAN, physical education educator; b. Dover, Del., Sept. 24, 1933; d. Edward and Viola H. (Chase) K. BS, Bridgewater Coll., 1955; MA, U. Md., 1961; PhD, U. Del., 1972. Tchr., coach Caesar Rodney H.S., Camden, Del., 1955-60, Claymont (Del.) H.S., 1961-62; from asst. prof. to assoc. prof. U. Del., Newark, 1967-88, prof., 1988—. Vis. lectr. All China Sports Fedn., Beijing, Xian and Shanghai, 1992. Author: Issues in Physical Activity Studies, 1993; contbg. author: The 20th Century: Great Athletes, 1992, 94, Wellness A Way of Life, 1992. Recipient Pathfinder award Nat. Assn. for Girls and Women's Sports, 1994, Internat. Pathfinder award 2003; named to Athletics Hall of Fame, U. Del., 2002. Mem. AAHPERD, Internat. Assn. for Phys. Edn. and Sports for Girls and Women (U.S. rep. 1994-2002), Del. Nature Soc., Del. Hist. Soc., Phi Kappa Phi (honoree), Psi Delta Kappa (honoree). Avocations: exercise, gardening. Office: U Del Carpenter Sports Bldg Newark DE 19716

KELLY, BARBARA SUE, psychologist; b. Somers Point, N.J., June 24, 1958; d. Joseph Raymond and Catherine Agnes Kelly. BA, Muhlenberg Coll., 1980; MA, Marywood Coll., 1983; PhD, Walden U., 2001. Lic. psychologist, Pa. Cmty. social worker Ctr. for Human Devel., Millville, N.J., 1984-87; counselor I Cape Counseling Svcs., Cape May Courthouse, N.J., 1987-88; biofeedback therapist Guardian Group, Inc., Plymouth Meeting, Pa., 1992-97; v.p. Psychol. Wellness Assocs., Deptford, N.J., 1996—. Fellow Biofeedback Cert. Inst. Am.; mem. APA, Pa. Soc. Behavioral Medicine and Biofeedback. Avocations: cooking, gardening, music, reading. Office: Psychol Wellness Assocs LLC PO Box 5025 Deptford NJ 08096-0025

KELLY, CAROL A. travel company executive; married; 3 children. BS in Computer Sci. Engring., Mich. State U.; MBA, U. Chgo. CPA. With COVIA, United Airlines; v.p., CFO Apollo Travel Svcs., Rolling Meadows, Ill.; v.p., corp. svcs. Sabre Holdings, Southlake, Tex., 1998—99, sr. v.p., corp. svcs., 1999, sr. v.p., chief info. officer, 1999—. Recipient Best Marriage of IT and Bus. Processes award, Salomon Smith Barney, 2001. Office: Sabre Holdings 3150 Sabre Dr Southlake TX 76092

KELLY, CAROL WHITE, company executive; b. Shreveport, La., Dec. 23, 1946; d. Verlin Ralph and Mary Louise (Humphries) White; m. James Patrick Kelly, June 6, 1968; children: Mary Louise, Christopher John. BA, Centenary Coll. La., Shreveport, 1968. Corp. sec., treas. Kelly Law Firm P.C., Atlanta, 1986—. Mem. NAFE, Ga. Baptist Med. Guild (life), Atlanta Hist. Soc., Atlanta Ballet Guild (life), Internat. Platform Assn., High Mus. Art, Episcopal Ch. Women (sec.-treas. 1976-80), Mil. and Hospitaller Order St. Lazarus of Jerusalem (life), Chi Omega Alumnae Assn. (pres. 1979-80). Avocations: travel, pub. speaking, collecting teapots. Office: Kelly Law Firm PC 200 Galleria Pkwy SE Ste 1510 Atlanta GA 30339-5946

KELLY, CAROLYN SUE, newspaper executive; b. Pasco, Wash., Oct. 25, 1952; d. Jerald Davin and Margaret Helen (Nibler) K. BBA, Gonzaga U., 1974; MBA, Seattle U., 1985. CPA, Wash., 1976. Acct. Brajcich & Loeffler, Spokane, Wash., 1972-74; auditor Peat, Marwick, Mitchell & Co., Seattle, 1974-77; fin. analyst Seattle Times, 1977-81, asst. circulation mgr., 1981-83, spl. project advt. mgr., 1983—87, dir. mktg. and new bus., 1987—89, v.p., CFO, 1989—95, sr. v.p., CFO, 1995—97, sr. v.p., gen. mgr., 1997—2001, pres., COO, 2001—. Mem. Fin. Execs. Avocation: running. Office: Seattle Times PO Box 70 Seattle WA 98111-0070*

KELLY, CHRISTINA, editor; BA in english and history, Colgate U. Contbg. editor US; editor Sassy, 1988—94; dep. editor/founding editor Jane Mag., 1997—2000; exec. editor YM Mag., 2000—01, editor-in-chief, 2001—04. Publisher: freelance articles include Rolling Stone, Spin, Premiere, The Rolling Stone Book of Women in Rock. Mem.: ASME. Office: YM Mag 15 E 26th St New York NY 10010

KELLY, CLEO PARKER, retired bank executive; b. Moreland, Ala., Feb. 25, 1918; d. Lee Reynold and Mittie Revis; m. Albert Francis Parker, Nov. 4, 1933 (dec. Nov. 15, 1983); 1 child, Brenda Faye Floyd ; m. Emmett

Smith Kelly, Oct. 8, 1985. AS in Banking, Broward C.C., Ft. Lauderdale, Fla., 1980; BA in Psychology, U. Miami, Fla., 1964. Sec., clk. Morgan County Office Dep. Sheriff, Decatur, Ala.; dep. cir. ct. clk. Morgan County Cir. Ct. Clks. Office, Decatur; legal sec. Hare, Wynn & Newell, Birmingham, Nichols, Gaither, Green, Frater & Beckham, Miami; numerous secretarial positions First Nat. Bank Miami; various positions Barnett Bank (now Bank Am.), Hollywood and Miami, Fla., asst. v.p. Vol. Hospice Broward County, Ft. Lauderdale, 1988, Hollywood Hills Meth. Ch., Fla., tchr. Sunday sch. Named Woman of Yr., Hollywood Bus. and Profl. Womens Club, 1977. Democrat. Methodist. Avocations: golf, walking. Home: 3300 Golf St Hollywood FL 33021

KELLY, DIANA KAY, counselor, educator; b. Shaw AFB, S.C., July 31, 1958; d. Donald I. and Georgianna Kelly; life ptnr. Mary L. Baldwin. BA in Sociology, U. N.Mex, Albuquerque, 1979; MA in Rehab. Counseling, Calif. State U., San Bernardino, 1995. Cert. rehab. counselor Commn. Rehab. Counselor Certification, 1995. Prof. City Colls. Chgo., Brunssum, Netherlands, 1979—80; test examiner U.S. Army, Brunssum, Netherlands, 1980—81; supr. FEDCO, Ontario, Calif., 1982—88; asst. mgr./title asst. World Title Co., Colton, Calif., 1989—94; title asst. Stewart Title Co., Riverside, Calif., 1994—95; counselor/asst. prof. Bakersfield (Calif.) Coll., 1996—. Mem. adv. bd. WorkAbility III, Bakersfield Coll., 1996—; counselor coord. Calif. C.Cs., Disabled Student Programs and Svcs., Region V, Fresno, Calif., 2002—03. Advisor, student club Students for the Ethical Treatment of Humanity, Bakersfield Coll., Bakersfield, Calif., 2000—02; presenter Nat. Orgn. for the Mentally Ill (NAMI), Bakersfield, Calif., 2002—02, Kern County Mental Health In-Service, Bakersfield, Calif., 2002—02, Calif. Placement Assn. (CPA) ann. Conf., Fresno, Calif., 2003—03, Multiple Sclerosis Soc., Bakersfield, Calif., 2003—03, Calif. State Dept. of Rehab., Bakersfield, Calif., 1997—2002. Mem.: Calif. Assn. for Counseling and Devel. (assoc.), Calif. Assn. for Postsecondary Edn. and Disability (CAPED) (assoc.), Nat. Rehab. Assn. (assoc.), Nat. Rehab. Counseling Assn. (assoc.), Chi Sigma Iota (assoc.; v.p., student club 1994—95), Phi Kappa Phi (life). Avocations: reading, travel. Office: Bakersfield Coll Support Svcs 1801 Panorama Dr Bakersfield CA 93305

KELLY, SISTER DOROTHY ANN, Ursuline Provincial college chancellor; b. Bronx, NY, July 26, 1929; d. Walter David and Sarah (McCauley) K. BA in History, Coll. New Rochelle, 1951; MA in Am. Ch. History, Cath. U., Washington, 1958; PhD in Am. Intellectual History, U. Notre Dame, 1970; LittD (hon.), Mercy Coll., Dobbs Ferry, N.Y., 1976; LLD (hon.), Nazareth Coll. of Rochester, N.Y., 1979; DHL (hon.), Coll. St. Rose, 1981, Manhattan Coll., 1979, LeMoyne Coll., 1990, St. Thomas Aquinas Coll., 1990, St. Joseph Coll., Conn., 1996, Iona Coll., 1997. Joined Order of St. Ursula, Roman Cath. Ch., 1952. Assoc. prof. history Coll. New Rochelle, N.Y., 1957—, chmn. dept. history, 1965-67, acad. dean, 1967-72, acting pres., 1970-71, pres., 1972-97, chancellor, 1997—. Mem. Interreligious Coun. New Rochelle, 1974—, exec. com., 1974-79, v.p., 1980-84, pres., 1984-88, mem. Commn. Ind. Colls. and Univs. State of N.Y., 1976-78, chmn. bd. trustees, 1978-80, mem. govt. rels. com., 1980-81; chmn. Com. Higher Edn. Opportunity, 1976-78; mem. commr. of edn. Adv. Coun. on Higher Edn. for N.Y. State, 1975-77, subcom. on postsecondary occupational edn., 1975-77; exec. com. Empire State Found. Ind. Liberal Arts Colls., 1975—, vice chmn., 1977-81, chmn., 1981—; trustee, mem. exec. com. Assn. Colls. and Univs. State of N.Y., 1976-80; mem. com. on purpose and identity Assn. Cath. Colls. and Univs., 1975-80; mem. steering com. Neylan Conf., 1978-81, mem. bishops and pres. com., 1979-84; mem. adv. coun. on fin. aid to students Office Edn., HEW, 1978-86; chmn. Women's Coll. Coalition, 1981-83; chmn. govt. rels. adv. com. Nat. Assn. Ind. Colls. and Univs., 1981-82, chair, 1987-88. Chair City-wide Confs., New Rochelle, 1977-79; bd. dirs. United Way Westchester, 1977-84, mem. planning, allocations, evaluation com., 1977-80, nominating and campaign coms., 1990—; bd. dirs. Westchester County Assn., 1980-90, New Rochelle Community Action Program, 1982-83, New Rochelle Cmty. Fund, 1989-91; mem. steering com. Westchester County Women's Hall of Fame, 1984-85; bd. dirs. Vis. Nurse Svcs. in Westchester, Inc., 1983-86, chair nominating com., 1985-86; trustee LeMoyne Coll., 1982-88, vice chairperson, 1984-87; mem. bd. govs. New Rochelle Hosp. Med. Ctr., 1987—; trustee United Student Aid Funds, 1980-90, Ursuline Sch., New Rochelle, 1988—, Cath. U. Am., 1988—, Am. Coun. on Edn., 1990—, Ind. Coll. Fund Am., 1982-85; mem. ofcl. U.S. del. to UN 4th World Conf. on Women in Beijing, 1995; mem. nat. adv. bd. Nat. Mus. Women in the Arts, 1996—. Recipient Medallion award Westchester C.C., 1978, Leadership award Am. Soc. Pub. Adminstrn., 1986, Sch. Svc. award Thornton-Donovan Sch., 1977, Henry D. Paley award, 1994, Father Theodore M. Hesburgh award, 1998, N.Y. State Gov.'s award for excellence, 1997; inducted into Westchester County/Avon Women's Hall of Fame, 1989; Paul Harris fellow, 1997. Mem. AAUP, AAUW, NCCJ (trustee 1989—), Am. Hist. Assn., Nat. Fedn. Bus. and Profl. Women, Am. Assn. Higher Edn., Nat. Assembly Women Religious, Am. Coun. Edn. (bd. dirs. 1990), Assn. Am. Colls. (bd. dirs. 1983-86), Tchrs. Ins. and Annuity Assn. Am. (trustee 1987—, fin. com. 1987-88, exec. com. 1988—, audit com. 1990—, products and svcs. com. 1990-91, nominating and pers. com. 1991), Assn. Colls. Mid-Hudson Area (pres. 1979-81, exec. com. 1982—).

KELLY, DOROTHY HELEN, pediatrician, educator; b. Fitchburg, Mass., July 29, 1944; BS in Nursing magna cum laude, Fitchburg State Co., 1966; BS with distinction, Wayne State U., 1968, MD with distinction, 1972. Diplomate Am. Bd. Pediatrics, Pediatric Pulmonology. Intern Children's Svc. Mass. Gen. Hosp., Boston, 1972-73, resident in pediatrics, 1973-75, fellow in pediatrics pulmonary medicine, 1976-79, co-dir. pediat. pulmonary lab., 1976—83, assoc. dir. pediatric pulmonary unit, 1983—95; teaching fellow Harvard Med. Sch., Boston, 1973-75, clin. fellow, 1972-75, instr. in pediatrics, 1975-81, asst. prof. pediatrics, 1981-89, assoc. prof. pediatrics, 1989-95, U. Tex., Galveston, 1995-97, Houston, 1995—; assoc. dir. S.W. SIDS Rsch. Inst. Meml. Herman S.W. Hosp., Houston, 1995—. Cons. Bur. Community Health Svcs., NEW, 1979-80, FDA, 1986, 88-92, ECRI, 1987-88, also others; chmn. apnea adv. com. Nat. Sudden Infant Death Syndrome Found., 1979-81; mem. com. anesthesiology and respiratory devices panel Ctr. for Devices and Radiol. Health, FDA, 1990-94; chmn. physicians' com. Nat. Assn. Apnea Profls., 1990-91, also others; reviewer numerous jours. in field. Contbr. numerous articles to profl. jours. Recipient Woman of Vision award Nat. Soc. for Prevention of Blindness, Mass. Affiliate, 1981, First Disting. Alumni award Fitchburg State Coll., 1984, grants in field. Mem. Am. Med. Woman's Assn., Am. Acad. Pediatrics (task force on prolonged apnea 1978), Am. Thoracic Soc., Soc. Pediatric Rsch., Internat. Pediatric Soc., Assn. for Psychophysiol. Study Sleep, Soc. for Pediatric Rsch., Tex. Thoracic Soc., Tex. Med. Assn., Tex. Pediatric Soc., Am. Autonomic Soc. Office: SW SIDS Rsch Inst Meml Hermann SW Hosp Houston TX 77030 E-mail: dkellymd@sbcglobal.net.

KELLY, GLENDA MARIE, state legislator; b. San Diego, June 3, 1944; d. Glenn Adrian and Donna Louise (Embrey) Molsberry; m. Ronald Worth Campbell, June 3, 1962 (div. 1969); children: Gina Marie, Chad Loren; m. Dennis Patrick Kelly, Sept. 18, 1970. BS in Sociology cum laude, Mo. Western State Coll., 1989. Legal sec. Stanley S. Kalender, St. Joseph, Mo., 1960-88; dep. mayor City of St. Joseph, 1986-89, mayor, 1989-94; mem. Mo. Ho. Reps. 27th Dist., Mo., 1995—. Mem. Buchanan County Social Welfare Bd., 1979-85; mem. steering com. YWCA Women's Abuse Shelter, 1980; vice chair, chair budget com. Citizen's Adv. Commn., 1980-81; mem. task force Mo-Kan Regional Food Bank, 1981-83, City St. Joseph Fair Housing, 1984, Pony Express Region Tourist Info. Ctr., 1982, bd. dirs., 1983; bd. dirs. Pony Express Hist. Assn., 1983-84, Econ. Opportunity Corp., 1984-85, YWCA, 1985-86, Mo. Mcpl. League, 1990-94, St. Joseph Hist. Soc., 1979-80, sec., 1979-80; mem. St. Joseph City Coun., 1986, Governance Coun. Cmty. Based Health Care for Children, 1994—. Recipient Outstanding Community Vol. award United Way, Civic Recognition award City St. Joseph, Vol. award VFW Aux., 1980, Recognition award St. Joseph's br. NAACP, 1990, James C. Kirkpatrick Good Govt. award Northwest Mo. Press Assn., Historic Preservation award for Leadership in Historic Preservation Issues St. Joseph Landmark Commn., 1993; named Woman of Month by YWCA, 7/93, Outstanding Woman of Yr. YWCA, 1993. Mem. LWV (bd. dirs. St. Joseph area, co-chair local govt. com. 1978-79, chair budget com. 1979-80, 1st v.p. 1981, chair drug awareness com. 1981, pres. 1985-86), St. Joseph Area C. of C. (urban action com. 1985, econ. devel. coun. 1988—, bd. dirs. 1994—). Democrat. Roman Catholic. Avocations: reading, writing, fishing, drawing. Office: Mo Ho of Reps State Capitol Building Rm 312 Jefferson City MO 65101-1556

KELLY, HOLLY ANDREA, real estate developer; b. Cin., Dec. 1, 1963; d. Jesse and Barbara (Byers) Robinson; children: Gretchen R., Kimberly B. BA, Xavier U., Cin., 1994; MPA, No. Ky. U., 1997. Cert. econ. devel. fin. profl., 1997. Mgr. residential svcs. Metro Mgmt., Inc., Cin., 1994-96; devel. officer City of Cin., 1996—. Notary Pub., Ohio, 1995—. Mem. LWV, Am. Soc. Pub. Adminstrn. (bd. dirs.), Nat. Coun. Negro Women. Democrat. Baptist. Avocations: reading, photography. Office: City Cincinnati Dept Econ Devel 805 Central Ave Cincinnati OH 45202-1972

KELLY, JANET G. retail executive; b. 1953; BA, Morehead State U.; JD, U. Ky. Bar: Ky. 1978. V.p., sr. counsel The Limited, INc.; exec. v.p., gen. counsel Kmart, Troy, Mich., 2001—. Office: Kmart Corp 3100 W Big Beaver Rd Troy MI 48084-3163

KELLY, JANET LANGFORD, lawyer; b. Kansas City, Mo., Nov. 27, 1957; BA, Grinnell Coll., 1979; JD, Yale U., 1983. Bar: N.Y. 1985, Ill. 1989. Law clerk to Hon. James J. Hunter III U.S. Ct. Appeals (3rd cir.), 1983-84; ptnr. Sidley & Austin, Chgo., 1984-89; sr. v.p., sec., gen. counsel Sara Lee Corp., Chgo., 1995-99; exec. v.p. corp. devel., gen. counsel, sec. Kellogg Co., Battle Creek, Mich., 1999—. Sr. editor Yale Law Jour., 1983. Bd. dirs. Am. Arbitration Assn., Constl. Rights Found.; mem. adv. bd. Chgo. Vol. Legal Svcs. Found. Office: Kellogg Co PO Box 3599 1 Kellogg Sq Battle Creek MI 49016

KELLY, KAREN DELORIS, addiction counselor, administrator; b. Cleve., Oct. 6, 1951; d. Lawrence Childs and Doris R. (Minter) Wilder; 1 child, Kendrick Lamar Kelly. BS, Park Coll., 1984; MS, Ctrl. Mich. U., 1988; postgrad., Grad. Sch. of Am., 1997—. Cert. addictions counselor. Pres., CEO Circle of Recovery, Inc., Decatur, Ga., 1982—; clin. dir. DHR/Atlanta West, 1986-87; program dir. DHR/McIntosh Trail Outpatient Substance Abuse Svcs., Griffin, Ga., 1987-90; statewide coord. State Bd. Pardons and Paroles, Atlanta, 1990-92; clin. dir. Cameron & Assocs., Atlanta, 1992-95; dir. addiction tech. transfer Ctr. More House Sch. of Medicine-Psychiatry, 1995—. Aftercare coord., cons. The Bradford, Atlanta, 1987-91; cons. More House Sch. of Medicine, 1990-95, Dept. Ga. of Corrections, Atlanta, 1990—; faculty U. of Ga., Athens, 1990—. Contbr. articles to profl. jours. Bd. dirs. Morris Brown Criminal Justice Coun., Atlanta, Changed Living, 1994; mem. Ray of Hope Christian Ch., Decatur, 1987—. Mem. Delta Sigma Theta. Avocations: outdoor activities, reading sports, theatre, travel. Home: 6064 Valley Green Rd Lithonia GA 30058-3169 Office: Morehouse Sch Medicine ATTC 720 Westview Dr SW Atlanta GA 30310-1458

KELLY, KATHERINE THERESA, psychologist, consultant; b. Englewood, Colo., Dec. 6, 1969; d. Edward James and Joyce Marie Kelly. PhD in Counseling Psychology, Ind. State U., Terre Haute, 1999; M in Pub. Health, U. Mo., 2000. Acad. fellow in family medicine dept. family medicine U of Mo., Columbia, 1999—2000; dir. behavioral sci. dept. family medicine Wake Forest U., Winston-Salem, NC, 2000—. Cons., Winston-Salem, NC, 2003—. Contbr. articles to profl. jours. Mem.: Assn. for Behavioral Sci. in Med. Edn. (assoc.), APA (assoc.), Soc. for Tchrs. of Family Medicine (assoc.). Independent. Office: Wake Forest Univ Sch of Medicine Dept Family Medicine Mec Ctr Blvd Winston-Salem NC 27157 E-mail: ktkelly@wfubmc.edu.

KELLY, KATHLEEN DENNIS, international government affairs consultant; b. Ann Arbor, Mich., Aug. 20, 1952; d. Edward Wimberly and Beatrice Forrest Dennis; children: Charlotte, John. BA in Polit. Sci., U. Tex., 1974. Pres. Interisk, Inc., Houston, 1981-85; cons. Russell Reynolds & Assoc., Houston, 1985-88; exec. dir., pres. Houston Internat. Protocol Alliance, Houston, 1988-94; pres. Internat. Protocol Advisors, Houston, 1994; hon. consul New Zealand, 1995—. Chair Houston Com. Fgn. Rels., 1997, mem. exec. com., 1997—. Author booklet: Consular Ball, 1993. Bd. dirs. Houston World Affairs Coun., 1996—, Bolivian Charity Found., Houston, 1997—; bd. dirs. world trade divsn. Greater Houston Partnership; mem. internat. rev. bd. Park Plz. Hosp., Houston, 1993-95; mem. exec. com. Consular Corps of Houston. Recipient Cert. of Appreciation, U.S. Dept. State, 1992, U.S. Secret Svc., 1992, Cert. Merit, Bolivian Govt., 1994. Mem. Bus. Coun. for Internat. Understanding. Republican. Presbyterian. E-mail: KathleenKell@sbcglobal.net.

KELLY, KATHLEEN S(UE), communications educator; b. Duluth, Minn., Aug. 6, 1943; d. Russell J. and Idun N. Mehrman; m. George F. Kelly, Apr. 29, 1961; children: Jodie A., Jennifer L. AA, Moorpark (Calif.) Coll., 1971; BS in Journalism, U. Md., College Park, 1973, MA in Pub. Rels., 1979, PhD in Pub. Communication, 1989. Accredited pub. rels.; cert. fundraising exec. Dir. pub. info. Bowie (Md.) State U., 1974-77; asst. to dean, instr. Coll. Journalism U. Md., College Park, 1977-79, assoc. dir. devel., 1979-82; v.p. Mt. Vernon Coll., Washington, 1982-83; dir. devel. U. Md., College Park, 1983-85, assoc. dean, lectr. Coll. Journalism, 1985-88, asst. dean Coll. Bus. and Mgmt., 1988-90; prof. U. La., Lafayette, 1991—2003; prof., chair dept. pub. rels. U. Fla., Gainesville, 2003—. Cons. NASA, NIH, Mt. St. Marys Coll., 1986—; lectr. CASE, Pub. Rels. Soc. Am., 1987—. Author: Fund Raising and Public Relations: A Critical Analysis, 1991, Building Fund-Raising Theory, 1994, Effective Fund-Raising Management, 1998. Named PRIDE Book award winner Speech Comm. Assn., 1991, article award winner 1994, John Grenzebach award winner for rsch. on philanthropy CASE and Am. Assn. Fund-Raising Coun., 1991, 98, PRIG award winner for outstanding dissertation Internat. Comm. Assn., 1990, winner 1995 Pathfinder award Inst. for Pub. Rels. Rsch. and Edn., Staley/Robeson/Ryan/St. Lawarence prize for rsch. on fund raising and philanthropy Nat. Soc. Fundraising Execs., 1998, Jackson, Jackson & Wagner Behavioral Sci. prize, Pub. Relations Soc. Am. Found., 1999. Fellow Pub. Rels. Soc. Am. (chmn. ednl. and cultural orgn. sect. 1989, pres. Md. chpt. 1986-87, Pres.' Cup 1981, nat. bd. dirs. 1994-96, Jackson Jackson and Wagner Behavioral Sci. prize 1999); mem. Nat. Soc. Fund Raising Execs. (mem. rsch. coun.), Coun. Advancement and Support of Edn. (women's forum 1983), Phi Kappa Phi. Democrat. Avocations: travel, reading. Home: 1922 NW 4th Ave Gainesville FL 32603 Office: U Fla Dept Pub Rels PO Box 118400 Gainesville FL 32611-8400

KELLY, KAY, social worker, administrator; B of Social Welfare, M of Social Welfare, U. Kans.; postgrad., Karl Menninger Sch. Psychiatry. Dir. social work Menninger, Topeka. Contbr. articles to profl. jours. Address: Menningers PO Box 809045 Houston TX 77280

KELLY, LEONTINE T. C. clergywoman; b. Washington; d. David D. and Ila M. Turpeau; m. Gloster Current (div.); children: Angella, Gloster Jr., John David; m. James David Kelly (dec.); 1 child, Pamela (adopted). Student W.Va. State Coll.; grad. Va. Union U., 1960; MDiv, Union Theol. Sem., Richmond, Va., 1976. Formerly sch. tchr.; former pastor Galilee United Meth. Ch., Edwardsville, Va.; later mem. staff Va. Conf. Council on Ministries; pastor Asbury United Meth. Ch., Richmond, 1976-83; mem. nat. staff United Meth. Ch., Nashville, 1983-84; bishop Calif.-Nev. Conf., San Francisco, 1984-88. Adj. prof. Pacific Sch. Religion, Berkeley, Calif., 1992—. Office: 316 N El Camino Real Apt 112 San Mateo CA 94401-2529

KELLY, LINDA L. prosecutor; Atty. U.S. Dept. Justice, Pitts., 1993-99, asst. U.S. atty., 1999—. Office: US Attys Office US Post Office & Courthouse 7th Ave & Grant Street Rm 633 Pittsburgh PA 15219

KELLY, LUCIE STIRM YOUNG, nursing educator; b. Stuttgart, Germany, May 2, 1925; came to U.S., 1929; d. Hugo Karl and Emilie Rosa (Engel) Stirm; m. J. Austin Young, Aug. 30, 1946 (div. Feb. 1971); m. Thomas Martin Kelly, 1972 (dec. Aug. 2003); 1 child by previous marriage, Gay Aleta (Mrs. Donald Meyer). BS, U. Pitts., 1947, MLitt, 1957, PhD, 1965; D in Nursing Edn. (hon.), U. RI, 1977; LHD (hon.), Georgetown U., 1983; DSc (hon.), Widener U., 1984; D of Pub. Svc. (hon.), Am. U., 1985; DSc (hon.), U. Mass., 1989; DHL (hon.), SUNY, 1996. Instr. nursing McKeesport (Pa.) Hosp., 1953-57, asst. adminstr. nursing, 1966-69; asst. prof. nursing U. Pitts., 1957-64, asst. dean, 1965; prof., chmn. nursing dept. Calif. State U., LA, 1969-72; co-project dir. curriculum rsch. Nat. League for Nursing, 1973-74; project dir. patient edn., office consumer health edn., also adj. assoc. prof. cmty. medicine Coll. Medicine and Dentistry N.J.-Rutgers Med. Sch., 1974-75; prof. pub. health and nursing Sch. Pub. Health and Sch. Nursing Columbia U., N.Y.C., 1975-90, prof. emeritus Sch Pub. Health, Sch. Nursing, 1990—, assoc. dean acad. affairs Sch. Pub. Health, 1988-90, hon. prof. nursing edn. Tchrs. Coll., 1977-93, acting head divsn. health adminstrn. Sch. Pub. Health, 1980-81, 86-88; on leave as exec. dir. Mid-Atlantic Regional Nursing Assn., 1981-82. Cons. U. Nev., Las Vegas, 1970-72, Ball State U., Ind., 1971, Long Beach (Calif.) Naval Hosp., 1971-72, Travis AFB, Calif., 1972, Brentwood VA Hosp., LA, 1971-72, Ctrl. Nursing Office VA, Washington, 1971-94, N.J. Dept. Higher Edn., 1974-78, John Wiley Pub., 1974-76, Sch. Nursing Am. U. Beirut; mem. spl. med. adv. group VA Dept. Medicine and Surgery, Washington, 1980-84, cons. nursing com. AMA, 1971-74, Citizen's Com. for Children, N.Y.C.; v.p. Pa. Health Coun., 1968-69; mem. adv. com. physicians assts. Calif. Bd. Med. Examiners, adv. com. Cancer Soc. L.A., 1970-72, com. nursing VA, Washington, 1971-74, chair 1975-90, regional med. programs, Pa., 1967-69, Calif. 1970-72; mem. spl. adv. com. on med. licensure and profl. conduct N.Y. State Assembly, 1977-79, mem. nat. adv. com. Encore (nat. YWCA post-mastectomy group rehab. project), 1977-83; assoc. mem. N.Y. Acad. Medicine, 1988-90; mem. ethics com. Palisades Med. Ctr., 1993—, bd. govs., 1995—, mem. profl. and quality rev. com., 1995—, chair, 1998—, exec. com., 1998-99; 2d vice chair N.Y. Presbyn. Healthcare Sys., Palisades Med. Ctr., 1999-2003, 1st vice chair 2003-; lectr., cons., guest Beijing Med. Coll., China, 1982, Aga Khan U., Pakistan, 1990; bd. visitors U. Pitts. Sch. Nursing, 1986-93; mem. editl. adv. bd. Am. Jour. Pub. Health, 1992, chair, 1993-97; nat. and internat. lectr. in field; chair adv. com. grad. program in pub. health U. Medicine and Dentistry of N.J., 1995-2000. Author: (textbooks) Dimensions of Profl. Nursing, 8th edit., 1999, The Nursing Experience: Trends, Challenges, Transitions, 4th edit., 2001; contbg. editor: (jour.) Jour. Nursing Adminstrn., 1975—82; columnist: jour. Nursing Outlook, editor-in-chief, 1982—91; mem. bd. advisors (jour.) Nurses Almanac, 1978, Nurse Manager's Handbook, 1979, Nursing Administration Handbook, 1992; editor (editl. bd.): (jour.) Am. Health, 1981—91; editl. bd. (jour.) Nursing and Health Care, 1991—95, Internat. Nursing Index, 1997—2001. Bd. dirs. ARC, LA, 1971-72; bd. dirs. Vis. Nurse Svc. N.Y., 1980-2001, mem. exec. com., chmn. human resources, 1989-2001; bd. dirs. Concern for Dying, 1983-89; trustee Calif. State Coll. LA Found., 1971-72, U. Pitts., 1984-90, mem. exec. com. 1988-90; chair bd. visitors U. Pitts. Sch. Pub. Health, 1988-90; bd. visitors U. Miami Sch. Nursing, 1986—; mem. health svcs. com. Children's Aid Soc., N.Y., 1978-84; v.p. Am. Nurses Found., 1980-82; mem. nat. adv. coun. on nurse tng. HRA, 1981-85; mem. nurses leadership coun. Chlorine Chemistry Coun., 1999-2003; hon. bd. dirs. NOVA Found., 1998—, Health Professions Panel, Am. Legacy Found., 2000—. Named Outstanding Alumna U. Pitts. Sch. Nursing, 1966, Pa. Nurse of Yr., 1967, Roll of Honor N.J. State Nurses Assn., 1990; named to Tchrs. Coll. Columbia U. Nursing Edn. Alumni Hall of Fame, 1999; recipient Disting. Alumna award U. Pitts. Sch. Edn., 1981, Shaw medal Boston Coll., 1985, Bicentennial Medallion of Distinction, U. Pitts., 1987, R. Louise McManus Medallion for Disting. Svc. to Nursing, Tchrs. Coll. Columbia U., 1987, Dean's Disting. Svc. award Columbia Sch. Pub. Health, 1995, Second Century award in health care, Columbia U. Sch. Nursing, 1996; fellow HEW, 1965. Fellow Am. Acad. Nursing (named Living Legend 2001); mem. ANA (dir. 1978-82, Hon. Recognition award 1992), APHA (Ruth Freeman Pub. Health Nursing award 1993), Pa. Nurses Assn. (pres. 1966-69), Nat. League Nursing (bd. govs. 1991-95), Nurses Ednl. Funds Bd., U . Pitts. Sch. Nursing Alumni (pres. 1959), Vis. Nurse Assn. Ctrl. Jersey (bd. dirs. 1999-2001, mem. bd. trustees), Am. Hosp. Assn. (com. chmn. 1967-68), Assn. Grad. Faculty Cmty. Health/Pub. Health Nursing (v.p. 1980-81), Sigma Theta Tau (sr. editor Image 1978-81, pres.-elect 1981-83, pres. 1983-85, nat. campaign chair Ctr. for Nursing Scholarship 1987-89, chair devel. com. 1989-95, spl. advisor 1995-97, planned giving task force 1998-2001, Mentor award 1985, 93, 97, Spirit of Philanthropy award 1997), Pi Lambda Theta, Alpha Tau Delta (Cert. of Merit 1968). Achievements include collection of papers in Mugar Library, Boston U. Home: 6040 Boulevard E Apt 11G West New York NJ 07093-3827

KELLY, MARILYN, state supreme court justice; b. Apr. 15, 1938; m. Donald Newman. BA, Ea. Mich. U., 1960, JD (hon.); postgrad., U. Paris.; MA, Middlebury Coll., 1961; JD with honors, Wayne State U., 1971. Assoc. Dykema, Gossett, Spencer, Goodnow & Trigg, Detroit, 1973-78; ptnr. Dudley, Patterson, Maxwell, Smith & Kelly, Bloomfield Hills, Mich., 1978-80; owner Marilyn Kelly & Assocs., Bloomfield Hills, Birmingham, Mich., 1980-88; judge Mich. Ct. of Appeals, 1989-96; justice Mich. Supreme Ct., 1997—. Tchr. lang., lit. Grosse Pointe Pub. Schs., Albion Coll., Ea. Mich. U.; past mem. rep. assembly, comms. com., family law coun. Mich. State Bar, now co-chair Open Justice Commn. Active Mich. Dem. Party, 1963—. Recipient Disting Alumni award Ea. Mich. U., Disting. Svc. award Mich. Edn. Assn. Mem. Soc. Irish-Am. Lawyers, Women Lawyers Assn. (past pres.), Oakland County Bar Assn. (past chair family law com.) Office: Mich Supreme Ct PO Box 30052 Lansing MI 48909

KELLY, SISTER MARY ELIZABETH, principal; b. N.Y.C., Nov. 13, 1934; d. Patrick Joseph Kelly and ELizabeth Christine Dinan. B, St. Joseph's Coll., 1966; postgrad., Fordham U., 1967, postgrad., 1971, SUNY, Plattsburgh, 1975. Tchr. 1st grade Cath. Schs. Diocese Bklyn., 1954—66; tchr. jr. high sch. Immaculate Heart Mary, 1966—70, prin. elem. sch., 1970—81; tchr. English Bishop Kearney High Sch, 1981—84; prin. elem. sch. St. Rose Lima Sch., 1984—. Mem. Mid. States Elem. Sch. Adv. Bd.; mem. diocesian assessment com. Cath. Schs. Diocese, 1998—2003, mem. elem. prin. adv. com., 1998—. Mem. sch. bd. Immaculate Heart Sch., 1970—81, St. Rose Lima Sch., 1984—. Recipient Thomas Cuite award, Ancient Order Hibernian. Roman Catholic.

KELLY, MAURA ANNE, reporter; b. Bridgeport, Conn., Apr. 2, 1971; d. Richard Francis and Margaret Mary Kelly. BA, Boston Coll., 1993; MS in Journalism, Northwestern U., 1994. Intern The Patriot Ledger, Quincy, Mass., 1993; corr. Conn. Post, Bridgeport, 1993; reporter Naugatuck bur. Waterbury (Conn.) Rep.-Am., 1994—95, edn. reporter, 1995, city hall reporter, 1995—96, state capitol reporter, 1996-99; reporter Chgo. Tribune, 2000—01, Associated Press, 2001—. Mem. reporters' roundtable discussion Conn. Jour. on Conn. Pub. TV, Hartford, 1998-99 and WFSB's CT '97, CT '98, Ct '99 in Hartford. Co-recipient Explanatory Reporting-Team Coverage, Pulitzer Prize, 2001. Mem. Soc. Profl. Journalists (Reporting awards Conn. chpt. 1998, 99, 2000), Investigative Reporters and Editors, Boston Coll. Alumni Assn., Northwestern U. Alumni Club Conn. Roman

Catholic. Avocations: photography, travel, skiing, tennis, swimming. Home: 2464 N Geneva Terr Apt 2D Chicago IL 60614 Office: Associated Press Ste 2500 10 S Wacker Dr Chicago IL 60606 E-mail: makelly42@hotmail.com.

KELLY, MAXINE ANN, retired property developer; b. Ft. Wayne, Ind., [illegible] 1931; d. [illegible] and Marguerite E. [illegible]; m. James Herbert Kelly, Oct. 4, 1968 (dec. Apr. 1974). BA, Northwestern U., 1956. Sec. Parry & Barns Law Offices, Ft. Wayne, 1951—52, Lincoln Nat. Bank and Trust Co., 1956—58; sr. clk. stenographer divsn. Mental Health Alaska Dept. Health, Anchorage, 1958—60; office mgr. Langdon Psychiat. Clinic, 1960—70; propr. A-1 Bookkeeping Svc., 1974—75; ptnr. Gonder-Kelly Enterprises and A-is-A Constrn., Wasilla, Alaska, 1965—92; sales assoc. Yukon Realty/Gallery of Homes, Wasilla, 1989; sec. Rogers Realty, Inc., Wasilla, 1989, MMC Constrn., Inc., 1992—96. Pres., treas. Libertarian Party, Anchorage, 1968—69, Alaska Libertarian Party, 1969—70; dir. Alaska Mental Health Assn., Anchorage, 1960—61. Mem.: AAUW (life), Whittier Boat Owners Assn. (treas. 1980—84), Anchorage C. of C. Home: 8653 Augusta Cir Anchorage AK 99504-4202

KELLY, MOIRA, actress; b. Queens, NY, Mar. 6, 1968; Student, Marymount Coll. Appeared in films The Boy Who Cried Bitch, 1991, Billy Bathgate, 1991, The Cutting Edge, 1992, Mr. Saturday Night, 1992, Chaplin, 1992, Twin Peaks: Fire Walk With Me, 1992, With Honors, 1994, Little Odessa, 1994, The Tie That Binds, 1995, (voice) The Lion King, 1994, Unhook the Stars, 1996, Entertaining Angels: The Dorothy Day Story, 1996, Changing Habits, 1997, Drive, She Said, 1997, Love Walked In, 1998, Dangerous Beauty, 1998, Hi-Life, 1998, Henry Hill, 1999, The Safety of Objects, 2001, (voice) The Lion King 1 1/2, 2004; TV movies include Monday After the Miracle, 1998; television appearances include (movies) Love Lies and Murder, 1991, Daybreak, 1993, To Have and To Hold, 1998, (series) The West Wing, 1999-2000. Office: care Gersh Agy 232 N Canon Dr Beverly Hills CA 90210-5302*

KELLY, NANCY FOLDEN, arts administrator; b. Fredericksburg, Va., Oct. 28, 1951; d. Virgil Alvis Jr. and Frances Virginia (DeShazo) Folden; m. Frank R. Kelly, Aug. 11, 1973; 1 child, Katherine Elizabeth Kelly. BA in Theatre Arts, Va. Poly. Inst. and State U., 1973; MFA in Theatre Directing, So. Meth. U., 1975. Coord. student programs Lincoln Ctr. Inst., N.Y.C., 1976-79; dir. N.Y.C. Opera Nat. Co. and edn. dept. Lincoln Ctr., 1979-93, mem. coun. on ednl. programs, 1979-93; mng. dir. Broadway Arts Theatre for Young Audiences, N.Y.C., 1994-96; dir. family and cmty. programs Ctrl. Park Conservancy, N.Y.C., 1996-98; fin. mgr., assoc. dir. devel. Film Soc. Lincoln Ctr., N.Y.C., 1999—. E-mail: nkelly@filmlinc.com.

KELLY, PAMELA B. lawyer; BA, U. Va., 1981; JD, UCLA, 1986. Bar: Calif. 1986. With Latham & Watkins, L.A., 1986—, ptnr., 1994—. Mem.: ABA (bus. law sect.), L.A. County Bar Assn., Calif. Bar Assn. Office: Latham & Watkins LLP 633 W Fifth St Ste 4000 Los Angeles CA 90071*

KELLY, PATRICIA ELLEN, information technology manager; b. Massena, N.Y., Apr. 16, 1958; d. John James and Edith Ellen (Veitch) Kelly. BS, SUNY, 1979; MS, Western Ill. U., 1980; BS, SUNY, 1986. Dir. athletic programs D'Youville Coll., Buffalo, 1981-83; project mgr. Buffalo & Eric County Pub. Libr., 1983-84; computer operator IBM, Kingston, 1986-87; computer ops. supervisor GTech Corp., Saugerties, N.Y., 1987-88; from computer programmer to adv. fin. analyst IBM, Poughkeepsie, NY, 1988—, fin. mgr., program mgr. developer rels. Recreation leader Mohonk Mountain Ho., New Paltz, NY, 1984—94; athletic adv. coun. SUNY, Cortland, 1975—76. Mem. registration com. Crop Walkathon for Hunger, New Paltz, 1994; mem. kids activities com. Taste of New Paltz, 1994; grounds team leader Christmas in Apr. project, Poughkeepsie, 1995; bd. dirs. Massena (N.Y.) Girls Softball League, 1974—76; site selection chair Ulster County Habitat for Humanity, Kingston, 1993—95; v.p. Ulster County Women's Golf Assn., 1999—2001. Mem.: YMCA, NOW, NAFE, Cortland State Athletic Club. Democrat. Roman Catholic. Avocations: golf, hiking, reading, dogs. Home: 748 Springtown Rd Tillson NY 12486-1100 E-mail: pekelly@hvc.rr.com.

KELLY, RITA MAE, academic administrator, researcher; b. Waseca, Minn., Dec. 10, 1939; d. John Francis and Agnes Mary (Lorentz) Cawley; m. Vincent Peter Kelly, June 2, 1962; children: Patrick, Kathleen. BA, U. Minn., 1961; MA, Ind. U., 1964, PhD, 1967; doctorate (hon.), U. Umeå, Sweden, 1998. Rsch. scientist Ctr. for Rsch. in Social Systems, 1968-70; sr. rsch. scientist Am. Inst. for Rsch., Inc., Kensington, Md., 1970-72; cons. OEO, 1972-73; pres. Rita Mae Kelly & Assocs., 1973-75; tenured prof. Rutgers U., 1977-79, prof., 1979-82; from tenured to full prof. Sch. Justice Studies Ariz. State U., Tempe, 1982-87, tenured prof. justice studies, pub. affairs, polit. sci. and women's study, 1987-96, chair, dir. Sch. Justice Studies, 1990-95; dean social scis. U. Tex., Dallas, 1996—. Mem. credentials com. U.S. Dem. Party, Atlanta, 1988; mem. state com. Ariz. Dem. party, Phoenix, 1988; dist. committeeman Tempe Dist. 27 Dem. Party, 1988; charter mem., hon. bd. dirs. Ariz. Women's Inst., 1988; founding mem. Inst. for Women's Policy Rsch., Washington, 1988, Ariz. Found. for Women, Inc., 1995—; bd. dirs. Ariz. Leadership 2000 Alumni Assn., 1993—; co-dir. Ariz. Leadership 2000 and Beyond, 1993—; co-chair Arizonians for a Healthy Future, 1994-95. Author: (with others) The Making of Political Women: A Study of Socialization and Role Conflict, 1978, Promoting Productivity in the Public Sector: Problems, Strategies, Prospects, 1988, Comparable Worth, Pay Equity, and Public Policy, 1988, (with Mary M. Hale) Gender, Bureaucracy, and Democracy: Careers and Equal Opportunity in the Public Sector, 1989, The Gendered Economy, 1991, Advances in Policy Studies Since 1950, 1992, Gender Power, Leadership and Governance, 1995, Gender, Globalization and Democratization, 2000; editor book series Women in Politics Series, 1981-88; editor: (with Dennis J. Palumbo) Sage Series in Public Policy, 1989-94; co-editor: Gender, Globalization and Democratization, 2001; editor Women & Politics Jour. Dep. gov. Am. Biog. Inst., 1995—; co-chair Airz. Women's Vote Project, 1996—; coord. scientific rsch. com. engendering globalization democratization internat. Social Sci. Coun., 1998—. Internat. Soroptimists of Phoenix, Inc. grantee, 1987, GTE Found. Rsch. grantee, 1988, Ind. U. Rsch. grantee, 1964-65; Ford Found. fellow, 1962-63; recipient Rutgers U. Outstanding Faculty merit award, 1979, All-Am. Women's award, 1985, YWCA Camden County award, 1980; Fulbright award to Brazil, 1991; recipient Aaron Wildovsky award for best book pub. policy, 1992, 93, Outstanding Mentor award Women's Caucus for Polit. Sci., 1991, 97, Miriam Mills award, 1995; U.S. Dept. Labor Step Out grantee, 1993-95. Mem. Am. Polit. Sci. Assn. (chair roundtable 1985, chair B. William Anderson award com. 1983-84, reviewer 1977-78, 83-84, head policy sect. 1989), APA Soc. for Psychol. Study of Social Issues (chair nat. task force on productivity in the pub. sector 1975-80), Am. Soc. for Pub. Adminstrn. (exec. coun. sect. on mgmt. sci. and policy analysis 1986-89, vice chair planning and evaluation com. 1985-86, Achievement award 1981, Disting. Rsch. award for rsch. on women 1991), Internat. Polit. Sci. Assn. (chair com. on status of women 1986-88), Western Polit. Sci. Assn. (pres. 1988-89), Policy Studies Orgn. (pres. 1988-89, Merriam Mills award 1995, Thomas R. Dye Svc. award 1997). Office: U Tex PO Box 830688 Richardson TX 75083-0688

KELLY, ROBIN L. state representative; b. New York, NY, Apr. 30, 1956; children: Kelly, Ryan. BA, Bradley Univ., 1977, MA, 1982; PhD (pending), No. Ill., 2002. State Rep. House of Rep., Dist. 38, 2002—; dir. Crisis Nursery, 1984—87; assoc. dir. The Youth Shelters, 1987—90; svc. Bradley Univ., 1990—92; dir. Multicultural Student; dir. of comm. affairs Village of Matteson, 1992—. Commr. Cook County Commn. on Human Rights, 1998—; bd. mem. Rich Twp. Food Pantry Bd., 1995—, Ill. Theatre Ctr., 1993—, Bradley Univ. Coun., 1998—. Democrat. Office: Capitol 252-W Stratton Office Bldg Springfield IL 62706 also: District 3649 West 183rd St, Suite 110 Hazel Crest IL 60429

KELLY, RUTH, state agency administrator; b. Mt. Vernon, N.Y. d. John Edwin and Ruth Elizabeth (Brady) Dowling; m. Paul Joseph Kelly Jr., June 27, 1964; children: Johanna, Paul Edwin, Thomas Martin, Christopher Mark, Heather Marie. BA, Seton Hall Coll., 1962; MA, Duke U., 1964. Assoc. tech. staff Bell Labs, N.Y., 1964-67; office mgr. Santa Fe Mountain Co., N.M., 1989-91, A.G. Edwards & Sons, Santa Fe, N.M., 1992-94; dir. Bds. and Commns. Office Gov., Santa Fe, 1995—. Chmn. Roswell Pub. Libr., N.M., 1975-76. Mem. bd. of Zia, Girl Scout Coun., Artesia, N.M., 1980; treas. Republican Party Santa Fe Co., 1993-94. Recipient Trustee of Yr. award, N.M. Libr. Assn., 1977. Mem. Federated Republican Women of Santa Fe. Avocations: reading, aerobics, golf, skiing, pub. affairs. Office: Office of Gov State Capitol Bldg 400 Santa Fe NM 87503-0001

KELLY, SUE W. congresswoman; b. Lima, Ohio, Sept. 26, 1936; m. Edward; 4 children. BA, Denison U., 1958; MA in Health Advocacy, Sarah Lawrence Coll., 1985. Rschr. New England Inst. Med. Rsch., 1958; tchr. John Jay Jr. H.S., 1962-63, Harvey Sch.; real estate rehabilitator, 1963—; campaign coord. Rep. Hamilton Fish, N.Y., 1971-72; intern Ruth Taylor Home, 1973-74; florist, owner Somerstown Flower Shop, 1978-79; patient advocate St. Luke's Hosp., 1984-87; adj. prof. of health advocacy Sarah Lawrence Coll., 1987-92; mem. 105th to 108th Congress from 19th N.Y. dist. U.S. Ho. of Reps., 1995—. Vice chmn. com. fin. svcs. U.S. Ho. Reps., mem. com. transp. and infrastructure, mem. com. small bus., mem. various subcoms. Republican. Home: 2025 Crompond Rd Yorktown Heights NY 10598 Office: US House Reps 1127 Longworth Bldg Washington DC 20515-3219

KELM, BONNIE G. art museum director, educator; b. Bklyn., Mar. 29, 1947; d. Julius and Anita (Baron) Steiman; m. William G. Malis; 1 child, Michael Darren. BS in Art Edn., Buffalo State U., 1968; MA in Art History, Bowling Green (Ohio) State U., 1975; PhD in Arts Adminstrn., Ohio State U., 1987. Art tchr. Toledo Pub. Schs., 1968—71; ednl. cons. Columbus (Ohio) Mus. Art, 1976—81; prof. art Franklin U., Columbus, 1976—88; legis. coord. Ohio Ho. of Reps., Columbus, 1977; pres. bd. trustees Columbus Inst. for Contemporary Art, 1977—81; tech. asst. cons. Ohio Arts Coun., Columbus, 1984—88; dir. Bunte Gallery Franklin U., Columbus, 1978—88; dir. art mus. Miami U., Oxford, Ohio, 1988—96, assoc. prof., 1988—96; dir. Muscarelle Mus. of Art Coll. William and Mary, Williamsburg, Va., 1996—2002, assoc. prof. art and art history, 1996—2002; dir. Univ. Art Mus. U. Calif., Santa Barbara, 2002—. Adj. prof. dept. art history U. Art Mus. U. Calif., Santa Barbara; grant panelist Ohio Arts Coun., Columbus, 1985-87, 91-95; art book reviewer William C. Brown Pub., Madison, Wis., 1985-92; mem. acquisitions adv. bd. Martin Luther King Ctr., Columbus, 1987-88; field reviewer Inst. Mus. Svcs., Washington, 1990—; chairperson grant panel Art in Pub. Places, 1992-95; trustee Ohio Mus. Assn., 1993-96; state apptd. mem. adv. com. Ohio Percent for Art, 1994-96; bd. dirs. U.S. Nat. Com. Internat. Coun. Museums, 1998—; bd. dirs., southeast rep. Assn. Univ. & Coll. Mus. Galleries, 1998—. Author, editor (mus. catalogues) Connections, 1985, Into the Mainstream: Contemporary Folk Art, 1991, Testimony of Images: PreColumbian Art, 1992, Collecting by Design: The Allen Collection, 1994, Photographs by Barbara Hershey: A Retrospective, 1995, Georgia O'Keeffe in Williamsburg, 2001; contbr. chpt. to book Modernism Gender & Culture, 1997, articles to profl. jours. Founding mem., mem. adv. coun. Columbus Cultural Arts Ctr., 1977-81; coord., curator Cultural Exch. Program, Honolulu-Columbus, 1980; mem. acad. women achievers YWCA, 1991—; guest spkr. 1991 Scholastic Arts Award, Cin., 1991; keynote spkr. Ohio Mus. Assn., ann. meeting, 1992; spkr. Internat. Coun. Mus. Triennial Conf., Quebec City, 1992, Internat. Coun. Mus. Triennial Congress, Barcelona, Spain, 2001, session chair; session chair Midwest Mus. Assn. ann. meeting, St. Louis, 1993; session chair Am. Assn. Mus. ann. meeting, Balt., 2000; presenter East-West Ctr. Internat. Conf., Honolulu, 2000. Recipient Marantz Disting. Scholar award Ohio State U., 1995, Gelpe award YWCA, 1987, Cultural Advancement of City of Columbus award, The Columbus Dispatch, 1984, Disting. Svc. award, Columbus Art League, 1984, Critic's Choice award Found. for Cmty. of Artists, N.Y., 1981; Fulbright scholar USIA, 1988 (The Netherlands); NEH fellow East-West Ctr., Honolulu, 1991. Mem. Am. Assn. Mus. (advocacy task force, surveyor mus. assessment program 1996—, nat. program com. 2001), Assn. of Coll. and Univ. Mus. and Galleries, Western Mus. Assn., Assn., Fulbright Assn., Coll. Arts Assn. (session chair, spkr. ann. meeting 2003), Internat. Coun. Mus., Calif. Assn. Mus. Office: Univ Art Mus U Calif Santa Barbara 1626 Arts Bldg Santa Barbara CA 93106 E-mail: bgkelm@uam.ucsb.edu.

KELMAN, LORI MACELLARO, biology educator, molecular biology researcher; b. N.Y.C., May 16, 1960; d. Charles John and Eleanor (Cacace) M.; m. Zvi Kelman, May 18, 1996. AB in Biochemistry, Mt. Holyoke Coll., 1982; MS in Biology, St. John's U., 1984; PhD in Molecular Biology, Cornell U., 1994; MBA in Mgmt., Iona Coll., 2000. Yeast molecular geneticist Sloan-Kettering Inst., N.Y.C., 1986-95; asst. prof. biology Iona Coll., New Rochelle, N.Y., 1991-96, assoc. prof., 1996—2001; prof. biotechnology Montgomery (Md.) Coll., 2001—. Editor Bios, 1998—. Mem. AAAS, Nat. Assn. Biology Tchrs. (coun. sci. editors), Am. Women in Sci., Genetics Soc. Am., N.Y. Acad. Scis. (chair biol. scis. sect. 1994-96). Office Phone: 301-601-6929. E-mail: lori.kelman@montgomerycollege.edu.

KELMAN, MARYBETH, health care consultant, health policy analyst; b. Aug. 16, 1944; AS in Nursing, Rutgers U., 1964; BA, Douglas Coll., 1977; MA, Rutgers U., 1988. Program dir. health promotion N.J. Hosp. Assn., Princeton, NJ, 1983-87; policy analyst N.J. Dept. Human Svcs., Trenton, NJ, 1988-89; exec. dir. Eye Screening Coord. Coun. N.J., Inc., Monmouth Junction, NJ, 1989-91; health care cons. N.J. Divsn. Pensions and Benefits, Trenton, NJ, 1992—. Chmn. bd. trustees Forums Inst. for Pub. Policy, Princeton, 1998—. Office: 50 W State St PO Box 295 Trenton NJ 08625-0295 Business E-Mail: mbkelman@att.net.

KELSCH, RAEANN, state legislator; m. Thomas D. Kelsch; 3 children. BBA, U. N.D. Mem. N.D. Ho. of Reps.; vice chmn. judiciary com.; mem. govt. and vets. affairs com. Bd. dirs. United Way; active AID, Inc. Republican. Home: 611 Craig Dr Mandan ND 58554-2353 Office: ND Ho of Reps State Capitol Bismarck ND 58505

KELSEY, ANN LEE, library administrator; b. Kokomo, Ind., June 20, 1946; d. Harry Willard and JoAnn Kelsey. BA in Anthropology and English cum laude, U. Calif., Riverside, 1968; MLS, UCLA, 1969. Adminstrv. libr. U.S. Army Spl. Svcs., Cam Ranh Bay, Vietnam, 1969-70; children's libr. Elmont (N.Y.) Meml. Libr., 1970-71; libr. Queensborough Pub. Libr., Jamaica, N.Y., 1971-73; children's libr. Upper Saddle River (N.J.) Pub. Libr., 1973-75; prin. libr. Morris County Libr., Whippany, N.J., 1975-83; assoc. dir. Learning Resource Ctr., County Coll. Morris, Randolph, N.J., 1983—. Networked assoc. fellow 60s workgroup Inst. for Advanced Tech. in Humanities, U. Va., 1994—; ptnr., cons. libr. automation and planning DocuMentors, Rockaway, N.J., 1985—; ind. cons. infosys., Whippany, 1978—. Co-author: Planning for Automation: A How-To-Do-It Manual for Librarians, 1993, 2d edit., 1997, Writing and Updating Technology Plans: A Guidebook with Sample plans in CD-ROM, 1999, Planning for Integrated Systems and Technologies, 2001; contbr. chpt. to: Insider's Guide to Library Automation, 1993; editor: Resources for Teaching the Vietnam War: An Annotated Guide, rev. edit., 1996; also articles. V.p. Project: Hearts and Minds, Inc., Greenwich, Conn., 1995; bd. dirs. N.J. Vietnam Vets. Oral History Project, Kean U., 1998; mem. edn. adv. com. N.J. Vietnam Vets. Meml. Found., Vietnam Era Ednl. Ctr., 1998; mem. Morris County Dem. com., 1992; bd. dirs. N.J. Vietnam Vets. Meml. Found., 2001. Named to honor roll Vietnam Women's Meml. Project, Washington, 1993; recipient award African Am. Cultural Coun. Virginia Beach, 1999. Mem. ALA (travel grantee 1988), Am. Soc. Info. Sci., Spl. Librs. Assn. (pres. N.J. chpt. 1989-90, chairperson cataloging com. 1992-93), N.J. Libr. Assn. (chairperson automated libr. svcs. sect. 1992-93, mem. pers. adminstrn. com. 1986-87, mem. pay equity task force 1985-86), Women's Overseas Svc. League (scholarship com. chair 2003-), UCLA Alumni Club (co-chmn. [illegible] N.J. [illegible]), Phi Beta Kappa. Avocations: bicycling, internet, gardening. Office: DocuMentors 7 Valley View Dr Rockaway NJ 07866-1506 E-mail: akelsey@ccm.edu.

KELSEY, FRANCES OLDHAM, government official; b. Cobble Hill, Vancouver Island, Can., July 24, 1914; came to U.S., 1936, naturalized, 1956; d. Frank Trevor and Katherine (Stuart) Oldham; m. Fremont Ellis Kelsey, Dec. 6, 1943; children— Susan Elizabeth, Christine Ann. B.Sc., McGill U., 1934, M.Sc., 1935; PhD, U. Chgo., 1938, MD, 1950. Instr., asst. prof. pharmacology U. Chgo., 1938-50; editorial assoc. AMA, Chgo., 1950-52; assoc. prof. pharmacology U. S.D., 1954-57; med. officer FDA, Washington, 1960-63, chief investigational drug br., 1963-66, dir. divsn. oncology and radiopharm. drug products, 1966-67; dir. divsn. sci. investigations Office of Compliance, FDA, Rockville, Md., 1967-95, dep. for sci. and medicine Office of Compliance, 1995—. Author: (with F.E. Kelsey, E.M.K. Geiling) Essentials of Pharmacology, 1960. Recipient Pres.'s award for Distinguished Fed. Civilian Service (refusal to approve coml. distbn. thalidomide in U.S.), 1962. National Women's Hall of Fame, 2000. Mem. Am. Soc. Pharmacology and Exptl. Therapeutics, Am. Med. Writers Assn., Teratology Soc., Sigma Xi, Sigma Delta Epsilon. Office: FDA Office of Compliance 7520 Standish Pl Rockville MD 20855-2730

KELSEY, LINDA JEAN, technologist, educator; b. Charleston, W.Va., Feb. 9, 1948; d. John Arliss and Frances Lorraine (Smith) Peters; m. George Daniel Kelsey, Apr. 29, 1977; 1 child, Ruth Ann. AA, St. Petersburg Jr. Coll., 1981; BA in Bus. Mgmt., Eckerd Coll., 1986; MA in Christian Counseling, Christian Internatl., 1991; MA in Counseling, Liberty U., 1995. Staff technologist Montefiore Hosp., Pitts., 1968-70, St. Margaret Meml. Hosp., Pitts., 1970-73; evening supr. Presbyn. Hosp., Pitts., 1973-77; staff technologist Palms of Pasadena Hosp., St. Petersburg, Fla., 1977-78; supr. Computerized Tomography scanning Suncoast Hosp., Clearwater, Fla., 1978; control supr. Morton Plant Hosp., Clearwater, Fla., 1978-86, staff technologist, 1988-95; clin. instr. radiology program St. Petersburg Jr. Coll., Pinellas Park, Fla., 1995—. Mem.: Am. Assn. Christian Counselors, Am. Counseling Assn., Office Radiation Control, Am. Registry Radiologic Technologists. Avocations: reading, exercise, crafts, travel. Home: 1994 Hastings Dr Clearwater FL 33763-4417

KELSEY, NORMA L. labor union administrator; b. Independence, Kans., Sept. 19, 1935; d. James Harrison Arnold and Mary Louise Harshman; m. Alfred J. Jones, Dec. 22, 1951 (div. Oct. 1961); m. Robert A. Kelsey, Oct. 18, 1961; children: Jack, Cathryn, James, David; stepchildren: Robert Jr., Larry Krepelka, Karen Metcalf; foster children: Patrick and Vernor Williams. Student, Am. River Coll., 1965-70. Sec. OPEIU #29, Sacramento, Calif., 1961-80, OPEIU #8, Seattle, Wash., 1980—. Bd. dirs., v.p. El Centro de la Raza, Seattle, 1986-98. Mem. Mensa (SIGHT coord. 1982-92), King County Union Retirees Coun. (pres. 1998—), King County Labor Coun. (trustee, exec. bd. 1997—), Office and Profl. Employees (sec.-treas. local #8 1985-89, pres. 1989—). Democrat. Avocations: travel, labor union activities. Home: 22316 11th Ave S Des Moines WA 98198-6923 Office: OPEIU #8 2800 1st Ave Seattle WA 98121-1182

KELSH, JANICE EILEEN, club executive; b. Hagerstown, Md., May 5, 1947; d. Robert Henry and Mary Ellen (Slaughter) K. Student, U. D.C., 1971-77. Exec. dir. Miniature Piano Enthusiast Club, Hagerstown, 1990—. Conv. coord. Miniature Piano Enthusiast Club, 1992, Rochester, N.Y., 1993, Akron, Ohio, 1994, Las Vegas, Nev., 1995, 98, Cedar Rapids, Iowa, 1996. Editor: (newsletter) Musically Yours, 1991—. Mem. Assembly Of God Ch. Avocations: collecting miniature pianos, drama, singing. Home: 633 Pennsylvania Ave Hagerstown MD 21740-3769 E-mail: mpec2000@hotmail.com.

KELSO, BECKY, former state legislator; b. 1948; m. Michael Kelso; 2 children. BA in Comm., U. Minn. Mem. Minn. Ho. of Reps., 1986-98; mem. capital investment com.; mem. edn. com.; mem. regulated industries and energy com.; mem. transp. and transit com. Home: 60 S Shannon Dr Shakopee MN 55379-8025

KELSO, CAROL, state legislator; b. May 26, 1945; BA, Iowa State U. Assemblywoman Wis. State Dist. 88. Pres. Brown County Planning Commn.; mem. Brown County Harbor Commn., 2020 Hwy. Coalition. Address: 416 E Le Capitaine Cir Green Bay WI 54302-5153

KELSO, GWENDOLYN LEE, silver appraiser, consultant; b. Washington, Jan. 5, 1935; d. Leon Hugh and Katherine Estelle (Henderson) K. Mgr. Shaw & Brown Co., Washington, 1967-71, Chas. Schwartz & Son, Washington, 1972-76; silver appraiser Washington, 1976—; ptnr. The Silver Lion, Washington, 1983-85; owner, mgr. The Rampant Lion, Washington, 1985—. Cons. FBI and law enforcement agys. and ctrs., 1982—; cataloguer, conservator his. silver belonging to USN and U.S. Naval Acad., 1987—; appraiser presentation silver aboard U.S. Naval vessels and at installations, 1986—; cataloguer, conservator silver Forbes mag. collection, N.Y.C., 1989; mem. USS Alexandria Commissioning Com., 1990, USS Maryland Commissioning Com., 1993; conservator State of Md. for preservation battleship USS Maryland presentation silver, 1990—; instr. USN pers. for care and maintenance preservation silver; guest curator Washington Nat. Cathedral, 1997-98; cons. in field. Author: God's Treasures At Risk?, 1999, United States Navy Presentation Silver-A History and a Manual for its Care and Preservation, 1989, Silver Reflections an American Naval History, 1991 (exhbn. catalogue) Silver for Sacred Spaces—Four centuries of Ecclesiastical Silver from the Judeo-Christian Tradition, Washington Nat. Cathedral, 1998. Mem. NAFE, Internat. Soc. Appraisers (scholar 1989), Am. Soc. Appraisers (sr.), Appraisers Assn. Am., N.Y. Silver Soc., Silver Soc. (London), U.S. Naval Inst., Navy League U.S., Newcomen Soc. U.S. Republican. Episcopalian. Avocations: writing, travel, sewing, volunteering. Home and Office: 3731 39th St NW Washington DC 20016-5522

KELSO, LINDA YAYOI, lawyer; b. Boulder, Colo., 1946; d. Nobutaka and Tai Ike; m. William Alton Kelso, 1968. BA, Stanford U., 1968; MA, U. Wis., 1973; JD, U. Fla., 1979. Bar: Fla. 1980. Assoc. Mahoney, Hadlow & Adams, Jacksonville, Fla., 1979-82, Commander, Legler, Werber, Dawes, Sadler & Howell, Jacksonville, 1982-86, ptnr., 1986-91, Foley & Lardner, L.L.P., Jacksonville, 1992—. Mem. ABA (bus. law sect.), Jacksonville Bar Assn., Phi Beta Kappa, Order of Coif. Avocations: music, gardening, cooking. Office: Foley & Lardner LLP PO Box 240 Jacksonville FL 32201-0240 Office Phone: 904-359-2000. E-mail: lkelso@foley.com.

KEM, KATHERINE FRANCES, urban planner; b. Raleigh, N.C., Apr. 2, 1958; d. Winfield Thomas and Iris Elaine (Pearce) Fisher; m. William Earl Baker Jr., July 7, 1979 (div. Dec. 1996); children: Ryan Thomas, Heather Nicole; m. Jackie David Kem, Jan. 10, 1997. BBA, U. Tex., 1982; MPA, Troy State U., Germany, 1988. Tax preparer H&R Block, Lubbock, Tex. and Fayetteville, N.C., 1990-93, 96; Protestant music dir. 425 Air Base Squadron, Izmir, Turkey, 1994-95, dependent schs. officer, 1994-95; clk. Cumberland County Planning, Fayetteville, 1996; planner City of Fayetteville, 1996—2001. Pres. Hardwick Elem. Sch. P.T.A., Lubbock, Tex., 1992-93; Bible drill tchr. Shadow Hills Bapt. Ch., Lubbock, 1992-93; bn. coord. Family Support Group, 319th Mi, Ft. Bragg, N.C., 1997; music dir. LaGrange Park Bapt. Ch., Fayetteville, 1995—. Recipient Comdr.'s award for pub. svc. Dept. of Army, 1997. Mem. Internat. Cake Exploration Soc.,

Am. Planners Assn., N.C. Am. Planners Assn. Republican. Baptist. Avocations: cake decorating, cross stitching, reading, snow skiing. Home: 445 Hithergreen Dr Lansing KS 66043 Office: City of Fayetteville 433 Hay St Fayetteville NC 28301-5537

KEMETHER, EILEEN, psychiatrist; b. Staten Island, N.Y., Mar. 25, 1952; d. Fred Martin and Patricia Elizabeth (Hough) K. BA cum laude, East Stroudsburg State U., 1972; MA, The New Sch., 1978; MS, Pace U., 1980; MD, Mt. Sinai Sch. Medicine, 1992. Receptionist to chmn. of bd. IBM, N.Y.C., 1969-70; sec. Pfizer, Inc., N.Y.C., 1970-72; office mgr. Canada Life, N.Y.C., 1974-75; receptionist, sec. Nat. Forge Co., N.Y.C., 1975-78; nurse practitioner Goldwater Meml. Hosp., Roosevelt Island, N.Y., 1980-88; intern in internal medicine Elmhurst Hosp., 1992; intern in neurology Bronx VA, 1992; intern in psychiatry Mt. Sinai Hosp., N.Y.C., 1993, resident in psychiatry, 1993-96; attending psychiatrist (part time) Mt. Sinai Hosp. Psychiat. Emergency Room, 1996-98; assoc. Mt. Sinai Sch. Medicine, N.Y.C., 1996-99; psychiatrist, rschr. Med. Rsch. Network, N.Y.C., 1997; rsch. fellow Pilgrim Psychiat. Ctr., 1998-99; pvt. practice N.Y.C., 1996—. Psychiatrist MTA Connections, 1999—, Project Renewal, 1999—; rsch. fellow Lab. Neuroanatomy and Morphomoteics, 1996—. Mem. Am. Psychiat. Assn. Office: 903 Park Ave Apt 2C New York NY 10021-0361

KEMMERER, SHARON JEAN, computer systems analyst; b. Sellersville, Pa., Apr. 11, 1956; d. John Musselman and Esther Jone (Landis) K. BS, Shippensburg U., 1978; MBA, Marymount U., 1982. Mgmt. analyst Navy Internat. Logistics, Phila., 1978-81; computer systems analyst Navy Supply Sys. Commn., Crystal City, Va., 1981-86, Nat. Inst. Stds. and Tech., Gaithersburg, Md., 1986—. Bd. dirs. ComSci, Derwood Sta., 1994-97; adult tutor, 1991-95; mem. diversity bd. Nat. Inst. Stds. and Tech., 1997—. Contbr. articles, poetry to newspapers; author publs. Moderator Lung Assn., Fairfax, Va., 1986; vol. Project Heart, Washington, 1986—87, Montgomery County Health Buddy, 1988—99, Stepping Stones Shelter for Homeless, 1989—91, Pets on Wheels, 1994—96, Avon 3 Day Breast Cancer 60 mile walk, 2000, Habitat for Humanity, Montgomery County, 2001—, Burgundy Crest Vols., 2002—; dir. Global Village Mission trips Habitat For Humanity Internat., 2003—; mem. Global Village Mission Trips, 2000—; deacon Alexandria (Va.) Ch., 1985—86, v.p. coun., 1985, ch. coun., 1995—2001; mem. adv. bd. to dean of edn. and human resources Shippensburg U., 2002—. Lutheran. Avocations: renovation, antiques, volleyball, power walking. Office: Nat Inst Stds and Tech Mfg Engring Lab Gaithersburg MD 20899-8260

KEMP, ANN, retired librarian; b. Providence, Ky., Aug. 2, 1941; d. Charlie and Rubye (Sigler) Kemp Page. BA, Belmont U., 1964; MLS, Vanderbilt U., 1965, postgrad., 1968-79. Cert. tchr. Ky. Libr. Nashville Pub. Libr., 1965, U. Louisville Libr., 1965-67, Dawson Springs (Ky.) Ind. Schs., 1967-93; instr. Murray (Ky.) State U., 1973-78. Instr. Murray (Ky.) State U., 1973-78. Author: Poem, The ABC's of Parthenon. Mem.: Ky. Libr. Assoc., Ky. Edn. Assoc., Nat. Edn. Assoc., The Parthenon Patrons. Baptist. Avocations: studying architecture and folklore, writing poetry. Home: 113 Woodlawn Dr Madisonville KY 42431-3254

KEMP, BETTY RUTH, retired librarian; b. Tishomingo, Okla., May 5, 1930; d. Raymond Herrell and Mamie Melvina (Hughes) K. BA in Libr. Sci., U. Okla., 1952; MS, Fla. State U., 1965. Extramural loan libr. U. Tex., Austin, 1952-53, libr. lit. and history dept. Dallas Pub. Libr., 1955-56, head Oaklawn Br., 1956-60, Walnut Hill Br., 1960-64; dir. Cherokee Regional Libr., Lafayette, Ga., 1965-74, Lee County Libr., Tupelo, Miss., 1975-92. Bd. libr. commrs. State of Miss., 1979-83, chmn., 1979-80. Chmn. Chickasaw Hist. Soc., 1994-96, bd. dirs., 1994-98; active Native Am. Chickasaw Nation, United Meth. Women. Mem. AAUW, ALA, Nat. Soc. Daus. Am. Colonists, Nat. Soc. U.S. Daus. of 1812, United Daus. of the Confedercy, Nat. Soc. Dames of Ct. of Honor, Am. Indian Cultural Soc., Am. Indian C. of C., First Families Twin Ters, Beta Phi Mu. Democrat. Home: 3313 Winchester Cir Norman OK 73072-2937 Office: Kemp Rsch & Cons Svc PO Box 720531 Norman OK 73070-4388

KEMP, RENE D. state legislator; b. July 15, 1935; Attended, Ga. Mil. Coll.; JD, U. Ga. Atty.; mem. Ga. Senate, 1977—; vice chair judiciary com.; mem. def. and vets. affairs; mem. natural resources and transp. coms. Home: PO Box 497 Hinesville GA 31310-0497 Office: Ga State Senate State Capitol Atlanta GA 30334 also: 311-A Legis Office Bldg Atlanta GA 30334

KEMP, SUZANNE LEPPART, elementary school educator, clubwoman; b. N.Y.C., Dec. 28, 1929; d. John Culver and Eleanor (Buxton) Leppart; m. Ralph Clinton Kemp, Apr. 4, 1953; children— Valerie Gale, Sandra Lynn, John Maynard, Renee Alison. Grad. Ogontz Jr. Coll., 1949; B.S., U. Md., 1952. Elem. sch. tchr. Mem. Nat. Soc. Women Descs. of Ancient and Hon. Arty. Co., Nat. Soc. Daus. of Founders and Patriots of Am. (corr. sec.), Nat. Soc. Sons and Daus. of Pilgrims, Nat. Soc. U.S. Daus. of 1812 (chpt. organizing Md. state pres. 1977-79, chpt. v.p. 1979—), Nat. Soc. New Eng. Women (colony pres. 1978-80, Nat. Soc. Colonial Dames XVII Century (state chmn. heraldry and coats of arms 1977-79), Nat. Soc. D.A.R. (chpt. regent 1970-73, chpt. v.p., Md. soc. chmn. transp. 1976-79), Md. State Officers Club, Md. Hist. Soc., Friends of Animals, Defenders of Animal Rights Inc., U. Md. Alumni, English Speaking Union, Star Spangled Banner Flag House Assn., Potter-Balt. Clayworks, Balt. Mus. Art, Walters Art Gallery, Dames of the Court of Honor, Kappa Delta Alumni. Clubs: Baltimore Country; Lago Mar (Ft. Lauderdale, Fla.); Roland Park Women's; Woodbrook-Murray Hill Garden Club, Federation Garden Clubs. Editor; The Spinning Wheel, 1973-76. Home: 7 Ruxton Green Ct Baltimore MD 21204-3548

KEMPER, CHRISTINA, small business owner, respiratory therapist, elementary school educator; b. St. Louis, Feb. 16, 1952; d. Edward James and Norma Helen (Renner) K.; m. Don Eichholz, Dec. 23, 1972 (div. Apr. 1994); children: Cherie L., Derek V. BS in Edn., U. Mo., St. Louis, 1976, MA in Polit. Sci., 1980; AAS in Respiratory Therapy, Maryville U., 1983. Registered respiratory therapist. Staff respiratory therapist respiratory care various hosps., St. Louis, 1974—. Tchr. Parish Sch. Religion, St. Joseph's Ch., Manchester, Mo.; leader Girl Scouts Am., St. Louis. Mem. NOW (treas.), Am. Assn. for Respiratory Care, Nat. Bd. for Respiratory Care, Kappa Delta Pi. Avocations: floral designing, reading, interior decorating. Home: 12930 Twin Meadow Ct Creve Coeur MO 63146-1803 E-mail: christiekemper@yahoo.com.

KEMPER, DORLA DEAN EATON (DORLA DEAN EATON), real estate broker; b. Calhoun, Mo., Sept. 10, 1929; d. Paul McVay and Jesse Lee (McCombs) Eaton; m. Charles K. Kemper, Mar. 1, 1951; children: Kevin Keil, Kara Lee. BS in Edn., Ctrl. Mo. State U., 1952. Tchr. pub. schs., Twin Falls, Idaho, 1950-51, Mission, Kans., 1952-53, Burbank, Calif., 1953-57; real estate sales, 1967-68, 1971-73, Deanie Kemper, Inc. Real Estate Brokerage, Loomis, Calif., 1974-76, pres., 1976-91; sr. couns. Capital holdong Corp., Louisville, 1991-93. Pres. Battle Creek Park Elem. Sch. PTA, St. Paul, 1966-67; mem. Placer County (Calif.) Bicentennial Commn., 1976; mem. Sierra Coll. Adv. Com., 1981—; active Placer County Hist. Soc. Named to Million Dollar Club (lifetime) Sacramento and Placer County bds. Realtors, 1978-94; designated Grad. Realtors Inst., Cert. Residential Specialist. Mem. Nat. Assn. Realtor, Calif. Assn. Realtors, Nat. Assn. Real Estate Appraisers, Placer County (mem. profl. stds. com.), Bds. Realtors, DAR (chpt. regent 1971-73, organizing chpt. regent 1977—, dist. dir. 1978-80, state registrar Calif. 1980-82, state vice regent 1982-84, state regent 1984-86, nat. resolutions com., nat. rec. sec. gen. 1986-89, nat. chmn. units overseas 1983-86, nat. pres. gen. 1995-98, hon. nat. pres. gen. 1998—, nat. chmn. WWII Meml. Campaign 1998-2001), Nat. Gavel Soc., Daus Am. Colonists, Colonial Dames Am., Internat. Platform Assn., Hidden Valley Women's (pres. Loomis club 1970-71), Auburn Travel Study (pres. 1979). Republican. Home: 8165 Morningside Dr Granite Bay CA 95746-8163

KEMPLEY, RITA A. film critic, editor; b. Frankfort, Ky., Sept. 12, 1945; d. Noah and Musaetta (Lathrem) Abrams; m. Edward Ronald Schneider, Aug. 11, 1986. BJ, U. Mo., 1967. Reporter Copley News Svc., La Jolla, Calif., 1967-68; assoc. editor John F. Holman & Co., Washington, 1968-71; reporter Graphic Arts Mag., Washington, 1972-75; freelance editor-writer Washington, 1975-76; mng. editor Washington Dossier, 1977-79; editor/critic Washington Post, 1979—. Commentator Sta. WETA, 1989-96, Sta. WBIG, 1997—. Host Washington Post Live on Line. Grantee Alicia Patterson Found. fellow, 2002. Mem. Kappa Tau Alpha. Office: The Washington Post 1150 15th St NW Washington DC 20071-0002

KENAN, BRUNETTE JOHNELLA, graphics designer; b. Charlottesville, Va., May 19, 1948; d. John Henry Blakey and Jeanette Bernice Carey; 1 child, Shameen Jamiqua. Student, Sch. Visual Arts, N.Y.C., 1994. Clk. Credit Bur. Greater N.Y., N.Y.C., 1964—65; clerical staff Met. Life Ins., N.Y.C., 1965—66; sec. The N.Y. Times, N.Y.C., 1967—77, market rschr., 1977—83, graphic designer, 1983—. Mem.: NAFE, Nat. Assn. Photoshop Profls., Type Dir. Club, Order Ea. Star (fin. sec.). Democrat. Avocations: dance, sewing, travel, interior decorating. Office: The New York Times 229 W 43rd St New York NY 10036

KENAS-HELLER, JANE HAMILTON, musician; b. Fond du Lac, Wis., June 17, 1951; d. Vern Aaron and Marilyn Jane (Bluemke) Kenas; m. Irwin L. Heller. MusB, U. Wis., Stevens Point, 1975; MA, Northeastern Ill. U., 1987. Staff accompanist dept. music Northeastern Ill. U., Chgo., 1982—. Music dir. USO Tour to Europe, Germany, 1973; music dir., composer Harlequin Players Theatre Co., Palatine, Ill.; accompanist Park Ridge (Ill.) Chorale; condr. Temple Beth El High Holiday Choir, Northbrook, Ill. Composer: (mus. play) The Adventures of Goldilocks, 1990; (one-act opera) Romance Novel, 1993. Organist Edgewater Presbyn. Ch., Chgo. Office: Northeastern Ill U 5500 N Saint Louis Ave Chicago IL 60625-4679

KENDALL, KAY LYNN, interior designer, consultant; b. Cadillac, Mich., Aug. 20, 1950; d. Robert Llewellyn and Betty Louise (Powers) K.; 1 child, Anna Renee Easter. BFA, U. Mich., 1973. Draftsman, interior designer store planning dept. Jacobson Stores, Inc., Jackson, Mich., 1974-79, sr. interior designer store planning dept., 1981-98; prin., pres. Kay Kendall Designs LLC (Kendall Interior Design and Devel.), Jackson, 1979—; sr. interior designer Maddalena's Inc., Jackson, 1998—2002; realtor Edward Surovell Realtors, Ann Arbor, Mich., 2000—. Cons. in field. Big sister Big Bros./Big Sisters Jackon County. Mem. Am. Soc. Interior Designers (profl. mem., assoc. Ctrl. Mich. chpt.), Nat. Assn. Realtors, Ann Arbor Area Assn. Realtors, Mich. Assn. Realtors. Avocations: tennis, golf, gardening, skiing. Home: 701 Church St Grass Lake MI 49240-9206 Office: Edward Surovell Realtors 1898 W Stadium Blvd Ann Arbor MI 48103 E-mail: kkendall@acd.net.

KENDALL, MARCIA S. literature educator, consultant; d. Roger Grover and Elizabeth Karnel. BA in English/Comm., Western Conn. State U., 1998, postgrad. Freelance writer, rschr., photographer, educator, Danbury, Conn., 1994—; dir. programming Orcamajes, Danbury, 2002—; dir. ESL, prof. Western Conn. State U., Danbury, 2002—. Bd. mem. Town Gown City of Danbury, 1998—; v.p. Environ. Impact Com., Danbury, 1998—2002; sec. Western Conn. State U. Alumni Assn., Danbury, 1998—2001; active Danbury Dems., 1998—; vol. coord. Com. to Re-Elect Lew Wallace, Danbury, 1998—2002. Recipient White Oak award for svc., The Nature Conservancy, 2000; grantee, N.Y. Scholarship Found., 2002—03. Mem.: So. New Eng. Golf Assn., WXCI Radio 91.7 FM (life; bus. mgr. 1996—98), Wamegos Ladies Golf Club. Unitarian. Avocations: hike leader/explorer, photography, creative writing, golf, collecting. Home: 125 Carol St Danbury CT 06810 Office: Western Conn State Univ 181 White St Danbury CT 06810

KENDALL, REBECCA O. lawyer, pharmaceutical company executive; BS, Ind. U., 1970, JD, 1975. Bar: Ind. 1975. Lectr. Ind. U. Sch. Bus., 1979-80; counsel Nat. Ins. Assn., 1980-81; atty. Eli Lilly and Co., Indpls., 1981-83, sec., gen. counsel Elanco Products co. divsn., 1983-88, sec., gen. counsel Pharm. divsn., 1988-93, dep. gen. counsel, asst. sec., 1993-95, v.p., gen. counsel, 1995-98, sr. v.p., gen. counsel, 1998—. Office: Eli Lilly and Co Lilly Corp Ctr Indianapolis IN 46285-0001

KENDALL, SUSAN HAINES, library director; b. Greenville, Ohio, Nov. 5, 1952; d. Kenneth Edward and Zelda Lucille (Delk) Haines; m. John Leroy Sweigart, May 25, 1974 (div. 1986); m. Patrick William Kendall, Nov. 28, 1986. BS in Edn., Wright State U., 1977; MLS, Ball State U., 1981. Cert. tchr., Ohio; cert. libr., Ohio. Libr. clk. Greenville (Ohio) Pub. Libr., 1971-77; libr. asst. Flesh Pub. Libr., Piqua, Ohio, 1977-78, Amos Meml. Pub. Libr., Sidney, Ohio, 1978-81; libr. dir. Preble County Dist. Libr., Eaton, Ohio, 1981—. Tech. task force Ohio Pub. Libr. Info. Network, Columbus, 1993-95, bd. dirs. 1995-2003. Editor Preble's Pride quar., 1986—; contbr. to Ohio Librs., 2000. Bd. dirs. Preble County Hist. Soc., 2000—. Mem. ALA, Ohio Libr. Assn. (mem. coun. S.W. chpt. 1984-86, asst. coord. 1986-87, coord. 1988-89), Miami Valley Librs. (coun. 1981—, v.p. 2002-2003), Commodore-Preble DAR, Preble County Genealogy Soc. (v.p. 2003-), Eaton/Preble County C. of C. Republican. Methodist. Avocations: genealogy, motorcycling. Office: Preble County Dist Libr 450 S Barron St Eaton OH 45320-2402 Office Phone: 937-456-4250. E-mail: skendall@infinet.com.

KENDLE, CANDACE, pharmaceutical executive; m. Christopher C. Bergen; 2 children. BS in Pharmacy, U. Cin., 1970, PhD in Pharmacy, 1972. Resident Cin. Children's Hosp. Med. Ctr., 1972; epidemiology fellow U. N.C. Sch. Pub. Health; dir. pharmacy The Children's Hosp. Phila., 1979—81; clin. asst. prof. Phila. Coll. Pharmacy and Scis., 1979—81; clin. assoc. prof. pediat. U. Pa. Sch. Medicine., 1979—81; co-founder, CEO Kendle Internat., Inc., Cin., 1981—, chmn., 1991—. Adj. assoc. prof. U. Cin. Sch. Pharmacy, 1982—84; bd. dirs. U. Cin., H.J. Heinz Co., Isabella Venture Fund, UMD Inc. Contbr. articles to profl. jours. Named one of Nations Top 25 Female CEO's, Worth Mag., 2001; recipient Entrepreneur of Yr. award, Cin. Mag., 1998, Disting. Alumni award, U. Cin. Dept. Women's STudies, 1999, Arthur C. Glasser Disting. Alumni award, U. Cin., Coll. Pharmacy, 2001, William Howard Taft medal for notable achievement, U. Cin., 2002. Mem.: Com. of 200, Assn. Clin. Rsch. Orgns. (founder). Office: Kendle Internat Inc 1200 Carew Tower 441 Vine St Cincinnati OH 45202*

KENDRICK-HOPGOOD, DEBRA JO, small business owner; b. Mount Vernon, Ill., June 26, 1958; d. L. John and B. Jean (Stovall) K.; m. Joseph Jefferson Hopgood Jr., Jan. 10, 1981; children: Jillian Denise, Ashley Erin. Owner Balloons and Tunes, 1985-90; with Kendrick Paper Stock Co., Mt. Vernon, Ill., 1980—; owner Shenanigans Restaurant, 1990—. Com. mem. Mt. Vernon Civic Ctr., 1983-86, Jefferson County Crime Stoppers, Mt. Vernon, 1984-85; chaperone Loiterers Club, Mt. Vernon, 1987; mem. adv. bd. Good Samaritan Hosp., 1988-93; bd. dirs. Mt. Vernon Twp. High Sch. Bd. Edn., 1986—, Mt. Vernon Women's Crisis Ctr., 1988-91, Jefferson County, 1988; bd. suprs. Jefferson County, 1988—; bd. dirs. Bright and Beautiful, 1989—; mem. Mt. Vernon Econ. Devel. Commn., 1997—; mem. adv. bd. Jefferson County Health Dept., 1995-98; asst. leader Girl Scouts USA, 1996—; mem. Mt. Vernon Econ. Devel. Commn., 1997—. Named Woman of Yr. Mt. Vernon Bus. and Profl. Women's Club, 1998, DBE of Yr. Ill. Dept. of Transp. Bus. of Small Bus. Enterprise, 1997, Trucker of the Month, Midwest Truckers Assn. Mem. Nat. Fedn. Female Execs., Bus. and Profl. Womens Club, People Against Violent Environments (bd. dirs.). Baptist. Avocations: collecting coins, reading, tennis, old movies. Office: Kendrick Paper Stock Co PO Box 1385 Mount Vernon IL 62864-0028

KENNAN, ELIZABETH TOPHAM, academic administrator, retired historian; b. Phila., Feb. 25, 1938; AB summa cum laude, Mt. Holyoke Coll., 1960; MA, Oxford (Eng.) U., 1962; PhD, U. Wash., 1966; LHD (hon.), Trinity Coll., 1978, Amherst Coll., 1980, St. Mary's Coll., 1982, Oberlin Coll., 1983; LLD (hon.), Smith Coll., 1984; LittD (hon.), Cath. U. of Am., 1985, U. Mass., Amherst, 1988. Asst. prof. history Cath. U., Washington, 1966-70, assoc. prof. history, dir. medieval and Byzantine studies, 1970-78, dir. program in early Christian humanism, 1970-78; pres. Five Colls. Inc., 1985-94; pres., prof. history Mt. Holyoke Coll., South Hadley, Mass., 1978-95, pres. emeritus, 1996. Bd. dirs. Coun. on Libr. Resources, 1980-95; mem. com. Folger Shakespeare Libr., 1994-2001; lead dir. N.E. Utilities, Hartford, Conn.; bd. dirs. The Putnam Funds, Boston, Talbots, Hingham, Mass. Co-author: (under pseudonym Clare Munnings) Overnight Float, 2000; contbr. articles to profl. jours. including Georgetown Univ. Press, Univ. of Wash. Press, Cath. Univ. of Am., Cath. Univ. Press, Cistercian Publs., Mem. Coun. on Econ. Devel., 1991-95; mem. bd. selectors Jefferson awards Am. Inst. for Pub. Svc., 1991-96; trustee U. Notre Dame, 1985-94, Miss Porter's Sch., 1980-85; mem. higher edn. program com. Dana Found., 1986-90, Indo-U.S. Subcommn. on Edn. and Culture, 1986-91; vice chmn. 1000 Friends of Mass., 1989-91, Mass Gov.'s Nominating Coun., 1990-91; trustee Trustees for the Reservations, 1999—, Centre Coll., Danville, Ky., 2001—, Midway Coll., Midway, Ky., Nat. Trust Hist. Preservation, 2004—. Marshall scholar, 1960; Woodrow Wilson fellow (hon.), 1960. Mem. Coun. Fgn. Rels. Home and Office: Cambus-Kenneth Farm PO Box 1989 Danville KY 40423

KENNAN, STEPHANIE ANN, policy advisor; b. Frankfurt am Main, Germany, Oct. 25, 1958; d. Ralph Hyde and Loretta (Pumphrey) K. BA in Am. Govt. and Fgn. Affairs, U. Va., Charlottesville, 1980; MA in Creative Writing, Johns Hopkins U., Balt., 1997. Legis. asst. Rep. Larry Smith, Washington, 1983-85; asst. dir. edn. Group Health Assn. Am., Washington, 1985-86; legis. rep. Am. Assn. Ret. Persons, Washington, 1986-89, Am. Coll. Emergency Physicians, Washington, 1989-94; dir. fed. rels. Md. Dept. Health, Balt., 1995-97; sr. policy advisor U.S. Senator Ron Wyden, Washington, 1998—. Mem. Montgomery Couty (Md.) Commn. on Aging, 1983-86. Co-author: Health Care Playbook, 1994; contbr.: Public Health Administration, 2000; contbr. articles to profl. jours., books. Mem. Nat. Press Club. Episcopalian. Office: 516 Hart Senate Office Bldg Washington DC 20510-0001

KENNARD, JOYCE L. judge; b. Bandung, West Java, Indonesia, May 6, 1941; AA, Pasadena City Coll., 1970, U. So. Calif., 1970, BA, 1971, MPA, JD, U. So. Calif., 1974, Pepperdine Sch. Law, 1989; LLD (hon.), Calif. Western Sch. Law, 1990, Southwestern U. Sch. Law, 1991, Whittier Law Sch., 1994, Northwestern Sch. Law, Lewis and Clark Coll., 1997, Lincoln Law Sch., 1997. Dep. atty. gen., LA, 1975—79; sr. atty. State Ct. Appeals, LA, 1979—86; judge LA County Mcpl. Ct., 1986—87; assoc. justice pro tempore State Ct. Appeal (divsn. three), LA, 1987; judge LA County Superior Ct., 1987—88; assoc. justice State Ct. Appeals (divsn. five), LA, 1988—89, Calif. Supreme Ct., San Francisco, 1989—. Named Justice Yr. 1991, Calif. Trial Lawyers Assn.; recipient Ernestine Stahlhut award, Women Lawyers' Assn., LA, 1990, award, San Fernando Valley Bar, 1990, Asian/Pacific Women's Network, LA, 1991, Atty. Gen. award, Asian and Pacific Islander Employee Adv. Com., Atty. Gen. Office, 1992, award, ABA Task Force on Opportunities for Minorities in the Judicial Adminstrn. Divsn. and Commn. on Opportunities for Minorities in the Profession, 1992, Margaret Brent Women Lawyers of Achievement award, ABA, 1993, Trailblazer award, Nat. Asian Pacific Am. Bar Assn. (NAPABA), 1994, St. Thomas More Medallion award, St. Thomas More Law Honor Soc. and Loyola Law Sch., 1995, 1996 Spirit Excellence award, ABA Commn. on Opportunities for Minorities in the Profession, award, San Francisco Women Lawyers Alliance, 1997, Asian Pacific Am. Legal Ctr. So. Calif., LA, 1997, Legal Impact award, Asian Law Alliance, San Jose, Calif., 2000, First Justice Rose Bird Meml. award, Calif. Women Lawyers San Francisco, 2001. Office: Calif Supreme Ct 350 Mcallister St San Francisco CA 94102-4783

KENNARD, LYDIA H. airport terminal executive; BA, Stanford U.; MS, MIT; JD, Harvard U. Former pres./prin.-in-charge KDG Devel. Constrn. Consulting, L.A.; former mem. L.A. Planning Commn.; dep. exec. dir. design and constrn. L.A. World Airports, 1994-99, interim exec. dir., 1999-2000, exec. dir., 2000—. Lawyer in real estate and constrn. law. Active UniHealth Found. Bd.; past mem. Calif. Med. Ctr. Found. Bd., Equal Opportunity Adv. Coun. So. Calif. Edison. Named Woman of Yr. L.A. chpt. Women's Trans. Seminar, 1995, Civic Leader of Yr. Nat. Assn. Women Bus. Owners-L.A., 2000. Office: LA World Airports PO Box 92216 Los Angeles CA 90009-2216

KENNARD, MARY ELIZABETH, lawyer; b. Phila., Dec. 1, 1954; d. Rodman Ramos and Mary Elizabeth Kennard. BAS, Boston U., 1976; JD, Temple U., 1980; LLM, George Washington U., 1982. Bar: Pa. 1980, R.I. 1988, D.C. 1988, U.S. Dist. Ct. (we. dist.) Pa. 1985, U.S. Ct. Appeals (3d cir.) 1985, U.S. Dist. Ct. R.I. 1988, U.S. Ct. Appeals (1st cir.) 1989, U.S. Dist. Ct. D.C. 1996, U.S. Supreme Ct. 1985. Assoc. Obermayer, Rebmannn, Maxwell & Hippel, Phila., 1979-80; asst. exec. dir. Nat. Assn. Coll. and Univ. Attys., Washington, 1981-83; asst. univ. counsel U. Pitts., 1984-85; asst. to v.p. for legal affairs Howard U., Washington, 1985-87; legal counsel U. R.I., R.I. Coll. and C.C. of R.I., Kingston, 1987-94; v.p., gen. counsel Am. U., Washington, 1995—. Bd. dirs. Washington Trust Bank, Washington metro area Am. Corp. Counsels Assn. Mem. Nat. Assns. Coll. and Univ. Attys., R.I. Black Lawyers Assn. Democrat. Avocation: golf. Office: American Univ 4400 Massachusetts Ave NW Washington DC 20016-8165

KENNE, LESLIE F. military officer; B in Aero. Engring., Auburn U., 1970; grad., Squadron Officer Sch., 1975; M in Procurement Mgmt., Webster Coll., 1979; grad., Armed Forces Staff Coll., 1981, Nat. War Coll., 1986, Def. Sys. Mgmt. Coll., 1988; advanced mgmt. program, U. N.H., 1993; nat. and internat. security mgmt., Harvard U., 1995. Cert. level III program mgmt., level III test and evaluation. Commd. 2d lt. USAF, 1971, advanced through grades to maj. gen., 1998; maintenance supr. 474th Orgnl. Maintenance Squadron, Takhli Royal Thai AFB, Thailand, 1973-74; project mgr., dep. test dir. range measurement sys. jt. test Tactical Fighter Weapons Ctr., Nellis AFB, Nev., 1975-78; program mgr. Office of Sec. of Def.-directed joint tests Air Force Test and Evaluation Ctr., Kirtland AFB, N.Mex., 1978-81; chief airborne sys. test br., chief elec. sys. test divsn. 324th Test Wing, Eglin AFB, Fla., 1982-85; dir. ops. and support Airborne Warning and Control Sys. Program Officer, Hanscom AFB, Mass., 1986-88; chief spl. projects divsn. directorate spl. programs Office of Asst. Sec. of Air Force for Acquisitions, Washington, 1988-90; dir. LANTIRN Sys. Program Office Aero. Sys. Divsn., Wright-Patterson AFB, Ohio, 1993-94; dep. dir. fighters and C2 and weapons programs Office of Asst. Sec. of Air Force for Acquisition, Washington, 1992-93; dir. F-16 Sys. Program Office Aero. Sys. Ctr., Wright-Patterson AFB, 1993-94, vice comdr., 1994-95, Sacramento Air Logistics Ctr., McClellan AFB, Calif., 1995-96; dep. dir. Joint Strike Fighter Program, Arlington, Va., 1996-97, dir., 1997-99; comdr. Electronics Sys. Ctr., Hanscom AFB, Mass., 1999—. Decorated Legion of Merit, Bronze Star, Meritorious Svc. medal with 2 oak leaf clusters. Office: Hanscom AFB ESC / CC Hanscom AFB MA 01731-5000

KENNEDY, ADRIENNE LITA, playwright; b. Pitts., Sept. 13, 1931; d. Cornell Wallace and Etta (Haugabook) Hawkins; m. Joseph C. Kennedy, May 15, 1953 (div. 1966); children: Joseph C., Adam. BS, Ohio State U.,

1953; student creative writing, Columbia U., 1954-56; student playwrighting, New Sch. Social Research, Am. Theatre Wing, Circle in the Sq. Theatre Sch., 1957-58, 62; doctorate (hon.), Ohio State U., 2003. Mem. playwriting unit Actors Studio, N.Y.C., 1962-65; lectr. Yale U., New Haven, 1972-74; CBS fellow Sch. Drama, N.Y.C., 1973; lectr. Princeton (N.J.) U., 1977; vis. assoc. prof. Brown U., 1979-80; Rep. to conf. Internat. Theatre Inst., Budapest, 1978; vis. lectr. Harvard U., 1990, 91, vis. prof., 1997—. Author: (plays) Funnyhouse of a Negro, 1964, Cities in Bezique, 1965, A Rat's Mass, 1966, A Lesson in Dead Language, 1966, The Lennon Plays, 1968, Sun, Cities of Bezique, 1969; A Movie Star Has To Star in Black and White, 1976, Ohio State Murders, She Talks to Beethoven, 1990, (with Adam Kennedy) Sleep Deprivation Chamber, 1995; (memoirs) People Who Led to My Plays, 1987 (Manhattan Borough Pres.'s award 1988), Letter to My Students, Lancashire Lad; commd. by Empire State Youth Inst., 1979, Onestes, Electra, Juilliard Sch. Music, 1980, Black Children's Day, Rites and Reason, Brown U., 1980; represented in numerous anthologies Norton Anthology of Am. Lit. Recipient Obie award, 1964, 96, Pierre Lecomte du Novy award Lincoln Ctr., 1994, award Am. Acad. Arts and Letters, 1994; fellow Guggenheim Found., 1968, Rockefeller Found., 1967-68, NEA, 1993, Lila Wallace Readers Digest, 1994, Yale U., 1974-75; grantee Nat. Endowment Arts, 1973, Rockefeller Found., 1974, Creative Artists Pub. Svc., 1974; Disting. lectr. U. Calif., Berkeley, 1980, 86. Mem. PEN (bd. dirs. 1976-77). Address: 325 W 89th St New York NY 10024

KENNEDY, BARBARA ELLEN PERRY, art therapist; b. Columbus, Ohio, Apr. 22, 1937; d. Donald Earl Perry and Elsie Irene (Strait) Perry Modglin; m. Marvin Roosevelt Kennedy, July 1, 1955 (div. Sept. 1969); children: Sherry Lynn Kennedy Anderson, Michelle Reneé Kennedy Byrd. AS in Mental Health Technology cum laude, Purdue U., 1975, BA in Psychology, 1976; MA in Art Therapy, Wright State U., 1990. Registered art therapist; cert. social worker; cert. marriage and family therapist. Probation officer intern Allen County Juvenile Probation Dept., Ind., 1975; prodn. supr. asst. Allen County Assn. for Retarded, Ft. Wayne, Ind., 1975, relief supr. semi-ind. living, 1975-76; occup. therapist asst. Logansport State Hosp., Ind., 1977; rehab. therapist Richmond State Hosp., Ind., 1977—, recreation therapy dir. acute intensive treatment unit, 1983-85, dir. art therapy dept., 1986—, art tchr., art therapist with MIDD, adolescent and geriatric, 1995—. Pvt. counselor, 1986—; counselor Mental Health Assn., Richmond, 1986; art therapy counselor Battered Women's Shelter, Richmond, 1986; counselor Dayton (Ohio) Pub. Sch., Family Svc. Assn., 1989-90, expressive therapy counselor with Mentally Ill Chemically Addicted population, 1993—; lectr. in field of mental health and art therapy. Author, editor: Mental Stimulation Activities, 1992. Mem. com. LWV, Richmond, 1977-80; publicity officer USCG Aux., Richmond, 1985; chairperson legis. group AAUW, Richmond, 1982-84; bd. dir. Community Coun. on Disabilities Awareness, Richmond, 1985-86; vol. ARC, Muncie, Ind. and Ft. Wayne, 1969-73; vol. tutor Adult Literacy Resource Ctr., 1991—; pres. Richmond Art Club, 1996-97; active Fountain City Wesleyan Ch. Recipient Merit scholarship Purdue U., 1971-76, Gov.'s Showcase award State of Ind., 1990. Mem. Am. Art Therapy Assn., Buckeye Art Therapy Assn., Ind. Art Therapy Assn. (v.p. 1992-95), Mensa. Mem. Wesleyan Ch. Avocations: sailing, hiking, piano, reading, art. Office: Richmond State Hosp 498 NW 18th St Richmond IN 47374-2898 Personal E-mail: barbiecutie47374@cs.com.

KENNEDY, BEVERLY (KLEBAN) BURRIS, financial advisor, television and radio personality; b. Pitts., Sept. 23, 1943; d. Jack and Ida (Davis) Kleban; m. Thomas E. Burris, Dec. 31, 1967 (div.); 1 child, Laura Danielle Burris; m. Ed A. Kennedy, Jan 14, 1984; stepchildren: Kathleen, Patricia, Thomas. BS, Pa. State U., 1964; postgrad., Va. Commonwealth U., 1967. Founder, exec. dir. Broward Art Colony, Inc., Broward County, Fla., 1978-80; dir. sales Holiday Inn, Plantation, Fla., 1980-81; agent, registered rep. Equitable Life Assurance Soc., Ft. Lauderdale, Fla., 1982—; pres. Fin. Planning Svcs. Assn., Inc., Ft. Lauderdale, Fla., 1984-86; owner, fin. cons. Beverly B. Kennedy & Assocs., Ft. Lauderdale, Fla., 1982—; republican nominee for U.S. Congress 19th Dist., Fla., 1996; dir. of rsch. tech. & grants adminstrn. Diversity Planning Instit., 2002—; pres., CEO Cosmetic Rejuvenation Svcs. Fla., LLC, 2004. Mem. adv. bd. Transflorida Bank, 1983-88; mem. bd. arbitration Nat. Assn. Securities Dealers, Inc., 1992-2004. Talk show host Sta. WWNN, 1992-93. Bd. dirs. Community Appearance Bd., 1988-89, Riverwalk, Ft. Lauderdale, 1988-89, First Charter Sch. of Excellence, Ft. Lauderdale, 1997-2003; trustee Police and Fireman Fund of Fort Lauderdale, 1990-91; appointed by gov. to Fla. State Bd. Profl. Engrs., 1988-91; cons. Com. on Fin. for Nat. Coun. examiners for Engring and Surveying, 1990-91; Rep. nominee for U.S. Congress 20th dist. Fla., 1992, 94, 19th dist., 1996; appointed to silver haired legis. of Fla., 1999-2003, exec. bd. coalition of condominiums and home owners assoc., 2001-2003. Named Woman of the Year (Bus. for Profit), Women in Communications, Broward County, 1986, Bus. & Profl. Women, 1988-89, Outstanding Alumni, Pa. State Univ. Coll . Edn., 1988-89, A Woman of History, Nova S.E. U., 2001. Mem. Internat. Assn. Fin. Planning, Nat. Assn. Life Underwriters, East Broward Fed. Women's Rep. Club (pres. 1992-93). Home and Office: 3240 Seaward Dr Lauderdale By The Sea FL 33062 E-mail: ekenn@bellsouth.net.

KENNEDY, CAROLINE See SCHLOSSBERG, CAROLINE

KENNEDY, CHERYL LYNN, museum director; b. Pekin, Ill., Nov. 25, 1946; d. Paul Louis and Ann Marie (Bingham) Wieburg; children: Kurt Alan, Kimberly Ann. Grad. high sch., Pekin, Ill.; BA, Eastern Ill. U. Prin., and profl. quilter, Mahomet, Ill., 1976-81; program coord. Early Am. Mus., Mahomet, 1981-85; dir. Early Am. Mus. Champaign County Forest Preserve, Mahomet, 1986—. Chmn. Ill. Quilt Rsch. Project Early Am. Mus. and Land of Lincoln Quilt Assn., 1986—, Ill. Historic Sites Adv. Coun., 2000—03 mem. adv. com. AAM Mus. Assessment Program, 2002--. Historian Meth. Local History Com., Mahomet, 1984-86. Mem. Assn. Midwest Mus., Am. Assn. Mus. (assessment adv. com.), Am. Assn. State and Local History, Ill. Assn. Mus. (past pres., advocacy chair), Ill. Heritage Assn., Ill. State Hist. Soc., Champaign County Hist. Soc., Nat. Quilt Assn., Am. Quilt Soc., Antique Quilt Study Group, Quilt Conservancy. Avocations: quilting, women's history, walking, gardening. Office: Early Am Mus PO Box 1040 Mahomet IL 61853-1040 E-mail: ckennedy@prairienet.org.

KENNEDY, CLAUDIA J. retired military officer; BA in Philosophy, Southwestern U.; grad., U.S. Army Command/Gen. Staff, U.S. Army War Coll. Commd. 2d lt. U.S. Army, 1969, advanced through grades to lt. gen., 1997, strategic intelligence officer 501st military intelligence, 1977; asst. ops. officer, ops. officer U.S. Army Field Sta., Augsburg, Germany, 1981-84; staff officer, dir. tng. Office of Dep. Chief of Staff for Ops. and Plans, Washington, 1984-86; comdr. San Antonio Recruiting Bn., 5th Recruiting Brigade, Ft. Sam Houston, Tex., 1988-90, 703d Mil. Intelligence Brigade, Kunia, Hawaii, 1991-93; dep. comdr. U.S. Army Intelligence Ctr. and Ft. Huachuca, Ariz., 1994-95; asst. dep. chief of staff for intelligence Office of Dep. Chief of Staff for Intelligence, U.S. Army, Washington, 1995-97. Author: (with Michael McConnell) Generally Speaking: A Memoir by the First Woman Promoted to Three-Star General in the United States Army, 2004. Decorated Legion of Merit with 3 oak leaf clusters, Def. Meritorious Svc. medal, Meritorious Svc. medal with 3 oak leaf clusters.

KENNEDY, COLLEEN MICHELLE, academic administrator, educator; d. Patrick Joseph and Charlotte Estelle Kennedy. BA in Psychology, Ill. Wesleyan U., 1995; MA in Behavior Analysis and Psychology, W.Va. U., 1998. Recycling coord. Ill. Wesleyan U., Bloomington, 1992—93; tchg. asst. W.Va. U., Morgantown, 1995—98; curriculum cons. Ulster Project, Bellefonte, Pa., 1999—2000; sr. sec. Roosevelt U., Schaumburg, Ill., 2001—, assessment proctor, 2002—. Mem. microlab. com. W.Va. U., Morgantown, 1997—98, student rep. animal lab. com., 1996—97; chair edn. com. environ. awareness force Ill. Wesleyan U., Bloomington, 1991—92, disc jockey WESN, 1991—92; adj. faculty Roosevelt U., Schaumburg, 2003—; presenter in field. Fellow, Nat. Inst. Occupl. Safety and Health, Morgantown, 1998—2001. Mem.: APA (assoc.), Southeastern Assn. Behavior Analysis, Scientists Ctr. Animal Welfare, Assn. Behavior Analysis, Am. Psychol. Assn., Psi Chi, Alpha Phi Omega. Achievements include Outstanding Employee Service Award 2002-2003; research in Behavior Analytic Research 1994-2001. Avocations: soccer, travel, tennis, reading, hiking.

KENNEDY, CORNELIA GROEFSEMA, federal judge; b. Detroit, Mich., Aug. 4, 1923; d. Elmer H. and Mary Blanche (Gibbons) Groefsema; m. Charles S. Kennedy, Jr. (dec.); 1 son, Charles S. III. BA, U. Mich., 1945, JD with distinction, 1947; LL.D. (hon.), No. Mich. U., 1971, Eastern Mich. U., 1971, Western Mich. U., 1973, Detroit Coll. Law, 1980, U. Detroit, 1987. Bar: Mich. bar 1947. Law clk. to Chief Judge Harold M. Stephens, U.S. Ct. of Appeals, Washington, 1947-48; assoc. Elmer H. Groefsema, Detroit, 1948-52; partner Markle & Markle, Detroit, 1952-66; judge 3d Judicial Circuit Mich., 1967-70; dist. judge U.S. Dist. Ct., Eastern Dist. Mich., Detroit, 1970-79, chief judge, 1977-79; circuit judge U.S. Ct. Appeals, (6th cir.), 1979-99, sr. judge, 1999—. Mem. Commn. on the Bicentennial of the U.S. Constitution (presdl. appointment). Recipient Sesquicentennial award U. Mich. Fellow Am. Bar Found.; mem. ABA, Mich. Bar Assn. (past chmn. negligence law sect.), Detroit Bar Assn. (past dir.), Fed. Bar Assn., Am. Judicature Soc., Nat. Assn. Women Lawyers, Am. Trial Lawyers Assn., Nat. Conf. Fed. Trial Judges (past chmn.), Fed. Jud. Fellows Commn. (bd. dirs.), Fed. Jud. Ctr. (bd. dirs.), Phi Beta Kappa. Office: US Ct of Appeals 6th Circuit 532 Potter Stewart US Courthouse 100 E Fifth St Cincinnati OH 45202

KENNEDY, DEBORAH, writer, editor, business owner; b. Wayland, Mass., Feb. 6, 1955; m. Leonard L. M. Coster (dec.). BA, MA, Boston U., 1978; M. of Theol. Studies, Harvard Divinity Sch., 1981; MA, Am. U., 1988. Instr. Dickinson Coll., Carlisle, Pa., 1985-86, Denison U., Granville, Ohio, 1986-87; asst. to dean Am. U., Washington, 1987-90; dir. ops. Lang. at Work, Washington, 1991-98; owner, prin. Key Resources, Washington, 1998—. Chair, bd. dirs. Thomas Cir. Singers, Washington, 1995-97, fund raising chair, 1995-2000; coord. concert series St. Columba's Ch., Washington, 1994-97. Mem. ASTD, Women's Nat. Book Assn., Tchrs. of English to Spkrs. of Other Langs., Washington Ind. Writers. Episcopalian. Avocations: singing, gardening. Home and Office: 245 Dockham Shore Rd Gilford NH 03249-6677 E-mail: drkennedy@netacc.net.

KENNEDY, DEBRA JOYCE, marketing professional; b. July 9, 1955; d. John Nathan and Drea Hannah (Lancaster) Ward; m. John William Kennedy, Sept. 3, 1977 (div.); children: Drea, Noelle. BS in Comm., Calif. State Poly. U., 1977; MA in Orgnl. Mgmt., U. Phoenix, 2003. Pub. rels. coord. Whittier (Calif.) Hosp., 1978—79, pub. rels. mgr., 1980; pub. rels. dir. San Clemente (Calif.) Hosp., 1979—80; dir. pub. rels. Garfield Med. Ctr., Monterey Park, Calif., 1980—82; dir. mktg. and cmty. rels. Charter Oak Hosp., Covina, 1983—85; mktg. dir. CPC Horizon Hosp., Pomona, 1985—89; dir. mktg. Sierra Royale Hosp., Azusa, 1989—90; mktg. rep. PacifiCare, Cypress, 1990—92; regional medicare mgr. Health Net, Woodland Hills, Calif., 1992—95; dist. sales mgr. Kaiser Permante Health Plan, Pasadena, Calif., 1995—. Contbr. articles to profl. jours. Mem.: Healthcare Pub. Rels. and Mktg. Assn., Healthcare Mktg. Assn., Am. Soc. Hosp. Pub. Rels., Covina and Covina West C. of C., Soroptimists, West Covina Jaycees. Republican. Methodist.

KENNEDY, ELIZABETH, health facility administrator; b. Binghamton, N.Y., Mar. 19, 1944; d. Robert D. and Doris Beverly (Bryde) Courtright; m. Leon C. Kennedy, Aug. 29, 1964; children: Andrew, Tracey, Brian, Kristie. AAS, Ind.-Purdue U., 1986; BSN, Ind. Wesleyan U., 1996. RN, Ind.; lifetime ARC nurse. DON Summit House, Ft. Wayne, Ind., 1986-87; staff nurse Mark Souder, M.D., Auburn, Ind., 1988; DON Kendallville (Ind.) Nursing Home, 1988-89, Lifecare Ctr., Lagrange, Ind., 1989-91; asst. DON Arbors at Ft. Wayne, Ind., 1991-92; nursing supr. Allen Home, Health Care & Hospice, 1993-95; DON Courtland Health and Rehab. Ctr., Ft. Wayne, 1996—; staff nurse Interim Health Care, Ft. Wayne, Ind., 1996-97; agy. nurse The Arc of N.E. Ind., 1997-98; DON The Cedars, Leo, Ind., 1998-99; RN cons. Prof. Nursing Svc., 1989-99; clin. educator Parkview Health Sys., Ft. Wayne, Ind., 1999-2000; case mgr. mr/dd In Case Mgmt., Indpls., 1999-2000; mgr. extended care unit Don Adams County Meml. Hosp. Decatur, Ind., 2000; dir. nursing Englewood Health and Rehab. Ctr., Ft. Wayne, Ind., 2001—02; nursing mgr. Wash. House Treatment Ctr., 2001—; dir. nursing Riverbend H.C., Ft. Wayne, 2001; RN coord. Ft. Wayne State Devel. Ctr., 2002—; asst. dir. nursing Univ. Park Nursing Ctr., Ft. Wayne, 2002—03; with Don Kendallville Manor, Kendallville, Ind. Instr. ARC., 1986, AHA CPR, 1998; assoc. faculty dept. nursing Purdue U., Ft. Wayne, 2000. Recipient Scottish Rite Nursing scholarship. Home: 8233 Red Shank Ln Fort Wayne IN 46825 E-mail: tishrn@comcast.net.

KENNEDY, EVELYN SIEFERT, foundation executive, textile specialist; b. Pitts., Nov. 11, 1927; d. Carmine and Assunta (Iacobucci) Rocci; m. George J. Siefert, May 30, 1953 (dec. 2000); children: Paul Kenneth, Carl Joseph, Ann Marie; m. Lyle H. Kennedy II, Oct. 12, 1974 (dec. 1990); m. Frederick J. Commentucci, Feb. 24, 2001. BS magna cum laude, U. R.I., 1969, MS in Textiles and Clothing, 1970. accredited appraiser of personal property, Internat. Soc. Appraisers. With Pitts. Pub. Schs., 1945-50, Goodyear Aircraft Corp., Akron, Ohio, 1950-54; clothing instr. Groton (Conn.) Dept. Adult Edn., 1958-68; pres. Sewtique, Groton, 1970—, Sewtique II, New London, Conn., 1986; v.p. Kennedy Capital Advisors, Groton, 1973-85, Kennedy Mgmt. Corp., Groton, 1974-85, Kennedy Intervest, Inc., Groton, 1975-85; pres., exec. dir. PRIDE Found., Inc., Groton, 1978—. Clothing cons. Coop. Ext. Svc., Dept. Agr.; internat. lectr. on clothing for disabled and elderly; adj. faculty U. Conn., Ea. Conn. State Coll., St. Joseph Coll.; hon. prof. U. R.I., assoc. prof., 1987—; fed. expert witness Care Label Law, FTC, 1976; mem. Major Appliance Consumer Action Panel, 1983-89. Author: Dressing With Pride, 1980, Clothing Accessibility: A Lesson Plan to Aid the Disabled and Elderly, 1983, Textiles Speak, 1996. Regional adv. coun. SBA Active corps Execs., Hartford, 1985—; bd. dirs. Sml. Bus. Devel. Ctr., 1989—, Easter Seal Rehab. Ctr. Southeastern Conn., Southeastern Conn. Women's Ctr., 1997—, Women's Ctr. New London County, 1997—; bus. adv. coun. U. R.I., 1979—, trustee, 1985—; active LWV; mem. Groton Vocat. Edn. Adv. Coun. Recipient award of distinction U. R.I., 1969, Adv. of Yr. SBA, 1984, Outstanding Svc. in Cmty., 1991; named Woman of Yr. Bus. and Profl. Women's Club, 1977, Conn. Home Economist of Yr., 1987. Mem. Internat. Sleep Coun. (consumer affairs rep., Sml. Bus. Adminstrn. award 1991), Internat. Soc. Appraisers (accredited appraiser personal property, panelist FMHA roster, farmer's credit mediator 1989—), Nat. Assn. Bedding Mfrs., Conn. Home Economists in Bus. (founder 1977, Women of Yr. 1987), Nat. Home Economists in Bus. (chmn. internat. rels., nat. fin. chmn. 1986), Am. Home Econs. Assn., Coll. and Univ. Bus. Instrs. of Conn., Am. Occupl. Therapy Assn. (resource cons. 1986—), Web-Re-Stor Assn. (wedding restoration specialist 1993-2000), Southeastern Women's Network, Fashion Group, Costume Soc. Am., New London Zonta Club, Bus. and Profl. Women's Club (Outstanding Women of Yr. 1977), Omicron Nu, Phi Kappa Phi. Office: 391 Long Hill Rd Groton CT 06340-3812 Office Phone: 860-445-7320. E-mail: textileappraisal@aol.com.

KENNEDY, FAYE, retired social worker, author; b. Kansas City, Mo., Apr. 3, 1931; d. Wiley Choice and Zella Rae (Jackman) K.; m. Patrick Joseph Daly, Jan. 7, 1961. AA, Pasadena City Coll., 1951; BA, Hunter Coll., 1955; cert., Alliance Francaise, Paris, 1956. Vocat. counselor N.Y. State Divsn. Employment, N.Y.C., 1957-65; social worker N.Y. State Div. Parole, N.Y.C., 1965-77. Author: Good-bye, Diane, 1976; assoc. editor Afro-Hawaii News, 1990-92. Hawaii adv. com. U.S. Civil Rights Commn., Honolulu, 1990—; active Hawaii State Commn. on Status of Women, Honolulu, 1993-95, Hawaii Civil Rights Commn., Honolulu, 1995-2003, Martin Luther King Jr. Commn., Honolulu, 1989-93; del. Hawaii Dem. Party State Cen. Com., 1994—, Dem. Nat. Conv., 1996, 2000; bd. dirs. Hawaii Literacy, Inc., 1987-97, Hawaii Youth at Risk, 1991-94, ACLU of Hawaii, 1999-2002; 1st v.p. NAACP-Hawaii, 2003, 2004. Recipient Gov.'s Cert. of Appreciation, State of Hawaii, 1989-93, Making of the King Holiday award Martin Luther King Jr. Commn., 1991, Outstanding Achievement award Hawaii Literacy, Inc., 1988, 92, Outstanding African Ams. citation Mahogany, 1996, Afro-Hawaii News, 1992, Hawaii Personalities Recognition citation RSVP mag., 1989, Lifetime Dedication to Pub. Svc. cert. Honolulu City Coun., 1996. Mem. Hawaii Women's Polit. Caucus (pres. 2003-), Hawaii Yacht Club. Democrat. Avocations: reading, writing, movies, gardening. Home: 3071 Felix St Honolulu HI 96816-1911

KENNEDY, GWENDOLYN DEBRA, artist, scriptwriter, playwright; b. Daly City, Calif., Nov. 18, 1960; d. Adolphus Brooks and Ella (Robinson) K.; children: Gwendolyn Fincher, Edward James, Jr. AA in Theater Prodn., City Coll. San Francisco, 1992. Artist Walt Disney Animation Art, 1991; artist animation and fine art www.blackpantherpartypress.tv, 1994—; owner Black Panther Party Press and Pub., 1993—. Owner mail order co. La Chateau D'Gwendolyn Kennedy Co., 1991—. Author: Billie Holliday Collection Book, 1993, Kane Kut Murder Trial, 1993, Poetic Justice, 1994, No Struggle No Progress, 1995, Nyami the Sky God, 1996. Recipient Journalist of Yr. award City News Svc., Mo., 1995. Lutheran. Avocations: guitar, ballet, art, track, piano, computers. Home: 285 Bellevue Ave Daly City CA 94014-1305 Office: PO Box 135 Daly City CA 94016-1305

KENNEDY, JERRIE ANN PRESTON, public relations executive; b. Quanah, Tex. Student, Sunset Sch. Preaching, Lubbock, Tex., 1975-78, Jo-Susan Modeling Sch., Nashville, 1984, Film Actors Lab., 1986. Coprodr. Vincent Cirrincione & Assocs., NY, 1986; paralegal Arlington Career Inst., 1998—; freelance internat. mktg. and pub. rels. exec. Military del. NATO Allies for The French Liaison, Ft. Hood, Tex., 1992, Vietnam War (Diplomatic immunity) 1972-1975. Author screenplay, fed. and cmty. pub. spl. events prodn. US Activist Women's Rights in the State of Tex., 2003. Recipient 1st and 3d pl. awards Modeling Assn. Am., NYC, 1985.

KENNEDY, JOANIE TISKA, artist, painter, sculptor; b. Pittsfield, Mass., July 12, 1950; d. Edward Frances and Jean Frances (Hayes) Tiska; m. Willard Lee Kennedy, May 25, 1974; children: Tiska Ann, Katherine Jean, Christine Ashley. Student, East Carolina U., 1968-71, N.C. State U., Raleigh, 1971-72, Lincoln Land Coll., 1976-79. Designer Stained Glass Assoc., Knightdale, N.C., 1971-74; prof. asst. Lincoln Land Coll., Springfield, Ill., 1977-79; artist Art Space Inc., Raleigh, N.C., 1984—; bd. dirs. Mem. Med. Soc. Alliance Book Club, Nat. Mus. Women in Arts (charter), Wake Visual, Charlotte Hilton Green Park Assn., Nature Conservancy. Avocations: gardening, walking, aerobics, water sports, writing.

KENNEDY, JUDITH PRICE, elementary school educator; b. Oakland, Calif., June 18, 1941; d. Forest Walter Price and Clelia Diana Spini; m. Jeffery Allen Kennedy, Aug. 11, 1973; children: Michael Richard Nova, Jeffrey Price Schmidt. BA U. Calif., Berkeley, 1963. Cert. tchr. Tchr. grade 3 San Mateo County, Calif.; tchr. grade 4 Riverdale Sch. Dist., Md., 1967—68, Champaign-Urbana, Champaign, Ill., 1965—67, Head-Royce Sch., Oakland, Calif., 1971—. Mem. KQED Ednl. TV, Oakland. Mem. Chabot Sci. Ctr., Oakland Mus. Mem.: Calif. Alumni Assn., Nat. Assn. Ind. Schs. Democrat. Avocations: hiking, travel, reading, gardening. Home: 5545 Taft Ave Oakland CA 94618 Office: Head-Royce Sch 4315 Lincoln Ave Oakland CA 94602

KENNEDY, KATHLEEN, film producer; m. Frank Marshall. Student, San Diego State U. With KCST, San Diego; pres. Amblin Entertainment, Universal City, Calif. Assoc. prodr.: (films) Poltergeist, 1982, Twilight Zone-The Movie, 1983, Indiana Jones and the Temple of Doom, 1984, Reform School Girls, 1986; prodr.: (films) E.T. The Extra-Terrestrial, 1982 (Academy award nomination for best picture 1982); (with Quincy Jones, Frank Marshall, and Spielberg) The Color Purple, 1985 (Academy award nomination for best picture 1985); (with Marshall and Art Levinson) The Money Pit, 1986; (with Marshall and Spielberg) Empire of the Sun, 1987, Always, 1989; (with Richard Vane) Arachnophobia, 1990; (with Marshall and Gerald R. Molen) Hook, 1991; (with Robert Watts) Alive, 1993; (with Molen) Jurassic Park, 1993, (with Marshall) Milk Money, 1994; (with Clint Eastwood) The Bridges of Madison County, 1995, Twister, 1996; (with Steven Spielberg), The Six Sense, 1999, Snow Falling on Cedars, 1999, A Map of the World, 1999, Artifical Intelligence: AI, 2001, Jurassic Park III, 2001, Seabiscuit, 2003; exec. prodr.: (films)Roller Coaster Rabbit, 1990, A Dangerous Woman, 1993, Schindler's List, 1993 (Academy award for best picture 1993), Trail Mix-Up, 1993, A Far Off Place, 1993, Balto, 1995, Congo, 1995, The Indian in the Cupboard, 1995; (with Marshall and Spielberg) Gremlins, 1984, The Goonies, 1985, Back to the Future, 1985, Young Sherlock Holmes, 1985, *batteries not included, 1987, Jurassic Park: The Lost World, 1997, Dad, 1989, Back to the Future Part II, 1990, Gremlins 2: The New Batch, 1990, Back to the Future Part III, 1990, Joe Versus the Volcano, 1990, Cape Fear, 1991, We're Back! A Dinosaur's Story, 1993, (with Marshall) Fandango, 1985; (with Marshall, Spielberg, and David Kirschner) An American Tail, 1986; (with Marshall, Spielberg, Peter Guber, and Jon Peters) Innerspace, 1987; (with Spielberg) Who Framed Roger Rabbit, 1988; (with Marshall, Spielberg, and George Lucas) The Land Before Time, 1988; (with Marshall and Lucas) Indiana Jones and the Last Crusade, 1989; (with Marshall and Kirschner) An American Tail: Fievel Goes West, 1991; (with Peter Bogdanovich) Noises Off, 1992; (with Marshall and Molen); (with Molen, Kirschner, William Hanna, and Joseph Barbera) The Flintstones, 1994, Olympic Glory, 1999, Signs, 2002; exec. prodr. TV Tummy Trouble, 1989, The Sports Pages, 2001

KENNEDY, KATHY KAY, library director; b. New Kensington, Pa., Oct. 21, 1942; d. Lawrence Michael Kennedy and Vivian Mae Smeltzer. BA in English, Thiel Coll., 1964; MSLS, Drexel Inst. Tech., 1967. Bibliographer Union Libr. Catalog, Phila., 1964-67; sci./tech. librarian Carnegie Libr. of Pitts., 1967-73, adult svcs. specialist, 1973-74; libr. dir. Peoples Libr., New Kensington, pa., 1974-87; adult svcs. librarian Monroeville (Pa.) Pub. Libr., 1987-89, asst. dir., 1989-93, dir., 1993—. Editor: Review of Iron and Steel Literature, 1972. Bd. dirs. Pa. Citizens for Better Librs., Greensburg, 1996—, Monroeville Arts Coun., 1989-91; mem. bd. assocs. Thiel Coll., 2002--. Mem. Pa. Libr. Assn. (pres. 1995, editor jour. 1976-78, Cert. of Merit 1982), Bus. and Profl. Women of Pitts. (pres. 1975-77), McKeesport Bus. and Profl. Women (Woman of Yr. 1999), Pa. Fedn. Bus. and Profl. Women (dist. dir. 1984-85), Allegheny County Libr. Assn. (bd. dirs. 1999-2001). Lutheran. Avocations: music, theater, reading, travel. Office: Monroeville Pub Libr 4000 Gateway Campus Blvd Monroeville PA 15146-3381

KENNEDY, LEILA, accounting educator; b. Murray City, Ohio, June 19, 1941; d. Carl Eugene and Jesse Marie (Mentzer) Wynegar; m. Gary Nelson Retterer, Sept. 28, 1958 (div. Jan. 1962); children: April Anne, William Eugene; m. Junior Everett Kennedy, May 31, 1963. BS in Acctg., Bluefield State Coll., 1989; MS in Acctg., Marshall U., 1992. Faculty Nat. Bus. Coll., Bluefield, Va., 1992; adj. faculty Bluefield State Coll., W. Va., 1991-92, instr. bus., 1992-93, asst. prof., 1993-98, assoc. prof., 1998—. Cons. in field. Avocations: crochet, knitting, reading. Office: Greenbrier Cmty Coll 101 Church St Lewisburg WV 24901-1303 E-mail: lkennedy@bluefieldstate.edu.

KENNEDY, LINDA MANN, neuroscience educator, researcher; b. Malden, Mass., July 29, 1939; d. Alfred William Mann and Etta May (Maglue) Stenquist; m. Richard Dearman Kennedy, Apr. 15, 1961; children: Pamela Lee, Ruth Alexander. Diploma in nursing, New England Deaconess Hosp., 1959; AB, Simmons Coll., 1975; PhD, Harvard U., 1980. RN, Mass. Staff nurse Lahey Clinic, Boston, 1959-61, various hosps., Mass., Ga., 1962-72; tchg. asst. Simmons Coll., Boston, 1972-75; vis. rsch. fellow Cornell U., Ithaca, NY, 1978-81; rsch. assoc. Worcester (Mass.) Found. Exptl. Biology, 1980-83; rsch. asst. prof. Clark U., Worcester, 1983-84, asst. prof., 1984-91, assoc. prof., 1991—, U. Mass. Med. Sch., 1995—2000. Co-founder, co-dir., dir. interdisciplinary neurosci. program Clark U., Worcester, 1984—97; vis. scientist Weizmann Inst. Sci., Rehovot, Israel, 1991—92; mem. adv. panel various programs, ADVANCE fellows program NSF, Washington, 1993—, vis. program dir. Sensory Sys. program, 2000—02; mem. study sections various programs NIH, 1988—. Mem. editl. com. Univ. Press New England, 1989-91; contbr. articles to profl. jour. Mem. conservation com. Town of Framingham, Mass., 1973-74. Recipient Grad. fellowship for women Danforth Found., 1975-79, Rsch. Svc. award NIH, 1980-83, multiple Rsch. grants NSF, NIH, 1978—. Mem. AAUP, New Eng. Psychol. Assn. (hon.), Assn. Chemoreception Sci. (exec. bd. councilor 1986-88), Soc. for Neurosci., Soc. for Values in Higher Edn., European Chemoreception Orgn., Internat. Brain Rsch. Orgn., Assn. for Women in Sci. Unitarian Universalist. Avocations: scuba diving, classical and jazz concerts, travel, reading mysteries. Home: 98 Waterford Dr Worcester MA 01602-3512 Office: Clark Univ Dept Biology Worcester MA 01610

KENNEDY, MARJORIE ELLEN, librarian; b. Dauphin, Man., Can., Sept. 14, 1946; d. Stanley Harrison and Ivy Marietta (Stevens) May; m. Michael P.J. Kennedy, Apr. 3, 1980. BA, U. Sask., Regina, 1972; BLS, U. Alta., Edmonton, 1974; BEd, U. Regina, 1981. Profl. A cert. edn., Sask. Elem. sch. tchr. Indian Head (Sask) Pub. Sch., 1965-66, Elgin Sch., Weyburn, Sask., 1967-68; tchr., libr. Ctrl. Sch., Prince Albert, Sask., 1970-71; elem. sch. tchr. Vincent Massey Sch., Prince Albert, 1969-70, 72-73; children's libr. J.S. Wood br. Saskatoon (Sask.) Pub. Libr., 1974-77, asst. coord. children's svcs., 1977-79; programme head, instr. libr. tech. Kelsey Inst., Saskatoon, 1979—; head libr. and info. tech. SIAST-Kelsey Campus, Saskatoon. Presenter workshops on reference materials for elem. sch. librs., storytelling and libr. programming for children, 1980—; vol. dir. Children's Lit. Workshops, Sask. Libr. Assn., 1979-80; mem. organizing com. Sask. Libr. Week, Saskatoon, 1988. Mem. Vanscoy (Sask.) and Dist. Agr. Soc., 1983-95. Named to Libr. Edn. Honor Roll ALA, 1987. Mem. Can. Libr. Assn. (instl. rep. 1984—), Sask. Libr. Assn. (insl. rep. 1984—, mem. children's sect. 1982-83), Sask. Assn. Libr. Techs. (instl. rep. 1984—), Can. Club (bd. mem. 1981-84). Mem. United Ch. Can. Avocations: antique doll restoration, porcelain doll making, antiques, pottery, gardening. Office: Kelsey Inst Box 1520 Libr Info Tech Program Saskatoon SK Canada S7K 3R5 E-mail: Kennedy@siast.sk.ca.

KENNEDY, MARLA CATHERINE, psychologist; b. Milw., June 28, 1935; d. Raymond G. and Catherine (Wimmer) Mueller; m. William Robert Kennedy, Mar. 2, 1957; children: Joseph, Timothy, Kristin, William, Daniel. BS, Alverno, Milw., 1956; MA, U. Minn., 1983, postgrad., 1983-1989. Lic. psychologist, lic. marriage and family therapist. Intern with mentally ill and mentally retarded Met. Clin., Mpls., 1984—85; pvt. practice psychology, marriage and family therapy Mpls., 1985—. Spkr. in field; part-time at Family Svc. Greater St. Paul, 1989-98; dir., co-counselor Adlerian Family Edn. Ctr., 1983-85. Contbr. articles to profl. jours. Bd. dirs. Books for Africa, 1997-2002; co-founder Community Line (now First Call for Help); pres. Legions of PTAs; active YWCA Shelter for Women, St. Paul; vol. Rams Juvenile Justice, 1985-2003. Mem. Am. Acad. Neurology Aux. (bd. dirs.), Minn. Assn. Marriage and Family Therapists, Minn. Assn. Group Psychotherapists (pres. 1998-00), Alfred Adler Assn. (bd. dirs. 1965-80), AAUW (bd. dirs.), New Century (bd. dirs.), Women's Investment Club (treas.), Mensa, Phi Lambda Theta. Unitarian Universalist. Avocations: swimming, tennis, reading.

KENNEDY, MARY SUSSOCK, artist; b. Liverpool, Eng., Oct. 29, 1926; came to U.S., 1951; d. Charles Archibald and Maria (Mullin) Sussock; m. Rogers Jack Kennedy, May 18, 1946 (dec. Jan. 1987); children: Jacollyn Fenny-Maria, Beverley Gillian, Kimberley Tara. AAS with highest honors, Fashion Inst. Tech., N.Y., 1975; BA summa cum laude, Montclair State Coll., 1977; postgrad., Montclair State Univ., 1977-78. Portrait, stage and wedding photographer Wilkinson and Kennedy, Liverpool, 1943-47; freelance artist Montville, Barnegat Light, NJ, 1956-73; freelance artist Key Largo, Fla., 1984—; grad. asst. in sculpture Montclair State Univ., Upper Montclair, NJ, 1977-78; diamond stylii maker Rogers Kennedy Inc., Saddle Brook, N.J., 1978-84. One woman show at Fashion Inst. Tech., N.Y., 1974; exhibited in group shows at Smithsonian Instn., Washington, 1963, Montclair Art Mus., 1964, U.S. Custom House, N.Y.C., 1979, also exhibit opened by Princess Grace in Monaco, 1960; sculpture exhibited in two person show at Montclair State Univ., 1977. Mem. Phi Kappa Phi. Democrat. Episcopalian. Avocations: anthropology, reading, travel, gardening. Home: PO Box 2560 Key Largo FL 33037-7560

KENNEDY, MARY VIRGINIA, diplomat; b. Pocatello, Idaho, Sept. 5, 1946; d. Charles Millard and Martha Lorissa (Evans) K. BA, U. Denver, 1968, MA, 1969; MAT, U. Idaho, 1971, JD, 2001. Tchr. cert. Idaho. Recreation aide ARC, South Vietnam, 1969-70; ops. officer State Dept. Ops. Ctr., Washington, 1977-78; spl. asst. amb. Philip Habib, Washington, 1979-80, Sec. State, Washington, 1980-81; econ. officer U.S. Embassy, Cairo, 1981-84; consul Am. Consulate, Adana, Turkey, 1985-88; Pearson fellow Office Cong. Bereuter Ho. Reps., 1988-89; exec. asst. Dept. Sec. State, Washington, 1989-91; dep. chief mission Dept. State U.S. Embassy, Kuwait, 1991-93; consul gen. Am. Consulate, Karachi, Pakistan, 1994-96; dean Sch. Profl. Area Studies, Fgn. Svc. Inst., 1996-98. Bd. trustees Idaho State Hist. Soc., 1999—2002. Mem. Am. Fgn. Svc. Protective Assn. (bd. dirs. 1988-91), Phi Beta Kappa, Mortar Bd. Home: 5137 Admiral Way SW Seattle WA 98116 Address: PO Box 16634 Seattle WA 98116-0634 E-mail: niact@aol.com.

KENNEDY, MAYDRA JANE PENISSON (J.P. KENNEDY), poet; b. New Orleans, Aug. 31, 1938; d. Charles Christopher and Clare Elda (Walter) Penisson Jr.; m. Jacob Louis Kennedy Sr., July 17, 1974 (dec. Nov. 1995); 1 child, Wendy Jane Kennedy. Grad., West Jefferson H.S., Harvey, La. Author of poetry and song lyrics. Inductee Internat. Poetry Hall of Fame, 1997. Mem. Internat. Soc. Poets (life), Am. Fedn. Police (mem. in good standing), Nat. Mus. Women in the Arts, Paralyzed Vets. Am. (hon.). Democrat. Lutheran. Avocations: oil painting, singing, gardening, creative activities. Home: 807 Monroe St Gretna LA 70053-2241

KENNEDY, MICHELE LYN, artist; b. Durham, N.C., Dec. 21, 1958; d. Michel Paul and Denise Francis Richard; children: John Paul Jones, Catherine Elizabeth. Student, New Paltz State U., 1976-78; cert. in jewelry design, Fashion Inst. Tech., 1980; BA, Geneseo State U., 1981; studies Robert Cormier, Fenway Studio, 1987-88; studied with Henry Hensche, Cape Cod Sch. Art, 1988. Owner Kennedy Gallery, Key West, 1988—. Painting published in Florida Art Digest, 1996, Tribute to Caruso Key West Music Festival, 1997, Profiles of Key West. Painting donations AIDS Help Art Auction, Key West, 1990-96. Recipient Best Gallery in Key West award Key West Citizen newspaper, 1993-98. Avocations: biking, tennis. Home and Office: Kennedy Gallery 61 Sunset Ln Osterville MA 02655-2043

KENNEDY, MURIEL, psychologist, consultant, educator; b. Bamberg, S.C., Mar. 29, 1965; d. Harold Lee Kennedy (dec.) and Virginia Morgan Kennedy Marion. BS, U. S.C., 1987; MS, Howard U., 1993, PhD, 1995. Lic. psychologist, Va., Md., D.C. Nuc. engr. Charleston Naval Shipyard, Charleston, S.C., 1987-90; psychology assoc. Child Advocacy Network, Balt., 1996-97; clin. psychologist Child and Family Therapy Ctr., Washington, 1997—. Clin. cons. Inst. for Life Enrichment, Washington, 1997—, Baraka Pastoral Counseling Ctr., Largo, Md., 1997—; adj. prof. Howard U., Washington, 1997—; exec. dir. Perico Inst. for Youth Devel. Entrepreneurship, Inc.; co-founder New Life Enrichment Ctr., Inc. Mem. Assn. Black Psychologists (treas. 1996-97, pres.-elect 1998-99, pres. 1999-2000, immediate past pres. 2000-2001), Psi Chi. Democrat. Baptist. Avocations: inspirational writing, listening to music, poetry, the arts, sports. Home: 116 Adams St NW Washington DC 20001-1611 E-mail: murielkenn@yahoo.com.

KENNEDY, RENEAU CHARLENE UFFORD, forensic psychologist, consultant; b. Weiser, Idaho, June 18, 1954; d. Eldon Luther and Iris Jean (Hetrick) Ufford; m. Allen Ken Kennedy (div. Apr. 1999). BS in Psychology and Speech, Willamette U., 1975; MS in Psychology, U. Oreg., 1981; EdD in Psychology, Boston U., 1994; postgrad., Harvard U., 1994-98. Lic. psychologist. Tchr., counselor Victorian Dept. Edn., Melbourne, Australia, 1975-78, 80; fellow in clin. and forensic psychology The McLean Hosp., Harvard Med. Sch., Belmont, 1986-87, fellow in neuropsychology dept. neurology, 1987-89; clin. fellow in forensic psychology Harvard Med. Sch./Mass. Gen. Hosp., Boston, 1992-98; cons. Mass. Dept. Youth Svcs., Boston, 1994-95, Ky. Justice Cabinet, Frankfort, 1995; pvt. practice Weston, Mass., 1996—, Honolulu, 1997—. Affiliate clin. tng. supr., course instr. Am. Sch. Profl. Psychology, Honolulu; dir. tng. Forensic and Behavioral Scis. Inst., Honolulu, 1998-2000, Honolulu Family Therapy Ctr., 2000—; clin. fellow MGH Law and Psychiatry Svc., 1992-98; cons., spkr. in field. Mem. Ky. Justice Cabinet Juvenile Task Force, Frankfort, 1994-96, Mass. Child Death Rev. Team, Boston, 1995-97, Mass. Ct. Subcom. on Risk Assessment, Dedham, 1995—; col., aide de camp Commr. of Ky. State Police, Frankfort, 1994, 95, 96. Predoctoral fellow Harvard Med. Sch., Boston, 1992-94; named to Hon. Order of Ky. Cols. Mem. APA, Soc. for Personality Assessment, Hawaii Psychol. Assn., Homicide Rsch. Working Group, Psi Chi, Phi Delta Kappa, Pi Lambda Theta. Avocations: scuba diving, triathlon events, exotic travel. Home and Office: 3001 Diamond Head Rd Honolulu HI 96815-4716 Fax: 808-923-2299. E-mail: rkennedy@lava.net.

KENNEDY, ROBINETTE, anthropologist, researcher; b. Reidsville, Ga, May 22, 1948; d. James Clifford and Dana Kate (Williams) Kennedy. BA in Journalism, U. Ga., Athens, 1970; MA in Humanistic Psychology, W.Ga. State U., Carrollton, 1973; PhD in Psychology, Saybrook Grad. Sch., San Francisco, 1981. Social worker Grady Hosp. Emory U. Dept. Medicine, Atlanta, 1970—71; rsch. asst. Dept. Family Rsch. Emory U., Atlanta, 1971—72; anthropology field work Ind. scholar, Crete, Greece, 1975—77; sr. rsch. assoc. Dept. Clin. Rsch. Ga. Mental Health Inst., Atlanta, 1978—80; pvt. practice Mountain City, Ga., 1981—. Co-author: Women's Friendship on Crete: A Pyschological Perspective in Gender and Power in Rural Greece, 1986. Achievements include first to document the structural role of women's friendships in a traditional culture. Home: PO Box W Mountain City GA 30562

KENNEDY, SUSAN MARIE, music educator; b. Attleboro, Mass., Apr. 29, 1951; d. Thomas E. and Irene K. Kennedy. MusB cum laude, U. Mass., Lowell, 1973; MA in Tchg. summa cum laude, Bridgewater (Mass.) State Coll., 1981; CAGS with honors, Fitchburg (Mass.) State Coll., 2003. Cert. music tchr. Dept. Edn., Mass., supr., dir. Dept. Edn., Mass., music tchr. Dept. Edn., Fla., Dept. Edn., Ga., Dept. Edn., RI, Dept. Edn., Conn., adminstr. Dept. Edn., Conn. Music tchr. Citrus County Pub. Schs., Inverness, Fla., 1973—76, Bourne (Mass.) Pub. Schs., 1976—81, Lee County Pub. Schs., Ft. Myers, Fla., 1981—82, Hernando Pub. Schs., Brooksville, Fla., 1982—95, Clayton County Pub. Schs., Jonesboro, Ga., 1995—99, New Bedford (Mass.) Pub. Schs., 1999—2002, Windham (Conn.) Pub. Schs., 2002—. Performing musician (electric piano) Jerry Rellman Orch., Sharon, Mass., 1969—73; accompanist Chelmsford (Mass.) Choral Soc., 1970—71; jazz and classical pianist Holiday Inn, Dedham, Mass., 1971—72; organist various chs., Spring Hill, 1973—76; performing musician (percussion) The Wave, Citrus County, 1973—88; classical pianist various restaurants, Crystal River, Fla., 1974—76; autoharp instr. Lee County Adult Edn., Ft. Myers, 1981—82; pvt. piano tchr., Brooksville, Fla., 1983—94; performing musician(synthesizer) Candlelight Orch., Brooksville, 1988—95. Composer: pieces for students; dir. and arranger pieces for steel band, dir., prodr. original musicals, dir. first elem. steel band, Ga., 1996. Performer benefit concerts Am. Cancer Soc., Ocala, Fla., 1988—95; animal abuse investigator Humane Soc., Brooksville, 1990—95. Nominee Outstanding Elem. Tchrs. Am., 1973; named Tchr. of Yr., Hernando County, Fla., 1982, Outstanding Grad. Student in Ednl. Leadership, Fitchburg (Mass.) State Coll., 2003; recipient award, Brooksville PTO, 1992—93; grantee, Grass Roots Fine Arts Orgn., 1996, Conn. Commn. on the Arts. Mem.: Music Educators Nat. Conf. (assoc.), Kappa Delta Pi (assoc.). Avocations: fine arts, farming, travel, animals, environment. Home: 37 Granite St Foxboro MA 02035 Personal E-mail: suekennedy@rcn.com.

KENNEDY, SYLVIA C. state representative; b. Barre, Vt., Apr. 26, 1932; 3 children. Ret.; rep. Vt. State Ho. Reps., 2001—. Chmn. Chelsea (Vt.) Rep. Town Com.; mem. Orange County Rep. Com, Gov.'s Parole Bd. Mem.: Bethel Christian Fellowship. Republican. Home: PO Box 158 Chelsea VT 05038

KENNEDY, YVONNE, state legislator; b. Jan. 8, 1945; BS, Ala. State U.; MA, Morgan State U.; PhD, U. Ala.; LLD (hon.), Lane Coll. Pres. Bishop State Jr. Coll.; rep. Ala. Ho. Reps., Montgomery, 1982—. Democrat. Episcopalian. Office: Ala State Ho 11 S Union St Rm 537-c Montgomery AL 36130-2103 also: 1205 Glennon Ave Mobile AL 36603-5224

KENNELLY, BARBARA B. former congresswoman, federal agency administrator; b. Hartford, Conn., July 10, 1936; d. John Moran and Barbara (Leary) Bailey; m. James J. Kennelly, Sept. 26, 1959 (dec. 1995); children: Eleanor Bride, Barbara Leary, Louise Moran, John Bailey. BA in Econs, Trinity Coll., Washington, 1958; grad., Harvard-Radcliffe Sch. Bus. Adminstrn., 1959; MA in Govt, Trinity Coll., Hartford, 1971. Mem. Hartford Ct. of Common Council, 1975-79; sec. of state State of Conn., Hartford, 1979-83; mem. 98th-105th Congresses from 1st Dist. Conn., Hartford, 1982-98; mem. ways and means com.; counselor, assoc. commr. Social Security Adminstrn., 1999-2000; sr. adv. Baker & Hostetler, Washington; currently pres. & CEO Nat. Com. to Preserve Social Sec. & Medicare. Trustee Trinity Coll., Hartford, Conn.; active in numerous polit., civic, and goft. orgns. Greater Hartford, Conn.; co-chair Ctr. for Democracy, Washington. Democrat. Roman Catholic. Office: Natl Com Preserve Social Security & Medicare 10 G St NE Ste 600 Washington DC 20002*

KENNELLY, SISTER KAREN MARGARET, retired academic administrator, church administrator, nun; b. Graceville, Minn., Aug. 4, 1933; d. Walter John Kennelly and Clara Stella Eastman. BA, Coll. St. Catherine, St. Paul, 1956; MA, Cath. U. Am., 1958; PhD, U. Calif., Berkeley, 1962. Joined Sisters of St. Joseph of Carondelet, Roman Cath. Ch., 1954. Prof. history Coll. St. Catherine, 1962-71, acad. dean, 1971-79; exec. dir. Nat. Fedn. Carondelet Colls., 1979-82; province dir. Sisters of St. Joseph of Carondelet, St. Paul, 1982-88; pres. Mt. St. Mary's Coll., L.A., 1989-2000, pres. emerita, 2000—; congl. dir. Sisters of St. Joseph of Carondelet, St. Louis, 2002—. Cons. N. Ctrl. Accreditation Assn., Chgo., 1974—84, Ohio Bd. Regents, Columbus, 1983—89; trustee colls., hosps., Minn., Mo., Wis., Calif., 1972—; chmn. Sisters St. Joseph Coll. Consortium, 1979—82. Editor, co-author: Am. Cath. Women, 1989; author (with others): Women of Minnesota, 1977; author: Women Religious and the Intellectual Life: The North American Achievement, 1996; co-editor: Gender Identities in American Catholicism, 2001; : Cath. Coll. Women in Am., 2002. Bd. dirs. Am. Coun. on Edn., 1997—99, Nat. Assn. Ind. Colls. and Univs., 1997—2000, Assn. Cath. Colls. and Univs., 1996—2000, Western Region Nat. Holocaust Mus., 1997—2000. Fellow Fulbright, 1964. Mem.: Western Assn. Schs. and Colls. (sr. commn. 1997—2000), Assn. Cath. Colls. and Univs. (exec. bd. 1996—2000), Am. Coun. Edn. (bd. dirs. 1997—99), Nat. Assn. Ind. Colls. and Univs. (bd. dirs. 1997—99), Am. Assn. Rsch. Historians Medieval Spain, Medieval Acad., Am. Cath. Hist. Assn. Avocations: skiing, cuisine. Office: Congl Ctr 2311 Lindbergh Blvd Saint Louis MO 63131 Office Phone: 314-966-4048.

KENNER, CAROL J. federal bankruptcy judge; b. 1950; BA, Syracuse U., 1972; JD magna cum laude, New Eng. Sch. Law, 1977; postgrad., NYU Sch. Law, 1976-78. Bar: Mass. 1977. With Weil, Gotshal & Manges, N.Y.C., 1977-78, Widett, Slater & Goldman, Boston, 1978-81; pvt. practice Herrick & Smith, Boston, 1981-86; judge U.S. Bankruptcy Ct., 1986—; chief judge U.S. Bankruptcy Ct., Dist. Mass., Boston, 1994-98. Adj. faculty mem. Suffolk U. Sch. Law, 1998—; mem. Jud. Nominating Com., 1982-86 Mem. Mass. Bar Assn. (bd. dirs. 1982-84), Womens Bar Assn. (founding mem., v.p., bd. dirs. 1979-81). Office: US Bankruptcy Ct Thomas P O'Neill Fed Bldg 10 Causeway St Rm 1101 Boston MA 02222-1009

KENNER, MARILYN SFERRA, civil engineer; b. Youngstown, Ohio, Oct. 16, 1959; d. Joseph James and Mary (Conti) Sferra; m. Walter Sherden Kenner, July 7, 1984. B in Engring., Youngstown State U., 1982. Registered profl. engr., Ohio. Design and constrn. engr. Mahoning County Engr.'s Office, Youngstown, 1982-89, chief dep. engr., 1989—. Mem. engring. dean search com. Youngstown State U. Mem. Mahoning Valley Soc. Profl. Engrs. (pres., v.p. 1990-93, treas. 1987-90). Democrat. Roman Catholic. Home: 6941 Lockwood Blvd Youngstown OH 44512-4014 Office: Mahoning County Engr Office 940 Bears Den Rd Youngstown OH 44511-1218 Office Phone: 330-799-1581.

KENNEY, BELINDA JILL FORSEMAN, technology company executive; b. Oak Ridge, Tenn., Dec. 18, 1955; d. Jack Woodrow and Betty Jean Forseman; m. Ronald Gene Kenney, Feb. 23, 1985; 1 child, Brandon. BS, U. Tenn., 1977, postgrad., 1977-78; MBA, Emory U., 2000. Sales rep. Xerox Corp., Nashville, 1978—82, maj. account sales mgr., 1982—83, region sales ops. mgr. St. Louis, 1984—86, dist. sales mgr. Overland Park, Kans., 1987—89, dist. mgr. San Antonio, 1989—95, v.p. Houston, 1995—97, v.p., region gen. mgr. Bus. Svcs. Atlanta, 1998—99, sr. v.p. region mgr. NASG, 2000—01; corp. v.p. worldwide mktg. and corp. strategy Storage Tech. Corp., Superior, Colo., 2001—04. Exec. in residence Leeds Sch. Bus. U. Colo. Patron M.D. Anderson Cancer Ctr.; bd. dirs. Wise Women's Coun.; exec.-in-residence Leeds Sch., U. Colo.; bd. dirs. Women's Vision Found., Denver, United Way Boulder County. Mem. Rocky Mountain MENSA. Lutheran. Avocations: jogging, reading, tennis, health and fitness. Office: 1 Storagetek Dr Louisville CO 80028-0001

KENNEY, COLLEEN M. lawyer; b. 1959; BS, No. Ill. U., 1981, MS, 1982; JD, U. Chgo., 1991. Bar: Ill. 1991. Ptnr. Sidley Austin Brown & Wood, Chgo., 2000—. Office: Sidley Austin Brown and Wood Bank One Plz 10 S Dearborn St Chicago IL 60603*

KENNEY, ESTELLE KOVAL, artist; b. Chgo., Feb. 15, 1928; d. Hyman English and Florence (Browman) Koval; B.F.A., Art Inst. Chgo., 1976, M.F.A., 1978; postgrad. Yale U., 1980; m. Herbert Kenney, Feb. 6, 1948; children— Carla, Robert. Art therapist Grove Sch., Lake Forest, Ill., 1973-78, New Trier High Sch. and Central High Sch., Winnetka, Ill., 1978-79, Mosely Sch., Chgo., 1979, Cove Sch., Evanston, Ill., 1979-82; dir. art therapy concentration, instr. painting and drawing Loyola U., Chgo., 1981— ; pres., art dir. Nuts on Clark Inc., Chgo.; one woman shows: Evanston (Ill.) Library, 1971, Zaks Gallery, Chgo., 1977, 79, 82, Renaissance Soc.-Bergman Gallery, U. Chgo., 1980; group shows include: Ill. State Mus., 1975, Women Artists, Here and Now, 1976, Chgo. Connections travelling exhbn., 1976-77, Nat. Women's Caucus for Art, 1977, Nancy Lurie Gallery, 1978, Marycrest Coll. Gallery, Davenport, Iowa, 1982, Chgo. Internat. Art Expo, 1981, 82, 83, Notre Dame U. Gallery, South Bend, Ind., 1982; represented in permanent collections: Ill. State Mus., Springfield, Union League Club of Chgo. Mem. Am. Art Therapy Assn., Ill. Art Therapy Assn. (pres. 1979—), Coll. Art Assn. Home: 3830 N Clark St Chicago IL 60613-2812 Office: Loyola University of Chicago Dept Fine Arts 6525 N She Ridan Rd Chicago IL 60626 E-mail: estellekenneynutsonclark@nutsonclark.com.

KENNEY, KRISTIE ANNE, ambassador; b. Wash. m. William R. Brownfield. M in Latin am. studies, Tulane U.; B in polit. sci., Clemson U.; attended, Nat. War Coll. Amb. Ecuador US Dept. State, Quito, Ecuador, 2002—; sr. adv. to asst. sec. Internat. Narcotics and Law Enforcement, 2001—; exe. sec. State Dept.; econ. cons. US Mission, Geneva; econ. off. US Embassy, Argentina, consular off.; dir. State Dept. Oper. Ctr., Wash.; mem. Nat. Security Coun.; polit. mil. officer Off. of NATO Affairs. Recipient Dist. Honor award, State Dept., Arnold Raphel Meml. award. Avocations: skiing, tennis. Office: Embassy of USA Avenida 12 de Octubre y Patria 120 Quito Ecuador

KENNEY, MARY R. software engineer; b. Richmond, Va., 1945; d. Thomas W. and Clara G. K.; m. Jeremy M. (div.). BS and MS in Math., Howard U., 1967; MS in Computer Sci., Steven's Inst., 1984. Sr. math. aide Ctr. Naval Analysis, Rosslyn, Va., 1967-77; sr. programmer analyst Control Data Corp., Rockville, Md., 1977-81; software quality engr. AT&T Bell Labs., Piscataway, N.J., 1981-84, Bellcore, Piscataway, 1984-99, Telcordia Techs., Piscataway, 1999—. Chair fundraising Youth in Sports Found., Piscataway, 1995-97; mem. fundraising com. Cmty. League Active Youth, New Brunswick, N.J., 1994, N.J. Rams, Newark, 1992-93. Mem. AAUW, NAFE, ACM, Am. Mgmt. Assn. Avocations: reading, crochet, bowling. Office: Telcordia Techs Inc 3 Corp Pl Piscataway NJ 08854

KENNON, GLORIA OLIVER, guidance counselor; b. Birmingham, Ala., Nov. 6, 1942; d. Leavy Winston Oliver and Lida Moore White; m. Rozmond Herron Kennon, Oct. 10, 1985. BS, St. Augustine's Coll., 1966; MS, Ala. A&M U., 1975. Lic. guidance counselor. Tchr. A. H. Parker Sch., Biringham, Ala., 1966-68, Morse Elem. Sch., Tarrytown, N.Y., 1968-70; cons. VII Human Rels. Desegregation U. S. Ala., Mobile, 1970; counselor Opportunities Indstrialization Ctr., Washington, 1971-73; teacher, counselor Sch. Cmty Anti Narcotic Program, N.Y.C., 1973-75; guidance counselor Birmingham Pub. Schs., 1975—80, Mpls. Pub. Schs., 1985—. Pres. Mpls Counselor's Forum, 1989-90. Mem. Minn. Sch. Counselors' Assn. (bd. dirs. 1989-90), Minn. Counseling and Devel. Assn., Am. Counseling Assn., The Links, Inc., Delta Sigma Theta. Avocations: dance aerobics, music, reading, snorkeling. Home: 5120 Lake Crest Cir Hoover AL 35226-5027

KENNY, DEBORAH, marketing professional, educator; b. N.J., Nov. 13, 1962; BA, U. Pa., 1983; MA, PhD, Columbia U., 1994. Publ. Dimension Mag., N.Y.C., 1987-90; pres. N.Am. opers. The Jerusalem Report, N.Y.C., 1994-97; v.p. mktg. Parenting group Time Warner, N.Y.C., 1998-99; pres. publ. divsn. Sesame St., N.Y.C., 1999—. Bd. dirs. Domestic Abuse Prevention Project. Fellow IWF-Harvard Leadership Found., 1997-98; recipient Clarion Advt. award, 1997, Echo Leader award Direct Mktg. Assn., 1989. E-mail: dkenny2222@aol.com.

KENNY, JANE MARIE, government agency administrator; b. Jersey City; m. Greg Myer; 3 children. B, Trinity Coll., Washington, 1974; M in English and Am. Lit., Rutgers U., 1982. Chief policy and planning Gov. Whitman, 1994—96; v.p. corp. cmty. affairs Beneficial Mgmt. Corp., Peapack, NJ, 1990—94; cabinet sec. Gov. Tom Kean, 1986—90; commr. NJ Dept. Cmty. Affairs, 1996—2001; regional adminstr. region 2 US EPA,

2001—. Recipient Nat. Pub. Svc. award, Women in Govt. award, Good Housekeeping. Fellow: Nat. Acad. Pub. Adminstrs. Office: US EPA Region 2 290 Broadway New York NY 10007-1866 Office Phone: 212-637-5000.

KENNY, SHIRLEY STRUM, academic administrator; b. Tyler, Tex., Aug. 28, 1934; d. Marcus Leon and Florence (Golenternek) Strum; m. Robert Wayne Kenny, July 22, 1956; children: David Jack, Joel Strum, Daniel Clark, Jonathan Matthew, Sarah Elizabeth. BA, BJ, U. Tex., 1955; MA, U. Minn., 1957; PhD, U. Chgo., 1964; LHD (hon.), U. Rochester, 1988, Chonnam U., 1996, Donguk U., 2000. Chair English dept. U. Md., College Park, 1973-79, provost Arts and Humanities, 1979-85; pres. CUNY Queens Coll., Flushing, 1985-94, SUNY, Stony Brook, 1994—; chair Brookhaven Sci. Assocs. Mem. regional adv. bd. Chase Manhattan Corp. Author: The Conscious Lovers, 1968, The Plays of Richard Steele, 1971, The Performers and Their Plays, 1982, The Works of George Farquhar, 2 vols., 1988, British Theatre and the Other Arts, 1984; contbr. articles to profl. jours. Bd. dirs. Goodwill Greater N.Y., L.I. Assn. Named Outstanding Woman, U. Md., 1983, Outstanding Alumnus, U. Tex. Coll. Comm., 1989, Disting. Alumna, U. Tex., 1999; recipient Disting. Alumnus award, U. Chgo. Club Washington, 1980, Svc. and Leadership award, N.Y. Urban League, 1988. Mem.: Boyer Comm. Educating Undergrads (chair), Assn. Am. Colls. and Univs. (bd. dirs. 1988—96). Office: SUNY 310 Adminstrn Bldg Stony Brook NY 11790-0701

KENOFER, DORIS DILLON See DILLON, DORIS

KENSEK, MAGDALENE AGNES, private school educator; d. Charles and Amalie Teresa Moravec; m. Edward Frank Kensek, June 24, 1972; children: Elizabeth Anne, Victoria Anne. BA in German, Coll. of St. Francis, Joliet, Ill., 1970. Cert. tchr. Ill., 1970. Social studies dept. head St. Daniel the Prophet Sch., Chicago, Ill., 1990—2000, gifted program advisor, 1995—2000; student coun. moderator St. Cletus Sch., LaGrange, Ill., 2000—. Recipient Heart of the Sch. award, Archdiocese of Chgo., 1999; grantee, Golden Apple Found. for Excellence in Tchg., 2001. Mem.: NSTA (assoc.), Nat. Coun. Tchrs. Math. (assoc.), Nat. Cath. Educators Assn. (assoc.). Roman Catholic. Avocations: gardening, reading, travel. Office: St Cletus School 700 West 55th St LaGrange IL 60525

KENT, AIMEE BERNICE PETERSEN, small business owner, interior designer, landscape architect, artist; b. North Vancouver, B.C., Can., Apr. 13, 1939; d. Samuel Nathaniel and Aimee Selena (Topping) Hadley; m. Gary Andrew Petersen, May 1, 1959; children: Todd William, Troy Andrew; m. Michael Douglas Kent, Aug. 1, 1998. Student, U. Wash., 1957—59, Edmonds (Wash.) C.C., 1967—74. Owner, designer The Designing Woman, Edmonds, 1979—. Pres. Ballinger Elem. PTA, 1969-71, Madrona Jr. H.S., 1973, 74; deaconess United Presbyn. Ch., Edmonds, 1967-75. Recipient Golden Acorn award Ballinger Sch. PTA, 1972; named Woman of Yr., Jr. Women Federated Women's, 1967. Mem. Nat. Fedn. Ind. Bus. People, Better Bus. Bur., Bus. and Profl. Women, Women Investing Now (founder 1991, pres. 1997-2000), Edmonds C. of C., Sons of Norway (Lodge 130 social chmn. 1987-93). Presbyterian. Avocation: artist. Home: 23807 113th Pl W Woodway WA 98020-5204 Office: 23807 113th Pl W Woodway WA 98020-5204

KENT, DEBORAH, automotive executive; div.; children: Jessica, Jordan. BA in Psychology, So. Ill. U.; MA in Indsl. Psychology, Washington U., St. Louis. Quality control supr., reliability engr. Ford Motor Co. Assembly Plant, Dearborn, Mich., area mgr. Wixom, Mich., 1987-92, mfg. mgr. Chgo., 1992-94, plant mgr. Avon Lake, Ohio, 1994—. Office: Ford Motor Co 650 Miller Rd Avon Lake OH 44012-2398

KENT, GEORGIA L. obstetrician-gynecologist, healthcare executive, educator; b. N.Y.C., May 30, 1950; d. Harry J. and Eva R. K. BS in Biology with honors, U. Pitts., 1971; MD, U. Pa., 1975; MBA, George Washington U., 1991. Diplomate Am. Bd. Obstetricians-Gynecologists; MD, Colo., Calif., N.Y., N.J., Pa. Sr. instr. ob-gyn. Hahnemann U., Phila., 1979-82; obstetrician-gynecologist Kaiser Group Health Assn., Washington, 1982-90; med. dir. Pacificare, Fountain Valley, Calif., 1991-93, Denver, 1993-94; v.p. med. svcs. The Prudential Ins. Co. of Am., Prudential Healthcare, Roseland, N.J., 1994-96; potter, healthcare cons. self employed, West Orange, N.J., 1997-99, Pitts., 1999—; coll. chair undergrad. bus. and mgmt. degree programs U. Phoenix-Pitts. Campus, 2000—. Guest lectr. U. Calif. Riverside, 1992-93, Denver U., 1993-94; adj. faculty Duquesne U., 1999—; dept. chair undergrad. bus. & mgmt. U. Phoenix, Pitts., 2000—. Contbg. author, featured in: (book) Women in Medicine and Management: A Mentoring Guide, 1995; exhibited in group shows at N.J. Ctr. for Visual Arts Mem. Show, 1997, 98, Sweetwater Art Ctr., 1999, North Hills Art Ctr., 2000 (hon. mention). Mem. AAUW, Am. Coll. Obstetricians and Gynecologists, Phi Beta Kappa, Beta Gamma Sigma. Avocations: greyhound rescue/adoption, potter, gardening, walking. Office: Penn Ctr West Four Ste 100 Pittsburgh PA 15276 E-mail: georgia.kent@apollogrp.edu.

KENT, JILL, midwife; b. Cottage Grove, Oreg., May 22, 1953; d. Laurence Durward and Laurel Naomi Kent; m. Mark Taylor White, June 15, 1974 (div. Nov. 12, 1987); children: Darcy Michelle Shargo, Kara Naomi White, Cameron St. John White, Brendan Morrison White; m. Stashenko Emil Hempeck, Aug. 26, 1989; 1 child, Duncan Alexandre Hempeck ; 1 child, Ethan Ambrosius. Grad., Van Horn H.S., Kansas City, Mo., 1971; student, Ctrl. Mo. State U., 1971—72, Moorhead (Minn.) State U., 1990—91. Lic. midwife Bd. Med. Practice, Minn., 2000, cert. profl. midwife N.Am. Registry Midwives. Midwife, owner, operator The Stork's Nest Birth Ctr., Moorhead, 1981—. Mem.: Minn. Assn. Midwives (pres. 1985—88), Minn. Midwives Guild (pres. 1988—94), Minn. Coun. Cert. Profl. Midwives (treas. 2000—03), Midwives Alliance N.Am. (midwest regional rep. to bd. 1985—88). Unitarian. Avocations: antiques, books, travel, gardening, music. Home: 520 32d Ave S #327 Moorhead MN 56560 Office: The Stork's Nest Birth Ctr 312 Hwy 75 N Moorhead MN 56560 E-mail: jk-cpm1@juno.com.

KENT, JULIE, ballet dancer, actress, model; b. Bethesda, Md., July 11, 1969; d. Charles Lindbergh and Jennifer Elsie Cox; m. Victor Barbee, 1996. Grad. high sch., Potomac, Md. Apprentice Am. Ballet Theatre, N.Y.C., 1985-86, mem. corps de ballet, 1986-1990, soloist, 1990-93, prin. dancer, 1993—. Starring role (films) Dancers, 1986, Center Stage, 2000; performed as a guest artist nationally and internationally. Recipient Prix de Lausanne Internat. Ballet competition, 1986, 1st prize at Erik Bruhn Competition in Toronto, 1993, Prix Benois de la Danse, Stuttgart, Germany, 2000; named one of 50 Most Beautiful People, People Mag., 1993. Office: Am Ballet Theatre 890 Broadway Fl 3 New York NY 10003

KENT, LINDA GAIL, dancer; b. Buffalo, Sept. 21, 1946; d. Jerol Edward and Dorismae (Kohler) K.; m. Nicholas Wolff Lyndon, June 9, 1996. BS, Juilliard Sch., 1968. Dancer Alvin Ailey Am. Dance Theater, 1968-74, then prin. dancer, 1970-74; prin. dancer Paul Taylor Dance Co., N.Y.C., 1975-89; dir. dance Perry-Mansfield Performing Arts Sch. and Camp, Steamboat Springs, Colo., 2001—. Faculty Juilliard Sch., 1984—; artist-in-residence Union Theological Seminary, N.Y. Mem. Am. Guild Mus. Artists, Actors Equity. Democrat. Unitarian Universalist. Home: 91 Payson Ave New York NY 10034-2722 Office: The Juilliard Sch Dance Divsn 60 Lincoln Center Plz New York NY 10023-6588

KENT, SUSAN, library director, consultant; b. N.Y.C., Mar. 18, 1944; d. Elias and Minnie (Barnett) Solomon; m. Eric Goldberg, Mar. 27, 1966 (div. Mar. 1991); children: Evan Goldberg, Jessica Goldberg; m. Rolly Kent, Dec. 20, 1991. BA in English Lit. with honors, SUNY, 1965; MS, Columbia U., 1966. Libr., sr. libr. N.Y. Pub. Libr., 1965-67, br. mgr. Donnell Art Libr., 1967-68; reference libr. Paedergaat br. Bklyn. Pub. Libr., 1971-72; reference libr. Finkelstein Meml. Libr., Spring Valley, N.Y., 1974-76; coord. adult and young adult svcs. Tucson Pub. Libr., 1977-80, acting libr. dir., 1982, dep. libr. dir., 1980-87; mng. dir. Ariz. Theatre Co., Tucson, Phoenix, 1987-89; dir. Mpls. Pub. Libr. and Info. Ctr., 1990-95; city libr. L.A. Pub. Libr., 1995—. Tchr. Pima CC, Tucson, 1978; grad. libr. sch. U. Ariz., Tucson, 1995—; panelist Ariz. Commn. Arts., 1981—85; mem. bd. devel. and fundraising Child's Play, Phoenix, 1983; reviewer pub. programs NEH, 1985, panelist challenge grants, 1986—89, panelist state programs, 1988; cons., presenter workshops Young Adult Svcs. divsn. ALA, 1986—88; bd. dirs., mem. organizing devel. and fundraising com. Flagstaff (Ariz.) Symphony Orch., 1988; cons. to librs. and nonprofit instns., 1989—90, 1992—; bd. advisors UCLA Grad. Sch. Edn. and Info. Scis., 1998—2001; presenter in field. Contbr. articles to profl. jours. Chair arts and culture com. Tucson Tomorrow, 1981—85; commr. Ariz. Commn. Arts, 1983—87; bd. dirs., v.p. Ariz. Dance Theatre, 1984—86; bd. dirs. Arizonans Cultural Devel., Ariz., 1987—89, YWCA Mpls., 1991—92; bd. dirs. women's studies adv. coun. U. Ariz., 1985—90; participant Leadership Mpls., 1990—91. Recipient Libr. of the Yr., Libr. Jour., 2002, Info. Assocs. Exec. Leadership award, UCLA Anderson Sch., 2001, Interfaith Leadership award, Archdiocese of L.A., 2004; fellow, Sch. Libr. Sci., Columbia U., 1965—66. Mem.: ALA (mem. membership com. S.W. regional chair 1983—86, mem. com. appts. 1986—87, gov. coun. 1990—98, planning and budget assembly del. 1991—93, chair conf. com. 1996—97, Joseph Lippincott award 2003), Coun. Libr. and Info. Resources (bd. dirs. 2000—, Libr. of the Yr. award 2002), Libr. Adminstrn. and Mgmt. Assn. (mem. John Cotton Dana Award com. 1994—95), Urban Librs. Coun. (mem. exec. bd. 1994—2001, treas. 1996—98, vice chair/chair elect 1998, 1999, chair 1999—2000), Calif. Libr. Assn., Pub. Libr. Assn. (mem. nominating com. 1980—82, v.p. 1986—87, pres. 1987—88, chair publs. assmebly 1988—89, chair nat. conf. 1994, chair legis. com. 1994—95). Office: LA Pub Libr 630 W 5th St Los Angeles CA 90071-2002 Office Phone: 213-228-7515. Business E-Mail: skent@lapl.org.

KENYON, CYNTHIA, medical researcher; BS in Chemistry and Biochemistry, U. Ga., 1976; PhD, MIT, 1981. Post-doctoral fellow Med. Rsch. Coun. Lab. Molecular Biology, Cambridge, England; prof. U. Calif., San Francisco, 1986—, Herbert Boyer Disting. prof. biochemistry and biophysics. Contbr. articles to profl. jours. Mem.: AAAS, NAS. Office: Dept Biochemistry and Biophysics U Calif Box 2200 Genentech Hall S312D San Francisco CA 94143

KENYON, DAPHNE ANNE, economics educator; b. Augusta, Ga., Aug. 14, 1952; d. Lawrence Austin and Shirley (Knaus) Kenyon; m. Peter George Kachavos, Oct. 22, 1988. BA, Mich. State U., 1974; MA in Econs., U. Mich., 1976, PhD in Econs., 1980. Asst. prof. Dartmouth Coll., Hanover, N.H., 1979-83; sr. analyst U.S. Adv. Commn. on Intergovt. Relations, Washington, 1983-85; fin. economist U.S. Treasury Dept., Washington, 1985-87; sr. research assoc. Urban Inst., Washington, 1987-88; Lincoln fellow Lincoln Inst. of Land Policy, Cambridge, Mass., 1988-89; asst. prof. econs. Simmons Coll., Boston, 1989-90, assoc. prof. econs., 1991-98, chair dept. econs., 1996-99, prof. econs., 1998-2000; pres. The Josiah Bartlett Ctr. for Pub. Policy, 1999—2002; prin. D.A. Kenyon & Assocs., 2002—. Cons. U.S. IRS Adv. Panel, Washington, 1987-99; appt. to Mass. Dept. of Revenue Adv. Group, 1991; bd. dirs. New Eng. Econ. Project, v.p., 1997-98, pres., 1999. Assoc. editor Urban Studies, 1988-93, mem. U.S. editl. adv. com., 1993—; co-editor: Coping with Mandates, 1990, Competition Among States and Local Governments, 1991; N.H. corr. State Tax Notes, 1990-93; mem. editl. bd. Mass. Benchmarks, 1997-99; columnist: State Tax Notes, 2003—; contbr. articles to profl. jours. Active NH Gov.'s Revenue Adv. Com., Concord, 1982, 98, N.H. State Consensus Revenue Estimating Panel, 2000-03, Windham NH Sch. bd., 2000-03, vice chmn. 2002-03. Fellow Grad. fellow, NSF, 1974. Mem. Am. Econ. Assn. (com. on the status of women in econs. profession 1995-98), Nat. Tax Assn. (bd. dirs. 1996-99, chair intergovernmental fiscal rels. com. 1996-98, program chair 1999), Nat. Tax Jour. (referee Ea. Econ. Jour.). Episcopalian.

KENYON, KAREN BETH SMITH, literature educator, writer; b. Oklahoma City, Sept. 4, 1938; d. Claude Emory and Evelyn Grace (Brown) Smith; m. Richard Bertram Kenyon, Feb. 14, 1963 (dec. Nov. 1978); 1 child, Richard Laurence. BA with honors, San Diego State U., 1977, MA in English, 1987. Instr. Mira Costa Coll., Cardiff, Calif., 1981—; instr. extended studies U. Calif., San Diego, 1982—; instr. San Diego State U., 1985—. Author: Sunshower, 1981, The Bronte Family, 2003; contbr. over 800 articles to profl. jours. Recipient Creativity award, San Diego Ctr. for Creativity, 1973, Poetry award, Atlantic Monthly, 1975. Mem.: Soc. Children's Book Writers and Illustrators, PEN. Democrat. Mailing: PO Box 12604 La Jolla CA 92039

KENYON, KENDRA SUE, organizational consultant; b. Boise, Idaho, Aug. 26, 1956; d. Francis Elwood and Patricia Ann (Sellars) K.; m. David Michael Bertsch, Feb. 16, 1972 (div. May 1979); 1 child, Shad I.; m. Curtis Sumner Van Inwegen, Sept. 1, 1997; 1 child, Cyprus Kenyon. BA in Comm., Boise State U., 1988; M in Psychol. Counseling, Idaho State U., 1991; PhD, U. Idaho, 1999. Nat. cert. counselor, N.Y.; lic. profl. counselor; cert. mediator. Sport psychologist Boise State U., 1990-91; dir. of therapy Northview Hosp., Boise, 1991-94; pvt. practice Boise, 1994—; pres. Orgnl. Performance Cons. Inc., Boise, 1995—. Adj. prof. Boise State U., 1991-93; counselor, conflict mediator, trainer State of Idaho, Boise, 1994—; cons. Hewlett Packard, Boise, 1997-98; mem. adv. bd. Indsl. Commn., Boise, 1997—. Legis. advisor Westerberg & Panter Assoc., Boise, 1995—; senate candidate Dem. Party Dist. 19, Boise, 1997; past mem. Parents and Youth Against Drug Abuse, Boise, 1990-91. Internat. Amb. scholar Rotary Internat., 1998—; doctoral fellowship Idaho State U., 1991. Mem. ASTD, Internat. Assn. of Univ. Women, Idaho Psychol. Assn., Internat. Soc. for Performance Improvement, Idaho Assn. on Counseling and Devel., Assn. for Multi-Cultural Counseling and Tng. Democrat. Avocations: white water rafting, travel, fly fishing, hiking, skiing. Address: 435 Carmel Creeper Pl Encinitas CA 92024-7706

KEOGH, HEIDI HELEN DAKE, advocate; b. Saratoga, N.Y., July 12, 1950; d. Charles Starks and Phyllis Sylvia (Edmunds) Dake; m. Randall Frank Keogh, Nov. 3, 1973; children: Tyler Cameron, Kelly Dake. Student, U. Colo., 1972. Reception, promotions Sta. KLAK, KJAE, Lakewood, Colo., 1972-73; acct. exec. Mixed Media Advt. Agy., Denver, 1973-75; writer, mktg. Jr. League Cookbook Devel., Denver, 1986-88; chmn., coord. Colorado Cache & Creme de Colorado Cookbooks, 1988-90. Speakers bur. Mile High Transplant Bank, Denver, 1983-84, Writer's Inst., U. Denver, 1988; bd. dirs. Stewart's Ice Cream Co., Inc., Jr. League, Denver. Contbr. articles to profl. jours. Fiscal officer, bd. dirs. Mile High Transplant Bank; blockworker Heart Fund and Am. Cancer Soc., Littleton, Colo., 1978—, Littleton Rep. Com., 1980-84; fundraising vol. Littleton Pub. Schs., 1980-98; vol. Gathering Place Assn., bd. dirs., 2003—, pres., 2003—, chmn. Brown Bag benefit, 1996; vol. Hearts for Life, 1991—, Oneday, 1992, Denver Ballet Guild, 1992—, Denver Ctr. Alliance, 1993—, Newborn Hope, 1980—, Girls, Inc., 1995—, Girls Hope, VOA Guild, 1996—, Le Bal de Ballet, 1998—, The Denver Social Register and Record, 1999—. Mem. Jr. League Denver (pub. rels. bd., v.p. ways and means 1989-90, planning coun./ad hoc 1990-92, sustainer spl. events 1993-94, found. 2002—), Community Emergency Fund (chair 1991-92), Jon D. Williams Cotillion at Columbine (chmn. 1991-93), Columbine Country Club, Gamma Alpha Chi, Pi Beta Phi Alumnae Club (pres. Denver chpt. 1984-85, 93-94, nat. conv. chmn. Denver 2001), Pi Beta Phi Found. (grantee 2000-05). Episcopalian. Avocations: traveling, skiing, golf, family activities. Home: 63 Fairway Ln Littleton CO 80123-6648

KEOGH, MARY CUDAHY, artist; b. Milw., Nov. 11, 1920; d. John and Katherine (Reed) Cudahy; m. Frank Stephen Keogh, Jan. 17, 1947 (dec. 1980); children: Mary K., Anne C., Patricia, Margaret E.; m. Warren Stringer, July 5, 1985. Student, Smith Coll., 1939-42; BFA, Milw. Downer Coll., 1944; postgrad., Parsons Sch. of Design, 1945. Artist, 1969—. Lect. Woman's Club of Wis., 1977, workshops, Omaha, 1978-80, demo. Cape Coral (Fla.) Art League, 1991. One and two person shows include Lee County Alliance for the Arts, 1988, 90, 96, Barbara Mann Hall, Ft. Myers, 1992, Phillips Gallery, Sanibel, Fla., 1993, Uihlein-Peters Gallery, Milw., 1994, Alliance for the Arts, 1996, Phillips Gallery Sanibel, 1997, Syzygy Gallery, 2000, Retro. Show Phillips Gallery, Sanibel, Fla., 2004; exhibited in group shows at Sarasota Visual Arts Ctr., 1995, Fla. Artists' Group, Winter Haven, 1996, Lee County Alliance for the Arts, 1996, Women's Caucus for Art, Longboat Key, Fla., 1997, Fla. Artists Group, Venice, 1997, Venice Biennial, 1997, Phillips Gallery, 1998; represented in permanent collections U. Utah, Cedar City, Northwestern Bell, Omaha, Health Park, Ft. Myers, The Endeavers Group, Milw., Wis. others; Retro. Art House, 2003. Named Best of Show, Nebr. Wesleyan Coll., Lincoln, 1988; recipient 3d place, Sarasota Visual Arts Ctr., 1995, Big Arts, Sanibel, 1995, honorable mention award, Venice (Fla.) Biennial, 1997, Fla. Artist Group award, Jacksonville Mus. Contemporary Art, 1998, Best of Show, Big Arts Sanibel, 2000, 2d award, Big Arts, 2000, award, Flag Ann. Exhbn., 2001, Flag Invitational, 2002. Mem. Women Contemporary Artists (Best of Show spring show), Nat. Mus. Women in the Arts (charter), Fla. Artists Group. Roman Catholic. Avocations: cooking, traveling. Home: 9439 Coventry Ct Sanibel FL 33957-4231 E-mail: wmstringer@comcast.net.

KEOHANE, NANNERL OVERHOLSER, university president, political scientist; b. Blytheville, Ark., Sept. 18, 1940; d. James Arthur and Grace (McSpadden) Overholser; m. Patrick Henry III, Sept. 16, 1962 (div. May 1969); 1 child, Stephan Henry ; m. Robert Owen Keohane, Dec. 18, 1970; children: Sarah, Jonathan, Nathaniel. BA, Wellesley Coll., 1961, Oxford U., Eng., 1963; PhD, Yale U., 1967. Faculty Swarthmore Coll., Pa., 1967—73, Stanford U., Calif., 1973—81, fellow Ctr. for Advanced Study in the Behavioral Scis., 1978—79, 1987—88; pres., prof. polit. sci. Wellesley (Mass.) Coll., 1981—93, Duke U., Durham, NC, 1993—. Bd. dirs. IBM. Author: Philosophy and the State in France: The Renaissance to the Enlightenment, 1980; co-editor: Feminist Theory: A Critique of Ideology, 1982. Trustee Colonial Williamsburg Found., 1988—2001, Nat. Humanities Ctr., 1993—, Doris Duke Charitable Found., 1996—. Named to National Women's Hall of Fame, 1995; recipient Marshall Medal, 2003; fellow Dissertation fellow, AAUW; scholar Marshall scholar, 1961—63. Fellow: Am. Philos. Soc., Am. Acad. Arts and Scis.; mem.: Coun. on Fgn. Rels., Watauga Club, Saturday Club, Phi Beta Kappa. Democrat. Episcopalian. Office: Duke Univ Box 90001 207 Allen Bldg Durham NC 27708-0001

KEOUGH, SHAWN, state legislator; b. Pompton Plains, N.J., Dec. 30, 1959; m. Mike Keough; children: Bryan, Daniel. Student, North Idaho Coll.; student in bus. mgmt., Lewis Clark State Coll. In pub. rels.; mem. Idaho Senate, Dist. 1, Boise, 1996—. Vice chair transp. com., mem. agrl. affairs, commerce and human resources, and edn. coms. Mem. Idaho Women in Timber, Greater Sandpoint (Idaho) C. of C. Republican. Protestant. Office: State Capitol PO Box 83720 Boise ID 83720-3720

KEPCHER, CAROLYN, real estate company executive; m. George Kepcher; children: Connor, Cassidy. Degree in bus. mktg., Mercy Coll. Dir. sales and mktg. Beck Summit Hotel Mgmt. Group, Boca Raton, Fla.; exec. v.p. The Trump Orgn.; gen. mgr., COO Trump Nat. Golf Club, Briarcliff, NY, Bedminster, NJ. Office: Trump Nat Golf Club 339 Pine Rd Westchester NY 10510*

KEPNER, RITA MARIE, sculptor, writer, editor, educator; b. Binghamton, N.Y., Nov. 15, 1944; d. Peter Walter and Helena Theresa (Piotrowski) Kramnicz; m. John C. Matthiesen; 1 child, Stewart J. Matthiesen. Student, Elmira Coll., 1962-63; BA, Harpur Coll. at SUNY, 1966; postgrad., Okla. U., 1988, Seattle Pacific U., 1991, Western Wash. U., 1991, 92; MA in Mgmt., City U., Seattle, 1998; diploma of merit (hon.), Acad. Bedriacense, Calvatore, Italy, 1984. Holder USCG capt. lic. for passenger carrying aux. sailing vessels up to 50 tons, 1980—. Instr. exptl. coll. U. Wash., 1972-74; instr. sculpture internship program Evergreen Coll., Olympia, Wash., 1974-78; informal visual arts amb. between U.S. and Poland, 1976-81; pres. fed. women's program coun. Seattle dist., 1985-86; fed. women's program mgr. Schweinfurt, Germany, 1986-87, Wiesbaden, Germany, 1988; artist-in-residence City of Seattle, 1975, 77-78; del. Internat. Sculptors Conf., Toronto, Ont., Can., 1978; writer, editor, pub. affairs specialist Seattle dist. U.S. Army Corps Engrs.; spokesperson Exxon Valdez oil spill clean-up ops.; pub. affairs officer Wiesbaden Milcom Hdqrs., 1987-88; editor Schweinfurt Crusader, 1986-87; instr., writing & editing for mgrs. Dept. of Navy, Bremerton, Wash., 1991-93. Apptd. disaster assistance spokesperson and pub. affairs reservist Hdqrs., Fed. Emergency Mgmt. Agy., Washington, mid-western floods U.S., 1993, So. Calif. firestorm, 1993, Northridge earthquake, Calif., 1994, States of Ga., Oreg., Wash. and Alaska, 1994, No. Calif. floods, 1995, Oklahoma City Bombing, 1995, W.Va. floods, 1995, Wash. State floods, 1996, N.Y. State snowstorms and floods, 1996, Pa. floods, 1996, Huricane Fran, N.C., 1996, severe storms and flooding Calif., 1997, Ohio, 1997, Ill., 1997, blizzards and floods, N.D., 1997, winter storms, N.H., 1998, El Nino earthslides and floods in Calif., 1998, Mass. floods, 1998, Hurricane Bonnie, N.C., N.Y. storms, Hurricane Georges, U.S.V.I., 1998, Okla. City tornadoes, 1999, Kans. tornadoes, 1999, Hurricane Brett, Tex., 1999, Salt Lake City tornado, 1999, Tropical Storm Floyd Floods, N.Y., 1999, Tropical Storm Floyd, Vermont, 1999, disaster response reservist; temp. reassignment to NTSB for work on flight 990 Egyptian Airline Crash, 1999, Los Alamos Fire, 2000, Mont. Fires, 2000, Arkansas ice Storm, 2001, Oklahoma Ice Storm, Windstorms, Tornadoes and Floods, 2001, Kans. Ice Storms, 2002, Ky. Hailstorms, Floods and Tornadoes, 2002, Tenn. Tornados and Floods, 2003, spl. assignment FEMA Reg. 3, Phila., 2004, others; trainer class for lead pub. affairs officers Emergency Mgmt. Inst., Emmitsburg, Md., 2003. One-woman shows include Willoughby Wallace Meml. Gallery, Branford, Conn., 1967, Penryn Gallery, Seattle, 1970, 73, 76, Haines Gallery, Seattle, 1975, Zoliborz Gallery, Warsaw, Poland, 1981, Yorkshire 510, Norman, Okla., 1988, Women's Ctr., Port Townsend, Wash., 1995, Bruskin Gallery, 1998, Turtle Bluff, Nordland, Wash., 2001; group shows include SUNY, Binghamton, 1966, 96, Manawata Art Gallery, Palmerston North, N.Z., 1976, Modern Art Mus., Seattle, 1976, Portland (Oreg.) Art Mus., 1976, Hajnowka (Poland) Gallery, 1977, Die Roemer Gallery, Wiesbaden, Fed. Republic Germany, 1988, Blue Heron Gallery, Port Hadlock, Wash., 1991-92, Quimper Arts, Bruskin Gallery, Port Townsend, Wash., 1993, 94, Port Townsend Women's Ctr., 1995, Ichikawa, Japan, 1997, Scott Milo Gallery, Anacortes, Wash., 2000-2003, Turtle Bluff Art Show, Marrowstone Island, Wash., 2001, Jefferson County Arts Alliance Gallery, Port Townsend, Wash., 2002, Quimper Arts, 2003, Gallery 9, 2004; major works include Peace Pipe, Zalaegerszeg, Hungary, Human Forms in Balance, City of Seattle, 1975, Unity, City of Znin, Poland, 1976, Rough to Smooth, Hard to Soft Man to Woman In Transition is Unity, Seattle Pub. Libr., 1978, The Surveyor, Savannah, Ga.; sculpture commn. U.S. Army Corps of Engrs., 1995, 96, Medicine Man-Cowlitz Indian Tribe, 2000; contbr. articles to N.W. Arts, Seattle Post-Intelligencer, Leonardo mag., Polska Panorama, Poland mag. Founder Bainbridge Island Arts and Humanities Coun., 1984; VISTA vol., 1982-84; bd. dirs. Aradia Med. Clinic, Seattle, 1972-74; founder Chimacum (Wash.) Sch. Dist. Learning Boosters, 1989; loaned exec. to govt. campaigns United Way, 1989; trainer for campaign coords. and key workers, 1989; 1st aid trainer Medic I, Seattle, 1989-91; elected chair Marrowstone Island Groundwater Com., 1989-94; mem. adv. com. Seawater Intrusion Team Dept. of Ecology, Wash. State; pres. Marrowstone Island Cmty. Assn., 1993-94; mem., sec. orgnl. task force to structure The Marrowstone Island Found., 2000, Pub. Affairs Officer (reservist) Dep. External Affairs Sect.

Chief Nat. Crisis Response Team, 2002; adv., cert. mem. Jefferson County Explorer Search and Rescue, 1990-2000. Recipient merit award for superior journalistic achievement U.S. Army CE, 1984, 85, 2d place news category competition award, 1985-86, Recognition letter, Nat. Trans. Safety Bd., 1999; suggestion award Dept. Army, 1984, ofcl. commendation Dept. of Army, 1985, 86, 87, 90, Dept. of Navy, Puget Sound Naval Shipyard, 1990, 91, Achievement cert. Washington Assn. Educators of the Talented and Gifted, 1990, Specialist Achievement award, 1991, Recognition cert. FEMA, 1993 (3), 1994, 95, 96, 97, 98, 99 (3), 2000, 2001, 2002, 2003; named Citizen of Yr., City of Marrowstone Island, Wash., 1994; Kosciuszko Found. grantee, 1975, 76, 79, 81; pres.'s scholarship City U., Bellevue, Wash., 1995-98. Mem. N.W. Multihull Assn. (commodore 1974), Marrowstone Island Cmty. Assn. (pres. 1983), Quimper Arts. Home and Office: 8643 Flagler Rd Nordland WA 98358-9600

KEPPLER, MARY LOUISE, elementary school educator; b. Altoona, Pa., Nov. 5, 1927; d. Oscar David and Florence Marie (DeViney) K. BS in Edn., Kutztown (Pa.) State Coll., 1949. Cert. tchr. Del. Classroom tchr. Newark (Del.) Sch. Dist., 1949-78, Christiana Dist., New Castle County, Del., 1978-80, ret., 1980. Tchr. pilot program open classroom, 1972-74; instr. tchg. students to aide kindergarten students Mini-Tchrs., 1972-78, literary braillist, divsn. visually impaired, Del., 1984-2000. Mem. adminstrv. bd. Meth. Ch., Newark, Del., 1975-80, 84-, chair status/role of women, 1984-96, mem. outreach com., 1999—, task force Winterthur Mus. Ednl. Found., Wilmington, 1972, energy conservation task force Hagley Mus., Wilmington, Del., 1976. Recipient Outstanding Elem. Tchr. of Am. award, 1975, Gov.'s award Vol. Braillist, 1994. Mem. NEA (life), Retired Tchrs. Assn., Delta Kappa Gamma (regional dir. N.E. region 1980-82, internat. chmn. membership 1986-88, charter mem., state pres. 1977-79, state parliamentarian 1999—, state rules com. 1999-2003, state nomination com. 1985-90, 2001-03), Libr. Assn., Nat. Braille Assn., Del. Ret. Sch. Personnel Assn. Republican. Methodist. Avocations: photography, poetry, short story book group, collecting books on local history. Home: 115 Townsend Rd Newark DE 19711-7905

KERA, TIIU, career officer; b. Balingen/Wuerttemberg, Germany; BA in Polit. Sci., Valparaiso U., 1967; M in Polit. Sci., Indiana U., 1969; grad. (disting.), Squadron Officer Sch. Maxwell AFB, Ala., 1976; student, Air Command, Staff Coll., 1982, Air War Coll., 1986; grad., Nat. War Coll., 1988. Commd. 2d. lt. USAF, 1973, advanced through grades to maj. gen., 1998; chief quality control sec. Bolling AFB, Washington, D.C., 1973-75; chief quality control sect., personnel utilization sect. 3245th Air Base Grp., Hanscom AFB, Mass., 1975-78; chief quality progression sect. 51st Combat support Grp., Osan Air Base, South Korea, 1978-79; air staff tng. program officer Hdqs. USAF, Washington, D.C., 1979-80; chief Airmen Base Support Assignments Br., Support Officer Assignments Br. Hdqs. Tactical Air Command, Langly AFB, Va., 1980-83; chief mil. pers. br. 1st. Tactical Command, Langly AFB, Va., 1983-84; chief pers. plans, dir. pers. mgmt. Hdqs. Space Divsn., Los Angeles, 1984-87; strategic planner, then chief Strategic Cconcepts Br., Washington, D.C., 1988-1990; fellow Harvard U., Cambridge, Mass., 1990-91; polit.-mil. affairs officer Hdqs. USAF, Washington, D.C., 1991-92; U.S. def. and air attaché Vilnius, Lithuania, 1993-95; dir. intelligence Hdqs. U.S. Stragetic Command, Offutt AFB, Neb., Lithuania, 1995-98; chief of staff, dep. dir. ops. Nat. Security Agency, Fort George G. Meade, Md., 1998-99, asst. dep. dir. ops., prodn. and strategic issues, 1998—, dep. Ctrl. Security Svc., 1999—. Decorated Def. Superior Svc. medal with oak leaf cluster, D.M.S. medal, Meritorious Svc. medal with three oak leaf clusters, AF Commendation medal with oak leaf cluster. Office: NSA/DCH CSS 9800 Savage Rd Ste 2w118 Fort George G Meade MD 20755-6000

KERBER, LINDA KAUFMAN, historian, educator; b. N.Y.C., Jan. 23, 1940; d. Harry Hagman and Dorothy (Haber) Kaufman; m. Richard Kerber, June 5, 1960; children: Ross Jeremy, Justin Seth. AB cum laude, Barnard Coll., 1960; MA, NYU, 1961; PhD, Columbia U., 1968; DHL, Grinnell Coll., 1992. Instr., asst. prof. history Stern Coll., Yeshiva U., N.Y.C., 1963-68; asst. prof. history San Jose State Coll., (Calif.), 1969-70; vis. asst. prof. history Stanford U., (Calif.), 1970-71; asst. prof. history U. Iowa, Iowa City, 1971-75, prof., 1975-85, May Brodbeck prof., 1985—. Vis. prof. U. Chgo., 1991-92. Author: Federalists in Dissent: Imagery and Ideology in Jeffersonian America, 1970, paperback edit., 1980, 97, Women of the Republic: Intellect and Ideology in Revolutionary America, 1980, paperback edit., 1986, Toward an Intellectual History of Women, 1997, No Constitutional Right to Be Ladies: Women and the Obligations of Citizenship, 1998, paperback edit., 1999 (Littleton-Griswold prize in legal history Am. Hist. Assn., Joan Kelley prize in womens history Am. Hist. Assn.); co-editor: Women's America: Refocusing the Past, 1982, 6th edit., 2004, U.S. History As Women's History, 1995; mem. editl. bd. Signs: Jour. Women in Culture and Society, Jour. Women's History; contbr. articles and book revs. to profl. jours. Fellow Danforth Found., NEH, 1976, 83-84, 94, Am. Coun. Learned Socs., 1975, Nat. Humanities Ctr., 1990-91, Guggenheim Found., 1990-91, Radcliffe Inst. for Advanced Study, 2003. Mem. Orgn. Am. Historians (pres. 1996-97), Am. Hist. Assn., Am. Studies Assn. (pres. 1988), Am. Soc. for Legal History, Berkshire Conf. Women Historians, Soc. Am. Historians, Japan U.S. Friendship Commn., PEN/Am. Ctr., Am. Acad. Arts and Scis. Jewish. Office: U Iowa Dept History Iowa City IA 52242

KERBIS, GERTRUDE LEMPP, architect; m. Walter Peterhans (dec.); m. Donald Kerbis (div. 1972); children: Julian, Lisa, Kim. BS, U. Ill.; MA, Ill. Inst. Tech.; postgrad., Grad. Sch. Design, Harvard U., 1949-50. Archtl. designer Skidmore, Owings & Merrill, Chgo., 1954-59, C.F. Murphy Assocs., Chgo., 1959-62, 65-67; pvt. practice architecture Lempp Kerbis Assocs., Chgo., 1967—; lectr. U. Ill., 1969; prof. William Rainey Harper Coll., 1970—95, Washington U., St. Louis, 1977, 82, Ill. Inst. Tech., 1989-91. Archtl. cons. Dept. Urban Renewal, City of Chgo.; mem. Northeastern Ill. Planning Commn., Open Land Project, Mid-North Community Orgn., Chgo. Met. Housing and Planning Council, Chgo. Mayor's Commn. for Preservation Chgo.'s Hist. Architecture; bd. dirs. Chgo. Sch. Architecture Found., 1972-76; trustee Chgo. Archtl. Assistance Ctr., Glessner House Found., Inland Architect Mag.; lectr. Art Inst. Chgo., U. N.Mex., Ill. Inst. Tech., Washington U., St. Louis, Ball State U., Muncie, Ind., U. Utah, Salt Lake City. Prin. archtl. works include U.S. Air Force Acad. dining hall, Colo., 1957, Skokie (Ill.) Pub. Library, 1959, Meadows Club, Lake Meadows, Chgo., 1959, O'Hare Internat. Airport 7 Continents Bldg, 1963; prin. developer and architect: Tennis Club, Highland Park, Ill., 1968, Watervliet, Mich. Tennis Ranch, 1970, Greenhouse Condominium, Chgo., 1976, Webster-Clark Townhouses, Chgo., 1986, Chappell Sch., 1993; exhibited at Chgo. Hist. Soc., 1984, Chgo. Mus. Sci. and Industry, 1985, Paris Exhbn. Chgo. Architects, 1985, Spertus Mus.; represented in permanent archtl. drawings collection Art Inst. Chgo. Active Art Inst. Chgo.. Recipient award for outstanding achievement in professions YWCA Met. Chgo., 1984 Fellow AIA (bd. dirs. Chgo. chpt. 1971-75, chpt. pres. 1980, nat. com. architecture, arts and recreation 1972-75, com. on design 1975-80, head subcom. inst. honors nomination); mem. Chgo. Women in Architecture (founder), Chgo. Network, Internat. Women's Forum, Arts Club Chgo., Cliff Dwellers (bd. dirs. 1987-88, pres. 1988, 89), Lambda Alpha. Office: Lempp Kerbis Assocs 172 W Burton Pl Chicago IL 60610-1310 E-mail: lk172@aol.com.

KERCHER, KELLI S. special education educator; b. Salt Lake City, Utah, Apr. 20, 1962; d. Ronald F. and Linda Halton Sevey; m. Steven A. Kercher; children: Britton James, Karsen Jean, Makellin Irene. BS, MEd, U. Utah. Cert. tchr. Utah, spl. educator Coun. for Exceptional Children. Instr./specialist Columbus Cmty. Ctr., Salt Lake, Utah, 1988—95; paraeducator Murray (Utah) Sch. Dist., 1989—90; educator Murray HS, 1990—98; transition specialist Murray Sch. Dist., 1998—99; educator Liberty Elem. Sch., Murray Sch. Dist., 1999—2000, Hillcrest Jr. HS, Murray Sch. Dist., Murray, Utah, 2000—; dist. specialist - severe and multiple disabilities Murray Sch. Dist., Murray, Utah, 1998—. Dept. chair-assisted edn. Murray HS, 1997—99; sponsoring tchr. Project ACT Grant U. of Utah, Salt Lake City, 1999—2003; model classroom Utah Model for Integration SCIP Grant, U. of Utah, Salt Lake City, 1994—98; dept. chair-spl. edn. Hillcrest Jr. HS, Murray, Utah, 2000—02; mem. Murray Cmty. Transition Coun., Murray, Utah, 1994—, facilitator, 1997—99; intermediate level trainer Mandt Sys., Salt Lake, Utah, 1993—2001; chairperson Wasatch Front Agy. InformationFair, Utah, 1999—99; advisor S.H.A.D.E. Club student chpt. Coun. for Exceptional Children, Murray, Utah, 1994—97; adj. faculty U. of Utah Coll. of Edn., Salt Lake City, 1994—96; mentor tchr. Murray Sch. Dist., Murray, Utah, 1995—; presenter confs. on spl. edn. Author (editor): (manual) Paraeducator Information Guide; contbr. articles to profl. jours. Adv. bd. Murray Disability Resource, Murray, Utah, 1998—2001; mem. bus. coun. Murray C. of C., Murray, Utah, 1998—99. Recipient Clarissa Hug Tchr. of the Yr. award, Coun. for Exceptional Children, 2002, Joanne Gilles Tchr. of the Yr. award, Utah Coun. for Exceptional Children, 2001, Ednl. All-Star award, Granite Credit Union, 1994, 1996. Mem.: NEA, Murray Edn. Assn., Utah Edn. Assn., Parent Tchr. Student Assn., Divsn. of Mental Retardation/Devel. Disabilities (treas. 1998—2001), Snowbird Chpt. Coun. for Excpetional Children (pres. 1999—2001), Utah Coun. for Exceptional Children, Coun. for Exceptional Children. Avocations: travel, bicycling, team sports, reading, sewing.

KERCKHOFF, SYLVIA STANSBURY, mayor; b. Toledo, June 7, 1928; d. Paul William Stansbury and Lass Elizabeth Hackney; m. Alan Chester Kerckhoff, June 11, 1949; children: Steven, Sharon. BS, U. Wis., 1950; MAT, Duke U., 1960. Kindergarten tchr. Madison (Wis.) Schs., 1950-52; rsch. asst. Vanderbilt U., Nashville, 1957-58; jr. and sr. h.s. tchr. City Schs., Durham, N.C., 1959-60, 69-81; mem. City Coun., City of Durham, 1981-93, mayor, 1993-99. Co-chair Violence Prevention Commn., Durham, 1993-97; mem. Chamber Commerce Bd., Durham, 1993-97; founder Mayor's Univ. Adv. Coun., Durham, 1993-97; co-chair City-County Com., Durham, 1993-97. Chair N.C. League Municipalities, Transp., Comm. and Pub. Safety, 1996-97; mem. Gov.'s Transit 2000 Commn., N.C., 1996; v.p. N.C. LWV, 1967-69, fin. chair, Durham LWV, 1960-70; co-chair Youth Coordinating Bd., 1998—; v.p. pres. bd. dirs. Durham United Way, 1990-2000, bd. dirs. Triangle United Way; co-chair Durham Cultural Master Plan, 2002—. Recipient Leadership award Duke U. med. Ctr., Durham, 1995, Durham County Women's Commn. Svc. award, 1993, Community Leadership in Arts award Durham Arts Coun., 1991; inductee DeVilbiss H.S. Hall of Fame, Toledo, 1998. Democrat. Presbyterian. Avocations: reading, tennis, music, hiking, travel. Home: 1511 Pinecrest Rd Durham NC 27705-5816

KERES, KAREN LYNNE, English language educator; b. Evanston, Ill., Oct. 22, 1945; d. Frank and Bette (Pascoe) K.; m. Walter Wilson Berg. BA, St. Marys Coll., 1967; postgrad., U. Notre Dame, 1967-68; MA, U. Iowa, 1969. Assoc. prof. English, humanities and fine arts William Rainey Harper Coll., Palatine, Ill., 1969-95, prof., 1995—, Palomar Coll., San Marcos, Calif., 1990-93. Cons. in field. Mem. MLA, Ill. Assn. Tchrs. English, Am. Fedn. Tchrs., Nature Conservancy, Mensa. Home: 222 Fairfield Dr Island Lake IL 60042-9622 Office: William Rainey Harper Coll Dept Liberal Arts Palatine IL 60067

KERKMAN, SAMANTHA, state representative; b. Mar. 6, 1974; BA, U. Wis., Whitewater, 1996. Former legis. aide Wis. State Legis., Madison; state assembly mem. Wis. State Assembly, Madison, 2000—, mem. joint com. on audit, mem. audit, fin. instns., govt. ops., judiciary, urban and local affairs, and ways and means coms. Mem.: Randall Fire Dept. Aux., Twin Lakes Chamber and Area Bus. Assn., Powers Lake Sportsmen Club, Twin Lakes Am. Legion Aux. Post 544. Republican. Office: State Capitol Rm 109 W PO Box 8953 Madison WI 53708-8953

KERKOC, RUTH ANN, Spanish educator; b. New Orleans, Aug. 24, 1930; d. Ernest Edward and Alta Mai (Jacobs) Clark; m. Anto Kerkoc, Sept. 3, 1966; 1 child, Kristina Maria. BA, Wellesley (Mass.) Coll., 1951; MA, Yale U., 1959, U. Calif., Berkeley, 1966. Cert. tchr., Calif. Adminstrv. asst. U.S. Govt., Washington, 1951-55; 2nd grade tchr. Karl C. Parrish Sch., Barranquilla, Colombia, 1955-57; Spanish and German tchr. Yorktown H.S., Arlington, Va., 1959-64; teaching assst. German U. Calif., Berkeley, 1964-66; tchr. Spanish Piedmont, Calif., 1966-67; tchr. German DeAnza Coll.q, Cupertino, Calif., 1968; tchr. Spanish part time West Valley Coll., Campbell, Calif., 1968-69; tchr. social studies Young Mothers Program, San Jose, 1969-84; tchr. Spanish Leland H.S., San Jose, 1984—. Mem. pacesetter Soanish Coll. Bd., N.Y.C., 1994—; nat. com. ednl. Testing Svc., Princeton, N.J., 1997—; trainer pacesetter Spanish Coll. Bd., 1995—. Named Fullbright Teaching Asst., Aachen, Germany, 1957-58. Mem. AAUW, Am. Coun. Teaching Fgn. langs., Calif. lang. Assn., Fgn. lang. Assn. Santa Clara County. Democrat. Episcopalian. Avocations: reading, travel, walking. Home: 6198 Cecala Dr San Jose CA 95120-2709 Office: Leland High School San Jose CA 95120

KERN, ANGELINE FRAZIER, educational administrator, guidance counselor; b. Jackson, Tenn., Apr. 27, 1939; d. William Raymond and Sarah Louise (Harris) Frazier; divorced; children: Tiffany Louise, Kevin James. BA, Lambuth Coll., Jackson, 1961; MA, Memphis State U., 1962; postgrad., U. Tenn., 1963. Cert. assessor trainer, Nat. Assn. Secondary Sch. Prins. Tchr. phys. edn. Jackson City Schs., 1960-62; tchr. English, guidance counselor Georgian Hills Jr. H.S., Memphis, 1962-65; guidance counselor Colonial Jr. H.S., Memphis, 1965-70; adminstrv. asst. Kingsbury H.S., Memphis, 1970-72; prin. Avon Elem. Sch., Memphis, 1972-77, Balmoral Elem. Sch., Memphis, 1977-93, Cordova Sch., 1993—. Mem. adv. bd. East Memphis YMCA, 1984-87; mem. Memphis City Beautiful Commn., 1985-89; pres. St. John's Creek Home and Garden Club, Memphis, 1968-70. Recipient Youth Svc. award YMCA, Memphis, 1983, Vol. Recognition award, 1986; finalist Rotary Club Prin. of Yr. award, 1989. Mem. NEA, NAESP, ASCD, Tenn. Assn. Elem. Sch. Prins. (mem. fall conf. planning com. 1985), Tenn. Assn. Mid. Schs. (Adminstr. of Yr. 1997), Memphis Pub. Sch. Prins. Assn. (auditing com. 1983-85), U. Memphis Tiger Club, Educators Bridge Club, Phi Delta Kappa, Delta Kappa Gamma (fin. chmn. Epsilon chpt. 1976-84, corr. sect. 1990-92). Republican. Roman Catholic. Office: Olive Br HS Olive Branch MS 38654

KERNAN, BARBARA DESIND, senior government executive; b. N.Y.C., Jan. 11, 1939; d. Philip and Anne (Feuer) Desind; m. Joseph E. Kernan, Feb. 14, 1973. BA cum laude, Smith Coll., 1960; postgrad. Oxford U., 1963; MA, Harvard U., 1963; postgrad. in edn. policy George Washington U., 1980. Editor Harvard Law Sch., 1960-62; tchr. English, Newton (Mass.) H.S., 1962-63; editor Allyn & Bacon Pubs., Boston, 1963-64; edn. assoc. Upward Bound, Edn. Assocs., Inc., Washington, 1965-68; edn. program specialist Title I, Elem. and Secondary Edn. Act, U.S. Office Edn., 1969-73; fellow Am. Polit. Sci. Assn., Senator William Proxmire and Congressman Alphonzo Bell, 1973-74; spl. asst. to dep. commr. for elem. and secondary edn. and dir. dissemination, sch. fin. and analysis, U.S. Office Edn., 1975-77, chief program analysis br. divsn. edn. for disadvantaged, 1977-79; chief grant program coordination staff Office Dep. Commr. for Ednl. Resources, 1979-80; chief priority concerns staff Office Asst. Sec. Mgmt., U.S. Dept. Edn., Washington, 1980-81; dir. divsn. orgnl. devel. and analysis Office of Dep. Undersec. for Mgmt., 1981-86; Sr. Exec. Svc. candidate on spl. project to improve status of women Sec. Transp., Washington, 1983-84; inducted Sr. Exec. Svc., 1986; assoc. adminstr. for adminstrn. Nat. Hwy. Traffic Safety Adminstrn., U.S. Dept. Transp., 1986-94, career devel. leader to presdl. mgmt. interns, 1989-91; trustee Capricorn Galleries, Bethesda, Md., 1996-97; owner Philip Desind Collection, Am. Realism Fine Arts, 1997—; pres. Capricorn Galleries, Potomac, Md., 1997—. Recipient awards U.S. Office Edn., 1969, 71, 77, U.S. Dept. Edn., 1981-86, U.S. Dept. Transp., 1991, 94, Small Agy. Coun., 1990; scholarships U. Mich., 1956-58, Smith Coll., 1958-60, Harvard U., 1962-63; Am. Polit. Sci. Assn. fellow, 1973-74; Sr. Exec. fellow John F. Kennedy Sch. Govt. Harvard U., 1983. Office: Capricorn Galleries 10236 River Rd Potomac MD 20854-4905 Office Phone: 301-765-5900. E-mail: bkernan@prodigy.net.

KERNEY, YOLONDA V. music historian; d. James Bell Kerney, Jr. and Nancy McKinney Kerney. MusB, Howard U., 1996, MMus, 2003. Music libr. U.S. Libr. Congress, Washington, 1995—. Chair Daniel Murray African Am. Culture Assn. of the Libr. of Congress, Washington, 1999—. Vol. tutor Met. Delta Adult Literacy Coun., Washington, 1996—2002. Recipient Outstanding Svc. citation, Met. Delta Adult Literacy Coun., 1999; fellow Jr. fellow, Libr. Congress, 1995. Mem.: Black Caucus of the ALA, ALA, Libr. Congress Pa., Music Libr. Assn., TransAfrica Forum. Republican. Episcopalian. Avocation: research of the negro spiritual and historical documents related to slavery in America. E-mail: yker@loc.gov.

KERNOCHAN, SARAH M. film director, scriptwriter, composer; b. N.Y.C., Dec. 30, 1947; m. James Lapine; 1 child, Phoebe. Student, Sarah Lawrence Coll., 1966—69. Writer Village Voice, N.Y.C. Co-prodr. and dir. : (films) Marjoe, 1972 (Acad. award best documentary); co-writer 9 1/2 Weeks, 1986; writer Dancers, 1987; writer, with James Lapine, Impromptu, 1991; writer Sommersby, 1993; dir.: The Hairy Bird (aka Strike, All I Wanna Do), 2000, Thoth, 2002 (Acad. award best documentary); story : What Lies Beneath, 2000; author: Dry Hustle, 1997; recording artist: House of Pain, 1973, Beat Around the Bush, 1974; score composer : Sleeparound Town, 1983.

KERNS, JOANNA DE VARONA, actress, writer, director; b. San Francisco, Feb. 12, 1953; d. David Thomas and Martha Louise (Smith) de V.; m. Richard Martin Kerns, Dec. 11, 1976 (div. Dec. 1986); 1 child, Ashley Cooper. Student, NYU, 1970-71. TV series include The Four Seasons, 1984, Growing Pains; TV includes A Wedding On Waltons Mountain, 1982, V, 1983, Stormin' Home, 1985, The Return of Marcus Welby, M.D., 1984, The Rape of Richard Beck, 1985, Mother's Day On Waltons Mountain, 1982, A Bunny's Tale, 1985, Robin Cook's Mortal Fear, 1994, Whose Daughter is She?, 1995, No One Could Protect Her, 1995, See Jane Run, 1995, Terror In the Family, 1996; movies include Cross My Heart, 1986, Mother Knows Best, 1997, Sisters and Other Strangers, 1997, Emma's Wish, 1998, Girl Interrupted, 1999. Democrat. Office: Creative Artists Agy 9830 Wilshire Blvd Beverly Hills CA 90212-1804

KERR, ALICE FORGY, state legislator; b. Aug. 30, 1954; BS, MA, We. Ky. U. Mem. Ky. Senate from 12th dist., Frankfort, 1999—. Bd. dirs. Ky. Bapt. Homes for Children; active United Way of Bluegrass; vol. in cmty. Mem. PEO Ednl. Sorority, Women in Leadership. Republican. Baptist. Office: 3274 Gondola Lexington KY 40513

KERR, BARBARA PROSSER, research scientist, educator; b. Asheville, N.C., Dec. 28, 1925; d. George Holcomb and Gertrude Berenice (Parker) Prosser; m. William Albert Kerr, June 18, 1950 (div. May 1959); 1 child, Diana. BA, U. Chgo., 1951; MSW, Ariz. State U., 1971. Cert. clin. social worker, psychiatry and mental health nursing. Exec. sec. Union Theol. Sem., N.Y.C., 1961-67; case worker Dept. Pub. Welfare, Wilmington, Del., 1967-69; psychiatric nurse St. Luke's Hosp. and Med. Ctr., Phoenix, 1969-70; emergency rm. social worker Maricopa Med. Ctr., Phoenix, 1971-82; dir. Kerr-Cole Sustainable Living Ctr., Taylor, Ariz., 1983—. Adv. Solar Cookers Internat., Sacramento, 1993—. Author: The Expanding World of Solar Box Cookers, 1991; inventor Solar Box Cooker, 1976, Solar Wall Oven, 1986. Home: PO Box 576 Taylor AZ 85939 E-mail: kerrcole@skyboot.com.

KERR, DARLENE DIXON, electric power company executive; b. Syracuse, N.Y., Nov. 26, 1951; d. James and Mary Dixon; children: E. Kaye, J. Craig. BA, SUNY, Potsdam, 1973; MBA, Syracuse U., 1984. V.p. sys. electric ops. Niagara Mohawk Power Corp., Syracuse, 1988-91, v.p. gas mktg. and rates, 1991-93, v.p. electric customer svc., 1993-94, sr. v.p. electric customer svc., 1994-95, sr. v.p. energy distbn., 1995—98, past mem. steering com. and past chmn. polit. action com., exec. v.p. energy delivery, 1998—99, exec. v.p., chief oper. officer, 1999—2000, pres., chief operating officer, 2000—01; sr. v.p. Nat. Grid U.S.A., 2001—, pres., Nat. Grid U.S.A. Svc. Co., 2001—. Former mem. adv. bd. Rural Metro; former mem. policy coun. Success by 6. Former trustee Onondaga C.C.; former bd. dirs. Cmty.-Gen. Hosp.; mem. Syracuse U. Thursday Morning Roundtable and Corinthian Found.; mem. task force Bus. Alliance for a New N.Y.; past pres. and bd. dirs. Onondaga Citizens League; past v.p. bd. dirs. Regional Learning Svcs., Inc.; past mem. policy and planning com. Leadership Grater Syracuse; former mem. Downtown Improvement Task Force; former committeewoman and vice chmn. Onondaga Rep. Com.; former mem. numerous campaign ad. coms. and Onondaga County Rep. task forces; mem. chmn.'s coun. and fin. com. Onondaga County Rep. Com.; bd. dirs. Farmers and Traders Life Ins. Co., Utilites Mutual Ins. Co., Greater Syracuse C.C., M&T Bank, N.Y. State Women in Comm. and Energy, former pres., LeMoyne Coll., Mktg. Execs. conf., Ctrl. N.Y. Regional Compact, Greater Syracuse Econ. Growth Coun., Syracuse 20/20. Named Mover and Shaker for bus. Syracuse Herald Am., 1990, Woman of Achievement for career Post-Std., 1991, Alumni of Distinction, SUNY, 1993, Citizen of Yr. Temple Adath Yeshurun, Syracuse, Woman of Achievement N.Y. State-Gov. Pataki, Extraordinary Woman Nat. Women's Hall of Fame, Seneca Falls, N.Y.; recipient Spirit Am. Women award Girls Inc. Ctrl. N.W., 1993, Multiple Sclerosis Soc. Crusaders for a Cure award, Zonta Crystal award. Office: National Grid USA 300 Erie Blvd W Syracuse NY 13202-4250*

KERR, JANET SPENCE, physiologist, pharmacologist, researcher; b. New Haven, May 30, 1942; d. Alexander Pyott and Janet Blake (Conley) Spence; m. Thomas Albert Kerr Jr., July 24, 1965; children: Sarah Patterson, Matthew Spence, Timothy Marden. BA, Beaver Coll., 1964; MS, Rutgers U., 1969, PhD, 1973. Asst. prof. Rutgers U., Camden, N.J., 1973-76; rsch. assoc. U. Pa. Sch. Medicine, Phila., 1976-79; asst. prof. U. Medicine and Dentistry N.J.-Rutgers Med. Sch., New Brunswick, 1979-84; prin. rsch. scientist DuPont Pharms. Co., Wilmington, Del., 1985—2001; prin. investigator ENANTA Pharms., 2002; sr. investigator Merck Pharm. Co., Inc., 2003—. Sec. Biochem. Pharmacology Discussion Group, 1997—; vis. scientist Med. Sch. Harvard U., 2002—03; sr. investigator Merck & Co., Inc., 2003—. Contbr. articles to profl. jours. Busch fellow Rutgers U. Mem. AAAS, Am. Heart Assn., Am. Fedn. Clin. Rsch., Am. Physiol. Soc., Am. Thoracic Soc., Am. Assn. Cancer Rsch., Inflammation Rsch. Assn. (bd. dirs. 1996-98), N.Y. Acad. Scis., Sigma Xi. E-mail: janetskerr@hotmail.com.

KERR, LINDA, executive secretary; b. Waco, Tex., Aug. 26, 1949; d. Carl and Ruth Harding; m. David Kerr, Feb. 14, 1969; children: Dean, Gabe. Grad. h.s., Wichita Falls, Tex. Sec. First Bapt. Ch., China Spring, Tex., 1984—88; adminstrv. assoc. dept. engring. Baylor U., Waco, 1988—.

KERR, LOU C. foundation administrator; b. Oklahoma City, Jan. 24, 1937; d. Lem C. and M. Mae (Beck) Coker; m. Robert S. Kerr, Jr., July, 1972; children: Steven S., Laura Kerr Ogle. BS in Edn. and Health, DHL, Oklahoma City U. V.p. The Kerr Found., Inc., Oklahoma City, 1985-99, pres., 1999—. Dir. UMB Bank, Oklahoma City, Okla. City U.; founder, dir. Red Earth, Inc., Oklahoma City; adv. com. Breast Cancer Prevention and Treatment, 1994—; mem. Commn. on the Status of Women, 1994-99, 2000—; mem. Gov.'s State White House Conf. on Aging; mem. selection com. for Truman Found. Scholars, 1991-2000; mem. Social Security

Disability Task Force; chair State Capitol Preservation Commn., 1990—; adv. coun. for gov. Okla. Environ. Concerns Coun., vice chair for gov., others; pres. Ind. Coll. Fund. Vice pres. fundraising campaign Allied Arts, 1985, v.p. exec. com., 1988-89, sec. exec. com., 1990—; bd. advisors ANSER-Ctr. for Internat. Aerospace Coop. 1995-98; mem. founder Atty. Gen's Community 111. Comm. founder BLCCH Libr. Soc., u. Okla., exec. com., v.p. Ctr. of the Am. Indian/Red Earth, 1983—; bd. dirs., exec. com. Ctrl. Okla. Coun. of World Affairs; bd. dirs. Am. Cancer Soc., Oklahoma County unit, 1995-97, Internat. Women's Forum, Washington, 1992—; founder, chair Okla. Internat. Women's Forum, 1990—; nat. trustee Nat. Symphony Orch., Washington, 1999—; trustee NPR Found., Washington, 2001—; chair State Capitol Preservation Commn., Oklahoma City, 1990—; women's leadership bd., exec. com. Harvard U., Cambridge, 1999—; nat. bd. Fund for Am., 1989—; 3d v.p. Red Lands coun. Girl Scouts U.S., 1993-97; v.p. Global Family Found.; adv. bd. Hazel K. Goddess Fund for Stroke Rsch. in Women, Internat. Found. of Fame, 1997—; exec. com. Lyric Theatre of Okla., Inc., 1992—; adv. bd. dirs. Okla. Brest Inst. 1992-97; adv. trustee Oklahoma City U., 2000, Okla. City Pub. Sch. Found. Wall of Fame, 2001.; knighted into The Byzantine Order of the Holy Sepulchre; recipient Vis A Tergo award Women's Bus. Ctr., 1997, Women Who Make a Difference award Internat. Women's Forum, 1994, Cert. of Merit Vol. Action Com. of Cmty. Coun., Okla. Tourism and Recreation Indsl. Gov.'s award, Nat. Others award Salvation Army, Kirkpatrick Petree award for outstanding cmty. svc. Oklahoma City U. Music Theatre Soc., 1988, Gov.'s Arts award Okla. State Arts Coun., 1988, Woman of Distinction award, Girl Scouts Red Lands Coun., 2002, Leading Lights award Internat. Women's Forum, 2003. Democrat. Methodist. Office: The Kerr Foundation Inc 12501 N May Ave Oklahoma City OK 73120 Fax: (405) 749-2877. E-mail: lkerr@thekerrfoundation.org.

KERR, NANCY HELEN, psychology educator; b. L.A., June 27, 1947; d. Edmund James and Sally (Byrd) K.; m. David Foulkes, Apr. 19, 1978. BA, Stanford U., 1969; PhD, Cornell U., 1974. Asst. prof. psychology U. Wyo., Laramie, 1974-78; vis. asst. prof. psychology Emory U., Atlanta, 1978-79, vis. asst. prof. psychiatry, 1979-82; vis. asst. prof. psychology Mercer U., Macon, Ga., 1982-83; asst. prof. to prof. psychology Oglethorpe U., Atlanta, 1983—, chair div. behavioral scis., 1989-96, interim acad. dean, 1996-97, provost, 1997—. Contbr. articles to profl. jours. Recipient James McKeen Cattell award, 1990. Mem. Psychonomic Soc. Office: Oglethorpe U 4484 Peachtree Rd NE Atlanta GA 30319-2797

KERR, NANCY KAROLYN, pastor, mental health services professional; b. July 10, 1934; d. Owen W. and Iris Irene (Israel) K.; m. Richard Clayton Williams, June 28, 1953 (div.); children: Richard Charles, Donna Louise. Student, Boston U., 1953; AA, U. Bridgeport, 1966; BA, Hofstra U., 1967; postgrad. in clin. psychology, Adelphi U. Inst. Advanced Psychol. Studies, 1968-73; MDiv, Associated Mennonite Bibl. Sems., 1986. Ordained pastor Mennonite Ch., 1987; apptd. pastor Kamloops Presbytery Ch., Can., 1992. Pastoral counselor Nat. Coun. Chs., Jackson, Miss., 1964; dir. teen program Waterbury (Conn.) YWCA, 1966-67; intern in psychology N.Y. Med. Coll., 1971-72, rsch. cons., 1972-73; coord. home svcs., psychologist City and County of Denver, 1972-75; cons. Mennonite Mental Health Svcs., Denver, 1975-78; asst. prof. psychology Messiah Coll., 1978-79; mental health cons., 1979-81; called to ministry Mennonite Ch., 1981; pastor Cin. Mennonite Fellowship, 1981-83, mem. Gen. Conf. Peace and Justice Reference Coun., 1983-85; instr. Associated Mennonite Bibl. Sems., 1985; tchg. elder Assembly Mennonite Ch., 1985-86; pastor Pulaski Mennonite Ch., 1986-89; exec. dir., pastoral counselor Bethesda Counseling Svcs., Prince George B.C., 1989-99; pvt. practice, 1999—. Spl. ch. curriculum Nat. Coun. Chs., 1981; mem. Cen. Dist. Conf. Peace and Justice Com., 1981-89; mem. exec. bd. People for Peace, 1981-83. Active Prince George Ministerial Assn., chmn. edn. and airport chapel coms., 1990—92; elder St. Giles Presbyn. Ch., 1996—2000; bd. dirs. Tri-County Counselling Clinic, Memphis, Mo., 1980—81, Boulder (Colo.) ARC, 1977—78, PLURA, B.C. Synod, 1995—98, Prince George Neighbor Link, 1995—99, Davis County Mins. Assn., v.p., 1988—89; mem. Waterbury Planned Parenthood Bd., 1964—67, MW Children's Home Bd., 1974—75; mem. crisis bd. ARC, 2000—; mem. Mennonite Disabilities Respite Care Bd., 1981—86, Prince George Children's Svcs. com., 1992—94; adv. com. Prince George Planning Coun., 1997—98; mem. housing Prince George adv. bd. Mennonite Cen. Com., 1998—99. Mem. APA (assoc.), Can. Psychol. Assn., Soc. Psychologists for Study of Social Issues, Christian Assn. Psychol. Studies, Soc. Bibl. Lit. & Exegesis, sec. Ft. Geo. Bd., 2004—. Office: Nancy Kerr Counselling Svcs 110-154 Quebec St Prince George BC Canada V2L 1W2

KERR, SYLVIA JOANN, science educator; b. Detroit, June 19, 1941; d. Frederic Dilmus and Maud (Dirst) Pfeffer; widowed; children: David, Kathleen. BA, Carleton Coll., 1963; MS, U. Minn., 1966, PhD, 1968. Asst. prof. Augsburg Coll., Mpls., 1968-71; instr. Anoka Ramsey Community Coll., Coon Rapids, Minn., 1973-74; from asst. prof. to full prof. Hamline U., St. Paul, 1974—. Contbr. numerous articles to profl. jours. NIH fellow U. Minn., 1972, 74-75. Office: Hamline U Dept Biology 1536 Hewitt Ave Saint Paul MN 55104-1205 E-mail: sKerr@piper.hamline.edu.

KERRIGAN, KELLY ANN, special education educator; b. Elizabeth, N.J., Mar. 18, 1974; d. Thomas and Kathleen Kerrigan. BSE magna cum laude, Seton Hall U., South Orange, N.J., 1996; MS, Seton Hall U., 2001. Cert. elem. tchr. N.J.; tchr. of handicapped N.J. Tchr. spl. edn. Edison Sch., Westfield, NJ, 1996, Jefferson Sch., Westfield, 1997—. Pvt. tutor; tchr. Westfield Summer Workshop, 2000; condr. tng. workshops in field. Co-author: Action Research, 1999—2001. Nominee Tchr. Hand award, Disney Co., 2000, 2004. Mem.: ASCD, Westfield Edn. Assh., N.J. Edn. Assn., Kappa Delta Pi.

KERRIGAN, NANCY, professional figure skater, former Olympic athlete; b. Woburn, Mass., Oct. 13, 1969; d. Daniel and Brenda Kerrigan; m. Jerry Solomon, 1995; 1 child, Matthew Eric Solomon. Bronze medalist World Championships, 1991, 92, Olympic Games, Albertville, France, 1992; U.S. nat. champion, 1993; silver medalist Olympic Games, Lillehammer, Norway, 1994. Numerous commls. and product endorsements including Walt Disney Co., Reebok, Northwest Airlines, Frosted Cheerios, Ray Ban, Revlon, Aetna U.S. Healthcare, Salvino Bammers, AquaTrend, Tostitos, sportsinstruction.com; author: In My Own Words, 1996, (with Mary Spencer) Artistry on Ice, 2002; choreographer Halloween on Ice; performer: (video) Fairy Tales on Ice, Champions on Ice Tour, 1992-04; host Lifetime TV, 2002-04; TV spls. incl. Dreams on Ice, Breaking the Ice, Nancy Kerrigan and Friends, Holiday Celebration on Ice, One Enchanted Evening, Divas on Ice, Nancy Kerrigan's Winter Wonderland, Colors of Winter, 2003; TV host Nancy Kerrigan's World of Figure Skating (host), 2002, Grand Prix of Figure Skating, ISU Grand Prix Lifetime TV, 2003-2004; released Shining Through as part of Reflections Off the Ice CD, 1999, Simply the Best as part of Tina Turner Tribute album, 2004; starred as Sandy in Grease on Ice, 1998-99, Broadway on Ice, Branson, Mo., 2000, Footloose on Ice, 2001; appeared in TV movies and shows including Boy Meets World, 1995, The Journey of Allen Strange, 1998, Ice Angel, Hollywood Squares, 2003, Family Feud, 2003, Lifetime Intimate Portrait, 2004. Spokesperson Lions Club, 1994, Children's Trust Fund, 1997, Spalding Rehab. Hosp., MADD, Fight for Sight; founder, benefactor Nancy Kerrigan Found.; hon. chair Nancy Kerrigan Golf Classic, 2000—; bd. dirs. Ice Castle Theatre, Myrtle Beach, S.C. Recipient Bronze medal World

Figure Skating Championships, 1991, Silver medal, 1992, Bronze medal U.S. Pro Championships, 1997, Bronze medal Goodwill Games, 2000, Outstanding Mother award Mother's Day Found., 2001, Henry Iba Outstanding Citizen-Athlete award Rotary Club, Tulsa, Okla., 2002. Office: care of StarGames Bldg 1 40 Salem St Lynnfield MA 01940 Office Phone: 781 224 3055.

KERR-NOWLAN, DONNA COURTNEY, pre-school administrator; b. Wellsboro, Pa., Sept. 25, 1940; d. Sylvan LaRue and Mildred Fowler Kerr; children from previous marriage: Craig Kerr Nowlan, Brent Fowler Nowlan. Cert., Jean Summers Bus. Sch., N.Y., 1956; student, Corning C.C., Mansfield (Pa.) State Tchrs. Coll., 1960. Owner, bridal cons. Bridal Bower, 1960—63; owner Victorian Fingerlakes Tour Guides, 1963—72; dir., owner Building Block Nursery & Pre-K, Elmira, NY, 1969—. Coord. Civil War prison camp Chemung County C. of C., Elmira, 2000—; pres. Hist. Near Westside Bd. Dirs. and Assn., 1985—89; mem. planning commnn. City of Elmira; mem. Chemung County Planning Bd.; dir. Found. for Ctrl. Diocese Episcopal Ch., Syracuse, NY, 1981. Named Woman of Achievement, Chemung County Coun. of Women, 1993; named to Legion of Honor, Chaplin of Four Chaplins, Valley Forge, Pa., 1994; recipient Cmty. Svc. award, Hist. Near Westside Neighborhood Assn., 1982, cert. of appreciation, Elmira Coll., 1985, 1994, Robert Goostrey award, Chemung County C. of C., 1990. Mem.: Twin Tier Jazz Soc. (bd. dirs. 1989—, pres. 2000—), Hal Roach Soc. (bd. dirs. 1987—), Soroptimist Internat. (pres. Elmira chpt. 1989—99, Outstanding Cmty. Svc. award 1994, Outstanding Club Mem. 1995, Outstanding Cmty. Vol. 1996, Outstanding Vol. Svc. award 1986). Republican. Episcopalian. Avocations: walking, gourmet cooking, reading, painting. Home: 715 Winsor Ave Elmira NY 14905 Office: Building Block Pvt Nursery Sch 308 College Ave Elmira NY 14901 E-mail: dnowlan@stny.rr.com.

KERSEY, TALANA S. mental health counselor; b. Joliet, Ill., May 5, 1947; d. Elgin L. and Virgil D. McMahon; m. Joel Allen Kersey, Dec. 7, 1991; children: Michelle Talana, Eric Charles, Kelly Brooke. BA in Edn., Ariz. State U., 1970; MS in Mental Health Counseling, Nova Southeastern U., 1996. Lic. mental health counselor, real estate salesman, Fla.; cert tchr. Fla. Secondry tchr. Orange County Schs., Orlando, Fla.; acad. instr. Brevard Start Ctr., Titusville, Fla.; eligibility specialist Ill. Aid to Families and Dependent Children, Apopka; tchr. C.H. Price Mid. Sch., Interlachen, Fla.; instr., job developer displaced homemaker program Santa Fe C.C., Gainesville, Fla.; therapist, mental health counselor Meridian Behavioral Healthcare, Inc., Gainesville, 1996—; Nick Ungson MD, P.A., Leesburg, Fla. Pvt. tutor, Gainesville, 1991-93. Vol. tchr. Head Start, Phoenix, 1970, Sparc, shelter for abused women, Gainesville, 1989; mem. planning bd. Gainesville Area Women's Network, 1990. Mem. ACA, NEA, Real Estate Edn. Assn. Avocations: piano, decorating, sewing. Office: Meridian Behavioral Healthcare 4300 SW 13th St Gainesville FL 32608

KERSTEN, MARY LOU, real estate broker; b. Milw., May 22, 1950; d. Oliver and Leocadia Coleman; m. David Moore Thomas, June 24, 1974 (div. 1981); m. Christian George Kersten, Jan. 5, 1985; 1 child, Hilary Coleman. BA, U. Wis., 1972. Dir. rsch. Am. U., Washington, 1974-76; dir. devel. Southeastern U., Washington, 1976-78; dir. conf. planning Coun. Advancement & Support of Edn., Washington, 1978-82; dir. ednl. programs Nat. Assn. Fund Raisers, Washington, 1982-85; administrv. asst. to headmaster Cate Sch., Ojai, Calif., 1985-87; real estate broker, owner Hillsdale (N.Y.) Country Realty, 1987—. Bd. dirs. Columbia County Bd. Realtors, Hudson, N.Y. Planning bd. Town of Hillsdale, 1996—; pres. bd. dirs. Friends Hillsdale Pub. Libr., 1994—95; pres. Columbia Green County Bd. Realtors, 2002—; bd. dirs. Hillsdale Pub. Libr., 2002—, Clarion Concerts Columbia County, Copake, NY, 1998. Recipient Realtor of Yr., Columbia Greene, 2003. Avocations: country walking, travel, biking, gardening. Office: Hillsdale Country Realty PO Box 400 Hillsdale NY 12529-0400

KERSTEN, SHARON, public relations executive, consultant; BA, Brandeis U.; MA, New Sch. Social Rsch. Owner Kersten Comm., Miami Beach, Fla., 1995—. Mem. Greater Miami Conv. and Visitors Bur., Miami, Fla. Comm. com. Voices for Children, Miami, Fla.; adv. Guardian Ad Litem, Miami, Fla., 2002. Named Woman Worth Knowing, City of Miami Beach. Mem.: Hispanic Mktg. and Comm. Assn. (founding mem.), Miami Beach C. of C. Office: Kersten Communications 1815 Bay Dr Miami Beach FL 33141

KERTH, ROBERTA JEAN, artist; b. Lucas, Kans., Jan. 16, 1936; d. Gerald Wayne and Georgia Lavaugh (Applegate) McNerney; m. Donald Adair Kerth, Feb. 7, 1954; children: Robbin Adair, Christopher Jay. Grad., Trego Cmty. High Sch., Wakeeney, Kans., 1954. Sec. Verbeck Lumber & Supply Co. Inc., Wakeeney, Kans., 1960—97, co-owner, 1970—97, La-Crosse (Kans.) Lumber Co., Inc., 1963—85, Becky's Hallmark, Camarillo, Calif., 1968—88; artist Brush Strokes by Bobbi Kerth, Wakeeney, 2003—. Art work featured in Hays Daily News, KSN-TV, Christmas Across Kansas, Diabetes Forecast Mag. Mem. choir 1st United Meth. Ch., Wakeeney. Recipient Art Search Winner, Am. Diabetes Assn., 2000, 2001, 2002. Mem.: PEO (pres. chpt. CT. 1988—90), Trego Arts Coun, Palco (Kans.) Art Club. Avocations: painting, gardening, golf. Home: RR # 1 Box 122 Wa Keeney KS 67672

KERZ, LOUISE, historian; b. N.Y.C., Sept. 16, 1936; d. Louis and Catharine Sohn; m. Leo Kerz, Apr., 1965 (dec. 1976); children: Jonathan, Antony; m. Al Hirschfeld, Oct. 1996 (dec. 2003). Student, Queens Coll., 1954-56, Marymount Coll., 1972-74. Theatre producer Leo Kerz Prodns., N.Y.C., 1960-74; theatrical curator N.Y. Cultural Ctr., N.Y.C., 1974, Theatre of Max Reinhardt, 1974, N.Y. Pub. Libr. Lincoln Ctr., N.Y.C., 1984, Calif. Mus. Sci. and Industry, L.A., 1985, The Demille Dynasty, 1984; rsch. cons. CBS: On the Air, 1978, Smith-Hemion TV Prodns., L.A., 1987—, The Phantom of the Opera, 1995. Dir. rsch. Greengage Prodns., Julie Andrews/Greengage Prodns., LA, 1988, Tony Awards Telecast 50th Anniversary Show, 1947—96; rsch. cons. TV Acad. Hall of Fame and Tony Awards telecasts, 1993—96; dir. rights and permissions The Line King (The Al Hirschfeld Story-nominated for Oscar 1996) NY Times, TV documentary; rsch. historian "Broadway", six-part TV series, 1997; spl. cons. The Demille Family-Documentary Am. Movie Channel, 1997; exec. cons., liaison Hirschfeld Exhbns., catalogs, books and events Mus. of City of NY, cons. Hirschfeld's NY exhibit, 2001; cons. Hirschfeld's Hollywood exhibit Acad. Motion Picture Arts & Scis., Beverly Hills, Calif., 2001; cons. catalogues to exhibits Pub. Harry N. Abrams, 2001. Assoc. prodr. on Broadway: Rhinoceros, 1961; contbg. editor: N.Y.C. Access, 1983; picture editor The DeMilles: An American Family, 1988, curator, dir. Exhibit Broadway, 1995, picture editor Al Hirschfeld: On Line, 1998, curator, photographer (exhibitions) Hirschfeld Celebration at Leica Gallery, N.Y.C., 2002; one-woman shows include The Leica Gallery, N.Y.C., 2002. Vol. Persian Gulf war Am. Jewish Congress, Israel, 1991; elected mem. Tony Awards nominating com. Am. Theatre Wing, 2000-2003; co-chair Al Hirschfeld Centennial, assoc. prodr. Al Hirschfeld 100th Birthday Salute, 2003. Mem. Theatre Libr. Assn. Democrat. Address: c/o Al Hirschfeld 122 E 95th St New York NY 10128-1705

KERZHNERMAN, IRINA, psychologist; b. Odessa, Ukraine, July 16, 1975; arrived in U.S., 1979; d. Isaak and Alla Kerzhnerman; m. David Neil Rubin, Apr. 25, 2003. BA magna cum laude, NYU, 1996; MA, Hahnemann U., 1999, PhD in Clin. Psychology, 2002. Mobile therapist Northwest Human Svcs., Phila., 1997—98; crisis therapist Renfrew Ctr., 1998—99, Parkview Hosp., 1999; therapist U. Pa., 1999—2000; intern U. Hawaii at Manoa, Honolulu, 2000—01; crisis therapist Sex Abuse Treatment Ctr., 2001—02; dual diagnosis therapist House of Hope, Inc., Ft. Lauderdale, Fla., 2002—. Rschr. Hahnemann U., Phila., 1996—2002. Crisis vol. Women Organized Against Rape, Phila., 1996—2000; vol. NYU Student

Svcs., N.Y.C., 1992—96, Ocean Watch, Ft. Lauderdale, 2003. Mem.: APA, Fla. Psychol. Assn., Psi Chi, Phi Beta Kappa. Avocations: scuba diving, cooking, Hawaiian quilting. E-mail: irenekerzhnerman@aol.com.

KES VIC'KI, museum director; d. Durrington Adair June 2, 1932; d. Gerald Vance and Marjorie Jean (Bush) George; m. Pieter A. Kes, Sr., Nov., 2002; children: Alissa Hubbard, Rebecca Hubbard. Office worker Mining Corp. of the South, Vance, Ala., 1978-79; artist, sign painter Bob's Sign Shop, Midfield, Ala., 1980—; dir. Iron & Steel Mus. of Ala., McCalla, 1980—. Program completion Office of Mus Programs, Smithsonian, Washington, 1987. Artist (book) Tannehill Crafts, 1982. Events Planner Ala. Reunion State of Ala., Montgomery, 1990. Recipient Top 20 Events in the South East award SE Tourism Soc., Atlanta, 1986-87, 88, 91, Head Start Vol. award, 1994. Mem. Ala. Preservation Alliance, Soc. Indsl. Archaeology, Nat. Trust for Hist. Preservation, Birmingham Area Mus. Assn., Am. Assn. State and Local History (program completion 1980), Am. Assn. Mus., Ala. Mus. Assn. (sec.-treas. 1983-85, chair com. Southeastern Museums Conf. 1999, co-chair com. 2000, Meritorious Svc. award 1983), Ala. State Employees Assn. (pres. Tannehill chpt. 1999). Democrat. Baptist. Avocations: pen, ink drawings, painting. Home: 258 Stipes Rd West Blocton AL 35184 Office: Tannehill Historical State Park 12632 Confederate Pkwy Mc Calla AL 35111-2620 E-mail: tannehillmuseum@att.net.

KESSEL, MONA, space physicist; married; 2 children. BS in Physics, Baker U.; PhD, U. Kans. Postdoctoral rsch. assoc. Mullard Space Sci. Lab., England, 1986-90; astronomy lectr. DeKalb Coll., Ga., 1990-91; sr. data acquistion scientist NASA Goddard Space Flight Ctr., Greenbelt, Md., 1991—93, astrophysicist. Avocations: cooking, reading. Office: NASA Goddard Space Flight Ctr Greenbelt MD 20771-0001*

KESSELRING, LINDA J. medical editor, writer; b. Waynesboro, Pa., Dec. 23, 1953; BA in Chemistry, Shippensburg U., 1975; MS in Profl. Writing, Towson U., 1994. Med. copy editor Harper & Row Pubs., Hagerstown, Md., 1975—81; editor Frederick Cancer Rsch. Facility Nat. Cancer Inst., Frederick, Md., 1981—84; tech. editor, writer Md. Inst. for Emergency Med. Svcs. Sys., Balt., 1984—94; tech. editor, writer emergency medicine U. Md. Sch. Medicine, Balt., 1994—. Mng. editor, TraumaCare, Internat. Trauma Anesthesia and Critical Care Soc., Balt., 1988—. Mem.: Am. Med. Writers Assn. (mid-Atlantic pres. 1996—97), Coun. Sci. Editors, Bd. Editors in Life Scis. Office: Emergency Medicine U Md Sch Medicine 419 W Redwood St Ste 280 Baltimore MD 21201 Office Phone: 410-328-7449. Personal E-mail: lkessel112@aol.com.

KESSINGER, MARGARET ANNE, medical educator; b. Beckley, W.Va., June 4, 1941; d. Clisby Theodore and Margaret Anne (Ellison) K.; m. Loyd Ernst Wegner, Nov. 22, 1971. MA, W.Va. U., 1963, MD, 1967. Diplomate Am. Bd. Internal Medicine and Med. Oncology. Internal medicine house officer U. Nebr. Med. Ctr., Omaha, 1967-70, fellow med. oncology, 1970-72, asst. prof. internal medicine, 1972-77, assoc. prof., 1977-90, prof., 1990—, assoc. chief oncology hematology sect., 1988-91, chief oncology hematology sect., 1991-99; assoc. dir. clin. rsch. U. Nebr. Med. Ctr./Eppley Cancer Ctr., Omaha, 1999—. Contbr. articles to profl. publs. Fellow ACP, Am. Assn. Cancer Edn.; mem. Am. Soc. Clin. Oncology, Am. Assn. Cancer Rsch., Internat. Soc. Exptl. Hematology, Am. Soc. Hematology, Sigma Xi, Alpha Omega Alpha. Republican. Methodist. Avocations: aviation, gardening, canning, skiing. Office: U Nebr Med Ctr 987680 Nebraska Med Ctr Omaha NE 68198-0001 E-mail: makessin@unmc.edu.

KESSLER, DIANE COOKSEY, religious organization administrator, minister; b. Jan. 8, 1947; BA in Religion, Oberlin Coll., 1969; MA in Religion and Soc., Andover Newton Theol. Sch., 1971, postgrad., 1979—; DD (hon.), Episcopal Divinity Sch., 2001. Ordained to ministry United Ch. of Christ, 1983. Assoc. dir. for strategy and action Mass. Coun. Chs., Boston, 1975-88, exec. dir., 1988—. Ind. preacher; speaker in field. Author: Parents and the Experts, 1974, God's Simple Gift: Meditations on Friendship and Spirituality, 1988; co-author Councils of Churches and the Ecumenical Vision, 2000; editor Together on the Way, 1999; co-editor Encounters for Unity, 1995; also articles; mem. editl. adv. bd. Theology and Pub. Policy, 1989, 98, Mid-Stream, 1995-98. Former mem. adv. bd. Mass. Dept. Revenue; active Wellesley Congl. Ch.; mem. coun. for ecumenism United Ch. of Christ, 1984-94, chairperson coun. 1988-89, 90-91; mem. Atty Gen.'s Adv. Com. on Pub. Charities, 1988—, World Coun. of Churches, Joint Working Group, 1998-2005; trustee Hancock Variable Series Trust I; bd. dirs. Howard Benevolent Soc., 1989-96, New Eng. Holocaust Meml. Com., 1st Ch. Legacy Fund. Recipient Outstanding Woman award Coll. Club, 1990, Focolare award, 1994, Social Action Ministries award, 1995, Patron of Christian Unity award, 1998. Mem. Valiant Woman award 1991), Boston Min.'s Club. Office: Mass Coun Chs 14 Beacon St Ste 416 Boston MA 02108-3704 E-mail: council@masscouncilofchurches.org.

KESSLER, GALE SUZANNE, psychologist, educator; b. Chgo., Sept. 5, 1940; d. George I. Alpert and Celia Larman-Alpert-Shaps; m. Marvin Charles Facktor, June 4, 1960 (dec.); children: Greg Facktor, Charles Facktor, Laura Meehan; m. John W. Kessler, Feb. 20, 1986 (dec. Apr. 4, 2001). BA in Edn., Roosevelt U., Chgo., 1961; MS in Orgnl. Behavior, Adminstrn., George Williams Coll., Aurora, Ill., 1980. Tchr. Chgo. Pub. Schs., 1961; dir. constituency rels. George Williams Coll., 1982—85; dir. alumni rels. U. Chgo. Grad. Sch. Bus., 1986; dir. devel. Nat. MS Soc., Chgo., 1986—87; tchr. Chgo. Pub. Schs., 1987; instr. Columbia Coll., Lake Ozark, Mo., 1993—95; exec. dir. Women's Coun., Mo., 1998—2001. Internat. liaison to human svcs. George Williams Coll., Downers Grove, Ill., 1982—85; advisor Inst. for Women's Policy Rsch., Washington, 2000—01. Columnist: Consultations, 1995—98; author: Male "Mid-Life Crisis In Relation To Job Change", 1980. Chair Elmhurst Citizens for Flood Control, Ill., 1987—90; pres. Arts Coun. Lake Ozark, Mo., 1991—93; candidate state rep. State of Mo., Lake Ozark, 1997—98. Recipient Key to City, City of Elmhurst, Ill., 1990. Fellow: World Affairs Coun. (Seattle); mem.: Women's Univ. Club (co-chair com. 2003, Seattle). Avocations: reading, travel, writing, golf, tennis. Home: 7905 W Mercer Way Mercer Island WA 98040

KESSLER, GLADYS, federal judge; b. 1938; BA, Cornell U., 1959; LLB, Harvard U., 1962. Staff atty. enforcement divsn. Nat. Labor Rels. Bd., 1962-64; legis. asst. Sen. Harrison A. Willians Jr., 1964-66, Rep. Jonathan B. Bingham, 1966-68; staff atty. office labor rels N.Y.C. Bd. Edn. 1968-69; ptnr. Berlin, Roisman and Kessler (and successor firms), 1969-77; assoc. judge D.C. Superior Ct., 1977-94; judge U.S. Dist. Ct. D.C., Washington, 1994—. Asst. lectr. law sch. George Washington U., 1971-73; del. to judicial adminstrn. divsn. D.C. Superior Ct., 1985-90; mem. adv. bd. Ctr. for Dispute Settlement Inst. for Judicial Adminstrn., State Justice Inst.; mem. adv. com. nat. judicial edn. project on domestic violence; mem BNA adv. bd. Alternative Dispute Resolution Report, 1987-90; mem. family law cirriculum planning com. Georgetown U.; lead judge permanency planning project Nat. Coun. Juvenile and Family Ct. Judges; chair Nat. Conf. on Bioethics, Family and the Law, D.C., 1991; mem. faculty Nat. Inst. Trial Advocacy; exec. com. Nat. Adult Jud. Divsn./Conf. of Federal Trial Judges, 1997-2000; with U.S. Jud. Conf. Com. on Ct. Adminstrn. and Mgmt., 1999. Contbr. articles to legal jours. Recipient Women Lawyer of Yr. award Women's Bar Assn., 1983, Svc. award D.C. Coalition Against Domestic Violence, 1987, Judicial Excellence award Trial Lawyers Assn. Washington, 1987. Fellow Am. Bar Found.; mem. ABA (judicial adminstrn. divsn., com. on bioethics and AIDS, adv. com. on youth, alcohol and drug problems, nat. adv. bd. on child support and criminal justice, individual rights and responsibilities sect.), Am. Judicature Soc. (bd. dirs. 1985-89), Nat. Assn. Women Judges (v.p. 1979-81, pres. 1981-82), Nat. Ctr. for State Cts. (bd.

dirs. 1984-87), Women's Legal Def. Fund (founding pres. 1971), Women Judges' Fund. for Justice (bd. dirs. 1980—), Found. for Women Judges (pres. 1980-82). Office: US Courthouse 333 Constitution Ave NW Washington DC 20001-2802*

KESSLER, INGRID ANDERSON, musician, music educator; b. North Platte, Nebr., Aug. 18, 1944; d. R. Cedric and Ruby (Peterson) Anderson; m. Robert Michael Kessler, May 23, 1971; children: Jeffrey Charles, Lynn Elizabeth. BA in English Lit., U. Iowa, Iowa City, 1966; MusB summa cum laude, Vanderbilt U., 1998. Pianist, 1980—; pvt. tchr., 1983—; founding faculty W.O. Smith Music Sch., Nashville, 1984—87. Mem.: Nashville Opera Guild, Nat. Guild Piano Tchrs. (v.p. 1995—96, various other offices 1985—2001), Nashville Area Music Tchrs. Assn. (various offices 1985—2001, pres. 1999—2001). Jewish. Avocations: photography, gardening, travel, physical fitness. Home: 1247 Saxon Dr Nashville TN 37215

KESSLER, JOAN F. lawyer; b. June 25, 1943; m. Frederick P. Kessler, Sept. 1967; 2 children. BA, U. Kans., 1961-65; postgrad., U. Wis., 1965-66; JD cum laude, Marquette U., 1968. Law clk. Hon. John W. Reynolds U.S. Dist. Ct. (ea. dist.) Wis., Milw., 1968-69; assoc. Warschafsky, Rotter & Tarnoff, Milw., 1969-71; pvt. practice Milw., 1971-74; assoc. Cook & Franke, S.C., Milw., 1974-78; U.S. atty. Eastern Dist. Wis., Milw., 1978-81; ptnr. Foley & Lardner, Milw., 1981—. Lectr. profl. responsibility U. Wis. Law Sch., Marquette U. Law Sch., Milw., 1994-96; mem. bd. govs. State Bar of Wis., 1985-89, 90-92, 93-95, chair, 1993, bd. dirs. family law sect., 1991-94; mem. Jud. Coun. Wis., Madison, 1989-92; mem. Milw. Bd. Attys. Profl. Responsibility, 1979-85. Bd. dirs. Legal Aid Soc., 1974-78, v.p., 1978, Urban League, 1980-82, Women's Bus. Initiative Corp., 1989-91, Girl Scouts U.S., Milw., 1994-96; bd. dirs., pres. Voters for Choice in Wis., 1989-93. Fellow Am. Matrimonial Lawyers (bd. govs. 1990-96, v.p. 1996-99), Am. Law Inst., Am. Bar Found.; mem. ACLU (Best Lawyers in Am. 1993-98). Office: Foley & Lardner 777 E Wisconsin Ave Ste 3800 Milwaukee WI 53202-5367

KESSLER, KENDALL SEAY FERIOZI, artist; b. Washington, Nov. 4, 1954; d. Dan John and Anne Fletcher (Trotter) Feriozi; m. Clyde Thomas Kessler, June 25, 1977; 1 child, Alan. BA in Art Edn., Va. Poly. Inst. and State U., 1976; MFA in Painting and Printmaking, Radford U., 1983. Tchr. art, Spanish Cherrydale Christian Sch., Arlington, Va., 1976-77; tchr. community arts sch. Radford (Va.) U., 1980-82, adminstr., 1982-83; tchr. art Fine Arts Ctr., Pulaski, Va., 1984; instr. art Radford U., 1985-87, 88-93, interim gallery dir., 1987-88, asst. prof. art, 2000—; freelance profl. artist, tchr. Radford, 1993—. Illustrator (poetry books) Shooting Creek, 1982, Dancing at Big Vein, 1987, Preservations, 1989; promotional book jacket illustrator: The Rosewood Casket by Sharon McCrumb, 1996; exhibited in group shows Agora Gallery, Soho, N.Y., 1994, 95; exhibited and represented by Framescapes, Roanoke, Va., Fine Art Ctr. for the New River Valley, Pulaski, Va., Art Pannonia, Blacksburg, Va. Officer PEO Sisterhood, Radford, 1992-94, mem., 1989—; mem. Lamplighters, Radford Pub. Libr., 1991—. Recipient Am. Artist award Pastel Soc. West Coast 4th Nat. Exhibit, Sacramento, Daniel Greene 1st place award for oils Paris (Tex.) Art Fair, 1991, Best in Show award Fincastle (Va.) Arts Festival, 1997. Mem. Nat. Mus. Women in Arts, Blacksburg Regional Art Assn., Lynwood Artists, Piedmont Arts Assn. Avocations: theatre, literature, music, skating. Home: PO Box 3612 Radford VA 24143-3612 Business E-Mail: kkessler@radford.edu.

KESSLER, LYNN ELIZABETH, state legislator; b. Seattle, Feb. 26, 1941; d. John Mathew and Kathryn Eisen; m. Keith L. Kessler, Dec. 24, 1980, children: William John Moore, Christopher Scott Moore, Bradley Jerome Moore, Jamie. Attended, Seattle U., 1958-59. Mem. Wash. Ho. of Reps., 1993—. Majority leader, mem. rules com., mem. appropriations com. Exec. dir. United Way Grays Harbor, 1984-92; mem. adv. coun. Head Start, 1986-89, Cervical Cancer Awareness Task Force, 1990-91, vocat. adv. coun. Hoquiam High Sch., 1991—, strategic planning com. Grays Harbor Community Hosp., 1991-92, Grays Harbor Food Bank Com., 1991-92, Grays Harbor Dem. Ctrl. Com.; vice-chair Grays Harbor County Shorelines Mgmt. Bd., 1988-90; chair Disability Awareness Com., 1988-90, Youth 2000 Com., 1990-91; pres. Teenage Pregnancy, Parenting and Prevention Adv. Coun., 1989-91; v.p. Grays Harbor Econ. Devel. Coun., 1990-92; trustee Grays Harbor Coll., 1991-2001, Aberdeen YMCA, 1991—. Mem. Aberdeen Rotary (pres. 1993-94). Home: 62 Kessler Ln Hoquiam WA 98550-9742 Office: Wash Ho of Reps Legislative Bldg 3rd Fl Olympia WA 98504-0001

KESSLER, MITZI LYONS, artist; b. Charleston, S.C., May 26, 1932; d. Albert Percy and Carlotta Albertina (Drews) Lyons; m. Robert Frederick Kessler, May 3, 1952; children: Karen, Elizabeth. Student, Hollins Coll. Exhbns. include LyMoyne Art Found., Tallahassee, 1982-92, Gallery of Art, Panama City, Fla., 1986-96, Signature Gallery, Tallahassee, 1998—. Bd. dirs. Monticello (Fla.) Opera Co., 1976-82, Tallahassee Symphony Orch., 1990-95, bd. dirs. Mus. of Art, Tallahassee, 1997-98, v.p. 1992-93; vice moderator Christ Presbyn. Ch., Tallahassee, 1997-98, moderator Christ Presbyn. Ch. Women, 1998—. Mem. So. Watercolor Soc., Fla. Watercolor Soc., Tallahassee Watercolor Soc., Town Club. Avocations: travel, gardening, walking, reading, music. Home: 512 Summerbrooke Dr Tallahassee FL 32312-6726

KESSLER-GILLESPIE, KATHLEEN E. psychotherapist; b. Cleve., Dec. 27, 1946; d. Nathan J. and Rebecca M. (Bronstein) Eaton; m. James E. Kessler, July 20, 1968 (div. May 1996); children: Brett E., Dale E.; m. Jason R.D. Gillespie, Aug. 17, 1997. BA, Prescott Coll., 1991; postgrad., Remuda Ranch Treatment Ctr., 1992; MA, Ottawa U., Phoenix, 1994. Cert. profl. counselor. Dir. art therapy Remuda Ranch, Wickenburg, Ariz., 1990-93; psychotherapist Living Dynamics, Phoenix, 1993-94, Arrowhead Psychol. Resources, Phoenix, 1994-95, Arrowhead Behavioral Health, Sun City, Ariz., 1996—. Psychotherapist Ariz. Bapt. Children's Svcs., Phoenix, 1994-97; cons. Arrowhead Hosp. Women's Ctr., Glendale, Ariz., 1994—; lectr. mental health Cmty. Colls. Phoenix, 1993—, Mil. Base; facilitator 12-Step Recovery Groups, Phoenix, 1993-97. Author: Southwest Splender, 1990. Mem. ACA, Am. Assn. Christian Counselors, Ariz. Counseling Assn. Avocations: art, jazz, theater, hiking, physical fitness. Office: 104 99421 W Bell Rd Sun City AZ 85351-1362

KESSLER-HODGSON, LEE GWENDOLYN, actress, corporate executive; b. Wellsville, NY, Jan. 16, 1947; d. James Hewitt and Reba Gwendolyn (Adsit) Kessler; m. Bruce Gridley, June 22, 1969 (div. Dec. 1979); m. Jeffrey Craig Hodgson, Oct. 31, 1987. BA, Grove City Coll., 1968; MA, U. Wis., 1969. Prof. Sangamon State U., Springfield, Ill., 1969-70; pers. exec. Bullock's, L.A., 1971-74; owner Brunnen Enterprises, L.A., 1982—. Author: A Child of Arthur, 1981; producer, writer play including Anais Nin: The Paris Years, 1986; appeared in TV movies, mini-series including Roots, 1978, Backstairs at The White House, 1979, Blind Ambition, 1980, Hill Street Blues, 1984-87, Murder By Reason of Insanity, 1985, Hoover, 1986, Creator, 1987, Our House, 1988, Favorite Son, 1988, Lou Grant 1983-84, Barney Miller, 1979, L.A. Law, 1990, Hunter, 1991, (screenplay) Settlers Way, 1988; (TV series) Matlock, L.A. Law others. Knapp Prize fellow U. Wis., 1969. Mem. AFTRA, SAG, Actors Equity Assn. Republican. Mem. Ch. Scientology. Avocations: singer, directing, motivational speaking. Home: 2717 Seville Blvd Apt 11101 Clearwater FL 33764-1174 E-mail: kesslerl@bww.com.

KESTER, GUNILLA THEANDER, poet, literature educator, music educator; b. Lund, Sweden, Jan. 28, 1958; arrived in U.S., 1982; d. Sten and Siv Theander; m. Daniel John Kester, June 19, 1988; children: Anya Rebecca, Shiri Sophia. BA, U. Stockholm, 1982, U. Lund, 1982; MA, Pa. State U., 1985; PhD, U. N.C., 1991. Adj. asst. prof. Franklin-Marshall Coll., Lancaster, Pa., 1995—96, Daemen Coll., Buffalo, 1997—; classical guitar tchr. Amherst Sch. Music, Buffalo, 1997—. Asst. festival dir. Rantucci Internat. Guitar Festival and Competition, Buffalo, 1997—. Author: Writing the Subject, 1995, 1997, articles and poems. Recipient first prize, Giral Press Tri-Lang. Competition in English, 2002; Fulbright scholar, 1982, Scandinavian-Am. fellow, 1986. Mem.: Am. Profl. Woman Writers, Buffalo Guitar Soc. (v.p. 1997—), Swedish Women's Ednl. Assn. Office: Daemen Coll 4380 Main St Amherst NY 14226

KETCHAM, SALLY ANN, historic site staff member, consultant; b. Norfolk, Nebr., Mar. 11, 1928; d. William Ralph and Sallie Gertrude (Marshall) Johnson; m. Richard W. Ketcham, Jan. 24, 1962; children: Sallie Jane, William Marshall. Student, Colo. Woman's Coll., 1946—47; BA, U. Nebr., 1950, MA, 1956. Curator of history Nebr. State Hist. Soc., Lincoln, 1951—60; furnishing curator U.S. Nat. Pk. Svc., Omaha, 1960—62, rsch. specialist San Francisco, 1962—64, Washington, 1962—67; contractor U.S. Nat. Pk. Svc. and others, 1968—96, U.S. Fish and Wildlife, Omaha, 1979. Restoration chmn. Gen. Crook House, Omaha, 1980—86, Avery House, Ft. Collins, 1985—; steering com. Amigos de la Romero House, Ft. Collins, 2001—02. Co-author: (book) Sautterhouse Five, 1983; contbr. articles to profl. jours. and newspapers. Mem. Landmark Preservation Com., Ft. Collins, 1984—90, Poudre Landmarks Fedn., Ft. Collins, 1986—2000, Colo. Hist. Soc.; v.p. Douglas County Hist. Soc., Omaha, 1980—86; pres. Ft. Collins Hist. Soc. Recipient Disting. Svc. award, Douglas County Hist. Soc., 1984, Award of Excellence, City of Ft. Collins, 1990, Superior Svc. award, Nat. Park Svc., Outstanding Cmty. Svc. award, PLF, 2003. Mem.: Ft. Laramie Assn. (hon.). Home: 1132 Lindenwood Dr Fort Collins CO 80524

KETCHUM, IRENE FRANCES, library director; b. Hammond, Ind., Jan. 19, 1914; d. Peter H. and Theresa C. (Weis) Young; m. Alden W. Ketchum, Sept. 17, 1936 (dec. 1973); 1 child, William H. Grad. high sch., Hammond, 1932. Cert. mcpl. clk. Mng. editor Herald Newspapers, Gary, Ind., 1950-55; clk.-treas. Town of Highland, Ind., 1956-79; trustee, bd. sec. Lake County Pub. Libr., Merrillville, Ind., 1980-95; past trustee, 1995—; pres., 1995. Active Ind. State Libr. Adv. Com., Indpls., 1988—90; treas. Highland Cmty. Events Coun., 1975—; mem. Friends of Ind. Librs., Friends of Lake County Pub. Libr., Lake County Pub. Libr. Found.; pres. Highland Women's Dem. Club, 1978, auditor Highland Dem. Club, 1980—89. Named Sagamore of the Wabash, 1996, Fraternalist of Yr., Fraternal Congress, 2002. Mem. Internat. Inst. Mcpl. Clks., Ind. League Mcpl. Clks. and Treas. (assoc., treas., sec., v.p., pres. 1967-68), Girl Scouts USA (life). Roman Catholic. Avocations: community service volunteer, reading, travel.

KETEFIAN, SHAKÉ, nursing educator; b. Beirut, Dec. 29, 1939; d. Krikor and Zaghganoush (Soghomonian) K. BSN, Am. U. Beirut, 1963; MEd, Columbia U., 1968, EdD, 1972. From asst. prof. nursing to prof. NYU Sch. Edn., Health, Nursing and Arts Professions, N.Y.C., 1972-84; dir. continuing edn. in nursing NYU, N.Y.C.; with U. Mich., 1984—; prof., assoc. dean for grad. studies, dir. doctoral and postdoctoral studies, dir. internat. affairs U. Mich. Sch. Nursing, Ann Arbor, acting dean, 1991-92. Contbr. articles to profl. jours. Fellow AAUW, Am. Acad. Nursing (governing coun.); mem. ANA, Am. Orgn. Nurse Execs., Midwest Nursing Rsch. Soc. (chair sci. integrity task force 1994-96, 2001-03), Mich. Nurses Assn., Assn. for Moral Edn., Internat. Network for Doctoral Edn. in Nursing (co-founder, chmn.), Sigma Theta Tau. Office: U Mich Sch Nursing 400 N Ingalls Ann Arbor MI 48109

KETTERLING, DEBRA M. secondary school educator; b. Lamoure, North Dakota, July 21, 1951; d. Harold E. and Hilda L. Weixel; m. Lynn Ketterling, Dec. 28, 1968; children: Darin, Dustin. EdM, U. Mary VCSU, Bismarck, N.D., 1974. Tchr., Killdeer, ND, Veblen, SD, White, SD, Richardton, ND, Bismarck, ND. Mem. coll. adv. bd. U. Mary Masters, Bismarck, ND, 1998; tchr., adv. bd. Century H.S., Bismarck, ND, 1989—. Home: 2905 Vancouver Ln Bismarck ND 58503 Office: Century HS 1000 Century Ave E Bismarck ND 58503

KETTERSON, ELLEN D. biologist, educator; b. Orange, N.J., Aug. 9, 1945; m. Val Nolan, Jr. BA in Botany, Ind. U., 1966, MA in Botany, 1968, PhD in Zoology, 1974. NIH fellow Wash. State U., 1975-77; asst. prof. biol. scis. Bowling Green State U., 1975-77; from vis. asst. prof. to asst. prof. biology Ind. U., Bloomington, 1977-84, from assoc. prof. to prof. biology, 1984—, co-dir. Ctr. for Integrative Study Animal Behavior, 1990—. Vis. scientist Purdue U., Lafayette, Ind., 1991, Rockefeller U., 1985, U. Va., 1984. Mem. editl. bd. Current Ornithology, 1989-94, editor, 1994-99; mem. editl. bd. Animal Behaviour, 1991-94, assoc. editor, 1997—; mem. editl. bd. Evolution, 1994, editor, 1994-99; editor: Jour. Avian Biology, 1999—. Grantee NSF, 1978—. Fellow Am. Ornithologists Union (v.p. 1995-96, coun. 1988-91, Elliot Coues award 1996), Animal Behavior Soc.; mem. AAAS, Internat. Ornithol. Com., Ecol. Soc. Am., Am. Soc. Naturalists, Animal Behavior Soc., Assn Field Ornithologists, Cooper Ornithol. Soc., Soc. Conservation Biology, Soc. Study of Evolution, Soc. Integrative and Comparative Biology, Soc. Behavioral Neuroendocrinology, Wilson Ornithol. Soc. (Margaret M. Nice award 1998), Sigma Xi. Office: Indiana U Dept Biology Bloomington IN 47405

KETTLE, SALLY ANNE, consulting company executive, educator; b. Omaha, Feb. 2, 1938; d. H. Eugene and Elaine Josephine (Winston) Smiley; m. William Frederick Kettle, July 20, 1968 (div. 1973); children: Christopher, Winston. BEd, U. Nebr., 1960, postgrad. Cert. tchr., S.C., Nebr. Tchr. Dist. 66 Pub. Schs., Omaha, 1966-72; owner, mgr. The Rick Rack, Ltd., Lakewood, Colo., 1974-75; coord. merchandising communications 3M, St. Paul, 1978-80, sr. coord. internat. corp. comm., 1981-83; corp. dir. communications Intran Corp., St. Paul, 1984; pres. Sally Kettle & Co., Bloomington, Minn., 1985-95, Apple Valley, Minn., 1994—. Mem. cmty. faculty Met. State U., Mpls., 1983-90, 97—, St. Olaf Coll., Northfield, Minn., 1992-94, asst. prof. econs., 2000-01; mem. adj. faculty U. Minn. Sch. Journalism and Mass Comm., Mpls., St. Thomas U., 1994-95, Northwestern Coll., 1998-2000. TV hostess City of Bloomington Cable TV, 1984-86. Co-founder Women's Resource Ctr., bd. dirs., mem. adv. bd., 1978-88; chair 13th Precinct, Bloomington, 1978-83; bd. dirs. 41st Sen. Dist., Bloomington, 1982-83; cable TV commr. Bloomington City Coun., 1984-85; pub. rels. com. U.S. Olympic Festival, 1989-90; bd. dirs. Minn. Prayer Breakfast Bd., 1984—; mem. Better Bus. Bur.; founder Ad Rev. Coun.; v.p. Christian Mgmt. Assn., Minn.; internat. com. bd. Carlson Grad. Sch. Mgmt., U. Minn.; mem. state ctrl. com. and platform commn. DFL, 1988-90; bd. dirs. Fellowship of Christian Athletes, 1988-89; pub. rels. com., vice chair bd. comms. '96 Billy Graham Minn. Crusade, 1996; bd. commrs. Shoreland Zoning Commn. Dakota County, Minn., 1996—, vice chair, 1998—. Named one of Outstanding Young Women of Am., 1965. Mem. Am. Advt. Fedn. (conf. com. 1985-87, pub. svc. com. 1986-88), Pub. Rels. Soc. Am., Advt. Fedn. Minn. (bd. dirs. 1982-86), Minn. Women's Econ. Roundtable, Internat. Platform Assn., Nat. Grad. Women's Honor Soc., Minn. Press Club (co-chair newsmaker com., bd. dirs. 1989-92), Phi Delta Gamma, Kappa Alpha Theta. Avocations: reading, sewing, entertaining, volunteering. Home: 13390 Gunflint Path Apple Valley MN 55124-7376

KEULEGAN, EMMA PAULINE, special education educator; b. Washington, Jan. 21, 1930; d. Garbis H. and Nellie Virginia (Moore) K. BA, Dumbarton Coll. of Holy Cross, 1954. Cert. tchr. elem. and spl. edn. Tchr. St. Dominic's Elem. Sch., Washington, 1954-56, Sacred Heart Acad., Washington, 1956-59, Our Lady of Victory, Washington, 1959-63, St. Francis Acad., Vicksburg, Miss., 1963-78, Culkin Acad., Vicksburg, 1978-91, substitute tchr. spl. edn., 1991—. Treas. PTA, Vicksburg, 1980; pres. Vicksburg Genealogical Soc., 1999. Mem.: DAR (chpt. regent 1967—69, sec. 1994, chpt. chaplain 1996, chpt. libr. 2002, chpt. membership chmn.), Daus. of United Confederacy (chpt. chaplain), Soc. Descs. of Knights of Most Noble Order of the Garter, Sovereign Colonial Soc. Am. Royal Descent, Soc. Magna Charta Dames and Barons (state chaplain 2001), Daus. of the War of 1812 (state chaplain 1998, hon. state pres. 2002, state pres. 2002—, hon. state pres. 2003), Daus. Am. Colonists (chaplain 1985—89, state pres. 1992—94, hon. state pres. 1994—), Colonial Dames 17th Century (state v.p. 1987—89, state pres. 1989, hon. state pres. 1991—), Internat. Reading Assn. (pres. Warren County chpt.), Vicksburg Geneal. Soc. (pres. 2003). Republican. Roman Catholic. Avocations: stamp and coin collecting, needlework, reading. Home: 215 Buena Vista Dr Vicksburg MS 39180-5612

KEWLEY, SHARON LYNN, systems analyst, consultant; b. Geneseo, Ill., Sept. 23, 1958; d. James Leslie and Geraldine (Myers) K. BBA with honors, U. Miami (Fla.), 1988. Gen. agt. Varvaris & Assocs., Cedar Rapids, Iowa, 1981-84; programmer, analyst U. Miami, Coral Gables, Fla., 1984-88; systems analyst Metro Dade County, Miami, Fla., 1988-91; sys. analyst Nat. Coun. on Compensation Ins., Boca Raton, Fla., 1991-93; owner Boca Byte, Boca Raton, 1993—. Mem. NAFE, Kendall Jaycees, Nat. Gold Key Honor Soc., PADI Divemaster. Republican. Lutheran. Avocations: cruising, world travel, scuba diving. Office: Boca Byte PO Box 7072 Boca Raton FL 33431-0072 E-mail: kewstan@aol.com.

KEY, ANNIE L. state representative; b. Camden, Ala. 1 child, Stephanie. Degree, Cuyahoga C.C., Cleve. State U. Mem. econ. devel. and small bus. com. Ho. Reps., mem. bus. com., mem. retirement and aging com., mem. trans. and pub. safety com. Mem. adv. bd. Hough Neighborhood Empowerment Zone; mem. Nat. Coun. Negro Women, Inc.; area v.p. St. Clair/Superior Coalition; mem. Sch. Cmty. Coun.; exec. bd. mem. Cuyahoga County Dem. Party; mem. Cuyahoga County Women's Polit. Caucus. Office: House of Representatives 77 South High St 10th Floor Columbus OH 43215 6111

KEY, FLEDA, administrative assistant; b. Sault Ste. Marie, Mich., Sept. 10, 1946; d. Orville Levi and Ethel Helen (Wilson) Izzard; m. Tommy Wayne Key, Aug. 10, 1964; 1 child: Michelle Denise. Cert., Draughn's Bus. Sch., Lubbock, Tex., 1968. With Furr's Cafeteria, Lubbock, 1964-66; sec., receptionist Kilpatrick Hardware, Lubbock, 1966-67; sec. Bob Hunter Constrn., Lubbock, 1967-68; sec., exec. sec., adminstrv. aide, adminstrv. asst. Harris County (Tex.) Pollution Control Dept., Pasadena, 1968—. Active United Way, Statue of Liberty Restoration Drive, March of Dimes, local blood drive campaign; bd. dirs. Cedar Bend Subdivsn. Home Owners Assn., Baytown, Tex., 1995, Paradise Acres Subdivsn., Onalaska, Tex., 1985—. Mem. Am. Bus. Women's Assn. (sec. 1981, treas. 1982, 85, v.p. 1980, pres. 1988, 95, chmn. registration chairperson for regional conv. 1988, Woman of Yr. 1988), Fedn. of Houston Profl. Women (trophy winner class C slow-pitch women's softball player, Woman of Excellence award 1996). Baptist. Avocations: travel, sewing, photography, genealogy, family.

KEY, HELEN ELAINE, accountant, educator, consulting company executive; b. Cleve., Jan. 16, 1946; d. Maud and Helen (Key) Vance. BS, W.Va. State Coll., 1968; MEd, Cleve. State U., 1977, PhD, 2003. Prin. Cleve. Bd. Edn., 1968—2004; pres. H.E. Key & Assoc., Cleve., 1983—. Instr. Cuyahoga C.C., Cleve., 1969—, Dyke Coll., Cleve., 1979-85; treas. BK4W Inc., Cleve., 1981; sec. Progressive Pioneers, Inc. Mem. AAUW, NAACP, NEA, Am. Assn. Notary Pubs., Women Bus. Owners Assn., Cleve. Area Bus. Tchrs., Toastmistress Club (sec. 1978), Pi Lambda Theta, Alpha Kappa Alpha. Democrat. Baptist. Home: 564 Wilkes Ln Cleveland OH 44143-2622 E-mail: hekey-clev@worldnet.att.net.

KEY, JANICE DIXON, physician, medical educator; b. Hickory, N.C., Aug. 14, 1954; d. Charles Dennis and Mary Louise (Edgerton) Dixon; m. L. Lyndon Key Jr., May 27, 1973; children: Rebecca Louise, Emily Edgerton. BS, U. N.C., 1976, MD, 1980. Clin. instr. Harvard Med. Sch., Boston, 1984-85; clin. assoc. prof. Sch. of Medicine, U. N.C., Greensboro, N.C., 1985-91; asst. prof. Med. U. of S.C., Charleston, S.C., 1991-98, assoc. prof. pediat., 1998—. Author: Ambulatory Pediatric Care, 1992, Sleepwell Series, vol. 3, 2003; contbr. articles to profl. jours. Pres. Charleston County Med. Soc., 2002—; com. mem. S.C. Adolescent Task Force, Charleston, 1993, S.C. Dept. Edn., Columbia, 1992, S.C. Sch. Health Advisory, Columbia, 1992; co-chair Sch. Health Com., Charleston, 1992—; cmty. adv. bd. Jr. League, Charleston, 1994 Recipient Faculty Rsch. award U. N.C., 1978. Fellow Am. Acad. Pediat.; mem. Am. Soc. Human Genetics, Soc. Adolescent Medicine (chpt. pres. 1991-98), Am. Med. Women's Assn., S.C. Med. Assn. (del., com. chairperson 1996—), S.C. Pediat. Med. Soc. (CME com. 1994-96), Alpha Omega Alpha, Phi Beta Kappa, Phi Eta Sigma. Democrat. Presbyterian. Office: 135 Rutledge Ave Charleston SC 29425-0001

KEY, OTTA BISCHOF, retired educator; b. Englewood, Colo., May 19, 1907; d. Herbert and Lulu Bonita (Kitterman) Bischof; m. Elra Richard Key, Aug. 21, 1938 (dec. June 1993); children: Paul, Kathryn. BFA, Kans. U., 1933; MA, Ctrl. Mich. U., 1967. Cert. Christian educator. Tchr., Luray, Kans., 1923; elem. tchr., 1924-26; tchr. jr. h.s. Russell, Kans., 1926-29; tchr. art Meml. H.S., Lawrence, Kans., 1934-38; instr. art edn. Maryville (Mo.) U., 1937-38, Saginaw (Mich.) Valley Coll., 1957-70; ednl. asst. Meml. Presbyn. Ch., Midland, Mich., 1958-73; ednl. asst. religion dept. Millikin U., Decatur, Ill., 1976-84. Student adviser Meml. H.S., Lawrence, 1934-38, dir. art exhibits, 1934-38; tchr. synod schs. Presbyn. Ch., 1955-58; mem. edn. City Ch. Coun., Decatur, Ill., 1978-84. Author: Teaching Volunteers Teachers, 1984. Cooperator Decatur Ch. coun., 1976-84, Ch. Women United, Decatur, 1974-93; supporter Am. United, Washington, 1970-97, Presbyn. Ch., 1973-93. Scholarships established McCormick Presbyn. Sem., Louisville Presbyn. Sem.; recipient award Presbyn. Ch., 1958-93. Mem. Assn. of Presbyn. Ch. Educators, Assn. of Great Lakes Ch. Educators. Democrat. Ecumenical. Avocations: reading current events, ecumenical activities, visual arts, family education. Home: 2025 E Lincoln St # 1221 Bloomington IL 61701-5995

KEYES, JOAN ROSS RAFTER, education educator, writer; b. Bklyn., Aug. 12, 1924; d. Joseph W. and Hermia (Ross) Rafter; m. William Ambrose, Apr. 26, 1947 (dec.); children: William, Peter, Dion, Kenzie. BA, Adelphi U., Garden City, N.Y., 1945; MS, Long Island U., Greenvale, N.Y., 1973. Prodn. asst. CBS Radio, N.Y., 1943-44; cub news reporter Bklyn. Daily Eagle, 1945-46; advt. copywriter Gimbel's Dept. Store, N.Y., 1946-47; adj. prof. L.I. U., Greenvale, N.Y., 1984—; tchr. Port Wash. Pub. Schs., N.Y., 1970-94. Lectr., cons. pub. sch. dists. nationwide, 1978—; workshop leader Tchrs. English to Speakers Other Langs. convs., 1981—. Author: Beats, Conversations in Rhythm, 1983, (video program) Now You're Talking, 1987, (computer program) Quick Talk, 1990, Oxford Picture Dictionary for Kids Program, 1998; contbr. articles to ednl. mags. Lectr., catechist Our Lady of Fatima Ch., Port Washington, 1987—; vol. Earthwatch, Mallorca, 1988. Australia/New Zealand ednl. grantee Port Washington Pub. Schs., 1992. Mem. Tchrs. of English to Speakers of Other Languages, Am. Fedn. of Tchrs., N.Y. State United Tchrs., Port Wash. Tchrs. Assn. Republican. Roman Catholic. Avocations: music, painting, travel, tennis, golf. E-mail: joanrosskeyes@aol.com.

KEYES, MARGARET NAUMANN, home economics educator; b. Mt. Vernon, Iowa, Mar. 4, 1918; d. Charles Reuben and Sarah (Naumann) K. BA, Cornell Coll., Mt. Vernon, 1939, LHD, 1976; MS, U. Wis., 1951; PhD (Ellen H. Richards grad. fellow), Fla. State U., 1965; H.H.D., Coe Coll., 1977. Tchr. home econs. Stanley (Iowa) High Sch., 1939-42, Washington Jr. High Sch., Clinton, Iowa, 1942-44, Clinton High Sch., 1944-50; instr. related art U. Iowa, Iowa City, 1951-57, asst. prof. related art dept. home econs., 1957-68, assoc. prof., 1968-75, prof., 1975-88; research prof. U. Iowa Found., 1971-74. Author: Nineteenth Century Home Architecture Iowa City, 1967, expanded edit., 1993, Old Capitol: Portrait of an Iowa Landmark, 1988; mem. editorial bd., Home Econs. Research Jour; contbr. articles to periodicals. Mem. Terr. Hill Planning Commn. for Iowa, Terr. Hill Authority for Iowa; mem. design rev. bd. Iowa City Urban Renewal Commn.; dir. research Old Capitol Restoration Com., 1971-75; dir. Old Capitol, 1975-88; mem. Iowa State Hist. Bd., vice chmn. 1986-90, chmn., 1990-92. Recipient Peterson/Harlan award State Hist. Soc. of Iowa, 1994, Nat. History Award medal DAR, 1996; named Dist. Friend of U. Iowa Alumni Assn., 1989. Mem. Am. Home Econ. Assn. (exec. bd., chmn. art sect.), Iowa Home Econs. Assn., AAUP, Soc. Archtl. Historians, Am. Soc. Interior Designers, Interior Design Educators Council, Iowa Soc. Preservation Hist. Landmarks (dir. 1970-75), Cornell Coll. Alumni Assn. (dir. 1970-73), Nat. Trust Hist. Preservation (bd. advs. 1974-77), Internat. Fedn. Home Econs. (individual), Victorian Soc. Am. (v.p., dir. 1974-80), Iowa Centennial Meml. Found., Altrusa Club (pres. 1969-70), Phi Beta Kappa, Omicron Nu, Omicron Delta Kappa. Democrat. Presbyterian.

KEYES, SAUNDRA ELISE, newspaper editor; b. Salt Lake City, June 28, 1945; d. Vernon Harrison and Mildred K.; m. William J. Ivey, June 13, 1969 (div. 1976). BA, U. Utah, 1966; MA, Ind. U., 1969, PhD, 1976. Tchr. Salt Lake City Pub. Schs., 1966-67; asst. prof. Fisk U., Nashville, 1971-76; reporter, city editor The Tennessean, Nashville, 1976-83; staff writer The Courier-Jour., Louisville, 1983-84; dep. mng. editor Orlando (Fla.) Sentinel, 1985-88; mng. editor Phila. Daily News, 1988-90; exec. editor, sr. v.p. Press-Telegram, Long Beach, Calif., 1991-93; mng. editor The Miami Herald, 1993-96, Contra Costa Times, 1996—2000; editor Honolulu Advertiser, 2000—. Ford Found. fellow, 1978. Office: Honolulu Advertiser 605 Kapiolani Blvd PO Box 3110 Honolulu HI 96802*

KEYS, ALICIA, vocalist, musician, songwriter; b. N.Y.C., Jan. 25, 1981; d. Craig Cook and Terri Augello. Student, Columbia U. Singer: (albums) Songs in A Minor, 2001 (Video Music Award, two Billboard Awards, two Am. Music Awards, two NAACP Image Awards, three Soul Train awards, two World Music Awards, an ECCHO award, five Grammy awards including Best New Artist, Song of Yr., Best R&B Vocal Performance, Best R&B Song and Best R&B Album), The Diary of Alicia Keys, 2003. Office: BMG Entertainment 1540 Broadway New York NY 10036

KEYS, ELIZABETH A. accountant, business executive; b. Grosse Pointe, Mich., Jan. 6, 1969; BS summa cum laude, Boston Coll., 1991. CPA, Mich. Audit asst. Deloitte & Touche, Detroit, 1991-93, audit sr., 1993-95, audit mgr., 1995, 1995-97; regional mgr. acctg. Gen. Motors Asia Pacific, Singapore, 1997-98, chief acctg. officer, 1998-2000; dir. investor rels. GM, Detroit, 2000—. Bd. dirs. Assn. for Retarded Citizens, Mich., 1995. Mem. AICPA, Mich. Assn. CPAs. Home: 1335 S Main St Royal Oak MI 48067-3267 Office: Gen Motors MC 482-C34-D71 PO Box 300/Renaissance Ctr Detroit MI 48265-3000 E-mail: beth.keys@gm.com.

KEZER, PAULINE RYDER, state government executive, management consultant; b. Boston, Feb. 4, 1942; d. Paul Washington and Madeline (Farmer) Ryder; m. Kenneth Ronald Kezer, Sept. 23, 1962; children: Anne Elizabeth, Pamela Lynne, Cynthia Karen. B in Psychology, Colby Coll., 1963; postgrad., Ctrl. Conn. State Coll., 1978, 83. Tutor sci. and humanities New Britain (Conn.) Schs. Teenage Parent Program, 1964-78; mem. Conn. Ho. of Reps., Hartford, 1979-85, asst. minority leader, 1981-84, asst. majority leader, 1985-86; sec. of state State of Conn., Hartford, 1991-94, asst. treas. intergovtl. affairs, 1998-99. Bd. dirs. New Eng. Caucus Women Legislators, 1983-84, chmn., 1985-86; CEO, Kezer Cons., 2000—; pres. Conn. Order Women Legislators, Hartford, 1981-82; mem. adv. com. Ctrl. Conn. State U. Polit. Inst., New Britain, 1983-84; mem. adv. bd. Coloniall Bank, Plainville, Conn., 1980-85; CEO Hartford Ballet, 1995-97; asst. treas., dir. unclaimed property divsn. State of Conn., 1998-99. Camp dir. Girl Scout Coun., 1972-81, assoc. chair, 1975-78, v.p., 1979-85, nat. bd. dirs., 1984-93; pres., v.p., treas., bd. dirs. YWCA, New Britain, 1971-79; chmn., sec. Inland Wetlands Com., 1972-79; chmn. State Employees Campaign for Charitable Giving, 1992; active Rep. Town Com., Plainville, 1977-84; exec. bd. Ea. region Coun. State Govts., Cmty. Health Charities of Conn., 1993—; vol. New Britain Cancer Soc., 1980-85; bd. dirs. Collaboration for Conn.'s Children, 1985—, Conn. Spl. Olympics, 1993-94, Am. Leadership Forum, 2001-; adv. bd. Tunxic C.C., 1984—; nat. rev. team Projects Hometown Am., 1986; hon. chair Conn. Citizen Bee, 1992; vice-chair Conn. Rep. Party, 1987-89; gov. chair, Greater Hartford United Way, 1993-94; co-chair, founder, bd. dirs. Conn. Race for the Cure, Susan G. Komen Found. for Breast Cancer Rsch., 1993-99; chmn. Conn. Sports Mus. Hall of Fame Dinner, 1994; Rep. candidate for Gov. of Conn., 1994; bd. nominating chair Conn. Combined Health Appeal, 1995-98; exec. bd. Cmty. Health Charities Conn., 1998-2001, nat. bd., 1999—; bd. dirs. Bishops Fund for Children, 1998—, trustee 1999-2002, pres. 2002-; bd. dirs., v.p. Women's Campaign Sch. at Yale, 1993-99; co-chair, bd. dirs. Conn. Komen Race for the Cure, 1994-99; nat. bd. dirs., vice-chair, 1999—; choir mem. St. Mark's Episcopal Ch., 1998-2002, chair planned giving com., 2000-. Harvard U. fellow Inst. Politics, 1990, Am. Leadership Forum fellow, 1991-92; recipient Thanks Badge and Conn. Yankee award Conn. Yankee Girl Scout coun., Farmington, 1982, 79, Women Helping Women award Soroptimists, 1984—, Women of Mert award, Conn. Valley Girl Scouts, 1993, DKG award, 1994; named Outstanding Citizen, Jaycees, Plainville, Conn., 1980, Outstanding Vol., New Britain YWCA, 1978, Legislator of Yr., Conn. Valley Girl Scout Coun., Hartford, 1984. Mem. Nat. Order Women Legislators (legis. chair 1986), Nat. Assn. Sec. State Regional V.P., Women Execs. in State Govt., Conn. Fedn. Rep. Women (2d v.p. 1992—), Ea. Region Coun. State Govts. (exec. bd. 1991-92), Nat. Assn. Secs. of State (exec. bd. 1991-92, Alpha Delta Pi. Republican. E-mail: pauline@kezerconsulting.com.

KEZLARIAN, NANCY KAY, marriage and family therapist; b. Royal Oak, Mich., Aug. 26, 1948; d. Barkev A. and Nancy (Israelian) K.; m. Robert S. Vinetz, M.D., Aug. 1995. Student, U. Vienna, Austria, 1969; BA, Albion Coll., 1970; MA in Theatre and TV, U. Mich., 1971; MA in Clin. Psychology, Pepperdine U., 1992. Cert. secondary tchr., Mich., Calif.; lic. marriage family therapist. Tchr. West Bloomfield Hills (Mich.) High Sch., 1971-76; tchr. ESL, L.A. Pub. Schs., 1976-80; personnel dir. Samuel Goldwyn Co., L.A., 1985-86; dir. adminstrn. and human resources (Norman Lear) Act III Communications, L.A., 1986-90; dir. programs Salvation Army Booth Meml. Ctr., L.A., 1993-94; asst. exec. dir. Florence Crittenton Ctr., L.A., 1994-96, exec. dir., 1996-2000; pvt. practice marriage and family therapy, 2000—. Owner, mgr. KAZ, hand painted clothing co., L.A., 1980-85; mem. Screen Actors Guild. Actress My Seventeenth Summer, The Big Blue Marble, 1979 (Emmy award for childen's TV programming). Bd. dirs. Calif. Assn. Children's Homes. Named Tchr. of Yr., West Bloomfield Hills High Sch., 1976. Mem. SAG, Pers. and Indsl. Rels. Assn. (legis. rep. dist. 5 1989, 90), Calif. Assn. of Marriage and Family Therapists, L.A. Group psychtherapy Soc., Rotary Internat., Psi Chi. Avocations: writing, world mythologies, theatre, abstract artist, vegetarian chef.

KHAN, ARFA, radiologist, educator; b. Srinagar, Kashmir, India, Dec. 4, 1943; came to U.S., 1966; d. Ghulam Rasool and Ruqia Hayat; m. Faroque A. Khan, Apr. 16, 1966; children: Arif O., Shireen. B of Medicine, B of Surgery, Govt. Med. Coll., Kashmir, 1964. Diplomate Am. Bd. Radiology. Intern Barberton (Ohio) Citizen Hosp., 1966-67; resident in radiology L.I. Jewish Med. Ctr., New Hyde Park, N.Y., 1967-70, from instr. to assoc. prof. radiology, 1970-93, prof., 1993—, assoc. chmn. radiology, 1994-2000; program dir., 1995. Contbr. 50 articles to radiology jours. Fellow Am. Coll. Radiology; mem. Am. Coll. Radiology, Am. Soc. Neuroradiology, Am. Soc. Head & Neck Radiology, Am. Soc. Thoracic Radiology, Radiol. Soc. N.Am. Democrat. Moslem. Avocations: cooking, tennis, aerobics, gardening, skiing. Fax: 718-343-7463. E-mail: khan@lij.edu.

KHAN, KAY, state legislator; BSN, Boston U., 1965, MS in Nursing, 1981. Staff nurse Boston Children's Hosp. Med. Ctr., 1965-67; clin. instr. Boston U. Sch. Nursing, 1967-68; asst. head nurse Goebler children's unit Met. State Hosp., 1978-79; nurse pvt. group practice, 1981—, mem. Mass. Ho. of Reps., Boston, 1995—. Mem. ANA, Mass. Nurses Assn., Mass. Assn. Mental Health (bd. dirs.), Nurses United for Responsible Svc. Office: 2000 Washington St Ste 402 Newton MA 02462-1602 also: Mass Ho of Reps State House Rm 22 Boston MA 02133

KHANBEGIAN, JEAN M. artist; arrived in U.S., 1953; d. John Joseph and Anne Genivieve MacNeil; m. Peter Khanbegian. Student, Sch. Visual Arts, N.Y.C., 1953—55, Parsons Sch. Design, 1955—56, Art Students League. Artist Khanbegian Studio, Bar Harbor, Maine, 1965—82; freelance artist Windham, NH, 1998—2003. Cover artist Readers Digest, 1973; graphic artist JJ Graphics, Windham, 1999—. One-woman shows include Backstage Gallery Fine Art, Derry, N.H., 2002, Jean Khanbegian Studio & Gallery; author: Painting Sea & Sky, 1968; editor: Artist Mag, 1965. Home: 7 Sharon Rd Windham NH 03087-2213

KHEDOORI, TOBA, artist; b. Sydney, Australia; BFA, San Francisco Art Inst., 1988; MFA, UCLA, 1994. Represented by David Zwirner Gallery, NYC. One-woman shows include Hirshhorn Mus., Mus. Contemporary Art LA, Walker Art Ctr., Whitechapel Art Gallery, London, Mus. Gegenawartskunst, Basel, exhibited in group shows at Mus. Moder Art, NYC, Mus. Contemporary Art, Chgo., Mus. Modern Art, Copenhagen. Fellow MacArthur Found. fellow, 2002. Address: David Zwirner Gallery 525 W 19th St New York NY 10011-2000

KHIDEKEL, REGINA P. art historian, curator, lecturer; b. Khmelnitsky, Russia, Apr. 11, 1946; d. Peter I. and Sophie M. (Sirota) Gezunterman; m. Mark L. Khidekel, Dec. 3, 1967; 1 child, Roman M. MA, Acad. Fine Arts, St. PEtersburg, Russia, 1969, PhD, 1978. Tchr., lectr. Leningrad (USSR) U. Architecture, 1972-85; art dir. Diaghilev Art Ctr., St. Petersburg, 1990-93; founder, pres. Russian-Am. Cultural Ctr., N.Y.C., 1998—. Author: "It's the Real Thing" Soviet & Post Soviet Sots Art and American Pop Art, 1998; contbr. to Art News mag., books and catalogs. Mem. Internat. Art Critics Assn., Russian Union of Artists (awards 1975, 79). Home: 500 E 77th St Apt 316 New York NY 10162-0001 E-mail: khidart@aol.com.

KHIN, DIANNE FAITH, urban planner; b. Muskegon, Mich., Oct. 15, 1971; d. Donald Frank and Gailenne Kay Pickel; m. Frederick Christopher Chit Khin, May 22, 1999; 1 child, Connor Christopher. BA, Vassar Coll., 1994; M of Regional Planning, U. N.C., 1998. Planner Village of Pinehurst, NC, 1998—99; sr. planner Town of Apex, NC, 1999—. Mem.: Am. Inst. Cert. Planners, Am. Planning Assn. (N.C. chpt.), Phi Beta Kappa. Democrat. Lutheran. Home: 304 Milky Way Dr Apex NC 27502 Office: Town of Apex 73 Hunter St Apex NC 27502

KHOL, CHAREL L. psychologist; b. Cleve., Apr. 2, 1943; divorced; children: Adrienne Marie, Matthew Philip. BS in Edn., Ohio State U., 1965; MS in Edn., Ohio U., 1969; PhD, Kent State U., 1982. Lic. psychologist, Ohio. Psychologist Kevin Coleman Ctr., Ravenna, Ohio, 1983-87; pvt. practice Ravenna and Kent, 1984—; psychologist Child Guidance Ctr., Akron, Ohio, 1987—. Cons., expert witness. Named Jennings Scholar for Tchr. Excellence, Jennings Trust, 1967. Mem.: APA, State U. Varsity O, Ohio Psychol. Assn. Avocations: reading, quilting, collecting. Office: 4130 St Rt 43 Ste 202 Kent OH 44240 also: Child Guidance Ctr 312 Locust Akron OH 44305-3838

KHOURY, COLLEEN A. dean; b. 1943; BA, Colby Coll., 1964; JD, Ill. Inst. Tech., 1975. Dir. info. and devel. pvt. child welfare agy., Chgo.; pub. info. dir. Cook County Dept. Pub. Aid; assoc. Bell, Boyd & Lloyd, 1975—83, ptnr., 1983; gen. counsel Ventrex Labs.; prof. U. Maine Sch. Law, Portland, 1985—, assoc. dean, 1991—93, dean, 1998—. Bd. dirs. Justice Action Group, Banknorth Group, Inc.; chair Commn. on Gender, Justice and Cts., Maine Supreme Jud. Ct., 1993—96. Corporator Boys and Girls Clubs Greater Portland, Maine; trustee Portland Symphony Orch.; vice chair bd. trustees Colby Coll. Recipient Caroline Duby Glassman award, Maine State Bar Assn., 1997, Deborah Morton award, U. New Eng., 2002, Margaret Brent Lawyers Achievement award, ABA, 2003. Mem.: Am. Law Inst., Maine Bar Found. (bd. dirs.). Office: Univ Maine Sch Law 246 Deering Ave Portland ME 04102*

KIANG, ASSUMPTA (AMY KIANG), brokerage house executive; b. Beijing, Aug. 15, 1939; came to U.S., 1962; d. Pei-yu and Yu-Jean (Liu) Chao; m. Wan-lin Kiang, Aug. 14, 1965; 1 child, Eliot Y. BA, Nat. Taiwan U., 1960; MS, Marywood Coll., Scranton, Pa., 1964; MBA, Calif. State U., Long Beach, 1977. Cert. fin. mgr. Data programmer IBM World Trade, N.Y.C., 1963; libr. East Cleve. Pub. Libr., 1964-68; lectr. Nat. Taiwan U., Taipei, 1971-73; reference libr. U.S. Info. Svc., Taipei, 1971-74; v.p., sr. fin. advisor Merrill Lynch, Santa Ana, Calif., 1977—, v.p., sr. fin. cons. Costa Mesa, Calif., 1996—. Author numerous rsch. reports in field. Founder Pan Pacific Performing Arts Inc., Orange County, Calif., 1987; pres. women league Calif. State. U., Long Beach, 1980-82. Mem. AAUW (treas. Newport-Costa Mesa br. 1996—), Chinese Bus. Assn. Soc. Calif. (chmn. 1987—, v.p. 1986-87), Chinese Am. Profl. Women's League (treas. 1993, pres. 1997—), Pacific Rim Investment and trade Assn. (vice-chair 1994-96), U.C.I. Chancellor's Club, Old Ranch Country Club, Ctr. Club (bd. dirs. exec. women's coun. Orange County 1998—). Democrat. Roman Catholic. Office: Merrill Lynch 650 Town Center Dr Ste 500 Costa Mesa CA 92626-1905 E-mail: AKiang@pclient.ml.com.

KIANG, CHING-HWA, chemical engineering educator; b. Taipei, Taiwan, Jan. 20, 1965; came to U.S., June 24, 1988; d. Song Kiang and Pi-Ying Huang; m. Michael William Deem, Sept. 2, 1995. BSChemE, Nat. Taiwan U., Taipei, 1987; PhD in Chemistry, Calif. Inst. Tech., 1995. Rsch. asst. Inst. Atomic and Molecular Scis. Academia Sinica, Taipei, Taiwan, 1987-88; postdoctoral assoc. dept. Physics MIT, 1995-96; vis. asst. prof. dept. Chemistry and Biochemistry UCLA, 1996—99, cram tchr.-scholar dept. Chemistry and Biochemistry, 1996—99, rsch. asst., physicist Dept. Physics and Astronomy, 2000—02, Rice U., Houston, 2002—. Grantee NIH, 1998, U. Calif. Energy, 1998. Mem. Am. Phys. Soc., Sigma Xi. Achievements include patent in field. Office: Dept Physics and Chemistry Rice U 6100 Main St MS 61 Houston TX 77005 E-mail: chkiang@rice.edu.

KIBBE, THANA M. pastor; b. North Bingham, Pennsylvania, Nov. 11, 1939; d. Landis Clair and Dora Cathern (Talbett) Kibbe; m. William F. Coons (div. Sept. 1960); children: Eric, Jeffery, Pamela. Cert. licensing sch., 1989; attended, Cmty. Coll. of Finger Lakes, 1989, AA in Human resources, 1990; Cert. of Attainment, Wesley Theological Seminary Course of Study, 1996—97; Ordination Sacred Order of Deacon, No. Ctrl. N.Y., 1999. Lic. practical nurse, N.Y., 1960. Fl. nurse Tioga Gen Hosp., 1962—64; charge nurse Hurlburt Nursing Home, 1972—74; working with families Family Counseling of Finger Lakes, NY, 1975—76; organizing programs and meetings, speaking in area churches Cert. Advanced Lay Spkr., NY, 1978—89; dir. auction setup Duane F. Gansz Auction and Reality, NY, 1979—82; taped Sunday Morning Svc. WACK Radio, Newark, 1984—85; charge nurse Wayne County Nursing Home, 1986—87; hospice care in the home Genesee Home Care, 1987—88; LPN Clifton Springs Hosp., 1987—88; counselor, provide support and supervision in the home Resident Home, 1987—88; internship devel. of programs for seperated, divorced, and widowed Cath. Diocese of Rochester, NY, 1987—89; performed min. duties United Meth. Ch., Freeville and Varna, NY, 1989—91, part time assoc. pastor Wollcott and North Wolcott, NY, 1993—96, performed all min. duties Moria, Brushton, and No. Bangor, NY, 1993—96, performed all min. duties, started Sunday Sch. programs, VBS, and Grief and Loss Program Thousand Island Parish, NY, 1996—; ordained deacon Newfield United Meth. Ch., NY, 2003—. Founding mem., treas. Orleans Coun. of Churches. Sponsor Gwen's Pantry, Orleans Clothing Outreach; treas. Crop Walk; dir. Single Parent Program at Camp Aldersgate, NY; mem. Race and Religion Com., NY. Recipient Donald Burgan Cmty. Svc. Award, 1989. Methodist. Avocations: music, sewing, antiques, gardening, doll collecting, nature. E-mail: tkibbe@usadatanet.net.

KIBBE-REED, TRUDIE, academic administrator; m. Willie Reed; children: Jason Christopher Preciphs, Joseph Cameron Preciphs. MSW, U. Tex.; MA, PhD, Columbia U. Assoc. gen. sec. Coun. on Ministries, Dayton, Ohio; sr. adminstr. Gen. Commn. Status and Role of Women, Evanston, Ill.; dir. leadership studies Columbia (S.C.) Coll.; pres. Philander Smith Coll., Little Rock, 1998—. Contbr. articles to profl. publs. Bd. dirs. Little Rock C. of C., Downtown Rotary, Ark. Symphony Orch., Nat. Kidney Found. Ark. Recipient Tribute to Women and Industry Diamond award YWCA, 1997. Mem. Nat. Assn. Ind. Colls. and Univs., Ark. Assn. Ind. Colls. and Univs. Office: Philander Smith Coll 812 W 13th St Little Rock AR 72202-3718

KIBBLE-CACIOPPO, MAXINE LORRAINE, recording company executive; b. Bklyn., July 3, 1950; d. Robert Langston and Arletha Cobb; m. Robert Francis Kibble, Oct. 4, 1979 (div.); 1 child, Vanessa; m. Victor V. Cacioppo, Aug. 7, 1998. BS, NYU, 1978. Sales assoc. Saks Fifth Ave., Bergdorf, N.Y.C., 1988-92; model Sch. Visual Arts, N.Y.C., 1993-96; exec. asst. Banco Inverlat, N.Y.C., 1996—; songwriter N.Y.C., 1998; owner Sable Records, N.Y.C., 1993-97. Choreographer (modern dance) Portrait of a Shadow, 1977. Bd. dirs. Andrew Janetti and Dancers, N.Y.C., 1995-97; dance tchr. Police Athletic League, N.Y.C., 1977; mem. Broadway Fights Back (AIDS Orgn.), N.Y.C., 1998; mem. PTA, Unity H.S., N.Y.C., 1998. Recipient Hon. award Andrew Janetti & Dancers, 1998. Mem. ASCAP, NAFE. Avocations: aerobics, gardening. Office: 1518 Vista Sierra Dr El Cajon CA 92019-3583

KIBILOSKI, CATHERINE KAY, real estate appraiser; b. Coldwater, Mich., Feb. 10, 1967; d. Dugald (Stepfather) and Carol Ann McCulloch, James Ralph and Patricia Hacker(Stepmother); m. James Allen Hacker, Sept. 8, 1999; children: Lyndsay Marie, Daniel James, Lindsey Danielle Adams. Cert. Form Appraiser, CF-A Mich. Real estate appraiser A-1 Appraisal Co., Inc., Battle Creek, Mich., 1992—2003; owner/pres. Catherines Appraisal Co., Inc, Coldwater, Mich., 1995—. Mem.: Nat. Assn. of Ind. Fee Appraisers (assoc.; mem. 1995—). R-Liberal. Avocations: private pilot, boating, motorcycling. Home: 448 Buck Road Coldwater MI 49036 Office: Catherines Appraisal Co Inc Coldwater MI Office Fax: 517-238-2269. Personal E-mail: catherinesa@earthlink.net.

KIBRICK, ANNE, retired nursing educator and university dean; b. Palmer, Mass., June 1, 1919; d. Martin and Christine (Grigas) Karlon; m. Sidney Kibrick, June 16, 1949; children: Joan, John. RN, Worcester (Mass.) Hahnemann Hosp., 1941; BS, Boston U., 1945; MA, Columbia Tchrs. Coll., 1948; EdD, Harvard U., 1958; LHD (hon.), St. Joseph's Coll., Windham, Maine, 1973. Asst. edn. dir. Cushing VA Hosp., Framingham, Mass., 1948—49; asst. prof. nursing Simmons Coll., Boston, 1949—55; dir. grad. div. Boston U. Sch. Nursing, 1958—63, dean, 1963—68, prof., 1968—70; chmn. dept. nursing Boston Coll. Grad. Sch. Arts and Sci., 1970—74; founding chmn. Sch. Nursing Boston State Coll., 1974—82; founding dean Sch. Nursing U. Mass., Boston, 1974—88, prof., 1988—93, prof. emeritus, 1993—. Mem. editl. bd. Mass. Jour. Cmty. Health. Mem. Brookline Town Meeting, 1995—2000; mem. nat. adv. bd. Hadassah Nurses Coun., 1996—; bd. dirs. Brookline Mental Health Assn., Met. chpt. ARC, Children's Ctr. Brookline and Greater Boston, Inc., 1984—89, Boston Health Care for Homeless, 1988—90, Landy-Kaplan Nurses Coun., 1992—, treas., 1994—96. Named to, Nursing Edn. Alumni Assn. Tchr.'s Coll., Columbia U. Hall of Fame, 1999. Fellow: Am. Acad. Nursing; mem.: Inst. of Medicine of NAS, Mass. Blueprint 2000, Mass. Orgn. Elder Ams. (bd. dirs. 1988—2000), Mass. Med. Soc. (postgrad. med. inst. 1983—96, bd. dirs. 1983—96, exec. com. 1989—96), Nat. Acads. of Practice, Mass. Nurses Found. (v.p. 1983—86), AIDS Internat. Info. Found. (founding mem. 1985), Mass. Nurses Assn. (dir. 1982—86, charter inductee to Hall of Fame 2000), Nat. Mass. League Nursing (pres. 1971—73), ANA, Pi Lambda Theta, Sigma Theta Tau. Home: # 312 130 Seminary Ave Auburndale MA 02466

KICKBUSCH, CONSUELO CASTILLO, educational association administrator, consultant, former military officer; b. Laredo, Tex. married; 5 children. BS in law enforcement, earned ROTC commn. as 2nd lt., Hardin-Simmons U.; advanced degree in Cybernetics, San Jose U.; grad., Army Command and Gen. Staff Coll.; exec. course in program mgmt., Dept. Defense. Founder, pres. Ednl. Achievement Svcs., Inc., 1996—. Prodr.: (edn. video) Porque No-Why Not?. Various positions U.S. Army, 1976—96, platoon leader U.S. Army, Fort Hood, Tex., tech. adv. U.S. Army, Sys. Integration Divsn. and Joint Command and Control Warfare Ctr. Decorated Nat. Def. medal, Legion Merit medal, Army Commendation medal, Army Achievement medal (twice); recipient Latina Leadership Excellence award, US Army and Hispanic mag., Uniformed Svc. award, Nat. Image Inc., 1993, Women at their Best award, Saturn and Glamour, 2002. Achievements include highest ranking Hispanic woman in combat support field, US Army; first woman commn. as ROTC officer in Tex. Office: Ednl Achievement Svcs Inc 11807 Jarvis Dr San Antonio TX 78253*

KICKISH, MARGARET ELIZABETH, elementary school educator; b. Atlantic City, N.J., Nov. 30, 1949; d. James Bernard and Margaret Elizabeth (Egan) Parlett; m. Robert Anthony Kickish, June 30, 1973; children: Eileen, Kathleen, Robert Jr. BS, Franciscan U., 1971; MEd, Coll. N.J., 1977. Cert. elem. tchr., learning disabilities tchr. cons. Tchr. Our Lady Star of the Sea Sch., Atlantic City, 1971-75, Weymouth Twp. Elem. Sch., Dorothy, NJ, 1975-89; curriculum coord. Port Republic (N.J.) Sch., 1990-91; tchr. Brigantine (N.J.) Bd. Edn., 1991-94, supr. curriculum and instrn., 1995—. Cognetics coach St. Joseph Sch., Somers Point, NJ, 1989—. Treas. PTA, Somers Point, 1987—89, pres., 1989—90; asst. coach Somers Point Softball Assn., 1991—; rec. sec. Parents Orgn. Mainland Regional HS, 2001—; mem. choir St. Joseph Ch., Somers Point, 1985—. Mem.: ASCD, NEA, AAUW, Assn. Learning Cons., Coun. Exceptional Children, Prins. and Suprs. Assn., N.J. Edn. Assn., S. Jersey Irish Cultural Soc., Seashore Mother of Twins Club, Phi Delta Kappa, Delta Zeta, Kappa Delta Pi. Democrat. Roman Catholic. Avocations: swimming, bicycling, reading, travel, crafts. Home: 526 9th St Somers Point NJ 08244-1458 Office: Brigantine Bd of Edn 301 E Evans Blvd Brigantine NJ 08203-3424 E-mail: mskick@aol.com.

KICZA, MARY E. federal agency administrator; Lead sys. engr. Centaur Engring. Support Group Kennedy Space Ctr., Fla., 1982; assoc. ctr. dir. space sci. programs Goddard Space Flight Ctr., Greenbelt, Md., assoc. ctr. dir.; dep. divsn. dir. Office of Space Sci. Solar Sys. Exploration Divsn., program mgr. Discovery program NASA, Washington, 1992—94, asst. assoc. adminstr. tech. Office Space Sci., 1994—96, assoc. adminstr. biol. and phys. rsch., 2002—. Office: NASA Mail Code U 300 E St SW Washington DC 20546

KIDD, DEBRA JEAN, communications executive; b. Chgo., May 13, 1956; d. Fred A. and Jean (Pezzopane) Winchar: m. Kim Joseph Kidd, July 22, 1978; children: Jennifer Marie, Michele Jean. AA in Bus. with high honors, Wright Jr. Coll., 1977. Legal sec. Sidley & Austin, Chgo., 1977-80; investment adminstr. Golder, Thoma & Co., Chgo., 1980-81, exec. asst., 1981-84; sales rep. Dataspeed, Inc., Chgo., 1984, midwestern regional mgr., 1985; comm. cons. Chgo. Comm., Inc., Chgo., 1986-88; owner, founder

Captain Kidd's Video, Niles, 1981-84. Editor: Lion's Roar, 1993-95. Vol. Am. Lung Assn., Chgo., 1979; vol. tchr. religious edn. Our Lady Mother of Ch., Norridge, Ill., 1981-83, St. Raymonds, Mt. Prospect, 1993-94, 2000—; vol. Parents Who Care, 1988-94, pres., 1991-93; vol. PTA Lion's Park Sch., 1993-95, bd. dirs., 1993-94; founder Young Journalist Club, 1994-95; leader Girl Scouts, 1992—, cons., 1994—, del., 1995—, registrar, 1996-97, organizer, 1996—, svc. unit mgr., 2000—; referee assignor Green White Soccer, 2001--; vol. Hearts Across Am., 2001--. Mem. NAFE, Nat. Assn. Bus. Women, Nat. Assn. Profl. Saleswomen, Phi Theta Kappa. Roman Catholic. Avocations: camping, skiing, snorkeling, sailing, reading. E-mail: dkidd739@aol.com.

KIDD, LOVETTA MONZA, music educator; b. Anniston, Ala., Jan. 13, 1943; d. Andrew Jackson and Velma Mildred (Duke) Traywick; m. Everett Wayne Kidd, Dec. 20, 1961 (dec. Dec. 1998); children: Michelle Kidd Belindo, Andy, David. Student, Okla. Coll. for Women, 1961-62, Southwestern Okla. State U., 1982-83. Pvt. piano tchr., Eva, Okla., 1967-69, Sickles, Okla., 1970-71, Dibble, Okla., 1971-78, Anadarko, Okla., 1979—. Pianist First Bapt. Ch., Anadarko, 1980's. Sec. Okla. Conservative Com., Norman, 1994-95; vice chmn. Caddo County (Okla.) Rep. party, 1995-97, chmn., 1997-99; alt. del. Nat. Rep. Convention, San Diego, 1996. Mem. Okla. Fedn. Rep. Women, Concerned Women for Am., Anadarko Eagle Forum (founder, pres. 1994—), Okla.'s First Ladies, Gen. Fedn. Women's Clubs Philomathic Club (sec. 1996-98, v.p. 1998—), Okla. Fedn. Music Clubs (dist. Gold Cup chmn. 1993—), Musical Key Club (founder, pres. 1981—). Avocations: reading, gardening, needlepoint, oil painting, drawing. Home: 701 W Alabama Ave Anadarko OK 73005-4636

KIDDOO, JEAN LYNN, lawyer; b. White Plains, N.Y., Apr. 30, 1953; d. Richard C. and Catherine (Schumann) K.; m. Timothy James Cooney, Aug. 20, 1988. BA, Colgate U., 1975; JD, Cath. U., Washington, 1980. Bar: D.C. 1980, U.S. Dist. Ct. D.C. 1981, U.S. Ct. Appeals (D.C. cir.) 1981, U.S. Supreme Ct. 1984, U.S. Ct. Appeals (2d cir.) 1995, U.S. Ct. Appeals (5th cir.) 1997. Assoc. Bergson, Borkland, Margolis & Adler, Washington, 1980-82, McKenna, Wilkinson & Kittner, Washington, 1982-85, Pepper, Hamilton & Scheetz, Washington, 1985-88; ptnr. Swidler Berlin Shereff Friedman, LLP, Washington, 1988—; pres. Fed. Com. Bar Assoc., Washington, currently. Mem. Fed. Comms. Bar Assn. (pres. 1999—). Address: Fed Com Bar Assoc 1020 19th St NW Ste 325 Washington DC 20036 6113

KIDMAN, NICOLE, actress; b. Honolulu, Hawaii, June 20, 1967; m. Tom Cruise, 1990 (div. 2001); children: Isabella Jane Kidman, Connor Antony Kidman. Film appearences include BMX Bandits, 1983, Bush Christmas, 1983, Wills & Burke, 1985, Archer's Adventure, 1985, Windrider, 1986, Watch the Shadows Dance (aka Nightmaster), 1986, Bit Part, 1987, Emerald City, 1989, Dead Calm, 1989, Days of Thunder, 1990, Flirting, 1991, Billy Bathgate, 1991 (Golden Globe Award nomination 1992), Far and Away, 1992, Malice, 1993, My Life, 1993, Batman Forever, 1995, Portrait of a Lady, 1996, To Die For, 1995 (Golden Globe award), The Peacemaker, 1997, Practical Magic, 1998, Eyes Wide Shut, 1999, The Others, 2001 (nominee Best Performance by Actress in Motion Picture-Drama Golden Globe award 2002, Best Actress KCFCC award 2001), Birthday Girl, 2001, Moulin Rouge, 2001 (Best Actress in Motion Picture Musical/Comedy Golden Globe award 2001, nominee Best Actress in Leading Role Acad. award 2002, Best Actress London Film Critics Cir. award 2001), The Hours, 2002 (Best Actress Academy award, 2003, Best Actress in Leading Role, British Acad. Film Award (BAFTA), 2003, Best Actress Golden Globe, 2003), Dogville, 2003, The Human Stain, 2003, Cold Mountain, 2003; prodr. (films) In the Cut, 2003; TV appearances include Five Mile Creek, 1983, Chase Through the Night, 1983, Matthew and Son, 1984, Bangkok Hilton, 1989 (Australian Film Inst. Best Actress in Miniseries), Vietnam, 1985 (Australian Film Inst. Best Actress in Miniseries); theatrical prodns. include The Blue Room, London, 1997-98, Broadway, 1998-99. Recipient ShoWest Dist. Decade Achievement award, 2002. Address: Creative Artists Agy 9830 Wilshire Blvd Beverly Hills CA 90212*

KIECOLT-GLASER, JANICE KAY, psychologist; b. Oklahoma City, June 30, 1951; d. Edward Harold and Vergie Mae (Lively) Kiecolt; m. Ronald Glaser, Jan. 18, 1980. BA in Psychology with honors, U. Okla., 1972; PhD in Clin. Psychology, U. Miami, 1976. Lic. psychologist, Ohio. Clin. psychology intern Baylor U. Coll. Medicine, Houston, 1974-75; postdoctoral fellow in adult clin. psychology U. Rochester, N.Y., 1976-78; asst. prof. psychiatry Ohio State U. Coll. Medicine, Columbus, 1978-84, assoc. prof. psychiatry and psychology, 1984-89, prof. psychiatry and psychology, 1989—, dir. divsn. health psychology, 1994—, active various coms. Mem. AIDS study sect. NIMH, 1988-91. Editl. bd. Brain, Behavior and Immunity jour., 1986—, Health Psychology jour., 1989—, Brit. Jour. Health Psychology, 1996—, Jour. Behavioral Medicine, 1994—, Psychosomatic Medicine, 1990—, Jour. Cons. and Clin. Psychology, 1992—, Jour. Gerontology, 1992—; reviewer Jour. Personality and Social Psychology, Psychiatry Rsch. jour.; author: Detecting Lies, 1997, Unconscious Truths, 1998, Handbook of Human Stress and Immunity, 1994; contbr. articles to profl. jours., chpts. to books. NIMH grantee, 1985—; recipient Merit award NIMH, 1993; Ohio State Disting. scholar, 1994, Devel. Health Psychology award, Divsn. Health Psychology and Adult Devel. and Aging, Norman Cousins award, Psychoneuroimmunology Rsch. Soc., 1998. Fellow Am. Psychol. Assn. (Outstanding Contbns. award 1988), Acad. Behavioral Medicine Rsch.; mem. Phi Beta Kappa, Inst. Medicine. Avocations: jogging, fiction writing. Office: Ohio State U Coll Medicine Dept Psychiatry 1670 Upham Dr Columbus OH 43210*

KIEFER, ANN MARIE, music educator; b. Queens, NY, July 20, 1968; d. Frank Joseph and Audrey Theresa LaCommare; m. Aron David Kiefer, Aug. 31, 2003. MusB, Crane Sch. Music, 1990; M in Elem. Edn., U. Buffalo, 1997. Tchr. orch. Williamsville (NY) Schs., 1993—. Violinist Amherst (NY) Symphony, Amherst, 1990—92. Mem.: Music Educators Assn., NY State Sch. Music Assn. Avocation: scrapbooks. Home: 25 Landings Dr Buffalo NY 14228 Office: Williamsville Ctrl Sch Buffalo NY 14221

KIEFFER, KATHLEEN CECIL, elementary school educator; b. Hastings, Minn., Sept. 23, 1931; d. William A. and Kathryn (Brummel) Schaffer; m. Ralph W. Kieffer, Aug. 11, 1956 (div. Jan. 1972); 1 child, Joseph W. BS, Coll. St. Teresa, Winona, Minn., 1953; MA, St. Thomas Coll., St. Paul, 1968. Cert. specific learning disabilities Minn. Elem. tchr. Mpls. Pub. Schs., 1953—68, specific learning disabilities resource tchr., 1968—93, vol. tchr. grade 4 Sheridan Sch., 1996—. Treas., pres. Mpls. Women in Edn., 1982—83, 1992—93. Del. to local, state and dist. convs. DFL Party, State of Minn., 1974—, mem. local, dist. and state ctrl. coms., 1984—; sec. DFL Senate Dist. 52 and 51, Ramsey County, Minn., 1992—; bd. mem. St. John's Ch., New Brighton, 1998—. Mem.: Mpls. Ret. Tchrs., We in Svc. to Edn. (v.p. 1994—), Minn. Assn. for Childhood Edn. Internat. (sec. 1977—80, v.p. 1988—89, pres. 1990—92, com. mem. 1994—, v.p. 2002—, Promoting the Well Being of Children award 2003), St. Vincent DePaul Soc., Delta Kappa Gamma (pres. 1980—82, legis. chmn. Gamma chpt. 1984—, comm. chmn. Tau State chpt. 1983—85, nominations com. Tau State chpt. 1989—90, Woman of Achievement award Gamma chpt. 1988). Roman Catholic. Home: 5180 Bona Rd New Brighton MN 55112

KIEFFER, MARCIA S. psychotherapist; b. Buffalo, N.Y., Mar. 29, 1951; d. Milford Shepherd and Doris Verna (Nerber) Smith; m. William Charles Kieffer, Nov. 25, 1972; children: Michelle L. Kieffer Kowalski. AA in Applied Sci., Hilbert Coll., 1988; BS, Buffalo State Coll., 1993; MS in Social Work, SUNY Buffalo, 1995. Cert. social work, N.Y., 1995. Teller, bookeeper Mfrs. & Traders Trust, Buffalo, 1969-71; accounts recieveable Peter J. Schmidt, Buffalo, 1971-72; booking Meyer SFS Niagara, Buffalo, 1972-73; teller Bank of N.Y., Buffalo, 1973-75; headcashier Tops, Markets, Buffalo, 1980-81; teller Evans Nat. Bank, Angola, N.Y., 1981-88; dir. care and devel. Luth. Svc. Soc., Buffalo, 1988; case mgr. Suburban Adult Svcs., Buffalo, 1988-95, Cmty. Concern, Derby, N.Y., 1995—. Student intern supr. St. Bonaventure, Hamburg, N.Y., 1999, Hilbert Coll., 1997 Vol. Salvation Army, Angola, N.Y., 1989—, Holy Cross Luth. Ch., Farnham, N.Y., 1988—. Recipient Franciscan award, Hilbert Coll., 1988, McGrath award Human Svcs, Hilbert Coll., 1988, Excellency in Social Work, award, Buffalo State Coll., 1993. Mem. Nat. Assn. Social Workers, 1992—. Avocations: qi gong, walking, reading, gardening, animals. Home: 6786 Wayne Dr Derby NY 14047-9737 Office: Cmty Concern Evans 6722 Erie Rd Derby NY 14047-9670

KIEFFER, SUSAN WERNER, geologist, educator, media consultant; b. Warren, Pa., Nov. 17, 1942; BS in Physics and Math., Allegheny Coll., 1964; MS in Geol. Scis., Calif. Inst. Tech., 1967, PhD in Planetary Scis., 1971; DSc (hon.), Allegheny Coll., 1987. Rsch. physicist UCLA, 1971-73, asst. prof. geology, 1973-79; geologist U.S. Geol. Survey, Flagstaff, Ariz., 1979-90; prof. geology Ariz. State U., Tempe, 1988—, Regents prof., 1991-93; prof., head dept. geol. sci. U. B.C., Vancouver, Canada, 1993-95; co-founder Kieffer & Woo, Inc., Palgrave, Ont., Can., 1996-2000; founder Kieffer Inst. for Devel. of Sci. Based Edn., 1997-99; Walgreen chair, prof. geology U. Ill., Urbana, 2001—. W.H. Mendnhall lectr. U.S. Geol. Survey, 1980. Editor (with A. Navrotsky): Microscopic to Macroscopic: Atomic Environments to Mineral Thermodynamics, 1985. Recipient Disting. Alumnus award, Calif. Inst. Tech., 1982, Meritorious Svc. award, Dept. Interior, 1986, Spendiarov award, Soviet Acad. Scis., 1990; Alfred P. Sloan Found. fellow, 1977—79, MacArthur fellow, 1995—. Fellow: Mineral Soc. Am. (award 1980), Meteoritical Soc., Geol. Soc. Am. (Arthur L. Day medal 1992), Am. Geophys. Union, Am. Acad. Arts and Scis.; mem.: NAS. Avocations: athletics, music. Office: U Ill Dept Geology MC 102 1301 W Green St Urbana IL 61801 E-mail: skieffer@uiuc.edu.

KIEL, MARTHA GUILLET, art educator; d. Nicholas Jesse and Mary Terry Guillet; children: Mary K., Bit, Drei. BS, Midwestern St. U., Tex., 1953; MEd, ACU, Tex., 1974. Art tchr. Abilene (Tex.) ISD, 1966—2000; chair art dept. Hardin Simmons U., Abilene, Tex., 2000—. Photographs, Big Country Art Assn., 2003. Trustee Grace Mus.; pres. Big Country Art Assn., 2001—03. Mem.: Tex. Art Edn. Assn. (sec. 1999—2001, treas. 2001—03, chair 2000—03). Home: 533 Sayles Blvd Abilene TX 79605 3101

KIEL, SHELLEY, state senator; b. Galesburg, Ill., Aug. 16, 1950; m. Gary Kiel, Mar. 11, 1989; children: Darien, Brien, Joseph MS, U. Nebr., Omaha, 1977. V.p. mktg. and ednl. design Flat Worl, Inc.; tchr.; state senator State of Nebr., Lincoln. Chmn. Metropolitan Cmty. Coll. (bd. govs.); mem. Save our LIbrs. STeering Com. Mem. Dundee Mem. Pk. Assn. (pres.), Omaha Neighborhood Courage, PTA bds. Lewis and Clark, Kennedy, Dundee schls., Omaha Libr. bd., Women's Fund.. Mem. Met. Cmty. Coll. Bd. Govs.,Pi Beta Phi House Corp. (pres.) Creighton U.; Leadership Omaha Alumni Assn. Congregationalist.

KIENITZ, LADONNA TRAPP, lawyer, librarian, municipal official; b. Bay City, Mich. d. Orlin D. and Mary (Stanford) Trapp; m. John Kienitz, Feb. 9, 1951 (div. Dec. 1974); children: John, Jim, Rebecca, Mary, Timothy, David. BA, Westmar Coll., 1951; MA in Libr. Sci., Dominican U., River Forest, Ill., 1970; M Mgmt., Northwestern U., 1984; JD, Western State U., Fullerton, Calif., 1995; LLM in Taxation, U. San Diego, 2004. Head libr. Woodlands Acad., Lake Forest, Ill., 1973-77; project officer North Suburban Libr. Sys., Wheeling, Ill., 1977-78; libr. dir. Lincolnwood (Ill.) Pub. Libr. Dist., 1978-86; city libr. City of Newport Beach, Calif., 1987—, dir. cmty. svcs., 1994—2002. Mem. ALA, ABA, Pub. Libr. Assn. (pres. 1995-96), State Bar Calif., Orange County Bar Assn. Office Phone: 949-759-0314. E-mail: ladonnakienitz@sbcglobal.net.

KIERNAN, MARGARET M. adult education educator; b. Ross, Calif., Feb. 18, 1944; d. William C. and Elizabeth K. Murray; m. John S. Kiernan, July 19, 1969; m. Robert K. Dwyer, June 11, 1966 (dec. July 15, 1967); children: Christopher S., Kathleen K. Dwyer, Sean R. BA in Psychology, Coll. New Rochelle, 1966; MS in Adult Edn., Old Dominion U., 1989. Postgrad. profl. tchg. lic. Commonwealth of Va., 1992. First grade tchr. St. Francis Xavier Sch., Washington, 1968—69; pre-school tchr. St. Francis Episcopal Sch., Charlotte, NC, 1971—73; ESL tchr. Virginia Beach (Va.) Adult Learning Ctr., 1980—87, ESL coordinating tchr., 1987—2002, ESL coord., 2002—. Pres. Virginia Beach (Va.) Coun. PTAs. Recipient Human Rights award, Virginia Beach Human Rights Commn., 2001. Mem.: Va. TESOL (pres. 1985—86, 1993—97, Pres. award 1990), Virginia Beach Assn. Secondary Prins., Va. Beach Reading Coun. (Literacy Tchr. of the Yr. 1991), TESOL (chair adult edn. interest sect. 2000—01), Virginia Beach Coun. PTAs (life; pres.). Avocations: reading, gardening. Home: 3812 Old Shell Rd Virginia Beach VA 23452 Office: Virginia Beach Adult Learning Ctr 4160 Virginia Beach Blvd Virginia Beach VA 23452 E-mail: mkiernan@vbcps.k12.va.us.

KIESSLING, LAURA LEE, chemist, researcher; b. Milw, Wis, Sept. 21, 1960; d. William E. and LaVonne V. (Korth) K. SB, MIT, 1983; PhD, Yale U., 1989. Teaching asst. MIT, Cambridge, Mass., 1982-83, Yale U., New Haven, 1983-84, rsch. asst., 1984-89; rsch. fellow Calif. Tech. U., Pasadena, Calif., 1989-91; asst. prof. chemistry U. Wis., Madison, Wis., 1991-97, assoc. prof., 1997-99, prof. chemistry, prof. biochemistry, 1999—. Cons. Ophidian, Inc., 1997-99, Alfred P. Sloan Found. Fellowships, 1997—; mem. bioorganic and natural products study sect. NIH, 1997-2000; Fellow, Am. Assoc. for the Advancement of Sci., 2003; elected Acad. of Arts and Sci., 2003; sci. adv. bd. Promega Corp., 1999—; selection com. for editor Jour. Organic Chemistry, 1999. Mem. editl. bd. Chemistry and Biology, 1997—, Organic Reactions, 2000—; contbr. articles to profl. jour. Recipient Dow Chems. New Faculty award, 1992, Shaw Scientist award, 1992-97, Nat. Young Investigator award NSF, 1993-98, Beckman Young Investigator award, 1994-96, Zeneca Excellence in Chemistry award, 1996, Dreyfus Tchr.-Scholar award Dreyfus Found., 1996; Postdoctoral fellow Am. Cancer Soc., 1989-91, MacArthur fellow John D. and Catherine MacArthur Found., 1999, Alfred P. Sloan Found. fellow, 1997. Mem. AAAS, Am. Chem. Soc. (Cope scholar 1999, Isbell award 2000), Soc. Glycobiology, Am. Soc. for Biochemistry and Molecular Biology, Sigma Xi, Phi Lambda Upsilon. Avocations: canoeing, rowing, running. Office: U Wis Dept Chemistry 1101 University Ave Madison WI 53706-1322 Fax: 608-265-0764.

KIFFMEYER, MARY, state official; b. Balta, N.D., Dec. 29, 1946; m. Ralph Kiffmeyer; children: Christina, Patrick, James, John. RN, St. Gabriel's Sch. Nursing, Little Falls, Minn.; student, Anoka Ramsey C.C. RN, Minn.; cert. election judge. Co-owner RK Anesthesia, Big Lake, Minn.; sec. of state State of Minn., St. Paul, 1999—. Republican. Office: 180 State Office Bldg 100 Dr Martin Luther King Jr Blvd Saint Paul MN 55155-1210*

KIGER, F. LOUISE, nursing administrator; b. El Paso, Tex., Aug. 5, 1938; d. LaVirgen Silva Grey; m. Charles R. Kiger, June 27, 1970; children: Stephanie, Jim, Derek. BSN, U. N.Mex., Albuquerque, 1959; MSN, U. Wash., 1979. Staff nurse Bataan Meml. Hosp., Albuquerque, 1959-60; advanced through grades to comdr. USN, various positions, 1960-71, USPHS and Indian Health Svc., 1979-93; capt. USPHS, 1993; dir., chief nurse Indian Health Svc. Divsn. of Nursing, Rockville, Md., 1993—. Recipient Bronze Star V, 1969. Mem. Nat. Alaska Native Am. Indian Nurses Assn., N.Mex. Indian Nurses Assn. Roman Catholic. Avocations: reading, gardening, travel. Office: US Dept Health and Human Svcs Indian Health Svc 5600 Fishers Ln Rockville MD 20852-1750

KIKEL, SUZANNE, patent agent; b. Pitts., Apr. 4, 1946; d. John George Kikel and Elizabeth Marie Pello; m. John Thomas Stauffer, Oct. 25, 1996. BA in Humanities, U. Pitts., 1972, BS in Mech. Engring., 1981; A in Chemistry, C.C. Allegheny County, Pitts., 1994. Registered patent practitioner U.S. Patent and Trademark Office, 1976. Patent agt. Wean United, Inc., Pitts., 1974-86, Eckert Seamans Cherin & Mellott, LLC, Pitts., 1986-95; intellectual property coord., patent agt. ECC Internat. Inc., Atlanta, 1995-99; patent agt. Calgon Corp., Pitts., 1999-2000, Pietrallo, Bosick & Gordon, Pitts., 2000—. Mem. Pitts. Intellectual Patent Law Assn., Pitts. Ski Club. Avocations: golfing, tennis, skiing, biking, photography. Office: Pietrallo Bosick and Gordon 38th Flr 1 Oxford Ct Fl Grant38 Pittsburgh PA 15219-1407

KILBANE, CATHERINE M. lawyer; b. Cleve., Apr. 10, 1963; BA cum laude, Case Western Res. U., 1984, JD cum laude, 1987. Bar: Ohio 1987. Ptnr. Baker & Hostetler, Cleve., 1997—. Mem. Delta Theta Phi. Office: Baker & Hostetler 3200 Nat City Ctr 1900 E 9th St Ste 3200 Cleveland OH 44114-3475

KILBANE, SALLY CONWAY, economics educator; b. Cleve., Nov. 11, 1942; d. John J. and May (Carlin) Conway; m. Thomas Stanton Kilbane, June 4, 1966; children: Sarah, Thomas, Eamon, James, Carlin. BSN, St. John Coll., 1964; MSN, Case Western Res. U., 1971, MA, 1982, PhD, 1987. Pub. health nurse City of Cleve., 1964-65; instr. nursing St. John Hosp., Cleve., 1965-67, 68-69; instr. econs. Case Western Res. U., Cleve., 1988-93; adj. asst. prof. econs. Cleve. State U., 1988—. Congl. candidate Rep. Primary 10th Dist., 1992. Home: 20000 Lorain Rd Apt 607 Cleveland OH 44126-3460

KILBOURNE, BARBARA JEAN, health and housing executive; b. Milw., Mar. 21, 1941; d. Burton Conwell and Marjorie Janet (Tufts) K.; m. Kenneth Keith Kauffman, Feb. 10, 1962 (div. 1983). BA, U. Minn., 1972; MBA, Coll. St. Thomas, St. Paul, 1980. Adminstr. Ebenezer Soc., Mpls., 1974-85; v.p., dir. housing Walker Residence and Health Svcs., Inc., Mpls., 1985-88; exec. v.p. Oblate Ministries Health and Aging, West St. Paul, Minn., 1988-94; cons., 1995—; pres. Barbara J. Kilbourne, Ltd., 1996—2002; exec. dir. Cath. Health Assn. Minn., 1997—2002; v.p. mem. svcs. and internal ops. Minn. Health and Housing Alliance, 2001—. Bd. dirs. CommonBond Communities, St. Paul, Villa Guadalupe, Chgo., Minn. Am. Red Cross Mpls. chpt., 1997-2002; chair Villa Guadalupe, 1999—, Minn. State Operated Svcs., 2000-02. Author: Family Councils in Nursing Homes, 1981. Chmn. bd. dirs. LifeWorks, Eagan, Minn., 1985-96, Minn. Assn. Homes for Aging, 1991-92, Sem. Plaza, Red Wing, 1995-97; project chair Dialog 2000, Dakota County, Minn., 1988-91; bd. dirs. ARC, Mpls., 1997-2002, Common Bond Cmtys., 1999-2002, Villa Guadalupe, Chgo chair 1999—. Mem. Minn. Rural Health Assn. (bd. dirs. 1998-2001). Episcopalian. Avocations: piano, golf, hiking. Home: 1021 Sibley Memorial Hwy Saint Paul MN 55118-6100 Office: 2550 University Ave Ste 350 S Saint Paul MN 55114

KILBOURNE, CLAIRE ANNE, retired gifted and talented education educator; b. Pt. Jervis, N.Y., Aug. 3, 1939; d. Eston Arthur and Elizabeth Anna (Coss) Garrison; m. Charles Warren Kilbourne, June 17, 1961; children: Caroline, Kevin Charles. BA, Trenton State Coll., 1961; postgrad., Rider U., 1980. Cert. tchr. secondary edn., N.J. Tchr. English, Hopewell, N.J., 1961-62; supplemental instr. Hamilton Twp., 1974-77; tchr. gifted edn. Grice Mid. Sch., Hamilton, N.J., 1977-89, Crockett Mid. Sch., Hamilton, 1989-97; ret., 1997. Workshop presenter Hamilton Sch. Dist., 1977-96; cons. gifted edn., N.J., 1977-95. Author: (anthologies) Best Poems of 1996, Expressions; author: (song lyrics) (CD) Leaving You, Great Am. Songs, The Best of Country Music USA, Country Music Favorites, 2002; author: (poem) (I Treasure You) Theatre of the Mind, 2003, (Too Much Hurt) Colours of the Heart, 2004. Mem., donor Lakota Indians, 1985-95; writing mentor, 1977-95; dep. gov. Am. Biog. Inst. Bd. Govs. Recipient plaque N.J. Assn. for Supervision and Curriculum Devel.; named Golden Poet of World, 1989-92, Most Admired Woman of Decade, 1994; grantee Kodak Cameras in the Curriculum, Hamilton Twp. Dist. Fellow: Archaeol. Inst. Am.; mem.: NEA, Hamilton Twp. Edn. Assn., Internat. Soc. Poets, Planetary Soc., Acad. Am. Poets, Famous Poets, Internat. Platform Assn. Avocations: creative writing, crafts, baking. Home: 200 Carlisle Ave Hamilton NJ 08620-1212

KILBOURNE, KRYSTAL HEWETT, retired rail transportation executive; b. Sandersville, Ga., Apr. 7, 1940; d. John Ray and Kathleen (Perkins) Hewett; m. Alan Arden Kilbourne, July 1, 1961 (div. May 1972); children: Arden Alan, Keith Ray. A, U. Ga., 1960. Tchr. Massey Bus. Coll., Jacksonville, Fla., 1968-72, editor, reporter, photographer, 1968-72; asst. to pres. Luter Advt. Agy., Jacksonville, Fla., 1973-74; asst. to dir. Leukemia Soc., Jacksonville, Fla., 1975-76; asst. to pres. TeleCheck Corp., Jacksonville, Fla., 1979; mgr. customer svc. railroad ops. CSX Transp., Jacksonville, Fla., 1980—2002; ret., 2002. Chair CSX Equal Employment Opportunity Coun., 1992-94. Tuition scholar U. Ga., 1958; recipient Transp. Workers Leadership award, 1995. Mem. Nat. Assn. Railway Bus. Women, Am. Coun. Railroad Women. Democrat. Presbyterian. Avocations: oil painting, poetry, snorkeling, traveling, reading. Home: 4856 Deermoss Way S Jacksonville FL 32217-9306

KILCHER, JEWEL See JEWEL

KILCULLEN, MAUREEN, librarian, educator; b. Canton, Ohio, Oct. 29, 1954; d. Thomas Vincent and Betty Jane (Rawley) Kilcullen. BA in History, Kent State U., 1981, MLS, 1984. Libr. reference/audiovisual Barberton Pub. Libr., Barberton, Ohio, 1985—90; assoc. prof., reference libr. Stark Campus Kent State U., Canton, Ohio, 1990—. Contbr. chapters to books, articles to profl. jours. Vol. Dublin Irish Festival, Dublin, Ohio, 1995—. Recipient Regional Campus Vice Provost award Outstanding Service, Kent State U. Regional Campuses, 1997. Mem.: ALA, Acad. Libr. Assn. Ohio, Assn. Coll. and Rsch. Librs. Democrat. Roman Catholic. Avocations: reading, gardening, genealogy, photography. Office: Kent State Univ Stark Campus 6000 Frank Ave Canton OH 44720 Office Fax: 330-494-6212. Personal E-mail: mkilcullen@stark.kent.edu. Business E-Mail: mkilcullen@stark.kent.edu

KILDE, SANDRA JEAN, nurse, anesthetist, educator, consultant; b. Eau Claire, Wis., June 25, 1938; d. Harry Milan and Beverly June (Johnson) K. Diploma, Luther Hosp. Sch. Nursing, Eau Claire, 1959; grad. anesthesia course, Mpls. Sch. Anesthesia, 1967; BA, Met. State U., St. Paul, 1976; MA, U. St. Thomas, 1981; EdD, Nova Southeastern U., 1987. RN, Wis., Minn. Oper. rm. nurse Luther Hosp., Eau Claire, 1959-61, head nurse oper. rm., 1961-63; supr. oper. rm. Midway Hosp., St. Paul, 1963-66; staff anesthetist North Meml. Med. Ctr., Robbinsdale, Minn., 1967-68, St. Joseph's Hosp., St. Paul, 1992-99, R.C. Shefland Anesthesia, Ltd., Bemidji, Minn., 2003—. Program dir. Mpls. Sch. Anesthesia, St. Louis Park, Minn., 1968-96; adj. assoc. prof. St. Mary's U., Winona, Minn., 1982-96, adj. prof., 1996-2004, program dir. Masters Degree Program, 1984-96; nurse anesthesia cons., 1996—; ednl. cons. chair reviewer Coun. on Accreditation of Nurse Anesthesia Ednl. Programs, Park Ridge, Ill., 1983-92, 99—, elected to coun., 1992-99, vice chmn., 1994-97, chmn., 1997-99; corp. mem. Aitkin Cmty. Hosp., Inc. dba Riverwood HealthCare Ctr., 2001—, bd. dirs., 2002—; presenter in field. Choir dir. Grace Luth. Ch., McGregor, Minn., 1988—, mem. ch. coun., 1992—97, 1998—2001, pres. ch. coun., 1992—97. Recipient Good Neighbor award Sta. WCCO, Mpls., 1980, Disting. Alumni Achievement award Nova Southeastern U., 1993, Lifetime Achievement for Excellence in Edn. award Mpls. Sch. Anesthesia Class of 1999, 1999, Cert. of Appreciation Aitkin County Bd. Commrs. and Aitkin County Health and Human Svc. Adv. Com., 2001. Mem. Am. Assn. Nurse

Anesthetists (pres. 1981-82, pres. and bd. dirs. Edn. and Rsch. Found., 1981-83, cert. profl. excellence 1976, Program Dir. of Yr. award 1992), Minn. Assn. Nurse Anesthetists (pres. 1975-76). Lutheran. Avocations: gardening, fishing, photography, choir directing, playing guitar and piano. Home and Office: PO Box 80 Palisade MN 56469-0080

KILGORE, CAROLYN HARRELL (CAROLYN LAWTON HARRELL), writer; b. Macon, Ga., Apr. 10, 1911; d. Furman Dargon and Mary Elliott (Nottingham) Lawton; m. Glover Futch Harrell, June 17, 1933 (dec. Oct. 1983); children: Mary Elliott Harrell Reeves, Carolyn Harrell Foley; m. Morris Ward Kilgore, Jan. 13, 1991 (dec. Jan. 1995). BA, Wesleyan Coll., 1933; cert. tech. writing, Rensselaer Poly. Inst., 1962. Newswriter Marine Corps Supply Ctr., Albany, Ga., 1957-59; tech. writer Thiokol Chem. Corp., Huntsville, Ala., 1960-63; publs. engr. Lockheed Aerospace Rsch. and Engring. Ctr., Huntsville, 1964-72. Author: (history) Kith and Kin: A Portrait of a Southern Family (1630-1934), 1984, When the Bells Tolled for Lincoln: Southern Reaction to the Assassination, 1997; contbr. numerous articles to mags. and newspapers. Recipient citation for outstanding performance in writing, editing and prodn. of four book-length volumes of classified documents pertaining to R & D of space vehicles, Lockheed-Huntsville Rsch. and Engring. Ctr., 1965. Mem. DAR, Nat. Soc. Colonial Dames, XVIII Century Huguenot Soc. S.C., Soc. 1st Families of S.C., Macon, Ga., Writers' Club (pres. 1957). Avocations: classical music, family history. Home: Round Top, Tex. Died Oct. 11, 2001.

KILGORE, NANCY, educational association administrator; BA, Sacramento State U. Dir. Edn. PTSD & Domestic Violence, Eugene, Oreg. Office: Edn on PSTD & Domestic Violence PO Box 26205 Eugene OR 97402

KILGUSS, ELSIE SCHAICH, artist, gallery owner; b. Manhattan, NY, Aug. 04; BS in Advt., Mktg., Bryant Coll.; studied with Charles Sovek, studied with Betty Cappelli, 1968, studied with Henry Hensche, Lois Griffel; grad., RISD; student, Cape Sch. Art. With Horton, Church & Goff, Advt. Agy., Providence; represented by Gallery at Chatham, Mass., 1990-99; owner, instr. Studio Zwei, Wickford, R.I., 1991—. Art instr. Wickford Art Assn., 1990-98, Warwick Art Mus., 1998-2000, Attleboro Mus., 2000—, South County Art Assn., 2000-02. One-woman shows include Wickford Art Festival, 1988—, Gallery at Chatham, 1990—99, Studio Zwei Gallery, Wickford, 1991—, Alfred Butler & Co., North Kingstown, 1992—, Fleet Bank, 1992—, R.I. State House, Providence, 1993—, Art in the Garden, 1995, 1997, 1999, Aszzo, 1998—99, Music on the Hill Anniversary Art Show, 1998, Cafe Gallery, 1998—99, Dodge House Gallery, Providence, 1999, 2001, 2003, Providence, 2001, 2003, Warwick Mus. Art, 2000; two-woman shows B&H Framing, 1987, Artists Gallery, Wickford, R.I., 1990, Maxwell Mays Gallery-Providence Art Club, 1991, 1997, Providence Art Club, 1993, 1995, 1997—98; Exhibited in group shows at Warwick (R.I.) Art Mus., 1987, 1989, 1991, 1997—99, Helme House, Kingston, R.I., 1990, 1993, 1995, 1997, 2000, 2002, Woods-Gerry Gallery, Providence, 1991, Wickford Art Assn. Gallery, North Kingstown, 1991, 1993, 1995, 1997, 1999, R.I. Sch. Design Mus., Providence, 1992, Spring Bull Gallery, Newport, R.I., 1993, 1999, Newport, RI, 2001—02, Newport ArtMus., 1990, 1993, 1995, 1997, 1999—2001, 2003, R.I. Watercolor Soc., Pawtucket, 1993, 1995, 1997, 2000, 2003, South County Helme House, 2001—02, Spring Bull Gallery, 2002—03, Represented in permanent collections Alfred Butler & Co., Carribean Villas, others; catalog covers Providence Mag., R.I. Sch. Design, Cape Cod Mag., North Kingstown Villager. Mem.: Nat. Mus. Women in Arts, Warwick Mus., Boston Mus. Fine Arts, RISD Mus., Attleboro Mus., Newport Mus., Copley Soc. (Boston), Creative Arts Ctr., Newport Artist's Guild, South County Art Assn., Wickford Art Assn. (art instr. 1990—91, 1998—99, past pres. 1991), R.I. Watercolor Soc., Am. Soc. Marine Artists (assoc.), Am. Watercolor Soc. (assoc.), Oil Painters Am. (assoc.), Providence Art Club. Studio: Studio Zwei Gallery 2 Main St North Kingstown RI 02852-5016 E-mail: ekilguss@aol.com., studiozwei.2main@aol.com.

KILIAN, PAMELA REEVES, journalist, writer; b. Chgo., July 27, 1946; d. Roy Hester and Marguerite (Shaw) R.; m. Michael D. Kilian, Oct. 17, 1970; children: Eric Shaw Kilian, Colin David Reeves Kilian. B in Journalism, U. Mo., 1969. From reporter to editor United Press Internat., Chgo., Washington, 1970-84; news editor Scripps Howard News Svc., Washington, 1984—2002, asst. mng. editor news, 2002—. Author: (children's book) What Was Watergate?, 1990 (Hon. Mention Va. Coll. Stotes Assn. 1991); (nonfiction) Ellis Island, 1991; (biography) Barbara Bush, 1992, Barbara Bush Matriarch of a Dynasty, 2002. Home: 1003 Heather Hill Ct Mc Lean VA 22101-2024 Office: Scripps Howard New Svc 1090 Vermont Ave NW Ste 1000 Washington DC 20005-4906

KILKELLY, MARJORIE LEE, state legislator, community development official; b. Hartford, Conn., Dec. 1, 1954; d. Bruce Hamilton and Corlys Lucille (Lux) Brewer; children: Jeffrey Jr. (dec.), Robert, Sarah A.E. BS in Human Svcs., MS in Cmty. Econ. Devel., N.H. Coll., 1986; postgrad., Harvard U., 1997. Asst. to dir. Lincoln County Summer Youth Employment Program, Wiscasset, Maine, 1978; coordinator Community Food & Nutrition Program Coastal Enterprises, Inc., Wiscasset, 1978-79, Coastal Econ. Devel. Corp., Wiscasset, 1979-80, dir. Head Start Program Bath, Maine, 1980-84; asst. instr. N.H. Coll., Manchester, 1985-86; dir. Jr. Tots Wiscasset Recreation Program, 1985-88; dir. food services Boothbay Sch. Dept., Boothbay Harbor, Maine, 1985-88; owner Hurricane Hill Catering Co., Wiscasset, 1989—; mem. Maine Ho. of Reps., Augusta, 1986-96; house chair com. on agr., forestry and conservation, 1995-96; co-chmn. coastal caucus Maine Ho. of Reps., Augusta, spkr. pro tem, 1996—, candidate for speaker of house, 1992, candidate for house majority whip, 1994, chmn. agr., forestry and conservation com., 1995—; candidate Maine Senate, 1996; state senator, chmn. agriculture conservation and forestry com., island fish and wildlife com. State of Maine, 1996-98, chmn. Nat. Conf. State Legislators agr. com., 1997—; mem. Harvard state and local govt. ofcls. program Kennedy Sch. Govt., 1997—; cmty. devel. dir. Island Inst., Rockland, Maine, 1997—, community devel. dir., 1997—. Treas. Coastal Enterprises, Inc., Rundlet Block, Wis., 1981-90; rep. to Internat. Conf. on Econ. Devel., New Delhi, 1983—; 3d Selectman Town of Wiscasset, 1993-97; dir. devel. Maine Hospice Coun., 2000; owner Hurrican Hill Cons.; dir. N.E. States Assn. for Agrl. Stewardship, 1996-02. Mem. planning com. Blaine House Conf. on Families, 1979-80; active Maine Human Svcs. Coun. Sta. 23, Augusta, 1980-88; Sunday sch. tchr., lectr. St. Philips Episcopal Ch., Wiscasset, 1984-85, chmn. coord. com. food bank, 1986-88, sr. warden, 1995-98; chmn. Wis. Dem. Com., 1986; nat. chmn. Schs. S.O.S. Nat. Hunger Awareness Program, Denver, 1986; mem. exec. com. Maine Rural Devel. Coun., 1995—; spkr. pro tempere 118th Legislature, 1996; candidate Main State Senate Dist. 16, 1996; chair comm. adv. panel on decommissioning Maine Yankee Nuclear Plant, 1997, mem. legis. select com.; bd. dirs. Miles Health Care, Damanscotta, Mass., 1996—, Mid Coast United Way; chmn. Citizens Adv. Panel on Decommissioning Maine Yankee Atomic Power Plant, 1997—; lay dep. Nat. Episc. Ch. Conv., 1996—. Recipient Good Governance award, Maine Merchants Assn., 2000; fellow New Eng. Rural, Coun. State Govts. Toll, Flemming fellow, Ctr. Policy Alternatives, 1999, Eisenhower Exch., 1999; grantee Maine Welfare Edn. Employment Tng. Program, 1983. Mem. Bus. and Profl. Women (Maine Young Career Woman award 1989), Huntoon Hill Grange Club, Lincoln County Pomona Grange Club, Sportsmans Alliance Club of Maine, Am. Coun. Young Polit. Leaders, United Way of Mid Coast Maine (bd. mem.), Miles Hlth. Care Bd., U. Maine Bd. of Agr., Northeast States Assn. for Agrl. Stewardship (chair). Clubs: Maine Farm Bur., Maine State Grange. Democrat. Episcopalian. Avocations: horseback riding, gourmet cooking, fishing. Office: Maine State Senate State Capitol Augusta ME 04333-0001 Home: 5 Mcobb Rd Dresden ME 04342-4023 E-mail: kilkelly@wiscasset.net.

KILLEBREW, ELLEN JANE (MRS. EDWARD S. GRAVES), cardiologist, educator; b. Tiffin, Ohio, Oct. 8, 1937; d. Joseph Arthur and Stephanie (Beriont) K.; m. Edward S. Graves, Sept. 12, 1970. BS in Biology, Bucknell U., 1959; MD, N.J. Coll. Medicine, 1965. Diplomate in cardiovasc. disease Am. Bd. Internal Medicine. Intern U. Calif., 1965-66, resident, 1966-68; cardiology fellow Pacific Med. Ctr., San Francisco, 1968-70; dir. coronary care Permanent Med. Group, Richmond, Calif., 1970-83; asst. prof. U. Calif. Med. Ctr., San Francisco, 1970-83, assoc. prof., 1983-93; clin. prof. medicine U. Calif., San Francisco, 1992—, mem. admissions panel, 1998—. Admissions panel joint med. program U. Calif. San Francisco/U. Calif. Berkeley, 1998—; expert med. reviewer Calif. Med. Br., 1999; expert med. reviewer Bd. of Med. Examiners Calif., 1999—. Contbr. chpt. to book. Recipient Physician's Recognition award continuing med. edn., Lowell Beal award excellence in tchg., Permante Med. Group/House Staff Assn., 1992; Robert C. Kirkwood Meml. scholar in cardiology, 1970. Fellow ACP, Am. Coll. Cardiology; mem. Fedn. Clin. Rsch., Am. Heart Assn. (rsch. chmn. Contra Costa chpt. 1975—, v.p. 1980, pres. chpt. 1981-82, chmn. CPR com. Alameda chpt. 1984, pres. Oakland Piedmont br. 1995—, bd. dirs. western affiliate). Home: 30 Redding Ct Belvedere Tiburon CA 94920-1318 Office: 280 W Macarthur Blvd Oakland CA 94611-5642 also: 901 Nevin Ave Richmond CA 94801-3143 E-mail: Ellen.Killebrew@k.p.org.

KILLEEN, ALBERTINA ELLEN, retail executive, consultant, personnel advisor; b. St. Louis, June 9, 1950; d. Elwood Spencer and Albertine Emma (Waltman) Strauser; m. Jerry Hitchcock (div. Jan. 1970); 1 child, Jerry Spencer Hitchcock; m. Harold Blandford (dec. Jan. 1980); 1 child, Kevin Wayne Blandford; m. John Michael Killeen, Sept. 25, 1981. Fin. analyst Dynascan Corp., Chgo., 1981-83; mgr. customer svc. Carson-Pirie-Scott, Inc., Champaign, Ill., 1984-88; personnel mgr. Venture Stores, Inc., Champaign, Ill., 1988-91; mgr. personnel/ops. Kohl's Dept. Stores, Champaign, Ill., 1991—. Cons. Recurrent Tng. Ctr., Savoy, Ill., 1989—. Author (play) Montage; contbr. articles to mags. Mem. Chanute Hist. Soc., Rantoul, Ill., 1996, 97. Recipient Curator's award State of Mo., 1968. Mem. Champaign-Urbana Personnel Assn., Berks County Geneol. Soc., Reynold County Geneol. Soc., Bedford County Geneol. Soc., DAR. Avocation: geneology. Home: 812 Arends Blvd Rantoul IL 61866-3608 Office: Kohls Dept Stores 109 Convenience Center Rd Champaign IL 61820-7812

KILLEEN, JOHANNE, small business owner; Degree, R.I. Sch. of Design; Doctorates in Culinary Arts (hon.), Johson and Wales Univ. Chef, co-owner Al Forno Restaurant, Providence, 1975—. Appearances (TV series), In Julia Child's Kitchen with Master Chefs, Baking with Julia, Martha Stewart Living, David Rosengarten's Grilling, Cooking Live Primetime (Sarah Moulton); co-author: CUCINA SIMPATICA:Robust Trattoria Cooking, 1999. Actively involved Providence Pub. Libr., R.I. Food Bank, R.I. Project Aids, R.I. Ballet. Co-recipient The Ten Best Chefs in Am., Food and Wine; named World's Best Restaurant for casual dining, Internat. Herald Tribune, Scholars-in Residence; named one of top twenty women chefs in the country, USA Today; recipient nearly every honor, award and pub. recognition for orginal, innovative cuisine, Disting. Restaurants of North Am., Conde Nast Traveler's, 1992—2003, Hall of Fame award, Nation's restaurant, Insegna del Ristrante Italiano, Italian Ministries of agr. and of Foriegn Trade, 1999. Achievements include has taught DeGustibus (Macy's N.Y.C.), Bristol Farms, Drager's, Fetzer Vineyards in Calif., La Varenne in W. Va., and in Italy teach regularly at the Capezzana Estate in Tuscany and Hotel Cipriani in V. Office: 577 S Main St Providence RI 02903

KILLEN, KATHLEEN ELIZABETH, systems engineer, retired military officer; b. Winnfield, La., Dec. 23, 1953; d. Walter Walden and Beatrice (Bright) K.; 1 child, Woodrow H. Kroll III. BSChE, La. Tech. U., 1983; BS in Aero. Engring., Air Force Inst. Tech., 1985, MS in Sys. Mgmt., 1992. Commd. 2d lt. USAF, 1983, advanced through grades to maj., 1995, armament engr. Maverick missile, 1985-88, chief global positioning system bus systems engr. L.A. AFB, Calif., 1988-91, program mgr. Spinal Cord Injury Transport Sys. Brooks AFB, Tex., 1992—96, instr. Systems Acquisition Sch., 1997—98, ret., 1998; assoc. rsch. engr. Tex. Engring. Experiment Sta., San Antonio, 1998—2003; quality engr. CACI Internat., San Antonio, 2003—. Petty officer 2d class USN, 1974-79. Decorated Achievement medal, Commendation medal, Joint Svc. Achievement medal. Mem. Tau Beta Pi, Sigma Iota Epsilon. Avocations: reading, crafts, sewing. Office Phone: 210-735-1903 256.

KILLIAN, CHRISTINE LYNN COE, art educator; b. Houston, Mar. 19, 1967; d. Robert Brooks and Glenda J. (Gammill) Coe; m. Daniel S. Killian, Oct. 15, 1994; children: Kaitlyn, Abigail, Meagan, Lauryn. AA, San Jacinto Coll., 1987; BA, U. Houston Clear Lake, 1988, MA, 1990. Cert. visual arts educator & home econ. Instr. Visual Arts Sam Rayburn H.S., Pasadena, Tex., 1991—2001, Whitehouse H.S., Tex., 2001—; cons. gifted and talented visual arts Pasadena Ind. Sch. Dist., 1997—2001. Named Outstanding Educator, Tex. A&M Alumni Assn. Mem.: Tex. Art Edn. Assn. (Nat. Art. Honor Soc. Sponsor of Yr. 1996), Nat. Art Edn. Assn., Delta Kappa Gamma. Avocations: scrapbooks, painting, travel. Office: Whitehouse High Sch 901 E Main Whitehouse TX 75791*

KILLINGBECK, JANICE LYNELLE (MRS. VICTOR LEE KILLINGBECK), journalist; b. Flint, Mich., Nov. 11, 1948; d. Leonard Paul and Ina Marie (Harris) Johnson; m. Victor Lee Killingbeck, Sept. 26, 1970; children: Deeanna Dawn, Victor Scott. BA, Mich. State U., 1970; postgrad., Delta Coll., 1971-72; MA in Humanities, Ctrl. Mich. U., 2002. Tourist counselor Mich. Dept. State Hwys., Clare, 1969; copy editor Mich. State News, East Lansing, 1969-70; gen. reporter Midland (Mich.) Daily News, 1970; substitute tchr. Saginaw (Mich.) Pub. Schs., 1971; pub. rels. teller 1st State Bank of Saginaw, 1971-75; crew leader spl. census in Buena Vista Twp. Detroit Regional Office, U.S. Bur. Census, 1976, interviewer ann. housing survey-std. met. statis. areas, 1977-78, interviewer on-going health surveys, 1979-85, Nat. Crime Survey, 1985-86; editor AMEN newsletter United Meth. Women, Saginaw, 1984-87, Bridgeport-Birch Run Weekly News, 1986-93; owner Have Camera Will Travel, 1993—. Accelerated reader para-profl. A.A. Claytor Elem. Sch. Buena Vista Sch. Dist., Saginaw, Mich., 1997, libr., 1998—. Mem. Women in Comm., Sigma Delta Chi. Methodist. Home: 4946 Hess Rd Saginaw MI 48601-6809 Office: 3200 Perkins St Saginaw MI 48601-6563 E-mail: killingbeckj@email.bvsd.k12.mi.us.

KILLORAN, CYNTHIA LOCKHART, retired educator; b. Collinsville, Ill., June 19, 1918; d. Hugh McLelland and Estelle (Jones) Lockhart; m. Timothy Thomas Killoran, Feb. 9, 1944 (dec. Mar. 1991); children: Margaret, Kathleen, Timothy P., Cynthia, Mary. BS, U. Ill., 1940, postgrad. Home econs. tchr. LaMoille (Ill.) H.S., 1940-41; home supr. Farm Security, Dept. Agr., Pittsfield, Ill., 1941-42; civilian instr. radio operating procedure USAAC, Sioux Falls, S.D., 1942-44, Batavia, Ill., 1944-69; kindergarten tchr. Batavia Sch. Dist. # 101, 1967-93; ret., 1993. Methodist.

KILNER, URSULA BLANCHE, genealogist, educator, writer; b. Chgo., Feb. 2, 1925; d. Frederic Russell and Blanche (Miller) Gamble; m. Glen Kilner, May 12, 1950 (dec. Feb. 1998). BA cum laude, Mt. Holyoke Coll., 1946; MA, Columbia U., 1947, postgrad., to 1951. Asst. to editor Grolier Pub., N.Y.C., 1947; mgr. Magnamusic Inc., Garrison, N.Y., 1954-55; publicity and fundraising Little Guild of St. Francis Inc., Cornwall, Conn., 1957-68; lectr. U. Conn., Torrington, 1964-66; genealogist Bird Bottom Genealogy, Salisbury, Conn., 1979—. Owner, mgr. The Tenth Muse, phonograph and stereo co., 1958-60; reporter The Comml. Record, 1960-61. Author, editor: A Revolutionary Cook Book, 1985, A Cook Book for All Seasons, 1994; columnist The Voice, 1993-2003; book reviewer Heritage Books; contbr. articles to profl. jours. Mem. Planning and Zoning Commn., Salisbury, Conn., 1981-82, N.Y. State Hist. Assn. Mem.: DAR (chpt. registrar Salisbury Arsenal), N.Y. State Hist. Assn., Ill. Geneal. Soc., N.Y. Hist. Assn., Essex (Mass.) Soc. Genealogists, Nat. Geneal. Soc., Soc. Genealogists, Conn. Gravestone Studies, Assn. Gravestone Studies, Vt. [illegible], Suffolk County Hist. Soc., Conn. Soc. Genealogists, Am. Coll. Genealogists (asst. nat. registrar 1990—91, cert. genealogist), N.H. Genealogy Soc. (life), Nat. Soc. Huguenots (life; adv. bd. 1993—2001, Conn. registrar 1998—2001), N.H. Soc. Genealogists (life), N.Y. Geneal./Biog. Soc. (life), New Eng. Hist./Geneal. Soc. (life), Salisbury Assn., Sons and Daus. First Settlers Newbury, Van Voorhees Family Soc., Greyhound Friends West, Inc., Nat. Soc. Colonial Dames XVII Century (organizing pres. Winthrop Fleet chpt. 1990, Conn. state registrar 1995—99, chpt. pres. 1999—2001, ret.), Sheffield Hist. Soc. (life), Morse Family Soc. (life), Piscataqua Pioneers N.H. (life), Kewanee (Ill.) Hist. Soc. (life), Andover (Mass.) Hist. Soc. (life), Nat. Soc. Daus. Am. Colonists (ret. Conn. registrar), Seeley Family Soc., Whitlock Family Soc., Ea. Star. Avocations: knitting, lecturing, saving greyhounds, greenhouse plants. Home and Office: Bird Bottom Farm RR 1 Salisbury CT 06068-9802

KILPATRICK, CAROLYN CHEEKS, congresswoman; b. Detroit, June 25, 1945; d. Marvell and Willa Mae (Henry) Cheeks; divorced; children: Kwame, Ayanna. AS, Ferris State Coll., Big Rapids, Mich., 1965; BS, Western Mich. U., 1972; MS in Edn., U. Mich., 1977. Tchr. Murray Wright High Sch., Detroit, 1972-78; mem. Mich. Ho. of Reps., Lansing, 1978-96, U.S. Congress from 13th Mich. dist. (formerly 15th), Washington, 1997—; mem. appropriations com. Del. Dem. Convs., 1980, 84, 88. Participant Mich. African Trade Mission, 1984, UN Internat. Women's Conf., 1986; del. participant Mich. Dept. Agr. to Nairobi (Kenya) Internat. Agr. Show, 1986. Recipient Anthony Wayne award Wayne State U., Disting. Legislator award U. Mich., Disting. Alumni award Ferris State U., Woman of Yr. award Gentlemen of Wall St., Inc., Burton-Abercrombie award 15th Dem. Congrl. dist. Mem. Nat. Orgn. 100 Black Women. Democrat. Office: House of Reps 1610 Longworth House Office Bldg Washington DC 20515-2215*

KILPATRICK, LAURA SHELBY, music educator; b. Des Moines, Feb. 27, 1961; d. Nicholas Ligear and Barbara Slezak Shelby; m. Mark Allen Kilpatrick, July 28, 1984; children: Jennifer Morgan, Mitchell Austin. BS in music edn., U. Mo., 1983; M in edn., Lesley U., 2001. Cert. tchg. Nat. Bd. Profl. Tchrs. Standards Bd. of Dirs., 2002. Exec. asst. Pebble Beach Co., Pebble Beach, Calif., 1985—91, Century Fin., Kans. City, Mo., 1992—94; office mgr. Space Developers, Callahan Constrn., Trinitas, Old Town Corp., Independence, Mo., 1994—96; children youth choir dir. Christ United Meth. Ch., Independence, 1993—2003; music tchr. Thomas Hart Benton Elem., Independence, 1996—2001; tchr. Bryant Elem., Independence, 2001—. Dir. Independence Sch. Dist. Wide Holiday Concert, Independence, 1999—2001, Kans. City Chorale Holiday Concert, Independence, 2002. Outstanding tchr. grant, Gov. Employees Hosp. Assn., 2003. Mem.: Music Educators Nat. Conf., Mo. State Tchrs. Assn. Methodist. Achievements include Nat. Anthem soloist for Kans. City Royals Baseball Team. Avocations: sports and health, movies and live performances. Home: 19209 E 34th St S Independence MO 64057 Office: Bryant Elem 827 W Coll Ave Independence MO 64050

KILPATRICK, MAUREEN, food service executive; Grad. cert., Calif. Culinary Acad. Worked with Lydia Shire Pignoli, Boston; co-creator with Ana Sortun and Moncef Medeb 8 Holyoke, Boston; co-developer with Rene Becker High-Rise Bread Co., Hi-Rise Pie Co.; owner Harvest, Boston; worked with Rene Michelena La Bettola, Boston; pastry chef Oleana, Cambridge, Mass. Office: Oleana 134 Hampshire St Cambridge MA 02139

KILRAIN, SUSAN, astronaut; b. Augusta, Ga., Oct. 24, 1961; d. Joe and Sue Still; m. Colin James Kilrain. BS in Aerospace Engring., GA. Inst. Tech., 1985; grad., Test Pilot Sch. Wind tunnel project officer Lockheed Corp., Marietta, Ga.; commd. ensign USN, 1985, advanced through grades to lt. comdr., flight instr. TA-4J Skyhawk; naval aviator EA-6A Electric Intruders for Tactical Electronic Warfare Sq. 33, Key West, Fla.; with NASA Johnson Space Ctr., Houston, 1995—, with Vehicle Sys. and Ops. Br. Astronaut Office, pilot STS-83, 1997, pilot STS-94, 1997, spacecraft communicator in mission control. Decorated Def. Superior Svc. medal, Navy Meritorious Svc. medal, Navy Commendation medal, Navy Achievement medal, (2) NASA Space Flight medals, Nat. Def. Svc. medal; recipient 10 Outstanding Young Ams. award U.S. Jr. C. of C., Good Scout award, 1997. Mem. Assn. Naval Aviation, Assn. Space Explorers, Ga. Tech. Found. Avocations: triathlons, martial arts, playing piano. Office: NASA Lyndon B Johnson Space Ctr Houston TX 77058*

KIM, CHARLOTTE CHUNG-SOOK, retired librarian, administrator; b. Seoul, Korea, Apr. 15, 1940; came to U.S., 1963; d. Soon Kyung and Un Yun (Kim) Hong; m. Samuel C. Kang, Dec. 19, 1964 (div. Aug. 1976); Ben H. Kim, Nov. 17, 1985; children: Patricia Jean, Claudia Suk-Jin. BA, Yonsei U., 1962; MEd, Duquesne U., 1967; MLS, U. Pitts., 1968. Children's libr. Whitehall (Pa.) Pub. Libr., 1965-67, Carnegie Libr. Pitts., 1969-71, br. head, 1971-76, divsn. head, 1976-85; br. head Chgo. Pub. Libr., 1986-88, chief N.W. dist., 1989-90, asst. commr., 1990—2004, ret., 2004—. Bd. trustees North Cen. Coll., Naperville, Ill., 1995-2001. Bd. dirs. YWCA Met. Chgo., 1996-97, Korean Am. Scholarship Found., Chgo., 1992—, Chgo. Libr. Sys., 1991-96; v.p. Korean Am. Sr. Ctr., Chgo., 1994-98, pres., 1998—; v.p. Korean Am. Comty. Svcs., Chgo., 1990-93, Korean YWCA Chgo., 1997-98, bd. pres., 1999-2003, pres.; mem. adv. coun. Dem. and Peaceful Unification Korea, 1999-2003, v.p.; del. White House Conf. on Libr. and Info. Svcs., 1991; pres. Korean Women's Internat. Network (ctrl. chpt. U.S. East region). Recipient Outstanding Pub. Svc. award Friends of Chgo. Pub. Libr, 1987, Disting. Pub. Svc. award Asian Human Svcs. of Chgo., 1992, Outstanding Comty. Svc. award Korean Am. Assn. Chgo., 1995, Asian Libr. of Yr. award Sec. Ill. State/Ill. State Libr., 1998, Outstanding Achievement Cmty. Leadership award YWCA Met. Chgo., 1998, Korean Presdl. award 1999, 2002, Kathy Osterman Superior Pub. Svc. award City of Chgo., 2003; named Man of Yr., Korea Cen. Daily of Chgo., 1988, One of 100 chgo. Women Making Difference, Today's Chgo. Woman, 1998. Mem. ALA (internat. rels. com. 1992—, councilor 1993-97), ALA/Ethnic Materials and Info. Exch. Round Table (bd. dirs. 1994-96), Ill. Libr. Assn., Asian/Pacific Am. Librs. Assn. (past pres. 1991-92). Democrat. Methodist. Avocations: travel, reading, opera, concerts, plays. Home: 6245 N Kirkwood Ave Chicago IL 60646-5066

KIM, CHRISTINA K.(YUNG), investment company executive; b. Seoul, Republic of Korea, Feb. 11, 1968; arrived in U.S., 1978; d. In H. and Young J. Kim; m. Enoch Kim. BA, Boston U., 1991. CFA, cert. Series 7 Nat. Assn. Securities Dealers . Product mgr. New Eng. Funds, Boston, 1992—99; asst. v.p. MFS, Boston, 1999—. Mem.: Boston Security Analysts Soc. Business E-Mail: ckim@mfs.com.

KIM, DONNA MERCADO, state senator; b. Honolulu, July 31, 1952; BA, Wash. State U., 1974. Recreation dir.; small bus. exec. dir.; comm. sales rep.; hotel catering sales rep.; pub. rels. dir. KUMU Radio; Dem. senator dist. 15 Hawaii State Senate. Past mem. Pres.'s Nat. Com. on Transp.; past mem. steering com. Nat. League Cities, Econ. Devel.; bd. dirs. Bank of Am. Hawaii; trained facilitator The Pacific Inst. Active Aliamanu unit Boys and Girls Club Honolulu, Hawaii's Jr. Miss, Inc., Planned Parenthood, YMCA Century Club; mem. Hawaii Korean Millenium Commn.; bd. trustees Palama Settlement. Named one of Three Outstanding Young Persons, Hawaii Jaycees, 1988; recipient Outstanding Alumni award Farrington H.S., 1997. Mem. ASPA (Outstanding City and County Adminstr. award 1997), Asian Pacific Am. Mcpl. Ofcls., Kaliki Bus. Assn., Hawaii Korean C. of C. (hon.), Filipino C. of C. Office: Hawaii State Senate State Capitol Rm 218 415 S Beretania St Honolulu HI 96813 Fax: 808 587-7205. E-mail: senkim@Capitol.hawaii.gov.

KIM, HYO SOOK, anesthesiologist; b. Republic of Korea, 1940; d. Kyu T. and Ki Won (Shin) Kim; m. Chong H. Kim, Nov. 23, 1968; children: Jeanne I. Kim, Katherine M. Kim, Riena Y. Kim. MD, Korea U. Med. Coll., Seoul, 1964. Diplomate Am. Bd. Anesthesiology. Intern St. Joseph's Hosp., 1965; resident U. Chgo. Hosp., 1966-67, Children's Meml. Hosp., Chgo., 1968, fellow, 1969-70; chief anesthesiologist Seaway Hosp., Trenton, Mich.; instr. Dept. Anesthesiology U. Chgo., 197-72; clin. asst. prof. Surgery Mich. State U., 1976-82. Fellow Am. Coll. Anesthesiologists; diplomat Am. Bd. Anesthesiologists; mem. AMA, Am. Soc. Anesthesiologists, Am. Soc. for Regional Anesthesia, Internat. Anesthesia Rsch. Soc., Am. Acad. Med. Acupuncture. Office: 18445 Vanhorn Woodhaven MI 48183

KIM, KYUNG-SUN, library and information scientist, educator; b. Seoul, South Korea, 1964; came to U.S., 1994; d. Jin-Guil and Ha-Woon (Ahn) K. BA, Duksung U., Seoul, 1987; MA, U. Montreal, 1994; PhD, U. Tex., Austin, 1998. Asst. prof. U. Mo., Columbia, 1998-2001, U. Wis., Madison, 2001—. Reviewer Interactive Learning and Info. Sys., 1999—, Jour. Libr. and Info. Sci. Edn., 2000—, Libr. Resources and Tech. Svcs., 2000—; contbr. articles to profl. jours. Mem. ALA, Assn. Computing Machinery, Assn. Libr. and Info. Sci. Edn., Am. Soc. Info. Sci. and Tech. Office: U Wis 4217 HC White Hall 600 North Park St Madison WI 53706

KIM, LILLIAN G. LEE, retired administrative assistant; b. Toishan, Canton, China, June 17, 1919; came to the U.S., 1921; d. Yick You and Lucy Yu Oy (Louie) Lee; m. Herman Hom Kim, Oct. 12, 1941. Cert., Ea. U., 1941. Stenographer, sec. Peabody Book Shop, Balt., 1937-38; sec. Prisoners Aid Assn., Balt., 1938-41; sec. Civilian Def. Exec. Office Balt. Mcpl. Govt., 1942-44, sec. to safety dir., 1944-48; sec.-stenographer, asst. supr. stenography divsn. Ctrl. Payroll Bur., 1948-64, adminstrv. sec., supr. adminstrv. and stenographic sect., 1946-63, supr. adminstrv. sect., 1964-77; ret., 1977. Ctrl. payroll councilwoman Classified Mcpl. Employee Assn., Balt., 1949-77, columnist Hall Light, 1950-77; chair ret. employee group CHICA-Combined Health/Industry Comb. Appeal and United Way, Balt., 1970-77; bd. dirs. Women's Civic League; pres., bd. dirs. AARP (Rodgers Forge Chpt. 2360), 1996-, publicity and pub. rels. officer, corr. sec., 1997-99; lectr. in field. Author: (with Lee Yick You and Louie Yu Oy) Early Baltimore Chinese Families, 1976, Chinese Americans-A Part of America, 1977; Letters to the Editor: (tribute to Marhsall Sisters) History of Grace & St. Peter's Chinese Ch. Sch., 1975, Tien Nien Poems, Lectures, and Speeches, Gnin-Gnin's China: Our Heritage, 1980, Grace and St. Peter's Chinese Church School (founders Frances L. and Florence M. "Daisy" Marshall), Chinese Traditions, Customs, and Festivals; author short stories, essays, 1960-70; edit. publ. Wah Kue Sim Mon (bilingual news bull.), 1998, Tien Nien Chatter, cmty. news columnist Towson Times, 1978—; freelance writer Senior Digest, 1990—; Gone But Not Forgotten: Nostalgic Maryland Memories, 1993, editor-pub. Tien Nien Chatter, 1946-60; contbg. writer Hall Light, 1950-77. Founder Chinese Young People's Fellowship, sec., mem. pub. rels. sect. 1946-60, pres., 1960-65; mem. Senator Charles McMathias Jr.s' Select. Immigration Com., 1960s; founder, exec. sec. Grace and St. Peter's Bilingual Chinese Lang. Sch., Balt., 1954-73, supr., 1964-85, dir., prin., 1974—, compiler evening prayer svc. and hymn book; vestrywoman Grace and St. Peter's Ch., Balt., mem. parish activity planning, 1969—, compiler bilingual evening prayer svc.; sec. bd. trustees Grace and St. Peter's Sch., Balt., 1980-86, trustee, 1987-90, exec. bd. Boy Scouts Am., 1978-95; bd. dirs. Women's Civic League, 1979-82, exec. bd., 1999; mem. Bishop's Guild, Diocese of Md., 1960-99; mem. Holly Tour Com., Inc. of Balt., 1975-85, sec., 1978-82; sec., pub. rels. Chinese Women's Assn. Balt., 1937-46; Chinese interpreter of Am. laws, social security taxes, federal and state taxes to Chinese; represented Chinese immigrants in cts. as a vol.; advocate Family Reunionifications, Canton, Balt., 1964; participant Testimonial Dinner Tribute to Councilman Leon A. Rubenstein, Senator Charles McMathias Retirement Dinner; spkr. Tribute to Senator Barbara A. Mikulski; del. to Md. Diocesan Conv., selected lay reader Diocesan Conv. Holy Eucharist Svc., St. Anne's Ch., Annapolis, numerous other diocesan activities; cmty. advocate Dept Justice, Immigration and Naturalization Svc., 1997—; initator, coord. Grace and St. Peter's Chinese Lunar New Yr., Balt.; compiler bilingual citizenship study guide; mem. exec. bd. Boy Scouts Am., 1978-1995; organizer Tiger Club program; apptd. to serve on Senator Charles McMathias Jr.'s select immigration com., 1960s. Recipient awards, including Spl. Baltimorean award, 1976, Balt.'s Best Blue and Silver awards, numerous times, award for outstanding svc. in promoting internat. rels., Carnation Volunteerism award, Balt. City Outstanding Woman of Yr. award, Baltimore County Exec. Proclamation, 1985, Balt. County Woman of Yr., 1986, GERI award, 1990, Baltimore County Execs.'s Baltimore County Exec. citation-Humanitarian award honoree, 1993, Gold 13 medal WJZ-TV, Exec. Citation Humanitarian award Baltimore County, Golden Rule award JC Penney's, Best of Towson, 1998, First Place Best Vol. award Readers of Towson Times, 1998; Congratulatory Honors award Club 88 Tchrs. of Lyndhurst Elem. Sch. No. 88), 1999, award for outstanding svc. tchg. and promoting lang., culture, tradition, and history Coordination Coun. for N.Am. Affairs, Dist. Svc. to Balt. Chinese Cmty. award Balt. chpt. Orgn. Chinese Ams., Outstanding Achievement award Dorothy G. Reddick, 1999, Feast of the Dedication cert. of appreciation Grace and St. Peter's Parish, 1999, My Most Significant Memory of 20th Century award Dept. Aging, 2000. Mem. AARP (pub. rels. dir., bd. dirs.), Episcopal Asiamerica Ministry (parish rep. 1975-93, diocesan rep. 1994—), DAR (medal of honr.), Walters Art Mus., Balt. Mus. Art, Md. Hist. Soc., Stars Spangled Banner Assn., Johns Hopkins Alumni Assn., UCLA Alumni Assn., Washington Nat. Episcopal Cathedral Assn., Ellis Island Found.-Statue of Liberty, Chinese Hist. Soc. Am. (life), Chinese Hist. Soc. So. Calif. (life), Assn. Chinese Schs., Chinese Lang. Tchrs. Assn., Crozier Soc., Md. Assn. of Deaf, Historic Towson, Inc., Balto Coun. Fgn. Affairs, Reagan Ranch, WYPR Radio News Sta., Friends of Nat. Parks at Gettysburg, U.S. Capitol Hist. Soc., Nat. Trust for Historic Presevation, Chesapeake Bay Found., Balt. City Hist. Soc., Enoch Pratt Free Libr./State Libr. Resource. Democrat. Episcopalian. Avocations: community service, gardening, bowling, reading. Home: 524 Anneslie Rd Baltimore MD 21212-2009 Office: Grace & St Peters Chinese Lang Sch 707 Park Ave Baltimore MD 21201-4703

KIM, MI JA, dean, academic administrator; b. Seoul, Republic of Korea, Jan. 23, 1940; came to U.S., 1966; d. Si Hyung and Jung Kwon (Ahn) Lee; m. Heung Soo Kim, Jan. 14, 1964; children: Yoon Hi and Joseph. BS in Nursing, Yon Sei U., Seoul, 1962; PhD in Physiology, U. Ill., Chgo., 1975; JD (hon.), North Park Coll., 1995. Staff nurse Severance Hosp., Seoul, 1962-63; health nurse Am. Embassy, Seoul, 1963-66; asst. prof. Coll. Nursing/Univ. Ill., Chgo., 1975-79, assoc. prof., 1979-84, prof., 1984—, assoc. dean for rsch. dir. of grad. studies and assoc. dean acad. affairs, 1984-88, acting dean, 1988-89, dean, 1989-95, vice chancellor for rsch. and dean of grad. coll., 1995-99, dir. Acad. of Internat. Leadership Devel., 2001—. Cons. Nat. Ctr. Nursing Rsch., Bethesda, Md., 1987-91, Bd. Regents Higher Edn., Boston, 1989, WHO, Geneva, 2000, Nat. Inst. Gen. Med. Scis., NIH, 2000; mem. nat. adv. coun. Nat. Ins Mem. adv. bd. Health of the Pub., PEW Charitable Trust, Robert Wood Johnson found., 1992-96; adv. coun. Ctr. Bioethics and Human Dignity, 1994—. Named 100 Most Influential Women in Chgo., Chgo. Tribune, 1991, Univ. Scholar, U. Ill., 1985-88, Outstanding Nurse Educator, Korean Nurses Assn., Seoul, 1983; recipient Disting. Health and Edn. award Midwest Cmty. Coun. Chgo., 1994, Book of Yr. award Am. Jour. Nursing, 1984, Golden Apple award, students of Coll. Nursing, U. Ill., 1976, 78; Fulbright scholar Yon Sei U., Seoul, 2001. Fellow Am. Acad. Nursing; mem. North Am. Nursing Diagnosis (bd. dirs. 1985-92), Am. Thoracic Soc., Chgo. Lung Assn. (bd. dirs. 1977-97, Leadership Recognition award 1996), Chgo. Heart Assn. (bd. govs. 1980-88), Am. Physiol. Soc., Internat. Leadership Inst. (adv. coun. 1998-99), Sigma Theta Tau (Disting. lectr. 1987, Mary Tolle Wright award for Excellence in Leadership, 1997). Avocation: golf. Office: U Ill Chgo Rm 1156 Coll of Nursing Chicago IL 60612-7350 Office Phone: 312-996-5275. Business E-Mail: mjkuic@uic.edu.

KIM, SOOK CHA, artist; b. Choong-Joo, Korea, Mar. 30, 1940; arrived in U.S., 1973; d. Kyung Nam Chai and Choon Yi Lim; m. Myung Hak Kim, Dec. 5, 1967; 1 child, Young Kyoon. BFA, Hong-Ik U., 1965, MFA, 1967. Owner Morning Star Art Gallery, Washington, 1995—2003. Featured artist New Art Internat. 1997 Edit.; group exhibits Gallery Close. Recipient Gold medal--Art Addiction Internat. prize Most Talented Artists Competition, Sweden, 1997, Cert. of Merit 6th Internat. Female Artist Art Exhbn. on Internet Art Mus., 1999. Home: 6540 Braddock Rd Alexandria VA 22312-2206

KIM, TONG RIM, art foundation administrator; b. Seoul, Korea, Jan. 20, 1916; came to U.S., 1964; d. Kuk Sun and Yoo Dang; m. Whanki Kim, May 1, 1944 (dec. July 1974); 1 child, Wha Young. Student, Ewha U., Seoul, 1934-36, U. Sorbonne, Paris, 1955-56, Ecole du Louvre, 1956-58. Dir. Whanki Found. Fine Arts for Young Artists, N.Y.C., 1979-99. Author: Life & Work, 1992, also essays. Founder Whanki Mus., Seoul. Home: 160 W 73rd St New York NY 10023-3012

KIMANI, GRACE ALEXANDRA, internist; b. Peterborough, England, May 16, 1963; d. Astley and Salome (Taylor) Brown; m. Anthony Philip Kimani, July 23, 1988; children: Destiny, Daniel. BS, Oral Roberts U., 1988; MD, Morehouse Sch. Medicine, Atlanta, 1994. Diplomate Am. Bd. Internal Medicine. Intern Ga. Bapt. Med. Ctr., Atlanta, 1995-96, resident, 1996-98; pvt. practice Crawford Long Hosp. Mem. ethics com. Ga. Bapt. Med. Ctr.; presenter in field. Mem. AMA, Am. Coll. Physicians. Avocations: playing piano, tennis, novels, traveling, languages. Home: PO Box 54712 Atlanta GA 30308-0712

KIMBALL, CATHERINE D. state supreme court justice; b. Alexandria, La., Feb. 7, 1945; m. Clyde W. Kimball; 3 children. JD, La. State U., 1970. Law clerk US Dist. Court, Western Dist. La., 1970; spec. coun. La. Attorney Gen. Office, 1971—73; gen coun. La. Commn. Law Enforcement & Admin. Crim. Just., 1973—81; priv. law prac., 1975—82; judge La. Dist. Ct. (18th dist.), 1982—92; assoc. justice Supreme Ct. of La., 1992—. Office: Supreme Ct of La 301 Loyola Ave New Orleans LA 70112-1814

KIMBALL, CHARLOTTE ELIZABETH, systems analyst, writer, retired military officer; b. Pinebluff, Ark., Aug. 27, 1953; d. William Clifford and Mary Charlotte Ruffin; m. Ira Hugh Hudson, Oct. 15, 1953; m. David Longley Kimball, July 17, 1979 (dec. Feb. 11, 1981); 1 child, Dustin Dean. BA, Northwestern State U., 1974; MS in Orgnl. Devel., E. Tex. State U., 1983. Mil. officer U.S. Army, 1973—95; sr. logistics analyst SYTEX, Inc., Alexandria, Va., 1996—2002, Ft. Buchanan, PR, 2002—. Author: (novel) Orchids in the Snow, Shades of Murder, Parent's Guide to Business Travel. Decorated Legion of Merit U.S. Army. Mem.: Women in the Mil. Svc. of Am., Nat. Mus. of Women in the Arts, VII Corps Desert Storm Vets. Assn., U.S. Army War Coll. Alumni Assn., Wash. Ind. Writers, Assn. of the U.S. Army. Avocations: scuba diving, travel, cooking. Home: 609 Longleaf Dr Minden LA 71055 Personal E-mail: charlie@charliehudson.net.

KIMBALL, DOROTHY JEAN, foundation executive; b. Riceville, Miss., Dec. 27, 1927; d. Hiram William and Norma Lucille (Wilson) Cutrer; m. Peter Nolan Kimball, Nov. 30, 1946; children: Donna Jean, Brenda Gail. Student, La. State U., 1947-48. With E.B. Badger & Sons Constrn. Co., Baton Rouge, 1944-45; sec. State of La. Dept. Edn., Baton Rouge, 1945-49; sec., bkpr. Better Bus. Bur. of Baton Rouge, Inc., 1950-52; pvt. sec., nat. comdt., mgr. nat. hdqtrs. Marine Corps League, Baton Rouge, 1952-54; sec., bookkeeper Louis B. Rogers Constrn. Co., Baton Rouge, 1954; sec. to pres. Crawford Corp., Baton Rouge, 1955-64; sec-v.p. Crofton (Md.) Corp., 1964-74; sec.-treas. W.H. Crawford, Baton Rouge, 1975-89; found. exec. Crawford Found., Baton Rouge, 1990-96. Notary pub. State of Md., 1964-74. Named Baton Rouge High Magnet Sch. Hall of Fame, 1999. Mem. Am. Legion Aux. (Post 38), City Club, Country Club of La., Rolls Royce Club (entertainment com. 1985-87). Republican. Baptist. Avocations: fishing, reading, dance. Home and Office: 1418 Applewood Rd Baton Rouge LA 70808-5905

KIMBERLY, SUSAN ELIZABETH, state legislative director, city program administrator; b. Tracy, Minn., July 23, 1942; d. Mervin Glen and Blanche Pontius (Lees) Sylvester. BA, U. Minn., Mpls., 1965. Coun. mem. City of St. Paul, Minn., 1974—78; v.p. Piper Jaffray, Mpls., 1978—82; self-employed cons. St. Paul, 1983—86; asst. to mayor City of St. Paul, 1987—88, dep. mayor, chief staff, 1999—2002; commr. Metro Waste Control, St. Paul, 1985—91; exec. dir. Coalition for Cmty. Devel., St. Paul, 1992—97; team leader St. Paul Planning Dept., 1997—98; program adminstr. City of St. Paul, 2002—03; state legis. dir. US Senator Norm Coleman, 2003—. Dir., pres. Minn. Film Bd., Mpls., 1987-98; dir. St. Paul Found., 1998-, Family Housing Fund, 1999-; commr. St. Paul Human Rights, 2001—; dir., Minn. Civil Liberties Union, Regions Hosp., 2003-. Republican. Episcopalian. Avocations: walking, running. Office: City of St Paul 25 W 4th St Ste 1300 Saint Paul MN 55102-1621 E-mail: susan.kimberly@usa.net.

KIMBLE, JUDITH E. molecular biologist, cell biologist; b. Providence, Apr. 24, 1949; BA, U. Calif., Berkeley, 1971; PhD, U. Colo., 1978; postgrad., MRC, Cambridge, Eng., 1978-82. Asst. prof. to assoc. prof. U. Wis., 1983-92; prof. molecular biology, biochemistry U. Wisc., Madison, 1992—, prof. med. genetics, 1994—. Investigator Howard Hughes Med. Inst., Md., 1994—. Mem. NAS, Am. Acad. Arts and Sci., Am. Soc. Cell Biology, Am. Soc. Biochemistry and Molecular Biology, Genetic Soc. Office: HHMI/Dept Biochemistry U Wisc-Madison 433 Babcock Dr Madison WI 53706-1544

KIMBLE, MELINDA LOUISE, environmental administrator; m. James R. Phippard; 4 stepchildren. B in Econs., M in Econs., U. Denver; MPA in Econs., Kennedy Sch. Fgn. svc. officer Dept. of State, Washington, 1971-89, sr. fgn. svc. officer, 1989-93, min. counselor, 1993-97, dep. asst. sec. Bur. Internat. Orgn. Affairs, 1993-97, prin. dep. asst. sec. Oceans and Internat. Environ. and Sci. Affairs, 1997-99; v.p. programs UN Found., Washington, 2000—03, sr. v.p. programs, 2003—. Recipient award Global Alliance for Women's Health, Internat. Honor award USDA, Disting. Honor award Dept. State, 2000. Office: 1225 Connecticut Ave NW 4th Fl Washington DC 20036-1815

KIMBRELL, DEBORAH ANN, geneticist, educator; b. San Angelo, Tex., July 22, 1950; d. Billy Lee and Dorothy (Babish) K.; m. S. Ingemar C. Olsson, June 15, 1991. BA in Biology and Psychology with honors, Mills Coll., 1972; PhD in Genetics, U. Calif., Berkeley, 1985. Rsch. technician dept. respiration physiology Max Planck Inst. Exptl. Medicine, Göttingen, Germany, 1973-74; NIH predoctoral trainee dept. genetics U. Calif., Berkeley, 1979-85; Am. Cancer Soc. postdoctoral fellow dept. genetics U. Cambridge, Eng., 1985-88; Swedish MRC vis. scientist fellow dept. microbiology U. Stockholm, 1988-90; asst. prof. dept. biology and Inst. Molecular Biology, U. Houston, 1991-98; sr. faculty fellow dept. biochemistry and cell biology Rice U., Houston, 1998—. Contbr. articles to profl. jours. Pres. Rsch. and Scholarship Fund grantee U. Houston, 1991, 92-93; grantee Houston Coastal Ctr., 1992-98, Am. Cancer Soc., 1993—. Mem. AAAS, Genetics Soc. Am. Home: 127 Sunnybrae Ct Martinez CA 94553-5800

KIMBRIEL-EGUIA, SUSAN, engineering planner, small business owner; b. San Francisco, July 22, 1949; d. Scott Slaughter and Kathleen (Edens) Smith; m. Floyd Thomas Kimbriel; children: John Thomas, Tammy Lee Petersen; m. Candelario Eguia, Feb. 14, 1991; 1 child, Daniel. Accredited Nat. Assn. Family Child Care. Engrng. planner, sys. adminstr. various mainframe and PC based sys. Northrop Aircraft, Hawthorne, Calif., 1982-91; owner, operator Susie's Day Care/PreSchool, Palmdale, Calif., 1995—. Mem.: Antelope Valley Child Care Assn., Nat. Assn. for Family Child Care. Avocations: handcrafts, gardening, computer graphics.

KIMBROUGH, LORELEI, elementary school educator; b. Chgo. d. Paul and Lina (Higgs) Bobbett; m. James Kimbrough; children: Denise, Devi, Paul, Jeri Lynn, Sandra, Diane, James III. BS in Edn., Ill. State U., 1947; postgrad., DePaul U., Chgo. U. Cert. tchr., Ill. Tchr. of Latin and English, Greensboro (N.C.) Pub. Schs.; spl. edn. tchr. Chgo. State Hosp./Reed Zone Ctr., Chgo., Jewish Children's Bur., Chgo.; elem. tchr. Chgo. Bd. of Edn., Pasadena (Calif.) H.S.; English tchr. Malala H.S., Madang, 1993-94; tchr. jr. H.S. Cathedral Chapel Cath. Sch., 1995-96, Holy Trinity Sch., L.A., 1998-2000. Tutor to fgn. students. Missionary worker L.A. Archdiocese, Papua New Guinea; vol. ARC, Solheim Luth. Home, Glendale Meml. Hosp. 4-year scholar State of Ill., Chgo. Musical Coll. award. Mem. Nat. Coun. Tchrs. of English, Ill. Coun. of Social Studies, Nat. Coun. Social Studies. Home: 86 S Daisy Ave Pasadena CA 91117 Mailing: 5209 Bentgrass Dr Raleigh NC 27610-2134

KIMERER, ALICE LOUISE, artist, educator; b. Dilley, Tex., Dec. 22; d. William Lee and Effie (Edwards) Crawford; m. Vincent Augustine Braun, Mar. 6, 1944 (div.); children: Vincent Braun Jr., Barbara Ann Braun; m. Perry Eugene Kimerer, Apr. 17, 1976; children: Candance, Toni. BFA in Art Edn., Our Lady of Lake U., 1942; MFA, Art Inst., Mex., 1960. Art tchr. Burbank Jr. H.S., San Antonio, 1943—44, San Antonio Boys Acad., 1950, Mus. Sci. and History, Ft. Worth, 1976; art instr., judge Carswell AFB, Ft. Worth, 1977; artist Left Bank Gallery, St. Simonis, Ga., 1998—99, Upwest Gallery, Ft. Worth, 1999—2001. Regional dir. Tex. Watercolor Soc., San Antonio, 1980. Artist oil paintings; one-woman shows include 6 shows, Represented in permanent collections chs., profl. offices, hosps., banks and homes. Recipient Arts award, USAF, 1972, Purchase prize, Tex. Watercolor Soc., 1975. Mem.: AAUW (art advisor 1999, art show judge 2001), Kimbell Mus. (patron 1974—), Dallas Mus. for Women, Nat. Mus. Women in Arts. Avocations: travel, teaching, sketching, workshops. Home: 6113 Valley View Dr Fort Worth TX 76116

KIMETHU, SUSAN WANJA, computer specialist, database manager; b. Nairobi, Kenya, Mar. 13, 1956; d. Samuel Kimama Ngaii and Mary Nyambura Kimama; m. Daniel Mburu Kimethu; children: Hosea Kimethu Mburu, Samuel Kimama Mburu, Esther Njeri Mburu. Diploma, Kenya Tech. Coll., 1983; MBA, Baldwin Wallace Coll., 1992; PhD in Bus. Adminstrn., Kennedy Western U., 2002. Cert. Oracle database adminstr.; h.s. tchr. Sr. acct. Ameritrust Bank, Cleve., 1993—94; sr. fin. analyst Key Bank, Cleve., 1994—98; instr. Sawyer Bus. Coll., Cleve., 1994—98; database mgr. Telesis Of Ohio, Cleve., 1997—99; sr. bus. analyst Emerald Health, Cleve., 1998—99; database mgr. Orbital Computers, Cleve., 2000—01; computer specialist United Labor Agy., Cleve., 2001—; tchr. Life Skills Ctr., Counmbus, 2003. Tchr. h.s., Columbus, Ohio, 2003. Author: Following & Obeying God in Your Youth, 2001, Kids, Let's Follow Christ, 2002, Kids, Let's Follow Christ Workbook, 2002. Mem.: Network Adminstrs., Oracle User Group. Office: Dansu Pubs LLC PO Box 937 Grove City OH 43123-0937 E-mail: skimethu@hotmail.com.

KIMMEL, ELLEN BISHOP, psychologist, educator; b. Knoxville, Tenn., Sept. 16, 1939; d. Archer W. and Mary Ellen (Baker) Bishop; divorced; children: Elinor, Ann, Jean, Tracy. BA summa cum laude, U. Tenn., 1961; MA, U. Fla., 1962, PhD, 1965. Asst. prof., rsch. assoc. Ohio U., 1965-68; asst. prof. U. South Fla., Tampa, 1968-72, assoc. prof., dean Univ. Studies Coll., 1972-73, prof. psychology and ednl. psychology, 1975-95, chair, 1992-94, disting. prof., 1996—2003, prof. emeritus, 2003—. Disting. vis. prof. psychology Simon Fraser U., Vancouver, B.C., Can., 1980-81; cons. numerous sch. systems, bus. and govt. Author books; contbr. articles to profl. jours., chpts. to books. Mem. Fla. Blue Ribbon Task Force on Juvenile Delinquency, 1976-77; mem. Fla. Gov.'s Commn. on Women, 1979-83; mem. adv. bd. Stop Rape, Good Govt., Inc.; bd. dirs. NCCJ. Recipient Outstanding Svc. award State of Fla., 1975, Outstanding Tchg. award U. South Fla., 1978, Career Achievement award U. Tenn., 1983, Professorial Excellence award Fla. State U. Sys., 1997, Disting. Sr. Scholar Spl. Commendation of Honor, AAUW, 2001; 17 rsch. grants. Fellow: APA (governing coun. 1982—85, pres. divsn. 1986—88, Disting. Leadership award 1993), Am. Assn. Applied and Preventive Psychology (bd. dirs. 1994—97, charter fellow, program chair 1991, Disting. Edn. award 1994), Am. Psychol. Soc. (charter fellow, conf. chair 1990); mem.: Southeastern Psychol. Assn. (pres. 1977—79), Assn. Women in Psychology (Disting. Publ. award 2000), Athena Soc., Omicron Delta Kappa, Delta Kappa Gamma, Sigma Xi. Democrat. Office: U South Fla EDU 162 Tampa FL 33620

KIMURA, DOREEN, psychology educator, researcher; b. Winnipeg, Man., Can. 1 child, Charlotte Vanderwolf. BA, McGill U., Montreal, Que., Can., 1956, MA, 1957, PhD, 1961; LLD (hon.), Simon Fraser U., 1993, Queen's U., 1999. Lectr. Sir George Williams U. (now Concordia U.), Montreal, 1960-61; rsch. assoc. otol. rsch. lab. UCLA Med. Ctr., 1962-63; rsch. assoc. Coll. Medicine, McMaster U., Hamilton, Ont., 1964-67; assoc. prof. psychology U. Western Ont., London, 1967-74, prof., 1974-98, coord. clin. neuropsychology program, 1983-97. Supr. clin. neuropsychology Univ. Hosp., London, 1975-83; vis. prof. psychology Simon Fraser U., 1998—. Author: Neuromotor Mechanisms in Human Communication, 1993, Sex and Cognition, 1999, French, Japanese, Swedish, Spanish edit.; contbr. numerous articles to profl. jours. Recipient Outstanding Sci. Achievement award Can. Assn. Women in Sci., 1986, John Dewan award Ont. Mental Health Found., 1992; fellow Montreal Neurol. Inst., 1960-61, Geigy fellow Kantonsspital, Zürich, Switzerland, 1963-64. Fellow Royal Soc. Can., Can. Psychol. Assn. (Disting. Contbns. to Sci. award 1985); mem. Soc. Acad. Freedom & Scholarships (founding pres. 1992-93, 98-2000). Office: Simon Fraser U Dept Psychology Burnaby BC Canada V5A 1S6 E-mail: dkimura@sfu.ca.

KINARD, AGNES DODDS, retired real estate company executive, historian, writer, lawyer; b. Pitts. d. Robert James Dodds and Agnes Julia Raw; m. Morton Frank, June 2, 1944 (div. 1958); children: Allan Dodds, Michael Robert, Marilyn Morton; m. James Pinckney Kinard, Dec. 27, 1961 (dec. Mar. 1994). BA in History cum laude, U. Pitts., 1936, LLB, 1939, JD, 1961; postgrad., Chatham Coll., 1980. Bar: Pa. 1940. Law researcher Reed, Smith, Shaw & McClay, Pitts., 1940-41; Lynne A. Warren, N.Y.C., 1940-41; exec. sec. Allegheny County War Price and Ration Bd., Pitts., 1941-44; British Colonies section chief, asst. to the deputy adminstr. Lend-Lease Adminstrn., Washington, 1944-46; women's editor, columnist Canton (Ohio) Economist, 1946-58; assoc. broker, sales Kelly Wood Real Estate, Pitts., 1959-72; broker, pres., co-owner Mountain Real Estate Co., Inc., Confluence, Pa., 1973-83. Author: Seasons of the Heart in Quest of Faith, 1989, Fanfare for Fifty Years, Pittsburgh Symphony Association, 1939-1989, 1989, Celebration of The Carnegie in Pittsburgh, 1982, Celebrating the First 100 Years of The Carnegie in Pittsburgh, 1995, booklets. Bd. dirs. Pitts. Plan for Art, Sch. Vol. Assn., Pitts. Youth Symphony Orch. Assn., Pitts. Symphony Assn.; co-founder, mem. Rachel Carson Homestead Assn.; founder, pres. Pioneer Crafts Coun. (now Touchstone Crafts Ctr.); mem. women's com. Carnegie Mus. Art. Recipient Award of Merit Pitts. History and Landmark Found., Three Rivers Environ. award, 1993; named No. 60 of the First 100 Women Lawyers in Allegheny County, Pa., 1992. Mem. Pitts. Civic Garden Ctr. (life), Nat. Coun. State Garden Clubs (life),

Nat. Soc. Arts and Letters (life, landscape design critic), Landscape Design Soc. Western Pa. (founding bd. dirs., past pres., Helen S. Hull plaque for lit. hort. interest 1986), Kappa Kappa Gamma.

KINBERG, JUDY, television producer, director; b. Freeport, N.Y., Sept. 15, 1948; d. Jack H. and Rose M. (Schwartz) K. BA, Hofstra U., 1970. Prodn. asst. various programs including Camera Three CBS TV, N.Y.C., 1970-75; assoc. producer PBS-WNET/Dance in America, N.Y.C., 1975-76, producer, 1977—. NBC co-producer: He Makes Me Feel Like Dancin', 1984 (Acad. award, Emmy award, Chgo. Internat. Film Festival Silver Hugo, CINE Golden Eagle award, Christopher awards); prodr., dir. Who's Dancin' Now? (AFI L.A. Internat. Film Fest. Audience award, Best Documentary, Cine Golden Eagle award, Parents' Choice award), 1999; producer: PBS Dance in America: The Feld Ballet, 1979, The Green Table (with Joffrey Ballet), 1982, The Magic Flute (with N.Y.C. Ballet), 1983, San Francisco Ballet: A Song for Dead Warriors, 1984, A Choreographer's Notebook: Stravinsky Piano Ballets by Peter Martins, 1984, Balanchine, Parts I and II, 1984 (27th Ann. Internat. Film and TV awards of N.Y., gold medal Chgo. Internat. Film Festival Silver Plaque Monitor award, Emmy nomination), San Francisco Ballet in Cinderella, 1985 (Internat. Film and TV Festival of N.Y. gold medal, CINE Golden Eagle award, Parent's Choice award), Mark Morris, 1986 (CINE Golden Eagle award, Am. Film & Video Festival Red Ribbon award), Choreography by Jerome Robbins, 1986 (Chgo. Internat. Film Festival Silver Hugo, CINE Golden Eagle award), Dance Theatre of Harlem in A Streetcar Named Desire, 1986 (Chgo. Internat. Film Festival Silver Hugo), In Memory of...A Ballet by Jerome Robbins, 1987 (Chgo. Internat. Film Festival Silver Hugo, CINE Golden Eagle award), Agnes, the Indomitable de Mille, 1987 (Emmy award, Chgo. Internat. Film Festival Silver Hugo, CINE Golden Eagle award), Paul Taylor: Roses and Last Look, 1988, Balanchine and Cunningham: An Evening at Am. Ballet Theatre, 1988, La Sylphide (with the Pa./Milw. Ballet), 1989, A Night at The Joffrey, 1989, (Emmy nomination, Gold medal Internat. Film and TV Festival of N.Y., Best Video Creation IMZ Video Danse Awards, Gold Hugo award Chgo. Internat. Film Festival), The Search for Nijinsky's Rite of Spring, 1989 (producer/dir., Best Documentary IMZ Video Danse Awards, Internat. Film & TV Festival N.Y. Bronze medal), Baryshnikov Dances Balanchine, 1989 (Emmy nomination, finalist Internat. Film and TV Festival of N.Y.), Paul Taylor's Speaking in Tongues (Gold medal Internat. Film and TV Festival N.Y. Gold Plaque award Chgo. Internat. Film Festival), 1991, The Hard Nut with Mark Morris Dance Group, 1992 (Gold medal Internat. Film and TV Festival of N.Y., Emmy nomination), Balanchine Celebration, 1993 (with N.Y.C. City Ballet, Emmy nomination), The Wrecker's Ball, Three Dances by Paul Taylor, 1996 (Rose d'or de Montreaux Festival finalist); producer, dir. Bob Fosse/Steam Heat, 1990 (Emmy award, Ohio State award, Chgo. Film Festival Silver Plaque, Festival Internat. du Film Sur L'Art, Festival Rose d'Or, Montreux), A Tudor Evening with Am. Ballet Theatre, 1990, Balanchine in Am. with the N.Y.C. Ballet, 1990, Ballerinas: Dances by Peter Martins, 1991, A Renaissance Revisited, 1996 (N.Y. Festivals finalist award), (documentary) Variety and Virtuosity/American Ballet Theatre Now, 1998 (Chris award Columbus Internat. Film & Video Festival), Am. Ballet Theatre in Le Corsaire, (Emmy award 2000)From Broadway: Fosse, 2001 (CINE Golden Eagle award); producer PBS Great Performances: Out of Our Fathers' House, 1978; co-producer PBS Dance in America: Pilobolus Dance Theatre, 1977, Trailblazers of Modern Dance, 1977 (1st pl. 9th Ann. Dance Film and Video Festival), San Francisco Ballet: Romeo and Juliet, 1978, Choreography by Balanchine, Part III, 1978 (Chgo. Internat. Film Festival Silver Plaque, Emmy nomination), Choreography by Balanchine, Part IV, 1979 (Emmy award), The Martha Graham Dance Company: Clytemnestra, 1979 (Chgo. Internat. Film Festival Golden Hugo), Two Duets with Choreography by Jerome Robbins and Peter Martins, 1980, Nureyev and the Joffrey Ballet: In Tribute to Nijinsky, 1981 (Peabody award 1981, Emmy nomination), The Tempest: Live with the San Francisco Ballet, 1981, L'Enfant et Les Sortileges, 1981, Paul Taylor: Three Modern Classics, 1982, Paul Taylor: Two Landmark Dances, 1982, Bournonville Dances (with mems. ofN.Y.C. Ballet), 1982; co-producer PBS Theater in America: When Hell Freezes Over I'll Skate, 1979; prodr., dir. PBS Great Performances: The World of Jim Henson, 1994 (Parents Choice honor, 1995, Emmy award), Born to Be Wild: The Leading Men of American Ballet Theatre, 2002 (Festival Rose d'Or Montreux, N.Y. Festivals Gold World medal, Parents' Choice Silver Honor, Berkeley Video and Film Grand Festival Winner, Chris Statuette 2003, Ojai Film Festival Jury award), 22nd Festival Internat. Du Film Sur L'Art, 4th Constellation Change Screen Dance Festival, London, (with Am. Ballet Theare) The Dream, 2004; prodr. PBS Stage on Screen: The Man Who Came to Dinner, 2000, The Women, 2002. Mem. Dirs.' Guild Am., Acad. TV Arts and Scis. Office: Thirteen/WNET/Dance In America 450 W 33rd St Fl 6 New York NY 10001-2603

KINCAID, JAMAICA, writer; b. St. John's, Antigua and Barbuda, May 25, 1949; came to U.S., 1966; d. Annie Richardson; m. Allen Shawn; 2 children. Student pub. schs., St. John's; hon. degree, Williams Coll., 1991, L.I. Coll., 1991, Amherst Coll., 1995, Bard Coll., 1997, Middlebury Coll., 1998. Author: At the Bottom of the River, 1983 (Morton Dauwen Zabel award Am. Acad. and Inst. of Arts and Letters 1984), Annie John, 1985, A Small Place, 1988, Lucy, 1990, Autobiography of My Mother, 1996, My Brother, 1997; editor: My Favorite Plant, 1998, My Garden.

KINCAID, JUDITH WELLS, electronics company executive; b. Tampa, Fla., July 1, 1944; d. George Redfield and Louise Wells (Brodt) K.; one child: Jennifer Wells Maben. A, Stanford U., 1966, MS in Indsl. Engring., 1978. Sci. programmer med. rsch. Stanford (Calif.) U., 1972-77; info. systems mgr. Hewlett Packard Co., Palo Alto, Calif., 1978-2001, mgr. strategic systems, 1985-91; direct mktg. mgr. Hewlett Packard Corp., Palo Alto, Calif., 1991-95, dir. customer relationship mgmt., 1995-2001; pres. JK Assocs., Palo Alto, Calif., 2001—. Author: (book) Customer Relationship Management: Getting It Right, 2003. Bd. dirs. Ecumenical Hungar Program. Mem. Inst. Indsl. Engrs., Dir. Mktg. Assn. (privacy program chair 1998—, bus. to bus. ops. coun. 1998—), Ecumenical Hungar Program (bd. dirs. 2004-). Office: JK Assocs LLC 445 Sherman Ste W Palo Alto CA 94306 E-mail: jkincaid@jk-associates.com.

KINCAID, MARILYN COBURN, medical educator; b. Bennington, Vt., July 14, 1947; d. E. Robert and Jean A. (Flagg) Coburn; m. William Louis Kincaid, Dec. 21, 1970. AB, Mt. Holyoke Coll., 1969; MD, St. Louis U., 1975. Cert. Am. Bd. Ophthalmology, Am. Bd. Pathology. Asst. prof. ophthalmology & pathology U. Tex., San Antonio, 1982-86; assoc. prof. ophthalmology & pathology U. Mich. Med. Sch., Ann Arbor, 1986-87, St. Louis U. Sch. Medicine, 1989-94, prof., 1994—. Bd. dirs. Singular Vision Outreach, St. Louis. Author (book) Intraocular Lenses, 1989; contbr. articles to profl. jours. Fellow Am. Acad. Ophthalmology (Honor award 1990), Coll. Am. Pathologists; mem. Am. Assn. Ophthalmic Pathologists (sec.-treas. 1983-86). Avocations: sewing, embroidery. Office: St Louis U The Eye Inst 1755 S Grand Blvd Saint Louis MO 63104-1540

KIND, PHYLLIS, art gallery owner; BS in Chemistry, U. Pa., 1954, PhD in Phys. Chemistry, 1956; MA in English, U. Chgo., 1965. Mem. staff mdse. control Macy's, New York, N.Y., 1948-53; social worker N.Y.C. Dept. Welfare, 1954; 3d grade tchr. N.Y.C. Bd. Edn., 1956-59; various positions Chgo. Bd. Edn., 1960-67; owner Phyllis Kind Gallery, Chgo., 1967, N.Y.C., 1975—. Office: Phyllis Kind Gallery 136 Greene St New York NY 10012-3202

KINDBERG, SHIRLEY JANE, pediatrician; b. Newark, Feb. 4, 1936; d. John Bertil and Mabel Jacoba (deJonge) Kindberg; m. Charles Dale Coln, May 12, 1962; children: Sara Goldstein, Eric Coln, Lois Thompson, Ruth Coln, Mary Kohn. BS, Wheaton Coll., 1957; MD, Baylor U., 1961. Intern Tex. Children's Hosp., Houston, 1961-62; resident Children's Med. Ctr., Dallas, 1962-63; fellow in pediat. pulmonary disease U. Tex. S.W. Med. Sch., Dallas, 1963-64, fellow in pediat. infectious disease, 1965-67; pvt. practice gen. pediat. Dallas, 1969-81; pvt. practice newborns, 1981—, Active N.W. Bible Ch., 1977; [illegible] Dallas Symphony Assn. Fellow Am. Acad. Pediat. (mem. sect. perinatal pediat.); mem.: Tex. Pediat. Soc. (com. fetus and newborn, com. on injury and environ. hazards). Republican. Avocations: cooking, travel, music, fitness. Office: 3600 Gaston Ave Ste 406 Dallas TX 75246-1804 E-mail: colnoma@sbcglobal.net.

KINDER, JOANN STEPHANIE LOVE, music educator; b. Oak Hill, W.Va., July 20, 1956; d. John Samuel and Catherine (Kitty) Virginia Love; m. John Bradley Kinder, Apr. 14, 1981; children: Crystal Lee, John David. MusB, Coll. Arts and Scis., U. Del., 1978. Cert. music tchr. grades K-12 Fla. Dept. Edn., 2000. K - 12 music tchr. Indian River Acad., Fort Pierce, Fla., 1987—88; MIS coord. Savannas Hosp., Port St. Lucie, Fla., 1988—99; dir. bands So. Oaks Mid. Sch., Port St. Lucie, 1999—. Pvt. lesson tutor, Port St. Lucie, 1972—; performer/flautist Treasure Coast Flute Choir, Stuart, Fla., 1992—; substitute flautist Treasure Coast Symphony, Fort Pierce, 1996—; mem./flautist Stuart Cmty. Band, 1997—, Indian River Pops Orch., Stuart, 2000—. Mem.: Music Educator's Nat. Conf., Fla. Bandmasters Assn. (dist. 13 sec. 2002—). Avocation: music. Home: 3755 SW Karin St Port Saint Lucie FL 34953 Office: Southern Oaks Middle School Band 5500 NE St James Dr Port Saint Lucie FL 34983

KINDER, SUZANNE FONAY WEMPLE, historian, educator; b. Veszprem, Hungary, Aug. 1, 1927; arrived in U.S., 1948; d. Ernest Fonay and Magda Mihalyfy (Fonay) Szechenyi; m. George Barr Wemple, June 17, 1957 (dec. Apr. 1988); children: Peter Holland Wemple, Stephen Barr Wemple, Carolyn Wemple Steffey; m. Gordon T. Kinder, May 26, 1990. B, English Sisters, Budapest, Hungary, 1945, U. Calif., Berkeley, 1953; MLS, Columbia U., 1955, PhD, 1967. Instr. Stern Coll. Women, N.Y.C., 1962-63; asst. prof. Tchrs. Coll., Columbia U., N.Y.C., 1964-66; from asst. prof. to prof. Barnard Coll., Columbia U., N.Y.C., 1966-92, ret., 1992. Author: Atto of Vercelli: Church, State and Christian Society, 1979, Women in Frankish Society, 1981, 1983 (Berkshire prize, 1981); co-editor: Women in Medieval Society, 1985; contbr. articles to profl. jours. and encys. Recipient grant NEH, 1975, 80, 81-85, Spivack summer grant Barnard Coll., 1970, 81, Fulbright grant, 1982. Mem.: NOW, AAUP. Home: 1285 Gulf Shore Blvd N Naples FL 34102-4911

KINDERWATER, DIANE, state official; BA in Broadcast Journalism, U. Wis. Promotions and mktg. dir., prodr., nat. sales mgr.; media advisor, press sec. N.Mex. Legislature; press sec. Office Gov. Gary Johnson, Santa Fe, 1994—. Office: Office Gov State Capitol Bldg Rm 400 Santa Fe NM 87503-0001 Fax: 505-986-4364.

KINDZRED, DIANA, communications company executive; b. Chgo., Apr. 13, 1946; d. Bernell and Katherine L. (Gee) K. BA in Edn., Northwestern U., 1970—73; cert. in bio-med. scis., U. Chgo. Med. Ctr., 1998; postgrad., DePaul U., 2004. Owner, pres. Kindzred & Co. Comm., Chgo., 1978—. Bd. dirs. WomanMade Gallery. Contbr. articles to profl. jours.; author numerous poems. Bd. dirs. Jewish United Fund/Comm., 1985-95; co-founder midwest divsn. Am. Sephardi Fedn., Evanston, Ill., 1990; coord. Amnesty Internat., Evanston, 1991. With U.S. Army, 1964-67. Recipient Award for Poetry Nat. Libr. of Poetry, 1996, Cmty. Svc. award Fred Hampton Scholarship Fund, 1990, Fundraising award Jewish United Fund, 1994. Democrat. Jewish. Avocations: international travel, writing, lecturing, art, art history. Home and Office: 1530 N Sedgwick St Apt 306 Chicago IL 60610-5856 E-mail: berdikind@hotmail.com.

KING, ALMA JEAN, retired physical education educator, healthcare educator; b. Hamilton, Ohio, Feb. 28, 1939; d. William Lawrence and Esther Mary (Smith) K. BS in Edn., Miami U., Oxford, Ohio, 1961; MEd, Bowling Green State U., 1963; postgrad., Fla. Atlantic U., 1969, '92, Nova U., Ft. Lauderdale, Fla., 1979. Cert. elem. and secondry tchr., Ohio, all levels incl. coll., Fla. Tchr. health, physical edn. Rogers Middle Sch., Broward County Bd. Pub. Instrn., 1963-64; assoc. prof. health, phys edn., recreation, dance Broward C.C., Fort Lauderdale, Fla., 1964-94; ret., 1994. Dir. Intramurals and Extramurals Boward C.C., Fort Lauderdale, Fla., 1964-67, chair person Women's Affairs, 1978, health and safety com., 1975, faculty evaluation com. 1980-85, mem. faculty ins. benefits com. 1993-94. Sponsor Broward County Fire Fighters, Police; active mem. Police Benevolent Assn.; Historical Soc. Grantee Broward C.C. Staff Devel. Fund, 1988. Mem. AAHPERD, NEA, Fla. Edn. Assn., Fla. Assn for Health, Physical Edn., Recreation and Dance, Am. Assn. for Advancement of Health Edn., United Faculty of Fla., Fla. Assn. of C.C., Order of the Eastern Star (past Worthy Matron), Order of Shrine. Avocations: concerts, theater, art, historic museums, recreational activities. Home: 4310 Buchanan St Hollywood FL 33021-5917

KING, AMY CATHRYNE PATTERSON, retired mathematics educator, researcher; b. Douglas, Wyo., Dec. 30, 1928; d. John Francis and Mabel Eloise (Wear) Patterson; m. Don R. King, Aug. 8, 1949 (dec. 1985). BS, U. Mo., 1949; MA, U. Wichita, 1960; PhD, U. Ky., 1970. Tchr. Goddard (Kans.) Pub. Schs., 1956-58, U. Wichita, 1960-62; asst. instr. U. Kans., Lawrence, 1962-65; instr. Washburn U., Topeka, 1966-67; teaching asst. U. Ky., Lexington, 1967-70; prof. math. Ea. Ky. U., Richmond, 1970-98; Found. prof. emeritus, 1998—. Presenter in field. Author: instr.'s manual for College Algebra, 1981; (with Cecil B. Read) Pathways to Probability, 1963; contbr. (with others) articles to profl. jours. Departmental rep. for United Way, 1983; pres. Cokesbury Sunday Sch., Centenary United Meth. Ch., 1995-96, tchr. 3-yr.-olds. Recipient Award in Teaching, Ea. Ky. U., Richmond, 1982, Ea. Ky. U. Found. Professorship, 1993. Mem. Am. Math. Soc., Math. Assn. Am. (mem. various coms., 1st award for Disting. Coll. or Univ. Teaching 1992), Nat. Coun. Tchrs. Math., Assn. for Women of Math., Ky. Coun. Tchrs. Math. (Maths. Edn. Svc. and Achievement award 1998), Women in Math. Edn., Ky. Acad. Computer Users' Group, AAUP (treas. local chpt. 1984-86), Pi Mu. Epsilon, Kappa Mu Epsilon, Pi Lambda Theta, Sigma Delta Pi, Delta Kappa Gamma (pres. Omicron chpt., 1994-96), Sigma Xi. Phi Kappa Phi. Methodist. Office: Ea Ky Univ Wallace Bldg # 114 Richmond KY 40475-3102

KING, BARBARA JEAN, nurse; b. Cape Girardeau, Mo., June 28, 1941; d. Otto Samuel and Goldie Elizabeth (Clover) Fowler; m. Charles Basil King, Jr., Sept. 4, 1972; children: Otto Samuel, Christopher Lee. Student, Weatherford Jr. Coll., 1965; nursing degree, John Peter Smith Hosp. Sch. Profl. Nursing, 1969. RN, Tex. Head nurse pediat. and isolation County Hosp.; also ICU and CCU, Small Gen. Hosp., Ft. Worth, 1969-72; dir. nursing svc. Jarvis Hts. Nursing Ctr., Ft. Worth, 1976-77; dir. nursing svcs. Ft. Worth Rehab. Farm, 1978-80; staff nurse, asst. supr. shift Decatur (Tex.) Cmty. Hosp., 1983-85; staff nurse and supr. Burdgeport Hosp., Tex., 1986—; mgr., CEO, King Cons. Group for Homecare Mgmt., 2003—. Clin. supr., patient care coord. Hospice of Tejas; instr. vocat. nursing Cooke County Coll., Gainesville, Tex., 1981; clin. care supr. home health dept. Faith Community Hosp., 1992, assoc. dir. 1993—; patient care coord. Family Svcs. Home Health Svcs., Inc., 1994, adminstrn. for choice Choice Home Health Svcs., Inc., Nocona Gen. Hosp. Home Health, 1995, asst. dir., 1999; cons. convalescent centers and hosps. Chmn. child care com. Women of Moose, 1997—; ch. organist Bethel Bapt. Ch., assoc. pianist, 1996. Served with M.C., USN, 1962-65. Mem. Dirs. of Nursing Homes Assn. Tarrant County (v.p.). Democrat. Home: 202 S Trappier St Alvord TX 76225-6015

KING, BARBARA LEWIS, minister, lecturer; b. Houston, Aug. 26, 1930; d. Lee Andrew Lewis and Mildred Marie (Jackson) Shackelford; m. Moses King, Sept. 8, 1966 (div. Sept. 1970); 1 child, Michael. BA, Tex. So. U., 1955; MSW, Atlanta U., 1957, postgrad.; DDiv, Bethune Cookman Coll., 1988. Exec. dir. South Chgo. Community Svc. Assn., Chgo., 1966-68; dean community rels. Malcolm X campus Chgo. City Coll., 1967-69; instr. Sch. Social Work Atlanta U., 1970-71; dir. South Cen. Community Mental Health Ctr., 1971-73; dean students Spelman Coll., 1973-74; founder, minister Hillside Internat. Truth Ctr., 1971—; founder, pres. Barbara King Sch. Ministry, 1977—. Host Sta. WVEU, Atlanta, 1987—, WXIA, Atlanta, 1980-85, Channel 8, Atlanta, 1980-85. Author: What is a Miracle?, 1973, Do I Need a Flood, 1983, Transform Your Little Book, 1989. Mem. nat. rules com. Dem. Nat. Conv., Ga., 1984; mem. State Com. on the Life and History of Black Georgians, Atlanta, 1986, Ethics Bd. Met. Atlanta, 1986, Joint Bd. Family Practice, Atlanta, 1986. Mem. Am. Mgmt. Assn., Internat. New Thought Alliance (v.p. 1972), Christian Coun. Met. Atlanta (trustee 1985), Internat. Congress Women Ministries (internat. pres. 1975), Acad. Cert. Social Workers, Nat. Assn. Social Workers, Women's C. of C. in Atlanta, Zeta Phi Beta. Office: Hillside Internat Truth Ctr 2450 Cascade Rd SW Atlanta GA 30311-3226

KING, BETSY, professional golfer; b. Reading, Pa., Aug. 13, 1955; Winner U.S. Open-Women, 1989, 1990, LPGA, 1992; 3d ranked woman LPGA Tour, 1992. LPGA tour victories include: Orlando Classic, 1984, Columbia Savings Classic, 1984, Henredon Classic, 1986, Rail Charity Classic, 1986, 88, Tucson Open, 1987, Dinah Shore Invitational, 1987, McDonald's Classic, 1987, Atlantic City Classic, 1987, Kemper Open, 1988, Cellular One-Ping Championship, 1988, Jamaica Classic, 1989, Nabisco Dinah Shore, 1990, U.S. Women's Open, 1989, 1990, Corning Classic, 1991, Mazda Championship, 1992, ShopRite Classic, 1995, Corestates Betsy King Classic, 1997, Solheim Cup, 1998. Inductee LPGA Hall of Fame, 1995. Achievements include LPGA leading money winner, 1984, 89, 93. Office: LPGA 100 International Golf Dr Daytona Beach FL 32124-1092

KING, BILLIE JEAN MOFFITT, former professional tennis player; b. Long Beach, Calif., Nov. 22, 1943; d. Willard J. Moffitt; m. Larry King, Sept. 17, 1965. Student, Calif. State U. at Los Angeles, 1961-64. Amateur tennis player, 1958-67; profl., 1968—84; mem. Tennis Challenge Series, 1977, 78; dir., ofcl. spokesperson World TeamTennis, Chgo., 1985—; commentator, analyst Wimbledon and other tennis events HBO, N.Y.C. Winner, Singles champion tournaments include: Wimbledon, 1966-68, 72, 73, 75, U.S. Open, 1967, 71, 72, 74, Australian Open, 1968, French Open, 1972; Doubles champion Wimbledon, 1961, 62, 65, 67, 68, 70-73, U.S. Open, 1965, 67, 74, 80, French Open, 1972; mixed doubles champion Wimbledon, 1967, 71, 73, U.S. Open, 1967, 71, 73, French, 1967, 70, Australian, 1968; winner 29 Virginia Slims singles titles, 1970-77, 4 Colgate titles, 1977, Fedn. Cup, 1963-67, 76-79, Wightman Cup, 1961-67, 70, 77, 78; World Tennis Team All-Star, 3 times; host Colgate women's sports TV spl. The Lady is a Champ, 1975; co-founder, dir. Kingdom, Inc., San Mateo, Calif.; sports commentator ABC-TV, 1975-78; co-founder, pub. WomenSports mag., 1974—; founder Women's Tennis Assn., 1973; first woman commr. (Team Tennis League) profl. sports history, 1984; TV commentator HBO-Sports Wimbledon coverage; capt. Fed. Cup for USA, 1995; cons. Virginia Slims World Championship Series; bd. dirs. Challenger Ctr.; amb. Adventures in Movement Charity; coach Fed. Cup Women's Tennis Team, 1995-96, USA Olympic Women's Tennis Team, 1996; nat. spokesperson Literary Vols. Am.; tennis tchr. to profls. Author: Tennis to Win, 1970, (with Kim Chapin) Billie Jean, 1974, (with Cynthia Starr) We Have Come a Long Way, The Story of Women's Tennis, 1988. Named Sportsperson of Yr., Sports Illustrated, 1972; Woman Athlete of Yr., A.P., 1967, 73, Top Woman Athlete of Yr., 1972; Woman of Yr., Time mag., 1976, One of 10 Most Powerful Women in Am., Harper's Bazaar, 1977, One of 25 Most Influential Women in Am., World Almanac, 1977, One of 100 Most Important Ams. of 20th Century, Life mag., 1990; named to Internat. Tennis Hall of Fame, 1987, Nat. Women's Hall of Fame, 1990; Lifetime Achievement award, March of Dimes, 1994. Office: Billie Jean King Ste 983 960 Harlem Ave Glenview IL 60025*

KING, BONNIE LA VERNE, education educator; b. Denver, Aug. 28, 1942; d. Carl A. and Myrtle Carlson; m. Hal K. King, Aug. 15, 1964 (dec. Nov. 1991); children: Mark, Christina, Peter. BA in Elem. Edn., U. Denver, 1964; postgrad., U. Colo.; MA in Ednl. Adminstrn., U. Hawaii, 1994. Tchr. Denver Pub. Schs., 1964-66, Cheyenne Mountain Pub. Schs., Colorado Springs, Colo., 1966-74, State of Hawaii Dept. of Edn., Maui, 1989—; lectr., instr. elem. reading and literacy U. Hawaii Sch. Edn., 1994—. Instr., lectr. McGill U., Montreal, 1997-98; real estate broker, Colo., 1976-89; coord. early childhood vision screening program. Contbr. poetry to anthologies. Vol. Colorado Springs Fine Arts Ctr., 1973-86; docent, art tchr. Montreal Museum of Fine Arts; vol., instr. Alzheimer's Assn.; chmn. vols. Spl. Olympics; U.S. figure skating judge, 1980—; ch. deacon; mem. Honolulu Symphony Choral. Recipient Gold Medal U.S. Figure Skating Competition, 1961. Mem. AAUW, Internat. Reading Assn. Avocations: swimming, skiing.

KING, CAROLE (CAROLE KLEIN), songwriter, singer; b. Bklyn., Feb. 9, 1942; m. Gerry Goffin; m. Charles Larkey; m. Rick Evers, 1977 (dec., 1978); m. Rick Sorensen, 1982; children: Louise, Sherry, Molly, Levi. Student, Queens Coll. Co-writer (with Gerry Goffin) numerous songs, 1960-68, including Will You Still Love Me Tomorrow?, He's a Rebel, Go Away, Little Girl, Up on the Roof, Natural Woman, The Locomotion, Take Good Care of My Baby, It's Too Late; albums include Tapestry, 1971 (4 Grammy awards), Simple Things, Pearls: Songs of Goffin and King, Music, 1971, Rhymes & Reasons, 1972, Fantasy, 1973, Wrap Around Joy, 1974, Really Rosie, 1975, Thoroughbred, 1976, Her Greatest Hits: Songs of Long Ago, 1978, One To One, 1982, Speeding Time, 1983, City Streets, 1989, Legacy, 1989, Colour Of Your Dreams, 1993, In Concert, 1994, A Natural Woman, 1994, The Carnegie Hall Concert, 1996, Pearls/Time Gone By, 1999, The Early Years, 2000, Super Hits, 2000, Love Makes the World, 2001; composer music for films Head, 1968, Murphy's Romance, 1985, The Care Bears Movie, 1985; assoc. prodr. film The Changeling, 1998; off-Broadway theater appearance in A Minor Incident, 1989; Broadway appearance in Blood Brothers, 1994; appeared in films Dynamite Johnson, 1978, Murphy's Romance, 1985, Russkies, 1987, TV film Hider in the House, 1989, TV series The Tracy Ullman Show. Inducted in Rock & Roll Hall of Fame, 1990. Office: Carole King Prodns 11684 Ventura Blvd 273 Studio City CA 91604*

KING, CAROLYN DINEEN, federal judge; b. Syracuse, N.Y., Jan. 30, 1938; d. Robert E. and Carolyn E. (Bareham) Dineen; children: James Randall, Philip Randall, Stephen Randall. AB summa cum laude, Smith Coll., 1959; LLB, Yale U., 1962. Bar: D.C. 1962, Tex. 1963. Assoc. Fulbright & Jaworski, Houston, 1962—72; ptnr. Childs, Fortenbach, Beck & Guyton, Houston, 1972—78, Sullivan, Bailey, King, Randall & Sabom, Houston, 1978—79; judge U.S. Ct. Appeals (5th cir.), Houston, 1979—99, chief judge, 1999—; with U.S. Jud. Conf., 1999—, exec. com., 2000—, chmn. exec. com., 2002—. Trustee, exec. com., treas. Houston Ballet Found., 1967—70; Houston dist. adv. coun. SBA, 1972—76; Dallas regional panel Pres.' Commn. White House Fellowships, 1972—76, mem. commn., 1977; bd. dirs. Houston chpt. Am. Heart Assn., 1978—79; nat. trustee Palmer Drug Abuse Program, 1978—79; trustee, sec., treas., chmn. audit com., fin. com., mgmt. com. United Way Tex. Gulf Coast, 1979—85; trustee, exec. com., chmn. bd. trustees U. St. Thomas, 1988—98. Recipient Smith Coll. medal, 1997, Outstanding Alumnus award, Phi Beta Kappa Alumni of Greater Houston, 1998; rsch. fellow, Ctr. for Am. and Internat. Law, 1989—. Mem.: ABA, Philos. Soc. Tex., Houston Bar Assn., State Bar

Tex., Am. Law Inst. (coun. 1991—, chmn. membership com. 1997—99), Fed. Bar Assn. Roman Catholic. Office: US Ct Appeals 11020 US Courthouse 515 Rusk Avenue Houston TX 77002-2694

KING, CLAUDIA LOUAN, film producer, lecturer; b. Merced, Calif., May 1, 1940; d. Alvin Cecil and Thelma May (Matthew) K.; m. Douglas McLean, July 10, 1965 (div. 1975); children: Kia Gabrielle, Kendra Sue. BA, U. Calif., 1963; MA, Ind. U., 1969. Lectr. U. Fla., Gainesville, 1969-70; asst. prof. U. Nev., Las Vegas, 1973-79; producer Source 17 Prodns., Santa Monica, Calif., 1979-85; freelance producer Chico, Calif., 1985—. Author: Life Mastery: A Self-Esteem Handbook for Adults and Children, 1994, (screenplays) The Garden of Eden, 1983, My Sister's Keeper, 1986, (documentary) The Evolution of Women, 1988, 92 (short stories) In the Realm of the Invisible, 1991; prodr.: Rape is Everybody's Concern, 1978, Los Angeles Personally Yours, 1986; pub. Light Paths Communications, 1994—; artist "Mandalas and Altar Pieces" Steam and Bean, Chico, Calif.; contbr. articles to art mags. Mem. Chico Annie's Com. for Dramatic Arts, 1996; v.p. Chico Dharma Study, 1998; mem. Chico Buddhist Coun.; mem. choir Calif. State U., 1996—; bd. dirs Chico Dharma Study. Carnegie grantee, 1969; Nev. Endowment for Humanities grantee, 1978. Mem.: CSU Chico Choir, Women in Film. Democrat. Avocations: camping, opera. Home: PO Box 3576 Chico CA 95927-3576 E-mail: litpaths@shocking.com.

KING, CORETTA SCOTT (MRS. MARTIN LUTHER KING JR.), educational association administrator, lecturer, writer, concert singer; b. Heiberger, Ala., Apr. 27, 1927; d. Obidiah and Bernice (McMurray) Scott; m. Martin Luther King, Jr., June 18, 1953 (dec. Apr. 1968); children: Yolanda Denise, Martin Luther III, Dexter Scott, Bernice Albertine. AB, Antioch Coll., 1951; Mus.B., New Eng. Conservatory Music, 1954, Mus.D., 1971; L.H.D., Boston U., 1969, Marymount-Manhattan Coll., 1969, Morehouse Coll., 1970; H.H.D., Brandeis U., 1969, Wilberforce U., 1970, Bethune-Cookman Coll., 1970, Princeton U., 1970; LL.D., Bates Coll., 1971. Voice instr. Morris Brown Coll., Atlanta, 1962; commentator CNN, Atlanta, 1980—; lectr., writer; founding pres., chief exec. officer Martin Luther King Jr. Ctr. for Nonviolent Social Change Inc. Chairwoman Martin Luther King, Jr. Fed. Holiday Commn.; mem. Black Leadership Forum, Black Leadership Roundtable. Author: My Life With Martin Luther King, Jr., 1969, The Words of Martin Luther King, 1983; contbr. articles to mags.; syndicated newspaper columnist N.Y. Times Syndication Sales Corp., 1986-90, United Features Syndicate, 1990-94; concert debut, Springfield, Ohio, 1948; numerous concerts throughout U.S., concerts, India, 1959, performances, Freedom Concert. Del. to White House Conf. Children and Youth, 1960; sponsor Com. for Sane Nuclear Policy, Com. on Responsibility, Moblzn. to End War in Viet Nam, 1966, 67, Margaret Sanger Meml. Found.; mem. So. Rural Action Project, Inc.; pres. Martin Luther King, Jr. Found.; chmn. Commn. on Econ. Justice for Women; mem. exec. com. Nat. Com. Inquiry; co-chmn. Clergy and Laymen Concerned about Vietnam, Nat. Com. for Full Employment, 1974; pres. Martin Luther King Jr. Center for Nonviolent Social Change; co chairperson Nat. Com. Full Employment; mem. exec. bd. Nat. Health Ins. Com.; active YWCA; bd. dirs. So. Christian Leadership Conf., Martin Luther King, Jr. Found. Gt. Britain; trustee Robert F. Kennedy Meml. Found., Ebenezer Bapt. Ch. Recipient Nat. Coun. Negro Women Ann. Brotherhood award, 1957, Outstanding Citizenship award Montgomery (Ala.) Improvement Assn., 1959, Merit award St. Louis Argus, 1960, Distinguished Achievement award Nat. Orgn. Colored Women's Clubs, 1962, Louise Waterman Wise award Am. Jewish Congress Women's Aux., 1963, Myrtle Wreath award Cleve. Hadassah, 1965, award for excellence in field human relations Soc. Family of May, 1968, Universal Love award Premio San Valentine Com., 1968, Wateler Peace prize, 1968, Dag Hammarskjold award, 1969, Pacem in Terris award Internat. Overseas Service Found., 1969, Leadership for Freedom award Roosevelt U., 1971, Martin Luther King Meml. medal Coll. City N.Y., 1971, Internat. Viareggio award, 1971, Eugene V. Debs award, 1982, numerous others; named Woman of Year Utility Club N.Y.C., 1962, Woman of Year Nat. Assn. Radio and TV Announcers, 1968, UAW Social Justice award, 1980. Mem. Nat. Council Negro Women (Ann. Brotherhood award 1957), Women Strike for Peace (del. disarmament conf. Geneva, Switzerland 1962, citation for work in peace and freedom 1963), Women's Internat. League for Peace and Freedom, NAACP, United Ch. Women (bd. mgrs.), Alpha Kappa Alpha (hon.) Baptist (mem. choir, guild adviser). Club: Links (Human Dignity and Human Rights award Norfolk chpt. 1964). Address: Martin Luther King Jr Ctr 449 Auburn Ave NE Atlanta GA 30312-1503*

KING, ELAINE A. curator, art historian, critic; b. Oak Park, Ill., Apr. 12, 1947; d. Casimir Stanley and Catherine Mary (Chmel) Czerwien. BS, No. Ill. U., 1968, MA, 1974; PhD, Northwestern U., 1986. Cert. Fine Arts Appraisal, 2002. Intern George Eastman House, Rochester, NY, 1977; lectr. history of photography Northwestern U., Evanston, Ill., 1977-81; curator Dittmar Meml. Gallery, Evanston, 1978-81; dir. Artemesia Gallery, Chgo., 1976-77; exec. dir., chief curator Carnegie-Mellon Art Gallery, Pitts., 1985—91; prof. critical theory and history of art Carnegie Mellon U., Pitts., 1981—. Bd. dirs. Mountain Lake Criticism Conf., Blacksburg, Va., 1982-91; ind. curator, 1991—; exhbn. rev. panel Pa. Coun. on Arts, 1991; exec. dir., chief curator Contemporary Art Ctr., Cin., 1993-95; guest curator Pitts. Cultural Trust, 1992, 93, 95, 96; 10 year Retrospective of Diane Samuels, Mus. of Art, Györ, Hungary, Györ, 1999, bd. dirs. Mid-Am. Coll. Art Assn.; panel chair Midwest CAA Conf., 1997, 2003; co-coord. Wats:ON Festival, 1996-2003; adj. prof. U. Cin., 1994; art critic-in-residence U. Ariz., Tucson; Am. guest curator Hungarian Bienale Exhbn. II, Györ, 1993, Master Graphic Arts Internat. Biennial, 1995, 97, 99, 2001, 03; pres. Internat. Jury, 2003; panelist NEA Visual Arts, 1993; grant reviewer Inst. Mus. Sci., Washington, 1994, Ohio Arts Coun. fellowship and grant evaluator, 1994-95; Internat. Rev. panel, AAUW internat. fellowships, Washington, D.C., 2000-03; mem. organizing com. Midwest Mus. Con., 1994-95; Am. rep. Inter Arts Spring 1996 Budapest (Hungary) Crossroads, Am. critic rep. AICA Conf. The Edge, Zagreb, Croatia, Chair Coll. Arts Assoc. Com. disting. exhbn. award, 1995-98, AICA XXXIV Congress Internat. Art Critics, Zagreb, AICA conf. ctrl. European cross-roads, 1996, 97, AICA Congress 2000, London, speaker XXXIII Congress Internat. Art Critics, Warsaw, Poland, 1999, XXXIV Congress Internat. AICA, London, 2000, XXXVII Congress Internat. AICA, Barbados, 2003; plenary spkr. Prague Triennial Symposium, Prague, Czech Republic, 2001; juror exhbn. 3rd Prague Internat; nominator 4th Prague Internat., 2004; spkr. in field. Curator, author: Crossing Borders: USA/Europe, Alleghany Coll. Art Galleries, 2000, Marking, 1999, The Figure As Fiction, 1993, Alfred DeCredico: Drawings, 1985-93, Emily Cheng: Monoprints, 1994, (exhbn. catalogues) Barry LeVa: 1966-88, Mel Bochner: 1973-85, Elizabeth Murray: Drawings: 1980-86, Michael Gitlin: Sculpture & Drawings, 1990, New Generations: Chgo., 1990, New Generations: N.Y., 1991, Magdalena Jetalová, 1991, Martin Puryear: Sculpture & Drawings, 1987, Abstraction/Abstraction, Tishan Hsu, Paintings, Drawings & Sculpture, 1987, N.Y. Painting Today, Michel Gerand: Drawings and Site Works, 1989, Drawings and Sculpture, 1990, Art in the Age of Information, 1993, Five Artists at the Airport: Insights into Public Art, 1992, Martha Rosler: In Place of the Public, 1994, Shari Zolla, 1997, Lyzabeth Sallan: 2 Installations, Light Into Art: From Video to Virtual Reality (also booklet), David Humphrey: Paintings and Drawings 1987-95 (also catalogue), others; author: The Misunderstood Patron, The National Endowment for the Arts; critic-in-residence Sch. Art, San Juan, PR; free lance art critic, Washington Post, Grapheion, Tema Celeste, & Sculpture, Cin. Enquirer; Grapheion; Art on Paper, Pitt. Post-Gazette, art critic in residence Delaware Contemporary Ctr. for the Arts, 1992, Mid-Atlantic Arts Fellow, 1991, No. Ill. U., 1997; corr. critic, regional editor Diaglogue, Columbus, Ohio, 1984-89; corr. critic Sculpture; contbr. articles to profl. jours. Active Dem. Party, Evanston, ward judge, 1977-78, precinct capt., 1977. Recipient Hunt Art award, 1977; Art Critics fellow Pa. Coun. on Arts, 1985, 89, 95, 99, 2000; rsch. fellow Smithsonian Inst., 1998, sr. rsch. fellow, 2000—; faculty rsch. grantee, 1985, 87, 89-90, 96-99, 2002, Grant Trust for Mut. Understanding, Rockefeller Found., 1994, Thendora Found., 1995; mem. tech. com., cmty. program scholar Pa. Humanities Coun., 1997; Nat. Mus. Am. Art, 2000, sr. rsch. fellow, short-term rsch. fellow Smithsonian Instn., Nat. Portrait Gallery, 2001; spl. initiatives grantee Pa. Coun. on Arts, 2000; grantee, IREX, 2000; rsch. fellow Inst. for Art History, Acad. Scis., Budapest, Hungary, 2002; fellow Ctrl. European Cultural Inst., 2002. Mem. Coll. Art Assn., Am. Assn. Mus., Assn. Historians Am. Art, Internat. Assn. Art Critics (Am. sect.), Art Table, Midwest Coll. Art Assn. Avocations: cooking, gardening, tennis, swimming, sailing. Office: Carnegie Mellon U Coll Fine Arts Pittsburgh PA 15213 E-mail: eaking13@yahoo.com.

KING, GWENDOLYN BAIR, former government staff member, public speaker; b. Hartsville, S.C., Oct. 27, 1915; d. William Parlor and Mary Margaret (Scurry) Bair; m. LaBruce Ward King, Dec. 26, 1937; children: John LaBruce King, Margaret Gwendolyn King Farrow. AB, Coker Coll., 1936. With asst. pers. office Libr. Congress, Washington, 1937-39; sec., dir. Libr. Congress, Union Catalog, Washington, 1939-43; asst. to appointments sec. for the President The White House, Washington, 1953-69, dir. correspondence for Pat Nixon, 1969-74; pub. speaker on White House career Calif., 1977—. Contbr. to Presidential Records, The Nat. Archives, Washington, 1988. Dir. Speakers' Bur., Home Hospice, Santa Rosa, Calif., 1985, cert. caregiver, 1982-84; mem. Oakmont Archtl. Com., Santa Rosa Symphony League. Named Paul Harris Fellow, Rotary Internat., 1983, Citizen of the Day, KABL, San Francisco, 1983. Mem. AAUW, Newcomers Club (pres. Santa Rosa chpt. 1977-78), Oakmont Book Club (chmn. 1981-82), Oakmont Golf Club (sec. 1986), Saturday Afternoon Club, Oakmont Classical Music Soc., PEO. Republican. Avocations: golf, bridge, gardening, travel. Home: 451 Pythian Rd Santa Rosa CA 95409-6346

KING, GWENDOLYN S. retired utility company executive, former federal official; b. East Orange, N.J. d. Frank M. and Henryne (Walker) Stewart; m. Colbert I. King. BA cum laude, Howard U., 1962; postgrad., George Washington U.; hon. doctorate, U. Md., 1990, U. New Haven, 1992. Legis. asst. to Sen. John Heinz, Washington, 1978-79; dir. Commonwealth of Pa. Office, Washington, 1979-86; dep. asst. to the pres. and dir. Office Intergovtl. Affairs, The White House, Washington, 1986-88; exec. v.p. Gogol & Assocs., 1988-89; commr. Social Security Adminstrn., Balt., 1989-92; sr. v.p. corp. and pub. affairs PECO Energy Corp., Phila., 1992-98; pres. Podium Prose, LLC, Washington. Bd. dirs. Lockheed Martin, Countrywide Fin. Corp., Marsh & McLennan Cos., Monsanto Corp. Mem. Pres.'s Commn. to Strengthen Social Security, 2001. Recipient Drum Major for Justice award So. Christian Leadership Conf., 1990, Disting. Alumni award Howard U., 1991, Black Achievement Bus. and Fin. award Ebony Mag., 1992. Mem. Assn. Corp. Dirs. (bd. dirs.). Office: Podium Prose LLC Ste 1012 1025 Connecticut Ave NW Washington DC 20036

KING, HEATHER ANN, freelance journalist; b. Waukegan, Ill., Oct. 27, 1939; d. Marion Vincent and Elaine Ann (Ramage) Warton; m. Peter Austin Randall, Feb. 29, 1964 (div. July 1982); children: Holly Elizabeth, Melissa Leigh; m. Richard Harding King, Aug. 11, 1984. BA, Macalester Coll., St. Paul, 1960; student, Cordon Bleu Sch. Cooking, 1964-65. Mgmt. trainee Dayton Co., Mpls., 1960-61; indsl. editor, pub. rels. Luth. Brotherhood Ins. Soc., Mpls., 1961-64; asst. regional adminstr. Jefferson County ARC, Lakewood, Colo., 1965-67; freelance writer, editor Mpls., 1970-80; feature writer Mpls. Star, 1980-82; freelance copywriter, editl. cons., pub. rels., mktg. Mpls., 1982—. Bd. dirs. ARC. Editor/copywriter: The Global Gourmet, Ten Thousand Tastes of Minnesota, Savor the Flavor, The Best of Byerly's Vol. I & II; awarded U.S. Patent for gift/gourmet bag in Oct. 1994. Bd. dirs. AAUW, Minn. Orch., Friends of the Mpls. Inst. Arts, Edina Art Ctr., Edina Newcomers, Jr. League Mpls.; adv. bd. Concordia Lang. Villages; past pres. Edina Federated Women's Club; house com., bulletin, Art Godfrey House, scholarship co-chair, food chair Bus. Women's Forum, Woman's Club of Mpls.; fundraising Twin Cities Pub. TV; comm., outreach, stewardship Westminster Presbyn. Ch.; group facilitator Metro Drug Awareness Program; mem. LWV, Blake Sch. Parents Assn. Recipient Nat. Book awards, Tabasco Cmty. Cookbook award McIlhenny Co., 1993. Mem. Nat. Assn. Female Execs., Macalester Coll. Alumni Assn. (fundraising, reunion com.), Mpls. Club, Interlachen Country Club, 1006 Summit Ave. Soc. Republican. Avocations: traveling, boating, reading, cultural events. Office: Copy à la King 4445 W 77th St Edina MN 55435-5133 Home: 5901 View Ln Minneapolis MN 55436-1824

KING, HELEN EMORI, dean; b. Stockton, Calif., Apr. 10, 1936; d. Susumu and Sumi Emori; m. William King, Aug. 5, 1973; children: Bill, Brian, Donna, Debbie. BS, Loma Linda U., 1959, MS, 1965; PhD, Boston U., 1973. Asst. prof. Boston U., 1973-75; dept. chmn., prof. Atlantic Union Coll., South Lancaster, Mass., 1978-81; dean sch. nursing Loma Linda (Calif.) U., 1981—. Mem. Nat. League Nursing, Sigma Theta Tau. Office: Loma Linda U Sch Nursing Loma Linda CA 92350-0001 E-mail: hKing@sn.llu.edu

KING, IMOGENE M. retired nursing educator; b. West Point, Iowa, Jan. 30, 1923; Diploma, St. John's Hosp., 1945; BSN, St. Louis U., 1948, MSN, 1957; EdD, Columbia U., 1961; PhD (hon.), So. Ill. U., 1980, Loyola U., Chgo., 1998. Instr. med.-surg. nursing, asst. DON St. John's Hosp., St. Louis, 1947-58; from asst. prof. nursing to assoc. prof. Loyola U, Chgo., 1961-66, prof., dir. grad. program in nursing, 1972-80; prof. U. South Fla., Tampa, 1980-90, dir. rsch., 1982-85, prof. emeritus, 1990—. Asst. chief rsch. grants br. div. nursing HEW, Washington, 1966-68; prof., dean sch. nursing Ohio State U., Columbus, 1968-72; mem. def. adv. com. on women in svcs. Dept. Def., 1972-75; adj. prof. U. Miami Sch. Nursing, 1986-89; cons. VA Hosp., health care agencies. Author: Toward a Theory for Nursing, 1971, transl. to Japanese, 1975, A Theory for Nursing: Systems, Concepts, Process, 1981, transl. to Japanese, 1983, transl. to Spanish, 1985, Curriculum and Instruction in Nursing, 1986; mem. editl. bd. Theoria: The Journal of Nursing Theorica, Malmo, Sweden; contbr. articles to profl. jours., chpts. to books. Alderman, chmn. fin. com. Ward 2, Wood Dale, Ill., 1975-79; bd. dirs. operation PAR Inc., Pinellas County, Fla., 1990-92. Recipient Founders award St. Louis U., 1969, Recognition of Contbns. to Nursing Edn. award Columbia U. Tchrs. Coll., 1983, Disting. Scholar award U. So. Fla., 1988-89, Award for Outstanding Cmty. Svc. U. Tampa, 1997, Imogene King Rsch. award U. Tampa, 1997, Fla. Gov.'s medal for contbn. to nursing and health care, 1997, Dirs. award Fla. League Nursing, 1997. Fellow Am. Acad. Nursing (hon.); mem. ANA (conv. lectr. 1996, Jessie M. Scott award 1996, Hall of Fame 2004), Ill. Nurses Assn. (highest recognition award 1975, award 19th dist. 1975), Fla. Nurses Assn. (life, dir. region 2 1981-83, 2d v.p. 1983-85, bd. dirs. 1997-2001, Nurse of Yr. 1984, Nursing Rsch. award 1985, Hall of Fame award 2003), Dist. IV Fla. Nurses Assn. (del. to Fla. Nurses Assn. 1981-96, pres.-elect 1982-83, del. to ANA conv. 1982-2003, pres. 1983-84, Advancing the Nursing Profl. award), Fla. Nurses Found. (sec. 1986-88, pres. 1988-91), Sigma Theta Tau (counselor Delta Beta chpt. 1981-83, pres.-elect 1986-87, pres. 1987-89, disting. lectr. 1990-91, co-chmn. biennial conv. 1991, nominating com. 1993-95, Founders award for excellence in nursing edn. 1989, life, Virginia Henderson fellow 1993) Sigma Theta Tau, Phi Kappa Phi (scholar award 1988).

KING, JANE CUDLIP COBLENTZ, volunteer educator; b. Iron Mountain, Mich., May 4, 1922; d. William Stacey and Mary Elva (Martin) Cudlip; m. George Samuel Coblentz, June 8, 1942 (dec. June 1989); children: Bruce Harper, Keith George, Mary Allison Coblentz Patch; m. James E. King, August 23, 1991 (dec. Jan. 1994). BA, Mills Coll., 1942. Mem. Sch. Resource and Career Guidance Vols., Inc., Atherton, Calif., 1965-69, pres., CEO, 1969—. Part-time exec. asst. to dean of admissions Mills Coll., 1994-99. Proofreader, contbr. Mills Coll. Quarterly mag. Life gov. Royal Children's Hosp., Melbourne, Australia, 1963—; pres. United Menlo Park (Calif.) Homeowner's Assn., 1994—; nat. pres. Mills Coll. Alumnae Assn., 1969-73, bd. trustees, 1975-83; bd. govs. Mills Coll. Alumnae Assn., 1966-73, 75-83, 98-2000, v.p., 2001—. Named Vol. of Yr., Sequoia Union H.S. Dist., 1988, Disting. Woman Mid-Peninsula (forerunner San Mateo County Women's Hall of Fame), 1975; recipient Golden Acorn award for Outstanding Cmty. Svc., Menlo Park C. of C., 1991. Mem. AAUW (Menlo-Atherton br. pres. 1994-96, v.p. programs 1996-97, editor Directory and Acorn, 1994—), Atherlons, Palo Alto (Calif.) Area Mills Coll. Club (pres. 1986), Phi Beta Kappa. Episcopalian. Avocations: reading, gardening.

KING, JANET CARLSON, nutrition educator, researcher; b. Red Oak, Iowa, Oct. 3, 1941; d. Paul Emil and Norma Carolina (Anderson) Carlson; m. Charles Talmadge King, Dec. 25, 1967; children: Matthew, Samuel. BS, Iowa State U., 1963; PhD, U. Calif., Berkeley, 1972. Dietitian Fitzsimmons Gen. Hosp., Denver, 1964-67; NIH postdoctoral fellow dept. nutrition sci. U. Calif., Berkeley, 1972-73, asst. prof. nutrition dept. nutrition sci., 1973-78, assoc. prof. nutrition dept. nutrition sci., 1978-83, prof. nutrition dept. nutrition sci., 1983—, chair dept. nutrition sci., 1988-94; dir. USDA Western Human Nutrition Rsch.Ctr., Davis, Calif., 1995—2002; sr. scientist Children's Hosp. Oakland Rsch. Inst., 2003—; prof. internal medicine U. Calif., Davis, 2003—. Frances E. Fischer Meml. nutrition lectr. Am. Dietetic Assn. Found., 1985, Lotte Arnrich Nutrition lectr. Iowa State U., 1985; Massee lectr. N.D., 1991, Lydia J. Roberts lectr. U. Chgo., 1995, Virginia A. Beal lectr. U. Mass., 1998; vis. prof. U. Calif., Davis, 1998—. Contbr. articles to Jour. Am. Diet. Assn., Am. Jour. Clin. Nutrition, Jour. Nutrition, Nutrition Rsch., Obstetrics and Gynecology, Brit. Jour. Obstetrics and Gynaecology. Recipient Lederle Labs. award in human nutrition Am. Inst. Nutrition, 1989, Internat. award in human nutrition, 1996. Mem. AAAS, Nat. Acad. Scis. Inst. Medicine, Am. Dietetic Assn., Am. Inst. Nutrition, Am. Soc. Clin. Nutrition. Office: Childrens Hosp Oakland Rsch Inst 5700 MKL Jr Way Oakland CA 94609 E-mail: jking@chori.org.

KING, JANEY HAMPTON, music educator, vocalist, educator; b. Port Saint Joe, Fla., Aug. 14, 1941; d. Howell Morton Hampton, Jr. and Mildred Francis Hampton; m. Richard Byron Robbins (div. Feb. 14, 1967); children: Richard Robbins, Michael Robbins; m. Fred Harlan King, Dec. 18, 1971. AA, Pensacola (Fla.) Jr. Coll., 1965—68; BA, U. W. Fla., Penscol, 1970; Master of Arts, University Of West Florida, Pensacola, Florida, 1976—78. Cert. tchr. Fla., 1970. Tchr.. choral dir. Pensacola (Fla.) Acad. of Arts and Scis., 1970—75; adjunct voice instr. U. West Fla., Pensacola, 1975—77; teacher/choral dir. Englewood HS, Jacksonville, Fla., 1979—89, Mayport Middle Sch., Atlantic Beach, Fla., 1988—99, LaVilla Sch. of the Arts, Jacksonville, 2000—; private voice tchr. Home, Various Cities, Fla., 1968—. Childrens, youth, and adult ch. choir dir. Fla. Chs., 1960—89; conductor/clinician Duval All County Elem. Chorus, Jacksonville, 1999; asst. conductor North Fla. Women's Chorale, Jacksonville, 1992—98; junior high/middle school coordinator Florida Vocal Association, Fl, 1997—99; conductor/ clinician Pasco County, New Port Richey, Fla., 2000, jr. high/ middle sch. coord. district 4 Fla. Vocal Assn., Jacksonville, 1999—. Singer: (opera) Don Giovanni, 1970; performer (singer): (with) Fla. Women's Chorale Group, 1992—96. Mem. adv. panel Jacksonville (Fla.) Childrens Chorus Fdn., 2000—01. Recipient Leadership Award, Pensacola Jr. Coll., 1968, Second Place, Rose Tensie-Palmer Opera Auditions, Mobile, Alabama, 1970, Choral Groups have been Awarded Outstanding Choirs in numerous national competitions, "Music in the Parks", "Music Festivals, USA", "Musicfest, Orlando", 1995,1996, 1997, 2001, Choral Group Invited to Sing in Washington, D.C. (did perform), Music Celebrations, Internat., 1998, Choral Group invited to Sing in England (did perfom), 1999, Current Choral Group invited to perform in Austria, 2001 - 2002. Mem.: Nat. Fellowship of Meth. Musicians (sec./treas. 1965—66), Fla. Vocal Assn., Fla. Music Educators Assn., Music Educators Nat. Conv., Nat. Assn. Tchrs. of Singing, Am. Choral Dirs. Assn. (life), Pensacola Oratorio Soc. (sec. 1965—66), Jacksonville Heritage Singers, Jacksonville Art Singers (pres. 1986—87). Presbyterian. Avocations: interior decorating, singing, travel. Home: 600 Pine Street Jacksonville FL 32266 Office: Lavilla Sch Of The Arts 501 North Davis Street Jacksonville FL 32202 Personal E-mail: soprano@bellsouth.net. Business E-Mail: king_j@firn.edu.

KING, JENNIFER ELIZABETH, editor; b. Summit, N.J., July 15, 1970; d. Layton E. and Margery A. (Long) K. BS in Journalism, Northwestern U., Evanston, Ill., 1992. Asst. editor Giant Steps Media, Chgo., 1992-93, assoc. editor Corp. Legal Times, 1993-94, dir. confs., 1994-95, mng. editor Corp. Legal Times, 1995-2001, v.p. editl. Corp. Legal Times, 2001—; acting mng. editor Ill. Legal Times, 1996-97; mng. editor U.S. Bus. Litig., 1997. Office: Corporate Legal Times LLC 656 W Randolph St # 500-e Chicago IL 60661-2114

KING, JOAN CALUDA, medical educator, neuroscientist; b. New Orleans, Mar. 6, 1938; BS, St. Mary's Dominican Coll., 1961; MS, U. New Orleans, 1970; PhD, Tulane U., 1973. Rsch. assoc. in neuroanatomy U. Iowa Coll. Medicine, Iowa City, 1973-74; NIH postdoctoral fellow (neuroscis.) Tulane U., New Orleans, 1974-76, rsch. assoc., vis. asst. prof. neurosci., 1976-79; asst. prof. anatomy Tufts U. Sch. Medicine, Boston, 1979-85, assoc. prof. anatomy and cellular biology, 1985-92, prof., chmn. anatomy and cellular biology, 1992-97, dir. reproductive ctr., 1992-97, prof. emeritus, 1997—. Mem. many nat. rev. coms., NSF, NIH, NICHD, 1979—. Co-author: Exploring the Basic Structures of the Brain, 1991, A Responsive Learning Environment for Medical Neurosciences: Sensory and Motor Pathways in the Spinal Cord, 1991; contbr. articles to profl. jours., chpts. to books; presenter in field; invited participant in numerous rsch. seminars and symposia; editl. bd. Biotechniques; ad hoc reviewer Science, Nature, Biology of Reproduction, Brain Rsch., Brain Rsch. Bull., Endocrinology, Jour. Histochemistry Cytochemistry, Jour. Neurosci., Neuroendocrinology, Neurosci., Peptides. Recipient Career Devel. award USPHS, 1979-84. Mem. Am. Assn. Anatomists, Internat. Soc. Psychoneuroendocrinology, Soc. Neurosci., Endocrine Soc. (animal welfare subcom. 1989), Kappa Delta Pi. Office: 14640 Swanson Ranch Rd Loveland CO 80538-9144

KING, JOY RAINEY, poet, executive secretary; b. Memphis, Aug. 5, 1939; d. Roy Henry and Margaret (Irvin) Rainey; m. Guy Robert King, Dec. 24, 1956; children: William Lonnie, Cheryl King Ramsey. Grad., Whitehaven H.S., Memphis, 1957. Sec. Gen. Telephone Co., Sumter, S.C., 1957-59; med. sec. L.H. Brisco, MD, Tupelo, Miss., 1963-69, James Ballard, MD, Tupelo, 1969-73; with First Nat. Bank of Southaven, Miss., 1973-79. Staff writer Majestic Records and Countrywine Pub. Co. Author: From the Gazebo, Wonder of Words, 2003 (Internat. Book of Gold prize, 2003), 12 poetry books; poem featured: in Baseball Hall of Fame, lyrics: songs America's New Hero, lyrics: songs; author: numerous poems. Recipient Editor's Choice award, 1993, 94, Nat. Libr. Poetry award, 1995-96, Pres.'s recognition lit. excellence Nat. Authors Registry, 1999-2000, Poet of Month award; named Author of Yr., Edizoni U., Trento, Italy, 1999; poem included in Best Poems and Poets of the 20th Century, Internat. Peace prize United Cultural Conv., 2002. Mem. Internat. Soc. Poets, Poets Guild, Internat. Poetry Hall of Fame, So. Ill. Writers Guild (sec. 1996-98), Top Recorders Songwriters Assn., Famous Poets Soc., Metverse Muse in India. Baptist.

KING, JOY RIEMER, art educator; d. Bjarne Viggo and Thora Yrsa Xenia (Riemer) Ferdinandsen; m. Charles Banks King, Jr. IV, July 4, 1992; stepchildren: Captain Charles Pat, Dorothy Marie 1 child, Nanette Joy Xenia Riemer. Diploma, Sorbonne, 1959; BA, Principia Coll., 1961; MA, Columbia U., 1968; art specialist diploma, Fla. Internat. U., 1999. Cert. tchr. Ill., 1961, Fla., 1972. Tchrs. aide Columbia U. Team, Kabul, Afghanistan, 1961—62; tchr., curriculum coord. Parents' Coop. Sch., Jeddah, Saudi Arabia, 1967—68; prin., tchr. Latin, French, civics, arts So. Acad., Miami,

1972—77; instr. art Internat. Fine Arts Coll., Miami, 1977—78; instr. French & English Internat. Sch. Langs., Miami Shores, 1978—79; mgr./artist Frances W. Cary Antiques, 1983—89; instr. French & Danish Inlingua, Coral Gables, 1989—90; tchr., art, French, U.S. history Dade County Pub. Schools, 1990—2002; art therapist St. Mary Cathedral Sch., 2002—. Dir. Paul Abrams Found., Miami, Fla., 1998—2001, So. Acad., 1972—77. Exhibitions include Jackie Hinckey Sipes Gallery, Dublin-Kitzen Fine Arts Gallery, Coral Gables, Fairchild Tropical Garden, Bok Tower Gardens, S.E. Pastel Soc., Salmagundi Club, N.Y.C., Hispanic C.C., Miami, Paula Insel Gallery, N.Y., Stern's Gallery, Roselyn Gallery, N.C., Art Works Gallery, Miami, Nat. Art Edn. Assn. Elec. Gallery, Washington; contbr. articles to profl. jours. Pub. rels. dir. Civitan, North Miami, 2000—01. Named in U.S. Congl. Record for art edn. program with at risk students, U.S. Congress, 1992; recipient Marge Pearlson award, Dade Coalition Cmty. Edn., 1997, award of Excellence, Goya Foods, Fla., 1996, cert. of Appreciation, Metro-Dade Police Dept, Northside Sta., 1996. Mem.: ASPCA, Southeastern Pastel Soc., Fla. Watercolor Soc., Nat. Art Edn. Assn., French Teachers Am., Alliance Francaise, Fla. Art Edn. Assn., Nat. Assn. Women Artists, Dade Art Educators Assn., The Nature Conservancy, Friends the Everglades, Nat. Wildlife Fedn., Smithsonian Instn., St. Joseph's Indian Sch., North Shore Animal League, Farm Sanctuary, World Vision, Friends Bok Tower, Internat. Fund for Animal Welfare, Navy League, Nat. Gardening Club (life). Avocations: travel, gardening, bird-watching, reading, swimming, painting, sculpting. Personal E-mail: joyscapes@aol.com.

KING, JUDITH MARIE, librarian, educator; b. Watertown, Wis., Oct. 24, 1939; d. Chester Roland and LaVerne Lydia (Schramm) Gauerke; m. Lewis King, Nov. 8, 1963 (dec. Mar. 16, 2000). BS in Edn., Wis. State Coll., 1962; MS in Edn., W. Maryland Coll., 1983. Libr. Plymouth HS, Wis., 1962—63; tchr. Waukesha sch. dist., Wis., 1963—65, Ctrl. Bucks sch. dist., Doylestown, Pa., 1965—67; libr. media specialist Ctrl. Bucks HS, Doylestown, 1967—69, Montgomery County pub. schs., Rockville, Md., 1970—95; libr. media specialist/audio video specialist Madison (Wis.) Meml. HS, 1995—97; dir. info. and libr. svcs. Madison Met. sch. dist., 1997—99; dir. program devel. Am. Libr. Assn., 2000—02, Am. Assn. Sch. Librs., 2000—02. Adjunct prof. Western Maryland Coll., 1985—; cons. Gale Rsch. UXL, Detroit, 1993—99, U. Wis., Madison, 1998—99. Editor: (sch. libr. media quar.jour.) Idea Exchange, 1979—82; contr. (ALA Yearbook), 1984, (sch. libr. media annual), 1984. Bd. adv. Cooperative Children's Book Ctr. U. Wis., 1997—2000. Mem.: Am. Assn. Sch. Librs. (pres. 1983—84, div. councilor 1994—99, publs. chair 2002—), Am. Libr. Assn., Maryland Ednl. Media Orgn. (life). Home: 5434 Westshire Cir Waunakee WI 53597

KING, KATHY COOPER, music educator; b. Ackerman, Miss., Jan. 12, 1954; d. Bobby Gene and Mary Lou (McGee) Cooper; m. Kenneth A. King, Aug. 1, 1976; children: Matthew Cooper, Katherine Elizabeth. B of Music Edn., 1976, M of Music Edn., 1983, Cert. in Gifted/Talented Music Edn., 1986, ArtsD of Music Edn., Vocal Pedagogy, 1996. Vocal, choral and piano tchr. Weir (Miss.) H.S., 1976—78; dir. of music Ackerman (Miss.) United Meth. Ch., 1978—98; vocal, choral and piano tchr. Ackerman H.S., 1976—96; choral music edn. instr. U. Miss., University, 1996—97; vocal, choral and classroom tchr. Holmes C.C., Goodman, Miss., 1997—. Featured in Making the Grade, WTVA, 1990. Recipient Outstanding Cmty. Leader in Edn., Choctaw County Econ. Devel. Coun., 1991, STAR Tchr. award, Miss. Econ. Devel. Coun., 1995, Tchr. of Yr. award, Choctaw County, 1995. Mem.: Miss. Music Educators Assn., Music Tchrs. Nat. Assn., Nat. Assn. Tchrs. of Singing, Music Educators Nat. Conf., Am. Choral Dirs. Assn., Phi Kappa Phi, Sigma Alpha Iota, Pi Kappa Lambda. Republican. Methodist. Avocations: gourmet cooking, travelling, interior decorating, fitness training. Home: PO Box 413 Ackerman MS 39735 Office: Holmes CC PO Box 369 Goodman MS 39079

KING, KAY SUE, investment company executive; b. Indpls., Sept. 14, 1948; d. George W. and Nadine M. K.; 1 child, Christopher G. Student, U. Ariz., 1966-70; BS in Edn., Ind. U., 1971; MA in Speech Communication, U. Hawaii, 1974. Tchr. Indpls. High Schs., 1971-1973; sec., treas. G. W. King Co., Indpls., 1974—; domestic sales mgr. Regal Travel, Indpls., 1975-90; pres., bd. dirs. K.S. King, Inc., Indpls., 1977—; mng. ptnr. K.S. King Co., Indpls., 1982—. Mem. pub. rels. com. Indpls. Zoolog. Xoc., 1976-85; vol. Indpls Humane Soc., 1966—, Indpls. Aid to Zoo Horse Show, 1974-78, Save the Ducks campaign, Indpls., 1978, Pan Am. Games Olympic Sports Com., Indpls., 1981-82; tchr. Sunday sch. Meridian St. Methodist Ch., Indpls., 1988-90. Elected Festival Princess 500 Festival Assn., Indpls., 1968. Mem. Internat. Assn. Bus. Communicators, Internat. Wildlife Fedn., Indpls. Zool. Soc. (charter), Indpls. Pub. Libr., Indpls. Children's Mus., Indpls. Ski Club, U. Ariz. Alumni Assn., Ind. Univ. Alumni Assn., Channel 20, Riviera Club, Lilly Pool, Meridian Hills Country Club, Delta Delta Delta. Avocations: swimming, reading, skiing, horseback riding, animals, children. Office: King Co 5665 N Meridian St Indianapolis IN 46208-1502 Home: PO Box 702 Indianapolis IN 46260-0582

KING, KAY WANDER, academic administrator, design educator, fashion designer, consultant; b. Houston, Oct. 16, 1937; d. Aretas Robert and Verna Elizabeth (Klann) Wander; m. George Ronald King, Feb. 21, 1960; 1 child, Collin Wander. BA, U. North Tex., 1959; M of Liberal Arts, Houston Bapt. U., 1991. Fashion designer Kabro Houston, Inc., 1959-66, Joe Frank, Inc., Houston, 1966-68; fashion dir. Foley's, Houston, 1968-70; prin. Kay King Designer/Cons., Houston, 1970—; chair fashion dept. Houston C.C., 1981-97, chair fashion and interior design dept., 1997—2003; cultural exch. prof. fashion design Jinan, China, 2000; interim dean workforce devel. Houston C.C., 2000—01, chmn. Dept. Applied Arts, 2003—. Mem. adv. bd. Spring (Tex.) Ind. Sch. Dist. Tech. Edn., 1990—; bd. dirs. Make it Yourself with Wool, Tex., nat. judge, Tex., 1997—2001; Tex. Workforce Edn. Course Manual Facilitator, 1997—2001; site evaluator Tex. Coord. Bd. for Higher Edn., 1994, 99, 2000. Designer Mrs. Am., 1966, Houston Oilers Cheerleaders, 1968-92, Astroworld and The Astrodome, 1968-69, Brian Boru Opera, 1991, Design Industries Found. Fighting AIDS, 1994-96, Houston Comets/Houston Rockets, 1997. Chair Gulf Coast area United Cerebral Palsy Telethon, 1981; chair Whiteley Endowment Scholarship Awards, Houston, 1990-93, Sickle Cell Found., Houston, 1995-2000; adminstr. Bedichek Faculty Devel. Grants, 1995-96; pres. Spring Br. Ind. Sch. Dist. Coun., PTAs, Houston, 1987-88; bd. dirs. Houston C.C. Found., 1988-93, Mus. Fine Arts Costume Inst., Houston, 1991—, acquisitions com., 1993—. Named Woman to Watch, Houston Woman mag., 1991, Woman of Excellence, Fedn. Houston Profl. Women, 1992; recipient Freedoms Found. at Valley Forge Nat. award, 2001, Exemplary Program awards for fashion design and fashion merchandising, Tex. Higher Edn. Coord. Bd., 2001, Yellow Rose of Tex., Gov. Tex., 1982, Nat. Inst. for Staff and Orgnl. Devel. Tchg. Excellence award, U. Tex., 1993, Award of Excellence, Houston C.C. Faculty Assn. Coun., 1995, Fin. Advisors' Excellence in Cmty. Leadership award, Am. Express, 1996, Innovation award, Houston C.C., 1996, Chancellor's Medallion award, 1996, Tony Chee Tchg. Excellence award, 1996, Bedichek Outstanding Cmty. Svc. award, 1997, Athena award, Sickle Cell Assn., 1997, Fine Arts Fashion award, Mus. Fine Arts Houston, 1999, Fashion Forum award, Foley's Dept. Store and Fashion Group Internat., 2000, Women's Archives honoree, U. of Houston, 1998—99; grantee Bedichek Faculty Devel. grantee, 1986, 1989, 1990, 1993, 1994. Mem. Nat. PTA (life, hon., coun. pres. 1987-88), Costume Soc. Am. (awards chair 1992-93, exec. bd. dirs., sec. 1993-99, v.p. 2000—), Tex. Jr. Coll. Tchrs. Assn. (sect. chair 1990-92), Fashion Group Internat. (bd. dirs. 1969—, cultural exch. chair 1965-71, regional dir. 1969-70, program dir., chair career conf. 1994, retail chair 1995, Keynote address 1997), Houston C.C. Women Adminstrs. Assn. (bd. dirs. 1993-95, v.p. 1994-95, Star award 1989, Keynote address 1996), Houston Fashion Designers Assn. (charter, publicity chair 1989-93, v.p. bd. dirs. 1993-97), Tex. Sheep and Goat Raisers Assn. (Achievement award 2003), Fedn. Houston Profl. Women (bd. dirs., program dir. 1993, adminstrv. sec. 1994, pres.-elect 1995, pres. 1996, past pres. 1997, travel chair 1998—, charter mem. Classy Clown Corps 1994-2000), Zeta Tau Alpha (charity showhouse chair 1985, Nat. Cert. of Merit 1986). Avocations: opera, ballet, travel, graphic computer design, professional football. Office: Houston CC System 1300 Holman St # 325A Houston TX 77004-3834

KING, LAURA JANE, librarian, genealogist; b. Pemberville, Ohio, Jan. 19, 1947; d. Richard D. and Jessie Florence (Brown) Zepernick; m. Bruce William King, June 17, 1972; 1 child, Christian Andrew. BA, Bowling Green (Ohio) State U., 1969, MEd, 1976; MLS, Kent State U., 1995. Cert. pub. libr. Cert. geneal. lectr. County ext. agt. home econs. Ohio Coop. Ext. Svcs., Paulding County, 1970-77; asst. dir., historian Pemberville (Ohio) Pub. Libr.; asst. dir., br. coord. Pemberville Pub. Libr.; mem. PRICE com., vocat. home econs. dept. Paulding Exempted Village, 1975—. Instr. genealogy Continuing Edn. Bowling Green State U., Eastwood Sch. Dist. Cmy. Edn. Mem. Paulding County Bicentennial Commn., 1975—77; state chmn. Friends of Libr., 1992—95; advisor 4-H; mem. Wood County Citizens Com. fo Bicentennial of U.S. Constn. and N.W. Ordinance; chmn. Pemberville com. Ohio Bicentennial; mem. Wood County Literacy Bd., Pemberville Sch. Adv. Com.; past pres. Eastwood Local Schs. Band Boosters; corr. docent DAR Mus., Washington; organist First Presbyn. Ch., Pemberville, ch. historian. Recipient Tenure award, Coop. Ext. Svc., 1975, Oustanding Svc. award, 4-H, 1999. Mem.: SAR (medal of appreciation), DAR (vice regent chpt. 1975—77, state vice chmn. pages 1978—80, regent chpt. 1979—83, state and divsn. outstanding jr. mem. 1980, state chmn. lineage rsch. 1980—87, state chmn. membership commn. 1983—87, registrar chpt. 1985—, state rec. sec. 1987—89, state corr. sec. 1989—92, area spkr.'s staff, state chmn. Friends of the Libr. 1992—95, chpt. libr. 1998—), ALA, Coun. Ohio Genealogists (v.p. 1992), Ohio Libr. Assn., Berks County Geneal. Soc., Ohio Geneal. Soc. (pres. Wood County chpt. 1978—80, chmn. pub. rels. com. 1982—83, state program chmn. ann. conf. 1991, state chmn. History Writing Contest 1993, state program chmn. ann. conf. 1995, trustee 1995—, chmn. First Families of Wood County com.), Libr. Adminstrn. and Mgmt. Assn., Flag of the U.S. of Am. (sr. state registrar 1994—, sr. state chmn. govt. studies 1998—, sr. state organizing sec. 2000—, sr. state chmn.), Mary Sherman Hayes Soc. (past sr. v.p.), Bus. and Profl. Women's Club (pres. Paulding 1975—76, v.p. 1974—75), Order Ea. Star, Colonial Order Crown of Charlemagne, Daus. Am. Colonists (chpt. regent 1986—, state chmn. pub. rels. 1987, chmn. mideast region pub. rels.), Colonial Dames 17th Century, Nat. Soc. Magna Charta Dames, Daus. Union Vets., First Families Ohio, U.S. Daus. of 1812 (chmn. state insignia), Palantines to Am., Children of Am. Revolution (past sr. state historian, sr. state rec. sec.). Home: 14553 N River Rd Pemberville OH 43450-9797 E-mail: lking@wcnet.org.

KING, LINDA, musician, music educator; b. Wichita Falls, Tex., July 30, 1940; d. Charles Ecford Jr. and Norma Reeda Collins; m. James Arthur King, Aug. 19, 1961; children: Linda Renée DeValois, James Arthur II, Jon Allen. Student, Tex. Christian U., 1958, 59, 60; MusM, Juilliard Conservatory, 1973. Judge Nat. Fedn. Music Clubs; adjudicator Nat. Guild Auditions, Austin, Tex., 1987—; founder, past pres. Piano Arts Assn., Denver, 1987; exec. dir. Rocky Mountain Duo Piano Competition, Colorado Springs, Colo., 1997-99; piano tchr., 1968—; founder, exec. dir. The Clementi Piano Festival, 1994-2000. Active Jr. League, Dallas, 1967-70; pres. Irving (Tex.) Women's Choral Club, 1968-73, PTO, Irving, 1970; bd. mem., actor Irving Cmty. Theatre, 1968-73; follies now girl Symphony Guild, Irving, 1970-73; children's choir dir. First Christian Ch., Irving, 1968; city choir dir. Girl Scouts, Irving, 1970. Named Outstanding Mem., South Suburban Christian Ch., Littleton, 1981. Mem. Am. Coll. Musicians (adjudicator), Nat. Music Tchrs. Assn., Colo. State Music Tchrs. Assn., Fedn. Music Clubs (state pres. 1998-2000), Colo. Fedn. Music Clubs (state pres. 1998-2000), Alpha Gamma Delta (pledge trainer 1962-63). Republican. Avocations: directing singing groups of high school students, teaching children piano who cannot afford lessons. Home: 6916 S Ogden Ct Littleton CO 80122-1370

KING, LINDA ORR, museum director, consultant; b. Washington, June 21, 1948; d. William Baxter and Jayne (Reiser) Orr; m. James McClain King (dec. Aug. 1997); children: David, Adam, Lindsay. BA, La. State U., 1970, MA in Fine Arts, 1971. Fine arts history asst. La. State U., Baton Rouge, 1967-70, grad. asst., 1970-71; assoc. curator La. State Mus., New Orleans, 1971-74; curator Coastal Ga. Hist. Soc./St. Simons Island Lighthouse Mus., St. Simons Island, 1984-87; dir. Coastal Ga. Hist. Soc., St. Simons Island, 1987-2000; dir. exhibitions and collections Atlanta Hist. Ctr., 2000-01; ind. mus. profl., 2001—. Romanian Mus. advisor U.S. State Dept., 2002. Co-editor: (photograph essay) George Francois Mugnier, 1975. Pres. Glynn County Soc. of St. Vincent de Paul, 1990-94; mem. Glynn County Courthouse Renovation Com., 1989-2000; Ga. state dir. S.E. Mus. Conf., 1990-94, also membership chair; mem. adv. coun. Brunswick Downtown Devel. Authority; mem. Leadership Glynn, 1992; mem. Commn. on Preservation of Ga. State Capitol; chmn. adv. coun. on hist. preservation Coastal Regional Devel. Ctr., 1987-98, chmn., 1996-98. Recipient Kellogg Career Enhancement award, Kellogg Found., 1989, Leadership award, Southeastern Mus. Conf., 1995, Nat. Mus. award, 1999, Ga. History Mus. Exhibit of 2002 award, 2002; fellow Internat. Partnership Among Mus. fellow to Sierra Leone, 1992. Mem. Ga. Assn. Mus. and Galleries (treas. 1987-89, Mus. Profl. of Yr. 1993), Coastal Mus. Assn. (treas. 1987-89), Am. Assn. Mus., Low Country Mus. Network (treas. 1993-99). Roman Catholic. Home: 3514 Paces Pl Atlanta GA 30327 : Office Phone: 404-495-0184. E-mail: lindaorrking@comcast.net.

KING, LYNDA, counselor; d. Kenneth Dodds and Emily Marie King. BA in Psychology, Tabor Coll., Hillsboro, Kans., 1995; MA in Profl. Counseling, Ottawa U., Phoenix, 2002. Dir. care staff Res-Care, Mesa, Ariz., 1998—; therapist Mental Health Agy., Apache Junction, Ariz., 2003—. Democrat. Avocations: hiking, rock climbing.

KING, LYNDEL IRENE SAUNDERS, art museum director; b. Enid, Okla., June 10, 1943; d. Leslie Jay and Jennie Irene (Duggan) Saunders; m. Blaine Larman King, June 12, 1965. BA, U. Kans., Lawrence, 1965; MA, U. Minn.-Mpls., 1971, PhD, 1982. Dir. Univ. Art Mus., U. Minn.-Mpls., 1979—; dir. exhbns. and mus. programs Control Data Corp., 1979, 80-81; exhbn. coordinator Nat. Gallery of Art, Washington, 1980. Recipient Cultural Contbn. of Yr. award Mpls. C. of C., 1978; Honor award Minn. Soc. Architects, 1979. Mem. Assn. Art Mus. Dirs. (chair art issues com. 1998-2000, chair tech. comm. com. 2000, bd. trustees 1998—), Art Mus. Assn. Am. (v.p. bd. dirs. 1984-89), Assn. Coll. and Univ. Mus. and Galleries (v.p. 1989-92), Am. Assn. Mus., Internat. Coun. Mus., Upper Midwest Conservation Assn. (pres. bd. dirs. 1980—), Minn. Assn. Mus. (steering com. 1982), Am. Fedn. Arts Bd. Home: 326 W 50th St Minneapolis MN 55419-1247 Office: Weisman Art Mus 333 E River Rd Minneapolis MN 55455-0367

KING, MARCIA GYGLI, artist; b. Cleve., June 4, 1931; d. Robert Prescott and Ruth (Farr) Gygli; m. Rollin White King, May 10, 1956 (div. 1974); children: Rollin White King Jr., Edward Prescott King. BA, Smith Coll., 1953; MFA, U. Tex., San Antonio, 1981. Docent Nat. Gallery Art, Washington, 1956-60; organizer, dir. docent program McNay Art Mus., San Antonio, 1964-76; art critic Express news, San Antonio, 1976-77; artist N.Y.C., 1979—. Lectr. Nat. Gallery Art, Washington, 1956-60, div. continuing edn. U. Tex., 1976, So. Meth. U., Dallas, 1984, McNay Art Mus., San Antonio, 1984, Washington Project for the Arts, 1985, Monserrat Coll. Art, Beverly, Mass., 1987, Whitney Mus., Phillip Morris, N.Y.C., 1988, Lehman Coll. CUNY, 1988, MTA Pub. Art Commn. for Creative Stations, N.Y., 1995; panelist Panel on Women in the Arts, Alexandria, Va., 1978, Washington Project for the Arts, 1985, Corpus Christi (Tex.) State U., 1986, Dallas Mus., 1991, New Mus., N.Y., 1993, Mus. Mod. Art, N.Y., 1995. One woman shows include McNamara O'Connor Mus., Victoria, Tex., 1975, Charleton Gallery, San Antonio, 1980, Douglas Coll. Rutgers U., New Brunswick, N.J., 1981, McNay Art Mus., San Antonio, 1984, Mattingly Baker Gallery, Dallas, 1984, White Columns, N.Y., 1985, Parker Smalley Gallery, N.Y., Manhattan Marymount, N.Y., 1986, Ferver Gallery, N.Y., 1987, Katzen Brown Gallery, N.Y.C., 1988, 90, Haines Gallery, San Francisco, 1988, Wallace Wentworth Gallery, Washington, 1988, U. N.C., 1989, Valerie Miller Gallery, Palm Desert, Calif., 1989, Cleve. Ctr. for Contemporary Art, 1989-90, Hal Katzen, N.Y., 1992, 94, Guild Hall Mus., N.Y., 1995, Renee Fotouhi Fine Art, N.Y., 1995, Arts Acad., Md., 1996, Kouros Gallery, N.Y., 1999, Parchman Stremmel Gallery, San Antonio, 2000, San Antonio Art League Mus., 2000, Bklyn. Botanic Garden, 2001, Gallery Camino, Real, Fla., 2002, Gallery 668, N.Y., 2003; represented in collections Bklyn. Mus., Cleve. Mus., Guggenheim Mus., Johnson Mus., Cornell U., Nat. Mus. Women in Arts, Newark Mus., Robert Coll., Istanbul, Ark. Art Ctr., Guild Hall, L.I., McNay Art Mus., San Antonio Art League. Recipient Internat. Women's Yr. Panel award, Tex., 1977, Artist of Yr., San Antonio, 2000, James Kirkeby Nat. Meml. award Tex. Watercolor Soc., 1976, Brewer's Digest award Lone Star Brewery Day, 1963, Annual Z.T. Scott award & cir. Tex. Fine Arts Assn., 1970, Ethel T. Drought Meml. award San Antonio Art League Exhbn., 1971, Best of Show award Tex. Watercolor Show, 1971, First Purchase Prize, Tex. Watercolor Show, 1972, First Purchase Prize, 17th Delta Annual, Ark. Art. Ctr., 1974; named Outstanding Woman in San Antonio, Women's Polit. Caucus, 1979. Avocations: swimming, bicycling. Office: 477 Broome St Apt 63 New York NY 10013-5311

KING, MARCIA JONES, potter, physicist, photographer; b. Oak Park, Ill., May 17, 1934; d. Walter Leland Jones and Florence W. (Dull) Anderson; m. James Craig King, Nov., 1953 (div. 1966); 1 child, James Craig King, Jr. BS, Johns Hopkins U., 1960, PhD, 1969. Elec. engr. Electronic Comm., Inc., Timonium, Md., 1959-63; rsch. assoc. theoretical particle physics Syracuse (N.Y.) U., 1969-72; asst. editor Phys. Rev. Brookhaven Nat. Lab., Upton, N.Y., 1972-74; physicist Argonne (Ill.) Nat. Lab., 1974-78; pvt. practice potter and physicist Syracuse, N.Y., 1978—. Contbr. articles to profl. jours.; exhibitor pots throughout Ctrl. N.Y.; one-woman photography shows in Ctrl. N.Y. and So. Calif.; author: Nature's Telling: Anza-Borrego Desert, 1996. Mem. AAAS, Am. Phys. Soc., Syracuse Ceramic Guild (pres. 1982-84), Phi Beta Kappa, Sigma Xi. Democrat. Home and Office: 228 Buckingham Ave Syracuse NY 13210-3024 E-mail: mking52701@aol.com.

KING, MARGARET ANN, communications educator; b. Marion, Ind., Feb. 27, 1936; d. Paul Milton and Janet Mary (Broderick) Burke; m. Charles Claude King, Aug. 25, 1956; children: C. Kevin, Elizabeth Ann, Paul S., Margaret C. Student, Ohio Dominican, 1953-56, U. Kans., 1980-81; BA in Communication, Purdue U., 1986, MA in Pub. Communication, 1990. Regional rep. Indpls. Juv. Justice Task Force, 1984-85; vis. instr. dept. communication Purdue U., West Lafayette, Ind., 1992-96; v.p. King Mktg. Cons., Inc., 1996—2002; adj. lectr. U. Cin., 2002—. Bd. dirs. Vis. Nurse Home Health Svcs.; adj. instr. U. Cin., 2002—. Contbr. chpt. to book. Grad. mem. Leadership Lafayette, 1983. Purdue U. fellow, 1986-87. Mem. AAUW, Ctrl. States Comm. Assn. (conf. presenter 1989), Golden Key, Phi Kappa Phi. Republican. Roman Catholic. Avocations: poetry writing, vocal and piano music. Home: 7938 Wild Orchard Ln Cincinnati OH 45242-4309

KING, MARGARET LEAH, history educator; b. N.Y.C., Oct. 16, 1947; d. Reno C. and Marie (Ackerman) King; m. Robert E. Kessler, Nov. 12, 1976; children: David King Kessler, Jeremy King Kessler. BA, Sarah Lawrence Coll., 1967; MA, Stanford U., 1968, PhD, 1972. Asst. prof. dept. history Calif. State Coll., Fullerton, 1969-70; asst. prof. Bklyn. Coll., CUNY, 1972-76, assoc. prof., 1976-86; prof. Bklyn. Coll. and Grad. Ctr., CUNY, 1987—, Claire and Leonard Tow disting. prof., 2000—02. Disting. guest prof. Centre for Reformation and Renaissance Studies, U. Toronto, 1995. Author: The Renaissance in Europe, 2004, (textbook) Western Civilization: A Social and Cultural History, 2d edit., 2002, Venetian Humanism in an Age of Patrician Dominance, 1986, Women of the Renaissance, 1991, The Death of the Child Valerio Marcello, 1994, The Renaissance in Europe, 2004; editor, translator: (with Diana Robin) Complete Works of Isotta Nogarola, 2004; co-editor series The Other Voice in Early Modern Europe; contbr. more than 20 articles to profl. jours. Recipient Howard R. Marraro prize, Am. Cath. Hist. Assn., 1986, Tow award for distinction in scholarship, Bklyn. Coll., 1994—95; fellow, Danforth Found., 1967—72, Woodrow Wilson Found., 1967—68, Am. Coun. Learned Socs., 1977—78, NEH, 1986—87, Leonard and Claire Tow Disting. fellow, 2000—; grantee, Am. Coun. Learned Socs., 1976, Gladys Krieble Delmas Found., 1977—78, 1980—81, 1990, Am. Philos. Soc., 1979, 1990, NEH, 1984. Mem. Am. Hist. Assn. (Howard and Helen Mararro prize 1996), Hist. Soc., Renaissance Soc. Am. (exec. dir. 1988-95, editor Renaissance Quar. 1984-88, 97-2002). Home: 324 Beverly Rd Little Neck NY 11363-1125 Office: CUNY Bklyn Coll Dept History 2900 Bedford Ave Brooklyn NY 11210-2814 Office Phone: 718-951-5303. E-mail: mking@nyc.rr.com.

KING, MARY LOU, artist, medical technologist; b. Vernon, Tex., Apr. 11, 1927; d. H. Raymond and Alma Vivian (Davenport) Hudson; m. Jack E. King, June 3, 1948 (dec. May 2002); children: Paul Hudson, Karen Anne, Julie Louise; m. Bert B. Thompson, July 11, 2003. BS in Biology and Med. Tech., N. Tex. State U., 1948; AS in Art, Midland (Tex.) Coll., 1987. Bd. cert. med. technologist Am. Soc. Clin. Pathologists. Dept. head Santa Rosa Hosp., San Antonio, Tex., 1948-49; lab. dir. Drs. Offices, San Antonio, 1949-50; artist pvt. practice, Midland, 1986—. One-woman shows include Silvers Gallery, Midland, Tex. State Capital Bldg., Austin, Gallery of the Woman's Club, Midland, Gallery Theatre Ctr., Midland; invitational shows in China, Norway and Japan; 20 commns.; featured in publs. including Artists of Texas, vol. II & IV, American Artists, Illustrated Survey of Leading Contemporary Watercolorists, Splash IV, The Splendor of Light, Contemporary Watercolorists, Keys to Painting Light and Shadow, 1999, Texas Watercolor Society: Fifty Years of Excellence, 1999, Watercolor (mag.), 1999, The Artist Sketch Book, 2001, Capturing Texture in Watercolors, 2002, Textuur Annbrengen, 2003. Bd. dirs. First United Meth. Ch., Midland, 1963-85, adult class leader and lay speaker, 1970—; Troop leader Girl Scouts U.S.A., Midland, 1958-75, officer, dir. coun., trainer, coord., 1968-80. Recipient Thanks award Girl Scouts Am., 1975, Life Membership award, 1990, Woman of Distinction award, 2000. Mem. Tex. Water Color Soc. (signature mem. 1987, regional del. 1988-89, mem. Purple Sage Soc. 1995), West Tex. Watercolor Soc. (signature mem. 1995), So. Watercolor Soc. (signature mem. 1993, regional del. 1995—), Midland Arts Assn. (bd. dirs., officer 1983—), Arts Assembly of Midland (chmn. visual arts, mem. planning coun. 1983-86, Outstanding Svc. award 1985), Watercolor USA Hon. Soc. Avocations: travel, dance, poetry. Home: 4513 Cardinal Ln Midland TX 79707-2203 E-mail: MLJKINGART@aol.com.

KING, MARY-CLAIRE, geneticist, educator; b. Evanston, Ill., Feb. 27, 1946; m. 1973; 1 child, Emily King Colwell. BA in Math., Carleton Coll., 1966; PhD in Genetics, U. Calif., Berkeley, 1973. Am. Cancer Soc. prof. medicine and genetics U. Wash., Seattle, 1995—. Mem. bd. sci. counselors Nat. Cancer Inst.; cons. Com. for Investigation of Disappearance of Persons, Govt. Argentina, Buenos Aires, 1984—. Contbr. more than 150 articles to profl. jours. Recipient Alumni Achievement award Carleton Coll.,

Basic Rsch. award Susan G. Komen Breast Cancer Found., 1999. Mem. AAAS, Am. Soc. Human Genetics, Soc. Epidemiologic Research, Inst. Medicine, Phi Beta Kappa, Sigma Xi. Office: U Wash 1959 NE Pacific St # 357720 Seattle WA 98195-0001*

KING, MURIEL EILEEN, secondary school educator; b. Georgetown, Demerara, Guyana, July 2, 1924; came to U.S., 1972; d. Egbert Sinclair Harvey and Edna Mollyneau; m. Rupert Oliver King, Aug. 4, 1944; children: Egbert Samuel, Aubrey, Ancil, Rawle Oliver, Dawn Allison. BA in English cum laude, L.I. U., Bklyn., 1975, MSc in Edn., 1977. Cert. tchr., Calif., Guyana, Can. Tchr. Washington High Sch., Georgetown, 1942-44, Enterprise High Sch., Georgetown, 1944-49, Mt. Zion Luth. Sch., Georgetown, 1949-56, Schepmoed Sch., Berbice, 1959-62, Tchrs. Tng. Coll., 1962-63, Ascension Luth. Coll., 1963-69, Kyle (Sask., Can.) Composite Sch., 1969-72, Epiphany High Sch., 1972-80, Straubemauller Jr. High. Sch., 1981. Sr. asst., Georgetown, 1963-69. Author: Juvenile Delinquency and the Part Education Can Play to Solve the Problem, 1964. Liaison officer, tchr. Aboriginal Indians, Homeless in the Mantinique Hotels, Prince George Hotel Homeless, Guyana, S.Am., 1949-56. NSF award, L.I.U., 1978-79. Avocations: art, painting, debating, needlecrafts. Home: 6075 Geremander Ave Rialto CA 92377-4023

KING, NANCY, communications educator; b. Blytheville, Ark., May 10, 1945; d. Willie Lee and Janie (Jones) Garrett; m. Perry King, June 17, 1967; children: Perry Jr., Tiffany, Christopher. BA in Speech Communication, Calif. State U., L.A., 1974, MA in Speech Communication, 1981; MA in Psychology, Chapman U., 1998. Asst. supr. Pacific Telegraph & Telephone, 1968-70; computer operator West Coast Community Exch. Fenton & Lavine, L.A., 1970-71, So. Gas Co., L.A., 1972-81, communication cons., 1982—; devel. lang. specialist Charles Drew Headstart Program, L.A.; prof. speech dept. Marymount Coll., Rancho Palos Verdes, Calif., 1986—. Speechwriter various regional ofcls.; instr. Calif. State U., L.A., 1979-86; mem. Calif. Libr. Svcs. Bd., 1984-94, pres., 1988-89, 90-91; mem. Calif. Libr. Networking Task Force, 1985-2000, Calif. Librs. Adv. Bd., 1984-94, Orange County Friends of Libr. Found., 1988-94, Calif. Alliance for Literacy Task Force, 1988, 92; faculty coord. Webster U., 1996—; intern counselor Am. Inst. Family Counselors, 1997, Human Options Counseling Ctr., 2000. Contbr. articles to profl. jours. Co-chmn. black coun. Orange County Hist. and Cultural Found., pres. bd., 1992, campaign mgr. Fran Williams for Santa Ana City Coun. Mem. NEA, Nat. Speech Communication Assn., Western Speech Communication Assn., Am. Fedn. Tchrs., AAUW, L.A. Southcentral Planning Coun. (bd. dirs.). Republican. Roman Catholic. Office: Marymount Coll 30800 Palos Verdes Dr E Palos Verdes Peninsula CA 90274 E-mail: nking@marymountpv.edu.

KING, NINA DAVIS, journalist; b. Coco Solo, Panama, May 7, 1941; d. James White and Ruth (Steele) Davis. BA in French, U. N.C., 1963, MA in Comparative Lit. (Chancellors fellow), 1967; PhD in English, Wayne State U., 1973. Lectr. Queens Coll., 1970-73; copy editor Newsday, L.I., N.Y., 1973-76, asst. news editor, 1976-77, asst. book rev. editor, 1977-79, book rev. editor, 1979-88; book editor The Washington Post, 1988-99, assoc. editor, 1999—. Author: (with R. Winks) Crimes of the Scene: A Mystery Novel Guide for the International Traveler, 1997. Mem. Nat. Book Critics Circle, Phi Beta Kappa. Office: The Washington Post 1150 15th St NW Washington DC 20071-0002 E-mail: kingn@washpost.com.

KING, NORAH MCCANN, federal judge; b. Steubenville, Ohio, Aug. 13, 1949; d. Charles Bernard and Frances Marcella (Krumm) McCann; married; 4 children. BA cum laude, Rosary Coll. (now Dominican U.), 1971; JD summa cum laude, Ohio State U., 1975. Bar: Ohio 1975, So. Dist. of Ohio 1980. Law clerk U.S. Dist. Ct., Columbus, Ohio, 1975-79, counsel Frost, King, Freytag & Carpenter, Columbus, Ohio, 1979-82; asst. prof. Ohio State U., Columbus, Ohio, 1980-82; U.S. magistrate judge U.S. Dist. Ct., Columbus, Ohio, 1982—, chief magistrate judge, 2000—. Recipient award of merit Columbus Bar Assn., 1990. Mem.: Columbus Bar Assn., Fed. Bar Assn., Coun. U.S. Magistrate Judges. Office: US Dist Ct 85 Marconi Blvd Rm 235 Columbus OH 43215-2837

KING, PATRICIA ANN, law educator; b. Norfolk, Va., June 12, 1942; d. Addison A. and Grayce (Wood) K.; m. Roger W. Wilkins, Feb. 21, 1981; 1 child, Elizabeth. BA, Wheaton Coll., 1963; JD, Harvard U., 1969. Bar: D.C. 1969, U.S. Supreme Ct. 1980. Spl. asst. to chair EEOC, Washington, 1969-71; dep. dir. civil rights office HEW, Washington, 1971-73; prof. law Georgetown Law Ctr., Washington, 1973—. Adj. prof. Sch. Hygiene and Pub. Health Johns Hopkins U., 1990—; bd. dirs. Wheaton Coll., Womens Legal Defense Fund. Co-author: Law, Science and Medicine, 1984; contbr. articles to profl. jours. Chmn. Redevelopment Land Agy., Washington, 1976-80. Fellow Hastings Ctr.; mem. Am. Soc. Law and Medicine, Am. Law Inst., Inst. Medicine. Office: Georgetown Law Ctr 600 New Jersey Ave NW Washington DC 20001-2075

KING, REATHA CLARK, community foundation executive; b. Ga. m. N. Judge King Jr.; children: N. Judge III, Scott. BS in Chemistry and Math., Clark Coll., 1958; PhD in Chemistry, U. Chgo., 1960; MBA, Columbia U., 1977; doctorate (hon.), Smith Coll., 1993, S.C. State U., 1995. Rsch. chemist Nat. Bur. Standards, Washington, 1963-68; mem. chemistry faculty York Coll. CUNY, Jamaica, 1968-77, assoc. dean divsn. natural scis. and math., 1970-74, assoc. dean acad. affairs, 1974-77; pres. Met. State U., St. Paul, Mpls., 1977-88; pres., exec. dir. Gen. Mills Found., Mpls., 1988—. Bd. dirs. Minn. Mut. Ins. Co., St. Paul, H.B. Fuller Co., St. Paul, N.W. Corp., Mpls.; cons., spkr. in field. Contbr. numerous articles to profl. jours. Bd. dirs. Coun. on Founds., Washington, Minn. Coun. on Found., H.B. Fuller Co. Found., St. Paul, Corp. Nat. and Cmty. Svc., vice-chair; chair corp. adv. coun. ARC; bd. overseers Clark Atlanta U.; mem. ministers and missionaries benefit bd. Am. Bapt. Ch., N.Y.C. Recipient Sisterhood award for disting. humanitarian svc. Nat. Conf. Christian and Jews, 1993, Woman of Distinction award St. Croix Valley Girl Scouts, 1995. Mem. NAACP (cmty. svc. award in edn. 1994), Delta Sigma Theta. Home: 110 Bank St SE Apt 2005 Minneapolis MN 55414-3905 Office: Gen Mills Found PO Box 1113 Minneapolis MN 55440-1113

KING, REBECCA JANE, nursing educator; b. Warsaw, Ind., Jan. 25, 1970; d. George Allen Chapman and Clematean Hinson Moore; m. Johnny Allen King; 1 child, Nathan John. Student, W.V. U., Morgantown, 1988—90; BSN, U. Charleston, 1994; MS in Adult Tech. Edn., Marshall U., 2002, postgrad., 2003—. Registered nurse W.Va., cert. BLS instr. W.Va., tchr. W.Va. Charge nurse cardiac unit Charleston Area Med. Ctr. Meml., Charleston, W.Va., 1994—96, Eye and Ear Clinic, Charleston, 1996—2001; practical nursing instr. Garnet Career Ctr., Charleston, 1999—2003; HIV/AIDS coord. W. Va. Dept. Edn., 2003—. CPR instr., Charleston, 1993—; vis. nurse Charleston Area Med. Ctr. Home Care, Charleston, 1997—2000. Organizer relay for life team Am. Cancer Soc., Charleston, 2001—; blood drive organizer ARC, Charleston, 2002—; clothing drive Mildred Mitchell Bateman Hosp., Huntington, W.Va., 2002—. Master: Sigma Theta Tau; mem.: Nat. Assn. State Sch. Nurse Cons., W. Va. Assn. Sch. Nurses, Am. Fedn. Tchrs. Avocations: walking, bicycling. Office: W Va Dept Edn Student Svc and Health Promotions Bldg 6 Rm 309 1900 Kanawha Blvd E Charleston WV 25305 E-mail: rjnking@earthlink.net.

KING, ROBERTA See CINCA, SILVIA

KING, ROSALYN MERCITA, social sciences educator, researcher; b. Jacksonville, Fla., Aug. 16, 1948; d. Morris Charles and Marie (Coleman) K. BS, Howard U., 1970, MA, 1972; EdD, Harvard U., 1979. Dir. police youth project NCCJ, Washington, 1970-73; placement coord. U. North Fla., Jacksonville, 1973-74, instr., student support counselor, 1973-75; career edn. program coord. Roxbury/Harvard Sch. Program, Cambridge, Mass., 1976; rsch. analyst Spl. Commn. on Unequal Ednl. Opportunity Mass. Ho. of Reps., Boston, 1977; program coord. Freedom House, Inc., Roxbury, Mass., 1977-78; sr. program assoc. Expand Assocs., Inc., Silver Spring, Md., 1979; sr. assoc., dir. rsch. Mark Battle Assocs., Inc., Washington, 1980; dir. planning, program devel. and tech. assistance PUSH-Excel Inst. Research and Tng., Washington, 1981; rsch. assoc. So. Ctr. Studies in Pub. Policy Clark Coll., Atlanta, 1981-84; pres. Info. Rsch. Network Svc., Alexandria, Va., 1984—, Bathshua's Greetings, Alexandria, 1988—. Chief racial stats. U.S. Bur. Census, Washington, 1988; vis. prof. psychology Coppin State Coll., Balt., 1989-90; faculty rsch. assoc. U. Md., College Park, 1990-91; adj. lectr. dept. psychology George Mason U., Fairfax, Va., 1991—; adj. prof. psychology Prince George's C.C., Andrews AFB, 1991-94, Mary Washington Coll., Fredericksburg, Va., 1992-93, Catonsville (Md.) C.C., 1991-96, lectr., 1994-96; sr. pub. health analyst Agy. for HIV/AIDS Comm. Pub. Health, Washington, 1992-94; from assoc. prof. to prof. psychology and chair Ctr. for Tchg. Excellence No. Va. Region, No. Va. C.C., Loudoun campus, Sterling, Va., 1996—. Contbr. articles to profl. jours. Mem. Am. Psychol. Soc., Am. Psychol. Assn., Soc. for the Tchg. of Psychology, Psi Chi, Phi Delta Kappa. E-mail: rosalynmercita.king@worldnet.att.net., roking@nvcc.edu.

KING, SHARON LOUISE, lawyer; b. Ft. Wayne, Ind., Jan. 12, 1932; AB, Mt. Holyoke Coll., 1954; JD with distinction, Valparaiso U., 1957; LLM in Taxation, Georgetown U., 1961. Bar: Ind. 1957, D.C. 1958, Ill. 1962. Trial atty. tax divsn. U.S. Dept. Justice, 1958-62; sr. counsel Sidley & Austin, Chgo. Bd. dirs. Lawyer's Com. for Better Housing, Inc. Fellow Am. Coll. Tax Counsel; mem. ABA (chmn. com. closely-held corps. taxation sect. 1979-81, regulated pub. utilities com. taxation sect. 1982-83, coun. dir. taxation sect. 1983-86), Chgo. Bar Assn. (bd. mgrs. 1973-75, chmn. fed. tax com. 1983-84), Ill. State Bar Assn. (counsel dir. sect. fed. taxation 1989-91), Women's Bar Assn. Ill. Found. (bd. dirs., v.p., dir. scholarship). Office: Sidley & Austin Bank One Plaza 10 South Dearborn Street Chicago IL 60603

KING, SHARON MARIE, consulting company executive; b. Clarksville, Ark., Sept. 16, 1946; d. Argie L. and Vida M. K.; m. Robert W. Warnke, Feb. 14, 1983; children: Michael R., Jenna L. AA, Coll. of Ozarks, Clarksville, 1966, BA summa cum laude, Calif. State U., Dominguez Hills, 1979. Sr. exec. asst. Computer Sci. Corp., El Segundo, Calif., 1973-79; office mgr., bookkeeper Internal Charter Brokers, Manhattan Beach, Calif., 1979-80; office mgr. Metal Box Can, Torrance, Calif., 1980-81; sec. to pres. Filtrol, L.A., 1981-82; owner, mgr. Select Secretarial Svc., Manhattan Beach, 1982-89; pres., CEO Chipton-Ross, Inc., El Segundo, Calif., 1989—. Mem. Calif. C. of C. Presbyterian. Office: Chipton-Ross Inc 1756 Manhattan Beach Blvd Manhattan Beach CA 90266-6220 E-mail: sking@chiptonross.com.

KING, SHEILA SUE, music educator, elementary school educator; b. Chgo., Ill., Aug. 23, 1949; d. Robert William and Bernette Lips; m. John W. King, June 12, 1976; 1 child, Sarah Rebecca. B in Music Edn., Mich. State U., 1971. Pvt. practice, Laramie, Wyo., 1971—75; music tchr. Houston Ind. Sch. Dist., Houston, 1975—76; pvt. practice Huntsville, Ala., 1976—80, Gaithersburg, Md., 1976—80; music tchr. Apollo Elem. Sch., Titusville, Fla., 1981—. Dir. music Good Shepherd Luth. Ch., Titusville, Fla., 1981—; mem. leadership team Brevard County Sch., Melbourne, Fla., 1983—. Bd. dirs. Brevard Symphony Youth Orch., 2002—. Mem.: Brevard Symphony Youth Orchestra (exec. bd. 2002), Am. Orff-Schulwerk Assn. (Ctrl. Fla. chpt. v.p. 1983—), Fla. Music Educators Assn. (music demonstration sch. 1996—99, 1999—, state chmn. 1999—), Music Educators Nat. Conf., Alpha Delta Kappa. Lutheran. Avocation: space coast clogger. Home: 3730 Oakhill Drive Titusville FL 32780 Office: Apollo Elementary 3085 Knox McRae Drive Titusville FL 32780 E-mail: pianoforte@mindspring.com.

KING, SUSAN BENNETT, retired glass company executive; b. Sioux City, Iowa, Apr. 29, 1940; d. Francis Moffatt Bennett and Marjorie (Rittenhouse) Sillin; m. Stephen P. Glantz. AB, Duke U., 1962. Legis. asst. U.S. Senate, Washington, 1963-66; dir. Nat. Com. for Effective Congress, Washington, 1967-71, Ctr. Pub. Financing of Elections, Washington, 1972-75; exec. asst. to chmn. Fed. Election Commn., Washington, 1975-77; chmn. U.S. Consumer Product Safety Commn., Washington, 1978-81; dir. consumer affairs Corning (N.Y.) Glass Works, 1982, v.p. corp. communications, 1983-86; pres. Steuben Glass, N.Y.C., 1987-92; sr. v.p. corp. affairs Corning Inc., 1992-94. Trustee Duke U., Durham, NC, 1987—2001, Nat. Pub. Radio Found.; chmn. bd. Making a Difference in Cmtys., Inc., 1995—, Triangle Cmty. Found., 2002—, trustee; bd. dirs. MPC, Inc., 1995—. Fellow Inst. Politics, Harvard U., 1981.

KING, SUSAN MARIE, special education educator; b. Cambridge, Mass., Feb. 10, 1956; d. V. James and Joan Frances Cannalonga; m. John Charles King, Apr. 27, 1975. Student, Valencia C.C., Kissimmee, Fla., 1996—97; student sign lang., Mid Fla. Tech, Orlando, Fla, 1987—92, Fla. Sch. for the Deaf and Blind, St. Augustine, Fla. Vocat. 7 Teaching Certificate Kissimmee, Fla., 1997, cert. QA Registry of Interpreters for the Deaf, completion Dale Carnegie. Belly dancer, Orlando, Fla., 1980—82; co-owner, mgr. Colonial Motel and Apts., St. Cloud, Fla., 1980—89; tchr. Master's Acad., St. Cloud, Fla., 1989—91, Heartland Christian Acad., Kissimmee, Fla., 1993—94, Kingsway Christian Sch., St. Cloud, Fla., 1994—95, Osceola Assn. for Retarded Citizens and Tech. Edn. Ctr. Osceola (TECO), Kissimmee, Fla., 1995—97; tchr., testing specialist TECO, Kissimmee, Fla., 1995—. Sales rep. Avon, 2000—; mystery shopper, 2003—. Co-dir. (variety shows) Variety Show; translator: (first person to interpret Nat. Anthem performance in sign lang.) Orlando Magic Game, 1990 (cert., 1990). Vol. Spl. Olympics, Kissimmee, Fla., 1994—96, Osceola Ctr.Arts, Kissimmee, Fla., 1995—96, Am. Bible Soc., New York, NY, 1984—89; interpreter Heartland Worship Ctr., Kissimmee, Fla., 1985—95. Recipient Second Pl. Nat. Essay Olympics, Assn. of Christian Sch. Internat., 1994. Mem.: Kissimmee Deaf Club (mem. 1988—91). Republican. Avocations: horseback riding, reading, puzzles and games. Office: Tech Edn Ctr Osceola-TECO 501 Simpson Rd Kissimmee FL 34744-4459 E-mail: www.teco.osceola.k12.fl.us.

KING, TABITHA, author; b. 1949; m. Stephen King. Author: (novels) Small World, 1981, Caretakers, 1983, The Trap, 1985, Pearl, 1988, One on One, 1993, The Book of Reuben, 1995, Survivor, 1997, (non-fiction) Mid-Life Confidential, 1994, (anthologies) Shadows 4, 1981, The Best of the Best, 1998, (short stories) The Blue Chair, 1981, Djinn and Tonic, 1998; actor: (films) Knightriders, 1981. Trustee The Stephen and Tabitha King Foundation. Office: The Stephen and Tabitha King Found 49 Florida Ave Bangor ME 04401 Office Phone: 207-990-2910. Office Fax: 207-990-2975.*

KING, TAMARA LYNN, counselor; b. Roanoke, Va., May 1, 1972; d. Terrence Lee and Theresa (Richardson) King. BS, Va. Tech., 1994; MA, U. Houston, 2000. Lic. profl. counselor Tex., specialist sch. psychology Tex. Counselor psychol. testing Child Study Clinic, Victoria, Tex., 2000—01; intern Victoria Ind. Sch. Dist., 2001—02; in home counselor, day treatment counselor Family Preservation Svcs., Roanoke, 2002—, day treatment coord., 2003. Mem.: APA, Phi Kappa Phi. Personal E-mail: tami.king@lycos.com.

KING, TAMARA POWERS, music educator, musician; b. Spartanburg, S.C., Dec. 29, 1959; d. Douglas Edgar and Patricia Elizabeth Powers; m. Bryan Ray King, June 23, 1985; 1 child, Caroline Dawn. MusB in Edn., So. Missionary Coll., Collegedale, Tenn., 1982; postgrad., Converse Coll., 2000—03. Customer svc. and sales Powers Printing Co., Inc., Spartanburg, 1982—2000; violin tchr. dept. pre-coll. Converse Coll., Spartanburg, 1982—84; violin and viola tchr. Spartanburg, 1996—, Alia Lawson Pre-Coll., Spartanburg, 2001—03; strings and orch. tchr. Spartanburg County Sch. Dist. 1, Inman, SC, 2002—. Violinist Spartanburg Symphony Orch., 1982—95, Greenville Symphony Orch., SC, 1985—87, Greater Spartanburg Philharm., 1995—97; violinist and violist Converse Symphony Orch., Spartanburg, 2000—. Mem. music com. Spartanburg Seventh Day Adventist Ch., 1985—2003, asst. choir dir., 2000. Mem.: Music Educator's Nat. Conf., Spartanburg Philharm. Music Club. Avocations: reading, birding and nature study, drawing, collecting musical instruments, painting. Home: 1099 Moore-Duncan Hwy Moore SC 29369

KING, VERNA ST. CLAIR, retired school counselor; b. Berwick, La.; d. John Westley and Florence Ellen (Calvin) St. C.; A.B., Wiley Coll., 1937; M.A., San Diego State U., 1977; m. Alonzo Le Roy King, Aug. 27, 1939 (dec.); children— Alonzo Le Roy, Joyce Laraine, Verna Lee Eugenia King Bickerstaff, St. Clair A., Reginald Calvin (dec.). Tchr., Morgan City, La., 1939-40; tchr. San Diego Unified Sch. Dist., 1955-67, parent counselor, 1967-78, counselor grades 1-9, 1978-86; cons. Tucson Sch. Dist., 1977—, dir. compensatory edn., 1983—. Mem. Calif. Democratic State Central Com., 1950—, Dem. County Central Com., 1972—, del. nat. conv., 1976, 84, mem. exec. bd. Dem. State Central Com., 1982—; mem. San Diego County Sander Adv. Commn., 1982; hon. life mem. PTA; bd. dirs. YWCA, 1983—, v.p., 1987-88; chair Dem. County Ctrl. fundraising, 1992—; del. Dem. Nat. Com., 1992. Recipient Key to City, Mayor C. Dail, 1955, cert. United Negro Coll. Fund dr., 1980, Urban League Pvt. Sector award, 1982, 4th Ann. Conf. on Issues in Ethnicity and Mental Health Participants award, 1982 ; named Woman of Dedication, Salvation Army, 1985, Citizen of Yr., City Club and Jaycees, 1985, Woman of Achievement, Pres.' Council, 1983, Henry Auerbach award San Diego Dem. Party Ctrl. Com., 1997; numerous other honors. Mem. NEA (women's council 1980-82), AAUW, Calif. Tchrs. Assn. (state council 1979—, area dir. 1985—), San Diego Tchrs. Assn. (dir. 1958, 64, sec. 1964-67), Nat. Council Negro Women, San Diego County Council Dem. Women (pres. 1986-88), Compensatory Edn. Assn. (area dir. 1982-87), Pres. Women, Inc., Alpha Kappa Alpha (pres. 1978-80), Delta Kappa Gamma. Methodist. Clubs: Women's Inc., Order Eastern Star. Home: 5721 Churchward St San Diego CA 92114-4011

KING, VIRGINIA SHATTUCK, painter, retired school nurse practitioner, educator; b. Bklyn., Feb. 8, 1921; d. Harold James Shattuck and Lillian Elizabeth Shatluck; m. Stuart G. King, May 26, 1946 (dec. July 1988); children: Richard D., Stuart George, Harold James, Douglas Louis. BS in Nursing, Columbia U. Sch. of Nursing, N.Y.C., 1944; grad. studies, Adelphi U., Garden City, N.J., SUNY, Stonybrook. RN N.Y., 1946; cert. sch. nurse tchr. N.Y., 1960. Head nurse, obstet. fl. Columbia - Presbyn. Hosp., N.Y.C., 1945—46; pub. health nurse Suffolk County, NY, 1959, sch. nurse, 1959—79, tchr. health edn., 1970—79, ret., 1979. Author: From Then...To Who Knows When, 1996; one-woman shows include Fla. Revisited, Maxwell C. King Ctr. Performing Arts, 2001—02, exhibitions include Artists Forum Juried Show, King Ctr. Performing Arts, 1993, Fla. State Soc. Nat. Soc. DAR Am. Heritage Art Competition, 1993 (hon. mention), Spacecoast Art League Spring Show, 1996 (hon. mention), Spacecoast Art League Fall Show, 1996 (3d pl.), Spacecoast Art League Spring Show, 1997 (2d pl.), Spacecoast Art League Fall Show, 1997 (2d pl.), Brevard Mus. of Arts and Scis. 19th Juried Show, 1997, Fla. Hist. Soc. Tebeau Libr., 1998, George Plimpton Zoo-to-Do, Cape Canaveral, 1998, Boundless Expressions, Moffitt Cancer Rsch. Ctr., 1999, Brevard Mus. Arts and Scis., 1999, Fla. Watercolor Soc. Juried Show, 1999, Charlotte Country Art Guild Nat. Exhibit 2000, 2000, Ridge Art League New Mem. Exhibit, 2000, Bayard Ho. Exhibit, 2000, Strawbridge Art League Ann. Juried Show, 2001, From Grandmother's Brush, Orlando Mus. of Art, 2001, Fla. Watercolor Soc., 2001 (Strathmore award), Patriotic Traveling Show, Strawbridge Art League, 2002, Southern Watercolor Show, Baton Rouge, La., 2002, So. Watercolor Soc., 2002, children's wall mural, Brevard County Libr., 2000, one-woman shows include King Center for Performing Arts. Secound v.p. Friends of Eau Gallie Pub. Libr., 1999—. Mem.: DAR, Brevard watercolor Soc., Strawbridge Art League, Ga. Watercolor Soc. (ribbon and prize 2003), So. Watercolor Soc., P-2 Fla. Watercolor Soc., N.Y. State Tchrs. Retired in Fla. Republican. Achievements include the Virginia Shattuck Archives at Health Scis. Divsn. of Columbia U. Avocations: watercolor artist, writing, swimming, tennis, music. Home and Studio: 2419 Apache Dr Melbourne FL 32935 Personal E-mail: hglartiste@aol.com.

KING, WILLARD FAHRENKAMP (MRS. EDMUND LUDWIG KING), Spanish language educator; b. Roswell, N.Mex., July 13, 1924; d. W.F. and Willard (Pickerill) Fahrenkamp; m. Edmund Ludwig King, Jan. 29, 1951. Student, Tex. Christian U., 1940-41; BA, U. Tex., 1943, MA, 1946; PhD, Brown U., 1957. Instr. Spanish U. Tex., 1946-47, 49-50; instr. Spanish Brown U., 1950-51, Bryn Mawr (Pa.) Coll., 1958-60, asst. prof., 1960-64, assoc. prof., 1964-70, prof. Spanish, 1970—, Dorothy Nepper Marshall prof. Hispanic studies, 1976—, chmn. dept. Spanish, 1964-89, dir. Hispanic studies program, 1971-92. Corporator Internat. Inst. in Spain, resident dir., 1991-93. Author: Prosa novelística y academias literarias en el siglo XVII, 1963, Juan Ruiz de Alarcón, letrado y dramaturgo, 1989; also articles; editor, translator: Lope de Vega, El Caballero de Olmedo, 1972; translator: Amèrico Castro, The Spaniards, 1971; editor, commentator Agustín Moreto, El desdén, con el desdén, 1996. Guggenheim fellow, 1965-66 Mem. MLA, Renaissance Soc. Am., Phi Beta Kappa. Home: 171 Western Way Princeton NJ 08540-7207 Office: Thomas Libr Bryn Mawr Coll Bryn Mawr PA 19010

KING-BARRUTIA, ROBBIE L. state senator; b. Waco, Tex., Jan. 10, 1959; m. Kevin Barrutia; children: Kandace, Kenzie. Student, Coll. So. Idaho. Legis. attache; Rep. rep. dist. 20 Idaho Ho. of Reps., 1992-96; Rep. senator dist. 20 Idaho State Senate, 1996—. Mem. commerce and human resources, health and welfare, judiciary and rules coms. Idaho State Senate. Mem. Owyhee County Cowbelles; mem. Mountain Home Mil. Affairs Com., Region IV Infant and Toddler Com., Idaho Rural Devel. Coun. With Idaho Air N.G. Mem. South Ctrl. Idaho Recreation and Tourism Devel. Assn., Owyhee County Cattlemens Assn., Mountain Home C. o C., Glenns Ferry C. of C. Roman Catholic. Office: PO Box 28 Glenns Ferry ID 83623 also: Idaho State Senate State Capitol PO Box 83720 Boise ID 83720-0081 E-mail: infocntr@lso.state.id.us.

KING CALKINS, CAROL COLEMAN, health sciences administrator; b. L.A., May 31, 1949; d. Harold S. and Gladys (Blumenthal) Coleman; 1 child, Katrina Elizabeth King; m. Michael Steven Calkins, Oct. 10, 1987. BA in Psychology, U. Colo., 1972, PhD in Pub. Affairs, 2000; MBA, U. No.Colo., 1982. Dir. group living Nat. Jewish Med. Ctr., Denver, 1980-82, dir. clin. support svcs., 1982-83, dir. spl. projects, 1983-84, asst. dir. adminstrv. svcs., 1984, dir. adminstrv. svcs., 1984-95; dir. facilities ops. U. Colo. Health Scis. Ctr., Denver, 1995—. Asst. adj. prof. U. Colo., Denver; chair purchasing and contract subcom. Denver Health and Hosps. New Authority, 1994—96; spkr. in field. Recorder improvement process coun. Jefferson County (Colo.) Schs., 1989. Mem.: ASTD, Rocky Mountain Assn. Higher Edn. Facilities Officers, Assn. Commuter Transp. (v.p. Rocky Mountain chpt. 1992), Am. Coll. Healthcare Execs., Colo. Hosp. Assn. Risk Mgrs., Pi Alpha Alpha (chpt. pres.). Avocations: weight training, horseback riding, hiking, snowboarding. Office: Fitzsimons Bldg 500 Mail Stop F410 PO Box 6508 Aurora CO 80045-0508

KING-COOPER, JENNIFER LAINE, social sciences educator; b. Pitts., Sept. 6, 1950; d. Donald Frederick and Nancy Elaine (Clark) King; m. Timothy Dean Cooper, Dec. 27, 1986. BA, Allegheny Coll., 1972; MA, Bowling Green State U., 1973; PhD, U. Pitts., 1986, The Union Inst., 1995. Residence hall dir. Bowling Green State U., Bowling Green, Ohio, 1973-77; asst. dir. student life svcs. Wilmington (Ohio) Coll., 1977-78; dir. residence life Allegheny Coll., Meadville, Pa., 1978-82; asst. to dean for student affairs U. Cin. Clermont Coll., Batavia, Ohio, 1983-86; lectr. psychology U. Cin., Batavia, Ohio, 1985-86; admissions coord. The Union Inst., Cin., 1987-94, adj. instr., 1987—; co-facilitator Domestic Safety Program, Marathon, Fla., 1995-96; instr. Sinclair C.C., Dayton, Ohio, 1996-2002, asst. prof., 2002. Part-time instr psychology of women U. Dayton, 1998-2003. Author: Explorations in Voice: Women's Psychosocial Development, 1995. Vol. Artemis Ctr. for Alternatives to Domestic Violence, Dayton, 1998—. Mem.: APA. Home: 70 Woods Rd Springboro OH 45066-1267 Office: Sinclair CC 444 W 3d St Dayton OH 45402

KINGERY, BRENDA L. artist, volunteer; b. Oklahoma City, Nov. 7, 1939; d. Jay B. Smith and June Stinnett Smith; m. Thomas Llyod Kingery, Feb. 28, 1939; children: Donald Scott, Karyn L. Kingery Lemons. BFA, Univ. Okla., 1961, MFA, 1970; grad. studies, Ryukyu Diaqaka Univ., Okinawa, Japan. Docent/arts Nat. Gallery Smithsonian, Washington, 1970—73; chmn. docent program McNay Mus., San Antonio, 1974; prof., painting, design Okinawan Folk Art History, Univ. Md., 1975—80; prof. art history San Antonio Coll., 1981—82; profl. artist, 1190—. Arts adv. coun. HeButt Found., Kerrville, Tex., 2000—03; cons. Cody Ctr. HEB Found., Kerrville, Leakey, Tex.; honors lectr. Tex. Tech Univ., Lubbock. Prin. works include Fletcher Gallery, SantaFe, Adair Margo Gallery, El Paso, Tex., Parchman Stremmel Gallery, San Antonio, Vandegriff-Marr Gallery, Chgo., Contemporary Southwest Gallery, Santa Fe, Eva Cohen Gallery, Chgo. Helping startup programs Cottage Industries; mission programs to 3rd world countries; city coun. foreign student programs; tapestry mission Women of third world countries, 1997—2003. Recipient Artist of the Yr., San Antonio, Tex, 1990, achievement recognition for Refugee programs, Okinawa, Japan, 1989—90.

KING HAUSER, ANN MARIE B. retired controller, artist; b. Manila, Nov. 7, 1951; d. Antonio G. and Dalisay B. King. BS in Hotel and Restaurant Mgmt., U. of the Philippines, Manila, 1972; MBA, Northwestern U., Evanston, Ill., 1977. Analyst Pacific Vegetable Oils, San Francisco, 1978—80; fin. analyst, sr. fin. mgr. Del Monte Corp., San Francisco, 1980—84, dir. fin. planning Internat. Grocery Products Divsn., 1984—86, dir. analytical svcs. U.S.A. divsn., 1986—87, mktg. controller USA divsn., 1987—90, dir. planning, 1990—92, controller Internat. Mkts., 1992. Featured spkr. Indonesian Batik paintings U. Philippines Alumnae Assn., Chgo., 1974. Joy Mag. website, 2001—03, one-woman shows include Philippine Consulate, San Francisco, exhibited in group shows at Blackhawk Gallery, Sebastopol Ctr. Arts, Calif., Danville Fine Arts Gallery, San Francisco Acad. Arts Gallery, 2002, Sacramento Arts Ctr., Represented in permanent collections N.W. Kellogg Sch. Bus. Dean's Office, Toshiba Corp. Mem.: Internat. Soc. Exptl. Artists, The Nat. Mus. Women in the Arts, Alamo Danville Artists Soc., Calif. Watercolor Assn. Roman Catholic. Avocations: tennis, bridge, music, opera, travel. Home: 707 Lakemont Pl #7 San Ramon CA 94583-1481

KINGMAN, ELIZABETH YELM, anthropologist; b. Lafayette, Ind., Oct. 15, 1911; d. Charles Walter and Mary Irene (Weakley) Yelm; m. Eugene Kingman, June 10, 1939; children: Mixie Kingman Eddy, Elizabeth Anne. BA, U. Denver, 1933; MA, 1935. Asst. in anthropology U. Denver, 1932-34; mus. asst. Ranger Naturalist Staff Mesa Verde Nat. Park, Colo., 1934-38; asst. to husband in curatorial work Indian art exhibits Philbrook Art Ctr., Tulsa, 1939-42, Joslyn Art Mus., Omaha, 1947-69; tutor humanities dept. U. Omaha, 1947-50; cjhn. bd. govs. Pi Beta Phi Settlement Sch., Gatlinburg, Tenn., 1969-72, Joslyn Art Mus., Omaha, 1947-50; tutor humanities dept. U. Omaha, 1947-50; chmn. bd. govs. Pi Beta Phi Settlement Sch., Gatlinburg, Tenn., 1969-72; asst. to husband in exhibit design mus. Tex. Tech. U., 1970-75; bibliographer Internat. Ctr. ARid and Semi-Arid Land Studies, 1974-75; libr. Sch. Am. Rsch., Santa Fe, N.Mex., 1978-86; rsch. assoc., 1986-98. V.p. Santa Fe Corral of the Westerners, 1985-86. Mem. AAUW, LWV, Archeol. Inst. Am. (v.p. Santa Fe chpt. 1981-83), Santa Fe Hist. Soc. (sec. 1981-83). Home: 604 Sunset St Santa Fe NM 87501-1118

KING-PIMENTEL, CARA SHANNON, music educator; b. Albuquerque, June 13, 1975; d. Gary Leon and Shelia Jolliff King. B of Music Edn., U. N.Mex., 1999. Orch., exploratory music, literacy tchr. Albuquerque Pub. Schs., 2000—; violin and viola tchr. Albuquerque, 2000—. Violist, founder Empire String Quartet, 1998—; mem. Knights team J. Carter Mid. Sch., Albuquerque Pub. Schs., 2000—01, mem. literacy study group J. Carter Mid. Sch., 2000—02, leader literacy study group J. Carter Mid. Sch., 2002—03. Musician (violist): San Juan Symphony, 2000—. Vol. U. N.Mex. Hosp., Carrie Tingley Children's Hosp. Mem.: Music Educators Assn., Am. String Tchrs. Assn., Chi Omega (song chair, activities chair 1995—99, Symphony award 1996). Avocations: study of psychology and music, water aerobics, reading, cross stitch, crochet. Home: 740 Terracotta Pl SW Albuquerque NM 87121 Office: J Carter Mid Sch 8901 Bluewater NW Albuquerque NM 87121

KINGSBURY, CAROLYN ANN, aerospace engineer, craftsman, writer; b. Newark, Ohio, Aug. 4, 1938; d. Cecil C. Layman and Orpha Edith (Hisey) Layman Dick; m. L.C. James Kingsbury, Apr. 25, 1959; children: Donald Lynn, Kenneth James. BS in Math. and Info. & Computer Scis., U. Calif., Irvine, 1979; postgrad., West Coast U., 1982-84. Systems engr. analyst Rockwell Internat., Downey, Calif., 1979-84; system and software engr. Northrop Corp., Pico Rivera, Calif., 1984-89; systems engr., rsch. engr. Hughes Aircraft Co., Long Beach, Calif., 1989-90, Fullerton, Calif., 1990—91; writer, 2001—. Pres. PTA, Manhattan Beach, Calif., 1971-73; Cub Scout den mother Boy Scouts Am., Manhattan Beach, 1972-73; mem. Fountain Valley Regional Hosp. Guild, 1993-96; radio reader Regional Audio Info. Svc. Enterprises, 1997-98; vol. computer cons. Henderson County Assessor's Office, 1997-98, Head Start program, 1998-99; with Blue Ridge Literacy Coun., 1998, 2002-03, Henderson County Pub. Libr., 2000-02. Recipient Svc. award Calif. Congress Parents and Tchrs., 1973, Leadership Achievement award YWCA, L.A., 1980, 84, NASA Achievement awards, 1983. Mem. NAFE, AAUW, Nat. Mgmt. Assn., Newtowners Club (pres. 1962). Republican. Home: 319 Mockingbird Dr Hendersonville NC 28792-6553 E-mail: kingsburys@bellsouth.net.

KINGSBURY, LISA R. instructional design consultant; b. McKeesport, Pa., Mar. 14, 1968; d. Frank A. and Frances V. Rendulic; m. Jeff N. Kingsbury, Aug. 9, 2003. BA in Comm., Calif. U. of Pa., 1990, MA in Comm., 1993. Sr. instructional designer Mellon Fin., Pitts., 1995—2001; instructional design cons. The Abreon Group, Pitts., 2002—. Grant writer Rostraver Libr., Pa., 1993—97; forensic judge Belle Vernon Area H.S., Pa., 1990—2001. Vol. Rostraver Pub. Libr., Pa., 1991—2000. Mem.: Toastmasters (Divsn. Gov. of Yr. - Dist. 13 2001). Avocations: reading, bicycling, interior decorating. Office: The Abreon Group Foster Plaza 10 Ste 500 680 Andersen Dr Pittsburgh PA 15220

KINGSLEY, KATHRYN ALEXIS KRAH, retired elementary school educator; d. Carl Alexis and Evelyn Brown Krah; m. Noel Draeger, June 12, 1966 (div. 1973); m. David A. Walsh, July 21, 1983. BS in Edn., No. Ill. U., 1966; MA in Multicultural Edn., Calif. State U., Dominguez Hills, 1976. Std. tchg. credential grades 7-12 Calif. Tchr, Sandwich (Ill.) Sch. Dist., 1966—67, El Monte (Calif.) Sch. Dist., 1967—9069; middle sch. tchr. Torrance (Calif.) Unified Sch. Dist., 1969—, ret., 2003. Rep. Nat. Edn. Assn. Conv., Portland, Oreg., 1974. Coord., editor: poetry Through the Ages, 1996—2003. Active So. Poverty Law Clinic, 1983—, ACLU, South Bay, Calif., 2002—, Dem. Party. Mem.: NEA, Torrance Tchrs. Assn. (bd. dirs. 1969—78, sch. rep. 1985—2003), Calif. Tchrs. Assn. (WHO award 2003). Avocations: theater, travel, reading, writing, dance. Home: 1533 Espinosa Cir Palos Verdes Estates CA 90274

KINGSLEY, PATRICIA, public relations executive; b. Gastonia, N.C., May 7, 1932; d. Robert Henry and Marjorie (Norment) Ratchford; m. Walter Kingsley, Apr. 1, 1966 (div. 1978); 1 child, Janis Susan. Student, Winthrop Coll., 1950-51. Publicist Fountainebleau Hotel, Miami Beach, Fla., 1952; exec. asst. ZIV TV, N.Y.C., 1953-58, publicist Rogers & Cowan L.A. and N.Y.C., 1960-71; pthr. Pickwick Pub. Rels., L.A., 1971-80, PMK Pub. Rels., L.A., 1980—. Adv. com. Women's Action for Nuclear Disarmament, Arlington, Mass., 1983—. Democrat. Office: PMK Pub Rels Inc 8500 Wilshire Blvd Beverly Hills CA 90211

KINGSOLVER, BARBARA ELLEN, writer; b. Annapolis, Md., Apr. 8, 1955; d. Wendell and Virginia (Henry) K.; m. Steven Hopp, 1993; 2 children. BA, DePauw U., 1977; MS, U. Ariz., 1981; LittD (hon.), DePauw U., 1994. Sci. writer U. Ariz., Tucson, 1981-85; free-lance journalist Tucson, 1985-87; novelist, 1987—. Book reviewer N.Y. Times, 1988—, L.A. Times, 1989—. Author: The Bean Trees, 1988 (ALA award 1988), Homeland and Other Stories, 1969 (ALA award 1990), Holding the Line: Women in the Great Arizona Mine Strike of 1983, 89, Animal Dreams, 1990 (PEN West Fiction award 1991, Edward Abbey Ecofiction award 1991), Another America, 1992, Pigs in Heaven, 1993 (L.A. Times Fiction prize 1993, Mountains and Plains Fiction award 1993, Western Heritage award 1993, ABBY Honor Book 1994), Essays, High Tide in Tucson, 1995, The Poisonwood Bible, 1998 (ABBY Honor Book 2000, PEN/Faulkner honoree 1999, Pulitzer runner-up 1999, Orange Prize short list 1999), Prodigal Summer, 2001, Small Wonder, 2002; co-author (with Annie Belt) Last Stand: America's Virgin Lands. Recipient Feature-writing award Ariz. Press Club, 1986; citation of accomplishment UN Nat. Coun. of Women, 1989; Woodrow Wilson Found./Lila Wallace fellow, 1992-93; Andrea Egan award Nat. Writers Union, 1998, Nat. Humanities Medal, 2000, Best Am. Sci. and Nature Writing, 2001, Gov.'s Nat. Award in the Arts, Ky., 2002, John P. McGovern award for Family, 2002, Nat. award Physicians for Social Responsibility, 2002. Mem. PEN Ctr. USA West, Nat. Writers Union, Phi Beta Kappa. Avocations: human rights, environmental conservation, gardening, natural history. Office: PO Box 31870 Tucson AZ 85751-1870 also: care Harper Collins 10 E 53rd St New York NY 10022-5244

KINGSTON, ALEX(ANDRA), actress; b. London, Mar. 11, 1963; m. Ralph Fiennes, 1993 (div. 1997); m. Florian Haertel, 1998; 1 child. Student, Royal Acad. Dramatic Arts. T.V. and movie actress. Appeared in T.V. films Foreign Affairs, 1993, The Infiltrator, 1995, Weapons of Mass Distraction, 1997; films include The Cook, The Thief, His Wife & Her Lover, 1989, Carrington, 1995, Virtual Encounters 2, 1998, Croupier, 1998, This Space Between Us, 2000, Moll Flanders, 1999, Essex Boys, 2000, Warrior Queen, 2003; T.V. series include The Knock, 1994, ER, 1997—. Recipient SAG award for Outstanding Performance by Ensemble in a Drama Series, 1994. Office: c/o The Gersh Agy 232 N Canon Dr Beverly Hills CA 90210-5302

KINGSTON, MAXINE HONG, writer, educator; b. Stockton, Calif., Oct. 27, 1940; d. Tom and Ying Lan (Chew) Hong; m. Earll Kingston, Nov. 23, 1962; 1 child, Joseph Lawrence. BA, U. Calif., Berkeley, 1962; D (hon.), Ea. Mich. U., 1988, Colby Coll., 1990, Brandeis U., 1991, U. Mass., 1991. Tchr. English, Sunset H.S., Hayward, Calif., 1965-66, Kahuku (Hawaii) H.S., 1967, Kahaluu (Hawaii) Drop-In Sch., 1968, Kailua (Hawaii) H.S., 1969, Honolulu Bus. Coll., 1969, Mid-Pacific Inst., Honolulu, 1970-77; prof. English, vis. writer U. Hawaii, Honolulu, 1977; Thelma McCandless Disting. Prof. Eastern Mich. U., Ypsilanti, 1986, Chancellor's Disting. Prof. U. Calif., Berkeley, 1990—. Author: The Woman Warrior: Memoirs of a Girlhood Among Ghosts, 1976 (Nat. Book Critics Cir. award for nonfiction; cited by Time mag., N.Y. Times Book Rev. and Asian Mail as one of best books of yr. and decade), China Men, 1981 (Nat. Book award; runner-up for Pulitzer prize, Nat. Book Critics Cir. award nominee 1988), Hawai' One Summer, 1987 (Western Books Exhbn. Book award, Book Builders West Book award), Tripmaster Monkey-His Fake Book, 1989 (PEN USA West award in Fiction), Through the Black Curtain, 1988, To Be The Poet, 2002, The Fifth Book of Peace, 2003 (Best Spiritual Book award, Spirituality and Health, 2003); editor: The Literature of California, 2001, (Commonwealth Club Book award 2001); To Be the Poet, 2002; contbr. short stories, articles and poems to mags. and jours., including Iowa Rev., The New Yorker, Am. Heritage, Redbook, Mother Jones, Caliban, Mich. Quarterly, Ms., The Hungry Mind Rev., N.Y. Times, L.A. Times, Zyzzyva; prodr. The Woman Warrior, Berkeley Repertory Co., 1994, The Huntington Theater, Boston, 1994, The Mark Taper Forum, L.A., 1995; host: (TV series) Journey to the West, 1994; subject of documentaries Talking Story, Stories My Country Told Me, Writers and Places; interviews on Dick Cavett, Bill Moyers, Ken Burns' The West, The News Hour with Jim Lehrer. Guggenheim fellow, 1981; recipient Nat. Endowment for the Arts Writers award, 1980, 82, Mademoiselle mag. award, 1977, Anisfield Wolf Book award, 1978, Calif. Arts Commn. award, 1981, Hawaii award for lit., 1982, Calif. Gov.'s award art, 1989, Major Book Collection award Brandeis U. Nat. Women's Com., 1990, award lit. Am. Acad. & Inst. Arts & Letters, 1990, Lila Wallace Reader's Digest Writing award, 1992, Spl. Achievement Oakland Bus. Arts award, 1994; named Living Treasure Hawaii, 1980, Woman of Yr. Asian Pacific Women's Network, 1981, Cyril Magnin award for Outstanding Achievement in the Arts, 1996, Disting. Artists award The Music Ctr. of L.A. County, 1996, Nat. Humanities medal NEH, 1997, Fred Cody Lifetime Achievement award, 1998, John Dos Passos prize for lit., 1998, Ka Palapola Po'okela award 1999, Profiles of Courage honor Swords to Plowshares, 1999, Alumna of Yr. award U. Calif.-Berkeley, 2000, Gold medal Calif. State Libr., 2002. Mem. Am. Acad. Arts and Scis.

KINKADE, JILL ANNETTE, writer; b. Evansville, Ind., Nov. 5, 1961; d. Jack Neal and Carolyn A. Kroeger; m. C. Lynn Kinkade, Oct. 10, 1987 (div.). BA summa cum laude, Hunter Coll., 1995; MA, U. Louisville, 1997. Owner Lady Day Cafe, Evansville, Ind., 1984-86; bookkeeper Alpha Lumber, Astoria, NY, 1987-89; mgr. gift shop Cabrini Med. Ctr., NYC, 1989-93; mktg. resources rep. Atlantic City C.C., 1995; English composition instr. U. Louisville, 1995-97; English and Humanities instr. U. So. Ind., 1997—2003; announcer WNIN Pub. Radio, 2004—. Mem. Phi Beta Kappa. Avocations: painting, weaving, building, baking. Home: 411 Washington Ave Evansville IN 47713-1526

KINLEY, CHRISTINE T. certified physician assistant; b. Carter County, Tenn. d. Lon Samuel and Mary (Johnson) Turbyfill; children: Amy Nikol, Michael Lon. Diploma, Johnson City Vocat. Tech. Sch., 1977; BSN, East Tenn. State U., 1988; Physician Asst., Trevecca Nazarene U., Nashville, 1997; postgrad., U. Health Scis., St. John's U., St. Lucia Sch. Medicine. LPN, RN, Tenn.; cert. physician asst. Charge nurse Four Oaks Health Care Ctr., Jonesborough, Tenn.; staff nurse VA Med. Ctr., Johnson, Tenn., nurse recruiter; physician asst. Johnson City Emergency Physicians, 1997-1999, emergency care coverage, 2000—; emegency care coverage Olde Towne Gen. Medicine, 2000—. E-mail: CKinley333@aol.com.

KINNAIRD, ELEANOR GATES, state legislator, lawyer; b. Rochester, Minn., Nov. 14, 1931; d. E. Vernon and E. Madge (Pollock) Gates; m. Richard W. Kinnaird, July 27, 1954 (div. June 1982); children: Robinson S., Michael G., Paul N. BA, Carleton Coll., 1953; MM, U. N.C., 1973; JD, N.C. Ctrl. U., 1992. Bar: N.C. 1992, U.S. Dist. Ct. (ea. and mid. dists.) N.C. 1992, U.S. Ct. Appeals (4th cir.) 1992. Staff atty. N.C. Prisoner Legal Svcs., Inc., Raleigh, 1993—; senator N.C. Gen. Assembly, 1997—. Mayor, Town of Carrboro, 1987-95. Mem. Phi Alpha Delta. Episcopalian. Avocations: political and civic activities, movies, reading, gardening. Home: 207 W Poplar Ave Carrboro NC 27510-1613 Office: NC Prisoner Legal Svcs Inc 224 S Dawson St Raleigh NC 27601-1306 E-mail: elliek@ncleg.net.

KINNE, FRANCES BARTLETT, academic administrator; b. Story City, Iowa; d. Charles Morton and Bertha (Olson) Bartlett; m. Harry L. Kinne, Jr. (dec.); m. M. Worthington Bordley, Jr. (dec.). Student, U. No. Iowa; B of Music Edn., M. of Music Edn., Drake U., DFA (hon.), 1981, hon. degree; PhD cum laude, U. Frankfurt, Fed. Republic of Germany, 1957; LHD (hon.), Wagner Coll., N.Y.; LLD (hon.), Lenoir Rhyne Coll.; DHL (hon.), Jacksonville U., 1995; LLD (hon.), Flagler Coll. Tchr. music Kelley (Iowa) Consol. Sch.; supr. music Boxholm (Iowa) [illegible] Sch.; Des Moines pub. schs.; sr. hostess Camp Crowder, Mo.; dir. recreation VA, Wadsworth, Kans.; lectr. music, English and Western culture Tsuda Coll., Tokyo; cons. music U.S. Army Gen. Hdqrs., Tokyo; mem. faculty Jacksonville (Fla.) U., 1958—, Disting. Univ. prof., 1961-62, prof. music and humanities, 1963—, dean, founder Coll. Fine Arts, interim pres., 1979, pres., 1979-89, chancellor, 1989-94; chancellor emeritus, 1995—. Past chmn. Ind. Colls. and Univs. Fla.; mem. adv. coun. Nat. Soc. Arts and Letters; hon. mem. staff Mayo Clinic, Jacksonville; corporator Charles Schepens Eye Rsch. Inst. of Harvard U., Cambridge, Mass.; mem. adv. bd. Women's Eye Task Force, Harvard. Author: A Comparative Study of British Traditional and American Indigenous Ballads, 1958, Iowa Girl: The President Wears a Skirt, 2000; contbr. chpt. to book and articles to profl. jours. Trustee Drake U.; bd. dirs., life mem. Jacksonville Symphony Assn., Bert Thomas Scholarship Found., Doug Milne Found., Jacksonville U.; bd. dirs., exec. com. Eye Rsch. Found.; mem., then chmn. adv. bd. Ronald McDonald House; past mem. bd. govs. Jacksonville C. of C., past v.p.; mem. pres.'s adv. coun. Flagler Coll. Recipient hon. awards Bus. and Profl. Women's Clubs, 1962, Disting. Svc. award Drake U., 1966, 1st Fla. Gov.'s award for achievement in arts, 1972, EVE award in edn., 1973, Arts Assembly Individual award, 1978-79, Roast award Soc. for Prevention of Blindness, 1980, Brotherhood award NCCJ, 1981, Top Mgmt. award Jacksonville Sales and Mktg. Execs., 1981, Alumni Achievement award U. No. Iowa, Ann. Burton C. Bryan award, Pub. Svc. award Physicians Edn. Network, Freedom Found. Valley Forge, Brotherhood of NCCJ award, Disting. Svc. award Fla. Soc. Ophthalmology, Women of Achievement award 1st Coast Bus. and Profl. Women's Club Jacksonville, Disting. Educator award Internat. Longshoremen's Assn., Hope award Nat. Multiple Sclerosis Soc., Disting. Am. award Nat. Football Fedn., Fla. State Mus. Tchrs. award, Outstanding Civic Leader award Civic Roundtable of Jacksonville, Vol. Jacksonville 2d Ann. Bernard Gregory Servant Leader award; named Eve of Decade, Elaine Gordon Lifetime Achievement award Fla. Fedn. Bus. and Profl. Women, 1996, Order of the South award So. Acad. Letters, Arts and Scis., Order of the South award Nat. Soc. Arts and Letters; inducted into Fla. Women's Hall of Fame, Outstanding Svc. to Theatre Edn. Fla. Assn. for Theatre Edn.; hon. mem. 3d Armored Divsn., U.S. Army; day named in her honor Women's Club of Jacksonville and other orgns.; one of six women featured on History Week posters apptd. by Mayor Jacksonville; bldgs. named in honor: Frances Bartlett Kinne Univ. Ctr. Jacksonville U., Frances Bartlett Kinne Alumni and Devel. Ctr. Drake U., Frances Bartlett Kinne Auditorium at Mayo Clinic, Jacksonville. Mem. AAUW, Nat. Music Tchrs. Assn., Fla. Music Tchr. Assn., Music Educators Nat. Conf., Fla. Music Edn. Assn. (past bd. dirs.), Assn. Am. Colls. (past bd. govs., exec. com.), Friday Musicale (life), Fla. Coll. Music Edn. Assn. (past pres., v.p.), Delius Assn. of Fla. (life), Nat. Assn. Schs. Music (past chmn. region 7), Fine Arts Forum (hon.), Ind. Colls. and Univs. of Fla. (past chmn., 1st woman chmn.), So. Acad. Letters, Arts and Scis., Internat. Coun. Fine Arts Deans (past chmn., 1st woman chmn.), Fla. Women's Hall of Fame (Gov.'s First award), Jacksonville Women's Network Inner Wheel, Nat. Soc. Arts and Letters (adv. coun.), P.E.O., Green Key (hon.), Ret. Officers Assn. (hon. mem. Mayport chpt.), St. John's Dinner Club (past pres.), Exch. Club (Golden Deeds award), River Club (1st woman mem.), Rotary (pres. 2000, one of 1st two women elected bd. dirs. Jacksonville chpt., Paul Harris fellow, 1st woman pres. Rotary Club Jacksonville, 2000—), Alpha Xi Delta, Mu Phi Epsilon (Elizabeth Mathias award, judge internat. music edn. award), Alpha Psi Omega (hon.), Alpha Kappa Pi (hon.), Alpha Kappa Psi (hon.), Beta Gamma Sigma, Omicron Delta Kappa (hon.), Alpha Xi Delta (Woman of Distinction award). Home: 4032 Mission Hills Cir W Jacksonville FL 32225-4635

KINNEY, BEVERLY JEAN, English language educator; b. Yakima, Wash., Apr. 17, 1926; d. Vesper Lewis and Ethel Annetta (Silvers) Cox; m. Lyle B. Kinney, Aug. 21, 1948. BA, Ctrl. Wash. U., 1948; MA in Reading, U. Mo., 1968; cert. in edn. adminstrn., Western Wash. U., 1976. Mem. dist. reading team Port Angeles (Wash.) Pub. Schs., 1969-75, prin. Franklin Elem. Sch., 1975-89, supr. student tchrs., 1968-90; instr. Peninsula Coll., Port Angeles, 1992; prin. Queets-Clearwater Sch. Dist. Ednl. Svcs. Dist., Bremerton, Wash., 1993-94; supr. student tchrs. Olympic Peninsula Ednl. Svcs. Dist., Bremerton, Wash., 2000—. Fellow Fla. Inst. Tech., Melbourne, 1983, Inst. for Devel. Ednl. Activities, Claremont, Calif., 1978-88; tchr. NEA Tchg. Corps, Sierra Leone, summers, 1965, 67; tchr. English, Shijiazhuang (China) Hebei Tchrs. Coll., 1990-91, 92-93, 94. Active YMCA, Port Angeles, 1956-61, Girl Scouts of U.S., Port Angeles, Women in Politics, Beijing, Shanghai, People to People, George Washington U. Recipient Friendship award People's Republic of China, 1994, Disting. Alumni award Coll. Edn. and Profl. Studies, Ctrl. Wash. U. Alumni Assn., 1997. Mem. AAUW, LWV, Delta Kappa Gamma, Soroptimists. Democrat. Methodist. Avocations: outdoors, gardening, hiking, walking, reading. Home and Office: 253 Cedar Park Dr Port Angeles WA 98362-8430

KINNEY, CAROLYN, executive secretary; b. Philipsburg, Pa., Feb. 18, 1957; MD, Boston U., 1981. Sec. Am. Bd. Phys. Medicine & Rehab.; staff Good Samaritan Regional Hosp. Med. Ctr., Phoenix, 1995—; phys. Health South Meridian Point Rehab., Scottsdale, Ariz., 1996—; resident Thomas Jefferson U. Hosp., Phila., 1982—84; intern Thomas Jefferson U. Hosp., Phila., 1981. Office: Am Bd Phys Medicine & Rehab 21 First St Ste 674 Rochester MN 55902-3092

KINNEY, CATHERINE R. stock exchange executive; BS magna cum laude, Iona Coll.; cert. advanced mgmt., Harvard Sch. Bus. Various positions N.Y. Stock Exch., 1974—86, mgr. trading-floor opers. and tech., 1986—95, group exec. v.p., 1995—2002, exec. vice chmn., pres. & co-COO, 2002—. Mem. office of chmn. N.Y. Stock Exch., co-chair mgmt. and oper. coms., bd. mem., MetLife Inc., Depository Trust & Clearing Corp., NYU Downtown Hosp., Securities Industry Automation Corp., 1988—97, mem. exec. com., 1994—97. Bd. regents Georgetown U.; trustee Iona Coll. Office: attn Ray Pellecchia NY Stock Exch 11 Wall St New York NY 10005

KINNEY, JANIS MARIE, librarian, consultant; b. Cresson, Pa., Dec. 26, 1935; d. Cecil and Ruth Ellen (Moyer) Powell; m. James Leroy Kinney; 1 child, Janis Cecilia. BS in Libr. Sci., Clarion U., 1957; MEd in Curriculum and Instrn., Pa. State U., 1987. Librarian N. Huntingdon Sch. Dist., Irwin, Pa., 1957-58, Greater Gallitzin (Pa.) Schs., 1959-61, Hollidaysburg (Pa.) Area Sch. Dist., 1961-90; storyteller Altoona, Pa., 1990—. Chair Allegheny Storytellers of Pa., 1991—; rostered artist Pa. Coun. on the Arts in Edn. Program; cons. various sch. dists.; cons. Old Bedford Village Storytelling Festival, Bedford, Pa., West Overton Village Tellabration; cofounder interdisciplinary arts group Stories in Motion. Author/producer audio cassettes; featured teller Corn Island Storytelling Festivals, Louisville; contbr. articles to profl. jours. Active Blair County Arts Found., Altoona, 1991—, Blair County Tourist & Conv. Bur., 1992—, Blair County Hist. Soc., 1994—; Pa. Rural Arts Alliance, 1992—. Recipient Disting. Educator award Hollidaysburg Alumni, 1996. Mem. Internat. Order E.A.R.S. (Disting. Svc. award 2001), Nat. Storytelling Assn., Allegheny Storytellers Pa. (founder). Avocations: reading, bicycling, hiking, music, travel. Home and Office: 1900 16th Ave Altoona PA 16601-2502 E-mail: jankin@pennswoods.net.

KINNEY, JEANNE KAWELOLANI, English studies educator, writer; b. Bayville, N.Y., Nov. 22, 1964; d. Robert Warren Stewart and Genevieve Lehuanani (Okilauea) Kinney. BA, Linfield Coll., 1986; MFA, Bowling Green State U., 1988. Tchr. Hawaii Bus. Coll., Honolulu, 1993-95; ESL tchr. GEOs Lang. Corp., Osaka and Kobe, Japan, 1996-97; English tchr. St. Joseph's H.S., Hilo, Hawaii, 2000. Poet-in-the-schs. Dept. Edn., Honolulu, fall 1994; sub. English tchr. St. Andrew's Priory, Honolulu, 1993; adj. English tchr. Chaminade U., Honolulu, spring 1993, 94; basic skills instr. Kamehameha Schs., Honolulu, 1991-92; English tchr., speech coach Punahou Sch., Honolulu, 1989-91. Contbr. to profl. publs. including Hawaii Rev., Kaimana, Ascent, Seattle Rev., Bamboo Ridge Press. Precinct ops. cood. Office Lt. Gov., Hawaii Elections Divsn., 1991-93, precinct worker trainer, 1989-91; v.p. Hawaii Lit. Arts Coun., Honolulu, 1990; pub. rels. officer Hawaii Speech League, Honolulu, 1991. Avocations: dance, swimming, writing, travel, foreign languages. Home: 10 Ululani St # 10 Hilo HI 96720-2979

KINNEY, KATHY, actress; b. Stevens Point, Wis., Nov. 3, 1954; d. Harold and Marian Kinney. Student, U. Wis. Actress playing Mimi Bobeck on The Drew Carey Show ABC-TV, 1995—. Appearances include (films) Parting Glances, 1986, Scrooged, 1988, Arachnophobia, 1990, Stanley and Iris, 1990, The Linguini Incident, 1991, Mr. Jones, 1993, This Boy's Life, 1993, (TV series) Newhart, 1989-90, Grand, 1990, (TV episodes) The Larry Sanders Show, 1992, Seinfeld, 1992, Lois and Clark: The New Adventures of Superman, 1996, (TV movies) Inherit the Wind, 1988, Promised a Miracle, 1988, (TV spls.) Tag Team, 1991, presenter The Eighteenth Ann. Cable Ace Awards, 1996; also various stage appearances. Avocations: restoring old lamps, reading. Office: care The Drew Carey Show Warner Bros TV 4000 Warner Blvd Burbank CA 91522-0001

KINNEY, LISA FRANCES, lawyer; b. Laramie, Wyo., Mar. 13, 1951; d. Irvin Wayne and Phyllis (Poe) Kinney; m. Rodney Philip Lang, Feb. 5, 1971; children: Cambria Helen, Shelby Robert, Eli Wayne. BA, U. Wyo., 1973, JD, 1986; MLS, U. Oreg., 1975. Reference libr. U. Wyo. Sci. Libr., Laramie, 1975-76; outreach dir. Albany County Libr., Laramie, 1975-76, dir., 1977-83; mem. Wyo. State Senate, Laramie, 1984-94, minority leader, 1992-94; with documentation office Am. Heritage Ctr. U. Wyo., 1991-94; assoc. Corthell & King, 1994-96, shareholder, 1996-99; owner Summit Bar Rev., 1987—; fin. planner VALIC, 2001—. Author: (with Rodney Lang) Civil Rights of the Developmentally Disabled, 1986; (with Rodney Lang and Phyllis Kinney) Manual For Families with Emotionally Disturbed and Mentally Ill Relatives, 1988, rev. 1991, 99, Lobby For Your Library, Know What Works, 1992, Understanding Mental Illnesses: A Family Legal Guide, 2004; contbr. articles to profl. jours.; editor, compiler pub. rels. directory of ALA, 1982. Bd. dirs. Big Bros./Big Sisters, Laramie, 1980-83, Children's Mus., 1993-97; bd. dirs. Am. Heritage Ctr., 1993-97, Citizen of the Century, 1997-99, govt. chmn. 1997-99; pres. Friends Cmty. Recreation Project, 2001—. Recipient Beginning Young Profl. award Mt. Plains Libr. Assn., 1980; named Outstanding Wyo. Libr. Assn., 1977, Outstanding Young Woman State of Wyo., 1980, Arts and Scis. Disting. Alumni award U. Wyo., 1997, Making Democracy Work award Wyo. LWV, 2000. Mem.: ABA, Nat. Conf. State Legislatures (various coms. 1985—90), Laramie Area C. of C. (bd. dirs. 1996—2000, mem. 1999, Top Hand award 1997), Zonta, Kiwanis. Democrat. Avocations: photography, dance, reading, travel, languages. Home: 1415 E Baker St Laramie WY 82072 Office: PO Box 1710 Laramie WY 82073-1710 Office Phone: 302-742-6644. E-mail: lfkl@aol.com.

KINNEY, STEPHANIE S. state agency administrator; b. Orlando, Fla., June 24, 1944; m. Douglas S. Kinney, June 27, 1970; 1 child. Student, U. Madrid, Spain, 1964-65; BA cum laude, Vassar Coll., 1966; MA, Harvard U., 1967; MS, Nat. Defense U., 1994. With foreign svc. Dept. State, 1983 86, desk officer, 1986-88, asst. cultural affairs officer, 1990-92; dep. dir. office of global change Dept. of State, 1992-93, dep. dir. office environ. policy, 1994-97, exec. dir. bureau of oceans, environ. and sci. Washington, 1997—. Recipient Superior Hero award 1992. Mem. Am. Foreign Svc. Assn., Vassar Club (Washington, D.C. chpt.), Women's Foreign Policy Group. Office: Bureau of Oceans Environ and Sci Dept of State 2201 C St NW Rm 7820 Washington DC 20520-0001

KINNIER, EMILY P. artist; d. Nelson Palmore and Elizabeth Bott; m. Eugene Howard Kinnier, Feb. 4, 1939. Grad., Pan Am. Bus. Coll., Richmond, VA, 1935; Studied, Art Students League, N.Y.C., 1953—70. Treas. patterson nj br. Nat. League of Am. Penwomen, Patterson, NJ, 1968—69; treas. Richmond br. Nat. League of Am. Pen Women (Hdgs.), Washington, 1977—78. Studied with Laura Glenn Douglas, Washington, 1950—50; studied with Vytlacil, Kantor, Hovannes, Ben Cunningham, Hale Art Students League, N.Y.C., 1953—72; studied with Burgoyne Diller Studio Atlantic Highlands, Atlantic Highlands, NJ, 1960—64; studied with Laura Pahris Richmond Printmaking Workshop, Richmond, Va., 1980—82. One-woman shows include Middle St. Gallery, Wash., Va., 1996—98, exhibited in group shows, 2000, 2002, exhibitions include Juried Show, Newark Mus., 1964 (Second Prize in Watercolor), State Juried Show, Montclair Mus., 1964 (2nd prize on watercolor), Montclair Mus., N.J., 1964, Jersey City Mus., 1965, Festival of Arts, Monmouth Coll., N.J., 1966, Middle St. Gallery, Wash., Va., 1995, 1708 Gallery, Richmond, Va., 1996—2004, Nations Bank Gallery, 1998. Arts bd. St. Pauls Episc. Ch., Richmond, Va., 1982—84. Mem.: Nat. League of Am. Pen Women Richmond Br., Art Students League N.Y.C. (life). Avocations: travel, gardening. Home: 812 N Tilden Richmond VA 23221-1517

KINSER, CYNTHIA D. state supreme court justice; b. Pennington Gap, Dec. 20, 1951; d. Morris and Velda (Myers) Fannon; m. H. Allen Kinser, Jr., March 17, 1974; children: Charles Adam, Terah Diane. Student, Univ. of Ga., 1970-71; BA, Univ. of Tenn., 1974; JD, Univ. of Va., 1977. Bar: Va. 1977, U.S. Dist. Ct. (we. dist.) Va. 1977, U.S. Ct. Appeals (4th cir.) 1977, U.S. Supreme Ct. 1988. Law clk. to Judge Glen M. Williams U.S. Dist. Ct., 1977-78; pvt. law practice, 1978-90; commonwealth's atty. Lee County, Va., 1980-83; magistrate judge U.S. Dist. Ct. (we. dist.) Va., Abingdon, 1990-98; justice Va. Supreme Ct., Richmond, 1998—. Trustee Chapter 7 Panel, U.S. Bankruptcy Ct., 1979-90. Mem. Va. Bar Assn., Va. Trial Lawyers Assn., Am. Bar Assn. Methodist. Office: Supreme Court 100 North 9th Street, 5th Floor Richmond VA 23219

KINSER, DIANE, communications educator, writer; b. Mpls., Oct. 14, 1943; d. Frank LaVerne and M. Elizabeth (Mechem) Fuller; m. Lonnie Paul Jenkins, Apr. 5, 1969 (div. Aug. 1979); children: Amy Elizabeth Jenkins, Amanda Erin Jenkins; m. Paul Richard Kinser, May 21, 1980. BA, Ohio U., 1965; MA, Ohio State U., 1969; postgrad., U. Dayton, 1974—76. 8-yr. profl. tchg. cert. Ohio. English tchr. Groveport (Ohio)-Madison H.S., 1969—71; sixth grade tchr. Columbus (Ohio) Torah Acad., 1974—78; owner, operator Diet Ctr., Ohio, 1978—88; instr. English and speech Bradford Sch., Columbus, 1987—90; instr. comm. Columbus State C.C., 1991—; instr. writing program Franklin U., Columbus, Ohio, 1994—; instr. English Ohio U., Lancaster, 1997—2001. Graduation cord. Bradford Sch., Columbus, 1987—90; adj. faculty com. Franklin U., Columbus, 1997—99; host writers conf. Columbus State C.C., 2003. Author: (novels) Magician's Wake, 2002, Legacy of Black Diamond, 2003. Pres., sec. Gahanna (Ohio) Area C. of C., 1981—89; pres., program chair Am. Bus. Women's Assn., Reynoldsburg, Ohio, 1983—94; bd. mem. Gahanna Mental Health Ctr., 1984—87. Named Woman of the Yr., Am. Bus. Women's Assn.-Reflection Chpt., 1990. Home: 3642 Melrare Ct Grove City OH 43123 Office: Columbus State CC 550 E Spring St Columbus OH 43123

KINSEY, DONNA LEE, music educator; b. Punxsutawney, Pa., Dec. 18, 1947; d. Donald Joseph White and Sarah Leona Gromley; m. William Robert Kinsey, Mar. 30, 1970; stepchildren: Sheryl Ann Mock, Merrilee Kay Saccol. BS in Music Edn., Ind. U. Pa., 1969; MusM, W.Va. Univ., 1979. Cert. tchr. W.Va. Organist/choir dir. St. John's Luth. Ch., Kittanning, Pa., 1969—71; music tchr. Latrobe Jr. High, Pa., 1971—72; pastoral musician St. Theresa's Roman Cath. Parish, Morgantown, W.Va., 1972—2003, St. Francis de Sales, 2004—; music tchr. Armstrong Sch. Dist., Kittanning, 1969—71, Monongalia County Schs., Morgantown, 1993—. Asst. organist, choir dir. 1st Presbyn. Ch., Greensburg, Pa., 1971—72; music tchr. St. Francis Ctrl. Sch., Morgantown, 1973—92; chair Music Commn. Diocese, Wheeling/Charleston, W.Va., 1973—99; program chair Nat. Pastoral Musicians Music Edn. Bd., 1992—2002. Mem. bd. W.Va. Children's Chorus Bd., 1992—95, 2003—. Mem.: Choristers Guild, Am. Guild Organists, Am. Guild English Handbell Ringers (chair 2002—03, mem. spl. events com.), Music Edn. Assn., Nat. Pastoral Musicians (Nat. Cath. Music Educator of the Yr. 2001—02), Am. Choral Dirs. Assn. Republican. Methodist. Home: 2594 Grafton Rd Morgantown WV 26508 Office: St Francis de Sales 1 Gutherie Ln Morgantown WV 26508

KINSLOW, MARGIE ANN, volunteer; b. Salt Lake City, Dec. 7, 1931; d. Diamond and Sarah (Chipman) Wendelboe; m. James Ferol Kinslow, Apr. 6, 1954 (dec. July 1982). Student, U. Utah, 1949—53. Jr. vol. chmn. various hosps., Okla., Mont., Colo., 1967—87; pres. Ch. Woman's Orgn., Bartlesville, Okla., 1968; fin. advisor, jr. v.p., vol. chmn. Swedish Med. Ctr., Englewood, 1971—92; pres. Delta Gamma Alumnae, Denver, 1975—76; jr. vol. chair Colo. Assn. Hosp. Aux., Denver, 1977—82, 2d v.p., 1982—84; transp. chair, master class chmn. Rocky Mountain Regional Auditions, Met. Opera, Denver, 1986—. Office vol. Rep. Office, Billings, Mont., 1969-70, Colo. Senator, Denver, 1974-76; vol. various polit. candidates, Denver, 1974-90; various offices Newcomers, Okla., Mont. and Colo., 1967-75; bd. dirs. Anchor Ctr. for Blind Children, 2000—, Denver Lyric Opera, 2002—. Recipient Stellar award, 1979, Cable award, 1991. Mem. PEO, Gen. Fedn. of Women's Clubs (bd. dirs. 1994—, corr. sec. Western region), Colo. Gen. Fedn. of Women's Clubs (pres. 1994-96, various offices 1986-94), Denver Lyric Opera Guild (bd. dirs. 2002—), Cherry Creek Woman's Club (pres. 1985, Hoby corp. bd. 1997—), Littleton Rep. Women's Club. Episcopalian. Avocations: bridge, travel, people, the arts.

KINSLOW, MONICA M. forensic scientist; b. Chgo., Feb. 19, 1956; d. Chris C. and Martha Stratton; m. Keith Kinslow, Mar. 8, 1975; children: Aisha Ebony, Naomi Alice, Miles Keith. BS in Chemistry, Chgo. State U., 1981. Criminalist Chgo. Police Dept., 1988-96; forensic scientist Ill. State Police, Chgo., 1996—. Mem. Midwestern Assn. Forensic Scientists, Am. Chem. Soc. Avocations: church activities, reading. Office: Ill State Police Forensic Sci Ctr 1941 W Roosevelt Rd Chicago IL 60608-1246

KINSLOW, NORMA JEAN, musician, educator; b. Cookeville, Tenn., Sept. 19, 1958; d. Norman and Mary Louise Whitewater; m. Stan M. Kinslow, Dec. 14, 1979; children: Kara, Kate, John. BS in Family Consumer Sci. Edn. and Merchandising, Tenn. Tech. U., Cookeville, 1981, MusB in Edn., 1998. Cert. Am. Bd. of Opticianry. Supr. jewelry dept. Harvey's Dept. Store, Cookeville, 1981—83; preschool tchr. Agape and Jefferson Ch., 1988—98; optician Dr. James Miller, 1995—98; cellist/violinist Cumberland String Quartet, Crossville, Tenn., 1998—; music specialist Cumberland County Schs., Crossville, 1999—. Condr. Children of Crossville Prep. Orch., 2002—; asst. condr. Children of Crossville Chamber Orch., 1998—. Mem.: NEA, Am. String Tchrs. Assn., Tenn. Music Educators Assn., Music Educators Nat. Conf. Mem. Ch. Of Christ. Avocations: needlecrafts, travel. Office: 1219 Cook Rd Crossville TN 38555

KINSMAN, SARAH MARKHAM, investment company executive; b. L.A., Oct. 1, 1951; d. Robert Starr and Barbara Ann (Yates) K.; m. Kevin H. Olsen, Oct. 15, 1984 (div.); 1 child, Robert Kinsman. AB, UCLA, 1973; MBA, Harvard U., Boston, 1976. Acct. officer Citibank's World Corp. Group, N.Y.C., 1976-79; fin. mgr. Union Pacific Corp., N.Y.C., 1980-86; v.p., sr. transactor Citibank, N.A., N.Y.C., 1986-88; v.p. Bank N.Y., N.Y.C., 1988-92; sr. v.p. GE Capital, N.Y.C., 1992—. Com. chmn. Jr. League, N.Y.C., 1988—; mem. women's com. Am. Cancer Soc., N.Y.C., 1988-90; den leader Boy Scouts Am. Mem. Assn. for Corp. Growth, Women's Harvard Bus. Sch. Club N.Y.C., Harvard Bus. Sch. Club N.Y.C., Harvard Bus. Sch. Club N.J., Phi Beta Kappa. Avocations: horseback riding, gardening, travel, reading, dance. Office: One World Fin Ctr 100 Liberty St 3d Fl New York NY 10281 Home: PO Box 1094 Flemington NJ 08822-1094

KINSOLVING, SYLVIA CROCKETT, musician, educator; b. Berkeley, Calif., Sept. 30, 1931; d. Harold Waldo and Louise (Effinger) Crockett; m. Charles Lester Kinsolving, Dec. 18, 1953; children: Laura Louise, Thomas Philip, Kathleen Susan. AA in Voice, Piano magna cum laude, No. Va. Community Coll., 1983; BA, U. Calif., Berkeley, 1953. Solo vocalist various chs., Va., 1982—; pvt. tchr. piano, 1983—. Singer, soloist Unity Ch., Oakton, Va., 1980—, St. Andrew's Anglican Ch., Alexandria, Va., 1985—; active numerous local musical prodns., 1959—. Tour leader Vienna Newcomers, 1980. Mem. PEO, U. Calif. Alumni Club, Fairfax West Music Fellowship (sec. 1990—), Phi Theta Kappa, Pi Beta Phi. Democrat. Episcopalian. Avocations: walking, swimming, music, reading. Home: 1517 Beulah Rd Vienna VA 22182-1417

KINTZING, JULIE ALEXANDRA, social worker; d. Bernard and Pilar Bundarin; m. William Michael Kintzing, Oct. 25, 1986; 1 child, Lauren 1 stepchild, Christof. BS in Social Work, Colo. State U., Ft. Collins, 1976, MS in Social Work, 1993. LCSW Colo., cert. State Bd. of Social Workers, Colo. Therapist I bilingual Larimer County Mental Health, Ft. Collins, Colo., 1976—78; temporary residential counselor Larico Youth Homes, Ft. Collins, 1979; social svc. dir. Columbine Manor, Wheat Ridge, Colo., 1987—88; bilingual caseworker Emergency Family Assistance Corp., Boulder, Colo., 1988—91; clin. therapist intern Mental Health Ctr. of Boulder County, Longmont, Colo., 1992—93; emergency bilingual caseworker Boulder County Dept. Social Svcs., Longmont, 1989—94; bilingual therapist Longmont Headstart Program, 1994; contract clin. therapist Mental Health Ctr. of Boulder County, LaFayette, Colo., 1994—95; rsch. asst. Inst. of Behavioral Genetics Colo. U., Boulder, 1995—96; bilingual caseworker III Boulder County Dept. Social Svcs., 1994—2002; pvt. practice. Mental health crisis - disaster counselor Am. Red Cross (mile hi chpt.), 2001—; vol. crisis counselor Roundhouse Ctr. Colo. State U., Ft. Collins, 1972—75. Recipient Eddie Schoech award, Boulder County Dept. Social Svcs., 1995. Achievements include development of liaison program between government and private service providers in the area of mental health; assisted in the development of treatment programs, halfway house and bilingual support. Avocations: skiing, music, theater, art, bicycling. Office: J Kintzing PO Box 20944 Boulder CO 80308-3944 Office Phone: 303-875-6207. E-mail: kintz53@msn.com.

KINZIE, CAROLE G. artist; b. Suffolk, Va., Nov. 8, 1944; d. Alfred Percy and Rebecca Inez (Chappell) Gillette; m. Richard Cline Kinzie Jr., Mar. 18, 1962; children: Rebecca Susan Kinzie Johnston, Edward Charles, Sharon Margaret. AA, Macon Coll., 1994; BA, Ga. Coll., 1996. Artist, tchr., Macon, Ga., 1996—97; owner Artel Art Craft Market, Payne, Ga. Dep. co-leader med. mission World Wide Svcs., Yemen, 1981—97. Mem.: Macon Art Assn., Ga. Watercolor Soc. (assoc.), Friends of Dard Hunter. Avocations: canoeing, reading, restoring furniture. Home: 522 Corbin Ave Macon GA 31204

KINZIE, JEANNIE JONES, radiation oncologist, nuclear medicine physician; b. Great Falls, Mont., Mar. 14, 1940; d. James Wayne and Lillian Alice (Young) Jones; m. Joseph Lee Kinzie, Mar. 26, 1965 (div. Sept. 1982); 1 child, Daniel Joseph; m. Johnson Wachira, Oct. 7, 1991. Student, Oreg. State U., 1960; BS, Mont. State U., 1961; MD, Washington U., 1965; MBA, U. Phoenix, 1997. Diplomate Am. Bd. Radiology; diplomate Am. Bd. Nuclear Medicine; cert. advanced master gardener Colo. State U., 1997. Intern. in surgery U. N.C., Chapel Hill, 1965-66; resident in therapeutic radiology Washington U., St. Louis, 1968-71, instr. in radiology, 1971-73; asst. prof. in radiology Med. Coll. of Wis., Milw., 1973-75, U. Chgo., 1975-78, assoc. prof. in radiology, 1978-80; assoc. prof. of radiation oncology Wayne State U., Detroit, 1980-85; prof. radiology U. Colo., Denver, 1985-95; dir. radiation oncology U. Hosp., Denver, 1985-91; fellow in nuclear medicine U. Colo., 1996-98, asst. clin. prof. nuclear medicine, 1998—; staff radiologist Denver Vets. Hosp., Denver, 2003—. Cons. Denver Vets. Hosp., 1985-98, Denver Gen. Hosp., 1985-95, Rose Med. Ctr., 1986-95, FDA Ctr. for Devices and Radiologic Health, 1986-2003; mem. sci. adv. bd. Cancer League Colo., 1985-88; examiner Am. Bd. Radiology, 1985-88; adv. physician Colo. Med. Found., 1988-98; chmn. faculty promotion com. U. Colo. Health Scis. Ctr., 1988-89. Assoc. editor Internat. Jour. Radiation Oncology Biology and Physics, 1985-95; contbr. articles to profl. jours.; chpts. to books. Mem. Faith Bible Chapel Ch. NIH grantee, 1973-75. Fellow Am. Coll. Radiology; mem. AMA, Am. Coll. Nuclear Physicians, Colo. Med. Soc., Denver Med. Soc. (del. to Colo. Med. Soc. Ho. of Dels. 1989—), Colo. Radiol. Soc., Soc. Nuclear Medicine, Rocky Mountain Oncology Soc. (bd. dirs. 1989-93, pres. 1991-93), Am. Soc. Therapeutic Radiologists, Am. Cancer Soc. (bd. dirs. Denver unit 1986-87), Wilderness Med. Soc. Republican. Avocations: stamp collecting, gardening, rug latching, mountain climbing. E-mail: jeannie.kinzie@worldnet.att.net.

KIPFERL, CHRISTIANA A. special education educator; b. Elmira, N.Y., June 6, 1953; d. Martin Joseph and RosaLea (VanMarter) Burke; m. H. LaVerne Kipferl, Aug. 9, 1986; stepchildren: Kevin, Keith, Kayla, Kerry, Kory, Kelly. AA, Corning C.C., 1973; BS, Mansfield State Coll., 1975, MEd, 1993. Sr. exec. sec., travel coord. Imaging & Sensing Technology Corp., Horseheads, N.Y., 1988-95; resource rm. tchr. Elmira (N.Y.) City Sch. Dist., 1995-96; affective educator Steuben-Allegany BOCES, Bath, N.Y., 1996-97; learning support resource rm. tchr. North Tioga Sch. Dist., Westfield (Pa.) Area Elem. Sch., 1997—. Sunday sch. tchr. Jackson Summit (Pa.) Bapt. Ch.; mem. Corning C.C. Alumni Chorus. Mem. Coun. Exceptional Children. Republican. Baptist. Avocations: fishing, music, camping, working with children, reading. Home: RR 1 Box 32K Millerton PA 16936-9712

KIPKE, MICHELE DIANE, education and social services administrator, former hospital director; b. Glendale, Calif., Mar. 4, 1962; d. Arthur Harold and Anne Stuart (Mills) K. BA, NYU, 1984; PhD, Yeshiva U., 1989. Rsch. asst. Montefiore Med. Ctr., Bronx, N.Y., 1984-86; psychology intern Albert Einstein Coll. Medicine, Bronx, 1986-87; dir. AIDS prevention Montefiore Med. Ctr., Bronx, 1987-89; coord. substance abuse program Childrens Hosp. L.A., Calif., 1990-92, assoc. dir. rsch. and evaluation, 1992-98; dir. bd. children, youth & families Nat. Res. Council, Washington, 1998—. Cons. HHS, SAMSA, HRSA, Washington, 1990—; coun. rep. elect Homeless Caucus, APHA, 1992-93; peer reviewer NIH, Washington, 1993—; cons. WHO/Mentor Found., Geneva, 1994—; spl. advisor Primary Health Care Initiative, Office of Treatment Improvement, Alcohol, Drug Abuse and Mental Health Adminstrn.; presenter in field. Reviewer AIDS Edn. and Prevention: An Interdisciplinary Jour., Jour. Adolescent Health Care; contbr. articles to profl. jours. Grantee Ctrs. for Disease Control (AIDS Evaluation of Street Outreach Project), 1992-95, Universitywide AIDS Rsch. Program (HIV Prevention Intervention Study with Seropositive Youth, 1993-95, Nat. Inst. on Drug Abuse (Investigation of Drug Use and HIV-Risk Sexual Behaviors Among Homeless Youth, 1993—, Substance Abuse and Mental Health Svc. Adminstrn./Ctr. for Substance Abuse Treatment, 1993—, Health Resources and Svcs. Adminstrn./Bur. Health Cre and Delivery and Assistance, 1993—, others. Mem. APA, Soc. Adolescent Medicine (ad hoc com. on health needs of homeless youth). Office: Childrens Hosp LA Mail Stop #2 PO Box 54700 Los Angeles CA 90054-0700

KIPPER, BARBARA LEVY, corporate executive; b. Chgo., July 16, 1942; d. Charles and Ruth (Doctoroff) Levy; m. David A. Kipper, Sept. 9, 1974; children: Talia Rose, Tamar Judith. BA, U. Mich., 1964. Reporter Chgo. Sun-Times, 1964-67; photo editor Cosmopolitan Mag., N.Y.C., 1969-71; vice chmn. Chas Levy Co., Chgo., 1984-86, chmn., 1986—. Trustee Spertus Inst. Jewish Studies, Chgo. Hist. Soc., Golden Apple Ind., Joffrey Ballet of Chgo.; bd. dirs. Lincoln Park Zoo, Chgo. Humanities Festival. Recipient Deborah award Com. Women's Equality, Am. Jewish Congress, 1992, Shapiro Human Rels. award The Anti-Defamation League of B'nai B'rith, Personal PAC's Leadership award, 1996, Disting. Cmty. Leadership award, ADL, 1999, Golden Sceptre award Ned. Found. Jewish Culture, 2004; named Nat. Soc. Fund Raising Execs. Disting. Philanthropist, 1995. Mem.: Chgo. Network, Chgo. Coun. on Fgn. Rels., Com. of 200, Coun. on Founds., Internat. Women's Forum, Econ. Club of Chgo., Execs. Club of Chgo., The Standard Club. Jewish. Office: Chas Levy Company 1930 George St Ste 1 Melrose Park IL 60160-1501

KIRBY, MARCIA KAREN, librarian; b. Williamsburg, Va., Oct. 23, 1952; d. Marion O. and Rita S. Smith; m. Garnett E. Kirby, Jr., Aug. 18, 1979; children: Jon-David G., Phillip E. Libr. clk. Williamsburg Regional Libr., Va., 1975—80; libr. tech. Navelex Tech. Libr., Portsmouth, Va., 1982—83; libr. clk. Hampton U. Libr., Va., 1985—87; libr. tech. Internat. Telephone Telegraph, Hampton, Va., 1987—91; libr. clk. Hampton U. Libr., Va., 1992—95; tchr. resource ctr. clk. Newport News Pub. Schs., Va., 1995—96; libr. clk. Gildersleeve Mid. Sch., Newport News, Va., 1995—97; libr. practitioner I Coll. of William & Mary Libr., Williamsburg, Va., 1997—. Mem.: Classified Staff Assn. (corr.; pres. 2000—01, sec. 2003). Avocations: reading, photography, videography, piano.

KIRCHHOFF, MARY VIRGINIA, city council member; b. Wilson Creek, Mo., Jan. 30, 1926; d. Ashley Chester and Ollie Flora (Alexander) Mixon; m. John Joseph Kirchhoff, May, 23, 1948; children: John E., Mary Karen. BA in Fine Arts, Tex. Christian U., 1969. Speaker Nat. Parkinson's Disease Assn., West Tex., Lubbock, Tex., 1996—; city council mem. Plainview, Tex., 1990—. Dep. chmn., Rep. Party State of Tex., elected senatorial # 30 com. woman State Rep. Com., 1972-78; elected to supts. cabinet Plainview Ind. Sch. Dist., 1990-92; city council rep. Canadian Mcpl. Water Authority, Plainview, Tex., 1995—; bd. dirs. Hale County Appraisal Dist., Plainview, 1995—; bd. dirs. Unger Meml. Lib., Plainview, 1992-96; advisor to chmn. dist. 18 State Bd. Edn., Tex., 1994, appointed by Commnrs. Ct. to the Plainview Hosp. Authority Bd., 1999—; spkr. in field. Contbr. articles to profl. jours. Organizer summer youth program SCOPE; officer Girl Scouts U.S., 1963-67; mem. airport bd., 1994-96; bd. dirs. Plainview Recycling Beautification, 1995—; elder 1st Christian Ch., 1997—; vol. reader/listener La Mesa Elem. Sch., 1998—; organizer Plainvew area Parkinson Diseases Support Group, Plainview Meth. Hosp., 1999—. Named Tex. Outstanding Rep. Woman, Rep. Party. Mem. Lions Club Internat., Retired Tchrs. Assn., Tex. Mcpl. League, DAR (Daughters of Amer. Revolution), West Tex. C. of C. (elected 1st woman to exec. bd. 1965), Jr. Svc. League (pres., 1953-62), Women's Club (pres., charter mem., 1953-63), Delta Kappa Gamma (organizer Kappa Xi chpt., pres. 1984), Pi Beta Phi (charter). Avocations: philanthropy, travel, writing. Home: 311 Hughes St Nacogdoches TX 75961-5025

KIRCHNER, BHARTI N. writer; d. Amiya Kumar and Anima Nandi; m. Thomas Brian Kirchner, July 13, 1976. BS, MS, Calcutta U., 1961; postgrad., U. Wash., 1990. Adv. systems engr. IBM, Seattle, 1984—89; systems mgr. Bank of Am., San Francisco, 1980—84. Author: 8 books, including novels and cookbooks. Vol./presenter APAWLI (Asian Pacific Am. Women's Leadership Inst.), Seattle, 1999—2000; vol./advisor/presenter Pacific N.W. Writer's Conf., Seattle, 2001—03. Lit. grantee, Artist Trust, 1995, Seattle Arts Commn., 1996, 1999. Mem.: Toastmasters Internat. (assoc.). Avocations: gardening, travel.

KIRCHNER, LISA BETH, actress, vocalist; b. L.A. d. Leon and Gertrude (Schoenberg) K. BA, Sarah Lawrence Coll., N.Y., 1975. Picture rschr. McGraw-Hill, 1985-87, John Wiley & Sons, 1988, Simon & Schuster/Globe Book Co., 1992—2000, Chelsea House Pubs., 1987-94, Oxford Univ. Press, 1997, Facts on File, 2001—02, Greenwood Pub. Co., 1997, Lazard Freres, 1998—, The Oryx Press, 1999—, Abbeville Press, 2001—02. Songwriter, BMI. Broadway appearances include The Threepenny Opera, 1975, The Human Comedy, 1985; off-Broadway appearances include the Radiant City, 1993, Hotel for Criminals, 1974, The American Imagination, others; TV shows include Songs From the Heart, Another World, The Guiding Light, As The World Turns, Out of Our Father's House; appearances at The White House and Gracie Mansion; performed as featured soloist and back-up singer with Judy Collins (numerous TV appearances); prodr., solo vocalist CD releases (Albany Records) entitled One More Rhyme, 1999, When Lights Are Low, 2002. Mem. AFTRA, SAG, BMI, Equity, Actor's Equity Assn. Avocations: painting, crafts, poetry. E-mail: kirchl@aol.com.

KIRCHNER, MARY KATHERINE, musician, educator; b. Omaha, Apr. 22, 1937; d. Ferdinand Anthony and Loretta Agnes (Brady) Dascher; m. John Edmund Kirchner, Jr., June 20, 1959; children: J. Kevin, Mark A., Patrick D., Edmund J., Thomas J. BA, Loretto Heights Coll., 1959. Pvt. voice tchr., Edina, Minn., 1982—. Voice tchr. Performing Arts Ctr., Edina, 1982—95; adj. faculty voice tchr. Edina HS, 1982—99; pres. Thursday Musical, Mpls., 1992—94. Sec. Rep. Senate Dist. 42, 1983—85. Mem.: Minn. Music Tchrs. Assn. (adminstr. non-keyboard programs 1987—89, cert.), Nat. Assn. Tchrs. Singing, Mu Phi Epsilon (pres. 1988—90, dist. dir. 1995—98). Roman Catholic. Avocations: reading, walking. Home: 7470 Cahill Rd Edina MN 55439 Personal E-mail: jkkirchner@msn.com.

KIRDANI, ESTHER MAY, school counselor; b. Nunda, N.Y., Aug. 27, 1936; d. Herbert Stewart and Sarah Edith (Veley) Stewart Kernahan; m. Rashad Y. Kirdani, Aug. 16, 1958; children: Lavinia Helen, Leila Andrea. BS in Home Econs. Edn., SUNY, Buffalo, 1958; EdM in Secondary Guidance, U. Buffalo, 1972. Permanent cert. home econs. edn. and secondary sch. guidance. Tchr. home econs. Royalton-Hartland (N.Y.) Ctrl. Sch., 1958-60; tchr. math. Grafton (Mass.) Jr. H.S., 1962-65, Clarence (N.Y.) Jr. H.S., 1967-68; sch. counselor West Seneca (N.Y.) Sch. Dist., 1973—2002; ret., 2002. Mem. ACA, Am. Sch. Counselor Assn., Western N.Y. Guidance Dirs. and Chairpersons (coord. 1987-94), Western N.Y. Sch. Counselors Consortium, Western N.Y. Sch. Counselors Assn. (Sch. Counselor of Yr. 2001-02). Avocations: gardening, travel, aerobics, sewing, doll collecting. Home: 44 Buttonwood Ln East Amherst NY 14051-1642

KIRILA, CAROL ELIZABETH, osteopathic physician, internist; b. Mount Clemens, Mich., Oct. 28, 1952; d. Andrew William and Mary Margaret (Schmeltz) K. Diploma, Rsch. Med. Ctr. Sch. Nursing, Kansas City, Mo., 1974; BS in Biology, U. Mo., Kansas City, 1987; DO U. Health Scis., Coll. Osteo. Medicine, 1991. RN Mo. Lab. asst. Lakeside Hosp., Kansas City, 1969-74, RN, inservice instr., 1976-87, part time staff nurse, relief supr., 1988-91; staff nurse Children's Mercy Hosp., Kansas City, 1974, U. Health Scis. Hosp., Kansas City, 1974-76, Rsch. Med. Ctr., Kansas City, 1976; part time staff nurse Kendallwood Pvt. Duty, 1988-91; intern Still Regional Med. Ctr., Jefferson City, Mo., 1991-92; resident internal medicine U. of Mo. Kansas City Sch. of Medicine, 1992-95; staff physician Internal Medicine Assocs. St. Joseph, Mo., 1995—96, Permante Med. Group, Kansas City, Mo., 1996-98; mem. faculty U. of Health Scis., Coll. Osteo. Medicine, 1998—. Catechumenate sponsor St. James Ch., Kansas City, 1982; mem. Manheim Park Neighborhood Assn., Kansas City, 1982-91. Recipient cert. of recognition U. Health Scis. Coll. Osteo. Medicine, 1988-89, Outstanding Svc. and Achievement award U. Mo.-Kansas City, 1986, Pres.'s award Mo. Assn. Osteo. Physicians and Surgeons, 2000, 02 Mem.: Mo. Assn. Osteo. Physicians and Surgeons (Medallion award 2002), Am. Osteo. Assn. Democrat. Episcopalian. Avocations: gardening, cooking, music.

KIRK, CARMEN ZETLER, data processing executive; b. Altoona, Pa., May 22, 1941; d. Paul Alan and Mary Evelyn (Pearce) Zetler. BA, Pa. State U., 1959-63; MBA, St. Mary's Coll. Calif., 1977. Cert. in data processing. Pub. sch. tchr. State Ga., 1965-66; systems analyst U.S. Govt. Dept. Army, Oakland, Calif., 1967-70; programmer analyst Contra Costa County, Martinez, Calif., 1970-76; applications mgr. Stanford (Calif.) U., 1976-79; pres. Zetler Assocs., Inc., Palo Alto, Calif., 1979—. Cons. State Calif., Sacramento, 1985-88. Office: Zetler Assocs Inc PO Box 50395 Palo Alto CA 94303-0395

KIRK, CAROL, lawyer; b. Henry, Ill., Dec. 23, 1937; d. Howard P. and Mildred Root McQuilkin; m. Robert James Kirk, Aug. 20, 1961; children: Kathleen, Nancy, Sally. BS in Music Edn., U. Ill., 1960; JD, Ind. U., Indpls., 1989. Bar: Ind. 1989. Pvt. piano tchr., 1957-85; pub. sch. music tchr., 1960-62; dir. Ind. State Ethics Commn., Indpls., 1989-97; atty. and investigator Disciplinary Commn., Supreme Ct. Ind., Indpls., 1997—. Pres. Coun. on Govtl. Ethics Laws, (Internat.), 1993-94. Exec. editor Articles & Prodn. Ind. Law Rev., 1988-89. Mem. Met. Devel. Commn., Indpls., 1982-87; chairperson Pub. Radio Adv. Bd., Indpls., 1983-84, treas. Cmty. Svc. Coun., Indpls., 1988-91. Invitee to Nat. 4H Congress, Chgo., 1956; named 4H Family of Yr., Washington Twp., 4-H, Indpls., 1980, Vol. of Week, Voluntary Action Ctr., Indpls., 1980. Mem. LWV (pres. Indpls. 1979-83), Ind. Bar Assn., Indpls. Bar Assn., Phi Alpha Delta, Mu Phi Epsilon. Avocation: choir singing. Office: Discip Commn Supreme Ct Ind 1165 South Tower 115 W Washington St Indianapolis IN 46204-3420 E-mail: rkirk1937@aol.com.

KIRK, CHARLOTTE LEIDECKER, director; b. Sheffield, Ala., Feb. 11, 1949; d. Boyd Frank and Mildred Wiley Leidecker; m. Clinton Dale Kirk, Sept. 8, 1967 (div. Mar. 1996); 1 child, Chad E. BS magna cum laude, Murray State U., 1976, MA in Edn., 1980, MA in Sch. Adminstrn., 1986. Kindergarten tchr. Crittenden County Bd. Edn., Marion, Ky., 1977—86; primary tchr. Ft. Thomas (Ky.) Bd. Edn., 1986—88, Harrodsburg (Ky.) Bd. Edn., 1988—89; spl. edn. cons. Ky. Dept. Edn., Frankfort, 1989—94; dir. state and fed. programs Hickman County Bd. Edn., Clinton, Ky., 1994—96; dir. spl. edn. McCracken County Bd. Edn., Paducah, Ky., 1996—2000; asst. supt. Hickman County Bd. Edn., Clinton, 2000—01; dir. spl. edn. Covington (Ky.) Bd. Edn., 2001—. Charter mem. Ky. Assn. Sch. Admin. Inst. for Women in Adminstrn., 1978—2002; pres., sec. Western Ky. Assn. Sch. Adminstr., Paducah, 1995—2000; mem. adv. bd. Ky. Dept. Juvenile Justice, Frankfort, 1998—2001; cons. Trimble County Bd. Edn., Bedford, Ky., 2003; com. mem. Devel. of Ky. Adminstrv. Regulations for Spl. Edn.; presenter Ky. Assn. Gifted Edn. Rec. sec. Marion (Ky.) Woman's Club, 1980—86. Mem.: Kappa Delta Phi, Phi Delta Kappa. Democrat. Baptist. Avocations: sailing, reading, golf. Home: 1204 Aspen Pines Dr Newport KY 41071 Office Phone: 859-392-1137.

KIRK, DEBORAH, piano teacher; b. Morehead City, N.C., Aug. 14, 1951; d. David Arthur Kirk Jr. and Judy Mann Hartford; m. Kenneth Hinso, Dec. 23, 1984. BM, U. N.C., Greensboro, 1973, MM, 1988. Nat. cert. music tchr.; cert. music tchr., N.C. Ind. piano tchr., Greensboro, 1986—. Piano tchr. Music Camp/U. N.C., Greensboro, 1997; adjudicator Raleigh Music Tchrs. Assn., 1996, Charlotte Piano Forum, NC, 1999, N.C. Fedn. Music Clubs, 1999; music specialist Peeler Open Sch. for Performing Arts. Concerto soloist Univ. Symphony Orch., Greensboro, 1973. Mem. Greensboro Music Tchrs. Assn. (v.p. 1995-98), N.C. Music Tchrs. Assn. (dist. festival chair 1996-99), Music Tchrs. Nat. Assn., Am. Coll. Musicians Guild. Avocation: feral cat management. E-mail: dkkirk@hotmail.com.

KIRK, FLORA KAY STUDE, artist, accountant; b. San Diego, Feb. 16, 1944; d. Lawrence Wilbur Stude and Lois Eileen (Johnson) Plunkett; m. Bobby Gene Kirkpatrick, Feb. 16, 1960 (div. 1974); children: Jeffery Lane, Ladina B.J. Kirkpatrick Wingfield; m. Charles Robert Kirk, June 11, 1977 (div.); 1 child, Robert Marcel. Student, Western Tex. Coll., 1973-74, Ft. Hays (Kans.) State Coll., 1974-75, U. Nebr., Kearney, 1988; AA, Mid-Plains C.C., North Platate, Nebr., 1987. Decorator, Snyder, Tex., 1960-73; bookkeeper, office mgr. Tri-State Constrn., Snyder, 1973-75; acct. Aid Feed Yard, Syracuse, Kans., 1975-77; agt., broker Woodmen Accident & Life Ins. Co., Lincoln, Nebr., 1977-92; owner, mgr., artist Kirk's Pottery and Painting Studio, North Platte, 1984—; acct., corp. sec.-treas. Profl. Ag Products, Inc., North Platte, 1988-93. Chmn. bd. Artists Coop. Art & Gift Gallery, North Platte, 1987-99; ceramics & painting instr. Mid Plains C.C., 1992—; mem. artist Artists in Embassies Program, Washington, 1991, 92; artist Carolyn Nelson Galleries, Pasadena, Calif., 1992, Robert Henri Mus., Conad, Nebr., 1996. One-woman show Art & Gift Gallery, 1987-96, Morin-Miller Galleries, N.Y.C., 1989, Gt. Plains Regional Med. Ctr., 1989-96, Bismark State Coll., Arroyo Theatre Gallery, L.A., 1993, 94, Pen & Brush Club, 1995, Broom St. Gallery, N.Y.C., 1995, U.S. Senate, 1995, Vanderbilt Mus., 1995, Noyes Gallery, Lincoln, Nebr., 1995-96, Robert Henri Mus., Crozad, Nebr., 1996; exhibited in group shows Fiske Planetarium, Boulder (recipient 1st place award 1992-94, 1st pl. in 1993-94), Nat. Arts Club, N.Y.C., 1987, ARiel Gallery, N.Y.C., 1988, Univ. Place Gallery, Lincoln, 1990-93, Gallery 525, Loveland, Colo., 1990, 91, C.W. Post Coll., L.I. U., 1990, U. Colo., 1990, Jacob Javits Fed. Bldg. Gallery, N.Y.C., 1991-92, U.S. Ho. Reps., Washington, 1992, 94, 95, Antiquarium Gallery, Omaha, Artel Gallery, White Crane Gallery, Omaha, 1993, Cork Gallery, Lincoln Ctr. Performing Arts, N.Y.C., Arroyo Theatre Gallery, L.A., 1993, 94, Santa Fe Ski Basin, New Mexico, 2001, Art & Live Art, 2001; represented in permanent collections Mus. Cultural Exch., Cairo, Prarie Peace Park, Lincoln, Bismark State Coll.; featured at Lincoln Benefit Auction, North Platte, Nebr., 1999. Chmn. North Platte Arts and Humanities Coun., 1991-92; vol. Kerry for Pres. Campaign, North Platte, 1992. Mem. Soc. Exptl. Artists, Nat. Soc. Painters in Casein and Acrylic (assoc.), Nat. Watercolor Soc. (assoc.), Visual Individual United (1st place award 1992), The Artel (merit award 1991), North Platte Art Guild, Platter Painters Art Club (pres. 1987-88, 1st place award 1987-91), Assn. Nebr. Art Clubs, Phi Theta Kappa. Democrat. Avocations: astronomy, physics, chemistry, writing, environmental causes. Home: 600 W Alameda Santa Fe NM 87501

KIRK, JANE SEAVER, municipal government administrator; b. Boston, May 12, 1928; d. Howard Wesley and Ruth (Seaver) K. BA, Duke U., 1950; MS, Springfield (Mass.) Coll., 1956. Ctr. dir. ARC, Korea, Japan, France, Morocco, 1951-60; dep. dir. internat. group YMCA of the U.S.A., Chgo., 1961-93; chair selectmen Town of Nelson, NH, 1997—2004. Bd. dirs. N.E. Delta Dental, Concord, NH, 1998—2005; incorp Monadnock Family Svcs., 2001—02. Trustee Hist. Soc. Cheshire County, Keene, NH, 1995—2001, Springfield Coll., 1973—2000; pres. Granite Lake Assn., Munsonville, NH, 1995—2000; bd. dirs. Duke Ctr. for Living, Durham, NC, 1995—2001. Recipient Fundraising Achievement award N.Am. YMCA Devel. Officers, 1991. Mem. AAUW, DAR, ARCOA, NAFYR, Daus. of Founders and Patriots, Order Eastern Star, Union League Club Chgo., Coll. Club of Boston, Descendants of Colonial Clergy, Women's Aux., Mass. Ancient and Honorable Artillery Co., Edmund Rice (1638) Assn., Boston Alliance, Ladies Charitable Soc., Internat. Assn. of Women, Bay State African Violet Soc., Walpole Hist. Soc., Am. Orchid Soc., Rotary Club of Keene (Paul Harris fellow), Phi Beta Kappa. Republican. Baptist. Avocations: photography, gardening, travel, walking. Home: 543 Granite Lake Rd Munsonville NH 03457-5121 Fax: 603-847-9647. E-mail: janekirk@msn.com.

KIRK, JILL, educational association administrator; BA, U. Oreg. Corp. dir. human resources/orgnl. devel. Tektonix, Inc., group human resources mgr.; dir. cmty. affairs Tektronix, Inc., 1994; exec. dir. Tektronix Found., 1991; founder The Kirk Group LLC, 1999—; ptnr. Lindberg/Kirk/Millar, 2000—. Mem. bd. dirs., exec. bd., govt. affairs com. Am. Electronics Assn.; bd. dirs. Associated Oreg. Industries; chair deputies com. Oreg. Bus. Coun., vice chair edn. com., mem. higher edn. task force, mem. pub. fin. com. Mem. Oreg. State Bd. Edn., 1996—, chairperson, 2001—, mem. exec. com., mem. joint bds. working group, mem. econ. devel. joint bds. working group; trustee Portland Art Mus., 1998—2001, 2001—; mem. adv. com. Portland Ctr. for the Performing Arts; bd. dirs. Portland Youth Philharm.; mem. strategic planning com. United Way Columbia-Willamette; active Oreg. Profl. Devel. Coun.; bd. chair Lintner Ctr. for Advanced Edn.; active Govs. Task Force on Higher Edn., Govs. Task Force on Quality Edn.; bd. dirs. Japanese Garden Soc., 2001—, STARS, Portland Edn. Network, N.W. Bus. for Culture and the Arts, Nat. Alliance Bus. Western Region. Mem.: Portland C. of C. (bd. dirs.). Office: Oreg Dept Edn 255 Capitol St NE Salem OR 97310-0203

KIRK, LYNDA POUNDS, biofeedback therapist, neurotherapist, counselor; b. Corpus Christi, Tex., Dec. 17, 1946; d. James Arthur and Elizabeth Pauline (Sanders) Pounds; children: Leslie Jennifer, Edward Christopher. BA, U. Tex., Austin, 1977; MA, St. Edwards U., 1996. Lic. profl. counselor. Therapist Austin (Tex.) State Hosp., 1977-80; dir. stress mgmt. The Hills Med./Sports Complex, Austin, 1980-82; founder, owner Austin Biofeedback Ctr., 1982—, Health Mastery Concepts, Austin, 1982—, Optimal Performance Inst., 2000—; CEO Healthy Life Options, Inc., Austin, 1998—. Cons. State of Tex., Austin, 1983—, City of Austin, 1985—, Lower Colo. River Authority, Austin, 1984—. Author: (book/cassette series) Regenerative Relaxation, 1981; Urological Applications of Biofeedback, Stress Mastery and Peak Performance, 1986. Bd. dirs. South Austin Civic Club, 1983—, pres., 1987; bd. dirs., treas. Texans for the Preservation of Hist. Structures, 1990—; bd. dirs. Austin Ctr. for Attitudinal Healing, 1992—. Fellow Biofeedback Cert. Inst. Am. (sr.), Internat. Soc. for Neuronal Regulation (pres. 1997-98); mem. Assn. Applied Psychophysiology and Biofeedback (pres. 2003—), Internat. Soc. for Study of Subtle Energies and Energy Medicine, Biofeedback Soc. Tex. (pres. 1995-97, exec. bd., citation award 1989), Behavioral Medicine Soc. Am., Am. Holistic Med. Assn., Assn. Cert. QEEG Technologists, Acad. Cert. Neurotherapists, Phi Beta Kappa. Episcopalian. Avocations: jogging, snorkeling, mountain biking, designs for world peace. Home: 420 Brady Ln Austin TX 78746-5502 Office: Austin Biofeedback Ctr 3624 N Hills Dr Ste B205 Austin TX 78731-3061 E-mail: lkirk@austinbiofeedback.com.

KIRK, NANCY A. state legislator, nursing home administrator; m. Henry Kirk. MSW, University of Kansas, 1976;BS, Illinois State University, 1964. Nursing home adminstr.; mem. from dist. 56 Kans. State Ho. of Reps., Topeka. Address: 932 SW Frazier Ave Topeka KS 66606-1948

KIRK, REA HELENE (REA HELENE GLAZER), special education educator; b. N.Y.C., Nov. 17, 1944; d. Benjamin and Lillian (Kellis) Glazer; 3 stepdaughters. BA, UCLA, 1966; MA, Ea. Mont. Coll., 1981; EdD, U. So. Calif., 1995. Life cert. spl. edn. tchr., Calif., Mont. Spl. edn. tchr., L.A., 1966-73; clin. sec. speech and lang. clinic Missoula, Mont., 1973-75; spl. edn. tchr. Missoula, Gt. Falls, Mont., 1975-82; br. mgr. YWCA of L.A., Beverly Hills, Calif., 1989-91; sch. adminstrn., ednl. coord. Adv. Schs. of Calif., 1991-94; dir. Woman's Resource Ctr., Gt. Falls, Mont., 1981-82, Battered Woman's Shelter, Rock Springs, Wyo., 1982-84, Battered Woman's Program, Sweetwater County, Wyo., 1984-88, San Gabriel Valley, Calif., 1988; with Spl. Edn., Pasadena, 1994-96, prin., 1995; asst. prof. U. Wis., Platteville, 1996—2003, assoc. prof., 2003—. Mem. Wyo. Commn. on Aging, Rock Springs; mem. Cmty. Action Bd. City of L.A. Pres., bd. dirs. battered woman's shelter, Gt. Falls; pres. Women's Resource Ctr., Gt. Falls, Religious Congregation, Rock Springs; founder, advisor Rape Action Line, Gt. Falls; founder Jewish religious svcs., Missoula; 4-H leader; hostess Friendship Force; Friendship Force ambassador, Wyo., Fed. Republic Germany, Italy; mem. YWCA Mont. and Wyo.; v.p. Coun. Devel. Disabilities, Wis.; bd. dirs. Coun. Children with Behavior Disorders, Wis., Family Advocates, Platteville, 1996—; organizer Women's Readers Theater, Platteville, Wis.; advisor Pioneer Svc. Club, Platteville. Recipient Gladys Byron scholar U. So. Calif., 1993, Dept. Edn. scholar U. So. Calif., 1994, honors Missoula 4-H, Underkoffler Tchg. Excellence award U. Wis., 2000, named advisor of yr., 2000; recognized as significant Wyo. woman as social justice reformer and peace activist Sweetwater County, Wyo.; nominated Wyo. Woman of the Yr., 1981, 82; honored by L.A. Mayor Bradley for Anti-Poverty work. Mem. Coun. for Exceptional Children (v.p. Gt. Falls 1981-82, bd. dirs., Professionally Recognized Spl. Educator 1998), Wis. Coun. Exceptional Children (bd. dirs., pres. S.W. region), Wis. Divsn. Mentally Retarded/Developmenally Disabled), Wis. Assn. Children with Behavior Disorders, Assn. for Children with Learning Disabilities (Named Outstanding Mem. 1982), Pioneer Svc. Club (adv.), Phi Delta Kappa, Delta Kappa Gamma (sec. 2002—), Kappa Delta Pi (co-counselor 2000—, sec. 2002—), Pi Lamda Theta. Office Phone: 608-342-1279. Business E-Mail: Kirkr@uwplatt.edu.

KIRK, RUTH M. state legislator; b. Balt., Feb. 2, 1930; m. Arthur F. Kirk, Jr.; 6 children. Tchr.'s asst. Balt. City Pub. Schs.; mem. Md. Ho. of Dels., Annapolis, 1983-94, 95—, mem. constl. and adminstrv. law com., 1983-90, mem. econ. matters com., 1991—, mem. house facility com., 1993—. Treas. Md. Black Caucus; mem. Urban Svc. Commn.; bd. dirs. Meals on Wheels; mem. Cmty. Orgn. to Improve Life, Citizens Dem. Action Orgn. Recipient Balt. Best Silver and Blue award, 1982, Frances Morton Forelicher Civic Statesmanship award, 1982, Golden Brick award Balt. Blueprint. Mem. Women Legislators of Md., Order Ea. Star. Office: Md Ho of Reps State Capital Annapolis MD 21401

KIRKER, LINDA, state representative, health facility administrator; b. Glen Ridge, N.J., Apr. 20, 1939; m. David J. Kirker (dec.); 2 children. Degree in nursing, U. Vt. Acct. exec. New Eng. region Am. Red Cross Blood Svcs.; state rep. State of Vt., 2001—, mem. pub. works and welfare com., 2001—02. Past mem. Essex Junction Cmty. Develop. Com., Bd. Civil Authority; sec. Chittenden County Rep. Com.; vice chair Essex Town Rep. Com.; deacon First Congregation Ch., Essex Juction, mem. missions com.; bd. dir. Friends of UVM Hockey; justice of peace. Mem.: Am. Legion (past pres.), Lions (fundraising com. Vet. Meml. Pk.). Republican. Office: 28 Villa Dr Essex Junction VT 05452

KIRKGAARD, VALERIE ANNE, media group executive, syndicated talk radio host, writer, producer, consultant; b. Merced, Calif., Aug. 18, 1940; d. Basil Stuart and Audrey (Thompson) Coghlan; m. Alonzo Bryson Kirkgaard, Oct. 6, 1962 (div. Aug. 1983); children: Jennifer Alexandra, John Erik. AA, Santa Monica City Coll., 1961; BA, UCLA, 1968; M of Counseling, Goddard Coll., L.A., 1982; M. of Enlightenment, Sci. of Mind Ch., San Diego, 1992; PhD, Harrington U., 1999. Bd. and care organizer Norwalk State Hosp., L.A., 1976-78; liaison to bd. dirs. Gay and Lesbian Cmty. Svcs. Ctr., 1976—79; therapist in pvt. practice Kirkgaard & Assocs, Pasadena, Pacific Palisades, Santa Monica, Calif., 1975—; pvt. practice matrimonial cons., 1976—; CEO Laughing Dragon Entertainment. Ear coning educator, mfr., 1992—; prodr., host radio and TV Waking Up In America, 1987—; radio prodr. Terry Cole Whittaker; radio prodr./host Open Forum, Waking Up In America, 2 programs for KFNX, Phoenix, Ariz., KTBC, Albuquerque; spkr. in field; also VoiceAmerica.com. Author: Breakfast At Bob's, 1982, Take Two Breaths and Call Me in the Morning, 1988, Making Room for Love: A Primer for Causing Powerful Relationships, 2001; environ. editor United Fitness Mag., 1992; columnist Hollywood Times, 1976, Century City News, 1990-92, Topanga Messenger, 1996—; author numerous articles; numerous appearances and interviews; inventor in field. Founder Golden Hearts Found. Olympic Torch bearer Olympic Com., Santa Fe Springs, Calif., 1984. Mem. Calif. Assn. Marriage Family and Child Counselors, Women's Mus. of Art, Los Angeles County Mus. Art, World Vision, State of the World Forum, The Hunger Project, Mus. of Tolerance, Greater L.A. Press Club, Scriptwriters Network, Pacific Palisades C. of C., Roar Found. Avocations: polo, horseback riding, hiking, racquetball, reading, gardening. Office: Kirkgaard & Assocs 869 Via De La Paz Ste F Pacific Palisades CA 90272-5202 Office Phone: 340-455-8623. E-mail: elvenears2@aol.com.

KIRKHAM, M. B. plant physiologist, educator; b. Cedar Rapids, Iowa; d. Don and Mary Elizabeth (Erwin) K. BA with honors, Wellesley Coll.; MS, PhD, U. Wis. Cert. profl. agronomist. Plant physiologist U.S. EPA, Cin., 1973-74; asst. prof. U. Mass., Amherst, 1974-76, Okla. State U., Stillwater, 1976-80; from assoc. prof. to prof. Kans. State U., Manhattan, 1980—. Guest lectr. Inst. Water Conservancy and Hydroelectric Power Rsch., Inst. Farm Irrigation Rsch., China, 1985, Inst. Exptl. Agronomy, Italy, 1989, Agrl. U. Wageningen, Inst. for Soil Fertility, Haren, The Netherlands, 1991, Massey U., New Zealand, 1991, Lincoln U., New Zealand, 1998, Environ. and Risk Mgmt. Group Hort. Rsch., 1998, Palmerston North, New Zealand, 1998, U. Hannover, Germany, 2003; William A. Albrecht seminar spkr. U. Mo., 1994; vis. scholar Biol. Labs., Harvard U., 1990; vis. scientist environ. physics sect. dept. sci and indsl. rsch., Palmerston North, New Zealand, 1991, The Horticulture and Food Rsch. Inst. New Zealand, Ltd., Crown Rsch. Inst., Palmerston North, 1998, Landcare Rsch., Lincoln, New Zealand, 1998; mem. peer rev. panel USDA/Nat. Rsch. Initiative, Washington, 1994; mem. rev. panel USDA Office Sci. Quality Rev. Water Quality Nat. Program, 2001, apptd. mem. U.S. Nat. Com. for Soil Sci. of NAS, 2001-04; participant confs. and symposia; spkr., presenter in field. Editor: Water Use in Crop Production, 1999; co-editor: (with I.K. Iskandar) Trace Elements in Soil, 2001; cons. editor Plant and Soil Jour., 1979-; mem. editl. bd. BioCycle, 1978-82, Field Crops Rsch. Jour., 1983-91, Soil Sci., 1997-, Jour. Crop Prodn., 1998-, Jour. Environ. Quality, 2002-; mem. editl. adv. bd. Internat. Agrophysics, 2000—; contbr. more than 220 articles and papers to sci. jours. Recipient Best Reviewer award, Water Resources Engring. divsn. Jour. Irrigation and Drainage Engring., ASCE, 1996, scholar award, 2000, grad. faculty tchg. award, Coll. of Agr., Kanas State Univ., 2001; fellow NSF postdoctoral fellow, U. Wis., 1971—73, NDEA fellow, E.I. du Pont de Nemours and Co. summer faculty fellow, 1976; grantee, NSF, USDA, U.S. Dept. Energy, Dept. Sci. and Indsl. Rsch., New Zealand. Fellow AAAS, Am. Soc. Agronomy (editl. bd. 1985-90), Soil Sci. Soc. Am. (travel grantee to internat. congress Japan 1990), Royal Meteorol. Soc., Crop Sci. Soc. Am. (editl. bd. 1980-84, 2004-); mem. Am. Soc. Plant Physiology (editl. bd. 1982-87), Am. Soc. Hort. Sci., Internat. Soil Tillage Rsch. Orgn., Internat. Union Soil Sci. (1st vice chmn. commn. soil physics 1994-98, sec. commn. on soils, food security and human health 2002—), Bot. Soc. Am., Am. Meteorol. Soc., Société Française de Physiologie Végétale, Japanese Soc. Plant Physiology, Scandinavian Soc. Plant Physiology, N.Y. Acad. Sci., Soc. for Exptl. Biology (London), Growth Regulator Soc. Am., Water Environment Fedn., Am. Phytopathol. Soc., Internat. Assn. Vegetation Sci., Am. Geophys. Union, Internat. Water Resources Assn., Royal Soc. New Zealand, Internat. Assn. Hydrolics Sci., Am. Phys. Soc., Am. Math. Assn., Am. Chem. Soc., Phi Kappa Phi (scholar award 2000), Gamma Sigma Delta (Disting. Faculty award Kans. State U. chpt., 2001), Sigma Xi (sec. chpt. 1997-99, Outstanding Sr. Scientist award 2002). Home: 1420 McCain Ln Apt 244 Manhattan KS 66502-4680 Office: Kans State U Dept Agronomy Throckmorton Hall Manhattan KS 66505-5501 E-mail: mbk@ksu.edu.

KIRKIEN-RZESZOTARSKI, ALICJA MARIA, academic administrator, researcher, educator; b. Lodz, Poland; came to U.S., 1965; d. Leszek Tadeusz and Francesca Irene (Mortkowicz) Kirkien. MSChemE, Polish U. Coll., London, 1951; PhD, U. London, 1955. Asst. prof. chemistry U. W.I., Jamaica, 1956-59, assoc. prof., 1959-61, Trinidad, 1961-65, Trinity Coll., Washington, 1966-68, prof. chemistry, 1968-92, chair chemistry dept., 1969-91, prof. emeritus, 1992—. Sr. rsch. assoc. George Washington U. Med. Ctr., Washington, 1984. One person show at Trinity Coll., Washington, 1994; watercolors and oils exhibited in show at Sorrento, Italy, 1994,

96, Karistos, Greece, 1993, Cade Gallery, Anne Arundel Coll., Arnold, Md., 1998; contbr. numerous articles to profl. publs. Sec., treas. Polish Vets. Assn., Washington, 1981-83. Named one of Outstanding Educators of Am., 1973, 75; sr. rsch. fellow Univ. Coll., 1965-66, 71, U. Calif., Santa Barbara, 1967. Fellow Royal Inst. Chem. (Gt. Britain); mem. Md. Fedn. Art (Critics Choice award for pottery 1992), Am. Chem. Soc. (adv. bd. Chem. and Engring. News 1978-81), Chem. Soc. Gt. Britain, Polish Inst. Arts and Scis. of N.Y., Phi Beta Kappa. Republican. Roman Catholic. Avocations: graphic painting, and ceramics. Home: 407 Buckspur Ct Millersville MD 21108-1764 Office: Trinity Coll 125 Michigan Ave NW Washington DC 20010-2916

KIRKLAND, BERTHA THERESA, project engineer; b. San Francisco; d. Lawrence and Theresa (Kanzler) Schmelzer; m. Thornton C. Kirkland, Jr., Dec. 27, 1937 (dec. July 1971); children: Kathryn Elizabeth, Francis Charles. Ed. pub. schs., Calif. Supr. hosp. ops. Am. Potash & Chem. Corp., Trona, Calif., 1953-54; office mgr., estimator T.C. Kirkland Elect. Contractor, San Bernardino, Calif., 1954-58, estimator, sec./treas., bd. dir., 1958-74; estimator design-installation engr. Add-M Electric, Inc., San Bernardino, 1972-82, v.p., 1974-82; estimator, engr. Corona (Calif.) Indsl. Electric, Inc., 1982-83; project engr. Fiscbach & Moore, Inc., L.A., 1984-91; project engr. cons. Fischbach & Moor, Inc., L.A., 1993-94. Home: 526 Sonora St San Bernardino CA 92404-1762

KIRKLAND, JUDY JOYLENE, computer specialist; b. Great Falls, Mont., June 16, 1952; d. Howard Harold and Marvelle Ann (Plummer) Scoones; m. Paul M. Kirkland, May 22, 1976 (div. Feb. 1982); 1 child, William Howard. Cert in Acctg. Data Processing, Helena (Mont.) Vo-Tech Ctr., 1975; BS in Home Econs., Mont. State U., 1986. Adminstrv. asst. State of Mont., Helena, 1979-82; work/study sec. Mont. State U., Bozeman, 1982-86; title ins. clk. Am. Title, Billings, Mont., 1986-87; legal sec. Corner Pockets of Am., Billings, 1987-89; word processing operator Mont. State U., Bozeman, 1989-92; temporary sec. Tenera, Idaho Falls, Idaho, 1992-94, Express Svcs./INEL, Idaho Falls, 1995-96; adminstrv./sales asst. TCI Media Svcs., Idaho Falls, 1996-97; customer svc. rep. fin. Idaho Innovation Ctr., Idaho Falls, 1997—, quickbooks profl. advisor, 1998—. Sec., dir. Musicians West Inc., Pocatello, Idaho, 1994—; computer trainer Computer Tng. Wheels, Idaho Falls, 1992-93; adminstrv. asst. Summer Music Festival, Pocatello, 1994-95. Graphic artist posters, brochures, programs Musicians West, 1st Presbyn. Ch., Idaho Falls Symphony Chorale, Mark Neiwirth, Brian Wilhour, 1992—. Crisis line counselor Bozeman Help Ctr., 1985-86; team mem. Life Tng. various locations, 1988-93; music vol. 1st Presbyn. Ch., Idaho Falls, 1996-97; adult CPR/1st aid cert. ARC, Idaho Falls, 1996—. Mem. Idaho Falls Symphony Chorale, Westminster Choir, Tau Pi Phi, Alpha Psi Omega. Avocations: piano, music theory, yoga, spirituality, reading. Office: Idaho Innovation Ctr 2300 N Yellowstone Hwy Idaho Falls ID 83401-1662 Home: Apt 8 573 S Curtis Rd Boise ID 83705-6425

KIRKLAND, NANCY CHILDS, secondary education educator, consultant; b. Ideal, Ga., July 20, 1937; d. Millard Geddings and Bessie Vioda (Forbes) C.; m. Allard Corley French, Jr., Apr. 22, 1961 (div. Dec. 7, 1978); children: Vianne Elizabeth French Ouzts, Nancy Alysia French Joyce; m. Clarence Nathaniel Kirkland, Jr., Dec. 12, 1987. AB in Speech and Religious Edn., LaGrange Coll., 1959; MS, Troy State U., 1977; EdD in Child and Youth Studies, Nova U., 1993. Cert. tchr. English, Religion; cert. instr. Profl. Refinements in Developing Effectiveness, Tchr. Effectiveness and Classroom Handling. Dir. Christian edn. First Meth. Ch., Thomson, Ga., 1959-61; tchr. English Flanagan (Ill.) Jr.-Sr. H.S., 1962-63; tchr. English and social studies Woodland Jr. H.S., Streater, Ill., 1963-64; tchr. 5th grade Sheridan Elem. Sch., Bloominton, Ill., 1964-65; tchr. English Samson (Ala.) H.S., 1965, Choctawhatchee H.S., Fort Walton Beach, Fla., 1966-68, Marianna (Fla.) H.S., 1972-77; dir. devel. reading lab. Chiefland (Fla.) H.S., 1979-82; tchr. English Buchholz H.S., Gainesville, 1982—. Co-founder, cons. KPS Leadership Specialists, Jonesboro, Ga., 1993—; chairperson Buchholz facilitis com., Gainesville, Fla., 1993—; instr. English Santa Fe C. C., Gainesville, Fla., 1982-87, 96; asst. chairperson Buchholz English Dept., Gainesville, Fla., 1989-92. Contbr. articles to profl. jours. Sec., co-chmn., mem. Buchholz sch. adv. coun., Gainesville, 1994-95; tchr., dir., tchr. trainer Sunday sch., vacation sch., Fla.; actress, dir. Little Theaters, ch. groups, Ill., Ga., Ala.; coord. Gainesville Sister Cities Youth Correspondence Program, 1991-93. Mem. AAUW, ASCD, Alachua Multicultural Coun. (grantee 1992), Nat. Coun. Tchrs. English, Fla. Coun. Tchrs. English, Altrusa Internat. Gainesville (sec. 2004-), Alachua Coun. Tchrs. English (v.p. 1991-92, pres. 1992-93), Gainesville C. of C., Altrusa Internat. Gainesville (sec. 2004-). Methodist. Avocations: crafts, sewing, fishing, travelling. Home: 1728 NW 94th St Gainesville FL 32606-5570 Office: Buchholz H S 5510 NW 27th Ave Gainesville FL 32606-6405

KIRKLAND, REBECCA TRENT, pediatric endocrinologist; b. Durham, N.C., Dec. 27, 1942; d. Josiah Charles Trent and Mary Duke (Biddle) Trent-Semans; m. John Lindsey Kirkland III, June 24, 1965. BA, Duke U., 1964, MD, 1968. Intern Baylor Coll. Medicine, 1968-69, resident in pediatrics, 1969-70, fellow in pediatric endocrinology, 1971-73, asst. prof. dept. pediatrics, 1975-81, assoc. prof., 1981-88, prof., 1988—, sr. assoc. dean med. edn., 2000; registrar Guy's Hosp., Hosp. for Sick Children, London, 1970; with U. Pa. Sch. Medicine, 1973-74, fellow, 1974-75. Asst. physician divsn. endocrinology Children's Hosp. Phila., 1973-75; mem. staff Tex. Children's Hosp., 1975—, Harris County Hosp. Dist., 1975—; head ambulatory svcs. Tex. Children's Hosp., 1984—, dir. jr. league outpatient dept., 1984—. Contbr. articles and revs. to profl. jours. Active Leadership Tex., Leadership Houston; pres. Greater Houston Women's Found., 1994—96; bd. dirs. AVANCE, Inc., 1992, YWCA, 1992; trustee Mus. Med. Sci., 1984—88; pres. Josiah C. Trent Meml. Found., Inc., 1983—, v.p., 1977—83; bd. dirs. Am. Leadership Forum, 1991, mem. selection com., 1989, 1990, sec. bd. dirs. Houston/Gulf Coast chpg., 1989, 1990, pres.-elect, 1991, pres., 1991—93; bd. dirs. Mus. Health and Med. Scis., 2001—. NIH fellow, 1971-73; recipient Alumnae award Baldwin Sch., 1983, Disting. Alumni award Durham Acad., 1984, Goodheart Humanitarian award B'nai B'rith, 1986, Disting. Svc. award Duke U. Med. Alumni Assn., 1992, Recognition award Ctr. for Interaction: Man, Sci. and Culture, 1993, One Voice for Children award Tex. Network for Medically Fragile and Chronically-Ill Children, 1993; named one of five Outstanding Women of Yr. Channel 13, Houston, 1984, Woman on the move Houston Post, 1989. Fellow Am. Acad. Pediatrics; mem. Endocrine Soc., Am. Fedn. For Clin. Rsch., So. Soc. for Pediatric Rsch., Lawson-Wilkins Pediatric Endocrine Soc., Houston Pediatric Soc., Tex. Pediatric Soc., Tex. Med. Assn., Soc. for Pediatric Rsch., Pediatric Endocrinology Soc. Tex., Ambulatory Pediatric Assn., Am. Pediatric Soc., Am. Acad. Pediatrics (pediatric endocrine sect.) 1990), Tex. Diabetes and Endocrine Assn. Office: Baylor Coll Medicine 1 Baylor Plz Houston TX 77030-3411

KIRKLEY, D. CHRISTINE, non-profit organization administrator; b. Horton, Ala., Aug. 28, 1932; d. Vester Boyd and Josephine Prumrytle (Parrish) K.; m. Jack Stanley I, July 4, 1952; 1 child, Jack Stanley II. Student, U. Ala., 1951-52, Samford U., 1963-65, Cathedral Coll., 1982. Svr. rep. South Ctrl. Bell, Birmingham, Ala., 1984—; dir. Helpline Christian Outreach Ministries Inc, Birmingham, 1991—. Area mgr. Operating Blessing, Birmingham, 1989—; mem. Christian Helplines Internat., 1990—, sec. exec. com., 1994—. Mem. Telephone Pioneers Am. (fund raiser 1976-78, pres. 1979, cmty. edn. coord. 1982-83, drug abuse chairperson 1982-83). Mem. Assemby of God Ch. Avocations: reading, bowling, crocheting, swimming. Office: Helpline Christian Outreach Ministries Inc 8 Roebuck Dr Birmingham AL 35215-8046 Office Phone: 205-833-7712.

KIRKLEY-BEY, MARIE LOPEZ, state legislator; b. New Britain, Conn. widowed. Grad. high sch., New Britain, Conn. Mem. Conn. Ho. of Reps., Hartford. Mem. exec. bd. Ctr. for Cmty. Change, Washington; mem. human svc. com. Nat. Conf. State Legislators; mem. econ. devel. com. Hartford Downtown Coun.; state dir. will NCSW Women's Network. Recipeint awards United Negro Coll. Fund, 1991, 96, Women in Leadership award Hartford YWCA, 1992, Cmty. Svc. award MiCasa, 1994, 99, award Hogar Crea Internat., 1994, award Alcohol and Drug Recovery Ctr., 1998, Cmty. Svc. award Chappell Garden, 1999. Mem. Nat. Black Caucus. Address: 39 Ashley St Hartford CT 06105-1402 Office: Conn Ho of Reps State Capitol Hartford CT 06106

KIRKPATRICK, ANNE SAUNDERS, systems analyst; b. Birmingham, Mich., July 4, 1938; d. Stanley Rathbun and Esther (Casteel) Saunders; children: Elizabeth, Martha, Robert, Sarah. Student, Wellesley Coll., 1956-57, Laval U., Quebec City, Can., 1958, U. Ariz., 1958-59; BA in Philosophy, U. Mich., 1961. Systems engr. IBM, Chgo., 1962-64; sr. analyst Commonwealth Edison Co., Chgo., 1981-97. Treas. Taproot Reps., DuPage County, Ill., 1977—80; pres. Hinsdale (Ill.) Women's Rep. Club, 1978—81. Mem.: Wellesley of Chgo. (bd. dirs. 1972-73). Home: 222 E Chestnut St Unit 8B Chicago IL 60611-2376 E-mail: a.kirkpatrick@sbcglobal.net.

KIRKPATRICK, DIANE YVONNE, retired speech pathology/audiology services professional; b. San Diego, Apr. 20, 1938; d. Claude Cliff Davis and Charlotte (Mulnix) Gibson; m. Richard John Prigge Sr., July 2, 1960 (div.); children: Richard John Jr., Tamsin Gail, Kimberly Ann; m. Lee Kingston Kirkpatrick, Aug. 24, 1985. BA, U. Calif., Santa Barbara, 1970, MA, 1973. Cert. clin. competency speech and lang. pathology; lifetime restricted tchg. credential, Calif. Speech pathologist Santa Barbara County Schs., 1972-98, ret., 1998. Mem. Beacon of Light Found., Santa Barbara, 1989—; elder 1st Presbyn. Ch., Santa Barbara, 1995-98; chpt. dir. Goldwing Roadriders Assn., Santa Barbara, 1997-98; mem. Santa Barbara Civil Grand Jury, 1999-2000; mem. Santa Barbara Women's Polit. Com. Mem.: Am. Speech and Hearing Assn. Home: 415 N Turnpike Rd Santa Barbara CA 93111-1932 E-mail: dyksb@cox.net.

KIRKPATRICK, EDITH KILLGORE, music educator, volunteer; b. Lisbon, La., Nov. 14, 1918; d. Thomas Morton and Bess Blanche (Melton) Killgore; m. Claude Kirkpatrick, Aug. 21, 1938; children: Claude Kent (dec.), Thomas Killgore, Edith Kay, Charles Kris. BA, La. Coll., 1938; grad., Juilliard Sch. of Music, 1938; MusM, La. State U., 1963; LLD (hon.), La. Coll., 1980. Pvt. voice tchr., Sulphur, Jennings, La., 1939-59; instr. music McNeese State U., Lake Charles, La., 1955-58; choir dir., ch. soloist Bapt. Ch., Sulphur, Jennings, Baton Rouge, 1938-95. Vis. asst. prof. La. State U., Baton Rouge, 1967-68; mem. State Bd. of Trustees for Higher Edn., Baton Rouge, 1975-77; mem. La. Bd. of Regents for Higher Edn., Baton Rouge, 1978-90. Contbg. editor La. Bapt. Message, 1970-75; chmn. editl. bd., writer, critic Music Clubs Mag., 1969-95; contbr. articles to mags. Mem. exec. bd. La. Bapt., Alexandria, 1969-75; chmn. woman's divsn. Gubernatorial candidate, Jennings, 1959, Baton Rouge, 1963; candidate State Bd. Edn., Baton Rouge, 1974; bd. drs. Baton Rouge Arts Coun. and Cmty. Fund for Arts, 1983-89, Red Cross, Baton Rouge, 1961-66, YMCA, Baton Rouge, 1961-66, PTA, Baton Rouge, 1961-66, Baton Rouge Symphony, 1961-2002; women's pres. U. Bapt. Ch., Jennings, 1992-95, 1st Bapt. Ch., Baton Rouge, 1964-68; founder, chmn. Baton Rouge (La.) Symphony Youth Orch., 1983-2002. Recipient Disting. Alumni award La. Coll., 1961, Vol. Activist award Speech and Hearing Baton Rouge, 1979, Brotherhood award Baton Rouge chpt. Conf. Christians and Jews, 1989, Disting. Alumni award La. State U., 1995. Mem. Nat. Fedn. Music (exec. bd. 1979-95), La. Arts in Edn., Baton Rouge Music Club (state pres. 1966-70), Bapt. Women's Missions (state pres. 1960-63), Mortar Bd., ODK, Sigma Alpha Iota, Phi Kappa Lambda, PEO, Phi Kappa Phi. Democrat. Avocations: cooking, gardening, reading.

KIRKPATRICK, JEANE DUANE JORDAN, political scientist, government official; b. Duncan, Okla. d. Welcher F. and Leona (Kile) Jordan; m. Evron M. Kirkpatrick; children: Douglas Jordan, John Evron, Stuart Alan. AA, Stephens Coll.; AB, Barnard Coll.; MA, PhD, Columbia U.; postgrad. (French govt. fellow), Inst. Polit. Sci., U. Paris; LHD (hon.), Georgetown U., U. Pitts., U. Charleston, Hebrew U., Colo. Sch. Mines, St. John's U., Universidad Francisco Marroquin, Guatemala, Coll. of William and Mary, U. Mich., Syracuse U.; hon. degree, Loyola U., Chgo., U. Rochester. Asst. prof. polit. sci. Trinity Coll., 1962-67; assoc. prof. polit. sci. Georgetown U., Washington, 1967-73, prof., 1973—, Leavey prof., 1978—2002, prof. emeritus, 2002—; sr. fellow Am. Enterprise Inst. for Pub. Policy Rsch., 1977—; mem. cabinet U.S. permanent rep. to UN, 1981-85; mem. Def. Policy Rev. Bd. (DPB), 1985-93; chair Commn. on Fail Safe and Risk Reduction (FARR), 1990-92; mem. Pres.'s Fgn. Intelligence and Adv. Bd. (PFIAD), 1985-89; head U.S. Delegation to Human Rights Commn., 2003. Author: Elections USA, 1956, Perspectives, 1962, The Strategy of Deception, 1963, Mass Behavior in Battle and Captivity, 1968, Leader and Vanguard in Mass Society; The Peronist Movement in Argentina, 1971, Political Woman, 1974, The New Presidential Elite, 1976, Dismantling the Parties: Reflections on Party Reform and Party Decomposition, 1978, The Reagan Phenomenon, 1983, Dictatorships and Double Standards, 1982, Legitimacy and Force (2 vols.), 1988, The Withering Away of the Totalitarian State, 1990; syndicated columnist, 1985-97; contbr. articles to profl. jours.; editor, contbr. various pubs. Trustee Helen Dwight Reid Ednl. Found., 1972—, pres., 1990—. Recipient Disting. Alumna award Stephens Coll., 1978, B'nai B'rith Humanitarian award, 1982, Award of the Commonwealth Fund, 1983, Gold medal VFW, 1984, French Prix Politique, 1984, Dept. Def. Disting. Pub. Svc. medal, 1985, Bronze Palm, 1992, Disting. Svc. medal Mayor of N.Y.C., 1985, Presdl. Medal of Freedom, 1985, Jamestown Freedom award, 1990, Centennial medal Nat. Soc. DAR, 1991, Disting. Svc. award USO, 1994, Laureate of the Lincoln Acad. of Ill., Medallion of Lincoln, 1996, Jerusalem 2000 award, 1996, Casey medal of hon., 1998, Tomas Garrigue Masaryk Order, 1998, Chauncey Rose award Rose-Hulman Inst. Tech., 1999, Hungarian Presdl. Gold medal, 1999, Living Legends medal Libr. Congress, 2000, Grand Officier du Wissam Al Alaoui medal King of Morocco, 2000; Kirkpatrick professorship of internat. affairs chair established in her honor Harvard U., 1999; Coun. on Fgn. Rels. established Jeane Kirkpatrick chair in nat. security, 2002. Mem. Internat. Polit. Sci. Assn. (exec. coun.), Am. Polit. Sci. Assn. (Hubert Humphrey award 1988), So. Polit. Sci. Assn. Office: Am Enterprise Inst 1150 17th St NW Washington DC 20036-4603 E-mail: jkirkpatrick@aei.org.

KIRKPATRICK, SHARON MINTON, nursing educator, college administrator; b. Independence, Mo., Aug. 31, 1943; d. Charles Russell and Minnetta (Brotherton) Minton; m. John P. Kirkpatrick; children: John Brent, Kraig Russell. Grad. in nursing, Ind. Sanitarium and Hosp., Independence, 1965; AA, Graceland Coll., Lamoni, Iowa, 1965; BSN, Calif. State U., Sacramento, 1976; M in Nursing, U. Kans., 1981, PhD in Nursing, 1988. RN, Mo., Iowa. Office coordinator Family Practice Physicians, Cupertino, Calif., 1965-67; head nurse Truman Med. Ctr. East, Kansas City, Mo., 1977-79; teaching asst. U. Kans. Med. Ctr., Kansas City, 1980; asst. prof. nursing Graceland Coll., 1980-86, chmn. div. nursing, 1986-94, prof., dean Independence Campus, 1990-94, v.p., dean. of nursing, 1994—. Dir. cmty. health projects Haiti, Dominican Republic, Jamaica, Zambia, Zaire and Malawi. Contbr. articles to profl. jours. Trustee Independence Sanitarium and Hosp., 1977-86; mem. corp. body Truman Neurol. Ctr., Kansas City, 1979-86. Mem. ANA (coun. on cultural diversity), Mo. Nurses Assn. (bd. dirs., pres. 1991-93), Profl. Nurses Assn. (pres. 1982-84), Collegiate Nurse Educators Greater Kansas City (pres. (1991-92), Jr. Women's Club Cupertino (past pres.), Sigma Theta Tau. Mem. Reorganized Lds Ch. Avocations: traveling, cultural studies, backpacking, boating, reading. Home: 5665 NE Northgate Xing Lees Summit MO 64064-1240 Office: Graceland Coll Lamoni IA 50140

KIRKSEY, AVANELLE, nutrition educator; b. Mulberry, Ark., Mar. 23, 1926; BS, U. Ark., Fayetteville, 1947; MS, U. Tenn., Knoxville, 1950; PhD, Pa. State U., 1961; postdoctoral, U. Calif., Davis, 1976; DSc honoris causa, Purdue U., 1997. Assoc. prof. Ark. Polytechnic U., Russellville, 1950-55; rsch. asst. Pa. State U., University Park, 1956-58, fellow Gen. Foods, 1958-60; assoc. prof. Purdue U., West Lafayette, Ind., 1961-69, prof. nutrition, 1970-85, disting. prof., 1985-96, disting. prof. emeritus, 1997. Prin. investigator nutrition project in rural Egypt; coord. nutrition program Indonesian Univs., 1987-91 Contbr. articles to profl. jours. Recipient Borden award Am. Home Econs. Assn., 1980. Fellow Am. Inst. Nutrition (Lederle award 1994); mem. N.Y. Acad. Scis., Phi Kappa Phi, Sigma Xi. Office: Purdue U Dept Food Nutrition West Lafayette IN 47907

KIRMSE, SISTER ANNE-MARIE ROSE, nun, educator, researcher; b. Bklyn., Sept. 23, 1941; d. Frank Joseph Sr. and Anna (Keck) K. BA in English cum laude, St. Francis Coll., 1972; MA in Theology with honors, Providence Coll., 1975; PhD in Theology, Fordham U., 1989. Joined Sisters of St. Dominic, Roman Cath. Ch., 1960; cert. elem. tchr., N.Y. Tchr. elem. sch. Diocese Bklyn., 1962-73; instr. adult edn. Diocese Rockville Centre, N.Y., 1974—; dir. religious edn. St. Anthony Padua Parish, East Northport, N.Y., 1975-83; dir. spiritual programs Diocese of Rockville Centre, 1979—. Demonstration tchr. Paulist Press, N.Y.C., 1968-70; cons. Elem. Sch. Catechetical Assocs., Bklyn., 1971-73; mem. adj. faculty grad. program Sem. Immaculate Conception, Huntington, N.Y., 1979-80; adj. instr. Molloy Coll., Rockville Centre, 1985, St. Joseph's Coll., Patchogue, N.Y., 1990-91; adj. asst. prof. Ignatius Coll., Bronx, N.Y., 1996-98; adj. assoc. prof. Fordham Coll. Liberal Studies, 1998—; asst. to Card. Avery Dulles, Fordham U., Bronx, 1988—, rsch. assoc. Laurence J. McGinley chair in religion and society, 1989-2003. Recipient Kerygma award Diocese of Rockville Centre, 1980; Dominican scholar Providence Coll., 1973, Presdl. scholar Fordham U., 1988; McGinley fellow Fordham U., 1988. Mem. Cath. Theol. Soc. Am., Coll. Theology Soc., Amnesty Internat., Kiwanis (pres. Fordham U. 1997-2000, Tablet of Honor 2000, Lt. gov. dist. chmn. Internat. Understanding/Student Exch., 2001-03, lt. gov. Bronx-Westchester South divsn. 2003—, KPTC fellow 2001). Democrat. Roman Catholic. Avocations: swimming, needlework, cooking, traveling, reading. Office: Fordham U Faber Hall 255 Bronx NY 10458 Office Phone: 718-817-4746. E-mail: kirmse@fordham.edu.

KIRNOS, DINA, technology support professional; b. Dushanbe, Russia, Oct. 6, 1953; came to the U.S., 1979; d. Sholom and Klara (Blitshteyn) Kirnos; children: Semyon Shnayderman, Mallory McCoy. BA, U. Dushanbe, 1974. Programmer Royal Ins. Co., N.Y.C., 1979-82; systems analyst Chem. Bank, N.Y.C., 1982-84, Securities Industry Automation Corp., N.Y.C., 1984-89; sr. systems analyst N.Y. Stock Exch., 1989-94, dir. support, 1994—. Mgr. customer svcs. N.Y. Stock Exch., Inc., 1994—. Mem. Assn. Info. Techs., Help Desk Inst. Republican. Jewish. Avocation: music. Office: NY Stock Exch Inc 20 Broad St New York NY 10005-2601

KIRSCH, ABIGAIL, culinary productions executive; b. Bklyn., Jan. 22, 1930; d. Joseph and Mollie (Langbert) Greenberg; m. Robert B. Kirsch, June 19, 1951; children: Richard, James, Billy, Jo-Ellen. BA, Adelphi U., 1951; culinary cert., Cordon Bleu, Paris, 1967, Culinary Inst. Am., 1968. Founder, owner, chef, instr. Abigail Kirsch Sch. Cookery, Chappaqua, N.Y., 1964-75; founder Abigail Kirsch Culinary Prodns., Ltd., Tarrytown, N.Y., 1975—; chef, owner Abigail Kirsch's Husband's Pl., Chappaqua, 1975; owner, operator Abigail Kirsch at Tappan Hill, Tarrytown, N.Y., 1989—. Author cookbooks: Teen Cuisine, 1968, The Bride and Groom's First Cookbook, 1996, Invitation to Dinner, 1998, The Bride and Groom's Menu Cookbook, 2002; contbr. articles to profl. publs.; appeared on TV programs on CNN, Food Network, Discovery, Our Home, 1996. Bd. dirs. Westchester County Assn., White Plains, N.Y., 1997-99, March of Dimes West Divsn., White Plains, 1989-90; mem. exec. bd. Food Patch of Westchester, Millwood, N.Y., 1993-97; ann. gala advisor Westchester C.C., Valhalla, N.Y., 1990. Recipient Small Bus. award for Women U.S. C. of C., 1987, Vol. of Yr. award March of Dimes, 1992, Headliner award Women in Comms., 1995, Woman of Distinction award roundtable for Women in Food Svc., 1995, Pacesetter award Nat. Roundtable of Women in Food Svc., 1996, Restaurateur of Yr. award N.Y. State Restaurant Assn., 1996, Silver Plate award Internat. Food Svc. Mfrs. Assn., 1997, Family of Yr. award Family Svc. of Westchester, 1997; named to New York's 100 Most Influential Women in Bus., Crain's N.Y. Bus., 1999. Mem. Culinary Inst. Am. (chair ednl. policies com. 1988-95, sec. 1991-93, vice chair 1993-95, trustee emeritus 1995—), Les Dames d'Escoffier Internat. (sec. N.Y. chpt. 1995-96, pres. 1996-98, internat. pres. 1999—). Avocations: reading, travel, swimming. Home: 18 Robin Hood Rd Pound Ridge NY 10576-2306 Office: Abigail Kirsch at Tappan Hill 81 Highland Ave Tarrytown NY 10591-4206*

KIRSCH, ROSLYN RUTH, art educator, painter, printmaker; b. N.Y.C., Dec. 30, 1928; d. Harry Morris and Lillian (Zemachson) Friedenberg; m. Louis Kirsch, Dec. 26, 1948; children: Libby Ann, Andrew Lawrence. Student, Queens Coll., 1946-48; BA, Hunter Coll., 1950. Art dir. Ladies' Ready-to-Wear Buying Office, N.Y.C., 1948-50; profl. artist, self employed, 1965—; art educator Armory Art Ctr., West Palm Beach, Fla., 1987—, Boca Raton Mus. Art Sch., Boca Raton, Fla., 1990—. One-person shows include J&W Gallery, New Hope, Pa., Capitol Gallery, Tallahassee, Fla., Peter Drew Galleries, Fla., Ken Elias, Habitat Gallery, West Palm Beach, Fla., Joel Kessler Gallery, Fla., Indigo Gallery, Fla., Palm Beach Internat. Airport; exhibited in group shows Ann. Hortt Exhbn., Mus. of Art, Ft. Lauderdale, 1994 (award), Nat. Assn. Women Artists, West Palm Beach, 1995 (award), Mus. Art (invitational exhibit), Ft. Lauderdale, 1998, Boca Raton Mus. Art, Fla., 1999; represented in permanent collections including Mus. Art., Ft. Lauderdale, Boca Raton Mus. Art. Recipient Honorable Mention award Mus. Art, Ft. Lauderdale, 1994, others. Mem. Nat. Assn. Women Artists, Boca Raton Mus. Artists Guild, others. Avocations: golf, fundraising. E-mail: kirschfineart@yahoo.com.

KIRSCHBAUM, PAMELA GALE, editor, writer; b. St. Louis, Jan. 16, 1941; d. David Canter Rosenfeld and Bee Gale; m. Barry B. Kirschbaum, June 8, 1965; children: Charles, Stephen. BA in Polit. Sci. (hons.), Washington U., St. Louis, 1962; MS in mass comm., Va. Commonwealth U., 1983. History/Govt. tchr. Brittany Jr. HS, St. Louis, 1966—67, St. Joseph's HS, Olongapo, Philippines, 1967—69, Herzliah HS, Montreal, Canada, 1969—70; dir. publs. and pub. rels. St. Catherine's Sch., Richmond, 1985—95; adj. faculty writing and editing publs. Va. Commonwealth U., Richmond, 1996—98; editor Am. Cmty. Gardening Assn. Mag., 1997—2003, Infoworks, Richmond, 1983—2003. Bd. mem. Beth Ahabah Temple Mus. and Archives, Richmond, 1995—2000. Recipient Publ. award, Nat. Fedn. Press Women, 1986—, Coun. for Advancement and Support of Edn., 1986, 1989, Va. Press Women, 1992. Democrat. Jewish. Avocations: swimming, fiber arts. Home: 10806 Chipewyan Dr Richmond VA 23233

KIRSCHENBAUM, LISA L. portfolio manager, financial advisor; b. N.Y.C., May 7, 1971; d. J. Michael and Paulenne Lydia (Roeske) K. BA, Brandeis U., 1994. Lic. portfolio mgr. Pres., CEO Financier's Internat. Inc., Mendham, N.J., 1992-95; account exec. T.R. Winston, Inc., Bedminster, N.J., 1994-95; Quantum Portfolio Mgr., Fin. Advisor Prudential Securities, N.Y.C., 1995-97; fin. cons. Chase Investment Svcs. Corp., N.Y.C., 1997-99; v.p., sr. fin. exec. CitiGold Pvt. Banking Group, N.Y.C., 1999—. Mem. Women's Rep. Com. Somerset County, 1994—. Mem. Internat. Platform Assn., N.Y. Health and Racquet Club, Mendham Raquet Club. Republican. Avocations: skiing, chess, deep sea fishing, boating, tennis. Home: 80 Chapin Rd Bernardsville NJ 07924-1102 Office: CitiGold Fin Ctr 666 5th Ave Frnt 5 New York NY 10103-0001

KIRSCHNER, BARBARA STARRELS, pediatric gastroenterologist; b. Phila., Mar. 23, 1941; m. Robert H. Kirschner (dec.). MD, Women's Med. Coll. Pa., 1967. Diplomate Am. Bd. Pediatrics; cert. in pediatric gastroenterology and nutrition. Intern U. Chgo., 1967-68, resident, 1968-70; mem. staff U. Chgo. Children's Hosp., 1977-83, asst. prof. pediatrics, 1984-88, prof. pediatrics and medicine, 1988—, mem. com. on nutrition and nutritional biology. Contbr. articles to profl. jours. Pediatric Gastroenterology fellow U. Chgo., 1975-77; recipient Davidson award in Pediatric gastroenterology Acad. Pediatrics, 1993, Joseph Brenneman award Chgo. Pediat. Soc., 2001. Mem. Am. Gastroenterologic Assn., N.Am. Soc. Pediatric Gastroenterology, Soc. Pediatric Rsch., Alpha Omega Alpha. Office: U Chgo Med Ctr 5839 S Maryland Ave # MC 4065 Chicago IL 60637-5417

KIRSCHNER, JOYCE, art dealer; b. L.A., Jan. 2, 1943; d. Alec and Marian Kirschner; m. Richard Aronson, Sept. 8, 1978. Bachelors Degree, Douglass Coll., 1963; Masters Degree, Hunter Coll., 1972. Adminstr. N.Y.C. Dept. for the Aging, 1973—90; art dealer Joyce Kirschner Fine Arts, 1992—. Office: Joyce Kirschner Fine Arts 146 Bank St New York NY 10014 E-mail: jknyart@aol.com.

KIRSCHSTEIN, RUTH LILLIAN, physician; b. Bklyn., Oct. 12, 1926; d. Julius and Elizabeth (Berm) Kirschstein; m. Alan S. Rabson, June 11, 1950; 1 child, Arnold. BA magna cum laude, L.I. U., 1947; MD, Tulane U., 1951, LLD, PhD, Tulane U., 1997; DSc (hon.), Mt. Sinai Sch. Medicine, 1984; LLD, Atlanta U., 1985; DSc (hon.), Med. Coll. Ohio, 1986; LHD (hon.), L.I. U., 1991; PhD (hon.), U. Rochester Sch. Medicine, 1998, Brown U., 1999; DSc (hon.), Spelman Coll., 2001, Georgetown U., 2001. Intern Kings County Hosp., Bklyn., 1951-52; resident pathology VA Hosp., Atlanta, Providence Hosp., Detroit, Clin. Ctr., NIH, Bethesda, Md., 1952-57; fellow Nat. Heart Inst. Tulane U., 1953-54; asst. dir. div. biologics standards NIH, 1971-72; dep. dir. Bur. Biologics, FDA, 1972-73, dep. assoc. commr. sci., 1973-74; dir. Nat. Inst. Gen. Med. Scis., 1974-93; acting assoc. dir. woman's health NIH, Bethesda, 1974-93, acting dir., 1993, 2000—, dep. dir., 1993—, acting dir., 2000, sr. advisor to dir., 2003—. Chmn. grants peer rev. study team NIH; mem. Inst. Medicine NAS, 1982—; co-chair, sec. Spl. Emphasis Oversight com. on Sci. and Tech., 1989—; mem. Office Tech. Assessment Adv. Com. on Basic Rsch., 1989—; co-chair PHS Coordinating Com. on Women's Health Issues, 1990—. Recipient Superior Svc. award, 1980, 1993, Presdl. Disting. Exec. Rank award, 1985, 1995, Pub. Svc. award, Fedn. Am. Soc.s Exptl. Biology, 1993, Nat. Pub. Svc. award, Am. Pub. Adminstrn./Nat. Acad. Pub. Adminstrn., 1994, Roger W. Jones award for exec. leadership, Am. U., 1994, Georgeanna Seegar Jones Women's Health Lifetime Achievement award, 1995, Albert Sabin Hero of Sci. award, 2000, Women Achievement award, Anti-Defamation League, 2001, J. Richard Nesson award, Harvard Med. Sch., 2002, Pub. Svc. award, Am. Soc. for Biochemistry and Molecular Biology, 2003. Mem.: NAS-IOM, AMA (Dr. Nathan Davis award 1990), Am. Acad. Arts and Scis., Am. Acad. Microbiology, Am. Assn. Pathologists, Am. Assn. Immunologists. Home: 6 West Dr Bethesda MD 20814-1510 Office: NIH 1 Center Dr Msc 0148 Rm 158 Bethesda MD 20892-0001 E-mail: rk25n@nih.gov.

KIRTLAND, MARIANNE MAIOCCO, psychologist; d. Vincent Carmine and Anna Teresa Maiocco; m. Walter Bramson, July 20, 1975 (div. Dec. 1985); children: Rachel Bramson, Lauren Bramson; m. Donald Robert Kirtland, Feb. 12, 2000; children: Robert, Marisa. BS, U. Calif., Irvine, 1976; MPA, Calif. State U., Long Beach, 1978; M in Psychology, US Internat. U. San Diego, 1991, PhD in Clin. Psychology, 1996. Lic. clin. psychologist Calif., 2001. Dir. patient rels., risk mgmt. San Bernardino (Calif.) Cmty. Hosp., San Bernardino, 1978—96; coord. outreach San Bernardino Cmty. Hosp., 1996—98; intern in psychology County San Bernardino, 1990—92, U. Calif. Riverside Counseling Ctr., 1993—95; asst. psychology Inland Psychiatric Med. Group, Redlands, Calif., 1997—2000; adolescent coord. teens with addictions Kaiser Permanente, Fontana, 2001—. Adj. prof. Calif. Bapt. U., Riverside, 2000. Com. Agewise, Rialto, Calif., 1996—98, Sch. Attendance Rev. Bd., San Bernardino, 1996—98; vol. Feed the Homeless, San Bernardino, 1998—2000; facilitator divorce recovery for kids Immanuel Bapt. Ch., Highland, Calif., 1997—98. Mem.: Am. Psychol. Assn. Avocations: travel, exercise, investing. Office: Kaiser Permanente 17046 Marygold Bldg 5 Fontana CA 92335

KIRTLEY, JANE ELIZABETH, law educator; b. Indpls., Nov. 7, 1953; d. William Raymond and Faye Marie (Price) K.; m. Stephen Jon Cribari, May 8, 1985. BS in Journalism, Northwestern U., 1975, MS in Journalism, 1976; JD, Vanderbilt U., 1979. Bar: N.Y. 1980, D.C. 1982, Va. 1995, U.S. Dist. Ct. (we. dist.) N.Y. 1980, U.S. Dist. Ct. D.C. 1982, U.S. Ct. Claims 1982, U.S. Ct. Appeals (4th cir.) 1982, U.S. Ct. Appeals (D.C. cir.) 1985, U.S. Ct. Appeals (10th cir.) 1996, U.S. Ct. Appeals (5th cir.) 1997, U.S. Ct. Appeals (6th cir.) 1998, U.S. Ct. Appeals (6th and 11th cir.) 1998, U.S. Supreme Ct. 1985. Assoc. Nixon, Hargrave, Devans & Doyle, Rochester, N.Y., 1979-81, Washington, 1981-84; exec. dir. Reporters Com. for Freedom of Press, Arlington, Va., 1985-99; Silha prof. media ethics & law U. Minn. Sch. Journalism & Mass Comm., Mpls., 1999—; dir. Silha Ctr. for Study of Media Ethics and Law, Mpls., 2000—; mem. affiliated faculty U. Minn. Law Sch., 2001—. Mem. adj. faculty Am. U. Sch. Comm., 1988-98; mem. affiliated law faculty U. Minn., 2001—. Exec. articles editor Vanderbilt U. Jour. Transnat. Law, 1978-79; editor: The News Media and the Law, 1985—, The First Amendment Handbook, 1987, 4th edit., 1995, Agents of Discovery, 1991, 93, 95, Pressing Issues, 1998-99; columnist NEPA Bull., 1988-99, Virginia's Press, 1991-99, Am. Journalism Rev., 1995—, W.Va.'s Press, 1997-99, Tenn. Press, 1997-99; mem. editl. bd. Comm. Law and Policy. Bd. dirs. Sigma Delta Chi Found., Indpls. Mem. ABA, N.Y. State Bar Assn., D.C. Bar Assn., Va. State Bar Assn., Sigma Delta Chi. Home: 3645 46th Ave S Minneapolis MN 55406-2937 Office: 111 Murphy Hall 206 Church St SE Minneapolis MN 55455-0488 E-mail: kirtl001@tc.umn.edu.

KIRTON, JENNIFER MYERS, artist; b. Berwick, Pa., Sept. 16, 1949; d. Fred H. and Jean I. Myers; m. Timothy Kirton, Aug. 8, 1970; children: Timothy James, Andrea Jolene, Andrew Joseph. Diploma, Orange Meml. Sch. Nursing, Orlando, Fla., 1970. RN. Galleries in Paris; represented by Mt. Dora Creative Framing Gallery, Met. Art and Antiques Gallery, art-exchang.com, IRRA Registry, Ormond Beach, Leesburg Ctr for Arts, NMWA Gallery Artisan Inn, Deland. Tchr. drawing Leesburg Ctr. Arts; overseas prodn. exhibitor, Paris, 1992—; lectr. in field; chair, judge juried art shows. Exhibited in group shows at Nat. Red Cross Scholastic (Nat. award, 1961), Apopka Art & Foliage (1st Place, 1975, 1982, Purchase award, 1978, 3rd Place, 1983, Hon. Mention, 1980, 1986), Winter Park Mall (Best of Show, 1977), Longwood ALOC/CFA (3rd Place, 1980), Colonial Plz. (Hon. Mention, 1982, 1st Place, 1988, 1989), Springs Plz. (Hon. Mention, 1983), Howell Branch Plz. (1st Place, 1984), Under the Trees (2nd Place, 1984, Special Judges award, 1985), Fashion Sq. (Hon. Mention, 1986), Artist League (Hon. Mention, 1986), Centrust (1st Place, 1988), Lake County Art Show (Hon. Mention, 1992), Working Area Artist, Altamonte Libr., Pine Hills, Fiesta in Pk., Art Addiction Sweeden, Mount Dora Ctr. Arts, MDCA Permanent Collection, Artists Fla., Vol. IV, 1994—95, one-woman shows include Meritor Bank, Seminole CC, 5th St., Overseas European Corp., Mayor's Show Apopka City Hall, Fruitland Park Libr., Biennial Deland Mus. Art, mural, Apopka H.S. Stadium, Represented in permanent collections City of Apopka, Mt. Dora Ctr. for Arts. Named Artist of Month, artexchange website, sunshine-arts website. Mem.: Internat. Registry Artist and Artwork, Art Exch., Leesburg Art Assn. (Artist of Month), Ctrl. Fla. Artists, Orange County League Artists (past pres.), Nat. Mus. Women Arts (mem. Fla. com., historian ecentfl.com, historian). Baptist. Avocation: collecting fine art. Home: 4700 Meadowland Dr Mount Dora FL 32757-9661 Personal E-mail: kirtonart@aol.com.

KIRWAN, BETTY JANE JANE, lawyer; b. Rockeville Center, N.Y., Feb. 4, 1947; d. Franklin Ira and Pearl Elias; m. Ralph D. Kirwan (div.); children: Katherine, Andrew, Kerrigan; m. John Terence Hanna, Sept. 15, 1985. AB, U. Calif., Berkeley, 1968, JD, 1971. Bar: Calif. 1972, U.S. Dist. Ct. (cen. dist.) Calif. Atty. McCutchen, Black, Verleger, Shea, L.A., 1972-85; founding ptnr. McClintock, Kirwan, Benshoof, Rochefort, Weston, L.A., 1985-89; environ. atty., chair dept. environment L.A. office Latham & Watkins, L.A., 1989—, ptnr., 1989—. Pres. Boalt Hall Alumni Assn., Berkeley, 1983-84; vice chair Hathaway Children's Svcs., L.A., 1984-89. Bd. dirs. Hathaway Children's Svcs., 1985-90, PLI Environ. Law Adv. Com., 1992—. Mem. ABA (vice chair air quality com. Natural Resource sect. 1980-88, chair environ. quality com. Natural Resource sect., chair environ. controls com. Bus. Law sect. 1986-90, coun. Bus. Law sect. 1990-94), Boalt Hall Alumni Assn. (pres. 1984). Home: 1480 Lomita Dr Pasadena CA 91106-4341 Office: Latham & Watkins 633 W Fifth St Ste 4000 Los Angeles CA 90071

KIRWAN, KATHARYN GRACE (MRS. GERALD BOURKE KIRWAN JR.), retail executive; b. Monroe, Wash., Dec. 1, 1913; d. Walter Samuel and Bertha Ella (Shrum) Camp; m. Gerald Bourke Kirwan Jr., Jan. 13, 1945. Student, U. Puget Sound, 1933-34; BA, BS, Tex. Woman's U., 1937; postgrad., U. Wash., 1941. Libr. Brady (Tex.) Sr. High Sch., 1937-38, McCamey (Tex.) Sr. High Sch., 1938-43; mgr. Milady's Frock Shop, Monroe, 1946-62, owner, mgr., 1962-93. Meml. chmn. Monroe chpt. Am. Cancer Soc., 1961-93; mem. Snohomish County Police Svcs. Action Coun., 1971; mem. Monroe Pub. Libr. Bd., 1950-65, pres. bd., 1964-65; mem. Monroe City Coun., 1969-73; mayor City of Monroe, 1974-81; commr. Snohomish County Hosp. dist. 1, 1970-90, chmn. bd. commrs., 1980-90; mem. East Snohomish County Health Planning Com., 1979-81; mem. Snohomish County Law and Justice Planning Com., 1974-78, Snohomish County Econ. Devel. Coun., 1975-81, Snohomish County Pub. Utility Dist. Citizens Adv. Task Force, 1983; sr. warden Ch. of Our Saviour, Monroe, 1976-77, 89, sr. warden, 1976-77, 89-90; mem. Monroe Breast Cancer Screening Project community planning group Fred Hutchinson Cancer Rsch. Ctrs., 1991-93. With USNR, 1943-46. Recipient Malstrom award for Hist. Homes and Bldgs. of Monroe, 2000, award of project excellence Washington Mus. Assn., 2000. Mem. AAUW, U.S. Naval Inst., Ret. Officers Assn., Naval Res. Assn., Bus. and Profl. Women's Club (2d v.p. 1980-82, pres. 1983-84), Washington Gens., Snohomish County Pharm. Aux., C. of C. (pres. 1972), Valley Gen. Hosp. Guild (pres. 1994, 95, 96), Valley Gen. Hosp. Found. (sec. 1993-97). Episcopalian. Home: 538 S Blakeley St Monroe WA 98272-2402

KIRY-RYAN, RITA IRENE, computer scientist, educator; b. St. Louis, July 12, 1960; d. Joseph and Annie Marie (Lorenz) Kiry; m. Thomas Ryan, May 26, 1989; children: Tommy Ryan, Jenny Ryan. BS in Mktg., St. Louis U., 1982, MBA in Internat. Bus., 1988. Maj. account rep. Konica Bus. Machines, St. Louis, 1988—90; store mgr. U.S. Shoe Corp., 1990—93, Charming Shoppes Inc., St. Louis, 1993—94; instr. Sterling Coll., St. Louis, 1996—97, Sanford Brown Coll., St. Louis, 1994—99, ITT Tech. Inst., St. Louis, 1996—, faculty advisor, 2001—. Vol. Long Elem. Sch., Crestwood, Mo.; mem. Celiac Sprue Assn., St. Louis, 2003. Mem.: Assn. Tchrs. Career and Tech. Edn., St. Louis U. Alumni Assn. Roman Catholic. Avocation: travel. Office: ITT Tech Inst 13505 Lakefront Dr Earth City MO 63045 Office Phone: 314-298-7800.

KISCADEN, SHEILA M. state legislator; b. St. Paul, Apr. 21, 1946; d. Harvey Richard and Bea Mae (Conway) Martineau; m. Richard Craig Kiscaden, Sept. 12, 1970; children: Michael, Karen. BS in Edn., U. Minn., 1969; MS in Pub. Adminstrn., U. So. Calif., L.A., 1986. Tchr. So. St. Paul Secondary Schs., Minn., 1969-70, Jobs 70, Rochester, Minn., 1970-71; regional coord. Planned Parenthood, Rochester, Minn., 1971-76; vol. svc. coord. Olmsted County, Rochester, Minn., 1977-80, human svc. planner, 1980-82, legis. liaison, 1982-85; prin. Cons. Collaborator, Rochester, Minn., 1987—; mem. Minn Senate from 30th dist., St. Paul, 1992—. Bd. dirs. Ability Bldg. Ctr. Found. Bd., Rochester, Minn., 1989-94, Dyslexia Inst. Minn., Rochester, Minn., 1989-94; team leader Global Vols., 1989—. Fulbright scholar, 1970. Mem. Phi Beta Kappa. Republican. Office: Minn State Senate 143 State Office Bldg Saint Paul MN 55155-0001

KISER, JO ANN, editor; b. Penny, Ky., Nov. 9, 1940; d. Ezra and Hazel (Bartley) Kiser. BA, CUNY, 1967; MA in English, U. Chgo., 1968, PhD in Comm. on Social Thought, 1993. Editl. asst. Charles E. Merrill Books, Columbus, Ohio, 1960—61; sec. Hawthorn Books, N.Y.C., 1962—63; typist, rschr., reader New Yorker mag., N.Y.C., 1963—78; manuscript editor U. Chgo. Press, 1989—97; instr. Morehead (Ky.) State U., 1997—98; quality editor Lexis-Nexis, Dayton, Ohio, 1999—2000; assoc. editor lit. Ency. Britannica, Chgo., 2000—03; copy editor Am. Jour. Sociology, 2003—. Book reviewer Whitesburg, Ky. Mountain Eagle, 1993—. Author: short stories, poems. Democrat.

KISER, MOLLY, musician; b. Dec. 15, 1971; d. Loren Hall and Yoko Tajima Kiser. Student, Tokyo Nat. U. of Fine Arts and Music, 1990; BM, Curtis Inst. Music, 1994; MM, New Eng. Conservatory, 1996; D of Mus. Arts, Juilliard Sch., 2003. Performer: Beethoven's 5th concerto "Emperor" with Rosenkranz Orch., Tchaikovsky's 1st Piano Concerto with NHK secondary Orch., Aspen Music Festival Student Orch., 1992, Salem Philharm. Orch., 1995, New Eng. Conservatory Symphony Orch., 1994, 1996, Ft. Collins Symphony Orch., 1996, Corpus Christi Symphony Orch., 1997, World Festival Orch., 1999, Westchester Symphony Orch., 2001, Tokyo City Orch., 2002. Recipient piano hons. audition, New Eng. Conservatory, 1991, winner concerto competition, Aspen Music Sch., 1992, New Eng. Conservatory, 1994, 1996, 1st prize, 41st Ft. Collins Symphony Orch. Young Artist Competition, 1996, 15th Kingsville Internat. Young Performers competition, 1996, Bronze medal, 6th San Antonio Internat. Piano competition, 1997, Silver medal, 47th Nina Widemann Piano competition, 1997, gold medal, World Piano competition, 1999, numerous others; fellow Tanglewood Music Festival fellow, 1993. Avocations: dancing, reading. Home: Apt 3F 33 Hamilton Ter New York NY 10031 Office: The Juilliard Sch 60 Lincoln Center Plz New York NY 10023

KISER, NAGIKO SATO, retired librarian; b. Taipei, Republic of China, Aug. 7, 1923; came to U.S., 1950; d. Takeichi and Kinue (Soma) Sato; m. Virgil Kiser, Dec. 4, 1979 (dec. Mar. 1981). Secondary teaching credential, Tsuda Juku U., Tokyo, 1945; BA in Journalism, Trinity U., 1953; BFA, Ohio State U., 1956, MA in Art History, 1959; MLS, cert. in library media, SUNY, Albany, 1974. Cert. community coll. librarian, Calif., cert. jr. coll. tchr., Calif., cert. secondary edn. tchr., Calif., cert. tchr. library media specialist and art, N.Y. Pub. rels. reporter The Mainichi Newspapers, Osaka, Japan, 1945-50; contract interpreter U.S. Dept. State, Washington, 1956-58, 66-67; resource specialist Richmond (Calif.) Unified Sch. Dist., 1968-69; editing supr. CTB/McGraw-Hill, Monterey, Calif., 1969-71; multi-media specialist Monterey Peninsula Unified Sch. Dist., 1975-77; librarian Nishimachi Internat. Sch., Tokyo, 1979-80, Sacramento City Unified Sch. Dist., 1977-79, 81-85; sr. librarian Camarillo (Calif.) State Hosp. and Devel. Ctr., 1985-93. Editor: Short Form Test of Academic Aptitude, 1970, Prescriptive Mathematics Inventory, 1970, Tests of Basic Experience, 1970. Mem. Calif. State Supt.'s Regional Coun. on Asian Pacific Affairs, Sacramento, 1984-91. Library Media Specialist Tng. Program scholar U.S. Office Edn., 1974. Fellow Internat. Biog. Assn. (life); mem. ALA, Am. Biog. Inst. (life, dep. gov. 1988—), Libr. Congress (nat. mem.), Calif. Libr. Assn., Med. Libr. Assn., Asunaro Shogai Kyoiku Kondankai (Lifetime Edn. Promoting Assn., Japan), The Mus. Soc., Internat. House of Japan, Matsuyama Sacramento Sister City Corp., Japanese Am. Citizens League, Japanese Am. Nat. Mus., Japanese Am. Cultural and Cmty. Ctr., Ikenobo Ikebana Soc. Am., L.A. Hototogisu Haiku Assn., Ventura County Archeol. Soc., Internat. Soc. Poets, AAUW, Ventura County Chpt. Mem. Christian Science Ch. Avocations: flower arranging, ballroom dance, classical music.

KISER-MILLER, KATHY JOY, humanities educator; b. Dayton, Ohio, Feb. 18, 1956; d. Fred Cecil and Joyce Arlene Kiser; m. Daniel Patrick Miller, Aug. 22, 1981; children: Alexander Ross Miller, Davis Noel Miller. BA, Otterbein Coll., 1978; MFA, U. Wis., 1981. Cert. secondary theatre. Sales-kitchen design Matercraft Industries, Boulder, Colo., 1981—83; sales Ford Mktg. Inst., Denver, 1983—84; assoc. prof. humanities Colo. Mountain Coll., Steamboat Springs, 1985—. Forensic dir. Colo. Mountain Coll., Steamboat Springs, 1989—95, theatre dir., 1995—, comm. and humanities discipline coord., Glenwood Springs, 1999—; humanities state chair Colo. State Faculty, 1999—2003; adjudicator Theatre Masters, Aspen, Colo., 2003—; judge scholarships Perry Mansfield Performing Arts Camp, Steamboat Springs; mem. adj. faculty Front Range C.C., Westminster, Colo., 1989—95, Regis U., Denver, 1990—94; artist in residence Boulder Valley Schs., 1987—88. Actor: Actors Theatre of Louisville, Midwest Playwright Lab., Germinal Stage, Nat. Pub. Radio-Shakespeare Series, The Changing Scene; mem. editl. adv. bd.: Collegiate Press, 1998—2001. Mem. performing arts guild Steamboat Springs Arts Coun., 1999—2000. Recipient Voice of Democracy Citation, VFW Womens Aux., 1990. Mem.: NEA, C.C. Humanities Assn., Colo. Edn. Assn., Nat. Women in the Arts, U.S. Ski Assn. (sec. 2002—), Theatre Comm. Guild, Kiwanis (pres. 2000—01, sec. 1998—99), Steamboat Springs Winter Sports Club (chair winter carnival sales 1999). Office: Colorado Mountain College 1330 Bob Adams Dr Steamboat Springs CO 80487 Office Phone: 970-870-4489.

KISLAK, JEAN HART, art director; b. 1931; d. Frank Ernest and Isabelle Tayor (Ellis) Hart; m. William I. Herendeen, Aug. 23, 1952 (div. Feb. 1956); m. Louis G. Johnson, Jan. 31, 1959 (div. Feb. 1975); 1 child, Jennifer Taylor Johnson; m. Jay Kislak, Apr. 7, 1985. Student, Peace Jr. Coll., Raleigh, N.C., Queens Coll., Charlotte, N.C. With Storer Broadcasting Co., Miami, Fla., S.E. Banks, N.A., Miami, 1974-84, art dir., 1974-84; mem. Gov. Fla. Panel Visual Arts, 1979-81; art cons., 1974—. Internat. rep. Christies, Inc., 1998—2001; mem. art and archtecture com. Libr. of Congress, Washington, 2003. Bd. dirs. Viscaya Mus., Miami, 1963, Beaux Arts, U. Miami, 1968, Theatre Art Patrons, Miami, 1968, Theatre Art Patrons, Miami, 1965, NEH, Fla., 1992; trustee Dade County Zool. Soc., 1988—, Miami Art Mus., Barry Coll. Charter Sch.; mem. Bacardi Imports Art Bd., 1983-89, 98—, Fla. State Bd. Art Coun., 1987, Miami Art Mus. (formerly Dade County Ctr. for the Arts Bd.), 1989-99; bd. dirs. Nat. Wildflower Assn., 1991; mem. exec. bd. Zool. Soc. Fla., 1994; mem. Fla. Humanities Bd., 1994; mem. visual arts com. Libr. Congress, 2002. Recipient Gov. Fla. award art, 1976, 79, Miami Dade Pub. Libr. award, 1978, Bus. Com. for Arts award, 1975-79, WPBT Pub. TV award, 1976, 77, 80, Lowe Gallery, U. Miami cert. recognition, 1980, Dade County Art in Pub. Places cert. recognition, 1981, 82. Mem. 1805 Club (London) (hon. v.p. 1993—), Kislak Found. (bd. dirs. 1997—). Address: 720 NE 69th St Miami FL 33138-5738

KISSINGER, KAREN G. energy executive; V.p., contr. UniSource Energy Corp., Tucson, 1997—. Office: UniSource Energy Corp PO Box 711 Tucson AZ 85702-0711

KISSLER, CYNTHIA ELOISE, geologist, consultant; b. Knoxville, Tenn., July 6, 1949; d. James Albert Jurney and Josephine Cassandra Ramsey-Jurney; m. Albert Donald Kissler, Apr. 16, 1994; children: Eric, T. Duff. AAS, Wenatchee Valley Coll., 1994; BS in Geology, Ctrl. Wash. U., 1996, postgrad. Geol. cons., E. Wenatchee, 1998. Mem. Am. Goephys. Union, Geol. Soc. Am., Wenatchee Applarians. Avocations: skiing, woodworking. Home and Office: 690 Degage St East Wenatchee WA 98802-4961 E-mail: kisslerc@nwi.net.

KISTIAKOWSKY, VERA, physics researcher, educator; b. Princeton, N.J., Sept. 9, 1928; d. George Bogdan and Hildegard (Moebius) K.; m. Gerhard Emil Fischer, June 16, 1951 (div. 1970); children: Marc Laurenz Fischer, Karen Marie Fischer. AB, Mt. Holyoke Coll., 1948, ScD (hon.), 1978; PhD, U. Calif., Berkeley, 1952. Staff scientist U.S. Naval Rsch. Def. Lab., San Francisco, 1952-53; fellow U. Calif., Berkeley, 1953-54; rsch. assoc. Columbia U., N.Y.C., 1954-57, instr., 1957-59; asst. prof. Brandeis U., Waltham, Mass., 1959-62, adj. assoc. prof., 1962-63; staff mem. MIT, Cambridge, 1963-69, sr. rsch. scientist, 1969-72, prof. physics, 1972-94, prof. emerita, 1994—. Author: Atomic Energy, 1959, One Way Is Down, 1967; contbr. articles on nuc. and elem. particle physics and astrophysics to profl. jours. Dir. Coun. for a Liveable World, 1983—, dir. Edn. Fund, 1983—2001, pres., 1997—2000. Recipient Centennial award Mt. Holyoke Coll., 1972. Fellow AAAS, Am. Phys. Soc. (councilor 1974-77); mem. Assn. for Women in Sci. (pres. 1982-83), Phi Beta Kappa (vis. scholar 1983-84, senator 1988-96), Sigma Xi (lectr. 1990-92). Office: MIT 77 Massachusetts Ave Rm 6-108 Cambridge MA 02139-4307 E-mail: verak@mit.edu.

KISTLER, LORETTA M. social worker, consultant; b. Lehighton, Pa., Oct. 1, 1960; d. Wayne R. Behler and Carolyn A. Walck, James E. Ahner and Maryellen L. Behler; m. John Kistler, Nov. 13, 1982 (div. Dec. 16, 1989). BA, Cedar Crest Coll., 1982; MSW, Marywood U., 1984. Lic. social worker Pa., LCSW N.J. Psychiat. social worker Wiley Ho., Bethlehem, Pa., 1984—88; adolescent addictions evaluator Good Samaritan Hosp., Pottsville, Pa., 1988—89; clin. coord. Renewal Centers, Quakertown, Pa., 1989—91, Vitae Ho., Glenmore, Pa., 1991—95; program coord., therapist Cath. Charities-Diocese of Metuchen, Perth Amboy, NJ, 1995—2002; chief social worker Easton (Pa.) Hosp., 2002—. Faculty liasion Marywood U., Scranton, Pa., 1995—2002; program developer Regional Devel. Corp., Pottsville, 1993; addictions group educator Bethesda Treatment Programs, Lehighton, Pa., 1984—89. Sec., past dir. LV K-9 Therapy Assn., Nazareth, Pa., 1997—2003. Mem.: NASW. Lutheran. Avocations: river rafting, camping, therapy dog community education and visiting, cooking. Office: Easton Hosp 250 21st St Easton PA 18042 Personal E-mail: rett60@yahoo.com.

KISVARSANYI, EVA BOGNAR, retired geologist; b. Budapest, Hungary, Dec. 18, 1935; arrived in U.S., 1957; d. Kalman and Ilona (Simon) Bognar; m. Geza Kisvarsanyi, July 3, 1956; 1 child, Erika G. Student, Eotvos Lorand U., Budapest, 1954-56; BS in Geology, U. Mo., Rolla, 1958, MS, 1960. Geologist Mo. Geol. Survey, Rolla, 1959-68; from rsch. geologist to sect. chief Mo. Dept. Natural Resources/Geol. Survey Program, Rolla, 1968-90; asst. dir. MODNR/Geol. Survey Program, Rolla, 1990-93; cons. Sarasota, Fla., 1993—; exec. dir. Hungarian-Am. Cultural Assn., Inc., 1995—; tchr. Sarasota County Pub. Sch. Sys., Sarasota, 1994-98; dir. comm. NEM, Inc., 1998—2001; ret., 2001. Editor: geol. guidebooks, 1976—; contbr. articles to profl. jours. Fellow: Soc. Econ. Geologists (mem. rsch. com. 1989—92), Geol. Soc. Am. (mem. rep. 1985—93); mem.: AAUW, Sigma Xi (pres. Rolla chpt. 1990—91). Avocations: travel, music.

KITAGAWA, AUDREY EMIKO, retired lawyer; b. Mar. 31, 1951; d. Yonoichi and Yoshiko Kitagawa. BA cum laude, U. So. Calif., 1973; JD, Boston Coll., 1976. Bar: Hawaii 1977, U.S. Dist. Ct. Hawaii 1977. Assoc. Rice, Lee & Wong, Honolulu, 1977-80; pvt. practice Honolulu, 1980-96; head Sri Ramakrishna Spiritual Family, 1992—. Advisor Office of Spl. Rep. of Sec. Gen. for Children and Armed Conflict (UN); mem. internat. adv. coun. Internat. Caring Comtys., Toda Inst. for Peace and Global Policy Rsch.; exec. coun. World Commn. Global Consciousness and Spirituality, Spiritual Caucus at UN. Coun. Global Action to Stop War; founder, dir. Vision for Humanity; bd. dirs. Wall St. Rotary, Apeader Children's Peace Ctr.; co-facilitator United Religions Initiative, UN Cooperation Circle;

co-dir. Mereon Inst. Mem.: ABA, Women in Internat. Security, Hawaii Bar Assn., Honolulu Club. Republican. Office: UN Hdqs Secretariat 3161B New York NY 10017 E-mail: dmaudrey@agk9.net.

KITAHATA-SPORN, AMY, movement educator; b. Kyoto, Sept. 1, 1957; came to U.S. 1960; d. Luke Masahiko and Carolyn Dawson (Massey) Kitahata; m. Lee Stuart Sporn, Sept. 26, 1981. BA, Oberlin Coll., 1979; tchrs. cert., Am. Ctr. for the Alexander Technique, 1983, Ctr. for Study of Authentic Movement, 1991. Pvt. practice in Alexander Technique, N.Y.C., 1983—; mem. faculty Am. Ctr. for Alexander Technique, N.Y.C., 1984-90, The Juilliard Sch., N.Y.C., 1984—; pvt. instr. creative movement N.Y.C., 1988—. Mem. Am. Ctr. for the Alexander Technique (bd. dirs. 1984-86), N.Am. Soc. Tchrs. of Alexander Technique, Nature Conservancy, Sierra Club. Avocations: yoga, authentic movement, hiking, biking, dance. Office: The Juilliard Sch Lincoln Ctr New York NY 10023

KITCHEN, SHIRLEY, state legislator, social worker; b. Augusta, Ga., Sept. 18, 1946; d. Ferman and Ruth Few. BA in Human Svcs., Antioch U., 1979; postgrad., Temple U. Mem. Pa. Senate, Dist. 3, Harrisburg, 1987-88, 96—; minority chmn. Pa. Senate, Harrisburg, mem. aging and youth com., mem. pub. health and welfare, mem. local govt. com., mem. intergovtl. affairs com., mem. state govt. com. Mem. exec. com. Phila. Dem., ward leader 20th ward; mem. adv. com. Calcutta House; bd. dirs. St. Joseph Hosp.; mem. North Phila. Housing Cmty. Devel. Corp., NAACP, East of Broad Coalition; mem. ex-officio North Ctrl. Empowerment Zone; co-sponsor, founder North Philly Dazzling Diamonds. Office: 1701 W Lehigh Ave Ste 104 Philadelphia PA 19132-2106

KITCHENS, JOYCE ELLEN, lawyer; b. Jesup, Ga., Oct. 8, 1948; d. Arthur Ellis and Ray Lucille (Burton) K.; m. Larry Keith Brumfield, Aug. 23, 1969 (div. July 1973); m. Jerry Baxter Barnes; stepchildren: Craig Randall Barnes, Suzanne Cynthia Barnes. BA in English Lit., Purdue U., 1970, MA in English Lit., 1972; JD, Emory U., 1982. Bar: Ga. 1982, U.S. Dist. Ct. (no. dist.) Ga. 1982, U.S. Dist. Ct. (mid. dist.) Ga. 1992, U.S. Ct. Appeals (11th cir.) 1982, U.S. Ct. Mil. Appeals 1996, U.S. Tax Ct. 1995, U.S. Ct. Appeals (fed. cir.), 1999. Staff atty. Dept. Vet. Affairs, Atlanta, 1982-89, asst. dist. counsel, 1989-91; pvt. practice Atlanta, 1991—. Adj. faculty Emory U. Sch. Law, 1996-2001. Mem. Fed. Bar Assn. (pres. Atlanta chpt. 1991-92, 11th cir. officer 1992-98, dep. sec. 1998-99, sec. 1999-2000, nat. pres. 2003--), Ansley Kiwanis (past pres. 1992-93, Disting. Svc. award 1991). Democrat. Methodist. Avocations: reading, travel, adventure. Office: 2973 Hardman Ct Atlanta GA 30305

KITE, MARILYN S. state supreme court justice, lawyer; b. Laramie, Wyo., Oct. 2, 1947; BA with honors, U. Wyo., 1970, JD with honors, 1974. Bar: Wyo. 1974. Mem. Holland & Hart, Jackson, Wyo., 1979—2000; justice Wyo. Supreme Ct., 2000—. Contbr. articles to profl. jours. Mem. ABA (nat. resources sect., litigation sect.), Wyo. State Bar. Address: Wyo Supreme Ct 2301 Capitol Ave Cheyenne WY 82002

KITSANTAS, ANASTASIA, educational psychologist; PhD in Edn. Psychology, CUNY, 1996. Asst. prof. James Madison U., Harrisonburg, Va., 1997—99, Fla. State U., Tallahassee, 1999—2000; asst. prof., edn. psychology program coord. George Mason U., Fairfax, Va., 2001—. Assoc. dir. Hellenic Inst. Psychology & Health, 1999—. Contbr. articles to profl. jours. Mem.: APA, Fla. Rsch. Assn., Am. Ednl. Rsch. Assn. (chair, spl. interest group officer 2001—). Office: George Mason Univ Grad Sch Edn MSN 4B3 Fairfax VA 22030-4444 Home: 2505 Popkins Ln Alexandria VA 22306-1815 Office Phone: 703-993-2688. Business E-Mail: akitsant@gmu.edu.

KITT, EARTHA MAE, actress, singer; b. St. Matthews, S.C., Jan. 17, 1927; d. John and Anna K.; m. William McDonald, June 1960 (div.); 1 child, Kitt Shapiro. Grad. high sch. Soloist with Katherine Dunham Dance Group, 1948; night club singer, 1949—, appearing in France, Turkey, Greece, Egypt, N.Y.C., Hollywood, Las Vegas, London, Stockholm; actress: (plays) Dr. Faustus, Paris, 1951, New Faces of 1952, N.Y.C., Mrs. Patterson, N.Y.C., 1954, Shinbone Alley, N.Y.C., 1957, Timbuktu, 1978, Blues in the Night, 1985, (films) including New Faces, 1953, Accused, 1957, Anna Lucasta, 1958, Mark of the Hawk, 1958, St. Louis Blues, 1957, Saint of Devil's Island, 1961, Synanon, 1965, Up The Chastity Belt, 1971, Dragonard, Ernest Scared Stupid, 1991, Boomerang, 1992, Fatal Instinct, 1993, Harriet the Spy, 1996, Ill Gotten Gains (voice), 1997, (TV) The Wild Thornberrys (voice), 1998, The Emperor's New Grove (voice), 2000, Feast of All Saints, 2001, Santa Baby!, 2001, Standard Time, 2002, Holes, 2003, also 2 French films, also numerous TV appearances including Cat Woman role in Batman series, (broadway shows) The Wizard of Oz, 1998, The Wild Party, 2000 (Tony nominee), Rodgers & Hammerstein's Cinderella, 2001; star: (documentary film) All By Myself, 1982; albums include In Person at the Plaza, 1987, My Way: A Musical Tribute to Rev. Dr. Martin Luther King Jr., 1987; author: Thursday's Child, 1956, A Tart Is Not a Sweet, Alone With Me, 1976, I'm Still Here, 1990, Confessions of a Sex Kitten, 1991; co-author: Down to Eartha, 2000, How to Rejuvenate: It's Not Too Late, 2000; albums: Best of Eartha Kitt, 1983, Miss Kitt, To You, 1992, Back in Business, 1994, Standard/Live, 1998, The Best of Eartha Kitt: Where Is My Man, 1998, Thinking Jazz, 1998, Purr-fect: Greatest Hits, 1999, Where Is My Man: The Best of Eartha Kitt, 1999. Named Woman of Yr. Nat. Assn. Negro Musicians, 1968; nominated 2 Grammys, 2 Tony awards, 1 Emmy. Office: care Provident Fin Mgmt 1185 Sixth Ave 19th Fl New York NY 10036

KITT, OLGA, artist; b. N.Y.C., July 29, 1929; d. Elias and Mary (Opiela) K.; m. Nicholas Rawluk, Aug. 6, 1955 (div. 1960); 1 child, Wade. BA, Queens Coll., 1951; MA, State U. Iowa, 1952; studied with Meyer Schapiro, N.Y.C., 1954; studied with Hans Hofmann, N.Y.C., Provincetown, 1954-55; postgrad., Inst. Fine Arts, NYU, 1955, NYU, 1960-62; studied with Robert Beverly Hale, N.Y.C., 1979. Gallery asst. Chappellier Gallery, N.Y.C., 1952—53; asst. to Walter Pach NY, 1953—56; tchg. asst. CCNY, 1953—58; tchr. art NY, 1962—80. One-woman shows include CCNY, 1957, Manhattan Coll., Riverdale, N.Y., 1980, Blackout Gallery, N.Y.C., 1997, Coll. Mt. St. Vincent, 2001, The Corridor Gallery of Riverdale Temple, 2001, 2002, The Corridor Gallery of Interchurch Ctr., 2002, exhibited in group shows at Whitney Mus., 1954, Bronx County Hist. Soc., 1978, Mus. Modern Art, N.Y.C., 1978, Art Students League, 1979, Bronx Mus. Arts, 1979, Coll. Mt. St. Vincent, 2000, Broome St. Gallery, N.Y.C., 2002, 2003, Represented in permanent collections Bronx Arts Ensemble, Riverdale Press, Riverdale YM-YWHA, U. Iowa, Iowa City, Fordham U., Fordham Prep. Sch., Hostos Coll., N.Y.C., Harris Sch. of Art, Tenn., numerous pvt. collections. Home: Apt 4D 5610 Netherland Ave Bronx NY 10471-1703 Studio: 495 S Broadway Yonkers NY 10705-3221 E-mail: olgakitt2@cs.com.

KITTELL, SARA BRANON, state legislator; b. Burlington, Vt., Nov. 8, 1945; m. William Kittell; three children. RN, Jeanne Mance Sch., Burlington, 1967; BSN, U. Vt., 1981. Nurse, sml. bus. owner; mem., Franklin County Vt. Senate, Montpelier, 1995—. Mem. Vt. Nurses Assn. Office: RR 1 Fairfield VT 05455-9801

KITTS, DEBORAH L. accountant; b. Olean, N.Y., May 1, 1966; d. Robert Earl and Anne Louise (Tyler) Wheaton; m. Dennis Dulane Kitts, Oct. 26, 2001; 1 child from previous marriage, Jessica Brianne Keiling. BBA cum laude, Radford (Va.) U., 1998. Front office supr., night mgr. Marriott Corp., 1986—94; fin. analyst, staff acct. Alliant Techsystems, Inc., Radford, 1998—2003; commencement coord. Radford (Va.) U., 2003. Mem.: Inst. Mgmt. Accts., Va. Soc. CPAs. Democrat. Episcopalian. Office: Radford U PO Box 6904 Registrar's Office Radford VA 24142 Home: 1552 Grayson Tpke Wytheville VA 24382-5877

KIVELSON, MARGARET GALLAND, physicist; b. N.Y.C., Oct. 21, 1928; d. Walter Isaac and Madeleine (Wiener) Galland; m. Daniel Kivelson, Aug. 15, 1949; children: Steven Allan, Valerie Ann. AB, Radcliffe Coll., 1950, AM, 1951, PhD, 1957. Cons. Rand Corp., Santa Monica, Calif., 1956-69; asst. to geophysicist UCLA, 1967-83, prof., 1983—, also chmn. dept. earth and space scis., 1984-87, acting dir. Inst. Geophys. Planet Phys., 1999—2000; prin. investigator of magnetometer, Galileo Mission, Jet Propulsion Lab., Pasadena, Calif., 1977—2004. Overseer Harvard Coll., 1977-83; mem. adv. coun. NASA, 1987-93; chair atmospheric adv. com. NSF, 1986-89, Com. Solar and Space Physics, 1977-86, com. planetary exploration, 1986-87, com. solar terrestial phys., 1989-92; mem. adv. com. geoscis. NSF, 1993-97; mem. space studies bd. NRC, 2002—. Editor: The Solar System: Observations and Interpretations, 1986; co-editor: Introduction to Space Physics, 1995; contbr. articles to profl. jours. Named Woman of Yr., L.A. Mus. Sci. and Industry, 1979, Woman of Sci., UCLA, 1984; recipient Grad. Soc. medal Radcliffe Coll., 1983, 350th Anniversary Alumni medal Harvard U. Fellow AAAS, NAS, Internat. Inst. Astronautics, Am. Geophys. Union, Am. Acad. Arts and Scis., Am. Phys. Soc., Royal Astron. Soc.; mem. Am. Astron. Soc. Office: UCLA Dept Earth & Space Scis 6847 Slichter Los Angeles CA 90095-0001 Office Phone: 310-825-3435. Business E-Mail: mkivelson@igpp.ucla.edu.

KIZER, CAROLYN ASHLEY, poet, educator; b. Spokane, Wash., Dec. 10, 1925; d. Benjamin Hamilton and M. (Ashley) K.; m. Stimson Bullitt, Jan., 1948 (div.); children: Ashley Ann, Scott, Jill Hamilton; m. John Marshall Woodbridge, Apr. 11, 1975. BA, Sarah Lawrence Coll., 1945; postgrad. (Chinese govt. fellow in comparative lit.), Columbia U., 1946-47; studied poetry with Theodore Roethke, U. Wash., 1953-54; LittD (hon.), Whitman Coll., 1986, St. Andrew's Coll., 1989, Mills Coll., 1990, Wash. State U., 1991. Specialist in lit. U.S. Dept. State, Pakistan, 1964-65; first dir. lit. programs Nat. Endowment for Arts, 1966-70; poet-in-residence U. N.C. at Chapel Hill, 1970-74; Hurst Prof. Lit. Washington U., St. Louis, 1971; lectr. Spring Lecture Series Barnard Coll., 1972; acting dir. grad. writing program Columbia U., 1972; poet-in-residence Ohio U., 1974; vis. poet Iowa Writer's Workshop, 1975; prof. U. Md., 1976-77; poet-in-residence, disting. vis. lectr. Centre Coll., Ky., 1979; disting. vis. poet East Wash. U., 1980; Elliston prof. poetry U. Cin., 1981; Bingham disting. prof. U. Louisville, Ky., 1982; disting. vis. poet Bucknell U., Pa., 1982; vis. poet SUNY, Albany, 1982; prof. Columbia U. Sch. Arts, 1982; prof. poetry Stanford U., 1986; sr. fellow in humanities Princeton U., 1986; vis. prof. writing U. Ariz., 1989, 90, U. Calif., Davis, 1991; Coal Royalty chair U. Ala., 1995. Participant Internat. Poetry Festivals, London, 1960, 70, Yugoslavia, 1969, 70, Pakistan, 1969, Rotterdam, Netherlands, 1970, Knokke-le-Zut, Belgium, 1970, Bordeaux, 1992, Dublin, 1993, Glasgow, 1994; sr. fellow humanities council Princeton U., 1986. Author: Poems, 1959, The Ungrateful Garden, 1961, Knock Upon Silence, 1965, Midnight Was My Cry, 1971, Mermaids in the Basement: Poems for Women, 1984 (San Francisco Arts Commn. award 1986), Yin: New Poems, 1984 (Pulitzer prize in poetry 1985), The Nearness of You, 1987 (Theodore Roethke prize, 1988); Proses: On Poems & Poets, 1994, Picking & Choosing: Prose on Prose, 1995, Harping On: Poems 1985-1995, 1996, The Complete Pro Femina, 2000, Cool, Calm and Collected Poems, 1960-2000; editor: Woman Poet: The West, 1980, Leaving Taos, 1981, The Essential Clare, 1993, 100 Great Poems by Women, 1995; translator Carrying Over, 1988; founder, editor: Poetry N.W., 1959-65; contbr. poems, articles to Am. and Brit. jours. Recipient award Am. Acad. and Inst. Arts and Letters, 1985, Pres.'s medal Ea. Wash. U., 1988, 5 Gov.'s awards State of Wash., 1965, 85, 95, 98, 2001, Silver medal Commonwealth Club, 1997, 2002, Aiken Taylor prize Sewanee Rev., 1998, Patterson prize, 2002, Western State Lifetime Achievement award, 2002, 1st prize Ind. Pub. Book award, 2002, L.A. Times Top Ten Books award, 2002, Acad. prize, 2003, Poets' prize, 2003. Mem. PEN, Amnesty Internat., Poetry Soc. Am. (Masefield prize 1983, Frost medal 1988). Episcopalian. Address: 19772 8th St E Sonoma CA 95476-3849

KIZER, NANCY ANNE, music educator, musician; b. Richmond, Calif., July 30, 1940; d. Benjamin Harrison and Doris Mabel (Myers) Pilgrim; children: Kevin John Keuning, Stephen Douglas Keuning. MusB, U. of the Pacific, Stockton, Calif., 1958—62. Spl. secondary tchg. credential in music (Life) K-14. Musician/violist Stockton Symphony Orch., Stockton, Calif., 1959—; music tchr./grades 7-9 Stockton Unified Sch. Dist., Stockton, Calif., 1962—64; music tchr./grades kindergarten-12 Lincoln Unified Sch. Dist., Stockton, Calif., 1983—95; coord./summer arts program Stockton Arts Commn., Stockton, Calif., 1987—2002; instr./string ensemble San Joaquin Delta Coll., Stockton, Calif., 1995—; music libr. Stockton Symphony Assn., Stockton, 1996—2002, pers. mgr., 1999—; instr./string ensemble San Joaquin Delta Coll., Stockton, Calif., 2002—; music tchr./HS Stockton Unified Sch. Dist., Stockton, Calif., 2002—. Recipient Music Honor Student, Santa Cruz HS, 1958. Mem.: Mortar Bd./Sr. Women's Honor Soc. (mem. 1962), Am. Fedn. Musicians, Nat. Educators Assn. (licentiate), Music Educators Nat. Conf. (licentiate), Mu Phi Epsilon/Nat. Music Fraternity (mem. 1959—). Home: 2424 North Center St Stockton CA 95204 Office: Stockton Symphony 46 West Freemont St Stockton CA 95202 Personal E-mail: vlanancy@inreach.com. E-mail: stocktonsymphony.org.

KIZZIAR, JANET WRIGHT, psychologist, writer, lecturer; b. Independence, Kans. d. John L. and Thelma (Rooks) Wright; m. Mark Kizziar. BA, U. Tulsa, 1961, MA, 1964, EdD, 1969. Sch. psychologist Tulsa Pub. Schs.; pvt. practice psychology Tulsa, 1969-78, Bartlesville, Okla., 1978-88. Lectr. univs., corps., health spas, 1989—. Co-host: Psychologists' Corner program, Sta. KOTV, Tulsa.; author: (with Judy W. Hagedorn) Gemini: The Psychology and Phenomena of Twins, 1975, Search for Acceptance: The Adolescent and Self Esteem, 1979. Sponsor Youth Crisis Intervention Telephone Center, 1972-74; bd. dirs. March of Dimes, Child Protection Team, Women and Children in Crisis, United Fund, YMCA Fund, Mental Health of Washington County, Alternative H.S.; edn. dir. appt. Gov.'s Commn. on Violence Against Women, Pub. Awarness Com., 1996, Women's Found. Fresh Start Women's Found., 1995. Named Disting. Alumni U. Tulsa, Outstanding Young Woman of Okla. Mem. APA, NOW, Internat. Twins Assn. (pres. 1976-77) Home: 9427 N 87th Way Scottsdale AZ 85258-1913 Office: PO Box 5227 Scottsdale AZ 85261-5227

KJELLBERG, ANN C. editor; b. Boston, Jan. 11, 1962; d. Raymond N. and Judith (Priestley) K.; 1 child, Sara Zerof. BA, Yale U., 1984. Asst. to exec. editor Farrar, Strauss & Giroux, N.Y.C., 1986-87, asst. editor, 1987; asst. to the editor N.Y. Rev. of Books, N.Y.C., 1988-93; Am. editor Artes, Stockholm, Sweden, 1993-95; asst. editor N.Y. Rev. of Books, N.Y.C., 1993—. Editor: Joseph Brodsky: Collected Poems in English, 2000. Mem. comms. com. Am. Friends Svc. Com., Phila., 1991-2000; lit. exec. Estate of Joseph Brodsky. Office: NY Rev of Books 1755 Broadway New York NY 10019-3743

KJOK, SOL, artist, art historian, linguist, translator; b. Lillehammer, Norway, Mar. 16, 1968; d. Erik and Ingunn (Haugsrud) K. BA in French Lit., U. Vienna, Austria, 1991; M in French Lit., U. Paris, 1992; MA in Romance Lang. and Lit., U. Cin., 1993, MA in Art History, 1996; MFA in Painting, Parsons Sch. Design, N.Y.C., 1998. Cert. govt. authorized translator and interpreter. Graphic designer Agence Karen, Paris, 1988; tchg. asst. art history U. Cin., 1995-96, dir. ind. studies of Norwegian lang./culture, 1993-96; resident Larroque Artists' Colony, Urt, France, 1997-98; tchg. asst. painting Parsons Sch. Design, N.Y.C., 1997-98. Lectr. in field. Contbr. articles to profl. jours.; translator: French/Norwegian, Paris, 1988; Spanish/Norwegian translator/interpretor Medellin, Bogota, Colombia, 1993; translator English, German novels, articles, short stories into Norwegian, various pub. houses, 1985—; one-woman shows include Brodie Gallery, Cin., 1996, Kreditkassen, Bagn, Norway, 1987, Tegnerforbundet Gallery, Oslo, 2001; exhibited in group shows at Gjensidigegården, Fagernes, Norway, 1985, Valdrestunet, Bagn, 1987, Art et Dessin, Paris, 1988, Mus. of U. Medellin, 1993, KZF Gallery, Cin., 1994, 840 Gallery, Cin., 1995, 96, Machina dell'Arte, Cin., 1996, Schoharie County Arts Coun., 1996, Gallery Alexy, Phila., 1996, Glenn Eure's Ghost Fleet Gallery, Nags Head, N.C., 1996, Amos Joseph Fine Art, Santa Fe, 1996, N.J. Ctr. Visual Arts, 1997, Pleiades Gallery, N.Y.C., 1997, Viridian Artists, Inc., 1997, Akademie der bildenden Künste Munich, 1997, A.I.R. Gallery, N.Y.C., 1997, Artists' Space, N.Y.C., 1997, Brenda Taylor Gallery, N.Y.C., 1998, Cmty. Cultural Ctr., Phila., 1998, Manefisken Galleri, Oslo, 1998, Valdres Kunstforening's Gallery, Norway, 1998, PS 122 Gallery, N.Y.C., 1998, Cameron/Weiland Gallery, N.Y.C., 1998, Galeri Steen, Oslo, Norway, 1999, Painted Bride Art Ctr., Phila., 2002, others; works in pvt. and pub. collections. Mem. Cin. Artists Group Effort, 1994—. Recipient Alpha Kappa Alpha Grad. Merit award; grantee Ga. Rotary Student Program, 1989, Lise & Arnfinn Heje's Legacy, Oslo, 1990, Thom Wilhelmsen's award, Oslo, 1991, Knut Hamsun's Legacy, Oslo, 1992, Olav and Lizzie Juvkam's legacy, 1990-94, Einar Storsveen's Legacy, 1992-94; Cin. Women's Club scholar, 1995, U. Cin. scholar, 1993-96, Parsons scholar, 1997-98; AAUW fellow, 1997-98; Joahn Jorgen Brochs Legat. grant, 1998, Rsch. grant Astrup-Fearnley, Oslo, 1996, Thesis Rsch. grant Astrup-Fearnley Found., Oslo, 1996, Artist grant Norwegian Ministry Culture, 1998; recipient Edwin Gould Found. award Nat. Arts Club, N.Y.C., 1998, Excellence in Drawing award Internat. Icarus Exhbn., 1998, Spl. Gallery prize Contemporary Realism III Exhibit, Phila., 1998, others. Mem. Internat. Assn. Univ. Women, Coll. Art Assn., Norwegian Soc. Young Artists, Norwegian Visual Artists, Drawing Assn. Norway. Avocation: long distance running. Home: 44 Eagle St Brooklyn NY 11222-1013 Personal E-mail: sol.kjok@rcn.com.

KJOS, VICTORIA, lawyer; b. Fargo, N.D., Sept. 17, 1953; d. Orville I. and Annie J. (Tanberg) K. BA, Minot State U., 1974; JD, U. N.D., 1977; MS, Ariz. State U., 2003. Bar: Ariz. 1978. Assoc. Jack E. Evans, Ltd., Phoenix, 1977-78, pension and ins. cons., 1978-79; dep. state treas. State of N.D., Bismarck, 1979-80; freelance cons. Phoenix, 1980-81, Anchorage, 1981-82; asst. v.p., v.p., mgr. trust dept. Great Western Bank, Phoenix, 1982-84; assoc. Robert A. Jensen P.C., Phoenix, 1984-86; ptnr. Jensen & Kjos, P.C., Phoenix, 1986-89; assoc. Allen, Kimerer & LaVelle, Phoenix, 1989-90, ptnr., 1990-91; dir. The Yoga and Fitness Inst., Phoenix, 1994-97; mem. faculty Maricopa County C.C., 1997—; pvt. practice Phoenix, 2003—04; assoc. Jensen Law Firm, Prescott, 2004—. Freelance cons., Phoenix, 1999—2003; lectr. in domestic rels. Contbr. articles to profl. jours. Bd. dirs. Arthritis Found., Phoenix, 1986-89, v.p. for chpt. devel., 1988-89; bd. dirs. Ariz. Yoga Assn., 1993-95, v.p., 1993-95. Mem. ABA, ATLA, Am. Coll. Sports Medicine, Am. Alliance Health, Phys. Edn., Recreation & Dance, Ariz. Bar Assn. (exec. coun. family law sect. 1988-91), Maricopa Bar Assn. (sec. family law com. 1988 89, pres. family law com. 1989-90, judge pro tem 1989-91), Ariz. Trial Lawyers Assn.

KLAGSBRUN, FRANCINE, writer, editor; b. N.Y.C. d. Benjamin and Anna Pike Lifton; m. Samuel Charles Klagsbrun, Jan. 23, 1955; 1 child, Sarah Devora. BA magna cum laude, Bklyn. Coll., 1952; B in Hebrew Lit., Jewish Theol. Sem., N.Y.C., 1952; MA, NYU, 1959; D of Hebrew Letters (hon.), Jewish Theol. Sem., 1999. Sr. editor World Book Ency., Chgo., 1957—62, mng. editor, 1962—63; exec. editor Ency. Americana, N.Y.C., 1963—65, Cowles Book Co., N.Y.C., 1965—68; editl. dir. Universal Edn. Co., N.Y.C., 1969—72. Author: (book) Sigmund Freud: A Biography, 1967, The First Book of Spices, 1968, Psychiatry: What It Is, What It Does, 1969, Freedom Now! The Story of the Abolitionists, 1972, Too Young to Die: Youth and Suicide, 1976, Voices of Widom: Jewish Ideals and Ethics for Everyday Living, 1980, Voices of Widom: Jewish Ideals and Ethics for Everyday Living, new edit., 2001, Married People: Staying Together in the Age of Divorce, 1985, Married People: Staying Together in the Age of Divorce, updated edit., 1992, Mixed Feelings: Love, Hate, Rivalry and Reconciliation Among Brothers and Sisters, 1992, Mixed Feelings: Love, Hate, Rivalry and Reconciliation Among Brothers and Sisters, paperback edit., 1993, Jewish Days: A Book of Jewish Life and Culture Around the Year, 1996, Jewish Days: A Book of Jewish Life and Culture Around the Year, paperback edit., 1998, The Fourth Commandment: Remember the Sabbath Day, 2002; editor: Assassination: Robert F. Kennedy, 1968, The First Ms. Reader, 1973, Free to Be...You and Me, 1974 (Graphic Arts award, 1974), Words of Women, 1975; contbr. articles to mags. and newspapers; columnist: Moment Mag., 1990—, Jewish Week, 1993—, bd. dirs.: Lilith Mag., mem. editl. bd.: Hadassah Mag. Mem. women's dialogue group Am. Jewish Com.; mem. task force Jewish woman United Jewish Appeal Fedn. Jewish Philanthropies; trustee Jewish Mus.; founding chair, bd. overseers Libr. Jewish Theol. Sem.; bd. dirs. Nat. Jewish Book Coun. Named Woman Who Made a Difference, Am. Jewish Congress, 2000; recipient Eternal Light medal, Jewish Theol. Sem., 1993, Outstanding Alumna award, 1996, Disting. Alumna award, Bklyn. Coll., 2000, Centennial award, Rabbinical Assembly Am., 2000, Stanley M. Isaacs Human Rels. award, Am. Jewish Com., 2000. Mem.: Phi Beta Kappa. Avocation: collecting early 20th century art. Office: Charlotte Sheedy Agy 65 Bleeker St New York NY 10012

KLAHRE, HEIDI LYNN, music educator; b. Clearville, Pa., Feb. 27, 1976; d. Kenneth Roy and Sandra Kay Klahre. BS in Edn., Millersville U., 1999; M in Sch. Libr. Sci. and Info. Tech., Mansfield U., 2003. Cert. tchr. Pa., 1999. Music educator Shade-Ctrl. City Sch. Dist., Cairnbrook, Pa., 2000—; music dir. First Christian Ch., Johnstown, Pa., 2003—. Mem.: NEA, Pa. State Libr. Assn., Pa. State Edn. Assn. Avocations: reading, working out, piano.

KLAMERUS, KAREN JEAN, pharmacist, researcher; b. Chgo., Aug. 10, 1957; d. Robert Edward and Jane Mary (Nawoj) Klamerus; m. Frederick P. Zeller. BS in Pharmacy, U. Ill., 1980; PharmD, U. Ky., 1981. Registered pharmacist Ky., Ill., Pa. Staff pharmacist Haggin Meml. Hosp., Harrodsburg, Ky., 1980-81, Regional Med. Ctr., Madisonville, Ky., 1982, critical care liasion, 1982; clin. pharmacist resident U. Nebr., Omaha, 1983; clin. pharmacist cardiothoracic surgery U. Ill., Chgo., 1983-88, clin asst. prof. dept. pharmacy practice, 1983-86, asst. prof., 1986-88, departmental affiliate dept. pharmaceutics, 1986-88; sr. pharmacokineticist Wyeth-Ayerst Rsch., Phila., 1988-91, asst. dir. clin. pharmacology, 1991-95, assoc. dir. clin. pharmacology, 1995-97; dir. med. rsch. Roche Global Devel., Palo Alto, Calif., 1997—2001; dir. clin. rsch. Vical, Inc., San Diego, 2002, Pfizer, 2002—. Fellow: Am. Coll. Clin. Pharmacology (indsl. rels. com. 1995); mem.: Mid-Atlantic Coll. Clin. Pharmacology (sec. 1991, pres. 1992—94), Am. Soc. Clin. Pharmacology and Therapeutics. Avocations: softball, scuba diving, gardening, sewing. Office: Pfizer-La Jolla 10777 Science Center Dr B95 San Diego CA 92121 E-mail: kjklamerus@yahoo.com.

KLANG, MARY MARGARET, secondary school educator; b. Butte, Mont., Mar. 22, 1949; d. James J. and Eileen T. O'Brien; m. Donald L. Klang; children: Evangeline, Alexia, Jesse. BA, San Francisco State U., 1974; Master Herbalist, Emerson Coll. Herbology Ltd., Mont., Que., Can., 1981. Cert. tchr. Mont., Calif. Tchr. Laguna Salada Sch. Dist., Pacifica, Calif., 1973—79; substitute tchr. Sch. Dist. 5, Kalispell, Mont., 1990—95; tchr., tutor Linderman Mid. Sch., Kalispell, 1995—2002; tchr. English and math. Linderman Sch., Kalispell, 2002—. Dir. summer sch. Linderman Sch., Kalispell, 1998—2002; pvt. tutor, Kalispell, 1995—2002. Author: (pamphlet) Steps to Success: A Tutoring Program, 1998, Seeing, 1985. Grantee travel grantee as mem. of Reading Delegation, China, Alpha Delta Kappa, 2001. Mem.: ASCD, Internat. Reading Assn., Phi Delta Kappa,

Alpha Delta Kappa (sec. 2002—02). Democrat. Avocations: literacy, gardening, travel. Office: Linderman Mid Sch 124 3rd Ave E Kalispell MT 59901 Personal E-mail: klang@digisys.net. Business E-Mail: klangm@sd5.k12.mt.us.

KLARK, DENISE J. special education educator, consultant; b. North Wilkesboro, N.C., May 9, 1967; d. Samuel Theron and Donna Lynn Jennings; m. John Fitzgerald Klark, Oct. 22, 1994; children: Jonathan Taylor and Brandon Tyler (twins). BA in Mental Handicaps, U. N.C., Charlotte, 1994; postgrad., Appalachian State U., 1997, 98, 99. Cert. tchf. B-K and K-12 spl. edn., N.C. Spl. edn. tchr. Wilkes County Schs., Wilkesboro, N.C., 1995-97; dir. Summer Program for Exceptional Children, North Wilkesboro, N.C., 1994—; preschool/spl. edn. tchr. Wilkes Devel. Day Sch., Wilkesboro, 1997—. Bd. dirs. Summer Program for Exceptional Children, 1994—. Office: Wilkes Devel Day Sch 1021 Welborn Ave Wilkesboro NC 28697-2223

KLASFIELD, ILENE, psychologist; b. N.Y.C., Aug. 23, 1943; d. Robert Louis and Laura Mersand; m. Jon Klasfeld, Dec. 24, 1962; children: Alan, Michael. BS, N.Y. State U., Old Westbury, 1978; MS, LaSalle U., Mandeville, La., 1998, PhD in Psychology, 2000. Acct., mgr. Almike Realty, Boca Raton, Fla.; therapist, psychologist, vol. JCC, Boca Raton, 1998—. Parent adv. com. Boca H.S., Boca Raton. Bd. dirs. Women's League for Peace, Queens, N.Y.; vol. Home for the Aged, Boca Raton; active Women for Alternative Medicine, 1993, Am. Cancer Soc., 1968-70, Mothers Against Drunk Driving, Boca Raton, 1990-98, United Cerebral Palsy Assn., Washington, 1990. Mem. Alzheimer's Assn. Democrat. Avocations: tai chi, writing, reading, hiking, gardening, tennis, yoga. Home: 701 NW 13th St Apt B1 Boca Raton FL 33486-2363

KLAVITER, HELEN LOTHROP, magazine editor; b. Lima, Ohio, Mar. 5, 1944; d. Eugene H. and Jean (Walters) Lothrop; m. Douglas B. Klaviter, June 7, 1969 (div. 1982); 1 child, Elizabeth. BA, Cornell Coll., Mt. Vernon, Iowa, 1966. Communication specialist Coop. Extension Service, Urbana, Ill., 1969-71; mng. editor Poetry Mag., Chgo., 1973—. Editorial cons. Harper & Row, N.Y.C., 1983-87. Bd. dirs. Ill. Theatre Ctr., 1989-95, St. Clement's Open Pantry, 1990—, Episc. Diocese of Chgo. Hunger Commn., 1992—, Comms. Commn., 1993—. Episcopalian. Office: Poetry Mag The Poetry Found 1030 N Clark St Ste 420 Chicago IL 60610 E-mail: hklaviter@poetrymagazine.org.

KLEE, ANN, lawyer; BA in Ancient History, Swarthmore Coll., 1983; JD, U. Pa., 1986. Assoc. Crowell & Moring, Washington, 1986—90; ptnr., chair environ. group Preston, Gates, Ellis & Rouvelas Meeds, Washington, 1990—95; chief counsel Senate Environment and Pub. Works Com., Washington, 1997—2001; counselor to sec. U.S. Dept. of Interior, Washington, 2001—. Office: US Dept Interior Office Sec 1849 C St NW Washington DC 20240

KLEE, CLAUDE BLENC, medical researcher; MD, U. Marsailles, France, 1959. Chief lab. chemistry, chief protein biochemistry sect. Nat. Cancer Inst., 1974—. Recipient Women's Excellence in Scis. award, Fedn. Am. Soc. for Exptl. Biology, 1997. Mem.: Inst. Medicine of NAS. Office: Nat Cancer Inst-Biochem Lab 9000 Rockville Pike Bethesda MD 20892-0001

KLEEFISCH, REBECCA, reporter; b. Waterville, Ohio; m. Joel Kleefisch. B Journalism, U. Wis. Anchor WIFR-TV, Rockford, Ill.; reporter, anchor WISN 12, Milw., 1999—. Office: WISN PO Box 0402 Milwaukee WI 53201-0402

KLEIKAMP, BEVERLY, poet, writer, publisher; b. Iron Mountain, Mich., Apr. 15, 1953; d. Hector Joseph and Lorraine Agnes (Frisque) Dugree; m. Vernon Lee Kleikamp, Feb. 5, 1972; children: Henry J., Richard V., Carl A. Freelance writer U.P. Horse News, Florence, Wisc., 1984-91; pub. North Star Pub., 1998—. Editor: (mag.) Northern Stars, 1997—; author: (book) Fifth Season, 1997, Of Higher Powers, 1998; pub.: (book) Best of 98 Anthology, 1999, Old Century/New Millennium Anthology, 2000, Shining Stars Anthology, 2001, Stars of Wonder Anthology, 2002, Stars I, 2003, Stars II, 2003 (book) Stories for Children, 2002. Tracy and The Shadow Horse (book), 2003. Recipient 8th Honorable Mention, Poets' RoundTable 59th Internat. Poetry Contest, 1999, 6th Hon. Mention 63d ann. contest, 2003. Mem. Upper Peninsula Publs./Authors Assn., Upper Peninsula Writers Assn. Avocations: camping, fishing, hunting, photograpy. Home: N17285 County Road 400 Powers MI 49874-9758

KLEIM, E. DENISE, city official; BA in Econs. cum laude, San Jose State U., 1975; MBA, Willamette U., 1982. Mgmt. asst. Urban Renewal Agy. City of Salem, Oreg., 1976-78, grant adminstr. dept. cmty. devel., 1978-80, asst. to dir. dept. cmty. devel., 1981-84, lobbyist, 1980-83; sr. mgmt. analyst Bur. Bldgs., City of Portland, Oreg., 1984-86, adminstrv. mgr., 1986-99, mgr. adminstrv. svcs. bur. devel. svcs., 1999—. V.p. Montclair After Sch. Care Assn., Portland, 1995-96; mem. Atkinson Soc., Salem, 1995-97. Office: City of Portland Bur Devel Svc 1120 SW 5th Ave Portland OR 97204-1912

KLEIMAN, DEVRA GAIL, zoologist, zoological park research scientist; b. N.Y.C., Nov. 15, 1942; BS in Biopsychology, U. Chgo., 1964; PhD in Zoology, U. London, 1969. Rsch. asst. Wellcome Inst. Comparative Physiology, Zool. Soc. London, 1965-69; NIMH postdoctoral fellow Inst. Animal Behavior, Rutgers U., N.J., 1970-71; rsch. assoc. Smithsonian Instn., 1970-72; reproduction zoologist Nat. Zool. Pk., Smithsonian Instn., Washington, 1972-79, acting head dept. zool. rsch., 1979-81, head dept. zool. rsch., 1981-96, acting asst. dir. animal programs, 1983-84, asst. dir. rsch. ednl. activities, 1984-85, asst. dir. rsch., 1985-96, sr. rsch. scientist, 1997-2001; dir. conservation planning Conservation Internat., Washington, 2001—. Adj. asst. prof. dept. Psychology George Washington U., 1974-77; adj. asst. prof. dept. Zoology U. Md., 1979-84, adj. prof., 1984—; studbook keeper International Studbook for Leontopithecus rosalia, 1974-84; grant reviewer NIMH, 1977, 81, NSF, 1978, 79; adj. prof. Biology George Mason U., Fairfax, Va., 1980-82; U.S. del. com. Internat. Ethological Conf., 1980-86; mem. bd. fellowships and grants Smithsonian Instn., 1982-84, chair rsch. policy com., 1984-86; mem. species survival plan mgmt. com. L. r. chrysomelas, 1985—, L. r. chrysopygus, 1986—; scientific adv. com. Jersey Wildlife Preservation Trust, 1986—; co-studbook keeper Giant Panda Ailuropoda melanoleuca, 1988-96; chair species survival plan giant panda, 1993-96; ad hoc reviewer behavioral and neurosci. studies sect. NIH, 1988; adv. bd. program on zoos Sta. WQED, 1990; presenter numerous confs. Mem. editorial bd. International Zoo Yearbook, 1977—, Carnivore, 1977-81, Zoo Biology, 1982-99; consulting editor Am. Jour. Primatology, 1983-91; chief editor Wild Mammals in Captivity, 1983-96; field editor Jour. Soc. conservation Biology, 1986—; contbr. articles to profl. jours. Bd. dirs. Scientists Ctr. Animal Welfare, 1984-86; trustee Dian Fossey Gorilla Fund, 1990-95. Recipient Women in Sci. and Engring. award NSF, 1987, award for Disting. Achievement Soc. Conservation Biology, 1988, Outstanding Svc. award Am. Zoo and Aquarium Assn., 1993. Fellow AAAS, Animal Behavior Soc. (sec. 1977-80, pres. 1983—); mem. Am. Assn. Zool. Pks. and Aquariums (species coord., internal mgmt. com. L. r. rosalia, species survival plan subcom. 1986-90, vice chair Giant Panda task force 1988-92, chair 1992-93, mem New World Primate TAG, Cheetah SSP, Brazil FIG, Reintro. adv. group, rsch. coord. group 1991—, chair behavior and husbandry adv. group 1992-93), World Conservation Union (mem. SSC primate specialist group 1983—, SSC reintro./specialist group 1988—, vice-chair primates 1989—), Consortium Aquariums, Univs. and Zoos (adv. com. 1986—), Internat. Soc. Endangered Cats (rsch. adv. bd. 1988-91), Sigma Xi. Office: Conservation Internat 1919 M St NW Washington DC 20036 E-mail: D.Kleiman@conservation.org.

KLEIMAN, EVAN, [illegible] kitchen mgr. Mangia; exec. chef Verdi Ristorante di Musica, Santa Monica, Calif.; owner, chef Angeli Caffe, L.A. Host "Good Food" KCRW, Santa Monica, Calif. Author (cookbooks): Cucina Fresca, 1983; author: Cucina Rustica, 1990, Angeli: Piza, Pasta and Panini, 1997. Office: 7274 Melrose Ave Los Angeles CA 90046

KLEIMAN, MARY MARGARET, lawyer; b. Norfolk, Va., May 26, 1959; d. William Edward and Patricia Mae Holste; m. David James Kleiman, June 29, 1991; children: Amanda Grace, Amy Elizabeth. BA in History summa cum laude, Marian Coll., Indpls., 1981; JD cum laude, Ind. U., Indpls., 1984. Bar: Ind. 1985, U.S. Dist. Ct. (no. and so. dists.) Ind. 1985. Bailiff, law clk. Marion County Mcpl. Ct., Indpls., 1983-84; counsel Am. Fletcher Nat. Bank (now Bank One, Ind. N.A.), Indpls., 1985-88; assoc. Krieg DeVault Alexander & Capehart, Indpls., 1989-95; ptnr. Krieg Devault Alexander & Capehart, Indpls., 1995-2000; v.p. and assoc. gen. counsel Federal Home Loan Bank of Indianapolis, 2000—. Bd. dirs. Ind. Bus. Devel. Corp., 1994-97; spkr. at banking confs. Contbr. articles to profl. jours. Pro bono atty. Cmty. Orgns. Legal Assistance Project, Indpls., 1994—; vol. com. chair, mem. client programs com. Ind. chpt. Nat. Multiple Sclerosis Soc., 1997-2001, trustee Ind. chpt., 1999-2001; mem. mission com. Castleton United Meth. Ch., Indpls., 1993-2000, acolyte coord., mem. worship com., 1998-99, mem. chancel choir, 1999—, chair staff-parish rels. com., 2000-02; bd. dirs. Circle Area Comm. Devel. Corp., 2000—, Downtown Area Comm. Devel. Corp., 2000—, Mass. Ave. Comm. Devel. Corp., 2000—, Naval Air Warfare Center Reuse Planning Authority. Recipient Leadership award Nat. Multiple Sclerosis Soc., 1998, Nat. Vol. of Yr. award Nat. Multiple Sclerosis Soc., 1999, Outstanding Vol. award Ind. Ronald McDonald House, 1990; named to Outstanding Young Women in Am., 1981, 87. Mem. ABA, Ind. State Bar Assn., Indpls. Bar Assn. (chair printed forms com. 1987), Phi Delta Phi. Democrat. Avocations: gardening, cross-stitch, reading science fiction, calligraphy. Office: Federal Home Loan Bank of Indianapolis PO Box 60 Indianapolis IN 46206 E-mail: mkleiman@fhlbi.com.

KLEIN, ANNE SCEIA, public relations executive; b. Phila., Apr. 25, 1942; d. Charles B. and Kathryn L. (Lucas) Sceia; m. Gerhart L. Klein, June 19, 1976. BS in Econs., U. Pa., 1964, MA in Communications, 1965. Promotion asst. S.E. Pa. Transit Authority, Phila., 1965; pub. rels. dir. Pa. Lung Assn., Phila., 1965-68; info. dir. H2L2 Architects, Phila., 1968; pub. rels. officer Girard Bank, Phila., 1969-76; acct. exec. Aitkin-Kynett Co., Inc., Phila., 1977; mgr. media rels. Sun Co., Radnor, Pa., 1978-80, mgr. exec. comm., 1980-82; pres. Anne Klein & Assocs., Inc., Mt. Laurel, NJ, 1982—. Mem. Ethics Com., Mt. Laurel, 1988-92; mem. Citizens Adv. Com., Mt. Laurel, 1988-92; chair, Lake Preservation initiative, Old Taunton Colony Club, Medford, N.J., 1995—. Recipient Super Communicator of 80's award Women in Comm., 1987, Tribute to Women in Industry award YMCA, 1990, Hale's Legacy award Women in Comm., 1996, Sarah award Women in Comm., 1998; named Small Bus. Person of Yr. So. N.J. C. of C., 1991, DeAnn White award, 2003; named to Phila. Pub. Rels. Assn. Hall of Fame, 2004. Fellow: Pub. Rels. Soc. Am. (accredited, pres. Phila. chpt. 1979, mid-Atlantic chmn. 1984, assembly del. 1980—82, 1988—94, exec. com. Counselors Acad. 1990—91, Coll. of Fellows 1991, Maxine Elkin award Phila. chpt. 2001, Pepperpot awards, PR Profl. of Yr. N.J. chpt. 2002); mem.: Forum Exec. Women (sec. bd. dirs. 1981—83), Pub. Rels. Profls. So. N.J. (chmn. 1987—, pres. 1985—87), Kappa Delta. Avocations: skiing, boating. Office: Anne Klein & Assocs 10 Lake Ctr Ste 108 Marlton NJ 08053-3424

KLEIN, BARBARA A. information technology executive; BS, Marquette U.; MBA, Loyola U., Chgo., 1977. CPA. Former exec. Pillsbury, Sears, Roebuck and Co.; former v.p., corp. contr. Ameritech Corp.; former v.p. fin., CFO Dean Foods Co.; sr. v.p., CFO CDW Computer Ctrs., Vernon Hills, Ill., 2002—. Mem.: AICPA. Office: CDW 200 N Milwaukee Ave Vernon Hills IL 60061

KLEIN, CATHY M. funeral director; b. BayShore, N.Y., Jan. 9, 1953; d. Harry and Marie Routledge; m. James Klein, May 20, 1979; children: Shannon, Chelsea. LPN, Hermann Hosp., 1980; AAS, Briarwood Coll., 1998. Funeral dir. Ch. & Allen Funeral Home, Norwich, Conn., 1998—2000, D'Esopo Funeral Home, Wethersfield, Conn., 2003—. Mem.: NFDA, CFDA, Columbia BOE. Home: 6 River Valley Rd Columbia CT 06237

KLEIN, CHARLOTTE CONRAD, public relations executive; b. Detroit, June 20, 1923; d. Joseph and Bessie (Brown) K. BA, UCLA, 1945. Corr. UPI, Los Angeles, 1945-46; staff writer CBS, Los Angeles, 1946-47; publicist David O. Selznick Studios, Culver City, Calif., 1947-49, Foladare and Assocs., Los Angeles, 1949-51; publicist to v.p. Edward Gottlieb & Assocs., N.Y.C., 1951-62; v.p. to sr. v.p. Harshe Rotman & Druck, N.Y.C., 1962-78; dir. press/govt. affairs Sta. WNET-TV, N.Y.C., 1978-79; pres. Charlotte C. Klein Assocs., N.Y.C., 1979-84; sr. v.p., group supr. Porter Novelli, N.Y.C., 1984-89; prin. Charlotte Klein Assocs., N.Y.C., 1989—. Adj. prof. pub. rels. NYU; bd. dirs. U.S. Trademark Assn., 1959-62, Am. Arbitration Assn., 1970-80 (exec. com. 1980-82); mem. adv. bd. Coll. and Cmty. Fellowship Grad. Ctr., CUNY, 2002—; cons. Ctr. for Advancement of Women, 2003—. Contbr. articles to profl. jours. Bd. dirs. Manhattan chpt. Am. Cancer Soc., 1988-92. Recipient Cine Golden Eagle, 1977, Matrix award Women in Communications, 1975. Mem. Pub. Rels. Soc. Am. (accredited; pres. N.Y. chpt. 1985-86, Silver Anvil award 1978, John Hill award 1988), Women's Forum (bd. dirs. N.Y. chpt. 1986-87, 96-98), Internat. Women's Forum (leadership com. chair dialogue for democracy 1993-98, co-chair task force on violence against women globally, 1998-2001), Women Execs. in Pub. Rels. (pres. 1965). Avocations: painting, stamp collecting, tennis, kite flying. E-mail: kleintravis@earthlink.net.

KLEIN, CHARLOTTE FEUERSTEIN, art consultant; b. Stoneham, Mass., June 3, 1931; d. Harold and Esther B. (Franks) Feuerstein; m. Philipp Hillel Klein, June 21, 1953; children— Joshua David, Daniel William, Jonathan Henry. B.S., Boston U., 1953. Tchr. pub. schs., Scotia, Schenectady, Niscayuna, N.Y., 1953-56, Newton, Mass., 1974, 75; prtnr., art cons. Washington Graphics, Washington, 1979-82; dir., art adviser CFK Assocs., Washington, 1982— . Mem. AFI Silver Theatre and Cultural Ctr., Washington Opera Soc., The Phillips Collection, Friends of Kennedy Ctr., Washington, Nat. Symphony Orch. Assn., Holocaust Mus., Textile Mus., Washington, Corcoran Gallery Art, Smithsonian Assn. Mem. Nat. Bldg. Mus.

KLEIN, ELAINE, advertising executive; b. Bklyn., Mar. 12, 1929; d. Sidney and Bertha (Smith) Laks; m. Melvin Klein, Dec. 23, 1951; children: Cyd Robin Klein Tomack, Amy Susan. Exec. sec. to pres. Muzak Corp., N.Y.C., 1949-55; expeditor The Van Ard Co., Forest Mills, N.Y., 1968-70; advt. sales mgr., West Coast advt. dir. Playbill mag., N.Y.C., 1970-95, L.A., 1995—. Mem. Nat. Assn. Exec. Women, The New Dramatists, Friars Club, Mus. of Natural History, Advt. Club of L.A. Democrat. Jewish. Office: Playbill Mag 6531 W 6th St Los Angeles CA 90048-4715

KLEIN, ELAINE CHARLOTTE, school system administrator; b. Herreid, S.D., June 14, 1939; d. Herman F. and Minnie (Weigum) Klein; 1 child, Erika Katherine. BA, U. Puget Sound, 1961; MA, U. Wash., 1964; cert. in adminstrn., Seattle U., 1976; postgrad., Western Wash. U., 1986. Cert. secondary sch. adminstr. Wash., K-12 tchr. Wash. Tchr. Edmonds Sch. Dist., Lynnwood, Wash., 1961-77; asst. prin. Meadowdale Jr. HS, Lynnwood, Wash., 1977-80, Mountlake Terrace (Wash.) HS, 1981-93, prin., 1993-97; exec. dir. cmty. svcs. Frederick (Md.) County Pub. Schs., 1997— Adj. faculty Heritage Inst., Antioch U., Seattle Pacific U., Western Wash U., [illegible] Mt. St. Mary's Coll., Emmitsburg, Md.; cons. Am. Coll. Testing Passport Portfolio, Iowa City, 1995—97; presenter in field. Co-author: (book) ACT Manual for Administrators, 1997; grant writer:. Pres. Pacific N.W. region Internat. Tng. Comm., Alaska, 1993—94. Named Wash. State Prin. of the Yr., 1997, Adminstr. of the Yr., Md. Assn. Edn. Office Pers., 1999, Friend of Edn., M. St. Mary's Coll., 1999, Outstanding Contbr., Hood Coll., 2002; recipient award for Excellence in Edn., Wash. State Legislature, 1997. Mem.: ASCD, Nat. Assn. Secondary Sch. Prins. and Affiliates, Am. Assn. Sch. Adminstrs., Rotary (Mountlake Terrace pres. 1996—97). Methodist. Avocations: public speaking, reading, travel, advocating for public schools. Office: Frederick County Pub Schs 115 E Church St Frederick MD 21701-5403 E-mail: elaine.klein@fcps.org.

KLEIN, EMILEE, professional golfer; b. Santa Monica, Calif., June 11, 1974; Student, Ariz. State U. With LPGA, 1994—; mem. U.S. Solheim Cup Team, 2002. Named two-time All-American, 1993, 94, Collegiate Player of the Year, 1994. Achievements include Winner PING/Welch's Championship, 1995, Weetabix Women's British Open, 1995; recorded four top-20 finishes in 1995; third place Rolex Rookie of the Year standings, 1995. Office: LPGA 100 International Golf Dr Daytona Beach FL 32124-1092 also: Callaway Golf 2285 Rutherford Rd Carlsbad CA 92008-8815

KLEIN, FREDA, retired state agency administrator; b. Seattle, May 17, 1920; d. Joseph and Julia (Caplan) Vinikow; m. Jerry Jerome Klein, Oct. 20, 1946; children: Jan Susan Klein Waples, Kerry Joseph, Robin Jo Klein. BA, U. Wash., 1942; MS, U. Nev., Las Vega, 1969, EdD, 1978. Owner, mgr. Smart Shop, Provo, Utah, 1958-60, Small Fry Shop, Las Vegas, 1961-66; vocat. counselor, test adminstr. Nev. Employment Security Dept., Las Vegas, 1966-77, local office mgr., 1978-95; ret., 1995. Contbr. articles to profl. jours.; screenwriter, 1995-98. Exec. bd. Pvt. Industry Coun., Las Vegas, 1988—, Interstate Conf. on Employment Security Agys., Nev., 1988—90, Area Coordinating Com. for Econ. Devel., Las Vegas, 1988—; vol. Ctr. for Bus. and Econ. Rsch., U. Nev., Las Vegas, 1995—. Recipient Achievement award Nev. Bus. Svc., 1990, Cert. of Spl. Congl. Recognition, 1992; named Outstanding Woman, Goodwill Industries sci. and rsch. divsn., 1977. Mem. AAUW, Internat. Assn. Pers. in Employment Security, U. Nev. Las Vegas Alumni Assn., Henderson C. of C. (exec. bd. 1986—), Soroptimist Internat. (pres. 1987-88), Phi Kappa Phi (scholastic hon.). Avocations: hiking, swimming, writing. Home: 2830 Phoenix St Las Vegas NV 89121-1312 E-mail: drfredai@aol.com.

KLEIN, GAIL BETH MARANTZ, freelance/self-employed writer, animal breeder; b. Bklyn., Dec. 1, 1946; d. Herbert and Florence (Dresner) Marantz; m. Harvey Leon Klein, Mar. 17, 1979. AB cum laude, U. Miami, Coral Gables, Fla., 1968, MEd, 1969, MBA, 1977. Cert. residential contractor, Fla.; notary pub. Asst. dir. student activities Miami-Dade Community Coll., 1969-79, instr. photography for mentally retarded adults, 1974, acting dir. student activities, 1976, acting advisor student publs., 1979; dog breeder Vizcaya Shepherds, Palm Beach Gardens, Fla., East Hampton, Conn., 1979—; trainer Dog Obedience and Conformation Show Handling, West Palm Beach, 1980—; owner, CEO Word Master Profl. Comm. Freelance writer WordMaster Profl. Comms.; mgr. proposal devel., specialist Profl. Food-Svc. Mgmt., Inc., 1994—97; spl. projects-ops. Chartwells, 1997—98; proposal and resource libr. mgmt., proposal writer Wackenhut Corp., Inc., 1998—2000; cons. Universal Staffing Svcs., 2001; sr. tech. cons. Belcan Corp., 2001—02; tech. publs. analyst-mil. engines Pratt & Whitney, 2002—; spkr. in field; appeared on various radio talk shows. Editor (booklet) 1978 Consumers Guide to Banking, 1978, (newsletter) Newsletter of German Shepherd Dog Club Ft. Lauderdale, Inc., 1980-83, Sunshine State Shepherd, 1988-89; contbr. articles to newspapers and mags. Chair spl. events com. Third Century U.S.A., Dade County, Fla., 1976; mem. adv. com., mktg. cons. YWCA of Greater Miami, 1976-79; mem. comty. rels. com. Greater Miami Jewish Fedn., 1976-79; mem. Met. Miami Art Ctr., 1977-79; vice chair, chair appeals bd. Palm Beach County Animal Care and Control, 1989-97, mem. pet overpopulation com., 1991-93; co-developer, co-adminstr. OFA Verifications for German Shepherd Dogs, 1985—; pub. info. coord. Am. Kennel Club, Palm Beach County, 1991-94. Recipient Job Training Partnership Act Employee of Yr. award State of Fla., 1994. Mem.: Am. Sewing Guild, Palm Beach Users Group, Conformation Judges Assn. Fla., Inc., Nat. Assn. Dog Obedience Instrs., Assn. Proposal Mgmt. Profls., Fla. Freelance Writers Assn., Hadassah (life), Wolf Song of Alaska (grant/proposal writer), Treasure Coast German Shepherd Dog Club (charter), Jupiter-Tequesta Dog Club, Inc. (pres. 1984—85, bd. dirs., various other offices, Gaines Sportsmanship award 1993), German Shepherd Dog Club of Can., Inc., German Shepherd Dog Club of Greater Miami (life; rec. sec. 1977—78, corr. sec. 1978—80, bd. dirs. 1981—82, 1989—94), German Shepherd Dog Club Am., Inc. (hip dysplasia/orthopedic com. 1987—89), German Shepherd Dog Club Eastern Conn., Obedience Tng. Club Palm Beach County, Inc. (AKC Cmty. Achievement Merit award 1994), Mortar Board, Phi Kappa Phi, Epsilon Tau Lambda, Alpha Lambda Delta. Republican. Jewish. Avocations: reading, computers, crafts, photography, sewing. Home: 12 Comstock Trl East Hampton CT 06424-2304

KLEIN, IRMA MOLLIGAN, career development educator, consultant; b. New Orleans, Jan. 5, 1929; d. Harry Joseph and Gesina Francis (Bauer) Molligan; m. John Vincent Chelena (dec. 1978); 1 child, Joseph William; m. Chris George Klein, Aug. 14, 1965; 1 step-son, Arnold Conrad Klein. BS in Bus., Augustine Coll.; postgrad., Mktg. Inst., Chgo., Loyola U., Realtors Inst., Baton Rouge. Mgr. Stan Weber & Assocs., Metairie, La., 1971-75, tng. dir., 1975-81; cons. Coldwell Banker Comml. Co., New Orleans, 1981; dir. career devel. Coldwell Banker Residential Co., New Orleans, 1982-85; pres. Irma Klein Career Devel., Inc., 1994-95, Klein Enterprises, Inc., 1994—. Instr. U. New Orleans, Realtors Inst., La. Real Estate Commn. Author: Career Development, 1982; Training Manual, 1978, Obtaining Listings, 1986, Participative Marketing, 1986, Marketing & Servicing Listings, 1987, Designing Training Curriculum, 1987, Participative Management. Mem. La. Hist. Assn. Meml. Hall Found. Mem. La. Realtors Assn. (bd. dirs. 1973-74, grad. Realtors Inst. 1976), Jefferson Bd. Realtors (v.p. 1984), Edn. and Resources (cert., pres. La. chpt.), Rsch. Club of New Orleans (pres. 1984-85), Realtors Nat. Mktg. Inst. (amb. Tex. and La. 1985—, Outstanding Achievement award 1985, cert. broker 1980, residential specialist 1977), Nat. Assn. Realtors (nat. conv. spkr. 1986), CRB (pres. La. chpt. 1982-83, chmn. edn.), CRS (pres. La. chpt. 1988-90), Am. Dental Assts. Assn., La. Dental Assts. Assn. (pres. 1964), Les Quarante Ecolieres (pres. 1994-96), Antique Study Group (pres. 2001-2003), Confederate Lit. (New Orleans, pres. 2001—), Rsch. Club (New Orleans), Metairie Woman's Club (sec. 1997-99, pres.-elect 1999, pres. 2000-01), Odyssey Ho. La. Republican. Roman Catholic. Avocation: antiques. E-mail: cgkimk@bellsouth.net.

KLEIN, JULIA MEREDITH, freelance journalist; b. Phila., Dec. 11, 1955; d. Abraham and Murielle (Pollack) K. BA magna cum laude, Harvard U., 1977. Copy editor J.B. Lippincott, Phila., 1977; features reporter The Oakland Press, Pontiac, Mich., 1978; freelance writer, researcher, editorial cons., 1978—; reporter, critic and editor The Phila. Inquirer, 1983-2000. Nat. Arts Journalism Program fellow, 1996-97, John J. McCloy fellow in journalism, 1998, Alicia Patterson Found. fellow, 2000, Western Knight Ctr. fellow for Specialized Journalism, 2001; Fulbright German Studies Seminar grantee, 2004. Mem. Soc. Profl. Journalists (2d Pl. award for criticism 1998, 3d Pl. award for criticism 1999), Am. Soc. Journalists and Authors, N.Am.

Travel Journalists Assn., Journalism and Women Symposium, Phi Beta Kappa. Home and Office: 307 Monroe St Philadelphia PA 19147-3211 Office Phone: 215-773-0761. E-mail: julklein@juno.com.

KLEIN, KAREN K. federal judge; Magistrate judge U.S. Dist. Ct. N.D., Fargo. Office: 655 1st Ave N Ste 440 Fargo ND 58102-4952 Fax: 701-297-7075.

KLEIN, LAURA, publishing executive; With Levine, Huntley, Schmidt & Beaver Advt., N.Y.C., 1985—86; nat. sales mgr. Andrew's Mag., 1986—89; acct. mgr. ELLE Mag., 1989—92; Ea. sales mgr. Woman's Day, N.Y.C., 1992—96, v.p., ad dir., 1996—2000, v.p., pub., 2002—; pub. Family Life, 2000. Office: Womans Day 1633 Broadway 42d Fl New York NY 10019

KLEIN, LISA CAROL, materials scientist, educator; b. Wilmington, Del., Dec. 7, 1951; d. Charles and Naomi (Rudman) K.; m. Timothy Francis Kinsella, May 24, 1984; 1 child, Martha Ann. BS, MIT, 1973, PhD, 1977. Asst. prof. Rutgers U., Piscataway, N.J., 1977-81, assoc. prof., 1981-87, prof., 1987—. Vis. faculty Sandia Nat. Labs., Albuquerque, 1983 summer, vis. assoc. prof. ENSEEG, Grenoble, France, 1984 summer, vis. scientist Hebrew U., Jerusalem, 1995 summer. Editor: Sol-Gel Technology, 1988, Sol-Gel Optics, 1994, Jour. Am. Ceramic Soc., 1998. Recipient N.J. Women of Achievement award N.J. Fedn. of Women's Club, 1992, Nat. Achievement award, Soc. Women Engrs., 1998. Fellow Am. Ceramic Soc. (Schwartzwarden-PACE award 1987). Achievements include patent for sol-gel electrochromic device; first woman hired and tenured by the Coll. Engrng. at Rutgers. Office: Rutgers U 607 Taylor Rd Piscataway NJ 08854-8065 E-mail: licklein@rci.rutgers.edu.

KLEIN, LUELLA VOOGD, obstetrics-gynecology educator; b. Walker, Iowa, Oct. 24, 1924; d. Elmer De Witt and Leah (Stunkard) Bare; m. Alfred O. Colquitt. BA, U. Iowa, 1947, MD, 1949. Diplomate Am. Bd. Ob-Gyn. Intern Western Res. U., Cleve., 1949—50; resident in medicine, surgery and ob-gyn Cleve. City Hosp., 1950—55; U.S. Sr. Fulbright Rsch. scholar U. London Postgrad. Med. Sch., 1955—57; obstetric cons. Ga. Dept. Pub. Health, Atlanta, 1958—60; pvt. practice Atlanta, 1960—65; asst. dir. clin. rsch. Bristol Labs., Syracuse, NY, 1965—67; prof., dir. maternal and infant care project Emory U. Grady Meml. Hosp., Atlanta, 1967—; co-dir. Regional Perinatal Ctr., Charles Howard Candler prof., chmn. dept. ob-gyn Emory U. Sch. Medicine, Atlanta, 1986—93. Gen. bd. dirs., bd. dirs. divsn. maternal-fetal medicine Am. Bd. Ob-Gyn.; bd. dirs. Alan Guttmacher Inst., N.Y.C., chmn., vice chmn.; Maternal and Child Health Care governing coun. Am. Hosp. Assn., Chgo.; chmn. FDA Ob-Gyn Device Com., Washington, 1986—88. Recipient Elizabeth Blackwell award, Am. Women's Med. Assn., 1986, Atlanta Woman History Maker award, Am. Women's Assn., 1987, Daggett Harvey award, Chgo. Maternity Ctr., Northwestern U., 1991, 40th Anniversary award, FIGO, 1994. Fellow: ACOG (pres., v.p., asst. sec. 1982—85, Disting. Svc. award 1994); mem.: AMA, Inst. Medicine, Med. Assn. Ga. (chair maternal and child health care com.), Atlanta Obstet. and Gynecol. Soc. (pres.), Ga. Obstet. and Gynecol. Soc. (pres.), Marietta (Ga.) Country Club. Office: Grady Meml Hosp Dept Gyn/Ob 69 Butler St SE Atlanta GA 30303-3033

KLEIN, LYNN ELLEN, artist; b. San Francisco, Apr. 14, 1950; BA in Studio Arts, U. Minn., 1974, MFA in Design, 1976. Instr. art edn. U. Minn., Mpls., 1976-78, lectr. in design, 1974-84; vis. artist U. Iowa, Ames, 1984—, Textile Ctr. of Minn., 2003. Resident Cité Internat. des Arts, Paris, summer 1998, vis. artist Textile Arts Ctr. of Minn., 2003. One woman shows include Rochester (Minn.) Fine Arts Ctr., 1976, Northrup Gallery, U. Minn., Mpls., 1976, Allrich Gallery, San Francisco, 1982, 88, Coffman Gallery, U. Minn., 1982, The Print Club, Phila., 1985, Foster-White Gallery, Seattle, 1989, Carolyn Ruff Gallery, Mpls., 1994, Robert Green Fine Arts, 2000; exhibited in group shows at Mpls. Inst. Arts, 1976, 88, Franklin Inst. Sci. Mus., Phila., 1984, Minn. Mus. Art, St. Paul, 1990, Textile Arts Internat., 1990, Vermillion edit., 1983, 92, San Francisco Bay Area Women Artists Mentors, San Francisco, 1994, USART San Francisco Internat. Art Expo, I. Wolk Gallery, St. Helena, Calif., 1996, Robert Green Fine Arts, Mill Valley, Calif., 1996, 2002, Craftsman's Guild and Calif. Heritage Gallery, 1998, Ren Brown Collection, Bodega Bay, Calif., 1998, Gensler Architecture-Material Matters, San Francisco, 1998, San Jose Mus. Art, Visible Rhythm, 2001, 2003, Achenbach Collection Fine Arts Mus., San Francisco, 2001, Wild Women Print Portfolios, 2001, Kala Art Inst., 2002, Pyramid Atlantic Book Arts Fair, Wash., 2002, N.Y. Print Fair, 2004, Brave New World, 2004; represented in permanent collections Mpls. Inst. Arts, Oakland (Calif.) Mus., Bibliotéque Nat., Dept. des Estampes et de lá Photographie, Paris, Phila. Mus. Art, Walker Art Ctr., Mpls., Achenbach Found., Fine Arts Mus. San Francisco, San Jose Mus. Art., Calif. Recipient J.D. Phelan award World Print Coun., 1983; Minn. State Arts Bd. Grantee, 1978; Photography fellow, St. Paul, 1984; Rockefeller Found. fellow, Am. Ctr., 1984-86, Jerome Found. Printmaking fellow, Kala Inst., Berkeley, 1989; Amity Art Found. grant, Woodbridge, Conn., 2003. Mem. Achenbach Graphic Arts Coun.

KLEIN, MARY ANN, special education educator; b. Ridgewood, N.J., Jan. 31, 1956; d. Julius R. and Nancy M. Pascuzzo; m. Thomas F. Klein, July 16, 1983. B in Elem. Edn. & Spl. Edn., Adelphi U., Garden City, N.Y., 1978; M in Spl. Edn. & Reading, Adelphi Univ., Garden City, N.Y., 1980. Cert. in spl. edn. Learning disabilities specialist Merrick UFSD, Merrick, NY, 1978—. Swimming instr. disabled children and adults Village of Garden City, 1974—79; pvt. piano instr., NY, 1978—82; clinician & diagnostician Adelphi U. Reading Clinic, Garden City, 1980—84; ednl. cons. BOCES of Nassau County, Merrick, NY, 1993—94, SETRC of Nassau County, Westbury, NY, 1995—96; founder peer tutoring program Birch Sch., Merrick, NY; spl. edn. rep. Birch Child Study Team, Merrick, NY. Co-author: (curriculum guide) Foundations for Learning, 1991; author: (resource guide) Strategies to Assist Learning Disabled Children in the Classroom Setting, 1995. Mem. Merrick PTA, 1978—, tchr. liaison, 1994—97; mem. Merrick SEPTA, 1983—, Com. on Spl. Edn., 1983—, Nassau Reading Coun., 1996—; co-founder Students Against Destructive Decision-Making, Birch Sch., Merrick, NY; apptd. Crisis Mgmt. Team, Birch Sch. Mem.: State Congress of Parents & Tchrs. (hon.), Coun. for Exceptional Children, Kappa Delta Pi. Avocations: piano, travel.

KLEIN, NANCY LYNN, fine jewelry company owner, consultant; b. Syracuse, N.Y., May 9, 1961; d. Irwin Lenard and Ann Betty (Ginsburg) K. BS in Journalism, Ohio U., 1985; grad., Gem. Inst. Am., N.Y.C., 1987. Advt. coord. Henry Birks Fine Jewelry, N.Y.C., 1985-87; brand mgr. N.W. Ayer Advt., N.Y.C., 1987-90; advt. dir. Honora Jewelry Co., N.Y.C., 1991-92; asst. jewelry buyer Finlay Co., N.Y.C., 1992-94, buyer fine jewelry Washington, 1994-95; sr. buyer fine jewelry QVC Network, West Chester, Pa., 1995-96; pres., owner Antica Design, Inc., N.Y.C., 1996—. Mem. Women's Jewelry Assn. Office: Antica Design Inc 19 W 44th St Fl 9 New York NY 10036-6001 E-mail: nk5037@aol.com.

KLEIN, REBECCA, commissioner; m. Dale Klien. BA Human Biology, Stanford U.; M Nat. Security Studies, Georgetown U.; JD, St. Mary's Univ., San Antonio. Assoc. dir. nat. security Office of Presdl. Personnel, Washington, 1989—92; asst. to dir. U.S. Trade & Devel. Agy., 1992—93; telecomms. law analyst Am. Enterprise Inst., Washington; sr. atty. Office Policy Devel. Pub. Utility Commn. Tex., 1997—99, commr., 2001—. Maj. USAF. Office: 1701 N Congress Ave PO Box 13326 Austin TX 78711-3326

KLEIN, RENNY, writer, columnist; b. N.Y.C., Sept. 29, 1935; d. Joseph Ferezy and Stella Benjamin; m. Harold Klein; children: Joseph Steven, Jeffrey Michael, Deborah Lynne. BA, San Fernando Valley State Coll., 1966, MA, 1970; postgrad., U. So. Calif., 1970—73, MFCC, 1973; PhD in Counseling Psychology, Pacific Western U., 2002. With Benjamin Rush Crisis Ctr., L.A., 1970—73, L.A. Psychiat. Clinic, 1970—73, Bay Cities Mental Health Ctr., L.A., 1970—73, pvt. practice, 1973—90, Camden Drive, Beverly Hills, Calif., 1973—90. Lectr., presenter in field. Author: The Joy of Eating, The Love of Eating, The Joy of Entertaining, The Joy of Eating French Food, Great Beginnings and Happy Endings, With Love from Darling's Kitchen, Easiest & Best Coffee Cakes and Quick Breads, Entertaining Fast & Fancy, The Moderation Diet, Cooking Great, Looking Great, Feeling Great, The New Joy of Eating, Happy Holidays & Great Celebrations, Vegetarian Fast & Fancy. Various positions including program chair and hospitality chair PTA, 1961—78; various positions including fundraiser, program chair Hadassah So. Calif., 1968—, pres., 1996—98; touring docent L.A. County Art Mus., 1980—85; founder leadership coun., chair fundraisers Technion U., 1985—91. Mem.: PEN. Avocations: art, music, literature. Home: 222 S Peck Dr Beverly Hills CA 90212

KLEIN, ROSALYN FINKELSTEIN, social worker; b. N.Y.C., Dec. 4, 1946; d. Philip and Hilda (Myers) Finkelstein; m. Edward R. Klein, June 14, 1970; children: Brian, Dana, Jennifer. BA, Hunter Coll., 1970; MA, NYU, 1973; MSW, Fordham U., 1983. Lic. clin. social worker, Conn.; diplomate Am. Bd. Examiners Clin. Social Work; cert. clin. supr. Acad. Cert. Social Workers; cert. speech and lang. pathologist. Speech pathologist N.Y.C. Bd. Edn., Bklyn., 1970-74, Princeton (N.J.) Med. Ctr., 1974-76; clin. supr. So. Conn. State U., New Haven, 1977; speech pathologist Easter Seal Rehab., Meriden, Conn., 1977-79; social worker Greenwich (Conn.) Dept. Social Svc., 1983—. Social worker Milford (Conn.) Mental Health Ctr., 1985-86, Jewish Family Svc., Greenwich, 1995-98; field instr. Fordham U., 1987—, Stamford (Conn.) Psychiatry and Geriat., 1998-2001; mem. future planning com., operating com., mem. supervisory com., conflict mediation com. Greenwich Dept. Social Svcs., 1995—. Mem. Hadassah, Orange, 1976-94, Dem. Town Com., Greenwich, 1996-97; treas. Sisterhood/Synagogue, Orange, 1984-86. Recipient Award of Excellence, Town of Greenwich, 1999. Mem. Conn. Soc. Clin. Social Workers. Avocations: walking, traveling, reading, theater.

KLEIN, SAMI WEINER, librarian; b. Worcester, Mass., July 6, 1939; d. Phillip and Barbara Rose (Ginsberg) Weiner; m. Eugene Robert Klein, Oct. 22, 1961; children: Pamela, Jeffrey, Elizabeth. BS, Simmons Coll., 1961; MLS, U. Md., 1973; postgrad., Johns Hopkins U., 1976-78. Chemist Hercules, Wilmington, Del., 1961-62, FDA, Washington, 1965-66; libr. NSWC, White Oak, Md., 1973-78; chief Hdqs. Libr. EPA, Washington, 1978-82; chief rsch. info. svcs. Nat. Inst. Svcs. and Tech., Gaithersburg, Md., 1982-95; chief rsch. libr. and info. program, rsch. libr. Nat. Inst. Stds. and Tech., Gaithersburg, Md., 1995-99; retired Nat. Inst. Svcs. and Tech., Gaithersburg, Md., 1999. Cons. in field; mem. librs. exec. coun. Met. Washington Coun. of Govts., 1981-82; elected mem. com. Fed. Libr. Info. Ctr., 1993-95, chair, budget and fin. working group, 1994-98. Editor OIS Sci.-Tech Info, 1982-95; mem. editorial bd. Assn. Ofcly. Analyt. Chemists, 1985-92, Sci. and Tech. Librs., 1996—. Fed. govt. rep. Inst. for Sci. Info. Internat. Users Group, 1985—86; mem. info. tech. com. Candlelight Concert Soc.; chmn. Howard County Holocaust Remembrance Program, 2003; 2d v.p. Bet Aviv Congregation; mem. edn. com. Fed. Libr. and Info. Ctr. Com., 1987—91. Recipient Gold medal Am. Soc. Chemists, 1961, Engrng. award Govt. Inidustry Data Exch. Program, 1997. Mem. ALA (sec.-treas. Fed. Librs. Round Table 1983-84, rep. to NTIS 1984-90, bd. dirs. 1986-89, v.p. 1991, pres. 1991-92, nominations chair 1992-93, scholar 1994-96, chair privatization com. 1995-97, chair co-awards com. 1996—, 1st FLRT Disting. Svc. award 1995), Spl. Librs. Assn. (treas. info.-tech. group 1986-87, student loan com. 1984-85), D.C. Law Librs. Soc. (NIST v.p. standards com. for women 1988, pres. 1989, bd. dirs. Comstar Credit Union 1994-2000), Fed. Libr. and Info. Network (exec. adv. com. 1989-91, sec. 1989, vice chair 1990-91), Jewish Mus. Md. (bd. dirs. 1999—), Beta Phi Mu. Democrat. Jewish. Home: 11041 Wood Elves Way Columbia MD 21044-1002 E-mail: swklein@comcast.net.

KLEIN, SHERI ROSE, art educator; b. Chgo. BFA, Sch. of Art Inst., Chgo., 1981, MFA, 1983; PhD, Ind. U., 1996. Prof. art edn. U. Wis.-Stout, Menomonie, 1993—. Editor: Case Studies for Pre-Service Art Education, 2003; contbr. articles to profl. jours.; exhibitions include Art Inst. Chgo., Albright-Knox Gallery, Buffalo, N.Y., and numerous other solo and group exhibits. Mem.: Internat. Soc. Edn. Through the Arts, Nat. Art Edn. Assn., Am. Fedn. Tchrs., Wis. Art Edn. Assn. (pres.-elect 2003—, mem. higher edn. bd. 1995—98, Outstanding Art Educator 2000). Avocations: photography, gardening, travel, folk art. E-mail: kleins@uwstout.edu.

KLEIN, SHIRLEY SNYDERMAN, retail executive; b. Balt., Oct. 23, 1929; d. Julius Herman and Fannie (Dannenberg) Snyderman; m. Ralph Lincoln Klein, Jan. 4, 1953; children: Andrew P., Michael J., Howard S. BA, Towson State Tchr.'s Coll., 1951. Office staff accts. receivable, jr. controller Klein's Tower Plz., Inc., Forest Hill, Md., 1952-60, jr. buyer, 1960-70, v.p., buyer children's, ladies, linens, 1970—; bd. mem. Ben Chesapeake Health Sys. (2 Hosp.), 1994; chmn. Upper Chesapeake Health Found., 1995—2001. Treas. Mortgage Svc. Co., Inc., 1956—64; v.p. Klein's Supermarkets, 1979—, Colgate Investments, 1970—; bd. dirs. Upper Chesapeake Health Systems, found. chair, 1993—2001. Pres. Hadassah Harford County, 1966-68; v.p.;. adv. bd. John Carroll Sch., Md. Diocese, 1967, bd. mem., 1970; chmn. Retinitis Pigmentosa Found., Harford County, Md., 1971; bd. dirs. Harfard Opera Theatre Guild, 1976-79; treas. Harford County Commn. for Women, 1977-82; v.p. Jewish Nat. Fund., Balt., 1990-95, bd. dirs., 1993-2000; vice chair Israel Bonds Balt., 1980-97. Recipient Goldie Myeir award, 1996. Mem.: LWV. Home: 109 W Jarrettsville Rd Forest Hill MD 21050-1319 Office: 2101 Rockspring Road Forest Hill MD 21050 Fax: 410-838-5592.

KLEIN, SUSAN ELAINE, librarian; b. Cedar Falls, Iowa, Aug. 5, 1952; d. Elmo Calvin and Mabel Audrey (Taylor) Boone; m. Richard Joseph Klein II, Oct. 16, 1982; children: Michael Joseph, Christopher James. BA, U. No. Iowa, 1974. Reporter The No. Iowan, Cedar Falls, summer 1972; res. desk clk. U. No. Iowa Libr., Cedar Falls, summer 1974; paralegal for migrant action program VISTA, Muscatine, Iowa, 1975-76; office asst. Cedar Falls Pub. Libr., 1976-77, libr. asst., 1977-78, cataloger, 1978-86, libr. asst., 1986-87, young adult libr., 1988—. Mem. Iowa Libr. Assn. (cert.). Democrat. Avocations: cooking, bicycling, gardening, canoeing, reading.

KLEIN, TONY, public relations executive, state representative; b. N.Y.C., Mar. 22, 1947; m. Jennifer F. Boyer; 2 children. BA, Am. U., 1969. Ptnr. Klein and Assocs.; rep. Vt. State Ho. Reps., 2003—. Chmn. U-32 Sch. Bd.; bd. dirs. Vt. Coun. on Humanities. Home: 95 Powder Horn Glen Montpelier VT 05602

KLEIN, WENDY LEE, music educator; b. Wilmington, RI, June 27, 1955; d. Charles and Naomi Ruth Klein; m. Alan Douglas Metnick, July 1, 1980; 1 child, Maggie Arin Metnick. Ba, Brown U., 1977; MusB, Berklee Coll. Music, 1982; MusM, New England Conservatory, 1990. Chairperson jazz dept. Music Sch. RI Philharm., Providence, 1986—; asst. prof. Berklee Coll. Music, Boston, 2000—. Composer, musician Joe Parillo Ensemble, Providence, 1985—2000; performer, musician Looking Glass Theatre, 1985—97; condr. RI Youth Jazz Ensemble. Composer: (albums) Almost Carefree, 1994, Black Island Summer, 1996, Little Songs For Little Ones, 2003, author. Named Phi Beta Kappa, Brown U., 1973; recipient Minnie Helen Hicks award, Brown U. Linquistics Dept., 1973; grantee Cirino fellow, RI Found., 1989—90. Mem.: Musicians Union, Internat. Assn. Jazz Educators. Democrat. Jewish. Home: 28 Dexterdale Rd Providence RI 02906 Office: Berklee Coll Music 1140 Boylston St Boston MA 02215

KLEIN-DAVIS, STEPHANIE ANN, photojournalist; b. Charlottesville, Va., Feb. 17, 1961; d. Richard Martin and Eleanor O. Klein; m. John Mathew Davis; children: Wyeth Alexander Davis, Aria Lilyana Davis. Student, Stanford U., 1981, Franklin Coll., 1982; BA in Comm., Tulane U., 1983; MA in Journalism, U. S.C., 1985. Staff photographer The Sun News, Myrtle Beach, SC, 1985—87; staff photographer, asst. editor The Roanoke (Va.) Times, 1987—2000, staff photographer, 2001—; prof. art photography Hollins U., Roanoke, 2000—01. Conv. chmn. Va. News Photography Assn., 1996; staff photographer Atlanta Com. Olympic Games, 1996; freelance photographer Klein-Davis Photography, Roanoke, 2000—01. Represented in permanent collections Am. Mus. Western Va. Mem.: Arts Coun. of the Blue Ridge, Nat. Press Photographers Assn. (regional v.p. 2002—03). Avocations: running, tennis, sailing, swimming, violin. Home: 5515 Yellow Mountain Rd Roanoke VA 24014 Office: The Roanoke Times 201 W Campbell Ave SW Roanoke VA 24010

KLEINE, ANDREA, playwright, actor, choreographer; b. Falls Church, Va., 1970; BFA, NY U. Dir.(also writer): (plays) Claude (Finalist, Jane Chambers Playwriting award, 2003), (also writer and choreographer) Memoir Never Was (secret tales from the annex), (also choreographer) Flesh Food; author: (plays) Leering; dir.: (films) Murmur (Ofcl. selection - Sundance Online Film Festival, 2002). Recipient NY Finalist, VI Rencontres Choregraphiques de Seine-St-Denis, 1997; Macdowell fellowship, The Macdowell Colony, 2003, Resident Artist, Mabou Mines, 2000, Movement Rsch., 1998—99, Playwrights Lab, The Women's Project Theatre, 2003—, NYC Dept. of Cultural Affairs Challenge grant, Dance Theatre Workshop, 2002, Artist grant, The Puffin Found., 2002, Bossak Heilbron Found., 2000, NY State Coun. on the Arts Commn. award, Performance Space 122, 1999, Jerome Found. Commn. award, 1996—97, Finalist, Nat. Mcknight fellowship, 2001. Mem.: Lincoln Ctr. Theater Directors Lab. Personal E-mail: akleine@echonyc.com.

KLEINER, DIANA ELIZABETH EDELMAN, art history educator, administrator; b. N.Y.C., Sept. 18, 1947; d. Morton Henry and Hilda Rachel (Wyner) Edelman; m. Fred S. Kleiner, Dec. 22, 1972; 1 child, Alexander Mark. BA magna cum laude, Smith Coll., 1969; MA, MPhil, Columbia U., 1970, 74, PhD, 1976; MA (hon.), Yale U., 1989. Lectr., asst. prof. U. Va., Charlottesville, 1975-76, 76-78; vis. asst. prof. U. Mass., Boston, 1979; Mellon faculty fellow Harvard U., Cambridge, Mass., 1979-80; asst. prof. Yale U., New Haven, 1980-82, assoc. prof., 1982-89; fellow Whitney Humanities Ctr., Yale U., New Haven, 1984-87; master Pierson Coll., Yale U., New Haven, 1986-87; dir. grad. studies dept. history of art Yale U., New Haven, 1988-90; prof. history of art and classics Yale U., New Haven, 1989-95, dir. grad. studies dept. classics, 1991-94, chair dept. classics, 1994-95, Dunham prof. classics and history of art, 1995—, dep. provost for the arts, 1995—2003; liaison for faculty programs AllLearn, 2000—. Adv. bd. Archaeol. News, Tallahassee, 1980—, Am. Jour. Archaeology, Boston, 1985-98; mem., chair program for ann. meetings com. Archaeol. Inst. Am., Boston, 1988-93. Author: Roman Group Portraiture, 1977, The Monument of Philopappos in Athens, 1983, Roman Imperial Funerary Altars with Portraits, 1987, Roman Sculpture, 1992, paperback edit., 1994; editor: I, Clavdia: Women in Ancient Rome, 1996, I Clavdia II: Women in Roman Art and Society, 2000, (electronic courses for AllLearn) eClavdia: Women in Ancient Rome, 2001—, Brainy and Battered Third-Century Women, 2003—, Pompeii!, 2004—. Bd. dirs. Westville Cmty. Nursery Sch., New Haven, 1989-90, The Foote Sch., New Haven, 1994-2000; regional rep. Deerfield (Mass.) Acad., 2001—, mem. parent's com., 2002—, trustee, 2004—. Grantee: Am. Coun. Learned Socs., 1979, NEH, 1980, 95, Am. Philos. Soc. 1982, The John Paul Getty Trust, 1992. Mem. Archaeol. Inst. Am., Am. Philol. Assn., Coll. Art Assn. Home: 102 Rimmon Rd Woodbridge CT 06525-1941 E-mail: diana.kleiner@yale.edu.

KLEINHENZ, NANCY ALISON, medical/surgical nurse; b. Dayton, Ohio, Mar. 10, 1960; d. William G. and Thelma J. Reeves. Diploma in nursing, Miami Valley Hosp., Dayton, 1982. RN, Ohio. Shift leader St. Elizabeth Hosp., Dayton, 1982—.

KLEINLEIN, KATHY LYNN, training and development executive; b. S.I., N.Y., May 2, 1950; d. Thomas and Helen Mary (O'Reilly) Perricone; m. Kenneth Robert Kleinlein, Oct. 30, 1983. BA, Wagner Coll., 1971, MA, 1974; MBA, Rutgers U., 1984; MA in Theology, Barry U., 1998. Cert. secondary tchr., N.Y., N.J., Fla. Tchr. English N.Y.C. Bd. Edn., S.I., 1971-74, Matawan (N.J.) Bd. Edn., 1974-79; instr. English Middlesex County Coll., Edison, N.J., 1978-81; med. sales rep. Pfizer/Roerig, Bklyn., 1979-81, mgr. tng. ops. N.Y.C., 1981-86; dir. sales tng. Winthrop Pharms. divsn. Sterling Drug, N.Y.C., 1986-87; dir. tng. Reuters Info. Sys., N.Y.C., 1987-90; pres., dir. tng. Women in Transition career counseling firm, 1990-98; pastoral min., dir. religious edn. St. Raphael's Ch., 1998-2001; diocesan dir. catechetical ministry Diocese of Venice (Fla.), 2001—. Pres. Kleinlein Cons.; pers. mgmt. officer USAR, N.J., 1981-86; cons. Concepts & Prodrs., N.Y.C., 1981-85; bd. regents Blessed Edmund Rice Sch. for Pastoral Ministry; bd. dirs. Campaign for Human Devel. Trainer United Way, 1982-83, mem. polit. action com., 1982—85; mem. Rep. Presdl. Task Force, Washington, 1983—; chair Sarasota Library Adv. Bd.; sec. Intracoastal Civic Assn.; mem. Reinventing Govt. Coun., Sarasota County Planning Commn., exec. bd. Edn. Found., St. Joseph Bon Secours Hosp.; mem. grievance com. Fla. Bar; bd. regents Blessed Edmund Rice Sch. for Pastoral Ministry. Mem. Sarasota County Sch. Bd., 2002—. Capt. U.S. Army, 1974—78. First woman in N.Y. N.G., 1974; first woman instr. Empire State Mil. Acad., Peekskill, N.Y., 1976. Mem.: Sarasota Women's Alliance, Rep. Women's Club, Alpha Omicron Pi. Republican. Roman Catholic. Office: Diocese Venice Cath Ctr 1000 Pinebrook Rd Venice FL 34292 Office Phone: 941-484-9546. Business E-Mail: kleinlein@dioceseofvenice.org.

KLEINMAN, LORI I. psychologist; b. Miami, Mar. 31, 1964; d. Burton and Jeanne Kleinman. MusB, U. Miami, 1986; MSc, Fla. State U., 1989; PhD, U. Miami, 2000. Lic. Psychologist Fla. Program therapist Caron Found., Harrisburg, Pa., 1989—90; therapist Mazziti and Sullivan/Taylor and Assoc., Harrisburg, 1989—92, Charter Hosp., Miami, 1992—93; program therapist Am. Day Treatment, Miami, 1993—94; Air Force psychologist USAF, 1998—2002; psychologist cons. various, Tampa, Fla., 2002—. Faculty intern US Air Force, Andrews AFB, Md., 1998—2000; disaster response team leader MacDill Air Force Base, Tampa, 2000—02. Author: (manuals) Diagnosis Psychoeducation manuals, 1994, Suicide Prevention Manual, 2000. Mem. Hands on Miami, 1995—97, Children's Youth Svcs. Citizens Adv. Com., Cumberland County, Pa., 1990—91; v.p., dir. US Jr. C of C, Camp Hill, Pa., 1989—97. Capt. USAF, 1997—2002. Decorated Achievement medal USAF, Commendation medal. Mem.: Fla. Psycho. Assn., Hands on Tampa. Avocations: music, sailing, theater, bicycling, dance.

KLEMENT, DIANE, educational assistant; b. Bronx, N.Y., Feb. 24, 1945; d. James Teller and Hilda (Artiano) Wright; m. Robert Francis Klement, Jan. 23, 1943; children: Debora Suzanne, James Robert. Student, Fairleigh Dickinson U., 1962-64. Tchr. aide Riverhead (N.Y.) Sch. Dist., 1976—. Pres., mem. Wildwood Acres Homeowners Assn., 1980-82, Wading River Fire Dept. Aux., 1979-81. Mem. Suffolk Ednl. Assn. (del. local 870 1989-92, v.p. 1992-95, pres. 1995—), Civil Svc. Employees Assn. (pres. Riverhead aides 1976-98; co-chairperson sch. dist. com. L.I. region I 1998—; mem. sch. rep. polit. action com. 1995-98, sen. liaison 1995—). Avocations: travel, boating, camping. Office: Civil Svc Employees Assn Suffolk Edn Local 870 1731D N Ocean Ave Medford NY 11763-2649

KLEMENT, VERA, artist; b. Gdansk, Dec. 14, 1929; d. Klement and Rose (Rakovchik) Shapiro; divorced; 1 son, Max Klement Shapey. Cert. in fine arts, Cooper Union Sch. Art and Architecture, 1950. Prof. art U. Chgo.,

1969—95. One woman shows include RoKo Gallery, N.Y.C., 1958, 60, Bridge Gallery, N.Y.C., 1965, Artemisia Gallery, Chgo., 1974, Chicago Gallery, 1976, Marianne Deson Gallery, 1979, 81, Goethe Inst., 1981, CDS Gallery, N.Y.C., 1981, 84, Roy Boyd Gallery, Chgo., 1983, 85, 87, 89, 90, 91, 92, 93, Spertus Mus., Chgo., 1987, retrospective exhbn., 1953-86, Renaissance Soc., Chgo., 1987, Brody's Gallery, Washington, 1992, Fassbender Gallery, Chgo., 1994, 95, 96, 97, Chgo. Cultural Ctr., 1999, retrospective exhbn., 1965-99, Fassbender, 1999, 2001, Ft. Wayne (Ind.) Mus. Art, 2001, Block Mus., Northwestern U., Evanston, Ill., 2001, U. Ariz. Mus. Art, Tucson, 2001, Tarble Arts Ctr., Ea. Ill. U., Charleston, 2002, Brauer Art Mus., Valparaiso (Ind.) U., 2002, Eric Yake Kenagy Gallery, Goshen (Ind.) Coll., 2003, Miami U. Mus. Art, Oxford, Ohio, 2004, Maya Polsky Gallery, Chgo., 2004; group shows include Mus. Modern Art, N.Y.C., 1954, 55, Bklyn. Mus., 1950-60, Dallas Mus. Fine Arts, 1954, Tate Gallery, London, 1956, Museo de Arte Moderno, Barcelona, Spain, 1955, Musee d'Arte Moderne, Paris, 1955, U. Ky., 1959, Art Inst. Chgo., 1967, Walker Art Ctr., Mpls., 1977, U. Mo., 1978, Detroit Inst. Arts, 1978, Ukrainian Inst. Art, Chgo., 1978, Jewish Mus., N.Y.C., 1982, Kunstverein, Munich, Germany, 1987, Amerika Haus, Berlin, 1987, Terra Mus. Am. Art, Chgo., 1988, Corcoran Gallery, Washington, 1994, Cultural Ctr., Chgo., 1994, former IBM Gallery, N.Y.C., 1995, Virginia Beach Ctr. Arts, 1995, Fischer Art Gallery U. So. Calif., 1995, Portland (Oreg.) Mus. Art, Evanston Art Ctr., Mus. Contemporary Art, Chgo., 1996, Block Gallery Northwestern U., Evanston, 1996, Ft. Wayne Mus. Art, 2001, Riva Yares Gallery, Santa Fe, 2002, Klein Artworks, Chgo., 2002, Maya Polsky Gallery, Chgo., 2002, Goshen (Ind.) Coll., 2003; represented in permanent collections Mus. Modern Art, N.Y.C., Phila. Mus. Art, Print Club, Phila., Ill. State Mus., Springfield, U. Tex., Nat. Mus. Am. Art, Washington, Jewish Mus., N.Y.C., Art Inst. Chgo., Philip Morris, N.Y.C., Smart Mus. U. Chgo., Sch. Social Svc. Adminstrn. U. Chgo., Mus. Contemporary Art, Chgo., Mary & Leigh Block Gallery, Evanston, Mus. Art U. Ariz., Tucson, Union Club League Chgo., Daum Mus. Contemporary Art, Sedalia, Mo.; also pvt. collections. Recipient Pollock/Krasner Found. award, 1998, others; Louis Comfort Tiffany Found. fellow, 1954, Guggenheim fellow, 1981-82, Nat. Endowment for the Arts fellow, 1987; Ill. Arts Coun. grantee, 1988. E-mail: veraklement@aol.com.

KLEMP, BARBARA ANNE, music educator; b. Morristown, N.J., Oct. 10, 1960; d. Carl William and Edith Nathalie Klemp. BA in Music Edn., Rutgers U., 1982, MusM, 2004. Cert. K-12 vocal/instrumental music comprehensive tchr. N.J. Tchr. music Shore Regional H.S., West Long Branch, NJ, 1982—84; tchr. elem. music Bartle Sch., Highland Park, NJ, 1986—88; tchr. music, dir. H.S. Choral Activities Sch. Dist. of Chathams, Chatham, NJ, 1988—. Choreographer, Chatham, 1990—; composer/arranger, Chatham, 1995—; clin. music edn., Chatham, 1991—. Composer ednl. choral publs. Vol. America Sings! Inc., Alexandria, Va., 1990—. Named conductor, Morris-Union Jointure Commn., 1992-1998; recipient Svc. and Leadership Recognition award, 1995. Mem.: Internat. Assn. Jazz Educators (condr. N.J. All-State Jazz Choir 2001), Am. Choral Dirs. Assn., Music Educators Nat. Conf., N.J. Music Educators Assn. (condr. All-N.J. Region I Choirs 1994, 2000), N.J. Edn. Assn. Republican. Avocations: bicycling, walking, rollerblading, reading. E-mail: bkjerzshore@aol.com.

KLENK, ROSEMARY ELLEN, pediatrician; b. Pitts., June 16, 1948; d. Joseph Albert and Frieda (Roppolo) Meisner; m. Kenneth Klenk, June 26, 1977; children: Kara, Jacob, Caitlin, David, Colin, Kevin. BA in History, U. Rochester, 1970; BSN, Columbia U., 1972; MD, Cornell U., 1980. Diplomate Nat. Bd. Med. Examiners, Am. Bd. Pediat.; RN. Ptnr., pvt. practice New England Pediat., Stamford, Conn., 1983—. Part-time instr. Coll. Physicians & Surgeons Columbia U., 1983—; attending physician Stamford Hosp. Contbr. articles to profl. jours. Fellow Am. Acad. Pediat.; mem. Conn. State Med. Soc., Fairfield County Med. Soc. Office: New England Pediatrics 166 W Broad St Ste 103 Stamford CT 06902-3661 also: 183 Cherry St New Canaan CT 06840-5409

KLEPPE, JOAN MARIE, entertainment executive; b. Lomira, Wis., Aug. 22, 1925; d. George Jacob and Susan Elizabeth (Welsch) Steiner; m. Albert Whitney Wellander, June 10, 1950 (div. Mar. 1960); children: Thomas A., Alan G., Barbara Sue; m. Willard Earl Kleppe, Sept. 18, 1978 (dec. Mar. 1988). Degree magna cum laude, Fond du Lac (Wis.) Comml Coll., 1943; BS in Music Edn., U. Wis., 1947; postgrad., Second City, Chgo., 1976-78. Cert. exec. sec., Ill. Adminstrv. asst. to pres. Canvas Products Corp., Fond du Lac, Wis., 1947-50; jr. exec. corp. offices Sears, Roebuck and Co., Chgo., 1950-54; exec. dir. Lake View Citizens' Coun., Chgo., 1963-67; exec. sec. Chgo. Police Dept., 1967-72, founder, dir. boys' a capella choir, 1970-72; polygraph interviewer, reporter Inst. Lie Detection, Chgo., 1972-75; exec. sec., adminstrv. asst. Electro Brand, Inc. importers, Chgo., 1975-80, Gen. Instrument Corp., Chgo., 1980-85; founder, exec. dir., musician Spring Valley Concert Band, Schaumburg, Ill., 1994—. Entertainer St. Andrew Players, Chgo., 1965-74; trombonist Ukrainian Cathedral Concert Band, Chgo., 1968-70; performer, dir., costumer St. Marcelline Prodns., Inc., Schaumburg, 1989-95; performer, bd. dirs. Silver Foxes Theatrical Troupe, Streamwood, Ill., 1992-96. Author, dir. children's theatrical prodns. Let Freedom Ring, 1966, A Fractured Fairy Tale, 1967; author: Kids 'n' Kops, 1997; writer, dir. musical comedy Talent, of Chorus, 1989, Puttin' on the Bits, 1990; composer music anthem Chgo.: I Will, 1970; columnist Chgo. police dept. publ. The Star, 1968-72. Coord. neighborhood groups Lake View Citizens Coun., Chgo., 1963-67; sec., youth liaison youth com. Chgo. Police Dept., 1967-72; founding mem. Schaumburg Arts Collective, 1996—; mem., liaison Schaumburg Sister Cities, 1995—; coord. benefit performances; bd. dirs. St. Marcelline Prodns.; mem. Prairie Center Arts Found., 1997—, Assn. Concert Bands, Inc., 1998—. U. Wis. scholar, 1943, Pi Rho Zeta scholar, 1942; named Vol. of Yr. Kiwanis, 1970, Most Valuable Civilian Employee Chgo. Police Dept., 1970. Republican. Roman Catholic. Avocations: acting in community theater, freelance writing, costume design, singing, fishing. Home: 716 Kemah Ln Schaumburg IL 60193-1420 Office: Spring Valley Concert Band Inc PO Box 68901 Schaumburg IL 60168-0901 Office Phone: 847-289-4227. E-mail: jkleppe1@aol.com.

KLEPPER, CAROL HERDMAN, mental health therapist; b. Wagner, S.D., July 17, 1933; d. Forrest Glenwood and Augusta Wilhamina (Mills) Herdman; m. Albert Raymond Klepper, May 14, 1955; children: James David, Leesa Lynn, Krista Patrice. BS in Psychology cum laude, South Oreg. State Coll., 1987; MS in Counseling, Oreg. State U., 1989. Nat. cert. counselor, lic. profl. counselor; cert. diplomate in psychotherapy. Dir. counseling Klamath Hospice, Klamath Falls, Oreg., 1990-91; staff therapist Klamath Mental Health Ctr., 1991-94; in-house counselor Wednesday's Child, 1995-2001, title 19 supv., 1996-99; pvt. practice Klamath Falls, Oreg., 2000—. Data rschr. Rich Pickett and Co., Klamath Falls, 1986—90; pre-commitment investigator Klamath Mental Health Ctr., 1991—94; EPSDT coord. County of Klamath, 1991—94; affil. Big Sage Counseling, 2000—02. Mem. youth svcs. team local mid-schs, Klamath Falls, 1992—94; juv. fire-setters network Klamath Falls Fire Dist. #1, 1992—95; head start health bd. Klamath Falls, 1991—2001; del. People to People Program, 2004; adv. bd. Klamath Falls Gospel Mission, 2000—; RAPP Team Mem., 1995—; program therapist KAP, 1995—2000; abuse therapist Klamath County Juvenile Dept., 2000—02; child and family counselor Head Start, 2000—01. Mem. Psi Chi. Home and Office: 8926 Highway 66 Klamath Falls OR 97601-9519 Office: 2960 Maywood Dr # 10 Klamath Falls OR 97602 E-mail: klepper@cvc.net.

KLEPPER, ELIZABETH LEE, physiologist; b. Memphis, Mar. 8, 1936; d. George Madden and Margaret Elizabeth (Lee) K. BA, Vanderbilt U., 1958; MA, Duke U., 1963, PhD, 1966. Research scientist Commonwealth Sci. and Indsl. Research Orgn., Griffith, Australia, 1966-68, Battelle Northwest Lab., Richland, Wash., 1972-76; asst. prof. Auburn (Ala.) U., 1968-72; Plant physiologist USDA Agrl. Research Service, Pendleton, Oreg., 1976-85, research leader, 1985-96. Assoc. editor Crop Sci., 1977-80, 88-90, tech. editor, 1990-92, editor, 1992-95, mem. edit. bd. Plant Physiology, 1977-92, Irrigation Sci., 1987-92, mem. edit. adv. bd. Field Crops Rsch., 1983-91; contbr. articles to profl. jours., chpts. to books. Marshall scholar British Govt., 1958-59; NSF fellow, 1964-66. Fellow AAAS, Crop Sci. Soc. Am. (fellows com. 1989-91, pres.-elect 1995-96, pres. 1996-97, past pres. 1997-98), Soil Sci. Soc. Am. (fellows com. 1986-88), Am. Soc. Agronomy (monograph com. 1983-90, bd. dirs. 1995-98); mem. Agronomic Sci. Found. (bd. dirs. 1993-99), Sigma Xi. Home: 1454 SW 45th Pendleton OR 97801 Office: USDA Agrl Rsch Svc PO Box 370 Pendleton OR 97801-0370 E-mail: klepperb@uci.net.

KLIEBHAN, SISTER M(ARY) CAMILLE, academic administrator; b. Milw., Apr. 4, 1923; d. Alfred Sebastian and Mae Eileen (McNamara) K. Student, Cardinal Stritch Coll., Milw., 1945-48; BA, Cath. Sisters Coll., Washington, 1949; MA, Cath. U. Am., 1951, PhD, 1955. Joined Sisters of St. Francis of Assisi, Roman Catholic Ch., 1945; legal sec. Spence and Hanley (attys.), Milw., 1941-45; instr. edn. Cardinal Stritch Coll., 1955-62, assoc. prof., 1962-68, prof., 1968—, head dept. edn., 1962-67, dean students, 1962-64, chmn. grad. div., 1964-69, v.p. for acad. and student affairs, 1969-74, pres., also bd. dirs., 1974-91, chancellor, 1991—. Mem. TEMPO, 1982—2001; bd. dirs., 1986—89; bd. govs. Wis. Policy Rsch. Inst., 1987—97; bd. dirs. Goals for Milw. 2000, 1980—83; treas. Wis. Found. Ind. Colls., 1974—79, 1987—90, v.p., 1979—81, pres., 1981—83; bd. dirs. DePaul Hosp., 1982—91, Sacred Heart Sch. Theology, 1983—, Viterbo Coll., 1990—98, Milw. Cath. Home, 1991—2001, St. Ann Ctr. for Intergenerational Care, 1991—99, Wis. Psychoanalytic Found., 1989—96, St. Coletta's of Mass., 1995—98, Internat. Inst. Wis., 1984—94, Milw. Achiever Program, Inc., 1983—2003, Franciscan Pilgrimage Programs, Inc., 1997—, Friends of Internat. Inst. Wis., 1994—, Mental Hea.th Assn. Milwaukee County, 1983—87, Pub. Policy Forum, 1987—90, Better Bus. Bur. of Wis., Inc., 1989—2001, YWCA Greater Milw., 1996—2001, St. Camillus Campus, 1996—2001, mem. adv. bd., 1989—96. Mem. Am. Psychol. Assn., Rotary Club of Milw. (v.p., pres. elect 1992-93, pres. 1993-94), St. Mary's Acad. Alumnae Assn., Phi Delta Kappa, Delta Epsilon Sigma, Psi Chi, Delta Kappa Gamma, Kappa Delta Pi.

KLIEN, KAREN ANN, speech pathology/audiology services professional; d. Arthur George and Arlene Naomi Klien. BS summa cum laude, Marywood Coll., 1983; MA in Hearing and Speech Sci., Ohio U., 1985. Speech-lang. clinician New Berlin (N.Y.) Ctrl. Sch., 1985—88; speech-lang. pathologist Albemarle Rehab. Svcs., Elizabeth City, NC, 1988—93, Devel. and Disability Svcs. Lebanon (Pa.) Valley, 1993—97, Harford County Pub. Schs., Bel Air, Md., 1997—. Cons. pre-kindergarten Edenton (N.C.)-Chowen Schs., 1990—93. Humanitarian aid worker Families-in-Tune Ministries, Almaty, Kazakhstan, 1999; vol. Operation Carelift Josh McDowell Ministry, Ivanova, Russia, 2001. Grantee, Klein Found., 2003. Mem.: Speech Pathologists Harford County, Am. Speech-Lang. Hearing Assn. (cert. speech-lang. pathologist). Avocations: travel, reading, writing, walking. Office: Halls Cross Roads Elem Sch 203 E Bel Air Ave Aberdeen MD 21001 Office Phone: 410-273-5524. E-mail: speechlady5000@aol.com.

KLIKA, CRISTINE M. state official; BS in Civil Engring., Purdue U. Registered profl. engr., Ind. With pvt. cons. firm designing rds. and bridges; county engr. Monroe County, Ind.; design engring. supr. Ind. Dept. Transp., cons. svcs. supr., design svcs. mgr. Design divsn., chief Tech. Svcs. divsn., mgr. Preliminary Engring. sect., to 1997, dep. commr. Office of Planning and Intermodal Transp., 1997—. Office: Ind Dept Transp 100 N Senate Ave Rm N755 Indianapolis IN 46204-2216

KLIMA, MARTHA SCANLAN, state legislator; b. Balt., Dec. 3, 1938; d. Thomas Moore and Catherine A. Scanlan; m. James Patrick Klima Jr., Apr. 8, 1961; children: Jennifer, J. Patrick III, Andrew. AA, Villa Julie Coll., 1958. Mem. appropriations com. Md. Ho. of Dels., Annapolis, 1982—. Sec. Cen. Md. Health Systems Agy., 1981-83; commr. State Planning Commn., State of Md., 1983—. Del. Rep. Nat. Conv. Dallas, 1984; bd. dirs. Greater Balt. Med. Ctr., Towson, 1986-91, Md. Spl. Olympics, 1987—. Named Freshman of Yr., Ho. of Dels., 1984, Woman of Yr. Towsontowne Bus. and Profl. Women's Club; recipient Gov.'s Citation for Outstanding Svc. to Citizens of Md., 1988, Pub. Svc. award for Outstanding Support to Balt. Assn. Retarded Citizens, Inc., 1994, 2001, Legis. award Balt. County Commn. on Disabilities, 1994, 2001. Mem. Am. Legis. Exchange Coun. (state chmn. 1987-97, chmn. Telecomm. and Info. Tech. Task Force, Outstanding State Legislator award 1994, 2001), Women Legis. Md., Congress of PTA's (hon. life), Balt. County C. of C. (Merit award 1981). Republican. Roman Catholic. Avocations: fishing, walking, boating. Home: 1403 Newport Pl Lutherville Timonium MD 21093-5920 Office: Ho Reps State Capital Annapolis MD 21401

KLIMAS, ELIZABETH JOLANTA, accountant, lawyer, economist; d. Anna Z. (Klimas) Sarwaryn. BSBA, Calif. State U. Northridge, Northridge, Calif.; BS bus. law. Cert. Acctg. Assn., 1992; Summa Pub./NY 1999, Summa Pub./NY 2000. Sr. acctg. staff Motion Picture Industry, Los Angeles, Calif., 1992—. Author: (poetry) The Best Poems & Poets Of 2001 (Internat. Poet Of Merit Award, 2002), Tender Moments (Bronze Commemorative Award Medallion, 2001), (law and taxation) IRS Revealed: Money For Sex, (articles) on taxation and tax law/Los Angeles Daily News, (book) The New World Book of Klimases, A Celebration of Klimases, The Klimases Since 1912. Silver leader DAV, Calif., 1996—2003; vol. Getty Mus., Los Angeles, Calif., 1999—2003; 1996 campaign advisor Rep. Senatorial Inner Cir., Washington DC, Md., 1996—96. Nominee For Appointment as Citizen of the Yr. 1994 for Outstanding Services and Contbn. to Internat. Affairs, H.R.H. Kevin, Prince Regent, Hutt River Province Principality, 1995; recipient Order of the Legion of Merit, The Rep. Senatorial Inner Cir., 1998, Rep. Senatorial Medal of Freedom, Rep. Senatorial Inner Cir., 1999. Mem.: The Smithsonian Instn. (assoc.; nat. assoc. mem. 1996—), So. Poverty Law Ctr. (assoc.; mem. 2001—03, Cert. for Outstanding Support of the work of the So. Poverty Law Ctr. & Tchg. Tolerance 2002), The Libr. of Congress (assoc.; mem. 1996—2003), ABA (assoc.; j.d. mem. 1996—2002), Rep. Presdl. Task Force (life; platinum mem. 1992—2003, Cert. of Membership 2003). Independent Thinkers. Catholic. Avocations: cmty. TV for So. Calif. KCET, Am. for fair taxation, natural history preservation, nat. wildlife federation/defenders of wildlife, guiding eyes for the blind/ASPCA. Home: PO Box 56944 Sherman Oaks CA 91413 Personal E-mail: elzaklimas@yahoo.com.

KLIMLEY, NANCY LEE, volunteer; b. Chgo. d. William Peter and Flora (Sutherland) Enzweiler; m. Francis Joseph Klimley; children: Lisa, Brooks. BA, St. Mary's Coll., Notre Dame, Inc., 1951. Asst. fashion coord., dir. Carson Pirie Scott, Chgo.; asst. social dir. Lake Shore Club, Chgo., editor mag. Chmn. women's divsn. Chgo. Heart Assn., 1958—, pres. women's coun., 3 times. Bd. dirs. Chgo. Boys and Girls Club, 1970—, Brookfield Zoo, 1982—, Libr. of Internat. Rels., 1980-92, Northwestern U. Settlement, 1962-78, Great Lakes Hosp. League, 1962, Boy Scouts Am., 1965, Aides to the Handicapped, 1965, ARC, Mus. of Scis.; bd. dirs. Children's Home and Aid Soc., 3-time pres. woman's bd., sponsor parent bd. 1962—; bd. dirs. Fashion Group, treas., 1958; bd. dirs. Am. Opera Soc., 1962-76, Ill. Opera Guild, 1962-76, Artists Adv. Coun., 1970-80, Republican Women Vols., 1958; bd. dirs., mem. exec. com. USO, 1980—, benefit chmn. 5 years, founder, pres. woman's adv. bd.; founding mem., benefit chmn. Joffrey Ballet, vice chmn. emeritus of benefits; chmn., hon. chmn. The Consular Ball. Recipient Golden Heart award, Heart of Yr. award Am. Heart Assn., Fund Raising award Children's Home and Aid Soc., Golden Eagle award USO, others. Mem. Chgo. Hist. Soc., Guild of the Chgo. Hist. Soc., Antiquarians of the Art Inst. (life), Woman's Athletic Club (bd. dirs.), Saddle and Cycle Club. Republican. Roman Catholic. Avocations: antiques, collecting and reading books, world of fashion as an art form, interior decorating. Home: 3240 N Lake Shore Dr Chicago IL 60657-3954

KLINCK, CYNTHIA ANNE, library director; b. Salamanaca, N.Y., Nov. 1, 1948; d. William James and Marjorie Irene (Woodruff) K.; m. Andrew Clavert Humphries, Nov. 26, 1983. BS, Ball State U., 1970; MLS, U. Ky., 1976. Reference/ young adult libr. Bartholomew County Libr., Columbus, Ind., 1970-74; dir. Paul Sawyier Pub. Libr., Frankfort, Ky., 1974-78, Washington-Centerville Pub. Libr., Dayton, Ohio, 1978—. Libr. bldg. cons.; libr. cons., trainer OPLIN Task Force. Contbr. articles to profl. jours. Bd. dirs. Bluegrass Comty. Action Agy., Frankfort, Ky., 1971-73; founder, bd. dirs. FACTS, Inc. (info. & referral), Frankfort, 1972-74; co-founder, bd. dirs. Seniors, Inc., Dayton, Ohio, 1980-81, 91—; trustee, officer South Comty., Inc. Mental Health Ctr., Dayton, 1980-89; pres. Miami Valley Librs.; mem. govt. affairs com., ann. conf. planning com., fin. resources task force conf. presenter Ohio Libr. Coun.; program presenter Ohio Libr. Coun. Confs.; del. to Am. Libr. Assn. Congress on Profl. Edn. Recipient Vol. of Yr. So. Metro Regional C. of C. Mem. ALA, Am. Soc. for Info. Sci., Am. Soc. for Pers. Adminstrn., Ohio Libr. Assn. (chmn. legis. com.), South Metro Regional C. of C. (exec. com., bd. dirs., chmn. edn. com., chair-elect), Rotary (bd. dirs.), Pub. Libr. Assn. Mng. for Results (trainer). Office: Washington-Centerville Pub Libr 111 W Spring Valley Rd Dayton OH 45458-3761 Office Phone: 937-435-7375.

KLINE, LINDA, employment consultant; b. Boston, Aug. 8, 1940; d. George and Eva (Weiner) Kline. BA in Biology, Boston U., 1962, postgrad. in Biochemistry, 1962—64. Pers. dir. Block Engring. Inc., Cambridge, Mass., 1964-66; brokerage mgr. Eastern Life Ins. Co. N.Y., Boston, 1966-68; mgr. direct placement Lendman Assocs., N.Y.C., 1968-72, Norfolk, Va., 1968—72; dir. women-in-mgmt. divsn. Roberts-Lund, Ltd., N.Y.C., 1972-77; exec. dir. Majority Money, women's network, 1976-79; tchr. fin. planning for women Marymount-Manhattan Coll., 1977; pres. Maxima Consulting, Inc., New York, 1978—80; prin. Kline-McKay, Inc. (name changed to Kline Cons., Inc. 1991), 1978-93; pres. Kline Consulting, Inc./Kline McKay, Inc., New York, 1980—93; pres., mng. dir. Ptnrs. in Human Resources Internat. (formerly the Arbor Group, Inc.), N.Y.C., 1993—98; pres. Bus. & Human Resources Consulting, Tannersville, NY, 1998—. Treas. Lower East Side Print Shop, N.Y.C., 1997-99, bd. advisors, 1999—; lectr. and/or cons. women's programs at several colls. and univs. and corps. Co-author: Career Changing: The Worry-Fee Guide, 1982. Bd. dirs. Women Bus. Owners Edn. Fund, 1982-86, Mom's Amazing, 1985-88; cmty. bd. dirs. Mt. Sinai Med. Ctr., 1984-1999; adv. counselor U.S. Small Bus. Adminstrn. WNET Program. Mem. Internat. Assn. Outplacement Profls., Women Bus. Owners N.Y. (bd. dirs. 1978-84), Nat. Coalition Women's Enterprise (adv. bd. 1988-89), Town of Hunter C. of C. (v.p. 1999—). Democrat. Avocations: antiques, gourmet cooking, reading, photography, travel. Office: Business & Human Resources Cons PO Box 124 Tannersville NY 12485

KLINE, MABLE CORNELIA PAGE, retired secondary school educator; b. Memphis, Aug. 20, 1928; d. George M. and Lillie (Davidson) Brown; 1 child, Gail Angela Page. Student, LeMoyne Coll.; BSEd, Wayne State U., 1948, postgrad. Tchr., Flint, Mich., 1950—51, Pontiac, Mich., 1953—62; tchr. 12th grade English Cass Tech. H.S., Detroit, 1962—95, coord. Study Skills program, mem. English book selection com., 1986—; ret., 1995. Mem.: ASCD, NEA (life), YWCA (life), NAACP (life), Nat. Coun. Tchrs. English, Am. Fedn. Tchrs., Sayne State U. Alumni Assn., Delta Sigma Theta. Episcopalian. Home: 555 Brush St Apt 1512 Detroit MI 48226-4354 Office: Cass Tech High Sch English Dept 2421 2nd Ave Detroit MI 48201-2697

KLINE, NANCY MEADORS, non-profit company executive, consulting executive, writer; b. Clovis, N.Mex., May 1, 1946; d. Max Irby and Edelweiss (Corbin) Meadors; m. Peter Lee Kline, Jan 27, 1972 (div. 1986); m. Christopher Alexander Spence, June 9, 1990. BA in Literature, Scripps Coll., Claremont, Calif., 1968. Tchr. Sandy Spring (Md.) Friends Sch., 1968-70, Madeira Sch., Greenway, Va., 1970-72; founding dir. Thornton Friends Sch., Silver Spring, Md., 1973-84, The Leadership Inst., Sandy Spring, 1984-92; pres. Time to Think, Inc., Oxfordshire, Eng., 1992—; dir. Leadership 2020, London, 1995—. Author: Physical Movement for the Theater, 1969, Enjoying the Arts: Dance, 1973, Women and Power: How Far Can We Go?, 1993; author BBC-TV program Breaking Glass: Women and Men in Leadership, 1995, Time to Think: Listening to Ignite the Human Mind, 1999. Mem. P.E.O. Women, Inst. Personal & Devel. In Practice (London), NOW. Democrat. Mem. Soc. Of Friends. Avocations: writing, gardening. Home: 63 Preston Crowmarsh Wallingford Oxfordshire OX10 6SL England Office: Time to Think Inc 6004 Rhode Island Ave Riverdale MD 20737-1936

KLINE, SUSAN ANDERSON, medical school official and dean, internist; b. Dallas, June 4, 1937; d. Kenneth Kirby and Frances Annette (Demorest) Anderson; m. Edward Mahon Kline, Dec. 26, 1964 (dec. July 1990). BA, Ohio U., 1959; MD, Northwestern U., 1963. Diplomate Am. Bd. Internal Medicine, Nat. Bd. Med. Examiners (bd. dirs. 1977-81). Asst. physician NY Hosp., 1967—68, physician-to-outpatients, 1968—69, electrocardiographer, 1968—70, asst. attending physician, 1969—76, physician-in-charge cardiopulmonary lab., 1970—71, dir. adult cardiac catheterizaion lab., 1970—71, dir. adult cardiac catheterization lab., 1971—79, assoc. attending physician, 1976—85, emeritus attending physician, 1985—, emeritus dir. adult cardiac catheterization lab., 1985—; assoc. dean student affairs Cornell U. Med. Coll., N.Y.C., 1974—78; assoc. dean admissions and student affairs Cornell Med. Sch., Ithaca, NY, 1978—80; mgr. occupl. med. programs GE Co., 1980—84; sr. assoc. dean student affairs N.Y. Med. Coll., Valhalla, 1984—94, interim dean, v.p. med. affairs, 1994—96, exec. vice dean acad. affairs, vice provost univ. student affairs, 1996—. Chmn. unmatched student com. Nat. Residency Matching Program, 1998—2000, chmn., second watch com., 2003—, mem. exec. com., 2003—; mem. test com. Ednl. Commn. on Fgn. Med. Grads., Phila., 1985—92; mem. U.S. Med. Licensing Exam test accommodations com. Nat. Bd. Med. Examiners, Phila., 1992—97; bd. dirs. Nat. Resident Matching Program, 1996—, bd. dirs., mem. exec. com., 2003—, chair 2nd match com., 2004; mem. Liaison Com. on Med. Edn., 1998—, chair ad hoc subcom. rev. accreditation stds., 2000—01, exec. com., 2002—; policy com. Liaiaon Com. on Med. Edn/, 2003—; chmn. adv. com. Electronic Residency Application Svc., 1996—2001. Bd. visitors Coll. Arts, Ohio U., Athens, 1981—91; bd. dirs. Burke Rehab. Hosp., White Plains, 1997—. Recipient Leaders of the Future award, Nat. Coun. Women, N.Y.C., 1978, Cert. of Appreciation, Ohio U., 1978. Fellow: ACP, Am. Soc. Internal Medicine, Am. Coll. Cardiology; mem.: Phi Kappa Phi, Am. Assn. Med. Colls. (chmn. 1989—93, chmn. N.E. group on student affairs, mem. sr. mgmt. adv. com. 2001—), N.Y. Cardiologists Soc., Am. Heart Assn. (fellow coun. on clin. cardiology), Cruising Club Am., Alpha Omega Alpha, Phi Beta Kappa. Avocation: sailing. Home: 561 Pequot Ave Southport CT 06490-1366 Office: NY Med Coll Sunshine Cottage Valhalla NY 10595 E-mail: kline@nymc.edu.

KLINE, SYRIL LEVIN, writer, educational consultant; b. Washington, Oct. 19, 1953; d. Irvin and Blanche (Hewitt) Levin; children: Seth Adam Lessans, Jonathan Rafael Lessans; m. Peter Lee Kline, Dec. 28, 1989. BS, U. Md., 1975. Cert. integrative learning master facilitator, 1990. Tchr. Hebrew Washington Hebrew Congregation, 1974-80; sec., realtor Colquitt-Carruthers Inc., Montgomery County, Md., 1974-80; adminstrv. asst. Bd. Jewish Edn., Silver Spring, Md., 1980-81; tchr. presch. and kindergarten Children's Learning Ctr., Rockville, Md., 1982-89; curriculum designer, dir. integrative learning Nat. Acad. Integrative Learning, Rochester, N.Y., 1990-92; ednl. cons. Integra Learning Systems, South Bend, Ind., 1992—;

free-lance radio and print writer South Bend, 1992—. Ednl. cons. Integrative Learning Systems, Damascus, Md., 1988-89; ind. cons., course designer Prince George's County (Md.) Libr., 1989, North Syracuse (N.Y.) Schs., 1989-92, Oswego (N.Y.) Cmty. Schs., 1989-92, Xerox, Rochester, N.Y., 1990-92, Eastman Kodak, Rochester, 1990-92, Penn Yann (N.Y.) Schs., 1991, Utica (N.Y.) Schs., 1991, City of Rochester Schs., 1991, Bellcore, Elizabeth, N.J., 1991, Alliant Tech Sys., St. Paul, 1991, Paramus (N.J.) Cmty. Schs., 1992, Govt. Can., 1992, Project Read, San Francisco, 1992, Sandia Labs, Santa Fe, 1992, City of Elkhart, Ind., 1992-94, Trinity Corp., Joliet, Ill., 1995, Scottsdale Mall, South Bend, 1995, Pathfinders, Plymouth, Ind., 1996; assessment designer Integra Learning Systems, 1995. Co-author: (novel) The Butterfly Dreams, 1998; featured commentator Sta. WVPE, 1995-98; reporter, staff writer Action Line column for South Bend Tribune; soprano Ind. Opera North; author: The Changeling, 2003, The Fortunate Unhappy, 2003. Spkr., presenter Little Bear Child Abuse Prevention Program, Madison Ctr. Hosp., South Bend, 1993-95; vol. fundraiser Jewish Fedn. St. Joseph Valley, South Bend, 1995-96; mem. com., writer, presenter Holocaust Commemoration; actress, dir. Osceola Players, South Bend Civic Theatre; cantorial soloist Temple Beth El, South Bend, 1997, poet, 1996. Mem. Hadassah (life, corres. sec. 1994-95), Omicron Nu. Democrat. Avocations: radio commercial voices, singing, theatre, pets, travel. Office: 1632 Orkney Drive South Bend IN 46614

KLINEFELTER, DONNA JEAN, secondary school educator; b. Sparta, Wis., Feb. 21, 1943; d. Donald Dean and Clara Lydia (Zietlow) Williams; m. Gerald Raymond Klinefelter, Aug. 29, 1964; children: Ann Katherine, Lisa Marie. BS with honors, U. Wis., Madison, 1965; MA, Cen. Mich. U., 1968. Bilingual cert. in Spanish, social studies. Tchr. Spanish, Janesville (Wis.) H.S., 1966-67, Midland (Mich.) Pub. Schs., 1967—2000; adj. instr. N.W. Mich. Coll., 2001—. Adj. instr. Spanish, Delta Coll., University Center, Mich., 1991-99, Northwest Mich. Coll., Traverse City, Mich.; presentor Cen. States Conf. on Tchg. of Fgn. Langs., 1992; mem. sch. improvement com. NE Intermediate, Midland H.S., strategic planning decision-making action team, 1991-92. Past pres., activity dir. People to People Internat., Midland, 1968—; homeowner's rep. on ad-hoc com. on storm water retention, Midland; vol. Com. to Elect Karen Sherwood, 1994, Creativity Ctr., Northwood U., Alden Dow Archtl. Tours. Recipient Gerstacker award for Excellence in Tchg., Midland, 1992. Mem. AAUW, Am. Assn. Tchrs. of Spanish and Portuguese, NEA, Mich. Edn. Assn., Midland City Edn. Assn. (bd. dirs., mem. profl. stds. com. 1967—); Mich. Fgn. Lang. Assn., Wis. Alumni Assn. Democrat. Methodist. Avocations: hiking, skiing, sailing, playing piano, archeology. Home: 1853 San Marino Trl Kewadin MI 49648-9354

KLINEFELTER, SARAH STEPHENS, retired division dean, radio station manager; b. Des Moines, Jan. 30, 1938; d. Edward John and Mary Ethel (Adams) Stephens; m. Neil Klinefelter. BA, Drake U., 1958; MA, U. Iowa, Iowa City, 1968; postgrad., Harvard U., July, 1984, U. Wis., Sept., 1987, Vanderbilt U., 1991-92. Chmn. humanities dept. High Sch. Dist. 230, Orland Pk., Ill., 1958-68; chmn. communications and humanities div. Kirkwood Community Coll., Cedar Rapids, Iowa, 1968-78; prof. English Sch. of the Ozarks, Point Lookout, Mo., 1978-86; gen. mgr. Sta. KSOZ-FM, Point Lookout, 1986-90; dean div. of performing and profl. arts Coll. of the Ozarks, Point Lookout, 1989-2001. Commr. Skaggs Cmty. Hosp., Branson, Mo., 1986—; chmn. Branson Planning and Zoning Commn., 1983; project dir. Mo. Humanities Bd.; commr., examiner North Cen. Assn. Higher Edn., 1978-85; commr. Iowa Humanities Bd., 1971-78; mem. Taney County Planning and Zoning Commn., 1989-98; pres. Branson Arts Coun., 1997—2002; co-chair Taney County Bd. Adjustment. Democrat. Presbyterian. Home: 182 Hensley Rd Forsyth MO 65653-5137 E-mail: sarahk@tri-lakes.net.

KLING, PHRADIE (PHRADIE KLING GOLD), small business owner, educator; b. N.Y.C., July 2, 1933; d. Samuel A. and Mary Leah (Cohen) Kling; m. Lee M. Gold, Sept. 5, 1955 (div. 1976); children: Judith Eileen, Laura Susan, Stephen Samuel, James David. BA, Cornell U., 1955; MA in Human Genetics, Sarah Lawrence Coll., 1971. Genetic counselor assoc. Coll. Medicine and Dentistry N.J., Newark, 1970—73; assoc. genetic counselor Sarah Lawrence Coll., Bronxville, NY, 1970—73; genetic counselor N.Y. Fertility Rsch. Found., N.Y.C., 1971—73; staff assoc., genetic counselor depts. pediatrics, ob-gyn and neurology Columbia U. Coll. Physicians and Surgeons, N.Y.C., 1973—78; asst. in genetics St. Luke's Hosp. Ctr., N.Y.C., 1977—79; health program assoc. Conn. Dept. Health Svcs., Hartford, 1978—84; edn. cons. Conn. Traumatic Brain Injury Assn., Rocky Hill, 1984—85; office mgr. Anderson Turf Irrigation Inc., Plainville, Conn., 1986—92; owner, mgr. KlingWorks, contract adminstrn., Avon, Conn., 1992—. Spkr., instr. health and health ethics issues, Conn., NY, NJ, 1971—85; dir. confs. genetics and traumatic brain injury, 1980—85; project dir. ednl. field testing Biol. Scis. Curriculum Study, 1981—83; scientist AAAS Sci.-by-Mail, 1991—2000. Active Farmington River Watershed Assn., Simsbury, Conn., 1988—; docent Sci. Mus. Conn., West Hartford, 1989—90. Recipient citation for dedicated svc., Conn. Safety Belt Coalition, 1985. Mem.: Conn. Assn. Jungian Psychology (bd. dirs.), Bus. and Profl. Microcomputer Users Group (bd. dirs.), Am. Human Genetics Soc., Am. Mensa (chpt. coord. gifted children 1985—), Cornell Club Greater Hartford. Home and Office: 33 Hunter Rd Avon CT 06001-3618

KLINGER, MARILYN SYDNEY, lawyer; b. N.Y.C., Aug. 14, 1953; d. Victor and Lillyan Judith Klinger. BS, U. Santa Clara, 1975; JD, U. Calif., Hastings, 1978. Bar: Calif. 1978. Assoc. Chickering & Gregory, San Francisco, 1978-81, Steefel, Levitt & Weiss, San Francisco, 1981-82, Sedgwick, Detert, Moran & Arnold, San Francisco and L.A., 1982-87, ptnr. San Francisco, 1988-98, L.A., 1998—. Guest lectr. Stanford U. Sch. Engrng. Vol. atty. Lawyers Commn. on Urban Affairs, San Francisco, 1978-80. Mem. ABA (tort and ins. practice sect., chair surety and fidelity com. 2003-04, constrn. forum, pub. contracts sect.), Internat. Assn. Def. Counsel (chmn. fidelity and surety com. 1996-98, chair-elect 2003-), Nat. Assn. Bond Claims (spkr.), Surety Claims Inst. (spkr.), No. Calif. Surety Underwriters Assn., No. Calif. Surety Claims Assn. (lectr., pres. 1989-90), Surety Assn. L.A. (spkr.). Avocations: reading, hiking, golf. Home: 939 15th St # 10 Santa Monica CA 90403-3146 Office: Sedgwick Detert Moran & Arnold 801 S Figueroa St Fl 18 Los Angeles CA 90017-2573

KLINGHOFFER, JUNE FLORENCE, physician, educator; b. Phila., Feb. 12, 1921; d. Harry and Esther (Uram) K.; m. Sidney U. Wenger, June 24, 1947; 1 child, Robert Klinghoffer Wenger. BA, U. Pa., 1941; MD, Woman's Med. Coll. Pa., Phila., 1945. Diplomate Am. Bd. Internal Medicine, Am. Bd. Rheumatology. Intern, then resident Albert Einstein Med. Ctr., Phila., 1945-47; fellow in pathology Woman's Med. Coll. Pa., 1947-48; prof. medicine Med. Coll. Pa., Phila., 1969—87, Ethel Russell Morris prof. medicine, 1987—2000, emeritus prof. medicine, 2000—. Contbr. articles to med. jours. Recipient Lindback award for disting. teaching, 1965, Alumnae Achievement award Med. Coll. Pa., 1978. Fellow ACP, Phila. Coll. Physicians; mem. AMA, AAUP, Am. Med. Women's Assn., Assn. Am. Med. Colls., Am. Coll. Rheumatology, Alpha Omega Alpha. Home: 356 Meadow Ln Merion Station PA 19066-1331 Office: Med Coll Pa 3300 Henry Ave Philadelphia PA 19129-1191

KLINGLER, GWENDOLYN WALBOLT, state representative; b. Toledo, May 28, 1944; d. L. Byron and Elizabeth (Brown) Walbolt; m. Walter Gerald Klingler, June 11, 1966; children: Kelly Michelle, Lance, Jeffrey. BA, Ohio Wesleyan U., 1966; MA, U. Mich., 1969; JD, George Washington U., 1981. Bar: Ill. Rsch. assoc. U. Mich., Ann Arbor, 1966-71; abstractor Year Book Med. Pub., Chgo., 1972-75; law clk. FDA, Rockville, Md., 1980; atty. Atty. Gen.'s Office State of Ill., Springfield, 1981-84, appellate prosecutor, 1984-92; ptnr. Boyle, Klingler & McClain, Springfield, 1992-95. Mem. Springfield Bd. of Edn., 1987-91, pres., 1988; alderman Springfield City Coun., 1991-95; Rep. Ill. Ho. of Reps., 100th Dist., 1995—. Recipient Woman of Achievement award in Govt., Women-in-Mgmt., 1994, Disting. Alumni award Leadership Springfield, 1996. Mem. AAUW, Cen. Ill. Women's Bar Assn. (chair membership com.), Sangamon County Bar Assn., Greater Springfield C. of C., Women-in-Mgmt. Republican. Presbyterian (elder). Home: 1600 Ruth Pl Springfield IL 62704-3362 E-mail: klingler@housegopmail.state.il.us.

KLINKE, LOUISE HOYT, volunteer; b. Rochester, N.Y., Nov. 16, 1933; d. Martin Breck Hoyt and Evelyn Louise Moone; children: Geoffrey P., David H., Debra L. Tice. AA, Rochester Bus. Inst., 1952. Dir. fin. and pers. Landmark Soc. Western N.Y., Rochester, 1965—85; ret., 1985. Vol. Landmark Soc. Preservation Issues Com., Nathaniel Rochester Soc., Rochester Inst. Tech., Arts and Cultural Coun. Devel. Com., Hillside's Campaign Com.; vol. chmn. Hillside's Bldg. Com.; mem. Meml. Art Gallery, Eastman House, Strong Mus., Nat. Trust for Hist. Preservation, Preservation League N.Y. State, Smithsonian Inst., Met. Mus., Rochester Area Cmty. Found.; treas. Rochester Contemporary; bd. dirs. Art Walk, Race and Reconciliation, Keuka Coll., 1982—, Hillside Children's Ctr., 1982—, treas.; former v.p. Hillside Children's Found., current treas.; bd. dirs. Women's Found. Genesee Valley, Rochester Hist. Soc., 1984—, former treas.; bd. dirs. Alzheimer's Assn., treas.; bd. dirs. Pyramid Arts Ctr., former treas.; bd. dirs. Opera Theatre Rochester, treas.; bd. dirs. Friends Eastman Opera, Garth Fagan Dance, 2001—. Mem.: BOA, Geva Theatre Rochester City Ballet, Assn. Fund Raising Profls., Chatterbox Club. Democrat. Episcopalian. Home: 35 Brunswick St Rochester NY 14607

KLINKER, SHEILA ANN J. state legislator, middle school educator; m. Victor Klinker; children: Kerri, Kevin, Kelly. BS in Edn., MS in Elem. Edn., MS in Adminstrn. and Supervision, Purdue U. Outreach liaison Purdue U. Sch. Edn., 1982—; state rep. Ind. Ho. of Reps., Indpls., 1982—. Mem. St. Mary's Cathedral Parish; 1st woman appointee Tippecanoe Area Plan Commn.; bd. dirs. Lafayette Symphony, Opera de Lafayette, Tippecanoe County Chid Care, Purdue Musical Orgn.; past chairwoman pub. svc. divsn. United Way. Recipient Outstanding Svc. award Ind. Advocates for Children, Legis. award Assn. of BPW's Outstanding Woman in Politics, Woman of Distinction award Sycamore Girl Scout Coun., Salute to Women in Politics award, Outstanding Svc. for Pub. Interest award Ind. Optometric Assn., Pres.'s Spl. Svc. award Ind. Soc. Profl. Land Surveyors, Spl. Recognition award Ind. Chpt. NASW, Legis. Efforts Recognition award Ind. Residential Facilities Assn., Ind. Assn. for Counseling and Devel., Tippecanoe Arts Fedn. award, Purdue U. Musical Orgn. Alumni award, Marriage and Family Therapists Svc. award, 1998, Social Workers Svc. award, 1998, Ind. Assn. for Gifted Leadership award, 1998. Mem. Bus. and Profl. Women's Assn., Lafayette C. of C. (edn. com.), Delta Kappa Gamma, Phi Delta Kappa, Kappa Alpha Theta (mem. adv. bd.). Democrat. Home: 633 Kossuth St Lafayette IN 47905-1444 Office: Ind Ho of Reps State House Third Fl Indianapolis IN 46204

KLINMAN, JUDITH POLLOCK, biochemist, educator; b. Phila., Apr. 17, 1941; d. Edward and Sylvia Pollock; m. Norman R. Klinman, July 3, 1963 (div. 1978); children: Andrew, Douglas. BA, U. Pa., 1962, PhD, 1966; PhD (hon.), U. Uppsala, Sweden, 2000. Postdoctoral fellow Weizmann Inst. Sci., Rehovoth, Israel, 1966—67; postdoctoral assoc. Inst. Cancer Rsch., Phila., 1968—70, rsch. assoc., 1970—72, asst. mem., 1972—77, assoc. mem., 1977—78; asst. prof. biophysics U. Pa., Phila., 1974—78; assoc. prof. chemistry U. Calif., Berkeley, 1978—82, prof., 1982—, prof. molecular and cell biology, 1993—, chair chem. dept., 2000—, Joel Hildebrand chair, 2002—03, Miller prof., 2003—04. Mem. ad hoc biochemistry and phys. biochemistry study sects. NIH, 1977—84, phys. biochemistry study sect., 1984—88. Mem. editl. bd.: Jour. Biol. Chemistry, 1979—84, Biofactors, 1991—98, European Jour. Biochemistry, 1991—95, Biochemistry, 1993—, Ann. Rev. Biochemistry, 1996—2000, Accts. Chem. Res., 1995—98, Current Opinion in Chemical Biology, 1997—, Chemical Record, 2000—, Advances in Physical Organic Chemistry, 2003—, Accts. Chem. Rsch., 1995—98; contbr. articles to profl. jours. Fellow, NSF, 1964, NIH, 1964—66, Guggenheim, 1988—89. Mem.: NAS, Am. Philos. Soc., Am. Soc. Biochemistry and Molecular Biology (membership com. 1984—86, pub. affairs com. 1987—94, program com. 1995, pres.-elect 1997, pres. 1998, past pres. 1999), Am. Acad. Arts and Scis., Am. Chem. Soc. (exec. coun. biol. divsn. 1982—85, chmn. nominating com. 1987—88, program chair 1991—92, Repligen award 1994), Sigma Xi. Office: U Calif Dept Chemistry Berkeley CA 94720-0001

KLOEFKORN, SHEILA, marketing professional, sales executive; d. Gary Kloefkorn and Holm Cherie; life ptnr. Jackie Eldridge; 1 child, Olivia Eldridge. BA in Polit. Sci., U. Wyo., 1991; MA in Coll. Student Pers. (Higher Edn. Adminstrn.), Bowling Green (Ohio) State U., 1993. Dir. ops. Network Event Theater, N.Y.C., 1995—97; v.p. ops. YouthStream Media Networks, N.Y.C., 1997—2002; v.p. mktg. and sales Cultural Experiences Abroad, Tempe, Ariz., 2002—03; pres. Team KEO Solutions, LLC, Tempe, 2003—. Bd. dirs. U. Wyo. Nat. Ambs., 2002—03. Mem.: Am. Mktg. Assn. (bd. dirs. 2003—). Home: 54 W Pecan Pl Tempe AZ 85284 Business E-Mail: Sheila@TeamKEO.com.

KLOSE, CHARLOTTE ANN, insurance agency owner; b. Mankato, Minn., Oct. 22, 1939; d. Jerome John and Drusilla Lucille (Wiegert) Kunkel; m. Gerhard Klose, Aug. 12, 1961; children: Karin Anne, Susan Marie. BA in English, Coll. St. Benedict, St. Joseph, Minn., 1961; MA in English, Nazareth Coll., Rochester, N.Y., 1967, MS in Edn., 1977. CLU, ChFC, The Am. Coll., Bryn Mawr, Pa., 1988; CPCU, CPCU Soc., Malvern, Pa., 1995. H.s. Latin and English tchr. Richfield (Minn.) Pub. Schs., 1961-63; h.s. English and reading tchr. Rochester City Schs., 1963-81; owner State Farm Ins. Agy., Penfield, N.Y., 1981—. Presenter regional conf. State Farm Ins. Cos., Albany, N.Y., 1997; presenter Nat. Conf. Students for Responsible Bus., Evanston, Ill., 1996; mem. adv. com. women and gender studies divsn. Colgate Rochester Divinity Sch., 1995—; presenter Theol. Inst., Colgate Rochester Divinity Sch., 1997. Contbr. articles to profl. jours. Mem. edn. coms. Penfield Schs., 1972-78; mem. steering com. Women's Resource Ctr., YWCA, Rochester, 1989-91; mem. Goals for a Greater Rochester, 1991-93; pres. Rochester Women's Network, 1991-92, bd. dirs. 1988-94; bd. dirs. Susan B. Anthony House, 1997—. Mem. CLU Assn. (bd. dirs. 1989-91), Rochester Life Underwriters Assn. (1994-96), CPCU Assn., Penfield Bus. Assn., Penfield Rotary (com. chair 1989-95). Roman Catholic. Avocations: travel, writing, reading, wine tasting, swimming. Home: 70 Thorntree Cir Penfield NY 14526-1224 Office: State Farm Ins Cos 1844 Penfield Rd Ste 3 Penfield NY 14526-1491

KLOSS, LINDA L. medical association administrator; Former sr. mgr. MediQual Systems, Inc., Mass., InterQual, Inc., Chgo.; exec. v.p., CEO Am. Health Info. Mgmt. Assn., Chgo., 1995—. Bd. dirs. Am. Health Info. Mgmt. Assn., 1980—86, pres. bd. dirs., 1985. Office: Am Health Info Mgmt Assn 233 N Michigan Ave Ste 2150 Chicago IL 60601-5519 Business E-Mail: lkloss@ahima.org.

KLOSTER, CAROL GOOD, book and magazine distribution company; b. Richmond, Va., Aug. 18, 1948; d. David William and Lucy (McDowell) Good; m. John Kenneth Kloster III, Feb. 15, 1975; children: John Kenneth IV, Amanda Aileen. AB, Coll. William and Mary, 1970. Personnel supr. Charles Levy Circulating Co., Chgo., 1974-75, warehouse supr., 1976-77, warehouse mgr., 1978-80, dir. sales, 1980-83, asst. v.p., dir. mktg., 1984; v.p., gen. mgr. Video Trend of Chgo., 1985-86; v.p. gen. mgr. Levy Home Entertainment, 1986-92; pres., CEO Chas Levy Co., 1992—. Mem. bd., Family Focus Inc. Recipient Algernon Sidney Sullivan award Coll. William and Mary, 1970. Presbyterian. Home: 619 W North St Hinsdale IL 60521-3152 Office: Charles Levy Co 1200 N North Branch St Chicago IL 60622-2493

KLOTH, CAROLYN, meteorologist; b. Lakewood, Ohio, Apr. 22, 1954; d. James Albert and Marian Lucille (Fiske) K. BS in Meteorology, Fla. State U., 1976; MS in Meteorology, U. Okla., 1980. Lic. pvt. pilot. Meteorologist intern Nat. Weather Svc., Louisville, 1980-82; meteorologist Nat. Severe Storms Forecast Ctr., Kansas City, 1982-95, Aviation Weather Ctr., Kansas City, 1995—. Part-time student scientist, coop. student Nat. Severe Storms Lab., Norman, Okla., 1977-80. Mem. Nat. Weather Assn. (Aviation Meteor. award 2000, co-chmn. aviation weather com. 1997-2002, v.p. 2002, chmn. publs. com. 2004-), Nat. Weather Svc. Employees Orgn. (sec. Kansas City chpt. mid 1980s), Am. Meteorol. Soc., 99s Internat. Women Pilots Orgn., Aircraft Owners and Pilots Assn., Am. Air Mus. in Britain (founding mem.), Fla. State U. Alumni Assn., U. Okla. Alumni Assn. Democrat. Avocations: gardening, needlework, reading, history. Office: Aviation Weather Ctr 7220 NW 101st Ter Rm 105 Kansas City MO 64153-2371

KLOTZ, FLORENCE, costume designer; b. N.Y.C., Oct. 28, 1928; d. Philip K. and Hannah Kraus. Student, Parsons Sch. Design, 1941. Designer: Broadway shows Take Her She's Mine, 1960, Never Too Late, 1962, Nobody Loves An Albatross, 1963, On An Open Roof, 1963, Owl and the Pussycat, 1964, One by One, 1964, Mating Dance, 1965, The Best Laid Plans, 1966, Superman, 1966, Paris Is Out, 1970, Norman Is That You, 1970, Legends, Follies, 1971 (Drama Desk award, Tony award), A Little Night Music, 1973 (Drama Desk award, Tony award), Side By Side Sondheim, 1975, Pacific Overtures, 1976 (Drama Desk award, Tony award, Los Angeles Critic Circle award), On the 20th Century, 1978 (Drama Desk award), Broadway Broadway, Dancin' In The Streets, 1982, Grind, 1984 (Tony award), Jerry's Girls, 1985; (ballet-jazz opus) Antique Epagraph, N.Y.C.; Broadway musicals Rags, 1986, Roza, 1987; Ctr. prodns. Carousel, 1956, Oklahoma, 1956, Annie Get Your Gun, 1956, 4 Baggatelle; movies Something for Everyone, 1969, A Little Night Music, 1976 (Oscar nomination, Los Angeles Critic Circle award); ice shows John Curry's Ice Dancing, 1979; Broadway musical A Doll's Life; ballet 8 Lines, 1986, I'm Old Fashioned (Jerome Robbins), Ives Songs (Jerome Robbins), City of Angels, 1989 (Tony award nominee, Outer Critics Circle award), Kiss of the Spider Woman, 1989 (Tony award 1989, Drama Desk award 1989), Show Boat, Toronto, Can., 1993, Broadway, 1994-95 (N.Y. Outer Critics Cirlce award 1995, Drama Desk award 1995, Tony award 1995, Theatre L.A. Ovation award 1997, Jessie award 1996), Whistle Down the Wind, 1996. Recipient Life Achievement award Theatre Crafts Internat., 1994, L.A. Ovation award, 1997, award NAACP, 1997, Dramalogue, 1997, L.A. Drama Desk, 1997; inducted into Theatre Hall of Fame, 1997, Patricia Zipprodt award, Fashion Inst. of Techn., 2002. Democrat. Home: 1050 Park Ave New York NY 10028-1031*

KLOTZ, LEORA NYLEE, retired music educator, vocalist; b. Canton, Ohio, Oct. 17, 1928; d. Clarence Karl and Nellie (Jacoby) Dretke; m. Kenneth Gordon Klotz, June 29, 1963. BMus and B.Pub. Sch. Music, Mount Union Coll., Alliance, Ohio, 1950; MA, Western Res. U., Cleve., 1954. Cert. vocal music tchr. Ohio. Elem. music supr. Canton City Schs., Ohio, 1950—60, h.s. vocal dir., 1955—60; elem. music tchr. Louisville City Schs., Ohio, 1960—71, h.s. vocal dir., 1960—81; adult choir dir. Perry Christian Ch., Canton, 1959—87; ret., 1987; mem. young artists competition com. Canton Symphony Orch. Bd., 1981—89; dir. Trirosis choir. Soprano soloist The Messiah Canton Symphony Orch., 1954—55; soprano soloist First Christian Ch., 1946—65, North Canton Cmty. Christian Ch., numerous vocal (solo) appearances N.E. Ohio. Composer choral octavos. Soprano soloist Rep. Civic Celebration, Canton, Ohio, 1950—60. Recipient Outstanding Young Ohio Composer, Ohioana Libr. Assn., 1959. Mem.: Mount Union Women, Canton Symphony League, Am. Guild Organists, ASCAP, Ohio Ret. Tchrs. Assn., Am. Choral Dirs. Assn. (life), Stark County Ret. Tchrs. Assn. (life), MacDowell Chorale (hon.), Canton Woman's Club, MacDowell Music Club (hon.), Order Ea. Star, PEO Sisterhood, Mu Phi Epsilon, Delta Kappa Gamma. Republican. Avocations: collecting Hummel figurines, reading, cooking. Home: 4009 Beechtree Cir NW Canton OH 44709

KLUGE, JANICE, art educator; b. Berwyn, Ill., July 25, 1952; d. Kenneth Leonard and Mildred Mary Kluge; m. George Cam Langley, June 30, 1984. BFA, U. Ill., 1974; MA, U. Wis., 1980, MFA, 1982. Instr., tchg. asst. U. Wis., Madison, 1977-82; asst. prof. art U. Ala., Birmingham, 1982-89, assoc. prof. art, 1989-2000, prof., 2000—, acting chair dept., 1993, dir. art edn., 1988—, interim dept. chair., 2000—. Dir. Samuel B. Barker Outdoor Scupture Competition, U. Ala., Birmingham, 1995—. Exhibited in solo show at Huntsville Mus. Art, 1998; group exhbns. at Columbus (Ga.) Mus. Art, 1998, Ormeau Baths Gallery, Belfast, No. Ireland, 1996, The Nat. Mus. for Women in the Arts, Washington, 2000, numerous others; featured in articles in Metalsmith mag., Sculpture mag. Recipient Individual Artist fellow Ala. State Coun. on Arts, 1988-89, 98-99; Andy Warhol Found. grantee Space One Eleven, Birmingham, 1997-98; U. Ala. Birmingham grantee, 1995-96, 97-98. Mem. Soc. N.Am. Goldsmiths Office: U Ala Birmingham Dept Art And Art History Birmingham AL 35294-0001 E-mail: kluge@uab.edu.

KLUGER, RUTH, German language educator, editor; b. Vienna, Oct. 30, 1931; came to U.S., 1947, naturalized, 1952; d. Viktor and Alma (Gredinger) Kluger Hirschel; m. Werner T. Angress, Mar. 1952 (div. 1962); children: Percy, Dan. BA, Hunter Coll., 1950; MA, U. Calif.-Berkeley, 1952, PhD, 1967. Asst. prof. German lang. and lit. Case Western Res. U., 1966-70; assoc. prof. U. Kans., Lawrence, 1970-73, U. Va., Charlottesville, 1973-75, prof., 1975-76, U. Calif.-Irvine, 1976-80, 86-88, dir. Göttingen Study Ctr., Edn. Abroad Program, 1988-90, prof. emeritus; prof. Princeton U., 1980-86; editor German Quar., 1977-84. Author: The Early German Epigram: A Study in Baroque Poetry, 1971, Weiter leben Eine Jugend, 1992, Katastrophen, Uber Deutsche Literatur, 1994, Frauen lesen anders, 1996; corr. editor Simon Wiesenthal Ctr. Ann., 1987; contbr. articles to profl. jous. Recipient Rauriser Literaturpreis, 1993, Grimmelshausen-Preis, 1993, Niedersachsen Preis, 1993, Marie-Louise-Kaschnitz preis, 1994, Heine-Preis, 1997, Thomas-Mann-Preis, 1999; ACLS fellow, 1978. Mem. MLA (exec. coun. 1978-82), Am. Assn. Tchrs. German (exec. coun. 1976-81), Deutsche Akademie für Sprache und Dichtung, Lessing Soc. (pres. 1977-79), PEN Club. Democrat. Jewish. Home: 62 Whitman Ct Irvine CA 92612-4066 Office: U Calif Dept German Irvine CA 92697-0001 E-mail: rkluger@uci.edu.

KLUKA, DARLENE ANN, human performance educator, researcher; b. Berwyn, Ill., Oct. 6, 1950; d. Aloysius Louis and Lillian (Malkovsky) K. BA, Ill. State U., 1972, MA, 1976; PhD, Tex. Woman's U., 1985. Educator, coach Fenton High Sch., Bensenville, Ill., 1972-73, New Trier East High Sch., Winnetka, Ill., 1973-80; coach Bradley Univ., Peoria, Ill., 1980-82; grad. teaching asst. Tex. Woman's Univ., Denton, 1982-85; prof. Newberry (S.C.) Coll., 1985-86; prof., rschr., dir. Human Performance Ctr., Grambling (La.) State U., 1986-90; asst. prof. human studies and sport adminstrn. U. Ala., Birmingham, 1990-94, rschr., dir. Motor Behavior and Sports Vision Lab., 1990-94; dir. grad. program U. Ctrl. Okla., Edmond, 1994-97; prof., coord. kinesiology and sport studies Grambling (La.) State U., 1997—. Head of del. Internat. Olympic Acad., Olympia Greece, 1990; dep. del. U.S. Olympic Com., 1996-2000; adv. bd. Women's Sports Found., 1992—; U.S.A. Volleyball Sports Medicine and Performance Commn., 1994—; bd. dirs. U.S.A. Volleyball, v.p. rels. and human resources, 1996-2000. Author: Visual Skill Enhancement for Sport Exercises, 1989, Volleyball Drills, 1990, Volleyball, 4th edit., 2000, Motor Behavior: From Learning to Performance, 1999; founding co-editor Internat. Jour. Sports Vision, 1991-97; founding editor Internat. Jour. Volleyball Rsch., 1997—, mem. editl. bd., Coaching Volleyball Jour., 1988—. Dir. Internat. Coun. Health, Phys. Edn., Recreation, Sport and Dance Girls and Women in Sport Commn., 1993—2001; mem. La. Gov.'s Coun. on Phys. Fitness and Sports, 2003—. Recipient Rsch. award So. Assn. Phys. Edn. Coll. Women, 1994, 96, USA

Volleyball Leader award, 1998, Joseph Andera Rsch. award Internat. Acad. of SportsVision, 1999, Disting. Svc. award AAALF Internat. Rels. Coun., 1999, Disting. Achievements award Ill. State U. Alumni Assn., 1997; LAHPERD scholar, 1999-2000, Honor award 2002, So. Dist. Honor award 2003; AAHPERD Honor award, 2004; Disting. Scholar in Sport award 1995, Internat. Coun. of Health Physical Edn., Recreation, Sport and Dance. Mem. AAHPERD (rsch. fellow, bd. govs. 1993-96, So. dist. scholar 2001, Honor award, 2004), AAUP (Disting. scholar award 1997), Nat. Assn. for Girls and Women in Sport (bd. dirs., exec. com. 1989-92, 93-96, pres. 1990-91, Honor award 1996), Internat. Coun. for Sport Sci. and Phys. Edn. (exec. bd. 1997-02, treas. 2002—, editl. bd. 1998—), Internat. Acad. Sports Vision (adv. bd. 1989-98, v.p. 1993-01), Am. Volleyball Coaches Assn. (mem. editl. bd. Coaching Volleyball Jour., 1988-, bd. dirs. 2003—, chmn. edn. and publs. com. 2003—, Excellence in Edn. award 1999), IAPESGW (Kluka/Love Young Rsch. Award named in her honor 2001), Am. Volleyball Coaches Assn., Hall of Fame inductee 2003, Women's Sports Found. (internat. coun. 1993—, edn. & rsch. coun. 1995—, Pres.'s award 1996, Darlene A. Kluka rsch. award named in her honor 2001), Internat. Assn. Phys. Edn. and Sports Girls and Women, Girls and Women in Sport (bd. cons. 2000—). Roman Catholic. Avocations: jogging, photography, collecting olympic games memorabilia, bicycling. Office Phone: 318-274-2602.

KLUNDER, JANICE MARIE, lawyer; b. Corvallis, Oreg., Mar. 3, 1958; d. Bruce W. Klunder and Joanne Klunder (Lehman) Hardy; m. Kollol Pal, June 23, 1984; children: Shonali Marie Pal, Anjali Joanne Pal. BA, Swarthmore Coll., 1980; PhD, MIT, 1987. Scientist Bristol Labs., Syracuse, N.Y., 1980-82; NIH postdoctoral fellow Johns Hopkins U., Balt., 1987-89; sr. scientist Boehringer Ingelheim, Ridgefield, Conn., 1989-93, prin. scientist, 1993-94; assoc. dir. chemistry, dir. patent affairs Pro Script, Inc., Cambridge, Mass., 1994—98; patent agt. Hale and Dorr LLP, Boston, 1998—2002, assoc., 2002—03; sr. patent atty. Millennium Pharms., Inc., Cambridge, 2003—. Co-author: Comprehensive Organic Synthesis, 1991; patentee in field; contbr. articles to profl. jours. Nat. Merit scholar, 1976. Mem. Am. Chem. Soc., Phi Beta Kappa. Office: Millennium Pharms Inc 75 Sidney St Cambridge MA 02139-4169

KLUSMAN, JUDITH ANDERSON, state legislator; b. Neenah, Wis., Dec. 14, 1956; m. Timothy A. Klusman; children: Charles, James. Student, Concordia Coll.; MDiv, Wartburg Theol. Sem., Dubuque, Iowa, 2004. Mem. from dist. 56 Wis. State Assembly, Madison, 1988—2000, asst. majority leader, co-chair joint survey com. retirement svc., mem. ways and means, assembly rules and orgn. coms. Mem. com. on agr. and internat. trade Nat. Conf. State Legislators; mem. task force on agr. and environ; mem. Legis. Coun. Spl. Com. on Child Custody, Support and Visitation Laws; mem. Legic. Coun. Spl. Com. on Remediation of Environ. Contamination. Mem. Outagamie County Local Emergency Planning Com.; mem. Wis. Rural Leadership Program; mem. World Dairy Ctr. Authority Bd. Recipient Key award 4-H, 1975, Outstanding Young Farm Couple award Winnebago County Farm Bur., 1983, Friend of Edn. award Neenah chpt. Wis. Edn. Assn., 1986-87, Friend of Agr. award Wis. Farm Bur. Fedn., 1990, 92, 94, Outstanding Alumni Wionnebago County 4-H, 1992, Buardian of Small Bus. award Fedn. of Ind. Bus., 1992. Mem. Rotary Internat., Wis. Rural Leadership Alumni. Address: 7547 Green Meadow Ave Oshkosh WI 54904-9405

KMIOTEK-WELSH, JACQUELINE, lawyer; b. Bklyn., Dec. 31, 1959; d. Casimir Edward and Anna Catherine Kmiotek; m. James Winfield Welsh III. BA, St. John's U., N.Y.C., 1981, JD, 1983; MBA, NYU, 1991. Bar: N.Y. 1984, U.S. Dist. Ct. (so. and ea. dists.) N.Y. 1984, U.S. Dist. Ct. (we. dist.) N.Y. 1992, U.S. Supreme Ct. 1989. Asst. counsel N.Y. Job Devel. Auth., 1984-85; assoc. Squadron, Ellenoff, Pleasant & Lehrer, N.Y.C., 1985; assoc. atty. N.Y. Power Authority, 1985-86, atty., 1986-90, sr. atty., 1990-99; prin., 1999—. Fellow N.Y. Bar Found., N.Y. State Bar Assn. (mem. Ho. of Dels. 1993-96, exec. com. young lawyers sect. 1993-97, pub. utility law com. 1994—, chair young lawyers sect., com. profl. svc. project on women subcom. 1994-96, chair young lawyers sect. com. on pub. svcs. and pro-bono project on disaster legal assistance 1994-95, mem. 1995-96, mem. com. 1995—, mem. internat. law and practice sect. com. on U.S.-Can. law 1994—, young lawyer divsn. pub. utility law com.), Am. Bar Found., young Lawyers Divsn.; mem. ABA (fellow young lawyers divsn., liaison pub. contract law sect. 1988-90, exec. com. 1988-89, vice-chmn. 1989-91, chmn. 1991—, young lawyers divsn. pub. utility law com., internat. law exec. com. 1989-91, mem. govt. lawyers exec. com. 1990-91, liaison coord. group on energy law 1990-92, coord. group energy law 1992-95, mem. com. sect. of real property, probate & trust law 1995-97, liaison ABA Jour. 1992-95, mem. Ho. of Dels. 1993-96, vice chair bylaws com. govt. and pub. sector lawyer's divsn. 1993-95, vice chmn. young lawyer divn. publs. com. 1995-96, vice chair women in the profession com. 1994-95, judge awards of achievement com. 1992-95, mem. exec. coun. young lawyer's divsn. 1993-95, 4th dist. rep., mem. membership com. sect. real property probate trust law, 1995-96, liaison, 1995-97, vice chair publ. com. 1995-96, mem. editl. bd. sect. pub. utility comm. transp. law 1996—), Fed. Energy Bar Assn., Phi Alpha Delta. Office: NY Power Authority 1633 Broadway New York NY 10019-6708

KNACKSTEDT, JUDY M. secondary school educator; b. Ill., Feb. 25, 1943; d. George John and Mae Ella Kastigar; m. Frank Rudolph Knackstedt, Oct. 11, 1970 (div. Mar. 1999); 1 child, Timothy Frederick. AA, Ill. Valley C.C., Oglesby, 1992; BS in Edn., Ill. State U., 1994, MS in Edn., 1998, admin. cert., 2002. Cosmetologist, Peru, Ill., 1968—70; singer, keyboard player various locations, 1970—78; realtor Malooley's Real Estate Agy., Peru, 1979—81; spl. edn. tchr.'s aide Peru Dist. #124, 1982—94; spl. edn. tchr. Midland H.S., Varna, Ill., 1994—. Tech. prep coord. Tech Prep Assn., Varna, Ill., 1998—; transfer mentor Ill. State U., Normal, 1994. Songwriter: Autumn of My Life, 1973. Telethon vol. Muscular Dystrophy Assn., LaSalle-Peru, Ill.; summer softball mgr., coach, league rep. Peru Girls' Softball, 1984—96, invitational tournament coord., dir., 1984—96. Scholar Spl. Edn. scholar, State of Ill., 1992. Mem.: Coun. for Exceptional Children, Ill. Prins. Assn., Golden Key, Alpha Chi, Red Tassel Mortar Bd. Avocations: computer research, home repair projects, furniture refinishing, hunting, singing. Home: 2330 Main St Peru IL 61354 Office: Midland High Sch 1830 State Rt 17 Varna IL 61375

KNACKSTEDT, MARY V. interior designer; b. Harrisburg, Pa., Oct. 26, 1940; d. Harry and Veronica Knackstedt. Student, Pratt Inst., 1957-59, Cooper Union, Phila. Coll. Art. Pres. Knackstedt Inc., Harrisburg, N.Y.C., 1958—. Mem. adv. bd. PNC Bank, N.A., Camp Hill, Pa., 1981—; pvt. practice cons.; speaker in field; lectr. bus. practices Harvard U., 1988—. Author: Interior Dsign for Profit, 1980, Profitable Career Options for Designers, 1985, The Interior Design Business Handbook, 1988, 92, Marketing and Design Services: The Designer Client Rlationship, 1993, Interior Design and Beyond, 1995; interior design projects include Hershey Med. Ctr., Milton Hershey Sch., founder's Hall, Hershey, Pa., The Hershey Pub. Libr. Bus. devel. program founder Riverfront Peoples Park, Harrisburg, 1980-90; bd. dirs. Harrisburg Symphony Assn., 1983-89; founder, pres. Profl. Cath. Women's Forum; devel. coun. Bishop McDevitt Sch., Harrisburg. Fellow Internat. Interior Design Assn., Am. Soc. Interior Designers (past officer); mem. Internat. Furnishings and Design Assn., Illuminating Engring. Soc. N.Am., Interior Design Soc., Pres.'s Assn., Am. Mgmt. Assn. Home and Office: 2901 N Front St Harrisburg PA 17110-1223 Address: 161 E 61st St New York NY 10021-8125

KNAPP, CANDACE LOUISE, sculptor; b. Benton Harbor, Mich., Feb. 28, 1948; d. Claire Warren and Frances Mary (Collins) K.; m. Björn Andrén, Mar. 3, 1988. BFA, Cleve. Inst. Art, 1971; MFA, U. Ill., 1974. Sculptures exhibited in numerous galleries; represented in permanent collections including Northwood Inst. Collection, West Palm Beach, Fla., Memphis Brooks Mus. Art, Mobil Oil Co., Stockholm, HageGården Music Ctr., Edane, Sweden, others; included in book Contemporary American Women Sculptors; numerous commns. including St. Peter and Paul Cath. Ch., Orlando, Fla., Padre Pio Found., Cromwell, Conn., Temple Emanuel, Dallas, West Haven, Conn., Tampa (Fla.) Gen. Hosp., Pub. Art Commn. City of St. Petersburg, Fla., Pub. Art Commn. Hillsborough County Courthouse, Tampa, Fla. Helen Greene Perry traveling scholar, 1971. Fax: 813-654-6572. E-mail: aok@andoknap.com.

KNAPP, DONNA LONG, music educator; b. Atlanta, May 20, 1950; d. Dallas Lloyd and Geraldine Mays Long, Sr.; m. Dale Howard Knapp, June 24, 1978; children: Deborah Lauren, Megan Marie. MusB in Edn. cum laude, U. of Ga., 1973; MusM in Edn., Ga. State U., 1976. Music tchr. Gwinnett County Sch. Sys., Lawrenceville, Ga., 1990—; clarinet tchr. Ga. Perimeter Coll., Clarkston, Ga., 2002—. Dir. Smoke Rise Handbells, Stone Mountain, Ga., 1997—2003. Choir mem., ensemble mem., orch. mem. Smoke Rise Bapt. Ch., Stone Mountain, Ga.; chairperson, founding bd. dirs. Smoke Rise Acad. Arts, 1993. Recipient Hutchenson Citizenship award, Rainbow Pk. Bapt. Ch., 1990. Mem.: Atlanta Orff Soc., Am. Choral Dirs. Assn., Ga. Music Educators Assn., Nat. Assn. for Music Edn., Kappa Kappa Iota (hon.; pres. 1987—88).

KNAPP, ELLEN M. financial company executive; 2 children. BS, U. SC, 1974. With Computer Scis. Corp. NASA Goddard Space Fligth Ctr.; with Booz-Allen & Hamilton; vice chmn., tech. Coopers & Lybrand, N.Y.C., 1992—98; chief knowledge officer, global CIO PriceWaterhouse Coopers, N.Y.C., 1998—. Mem. bd. assessment Nat. Rsch. Coun.; session chmn. Internat. Conf. on Future of Industry in Advanced Socs. MIT; guest lectr. Columbia U., Dartmouth U., Oxford U.; juror Lemelson-MIT award for Invention and Innovation, 1996, 97; keynote spkr. 10 Anniversary Symposium computer sci. and telecomms. bd. NAS, 1996; keynote spkr. numerous confs. Co-author: Every Manager's Guide to Business Processes, 1995; contbr. articles, chapters to books. Office: PriceWaterHouseCoopers 1301 Ave of Ams New York NY 10019-6022*

KNAPP, MILDRED FLORENCE, retired social worker; b. Detroit, Apr. 15, 1932; d. Edwin Frederick and Florence Josephine (Antaya) K. BBA, U. Mich., 1954, MA in Cmty. and Adult Edn., 1964, MSW, 1967. Dist. dir. Girl Scouts Met. Detroit, 1954-63; planning asst. Coun. Social Agys. Flint and Genessee County, 1965; sch. social worker Detroit Pub. Schs., 1967-98; field instr. grad. social workers. Mem. alumnae bd. govs. U. Mich., 1972-75, scholarship chmn., 1969-70 76-80, chair spl. com. women's athletics, 1972-75, class agt. fund raising Sch. Bus. Adminstrn., 1978-79; mem. Founders Soc. Detroit Inst. Art, 1969—, Friends Children's Mus. Detroit, 1978— Women's Assn., Detroit Symphony Orch., 1982-89, Mich. Humane Soc., 1991—; vol. Coun. Detroit Symphony Orch., 1990—; trustee, fin. chmn. Children's Mus. Recipient Appreciation cert.; Mott Found. fellow, 1964; HEW grantee, 1966. Mem. NASW, Acad. Cert. Social Workers, Nat. Cmty. Edn. Assn. (charter), Sch. Social Work Assn. Am. (charter), Outdoor Edn. and Camping Coun. (charter), Mich. Sch. Social Workers Assn. (pres. 1980-81), Detroit Sch. Social Workers Assn. (past pres.), Detroit Assn. U. Mich. Women (pres. 1980-82), Detroit Fedn. Tchrs., Madame Alexander Doll Club. Methodist. Home: 702 Lakepointe St Grosse Pointe Park MI 48230-1706

KNAPP, ROSALIND ANN, lawyer; b. Washington, Aug. 15, 1945; d. Joseph Burke and Hilary (Eaves) K. BA, Stanford U., 1967, JD, 1973. Bar: Calif. 1973, D.C. 1980. With U.S. Dept. Transp., Washington, 1973—, asst. gen. counsel legislation, 1979-81, dep. gen. counsel, 1981—. Mem. D.C. Bar Assn., Calif. Bar Assn. Office: Dept Transp Office of the General Counsel 400 7th St SW Washington DC 20590-0003 E-mail: lindy.knapp@ost.dot.gov.

KNAPP, VIRGINIA ESTELLA, retired secondary education educator; b. Washington, May 11, 1919; d. Bradford and Stella (White) Knapp; BA, Tex. Tech. U., 1940; MA, U. Tex. 1948; postgrad. Sul Ross Coll., 1950, Stephen F. Austin U., 1964-68. Tchr. journalism, high schs., Silverton, Tex., 1940-41, Electra, Tex., 1941-42, Joinerville, Tex., 1942-60, Carthage, Tex., 1961-69; tchr. history and journalism Longview (Tex.) High Sch., 1969-80; instr. Trinity U., San Antonio, summer 1972; fellowship tchr. Wall St. Jour., Tex. A&M U., College Station, summers 1964-67. Chmn., Rusk County (Tex.) Hist. Commn., 1980—2002; pres. Rusk County Hist. Found.; mem. Henderson Main St. Bd. Recipient Wall St. Jour. award Outstanding Journalism Tchrs. of Yr., 1965-66; Trail Blazer award Tex. High Sch. Press Assn., 1980; Woman of Yr. award, 1983. Mem. Tex. State Tchrs. Assn., Classroom Tchrs. Assn., Tex. Assn. Jour. Dirs., Rusk County Heritage Assn., Rusk County Hist. Commn., Women in Communications (pres. Longview chpt. 1972-74, Service award 1975), Tex. Press Women, bd-.member Gaston Mus. (finance chmn.) . Episcopalian. Contbr. hist. writing to Ala. Rev., Progressive Farmer, Rusk County C. of C. Brochure, Rusk County Heritage, numerous others. Home: 1802 Elm St Apt 301 Henderson TX 75652-6256 Office: 514 N High St Henderson TX 75652-5912

KNAUER, VIRGINIA HARRINGTON (MRS. WILHELM F. KNAUER), consumer consultant, former government official; b. Phila., Mar. 28, 1915; d. Herman Winfield and Helen (Harrington) Wright; m. Wilhelm F. Knauer, Jan. 27, 1940; children: Wilhelm F., Valerie H. (Mrs. I. Townsend Burden III). BFA, U. Pa., 1937; grad., Pa. Acad. Fine Arts, 1937; postgrad., Royal Acad. Fine Arts, Florence, Italy, 1938-39; LL.D. (hon.), Phila. Coll. Textiles and Sci., St. Francis de Sales, Widener Coll., Chester, Pa., Tufts U.; Litt.D. (hon.), Drexel U.; L.H.D. (hon.), Russell Sage Coll., Pa. Coll. Podiatric Medicine; L.H.D., Jacksonville U.; LLD (hon.), U. Pa., 1971. Dir. Pa. Bur. Consumer Protection, 1968-69; spl. asst. to Pres. for consumer affairs The White House, 1969-77; dir. U.S. Office Consumer Affairs, Washington, 1971-77, 81-88; spl. adv. to Pres. for consumer affairs The White House, 1981-88; chair ABRH Inc., Washington, 1988-91; consumer cons. Haney and Knauer, Inc., Washington, 1991-93. Pres. Virginia Knauer & Assocs., Inc., Washington, 1977-81; chmn. Coun. for Advancement of Consumer Policy, 1979-81; U.S. rep., vice chmn. consumer policy com. OECD, 1970-77, 81-88; mem. Coun. Wage and Price Stability, 1974-77; vice-chmn. Philadelphia County Rep. Com., 1958-77; pres. Phila. Congress Rep. Women's Councils, 1958-77; dir. Pa. Coun. Rep. Women, 1963-80; founder N.E. Phila. Coun. Rep. Women, pres., 1956-68 Bd. dirs. Hannah Penn House, 1956—, v.p., 1971; chmn. Knauer Found. Hist. Preservation, 1963—; nat. chmn. to promote no fault automobile ins. Project New Start, 1988-91; bd. dirs. Nat. Coalition for Cancer Survivorship; mem. city coun., Phila., Pa., 1960-68. Recipient Gimbel-Phila. award, 1977, Ind. Achievement in Govt. award Soc. Consumer Affairs Profls., 1983; named Disting. Dau. Pa., 1969; named to Disting. Women's Com., Northwood U., 1997. Mem. Nat. Trust Hist. Preservation, Am. Assn. Ret. Persons, Internat. Neighbors Club, Exec. Women in Govt., Penn Women (trustees coun.), Consumers for World Trade (bd. dirs.), Zeta Tau Alpha, Kappa Delta Epsilon (hon.). Episcopalian.

KNEAVEL, ANN CALLANAN, humanities educator, communications consultant; b. Balt., Oct. 29, 1946; d. James Michael and Ann (Ijams) Callanan; m. Thomas Charles Kneavel, Jr., Dec. 18, 1970; children: Meredith Elizabeth, Thomas Charles III, Rebecca Ann. BA, Coll. Notre Dame Md., 1968; MA in Am. Lit., U. Md., 1970; PhD in Modern Brit. Lit., U. Ottawa, Ont., Can., 1979. Instr. U. Md., College Park, 1968-71, U. Ottawa, 1971-72, Wilmington (Del.) Coll., 1976-79, Del. Tech. and C.C., Dover, 1975-79; asst. prof. Widener U., Chester, Pa., 1981-82; prof. Goldey-Beacom Coll., Wilmington, Del., 1981—; dir. satellite campuses Total Quality Master's Program, Falmouth, Mass., 1995—. Contbr. articles to profl. jours. Trustee Hockessin (Del.) Pub. Libr., 1981-93, Alpha Tau Omega Fraternity, Wilmington, 1994—; mem. Friends of Hockessin Libr., 1981—. Mem. MLA, Nat. Coun. Tchrs. English, Conf. on Christianity and Lit., Am. Culture Assn., C.C. Humanities Assn., Alpha Chi (faculty sponsor, Svc. award 1994, v.p. region VI 2000-02, pres. region VI, 2002-04, nat. coun. 2003—), Nat. Coun. 2003-. Roman Catholic. Home: 7 Arthur Dr Hockessin DE 19707-1012 Office: Goldey-Beacom Coll 4701 Limestone Rd Wilmington DE 19808-1927 E-mail: kneavela@gbc.edu

KNEE, RUTH IRELAN (MRS. JUNIOR K. KNEE), social worker, health care consultant; b. Sapulpa, Okla., Mar. 21, 1920; d. Oren M. and Daisy (Daubin) Irelan; m. Junior K. Knee, May 29, 1943 (dec. Oct. 1981). BA, U. Okla., 1941, cert. social work, 1942; MA in Social Svcs. Adminstrn., U. Chgo., 1945. Psychiat. social worker, asst. supr. Ill. Psychiat. Inst., U. Ill., Chgo., 1943-44; psychiat. social worker USPHS Employee Health Unite, Washington, 1944—49; social work assoc. Army Med. Ctr., Walter Reed Army Hosp., Washington, 1949-54; psychiat. social work cons.. HEW, Region III, Washington, 1955-56; with NIMH, Chevy Chase, Md., 1956-72; chief mental health care adminstrn. br. Health Svcs. and Mental Health Adminstrn., USPHS assoc. dep. adminstr., 1972-73; dep. dir. Office of Nursing Home Affairs, 1973-74; long-term mental health care cons.; mem. com. on mental health and illness of elderly HEW, 1976-77; mem. panel on legal and ethical issues Pres.'s Commn. on Mental Health, 1977-78; liaison mem. Nat. Adv. Mental Health Coun., 1977-81. Mem. editl. bd. Health and Social Work, 1979-81. Bd. dirs. Hillhaven Found., 1975-86, governing bd. Cathedral Coll. of the Laity, Washington Nat. Cathedral, 1988-94, Cathedral Fund Com., 1997—,bd. of visitors sch. of social work, Univ. of Okla., 2000— Recipient Edith Abbott award, U. Chgo. Sch. Social Svc. Adminstrn., 2001, Disting. Alumna award, U. Okla. Coll. Arts and Scis., 1999. Fellow APHA (sec. mental health sect. 1968-70, chmn. 1971-72), Am. Orthopsychiat. Assn. (life), Gerontol. Soc. Am., Am. Assn. Psychiat. Social Workers (pres. 1951-53); mem. Nat. Conf. Social Welfare (nat. bd. 1968-71, 2d v.p. 1973-74), Inst. Medicine/NAS (com. study future of pub. health 1986-87), Coun. on Social Work Edn., Nat. Assn. Social Workers (sec. 1955-56, nat. dir. 1956-57, 84-86, chmn. competence study com., practice and knowledge com. 1963-71, presdl. award for exemplary svc. 1999), Acad. Cert. Social Workers (NASW Found. co-chair social work pioneers 1993—), Am. Pub. Welfare Assn., DAR, U. Okla. Assocs., Woman's Nat. Dem. Club (mem. gov. bd. 1992-95, ednl. found. bd. 1992-2000), Cosmos Club (Washington, chair program com. 1998-2001), Phi Beta Kappa (fellow), Psi Chi. Address: 8809 Arlington Blvd Fairfax VA 22031-2705

KNEPEL, NANCY, school librarian; m. Robert Knepel, Dec. 31, 1976. BA, U. Wis., Oshkosh, 1973; MLIS, U. Wis., Milw., 1978. Libr. Ethan Allen Sch., Wales, Wis., 1974—80; cons. Colo. State Libr., Denver, 1980—83; dir. High Plains Regional Libr. Sys., Greeley, Colo., 1983—99; sch. libr. media specialist Northglenn (Colo.) Mid. Sch., 1999—. Office: Northglenn Middle Sch 1123 Muriel Dr Northglenn CO 80233

KNEZO, GENEVIEVE JOHANNA, science and technology policy researcher; b. Aug. 8, 1942; d. John and Genevieve (Sadowski) K.; 1 child, Alexandra M. AB in Polit. Sci., Rutgers U., 1964; MA in Sci., Tech. and Pub. Policy, George Washington U., 1981; grad., Nat. Def. U., 1989. With Congl. Rsch. Svc. Libr. of Congress, Washington, 1967—, specialist in sci. and tech., 1979—, head sci., rsch. and tech. sect., 1986-88, sr. level specialist in sci. and tech. policy, 1991—. Author profl. publs. Mem. Phi Beta Kappa, Pi Sigma Alpha. Avocations: white-water canoeing, hiking, gymnastics, classical music, community volunteer activities. Home: 606 Oakley Pl Alexandria VA 22302-3611 Office: Libr of Congress Congl Rsch Svc Resources Sci/Indust Divsn Washington DC 20540-7450 E-mail: gknezo@crs.loc.gov.

KNICKEL, CARIN S. oil industry executive; b. Powell, Wyo. BA in Mktg. and Stats., U. Colo.; M.Mgmt., MIT. Mktg. account mgr. Conoco-Phillips, 1979—87, area dir. light oil sales product supply and trading, 1987, gen. mgr. bus. develop. for refining and mktg. in Europe, gen. mgr. refining, mktg., and transp., pres. specialty bus. divsn., 2001—03, v.p. human resources, 2003—. Chmn. rodeo run com. ConocoPhillips; bd. dirs. Colo. Spl. Olympics. Office: ConocoPhillips 600 N Dairy Ashford Rd Houston TX 77079*

KNIERIEM, BEULAH WHITE, retired elementary school educator, minister; b. Appomattox, Va., Oct. 31, 1930; d. George Harrison and Virgie Ade (Kestner) White; m. Robert William Knieriem, July 11, 1953; children: Shawn, Roxanne (dec.), Roberta. AA, Mars Hill (N.C.) Coll., 1950; BA, Lynchburg (Va.) Coll., 1952; student, Baldwin-Wallace Coll., 1964-69, Ashland Sem., 1992-93. Lic. elem. tchr., Ohio; lic. to ministry, 1995. Tchr. Bd. Edn., Cleve., 1966-79; lifetime Stephen min. United Ch. of Christ, Cleve., 1990—; interim min., 1997—99; pastor Litchfield United Ch. of Christ, Ohio, 1999—. Min. nursing homes, Cleve., 1990—; chaplain Ky. Cols., 1990—. Democrat. Avocation: running. Home: 7324 Grant Blvd Cleveland OH 44130-5351

KNIESER, CATHERINE, music educator; b. Seoul, Republic of Korea, Aug. 12, 1974; d. Thomas and Susan Knieser. MusB, U. Del., 1997; MusM, Ithaca Coll., 2000. Cert. tchr. N.Y., Nat. Bd. Early Adolescent through Young Adulthood, 2003. Tchr.-in-charge, secondary music Wappingers Ctrl. Sch. Dist., Wappingers Falls, NY, 1999—. Grantee Latin Percussion Mini grant, Wappingers Ctrl. Sch. Dist., 1998—99, African Music Mini grant, Mid Hudson Tchr. Ctr., 1999—2000, Tech. Digital grant, Wappingers Ctrl. Sch. Dist., 2002—. Mem.: N.Y. State Sch. Music Assn., Music Educators Nat. Conf., Am. Orff-Schulwerk Assn., Sigma Alpha Iota (life). Personal E-mail: krabaple@vh.net.

KNIFFIN, PAULA SICHEL, insurance sales executive; b. N.Y.C., Oct. 2, 1941; d. Harold M. and Edith (Sachnoff) Sichel; m. Richrd G. Kniffin, Aug. 3, 1963; children: Douglas, Kelly. BA, Bucknell U., 1963. CLU; cert. fin. planner. Tchr. New Cumberland (Pa.) Jr. High Sch., 1963-64, Meadowbrook Jr. High Sch., East Meadow, N.Y., 1964-67; real estate salesperson Claire Sobel Real Estate, Syosset, N.Y., 1979-80; sales force recruiter Mut. of N.Y. Life Ins. Co., Jericho, 1981-82; head of life and health ins. dept., employee benefit cons. The Viking Agy., Inc., Syosset, N.Y., 1983—. Mem. Soc. Fin. Svc. Profls., Fin. Planning Assn., Women Life Underwriters Conf. (pres. 1988-89), Nat. Assn. Ins. and Fin. Advisors (bd. dirs. 1988-89), Nat. Assn. Ins. and Fin. Advisors, Ladies Golf Com. (chair 1990-93), Nassau Country Club, Mayacoo Lakes Country Club. Republican. Avocations: golf, tennis, bridge, reading. Office: The Viking Agy 117 Oak Dr Syosset NY 11791-4625 E-mail: paula@vikingagency.com.

KNIGHT, ATHELIA WILHELMENIA, journalist; b. Portsmouth, Va., Oct. 15, 1950; d. Daniel Dennis and Adell Virginia (Savage) K. BA with honors in English, Norfolk State Coll., 1973; MA with honors in Journalism, Ohio State U., 1974. Cert. tchr., Va. Aide D.C. Coop. Extension Service, 1969-72; sub. tchr. Portsmouth Pub. Schs., 1973; reporter Virginian Pilot, Norfolk, 1973, Chgo. Tribune, 1974; met. desk reporter Washington Post, 1975-81, investigative reporter, 1981-94, sports writer, 1994-2000; asst. dir. Washington Post Young Journalists, 2000—03, dir., 2003; adj. prof. Georgetown U., 2002—. Vis. prof. journalism Hampton U., 2001. Mem. Herb Block Found. Recipient Mark Twain award, 1982, 87, Front Page award Washington-Balt. Newspaper Guild, 1982, Nat. award for edn. Edn. Writers Assn., 1987, Pub. Svc. award Md.-Del.-D.C. Press Assn., 1990, 93, 1st Pl. award for spot news, 1997; Ohio State U. fellow, 1974, Nieman fellow Harvard U., 1985-86. Maynard Mgmt. at the Kellogg Sch. of Mgmt. N.W. U., 2003. Mem.: Assn. Women in Sports Media, Investigative Reporters and Editors, Nat. Assn. Black Journalists, Women in Comm. Methodist. Office: Washington Post 1150 15th St NW Washington DC 20071-0002

KNIGHT, BETTY ANN, county commissioner; b. Brunswick, Mo., Sept. 2, 1947; d. George William and Elizabeth (Miles) James; m. William M. Knight, Jan. 26, 1969; children: Michelle Ann, Carrie Shea. BS, U. Mo., 1969. Cert. real estate agt., Mo.; cert. securities specialist Nat. Assn. Securities Dealers; cert. ins. agt., Mo. Real estate agt. ERA MH Realty, Platte City, Mo., 1984-85; paraplanner IDS Fin. Svcs., Platte City, Mo., 1986-89; dep. treas. Platte County, 1989-94, presiding commr., 1995—. Treas., bd dirs. James' Pecan Farms, Inc., Brunswick, Mo., 1969—; bd. dirs. U. Mo. Ext. Coun., Platte City, 1995-99, Kansas City Internat./Northland C. of C., Kansas City, Clay/Platte Devel. Coun., Kansas City; chmn. Emergency Preparedness, Platte County, 1995—; bd. dirs. Mid-Am. Regional Coun., Kansas City, 1995—, 1st vice chair, 1997-98, chair, 1999—; bd. dirs. Mo. Assn. Counties, Jefferson City, 1995—, treas., 1998, 3d v.p., 1999. Arts chmn. Platte City Elem. PTA, 1984-89; leader Brownie Troop, Platte City, 1985-86; mem. Platte City Bus. and Profl. Women, 1987-90; mem. Mo./Nat. Rep. Parties, 1989—, Federated Rep. Women, Platte County, 1990—, Platte Rep. Assn., 1989—, Eleemonsynary Soc., Platte County, 1993—; bd. dirs. Platte County Econ. Devel. Coun., Kansas City, 1995—, Platte County Sch. Bd., 1992-95, Platte City Plan and Zoning, 1991; bd. dirs., sec. Platte City Ath. Assn., 1990-92; active Synergy Svcs. Comm. Adv. Bd., St. Luke's Northland Strategic Planning Adv. Bd. Mem. Mo. County Commrs., N.W. Commrs., Platte County Women's Exch. (pres., treas. 1989—, Leadership award 1992, Woman of Yr. 1993), Platte County Hist. Soc., Parkville Rotary, 1st Class County Caucus, U. Mo. Alumni Assn., Parkville Fine Arts Assn. Methodist. Avocations: collector (eggs, elephants, Republican memoribilia), travel, sports (Kansas City Chiefs and Univ. Mo. Tigers). Home: PO Box 1188 Platte City MO 64079-1188

KNIGHT, CONSTANCE BRACKEN, writer, realtor, corporate executive; b. Detroit, Oct. 30, 1937; d. Thomas Francis and Margaret (Kearney) Bracken; m. James Edwards Knight, June 14, 1958 (div. Feb. 1968); children: Constance Lynne Knight Campbell, James Seaton, Keith Bracken. Student, Barry Coll., 1955-56, Fla. State U., 1958-60; AA, Marymount Coll., 1957. Columnist, feature writer Miami Herald, Ft. Lauderdale, Fla., 1954-55, 79-80; pub. rels. dir. Lauderdale Beach Hotel, 1965-67; columnist, feature writer Ft. Lauderdale News/Sun-Sentinel, 1980-81; owner Connie Knight and Assoc. Pub. Rels., Ft. Lauderdale, 1981-85; editor, pub. Vail (Colo.) Mag., 1986-89, contbg. freelance writer, 1989—; editorial cons. Vail Valley Mag., 1993; pres. Knight Enterprises, Vail, 1994—; photojournalist Denver Post, 1999—. Instr. Colo. Mountain Coll., Vail, 1979. Mem. Planning and Environ. Commn., Vail, 1990-92, Vail Licensing Authority, 1995—. Mem. N.Am. Snowsport Assn. Journalists (treas. 1990-93). Office: 385 Gore Creek Dr Ste 201 Vail CO 81657-3606 E-mail: cknight@vail.net.

KNIGHT, GLADYS (GLADYS MARIA KNIGHT), singer; b. Atlanta, May 28, 1944; d. Merald and Elizabeth (Woods) Knight, Sr.; m. Barry Hankerson, Oct. 1974 (div. 1979); 1 child, Shanga Hankerson ; m. William McDowell, Apr. 2001. Grad. coll.; degree (hon.), Shaw U. Author: lyrics Way Back Home, others; first pub. recital, Mt. Mariah Bapt. Ch., Atlanta, 1948, toured with Morris Brown Choir, 1950-53, recitals local chs. and schs., 1950-53; winner grand prize Ted Mack's Amateur Hour 1952; jazz vocalist, Lloyd Terry Jazz Ltd., 1959-61, mem. Gladys Knight and the Pips (formerly Pips Quartet), 1953—, concert appearances in Eng., 1967, 72, 73, 76, Australia, Japan, Hong Kong, Manila, 1976; rec. artist, Brunswick, 1957-61, Fury, 1961-62, Everlast, 1963, Maxx and Bell, 1964-66, Motown, 1966-73, Buddah, Capitol, Columbia, MCA, 1988; albums with the Pips include Best of Gladys Knight and the Pips, All the Great Hits, If I Were Your Woman, 1989, Soul Survivors: The Best of Gladys Knight and the Pips 1973-1988, 1990, Blue Lights in the Basement, 1996, Imagination, 1996, The Lost Live Albums, 1996; solo album Good Woman, 1991; TV appearance Charlie & Co., 1985; produced, appeared in HBO film Sisters in the Name of Love, 1986. Winner 6 gold Buddah records, 1 gold, 1 platinum Buddah album; 4 Grammy awards; named Top Female Vocalist, Blues and Soul mag. 1972; spl. award Washington City Coun. for inspiration to youth in city, 1972; other awards include Clio, AGVA, NAACP Image, Ebony Music, Cashbox, Billboard, Record World, Rolling Stone, Ladies Home Jour., Am. Music award (with Pips), 1984, 1988, Core award B'nai B'rith award; inducted into Rock and Roll Hall of Fame, 1996. Address: Care Shakeji Inc 3221 LaMirada Ave Las Vegas NV 89120

KNIGHT, KAREN ANNE MCGEE, artist, educator; b. Florence, Ala., July 5, 1956; d. Glenn Houston and Juanita May (Fowler) McGee; m. Charles Ronald Knight, June 3, 1980; 1 child, Lara-Elizabeth. AA, Fla. Coll., 1976; BS, U. N. Ala., 1978, MA in Edn., 1994. Cert. tchr., Tenn., Ala. Title I reading aide Florence City Schs., 1978—79, 1st grade tchr., 1980—83; pre-kindergarten tchr. Belmont Weekday Sch., Nashville, 1984—85; kindergarten tchr. Metro-Davidson County Schs., Nashville, 1985—87; freelance watercolorist Shoals Artist's Guild, Florence, 1992—, Westat/quality control monitor, 1997—98, Westat/assessment adminstr., 1998—2001, Westat/field supr., 2001—. Chair Shoals Artists Guild, 1993—, v.p., 1996, pres., 1998. Sunday sch. tchr. Placed in watercolor competition N. Ala. State Fair, 1993. Mem. Nat. Mus. Women in Arts, Watercolor Soc. Ala. (N.W. Ala. area rep. 1996—), Tenn. Valley Art Assn., So. Watercolor Soc., Tenn. Valley Art Assn. Guild. Avocations: herb and perennial gardening, genealogy. Home: 111 Snell Dr Florence AL 35630-6257

KNIGHT, LINDA K. financial company executive; With Fed. Nat. Mortgage Assn., Washington, 1982—, v.p., asst. treas., 1986—92, sr. v.p., treas., 1993—. Office: Fed Nat Mortgage Assn 3900 Wisconsin Ave NW Washington DC 20016-2806

KNIGHT, NORMAH LOUISE, artist; b. Dallas, July 25, 1910; d. Edward Elbert Alcott and Floy Effie Hamilton; m. Bob Moore Knight, Mar. 11, 1929 (dec.); children: Bob, Roberta Knight Fogle. Student, Dallas Acad. Fine Art, 1927, So. Meth. U., 1930-31, Julian Acad., Paris, 1955, Schuler Sch. Fine Art, Balt., 1988-91. Tchr. art Harlingen (Tex.) Pub. Schs., 1931-32; artist head Cultural Arts Program for Tex. in Rio Grande Valley, 1934-44; owner, operator art gallery and sch., Harlingen, 1948-68; represented by Normah Knight Art Gallery Sch. of Art, 1949—. One woman shows at Elisbet Ney Mus., 1941, Coun. Am. Artists, 1966, Tex. Fedn. Women's Club, 1959; exhibited in group shows Smithsonian Instn., Washington, World's Fair, Brussels; mural executed San Benito Bank and Trust Co., Harlingen, 1951; represented in permanent collection VA, Washington; also cos. Mem. Am. Profl. Artists League, Rio Grande Valley Art League (founder). Home: 2101 Treasure Hills Blvd Harlingen TX 78550-8714

KNIGHT, PATRICIA MARIE, medical device researcher, consultant; b. Schnectady, N.Y., Jan. 25, 1952; BS in Engring. Sci., Ariz. State U., 1974, MSChemE, 1976; PhD in Biomed. Engring., U. Utah, 1983. Teaching and rsch. asst. Ariz. State U., Tempe, 1974-76; product devel. engr. Am. Med. Optics, Irvine, Calif., 1976-79, mgr. materials rsch., 1983-87; rsch. asst. U. Utah, Salt Lake City, 1979-83; dir. materials rsch. Allergan Surg. Products, Irvine, 1987-88, dir. rsch., 1988-91, v.p. rsch., devel. and engring., 1991—2002; v.p. rsch., devel. Advanced Med. Optics, Santa Ana, Calif., 2002—03; cons. biomed. product rsch. and devel. Laguna Niguel, Calif., 2003—. Contbr. articles to profl. jours. Mem. Soc. Biomaterials, Am. Chem. Soc., Soc. Women Engrs., Assn. Rsch. in Vision and Opthalmology, Biomed. Engring. Soc. E-mail: pkbiomed@cox.net.

KNIGHT, SHERRY ANN, art educator; b. Wash., Pa., July 8, 1955; d. Bernard P. and Angela Bernotas Miller; m. Kent Richard Knight, Jan. 2, 1980. BA, Carlow Coll., Pitts., 1977; EdM, U. Pitts., 1979. Cert. secondary principal Pa. Adj. prof. C.C. Allegheny County, Pitts., 1982—89; tchr. visual arts Trinity HS, Wash., Pa., 1977—. Sec. Pa. Coalition Arts in Edn., 1992—98; advisor and sec. Warhol Mus., Pitts., 2002—. Contbr. photographs Dog Fancy mag., 1998, articles to art pubs. Bd. sec. Pa. Crimestoppers, Wash., Pa., 1994—98; pres. bd. dirs. Pet Search, Wash., Pa., 1996—, People Animal Welfare, Wash., Pa., 1986—96. Named Outstanding Art Educator, Pa. Coalition Arts in Edn., 1996. Mem.: Assn. Artists of Pa., Pa. Coun. Arts, Pa. Arts Edn. Assn. (registration chair 1977—, Secondary Art Educator 2001). Democrat. Roman Catholic. Achievements include 4 copyrights for art. Avocations: animals, skiing, reading, museums, gardening. Home: 257 Point View Dr Washington PA 15301 Office: Trinity Area HS 231 Park Ave Washington PA 15301 E-mail: ksam10@pulsenet.com.

KNIGHT, SHIRLEY, actress; b. Goessel, Kans., July 5, 1936; d. Noel Johnson and Virginia (Webster) K.; m. John R. Hopkins; children: Kaitlin, Sophie. D.F.A., Lake Forest Coll., 1978. Actress theatre and films. Theater debut in Look Back in Anger, Pasadena (Calif.) Playhouse, 1958, N.Y.C. debut in Journey to the Day, 1963; other N.Y.C. theater appearances include The Three Sisters, 1964, Rooms, 1966, We Have Always Lived in the Castle, 1966, The Watering Place, 1969, Kennedy's Children, 1975 (Tony award), Happy End, 1977; with Bristol (Eng.) Old Vic Theatre in And People All Around, 1967; other appearances in Eng. include A Touch of the Poet, 1970, Antigone, 1971, Economic Necessity, 1973; other U.S. theater appearances include A Streetcar Named Desire, Princeton, N.J., 1976, Happy End, N.Y.C., 1977, Landscape of the Body, Chgo., then N.Y.C., 1977, A Lovely Sunday for Creve Coeur, Charleston, S.C., then N.Y.C., 1979, Losing Time, N.Y.C., 1979, I Won't Dance, Buffalo, 1980, Come Back Little Sheba, N.Y.C., 1984, Women Heroes, N.Y.C., 1986, The Depot, N.Y.C., 1987; film appearances include Five Gates to Hell, 1959, The Dark at the Top of the Stairs, 1960, Sweet Bird of Youth, 1962, House of Women, 1962, Flight from Ashiya, 1964, The Group, 1966, Petulia, 1966, Dutchman, 1967, The Rain People, 1969, The Counterfeit Killer, 1970, Juggernaut, 1974, Beyond the Poseidon Adventure, 1979, Endless Love, 1981, The Sender, 1982, Diabolique, 1996, As Good as it Gets, 1997; TV films include The Outsider, 1967, Shadow Over Elveron, 1968, Friendly Persuasion, 1975, Medical Story, 1975, Return to Earth, 1976, The Defection of Simas Kudirka, 1978, Champions: A Love Story, 1979, Playing for Time, 1980, With Intent to Kill, 1984, Indictment: The McMartin Trial, 1995 (Emmy award). Active Com. for Handgun Control, nat. civil rights orgns., worker for peace. Recipient Tony award (Antoinette Perry for Supporting or Featured Actress), 1976, Emmy award for Outstanding Guest Performer in Comedy Drama or Series, 1988, Emmy award for Outstanding Guest Performer in a Drama Series (NYPD Blue), 1995. Office: Gersh (New York) 130 W 42nd St Ste 1804 New York NY 10036-7901

KNIPP, JENNY L. science educator; b. Morehead, Ky., Feb. 9, 1968; d. Tommy R. Kiser and Billye L. Hawes; m. Charles R. Knipp, May 23, 1992; children: Tyberius, Alexandria. BA, Morehead State U., 1991, MEd, 1998, postgrad., 2003. Tchr. sci. Gallatin County Mid. Sch., Ky., 1992—93, McKell Mid. Sch., Greenup, Ky., 1996—98, West Carter Mid. Sch., Olive Hill, Ky., 1998—. Mem.: NSTA. Home: PO Box 1166 Olive Hill KY 41164*

KNIPPERS, DIANE LEMASTERS, association executive; b. Rushville, Ind., Jan. 6, 1952; m. Edward C. Knippers, Jr. BA in History, Asbury Coll., 1972; MA in Sociology, U. Tenn., 1974. Teaching asst. U. Tenn., 1972-73; assoc. editor, asst. editor, editorial asst. Good News Mag., 1974-80, assoc. exec. sec., editor, 1980-82; exec. v.p., deputy dir., program dir., dir. orgn. IRD, 1982-93; pres. Inst. Religion and Democracy, 1993—. Office: Inst Religion and Democracy 1110 Vermont Ave NW Ste 1180 Washington DC 20005-3544

KNIPPLE, MICHELLE BUSOWSKI, musician, educator; b. Braddock, Pa., Mar. 23, 1955; d. Peter Michael and Antoinette Payne Busowski; m. Daniel L. Knipple, Aug. 4, 1979. BS in Edn., Ind. U., Pa., 1977; MS in Edn., Old Dominion U., 1999. Lic. collegiate profl. State Bd. Edn. Va. Band dir. Hampton (Va.) Christian Schs., 1979—88, Trinity Luth. Sch., Newport News, Va., 1980—88, Williamsburg (Va.)-James City County Pub. Schs., 1988—. Musician: Spl. Music Trio, 1994—; musician: (clarinetist) Va. Wind Symphony, 1999—. Music dir. Immaculate Conception Cath. Ch., Hampton, 1990—96; music min. Our Lady of Mt. Carmel Cath. Ch., Newport News, 1998—. Mem.: NEA, Va. Edn. Assn., Va. Band and Orch. Dirs. Assn., Nat. Pastoral Musicians, Music Educators Nat. Conf., Internat. Clarinet Soc. Roman Catholic. Avocations: cooking, reading, listening to classical music, cats. Home: 114 Derosa Dr Hampton VA 23666

KNIZESKI, JUSTINE ESTELLE, insurance company executive; b. Glen Cove, N.Y., June 4, 1954; d. John Martin and Elsie Beatrice (Gozelski) Knizeski. BA, Conn. Coll., 1976; M in Mgmt., Northwestern U., 1981. Customer svc. supr. Brunswick Savs., Freeport, Maine, 1977-79; investment analyst Bankers Life and Casualty Co., Chgo., 1980-83, dir. corp. planning and analysis, 1983-87; dir. budgets, cost acctg. Blue Cross/Blue Shield of Ill., 1987-97, dir. planning, budgets and analysis, 1997—, exec. dir. budgets and analysis, 2002—, divsn. v.p. budgets and procurement, 2003—. Chmn. bd. dirs. Alternatives, Inc., Chgo., 1984—87, vice chmn., 1987—91, 2002—, sec., 1991—92, bd. dirs., 1983—84, 2001—02, mem. ad hoc fin. com., 1998—2001; mem. Chgo. Coun. Fgn. Rels., 1984—85, 2002—; bd. dirs. Non-Profit Fin. Ctr., 2000—03, treas., 2002—03. Mem.: Planning Forum. Avocations: travel, sailing, bicycling, traveling, painting. E-mail: knizeskij@bcbsil.com.

KNOBLAUCH, MARY REILLY (MARY LOUISE REILLY), retired music educator, writer; b. Montrose, Mo., Feb. 21, 1922; d. John Henry Welling and Sylvesta Lesmeister; m. Charles A. Knoblauch, Apr. 7, 1996; m. Barney E. Reilly, Dec. 28, 1946 (dec. July 30, 1991); 1 child, Marguerite Ann. BS in Music Edn., St. Mary Coll., Leavenworth, Kans., 1944; MA in Edn., Immaculate Heart Coll., L.A., Calif., 1956; LHD (hon.), St. Mary Coll., Leavenworth, Kans., 2002. Tchr. music French Inst. Notre Dame De Sion, Kansas City, Mo., 1944—46, L.A. City Schs., 1946—54, supr. music ctrl. dist., 1954—55; asst. prof. music L.A. State Coll., 1955—57; assoc. prof. music San Fernando State Coll., Northridge, Calif., 1957—74; prof. music Calif. State U., Northridge, 1975—92, prof. emeritus, 1992. Music cons. L.A. Parochial Schs., 1963—73; adv. bd. Cultural Ctr., Woodland Hills, Calif., 1960; v.p. edn. Opera Guild, L.A., 1970. Author: (tchr.'s materials) It's Time for Music, 1985, (textbooks) World of Music K-6, 1988, Music Connection Series K-6, 1995—98. Grant dir. L.A. Mcpl. Arts, 1978; mem. Liturgical Music Commn., L.A., 1972—79; dir. Docent Ministry, St. Francis of Assisi, 1999—; mem. Comprehensive Arts Ctr. State Dept. of Edn., Sacramento, 1976. Recipient Disting. Prof. award, Calif. State U., 1979, St. Cecilia's award Docent Ministry, 2002, Lifetime Achievement award, Calif. Music Educators Hall of Fame, 2002. Mem.: La Quinta Arts Found., Sigma Alpha Iota (award of Honor 1961), Delta Kappa Gamma (grad. scholarship 1955). Achievements include development of music framework for Calif. schs., State Dept. Edn., 1970. Avocations: reading, piano, dance, gardening. Home: 48 605 Vista Tierra La Quinta CA 92253

KNOEBEL, SUZANNE BUCKNER, cardiologist, educator; b. Ft. Wayne, Ind., Dec. 13, 1926; d. Doster and Marie (Lewis) Buckner. AB, Goucher Coll., 1948; MD, Ind. U.-Indpls., 1960. Diplomate: Am. Bd. Internal Medicine. Asst. prof. medicine Ind. U., Indpls., 1966-69, assoc. prof., 1969-72, prof., 1972-77, Krannert prof., 1977—. Asst. dean rsch. Ind. U., Indpls., 1975-85; assoc. dir. Krannert Inst. Cardiology, Indpls., 1974-90; asst. chief cardiology sect. Richard L. Roudebush VA Med. Ctr., Indpls., 1982-90; editor-in-chief ACC Current Jour. Rev., 1992-2000. Fellow Am. Coll. Cardiology (v.p. 1980-81, pres. 1982-83); mem. Am. Fedn. Clin. Research, Assn. Univ. Cardiologists Office: Krannert Inst 1701 N Senate Ave Indianapolis IN 46202 E-mail: sknoebel@iupui.edu.

KNOLL, FLORENCE SCHUST, architect, designer; b. Saginaw, Mich., May 24, 1917; d. Frederick E. and M. Haisting Schust; m. Hans G. Knoll, July 1, 1946 (dec. 1955); m. Harry Hood Bassett, June 22, 1958 (dec. 1991). Student, Cranbrook Art Acad., Bloomfield Hills, Mich., 1935-37, Archtl. Assn., London, 1938-39; B.Arch., Ill. Inst. Tech., Chgo., 1941; D.F.A. (hon.), Parsons Sch. Design, 1979. Archtl. draftsman, designer Gropius & Breuer, Boston, 1941; design dir. Knoll Planning Unit, 1942-55; pres. Knoll Internat., N.Y.C., 1955-65; pvt. practice architecture and designer Coconut Grove, Fla., 1965—. Named to Ill. Inst. Tech. Hall of Fame, 1982; recipient Athena award R.I. Sch. Design, 1982, Nat. Medal Arts award NEA, 2003. Mem. AIA (Gold medal 1961), Indsl. Designers Am. (hon.)

KNOLL, JEANNETTE THERIOT, state supreme court justice; b. Baton Rouge; m. Jerold Edward Knoll; children: Triston Kane, Eddie Jr., Edmond Humphries, Blake Theriot, Jonathan Paul. BA in Polit. Sci., Loyola U., 1966, JD, 1969; LLM, U. Va., 1996; studied with Maestro Adler, Mannes Coll. of Music, 1962-63. Criminal defense atty., first asst. dist. atty. Twelfth Jud. Dist. Ct. Avoyelles Parish, 1972-82; gratuitous atty., advisor U.S. Selective Svc., Marksville, La.; judge (3d cir.) U.S. Ct. of Appeal, 1982-93; justice La. Supreme Ct., 1997—. Instr. La. Jud. Coll.; chair CLE La. Ct. of Appeal Judges; mem. vis. com. Loyola U. Sch. of Law, Loyola Music Sch.; bd. dirs. Loyola U. Alumni Assn.; former mem. state bd. of La. commn. on law enforcement and criminal justice. Past pres. Bus. and Profl. Women's Club; Marksville C. of C.; active Am. Legion Aux. Recipient scholarship Met. Opera Assn., New Orleans Opera Guild. Office: La Supreme Ct 301 Loyola Ave New Orleans LA 70112-1814

KNOOP, MAGGIE PEARSON, language educator; b. Pitts., July 5, 1945; d. Lawrence Thomas and Marie Barnes Pearson; m. Michael Francis Knoop, Apr. 10, 1970 (div.); children: Jamie Michael, Meagan Pearson. BA, U. South Fla., 1971, MA, 1982. Tchr., coach Acad. Holy Names, Tampa, Fla., 1971—74, Shorecrest Prep. Sch., St. Petersburg, Fla., 1974—87; assoc. prof. St. Petersburg Coll., Clearwater, Fla., 1989—. Area dir. publicity Women's State Track Honor Roll, Fla., 1981—82; exercise specialist and fitness cons. Group W Cable, St. Petersburg, 1982—86; dir., fitness cons. Suncoast Nautilus, Clearwater, 1981—83; chmn. Divsn. Girl's and Women's Sports Fla. Assn. of Health, Phys. Edn., Recreation and Dance, Fla., 1986—87; presenter in field. Co-author: (pub.svc. announcements) Drug Abuse. Mem.: NOW, AAUW, Bay Area Regional Tchrs. Second Lang. Learners, Planned Parenthood Fedn. Am., NARAL Pro Choice. Democrat. Avocations: wellness, travel, literature. Home: 610 Island Way 105 Clearwater FL 33767 Office: St Petersburg College 2465 Drew Street Clearwater FL 33765 Personal E-mail: mknoop@tampabay.rr.com. Business E-Mail: knoopmaggie@spcollege.edu.

KNOPF, TANA DARLENE, counselor, music educator; b. Des Moines, Oct. 19, 1951; d. Charles D. Sr. and Edith D. Smith; m. James E. Knopf, Aug. 7, 1982; children: Daniel P., Chandra D. BA, Met. State Coll., Denver, 1974; MEd, U. Colo., Denver, 1983. Instrumental music tchr. Denver Pub. Schs., 1974—2000, counselor, 2001—. E-mail: tana-kropf@dpskiz.org.

KNOPMAN, DEBRA SARA, environmental scientist, director, hydrologist, policy analyst; b. Phila., Aug. 13, 1953; d. Harold L. and Minnette (Smulyan) Knopman; m. Donald Weightman, Sept. 29, 1985; children: Leah Alana, David Atwood. BA, Wellesley Coll., 1975; MSCE, MIT, 1978; PhD, Johns Hopkins U., 1986. Sci. writer and editor, Washington, 1975-78; legis. asst. Daniel P. Moynihan, Washington, 1979-80; prof. staff mem. U.S. Senate Com. on Environ. and Pub. Works, Washington, 1980-83; student asst., office of groundwater U.S. Geol. Survey, Reston, Va., 1984-85, rsch. hydrologist, nat. rsch. program, 1985-86, hydrologist, br. of systems analysis, 1987-91, chief, br. or systems analysis, 1991-93; dep. asst. sec. water and sci. Dept. Interior, 1993-95; dir. Progressive Policy Inst. Ctr. for Innovation and Environ., 1995—. Mem. Nuclear Waste Tech. Rev. Bd., 1997—. Editor: Scientific Research in Israel, 1976; editor Geophysics News, 1990-92; contbr. articles to profl. jours. Mem. commn. on geoscis., environment and resources NRC, 1995-98. Henry R. Luce Found. scholar, Taiwan, 1978-79. Mem. Am. Geophys. Union (chair pub. info. com. 1990-92). Democrat. Jewish. Address: Progressive Policy Inst 600 Pennsylvania Ave SE Ste 400 Washington DC 20003-4350

KNOTTS, CLARA JEAN, music educator; b. New Martinsville, W.Va., May 14, 1977; d. James Franklin and Linda Ann Knotts. BME, Stetson U., DeLand, Fla., 1999. Gen. music tchr. Volusia County Sch. Bd., DeBary, Fla., 2000—; pvt. violin tchr. Fla., 1995—. Violinist and singer in praise and worship band Sanctuary DeLand Ch. of God, Fla., 2002—03. Mem.: FOA, Fla. Music Educators Assn., Music Educators Nat. Conf. Christian. Personal E-mail: knottsland99@yahoo.com. E-mail: knottsland99@yahoo.com.

KNOTT-TWINE, LAURA MAE, director; b. Hartford, Conn., Nov. 11, 1946; m. Richard Graham Twine, Jan. 26, 1973; children: Edward Dean, Susan Helene. BA, Norwich U., 1996—98, MA, 1998—99. Pres. and owner Orchard Ho. Weavers, Windham Ctr., 1980—85; founder, exec. dir. & ceo Windham Textile and History Mus., Inc., 1980—95; dirctor of SBA Women's Bus. Ctr. U. of Hartford, Conn., 2000—; faculty- undergraduate Union U./Vt. Coll., Monpelier, Vt., 2002—. Pres., v.p. & sec. Handweavers Guild of Conn., Glastonbury, Conn., 1979—84; v.p. NE CT Tourism Dist., Windham, Conn., 1984—86; advisor Nat. Heritage Corrior Pk. Bd., Hartford, Conn., 1988—95; paliamentarian Assn. of Girl Scouts Exec. Staff, North Haven, Conn., 1997—98; mem. Windham, Conn. Econ. Devel. Com., Windham, Conn., 1988—95; founder Windham Textile and History Museum, Inc.; instr. bus. Vermont Coll. Handweaver, Colonial Handweaving. Mem. Nat. Heritage Corridor Bd., Hartford, Conn., 1988—95; advisor Nat. Inst. of Puppetry at U. of Conn., Storrs, Conn., 1990—96; mem. Assn. of Women's Bus. Centers, Boston, 2000—03; program officer Museums of NE Conn. Assn., 1989—95; mem. SBA Women Bus. Advocate, Conn., 2002; life mem. Girl Scouts of Am., NYC, 1998—2003. Independent. Catholic. Avocations: handweaving, handspinning, reading, travel. Home: 32 Gray Pine Common Avon CT 06001 Office: The Entrepreneurial Center U Hartford 50 Elizabeth St Hartford CT 06105 Office Phone: 860-768-5663. Personal E-mail: rltwine@comcast.com. E-mail: knotttwin@hartford.edu.

KNOUS, PAMELA K. wholesale distribution executive; Student, Carleton Coll.; Degree in Math., Bus. Adminstrn., Acctg., U. Ariz. Ptnr. KPMG Peat Marwick, L.A.; group v.p. finance The Vons Companies, Inc., 1991—94; sr. v.p., CFO The Vons Companies, Inc., 1994; exec. v.p., CFO The Vons Companies, Inc., 1995—97, Supervalu Inc., Mpls., 1997—. Office: Supervalu Inc PO Box 990 Eden Prairie MN 55344

KNOWLES, BEYONCÉ GISELLE See BEYONCÉ

KNOWLES, ELIZABETH PRINGLE, museum director; b. Decatur, Ill., Jan. 9, 1943; d. William Bull and Elizabeth E. (Pillsbury) Pringle; m. Joseph E. Knowles; 1 child, Elizabeth Bakewell. BA in Humanities with honors, Stanford U., 1964; MA in Art History, U. Calif., Santa Barbara, 1968; grad., Mus. Mgmt. Inst., 1984; MBA, Rensselaer Poly. Inst., 1999. Cert. jr. coll. tchr. Calif. Instr. art history Murray State U., Murray, Ky., 1967-68; instr. Santa Barbara Art Inst., 1969, Santa Barbara City Coll., 1969-70, 76-78, instr. cont. edn., 1973-86; from staff coord. docents to curator edn. Santa Barbara Mus. Art, 1974-86; assoc. dir. Meml. Art Gallery, Rochester, N.Y., 1986-88; instr. mus. studies Calif. State U., Long Beach, 1989; exec. dir. Lyman Allyn Art Mus., New London, Conn., 1989-95; pres. Only In Conn. Spl. Interest Tours, Chester, 1995-97; supr. mus. edn. programs Mystic (Conn.) Seaport Mus., 1996-2001; exec. dir. Wildling Art Mus., Los Olivos, Calif., 2001—. Instr. continuing edn. Santa Barbara City Coll., 1973—86.

Contbr. essays to art catalogues. Bd. dirs., chmn. Met. Transit Dist., Santa Barbara, 1978—80; commr. Santa Barbara City Planning Commn., 1975—77; founding pres. Santa Barbara Contemporary Arts Forum, 1976—78. Fellow Kellogg Found., Smithsonian Inst., 1985. Mem.: New Eng. Mus. Assn. (v.p. 1993—95), Coll. Art Assn., Am. Assn. Mus. (treas. edn. com. 1986—88). E-mail: Ronny@wildlingmuseum.org.

KNOWLES, JULIE NALL, secondary school educator; b. Webb, Ala., Nov. 5, 1941; d. Ealie Edward and Creola (Carter) Nall; m. William Durwood Knowles, Jan. 17, 1970. BS in Edn. magna cum laude, Troy State U., 1965; MA in English, Samford U., 1969; PhD in English, Auburn U., 1980; AA in Music, Chattahoochee Valley C.C., Phenix City, Ala., 1999. Cert. tchr. Ala., Ga., Fla. Tchr. Ahrens High Sch. Jefferson County Schs., Louisville, Ky., 1975-76; instr. Auburn (Ala.) U., 1981-82; assoc. prof. Stillman Coll., Tuscaloosa, Ala., 1983-85; asst. prof. Mercer U., Macon, Ga., 1986-87; prof. Troy State U., Phenix City, Ala., 1987-99; tchr. Camden County High Sch. Camden County Schs., Kingsland, Ga., 1999-2000; tchr. Paxon Sch. Advanced Studies Duval County Sch. Sys., Jacksonville, Fla., 2000—. Editor, creator: The Chariot, 1988-91; contbr. articles to mags. Ch. pianist Turners Station (Ky.) Bapt Ch., 1973—76, Union Grove Bapt. Ch., Opelika, Ala., 1976—82, Hatchechubbee (Ala.) Bapt. Ch., 1988—95; mem. choir Folkston (Ga.) Bapt. Ch., 2000—. Rsch. grantee Troy State U., 1992; recipient Woodrow Hale Meml. Prize # 1 Green River Writers, 1996. Mem. Profl. Assn. Ga. Educators, Phi Theta Kappa, Phi Kappa Phi, Kappa Delta Pi (counselor Rho Phi chpt. 1989-92, Point of Excellence award 1993). Democrat. Southern Baptist. Avocations: motorcycling, piano, fishing. Home: Rte 2 Box 1785 Folkston GA 31537

KNOWLES, MARIE L. transportation executive; Sr. fin. analyst Arco Transp. Co., Long Beach, Calif., 1972-1986; asst. treas. for banking, 1986-1988; v.p. of fin., planning and control ARCO Internat. Oil and Gas Co., 1988-90; v.p. and controller ARCO, 1990-93; sr. v.p. and pres. ARCO Transp. Co., 1993-96, exec. v.p., CFO, 1996—. Office: Atlantic Richfield 515 S Flower St Ste 3700 Los Angeles CA 90071-2201

KNOWLES, MARJORIE FINE, lawyer, educator, dean; b. Bklyn., July 4, 1939; d. Jesse J. and Roslyn (Leff) Fine; m. Ralph I. Knowles, Jr., June 3, 1972. BA, Smith Coll., 1960; LLB, Harvard U., 1965. Bar: Ala., N.Y., D.C. Teaching fellow Harvard U., 1963-64; law clk. to judge U.S. Dist. Ct. (so. dist.), N.Y., 1965-66; asst. U.S. atty. U.S. Atty.'s Office, N.Y.C., 1966-67; asst. dist. atty. N.Y. County Dist. Atty., N.Y.C., 1967-70; exec. dir. Joint Found. Support, Inc., N.Y.C., 1970-72; asst. gen. counsel HEW, Washington, 1978-79; insp. gen. U.S. Dept. Labor, Washington, 1979-80; assoc. prof. U. Ala. Sch. Law, Tuscaloosa, 1972-75, prof., 1975-86, assoc. dean, 1982-84; law prof., dean Ga. State U. Coll. Law, Atlanta, 1986-91, law prof., 1986—. Cons. Ford Found., N.Y.C., 1973-98, 2000-03, trustee Coll. Retirement Equities Fund, N.Y.C., 1983-2002; mem. exec. com. Conf. on Women and the Constn., 1986-88; mem. com. on continuing profl. edn. Am. Law Inst.-ABA, 1987-93. Contbr. articles to profl. jours. Am. Council Edn. fellow, 1976-77, Aspen Inst. fellow, Rockefeller Found., 1976. Mem. ABA (chmn. new deans workshop 1988), Ala. State Bar Assn., N.Y. State Bar Assn., D.C. Bar Assn., Am. Law Inst., Tchrs. Ins. Annuity Assn. (trustee 2003-). Office: Ga State U Coll Law University Plz Atlanta GA 30303

KNOWLTON, GRACE FARRAR, sculptor, photographer, painter; b. Buffalo, Mar. 15, 1932; d. Frank Neff and Esther Sargeant (Norton) Farrar; m. Winthrop Knowlton, July 8, 1960 (div. 1980); children: Eliza, Samantha. BA, Smith Coll., 1954; MA, Columbia U., 1981. Asst. to curator of graphic arts Nat. Gallery of Art, Washington, 1955-57; tchr. art Arlington (Va.) Pub. Schs., 1957-60; sculptor, photographer, painter, 1960—; tchr. art Art Students League, N.Y.C., 1999—. Home: 67 Ludlow Ln Palisades NY 10964-1606

KNOWLTON, NANCY, biologist; b. Evanston, Ill., May 30, 1949; d. Archa Osborn and Aline (Mahnken) K.; m. Jeremy Bradford Cook Jackson; 1 child, Rebecca Knowlton. AB, Harvard U., 1971; PhD, U. Calif., Berkeley, 1978. Asst. prof. biology Yale U., New Haven, 1979-84, assoc. prof., 1984; biologist Smithsonian Tropical Rsch. Inst., Panama, Republic of Panama, 1985—; prof. Scripps Instn. Oceanography U. Calif., San Diego, 1997—. Panelist animal learning and behavior NSF, Washington, 1989-92; vis. scholar Wolfson Coll., Oxford (Eng.) U., 1990-91, Zoology Inst., U. Basel, Switzerland, 1996-97. Editor Am. Scientist, 1981-90, Evolution, 1995-97. NATO postdoctoral fellow NSF, Liverpool, Cambridge, Eng., 1978-79; Aldo Leopold Leadership fellow, 1999. Mem. AAAS (coun. del. sect. on biol. scis., com. on coun. affairs), Ecol. Soc. Am., Soc. Study Evolution. Office: U Calif San Diego La Jolla CA 92093

KNOX, CAROL B. biologist, educator; b. Pitts., Feb. 26, 1941; d. Ellsworth Reid and Marian Ruth (Emmert) Baumann; m. Walter E. Knox, Jr., Apr. 14, 1962; children: Deborah, Walter T. BS cum laude, Chatham Coll., 1962; MS, Rutgers U., 1964. Rsch. asst. Zoology dept. U. Mass., Amherst, 1964—68; tchr. botany and biology Northfield (Mass.) Mt. Hermon Sch., 1969—, head sci. dept., 1984—89. Reviewer sci. books and films, Washington, 1980—; lectr. tchrs. course Sea Edn. Assn., Falmouth, Mass., 2003. Author: Problems in Biology, 1980; exhibitions include Woods Hole (Mass.) Cmty. Art Show, 2001, 2003, Schaulter Libr. Gallery, Northfield, 2003. Active Gill (Mass.) Conservation Commn.; investigator, vol. 300 Com., Falmouth, 2002—03. Grantee, GTE Corp., 1982; faculty fellow, Northfield Mt. Hermon Sch., 1984, 1992. Mem.: Nat. Sci. Tchrs. Assn., New Eng. Wildflower Soc., Phi Beta Kappa. Republican. Methodist. Avocations: cello, kayaking, bicycling, pipe organ, painting. Home: 159 Racing Beach Ave Falmouth MA 02540 Office: Northfield Mt Hermon Sch 7 Bolton Rd Northfield MA 01360 E-mail: cknox@nmhschool.org.

KNOX, GERTIE R. company executive, accountant; b. Rossville, Tenn., Feb. 2, 1960; d. Columbus and Mabel (Strickland) K.; m. Micheal F. Coley, Sept. 1, 1990. BBA, U. Memphis, 1982; MBA, Colo. State U., 1998. CPA, Calif. Contracts and fin. adminstr. Textron Aerostructures, Nashville, 1983-86; ptnr. PricewaterhouseCoopers LLP, Irvine, Calif., 1986-2001; COO, Global Social Compliance LLC, L.A., 2001—. Mem.: AICPA. Avocations: reading, travel. Home: Irvine CA 92606 Office: Global Social Compliance LLC 801 S Figueroa St Ste 850 Los Angeles CA 90017 Fax: 213-362-6012. E-mail: gknox@gsocialc.com.

KNOX, HAVOLYN CROCKER, financial consultant; b. Charlotte, N.C., Oct. 20, 1937; d. Earl Reid and Etta Lorain (Wylie) Crocker; m. Charles Eugene Knox, July 20, 1963 (div. 1981); children: Charles Eugene Jr., Sandra Leigh. Cert. Stenography, U. N.C., Greensboro, 1956. ChFC, CLU. Exec. sec. Stellings-Gossett Theatres, Inc., Charlotte, 1956-57; legal sec. McDougle, Ervin, Horack & Snepp, Charlotte, 1957, Pierce, Wardlow, Knox & Caudle, Charlotte, 1957-63; adminstrv. asst. Charlotte-Mecklenburg Planning Commn., 1980; exec. asst. Conn. Mut. Life Ins. Co., Charlotte, 1981-86; assoc. The Hinrichs Fin. Group, Charlotte, 1986-91, Lyn Knox & Assocs., Charlotte, 1991—. Ops. dir. Eddie Knox for Mayor campaign, Charlotte; campaign mgr. Herb Spaugh for City Coun., Charlotte, 1981, 83, 85; registration chmn. Kemper Open Golf Tournament, Charlotte, 1976-79; pres. The Legal Aux., Charlotte, 1972-73; bd. dirs. Oratorio Singers of Charlotte, 1986-93. Recipient William Danforth Found. award, 1955. Mem. Am. Soc. CLU and ChFC (bd. dirs. Charlotte chpt. 1994-95). Republican. Presbyterian. Avocations: piano, reading, golf. Home and Office: 2331 Carmel Rd Charlotte NC 28226-6322

KNOX, TERESA LOUISE, entrepreneur, small business owner; b. Tulsa, Okla., Jan. 31, 1969; d. Richard L. and Virginia J. Knox; m. Ivan David Acosta, July 25, 1998; children: Lilliana Acosta, Ronnie Carlson, Annabel Acosta. CEO, Cmty. Care Coll., Tulsa, 1995—, Knox Lab., Tulsa, 1998—. Republican. Avocations: travel, music, books. Office: Community Care Coll and Knox Lab 4242 S Sheridan Tulsa OK 74145

KNOX, VENERRIA L. city official; BS in Journalism, Northwestern U., 1970, M in Adminstrn., Willamette U., 1980. Asst. to dep. treas. Treasury Dept. State of Oreg., Salem, 1979-80; fin. analyst Pacific Power, Portland, Oreg., 1980-83; fin. officer Security Pacific Bank, Seattle, 1983-85; legis. analyst City of Seattle, 1985-87, mgr. fin. and govt. ops., 1987-91, dep. dir., program support divsn. dir. Dept. Housing and Human Svcs., 1991-93, dir. Dept. Housing and Human Svcs., 1994-99, dir. human svcs. dept., 1999—. Mem. U.S. Conf. City Human Svc. Ofcls., Nat. Cmty. Devel. Assn., Nat. Forum Black Pub. Adminstrs. Office: Human Svcs Dept Dept Housing & Human Svcs 618 2nd Ave Fl 6 Seattle WA 98104-2289

KNUDSEN, LAURA GEORGIA, linguist; b. Kenosha, Wis., Sept. 21, 1969; d. Richard Dennis and Georgia Elizabeth (Perrin) Wright; m. Martin Christian Knudsen, Aug. 20, 1994. BA in Linguistics, Ind. U., 1991, MA in Linguistics, 2001. Linguist Ind. U., Bloomington, 1987—, tchr. ESL, Ctr. for English Lang. Tng., 1995—; tchr. ESL Aichi U., Toyohashi, Japan, 1998, Ind. U./ Purdue U. Indpls., 2002; tchr. Aikido Ind. U., 2001—. Presenter in field Contbr. articles to profl. jours. Fulbright scholar IIE, Budapest, 1996-97; FLAS fellow U.S. Dept. Edn., Ind. U., 1993-94, GANN fellow, 1991-92. Mem. Linguistic Soc. Am., Ind. U. Linguistic Club (sec. 1996, pres. 1998), INTESOL (student rep. 1999, rec. sec. 2002-03). Avocation: Aikido. Office: Ind U Ctr English Lang Tng Meml Hall 317 Bloomington IN 47405

KNUDSON, RUTHANN, environmental consultant; b. Milw., Oct. 24, 1941; d. Sidney Olaus and Clara Ruth (Tappe) K. BA magna cum laude, U. Minn., 1963, MA, 1966; PhD, Wash. State U., 1973; postgrad., U. Idaho, 1988. Seasonal ranger Nat. Park Svc., Bandelier Nat. Monument, N.Mex., 1963; instr. U. No. Colo., Greeley, 1966-68; asst. rsch. prof. U. Idaho, Moscow, 1974-79, assoc. rsch. prof., 1979-81; dir. cultural resource svcs. Woodward Clyde Cons., San Francisco, 1981-86, v.p., shareholder, 1985-88; arch. Nat. Park Svc., Washington, 1990—96; supr. Agate Fossil Beds Nat. Monument, 1996—; prin. Knudson Assoc. (formerly Paleo-Designs), 1974—. Vis. asst. prof. Wright State U., Dayton, Ohio, 1974; cons. Am. Folklife Ctr., Washington, 1981-83, NRC, Washington, 1982, 83; resource cons. Calif. Heritage Task Force, 1983-94, Office Tech. Assessment, Washington, 1986; Woodward lectr., 1985; mem. Nebr. Panhandle Tourism Coalition, 1996—; mem. Friends of the Intertribal Gathering, 2002—. Author: Cambria Village Ceramics, 1967, Organizational Variability in Late Paleo-Indian Assemblages, 1983, Contemporary Cultural Resource Management, 1986; co-editor: The Public Trust and the First Americans, 1995, The 10,000 year old Lubbock Artifact Assemblage, 1998, Using Cultural Resources to Enhance Ecosystem Management, 1999, Using the Past to Shape National Park Service Policy for Wildlife, 1999, Cultural Resource Management in Context, 2000, Medicine Creek is a Paleoindian Cultural Ecotone: The Red Smoke Assemblage, 2002. Bd. dirs. Preservation Action, Washington, 1980-85, 89-90, Californians for Preservation Action, 1981-82; sec.-treas. Idaho NOW, 1977-78; co-chmn. Nebr. Panhandle Tourism Coalition, 2000-01. Recipient Preservation award Nat. Conf. State Historic Preservation Officers, 1981, Conservation award Am. Soc. Conservation Archaeology, 1981. Mem. Plains Anthropol. Soc. (bd. dirs. 2003—), Soc. Applied Anthropology, Am. Anthropol. Assn. (Margaret Mead award 1983), Soc. Am. Archaeology (exec. bd. 1979-81, exec. com. 1983-85, legis. coord. 1979-82, chmn. com. pub. archaeology 1980-82, 84-85), Women's Coun. Energy and Environ. (bd. dirs. 1994-96), Soc. Vert. Paleontology, Geol. Soc. of Am., Phi Beta Kappa. Home: 343 River Rd Harrison NE 69346-2734 Office: Agate Fossil Beds Nat Monument 301 River Rd Harrison NE 69346-2734 Office Phone: 308-668-2211. Personal E-mail: paleoknute@aol.com.

KNUPP, JUDI BULKOWSKI, nutritionist; b. Newark, N.J., Dec. 22, 1950; d. Frank Adam and Catherine (Johnson) Bulkowski; children: Jeffrey Christopher, Lindsay Blaire. BS, Drexel U., 1972, MS, 1997. Registered dietitian. Clin. dietitian Presbyn. Med. Ctr., Phila., 1972-73, VA Hosps., Phila., Wilmington, Del., 1973-79; rsch. asst. dept. surgery U. Pa., Phila., 1979-80; from dir. nutrition & food svcs., nutrition cons. Linwood (N.J.) Convalescent Ctr., 1980-90; pub. rels. coord. Cape May County Tech. Sch. Dist., Cape May Court House, N.J., 1992-94; tchg. & rsch. assoc. Drexel U., Phila., 1994-96; dir. nutrition edn. Allegheny U. Health Scis., Phila., 1995—. Mem. Am. Dietetic Assn., Dietetics Edn. Cons. Network (invited), N.J. Dietetic Assn., Phila. Dietetic Assn., Sports & Cardiovasc. & Wellness. Avocations: tennis, international travel, art, theater, music. Home: 10 Dispatch Dr Washington Crossing PA 18977-1174

KNUTH, MARYA DANIELLE, special education educator; b. Bowling Green, Ohio, Apr. 27, 1971; d. Kerry Lee and Sandra Jean Knuth. BEd, U. Toledo, 1997; MEd (hon.), U Toledo, 2002; cert. in reading (hon.), U. Toledo, 2002. Cert. in tchg. Tchr. spl. edn. Jefferson Jr. H.S., Toledo, 1997—98, Washington Jr. H.S., Toledo, 1998—; promotion coord. J&L Mktg., 2002—. Coach intramurals Washington Local Schs., Toledo, 1998—2002; chairperson bldg. beautification com. Washington Jr. H.S., Toledo, 2001—, chairperson best practice com.; dem. exch. program Ohio - Ukraine- Hungary Ednl. Exch. Program in the Pub. Sch. Setting, Toledo, 1999—2000; reading tutor Read for Lit., Toledo, 2000—; co-chairperson 100% Homework Club, Washington Jr. High, 2002—03; promotion coord. J&L Mktg., 1999—; head coach freshman girls Whitmer HS. Author (editor): A Netherland Tour, 1998. Mem. Build Your Sch. Garden Com., 2003—; head coach freshman Broomball Team, Toledo, 2003—; mem. Sister Cities of Toledo, 2000—. Recipient Best Lesson Plans award, Teachers Orgn., 2000. Mem.: ASCD, Coun. Exceptional Children. Republican. Avocations: tutoring, travel, rollerblading. Home: 4812 W Bancroft St Apt 30 Toledo OH 43615 Office: Washington Jr HS 5700 Whitmer Dr Toledo OH 43613 Personal E-mail: MaryaK1999@aol.com.

KNUTH FISCHER, CYNTHIA STROUT, environmental consultant; b. Walpole, Mass. d. Harold A. and Doris A. (Kendall) Strout; m. Adam Knuth (dec.); m. Charles S. Fischer. BA, Middlebury Coll., 1948; MA in Internat. Law and Govt., NYU, 1965. Adminstrv. asst. FAO Mission to Iraq, Baghdad, 1950—53; internat. conf. precis-writer Copenhagen, 1954—56; exec. sec. to UN legal counsel, 1956—62; exec. sec. to pres. Gen. Assembly UN, N.Y.C., 1962—63; exec. sec. UN Devel. Program, N.Y.C., 1964—69; with Ctr. for Internat. Affairs, Harvard U., Cambridge, Mass., 1976—82; founder, pres. Friends of Native Ams., 1986—. Founder Menotomy Indian Day, Arlington, Mass., 1991, Aberjona Indian Day, Winchester, Mass., 1992; founder, pres. Ctr. for Environ. Edn., East Coast, 1990—; dir. Coalition for a Strong UN, 2001—; sec. to bd. dirs. UN Assn. Greater Phila., 1998—2002; publicity chair, bd. dirs. Valley Forge Audubon Soc., 1996—2000; environ chair Lions Club of West Chester, Pa., 1996. Vol. Chadds Ford Hist. Soc., Second Reading Bookstore to benefit Sr. Ctr. of West Chester, 1998—; founder Friends of Indigenous Peoples, 2000—; rep. Phila. Hospitality, 2002—; dir. Coalition Strong UN, 2001—; vol. Meals on Wheels CC Hosp., 2003—. Mem. Common Cause (exec. bd. Mass. 1986), Mass. UN Assn. (exec. bd. 1970), Boston Jazz Soc. (exec. bd. 1975), Mystic River Watershed Assn. (exec. bd. 1991), Phi Delta Kappa (2d v.p. Harvard U. chpt. 1990-92), Sierra Club/Thoreau Group (chair 1993), Walden Forever Wild (exec. bd. 1993-95). Home: 956 Conner Rd West Chester PA 19380-1810

KNUTSON, BONNIE RAE, secondary education educator, commercial artist; b. Perryton, Tex., Nov. 1, 1949; d. Vernon Ray and Imogene Marie Fronk; 1 child, Michael Shane. BS in Art, West Tex. A&M U., Canyon, 1972. Cert. tchr. emotionally disturbed. elem. and gen. elem., art Tex. Comml. artist KGNC Radio and TV, Amarillo, Tex., 1972-73, Traftin & Autry Printers, Amarillo, 1973-74; secondary tchr. Amarillo Ind. Schs., 1974—. Advisor La Airosa, Amarillo H.S., 1989-93. Designer, editor cookbook Something Different, 1995; designer T-shirts, golf towels, presentations, comml. artist monthly publs. Accent West, Grain Producers News, N.Mex. Stockman, Panhandle, 1973-74. Mem. Delta Kappa Gamma, Kappa Pi. Republican. Christian. Avocations: drawing and painting, commercial art and design, interior decorating, gardening. Office: Tascosa HS 3921 Westlawn St Amarillo TX 79102-1795

KNUTZEN, MARTHA LORRAINE, lawyer; b. Bellingham, Wash., Aug. 28, 1956; BA in Polit. Sci., Scripps Coll., 1978; MA in Polit. Sci, Practical Politics, JD, U. San Francisco, 1981. Bar: Calif. 1981. Lawyer, mgr. legal computer support svcs., San Francisco, 1981—. Mem. San Francisco Citizens' Adv. Com. on Elections, 1994-96; 3d vice chair Dem. Party, San Francisco, 1996-2000, mem. Resolution Com., Calif. Dem. Party, 2001—; chair San Francisco Human Rights Commn., 1996—; cmty. organizer. Recipient Civil Rights Leadership award Calif. Assn. Human Rights Commn., 1996. Office: Office Atty Gen 455 Golden Gate San Francisco CA 94102-2230 Home: Apt 44 601 Van Ness Ave San Francisco CA 94102-3263

KOART, NELLIE HART, real estate investor and executive; b. San Luis Obispo, Calif., Jan. 3, 1930; d. Will Carleton and Nellie Malchen (Cash) Hart; m. William Harold Koart, Jr., June 16, 1951 (dec. 1976); children: Kristen Marie Kittle, Matthew William. Student, Whittier Coll., 1947-49; BA, U. Calif., Santa Barbara, 1952; MA, Los Angeles State Coll., 1957. Life diploma elem. edn., Calif. Farm worker Hart Farms, Montebello, Calif., 1940-48; play leader Los Angeles County parks and Recreation, E. Los Angeles, Rosemead, Calif., 1948-51; elem. tchr. Potrero Heights Sch. Dist., South San Gabriel, Calif., 1951-55, vice prin., 1955-57; real estate salesman William Koart Real Estate, Goleta, Calif., 1963-76; real estate investor Ko-Art Enterprises, Goleta, 1976—; pres. Wm. Koart Constrn. Co., Inc., Goleta, 1975-91; real estate salesperson Joseph McGeever Realty Co., Goleta, 1976-91. Adv. bd. Bank of Montecito, Santa Barbara, Calif., 1983—. Editor: Reflections, 1972. Charter mem. Calif. Regents program Calif. Fedn. Republican Women, 1989; treas. Santa Barbara County Fedn. Republican Women, Alamar-Hope Ranch, 1981-82, treas. County Bd., 1983-84, auditor, 1985, 96, 97; treas. Com. to Recall Hone, Maschke and Shewczyk, Goleta, 1984; treas. Santa Barbara County Lincoln Club, 1983-87, bd. dirs., 1983-93; assoc. mem. state cen. com. Calif. Republican Party, 1985-87. Mem.: Santa Barbara County Tax-Payers Assn., Serena Cove Owners Assn. (sec.-treas., bd. dirs. 1990—2002), Santa Barbara Apt. Assn., Santa Barbara County Lincoln Club, Antique Automobile Club of Am. (sec. treas. Santa Barbara 1980—84). Avocations: swimming, coin collecting/numismatics, genealogy, gardening, football. Office: KO-ART Enterprises PO Box 310 Goleta CA 93116-0310

KOBBEROE, BIRTHE, corporate financial executive, accountant; b. Copenhagen, June 17, 1937; arrived in U.S., 1983, permanent resident, 1996; d. Gustav Carl Andersen and Britta Madsen; m. John Kobberoe, Mar. 4, 1961; children: Michael, Lise. Student, Nelholt & Son, 1954—58; diploma, Copenhagen Trade Sch., Denmark, 1955; diploma in English, Berlitz Sch. Lang., 1956, U. Nev., Las Vegas, 1984. Acct. Hoffman & Sons, Copenhagen, 1958, Jens Pedersen Forwarder, Copenhagen, 1958—59, Nordic Antenna Man, Copenhagen, 1959—63; acct., CFO Ratel Radio, Copenhagen, 1963—83, Ratel Radio, Cons., Las Vegas, 1983—. Editor bi-monthly Danish Am. newspaper; pub. (CD with Poems), 2002; author (Poet): (book of poetry) A Lifetime of Poetry, 2003. Culture leader Scandinavian Club of Las Vegas, 1986—90. Mem.: The Great Book Found., Nev. State Garden Club (envirionment chmn. 1988—90, auditor), Sunset Garden Club. Republican. Lutheran. Avocations: swimming, oil painting, writing books, poetry, piano. Home: 1995 Hallwood Dr Las Vegas NV 89119 E-mail: susdane@kobberoe.com.

KOBE, LAN, medical physicist; b. Semarang, Indonesia; naturalized; d. O.G. and L.N. (The) Kobe. BS in Physics, IKIP U., Bandung, Indonesia, 1964; MS in Physics, IKIP U., 1967; MS in Med. Physics and Biophysics, U. Calif.-Berkeley, 1975. Physics instr. Sch. Engring. Tarumanegara U., Jakarta, Indonesia, 1968-72; rsch. fellow dept. radiation oncology U. Calif.-San Francisco, 1975-77; clin. physicist in residence dept. radiation oncology UCLA, 1977-78, asst. hosp. radiation physicist, 1978-80, hosp. radiation physicist, 1980—. Instr. radiation oncology physics to resident physicians and med. physics grad. students. Contbr. sci. papers to profl. publs. Newhouse grantee U. Calif.-Berkeley, 1974-75, grantee dean grad. divsn. U. Calif.-Berkeley, 1975; recipient Pres. Work Study award U. Calif., Berkeley, 1974-75, Outstanding Svc. award, 1986, devel. Achievement award, 1988, Ptnrs. in Excellence award UCLA, 1996. Mem. Am. Soc. for Therapeutic Radiology and Oncology, Am. Assn. Physicists in Medicine (nat. and So. Calif. chpts.), Am. Bd. Radiology (cert.), Am. Assn. Individual Investors (life). Office: UCLA Dept Radiation Oncology Los Angeles CA 90095-6951

KOBE, LISA MARIE, quality assurance professional, consultant; b. Cleve., Apr. 3, 1973; d. Victor Allen and Marie Rose Kobe; m. Kevin David Cross, Dec. 31, 2003. BA in Psychology, Ohio U., 1995; MA in Psychology, U. Nebr., Omaha, 1999; PhD in Indsl./Orgnl. Psychology, U. Nebr., 2001. Sr. skills analyst SkillsNET Corp., Waxahachie, Tex., 1997—2001; cons. SilverStone Group, Inc, Omaha, 2000—01; sr. pers. mgmt. cons. CPS Human Resource Svcs., Sacramento, 2001—03, quality mgmt. and bus. process mgr., 2003—. Presenter in field. Contbr. articles to profl. jours. Grantee, U. Nebr. Omaha, 1998—2001; scholar, 2000, 2001; Paul Beck scholar, 1998—99. Mem.: APA, Project Mgmt. Inst., Soc. for Human Resource Mgmt., Soc. for Indsl./Orgnl. Psychology, Soc. for I/O Psychology at UNO (tri-chair 1995—97), Psi Chi, Phi Gamma Mu, Golden Key Honor Soc., Phi Beta Kappa, Psi Chi Ohio U. (pres. 1993—95), Phi Kappa Phi (life). Office: CPS Human Resource Services 241 Lathrop Way Sacramento CA 95815

KOBER, ARLETTA REFSHAUGE (MRS. KAY L. KOBER), supervisor; b. Cedar Falls, Iowa, Oct. 31, 1919; d. Edward and Mary (Jensen) Refshauge; m. Kay Leonard Kober, Feb. 14, 1944; children: Kay Mary, Karilyn Eve. BA, State Coll. Iowa, 1940; MA, U. No. Iowa. Tchr. HS, Soldier, Iowa, 1943—50, 1965—67; coord. Office Edn. Waterloo (Iowa) Cmty. Schs., 1967—84; head dept. coop. career edn. West HS, Waterloo, 1974—84. Mem. Waterloo Sch. Health Coun.; mem. nominating com. YWCA, Waterloo; Black Hawk County chmn. Tb Christmas Seals; ward chmn. ARC, Waterloo; co-chmn. Citizen's Com. Sch. Bond Issue; pres. Waterloo PTA Coun., Waterloo Vis. Nursing Assn., 1956—62, 1982—, Kingsley Sch. PTA, 1959—60; v.p. Waterloo Women's Club, 1962—63, pres., 1963—64, trustee bd. clubhouse dirs., 1957—58; mem. Gen. Fedn. Women's Clubs, Nat. Congress Parents and Tchrs.; bd. dirs. United Svcs. Black Hawk County, Broadway Theatre League, St. Francis Hosp. Found., Black Hawk County Rep. Women, 1952—53; del. Iowa Rep. Convs., 1996, 1998; Presbyterial world svc. chmn. Presbyn. Women's Assn.; deacon Westminster Presbyn. Ch., 1995—98. Mem.: LWV (dir. Waterloo 1951—52), NEA, AAUW (v.p. Cedar Falls 1946—47), Black Hawk County Hist. Soc. (charter), Internat. Platform Assn., Town Club (dir.), P.E.O., Elklets, Dleta Kappa Gamma, Delta Pi Epsilon (v.p. 1966—67). Home: 3436 Augusta Cir Waterloo IA 50701-4608 Office: 503 W 4th St Waterloo IA 50701-1554

KOBER, JANE, lawyer; b. Shamokin, Pa., May 17, 1943; d. Jeno Daniel and Angela Agnes (Kogut) DiRienzo; m. Arthur Kober, June 20, 1970 (div. 1975). AB, Pa. State U., 1965; MA, U. Chgo., 1966; JD, Case Western Res. U., 1974. Bar: Ohio, N.Y. Lectr. U. Baghdad, Iraq, 1966-67; editor, cons. Ernst & Young, Washington, 1968-70; law clk. to Hon. William K. Thomas, U.S. Dist. Ct. for No. Dist. Ohio, Cleve., 1974-75; atty., ptnr. Squire,

Sanders & Dempsey, Cleve. and N.Y.C., 1975-87; ptnr. Shea & Gould, N.Y.C., 1987-89, LeBoeuf, Lamb, Greene & MacRae, L.L.P., N.Y.C., 1989-98; sole practitioner, 1998—; sr. v.p., gen. counsel, sec. Biopure Corp., Cambridge, Mass., 1998—. Mem. vis. com. Case Western Res. U. Sch. Law, Soc. of Benchers. Office: Jane Kober Law Offices 125 W 55th St New York NY 10019-5369 also: Biopure Corp 11 Hurley St Cambridge MA 02141-2110 E-mail: jkober@biopure.com.

KOBZA, JULIA COLLEEN, drafter, building designer; b. Grand Rapids, Mich., Sept. 21, 1966; d. Thomas Theodore K. and Joyce Colleen (Stephens) Kelly; m. Randy Thomas Van Blaricum, Oct. 12, 1985 (div. July 1992); children: Aimee Colleen, Codie Leigh. Student, Grand Valley State U., 1984-85, Northwestern Mich. Coll., 1994-95. Waitress Timberlanes Bowling Alley, Traverse City, Mich., 1991-92, 626 Family Restaurant, Traverse City, Mich., 1992; customer svs. Meijers, Traverse City, Mich., 1992; adminstrv. asst. MAM Contracting, Traverse City, Mich., 1991-92; office adminstr. Builders' Arch. Woodworking, Traverse City, Mich., 1992; acctg. asst. Brown Lumber, Traverse City, Mich., 1992-93; adminstrv. asst. Brown Mfg., Traverse City, Mich., 1993; owner, designer Art 'N' Texture Building Design, Traverse City, Mich., 1993. Planning commr. Elmwood Twp., Traverse City, 1997. Mem. NAFE, Mich. Soc. Planning Ofcls., Congress for New Urbanism, Bldg. Ofcls. Code Adminstrs. Internat. Avocations: reading, clarinet, family, volunteering.

KOCH, CATHERINE ANN, music educator, musician; b. Manchester, N.H., July 27, 1953; d. David Milton and Clarice Joyce Cargill; children: Christopher Lawrence, Gretchen Renate. B in Music Edn., Bucknell U., Lewisburg, Pa., 1975; MS in Music Edn., Syracuse U., 1976. Cert. tchr. N.Y. Pvt. piano, voice and guitar tchr., Fayetteville, NY, 1975—; choral and gen. music tchr. Smith Rd. Sch., N. Syracuse, NY, 1976—81, Manlius Pebble Hill Sch., DeWitt, NY, 1981—89, Eagle Hill Middle Sch., Manlius, NY, 1989—. Substitute organist, soloist various chs., NY, 1993—; organist U. Meth. Ch., Manlius, 1976—93; jr. choir dir. DeWitt Cmty. Ch., 1993—2000; accompanist Syracuse U. Oratorio Soc., 1975—82; mgr., accompanist Jr. High All-County Chorus, Onondaga County, NY, 1992, Onondaga County, 95, Onondaga County, 98, Onondaga County, 2001; chmn. elem. and jr. high vocal task com. Elem. and Jr. High Schs., Onondaga County, 2001—03. Author: (pocket card) Student's Prayer, 1995; musician (pianist): Purely Percussion, 1993, 1995. Recipient Music Masters Harmony award, Soc. Preservation and Encouragement Barbershop Quartet Singing in Am., 2003. Mem.: Am. Choral Dirs. Assn., Onondaga County Music Educators Assn. (pres.), N.Y. State Sch. Music Assn. (presenter 1997, Presdl. Citation for Fayetteville-Manlius music program 1997), Music Educators Nat. Conf. Avocations: reading, swimming, biking. Home: 320 Highbridge St Fayetteville NY 13066 Office: Eagle Hill Middle Sch 4645 Enders Rd Manlius NY 13104

KOCH, CHRISTINE, legislative aide; b. Moline, ill. d. Clarence Albert and Bernadine Jeanette Grams; m. Allan Craig Koch, July 11, 1965; children: David Craig, Brian Michael. Student, U. Ill., 1963-65, Wayne State U., 1965-67. Tchr. Harper Woods Publ. Sch., Harper Woods, Mich., 1967-74; admin. asst. Congressman David E. Bonior, Mt. Clemens, Mich., 1977—2001. Pres. Comprehensive Youth Svcs., Mt. Clemens, Mich., Clinton Twp. Dem. Club; sect. Salvation Army Adv. Bd., Downtown Devel. Authority, Mich. Housing Counselors, Mt. Clemens, Mich.; recording sect. tenth dist. Dem. Com. Democrat. Methodist. Avocations: reading, gardening.

KOCH, EDNA MAE, lawyer, nurse; b. Terre Haute, Ind., Oct. 12, 1951; d. Leo K. and Lucille E. (Smith) K.; m. Mark D. Orton. BS in Nursing, Ind. State U., 1977; JD, Ind. U., 1980. Bar: Ind. 1980, U.S. Dist. Ct. (so. dist.) Ind. 1980. Assoc. Dillon & Cohen, Indpls., 1980-85; ptnr. Tipton, Cohen & Koch, Indpls., 1985-93, LaCava, Zeigler & Carter, Indpls., 1993-94, Zeigler Cohen & Koch, Indpls., 1994—. Leader seminars for nurses, Ind. U. Med. Ctr., Ball State U., Muncie, Ind., St. Vincent Hosp., Indpls., Deaconess Hosp., Evansville, Ind., others; lectr. on med. malpractice Cen. Ind. chpt. AACCN, Indpls. "500" Postgrad. Course in Emergency Medicine, Ind. Assn. Osteo. Physicians and Surgeons State Conv., numerous others. Mem. ABA, ANA, Ind. State Bar Assn., Indpls. Bar Assn., Am. Soc. Law and Medicine, Ind. State Nurses Assn. Republican. Office: Zeigler Cohen & Koch 9465 Counselors Row Ste 104 Indianapolis IN 46240-3816 Business E-Mail: ekoch@zcklaw.com.

KOCH, KATHERINE ROSE, communications executive; b. Pitts., Apr. 21, 1949; d. Irving Samuel Stapsy and Betty Ruth (Sachs) Blake; m. Stanley Christopher Brown, July 26, 1986; 1 child, Matthew. BFA, Rochester Inst. Tech., 1973. Instr. Ivy Sch. Profl. Art, Pitts., 1973-74; advt. dir. Buhl Optical Co., Pitts., 1974-77; pres., creative dir. Ambit Mktg. Comm., Ft. Lauderdale, Fla., 1977—. Instr. Point Park Coll., Pitts., 1977-78. Bd. dirs. United Way, Broward County, 1995—, Broward C.C. Found., 2002, Broward Coordinating Coun., 1994—, Broward Alliance, Ft. Lauderdale Mus. Art. Mem.: Tower Forum (bd. dirs. 1995—), Womens Exec. Club (pres. 1995—96). Office: Ambit Mktg Comm 2455 E Sunrise Blvd Ste 711 Fort Lauderdale FL 33304-3110

KOCH, KATHLEEN DAY, lawyer; b. St. Louis, Nov. 27, 1948; d. Edward J. and Margaret (Beckmeier) D.; children: Stefan, Martha, Rebecca. Student, Concordia Coll., River Forest, Ill., 1966-69; BS in Edn., U. Mo., 1971; JD, U. Chgo., 1977. Bar: Ill. 1977, D.C. 1978. Atty. HUD, Washington, 1977-79, U.S. Merit Sys. Protection Bd., Washington, 1979-84; sr. atty. U.S. Dept. Commerce, Washington, 1984-87; assoc. counsel to pres. White House, Washington, 1987-88; gen. counsel Fed. Labor Rels. Authority, Washington, 1988-91; spl. counsel Office Spl. Counsel, Washington, 1991-97; chief OEEOA FBI, Washington, 1997—. Recipient Disting. Alumni award U. Mo., St. Louis, 1990. Office: FBI 935 Pennsylvania Ave NW Rm 7901 Washington DC 20535-0001

KOCH, LINDA BROWN, utility administrator; b. Clay County, Tenn., Nov. 1, 1947; d. Verne Robert and Erma A. Cherry; m. James M. Brown, Sept. 4, 1966 (dec. Jan. 1994); children: Melissa Brown LaFoe, James K. Brown; m. Ronald W. Koch, Oct. 26, 1996. ASA in Bus. Mgmt., Ind. U./Purdue U., Indpls., 1990; BA in Bus. Mgmt. magna cum laude, Ind. Wesleyan U., 1995; MA in Pub. Rels., Ball State U., 1999. Exec. sec. to sr. v.p. corp. affairs Indpls. Power & Light, 1984-89, cmty. investment mgr., 1989-97, dir. cmty. rels., 1997—. Bd. dirs. Flanner House, Indpls., 1992—, Girls Inc. of Indpls., 1993-98, IPL Employee Credit Union, Indpls., 1992-98; mem. children and youth impact coun. United Way Ctrl. Ind., 1999—. Recipient Keystone award IPL Women's Club, 1992. Mem. Pub. Rels. Soc. Am. (chpt. chair, Keystone award 1999-00), Ctrl. Ind. Corp. Vol. Coun. (founder, pres. 1999—), Exch. Club. (bd. dirs. 1996—). Home: 680 Hillcrest Dr Greenwood IN 46142-1827 Office: Indpls Power & Light Co PO Box 1595 1 Monument Cir Indianapolis IN 46204-2900 E-mail: lkoch@ipalco.com.

KOCH, LISA MICHELLE, psychologist; b. Phoenix, June 20, 1971; d. Donald Gregory and Sandra Lee Koch; m. Russell Leo Kolts, May 20, 2003. BA, U. Calif. San Diego, La Jolla, 1993; MA, U. Miss., Oxford, 1996; PhD, U. MIss., Oxford, 1999. Lic. clin. psychologist Wash. APA intern Spokane (Wash.) Mental Health, 1998—99, staff psychologist, 1999—2001, psychologist supr., 2001—, APA internship tng. dir., 2001—. Cons. Head Start, Spokane, 1998—. Contbr. chapters to books, articles to profl. jours. Mem.: APA, Western Psychol. Soc. Avocations: hiking, kayaking, reading. Office: Spokane Mental Health 131 S Division Spokane WA 99203

KOCH, LORETTA PETERSON, librarian, educator; b. Anna, Ill., Mar. 5, 1951; d. Vance G. and Dorothy M. (Cline) Peterson; m. David Victor Koch, Aug. 25, 1979; 1 child, Elizabeth; stepchildren: John, Victor. AB in English with high honors, U. Ill., 1973, MS in LS, 1974; postgrad., So. Ill. U., Carbondale, 1976. Adult svcs. libr. Carbondale Pub. Libr., 1974-81; owner, operator L. Koch-Words, editing and word processing, Carbondale, 1981-85; rsch. asst. So. Ill. U., 1973, asst. humanities libr., 1985-86, libr. tech. asst. III humanities div., 1986-89, asst. humanities libr., 1989-92, acting humanities libr., 1992-93, humanities libr., 1993—, asst. prof. libr. affairs, 1989-95, assoc. prof. libr. affairs, 1995—, mem. faculty exec. bd., 1989-91. Participant confs. and workshops; presenter in field; field reader grant proposals Ill. Coop. Collection Mgmt. Coordinating Com., 1993. Contbr. articles to profl. publs. Divsn. coord. fund drive United Way, 1989, 90; room parent Lakeland Sch., 1993-94, Parrish Sch., 1994-95, 95-96, 96-97, Thomas Sch., 1998-99, 99-2000; asst. leader troop 813, Girl Scouts U.S.A., 1993-94. Mem. ALA (chmn. poster session abstracts booklet com. 1993-94), Assn. of Col. and Rsch. Libr. (comm. com. women's studies sect. 1993-95), Libr. Adminstrn. and Mgmt. Assn. (using stats. for libr. evaluation com.), Reference and adult svcs. divsn. Ill. Libr. Assn. (nominations com. resources and tech. svcs. forum 1993-94), Margaret Atwood Soc., Midwest Assn. for Can. Studies, Assn. for Can. Studies in U.S., Beta Phi Mu. Home: 2800 W Sunset Dr Carbondale IL 62901-2046 Office: So Ill U Humanities Div Morris Libr Carbondale IL 62901 E-mail: lkoch@lib.siu.edu.

KOCH, MARGARET RAU, writer, artist, historian; b. Sacramento; d. George James Rau and Callista Marie Martin; children: Edward James, Kathleen, Thomas C. Student, U. Calif., Berkeley, 1936-38. Mem. editl. staff Santa Cruz (Calif.) Sentinel, 1958-76. Author: Santa Cruz County, Parade of the Past, 1973, 74, 77, 81, 91, 99, They Called It Home, 1974, Walk Around Santa Cruz, 1978, Going To School in Santa Cruz County, 1978, The Pasatiempo Story, 1990, Santa Cat-Behind the Lace Curtains, 2001; exhibited in group shows at Sedona Arts Ctr., Yavapai County Arts Fair, Ft. Verde Art Show, 1997, 98, 99, 2000. Organizer, first pres. Santa Cruz Hist. Soc. Recipient 3 Mixed Media Watercolor awards Yavapai County Art Fair, Ariz., 2 Watercolor awards Fort Verde Art Show, Ariz. Mem. No. Ariz. Watercolo Soc., Pen Women, Santa Cruz Art League, Sedona Art Ctr. Home: 2307 Town Center Dr Klamath Falls OR 97601-7142

KOCH, SUZANNE M. interior designer; b. Greenbay, Wis., June 24, 1966; d. John Andrew and Mary Ann Hager; m. David Peter Koch, Oct. 14, 2000. BS in Interior Design, U. Wis., 1988. Registered interior designer Wis., cert. Nat. Coun. Interior Design Qualifications. Interior designer Sturgeon Interiors, Milw., 1988—89; facilities planner Milw. Ins., 1989—93; sr. interior designer Bldg. Svc. Inc., Milw., 1993—98; design svcs. mgr. Creative Bus. Interiors, Milw., 1998—. Mem. adv. bd. Waukesha (Wis.) Area Tech. Coll., 1999—, Milw. Area Tech. Coll., 2000—; design student mentor Mount Mary Coll., Milw., 2001—; guest spkr. in field. Mem.: Am. Soc. Interior Designers. Avocations: jewelry beading, traveling, softball. Office: Creative Bus Interiors 11217 W Becher St West Allis WI 53227

KOCHER, JEANNINE M. art educator; b. Yonkers, N.Y., Feb. 10, 1971; d. Merrill and Marilyn Kocher. AA, Coll. of New Rochelle, N.Y., 1991; BA, Coll. of New Rochelle, 1993, MA, 1991. Cert. tchr. art N.Y. Tchr. art St. Mary Star of the Sea, City Island, N.Y., 1991—96, Sacred Heart Elem. Sch., Yonkers, 1993—96, Villa Maria Acad., Bronx, 1996—99, Montessori 27/Yonkers Pub. Schs., 1999—. Avocations: travel, theater, movies.

KOCHER, JUANITA FAY, retired auditor; b. Falmouth, Ky., Aug. 9, 1933; d. William Birgest and Lula (Gillespie) Vickroy; m. Donald Edward Kocher, Nov. 18, 1953. Grad. high sch., Bright, Ind. Cert. internal auditor and compliance officer. Bookkeeper Mchts. Bank and Trust Co., West Harrison, Ind., 1952-56, teller, asst. cashier, 1962-87, br. mgr., 1979-87, internal auditor, 1987-96, ret., 1996; bookkeeper Progressive Bank, New Orleans, 1956-58; with proof dept. 1st Nat. Bank, Cin., Ohio, 1958-59, teller Harrison, Ohio, 1959-62. Bookkeeper Donald E. Kocher Constrn., Harrison, 1981—. Mem. Am. Bankers Assn., Ind. Bankers Assn. Home: 11277 Biddinger Rd Harrison OH 45030

KOCSIS, JOAN BOSCO, elementary education educator, administrative assistant, assistant principal; b. Phillipsburg, N.J., Feb. 6, 1941; d. Frederick B. and Frances (Marina) Bosco; m. Gerald S. Kocsis Sr., Dec. 30, 1961; children: Gerald S. Jr., Jacqueline Kocsis Morgan. BA, Trenton State Coll., 1962; MEd, U. N.C., Charlotte, 1987. Cert. kindergarten-4 tchr., early childhood edn., lang. arts kindergarten-12, social studies 7-12, adminstrn., supervision and curriculum, N.C. Tchr. grades kindergarten, 1, 3 Hamilton Twp. (N.J.) Bd. Edn., 1962—68; tchr. grades kindergarten, talented and gifted Hopewell Valley Bd. Edn., Pennington, 1976—79; tchr. grades 4, 2, 3 Union County Pub. Schs., Monroe, 1981—88; tchr. grade 1 Charlotte (N.C.)-Mecklenburg Pub. Schs., 1988—89; tchr. grades 1, 2 Union County Pub. Schs., Monroe, 1989—. Presenter (TV show) "Positively for Parents", 1992. Recipient Presdl. award for excellence in tchg. sci. and math. NSF, 1994. Mem. NEA, NSTA, N.C. Sci. Tchrs. Assn., Assn. Presdl. Awardees in Sci. Tchg., Internat. Reading Assn. (Union-Monroe coun. treas. 1993—). Home: 309 Auckland Ln Matthews NC 28104-7867

KODA-KIMBLE, MARY ANNE, medical educator, pharmacologist, dean; PharmD, U. Calif., San Francisco, 1969. Lic. pharmacist Calif., 1969, cert. diabetes educator. Faculty U. Calif., San Francisco, 1970—, prof., dean Sch. Pharmacy, Thomas J. Long Endowed chair in Chain Pharmacy Practice. Mem. nonprescription drugs adv. com. FDA; mem. Calif. State Bd. of Pharmacy; lectr. and cons. in field. Co-editor (with others): Applied Therapeutics for Clinical Pharmacists, 1975, 1978, Basic Clinical Pharmacokinetics, 1980, Applied Therapeutics: Clinical Use of Drugs, 1988, Basic Clinical Pharmacokinetics, 1988, Handbook of Applied Therapeutics, 3d edit., 1996; contbr. numerous articles to profl. jours., chpts. to books.; editl. bd. Internat. Jour. Clin. Pharmacology, 1979—82, Drug Interactions Newsletter and Update, 1981, Diabetes Forecast, 1986—89, referee various jours. Numerous others. Named to Hall of Fame, CPhA; recipient Disting. Alumna award, U. Calif.-San Francisco. Mem.: Nat. Acad. of Practice in Pharmacy (founding mem., Disting. Practitioner), Am. Coun. on Pharm. Edn., Am. Coll. Clin. Pharmacy (bd. dirs., Edn. award), Calif. Soc. Health-System Pharmacists (bd. dirs., Pharmacist of the Yr.), Am. Pharm. Assn. (task force on edn.), Am. Assn. Colls. of Pharmacy (pres., commn. to implement change in pharm. edn.), Inst. of Medicine of NAS. Office: Sch Pharmacy C-152 Box 0622 521 Parnassus Ave San Francisco CA 94143-0622

KOEBEL, SISTER CELESTIA, health care system executive; b. Chillicothe, Ohio, Jan. 12, 1928; BS, Coll. of Mount St. Joseph, 1958; MHA, St. Louis U., 1964; D, U. Albuquerque, 1976. Asst. dir. nursing svcs. Good Samaritan Hosp. & Health Ctr., Dayton, Ohio, 1961-62; adminstrv. resident Providence Med. Ctr., Seattle, 1963-64; pres. St. Joseph Healthcare Corp., Albuquerque, 1964-85, Sisters of Charity Health Care Systems, Cin., 1985-96; hon. offcl. Cath. Health Initiatives, Denver, 1996—. Mem. Am. Hosp. Assn. (adv. coun., 1987-88), N.Mex. Hosp. Assn. (treas. 1968-69, v.p. 1970, pres. 1972). Office: 345 Neeb Rd Cincinnati OH 45233-5102

KOEHL, CAMILLE JOAN, accountant; b. Chgo., Nov. 9, 1943; d. Alfonse James and Genevieve V. (Riche) Daurio; children: David A., Laura L., Robert M., Karen M. BS in Acctg., De Paul U., 1976; postgrad., Roosevelt U., 1987—. CPA, Ill.; CFP. Treas. Meritex Corp., Carpentersville, Ill., 1966-68; contr. Di Com Corp., Glenview, Ill., 1968-72; v.p., treas. Ridge Road Co., Northbrook, Ill., 1982-87, Decker Gardens, Inc., Northbrook, 1979-87, S&L Engring. Co., Northbrook, 1972-87; ptnr. HJS Constrn. Co., Barrington Hills, Ill., 1979—; pres. Lé Tan Ltd., Palatine, Ill., 1984—, CJK Enterprises Ltd., Lakemoor, Ill., 1985—; owner Camille J. Koehl & Assoc., Lakemoor, 1978—; pres. Koehl Constrn. and Devel. Corp., Lakemoor, 1990—, Pressing Matters Ltd., McHenry, Ill., 1990—. Mem. Internat. Bd. Cert. Fin. Planners, Ill. CPAs. Avocations: golf, reading. Home and Office: 2020 W Il Route 120 # A Mchenry IL 60050

KOEHN, TORI JOANN, music educator; b. Texarkana, Tex., Aug. 17, 1980; d. Steven Joseph and Shelly Joan Graff; m. Jason Lee Koehn, June 16, 2001. MusB Edn., U. Kans., Lawrence, Kans., 2001. Cert. tchg. Kans., 2002. Accompanist/asst. dir. Bel Canto Choir-Southwest Jr. High, Lawrence, Kans., 2000—01; children's choir dir. Plymouth Congl. Ch., Lawrence, Kans., 2001—02; vocal music instr. USD 467 - Wichita County Sch., Leoti, Kans., 2002—. Music and arts camp dean Camp Lakeside United Meth. Ctr., Scott City, Kans., 1999—; pianist St. Mary's Cath. Ch., Marienthal, Kans., 2002—. Mem. St. Mary's Altar Soc., Marienthal, Kans., 2002; bd. mem. Wichita County Arts Alliance, Leoti, Kans., 2003. Recipient Grad. with Highest Distinction, U. Kans., 2001. Mem.: Nat. Assn. for Music Edn., Am. Choral Directors Assn. Roman Cath. Avocations: cooking, gardening, scrapbooks, reading, spending time with family. Home: Route 1 Box 94 Leoti KS 67861 Personal E-mail: tjkoehn@wbsnet.org.

KOEL, JENNIFER JO WEBER, music educator; b. Quinter, Kans., Oct. 31, 1972; d. James and Sue Weber; m. Jeff Koel, Dec. 19, 1997; children: Leighton, Elizabeth. B of Music Edn., Ft. Hays State U., Kans., 1995. Cert. music tchr., drivers edn. tchr. Kans. Band tchr. Quinter Schs., Kans., 1996; music tchr. USD # 275, Winona, Kans., 1996—98, Herndon Schs., Kans., 1998—2000, USD # 315, Colby, Kans., 2000—. Chaplain VFW-Ladies Aux., Barnett Post, Kans., 2001—02. Grad. spkr., Herndon H.S., 2003. Mem.: Kans. Safety and Driver Edn. Assn., Kans. Music Edn. Assn. Republican. Roman Catholic. Avocations: gardening, crafts. Office: Colby Grade Sch 210 N Grant Colby KS 67701 Office Phone: 785-460-5100 x1104.

KOELINER, LAURETTE, manufacturing executive, human resources specialist; b. Bklyn, Oct. 21, 1954; BA Bus. Mgmt., U. Ctrl. Fla.; MBA, Stetson U., Deland, Fla. From contract analyst to mgr. contracts and pricing for Missile Systems Co. McDonnell, Douglas, Titusville, Fla., 1978—88, bus. mgr. Tomahwk Cruise Missile Program, 1988—89, dir. strategic and bus planning Tomahawk, 1989—90, head internal support and service ops., 1990—92, dir. structuring and managinoverhead budget St. Louis, 1992—94, dir. human resources, security, 1994—96; dir. internal audit, mgmt. control systems and exec. devel. McDonnell Douglas-Boeimg, St. Louis, 1996—99; v.p. corp. controller Boeing Co., Seattle, 1999—2002; exec. v.p., chief people and adminstn. officer The Boeing Co., Chgo., 2002—. Bd. dirs. Sara Lee Corp. Mem. Adv. Coun. U. Portland (Oreg.)., New Leaders for New Schs., Chgo.; Intiman Theater Seattle. Named to Hall of Fame, U. Ctrl. Fla. Coll. Bus. Adminstrn., 2003. Mem.: Soc. for Human Resource Mgmt., Econ. Club Chgo., Chicagoland C. of C. (bd. dirs.), Nat. Contracts Mgmt. Assn. Office: The Boeing Co 100 N Riverside Pla Chicago IL 60606

KOELLINER, LAURETTE T. aerospace transportation executive; b. Bklyn., Oct. 21, 1954; BS in Bus. Mgmt., U. Ctrl. Fla.; MBA, Stetson U., Deland, Fla. Contracts analyst McDonnell Douglas, 1978—80, mgr. contracts and pricing Missile Systems Co., Titusville, Fla., 1986—88, bus. mgr. Tomahawk Cruise Missile Program, Titusville, 1988; dir. strategic and bus. planning Missile Systems Co., Titusville, 1989—90, dir. internal support and svcs. ops., 1990 92; dir. structuring and overhead mgmt. McDonnell Douglas Aerospace, St. Louis, 1992—94, dir. human resources divsn., 1994—96, dir. internal audit, mgmt. control systems and exec. devel., 1996—99; v.p., corp. controller Douglas -Boeing, St. Louis, 1999—2000; pres. shared svcs. group The Boeing Co., 2000—00, exec. v.p., 2002—. Bd. dirs. Sara Lee, Chgo., Exostar. Mem. adv. coun. Univ. Portland, Oreg.; bd. dirs. Intiman Theater, Seattle. Mem.: Econ. Club Chgo., Chicagoland C. of C. Office: The Boeing Co 100 N Riverside Plz Chicago IL 60606-2609*

KOELMEL, LORNA LEE, data processing executive; b. Denver, May 15, 1936; d. George Bannister and Gladys Lee Steuart; m. Herbert Howard Nelson, Sept. 9, 1956 (div. Mar. 1967); children: Karen Dianne, Phillip Dean, Lois Lynn; m. Robert Darrel Koelmel, May 12, 1981; stepchildren: Kim, Cheryl, Dawn, Debbie. BA in English, U. Colo., 1967. Cert. secondary English tchr. Substitute English tchr. Jefferson County Schs., Lakewood, Colo., 1967—68; sec. specialist IBM Corp., Denver, 1968—75, pers. administr., 1975—82, asst. ctr. coord., 1982—85, office systems specialist, 1985—87, backup computer operator, 1987—; computer instr. Barnes Bus. Coll., Denver, 1987—92; owner, mgr. Lorna's Precision Word Processing and Desktop Pub., Denver, 1987—89; computer cons. Denver, 1990—. Editor newsletter Colo. Nat. Campers and Hikers Assn., 1992-94. Organist Christian Sci. Soc., Buena Vista, Colo., 1963-66, 1st Ch. Christ Scientists Thornton Westminster, Thornton, Colo., 1994—; chmn. bd. dirs., 1979-80. Mem. NAFE, Nat. Secs. Assn. (retirement ctr. chair 1977-78, newsletter chair 1979-80, v.p. 1980-81), Am. Theatre Organ Soc. (Rocky Mountain chpt.), Am. Guild Organists, U. Colo. Alumni Assn., Avon Ind. Sales Rep and Pres. Club, Alpha Chi Omega (publicity com. 1986-88). Clubs: Nat. Writers. Lodges: Job's Daus. (recorder 1953-54). Republican. Avocations: quilting, piano, bridge, logic problems, golf.

KOENIG, ELIZABETH BARBARA, sculptor; b. N.Y.C., Apr. 20, 1937; d. Hayward and Selma E. (Rosen) Ulman; m. Carl Stuart Koenig, Sept. 10, 1961; children: Katherine Lee, Kenneth Douglas. BA, Wellesley Coll., 1958; MD, Yale U., 1962; postgrad., Art Students League N.Y., 1963-64, Corcoran Sch. Art, 1964-67. One-woman shows include St. John's Coll., Annapolis, Md., 1974, Foxhall Gallery, Washington, 1977, 85, 99, also solo retrospectives Lyman Allyn Mus., New London, Conn., 1978, Rotunda of Pan-Am. Health Orgn., Washington, 1978, Gallery Metayer, Paris, 1999; exhibited in group shows at Internat. Dedication Nat. Bur. Stds., Gaithersburg, Md., 1966, Textile Mus., Washington, 1974-75, No. Va. Mus., Alexandria, 1975, Meridian House Internat., Washington, 1980; commd. works include Free Spirit marble carving Washington Hebrew Congregation, 1978, Monumental Torso bronze for grounds George Meany Ctr. for Labor Studies, 1982, desert stone marble carving Regional Ctr. for Women in Arts, Westchester, Pa., 2003; represented in pvt. collections, U.S. and Europe. Recipient 1st prize sculpture Tri-State Regional Exhbn., Md., 1970, 2d and 3d prize sculpture, 1971. Mem. Artists Equity Assn. (v.p. Washington 1977-83), Art Students League N.Y. (life), Internat. Sculpture Ctr., New Arts Ctr. Avocations: reading, gardening. Home: 9014 Charred Oak Dr Bethesda MD 20817-1924

KOENIG, HEIDI MARGRET, medical educator; b. Newman Grove, Nebr., Apr. 8, 1958; d. Paul Fritz and Barbara Ann (Kaempf) K.; m. William Walter Holt, May 21, 1993; children: William Paul Holt, Samuel Koenig Holt. BS, Wayne State Coll., Wayne, Nebr., 1980; MD, U. Nebr. Med. Ctr., Omaha, 1985. Intern S.W. Mich. Area Health Edn. Ctr., Kalamazoo, 1985-86; resident in surgery Michael Reese Hosp., Chgo., 1986-89; resident in anesthesiology U. Ill., Chgo., 1989-92, fellow in neuroanesthesiology, 1992-93; asst. prof. anesthesiology U. Ill. Chgo., Michael Reese Hosp., 1993—. Co-author: (chpt. in book) International Anesthesiology Clinics, 1996; contbr. articles to profl. jours. Recipient FY94 grant Michael Reese Hosp., 1994-95, 96-97, nat. grant Am. Heart Assn., 1996—. Mem. AAAS, Am. Soc. Anesthesiology, Internat. Anesthesia Rsch. Soc., Ill. Soc. Anesthesiology, Chgo. Soc. Anesthesiology, Soc. Neuroanesthesia and Critical Care. Office: U Ill at Chgo Dept Anesthesiology 1740 W Taylor St Ste 3200 Wes Chicago IL 60612-7232

KOENIG, LEAH, marriage and family therapist; b. Bklyn., Oct. 8, 1927; d. Abraham Hirsch and Rose Siderowitz; m. Irving Koenig, May 16, 1949 (dec. Apr. 15, 1998); children: Karen Schochet, Anne. BA, Bklyn. Coll., 1947; MA in French Lit., Columbia U., N.Y.C., 1950; MS in Guidance, Bklyn. Coll., 1969, Advanced Cert. Adminstrn. and Supervision, 1977; Advanced Cert. Family Systems Therapy, Hunter Coll. Social Work, N.Y.C., 1986. Cert. tchr., guidance counselor, ednl. adminstr., prin. N.Y.C. Bd. Edn. Exec. dir. Young Zionist Actions Com., N.Y.C., 1947—49; tchr. Ramaz, N.Y.C., 1951—55, PS 186, Bklyn., 1952—55; thcr., guidance counselor JHS 285, Bklyn., 1954—55, 1961—93; dir. Substance Abuse Prevention Project Concern, Bklyn., 1971—93; family therapist EFCC-Project Concern, Bklyn., 1993—. Pub. (songbook): Songs of Israel, 1949. Recipient Cmty. Svc. award, Samuel and May Rudin, 1990, Excellence in Edn. award, Canarsie Mental Health, 1990, Leadership in Edn. award, Jewish Tchrs. Cmty. Chest, 1992. Achievements include development of curricula in substance abuse prevention for Bd. Edn. and NYU; curricula for in-svc. tng. of tchrs. in human rels. Avocations: Hebrew, opera, theater, great books, crossword puzzles. Home: 2777 Bedford Ave Brooklyn NY 11210

KOENKER, DIANE P. history educator; b. Chgo., July 29, 1947; m. Roger Koenker; 1 child. AB in History, Grinnell Coll., 1969; AM in Comparative Studies in History, U. Mich., 1971, PhD in History, 1976. From asst. prof. to assoc. prof. in history Temple U., Phila., 1976-83; asst. prof. history U. Ill., Urbana-Champaign, 1983-86, assoc. prof., 1986-88, prof. history, 1988—, dir. Russian and East European Ctr., 1990-96, editor Slavic Rev., 1996—. Vis. lectr. history U. Ill., Urbana-Champaign, 1975; vis. fellow Australian Nat. U., 1989; Fulbright-Hays Faculty Rsch. Abroad, 1993; active Study Group on Russian Revolution, Study Group on Internat. Labor and Working-Class History; lectr. in field. Author: Moscow Workers and the 1917 Revolution, 1981, paperback edit., 1986, (with William G. Rosenberg) Strikes and Revolution in Russia 1917, 1989, editor: Tret'ya Vserossiiskaya Konferentsiya Professional'nykh Soyuzov 1917, 1982, (with William G. Rosenberg and Ronald Grigor Suny) Party, State and Society in the Russian Civil War: Explorations in Social History, 1989, (with Ronald D. Bachman) Revelations from the Russian Archives, 1997; editor, translator: (with S.A. Smith) Notes of a Red Guard, 1993; mem. editl. bd. Cambridge Soviet Paperbacks; mem. adv. bd. Soviet Studies in History, 1986-89; book reviewer to numerous jours.; contbr. articles to profl. jours. Rsch. fellow Temple U., 1977, 82, Sr. fellow Russian Inst.-Columbia U., 1977-78, Individual fellow NEH, 1983-84, Rsch. fellow NEH, 1984-85, 94-95, MUCIA Exch. fellow Moscow State U., 1991; grantee Am. Coun. Learned Socs.-Social Sci. Rsch. Coun., 1977-78, Temple U., 1979-81, 82-83, William and Flora Hewlett Internat. Rsch. grantee, 1986, 91, Nat. Coun. for Soviet and East European Rsch. grantee, 1989, IREX Travel grantee, 1993; recipient Fulbright-Hays Faculty Rsch. award for USSR, 1989, Arnold O. Beckman Rsch. Bd. award, 1990-91, 2002-. Mem. Am. Hist. Assn. (mem. membership com. 1996-98, European History sect. chair 2001, Chester Higby prize European sect. 2003), Am. Assn. Advancement Slavic Studies (bd. dirs. 1996—), Midwest Workshop of Russian and Soviet Historians, Assn. Women in Slavic Studies. Office: U Ill Slav Rev 57 E Armory Ave Champaign IL 61820-6601 also: U Ill Dept History 309 Gregory Hall 810 S Wright St Urbana IL 61801-3644

KOEPP, DONNA PAULINE PETERSEN, librarian; b. Clinton, Iowa, Oct. 8, 1941; d. Leo August and Pauline Sena (Outzen) Petersen; m. David Ward Koepp, June 5, 1960 (div. June 1984). BS in Edn., U. Colo., 1967; MA in Libr., U. Denver, 1974; postgrad., U. Colo., 1984-85. Subject specialist govt. publs., map dept. Denver Pub. Libr., 1967-85; head govt. documents, map libr. U. Kans., Lawrence, 1985-2000, map and geomedia svcs. libr., 2000—02. Head govt. document, microforms, reference instrn. Soc. Sci. Program Harvard U., 2002-; apptd. Fed. Depository Libr. Coun. to Pub. Printer, 1998-2001. Prodn. mgr. Meridian Jour., 1988-93, 96-99; editor: Index and Carto-Bibliography of Maps, 1789-1969, 1995. Recipient Documents to the People award Congl. Info. Svc./Govt. Documents Round Table/ALA, 1999. Mem. Map & Geography Round Table of Am. Libr. Assn. (chmn. 1986-87, Outstanding Contbn. to Map Librarianship 1991), Govt. Documents Round Table of Am. Libr. Assn., Western Assn. Map Librs. (sec. 1983-84). Office: Govt Documents Microforms Libr Lamont Libr Lower Level U Harvard College Libr Cambridge MA 02138- E-mail: koepp@fas.harvard.edu.

KOEPPEL, HOLLY, electric power industry executive; b. Pitts. married; 2 children. BS in Bus., Ohio State U., Columbus; MS in Bus., Ohio State U. From mgr. to v.p. Asia-Pacific Ops. Consolidated Natural Gas, Sydney, Australia, 1984—2000; v.p. new ventures for corp. devel. Am. Electric Power Co., Columbus, Ohio, 2000—02, exec. v.p. comml. ops., 2002—. Office: Am Elec Power Co ! Riverside Plz Columbus OH 43215-1000

KOEPPEL, MARY SUE, communications educator, writer; b. Phlox, Wis., Dec. 12, 1939; d. Alphonse and Emma Petronella Marx Koeppel; m. Robert B. Gentry, May 31, 1980. BA, Alverno Coll., 1962; MA, Loyola U., Chgo., 1968; postgrad., U. Wis., St. Louis U., U. N.H., U. Calif., U. North Fla., U. Minn., Jacksonville U. Tchr. St. Joseph H.S., Milw., 1962-68, Pius XI H.S., Milw., 1968-72; instr., head dept. comms., dir. learning ctr. Waukesha County Tech. Inst., Pewaukee, Wis., 1972-80; pres., exec. bd. West Suburban Coun. Tchg. Profession, 1976-80. Adv. Waukesha chpt. Parents Without Partners, 1975—80; cons. Learning Ctrs., 1976—, Coll. and Univ. Faculties; instr. comm. Fla. C.C., Jacksonville, 1980—; instr. (summers) Inst. for Tchrs. of Writing Westbrook Coll., Portland, Maine, 1980—84, instr. (summers) nat. master tchr. seminar, 1982—, TV interviewer, 1989—; instr. Nat. Inst. for Tchrs. Writing, Greenfield, Mass., 1987—94. Editor (-in-chief): Kalliope Jour. Women's Lit. and Art, 1988—, Lollipops, Lizards and Literature, 1994—; editor: Instructional Network Notes, 1982—85; co-editor: Women of Vision, 2000; author: Writing Resources for Conferencing and Collaboration, 1989, Writing Strategies Plus Collaboration, 1997, Writing Strategies Plus Collaboration. 4th edit., 2004, Write Your Life-The Memory Catcher, 1998, In the Library of Silences, Poems of Loss, 2001; contbr. ; contbg. editor: State St. Rev., 1992—. Mem. Sherman Park Cmty. Ctr., 1975—80; co-founder, bd. dirs. Instrnl. Network for coll. Faculty, 1981—85. Recipient Red Schoolhouse award for tchg. excellence, Assn. Fla. C.C., 1983, Faculty Excellence award, 2000, Frances Buck Sherman award, 2001, Educator of Yr. award, Cultural Coun. of Greater Jacksonville, 2002, Bd. Trustees award for Cmty. Svc., Fla. C.C. at Jacksonville, 2003; grantee, NDEA, 1968, Art Ventures, 1992, Tchg. and Learning Ctr., 1999; scholar, Fla. Humanities Coun., 1999. Mem.: Am. Pen Women, Nat. Coun. Tchrs. of English. Office: Kalliope 11901 Beach Blvd Jacksonville FL 32246 E-mail: skoeppel@fccj.edu.

KOERBER, DOLORES JEAN, music educator, musician; b. Martins Ferry, Ohio, Apr. 7, 1936; d. Clarence Donald and Bertha Gail (Palmer) K. B in Religious Edn., Malone Coll., 1958, BS, 1965; MEd, Kent State U., 1972; D in Religious Edn., Massillon Baptist Coll., 2000. Cert. tchr. music grades K-12, Ohio. Tchr. Coun. Religious Edn., North Canton, Ohio, 1958-60, Shelby, Ohio, 1960-62, Garaway Local, Sugarcreek, Ohio, 1965-71, Fairless Local, Justus, Ohio, 1971-73, Massillon (Ohio) Christian Sch., 1973-75; prof. Massillon Bapt. Coll., 1973—. Choir dir. Evang. United Brethren Ch., Sugarcreek, 1965-68, Westminster Presbyn., Canton, 1973-75, organist, 1981-85, Christ United Meth., Louisville, Ohio, 1985-92, St. Paul's United Meth., Canton, 1993—. Performer in programs for schs., clubs and chs. Named first native Cantonian to graduate from Malone Coll. after its relocation in Canton, 1958. Mem. Fortnightly Music Club (pres. 1970-71), MacDowell Music Club (rec. sec. 2001-03, 1st v.p. 2003—), Am. Guild Organists. Republican. Avocations: doll collecting, handwork, swimming.

KOERBER, MARILYNN ELEANOR, gerontology nursing educator, consultant, nurse; b. Covington, Ky., Feb. 1, 1942; d. Harold Clyde and Vivian Eleanor (Conrad) Hilge; m. James Paul Koerber, May 29, 1971. Diploma, Christ Hosp. Sch. Nursing, Cin., 1964; BSN, U. Ky., 1967; MPH, U. Mich., 1970. RN, Ohio, S.C.; cert. gerontologist. Staff nurse premature and newborn nursery Cin. Gen. Hosp., 1964-65, staff nurse, hosp. discharge planner Vis. Nurse Assn., Cin., 1967-69, asst. dir. Atlanta, 1976-78; instr. Coll. Nursing, U. Ky., Lexington, 1970-71; supr. Montgomery County Health Dept., Rockville, Md., 1971-74; asst. prof. Coll. Nursing, U. S.C., Columbia, 1979-86, instr., 1987-89; alzheimer's project coord. S.C. Commn. on Aging, Columbia, 1988-90; dir. edn. and tng. Luth. Homes S.C., White Rock, 1988-91; grad. asst. U. S.C. Sch. of Pub. Health, 1991-94; trainer for homemakers home health aides S.C. Divsn. on Aging, 1991-97; coord. to train homemakers home aides nursing assts. State Pilot Program, DSS and Divsn. on Aging, 1993-95; Alzheimer's trainer office aging, nurse mgr. Beaufort-Jasper Hampton Comprehensive Health, 1998—2003; allied health program mgr. Tech. Coll. of the Lowcountry, 1997—. Mem. utilization rev. bd. Palmetto Health Dist., Lexington, 1984-2000; test item writer, nurse aide cert. Psychol. Corp., San Antonio, 1989, 91, 92; bd. examiners Nursing Home Adminstrn. and Community Residential Care Facility Adminstr., chmn. of edn. com., Columbia, S.C., 1990-93; presenter gerontol. workshops and residential care facilities adminstrn. Contbg. editor: (handbook) Promoting Caregiver Groups, 1984; reviewer gerontology textbooks, 1983-91; contbr. tng. video and manuals on Alzheimers, 1988 (hon. mention Retirement Rsch. Found. 1989). Del. S.C. Gov. White House Conf. on Aging, Columbia, 1981; chmn. ann. meeting S.C. Fedn. for Older Ams., Columbia, 1989—91; v.p. Alzheimer's Family Services of Greater Beaufort, 1998—99, mem. adv. bd., 2002—; bd. dirs. Sr. Svcs. of Beaufort County, 1997—2002, Alzheimer's Family Services of Greater Beaufort, 1997—2002. USPHS trainee, 1965-67, Adm. on Aging trainee, 1969-70. Mem. ANA (cert. gerontol. nurse, cmty. health nurse), S.C. Nurses Assn., So. Gerontol. Soc., Gerontol. Soc. Am., S.C. Gerontol. Soc. (treas. 1989-91, Rosamond R. Boyd award 1986, Pres. award Mid State Alzheimers Chpt., 1993, Macy Scally Alzheimers award 2000), Soc. for Pub. Health Edn., Am. Soc. on Aging, Alzheimers Assn. (bd. dirs. Columbia chpt. 1988-93, sec. 1992, chmn. nominating com. 1991-92; bd. dirs. S.C. combined health appeal 1991-93), Nat. Coun. on Aging, Nat. Gerontol. Nursing Assn. Democrat. Unitarian Universalist. Avocations: interior decorating, wine tasting.

KOESTER, JOLENE, academic administrator; BA magna cum laude, U. Minn., 1970; MA in Communication Arts, U. Wis., Madison, 1971; PhD in Speech Communications, U. Minn., 1980. Asst. prof. speech and drama U. Mo., Columbia, 1980—83; asst. prof. communication studies Calif. State U., Sacramento, 1983—85, assoc. prof. communication studies, 1985—89, dept. chair communication studies, 1986—89, prof. communication studies, 1989—2000, asst. v.p. academic affairs, 1989—91, assoc. v.p. academic affairs, 1991—93, v.p. academic affairs, 1993—2000, provost, 1996—2000; pres. Calif. State U. Northridge, 2000—. Office: Calif State U UN 200 18111 Nordhoff St Northridge CA 91330-8230*

KOESTER, LISA, educational administrator, consultant; b. Sioux City, Iowa, July 31, 1957; d. Clifford Duane and Janet Anne Hansen; m. David John Koester, June 9, 1979; children: Andrew John, Amy Lynn. BS, Iowa State U., 1979, MS, 1994. Cert. administrator, evaluator, Iowa. Tchr., coach South Tama County Schs., Toledo, Iowa, 1979-82, 88-92, Gladbrook (Iowa) Cmty. Schs., 1982-84; grad. rsch. asst. Iowa State U., Ames, 1992-94; mid. sch. assoc. prin. Marshalltown (Iowa) Cmty. Schs., 1994-98; h.s. prin. Gladbrook-Reinbeck Cmty. Schs., Reinbeck, Iowa, 1998—. Ednl. cons., Gladbrook, 1994—. Mem. Sch. Bd., Gladbrook Cmty. Schs., 1983-86. Mem. ASCD, Nat. Assn. Secondary Sch. Prins., Alpha Delta Kappa, Phi Kappa Phi, Phi Delta Kappa. Republican. Methodist. Avocations: sports, reading, gardening, computers. Home: 513 6th St Gladbrook IA 50635-9411 Office: Gladbrook-Reinbeck HS 600 Blackhawk St Reinbeck IA 50669-1312

KOESTNER, CAROL ANN, information technology manager, consultant; d. Edward Richard and Ileita P. Koestner; adopted children: Tamera A. Hough, Sheryl D. Fox, Charles R. Shumate. BA in Math., U. of South Fla., 1969, Roanoke Coll., 1967. Programmer May Plant DuPont Data Sys., Camden, SC, 1969—71; analyst May Plant Nylon Info. Sys., Camden, 1971—74; from sr. analyst to sr. specialist DoPunt Nylon Info. Sys., Camden, 1974—84, sr. specialist, 1984—89; sys. cons. DuPont Textiles & Interiors Nylon Info. Sys., Camden, 1990—. Bus. cons. applied economics class Jr. Achievement Camden (S.C.) HS, 1987—99. Musician at various venues songs. Pres. band booster club Camden (S.C.) HS, 1979—80; campaign leader breast cancer Am. Cancer Soc., Columbia and Camden, SC, 2001—02; mem. coun. on ministries Lyttleton St. United Meth. Ch., Camden, 1980—83; vol. grant writer. Vet.'s Formation, Columbia, SC, 2002—03. Recipient Jake Watson award, United Way of Kershaw County, 1987, 1993, Svc. award, Jr. Achievement. Republican. Methodist. Avocations: travel, volunteer work, crafts. Home: 2204 Elkridge Drive Camden SC 29020-2016 Office: DuPont Textiles & Interiors PO Drawer 7000 Camden SC 29020-7000 Personal E-mail: ckoestner@aol.com.

KOFF, SHIRLEY IRENE, writer; b. Oakland, Calif., Aug. 31, 1948; d. Lawrence Ray and Stella Pauline (Durham) Butler; m. Robert Allen Koff, June 12, 1971; children: Jennifer, Katherine. BA, Calif. State U., 1971, MA, 1972. Adj. prof. Pellissippi State U., Knoxville, 1989-93; asst. mgr. Adolfo II, Pigeon Forge, Tenn., 1994-98. Poet, writer; tchr. adult religious edn. classes and seminars; expert info. provider internet resource AskAnything-.com. Tchr., lay min., bd. dirs. First Assembly of God Ch., Sevierville, 1996-99; core group leader, founding mem. Wellspring Congregation, United Meth. Ch., 1999-2001. Mem.: AAUW, Knoxville (Tenn.) Writers Guild, Tenn. Writers Alliance, Appalachian Writers Assn., Mensa. Democrat. Avocations: writing, speaking, teaching. Home: 1214 Amber Ln Sevierville TN 37862-6101 E-mail: skoff@ix.netcom.com.

KOFNOVEC, DONNA ANN See HANOVER, DONNA

KOGELSCHATZ, JOAN LEE, psychologist, psychotherapist; b. Detroit, Nov. 26, 1940; d. Edgar Rolfe and Helen Josephine (York) K.; B.A., U. Fla., 1963; M.S.W., Fla. State U., 1967, Ph.D., 1976. Intern, VA Hosp., Bay Pines, Fla., 1966, div. child and adolescent psychiatry, dept. psychiatry U. Fla. Med. Center, Gainesville, 1966; instr. psychiatry div. child Adolescent psychiatry U. Fla. Med. Center, Shands Teaching Hosp. & Clinics, Gainesville, 1967-72; field supr., instr. Fla. State U., 1973, field supr., instr. Psychiatric Social Work, 1973-74; pvt. practice psychology, Dothan, Ala., 1975—; guest lectr. Shands Teaching Hosp. & Clinics, 1975, Neurosis Inst., Moscow, 1992, Siriraj/Bumrongrad Hosps., Bangkok, Thailand, others; cons. Lyster Army Hosp., Ft. Rucker, Ala., 1975-78; guest lectr. Dept. Mental Health, Ft. Rucker, 1975; lectr. in field; asst. prof. U. Ala., 1976-77; cons. Bd. dirs. Ala. Soc. Crippled Children and Adults, 1981—, cons., 1981—, fin. chmn., 1983—; apptd. to adv. bd. Law Enforcement Planning Agy. Ala., State of Ala., 1980—, State of Ala. Child Abuse and Neglect Prevention, pres., chmn., 1985-91; chmn., pres. State of Ala. Children's Trust Fund Council, 1984-86, pres. Ala. 2d Congl. Dist., 1985. Diplomate Am. Bd. Psychotherapy, Am. Bd. Medical Psychotherapy, Am. Bd. Pain Mgmt., Am. Bd. Med. Psychotherapists, Am. Bd. Sexologist; lic. profl. counselor, Ala.; lic. marriage and family therapist, Ala.; lic. psychologist, Fla.; lic. clin. psychiat. social worker, Ala.; cert. emergency therapist, Fla. State U.; bd. cert. emergency crisis response, traumatic stress expert, Am. Acad. Experts in Traumatic Stress; bd. certified traumatologist, Traumatology Inst. Fla. State U.; bd. dirs. Dothan Child Abuse Prevention Bd., S.E. Ala. BBB, S.E. Ala. Symphony Assn., Ala.Soc. Crippled Children and Adults, Girls Club Dothan, S.E. Ala. Rehab. Bd., chmn. legis. com.; bd. dirs., cons. Fibromyelgia and Chronic Fatigue Support Group, Compassionate Friends, Adam Group; chmn. com. mem., bd. dirs. Landmark Found.; exec. bd. mem., chmn. judges com. Nat. Peanut Festival. Host. An Hour With Dr. Joan WWNT, WTKN-Talk Radio, 1995. Named Woman of Yr., Nat. Fedn. Bus. and Profl. Women, 1984, Model Woman of Yr., Girls Clubs of Dothan, 1998; recipient Sm. Bus. of Yr. Profl. Divsn. award Dothan C. of C., 1994, Leadership Dothan award, 1989, Treasurer, Leadership Dothan Alumni Coun., 1990. Mem. Am. Acad. Clin. Sexologists (founding clin. fellow), Am. Psychol. Assn., Acad. Psychosomatic Medicine, Am. Acad. Pain Mgmt. (cert.), Am. Orthopsychiat. Assn. (life), Am. Assn. Psychiat. Services for Children (chmn. pub. edn. com. 1984), Internat. Assn. Trauma Counselors, Internat. Soc. Clin. Hypnosis, Am. Soc. Clin. Hypnosis (cert.), Am. Assn. Marriage and Family Therapists, Nat. Assn. Social Workers, Acad. Cert. Social Workers, Nat. Council Family Relations, Southeastern Council on Family Relations, Assn. Traumatic Stress Specialists, Internat. Critical Incident Stress Found., Am. Assn. Sex Therapists, Fla. Assn. Practicing Psychologists, Counselors and Therapists, Gulf Coast Assn. Marriage and Family Therapy, Alpha Kappa Delta. Contbr. articles to profl. jours. Office: 921 Honeysuckle Rd Dothan AL 36305-1934

KOHL, JOAN, non-profit administrator, social worker; b. N.Y.C., Mar. 28, 1952; d. Michael and Victoria Lucas; m. Donald Kohl, Aug. 12, 1978. BA, CUNY, 1974, MSW, 1978. Cert. social worker, N.Y.; cert. wildlife rehabilitator. Recreation specialist Lt. Joseph P. Kennedy Jr. Home, Bronx, N.Y., 1975-78; social worker Rofay Nursing Home, Bronx, 1978-81; dir. social svc. New Rochelle (N.Y.) Hosp. Med. Ctr., 1981-84; pres., founder Coral Springs (Fla.) Nature Ctr. and Wildlife Hosp., 1992—. Adv. bd. mem. Coral Springs Growth Mgmt. and Environ. Protection Commn., 1991—, Fla. Wildlife Rehab. Assn., Miami, 1996—, Sawgrass Springs Middle Sch., Coral Springs, 1996—; pres. bd. dirs. Wildlife Care Ctr., Inc., 1985-95. Recipient Outstanding Personal Contbn. awad Keep Fla. Beautiful, 1998, 1st Annual Legacy award Nature Conservancy, Fla., 1999; Forestry grantee Fla. Dept. Agr., 1998. Mem. Leadership Broward Found., Leadership North Broward (alumni, environ. chair 1993-94), Coral Springs C. of C. (founder 1995, Rookie of the Yr. 1997). Avocations: wildlife preservation, birding, photography, gardening, aviculturist. Office: Coral Springs Nature Ctr 3916 NW 73rd Ave Coral Springs FL 33065-2140

KOHLER, LAURA E. human resources executive; married; 2 children. Grad., Duke U., 1984; MFA, Cath. U., 1987. Past tchr. Chgo. Pub. Schs.; past corp. team facilitator; past mgr. Nat. Players, Washington; past residence mgr. Olney (Md.) Theatre; founder Address Unknown, Chgo.; past exec. dir. Kohler Found., Inc.; v.p. human resources Kohler Co., 1994—. Office: Kohler Co 444 Highland Dr Kohler WI 53044-1500

KOHLER, NORA HELEN, music educator; b. Missoula, Mont., Sept. 17, 1950; d. Edwin Gibbs and Helen (Oktabec) Linderman; m. Allen L. Kohler, Jr., Aug. 23, 1969; children: Oralee, Robert, Jennifer, Benjamin, Keri. BS cum laude in Elem. Edn., We. Mont. Coll., 2001. Music aid Ramsay (Mont.) Sch. Dist., 1996—98; tchr. Powell County HS, Deer Lodge, Mont., 2001—02, coach pep band, 2001—02; tchr. music Sch. Dist. 1, Butte, Mont., 2002—. Bd. dirs. Young Musicians Club, Butte. Co-dir. City YMCA Benefit Concert, Butte, 1996—98; co-leader Brownie Girl Scouts, 1980—81; leader dist. Boy Scouts, 1976—78; active various positions Cub Scouts, 1983—91; active LDS Ch., 1969—. Named Den Leader of Yr., Viligante Coun. Boy Scouts Am., 1985. Mem.: Mont. Fedn. Tchrs., Mont. Edn. Assn., Mont. Gen. Music Tchrs. Assn., Music Educators Nat. Conf. Mem. Lds Ch. Avocations: fishing, hunting, sewing, grandchildren. Office: School Dist 1 Whittier School 2500 Sherman Butte MT 59701

KOHLER, SHEILA M. humanities educator, writer; b. Johannesburg, Nov. 13, 1941; arrived in U.S., 1981; d. Max Kohler and Sheila M. Bodley; m. William M. Tucker; children: Sasha T., Cybele, Brett. BA, Sorbonne, Paris; MA, Inst. Catholique, Paris; MFA, Columbia U., 1983. Prof. New Sch., N.Y.C., 1996—99, CCNY, 2001, Bennington Coll., 2001—03. Author: The Perfect Place, 1987, Crossways, 2004 (Best Am. award Houghton Mifflin, 1999), 2d edit., 2004, Miracles in America, 1990, The House on R Street, 1994, Cracks, 1999, The Children of Pithiviers, 2001, One Girl, 1999, Stories From Another World, 2002. Recipient O'Henry Prize, 1989; Lewis B. Cullman Libr. Fellowship, N.Y. Pub. Libr. Ctr. for Scholars and Writers, 2003—.

KOHLER, SUE A. architectural historian; b. Grand Rapids, Mich., Nov. 27, 1927; d. Leon Burns Snyder and Harriet Sarah Shoemaker; m. Carl Raymond Kohler, Mar. 2, 1953 (dec. Dec. 1987); children: Lisa, Peter, Eric. BA in History, U. Mich., 1949, MA in History of Art, 1950. Rsch. asst. Mus. of the Cranbrook Acad. of Art, Bloomfield Hills, Mich., 1951—53; lectr. Grand Rapids Art Gallery, Grand Rapids, Mich., 1956—58; rschr. archtl. history and urban planning Chloethiel Woodard Smith & Assoc. Architects, Washington, 1967, Douglas Haskell FAIA, N.Y.C., 1968; historian U.S. Commn. of Fine Arts, Washington, 1974—. Lectr. on Washington arch. various orgns. Author: The Commission of Fine Arts: A Brief History, 1996; co-author: Massachusetts Avenue Architecture, Vol. 2, 1975, Sixteenth Street Architecture, Vol. 1, 1978, Sixteenth Street Architecture, Vol. 2, 1988; contbr. chpts. to books. Mem.: Potomac Bonsai Assn., Nat. Trust for Historic Preservation, Hist. Soc. of Washington, Victorian Soc. Am. (v.p. local chpt. 1979—80), Soc. of Archtl. Historians, Phi Kappa Phi, Phi Beta Kappa. Avocations: travel, photography, gardening, sewing. Office: US Commn of Fine Arts National Bldg Mus 401 F St NW #312 Washington DC 20001-2728

KOHLHORST, GAIL LEWIS, librarian; b. Phila., Dec. 5, 1946; d. Richard Elliott and Lucille (Lampkin) Lewis; m. Allyn Leon Kohlhorst, Feb. 14, 1974; 1 child, Jennifer Marion. BA in Govt, Otterbein Coll., Westerville, Ohio, 1969; MS in L.S, Cath. U. Am., 1977. Info. classifier U.S. Ho. of Reps. Commn. on Internal Security, Washington, 1969-70; adminstrv. asst. Office of Gen. Counsel, GSA, Washington, 1971-76; chief tech. services sect. GSA Libr., Washington, 1976-79; chief GSA libr., 1979-88; acting chief, div. info. and libr. svcs. U.S. Dept. Interior, Washington, 1988-89; chief libr. svcs. br. GSA, Washington, 1989-96; chief mgmt. analysis FDA, Rockville, Md., 1996, dir. mgmt. sys. and policy, 1996-99, dir. divsn. mgmt. programs, 1999—. Author: Art and Architecture: An Annotated Bibliography, 1986, Total Quality Management: An Annotated Bibliography, 1990, 91, 93, Federal Librarians Round Table, ALA, Yearbook, 1989, Federal Librarian, 1991-94; contbr. Calendar Commn. on the Bicentennial for the U.S. Constn. Chair Trinity Evangelism Com., 2001—. Recipient Outstanding Performance awards, 1973, 75, 76, 79, 81-86, 88-89, 91-96, Spl. Achievement awards, 1982-84, Commendable Svc. award, 1984, Nat. Capital Performance award, 1985, Meritorious Svc. award, 1992, Disting. Svc. award, 1995, Dep. Commr.'s Spl. Achievement award, 1999, award of Merit, 2001. Mem. ALA (Fed. Libr.'s Achievement award 1995), Fed. Librs. Round Table (pres. 1990-91, membership chair 1994-96), Fed. Libr. and Info. Ctr. (observer 1984-96, exec. bd. 1992-94, chair 1994, membership and governance com.), Fed. Pre-Conf. on the White House Conf. on Librs. and Scis. (del. 1990), Fedlink Adv. Coun. (chair exec. adv. coun. 1988-90), Pub. Employees Roundtable (bd. dirs. 1994-96), D.C. Libr. Assn., United Meth. Women (mem. Dulin outreach com. 1994-96, pres. Joshua's Way 1995-96, mem. Naomi Circle Trinity 2001—, chair Trinity Evangelism 2001—), Beta Phi Mu. Methodist. Home: 1830 Opalocka Dr Mc Lean VA 22101-5445 Office: FDA 5600 Fishers Ln HFA 300 Rm 4B-03 Parklawn Bldg Rockville MD 20852-5600

KOHLSTEDT, SALLY GREGORY, history educator; b. Ypsilanti, Mich., Jan. 30, 1943; BA, Valparaiso U., 1965; MA, Mich. State U., 1966; PhD, U. Ill., 1972. Asst. prof. Simmons Coll., Boston, 1971-75; assoc. prof. to prof. Syracuse (N.Y.) U., 1975-89; prof. history of sci. U. Minn., Mpls., 1989—; dir. Ctr. for Advanced Feminist Studies, 1997-98. Vis. prof. history of sci. Cornell U., 1989, Amerika Inst. U. Munich, 1997, Calif. Inst. Tech., 2004;

lect. univs. in U.S. and abroad; mem. nat. panels. Author: The Formation of the American Scientific Community: AAAS, 1848-1860, 1976; editor: (with Margaret Rossiter) Historical Writing on American Science, Osiris, 2d Series, 1, 1985, (with R.W. Home) International Science and National Scientific Identity: Australia between Britain and America, 1991, The Origins of Natural Science in the United States: The Essays of George Brown Goode, 1991, (with Barbara Haslett et al.) Gender and Scientific Authority, 1996, (with Helen Lonino) The Women, Gender, and Science Question, 1997, The History of Women in Science: An Isis Reader, 1999, (with Bruce Leavenstein and Michael Sokal) The Establishment of Science in America: The American Association for the Advancement of Science, 1999; contbr. articles to profl. jours.; mem. editl. bd. Signs, 1980-88, 90-93, Sci., 1980-81, News and Views: History of Am. Sci. Newsletter, 1980-86, Sci., Tech. and Human Values, 1983-90, Syracuse Scholar, 1985-88, chair, 1988, Isis, 2002-; assoc. editor Am. Nat. Biography, 2d edit., 1988-98, consulting edit., 1993—; Gruphon Press Reprints in the History of Science, 1993-98; reviewer books, articles, proposals for NSDF, NEH, U. Chgo. Press, numerous other pub. cos.; editor sci. biography series Cambridge U., 1997—. NSF grantee, 1969, 78-79, 84, 93-95, Smithsonian Instn. predoctoral fellow, 1970-71, Danforth Assoc., 1975-82, Syracuse U. grantee, 1976, 82, Am. Philos. Soc. rsch. grantee, 1977, Haven fellow Am. Antiquarian Soc., 1982, Fulbright Sr. fellow U. Melbourne, Australia, 1983, Woodrow Wilson Ctr. fellow, 1986, Smithsonian Instn. Sr. fellow, 1987. Fellow AAAS (nominating com. 1980-83, 96-98, sect. chair 1986, bd. dirs. 1998-2002, coun. 2004—), Am. Hist. Assn. (profl. com. 1974-76, rep. U.S. Nat. Archives Adv. Coun. 1974-76), Berkshire Conf. Women Historians (program com. 1974), Forum on the History Sci. in Am. (coord. com. 1980-86, chair 1985, 86), History of Sci. Soc. (sec. 1978-81, coun. 1982-84, 89-91, 94-96, com. on publs. 1982-87, chair nominating com. 1985, 99, women's com. 1972-74, vis. lectr. 1988-89, chair edn. com. 1989, pres. 1992, 93), Internat. Congress for History of Sci. (U.S. del. 1977, 81, vice chair 1985) Orgn. Am. Historians (chair com. on status of women 1983-85, endowment fund drive, auction subcom. 1990-91). Lutheran. Home: 4140 Edmund Blvd Minneapolis MN 55406-3646 E-mail: sgk@tc.umn.edu.

KOHN, JEAN GATEWOOD, retired health facility administrator, pediatrician; b. Chgo., July 8, 1926; d. Gatewood and Esther Lydia (Harper) Gatewood; m. Martin M. Kohn, Feb. 10, 1951; children: Helen, Joel, Michael, David. BS, U. Chgo., 1948, MD, 1950; MPH, U. Calif., Berkeley, 1973. Diplomate Am. Bd. Pediatrics. Physician Permanente Med. Group, San Leandro, Calif., 1953-60; pediatric cons. Calif. Children Svcs., 1961-72; lectr. maternal and child health U. Calif., 1973-91; med. advisor rehab. engrng. ctr. Packard Children's Hosp. at Stanford, Calif., 1976-97, med. dir. child prosthetic clinic, 1977-97, ret., 1997, pediatrician Mary L. Johnson Infant Devel. Unit, 2000—. Asst. neurologic diagnostic ctr. U. Calif., San Francisco, 1960-72; pediatric cons. Project HOPE, Nicaragua, 1966, Peru, 1962; pediatric cons. sch. pub. health U. Hawaii, Okinawa, 1975. Contbr. chpts. to books and articles to profl. jours. Mem. adv. panel State of Calif. Dept. Spl. Edn., Calif. Children Svcs.; bd. dirs. Mental Health Assn., United Cerebral Palsy Assn., Head Start, San Mateo County, 1993—. Recipient Lyda M. Smiley award Calif. Sch. Nurses Orgn., 1987. Fellow Am. Acad. Pediats., Am. Acad. Cerebral Palsy and Devel. Medicine; mem. Project HOPE Alumni Assn. (pres. 1988-92).

KOHN, KAREN JOSEPHINE, graphic and exhibition designer; b. Muskegon, Mich., Jan. 8, 1951; d. Herbert George and Catherine Elizabeth (Johnson) K.; m. Robert Joseph Duffy Jr., July 10, 1982; children: Megan Kathleen, Sarah Evelyn. BFA cum laude, U. Mich., 1973; MFA, Sch. Art Inst., Chgo., 1975. Free-lance designer, Chgo., 1976-77; designer Stevens Exhibits, Chgo., 1977-78; artist-in-residence Chgo. Coun. Fine Arts, 1978-79; designer Chgo. Hist. Soc., 1979-81, dir. design, 1981-84; prin. Karen Kohn & Assocs. Ltd., Chgo., 1985—2000; sr. art dir. Carus Pub., 2000—. Work appeared in Mus. News, Kraft Gen. Foods hdqrs. Recipient Superior Achievement award for temporary exhbn. Congress of Ill. Hist. Socs. and Mus., 1985, Superior Achievement award for permanent exhbn., 1989, Cert. Excellence Strathmore Graphics Gallery, 1990, award of Merit Ill. Assn. Bus. Comm., 1993, Motorola Pinnacle award, 1994. Mem. Am. Assn. Mus. (Distinctive Merit awards 1982-84, 92), Am. Ctr. Design, Chgo. Women in Pub. (1st prize Individual Excellence in Design 1995, 97, 1st prize in sci. and tech. publs. 1995, 1st prize Self Pub. Books 1996, 98, 1st prize Juvenile Non-fiction 1998, 1st prize Brochures 1998, 2d prize Brochures Acad. Jours. 1999).

KOHN, MARY LOUISE BEATRICE, nurse; b. Yellow Springs, Ohio, Jan. 13, 1920; d. Theophilus John and Mary Katherine (Schmitkons) Gaehr; m. Howard D. Kohn, 1944; children: Marcia R., Marcia K. Epstein. AB, Coll. Wooster, 1940; M in Nursing, Case Western Res. U., 1943. Nurse, 1943-44, Atlantic City Hosp., N.J., 1944, Thomas M. England Gen. Hosp., U.S. Army, Atlantic City, N.J., 1945-46, Peter Bent Brigham Hosp., Boston, 1947, Univ. Hosps., Cleve., 1946-48; mem. faculty Frances Payne Bolton Sch. Nursing Case We. Res. U., Cleve., 1948-52; vol. nurse Blood Svc. ARC, 1952-55; office nurse Cleve., 1955-94; freelance writer. Author: Berry and Kohn's Operating Room Technique, 10th edit., 2003; asst. editor: Cleve. Physician Acad. Medicine, 1966-71. Bd. dirs. Aux. Acad. Medicine Cleve., 1970-72, officer, 1976; mem. Cleve. Health Mus. Aux., Am. Cancer Soc. vol.; mem. women's com. Cleve. Orch., 1970; mem. women's com. Sta. WVIZ-TV. Mem. ANA, Ohio, Greater Cleve. Nurses Assn., Alumni Assns. Wooster Coll., Frances P. Bolton Sch. Nursing (pres. 1974-75, bd. dirs. 1997-2000), Assn. Oper. Rm. Nurses, Assn. Oper. Rm. Nurses of Greater Cleve. (charter; 30-yr. leadership plaque 2004), Antique Automobile Assn. Am., Western Res. Hist. Soc., Am. Heart Assn., Cleve. Playhouse, Internat. Fund for Animal Welfare, Cleve. Animal Protective League, U.S. Humane Soc., Friends of Cleve. Ballet, Smithsonian Instn., Coun. World Affairs, Cleve. Children's Mus., Cleve. Zool. Soc., Cleve. Racquet Club (social com. 1999-2000), Women's City Club (Jewel award 1992), Internat. Honor Soc. Nursing. Home: 28099 Belcourt Rd Cleveland OH 44124-5615

KOHNEN, CAROL ANN, librarian; b. St. Louis, Apr. 8, 1948; d. Joseph William and Josephine (Strenfel) Licavoli; m. Richard Joseph Kohnen, May 9, 1970; children: Jill Patricia, Douglas Richard. BA, St. Louis U., 1970; MA in Libr. Sci., U. Mo., 1994. Cert. tchr., secondary English Mo., libr. K-12 Mo. Programmer, cons., Creve Coeur, Mo., 1981-90; audio-visual technician Parkway Schs., Chesterfield, 1989-92; libr. St. Joseph's Acad., Frontenac, 1992-98, Parkway No. HS, 1998—. Co-chair telecomms, users group Coop. Sch. Dists., St. Louis County, 1995—99; dept. leader Parkway No. HS, 1999—; mem. Profl. Devel. com., 2000—, Parkway Sch. Dist. Tech. Coun., 2002—, 2002. Am. memory fellow, Libr. Congress, 1998—99. Mem.: Mo. Assn. Sch. Librs., St. Louis Suburban Sch. Librs. Assn. (sec. 1993—95, membership chmn. 2001—03), Parkway Sch. Dist. Librs. Tech. Com. (chmn. 1999—), Mo. Assn. Sch. Librs. (Webmaster, bd. dirs. 2003—), Am. Assn. Sch. Librs., ASCD, ALA, Beta Phi Mu, Phi Beta Kappa. Avocations: reading, genealogy, web browsing. Office: Parkway North HS 12860 Fee Fee Rd Saint Louis MO 63146-4431 E-mail: ckohnen@pkwy.k12.mo.us.

KOHNSTAMM, ABBY E. marketing executive; married; 2 children. BA, Tufts U.; MA in Edn., MBA, NYU. With Am. Express, 1979-1993, exec. asst. to the pres., 1986-87, sr. v.p. cardmember mktg.; v.p. corp. mktg. Internat. Bus. Machines Corp., Armonk, NY, 1995—. Bd. dirs. Overseers Arts & Sci. Tufts U., IBM Credit Corp. Mem. Assn. Nat. Advertisers. Avocations: family acitivies, music, theater. Office: Internat Bus Machines Corp New Orchard Rd Armonk NY 10504-1722

KOHR, MELINDA ANN, psychologist, educator; b. Washington, May 30, 1961; d. Richard Allen and Patricia Ann Kohr. BA, U. Md., 1983; MA, So. Ill. U., 1986; MEd, Temple U., 1991, PhD, 1996. Cert. sch. psychologist Pa., 1991, N.J., 1993. Dir. outpatient services CARE Hawaii, Honolulu, 1999—2001; clin. psychologist Behavioral Health Ctr., Inc., Honolulu, 2002—, pres., 2002—. Adj. faculty Argosy U., Honolulu, 1997—; instr. MCH Lend U. of Hawaii, Honolulu, 1999—; clin. psychologist Related Svcs. Assts. Micronesia, Honolulu, 2001—. Vice commodore Hawaii Women's Yatch Racing Assn., Honolulu, 1996—2001. Mem.: APA (corr.), Hawaii Women's Yacht Racing Assn. (vice commodore 1996—2001), Jr. League of Honolulu, Hawaii Yatch Club (corr.). Office: Behavioral Health Center Inc 2875 South King Street Suite 203 Honolulu HI 96826

KOHWI-SHIGEMATSU, TERUMI, research scientist; b. Tokyo, Aug. 30, 1949; d. Teruhiko and Futaba (Takamatsu) Shigematsu; m. Yoshinori Kohwi; 1 child, Minoree. BS magna cum laude, Washington Coll., 1971; MA, John Hopkins U., 1973; PhD, U. Tokyo, 1978. Sci. fellow Japan Soc. for Promotion, Tokyo, 1978-79; rsch. scientist Inst. Tuberculosis and Cancer, Sendai, Miyaginken, Japan, 1979-81; postdoctoral fellow Fred Hutchinson Cancer Rsch. Ctr., Seattle, Wash., 1981-84; asst. staff scientist La Jolla (Calif.) Cancer Rsch. Found., 1984-88, staff scientist, 1988-94, sr. staff scientist, 1994-96; sr. staff scientist life scis. divsn. Lawrence Berkeley Lab.-U. Calif., Berkeley, 1996—. NIH Fogarty Internat. fellow, 1981-82, Leukemia Soc. Am. spl. fellow, 1983-85. Mem. NIH (chem. pathology study sect. 1992-96), Am. Cancer Soc. (Faculty award 1988-93). Office: Lawrence Berkeley Lab Univ Calif Berkeley CA 94720-0001 Home: 2620 Arlington Blvd El Cerrito CA 94530-1506

KOKEN, M. DIANE, commissioner, state; b. Lancaster, Pa., Dec. 29, 1952; d. James E. Koken and Helen Sotiro; m. John K. Herr III; children: Kathryn, Rebecca. BS magna cum laude, Millersville U., 1972; JD, Villanova U., 1975. Counsel, v.p., corp. sec. Provident Mutual Ins. Co., Harrisburg, Pa., 1975-97; commr. Pa. Ins. Dept., Harrisburg, 1997—. Bd. dirs. endowments and capital campaign com. Millersville U. Mem. ABA, Internat. Claims Assn., Am. Coun. Life Ins. (state v.p.), Am. Life Ins. Counsel, Am. Corp. Counsel Assn., Am. Trial Lawyers Assn., Phila. Bar Assn. Office: Pa Insurance Dept 1326 Strawberry Sq Harrisburg PA 17120-0046

KOKORAS, VICTORIA, retired elementary school educator; b. Peabody, Mass., Aug. 13, 1927; d. Nicholas and Theodora (Triantafillou) K.; m. Francis Edward Quinn (div.). BA cum laude, Boston U., 1955; MA, NYU, 1968; student in Reiki, Northshore C.C., 2003—. Exec. sec. Com. for the Study of Mankind, Chgo., 1956-59; elem. sch. tchr. N.Y.C. Pub. Schs., 1966-67, Peabody Schs., 1968-92. Guest reader Peabody Pub. Schs., 1998; founder, developer Peabody Arts Assn., 1970-75. Founder, chair Peabody Coalition for Nuclear Freeze, 1982-86; mem. Ralph Nader Pub. Citizens, 1992—, People for the Am. Way, 1987—, So. Poverty Law Ctr., Montgomery, Ala., 1994-95. Horace Mann grantee, 1988-89. Mem. AAUW, ACLU, Nat. Women's History Project, Peabody Essex Mus., Friends of Peabody Inst. Libr., WGBH. Democrat. Avocations: creative writing, acting, opera, tai chi, yoga. Home: 20 Greenwood Rd Peabody MA 01960-6316

KOLAKOSKI, DAWN LAYMOND, education educator, consultant, music educator; d. Robert F. and Marjory M. Laymond; children: Kathryn Turana, Rebecca Ashley. BS, Coll. of St. Rose, Albany, NY, 1981, MS. in Edn, 1984, MS in Early Childhood Edn., 1993; EdD, Nova Southeastern U., Ft. Lauderdale, FL, 2001. Cert. tchr. music K-12 N.Y., 1981. Music tchr. Bethlehem Ctrl. Sch. Dist., Delmar, NY, 1980—83; owner/dir. The Magic of Music, Delmar, NY, 1982—97; adj. prof. Maria Coll., Albany, 1989—97; assoc. prof. Hudson Valley C.C., Troy, 1991—; adj. prof. Lesley U., Boston, 2003—. Owner and cons. Resources for Ednl. Tng., Delmar, NY, 1993—. Author: (textbook) Write It Down: A Guided Jour. of Ideas, Strategies, and Reflection for Beginning Tchrs., 2004. Mem.: N.Y. State Am. Assoc. Degree Early Childhood Educators (pres. 1999—2003).

KOLAKOWSKI, DIANA JEAN, county commissioner; b. Detroit, Aug. 28, 1943; d. Leo and Genevieve (Bosh) Zyskowski; m. William Francis Kolakowski, Jr., Oct. 22, 1966; children: Wiliam Francis III, John. BS, U. Detroit, 1965. Lab. asst. chemistry dept. U. Detroit, 1961-65; rsch. chemist Detroit Inst. Cancer Rsch., Mich. Cancer Found., 1965-70; substitute tchr. Warren (Mich.) Consol. Schs., 1979-81; mem. Macomb County Bd. Commrs., Mt. Clemens, Mich., 1983—, vice chmn., 1993-95, chmn., 1995-97. Dir. S.E. Mich. Transp. Authority, Detroit, 1983—85; trustee Macomb County Ret. System, Mt. Clemens, 1988—91, 1992—95; chmn. Regional Transit Coord. Coun., 1995—97; del. S.E. Mich. Coun. Govts., Detroit, 1987—, vice chmn., 1995—99, chmn., 1999—2000, Regional Transit Coord. Coun., 1995—97; bd. dirs. Creating a Healthier Macomb, 1996—2001, Macomb Bar Found., 1996—; trustee Macomb County Ret. System, Mt. Clemens, 2003—. Contbr. articles to sci. jours. Trustee Myasthenia Gravis Found., Southfield, Mich., 1964-71; dir. Otsikita coun. Girl Scouts Am., 1995-96; mem., sec. Sterling Heights (Mich.) Bd. Zoning Appeals, 1978-83; mem. Macomb County Dem. Exec. Com., Mt. Clemens, 1982—, 10th and 12th Dem. Congl. Dist. Exec. Com., Warren, 1982—, del. 1996 Dem. Nat. Conv.; mem. behavioral medicine adv. coun. St. Joseph Hosp. GM scholar U. Detroit, 1961-65; named Woman of Distinction Macomb County Girl Scouts U.S.A., 1996; recipient Leadership award Cath. Social Svcs. Macomb, 1997, Polish Pride award Polish Am. Citizens for Equity, 1997, Excellence in County Govt. award, 1997, others. Mem. Nat. Assn. Counties, Mich. Assn. Counties, Mich. Assn. Planning Ofcls., Am. Polish Cultural Ctr., Polish Am. Congress, Alpha Sigma Nu. Roman Catholic. Avocations: singing, piano, crossword and jigsaw puzzles. Home: 33488 Breckenridge Dr Sterling Heights MI 48310-6082 Office: Office Bd Commrs Macomb Co Adminstrn Bldg 1 S Main St Fl 9 Mount Clemens MI 48043-2306

KOLB, DOROTHY GONG, elementary school educator; b. San Jose, Calif. d. Jack and Lucille Gong; m. William Harris Kolb, Mar. 22, 1970. BA with highest honors, San Jose State U., 1964; postgrad., U. Hawaii, Calif. State U., L.A.; MA in Ednl. Tech., Pepperdine U., 1992. Cert. in elem. edn., edn. for mentally retarded, edn. for learning handicapped pre-sch., adult classes, resource specialist, English lang. devel., specially designed acad. instrn. in English, 2000, 2003. Tchr. Cambrian Sch. Dist., San Jose, 1964-66, Ctrl. Oahu Sch. Dist., Wahiawa, Hawaii, 1966-68, Montebello (Calif.) Unified Sch. Dist., 1968—. Recipient Very Spl. Person award, Calif. PTA, 1998, Hon. Svc. award, 2003; Walter Bachrodt Meml. scholar. Mem.: Tau Beta Pi, Pi Tau Sigma, Kappa Delta Pi, Pi Lambda Theta.

KOLB, JENNIFER AKRIDGE, special education educator; b. Mobile, Ala., Jan. 2, 1971; d. Neil Thomas and Jerrie Knight Akridge; m. Douglas Calvin Kolb, Nov. 3, 1968. BS in Speech Pathology and Audiology, U. of South Ala., 1993; BS Edn. of Deaf and Hard-of-Hearing, U. of Montevallo, Ala., 1999. Hearing-impaired tchr. Homewood City Schs., Homewood, Ala., 1999—. Home: 105 Roy Ct Helena AL 35080 Office: Hall-Kent Elem Sch 213 Hall Ave Homewood AL 35209 Personal E-mail: jenniferkolb@hotmail.com.

KOLB, JIMMIE LOIS, marriage and family therapist; b. Calhoun City, Miss., Sept. 9, 1938; d. Johnny Buford and Maylene Spruill; m. Denis E. Kolb, Apr. 16, 1994; m. Robert E. Maddox, Nov. 26, 1955 (div. Mar. 1994); 1 child, alena Gale. BS in Bus. Adminstrn., BA in Psychology, Drury Coll., 1982, MEd, 1985; PhD, Forest Inst. Profl. Psychology, 1989. Dir. army cmty. svc. Chapel Army, Germany, 1972—74; dir. edn. Ft. Leonard Wood (Mo.) Chapel, Ft. Leonard Wood, Mo., 1972—74; counselor drugs and alcohol U.S. Army, Ft. Leonard Wood, 1984—85; family counselor Assocs. Counseling, Springfield, Mo., 1986—97; pvt. practice Seneca, Mo., 1997—. Counselor Agape Pregnancy Ctr., Miami, Okla., 2000, 2003; edn. dir. Springfield (Mo.) C. of C., 1980—85. Named Woman of Yr., Lt. Gov. Mo., 1982. Baptist. Avocations: animal counseling, fishing, public speaking, reading. Home: PO Box 276 Seneca MO 64865 Office: Riverbend Mental Health 920 B Cherokee Seneca MO 64865

KOLB, NANCY DWYER, museum director; b. Albany, N.Y., Nov. 23, 1940; d. Edward James and Elizabeth (McLachlan) Dwyer; m. W. Roy Kolb, June 16, 1962; children: Amy Elizabeth, William Roy, E. Anders. BA, Bucknell U., 1962. Social studies tchr. Abington (Pa.) Sch. Dist., 1962-65; editor Bucks County Chronicles, Doylestown, Pa., 1974-76; cons. in history, 1976-77; dir. Pennsbury Manor Historic Site, Morrisville, Pa., 1977-82; asst. exec. dir. Pa. Hist. and Mus. Commn., Harrisburg, 1982-87; dir. Bur. Historic Sites and Mus., Harrisburg, 1987-88; pres. Please Touch Mus., Phila., 1988—. Contbr. articles to profl. jours. Bd. dirs. Phila. Soc. for Preservation of Landmarks, 1990-94, Friends of Ft. Mifflin, Phila., 1990-93, Parents Network, Ft. Washington, 1993—; exec. com. Fairmount House Adv. Commn., Phila., 1987-93; bd. dirs. Big Sisters Phila., 1989-93. Mem. Mus. Trustee Assn., Pa. Hort. Soc., Assn. Youth Mus. (regional rep. 1990), Bucks County Hist. Soc. (bd. dirs. 1970-79, treas. 1976-79), Am. Assn. Mus. (bd. dirs. 1991-94), Am. Assn. for State and Local History (coun. 1988-92, sec. 1992-94), Mid-Atlantic Assn. Mus. (bd. govs.), Assn. Youth Mus. (bd. dirs. 1994—). Avocations: horticulture, golf. Office: Please Touch Mus 210 N 21st St Philadelphia PA 19103-1088

KOLB, VERA M. chemist, educator; b. Belgrade, Yugoslavia, Feb. 5, 1948; arrived in U.S., 1973; d. Martin A. and Dobrila (Lopicic) Kolb; m. Cal Y. Meyers, 1976 (div. 1986); m. Michael S. Gregory, 1997 (div. 1999). BS, Belgrade U., 1971, MS, 1973; PhD, So. Ill. U., 1976. Fellow So. Ill. U., Carbondale, 1977-78, vis. faculty lctr., 1978-85; assoc. prof. chemistry U. Wis., Parkside, 1985-90, prof. chemistry, 1990—, dept. chair, 1995-97. Vis. scientist Salk Inst. Biol. Studies U. Calif., San Diego, 1992—94; faculty San Francisco State U., 1997; vis. scholar Northwestern U., 2002—03. Editor: (book) Teratogens, Chemicals which Cause Birth Defects, 2nd edit., 1993, 1988; contbr. articles to profl. jours.; musician (violinist): Racine (Wis.) Symphony Orch. Assoc. dir. higher edn. Wis. Space Grant Consortium, 1995—97, assoc. dir. for special initiatives, 2002—; violinist Racine (Wis.) Symphony Orch., Parkside Cmty. Orch. Recipient Higher Edn. awards, Wis. Space Grant Consortium, 1999—2003, Hall of Fame, Southeastern Wis. Educators, 2002; fellow NASA, 1992—94; grantee Fulbright, 1973—76, NIH, 1984—87, Am. Soc. Biochemistry and Molecular Biology, 1988. Mem.: Am. Chem. Soc. (task force occupl. safety and health 1980—94). Achievements include patents in field. Office: Univ Wis Parkside Dept Chemistry PO Box 2000 Kenosha WI 53141-2000 E-mail: kolb@uwp.edu.

KOLBERT, KATHRYN, lawyer, educator; b. Detroit, Apr. 8, 1952; d. Melvin and Rosalie Betty (Frank) K.; children: Samuel Kolbert-Hyle, Kate Kolbert-Hyle. BA, Cornell U., 1974; JD, Temple U., 1977. Bar: Pa. 1977, U.S. Dist. Ct. (ea. dist.) Pa. 1977, U.S. Ct. Appeals (3d cir.) 1977, U.S. Supreme Ct. 1985, U.S. Dist. Ct. N.D. 1991, U.S. Ct. Appeals (5th cir.) 1991, U.S. Ct. Appeals (10th cir.) 1994, U.S. Ct. Appeals (8th cir.) 1994. Atty. Community Legal Svcs., Phila., 1977-79, Women's Law Project, Phila., 1979-88; co-founder, dir. policy Women's Agenda, Phila., 1984-88; atty. pvt. practice, Wyndmoor, Pa., 1997. Cons. Planned Parenthood Fedn., N.Y.C., 1988-89, Nat. Abortion Rights Action League, Washington, 1987; cons. reproductive freedom project ACLU, N.Y.C., 1988-89, state coordinating counsel, 1989-92; v.p. Ctr Reproductive Law & Policy, N.Y., 1992-97; lectr. dept. women's studies U. Pa., 1978-86, 90-91, lectr. Sch. Law, 1989-91, sr. rsch. adminstr. Annenberg Pub. Policy Ctr., 1998—, Open Soc. Inst. fellow, 1998-2000. Exec. prodr. (radio series on constnl. law) Justice Talking; pilot host Justice Talking Live!; contbr. chpts. to books. Founder, Commn. to Elect Women Judges, Women Judges Pac, Phila, 1984; bd. dirs. Com. to Elect the Coscy 5, Phila. Recipient Dedicated Advocacy award Nat. Abortion Rights Action League Pa., 1986, Pa. Coalition Against Domestic Violence, 1986, Luth. Settlement House Women's Program, 1987, Am. Dem. Action award, 1989, honoree Women's Way, 1991; named One of 100 Most Influential Lawyers in Am., Nat. Law Jour. Democrat. Jewish. E-mail: KKOLBERT@asc.upenn.edu.

KOLBESON, MARILYN HOPF, holistic practitioner, educator, artist, poet, advertising executive, poet; b. Cin., June 9, 1930; d. Henry Dilg and Carolyn Josephine (Brown) Hopf; children: Michael Llen, Kenneth Ray, Patrick James, Pamela Sue Kolbeson Lang, James Allan. Student, U. Cin., 1947-48, 50. Cert. holistic memory release practitioner. Interior decorator Metro Carpet, 1971-77; sales and mktg. mgr. Cox Patrick United Van Lines, 1977-80; sales mktg. mgr. Creative Incentives, Houston, 1980-81; pres. Ad Sense, Inc., Houston, 1981-87, M.H. Kolbeson & Assocs., Houston, 1987, Seattle, 1987—, The Phoenix Books, Seattle, 1987-90, METASELF Healing, Seattle, 1999—. Bd. dirs. Umbrella Prodns.; cons. N.L.P. Practitioner and Cons.; Aircraft bus. mgmt. cons., Seattle, 1988—90; holographic memory release practitioner, 1996—; cooking demonstrator, nutritional advisor Puget Consumers Coop., Seattle, 1991—2002; lectr., cons. in field. Pub.: You Make the Difference in Nat. Lit. Poetry Anthology, Morning Song, 1996, : Moving On in Nat. Libr. Poetry, 1998; contbr. poetry to A Place at the Table, 1999; originator : Heart Button Technique, 1995; mgr., assoc. prodr. (mus. comedy) Times Three, 1999; prodn. mgr. Of a Certain Age, 2002; Green Scythe; instrument keeper (group shows) Gentle Wind Project, 1999—; Om Art angel meditation balls, 2002; bus. mgr. : Green Seythe, 2004. Vol. Seattle Pub. Schs., 1992—; mem. citizens adv. bd. Arcola (Ill.) Sch. Dist., 1964—66; mem. ARC, Seattle; charter mem. Rep. Task Force; mem. adv. bd. Alief Ind. Sch. Dist., 1981—87, pres., 1983—84; bd. dirs. Santa Maria Hostel, 1983—86, v.p., 1983—84; mem. citizen's adv. bd. Am. Inst. Achievement, 1986—87; bd. dirs. Breighton Found. Sr. Housing Devel., Seattle, 2000—, S.E. Seattle Sr. Found., 2000—; founder, pres. Mind Force, Houston, 1978—87, Seattle, 1987—95; founder META Group, Seattle, 1991—, Meta-Self Healing Ministries, Seattle, 1997—. Mem.: Internat. Soc. Poets, Inst. Noetic Scis., Houston Advt. Splty. Assn. (bd. dirs. 1984—87, treas. 1985, v.p. 1986—87), Internat. Platform Assn., World Future Soc., Nat. Assn. Mentally Ill. (Wash.), Galleria Area C. of C. (bd. dirs. 1986—87), Toastmasters (area gov. 1978), Fair and Tender Ladies Book Group, Lakewood Seward Park Cmty. Club (bd. dirs.), Grand Club (v.p. 1986). Republican. Universalist. Office: 5253 S Brandon St Seattle WA 98118-2522 Office Phone: 206-723-3588. E-mail: mhk99@comcast.net.

KOLBYE, MELANIE DAWN BOWMAN, physical education educator, special education educator; b. Paris, Tex., Feb. 20, 1961; d. Thomas Boyd and Juanita (Powers) Bowman; m. Jack L. Kolbye, July 22, 1996. BS, East Tex. State U., 1983, MEd, 1990. Cert. tchr., Tex. Tchr. phys. edn. Garland (Tex.) Ind. Sch. Dist., 1984-87, 91, tchr. adapted phys. edn., 1991-96, Plano (Tex.) Ind. Sch. Dist., 1996—99, spl. edn. and phys. edn. tchr., 1999—2002, sch. counselor, 2002—. Coach Spl. Olympics, Garland, 1991. Mem. Tex. APHERD, Am. Sch. Counselor Assn., PTA, DAR of Tex., Phi Beta Kappa. Republican. Baptist. Avocations: reading, cooking, travel, fishing.

KOLE, JANET STEPHANIE, lawyer, writer, photographer; b. Washington, Dec. 20, 1946; d. Martin J. and Ruth G. (Goldberg) K. AB, Bryn Mawr Coll., 1968; MA, NYU, 1970; JD, Temple U., 1980. Bar: Pa. 1980, N.J. 1994, N.Y. 2000. Assoc. editor trade books Simon & Schuster, N.Y.C., 1968-70; publicity dir. Am. Arbitration Assn., N.Y.C., 1970-73, freelance photojournalist, 1973-76; law clk. Morgan Lewis & Bockius, Phila., 1977-80; assoc. Schnader, Harrison, Segal & Lewis, Phila., 1980-85; ptnr. Cohen, Shapiro, Polisher, Shiekman & Cohen, Phila., 1985-95; ptnr., chmn. environ. practice group Klehr, Harrison, Harvey, Branzburg & Ellers, Phila., 1995-97; pvt. practice, 1997-2001; chmn. environ. dept. Cooper, Levenson, April, Niedelman & Wagenheim, Atlantic City/Cherry Hill, NJ, 2001—03; shareholder Flaster Greenberg, PC, Cherry Hill, NJ, 2003—. Author: Post Mortem, 1974; editor Environmental Litigation, 1991, 99; contbr. numerous articles to profl. jour.; past mem. editl. bd. New Am. Rev. Mem. Mayor's

Task Force on Rape, N.Y.C., 1972-77; adv. Support Ctr. Child Advs., Phila., 1980—; mem. Phila. Vol. Lawyers for Arts. Fellow Acad. Advocacy, Am. Bar Found.; mem. ABA (former co-chair individual and small firm, former co-chair environ. litigation com., former dir., publs., former coun. mem. sect. litigation, dir. publs., former co-divsn. dir. substantive areas litigation, former editor litigation news, former chmn. [illegible] monographs and unpublished papers, com. spl. pubs., co-chair electronic publ. com., vice-chair, special com. on smart growth and urban policy), ATLA. Office: 3d Fl 1810 Chapel Ave West Cherry Hill NJ 08002 Office Phone: 856-382-2230. Business E-Mail: janet.kole@Flastergreenberg.com.

KOLKER, SONDRA G. fund raising, special events executive; b. N.Y.C., Nov. 30, 1933; d. Morris Henry and Alice (Cohen) Budow; m. Justin William Kolker, Aug. 23, 1953 (div.); children: Lawrence Paul, David Brett; m. David Kern, July 2000 (dec. Sept. 10, 2003). Student, Hofstra U. Dir. N.Y.C. Office N.Y. State Dem. Com., 1977-79; v.p., exec. dir. Fund for Higher Edn., N.Y.C., 1980-88; pres. Sondra Kolker & Assocs., Halesite, N.Y., 1988-96, Miami, Fla., 1996-98, Ft. Lauderdale, Fla., 1998—. Spl. cons. Internat. Devel. Svcs. subs NMP of Am., Inc., 1989-90; dist. rep. Congressman Robert J. Mrazek, 1990-93. Speechwriter for numerous speakers at corp. banquets, 1980-88. Bd. dirs. Huntington (N.Y.) Townwide Fund, 1978-96, Single Family Homes at Sawgrass, treas., 1999--; mem. adv. bd. Julia's Fund (divsn. Gilda's Club), 1999—; active Huntington Hosp. Aux., 1965-96, Great Gatsby Soc. for Multiple Sclerosis, 1988-96, Marble Hills Civic Assn., Halesite, 1955-96; committeewoman Huntington Dem. Com., 1974-82; fundraiser/dist. rep. Congressman Robert J. Mrazek, L.I., N.Y., 1991-93; banquet planner Temple Adath Or; active Temple Kol Ami; mem. Broward Guild, Miami City Ballet. Recipient Meritorious Svc. award Huntington Twp. C. of C., 1974, 76, 77, 78, Bicentennial Citation Town of Huntington, 1977. Mem. NAFE, MOMA, Met. Mus. Art, Nat. Mus. Women in the Arts, L.I. Crafts Guild, Huntington Twp. C. of C., Women's Econ. Round Table, Huntington Bus. and Profl. Women, Nature Conservancy, Sierra Club, World Wildlife Fund. Jewish. Avocations: fabric painting, writing poetry, nature study, travel, opera. Home and Office: Sondra Kolker & Assoc 12683 NW 11th Pl Sunrise FL 33323-3119

KOLLAR-KOTELLY, COLLEEN, federal judge; b. Apr. 17, 1943; m. John T. Kotelly. BA, Cath. U., 1965, JD, 1968. Law clerk to Hon. Catherine Kelly, Dist. Columbia Ct. Appeals, 1968—69; atty. criminal divsn. US Dept. Justice, 1969-72; chief legal counsel St. Elizabeth's Hosp., 1972-84; judge DC Superior Ct., 1984-97, dep. presiding judge, criminal divsn., 1995—97; dist. judge US Dist. Ct. DC, 1997—. Apptd. mem. Judicial Conf. Com. Fin. Disclosure by Chief Justice Rehnquist, 2000—02; apptd. to presiding judge US Foreign Intelligence Surveillance Ct. by Chief Justice Rehnquist, 2002—09; adj. prof. joint tchg. program on mental health and the law Georgetown U. Sch. Medicine, chair bd. art trust for superior ct. Fellow: ABA; mem.: Thurgood Marshall Inn of Ct. (founding mem.). Office: 333 Constitution Ave NW Washington DC 20001-2802

KOLLER, BERNEDA JOLEEN, library administrator; b. Marion, S.D., Dec. 23, 1935; d. Theodore Jacob Poppe and Clara Johanna Goertz; m. Dennis Eugene Koller, May 8, 1955; children: Kim Denise, Kerry Tay, Kecia Rae. BA, Augustana Coll., 1974; postgrad., U. S.D., 1976-77. Cert. pub. libr. mgmt., S.D. Sec. Turner County Soil Conservation Dist., Parker, S.D.; tchr. Freeman (S.D.) Pub. H.S., 1974-81; sec. State Farm Ins., Freeman, 1982-90; libr. dir. Freeman Pub. Libr., 1990—. Spkr. hist. lectrs., 1984—. Author: (book) Ironic Point of Light, 1994; columnist Freeman Courier, 1983-88. Pres. Parker (S.C.) Alumni Assn., 1959; sec. S.D. Assn. German-Russians, Pierre, 1989—; dir. Musicals at Schmeckfest, Freeman, 1976, 82, 86; mem. Am. Hist. Soc. of Germans from Russia, Lincoln, Nebr., 1986—, German Russian Hist. Soc., Bismarck, N.D., 1994—; pres. Homestead chpt. Am. Hist. Soc. of Germans from Russia, Freeman and Yankton, 1988—; historian, sec., chairperson Dorcas Soc., Freeman, 1976-96; tour guide Freeman Devel. Corp., 1997—; pres., sec., mem. Freeman Area Arts Coun. and Freeman Area Arts Alliance, 1998—; ch. del. Wellspring Wholistic Care Ctr., Freeman, 1997—. Recipient Best Local Column award S.D. Press Assn., 1985, 2d pl. statewide. Mem. S.D. Libr. Assn. Democrat. Mennonite. Avocations: writing, genealogy, traveling, knitting, guitar. Office: Freeman Pub Libr 185 E 3d St Freeman SD 57029 Fax: 605-925-7127. E-mail: bkoller85@hotmail.com.

KOLLSTEDT, PAULA LUBKE, communications executive, writer; b. Cin., Aug. 27, 1946; D. Elmer George and Mary Margaret (Kelly) Lubke; m. Stephen Leonard Kollstedt, Jan. 21, 1968; children: Kelly, Lance, Stacey, Jonathan. BA, Xavier U., 1968, MEd, 1982. Cert. secondary tchr., Ohio. Editor, writer Shillito's Dept. Store, Cin., 1966-69; freelance writer Cin., 1969-74; pub. info. coord. Prince William County Parks and Recreatoin Com. (Va.), 1974-75; comm. coord. City of Cin. Recreation Com., 1975-78; cons. Warner Amex Cable TV, Cin., 1982-84, Moellers Assocs., Cin., 1982-84; writer Cin. Enquirer, 1982-83; exec. comm. specialist Gen. Electric Aircraft Engines, 1984-87, employee comm. specialist, 1987-90, mgr. comm., 1990-96, mgr. employee comm., 1996-99, mgr. cmty. and pub. rels., 1999—. Spkr. Cin. Presch. Coops., 1981, Cin. Women's Conf., 1984, lectr., presenter workshops on self-esteem for parents, 1975-86; lectr. bus. comm., 1992—. Author: Surviving the Crisis of Motherhood, 1982; contbr. articles to newspapers; writer, prodr. multi-media presentation Comm. Cin. (Unique Program award Ohio Parks and Recreation), 1978. Recipient Prism award Pub. Rels. Soc. Am., 1983, 85, 86, 87, 88, 92, 94, 95, 96, Pres.' award, 1995, 97, 98, Bronze Quill award Internat. Assn. Bus. Communicators, 1986, 87, 88, 90, 92, 95, 96, 97, 98, 99, Silver Quill award, 1989. Mem. Women in Comm. (v.p. programs 1981-82, v.p. corp. sponsorship 1998, 99, 2000, Gt. Lakes regional 1st pl. award 1984, 86, 87, 88, 95, recipient Nat. Clarion awards 1990, 98, Gem award 1992, Outstanding Communicator of Yr. 1999). Roman Catholic. Home: 5391 Haft Rd Cincinnati OH 45247-7419 Office: GE Aircraft Engines One Neumann Way Cincinnati OH 45215-1915

KOLOSVARY-STUPLER, EVA, sculptor; b. Budapest, Hungary, May 14, 1937; arrived in U.S., 1961; d. Alexander Stein and Anna Herczog; m. Paul Kolosvary, July 24, 1955 (dec. Dec. 2, 1995); 1 child, Judy ; m. Harvey Stupler, June 6, 1997. BA, Calif. State U., Long Beach, 1972, MA, 1974, MFA, 1980. Art instr. Palos Verdes Art Ctr., Rancho Palos Verdes, Calif., 1972—93; prof. art Orange Coast Coll., Costa Mesa, Calif., 1976—79; v.p. Palko Advt., Inc., Lomita, Calif., 1993—96. Catalog, Reflections, 2002; poetry included in anthology: When a Lifemate Dies, 1997; Represented in permanent collections San Jose Mus. Art, Downey (Calif.) Mus. Art, Santa Monica Coll., Huntsville (Ala.) Mus. Art, Owensboro (N.Y.) Mus. Fine Art, Brand Art Ctr., Glendale, Calif., Mucsarnok Mus., Budapest, exhibitions include Calif. State U., L.A., 2000, City of Brea (Calif.) Gallery, 2000, Long Beach (Calif.) Arts, 2000 (1st prize, 2000), 2001 (3d prize, 2001), Long Beach (Calif.) Arts., 2002, Orange County Ctr. Contemporary Art, 2000, Eye Five Gallery, L.A., 2001, Ventura Coll., Calif. (Award of Excellence, 2001), A Shenere Velt Gallery, L.A., 2001, LA Artcore, 2001, one-woman shows include Don O'Melveny Gallery, L.A., 2002, exhibitions include Folk Tree Gallery, Pasadena, Calif., 2002, Loft Gallery, San Pedro, Calif., 2002, U. Judaism, Bel Air, Calif., 2002, Orlando Gallery, Tarzana, Calif., 2003, Long Beach Mus. Art, 2003, El Camino Coll., Torrance, Calif., 2003, Angels Gate Gallery, San Pedro, Calif., 2003. Mem.: L.A. Printmaking Soc. (pres. 1980), L.A. Assemblage Group (founding mem.). Home: 30211 Via Rivera Rancho Palos Verdes CA 90275 E-mail: eva@kolosvary.com.

KOLSTAD, CANDICE (CANDY) CAROL, pre-school educator, special needs coordinator; b. Billings, Mont., Dec. 24, 1951; d. Clarence Henry and Edna Pearl Hein; m. Keith Keenan Kolstad, Aug. 18, 1973; children: Kelsey Larson, Kristofer Andrew, Heather Lynn. MS Edn. magna cum laude, Early childhood education, Mont. State U., Billings, Mont., 1975—79, BS cum laude, elem. edn., 1970—74. Cert. Class 1 Profl. Tchg. Office of Pub. Instrn./Mont., 1979, Class 2 Profl. Tchg. Office of Pub. Instrn./Mont., 1974, Profl. Edn. SPI Office of Profl. Certification/Wash., 1988, Occupl. Hearing Conservationist Coun. for Accreditation in Occupl. Hearing Conservation, 2001. Kindergarten tchr. Lockwood Pub. Schools, Billings, Mont., 1974—78, title 1 para profl. Billings Pub. Schools, Billings, Mont., 1980—81; tchr./home visitor Head Start, Inc, Billings, Mont., 1989—97, spl. needs coord., 1997—; preschool day treatment program tchr. Head Start, Inc/Yellowstone Boys and Girls Ranch, Billings, Mont., 2003—. Mem. Comprehensive Sys. of Pers. Devel. Coun., Billings, Mont., 1999—; assoc. bd. mem. Parents Lets Unite for Kids (PLUK), Billings, Mont., 2001—. V.p. Parent Tchr. Assn., Alkali Creek Sch., Billings, Mont., 1985—86; Cub Scout den leader Boy Scouts of Am., Billings, Mont., 1987—88, troop coun. mem., 1989—96; Daisy Girl Scout leader Girl Scouts of Am., Billings, Mont., 1990—91. Mem.: Mont. Assn. for the Edn. of Young Children, Coun. for Exceptional Children, Early Childhood Divsn., Behavior Disorders Divsn., Billings Assn. for the Edn. of Young Children, Nat. Assn. for the Edn. of Young Children. Avocations: sewing, reading, embroidery. Home: 1808 Miles Avenue Billings MT 59102-4949 Office: Head Start Inc 615 North 19th Street Billings MT 59101-4949 Office Phone: 406-245-7233. Personal E-mail: candyk_ychs@yahoo.com. E-mail: candyk@billingsheadstart.org.

KOMP, BARBARA ANN, writer; b. La Porte, Ind., Nov. 3, 1954; d. Gerald Lee and Betty Mae (Schelin) K. BA in Elem. Edn., Ball State U., 1977; cert. in lang. arts/reading competencies, 1977. Quality control insp. Foreman Mfg. Co., Rolling Prairie, Ind., 1978-80; quality control inspector Weil-McLain, Michigan City, Ind., 1980-81, jr. quality control engr., 1981-84, tech. writer, 1984-88, mgr. tech. pubs., 1988-97, mktg. comms. specialist, 1997-2000; tech. writer C E Niehoff & Co., Evanston, Ill., 2000—. Advisor Jr. Achievement, Michigan City, 1982-84; mem. bd. dirs. Mich. City YMCA, 1992-93; mem. bd. dirs. Christmas-in-April, Michigan City, chair in-kind donations com., 1993-95, bd. sec. 1994-95. Mem.: Soc. Tech. Comm. (sr.; competition judge 1994, Tech. Manual Achievement award 1986, 1996, Tech. Manual Merit award 1990, 1992, 1993, 1996, Tech. Manual Excellence award 1996), Mensa. Avocations: jazz aerobics, photography, volleyball. Office: C E Niehoff & Co 2021 Lee St Evanston IL 60202 E-mail: bkomp@ceniehoff.com, centwriter11@comcast.net.

KONDAS, PATRICIA ANN, film studies educator; b. Rock Springs, Wyo., July 14, 1947; d. Steve Kondas and Anne Marie Lucero; m. Thomas Mullin, Dec. 7, 1983; 1 child, Larkin Marie Mullin. BA, U. Wyo., 1971, MA, 1984; MFA, Ea. Wash. U., 1994. Instr. Spokane Falls C.C., Spokane, Wash., 1997—2000; instr. film studies Ea. Wash. U., Cheney, 2002—. Office: Ea Wash U RTV 104 Cheney WA E-mail: pkondas@ewu.edu., pkondas@centurytel.net.

KONDRICK, LINDA CAROL, science educator; b. St. Charles, Mo., Oct. 31, 1949; d. James Forrest and Catherine Clara Bushdiecker; m. Joseph Robert Kondrick, Aug. 28, 1968; 1 child, Melissa. BS, U. of the Ozarks, 1988; MEd, Ark. Tech. U., 1992; EdD, U. Ark., Little Rock, 2002. Secondary tchr. math. and sci. Lamar (Ark.) Pub. Schs., 1988—2002; asst. prof. phys. sci. Ark. Tech. U., Russellville, 2002—. Fellow: Mid-South Ednl. Rsch. Assn. (bd. dirs. 2002—03), Assn. for Women in Sci. Home: 445 Forest Service Oark AR 72852 Office: Ark Tech Univ North Ark Ave Russellville AR 72801

KONECKY, EDITH, writer; b. N.Y.C., Aug. 1, 1922; d. Harry and Elizabeth (Smith) Rubin; m. Murray Leon Konecky, May 14, 1942 (div. 1963); children: Michael, Joshua. Student, NYU, 1938-41. Author: Allegra Maud Goldman, 1976, reprinted 1978, 87, 90, 93, 2001, A Place at the Table, 1989, reprinted 1990, Past Sorrows and Coming Attractions, 2000; contbr. short stories to various mags. and anthologies, including Best American Short Stories of 1964; contbr. poetry to various mags. and anthologies, and essays to The Writer's Handbook, 1991, 2000; work discussed in Her Testimony, 1994 and Jewish-American Women Writers. 1994; co-prodr. Yiddish Book Ctr., KCRW, 1995. N.Y. Found. for the Arts fellow 1992; Yaddo fellow, 1962-88; MacDowell Colony fellow, 1971-98; Helene Wurlitzer Found. fellow, 1973; VCCA fellow, 1981, Djerassi Found. fellow, 1987; Blue Mountain Ctr. fellow, 1983-88; Leighton Artist Colony at the Banff Ctr. for Fine Arts fellow, 1990; recipient Mabel Louise Robinson prize for best short story of yr., Columbia U., 1961; recipient Quill award for best fiction, 1963, Mass. Rev.; recipient citations ALA, 1976, Sch. Libr. Jour., 1977 (Best Young Adult books). Mem. Authors' Guild, PEN, Poets and Writers.

KONECNY-COSTA, JENNIFER, computer company executive; B in Political Sci., M in Counseling Psychology, Santa Clara U. Various mgmt. positions Hewlett-Packard; campus min. U. Santa Clara; v.p. human resources Silicon Graphics, Wilson Sonsini Goodrich & Rosati; sr. v.p. human resources Novell, Inc., Provo, Utah, 1996—. Active HR Consortium, Calif. Leadership Coun., Bay Area Human Resources Exec. Com., Am. Electronics Assn. Human Resource Com.; del. to Russia Soc. Human Resource Mgmt., 1991, 92; bd. trustees Santa Clara U.; exec. com. mem. Tech. Mus. Innovation Bd. Dirs.; bd. dirs. San Jose Repertory Theater. Office: Novell Inc 122 E 1700 S Provo UT 84606-6194 Fax: 801-228-7077.

KONEFAL, MARGARET MOORE, health facility administrator, critical care nurse, nursing consultant, educator; b. N.Y.C., Apr. 20, 1939; d. James G. and Virgene M. (Allen) Moore; m. Walter A. Konefal, Dec. 30, 1961 (div. 1992); children: Douglas, David, Jesse, Benjamin; m. James J. Gallagher, Feb. 15, 2003. BSN, Incarnate Word Coll., 1961; MSN, Cath. U. of Am., 1969; PhD, Old Dominion U., 1991. RN Tex., cert. nurse adminstr., advanced. Clin. nurse specialist, clin. coord. newborn svcs. Children's Nat. Med. Ctr., Washington, 1972-77; assoc. DON Children's Hosp. of the King's Daus., Norfolk, Va., 1977-82; asst. prof. Norfolk State U., 1982-91; dir. critical care nursing Children's Hosp., Columbus, Ohio, 1991-94; dir. Meml. Children's Hosp., Savannah, Ga., 1994—95; dir. clin. edn. and performance devel. Meml. Healthcare Sys., Savannah, 1995—97; adminstrv. dir. child and adolescent ctr. U. Tex.-M.D. Anderson Cancer Ctr., Houston, 1997—99; sr. mgr. and healthcare industry leader Internal Audit Svcs., Gulf Coast Area, Ernst & Young LLP, 1999-2000; dir. women and infant svcs. Ben Taub Gen. Hosp., Houston, 2000—. Adj. faculty Ohio State U., 1992—94. Mem. ANA, Am. Coll. Healthcare Execs., Healthcare Fin. Mgmt. Assn., Houston Orgn. Nurse Execs., Assn. Healthcare Internal Auditors, Nat. Assn. Neonatal Nurses, Nat. Perinatal Assn., Assn. Womens Health, Obstetric and Neonatal Nurses, Tex. Forum on Health Safety, Sigma Theta Tau. Home: 5743 Cheena Dr Houston TX 77096-5911 Office: Ben Taub Gen Hosp Harris County Hosp Dist 1504 Taub Loop Houston TX 77030 E-mail: Margi1@ix.netcom.com., Margaret_Konefal@hchd.tmc.edu.

KONERSMAN, ELAINE REICH, nursing administrator; b. Macon, Ga., Aug. 12, 1949; d. Edward Allen Reich and Martha Alberta (Bridges) Kirkpatrick; m. Elijah Arlington Scott, Aug. 4, 1967 (dec. Nov. 1970); 1 child, Michael Arlington Scott; m. Gregory Lee Konersman, Mar. 29, 1985. ADN, Macon Coll., 1983. RN, Ga. Floor nurse supr. Perry (Ga.)-Houston County Hosp., 1983-85, Mangum (Okla.) City Hosp., 1985-87, Tillman County Hosp., Frederick, Okla., 1987-88; traveling nurse Kahu Malama Nurses, Honolulu, 1989-90; charge nurse nursery, fl. nurse ICU nursery Tripler Army Med. Ctr., Honolulu, 1990-92; coord. endocrinology clinic MacDill AFB, Tampa, Fla., 1991-93; clin. nurse pediat. unit South Fla. Bapt. Hosp., Plant City, 1993-96; clin. coord. nursing Pediatric Svcs. Am., Inc., Macon, 1997—. Gail Burdsall Cowan scholar Macon Coll., 1982-83. Baptist. Avocations: reading, grandchild, stock car racing, computer programmer. Home: 7200 Houston Rd Macon GA 31216-7336

KONIGSBURG, ELAINE LOBL, writer; b. N.Y.C., Feb. 10, 1930; d. Adolph and Beulah (Klein) Lobl; m. David Konigsburg, July 6, 1952; children— Paul, Laurie, Ross. BS, Carnegie Mellon U., 1952; postgrad., U. Pitts., 1952-54; DHL (hon.), U. North Fla., 2001. Author: juveniles Jennifer, Hecate, Macbeth, William McKinley and Me, Elizabeth, 1967 (Newbery Honor Book), From The Mixed-Up Files of Mrs. Basil E. Frankweiler, 1967 (Newbery medal 1968), About the B'nai Bagels, 1969, (George), 1970, Altogether, One at a Time, 1971, A Proud Taste for Scarlet and Miniver, 1973 (Nat. Book award nominee), The Dragon in the Ghetto Caper, 1974, The Second Mrs. Giaconda, 1975, Father's Arcane Daughter, 1976, Throwing Shadows, 1979 (Am. Book award nominee), Journey to an 800 Number, 1981, Up From Jericho Tel, 1986, Samuel Todd's Book of Great Colors, 1990, Samuel Todd's Book of Great Inventions, 1991, Amy Elizabeth Explores Bloomingdale's, 1992, T-backs, T-shirts, COAT and Suit, 1993, TalkTalk, 1995, The View From Saturday, 1996 (Newbery medal 1997), Silent to the Bone, 2000. Recipient Regina medal, Cath. Libr. Assn., 2001; named to State of Fla. Hall of Fame, 2000.

KONNER, JOAN WEINER, academic administrator, educator, television producer, writer; b. Paterson, N.J., Feb. 24, 1931; d. Martin and Tillie (Frankel) Weiner; children: Rosemary, Catherine (dec.); m. Alvin H. Perlmutter. Student, Vassar Coll., 1948—49; BA, Sarah Lawrence Coll., 1951; MS, Columbia U., 1961. Editl. writer, columnist, reporter Hackensack (N.J.) Record, 1961-63; prodr., reporter WNDT Ednl. Broadcasting Corp., N.Y.C., 1963-65; prodr., writer, reporter NBC News, N.Y.C., 1965-77; exec. prodr. nat. pub. affairs programs WNET Ednl. Broadcasting Corp., N.Y.C., 1977-78, exec. prodr. Bill Moyers Jour., 1978-81, v.p. met. programming, 1981-84; exec. prodr., pres. Pub. Affairs TV with Bill Moyers PBS; prof. broadcast and journalism, dean Grad. Sch. Journalism Columbia U., N.Y.C., 1988-97, pub. Columbia Journalism Rev., 1988-99. Prof. Grad. Sch. Journalism, Columbia U., N.Y.C., 1988—. Bd. dirs. Hudson River Found., Contemplative Mind in Society; past trustee Providence Jour., Columbia U., Rockland Ctr. for Arts, Sarah Lawrence Coll., Religion Writers Found., Radio and TV News Dirs. Found., Pulitzer Prize Bd. Recipient 16 Emmy awards NATAS, Columbia-du Pont award, Peabody award, Gavel award ABA, Edward R. Murrow award, others. Mem. Dirs. Guild, Writers Guild, Soc. Profl. Journalists, Newspaper Women's Club of N.Y.C., Century Assn., Cosmopolitan Club. Office: Columbia U Grad Sch Journalism Journalism Bldg New York NY 10027

KONON, NEENA NICHOLAI, design strategist; b. Chgo., Dec. 4, 1951; d. Nicholas Alexander and Marie G. (Korotkoff) K. BFA cum laude, Ohio U., 1973. Interior designer Architectonics, Inc., Chgo., 1973-75, sr. interior designer, 1978-82; interior designer Space Mgmt. Assoc., Inc., Chgo., 1975-78; design prin. Borkon & Konon Assoc., Inc., Chgo., 1982-84; dir. interiors Perkins & Will, Chgo., 1984-91; pres. Nicholai Ltd., Chgo., 1991—; assoc. Woman Bus. Enterprise (WBE), Chgo. Founding mem. Orthodox Christian Synergy, 1988—. Mem. Chgo. Real Estate Exec. Women. Republican. Avocations: drawing, gourmet cooking. E-mail: neena@nicholaistudio.com.

KONRAD, AGNES CROSSMAN, retired real estate agent, retired educator; b. Rutland, Vt., Nov. 26, 1921; d. Warren Julius and Susan Anna (Cain) Crossman; children: Suzanne Martha, Dianna Marie; m. Henry Konrad, Nov. 27, 1954. Assoc. degree in Edn., Castelton Coll., 1943; BS in Edn., Castelton State Coll., 1951; postgrad., SUNY, New Paltz, 1969-70, Fla. Atlantic U., 1973; grad., Realtors Inst. Fla., 1981. Cert. realtor. Tchr. 1st to 8th grades Pittsford (Vt.) Pub. Schs., 1943-44, tchr. 1st grade, 1950-52; tchr. 3d grade Ralph Smith Sch.-Hyde Park (N.Y.) Ctrl. Schs., 1952-69, Violet Ave. Sch.-Hyde Park Sch. Sys., 1969-73; realtor Four Star Realty of Boca Raton (Fla.), 1974-93; ret., 1993. Inducted into Golden Alumni Soc. of Castleton State Coll., 2001. Mem. AAUW (life), N.Y. State Ret. Tchrs. Assn. (life), Castleton Vt. State Coll. Alumni. Avocations: painting, travel, reading, poetry, computer art painting. Home: 1229 SW 13th St Boca Raton FL 33486-5307 E-mail: Henag40@aol.com.

KONTOS, CAROL A. state senator, educator; b. Dec. 5, 1946; m. Gregory Kontoss; 2 children. BA, U. Iowa, 1969; MA, U. Maine, 1981. Assoc. prof. U. Maine; mem. from dist. 37 Maine State Ho. of Reps., 1995-98, mem. housing and econ. com., mem. utilities com.; mem. dist. 26 Maine Senate, Augusta, 1998—. Mem. Maine Tchrs. Assn., Nature Conservancy. Home: 22 Woldbrook Dr PO Box 1785 Windham ME 04062-1785 Office: Maine Senate 3 State House Station Augusta ME 04333

KOOB, KATHRYN LORAINE, religious studies educator; b. Independence, Iowa, Oct. 8, 1938; d. Harold Frederick Koob and Elsie Muriel Woodward. BA, Wartburg Coll., 1962; MA, U. Denver, 1968; MA Religion, Lutheran Theol. Sem., Gettysburg, Pa., 1998; LHD (hon.), Gwynedd-Mercy Coll., Gwynedd Valley, Pa., 1981, Upsala Coll., 1983. Dist. parish worker Am. Luth. Ch., Denver, 1958—60; tchr. St. Paul's Luth. Sch., Waverly, Iowa, 1962—64, Newton (Iowa) Pub. Schs., Newton, 1964—68; fgn. svc. officer U.S. Info. Agy., Washington, 1969—96; motivational spkr. Waverly, Iowa, 1981—. Co-chair Nat. Adv. Bd. for Comm. Arts Dept. Wartburg Coll., Waverly, Iowa, 2001—. Author: Guest of the Revolution, 1982 (Gold Medallion Book Award presented by Evang. Christian Pub. Assn., 1984); contbr. chapters to books Heroes, 1983, articles to profl. jours. and newspapers. V.p. Wartburg Cmty. Symphony Bd., Waverly; bd. dirs. Iowa Divsn. UN Assn.-U.S.A., Iowa City, 1999—; sec. bd. dirs. ASPIRE-Therapeutic Riding Program, Waterloo. Recipient medal of valor, U.S. Dept. State, 1981, Governor's medal of valor, Iowa State Gov., 1981, Woman of Yr. award, Am. Legion Women's Aux., 2002. Mem.: AAUW (Waverly chpt.), U.S. Info. Agy. Alumni Assn. (life), Am. Fgn. Svc. Assn. (life), Rotary, Kappa Delta Gamma. Lutheran. Avocations: travel, opera, reading. Home: 608 3rd Ave NW Waverly IA 50677-2331 Office: Wartburg Coll 100 Wartburg Blvd PO Box 1003 Waverly IA 50677 Business E-Mail: kathryn.koob@wartburg.edu.

KOOIJ, NINA MICHAELA, editor; b. La Spezia, Italy, May 11, 1964; came to U.S., 1968; d. Theo Kooij and Johanna Veronica (Hol) Crighton. BA, U. Va., 1986; MA, Columbia U., 1987. Editor-in-chief Pelican Pub. Co., Inc., Gretna, La., 1987—. Avocations: travel, music, cooking.

KOOIMA, LINDA KAY, neonatal and pediatrics nurse; b. Rock Valley, Iowa, Aug. 26, 1948; d. Thomas and Frances Mae (Harmelink) K.; m. Orlando Sabas Arroyo, Apr. 12, 1976; children: Annie Josephine, Solomon Jordan. Dipl. nursing, Northwestern U., 1969; BA in Spanish, S.D. State U., 1989. RN, Ill., S.D., Ariz., Calif., Fla. Critical care nurse Children's Meml. Hosp., Chgo., 1969-70; nurse neonatal ICU, Moffitt Hosp. U. Calif., San Francisco, 1970-76; clinic nurse S.D. State U., Brookings, 1985-88; mother and baby nurse Santa Barbara (Calif.) Cottage Hosp., 1988-89; neonatal nurse Santa Ana (Calif.) Hosp. and Med. Ctr., 1990, Hoag Presbyn. Meml. Hosp., Newport Beach, Calif., 1991; pediatric camp nurse Camp Gulliver, Coral Gables, Fla., 1993-95; utilization rev. nurse Initial Health Care, Miami, 1995-98; travel nurse mother/baby Star-Med Co., 1998-99, U.S. Nursing Corp., 2000—. Travel nurse mother-baby unit Cedars-Sinai Med. Ctr., L.A., 2002—03. Mem. Assn. Camp Nurses. Republican. Avocation: scuba diving. Home: 13890 SW 100th Ln Miami FL 33186-6989

KOOLURIS DOBBS, LINDA KIA, artist; b. Orange, N.J., Jan. 28, 1949; m. Kildare Dobbs, May 7, 1981. AA, Pine Manor Coll., 1968; Cert., Sorbonne, 1968-69; BFA with honors, Sch. Visual Arts, 1972. Tchg. staff various colls., 1975—; tchg. staff fashion dept/ Ryerson U., 1980—2003; tchg. staff Ave. Rd. Art Sch., 1999—. Exhibitions include Mus. of Textiles, Toronto, ArtCanadiana.com, Gallery Sheila Roth, Bronxville Art and Frame Gallery, Atrium Gallery, Chubb Group of Ins. Cos., Warren, N.J., Vancouver Art Gallery, Newbury Fine Arts, Boston and Edgartown, Mass., Art Gallery of Hamilton, Toronto Watercolour Soc., Vancouver Maritime Mus., Ceperley House of Visual Arts Burnaby, B.C., Sutton Gallery, Carrier Gallery, Columbus Ctr., First Canadian Pl. Gallery, Toronto, Harry Ransom Humanities Rsch. Ctr., U. Tex., Austin, Represented in permanent collections AT&T, Artform, Norway, Glaxo Wellcome Inc., Inland Pacific Enterprises, Temple Scott & Assocs., Uniglobe, Advance Travel, AGF Mgmt. Ltd., Toronto Stock Exch., Ont. Govt. Art Collection, Parliament Bldg., Queen's Park, Pine Manor Coll., U.S., Mt. Sinai Hosp., Merrill Lynch, Aon Reed Stenhouse, U. Toronto, Scotia McLeod, Probyn & Co., numerous others, prin. works include portrait commns. the Hon. Henry N. R. Jackman, the Hon. Edwin A. Goodman, the Hon. Barbara McDougall, others, the Hon. David Peterson ; contbr. to art periodicals and publications; featured in water color books, Splash 3, 4, 5 & 8; photographer The Nat. Post, The Fin. Post., Verve Mag. Recipient Ann. Art Purchase prize Pine Manor Coll., 1968, 2d prize Fin. Post Ann. Reports awards, 1981. Mem. Toronto Watercolour Soc. (Hon. Mention, Ann. Fall Show 1991, Best in Architecture 1994). Address: 484 Avenue Rd Ste 609 Toronto ON Canada M4V 2J4

KOOR, MARGARET P. medical/surgical nurse, deacon, obstetrical nurse; b. Westerly, R.I., July 27, 1944; d. Thomas Alfred and Mildred Esther Platt; children: Jennifer Walke, Melissa Mattes, Jeffrey. Degree in health ministry, Eddison Coll., Ft. Myers, Fla., 1999, Nat. Health Ministry, N.Y., 2001. RN Conn., cert. psychiatric nurse, Conn., 1968; ordained deacon Episcopal Ch., 1992. Nurse Westerly Hosp., 1968—74, Sarasota (Fla.) Meml. Hosp., 1974—; resident dir. Noel House, deacon Sarasota-Pregnancy Crisis, 1996—99; deacon Episcopal Ch., North Port, Fla. Mem.: Julian of Norwich (OBIATE). Episcopalian. Avocations: knitting, scrapbooks, music. Home: 4017 Heaton Terr North Port FL 34286 E-mail: mpkoor@aol.com.

KOPENHAVER, PATRICIA ELLSWORTH, podiatrist; Student, Columbia U., 1950-53; BA, George Washington U., 1954; MA, Columbia U., 1956; Dr. Podiatric Medicine, N.Y. Coll. Podiatric Medicine, 1963, postgrad., 1980; LLD (hon.), Barry U., 1998; MD (hon.) (hon.), Internat. U. Health Scis. Sch. Medicine, 2001; MD (hon.), Internat. Univ. of the Hlth. Sci., 2001. Diplomate Nat. Bd. Podiatry Examiners. Pvt. practice podiatry, Greenwich, Conn., 1964—; staff podiatrist Havenhealth Care Ctr., Greenwich, 2003—. Mem. staff Laurelton Convalescent Hosp., Greenwich; trustee N.Y. Coll. Podiatric Medicine, 1998. Bd. dirs. Monmouth Opera Guild, 1965, trustee Monmouth Opera Festival, 1966, v.p., 1964; mem. Greenwich Arts Coun.; program chmn. Greenwich Women's Rep. Club, 1983-84, 4th dist. rep., 1984-85, 87—; trustee N.Y. Coll. Podiatric Medicine, 1998—. Recipient Hosp. Fund award for med. research translations ARC, Alumni award of distinction N.Y. Coll. Podiatric Medicine, 1997; scholarship named in her honor N.Y. Coll. Podiatric Medicine, 1997. Mem. AAUW (v.p. 1991, pres. Greenwich br. 1992-94, bd. dirs. 1996), NOW, Conn. Podiatric Med. Assn., Hist. Soc., Asian Soc., Fairfield Podiatry Assn., Am. Assn. Women Podiatrists (founding charter pres. 1969-78), Acad. Podiatry, Am. Podiatry Coun., UN Assn. U.S.A., Acad. Podiatric Medicine (chmn. nominating com. 1981, 1st v.p. 1983-84, chmn. fundraising 1984-85, chmn. women's issues 1985, chmn. cmty. edn. 1989), Am. Acad. Sports Medicine, Am. Acad. Podiatric Sports Medicine (assoc. 1989), George Washington U. Alumni Assn., Columbia Alumni Assn., Fairfield County Alumni Assn. Columbia U., Coast Soc. of Founders Barry U. (treas. 1998), Nat. Fedn. Rep. Women, Bruce Mus., Nature Conservancy, Federated Garden Clubs Conn., St. Mary Ladies Guild, Greenwich Gardeners, Womans' Club (ways and means com. 1989, pres.), English Speaking Union, Soroptimist Internat. Am. (pres. Greenwich br. 1990—, bd. dirs. 1997-98), Inc. (vice chmn. program com. 1985—, regional med. scholarship chmn. 1987, med. scholarship chmn. N.E. region 1988, program dir. 1988—, pres. Greenwich br. 1990-92), Toastmasters, Travel Club (program com. 1984—), Soroptimist (bd. dirs. 1997, 2000—), Greenwich Woman's Club (chair gardeners judges 2001—), Pi Epsilon Chi. Home: 2 Sutton Pl S New York NY 10022-3070 Office: 8 Dearfield Dr Greenwich CT 06831-5348 Office Phone: 203-661-9311. Office Fax: 203-869-5096.

KOPF, RANDI, family and oncology nurse practitioner, lawyer; b. Jersey City, Mar. 30, 1953; d. Soloman and Sydell Kopf. BS, MS, SUNY, Stony Brook, 1978; JD, U. Md., Balt., 1989. Bar: Md., 1989, D.C., 1991; cert. family nurse practitioner. Pvt. practitioner allergy and dermatology, 1982-83; pvt. cons. practice as oncology nurse practitioner; legal intern Office of Gen. Counsel, NIH, 1988; legal assoc., health svcs. group Nixon, Hargrave, Devans & Doyle, Washington, 1990-93; prin. atty., founder Kopf Health-Law Group, Bethesda, Md., 1995; pvt. law practice, 1995—. Lectr., cons. Am. Cancer Soc.; mem. faculty Georgetown U., U. Md., Adelphi U.; nat. lectr. on med. legal topics. Author: Handbook of Nursing Physical Assessment, 1987, Before You Sign...Managed Care Contract Review for Health Care Providers, 1996; editor, contbg. author Jour. Nursing Law, 1993—; contbr. articles to nat. profl. jours. Recipient Alumni award for Outstanding Volunteerism, Cornell U., 1998. Mem. D.C. Bar Assn., Md. Bar Assn., Am. Hosp. Atty. Assn., Chesapeake Nurse Atty. Assn. (pres., bd. dirs.), Am. Health Lawyers Assn.

KOPLOVITZ, KAY, television network executive; b. Milw, Apr. 11, 1945; d. William E. and Jane T. Smith; m. William C. Koplovitz Jr., Apr. 17, 1971. BS, U. Wis., 1967; MA in Comms., Mich. State U., 1968. Radio and TV producer, dir. Sta. WTMJ-TV, Milw., 1967; editor Comm. Satellite Corp., Washington, 1968-72; dir. cmty. svc. UA Columbia Cablevision, Oakland, NJ, 1973-75; v.p., exec. dir. UA Columbia Satellite Services Inc., Oakland, NJ, 1977-80; founder, chmn., CEO USA Networks and Sci-Fi Channel, NYC, 1977—98; CEO Koplovitz & Co., NYC, 1998—; chmn. bd Reality Central, 2003—. Founder Springboard 2000; bd. dirs. Springboard Enterprises, Liz Claiborne, Instinet. Mem. bd. overseers NYU Grad. Sch. Bus., 1984-90; bd. dir. Nat. Jr. Achievement, 1986-1996. Named Entrepreneur of Yr., Babson Coll., 2001; named to Cable Hall of Fame, 2001, Broadcasting Mag. Hall of Fame, 1992; recipient Outstanding Alumnus award, Mich. State U. Grad. Sch. Bus., 1985, Oustanding Corp. Social Responsibility, CUNY, 1986, Women Who Run the World award, Sara Lee Corp., 1987, Muse award, N.Y. Women in Film and TV, 1992, Ellis Island medal of honor, 1993, Crystal award, Women in Film, 1993. Mem.: Com. of 200, Nat. Acad. Cable Programming (bd. dirs. 1984—87), Cable Advt. Bur. (bd. dirs., exec. com., treas. 1981—87, Chmn.'s award for leadership 1987), Women in Cable (founding bd. dirs., membership chmn. 1979—80, v.p. 1981—82, pres. 1982—83), Nat. Acad. TV Arts and Scis. (chmn. 1994—97, bd. dirs. 1984—93), Internat. Coun., Advt. Coun. Inc. (chmn. 1992—93, bd. dirs. 1985—94), Nat. Cable TV Assn. (bd. dirs. 1984—98), N.Y.C. Partnership (bd. dirs. 1987—), Womens Forum. Avocations: tennis, skiing, travel. E-mail: kay@koplovitz.com.

KOPP, NANCY KORNBLITH, state official; b. Coral Gables, Fla., Dec. 7, 1943; d. Lester and Barbara M. (Levy) Kornblith; m. Robert E. Kopp, May 3, 1969; children: Emily, Robert E. III. BA with honors, Wellesley Coll., 1965; MA, U. Chgo., 1968; LittD (hon.), Hood Coll., 1988; LHD (hon.), Towson U., 2001; JD (hon.), U. Md., Balt., 2001. Instr. polit. sci. U. Ill., 1968-69; staff spl. subcom. on edn. U.S. Ho. of Reps., Washington, 1970-71; legis. staff Md. Gen. Assembly, Annapolis, 1971-74; mem. Md. Ho. of Dels., 1974—2002, spkr. pro tem, 1991-93, chmn. appropriations subcom on edn. and devel., chmn. spending affordability joint com.; state treas. State of Md., Annapolis, 2002—. Chmn. Md. Coll. Savings Plans. Mem. exec. com. So. Regional Edn. Bd. Mem.: N.E. State Treas. Assn. (chmn. capital debt affordability bd., vice chmn. state ret. and pension bd.). Democrat. Jewish. Office: Treasury Building 80 Calvert St Annapolis MD 21401 Office Phone: 410-260-7160. E-mail: nkopp@treasurer.state.md.us.

KOPP, WENDY, teaching program administrator; b. Austin, Tex., June 29, 1967; BA, Princeton U., 1998; degree (hon.), Conn. Coll., Drew U. Pres. and founder Teach For America, 1989—. Bd. dirs. New Tchr. Project, The Learning Project, Kipp Acad. Recipient Nat. Acad. fellow, 1990, Jefferson Award for Pub. Svcs., Woodrow Wilson award, 1993, Aetna's Voice of Conscience award, 1994, Citizen Activist award, 1994, Kilby Young Innovator award; named to Time Mag. Roster of Am. Most Promising Leaders Under 40, 1994, Woman of Yr. Glamour mag., 1990. Office: Teach For America 315 W 36th St Fl 6 New York NY 10018-6404

KOPPELMAN, DOROTHY MYERS, artist, consultant; b. N.Y.C., June 13, 1920; d. Harry Walter and May (Chalmers) Myers; m. Chaim Koppelman, Feb. 13, 1943; 1 child, Ann. Student, Bklyn. Coll., 1938-42, Am. Artists Sch., 1940-42, Art Students League, 1942; student of Aesthetic Realism, with Eli Siegel, 1942-78, with Ellen Reiss, 1978—. Instr. art Bklyn. Coll., 1952-75; dir. Terrain Gallery, N.Y.C., 1955-83, Visual Arts Gallery., Sch. Visual Arts, 1961-62; pres. Aesthetic Realism Found., 1973-85, cons., 1973—. Instr. Nat. Acad. Sch. of Design, 1988-89, 96, 98. One-woman shows include Terrain Gallery, 1961, Rina Gallery, Jersey City, 1963, Atlantic Gallery, 1999; exhibited in group shows at Mus. Modern Art, N.Y.C., 1962, Balt. Mus., 1962, Bklyn. Mus., 1962, N.J. State Mus., Jersey City, 1959, Butler Art Inst., Youngstown, Ohio, San Francisco Art Inst., 1961-62, 65, Nat. Acad. of Design Juried Ann., 1986, 90, 99, 2000, Swiss Inst., N.Y.C., Susan Teller Gallery, N.Y.C., 1993, 95, Drawing Ctr., N.Y.C., Audubon Soc. ann., N.Y.C., 1995-96, 98, Chuck Levitan Gallery, N.Y.C., 1996, Washington Square East Gallery, N.Y.C., 1992, 96, Am. Soc. Contemporary Artists Anns., 1994-96, 97, 98, 99, 2000, 01, 02, Atlantic Gallery, 1998—, Beatrice Conde Gallery, 2000, Terrain Gallery, 2001, Sarah Lawrence Gallery, 2001, Denise Bibro Gallery, 2001, Terrain Gallery, 2002, 2003; represented in permanent collections Hampton Inst., Nat. Mus. Women in the Arts, Mus. Jewish Family, Durham, N.C., Savannah Coll. Art and Design, Washington County Mus. Art, Md.; author Poems and Prints, 2000; co-author: Aesthetic Realism: We Have Been There - Six Artists, 1969; illustrator Children's Guide to Parents (by Eli Siegel), 1971, 2d edit., 2003. Recipient Theresa Lindner award for painting ASCA, 1996, Clara Shainness award for painting, 1999, Tiffany grantee for painting, 1965. Home: 498 Broome St New York NY 10013-2213 Office: Aesthetic Realism Found Inc 141 Greene St New York NY 10012-3201 Personal E-mail: pierodella@aol.com.

KOPPER, MARY CARLL, director; b. Balt., Apr. 12, 1944; d. Jesse Whilden and Jane Connelly Carll; m. Jeffrey Hallett, Aug. 2, 1964 (div.); children: Christopher Fitzrandolph Hallett, Jonathan Talbot Hallett, Andrew Carll Hallett; m. Philip Dana Kopper, Sept. 22, 1979; 1 child, Timothy D.B. BA magna cum laude with honors in lit. studies, Am. U., 1979. Writer Crowley Comm., Wash., DC, 1986—91; regional dir. The Worth Collection, Wash., 1991—93; program dir. Inst. for Immunology and Aging, Wash., 1993—97; dir. of devel. The Nat. Mus. of Women in the Arts, Wash., 1999—2001, The Wash. Ballet, 2001—02; dir. Am. U., Campaign for the Arts, Wash., 2002—. Editor (art): A Christmas Testament, 1982; dir.: (plays) Equus, 1978. Trustee Crafts Ctr., Wash., 2002—, Kid Power DC, Wash., 2002—. Mem.: Nat. Mus. Women in the Arts, The Wash. Ballet, Wash. Area Women's Found. Office: Am U 4400 Mass Ave NW Washington DC 20008

KOPP-KELLY, JENNIFER LEE, technical illustrator; b. Phoenix, May 30, 1949; d. Leonard Owen and Gloria Belle (Shaffer) Kelly; student Los Angeles Pierce Coll., 1976-78, Moorpark Coll., 1981-83; m. Glenn Robert Kopp, Sept. 7, 1969; children— M. Scott, G. Douglas (dec.). Supr., Volt Tech Corp., Van Nuys, Calif., 1977-78, project coordinator, El Segundo, Calif., 1979-80; checker in drafting Mainstream Engring., Sherman Oaks, Calif., 1978-79; sr. tech. illustrator Dynaction Resources, Chatsworth, Calif., 1979; sr. tech. illustrator Litton Data Command Systems, Agoura Hills, Calif., 1980-86. Dir. North Shore chpt. Gt. Salton Sea Experience, 1986; dir. Salton Sea Legal Def. Group Systems, Agoura Hills, Calif., 1986-87; firefighter, sec.-treas. North Shore Vol. Fire Co., 1985-86; docent Living Desert, 1986-88. Recipient Presdl. Sports award Pres.'s Council on Phys. Fitness, 1973, 4 awards of Merit for sports L.A. Pierce Coll., 1977, Sportsmanship award Women's Internat. Motorcycle Assn., 1976, Citizenship award, 1978. Mem. North Shore C. of C. (founder 1987, pres., exec. dir. 1987-88), North Shore Litton Data Command Systems Rod and Gun Club (pres. 1982-83, v.p. 1984-85). Office: PO Box 3197 North Shore CA 92254-0980 Address: PO Bx 133 La Quinta CA 92253

KOPROWSKA, IRENA, cytopathologist, cancer researcher; b. Warsaw, May 12, 1917; came to U.S., 1944; d. Henryk and Eugenia Grasberg; m. Hilary Koprowski, July 14, 1938; children: Claude, Christopher. BA, Popielewska/Roszkowska, Warsaw, 1934; MD, Warsaw U., 1939. Cert. Am. Bd. Pathology, Internat. Bd. Cytology. Intern in medicine Villejuif Lunatic Asylum, Seine, France, 1940; asst. pathologist Rio de Janeiro City Hosp., Miguel Couto, Brazil, 1942-44; rsch. fellow dept. pathology Cornell U. Med. Coll., N.Y.C., 1945-46, rsch. asst. dept. pharmacology, 1949-50, rsch. fellow dept. of anatomy, 1949-54; rsch. fellow applied immunology Pub. Health Rsch. Inst. of The City of N.Y., 1946-47; asst. pathologist N.Y. Infirmary for Women and Children, N.Y.C., 1947-49; asst. prof. dept. pathology SUNY Downstate Med. Ctr., Bklyn., 1954-57; assoc. prof. pathology, dir. cytology lab./Sch. Cytotech. Hahnemann Med. Coll., Phila., 1957-64, prof. pathology dir. cytology lab., sch. cytotechnology, 1964-70; prof. pathology, dir. cytology lab. Temple U. Sch. Med., Phila., 1970-87, prof. emerita, 1987—. Cons. WHO, Switzerland, Egypt, Iran, Latin Am., India, 1960-85, Armed Forces Inst. Pathology, Air Force Cytology Rescreen Project, 1979-80. Author: Woman Wanders Through Life and Science, 1997; contbr. articles on cancer rsch. to profl. and sci. jours. Named Woman Physician of Yr., Polish Am. Med. Assn., 1977; grantee USPHS-Nat. Cancer Insts., 1954-75, rsch. grantee Bender Co., Vienna, Austria, 1983-89. Fellow Am. Soc. Clin. Pathologists (emeritus), Coll. Am. Pathologists (emeritus), Coll. Physicians of Phila., Internat. Acad. Cytology (hon.), Internat. Acad. Pathology (emeritus); mem. Am. Assn. for Cancer Rsch. Inc. (emeritus), Am. Assn. Pathologists Inc. (emeritus), Am. Med. Women's Assn., Am. Soc. Cytology (life, Papanicolaou award 1985), Am. Soc. Exptl. Pathology, Argentinian Soc. Cytology (hon.), Path. Soc. Phila. Avocations: reading, writing. Home: 334 Fairhill Rd Wynnewood PA 19096-1804

KORANDO, DONNA KAY, journalist; b. Chester, Ill., Mar. 31, 1950; d. Samuel L. and Dorothy L. (Meyer) K.; m. James J. Heidenry, Nov. 28, 1981; children: Reid Samuel, Rachel. BA, So. Ill. U., 1972; MSL, Yale U., 1980. Tchr. journalism Lincoln H.S., Manitowoc, Wis., 1972-73; copy editor St. Louis Post-Dispatch, 1973-77, editorial writer, 1977-86, editor commentary page, 1986—. Mem. Lafayette Square Restoration Com., St. Louis, 1981—. Mem. Assn. Opinion Page Editors (bd. dirs.). Roman Catholic. Avocations: children, literature. Office: St Louis Post Dispatch 900 N Tucker Blvd Saint Louis MO 63101-1099

KORB, CHRISTINE ANN, music therapist, researcher, educator; b. Milw., Aug. 9, 1943; d. Carl William and Lucille (Bell) Knoernschild; m. Mark Lee Korb, June 3, 1967 (div. May 1991); children: Tracy Lee, Amy Elizabeth. BS, Mt. Mary Coll., Milw., 1965; MMus in Music Therapy, Colo. State U., Ft. Collins, 1988. Registered and bd. cert. music therapist. Field dir. Girl Scouts of Am., Ill, Wis., 1965-69; contractual swimming tchr. YMCA, Janesville, Wis., 1970-76; contractual music tchr. YWCA, Janesville, Wis., 1971-76; music therapist inpatient/outpatient psychiat. unit Poudre Valley Hosp., Ft. Collins, 1989-92; music therapist Mary Hill Retirement Ctr., Milw., 1992-93, VA Med. Ctr., Milw., 1992-98; vis. asst. prof. music therapy Willamette U., Salem, Oreg., 1998—2000; dir of music therapy Marylhurst Univ., Oreg., 2000—. Composer (musical works) Namasté, 1988 (Art of Peace award 1985), We Are Your People of Love, 1981 (hon. mention Am. Song Festival 1981), Windseeker, 1988, Merry Christmas Day, 1994. Founding mem. Women in the Arts, Ft. Collins, 1987-88. Rsch. for music therapy grantee Helen Bader Found., Milw., 1994-95. Mem. Am. Music Therapy Assn., Music Tchrs. Nat. Assn., Amnesty Internat., Mu Phi Epsilon, Am. assoc. of univ. women. Democrat. Avocations: reading, spirituality, hiking, cross-country skiing, canoeing. Home: 13538 SW 63rd Pl Portland OR 97219-8122

KORB, JOAN, lawyer; b. Fond du Lac, Wis., Jan. 22, 1953; d. Allen Dale Korb and Evelyn A. Schmitz-Korb; m. Frederic B. Will, June 19, 1983. BS in Biology, U. Wis., Oshkosh, 1975; JD, John Marshall Sch. Law, Chgo., 1985. Bar: Wis. 1985, Ill. 1985. Asst. corp. counsel Racine County, Racine, Wis., 1985-89, asst. dist. atty., 1990-99, Door County, Sturgeon Bay, Wis., 1999—. Commentator on fetal abuse on TV, radio, in newspapers. Author novels. Mem. Mt. Pleasant (Wis.) Zoning Bd. Appeals, 1987-99; past pres. Wis. Profl. Soc. on Abuse of Children, Milw.; treas. Bd. Children Law Sec. of State Bar of Wis., 1998-2003. Mem. NOW, AAUW (pub. policy chmn. Racine 1995-99), Sierra Club (life). Avocations: lectr. children and legal issues, reading, scuba diving, sailing, travel. Office: Door County Dist Atty's Office 421 Nebraska St Ofc Sturgeon Bay WI 54235-2249 Office Phone: 920-746-2284.

KORCHIN, JUDITH MIRIAM, lawyer; b. Kew Gardens, N.Y., Apr. 28, 1949; d. Arthur Walter and Mena (Levisohn) Goldstein; m. Paul Maury Korchin, June 10, 1972; 1 son, Brian Edward. BA with high honors, U. Fla., 1971, JD with honors, 1974. Bar: Fla. 1974, U.S. Ct. Appeal (2d, 5th and 11th cirs.), U.S. Dist. Ct. (so., mid. and no. dists) Fla. Law clk. to judge U.S. Dist. Ct., 1974-76; assoc. Steel, Hector & Davis, Miami, Fla., 1976-81, ptnr., 1981-87, Holland and Knight, Miami, 1987—. Author, exec. editor U. Fla. Law Rev., 1973-74. Mem. U. Fla. Law Ctr. Coun., 1980-83; pres. alumni bd. U. Fla. Law Rev., 1983; bd. dirs. Fla. Film & Rec. Inst., 1982-84. Recipient Trail Blazer Award The Women's Com. of 100, 1988. Fellow: Fla. Bar Found. (subcom. legal assistance for poor 1988—90), Am. Bar Found.; mem.: ABA (sect. alternative dispute resolution, vice chmn. 1994—95, co-chmn. fed. ct. mediation com. 1995, sect. labor and employment law, sect. litig.), Fla. Bar Assn. (vice chmn. jud. nominating procedures com. 1982, civil procedure rules com. 1984—89, 1993—95), Nat. Assn. Bank Women (TV panelist greater Miami chpt. 1987), Nat. Assn. Women Bus. Owners (adv. coun. 1987—88), Dade County Bar Assn. (bd. dirs. 1981—82, treas. 1982, sec. 1983, 3d v.p. 1984, 2d v.p. 1985, 1st v.p. 1986, pres. 1987), CPR Inst. for Dispute Resolution (nat. panelist 1994—, exec. com. 2003—), Am. Arbitration Assn. (employment law panel, s.e. 1993—, comml. law panel 1993—), Greater Miami C. of C. (com. profl. devel. 1988—90), Rabbinical Assn. Greater Miami (TV panelist Still Small Voice 1987), City Club (bd. dirs. 1988—93), Phi Kappa Phi, Phi Beta Kappa, Order of Coif. Office: Holland & Knight PO Box 015441 701 Brickell Ave Ste 3000 Miami FL 33131-2898 Office Phone: 305-789-7764.

KORDALEWSKI, LYDIA MARIA, news correspondent, municipal employee; b. Detroit, Oct. 19, 1956; d. Zygmunt and Maria Kordalewski. AA, East Los Angeles Coll., 1979. Police svc. rep. L.A. Police Dept., 1979—88; actress, casting asst. Miami, Fla., 1988—99; news corr. Polish News, Polish Am. Jour., various others, 1999—; mcpl. asst. enforcement, dir. park and recreation Bal Harbour City Hall, Fla., 2001—. Media spokesperson Haitian-Am. Law Enforcement Officers Assn., Fla., 2001—. Mem. Hall of Fame Selection Com., North Miami, Fla., 1999—; advocate mem. Fla. Local Advocacy Coun., 1999—; assoc. councillor Atlantic Coun. of U.S., Washington, 1999—; sec. Polish Am. Congress, Fla., 1999—; chair audience devel. com. Mus. Contemporary Art, 1999—; organizer, founder internat. NATO European Balls, 1999—2001; candidate for city coun. City of North Miami, 2001. Named Woman of Yr., Polish Am. Congress, Fla., 2001; recipient cert. of achievement, White Ho. Comm. Agy., Miami, 1994, cert. award, Eckerd's Salute to Women, Miami, 2000. Mem.: Am. Inst. Polish Culture, Polish-Am. Club (dir. pub. rels. 1999—). Democrat. Roman Catholic. Avocations: travel, photography, volunteering, languages. Home: 11550 NE 22nd Dr North Miami FL 33181

KORDESTANI, KAYVON KIM, music educator, choreographer; b. St. Louis, Sept. 22, 1967; d. George Houshang and Nancy Louise (Nitz) Kordestani. BA, U. of the Pacific, 1990. Cert. tchr. music, English, elem. edn. Kindergarten tchr. Cambrian Sch. Dist., San Jose, Calif., 1990—; dir., choreographer San Jose Children's Mus. Theater, San Jose, 1991—; vocal dir. Am. Zoetrope, San Francisco, 1993; artistic mgr. San Jose Children's Mus. Theater, 1998; choreographer Sunnyvale (Calif.) Comty. Players, 2002, Freemont H.S., Sunnyvale, 2003, Saratoga (Calif.) Drama Group, 2003. Recipient Dedication to Tchg. Excellence award, Target, 1999. Mem.: Panehellenic Coun. (pres. 1989), Alpha Lambda Delta, Delta Gamma. Republican. Lutheran. Avocations: theater, dance. Office: Sartorette Elem 3850 Woodford Dr San Jose CA 95124

KORDINAK, IRMA L. piano teacher, musician; b. Buffalo, Feb. 27, 1930; d. Paul Eugene Kompalla and Pauline Beuter; m. Albert Andrew Kordinak, July 18, 1964. BM, Oberlin Coll. Consevatory Music, 1953; postgrad, Eastman Sch. Music, Rochester, N.Y., 1962. Nat. cert. tchr. music Music Tchrs. Nat. Assn. Pianist, singer Hormel All-Girl Orch., 1953—54; piano faculty Cmty. Music Sch., Buffalo, 1954-64; piano tchr. pvt. practice, 1954—. Pres. Music Forum for Piano Tchrs. of Western N.Y., 1970—72, social chmn., 2002—; bd. dirs. Music Forum for Piano Tchr. of Western N.Y., 1959—91, 2002—, hon. mem., 2003; pres. dist. 8 N.Y. Fedn. Music Clubs, 1970—76; pres.-elect Amherst (N.Y.) Symphony Orch. (Women's Com.), 1999—2000, co-chair scholarship com., 2000—03; chmn. dist. 10 N.Y. State Music Tchrs. Assn., Buffalo, 1987—; bd. dirs. QRS Arts Found., Buffalo, 1991—98. Mem.: Music Tchrs. Nat. Assn., Am. Liszt Soc., Friends of Vienna in Buffalo, Opera Buffs of Western N.Y., Chromatic Club (hon.; life, past. pres. 1967—68). Avocations: photography, theater, concerts. Home and Office: Buffalo-Niagara Frontier MTA 265 Countryside Ln Buffalo NY 14221-1523

KOREMAN, DOROTHY GOLDSTEIN, physician, dermatologist; b. Bklyn., Nov. 1, 1940; d. Benjamin and Ida (Krenick) Goldstein; m. Neil M. Koreman, Aug. 16, 1964; children: Elizabeth Koreman Landau, Robert Stephen. BA, Bklyn. Coll., 1961; MD, SUNY, Bklyn., 1965. Diplomate Am. Bd. Dermatology. Intern pediatrics Kings County Hosp. Ctr., Bklyn., 1965-66; resident dept. dermatology Wayne State U. Sch. Medicine, Detroit, 1966-69; clin. instr. dermatology Sch. Medicine Wayne State U., Detroit, 1969-71; asst. clin. prof. dermatology U. Miami, 1971-75, assoc. clin. prof. dermatology, 1975-82, clin. prof. dermatology and cutaneous surgery, 1982—. Mem. Miami Dermatol. Soc. (pres. 1978-79). Avocations: traveling, cooking, reading, skiing, needlepoint. E-mail: skinkor40@aol.com.

KORENIC, LYNETTE MARIE, librarian; b. Berwyn, Ill., Mar. 29, 1950; d. Emil Walter and Donna Marie (Harbutt) K. m. Jerome Dennis Reif, Dec. 31, 1988. BS in Art, U. Wis., 1977, MFA, 1979, MA in LS, 1981, MA in Art History, 1984. Asst. art libr. Ind. U., Bloomington, 1982-84; art libr. U. Calif., Santa Barbara, 1984-88, head Arts Libr., 1988-99; art libr. U. Wis., Madison, 1999—. Author articles. Mem. Art Librs. Soc. N.Am. (sec. 1983-84, v.p. 1989, pres. 1990), Beta Phi Mu. Office: U Wis Kohler Art Libr Madison WI 53706 E-mail: lkorenic@library.wisc.edu.

KORF, JEAN PRINZ, retired theater educator; b. New Albany, Ind., Oct. 28, 1925; d. Winfield Henry and Waneta Sadler Prinz; m. Leonard Lee Korf, Aug. 15, 1949; children: Kerry Lee, William Milton, Geoffrey Leonard. BA, UCLA, 1947, MA, 1953; MS in Edn., U. So. Calif., 1963. Theater prodn. mgr. Whittier (Calif.) H.S., 1949-52; drama tchr. Calif. H.S., Whittier, 1953-66; theater arts prof. Rio Hondo Coll., Whittier, 1966-90. Founder TheaterCreations Unltd., 1990—; guest dir. La. State U., Baton Rouge, 1990, 91, St. Barts Playhouse, N.Y.C., 1992, U.S. State Dept. Arts Am., Bialystok, Poland, 1993. Commr. Whittier Cultural Arts Commn., 1993-2005; bd. dirs. Whittier Cultural Arts Found., 1990—. Fellow Coll.

Fellows Am. Theater (dean 1994-96), Rio Hondo Coll.; mem. Los Angeles County Mus. Art, Nat. Mus. Women in the Arts, UCLA Theater Film & TV Alumni Assn. (bd. dirs. 1991-2000), Nat. Theatre Conf., Nature Conservancy, World Wildlife Fund. Democrat. Unitarian Universalist. Avocations: theatre going, attending cultural events, conservation, travel, genealogy. Home: 9811 Pounds Ave Whittier CA 90603-1616 E-mail: jeankorf@aol.com.

KORFF, PHYLLIS G. lawyer; b. N.Y.C., 1943; BA, Bklyn. Coll., 1964; EdM, Boston U., 1967; JD, NYU, 1981. Bar: N.Y. 1982. Ptnr. Skaden, Arps, Slate, Meagher & Flom, N.Y.C., 1990. Office: Skadden Arps Slate Meagher & Flom 4 Times Sq Fl 24 New York NY 10036-6595

KORN, JESSICA SUSAN, research scientist, educator; b. L.A., Aug. 16, 1968; d. Lester B. and Carolbeth (Goldman) K. BA in Sociology, UCLA, 1990, MA in Edn., 1992, PhD in Philosophy, 1996. Actor Curb-Esquire Films, Burbank, Calif., 1984; exec. asst. Korn Capital Group, Inc., L.A., 1991; tchg. asst. Grad. Sch. Edn. and Info. Studies UCLA, 1995, rsch. analyst Grad. Sch. Edn. and Info. Studies, 1992-96, postdoctoral fellow Higher Edn. Rsch. Inst., 1996-97, tchg. assoc., 1997; rsch. scientist, affiliate asst. prof. U. Wash., 1997-99; v.p. instnl. rsch. Eckerd Coll., St. Petersburg, Fla., 1999—. Internat. election observer Orgn. for Security and Cooperation in Europe, 1997, 98, 2000, 02. Contbr. articles to profl. jours. Jr. assoc. Big Sisters Am., L.A., 1994-98. Mem. AAUW, Am. Ednl. Rsch. Assn., Assn. Study of Higher Edn., Assn. for Instnl. Rsch., Nat. Coun. Rsch. on Women, Screen Actors Guild Am. Avocations: working with rape and other trauma survivors, humanitarian aid, travel, writing, yoga, acting. E-mail: kornjs@eckerd.edu.

KORN, NAOMI S. social worker, consultant; b. Johnson City, N.Y., Oct. 28, 1940; d. Anthony Shary and Theodora Shary-Pluta; m. Saul Burton Korn, Dec. 25, 1968; children: Daniel Evan McMartin, Shoshanna Shary Korn-Meyer, Uri Maximilian. BA, D'Youville Coll., Buffalo, 1962; MSW, SUNY, Buffalo, 1964. Diplomate Am. Bd. Clin. Sexology, Am. Bd. Clin. Social Work, diplomate in clin. social work NASW, cert. therapist EMDR Internat. Assn. Co-dir. Poplar Sch., Chestnut Hill, Mass., 1973—78; dir. svc. to mil. families ARC, St Petersburg, Fla., 1979—81; dir. adopt-a-grandchild program Gulf Coast Jewish Family Svcs., Clearwater, Fla., 1981—83; dir. social work, adminstr. hosp. therapists Horizon Hosp., Clearwater, 1987—89; sch. social worker Pinellas County Sch. Bd., Pinellas Park, Fla., 1989—91; ind. psychotherapist St Petersburg, 1991—; coord. Cmty. Alliance of Pinellas for AIDS/ Children's Mental Health Project, St Petersburg, 1994—97. Clin. cons. PACE Ctr. for Girls, Pinellas Park, 1999—2002; cons. Meridien Rsch., St Petersburg, 2000—03. Vol. bereavement counselor Temple Beth El, St Petersburg, 1998—2000. Jewish. Avocations: travel, bicycling, reading, sewing. Office: 535 Central Ave Ste 316 Saint Petersburg FL 33701 Personal E-mail: kornkorn@tampabay.rr.com. E-mail: naomi.korn3@verizon.net.

KORN, THERESA MARIE, former electrical engineer, consulting firm co-owner, technical writer; b. St. Louis, Nov. 5, 1926; d. William John McLaughlin and Mary Rose Heinz; m. Granino Arthur Korn, Sept. 3, 1948; children: Anna M. and John M. BSEE, Carnegie Inst. Tech., 1947; MSEE, UCLA, 1954. Lic. comml. radio transmission engr., 1942. Elec. engr. Curtiss-Wright Aircraft Co, Columbus, Ohio, 1947-49, Boeing Airplane Co., Seattle, 1949-50; tech. writer, co-owner G.A. & T.M. Korn Indsl. Cons., Tucson, 1952-92, Chelan, Wash., 1992—. Expert witness Ariz. Corp. commn., Tucson, 1971; mem. gov.'s adv. commn. on environ. State of Ariz., 1974-76; mem. Master Tech. com. City of Tucson, 1975-76. Co-author (with E.P. Korn) Trailblazer to Television, 1950; (with G.A. Korn) Electronic Analog Computers, 1952, 2d edit., 1956, Electronic Analog and Hybrid Computers, 1964, 2d, edit., 1974, Mathematical Handbook for Scientists and Engineers, 1961, 2d edit., 1968, Manual of Mathematics, 1968. Active, vol. engr. Tucson Consumer's coun., 1970-76; active Ariz. Consumer's coun., 1970-76, Profl. Women's coalition, Tucson, 1988-91, Nat. Women's Polit. Caucus; citizen's adv. bd. Tucson E. Cmty. Mental Health Ctr., 1974-76; bd. dirs., treas., risk mgr. Planned Parenthood of So. Ariz., Tucson, 1983-89; mem. ad hoc com. Establishing Tucson Women's Commn., 1975-76. Warrant officer Pa. Wing USNG Civil Air Patrol, 1941-43. Named Woman on the Move YWCA, 1976; recipient plaque, with Granino A. Korn, as Pioneers in Analog and Digital Computation, 1998, Computer Engrng. Rsch. Lab., Dept. Elec. and Computer Engrng., U. Ariz., Tucson. Mem. Soc. Women Engrs. (co-founder Tucson chpt., former v.p.), AAUW, Quarter Century Wireless Assn., Quarter Century Wireless Women, Young Ladies' Radio League. Avocations: amateur radio, flying, photography, travel, genealogy. Office: Korn Indsl Cons 7750 S Lakeshore Rd Unit 15 Chelan WA 98816-9328

KORNBLAU, BARBARA L. physical therapist; BS in Occupl. Therapy, U. Wis., 1977; JD, U. Miami, 1984. Diplomate Am. Acad. Pain Mgmt.; lic. O.T. Fla., Tex., rehab. svcs. provider/rehab. counselor, cert. disability mgmt. specialist, case mgr. Occupl. therapist Kuakini Med. Ctr., Honolulu, 1978, Rock County Health Care Ctr., Janesville, Wis., 1978—79, Coop. Edn. Svc. Agy. #17, Janesville, Wis., 1979—80; contract occupl. therapist Prince George County Pub. Health Dept., Md., 1980; asst. to coord. disabled students affairs Cath. U., Washington, 1980; occupl. therapist South Miami Hosp., 1980—85; dir. clin. svcs., owner Innovative Therapeutics, 1985—87; assoc. dir. Occupl. Therapy Resource Svcs., Inc., 1985—87; chief occupl. therapist Bapt. Hosp. of Miami, Fla., 1986—87; cons. in rehab. and occupl. therapy svcs., 1982—; pres. ADA Cons., Inc., 1991—; pvt. practice law, 1985—; adj. prof. Fla. Internat. U., 1986, adj. prof. occupl. therapy, 1992, vis. lectr. occupl. therapy, 1992—93; prof. occupl. therapy and pub. health Nova Southeastern U., Ft. Lauderdale, Fla., 1994—. Cons. in field. Contbr. numerous articles to profl. jours., chpts. to books; co-author (with Karen Jacobs): Principle and Practices of Work, 2001; co-author: (with Shirley Starling) Ethics in Rehabilitation, 2000; mem. editl. bd. Am. Jour. Pain Mgmt., Occupl. Therapy in health Care, Prevention Plus Newsletter, Advance for Occupl. Therapists, peer rev. panel mem. Jour. of Care Mgmt. Founder, former dir. Pro Bono Law Project for the Deaf; mem. atty.'s dvsn. ACLU; vol. Dade County Bar Assn. Vol. Lawyers Program; numerous other civic activities; mem. instnl. rev. bd. and ethics com. Deering Hosp.; past bd. dirs. Bus. Coalition for Ams. with Disabilities; former edn. com. mem. Multiple Sclerosis Soc.; bd. dirs., chair S.E. br. Fla. chpt. Arthritis Found., 1998—2000, sec., 1999—2000, chpt. del. to nat. ho. of dels., 1999—2000, exec. com., 1999—2000; past steering com. ann. jud. reception Greater Miami Jewish Fedn. Named Young Achiever, Wis. State Jour., 1976, Disting. Lectr., Maine Tech. Coll. Sys., 1993, Outstanding Alumni, U. Wis.-Madison Sch. Edn., 1999; recipient Outstanding Sr. award, U. Wis., 1977, Svc. award, Fla. Occupl. Therapy Assn., 1994—97, Presdl. Recognition Award for outstanding svc. to families and communities, Rotary Internat., 1995—96, Vol. of the Yr. award, Arthritis Found., 1998, Award of Excellence, Fla. Occupl. Therapy Assn., 1998; fellow DeWitt Wallace fellow, NYU Inst. Rehab. Medicine, 1973; scholar Wis. State Legis. scholar, 1974—77, Henry B. Herman Meml. scholar, 1975. Fellow: Am. Occupl. Therapy Assn. (chair stds. and ethics comm. 1998—, pres., chair bd. dirs. 2001—, pres.-elect, exec. bd. dirs., chair stds. and ethics commn., past chair work programs spl. interest sect., paper reviewer ann. conf., Svc. award 1996, 2000); mem.: U. Wis. Alumni Assn. (former pres. and founding mem. S. Fla. chpt.), Fla. Bar Assn. (employment, workers' compensation and elder law sects.), Am. Soc. for Law, Medicine and Ethics, ABA (labor sect.), Nat. Assn. Rehab. Providers in the Pvt. Sector, Case Mgmt. Soc. Am., N.Am. Cervicogenic Headache Soc., Fla. Occupl. Therapy Assn. (legal cons., conf. planning com. mem., paper peer reviewer, legis. impact team capt.), Autism Soc. Am., APHA, Am. Bd. Disability Analysts, Am. Acad. Pain Mgmt. (adv. bd.), South Miami Rotary Club (Paul Harris fellow, sec. and pres.-elect, numerous other com. positions), U. Miami Hurricane Club. Office: Nova Southeastern Univ 3200 S University Dr Fort Lauderdale FL 33328

KORNBLEET, LYNDA MAE, insulation, fireproofing and acoustical contractor; b. Kansas City, Kans., June 15, 1951; d. Seymour Gerald Kornbleet and Jacqueline F. (Hurst) Kornbleet Malka. BA, U. St. Thomas, Houston, 1979. Lic. real estate salesperson; Disadvantaged Bus. Cert., State of Tex. Temporary counselor Lyman's Pers., Houston, 1974-75; real estate salesperson Coldwell Banker, Houston, 1975-77; sales, office mgr. Acme Insulation, Dallas, also Houston, 1977-79; owner, pres. Payless Insulation Inc., Houston, 1979—; contractor City of Houston, 1985—; owner, founder Superior Air Ducts, Houston, 2002—. Active Houston Ind. Sch. Dist., 1989—. Recipient award Internat. Cellulose 7,000,000 sq. ft., 2002; named Contractor of Yr., Sears Home Improvement, 1988. Mem. Houston Air Conditioning Coun. (bd. dirs. 1982-83), Cellulose Insulation Contractors (chmn. Houston 1981-82), Houston Bus. Coun., Insulation Contractors Assn. Greater Houston (pres. 1991-94, award for Top 50 Woman-Owned Cos. 1995), Women in Constrn. (bd. dirs. 1998-2000, sec.). Democrat. Avocations: bridge, golf. Office: Payless Insulation 1331 Seamist Dr Houston TX 77008-5017

KORNBLEUTH, MICHELLE LORRAINE, psychologist; b. Bronx, N.Y., Nov. 26, 1968; d. Norman Stewart and Babette Kornbleuth. BA, U. Hartford, 1991; MS, Springfield Coll., 1993; PhD, Ill. Inst. Tech., 1998. Lic. psychologist N.Y. Project psychologist Mt. Sinai Med. Ctr., N.Y.C., 1999—2000; sr. staff psychologist Lenox Hill Hosp., N.Y.C., 2000—; pvt. practice N.Y.C., 1999—. Adj. faculty Mt. Sinai Sch. Medicine, N.Y.C., 1999—; cons. IQ Toys, N.Y.C., 1999—2001; adj. faculty Hunter Coll., N.Y.C., 2000—02. Contbr. articles to profl. jours. Grantee Rehab. Svc. Adminstrn. grant, 1993. Mem.: APA. Avocations: ceramics, skiing.

KORNER, BARBARA OLIVER, academic administrator; b. Kansas City, Mo., July 26, 1950; d. Robert C and Vonda F (Jenkins) Oliver; m. James Richard Korner, July 7, 1979. PhD, Ohio U., Athens, Ohio, 1983. Assoc. dean Coll. of Fine Arts, U. Fla., Gainesville, Fla., 2000—; dean Fine and Performing Arts, Seattle Pacific U., Seattle, 1990—99; asst. dir. Sch. of Fine Arts, U. Mo., Columbia, Mo., 1988—90; spl. asst. to the chancellor U. Mo., Columbia, Mo., 1985—88; asst. to the dean U. Coll., Ohio U., Athens, Ohio. V.p. for adminstrn. Assn. for Theatre in Higher Edn., Downers Grove, Ill., 1993—99; speakers' bur. Wash. Commn. for the Humanities, Seattle; spkr. Mo. Humanities Coun., St. Louis; dir. Leadership Inst., Assn. for Theatre in Higher Edn., Downers Grove, Ill. Editor: (book) Hardship and Hope: Mo. Women Writing About their Lives; actor: Responding to the Call: Women of Spiritual Action, Hardship and Hope: Heroines in Life and Art (Grant: Mo. Humanities Coun.), Creating Sacred Spaces. Bd. dir. Duval Sch. Arts Coun., Gainesville, Fla.; pres. Kiwanis Club, Seattle; lay spkr. United Meth. Ch. Mem.: Nat. Storytelling Assn., S.E. Theatre Conf., Assn. for Theatre in Higher Edn. (v.p. for adminstrn. 1993—99), Kiwanis (Outstanding Leadership Award 1998). United Meth. Ch. Office: University of Florida PO Box 115800 Fine Arts A Gainesville FL 32611-5800 E-mail: bkorner@arts.ufl.edu.

KORNFIELD, JULIA ANN, chemical engineering educator; b. Oakland, Calif., July 2, 1962; BA, Calif. Inst. Tech., 1983; MS, Stanford U., 1984, PhD in Chemical Engrng., 1988. Rsch. asst. Calif. Inst. Tech., 1983-84, asst. prof. chemical engrng., 1990—; rsch. asst. chem. engrng. Stanford U., 1984-88, tchg. asst. appl. math., 1986, 87. NSF/NATO fellow chem. engrng. Max-Planck Inst., 1989. Mem. AIChE, Am. Phys. Soc. (John H. Dillon medal Rsch. in Polymer Physics 1996), Am. Chem. Soc., Soc. Rheology. Office: Calif Inst Tech Dept Chem Engrng 206-41 1201 E California Blvd Pasadena CA 91125-0001

KORNS, LEOTA ELSIE, writer, mountain land developer, insurance broker; b. Canton, Okla., Jan. 19, 1916; d. James Abraham and Ida Agnes (Engel) Klopfenstine; m. Richard Francis Korns, July 1, 1943 (wid. Dec. 17, 1988); 1 child, Michael Francis. BS, Pitts. State U. of Kans., 1966. Sec. various firms, Kans. City, Mo., 1937-45; cons. Electrolux Corp., St. Paul, 1946-49; sec. health, safety and waste IAEA, Vienna, Austria, 1959-60; tchr. Montezuma-Cortez H.S., Cortez, Colo., 1966-67; ins. agent Korns Ins. Agy., Durango, Colo., 1968—; owner, pres. Korns Investments, Inc., Durango, Colo., 1970—. Bd. dirs. LaPlata County Landowners Assn., Durango, 1981-87; writer, instr. women's history course U. N.Mex., Albuquerque, Ft. Lewis Coll., Durango, Colo., and Mesa (Ariz.) C.C., 1970-75; also spkr. in field. Author: (novels) Yesterday Should Have Been Over, 1965, Somewhere Out in the West, 2002; (play) Angry Young Men, 1957; writer numerous short stories including The Combine, 1947. Convenor, mem. NOW, Durango, 1970—; precinct capt. La Plata County Rep. Party, 1981—. Mem. Unity Sch. Christianity, Trimble Hot Springs. Avocations: mountain walking, swimming, piano, cross-country skiing. Home: 556 2d Ave Durango CO 81301-5604 Office Phone: 970-247-0532. E-mail: leotakorns@frontier.net.

KOROLOGOS, ANN MCLAUGHLIN, public policy, communications executive; b. Newark, N.J., Nov. 16, 1941; d. Edward Joseph and Marie (Koellhoffer) Lauenstein; m. John McLaughlin, 1975 (div. 1991); m. Tom C. Korologos, 2000. Student, U. London, 1961-62; BA, Marymount Coll., 1963; postgrad., Wharton Sch., 1987. Supr. network comml. schedule ABC, N.Y.C., 1963-66; dir. alumnae relations Marymount Coll., Tarrytown, N.Y., 1966-69; account exec. Myers-Infoplan Internat. Inc., N.Y.C., 1969-71; dir. comm. Presdl. Election Com., Washington, 1971-72; asst. to chmn. and press sec. Presdl. Inaugural Com., Washington, 1972-73; dir. Office of Pub. Affairs, EPA, Washington, 1973-74; govt. rels. and comm. exec. Union Carbide Corp., N.Y.C. and Washington, 1974-77; pub. affairs, issues mgmt. counseling McLaughlin & Co., 1977-81; asst. sec. for pub. affairs Dept. of Treasury, Washington, 1981-84; under sec. Dept. of Interior, Washington, 1984-87; cons. Ctr. Strategic and Internat. Studies, Washington, 1987; sec. labor Dept. of Labor, Washington, 1987-89; vis. fellow Urban Inst., 1989-92; pres., CEO New Am. Schs. Devel. Corp., 1992-93; ret., 1993. Mem. def. adv. com. Women in the Svcs., 1973—74; mem. Am. Coun. Capital Formation, 1976—78; mem. environ. edn. task force HEW, 1976—77; chair Pres.'s Commn. Aviation Security and Terrorism, 1989—90; bd. dirs. Fannie Mae, Kellogg Co., Host Marriott Corp., Am. Airlines, AMR Corp., Harman Internat. Industries, Inc., Microsoft; pres. Fed. City Coun., 1990—95; chair Aspen Inst., 1996—2000, vice-chair, 1996; chmn. RAND. Bd. dirs. Charles A. Dana Found., Conservation Fund; mem. bd. overseers Wharton Sch. U. Pa. Mem.: Sulgrave Club, Met. Club, Cosmos Club. Republican. Roman Catholic.

KOROPSAK-BERMAN, ELIZABETH A. psychologist, consultant; d. Stanley Francis and Ann Mary Koropsak; m. Richard David Berman, July 1, 1970; 1 child, Jacob Rama Berman. PhD, W.Va. U., 1997; MS, Fla. State U., 1968; BA, Washburn U., 1965. Licensed Psychologist State Bd. Psychology DE, 2003, State Bd. Psychology Pa., 2000, State Bd. of Psychology, W,Va., 1998, Cert. Family Mediator State of Fla., 1991, Licensed Marriage & Family Therapist State of Fla., 1986. Sr. rsch. asst. Stein Gerontology Inst., Miami, Fla., 1982—85; pvt. practice psychologist Miami, Fla., 1985—93. Psychologist HRS State of Fla., Miami, 1985—87; psychologist, tchr. Fairmont State Coll., W.Va., 1995—96; intern U. Rochester Sch. Medicine, NY, 1996—97; psychologist Health South Rehab. Hosp., Morgantown, W.Va., 1997—99, Elwyn, Inc., Elwyn, Pa., 2000—03, Maternal/Child Svcs., Bensalem, Pa., 2001—. Co-author (chapter in edited book) Longitudinal Course of Bereavement in Older Adults. Vol. Food Bank, Wilmington, Del., 2000—03, SPCA, West Chester, Pa., 2001—03, Pa. Autism Task Force, WMCA, Brandywine, Del. Winifred South Knutti Grad. Scholarship Dept. Women's Studies, W.Va. U., 1996, Arlene & Louis Swigger Fellowship, 1995. Fellow: Pa. Psychology Assn.; mem.: APA. Achievements include Mentoring Young Psychologists; integrating eastern traditions into western psychology; development of mind/body programs in cmty. Avocations: painting, gardening, travel, creating wildlife habitate. Home and Office: 200 Prospect Drive Wilmington DE 19803 Office Phone: 302-477-9488. Personal E-mail: eberman@comcast.net.

KOROT, BERYL, artist; b. N.Y.C., Sept. 17, 1945; d. George and Frieda (Braunstein) K.; m. Steve Reich, May 30, 1976; 1 child, Ezra. Student, U. Wis., 1963-65; BA, Queens Coll., 1967. Chief, co-founder Radical Software, 1970-73; co-editor Video Art, 1976. Exhibitions include 4 channel video work Dachau, exhibitions include 5 channel video work, weavings, drawings Text and Commentary, Kitchen, N.Y.C., 1975, exhibitions include Everson Mus. Art, Syracuse, N.Y., 1975, 1977, Documenta 6, Kassel, Germany, 1977, Videopoints, Mus Modern Art, N.Y.C., 1978, Mickery Theatre, Holland, 1978, Whitney Mus., N.Y.C., 1980, San Francisco Art Inst., 1981, Leo Castelli Gallery, N.Y.C., 1977, Mus. Fine Arts, Montreal, 1979, John Weber Gallery, 1986, Jack Tilton Gallery, 1987, Carnegie Mus. Art, 1990, Long Beach Mus. Art, 1988, Jewish Mus., N.Y.C., 1988, Video Skuptur, Kunstverein, Koln, 1989, The Cave, 1993, Reina Sofia Mus., Madrid, 1993—94, Dusseldorf Kunsthalle, Whitney Mus. Am. Art, N.Y.C., Carnegie Mus. Art, ICC Gallery, Tokyo, 1997, Hindenburg, 1998, Bklyn. Acad. Music, 1998, Spoleto Festival, 1998, Mass. Coll. Art, 1999, Historischen Mus., Frankfurt, 2000—01, Whitney Mus., N.Y.C., 2000, 2001, Jewish Mus. Paris, 2002—03, short commd. work, Art 21, PBS, 2002; cinematographer: (video opera) The Cave, 1993, Three Tales, 2002. Montgomery fellow Dartmouth Coll., 2000. Artist fellow NEA, 1975, 77, 79, N.Y. State Coun. on Arts, 1978, Creative Artist Pub. Svc., 1975, 79, Guggenheim fellow, 1995; grantee Rockefeller Found., 1989, 98, Andy Warhol Found., 1991, NEA, 1991-92. Home: 258 Broadway New York NY 10007-2315

KOROW, ELINORE MARIA, artist, educator; b. Akron, Ohio, July 31, 1934; d. Alexander and Elizabeth Helen (Doszpoly) Vigh; m. John Henry Korow, Sept. 28, 1957 (div. Oct. 1980); children: Christopher, David, Daniel; m. Harry Edward Bieber, Aug. 1, 1982 (dec. May 1994). Student, Siena Heights Women's Coll., 1952-53; four yr. diploma, Cleve. Inst. Art, 1957; diploma, Sawyer Coll. Bus., 1976. Staff artist Am. Greetings Corp., Cleve., 1957-58, designer, 1970-73; owner Elinore Korow: Portraits, Shaker Heights, Ohio, 1973-94, Akron, 1994—. Painting instr. Cuyahoga C.C., Cleve., 1979—, chmn. sr. excellence in art exhbn., 1985-96; painting instr. U. Akron, 1995—. Represented in permanent collections Blue Cross/Blue Shield of N.E. Ohio, Am. Greetings Corp., U. Akron Alumni Ctr., Cleve. Playhouse, Temple Emanuel, Cleveland Heights, Ohio, Kent State U., First Congrl. Ch., Akron, Ohio; one woman-shows include Akron (Ohio) Woman's City Club, 1996, Cuyahoga Valley Art Ctr., Cuyahoga Falls, Ohio, 1995, others; group shows include Ohio Regional Painting Exhbn., 1993, Beck Ctr. for the Cultural Arts, Lakewood, Ohio, 1993, 17th Ann. Russell Art Exhibit, Novelty, Ohio, 1992, Canton Art Inst., Butler Inst. Am. Art, Youngstown, Nat. Acad. Design, NYC, others. Women's com. Cleve. Orchestra, 2002; rep. Women's Art League to the Akron Area Arts Alliance, 2001; charter mem. Alliance for The Visual Arts, 1999—2000; bd. mem. Akron Soc. of Artists and Women's Art League, 2001—. Recipient 2d place 17th Annual Russell Show, Novelty, Ohio, 1992, first place 17th Annual Russell Show, Novelty, 1993, third place Valley Art Ctr., Cuyahoga Falls, Ohio, 1994, First Prize cash award, AIDS Benefit, Ohio, 2000, First Prize All Mem. Show, 2001, First Place Beginnings, Lawrence Churski Gallery, 2002. Mem. Am. Soc. Portrait Artists (assoc.), Women's Art League (past pres. 1999-2000, Best in Show award 2000), Women's Art Club Cleve. (past pres. 1970-71), Ohio Watercolor Soc. (charter), Akron Soc. Artists (signature), Women's Network, Boardroom Group. Avocations: music, world travel, teaching courses on gems and minerals. Home: 923 Mayfair Rd Akron OH 44303-1317

KORR, MARLA, artist; b. N.Y.C., N.Y., Dec. 14, 1950; d. Morris Korr and Irene Berlin; m. Richard Dominique, June 25, 1995. BA, Bklyn. Coll., 1972, MFA, 1979; postgrad., Stevenson Acad. Art, 1984—87, N.Y. Acad. Art, 1986. Tchr. Korr Atelier, N.Y.C., 1986—. Prin. works include Stevenson New Renaissance Gallery, Sea Cliff, N.J., 1990—, Edgartown Gallery, Martha's Vineyard, Mass., 1999—, Willoughby Fine Art, 1999—, Cavalier Galleries, Nantucket, Mass., 2000—, RVS Gallery, South Hampton, N.Y., 2000—, Windham Fine Art, N.Y., —, exhibitions include Bergen Mus. Art, N.J., Olana, State Hist. Site, N.Y., Barrett House, Broome St. Gallery, N.Y.C., The Rice Gallery, Albany Inst. Art, Nat. Arts Club, N.Y.C., Ven Vlecjk Mus., N.J., Clinton West Corp., Ithaca, N.Y. Recipient Bronze medal, Nat. Art League, N.Y., 1993. Mem.: Maritime Artists Am., Nat. Arts Club, Catharine Lorillard Wolfe Art Club (Mae Bolind Bach award 1997).

KORSAK, BARBARA A. geriatrics nurse; b. Coplay, Pa., Sept. 17, 1940; d. Paul Alexander and Angela Theresa (Deutsch) Korsak; 1 child, Alisa R. Student, Sacred Heart Coll., Allentown, Pa., 1961—63; A, Mary Roger's Coll., 1965; BS in Health Arts, St. Franci's Coll., Joliet, Ill., 1998. Lic. nurse N.J., N.Y. Staff nurse Sacred Heart Hosp., Allentown, 1961—62; staff nurse, charge nurse Mt. Sinai Hosp., N.Y.C., 1961—68; staff nurse ICU and critical care unit, emergency room Allentown Hosp., 1969—87; staff nurse then charge nurse emergency room Easton (Pa.) Hosp., 1987—2000; case mgr. Spruce Monor Nursing Home, Reading, Pa., 2000—01; supr. charge nursing dept. Holy Family Villa, Bethlehem, Pa., 2001—. Vol. St. John's, Whitehall, Pa., 1987—92, St. Nicholas, Walnutport, Pa., 1980—. Mem.: Sacred Heart Hosp. Alumni Assn. Roman Catholic. Avocations: reading, gardening, crossword puzzles, travel. Office: Holy Family Villa 1325 Prospect Ave Bethlehem PA 18018

KORSCH, BARBARA M. pediatrician; b. Jena, Germany, Mar. 30, 1921; arrived in U.S., 1936; 1 child. BA, Smith Coll., 1941; MD, Johns Hopkins U., 1944. Cert. Am. Bd. Pediat. Asst. resident Bellevue Hosp., 1945, Mary Imogene Basset Hosp., 1946, N.Y. Hosp., 1947, fellow Inst. Child Devel., 1948—49; asst. pediats. Med. Coll. Cornell U., 1949—50, from instr. to assoc. prof., 1950—61; assoc. clin. prof. preventive medicine Sch. Medicine UCLA, 1961—64; assoc. prof. Keck Sch. Medicine, U. So. Calif., L.A., 1964—69, prof. pediats. Sch. Medicine, 1969—. George Armstrong lectr. Ambulatory Pediatric Assn., 1973; Katherine D. McCormick Disting. lectr. Stanford U., 1977; Kathy Newman Meml. lectr. Tulane U., 1987; asst. outpatient pediatrician N.Y. Hosps., 1949—50, asst. attending pediatrician, 1950—55, clin. dir. pediatric outpatient dept., 1950—61, assoc. attending pediatrician, 1955—61; pediatric cons. Dept. Health, NY, 1949—51, Hosp. Spl. Surgery, 1955—61, Gen. Pediatric Childrens Hosp., L.A., 1961—65, Med. Ctr., U. So. Calif., 1969—74; coord. pediatric rehab. program Nat. Found. Infantile Paralysis, 1953—61; pediatric dir. Obs. Clinic Children L.A., 1961—64; assoc. attending pediatrician Cedars of Lebanon Hosp., 1961—; vis. prof. numerous U.S. and fgn. univs., 1973—89; hon. staff mem. dept. pediat. Cedars-Sinai Med. Ctr., 1976—; attending pediatrician, dir. behavioral and devel. program, dir. dr.-patient comm. project Children's Hosp. L.A.; Philip Rothman fellow, 1999—. Author: Intelligent Patient's Guide to the Doctor-Patient Relationship, 1997; contbr. articles to profl. jours. Chmn. coun. Bayer Inst. for Health Comm., 1989—98. Recipient Disting. Career award, Ambulatory Pediatric Assn., 1991. Mem.: Soc. Pediatric Rsch., Soc. Behavioral Pediat. (pres. 1985), Am. Pediatric Soc., Am. Acad. Pediat. (C. Anderson Aldrich award 1988, Genesis award for med. ethics 1998), Inst. Medicine NAS, Sigma Xi. Office: Childrens Hosp Divsn Gen Pediats MB # 76 4650 W Sunset Blvd Los Angeles CA 90027-6062 E-mail: bkorsch@chla.usc.edu.

KORSGAARD, CHRISTINE MARION, philosophy educator; b. Chgo., Apr. 9, 1952; d. Albert and Marion Hangaard (Kortbek) K.; m. Timothy David Gould, June 1980 (div. Sept. 1984). BA, U. Ill., 1974; PhD, Harvard U., 1981. Instr. Yale U., New Haven, 1979-80; asst. prof. U. Calif., Santa

Barbara, 1980-83; from asst. prof. to prof. U. Chgo., 1983-91; prof. Harvard U., Cambridge, Mass., 1991—, chair philosophy dept., 1996—2002. Vis. assoc. prof. Berkeley, 1989, UCLA, 1990; Tanner lectr. human values, 1992, Locke lectrs., 2002. Author: The Sources of Normativity, 1996, Creating the Kingdom of Ends, 1996; editor: (with Andrews Reath and Barbara Herman) Reclaiming the History of Ethics: Essays for John Rawls, 1997; contbr. chpts. to books, articles to profl. jours. Whiting fellow, 1978-79; Ctr. for Human Values fellow, 1995-96. Fellow AAAS; mem. Am. Philos. Assn., N.Am. Kant Soc., Hume Soc., Am. Soc. for Polit. and Legal Philosophy.

KORSHAK, YVONNE, art historian; b. Chgo., May 30, 1936; d. Donald Korshak and Irma B. Jaffe; m. Robert J. Ruben; 1 child, Karin. BA cum laude, Radcliffe Coll., Cambridge, Mass., 1958; MA, U. Calif. Berkeley, 1966; PhD, U. Calif., 1973. Asst. prof. U. Md., College Park, 1972-74, Fordham U., N.Y.C., 1974-75; from asst. prof. to prof. Adelphi U., Garden City, N.Y., 1975—, chairperson Dept. Art and Art History, 1978-81, dir. honors program, dir. mus. studies, 1979—. Project dir. seminar on the modern condition NEH, 1990. Author: Frontal Faces in Attic Vase Painting, 1987, co-editor: Selections from Permanent Collection, 1983. Recipient Pres.'s award for excellence in teaching, 1990. Mem. Coll. Art Assn. Am., Archaeological Inst. Am., Long Island Art Historians Assn., American Soc. for Eighteenth Century Studies, American Philological Assn. Office: Adelphi U Dept Art And Art History Garden City NY 11530 E-mail: ykorshak@aol.com.

KORSLUND, ANNETTE, administrative assistant, translator, interpreter, writer; b. Falls City, Nebr., Sept. 5, 1953; d. John Granger and Yvonne Piel K. AA, Am. Coll. in Paris, 1973; BA, George Washington U., 1976. Cert. bus. French, French C. of C. Profl. translator OEA, Inc., Denver, 1988-89, Ceric, USA, Denver, 1989-90; adminstrv. asst. Dept. Edn., Denver, 1991-95, Bd. Acctg., Denver, 1995-96, Bd. Nursing, Denver, 1996—. Campaigner Dem. Party, Denver, 1992; vol. translator/hostess G-8 Summit, Denver, 1997; vol. mem. Gov.'s Diversity Coun., Denver, 1997; vol. elem. sch. pen pal Dept. Regulatory Agys., 1997. Named for Disting. Svc., Sch. Architecture, U. Denver, 1988; recipient cert. appreciation World Youth Day, Denver, 1993. Mem. Alliance Francaise, French Conversation Group (leader, founder 1988—). Roman Catholic. Avocations: writing, tennis, travel, praying, reading. Office: Bd Nursing 1560 Broadway Ste 880 Denver CO 80202-5141 Home: 1010 S Oneida St Apt C208 Denver CO 80224-3593 E-mail: annette.korslund@dora.state.co.us.

KORT, BETTY, secondary school educator; English tchr. Hastings (Nebr.) Sr. High Sch., 1979—. Named Nebr. State English Tchr. of Yr., 1993. Office: Hastings Sen High Sch 1100 W 14th St Hastings NE 68901-3064

KORTH, CHARLOTTE WILLIAMS, furniture and interior design firm executive; b. Milw.; d. Lewis C. and Marguerite Peil Brooks; m. Robert Lee Williams, Jr., Oct. 25, 1944 (dec.); children: Patricia Williams, Melissa Williams O'Rourke, Brooks Williams; m. Fred Korth, Aug. 23, 1980. Student, U. Wis., 1941. Owner Charlotte's Inc., El Paso, Tex., 1951—, chmn., CEO, 1979—; pres. Paso del Norte Design, Inc., El Paso, 1978-81; mem. adv. com. for interior design program El Paso C.C., 1981—; mem. adv. bd. S.W. Design Inst., 1982—; ptnr. Wilko Partnership, 1981-98; mem. adv. bd. Mountain Bell Telephone Co., 1976-79; mem. Sch. Architecture Found. Adv. Coun. U. Tex. Austin, 1985-91. Charter mem. Com. of 200, 1982—, Nat. Mus. Women in the Arts, 1985—; mem. Renaissance 400, El Paso, El Paso Women's Symphony Guild, El Paso Mus. Art. Recipient of Silver plaque Gifts and Decorative Accessories Mag., 1978; named Woman of Yr. by El Paso Am. Bus. Women's Assn., 1978, Outstanding Woman of Yr. by Women's Polit. Caucus, 1979. Mem. Am. Soc. Interior Designers (bd. dirs. Tex. chpt. 1977-82), El Paso Women's C. of C. (hon.), El Paso C. of C. (dir. 1976-82), Coronado Country Club, Internat. Club, El Paso Country Club, Santa Teresa Country Club (N.Mex.). Avocations: travel, antiques, collectibles. Home: 6041 Torrey Pines Dr El Paso TX 79912-2029 Office: Charlotte's Inc 5411 N Mesa St Ste 7 El Paso TX 79912-5495

KORTHALS, CANDACE DURBIN, lawyer; b. Tampa, Fla., Oct. 3, 1948; d. Robert F. and Geraldine B. Durbin; children: John Kristofor, Kathryn Elizabeth. BA in Internat. Studies, Ohio State U., 1969, BS in Edn., 1970; JD cum laude, Nova U., 1982. Bar: Fla. 1982. Tchr. Palatka (Fla.) Mid. Sch., 1970-72, Dillard H.S., Ft. Lauderdale, Fla., 1974-79; atty. Broward County Pub. Defenders, Ft. Lauderdale, 1982-84, Grimmett & Korthals, Ft. Lauderdale, 1984-90, Gunther & Whittaker, Ft. Lauderdale, 1990-94, Law Office of John Camillo, Ft. Lauderdale, 1994-99, Neale & De Almeida, Ft. Lauderdale, 1999-2000, Heinrich, Gordon, Hargrove, Weihe & James, Ft. Lauderdale, 2000—02, Barnett & Barnard, Hollywood, Fla., 2002—. Staff mem. Nova Law Rev., 1981, 82. Office: Barnett & Barnard 4601 Sheridan St #505 Hollywood FL 33021 Business E-Mail: ckorthals@bbslawfirm.com.

KORY, MARIANNE GREENE, lawyer; b. N.Y.C., 1931; d. Hyman Louis and Belle (Rome) Greene; children: Erich Marcel, Lisa. BA, CCNY, JD, N.Y. Law Sch., 1976; LLM, U. Wash., 1986. Bar: Ohio 1977, D.C. 1979, N.Y. 1983, Vt. 1994, U.S. Dist. Ct. (so. and ea. dists.) N.Y. 1983, U.S. Dist. Ct. Vt. 1994. Hearing examiner Ohio Bd. Employee Compensation, Columbus, 1977; atty. advisor Office Hearings and Appeals Social Security Adminstrn., Cin. and N.Y.C., 1977-78; gen. atty. labor Office of Solicitor U.S. Dept. of Labor, N.Y.C., 1978-82; pvt. practice N.Y.C., 1983—; adminstrv. Seattle, 1989-91, Burlington, Vt., 1994—. Founder Cin. chpt. Amnesty Internat., 1977. Alvin Johnson fellow in Philosophy; grad. faculty New Sch. for Social Rsch. Mem. Nat. Abortion Rights Action League, Feminist Majority Found., Vt. Bar Assn., Planned Parenthood, Wilderness Soc., Defenders of Wildlife, Ctr. for Marine Conservation, Nat. Wildlife Fedn., Audubon Soc., Emily's List, Phi Beta Kappa. Office: 1361 S Ocean Blvd #202 Pompano Beach FL 33062-8022 Office Phone: 954-781-2820. E-mail: mariannekory@aol.com.

KOSA, JAYMIE REEBER, middle school educator; b. N.J., Oct. 19, 1967; BA in English Lit., U. Md.; EdM, Rutgers U., 1991. Nat. bd. cert. tchr. 1999. Tchr. The Newgrange Sch., Trenton, NJ, 1991—92, West Windsor-Plainsboro Middle Sch., Plainsboro, NJ, 1991—99, Thomas Grover Middle Sch., West Windsor, NJ, 2001—; adj. prof. Fairleigh Dickinson U., Teaneck, NJ, 2000—01. Mem.: Nat. Bd. for Profl. Tchg. Stds. (bd. mem.), Phi Beta Kappa.

KOSCIK, ELLA M. company executive; With sales dept., 1986—; with IT Cons., 1988—; CEO Mgmt. Decision Inc. Mem. Ga. Assn. Pers. Svcs. (bd. dirs.), Nat. Assn. Women Bus. Owners (founder Atlanta chpt.). Office: Mgmt Decisions Inc Ste 310 4940 Peachtree Industrial Blvd Norcross GA 30071-1568 Fax: 770-416-7323. E-mail: mdi@america.net.

KOSEL, RENÉE, state representative; b. Chgo., Apr. 3, 1943; m. Alfred Kosel; 3 children. BS in Edn., Western Ill. U. Bd. dirs. Lincoln-Way H.S. Dist. Recipient Ednl. Excellence award, Lincoln-Way Found., New Lenox Twp. Steering Com. award, United Way. Mem.: Ill. Assn. Sch. Bds. (dir.), Edn. Commn. States (commr.), Nat. Sch. Bd. Assn. (fed. rels. rep.). Republican. Lutheran. Office: 221-N Stratton Office Bldg Springfield IL 62706 Address: 19201 S LaGrange Rd Ste 204B Mokena IL 60448

KOSHIMITSU, KEIKO, artist; b. Tokyo, Sept. 21, 1958; arrived in U.S., 1984; d. Minoru and Sumiko Koshimitsu; m. Aldo E. Garay, June 1, 1995; children: Kazuki Aldo Garay Jr., Rina Angelica Garay. BFA, Tama Art U., Tokyo, 1981; MA in Edn., Yokohama (Japan) Nat. U., 1983. Supr. The Bank of Yokohama, N.Y.C., 1997—2002, asst. v.p., 2003. One-woman shows include JTB Equitable Ctr., N.Y., 1992, exhibitions include Tokyo Prefecture Mus., 1979, 1980, 1982, Bronx Mus., N.Y., 1994, exhibited in group shows at Sanaa Gallery, Tokyo, 1981, Sumitomo Bldg. Gallery, 1981, Kanagawa Prefecture Gallery, Yokohama, 1982, Yokohama Gallery, 1982, 1983, 1984, 1985, 1986, Mitsubishi Gallery, Tokyo, 1983, Cast Iron Gallery, N.Y., 1992, 1996, El Bohio C.C., 1992, Tenri Gallery, 1992, Klein Landaw Fine Arts, 1992, Japan Consulate, 1993, 2004, Walter Wickiser Gallery, N.Y., 1993, 1995, 1999, 2000, 2001, Gallery One Twenty Eight, 1994, Liver House, 1994, Krasdale Gallery, 1995, Ise Gallery, 1996, 1997, Kaoru Gallery, Tokyo, 1997, Broome St. Gallery, N.Y., 1999, New Century Artist Gallery, 2000, Caelum Gallery, 2001, Tenri Gallery, 2001, 2002, 2003, 2004. Mem.: Japanese Artists Assn. (treas. 1991—99, pres. 2000—), Tama Art U. Alumni Assn. (v.p., treas. 2003). Home: 175 Maplewood Ave Bogota NJ 07603 Office: Japanese Artist Assn NY Inc 175 Maplewood Ave Bogota NJ 07603 E-mail: keikokoshimitsu@optonline.net.

KOSKI, DONNA FAITH, poet; b. Wildwood, NJ, Aug. 18, 1935; d. Sebastian and Mildred (Shastany) Rossitto; m. Paul A. Koski, May 5, 1968 (div. June 1982); children: Danita Swift-Stearns, Darla Swift, Deanna Swift-Everett, Deena Swift Bauer, Charles Swift. Student, San Diego Jr. Coll., 1955-58, Mesa Jr. Coll, San Diego, 1993. With Pacific Telephone, San Diego, 1954-68; credit clk. Norwich (Conn.) Gas & Lights, 1968-70; clk. Navy Exch., New London, Conn., 1969-70; front desk clk. Del Webb's, San Diego, 1971-72; payroll clk. U.S.I.U., San Diego, 1974-76; facility mgr. Price Costco, San Diego, 1978-94, Price Enterprises, Inc., San Diego, 1994-97, Price Smart Vacations (Costco Travel), 1997—99; facility and maintenance mgr. The Price Club, 1999—2000; quality control and support agent Club 4 U. Worker Diversified Copier Products in San Diego, Price's, PAcific bell, Westgate (C Arnolt Smith), Alvin Strep Interiors, USIU, Norwich Gas and Electric, John Myers of Norwich, Navy Exch.-New London, Conn, several hotels and motels. Author: The Power of Love, 1995, Nights in Sedona, 1995, Faces in the Clouds, 1994, Dream Catcher, 2001, The New Heros, 2003, numerous poems, (book) Theatre of the Mind, 2003, Celebrate Poets Speak Out, 2003. Vol. Nat. Multiple Sclerosis Soc., San Diego, 1995, React-Telecom. Emergency Svcs., San Diego, 1985-93, Perot Hdqrs., San Diego, 1992, 96, Social Svcs., San Diego, 1980-82, Project Oz (runaway kids). Recipient Editor's Choice award Nat. Libr. of Poetry, 1995, Accomplishment of Merit, Creative Arts and Sci., 1994, 1st Pluto Browning Competition award Iliad Press, 1998, Presdl. Recognition award, 1998-99, Outstanding Achievement in Poetry award Famous Poets Soc., 1998, others. Mem. Internat. Soc. Poets, Internat. Soc. Authors and Artists, Blind Soc., Multiple Sclerosis Soc., Moose. Mem. Unity Ch. Avocations: writing, poetry, computers, music, sports. Home: 8661 Winter Gardens Blvd SP 45 Lakeside CA 92040 E-mail: koskidonna@aol.com., k78@yahoo.com.

KOSKINIEMI, DONNA LOUISE ROGERS, elementary school educator, music educator; d. Donald W. and Mary Lou Barbara Rogers; m. Gary Michael Koskiniemi, Aug. 22, 1975; children: Michael Rogers, Valerie Louise. MusB, No. Mich. U., Marquette, Mich., 1989, EdM, 2004. Cert. tchg. Mich., 1989. Music tchr. pvt., Marquette, Mich., 1978—93; youth choir dir. Grace United Meth. Ch., Marquette, Mich., 1979—83; music tchr. Ishpeming (Mich.) Sch. Dist., 1991—93, Marquette Area Pub. Sch., Mich., 1993—. Supr. for student teachers No. Mich. U., Marquette, Mich., 2000—02; mentor tchr. Marquette Area Pub. Schools, Mich., 2002—03. Recipient Who's Who in Am. High Sch., Marquis Who's Who, Calumet, Mich., 1973. Mem.: Music Educators Nat. Conf. Methodist. Avocations: reading, golf, walking, bicycling, sewing. Office: Marquette Area Pub Sch 1201 W Fair Ave Marquette MI 49855

KOSLOW, SALLY, editor-in-chief; BA, U. Wis. Editor-in-chief McCall's mag., N.Y.C., 1994—2001; editor-in-chief Lifetime mag. The Hearst Corp., N.Y.C., 2002—, editor Mary Emmerling's Country, 2002—. Office: Lifetime mag The Heart Corp 1790 Broadway New York NY 10019

KOSMAS, SUZANNE, state legislator, real estate company executive; b. Washington, Feb. 25, 1944; Student, Pa. State U., 1961-63, George Mason U., 1971-73, Stetson U., 1989-96. Owner, broker Prestige Properties of New Smyrna Beach (Fla.); mem. Fla. Ho. of Reps., Tallahassee, 1996—. Mem. Select Com. on Ednl. Facilities, Com. on Cmty. Affairs Govtl. Responsibility Coun., 1996-97, Com. on Corrections Justice Coun., 1996-97, Com. on Edn. K-12 Acad. Excellence Coun., 1996-97. Mem. Indian River Lagoon Nat. Estuary Program, Volusia County Planning and Zoning Bd., East Ctrl. Fla. Regional Planning Coun.; chair Southeast Volusia Zoning Bd.; chair Volusia County Environ. and Natural Resource Adv. Coun.; chair bus. intern com. Futures, Inc.; chair bd. United Way Volusia County; mem. exec. bd. Volusia Vision; adv. bd. Habitat for Humanity, Volusia County Cultural Arts; trustee Atlantic Ctr. for the Arts. Named Vol. of Yr. Ctr. of Cmty. Involvement, 1996. Mem. Nat. Assn. Realtors, Fla. Assn. Realtors, Volusia County Assn. Responsible Developers, Volusia County Bus. Devel. Corp. Methodist. Avocations: tennis, jogging, reading, school, grandchildren. Home: 403 Canal St New Smyrna Beach FL 32168-7009 Office: Fla Capitol 402 S Monroe St Tallahassee FL 32399-6526 E-mail: kosmas.suzanne@leg.state.fl.us.

KOSOWSKI, MARY, artist, educator; b. Pawtucket, R.I., Dec. 7, 1927; d. Marlin Padykula and Constance Trzuskowski; m. Alfred Kosowski, Oct. 14, 1950 (dec. July 1989); children: Eileen, Linda. BFA, R.I. Sch. Design, 1949; B in Tchg., R.I. Coll., 1970. Fabric designer Decorative Fabrics, Pawtucket, R.I., 1949-52; children's wear designer Healthtex, Pawtucket, 1964-67; tchr. Cumberland (R.I.) Sch. System, 1967-90. Mem. pres. club R.I. Sch. Design, 1996—. Recipient many awards for art works. Mem. Rockport Art Assn., Attleboro Mus., Providence Art Club (mem. providence art on art qualifications com. 1975—), Met. Mus. Art, Nat. Mus. for Women in Arts, Boston MFA, Copley Soc., others. Avocation: travel. Home: 76 Orchard Meadows Dr Smithfield RI 02917-1846

KOSTECKI, MARY ANN, financial tax consultant, small business consultant; b. St. Louis, Jan. 6, 1941; 4 children. Student, Forest Park Jr. Coll., 1969-72, Washington U., 1973-77. Dem. candidate for U.S House 2nd Dist., Mo., 1996. Office: 7446 Sieloff Dr Ste G Hazelwood MO 63042-2250

KOSTER, BARBARA, insurance company executive; Acct. Chase Manhattan Bank, 1976, v.p. fin. sys.; chief info. officer Prudential Individual Ins., Newark. Recipient award Women in Sci. & Tech., 1999. Office: Prudential Ins Co Am 751 Broad St Newark NJ 07102-3714

KOSTER, ELAINE LANDIS, publishing executive; b. N.Y.C. BA, Barnard Coll., 1962. Pres., pub. Dutton Signet, N.Y.C.; head Elaine Koster Literary Agy. LLC, N.Y.C. Office: Elaine Koster Literary Agy LLC 55 Central Park W Ste 6 New York NY 10023-6003

KOSTICK, ALEXANDRA, ophthalmologist; BSc, MD, U. Man., Winnipeg, Can., 1990. Surg. intern St. Boniface Hosp./U. Man., Winnipeg, 1990-91; rsch. fellow in ocular pathology Storm Eye Inst./Med. U. S.C., Charleston, 1991-92; resident in ophthalmology U. Sask., Saskatoon, Can., 1992-95; fellow corneal diseases U. Mo., Columbia, 1995-96; practice ophthalmology specializing in cornea and external diseases, Ormond Beach, Palm Coast, Fla., 1996—. Contbr. articles to profl. jours. Fellow ACS, Am. Acad. Ophthalmology; mem. Am. Soc. Cataract and Refractive Surgeons, European Soc. Cataract and Refractive Surgeons, Royal Coll. Physicians and Surgeons Can., Castroviejo Corneal Soc., Paton Eye Bank Soc., Can. Ophthalmology Soc., Royal Acad. Dancing (London). Office Phone: 386-446-9590.

KOSUB, JANE STEVENS, marriage and family therapist, consultant; b. Alpine, Tex., July 10, 1948; d. Bedford Peyton and Alta Stevens Cain; m. James Albert Kosub, Aug. 11, 1979; children: Kathryn Lauren, Nicholas Anthony Kosub (deceased) 1 stepchild, James Albert Jr. BA, Angelo State U., 1969; MEd, Trinity U., 1978; postgrad., Kennedy Western U., 2001—03. Cert. tchr. Tex. Edn. Agy., 1969, counselor Tex. Edn. Agy., 1976, lic. profl. counselor Tex. State Bd. of Examiners, 1984, marriage and family therapist Tex. State Bd. of Examiners, 1986. Tchr., counselor San Antonio (Tex.) Ind. Sch. Dist., 1969—79; counselor Judson Ind. Sch. Dist., Converse, Tex., 1982—94; pvt. practice behavioral cons. Eldorado, Tex., 1998—. Chmn. Edwards Plateau Cmty. Resource Coop. Group, Eldorado, 1995—2000. Mem.: Am. Assn. of Marriage and Family Therapists. Democrat. Episc. Avocations: ranching, breeding horses. Home and Office: Office of Jane S Cain Kosub 105 South Main Eldorado TX 76936 E-mail: jane1998@aol.com.

KOT, HEATHER A. (HEATHER A. OLIVER), soprano, educator; b. Warrensville Heights, Ohio, Feb. 12, 1977; d. John E. and Gail S. Oliver; m. David A. Kot; 1 child, Chloe H. BA in Music, Dickinson Coll., 1999; MusM in Voice Performance and Pedagogy, Pa. State U., 2001. Residency asst. Eaken Piano Trio, Carlisle, Pa., 1998—99; edn. dept. asst. adminstr. Eisenhower Ctr. for the Arts, State College, Pa., 1999—2000; pvt. voice and piano instr. Heather A. Kot Voice & Piano Studio, Carlisle, 2001—. Choral condr. LDS Ch., Mechanicsburg, Pa., 1998—99, 2001, State College, 1999—2000; contbg. soloist Jubilate, Camp Hill, Pa., 2003—. Composer: (song cycle) Scarlet Tides; singer: Requiem (Mozart), Roman Fever, (symphony) Te Deum (Dvorak). Named Most Outstanding Woman, Wheel & Chain Honor Sorority, 1998; recipient 1st prize in regional adult soprano competition, Nat. Assn. Tchrs. of Singing, 2000. Mem.: Cantate Carlisle (soprano soloist 2001—), Pa. Music Educators Assn. Republican. Mdm. Lds Ch. Avocations: interior decorating, architecture, reading, travel. Office: Heather Kot Voice and Piano Studio 1-C Mel-Ron Ct Carlisle PA 17013

KOTCHER, SHIRLEY J. W. lawyer; b. June 6, 1924; m. Harry A. Kotcher; children: Leslie Susan, Dana Anne. BA, NYU; JD, Columbia U. Bar: N.Y. In-house counsel Booth Meml. Med. Ctr., Flushing, N.Y., 1975-83, gen. counsel, 1983-91; v.p., gen. counsel the N.Y. Hosp. Med. Ctr. Queens, 1991-97; advisor health care Borough Pres. Queens, 1978. Author: Hidden gold and Pitfalls in New Tax Law, 1970. Mem. North Hempstead Sr. Citizen Commn., Manhasset, NY, 1999—; mem. affordable sr. housing endowment adv. com. Town of North Hempstead, 1999—; bd. dirs. Denton Green Housing Co. Inc., Garden City Park, NY, 1999—. Mem. ABA (health law forum com.), Nat. Health Lawyers Assn., Am. Acad. Hosp. Attys., Am. Soc. Law and Medicine, Am. Soc. Health Care Risk Mgmt., Assn. for Hosp. Risk Mgmt. N.Y., Greater N.Y. Hosp. Assn. (legal adv. com. 1976-97).

KOTCHIAN, SARAH BRUFF, municipal official; MEd, Harvard U., 1977; MPH, U. Wash., 1985. Dir. dept. environ. health City of Albuquerque, 1982—. Office: City of Albuquerque Environ Health Dept PO Box 1293 Albuquerque NM 87103-1293

KOTEFF, ELLEN, periodical editor; b. Harvey, Ill. d. Walter Peter and Florence (Walz) K. BS in Journalism, U. Fla. Editor Palm Beach (Fla.) Daily News; met. editor Daily Record, Parsippany; exec. editor Nation's Restaurant News, N.Y.C. Bd. dirs. Women's Foodservice Forum; v.p. Internat. Foodservice Editl. Coun. Bd. dirs. Women's Foodservice Forum, 2003. Recipient Jesse H. Neal award, 2002, McAllister Editl. fellowship award, 2002. Office: Nations Restaurant News 425 Park Ave New York NY 10022-3506 Office Phone: 212-756-5186.

KOTHERA, LYNNE MAXINE, clinical psychologist; b. Cleve., Dec. 18, 1938; d. Leonard Frank and Lillian (Shackleton) K.; m. Richard Litwin, Oct. 24, 1965 (dec.). BA with hons., Denison U., Granville, Ohio, 1960; MA, NYU, 1983; PhD, L.I. U., Bklyn., 1989; postgrad. psychotherapy/psychoanalysis, NYU, 2003. Dancer Martha Graham Dance Co., N.Y.C., 1961-62, Carmen DeLavallade Dance Co., N.Y.C., 1965-68, Glen Tetley Dance Co., N.Y.C., 1965-69; prin. dancer John Butler's, N.Y.C., 1971; artist-in-residence Boston High Schs. - Title III, 1969-71, Hobart-Smith Coll./Denison U., 1973; auditor N.Y. State Council of the Arts, N.Y.C., 1974-78; predoctoral fellow clin. psychology Yale-New Haven Hosp., 1987-88; postdoctoral fellow neuropsychology Inst. of Living, Hartford, Conn., 1989-91; with dept. rehab. medicine Mt. Sinai Med. Ctr., N.Y.C., 1991—, co-dir. tng. in-patient, 1995—; adj. asst. prof. Hunter Coll., N.Y.C., 1998-99. Mem.: APA. Democrat. Avocation: the arts. Home: 23 E 11th St New York NY 10003-4450 Office: Mt Sinai Med Ctr Rehab Med KCC-365-G PO Box 1674 1 Gustave L Levy Pl New York NY 10029-6500 Office Phone: 212-241-4196. Business E-Mail: lynne.kothera@msnyuhealth.org.

KOTLER, WENDY ILLENE, art educator, social studies educator, grants coordinator; b. Chgo., Mar. 4, 1947; d. Robert and Florence (Rabin) Abrams; m. Neil G. Kotler, Dec. 17, 1971; 1 child, Jena Julianne. BFA, U. Ill., 1969; MEd, U. Va., 1982, PhD, 1991. Cert. NK-12 art tchr., gifted and talented edn., mid., elem. and secondary sch. supr. and prin. Tchr. Sch. Dist. 109 and 23, Cook County, Ill., 1969-71; tchr. art, supr. Supervisory Union 32, N.H., 1972-74; tchr., curriculum developer Austin (Tex.) Ind. Sch. Dist., Hanover, N.H., 1974-75; staff devel. trainer, program developer Fairfax County (Va.) Pub. Schs., 1975-76, tchr., curriculum developer, 1979-85, program coord., art and mid. sch. resource tchr., 1985-92; mem. adj. faculty No. Va. Ext., U. Va., Fairfax, 1985—; adj. faculty George Mason U. Program developer, tchr. trainer Regional Ctr. for Ednl. Tng., Wilson Mus., Dartmouth Coll., Hanover, N.H., 1972-74; workshop presenter in field to regional, state, nat. and sch. confs.; curriculum and instrn. cons.; adj. faculty George Mason U. Contbr. articles to profl. publs. Recipient commendation for profl. excellence Fairfax County Pub. Schs., 1989, 92. Mem. NEA, ASCD, NCSS, Va. Edn. Assn., Fairfax Edn. Assn., Nat. Art Edn. Assn. (Southeastern Elem. Art Educator of Yr. award 1991, Nat. Elem. Art Educator of Yr. award 1992), Va. Art Edn. Assn. (bd. dirs. 1989, 93, Va. Elem. Art Tchr. of Yr. award 1989, cert. of commendation 1990), No. Va. Art Edn. Assn. (pres. 1993, No. Va. Art Tchr. of Yr. award 1988, 89), Phi Delta Kappa. Home: 507 Roosevelt Blvd Apt C403 Falls Church VA 22044-3156

KOTT, BEVERLY PARAT, financial counselor, community activist; b. Chgo., Sept. 7, 1936; m. Russell Kott; children: Vinson V., Donna M., James L., Michael A. Grad., Life Underwritr Tng. Coun., Washington, 1977. Mem. mgmt. ea. region Met. Life Ins. Co., Balt., 1977; ins. broker, 1979-85; pres. Kott & Assocs. Fin. Counseling Svc., Joppa, Md., 1985—. Fin. counselor coop. extension svc. U. Md., Bel Air, 1987-2000, mem. Harford extension adv. coun., 1988-93; dir. Prison Ministry, 1983—; lay minister Roman Catholic Ch., 1995—. Commr. Harford County Commn. for Women, Bel Air, 1981-87; v.p. Joppa Friends of the Libr., 1988—; mem. Rumsey Island Civic Assn., 1980—; dir. Joppatowne Civic Assn., Joppa, 1990—, Padre Rio Rosary Makers, 1993—, Postal Adv. Coun., 1992-2000; sec. Harford County Libr. Coun., 1999—. Named one of Most Beautiful People, Harford County, 1990. Mem. Hunt Valley Bus. and Profl. Woman's Club (charter), Aux. VFW (pres. 1988-90, legis., youth, publicity and cancer aid coms. 1989, 90), Mensa Internat. Roman Catholic. Avocations: chess, bridge, writing, travel, volunteering. Office: 661 Towne Center Dr Joppa MD 21085-4439 E-mail: kottbev@aol.com.

KOTUK, ANDREA MIKOTAJUK, public relations executive, writer; b. New Brunswick, N.J., Oct. 19, 1948; d. Michael and Julia Dorothy (Muka) Mikotajuk. BA, Douglass Coll., Rutgers U., 1970. Pub. relations asst. Wall St. Jour. Newspaper Fund, Princeton, N.J., 1970; editorial asst. Redbook mag., N.Y.C., 1970-71; asst. pub. relations dir. Children's Aid Soc., N.Y.C.,

1971-75; assoc. pub. relations dir. Planned Parenthood, N.Y.C., 1975-80; pres. Andrea & Assocs., N.Y.C., 1980—. Writer publicist for non-profit agys.; contbg. editor Arts Mag., 1970-75. Office: Andrea & Assocs 112 E 23rd St New York NY 10010-4518

KOUBA, SHARI L. retired federal official; d. Joseph Frank and Ferne Dorothy Kouba. BS, U. Ill., 1968; MA, U. Colo., 1973. Tchr. Robert Frost Jr. High, Schaumburg, Ill., 1968—69, Niles Twp. H.S., Skokie, Ill., 1969—79; spl. agent FBI, Chgo., 1979—2000; ret. Mem.: Soc. Former SA (treasurer), Sq. Spares Dance Club, 400 Ski Club. Protestant. Avocations: theater, skiing, reading, travel. Home: 9135 National Morton Grove IL 60053

KOURIDES, IONE ANNE, endocrinologist, researcher, educator; b. N.Y.C., Sept. 1, 1942; d. Peter T. and Anne E. (Spetseris) K.; m. Charles G. Zaroulis, Nov. 30, 1974; children: Anna Larisa, Andrew, Christina, Peter. BA, Wellesley Coll., 1963; MD, Harvard U., 1967. Diplomate Am. Bd. Internal Medicine, Am. Bd. Endocrinology and Metabolism. Intern Jewish Hosp., Washington U., St. Louis, 1967-68; resident Montefiore, Albert Einstein Med. Sch., Bronx, NY, 1968-69; fellow Beth Israel, Harvard U., Boston, 1970-72; assoc. prof. medicine Cornell U. Med. Coll., N.Y.C., 1981—; sr. med. dir., worldwide team leader endocrine care team Pfizer Inc., N.Y.C., 1990—, team leader, 1990—. Mem. editl. bd. Endocrinology, Jour. Clin. Endocrinol Metabolism, also others; contbr. over 100 articles to sci. jours., chpts. to books. Mem. nat. campaign Harvard Med. Sch., Boston, 1986-92; nat. bd. dirs. Philoptochos Soc. Greek Orthodox Archdiocese. Grantee NIH, 1979-84. Fellow ACP; mem. Am. Soc. Clin. Investigation, Am. Assn. Physicians, Am. Thyroid Assn. (coms.), Endocrine Soc. (coms.). Achievements include discovery of alpha-secreting pituitary tumors; demonstrated that measurement of amniotic fluid thyroid stimulating hormone can be used to diagnose hypthyroidism in utero; development of insulin secretagogue Glucotrol XL. Home: 1070 Park Ave New York NY 10128-1000 Office: Pfizer Inc 235 E 42nd St New York NY 10017-5755 Business E-Mail: kourii@pfizer.com.

KOURLIS, REBECCA LOVE, state supreme court justice; b. Colorado Springs, Colo., Nov. 11, 1952; d. John Arthur and Ann (Daniels) Love; m. Thomas Aristithis Kourlis, July 15, 1978; children: Stacy Ann, Katherine Love, Aristithis Thomas. BA with distinction in English, Stanford U., 1973, JD, 1976; LLD (hon.), U. Denver, 1997. Bar: Colo. 1976, D.C. 1979, U.S. Dist. Ct. Colo. 1976, U.S. Ct. Appeals (10th cir.) 1976, Colo. Supreme Ct., U.S. Ct. Appeals (D.C. cir.), U.S. Claims Ct., U.S. Supreme Ct. Assoc. Davis, Graham & Stubbs, Denver, 1976-78; sole practice Craig, Colo., 1978-87; judge 14th Jud. Dist. Ct., Craig, Colo., 1987-94; arbiter Jud. Arbiter Group, Inc., 1994-95; justice Colo. Supreme Ct., 1995—. Water judge divsn. 6, 1987-94; lectr. to profl. groups. Contbr. articles to profl. jours. Chmn. Moffat County Arts and Humanities, Craig, 1979; mem. Colo. Commn. on Higher Edn., Denver, 1980-81; mem. adv. bd. Colo. Divsn. Youth Svcs., 1988-91; mem. com. civil jury instructions, 1990-95, standing com. gender and justice, 1994-97, chair jud. adv. coun., 1997-2002, chair com. on jury reform, 1996—, chair com. family issues, 2002—; co-chair com. on atty. grievance reform, 1997-2002; mem. long range planning com. Moffat County Sch., 1990; bd. visitors Stanford U., 1989-94, Law Sch. U. Denver, 1997-2002; trustee Kent Denver Sch., 1996-2002. Named N.W. Colo. Daily Press Woman of Yr., 1993; recipient Trailblazer award AAUW, 1998, Mary Lathrop award Colo. Women's Bar Assn., 2001, Jud. Excellence award Acad. Matrimonial Lawyers, 2002, Champion for Children award Rocky Mountain Children's Law Ctr., 2003, Friend of Children award Adv. for Children, 2003. Fellow: Colo. Bar Found., Am. Bar Found.; mem.: N.W. Colo. Bar Assn. (Cmty. Svc. award 1993—94), Dist. Ct. Judges' Assn. (pres. 1993—94), Colo. Bar Assn. (bd. govs. 1983—85, mineral law sect. bd. dirs. 1985, sr. v.p. 1987—88), Rocky Mountain Mineral Found. Office: State Jud Bldg 2 E 14th Ave Denver CO 80203-2115

KOURNIKOVA, ANNA, professional tennis player; b. Moscow, June 07; d. Sergei and Alla Kournikova. Player Russian Fed Cup team, 1996—97, 2000, Russian Olympic Team, 1996; founder Physical Culture Russian Acad., 1997. ITF Jr. World champion, 1995, ITF Women's Cir. Satellite Event, Midland, Mich., 1996, title ITF Women's Cir. Satellite, Rockford, Ill.; winner Orange Bowl, 1995, Italian Open Jrs., 1995, European Champaionships, 1995; semi-finalist Wimbledon Jrs., 1995, quarter finalist French Open Jrs.; recipient (with Martina Hingis) WTA Tour Doubles Team of the Year award, 1999; named 1 or top 10 Most Marketable Female Athletes, Sports Business Daily, 2003. Achievements include won 16 career WTA doubles titles including Australian Open, 1999, 2000. Office: c/o Bollettieri Tennis Acad 5500 34th St W Bradenton FL 34210-3506

KOURY, AGNES LILLIAN, real estate property manager; b. Denver, Oct. 16, 1935; d. John Joseph and Lucy Maria (Plomteaux) K.; m. William L. May, July 21, 1958 (div. 1961); 1 child, Tia Leslie Koury. BSBA, U. Denver, 1958; protocol cert., Southeastern U., 1964; paralegal cert., Georgetown U., 1978; MA, Marymount U., 1991. Registered profl. realtor, Va. Com. sec. N.Mex. Ho. of Reps., Santa Fe, 1959; contracts sec. Atomic Energy Commn., Albuquerque, 1959-63; ptnr. legal sec. Sughrue, Rothwell, Washington, 1963-65; legal asst. McClure & Trotter, Washington, 1965-67; case worker U.S. Ho. of Reps., Washington, 1968; adminstrv., rsch. asst. Harvard U., Washington, 1969-73; asst. mgr. Koury's Real Estate, Sant Fe, 1974-85; owner, mgr. various realty properties, Santa Fe and Arlington, 1985—. Pres. Yorktown Condominium, Arlington, 1972-74, bd. dirs.; treas. Birches Homeowners Assn., Arlington, 1987-90; chmn., vol. spkrs. bur. Hospice of No. Va., Arlington, 1993-2003, spkrs. bur., 1985—, 20th anniversary com., 1996-97, chmn. Tree of Lights event, 1999; bd. dirs. Arlington Symphony Assn., 1990-99; womens com. mem. chmn. music scholarship competition for No. Va., 1994-2003; bd. dirs. Mt. Vernon Orch., 2003-04, Wahington Symphony Orch. Assn., 2004-; chmn. music scholarship competition for Washington met. area, 2003—. Mem. Delta Sigma Epsilon, Phi Gamma Nu (Outstanding Mem. 1958). Roman Catholic. Avocations: travel, writing, poetry, playing piano, picture puzzles. Home and Office: 4741 23rd St N Arlington VA 22207-3408 Office Phone: 703-527-4456.

KOUZEL, MILDRED, artist; b. New Haven, Dec. 21, 1922; d. Samuel Goldberg (dec.) and Martha Mitzen-Hendler (dec.); m. Bernard Kouzel, June 20, 1948 (dec. Nov. 1993); children: Ilene, Janet, Lynn. RN, Grace Hosp. Sch. Nursing, New Haven, 1944; student, NYU, 1946-48; MA, Calif. State U., 1972. Pub. health nurse Lehigh Valley Pub. Health Nursing Assn., Allentown, Pa., 1948-49. One-woman shows include Fullerton (Calif.) Libr., 1977, Brand Librs. Art Gallery, Glendale, Calif., 1982, Agoura Hills (Calif.) Mcpl. Gallery, 1984, Orange County Ctr. for Contemporary Art, Santa Ana, Calif., 1986, 88, Techline Studio, L.A., 1990, Jewish Comty. Ctr., Costa Mesa, Calif., 1996, L.A. Art Core Brewery Annex, 1997, U. of Judaism, Platt Gallery, L.A., 1997, Grand Ctrl. Gallery, Santa Ana, Calif., 2002; group exhbns. include Del Mar Coll., Corpus Christi, Tex., 1976, Century Gallery, Sylmar, Calif., 1983, Brea (Calif.) Civic Gallery, 1985, Peter Strauss Ranch, Agoura, CAlif., 1985, Seasoned Eye Nat. Traveling Exhibit AARP, Washington, N.Y.C., others, 1986, UN World Conf. on Women, Nairobi, Kenya, 1986, So. Calif. Prints and Drawings, Saddleback Coll., Calif., Downey (Calif.) Mus., 1987, Anaheim (Calif.) Cultural Ctr., 1988, Pine St. Lobby Gallery, San Francisco, 1990, Koll Ctr. Newport, Newport Beach, Calif., 1991, Orange County Ctr. for Contemporary Art, Santa Ana, Calif., 1994, Wignal Mus./Gallery, Chaffey Coll., Rancho Cucmonga, Calif., 1994, Maynard Walker Art Collection, Garnet Kans., 1995, Chapman U., So. Calif. Artists, Orange, 1998, Calif. State U., Fullerton, 1998, Anaheim Cultural Ctr., 1999, Palos Verdes Art Ctr., Calif., 2002; pub. art projects include John Wayne Airport, Newport Beach, 1990, Calif. State U., Fullerton, 1990, Fullerton Mus. Ctr., 1991, 92, City of Brea Bus Shelter Program, Brea, 1992, Hunt Libr., Fullerton, 1999; commd. works for Temple Beth Tikvah, Fullerton, 1982, 84, Temple Beth Sholom, Whittier, Calif., 1985, Home Savs. Bank, Irwindale, Calif., 1988; represented in numerous pvt. collections. Mem. scholarship fund bd. Calif. State U., Fullerton, 1994, 95. 1st lt. U.S. Army Nurse Corps, 1945-46. Fellow So. Calif. Artists, Women's Caucus for the Arts. Democrat. Jewish. Avocations: folk dancing, writing memoirs, watching films, listening to jazz.

KOVACHEVICH, ELIZABETH ANNE, judge; b. Canton, Ill., Dec. 14, 1936; d. Dan and Emilie (Kuchan) Kovachevich. AA, St. Petersburg Jr. Coll., 1956; BBA in Fin. magna cum laude, U. Miami, 1958; JD, Stetson U., 1961, LLD (hon.), 1993. Bar: Fla. 1961, U.S. Dist. Ct. (mid. and so. dists.) Fla. 1961, U.S. Ct. Appeals (5th cir.) 1961, U.S. Supreme Ct. 1968. Rsch. and adminstrv. aide Pinellas County Legis. Del., Fla., 1961; assoc. DiVito & Speer, St. Petersburg, Fla., 1961—62; house counsel Rieck & Fleece Builders Supplies, Inc., St. Petersburg, 1962; pvt. practice St. Petersburg, 1962—73; judge 6th Jud. Cir., Pinellas and Pasco Counties, Fla., 1973—82, U.S. Dist. Ct. (mid. dist.) Fla., Tampa, 1982—96, chief judge, 1996—. Chmn. St. Petersburg Profl. Legal Project-Days in Ct., 1967, Supreme Ct. Bicentennial Com. 6th Jud. Cir., 1975—76. Prodr., coord. (TV prodn.) A Race to Judgement. Bd. regents State of Fla., 1970—72; legal advisor, bd. dirs. Young Women's Residence, Inc., 1968; mem. Fla. Gov.'s Commn. on Status of Women, 1968—71; mem. Pres.'s Commn. on White House Fellowships, 1973—77; mem. def. adv. com. on Women in Svc. Dept. Def., 1973—76; Fla. publicity chmn. 18th Nat. Rep. Women's Conf., Atlanta, 1971; lifetime mem. Children's Hosp. Guild, YWCA of St. Petersburg; charter mem. Golden Notes, St. Petersburg Symphony; hon. mem. bd. of overeers Stetson U. Coll. of Law, 1986. Recipient St. Petersburg Panhellenic Appreciation award, 1964, Pinellas United Fund award in recognition of concern and meritorious effort, 1968, Disting. Alumni award, Stetson U., 1970, Woman of Yr. award, Beta Sigma Phi, 1970, 1970, Am. Legion Aux. Unit 14 Pres. award cmty. svc., 1970, Dedication to Christian Ideals award and Man of Yr. award, KC Dists. 20-21, 1972, USN Recruiting Command Appreciation award, 1975, Woman of Yr. award, Fla. Fedn. Bus. and Profl. Women, 1981, ann. Ben C. Willard Meml. award, Stetson Lawyers Assn., 1983, Alumni of Yr. award, St. Petersburg Jr. Coll., 1994, Cath. Law Person of Yr., Greater Tampa Cath. Lawyer's Guild, 1998, Disting. Svc. award, Fla. Coun. on Crime and Delinquency, 1999, J-Ben Watkins award, Stetson U. Coll. of Law, 1999, Woman of Achievement award, Delta Delta Delta, 2000, Outstanding Jurist award, Hillsborough County, 2000—01, Pub. Svc. award, William Reece Smith, Jr., 2001, Mrs. Charles Ulrick Bay award, St. Petersburg Rotary award, St. Petersburg Quarterback Club award, President's Award, Fed. Bar. Assn., 2001, Presidential Special Recognition Award, 2002. Mem.: ABA, St. Petersburg Bar Assn. (chmn. bench and bar com., sec. 1969), Am. Judicature Soc., Pinellas County Trial Lawyers, Fla. Bar Assn., ATLA. Office: US Dist Ct Fl 17 801 N Florida Ave Tampa FL 33702-3849

KOVACIK, KAREN MARIE, English literature educator; b. East Chgo., Ind., July 21, 1959; d. Peter John and Frances Marie Kovacik; m. Daniel Carter Bourne, Dec. 10, 1983 (div. Dec. 1991). BA, Ind. U., 1981; cert., Sch. Art Inst. Chgo, 1988; MA, Cleve. State U., 1990; PhD, Ohio State U., 1997. Asst. prof. English Ind. U./Purdue U., Indpls., 1997—2003, assoc. prof. English, 2003—. Presenter in field. Author: Return of the Prodigal, 1991 (Poetry Atlanta prize, 1990), Nixon and I, 1998, Beyond the Velvet Curtain, 1999 (Wick prize, 1998). Sec. Etheridge Knight Poetry Festival Bd., Indpls., 2001—02. Recipient Fall Poetry Open prize, Glimmer Train, 1999, Fiction prize, Chelsea, 2001, Very Short Story award, Glimmer Train, 2002, Barbara Mandigo Kelly Peace Poetry prize, 2002; fellow in poetry, U. Wis. Inst. Creative Writing, 1991—92; Fulbright Rsch. grant, Poland, 2004—. Mem.: MLA, Acad. Am. Poets, Poets and Writers. Home: 1002 N New Jersey Street Indianapolis IN 46202 Office: IUPUI English Dept CA 502L 425 University Blvd Indianapolis IN 46202

KOVACS, BEATRICE, library studies educator; b. Seekirchen, Austria, June 2, 1945; came to U.S., 1948; d. Lorand and Helen (Magyary-Kossa) K.; m. Thomas Gordon Basler, Apr. 20, 1969 (div. 1979); m. Louis Edward Mitchum, Jan. 10, 1994. AB in English, Syracuse U., 1966; MLS, Rutgers State U., 1967; DLS, Columbia U., 1983. Libr. Nassau Acad. Medicine, Garden City, N.Y., 1967-70; cataloger, asst. acquisitions libr. Augusta (Ga.) Regional Libr., 1974-78; collection devel. libr. Med. Coll. Ga., Augusta, 1978-80; acct. specialist Readmore Publs., N.Y.C., 1982-83; chief collection devel. U. N.Mex. Med. Ctr. Libr., Albuquerque, 1984-85; asst. prof. U. N.C., Greensboro, 1985-91, assoc. prof., 1991—. Vis. instr. Pratt Inst. Grad. Sch. Libr., Bklyn., 1982-83; adj. prof. U. N.C. Chapel Hill Sch. Info. and Libr. Sci., 1997-98. Author: Decision-Making Process for Library Collections, 1990, ALA Fingertip Guide to National Health-Information Resources, 1995; co-author: Health Sciences Librarianship, 1977, Using Science and Technology Information Resources, 1991; contbr. articles to profl. jours. Bishop scholarship Med. Libr. Assn., 1966. Mem. ALA, N.C. Libr. Assn., Spl. Librs. Assn., N.C. Spl. Librs. Assn. (pres. 1992-93), Assn. Libr. & Info. Sci. Educators. Office: U NC Sch Edn PO Box 26170 Greensboro NC 27402-6170 E-mail: bea_kovacs@uncg.edu.

KOVACS, ROSEMARY, newpaper editor; BS in Journalism, Bowling Green State U., 1968. Mng. editor prodn. The Plain Dealer, Cleve., 1990—. Named to Bowling Green State U. Journalism Hall of Fame, 1988. Mem. Press Club of Cleve. (pres.). Office: Plain Dealer Pub Co 1801 Superior Ave Cleveland OH 44114-2198

KOVAT, ROBIN M. secondary school educator; b. Bklyn., Sept. 8, 1957; d. Robert Sanford and Marilyn Kovat. BA in Politics and Sociology, Brandeis U., 1978; grad. cert. in arts mgmt., Adelphi U., 1982; MS in Journalism, Poly. Inst. U., Bklyn., 1991. Asst. to borough pres. Bklyn. N.Y. Borough Pres. Office, 1979—82; freelance writer, 1982—92; tchr. Riker's Island, N.Y.C. Bd. Edn., Elmhurst, 1992—95; scheduling coord., tchr. Job Corps, Bklyn., 1995—97; adj. prof. Touro Coll., N.Y.C., 1996—98; tchr. Sheepshead Bay H.S., Bklyn., 1998—, coord. rsch. program and law program, coach moot ct. and mock trial teams. Dir. cultural devel. and women's issues Bklyn. Borough Pres. Office, 1979—82; advisor Sheepshead Angels svc. orgn.; campaign coord. Judge Lila Gold, Bklyn., 1991—92; Bd. dirs. Rebecca Kelly Dance Co., N.Y.C., 1985—87. Recipient Sterling Quality of Life award, 2003. Democrat. Jewish. Avocations: running, reading, writing, bicycling, traveling. Home: 2662Ford St Brooklyn NY 11235 Office: Sheepshead Bay H S 3000 Ave X Brooklyn NY 11235

KOVE, MIRIAM, psychotherapist; b. Chotin, Romania, Feb. 17, 1941; came to U.S., Sept. 12, 1962; d. Avrum and Riva (Nussenbaum) Wolkove; m. Marc L. Kouffman, Aug. 16, 1964 (div. Oct. 24, 1989); children: Avra, Paulette. BA in English Lit., Sir George Williams U., 1962; MA in Early Childhood, Hunter Coll., 1975; Cert. in Psychoanalytic Psychotherapy, New Hope Guild, N.Y.C., 1979; MSW, Adelphi U., 1983. Tchr. various pub. schs., Montreal, Can., 1957-58; actress N.Y.C., 1962—; tchr. early childhood Emanuel Nursery Sch., N.Y.C., 1964-74; adj. lectr. early childhood Cmty. Coll., Bklyn., 1974-75; psychotherapist, clinician New Hope Guild Ctr., N.Y.C., 1979-81; intake dir., clinician Insts. of Religion and Health, N.Y.C., 1983-84; pschotherapist N.Y.C., 1984—; faculty, supr. New Hope Guild Ctr., N.Y.C., 1990—; dir. day care on-site therapy program C.I.S. Counseling Ctr., N.Y.C., 1992-94. Author: (book) Myths and Madness. Mem. People for the Am. Way, Warsaw Gathering of Holocaust Survivors. Recipient Hebrew prize Sir George Williams U., 1962; recommended for English prize Concordia U. Fellow Nat. Orgn. Social Work, Soc. for Clin. Social Work Psychotherapists (edn. com.); mem. New Hope Grad. Soc. (steering com.), Am. Bd. Examiners in Clin. Social Work. Jewish. Home and Office: 320 E 25th St Apt 8ee New York NY 10010-3100

KOVEL, TERRY HORVITZ (MRS. RALPH KOVEL), writer, antiques authority; b. Cleve. d. Isadore and Rix Horvitz; m. Ralph Kovel; children: Lee R., Karen. BA, Wellesley Coll., 1950. Tchr. math. Hawken Sch. for Boys, Shaker Heights, Ohio, 1961-71; now pres. Antiques Inc.; past tchr. course in antiques Western Res. U., John Carroll U. Writer: (with Ralph Kovel) syndicated column Kovels Antiques and Collecting, 1955—, Ask the Experts, House Beautiful, 1979-2000, Medio, CD-Rom mag., 1995, The Kovels on Collecting, Forbes Mag., 2000-02; editor: monthly newsletters Kovels on Antiques and Collectibles, 1974—, Kovels Sports Collectibles, 1992-97; TV series Know Your Antiques, Pub. TV, 1969-70; syndicated TV Series Kovels on Collecting, 1981, 87, Collector's Journal TV, 1989-93, Flea Market Finds with the Kovels HGTV, 2000—; numerous appearances on radio and TV talk shows; author: (with Ralph Kovel) Kovels' Dictionary of Marks-Pottery and Porcelain, 1953, rev. edit., 1995, Directory of American Silver, Pewter and Silver Plate, 1958, American Country Furniture, 1780-1875, 1963, Kovels' Know Your Antiques, rev. edit, 1993, Kovels' American Art Pottery, 1993, Kovels' Antiques and Collectibles Price List, 36th edit., 2004, Kovels' Know Your Collectibles, 1981, 1992, Kovels' Bottle Price List, 12th edit., 2002, Kovels' Organizer for Collectors, 1978, revised, 1983, Kovels' Price Guide for Collector Plates, Figurines, Paperweights and Other Limited Editions, 1978, Kovels' Collector's Guide to American Art Pottery, 1974, Kovel's Collector's Guide to Limited Editions, 1974, Kovels' Price Guide to Depression Glass and Dinnerware, 7th edit., 2001, Kovels' Illustrated Price Guide to Royal Doulton, 2d edit., 1984, Kovels' Collectors' Source Book, 1983, Kovels' New Dictionary of Marks Pottery and Porcelain, 1850 to the Present, 1986, Kovels' Advertising Collectibles Price List, 1986, Kovels' Guide to Selling Your Antiques and Collectibles, 1987, 2d edit., 1990, Kovels' Book of Antique Labels, 1982, Kovels' American Silver Marks 1650 to the Present, 1989, Kovel's Antiques and Collectibles Fix-It Source Book, 1990, Kovels' Guide to Selling, Buying and Fixing Your Antiques and Collectibles, 1995, Kovels' Quick Tips: 799 Helpful Hints on How To Care for Your Collectibles, 1995, The Label Made Me Buy It, 1998, Kovels' Yellow Pages, 2d. edit., 2003, Kovels' Bid, Buy and Sell Online, 2001; (Video tape series) Kovels Picture-A-Day-Collectibles Calendar, 199, 91, Collecting With the Kovels, 1995, Art Pottery I, Art Pottery II, 2003, Kovels Antiques and Collectibles 2003 Day-At-A Time-Calendar; contbr. numerous articles on antiques to profl. publs. Trustee Hiram Coll., 1989-99, hon. trustee, 2000; bd. mem. Shaker Hist. Soc. Hiram fellow; recipient Peirce award for outstanding cmty. svc. Sta. WVIZ-TV, 1980, Cleve. Emmy award for best entertainment, 1971, Cleve. Emmy award for cultural affairs programming, 1987; Laurel Sch. Alumanae of Yr. Office: PO Box 22200 Cleveland OH 44122-0200

KOVNER, KATHLEEN JANE, civic worker, portrait artist; b. Cambridge, Mass., Nov. 25, 1919; d. David Leo and Kathleen Elizabeth (Lalley) Lane; m. Benjamin Kovner (dec.), June 20, 1938; children: Kathleen Barbara (dec.), Michael Anthony, Peter Christopher. Student, Art Students League, N.Y.C., 1937-40. Owner, CEO Helen Bennett Ltd., Stamford, Conn., 1948-59; cons. Bride's Mag., N.Y.C., 1967-70; co-chair membership com. Women's Nat. Rep. Club, N.Y.C., 1980-81, chmn. membership com., 1981-87, v.p., 1986-87, also bd. dirs. Ltd. ptnr. 519 8th Ave Corp., N.Y.C., 18-19th St. Corp., N.Y.C., Kaufman Arcade Bldg., N.Y.C., 19th St. Assn., N.Y.C., dir. Nelson Tower Assoc., N.Y.C., 1998, ptnr. 450 Seventh Ave Assoc., N.Y.C. Portrait artist in oils, with various portraits in pvt. collections. Fundraiser St. Ignatius Loyola, N.Y.C., 1960-61, Jeanine Pirro-Campaign for Dist. Atty., Westchester County, N.Y., 1993, 97. Republican. Roman Catholic. Home: 62 Brookridge Dr Greenwich CT 06830-4830 also: 923 5th Ave New York NY 10021-2649

KOWAL, RUTH ELIZABETH, library administrator; b. Amherst, Mass., Mar. 16, 1948; d. Alfred Alexander and Mary Arandale (Tomlinson) Brown; m. Harold F. Kowal, June 19, 1989; children: Elizabeth Ann, Susannah Terry. BS, Syracuse U., 1970; MLS, Simmons Coll., 1971. Reference libr. Falmouth (Mass.) Pub. Libr., 1971-74; sch. libr. Nauset High Sch., Eastham, Mass., 1974-75; asst. dir. Plymouth (Mass.) Pub. Librs., 1975, dir., 1976-83; exec. dir. Southeastern 3R's, Highland, N.Y., 1983-86; regional adminstr. Ctrl. Mass. Libr. System, Worcester, 1987-91, Ea. Mass. Libr. System, Boston, 1991-97, Boston Pub. Libr., 1997—, asst. dir., 1997-99; dir. ops. Boston Pub. Libr., 1999—. Instr. Northeastern U., Boston, 1980-83, SUNY, Albany, 1984-86. Mem. ALA. Office: Boston Pub Libr 700 Boylston St Boston MA 02117

KOWALSKA, MARIA TERESA, research scientist, educator; b. Wielun, Poland, June 8, 1932; arrived in U.S., 1982, naturalized, 1991; d. Jozef Ozmina and Zofia Elzbieta Pecherska; m. Wielislaw Kowalski, Apr. 19, 1954 (dec. Nov. 1991); children: Jacek Kowalski, Beata Kowalska-Ellington. BA, Lyceum Gen. Edn., Lodz, Poland, 1950; MS in Pharmacy, Med. Acad., Poznan, Poland, 1954, PhD in Pharmacy, 1964; Dr. Hab., Med. Acad., Lodz, 1978. Asst. prof. pharmacy Med. Acad., Poznan, 1955—69; postdoctoral fellow in pharmacy U. Paris, 1969—70; assoc. prof. Acad. Agr., Poznan, 1970—80; prof. pharmacognosy Nat. U. Kinshasa, 1980—82; rsch. assoc. Rsch. Ctr. Fairchild Frop Garden, Miami, Fla., 1985—90. Adj. asst. prof. dept. biochemistry and molecular biology Sch. Medicine U. Miami, 1990—2000; counselor students Acad. Agr., Poznan, 1975—80; prin. investigator on grant Internat. Palm Soc., Miami, 1986, Miami, 87, World Wildlife Fund, Washington, 1988. Appeared (TV) ABC Miami News, 1992, CNN News, 1993; contbr. articles to profl. jours. Avocations: music, skiing, mountain climbing. Home: 6421 SW 106 St Miami FL 33156

KOWALSKI, KATHE A. art educator, photographer; b. Paterson, N.J., Nov. 18, 1945; d. Jacob Lawrence and Rose Levenson Bernstein; children: Nathan Joseph, Jacob Matthew. BA, NYU, 1967; BFA, Ea. Mich. U., 1980, MFA, 1985. Asst. prof. Edinboro (Pa.) U., 1989—96, assoc. prof., 1996—2003, full prof., 2003—. Publication, Masquerade - Women's Contemporary Portrait Photography, La Fotografia Actual, exhibition, Art of the State. Pennsylvania (Second Prize Photography, 2003), Appalachian Corridors, Rural Poverty: Women Living Without. Recipient Award of Excellence, Magic Silver Show, 1998, Juror's award, 78th Ann. Spring Show of the Erie Art Mus., 2001, Donald Robinson award, Associated Artists Pitts. 92nd Ann. Exhbn., 2002; grantee Black Looks: Race and Representation, Pa. Humanities Coun., 2000, Faculty Profl. Devel. Coun. Grants, State Sys. of Higher Edn., 1997—98, 1999—2000. Office: Edinboro Univ Art Dept Doucette Hall Edinboro PA 16444 Personal E-mail: kathek1@earthlink.net. E-mail: kkowalski@edinboro.edu.

KOWLESSAR, MURIEL, retired pediatric educator; b. Bklyn., Jan. 2, 1926; d. John Henry and Arene (Driver) Chevious; m. O. Dhodanand Kowlessar, Dec. 27, 1952; 1 child, Indrani. AB, Barnard Coll., 1947; MD, Columbia U., 1951. Diplomate Am. Bd. Pediatrics. Instr. Downstate Med. Ctr., Bklyn., 1958-64, asst. prof., 1965-66; asst. prof. clin. pediatrics Temple U., Phila., 1967-70; assoc. prof. Med. Coll. Pa., Phila., 1971-83, dir. pediatric group svcs., 1975-90, acting chmn. pediatrics dept., 1981-83, vice chair pediatrics dept., 1982-91, prof., 1983-91, prof. emeritus, 1991—. Contbr. articles to med. jours. Mem. Pa. Gov.'s Task Force on Spl. Supplemental Food Program for Women, Infants and Children, Harrisburg, 1981-83, Phila. Bd. Health, 1982-86; vol. Phila. Com. for Homeless, 1991-92, Gateway Literacy Program, YMCA, Germantown Bridge, Pa., 1992-93. Fellow Am. Acad. Pediatrics (emeritus); mem. Phila. Pediatric Soc., Cosmopolitan Club Phila., Phi Beta Kappa. Democrat. Avocations: ballroom dancing, opera.

KOWROSKI, MARIA, dancer; b. Grand Rapids, Mich. Student, Sch. Grand Rapids Ballet, Sch. Am. Ballet, 1992. Apprentice N.Y.C. Ballet, 1994—95, mem. corps de ballet, 1995—97, soloist, 1997—99, prin., 1999—. Dancer (ballets) Agon, Apollo, Firebird, A Midsummer Nights Dream, The Nutcracker, Prodigal Son, Swan Lake, La Valse, The Waltz

Project, Dances at a Gathering, Schoenberg/Wuorinen Variations, Sonatas and Interludes, Them Twos, Organon, Variations Sériuses. Recipient Princess Grace award, 1994. Office: NYC Ballet NY State Theatre 20 LIncoln Ctr Plz New York NY 10023-6913

KOWULICH, BARBARA ANN, physician assistant; b. Elmira, N.Y., Apr. 2, 1944; d. William and Elizabeth Simmonds Kowulich; 1 adopted child, Wendy Elizabeth. Student, Alfred (N.Y.) Tech., 1966, U. Rochester, 1975; BS, Johns Hopkins U., 1978. Med. sec. Strong Meml. Hosp., Rochester, NY, 1966—73; asst. registrar Med. Sch. U. Rochester, 1973—76; physician asst. Tri County Family Medicine, Cohocton, NY, 1978—, Skilled Nursing Facility, Geneseo, NY, 2001—. Asst. clin. prof. Rochester (N.Y.) Inst. Tech., 1990—. Reviewer: Jour. Nat. Acad. Physician Assts., 1990—; contbr. articles to profl. jours. Vol. Benincasa Hospice, Mendon, NY, Spl. Olympics, Rochester. Mem.: Am. Assn. Physician Assts. Democrat. Episc. Avocations: travel, quilting. Home: 4 Nicole Capri Way West Henrietta NY 14586 Office: Tri County Family Medicine 25 Park Ave Cohocton NY 14826

KOZAK, HARLEY JANE, actress, writer; b. Wilkes-Barre, Pa., Jan. 28, 1957; d. Joseph Aloysius and Dorothy (Taraldsen) K.; m. Gregory Aldisert, 1997; children: Audrey, Lorenzo and Gianna. Cert., NYU, 1980. Appeared in films Parenthood, 1989, Arachnophobia, 1990, The Taking of Beverly Hills, 1990, The Favor, 1990, Necessary Roughness, 1991, All I Want for Christmas, 1991, Magic in The Water, 1995, TV series Harts of the West, 1993-94, Bringing Up Jack, 1995, You Wish, 1997; author: (novel) Dating Dead Men, 2004. Office: Renee Zuckerbrot Lit Agy 115 W 29th St 10th Fl New York NY 10001 Office Phone: 310-967-0072.

KOZAKIEWICZ, SANDI, bank executive; b. Paris, Ark., June 17, 1947; d. John Harley and Joyce Mae (Adams) Wooten; m. Chris Kozakiewicz, Dec. 9, 1970. BA, Calif. State U., 1970. Registered rep. Nat. Assn. Security Dealers. Supr. Marina Fed. Savs. & Loan, Westchester, Calif., 1971-74; teller new accounts Bank of Tokyo, Gardena, Calif., 1974-78; with fin. svcs. dept. Calif. 1st Bank, Gardena, 1978-84, mgr., 1985-89; asst. v.p. regional sales office Union Bank, L.A., 1989-91, v.p., mgr. Lakewood, Calif., 1991—. Spkr. statewide conf. on women, 1987; mem. telesvcs. task force Union Bank, L.A., 1990-91, tng. auditor, 1990-91; seminar spkr. various C. of C., Lakewood, 1991—. Commr. City of Stanton Redevel. Commn., 1988-89; chair Youth Citizenship Award Commn., Lakewood, 1996—; dir., treas. S.E. Area Bus. for Effective Reuse, Lakewood, 1994-95; vol. Pathways Vol. Hospice, 1996—. Mem. Prospector's Networking Orgn. (chair 1992—, dir./v.p. 1998—), Lakewood C. of C. (pres., dir. 1992-95), Soroptimist Internat. (dir., treas. 1997-98). Democrat. Avocations: historic research, tap dancing, theater, travel, star trek. Office: Union Bank Calif 5910 South St Lakewood CA 90713-1310

KOZBERG, DONNA WALTERS, rehabilitation administration executive; b. Milford, Del., Jan. 1, 1952; d. Robert Glyndwr and Gailey Ruth (Bedorf) Walters; m. Ronald Paul Kozberg, June 8, 1974; 1 child, Mariel Gailey. BA, U. Fla., 1973, M in Rehab. Counseling, 1974; MFA, CUNY, 1979; MBA, Rutgers U., 1986. Cert. rehab. counselor. Rehab. counselor Office Vocat. Rehab., N.Y.C., 1975-81; area dir. Lift, Inc., Staten Island, N.Y., 1981-83, ea. region dir. pub. relations, advt. Mountainside, N.J., 1983-85, v.p., 1985—, v.p., chief fin. officer, 1988, exec. v.p., 1991-93, pres., 1993; co-founder, mng. dir. Expert Strategies Inc., Mountainside, N.J., 1992—; self-employed writer, editor, 1975—. Adv. bd. Rutgers Exec. Master Bus. Adminstrn. Contbr. articles to profl. jours.; assoc. editor Parachute mag., 1978; editor-in-chief (newsletter) Counselor Adv, 1980. Pres. Com. on Employment of People with Disabilities; trustee Ctr. for Creative Living; bd. dirs. N.J. Adv. Coun. for Independent Living, adv. panel NYU. Mem. Nat. Rehab. Assn. (Spl. citation 1974, grantee 1973), Nat. Rehab. Adminstrs. Assn., Nat. Rehab. Counselors Assn., N.J. Rehab. Counselors Assn. (pres. 1996), Poets and Writers. Avocations: Tennis, English lit., Tae Kwon Do.. Home: 45 Dug Way Watchung NJ 07069-6011 Office: Lift Inc PO Box 4264 Warren NJ 07059-0264 E-mail: dwkozberg@aol.com.

KOZIK, SUSAN S. information technology executive; Grad., Bates Coll. With Cigna Corp.; sr. v.p., chief tech. officer Penn Mut. Life Ins. Co.; v.p. info. tech. ops. and svcs. Lucent Techs.; exec. v.p., chief tech. officer TIAA-CREF, N.Y.C., 2003—. Active, former trustee Bates Coll. Recipient 1st Distinug. Young Alumni award, Bates Coll. Office: TIAA-CREF 730 3d Ave New York NY 10017

KOZLOFF, JESSICA S. university president; b. San Antonio, Mar. 29, 1941; d. Robert John and Ann (Acklen) Sledge; m. Stephen R. Kozloff, June 12, 1965; children: Kyle Schaller, Rebecca Esther. BS, U. Nev., 1963, MA, 1964; PhD, Colo. State U., 1983. Prof. polit. sci. U. Northern Colo., Greeley, 1976-89, exec. asst. to pres., 1985-89; v.p. acad. affairs State Colls. in Colo., Denver, 1989-94; pres. Bloomsburg U., 1994—. Mem. Middle States Commn. on Higher Edn., 2000—. Bd. dirs. United Way, Bloomsburg, 1994—2000, Boy Scouts Am., Bloomsburg, 1994—2000. Acad. Adminstrn. fellow Am. Coun. on Edn., 1985. Mem.: Bloomsburg C. of C., Nat. Collegiate Athletics Assn. (mem. pres. commn. 1996—2001), Am. Assn. State Colls. and Univs. (mem. Pa. campus compact bd. dirs. 1998—2001, bd. dirs. 2004—), Bloomsburg Rotary Club. Avocations: golf, tennis, skiing, biking, travel. Office: Bloomsburg U 400 E 2nd St Bloomsburg PA 17815-1399

KOZLOW, BEVERLY KAY, physical therapist, psychologist, realtor; b. Detroit, Aug. 10, 1931; d. Samuel and Genevieve Ione (Griffin) K.; m. Roy Carl Gleaves, Apr. 16, 1959 (div. 1975). BS, Eastern Mich. U., 1953; MS, UCLA, 1959; PhD, Sierra U., 1987. Registered physical therapist. Phys. therapist Walter Reed Army Med. Ctr., Washington, 1953-55, Crippled Children's Soc., Rockville, Md., 1955-56, San Bernardino (Calif.) County Hosp., 1957-59; coord. phys. therapy program UCLA, 1959-67; home health phys. therapist Vis. Nurses Assn. L.A., 1967-68; from staff to dir. phys. therapy L.A. County Med. Dept., 1968-73; dir. in-patient/out-patient acute and rehab. svcs. Valley Med. Ctr., Van Nuys, Calif., 1973-81; contract phys. therapist L.A., 1981-89; home health phys. therapist Vis. Nurses Assn., Stuart, Fla., 1992-96; CPS Great River Property, Guerneville, Calif., 1997—. Adj. faculty U.S. Army Command and Gen. Staff Coll., Ft. Leavenworth, Kans., 1986-92. Ret. col. U.S. Army. Mem. Am. Physical Therapy Assn. (life), Ret. Officers Assn., Am. Legion. Democrat. Jewish. Avocations: reading, traveling, gardening. Home: 14740 Old Cazadero Rd Guerneville CA 95446-9004 E-mail: bkoz@ap.net.

KOZLOWSKI, CHERYL M. principal; b. Boston, July 19, 1974; d. Leo Dennis and Angeles Zenaida BA, Middlebury Coll., 1996; postgrad., Harvard Bus. Sch., 2000—02. Lic. pilot. Fin. analyst Merrill Lynch, N.Y.C., 1996-1998; prin. Clayton, Dubilier & Rice, Inc., N.Y.C., 1998-2000. Equity analyst Am. Express, 2002—. Treas. The Friends of Tolstoy Found., 1998—; chmn. Young New Yorkers of N.Y. Philharmonic, 1999—2002; bd. dirs. Shackleton Schs., 2000—. Avocation: skiing. Home: 610 Park Ave Apt 14A New York NY 10021-7080 E-mail: ckozlowski@mba2002.hbs.edu.

KRA, PAULINE SKORNICKI, French language educator; b. Lodz, Poland, July 30, 1934; arrived in US, 1950, naturalized, 1955; d. Edward and Nathalie Skornicki; m. Leo Dietrich Kra, Mar. 10, 1955; children: David Theodore, Andrew Jason. Student, Radcliffe Coll., 1951-53; BA, Barnard Coll., 1955; MA, Columbia U., 1963, PhD, 1968; MA, Queens Coll., 1990. Lectr. Queens Coll., CUNY, 1964-65; asst. prof. French Yeshiva U., N.Y.C., 1968-74, assoc. prof., 1974-82, prof., 1982-99, prof. emerita, 1999—; sr. programmer analyst Dept. Biomed. Informatics Columbia U., N.Y.C., 1998—. Author: Religion in Montesquieu's Lettres persanes, 1970; contbr. articles to profl. jours. Mem. MLA, Am. Assn. Tchrs. French, Am. Soc. 18th Century Studies, Société Française d'étude du XVIII Siècle, Soc. Montesquieu, Assn. for Computers and Humanities, Assn. for Lit. and Linguistic Computing, Phi Beta Kappa. Home: 10914 Ascan Ave Forest Hills NY 11375-5370 E-mail: kra@ymail.yu.edu.

KRAEMER, HELENA ANTOINETTE CHMURA, psychiatry educator; Degree, Stanford U., 1963. Prof. biostats. in psychiatry, Dept. Psychiatry and Behavioral Scis. Stanford U. Recipient Harvard award in psychiat. epidemiology and biostats., 2001. Mem.: Inst. Medicine. Office: Stanford U Dept Psychiatry and Behavioral Scis 300 Pasteur Dr Stanford CA 94305 Business E-Mail: hck@stanford.edu.*

KRAEMER, LILLIAN ELIZABETH, lawyer; b. N.Y.C., Apr. 18, 1940; d. Frederick Joseph and Edmee Elizabeth (de Watteville) K.; m. John W. Vincent, June 22, 1962 (div. 1964). BA, Swarthmore Coll., 1961; JD, U. Chgo., 1964. Bar: N.Y. 1965, U.S. Dist. Ct. (so. dist.) N.Y. 1967, U.S. Dist. Ct. (ea. dist.) N.Y. 1971. Assoc. Cleary, Gottlieb, Steen & Hamilton, N.Y.C., 1964-71, Simpson Thacher & Bartlett, N.Y.C., 1971-74, ptnr., 1974-99, of counsel, 2000—. Mem. vis. com. U. Chgo. Law Sch., 1988-90, 91-94, 97-99. Bd. mgrs. Swarthmore Coll., 1993—; warden St. Francis Episcopal Ch., Stamford, Conn., 2001—. Fellow Am. Coll. Bankruptcy; mem. Lawyers Alliance for N.Y. (bd. dirs. 1996-2001, co-chair capital campaign 2003—), Assn. of Bar of City of N.Y. (mem. various coms.), Coun. on Fgn. Rels., N.Y. State Bar Assn., Order of Coif, Phi Beta Kappa. Democrat. Avocations: travel, reading, word games. Home: 2 Beekman Pl New York NY 10022-8058 also: 62 Pheasant Ln Stamford CT 06903-4428 E-mail: lkraemer@stblaw.com.

KRAEMER, SYLVIA KATHARINE, government official, historian; b. Neisse, Silesia, Germany, Feb. 24, 1944; came to U.S., 1948; d. Thomas Paramore and Dorothea Freihube (Kraemer) Doughty; m. Russell Inslee Fries, Apr. 11, 1970 (div. Nov. 1991); children: Thomas Mount, Gwyneth Buchanan. BA in English, Hollins Coll., 1965; PhD in History, Johns Hopkins U., 1969. Instr. Johns Hopkins U., Balt., 1969; asst. prof. history Vassar Coll., Poughkeepsie, N.Y., 1969-70, So. Meth. U., Dallas, 1970-73; rsch. assoc. prof. U. Maine, Orono, 1975-78; mem. vis. faculty Bangor (Maine) Theol. Sem., 1981-83; chief historian NASA, Washington, 1983-89, dir. Office Spl. Studies, 1989-98, mem. adv. coun., 1981-83, dir. policy devel., 1998—. Author: Urban Idea in Colonial America, 1977, NASA Engineers in the Age of Apollo, 1992; also essays. Mem. Maine Humanities Coun., 1979-83; cons. on edn. issues, Va., 1993—. Fellow Coun. Humanities, So. Meth. U., 1973; rsch. grantee NSF, 1978-80. Fellow Internat. Acad. Astronautics; mem. Women in Aerospace, Exec. Women in Govt., Soc. for History in Fed. Govt. (exec. coun. 1988-91, James Madison award 1989), AAUW. Avocations: visual arts, writing, gardening. Office: NASA 300 E St SW Washington DC 20546-0005 Home: 80 Oak St Boothbay Harbor ME 04538-1814

KRAEMER-BATACAN, KRISTI ANN, not-for-profit fundraiser, actress; b. Torrance, Calif., July 28, 1975; d. Steven Roy and Theresa Farese Kraemer; m. Atticus Charles Batacan, July 14, 2001. BA in Theatre Arts, UCLA, 1997; MA in Theatre Arts, San Jose (Calif.) State U., 2002. Exec. dir. Calif. Children's Cmty., Cupertino, Calif., 1998—99; asst. mng. and artistic dir. San Jose (Calif.) Repertory Theatre, 1999—2001; asst. dir. of stewardship Stanford (Calif.) U., 2001—02; stewardship mgr. Pepperdine U., Malibu, Calif., 2002—03; donor rels. mgr. UCLA, 2003—. Mem. Knightsbridge Theatre Co., LA, 2003—, Meh-tropolis Dance Theatre, LA, 2003—. Actor: (plays) Godspell, Into the Woods; (plays) Mame, Rumors, Jesus Christ Superstar; contbr. (plays) Art; actor: (plays) The Boyfriend, West Side Story, Anything Goes, A Chorus Line. Scholar, LA (Calif.) AFB Officer's Wives Club, 1993—94. Mem.: UCLA Alumni Assn. Democrat. Roman Catholic. Avocations: dance, singing.

KRAETZER, MARY C. sociologist, educator, consultant; b. N.Y.C., Sept. 12, 1943; d. Kenneth G. and Adele L. Kraetzer; m. Kestas E. Silunas. AB, Coll. New Rochelle, 1965; MA, Fordham U., 1967, PhD, 1975. Instr. Mercy Coll., Dobbs Ferry, N.Y., 1969-70, asst. prof., 1970-75, assoc. prof., 1975-79, prof., 1979—, program dir. behavioral sci., 1997—, program dir. grad. programs in health svc. mgmt., 2001—. Rsch. asst. Fordham U., Bronx, N.Y., 1965-67, tchg. asst., 1967-68, tchg. fellow, 1968-69, adj. instr., 1971-75, adj. asst. prof., 1975-76; adj. assoc. prof. L.I. U. Grad. br. Campus Mercy Coll., 1976-79, adj. prof., 1979-81, coord. MS in Cmty. Health Program, 1976-81, adj. prof. Westchester campus, 1988-94; rsch. cons. elem. schoolbooks Nat. Coun. Chs./Ch. Women United Task Force on Global Consciousness, N.Y.C., 1971; mem. adv. com. edn. and society div. Nat. Coun. Chs., 1975-78; mem. evaluation team Middle States Assn. Colls. and Secondary Schs. Commn. on Higher Edn., Monmouth, N.J., 1976; presenter in field. Contbr. chpts. to books, articles to profl. jours. Recipient Tchg. Excellence award Mercy Coll., 1999; Bd. Regents scholar, 1961-65, 65-69; Fordham U. scholar, 1965-68; Fordham U. fellow, 1968-69; Mercy Coll. grantee, 1984, 85, 86, 88, 92; Mercy Coll. Faculty Devel. grantee, 1999; NSF summer intern, 1967. Mem. APHA (conf. presenter), Am. Sociol. Assn. (presenter). Office: Mercy Coll 555 Broadway Dobbs Ferry NY 10522-1134

KRAFKA, MARY BAIRD, lawyer; b. Ottumwa, Iowa, Jan. 4, 1942; d. Glenn Leroy and Alice Erna (Krebill) B.; m. Jerry Lee Krafka, Oct. 14, 1962; children: Lisa Krafka Piper, Gregory D., Jeffrey A., Amy Krafka Pittman. BA in English and Human Rels., William Penn Coll., Oskaloosa, Iowa, 1990; JD, U. Iowa, 1993. Bar: Iowa 1993. Vol. lawyer Legal Svcs. Corp., Ottumwa, 1993-94; pvt. practice, Ottumwa, 1994—. Mem. AAUW, ABA, Iowa Bar Assn., Wapello County Bar Assn., PEO Sisterhood (Iowa chpt. HC 1973). Lutheran. Avocations: sewing, walking and running, interior designing, church activities, reading. Home: 931 W Mary St Ottumwa IA 52501-4904 Office: 101 S Market St Ste 203 Ottumwa IA 52501-2933

KRAFT, ELAINE JOY, community relations and communications official; b. Seattle, Sept. 1, 1951; d. Harry J. and Leatrice M. (Hanan) K.; m. Lee Somerstein, Aug. 2, 1980; children: Paul Kraft, Leslie Jo. BA, U. Wash., 1973; MPA, U. Puget Sound, 1979. Reporter Eastside Jour., Bellevue, Wash., 1972-76; editor Jour./Enterprise Newspapers, Wash. State, 1976; mem. staff Wash. State Senate, 1976-78, Wash. Ho. of Reps.,1978-82, pub. info. officer, 1976-78, mem. leadership staff, asst. to caucus chmn., 1980—; ptnr., pres. Media Kraft Communications; mgr. corp. info., advt. and mktg. communications Weyerhaeuser Co., 1982-85; dir. comms. Weyerhaeuser Paper Co., 1985-87; dir. cmty. rels. N.W. region Coors Brewing Co. 1987-95; comms. dir. King County exec. King County Ct. House, 1996—. Recipient state and nat. journalism design and advt. awards. Mem. Nat. Fedn. Press Women, Women in Comms., Wash. Press Assn. Home: 14329 SE 63d St Bellevue WA 98006-4802 Office: King County Courthouse 516 3d Ave Seattle WA 98104-2312

KRAFT, JANICE KAY, accounting educator; b. Casper, Wyo., Mar. 8, 1947; d. Milo Todd and Margaret Leary Buckingham; m. Edwin David Kraft, June 26, 1965; children: Brad, Brian. BS in Bus. Edn., U. Wyo., 1974, MBA with Acctg. Emphasis, 1976. Instr. U. Wyo., Laramie, 1974-76, staff prof., 1978-80; prof. Casper Coll., 1976-77; adj. prof. Ea. Mont. Coll., Billings, 1982-83; assoc. prof. acctg. S.W. State U., Marshall, Minn., 1984—98; assoc. prof. N.W. Coll., Powell, Wyo., 1998—. Coach Marshall Little League, 1985-91; treas. AAU Baseball, Marshall, 1992-94; mem. parent coun. Marshall Sr. H.S., 1995-96; mem. Marshall Music Booster, Marshall Speech Booster. Mem. Inst. Mgmt. Accts. (cert.), Minn. Coun. Acctg. Educators (treas.). Avocations: furniture refinishing, antique book collecting, cooking, dogs, horses. Home: 76 Lane 17 Cody WY 82414-9688

KRAFT, ROSEMARIE, dean, educator; b. Franklin, Pa., Nov. 18, 1936; d. Jack B. Harter and Romaine B. Shick; m. Louis R. Kraft; children: Louis W., Jack C. PhD, Ohio State U., 1976. Prof. U. Calif., Davis, 1977—, assoc. dean, 1994—. Dir., prof. for future fellowship U. Calif., Davis, 1995—. Author: Individual Differences in Cognition, 1998. Recipient McNair Scholars grant, U.S. Dept. Edn., 1995, 1999. Avocations: hiking, reading, traveling. Home: 1315 Lake Blvd Davis CA 95616 Office: U Calif Davis One Shields Ave Davis CA 95616

KRAFT, YVETTE, art educator; b. Washington, Jan. 17, 1945; d. Alvin Abraham and Rena Zlotnick Kraft. Studied with Master Painter Leon Berkowitz, 1982—87; student, Corcoran Coll. of Art and Design, 1992—. Art dir. after-sch. program Georgetown Montessori Sch., 1988; art instr. Washington Home, Sr. Citizen Care Facility, 1989—90; art instr. students with spl. needs Horace Mann Elem. Sch., 1990; art instr. Southeast Asian Refugee Children, 4-H, Arlington, Va., 1989—90; pvt. art instr. ages 2-17, 1990—92; art instr. Janney Elem. Sch., 1991, 1998, 1999, Ben Murch Elem. Sch., 1991; artist-in-residence Anne Beers Elem. Sch., 1992—93; art instr. children and adolescents with emotional disorders Clara Aisenstein, MD, Child Psychiatrist, 1993—96; art instr. Randle Highlands Elem. Sch., 1994, Naylor Rd. Elem. Sch., 1997, Bethany Woman's Shelter, 1998—2000; conduct art classes N St. Village, Washington, 2003—. Fine arts com. Washington Hebrew Congregation, 1979—82; adv. bd. New Art Examiner Mag., Washington, 1985—86; asst. mgr. Americana West Gallery; founder, dir. Project City People, 1992, 93; edn. dir. Fondo del Sol Visual Arts Ctr., 1992—93. One-woman shows include Maret Sch., Washington, DC, 1987, Georgetown Montessori Sch., 1988, Horace Mann Sch., 1989, Fillmore Sch. of Arts, 1991, NIH, Clin. Ctr. Gallery, Bethesda, Md., 1995, Fondo de Sol Visual Arts Ctr., Washington, DC, 1996, DC Arts Ctr., 1999, Nat. Coalition for Homeless, 2001, exhibited in group shows at Am. Art League, 1982—85, Highlights of the Yr. Exhbn., Martin Luther King Libr., 1986—87, Washington Hebrew Congregation, 1986—87, 2002—03, Capricorn Gallery, Bethesda, Md., 1987, Ctr. for Collaborative Art and Visual Edn., Washington, DC, 1999, Capital Children's Mus., 1999, Eight Is An Octive, Nat. Theatre, 2000, Am. Oh Yes Folk Art Gallery, 2000—03, Joy of Motion, 2001, Rockville Arts Pl., Md., 2003. Grantee grant, Cafritz Found., 1990, 1991, Hattie M. Strong Found., 1991, George Preston Marshall, 1991. Independent. Jewish. Avocations: jazz, walking, art museums, sketching, clothing design and coordination.

KRAKOFF, DIANE ELIZABETH BUTTS, medical/surgical nurse; b. Columbus, Ohio, July 1, 1955; d. Edwin Joseph and Mary Lee (Fenstermaker) B. BSN, Ohio State U., 1978; MSN, U. Cin., 1984. Cert. critical care RN, CDE. Staff RN Riverside Meth. Hosp., Columbus, 1978-83; grad. asst. U. Cin., 1984; endocrinology clin. nurse specialist Mt. Carmel Med. Ctr., Columbus, 1985-90; rsch. assoc. II Ohio State U. Hosp., Columbus, 1990-92; diabetes nurse educator St Vincent's Hosp., Indpls., 1992-94; case mgr. Mount Carmel Health, Columbus, 2000—. Presenter in field. Contbr. articles to profl. jours. Mem. Cen. Ohio Assn. Diabetes Educators (past pres., sec. 1989-90), Am. Assn. Diabetes Educators (ann. program and meeting planning com., chairperson mini-sessions com. ann. meeting), Cen. Ohio Clin. Nurse Specialist Support Group (founder), Cen. Ohio Diabetes Assn., Am. Diabetes Assn., AACN (instr. cen. Ohio core curriculum rev. course edocrinology model 1986, 87, 89, 91). Home: 1400 Candlewood Dr Columbus OH 43235-1620 Office: 793 W State St Columbus OH 43222-1551

KRAKORA-LOOBY, JANICE MARIE, pediatrician; b. Chgo., Jan. 11, 1951; d. Joseph George and Marie Adele (Doleshek) Krakora; m. John Augustus Looby III, July 21, 1979; children: Eileen Loretta, John Augustus IV, James Patrick. BS with honors, Mich. State U., 1972, DVM with honors, 1973; MD with honors, Rush Med. Coll., Chgo., 1987. Diplomate Am. Bd. of Pediatrics. Assoc. vet. Kohn Animal Hosp., Highland Park, Ill., 1973—75, Libertyville (Ill.) Animal Hosp., 1976—77, hosp. dir., 1977—82; assoc. vet. Mundelein (Ill.) Animal Hosp., 1982—85; intern and resident in pediatrics Rush-Presbyn.-St. Luke's Med. Ctr., Chgo., 1987—90; pediatrician Vernon Hills (Ill.) Pediatric Assoc. Ltd., 1990—2001; assoc. prof. Rush Med. Coll., Chgo., 1996—; pediatrician Fairview Pediat. LLC, Grayslake, Ill., 2001—; vice chmn. dept. pediat. Lake Forest (Ill.) Hosp., 2000—03, chmn. dept. pediat., 2004—. Bd. dirs. Sun Room, Inc., Lake Forest. Editor newsletter St. Mary Parish Coun., 1991-94, sch. parents club, 1994-96. Paul Harris fellow Rotary, 1988. Fellow Am. Acad. Pediatrics; mem. AMA, Am. Med. Women's Assn., Chgo. Med. Soc., Ill. Med. Assn., Chgo. Pediatric Soc., Lake County Pediatric Soc., Am. Coll. Sports Medicine, Rotary Club Lake Forest/Lake Bluff. Home: 1764 Bowling Green Dr Lake Forest IL 60045-3504 Office: Fairview Pediat LLC 15 Commerce Dr # 108 Grayslake IL 60030-7807

KRALL, DIANA, musician; b. Nanaimo, BC, Can., Nov. 16, 1964; Student, Berklee Coll. Music, 1982—84; degree (hon.), U. Victoria. With Justin Time Records, Montreal, Canada, 1993, GRP, Verve Records. Musician: (albums) Stepping Out, 1993, Only Trust Your Heart, 1995, All For You, 1996, Love Scenes, 1997, When I Look In Your Eyes, 1999 (Grammy award for Best Jazz Vocal Performance, 2000, Grammy award nomination for Album of Yr., 2000, Cert. Platinum, U.S. and Portugal, Double Platinum in Can., Gold, France, Juno award Best Vocal Jazz Album), The Look of Love, 2001 (Quadruple Platinum, Can., Platinum, Australia, New Zealand, Poland and Portugal, Gold, France, Singapore, Eng., Juno award for Best Artist, Best Album, Best Vocal Jazz Album, Record of Yr. award Nat. Jazz Awards), Live in Paris, 2002 (Grammy award for Best Jazz Vocal Album), Heartdrops: Vince Benedetti Meets Diana Krall, 2003, The Girl in the Other Room, 2004. Named Musician of Yr., Nat. Jazz Awards, Internat. Musician. Office: Macklam/Feldman Mgmt 1605 W 2d Ave Ste 200 Vancouver BC Canada V6H 3Y4*

KRAM, SHIRLEY WOHL, federal judge; b. N.Y.C., 1922; Student, Hunter Coll., 1940-41, CUNY, 1940-47; LLB, Bklyn. Law Sch., 1950. Atty. Legal Aid Soc. N.Y., 1951-53, 1962-71; assoc. Simons & Hardy, 1954-55; pvt. practice law, 1955-60; judge Family Ct., N.Y.C., 1971-83, U.S. Dist. Ct. (so. dist.) N.Y., N.Y.C., 1983-93, sr. judge, 1993—. Author: (with Neil A. Frank) The Law of Child Custody, Development of the Substantive Law Office: US Dist Ct US Courthouse 40 Foley Sq Rm 2101 New York NY 10007-1502

KRAMER, ANDREA S. lawyer; b. Chgo., Mar. 15, 1955; BA summa cum laude with high distinction, U. Ill., 1975; JD cum laude, Northwestern U., 1978. Bar: Ill. 1978, U.S. Tax Ct. 1980, U.S. Ct. Claims 1982. With Coffield, Ungaretti & Harris, Chgo. Author: Taxation of Securities, Commodities and Options, 1986, Financial Products: Taxation, Regulation and Design, rev. edit., 1991; mem. editorial bd. Jour. Criminal Law and Criminology, 1976-78; contbr. articles to profl. jours. Mem. Am. League Lobbyists, Internat. Bar Assn., Chgo. Bar Assn. (sect. taxation), Lawyers Guild, Nat. Women's Law Ctr., Chgo. Fin. Exchange, Bronze Tablet, Alpha Lambda Delta, Phi Alpha Theta, Phi Beta Kappa, Phi Kappa Phi. Office: Coffield Ungaretti & Harris 3500 Three 1st Nat Plz Chicago IL 60602

KRAMER, CAROL GERTRUDE, marriage and family counselor; b. Grand Rapids, Mich., Jan. 14, 1939; d. Wilson John and Katherine Joanne (Wasdyke) Rottschafer; m. Peter William Kramer, July 1, 1960; children: Connie R. Kramer Sattler, Paul Wilson Kramer. AB, Calvin Coll., 1960; MA, U. Mich., 1969; PhD, Holy Cross Coll., 1973; MSW, Grand Valley State U., 1985. Diplomate Internat. Acad. Behavioral Medicine, Counseling and Psychotherapy, cert. addictions/substance abuse counselor Mich., hypnotherapist/psychotherapist, clin. certified forensic counselor 2001. Elem. tchr. Jenison (Mich.) Pub. Sch., 1960-65; sch. social worker Grand Rapids Pub. Sch., 1964-81; pvt. practice marriage and family counselor Grand Rapids, 1973—; v.p. Human Resource Assocs., Grand Rapids,

1983-88; pres. bd. dirs. Telecounseling, 1996-99. Guest lectr. Calvin Coll., Mich. State U., Grand Valley State U., 1975-85; presenter in field. Co-author: Parent Involvement Program, 1993, Stop Sexual Abuse for Everyone, 1996. Ruling elder 1st Presbyn. Ch., Grand Rapids, 1975-78; mem. Gerald R. Ford Rep. Women, Grand Rapids, 1980-87; co-chair pastoral rels. com. Gun Lake Community Ch., 1989-91, v.p. consistory, 1991-93; apptd. fellow State Mich. Bd. Marriage Counselors, 1985-87; pres. bd. dirs. Stop Sexual Abuse for Everyone. Named one of Outstanding Young Women in Am., 1974; recipient Meritorious Svc. award Kent County Family Life Coun., 1983.. Fellow Am. Assn. Marriage and Family Therapist; mem. NASW, Mich. Assn. Marriage Counselors (awards com. 1988, chmn. 1991, nominations com. 1992-95), Kent County Family Life Coun. (pres. 1975), Voters Against Sexual Abuse (pres., bd. dirs. 1992—). Home: 12622 Park Dr Wayland MI 49348-9085 Office: 1251 Century Ave SW Ste 107 Grand Rapids MI 49503-8047

KRAMER, CAROLE REE, retired special education educator; d. Peter and Luetta Marie (Wallace) Mihay; m. Donald Louis Kramer, Nov. 23, 1979; 1 child, Jenée Marie. BA in Elem. Edn., Mich. State U., 1964; M in Spl. Edn., Oakland U., 1981. Elem. tchr. Waverly (Mich.) Sch. Dist., 1964—65, Hayward (Calif.) Unified Sch. Dist., 1965—71, Waterford (Mich.) Sch. Dist., 1971—81, spl. edn. tchr., 1982—95; ret., 1995. Exhibitions include, Raleigh, N.C., 2003. Mem.: Morganton New Comers Club (pres. 1999—2002).

KRAMER, CECILE E. retired medical librarian; b. NYC, Jan. 6, 1927; d. Marcus and Henrietta (Marks) K. BS, CCNY, 1956; MS in L.S., Columbia U., 1960. Reference asst. Columbia U. Health Scis. Library, N.Y.C., 1957-61, asst. librarian, 1961-75; dir. Health Scis. Libr. Northwestern U., Chgo., 1975-91, asst. prof. edn., 1975-91, prof. emeritus, 1991—. Instr. library and info. sci. Rosary Coll., 1981-85 ; cons. Francis A. Countway Library Medicine, Harvard U., 1974. Pres. Friends of Libr., Fla. Atlantic U., Boca Raton. Fellow Med. Libr. Assn. (chmn. med. sch. librs. group 1975-76, editor newsletter 1975-77, instr. continuing edn. 1966-75, mem. panel cons. editors Bull. 1987-90, disting. mem. Acad. Health Info. Profls. 1993—); mem. Biomed. Comm. Network (chmn. 1979-80). Home: 9184 Flynn Cir Apt 4 Boca Raton FL 33496-6675 E-mail: kramer@fau.edu.

KRAMER, ELAINE, editor; m. Joel Shaul; 2 children. BS in Journalism, Northwestern U., 1979. With Peace Corps, Sierra Leone, 1980; reporter Belleville (Ill.) News-Dem.; copy editor Courier-Jour., Louisville, Hartford (Conn.) Courant, 1987, news editor, asst. to pub.; mng. editor Morning Call, Allentown, Pa., 1998—2000, editor, v.p. news, 2000—01; mng. editor Orlando (Fla.) Sentinel, 2001—. Recipient nat. writing award, Assn. Sunday Mags., 1990. Office: Orlando Sentinel 633 N Orange Ave PO Box 2833 Orlando FL 32801-2833*

KRAMER, ELEANOR, retired real estate broker, tax practitioner, financial consultant; b. N.Y.C., Feb. 18, 1939; d. Herman I. Kramer and Fay (Berger) Kramer-Levy; m. Richard H. Fitz-Gerald III, Dec. 24, 1959 (div.); m. Gregory F. Navarro, Oct. 1, 1975 (div. Mar. 1996); children: Brad, Cindy. BA in Speech and Theater, Bklyn Coll., 1975; MS in Urban Affairs, CUNY, Hunter Coll., 1976. Tchr. cultural arts Bronx (N.Y.) Bd. Edn., 1966-70; real estate broker, pres. Tritown Realty Corp., Mamaroneck, N.Y., 1978-83; pvt. practice tax cons. Mamaroneck, 1983—. Adj. prof. sociology Rockland Community Coll., Suffern, N.Y., 1979-85, Westchester Community Coll., Valhalla, N.Y., 1979-85; founder dance therapy St. Vincent's Hosp., N.Y.C.; lectr., demonstrator N.Y.C. Pub. Schs., author, producer, performer, co-creator child edn. programs, 1967-77. Mem. pub. relations com. Bicentennial commn. Village of Mamaroneck, 1976; bd. dirs. Community Action Program, Mamaroneck, 1977-79. Mem.: LWV (bd. dirs. 1977—80), NOW (ad hoc chmn. 1970, co-chair, co-author women's ednl. seminar Libr. of Congress), Nat. Soc. Tax Preparers, Lions (Larchmont, NY). Avocations: puzzles, tennis, antiques, jazz, theater. Office: PO Box 172 Bronx NY 10464-0172

KRAMER, ELISSA LIPCON, nuclear medicine physician, educator; b. N.Y.C., Feb. 22, 1951; d. Jules and Esther Ruth (Wagner) L.; children: Rachel, Aaron. BA, U. Pa., 1973; MD, NYU, 1977. Diplomate Am. Bd. Nuc. Medicine, Am. Bd. Radiology. Ob-gyn. intern Bellevue Hosp. Ctr./NYU Med. Ctr., 1977-78, resident in radiology, 1978-80, fellow in nuc. medicine, 1980-82; asst. prof. clin. radiology NYU, 1982-89, assoc. prof. clin. radiology, 1989-96, prof. clin. radiology, 1996—. Assoc. prof. radiology Cornell U. Med. Ctr., Ithaca, N.Y., 1989-90; assoc. Sloan-Kettering Cancer Ctr., N.Y.C., 1989-90; assoc. dir. nuc. medicine Tisch Hosp., N.Y.C., 1989-99; assoc. attending physician Tisch Hosp., 1990-99, Bellevue Hosp., N.Y.C., 1990—; dir. nuclear medicine Tisch Hosp./Bellevue Hosp., 1999—; master Lewis Thomas Soc. for the Arts and Humanities in Medicine, NYU Sch. Medicine. Author, editor: (book) Clinical SPECT Imaging, 1995; contbr. articles to profl. jours. Nat. Cancer Inst./NIG Rsch. grantee, 1993—. Mem. Am. Coll. Radiology, Am. Assn. Women Radiologists, Radiology Soc. N.Am., Soc. Nuc. Medicine (mem. brain imaging coun. 1982—, mem. bd. dirs. 1992-93). E-mail: elissa.kramer@med.nyu.edu.

KRAMER, JANE, writer; b. Providence, Aug. 7, 1938; d. Louis Irving and Jessie (Shore) K.; m. Vincent Crapanzano, Apr. 30, 1967; 1 dau., Aleksandra. BA, Vassar Coll., 1959; MA, Columbia U., 1961. Founder, writer Morningsider, N.Y.C., 1961-62; writer Village Voice, N.Y.C., 1962-63, New Yorker, N.Y.C., 1964—. Cons. German Marshall Fund; bd. dirs. East and Central European Pub. Project; mem. bd. adv. Daedalus. Author: Off Washington Square: A Reporter Looks at Greenwich Village, 1963, Allen Ginsberg In America, 1969, Honor to the Bride Like the Pigeon That Guards Its Grain Under the Clove Tree, 1970, The Last Cowboy, 1978, Unsettling Europe, 1980 (Am. Book award for non-fiction 1981), Europeans, 1988, Whose Art Is It?, 1994 (Nat. Mag. award 1993, Prix Européan de l'Essai 1993), Lone Patriot: The Short Career of an American Militiaman, 2002; contbr. to periodicals including N.Y. Times Book Rev., N.Y. Rev. of Books, others. Recipient Front Page award New Yorker, 1977, Overseas Press Club Am. award, 1979; named Woman of Yr. Mademoiselle, 1968. Mem. Council Fgn. Relations, Com. to Protect Journalists (bd. dirs.), Environ. Def. Fund, Authors Guild and League, Writers Guild, Nat. Book Critics Circle, Goethe Inst. (bd. dirs.). Office: New Yorker 25 W 43rd St New York NY 10036-7406

KRAMER, KAREN SUE, mind-body psychologist; b. L.A., Sept. 6, 1942; d. Frank Pacheco Kramer and Velma Eileen (Devlin) Moore; m. Stewart A. Sterling, Dec. 30, 1965 (div. 1974); 1 child, Scott Kramer Sterling. BA, U. Calif., Berkeley, 1966; MA, U.S. Internat. U., 1976; PhD, Profl. Sch. Psychology, 1980; MA in Asian Studies, U. San Francisco, 2003. Psychometrist U. Calif. Counseling Ctr., Berkeley, 1966-67; social worker Alameda County Welfare Dept., Oakland, Calif., 1967-69; vol. coord. San Diego County Probation Dept., 1971-73; officer San Diego County Probation Dept., 1973-76; counselor and coord. clin. and outreach programs Western Inst., San Diego, 1976-77; program coord. and counselor Women's Resource Ctr., Oceanside, Calif., 1977-78; pvt. practice psychology San Diego, 1978-81; planner/analyst San Diego County Dept. Health Svcs., 1979-81; prof. psychology Nat. U., San Diego, 1979-81; social svcs. program cons. Calif. Dept. Social Svcs., Emeryville, 1981-83; affirmative action officer State Compensation Ins. Fund, San Francisco, 1983-87; cmty. psychologist Calif. Dept. Mental Health, 1987-89; pvt. practice psychology Berkeley, 1990—. Personal analyst State Comp. Ins. Fund, 1989-91; regional property mgr. State Compensation Ins. Fund, San Francisco, 1991-95; prof. Nat. U. San Diego, 1979-81; pres. North County Coun. Social Concerns, Vista, Calif., 1977-78; advisor USMC Camp Pendleton Human Svcs., 1977-79; mem. adv. bd. Chinatown Resources Devel. Ctr., San Francisco, 1984-87, 2000—, San Francisco Rehab., 1984-87; bd. dirs. Network Cons. Svcs., Napa, Calif.; founder QiGong in China Ednl. Svcs. Travel/Study Programs, 1999; asst. dir. QiGong for Children, Am. Found. Traditional Chinese Medicine; cons. Success Strategies, programs for Health, Sports, Tests, Life; prof. Psychology, Am. Coll. TCM, 1999; pub. chmn. Intuition Network Conf., 1997; advisor Calif.-Hawaii Inst., 1998 . Editl. advisor (website) Alternative Medicine, 1998. Clin. dir. Pathways to Wellness Clinics, Oakland, Calif., 2002—; chmn. pub. awareness com. Alameda County Mental Health Bd., 2000—03. Mem. Calif. Peer Counselors Assn. (adv. bd. 1987-90), Calif. Prevention Network (bd. dirs. 1989-93, editl. advisor jour. 1992-93). E-mail: K.Kramer@comcast.net.

KRAMER, LORA L. executive assistant; b. East Patchogue, N.Y., Aug. 11, 1966; d. Oscar Emmett and Marylin Emily Blevins; m. Eric A. Kramer, Aug. 22, 1993; children: Jake Theodore, Isabella Camille. AAS, Suffolk C.C., Selden, N.Y., 1987; student, Inst. de Touraine, Tours, France, 1988; BS in French, SUNY, Brockport, 1988. Exec. asst. U.S. Arctic Rsch. Commn., Fairbanks, Alaska, 1989; sr. editl. asst. Am. Phys. Soc., Ridge, N.Y., 1985-87, 90-95; exec. asst. The Ulanov Partnership, Princeton, N.J., 1995—. Mem. DAR (jr. mem.; registrar 1998—02), Steuben Soc. Am., Historian, 2002. Avocations: piano, sailing. E-mail: kramer@ulanov.com.

KRAMER, MARLENE DIXIE, dietician; b. Matewan, W.Va., Mar. 5, 1952; d. Starling Hull and Martha Elizabeth K. AS, Brunswick (Ga.) Coll., 1970-72; BS in Home Econs., U. Ga., 1972-75; grad. dietetic traineeship program, Greenville (S.C.) Hosp. System, 1975-76. Registered and lic. dietitian. Dietitian Greenville Hosp. System, 1976; mgr. nutritional svcs. Citrus Meml. Hosp., Inverness, Fla., 1976—. Ombudsman coun. State of Fla. Long Term Care, Inverness, 1988-90; culinar arts cons. Withlacoochee Tech. Inst., Inverness, 1984—; adj. instr. Cen. Fla. Community Coll., Ocala, 1993. Mem. Am. Dietetic Assn., Am. Hosp. Food Svc. Adminstrs. Home: 911 E Harvard St Inverness FL 34452-6726

KRAMER, MARSHA LOUISE ENDAHL, psychotherapist; b. Davenport, Iowa, Feb. 18, 1948; d. John Charles Sr. and Etta M. (Johnson) Endahl; m. Hugh Thomas Kramer, July 10, 1983; children: Jennifer Michelle Cressy, Jillian Nicole Cressy. Student, U. Minn.; diploma in social welfare, Ryerson Inst., 1969; BA in Sociology, U. Toronto, 1978; MS in Counseling, U. Bridgeport, 1986. Counselor Family Svc. Assn., Toronto, Ont., Can.; pvt. practice New Canaan, Conn.; psychotherapist Christian Counseling Ctr., Norwalk, New Canaan, Conn.; dir. congregational care First Presbyn. Ch., Boca Raton, Fla., 1995—. Cons. in field. Author: (with Fowler) Guide to Homemade Toys; also articles in field. Officer 1st Presbyn. Ch. Mem. AACD, ACA (bd. dirs.), AAUW (bd. dirs.), Adult Devel. Assn., Alpha Delta Pi Alumnae Assn. (bd. dirs.). Address: 23371 Water Cir Boca Raton FL 33486-8542

KRAMER, MARY ELIZABETH, state legislator, health services executive; b. Burlington, Iowa, June 14, 1935; d. Ross L. and Geneva M. (McElhinney) Barnett; m. Kay Frederick Kramer, June 13, 1958; children: Kent, Krista. BA, U. Iowa, 1957, MA, 1971. Cert. tchr., Iowa. Tchr. Newton (Iowa) Pub. Schs., 1957-61, Iowa City Pub. Schs., 1961-67, tchr., asst. supt., 1971-75; dir. pers. Younkers, Inc., Des Moines, 1975-81; v.p. Wellmark, Inc., Des Moines, 1981-99; mem. Iowa Senate from 37th dist., Des Moines, 1990—2004; pres. of the senate, 1997—2004; U.S. amb. to Island of Ea. Caribbean, 2004—. Mem. Olympic adv. com. Blue Cross and Blue Shield Assn., Chgo., 1988—92; presdl. appointee White House Commn. on Presdl. Scholars, 2001, now chmn.; Bd. dirs. Polk County Child Care Rsch. Ctr., Des Moines, 1986—96, YWCA, Des Moines, 1989—94. Named Mgr. of Yr. Iowa Mgmt. Assocs., 1985, Woman of Achievement YWCA, 1986, Woman of Vision Young Women's Resource Ctr., 1989. Mem. Soc. Human Resource Mgmt. (Profl. of Yr. 1996), Iowa Mgmt. Assn. (pres. 1988), Greater Des Moines C. of C. (bd. dirs. 1986-96), Nexus, Rotary Internat. Republican. Presbyterian. Avocations: music, public speaking. Home: 13598 Village Ct Clive IA 50325 Office: Iowa State Senate State Capitol Des Moines IA 50319-0001 E-mail: mkramer@legis.state.ia.us., kaynmary@aol.com.

KRAMER, MICHELLE, reporter; City hall bur. chief N.Y. Daily News, N.Y.C.; chief investigative/polit. reporter Sta. WCBS-TV, N.Y.C., 1990—, host Sunday Edit. Recipient Peabody award, Edward R. Murrow award, Emmy, Golden Typewriter award. Office: CBS 524 W 57th St New York NY 10019

KRAMER, NORMA DOMENICA ANDREA, artist; m. Vernon V. Kramer, 1966. Student, Traphagen, 1946-47, Pratt Inst., N.Y.C., 1948-50, CCNY, 1951-52, Art Students League, 1979-87, Nat. Acad. Design, N.Y.C., 1988-89. In mdse. mgmt. and sales Henri Bendel, Mainbocher, Macy's, N.Y.C., 1946-50; publs. mgr. Met. Mus. of Art, N.Y.C., 1951-58; editl. asst., exhbn. asst., registrar Am. Fedn. Arts., N.Y.C., 1958-65; asst. to Harold Rosenberg, poet, art critic, editor, campaigns mgr., dir. rsch. The Advt. Coun., N.Y.C., 1965-89; exhbn. chmn. 3 Arts Club Homeland, 2000—04, art instr., 2003—. One-man shows include 3 Arts Club Homeland, Balt., 1998, Pearl Gallery, 1999, Preston's 500, 2001, exhibited in group shows at Nat. Inst. Architects, 1949, Met. Mus. Art, 1957, Epiphany Ch., N.J., 1983, Am. Watercolor Soc., 1984, Nat. Acad. Design, 1988, Cork Gallery, Lincoln Ctr., 1986, Nat. Arts Club, 1987, Pearl Gallery, 1996—, Old Forge Art Ctr., 1985—, Art Dirs. Club, 1999—, Hubbard Telescope Space Ctr., John/Hopkins, 1999—, Represented in permanent collections. Recipient Traphagen award, 1947, 1st prize Pratt Inst., 1950, concours prizes, purchase award, Art Students League, 1984—87, award Excellence solo watercolor exhbt., 2d Ave Fair, N.Y.C., 1980, 2nd prize award, Rose Soc. Md., 1998, 2001. Mem. Three Arts Club of Homeland, Art Students League (life). Studio: The Pearl Gallery 815 W 36th St Baltimore MD 21211-2508 Office Phone: 410-467-2260.

KRAMER, SUSAN ROSE, small business owner, skier, educator; b. Paterson, N.J., Feb. 7, 1966; d. George Jay and Carole Arch Kramer; m. George Courtney Glass IV, Sept. 24, 1989 (div. July 1998); m. J. Eric Diaz, Dec. 31, 2000; stepchildren: Dan Diaz, Emily Diaz. BA in Studio Art and Environ. Studies, U. Vt., 1988; MS in Art Edn., Ctrl. Conn. State U., 1993. Children's program dir. Bromley Learning Ctr., Peru, Vt., 1993—2000, ski sch. staff trainer, 2000—03; owner pottery bus. SRK Studio, Peru, 1997—2003. Named one of Top 100 Ski Pros, Bergie's Best, 2000, Ski Mag., 2003. Mem.: Profl. Ski Instrs. Am. (staff clinician 1997—2003, asst. chair children's com. 2001—03, advanced children's educator 2002—03). Independent. Jewish. Avocations: gardening, Afro-Cuban drumming.

KRAMER, WEEZIE CRAWFORD, former broadcast executive; Student, U. Ky., 1977, Wheaton Coll. Sales/local sales mgr. WKQQ, Lexington, Ky., 1977-80; local sales mgr. WHBQ, Memphis, 1980-81; gen. sales mgr. KBPI/KNUS, Denver, 1981-85, WFYR, Chgo., 1985-88, WMAQ All News 67, Chgo., 1988-94, sta. mgr., 1994, v.p., gen. mgr., 1994-99. Office: WMAQ-AM 455 N Cityfront Plaza Dr Chicago IL 60611-5503

KRANCEVICH-SHAW, CYNTHIA ANN, health facility professional; d. Joseph Krancevich and Patti Yvonne Ebbett-Krancevich. BS in Nursing, Lake Superior State U., 1981. RN, Mich., Colo., Ont. Nurse clinician cardiology No. Mich. Hosp., Petoskey, Mich., 1995—2002, bus. assoc. heart & vascular svcs., 2002—. Nursing adv. com. Lake Superior State U., Sault Se. Marie, Mich., 2003—. Mem. alumni bd. Lake Superior State U., 2002—03. Mem.: Kiwanis (v.p. elect 2003—). Presbyterian. Avocations: downhill skiing, gardening. Office: Northern Mich Hosp 416 Connable Ave Petoskey MI 49770 E-mail: ckshaw@northernhealth.org.

KRANE, JESSICA (AIDA JESSICA KOHNOP-KRANE), writer, educator; d. Samuel Rubenstein and Esther Ginsburg; m. Louis Kohnop, Jan. 11, 1956. Student, Roosevelt U. Writer, concert pianist, lectr. Appearances on varous TV programs including The Tonight Show, To Tell the Truth, The Today Show. Author: Face-O-Metrics, 1968, The Sensuous Approach to Looking Younger, 1969, How to Use Your Hands to Save Your Face, 1978; contbr.: memoir Born Again Vision, 1974—90, debut as pianist: Orchestra Hall, 1956; musician: toured U.S. and Canada with Louis Kohnop, Bklyn. Mus., WNYC, NY Town Hall, cmty. concerts. Avocation: fashion design. Home: 4400 Hillcrest Dr Apt 720 Hollywood FL 33021

KRANKING, MARGARET GRAHAM, artist, educator; b. Dec. 21, 1930; d. Stephen Wayne and Madge Williams (Dawes) Graham; m. James David Kranking, Aug. 23, 1952; children: James Andrew, Ann Marie Kranking Eggleton, David Wayne. BA summa cum laude (Clendenin fellow), Am. U., 1952. Asst. to head publs. Nat. Gallery Art, Washington, 1952-53. Tchr. art Woman's Club, Chevy Chase, Md., 1976-88, 98—; guest instr. Amherst Coll., 1985, The Homestead, Hot Springs, Va., 1997; judge The Miniature Painters, Sculptors and Gravers Soc. Washington, 69th Ann. Internat. Exhbn., 2002, Bethesda, Md. One-woman shows include Spectrum Gallery, Washington, 1974, 76, 78-79, 83, 85, 87, 90, 92, 95, 97, 2000, Philip Morris, U.S.A., Richmond, Va., 1982-83, 86, Forence (S.C.) Mus., 1991, Lombardi Cancer treatment Ctr., Washington, 1992, Capital Gallery, Frankfort, Ky., 1993, Acad. Arts, Easton, Md., 1999, Warm Springs (Va.) Gallery, 1997-98; exhibited in group shows at Balt. Mus., 1974, 76, Corcoran Gallery Art, Washington, 1952, 72, USIA Traveling Exhbt., C.Am., 1978-79, AARP Traveling Exhbn., 1986; represented in permanent collections U. Va., Philip Morris U.S.A., USCG, AT&T, Freddie Mac, Florence Mus., S.C., Navy Fed. Credit Union Hdqs., Vienna, Va., Marsh and McClennan Co., Washington, The Washington Hilton, D.C.; traveling exhbn. Nat. Watercolor Soc., Watercolor U.S.A., Am. Watercolor Soc., Am. Artist mag., North Light mag., Adirondacks Nat. Exhbn. of Am. Watercolor, Artitude Internat. Art Competition, N.Y., Shada Gallery, Riyadh, Saudi Arabia, Belle Grove Plantation Invitational, Middletown, Va., Strathmore Hall Arts Ctr., North Bethesda, Md., Wash. Woman mag., Am. Speech-Lang. Hearing Assn., mag., Govt. House, Annapolis, Md. Invitational, 1997-99, Strathmore Hall Arts Ctr., North Bethesda, Md., Montgomery Coll. Invitational, Md., Glen View Mansion Invitational, Rockville, Md., 2000; ofcl. artist USCG; contbr. reproductions and text to numerous books. Recipient George Gray award USCG Art Program, N.Y., 1991, 98. Mem.: Am. Watercolor Soc., Washington Soc. Landscape Painters, Potomac Valley Watercolorists (pres. 1981—83), Washington Watercolor Assn., So. Watercolor Soc., Ga. Watercolor Soc., Southwestern Watercolor Soc., Midwest Watercolor Soc., Nat. Watercolor Soc. Roman Catholic. Home: 3504 Taylor St Chevy Chase MD 20815-4022

KRANOWITZ, CAROL STOCK, pre-school educator, writer; b. New Haven, Conn., Dec. 3, 1945; d. Herman Edward and Doris Baker Stock; m. Alan Michael Kranowitz, June 25, 1967; children: Jeremy Lewis, David Stock. BA, Barnard Coll., N.Y., 1967; MA in Edn. and Human Devel., George Wash. U., Washington, 1995. Preschool tchr. St. Columba's Nursery Sch., Washington, 1976—2001; lectr. Sensory Processing Disorder, Md., 1998—. Editor in chief S.I. Focus Mag., 2004—; coord. Wise and Wonderful intergenerational program, Washington, 1994—2001. Author: The Out-of-Sync Child: Recognizing and Coping with Sensory Integration Dysfunction, 1998, The Out-of-Sync Child Has Fun, 2003 (Therapeutic Contbn. Award, Devel. Delay Resources (DDR), 2003), 101 Activities for Kids in Tight Spaces, 1995; co-author: (manual) Answers to Questions Teachers Ask About Sensory Integration, 2001, Balzer-Martin Preschool Screening, 1992, (teachers' guidebook) Hear, See, Play! Music Discovery Activities for Young Children, 1989; speaker (infor. videos) The Out-of-Sync Child, (infor. video) Getting Kids in Sync: Sensory-Motor Activities to Help Children Develop Body Awareness and Integrate Their Senses, 2002, interviewer (infor. audio) Teachers Ask About Sensory Integration. Adv. bd. Devel. Delay Resources, Bethesda, Md., 1998—, Nonverbal Learning Disorders Assn., West Hartford, Conn., 2000—, S.I. Challenge, Dallas-Ft. Worth, Tex., 2000—03. Judaism. Avocations: cello, chamber music.

KRANTZ, JUDITH TARCHER, novelist; b. N.Y.C., Jan. 9, 1928; d. Jack David and Mary (Brager) Tarcher; m. Stephen Falk Krantz, Feb. 19, 1954; children: Nicholas, Anthony. BA, Wellesley Coll., 1948. Fashion publicist, Paris, 1948-49; fashion editor Good Housekeeping mag., N.Y.C., 1949-56; contbg. writer McCalls, 1956-59, Ladies Home Jour., 1959-71; contbg. west coast editor Cosmopolitan mag., 1971-79. Author: Scruples, 1978, Princess Daisy, 1980, Mistral's Daughter, 1982, I'll Take Manhattan, 1986, Till We Meet Again, 1988, Dazzle, 1990, Scruples Two, 1992, Lovers, 1994, Spring Collection, 1996, The Jewels of Tessa Kent, 1998, Sex & Shopping: Confessions of a Nice Jewish Girl, 2000. Office: St Martin Press 175 5th Ave New York NY 10010*

KRANTZ, LINDA LAW, librarian; b. Princeton, N.J., June 19, 1943; d. Harold Bell and Ruth Workman Law; m. David Walter Krantz, July 29, 1967. Student. Mt. Union Coll., 1961-63; BA in French Lit., U. Rochester, 1965; MLS, Rutgers State U., 1967. Libr. asst. Fine Hall Libr. Math. and Physics Princeton U., 1962—66; reference libr. Princeton Pub. Libr., 1966-67; cataloger NASA Lewis Rsch. Ctr., Cleve., 1967; reference libr. sci.-tech. Cleve. Pub. Libr., 1968-69; reference libr. Wright State U. Libr., Dayton, Ohio, 1969-73; libr. dir. Rockbridge Regional Libr., Lexington, Va., 1974—. Bd. dirs. Kendal, sec., 2003—. Musician (violinist): Rockbridge Orch., 1975—96, 1999—, Allegheny-Highlands Symphony Orch., 1997—. Mem.: ALA, Va. Pub. Libr. Dirs. Assn. (pres. 2002—03), Va. Libr. Assn. (legis. co-chair 1997—99, George Mason award 1995), Lexington Rotary Club (bd. dirs. 1997, Paul Harris fellow 1996), Omicron Delta Kappa. Avocations: music, nature, reading, cats. Home: 151 Elliots Hill Ln Lexington VA 24450-7203 Office: Rockbridge Regional Libr 138 S Main St Lexington VA 24450-2316 Office Phone: 540-463-4324 1000. E-mail: lkrantz@cfw.com., lkrantz@rrlib.net.

KRANZ, KATHLEEN NEE, pianist, music educator; b. Fontana, Calif., May 31, 1951; d. Bruce Lester Brown and Margaret JoAnne Nee; m. Tomas Patten Kranz, July 4, 1978; 1 child, Michael Alexander. AB in Music, Fla. State U., 1973, MusM in Piano Performace, 1977; PhD in Music Theoretical Studies, U. Calif., San Diego, 1985. Mus. dir. Actor's Theater of Louisville, 1973—74, Asolo State Theater, Sarasota, Fla., 1974—75; mem. faculty, piano instr. U. Calif., San Diego, 1983—87; pvt. studio tchr. piano San Diego, 1978—; prof. piano, head theory dept. Fairbanks Sch. Performing Arts, Rancho Santa Fe, Calif., 1988—. Profl. accompanist Fairbanks Sch. for the Performing Arts, 1988—97; music theory tchr. Suzuki Assn., Calif., 1984—88; performer chamber music, San Diego, 1978—; master tchr. Am. Music Scholarship Assn., Cin., 1984—86, Batiquitos Festival, Del Mar, Calif., 1988; master accompanist, coach San Diego Children's Choir, 2003—. Contbr. articles to profl. jours. Recipient award, Fla. Fedn. Music Clubs, 1976, Alice Hohn scholarship, U. Calif., San Diego Grad. Sch., 1981; fellow, U. Calif., San Diego, 1981. Mem.: Music Tchrs.' Assn. Calif. (H.S. credit chmn., chmn. Bach Festival, chmn. Goodlin scholarship, chmn. composition contest), Music Tchrs.' Nat. Assn., Nat. Fedn. Music Clubs (judge 2004). Home: 3543 1/2 Myrtle Ave San Diego CA 92104-4250 Office: Calif Inst Music PO Box 9401 Rancho Santa Fe CA 92067 E-mail: drkathleenkranz@yahoo.com.

KRAPF, VERONICA LYNNE BENEFIELD, elementary school educator; b. Oneonta, Ala., May 8, 1965; d. Ronald Davis Benefield and Billie Jealene (Baty) Harp; m. Glen Barry Krapf; 1 child, Ethan Cole. BS in Psychology, Econs. and Bus. Adminstrn., Troy State U., 1988; tchr. cert., Kennesaw State U., 1993, EdM, 1997. 5th grade tchr. Fulton County Bd. Edn.-Crabapple Crossing Elem., Alpharetta, Ga., 1993—97; coll. supr. edn. dept. Kennesaw (Ga.) State U., 1998—2001; 5th grade tchr. The Davis Acad., Atlanta, 2003—. Pvt. practice tutor, Roswell, Ga., 1997—2003. Fundraiser Make A Wish Found., Atlanta, 2000—, Children's Wish,

Atlanta, 2000—, Camp Horizon, Atlanta, 2001—. Mem.: Kappa Delta Pi, Delta Kappa Gamma, Chi-Omega (2nd v.p.). Avocations: singing, music, literature. Home: 635 Garden Wilde Pl Roswell GA 30075

KRASKEY, CAROLYN RENEÉ, small business owner; b. Mpls., Feb. 25, 1940; d. Elmer Lincoln and Celeste Genevie Lukens; m. John Michael (Lukens) Kraskey, Aug. 22, 1959; children: Timothy, Jerome, Kimberley, Matthew, Reneé, Christine, Phillip, Nicholas. BA, U. Minn., 1984, MA, 1989; student, The Nat. Inst. Cosmetics, 1992; PhD, Capella U., 1994. Sch. dir. Maxines Current Regency, Blaine, Minn.; dir. sch. edn. Scot Lewis, Bloomington, Minn.; mgr. Hi Tech Beauty Acad., Mpls.; prin., owner Ctrl. Beauty Sch., Eagan, Minn. Mem.: Women's Club Ch. Roman Cath. Avocations: dog showing, theater, music, sewing, painting. Office: Central Beauty School 3906 Cedar Grove Pkwy Eagan MN 55122

KRASNY, PAULA J. lawyer; b. Phila., Pa., Sept. 29, 1963; Student, Harvard U., 1984; AB, Vassar Coll., 1985; JD, Northwestern U., 1988. Bar: Ill. 1988. Atty. McDermott, Will & Emery, Chgo., ptnr., 1995—99, Baker & McKenzie, Chgo., 1999—. Mem. adv. bd. Northwestern Jour. Tech. and Intellectual Property; bd. dir. Frances Lehman Loeb Art Ctr. Vassar Coll. Mem.: ABA, Internat. Trademark Assn., Am.-Israel C. of C. Office: Baker & McKenzie One Prudential Plz 130 East Randolph Dr Chicago IL 60601*

KRATOVIL, JANE LINDLEY, think tank associate, developer/fundraiser; b. Boston, Nov. 25, 1952; 1 child, Lindley. BA, Lynchburg Coll., 1974. Various positions U.S. Ho. of Reps., Washington, 1974-77, The Pittston Co., Greenwich, Conn., 1977-79; assoc. dir. City Sports Mgmt. Inc., Washington, 1979-82; adminstrv. asst. to spl. asst. to pres. for adminstrn. The White House, Washington, 1982-85; exec. asst. to gen. and dep. gen. counsel U.S. Dept. Treasury, Washington, 1985-88; exec. dir., sec. Eisenhower World Affairs Inst., Washington, 1988-2000; pres. Lindley & Assoc., Springfield, Va., 2000—. Office: 8340 Wickham Rd Springfield VA 22152-1739 E-mail: jkratovil@earthlink.net.

KRATZNER, JUDITH EVELYN, program manager; b. Fairmont, Minn., Sept. 4, 1942; d. Vernon W. and Evelyn B. (Jagodzinske) Schuler; m. Roland Ray Kratzner, Aug. 18, 1962; children: Mark V., Julie Ann, Jonathan R. BEd, Ill. State U., 1964; MEd, Ball State U., 1974; MS in Adminstrn., U. Notre Dame, 1986. Tchr. Sch. Dist. 117, Jacksonville, Ill., 1966-69, Harrison-Washington Sch. Dist., Gaston, Ind., 1970-73; dir. vols. St. John's Health Sys., Anderson, Ind., 1974-77, dir. human resource devel., 1977-84, asst. corporate staff, 1984-87, dir. cmty. svcs., 1987-93, dir. adult day care, 1993-96; exec. dir. Ind. Assn. Area Agys. Aging, Indpls., 1997-99; dir. ret. and sr. vol. program Anderson Pub. Libr., 1999—. Chair Ind. ElderCare Coalition, Indpls., 1993, 94; bd. dirs. Life Stream Svcs. Inc., 2000—, chair, 2002—. Pres. Anderson/Madison County YWCA, 1989, 90; pres. Mgmt. Club of Madison County, 1983-84; pres. Hist. West 8th St. Neighborhood Assn., Anderson, 1992-94; pres. LWV, Muncie, Ind., 1971-73. Recipient Women of Worth award Anderson Coun. of Women, 1994, YWCA Vol. of Yr. award, Anderson, 1992, Svc. Cmty. award Cmty. Svc. Coun., Anderson, 1989, Disting. Svc. award Internat. Mgmt. Coun., Anderson, 1987. Mem. Nat. Coun. on Aging (Nat. Adult Day Care Svcs. Assn. unit 1985), Nat. Adult Day Care Svcs. Assn. (region V. rep. 1991-96, nat. sec. 1996-98), Ind. Assn. Adult Day Care Svcs. (pres. 1986, 87). Avocations: historic preservation, photography. Home: 421 W 8th St Anderson IN 46016-1373 Office: RSVP Anderson Pub Libr 111 E 12th St Anderson IN 46016 E-mail: jkratzner@and.lib.in.us.

KRAUS, HILDA, designer, artist; b. N.Y.C., Jan. 26, 1915; d. Isaac and Sadie (Langer) K. BA, Hunter Coll., 1935; postgrad., Internat. Acad. Art, Salzburg, Austria, 1967, 72, 77. Jewelry, enamels and metalwork designer, 1935—. Tchr., instr. Brookfield (Conn.) Craft Ctr., 1965, 87, Silvermine Coll., New Canaan, Conn., 1975-76, Stamford (Conn.) Mus., 1979. Exhibited in shows at Cork Gallery, N.Y.C., Phila. Art Alliance, Gesellschaft fur goldschmiedekunst, Hamburg, Germany, Slater Meml. Mus., Norwich, Sarah Squeri Gallery, Cin., Mattatuck Mus., Waterbury, Conn., 1990, Berkshire Mus., Pittsfield, Mass., 1993, Worcester (Mass.) Ctr. for Crafts, 1993, Fuller Mus., Brockton, Mass., 1993, Silvermine Guild Arts Ctr., 1995, 2003. Coburg Germany, 1995, Ctr. for Arts, Wichita, Kans., 1995. Westport Art Ctr., 2003. Vol. Conn. Literacy, Norwalk, 1985—. Recipient Purchase prize Cooper-Hewitt Mus., 1969, Slater Meml. Mus., 1997, Del. Art Ctr., Best in Show award Art on the Mountain, Wilmington, Vt., 1985, Pen and Brush Club, N.Y.C., 1965-76, 1st prize Craftsman of N.Y., 1974, 76, 91, Medaille de la Ville de Limoges (France) Troisieme Biennale internat., 1975. Mem. Soc. Conn. Craftsmen (bd. dirs. 1950-70), Enamel Guild N.E., Silvermine Guild of Artists (bd. dirs. 1970's), Soc. Am. Craftsmen, Brookfield Crafts Ctr. Avocations: creative writing, making and flying kites, creative stitchery, travel, reading. Office: PO Box 305 Westport CT 06881-0305

KRAUS, LISA MARIE WASKO, music educator, composer, musician; b. Phila., Oct. 10, 1969; d. Raymond and Muriel Joan Wasko; m. Timothy J. Kraus, Nov. 23, 2002. AA in Music, Phila. CC, 1987; MusB Magna Cum Laude, Temple U., 1993; MusM Suma Cum Laude, Duquesne U., 2001. Cert. Music K-12 PA, 1993. Tchr. music, art, lit. tchr., program dir. Blair Christian Acad., 1993—95; tchr. orch., choir, music theory Archdiocese of Phila. St. Maria Goretti H.S., 1995—96; tchr. music Bristol Twp. Sch. Dist., Levittown, 1996—. Studio musician Various Studios, 1987—; composer, arranger She Writes Music, 2001—, Martial Arts Channel, Breakthrough Comm., 2003—. Performer: Pipes and Drums of the Delaware Valley, 1987—2003, Artists Conf., 2001—02. Recipient Musical Achievement Citation, Sen. Tommy Tomlinson, 2001, Performing Arts award, Mayor Bristol Twp., 2000, 2001; scholar Ednl. scholarship, St. Albain Swain Masonic Lodge #529, 2000. Master: TRI M Music Honor Soc. (corr.; soc. sponsor 2001—, Cert. Recognition 2002); mem.: Found. Ednl. Excellence (Recognition award 1997), Am. Choral Dirs. Assn., Music Educators Nat. Conf. (assoc.; collegiate chpt. treas. 1991—92), Nat. Acad. Recording Arts and Scis. (assoc.). Avocations: electronic music, cross stiching, antiquing, dog show training, cell painting.

KRAUS, MARGERY, management consultant, communications company executive; b. Franklin, N.J., May 20, 1946; d. Soland Lily (Cvern) Rosen; m. Stephen Kraus, Sept. 4, 1966; children: Lisa, Evan, Mara. BA in Polit. Sci., Am. U., 1967, MA in Govt., 1970. With Close Up Found., Arlington, Va., 1971-84, v.p., 1976-84; exec. v.p. APCO Assocs., Inc., Washington, 1984-88, pres., CEO, 1988—. Bd. dirs. Internat. Mgmt. and Devel. Inst.; chair, Northwestern Mutual Financial Network, Govt'l Rels. Com., chair, Coun. of PR Firms, Pub. Affairs Coun., Catherine B. Reynolds Found., Interat. Mgmt. and Devel. Inst., Inst. for Public Rels., The Creative Coalition, Meridian Internat. Ctr.; previously served as bd. dirs., Rsch. Inst. of the Children's Nat. Medical Ctr., Washington, D.C.; cons., speaker in field; adv. bd. Kellogg Sch. Mgmt. Bd. dirs. Close Up Found., Pub. Affairs Coun. Washington Businesswoman of the Year, 1998, PR Professional of the Year, 1997, named Internat. Pub. Rels. Profl. of Yr., 2001. Mem., Adv. Bd., Terry Sanford Inst. of Public Policy, Duke Univ, Coun. on Am. Politics, George Washington Univ. Grad. Sch. of Political Mgmt. Home: 9609 Whitecedar Ct Vienna VA 22181-5423 Office: APCO Worldwide 1615 L St NW Ste 900 Washington DC 20036-5623

KRAUS, NAOMI, retired biochemistry educator; b. Budapest, Hungary, July 4, 1933; came to U.S., 1965; d. Jacob and Vilma (Schwartz) K.; (div.); 1 child, Daphna. MS, Hebrew U., Jerusalem, Israel, 1960; PhD, Hebrew U., 1966. Instr. U. Pa., Phila., 1968-74; asst. prof. U. Tex. Sch. Medicine, Houston, 1974-76, assoc. prof., 1976-86, prof., 1986—2000; ret., 2000. Editor: Hormonal Control of Gluconeogenesis, 1986. Pres. Assn. Women in Sci. (Gulf Coast chpt.), 1974-76, v.p., 1989-90. Recipient grants from NIH, NSF. Mem. AAAS, Am. Soc. Cell Biology. Achievements include pioneering experiments on role Ca 2+ plays in the transduction of hormonal signals. Mailing: 360 Queen Anne Dr Seattle WA 98109 E-mail: naomik@mindspring.com.

KRAUS, NORMA JEAN, industrial relations executive; b. Pitts., Feb. 11, 1931; d. Edward Karl and Alli Alexandra (Hermanson) K. BA, U. Pitts., 1954; postgrad., NYU, 1959-61, Cornell U., 1969-70. Pers. mgr. for several cos., 1957-70; corp. dir. pers. TelePrompter Corp., N.Y.C., 1970-73; exec. asst., speech writer to Lt. Gov. N.Y. Office of Lt. Gov., Albany, 1974-79; exec. officer, v.p. human resources, labor rels. and stockholder rels. Volt Info. Scics., Inc., N.Y.C., 1979—. Co-founder Manhattan Women's Polit. Caucus, 1971; co-founder N.Y. State Women's Polit. Caucus, 1972, vice chair, 1978; bd. dirs. Ctr. for Women in Govt., 1977-79. Lt. (s.g.) USNR, 1954-57. Pa. State Senatorial Scholar, 1950-54. Mem. Women's Econ. Roundtable. Democrat. Avocations: politics, women's rights. Office: Volt Info Scis Inc 560 Lexington Ave Fl 15 New York NY 10022-6828 E-mail: njkideas@aol.com., nkraus@volt.com.

KRAUS, PANSY DAEGLING, gemology consultant, editor, writer; b. Santa Paula, Calif., Sept. 21, 1916; d. Arthur David and Elsie (Pardee) Daegling; m. Charles Frederick Kraus, Mar. 1, 1941 (div. Nov. 1961). AA, San Bernardino Valley Jr. Coll., 1938; student, Longmeyer's Bus. Coll., 1940; grad. gemologist diploma, Gemol. Inst. Gt. Britain, 1960, Gemol. Inst. Am., 1966. Clk. Convair, San Diego, 1943-48, San Diego County Schs. Publs., 1948-57; mgr. Rogers and Boblet Art-Craft, San Diego, 1958-64; part-time editl. asst. Lapidary Jour., San Diego, 1963-64, assoc. editor, 1964-69, editor, 1970-94, sr. editor, 1984-85; pvt. practice cons. San Diego, 1985—. Lectr. gems, gemology local gem, mineral groups; gem & mineral club bull. editor groups. Author: Introduction to Lapidary, 1987; editor, layout dir.: Gem Cutting Shop Helps, 1964, The Fundamentals of Gemstone Carving, 1967, Appalachian Mineral and Gem Trails, 1968, Practical Gem Knowledge for the Amateur, 1969, Southwest Mineral and Gem Trails, 1972, Introduction to Lapidary, 1987; revision editor Gemcraft (Quick and Leiper), 1977; contbr. articles to Lapidary jour., Keystone Mktg. catalog. Mem. San Diego Mineral and Gem. Soc., Gemol. Soc. San Diego, Gemol. Assn. Gt. Britain, Mineral. Soc. Am., Gemol. Inst. Am., Epsilon Sigma Alpha. Home and Office: 6127 Mohler St San Diego CA 92120-3515

KRAUS, ROZANN B. performing company executive; b. Dayton, Ohio, Oct. 7, 1952; m. Daniel Michael Epstein, Oct. 25, 1970; children: Jennah Buckaroo EpsteinKraus, Connor Bagel EpsteinKraus. MA, SUNY, Brockport, 1973. Pres./founder The Dance Complex, Cambridge, Mass., 1991—. Artistic dir./choreographer KRAUSAND..., Cambridge, Mass., 1974—98. Performer (dance concert) Paul Robeson award (Creative and Concerned Participation in the Arts in the Cmty., 1982). Democrat. Avocations: running, swimming, bicycling, political activism, writing. Office: The Dance Complex 536 Massachusetts Ave Cambridge MA 02139

KRAUSE, CAROLYN H. state legislator, lawyer; m. David Krause. BA, U. Wis.; JD, IIT. Assoc. Foss, Schuman & Drake, Chgo., 1966-73; lawyer, solo practice Mt. Prospect, Ill., 1973-76; pvt. practice Krause & Krause, Mt. Prospect, Ill., 1976—; mayor Mt. Prospect, 1973-76; Dist. 56 rep. Ill. Ho. Reps., Springfield, 1993—. Spokesman appropriations, gen. svcs., cities and villages, fin. instns., healthcare, and human svcs. coms., Ill. Ho. Reps. Apptd. by Gov. James Thompson (Ill.) to local govt. fin. study commn., 1980, criminal justice info. authority, 1985-87; past dir. Clearbrook Ctr.; chair Mcpl. Conf.; dir. Pub. Action to Deliver Shelter of Northwest Cook County. Mem. Ill. and Chgo. Bar Assns. Home: 204 S George St Mount Prospect IL 60056-3430 Office: Ill Ho of Reps State Capitol Springfield IL 62706-0001 Also: 111 E Busse Ave Ste 605 Mount Prospect IL 60056-3249

KRAUSE, GLORIA ROSE, music educator; b. Milw., Oct. 30, 1922; d. Carl Fred and Rose (Bremeier) Runge; m. George Tanner Krause Jr., June 24, 1960; 1 child, George Henry. MusB, U. Rochester, 1946; MusM, Northwestern U., 1954. Music tchr. Livington Manor (N.Y.) Cen., 1946-59, Monticello (N.Y.) Cen. Sch., 1959-61, Liberty (N.Y.) Cen. Sch., 1966-67, Livingston Manor Sch., 1968-79, Narrowsburg (N.Y.) Ctrl. Sch., 1979-87. Dir. Ill. Winds Chamber Ensemble, Narrowsburg, N.Y., 1975—; gen. mgr. Delaware Valley Opera, Narrowsburg, 1986—. Music dir.: (operas) HMS Pinafore, Mikado, Pirates of Penzance, Princess Ida, Patience, Amahl and Night Visitors, The Medium, Gondoliers, Marriage of Figaro, Don Pasquale, Die Fledermaus, Gypsy Baron, The Beggars Opera, La Traviata, Madame Butterfly, La Boehme, The Medium, The Merry Widow, The Barber of Seville (Rossini), Student Prince, Orphans in the Underworld, Hansel and Gretel; bassoonist with Highland Symphony Orch., Middletown, NY, 1986-90, New Sussex Cmty. Orch., Sparta, NJ, 1984-90. Pres. Del. Valley Arts Alliance, 1980—; bd. dirs. Tusten-Cochecton Libr., Narrowsburg, 1988—. Recipient Svc. award Siddha Meditation Ashram Found., South Fallsburg, NY, 1990, Recognition award Alliance NY State Arts Coun., 1995; named Woman of Yr., Catskill Mountain Bus. and Profl. Women, 1995; Gloria R. Krause Recital Hall named in her honor Del. Valley Arts Alliance, 2002 Office: Del Valley Opera PO Box 188 Narrowsburg NY 12764-0188

KRAUSE, HEATHER DAWN, data processing executive; b. Kansas City, Kans., May 6, 1956; d. Jack E. Firth and Bonnie Jo (Reeves) Cupps; m. Kerry Murray Krause, May 23, 1981. Cert., Kansas City Skill Ctr., 1980; BS in Computer Info. Sys., Friends U., Wichita, 2003. Cert. drafting tchr.; cert. in bus. supervision; cert. in Novell Netware system adminstrn. Assoc. drafter Black & Veatch, Kansas City, Mo., 1980; technician mech. design Wilcox Electric, Kansas City, 1980; network adminstr. Smith & Loveless, Inc., Lenexa, Kans., 1980—; owner Digital Design Technologies, Kansas City, Mo., 1989—; tech. editor Que Books Macmillan Computer Pub., 1994—. Instr. Longview C.C., Lee's Summit, Mo., 1987-93. Mem.: Phi Theta Kappa. Democrat. Avocations: camping, fishing, hiking, skiing, web site development. Home: PO Box 11319 Kansas City MO 64112-0319 E-mail: hkrause@krausehouse.com.

KRAUSE, HELEN FOX, otolaryngologist; b. Boston, Mar. 20, 1932; d. Nathan and Frances Lena (Rich) Fox; children: Merrick Eli, Beth Riva Harper, Kim Debra Codd. BS, U. Maine, 1954; MD, Tuft U., 1958. Diplomate Am. Bd. Otolaryngology. Intern Health Ctr. Hosps. Pitts., 1958-59; resident Eye & Ear Hosp., Children's Hosp., VA Hosp., 1959-62; pvt. practice Pitts., 1962—. Mem. otolaryngology adv. bd. U.S. Pharmacopea, 1991-96, 2000—, chmn., 1995-2000; clin. assoc. prof. U. Pitts. Sch. Medicine; vis. prof. Pan Hellenic Otorhinolaryngology Soc., Crete, Greece, 1993, Panama, Argentina, 1998, China, Hong Kong, 1999, Thailand, China, Taiwan, 2000, Pan Am. Oto Soc., 2000; assoc. clin. prof. U. Pitts. Sch. Medicine; pres., dir. 1st World Congress of Otorhinolaryngologic Allergy, Endoscopy and Laser Surgery, Athens, 1998, 2001; bd. dirs. Bayer Pharm. Women's Health Initiative; vis. prof. Thailand, Sigapore; lectr. 2nd World Congress Otolaryngology, Allergy and Immunology, 2001. Author, editor: Otolaryngic Allergy and Immunology, 1989; lectr., vis. prof. Singapore, Bangkok, Hong Kong (multiple tng. programs 1990); contbr. chpts. to books and articles to profl. jours. Pres. North Hills Jewish Community Ctr., Pitts., 1973-74; cons. North Allegheny Sch. Bd., Pitts., 1977; lectr. North Allegheny Sr. High Sch., Wexford, 1979-84; chmn. Desert Storm Project, North Hills Bus. and Profl. Women, 1991. Recipient Disting. Svc. award, Pa. Acad. Otolaryngology, 1993, Hon. Achievement award, Am. Acad. Otolaryngology Head and Neck Surgery, 1993, Bd. govs. Chair award, 2000, award, Panhellenic Soc. ORL-HNS, 2001; scholar Jackson Meml. Labs., Bar Harbor, Maine, 1954. Fellow ACS, Am. Acad. Otolaryngology Head and Neck Surgery (bd. govs. 1982-89, 90—), Am. Acad. Otolaryngologic Allergy (pres. 2984-85), Svc. award 1990, cert. appreciation 1991, Pres.'s award 1997, Spl. Achievement award 1997), Am. Acad. Facial Plastic and Rsch. Surgery; mem. Pa. Acad. Otolaryngology (pres. 1989-90), Internat. Soc. Otorhinolaryngic Allergy and Immunology (pres. 1995-98), Pitts. Otological Soc. (pres. 1983-85), Phi Beta Kappa, Phi Kappa Phi. Office: 1301 Aviara Pl Gibsonia PA 15044-8042 E-mail: hfk@nauticom.net.

KRAUSE, LOIS RUTH BREUR, chemistry educator; b. Paterson, N.J., Mar. 26, 1946; d. George L. and Ruth Margaret (Farquhar) Breur; m. Bruce N. Pritchard, 1968 (div. May 1982); children: John Douglas, Tiffany Anne,; m. Robert H. Krause, June 16, 1990. Student, Keuka Coll., 1964-65; BS in Chemistry cum laude, Fairleigh Dickinson U., 1980, MAT summa cum laude, 1994; postgrad., Stevens Inst. Tech.; PhD, Clemson U., 1996. With dept. R & D UniRoyal, Wayne, N.J., 1966-68, Jersey State Chem. Co., North Haledon, 1968-69, Inmont, Clifton, N.J., 1969; from chemist to sr. analyst Lever Bros., Edgewater, N.J., 1976-80; process engr. Bell Telephone Labs., Murray Hill, N.J., 1980-84, RCA, Somerville, N.J., 1984-86; sr. engr. electron beam lithography ops. Gain Electronics Corp., Somerville, 1986-88; ind. tech. cons. Pritchard Assocs., Budd Lake, N.J., 1988-92; tchr. of math. and scis. Mt. Olive Bd. Edn. (temporary assignments), 1990-92; tchr. chemistry Morris Hills Regional Dist., 1992-93; vis. asst. prof. edn. Clemson U., 1994—95, instr. chem. labs., 1994-96, vis. asst. prof. edn., 1995-96, vis. asst. prof. chemistry, 1996-98, lectr. phys. scis. dept. geol. scis., 1998—. Faculty fellow Office of Tchg. Effectiveness and Innovation Clemson U., 1999-2000; presenter workshops and profl. papers for profl. confs. Author: How We Learn and Why We Don't: Student Survival Guide, 1999, 2003; contbr. articles to profl. jours. Troop leader, trainer, cons. Bergen County council Girl Scouts U.S., 1969-80, troop leader Morris Area council, 1980-83, head com. Mt. Olive twp., 1980-81; den leader, den leader coach, trainer Boy Scouts Am., 1973-76. Peter Sammartino scholar, 1994. Fellow: Soc. Antiquaries (Scotland), Am. Inst. Chemists; mem.: AAUW, APA, ASCD, NRA (endowment mem.), IEEE (sr.), AAAS, Nat. Sci. Tchrs. Assn., N.Y. Acad. Scis., Assn. Women in Sci., Law Enforcement Alliance Am. (life), Am. Chem. Soc., Soc. Women Engrs., Am. Soc. Quality Control, Supreme Mil. Order of Temple of Jerusalum, Order Ea. Star, Single Action Shooting Soc., Catawba Valley Scottish Soc. (life patron), Clan Farquharson U.S.A. (asst. commr. for S.C. 1997—98, commr. Carolinas region 1998—99, clan genealogist 1999), Clan Morrison Soc. N.Am. (life), 2d Amendment Found. (life), Nat. Woodlot Owners Assn., Arbor Day Found., Mensa (cert. proctor 1999—), Clan Stewart Soc. of Am., Scottish Am. Mil. Soc. (color guard), 2d. Amendment Sisters, Marine Corps League Aux., Alpha Epsilon Lambda, Phi Delta Kappa (editor Clemson Kappan 1995—2000), Phi Omega Epsilon. Republican. Achievements include work in ultra fine line electron beam lithography, statis. process control, rsch. in learning and cognition; designed graduate course of student centered instruction. Home: 303 Cherokee Hills Dr Pickens SC 29671-8619 Office: Clemson U 442 Brackett Hl Clemson SC 29634-0001 Office Phone: 864-898-5113. E-mail: krause@clemson.edu., krause@cognitiveprofile.com., L_krause@bellsouth.net.

KRAUSE, MARCELLA ELIZABETH MASON (MRS. EUGENE FITCH KRAUSE), retired secondary education educator; b. Norfolk, Nebr.; d. James Haskell and Elizabeth (Vader) Mason; student Northeast C.C., 1928-30; B.S., U. Neb., 1934; M.A., Columbia, 1938; postgrad. summers U. Calif. at Berkeley, 1950, 51, 65, Stanford, 1964, Creighton U., 1966, Chico (Calif.) State U., 1967; m. Eugene Fitch Krause, June 1, 1945; 1 dau., Kathryn Elizabeth. Tchr., Royal (Nebr.) pub. schs., 1930-32, Hardy (Nebr.) pub. schs., 1933-35, Omaha pub. schs., 1935-37, Lincoln Sch. of Tchrs. Coll., Columbia, 1937-38, Florence (Ala.) State Tchrs. Coll., summer 1938, Tchrs. Coll., U. Nebr., 1938-42, Corpus Christi (Tex.) pub. schs., 1942-45, Oakland (Calif.) pub. schs., 1945-83. Bd. dirs. U. Nebr. Womens Faculty Club, 1940-42, mem. Nebr. State Tchrs. Conv. Panel, 1940-; mem. U. Nebr. Reading Inst., 1940; speaker Iowa State Tchrs. Conv., 1941; reading speaker Nebr. State Tchrs. conv., 1941; lectr. Johnson County Tchrs. Inst., 1942; chmn. Reading Survey Corpus Christi pub. schs., 1943; chmn. Inservice Reading Meetings Oakland pub. schs., 1948-57. Mem. Gov.'s Adv. Commn. on Status Women Conf., San Francisco, 1966; service worker ARC, Am. Cancer Soc., United Crusade, Oakland CD; Republican precinct capt., 1964-70; v.p. Oakland Fedn. Rep. Women. Ford Found. Fund for Advancement Edn. fellow, 1955-56; scholar Stanford, 1964; Calif. Congress PTA scholar U. Calif., 1965, Norfolk (Nebr.) Hall of Success Northeast C.C., 1990; recipient award of Excellence, U. Nebr. Tchrs. Coll., 1998. Mem. Nat. Council Women, AAUW (dir.), Calif. Tchrs. Assn., Oakland Mus. Assn., U. Nebr. Alumni Assn. (Alumni Achievement award 1984), Californians for Nebr., Ladies Grand Army Republic, 1960, 1986-87 Ruth Assn., Martha Assn. (pres. East Bay chpt. 1979), Sierra DAR (regent), Eastbay DAR Regents Assn. (pres.), Nebr. Alumni Assn. (life, alumni achievement award 1984), Grand Lake Bus. and Profl. Women, Internat. Platform Assn., Eastbay Past Matrons Assn., P.E.O., Pi Lambda Theta (pres. No. Calif. chpt.), Alpha Delta Kappa. Methodist. Mem. Order Eastern Star (past matron). Contbr. articles to profl. jours. Home: 5615 Estates Dr Oakland CA 94618-2725

KRAUSE, MARJORIE N. biochemist; b. Chgo., July 25, 1937; d. Robert Mortimer Krause and Eleanor Driese. BS, Mich. State U., 1959; MS, Cleve. State U., 1986. Cert. tchr., Mich.; cert. medical technologist in hematology Am. Soc. Clinical Pathologists. Technician Dartmouth Coll., Hanover, N.H., 1960-66, U. Vt., Burlington, 1966-70; technologist Case We. Res. U., Cleve., 1971-75, 89-93, U. Hosps., Cleve., 1975-79; lab technologist, med. technologist Cleve. Clinic Found., 1979-89; computer lab technician Lakeland C.C., Kirtland, Ohio, 1996-97, 99; narrator Sea World Ohio, Aurora, 1998, info. technologist, 2000. Judge youth sci. fair Ohio Acad. Scis., Columbus, Ohio, 1995, 96. Vol. Cleve. Orch., 1972—, Playhouse Sq. Found., Cleve., 1988—, Hunter Jumper Classic, 1999, 2000, 01, 02. Recipient Cert. Recognition, Playhouse Sq. Found., 1995, 96, 98. Avocations: natural history, bird watching, opera, theater, classical music. Home: 27500 Bishop Park Dr Apt 316 Wickliffe OH 44092-2757

KRAUSE, SONJA, chemistry educator; b. St. Gall, Switzerland, Aug. 10, 1933; came to U.S., 1939; d. Friedrich and Rita (Maas) K.; m. Walter Walls Goodwin, Nov. 27, 1970 BS, Rensselaer Poly. Inst., 1954; PhD, U. Calif., Berkeley, 1957. Sr. phys. chemist Rohm & Haas Co., Phila., 1957-64; vol. U.S. Peace Corps, Nigeria, 1964-65; asst. lectr. Lagos U.; asst. prof. Gondar Health Coll. U.S. Peace Corps, Ethiopia, 1965-66; vis. asst. prof. U. So. Calif., L.A., 1966-67; chemistry faculty Rensselaer Poly. Inst., Troy, N.Y., 1967—, prof., 1978—. Mem. coun. Gordon Rsch. Conf., 1981-83; mem. com. on polymers and engring. NRC, 1992-94; sabbatical Inst. Charles Sadron, Ctr. Rsch. on Macromolecules, Strasbourg, France, 1987. Author: (with others) Chemistry of Environment, 1978, 2d edit., 2002; editor: Molecular Electro-Optics, 1981; mem. editorial adv. bd. Macromolecules, 1982-84 Bd. dirs. Nat. Plastics Ctr. and Mus., Leominster, Mass., 1996-2000. Fellow Am. Phys. Soc. (coun. divsn. biol. physics 1980-93); mem. IUPAC (assoc.), Am. Chem. Soc. (chmn. ea. N.Y. sect. 1981-82, councillor 1993-95, adv. bd. petroleum rsch. fund 1979-81, assoc. mem. com. on edn. 1993-95, assoc. mem. internat. com. 1996), Biophys. Soc. (coun. 1977), N.Y. Acad. Scis., Sigma Xi (pres. Rensselaer Poly Inst. chpt. 1984-85). Office: Rensselaer Poly Inst Dept Chemistry Troy NY 12180 Business E-Mail: krauss@rpi.edu.

KRAUSS, ALISON, country musician; b. Champaign, Ill., July 23, 1971; d. Fred and Louise Krauss; m. Pat bergeson, Nov. 8, 1997. Albums Too Late to Cry, 1987, Two Highways, 1989, I've Got That Old Feeling, 1990, Every Time You Say Goodbye, 1992, I Know Who Holds Tomorrow, 1994 (Grammy award Best Southern, Country or Bluegrass Gospel album), Now That I've Found You, 1995, Forget About It, 1999, New Favorite, 2001, Live, 2002, (with Union Sta.) So Long So Wrong, 1997. Named to Grand Ole Opry, 1993; recipient Female Vocalist of Yr. award, Internat. Bluegrass Music Assn., 1990—91, 1993, 1995, Entertainer of Yr. award, 1991, 1995, Rising Video Star of Yr.-Europe award Country Music TV, 1995, Single of Yr. award, Country Music Assn, 1995, Vocal Event of Yr., 1995, Horizon award, 1995, Female Vocalist of Yr., 1995, Best New Country Artist Tour award Pollstar, 1995, Americana Artist of Yr. award Gavin, 1995, Country Artist of Yr. Rolling Stone, 1995, Grammy award Best Bluegrass Recording, 1992, Grammy award Best Country Collaboration with Vocals, 1995, Grammy award Best Female Country Vocal Performance, 1996, Bluegrass/Old-Time Music Album award, 1996, Best Female Vocalist, 1996, Grammy award Best Country Instrumental Performance, 1998, Grammy award Best Bluegrass Album, 1998, Grammy award Best Country Performance by a Duo or Group with Vocals, 1998. Office: Rounder Records 1 Camp St Cambridge MA 02140*

KRAUSS, JUDITH BELLIVEAU, nursing educator; b. Malden, Mass., Apr. 11, 1947; d. Leo F. and Dorothy (Conners) Belliveau; m. Ronald L. Krauss, Sept. 5, 1970; children: Jennifer Leigh, Sarah Elizabeth. BS, Boston Coll., 1968; MSN, Yale U., 1970. RN, Conn. Clin. specialist Conn. Mental Health Ctr., New Haven, 1971-73; clin. instr. Yale Sch. Nursing, New Haven, 1971-73; asst. prof. rsch. Yale U. Sch. Nursing, New Haven, 1973-78, assoc. dean, 1978-85, prof., dean, 1985-98, prof., 1998—; master Yale U. Silliman Coll., 2000—. Cons. pharm. and pub. cons., sch., govt. agys. Author: The Chronically Ill Psychiatric Patient and the Community, 1982 (Am. Jour. Nursing Book of Yr. 1982); editor Archives of Psychiat. Nursing, 1986—; mem. editl. bd. Psychiat. Rehab., Psychiat. Svcs.; contbr. articles to profl. jours. Trustee Boston Coll., 1991-99, trustee assoc., 2000—. Am. Nurses Found. scholar, 1978; recipient Chamberlain award Soc. Edn. and Rsch. in Nursing, 1994; named Disting. Alumna Yale Sch. Nursing, 1984; Am. Acad. Nursing/Inst. of Medicine sr. scholar-in-residence, 1998-99. Mem. ANA (Disting. Contbn. to Psychiat. Nursing award 1992, Leadership citation 2002), Am. Acad. Nursing, Conn. Nurses Assn. (mem. cabinet on edn. 1987-89, bd. dirs. 1988-91, rep. to ANA house of dels. 1988-91, Josephine Dolan award 1989), Sigma Theta Tau (Disting. Lectr. award 1987), Delta Mu (Founders award 1987). Avocations: tennis, golf, hiking, skiing. Office: Yale U Sch Nursing Ste 200 100 Church St S New Haven CT 06536-0740 E-mail: judith.krauss@yale.edu.

KRAUSS, JUDITH SCHEER, art dealer; b. Budapest, Hungary, Feb. 17, 1945; arrived in U.S., 1948; d. George and Magda (Kozma) Scheer; m. Alvin Krauss, June 4, 1966; children: Naomi, David, Sandor, Gabrielle. BA in Art History, C.W. Post Coll., 1986. Owner, ptnr. Steinbaum Krauss Gallery, N.Y.C., 1987—. Mem. com. Pub. Art Found., Greenvale, N.Y., 1989—; bd. overseers Hillwood Mus., Greenvale, 1992—. Mem. benefit com. City Arts, N.Y.C., 1994; active N.Y. Naral, 1990—, NOW, 1990—. Office: 132 Greene St New York NY 10012-3242

KRAUT, JOANNE LENORA, computer programmer, analyst; b. Watertown, Wis., Oct. 29, 1949; d. Gilbert Arthur and Dorothy Ann (Gebel) K. BA in Russian, U. Wis., 1971, MS in Computer Sci., 1973. Computer programmer U. Wis. Sch. Bus., Madison, 1969-72, Milw. Ins. Co., 1973-74; tech. coord. Wis. Dept. Justice, Madison, 1974-83; tech. svcs. supr. CRC Telecomm. (formerly Benchmark Criminal Justice Systems), New Berlin, Wis., 1983-89; sr. programmer/analyst Info. Comm. Corp., Pub. Safety Software, Inc., 1989-91; advanced systems engr. EDS, 1991-93; tech. specialist Time Ins., Milw., 1993-96; staff analyst Exacta Corp., Brookfield, Wis., 1996-98; prin. engr. Johnson Controls, Inc., 1998—. Mem. Lakewood Gardens Assn. (dir. 1981-83), Dundee Terrs. Condominium Assn. (officer 1983-99), Hartland Police & Fire Commn. (1998-99). Mem. AAUW, Phi Beta Kappa. Home: 37836 Division St Oconomowoc WI 53066-8910 Office: Johnson Controls Inc 507 E Michigan St Milwaukee WI 53202-5211

KRAUTER, LANA CAIN, retail executive; Pres., chief merchandising officer Goody's Family Clothing Inc., Knoxville, 2000—. Office: Goody's Family Clothing Inc 400 Goody's Ln Knoxville TN 37922

KRAVEC, CYNTHIA VALLEN, microbiologist; b. Newark, Sept. 8, 1951; d. William George and Elizabeth Irene (VanAllen) K. BS, Syracuse (N.Y.) U., 1974; MS, Seton Hall U., S. Orange, N.J., 1980; MBA, Monmouth Coll., W. Long Branch, N.J., 1986. Registered microbiologist. Sr. technician GIBCO/Invenex, Millburn, N.J., 1974-79; rsch. scientist Wampole Labs. div. Carter-Wallace Inc., East Windsor, N.J., 1979-90; scientist Roche Diagnostic Systems subsidiary Hoffmann-LaRoche, Inc., Nutley, N.J., 1990-98, Schering-Plough, Kenilworth, N.J., 1998—. Contbr. articles to profl. jours. Mem. Am. Soc. Microbiology, Tissue Culture Assn., Soc. of Indsl. Microbiology. Home: 1006 Coolidge St Westfield NJ 07090-1215 Office: Schering-Plough Rsch Inst 2015 Galloping Hill Rd Kenilworth NJ 07033-1300

KRAVETZ, KATHARINE, law educator; b. Houston, July 18, 1947; d. Frederick and Emily (Hollander) Kunreuther; m. Eric Stuart Kravetz, Aug. 25, 1974; children: Rachel, Daniel. BA, Harvard U., 1968; JD, Georgetown U., 1975. Bar: D.C. 1975, Md. 1981. Placement specialist TransCentury Corp., Washington, 1971—72; atty. Pub . Defender Svc. D.C., 1975—79, Law Offices of Katharine Kravetz, Washington, 1979—91; adj. prof. justice Am. U., Washington, 1979—82, adj. prof. law, 1988—91, asst. prof. justice, law and soc., 1991—94, 1998—2003, academic dir. Study Abroad, 1994—98. Mem. faculty senate Am. U., 2001—02; mem. steering com. on ex-offenders D.C. Govt./Non-Profit Coalition, Washington, 2000—02. Contbr. articles to profl. jours. Vol. U.S. Peace Corps, Rezaiyeh, Iran, 1968—70; mem., study circles D.C. Prisoners Legal Svcs. Project, 2000. Avocations: running, reading.

KRAVITCH, PHYLLIS A. federal judge; b. Savannah, Ga., Aug. 23, 1920; d. Aaron and Ella (Wiseman) K.. BA, Goucher Coll., 1941; LLB, U. Pa., 1943; LLD (hon.) (hon.), Goucher Coll., 1981, Emory U., 1998. Bar: Ga. 1943, U.S. Dist. Ct. 1944, U.S. Supreme Ct. 1948, U.S. Ct. Appeals (5th cir.) 1962. Practice law, Savannah, 1944—76; judge Superior Ct., Eastern Jud. Circuit of Ga., 1977—79, U.S. Ct. Appeals (5th cir.), Atlanta, 1979—81, U.S. Ct. Appeals (11th cir.), 1981—, sr. judge, 1996—. Mem. Jud. Conf. Standing Com. on Rules, 1994—2000. Trustee Inst. Continuing Legal Edn. in Ga., 1979—82; mem. Bd. Edn., Chatham County, Ga., 1949—55; mem. coun. Law Sch., Emory U., Atlanta, 1985—; mem. vis. com. Law Sch., U. Chgo., 1990—93; bd. visitors Ga. State U. Law Sch., 1994—; mem. regional rev. panel Truman Scholarship Found., 1993—2000; mem. vis. com. Goucher Coll., 2000—. Recipient Hannah G. Solomon award, Nat. Coun. Jewish Women, 1978, Trailblazer award, Greater Atlanta Hadassah, 2000, James Wilson award, U. Pa. Law Alumni Soc., 1992, Kathleen Kessler award, Ga. Assn. Women Lawyers, 2001, Shining Star award, Atlanta Women's Found., 2002. Fellow: Am. Bar Found.; mem.: ABA (Margaret Brent award 1991), Nat. Assn. Women Lawyers (Arabella Babb Mansfield award 1999), U. Pa. Law Soc., Am. Law Inst., Am. Judicature Soc. (Devitt award com. 1998—99), State Bar Ga., Savannah Bar Assn. (pres. 1976). Office: US Ct Appeals 11th Cir 56 Forsyth St NW # 202 Atlanta GA 30303-2205

KRAVITZ, ELLEN KING, musicologist, educator; b. Fords, N.J., May 25, 1929; d. Walter J. and Frances M. (Prybylowski) Kokowicz; m. Hilard L. Kravitz, Jan. 9, 1972; children: Julie Frances, Heather Frances stepchildren: Kent, Kerry, Jay. BA, Georgian Ct. Coll., 1964; MM, U. So. Calif., 1966, PhD, 1970. Tchr. 7th and 8th grade music Mt. St. Mary Acad., North Plainfield, NJ, 1949-50; cloistered nun Carmelite Monastery, Lafayette, La., 1950-61; instr. Loyola U., L.A., 1967; asst. prof. music Calif. State U., L.A., 1967-71, assoc. prof., 1971-74, prof., 1974—99, emeritus prof., 1999—. Founder Friends of Music Calif. State U., L.A., 1976. Mem. editl. adv. bd.: Jour. Arnold Schenberg Inst., 1977—87; editor: Jour. Arnold Schoenberg Inst., Vol. I, No. 3, 1977, Jour. Arnold Schoenberg Inst., Vol. II, No. 3, 1978; author (with others): Catalog of Schoenberg's Paintings, Drawings and Sketches; author: (book) Music in Our Culture, 1996. Guest lectr. Schoenberg Centennial Com., 1969—, mem., 1974. Mem.: Hist. Assn. L.A. Music Ctr., Am. Musicol. Soc., L.A. County Mus. Art, Pi Kappa Lambda, Mu Phi Epsilon.

KRAWCHECK, SALLIE L. investment company executive; b. 1966; BA, U. N.C., Chapel Hill; MBA, Columbia U., N.Y.C. Fin. analyst Salomon Brothers, Inc.; assoc. corp. fin. dept. Donaldson, Lufkin & Jenrette; sr. rsch. analyst Sanford C. Bernstein, 1994—98, dir. rsch., 1999—2001; exec. v.p. Alliance Capital Mgmt. L.P., 2001—02; chmn. and CEO Sanford C. Bernstein, 2001—02, Smith Barney, 2002—. Mem. Citigroup Mgmt. com., Citigroup Bus. Heads com. Office: Citigroup Global Mkts Holdings Inc 38th Fl 388 Greenwich St New York NY 10013*

KRAWCZYK, JUDY, state representative; b. Green Bay, Wis., Jan. 24, 1939; married; 3 children. Grad., Joseph Acad. H.S., 1957. Owner supper club; state assembly dist. 88 mem. Wis. State Assembly, Madison, 2000—, mem. colls. and univs., health, natural resources, small bus. and consumer affairs, state affairs, and vets. and mil. affairs coms. Mem.: Nat. Assn. Sportsmen Legislators, YWCA of Green Bay, Wis. Restaurant Assn., Zool. Soc. Inc. Brown County. Republican. Office: State Capitol Rm 9 N PO Box 8952 Madison WI 53708-8952

KREAGER, EILEEN DAVIS, administrative consultant; b. Caldwell, Ohio, Mar. 2, 1924; d. Fred Raymond and Esther (Farson) Davis. BBA, Ohio State U., 1945. With accounts receivable dept. M & R Dietetic, Columbus, Ohio, 1945-50; complete charge bookkeeper Magic Seal Paper Products, Columbus, 1950-53, A. Walt Runglin Co., L.A., 1953-54; office mgr. Roy C. Haddox and Son, Columbus, 1954-60; bursar Meth. Theol. Sch. Ohio, Delaware, 1961-86; adminstrv. cons. Fin. Ltd., 1986—. Ptnr. Coll. Administrv. Sci., Ohio State U., 1975-80; seminar participant Paperwork Systems and Computer Sci., 1965, Computer Systems, 1964, Griffith Found. Seminar Working Women, 1975; pres. Altrusa Club of Delaware, Ohio, 1972-73. Del. Altrusa Internat., Montreal, 1972, Altrusa Regional, Greenbrier, 1973. Mem. AAUW, Assoc. Am. Inst. Mgmt. (exec. coun. of Inst. 1979), Am. Soc. Profl. Cons., Internat. Platform Assn., Ohio State U. Alumna Assn., Columbus Computer Soc., Air Force Assn., Fraternal Order of Police Ohio, Motts Mil. Mus., Innovation Alliance, Toastmasters Internat., Ohio State U. Faculty Club, Univ. Club Columbus, Capital Club, Delaware Country Club, Columbus Met. Club, Friends Hist. Costume & Textile Collection Ohio State U., Internat. Order Police Ohio, Inc., Kappa Delta. Methodist. Home: PO Box 214 Columbus OH 43085-0214

KREBS, MARGARET ELOISE, publishing executive; b. Clearfield, Pa., Apr. 20, 1927; d. Henry Louis and Delia Louise (Beahan) Krebs. Grad. high sch. With Progressive Pub. Co., Inc., Clearfield, 1945—, bus. office mgr., 1959—60, bus. mgr., 1960—63, asst. to pub., 1963—69, dir., exec. v.p., 1969—77, pres., 1977—, assoc. pub., 1981—. V.p., sec. Clearfield Broadcasters, Inc., Stas. WCPA-AM and WQYX-FM, 1965—, dir., 1971—. Mem.: Pa. Newspaper Women's Assn., Lake Glendale Sailing Club (sec. 1966—), Clearfield Bus. and Profl. Women's Club (pres. 1952—53, dist. membership chmn. 1952—53). Democrat. Roman Catholic. Home: 526 Ogden Ave Clearfield PA 16830-2146 Office: 206 E Locust St Clearfield PA 16830-2423

KREBS, MARTHA, physicist, federal science agency administrator; PhD in Theoretical Physics, Cath. U. America, Washington, D.C., 1975. Staff dir. House subcommittee on energy development and applications, Washington, 1977-83; assoc. dir. planning and devel. Lawrence Berkeley Lab., 1983-93; dir. office of sci. Dept. of Energy, 1993-99; sr. fellow Inst. Def. Analyses. Office: Inst Def Analyses 1801 N Beauregard St Alexandria VA 22311-1701

KREBS, MARY, art educator; d. Andrew and Mary McCaffrey; m. Richard Krebs, May 11, 1980; 1 child, Michael. BS in Art Edn., SUNY, 1972; MBA in Mktg., Adelphi U., 1980; MEd in Elem. Edn., L.I. U., 1993. N.Y. State tchg. cert. elem. edn. (N-6), N.Y. State tchg. cert. art Eedn. (K-12). Buyer Bloomingdales, New York City, NY, 1973—80; dir. of customer svc. El Greco Leather (Candie's Shoes), Pt. Washington, NY, 1980—81; divisional mdse. mgr. Federated Dept. Stores, New York City, NY, 1981—83; graphic artist/sculptor Self Employed, Massapequa, NY, 1983—; tchr. - pre -sch. Cmty. Meth. Sch. & Our Lady of Assumption, Massapequa, NY, 1986—93; tchr. - elem. Massapequa Schools - Birch Ln./Unqua, Massapequa, NY, 1993—95; tchr. - art secondary Massapequa Schools - Berner Mid. Sch., Massapequa, NY, 1995—. Book, Rachel's Star of David. Bldg. rep. Massapequa Fedn. Tchrs., 2003. Named Outstanding Vol., YES Cmty. Counseling Ctr., 1996; named to Wall of Tolerance, Rosa Parks, Nat. Campaign for Tolerance, So. Poverty Law Ctr., Ala., 2003; recipient Cert. of Merit, Massapequa Bd. of Edn., 2002; M-TRACT and LINC-IT grants, NY Tchr. Ctr., Tech. Grants, 2000, 2001, Richard Gazzola Tchr. fellow, N.Y. State PTA, 2001. Mem.: Green County Coun. Arts, Massapequa S.D. (advisor 1993—), N.Y. State Art Tchr.'s Assn. (conf. presenter, spkr.'s bur. 1995—), N.Y. State PTA (life; chairperson 1985—2001, Hon. Life 2001), Massapequa PTA Coun. (life; mem. 1985—2001, Disting. Svc. 2001), Massapequa PTA (life; pres./mem. 1985—2001, tchr. rep. 1990, Hon. Life 1996). Avocations: sculpting, bowling, tennis. E-mail: mck_art@optonline.net.

KREBSBACH, KAREN K. state legislator; m. Paul Krebsbach; 2 children. BS, Minot State U. Corp. sec. Krebsbach's, Inc.; mem. N.D. State Senate from 40th and 50th dists., 1989-. Mem. adv. bd. SBA. Bd. dirs. Trinity Med. Ctr. Mem. Minot (N.D.) C. of C., Kiwanis Club, Trinity Med. Ctr. Republican. Home: PO Box 1767 Minot ND 58702-1767

KREDELL, CAROL RUTH, artist; b. Paterson, N.J., Oct. 20, 1924; d. Robert Blee and Stella Wilhelmina (Heffelfinger) K. BS, Pratt Inst., Bklyn., 1946; MS in Home Econs., U. Wis., 1957; MS in Art Edn., Syracuse U., 1968. Extension home economist York County/Pa. State U., State College, 1946-60; asst. prof. interior design Cornell U., Ithaca, N.Y., 1960-65; lectr. home econs. Syracuse (N.Y.) U., 1965-67; tchr. art and home econs. Ithaca City Sch. Dist., 1968-88; artist, vol. Trumansburg (N.Y.) Conservatory of Fine Arts, 1982—. Disaster vol. Tompkins County ARC, Ithaca, 1993—; vol. Trumansburg Conservatory fine arts and other shows, 1982—. Mem. Young Ladies Radio League, Second Area Young Ladies Amateur Radio Club, Tompkins County Amateur Radio Club (operator for disasters), Epsilon Sigma Phi. Republican. Presbyterian. Home: 1 Sunrise Ter Trumansburg NY 14886-9102

KREEK, MARY JEANNE, physician; b. Washington; d. Louis Francis and Esperance (Agee) K; m. Robert A. Schaefer, Jan. 24, 1970; children: Robert A., Esperance Anne. BA, Wellesley Coll., 1958; MD, Columbia U., Coll. Physicians and Surgeons, 1962; D honoris causa (hon.), Uppsala U., Sweden, 2000. Med. rschr. NIH, Bethesda, Md., 1957-62; intern, resident Cornell N.Y. Hosp. Med. Ctr., N.Y.C., 1962-65, fellow, 1965-67; instr. medicine Cornell Med. Coll., 1966-67; acad. medicine specializing in internal medicine, endocrinology, gastroenterology, clin. pharmacology, neuroscience, molecular genetics N.Y.C., 1966—. Mem. staff N.Y.-Presbyn. Hosp.-Weill Sch. Medicine of Cornell U., 1968—77, clin. asst. prof., asst. attending physician, now assoc. attending physician, adj. assoc. prof.; asst. prof. Rockefeller U., 1967—72, sr. rsch. assoc., physician, 1972—83, assoc. prof., physician, 1983—94, prof., sr. physician, head of lab., 1994—; head Ind. Lab. on Biology of Addictive Disease, 1975—94, head of lab., 1994—; sr. physician Rockefeller U. Hosp., 1994—; adj. prof. Beijing Med. U., 1996—2000, Peking U., 2000—, Karolinska Inst., 2001; mem. gen. medicine study sect. NIH, 1973—77; co-chmn. John E. Fogarty (NIH) Internat. Conf. Hepatotoxicity Due to Drugs and Chems., 1977, charter mem. peer rev. oversight group, 1996—2000; vis. prof. Pahlavi U., Shiraz, Iran, 1977; spl. adv. Nat. Inst. Drug Abuse, 1976—86, mem. nat. adv. coun., 1991—95, mem. molecular genetics consortium, 1999—; prin. investigator Rsch. Ctr. Biol. Basis Addictive Diseases, 1987—; mem. gastroenterology adv. com. FDA, 1975—79, 1992—96, NIH Gen. Clin., mem. gen. rsch. ctr. study sect. NIH, 1979—83, chmn., 1982—83, mem. exec. com. Coll. Problems Drug Dependence, 1982—87, 1989—94, chmn. exec. com., 1985—87, chair sci. program com., 1991—96; fellow CPDD, 1992—; dir. NIH-Nat. Inst. Drug Abuse Rsch. Ctr., 1987—. Recipient Borden Rsch. award, 1962, Career Scientist award Health Rsch. Coun. City N.Y., 1974-75, Dole/Nyswander award, Rsch. Scientist award NIH Gen. Clin. sect., 1978—, Mentor of Mentors award Am. Soc. Addiction Medicine, 1995, Assn. for Med. Edn. and Rsch. in Substance Abuse-Betty Ford award for outstanding rsch., 1996, R. Brinkley Smithers Disting. Scholar award Am. Soc. Addiction Medicine, 1999, Nathan B. Eddy award, Lifetime Rsch. award Coll. on Problems of Drug Dependence, 1999. Fellow: ACP, N.Y. Acad. Scis., Am. Fedn. for Clin. Rsch., Am. Coll. Neuropsychopharmacology; mem.: Assn. Am. Physicians, Coun. Fgn. Rels. (permanent mem. 2001—), Soc. on Neuroscis., Rsch. Soc. on Alcoholism, Internat. Narcotic Rsch. Conf. Group (exec. com. 1993—97, pres.-elect 2001—02, pres. 2002—), Internat. Assn. Study Liver, Am. Assn. Study Liver Diseases, Endocrine Soc., N.Y. Gastroent. Assn. (pres. 1987), Am. Gastroent. Assn., Shakespeare Soc. of Wellesley, Sigma Xi, Phi Beta Kappa. Office: Rockefeller U New York NY 10021

KREHTINKOFF-YARLOVSKY, NINA, nursing administrator, medical-legal consulting firm owner; b. Flin Flon, Man., Can., Oct. 5, 1955; d. Vasyl Nicolov and Milka Georgi (Krehtinkoff) Yarlovsky; m. Jay Richard Fisherman, June 26, 1983 (div. Dec. 1996). BS, Roanoke Coll., 1977; postgrad., Autonomous U. Guadalajara, 1977-79; MS, Pace U. Grad. Sch. Nursing, 1982. Legal nurse cons., cert. profl. in utilization rev., profl. in utilization mgmt. Staff nurse oncology Yonkers (N.Y.) Gen. Hosp., 1982-83, Montefiore Med. Ctr., Bronx, N.Y., 1984-85; br. mgr., nursing supr. Staff Builders, Health Care Svcs., Inc., Flushing, N.Y., 1985-88; inpatient nurse mgr. Ritter-Scheuer Hospice, Bronx, 1988-90; supr. home care Jacob Perlow Hospice, Beth Israel Med. Ctr., N.Y.C., 1990; patient care mgr. Westmoreland Hospice, Greensburg, Pa., 1992-93; dir. clin. svcs. Olsten Kimberly Quality Care, Inc., White Plains, N.Y., 1993-94; utilization review supr. Staff Builders, Health Care Svcs., Inc., Washington, 1994-95; sr. utilization rev. nurse ADP Integrated Med. Solutions, Rockville, Md., 1996—2003; pres., owner Med-Law Analysis, Inc., 2001—; clin. care mgr. Am. Healthways, Columbia, 2004—. Presenter AIDS conf. Mem.: Am. Bd. Quality Assurance and Utilization Rev. Physicians (diplomate 1997—), Nat. Alliance Cert. Legal Nurse Cons. (mem. 2001—). E-mail: medlaw@adelphia.net.

KREIBICH, ROBIN G. state legislator; b. June 4, 1959; BA, U. Minn.; postgrad., Brown Inst. Broadcasting. Former TV anchorman; former media specialist U. Wis., Eau Claire; mem. from dist. 93 Wis. State Assembly, Madison, 1992—. Address: 3437 Nimitz St Dr Eau Claire WI 54701-7200

KREINHEDER, HAZEL FULLER, genealogist, historian; b. Northampton, Mass., Aug. 27, 1935; d. John Herbert and Hazel Gertrude (Lamica) Fuller; m. Robert Frederick Kreinheder, Nov. 14, 1959; children: John Frederick, Paul Robert. BA, U. Mass., 1957. Lab. asst. dept. chemistry Amherst (Mass.) Coll., 1952-57; rsch. analyst Dept. Def., Fort George G. Meade, Md., 1957-63; libr. staff mem. Columbia Hist. Soc., Washington, 1976-77; hist. rschr. Washington, 1977-81; staff genealogist DAR, Washington, 1981-85, corrections genealogist, 1985-2001, ethnic and minority genealogist, 1997—, asst. dir. genealogy divsn., 2001—. Hist./geneal. cons. Washington Perspectives, Inc., 1977—90. Co-author/author: 5 booklets. Mem. exec. bd. Capitol Hill Babysitting Coop., 1966—68; mem. Com. 100 Fed. City, 1978—, mem. hist. preservation com., 1978—81; vol. pre-sch. vision screening program Prevention Blindness Soc., 1969—72; mem. Oldest Inhabitants DC, 1999—, Bryan Sch. Neighborhood Assn., 1995—, Nat. Bldg. Mus., 1999—; vol. Friends of Libr./U. Mass.; mem. Cir.-on-the-Hill, treas., 1964—65. Named Hon. Ky. Col., 2003; recipient Capitol Hill Citizen of the Yr., Capitol Hill Restoration Soc., 1970. Mem.: DAR (life; nat. vice chmn.'s assn., vice chair patriot index com. 1992—95, Mary Mattoon chpt. libr. 1996—, vice chair minority rsch. lineage rsch. com. 1998—), Soc. Genealogique Canadienne-Francaise, Soc. Genealogy Que., Nat. Geneal. Soc., Am. Hist. Assn., Orgn. Am. Historians, Capitol Hill Restoration Soc. (sec. 1967—68, treas. 1968—70, co-chmn. hist. preservation com. 1979—81, chmn. ho. com. 1979—81), Friends of Evergreens, Friends of Libr., Nat. Assn. Rail Passengers, Nat. Mus. Am. Indian (charter mem.), Nat. Inst. Geneal. Rsch. Alumni Assn., Mass. Soc. DAR. Republican. Lutheran. Avocations: civic activities, reading, needlework. Home: 113 Kentucky Ave SE Washington DC 20003-1447 Office: Nat Soc DAR 1776 D St NW Washington DC 20006-5303

KREISSMAN, STARRETT, librarian; b. N.Y.C., Jan. 4, 1946; d. Bernard and Shirley (Relis) K.; m. David Dolan, Apr. 13, 1985; 1 child, Sonya. BA, Grinnell Coll., 1967; MLS, Columbia U., 1968. Asst. circulation libr. Columbia U., N.Y.C., 1968-70; sci. libr. N.Y. Pub. Libr., N.Y.C., 1970-71; outreach libr. Stanislaus County Free Libr., Modesto, Calif., 1971-73, Oakdale libr., 1974-79, acquisitions libr., 1979-85, br. supr., 1985-92, county libr., 1992—99; libr. dir. Ventura County Libr., 1999—. Writer book revs. Stanislaus County Commn. on Women. Mem. ALA, Pub. Libr. Assn., Calif. Libr. Assn. (legis. com. 1993-95, 2003—, Libr. of Yr. 1998), Rotary. Office: Ventura County Library 646 County Square Dr Ste 150 Ventura CA 93003

KREIZMAN-RECZEK, KAREN INGRID, librarian; b. Phila., Pa., Jan. 19, 1965; d. Bernard Kreizman and Marilyn Ann Lieberman; m. Peter R. Reczek, Aug. 28, 1999. BS in Social Sci. and Humanities, Clarkson U., 1985; MLS, SUNY, Buffalo, NY, 1987. Libr. technician R&D Devel. Ctr., Occidental Chem. Corp., Grand Is., NY, 1987-88; asst. libr. Pharm. Rsch. Inst., Bristol-Myers Squibb Co., Buffalo, 1988-90, rsch. libr., 1990-91, info. scientist, 1991-93, sr. info. scientist, 1993-96; global info. specialist Bureau Veritas, Buffalo, 1996-97, mgr., 1997—. Author: Establishing an Information Center: A Practical Guide, 1999; contbr. articles to profl. jour. Mem. Med. Libr. Assn. (sr.), Soc. of Competitive Intelligence Profls., Spl. Librs. Assn. (bull. editor 1993-95, chair elect 1994-95, chair pharm. divsn. 1995-96, bd. dir. 2001-2003, profl. devel. com. 2003—, pres.-elect 2003—), Western NY Health Sci. Librs. (past-pres. 1995-96, pres. 1994-95, v.p. 1993-94, newsletter editor 1992-94, exec. bd. 1990-91, 92-93), Western NY Libr. Resources Coun. (continuing edn. chair 1992-93, regional automation chair 1993-95, bd. trustees 2000—, pres. 2003), Beta Phi Mu. Home: 22 Towhee Ct East Amherst NY 14051-1606 Office: Bureau Veritas 100 Northpointe Pkwy Buffalo NY 14228-1884

KREMENTZ, JILL, photographer, author; b. N.Y.C., Feb. 19, 1940; d. Walter and Virginia (Hyde) Krementz; m. Kurt, Jr. Vonnegut, Nov. 1979; 1 child, Lily Vonnegut. Student, Drew U., 1958—59; attended Art Students League. With Harper's Bazaar mag., 1959—60, Glamour mag., 1960—61; pub. rels. staff Indian Industries Fair, New Delhi, 1961; reporter Show mag., 1962—64; staff photographer N.Y. Herald Tribune, 1964—65, staff photographer Vietnam, 1965—66; assoc. editor Status-Diplomat mag., 1966—67; contbg. editor N.Y. mag., 1967—68; corr. Time-Life Inc., 1969—70; contbg. photographer People mag., 1974—; chancellor Nat. Portrait Gallery. Contbr. photography numerous U.S. and fgn. periodicals; one-woman shows include Madison (Wis.) Art Ctr., 1973, U. Mass., Boston, 1974, Nikon Gallery, N.Y.C., 1974, Del. Art Mus., Wilmington, 1975, Newark Mus., 1994, Staley-Wise Gallery, 1996, The Margaret Mitchell House, Atlanta, 1999, The Nat. Portrait Gallery, Represented in permanent collections Mus. Modern Art, Libr. of Congress, The Face of South Vietnam (text by Dean Brelis), 1968, Words and Their Masters (text by Israel Shenker), 1974; author (photographer): Sweet Pea: A Black Girl Growing

Up in the Rural South (foreword by Margaret Mead), 1969, A Very Young Dancer, 1976, A Very Young Rider, 1977, A Very Young Gymnast, 1978, A Very Young Circus Flyer, 1979, A Very Young Skater, 1979, The Writer's Image, 1980, How It Feels When a Parent Dies, 1981, How It Feels to be Adopted, 1982, How It Feels When Parents Divorce, 1984, The Fun of Cooking, 1985, Lily Goes to the Playground, 1986, Jack Goes to the Beach, 1986, Katherine Goes to Nursery School, 1986, Jamie Goes on an Airplane, 1986, Tanya Goes to the Dentist, 1986, Benjy Goes to a Restaurant, 1986, Holly's Farm Animals, 1986, Zachary Goes to the Zoo, 1986, A Visit to Washington, D.C., 1987, How It Feels to Fight for Your Life, 1989, A Very Young Skier, 1990, A Very Young Musician, 1990, A Very Young Gardener, 1990, A Very Young Actress, 1991, How It Feels to Live With a Physical Disability, 1992, The Writer's Desk, 1996, The Jewish Writer, 1998. Recipient Nonfiction award, Washington Post/Children's Book Guild, 1984, ACCH Joan Fassler Meml. Book award, 1990, Equality, Dignity, Independence award, Nat. Easter Seals, 1992. Mem.: PEN. Address: care Alfred A Knopf Inc 201 E 50th St New York NY 10022-7703

KREMER, HONOR FRANCES (NOREEN KREMER), real estate broker, small business owner; came to U.S., 1961; m. Manny Kremer; 1 child, Patrick David. BS, CUNY; MS, Baruch Coll. Group sec. Bentalls, Ltd.; office mgr. Aschner Assocs., N.Y.C., 1961-63; pub. rels. asst. McMaster U., Hamilton, 1963-64; office mgr. Packaging Components, N.Y.C., 1965-67; head acctg. Shaller Rubin Assocs., N.Y.C., 1967-72, v.p. fin. and adminstrn., 1979-82, sr. v.p., mem. exec. com., 1982—, sec.-treas. multimedia divsn., 1972-75. Pvt. practice bus. cons., 1986-89; sr. v.p., exec. v.p., fin. officer Lewis & Gace Med. Advt., N.Y.C., 1989-91; broker, owner Malone Kremer Realty, Leonia, N.J., 1991—; bus. cons., 1991—. Mem. Nat. Assn. Realtors, N.J. Assn. Realtors, Nat. Fedn. Bus. and Profl. Women (bd. dirs., v.p.), Advt. Fin. Mgmt. Group. Roman Catholic.

KRENDL, CATHY STRICKLIN, lawyer; b. Paris, Tex., Mar. 14, 1945; d. Louis and Margaret Helen (Young) S.; m. James R. Krendl, July 5, 1969; children: Peggy, Susan, Anne. BA summa cum laude, North Tex. State U., 1967; JD cum laude, Harvard U., 1970. Bar: Alaska 1970, Colo. 1972. Atty. Hughes, Thorsness, Lowe Gantz & Clark, Anchorage, 1970-71; adj. prof. U. Colo. Denver Ctr., 1972-73; from asst. prof. to prof. law, dir. bus planning program U. Denver, 1973-83; ptnr. Krendl, Krendl, Sachnoff & Way, Denver, 1983—. Author: Colorado Business Corporation Act Deskbook, 2003-4; editor: Colorado Methods of Practice, 8 vols. 1983-2004, Closely Held Corporations in Colorado, vols. 1-3, 1981; contbr. articles to profl jours. Named Disting. Alumna North Tex. State U., 1985. Mem. Colo. Bar Assn. (bd. govs. 1982-86, 88-91, chmn. securities subsect. 1986, bus. law sect. 1988-89, Professionalism award), Denver Bar Assn. (pres. 1989-90). Avocation: reading. Home: 1551 Larimer St Apt 1101 Denver CO 80202-1630 E-mail: csk@krendl.com.

KRENDL, KATHY, dean; BA in english, Lawrence U., 1972; MA in journalism, Ohio St. U., 1977; Ph.D in comm., U. Mich., 1982. Dean Ind. U., Sch. of Continuing Studies, 1994—96, Ohio U. Coll. Comms., Athens, 1996—. Office: Ohio U Coll Comm RTVC 483B Athens OH 45701-2905

KRENEK, DEBBY, newspaper editor; d. Ernest Reed and Elizabeth Pendleton (Brown) K.; m. James C. Roberts Jr., Feb. 28, 1987; children: Christine Elizabeth Roberts, Taylor James Roberts. BJ, Tex. A&M Univ., 1978. Copy editor Corpus Christi (Tex.) Caller-Times, 1978-81; news editor Dallas Times Herald, 1981-85, asst. bus. editor, 1985-86, exec. news editor, 1986-87; dep. news editor N.Y. Daily News, 1987-88, dep. mng. editor, 1988-91, mng. editor, 1991-93, exec. editor, 1993-97, editor-in-chief, 1997-2000; assoc. editor Newsday, 2001—. Chief creative officer Petplace.com, 2000—01. Named to Acad. of Women Achievers YWCA, N.Y., 1992. Avocations: photography, tennis, home renovation. Office: Newsday 235 Pinelawn Rd Melville NY 11747-4250*

KRENEK, MARY LOUISE, political scientist, researcher; b. Wharton, Tex., Dec. 8, 1951; d. George P., Jr. and Vlasta (Zahn) Krenek. AA, Wharton County Jr. Coll., 1972; BA, Tex. A&I U., Corpus Christi, 1974; MA, St. Mary's U., San Antonio, 1992; Czech lang. cert., Charles U., Prague, Czech Republic, 1994. Cert. secondary and elem. tchr. Tex. Polygraph examiner, San Antonio, 1979-81; ind. contractor market, polit. and social rschr. San Antonio, Houston, 1982—. Substitute tchr., tchr. San Antonio Ind. Sch. Dist., 1981—82, Houston Ind. Sch. Dist., 1991—98, 2002—; instr. govt. Wharton County Jr. Coll., 1997—99; assoc. J.C. Penney Co., Inc., 1994—2000; with Am. Acad. Excellence, Houston. Sec. Egypt Plantation Mus., 2003; del. Tex. Dem. Conv., 1971—72. 1st lt. U.S. Army, 1975—78, lt. col. USAR, 1978—2003, ret. USAR, 2003. Mem.: CESAT, Am. Polit. Sci. Assn., Nat. Assn. Self-Employed, Point/Counterpoint (Houston chpt.), Women in Mil. Svc. Am. Meml. Found. (charter), Houston Czech Cultural Ctr., Wharton County Hist. Mus. Assn. (assoc.), Res. Officers Assn. (sec.-treas. Alamo chpt., jr. v.p. Dept. Tex., sec. Greater Houston chpt., ROTC coord.), St. Mary's U. Alumni Assn., Am. Legion, Pi Sigma Alpha. Roman Catholic. Avocations: reading, writing, travel. Home: 10502 Fountain Lake Dr Stafford TX 77477-3711 also: PO Box 310 Egypt TX 77436-0310 Personal E-mail: marykrenek01@aol.com.

KRENTZ, JANE, state legislator, elementary school educator; b. Mpls., Dec. 24, 1952; children: Leah, Sarah, Jeremy. BA, Hamline U., 1971; MEd, U. Minn., 1996. Elem. sch. tchr.; mem. Minn. Senate from 51st dist., St. Paul, 1993—. Mem. C. of C. Stillwater, Forest Lake, Anoka County (all Minn.). Home: 14177 Paris Ave N Stillwater MN 55082-8523 Office: Minn State Senate 234 State Capitol Saint Paul MN 55155-0001

KREPS, JUANITA MORRIS, economics educator, former government official; b. Lynch, Ky., Jan. 11, 1921; d. Elmer M. and Cenia (Blair) Morris; m. Clifton H. Kreps, Jr., Aug. 11, 1944; children: Sarah, Laura, Clifton. AB, Berea Coll., 1942; MA, Duke U., 1944; PhD, 1948; LLD (hon.), Bryant Coll., 1972, U. N.C. at Chapel Hill, 1973, Tulane U., Colgate U., 1980, Trinity Coll., 1981, U. Rochester, Grove City Coll., 1984, Davidson Coll., 1990, Lenoir-Rhyne Coll., 1991, U. Notre Dame, 1992, Duke U., 1993; LittD (hon.), Cornell Coll., 1973, Western Md. Coll., 1982; LHD (hon.), Denison U., 1973, U. Ky., Queens Coll., St. Lawrence U., 1975, Wheaton Coll., 1976, Claremont Grad. Sch., Berea Coll., 1979. Instr. econs. Denison U., 1945-46, asst. prof., 1948-50; mem. faculty Duke U., 1955-77, assoc. prof., 1962-68, prof. econs., 1968-77, James B. Duke prof., 1972-77, James B. Duke prof. emerita, 1979—, asst. provost, 1969-72, v.p., 1973-77, v.p. emerita, 1979—; sec. U.S. Dept. Commerce, 1977-79. Mem. adv. com. Congl. Commn. for the Future of Worker Mgmt. Rels., Secs. of Commerce and Labor, 1993-94. Author: (with C.E. Ferguson) Principles of Economics, 2d rev. edit, 1965, Lifetime Allocation of Work and Income, 1971, Sex in the Marketplace: American Women at Work, 1971, Women and the American Economy, 1976; co-author: (with Richard Perlman and Gerald Somers) Contemporary Labor Economics, 1973; Editor: Employment, Income and Retirement Problems of the Aged, 1963, Technology, Manpower and Retirement Policy, 1966, Sex, Age and Work, 1975. Bd. dirs. Am. Coun. on Germany, Rsch. Triangle Found., Ednl. Testing Svc., 1972-77; mem. Nat. Manpower Policy Task Force; trustee Berea Coll., 1972-78, 80-98, Duke Endowment, 1979—. Nat. Humanities Ctr., 1983-86, U. N.C., Wilmington, 1993-2001, Humrro, 1980-83, Coun. Fgn. Rels., 1983-89, Kenan Inst. Pvt. Enterprise of U. N.C., Chapel Hill, 1995—; pres. bd. overseers Tchrs. Ins. and Annuity Assn., 1992-96; bd. dirs. TIAA, 1968-72, 85-96, Coll. Retirement Equities Fund, 1972-77. Named to Presl. Commn. on Nat. Agenda for the 80's, 1979; recipient N.C. Pub. Svc. award, 1976, Stephen Wise award, 1978, Woman of Yr. award Ladies Home Jour., 1978, Duke U. Alumni award, 1983, Haskins award Coll. Bus. and Pub. Adminstrn., NYU, 1984, First Corp. Governance award Nat. Assn. Corp. Dirs., 1987, Dir.'s Choice Leadership award Nat. Women's Econ. Alliance Found., 1987, Disting. Meritorious Svc. medal Duke U. Alumni, 1987. Fellow Gerontol. Soc. (v.p. 1971-72), Am. Acad. Arts and Scis.; mem. AAUP, AAUW (Achievement award 1981), Am. Econ. Assn. (v.p. 1983-84), So. Econ. Assn. (pres. 1975-76), Indsl. Rels. Rsch. Assn. (exec. com.).

KRESS, JILL CLANCY, human resources professional, consultant; b. Washington, Oct. 11, 1949; d. John William and Barbara Lois (Smith) Costello; m. Paul W. Combs, July 27, 2001; 1 child from previous marriage, Jason Patrick. BS in Edn., Jacksonville U., 1971. Tchr. Duval County Pub. Sch., Jacksonville, Fla., 1971—73; dir. Nat. Exec. Search, Washington, 1976—85; dir. human resources Cellmark Diagnostics, Germantown, Md., 1986—89, Life Technologies, Inc., Gaithersburg, Md., 1989—97; cons. HR Concepts, LLC, 1997—98; pres. HR Concepts, 2002—; v.p. Human Resources Am. WholeHealth, Reston, Va., 1998—2000; sr. dir. Conservation Internat., Wash., 2000—02; pres. HR Concepts LLC, 2002—. Workshop trainer Va. Tech., Blacksburg, 1992—, Md. U., College Park, 1991—, Hood Coll., Frederick, 1994—; biotech. adv. bd. Montgomery Coll. Mem. Soc. for Human Resources Mgmt., Biotechnology Indsl. Orgn. (steering com. mem.), Montgomery County High Technology Coun. (steering com.), Middle Atlantic Placement Assn. (adv. bd.). Republican. Roman Catholic. Avocations: racquetball, tennis, guitar. Office: Ste 307 301 High Gables Dr Gaithersburg MD 20878 Office Phone: 301-977-3776. E-mail: clancykio@comcast.net.

KRESS, MARY ELIZABETH, retired newspaper editor; b. Richmond, Va., Oct. 25, 1951; d. Samuel Kemp and Mary Elizabeth (King) Moody; m. Dean Herbert Kress, Jan. 20, 1973 (div. Feb. 1981); m. Ronald Lee Littlepage, Dec. 10, 1982: children: Ronald Kemp, Bramley Elizabeth. BS, Va. Commonwealth U., 1973. Editor M/G Fin. Weekly, Richmond, 1973-74, Richmond News-Leader, 1974-75, Petersburg (Va.) Progress-Index, 1975-77, The Fla. Times-Union, Jacksonville, 1977-92, now mng. editor, 1992-99; ret. Guest speaker Gannet Ctr. for Media Studies, N.Y.C., 1987. Active Riverside-Avondale Preservation, Inc., Jacksonville, 1987—; dir. Fla. Ballet at Jacksonville, 1980-81. Recipient Twin award YMCA, 1989. Mem. Investigative Reporters and Editors, Am. Soc. Bus. Writers and Editors, Ponte Vedra (Fla.) Inn Club. Home: 3331 Fitch St Jacksonville FL 32205-7824 Office: The Fla Times-Union 1 Riverside Ave Jacksonville FL 32202-4904

KRESS, NANCY, writer; b. Buffalo, Jan. 20; d. Henry Francis and Angelina (Canale) Konnigsor; m. Michael Joseph Kress, July 14, 1973 (div. 1986); children: Kevin Michael, Brian Stephen. BS in Edn., SUNY, Plattsburgh, 1969; MEd, SUNY, Brockport, 1978, MA in English, 1979. Cert. tchr. N.Y. K-6 and English 7-12. Grade 4 tchr. Penn Yan (N.Y.) Schs., 1970-73; tchr. grade 9 English Holley (N.Y.) Ctrl. Schs., 1979-80; instr. SUNY, Brockport, 1980-83; copywriter Stanton & Hucko, Inc., Rochester, N.Y., 1984-89; freelance writer, 1990—. Author: (novels) An Alien Light, 1988, Beggars in Spain, 1993, Beggars and Choosers, 1995, Beggars Ride, 1996, Oaths & Miracles, 1996, Maximum Light, 1997, Stinger, 1998, Yanked, 1999, Probability Sun, 2001, Probability Spun, 2002, Crossfire, 2003; columnist Writer's Digest mag., 1992—, Dynamic Characters, 1998, The Aliens of Earth, 1998, Breaker's Dozen, 1998, Probability Moon, 2000. Winner 1997 Nebula awd for Flowers of Aulit Prison. Mem. Sci. Fiction Writers Am. (nebula awards for best short story 1985, best novella 1991, hugo award for best novella 1992). Office: c/o Tor Books 14th Fl 175 5th Ave Fl 14 New York NY 10010-7703

KRETZSCHMAR, ANGELINA GENZER, small business owner, paralegal; b. San Antonio, Tex., July 19, 1946; d. Louis J. Genzer and Alma M. (Krause) Haase; m. Charles H. Kretzschmar, July 31, 1971. BBA cum laude, St. Mary's U., San Antonio, 1974. Budget analyst Fed. Govt., San Antonio, 1974-92, EEO specialist, 1992-96; owner, operator Kretzschmar Prop., San Antonio, 1971—. Fed. women's program mgr. Fed. Govt., San Antonio, 1992-96. Campaign treas. Citizens for Open Govt., San Antonio, 1988; polit. action com. Women's Polit. Caucas, San Antonio, 1993. Mem. Bus. & Profl. Women Inc. (com. chair), AAUW (public policy com. 1994), San Antonio Coun. of Fed. Womans Program Mgrs. (sec.), Federally Employed Women, Inc. (legis. chair). Democrat. Lutheran. Avocations: traveling, reading, political issues. Home and Office: 130 Navato Blvd San Antonio TX 78232-2255

KREUTER, GRETCHEN V. academic administrator; b. Mpls., May 7, 1934; d. Sigmund and Marvyl (Larson) von Loewe; m. Robert L. Sutton, 1993; children: David Karl, Betsy Ruth Rymes. BA, Rockford Coll., 1955; MA, U. Wis., 1958, PhD, 1961; LLD (hon.), Rockford Coll., 1992, Coll. St. Mary, 1994. Lectr. in Am. Studies Colgate U., Hamilton, N.Y., 1962-67; lectr. in history Coll. St. Catherine, St. Paul, 1969-71, Hamline U., St. Paul, 1971-72; prof. of history Macalester Coll., St. Paul, 1972-73, St. Olaf Coll., Northfield, Minn., 1975-80; asst. to pres. Coll. St. Catherine, St. Paul, 1980-84; asst. to v.p. acad. affairs U. Minn., Mpls., 1984-87; pres. Rockford Coll., Ill., 1987-92, Olivet (Mich.) Coll., 1992-93; sr. fellow Am. Coun. Edn., Washington, 1993-94; hon. fellow Inst. for Rsch. in Humanities U. Wis., Madison, 1994—; interim pres. Coll. of St. Mary, Omaha, 1995-96. Mem., chmn. Minn. Humanities Coun., St. Paul, 1974-83; mem. Mich. Humanities Coun., 1993, bd. dirs. Nat. Assn. State Humanities Commn., Washington, 1984-86. Author: An American Dissenter, 1969 (McKnight prize 1978), Running the Twin Cities: editor: Women of Minnesota, 1977, 2d edit., 1998, Two Career Family, 1978, Forgotton Promise: Race and Gender Conflict on a Small College Campus: A Memoir, 1996. Bd. dirs. Kobe Coll. Corp., Rockford Mus. Ctr., ACE Commn. on Minorities in Higher Edn., 1991-92, Mich. Humanities Coun., 1993-94. Address: 1666 Coffman St Apt 123 Falcon Heights MN 55108-1326 E-mail: gkreuter@facstaff.wisc.edu.

KREVSKY, MARGERY BROWN, talent agency executive; b. Phila., Oct. 24, 1944; d. John Lewis and Margery Jane (Moss) Brown; m. Joseph Langdon Stearns, Oct. 19, 1968 (div. Nov. 1979); 1 child, Joseph Leland Stearns; m. Seymour Krevsky, Feb. 11, 1981. BS in Elem. Edn., Lock Haven U., 1966; MFA in Retail Adminstrn., Tobe-Colburn, 1968. Tchr. 1st grade Yardley (Pa.) Sch. Sys., 1966-67; buyer Macy's Herald Sq., N.Y.C., 1968-69; asst. editor Glamour mag. Conde-Nast Publs., N.Y.C., 1969-71; mgr. fashion bur. Hudsons, Detroit, 1971-74; fashion merchandise mgr. Alvin's, Pontiac, Mich., 1974-81; pres., CEO Prodns. Plus, Birmingham, Mich., 1981—. Bd. dirs. Northwood U., Midland, Mich., Wayne State U., Detroit. Mem. Oakland Execs. Assn. (bd. dirs. 1990—), Adcrafters, Fashion Group, Women in Comm. Avocations: cooking, reading, aerobics. Office: Prodns Plus 30600 Telegraph Rd Ste 2156 Bingham Farms MI 48025-4532

KRIDLER, JAMIE BRANAM, children's advocate, social psychologist; b. Newport, Tenn., Jan. 23, 1955; d. Floyd A. and Mary Leslie (Carlisle) Branam; m. Thomas Lee Kridler, Mar. 19, 1989; children: Brittani Audra, Houston Scott, Clark Eaton, Sabrina Morrow. BS, U. Tenn., 1976, MS, 1977; PhD, Ohio State U., 1985; cert. interior design, retailing, profl. modeling, Bauder Fashion Coll., Atlanta, 1973. Fashion coord. Bill's Wear House, Newport, Tenn., 1969-77; buyer Shane's Boutique, Gatlinburg, Tenn., 1977-78; instr. Miami U., Oxford, Ohio, 1978-81; asst. prof. U. Tenn., Knoxville, 1985-89; mktg. dir. Profitt's Dept. Stores, Alcoa, Tenn., 1989-90; mktg. cons. Kridler & Kridler Mktg., Newport, Tenn., 1990-93; children's advocate Safe Space, Newport, Tenn., 1993-95. Adj. faculty U. Tenn., Knoxville, 1990-94, Walters State Coll., Morristown, Tenn., 1990-96, Carson Newman Coll., Jefferson City, Tenn., 1993-99; prof., FACS dept. chair East Tenn. State U., 1996—; founding mem. Cmty. House Coop., 1995—; mem., Tenn. evaluator Nation Funding Collaborative on Violence Prevention; participant Children's Def. Fund, Washington, 1992—; founding mem. Cmty. House Co-op; mem. Gov.'s Prevention Initiative and Family Needs Task Force. Costume designer Newport Theatre Guild: Guys and Dolls, Carousel, Fiddler on the Roof, Music Man, Crimes of the Heart, Rumors, Come Back to the Five and Dime, Jimmy Dean, Oliver, The Odd Couple, The Sunshine Boys, Harvey, Miami U. Dance Theatre, Ice Show. Bd. dirs. Safe Space, 1991-92; v.p. Newport Theatre Guild, 1991-92, pres., 1992-96, bd. dirs., 1990-97; dir. Cast and Crew Youth Theatre; creator Looking Glass Players. Named Outstanding Tchr., Miami U., Oxford, 1981, Outstanding Educator, U. Tenn., Knoxville, 1989; recipient numerous grants from univ. and non-profit orgns. Mem. NAACP, Lioness Club, Kappa Omicron Nu. Democrat. Lutheran. Avocations: yogi exercise, fashion design, dance, family activities. Home: 112 Woodlawn Ave Newport TN 37821-3031

KRIEBEL, DAWN KASTANEK, psychologist, educator, researcher; d. George Ronald and Helen Canci Kastanek; m. Jeffrey Coates Kriebel, July 15, 2000. BA in Philosophy and Psychology, West Chester U., 1996; PhD in Human Devel., U. Md., 2002. Instr./rschr. U. Md., College Park, 1997—2002; asst. prof. psychology Immaculata (Pa.) U., 2002—. Contbr. articles to profl. jours. Grantee, NIH/Immaculata U., 2003. Mem.: APA, Soc. for Rsch. in Child Devel. Achievements include research in socio-emotional adjustment of foster and adoptive children. Avocations: hiking, baking, reading. Office: Immaculata Univ 1145 King Rd Immaculata PA 19345 E-mail: dkriebel@immaculata.edu.

KRIEG, NANCY KAY, social worker, poet, musician; b. Jefferson City, Mo., Oct. 11, 1954; d. Arlin Darrell and Doris Lee Basinger; m. Russell Hugh Krieg, Mar. 15, 1975 (div. Aug. 18, 1988). BA in Psychology, Columbia Coll., 1994. Co-owner The Melody Shop, Jefferson City, Mo., 1975—85; co-mgr. Premiere Video, Osage Beach, 1991—94; social worker Miller County Psychol. Svcs., Eldon, 1994—95; substitute tchr. Eldon Pub. Schs., 1995; tchg. counselor, supr. Overland Pk., Kans., 1995—96; substitute tchr. Oak Hill Day Sch., Gladstone, Mo., 1997—98; tchg. counselor Concerned Care, Inc., Kansas City, 1998—. Author poetry. Recipient Mo. Writers' Week award for Poetry, Mo. Writers Guild, 1994, 1995, 1996, 1997. Mem.: Am. Fedn. Musicians, Acad. Am. Poets, The Writers Pl. Avocations: jazz drummer/percussion, mandolin, guitar, songwriting, poetry. Home: 1236 E 25th Ave Kansas City MO 64116

KRIEGE, KAREN THERESE, music educator; b. Oshkosh, Wis., Aug. 24, 1974; d. Thomas Paul and Mary Joyce Kriege. MusB with high honors, U. Wis., Stevens Point, 1996. Cert. tchr. Wis. Dir. bands Carl Traeger Mid. Sch., Oshkosh, 1997—; head counselor Am. Suzuki Inst., Stevens Point, 1997—. Bass clarinetist Ctrl. Wis. Symphony, Stevens Point, 1993—96, Oshkosh Symphony Orch., 1996—; sectional coach Oshkosh Youth Symphony, 1998—. Youth group leader Oakbrook Ch., Oshkosh, Wis., 2001—. Scholar, Dorothy Vetter Found., Stevens Point, 1993—95, Delta Omicron, 1993—95; Gov.'s Scholastic scholar, State of Wis., 1992—96. Mem.: Music Educators Nat. Conf., Delta Omicron, Pi Kappa Lambda. Avocations: travel, bicycling.

KRIEGER, BARBARA ANNE, broadcast technician, make-up artist, photographer, small business owner; b. Washington, Feb. 14, 1953; d. Sidney and Anne Krieger. BA in Childhood Edn., U. Md., 1975. Freelance photographer, Washington, 1971 ; tech. engr. Mut. Broadcasting, Washington, 1975—78, Sta. NBC/WRC/WKYS, Washington, 1979—80, Network Radio - NBC, Washington, 1980—87; makeup artist Sta. WRC-TV, Washington, 1987—93, video tape engr., 1993—2003; freelance tech. engr. Washington, 2003—. Cons., Washington, 2003—. Recipient 1st pl. photography, Washington Post, 2d pl. photography, Farmers Bank, 1st pl. photography, Silverspring Dist. Com., 3d pl. photography. Mem.: Nat. Assn. Broadcast Engrs. and Technicians - Comm. Workers Am. (v.p. local 31 2002—). Avocations: crafts, swimming, jewelry design. Personal E-mail: LocalSky@aol.com.

KRIEGER, LOIS B. retired state agency administrator; b. Merritt, B.C., Can., Nov. 4, 1917; came to the U.S., Feb. 1918; d. Howard Irving and Selma (Nelson) Boylan; m. James H. Krieger, 1938 (dec. 1975); children: James B.(dec.), Tor, Terra, Lex D., W. Heath, A. Kim. Cert., U. Calif., Berkeley, 1937. Bd. dirs. The Met. Water Dist. So. Calif., 1976-2001, ret., 2001. Chairperson MWO, So. Calif., 1989-92. Trustee U. Calif., Riverside, 1978—. Mem. Assn. Calif. Water Agys. (pres. 1987-89, mem. adv. com.), Assn. State Water Agys. (life). Avocations: reading, family activities. Home: 1035 Scott Dr Apt 402 Prescott AZ 86301-1776 E-mail: lois@primenet.com.

KRIEGER, MARCIA SMITH, federal judge; b. Denver, Mar. 3, 1954; d. Donald P. Jr. and Marjorie Craig (Gearhart) Smith; m. Michael S. Krieger, Aug. 26, 1976 (div. July 1988); children: Miriam Anna, Matthias Edward; m. Frank H. Roberts, Jr., Mar. 9, 1991; stepchildren: Melissa Noel Roberts, Kelly Suzanne Roberts, Heidi Marie Roberts. BA, Lewis & Clark Coll., 1975; JD, U. Colo., 1979. Bar: Colo. 1979, U.S. Dist. Ct. Colo. 1979, U.S. Ct. Appeals (10th cir.) 1979. Rotary grad. fellow U. Munich, Germany, 1975—76; assoc. Mason, Reuler & Peek, P.C., Denver, 1976-83, Smart, DeFurio Brooks, Eklund & McClure, Denver, 1983-84; ptnr. Brooks & Krieger, P.C., Denver, 1984-88, Wood, Ris & Hames, P.C., Denver, 1988-90; pvt. practice U.S. Bankruptcy Court, 10th Circuit, Denver, 1990-94; judge U.S. Bankruptcy Ct., 10th Circuit, Denver, 1994-2000; chief judge U.S. Bankruptcy Ct., Denver, 2000—. Lectr. U. Denver Grad. Tax Program, 1987—, Colo. Soc. CPA's, Denver, 1984-87, Colo. Continuing Legal Edn., Denver, 1980—, Colo. Trial Lawyers Assn., Denver, 1987—; adj. instr. U. Colo. Sch. Law, 1999-2001; spkr. in field. Contbr. articles to profl. publs. Vestry person Good Shepherd Episcopal Ch., Englewood, 1986—, judge and coach for H.S. mock trial. Mem. Colo. Bar Assn. (past chair Com. Court Reform; past mem. Professionalism Com.), Arapahoe Bar Assn., Arraj Inn of Ct. (v.p.), Nat. Conf. Bankruptcy Judges (past chair Internat. Law Rels. Com, Ethics Com.; past mem. Newsletter Com., Program Com.), Littleton Adv. Coun. for Gifted and Talented education, Alfred A. Arraj Inn of Court (past pres.), Colo. Jud. Coordinating Coun., Kenya Children Found. (bd. dirs.). Republican. Avocations: international relations, travel, marksmanship. Office: US Dist Ct Dist Colo Alfred J Arraj US Courthouse 901 19th St A-941 Denver CO 80294

KRIEGSMAN, SALI ANN, arts executive, artistic director, writer, consultant; b. N.Y.C., Apr. 16, 1936; d. Aaron and Charlotte (Pomeranz) Ribakove; m. Alan M. Kriegsman, Nov. 28, 1957. MA, Goddard Coll., 1976. Rsch. assoc. Scripps Clinic and Rsch. Found., La Jolla, Calif., 1961-65; exec. editor Am. Film Inst., Washington, 1969-74; asst. prof. George Washington U., Washington, 1979-80; dance cons. Smithsonian Instn., Washington, 1979—84; dir. dance program NEA, Washington, 1986-95; exec. dir. Jacob's Pillow Dance Festival, Becket, Mass., 1995-98. Writer An Evening of Dance, In Performance at the White House, Sta. WETA-TV, 1998; mem. arts acad. adv. com. Coll. Bd., 1996-97; mem. nat. dance and media project leadership group UCLA, 1996-2000; mem. steering com. Am. Assembly Art, Tech. and Intellectual Property, 2000-02; sr. advisor Digital Dance Libr., 2002-03. Author: Modern Dance in America: The Bennington Years, 1981; contbr.: Britannica Book Of The Year, 1984-86; contbg. author: International Encyclopedia of Dance, 1998. Bd. dirs. Mass. Mus. Contemporary Art, 1995-97, Meredith Monk/The House Found., 2001—; pres. Dance Heritage Coalition, 1999-2000. Recipient Flo-Bert award N.Y. Com. To Celebrate Nat. Tap Dance Day, 1997, Oklahoma City U. Preservation of Heritage Am. Dance award, 1999, Tap Preservation award, N.Y.C. Tap Festival, 2002; fellow Va. Ctr. for Creative Arts, 2003. E-mail: salann@verizon.net.

KRINER, SALLY GLADYS PEARL, artist; b. Bradford, Ohio, Jan. 29, 1911; d. Henry Walter and Pearl Rebecca (Brubaker) Brant; m. Leo Louis Kriner, Feb. 28, 1933; children— Patricia Staab, Jane Palombo. Grad. Arsenal Tech. sch. Indpls.; student Ind. U.-Indpls., 1954, Herron Sch. Art, Indpls., 1958. Exhibited in one woman shows Hoosier Salon, Indpls., 1960,

Village Art Gallery, Southport, Ind., 1967, 70, 73, Brown County Art Guild, Nashville, Ind., 1970, 74, 77, 80, 83, 87, 92; group shows include South Side Art League, Indpls., 1959-74, Indpls. Art League, 1959-64, Brown County Art Guild, 1969—, Hoosier Salon, 1961, 65, 67, 68, 73, 75, 76, 77, 82, 86, 87, 91, 95, Frames and Things Gallery, 1995; represented in permanent collections Riley Hosp., Indpls., others. Founder Southside Women's Symphony Com., Indpls., 1958; treas. Perry Twp. Republican Club, Ind., 1960-65; pres. State Assembly Women's Club, 1965-67; bd. dirs. ARC, Indpls., 1942-45, Southside Civic Orgn., Indpls., 1954, Clowes Hall Women's Com., Indpls., 1963. Recipient citation ARC, 1946; citation Marion County Meritorious Service Award, 1959; citation Greater Southside Civic Orgn., 1961; Art award Kappa Kappa Kappa, 1967, 68, 70, 71. Fellow Indpls. Art League Found. (numerous awards 1960-66); mem. Southside Art League, Inc. (pres. 1964-65, numerous awards 1964-75, founder), Ind. Artists Club, Inc. (Purchases award 1978), Ind. Heritage Arts, Inc., Rutland Art Assn., Brown County Art Guild (pres. 1980-83, v.p. 1983—), Ind. fedn. Arts Clubs (bd. dirs. 1963-73), Ind. Artist (chmn. prize fund 1974-75), Consignment and appraisal of fine arts, Hoosier Salon, Indpls. Mus. Arts, Nat. Soc. Arts and Letters, Nat. Mus. Women in Arts, Hoosier Group Women in Arts, Oil Painters of America (Master of Art award for contbg. to heritage Brown County Indiana Art Colony 1997). Presbyterian. Avocation: growing flowers. Home: 394 E Freeman Ridge Rd Nashville IN 47448-8871

KRINGEL, DEANNA LYNN, music educator; b. Dundalk, Md., Mar. 18, 1974; d. Arthur Dale and Dorothy Ann Kringel. BA, James Madison U., 1996. Lic. tchr. Va., 1996. Tchr., band dir. Fairfax County Pub. Schs., Springfield, Va., 1996—97; tchr., orch. dir. Roanoke (Va.) City Pub. Schs., 1998—99, Hanover County Pub. Schs., Ashland, Va., 1999—2000, Chesapeake (Va.) City Pub. Schs., 2000—; condr. Williamsburg (Va.) Youth Orch., 2000—; dir. Chesapeake (Va.) All-City Promenade Strolling Strings, 2000—. Pvt. music tchr., Chesapeake, 2000—; freelance profl. violinist, violist and flutist, Chesapeake, 1996—; cons. in field. Musician: Gov. Del.'s Inaugural Banquet, 1986, Gov.'s Sch. Excellence, 1990. Vol. musician Local Chs. and Hosps., Va., 1992—2003. Scholar Ben Wright Music scholarship, James Madison U., 1992, Second Pl. award Littman Music Competition, Concordia Coll., Bronxville, N.Y., 1992. Mem.: NEA, Nat. Flute Assn., Am. String Tchrs. Assn., Music Educators Nat. Conf., Chesapeake Educators Assn., Va. Band and Orch. Dirs. Assn., Va. Music Educators Assn., Kappa Delta Pi, Golden Key Nat. Honors Soc., Sigma Alpha Iota. Lutheran. Avocations: fitness training, music. Home: 724 Greentree Circle Apartment 103 Chesapeake VA 23320 Office: Oscar F Smith High School 1994 Tiger Drive Chesapeake VA 23320 E-mail: deannak770@aol.com.

KRINSKY, CAROL HERSELLE, art history educator; b. N.Y.C., June 2, 1937; d. David and Jane (Gartman) Herselle; m. Robert Daniel Krinsky, Jan. 25, 1959; 2 children. BA, Smith Coll., 1957; MA, NYU, 1960, PhD, 1965. Mem. faculty NYU, 1965—, assoc. prof. art history, 1973-78, prof., 1978—; Frederic Lindley Morgan prof. U. Louisville, 2001. Author: Vitruvius de Architectura, 1521. 1969, Rockefeller Center, 1978, Synagogues of Europe, 1985, rev. edit., 1996, Gordon Bunshaft of Skidmore, Owings & Merrill, 1988, Europas Synagogen, 1988, Contemporary Native American Architecture, 1996; contbr. articles to profl. jours. Bd. dirs. Internat. Survey Jewish Monuments, Syracuse, N.Y., 1981—, Soc. Archtl. Historians, 1978-80, 86-89, The Mac Dowell Colony, Inc., 1989—, Jewish Heritage Coun. World Monuments Fund; co-chair seminar on the city Columbia U., 1993-95. Am. Coun. Learned Socs. grantee, 1981, Nat. Endowment for the Arts grantee, 1993; recipient Arnold Brunner award N.Y.C. chpt. AIA, 1990. Fellow Soc. Archtl. Historians (pres. 1984-86, pres. N.Y.C. chpt. 1977-79); mem. Coll. Art Assn. (Disting. Tchg. of Art History award 2004), Planning History Group, Am. Urban History Assn., Women's City Club, Century Assn., Phi Beta Kappa. Office: NYU Dept Fine Arts 100 Washington Sq E New York NY 10003-6688 Office Phone: 212-998-8186. E-mail: chk1@nyu.edu.

KRINSKY, SHARON FRANCES, librarian, editor, writer; b. Bronx, NY, June 5, 1945; d. Nathan and Dorothy (Rosen) K. BA, Queens Coll., 1966; MLS, Pratt Inst., 1993. Registration supr. New Sch. Social Rsch., NYC, 1975-78; editl. svcs. Everette Sch., 1980—; ind. contractor editl. svs., 1990—; asst. editor H.W. Wilson Co., Bronx, 1993-98; libr. Mercy Coll, NYC, 1999—2000; reference libr. NY Inst. Tech., 2000—02, Channel Thirteen, WNET, 2002—03. Author: The Ruddy Duck, 1995; contbr. Best American Poetry of 1992; contbr. poetry to jours.; contbg author: Twenty Stories by Eighteen Authors, 1996. Vol. Am. Coun. Arts Libr., 1990-91, Poets House, 1992. Mem. ACRL, EFA, Internat. Women's Writing Guild, Editl. Freelancers Assn. Avocations: multi-media artist, poetry performance.

KRISE, PATRICIA LOVE, automotive industry executive; b. Indpls., July 28, 1959; d. John Bernard and Ann (Emmons) Love; m. Thomas Warren Krise, Sept. 5, 1987. BA magna cum laude, Hanover Coll., Ind., 1981; MBA with hons., Miami U., Oxford, Ohio, 1982. Substitute tchr. Henry County Sch. Dist., Knightstown, Ind., 1982-83; project mgr. Servaas Labs., Inc., Indpls., 1983-84; sales analyst Ford Motor Co., Mpls., 1984, outstate field mgr., 1984-86, met. field mgr., 1986-87, truck merchandising mgr., 1987-88, merchandising mgr., 1988-89, met. field dir. Denver dist., 1989, market representation specialist Denver dist., 1990-91; regional market rep. mgr. Infiniti divsn. Nissan Motor Corp., Naperville, Ill., 1991-92, regional merchandising mgr., 1992-93, dealer ops. cons., 1993—97, dealer ops. mgr., 1995-97; adminstrv./remktg. mgr. Fairlane Credit subsidiary Ford Motor Credit, Colorado Springs, 1997—99, mgr. nat. expansion, remktg. and adminstrn., 1999; acct. svcs. mgr. Ford Motor Credit, Colorado Springs, 2000—. Advisor/presenter Ford Dealer Advt. Fund, Mpls., 1987-88. Nat. sponsorship liaison Race for the Cure, Colorado Springs, 2002—04; vol. Marian House Soup Kitchen, 1997—2000; adult literacy tutor Jr. Achievement, 1998; mem. fund-raising com. Race for the Cure, Colorado Springs, 1999, co-chair ops. com., 2001; bd. dirs. Jr. Achievement, Colorado Springs, 2001—04. Recipient Outstanding Mktg. award Ctrl. Region Ford Motor Co., 1987, Wall St. Jour. award, 1982; named Internat. Woman of Yr., 1992. Mem. Twin Cities Sales Mgrs. Club, Hanover Coll. Alumni Assn., Women's Athletic Assn. (treas. 1979-80), Pre-Law Club (pres. 1980-81), Nat. Assn. Female Execs., Alpha Delta Pi., co-chair Race for the Cure for Fairlane Credit, 1998. Republican. Roman Catholic. Avocations: running, sailing, yoga. E-mail: PKrise@Ford.com., pkrise@peoplepc.com.

KRISHNAN, RANJANI, finance educator; b. Calcutta, West Bengal, India, Aug. 2, 1965; d. S. S. Ananthakrishnan and Anandi Krishnan; m. Satish Joshi; children: Prithvi Joshi children: Tanvi Joshi. AA, Inst. Cost and Works Accts., India; MBA, U. Pitts., PhD, 1998. Assoc. prof. Mich. State U., East Lansing, 1998—. Contbr. articles to profl. jours. Mem.: Am. Acctg. Assn. (exec. com. 2001—02). Office: Mich State Univ Eli Broad Sch Mgmt East Lansing MI 48824 Business E-Mail: krishn15@msu.edu.

KRISSEL, SUSAN HINKLE, transportation company executive; b. Miami, Nov. 21, 1947; d. Jack Boyd and Carolyn (Frates) Hinkle; m. Richard Krissel, Mar. 19, 1972; children: John Boyd, Carolyn Frates. BA, U. Miami, 1970, MEd, 1977. Grad. admissions counselor Fla. Internat. U., Miami, 1971-74, budget coord. external degree program, 1974-78, transcript officer, 1978-82; owner, dir. Southeastern Consolidated Industries, Inc., 1982—. Bd. dirs. Jr. League Miami, 1985-86, Beaux Arts, U. Miami, Coral Gables, 1980-84, Parents Assn. Trinity Episcopal Sch., Miami, 1988-91; pres. Woman's Cancer Assn., U. Miami, 1980-81, Palmer Trinity Parents Assn., 1992-93; trustee Palmer Trinity Sch., 1992-93; mem. Young Patronesses of the Opera, bd. govs., 1999—. Mem. The Flamingo Forum, Jr. League Miami, Beaux Arts. Episcopalian. Avocations: reading, boating, travel, needlepoint, golf. Home: 8750 SW 63rd Ct Miami FL 33143-8069

KRISTENSEN, KATHLEEN HOWARD, music educator; b. Salt Lake City, May 10, 1939; d. Erin Neils and Verdis Eliza (Berrett) Howard; m. Karl G. Topham (div. 1968); children: Stephanie T. Fullmer, Amelia T. Curtis, Suzanne T. Jones, David Howard Topham; m. Paul Kristensen, June 21, 1983. Student, Brigham Young U., 1957-59, U. Utah, 1970-72. Mem. Mormon Tabernacle Choir, 1972-79, 87-2000. Mem. Am. Guild Organists (sub-dean), Nat. Assn. Tchrs. Singing, Nat. Assn. Music, Utah Music Tchrs. Republican. Mem. Lds Ch. Home: 2146 E 7420 S Salt Lake City UT 84121-4925

KRISTIN, KAREN, artist; b. L.A., Aug. 27, 1943; d. Earle Barnard and Ann Maxine (Taylor) Immel; m. Richard Edward Amend, Aug. 21, 1976 (div. Aug. 1981); m. Gary Marchal Lloyd, Oct. 1, 1985 (div. Sept.1989). Student, Art Ctr. Coll. Design, 1961, Valley Jr. Coll., 1962, Pierce Jr. Coll., 1967, 68, UCLA, 1969, 70. Lectr. UCLA Ext. Program, 1973-76; scenic artist Hollywood, Calif., 1978-83; ptnr., designer, lead painter Sky Art Scenic Art Svcs., Hollywood, Calif., 1983-88; owner, pres., lead painter, designer Sky Art Karen Kristin, Inc., Englewood, Colo., 1989—. Spkr., lectr. in field. Co-author (under Karen Kristin Amend): Handwriting Analysis: The Complete Basic Book, 1980, Achieving Compatbility with Handwriting-Analysis, vol. I, Understanding Your Emotional Relationships, 1992, vol. II, Exploring Your Sexual Relationships, 1992; prin. murals include The Cirque Du Soleil Theater, Las Vegas, 1993, N.Mex. Mus. Natural History, 1989, 90, Forum Shops at Caesars, Las Vegas, 1992, 97, Kansas City Station Hotel and Casino, Kansas City, Mo., 1996, Sunset Station Hotel and Casino, Las Vegas, 1997, Venetian Hotel Grand Canal Shoppes, Las Vegas, 1998, Chaitanya Joti Mus., Puttaparthy, India, 2000, Hyatt Casino, Blackhawk, Colo., 2001, Argosy Casino, Kans. City, Mo., 2003, Rangeeli Mahal, Barsara, India, 2003, Boulder Sta. Casino, Las Vegas, 2004; sky art backdrops for numerous movies, commls., and TV. Mem. Am. Assn. Handwriting Analysts (spkr. 1991—), Am. Handwriting Analysis Found. (sprk. 1991—), Human Graphics Ctr., Graphex Internat. and Gold NIBS, Universal Soc. of Integral Why (mentor 1994—). Democrat. Avocations: photography, reading, traveling, camping, fishing. Office: Sky Art Karen Kristin Inc 3051 S Broadway Englewood CO 80113 E-mail: skyartkk@aol.com.

KRISTOF, CINDY, librarian, educator; b. Lakewood, Ohio, Nov. 15, 1965; d. John J. and Ruth M. Kristof; m. R. Carmean, Sept. 29, 1990. BA in English, Ohio State U., 1989; MLS, Kent State U., 1995. Program asst. Eisenhower Nat. Clearinghouse, Columbus, Ohio, 1994-95, reference libr., 1995-96; assoc. prof. document delivery and distance learning libr. Kent (Ohio) State U., 1996—. Author: (book) Electronic Reserve Operations in ARL Libraries: A SPEC Kit, 1999, (chpt.) The Role and the Impact of the Internet on Library and Information Services, 2001, (chpt.) Eletronic Reserves, Encyclopedia of Library and Information Science, 2003. Mem. ALA, AAUP, Assn. of Coll. and Rsch. Librs., Libr. and Info. Tech. Assn. (chair distance learning interest group), Acad. Libr. Assn. Ohio (bd. dirs. 2000—), Beta Phi Mu. Office: Kent State U Librs PO Box 5190 Kent OH 44242 E-mail: ckristof@kent.edu.

KRISTOF, KATHY M. journalist; b. Burbank, Calif., Feb. 4, 1960; d. Joseph E. and Frances S. Kristof; m. Richard R. Magnuson, Jr., Jan. 4, 1986 (div.); 2 children. BA, U. So. Calif., L.A., 1983. Reporter L.A. Bus. Jour., 1984-88, Daily News, Woodland Hills, Calif., 1988-89, L.A. Times, 1989—; syndicated columnist L.A. Times Syndicate, 1991—. Author: Kathy Kristof's Complete Book of Dollars and Sense, 1997, Investing 101, 2000, Taming the Tuition Tiger, 2003; contbr. articles to mags. and profl. jours. Recipient John Hancock Fin. Svcs. award, 1992, Personal Fin. Writing award ICI/Am. U., 1994, Consumer Adv. of Yr., Calif. Alliance for Consumer Edn., 1998. Mem. Soc. Bus. Editors and Writers (pres. 2003), Calif. Newspapers Pubs. Assn. (2nd pl. Bus. and Fin. Story award 1999). Office: Los Angeles Times 202 W 1st St Los Angeles CA 90012 E-mail: kathy.kristof@latimes.com.

KRIZER, JODI, performing arts executive; Mng. dir. Bill T. Jones/Arnie Zane Dance Co., N.Y.C., exec. dir. Office: Bill T Jones/Arnie Zane Dance Co Arnie Zance Dance Co 853 Broadway Ste 1706 New York NY 10003-4703

KROBATH, KRISTA ANN, pharmacist; b. Pottsville, Pa., July 8, 1962; d. James Joseph and Gaye Diane (Anderson) E.; m. Gilbert Krobath. BS in Pharmacy, Temple U., 1985. Registered pharmacist. Pharmacist People's Drug, Harrisburg, Pa., 1985-86; pharmacist, mgr. Amcare Health Svcs., Harrisburg, 1986-96; pharmacist Pharmerica, Harrisburg, 1996-99, CFI Pharmacy, Harrisburg, 1999—. Mem.: Capital Area Pharm. Assn., Pa. Pharm. Assn.

KROEGER, BROOKE W. journalist, writer; b. Kansas City, Mo., Feb. 18, 1949; d. David S. and Helen (Bratt) Weinstein; m. John C. Kroeger, Jan. 29, 1972 (div. 1983); children: Brett S. Kroeger; m. Alexander M. Goren, June 24, 1984; stepchildren: Andrea Goren, Elisabeth J. Goren. BS in Journalism, Polit. Sci., Boston U., 1971; MS in Journalism, Columbia U., 1972. UN corr. N.Y. Newsday, N.Y.C., 1984-85; dep. met. editor New York Newsday, N.Y.C., 1985-86; editor Europe, Middle East and Africa UPI, London, 1983-84, bureau chief Israel Tel Aviv, 1981-83, corr., 1979-81, London, 1978-79, Brussels, 1977, Chgo., 1973-76. Assoc. prof. journalism NYU, 1998—. Author: Nellie Bly: Daredevil, Reporter, Feminist, 1994, FANNIE: the Talent for Success of Writer Fannie Hurst, 1999, PASSING: When People Can't Be Who They Are, 2003; contbr. articles to local newspapers and popular mags. Home: 1175 Park Ave New York NY 10128-1211

KROEGER, CATHERINE C. writer, educator, editor; b. St. Paul, Minn., Dec. 12, 1925; d. Homer Pierce Clark and Elizabeth Turner Dunsmoor; m. Richard Clark Kroeger, Dec. 22, 1950; children: Paul, Robert, Elizabeth, Marjorie, Mary. AB, Bryn Mawr Coll., 1947; MA, U. Minn., 1982, PhD, 1987. Founding pres. Christian for Bibl. Equality, Mpls., 1987-95; pres. emerita Christians for Bibl. Equality, Mpls., 1995—; Protestant chaplain Hamilton Coll., Clinton, N.Y., 1987-88; adj. assoc. prof. Gordon Conwell Theol. Sem., South Hamilton, Mass., 1992—. Founding organizer Women in the Bibl. World sect. Soc. Bibl. Lit., 1980-89. Author, editor: Women, Abuse and the Bible, 1996, Healing the Hurting, 1998; co-editor: Study Bible for Women, 1996; editor: InterVarsity Press Women's Bible Commentary, 2002; mem. editl. bd.: Jour. Religion and Abuse, 1999—; co-author (with Nancy Nason-Clark): No Place for Abuse: Biblical and Practical Resources to Counteract Domestic Violence, 2001; co-author: (witn Nancy Nason-Clark) Beyond Abuse, 2004; author: I Suffer Not A Woman, 1992. Bd. dirs. St. Paul Philharm Soc., 1964-66, Evangels. for Social Action, Phila., 1987-93; bd. dirs., pres. Minn. Sch. Missions, St. Paul, 1959-79; bd. dirs. emerita Whitworth Coll., Spokane, Wash; pres. Peace and Safety in the Christian Home. Fellow Inst. Bibl. Rsch. (exec. bd. 1995-97); mem. Am. Acad. Religion/Soc. Bibl. Lit., Women's Classical Caucus, Archaeol. Inst. Am., Am. Philological Assn. Presbyterian. Avocations: grandchildren, conducting study tours. Home: 1073 Stony Brook Rd Brewster MA 02631-2448 Office: Gordon Conwell Theol Sem 130 Essex St South Hamilton MA 01982-2317 E-mail: ckroeger@world.std.com.

KROEGER SMITH, MARILYN BETH, adult education educator, researcher; d. Bernard F. and Betty H. Kroeger; m. Steven R. Koepke (div. Sept. 1994); children: Jason M. Koepke, Kristina L. Koepke, Kari E. Koepke; m. Richard H. Smith, Oct. 14, 1995. BA, St. Olaf Coll., Northfield, Minn., 1973; PhD, U. Nebr., 1978. Scientist I and II NCI- Frederick, Md., 1978—98; lectr. McDaniel Coll., Westminster, Md., 1998—. Rsch. anti-AIDS drugs, cancer, chem. rsch. toxicology. Author: (jour. articles) J. Med. Chem., and PNAS. Recipient Ill. State Scholar, Ill. Edn. Assn., 1969. Mem.: Am. Chem. Soc. Office: McDaniel Coll 2 Coll Hill Westminster MD 21157 E-mail: msmith@mcdaniel.edu.

KROEHLER, BETH ANN, librarian; b. Freeport, Ill., Sept. 1, 1955; d. Ralph Senf and Marjorie Ann Kroehler. BE, U. Wisc.-Whitewater, Whitewater, Wisc., 1977; MA Libr. Sci., U. Wisc.-Madison, Madison, Wisc., 1981; MA Exec. Devel. for Pub. Svc., Ball State U., Muncie, Ind., 1987. Cert. Librarian II Ind., 1986. Libr./av Wild Rose and Pleasant View Elem. Sch., Wild Rose, Wis., 1977—80; h.s. libr. Northland Pines Sch. Dist., Eagle River, Wis., 1980—81, dist. audio-visual coord./lib. h.s., 1981—82; reference asst./young adult libr. Muncie Pub. Libr., Muncie, Wis., 1983—87, spl. projects libr., 1987—93, coord. of circulation and computer services, 1993—95, asst. supr. tech. dept., 1995—. Presenter Pub. Libr. Assn. Conf., 1988, CODI Nat. Conf., 2000, 01. Contbr. articles to profl. jour.; editor: (booklet) Way to Go. Pres. and organizer Campus Girl Scouts U. Wisc.-Whitewater, Whitewater, Wis., 1973—74; organizer Laubach Literacy Coun., Eagle River, Wis., 1981, Whitewater City Laubach Literacy Coun., Whitewater, Wis., 1976—76; mem. LRC Adv. Com., Ind. Vocat. Tech. Coll., Muncie, Ind., 1983—85; treas. Ind. Literacy Coordinating Com., Ind., 1990—98; mem. Ctrl. Wis. Uniserv Coun., Wis., 1978—80; rec. sec. White Pines Cmty. Broadcasting Devel. Group, Wis., 1982—82; mem. Moore-Youse Hist. Mus., Muncie, Ind., 1985—87; trainer Laubach Literacy Action, 1982—90. Recipient Meritorious Svc. Award, Palatines to Am., 2003. Mem.: ALA, Ind. Libr. Fedn., Del. County Hist. Soc. (various positions 1984—2001), Ind. State Hist. Soc., Palatines to Am. (various positions 2000—, 2nd chpt., v.p. 1992—94, pres. 1994—98, nat. chpt., pres. 1996—2000), Phi Alpha Theta. Avocations: needlecrafts, travel, reading, post card collecting. Home: 301 W Charter Dr Muncie IN 47303 Office: Muncie Pub Libr 2005 S High St Muncie IN 47302 Personal E-mail: kroehler@juno.com.

KROHLEY, PATRICIA ANNE, marketing professional; b. N.Y.C., Feb. 13, 1954; d. Casper and Ann Marie (Calise) Inzerillo; m. Richard John Krohley Sr., June 10, 1977 (div. 2001); 1 child, Richard John Jr. Grad., Bklyn. Mus. Art Sch., 1971; student, Queens Coll., 1972, Fashion Inst. Tech., 1974. Lic. real estate salesperson, N.Y. Realtor Re/Max Bonus RE, Woodhaven, N.Y., 1988-96, Re/Max Liberty Realty, Ozone Park, N.Y., 1996; account exec. Metropolitan Life Ins. Co., Lake Success, NY, 1996—98; inside sales rep. GE Plastics, 1998—2001; account exec. Laird Plastics, Westbury, NY, 2001—03; dir. mktg. Corcon Developers, West Hempstead, NY, 2003—. Mem. Agt. Adv. Panel, Century 21 Broker's Coun., L.I., NY, 1990; with Key Communicator Re/Max Bonus Realty, Woodhaven, 1993—96. Recipient scholarship Bklyn. Mus. Art, 1971. Mem. Nat. Assn. Life Underwriters, Nat. Assn. Realtors, N.Y. State Assn. Realtors, N.Y.C. Assn. Life Underwriters, L.I. Bd. Realtors, Women in Transition (founder, pres. 1993—), Nat. Art League, Alliance of Queens Artists. Avocations: environmental and social issues, children's advocate, writing, swimming, painting. Office: care of Corcon 327 Hempstead Ave West Hempstead NY 11552 Office Phone: 516-505-2700.

KROIS, AUDREY, artist; b. Boston, Mar. 14, 1934; d. Henry and Lillian Marie (Mueller) Haeberle; m. Richard Gamage, May 14, 1966 (div. Mar. 1975); m. Joseph E. Krois Jr., June 17, 1978. BA, Syracuse U., 1956; MSW, Columbia U., 1958; postgrad., Fashion Inst. Tech., 1964-66, Art Students League, 1973-76. Social worker Pleasantville (N.Y.) Cottage Sch., 1958-62; cons. to UNICEF UN, Bangkok, Thailand, 1963; supr. vol. program Henry St. Settlement, N.Y.C., 1964-66; dir. cmty. devel. program Anti Poverty Funding, N.Y.C., 1966-68; supervising dir., asst. v.p., cons. Divsn. Homemaker, Home Health Care, G.H.I., Inc., N.Y.C., 1969-78. One-woman shows include Clayton Liberatore Gallery, Bridgehampton, N.Y., 1995, 1996, 1999, 2002, South Palm Beach Town Hall Gallery, 1998, Southampton Town Hall, 1998, exhibited in group shows at Access to the Arts, Jamestown, N.Y., 1981, Embroiderers Guild Abigail Adams Smith Mus., N.Y.C., 1982, Arrowmont Sch., Gatlinburg, Tenn., 1982, Gayle Wilson Gallery, Southampton, N.Y., 1983, 1988, Discovery Art Gallery, Glen Cove, N.Y., 1989, Decatur House, Washington, 1990, Mus. Am. Quilter Soc., Paducah, Ky., 1992, Vanderbilt Mus., Centerport, N.Y., 1992, 1994, Wellspring Gallery, Santa Monica, Calif., 1993—94, Aullwood Audubon Ctr., Dayton, Ohio, 1996 (Best of Show), South Fla. Fair, 2002, Northern Trust Bank, 2002, Everglades Vis. Ctr., 2002, Water Mill Mus., Water Mill, N.Y., 2002, West Palm Beach Internat. Airport, 2002—03. Recipient 2d Pl. award Brookhaven Arts and Humanities Coun., 1997, 2d Pl. award East End Arts Coun., 1998. Mem. South Fork Craft Assn., Southampton Artists Assn. (bd. dirs. 1990-96, fin. dir. 1992-93, pres. 1994, Award of Excellence in Watercolor, 1994-96), Goodman Design Gallery (Award of Merit in Watercolor 1993), Palm Beach Watercolor Soc. Home: PO Box 2482 Palm Beach FL 33480-2482 also: PO Box 960 Southampton NY 11969-0960

KROKEN, PATRICIA ANN, health science association administrator; b. Sturgis, Mich., June 26, 1947; d. Jesse W. and Dorothy Beth (Hollister) Penn; m. Bruce Edward Kroken, Jan. 28, 1967; children: Christina, Jennifer. BS in English cum laude, No. Mich. U., 1970. V.p., account supr. Rick Johnson & Co., Albuquerque, 1984-87; expansion sales mgr. Bueno Foods, 1987-89; bus. devel. dir. Radiology Assocs., Albuquerque, 1990-93, exec. dir., 1993-2000; v.p. compliance solutions div. Telemedix, Inc., Albuquerque, 2000—01; pres. Healthcare Resource Providers, LLC, 2001—. Adj. prof. U. N.Mex., Albuquerque, 1983—94; spkr. in field. Contbr. articles to various jours. Lectr. N. Mex. Womens Polit. Caucus, Albuquerque, 1986. Fellow Am. Coll. Med. Practice Execs.; mem. Radiology Bus. Mgmt. Assn. (chair publs. com. 1997-99, pres. 1999, Calhoun award 1996, 99), N.Mex. Med. Group Mgmt. Assn. (pres. 1995). Avocations: writing, horseback riding, public speaking. Home: 12501 Oakland Ave NE Albuquerque NM 87122-2274

KROLEWSKI, BOZENA K. molecular biologist, researcher, cell biologist; b. Warsaw, Jan. 18, 1949; came to the U.S., 1981; d. Stefan and Zdzislawa M.S. (Zabielski) Checinski; m. Andrzej S. Krolewski, June 3, 1972; children: Martin A., Adam W. BA, Warsaw Med. Sch., 1971, MS, 1972, PhD, 1979. Rsch. asst. Warsaw Med. Sch., 1972—74; vis. fellow Harvard Sch. Pub. Health, Boston, 1981-84, rsch. fellow, 1984-87, scientist, 1987-92, sr. scientist, 1992—; rsch. assoc., cons. Joslin Diabetes Ctr., Boston, 1992—. Contbr. articles to profl. jours. Recipient Rsch. award NIH, Boston, 1984. Mem. Radiation Rsch. Soc., Cancer Rsch. Soc. Roman Catholic. Avocations: collecting antiques, walking, climbing, history, politics. Home: 639 Great Plain Ave Needham MA 02492 Office: Joslin Diabetes Ctr Genetics/Epidemiology 3d Flr One Joslin Pl Boston MA 02215 Office Phone: 617-732-2668.

KROMINGA, LYNN, cosmetic and health care company executive, lawyer; b. L.A., May 16, 1950; d. Dale E. and Phyllis M. Krominga; m. Amnon Shiboleth, Apr. 9, 1992; 1 child, Karen Lee Shiboleth. BA in German, U. Minn., 1972, JD, 1974. Bar: Minn. 1974, N.Y. 1976. Assoc. firms in Mpls. and N.Y.C., 1974-77; assoc. counsel Am. Express Co., N.Y.C., 1977-80; sr. internat. counsel Revlon, Inc., N.Y.C., 1981-92, v.p. law, 1988-92, gen. counsel to exec. com., 1991-92, pres. licensing divsn., 1992-98, mem. exec. com., 1993-94, 97-99, exec. v.p. bus. devel., 1998-99; mem. bd. advisors MakeoverStudio.com, 1999—2001; bd. advisors Salonforce.com., 1999—2002; CEO Fashion Wire Daily, Inc., 2002; ptnr. KLS Mgmt. LLC, 2002—. Bd. dirs. StructuredWeb.com., 2000-02. Mem. ABA, Internat. Bar Assn. Cosmetic, Toiletry and Fragrance Assn. (vice chmn. govt. rels. com. 1991-92), Am. Arbitration Assn. (corp. counsel 1986-92, panel of arbitrators for large complex cases 1993-94, internat. panel of arbitrators 1997—), Phi Beta Kappa. Home: 180 Riverside Blvd Apt 21A New York NY 10069-0814

KROMMINGA, AN-MARIE, special education educator; b. Yakima, Washington, Mar. 23, 1936; d. Fred Henry and Edith Bessie Jackson; m. William Reynold Kromminga, Aug. 23, 1956. BA in Edn., Walla Walla College, 1958. Cert. profl. educator K-12 spl. edn., K-8 elem. edn., P-3 early childhood spl. edn., early childhood edn. Washington. Tchr. grades 1-7 Upper Columbia Conf. of Seventh-Day Adventist, Toppenish, Wash., 1955—56, tachr. grades 1-4 Wapato, Wash., 1959—60; tchr. grades 5-6 Ill. Conf. of Seventh-Day Adventist, Aurora, 1963—64, tchr. grades 1-8 Canton, 1972—74; substitute and homebound tchg. various schs., Ill., 1974—79; homemaking skills tchr. Ill. Dept. Children and Family Svcs., Sterling, 1979—81; home products ind. dealer, unit sales leader, to dist. leader Stanley Home Products Inc., Ill. and Wash., 1975—; presch./kindergarten tchr. Upper Columbia Conf. of Seventh-Day Adventists, Pasco, Wash., 1986—90; life skills spl. edn. tchr. Kiona-Benton Sch. Dist. 52, Benton City, Wash., 1990—. Chair Work Opportunities for Rural Kids, Benton City, 1990—96, Spl. Edn. Parent Group, Benton City, 1990—96; mem. Tri-Cities (Wash.) Transition Team, 1990—. Author: History of Benton City, Washington, 2000; contbr. articles to ch. newsletters and publs. Active disaster relief and cmty. svc. Seventh-Day Adventist Ch., 1963—79; leader for children's clubs and recreation programs for cmty. and ch., 1963—79. Recipient Tri City Crystal Apple award for excellence in edn., various cmty. svc. groups, bus., and orgns., 2002. Mem.: Coun. for Exceptional Children. Seventh Day Adventist. Avocations: dolls, music boxes, leathercraft, travel. Home: 1004 Frontier PR NE Benton City WA 99320

KRONEGGER, MARIA ELISABETH, French and comparative literature educator; b. Graz, Austria, Sept. 23, 1932; came to U.S., 1962, naturalized, 1968; d. Karl and Josefine (Sparovitz) K. Grad., Karl-Franzens U., Austria, 1960; postgrad., U. Sorbonne, Paris, 1953-55; MA in English and Am. Lit., Kans. U., 1958; PhD in French and Humanities, Fla. State U., 1960. Instr. French, German and Humanities Fla. State U., 1958-60; mem. faculty Internat. Coll., St. Gallen, Switzerland, 1961-62; asst. prof. Hollins Coll., Va., 1962-64; asst. prof. French and comparative lit. Mich. State U., East Lansing, 1964-67, assoc. prof., 1967-70, prof., 1970—. Author: James Joyce and Associate Image Makers, 1968, Impressionist Literature, 1973, The Life Significance of French Baroque Poetry, 1988; editor: Phénoménologie et Littérature: L'origine de l'oeuvre d'art, Hommages à A.-T. Tymieniecka, 1986, Phenomenology and Aesthetics: Approaches to Comparative Literature and the Other Arts, 1990, Dordrecht (Kluwer) vol. XXXIII of book series Analecta Husserliana, 1990; editor: Esthétique Baroque et Imagination Créatrice, 1997, Allegory Old and New in Literature, the Fine Arts, Music and Theatre, and its Continuity in Culture, 1994; co-editor: Life, The Human Quest for an Ideal, 1996, Life Differentiation and Harmony: Vegetal, Animal, Human, Analecta Husseliana LVII, 1998; contbr. more than 135 articles on 17th and 20th century French and English lit., lit. and the fine arts, lit. and phenomenology to scholarly publs., anelecta Husseliana LVII, 1998. Bd. dirs. World Inst. Phenomenology, 1980—; pres. Internat. Soc. Phenomenology and Lit., Internat. Soc. Phenomenology, Fine Arts and Aesthetics; exec. v.p. World Inst. for Advanced Phenomenological Rsch. and Learning. Fulbright scholar, 1957-60; Ford Found. grantee, 1965-66 Mem. MLA, AAUP, Am. Soc. Aesthetics, Am. Comparative Lit. Assn., Semiotic Soc. Am., Chinese Comparative Lit. Assn., Internat. Soc. for Phenomenology and Lit. (pres. 1985—), Internat. Comparative Lit. Assn., Internat. Soc. Civilization, Internat. Semiotic Soc., South Atlantic MLA, Société Paul Claudel, Am. Assn. Tchrs. French, Fédération Internationale de Langues et Littératures Modernes, Golden Key Soc. (hon., Rsch. award). Roman Catholic. Office: Mich State U Old Horticulture East Lansing MI 48824 Home: 615 N Capitol Ave Lansing MI 48933-1230 E-mail: kronegger@pilot.mus.edu.

KRONENBERG, JANET LOIS, lawyer; b. Cleve., Jan. 13, 1948; d. Louis David and Shirley Evelyn (Weiskopf) K. Student, George Washington U., 1966-68; BA, NYU, 1970, MPA, 1976; JD, Cleve. State U., 1978. Bar: Ohio 1979, U.S. Dist. Ct. 1979, U.S. Ct. Appeals 1983, U.S. Supreme Ct. 1988. Rsch. asst. Cleve. State U., 1977-78, adj. lectr. law, 1980-91; dep. treas. Cuyahoga County, Cleve., 1977-78; ptnr. Kronenberg & Kronenberg, Cleve., 1979—2000; program officer Cuyahoga County Bd. Commrs., 2000—, atty., 2000—. Asst. to sr. v.p. Curtis Brown, Ltd., N.Y.C., 1970-75; presenter various continuing edn. programs; life del. 8th Jud. Conf., Cleve. Pres., trustee Ctr. for Prevention Domestic Violence, Cleve., 1981-89, N.E. Ohio Health Svcs., Cleve., 1992-95; trustee Womenspace, Cleve., 1989-91, N.E. Ohio Health Svcs., 1990-93; mem. citizens adv. bd. Broadview Devel. Ctr., Broadview Heights, Ohio, 1990-91; mem. Cuyahoga County Child Protection Coun., Cleve., 1993-95; mem. Cuyahoga County Women's Polit. Caucus. Named Vol. Lawyer of Yr., Legal Aid Soc., Cleve., 1987, honoree Coalition To End Domestic Violence, Cleve., 1989; recipient Legacy award Domestic Violence Ctr., Cleve., 2003. Mem. Ohio Bar Assn., Cuyahoga County Bar Assn. (trustee), Cuyahoga County Bar Found. (trustee). Avocation: travel. Home: 339 Claymore Blvd Richmond Hts OH 44143-1712 Office: 339 Claymore Blvd Cleveland OH 44143-1712

KRONICK, SUSAN D. retail executive; b. N.Y.C. Grad., Conn. Coll. Exec. trainee Bloomingdale's Federated Dept. Stores, N.Y.C., 1973—85, operating v.p., divsn. merchandise mgr. Bloomingdale's, 1985—88, sr. v.p., divsn. merchandise mgr. Bloomingdale's, 1988—90, exec. v.p., gen. mgr. Bloomingdale's, 1990—91, sr. v.p. dir. stores, Bloomingdale's, 1991—93, pres. RLG Divsn., 1992—97; chmn. Burdines, Federated Dept. Stores, Fla., 1997—2000; group pres. regional dept. stores Federated Dept. Stores, Cin., 2001—03, vice chmn. Cin, 2003—. Bd. dirs. Pepsi Bottling Group. Recipient Nat. Human Rels. award, Am. Jewish Com., 1999. Office: Federated Dept Stores Inc 7 W Seventh St Cincinnati OH 45202

KRONOWITZ, PAMELA RENEE, music educator; b. Manhattan, N.Y., Dec. 3, 1954; d. Harold Arthur and Frieda (Kahn) Simmons; children: Lauren, Damon. BA, York Coll., 1976; MA, Queens Coll., 1978. Orch. tchr. Massapequa Pub. Schs., NY, 1994—. Coach Gemini Youth Orch., 1995—97; adjucator N.Y. State Sch. Music Assn. Home: 6 David Ave Hicksville NY 11801

KROP, LOIS PULVER, psychologist; b. Scranton, Pa., Dec. 24, 1930; d. Samuel Max and Esther Golden Pulver; m. Michael Morris Krop, June 14, 1953; children: Pamela Sue, Daniel Steven, Judith Mary, David Ralph. BA, Pa. State U., 1952; MSW, U. Pa., 1954; PhD, Nova Southeastern U., 1976. LCSW; lic. sch. psychologist Fla., cert. family ct. mediator Fla., lic. marriage and family therapist Fla., 1986, cert. clin. hypnotherapist, sports counselor, hypnotherapist 1995. Family therapist Alexandria Family Svcs., Va., 1954—58; treatment specialist Cath. Family Svcs., Miami, Fla., 1960—85; pvt. practice Marriage and Family Svcs., Inc., Aventura, Fla., 1985—; qualified supr. MFT-CSW and MHL, Tallahassee, 2000—. Prof. acad. lifelong learning Fla. Internat. U., Miami, Fla., 1998—; cons. Mgmt. Tng. Inst., Ft. Lauderdale, 1996—; lectr. Inst. for Ret. Profls., U. Miami, 2002—; prof. Univ. Miami Inst. for Ret. Profl., 2001—. Author: (book) Family Hour/Family Power, 2000; contbr. articles to profl. jours. Bd. trustees U. Pa. Dade Alumni, Miami, Fla., 1985—; pres. Majestic Towers, Bal Harbour, Fla., 1999—, Hadassah Chai Chpt., Miami, 1990—92. Mem.: NASW (pres. 1965), Barry U. Field Instrs. (pres. 1985—87), Assn. of Fla. Sch. Psychologists, Mensa (cert. sports instr. 1998—), Phi Beta Kappa, Mortar Bd., Phi Kappa Phi. Avocations: tennis, scuba diving, bridge, reading, travel. Home: 9601 Collins Ave #1710 Bal Harbour FL 33154 Office: 19495 Biscayne Blvd #203 Aventura FL 33180

KROPF, SUSAN J. cosmetics company executive; married. BA in English, St. John's U.; MBA in Fin., NYU. Adminstrv. asst. Avon Products, Inc., N.Y.C., 1970, various mgmt. positions, 1970-85, v.p. purchasing and package devel., 1985-90, v.p., sr. officer product devel., 1990-92, v.p. R&D and mfg., 1992-97, sr. v.p. global ops. and bus. devel., 1992-97, exec. v.p., 1998-99, COO N.Am. & Global Bus. Ops., 1999—. Bd. dirs. Green Point Savs. Bank. Mem.: Fashion Group Internat., Cosmetic Exec. Women. Office: Avon Products Inc Ste C2-04 1251 Avenue Of The Americas New York NY 10020-1196

KROPP, STACY ANNE, small business owner; b. Bklyn., Jan. 22, 1964; d. Alan Marc and Sheila Harriet (Friend) G.; 1 child, Ryan. Student, Suffolk C.C., 1981, Valencia C.C., 1982; grad., Fla. Coll. Natural Health, 2002. Lic. real estate agt., Fla., 1986. Owner, CEO Expert Restoration Techs., Inc., Sunrise, Fla., Bright Solutions, Inc.; ptnr., v.p. ops. Color All Techs. Inernat., Pompano Beach; owner Account Mgmt. Svcs., Inc., Ft. Lauderdale, Fla.; CEO Gold Power Supplements, Ft. Lauderdale; divsn. mgr. Alice Edwards Realty, Pembroke Pines, Fla.; gen. mgr. Gen. Accounts Svcs., Inc. Mem. NAFE, Nat. Assn. Self-Employed, Nat. Nutritional Foods Assn., Greater Miami Credit Assn., Am. Collectors Assn., Fla. Collectors Assn., Women in Network. Home: 14130 Langley Pl Fort Lauderdale FL 33325-6413

KROTINGER, SHEILA M. educator; b. Pitts., May 28, 1930; d. Michael N. and Rose Irene Lutsky; m. Nathan J. Krotinger, Mar. 7, 1949; children—Eve, Michelle. A.A. summa cum laude, East Los Angeles Coll., 1956; B.A. magna cum laude, Calif. State U.-Fullerton, 1966. Cert. life credential, Calif. Tchr. Norwalk-La Mirada Unified Sch. Dist., Calif., 1968— . Contbr. articles to profl. jours. Editor, producer, dir. cable TV shows. Bd. dirs. La Mirada Festival of Arts, 1981, 82, publicity dir., 1982— ; publicity dir. La Mirada Friends of Theatre, 1982— ; v.p. La Mirada Democratic Club, 1983; bd. dirs. Friends of McNally Ranch, La Mirada, 1984; mem. by-laws com., co-chmn. Hist. Com. Friends of La Mirada Civic Theatre, 1983; mem. initiative com. Californians for Non-Smokers Rights, 1980; founder Temple Beth Shalom, Whittier, Calif., 1952, Temple Beth Ohr, La Mirada, 1960; chmn. City of La Mirada Hist. Heritage Commn., 1991-94; founder Heritage Coalition of South Calif., 1992, chmn., 1992-96, emeritus bd. dir.; bd. dir. Sr. Net Learning Ctr., La Mirada, Calif. Recipient Vol. in Action Award of Excellance, Innovation, 1998. Mem. Mensa. Home: 15310 Talbot Dr La Mirada CA 90638-5469

KROUPA, DIANE LYNN, federal judge; b. Mitchell, S.D., Oct. 12, 1955; d. Edwin Raymond and Delores Ilene (Duncan Burg) K.; m. Robert Eugene Fackler, Sept. 12, 1981; children: Erin Elizabeth, Sara Marie. BS in Fgn. Svc., Georgetown U., 1978, postgrad., 1981-83; JD, U. S.D., Vermillion, 1981. Bar: S.D. 1981, D.C. 1984, Minn. 1986. Atty., advisor IRS legis. and regulation divsn. Office of Chief Counsel, Washington, 1981-84; atty., advisor to Judge Joel Gerber U.S. Tax Ct., Washington, 1984-85; assoc. Dorsey & Whitney, Mpls., 1985-87, Parsinen Bowman Levy, Mpls., 1987-90, ptnr., 1990-95; judge Minn. Tax Ct., St. Paul, 1995—2001, chief judge, 1998—2001; judge U.S. Tax Ct., Washington, 2003—. Chair tax sect. Hennepin County Bar, Mpls., 1985—; mem. adv. bd. Hamline U., St. Paul, 1995—. Editor multi-vol. treatises on corps., 1995; contbr. articles to profl. jours. Legal advisor Minn. Women's Polit. Caucus, Minn. Women's Edn. Coun., St. Paul, 1989-91, Jr. League Mpls., 1991-93. Recipient Volunteer of Year Award, Jr. League of Minn., 1993. Mem.: Am. Judicature Soc., Nat. Assn. of Women Judges, Minn. State Bar Assn. (Disting. Service Award 2001, Cmty. Vol. of Year 1998), ABA. Avocations: children activities, computers, furniture refinishing, reading. Office: US Tax Ct 400 Second St Washington DC 20217*

KRUBITZER, LEAH, psychology educator, neuroscientist; b. Wilkes-Barre, Pa., 1961; BS, Pa. State U., 1983; PhD, Vanderbilt U., 1989. Asst. prof. psychology U. Calif., Davis, 1995—, tchr. Ctr. for Neurosci. Presenter in field. Contbr. articles to profl. jours. MacArthur fellow John D. and Catherine T. MacArthur Found., 1998. Achievements include cross-species comparative studies to show the relationship between brain organization and brain function, providing new insights into the cerebral cortex development and the evolutionary forces responsible for brain adaptation. Office: U Calif Ctr Neurosci One Shields Ave Davis CA 95616

KRUC, ANTOINETTE CAMPION, family physician; b. Scranton, Pa., May 9, 1939; d. Robert Francis and Mary Elizabeth (Boyle) Campion; m. Peter John Kruc, Mar. 2, 1962 (div. Sept. 1973); children: Kathryn Anne, David Campion. BS, Phila. Coll. Pharmacy & Sci., 1961; DO, Phila. Coll. Osteo. Medicine, 1977. Rotating intern Osteo. Hosp., Phila.; physician/owner Spruce Hill Med. Assocs., Phila., 1978-95, Kruc/Palmerio Part, Phila., 1982-94; physician Allegheny Health Edn. and Rsch. Found., Phila., 1995—. Corp. mem. Pa.Blue Shield, Harrisburg, 1995—. Bd. dirs. West Cath. H.S., Phila., 1994—; spkr. Optimists-Overbrook, Phila., 1985—. Recipient Cmty. Svc. award Pa. House of Reps., 1983, Optimists Internat., 1993. Mem. POMA, POFPS, AC of GP, PCOS, Alpha Omega Alpha. Avocations: antiques and collectibles, sports memorabilia, reading, hiking. Office: 208 N 65th St Philadelphia PA 19139-1006

KRUCK, DONNA JEAN, special education educator, consultant; b. Peoria, Ill., Jan. 26, 1930; d. Walter George and Lois Irene (Newburn) Hagemeyer; m. Michael Roy Kruck Jr., June 27, 1948; children: Pamela Ann Kruck Hokanson, Michael Roy III, Quentin Robert; m. Somran Sirironrong, May 19, 1998. BS, Ill. State U., 1961; MEd, U. Ill., 1968. Cert. spl. edn. tchr. and adminstr., Ill. Tchr. New Lenox Dist. 122, Ill., 1956-61; tchr. spl. edn. Lincoln Way Area Joint Agreement, New Lenox, 1961-66; tchr. spl. edn., coord. Joliet Twp. High Sch. Dist. 204, Ill., 1966-86; pvt. practice cons. and diagnostician New Lenox, 1986-92. Child adv. New Lenox Dist. 122, 1986-88; instr. Chapel Christian U., 1994-96; LCMS missionary, ESL tchr., Bangkok, 1997—. Author: Let's Learn to Cook, 1971. Pres. Joliet Twp. Edn. Assn., 1971-76; donar Aurora Area Blood Bank, Joliet, 1974-90; v.p. Island Lakes Homeowners Assn., 1994-96; v.p. Luth. Women's Missionary League, 1993, pres., 1994-97; pres. Aid Assn. for Luths., 1995-97. Mem. AAUW, NEA (life), Nat. Ret. Tchr. Assn., Am. Assn. Retired Persons, Am. Assn. Mental Retardation, Am. Bus. Women's Assn., Coun. Exceptional Children (life), Coun. Adminstrs. Spl. Edn., Christian Edn. Assn., Ill. Edn. Assn. (life), Ill. Div. Learning Disabilities, Coun. for Ednl. Diagnostic Svcs. (div. learning disabilities), Lutherans for Life, Kappa Delta Pi, Delta Kappa Gamma. Lutheran. Avocations: traveling, presenting travelogues. Office: Concordia Gospel Ministry 205/20 Soi Chairyakiat 1 Ngam Wong Wan 10210 Bangkok Thailand Home: 1/121 Soi Chinnakhet 1/21 Ngam Wong Wan Rd Bangkok 10210 Thailand

KRUEGER, ANNE O. international agency executive, economist; b. Endicott, N.Y. BA, Oberlin (Ohio) Coll., 1953; MS, U. Wis., 1956, PhD, 1958, Georgetown U., 1992; PhD (hon.), Hacettepe U., Ankara, Turkey, 1990, Monash U., 1995. Asst. prof. econs. U. Minn., Mpls., 1959-63, assoc. prof. econs., 1963-66, prof. econs., 1966-82; v.p. econs. and rsch. The World Bank, Washington, 1982-86; art and scis. prof. econs. Duke U., Durham, N.C., 1987-93; Herald and Caroline L. Ritch prof arts and scis. in econs. Stanford (Calif.) U., 1993—, dir. Ctr. Rsch. Econ. Devel. and Policy Reform, 1996-2001; 1st dep. mng. dir. IMF, 2001—, acting mng. dir., 2004—. Bd. dirs. Nordson Corp., Westlake, Ohio; mem. vis. com. Econs. Dept. Harvard U., 1990-98; sr. non-resident fellow Brookings Inst.; rsch. assoc. Nat. Bur. Econ. Rsch. Author: Trade Policies and Developing Nations, 1995, Economic Policies at Cross Purposes, 1993, Economic Policy Reform in Developing Countries, 1992, The Political Economy of Agricultural Pricing Policy, Vol. 5: A Synthesis of the Political Economy in Developing Countries, 1992, Economic Policy Reform: The Second Stage, 2000; co-author (with O. Aktan): Swimming Against the Tide: Turkish Trade Reform in the 1980s, 1992; editor: (with R.H. Bates) Political and Economic Interactions in Economic Policy Reform, 1993, The World Trade Organization as an International Institution, 1998, Economic Policy Reform: Second Stage, 2000, A New Approach to Sovereign Debt Restructuring, 2002, Economic Policy Reform and the Indian Economy, 2003, (with Jose Antonio Gonzales, Vittorio Corbo and Aaron Tornell) Latin American Macroeconomic Reform: The Second Stage, 2003, (with Sajjid Z. Chinoy) Reforming India's Economic, Financial and Fiscal Policies, 2003. Mem. N.Y. State Regents Commn. on Higher Edn., 1992-93. Recipient Robertson prize NAS, 1984, Bernhard Harms prize Inst. for World Economy, Kiel, 1990, Enterprise award Kenan Inst., 1990, Seidman prize, 1994. Fellow AAAS, Econometric Soc. (award 1984); mem. NAS, Am. Econ. Assn. (disting. fellow, chmn. com. rsch. 1988-92, chmn. commn. on grad. edn. in econs. 1989-90, v.p. 1977, pres.-elect 1995, pres. 1996, rep. to Internat. Econ. Assn. and mem. IEA exec. com. 1992-98, v.p. Internat. Econ. Assn. 1994-98). Office: Internat Monetary Fund 700 19th St NW Washington DC 20431*

KRUEGER, BETH ANN, academic administrator; d. George C. and Ann D. Krueger. BS, U. Tampa, 1988; MS, U. Rochester, 1992; postgrad., U. Tex., 2000—03. Asst. prof. biology Monroe C.C., Rochester, NY, 1993—2000; dir. Ctr. for Distance Learning Laredo (Tex.) C.C., 2002—03; dir. distance learning Onondaga C.C., Syracuse, NY, 2003—. Freelance writer and photographer, 1995—. Author: (textbook) Laboratory Manual for Life Sciences; contbr. articles to jours. Mem.: N.Mex Steam Locomotive and RR Hist. Soc., Nat. Rlwy. Hist. Soc. Avocations: snowshoeing, photography, writing, hiking. Personal E-mail: yardengine1919@hotmail.com.

KRUEGER, BETTY ADEL, county official; b. Bellville, Tex., May 31, 1934; d. Roland Christian Krueger and Flora Margaret Stalbaum. Student, Blinn Jr. Coll., Tex. A&M U. Adminstrv. asst. to county sch. supt., Bellville, Tex., 1952-78; adminstrv. asst. to county judge, 1979-83; county treas. Austin County, Bellville, 1983—. Pres. Bellville Pub. Libr. Bd., 1992—; mem. Austin County Civic Chorale, 1989—. Named Woman of Yr. Bus. and Profl. Women Dist. 3, 1981. Mem. Pilot Club of Bellville (sec., pres. 1986—), Bellville VFW Aux., Woodmen of the World (dir.). Democrat. Lutheran. Avocations: bowling, playing cards, dominos, traveling. Home: PO Box 723 Bellville TX 77418-0723

KRUEGER, BETTY JANE, telecommunications company executive; b. Indpls., Oct. 4, 1923; d. Forrest Glen and Hazel Luellen (Taylor) Burns; m. Alan Douglas Krueger, Apr. 4, 1975; 1 son by previous marriage--Michael J. Vornehm. Student, Butler U., 1948-49. Supr., instr. Ind. Bell Telephone Co., Indpls., 1941-54; supr. communications Jones & Laughlin Steel Co., Indpls., 1954-56, Ford Motor Co., Indpls., 1956-64, U.S. Govt., Camp Atterbury, Ind., 1964-66; dir. communications Meth. Hosp. of Ind., Indpls., 1966-79; pres., owner Rent-A-Radio, Inc. of Ind., Indpls., after 1979; sec.-treas. Communications Unltd., Inc. Former pres. Am. Legion Aux.; chmn. for Ind., Girls State U.S.A., 1972-77; probation officer vol., 1973-74; suicide prevention counselor, 1972-73; mem. Nat. Wildlife Fund. Recipient award for outstanding community service Ford Motor Co., 1961. Mem. Am. Soc. Hosp. Engring., Am. Hosp. Assn., Nat. Assn. Bus. and Ednl. Radio, Inc., Nat. Mus. Women in Arts, Internat. Teletypewriters for the Deaf, Assn. Public Safety Communications Officers, Inc., Am. Bus. Women. Methodist. Home: 6242 N 575 E Franklin IN 46131-8759 Office: 4545 Southeastern Ave Indianapolis IN 46203-2307

KRUEGER, BONNIE LEE, editor, writer; b. Chgo., Feb. 3, 1950; d. Harry Bernard and Lillian (Soyak) Krueger; m. James Lawrence Spurlock, Mar. 8, 1972. Student, Morraine Valley Coll., 1970. Adminstrv. asst. Carson Pirie Scott & Co., Chgo., 1969-72; traffic coord. Tatham Laird & Kudner, Chgo., 1973-74, J. Walter Thompson, Chgo., 1974-76, prodn. coord., 1976-78, editor-in-chief Assoc. Pubs., Chgo., 1978—, Sophisticate's Hairstyle Guide, 1978—, Sophisticate's Beauty Guide, 1978—, Complete Woman, 1981—; pub., editorial svcs. dir. Sophisticate's Black Hair Guide, 1983—, Sophisticate's Soap Star Styles, 1994-95. Active Statue of Liberty Restoration Com., NYC, 1983, Chgo. Architecture Found.; campaign worker Cook County State's Atty., Chgo., 1982; poll watcher Cook County Dem. Orgn., 1983. Recipient Exceptional Woman in Pub. award, Women in Periodical Pub., 2000, Communicator of Yr. award, Am. Health and Beaty Aids Inst. Mem. Soc. Profl. Journalists, Am. Health and Beauty Aids Inst. (assoc., Communicator of Yr. award), Lincoln Park Zool. Soc., Landmarks Preservation Coun. of Ill., Art Inst. Chgo., Chgo. Hist. Soc., Mus. Contemporary Art, Peta, Headline Club, Sigma Delta Chi. Lutheran. Office: Complete Woman 875 N Michigan Ave Chicago IL 60611-1803 Office Phone: 312-266-8680. Business E-Mail: krueger@associatedpub.com.

KRUEGER, DEBORAH A. BLAKE, school psychologist, consultant; b. Chgo., Aug. 22, 1954; d. Stanley Walter and Maryanne Lois Blake; m. Darrell George Krueger, May 31, 1986; children: Sarah, Joshua. BA, DePaul U., 1976, MEd, 1980; PhD, Loyola U., 1998. Lic. psychologist, Ill. Learning disabilities specialist Assocs. in Family Therapy, Lake Bluff, Ill., 1980-85; reading and learning disabilities specialist Proviso West H.S., Hillside, Ill., 1980-82; edn. therapist Hartgrove Hosp., Chgo., 1982-85; dir. spl. edn. Old Orchard Hosp., Skokie, Ill., 1985-87; program coord. One-to-One Learning Ctr., Northfield, Ill., 1995-98; sch. psychologist Winnetka (Ill.) Pub. Schs., 1997—. Cons. Naperville and Woodridge Schs., 1998—; lectr. Loyola U., Chgo., 1997—; pvt. practice, Northbrook, Ill., 2000—; third-party cons. Hartgrove Psychol. Hosp., Chgo., 1985-88, Old Orchard Psychol. Hosp., Skokie, 1987-89; co-founder Baby N'Me Mother-Infant Dyad Groups, 1991; spkr. Resolve Orgn., Good Samaritan Hosp., Downers Grove, Ill., 1991. Founder Living with Infertility and Experimentation (L.I.F.E.), Evanston, Ill., 1990-96; mem. steering com. Resolve for L.I.F.E. Group, Evanston, 1990-94. Grantee Loyola U., 1996. Mem. APA, Assn. for Advancement Therapeutic Edn., Nat. Assn. Sch. Psychologists, Soc. Personality Assessment, Ill. Sch. Psychol. Assn., Ill. Assn. for Infant Mental Health. Avocations: piano, fitness, personal reading, local school involvement. Home: 2434 Ridgeway Ave Evanston IL 60201-1858 Office: Winnetka Pub Schs 520 Glendale Ave Winnetka IL 60093-2135 also: 910 Skokie Blvd Northbrook IL 60062 Office Phone: 847-604-4160. E-mail: DbKrueger@aol.com.

KRUEGER, JANET EAGER, artist, educator; MFA in Painting, U. Tex., San Antonio, 1998; BFA in Art History, U. Tex. Assoc. prof. art Tex. A&M Internat. U., Laredo, 1998—. Developer BA art and studio art program Tex. A&M Internat. U., Laredo. Prin. works include 8 drawings USAA, 2001, prin. works include 7 paintings SBC Ctr., San Antonio, Tex., 2002. Pres. Hecho en Encinal, Tex., 1999—2003. Youth Arts grantee, Nat. Endowment Arts, 2001—02, 2001—03. Office: Texas A&M Internat U 5201 University Blvd Laredo TX 78041-1900 E-mail: jkrueger@tamiu.edu.

KRUEGER, KATHLEEN SUSAN, special education administrator; b. Cape Girardeau, Mo., Jan. 21, 1951; d. Robert Settle and Myldred Frances (Jones) K. BS in Edn., Athens Coll., 1973; MEd, Ala. A&M U., 1980. Classroom tchr. Limestone County Schs., Athens, Ala., 1973-74; spl. edn. tchr. Huntsville (Ala.) City Schs., 1974-95, spl. edn. coord., 1995—. Mem. city-wide policy com. Huntsville City Schs., 1987-89, profl. devel. coord., 1986-95, dept. chair for spl. edn., 1993-95. Bd. dirs. H-Vote, Huntsville, 1989; vol. ARC, 1981-82; tchr. Sunday Sch., First United Meth. Ch., Huntsville, 1983-85, sec., 1985-86, mem. choir, 1985-89, hon. treas. for State of Ala., 1988. Mem. NEA (PAC), Ala. Edn. Assn., Huntsville Edn. Assn. (bldg. rep. 1992-95, treas. 1989, sec. 1992-93), Coun. for Exceptional Children, Ala. Coun. for Sch. Adminstrn. and Supervision, Phi Delta Kappa, Phi Mu (membership dir. 1970-71, treas. 1971-72). Home: 7801 Regent Pl SW Apt 8 Huntsville AL 35802-1471

KRUEGER, LIZ, state legislator; m. John E. Seley. BS in Social Policy and Human Devel., Northwestern Univ.; MS, Univ. Chgo. Assoc. dir. Cmty. Food Resource Ctr.; state sen. State of N.Y., 2002—. Founding dir. N.Y.C. Food Bank; bd. dirs. Am. Jewish Com. Chair N.Y.C. Food Stamp Task Force; co-facilitator N.Y.C. Welfare Reform Network; bd. dirs. City-Wide

Task Force on Housing Ct., N.Y.C., N.Y.C. Fed. Emergency Mgmt. Agy. Emergency Food and Shelter Program/United Way of N.Y. Recipient Disting. Svc. award, Hunger Action Network, N.Y., Inst. on Law and Rights of Older Adults, Brookdale Ctr. on Aging of Hunter Coll., 1997, Media Advocacy award, Pub. Health Assn. of n.Y., 1998. Democrat. Office: 302 Legis Ofc Bldg Albany NY 12247

KRUEGER, MARLO BUSH, retired lawyer; b. Little Rock, Ark., Sept. 5, 1956; d. James Shepherd Bush and Frances Rosannah Davidson; m. James Robert Krueger, Sept. 15, 2001. BS in Pub. Adminstrn., U. Ark., Fayetteville, 1978, JD, 1981. Bar: (Ark.) 1981. Asst. reporter decisions Ark. Supreme Ct. and Ct. of Appeals, Little Rock, 1982—88, reporter decisions, 1988—95. Articles editor (jour.) The Saline (Best Edited Documentary award, 1994, Dale Bumpers award for best Civil War article, 1994, Best Comty. History Pub. in Local Jour. award, 2000). Mem., sec. Saline County History and Heritage Soc., 1994—95; mem. various bds. and coms. 1st Meth. Ch., Benton, 1984—89, 1992—93. Mem.: Ark. Bar Assn., Assn. Reporters of Jud. Decisions (various coms., exec. bd. 1987—94, pres. 1992—93, Devoted Svc. award 1995), Phi Delta Phi (life; clk. 1980—81). Methodist. Avocations: genealogy, fishing, computers, photography, history. Home: 4011 Hwy 5 Benton AR 72015-8277

KRUEGER, NANCY ASTA, physical therapist; b. Manhattan Beach, Calif., Jan. 8, 1947; d. Henry Adolph and Asta Ida (Harrison) Graef; m. Gary Patrick Krueger, June 14, 1969. Student, Lewis & Clark Coll., 1964-66; BS, U. So. Calif., L.A., 1969; postgrad., U. So. Calif., Downey, 1980-81. Cert. orthopedic specialist, hand therapist. Staff phys. therapist Los Angeles County-U. So. Calif. Med. Ctr., L.A., 1969-71, Stockton (Calif.) State Hosp., 1971; pediatric phys. therapist Calif. Childrens Svcs.-San Joaquin County, Stockton, 1972-73; sr. phys. therapist Calif. Childrens Svcs.-San Diego County, San Diego, 1974-80; mng. dir. therapy svcs. Sharp-Cabrillo Hosp., San Diego, 1981-83; sr. phys. therapist El Cajon (Calif.) Valley Hosp., 1983-84; prin. El Cajon Therapy Assocs., 1984—. Cons. Teledyne Ryan Aero., San Diego County, 1984—, San Diego Marriott Hotel, 1995—; speaker in field. Singer Old Globe Madrigal Singers, 1983; vice chair adv. com. Maternal, Child and Adolescent Health, San Diego County, 1987-89; active local polit. campaigns; advisor Mesa Coll., 1985—; mem. edn. and sci. com. Arthritis Found., 1986-87; chairperson adv. com. Mesa Coll., 1992-96. Fellow Am. Acad. Sports Medicine, Orthopedic Soc.; mem. Am. Phys. Therapy Assn. (chmn. San Diego dist. 1977-78, bd. dirs. Calif. chpt. 1983-84, mem. nominating com. 1989-91, chmn. 1991, v.p. 1994-97, fin. com. Orthopedic sect. 1993-97), Aux. Am. Optometric Assn., Am. Soc. Hand Therapists, Arthritis Health Profls. Assn. (v.p. 1991-93), Jrs. of Social Svc. (treas. 1991-93), Soroptimists (sec. El Cajon chpt. 1982, chmn. 1994), Rotary Internat. (bull. editor), Acupational Health SIG (treas. 1997-99). Republican. Episcopalian. Avocations: skiing, boating, reading, needlework. Home: 4657 Rancho Park Ave San Diego CA 92120 Office: El Cajon Therapy Assocs 590 S Magnolia Ave El Cajon CA 92020-6011

KRUEGER, PATRICIA, state representative; b. Bayonne, N.J., Dec. 22, 1941; BS, Georgetown U., 1963; MEd, Keene State Coll., 1981. Former RN, educator and supt. of schs.; rep. dist. 16 N.H. Ho. of Reps. Del. Rep. Nat. Conv., 1996; mem. Nat. Rules Com., 1996; mem. Elec. Law Com.; owner Arbutus Farm. Mem. Montuchusset Vocat. Tech. Sch. Bd., 1980—. With USNR Nurse Corps. Address: 1850 Front St Apt 5 Manchester NH 03102-8983

KRUEGER-HORN, CHERYL, apparel executive; B in Home Econs. and Bus., Bowling Green State U., 1974. Buyer Burdine's Dept. Store, 1974-76; mdse. mgr. The Limited, 1976; v.p. sale Chaus Sportswear, CEO, until 1985; owner Cheryl's Cookies; pres., CEO Cheryl & Co. Bd. dirs. Bob Evans. Recipient Columbus Area Small Bus. Person of Yr. award Small Bus. Adminstrn., 1986, Woman of Achievement award YWCA, 1992, Outstanding Innovation Achievement award Innovation Alliance, 1992, Ctrl. Ohio Entrepreneur of Yr. award Inc. Mag. and Ernest & Young, 1994, Salesperson of Yr. award Columbus C. of C. Sales Exec. Club, Businessperson of Yr. award Ohio State U., Rosabeth Moss Kantor Excellence in Enterprise award Ohio Dept. Devel., 1996. Mem. Young Pres. Orgn. Office: 646 Mccorkle Blvd Westerville OH 43082-8778

KRUG, ELLEN J. social worker, medical educator; d. Theodore Krug and Beatrice Schreiber Krug; m. Denis J. Meadows, June 7, 1980; children: Kieran Krug-Meadows, Kyla Krug-Meadows. BA, Bard Coll., Annandale-on-Hudson, NY, 1975; MSW, Hunter Coll. Sch. of Social Work, N.Y.C., 1980. LCSW NY; cert. CE AAHCC, Calif. Clin. social worker Choiceful Birth and Parenting, Bklyn., 1984—; from social worker to sr. social worker Teen Choice program Inwood House, NYC, 1983—98, clin. dir. Teen Choice program, 1998—; adj. faculty, field advisor Columbia U. Sch. Social Work, NYC, 1998—99. Contbr. article Counseling, Psychological and Social Services in Partners in Prevention: Coordinated School Health Programs to Prevent Adolescent Pregnancy and STDs. Parent rep., sch. leadership team & parent exec. bd. Stuyvesant H.S., N.Y.C., 2000—03. Avocations: cooking, homeopathy, knitting, yoga, dance, working out, travel.

KRUG, SHIRLEY, state legislator; b. Milw., Jan. 29, 1958; BS, U. Wis., Milw., 1981, MA, 1983. Mem. from dist. 13 Wis. State Assembly, Madison, 1984-96, mem. from dist. 12, 1984—. Former adj. prof. econs. U. Wis., Parkside. Commr. Mils. Met. Sewerage Dist.; former v.p. Jobs with Peace. Office: Wis State Assembly State Capitol PO Box 8952 Madison WI 53708-8952 Address: 9352 W Terra Ct Milwaukee WI 53224-2949

KRUGER, FRANCES PETRONELLE, lawyer; b. Sasolburg, South Africa, July 14, 1967; came to U.S., 1993; d. Paul du Plessis and Gina (Claassen) K. LLB, U. Orange Free State, South Africa, 1990; LLM, Georgetown Law Ctr., Washington, 1994. Bar: South Africa 1992, N.Y.C. 1996. Assoc. Hofmeyer Inc., Johannesburg, South Africa, 1991-93; sr. assoc. Trinity Assocs., Greenwich, Conn., 1994-96, The Sloane Group, Greenwich, Conn., 1997-98; v.p. mktg., dir. legal affairs Innovative Marble & Tile Inc., Hauppauge, N.Y., 1998—. Avocations: sailing, skiing, diving, hiking. Office: Innovative Marble & Tile 130 Motor Pkwy Hauppauge NY 11788-5107

KRUGER, LOUISE VIRGINIA, sculptor; b. L.A., Aug. 5, 1924; d. Otto H. and Elizabeth Mary (Spinner) K. Student, Scripps Coll., Claremont, Calif., 1942-45, Art Students League, N.Y.C., 1945-46, Guastini Foundry, Pistola, Italy, 1957-58, Chief Opoku Dwumfuor, Kumasi, Ghana, 1969-70. Sculptor: one-woman shows include Artists' Gallery, N.Y.C., 1949, Brown U., Mass., Farnsworth Mus., Maine, Martha Jackson Gallery, N.Y.C., Schoelkopf Gallery, N.Y.C., Bowdoin Mus., Maine, Martin Sumers Gallery, N.Y.C.; represented in group exhibitions Mus. Modern Art, N.Y.C., Whitney Mus., N.Y.C., Met. Mus., N.Y.C., Bklyn. Mus., Modern Mus., Sao Paulo, Kunsthaus, Zurich, Riksgalleriet, Oslo, Libr. Congress, Washington, Chgo. Art Inst.; included in collections Mus. Modern Art, N.Y.C., Prudential Ins. Collection, Rutgers U., New Britain Mus. Am. Art, Conn., Bowdoin Mus., Maine, N.Y.C. Pub. Libr. Home: 30 E 2nd St New York NY 10003-8906 Office: Lori Bookstein Fine Art 37 W 57th St New York NY 10019

KRUGER, NANCY R. university program director, nurse; BS in Nursing, Skidmore Coll., 1967; MA in Parent-Child Health in Nursing, NYU, 1971; D of Sci. in Nursing, U. Pa., 1983. Staff nurse surgery SUNY Downstate Med. Ctr., Bklyn., 1967-68; staff nurse recovery room NYU Med. Ctr., 1968-70; clin. specialist, supr. critical care Mercer Med. Ctr., Trenton, N.J., 1971-81; clin. dir. U. Pa. Hosp., Dept. Med. Nursing and Emergency Svcs., Phila., 1981-84; asst. exec. dir., chief nursing officer Wills Eye Hosp., Phila., 1984-86; dir. nursing, chief nursing officer Pa. State U. Hershey Med. Ctr., Univ. Hosps., Hershey, Pa., 1986—, nurse practitioner cardiothoracic surgery, 1990-91; clin. instr. Sch. Nursing U. Pa., 1979-83; clin. prof. Coll. Allied Health Thomas Jefferson U., Sch. Nursing, Phila., 1985-89; adj. asst. prof. grad. faculty Pa. State U., Harrisburg, Pa., 1987—, co-dir. Quality Assurance Program, Grad. Pub. Adminstrn., 1987—. Various univ. com. memberships including clin. investigation com., 1986-89, strategic study group for nursing, 1987, planning com. for employee performance evaluation, 1993, search com. for chmn. pediatrics dept., 1989, others; cons. Commonwealth of Pa., Dept. Health, mem. application steering com. RWJ Found. Grant program, 1992. Contbr. articles to profl. jours. Bd. dirs. Harrisburg Opera Co., 1994-95; adv. com. Lion's Eye Bank of Ctrl. Pa., 1989—; mem. exec. com. Children's Miracle Network Telethon, 1986—. Mem. AACN, Am. Orgn. Nurse Execs., Nat. League for Nursing, Pa. Orgn. Nurse execs. (exec. com. 1988-92, chmn. nursing practice com. 1989, chmn. legis. com. 1992, pres. 1991, chmn. PONE nurse educators task force 1992—), South Ctrl. Orgn. Nurse Execs. (pres. 1989), Phila. Assn. Clin. Trials (human rsch. rev. bd. 1984-91), Coun. Health Profns. Edn. Hosp. Assn. Pa. (chmn. 1995), Am. Coun. Transplantation (bd. dirs. 1987-91), Sigma Theta Tau. Office: Pa State U Hershey Med Ctr 500 University Dr Hershey PA 17033-2360

KRUGER, PAULA, telecommunications industry executive; b. Bklyn., July 31, 1950; d. Jean Jacques Kruger and Jo Campione; m. Lawrence C. Heller; children: Michael, Tracy, Jessica. BA, CW Post, 1972, MBA, 1976. V.p. customer rels. Cablevision, Woodbury, NY, 1994—97; corp. v.p. customer svc. Am. Express, N.Y.C., Citibank, N.Y.C., v.p. devel. divsn.; v.p. consumer svcs. group South Korea; v.p. teleservices Excel Comm., 1997—99, exec. v.p., customer and independent representative ops., 1999; gen. mgr. customer relationship mgmt. service line Electronic Data Systems Corp., 2002—03; exec. v.p. consumer markets group Qwest Comm., 2003—. Office: Qwest Comm Internat 1801 California St Denver CO 80202

KRUKS, SONIA R. social sciences educator, researcher; b. London, Feb. 15, 1947; arrived in U.S., 1980; d. Leo Kruks and Sima Horn; m. Benjamin G. Wisner, Jr., Feb. 9, 1978; 1 child, Gabrielle Kruks-Wisner. BA hons., Leeds U., England, 1968; MSc Econs., London Sch. Econs., 1970, PhD, 1977. Lectr. in politics City of London Polytechnic, 1971—77; asst., assoc. prof. politics Grad. Fac. New Sch. For Social Rsch., N.Y.C., 1981—90; Danforth prof. politics Oberlin (Ohio) Coll., 1990—. Author: Political Philosophy of Merlean-Ponty, 1981, Situation and Human Existence, 1990, Retrieving Experience, 2001; mem. editl. bd. Polity, 1989—95, Sartre Studies, 1997—, Hypatia, 2000—. Mem.: Am. Philosophical Assn., Am. Polit. Sci. Assn. (sect. treas. 1992—95, sect. sec. 1993—95, best paper award women and politics sect. 1992). Avocations: ceramics, walking, music. Office: Oberlin Coll Politics Dept Oberlin OH 44074

KRULEWICZ, RITA GLORIA, special education educator; d. Charles Lewis and Gloria Edna Perrine; m. Donald Jospeh Krulewicz; 1 child, Clare. BS, Coll. Misericordia, 1976; MEd, Trenton State Coll., 1979. Multihandicapped tchr. The Woods Sch., Langhorne, Pa., 1976-79, Mercer County Spl. Svcs. Sch. Dist., Hamilton, NJ, 1979-86; resource ctr. tchr. Princeton (N.J.) Regional Sch. Dist., 1992—, John Witherspoon Mid. Sch., Princeton, 1992—. Worker Dem. Orgn., Pa., 1976—; mem. Morrisville Hist. Soc., 1976—. Named Tchr. of Yr. Mercer County Spl. Svcs., 1986. Mem.: NEA, Coun. Exceptional Children (professionally recognized spl. edn. 1999—), N.J. Edn. Assn., Kappa Delta Pi. Roman Catholic. Avocations: reading, gardening, surfing the net, going to movies, traveling. Home: 136 Carlisle Ave Yardville NJ 08620-1244 Office: John Witherspoon Mid Sch 217 Walnut Ln Princeton NJ 08540-3484

KRULFELD, RUTH MARILYN, anthropologist, educator; m. Jacob Mendel Krulfeld, 1964; 1 child, Michael David. BA cum laude, Brandeis U., 1956; PhD, Yale U., 1974. Field rschr. micro-geog. rsch. farms, Singapore, Malaya, 1951-53; anthrop. rschr., Jamaica, 1957, 1958, 1960—63, 1993; anthrop. rschr. S.E. Asian refugees to U.S., 1981—; anthrop. rschr., Lombok, Indonesia and N.E. Thailand, 1993; asst. prof. anthropology, dir. grad. students George Washington U., Washington, 1964-72, 93-97, assoc. prof., 1973-76, prof., 1976-2000, chmn. dept. anthropology, 1984-87, founder spl. grad. program in internat. world devel., prof. anthropology, internat. affairs, prof. emeritus anthropology, human scis., internat. affairs, 2000—. Bd. dirs. No. Va. Humanities Coun.; rschr. Laotian refugees in U.S., 1981—, also rschr. on culture change in villages in Indonesia; mem. adv. bd. Successful New Ams. Project of S.E. Asian Resource Action Ctr.; advisor to bd. Newcomers Cmty. Svc. Ctr., Lao-Am. Women's Assn., Lao Cmty. Forum; mem. faculty Semester At Sea, 1999, 2003. Co-author: Reconstructing Lives, Recapturing Meaning: Refugee Identity, Gender and Culture Change, 1994, Beyond Boundaries: Selected papers on Refugees and Immigrants, 1997, Power, Ethics, and Human Rights: Anthropological Studies of Refugee Research and Action, 1998; contbr. articles to profl. jours.; editl. bd. com. on refugees and immigrants. Bd. dirs. No. Va. Regional Humanities Coun. Currier scholar Yale U., 1958; Ford fellow, 1960-62; grantee Found. for Study of Man, 1957, Am. Coun., 1963, Cotlow faculty rsch. grantee, 1992-93, faculty rsch. grantee George Washington U., 1992-93, rsch. grantee Va. Found. for Humanities and Pub. Policy, 1995-96; recipient Banneker award Ctr. for Washington Area Studies, 1996, George Washington U. award, 2000. Mem. AAAS (bd. dirs., com. on sci. freedom and responsibility), Anthrop. Soc. Washington, Am. Anthrop. Assn. (nominating com., com. on refugee issues gen. anthropology divsn., vice chair com. on refugees issues 1992-94, gen. anthropology divsn. 1993-94, exec. bd. com. on refugees and immigrants 1994-99, CORI editl. bd. 1998-99, CORI award for best paper on refugees issues 1992, Pedagogical Rsch. and Innovative Devel. in Edn. award 1994, award for leadership and contbn. to refugee studies com. on refugees and immigrants 2000). Office: George Washington U Dept Anthropology Washington DC 20052-0001

KRULIK, BARBARA S. director, writer, curator; b. N.Y.C., June 13, 1955; d. Herbert Arnold and Irene Sylvia K. BA in Art History, Pa. State U., 1976; MA in Museology, Reinwardt Acad., Amsterdam, The Netherlands, 2000. Asst. to dir. Nat. Acad. of Design, N.Y.C., 1976—78; acting dir. NAD, N.Y.C., 1977-78, coord. exhbns., 1978-83, asst. dir., 1983-89, interim dir., 1989-90, dep. dir., 1990-92; assoc. dir. Forum Gallery, N.Y.C., 1992-94; dir. Grad. Sch. Figurative Art New York Acad. Art, N.Y.C., 1994-97; owner, dir. KCCS (Krulik Cultural Cons. Svs.), 2001—; mgr. Mugpre Music Dance Co., Amsterdam, Netherlands, 2003—; mem. steering com. Found. Exhibn. Man., Amsterdam, Netherlands, 2004—. Ind. curator, 1997—; cons., 1997—. Author, editor exhbn. catalogues. Mem. Am. Assn. Mus. (curators and registrars coms.), Internat. Coun. on Mus. E-mail: b.krulik@chello.nl.

KRULL, KATHLEEN, writer; b. Ft. Leonard Wood, Mo., July 29, 1952; d. Kenneth Owen and Helen (Folliard) K.; m. Loyal D. Cowles, Dec. 14, 1974 (div. May 1982); m. Paul W. Brewer, Oct. 31, 1989; stepchildren: Jacqui, Melanie. BA in English magna cum laude, Lawrence U., 1974. Editl. asst. Harper & Row, Evanston, Ill., 1973-74; assoc. editor Western Pub./Golden Books, Racine, Wis., 1974-79; mng. (acquiring) editor Raintree Pubs., Milw., 1979-82; sr. editor Harcourt Brace Jovanovich, San Diego, 1982-84; freelance writer and reviewer children's books, 1984—. Frequent speaker at confs., workshops and univs. Author: Golden Everything Workbook Series, 1979, Beginning To Learn (24 books transl. into 5 langs. 1979-82), Sometimes My Mom Drinks Too Much, 1980 (Outstanding Social Studies Trade Book award 1980), Trixie Belden and the Hudson River Mystery, 1979, Twelve Keys to Writing Books That Sell, 1989, Songs of Praise, 1989, Alex Fitzgerald, TV Star, 1990, Alex Fitzgerald's Cure for Nightmares, 1991, Gonna Sing My Head Off; American Folk Songs for Children, 1992, World of My Own (4 books 1994, 95), Lives of the Musicians: Good Times, Bad Times...And What the Neighbors Thought, 1993, Maria Molina and the Days of the Dead, 1994, Lives of the Writers: Comedies, Tragedies (And What the Neighbors Thought), 1995, V is for Victory: America Remembers World War II, 1995, Lives of the Artists, 1995, Wilma Unlimited, 1996, Wish You Were Here, 1997, Lives of the Athletes, 1997, Lives of the Presidents, 1998, Lives of the Musicians: Good Times, Bad Times: (And What the Neighbors Thought), 1998, Alex Fitzgerald's Cure for Nightmares, 1999, Gonna Sing My Head Off!: American Folk Songs for Children, 1999; also articles and revs. Recipient Celebrate Literacy award Greater San Diego Reading Assn., 1994, also numerous awards for writing, including Boston Globe/Horn Book honor award, PEN West children's lit. award, 1994, nonfiction award So. Calif. Coun. on Lit. for Children and Young People, ALA Notable Book awards, Tchrs.' Choice award Internat. Reading Assn., Best Book of 1993 award Pubs. Weekly. Mem. Soc. Children's Book Writers and Illustrators (bd. dirs. 1995—, Golden Kite honor award for nonfiction). Avocations: quilting, gardening, singing, playing piano, travel. Office: c/o Harcourt Brace & Co Childrens Books 525 B St Ste 1900 San Diego CA 92101-4495

KRUMHOLZ, MIMI, human resources administrator; b. N.Y.C., Aug. 7, 1954; d. Jack Walter and Ida Judith (Intrator) Jerome; m. Andrew Jay Krumholz, Aug. 15 1991; children: Matthew, Aaron, Paul. BA in Edn., BS in Psychology, SUNY, Stony Brook, 1976; MS in Clin. Psychology, Towson State U., Md., 1982. Paralegal Donovan, Leisure, N.Y.C., 1976-77; human resource mgr. Dynatech Data sys., Springfield, Va, 1977-80; human resource dir. Calif. Milling Corp., L.A., 1980-81, Providence Ctr., Arnold, Md, 1986-88, Dewey, Ballantine, Washington, 1988-90; legal adminstr. Latham & Watkins, Washington, 1990—, dir. profl. devel., 1999—, dir. human resources, 2000—. Mem. Assn. Legal Adminstrs, Soc. Human Resources Mgmt., Am. Soc. Training and Devel. Avocations: reading, swimming, writing. Office: Latham & Watkins Ste 1300 1001 Pennsylvania Ave NW Washington DC 20004-2585 E-mail: mimi.krumholz@lw.com.

KRUMSIEK, BARBARA J. investment company executive; B in math., Douglass Coll., Rutgers U.; M in math., Courant Inst. Math. Scis., NYU; LHD honoris causa (hon.), Georgetown U., 2002. With Alliance Capital Mgmt., LP (formerly Equitable), 1974—97, sr. v.p., mng. dir. mutual funds divsn.; pres., CEO, co-chairperson Calvert Group, Ltd., 1997—. Bd. Greater DC Cares, Trickle Up Found., Cultural Alliance, Wash., DC; bd. vis. Howard U. Sch. Law; exec. com. Greater Wash. Bd. Trade. Named Outstanding CEO Yr., Women's Bus. Ctr. Wash. DC, 2001; named one of 100 Most Powerful Women, Washingtonian mag., 2001; named to Hall Disting. Alumni, Rutgers U. Alumni Fedn., 2000, Douglass Soc., Douglass Coll. and Assoc. Alumnae, 2000; recipient CEO Diversity award, Diversity Best Practices, 2002. Mem.: Phi Beta Kappa. Office: Calvert Group Ltd 4550 Montgomery Ave Bethesda MD 20814 Office Phone: 800-368-2748.*

KRUPANSKY, ETHEL BLANCHE, retired judge; b. Cleve., Dec. 10, 1925; d. Frank and Ann K.; m. Frank W. Vargo, Apr. 30, 1960. AB, Flora Stone Mather Coll., 1943-47; JD, Case Western Res. U., 1948, LLM, 1966. Bar: Ohio 1949. Gen. practice law, 1949-61, 83-84; asst. atty. gen. State of Ohio; asst. chief counsel Ohio Bur. Workmen's Compensation; judge Cleve. Mcpl. Ct., 1961-69; judge Common Pleas Ct. Cuyahoga County, 1969-77, Ct. Appeals Ohio 8th Appellate Dist., 1977-81; justice Supreme Ct. Ohio, 1981-83; judge 8th Dist. Ct. Appeals, 1983-95, chief justice, 1991; ret., 1995. Vis. com. Case Western U. Law Sch., 1974-78, bd. govs., 1975-76 Recipient Outstanding Jud. Service award Supreme Ct. Ohio, 1972-76, Law Book scholar award Cuyahoga Women's Polit. Caucus, 1981, outstanding contbn. to law award Ohio Assn. Civil Trial Attys., 1982, Disting. Alumna award, 1982, Disting. Service award Women's Space, 1982, award Democratic Women's Caucus, 1983, award Women's Equity Action League Ohio, 1983; Personal Achievement and Community Svc. award Case We. Res. U., 1988, Margaret Ireland award Women's City Club, 1984; named Woman of Achievement Inter-Club Council Cleve., 1969; inducted into Ohio Women's Hall of Fame, 1981 Mem. Nat. Assn. Women Lawyers, Nat. Assn. Women Judges, Ohio Bar Assn. (Cronise Lutes award 1997), Bar Assn. Greater Cleve., Cuyahoga County Bar Assn., Cleve. Women Lawyers, LWV, Ohio Ctrs. of Appeals Assn., Ohio Assn. Attys. Gen., Ohio Appellate Judges Assn., Soc. of Benchers (chair 1994-95), SAR (Silver Medal award 1995). Republic. Roman Catholic. Club: Woman's City (Woman of Achievement award 1981) (Cleve.).

KRUPAT, KITTY WEISS, writer, educator; b. N.Y.C., Feb. 9, 1938; d. Paul and Magda (Neumann) Weiss; m. Arnold Krupat, Aug. 1962 (div. 1968). BA, NYU, 1961, Master's, 1998, postgrad., 1999—. Rsch. editor Esquire mag., N.Y.C., 1966-70; mng. editor pocket books Simon & Schuster, N.Y.C., 1970-74; organizer, edn. dir. dist. 65 UAW, N.Y.C., 1974-89; organizer grad. student organizing com. NYU, N.Y.C., 1996—; edn. dir. Internat. Ladies' Garment Workers Union, N.Y.C., 1989-95; instr. Cornell U., N.Y.C., 1997—; tchg. asst. NYU, 1995—2003; assoc. dir. Queen's Coll. Labor Resource Ctr. CUNY, 2002—. Instr. Queens Coll., CUNY. Co-editor (anthology) Out at Work: Building A Gay Labor Alliance, 2001; contbr. articles to profl. jours. Organizer No Sweat Coalition NYU, 1996—. Mem. MLA, Am. Studies Assn., Labor at the Crossroads (bd. dirs. 1989—), Wagner Labor Archives (bd. dirs. 1987—), United Assn. Labor Educators (bd. dirs. 1981—), Nat. Writers Union. Avocations: music, art, theater, gardening, movies.

KRUPCHAK, TAMARA, artist; b. Lake Station, Ind., Apr. 15, 1956; d. John Charles Krupchak and Rose Marie Maretich-Krupchak. BS, Ball State U., 1978. Artist, spkr., creativity coach Tamara Krupchak Fine Art, San Diego, 1988—. Group shows include San Diego Tijuana Yokohama Art Exchange, 1992, San Diego Mus. Art, 1994, 97, 98, 99; artist (book) Getting Exposure, 1995. Bd. dirs. artist guild San Diego Mus. Art, 1994-97, trustee, 1996-97; mem. nat. devel. com. Coll. Fine Arts, Ball State U., 2001. Recipient art commn. St. Mary's Health and Learning Ctr., Grand Rapids, Mich., 1998, Sunland Christian Sci. Healing Ctr., San Diego, 1998. Mem. Toastmasters Internat. (winner Area 21 Internat. Speech Contest 1998). Office: 1090 University Ave Ste 201A San Diego CA 92103-3362

KRUSA-DOSSIN, MARY ANN, military officer; m. Paul F. Dossin; 1 child, Michael. BA in Psychology and Sociology, Tex. Christian U., 1974; MS in Human Rels., Golden Gate U., 1981; MS in Nat. Resource Planning, Nat. Def. U., 1995. Commd. 2d lt. USMC, 1975, advanced through grades to brig. gen., platoon comdr. security dept. MCAS El Toro, 1976—79, tng. and human affairs officer Aircraft Group 15, 1st Marine Aircraft Wing, 1979—81, ops. officer provost marshal's office, 1979—81, dir. family svc. ctr. Camp Lejeune, 1981—84, with provost marshal's office, 1984—85, provost marshal MCAS, 1988—91, exec. offider Hdqrs. and svc. battalion MCB Camp Smedley D. Butler Okinawa, Japan, 1992—93, comdr., 1993—96, action officer joint staff J-7 operational plans and interoperability directorate Pentagon, 1996—98, comdr. security battalion MCB Camp Pendleton, 1998—2000, asst. chief of staff cmty. svcs. MCB Camp Pendleton, 2000—02, dep. dir. Marine Corps Pub. Affairs, 2002—03, dir. Marine Corps. Pub. Affairs, 2003—. Decorated Legion of Merit. Home: 1200 Crystal Dr Apt 412 Arlington VA 22202-4305*

KRUSCHKE, CANDY LYNN, music educator; b. Buffalo, N.Y., Oct. 26, 1962; d. Elwood Albert and Lucille (Altrogge) Kruschke. MusB, SUNY, Fredonia, 1984; MS, SUNY, Buffalo, 1989. Cert. tchr. music grades K-12 and math. grades 7-12 N.Y. Music tchr. Alden (N.Y.) Ctrl. Sch., 1985—89, Akron (N.Y.) Ctrl. Sch., 1990—, summer sch. math. tchr., 1993—. Title clk. Auto Dealers Exch. Sys. Am. Auction of Buffalo, 1993—; music competition judge Six Flags Darien Lake, Corfu, NY, 1996—; ch. and choir pianist Trinity Evang. Luth. Ch., Akron, 1997—; accompanist jr. high chorus Erie County Music Educators Assn., Buffalo, 2001—. Coun. mem. Trinity

Evang. Luth. Ch., Akron, 2000, chair worship and music com., 2000—. Mem.: N.Y. State Sch. Music Assn. (cert. piano judge), Music Educators Nat. Conf., Sigma Alpha Iota. Republican. Avocations: sewing, embroidery.

KRUSE, ANN GRAY, computer programmer; b. Oklahoma City, Jan. 4, 1941; d. Floyd and Bernice Florence (Follansbee) Gray; m. Roy Edwin Kruse, Mar. 20, 1971 (dec.). AB, Randolph Macon Woman's Coll., 1963; MBA, U. Chgo., 1973. Programming mgr. Ind. Info. Controls, Valparaiso, Ind., 1966-67; systems programmer Am. Steel Foundries, Hammond, Ind., 1970-73; engr. applications programming Bell Helicopter Textron, Fort Worth, 1974-76; lead systems programmer Harris Data Communications, Dallas, 1976-81; sr. systems programmer Lone Star Gas Co., Dallas, 1981-82; sr. software specialist Raytheon, Dallas, 1982—. Republican. Episcopalian. Home: 6128 Black Berry Ln Dallas TX 75248-4909 Office: PO Box 660023 Dallas TX 75266-0023 E-mail: akruse@gsb.uchicago.edu.

KRUSE, MARGARET M. art educator; b. Cape Girandeau, Mo., June 9, 1935; d. Arthur Lawrence Fuerth and Corona Ann Heisserer; m. Frederic Wallace Kruse, Nov. 25, 1960; children: Constance Katheryn, Valerie Anne. BS in Secondary Edn., State U. S.E. Mo., 1957; MEd in Art, Webster U., 1994. Tchr. art St. Charles (Mo.) HS, 1958—59, Bayless HS, St. Louis, 1959—66, Parkway S. Jr. HS, St. Louis, 1967—69, Ladue Sch. Dist., St. Louis, 1969—73, Immacotata Sch., St. Louis, Our Lady of Pillar, St. Louis, 1985—. Mem.: Nat. Cath. Edn. Assn., Mo. Art Edn. Assn., Nat. Art Edn. Assn. Home: 164 Saddleford Dr Chesterfield MO 63017

KRUSICK, MARGARET ANN, state legislator; b. Milw., Oct. 26, 1956; d. Ronald J. and Maxine C. K. BA, U. Wis., 1978; postgrad., U. Wis., Madison, 1979-82. Legal asst. Milw. Law Office, 1973-78; teaching asst. U. Wis., Milw., 1978-79; staff mem. Govs. Ombudsman Program for the Aging & Disabled, Madison, Wis., 1980; administrv. asst. Wis. Higher Edn. Aids Bd., Madison, 1981, legis. aide Wis. Assembly, Madison, 1982-83, state rep., 1983—. Author: Wisconsin Youth Suicide Prevention Act, 1985, Wisconsin Nursing Home Reform Act, 1987, Wisconsin Truancy Reform Act, 1988, Elder Abuse Fund, 1989, Stolen Goods Recovery Act, 1990, Fair Prescription Drug Pricing Act, 1994, Anti-Graffiti Act, 1996, Caregiver Criminal Background Checks and Abuse Prevention Act, 1997, Child Abuse Prosecution Act, 1998, Nursing Home Resident Protection Act, 1998. Mem. St. Gregory Great Cath. Ch., Milw., 1960—, Dem. Party, Milw., 1980—, bd. dirs. Alzheimer's Assn., 1986-88. Named Legislator of Yr. award Wis. Sch. Counselors, Madison, 1986, Wis. County Constnl. Officers Legislator of Yr., 1999; recipient Sr. Citizen Appreciation Allied Coun. for Sr. Milw., 1987, Crime Prevention award Milw. Police Dept., Milw., 1988, Cert. Appreciation, Milw. Pub. Sch., 1989, Friends of Homecare award, 1989, Environ. Decades' Clean 16 award, 1986-90, 95-96, Badger State Sheriff's Law and Order award, 1993, Appreciation award Coalition of Wis. Aging Groups, 1998. Mem. Jackson Park Neighborhood Assn., U. Milw. Alumni Assn. (trustee 1986-90). Home: 3426 S 69th St Milwaukee WI 53219-4037 Office: Wis Assembly State Capitol Madison WI 53702-0001

KRUTSCH, PHYLLIS, academic administrator; MS, U. Wis. Regent U. Wis., 1990—97, 2000—, chmn. edn. com., 1994—97, chmn. com. bd. effectiveness. Grantee, Bradley Found. Mailing: 727 Superior Ave Washburn WI 54891

KRYSIAK, CAROLYN, state legislator; b. Balt., Aug. 9, 1939; married; 5 children. Student, U. Md., Cmty. Coll. of Balt. Del. Dist. 46 Md. State Delegation, 1991—, dep. majority whip, mem. judiciary com., 1991-92, mem. econ. matters com., 1992—; supr. dept. fin. City of Balt. Mem. Dem. State Ctrl. Com., 1984-90; bd. dirs. S.E. Cmty. Orgn., S.E. Devel., Inc.; mem. Second Ward Dem. Club, Joseph Lee Cmty. Orgn. Mem. Polish Am. Congress, Polish Women's Alliance, Polish Home Club. Home: 364 Cornwall St Baltimore MD 21224-2710 Office: Md Ho of Reps State Capitol Annapolis MD 21401

KRZYZAN, JUDY LYNN, automotive executive; b. Buffalo, Sept. 1, 1951; d. James Lambert and Janet Lucille (Grabau) McKellar; m. Ronald Edward Krzyzan, Dec. 21, 1974 (div. Jan. 1989); 1 child, Brian Edward. Student, Erie C.C., 1969-70. With counter and delivery M & H Auto Supply, Orchard Park, N.Y., 1973-75; parts counter person Crest Dodge Inc., Orchard Park, 1975-81; parts mgr. Case Chrysler Plymouth, Hamburg, N.Y., 1981-87, Mancuso Chrysler Plymouth, Hamburg, 1987-91, Transitowne Dodge, Williamsville, N.Y., 1991—. Supr. Profl. Inventory Assn., N.H., 1976-85. Named Mopar Parts Master, 1996. Mem. Chrysler Parts and Svc. Mgrs. Guild (v.p., sec. 1986-87, 89-92), The Greater Buffalo Auto Body Guild. Avocations: scuba diving, horseback riding, downhill skiing, cross-country skiing, trap shooting. Home: 2801 Creek Rd Hamburg NY 14075 Office: Transitowne Dodge 7408 Transit Rd Williamsville NY 14221-6091 E-mail: partzladi@aol.com.

KUBIDA, JUDITH ANN, museum administrator; b. Chgo., Aug. 29, 1948; d. William and Julia Ann (Kun) K.; m. Benjamin Kocolowski, Nov. 22, 1980. Attended, Southeast Coll. Adminstrn. asst. in vis. svcs. and sci. and edn. depts. Mus. Sci. and Industry, Chgo. Columnist monthly community newspaper Pullman Flyer. Vice-pres. pub. rels. Hist. Pullman Found., Hist. Pullman Dist., Chgo., editor quarterly newsletter Update, create publicity brochures, liaison with Ill., Chgo. Film Offices, publ. chmn., mem. annual house tour com., prodr. commemorative plate. Democrat. Home: 11334 S Langley Ave Chicago IL 60628-5126 Office: Hist Pullman Found Hotel Florence 11111 S Forrestville Ave Chicago IL 60628-4649

KUBIE, RACHEL, librarian, writer; b. Saint Louis, Missouri, Oct. 22, 1968; d. Robert Hoch Kubie and Joan Skinner; m. Joseph Welty, May 9, 1999; 1 child, Billie Jupiter. BA, U. Mo., St. Louis, 1991; MA, Johns Hopkins U., Balt., 1996; MLS, Cath. Univ. Am., Washington, 1998. Libr. Enoch Pratt Free Libr., Balt., 1997—. Editor: A Brite Guide to Reference Services, 2000; author: (poems) in various lit. jour. E-mail: rkubie@epfl.net.

KUBISTAL, PATRICIA BERNICE, educational consultant; b. Chgo., Jan. 19, 1938; d. Edward John and Bernice Mildred (Lenz) Kubistal. AB cum laude, Loyola U., Chgo., 1959, AM, 1964, AM, 1965, PhD, 1968; postgrad., Chgo. State Coll., 1962, Ill. Inst. Tech., 1963, State U. Iowa, 1963, Nat. Coll. Edn., 1974-75. With Chgo. Bd. Edn., 1959-93, tchr., 1959-63, counselor, 1963-65, adminstrv. intern, 1965-66, asst. to dist. supt., 1966-69, prin. spl. edn. sch., 1969-75; prin. Simpson Sch., 1975-76, Brentano Sch., 1975-87, Roosevelt H.S., 1987, Haugan Sch., 1989; prin. Cook County Juvenile Temporary Detention Ctr. Sch. Jones Met. H.S. Bus. and Commerce, 1989-90, adminstr. dept. spl. edn., 1990-93; supr. Lake View Evening Sch., 1982-92, ednl. cons., 1993—. Lectr. Loyola U. Sch. Edn., Nat. Coll. Edn. Grad. Sch., Mundelein Coll., 1982-91, DePaul U., 1998-99; coord. Upper Bound Program of U. Ill. Circle Campus, 1966-68. Book rev. editor of Chgo. Prins. Jour., 1970-76, gen. editor, 1982-90. Active Crusade of Mercy; mem. com. Ill. Constnl. Conv., 1967-69; mem. Citizens Sch. Com., 1969-71; mem. edn. com. Field Mus., 1971; ednl. advisor North Side Chgo. PTA Region, 1975; gov. Loyola U., 1961-87; pres. St. Matthews Parish Coun., 1995-98. Recipient Outstanding Intern award Nat. Assn. Secondary Sch. Prins., 1966, Outstanding Prin. award Citizen's Sch. Com. of Chgo., 1986; named Outstanding History Tchr., Chgo. Pub. Schs., 1963, Oustanding Ill. Educator, 1970, one of Oustanding Women of Ill., 1970, St. Luke's Logan Sq. Cmty. Person of Yr., 1977; NDEA grantee, 1963, NSF grantee, 1965, HEW Region 5 grantee for drug edn., 1974, Chgo. Bd. Edn. Prins.' grantee for study robotics in elem. schs.; U. Chgo. adminstrv. fellow 1984. Mem. Ill. Personnel and Guidance Assn., NEA, Ill. Edn. Assn., Chgo. Edn. Assn., Am. Acad. Polit. and Social Sci., Chgo. Prins. and Adminstrs. Assn. (pres. aux.), Nat. Coun. Adminstrv. Women, Chgo. Coun. Exceptional Children, Loyal Christian Benevolent Assn., Kappa Gamma Pi, Pi Gamma Mu, Phi Delta Kappa, Delta Kappa Gamma (paliamentarian 1979-80, pres. Kappa chpt. 1988-90, Lambda state editor 1982-92, chmn. Lambda state comm. com. 1992, Internat. Golden Gift Fund award), Delta Sigma Rho, Phi Sigma Tau. Home and Office: 5111 N Oakley Ave Chicago IL 60625-1829

KÜBLER-ROSS, ELISABETH, physician; b. Zurich, Switzerland, July 8, 1926; came to U.S., 1958, naturalized, 1961; d. Ernst and Emma (Villiger) K.; m. Emanuel Robert Ross, Feb. 7, 1958; children: Kenneth Lawrence, Barbara Lee. MD, U. Zurich, 1957; D.Sc. (hon.), Albany (N.Y.) Med. Coll., 1974, Smith Coll., 1975, Molloy Coll., Rockville Centre, N.Y., 1976, Regis Coll., Weston, Mass., 1977, Fairleigh Dickinson U., 1979; LL.D., U. Notre Dame, 1974, Hamline U., 1975; hon. degree, Med. Coll. Pa., 1975, Anna Maria Coll., Paxton, Mass., 1978; Litt.D. (hon.), St. Mary's Coll., Notre Dame, Ind., 1975, Hood Coll., 1976, Rosary Coll., River Forest, Ill., 1976; L.H.D. (hon.), Amherst Coll., 1975, Loyola U., Chgo., 1975, Bard Coll., Annandale-on-Hudson, N.Y., 1977, Union Coll., Schenectady, 1978, D'Youville Coll., Buffalo, 1979, U. Miami, Fla., 1976; D.Pedagogy, Keuka Coll., Keuka Park, N.Y., 1976. Rotating intern Community Hosp., Glen Cove, N.Y., 1958-59; rsch. fellow Manhattan State Hosp., 1959-62; resident Montefiore Hosp., N.Y.C., 1961-62; fellow psychiatry Psychopathic Hosp., U. Colo. Med. Sch., 1962-63; instr. psychiatry Colo. Gen. Hosp., U. Colo. Med. Sch., 1962-65; mem. staff LaRabida Children's Hosp. and Rsch. Ctr., Chgo., 1965-70; asst. prof. psychiatry, asst. dir. psychiatric consultation and liaison service Billings Hosp., U. Chgo., 1965-71; chief cons. and rsch. liaison sect. LaRabida Children's Hosp. and Rsch. Ctr., 1969-70; med. dir. Family Service and Mental Health Ctr. S. Cook County, Chicago Heights, Ill., 1970-73; pres. Ross Med. Assos. (S.C.), Flossmoor, Ill., 1973-77; pres., chmn. bd. Shanti Nilaya Growth and Health Ctr., Escondido, Calif., 1977—. Consulting psychiatrist Chicago Lighthouse for the Blind, 1965-71; consultant Peace Corps, 1965-71, Illinois State Psychiatric Inst., 1965-71; mem. numerous adv., cons. bds. in field. Author: On Death and Dying, 1969, Questions and Answers on Death and Dying, 1972, Death: The Final Stage, 1974, To Live Until We Say Goodbye, 1978, Working It Through, 1981, Living With Death and Dying, 1981, Remember The Secret, 1981, On Children and Death, 1985, AIDS: The Ultimate Challenge, 1988, On Life After Death, 1991, The Tunnel and The Light: On Life, Death and Life After Death, 1994, The Wheel of Life: Autobiography, 1997, Life Lessons, 2000, Real Taste of Life, 2002; contbr. articles to profl. jours., chapters to books. Named Woman of the Decade, Ladies Home Jour., 1979, One of the 100 Greatest Thinkers of the Century, Time Mag., 2000; recipient Teilhard prize, Teilhard Found., 1981, Golden Plate award, Am. Acad. Achievement, 1980, Modern Samaritan award, Elk Grove Village, Ill., 1976, numerous others. Mem. AAAS, Am. Holistic Med. Assn. (founder), Am. Med. Women's Assn., Am. Psychiat. Assn., Am. Psychosomatic Soc., Assn. Cancer Victims and Friends, Ill. Psychiat. Soc., Soc. Swiss Physicians, Soc. Psychophysiol. Research, Second Attempt at Living. Address: PO Box 6168 Scottsdale AZ 85261-6168

KUBY, BARBARA ELEANOR, personnel director, management consultant; b. Medford, Mass., Sept. 1, 1944; d. Robert William and Eleanor (Frasca) Asdell; m. Thomas Kuby, July 12, 1969. BS in Edn./ Psychology, Kent State U., 1966, MEd, 1987. Tchr. Nordonia/Euclid (Ohio) Pub. Schs., 1966-78; chief tng. officer United Bldg. Factories, Manama, Bahrain, 1979-81; mgr. tng. and devel. Norton Co., Akron, Ohio, 1981-85; v.p. Kuby and Assocs. Inc., Chagrin Falls, Ohio, 1973-91, pres., 1992—2002; corp. dir. human resource devel. and systems TransOhio Savs. Bank, Cleve., 1985-88; asst. v.p. human resources and adminstrv. sys. Leasing Dynamics, Inc., Cleve., 1988-90; dir. human resources, orgnl. devel. GOJO Industries, Akron, 1990-93, v.p. human resources and orgnl. devel., 1993—. Adj. faculty cons. Buffalo State U., 1972—92, Lake Eric Coll., Cleve., 1985—95; lectr., cons. Cleve. State U., 1978—2000; program dir. Ctr. Profl. Advisors, East Brunswick, NJ, 1978—99. Cons., lectr. Girl Scouts U.S., Cleve., 1981—90; colleague Creative Edn. Found.; cons. project bus. Jr. Achievement, 1992—93; trustee Ohio Ballet, 1996—2002; bd. dirs. Apollo's Fire Baroque Orch. Friends Bd., 2003—. Recipient Svc./Commitment award, Creative Edn. Found., 2001, Athena Award Finalist, 2003. Mem.: ACLU, Gestalt Inst. Cleve., Soc. Orgnl. Learning, Human Resource Planning Soc., Holocaust Meml. Mus., Greenpeace. Avocations: travel, gardening, photography. Home: 7236 Chagrin Rd Chagrin Falls OH 44023-1102

KUCK, LEA HABER, lawyer; b. Lockport, N.Y., 1965; AB magna cum laude, Hamilton Coll., 1987; JD, NYU, 1990. Bar: N.Y. 1991, U.S. Dist. Ct. (ea. dist.) Mich. 1992. Law clk. HOn. Steven D. Pepe U.S. Dist. Ct. (ea. dist.) Mich., 1990—92; atty. Skadden, Arps, Slate, Meagher & Flom LLP, N.Y., 1992—98, ptnr., 1998—. Office: Skadden Arps Slate Meagher & Flom LLP Four Times Square New York NY 10036*

KUDDES, KATHRYN M. fine arts director; b. Midland, Tex., July 11, 1960; d. Fred M. and Dale M. Springer; m. Kenton C. Kuddes. MusB, Millikin U., 1983; Master in Music Edn., U. North Tex., 1995. Cert. provisional all-level music tchr. Tex., tchr. Kodály tng. Tex., profl. supr. Tex. . Choral dir. 6-12 Stafford Mcpl. Sch. Dist., Stafford, Tex., 1983—86; elem. music specialist Killeen Ind. Sch. Dist., Killeen, Tex., 1986—89, Coll. Sta. Ind. Sch. Dist., College Station, Tex., 1989—94; grad. tchg. fellow U. North Tex., Denton, Tex., 1994—95; elem. music specialist Plano Ind. Sch. Dist., Plano, Tex., 1995—98, K-12 coord. vocal music, 1998—2000, dir. fine arts. V.p. Kodály Educators Texas, 1992—97; pres. so. divsn. Orgn. Am. Kodály Educators, 1997—2001. Editor: (profl. newsletter) KET Encounter, 1997. Mem. P.E.O. Sisterhood, Allen, 1987—2002. Named nationally registered music educator, Music Educators Nat. Conf., 1993. Mem.: Assn. Supervision and Curriculum Devel., Am. Orff-Schulwerk Assn., Texas Music Adminstrs. Conf., Orgn. Am. Kodály Educators (pres. so. divsn. 1997—2001), Kodály Educators Tex. (v.p. 1992—97), Am. Choral Dirs. Assn., Tex. Choral Dirs. Assn., Music Educators Nat. Conf., Tex. Music Educators Assn. Avocations: music, folk instruments, travel. Office: Plano Ind Sch Dist 2700 W 15th St Plano TX 75075 Office Fax: 469-752-8039. Business E-Mail: kkuddes@pisd.edu.

KUDO, EMIKO IWASHITA, former state official; b. Kona, Hawaii, June 5, 1923; d. Tetsuzo and Kuma (Koga) Iwashita; m. Thomas Mitsugi Kudo, Aug. 21, 1951; children: Guy J.T., Scott K., Candace F. BS, U. Hawaii, 1944; MS in Vocat. Edn., Pa. State U., 1950; postgrad., U. Hawaii, U. Oreg. Tchr. jr. & sr. h.s., Hawaii, 1945-51; instr. home econs. edn. U. Hawaii Tchrs. Coll., Honolulu, 1948-51, Pa. State U., State College, 1949-50; with Hawaii Dept. Edn., Honolulu, 1951-82, supr. sch. lunch svc., 1951-64, home econs. edn., 1964-68, adminstr. vocat.-tecy. edn., 1968-78; dep. supt. State Dept. Edn., Honolulu, 1978-82, cons. Am. Samoa vocat. edn. state plan devel., 1970-71; vocat. edn. U. Hawaii, 1986. Internat. secondary program devel. Ashiya Ednl. Sys., Japan, 1986-91; cons. to atty. gen. mental health svcs. for children and adolscents State of Hawaii, 1994; chief planner devel. State of Hawaii Children & Adolscents Mental Health Svcs. Implementation Plan, 1994-95; state coord. industry-labor-edn., 1972-76; mem. nat. task force edn. and tng. for minority bus. enterprise, 1972-73; mem. steering com. Career Info. Ctr. Project, 1973-78; co-dir. Hawaii Career Devel. Continuum project, 1971-74; mem. Nat. Accreditation and Instl. Eligibility Adv. Coun., 1974-77, cons., 1977-78; mem. panel Internat. Conf. Vocat. Guidance, 1978, 80, 82, 86, 88; state commr. edn. commn. of the states, 1982-90; mem. Hawaii edn. coun., 1982-90. Author handbooks and pamphlets in field. Dir. Dept. Parks and Recreation, City and County of Honolulu, 1982-84; bd. dirs. Honolulu Neighborhood Housing Svcs., 1991—; exec. bd. Aloha coun. Boy Scouts Am., 1978-88; bd. trustees St. Louis H.S., 1988-95; mem. Gov.'s Commn. on Sesquicentennial Observance of Pub. Edn. in Hawaii, 1990-91; mem. Commn. State Rental Housing Trust Fund, 1992-98; mem. steering com. Hawaii Long Term Care Coalition, 1992—. Japan Found. Cultural grantee, 1977; Pa. State U. Alumni fellow, 1982; named to Konawaea H.S. Hall of Fame, 1997. Mem. ASCD, NEA, Am. Assn. Retired Persons (mem. state legis. com. 1990-92), Pa. State U. Disting. Alumni, Western Assn. Schs. and Colls. (accreditation team mem. Ch. Coll. of Hawaii 1972-73), Am. Vocat. Assn., Hawaii Vocat. Assn., Hawaii Edn. Assn. (trustee 1992—), Hawaii State Ednl. Officers Assn., Am. Family Consumer Sci. Assn., Hawaii Assn. Curriculum & Devel., Am. Tech. Edn. Assn., Hawaii Recreation and Park Assn., Omicron Nu, Pi Lambda Theta, Phi Delta Kappa, Delta Kappa Gamma. Home and Office: 217 Nenue St Honolulu HI 96821-1811

KUDO, IRMA SETSUKO, not-for-profit executive director; b. Ica, Peru, Feb. 25, 1939; arrived in U.S., 1944; d. Seiichi and Angelica (Yoshinaga) Higashide. Asst. dir. coun. annual session ADA, Chgo., 1971-80; exec. dir. Am. Assn. of Endodontists, Chgo., 1980—. Recipient Warren Wakai medal Japan Endodontic Assn., 1992. Mem. ADA Alumni Assn. Student Clinicians (hon.), Am. Assn. Endodontists (hon.), Am. Soc. of Assn. Execs., Profl. Conv. Mgmt. Assn., Assn. Forum Chicagoland. Office: Am Assn of Endodontists 211 E Chicago Ave Ste 1100 Chicago IL 60611-2687 E-mail: ikudo@aae.org.

KUDROW, LISA (LISA MARIE DIANE KUDROW), actress; b. Encino, Calif., July 30, 1963; d. Lee and Nedra Kudrow; m. Michael Stern, May 27, 1995; 1 child, Julian. BS in Biology, Vassar Coll., Poughkeepsie, N.Y., 1985. Actress (TV series) Mad About You, 1991-99, Friends, 1994-2004 (Emmy award outstanding supporting actress, 1998, SAG award outstanding performance female, 2000, Am. Comedy award, 2000, Golden Satellite award best actress, 2000); (TV guest appearances) Cheers, 1989, Newhart, 1990, Life Goes On, 1990, Coach, 1993-94, Flying Blind, 1993, Hope & Gloria, 1996, The Simpsons (voice), 1998; (films) The Crazysitter, 1995, Romy and Michele's High School Reunion, 1997, Clockwatchers, 1997, The Opposite of Sex, 1998 (NY Film Critics Circle award, 2000), Hercules (voice) 1998, Analyze This, 1998, Hanging Up, 2000, All Over the Guy, 2001, Dr. Dolittle 2 (voice), 2001, Analyze That, 2002, Marci X, 2003, Wonderland, 2003; (music video) The Rembrandts I'll Be There For You, 1995. Mem.: Th Groundlings Improv Group.*

KUDRYASHEVA, ALEKSANDRA A. scientist, researcher, educator; b. Tula, Russia, Jan. 1, 1934; d. Andrew P. and Neonila K. (Volkonogova) Chernozhukov; m. Michael N. Kudryashev (dec.); m. Dan B. Chopyk, Dec. 19, 1990. BS in Biology, All-Union Inst. Food Industry, Moscow, 1965, DSc, 1969; PhD in Tech. Biol. Scis., Russia, 1983; PhD (hon.), Volgograd Tech. Inst., 1996. Technologist Glavkonserv Food Ministry, Govt. of USSR, Eisk, Krasnodar Region, 1954-61, head. of lab. irradiation microbiology Tula, 1962-71; from asst. prof. to prof. Russian Acad. Economy, Moscow, 1971-93, dean tech. and commodities, 1983-85, head dept. biotech., 1985-93; head food resources Inst. of Human Ecology, Moscow, 1993-97; pres. Internat. Ctr. Nutrition and Health Rehab., Toms River, N.J., 1997—; cons. UNO, 2001—03. V.p. radiology of food products, Russian Acad. Agr., Moscow, 1976-89; pres. Assn. of Commodities Specialists of USSR, 1985-91; chmn. cert. com. Coun. of Ministers of USSR, 1989-96; sec. commodities sect. Ministry of Edn., Govt. of USSR, 1978-85. Contbr. more than 400 articles to sci. and profl. jours., books; holder more than 50 patents. Mem. Russian Acad. Natural Scis. (silver medal), Union of Concerned Scientists, N.Y. Acad. Scis., Internat. Info. Acad. (internat. prize 1996). Achievements include radiobiological and microbiological methods of food preservation; new technologies of manufacture and application of natural bio-correctors for food, medicine, agriculture and ecology. Avocations: travel, photography, ethnic cooking, poetry. Home and Office: 106 Guadeloupe Dr Toms River NJ 08757

KUECKER, LIZA LOUISE, sociology educator; b. La Crosse, Wis., Aug. 19, 1955; d. Duane Albert and Jacqueline Ardith (Major) K. BS in Sociology and Spanish, U. Wis., La Crosse, 1976; MA in Sociology, U. Oreg., 1979, PhD in Sociology, 1985. Asst., then assoc. prof. sociology U. S.C., Spartanburg, 1986-94; assoc. prof. Mont. State U., Billings, 1994—, mem. bd. career svcs., 1994—. Contbr. articles and book revs. to profl. jours. Mem., chmn. New Horizons Fask Force on Fair Housing, Spartanburg, 1988-93; presenter Spartanburg Human Rights Commn., 1993, Coun. Concerned Citizens, Billings, 1996; mem. minority edn. del. to China, Citizen Amb. Program, 1995. Mem. Am. Sociol. Assn., Sociologists for Women in Soc., Pacific Sociol. Assn., So. Sociol. Soc., Nat. Women's Polit. Caucus, Older Women's League. Avocations: knitting, gardening, walking, cycling.

KUEHL, SHEILA JAMES, state legislator; b. Tulsa, Feb. 9, 1941; d. Arthur Joseph and Lillian Ruth (Krasner) K. BA, UCLA, 1962; JD, Harvard U., 1978. Actress, 1950-65; assoc. dean of students UCLA, 1969-75; pvt. practice L.A., 1978-85; law prof. Loyola U. of L.A., 1985-89; mng. atty. Calif. Women's Law Ctr., L.A., 1989-93; mem. Calif. State Assembly, Sacramento, 1995-2000, spkr. pro tem, 1997-99, chair jud. com., 1999-2000; mem. Calif. State Senate, 2001—, chmn. natural resource com., 2001—. Appeared in TV series Broadside, 1964-65, as Zelda Gilroy in Dobie Gillis, 1959-63, as Jackie Erwin in Trouble with Father, 1950-56. Mem. gender bias adv. com. Calif. Supreme Ct., 1985-91; bd. overseers Harvard U., 1997—. Named One of 20 Most Fascinating Women in Politics, George Mag., 1996, named One of 100 Most Influential Attys. in Calif., Calif. Law Bus., 1998; recipient Barry Goldwater Human Rights award, 1998, Legislator of Yr., Calif. Pks. and Recreation Soc., 1999, Pub. Svc. award UCLA Alumni Assn., 2000, Liberty award Lambda Legal Def. Edn. Fund, 2002, Women in Govt. award Good Housekeeping, 2003. Mem. Women Lawyers' Assn. of L.A. (pres. 1986-87). Office: State Capitol Sacramento CA 95814-4906

KUEHN, MILDRED MAY, retired social worker; b. Milw., June 24, 1933; d. Frederick Kuehn and Mildred Leona Josslyn; m. Donald Tebay, Feb. 28, 1953 (div. June 22, 1994); children: Kim Tebay, Leslie Tebay, Jennifer Tebay. BS, U. Wis., Milw., 1981. Social worker Heritage Nursing Home, Port Washington, Wis., 1984—85; tchr.'s aide Grafton (Wis.) H.S., 1985—87, ret., 2003—. Mem. Jewish Cmty. Ctr., 1997—. Mem.: Nat. Trust for Hist. Preservation, U. Wis. Alumni. Methodist. Avocations: painting, reading, guitar, sewing, Sheepshead and Bridge.

KUEHNE, KELLI, professional golfer; b. Dallas, May 11, 1977; Student, U. Tex. Profl. golfer, 1998—; tied for 20th pl. First Union Betsy King Classic, 1998; participant 24 tournaments, 1998. Named 6th in standings Rolex Rookie of Yr., 1998; placed 1st Corning Classic. Avocations: fishing, hunting. Office: care LPGA 100 International Golf Dr Daytona Beach FL 32124-1082

KUEHNER, DENISE ANN, music educator, musician; b. Evanston, Ill., July 6, 1953; d. Alice Catherine Langan and Albert Edward Delgado; m. Eric Lee Kuehner, Oct. 26, 1954; children: Jeffrey Allen, Katherine Elizabeth. BME, Valparaiso U., 1973—77; MM in cello performance and lit., U. of Notre Dame, 1982—84. Tchr., string specialist South Bend Cmty. Sch. Corp., Ind., 1984—; lectr./adj. faculty St. Mary's Coll., Notre Dame, Ind., 1986—. Sect. cellist NW Ind. Symphony, Gary, Ind., 1972—83; cellist Carlson String Quartet, South Bend, 1978—; sect. cellist SW Mich. Symphony, St. Joseph, Mich., 1979—84, South Bend Symphony Orch., Ind., 1981—; choir dir. St. Paul Luth. Ch., South Bend, Ind., 1984—; acad. youth orch. dir. Ind. U. at South Bend, South Bend, Ind., 1986—; guest conductor-indiana all-region orch. Am. String Teachers Assn. (ASTA), La Porte, Ind., 1987; sect. cellist/soloist Borderline Philharm. and Chamber Music Festival, Waubun, Minn., 1989—2003; cellist Whitewater String Trio, South Bend, 1996—; orch. guest condr. Gt. Lake Music Camp, Ind., 1998; orch. dir. Summer Symphonette, South Bend, Ind., 2000—; condr.

SBCSC Firefly Productions, South Bend, Ind., 2000—. Editor: (newsletter) Michiana Cello Society News of Note. Worship com. St. Paul Ch., South Bend, Ind., 1990—2003. Mem.: Nat. Educators Assn., Ind. Music Educators Assn., Nat. Sch. Orch. Assn., Am. String Teachers Assn., Sigma Alpha Iota (musical dir. 1975—76, Sword of Honor 1976). Lutheran (Ms). Avocations: reading, art appreciation, attending arts events (music/drama), dancing (in nutcracker ballet), singing for church, wedddings and parties. Home: 19576 Paxson Drive South South Bend IN 46637 Office: Clay High School 19131 Darden Rd South Bend IN 46637 Personal E-mail: dkuehner@sbcsc.k12.in.us. E-mail: dkuehner@sbcsc.k12.in.us.

KUENN, MARJORIE ASP, music educator; b. Moorhead, Minn., Dec. 26, 1951; d. Robert Louis and Violet Rose Asp; m. Brent Jay Kuenn, Feb. 25, 1978 (div. Jan. 2001). EdB in Violin, U. So. Miss., 1973, EdM, 1974. Violinist Fargo-Moorhead Symphony, 1967—69, Meridian (Miss). Symphony, 1969—79, Jackson (Miss.) Symphony, 1969—79, Jackson Mini-Orch., 1969—79, Miss. Opera South, 1969—79, Miss. Opera, 1969—79, Gulfcoast (Miss.) Symphony, 1969—79, Miss. Ballet Orch., 1969—79, Mobile (Ala.) Opera, 1969—79, Tupelo (Miss.) Symphony, 1969—79, Greenville (Miss.) Symphony, 1969—79, Monroe (La.) Symphony, 1969—79, U. So. Miss. Symphony, Opera, Chamber & Ensemble, 1969—74; tchr. Jackson Symphony Orch., 1974—79; dir. orch. Hickman Mills Sch. Dist., Kansas City, Mo., 1979—; chair dept. music Smith-Hale Mid. Sch., Kansas city, 1990—. Author: Vocal techniques, 1998, Vocal Techniques, 2003, Choir Warm-up Exercises, 2002. Music scholar, U. So. Miss., 1969—73, Grad. Music Studies fellow, 1973—74. Mem.: U. So. Miss. Alumni Assn., Am. Fedn. Tchrs., Music Educators Nat. Conf., Mu Phi Epsilon, Alpha Lambda Delta. Avocations: sewing, reading, exercise. Office: Smith-Hale Mid Sch 8925 Longview Rd Kansas City MO 64134

KUETHER, ANNIE, state representative; b. St. Louis, Mar. 20, 1952; 2 children. Student, Bowling Green State U. Bd. dirs. Topeka City Homes. Mem.: Nat. Woman's Polit. Caucus, Topeka Conv. Visitor's Bur., Topeoka Arts Coun. (bd. dirs.), Topeka Bar Aux., Mulvane Art Mus., Friends Topeka Zoo. Democrat. Episcopalian. Office: 279-W State Capitol 300 SW 10th Ave Topeka KS 66612 Home: 1346 SW Wayne Ave Topeka KS 66604

KUGELMAN, STEPHANIE, advertising executive; married; 1 child. BA in Psychology and Sociology, Elmira Coll., 1968. With creative rsch. group Young & Rubicam N.Y., 1971—, dir. insights group, 1991, mng. dir., vice chmn., mng. ptnr., dir. br. planning group, chmn., CEO, 1999—. Office: Young & Rubicam 285 Madison Ave New York NY 10017-6486

KUH, CHARLOTTE VIRGINIA, economist; b. Apr. 13, 1944; d. Peter Greenebaum and Frederica Angela (Coerr) K.; m. Roy Radner, Jan. 22, 1978; children: Siobhan Frederica, Michael Edwin. BA magna cum laude, Radcliffe Coll., 1967; MPhil (Univ. fellow), Yale U., 1969, PhD (Dept. Labor grantee), 1976. Rec. sec.-treas. Econometric Soc., New Haven, 1970-75; acting asst. prof. engring. econ. systems Stanford U., 1974-76; asst. prof. Harvard U. Grad. Sch. Edn., 1976-79; staff mgr., dist. mgr. AT&T Corp., 1979-87; exec. dir. grad. records exams program Ednl. Testing Svc., 1987-95; exec. dir. Office of Sci. and Engring. Personnel Nat. Rsch. Coun., 1995—2001; dep. exec. dir. policy & global affairs divsn. Nat. Rsch. coun., Washington, 2001—. Mem. rev. panel NSF, 1979, 81, mem. adv. panel policy rsch. and sci. resource studies, 1983-87; mem. rev. panel Nat. Inst. Edn., 1978-85; mem. com. study nat. needs for biomed. and behavioral research pers. NRC, 1980-85, mem. adv. panel Office Sci. and Engring. Pers., 1983-90, mem. panel on stats. on supply and demand for precoll. sci. and math. tchrs., com. on nat. stats., 1986-89, mem. com. Women in Sci. and Engring. NRC, 1991-95, vice chair, 1993-95, mem. com. to study strategies to strengthen excellence of the N.I.H. Intramural Research Program, Inst. of Medicine, 1988; mem. exec. com. of dels. Am. Coun. Learned Socs., 1999—2002, chmn. 2001-02, treas., bd. dirs., 2002—; mem. adv. com. Bunting Inst., Radcliffe Coll., 1998—2001; cons. in field. Author articles in field. Grantee Carnegie Coun. Higher Edn., Ford Found., Spencer Found. Fellow Assn. Women in Sci.; mem. Am. Econ. Assn., Econometric Soc. Office: Natl Research Council 500 5th St Washington DC 20001 E-mail: ckuh@nas.edu., cvkuh@earthlink.net.

KUHL, TONYA L. science educator; BS Chem. Engring., U. Ariz., 1989; PhD Chem. Engring., U. Calif., Santa Barbara, 1996. Postdoctoral fellow U. Calif., Santa Barbara, 1996—97, asst. rsch. engr., 1997—2000, asst. prof. chem. engring. Davis, Calif. Office: One Shields Ave Davis CA 95616

KUHLER, DEBORAH GAIL, grief therapist, former state legislator; b. Moorhead, Minn., Oct. 12, 1952; d. Robert Edgar and Beverly Maxine (Buechler) Ecker; m. George Henry Kuhler, Dec. 28, 1973; children: Karen Elizabeth, Ellen Christine. BA, Dakota Wesleyan U., 1974; MA, U. N.D., 1977. Outpatient therapist Ctr. for Human Devel., Grand Forks, N.D., 1975-77; mental health counselor Community Counseling Services, Huron, S.D., 1978-88, 91-93; owner, dir. bereavement svcs. Kuhler Funeral Home, Huron, 1978—; adj. prof. Huron U., 1979—83, 1990—2002; mem. from dist. 23 S.D. Ho. Reps., Pierre, 1987-90; mem. House Judiciary com., chair House Health and Welfare Com., Pierre, 1990. Active First United Meth. Ch. Named Young Alumnus of the Yr., Dakota Wesleyan U., 1989, Bus. and Profl. Women, 1989. Mem. ACA, AAUW (Achievement in Politics award 1987), PEO, Am. Mental Health Counselors Assn., Assn. for Death Edn. and Counseling. Avocations: reading, breadmaking, sewing, piano.

KUHLMANN-WILSDORF, DORIS, materials scientist, educator; b. Bremen, Germany, Feb. 15, 1922; came to U.S., 1956. d. A. Friedrich and Elsa S. (Dreyer) K.; m. Heinz G.F. Wilsdorf, Jan. 4, 1950; children: Gabriele, Michael. BS in Physics, U. Göttingen, Germany, 1944, MS, 1946, PhD in Materials Sci., 1947; DS in Physics-Materials Sci., U. Witwatersrand, South Africa, 1954; DSc in Physics honoris causa, U. Pretoria, South Africa, 2004. Postdoctoral fellow U. Göttingen, 1947-48; postdoctoral fellow in physics U. Bristol, Eng., 1949-50; lectr. physics U. Witwatersrand, Johannesburg, 1950-56; from assoc. prof. metall. engring. to prof. U. Pa., Phila., 1957-63; prof. engring. physics U. Va., Charlottesville, 1963-66, univ. prof. applied sci., 1966—. Co-founder, co-owner HiPerCon; inventor in field. Editor: 4 materials sci. books; contbr. articles to profl. jours. Recipient J. Shelton Horsley award Va. Acad. Sci., 1966, Americanism medal DAR, 1966, Heyn medal German Metall. Soc., 1988, Achievement award Soc. Women Engrs., 1989, Ragnar Holm Sci. Achievement award IEEE, 1991. Fellow Am. Soc. Materials Internat. (life, Edward DeMille Campbell Meml. lectr. 2002), Am. Phys. Soc.; mem. Am. Soc. Women Engrs. (life), Am. Soc. Engring. Edn. (medal for excellence 1965, 66), AIME Metall. Soc., Nat. Acad. Engring. Achievements include development of metal fiber brushes; patents in field. Office: U Va Dept Physics Charlottesville VA 22904-0001 Mailing: HiPerCon 717 Albermarle St Charlottesville VA 22903 E-mail: dw@virginia.edu.

KUHN, HANS HEINRICH, retired chemist; b. Uzwil, St. Gallen, Switzerland; came to U.S., 1957; d. Werner and Gretchen (Haeberle) K.; m. Edith Lilly Peyer, Aug. 28, 1954; children: Johann Heinrich, Barbara Edith. Degree in Chem. Engring., Swiss Fed. Inst. Tech., Zürich, 1949, Doctor in Sci. Tech., 1954. Postdoctoral researcher Swiss Fed. Inst. Tech., Zürich, 1954-57; rsch. chemist Dewey & Almy, Div. W.R. Grace, Cambridge, Mass., 1957-60; group leader Deering Milliken Rsch. Co., Spartanburg, S.C., 1960-61, sect. leader, 1961-65, dep. mgr., 1965-80; sr. scientist Milliken Rsch. Co., Spartanburg, S.C., 1980-95, rsch. fellow, 1995-2000; ret., 2000. Contbr. articles to profl. jours. Consul of Switzerland for S.C. and N.C., Spartanburg, 1970-94. Recipient Olney medal Am. Assn. Textile Chemists and Colorists, 1997. Mem. Am. Chem. Soc., Swiss Chem. Soc., Rotary. Presbyterian. Home: 176 W Park Dr Spartanburg SC 29306-5045

KUHN, JOLYN, artist; b. Newark, Dec. 12, 1946; d. Joseph Roger and Evelyn Dorothy (Raimando) Tartaglia; m. Richard Francis Kuhn, July 16, 1966; children: David, Daniel, Chalena, Athena, Richard. Student, Newark Sch. Fine/Indsl. Arts, 1966; BFA, Md. Inst. Coll. At, Balt., 1989; student, Anne Arundel C.C., Arnold, Md., 1988, Schuler Sch. Fine Art, 2001. Fashion illustrator Banbergers, Newark, 1966; photographer Siegal Majestic, Catonsville, Md., 1980s; sports photographer The Picture Man, Md., 1990s; owner Kuhns Photography, Pasadena, Md., 1989—; freelance artist, 1969—. Substitute tchr. Anne Arundel Pub. Sch. Sys., 1973-87; dir. Parks and Recreation Dept., 1980-86. Works include clay sculpture, jewelry, stained glass windows, etchings, prints, portraits. Recipient numerous awards for artwork. Avocations: painting, sewing, bicycling, swimming, gardening. Home: 616 Riverside Dr Pasadena MD 21122-5046 E-mail: Jolyndk@aol.com.

KUHN, KATHLEEN JO, accountant; b. Springfield, Ill., Aug. 9, 1947; d. Henry Elmer and Norma Florene (Niehaus) Burge; m. Gerald L. Kuhn, June 22, 1968; children: Gerald Lynn, Brett Anthony. BS in Bus., Bradley U., 1969. CPA Ill. Contr. Byerly Music Co., Peoria, Ill., 1969—70; staff acct. Clifton Gunderson & Cjo., Columbus, Ind., 1970—71; acct. Dept. of Transp., State of Ill., Springfield, 1972—76, Gerald L. Kuhn & Assocs., Springfield, 1976—78, ptnr., 1979—, quality control mgr., 1990—. Grad. asst. Dale Carnegie courses, 1979—80; writer, editor co. policy guideline, 1979—80; editor co. quality control manual, 1990. Pianist Trinity Luth. Ch. Recipient Attendance award, Continuing Profl. Edn. for Accts., 1979—. Mem.: AICPA, Nat. Bus. & Motivational Assn., Am. Woman's Soc. CPAs, Ill. Soc. CPAs, Met. Federated Jr. Women's Club, Springfield Art Assn., Olympic Swim Club. Lutheran. Home: 2511 Westchester Blvd Springfield IL 62704-5406 Office: 2659 Farragut Dr Springfield IL 62704-1462

KUHN, MELANIE R. literature educator, consultant; d. Emma Gertrude and Raymond Joseph Kuhn; m. Jason Edward Chambers, Mar. 18, 2003. BA magna cum laude, Boston Coll., 1984; EdM, Harvard Grad. Sch. of Edn., Cambridge, MA, 1988; MPhil, Cambridge U., Eng., 1993; PhD, U. Ga., Athens, 2000. Clinician Ctr. Acad., London, 1989—92; asst. prof. literacy edn. Rutgers Grad. Sch. of Edn., New Brunswick, NJ, 2000—. Author: (chapter) Theoretical Models and Processes (in press), Literacy: Major Themes in Education (in press); contbr. articles to profl. jours. and books. Reviewer Am. Ednl. Rsch. Assn., 1997, Nat. Reading Conf., 1999—2003; com. mem. Internat. Reading Assn., Newark, Del., 2002—04; reviewer Jour. of Ednl. Psychology, 2002, Internat. Reading Assn., Newark, Del., 2001—03. Recipient Finalist, Outstanding Dissertation of the Yr., Internat. Reading Asscociation, 2002, Finalist, Outstanding Student Rsch., Nat. Reading Conf., 2000; grantee full Grant for study at Cambridge U., ESRC, 1992-93, Eisenhower Grant for Profl. Devel. Across Districts, NJ. Dept. of Edn., 2001-03. Mem.: Assn. of Reading Grad. Students (assoc.; pres. 1995—96), Nat. Reading Conf. (assoc.), Am. Ednl. Rsch. Assn. (assoc.), Internat. Reading Assn. (assoc.), Alpha Upsilon Alpha (assoc.). Independent. Catholic. Achievements include research in IERI Grant The Development of Fluent and Automatic Reading: Precursor to Learning from Text. Avocations: swimming, travel, walking. Office: Rutgers Univ 10 Seminary Pl New Brunswick NJ 08901-1183 E-mail: melaniek@rci.rutgers.edu.

KUHN, ROSEANN, sports association administrator; Staff mem. Women's Internat. Bowling Congress, Greendale, Wis., 1974-96, exec. dir., 1996—. Office: Womens Internat Bowling Congress (WIBC) 5301 S 76th St Greendale WI 53129-1128

KUHNE, ALICE, oil industry executive; b. 1953; BA, Boston U., 1973, MBA, 1978. Mem. staff Helix Tech. Group, 1978-82; controller Northeast Petroleum, 1982-86; treas., controller Gulf Oil, L.P., Chelsea, Mass., 1986—. Office: Gulf Oil Ltd Partnership 90 Everett Ave Chelsea MA 02150

KUHRT, SHARON LEE, nursing administrator; b. Denver, July 20, 1957; d. John Wilfred and Yoshiko (Ueda) Kuhrt. BSN, Loretto Heights Coll., 1982; MSN, Regis U., 1992. RN Colo., Mass., Maine. RN level III Porter Meml. Hosp., Denver, 1981-87; transport supr. Kapiolani Med. Ctr. Women & Children, Honolulu, 1987-89; dir. patient care unit Aspen Valley Hosp., Colo., 1989-91; dir. clin. practice Ctrl. Maine Med. Ctr., Lewiston, 1991-2000, dir. Sch. Nursing, 1998—. Home: 873 Oak Hill Rd North Yarmouth ME 04097-6242 E-mail: skhurts@cmhc.org.

KUJAWA, SISTER ROSE MARIE, academic administrator; b. Detroit; d. Francis and Anne Kujawa. BS in math., Madonna U., Livonia, Mich., 1966; MS in edn. and math., Wayne State U., Detroit, 1971, PhD in higher edn. adminstrn., 1979. Dept. chair math. Bishop Borgess H.S.; asst. prin. and curriculum coord. Ladywood H.S.; prof. Madonna U., Livonia, Mich., 1975, academic dean, academic v.p., acting dean Coll. of Arts and Sci., pres., 2001—. Office: Madonna U 36600 Schoolcraft Rd Livonia MI 48150-1173*

KUK, MARY HALVORSON, secondary school educator; b. Puyallup, Wash., Oct. 31, 1954; d. Raymond W. and Ruth A. Halvorson; m. Gregory L. Kuk, Feb. 5, 1983. BA, Ea. Wash. U., 1977; EdM in Health Edn., Oreg. State U., 1988. Educator South Umpqua Sch. Dist., Myrtle Creek, Oreg., 1977—. First aid/CPR instr. ARC, Roseburg, Oreg., 1995—; mem. Prevention Coalition, Roseburg, 1999—. Mem.: NEA, Nat. Multiple Sclerosis Soc., South Umpqua Edn. Assn. (bldg. rep.). Avocations: camping, photography, sewing, reading. Home: 425 W Maple Roseburg OR 97470-2926 Office: S Umpqua Sch Dist 501 NW Chadwick Myrtle Creek OR 97457

KUKLA, MAIJA MEIJER, research scientist, educator; b. Riga, Latvia, May 10, 1965; d. Meijer Girsh and Iraida Ivanovna Kukla; children: Anna Belak, Mark Belak. BS, MSc, U. Latvia, Riga, 1988, DSc (hon.), 1996. Cert. lead rsch. scientist title. Vis. rschr. Zelinsky Inst. Organic Chemistry, Moscow, 1988—89; rsch. assoc. Inst. Chem. Physics, Riga, 1991—96, sr. rsch. assoc., 1996—98, lead rsch. scientist, 1998—2002; program dir. U.S. NSF, Arlington, Va., 2002—. Invited scientist UNESCO Internat. Ctr. Theoretical Physics, Trieste, Italy, 1994; Office Naval Rsch. postdoctoral fellow Mich. Technol. U., Houghton, 1997—2000, rsch. faculty, 2000—01; rsch. scientist U. Md., College Park, 2001—02, Naval Warfare Ctr., Indian Head, Md., 2001—; reviewer Jour. Am. Ceramic Soc., Jour. Applied Physics, NATO Rsch. Series, Thermochimica Acta, Physica Status Solidi, MRS Procs.; presenter in field. Contbr. articles to profl. jours. Mem.: Am. Phys. Soc., Materials Rsch. Soc., Am. Chem. Soc.

KUKLIN, SUSAN BEVERLY, law librarian, lawyer; b. Chgo., Nov. 25, 1947; d. Albert and Marion (Goodman) K. BA in English and History with honors, U. Ariz., 1969, JD, 1973; MLS, Ind. U., 1970; LLM in Taxation, DePaul U., 1981. Bar: Ariz. 1973, Ill. 1980, Calif. 1984, U.S. Dist. Ct. (no. dist.) Ill. 1980. Asst. city atty. City of Phoenix, 1974-75; dep. county atty. County of Pima, Ariz., 1975-76; polit. sci., law libr. asst. prof. law No. Ill. U., 1976-78; law libr., assoc. prof. U. S.D., 1978-79; dir. law libr., asst. prof. DePaul U., 1979-83; law libr. Santa Clara County, San Jose, Calif., 1983—. Sec. bd. trustees Law Library Santa Clara County. Mem. Am. Assn. Law Libr. (cert. law libr.), Coun. Calif. County Law Libr. (newsletter editor 1983-84), No. Calif. Assn. Law Libr., Phi Beta Kappa, Phi Kappa Phi, Alpha Lambda Delta, Phi Alpha Theta, Phi Delta Phi. Office: Santa Clara County Law Library 360 N 1st St San Jose CA 95113-1004

KUKURA, RITA ANNE, pre-school educator; b. Tulsa, July 18, 1947; d. James Albert and Carmen Alberta (Parsons) Hayden; m. Joel Richard Graft, Oct. 28, 1967 (dec. Apr. 1969); m. Raymond Richard Kukura, Dec. 18, 1971 (div. 1981); children: Tiffany Carmen Noel, Austin Raymond. BS, Kent. State U., 1971; MS, Okla. State U., 1991. Cert. early childhood, nursery, elem. tchr., Okla., spl. edn. tchr. for emotionally disturbed. Tchr. kindergarten Southlyn Elem. Sch., Lyndhurst, Ohio, 1971-73; elem. tchr. Wakefield Acad., Tulsa, 1981-83, tchr. kindergarten, 1983-87; reg. early intervention coord. Okla. Dept. Edn., Tulsa, 1990-92; tchr. devel. delayed children, coord. integrated program Child Devel. Inst. Children's Med. Ctr., Tulsa, 1992-93; tchr. elem. sch. Prue (Okla.) Schs., 1993-95, Tulsa Pub. Schs., 1995—. Manuscript reviewer for profl. orgns., 1989-91; mem. human rights com. Ind. Opportunities of Okla., 1995—; Oklahoma Edn. Assn. Leadership Acad., 1998; del. Okla. Edn. Assembly, 1995; grant reviewer for spl. grants State Dept. Edn., 1996; presenter and lectr. in field. Den leader Cub Scouts Am., Tulsa, 1984-88; com. mem. Boy Scouts Am., Tulsa, 1984-88; vol. office worker Met. Tulsa Citizen Crime Commn., 1986; adv. com. Latchkey Project, Tulsa County, 1985; ad hoc task force on day care Interagy. Coord. Coun., 1989-91; nat. rep. Tourette Syndrome Assn. to Nat. Broadcasting Assn. AERho, 1990-93; mem. resource com. Ronald McDonald House, 1990-92, vol. Tulsa area, 1991-97, STARBASE, 1993—, Drug Edn. for Youth, 1994; mem. adv. bd. Tulsa Regional Coordinating Coun. for Svcs. to Children and Youth and Families, 1991-92; planning com. symposium Magic Coun. Girl Scouts Am., 1991-93; lt. sr. mem. Tulsa Composite Squadron CAP, 1992-94; presenter numerous confs.; workshop participant Alternatives to Violence Project, 1996. Recipient Den Leader Tng. award Boy Scouts Am., 1988, State Commendation medal Air N.G., 1993. Mem. AAUW (bd. dirs. Tulsa county chpt. 1991-93, mem., 1997-2000, 2003), Nat. Assn. Early Childhood Tchr. Educators, Nat. Tourette Syndrome Assn. (state pres. 1987-92, state dir. 1992-93, hon. mem. bd. dirs. 1993, area coord., fundraiser 1988-90), Gold Star Wives Am., Tulsa Classroom Tchrs. Assn. (bldg. del. 1997-98), Okla. Edn. Assn. (leadership acad. 1998), Okla. Edn. Assn. (mem. resolution com. 1998-2000), Kappa Delta Pi, Omicron Nu, Alpha Epsilon Rho (hon. mem. S.W. region 1990-93), Phi Delta Kappa. Roman Catholic. Avocations: piano, exercising, reading. Office: Burroughs Elem Sch 1927 N Cincinnati Tulsa OK 74106 E-mail: kukurri@tulsaschools.org.

KULIG, MARTHA, stage manager; d. Celia A. and Stanley B. Kulig. BA, New Eng. Coll., Henniker, NH, 1980. Stage mgr. Guthrie Theater Found., Mpls., 1989—. Mem.: Actor's Equity Assn. Office: Guthrie Theater Foundation 725 Vineland Place Minneapolis MN 55403 E-mail: marthak@guthrietheater.org.

KULIK, ROSALYN FRANTA, food company executive, consultant; b. Wilmington, Del., Aug. 29, 1951; d. William Alfred and Virginia Louise (Ellis) Franta. BS in Voc. Home Econs. Edn., Purdue U., 1972, MS in Foods and Nutrition, 1974; postgrad. in advanced mgmt. program, Harvard Bus. Sch., 1990. Registered dietitian. Home economist Kellogg Co., Battle Creek, Mich., 1974-75, nutrition and consumer specialist, 1975-77, mgr. advt. to children, 1977-79, corp. adminstrv. asst., 1979, dir. nutrition, 1979-82, dir. nutrition and analytical services, 1982, v.p. nutrition and chemistry, 1983, v.p. quality and nutrition, 1983-87, v.p., asst. to chmn., 1987-88; exec. v.p., gen. mgr. Fearn Internat., Franklin Park, Ill., 1988-90; cons., 1991—. Adj. faculty U. Tampa, Fla., 2001—. Contbr. articles on food sci. and nutrition to profl. jours. Regional coord. Camp Invention, Inc., 2004—; mem. ch. coun. Grace Luth. Ch., Tampa, Fla., 2000—; bd. dirs. State Arthritis Found., County Vol. Ctr., Homeowners Property Assn. Avila, Neighborhood Property Owners Assn., 2002—. Recipient Ada Decker Malott Meml. scholarship, Purdue U., 1970, disting. alumna Purdue U. Sch. of Consumer and Family Sci. Fellow Am. Dietetic Assn. (cofounder, exec. officer nutrition in complementary care dietetic practice group 1998-2004, chair 2002-03); mem. Inst. Food Technologists (profl. mem.), Am. Dietetic Assn., Phi Kappa Phi, Gamma Sigma Delta, Omicron Nu, Alpha Omicron Pi. Republican. Lutheran. Avocations: music, church work, travel, Jr. League volunteerism.

KULISH, CARMA C. music educator; b. Dickinson, ND, Jan. 21, 1957; d. Fred and Cleo Catherine Kulish. BA in Music Edn., Northwestern Coll., 1980; MA in Music Edn., U. St. Thomas, 1998. Tchr. music Regent Pub. Sch., ND, 1981—83, Gwinner Pub. Sch., ND, 1983—84, Pan Am. Christian Acad., Sao Paulo, Brazil, 1986—88, Choiefat Sch., Al Ain, United Arab Emirates, 1989—90, Harding County Sch., Buffalo, SD, 1990—94, Colome Pub. Sch., SD, 1995—96, Rhame Pub. Sch., ND, 2001—. Mem.: ND Music Tchrs. Assn. (chair state jr. festival 2002—, directory/handbook editor 2001—03), Am. Guild Piano Tchrs., ND Fedn. Music Clubs (St. Cecelia Music Club pres. 1999—2001), Nat. Fedn. Music Clubs (life). Republican. Baptist. Avocations: piano, reading, cross stitch, movies. Home: 1431 1st St W Dickinson ND 58601-4613 Office: Rhame Pub Sch 402 4th Ave E PO Box 250 Rhame ND 58651-0250

KULLEN, SHIRLEY ROBINOWITZ, psychiatric epidemiologist, consultant; b. Balt., Sept. 6, 1922; d. Joseph and Rose (Collins) Robinowitz; m. Joseph Stephen Reff, Sept. 14, 1941 (div. 1958); children: Richard Brian, Robert Alan; m. Sidney Irving Margolis, Oct. 28, 1973 (dec. Dec. 1988); m. Sol Kullen, Jan. 10, 1993. BS, Am. U., 1959, MBA, 1961, PhD, 1972. Statistician NIMH, Bethesda, Md., 1964-72, health scientist adminstrn., 1972-93; cons. psychiatric epidemiologist, Chevy Chase, Md., 1993—. Lectr. Am. U. Washington, 1961, 69, 70, 74, 87, seminar developer, 1987; lectr. Howard U., Washington, 1963-67. Bd. dirs. Jewish Cmty. Ctr. Greater Washington, Rockville, Md., 1979—90, Hebrew Home Washington, Rockville, 1980—85, Fed. Credit Union, Rockville, 1987—93; exec. v.p. S-K Family Partnership, 1996—. Mem. APHA (adv. bd. mental health sect. 1990-93), AAUW. Avocations: golf, music, writing. Home: 2100 S Ocean Blvd Apt 202N Palm Beach FL 33480-5201 Office: 5610 Wisconsin Ave Chevy Chase MD 20815

KULLMAN, ELLEN J. manufacturing executive; m. Michael Kullman; 3 children. BS in Mech. Engring., Tufts .; MBA, Northwestern U. Various bus. devel., mktg. and sales positions GE; mktg. mgr. med. imaging DuPont, 1988, bus. dir. x-ray film, global bus. dir. electronic imaging Printing & Pub., global bus. dir. White Pigment & Mineral Products, 1999, v.p., gen. mgr. White Pigment & Mineral Products, 2000, group v.p. DuPont Safety & Protection, 2002—. Trustee Christiana Care Corp.; bd. dirs. Del. Symphony, Wellness Comty. Office: DuPont Bldg 1007 Market St Wilmington DE 19898*

KULP, BETTE JONEVE, retired educator, wallpaper installation business owner; b. Pomona, Calif., Jan. 5, 1936; d. John M. and Eva Kathleen (Lynch) Beck; m. Edwin Hanaway Kulp, Sept. 12, 1957 (div. Apr. 1972); m. Frank Harold Little, Oct. 8, 1977. BS in Home Econs., UCLA, 1957, GPPS credential, 1972. Credential C.C. counselor, gen. pupil personnel svcs., tchr. homemaking. Social worker L.A. County DPSS, 1957-59; tchr., counselor L.A. City Sch. Dist., 1959-81; wallpaper installer West Los Angeles, Calif., 1981-87. Mem. UCLA Scholarship Com. West L.A., San Luis Obispo, Calif., 1978—; judge Acad. Decathalon, San Luis Obispo County, 1989-90, 92, 98-2003. Vol. Daffodil Days Am. Cancer Soc., San Luis Obispo, 1992—, Am. Heart Assn., San Luis Obispo, 1992, Sr. Nutrition Program, San Luis Obispo, 1993-2002; runner Spl. Olympics, San Luis Obispo, 1992; participant Audubon Bird-A-Thon, San Luis Obispo, 1993; locator nesting birds Audubon Breeding Bird Atlas, San Luis Obispo, 1992; fundraiser Womens Shelter Program, San Luis Obispo, 1993-94; precinct clk., judge San Luis Obispo County Election Bd., 1989—; mem. Sch. Dist. Orgn. Com. San Luis Obispo County Schs., 1995—; aide Dist. 3 San Luis Obispo County Bd. Suprs., 1994-96; campaign com. Marie Kiersch for Cuesta Coll. Bd. Trustees, 1994; vol. 22nd Congl. Dist., 1997, Neighborhood Vol. March of Dimes, 1998. Recipient Appreciation award Women's Shelter Program, 1993, Unsung Heroine award San Luis Obispo Commn. Status Women, 1995. Mem. AAUW (treas. San Luis Obispo br. 1989-91, pres.-elect 1991-92, pres. 1992-93, bylaws revision com. 1993, San Luis Obispo Interbr. chair 1993-94, chair state resolutions 1994-95, Grant Honoree 1994, 2000, membership co-v.p. 1994-95, herstory coord., 1995-96, Cuesta scholarship chair 1995-96,scholarship treas. 2000—, parliamentarian 1993-94,interbranch rep., 2003-04; dual mem. five cities Pismo 1994, endorsement com. 1995, scholarship com. 1995—, chair 1996-2002,2003-04, bylaws chair 1996-97, 99, 2001, co-pres. 1998-99, scholarship treas. 2000—, tech. trek com. 2001, scholarship fundraising v.p., 2002-03, interbranch rep., 2003—), Santa Lucia Bridge Club, Phi Mu Alumnae (founder Calif. Ctrl. Coast chpt.), Newcomers Club, Morro Coast Audubon Soc. Avocations: bridge, birding, travel, reading, puzzles. Home: 2362 Meadow St San Luis Obispo CA 93401-5628

KULP, SHERRILL IRENE, business educator, consultant; b. Lebanon, Kans., Jan. 27, 1944; d. Richard E. and Dorothy I. (Weems) Fisher; m. John W. Rabe Jr., Sept. 4, 1965 (div. June 1995); 1 child, Natasha R.; m. Edwin H. Kulp, Aug. 26, 1995. BA in Bus., Western State Coll., Gunnison, Colo., 1966, MA in Bus. Edn., 1968. Total quality mgmt. cert. Tchr. bus. Woodland (Calif.) H.S., 1967-84; prof. bus. Los Rios C.C., Sacramento, 1984—; prof. computer sci. Am. River Coll. Author: Macintosh Lab Manual, 1989—. Recipient Outstanding Teaching award Bd. Trustees of City of Woodland, 1983. Mem. Calif. Bus. Edn. Assn. (legis. com.), Delta Kappa Gamma (pres.). Democrat. Methodist. Avocations: golf, theatre. Office: American River College 4700 College Oak Dr Sacramento CA 95841-4286

KULT, AMY ELAINE, marketing consultant; b. Lafayette, Ind., Nov. 7, 1972; d. Jerry Lynn and Gayle Ann (Neal) Biggs; m. Troy Mathew Kult, My 12, 1995. BFA, Purdue U., 1996. Asst. sales mgr. Claire's Boutique, Lafayette, 1995-96; intern Lafayette Mus. of Art, Lafayette, 1996; sales Lafayette Bank & Trust, Lafayette, 1996-97; account rep. Dontech-Yellow Pages, Hillside, Ill., 1997; program mgr. Sunflower Group, Des Plaines, Ill., 1997-99; mktg. cons. Bounty SCA Worldwide, Chgo., 1999—; account exec. EURO RSCGIMAPCT, 2002—. Artist numerous posters. Recipient scholarship Ball State U., Muncie, 1991-93. Mem. Nat. Mus. of Women in the Arts, Nat. Trust for Hist. Preservation, Delta Phi Delta (sec. 1993-96). Democrat. Avocation: artwork.

KULYK, KAREN GAY, visual artist; b. Toronto, Can., July 19, 1950; d. Joseph and Natalie Melanie (Solowski) K. BFA with honors, York U., 1973. Founder, curator Seedlings Gallery, Toronto, 1973-75; established studios worldwide, 1975—. Tchr. various instns., Can., Thailand, Bermuda, and Eng. Solo exhbns. include Kitchener-Waterloo Art Gallery, 1994, Rodman Hall, St. Catharines, Ont., 1995, Harbinger Gallery, 1994—, Marianne Friedland Gallery, 1974-1996, Masterworks Found. Gallery, Hamilton, Bermuda, 1997, Henry Dyson Fine Art, London, 1996—, Carnegie Gallery, Dundas, Ont., Can., 1996, Nancy Poole's Studio, Toronto, 1996-99, Gallery on the Bay, Hamilton, Ont., 1997—, Wallack Gallery, Ottawa, Can., 1996—, Zwicker Gallery, Halifax, N.S., Can., 1999—, Nat. Gallery Thailand, Grey Coll. U. Durham, Eng., 2000; exhibited in group shows at Harbinger Gallery, Waterloo, Ont., Touchstone Gallery, Hong Kong, Marianne Friedland Gallery, Fla., Sotheby's, Toronto, Chgo. Internat. Art Exhbn., York U., U. Toronto, Offices of Gov. Gen. of Can., Carleton U. Art Gallery, numerous others; represented in collections at Kitchener-Waterloo Art Gallery, Wilfred Laurier U., Waterloo, Art Gallery of Hamilton, Carleton U., York U., Agnes Etherington Art Gallery, Nat. Gallery of Bermuda, Hartford Coll., Md., Can. Trust, Dominion Trust, Shell Can., Thai Airways Internat., Can. Airlines Internat., Dalhousie U., N.S., others, pvt. collections; illustration: Orff, 27 Dragons and a Snarkel; subject of several newspaper articles. Recipient Grollo d'Oro, award Treviso Internat. Art Competition, 1983; grantee Sheila Hugh Mackay Found., 1996. Home and Office: 5270 Morris St Halifax NS Canada B3J 1B4

KUMANYIKA, SHIRIKI K. nutrition epidemiology researcher, educator; b. Balt., Mar. 16, 1945; m. Christiaan B. Morssink; children: Chenjerai, Annoesjka. BA, Syracuse U., 1965; MS in Social Work, Columbia U., 1969; PhD in Human Nutrition, Cornell U., 1978; MPH, Johns Hopkins U., 1984. Asst. prof. nutrition Cornell U., Ithaca, N.Y., 1977-84; from asst. prof. to assoc. prof. epidemiology Johns Hopkins U. Sch. Hygiene and Pub. Health, Balt., 1984-89, asst. prof. internat. health, 1984-89; assoc. prof. nutritional epidemiology Pa. State U., University Park, 1989-92, prof. epidemiology, 1993-96; assoc. dir. for epidemiology Pa. State U. Coll. Medicine, Hershey, 1992-96; prof. epidemiology, prof. human nutrition and dietetics U. Ill. at Chgo., 1996-99, head dept. human nutrition and dietetics, 1996-99; chief of svc. U. Ill. Hosp. Nutritional Svcs., 1996-99; prof. epidemiology U. Pa. Sch. Med., Phila., 1999—, assoc. dean health promotion and disease prevention, 1999—. Adj. prof. epidemiology dept. health evaluation scis. Coll. Medicine, Pa. State U., Hershey, 1996-99; mem. adv. bd. Women's Health Alliance. Contbr. articles to profl. jours. Bd. dirs. Nat. Black Women's Health Project, 1994-99, Nat. Rural Ctr., 1978-82; active WHO. NIH grantee; recipient Bolton L. Corson medal Franklin Inst., 1997. Fellow Am. Coll. Epidemiology, Am. Coll. Nutrition; mem. AAUP, APHA, Am. Diabetes Assn., Am. Dietetic Assn., Am. Inst. Nutrition, Am. Soc. for Clin. Nutrition, Assn. Black Cardiologists, Internat. Soc. on Hypertension in Blacks, Nat. Med. Assn., N.Am. Assn. Study of Obesity, Soc. for Epidemiol. Rsch., Soc. for Nutrition Edn., Internat. Soc. and Fedn. Cardiology, others. Office: Ctr Clin Epidemiology and Biostats U Pa Sch Med 8th Fl Blockley Hall 423 Guardian Dr Philadelphia PA 19104-4209

KUMAR, FAITH, clinical professional counselor; b. South Haven, Mich., May 12, 1960; d. Norris Kendall and Verna Ann (Jeffries) Curtis BS, Western Mich. U., 1990, M Counseling Psychology, 1993. Lic. clin. profl. counselor, Ill. Nursery supr. Child Devel. Ctr., Kalamazoo, 1988-90; tchr. Kalamazoo Pub. Sch. Sys., 1990-93; supr. Victor C. Neuman, Chgo., 1993-94; mentor counselor IL Mentor, Schaumburg, Ill., 1994-97; pvt. practice Chgo., 1997—. Counselor Lakeside Boys and Girls Home, Kalamazoo, 1990-93; therapist Ctrl. Bapt. Family Svcs., Chgo., 1994; peer supr. for pvt. therapists, Chgo., 1998—. Author: (juvenile) Legend of Hun, 1986. Vol. Big Bros.-Big Sisters, Kalamazoo, 1989-93; vol. probation officer, Kalamazoo, 1989-92. Avocations: swimming, dance, travel, reading, stamp collecting. Office: 2524 N Lincoln Ave Ste 215 Chicago IL 60614-2326 Home: 1412 Vintage Dr Joliet IL 60431-8418

KUMIN, LIBBY BARBARA, speech language pathologist, educator; b. Bklyn., Nov. 11, 1945; d. Herbert H. and Berniece (Shuch) K.; m. Martin J. Lazar, Jan. 18, 1969; 1 child, Jonathan Kumin Lazar. BA summa cum laude, LIU, 1965; MA, NYU, 1966, PhD, 1969. Lic. speech pathologist, pathology. Asst. prof. speech pathology U. Md., College Park, 1972-76, cons., 1976-80; assoc. prof. Loyola Coll., Balt., 1980-88, prof., 1988—, chmn. dept. speech and lang. pathology, 1993-99, dir. MS program, 1983—2003, dir. grad. programs, 1999—2003. Adj. prof. Loyola Coll., 1976-80; specialist in speech and language in Down Syndrome; mem. profl. adv. bd. Nat. Down Syndrome Cong.; leader of parent and profl. seminars; mem. Down Syndrome Med. Interest Group. Author: Aphasia, 1978, Classroom Language Skills in Children with Down Syndrome, 2001, Early Communication Skills for Children with Down Syndrome, 2003; therapies editor: Down Syndrome Quar.; contbr. articles to profl. jours. Recipient Outstanding Individual of Yr. award Howard County Assn. Retarded Citizens, Nat. Meritorious Svc. award Nat. Down Syndrome Congress, 1987, Svc. Learning award Shriver Ctr., 1996-98, 2002, Summer Rsch. award Loyola Coll., 1983, 91, 97, 99, 2002; Aaron and Little Straus Found. grantee, 1983-89, 99—, Columbia Found. grantee, Joseph P. Kennedy Found. Faculty Innovation grantee, 1995, 2002. Mem. Nat. Down Syndrome Soc., Nat. Down Syndrome Congress, Am. Speech/Lang./Hearing Assn. (cert.), Md. Speech and Hearing Assn., ARC, Sigma Tau Delta, Pi Lambda Theta. Office: Loyola Coll Dept Speech Pathology 4501 N Charles St Dept Speech Baltimore MD 21210-2601 E-mail: lkumin@loyola.edu.

KUMIN, MAXINE WINOKUR, poet, writer; b. Phila., June 6, 1925; d. Peter and Doll (Simon) Winokur; m. Victor Montwid Kumin, June 29, 1946; children: Jane Simon, Judith Montwid, Daniel David. AB, Radcliffe Coll., 1946, MA, 1948; LHD (hon.), Centre Coll., 1976, Davis and Elkins Coll., 1977, Regis Coll., 1979, New England Coll., 1982, Claremont Grad. Sch., 1983, U. N.H., 1984. Instr. Tufts U., Medford, Mass., 1958-61, lectr. English, 1965-68. Scholar Radcliffe Inst. for Ind. Study, 1961-63; vis. lectr. U. Mass., Amherst, 1973, Princeton U., 1977, 79, 81-82; adj. prof. Columbia U., 1975; Fannie Hurst prof. of literature Brandeis U., 1975, Wash. U., St. Louis, 1977; Carolyn Wilkerson Bell vis. scholar Randolph-Macon Woman's Coll., 1978; poet in residence Bucknell U., 1983; vis. prof. MIT, 1984, U. Miami, 1995, Pitzer Coll., 1996; McGee prof. of writing Davidson Coll., 1997; writer in residence Fla. Internat. U., 1998-2000; master artist Atlantic Ctr. for Arts, New Smyrna Beach, Fla., 1984-2002; staff mem. Bread Loaf Writers' Conf., 1969-71, 73, 75, 77; poetry cons. Library of Congress, 1981-82; elector The Poet's Corner, The Cathedral of St. John the Divine, 1990—; mem. staff Sewanee Writer's Conf., 1993-94, Bucknell U. visiting poet, 2001. Author: (poetry) Halfway, 1961, The Privilege, 1965, The Nightmare Factory, 1970, Up Country: Poems of New England, 1972 (Pulitzer Prize for poetry 1973), House, Bridge, Fountain, Gate, 1975, The Retrieval System, 1978, Our Ground Time Here Will Be Brief, 1982, Closing the Ring, 1984, The Long Approach, 1985, Nurture, 1989, Looking for Luck, 1992, Connecting the Dots, 1996, Selected Poems 1960-1990, 1997, The Long Marriage, 2001; (novels) Through Dooms of Love, 1965, The Passions of Uxport, 1968, The Abduction, 1971, The Designated Heir, 1974; (essays) To Make A Prairie: Essays on Poets, Poetry, and Country Living, 1980, In Deep: Country Essays, 1987, Women, Animals and Vegetables: Essays and Stories, 1994; (short stories) Why Can't We Live Together Like Civilized Human Beings?, 1982; (juvenile) Sebastian and the Dragon, 1960, Spring Things, 1961, A Summer Story, 1961, Follow the Fall, 1961, A Winter Friend, 1961, Mittens in May, 1962, No One Writes a Letter to the Snail, 1962, Archibald the Traveling Poodle, 1963, (with Sexton) More Eggs of Things, 1964, Speedy Digs Downside Up, 1964, The Beach Before Breakfast, 1964, Paul Bunyan, 1966, Faraway Farm, 1967, The Wonderful Babies of 1809 and Other Years, 1968, When Grandmother Was Young, 1970, When Great-Grandmother Was Young, 1971, (with Sexton) Joey and the Birthday Present, 1971, (with Sexton) The Wizard's Tears, 1975, What Color Is Caesar?, 1978, The Microscope, 1984; contbr. poems to nat. mags. Recipient Lowell Mason Palmer award, 1960, William Marion Reedy award, 1968, Eunice Tietjens Meml. prize Poetry Mag., 1972, Borestone Mountain award, 1976, Radcliffe Coll. Alumnae Recognition award, 1978, Am. Acad. and Inst. Arts and Letters award for excellence in literature, 1980, Levinson award Poetry mag., 1987, The Poets' prize, 1994, Aiken Taylor Poetry prize, 1995, Centennial award Harvard Grad. Sch. Arts and Scis., 1996; grantee Nat. Endowment for the Arts, 1966; fellow Nat. Coun. on Arts and Humanities, 1967-68; fellow Acad. Am. Poets, 1986; fellow Woodrow Wilson, 1979-80, 91-93. Mem. Acad. Am. Poets (chancellor), Poetry Soc. Am., PEN Am., Authors Guild, The Writers Union.*

KUMMER, KAREN LANG, historian, consultant, architecture educator; d. Gerhard Paul and Elsie Reese Lang; m. Rex Kummer, Aug. 1975. BA magna cum laude, U. Mo., Columbia, 1970—74; MA in Archtl. History, U. Va., Charlottesville, 1979—81. Cert. in Hist. Preservation, U. Va., 1981. Rsch. cons. Hist. Richmond Found., Va., 1979—80; intern Va. Hist. Landmarks Commn., Richmond, Va., 1980; exec. dir. Preservation & Conservation Assn. Champaign County, Champaign, Ill., 1982—; vis. rsch. assoc. Small Homes Coun./Bldg. Rsch. Coun., Champaign, Ill., 1988—91, asst. editor, 1991—92; cons. The URBANA Group, Urbana, Ill., 1988—95; archtl. historian, ptnr. ArchiSearch, Urbana, Ill., 1995—. Adj. lectr. U. Ill., Urbana, 1987—97. Pres. Soc. for the Preservation of Greek Housing, Champaign, Ill., 2000—04. Mem.: Nat. Trust for Hist. Preservation, Phi Kappa Phi, Phi Beta Kappa. Office: Preservation & Conservation Assn PO Box 2575 Station A Champaign IL 61825-2575

KUMMETH, PATRICIA JOAN, nursing educator; b. Libertyville, Ill., Mar. 7, 1949; d. Francis Alphonse Kummeth, Elizabeth Claire Kummeth. BSN, Coll. St. Teresa, 1970; MSN, U. Wis., Eau Claire, 1988. Registered nurse. Staff RN med. Saint Marys Hosp., Rochester, Minn., 1970—72, clin. insvc. educator, 1972—76, head nurse med., 1976—78, staff RN hematology/nephrology, 1978—81; nursing edn. specialist Mayo Clinic Hosp., Rochester, 1982—. Nursing continuing edn. appraiser Am. Nurses' Credentialing Ctr., Washington, 1998—. Author: (booklet) Problem-Oriented Charting: A Study Guide, 1976; developer (nursing asst. model in jour.) Med.-Surg. Nursing, 2001. Sec. Rochester Women's Softball Assn., 1994—98. Recipient Breaking Barriers award, Minn. Coalition to Promote Women in Athletic Leadership, 2001. Mem.: ANA (congress on nursing practice and economics 1998—2002), Minn. Nurses Assn. (commn. nursing practice 1999—2003, sec. 1992—93, commn. on edn. 1991—92), Acad. Med.-Surg. Nurses (sec. Upper Miss. River Valley chpt. 1999—2001), Am. Soc.Healthcare Educators and Trainers (info. mgr. Minn. affiliate 1993—95), Minn. Nurses Assn. (pres. 6th dist. 1988—92, sec. 1995—99, dir. 2000—02), Sigma Theta Tau (Kappa Mu chpt.), American Nurses' Credentialing Center (Commn. Accreditation 1998—2002). Roman Catholic. Avocations: reading, golf, travel. Office: Mayo Clinic Hosp 1216 Second St SW - 7 Marian Hall Rochester MN 55902 Home: 5162 3rd St NW Rochester MN 55901-4418

KUMPFER, KAROL LINDA, research psychologist; b. Neptune, N.J., July 30, 1943; d. Beverly Donald and Mary Belle (Campbell) K.; m. Henry Overton Whiteside, Mar. 6, 1978; 1 child, Jane H. BA, Colo. Women's Coll., 1966; MA, U. Utah, 1970, PhD, 1972; postdoctoral, U. Minn., 1975. Lic. psychologist, Utah. Asst. prof. psychology Oberlin (Ohio) Coll., 1971-73; research assoc. Inst. Child Devel. U. Minn., Mpls., 1975-76; asst. prof. Colo. Women's Coll., Denver, 1976-78; psychologist Salt Lake County Mental Health Dept., 1979-80; dep. dir. State Div. Alcoholism and Drugs, Salt Lake City, 1980-84; vis. assoc. prof. Grad. Sch. Social Work U. Utah, Salt Lake City, 1983—88, asst. prof. psychiatry, 1986—88, assoc. prof. dept. health promotion and edn., 1988—; dir. Ctr. Substance Abuse and Prevention, Washington, 1998—2000; author, dir. Strengthening Families Program, Salt Lake City, 1982—; coordinating scientist Center for Disease Control, 2000—03. Editor/author: Childhood and Chemical Abuse: Prevention and Intervention, 1986. Bd. dirs. Repetory Dance Theatre, Salt Lake City, 1983-86, Western Assn. Concerned Adoptive Parents, Salt Lake City, 1985-90, Utah Alliance for Mentally Ill, Salt Lake City, 1979-80, Indian Walk-in Ctr., 2000—; pres. U. Utah. Faculty Women's Club, 1974-75. Grantee Utah Dept. Social Services, Salt Lake City, 1984-1986, Dept. Justice Office Juvenile Justice and Juvenile Delinquency Prevention, 1987-2003, Nat. Inst. on Drug Abuse, 1998-2004, Ctr. for Substance Abuse Prevention, 1997-2002; recipient SAMNSA/CSAP Model Prevention Program award, 2000, White House Office Nat. Drug Control Policy Dirs. award for Distinguished Svc., 2000, Luther Teryy Lectr. award U.S. Commds. Officers Assn., 2000. Mem.: APHA, AAAS, APA, Soc. for Prevention Rsch. (pres. 1997—99, bd. dirs. 1995—2002), US Commd. Officer Assn., Nat. Inst. Drug Abuse (spl. task force 1985—, grantee 1982—86, 1998—), Utah Mental Health Assn. (bd. dirs.), Coun. on Social Work Edn., Nat. Inst. Alcoholism and Alcohol Abuse (spl. task force 1985—, grantee 1980, 2000—), Am. Acad. Child Psychiatry (spl. task force 1986—88), Utah Psychol. Assn. (bd. dirs. 1985—88), Nat. Coun. Social Work Edn., Am. Pub. Health Assn. (mem. 1996—), Utah Psychologists in Pvt. Practice Assn. (pres. 1985—90), Sigma Xi. Democrat. Unitarian Universalist. Avocations: skiing, sailing, travelling. Office: Health Promotion Edn U Utah 250 S 1850 East Salt Lake City UT 84112-0920 Office Phone: 801-581-7718.

KUN, REBECCA, information technology executive; b. Spokane, Wash., Feb. 2, 1971; AA, Ane Arundel C.C., 1993; BSBA, Oreg. State U., 1999. Intern iinfo. tech. svcs. Internat. Ctr. Rsch. Agro Forestry, Nairobi, Kenya, 1998—99; programmer analyst Micron Technologies, Boise, 1999—2000; info. tech. project lead Supply Chain Services, Boise; nfo. tech. project lead IPG-IT, 2001—02; bus. analyst new & emerging bus. Hewlett Packard, Boise, 2002—. Mem. Idaho Dem. Womens Caucus, Boise. Mem.: Soc. Hispanic Profl. Engrs. (v.p. 1999—2000, pres. 2000—03). Jewish. Avocations: land sailing, travel, languages. Personal E-mail: rkun@lifetime.oregonstate.edu.

KUNDERT, CANDICE JEAN, psychotherapist, social worker, educator; b. Davenport, Iowa, Jan. 23, 1952; d. William Wayne and Lois Jean (Johnson) Thomas; m. George Joseph Burden, Nov. 9, 1968 (div. July 1981); children: Katherine Jean DeLaney, Michael Joseph Burden; m. Richard Allen Kundert, Feb. 12, 1982. AA magna cum laude, Black Hawk Coll., 1986; BA magna cum laude, Marycrest U., 1987; MSW, U. Iowa, 1995. LCSW Ill., lic. ind. social worker Iowa. Pvt. home health aide, 1983—86; family social worker Bethany Homes, Inc., 1986—87; supr. child abuse/neglect Iowa Dept. Human Svcs., Davenport, Clinton, Iowa, 1987—96; mental health therapist Clinton (Iowa) Sch. Dist., 1996—97; family therapist Psychology Assocs., Davenport, Clinton, Iowa, 1996—; lic. social worker-therapist New Hope Behavioral Health Svc., Inc., Moline, Ill., 2002—. V.p. student social work orgn. Marycrest Coll., Davenport, Iowa, 1986; tchr. Clinton C.C. and Scott C.C., 1989—; therapist Family Resources, Inc., Bettendorf, Iowa, 1995—; adj. faculty Black Hawk Coll., 1995—98; presenter in field. Mem.: NASW, Phi Theta Kappa (v.p. 1985—86), Psi Beta (pres. 1983—86). Democrat. Methodist. Avocations: reading, raising llamas, fishing. Home: 8495 Grennan Rd Fenton IL 61251 Office: New Hope Behavioral Health Inc 3302 41st St Moline IL 61265

KUNES, ELLEN, editor-in-chief; Cons. editor Mademoiselle Mag.; contbg. editor Omni Mag.; sr. editor Self Mag.; lifestyle dir. McCalls, 1991—94; exec. editor Redbook Mag., 1994—98; editor O Mag., 1999; editor-in-chief Redbook Mag., 2001—. Author: Living Well - Or Even Better, 1991. Office: Redbook 224 W 57th St New York NY 10019

KUNIN, JACQUELINE BARLOW, art educator; b. Harrisburg, Pa., Apr. 20, 1941; d. Rodney Kipton and Marie (Trunk) Barlow; m. Richard Henry Kunin, June 17, 1967. BFA, Pratt Inst., 1963; MEd, Temple U., 1967. Comml. artist Dock and Kinney Co., N.Y.C., 1963-64; art libr. Norcross, Inc., N.Y.C., 1964; tchr. graphic arts Jones Jr. H.S., Phila., 1964-66; tchr. art John Bartram H.S., Phila., 1966-86; tchr. painting and drawing H.S. for Creative and Performing Arts, Phila., 1986—. Named Disting Tchr. White House Commn. Presdl. Scholars, Washington, 1994, Outstanding Educator award Phila. Coll. Textiles and Sci., 1997. Mem. AAUW, Pa. Art Edn. Assn., Victorian Soc. Am. (Phila. chpt. bd. dirs. 1986-96), Valley Forge Civic Assn. Avocations: painting, collecting american costumes 1850-1950.

KUNIN, MADELEINE MAY, former ambassador to Switzerland, former governor; b. Zurich, Switzerland, Sept. 28, 1933; came to U.S., 1940, naturalized, 1947; d. Ferdinand and Renee (Bloch) May; children: Julia, Peter, Adam, Daniel BA, U. Mass., 1956; MS, Columbia U., 1957; MA, U. Vt., 1967; numerous hon. degrees. Newspaper reporter Burlington Free Press, Vt., 1957-58; guide Brussels World's Fair, Belgium, 1958; TV asst. producer Sta. WCAX-TV, Burlington, 1960-61; freelance writer, instr. English Trinity Coll., Burlington, 1969-70; mem. Vt. Ho. of Reps., 1973-78; lt. gov. State of Vt., Montpelier, 1979-82, gov., 1985-91; disting. vis. in Pub. Policy Bunting Inst., Cambridge, Mass., 1991-92, Dartmouth Coll., Hanover, N.H., 1992; dep. sec. edn. Dept. Education, Washington, D.C., 1993-96; U.S. amb. to Switzerland, 1996-99; scholar in residence Middlebury Coll., 1999; disting. vis. prof. St.Michael's Coll. and U. Vt., 2003—. Fellow Inst. Politics, Kennedy Sch. Govt., Harvard U., 1983; lectr. Middlebury Coll., St. Michael's Coll., 1984; disting. pub. policy visitor Rockefeller Ctr., Dartmouth Coll., 1992; pub. policy fellow Bunting Inst., Radcliffe Coll., Harvard U., 1991-92; Vt. Joint Fiscal Com., 1977-78; mem. exec. com. Nat. Conf. Lt. Govs., 1979-80; founder, pres. Inst. Sustainable Cmtys., Montpelier, Vt., 1991—; mem. 3 person com. to recommend v.p. to Bill Clinton; mem. transition team, co-chair nat. com. Women for Clinton, 1992; scholar-in-residence Middlebury (Vt.) Coll., 1999-2003; disting visitor U. of Vt. and St. Michael's Coll., 2003—. Author: Living a Political Life: A Memoir, 1994, The Big Green Book, 1976; contbr. articles to profl. jours., mags. and newspapers. Commentator Vt. Pub. Radio. Scholar in residence Middleberg Coll., 1999—; Named Outstanding State Legislator, Eagleton Inst. Politics, Rutgers U., 1975; Montgomery fellow Dartmouth Coll., 1991. Fellow Am. Acad. Arts & Scis.; mem. Nat. Gov.'s Assn. (mem. exec. com.), Nat. Govs.' Conf. (chair com. on energy and the environ.), New Eng. Gov.'s Conf. (chairperson). Democrat. Office: Univ Vt Burlington VT 05401 E-mail: mkunin@middlebury.edu.

KUNKEL, GEORGIE BRIGHT, freelance writer, retired school counselor; b. Chehalis, Wash. d. George Riley and Myrtia (McLaughlin) Bright; m. Norman C. Kunkel, Apr. 25, 1946; children: N. Joseph D.C.(dec.), Stephen Gregory, Susan Ann, Kimberly Jane Waligorska. BA in Edn., Western Wash. U., 1944; MEd, U. Wash., 1968. Tchr. pub. schs., Vader, Centralia, Seattle, Wash., 1941-67; counselor Highline Pub. Schs., Seattle, 1967-82; pvt. cons., Seattle, 1970—. Sch. counselor rep. State of Art Conf., Balt., 1980; co-presenter programs on the Holocaust. Author: You're Damn Right I Wear Purple! Color Me Feminist, 2000; editor: Women and Girls in Edn., 1972—75; columnist: Northwest Prime Time; contbr. articles to profl. jours. Organizer Women and Girls in Edn., Wash. State, 1971; pres. Wash. State NOW, 1973; past pres. West Seattle Dem. Women's Club. Named Woman of Yr. in Wash. State, Women's Fedn. for World Peace, 1998; grantee Women Adminstrs. Wash. State, 1971, Edn. Svc. Dist., Seattle, 1980; recipient Woman of Achievement award Past Pres. Assembly, 2000; winner essay contest and appeared on Oprah show. Mem. NEA (sec. pub. rels.), ACA (pres. state br. 1982-83), Am. Sch. Counseling Assn. (pres. state divsn. 1980-81), Seattle Counselors Assn. (organizer, past pres. office exec., Counselor of Yr. award 1990). Unitarian Universalist. Avocations: singing with Raging Grannies, doing "open mike" standup comedy. Home and Office: 3409 SW Trenton St Seattle WA 98126-3743 E-mail: gnkunkel@juno.com.

KUNKEL-CHRISTMAN, DEBRA ANN, educator; b. Palmerton, Pa., Sept. 11, 1967; d. Rosalie Meridith and Eugene William Kunkel; m. Kevin Douglas Christman, Aug. 9, 1997. EdM(hon.), Kutztown U., 2000. Cert. tchr. Pa., 1991. Tchr. Saucon Valley Sch. Dist., Hellertown, Pa., 1994—2003. Mem.: Coun. Exceptional Children. Home: 2127 Belmont St Allentown PA 18104 Office: Saucon Valley Sch Dist 20950 Polk Valley Rd Hellertown PA 18055

KUNKLE, MARY LOU, counselor; b. Norborne, Mo., Aug. 22, 1937; d. William J. and Hazel Irene (Lungren) McLaughlin; m. John K. Kunkle, Jan. 27, 1956; children: Cindy Canzanella, John W., Karen Reynolds, Nancy Harvest. BA, Millersville U., 1984, MS, 1988; PhD, Walden U., 1994. Cert. addictions counselor, diplomate Pa. Chem. Abuse Cert. Bd. Legal sec. Stein, Storb, Mann & O'Brien, Lancaster, Pa., 1970—74; city treas. City of Estell Manor, NJ, 1977—78; with Estell Mann Ch., 1974—78; legal sec. Shremer & Patterson, Lancaster, Pa., 1978—81; sec. RR Donnelly & Sons. Co., 1981—89; counselor Christian Counseling Svcs., Ephrata, 1988—94, Pa. Counseling Svcs., East Potersburg, 1994—. Cons. Manor Care Nursing Care, Dallastown, Pa., 1999. Avocations: choir, music. Home: 2487 Carriage Dr Lancaster PA 17601 Office: Pa Counseling Svcs 6079 Main St East Petersburg PA 17520

KUNSTADTER, GERALDINE SAPOLSKY, foundation executive; b. Boston, Jan. 6, 1928; d. Harry Herman and Nettie Sapolsky; m. John W. Kunstadter, Apr. 23, 1949; children: John W., Lisa, Christopher, Elizabeth Student, MIT, 1945-48. Draftsman U. Chgo. Cyclotron Project, 1948; engring. asst. Gen. Electric Corp., Lynn, Mass., 1948-49; pres. Capricorn

Investments Corp., 1971—; chmn., pres., dir. A. Kunstadter Family Found., N.Y.C., 1966—. Host family program dir. N.Y.C. Commn. for UN, 1971-86; pres. Nat. Inst. Social Scis., 1979-81; adv. coun. hospitality com. UN Delegations. Mem. internat. hospitality com. Nat. Coun. Women; chmn. N.Y.-Beijing Sister City Com.; mem. Com. Mgmt. of Network 20/20; bd. dirs. Bridge to Asia Found., Atlantic Coun. of U.S., Ballets Tech. Found., N.Y.C., Ctr. US.-China Arts Exch., Inst. World Affairs. Recipient Windham award, 1970, Silver medal, Nat. Inst. Social Sci., 1981, Pres.'s medal, Archtl. Soc. China, 2001. Mem. Inst. Current World Affairs, Coun. on Fgn. Rels., Am. Women's Club, Hurlingham Club, Lansdowne Club (London), Cosmopolitan Club N.Y.(Internat. com.).

KUNTZ, CAROL B. psychologist, educator; b. Dickinson, N.D., Oct. 13, 1952; d. John Nick Kuntz and Veronica Decker; divorced; children: Rick, Jess, Kristy. ADN, Dickinson State U., 1983; BS in Psychology, U. N.D., 1988; MA in Psychology, Ctrl. Mich. U., 1990, D in Psychology, 1993. Diplomate Am. Pyschotherapy Assn., cert. profl. qualification psychology Assn. State and Provincial Psychology Bd. RN St. Joseph's Hosp., Dickinson, ND, 1983, Minot, ND, 1983—86, United Hosp., Grand Forks, 1987—88, Ctrl. Mich. Hosp., Mt. Pleasant, 1988—92; rsch. asst. to Dr. David Stein U. N.D., Grand Forks, ND, 1987—88; psychologist Cath. Family Svcs., Mt. Pleasant, 1991—92; clin. psychologist Univ. Physicians, Sioux Falls, SD, 1993—2002, Avera McKennan Hosp., Univ. Health Ctr., Sioux Falls, 2002—. Cons. Healthy Solutions, Sioux Falls, 1992—93; asst. prof. U. S.D., Sioux Falls, 1994—, supr. psychiatry resident, 2002—; presenter in field. Mem.: APA, Am. Assn. Marriage and Family Therapy, Am. Psychol. Assn. Clin. Psychology, Am. Psychotherapy Assn., Am. Bd. Disability Analysts (diplomate), Internat. Neuropsychological Soc., Nat. Acad. Neuropsychology, S.D. Psychol. Assn., Clin. Neuropsychology, Psychology of Women, Nat. Register health SVc. Providers Psychology, Psi Chi. Roman Catholic. Avocations: ceramics, painting, poetry, bicycling, hiking. Office: Univ Psychiatry Assocs 1001 E 21st St Ste 2000 Sioux Falls SD 57105 Office Phone: 605-322-5700. Personal E-mail: drcbk52@aol.com.

KUNTZ, JANET RUTH, musician, music educator; b. Clearwater, Fla., Aug. 3, 1963; d. Grant Edgar and Barbara Lou Estep; m. Jeffrey Michael Kuntz, Dec. 28, 1985. MusB in Edn., Furman U., 1985; MusM, U. South Fla., 1997. Cert. profl. tchg. S.C. Dept. Edn., 1985, Fla. Dept. Edn., 1988. H.s. asst. band dir.. Spartanburg (S.C.) Sch. Dist. 7, 1985—86; h.s. asst. band dir. Columbia (Miss.) City Schs., 1986—88; band, choral dir. Pinellas County Schs., Largo, Fla., 1988—99; band dir. Fairforest mid. sch. Spartanburg (S.C.) Sch. Dist. 6, 1999—. Mem. of applied tchg. faculty Calvary Bapt. Musical Arts Sch., Clearwater, Fla., 1992—99; prin. flutist Tampa (Fla.) Bay Symphony, 1992—93; dean students Furman U. Summer Music Camp, Greenville, SC, 1994—2001. Musician (conductor): The Marriage of Figaro. Instrumental and vocalist soloist Prince of Peace Luth. Ch., Largo, Fla., 1989—99; instumental soloist, choir mem. First Presbyn. Ch., Spartanburg, 2001—. Named Kappa Delta Epsilon Outstanding Educator, Furman U., 1985; recipient Vince Perone Outstanding Bandsman Award, 1985, All Am. Collegiate Scholar, U. South Fla., 1997. Mem.: S.C. Band Dirs. Assn., S.C. Music Educators Assn., Music Educators Nat. Conf., Phi Kappa Phi. Presbyterian. Avocations: music, travel, creative projects. Home: 174 Bradford Crossing Dr Roebuck SC 29376 Office: Fairforest Mid Sch 4120 N Blackstock Rd Spartanburg SC 29301 E-mail: kuntzjr@spartanburg6.k12.sc.us.

KUNTZ, MARION LUCILE LEATHERS, classicist, educator, historian; b. Atlanta, Sept. 6, 1924; d. Otto Asa and Lucile (Parks) Leathers; m. Paul G. Kuntz, Nov. 26, 1970; children by previous marriage: Charles, Otto Alan (Daniels). BA, Agnes Scott Coll., 1945; MA, Emory U., 1964, PhD, 1969. Lectr. Latin Lovett Sch., Atlanta, 1963-66; mem. faculty Ga. State U., 1966[00bf], assoc. prof., 1969-73, prof. Latin and Greek, 1973[00bf], Regents' Prof., 1975—, chmn. dept. fgn. langs., 1975-84, rsch. prof., 1984[00bf], Fuller E. Callaway disting. prof., 1985[00bf], alumni disting. prof., 1994. Author: Colloquium of the Seven About Secrets of the Sublime of Jean Bodin, 1975, Guillaume Postel, Prophet of the Restitution of All Things: His Life and Thought, 1981, Jacob's Ladder and the Tree of Life: Concepts of Hierarchy and the Great Chain of Being, 1987, Postello, Venezia e Il Suo Mondo, 1988, Venice, Myth and Utopian Thought, 1999, The Anointment of Dionisio: Prophecy and Politics in Renaissance Italy, 2002; also scholarly articles; mem. editl. bd. Library of Renaissance Humanism. V.p. acad. affairs Am.-Hellenic Found. Named Latin Tchr. of Yr. State Ga., 1965; Am. Classical League scholar, 1966, Gladys Krieble Delmas scholar, 1991; Am. Coun. Learned Socs. grantee, 1970, 73, 76, 81, 87, 90; recipient medal for excellence in Renaissance studies Pres. of Coun. Gen., Tours, France, 1995, Disting. Career Alumna award Agnes Scott Coll., 1995. Master: Soc. for Values in Higher Edn., Philosophy and Religion; mem.: Am. Cath. Hist. Soc., Classical Assn. Midwest and South (Semple award 1965), Am. Philol. Assn., Archaeol. Inst. Am., Soc. di Philosophique Medievale, Soc. Medieval and Renaissance Philosophy (exec. bd. 1988—), Medieval Acad. Soc. de Culture Europèenne, Soc. des Seizièmistes, Soc. Christian Philosophers (exec. bd. 1987—), Internat. Soc. Neo-Latin Studies, Internat. Soc. Neo-Platonic Studies, Am. Hist. Assn., Am. Soc. Ch. History, Am. Cath. Philos. Assn., Am. Soc. Aesthetics, Renaissance Soc. Am. (coun. 1994—97, trustee 2003—, 2003—), Cath. Hist. Soc., Friends of the Vatican Libr., Italia Nostra, Fondazione Ambiente Italiana, Amici di Querini-Stampalia Galleria e Biblioteca, Coun. Amici di Biblioteca Nazionale di San Marco, Italian Cultural Soc., Nat. Trust Hist. Preservation, Atlanta Hist. Soc., High Mus. of Art (patron), Friends of the Warburg Inst., Am. Acad. Rome (sec.-treas. 1970—74), World Monuments Fund, The Atlanta Symphony (patron), Atlanta Opera, The Commerce Club, Omicron Delta Kappa, Phi Kappa Phi, Phi Beta Kappa. Roman Catholic. Home: Villa Veneziana 1655 Ponce De Leon Ave Atlanta GA 30307 also: Castello 6817 Venice Italy Office Phone: 404-651-2265. E-mail: marion@gsu.edu.

KUNZ, APRIL BRIMMER, state legislator, lawyer; b. Denver, Apr. 1, 1954; divorced. AA, Stephens Coll., 1974; BS, U. So. Calif., 1976; JD, U. Wyo., 1979. Bar: Wyo. Pres. K and R Enterprises; mem. Wyo. Ho. Reps., Cheyenne, 1985-86, 90-92, Wyo. Senate, Cheyenne, 1992—, chair jud. com., pres., 2003—. Mem. Women's Civic League; mem. Laramie County Rep. Women's Club. Mem. ABA, Wyo. State Bar Assn, Laramie County Bar Assn. Republican. Office: PO Box 285 Cheyenne WY 82003-0285 also: Wyo Senate State Capitol Cheyenne WY 82002-0001

KUO, CHARLENE, finance professional; b. Taiwan, July 11, 1964; d. Kirk H. and Stella S. Kuo. BS, U. Calif., Berkeley, 1986; MS, MIT, 1989; JD, Coll. William & Mary, 1994. Cons. Standard & Poor's, N.Y.C., 1994-95; sr. cons. Summit Systems, Inc., N.Y.C., 1995-97; v.p. Goldman Sachs & Co., N.Y.C., 1997—. Vol. N.Y.C. Jr. League, 1996—, Nat. Dem. Com., N.Y.C., 1999—; mem. N.Y.. Met. Mus., 1998—. ITT scholar, U. Calif., 1982-86. Mem. Princeton Club N.Y., Tau Beta Pi, Eta Kappa Nu. Avocations: painting, music. Office: Goldman Sachs & Co 85 Broad St New York NY 10004-2456

KUPERMAN, FRANCES PERGERICHT, lawyer; b. Cleve., June 4, 1952; d. Joseph and Ann Pergericht; m. Roman G. Kuperman, Feb. 24, 1982; 1 child, Natalie Jill. BA magna cum laude, Case Western Res. U., 1974; JD, Washington U., St. Louis, 1978. Bar: N.H. 1979, Ill. 1981. Law clk. presiding justice U.S. Dist. Ct. No. Dist. Ill., Chgo., 1979-81; assoc. Jenner & Block, Chgo., 1981-83; asst. regional atty. Dept. Health and Human Svcs., Chgo., 1983-96, sr. counsel Office of Counsel to the Inspector Gen. Washington, 1996—. Topics editor Washington U. Law Quar., 1977-78. Mem. Phi Beta Kappa. Office: Office of Inspector Gen Dept Health and Human Svcs 330 Independence Ave SW Washington DC 20201-0003 E-mail: frankuperman@comcast.net.

KUPIEC, SUZANNE L. utilities executive; BBA in Fin. and Acctg., Tex. A&M U. CPA Tex. Joined Ernst & Young, LLP, 1989, ptnr.; v.p., chief risk and corp. compliance officer Reliant Resources, Inc., Houston, 2003—. Mem.: AICPA, Tex. State Soc. CPA. Office: Reliant Energy Exec Offices PO Box 2286 Houston TX 77252-2286

KUPPER, KETTI, artist; b. L.A., Oct. 14, 1951; d. Charles Parnell Kupper and Donna Corrine Callen; m. Steven Robert Ford Feb. 9, 1978 (div. Mar. 1994); children: Ashley Elizabeth, Kimberly Brianna. BS, Brigham Young, 1974; student, Acad. Art, San Francisco, 1974-76; MFA in Visual Art, Norwich U., 1994. Freelance painter, illustrator, 1980—; prin., co-owner Fordesign Mktg., Wilton, Conn., 1990-93; chmn. of art U. Bridgeport, 1991-96; ind. cons. Milford, Conn., 1994-98; mentor, tchr. Conn. Commn. Arts, Hartford, Conn., 1996-98; non resident studio tchr. Vt. Coll., Montpelier, 1998—; pres. Ketti Kupper's Art & Design Inc., L.A. Commd. paintings include portrait Clint Murchison for Dallas Times Herald Mag., 1984, Am. Express Olympiadas Barcelona for commercial, 1992, portrait U. Bridgeport Pres. Edwin Eigel, 1995; collections include: Nestle Corp., Ptnrs. Nat. Health Plans, Tex. Instruments; designer, Romantic Backyard Getaway (winning designer, HGTV Landscaper's Challenge); art pub. in Times, Newsweek, Conn. Mag., Dallas Life Mag., Readers Digest. Curator Focus on Environ. U. Bridgeport Coll.; cmty. environ. activist Bridgeport Area Arts Coun.; dir. contest Smithsonian Nat. Mus. Am. Indian, N.Y.C., 1994; grantwriter, mural dir. Conn. commn. Arts, 1995; bd. dirs. Women's Caucus for Art, L.A. Recipient Addy 14th Dist. Region award Am. Adv. Fedn., 1984, Painting award The Discovery Mus., 1995, Painting award Silvermine Artists Guild, 1996, Painting award Artworks Gallery, 1997. Mem. AIA, Coll. Art Assn., Women's Caucus for Arts (chpt. pres. 1996-98), N.Y. Soc. Illustrators, Calif. Lawyers for Arts, Nat. Art Educators Assn., Assn. Profl. Landscape Designers. Democrat. Avocations: writing, gardening, remodeling, construction design. Office: 4208 1/2 Camero Ave Los Angeles CA 90027-4519 E-mail: ketti@KettiKupper.com.

KUPPERS, PETRA, art educator, artist; arrived in U.S., 2001; d. Hans Leo and Kathe Kuppers; m. R. Platt. MA in Film Studies, Warwick U., Eng., 1993; MA in Germanistik, U. of Cologne, Germany, 1994; diploma in health and social welfare studies, Open U., Eng., 1998; PhD, Falmouth Coll. of Arts, Eng., 1999. Asst. prof. of performance studies Bryant Coll., Smithfield, RI, 2001—. Artistic dir. Olimpias Performance Rsch. Series. Author: (acad. study) Disability and Contemporary Performance: Bodies on Edge; dir.: (creative CD ROM/digital media work) Sleeping Giants (Nat. Endowment for Sci., Tech. and the Arts, 2002). Sec. Performance Studies Internat. Achievements include research in Disability Arts. E-mail: pkuppers@bryant.edu.

KUPST, MARY JO, psychologist, researcher; b. Chgo., Oct. 4, 1945; d. George Eugene and Winifred Mary (Hughes) K.; m. Alfred Procter Stresen-Reuter Jr., Aug. 21, 1977. BS, Loyola U., 1967, MA, 1969, PhD, 1972. Lic. psychologist, Ill., Wis. Postdoctoral fellow U. Ill. Med. Ctr., Chgo., 1971—72; rsch. psychologist Children's Meml. Hosp., Chgo., 1972—89; assoc. prof. psychiatry and pediatrics Northwestern U. Med. Sch., Chgo., 1981—89; prof. pediatrics Med. Coll. Wis., Milw., 1989—, dir. pediatric psychology, 1995—. Practice clin. psychology, Chgo., 1975-89, McHenry, Ill., 1987-89; co-chair pediat. oncology group psychology com., 1995-2001, vice chair psychology discipline Children's Oncology Group, 2002—. Editor: (with others) The Child with Cancer, 1980; contbr. articles to profl. jours. V.p. McHenry County Mental Health Bd., 1997—2001. Fellow: APA (charter fellow, pres. divsn. 54 2004—); mem.: Wis. Psychol. Assn. Office: Med Coll Wis Dept Pediats 8701 W Watertown Plank Rd Milwaukee WI 53226-3548 E-mail: mkupst@mail.mcw.edu.

KURIAN, MARIAN, surgeon; b. Germany, Apr. 16, 1966; arrived in US, 1970; m. David O'Connor; 2 children. MD, Albany Med. Coll., 1990. Clin. laparoscopic fellow Mt. Sinai Minimally Invasive Clin. Ctr., 1999—2000; assoc. dir. surgical edn. Lenox Hill Hosp., NYC. Mem.: Assn. Women Surgeons, Am. Soc. Bariatric Surgery, Am. Gastroent. and Endoscopic Surgeons (SAGES). Achievements include pioneer in minimally invasive gastric bypass surgery. Office: Lenox Hill Hosp 130 E 77th St Black Hall 13th Fl New York NY 10021*

KURIANSKY, JUDY, television personality, radio personality, reporter, psychologist, writer, educator; b. N.Y.C., Jan. 31, 1947; d. Abraham and Sylvia (Feld) Brodsky; m. Edward Kuriansky, Aug. 24, 1969. BA, Smith Coll., 1968; EdM, Boston U., 1970; PhD, NYU, 1980. Reporter Sta. WABC-TV, N.Y.C., 1980-82, Sta. WBZ-TV, Boston, 1981-82, Sta. WCBS-TV, 1982-86, 1986-88, Sta. WPIX-TV, N.Y.C., 1987-89, Sta. CNBC-TV, Ft. Lee, NJ, 1989-93; host Total Wellness for Women program Sta. WDBB-TV, Birmingham, Ala., 1988-89; program host Sta. WABC-AM, N.Y.C., 1980-87, Sta. WOR-AM, 1987-88; temp. program host ABC Talk Radio, N.Y.C., 1988-90; host Modern Satellite Network, 1981; TV host J.C. Penney Golden Rule Network, Dallas, 1988-90; feature contbr. Attitudes Show LifeTime, 1992-94; host Love Phones, nat. syndicated Premiere Radio Networks, N.Y.C., 1992-97; host Dr. Judy Show, Winstar Radio, 1998-99. Spokesperson Universal Studios Fla., 1993—94, Church and Dwight, 2000—01; cons. Lily of France, Val Mode Lingerie, Charles of the Ritz, The Rolland Co., Taylor-Gordon Arons Advt., Clairol, Durex, London Internat., 1995, Organon, 1999—; tchr. Columbia U. Med. Sch., 1974—79, Inst. for Health and Religion, 1980—82; adj. prof. clin. psychology NYU, 1993—95; adj. prof. psychology Columbia U. Tchrs. Coll., 2001—; vis. prof. Beijing U. Health Sci. Ctr., 2002—; judge Most Unforgettable Women contest Revlon, 1990; judge Close-Up N Roll Contest, 1993, Cooney Waters P.R., Herpes Awareness Contest, 1996; therapy coord. Nat. Inst. for Psychotherapists, 1977—79; therapist Ctr. for Marital and Family Therapy, 1986—; cons. Shanghai Inst. Reproductive Health Instrn., China, 1999—; trainer marital cons. China Sexology Assn., 2000—; v.p. Quezon Corp., 1978—79; sr. rsch. scientist N.Y. State Psychiat. Inst., 1970—78; lectr. Blanton Peale Inst., 1979—81; mem. adv. bd. Single Living mag., 1997—98, Lane Bryant, 1997—98; cons. Ky. Married for Life Survey, 2003—; adj. prof. psychology Yeshiva Univ., 2003—; asst. clin. prof. psychiatry Columbia Med. Ctr., 2003—. Author: Sex, Now That I've Got Your Attention, Let Me Answer Your Questions, 1984, How to Love a Nice Guy, 1990, Italian and Japanese transls., Generation Sex, 1995, The Complete Idiots Guide to Dating, 1996, 2d edit., 1999, 3rd edit., 2003, The Complete Idiots Guide to a Healthy Relationship, 1997, 2d edit., 2001, The Complete Idiots Guide to Tantric Sex, 2001, China Reproductive Health Hotline Professionals Solve Problems on Sex and Emotions, 2001; columnist Family Circle mag., 1984—89, Whole Life Times, 1986—87, King Features Newspaper, 1984—86, N.Y. and L.I. Newsday, 1993—2000, Penthouse mag., 1995—, Soap Opera Update, 1995—96, Telluride Daily Planet, 1995—98, Cosmo Girl mag., 2001—03, N.Y. Daily News website, 2004—, writer New Woman, Ad Age, Boardroom Reports, Am. Advt. Fedn. mag., Chgo. Tribune Woman News, South China Morning Post, 2001—, columnist Singapore Straits Times, 2002—; contbg. editor: Beauty Mag., 1989—90; guest editor Ladies Home Jour., 1993, AOL On-Line Show, Keyword: Dr. Judy, 1996—97, www.cameraplanet.com, 2001—02, www-.matureamerica.com, 2002—03, mem. adv. bd. Single Living mag., 1997—99; author: Goodbye My Troubles, Hello My Happiness, 1997. UN del. Internat. Assn. Applied Psychology and World Coun. for Psychotherapy, 2004—; bd. dirs. Scientists Com. for Pub. Info., 1977—79; mem. adv. bd. N.Y. City Self Help Orgn., 1983—85; mem. benefits com. Mental Health Svcs. for Deaf, 1980—82; bd. advisors Planned Parenthood, 1998—. Recipient Civilian Commendation, N.Y.C. Police Dept., 1984, Cert. for Unique Pub. Svc. AWRT, 1984, Star award for individual achievement in radio, 1997, Sabo Media Programming Visionary award, 1984, Maggie award Planned Parenthood, 1985, 93, Freedoms Found. award Children for a Better Soc., 1986, Olive award Coun. of Chs., 1986, Mercury award Larimi Comm., 1987. Fellow APA; mem. Am. Women in Radio and TV (pres. N.Y. chpt. 1988-89, nat. found. vice chair 1988-90, nat. bd. treas. 1995-98, Internat. Outreach award 2003), Soc. Sex Therapy and Rsch. (charter), TV Acad. of N.Y. (gov. 1987-91), Friars Club.

KURITA, ROSALIND, state legislator; b. Sept. 24, 1947. Mem. Tenn. Senate 100th Gen. Assemblies. Democrat. Office: 6 Legislative Plaza Nashville TN 37243 E-mail: sen.rosalind.kurita@legislature.state.tn.us.

KURKUL, WENYI WANG, musician, educator, administrator; b. Taipei, Taiwan, Oct. 30, 1964; arrived in U.S., 1986; d. Shih-Ming and Hsieh-Chu Wang. MusM, Ohio U., 1988; MusD, U. Mo., 1995; D in Music Edn., Ind. U., 2000. Prof., adminstr. Sch. Music Tainan (Taiwan) Coll., 1989-92; prof. Nat. Taiwan Acad. Arts, 1989-92, Nat Sun Yat-Sen U., Kaohsiung, Taiwan, 1990-92; mem. vis. faculty Sch. Music Ind. U., Bloomington, 1999—2000; prof. dept. music George Mason U., 2000—03, dir. music edn. dept. music Coll. Visual and Performing Arts, 2001—03, exec. dir. Orff Schulwerk Tchr. Tng. and Cert. Program, 2001—03. Soloist-in-residence Nat. Chiang Kai Shek Cultural Ctr., Taipei, 1991-94; flutist Asian Composers League, Taipei, 1990-92; asst. prin. flutist Taiwan Symphony Orch., Taichung, 1984-86; contbr. articles to profl. publs. Nat. Art and Sci. Coun. scholar, Taiwan, 1989-92; Nat. rsch. grantee Ministry of Edn., Taiwan, 1989-92; named New Performing Star of Yr. Nat. Theatre and Concert Hall Planning and Mgmt. Coun., Taiwan, 1991. Mem.: APA, AAUP, Nat. Assn. Student Personnel Adminstrs., Nat. Assn. Student Affairs Profls., Internat. Soc. Philosophy Music Edn. (founding), Pub. Rels. Soc. Am., Am. Edml. Rsch. Assn., Am. Orff-Schulwerk Assn., Internat. Soc. for Music Edn. (Eng.), European Recorder Tchrs. Assn., Soc. for Rsch. in Music Edn., Music Edn. Nat. Conf., Coll. Music Soc., Nat. Flute Assn. (life), Am. Symphony Orch. League, Phi Kappa Lambda. Home: 403 Misty Knoll Dr Rockville MD 20850-2879 E-mail: wenyi.kurkul@verizon.net.

KURMAN, JUTA, music educator; b. Wändra, Parnu, Estonia, Nov. 7, 1912; d. August and Maria (Reier) Tomberg; m. Alexander Pooman, Sept. 17, 1938 (dec. 1938); m. Hugo Kurman, Jan. 18, 1940; children: Jaan, Juri-George. Tchrs. Lic., Tchrs. Sem., Estonia, 1934; Artist Dipl., State Conservatory of Music, Estonia, 1940, N.Y. Coll. of Music, 1952. Tchr. Tallinn (Estonia) Pub. Schs., 1934-38; performing artist concerts, state radio, and theater Estonia, 1932-40; TV voice soloist Maj. Bowes Original Amateur Hour, Radio City, N.Y., 1949-50; with Claire Mann Show, Channel 5, N.Y.C., 1952; pres. Estonian Music Ctr., N.Y.C., 1973—. Club and ch. soloist; lectr in field; music critic Free Estonian Word, 1948—, Baltic Papers. Co-editor: Haapsalu Shawl, 1972, Kompiling Mart Saar VocalAlbum, 1965, Kompiling Kaljo Raid Estonian Volksongs Album, 1991; contbr. articles to profl. jurs. Sustaining mem. Rep. Nat. Com., 1990—; sustaining sponsor Ronald Reagan Presdl. Found., 1987—. Decorated White Star with V, Order Estonian Republic; named Laureate of Estonian Letters and Scis. Found.; N.Y. Coll. Music grantee, 1948. Mem. Estonian Music Sorority (pres. 1951-63), Estonian Women's Club of N.Y. (pres.), Estonian Ednl. Soc. (hon. mem. elders coun.), World Fedn. Estonian Women's Clubs in Exile (West) (founding pres. 1966—). Republican. Lutheran. Avocations: music, poetry, writing, gardening. Home: 68-50 Juno St Forest Hills NY 11375-5728 Office: Estonian Music Ctr 243 E 34th St New York NY 10016-4852

KURONYA, CAROL GASCO, tour guide; b. Trenton, N.J., Dec. 23, 1935; d. Daniel A. and Amelia M. (Kovacs) Gasco; m. Géza Charles Kuronya, July 8, 1961; children: Kimberly Krajci, Thomas Daniel, Robert Charles. BA, Rutgers U., 1959; Tchr. Cert., Trenton State Coll., 1960. Lab. tech. N.J. State Health Dept., Trenton, 1956-59; tchr. Trenton Schs., 1959-62; owner, designer 18th Century Bouquet, Trenton, 1981-87; tour guide The Contemporary & Others, Bucks County, Pa., 1991—. Apptd. mem. Morrisville (Pa.) Econ. Devel. Corp., 1993-96; mem. edn. com. Mayor's Cultural Resource Com., Trenton, 1994—; pres. The Contemporary of Trenton, 1976-80, 96-2000. Mem. N.J. Children's Home Soc. (program policies chmn. 1990-93, mem.adv. bd. 1998), Morrisville Bus. Assn. (pres. 1992-96),Bucks County Children's Home Soc. Aux. (pres. 1972-74), Historic Morrisville Soc. (bd. dirs., pres. 2000-02). Home: 1230 Evergreen Rd Morrisville PA 19067-7343

KURTH, PATSY ANN, state legislator; b. Washington, Mo., Feb. 2, 1941; m. Alan Kurth; children: Dawn (dec.), Wendy, Martha, Sara. Student, S.W. Mo. State Tchrs. Coll., Brevard C.C. Real estate broker; senator 15th dist. Fla. State Legislature, 1990—. Mem. commerce and econ. opportunities com., cmty. affairs com., govtl. reform and oversight com., natural resources com., ways and means com., human svcs. subcom. Fla. State Senate. Mem. Brevard County Planning and Zoning Bd., Planning and Zoning Bd. for Town of Malabar. Recipient Sustained Support award East Ctrl. Fla. Memory Disorder Clinic, 1992, 94, Leadership award Fla. C. of C.-Chmn. Internat. Trade, Econ. Devel. and Tourism, 1992, Legislator of Yr. award Fla. Restaurant Assn., Fla. Assn. Realtors, 1993, Fla. Econ. Devel. Adv. Coun., 1993, 95, Brevard County Assn. Retarded Citizens, 1994, Area Assn. of Retarded Citizens, Brevard, 1995, Fla. Network of Youth and Family Svcs., 1995, 96, Rainbow Alliance for Mentally Ill, 1996, Fla. Alcohol and Drug Abuse Assn., 1996, Marjorie Olsen Child Advocacy award Child Care Assn. of Brevard County, 1994, Outstanding Senator award Fla. Nurses Assn., 1994, award for oustanding advocacy of children's causes Fla. Pediat. Assn., 1996, R. David Thomas Child Advocate of Yr. award Children's Home Soc., 1996, Fla. Senator of Yr. award Area Assn. of Retarded Citizens/ARC, 1996. Mem. LWV, South Brevard Dem. Women's Club. Methodist. Avocations: fishing, walking, quilting, antique collecting. Office: State Capitol 404 S Monroe St Tallahassee FL 32399-6526 also: 2540 Rocky Point Rd Malabar FL 32950-4603

KURTZ, DOLORES MAY, civic worker; b. Reading, Pa., Oct. 27, 1933; d. Harry Claude and Ethel Gertrude (Fields) Filbert; m. William McKillips Kurtz, Oct. 26, 1957. Sec. cert., Pa. State U., 1980. Legal sec. Snyder, Balmer & Kershner, Reading, 1951-53; head teletype operator E.. duPont de Nemours, Reading, 1953-56; exec. sec. Ford New Holland (Pa.) Inc. (formerly Sperry New Holland), 1956-91; ret., 1991. Active Lancaster County Rep. Com., 1983-85; pres. New Holland Area Womans Club, 1982-84; bd. dirs. Cmty. Meml. Park Assn., New Holland, 1957-82, Lancaster County Fedn. Womens Clubs, 1982—, 2d v.p., 1984-86, 1st v.p., 1986-88, pres. 1988-90; founding mem. Summer Arts Festival, New Holland, 1980—, bd. dirs., 1985-91; membership chair S.E. dist. Pa. Fedn. Womens Clubs, 1984-86; area rep., bd. dirs. Womens Rep. Club Lancaster County, 1982-84; com. mem. New Holland Boro, 1983-85; v.p. Lancaster-Lebanon Arthritis Found. Guild, 1992, pres., 1993. Recipient Outstanding Vol. for Pa. award Pa. Fedn. Womens Clubs, 1984, Woman in the Arts award, 1998. Mem. Gen. Fedn. Womens Clubs Pa. (conservation divsn. chair 1996-98, credentials com. 1998-2000, chmn. Caps for Kids project Lancaster County chpt. 1999-2004). Methodist. Avocations: arts and crafts, travel, photography.

KURTZ, ELLEN R. journalist; b. Bklyn., May 22, 1934; d. George and Gertrude (Troiansky) Rabinowitz; m. Raymond J. Kurtz, June 26, 1954 (dec. May 1988); children: Jill A., Michael S., Jack L.; m. Sol T. Horowitz. BA, Bklyn. Coll., 1955. Tchr. N.Y.C. Pub. Schs., 1955-56; lectr. Weight Watchers of N.J., Livingston, 1969-83; owner, dir. Livingston Coll. Bd. Rev., 1975-83; mng. editor On the Scene, Livingston, 1984-86; editor Regional Weekly News, East Hanover, N.J., 1986; writer spl. sects. Star-Ledger, Newark, 1987—2000. Cons. editor Hosp. News of N.J., Colonia, 1989—90; feature writer Drew U., Madison, NJ, 1996—2000; publicist Drew U. Ctr. for Holocaust Study, 1997—98; instr. The Adult Sch. of the Chathams, Madison and Florham Park, 1999; Holocaust coun. MetroWest, 2001—; lectr. Jewish Edn. Assn. MetroWest NJ, 2000—. Contbr. articles to newspapers, mags. Judge essay contest B'nai Brith/Albert Adler Meml. Scholarship Fund, Livingston, 1987—2002;

active Vols. for Israel, 1989. Mem.: Livingston Writers' Group, N.J. Press Women (office holder, com. chairperson, Communicator of Achievement award 1997). Jewish. Avocations: travel, aerobics, reading, bowling. Home and Office: 1305 Bush Circle Rockaway NJ 07866

KURTZ, GILLIAN L. medical/surgical nurse; d. Richard and Donna Kurtz. BSN, U. Pitts., 2002. Cert. EMT Pa., 1995; RN Pa., 2002. EMT Ctrl. Bucks Ambulance, Doylestown, Pa., 1997—2000; patient care assoc. UPMC, Pitts., 1999—2002, RN, 2002—03. Vol. EMT Upper Perkiomen Valley Ambulance, Red Hill, Pa., 1995—2000. Recipient Adda Eldridge award, Sigma Theta Tau, Eta Chpt., 2002. Mem.: Internat. Assn. Forensic Nurses (assoc.). Avocations: travel, swimming, reading, painting.

KURTZ, MAXINE, personnel consultant, lawyer; b. Mpls., Oct. 17, 1921; d. Jack Isadore and Beatrice (Cohen) K. BA, U. Minn., 1942; MS in Govt. Mgmt., U. Denver, 1945, JD, 1962; postdoctoral student, U. Calif., San Diego, 1978. Bar: Colo. 1962, U.S. Dist. Ct. Colo., 1992. Analyst Tri-County Regional Planning, Denver, 1945-47; chief rsch. and spl. projects Planning Office, City and County of Denver, 1947-66; dir. tech. and evaluation Model Cities Program, 1966-71; pers. rsch. officer Denver Career Svc. Auth., 1972-86, dir. pers. svcs., 1986-88, sr. pers. specialist, 1988-90, pub. sector pers. con., 1990-95, atty., 1990—, pers. and human resources cons., 1996-98. Expert witness nat. com. on urban problems U.S. Ho. of Reps., U.S. Senate. Author: Law of Planning and Land Use Regulations in Colorado, 1966; co-author: Care and Feeding of Witnesses, Expert and Otherwise, 1974; bd. editors: Pub. Adminstrn. Rev., Washington, 1980-83, 88-92; editl. adv. bd. Internat. Pers. Mgmt. Assn.; prin. investigator: Employment: An American Enigma, 1979. Active Women's Forum of Colo., Denver Dem. Com.; chair Colo. adv. com. to U.S. Civil Rights Commn., 1985-89, mem. 1989-2002. Sloan fellow U. Denver, 1944-45; recipient Outstanding Achievement award U. Minn., 1971, Alumni of Notable Achievement award, 1994. Mem. ABA, Am. Inst. Planners (sec. treas. 1968-70, bd. govs. 1972 75), Am. Planning Assn., Am. Soc. Pub. Adminstrn. (nat. coun. 1978-81, Donald Stone award), Colo. Bar Assn., Denver Bar Assn., Order St. Ives, Pi Alpha Alpha. Jewish. Home and Office: 2361 Monaco Pky Denver CO 80207-3453

KURTZ, ROSEMARY, state representative; b. Richmond, Ind., Aug. 11, 1930; m. James Kurtz (dec.); children: Jennifer, Donna, Tamara. BA, U. Okla., 1952; MA, U. Kans., 1955; postgrad., U. Iowa, 1968—70. Tchr., Phoenix, St. Louis, 1953—65; instr. McHenry County Coll., 1970—77; tchr. High Sch. Dist. 155, 1978—90; mem. Ill. Ho. of Reps., 2001—. Asst. instr. U. Kans., 1953—55. Appointee Zoning Bd. Appeals, Crystal Lake, 1978—98; treas. City of Crystal Lake, 1997—2001; appointee Firefighters Pension Bd., 1997—2001; Rep. election judge, 1994—97. Recipient, Women in Mgmt., 1997—2000. Mem.: Delta Gamma Found. for Blind. Republican. Roman Catholic. Office: 200-3N Stratton Office Bldg Springfield IL 62706 Address: 1301 Pyott Rd Ste 201c Lake In The Hills IL 60156

KURTZ, SWOOSIE, actress; b. Omaha, Sept. 6, 1944; d. Frank and Margo (Rogers) K. Student, Acad. Music and Dramatic Art, London, U. So. Calif. Appeared on TV series As the World Turns, 1956, Mary, 1978, Love, Sidney, 1981-83 (nominated Best Actress in Comedy Series 1982-83), Sisters, 1991-96 (Emmy nominee Lead Actress in Drama 1993, 94, SAG award nominee 1995), Suddenly Susan, 1996, 97, Touched by an Angel, 1997, ER, 1998, Love and Money. 1999; (TV films) Ah, Wilderness!, 1976, Walking Through the Fire, 1979, Uncommon Women and Others, 1979, Marriage is Alive and Well, 1980, The Mating Season, 1980, Fifth of July, 1982, A Caribbean Mystery, 1983, Guilty Conscience, 1985, A Time to Live, 1985, The House of Blue Leaves, 1987, Baja Oklahoma, 1988 (Golden Globe nominee 1987), Terror on Track 9, 1992, The Image (Emmy nominee, Ace award nominee), 1990, The Positively True Adventures of the Alleged Texas Cheerleader-Murdering Mom, 1993, And the Band Played On, 1993 (Emmy award nominee 1994, Ace award nominee), One Christmas, 1994, Betrayed: A Story of Three Women, 1995, A Promise to Carolyn, 1996, Little Girls in Pretty Boxes, 1997, More Tales of the City, 1998, My Own Country, 1998, Harvey, 1999, The Wilde Girls, 2001; TV guest appearances on Kojak, Carol and Co. (Emmy award); (films) Slap Shot, 1977, The World According to Garp, 1982, Against All Odds, 1984, Wild Cats, 1986, True Stories, 1986, Vice Versa, 1988, Bright Lights, Big City, 1988, Dangerous Liaisons, 1988, Stanley and Iris, 1989, A Shock to the System, 1990, Reality Bites, 1994, Citizen Ruth, 1996, Liar, Liar, 1997, Outside Ozona, 1999, Cruel Intentions, 1999, The White River Kid, 2000, Sleep Easy, Hutch Rimes, 2000, Get Over It, 2001, Bubble Boy, 2001, The Rules of Attraction, 2002, Duplex, 2003; (theater) Ah Wilderness!, 1975, Children, 1976, Tartuffe, 1977 (Tony award nominee), A History of the American Film, 1978 (Drama Desk award), Uncommon Women and Others, 1978 (Obie award, Drama Desk award), Who's Afraid of Virginia Woolf, 1980, Summer, 1980, Fifth of July, 1980-82 (Tony award, Drama Desk award, Outer Critics Circle award), Michael Bennett's Scandal, 1985, Beach House, 1986, The House of Blue Leaves, 1986-87 (Tony award, Obie award), Hunting Cockroaches, 1987 (Drama Logue award nominee), Love Letters, 1989-90, Six Degrees of Separation, 1990, Lips Together, Teeth Apart, 1991, The Mineola Twins, 1999 (Obie award, Drama Desk award nominee, Outer Critics Circle nominee), The Vagina Monologues, 2000, Imaginary Friends, 2002-03, Frozen, 2004 (Tony award nominee, Best Actress in a Play). Office: 1900 Ave Of Stars Ste 1640 Los Angeles CA 90067-4407*

KURTZBERG, JOANNE, pediatrics educator; b. N.Y.C., Nov. 18, 1950; d. Lawrence Kurtzberg; m. Henry S. Friedman; children: Joshua, Sara. BA, Sarah Lawrence Coll., 1972; MD, N.Y. Med. Coll., 1976. Intern in pediats. Dartmouth Med. Ctr., Hanover, N.H., 1976-77; resident in pediats. Upstate Med. Ctr., Syracuse, N.Y., 1977-79, clin. rsch. fellow in pediat. hematology/oncology, 1979-80; mem. faculty Duke Comprehensive Cancer Ctr., Durham, N.C., 1983—; sr. rsch. fellow in pediat. hematology/oncology Duke U. Med. Ctr., Durham, 1980-83, asst. prof., assoc. prof. pediat., 1983-88, prof., 1994—, dir. pediatric bone marrow lab., 1989—, dir. pediat. bone marrow transplant program, 1989—, mem. grad. faculty Grad. Sch. pathology dept., 1993—, assoc. prof. pathology, 1991—. Recipient R. Wayne Rundles award for excellence in cancer rsch., 1993, Basil O'Connor Starter Scholar Rsch. award, 1985-87. Fellow Leukemia Soc. Am. (spl. fellow, scholar 1986-89); mem. Internat. Soc. for Hematotherapy and Graft Engring., Am. Soc. for Blood & Marros & Transplantation, Am. Soc. Pediat. Hematology/Oncology, Am. Soc. Hematology, Soc. for Pediat. Rsch., Pediat. Oncology Group, Alpha Omega Alpha. Home: 1808 Faison Rd Durham NC 27705-2439 Office: Duke U Med Ctr PO Box 3350 Durham NC 27702-3350

KURTZIG, SANDRA L. software company executive; b. Chgo., Oct. 21, 1946; d. Barney and Marian (Boruck) Brody; children: Andrew Paul, Kenneth Alan; BS in Math., UCLA, 1968; MS in aeronaut. engring., Stanford U., 1968. Math analyst TRW Systems, 1967-68; mktg. rep., Gen. Electric Co., 1969-72; chmn. bd., CEO, pres. ASK Computer Systems, Mountain View, Calif., 1972-85, chmn. bd., 1986-89; founder The ASK Group, 1972—, chmn., pres., CEO, 1989-93; chmn. emeritus, 1993—, chmn. E-Benefits, 1996—. bd. dirs. Hoover Instn., Harvard Bus. Sch., Stanford Sch. of Engring., UCLA Anderson Grad. Sch. Mgmt. Author: CEO: Building a $400 Million Company from the Ground Up, 1991, 94. Cited one of 50 most influential bus. people in Am., Bus. Week, 1985. Office: 2420 Sand Hill Rd Ste 201 Menlo Park CA 94025-6942

KURTZMAN, SUSAN JOAN, school system administrator, speech pathology/audiology services professional; b. Bklyn, NY, May 24, 1952; d. Bernard and Rosalyn Novick; m. Richard Allan Kurtzman, May 3, 1991. MS, Columbia U., Teachers Coll., 1975—79. Cert. of Clinical Competence Am. Speech Lang. and Hearing Assn., 1982, Speech Pathologist NY State Edn. Dept., 1982, Speech-Language Pathologist State of NJ. Dept. of Law and Pub. Safety, 1997. Tchr. of speech-language and hearing impaired NYC Dept. of Edn., Bklyn, NY, 1974—77, speech-language and edn. evaluator, 1977—79, asst. chairperson, com. on spl. edn., 1979—88, chancellor's monitor, 1988—91, clin. supr., com. on spl. edn., 1991—2003, regional adminstr. of spl. edn., 2003—. Speech and lang. pathologist Pvt. Practice, NYC, 1978—. Mem.: Coun. for Exceptional Children, NJ. Speech and Hearing Assn., Am. Speech-Language-Hearing Assn. Office: New York City Dept of Education 22 East 28th St New York NY 10016 Personal E-mail: susankk@comcast.net.

KURZ, MARY ELIZABETH, lawyer; b. Scranton, Pa., May 13, 1944; m. William H. Bright III. Student, U. Paris, Sorbonne, summer 1965; BA in French magna cum laude, Marywood Coll., 1966; postgrad., U. Md., 1966-67, U. N.C., 1967, U. Wis., 1969; JD with honors, U. Md., 1971. Bar: Md. 1972, D.C. 1978, Mont. 1982, Mich. 1988, Tex. 1994, N.C. 1996, U.S. Dist. Ct. (we. dist.) Mich., U.S. Supreme Ct., U.S. Ct. Appeals (4th, 6th, D.C. cirs.), U.S. Dist. Ct. Mont. Law clk. to presiding justice Ct. Spl. Appeals Md., 1971-72; asst. atty. gen. criminal div. State of Md., 1972-74, asst. legis. officer to gov., 1974-75, asst. atty. gen. representing U. Md., 1975-82; legal counsel U. Mont., Missoula, 1982-87; gen. counsel, v.p. legal affairs Mich. State U., East Lansing, 1987-94; vice chancellor and gen. counsel Tex. A&M U. System, 1994-96; vice chancellor, gen. coun. N.C. State U., Raleigh, 1996—. Speaker numerous confs. and profl. meetings; mem. Commn. to Study Sovereign Immunity, 1975. Mem. staff Md. Law Rev. Reginald Heber Smith fellow, 1969. Mem. ABA, Nat. Assn. Coll. and Univ. Attys. (mem. numerous coms., chmn. com. site selection 1985-86, chmn. com. continuing legal edn. 1986-89, bd. dirs. 1985-88, 2d v.p. 1989-90, 1st v.p. 1990-91, pres.-elect 1991-92, pres. 1992-93) Home: 102 King George Loop Cary NC 27511-6334 Office: NC State U 3rd Fl Holladay Hall Raleigh NC 27695

KURZWEIL, EDITH, sociology educator, editor; b. Vienna; d. Ernest W. and Wilhelmine M. (Fischer) Weiss; m. Charles H. Schmidt, June 24, 1945 (div. 1958); children: Ronald J., Vivien A.; m. Aug. 2, 1958 (widowed 1966); 1 child, Allen J. BA, Queens Coll., CUNY, 1967; MA, New Sch. Social Rsch., 1969, PhD, 1973. Asst. prof. sociology Hunter Coll., N.Y.C., 1972-75, Montclair State Coll., Upper Monclair, NJ, 1973-78; assoc. prof. sociology Rutgers U., Newark, 1979-85, prof. sociology, chmn., 1985-92; Disting. Olin. Prof. Adelphi U., 1993, univ. prof., 1994—2001, univ. prof. emeritus, 2001—. Vis. prof. Goethe U., 1984. Author: The Age of Structuralism, 1980, Italian Entrepreneurs, 1983, The Freudians: A Comparative Perspective, 1989, Freudians and Feminists, 1995, Briefe aus Wien: Nazi Laws & Jewish Lives, 1999, 2d edit., 2004, The Partisan Century: 60 Years of Partisan Review, 1996, (with others) Literature and Psychoanalysis, 1983, Writers and Politics, 1983, Cultural Analysis, 1984; exec. editor Partisan Rev., Boston, 1978 94, editor, 1994-2003; mem. editl. bd. Psyche, 1990—, Psychoanalytic Books, 1990-2000; series editor Psychiatry and Psychology Transaction, 1995—. Bd. govs. New Sch. Univ., 1999—; adv. bd. N.Y. Civil Rights Coalition, 2001—. Recipient Nat. Humanities medal, 2003; Rockefeller Humanities fellow, 1982-83, NEH fellow, 1987-88; NEH grantee, 1989-90, 91-92; NYCH grantee, 1995. Mem. Am. Sociol. Assn., Tocqueville Soc., Internat. Assn. History of Psychoanalysis, Internat. Sociol. Assn., Women's Freedom Network (bd. dirs. 1994—), PEN. Home: 1 Lincoln Plz New York NY 10023-7129 E-mail: ekurzweil@rcn.com.

KUSAKA, MARYANNE WINONA, mayor; b. Kamuela, Hawaii, Sept. 11, 1935; BA in Elem. Edn., U. No. Colo. Mayor City of Lihue, Hawaii, 1994—. Office: County of Kauai Mo'ikeha Bldg 4444 Rice St Ste 235 Lihue HI 96766-1340

KUSHINSKY, JEANNE ALICE, humanities educator; b. Reading, Pa, Jan. 12, 1937; d. Otis Jacob and Alice Elizabeth (Kurtz) Rothenberger; m. Sheldon Melvin Wallerstein, May 9, 1959 (div. July 1978); children: Seth, Gail Wallerstein Melichar; m. David Lazar Kushinsky, Apr. 11, 1987. BS, Cedar Crest Coll., 1958; postgrad., Kean U. N.J., 1978—92, Rutgers U., 1993. Tchr. East Orange Bd. Edn., NJ, 1958—60; editor Dept. Testing and Assessment State Dept. Edn., Trenton, NJ, 1974—76; tchr. Edison Township Bd. Edn., NJ, 1974—2000; pvt. tutor SAT verbal sect. Edison, NJ, 1980—. Mem. Citizen's Adv. Coun. Edn., Edison, NJ, 1991—93. Fashion show com. Rahway Hosp. Found., 2002—; chairperson gala Edison Arts Soc., 2003—, bd. trustees, 2000—; active Dist. VIII Middlesex County Bd. Atty. Ethics, Trenton, NJ, 2000—. Grantee grant, N.J. Coun. for Humanities, 1996. Mem.: Brandeis Univ. Nat. Women's Comm., NJ Edn. Assn., NEA, Metuchen-Edison Hist. Soc., Proprietary House, Nat. Trust for Hist. Preservation, Borough Improvement League. Democrat. Jewish. Avocations: historic preservation architecture, feminist issues, mentoring young people, film studies, reading. Home: 119 Turner Ave Edison NJ 08820

KUSHLIS, PATRICIA HOGIN, foreign affairs writer, analyst; b. Fall River, Mass., Oct. 5, 1944; d. James Edgar and Frances Marston Hogin; m. William Joseph Kushlis, Apr. 3, 1971; 1 child, Christopher James. BA in Liberal Arts, U. of the Pacific, 1965; MA in Internat. Rels., Syracuse U., 1969, PhD in Polit. Sci., 1978. U.S. fgn. svc. officer U.S. Info. Agy. (now U.S. Dept. State), Athens, Greece, 1970—71, 1981—84, Bangkok, 1972—75, Moscow, 1978—80, Helsinki, Finland, 1988—92; adj. prof. U. N.Mex., Albuquerque, 1999—; N.Mex. state mgr. Voter News Svc., Albuquerque, 2000—02; U.S. fgn. svc. officer U.S. Info. Agy. (now U.S. Dept. State), Manila, Philippines, 1992—94. Asst. editor: quarterly mag. Dialogue, 1976; editor: (internet mag.) U.S. Fgn. Policy Agenda, 1996—98. Bd. mem. U.S.-Philippine Fulbright Commn., Manila, 1992—94. Mem.: Albuquerque Com. on Fgn. Rels. (bd. dirs. 2001—), Santa Fe Coun. on Internat. Rels. (bd. mem. 1998—2000), Am. Fgn. Svc. Assn. Avocations: skiing, music, travel. Home: 12704 Osito Ct NE Albuquerque NM 87111

KUSHNER, EVE, writer; b. Winston-Salem, N.C., Sept. 22, 1968; d. Jack and Annetta Esther (Horwitz) Kushner; m. Haroon Khalid Chaudhri, Apr. 12, 1992. Student, U. Calif., San Diego, 1988, U. London, 1988-89, U. Denver, 1990; BA summa cum laude, Dartmouth Coll., 1990. Proofreader Dharma Enterprises, Oakland, Calif., 1991-92; pres. Spruced Up Manuscripts, Berkeley, Calif., 1991—99, Profiles and More, Berkeley, 1999—. Author: Experiencing Abortion: A Weaving of Women's Words, 1997. Dartmouth Gen. Award Com. fellow, 1991. Mem. Phi Beta Kappa. Office: Profiles and More 1730 Martin Luther King Jr Way Berkeley CA 94709

KUSSROW, NANCY ESTHER, educational association administrator; BA, Valparaiso U., 1952; MA, U. N.C., 1954. Exec. dir. Nat. Assn. prins. of Schs. for Girls; ret., 1996.

KUSTER, DIANE M. computer technician; b. Lakewood, N.J., May 12, 1961; d. Robert Joseph and Doris M. Kuster. AA, Ocean County Coll., 1981; BS, Georgian Ct. Coll., 1985. Data svcs. supr. Barnes & Noble, Inc., Jamesburg, NJ, 1996—2003; AS/400 adminstr. Equity One, Inc., Marlton, NJ, 2003—. Registrar Mid-Atlantic Germanic Soc., 2001. Mem.: Nat. Geneal. Soc. (life). Home: 251 Serpentine Dr Bayville NJ 08721-3261 Office: Equity One Inc 301 Lippincott Dr Marlton NJ Personal E-mail: kusterdm@cs.com., dmkuster@comcast.net.

KUSTER, DOREEN K. accountant; b. Amherst, Ohio, Feb. 26, 1956; d. Kenneth Edward and Doris Jean Mary Williams; m. Richard J. Kuster, Sept. 14, 1985. B.Acctg., Kent State U., 1978. CPA, Ohio; CMA. Sr. acct. gen. products divsn. Goodyear Tire & Rubber Co., Akron, Ohio, 1980-86, computer analyst, 1986-87, fin. analyst tire divsn., 1987-94, sect. mgr. payroll tax and acctg., 1994-95, bus. fin. mgr. Brook Park, Ohio, 1995—98, mgr. customer acctg. and ops., 1998—2003; acctg. mgr. Twin Sisters Prodns., LLC, Akron, 2003—. Chairperson Heather Hills Woman's Club, Stow, Ohio, 1990-96. Mem. Inst. Mgmt. Accts. (dir. newsletter), Am. Soc. Women Accts. (v.p. publicity), Leadership Akron. Avocations: needlework, cycling. Home: 1341 Whippoorwill Trl Stow OH 44224-2327 Office: Twin Sisters Prodns Inc W Market St Akron OH 44333

KUTLAR, FERDANE, genetics educator, researcher; b. Turkey, Apr. 15, 1945; came to U.S., 1984; d. Mehmet and Sidika Tanrikulu; m. Abdullah Kutlar, Feb. 7, 1975. MD, Istanbul (Turkey) Med. Sch., 1971. Bd. cert in internal medicine, Turkey, 1976. Resident in internal medicine Istanbul U. Sch. Medicine, 1972-76; chief resident dept. medicine Istanbul Hosp., 1977-81; rsch. fellow Med. Coll. Ga., Augusta, 1982; hematology fellow Istanbul U. Sch. Medicine, 1983; rsch. fellow Med. Coll. Ga., Augusta, 1984, asst. prof., 1985-99, assoc. prof. medicine, 1999—. Dir. DNA lab. Med. Coll. Ga., Augusta, 1994—; presenter in field. Contbr. articles to profl. jours. Mem. Am. Soc. Hematology, Am. Soc. Human Genetics, Med. Coll. Ga. Pres.'s Club. Avocations: oil painting, gardening, decorating, chess. Home: 623 Sawgrass Dr Martinez GA 30907-9137 Office: Med Coll Ga Dept Medicine 15th St AC-1000 Augusta GA 30912-2100 E-mail: fkutlar@mail.mcp.edu.

KUTLICH, ANNA, writer; b. Detroit, Nov. 12, 1948; d. Nikola and Sophie (Bulat) Kutlich. BA in English, Oakland U., 1983. Reporter Oakland Press, Pontiac, Mich., 1980—83; copywriter, copyeditor Leo Burnett Advt., Southfield, Mich., 1984—85; tech. writer Time Engring., Troy, Mich., 1986; documentation analyst Henry Ford Hosp. Data Ctr., Rochester Hills, Mich., 1986—88; reporter Reminder Newspaper, Clarkston, Mich., 1989; project leader, copywriter, editor Electronic Data Systems, Troy, Mich., 1989—93; tech. writer VSE Corp., Sterling Heights, Mich., 1993—94; substitute tchr. Madison Dist. Pub. Schs., Madison Heights, Mich., 1994—95; process mgr., writer, editor U.S. Coun. Automotive Rsch., Southfield, 1995—99; engring. tng. coord. DaimlerChrylser Corp., Auburn Hills, Mich., 1999—2000; documentation specialist, trainer Ford Motor Co., Dearborn, Mich., 2000—01. Author (as Candy Stevans): (book) Eight O'Clock Blues, 2001. Precinct del., Rochester, Mich., 1996—98. Avocations: swimming, bicycling, walking. Business E-Mail: Candystevans@aol.com.

KUTNER, JANET, art critic, book reviewer; b. Dallas, Sept. 20, 1937; m. Jonathan D. Kutner, Jan. 15, 1961. Student, Stanford U., 1955-57; BA in English, So. Meth. U., 1959. Asst. dir. Dallas Mus. Contemporary Arts, 1959-61; art critic, book reviewer Dallas Morning News, 1970—; Dallas/Ft. Worth corr. ARTnews Mag., 1975—. Mem. arts adv. panel Dallas Mcpl. Libr., 1981-91; mem. adv. bd. Arts Magnet H.S. of Dallas, 1980-92; mem. adv. com. Sch. Architecture and Environ. Design, U. Tex., Arlington, 1985-87; mem. long range planning com. Dallas Mus. Art, 1985 86; mem. visual arts and architecture adv. panel Tex. Com. on Arts, 1980-82. Contbr. articles to profl. jours.; juror various art exhbns. Bd. trustees Greenhill Sch., Dallas, 1980-81. Art critic's grantee Nat. Endowment for Arts, 1976-77, art critic's fellow Nat. Gallery Art, 1991—. Mem. Am. Assn. Museums, Dallas Mus. Art, Internat. Coun. Museums, ArtTable, Dallas Press Club (Critics award 1997). Office: Dallas Morning News PO Box 655237 Dallas TX 75265-5237

KUTOSH, SUE, artist; b. Elizabeth, N.J., Dec. 25, 1947; d. Stephen and Irene (Ribecky) K. BFA, Carnegie-Mellon U., 1971; MA, Kent State U., 1973. One-woman shows include Keane Mason Gallery, N.Y.C., 1978, West Broadway Gallery, N.Y.C., 1981, Kristen Richards Gallery, N.Y.C., 1983, Mussavi Arts Gallery, N.Y.C., 1987, N.Y. Bot. Garden, Bronx, 1992, Montserrat Gallery, N.Y.C., 1996, Pleiades Gallery, N.Y.C., 1997; art included in books: The Films of Jane Fonda, 1981, Hispanic Hollywood, 1990, The Lavender Screen, 1993, Hollywood Babble On, 1994, New Art Interna., 1998-2000; scenic art contbns. Sesame Street. Recipient Daytime Emmy for Seseame Street, 1993-94. Mem. United Scenic Artists, Local 829, Catharine Lorillard Wolfe Art Club, N.Y. Artists Equity, Nat. Assn. Women Artists. Avocation: photography. Home: 200 E 16th St Apt 2-d New York NY 10003-3708

KUTSCHINSKI, DOROTHY IRENE, elementary school educator; b. Denison, Iowa, Feb. 19, 1922; d. Gustave Waldemar and Wilhelmina Louisa (Stahl) Wiese; m. Alvin Otto Kutschinski; children: Karen E. Kutschinski Christensen, Linda K. Kutschinski Nepper. BA, Morningside Coll., 1965, MA in Teaching, 1970. Tchr. Crawford County (Iowa) Rural Schs., 1940-53, Charter Oak (Iowa) Community Schs., 1953-90; substitute tchr., 1990—. Apptd. to Crawford County Coun. Local Govt. for Hist. Preservation, 1992—, chair 1996—; tchr. Bible class St. John Luth. Ch., Charter Oak, Iowa, 1956—; sec. Crawford County Rep. Ctrl. Com., 1980-91, 98—; pres. Crawford County Rep. Women, 1978-86 trustee Iowa N.W. Regional Libr., 1991-2001; co-founder, sec., charter Oak-Ute Cmty. Sch. Edn. Found., 1994—, apptd. to adv. com., sec., 1993-2001. Named Outstanding Elem. Tchr. of Am., 1973; recipient Tchr. of Yr. award, Denison Newspapers, 1985, Women of Excellence award, Women Aware, Inc., 2001. Mem. AAUW (treas. 1985-90, pres. 1991-93), Iowa State Hist. Soc., Crawford County Hist. Soc. (life), The Smithsonian Assocs., The Audubon Soc., Living History Farms, Iowa Natural Heritage, Crawford County Arts Assn. (pres. 1986-88, bd. dirs. 1972—, sec. 1996—), Delta Kappa Gamma, Alpha Delta (sec. 1984—). Avocations: reading, sewing, bird watching, walking, writing. Home: 103 Pine Ave Charter Oak IA 51439-7453

KUTZ, MARGARET, minister; b. Butler, Pennsylvania, May 3, 1948; d. Kenneth Richard and Nancy Jane (McKinney) Tack; m. Robert L. Kutz, Apr. 1, 1972; children: Robert K., Jennifer L. EdB, Clarion Univ., Clarion, Pa., 1971; MDiv, Wesley Theological Seminary, Washington, D.C., 1976. Pastor United Meth. Ch., Va., 1976—; prof. Field Edn., Wash., 1980—83. Author: (articles) Net Results, 1998—2002. Prayer of Invocation State Assembly, Richmond, Va., 2001. Recipient Race Rels., All Together, Williamsburg, Va., 2001. Methodist.

KUTZNER, PATRICIA LOU, cultural organization administrator, consultant; b. Billings, Mont., Jan. 27, 1930; d. Clyde Mondelle Kutzner and Nelle Pearson. BA, U. Calif., Berkeley, 1952, Gen. Secondary Credential, 1953; MA, Stanford U., 1962, PhD, 1972. Social studies tchr. Campbell (Calif.) HS, 1953—56; English asst. Nicolaus Cusanos Gymnasium, Bad Godesberg, Germany, 1957—58; social studies tchr. Cubberley HS, Palo Alto, Calif., 1958—59; German tchr. San Mateo (Calif.) HS, 1959—60; acting instr., German dept. Stanford U., Palo Alto, 1960—63; acting dir. Bridge Mountain Found., Ben Lomond, Calif., 1965—66; asst. prof. German Lone Mountain Coll., San Francisco, 1967—73; devel. edn. cons. N.Y.C. Nat. Programs of Episc. and United Meth. Chs., 1974—76; exec. dir., founder World Hunger Edn. Svc., Washington, 1976—96; cmty. devel. planner and trainer Torreon/Starlake chpt. Navajo Nation, Cuba, N.Mex., 1996—. Bd. trustees Right Sharing of World Resources, Inc., Cin., 1998—2000; co-founder U.S. Nat. Com. for World Food Day, Washington, 1980; mem. U.S. delegation to World Conf. on Agrarian Reform and Rural Devel. U.S. Dept. State, Rome, 1979. Editor and author: World Hunger: A Reference Handbook, 1991, founder, editor: Hunger Notes (jour.), 1975—95; editor: Who's Involved with Hunger: An Organization Guide for Education and Advocacy, 6th edit., 1995; contbr. articles to profl. publs. Mem. Rio Puerco Mgmt. Com., Albuquerque, 1999—2003, Interreligious Task Force on U.S. Food Policy, Washington, 1975—80. Rsch. fellow, Am. Coun. Learned Socs., 1972—73. Mem.: Native Am. Rights Fund, Phi Beta Kappa. Mem. Soc. Of Friends. Avocations: gardening, music, nature study, hiking, wilderness camping.

KUYKENDALL, CRYSTAL ARLENE, educational consultant, lawyer; b. Chgo., Dec. 11, 1949; d. Cleophus Avant and Ellen (Campbell) Logan; m. Roosevelt Kuykendall, Apr. 10, 1969 (dec. Aug. 1972); children: Kahlil, Rasheki, Kashif. BA, Southern Ill. U., 1970; MA, Montclair State U., 1972; EdD, Atlanta U., 1975; JD, Georgetown U., 1982; LHD (hon.), Lewis and Clark Coll., Portland, 2002. Bar: D.C. 1988. Instr. Seton Hall U., South Orange, N.J., 1971-73; adminstrn. intern D.C. Pub. Schs., 1974-75; dir. citizens tng. inst. Nat. Com. for Citizens in Edn., Washington, 1975-77; dir. urban and minorities rels. dept. Nat. Sch. Bd. Assn., Washington, 1977-79; edn. dir. PSI Assocs., Inc., Washington, 1979-80; exec. dir. Nat. Alliance of Black Sch. Educators, Washington, 1980-81; dir. mktg. Roy Littlejohn Assoc., Inc., Washington, 1983—; pres., gen. counsel K.I.R.K., Inc. (Kreative and Innovative Resources for Kids), Washington, 1981—. Cons. to Ministry of Sport and Recreation, Western Australia Govt., 1990; chmn. U.S. Pres. Nat. Adv. Coun. on Continuing Edn., Washington, 1978-81; cons. U. Pitts. Race Desegregation Assistance Ctr., 1982-87, J.H. Lowry Assn., Chgo., 1982, U.S. Dept. of Edn. Transition Team, Washington, 1980. Author: Developing Leadership for Parent/Citizen Groups, 1975, You & Yours: Making the Most of this School Year, 1987, Improving Black Student Achievement by Enhancing Self Image, 1989, From Rage to Hope: Strategies for Reclaiming Black and Hispanic Students, 1992, rev. edit., 2003, Dreaming of a PHAT Century, 2000, 2nd edit., 2003. Mem. adv. bd. Inst. of the Black World, Atlanta, 1975-81; mem. steering com. Nat Conf. on Parental Involvement, Denver, 1977-78; mem. edn. task force Martin Luther King Jr. Ctr. for Social Change, Atlanta, 1978-80; mem. bd. dirs. Health Power, Inc., 1995-2001; chairperson, bd. dirs. Henry C. Gregory III Family Life Ctr. Found. of Shiloh Bapt. Ch. of Washington, 2003—, bd. mem., 1996—. Named Honorary Citizen of New Orleans, Mayor's Office, 1976; Ford found. fellow, 1973-74; Honorary Ky Colonel award, 1993, 99, 2002; Cert. Congl. Recognition, 2001. Mem. Nat. Bar Assn., Nat. Alliance of Black Sch. Edn., Alpha Kappa Alpha. Democrat. Baptist. Avocations: poetry writing, card playing, swimming, jogging, skiing. Office: KIRK Inc PO Box 60115 Potomac MD 20859-0115

KUYKENDALL, TEMPEST ANNE, elementary school educator; b. Waverly, Iowa, Jan. 12, 1949; d. Arlo M. and Dorothy F. (Munson) Baker; m. David Erwin Kuykendall, Aug. 3, 1974; children: Carrie Anne Johnston, Cory David. BFA, Mpls. Coll. Art and Design, 1971; tchg. cert., Wartburg Coll., 1972; MA in Art and Design, Iowa State U., 1994. Lic. tchr., Iowa. Tchr. art Webster City (Iowa) Schs., 1972-78, Roland (Iowa)-Story Schs., 1979—. Participant new art basics pilot program Iowa State U., Ames, 1986—, mem. new art basics adv. bd., 1989—, coop. pub. sch. art tchr. in conjunction with tchr. edn. program, 1973-77. Recipient God and Country award Girl Scouts U.S.A., Waverly, 1967. Mem. Nat. Art Edn. Assn., Iowa Edn. Assn., Art Educators Iowa (lectr., presenter state confs. 1973-94, membership chmn. 1979-81, elem. rep. 1981-83, Iowa Christmas Seals rep. 1974-75, ctrl. rep. 1976-78, Presdl. citation for outstanding svc. 1976, Iowa Elem. Art Tchr. of Yr. award 1988). Republican. Lutheran. Avocations: weaving, spinning, basketry, drawing, handbuilt pottery. Home: 12652 590th Ave Roland IA 50236-9740

KUZAN, KATHLEEN, speech pathology services professional, educator; b. East Orange, N.J., July 2, 1955; d. James and Angela (Poeta) Massotto; m. Roman Michael Kuzan, Aug. 14, 1977; children: Larissa Marie, Michael Nicholas. BA, Montclair U., Upper Montclair, N.J., 1977, MA, 1983. Cert. speech lang. pathologist, speech lang. specialist, tchr. of the handicapped, reading tchr., CCC. Supplemental speech correctionist Bd. of Edn., Union, NJ, 1977—78, reading tchr. Irvington, 1978—80, speech cons. pre-sch. summer screening Union Twp., 1978—90; adj. prof. Kean U., Union, 1990—94; speech - lang. pathologist Bd. of Edn., Union Twp., NJ, 1980—. Supr. clin. fellowship yr. ASHA - Union Twp. Schs., 2001—02; speech lang. pathologist pvt. practice, 1985—. Mem. Holy Spirit Ch., Union, religion tchr., 1996—. Mem.: N.J. Edn. Assn., Am. Speech Lang. Hearing Assn., Alpha Delta Kappa (epsilon chpt.) (sec. 1998—), Phi Kappa Phi. Achievements include development of k-12 curriculum guide for speech and language svcs; program integrating speech and lang. svcs. in self-contained and regular classrooms. Avocations: reading, needlepoint, soccer mom. Office: Union Twp Bd of Edn Wash Sch Washington Ave Union NJ 07083

KUZIEMSKI, NAOMI ELIZABETH, educational consultant, counselor; b. Phila., Dec. 22, 1925; d. Andrew Raymond and Elizabeth M. (Graham) Hartman; m. Walter William Kuziemski, Dec. 28, 1943 (dec. Feb. 2000); children: Nancy Kuziemski Simpson, Sandra Ruth McElroy. BS in Bus. Edn., Temple U., 1945, MS in Counseling, 1949. Tchr. Sch. Dist. Phila., 1945-58; coll. counselor Phila. H.S. for Girls, 1958-96; ednl. cons., 1996—. V.p. Nat. Assn. Coll. Admissions Counselors, Alexandria, Va., 1985-87, dir. Tools of the Trade workshop, 1992-95; pres. Pa. Assn. Coll. Admissions Counselors, 1991-93; focus group mem. U.S. News and World Report, Washington, 1995-96; panelist and presenter in field. Del., instnl. rep. Coll. Bd., N.Y., 1978-96. Recipient Bernard P. Ireland award Coll. Bd., Phila., 1996, Gayle C. Wilson award Nat. Assn. Coll. Admission Counselors, Alexandria, 1996, Recognition award PASSCAC, 1998; named Counselor of the Yr., Inroads, Phila., 1982. Mem. AAUW (Phila. br., v.p. 1997-99), Coll. Bd.-Middle States (planning com. 1995-97). Home: 7 Lawnside Rd Cheltenham PA 19012-1812 Personal E-mail: naomikuz@aol.com.

KUZMIN-NICHOLS, NICOLE A, biotechnology research and development company executive; d. Alexander and Mary K. Kuzmin; m. Tann A. Nichols, June 26, 1999. BS, Case Western Res. U., 1995; MBA, Case Western Res. U., Cleve., Ohio, 1999. Cert.: US Patent & Trademark Office (patent agent) 2003. Rsch. asst. Case Western Res. U., Cleve., 1991—2000; dir., bus. devel. & ops. ChanTest, Inc., Cleve., 2000—01; v.p., bus. devel. & ops. Saneron CCEL Therapeutics, Inc., Tampa, Fla., 2001—. Office: Saneron CCEL Therapeutics Inc 13101 Telecom Dr Ste 105 Tampa FL 33637 E-mail: nkn@saneron-ccel.com.

KUZMOWYCH, CHRYSTYNA PRYTULA, optometrist; d. Wasyl and Myroslawa (Ziniuk) Prytula; m. Truvor Vadym Kuzmowych, June 5, 1971. BS, Pa. Coll. of Optometry, 1968; BA, SUNY, Binghamton, 1967; O.D., Pa. Coll. of Optometry, 1971; Mgmt. Trainee, Group Health, Washington, 1986-94. Ind. contractor, Great Falls, Va., 1997-99; optometrist Group Health Assoc., Washington, 1972-86, 95-97; chief Group Health/Humana, Washington, 1986-95; U. Ophthalmic Cons. of Washington Univ. Vision Ctrs., 1999—. U. Ophthalmic Cons. of Wash., 1999—, U. Vision Ctrs., 1999—, exec. bd. mem. Va. Optometric Assn., 1998—, N. Va. Optometric Assn., 1998—; panelist Optometric Coun. of D.C., U. of Md.; lectr. Am. Acad. of Optometry; participant Clek Study of Keratoconus, 1990; dir. Group Health Assoc. Ann., C.L. Seminar, 1987-94. Mem. AAUW, Nat. Mus. of Women in the Arts, Washington Performing Arts Soc., Ukrainian Nat. Women's League of Am., Nat. Symphony Orchestra, Va. Optometric Assn. (sec. 1978-80, bd. dirs. 1998—), D.C. Optometric Assn. (officer and exec. com. 1972-78), N. Va. Optometric Assn. (bd. dirs. 1998—). Avocations: music, gardening.

KUZNESOF, ELIZABETH ANNE, history educator; BA, U. Wash., 1961, MA, 1968; PhD, U. Calif., Berkeley, 1976. Vis. prof. history U. Kans., Lawrence, 1976-77, asst. prof. history, 1977-80, assoc. prof., 1980-85, prof., 1985—, asst. prof. history, 1977-80, assoc. prof., 1981-87, prof., 1987—, dir. L.Am. Studies, 1992—. Author: Household Economy and Urban Development in Sao Paulo 1765 to 1836, 1986; guest editor, author Jour. Family History, 1985; contbr. articles to profl. jours. Numerous fellowships and grants NEH, 1980, 91, Social Sci. Rsch. Coun., 1991-92, Fulbright/S.Am. Today Grant, 1986, Fulbright Tchg. Rsch. Grant to Brazil, 1988; Tinker fellow, 1981-82; John Carter Brown Libr., Hall Found. for Humanities, 1985-86, Utah Eccles Fellowship, 1991-92. Office: Univ of Kansas Ctr Latin Am Studies Lawrence KS 66045-0001

KVALHEIM, ETHEL M. (MARGETE), artist; b. Pleasant Springs, Wis., Mar. 5, 1912; d. John Nelson and Martha Bertina Larson; m. Arthur Peter Kvalheim, May 21, 1933 (dec. Nov. 1980); children: Keith Arthur, Gary Douglas. Student art classes, Vesterheim Mus., Decorah, Iowa. Represented in permanent collections Vesterheim Mus., Nelson Industries, Home Savs., Mt. Horeb Bank, Wis. Hist. Mus., Little Norway; featured (video) Ethel Kvalheim, Rosemaler, 1992, Art of Ethel Kvalheim, 2002, (TV broadcast) Wis. Pub. TV, (poster) Dane County Cultural Affairs Commn., 1989. Recipient King Olav V. medal, Norwegian Govt., 1971; Nat. Heritage fellow, Nat. Endowment Arts, 1989. Mem.: Wis. State Rosemalers Assn., Vesterheim Mus. (life; fund raiser, Gold medal 1969). Avocations: gardening, reading.

KVETKO, COLLEEN M. bank executive; m. Kirk Kvetko. From nat. comml. lender to pres. Fifth Third Bank, Fla., Naples, Fla., 1987—2002, pres., 2002—. Bd. dir. NCH Found. Chmn. YMCA Collier County, Econ. Devel. Coun. Collier County; campaign chmn. United Way Collier County. Named 10th Most Powerful Woman in Banking, U.S. Bankers Mag., Vol. of Yr., YMCA Collier County, 1998, Businesswoman of Yr., Gulfshore Bus. Mag. Mem.: Fla. Bankers Assn. (bd. dir.), Naples C. of C. Office: Fifth Third Bank Fla 4099 Tamiami Trail PO Box 41321 Naples FL 33941-3021*

KWAK, EUN-JOO, concert pianist, music educator; b. Seoul, Korea; d. Wan-Shin and Yi-Soon (Shin) Kwak; m. James F. Crowley, June 6, 1998. BMusic, Seoul Nat. U., 1987; MMusic, Roosevelt U., Chgo., 1990; DMusic, Northwestern U., 1995. Mem. piano faculty Northwestern U., Evanston, Ill., 1995-96, N.E. Mo. State U., Kirksville, 1995-96, Truman State U., Kirksville, 1996-98, Coll.of DuPage, Glen Ellyn, Ill., 1998-99; dir. piano studies New Canaan Conservatory of Music, Glenview, Ill., 1998—2000, program mgr., bd. dirs., 1998—2000; mem. piano faculty Cardinal Stritch U., Milw. Solo pianist : live recital and radio broadcast Dame Myra Hess Meml. Concerts, WFMT, 1998, duo pianist, prodr.: CD The Cheng and Kwak Piano Duo, 1997, solo pianist: radio broadcast Young Artists Live Concert Series, KBS-FM, 1994, ensemble performacne radio broadcast Musical Garden Christian Radio Taiwan, 2001; performer: (chamber music performance) Pine Mountain Music Festival, 2000; solo and duo pianist: recitals and performances with orchs. Recipient Bronze medal Tokyo Internat. Piano Duo Competition, 1994, Emily Boettcher Artists award Northwestern U., 1994, Theodor Bohlman award Internat. Beethoven Sonata Competition, Memphis, 1990; Korean Embassy scholar, 1991. Mem. Steinway Soc., Music Tchrs. Nat. Assn., Coll. Music Soc., Sigma Alpha Iota. Avocations: movies, drawing, interior decoration. Office: Cardinal Stritch U 6801 N Yates Rd Milwaukee WI 53217-4569

KWAKO, GENEVIEVE, civic worker; b. Evansville, Minn., Dec. 22, 1921; d. Carl Alfred and Agnes Estella (Bergen) Johnson; m. Fred John Kwako, Mar. 2, 1946 (dec. Sept 1978); children: Jon Thomas, Mary Jo (dec.), Kathryn Ann, Freddra Marie (dec.). BS in Edn. and Geography, Moorhead State U., 1943. Elem. sch. tchr., ElbowLake, Minn. and Fargo, N.D., 1943-45; secondary sci. tchr. Hoffmar, Minn., 1945-46. Mem. sr. adv. bd. First Nat. Bank of Detroit Lakes, 1989—. Mem. com. Downtown Redevel., Detroit Lakes, 1984—; mem. Citizens Adv. Group on Law Enforcement Ctr., Detroit Lakes, 1988; former mem. nursing bd. Ottertail County, Minn., Cath. Daus., Christian Mothers; Eucharistic minister and lectr.; former bd. dirs. United Way, Am. Cancer Assn.; sec., pres. PTA, 1946-57; mayoral candidate Pelican Rapids, Minn.; pres. altar soc., ch. organist; chmn. St. Mary's Hosp. Found., Detroit Lakes, Minn.; bd. dirs. Centennial com. Holy Rosary Parish. Recipient Award Merit ARC, 1957; named Local Cath. Day of Yr., 1992-93. Mem. Detroit Lakes C. of C. (pres. Women's div. 1950), Minn. Federated Womens Club (state credentials com. 1954-60, pres. Ottertail County chpt. 1954, 55, 56, North dist. 1957-60, State award for dedicated svc. to dist.), Damien Sorority (past pres., sec., treas.) Roman Catholic.

KWAN, KAREN, professional figure skater; b. Torrance, Calif., June 1, 1978; Student, Boston U. Competitive history includes 7th place at Nat. Sr., 1997, 7th place Lalique trophy, 1996, 4th place Vienna Cup, 1996, 3rd place Nebelhorn trophy, 1996, 5th place World Jr. Selections Competition, 1997, 5th place Nat. Sr., 1996, 4th place Pacific Coast Sr., 1996, 4th place World Jr. Selections Competition, 1996, others. Avocations: photography, modeling, music. Office: 20 1st St Colorado Springs CO 80906-3624

KWAN, MICHELLE, professional figure skater; b. Torrance, Calif., July 7, 1980; Grad. H.S. Nat. spokesperson Children's Miracle Network, co-chair ProKids program. Recipient Skating Mag. Readers' Choice award for figure skater of the year, 1993-94, 95-96, Dial award, 1997, Skating Mag. Reader's Choice award, 2003; named 1996 Female Athlete of Yr., U.S. Olympic Com, finalist, Women's Sports Found. Sportswoman of the Yr., 2003 Achievements include being the youngest World Champion in U.S. history; third youngest World Champion; victories include: World Junior Championships, 1994, 96, Nations cup, 1995, U.S. Postal Svc. Challenge, 1995, State Farm U.S. Championships, 1996, 1999, 2001, 2003, Champions Series Final, 1996, Japan Open, 1997, 99, Skate Am., 1995, 1997, 1999, 2000, Skate Can., 1995, 1997, 1999, U.S. Championships, 1996, 1998-2004, World Championships, 1998, 99, 2000, 2001, 2003, Goodwill Games, 1998, 1998 Ultimate Four, 1998, Grand Slam Figure Skating, 1998, U.S. Pro Classic, 1998, Masters of Figure Skating, 1999, 1998, 1999, 2000, Silver Medal, Olympics, 1998, Bronze Medal, 1996. Office: USFSA 20 1st St Colorado Springs CO 80906-3624*

KWAN, NESITA, newscaster; b. Canada; BA English, U. Va. Reporter Sta. WINA-AM, Charlottesville, Va., 1986; anchor, reporter Sta. WDBJ-TV, Roanoke, Va., 1987—90; co-anchor, reporter Sta. WVEC-TV, Norfolk, Va., 1990—92; co-anchor weekend news Sta. KHOU-TV, Houston, 1992—94; co-anchor weekend evening edition NBC 5 Chgo. News, 1994, co-anchor weekday morning show, anchor late night news. Office: NBC 454 N Columbus Dr Chicago IL 60611

KWIATKOWSKI, JONNA M. research scientist; b. Toledo, Nov. 11, 1971; d. Frank and Mary Kwiatkowski. PhD, U. Maine, Orono, 2002. Human factors specialist Anderson Consulting (now Accenture), Chgo., 1994—96; tchg. fellow psychology dept. U. Maine, Orono, 1996—2000; postdoctoral assoc. Yale U., New Haven, 2000—03, assoc. rsch. scientist, 2003—. Project dir. - transitions in the devel. of giftedness Yale U., New Haven, 2000—; project dir. - provision of tech. assistance and quality assurance for the bessip program in zambia: sch. health and nutrition component Successful Intelligence, New Haven, 2001—; project dir. - project rainbow Yale U., New Haven, 2003—. Contbr. chapters to books, articles to profl. jours. Humanities Travel grantee, U. Maine, 1999. Mem.: APA, Internat. Assn. Empirical Aesthetics, Am. Psychol. Soc. Achievements include research in neurophysiology of creativity. Avocation: sculpting. Office: Yale University PO Box 208358 New Haven CT 06520-8358

KWIK-KOSTEK, CHRISTINE IRENE, physician, retired military officer, medical officer; b. Lvov, Poland, Sept. 12, 1939; d. Karol Stanislaus and Leonarda Fryderica (Seniuk) Kostek; widowed; children: Christine and Catherine. Grad. summa cum laude, Med. Acad. Cracow, Poland, 1956-62; grad. primary flight medicine, Brooks AFB, Tex., 1985; completed chief of profl. staff, Sheppard AFB, Tex., 1988. Diplomate Am. Bd. Emergency Medicine, Am. Bd. Internal Medicine, Poland; cert. Ednl. Coun. Fgn. Med. Grad.; re-cert. Extended Allergy Care Provider. Intern. Med. Acad., Cracow, Poland, 1962-63; residency internal medicine II Clinic Internal Diseases, Cracow, Poland, 1963-66; staff II Clinic of Internal Diseases, Cracow, Poland, 1966-69; gen. med. officer Gen. Hosp., Sokoto, Nigeria, 1969-72; intern. Frankford Hosp., Phila., 1972-73; house physician Holy Redeemer Hosp., Meadowbrook, Pa., 1973-74; emergency room physician John F. Kennedy Hosp., Phila., 1974-76, Emergency Rm. dir., 1976-78; commd. capt. USAF Med. Corp, 1978, advanced through grades to colonel, 1993; primary care physician USAF Clinic Emergency Rm., Ramstein, Germany, 1978-81; officer in charge Emergency Rm. and Gen. Practice Clinic, Peterson Field, Colo., 1981-84; primary care physician Malcolm Grow Med. Ctr., Andrews AFB, Md., 1984-88; chief clinic svc. 63d Med. Group/SGH, Norton AFB, Calif., 1988-93; staff physician 60h Med. Group, Travis AFB, Calif., 1993-96, Occupl. and Environ. Health and Safety Svc., Ft. George Meade, Md., 1996-99; ret. USAF, 1999—; regional med. officer Dept. of State. Asst. tchr., sr. asst. tchr. Inst. Descriptive Anatomy, Cracow, Poland 1963-69; emergency physician on call First Aid Sta., Cracow, Poland 1966-69. Fellow Am. Coll. Emergency Physicians; mem. AMA; Am. Coll. Emergency Physicians; World Med. Assn. Avocations: photography, travel, gourmet cooking. E-mail: kwikci@state.gov.

KWOLEK, STEPHANIE LOUISE, chemist, researcher; b. New Kensington, Pa., July 31, 1923; d. John and Nellie (Zajdel) Kwolek. BS, Carnegie-Mellon U., 1946; DSc (hon.), Worcester Poly. Inst., 1981, Clarkson U., 1997, Carnegie Mellon U., 2001. Chemist E.I. duPont de Nemours & Co., Inc., Wilmington, Del., 1946—59, rsch. chemist, 1959—67, sr. rsch. chemist, 1967—74, rsch. assoc., 1974—86, cons. in polymer chemistry, 1986—. Contbr. articles to profl. jours.; prodr.:. Named a Women in Tech. Internat., 1996; named to U. Akron Polymer Processing Hall of Fame, 1985, Dayton, Ohio Engring. and Sci. Hall of Fame, 1992, Nat. Inventors Hall of Fame, 1995; recipient award for contbns. to Kevlar, Am. Soc. Metals, 1978, Engring./Tech. award, Soc. Plastics Engrs., 1985, Harold deWitt Smith award, ASTM, 1988, George Lubin Meml. award, SAMPE, 1991, Medal of Excellence in composite materials, U. Del., 1992, Jack Kilby award, Kilby Awards Found., 1994, Am. Innovation award, Patent and Trademark Office, 1995, Achievement award, Indsl. Rsch. Inst., Inc., 1996, Nat. Medal of Tech. award, U.S. Dept. of Commerce Tech. Adminstrn., 1996, Perkin medal, Soc. Chem. Industry, 1997, Commonwealth award, Commonwealth Trust and PNC Bank, 1998, Lemelson-MIT Lifetime Achievement award, 1999, Henry E. Millson award, AATCC, 2001. Mem.: Phi Kappa Phi, Franklin Inst. Phila. (Howard N. Potts medal 1976), Nat. Acad. Engring., Am. Inst. Chemists (Chem. Pioneer award 1980), Am. Chem. Soc. (award for creative invention 1980), Carnegie Mellon U. Alumni Assn. (Merit award 1983, Disting. Achievement award 1998), DuPont Country Club, Phi Beta Kappa, Sigma Xi. Achievements include patents in field. Home and Office: 312 Spalding Rd Wilmington DE 19803-2422

KWONG, EVA, artist, art educator; b. Hong Kong, 1954; came to the U.S., 1967; d. Tony and Ivory Kwong; m. Kirk Mangus, 1976; children: Una, Jasper. BFA, RISD, 1975; MFA, Tyler Sch. Art/Temple U., Phila., 1977. Vis. artist, 1977—; vis. faculty Cleve. Inst. Art, 1982-83; part-time faculty U. Akron, Ohio, 1987, 89, 95, Kent (Ohio) State U., 1990—. Lectr. in field. Works in over 300 exhbns. Visual Arts Regional fellow Arts Midwest, Mpls., 1987, Visual Arts fellow Nat. Endowment for the Arts, Washington, 1988, Ohio Arts Coun., Columbus, 1988, 94, 99, 2004, Ohio Arts Coun. fellow in visual arts, 2004; recipient Internat. award China NCECA, 2003. Mem. Nat. Coun. on Edn. for the Ceramic Arts (dir.-at-large 1995-97).

KWONG, JENNIFER, writer; Experiment support scientist space life scis. divsn. NASA Astrobiology Inst., tech. writer, web site coord. edn. and pub. outreach dept., 1999—. Office: NASA Ames Rsch Ctr Bldg 240 Rm 102 Moffett Field CA 94035*

KYBAL, ELBA GOMEZ DEL REY, economist, non-profit organization executive; b. Santa Fe, Argentina, Apr. 1, 1915; came to U.S., 1942; d. J. Ignacio and Concepción (del Rey) Gómez; m. Milic Kybal, July 16, 1950 (dec. July 1977); children: Cynthia, Alexander. BA in Internat. Rels., U. Litoral, Rosario, Argentina, 1940; MA in Econs., Harvard U., 1945, PhD in Econs., 1946. Economist Fed. Res. Bank, N.Y.C., 1946-47; economist, polit. affairs officer UN, N.Y.C., 1947-56, sr. economist; head specialized conf., chief L.Am. econ. integration Orgn. Am. States, Washington, dir. under secretariat for econ. and social affairs, 1956—80. Cons. Argentine Govt., Buenos Aires. Contbr. articles to profl. jours. Advisor InterAm. com. of women OAS, Washington, 1960—80; vol. cons. Pan Am. Devel. Found., Washington, 1980—82; vol. Argentine, Ecuadorian and Peruvian Found., Washington, 1988—90; pres. Pan Am. Roundtable, Washington, 1999—2001, Pan Am. Liaison Com. of Women's Orgns., 1995—99, 2003, Retirees Assn. Orgn. Am. States, Washington, 2001—03; bd. dirs. Gala Hispanic Theatre, Washington, 1997—2001. Named Vol. of the Yr., Pan Am. Devel. Found., 1981, Bus. and Profl. Women's Club, 1984. Mem.: Phi Beta Kappa. Roman Catholic. Avocation: travel. Home: Watergate South # 801 700 New Hampshire Ave NW Washington DC 20037-2406

KYER, MAUREEN MARY, protective services official; d. William Louis Kyer and Geraldiine Francis Balfe. BA, Coll. of the Holy Names, Oakland, Calif., 2003. Adminstr. Oakland Police Dept., Calif., 1977—. Cons., ct. liaison adminstrn. Oakland Police Dept., 1996—. Union organizer Svc. Employees Internat. Union, Chgo., 1983—84; youth group coord. St. Leanders Cath. Ch., San Leandro, Calif., 1982—83, ann. ecumenical hunger walk, 1982—84; bd. dirs. Labor - Mgmt. Adv. Com., Oakland, Calif., 1981—85. Mem.: Pi Gamma Mu, Theta Alpha Kappa. Catholic. E-mail: mkyer@oaklandnet.com.

KYGER, BRENDA SUE, intravenous therapy nurse; b. Balt., Nov. 18, 1947; d. Charles and Betty (Weese) Reynolds; m. William H. Kyger, Jan. 30, 1967; children: Jennifer Lee, Jeffrey Lee. Grad., Balt. City Hosps., 1966; ADN, Essex Community Coll., Balt., 1970; BSN, U. Md., Balt., 1991; MSN, U. Md., 1997. Cert. intravenous nurse; PICC certification. Nurse Balt. City Hosps., 1966-70, nurse, head nurse, 1970-71; staff nurse CCU/ICU Franklin Sq. Hosp., Balt., 1971-72, staff nurse intravenous therapy, 1972-92, instr. IV therapy, 1976—, clin. leader, 1988-90, clin. care coord. of IV therapy, 1998—, patient care coord. for IV therapy, 1999—. Active Clin. Practice Coun., 1988-90, 94—, quality assurance coun. Franklin Sq. Hosp. Ctr., 1991-93, Nursing Edn. Coun. Contbr. articles to profl. jours. Former mgr. girls under 16 soccer team Sharp Shooters II; former registrar Md. State Youth Soccer Assn., Inc.; past sec. Recreation and Parks Coun. Baltimore County; past. sec. Balt. Metro Soccer League. Mem. Intravenous Nurses Soc., Am. Soc. Parenteral and Enteral Nutrition, Nat. Assn. Vascular Access Networks, Oncology Nursing Soc., Sigma Theta Tau. Avocations: gardening, writing. Home: 23 Propeller Dr Baltimore MD 21220-4545 Office: Franklin Sq Hosp Ctr Franklin Square Dr Baltimore MD 21237 E-mail: DaisyJ3250@aol.com.

KYHOS, M. GAITHER GALLEHER, private school educator; b. Durham, N.C., Sept. 17, 1955; d. Earl Potter Jr. and Martha Hungerford (Wheelwright) Galleher; m. Thomas Flynn Kyhos, Sept. 4, 1982; children: Jennifer Chalfant, Patrick Flynn, Justin Farleigh. BA in Polit. Sci. cum laude, St. Lawrence U., 1977. Layout and prodn. asst. Nat. Geographic Mag., Washington, 1977-80, illustrations rschr., 1980-82, sr. rschr., 1982-85, sr. rschr./writer, 1985-88, sr. rschr./compiler, 1988-94; asst. tchr., social studies-resource St. Patrick's Episcopal Day Sch., Washington, 1994-97, co-head tchr., 1997—. Mem. internat. adv. bd. Sellinger Sch., Loyola Coll. in Md., Balt., 1992-96; presenter in field. Author map supplements for Nat. Geographic Mag. Bd. dirs. Lt. Joseph P. Kennedy Inst., Washington, 1993-95; Vice Presdl. advance person The White House, Washington, in Ivory Coast, 1991, in Estonia, 1992. Mem. Nat. Coun. for Social Studies, Spinal Cord Injury Network, Ednl. Alliance/Nat. Geog. Soc., So. Poverty Law Ctr. Avocations: travel, biking, yoga, reading, golf. Office: St Patrick's Episc Day Sch 4700 Whitehaven Pkwy NW Washington DC 20007-1554

KYLE, GENE MAGERL, merchandise presentation artist; b. Phila., Oct. 11, 1919; d. Elmer Langham and Muriel Helen (Magerl) Kyle. Student, Ctr. for Creative Studies, Detroit, 1938—45. Mdse. presentation artist D.J. Healy Shops, Detroit, 1946—50; Saks Fifth Ave., Detroit, 1950—58, J.L. Hudson Co., Detroit, 1958—84, Grosse Point, Mich., 1989—95; freeland mdse. presentations for windows Grosse Point, 1989—. Papercraft work Detroit Artists Mkt. Holiday Shows, 1997—2003; tchr. workshop classes. Exhibited in group shows at Mich. Watercolor Soc., 1944, 1953, 1974, Mich. Artists Exhbn., 1962, 1964, Scarab Club, 1948—49, 1952, Detroit Artist Mkt., 1946—97, Mich. Gallery, 1989—92, Coach House Gallery, 1980, 1990, Cmty. House, Birmingham, Mich., 1993—94, First Fed. Mich. Bank, 1994, 1995, Swann Gallery, 1996—97, Detroit Artists Mkt., 1997—2000. Vol. presentation work. Recipient various art awards. Mem.: Windsor Art Gallery, Mich. Watercolor Soc., Detroit Inst. Arts Founders Soc.

KYLE, SARA, state agency administrator; b. Norton, Va., Oct. 21, 1952; d. Bruce Young and Ema Gene (Clement) Perry; m. James F. Kyle Jr., Nov. 7, 1987; children: Sarah, Mary, Jim III. B of Elem. Edn., Austin State U., 1975; JD, Nashville Sch. of Law, 1987. Bar: U.S. Supreme Ct. Tchr. Clarksville (Tenn.) Pub. Schs., 1975-76; legis. aide Tenn. Legislature, NAshville, 1976-85; law clk. Tenn. Atty. Gen., NAshville, 1985-87; atty. Chambers, Kyle &Durham, Memphis, 1989-91; asst. pub. defender Shelby County Pub. Defender, Memphis, 1990-91; judge Memphis City Ct., Memphis, 1991-94; commr. Tenn. Pub. Svc. Commn., Nashville, 1995—. Mem. Dem. Women Tenn., Tenn. Women in Govt.; bd. dirs. Neighborhood Watch, Memphis, Immunization Coun., Memphis. Mem. ABA, Tenn. Bar Assn., Tenn. Lawyers Assn. for Women, Memphis Bar Assn., Kiwanis. Presbyterian. Office: TPSC 460 James Robertson Pkwy Nashville TN 37243-9021

KYLES-OMARI, CYNTHIA LEE, editor, career consultant; b. San Francisco, Feb. 1, 1965; d. Troy and Nancy Lee Kyles; m. Omar Ali Omari, Feb. 21, 1997; 1 child, James Jamil. BA in Polit. Sci., Cambridge State U., 2001. Dir. John Robert Powers, L.A., 1988-89; career cons. U. Sound Arts, Hollywood, Calif., 1989-90, Banking Inst., L.A., 1991-92, Barbizon Models, L.A., 1992-93; lobbyist Ga. Trial Lawyers, Atlanta, 1995; campaign asst. Re-Elect Willie Brown Campaign, San Francisco, 1999, legis. editor State Net, Sacramento, 2000—01; bd. dirs. Oreg. Coun. for Multiracial Affairs, 2001—02. Co-founder Orgn. for Bi-Racial Studies, Portland, Oreg., 1981; campaign worker Tom Torlakson for Senate, Martinez, Calif., 2000. Mem. Multi-Racial Ams. So. Calif. (bd. dirs. 1988-89). Democrat.

KYLLONEN, FRANCES THOMPSON, retired educator; b. Omaha, Oct. 24, 1915, d. Jacob S. and Effie Anna (Robinson) Thompson; m. Toimi E. Kyllonen, Dec. 31, 1940 (dec.); children: Roger L. (dec.), Julie F. Rose. AA, Stephens Coll., 1936; BA, U. Mo., 1941, MA, 1946, MEd, 1968. Cert. tchr. social studies and art, Mo. Secondary art instr., art coord. kindergarten-12th grades Columbia (Mo.) Pub. Schs. Recipient award for outstanding contbns. to the profession of art edn. Mo. Art Edn. Assn., 1982. Mem. Nat. Art Edn. Assn. (chair retired art educator affiliate 1991-93), Pi Lambda Theta, Delta Kappa Gamma. Home: 604 Westmount Ave Columbia MO 65203-3471

KYRIAKOU, LINDA GRACE, communications executive; b. N.Y.C. d. Frank T. and Dolores Helen Lagamma; m. Konstantinos G. Kyriakou, 1 child, Christina Elena. BA, Hunter Coll. Asst. acct. exec., dir. rsch. Books and Co., N.Y.C., 1969-75; mgr. pub. rels. CIT Fin. Corp., N.Y.C., 1975-79; dir. corp. comm. Sequa Corp., N.Y.C., 1979-88, v.p. corp. comm., 1988—. Recipient Twin award, 1985. Mem. Pub. Rels. Soc. Am., Nat. Investor Rels. Inst. (bd. dirs. 1981-82, Sr. Roundtable), Women's Bond Club N.Y. (bd. govs. 1978-80). Office: Sequa Corp 200 Park Ave Rm 4401 New York NY 10166-4400 E-mail: Linda_Kyriakou@sequa.com.

KYTE, SUSAN JANET, lawyer, consultant; b. Riverhead, N.Y., Nov. 17, 1956; d. Bruce Whiteman Kyte and Barbara Jean (Clark) Goldberg. BA cum laude, Southampton Coll. divsn. L.I. U., 1978; JD, Capital U., 1984. Bar: Ohio, 1984. Assoc. atty. Matan & Smith, Columbus, Ohio, 1984-90; econ. devel. dir. City of Columbus, 1990-91; chief counsel, legis. dir. Ohio Sec. State, Columbus, 1991-95; pvt. practice Columbus, 1996—. Del. Am. Coun. Young Polit. Leaders, Columbus, 1997; mgr. Drake for Congress, 1998; founder JoAnn Davidson Ohio Leadership Inst., 1999. Vice-chair Franklin County Rep. Party, Columbus, 1992—, chair doorbbell blitz, 1988-90; founder, 1st pres. Ohio Rep. Womens Campaign Fund, Columbus, 1994—, treas., 1997—; bd. dirs. Actors Theater, Columbus, 1996—; vol. Rinehart for State Treas., Columbus, 1982, Rinehart for Mayor of Columbus, 1983, Race for the Cure, Columbus, 1995—; coord. Franklin County coalitions Voinovich for Senate, Columbus, 1988, co-chair, 1997—; treas. Keep Ohio Working Ballot Issue Commn., 1997, Every Child Counts Ballot Issue Commn., 1998, Deters for Ohio's Future, 1998—; legal counsel Teater for Mayor, 1999; treas. Tanner for City Coun., 1999; co-mgr. Browell for Judge, Columbus, 1997—; policy com. Pryce for Congress, Columbus, 1992, 94; coord. Taft for Sec. of State, Columbus, 1990; trustee Cap City Young Rep., 1984-96; active Com. for 2000, 1993; asst. legal counsel Young Rep. Nat. Fedn., 1993-95; rep. Renews Congrl. Adv. Com., D.C., 1995, 97; v.p. Columbus Literacy Coun., Columbus, 1984-92; chair comm. com. Oktoberfest, Columbus, 1992-96; steering com. Kaleidoscope Conf. for Women, Columbus, 1994—; state coord. McCain 2000 Campaign, 2000. Mem. ABA, Columbus Bar Assn., Nat. Fedn. Ind. Businesses, Nat. Assn. Polit. Cons., Ohio State Bar Assn., Coun. Govt. Ethics Lawyers. Republican. Lutheran. Avocations: cooking, travel, reading, politics. Office: 57 E Gay St Ste 300 Columbus OH 43215-3103 E-mail: suekyte@aol.com.

LABAJ, PAMELA JOAN, lawyer; b. Newark, N.J., Oct. 3, 1963; d. Edward Joseph and Joan Mary L. BA in Comms., Montclair State U., 1985; JD, Widener U., 1989. Bar: N.J., 1990, N.Y., 1991, Pa., 1992, U.S. Dist. Ct. N.J. 1990, U.S. Dist. Ct. (so. dist.) N.Y. 1997, U.S. Ct. Appeals (3rd cir.) 1997, U.S. Supreme Ct. 1997. Jud. clk. N.J. Supreme Ct., Jersey City, 1990; lawyer Comml. Union Ins., Florham Park, N.J., 1991, Bivona Cohen Kunzman et al., Warren, N.J., 1991-93, Curtis, Mallet-Prevost, N.Y., N.J., 1993—. Officer Essex County Women Lawyers. Mem. Fed. Bar Assn., N.Y. State Bar Assn., N.J. State Bar Assn., N.J. Cares. Avocations: golf, scuba diving. Home: 751 Evergreen Pkwy Union NJ 07083-8731 Office: Curtis Mallet Prevost Colt & Mosle 1 Gateway Ctr Ste 403 Newark NJ 07102-5315 also: 101 Park Ave New York NY 10178-0002

LABARGE, MARGARET WADE, medieval history educator; b. N.Y.C., July 18, 1916; arrived in Can., 1940; d. Alfred Byers and Helena (Mein) Wade; m. Raymond C. Labarge, June 20, 1940 (dec. May 1972); children: Claire Labarge Morris, Suzanne, Charles, Paul. BA, Radcliffe Coll., 1937; LittB, Oxford (Eng.) U., 1939; LittD (hon.), Carleton U., Ottawa, Ont., Can., 1976; LLD (hon.), U. Waterloo, Ont., Can., 1993; HHD (hon.), Mount St Vincent U., Halifax, N.S., 2003. Lectr. history U. Ottawa, Carleton U., 1950-62; adj. prof. history Carleton U., Ottawa, 1983—. Author: Simon de Montfort, 1962, A Baronial Household, 1965, Gascony, 1980, A Small Sound of the Trumpet, 1987, A Medieval Miscellany, 1997, others; contbr. articles to profl. jours. Bd. dirs. St. Vincent's Hosp., Ottawa, 1969-81; chmn. 1977-79; pub. rep. bd. dirs. Can. Nurses Assn., 1980-83; bd. dirs. Carleton U., 1984-93, Coun. on Aging, 1986-93 (pres., 1989-91). Recipient Alumnae Recognition award Radcliffe Coll., 1987, Founders award, Carleton U., 2001 Fellow Royal Soc. Can.; mem. Medieval Acad., Soc. of Can. Medievalists (pres. 1993-94), Order of Can., Phi Beta Kappa. Roman Catholic. Avocations: traveling, reading, walking. Home and Office: 402-555 Wilbrod St Ottawa ON Canada K1N 5R4 E-mail: mwlabarge@sympatico.ca.

LABBE-WEBB, ELIZABETH GERALYN, freelance stage manager, educator; b. Akron, Ohio, Oct. 7, 1966; d. Edward James and Ruth Carolyn (Petree) L. BA in Theatre Arts, Kent State U., 1989; MBA in Mktg. and Strategic Leadership, Ohio State U., 2003. Contract prodn. technician Players' Theatre Columbus, Ohio, 1989-91; asst. prodn./co. mgr. Phila. Festival Theatre, 1991-92; costume asst. Am. Music Theatre Festival, Phila., 1991-92; office asst. Players' Theatre Columbus, 1992-93; audio description coord. Ohio Theatre Alliance, Columbus, 1993-94; sr. devel. assoc., grants mgr. Opera Assn. Ctrl. Ohio, Columbus, 1994-99, assoc. dir. devel., 1998-2000; freelance stage mgr., freelance acting tchr., 1994—; project mgr. The Bus. of Art, 2000—02. V.p. Rosebriar Shakespeare Co., Columbus, 1995-96, pres. 1997-98. Chpt. leader, chpt. arts officer Soc. for Creative Anachronism, 1995-2002; adv., vol. Canine Companions for Independence; creative cons. Found. for Environ. Edn., 2001-02; fundraising cons. Columbus Light Opera, 2000-2001. Personal Devel. grant Jefferson Ctr. for the Arts, 1994. Mem. Ohio Prospect Rsch. Network (bd. dirs. 1997-2001).

LABELLE, GINGER SULLIVAN, pediatric nurse practitioner; b. Jamaica, N.Y., Apr. 28, 1950; d. Thomas Robert and Betty (Steeg) Sullivan; m. James D. LaBelle (dec. 1988); children: Erin, Sean. BSN, Georgetown U., Washington, 1972; practitioner cert., U. Va., 1974. Cert. pediat. nurse practitioner. Sr. nurse practitioner Duke Med. Ctr., Durham, N.C., 1978—. Adj. faculty Sch. Nursing Duke U., NC. Mem. Nat. Assn. Pediat. Nurse Assocs. and Practitioners (pres. N.C. chpt. 1987-91, treas. 1991-96). Home: 413 Lochside Dr Cary NC 27511-9787

LABELLE, PATTI (PATRICIA LOUISE HOLT), singer, entertainer; b. Phila., May 24, 1944; d. Henry and Berha Holte; m. Armstead Edwards, 1969 (div. 2000); 3 children. Singer Patti LaBelle and the Bluebelles, 1962-70; lead singer musical group LaBelle, 1970-76; solo performer, 1977—; entrepreneur Patti LaBelles Frances & Cosmetics, 1995. Albums include Over the Rainbow, 1966, La Belle, 1971, Moon Shadows, 1972, Pressure Cookin', 1973, Chameleon, 1976, Patti LaBelle, 1977, Live at the Apollo, 1980, Gonna Take A Miracle-The Spirit's in It, 1981, I'm in Love Again, 1983, Winner in You, 1986, The Best of Patti LaBelle, 1987, Patti, 1985, Be Yourself, 1989, Burnin', 1991, Live (Apollo Theater), 1992, Gems, 1994, Live! One Night Only, 1998 (Grammy, 1999), Greatest Hits, 1996, Flame, 1997, When a Woman Loves, 2000; appeared in films A Soldier's Story, 1985, Beverly Hills Cop, 1985, appeared in TV movie Unnatural Causes, 1986, Santa Baby (voice), 2001, The O.Z., 2002; TV series A Different World, Out All Night, 1992; author: Don't Block the Blessings: Revelation of a Lifetime, 1997, LaBelle Cuisine: Recipes to Sing About, 1999, Patti's Pearls: Lessons in Living Genuinely, Joyfully & Generously, 2001. Recipient award of Merit, Phila. Art Alliance, 1987.Recipient Grammy award: best Rhythm & Blues vocal for "Burnin'", 1991, Grammy nomination (Best Rhythym & Blues Female Vocal, 1994) for "All Right Now", Entertainer of Yr. Image award NAACP, 1992, Walk of Fame honoree Black Entertainment TV, 2000. Home: 8730 W Sunset Blvd Ph W Los Angeles CA 90069 2210 Office: c/o MCA Records Inc 2220 Colorado Ave Santa Monica CA 90404 also: Azoff Mgmt care Susan Markheim/Danny Meier 100 Glendon Ave Ste 2000 Los Angeles CA 90024

LABENSKY, SARAH ROSS, culinary educator; b. Murray, Ky., Mar. 16, 1958; d. James Mason and Lucille Thomson Ross; m. Steven Jay Labensky, Oct. 14, 1983 (div. May 1995); m. Louis David Moline, Sept. 3, 1995 (dec. Aug. 2003) BS, Murray (Ky.) State U., 1980; JD, Vanderbilt U., 1983; cert., Scottsdale C.C., 1986. Atty. Hocker and Axford, Tempe, Ariz., 1983-85; cook/chef Phoenix, 1985-90, prof. Scottsdale C.C., 1990-98; dir. Miss. U. for Women Culinary Arts Inst., Columbus, 1998—. Author: On Cooking, 1995, 3d edit., 2003, Webster's N.W. Dictionary of Culinary Arts, 1997, 2d edit., 2000, Applied Math for Food Service, 1998, Complete Idiot's Guide to Cooking Techniques and Science, 2002, On Baking, 2004. Mem.: Internat. Assn. Culinary Profls. (cert., bd. dirs. 1999—, sec.-treas. 2002, v.p. 2003, pres. 2004), Am. Culinary Fedn. Office: Miss Univ for Women Box W-1639 Columbus MS 39701

LABENZ-HOUGH, MARLENE, dispute resolution professional; b. St. Edward, Nebr., May 25, 1954; d. Ralph Labenz and Lorene (Laudenklos); m. Jeff Hough, Mar. 5, 1983. Assocs., Platte Coll., 1974; BS in Social Work magna cum laude, U. Nebr., 1976; MA in Clin. Psychology, Trinity U., 1980. Adminstrv. asst., mgmt. analyst II City of San Antonio Dept. Human Resources and Svcs., 1980, adminstrv. asst. II, 1980-82, casework supr., Victims of Crime Program, 1982-89, program coord., Children's Resources Dvsn., 1989-90; asst. dir. Bexar County Dispute Resolution Ctr., San Antonio, 1990-92, dir., 1992—. Bd. dirs. KidShare, 1993-96, YWCA, 1990-93; mem. ADR sect. coun. State Bar Tex., 1996-99. Recipient Liberty Bell award, San Antonio Young Lawyers Assn., 2003. Mem.: ABA (chmn. conf. com. ADR sect. 2002), Tex. Bar Assn. (ADR sect.), Assn. Family and Conciliation Cts., Tex. Mediators Credentialing Assn., Alamo Area Mediators Assn., Tex. Dispute Resolution Ctrs. Dirs. Coun., Tex. Mediation Trainers' Roundtable, Assn. Conflict Resolution, Conflict Resolution and Peer Mediation Coun., Nat. Assn. Cmty. Mediation (founding dir.), Soc. Profls. in Dispute Resolution (co-chair S.W. region chpt. 1993, co-chair nat conf. 1995, Profl. Dedication award 1994), Acad. Family Mediators, Tex. Assn. Mediators (chair conf. 1998, bd. dirs. 1998—2001), Alpha Xi Delta. Home: 2518 Ashton Village Dr San Antonio TX 78248-2200

LABINER, CAROLINE, architect; b. Los Angeles, CA, Mar. 29, 1958; d. Gerald Wilk and Suzanne Solov Labiner; m. Franklin George Moser, Aug. 29, 1984; children: Claire, Julia. AB, Harvard Coll., 1980; MArch, MIT, 1984. Designer Kohn Pederson Fox, N.Y.C., 1983; architect Kohn Pederson Fox Conway, N.Y.C., 1984—85; project architect The Entrenkrantz Group & Eckstot, N.Y.C., 1985—86; owner, designer CSLM Design/Big Pink Hair, Los Angeles, 1984—; owner, architect Caroline Labiner Architect, Los Angeles, Calif., 1993—.

LABOUFF, JACKIE PEARSON, personal care industry executive, educator; b. Wilmington, Calif., June 26, 1936; d. Maurice Emerson and Juanita Armstrong Pearson; m. John Robert LaBouff, Oct. 5, 1957; children: Margaret C., Mark J., Thomas F., Joan. BA, Calif. State U., Domingez Hills, 1972, MA, 1987. Tchg. credential Calif., 1982, counseling credential Calif., 1987. Flight attendant Am. Airlines, LA, 1956—57; pre-sch. tchr. Hickory Tree, Torrance, Calif., 1972—77; adult edn. tchr. Torrance (Calif.) Unified Sch Dist., 1977—84, Calif. State U., Domingez Hills, 1984—94; grant dir. Lawndale (Calif.) Sch. Dist., 1991—95; exec. dir. Project Touch, Hermosa Beach, Calif., 1996—2003. Adult edn. anger mgmt. tchr. Beach Cities Health Dist., Redondo Beach, Calif., 2000—03; sch. bd. candidate Torrance (Calif.) Unified Sch. Dist., 1995. Commr. Cmty. Svcs. Commn., Torrance, Calif., 1991—99. Recipient Magnificent Woman, Carson Coord. Co., 2003. Mem.: Am. Assn. Univ. Women (pres. 1991—94, Ednl. Found. Honor award 1994). Democrat. Roman Catholic. Avocations: travel, knitting, crocheting, needlecrafts. Home: 3810 W 173 St Torrance CA 90504 Office: Project Touch 710 Pier Ave Hermosa Beach CA 90254 E-mail: sticher61@hotmail.com.

LABOVITZ, DEBORAH ROSE RUBIN, occupational therapist, educator; b. Phila., Oct. 13, 1942; d. Samuel Frank and Clara (Blank) Rubin; m. Judah Isaiah Labovitz, June 3, 1962; children: Gail Susan Labovitz Seligman, Bruce Joel, Daniel Mark. BS in Occupational Therapy, U. Pa., 1963, Ma in Sociology, 1974, PhD in Sociology, 1979. Lic. occupl. therapist Nat. Bd. for Cert. of Occupl. Therapy. Dir. occupational therapy Mercy Douglas Hosp., Dept Psychiatry, Univ. Pa., Phila., 1963-66; adj. lectr. U. Pa., Phila., 1967-69, adj. instr., 1971-72, instr., 1972-76, asst. prof., 1976-80; prof. and chair dept. occupational therapy NYU, N.Y.C., 1980—. Cons. Ea. Pa. Psychiatric Inst., 1967-69, to pres. Beaver Coll., Phila., 1980; adj. lectr. U. Pa., 1980-81; mem. NYU Faculty Senate (acad. affairs com. 1987-88, faculty coun. exec. com. 1988-89, acad. affairs com. 1989=90, mandatory retirement subcom., 1988-92, fin. affairs com., 1988-90), Faculty Resource Network, Minority Conf. Com., 1991-92; Sch. of Edn. Budget Adv. Com., 1985—, chair 1992-93; Sch. of Edn. Instl. Planning and Devel. Com., 1986—, chair 1992-93; chair Sch. of Edn. Senate and Faculty Coun.; other coms. and offices. Contbr. articles to profl. jours.; presenter at numerous profl. confs. and ednl. meetings. Alt. del. Dem. Nat. Conv., Miami Beach, Fla., 1972. Grantee: N.Y.C. Bd. Edn., 1990-93, 93-96, MCH grant project, RSA long term tng. grantee, 1984-87, 87—, AOA, 1988-90, NYU Challenge grant, 1990, and others. Fellow Am. Occupational Therapy Assn. (vice chair commn. on edn. steering com. 1991-93; reviewer conf. papers, rsch. grants, postdoctoral fellowships, various books and articles, many other coms. and com. offices, Svc. award 1986, 89, 93, Cert. of Appreciation 1991); mem. AAUP, Pa. Occupational Therapy Assn. Dist. V., World Fedn. of Occupational Therapists, N.Y. State Occupational Therapy Assn. (mem. chief's group met. N.Y. dist., Cert. Appreciation 1987). Office: NYU Dept Occup Therapy 35 W 4th St Fl 11 New York NY 10012-1172

LABRIOLA, ANGELINA MARIE, librarian; b. Jersey City, N.J., Nov. 24, 1946; d. Pasquale Michael and Antonia Maria (DeFelice) L. AA, Felician Coll., 1996, BA in English, 2002. Cardiology tech., nursing asst. St. Joseph Hosp., Phila., 1984-88; nursing asst., aide Our Lady of Lourdes Infirmary, Lodi, NJ, 1988-92; receptionist St. ignatius Home, Phila., 1992-93; libr. Immaculate Conception High Sch., Lodi, 1993-98; asst. to curriculum libr. Felician Coll., 1998—2002, dir. curriculum lib., 2002—. Mem. Felician Sisters, 1981—. Roman Catholic. Avocations: reading, writing, praying, walking, tutoring.

LABTIS-JARDIM, ODESSA, import/export company executive; d. William Labtis and Chit Pascua; m. Francisco Jardim, Jan. 28, 2000. BS in Internat. Studies, Miriam Coll., 1996. Pres. Odessa Trade Group, Inc., Radcliff, Ky., 2000—. Import/export cons. Yellowbulb, Inc., N.Y.C., 2002—. Achievements include development of a B2B site www.odessatradegroup.com where businesses can purchase direct from importers; Baby Bel & Prince Bel Children Apparel. Office: Odessa Trade Group Inc PO Box 544 Radcliff KY 40159 E-mail: info@odessatradegroup.com.

LABUDDE, BESSIE FREEMAN, retired small business owner, retired director; b. Horse Shoe, N.C., Oct. 17, 1931; d. Charles Marion Freeman, Sr. and Lura Ethel Maynard; m. John Arthur LaBudde, Aug. 10, 1955 (div. Feb. 1984); children: Samuel, Benjamin, Sarah, Nathan. BA in Biology, U. N.C., Greensboro, 1953; MS in Botany, U. Wis., 1956; BS in Psychology, U. Evansville, 1981, MA in Counseling, 1986. LCSW Ind. Lab. rsch. biologist U. N.C. and U. Wis., 1953—58; health com. outreach coord. PBS, Evansville, Ind., 1973—75; edn. program dir. Alcohol Med. Edn. Program, Evansville, 1974—75; dir. external studies program, summer sessions coord., industry and bus. outreach, publs. developer U. Evansville, 1976—84; lead counselor for displaced worker's retraining Ind. Vocat. Coll., Evansville, 1984—93; small bus. owner Testing and Career Svcs., Evansville, 1994—2002; ret., 2003—. Mus. art edn., UU social action chair Boise (Idaho) Art Mus., 2003—; grant writer, site guide developer, UU officer, bd. dirs. Friends Angel Mounds, Evansville. Wis. Alumni Rsch. Found. grantee, U. Wis., 1954—56. Mem.: Alpha Sigma Lambda, Psi Chi, Beta Beta Beta, Phi Beta Kappa. Unitarian-Universalist. Avocations: museums, plant finding, reading, walking, Cherokee history.

LACEY, DOROTHY ELLEN, theology studies educator, religious organization administrator; b. Urbancrest, Ohio, Feb. 24, 1931; d. Charles Franklin Nesbitt and Clifford (Dickerson); m. Joseph W. Lacey; 1 child, Michael Clifford. B in Christian Edn., M in Christian Edn., Grace Internat. Coll., 1996, ThD, D in Christian Edn., Adminstrn. and Org., Grace Internat. Coll., 2002. Ednl. dir. Emmanuel Tempe Ch. of Rochester N.Y., Inc., 1962—, adminstr., 1985—. Women's ministry evangelistic seminar tchr. Pentecostal Assemblies of the World, Indpls., 1960—; pres., founder Lacey's Travel Agy., Rochester, 1983—88; pres. women's ministry N.Y. Coun., 1990—96; bd. trustees Grace Internat. Coll., 2003—; dean of ministries Grace Coll., 2000. Pres. of trustee bd. Emmanuel Temple Ch. of Rochester, N.Y., 1962—. Mem.: NAACP, Profl. Bus. Women, Urban League. Pentecostal Assemblies. Avocations: singing, playing musical instruments. Home: 3500 Brown Rd PO Box 148 Caledonia NY 14423 Office: Emmanuel Temple Ch Rochester 1 Seneca Pkwy Rochester NY 14613

LACEY, ELLA MAE PHILLIPS, volunteer; b. Hayti, Mo., July 13, 1940; d. James Biven and Viola Walker Phillips; m. Jerome Lacey, Mar. 18, 1962 (dec.); children: Michael, Carmen, Deidre, Sherwin. BA, So. Ill. U., 1964, MS, 1972, PhD, 1979. In-tng. counselor Manpower Tng. and Devel., West Frankfort, Ill., 1964—66; rehab. counselor Ill. Vocat. Rehab., Carbondale, 1966—70; field coord. So. Ill. U., Carbondale, 1972—77, program coord., 1977—79, asst.-assoc. prof. Sch. Medicine, 1979—94; vol. U.S. Peace Corps, Zomba, Malawi, 1995—97; English vol. So. Ill. U., Nakajo, Japan, 2000; STOP team vol. U.S. Ctrs. for Disease Control, Bihar, India, 2000—01, Accra, Ghana, 2002, Cairo, 2002, Addis Ababa, Ethiopia, 2003. Cons., reviewer Nat. Heart and Lung Inst., Washington, 1987, U.S. Dept. Edn., Washington, 1992, Washington, 93, Washington, 94; mem. adv. com. U.S. FDA, Rockville, Md., 1999—2003. Contbr. articles to profl. jours. Grantee, Ill. Dept. Pub. Health, 1976, Egyptian Area Agy. on Aging, 1984, Soc. for Pub. Health Edn., 1978. Fellow: Rotary Internat. (Paul Harris fellow 2003); mem.: APHA, Delta Sigma Theta (life; nat. chair 1988—90). Avocations: exploration, travel.

LACEY, TRUDI, professional athletics coach; Grad., N.C. State U., 1981. Asst. coach Manhattan Coll., 1981, James Madison Coll., 1982, N.C. State U., 1983—84; head coach Francis Marion Coll., SC, 1987—88, U. South Fla., 1989—96; asst. coach U. Md., 1996—97; asst. dir. women's program USA Basketball, 1997—2003; head coach, asst. gen. mgr. Charlotte Sting, NC, 2003—. Mem. women's player selection com. USA Basketball, 1993—96; asst. coach R. William Jones Cub team, 1995, Olympic Festival East team, 1994; participant USA Select Team, 1978, World U. Games team, 1981, USA Nat. eam, 1982, USA World U. Games Team, 1983; profl. player, Italy, 1985—87; founding pres. Life Coach Designs, LLC. Named Sun Belt Conf. Coach of the Yr., 1989; recipient All-ACC honoree. Office: Charlotte Sting 100 Hive Dr Charlotte NC 28217*

LACEY, VERA LAVONNE, secondary school educator, researcher, retired minister; b. Spokane, Wash. d. Benjamin Franklin and Mina Strobridge Fox; m. Derald Eugene Lacey, Aug. 3, 1950; children: Diana Duerr, Kathleen Bezinover, Andrew. BA English, Eastern Oreg. Univ., LaGrande, Oreg., 1970, MEd, 1975. Cert. tchr. Oreg., 1970, reading splt. Oreg., 1980. English tchr. LaGrande Jr. H.S., Oreg., 1970, Pendleton Jr. H.S., Oreg., 1970—85, reading specialist, 1979—84; pastor United Meth. Ch., Fossil, Oreg., 1985—91. Evaluator (books) reading program, United Meth. Women, 1994—. Dist. team mem. United Meth. Women Ctrl. Dist., 1993—99, 2002—; Conf. officer United Meth. Women Oreg., Idaho, 1968—70; bd. dir. Fossil Sch. Dist., Oreg., 1999—2003, Haven House Ret. Ctr., Oreg., 1986—89; bd. mem. Paleo Project, Oreg., 1999—2003, Fossil Sch. Cmty. Sch., Oreg., 2001—03. Democrat. Meth. Avocations: reading, physics, quilting, volunteer, watercolorist.

LACEY-PARKS, RENA ELIZABETH, secondary school educator; b. Columbus, Ohio, Mar. 04; d. Benjamin Shepherd and Edna Courtney (Henry) Lacey; m. James Creswell Parks. BS in Edn., Cen. State Coll.; MEd in Adminstrn. and Supervision, Xavier U., 1973; PhD in English and Humanities Edn., Ohio State U., 1981. Tchr. English and French Columbus Pub. Schs.; tech. writing instr. for engrs. Bell Labs., Columbus; tchr. Keiller Mid. Sch., San Diego. Advisor French Club, Keiller Mid. Sch., San Diego, newspaper advisor, past ASB advisor. Editor: (book of poetry) Black Experience, 1971. Mem. Episcopal Comty. Svcs., San Diego, 1981-99, First United Meth. Ch., Chula Vista, 1999—; mem. Friends of Hallie Q. Brown Libr., Ctrl. State U. Mem. NEA, Calif. Edn. Assn., Calif. Tchrs. Assn., Ohio Edn. Assn., San Diego Tchrs. Assn., Nat. Coun. Tchrs. of English, CSN Booster Club, Ohio State U. Alumni Assn., Cal. State U. Alumni Assn., Alpha Kappa Alpha (Cert. Recognition award, 1996). Avocations: gardening, writing, running, teaching, traveling. Office: Keiller Mid Sch 7270 Lisbon St San Diego CA 92114-3007

LACH, ALMA ELIZABETH, food and cooking writer, consultant; b. Petersburg, Ill. d. John H. and Clara E. Satorius; m. Donald F. Lach; 1 child, Sandra Judith. Diplome de Cordon Bleu, Paris, 1956. Feature writer Children's Activities mag., 1954-55; creator, performer childrens cooking TV show Let's Cook, 1955; food editor Chgo. Daily Sun-Times, 1957-65; hostess weekly food program on CBS, 1962-66; pres. Alma Lach Kitchens, Inc., Chgo., 1966—; performer TV show Over Easy, PBS, 1977-78. Dir. Alma Lach Cooking Sch., Chgo.; lectr. U. Chgo. Downtown Coll., Gourmet Inst., U. Md., 1963, Modesto (Calif.) Coll., 1978, U. Chgo., 1981; resident master Shoreland Hall, U. Chgo., 1978-81; food cons. Food Bus. Mag., 1964-66, Chgo.'s New Pump Room, Lettuce Entertain You, Bitter End Resort, Brit. V.I., Midway Airlines, Flying Food Fare, Inc., Berghoff Restaurant, Hans' Bavarian Lodge, Unocal '76, Univ. Club Chgo. Author: A Child's First Cookbook, 1950, The Campbell Kids at Home, 1953, Let's Cook, 1956, Candlelight Cookbook, 1959, Cooking a la Cordon Bleu, 1970, Alma's Almanac, 1972, Hows and Whys of French Cooking, 1974, reprint, 1998; contbr. to World Book Yearbook, 1961-75, Grolier Soc. Yearbook, 1962; columnist Modern Packaging, 1967-68, Travel & Camera, 1969, Venture, 1970, Chicago mag., 1978, Bon Appetit, 1980, Tribune Syndicate, 1982; inventor: Curly-Dog Cutting Bd., 1995, Alma's Walker Tray, 1996; one woman show: 50 pixellist art pictures, 1999, Tavern Club, Chgo., 2002-2003. Recipient Pillsbury award, 1958, Grocery Mfrs. Am. Trophy award, 1959, certificate of Honor, 1961, Chevalier du Tastevin, 1962, Commanderie de l'Ordre des Anysetiers du Roy, 1963, Confrerie de la Chaine des Rotisseurs, 1964, Les Dames D'Escoffier, 1982, Culinary Historians of Chgo., 1993. Mem. Am. Assn. Food Editors (chmn. 1959), Tavern Club, Quadrangle Club (Chgo.). Home and Office: 5750 S Kenwood Ave Chicago IL 60637-1744 Fax: 773-363-2875. E-mail: alma@almalach.com.

LACHANCE, JANICE RACHEL, educational association administrator, former federal agency administrator, lawyer; b. Biddeford, Maine, June 17, 1953; d. Ralph L. and Rachel A. (Desnoyers) L. BA, Manhattanville Coll., 1974; JD, Tulane U., 1978. Bar: Maine 1978, D.C. 1982, U.S. Supreme Ct. 1999. Staff dir. subcom. on antitrust Ho. of Reps., Washington, 1982-83; adminstrv. asst. Congresswoman Katie Hall, 1983-84; asst. pres. sec. Mondale-Ferraro Campaign, Washington, 1984; press sec. Congressman Tom Daschle, 1985; ptnr. Lachance and Assocs., Washington, 1985-87; dir. communications and polit. action Am. Fedn. Govt. Employees (AFL-CIO), Washington, 1987-93; dir. policy and communications U.S. Office Pers. Mgmt., Washington, 1993-96, chief of staff, 1996-97, dep. dir., 1997, dir., 1997—2001; mgmt. consultant Analytica Inc., Alexandria, Va., 2001; exec. dir. Spl. Libraries Assn., Washington, 2003—. Vis. scholar Cornell U., 1972-73. Editor newsletter Govt. Standard, 1987-93. Mem. Delta Delta Delta, Phi Alpha Delta; fellow Nat. Acad. Pub. Admin. Democrat. Roman Catholic. Office: Spl Libraries Assn 1700 Eighteenth St NW Washington DC 20009-2514*

LACHENICHT-BERKELEY, ANGELA MARIE, marketing professional; b. St. Louis, Feb. 3, 1955; d. Bernard J. and Dolores B. (Vaughn) L.; m. David L. Fuller, Sept. 6, 1974 (div. Mar. 1987); m. John Berkeley, Apr. 22, 1991. A in Bus. Adminstrn., Meremac Community Coll., St. Louis, 1983; chancellor cert., U. Mo., St. Louis, 1989; cert. of tng. in employment law, U. Mo. St. Louis, St. Louis, 1990. P.B.X. operator Arthur Enterprises, St. Louis, 1971-73; credit mgr. Watson Furniture, St. Louis, 1973-80; owner, operator Action Video World, St. Louis, 1980-85; regional dir. retention and telemktg. Charter Comms., St. Louis, 1985—. Coord. Am. Cablevision, St. Louis, 1988; cons. Thomas Construction, St. Louis, 1987-90. Author, editor: (guide) Cencom Insider, 1989-91. Telemarketing coord. Comic Relief/Health Care for Homeless Coalition, St. Louis, 1988-92; cons. Non-Profit Employment Liaison Com., St. Louis, 1989-90. Recipient Emmy award, St. Louis chpt. NATAS, 1988, Civic Commendation, Health Care for the Homeless Coalition, St. Louis, 1989, 90, 91, 92. Mem. Women in Cable, Nat. Cable TV Assn. Democrat. Roman Catholic. Avocations: reading, creative writing, traveling, gourmet cooking, dance. Office: Charter Comms 941 Charter Commons Town And Country MO 63017-0609

LA CHIUSA, CAROL See **DISANTO, CAROL L.**

LACHOWICZ, RACHEL, artist, art educator; b. San Francisco, 1964; BFA, Calif. Inst. Arts, 1988. Adj. faculty art Claremont (Calif.) Grad. U., 1996—. One-woman shows include Dennis Anderson Gallery, L.A., 1989, 1991, Krygier/Landau Contemporary Art, Santa Monica, Calif., 1989, 1990, Shoshana Wayne Gallery, Santa Monica, 1991, 1993, 1996, Fawbush Gallery, N.Y.C., 1992, 1995, Newport Harbor Art Mus., Newport Beach, Calif., 1992, Rhona Hoffman Gallery, Chgo., 1993, Magazin 4 Vorarlberger Kunstverein, Bregenz, Austria, 1995, Dogenhaus Galerie, Berlin, 1997, Cristinerose Gallery, N.Y.C., 1998, Peggy Phekps Gallery, Claremont (Calif.) Grad. U., 1999, Kapinos Galerie for Zeitgenossische Kunst, Berlin, 2000, Cryo-Field Snap, L.A., 2001, Represented in permanent collections Denver Art Mus., Israel Mus., Jerusalem, L.A. County Mus. Art, Mus. Fine Art, Boston, Mus. Contemporary Art, L.A., Mus. Moderner Kunst, Palais Lichtenstein, Vienna, Orange County Mus. Art, Newport Beach, Whitney Mus. Am. Art, N.Y.C. Recipient Louis Comfort Tiffany Found. award, 1997; fellow, Skowhegan Sch. Painting and Sculpture, John Simon Guggenheim Meml. Found., 2003. Office: Claremont Grad Univ Art Dept 251 E Tenth St Claremont CA 91711

LA CIVITA, JENNIFER, artist, columnist, cultural organization administrator; b. Chgo., Dec. 23, 1965; d. Nicholas Joseph and Michaeleen Loretta (Fabianski) LaCivita; m. Brian Mitchell Kimbrough, Sept. 2, 1989 (div. 2002); children: Emily Rose, Eric. BA in Art and English, St. Mary of the Woods Coll., Terre Haute, Ind., 1988; postgrad., Adler Sch. Profl. Psychology. Artist S. Mark Graphics, Chgo., 1988; corr. Commerce Clearing House, Chgo., 1988-89; dir. devel./recruitment/pub. rels. Good Counsel H .S., Chgo., 1989-92; wedding cons. Photo By Robert, Chgo., 1991-92; weekly columnist Lerner Comm., Chgo., 1992-96; freelance artist, writer Chgo., 1992—; with Magic Tree Bookstore, Oak Park, Ill., 1997—; founder, exec. dir. Portage Park Ctr. for the Arts. Bd. dirs. Woman Made Gallery, Chgo., 1995-97. Mem. Chgo. Artists' Coalition, St. Mary of the Woods Coll. Alumnae Club (pres. 1992—). Home: 5304 W Belle Plaine Ave Chicago IL 60641-1336

LACK, PATRICIA ANN, drilling and pumping company executive, consultant; b. Phoenix, Oct. 15, 1946; d.J.V. and Vivian Margaret Henry; m. Ronald Lee Jackson, Mar. 6, 1964 (div. May 1969); 1 child, Vicki Marie Snyder; m. Larry Henry Lack, Aug. 19, 1978. Student, Glendale (Ariz.) C.C., 1985-86. Enlisted USAF, 1973, advanced through grades to E-6, 1984; equipment mgr. Supply Squadron, Eglin AFB, Fla., 1973-74; supr. inventory mgmt. 3d Supply Squadron, Clark Air Base, The Philippines, 1974-77; chief supply sr. advisor 443d Supply Squadron, Altus AFB, Okla., 1977-79; instr., br. chief curriculum devel. SAC Non-Commd. Officers Acad., Barksdale AFB, La., 1979-84; resigned, 1984; pres. Lack Industries, Inc., Phoenix, 1984-90; chmn. bd. Stellar Innovations, LLC, Phoenix, 1996—. Freelance cons. and trainer, Phoenix, 1984-90; sexual discrimination recognition, protection, prevention trainer Glendale C.C. and to cos., Phoenix, 1984-90; cons. on career motivation enhancement to bus., Phoenix, 1984-95; counselor sexual assault recovery workshops, Phoenix, 1993—. Author: (novel) Willowman, 1993. Pub. spkr. to various women's groups and bus., Phoenix, 1990—. Mem. DAV (life), NRA (life), NRA Inst. for Legis. Action (life, honor roll 1995), Women Entrepreneurs Ariz. Republican. Avocations: flying, scuba diving, sport shooting, reading, camping. Office: Stellar Innovations LLC PO Box 7632 Phoenix AZ 85011-7632 Home: 4317 W Waltann Ln Glendale AZ 85306-2709

LACKEY, KAYLE DIANN, elementary school educator; b. Willard, Ill., Oct. 22, 1937; d. Lon Edward and Eldora Grace (Pecord) Ogborn; m. Joseph Donald Lackey, Nov. 29, 1958; 1 child, Dana Lyn Embree. BA in History, Asbury Coll., Wilmore, Ky., 1958; MA with honors, Webster U., 1975, cert. reading specialist, 1977; cert. gifted and talented educator, So. Ill. U., Edwardsville, 1990. Ltd. cert. elem. edn., Ill; cert. pub. sch. tchr. (life), Mo.; cert. reading specialist, Mo.; registered profl. real estate salesperson, Mo. Tchr. kindergarten Dist. # 196, Dupo, Ill., 1959-63, reading specialist, 1973-79, tchr. 2d grade, 1979-84, tchr. 4th grade, 1985-93, tchr. gifted and talented, 1990-92; tchr. 1st grade Mehlville R-9 Dist., St. Louis, 1963-65, substitute tchr., 1965-72, 1993—. Clin. coop. tchr. So. Ill. U., Edwardsville, 1989; salesperson Coldwell Banker Real Estate, St. Louis, 1985-2000. Rep. for tchrs. Am. Fedn. Tchrs., Dupo, 1975-77, negotiation com., 1981; tchr. US Divsn. Laubach Literacy Internat., St. Louis, 1987-89; author, tchr. gifted and talented enrichment summer program, 1991; participant Asbury Coll. travel seminar on Near-Eastern studies, 1985; rep. ecumenical com. Cmty. Resource Svcs., 1986-89, trustee 2000-02; chmn. bd. edn. presch. Zion United Meth., St. Louis, 1987-88, 2000-02, trustee, 1986-90, adminstrv. bd. religion and race, ch. and soc., 1989-93, fin. sec., 1999, bd. dirs., 2000; active Ill. Tchrs. Retirement Sys., 1993—. Met. Congregations United of St. Louis, 2001-04, Gephardt for Congress, St. Louis, 1993-95; vol. Am. Cancer Soc., 2000, 04. Recipient Appreciation for Tchg. Excellence award Bd. Edn., Dupo, 1993, Ill. Math. and Sci. Acad. award of Excellence, 1999. Mem.: St. Louis Art Mus., Mo. Bot. Soc., St. Louis Zoo Soc. Avocations: piano, travel, writing, reading, political campaign volunteerism. Home: 6511 Towne Woods Dr Saint Louis MO 63129-4521

LACKEY, MARY MICHELE, physician assistant; b. Johnson City, N.Y., Dec. 22, 1955; d. Joseph Charles and Jane Ann (Weston) Reardon; m. Donald V. Lackey Jr., Oct. 27, 1979 (div. Nov. 1995); m. Shane R. Russell, Mar. 27, 1999. AAS in Nursing, Broome Community Coll., Binghamton, N.Y., 1978; cert. family nurse practitioner, Albany Med. Coll., 1982; BS in Psychology and Sociology, U. State of N.Y., Albany, 1989. Cert. physician asst., family nurse practitioner, nurse midwife; RN, N.Y., Conn. Physician asst. Streit, Hickey & Lasky MD, P.C., Saratoga Springs, NY, 1982—85, Litchfield Hills Ob/Gyn., Sharon, Conn., 1986—89, Dutchess Med. Practice, PC, Amenia, NY, 1991—. Physican asst. Vassar Coll. Health Svcs., Poughkeepsie, N.Y., 1990—. Leader, instr. Girl Scouts U.S.A., Dutchess County, N.Y., 1990-98. Lt. col. U.S. Army, 1975-98 (ret.). Fellow: Am. Coll. Nurse Midwives, Am. Acad. Physician Assts.; mem.: Militia Assn. N.Y., N.G. Assn. U.S., Phi Theta Kappa. Roman Catholic. Avocations: breeding exhbn. poultry and geese, gourmet cooking, collect early med. books and equipment. Home: 262 Davis Rd Salt Point NY 12578-3122

LACOMB-WILLIAMS, LINDA LOU, community health nurse; b. Galion, Ohio, Oct. 1, 1948; d. Horace Allen and Roberta May (Black) Braden; m. Robert Earl LaComb, Feb. 1, 1970 (div. Aug. 1984); children: Robin Marie, Patrick Alan; m. Robert Allen Williams, Aug. 30. 1991; children Erin, Megan. BSN, Capital U., 1970; MPH, U. South Fla., 2002. RN, Fla., Ohio; cert. health edn. specialist. Staff nurse St. Anne's Hosp., Columbus, Ohio, 1970; pub. health nurse Hillsborough County Dept. Health, Tampa, Fla., 1970-80, community health nurse supr., 1980-87; sr. community health nurse Polk County Dept. Health, Lakeland, Fla., 1987-88; sr. RN supr. Children's Med. Svcs., Tampa, 1988-91, Lakeland, 1991-99; sr. cmty. health nurse supr. Polk County Health Dept., Lakeland, Fla., 1999—2003; sr. cmty. health nurse Joyce Ely Health Ctr. Hillsborough County Health Dept., Ruskin, Fla., 2003—. 1st lt. flight nurse res. USAF, 1971-75. Recipient Boss of Yr. award, Straberry chpt. Am. Bus. Women's Assn., 1985. Mem.: ARC, ANA, Fla. Nurses Assn. (grievance rep. state employees profl. bargaining unit 1976, pres. 1984—87, 1st v.p. 1989—91, dist. 2d v.p. 1998, Undine Sams award 1987, Nurse of Yr. award Dist. Four 1987), Eta Sigma Gamma, Sigma Theta Tau, Phi Kappa Phi. Republican. Presbyterian. Avocations: walking, nurses' rights, writing. Home: PO Box 1491 Valrico FL 33595-1491 Office: Hillsborough County Health Dept Joyce Ely Health Ctr 205 14th Ave SE Ruskin FL 33570 E-mail: lacombwilliams@aol.com.

LACROIX, SOPHIA MARIE, artist; b. Port-au-Prince, Haiti, Mar. 1, 1969; arrived in U.S., 1984; d. Felix and Yanick Lorette LaCroix. BS Natural Scis., U. Fla., 1992. Pub. assistance specialist Fla. Dept. Children & Families, Miami, 1993—; artist, 1993—. Exhibitions include Afrika Fete, Miami, Fla., 1994, Coral Gables Internat Arts and Crafts Festival, Fla., 1994, Gallier Hall, New Orleans, 1995, exhibited in group shows, Queens, N.Y., 1995, exhibitions include Nat. urban League Conf., Miami, 1995, Young, Bowers and Brown Cultural Art Ctr., Opa Locka, Fla., 1995, Nat. Black Arts Festival, Atlanta, 1996, PIAA Regional Fina Art Juried Exhibition, Gulf Shores, Ala., 1997, Zora Neal Hurston Festival, Orlando, Fla., 2000, Nat. Black Fine Art Show, Manhattan, N.Y., 2001, one-woman shows include Old Capitol Complex, Tallahassee, Fla., exhibitions include numerous others. Recipient Proclamation by Miami, Fla. declaring October 26, 2000 as Sophia LaCroix Day. Mem.: KUUMBA Artist Assn. Miami, Alliance African Am. Artists, Art on Tour, LLC.

LACY, DONA PAULETTE, librarian, writer; b. Louisville, Oct. 29, 1970; d. Morris Ford Lacy and Phyllis John Susnick-Lacy. BA in Humanities, St. Mary of-the-Woods Coll., Ind., 1993. Libr. Scott. County Pub. Libr. Sys., Scottsburg, Ind., 1997—. Author: (poetry collection) Through The Hourglass, Best Poems of 1997. Logistics coord. Habitat For Humanity, Americus, Ga., 1993—94. Recipient Aurora award, 1992. Mem.: Phi Beta Psi Sorority (sec. 2003—, reporter 2000—01). Independent. Catholic. Avocations: hiking, doll collecting, reading. Office: Austin Public Library 26 Union Ave Austin IN 47102 Personal E-mail: lacyblue30@aol.com.

LACY, ELIZABETH BERMINGHAM, state supreme court justice; b. 1945; BA cum laude, St. Mary's Coll., Notre Dame, Ind., 1966; JD, U. Tex., 1969; LLM, U. Va., 1992. Bar: Tex. 1969, Va. 1977. Staff atty. Tex. Legis. Coun., Austin, 1969-72; asst. atty. Office of Atty. Gen., State of Tex., Austin, 1973-76; legis. aide Va. Del. Carrington Williams, Richmond, 1976-77; dep. atty. gen. jud. affairs div. Va. Office Atty. Gen., Richmond, 1982-85; mem. Va. State Corp. Commn., Richmond, 1985-89; justice Supreme Ct. Va., Richmond, 1989—. Office: Va Supreme Ct 100 North 9th Street, 5th Floor Richmond VA 23219*

LACY, ELSIE, state legislator; b. Las Animas, Colo., May 22, 1947; m. Duane Lacy. Mem. Colo. State Senate, 1992—, chair appropriations com., chair joint budge com. Fund raising coord. YMCA; pres. PTO; dist. chair Cancer Crusade; mem. Aurora City Coun., 1983-87, 89-92; mayor pro tem Aurora, 1991; active Denver Regional Coun. Govts., Transp. Fin. Task Force; vice-chair Aurora Econ. Devel. Coun. Mem. Aurora C. of C. Republican. Home: 11637 E Mexico Ave Aurora CO 80012-5213 Office: State Capitol 200 E Colfax Ave Ste 346 Denver CO 80203-1716

LADANYI, BRANKA MARIA, chemist, educator; b. Zagreb, Croatia, Sept. 7, 1947; arrived in U.S., 1969; d. Branko and Nevenka (Zilic) Ladanyi; m. Marshall Fixman, Dec. 7, 1974. BSc, McGill U., Montreal, Can., 1969; M in Philosophy, Yale U., 1971, PhD, 1973. Vis. prof. of chemistry U. Ill., 1974; postdoctoral research assoc. Yale U., 1974-77, research assoc., 1977-79; asst. prof. chemistry Colo. State U., Ft. Collins, 1979-84, assoc. prof. chemistry, 1985-87, prof. chemistry, 1987—. Vis. fellow Joint Inst. for Lab. Astrophysics, 1993—94. Contbr. articles to profl. jours. Fellow, Sloan Found., 1982—84, Dreyfus Found., 1983—87; grantee, NSF, DOE, NATO, 1983—89. Fellow: Am. Phys. Soc.; mem.: AAAS, Assn. Women in Sci., Am. Chem. Soc. (PRF grant 1979—82, 1989—91, 1995—98), Sigma Xi. Office: Colo State U Dept Chemistry Fort Collins CO 80523-1872 E-mail: bl@lamar.colostate.edu.

LADD, DIANE ROSE, actress; b. Meridian, Miss., Nov. 29, 1942; m. Bruce Dern (div.); 1 child, Laura; m. William Shea, Jr. (div.); m. Robert C. Hunter, Feb. 14, 1999; step-children: Brandon Hunter, Amy Oleson, Emily Hunter. Grad., St. Aloysius Acad. Appearances include (films) The Wild Angels, 1966, The Reivers, 1969, Macho Callahan, 1970, Rebel Rousers, 1970, WUSA, 1970, White Lightning, 1973, Alice Doesn't Live Here Anymore, 1974, Chinatown, 1974, Embryo, 1976, The November Plan, 1976, All Night Long, 1981, Something Wicked This Way Comes, 1983, Black Widow, 1987, Plain Clothes, 1988, National Lampoon's Christmas Vacation, 1989, Wild at Heart, 1990, A Kiss Before Dying, 1991, Rambling Rose, 1991, Cemetery Club, 1992, Hold Me, Thrill Me, Kiss Me, 1992, Code Name: Chaos, 1992, Carnosaur, 1993, Father Hood, 1993, Spirit Realm, 1993, Obsession, 1994, Mrs. Munck (also dir., writer, co-prodr.), 1994, The Haunted Heart, 1995, Raging Angels, 1995, Ghosts of Mississippi, 1996, Mother (also exec. prodr.), 1996, Citizen Ruth, 1996, James Dean: Race With Destiny, 1997, Primary Colors, 1998, Daddy N Them, 1999, 28 Days, 2001, Rain, 2001, Law of Enclosures, 2001, Charlies War, 2002; (TV series) Alice, 1980-81; (TV movies) The Devil's Daughter, 1973, Thaddeus Rose and Eddie, 1978, Black Beauty, 1978, Willa, 1979, Guyana Tragedy: The Story of Jim Jones, 1980, Desperate Lives, 1982, Grace Kelly, 1983, I Married a Centerfold, 1984, Crime of Innocence, 1985, Celebration Family, 1987, Bluegrass, 1988, The Lookalike, 1990, Rock Hudson, 1990, Shadow of a Doubt, 1991, Hush Little Baby, 1994, Ruby Ridge: An American Tragedy, 1996, Breach of Faith: Family of Cops II, 1997, The Waiting Game, 1997, The Staircase, 1998; (TV mini-series) Cold Lazarus, 1996, Aftermath, 2001, Damage Care, 2001, Kristy, James Van Praag Story, (15 hour TV spl.) Stephen King's Kingdom Hospital, ABC, 2003. Recipient award Brit. Acad., Spirit award, Golden Globe award, 3 Acad. award nominations, 4 Golden Globe nominations, 3 Emmy nominations for Guest Actress in a Series (Grace Under Fire), 1994, Dr. Quinn, Medicine Woman, Touched by an Angel; named Woman of Yr. City of Hope, 1992; recipient Achievement award Women in Film, 1992, PATH Angel award, 1992, Dist. Artist award L.A. Music Ctr., 1994, Hollywood Legacy award, 1994, 1st Time Dir. award Dla. Film Festival, 1996, Tribuate award Newport Festival, 1996.

LADD, LOUISE, writer; b. Montclair, N.J. d. Chester Reed and Marion Louise Ladd; m. Doug Taylor; m. Calvin E. Cordulack, June 14, 1965 (div. Mar. 1977); children: Julianne Louise Gemmell, Christopher Donald Cordulack, Jeffrey Joseph Cordulack. BA, Wellesley Coll., 1965; student, actors workshop, Fairfield U., 1975—84. Prodr. Conn. Ctr. Acting Ensemble, Fairfield, 1976—95; tchr., Writers' Workshop Fairfield (Conn.) U. Sch. Continuing Edn., 1990—; part-time librarian Darien (Conn.) Pub. Libr., 1985—93, Fairfield Pub. Libr., 1993—96; freelance editor Fairfield, 1993—. Spkr. various schs., orgns. and confs., Fairfield County, 1987—. Author: Miracle Island, 1995, Castle in Time, 1995, Lost Valley, 1996, Cherry Blossom Moon, 1996, Call Me Just Plain Chris, 2003, The Wrangler's Secret, 2003, Prize-Winning Horse--Maybe, 2003, The Perfect Horse, 2003, Home for Christmas, 2003, Rodeo!, 2003, Me, My Mare and the Movie, 2003, Belle's Foal, 2003, Stage Fright, 1993, Island of Secrets, 1994, Captive Heart, 1995; editor (with Doug Taylor): Sandy Dennis: A Personal Memoir, 1997; author: A Whole Summer of Weird Susan, 1987, The Double Fudge Dare, 1989; contbr. chapters to books, articles to mags. Mem.: Women Writing the West, Authors Guild, Sc. Childrens Book Writers and Illustrators, Nat. League PEN Women. Democrat. Avocations: reading, gardening, ice skating, snorkeling. Home and Office: 27 Bloomfield Dr Fairfield CT 06825

LADD, MARCIA LEE, medical equipment and supplies company executive; b. Bryn Mawr, Pa., July 22, 1950; d. Edward Wingate and Virginia Lee (McGinnes) Mullinix; children: Joshua Wingate, McGinnes Lee; m. Leroy D. Werley, III, Aug. 5, 2000. BA, U. Pa., 1972; MEd, U. Va., 1973; MA, Emory U., 1979. Rsch. assoc. N.C. Tng. and Standards Coun., Raleigh, 1973-75; dir. counseling svc. N.C. State Youth Svcs. Agy., Raleigh, 1975-76; acad. dean Duke U., Durham, N.C., 1976-77; prin. Ladd & Assocs. Mgmt. Cons., Chapel Hill, N.C., 1979-88; v.p. adminstrn. CompuChem Corp., Research Triangle Park, N.C., 1988-91; v.p. mktg. Prentke Romich Co., Wooster, Ohio, 1991-94; v.p. ops. Exec. Staffing Svcs., Inc., Cary, N.C., 1994; pres., CEO, owner Triangle Aftercare, Durham, N.C., 1994—. Bd. dirs. Home Med. Svcs., 1997—. Bd. dirs. Oackwood Hist. Soc., Raleigh, 1981—84; mem. bd. vis. Carolina Friends Sch., Durham, 1986—89; bd. dirs. Orange Enterprises, 2000—; Stephen min. Univ. Presbyn. Ch., Chapel Hill, 1994—97, 2003—, youth group leader, 1995—97, 2000—02, trustee, 1998—2000; bd. dirs. Wayne County Arts Coun., Wooster, 1992, Stoneridge/Sedgefield Swim/Racquet Club, Chapel Hill, 1985—88. Decorated Order of Long Leaf Pine Gov. of N.C., 1976; named one of Impact 100 Most Influential People, Research Triangle, N.C., 1997. Presbyterian. Office: Triangle Aftercare 105 W NC Hwy 54 Ste 267 Durham NC 27713

LADERER, PATRICIA M. career planning administrator; d. Robert Hall Pancoast and Helen Good; m. John Edward Laderer, June 8, 1968 (dec. Oct. 2001); children: Lisa Mae, James P. AS summa cum laude, Roane State C.C., Harriman, Tenn., 1986; BA magna cum laude, U. Tenn., Chattanooga, 1989. Cert. vol. mgmt. sys. First Link. Dir. vols. Hospice of Chattanooga, 1989—90, Westminster-Thurber Cmty., Columbus, Ohio, 1990—92; vol. coord. Hospice of Columbus, 1992—94; asst. vol. coord. Hospice at Riverside and Grant, Columbus, 1994—98; vol. coord. Ctr. for New Directions, Columbus, 1998—2001; intake specialist/vol. coord. Jewish Family Svcs., Columbus, 2001, career and workforce devel. cons., 2001—. Mem. Connect Columbus Svc. Bd., 1998—2000. Contbg. author: Quilts are Forever, 2002. Co-founder Westside F.I.S.H., Columbus, 1972—74; mem. exec. com. Muscular Dystrophy Assn., Columbus, 1997—2001. Named Woman of the Yr., Women's Assn. First Presbyn. Ch., 2003; scholar, PEO, 1989. Mem.: Vol. Adminstrs. Network (bd. sec. 1994), Creative Non-fiction Group (facilitator 2001—03). Presbyterian. Avocations: gardening, pressed flower designing, quilting, writing. Office: Jewish Family Svcs 1151 College Ave Columbus OH 43209

LADUKE, NANCIE, lawyer, corporate executive; b. Mayfield, Ky. m. Daniel E. LaDuke, 1978. BA, Wayne State U., 1962; JD, U. Detroit, 1976. Pvt. practice, Detroit, 1976; atty. Kmart Corp., Troy, Mich., 1977-84, comml. law counsel, 1984-90, v.p., sec., 1991-2001; ret. Office: Kmart Corp 3100 W Big Beaver Rd Troy MI 48084-3163

LADWIG, BONNIE L. state legislator; b. Dec. 11, 1939; married. Student, U. Wis. Mem. from dist. 63 Wis. State Assembly, Madison, 1992—. Mem. Racine County and Coastal Mgmt. Coun.; mem. County Human Svc. Bd., past chmn. Office: 6437 Norfolk Ln Racine WI 53406-1859

LAETHEM, FERN MELODY, lawyer; b. N.Y.C., Jan. 11, 1946; d. Herbert Irving and Cherie Claire (Stern) Lifton; m. Robert Malcolm Segal, Oct. 8, 1980 (div.); children: David Benjamin Laethem, Jared Matthew Laethem. BA in Econs., CUNY, 1968; JD, U. of the Pacific, 1976. Bar: Calif., 1976. Dep. dist. atty. Dist. Atty.'s Office, Sacramento, 1976-79; asst. U.S. atty. U.S. Atty.'s Office, Sacramento, 1979-80; pvt. practice Sacramento, 1981-89; state pub. defender of Calif. Office of the State Pub.

Defender, Sacramento, 1989—99; exec. dir. Sacramento County Conflict Defenders, 1999—. Co-chair Justice and Technology Forum, Sacramento, 1994-96; adv. bd. Citizen and Law-Related Edn. Ctr., Sacramento, 1995-96; mem. Calif. Commn. on Spl. Edn., 2003—. Active Cub Scouts Am., Sacramento, 1994-96. Recipient Profl. Achievement award McGeorge Sch. of Law Alumni Assn., 1989. Mem. Calif. Coun. on Criminal Justice (bd. dirs. 1989—), Calif. Pub. Defenders Assn., Nat. Legal Aid and Defender Assn. Democrat. Jewish. Office: Conflict Criminal Defenders 901 M St #409 Sacramento CA 95814

LAFARGUE, MELBA FAYE FULMER, credit manager, realtor; b. Baton Rouge, July 13, 1937; d. Harry Geon and Alice (Peters) Fulmer; m. Leo Wallace LaFargue, Aug. 13, 1953 (div. Aug. 1983). BS in Acctg., La. State U., 1959; postgrad., Am. Sch. Banking, 1962. Cert. fin. mgr., realtor. Co-owner Newspaper Crossroads, Kinder, La., 1958-74; loan officer Great So. Mktg. and Loan, 1959-60; office mgr. Savant Constrn. Co., Kinder, 1960-74; cons. Baton Rouge Recreation and Park Commn., 1975-77; realtor Sherwood Realty, Inc., Baton Rouge, 1974—; service mgr. Campus Fed. Credit Union, Baton Rouge, 1980—. Fin. counselor Displaced Homemakers, Baton Rouge, 1983. Mem. Women in Politics, Baton Rouge; cons. fin. Cath. Daus. Am., 1960—. Mem. Nat. Assn. of Bank Women, Nat. Assn. Realtors, Am. Mgmt. Assn., Investors Assn. Democrat. Roman Catholic. Office: AmSouth Investment Svcs Inc 201 NW Railroad Ave Hammond LA 70401-3249 Home: 6323 Westridge Dr Baton Rouge LA 70817-3452

LAFAYETTE, KAREN MORAN, state legislator; b. Burlington, Vt., Aug. 21, 1954; m. Paul Lafayette; children: Eddie, Daniel. BS summa cum laude, Trinity Coll. of Vt. Past vice-chair Burlington Dem. Com.; mem. Chittenden County Dem. Com.; co-pub., distbr. The Burlington Dem.; Vt. house rep. rules ways and meanss, 1993—. Mem. Project Renaissance, Inc., 1988-91. Mem. Kappa Gamma Pi. Address: 109 Caroline St Burlington VT 05401-4811

LAFEVOR, KIMBERLY ANN, human resources specialist, educator; b. Detroit; d. Robert Lee and Mary Kathleen Calloway; m. Paul Earle Lafevor; children: Lauren, Meghan. B in Psychology and Pers. Psychology, Athens State U.; MS in Human Resource Mgmt., Troy State U.; D in Bus. Adminstrn. and Edn., U. Sarasota; cert. in human resources, Human Resource Cert. Inst. Human resources mgr. Saturn Corp./Gen. Motors, Spring Hill, Tenn., leadership develop. advisor, tng. & develop. team leader. Adj. faculty Columbia State Cmty. coll., Athens State U.; sr. human resources cons. Helton, Umberger & Assoc., Nashville. Contbr. articles to profl. jours. Leader Girl Scouts Am., Cumberland Valley Coun., Nashville. Mem.: Tenn. Employment Rels. Rsch. Assn., Indsl. Rels. Rsch. Assn., Soc. Human Resources Mgmt., Rotary. Avocations: softball, travel. Office: Saturn Corp PO Box 1500 100 Saturn Pkwy Spring Hill TN 37174 1500

LAFFERTY, JOYCE G. ZVONAR, retired elementary school educator; b. Balt., July 9, 1931; d. George S. and Carolyn M. (Bothe) Greener; children: Barbara Z. Gunter, John G. Zvonar, David A. Zvonar. BS, Towson State, 1963; M. equivalent, Md. Inst. Coll. of Art, 1978. Cert. tchr., Md. Tchr., dept. chmn. Hampstead Hill. Jr. High Annex, Balt.; tchr. Forest Park Sr. High, Balt.; tchr., dept. chmn. Roland Park Mid. Sch., Balt. Mem. Nat. Art Edn. Assn., Internat. Soc. Artists, Balt. Tchrs. Union. Home: 1225 Tetbury Ln Austin TX 78748

LAFOREST, LANA JEAN, lawyer; b. Providence, Apr. 14, 1952; d. Harold Joseph Ecker and Nettie Jean (Starks) Page; children: Timothy Charles, Tisha DeAnne. AA in Humanities and Social Scis., Niagara County C. C., 1989, BA in English Lit. magna cum laude, Buffalo State Coll., 1990, MA in English Lit., 1999; JD, SUNY Buffalo Sch. Law, 1994. Bar: Fla. Property mgr. Personal Income Property Mgmt., Lockport, 1976—; sales assoc. John F. Collins Realty, Lockport, 1979-83, Town Crier Clark Nodine Realty, Lockport, 1983-90, McKnight, Hogan & Noonan, Lockport, 1990-91, H. Potter Realty, Lockport, 1991-93; advocate Family Court Resource Project Haven House, 1994-99; advocate domestic violence clinic U. Buffalo Law Sch., 1994; pvt. practice East Amherst, N.Y., 1994—. Owner, operator Custom Crafts by Lana, Lockport, 1975-79; adv. domestic violence clinic U. Buffalo Law Sch., 1994. Editor: (lit. mag.) Writer's Revue, 1989; corr. Union-Sun and Jour., summer 1989. Girl scouts coord. Niagara County Coun. Girl Scouts, Sanborn, N.Y., 1978-84; clover clan 4-H club leader Niagara County Coop. Extension, Lockport, 1984-87; with Project Dandelion, Neighborhood Legal Svcs., 1994-96. Mem. ABA, MLA, Mensa, N.Y. State Bar Assn., Niagara Linguistics Soc., Nat. Assn. Realtors, Univ. Buffalo Law Sch. Alumni Assn., Buffalo State Coll. Alumni Assn., Niagara County Community Coll. Alumni Assn., U. Buffalo Assn. Women Law Students, Erie County Bar Assn., Women's Bar Assn. Erie County, Phi Alpha Delt. Avocations: writing, sewing, gourmet cooking, painting. Address: 2705 29th Ave W Bradenton FL 34205-3723 Fax: 941-753-3636. E-mail: Lana@unforgettable.com.

LAFORGIA, JEANNE ELLEN, performing arts educator; b. Ho-Ho-Kus, NJ; d. Jerry and Eileen LaForgia; m. James Joseph Zambuto. High Honors, Phillips Exeter Acad., 1988; BA in English and Drama with honors, Dartmouth Coll., 1992; MM in Vocal Performance, Boston U., 1995; vocal studies with Metropolitan Opera soprano Phyllis Curtin. Stage dir. and voice tchr. BU Tanglewood Inst., Lenox, Mass., 1994—97; head of drama Convent of the Sacred Heart, Greenwich, Conn., 1996—99; head of performing arts Boston U. Acad., 1999—. Singer: (cd recording) Night at the Moulin Rouge (Boston Globe Calendar Pick), Our Kinda Guys: the Music of Sinatra, Chevalier, and Montand (Boston Globe Critics Choice), (Operas) Aspen Music Festival, Tanglewood Music Ctr., Manhattan Sch. Music, Moscow Art Theater Sch. Dramatic Studies. Roman Catholic. Home: 8 Wellington Rd Winchester MA 01890 Office: Boston U Acad 1 University Rd Boston MA 02115

LAFRAMBOISE, JOAN CAROL, middle school educator; b. Bklyn., June 23, 1934; d. Anthony Peter and Nellie Eva (Zaleski) Ruggles; m. Albert George Laframboise, Aug. 5, 1961; children: Laura J., Brian A. BS in Edn., Springfield (Mass.) Coll., 1956. Cert. tchr. social sci., and mid. sch.; cert. tchr. support specialist; cert. tchr. gifted. Tchr. Meml. Jr. H.S., Wilbraham, Mass., 1956-61, Midland Park (N.J.) Jr./Sr. H.S., 1961-63, Luke Garrett Middle Sch., Austell, Ga., 1983-93; tchr. lang. arts Pine Mountain Middle Sch., Kennesaw, Ga., 1993-2001; ret., 2001. Coun. pres. Knights of Lithuania, Westfield, Mass., 1973-75, Holyoke, Mass., 1975-76, New Eng. dist. pres., 1976-77; mem. Wistariahurst Mus. Assocs., Holyoke, 1975-77. Jr. League mini-grantee, 1991. Mem. ASCD, NEA, Ga. Assn. Educators, Cobb County Assn. Educators, Nat. Coun. Tchrs. English, Nat. Coun. Social Studies. Home: 2891 Dara Dr Marietta GA 30066-4009

LAGANGA, DONNA BRANDEIS, sales and marketing executive, management/educational administrator; b. Bklyn., June 27, 1950; d. Sidney L. and Sylvia (Herman) Brandeis; m. Thomas LaGanga, Aug. 11, 1974. BS in Bus. Edn., Ctrl. Conn. State Coll., 1972, MS, 1975; EdD in Ednl. Adminstrn.-C.C. Leadership, U. Tex., 1999. Various secretarial positions, 1969-72; tchr. bus. Lewis S. Mills Regional H.S., Burlington, Conn., 1972-78; cons. nat. accounts Southwestern Pub. Co., Pelham Manor, N.Y., 1978-84, dist. sales mgr., 1984-89; pres. DBL Industries, Inc., Torrington, Conn., 1989—. Nat. accounts mgr. South-Western Pub. Co., Cin., 1989—93, from sr. sales and mktg. mgr. to nat. career sch. mgr., 1993—95; dir. admissions and records Tunxis C.C.-Bristol Career Ctr., Farmington, Conn., 1995—, dir. cmty. alliances, 1992—2002, dir. continuing edn. and workforce devel., 2002—; v.p. adminstrv. svcs. Human Resource Devel. Assocs., 1996—; co-owner Colonial Welding Svc., seminar condr., 1980—; pres. DBL Industries, Inc.; mem. adv. bd. secretarial sci. dept. LaGuardia C.C., L.I. City, NY, 1982—95; mem. adv. bd. Krissler Bus. Inst. EDPA grantee, 1973; mem. non-partisan ednl. reform task force Pres. George Bush; dir. continuing edn. and workforce alliances, 2002—. Mem. NAFE, Assn. Info./Sys. Profls., Am. Mgmt. Assn., Nat. Bus. Edn. Assn., Profls. Secs. Internat., Eastern Bus. Edn. Assn., Conn. Bus. Edn. Assn., New Eng. Bus. Edn. Assn., Profl. Secs. Assn., N.Y., Nat. Assn. Cert. Profls. Secs. (cert. profl. sec.), U.S. Golf Assn., Delta Pi Epsilon, Phi Kappa Phi. Avocations: reading, bicycling, golf. Home: 2929 Torringford St Torrington CT 06790-2332 Office: 430E N Main St Bristol CT 06010

LAGARDE, CHRISTINE, lawyer; b. Paris, Jan. 1, 1956; d. Lallouette Robert and Carre Nicole; m. Wilfrid Lagarde, June 17, 1982 (div. Apr. 1992); children: Pierre-Henri, Thomas. BA, U. Avignon, France, 1979; M of Law, U. Paris, 1979; M Polit. Scientist, Polit. Scis. Inst., 1977. Assoc. Baker McKenzie, Paris, 1981-87, ptnr., 1987-91, mng. ptnr., 1991-95, chmn. Chgo., 1999—, chmn. of the firm, 1999—. Author: Breaking New Ground, 1991, Into France, 1993. Mem. French Prime Min. Adv. Bd. on Attractivity of France. Decorated chevalier de la Legion d'Honneur. Mem. Cercle Foch (Paris), Athenaeum Club (London), Exec. Club (Chgo.). Office: Baker & McKenzie One Prudential Plaza 130 E Randolph St Fl 2500 Chicago IL 60601 Office Phone: 312-861-7606.

LAGOMASINO, MARIA ELENA, bank executive; b. Havana, Cuba, 1949; B in French Lit., Manhattanville Coll.; MLS, Columbia U.; MBA, Fordham U. Joined Citibank, 1976, v.p., 1977—83; mgr., divsn. exec. Chase Pvt. Banking Internat., 1983—89, mgr. Western Hemisphere ops., 1989—94, mktg. exec. Ams. region, 1994—97; sr. mng. dir. Chase Manhattan Pvt. Bank, 1997—2000; chmn., CEO J.P. Morgan Pvt. Bank, N.Y.C., 2001—. Bd. dirs. Philips-Van Heusen, Avon Products, Coca-Cola, 2003—; trustee Synergos Inst. Mem. dean's coun. John F. Kennedy Sch. Govt., Harvard U. Named one of 25 Women to Watch, US Banker Mag., 2003; named to 2004 Hispanic Bus. Corp. Elite, Hispanic Bus. Mag., 2004. Mem.: Com. of 200, Coun. on Fgn. Rels. Office: JP Morgan Pvt Bank 345 Park Ave New York NY 10154-1002*

LAGORIA, GEORGIANNA MARIE, curator, writer, editor, visual art consultant; b. Oakland, Calif., Nov. 3, 1953; d. Charles Wilson and Margaret Claire (Vella) L.; m. David Joseph de la Torre, May 15, 1982; 1 child, Mateo Joseph. BA in Philosophy, Santa Clara U., 1975; MA in Museology, U. San Francisco, 1978. Exhbn. coord. Allrich Gallery, San Francisco, 1977-78; asst. registrar Fine Arts Mus., San Francisco, 1978-79; gallery coord. de Saisset Mus., Santa Clara, Calif., 1979-80, asst. dir., 1980-83, dir., 1983-86, Palo Alto (Calif.) Cultural Ctr., 1986-91; ind. writer, editor and cons. mus. and visual arts orgns., Hawaii, 1991-95; dir. The Contemporary Mus., Honolulu, 1995—. V.p. Non-Profit Gallery Assn., San Francisco, 1980-82; bd. dirs. Fiberworks, Berkeley, Calif., 1981-85; field grant reviewer Inst. Mus. Svcs., Washington, 1984, 85, 97, 98; adv. bd. Hearst Art Gallery, Moraga, Calif., 1986-89, Womens Caucus for Art, San Francisco, 1987—; mem. adv. bd. Weigand Art Gallery, Notre Dame Coll., Belmont, Calif. Curator exhbns. The Candy Store Gallery, 1980, Fiber '81, 1981; curator, author exhbn. catalogue Contemporary Hand Colored Photographs, 1981, Northern Calif. Art of the Sixties, 1982, The Artist and the Machine: 1910-1940, 1986; author catalogue, guide Persis Collection of Contemporary Art at Honolulu Advertiser, 1993; co-author: The Little Hawaiian Cookbook, 1994; coord. exhbn. selections Laila and Thurston Twigg-Smith Collection and Toshiko Takaezu ceramics for Hui No'eau Visual Arts Ctr., Maui, 1993; editor Nuhou (newsletter Hawaii State Mus. Assn.), 1991-94; spl. exhbn. coord. Honolulu Acad. Arts, 1995; dir. The Contemporary Mus., Honolulu, 1995—. Mem. Arts Adv. Alliance, Santa Clara County, 1985-86; grant panelist Santa Clara County Arts Coun., 1987; mem. art adv. bd. Kapiolani C.C., 1994—. Exhbn. grantee Ahmanson Found., 1981, NEA, 1984, Calif. Arts Coun., 1985-89 Mem. Am. Assn. Mus., ArtTable, 1983—, Calif. Assn. Mus. (bd. dirs. 1987-89), Assn. Art Mus. Dirs., Hawaiian Craftsmen (bd. dirs. 1994-95), Honolulu Jr. League, Key Project (bd. dirs. 1993-94). Democrat. Roman Catholic. Avocations: dance, fiction writing. Home and Office: 47-665 Mapele Rd Kaneohe HI 96744-4918

LAGOWSKI, BARBARA JEAN, writer, book editor; b. Adams, Mass., Nov. 9, 1955; d. Frank Louis and Jeanette (Wanat) L.; m. Richard Dietrich Mumma III, Oct. 11, 1980; 1 child, Adam Dietrich. BA, U. South Fla., 1977; MA, Johns Hopkins U., 1978. Asst. editor Fred Jordan Books Grossett and Dunlap Pubs., N.Y.C., 1978-80; mng. editor Methuen Inc., N.Y.C., 1980-81; mng. assoc., sr. editor Bobb-Merrill Co Inc., N.Y.C., 1981-84; editor New Am. Libr., N.Y.C., 1984-85. Poet-in-the-schs. Hillsborough County Arts Council, Tampa., Fla., 1976-77; poet-in-residence Cloisters Children's Mus., Balt.., 1977-78 Author: Silver Skates series, 1988—89; co-author: Good Spirits, 1986, Teen Terminators, 1989, How to Get the Best Public School Education for Your Child, 1991, The Sports Curmudgeon, 1993, How to Attract Anyone, Anytime, Anyplace, 1993, Daily Negotiations: A Malcontent's Book of Meditations for Every Interminable Day of the Year, 1996, 101 Ways to Flirt: How to Get More Dates and Meet Your Mate, 1997, Cyberflirt: How to Attract Anyone, Anywhere on the World Wide Web, 1999; singer: Angel Signs: A Celestial Guide to the Powers of Your Own Guardian Angel, 2002. Mem. Authors Guild, Phi Kappa Phi Home: 237 Lenox Ave Long Branch NJ 07740-5022 E-mail: blagowski@aol.com.

LAGRECA, CARLA IRENE, activist; b. Poughkeepsie, N.Y., Jan. 5, 1952; d. Anthony Salvatore LaGreca and Gloria Marie Carloss. BA cum laude in English, Marist Coll., 1974; MA in English Lit., Fordham U., 1980. Shop steward, clk. Am. Postal Workers Union, Wappingers Falls, NY, 1980—82; change agent U.S. Postal Svc., Wappingers Falls, 1984—. Postmasters equal opportunity adv. bd. U.S. Postal Svc., Poughkeepsie, 1985; adj. prof. english dept. Marist Coll., Poughkeepsie, 1986—. Campaign vol. Labor 2000 for Hillary Clinton, NY, 2000, Ulster County Dem. Party, Ulster County, NY, 2001. Mem.: ACLU, Inst. Noetic Sci., Global Edn. Assoc., Pub. Citizen, Women's Action Coun., Amnesty Internat. Avocations: literature, theater, films, fitness. Home: PO Box 2434 Poughkeepsie NY 12603 Office: Marist College Sch of Liberal Arts North Rd Poughkeepsie NY 12601

LAGRONE, LAVENIA WHIDDON, chemist, real estate broker; b. Feb. 27, 1940; d. James Lewis and Cora Lee (DeLuish) Whiddon; m. Doyle W. LaGrone, June 26, 1959 (div. Sept. 1965); 1 child, Russell Randal. AA, Kilgore Coll., 1960; BS, North Tex. State U., 1962. Grad. med. tech. Baylor U. Med. Ctr., Dallas, 1962, sr. technologist spl. chemistry, 1962—63; rsch. chemist, supr. labs., cardiovasc. surgery Southwestern Med. Sch., Dallas, 1964—69, Upstate Med. Ctr., SUNY, Syracuse, 1969—70; rsch. assoc. supr. lab. dept. surgery U. Tex. Med. Br., Galveston, 1970—74, rsch. assoc. supr. labs. pediat. nephrology, 1974—95, rsch. assoc., supr. trauma rsch. lab., 1995—; mem. chem. safety com., 1984—87. Real estate broker DeLanney & Assocs. Realtors, 1979—83; owner LaGrone & Assocs. Realtors, 1983—. Contbr. articles to profl. jours. Chmn. student activities PTA, Galveston, Tex., 1976—77. Named Broker's Excellence award, 1980, Top Real Estate Commn. award, 1980; recipient Million Dollar Prodr. award, 1980—91. Mem.: Multiple Listing Svc. (budget com., MLS com.), Galveston Bd. Realtors, Tex. Assn. Realtors, Nat. Assn. Realtors, Am. Soc. Clin. Pathologists (registered med. technologist), Bus. and Profl. Women's Club (pub. rels. officer 1985—86, chmn. Young Careerist award 1987, chmn. Woman of Yr. award 1989, scholar com. 1988), Phi Theta Kappa. Home: 142 San Fernando Dr Galveston TX 77550-5712 Office: U Tex Med Br 301 University Blvd Galveston TX 77555-5302 Office Phone: 409-762-2679. Business E-Mail: llagrone@utmb.edu.

LAHAYE, BEVERLY, cultural organization administrator; m. Tim LaHaye; 4 children. Founder, chmn. Concerned Women for Am., Washington, 1979—; founder, radio talk show host Beverly LaHaye Live (now Concerned Women Today). Author: The Spirit Controlled Woman, The Desires of A Woman's Heart, Who Will Save Our Children?; co-author (with Dr. Janice Crouse): The Strength of a Godly Woman, 2001; co-author: (with Terry Blackstock) (fiction series) Seasons Under Heaven. Bd. dirs. Internat. Right to Life Fed., Liberty U., Childcare Internat. Recipient Christian Woman of the Year, 1984, Church Woman of the Year, 1988, Religious Freedom Award, S. Baptist Convention, 1991, Thomas Jefferson award, 2001.

LAHAYE, LAURA LAUNEY, medical/surgical nurse; b. Ville Platte, La., July 9, 1951; d. Donald Jerome Launey, Sr. and Mary Ramona Soileau; m. John B. LaHaye, Jr., Aug. 19, 1972 (div. 1987); children: Maria Louise, John Seth. RN, La. State U., Eunice, 1976. RN La.; nat. cert. Cath. youth min. Cath. Ctr. for Ministry Devel. Emergency rm. and ICU nurse Savoy Meml. Hosp., Mamou, La., 1976—79, charge nurse emergency rm., 1979—80, pub. rels. dir., 1980—84; emergency rm. nurse various hosps., La., 1984—86; RN alcohol/drug unit Cypress Hosp., Lafayette, La., 1986—87; nurse Our Lady of Lourdes Regional Med. Ctr., Lafayette, 1995—; mem. adminstrv. staff Steubenville South Youth Conf., 1999—. Assisted in founding Lourdes Med. Clinic for Homeless and Poor, 2003; founder First Saturday Cath. Teen Ministry, 1998—. Youth min. Holy Cross Cath. Ch., Lafayette, 1988—94, St. Pius X Cath. Ch., Lafayette, 1995—98; exec. dir. Soldiers of Christ, Inc., Lafayette, 1999—2001; youth adult min., teen ministry advisor Cathedral St. John the Evangelist, Lafayette, 1999—; founder, dir. VERITAS Retreat, Lafayette, 1989—; founder, coord. CORAM DEO, Lafayette, 1990—, H.S. Teen Peace Rally, Lafayette, 2000. Republican. Roman Catholic. Avocations: painting, gardening, reading, music. Home: 100 Oren St Lafayette LA 70506

LAHDELMA, GLADYS LINDA, elementary school educator; b. Higginb, Minn., Jan. 13, 1950; d. Uno Adolph Lahdelma and Linnea Helena Heikkila; m. Merlin Dwayne Sundberg, June 20, 1998 (div. Feb. 2, 2000); children: Swen Sundberg, Kristina Sundberg, Thorsten Sundberg. AA, Hibbing (Minn.) Jr. Coll., 1970; BS in Elem. Edn., U. Minn., Duluth, 1972; M in Curriculum and Instrn., Bemidji State U., 1991; degree in real estate, Naples (Fla.) Sch. Real Estate. Tchr. Ind. Sch. Dist. #701, Hibbing, 1972—. V.p. Iron Range Svc. Unit, Hibbing, 2001—. Scholar, U. Minn., Duluth, 1970. Mem.: Hibbing United Educators (sec. 1995—), Finnish Am. Club, Ladies of Kaleva, Delta Kappa Gamma. Democrat. Lutheran. Avocations: crafts, foreign languages, travel. Home: 2406 5th Ave E Hibbing MN 55746

LAHEY, BONITA LOUISE, marketing and operations consultant; BS, Colo. Coll., 1969; postgrad., U. Colo., 1971—73; MBA, U. Denver, 1977. Geologist, Denver, 1970—75; exec. U S West, Denver, 1977—95; v.p. Pacific Enterprises, L.A., 1995—97; asst. gen. mgr. L.A. Dept. Water and Power, 1998—99; COO, CMO CH2M Hill, Englewood, Colo., 2000—02; pres. B. L. Lahey Consulting, Inc., Denver, 2002—. Pres. Utility and Telecom. Advisors, Denver, 2002—. Vice chair fund devel. ARC-Mile High Chpt., Denver, 2001—; chair allies com. Womens Vision Found., Denver, 2001—. Avocation: singing. Office: BL Lahey Consulting Inc 1600 Cook St Denver CO 80206

LAHIFF, MARILYN J. nursing administrator; b. Youngstown, Ohio; d. Jack L. and Lila J. (Webb) Mills; m. Lawrence C. Lahiff, Apr. 26, 1974. AAS, Lorain County C.C., Elyria, Ohio, 1973; student, Youngstown U., 1960-61. RN, Fla., Ohio; lic. rehab. svc. provider, Fla.; cert. rehab. nurse, cert. ins. rehab. specialist; cert. case mgr. Team leader pediatrics Lakewood (Ohio) Hosp., 1973-75; adminstr. Upjohn HealthCare Svcs., Reno, N.Y., 1977-78, 83-84; occupational health/sch. nurse Medina (Ohio) County Achievement Ctr., 1979-83; regional mgr. Beverly Enterprises, Torrance, Calif., 1984-87; program mgr. RehabCare Corp., Cleve., 1988-89; supr. med./vocat.rehab Feisco, Sarasota, Fla., 1989-92; cons., med. case mgmt. Riscorp, Sarasota, 1993-94; chief operating officer Prime Managed Care Svcs., Inc., Sarasota, 1994—. Mem. editl. bd. Directions in Rehab. Counseling, 1994. Mem. Assn. Rehab. Nurses, Fla. State Assn. Rehab. Nurses, Phi Theta Kappa. Avocations: boating, reading. Home: 30051 Center Ridge Rd Apt C Westlake OH 44145-5163

LAHIRI, JHUMPA, writer; b. London, Eng., July 1967. BA in English Lit., Barnard Coll.; MA in English, MA in Creative Writing, MA in Comparative Lit., PhD in Renaissance Studies, Boston U. Author: (short stories) The New Yorker, 1998, (collection of short stories) Interpreter of Maladies, 1999 (O. Henry award, Pulitzer prize for fiction, 2000), (photography collection) India Holy Song, 2000, The Namesake: A Novel, 2003. Office: c/o Houghton Mifflin 222 Berkeley St Boston MA 02116*

LAHOOD, JULIE ANN, small business owner; b. Martins Ferry, Ohio, May 31; d. Joseph Noah LaHood and Thelma Marie Rafful. Student, Ray Coll. Design, Chgo., 1954—55, Loyola U., 1974—79. Jr. exec. Bonwit Teller, Chgo., 1959—62; asst. dept. mgr. Saks Fifth Ave., Chgo., 1962; owner Historic Properties, Monroe, Mich., Julie's Trading Post, Monroe, St. Charles, Ill. Contbr. poetry to profl. jours. Mem Monroe County Hist. Soc., Mich., Nat. ProLife Alliance, Washington, 2001—; humane amb. Neglected Animals, St. Charles, 1999. Named to Internat. Libr. of Poetry, 2001—02; recipient Editor's Choice award best poems and poets, Internat. Libr. Poetry, 2002, Best Poems and Poets, Internat. Soc. Poets, 2002, 2003. Mem.: Nat. Trust for Historic Preservation, Chgo. Hist. Soc. Republican. Roman Catholic. Avocations: gardening, cooking, poetry, music. Home: 707 Monroe Ave Saint Charles IL 60174

LAHTI, CHRISTINE, actress; b. Detroit, Apr. 5, 1950; d. Paul Theodore and Elizabeth Margaret (Tabar) L.; m. Thomas Schlamme, Sept. 4, 1983; 1 child, Wilson Lahti. BA in Speech, U. Mich., 1972; postgrad., Fla. State U., 1972-73; studies with William Esper, Uta Hagen, Herbert Berghof Studios. Actress: (stage prodns.) The Woods, 1978 (Theater World award 1979), Division Street, 1980, Loose Ends, 1981, Present Laughter, 1983, Landscape of the Body, 1984, The Country Girl, 1984, Cat on a Hot Tin Roof, 1985, Little Murders, 1987, The Heidi Chronicles, 1989, Three Hotels, 1993; regular mem. cast (TV series) Dr. Scorpion, 1978, The Harvey Korman Show, 1978, Chicago Hope, 1995-1999, (TV films) The Last Tenant, 1978, The Henderson Monster, 1980, The Executioner's Song, 1982, Single Bars, Single Women, 1984, Love Lives On, 1985, Amerika, 1987, No Place Like Home, 1989, Crazy from the Heart, 1991, The Fear Inside, 1992, The Good Fight, 1985, The Four Diamonds, 1995, Subway Stories: Tales from the Underground, 1997, Hope, 1997, An American Daughter, 2000, The Pilot's Wife, 2002, Out of the Ashes, 2003 (feature films) And Justice For All, 1979, Whose Life Is It, Anyway?, 1981, Swing Shift, 1984 (N.Y. Film Critics Circle award for best supporting actress 1985, Acad. award nominee 1985, Golden Globe award nominee 1985), Ladies and Gentlemen: The Fabulous Stains, 1985, Just Between Friends, 1986, Housekeeping, 1987, Season of Dreams, 1987, Stacking, 1988, Running on Empty, 1988, Gross Anatomy, 1989, Miss Firecracker, 1989, Funny About Love, 1990, The Doctor, 1991, Leaving Normal, 1992, Hideaway, 1995, Pie in the Sky, 1995, A Weekend in the Country, 1996; prodr. short action film, actress: Lieberman in Love, 1995 (Acad. award nominee for best live action short film 1996). Recipient Golden Globe award for Best Actress in a Miniseries or Motion picture Made for TV. Office: ICM c/o Toni Howard 8942 Wilshire Blvd Beverly Hills CA 90211-1934

LAHTINEN, SILJA LIISA, artist; b. Lumivaara, Finland; came to U.S., 1978; d. Vaino Lambertinpoika and Katri Elisa (Tirri) Talikka; m. Pentti Kalervo Lahtinen; children: Karoliina, Katriina, Antti. BFA, MA, U. Helsinki, Finland, 1969; BFA, Atlanta Coll. Art, 1983; MFA, Md. Inst. Coll. Art, 1986. Tchr. Teknillinen Oppilaitos, Lahti, Finland, 1969-78; teaching asst. Md. Inst., Coll. of Art, Balt., 1986; artist, owner Siljas Fine Art Studio, Marietta, Ga., 1987—. V.p., creative advisor Pentec Internat. Inc., Marietta,

Ga., 1994—; tchr. etching, painting Atlanta Coll. Art, 1997—. Solo exhbns. include Ariel Gallery, N.Y.C., 1987, 350th Anniversary Swedish/Finnish Art, Atlanta, Ga., 1988, Callanwolde Arts Ctr., Atlanta, 1988, Morin-Miller Gallery, N.Y.C., 1989, La Chapelle de la Sorbonne, Paris, 1990, TaideArt Gallery Helsinki, 1987, 88, 91, 92, Internat. Exhbn., Ward-Nasse Gallery, N.Y.C., 1991, Pihagalleria, Lahti, Finland, 1995, Ars Arrakoski, Padasjoki, Finland, 1999, 2000, Nuutti Galleria, Virrat, Finland, 2002 Ward-Nasse-Chelsea, NYC, 2003; group exhbns. include Scandinavian Artists, Savannah Coll. Art & Design, 1989, La Chapelle de la Sorbonne, Paris, 1990, Ariel Gallery Group Exhbns., N.Y.C., 1987, 89, 90, Med. Coll. Ga., Augusta, 1992, 93, 94, Abney Gallery, N.Y.C., 1993, U. Alaska, Anchorage, 1993, Ward-Nasse Gallery, N.Y.C., 1989-99, Ward-Nasse Gallery Yr. Round Salon, 1999-2002, New Visions Gallery, Atlanta, 1993, Seaside Art Gallery, Nags Head, N.C., 1993, Spruill Ctr. Gallery, Atlanta, 1993, New Ams. Selected by Coca Cola Co., 1996, Telfair Mus. Art, Savannah, 1995, Albany Mus. Art, 1994, San Bernardino Art Mus., 1995, Orgn. of Ind. Artists, N.Y.C., 1995, Rutgers Nat., 1994, Stedman Gallery, City of Atlanta Gallery, Chastain Pk., 1994, Rolling Stone Press Gallery, Printmakers Renaissance, 1996, Atlanta Coll. of Art Juried Alumni Exhbn., 1987, 96, Chattahoochee Valley Art Mus., La Grange, Ga., 1997, Barbara Archer Gallery, Atlanta, 2001, Fabulous Finishes, Inc. and Biasucci Co., 2002, Seminole Coll., Sanford, Fla., 2003 (Award of Merit 2003), Greenbelt (Md.) C.C., 2003, Kennesaw State U., Atlanta, 2003, other shows; selected collections include Barbara Archer Gallery, 2001, Trinity Sch., Dr. Weisman Ctr., Lahden Rautateollisuus, Rauma, Vuorineuvos Tauno Matomaki, Helsinki, Pentec Internat. Inc., Markku af Herlin, Helena Jaakonmaki Collection, Hugh and Sirkka Barbour, Boston and others; contbr. various articles to profl. jours. Recipient Internat. Art Competition, Cert. of Excellence in Printmaking, N.Y.C., 1988, Award from FINNAIR to transport exhibit round trip Finland/USA, The State of Ga. award for achievement Ga. Women in the Visual Arts, 1997, Avery Gallery, 2 Painting awards, 1988. Mem.: Womens Caucus Art, Ward Nasse Gallery, Four Winds Soc., Roswell Fine Arts Alliance, Orgn. Ind. Artists, Am. Art Therapy Assn. Lutheran. Avocations: shamanism, trance dance, zen buddhism, haiku, yoga. Office: Siljas Fine Art Studio 5220 Sunset Trl Marietta GA 30068-4740

LAI, FENG-QI, instructional designer, educator; b. Shanghai, Mar. 25, 1948; came to U.S., 1992; d. Zheng-Zhong Lai and Yao-Zhang Zhu; m. Qun Zhang, Oct. 22, 1984. BA, Changsha (China) Railway Inst., 1982; MS, Purdue U., 1994, PhD, 1997. Asst. lectr. Shanghai Tiedao U., 1982-86, lectr., assoc. dir., 1986-91; instrnl. designer Nat. Edn. Tng. Group, Naperville, Ill., 1998; sr. instr., dir. tng. Advanced Tech. Support, Inc., Schaumburg, Ill., 1998-2000; sr. instrnl. designer Cognitive Concepts, Inc., Evanston, Ill., 2000—02; asst. prof. Ind. State U., Terre Haute, Ind., 2002—. Transl.: Writing Scientific Papers in English, 1983; co-author: Applied Cryptography, 1999. Mem. Phi Kappa Phi. Avocations: music, reading, Chinese poetry, photography, crafts.

LAI, LIWEN, molecular geneticist, educator; b. Taipei, Taiwan, 1957; d. Kwan-Long Lai. BS, Nat. Taiwan U., 1980; MS, U. Calif., San Francisco, 1983; PhD, U. Tex., Dallas, 1987. Diplomate Am. Coll. Med. Genetics. Postdoctoral fellow NIH, Bethesda, Md., 1987-89; asst. rsch. sci. U. Ariz., Tuscon, 1990-94, asst. dir. Molecular Diagnostic Lab., 1992—, rsch. asst. prof., 1995-97; rsch. assoc. prof., 1997—2003; rsch. prof., 2003—. Rsch. grantee Elks, 1994-96, Dialysis Clinic Inc., 1994-96, So. Ariz. Found., 1996—, NIH, 1997—. Mem. Am. Soc. Human Genetics, Am. Soc. Gene Therapy, Am. Soc. Nephrology, Am. Soc. Cell Biology. Office: U Ariz Dept Medicine 1501 N Campbell Ave Tucson AZ 85724-0001

LAINCZ, BETSY ANN, nurse; b. Phila., Feb. 7, 1949; d. Harry Ellsworth and Betty Mary (Minton) Henderson; m. Douglas Dardaris, 1968 (div. 1975); children: Amy, Christopher; m. Fred J. Laincz, Jan. 12, 1982; children: Joshua, Emily, Michael. Student, Bucks County C.C., Newtown, 1969—87, Temple U., Phila., 1973, Upper Bucks Sch. of Nursing, Perkasie, 1983, Internat. Sch. of Shiatsu, Doylestown, 1995—96, LaSalle U., 2000—. Lic. nurse, Pa. Staff nurse, mental health technician Doylestown (Penn.) Hosp., 1983-85, data abstractor med. records, 1988-89; nurse, coun., asst. mgr. NutriSystem, Warrington, Pa., 1985-88; nurse Independence Court, Quakerstown, Pa., 1991; health svcs. supr. Bucks County Assn. Retarded Citizens, Quakerstown, 1992-95; nurse Penn Found. Drug and Alcohol Recovery Ctr., 1996-2000; owner, founder, operator Willow Agy., Perkasie, Pa., 1996—. Mem. supports and standards com. Bucks County Assn. Retarded Citizens, 1995; territory mgr. Healthskil, Fairless Hills and Conshohocken, Pa., 2000—, regional mgr., 2001—03; staff nurse Penn Found., 2003—, Horsham (Pa.) Clinic, 2003—, Rockhill (Pa.) Mennonite Cmty., 2003—. Editor (newsletter) Serendipity, 1996-98. Mem. United Friends Sch., co-chair fundraising, 1989-97, nominating com., 1995-2000, ann. auction com. 1990-97, devel. com, 1991-92, 98-2003; active Individual's Person Centered Planning Team, 1994-96, Inst. of Noetic Scis., 1993—. Mem. Buck Womens Investment Club (v.p. 1995-2002), The Smithsonian Instn., Libr. of Congress Assn., Co-op Am. Republican. Soc. Of Religious Friends. Avocations: reading, writing, art, antiques. Home: 78 N Main St Quakertown PA 18951-1114 Office Phone: 215-538-4004. E-mail: laincz1@comcast.net.

LAINE, CLEO (CLEMENTINA DINAH DANKWORTH), singer; b. Southall, Middlesex, Eng., Oct. 28, 1927; d. Alexander and Minnie (Bullock) Campbell; m. George Langridge, 1947 (div.); m. John Philip William Dankworth, 1958; children: Stuart, Alec, Jackie MA (hon.), Open U., 1975; MusD (hon.), Berklee Coll. Music, 1982. Vocalist Dankworth Orch., 1953-58; lead role in Seven Deadly Sins, Edinburgh, Scotland Festival and Sadlers Wells, 1961, in Showboat, 1972; acting roles Edinburgh Festival, 1966, 67, Colette, 1980; appeared in A Time to Laugh, Hedda Gabler, The Women of Troy, The Mystery of Edwin Drood, 1986 (Theatre World award, Tony award nomination), Into the Woods, 1989 (L.A. Drama Critics award nomination); guest appearances symphony orchs. Eng. and abroad; numerous TV appearances and record albums; most recent albums That Old Feeling, 1985, Cleo Sings Sondheim, 1988, Woman to woman, 1989, Jazz, 1991, Nothing Without You (with Mel Torme), 1992, Smilin' Through (with Dudley Moore), 1992, Cleo at Carnegie, 1993, Born on Friday, 1993, A Beautiful Thing, 1994, Blue and Sentimental, 1994, Solitude (with John Dankworth), 1997, The Very Best of Cleo Laine, 1999, A Quintessential Cleo, 2001, Live in Manhattan, 2001; gold records: Feel the Warm, I'm a Song, Live at Melbourne; Platinum records: (with James Galway) Best Friends, Sometimes When We Touch; author: Cleo, an autobiography, 1994. Decorated Order Brit. Empire, Dame Brit. Empire; recipient Golden Feather award L.A. Times, 1973, Edison award, 1974, Grammy award for best female jazz vocal, 1985, Theatre World award, 1986; named Show Bus. Personality of Yr., Variety Club, 1977, Singer of Yr., TV Times, 1978; Tony nominee, 1986; recipient Theatre World award, 1986, Lifetime Achievement award N.A.R.M., 1990, Brit. Jazz award for best female vocalist, 1990. Office: care Sonoma-Hope Inc PO Box 250 Rockaway NJ 07866

LAINE, IRIS RUTH, minister, public relations/advertising executive; b. Aurora, Ill., Feb. 8, 1925; d. Herman Carl Butke and Ella Stallman; m. Steven Laine, Nov. 4, 1970; 1 child, Leah Reich; stepchildren: Karen McGivney, David, Mark. BA, Fla. Atlantic U., 1981; postgrad., Harvard Div. Sch., 1983, St. Vincent de Paul Sem., 1985-86; MDiv, Luth. Sem., 1988. Ordained to ministry Evangelical Luth. Ch., 1988. Advt. writer, prodr. Chgo. Advt. Agys. and Sears Roebuck & Co., Chgo., 1950—61; promotion copy chief Chgo. Sun-Times/Daily News, 1962—65; trade rels. dir. Smith, Bucklin & Assocs., Inc., Chgo., 1966—78; v.p., treas. Stirco, Inc., Boca Raton, 1979—82; pastor, preacher Evang. Luth. Ch. in Am., Fla., 1987—95. Author: Getting to Know God, 2001; co-author: Promotion in Foodservice, 1972. Mem. Cmty. Interfaith Coalition, Boca Raton, 1992-94, Women in Ministry, Boca Raton, 1988-90, Tradewinds Conf. Mins., Palm Beach/Martin counties, Fla., 1987-92, Synodical Coun., Evang. Luth. Ch. in Am., Fla., 1989-90; dir. Coun. on Hotel, Restaurant and Instnl. Edn., 1969; dir., sec. Internat. Food Editl. Coun., Nat. Orgn., 1968; vol. Rep. Orgns., Palm Beach County, 1996—. Recipient Award Art Dirs. Club of Chgo., 1964; named Top Ten in TV Pharms. award Am. TV Commls. Festival, 1960. Mem. Rotary Internat., Phi Kappa Phi, Alpha Sigma Lambda. Avocations: writing, social service. Home: 500 S Ocean Blvd Apt 904 Boca Raton FL 33432 Fax: 561-392-4822. E-mail: irislaine@aol.com.

LAING, ERIKA QUALLS, psychologist; b. Andrews Airforce Base, Md., Dec. 7, 1972; d. Johnnie J. and Peggy June Qualls; m. Mark Alexander Laing, Nov. 11, 2000. BA in Psychology cum laude, U. Ark., 1995; MS in Clin. Psychology, Pacific U., 1998, D in Psychology, 2002. Counselor Vanderbilt Summer Treatment Program, Nashville, 1995—95; residential treatment specialist Habberton House-Ozark Guidance Ctr., Springdale, Ark., 1995—95; psychiat. technician children's unit Charter Behavioral Health Care, Fayetteville, Ark., 1995—96; treatment counselor Parry Ctr.-Williams Group Home, Portland, Oreg., 1997—98; psychology practicum student Psychol. Svc. Ctr., Portland, 1997—98, Network Behavioral Heath Care, Portland, 1998—99; psychology intern N.W. Ga. Regional Hosp., Rome, 2001—02, Lookout Mountain Cmty. Mental Health, Summerville, Ga., 2001—02, Murphy Harpst Children's Ctr., Cedartown, Ga., 2001—02; psychology postdoctoral fellow Medlin Treatment Ctr., Marietta, Ga., 2002—. Clin. specialist II Protocall Svcs., Portland, 2000—01; presenter in field. Vol. Head Start, Fayetteville, 1992—93, N.W. Ark. Crisis Intervention Ctr., Springdale, 1994—95. Scholar, Pacific U. Sch. Profl. Psychology, 1996—2000. Mem.: APA, Ga. Psychol. Assn. Achievements include research in effect of testifying on sexually abused children; examination of stage of change, partnering and exercise adherence. Personal E-mail: erikaq@bellsouth.net.

LAING, JENNIFER, advertising executive; Chmn., CEO Saatchi & Saatchi N. Am., N.Y.C. Office: Saatchi & Saatchi 375 Hudson St 16th Floor New York NY 10014-3658

LAING, KAREL ANN, magazine publishing executive; b. Mpls., July 5, 1939; d. Edward Francis and Elizabeth Jane Karel (Templeton) Hannon; m. G. R. Cheesebrough, Dec. 19, 1959 (div. 1969); 1 child, Jennifer Read; m. Ronald Harris Laing, Jan. 6, 1973; 1 child, Christopher Harris Grad., U. Minn., 1960. With Guthrie Symphony Opera Program, Mpls., 1969-71; account supr. Colle & McVoy Advt. Agy., Richfield, Minn., 1971-74; owner The Cottage, Edina, Minn., 1974-75; salespromotion rep. Robert Meyers & Assocs., St. Louis Park, Minn., 1975-76; cons. Webb Co., St. Paul, 1976-77, custom pub. dir., 1977-89; pres. K.L. Publs., Inc., Bloomington, Minn., 1989—. Contbr. articles to profl. jours. Community vol. Am. Heart Assn., Am. Cancer Soc., Edina PTA; charter sponsor Walk Around Am., St. Paul, 1985 Mem. Bank Mktg. Assn., Fin. Instn. Mktg. Assn., Advt. Fedn. Am., Am. Bankers Assn., Direct Mail Mktg. Assn., Minn. Mag. Pub. Assn. (founder, bd. govs.), St. Andrews Soc. Republican. Presbyterian. Avocations: painting; gardening; reading; traveling. Office: KL Publs 2001 Killebrew Dr Minneapolis MN 55425-1865

LAIOU, ANGELIKI EVANGELOS, history educator; b. Athens, Greece, Apr. 6, 1941; came to U.S., 1959; d. Evangelos K. and Virginia I. (Apostolides) Laios; m. Stavros B. Thomadakis, July 14, 1973; 1 son, Vassili N. BA, Brandeis U., 1961; MA, Harvard U., 1962, PhD, 1966. Asst. prof. history Harvard U., Cambridge, Mass., 1969-72, Dumbarton Oaks prof. Byzantine history, 1981—; assoc. prof. Brandeis U., Waltham, 1972-75; prof. Rutgers U., New Brunswick, N.J., 1975-79, disting. prof., 1979-81; chmn. Gennadeion com. (Am. Sch. Classical Studies), Athens, Greece, 1981-84; dir. Dumbarton Oaks, 1989-98; prof. history Harvard U., Cambridge, 1998—. Mem. Greek Parliament, 2000-2002; dep. min. fgn. affairs, Greece, 2000. Author: Constantinople and the Latins, 1972, Peasant Society in the Late Byzantine Empire, 1977, Mariage, amour et parenté à Byzance, XIe-XIIIe siècles, 1992, Gender, Society and Economic Life in Byzantium, 1992, The Economic History of Byzantium, 2002. Guggenheim Found. fellow, 1971-72, 79-80, Dumbarton Oaks sr. fellow, 1983—, Am. Coun. Learned Socs. fellow, 1988-89. Fellow Am. Acad. Arts and Scis., Medieval Acad., Acad. Athens; mem. Am. Hist. Assn., Medieval Acad. Am., Greek Com. Study of South Eastern Europe. Office: Harvard U Dept History Cambridge MA 02138 E-mail: laiou@fas.harvard.edu.

LAIRD, DORIS ANNE MARLEY, humanities educator, musician; b. Charlotte, N.C., Jan. 15, 1931; d. Eugene Harris and Coleen (Bethea) Marley; m. William Everette Laird Jr., Mar. 13, 1964; children: William Everette III, Andrew Marley, Glen Howard. MusB, Converse Coll., Spartanburg, S.C., 1951; opera cert., New Eng. Conservatory, Boston, 1956; MusM, Boston U., 1956; PhD, Fla. State U., 1980. Leading soprano roles S.C. Opera Co., Columbia, 1951-53, Plymouth Rock Ctr. of Music and Art, Duxbury, Mass., 1953-56; soprano Pro Musica, Boston, 1956, New Eng. Opera Co., Boston, 1956; instr. Stratford Coll., Danville, Va., 1956-58, Sch. Music Fla. State U., Tallahassee, 1958-60, dept. humanities, 1960-68; tchr. Fla. State U., 1973-79; asst. prof. Fla. A&M U., Tallahassee, 1979-89, assoc. prof., 1990—2002; ret., 2002. Vis. scholar Cornell U., 1988; participant So. Conf. on Afro-Am. Studies, Inc. Author: Colin Morris: Modern Missionary, 1980; contbr. articles to profl. jours. Soprano Washington St. Meth. Ch., Columbia, S.C., 1951-53, Copley Meth. Ch., Boston, 1953-56; soloist Trinity United Meth. Ch., Tallahassee, 1983—; mem. Saint Andrews Soc., Tallahassee, 1986—; judge Brain Bowl, Tallahassee, 1981-84; mem. alumnae bd. Converse Coll., 2004—. Named subject of article, Glamour mag., 2001, Self mag., 2003; recipient NEH award, 1988, Disting. Alumna award, Converse Coll., 2001; scholar Phi Sigma Tau, 1960. Mem. AAUP, AAUW, Nat. Art Educators Assn., Tallahassee Music Tchrs. Assn., Tallahassee Music Guild, Am. Guild of Organists, DAR (mus. rep. 1984-85), Colonial Dames of 17th Century (music dir. 1984-85), Nat. Assn. Humanities Edn., U. Wyo. Women's Club, Woman's Club Tallahassee (v.p. 2004), Converse Coll. Alumni (bd. dir. 2003—). Democrat. Achievements include subject of article Self Magazine, 2004. Avocations: travel, dance, music. Home: 1125 Mercer Dr Tallahassee FL 32312-2833 Personal E-mail: wlaird@garnet.acns.fsu.edu.

LAIRD, JEAN ELOUISE RYDESKI (MRS. JACK E. LAIRD), author, adult education educator; b. Wakefield, Mich., Jan. 18, 1930; d. Chester A. and Agnes A. (Petranek) Rydeski; m. Jack E. Laird, June 9, 1951; children: John E., Jayne E., Joan Ann P., Jerilyn S., Jacquelyn T. Bus. Edn. degree, Duluth (Minn.) Bus. U., 1948; postgrad., U. Minn., 1949-50. Tchr. Oak Lawn (Ill.) H.S. Adult Evening Sch., 1964-72, St. Xavier Coll., Chgo., 1974—. Lectr., commencement address cir.; writer newspaper column Around The House With Jean, A Woman's Work, 1965-70, Chicagotown News column The World As I See It, 1969, hobby column Modern Maturity mag., travel column Travel/Leisure mag., beauty column Ladycom mag., Time and Money Savers column Lady's Circle mag., consumerism column Ladies' Home Jour. Author: Lost in the Department Store, 1964, Around the House Like Magic, 1968, Around the Kitchen Like Magic, 1969, How to Get the Most from Your Appliances, 1967, Hundreds of Hints for Harassed Homemakers, 1971, The Alphabet Zoo, 1972, The Plump Ballerina, 1971, The Porcupine Story Book, 1974, Fried Marbles and Other Fun Things to Do, 1975, Hundreds of Hints for Harassed Homemakers: The Homemaker's Book of Time and Money Savers, 1979, Homemaker's Book of Energy Savers, 1981; also 427 paperback booklets; contbr. articles to mags. Mem.: Marist, Mt. Assissi Acad., St. Linus Guild, Queen of Peace Parents Clubs, Oak Lawn Bus. and Profl. Women's Club, Canterbury Writers Club Chgo. Roman Catholic. Home: 10540 Lockwood Ave Oak Lawn IL 60453-5161 also: Vista De Lago Lake Geneva WI 53147 also: Harbor Towers Yacht Club Siesta Key FL 34242

LAIRD, MARY See WOOD, LARRY

LAJE, ZILIA L. writer, publisher, translator; b. Havana, Cuba, Feb. 1, 1941; came to U.S., 1961; d. Luis B. Laje and Zilia Isabel Bello; divorced; 1 child, Alberto Luis Dominguez. Comml. acct., Escuela Profl. de Comercio, Havana, 1959-61; AA in Bus. Adminstrn., Miami-Dade C.C., 1989. Export documentation clk. Pittsburgh Plate Glass Internat., Havana, 1959-60; agy. sec. Occidental Life Ins. Co., Miami, 1962-67; sec. to v.p./br. mgr. Chgo. Title Ins. Co., Miami, 1972-76; corp. banking asst. S.E. Bank, N.A., Miami Springs, Fla., 1978-90; writer, transl. Miami, 1991—. Exhibitor Miami Book Fair Internat., 1995—. Author: (novels) La Cortina de Bagazo, 1995, The Sugar Cane Curtain, 2000, Cartas Son Cartas, 2001, Love Letters in the Sand, 2002, Divagaciones, 2003. Mem.: PEN Ctr. for Writers in Exile, Writer's, N.Y., Cuban Writers in Miami (founder, assoc.), Women's Nat. Book Assn. (corr.), Alliance Française de Miami. Republican. Roman Catholic. Avocations: needlepoint, photography, travel. Office: Escritores Cubanos de Miami PO Box 45-1732 Miami FL 33245-1732 E-mail: guarinapub@juno.com.

LAJOUX, ALEXANDRA REED, editor, educator; b. Washington, Mar. 4, 1950; d. Stanley Foster and Stella Swingle Reed; m. Bernard Jacques Lajoux, Aug. 14, 1982; 1 child, Franklin Alberto; stepchildren: Valerie Corinne, Sylvia Patricia. BA, Bennington Coll., 1972; MA, Princeton U., 1974, PhD, 1978; MBA, Loyola Coll., Balt., 1981. Asst. prof. French lang. and lit. SUNY Coll. Oswego, N.Y., 1977-78; sr. editor Dirs. and Bds. Info. for Industry, McLean, Va., 1978-80; editor Mergers and Acquisitions The Hay Group, Phila., 1980-83; editor Export Today Export Info. Group, Washington, 1983-87; editor-in-chief Nat. Assn. Corp. Dirs., Washington, 1987—, dir. rsch. and publs., 1992-2000, sr. rsch. analyst, 2001—. Pres. Alexis & Co., Arlington, Va., 1987—; Washington bur. co-chief N.E. Internat. Bus., Washington, 1987-90; dir. M&A rsch. E-Know, Inc., Arlington, 2000-01. Author: The Art of M&A Integration, 1997; co-author (with J.F. Weston): The Art of M&A Financing and Refinancing, 1999; co-author: (with S.F. Reed) The Art of M&A: A Merger/Acquisition/Buyout Guide, 3d edit., 1999; co-author: (with C.M. Elson) The Art of M&A Due Diligence, 2000; co-author: (with H.P. Nesvold) The Art of M & A Structuring, 2004; editor-in-chief: HR Dir.: The Arthur Andersen Guide to Human Capital, 1998, 1999, 2000, 2001; contbr. articles to profl. jours. Co-dir. Gunston Mid. Sch. Chorus, 2000; drama and music tchr. Commonwealth Acad., Falls Church, Va., 2000—02, music tchr., spring, 2003; music tchr. Lab Sch., Washington, 2003—; cantor, children's music asst. St. Ann Cath. Ch., Arlington, 1988—, catechist, 1999—2001; alto sect. leader St. James Ch., Falls Church, 2001—; bd. dirs. Arlington Little League, 1992—94. Princeton fellow, 1972-74, French Govt. fellow, 1975-76, Mrs. Giles Whiting fellow, 1976-77. Mem. Toastmasters Internat. (v.p. local club membership 1999-2000), Assn. Princeton Grad. Alumni (trustee 1999-2002), Inst. Indsl. Engrs., Music Educators Nat. Conf. Republican. Roman Catholic. Avocations: singing and composing music, organizing musical performances, writing poetry and fiction, learning foreign languages, teaching children and teens. Home: 2256 N Nottingham St Arlington VA 22205-3344 Office: Nat Assn Corp Dirs 1828 L St NW Ste 801 Washington DC 20036 E-mail: arlajoux@aol.com.

LAKATOS, SUSAN CAROL, investment banker, artist; b. N.Y., 1960; BA, Georgetown U., 1981; MBA, Columbia U., 1989. CFA. Economist Washington Analysis Corp., 1980-84; v.p., economist Kidder, Peabody & Co., Inc., N.Y.C., 1984-89, investment strategist, 1989-92; pres. Ananda Advisors, 1992-2000; dir. rsch. Veronis Suhler, N.Y.C., 2000—. Bd. dirs., chair com. on prices, Bus. Rsch. Adv. Coun., Washington, 1983-92. One person shows include Stables Art Ctr., Taos, 1996-98, Bareiss Gallery, Taos, 1998. Mem. fin. com. Columbia Bus. Sch. Mem. Assn. Investment Mgmt. and Rsch., N.Y. Soc. Securities Analysts, Fin. Womens Assn. N.Y. Office: 350 Park Ave New York NY 10022-6022

LAKE, CAROL LEE, anesthesiologist, physician executive, educator; b. Altoona, Pa., July 14, 1944; d. Samuel Lindsay and Edna Winifred (McMahan) L. BS, Juniata Coll., 1966; MD, Med. Coll. Pa., 1970; MBA, U. Calif., Irvine, 1997; MPH, U. Mich., 2000. Intern Mercy Hosp., Pitts., 1970-71, resident in anesthesiology, 1971-73; staff anesthesiologist Pitts. Anesthesia Assocs., 1973-75; asst. prof. anesthesiology U. Va., Charlottesville, 1975-80, assoc. prof., 1980-89, prof. anesthesiology, 1989-94; prof. anesthesiology, chair U. Calif., Davis, 1994-95, prof. clin. anesthesiology, 1996; chief of staff Roudebush VA Med. Ctr., 1997-99; asst. dean, prof. anesthesia Ind. U., Indpls., 1997-99; prof. anesthesiology, chair U. Louisville, 1999—, assoc. dean for continuing med. edn., 1999—, asst. v.p. for health affairs/continuing edn., 2002—. Sr. assoc. examiner Am. Bd. Anesthesiology, 1981—. Author: Cardiovascular Anesthesia, 1985; editor: Pediatric Cardiac Anesthesia, 1988, 4th edit., 2004; Clinical Monitoring, 1990, 2d edit., 2000; editor Seminars in Cardiothoracic and Vascular Anesthesia, 1999—; co-editor: Blood: Hemostasis, Transfusion and Alternatives in the Perioperative Period, 1995; editor Advances in Anesthesia, 1993—. Fellow Am. Coll. Cardiology; mem. Assn. Cardiac Anesthesiologists (pres. 1987-88), Soc. Cardiovascular Anesthesiologists (bd. dirs. 1988-92), Assn. Univ. Anesthesiologists, Am Coll. Physician Execs., Alpha Omega Alpha. Presbyterian. Avocations: music, entomology, gardening. Office: U Louisville Dept Anesthesiology and Perioperative Me 530 S Jackson St Louisville KY 40202-1675 E-mail: cllake01@louisville.edu.

LAKE, CONSTANCE WILLIAMS, psychologist, public health administrator; b. Cleve., Aug. 16, 1949; d. Fredrick and Helen (Martin) Williams; m. Michael J. McCargo, Sept. 1, 1973 (div. Oct. 1989); children: Courtney McCargo, Jarad McCargo; m. Kenneth Paul Lake, Sept. 7, 1997. BA, Elmhurst (Ill.) Coll., 1971; MA, U. Conn., 1973; PhD, Kent State U., 1983. Psychologist Mile Sq. Health Ctr., Chgo., 1984-86, exec. dir., 1986-90; clin. assoc. Cmty. Mental Health Ctr., Chgo., 1985-90; AIDS cons. Assn. Black Psychologists, 1988—; instr. psychology Northeastern U., Chgo., 1989; dir. cmty. svc. Binghamton (N.Y.) Psychiat. Ctr., 1990-91; clin. assoc. Ramey & Assocs., Atlanta, 1991-92; bur. chief mental health City of Chgo. Joint Commn. Health Care Orgns., 1999—. V.p. profl. devel. Hamilton Behavioral Health, Chgo., 1992; cons./trainer Wells Cmty. Initiative, Chgo., 1992-93; trainer HIV Office, APA, Chgo., 1993—. Mem. long range planning bd. dirs. Trinity United Ch. of Christ, Chgo., 1992-99; mem. Renaissance Women, 1985-97. Honoree, Alpha Gamma Pi, Chgo., 1995; Woman of Achievement honoree broome County Status of Women, Binghamton, 1992. Mem. APA, APHA, Assn. Black Psychologists (conv. chair 1996-97), Delta Sigma Theta. Avocations: film, theater, dance. Office: Chgo Dept Pub Health 333 S State St Chicago IL 60604-3900 Home: # 1D 2211 E 68th St Chicago IL 60649-1212

LAKE, KATHLEEN COOPER, lawyer; b. San Antonio, Jan. 11, 1955; d. Herschel Taliaferro and Virginia Mae (Hylton) Cooper; m. Randall Brent Lake, Apr. 9, 1977; 1 child, Ethan Taliaferro. AB in Polit. Sci. magna cum laude, Middlebury Coll., 1977; JD with high honors, U. Tex., 1980. Bar: Tex. 1980, U.S. Ct. Appeals (5th cir.) 1981, U.S. Ct. Appeals (D.C. and 3rd cirs.) 1984. Assoc. atty. Vinson & Elkins, Houston, 1980-88; ptnr. Vinson & Elkins, LLP, Houston, 1989—. Bd. advisors, columnist Utilities, Y2K Advisor, 1998-99. Adult leader, com. mem. Sam Houston Area Coun.-Golden Arrow dist. Boy Scouts Am., 1993—, chair troop com., 1998-2001. Recipient Unit Svc. award Sam Houston Area Coun.-Golden Arrow dist. Boy Scouts Am., 1996, 98. Fellow Tex. Bar Found. (life), Houston Bar Found.; mem. ABA (vice-chair com. 1997-99), Energy Bar Assn., State Bar Tex., Tex. Law Rev. Assn. (life), Houston Bar Assn., Middlebury Coll. Alumni Assn. (com. mem. 1980-2000, Houston com. chair 2001—), Order of Coif, Phi Beta Kappa, Phi Kappa Phi. Office: Vinson & Elkins LLP 2300 First City Tower 1001 Fannin St Houston TX 77002-6760 E-mail: klake@velaw.com.

LAKE, MARILYN HOPE (WAIDE) WARN, artist; b. Alton, Ill., Dec. 3, 1941; d. Frank Joseph Waide, Sr. and Hope Helen (Lane) Waide; m. George William Lake, Feb. 17, 1964 (div. Sept. 8, 1975); children: David Ray, Amy Kate Heuer; m. Denton D. Warn, Jan. 1, 2002. BA in English, magna cum laude, Indiana U. Pa., 1971; MPA, U. Mo., Columbia, 1987, MA in Creative Writing, 1994, PhD in Creative Writing, 2003. Permanent cert. secondary English tchr. Mo., 1972, cert. assn. exec. Am. Soc. of Assn. Executives, 1981. Exec. coord. Mo. Libr. Assn., Columbia, Mo., 1974—79; exec. dir. Mo. Assn. of Cmty. and Jr. Colls., Columbia, Mo., 1979—82; pub. info. officer Coordinating Bd. for Higher Edn., Jefferson City, Mo., 1983—86; continuing edn. coord. Mo. Dept. of Health and U. Mo.-Columbia, Columbia, Mo., 1986—90, creative writing instr., English dept. and Mo. U. Direct, 1993—98, assoc. state bus. and industry specialist, Small Bus. Devel. Ctr., Coll. Bus., 1990—2001. Steering com. for 1985 seminar State Higher Edn. Exec. Officers, Comm. Officers, Jefferson City, Mo., 1985; del. White Ho. Conf. on Libraries and Info. Sciences, Washington, 1979; adv. com. Governor's Conf. on Libraries and Info. Svcs., Jefferson City, Mo., 1978; adminstr. Am. Small Bus. Devel. Centers/IBM/Lotus Learning Ctr., Columbia, Mo., 1991—94. Editor (and copy writer): (text book) Entrepreneurship: Changing the Odds, 1998; author (contributor to edited collection): (book) Missouri Women Writers, 1984; author: (short stories) Our Mothers' Ghosts, 2003; contbr. stories and poems to lit. jours. and anthology (Avila Coll. Fiction Writers' prize, 1987). Bd. trustees Boone County Regional Sewer Dist., Columbia, Mo., 1977—79; mem. ex-officio com. Mo. State Libr. Network; pres., bd.dirs. Highfield Acres Neighborhood Assn., Columbia, Mo., 1974—78. Mem.: U. of Mo.-Columbia Alumni Assn., U. Mo.-Columbia Faculty Retirees Assn. Democrat. United Methodist. Avocation: photography. Personal E-mail: lakehope@msn.com.

LAKE, MARTHA M. engineer; b. Henning, Tenn., Jan. 2, 1951; d. James Wesley and Warlean Thornton; children from previous marriage: Marshall, Michael, Deborah, Justin. AAS in Bus. Adminstrn., Dyersburg, Tenn., 1998; BS, Christian Bros. U., Memphis, Tenn., 2000—04. Sr. engring. document clk. Wright Med. Tech., Arlington, Tenn., 1998—2000, engring. document adminstrn. ofcl., 2000—. Office: Wright Med Tech 5677 Airline Rd Arlington TN 38002

LAKE, NANCY JEAN, nursing educator, medical/surgical nurse; b. Sandborn, Ind., May 13, 1942; d. Thomas Malone and Vivian Pearl (Meek) Wills; divorced; children: Brian, Deanna, Patrick. AS, Cleve. State Community Coll., 1972. RN, Ky., Ind., N.Y., Ark. Staff nurse geriatric unit Regional Hosp., Ft. Smith, Ark., 1973-74; pub. health staff nurse Ft. Smith, Ark., 1974; staff nurse Bradley County Hosp., Cleveland, Tenn., 1972-73; staff nurse recovery room and oper. room St. Anthony Hosp., Terre Haute Regional Hosp., Terre Haute, Ind., 1974-76; staff nurse oper. room, emergency room, med.-surg. fl. Washington County Hosp., Salem, Ind., 1976-77; oper. room. staff nurse Floyd County Hosp., New Albany, Ind., 1977-78; staff nurse oper. room Good Samaritan Hosp., Vincennes, Ind., 1978-82; staff nurse oper. room and thoriac cardio vascular coord. Winthrope Univ. Hosp., Mineola, N.Y., 1982-86; staff nurse oper. room Humana Hosp., Audubon, 1986-92; staff nurse oper. rm. Jewish Hosp. Healthcare Ctr., 1990—, staff nurse, organ retrivial nurse, nurse in sterile processing, 2000—. Home: 515 S Chestnut St Seymour IN 47274-3043

LAKE, RICKI, talk show host, actress; b. N.Y.C., Sept. 21, 1968; m. Rob Sussman; 2 children. Syndicated talk show host Ricki Lake, 1993—. Movie appearances include: Hairspray, 1988, Working Girl, 1988, Cookie, 1989, Cry-Baby, 11990, Last Exit to Brooklyn, 1989, Where the Day Takes You, 1992, Inside Monkey Zetterland, 1993, Serial Mom, 1994, Cabin Boy, 1994, Skinner, 1995, Mrs. Winterbourne, 1996; TV appearances include (series) China Beach, 1990, Kate and Allie, Fame, (spls.) A Family Again, 1988, Starting Now, 1989, Gravedale High, 1990, (movies) Babycakes, 1989, The Chase, 1991, Basedon an Untrue Story, (pilot) Starting Now; stage actress: A Girl's Guide to Chaos, 1990, (off-Broadway) The Early Show, Youngsters, 1983. Recipient Gracie Allen award, Am. Women in Radio & TV, 2001, Angel award (2), Excellence in Media. Office: Entrada Prodns 401 5th Ave Fl 7 New York NY 10016-3317 also: WMA 151 S El Camino Dr Beverly Hills CA 90212-2704 also: 8530 Wilshire Blvd 90211

LAKE, SUZANNE, singer, music educator; b. Palisade, N.J., June 26, 1929; d. Mayhew Lester and Suzanne Louise (Robin) L.; m. George A. De Vos, Nov. 19, 1974. Pvt. tchr., Oakland, Calif., 1976-86, univ. extension U. Calif., Sacramento State U., 1981-84. Featured roles opera, N.Y.C., 1948-51; appeared in Broadway plays The King and I, 1951-54, History of Musical Comedy with Leonard Bernstein, 1957, Flower Drum Song, 1960-61; featured singer with Guy Lombardo, 1964, 65, Experiencing Music, Expressing Culture, Oxford U. Press; concert and supper club appearances in U.S., Can., Carribbean, Japan, Republic of Korea, Taiwan and Europe, 1955-91, recs. include the Soul of Chanson, Potpourri, others; also TV appearances. Mem. Actors Equity, AFTRA, Am. Guild Mus. Artists, Am. Guild Variety Artists. Home: 2835 Morley Dr Oakland CA 94611-2547

LAKIN, JOAN FIELD, retired water treatment plant manager; b. Long Branch, N.J., Dec. 29, 1949; d. Norman J. and Gladys (Katz) Field; m. Alan Ray Lakin, June 6, 1971; children: Brian Matthew, Sara Lorraine. BA in Psychology, Wells Coll., 1971; MS in Environ. Sci., U. New Haven, 1992. Lic. water treatment plant operator class IV, State of Conn. Dept. Health Svcs., lic. distbn. sys. operator class II, State of Conn. Dept. Health Svcs. Collections rep. Regional Water Authority, New Haven, 1982-84, water quality control technician, 1984, water treatment plant operator, 1985—2000, ret., 2000. Commr., Planning and Zoning Commn., Hamden, Conn., 1982-86, chairperson planning sect., 1984-85; mem. Local Emergency Planning Commn., East Haven, Conn., 1985-2000; bd. trustees Congregation Mishkan Israel, Hamden, 1994—, pres., 2002—; pres. LWV, 1981-83; mem. charter revision commn., Hamden, 1980-81; mem. Town Plan Update Task Force, Hamden, 1980-81. Mem. LWV (pres., natural resources chairperson), Am. Water Works Assn. Home: 182 Eramo Ter Hamden CT 06518-2013

LA LIBERTE, ANN GILLIS, graphic artist, consultant, designer, educator; b. St. Paul, Nov. 10, 1942; d. Edward Robert and Frances Caroline (S.) Gillis; m. Paul Henry La Liberte, Aug. 22, 1964; children: Paul E., Elizabeth La Liberte Collins, Stephen A., Helen La Liberte Gallagher, Peter N., Marc H. Student, Am U., Washington D.C., 1963-64, Cardinal Stritch Coll., Milw., 1960-63; BA, Coll. St. Catherine, St. Paul, 1985. Artist, owner Ann La Liberte Papers and Posters, Minnetonka, Minn., 1968-71, A.L. Graphic Design and Drawings, Minnetonka, Minn., 1987-2001; artist-in-residence Tara Tonka Studio, Minnetonka, 1987-2001, Tara Claire Studio, Gordon, Wis., 2001—. Artist Arts in Schs., Minn., 1985-2001; pvt. art tchr., dir. creativity and problem solving seminars, 1991—. Liturgical design cons. Midwest, 1977—; paintings, drawings, photography and sculpture exhibited Mpls. and St. Paul area, 1983—; sculpture Life Exhibit, Paul VI Inst. for the Arts, Washington, 1988, on tour Vt., Ohio, Mo., Ill., Wis., 1988. Del. Minn. Ind. Reps., 1969, vice chmn. Minnetonka, 1970; promotional artist Soc. for Preservation Human Dignity, Palatine, Ill., 1973, Minn. Citizens Concerned for Life, 1980-88, Secular Franciscans, St. Paul, 1985; deanery rep. Pastoral Coun. Archdiocese of St. Paul and Mpls., 1978-82; chmn. devel. task force out-reach program Resurrection Ch., Mpls., 1980-81, cons. artist, 1983-87; dir. liturg. design Ch. of Immaculate Heart of Mary, Minnetonka, 1989-2001; liturgical art and environ. cons. Mem. Nat. Assn. Liturgical Mins., Mpls. Inst. of Arts, Nat. Mus. Women in Arts (charter), Walker Art Ctr., Coll. of St. Catherine Alumna Assn., Artists for Life Nat. Slide Registry, Delta Phi Delta. Roman Catholic. Avocations: art history, swimming, hiking, travel, sculpture. Studio: Tara Claire Studio 13709 S Fowler Cir Gordon WI 54838-9039 E-mail: taraclaire01@hotmail.com.

LA LIME, HELEN R. MEAGHER, ambassador; married; 2 children. BS, Georgetown U.; MS, Nat. Def. U. Consul gen., Zurich, Switzerland, 1993; with Bur. Internat. Orgnl. Affairs in Dept. of State, 1993—95; dep. chief of mission U.S. Embassy, N'djamena, Chad, 1996—99, dir. office of ctrl. African affairs, 2000—01, dep. chief of mission, 2001—03; U.S. amb. to Mozambique, 2002—. Office: Am Embassy Avenida Kenneth Kaunda 193 Maputo Czixa Postal 783 Mozambique Fax: (258) 1 49 01 14.*

LALLY, NORMA ROSS, retired federal agency administrator; b. Crawford, Nebr., Aug. 10, 1932; d. Roy Anderson and Alma Leona (Barber) Lively; m. Robert Edward Lally, Dec. 4, 1953 (div. Mar. 1986); children: Robyn Carol Murch, Jeffrey Alan, Gregory Roy. BA, Boise (Idaho) State U., 1974, MA, 1976; postgrad., Columbia Pacific U., 1988—. With grad. admissions Boise State U., 1971-74; with officer programs USN Recruiting, Boise, 1974; pub. affairs officer IRS, Boise and Las Vegas, 1975-94; ret., 1994. Speaker in field, Boise and Las Vegas, 1977—. Contbr. articles to newspapers. Mem. task force Clark County Sch. Dist., Las Vegas, 1986-96, Las Vegas Art Mus. Staff sgt. USAF, 1950-54. Mem.: NAFE, Women in Mil. Svc. Am. (charter), Mensa, Marine's Meml. Club (life), Am. Legion (life). Avocations: writing, music, swimming, travel. Home: 3013 Hawksdale Dr Las Vegas NV 89134-8967 Personal E-mail: norlally@aol.com.

LALONDE, FRANCINE, member of parliament; b. Ste.-Hyacinthe, Que., Aug. 24, 1940; children: Dominique, Philippe, Julien. Degree in edn. psychology, École normale Cardinal-Lé; lic. in history, U. Montreal. Instr. occupl. health and safety, history and adminstrn. U. Montreal, U. Que., Montreal, Chicoutimi, école Hautes Études Commls.; mem. Can. Parliament for Bloc Québécois for Mercier, 1993—. Ofcl. opposition critic on human resources and lit., v.p. standing com. on human resources devel., 1993-97; critic on industry, employment and econ. devel. Bloc Québécois, 1997-99, critic on fgn. affairs, mem. standing com. fgn. affairs and internat. trade, 1999—. Dir. info. and prs. CEGEP sect. CSN, 1969-83, 1st woman v.p., pres. Nat. Tchrs.' Fedn., chair coordinating com. pvt. sector fedns.; coord. Soc. Coop. Produits Électriques et Moteurs, 1984; minister responsible for status of women Govt. Que., 1985; cand. for presidency Parti Québécois, 1985, mem. nat. exec. coun., 1988, program advisor, 1991. Office: House of Commons 211 Justice Bldg Ottawa ON Canada K1A 0A6 E-mail: lalonf@parl.gc.ca.

LAM, CAROL C. lawyer; b. N.Y. m. Mark Burnett; 4 children. BA, Yale U., 1981; JD, Stanford U., 1985. Asst. pros. atty. So. Dist. Calif., 1986—90, chief, Major Fraud Sect., 1997—2000; judge Calif. Superior Ct., 2000—02; U.S. atty. So. Dist. Calif., 2002—. Office: So Dist Calif 880 Front St Rm 6293 San Diego CA 92101-8893

LAM, PAULINE POHA, library director; b. Hong Kong, Oct. 21, 1950; came to U.S., 1971; d. Cheung and Kam-Chun (Mo) Li; m. Frank Sung-Lun Lam, Nov. 28, 1973; children: Candace See-Win Lam, Megan See-Kay Lam. BA, U. B.C., 1977; MLS, U. Tex., 1980; cert. City Mgmt. Acad., Austin C.C., 1994. Libr. dir. City of Cedar Park (Tex.). Bd. dirs. Cedar Park Pub. Libr. Found., 1994—. Mem. Work Force Literacy Com. Literacy Coun. of Williamson County, 1995; bd. dirs. ARC of Ctrl. Tex., Austin, 1995-97. Mem. ALA, Tex. Libr. Assn., Tex. Mcpl. League Libr. Dir. Assn. Avocations: reading, crocheting, painting. Office: Cedar Park Pub Libr 550 Discovery Blvd Cedar Park TX 78613-2200

LAMANET LALONDE, SHARI, artist; b. San Francisco, Sept. 29, 1949; d. Alfred Paul and Marjorie Theodora (Hibschle) L.; m. Philip Martin Lalonde, Sept. 28, 1974; children: Sydney Lamanet, Paul Braque. BFA, San Francisco Art Inst., 1971, MFA, 1979. Mem. painting faculty San Francisco Art Inst., 1981—. Group shows include Emmanuel Walter Gallery San Francisco Art Inst., 1980, 83, 87, Rental Gallery San Francisco Mus. Modern Art, 1980, 93, 96, Sierra Nevada Mus. Art, Reno, Nev., 1980, Minot (N.D.) State Coll., 1981 (Hon. Mention), San Francisco Mus. Modern Art, 1981, Stedman Art Gallery Rutgers U., Camden, N.J., 1981-82, So. Exposure Gallery, San Francisco, 1983, Slant Gallery, San Francisco, 1984, Alternative Mus., N.Y.C., 1984, Ian Birkstad Gallery, London, 1985, Musavi Gallery, N.Y.C., 1985 (First Place Drawing), ARCO Visual Arts Ctr., Anchorage, Alaska, 1985-86, Fairbanks (Alaska) Art Assn., 1985-86, Alaska State Mus., Juneau, 1985-86, Koslow Gallery, L.A., 1988, 89, Camerawork Gallery, San Francisco, 1988 (Phelan award 1987), Downey Mus. Art, L.A., 1989, John Michael Kohler Arts Ctr., Sheboygan, Wis., 1990, U. San Diego, 1990, Redding (Calif.) Mus. Art and History, 1991, San Francisco Art Inst., 1992, 93, 96, Opts Arts, San Francisco, 1994, Ctr. Visual Arts, Oakland, Calif., 1994, Jernigan Wicker Gallery, San Francisco, 1997, numerous others; one person shows include Bruce Velick Gallery, San Francisco, 1984, 86, 88, Sheppard Gallery, U. Nev., Reno, 1984, Slant Gallery, 1985, Monterey (Calif.) Mus. Art, 1986. Bd. dirs. San Francisco Children's Art Ctr., 1990-92; mem. fine arts com. Schs. of the Sacred Heart, San Francisco, 1995-96. Home: 2475 Pacific Ave San Francisco CA 94115-1237 Office: San Francisco Art Inst 800 Chestnut St San Francisco CA 94133-2206

LAMB, BEATRIZ DOMINGUEZ, home health agency administrator; d. Efrain and Maria Dominguez; m. Charles Lamb, June 11, 1983; 1 child, Anna Marie. BSN, U. of Md., Balt., 1978; MBA, Ind. Wesleyan U., Marion, 2002. RN Ind. Dir. Home Health of Ancilla Health Care, Mishawaka, Ind., 1998—2001; exec. dir. St. Joseph VNA Home Care, Mishawaka, 2001—. Youth bd. Christ the King Luth. Ch., South Bend, Ind., 2000—03; mem. Alick's Home Med. Equipment, Elkhart, Ind., 2003. Capt. U.S. Army, 1974—84. Mem.: Ind. Assn. for Home and Hospice Care. Office: St Joseph VNA Home Care 810 E Park Pl Mishawaka IN 46545 Office Fax: 574-6501. E-mail: lambb@sjrmc.com.

LAMB, DARLIS CAROL, sculptor; b. Wausa, Nebr. d. Lindor Soren and June Berniece (Skalberg) Nelson; m. James Robert Lamb; children: Sherry Lamb Sobh, Michael, Mitchell. BA in Fine Arts, Columbia Pacific U., San Rafael, Calif., 1988, MA in Fine Arts, 1989. Exhibitions include Nat. Arts Club, N.Y.C., 1983 (Catherine Lorillard Wolfe award sculpture, 1983, 1997, C.L. Wolfe Horse's Head award, 1994, Anna Hyatt Huntington cash award, 1995, honorable mention, 1996, medal of honor, 1998, Anna Hyatt Huntington bronze medal, 2000, Paul Manship Meml. award, 2001, Harriet W. Frishmuth Meml. Sculpture award, 2002), 1985, 1989, 1991—93, 1995—97, 1998, 2000, 2001, 2002, 2003, N.Am. Sculpture Exhibit, Foothills Art Ctr., Golden, Colo., 1983—84 (Pub. Svc. Co. of Colo. sculpture award, 1990), 1986—87, 1990—91, Nat. Acad. of Design, 1986, Nat. Sculpture Soc., 1985 (C. Percival Dietch Sculpture prize, 1991), 1991, 1995, 1997, 2003, exhibitions include Loveland Mus. and Gallery, 1990—91, Audubon Artists, 1991, Allied Artists Am., 1992, 1995, Pen and Brush, 1993 (Roman Bronze award, 1995), 1995—97, 1999, 2000, 2001, Colorado Springs Fine Arts Mus., 1996 (Award of Merit), 1998, 2000, All Colo. Exhibit, 2001 (1st prize sculpture), Represented in permanent collections Nebr. Hist. Soc., Am. Lung Assn. of Colo., Benson Park Sculpture Garden, Loveland, U.S. Space Found., Colorado Springs Osteo. Found., Thomas Jefferson H.S., Council Bluffs, Iowa, one-woman shows include Curtis Arts & Humanities Ctr., Greenwood Village, Colo., 2002. Named to Hall of Fame, Thomas Jefferson H.S., 2004. Mem. Catherine Lorillard Wolfe Art Club, N.Am. Sculpture Soc. Office: PO Box 9043 Englewood CO 80111-8000 Office Phone: 303-779-4527. E-mail: dlambsculpture@usa.net.

LAMB, IRENE HENDRICKS, medical researcher; b. Ky., May 9, 1940; d. Daily P. and Bertha (Hendricks) Lamb. Diploma in nursing, Ky. Bapt. Hosp., Louisville; student, Berea (Ky.) Coll., Calif. State U., L.A. RN, Ky. Charge nurse, head nurse acute medicine, med. ICU, surgical ICU, emergency room various med. ctrs., 1963-67; staff nurse rsch. CCU U. So. Calif./L.A. County Med. Ctr., 1968; nurse mgr. clin. rsch. ctr. U. So. Calif./Los Angeles County Med. Ctr., L.A., 1969-74; sr. rsch. nurse cardiology Stanford (Calif.) U. Sch. Medicine, 1974-85, rsch. coord. pvt. clin., 1988; dir. clin. rsch. San Diego Cardiac Ctr., 1989-92; sr. cmty. health nurse Madison County Health Dept., Berea, 1993-97; sr. clin. rsch. mgr. stroke program U. Ky. Coll. Medicine, Lexington, 1997-2001. Co-contbr. numerous articles to med. jours.; contbr. articles to nursing jours., chpts. to med. books. Bd. dirs. Ky. Stroke Assn., 1998—2000. Home: 107 Lorraine Ct Berea KY 40403-1317

LAMB, ISABELLE SMITH, manufacturing executive; b. Charteris, Que., Can., Dec. 14, 1922; came to U.S., 1948; d. Gordon R. and Beatrice L. (Dale) Smith; married, Oct. 2, 1948 (dec.); 1 child, David E. Student, Gowling Bus. Coll., Ottawa, Ont., 1939, Carleton U., 1940-42. Sec. Gatineau Power, Ottawa, 1942; sec. to city treas. Ottawa, 1943; sec. Can. Internat. Paper, Gatineau, Que., 1943-48; adminstrv. asst. to C/B Enterprises Internat., Inc., Hoquiam, Wash., 1948-84, pres., 1984—2000, br. chmn., 2001—. Bd. dirs. U.S. Bank Washington, Seattle, Export Assistance Ctr. Wash., Seattle, N.W. Burn Found., Seattle, Wash. Coun. for Econ. Edn., Seattle, Ind. Colls. of Wash., Seattle. Participant spl. gifts United Way, Aberdeen, Wash., 1988—; active scholarships and philanthropic causes E.K. and Lillian Bishop Found., Seattle, 1985—. Avocations: reading, horseback riding. Office: Enterprises Internat Inc Blaine And Firman St Hoquiam WA 98550

LAMB, SLOANE TRELLES, finance company executive; b. Portland, Oreg., Feb. 14, 1969; d. Neven Patterson Lamb and Marcia Ann Judd; m. Karl Howard Smith, Aug. 25, 2001. Grad., Phillips Exeter Acad., 1986; BA, Columbia U., 1991. V.p. and prin. Sanford C. Bernstein & Co., Inc., New York, NY, 1993—2000; v.p. Alliance Capital, New York, NY, 2000—.

LAMBERT, ALYSIA CONNELL, music educator; b. Atlanta, Jan. 15, 1977; d. Flem Jackson and Tina Ferrell Connell; m. Bobby Lambert, June 30, 2001. BS in Edn., Western Carolina U., 1999; MusM, Ill. State U., 2001. Cert. tchr. Ill. Grad. tchg. asst. Ill. State U., Normal, 1999—2001; music tchr. Flossmoor (Ill.) Hills Elem., 2001—02; choral dir. Lincoln-Way East H.S., Frankfort, Ill., 2002—. Mem.: NEA, ACDA, Music Educators Nat. Conf. Home: Apt 107 306 W 34th St Steger IL 60475 Office: Lincoln-Way East HS 201 Colorado Ave Frankfort IL 60423

LAMBERT, CHRISTINA, telecommunications executive; b. Panama; m. Jim Lambert; children: Bill, Christine, Monica. BA in bus. mgmt., Ind. U.; M in bus. adminstrn., Ind. Wesleyan U. Joined Contel (merged with GTE in 1991), 1974; asst. v.p. process planning GTE, asst. v.p. customer care; v.p., gen. mgr. wireline svcs. PR Telephone, 1999—2003, pres., CEO, 2003—. Office: Telecommunicaciones de Puerto Rico Inc 1515 FD Roosevelt Ave Guaynabo PR 00968*

LAMBERT, CRISTINA, telecommunications executive; b. Panama; m. Jim Lambert; children: Bill, Christine, Monica. BA, U. Ind.; MBA, Ind. Wesleyan U. Various positions including cashier, trainer, coord., customer svc. mgr., state mgr., gen. mgr. Contel/GTE, Ill., 1974—91; asst. v.p. process planning GTE, 1991—99, asst. v.p. customer care, 1991—99; v.p., gen. mgr. wireline svcs. PR Telephone (Verizon), 1999—2003, pres., CEO, 2003—. Named one of Top 5 Elite Women, Hispanic Bus. mag., 2004. Achievements include positioned PR Telefonica Long Distance as the number one long distance provider on PR; led the acquistion of Coqui.net and its integration with PRT.net creating the largest internet svc. provider in Caribbean; responsible for deploying several new products such as VoIP, IP-Virtual Pvt. Networks, Frame Relay, and Asynchronous Transfer Mode capabilities. Office: PR Long Distance PO Box 360998 San Juan PR 00936-0998 Office Phone: 787-775-4000. Office Fax: 787-277-9234.*

LAMBERT, DEBORAH KETCHUM, public relations executive; b. Greenwich, Conn., Jan. 22, 1942; d. Alton Harrington and Robyna (Neilson) Ketchum; m. Harvey R. Lambert, Nov. 23, 1963 (div. 1985); children: Harvey Richard Jr., Eric Harrington. BS, Columbia U., 1965. Researcher, writer The Nowland Orgn., Greenwich, Conn., 1964-67; model Country Fashions, Greenwich, Conn., 1964-67; freelance writer to various newspapers and mags., 1977-82; press sec. Va. Del. Gwen Cody, Annandale, Va., 1981-82; assoc. editor Campus Report, Washington, 1985—; adminstrv. asst. Accuracy in Media, Inc., Washington, 1983-84, dir. pub. affairs, 1985—. TV producer weekly program The Other Side of the Story, 1994—; bd. dirs. Accuracy in Academia, Washington; film script cons. The Seductive Illusion, 1988-89. Columnist: The Eye, The Washington Inquirer, 1984—, Squeaky Chalk, Campus Report, 1985—; contbr. articles to various mags.; producer: The Other Side of the Story, 1993—. Co-founder, mem. Va. Rep. Forum, McLean, 1983—; mem. Rep. Women's Fed. Forum. Mem. Am. Bell Assn., Pub. Rels. Soc. Am., DAR., World Media Assn., Am. Platform Assn. Republican. Presbyterian. Home: 809 Gatestone St Gaithersburg MD 20008 Office: Accuracy in Media Inc 4455 Connecticut Ave NW Washington DC 20008-2328 E-mail: DLam530483@aol.com.

LAMBERT, DEBORAH SUE, data processing professional; b. Dayton, Ohio, Apr. 13, 1952; d. Walter Robert and Charlotte Marie (Rogers) L.; m. Thom Greer, Sept. 3, 1978 (div. 1980); children: Douglas Allen Byrd, Deborah Lynne Byrd. BA, Sinclair Coll., 1983. Teller Wright-Patt Credit Union, Fairborn, Ohio, 1977, auditor, 1977-78, interviewer sr. loan, 1978, loan officer, 1978-79, from asst. mgr. to mgr. remote mem. services, 1979-82, data coordinator, 1982-84; mgr. system quality assurance Summit Info. Systems Inc., Corvallis, Oreg., 1984-87, dir. product mgmt., 1988-89, v.p. on-line svcs., 1989-91; sr. v.p. svcs. div. Summit Info. Systems, Inc., Corvallis, 1991-93; pres. Deb Lambert Consulting Svcs. Inc., 1993-96; sr. v.p. Fiserv Inc., 1996—. Mem. Nat. Credit Union Adminstrn. (cert.), Nat. Assn. Female Execs., Am. Bus. Women's Assn., Ohio Credit Union League (cert. ops.). Avocations: bowling, softball, volleyball. Home: 561 N Hart Blvd Orlando FL 32818-6833 Office: Summit Info Systems 850 SW 35th St Corvallis OR 97333-4046

LAMBERT, JEAN MARJORIE, health care executive; b. Bay City, Mich., Mar. 19, 1943; d. Richard William and Fidelis Rena (LeVasseur) Lambert. BA, Madonna U., Livonia, Mich., 1967; MA, Ea. Mich. U., 1975. Cert. Shiatsu, reflexology. Dir. religious edn. Archdiocese of Detroit, 1970-75, dir. evaluation, 1975-77; assoc. dir. programming Intermedia Found., Santa Monica, Calif., 1977-78; acad. dean St. John Provincial Sem., Plymouth, Mich., 1978-84; asst. dir. quality mgmt. Sisters of Mercy Health Corp., Farmington Hills, Mich., 1984-87; sr. cons. Mercy Collaborative, Livonia, mich., 1987-88; v.p. Mission Mercy Health Sys., Cin., 1988-91, Mission Sisters Providence Health Sys., Springfield, Mass., 1991-99; sr. v.p. Mission Integration Humility of Mary Health Ptnrs., Youngstown, Ohio, 1999—; corp. dir. Mission Integration, Cath. Health Care Ptnrs., Youngstown, Ohio, 2004—. Asst. prof. homiletics St. John Sem., Plymouth, Mich., 1978—85, St. Mary of the Woods Coll., Terre Haute, Ind., 1985, St. Meinrad Sem., Ind., 1984; bd. dirs. Combined Health Appeal of Mass., Providence Ministries, New Eng. Conf. Cath. Healthcare; mem. Am. Reflexology Cert. Bd.; reflexology and therapeutic touch practitioner. Editor: Religious Edn., 1975—77. Bd. adv. Migrant Workers Diocese of Youngstown. Nat. Cath. edn. Assn.-Assn. Theol. Schs. for U.S. and Can. grantee, 1983. Mem.: NAFE, Providence Ministries, Acad. Leadership in Cath. Health Care, Cath. Health Assn. (bd. dirs. New Eng. Conf., mission adv. bd.), Mental Health Assn., Am. Mgmt. Assn., Am. Hosp. Assn., Network, Groundwork, Lions Club of Youngstown (bd. dirs.). Roman Catholic. Avocations: woodcarving, photography, continuing education, shiatsu, reflexology. Office: Humility of Mary Health Ptnrs 1044 Belmont Ave Youngstown OH 44504-1006

LAMBERT, JUDITH A. UNGAR, lawyer; b. N.Y.C., Apr. 13, 1943; d. Alexander Lawrence and Helene (Rosenson) Ungar; m. Peter D. Leibowits, Aug. 22, 1965 (div. 1971); 1 child, David Gary. BS, U. Pa., 1964; JD magna cum laude, U. Miami, 1984. Bar: N.Y. 1985, Fla. 1990. Assoc. Proskauer Rose Goetz & Mendelsohn, N.Y.C., 1984-86, Taub & Fasciana, N.Y.C., 1986-87, Hoffinger Friedland Dobrish Bernfeld & Hasen, N.Y.C., 1987-88, pvt. practice N.Y.C., 1988—. Mem. ABA, N.Y. State Bar Assn., Assn. Bar of City of N.Y., N.Y. Women's Bar Assn. (family law and trusts and estates com.), N.Y. County Lawyers Assn. Avocations: travel, music, theater. Office: 245 E 54th St New York NY 10022-4707 Office Phone: 212-888-7727.

LAMBERT, MEG STRINGER, construction executive, architect, interior designer; b. Selma, Ala., Aug. 10, 1941; d. John Bryant and Margaret Vandiver (Clark) Stringer; m. George Edward Buchner, June 30, 1962 (div. 1972); children: Susan Mayo Buchner, George Bryant Buchner, Robert Carson Buchner; m. Joseph Smith Lambert, June 20, 1975. BS, Auburn U., 1961, postgrad., 1972-73. Lic. real estate broker Ala., home builder Ala., master builder cert. Nat. Assn. Home Builders, cert. constrn. assoc. Nat. Assn. Women in Constrn. Math tchr. Selma (Ala.) Pub. Sch., 1961-62, Oscoda (Mich.) Pub. Sch., 1963-64; real estate sales Stower's Gallery of Homes, Montgomery, Ala., 1974-75; constrn. mgr. Lambert Constrn. Co., Inc., Montgomery, 1975-80, home builder, designer Prattville, Ala., 1984—; sec. estimating dept. Aesco Steel Co., Montgomery, 1981-82; steel bridge estimator and sales assoc. Trinity Industries, Montgomery, 1983-84; pres. Home Touch Builders, Inc., 2000—. Chmn. parade homes Prattville/Millbrook chpt. Home Builders, 1985—87, program chmn., 1985—90; masonry adv. bd. Prattville Vocat. Sch., Prattville, 1994—2001. Author: (book) A History of the Pleasant Hill Baptist Church (1840-1990), 1990. Vice-chmn. Prattville Planning Commn., 1992—95; mem. land use com. City Comprehensive Plan, Prattville, 1994—95; mem. leadership steering com. Autagua County, 1995—98, bd. equalization, 1995—99; chmn. health and welfare com. 1st United Meth. Ch., 1993; mem. beautificiation com. Prattville C. of C., 1992—95; pres. Pleasant Hill Cemetary Assn., 1990—98, 2000—02, South Dallas Hist. Preservation Assn., 2002—. Named Woman of the Yr., Montgomery chpt. Nat. Women in Constrn., 1990. Mem.: Greater Montgomery Home Builders Assn. (mem. longe range planning com. 1986, bd. dirs., exec. com. 2001, Named Builder of the Yr. 1989), Autauga County Heritage Assn. (pres. 1992). Republican. Avocations: genealogy, painting, historical preservation activities, working in political campaigns. Home: 394 Kingston Ridge Rd Prattville AL 36067-1725 Office: Lambert Construction Co Inc PO Box 680656 Prattville AL 36068-0656

LAMBERT, NADINE MURPHY, psychologist, educator; b. Ephraim, Utah; m. Robert E. Lambert, 1956; children[00bf] Laura Allan, Jeffrey. PhD in Psychology, U. So. Calif., 1965. Diplomate Am. Bd. Profl. Psychology, Am. Bd. Sch. Psychology. Sch. psychologist Los Nietos Sch. Dist., Whittier, Calif., 1952-53, Bellflower (Calif.) Unified Sch. Dist., 1953-58; research cons. Calif. Dept. Edn., Los Angeles, 1958-64; dir. sch. psychology tng. program U. Calif., Berkeley, 1964—, asst. prof. edn., 1964-70, asso. prof., 1970-76, prof., 1976—, assoc. dean for student svcs., 1988-94. Mem. Joint Com. Mental Health of Children, 1967-68; cons. state depts. edn., Calif., Ga., Fla.; cons. Calif. Dept. Justice; mem. panel on testing handicapped people Nat. Acad. Scis., 1978-81. Author: School Version of the AAMD Adaptive Behavior Scale, 3d edit., 1993; co-author: (with Wilcox and Gleason) Educationally Retarded Child: Comprehensive Assessment and Planning for the EMR and Slow-Learning Child, 1974, (with Hartsough and Bower) Process for Assessment of Effective Functioning, 1981, (with Windmiller and Turiel) Moral Development and Socialization -- Three Perspectives, 1979; assoc. editor Am. Jour. Orthopsychiatry, 1975-81, Am. Jour. Mental Deficiency, 1977-80, (with McCombs) How Students Learn-Reforming Schools Through Learner-Centered Education, 1998, (with Hylander and Sanoval) Consultee-Centered Consultation, 2004, others. With Hartsough and Sandoval Children's Attention and Adjustment Survey, 1990. Recipient Dorothy Hughes award for outstanding contbn. to ednl. and sch. psychology NYU, 1990, Tobacco Disease Related Rsch. award U. Calif., 1990-94, NIDA, 1994-2001; grantee NIMH, 1965-87, Calif. State Dept. Edn., 1-72, 76-78, NHSTE Dept. Transportation, 1995. Fellow APA (coun. reps. divsn. sch. psychologists, bd. dirs. 1984-87, mem. bd. profl. affairs 1981-83, bd. ednl. affairs 1991-94, chmn. 1992-94, exec. com. divsn. sch. psychology 1994-96, mem. commn. for recognition of specialities in psychology 1993-97, Disting. Svc. award 1980, award for disting. profl. contbns. 1986, award for disting. career contbns. of applications of psychology to edn. and tng. 1999), Nat. Assn. of Sch. Psychologists (hon., Legend in Sch. Psychology 1998), Am. Orthopsychiat. Assn.; mem. NEA, Calif. Assn. Sch. Psychologists (pres. 1962-63, Sandra Goff award 1985). Office: U Calif Dept Education Berkeley CA 94720-1670 E-mail: nlambert@socrates.berkeley.edu.

LAMBERT, REBECCA FOTOUHI, investment company executive; b. Binghamton, N.Y., Jan. 31, 1947; d. Abol Hassan and Eleanor Margaret (Page) Fotouhi; m. Edward S. Bent, June 20, 1987; 1 child, Maxwell S. Attended, Simmons Coll., 1965—68; BA, Williams Coll., 1969; A.M.P., Harvard U., 1982. Adminstrv. asst. Nat. Rep. Senatorial Com., 1975-76, Wallop for U.S. Senate Campaign, Washington, 1976—77; chief of staff Senator Malcolm Wallop, Washington, 1977—80; dep. asst. sec. U.S. Dept. Energy, Washington, 1981—82; assoc. dep. sec. U.S. Dept. Commerce, Washington, 1982—83; dir. corp. comm. CBS Inc., N.Y.C., 1983, Wiley & Rein, 1984—85; pres. Lambert Broadcasting, Inc., N.Y.C., 1985—88; chmn., CEO Lambert Comm., Inc., N.Y.C., 1988—95; fin. exec. Shaker Investments, N.Y.C., 2001—02, Verus Investment Mgmt., LLC, Washington, 2003—. Mem. Reagan Transition Team, 1980, Am. Coun. Young Polit. Leaders; pres., Bellevue Hosp. Assn., 1986-1994. Van Lear fellow, 1978 Episcopalian. E-mail: rlambert@verusinvestment.com.

LAMBERT, SHIRLEY ANNE, marketing professional, publisher; b. Dayton, Ohio, Sept. 28, 1945; d. Norman Frank and Muriel Noreen (Atkinson) Best; m. Joseph Calvin Lambert, Apr. 27, 1968 (div. 1986); children: Joseph Calvin III, James Edward, Kristin Carole. BA in Polit. Sci., Wellesley Coll., 1967; degree in French, Universite de Paris, 1966; MLS, Simmons Coll., 1980. Mktg. asst. G.K. Hall and Co., Boston, 1969-73; cons. Info. Dynamics Corp., Reading, Mass., 1973-75, Pergamon Press, Elmsford, N.Y., 1979-82; computer lab. coordinator Cherry Creek Schs., Aurora, Colo., 1983-85; mktg. dir. Libraries Unltd., Littleton, Colo., 1985—. Author: Clip Art and Dynamic Designs for Libraries and Media Centers, vol. 1; reviewer Am. Reference Books Ann., 1987-88, Library and Info. Sci. Ann., 1986-88. Host parent Am. Field Service, N.Y., 1986-87; selection chmn. Ams. Abroad; Returnee, 1962. Mem. ALA, Rocky Mountain (Colo.) Dressage Assn. (local chpt. sec. 1984-85), Colo. Hunter/Jumper Assn., Phi Beta Kappa, Beta Phi Mu. Republican. Congregationalist. Avocations: horse breeder, duplicate bridge. Office: Librs Unltd PO Box 3988 Englewood CO 80155-3988

LAMBERT, VICKIE ANN, dean emerita, international nursing consultant; b. Hastings, Nebr., Oct. 28, 1943; d. Victor E. and Edna M. (Hein) Wagner; m. Clinton E. Lambert, Jr., June 30, 1974; 1 child, Alexandra. Diploma, Mary Lanning Sch. Nursing, 1964; BSN, U. Iowa, 1966; MSN, Case Western Res. U., 1973; DNSc, U. Calif., San Francisco, 1981. RN, Ga. Acting chair dept. nursing adminstrn. Med. Coll. Ga., Augusta, 1982-84, coord. doctoral program nursing, 1984-85, George Mason U., Fairfax, Va., 1986-88; assoc. dean Case Western Res. U., Cleve., 1989-90; dean Sch. Nursing Med. Coll. Ga., Augusta, 1990-2001. Contbr. articles to profl. jours. Fellow Am. Acad. Nursing; mem. ANA, Sigma Theta Tau, Sigma Xi. Home: 7216 Deborah Dr Falls Church VA 22046-3721 E-mail: Vlambert@mcg.edu.

LAMBERT, WILLIE LEE BELL, mobile equipment company owner, educator; b. Texas City, Tex., Oct. 23, 1929; d. William Henry and Una Oda (Stafford) Bell; m. Eddie Roy Lambert, July 2, 1949; (dec. Mar. 1980); children: Sondra Kay Lambert Bradford, Eddie Lee. Degree in bus., Met. Bus. Coll., 1950; AAS, Coll. of Mainland, 1971; BS, Sam Houston U., 1976. Cert. hand and foot reflexologist, Hatha Yoga instr. Sec. Judges Reddell & Hopkins, Texas City, 1945-47, Union Carbide Chemicals, Texas City, 1947-48, John Powers Modeling, 1948—49, Charles Martin Petroleum, Texas City, 1948-50; acct. Goodyear Co., La Marque, Tex., 1968-70; instr. Coll. of the Mainland, Texas City, 1970—, serials libr., 1970-77, instr., 1970; exec. dir., office mgr. Mobile Air Conditioning, La Marque, 1977-80; owner Kivert, Inc., La Marque, 1982—; ptnr., exec. dir. A/C Mobile Equipment Corp., La Marque, 1988—94. Owner Star Bell Ranch, 1985—. Vol. Union Carbide Chems., Texas City, 1970—, Carbide Retiree Corp., Inc., Texas City, 1980—, Hospice, Galveston, Tex., 1985—, various polit. campaigns, Texas City, 1951-62, MD Anderson Cancer Inst., U. Tex., 1995—; v.p. Coalition on Aging Galveston County, Tex. City, 1990-92; vol. Baylor Coll. Medicine, Houston, 1990—; mem. adv. coun. bd. Galveston County Sr. Citizens, Galveston, 1990—; mem. planning bd. Heart Fund and Cancer Fund, Texas City, 1953-62, Santa Fe (Tex.) St. Citizens, 1990—; benefactor mem. Mainland Mus., Texas City, Tex., 1994—; sec. YMCA, 1947-55; sec. Ladies VFW, 1950-59; leader Girl Scouts Am., 1958-65; v.p. PTA, 1957-60; counselor Bapt. Ch. Camp, 1960-64; v.p. Santa Fe Booster Club, 1963-67; mem. Internat. Platform Assn., 1995—. Named Vol. of Yr., Heights Elem. Sch., Texas City Sch. Dist., 1959, Most Glamorous Grandmother, 1985, Mother of Yr., Texas City/La Marque C. of C., 1990, Unsung Hero award Texas City, 1995, 96, 97, 99, 2001, 02, 03, 04; named to Tex. Women's Hall of Fame, 1984. Mem. Internat. Platform Assn. Republican. Baptist. Avocations: making porcelain dolls and soft sculpture dolls, painting china portraits, sewing, needlework, volunteer work. Home: PO Box 1253 Santa Fe TX 77510-1253

LAMBERTI, DEBORAH LOUISE, psychotherapist; b. New Haven, Conn., May 1, 1953; d. James C. and Eugenia P. Lamberti; m. Akira Odani; stepchildren: Minoru, Shigeru. BA, Wheaton Coll., 1975; MSW, NYU Grad. Sch. of Social Work, 1977. LCSW, cert. social worker, Psychotherapist Greenwich Inst. of Psychoanalytic Studies, 1985. Pvt. practice, 1977—; dir. Fifth Ave Ctr. for Counseling of Psychotherapy, N.Y.C., 1977—2001; adj. faculty NYU, 1979—2001; adj. prof. Fordham U., N.Y.C., 1980—2001; adj. faculty Yeshiva U., N.Y.C., 1980—2001, Hunter Coll., N.Y.C., 1980—2000; cons. Gilda's Club, N.Y.C., 1996—, Internat. Neuroscience Found., N.Y.C., 2001—. Contbr. articles to various profl. jours. Bd. of Dirs. Boys and Girls Village, Milford, Conn., 2000—. Mem.: NY State Soc. Clin. Social Work Psychotherapy, Nat. Assn. Social Workers, Nat. Honor Soc. Avocations: sailing, swimming, cross country skiing, ice skating, photography. Home: 94 Southfield Ave Unit 605 Stamford CT 06902 Office Phone: 212-243-2292.

LAMBERTI, MARJORIE, retired social studies educator; b. New Haven, Sept. 30, 1937; d. James and Anna (Vanacore) L. BA, Smith Coll., 1959; MA, Yale U., 1960, PhD, 1965. Prof. history Middlebury Coll., Vt., 1964—84, Charles A. Dana prof., 1984—2002, ret., 2002, full-time scholar, 2002—. Author: Jewish Activism in Imperial Germany, 1978, State, Society and the Elementary School in Imperial Germany, 1989, The Politics of Education: Teachers and School Reform in Weimar Germany, 2002; mem. editl. bd.: History of Edn. Quar., 1992—94; contbr. articles to profl. jours. Mem. exec. com. Friends of Smith Coll. Librs., 1995—2001. NEH fellow, 1968-69, 81-82, Inst. for Advanced Study, Princeton, 1992-93, The Woodrow Wilson Ctr., Washington, 1997-98; German Acad. Exch. Svc. rsch. grantee, 1988, Rockefeller Archive Ctr. rsch. grantee, 2003. Mem. Am. Hist. Assn., Conf. Group for Ctrl. European History, Leo Baeck Inst., Phi Beta Kappa. Home: 8 S Gorham Ln Middlebury VT 05753-1002 Office: Middlebury Coll Library Middlebury VT 05753

LAMBIRD, MONA SALYER, lawyer; b. Oklahoma City, July 19, 1938; d. B.M. Jr. and Pauline A. Salyer; m. Perry A. Lambird, July 30, 1960; children: Allison Lambird Watson, Jennifer Salyer, Elizabeth Gard, Susannah Lambird Collier. BA, Wellesley Coll., 1960; LLB, U. Md., 1963. Bar: Okla. 1968, Md. Ct. Appeals 1963, U.S. Supreme Ct. 1967. Atty. civil div. Dept. Justice, Washington, 1963-65; sole practice law Balt. and Oklahoma City, 1965-71; mem. firm Andrews Davis Legg Bixler Milsten & Price, Inc. and predecessor firm, Oklahoma City, 1971—. Minority mem. Okla. Election Bd., 1984-99, vice chmn., 1990-94; mem. profl. responsibility tribunal Okla. Supreme Ct., 1984-90; Master of Bench, Luther Bohanan Am. Inn of Ct., Oklahoma City, 1986-98, pres., 1994. Editor: Briefcase, Oklahoma County Bar Assn., 1976. Profl. liaison com. City Oklahoma City, 1974-80; mem. Hist. Preservation of Oklahoma City, Inc., 1970— ; del. Oklahoma County and Okla. State Republican Party Conv., 1971— ; Okla. City Orch. League Inc., legal advisor, 1973—, bd. dirs., 1973— ; incorporator, bd. dirs. R.S.V.P. of Oklahoma County, pres., 1982-83; bd. dirs. Congregate Housing for Elderly, 1978—, Vis. Nurses Assn., 1983-86, Oklahoma County Friends of Library, 1980-91, The Support Ctrs., Inc., 1989-97; trustee Okla. Found. Excellence, 1997—, Okla. Breast Inst., 1997—, Okla. Humanities Coun., 1997—, YMCA, 1998—, Leadership Okla., 1998—. Mem. Okla. Women's Hall of Fame, 1995. Fellow Am. Bar Found.; mem. ABA, Am. Arbitration Assn. (bd. dirs. 1998—, chair Okla. adv. coun. 1997—), Am. Judicature Soc. (trustee 1994-98), Okla. Bar Assn. (pres. labor and employment law sect., bd. govs. 1992-94, pres. 1996), Oklahoma County Bar Assn. (bd. dirs. 1986—, pres. 1990), Oklahoma County Bar Found. (pres. 1988), Jr. League Oklahoma City (bd. dirs. 1973-76, legal advisor), Oklahoma County and State Med. Assn. Aux. (bd. dirs.), Leadership Okla., Class X, Seven Sisters Colls. Club (pres. 1972-76), Women's Econ. Club (steering com. 1981-86). Methodist. Office: 500 W Main St Oklahoma City OK 73102-2253 Home: 688 Glenneyre St Laguna Beach CA 92651-2420

LAMEL, LINDA HELEN, professional society executive, former insurance company executive, former college president, lawyer; b. N.Y.C., Sept. 10, 1943; d. Maurice and Sylvia (Abrams) Treppel; 1 child, Diana Ruth Sands. BA magna cum laude, Queens Coll., 1964; MA, NYU, 1968; JD., Bklyn. Law Sch., 1976. Bar: N.Y. 1977, U.S. Dist. Ct. (3d dist.) N.Y. 1977. Secondary sch. tchr. Farmingdale Pub. Sch., NY, 1965-73; curriculum specialist Yonkers Bd. Edn., Yonkers, 1973-75; program dir. Office of Lt. Gov., Albany, 1975-77; dep. supt. N.Y. State Ins. Dept., N.Y.C., 1977-83; pres. CEO Coll. of Ins., 1983-88; v.p. Tchr.'s Ins. and Annuity Assn., 1988-96; exec. dir. Risk and Ins. Mgmt. Soc., 1997-2000; CEO Claims on Line, Inc., 2000—02; exec. counsel Anderson Kill Loss Advisors, 2002—. Contbr. articles to profl. jours. Campaign mgr. lt. gov.'s primary race, N.Y. State, 1974; v.p. Edl. Found., 1997-2000. Mem. ABA (tort and ins. sect. com. chmn. 1985-86), N.Y. State Bar Assn. (exec. com. ins. sect. 1984-88), Assn. of Bar of City of N.Y. (chmn. med. malpractice com. 1989-91, ins. law com. 1997-98), Am. Mgmt. Assn. (ins. and risk mgmt. coun.), Am. Soc. Workers Compensation Profls. (bd. dirs. 1999—), Fin. Women's Assn., Assn. Profl. Ins. Women (bd. dirs. 2002—, Woman of Yr. 1988), Bklyn. Law Sch. Alumni Assn. (pres.-elect), Phi Beta Kappa Assocs. (bd. dirs. 1992—2002).

LAMI, JUDITH IRENE, advertising executive; b. St. Louis, Nov. 4, 1949; d. Melvin Charles William and Mildred Neva (Kayhart) Linders; m. William George Tomkiel, Dec. 15, 1972 (div.); children: Soteara Tomkiel, William Tomkiel, Kimberli Tomkiel, Jennifer Tomkiel, Christopher Tomkiel; m. Craig Harmon Lami, Apr. 22, 2003. Order filler Baker & Taylor Co., Sommerville, N.J., 1972-74; owner, founder Idea Shoppe, Garden Grove, 1983-90; seamstress, crafts person Cloth World, Anaheim, Calif., 1987-89; mgr. S.M.T. Dental Lab., San Clemente, Calif., 1990-94, pres., 1994—; founder, owner Creative Realm. Author: numerous poems; pub., editor: newsletter Shoppe Talk, 1987—90; editor: Perfectional Smiles, 1999; pub.: Fakatale, 1988. Vol. Reading is Fundamental Program, Garden Grove, 1988—89; freedom writer Amnesty Internat., Garden Grove, 1988—91. Fellow: World Lit. Acad.; mem.: NAFE, Dental Lab Owners Assn., Soc. Scholarly Pub., Nat. Writer's Club, Women, Inc. Avocations: sewing, writing, music, printmaking, gardening.

LAMM, CAROLYN BETH, lawyer; b. Buffalo, Aug. 22, 1948; d. Daniel John and Helen Barbara (Tatakis) L.; m. Peter Edward Halle, Aug. 12, 1972; children: Alexander P., Daniel E. BS, SUNY Coll. at Buffalo, 1970; JD, U. Miami (Fla.), 1973. Bar: Fla., 1973, D.C., 1976, N.Y. 1983. Trial atty. frauds sect. civil div. U.S. Dept. Justice, Washington, 1973-78, asst. chief comml. litigation sect. civil div., 1978, asst. dir., 1978-80; assoc. White & Case, Washington, 1980-84, ptnr., 1984—. Mem. Sec. State's Adv. Com. Pvt. Internat. law, 1987-2002, Secs. Study Com. on Proposal Hague Conv. on Jurisdiction and the Enforcement of Judgements, 1992-2002; arbitrator U.S. Panel of Arbitrators, Internat. Ctr. Settlement of Investment Disputes, 1995-2002; mem. com. on pvt. dispute resolution NAFTA. Mem. editl. adv. bd. Inside Litigation; contbg. editor: Internat. Arbitration Law Rev., 1997—; contbr. articles to legal publs. Fellow Am. Bar Found., Am. Coll. Trial Lawyers; mem. ABA (chmn. young lawyers divsn., bd. govs. 2002—, rules and calendar com., chmn. house membership com., chmn. assembly resolution com., sec. 1984-85, chmn. internat. litigation com. coun. 1991-94, sect. litigation, ho. dels. 1982—, nomination com. 1984-87, chair 1995-96, past D.C. Cir. mem., standing com. fed. judiciary 1992-95, chmn. com. scope and correlation of work 1996-97, commn. on multidisciplinary practice, bd. govs. 2002-), Am. Arbitration Assn. (bd., arbitrator, adv. com. internat. arbitration, exec. com.), Fed. Bar Assn. (chmn. sect. on antitrust and trade regulation), Bar Assn. D.C. (bd. dirs., sec., found. bd.), D.C. Bar (pres. 1997-98, bd. govs. 1987-93, steering com. litigation sect.), Am. Law Inst. (coun., named Women Laywer of the Yr., 2002), Women's Bar Assn. D.C., Am. Soc. Internat. Law, Am. Indonesian C. of C. (bd. dirs.), Am. Uzbekistan C. of C. (bd. dirs., sec., gen. counsel), Am. Turkish Friendship Coun. (bd. dirs., chair), Nat. Women's Forum, Columbia Country Club, Manchester Country Club, Stratton Mountain Club. Democrat. Home: 2801 Chesterfield Pl NW Washington DC 20008-1015 Office: White and Case 601 13th St NW Washington DC 20005-3807 E-mail: clamm@whitecase.com.

LAMMA, CANDACE MCDANIEL, guidance counselor, primary school educator, elementary school educator; b. Warrenton, Va., Oct. 1, 1955; d. Roy Franklin and Bette Anne (Slusher) McD.; m. Philip Daniel Lamma, Jan. 2, 1988; children: Anne-Ashleigh, Paige. BS, Longwood Coll., 1977; MA, Va. Tech., 1991. Cert. elem. tchr. K-3, Va., elem. guidance counselor. Tchr. Craig County Schs., New Castle, Va., 1977-79, Rappahannock County Schs., Washington, Va., 1979-88, counselor, 1989—. Chmn. gifted and talented screening com., Rappahannock County Schs., Washington, Va., 1989—, mem. gifted and talented adv. bd., 1989—, cons., 1989—, chmn. food drive, 1989—, child study team, 1989, virtue curriculum com., 1994—. Mem. choir Flint Hill (Va.) United Methodist Ch., 1982, Sunday sch. tchr., 1983—, supt., 1986—, pres. Women's Mission Group, 1995—; asst. leader 4-H Cloverbuds, Rappahannock County, 1992—; com. mem. 10K Fodderstack Race Rappahannock County, 1983—; helper Brownies, Flint Hill, Va., 1994—. Mem. Am. Counseling Assn., Va. Counseling Assn., Va. Sch. Counseling Assn., Apple Valley Counseling Assn., Rappahannock County Heart Assn. (resdl. chmn. 1992-94), Alpha Delta Kappa (recording sec. 1994—), Alpha Delta Pi. Methodist. Avocations: gardening, collecting bears, water sports, crafts, reading. Home: PO Box 368 Flint Hill VA 22627-0368 Office: Rappahannock County Elem Sch 34 School House Rd Washington VA 22747-1907

LA MONICA, PATRICIA C. real estate broker; d. Harold L. and Beatrice L. Carey; children: Shelley, Joseph Jr. Grad. h.s., Rochester, N.Y. Realtor Allen Tate Realtors, 1989—2000, Re/Max Lake and Land, 2000—01; prin., owner Keller Williams Realty, NC, 2001—. Owner KW.com; mem. nominating com. Charlotte Bd. Realtors, NC, 2002—03. Mem. bus. adv. com. Nat. Rep. Congl. Com., hon. chmn. Recipient Nat. Leadership award, Nat. Rep. Congl. Com., 2003. Home: 1307 Torrence Cir Davidson NC 28036 Office: Keller Williams Realty 514 Williamson Rd Ste 114 Mooresville NC 28117 Office Phone: 704-799-3700. Business E-Mail: patlamonica@kw.com.

LAMONT, LEE, music management executive; b. Queens, N.Y. m. August Tagliamonte, Apr. 30, 1951; 1 child, Leslie Lamont. With Nat. Concerts & Artists Corp., N.Y.C., 1955-58; asst. Sol Hurok Concerts, N.Y.C., 1958-67; person rep. for concerts, rec. and TV Isaac Stern, N.Y.C., 1968-76; v.p. ICM Artists Ltd., N.Y.C., 1976-85; pres. ICM Artists Ltd. and ICM Artists (London) Ltd., N.Y.C., 1985-95, chmn. bd. dirs., 1995—2002, chmn. emeritus, 2002—. Former mem. adv. com. Hannover (Germany) Internat. Violin Competition. Former mem. bd. overseers Curtis Inst. Music. Mem. Ams. for the Arts, Japan Soc., Asia Soc., Am. Symphony Orch. League (bd. dirs.), Bohemian Club. Avocations: painting, sculpture. Office: ICM Artists Ltd 40 W 57th St Fl 16 New York NY 10019-4098 E-mail: llamont@icmtalent.com.

LAMONT, ROSETTE CLEMENTINE, Romance languages educator, theatre journalist, translator; b. Paris; arrived in US, 1941, naturalized, 1946; d. Alexandre and Loudmilla (Lamont) L. BA, Hunter Coll., 1947; MA, Yale U., 1948, PhD, 1954. Tutor Romance langs. Queens Coll., CUNY, 1950-54, instr., 1954-61, asst. prof., 1961-64, assoc. prof., 1965-67, prof., 1967-96; mem. doctoral faculties, comparative lit., theatre, French and women's studies cert. program CUNY, 1968-96, prof. emeritus PhD program in theater, 1996—. State Dept. envoy Scholar Exch. Program, USSR, 1974; rsch. fellow, 1976; lectr. Alliance Francaise, Maison Francaise of NYU; vis. prof. Sorbonne, Paris, 1985-86; vis. prof. theatre Sarah Lawrence Coll., 1994—. Author: The Life and Works of Boris Pasternak, 1964, De Vive Voix, 1971, Ionesco, 1973, The Two Faces of Ionesco, 1978, Ionesco's Imperatives: The Politics of Culture, 1993, Women on the Verge, 1993; translator: Days and Memory, 1990, Auschwitz and After, 1995 (ALTA prize), Brazen, 1996, The Storm, 1999; also contbr. to various books; author, guest editor The Metaphysical Farce issue Collages and Bricolages, 1996-97; mem. editl. bd. Western European Stages, also contbg. editor; European corr. Theatre Week: Columbia Dictionary of Modern European Literature; fgn. corr. Stages; reviewer France-Amérique-Le Figaro. Decorated chevalier, then officier des Palmes Academiques, officier des Arts et Lettres (France); named to Hunter Coll. Hall of Fame, 1991; Guggenheim fellow, 1973-74; Rockefeller Found. humanities fellow, 1983-84. Mem. PEN, MLA, Am. Soc. Theatre Research, Internat. Brecht Soc., Drama Desk (voting mem.), Internat. Assn. Theatre Critics, Phi Beta Kappa, Sigma Tau Delta, Pi Delta Phi. Clubs: Yale. Home: 260 W 72nd St Apt 9D New York NY 10023-2822

LAMOTTA, CONNIE FRANCES, communications consultant, executive coach; b. Bronx, N.Y., Oct. 10, 1942; d. Salvatore Charles and Mary Moscatiello LaMotta; children: Raphael, Peter, David. BA, SUNY, Albany, 1969. Activities coord. San Diego Assn. for the Retarded, 1970-72; edn. program dir. Edn. Ctrs. of Newark Archdiocese, 1973-79; dir. comm. tng. Riverside Eating Disorder Clinic, Secaucus, N.J., 1979-84; comm. coord. Sun Chem. Corp., N.Y.C., 1984-86; pub. rels. dir. Nat. Coffee Assn., N.Y.C., 1986-87; v.p. pub. rels. comms. Direct Mktg. Assn., N.Y.C., 1987-99, sr. v.p. pub. rels. comms., 1987-99; pres. La Motta Strategic Comms., Inc., N.Y.C., 1999—. E-mail: connie@lamottastrategic.com.

LAMOTTE, JANET ALLISON, retired management specialist; b. Norfolk, Va., Mar. 3, 1942; d. Charles Nelson Jr. and Geneva Elizabeth (Baird) Johnson; m. Larry LaMotte, Aug. 30, 1964 (div. Aug. 1979); children: Lisa Renee LaMotte Buchholz, Lori Louise. AA, Rose State Coll., 1982; BA, U. Ctrl. Okla., 1984; MA in Human Rels., U. Okla., 1986. Clk./typist U.S.

Army, Washington, 1960, Fort Belvoir, Va., 1961, Dallas, 1961, IRS, Dallas, 1962, Richmond, Va., 1962-63, sec., 1963-64; pers. asst. State Bd. Control, Austin, Tex., 1964-65; procurement clk. FAA, Oklahoma City, 1965-66; clk./typist DLA, Alexandria, Va., 1978, IRS, Oklahoma City, 1978-79, Tinker AFB, 1979; acctg. clk., 1980-81; clk./stenographer, 1980-81; sec., 1981-82; supply specialist, 1982-87; worldwide inventory mgmt. specialist, 1987-98. Safety chmn. Kensler Elem. Sch. PTA, Wichita, 1974-75; vol. CONTACT Crisis Helpline, 1986-89. Federally Employed Women scholar, 1984. Mem.: AARP, AAUW, Tinker (Okla.) Mgmt. Assn. (membership, ticket monitor 1994—98, scholar 1981—85), Okla. Air Force Assn. (v.p. comms. 1995—97, exec. sec. 1996—97, Okla. Mem. of Yr. 1996, Nat. Exceptional Svc. award 1996), Air Force Assn. (v.p. pub. rels. Gerrity chpt. 1994, v.p. comm. 1995—98, Nat. medal of Merit 1995, Nat. Exceptional Svc. award 1996, Chpt. Exceptional Svc. award 1998), Nat. Assn. Ret. Fed. Employees, Am. Bus. Women's Assn. (v.p. membership downtown reflections chpt. 1992—93), Okla. Geneal. Soc., Nat. WWII Meml. (charter mem.), Okla. Hist. Soc., Toastmasters (edn. v.p. 1988, pres. Tinker chpt. 1989, area gov. 1991—92, area editor K-3 Newsletter 1992—93, awards), Rural Retreat (Va.) Hist. Soc., Morrow County (Ohio) Geneal. Soc., Pulaski County (Ky.) Hist. Soc., Nat. Trust for Hist. Preservation. Methodist. Avocations: history, writing, genealogy, computer, reading. Home: 9525 Ridgeview Dr Oklahoma City OK 73120-3419 E-mail: jlamott99@msn.com.

LAMOUREUX, GLORIA KATHLEEN, nurse, consultant, retired military officer; b. Billings, Mont., Nov. 2, 1947; d. Laurits Bungaard and Florence Esther (Nielsen) Nielsen; m. Kenneth Earl Lamoureux, Aug. 31, 1973 (div. Feb. 1979). BS, U. Wyo., 1970; MS, U. Md., 1984. Staff nurse, ob-gyn DePaul Hosp., Cheyenne, Wyo., 1970; enrolled USAF, 1970, advanced through grades to col.; staff nurse ob-gyn dept. 57th Tactical Hosp., Nellis AFB, Nev., 1970-71, USAF Hosp., Clark AB, Republic Philippines, 1971-73; charge nurse ob-gyn dept. USAF Regional Hosp., Sheppard AFB, Tex., 1973-75, staff nurse ob-gyn dept. MacDill AFB, Fla., 1976-79; charge nurse ob-gyn dept. USAF Med. Ctr., Andrews AFB, Md., 1979-80, MCH coord., 1980-82; chief nurse USAF Clinic, Eielson AFB, Alaska, 1984-86, Air Force Systems Command Hosp., Edwards AFB, Calif., 1986-90; comdr. 7275th Air Base Group Clinic, Italy, 1990-92, 42d Med. Group, Loring AFB, Maine, 1992-94; 347th Med. Group, Moody AFB, Ga., 1994-96; chief nursing svcs. divsn. Hdqrs. Air Edn. and Tng. Command, Randolph AFB, Tex., 1996-2000. Ind. cons. Customers First Cons., Universal City, 2000—, v.p., 2000—; sr. cons. Karta Tech., Inc., San Antonio, 2002—. Mem. Assn. Women's Health, Obstetric, and Neonatal Nurses (sec.-treas. armed forces dist. 1986-88, vice-chmn. armed forces dist. 1989-91), Air Force Assn., Bus. and Profl. Women's Assn. (pub. rels. chair Prince George's County chpt. 1981-82), Sigma Theta Tau. Republican. Lutheran. Avocations: reading, needlework, piano, photography. Home: 13515 Thessaly Universal City TX 78148-2810 E-mail: glamoureux@karta.com.

LAMPERT, ELEANOR VERNA, retired human resources specialist; b. Porterville, Calif., Mar. 23, d. Ernest Samuel and Violet Edna (Watkins) Wilson; m. Robert Mathew Lampert, Aug. 23, 1935; chidren: Sally Lu Winton, Lary Lampert, Carol R. John. Student in bus. fin., Porterville Jr. Coll., 1977-78; grad., Anthony Real Estate Sch., 1971; student, Laguna Sch. of Art., 1972, U. Calif., Santa Cruz, 1981. Bookkeeper Porterville (Calif.) Hos., 1956-71; real estate sales staff Ray Realty, Porterville, 1973; sec. Employment Devel. Dept. State of Calif., Porterville, 1973-83; orientation and tng specialist CETA employees, 1976-80. Sec. Employer Adv. Group, 1973-80, 81—. Author: Black Bloomers and Han-Ga-Ber, 1986. Mem. U.S. Senatorial Business Adv. Bd., 1981-84, Rep. Nat. congl. Com., 1982-88, Sierra View Hosp. Vol. League, 1988-89 (pres.); charter mem. Presdl. Republican Task Force, 1981—, Republican National Committee; vol. Calif Hosp. Assn., 1983-89, Calif. Spl. Olympics Spirit Team, Sonora Cmty. Hospital Oak Plus League, Special Olympics Northern Calif. partner. Recipient Merit Cert., Gov. Pat Brown, State of Calif., 1968. Mem. Lindsay Olive Growers, Sunkist Orange Growers, Am. Kennel Club, Internat. Assn. Personnel in Employment Security, Calif. State Employes Assn. (emeritus Nat. Wildlife Fedn., NRA, Friends of Porterville Library, Heritage Found., DAR (Kaweah chpt. rec. sec. 1988—), Internat. Platform Assn., Dist. Fedn. Women's Clubs (recording sec. Calif. chpt. 1988—), Ky. Hist. Soc., Women's Club of Calif. (pres. Porterville chpt. 1988-89, dist. rec. sec. 1987-89), Mo. Rep. Women of Taney County, Internat. Sporting and Leisure Club. Ladies Aux, VFW (No. 5168 Forsyth,Mo.), Ozark Walkers League, Women of the Moose Lodge, Humane Soc. U.S. Republican.

LAMPERTI, CLAUDIA JANE MCKAY, editor; b. Gooding, Idaho, Jan. 29, 1934; d. Francis Howard and Georgia Irene (Moore) McKay; m. John Williams Lamperti, Aug. 17, 1957; children: Matthew, Steven, Aaron, Noelle. BA, UCLA, 1955. Printer, publisher New Victoria Printer & Publisher, Lebanon, N.H., 1975-85; editor New Victoria Publisher, Norwich, Vt., 1976—. Author: Promise of the Rose Stone, 1986, Kali Connection, 1995, Twist of Lime, 1997; editor: Woman Space, 1980. Office: PO Box 27 Norwich VT 05055-0027

LAMPING, KATHRYN G. medical educator, medical researcher; BS in Biology, U. Ill., 1976; MS in Pharmacology, Med. Coll. Wis., 1982, PhD in Pharmacology, 1983. Postdoctoral rsch. fellow Dept. Internal Medicine, U. Iowa, Iowa City, 1983-86, asst. rsch. scientist, 1986-89, adj. asst. prof., 1989-95, asst. prof., 1995—. Contbr. articles to profl. jours. Mem. Am. Heart Assn. (Established Investigator award 1995), Am. Physiol. Soc., Microcirculatory Soc. Office: U Iowa Ctr on Agin 2159 Westlawn S Iowa City IA 52242-1100

LAMPL, PEGGY ANN, public policy administrator; b. N.Y.C., Dec. 12, 1930; d. Joseph and Alice L. BA, Bennington Coll., 1952. Dir. program devel. dept. mental health AMA, Chgo., 1962-66; spl. asst. NIMH, HEW, Washington, 1967-69; public relations dir. LWV, Washington, 1969—73, exec. dir., 1973—78; dep. asst. Sec. of State for congressional relations Dept. State, Washington, 1978-81; dep. dir. Iris Systems Devel., 1982-83; exec. dir. Children's Def. Fund, Washington, 1984-89, LWV, Washington, 1989—90; project mgr. Crimes of War, W.W. Norton, 1999; founder Project Vote Smart, Washington, 1993—; bd. dirs. Crimes of War Project, Washington, 1998—. Home: 2500 Q St NW Washington DC 20007-4373

LAMY, M(ARY) REBECCA, consultant, land developer, government official; b. Ft. Bragg, N.C., Nov. 21, 1929; d. Charles Joseph and Sarah Esther (Koonce) Lamy. BA, U. N.C., Greensboro, 1952. Procurement analyst Air Force Mil. Interdept. Purchase Request Mgmt. Office, Washington, 1958-60, procurement and fiscal officer, 1960-68; budget analyst Naval Air Sys. Command, Washington, 1968-69, indsl. specialist, 1969-71, Armament Devel. and Test Ctr., Eglin AFB, Fla., 1971-74, Def. Logistics Agy., Alexandria, Va., 1974-81; logistics mgmt. specialist Strategic Sys. Project Office, Dept. Navy, Washington, 1981-82; procurement analyst Hdqrs. Dept. Army, Washington, 1982-85. Emeritus mem. Onslow Mus. Found. Bd., Richlands, NC, Onslow Meml. Hosp. Aux., Jacksonville, NC, 1985—91. Recipient Outstanding Performance awards USAF, 1956, 65, 72, 73, Quality award Def. Logistics Agy., 1979, Outstanding Performance award, 1978, 79, Exceptional Svc. award, 1983, 84, 85, Comdr.'s award Hdqrs. Dept. Army, 1985, others. Mem. U. N.C. at Greensboro Alumni Assn.. Harriet Elliott Soc., Unbroken Band.

LANAM, LINDA LEE, lawyer; b. Ft. Lauderdale, Fla., Nov. 21, 1948; d. Carl Edward and Evelyn (Bolton) L. BS, Ind. U., 1970, JD, 1975. Bar: Ind. 1975, Pa. 1979, U.S. Dist. Ct. (no. and so. dists.) Ind. 1975, U.S. Supreme Ct. 1982, Va. 1990. Atty., asst. counsel Lincoln Nat. Life Ins. Co., Ft. Wayne, Ind., 1975-76, 76-78; atty., mng. atty. Ins. Co. of N.Am., Phila., 1978-79, 80-81; legis. liaison Pa. Ins. Dept., Harrisburg, 1981-82, dep. ins. commr., 1982-84; exec. dir., Washington rep. Blue Cross and Blue Shield Assn., Washington, 1984-86; v.p. and sr. counsel Union Fidelity Life Ins. Co., Am. Patriot Health Ins. Co., etc., Trevose, Pa., 1986-89; v.p., gen. counsel, corp. sec. The Life Ins. Co. Va., Richmond, 1989-97, sr. v.p., gen. counsel, corp. sec., 1997-98, also bd. dirs.; v.p., dep. gen. counsel Am. Coun. Life Insurers, Washington, 1999—. Chmn. adv. com. health care legis. Nat. Assn. Ins. Commrs., 1985-87, chmn. long term care, 1986-87, mem. tech. resource com. on cost disclosure and genetic testing, 1993-98; mem. tech. adv. com. Health Ins. Assn. Am., 1986-89; mem. legis. com. Am. Coun. Life Ins., 1994-96, mem. market conduct com., 1997-98. Contbr. articles to profl. jours. Pres. Phila. Women's Network, 1980—81; chmn. city housing code bd. appeals Harrisburg, 1985—86; bd. dirs. Shakespeare Theatre Guild, 2001—. Mem. ABA, Richmond Bar Assn. Republican. Presbyterian. Office: Am Coun Life Ins 1001 Pennsylvania Ave NW Washington DC 20004-2505

LANCASTER, JEANETTE (BARBARA LANCASTER), dean, nursing educator; BSN, U. Tenn.; MSN, Case Western Res. U.; PhD, U. Okla. Staff nurse U. Tenn.; nurse clinician Univ. Hosps. of Cleve.; assoc. prof. psychiat. nursing Tex. Christian U.; coord. cmty. health nursing U. Ala., Birmingham, chair master's degree program Sch. Nursing; dean, prof. Sch. Nursing Wright State U., Dayton, Ohio; now dean, prof. nursing U. Va., Charlottesville; assoc. dir. patient care svcs. U. Va. Health Scis. Ctr., Charlottesville. Former chmn. bd. dirs. Va. Statewide Area Health Edn. Ctr.; former pres. Charlottesville and Albemarle divsn. Am. Heart Assn.; presenter in field. Author: Community and Public Health Nursing: Nursing Issues in Leading and Managing Change; editor: Family and Cmty. Health; contbr. Bd. dirs. U. Va. Women's Ctr., Hospice of the Piedmont. Recipient Disting. Alumni award Frances Payne Bolton Sch. Nursing, Case We. Res. U., 1984, Outstanding Alumni award, U. Tenn. Coll. Nursing, 1985, honored with establishment of Jeanette Lancaster Professorship in Nursing, 1999. Fellow: Am. Acad. Nursing; mem.: Am. Assn. Colls. Nursing and Hospice Piedmont (bd. dirs.). E-mail: lancaster@virginia.edu.

LANCASTER, JOAN ERICKSEN, state supreme court justice; b. 1954; BA magna cum laude, St. Olaf Coll., Northfield, Minn., 1977; spl. diploma in social studies, Oxford U., 1976; JD cum laude, U. Minn., 1981. Atty. LeFevere, Lefler, Kennedy, O'Brien & Drawz, Mpls., 1981-83; asst. U.S. atty. Dist. Minn., Mpls., 1983-93; shareholder Leonard, Street and Deinard, Mpls., 1993-95; dist. ct. judge 4th Jud. Dist., Mpls., 1995-98; assoc. justice Minn. Supreme Ct., 1998—2002; judge U.S. Dist. Ct., St. Paul, 2002—.

LANCASTER, KARINE R. city health department administrator; b. Australia; MPH, U. Tex. Health Sci. Ctr., Houston, 1994. Pvt. practice, pediatrician, Dallas, 1978—; med. dir., health authority Dallas Co. Dept. Health and Human Svcs., Dallas, 1997—. Office: Dallas Co Dept Health and Human Svcs 2377 N Stemmons Fwy Dallas TX 75207-2710

LANCASTER, SALLY RHODUS, retired non-profit executive, consultant; b. Gladewater, Tex., June 28, 1938; d. George Lee and Milly Marie (Meadows) Rhodus; m. Olin C. Lancaster, Jr., Dec. 23, 1960; children: Olin C. III, George Charles, Julie Meadows. BA magna cum laude, So. Meth. U., 1960, MA, 1979; PHD, Tex. A&M, Commerce, 1983. Tchr. English pub. schs., 1960-61, 78-79; exec. v.p., sr. advisor Meadows Found., Inc., Dallas, 1979-96, also trustee and dir. Trustee So. Meth. U., 1980—88, East Tex. State U., regent, 1987—93; Tex. del. White House Conf. on Tourism, 1995; dir. Inst. Nautical Archaeology, 1988—2001; dir. emeritus Meadows Found.; mem. adv. bd. Cmtys. Found. Tex., 1987—2002. Named Disting. Alumni, So. Meth. U., Tex. A&M Commerce; recipient Ruth Lester award Tex. Hist. Commn., 1998; grantee-making and evaluations coms. Jacksonville Cmty. Found., 2000-01. Mem. Plantation Ladies Assn. (pres. 2000-01), Philos. Soc. Tex., Phi Beta Kappa. Presbyterian. E-mail: srhodusl@aol.com.

LANCIOTTI, JUDI D. art educator; d. Nicholas Salvatore Incaprera and Margaret Mary McLaughlin-Incaprera; m. Victor A. Lanciotti; children: Stephen A., Jason V., Nicole Rae Mary. BS, Towson State U., 1978; MA, Coll. Notre Dame, 1999. Art educator St. William of York Sch., Balt., 1991—96, Howard County Ctr. for the Arts, Ellicott City, Md., 1993—99, St. Louis Sch., Clarksville, Md., 1995—2000, St. Augustine Sch., Elkridge, Md., 1999—2000; art educator, fine arts chairperson Mount de Sales Acad., Catonsville, Md., 2000—. Mem. steering com. Celebration of the Arts, Balt., 2001—. Author: Prayers with Pizzazz, 1995. Mem.: Nat. Art Educators Assn. Roman Catholic. Avocations: art, writing. Home: 415 Rockway Rd Catonsville MD 21228

LAND, IRENE STOKVIS, marketing executive; b. N.Y.C., Sept. 29, 1939; d. Joseph William and Beatrice Winifred (Turetsky) Stokvis; m. Paul Ivan Land, Nov. 5, 1965; 1 child, Jonathan Brock. BA, CUNY, Queens, 1961. Assoc. book rev. editor Library Jour., N.Y.C., 1961-76; mgr. advt. and promotion Elsevier Sci. Pub. Co., N.Y.C., 1980-86; mgr. promotion Springer-Verlag, N.Y.C., 1986-88; freelance personal mgr. for actors, 1988-92; freelance mktg. and media comm., 1992—. Avocations: painting, piano, writing. Home: 401 E 34th St Apt N5B New York NY 10016-4921

LAND, JUDITH BROTEN, stockbroker; b. Newark, July 27, 1951; d. Robert Allan and Marjorie (Frederickson) Broten; m. Andre Paul Land, Jan. 6, 1973; children: Ian Sherard, Margo Caryn. Student, Hood Coll., 1969-70, Denver U., 1970-71, Monmouth Coll., 1971-72, Fla. Atlantic U., 1976-77. Lic. ins. agent Fla. Brokerage ops. Fahnestock & Co., Red Bank, NJ, 1973; with ops. dept. Thomson McKinnon, South Orange, N.J., 1973-75, Boca Raton, Fla., 1977-80; sales trainee Butcher & Singer Inc., Boca Raton, 1980-81, stockbroker, 1981-85, A.G. Edwards & Sons, Inc., Boca Raton, 1985—. Lectr. Palm Beach County Schs., Boca Raton, 1987-95, Palm Beach County Librs., 1990-91; daily stock market radio reporter Sta. WDBF-AM, Delray Beach, Fla., 1979-81. Cmty. theater performer, song composer; mem. Singing Pines Children's Mus., Boca Raton, Fla., 1989, Young Women of the Arts, Boca Raton, 1989, C. of C., 1990—92, Guardianship Assn., Palm Beach, 2001—03, C. of C., 2004. Republican. Episcopalian. Avocations: golf, photography. Office: AG Edwards & Sons Inc 1900 Glades Rd Ste 451 Boca Raton FL 33431-8548

LAND, JUDY M. real estate broker; b. Phoenix, Oct. 6, 1945; d. Sanford Karl Land and D. Latanne (Hilburn) Land Krauss; divorced; children: Neal McNeil III, Latanne. AA in Econs., Merritt Coll., 1967; MBA, Brklyn Bus. Sch., 1984. Cert. real estate developer, broker and appraiser. With real estate sales dept. Odmark/Welch Co/Mesa Realty, San Diego, 1971-76; v.p. Brehm Communities, San Diego, 1977; mgr. investment div. Ayers Realty, Encinitas, Calif., 1978-79; asst. v.p. Harry L. Summers Inc., La Jolla, Calif., 1982-85; pres. The Land Co., Carlsbad, Calif., 1979-90; nat. mktg. dir. Nat. Safety Assocs., San Diego, 1990—93; pres. Land Divsn. Prudential Calif. Realty, Rancho Santa Fe, Calif., 1996—. Fundraiser Hunger Project, 1979-86, Youth at Risk, 1984-86, Multiple Sclerosis Soc., 1984; mem. exec. com. U.S. Olympics, 1984; bd. dirs. Polit. Policies Com., San Diego, 1986. Mem. Nat. Assn. Real Estate Appraisers, Nat. Assn. Women Execs., Nat. Assn. Home builders, Home Builders Council (pres. 1985), Building Industry Assn. San Diego (bd. dirs. 1985, sale and mktg. coun.), Econ. Devel. Corp. San Diego (membership com. 1984), Women Comml. Real Estate, Life Spike Club. Avocations: tennis, skiing, swimming. Home: PO Box 676114 Rancho Santa Fe CA 92067-6114

LAND, TERRI LYNN, state official; m. Dan Hibma; children: Jessica Hibma, Nicholas Hibma. BA in Political Sci., Hope Coll., Holland, MI. Clerk Kent County, 1992—2000; sec. of state State of Mich., 2003—. Atty. Grievance Commn., 1999—2002; sec. Atty. Grievance Commn., 2001—02; mem. Secchia Millennium Commn., 2000, Cmty. Archives & Rsch. Ctr., 1997—, 54 Jefferson Study Com., 1997—. Mem. Grandville Rotary, 1990—99; mem. bd. dirs. Am. Heart Assn., 1995—99, Junior Achivement Alumni Bd., 1997—99, Project Rehab Found., 1997—98. Mem.: Mich. Supreme Ct. Hist. Soc., US Supreme Ct. Hist. Soc., Women's Resource Ctr. (v.p., bd. of dirs. 2001—02), Grand Rapids Pub. Mus. Found. Bd., Grand Rapids Rotary, Grand Rapids Early Morning Riser's Club, Friends of John Ball Zoological Park, Byron Ctr. Fine Arts Found. (pres. 1999—), Friends of Van Andel Mus., Frederick Meijer Gardens, Grand Rapids C. of C., Byron Ctr. Hist. Soc. (pres. 1990—92), Byron Ctr. Cmty. Fine Arts Coun., Potters House Found. (mem., bd. dirs. 1997—). Office: Treasury Bldg 430 West Allegan St 1st Fl Lansing MI 48918

LANDAU, LAURI BETH, accountant, tax consultant; b. Bklyn., July 21, 1952; d. Jack and Audrey Carolyn (Zuckernick) L. BA, Skidmore Coll., 1973; postgrad., Pace U., 1977-79. CPA, N.Y. Mem. staff Audrey Z. Landau, CPA, Suffern, N.Y., 1976-78, Ernst & Whinney, N.Y.C., 1979-80, mem. sr. staff, 1980-82, supr., 1982-84; mgr. Arthur Young & Co., N.Y.C., 1984-87, prin., 1987-89; sr. mgr. Ernst & Young, N.Y.C., 1989-92; ptnr. Landau & Landau, Pomona, N.Y., 1992—. Ptnr. Audrey Z. Landau & Co., Wilmington, Vt., 1995—; spkr. World Trade Inst., N.Y.C., 1987—, Nat. Fgn. Trade Coun., N.Y.C., 1989—. Composer songs. Career counselor Skidmore Coll., Saratoga Springs, N.Y., 1977—; mem. leadership com. Class of 1973, 83-85, pres., 1985-93, fund chmn., 1987-88, mem. planned gift com., 1989—. N.Y. State Regents scholar, 1970. Mem. Nat. Conf. CPA Practitioners, N.Y. State Soc. CPAs, Rockland Bus. Assn., Skidmore Coll. Alumni Assn. (mem. nominating com. 1989-92). Skidmore Alumni Club. Democrat. Avocations: music, ballet, photography, sports. Office: 26 Firemans Memorial Dr Pomona NY 10970-3553 E-mail: lauri@landauandlandau.com.

LANDAU-CRAWFORD, DOROTHY RUTH, retired social services administrator; b. Staten Island, NY, Oct. 5, 1957; d. Robert August and Dorothy Faith (Schaut) Landau; m. John W. Crawford, Oct. 21, 1989; 1 child, Jacqueline Lauren. AS, SUNY, Farmingdale, 1977; BS in Biology, Wagner Coll., 1979. Sci. tchr. Bais Yaakov, S.I., 1979-81; dental asst. Dr. Marvin Freeman, S.I., 1981-82; office mgr. Dr. Bennett C. Fidlow, S.I., 1982-85; polit. aide to S.I. Borough Pres. S.I. Borough Pres., 1985-89; exec. dir. Richmond Sr. Svcs. Project Share, 1990—2000; ret., 2000. V.p. N.J. Shared Housing Assn., regional dir. Nat. Shared Housing Resouces Ctr., 1995—; environ. chmn. S.I. League for Better Govt., 1984—; pres. Tottenville Improvement Council Inc., Staten Island, 1985—. Dem. candidate N.Y. State Assembly 60th Dist., 1986, dist. leader; dir. cmty. bds. S.I. Borough Pres.'s Office; founder, pres. environ. group S.I.L.E.N.T., S.I., 1985; 1st v.p. 123d Cmty. Coun., L.I., 1986; social chmn. South Shore Dem. Club; founding mem. Friends of Clay Pit Pond Park; active Protectors of Pine Oak Woods Inc., Roserio Alliotta Dem. Club, Dem. Orgn. Richmond; trustee S.I. Bd. Leukemia Soc. Am., 1988—, chair Celebrity Waiters Luncheon; spl. election candidate for 51st Councilmatic Dist., 1994. Recipient Cmty. Activist award Office of pres. S.I. Borough, 1987. Mem. NAFE, Bus. and Profl. Women (young careerist for S.I.). Avocations: photography, sports, ceramics, youth programs. Home: 370 Jackson Mills Rd Jackson NJ 08527-4446

LANDAUER, ELVIE ANN WHITNEY, humanities educator, writer; b. Detroit, Dec. 10, 1937; d. Augustus and Leona (Green) Moore; m. Thomas Whitney, 1963 (div. 1978); m. Ernest Landauer, Dec. 31, 1987. BA, Calif. State U., L.A., 1978; MA, San Francisco State U., 1989; postgrad., U. N.Mex. Dep. dir. Calif. Arts Coun., Sacramento, 1976-79; exec. dir. Mothers Emergency Svc., Sacramento, 1979-82; assoc. dir. San Francisco Cmty. Bds., 1982-83; adminstr. San Francisco Rsch. Project, 1983-86, exec. dir. East Bay Ctr. for Performing Arts, Richmond, Calif., 1987-89; instr. English Calif. C.C.s, Pittsburg, Fremont & Hayward, 1990-93; instr. Am. studies U. N.Mex., Alburg, 1993-94; instr. humanities New Coll., San Francisco, 1994-95. Bus. owner, pres., pub. Academics of Course Inc., Vallejo, Calif., 1997—; rschr. L.A. Cmty. Arts Alliance, 1972. Author: (drama anthology) The Disinherited, 1971, The Uptown Mrs. Carrie, 1989; prodr.: Meat Theater Co., 1970—72. Bd. dirs. Richmond (Calif.) Arts Coun., 1986-89; workshop coord. L.A. Writers Workshop, 1966-69, Sacramento Civic Theater, 1980; project coord. City Spirit Project, Pasadena, Calif., 1972-75. With USN, 1958-61. Recipient Woman of Yr. award Iota Phi Lambda, Sacramento, 1981. Home: 100 Kathy Ellen Ct Vallejo CA 94591-

LANDAUER, SUSAN E. art historian; b. Oakland, Calif., July 31, 1958; BA, U. Calif., Berkeley, 1982; MA in History of Art, Yale U., 1984, PhD in History of Art, 1992. Ind. curator/author, 1992—96; asst. curator Los Angeles County Mus., L.A., 1996; founding co-dir. San Francisco Ctr. for the Book, 1996—97; Katie and Drew Gibson chief curator San Jose Mus. of Art, Calif., 1999—. Author: Obatas Yosemite, 1993, The San Francisco Sch of Abstract Expressionism, 1996, California Impressionists, 1996, The Lighter Side of Bay Area Figuration, 2000, Elmer Bischoff: The Ethics of Paint, 2001, The Not-So-Still Life: A Century of California Painting and Sculpture, 2003, Tino Rodriguez: The Darkening Garden, 2003. Office: San Jose Mus of Art 110 S Market San Jose CA 95113

LANDER, JOYCE ANN, nursing educator, medical/surgical nurse; b. Benton Harbor, Mich, July 27, 1942; d. James E. and Anna Mae Remus LPN, Kalamazoo Practical Nursing, Ctr., 1967; AAS, Kalamazoo Valley C.C., 1981, Grad. Massage Therapy Program, 1995. LPN-RN Bronson Meth. Hosp., Kalamazoo, 1972-82; RN med./surg. unit Borgess Med. Ctr., Kalamazoo, 1982-84; RN pediat. Upjohn Home Health Care, Kalamazoo, 1984-88; supr. nursing lab Kalamazoo Valley Comm. Coll., 1982—. Therapeutic massage therapist in client homes with Business Kneading Peace Therapeutic Massage, Kalamazoo, 1995—; nursing asst., instr. State of Mich. Observer, 1990-96. Author: What Is A Nurse, 1980. Address: 3300 Woodstone Dr E Apt 108 Kalamazoo MI 49008-2548

LANDER, RUTH A. medical group and association administrator; b. Fitchburg, Mass., Dec. 13, 1948; d. H. Allison and Violet K. (Erickson) Linné; m. C. Stephen Lander, June 28, 1968; children: Timothy, Mary. BA, Ohio State U., 1978; postgrad., Kennedy-Western U., 1995—. Dir. fin. Luth. Svc. Assn. New England, Natick, Mass., 1973-76; gen. mgr. Logos, Columbus, 1976-87; practice adminstr. Columbus Oncology Assocs., Inc., 1987—. Sec., treas. Adminstrs. in Oncology Hematology Assembly, Englewood, Colo., 1994-95, legis. liaison, 1994-95, pres.-elect, 1995-96, pres., 1996-97; spkr. on med. group mgmt. issues. Editor Administrs. in Oncology Hematology Assembly News, 1994-95; mem. editl. bd. Oncology Issues Mag., 1998-2000; mem. editl. adv. bd. for coding and reimbursement Oncology & Hematology, 2001; contbr. articles to profl. jours. Mem. Vineyard Christian Fellowship, Westerville, Ohio; grass roots legis. group Ohio Med. Group Mgmt. Assn., Columbus, 1994—. Fellow Med. Group Mgmt. Assn., Am. Coll. Med. Practice Execs. (nat. chair membership devel. com. 1999, nat. bd. dirs. 2003—); mem. Nat. Oncology Soc. Network, Ctrl.-Ohio Med. Group Mgmt. Assn. (pres. 1993-94, sec. 1992-93, program dir. 1991-92, exec. com. 1990-97), Assn. Cmty. Cancer Ctr. (mem. editl. bd. mag. 1998-2000), Ohio Med. Group Mgmt. Assn. (exec. com. 1994-2001, sec. 1995-96, pres.-elect 1997, pres. 1998, rep. to Medicare PCOM adv. group, 2003-2004), Ohio Oncology Med. Group Mgmt. Assn. (pres. 1997), Ohio State Med. Assn. (mem. group practice task force 2000—), Columbus Med. Assn. (group practice mgrs. task force 2002—). Republican. Avocations: reading, computers, crafts, knitting, bible study. Office: Columbus Oncology Assocs 810 Jasonway Ave Ste A Columbus OH 43214-2329

LANDERS, AUDREY, actress, singer; d. Ruth Landers. BA, Barnard Coll. Records singles and albums with sister Judy Landers. Appeared in (films) A Chorus Line, 1985, Getting Even, 1986, (TV) The Merv Griffin Show, The Secret Storm, Somerset, Dallas; singer U.S., European tours. Office: care Jo-Ann Geffen & Assocs 3131 Cahuenga Blvd W Ste 235 Los Angeles CA 90068-1749

LANDERS, PATRICIA BURNEICE, writer; b. Evanston, Ill., Feb. 1, 1929; d. Oscar Jay Larson and Mildred Auriel Hansen; m. John Ainsworth Salisbury (div.); children: Clark Salisbury, Carey Salisbury; m. Forest Wayne Landers (dec.); 1 child, Kent. BA, Portland State U. Sales clk. Marshall Field, Chgo.; rsch. interviewer McGraw Hill, N.Y.C., Starch Hooper, N.Y.C.; investigator State Bur. Labor, Portland, Oreg.; seminar developer, presenter Oreg. Bur. Labor, Portland; writer Portland. Author: My Life As a Mollusk, 2000, Handbook of Wage and Hour Rates, 1998. Democrat. Avocations: reading, golf, swimming. Home: 7025 Valley View Dr Gladstone OR 97027-1125*

LANDERS, PATRICIA GLOVER, reading specialist; b. Pine Bluff, Ark., Nov. 15, 1945; d. Maurice Alexander Glover and Ruth Wells-Glover Wimberly; 1 child, Wendolynn. BS in Edn., Ark. State U., 1967; MS in Edn., OBU, 1976; postgrad., U. of Ark., 1980—81, U. of Ariz., 1980—81, Ariz. State U., 1983—88, U. Phoenix, 1988—89. Cert. tchr. English, reading specialist K-12 Ariz., C.C., English, lang. arts, composition Ariz. Elem. music supr. Greene County Tech. Schs., Paragould, Ark., 1967—68; band & choir dir. Naylor (Mo.) Schs., 1968—70; elem. tchr. Poughkeepsie (Ark.) Schs., 1970—72; reading specialist Sheridan (Ariz.) Schs., 1975—82, Casa Grande Union High Sch., Casa Grande, Ariz., 1982—; assoc. prof. Pima C.C., Tucson, 1982—94, Centra Ariz. Coll., Coolidge, Ariz., 1983—93; English tchr. Casa Granda Regional Med. Ctr. Alternative, Casa Grande, 1994—2001; owner Landers' Tutoring Svc., Casa Grande, 2001—. Test supr. SAT, ACT Testing Svcs., Casa Grande, 1997—. Author: Making English Make Sense, 1996. Invited rep. U.S. to China People to People Amb. Program, 2000; French hornist CAC Cmty. Concert Band, Coolidge, Ariz., 1984—2000; organist North Trekell Bapt. Ch., Casa Grande, 1996—, founder instrumental music founds. group, 2001; chair babysitting com. Casa Grand Regionl Med. Ctr., Casa Grande, 1995—98. Mem.: NEA, Ark. Reading Coun., Ctrl. Ariz. Reading Coun., Ariz. Reading Coun., Ariz. Edn. Assn., Casa Grande Edn. Assn. (pres. 1985—86, Outstanding Svc. award 1985—86), Sheridan Ednl. Assoc. (pres. 1978—79), Internat. Reading Assoc., CGRMC Aux. (com. chairperson 1995—98, Vol. of Month 1995). Democrat. Baptist. Avocations: reading, jogging, musical instruments. Home: PO Box 589 Arizona City AZ 85223 Office: CGUHS 2730 N Trekell Rd Casa Grande AZ 85222 Personal E-mail: patriciaglove90@hotmail.com. Business E-Mail: planders@cguhs.org.

LANDERS, SUSAN MAE, psychotherapist, professional counselor; b. Houston; d. James Edward and Frances Pauline (Braunagel) L. BS in Advt., U. Tex.; MS in Psychol. Counseling, U. Houston, Clearlake, 1994; cert. in sales, Dale Carnegie Inst. Lic. profl. counselor. Mktg. rep. K.C. Products, Houston, 1981-83; account exec. Williamson County Express, Austin, Tex., 1984; advt. cons. Stas. KMMM/KOKE, Austin, 1985; key account sales rep. GranTree Furniture Rental, Austin, 1986-89; individual habilitation counselor Ctr. for the Retarded Inc., Houston, 1990; case mgr. Mental Health and Mental Retardation Authority Harris County, Houston, 1991-92; primary therapist Riceland Psychiat. Hosp., 1994-96, Planned Behavioral Healthcare Inc., 1996-98, Continuum Healthcare, Houston, 1998—2000; pvt. practice, 1998—. Mem.: ACA, Am. Mental Health Counselors Assn. Avocation: photography. Home: 7915 Westbank Ave Houston TX 77064-8048

LANDERS, TERESA PRICE, librarian; b. N.Y.C., Dec. 28, 1954; d. Stanley and June Ethel (Novick) Price; m. Gary David Landers, Sept. 2, 1979; children: Joshua Price, Alisha Rose. BA in History cum laude, Williams Coll., 1976; MA in LS, U. Denver, 1978; postgrad., Ctrl. Wash. U., 1980; MA in Orgnl. Mgmt., U. Phoenix, 1999. Libr., asst. analyst Earl Combs, Inc., Mercer Island, Wash., 1979; reference libr. Yakima (Wash.) Valley Regional Libr., 1981-83, coord. youth svcs., 1983-84; libr. Tempe (Ariz.) Pub. Libr., 1984-85; supervisory libr. Mesa (Ariz.) Pub. Libr., 1985-90; head telephone reference Phoenix Pub. Libr., 1990-91, head bus. and scis., 1991-95, info. svcs. mgr., 1995-99; dep. dir. Corvallis-Benton County Pub. libr., 1999—. Cons. Fed. Dept. Corrections, Phoenix, 1993. Mem. ALA, Oreg. Libr. Assn., Nat. Wildlife Fedn. (life), Altrusa, Beta Phi Mu. Democrat. Unitarian Universalist. Avocations: cooking, horseback riding, gardening. Office: Corvallis-Benton County Pub Libr 645 NW Monroe Ave Corvallis OR 97330-4722 E-mail: teresa.landers@ci.corvallis.or.us.

LANDERS, VERNETTE TROSPER, writer, educator, association executive; b. Lawton, Okla., May 3, 1912; d. Fred Gilbert and LaVerne Hamilton (Stevens) Trosper; m. Paul Albert Lum, Aug. 29, 1952 (dec. May 1955); 1 child, William Tappan; m. 2d Newlin Landers, May 2, 1959 (dec. Apr. 1990); children: Lawrence, Marlin. AB with honors, UCLA, 1933, MA, 1935, EdD, 1953; Cultural doctorate (hon.), Lit. World U., Tucson, 1985. Tchr. secondary schs., Montebello, Calif., 1935-45, 48-50, 51-59; prof. Long Beach City Coll., 1946-47; asst. prof. L.A. State Coll., 1950; dean girls Twenty-Nine Palsm (Calif.) H.S., 1960-65; dist. counselor Morongo (Calif.) Unified Sch. Dist., 1965-72, coord. adult edn., 1965-67, guidance project dir., 1967; clk.-in-charge Landers (Calif.) Post Office, 1962-82, ret., 1982. Participant Yucca Valley Cowboy Poetry and Music Gathering, 1996, 98; grand marshall Yucca Valley Grubstake Parade, 1999. Author: Impy, 1974, Talkie, 1975, Impy's Children, 1975, Nineteen O Four, 1976, Little Brown Bat, 1976, Sio-Go, 1977, Owls Who and Who Who, 1978, Sandy, The Coydog, 1979, The Kit Fox and the Walking Stick, 1980; contbr. articles to profl. jours., poems to anthologies. V.p., sec. Landers Assn., 1965—; sec. Landers Vol. Fire Dept., 1972—; life mem. Hi-Desert Playhouse Guild, Hi-Desert Meml. Hosp. Guild; bd. friends Copper Mountain Coll., 1990-91; bd. dirs., sec. Desert Emergency Radio Svc.; mem. Rep. Senatorial Inner Cir., 1990-92, Regent Nat. Fedn. Rep. Women, 1990-92, Nat. Rep. Congl. Com., 1990-91, Presdl. Task Force, 1990-92; lifetime mem. Girl Scouts USA, 1991. Recipient internat. diploma Creativity award Internat. Pers. Rsch. Assn., 1972, award Goat Mt. Grange No. 818, 1987; cert. of merit for disting. svc. to edn., 1973; Order of Rose, 1978, Order of Pearl, 1989, Alpha Xi Delta; poet laureate Ctr. of Internat. Studies and Exchanges, 1981; diploma of merit in letters U. Arts, Parma, Italy, 1982; Golden Yr. Bruin UCLA, 1983; World Culture prize Nat. Ctr. for Studies and Rsch., Italian Acad., 1984; Golden Palm Diploma of Honor in poetry Leonardo Da Vinci Acad., 1984; Diploma of Merit and titular mem. internat. com. Internat. Ctr. Studies and Exchanges, Rome, 1984; Recognition award San Gorgonio coun. Girl Scouts USA, 1984—; Cert. of Appreciation Morongo Unified Sch. Dist., 1984, 89; plaque for contbn. to postal svc. and cmty. U.S. Postal Svc., 1984; Biographee of Yr. award for outstanding achievement in the field of edn. and svc. to cmty. Hist. Preservation of Am.; named Princess of Poetry of Internat. Ctr. Cultural Studies and Exchange, Italy, 1985; cmty. dinner held in her honor for achievement and svc. to cmty., 1984; Star of Contemporary Poetry Masters of Contemporary Poetry, Internat. Ctr. Cultural Studies and Exchanges, Italy, 1984; named to honor list of leaders of contemporary art and lit. and apptd. titular mem. of Internat. High Com. for World Culture & Arts Leonardo Da Vinci Acad., 1987; named to honor list Foremost Women 20th Century for Outstanding Contbn. to Rsch., IBC, 1987; Presdl. Order of Merit Pres. George Bush-Exec. Coun. of Nat. Rep. Senatorial Com., Congl. cert. of Appreciation U.S. Ho. of Reps.; other awards and certs. Guest of hon. ground breaking ceremony Landers Elementary Sch. 1989, dedication ceremony, 1991. Fellow Internat. Acad. Poets (life), World Lit. Acad.; mem. Am. Pers. and Guidance Assn., Internat. Platform Assn., Nat. Ret. Tchrs. Assn., Calif. and Nat. Assn. for Counseling and Devel., Am. Assn. for Counseling and Devel. (25-Yr. Membership pin 1991), Nat. Assn. Women Deans and Adminstrs., Montebello Bus. and Profl. Women's Club (pres.), Nat. League Am. Pen Women (pres. 1985-86), Leonardo Da Vinci Acad. Internat. (Winged Glory diploma of honor in letters 1982), Landers Area C. of C. (pres. 1985-86, Presdl. award for Outstanding Svcs., Internat. Honors Cup 1992-93), Desert Nature Mus., Whittier Toastmistress Club (Calif.) (pres. 1957), Homestead Valley Women's Club (Landers), Soroptimists (sec. 29 Palms chpt. 1962, life mem. 1983, Soroptimist of Yr. local chpt. 1987-88), Phi Beta Kappa, Pi Lambda Theta (Mortar Bd., Prytanean UCLA, UCLA Golden Yr. Bruin 1983), Sigma Delta Pi, Pi Delta Phi. Home: PO Box 3839 Landers CA 92285-0839

LANDGREBE, MARILYN ANN, nutritionist, electrochemical company executive; b. N.Y.C., June 8, 1935; d. Charles J. and Marie L. Osterwald; m. Albert R. Landgrebe, June 14, 1958; children: Marie Pilz, Albert C. PhD, U. Md., 1977. Nutritionist Children's Brain Rsch. Clinic, Washington, 1974-80; dir. rsch. Almar Rsch. Lab., Beltsville, Md., 1980-88; v.p. Internat. Electrochem. Systems & Tech., Long Neck, Del., 1990—. Cons. Autistic Soc., 1974-77. Contbr. articles to profl. jours. Pres. PTA, Calverton, Md., 1967. Mem. Am. Assn. Ret. Persons, Mariner's Cove Assn. (beautiful and landscape com. 1999). Avocations: gardening, boating, reading, travel. Home and Office: Internat Electrochem Systems & Tech B14 Sussex Ln Long Neck DE 19966-9634 E-mail: albert@dmv.com.

LANDGREN, KARIN ELISABETH, advocate; b. San Francisco, Calif., Oct. 13, 1957; d. Lars Elmer and Ruth Lydia Landgren; m. John Joseph Mills, Nov. 16, 1985 (dec. Feb. 1, 2001); children: Elinor Ingrid Landgren Mills, Benedict Stefan Landgren Mills. BSc, London Sch. of Economics, 1975—78, LLM in internat. law, 1978—79. Vol. Amnesty Internat., London, 1976—79; chief of standards and legal advice UNHCR, Geneva, 1994—98; chief of child protection UNICEF, New York, NY, 1998—; intern European Human Rights Commn., Strasbourg, France (incl. Monaco), 1978; assoc. legal officer (europe) UNHCR, Geneva, 1980—83, legal officer New Delhi, 1983—86, dep. rep. Manila, Philippines, 1986—88, rep., 1988—90, exec. asst. to the dep. high commr., 1990—92, chief of mission Asmara, Eritrea, 1992, 1992—93. Contbr. articles to jours. Mem.: Am. Soc. of Internat. Law.

LANDIS, DONNA MARIE, nursing administrator, women's health nurse; b. Lebanon, Pa., Sept. 5, 1944; d. James O.A. and Helen Joan (Fritz) Muench; m. David J. Landis, Jan. 1, 1967 (div. Jan. 1985); children: Danielle M. Landis Barry, David J., Derek J.; m. John C. Broderick, Jan. 1, 1990 (div. Jan. 1995). Diploma, St. Joseph's Hosp. Sch. Nursing, Reading, Pa., 1965. RN Md., cert. densitometry technologist. Head nurse med.-surg. unit Hosp. of U. Pa., 1965-67; nurse various hosps. and physician's offices, Md., Pa., 1965-85; clin. dir., clin. rsch. coord., DXA technologist Osteoporosis Diagnostic and Monitoring Ctr., Laurel, Md., 1985-95, owner, 1995—; clin. dir., clin. rsch. study coord. Osteoporosis Assessment Ctr., Wheaton, Md., 1985-95; clin. dir./owner Women's Health Rsch. Ctr., Laurel, Md., 1996—. Cons. Nat. Nurses Alliance for Better Bone Health, 1998—2001; osteoporosis and women's wellness cons. to numerous pharm. cos. Mem. task force on osteoporosis State of Md., 1996—; vol. Family Crisis Ctr. Prince George County. Named one of Md.'s Top 100 Women in Bus., 2002. Mem.: Nat. Osteoporosis Risk Assessment Project (specialist practice and lead technologist trainer 1997—98), Allied Health Profls./Arthritis Found., Nat. Osteoporosis Found. (pub. policy contact), Internat. Soc. Clin. Densitometry (steering com. 1993—94, contbg. editor SCAN newsletter 1994—2002, cert. and credentialing com. technologists and physicians 1995—2000, sci. adv. com. 1996—, trustee 1999—2002, technologist edn. subcom. 2000—, accreditation com. 2003—), St. Joseph's Hosp. Alumni Assn., Kiwanis Club (bd. dirs. 1997—2002, pres. Prince George's County 2000—01, capital dist. lt. gov. 2003—), Balt. Bone Club, Washington Met. Bone Club (steering com. 1996, bd. dirs. 1999—2001, sec. 1999—2001). Office: 14201 Laurel Park Dr Laurel MD 20707-5203 E-mail: dmlandis@whrc.net.

LANDIS, ELLEN JAMIE, art curator; b. Chgo., May 6, 1941; d. Alvin and Sadie (Reingold) L.; m. Frederick Cohn, Nov. 4, 1984; 1 child, David. BA, U. Calif., Berkeley, 1962; student, U. Vienna (Austria, 1960-61; MA, NYU, 1965. Asst. curator exhbns. and publs. L.A. County Mus. of Art, L.A., 1967-68; curator B.G. Cantor Collection & Art Found., Beverly Hills, Calif., 1968-70; curatorial cons. Robert Gore Rifkind Art Collection, Beverly Hills, 1970; curator painting and sculpture Balt. Mus. of Art, 1970-71; curator Robert Gore Rifkind Art Collection, Beverly Hills, 1974-75; instr. art history and appreciation Yuba Coll., Marysville, Calif., 1976-77; curator art Albuquerque Mus., 1977—2003; ind. curator, 2004—. Author: (exhbn. catalogs) Here & Now, 1981, West/Southwest, 1982; editor: (exhbn. catalogs) Hiroshige, 1983, Printers' Impressions, 1990; adv. bd. Artspace Mag., 1978—; exhibitions include Serenity Studies: Photographs by Diana Schoenfield, 1990, I Dream a World: Portraits of Black Women Who Changed America, 1990, Zones of Experience: The Art of Larry Bell, 1997, The American Rockies: Photographs by Gust Foster, 1999, Cast of Charactersd: Figurative Sculpture, 2000, Anderson Collection of Temporary Art, 2002, New Mexico Women in the Arts: Traces of the Journey, 2003, A Change of Mind: An Alzheimer's Portrait, A Photographic Memoir by Joyce Culver, 2003; several others. Juror Art in Pub. Places, Albuquerque, 1981, One Percent for Art, Albuquerque, 1978, N.Mex. Women in the Arts, Albuquerque, 1979, Suntran, Albuquerque, 1980; bd. trustees Comprehensive Art Publs., Ohio, 1980—; bd. dirs. Performing Arts Collective, Albuquerque, 1979-81. Recipient Chris award Film Coun. Greater Columbus (Ohio), 1969. Mem. Am. Assn. Museums, N.Mex. Assn. Museums, ICOM, Coll. Art Assn., Sculpture. Home: 7112 Osuna Rd NE Albuquerque NM 87109-2945 Office: Albuquerque Museum 2000 Mountain Rd NW Albuquerque NM 87104-1459

LANDIS, STORY C. neurobiologist; BA, Wellesley Coll.; PhD, Harvard U. Former faculty mem. in neurobiology Harvard Med. Sch.; faculty Dept. Pharmacology Case Western Res. U. Sch. of Medicine, Cleve., 1985—90, chair Dept. Neuroscis., 1990—95; sci. dir. of intramural program NINDS, 1995—2003, dir., 2003—. Contbr. articles to profl. jours. Fellow: AAAS, Acad. of Arts and Scis. Achievements include research in the study of the developmental interactions required for the formation of functional synapses. Office: Office of the Director NINDS Bldg 31 Rm 8A52 36 Convent Dr MSC 4150 Bethesda MD 20892-4150

LANDMAN, BETTE EMELINE, academic administrator; b. Piqua, Ohio, July 18, 1937; d. Wilson Richard and Lois (Wilson) L. BS, Bowling Green State U., 1959; MA, Ohio State U., 1961, PhD, 1972. From instr. to asst. prof. anthropology Springfield (Mass.) Coll., 1963-67; asst. prof. Temple U., 1967-71; asst. prof. anthropology Beaver Coll., Glenside, Pa., 1971-76, dean, 1976-85, v.p. acad. affairs, 1980-85, acting pres., 1982-83, 85, pres., 1985—. Bd. dirs. Abington (Pa.) Meml. Hosp., 1986-93, 95—, Abington Meml. Hosp. Found., 1993-95; mem. blood donor campaign ARC, chair Pa.-Jersey Region Higher Edn., 1990-91; bd. advisors Coll. Physicians of Phila., 1994—. Recipient Disting. Teaching award Christian R. and Mary F. Lindback Found., 1973; NSF fellow, 1961-63, Wenner-Gren Found. for Anthrop. Rsch. fellow, 1965-66; named Disting. Dau. of Pa., 1992, Educator of Yr. Boy Scouts Am., 1996; Ann. Pa. Am. Coun. on Edn.-NIP award established in her honor, 1992. Mem. Am. Coun. Edn. (state coord. 1980-84, commn. on leadership devel. 1989-94, chmn. 1991-92, bd. dirs. 1993-97), Assn. Am. Colls. (bd. dirs. 1986-91, vice chair 1989-90, chair 1990-91), Assn. Presbyn. Colls. and Univs. (exec. com. 1988-93, 95—, sec. 1989-90, v.p. 1990-91, pres. 1991-92), Pa. Assn. Colls. and Univs. (exec. com. 1992-93), Nat. Assn. Ind. Colls. and Univs. (commn. on campus concerns 1991—, vice chmn. 1992, chmn. 1993), NCAA Divsn III Pres. Coun., Southeastern Pa. Consortium Higher Edn. (chair 1996-98), Sigma Xi, Phi Kappa Phi, Kappa Delta Pi. Office: Beaver Coll Office of Pres 450 S Easton Rd Glenside PA 19038-3215

LANDMAN, DEBORAH TRACY, real estate company executive, small business owner, fitness trainer; b. Weymouth, Dorset, Eng., Aug. 24, 1969; came to U.S., 1997; d. Charles Denison and Helen Joy Bate; m. Michael Trevor Webb, May 31, 1992 (div.); m. William Scott Landman, Aug. 30, 1997. Pers. adminstr. RAF, Uxbridge, 1987—92; pres. Bodytalk Fitness, Ltd., Haslemere, Eng., 1992-97, Elite Retail Leasing, Inc., Parkland, Fla., 1997—; owner Journey's End Farm (dressage facility). Actress, model, TV presenter. Editor: (other) Flying Changes Publ.; prodr.: (workout video) Bodytalk Step Workout Video, 1992; contbr. articles on fitness to mags. Organizer charity events Starlight Found., 1995. Mem. Aerobics Orgn. Gt. Britain, Fitness Profls. U.K., Nat. Register Personal Trainers, IDEA Fitness Profls. Anglican. Avocations: fitness, horseback riding, dressage, travel, running. Office: Elite Retail Leasing Inc 5251 NW 80th Ter Parkland FL 33067-1137 E-mail: elitelease@aol.com., ukactress@aol.com.

LANDON, HELEN ZIELINSKI, psychologist; b. LA, June 22, 1962; d. Natan and Ann Baum Zielinski; m. Louis W. Landon, May 23, 1999; 1 child, Natasha Diane. BA in Psychology, UCLA, 1985; MA in Psychology, Pepperdine U., 1987; PhD in Clin. Psychology, Alliant Internat. U., 1995. Lic. psychologist Calif., 1998. Pvt. practice, Santa Monica, Calif., 1999—. Democrat. Jewish. Avocations: needlepoint, reading, walking, being a mother. Office: 1421 Santa Monica Blvd 106 Santa Monica CA 90404

LANDON, SUSAN MELINDA, petroleum geologist; b. Mattoon, Ill., July 2, 1950; d. Albert Leroy and Nancy (Wallace) L.; m. Richard D. Dietz, Jan. 24, 1993. BA, Knox Coll., 1972; MA, SUNY, Binghamton, 1975. Cert. profl. geologist; cert. petroleum geologist. Petroleum geologist Amoco Prodn. Co., Denver, 1974-87; mgr. exploration tng. Amoco, Houston, 1987-89; ind. petroleum geologist Denver, 1990—. Editor: Interior Rift Basins, 1993. Mem., chmn. Colo. Geol. Survey Adv. Com., Denver, 1991-98; mem. Bd. on Earth Sci. and Resources-NRC, 1992-97, chair com. on earth resources, 1998-2003; mem. Nat. Coop. Geologic Mapping Program Fed. Adv. Com., 1997—. Recipient Disting. Alumni award Knox Coll., 1986, Disting. Svc. award Rocky Mountain Assn. Geologists, 1986, Disting. Pub. Svc. to Earth Sci. award Rocky Mountain Assn. Geologists, 1998. Mem. Am. Assn. Petroleum Geologists (hon., treas., Disting. Svc. award 1995), Am. Inst. Profl. Geologists (pres. 1990, Martin Van Couvering award 1991, Ben H. Parker medal 2001), Am. Geol. Inst. (pres. 1998), Rocky Mtn. Assn. Geologists (pres. 2000). Achievements include frontier exploration for hydrocarbons in U.S. Home: 780 Ballantine Rd Golden CO 80401-9503 Office: Thomasson Ptnr Assocs 1410 High St Denver CO 80218-2609 E-mail: susanlandon@att.net.

LANDON, SUSAN N. volunteer, poet; b. Pittsburgh, Feb. 20, 1946; d. Kenneth L. and Nina H. Landon. BA, Tufts U., 1967; MA in Counseling Psychology, Lesley U., 1988. Sr. mem. of tech. staff (software engring.) Draper Lab., Cambridge, Mass., 1995—98; freelance journalist, 1991—95; compiler group mgr. (sofware engring.) Boston Systems Office, Waltham, Mass., 1985—86; program office mgr. (software engring.) Intermetrics, Inc., Cambridge, Mass., 1981—85; tech. staff mem. (software engr.) Adaptive Optics, Cambridge, Mass., 1978—81; assoc. staff mem. (software engring.) MIT Lincoln Lab., Cambridge, Mass., 1967—78. Founder & pres. Data Acquisition & Lab. Control SIG of Data Gen. Users Group, 1979—82; founder Intermetrics Women's Network, Cambridge, Mass., 1984—85; self-image subgroup leader MIT Lincoln Lab. Women's Forum, Lexington, Mass., 1973—78. Contbr. poetry anthology Wedding Blessings, poetry anthology Mothers and Daughters, poetry anthology Rising to the Dawn, A Rape Survivor's Journey into Healing, poetry anthology Freedom's Just Another Word, poetry anthology We Speak for Peace, poetry anthology Out of the Blue Writers Unite. Vol. tutor Somerville Cmty. Adult Learning Experiences, Somerville, Mass., 1998—2001; com. mem. Hoyt-Sullivan Com., Somerville, Mass., 1999—2001; writer for cmty. newspaper funded to stabilize the neighborhood after subway expansion disrupted it. North Cambridge News, Cambridge, Mass., 1991—92; clk. First Congl. Ch. of Somerville, Somerville, Mass., 1997—98; writer for Boston newsletter NOW (Nat. Orgn. Women), Cambridge, Mass., 1982—85; internat. friendship del. to Egypt: women in soc. trip People to People Internat., Kansas City, Mo., 2000—00, internat. friendship del., a mission in understanding to Cuba, 2002—02; transcendental meditation tchr. Students Internat. Meditation Soc., Cambridge, Calif., 1971—75; vol. computer aide Somerville Cmty. Computer Ctr., Somerville, Mass., 1998—2004; activist Mass. Choice, Cambridge, Mass., 1979—81; vol. computer cons. Cambridge Multicultural Arts Ctr., Cambridge, Mass., 1999—2004; vol. Ten Thousand Villages, Cambridge, Mass., 1999—2004. Named to Wall of Tolerance, So. Law Poverty Ctr., 2002; recipient Poetry prize, Spare Change News, 2001, Cambridge Poetry award, Cambridge Ctr. Adult Edn. (now by Cambridge Poetry Awards), 2004. Mem.: New Eng. Poetry Club. Avocations: travel, reading, languages. Office: PO Box 441203 Somerville MA 02144 Personal E-mail: landon_susan@hotmail.com.

LANDOVSKY, ROSEMARY REID, figure skating school director, coach; b. Chgo., July 26, 1933; d. Samuel Stuart and Audrey Todd (Lyons) Reid; m. John Indulis Landovsky, Feb. 20, 1960; children: David John, Linette. BA in Psychology, Colo. Coll., 1956. Profl. skater Holiday on Ice Touring Show, U.S., Mex., Cuba, 1956-58; skating dir. and coach Paradice Arena, Birmingham, 1958-62, Les Patineurs, Huntsville, Ala., 1960-62; coach competitive (Ice Skating Inst. Am., U.S. Figure Skating Assn.) Michael Kirby and Assocs., River Forest, Chgo., Ill., 1962-63; rink mgr., skating dir. Lake Meadows Ice Arena, Chgo., 1963-68; coach (ISIA, USFSA) Rainbo Arena, Chgo., 1968-73; skating dir. Northwestern U. Skating Sch., Evanston, Ill., 1968-73, Robert Crown Ice Ctr., Evanston, 1973-75; dir. instl. programs Skokie (Ill.) Park Dist., 1975-87. Competition dir. ISIA All America Competition, 1985-86. Dir., producer, choreographer Ice Show: Nutcracker Ballet, 1973, Ice Extravaganza III, 1985, Ice Lights '86, '87. Election judge, worker, Ind. Dems., Chgo., 1964-68. Mem. AAUW, Profl. Skaters Guild, Ice Skating Inst. Am., Coll. Coll. Alumni Assn., Gamma Phi Beta. Avocations: building cabin, travel, golf, tennis, hiking. Personal E-mail: rodysk8@earthlink.netm.

LANDOW-ESSER, JANINE MARISE, lawyer; b. Omaha, Sept. 23, 1951; d. Erwin Landow and Beatrice (Hart) Appel; m. Jeffrey L. Esser, June 2, 1974; children: Erica, Caroline. BA, U. Wis., 1973; JD with honors, George Washington U., 1976. Bar: Va. 1976, DC 1977, Ill. 1985. Atty. U.S. Dept. Energy, Washington, 1976-83, Bell, Boyd & Lloyd, Chgo., 1985-86, Seyfarth, Shaw, Fairweather & Geraldson, Chgo., 1986-88, Holleb & Coff, Chgo., 1988-2000, Quarles & Brady, Chgo., 2000—. Contbr. articles to profl. jours. Bd. dirs. Bernard Zell Anshe Emet Day Sch. Parent-Tchr. Orgn., 1991-95. Mem. ABA, Chgo. Bar Assn. (vice chmn. environ. law com. 1990-91, chmn. 1991-92), Am. Jewish Congress (bd. dirs., pres. Midwest Region 2001-04). Office: Quarles & Brady 500 W Madison St Ste 3700 Chicago IL 60661-2592 Office Phone: 312-715-5055. E-mail: je3@quarles.com.

LANDRAM, CHRISTINA LOUELLA, librarian; b. Dec. 10, 1922; d. James Ralph and Bertie Louella (Jordan) Oliver; m. Robert Ellis Landram, Aug. 7, 1948; 1 child, Mark Owen. BA, Tex. Woman's U., 1945, BLS, 1946, MLS, 1951. Preliminary cataloger Libr. of Congress, Washington, 1946-48; cataloger U.S. Info. Ctr., Tokyo, 1948-50, U.S. Dept. Agr., Washington, 1953-54; libr. Yokota (Japan) AFB, 1954-55, St. Mary's Hosp., West Palm Beach, Fla., 1957-59, Jacksonville (Ark.) H.S., 1959-61; coord. Shelby County Librs., Memphis, 1961-63; head catalog dept. Ga. State U. Libr., 1963-86, libr., assoc. prof. emeritus, 1986—. Contbr. articles to libr. jours. Mem. ALA (chmn. cataloging norms 1979-80, nominating com.

1977-78), Ga. Libr. Assn. (chmn. resources and tech. svcs. sect. 1969-71), Metro-Atlanta Libr. Assn. (pres. 1967-68), Southeastern Libr. Assn. (mem. govtl. rels. com. 1975-78, intellectual freedom com. 1984-86, mem. Rothrock awards com. 1987-90). Presbyterian. Home: 15201 Olive Blvd Apt 495 Chesterfield MO 63017-1819 Personal E-mail: bobland2@juno.com.

LANDRETH, KATHRYN E. lawyer; U.S. atty. Dept. Justice, Las Vegas, 1993—2001; chief of policy and planning Met. Police Dept., Las Vegas, Nev., 2001—02; metro counsel Las Vegas, 2003—. Office: Las Vegas Metro Police Dept 400 E Stewart Ave Las Vegas NV 89101

LANDRIEU, MARY L. senator; b. Nov. 23, 1955; m. E. Frank Snellings. BA, La. State U., 1977. Real estate agt.; La. state rep. from dist. 90, 1979-89; La. state treas., 1987-95; U.S. senator from La., 1997—; mem. small business com.; mem. energy and natural resources com.; mem. appropriations com. Del., Dem. Nat. Conv., 1980 Mem. LWV, Women Execs. in State Govt., Fedn. Dem. Women, Delta Gamma. Democrat. Roman Catholic. Office: 724 Hart Senate Off Bldg Washington DC 20510-0001

LANDRUM-BITTLES, JENITA, artist, educator; b. Jackson, Mich., Dec. 25, 1959; d. Bennie C. Landrum and Maxine A. Johnson; m. Roland Bittles, June 28, 1995; 1 child, Cory Mychal. BFA, Ariz. State U., 1991; MFA, Ohio State U., 1997. Art coord., grad. tchg. asst. Ohio State U., Columbus, 1997-98, vis. lectr., 1997—. Instr. art Columbus State Coll., 1997—, Cultural Arts Ctr., Columbus, 1997, Columbus Mus. Art, 1997; artist in residence Fort Hays Visual Arts Sch., Columbus, 1997, Skowhegan, N.Y.C., 1996. Solo exhbns. include Maine Daily News, 1996, The Lantern, 1996, 97, Ft. Hayes Shot Tower Gallery, Columbus, 1997, ACE Gallery, Columbus, 1998; contbr. articles to profl. jours. Grantee Liquitex, 1995, Edith Fergus Gilmore, 1997; Albert Murray Family scholarship, 1995-97; Ohio State U. fellow, 1997. Mem. Nation Women's Art Caucus, Black Women's Task Force (chairperson 1994—), Coll. Art Assn. Address: 3789 Towne Center Blvd Columbus OH 43219-3106

LANDRY, ABBIE VESTAL, librarian; b. Martinsville, Va., Oct. 29, 1954; d. Samuel Raynor and Grace Loraine (Cochrane) Vestal; m. Michael Ray Landry, Aug. 4, 1979. Assoc. Gen. Edn., Patrick Henry C.C., Martinsville, Va., 1975; BA in History, Longwood Coll., Farmville, Va., 1977; M in Libr. and Info. Sci., U. Tenn., Knoxville, 1981. Grad. asst. history dept. U. Tenn., Knoxville, 1977-78, grad. teaching asst., 1978-80, grad. asst. libr. and info. sci., 1980-81; reference libr., coord. online svcs., coord. biog. instrn. Watson Libr., Northwestern State U., Natchitoches, La., 1981-87, head reference divsn., supr. reference, 1987—, interim dir., 2000—01. Mem. adv. bd. Bowker Publ. Topical Reference Books, Princeton, N.J., 1988-89, sec. La. Assn. for Acad. Competition, 1991—; chmn. faculty-staff devel. com. Watson Libr., 1983-88, chmn. devel. com. collection, 1988-89, chmn. quiz bowl com., 1989—, mem. automated circulation sys. com., 1984-85, mem. centennial com. 1983-84, chmn. libr. evaluation com., 1997—; cons. Best Books for Academic Librs. Vol. 4, American History. Contbg. author: Booktalking the Award Winners, Vols. 1, 2, 3; mem. editl. bd. Alumni Reviewer for Reference Books Bull., 1991—, mem. edit. bd., 1987-91; co-editor newsletter Libr. Users Edn., 1991-92; editor Online Svcs. Interest Group Newsletter, 1986-87; editor Watson Libr. Newsletter Ex Libris, 1983-93; contbr. articles to profl. jours. and encys. Mem. Assn. for Preservation Historic Natchitoches, 1985—, Natchitoches Humane Soc., 1983—. Recipient Sigma Xi award, Natchitoches, 1986. Mem. ALA, La. Libr. Assn. (vice chair acad. sect. 1988-89, chair 1989-90, mem. exec. bd. 1988 90, coord. online svcs. interest group 1985-86), Southeastern Libr. Assn., Apple Libr. Users Group, Phi Kappa Phi, Beta Phi Mu, Phi Alpha Theta. Episcopalian. Avocations: reading, needlework, travel. Office Phone: 318-357-4574.

LANDRY, SARA GRIFFIN, social worker; b. Thomaston, Ga., Sept. 17, 1920; d. John Carl and Mary Thelma (Abercrombie) Griffin; m. Thomas Leonard Perkins, Dec. 22, 1939 (dec. Jan. 27, 1945); 1 child, Thomas Leonard Perkins Jr.; m. George Kimball Landry, Dec. 19, 1949 (dec. Aug. 30, 1971). AB in Social Work magna cum laude, Wesleyan Coll., 1980; MS in Family Counseling, Mercer U., 1981. Receptionist Social Security Adminstrn., Macon, Ga., 1945—50, clerical, 1960—65, svc. rep., 1965—78; dir., organizer Bibb County Foster Grandparent Program, Macon, Ga., 1981—84; coord. rsch. project Med. Ctr. of Ctrl. Ga., Macon, Ga., 1986—87; social worker, bd. dirs. Bibb County Sr. Citizens Inc., Macon, Ga., 1984—; sec. bd. dirs. Bibb County Sr. Citizens, Inc., Macon, Ga., 1989—90, pres. bd. dirs., 1990—91. Bd. dirs. grant chmn. Family Counseling Ctr., Macon, 1986-92, 94-97. Contbr. articles, poems and various short stories to profl. jours. Bd. dirs., v.p., com. chmn. Am. Cancer Soc., Macon, 1956—, hon. life mem., 1993—; sec., com. chmn. Dem. Women Bibb County, 1979—; mem., sec. Civic Woman's Club, Macon, 1955-61; mem. Coun. Cath. Women, St. Joseph's Parish, pres., 1956-58; mem., bd. dirs. Savannah Diocesan Coun. Cath. Women, 1957-59; bd. dirs. Macon Little Theatre, 1994-96. Recipient Disting. Alumnae award for cmty. svc. Wesleyan Coll., 1996, Svc. to Mankind award Sertoma Club of Macon, 1995; named Vol. of Yr., Bibb County Sr. Citizens, Inc., 1988, Am. Cancer Soc., 1987-88, Cherry Blossom Sr. Queen for Cmty. Svc., 1986; Fundraiser honoree Am. Cancer Soc., 1991; Sara Landry Day proclaimed in her honor Mayor of Macon, 1991. Mem. LWV, AAUW (pres. 1991-93), Wesleyan Coll. Alumnae Assn. (Sara Griffin Perkins Landry scholarship established for non-traditional age students 1994, Disting. Alumnae award for cmty. svc. 1996), Nat. Honor Soc., Macon Little Theatre. Democrat. Roman Catholic. Avocations: reading, swimming, travel, theater. Home: 3807 Drury Dr Macon GA 31204-1313

LANDSBERG, JILL WARREN, lawyer, educator, arbitrator; b. N.Y.C., Oct. 11, 1942; d. George Richard and Evelyn (Schepps) Warren; m. Lewis Landsberg, June 14, 1964; children: Alison, Judd Warren. BA, George Washington U., Washington, 1964; MAT, Yale U., 1965; JD, Boston Coll., 1976. Bar: Mass., 1977, Ill., 1991. Assoc., dir. (ptnr.) Widett, Slater & Goldman PC, Boston, 1976-90; pvt. practice Chgo., 1991-94; faculty Med. Sch. Ethics and Human Values Dept. Northwestern U., Chgo., 1991-94; exec. asst. spl. counsel for child welfare svcs. Office of the Gov., Chgo., 1994-95, acting spl. counsel for child welfare svcs., 1995-96; cons. in field, 1996—2002; adj. prof. law Northwestern U., 2000—. Govt. agys. cons.; mem. Legis. Com. on Juvenile Justice, Chgo., 1995—96, Task Force on Violence Against Children, Chgo., 1995—99, Citizens Com. on the Juvenile Ct., Chgo., 1995—. Tutor Ptnrs. in Edn., 4th Presbyn. Ch., Chgo., 1993—; mem. steering com. Ill. Ct. Improvement Program, 1995-99; Ill. Jud. Inquiry Bd., 2000—; adv. bd. Libr. Internat. Rels., Chgo., 1993-94; bd. trustees Children's Home and Aid Soc. of Ill. Mem. Chgo. Bar Assn., Ill. State Bar Assn.,, Am. Arbitration Assn. (cons. 1989—),Phi Beta Kappa, Order of the Coif. Home and Office: 70 E Cedar St Chicago IL 60611-1179

LANDSKE, DOROTHY SUZANNE (SUE LANDSKE), state legislator; b. Evanston, Ill., Sept. 3, 1937; d. William Gerald and Dorothy Marie (Drewes) Martin; m. William Steve Landske, June 1, 1957; children: Catherine Suzanne Jones, Jacqueline Marie Basilotta, Pamela Florence Snyder, Cheryl Lynn Boisson, Eric Thomas. Student, St. Joseph Coll., Ind. U., U. Chgo. Owner, operator Sues Bridal House, 1967-75; dep. clk.-treas. Cedar Lake, 1975; chief dep. twp. assessor Center Twp., Crown Point, Ind., 1976-78, twp. assessor, 1979-84; mem. Ind. Senate, 1984—. Asst. pres., chair elections protem-senate. Vice chair Lake County Rep. Cen. Com., 1978-89, 97—. Lt. col. NG Res. Mem. LWV, Coun. State Govts., Nat. Order Women Legislators, Nat. Coun. State Legislators, Bus. and Profl. Women, Grange Ind. Farm Bur. Roman Catholic. Office: Ind Senate Dist 6 200 W Washington St Indianapolis IN 46204-2728

LAND-WEBER, ELLEN, photography educator; b. Rochester, N.Y., Mar. 16, 1943; d. David and Florence Epstein; 1 child, Julia. BA, U. Iowa, 1965, MFA, 1968. Faculty mem. UCLA Extension, 1970-74, Orange Coast Coll., Costa Mesa, Calif., 1973, U. Nebr., Lincoln, 1974; asst. prof. photography Humboldt State U., Arcata, Calif., 1974-79, assoc. prof., 1979-83, prof., 1983—. Photographer Seagram's Bicentennial Courthouse Project, 1976-77, Nat. Trust for Hist. Preservation/Soc. Photographic Edn., 1987. Author: The Passionate Collector, 1980, To Save a Life: Stories of Holocaust Rescue, 2000; contbr. sects. to books; photographs pub. in numerous books and jours. Nat. Endowment for Arts fellow, 1974, 79, 82; Artist's support grantee Unicolor Corp., 1982, Polaroid 20X24 Artist's support grantee, 1990, 91, 93, 94; Fulbright sr. fellow, 1993-94. Mem. Soc. for Photog. Edn. (exec. bd. 1979-82, treas. 1979-81, sec. 1981-83) Avocation: weaving. Office: Humboldt State U Art Dept Arcata CA 95521

LANDY, JOANNE VEIT, foreign policy and health policy reform analyst; b. Chgo., Oct. 15, 1941; d. Fritz and Lucille (Stearns) Veit; m. Seymour Landy, Mar., 1959 (div. 1962); m. Nelson Lichtenstein, Mar., 1972 (div. 1976). BA in History, U. Calif., Berkeley, 1968, MA in History, 1970; MPH, Columbia U., 1982. Dir. N.Y. Met. Office, U. Chgo., N.Y.C., 1977-80; co-dir Campaign for Peace and Democracy, N.Y.C., 1982—; exec. dir. Physicians for a Nat. Health Program NY Chpt., 2000—. Editor: Peace and Democracy, 1984-1996; mem. editl. bd. New Politics, 1986—. Recipient grant for rsch. and writing John D. and Catherine T. Mac Arthur Fedn., Program on Peace and Internat. Cooperation, Chgo., 1990-91. Mem. Phi Beta Kappa. Home: 2785 Broadway Apt 7A New York NY 10025-2850

LANDY, LISA ANNE, lawyer; b. Miami, Fla., Apr. 20, 1963; d. Burton Aaron and Eleonora Maria (Simmel) L. BA, Brown U., 1985; JD cum laude, U. Miami, 1988. Bar: Fla. 1988, U.S. Dist. Ct. (so. dist.) Fla. 1988. Atty. Paul, Landy, Beiley & Harper, P.A., Miami, Fla., 1988-94, Steel Hector & Davis, Miami, Fla., 1994-97, ptnr., 1996-97; shareholder Akerman Senterfitt & Eidson P.A., Miami, 1997—. Bd. dirs. Miami City Ballet, 1992-97, pres., 1996; bd. dirs. Women in Internat. Trade, Miami, 1992—, pres., 1994; bd. dirs. Orgn. Women in Internat. Trade, 1994—, v.p., 1997, 98, pres. 1998-2000; bd. dirs. Women in Tech. Internat. South Fla, The Next Step Youth Cmty. Ctr., Inc., IT Women, Inc., 2002—. Mem. ABA, Inter-Am. Bar Assn. (asst. sec. 1997-2000). Avocations: sports, arts, languages.

LANE, ANN JUDITH, history and women's studies educator; b. N.Y.C., July 27, 1931; d. Harry A. and Elizabeth (Brown) Lane; children: Leslie Patricia, Joni Alexandra. BA, Bklyn. Coll., 1952; MA, NYU, 1958; PhD, Columbia U., 1968. Mng. editor Challenge Mag., NYU, 1953-56; asst. prof. Douglass Coll., Rutgers U., New Brunswick, N.J., 1968-71; prof. John Jay Coll., SUNY, 1971-83; vis. prof. Wheaton Coll., Norton, Mass., 1981-82; prof. history, dir. women's studies Colgate U., Hamilton, N.Y., 1983-90, U. Va., Charlottesville, 1990—. Author: To Herland and Beyond, 1990, Mary Ritter Beard: A Sourcebook, 1977, 2d edit., 1988, The Brownsville Affair, 1971; editor: Charlotte Perkins Gilman Reader, 1980, Herland: A Lost Utopian Novel, 1979. Chair Com. on Status of Women in the Profession, Orgn. of Am. Historians, 1992-95; dir. History Tchr. Inst., N.Y. Coun. for Humanities, summer 1985; mem. historians adv. com. Nat. Women's Hall of Fame, 1986—; bd. dirs. Louis M. Rabinowitz Found., 1972-76. Fellow, Berkshire Conf. Women Historians, 1988, Ford Found., 1981-82, Nat. Endowment for Humanities, 1980-81, Lilly Endowment, Inc., 1977-79, AAUW, 1959-60. Mem. AAUP (mem. com. on women 1987—), Orgn. Am. Historians (mem. Frederick Jackson Turner prize com. 1979), Women in Hist. Profession (exec. bd., coordinating com. 1971-74). Home: 2603 Jefferson Park Cir Charlottesville VA 22903-4133

LANE, BARBARA MILLER (BARBARA MILLER-LANE), humanities educator; b. N.Y.C., Nov. 1, 1934; d. George Ross Rede and Gertrude Miller; m. Jonathan Lane, Jan. 28, 1956; children: Steven Gregory, Eleanor. BA, U. Chgo., 1953, Barnard Coll., 1956; MA, Radcliffe Coll., 1957; PhD, Harvard U., 1962. Tutor history and lit. Harvard U., Cambridge, Mass., 1960-61; lectr. to prof. history Bryn Mawr Coll., Pa., 1962-75, dir. Growth and Structure of Cities Program, 1971-89, Andrew W. Mellon prof. humanities, 1981-99, Katherine McBride emeritus prof., 1999—, dr. grad. group in archaeology, classics and history of art, 2004—. Vis. prof. architecture Columbia U., 1989; cons. NEH sr. fellowships, Washington, 1971-73, Time-Life Books, N.Y.C., 1975; advisor Macmillan Ency. of Architects, N.Y.C., 1979-82; vis. examiner U. Helsinki, 1991; vis. lectr. Technische Universität, Berlin, 1991, Royal Inst. Tech., Stockholm, Sweden, 2002. Author: (books) Architecture and Politics in Germany, 1968, 1985, National Romanticism and Modern Architecture in Germany and the Scandinavian Countries, 2000; co-author: Nazi Ideology Before 1933, 1978; author (contbg.): Growth and Transformation of the Modern City, 1979, Macmillan Encyclopedia of Architects, 1982, Urbanisierung im 19. und 20. Jahrhundert, 1983, Perspectives in American History, 1984, The Evidence of Art: Images and Meaning in History, 1986, Art and History, 1988, Nationalism in the Visual Arts, 1991, Moderne Architektur in Deutschland: Expressionismus und Neue Sachlichkeit, 1994, Ultra terminum vagari: Scritti in onore di Carl Nylander, 1997; contbg. editor: Urbanism Past and Present, 1980—85; bd. editors Archtl. History Found., 1988—, (journal) Ctrl. European History, 1992—97; contbr. articles to profl. jours. Co-founder, dir., chmn. bd. dirs. New Gulph Child Care Ctr., Bryn Mawr, 1971-75; mem. Middle Atlantic Regional Com., Mellon Fellowships in the Humanities, 1985-87; mem. vis. com. Harvard U. Dept. History, 1986-92, Berlin Stadtforum (adv. coun. to Senator for Urban Devel. and Environment), 1991-96; mem. nat. screening com. Inst. Internat. Edn., 1999-2004; mem. com. NEH sr. fellowships, 2002. Recipient Lindback award for excellence in tchg., 1988, medal of honor U. Helsinki, 1996; fellow AAUW, 1959-60, Fels Found., 1961-62, Am. Council Learned Socs., 1967-68, Guggenheim Found., 1977-78, sr. fellow Ctr. for Advanced Study in Visual Arts, Nat. Gallery Art, Washington, 1983; Am. Scandinavian Found. fellow, 1989, Wissenschaftskolleg zu Berlin fellow, 1990-91; NEH grantee, summer 1989; NEH sr. fellow, 1998. Mem. Soc. Archtl. Historians (bd. dirs. 1977-80, Alice Davis Hitchcock award 1968, chmn. awards coms. 1976, 82, chmn. jour. com. 1982-83), Conf. Group on Central European History (bd. dirs. 1977-79, chmn. awards com. 1987), Am. Hist. Assn. (mem. coun. 1979-82, chmn. com. on Popular Mag. of History 1982), Coll. Art Assn., Phi Beta Kappa. Office: Bryn Mawr Coll Bryn Mawr PA 19010

LANE, CAROLYN BROOKS, school counselor; b. Phila., Nov. 11, 1948; 1 child, Brett A. BS, Millersville U., 1970; MEd, Xavier U., 1976; EdS, U. Ga., 1993. Nat. cert. counselor. Adminstrv. asst. State Govt., Harrisburg, Pa., 1970-71, Cen. Mich. U., Mt. Pleasant, Mich., 1971-72; reading specialist Princeton City Schs., Cin., 1972-79, Hamilton County Bd. of Edn., Cin., 1979-85, DeKalb County Schs., Ga., 1985-92; sch. counselor Gwinnett County Schs., Ga., 1992—. Level chair M.S. Sch. Counselors, Gwinnett County, 1995-96; mem. peer leadership conf. steering com. Gwinnett County Schs., 1993-95. Vol. Christ Hosp., Cin., 1980-82. Named Counselor of Yr., Gwinnett County Mid. Sch., 1997, Elem.Sch. Counselor of Yr., 2003 Gwinnett County, Ga. Region 2 Mid. Sch., 1997, Ga. Student Assistance Profls. Assn., 1998. Mem. ASCA, AAUW, Am. Sch. Counselor Assn., Ga. Sch. Counselor Assn. (editl. bd. Beacon, chair Gwinett County Elem. Counselors, 2001-02), Phi Kappa Phi. Avocations: travel, reading, interior design, collecting antiques. Office: Bethesda Elem Sch 525 Bethesda Sch Rd Lawrenceville GA 30044

LANE, CARRIE BELLE (HAIRSTON), retired music educator; b. Columbus, Ohio, Nov. 12, 1936; d. Samuel Arthur and Carrie Belle Hairston; m. LeRoy Elsworth Lane, June 27, 1964; children: Peter Kevin, Samuel Elsworth, Todd Lucien. BS in Edn., Ohio State U., 1960. Cert. music tchr. Ohio, Wash., N.J., 1960. Music tchr. Ctrl. Local Schs., Farmer, Ohio, 1961—64, Cleve. Pub. Schs., 1964—66, Clover Pk. Pub. Schs., Tacoma, 1969, Columbus Pub. Schs., 1968—69, Mt. Laurel Pub. Schs., NJ, 1967, Pemberton Twp. Schs., NJ, 1974—77, Willingboro Pub. Schs., NJ. Pvt. voice and piano tchr., Willingboro, 1977—2002, Delanco, NJ, 2004—. Charter mem. and sec., v.pres. Willingboro Chpt. NAACP, 1977—88; v.p. Willingboro Dem. Com., 1982; pres. Willingboro Zoning Bd. of Adjust., 1978—94; committeewoman dist. 26 Willingboro Dem. Club, 1992—94; sr. soloist and dir. Willingboro Presbyn. Ch., 1977—90; soloist and asst. dir. Christ Bapt. Ch. Sr. Choir, Burlington, NJ, 1991—. Recipient Cmty. and Edn. award, Willingboro NAACP, 1982, Ft. Dix Mil. Wife of the Yr., Ft. Dix Post Comdr. and Cmty., 1974. Mem.: N.J. Ret. Edn. Assn., NEA Ret. Tchrs. (assoc.), N.J. Edn. Assn. (assoc.; union rep. jr. h.s. 2001—02), Alpha Kappa Alpha (assoc.; charter mem. treas. 1978—). Democrat-Npl. Baptist. Avocations: reading, travel, singing, teaching, directing. Home: 11 Shipps Way Delanco NJ 08075

LANE, CHARLOTTE, lawyer; b. 1948; AB, Marshall U., 1966—69; JD, W.Va. U., 1969—72. Bar: W.Va. 1972. Delegate W.Va. House of Delegates, 1978—80, 1990—92; commr. W.Va. Pub. Svc. Commn., 1985—89, chmn., 1997—2001, commr., 2001—. Mem. W.Va. Bar Assn. (pres.-elect), Charleston Chamber of Commerce (bd. dirs.), Charleston Rotary (bd. dirs.), former mem. W. Va. Ho. Del., 1978-80, chmn. Public Svc. Commn. 1997-2001 Office: Public Svc Comm 201 Brooks St Charleston WV 25301

LANE, DIANE, actress; b. N.Y.C., Jan. 22, 1965; d. Burt Lane and Colleen Farrington; m. Christopher Lambert, Oct. 1988 (div. Mar. 1994); 1 child, Eleanor. Actress: (stage prodns.) Medea, 1972, Agamemnon, 1977, The Cherry Orchard, 1977, Runaways, 1978, Electra, The Trojan Woman, As You Like it, The Good Woman of Setzuan, (feature films) A Little Romance, 1979 (Young Artist Award for best juvenile actress motion picture, 1980), Cattle Annie and Little Britches, 1981, National Lampoon Goes to the Movies, 1981, Six Pack, 1982, Ladies and Gentlemen, The Fabulous Stains, 1982, The Outsiders, 1983, Rumble Fish, 1983, The Cotton Club, 1984, Streets of Fire, 1984, Lady Beware, 1987, The Big Town, 1987, Vital Signs, 1990, Chaplin, 1992, Knight Moves, 1992, Indian Summer, 1993, Wild Bill, 1995, Judge Dredd, 1995, Jack, 1996, Mad Dog Time, 1996, The Only Thrill, 1997, Murder at 1600, 1997, Over the Moon, 1998, GunShy, 1998, A Walk on the Moon, 1999, The Setting Sun, 1999, My Dog Skip, 1999, The Perfect Storm, 2000, Hard Ball, 2001, The Glass House, 2001, Unfaithful, 2002 (Acad. Award nomination for best actress, 2003, Golden Satellite award for best actress, 2003, Nat. Soc. of Film Critics award for best actress, 2003, NY Film Critics Circle award for best actress, 2003), Under the Tuscan Sun, 2003; (TV movies) Child Bride of Short Creek, 1981, Miss All-America Beauty, 1982; appeared in TV miniseries, Lonesome Dove, 1989, The World's Oldest Living Confederate Widow Tells All, 1994, A Streetcar Named Desire, 1995, Grace and Glorie, 1998. Named Actress of Yr., Hollywood Film Festival, 2003. Mem. Actors' Equity Assn., AFTRA.*

LANE, DOROTHY SPIEGEL, preventive medicine physician; b. Bklyn., Feb. 17, 1940; d. Milton Barton and Rosalie (Jacobson) Spiegel; m. Bernard Paul Lane, Aug. 5, 1962; children: Erika, Andrew, Matthew. BA, Vassar Coll., 1961; MD, Columbia U., 1965, MPH, 1968. Diplomate Am. Bd. Preventive Medicine, Am. Bd. Family Practice. Resident in preventive medicine N.Y.C. Dept. Health Dist., 1966-68, project dir. children and youth project Title V, HHS, 1968-69; med. cons. Maternal and Child Health Svc. HHS, Rockville, Md., 1970-71; asst. prof. preventive medicine Sch. Medicine SUNY, Stony Brook, 1971-76, assoc. prof., 1976-92, prof., 1992—2002, Disting. Svc. prof., 2002—, assoc. dean, 1986—; chair dept. cmty. medicine, dir. med. edn. Brookhaven Meml. Hosp. Med. Ctr., Patchogue, N.Y., 1972-86. Contbr. articles to profl. jours. Exec. com. L.I. divsn. Am. Cancer Soc., 1975—96, pres. L.I. divsn., 1982, mem. nat. assembly, 1996—2001, nat. bd. dir., 1994—96; corp. mem. Nassau Suffolk Health Sys. Agy, 1977—97; bd. dir. Cmty. Health Plan Suffolk, Hauppauge, NY, 1986—91. Grantee, HHS-USPHS, 1977—2001, Nat. Cancer Ins., 1987—. Fellow: APHA, Am. Bd. Preventive Medicine (trustee 1991—2000, chair 1998—2000), NY Acad. Medicine, Am. Acad. Family Physicians, Am. Coll. Preventive Medicine (regent 1988—96, sec.-treas. 1994—96, pres.-elect 1998—2001, pres. 2001—03, immediate past pres. 2003—), Assn. Tchrs. Preventive Medicine (pres. 1996—98); mem.: Accreditation Coun. for Continuing Med. Edn. Office: SUNY at Stony Brook Sch Medicine Health Scis Ctr L 4 Stony Brook NY 11794-0001

LANE, ELIZABETH ANN, music educator; b. Amityville, N.Y., Jan. 24, 1977; d. James August and Corinne Ann Lane. MusB in Edn., Mansfield (Pa.) U., 1999; MEd, Ind. Wesleyan U., 2003. Child care worker St. Michael's Sch. for Boys, Tunkhannock, Pa., 1999; prin., owner Elizabeth Ln. Musical Svcs., Sayre, Pa., 1999—; music tchr. Athens (Pa.) Area Schs., 1999—; prin., owner. Creative Memories Consulting, St. Cloud, Minn., 2003—. Flutist The Windwood Trio, Sayre, 2002—. Scholar Kreucher scholarship, Mansfield U., 1998, Presser scholarship, 1999. Mem.: Bradford County Music Educators Assn. (assoc.), Music Educators Nat. Conf. (assoc.). Democrat. Avocations: scrapbooks, bowling, bell choir, flute. Home: 7 Hemlock Road Sayre PA 18840 Office: Athens Area School District 0 Pennsylvania Ave Athens PA 18810 Personal E-mail: lizlane98@yahoo.com.

LANE, GLORIA JULIAN, foundation administrator; b. Chgo., Oct. 6, 1932; d. Coy Berry and Katherine (McDowell) Julian; m. William Gordon Lane (div. Oct. 1958); 1 child, Julie Kay Rosewood. BS in Edn., Cen. Mo. State U., 1958; MA, Bowling Green State U., 1959; PhD, No. Ill. U., 1972. Cert. tchr. Assoc. prof. William Jewell Coll., Liberty, Mo., 1959-60; chair forensic div. Coral Gables (Fla.) High Sch., 1960-64; assoc. prof. No. Ill. U., DeKalb, 1964-70; prof. Elgin (Ill.) Community Coll., 1970-72; owner, pub. Lane and Assocs, Inc., San Diego, 1972-78; prof. Nat. U., San Diego, 1978-90; pres., chief exec. officer Women's Internat. Ctr., San Diego, 1982—. Founder, dir. Living Legacy Awards, San Diego, 1984—. Author: Project Text for Effective Communications, 1972, Project Text for Executive Communication, 1980, Positive Concepts for Success, 1983; editor Who's Who Among San Diego Women, 1984, 85, 86, 90—, Systems and Structure, 1984. Named Woman of Accomplishment, Soroptimist Internat., 1985, Pres.'s Coun. San Diego, 1986, Center City Assn., 1986, Bus. and Profl. Women, San Diego, 1991, Woman of Yr., Girls' Clubs San Diego, 1986, Woman of Vision, Women's Internat. Ctr., 1990, Wonderwoman 2000 Women's Times Newspaper, 1991; recipient Angel in Action award, 1999, Independence award Ctr. for Disabled, 1986, Founder's award Children's Hosp. Internat., Washington, 1986, Making Difference for Women award, Soroptimist Internat., 1998, Women Who Mean Business Courage Award San Diego Bus. Jour., 1998. Avocations: computers, painting, writing. Home and Office: 6202 Friars Rd Unit 311 San Diego CA 92108-5000

LANE, HANA UMLAUF, editor; b. Stockholm, Mar. 14, 1946; came to U.S., 1951, naturalized, 1957; d. Karel Hugo Antonin and Anatolia (Spitel) Umlauf; m. John Richard Lane, Feb. 16, 1980; 1 stepchild, Matthew John AB magna cum laude, Vassar Coll., 1968; AM in Russian and East European Studies, Yale U., 1970. Asst. to exec. editor Newspaper Enterprise Assn., N.Y.C., 1970-72, sr. asst., assoc. editor World Almanac divsn., 1972-75, assoc. editor World Almanac, 1975-80, spl. project editor, 1977-80; editor World Almanac and World Almanac Publs., N.Y.C., 1980-85; editor in chief Pharos Books, N.Y.C., 1984-91, sr. editor, 1991-93, John Wiley & Sons, 1993—. Editor: World Almanac Book of Who, 1980, World Almanac and Book of Facts, 1981-85; (with others) The Woman's Almanac, 1977 Democrat. Home: 140 Fairview Ave Stamford CT 06902-8040

LANE, HOLLY DIANA, artist; b. Cleve., Sept. 13, 1954; d. Edwin Joseph and Ursula Anna (Neustadt) Selyem; m. L.A. Lane, Apr. 20, 1975. AA in 2-Dimensional Art, Cuesta Coll., San Luis Obispo, Calif., 1982; BFA with great distinction, San Jose State U., 1986, MFA in Pictorial Art, 1988.

One-woman shows include Ivory/Kimpton Gallery, San Francisco, 1989, Rutgers Barclay Gallery, Santa Fe, 1990, Bingham Kurts Gallery, Memphis, 1992, (solo survey show with catalog) Art Mus. S.E. Tex., Beaumont, 1995, Natalie & James Thompson Gallery, San Jose State U., 2001, Yellowstone Art Museum, 2001, Lyman Allyn Mus. Art, 2001, Schmidt Bingham Gallery, NYC, 1991, 93, 95, 97, 99, 2001, Forum Gallery, NYC, 2003, exhibited in group shows at Eiteljorg Mus., Indpls., 1995, 2000, Yerba Buena Ctr. for the Arts, San Francisco, 1994, Knoxville (Tenn.) Mus. Art, 1993-94, Fine Arts Ctr. U. RI, Kingston, 1992, Contemporary Mus., Honolulu, 1993, 2002, Boise (Idaho) Art Mus., 1994, Castle Gallery-Coll. New Rochelle, NY, 1996, Kennedy Mus. Am. Art, Athens, Ohio, 1996, Calif. Ctr. for the Arts Escondido Mus., 1996, Samuel P. Harn Mus., U. Fla., Gainesville, 1996, Whitney Mus. Am. Art, Champion, Conn., 1997-98, Arnot Art Mus., Elmira, NY, 1997-98, Susan H. Arnold Art Gallery Lebanon Valley Coll., Anneville, Pa., 1997-98, Pelham (NY) Art Ctr, 1998, Art Mus. Western Va., 1999-2000, San Jose Mus. Art, 1999-2000, Art Mus. Western Va., 1999-2000, Santa Cruz Art Mus., 2000, Brevard Mus. Art and Sci., Melbourne, Fla., 2000, Gallery of Contemporary Art, Sacred Heart U., Fairfield, Conn., 2002, NJ Ctr. For Visual Arts, Summit, 2002, Jarvic Ctr., NYC, 2002; represented in permanent collections Art Mus. S.E. Tex., Contemporary Mus., Honolulu, A.R.A. Svcs., Phila., Dow Jones & Co., NYC, Detroit Zool. Gardens, Prin. Fin. Group, Des Moines, IDS, Mpls., Memphis Cancer Ctr., Seven Bridges Found., Greenwich, Conn.; works reproduced in books, mags., calendars, jours., including ARTNews, Art in America, N.Y. Times, Art Papers, Art & Antiques, New Yorker Mag., Artweek, Christian Sci. Monitor, Pvt. Arts, Forensic Examiner, NYarts Mag., The Wilson Quar., Review Mag., NYC, 1999, Women Artists calendar 1996-98, San Raphael, Calif., The Sciences, NY Acad. Scis., 1992-93, (textbook) Artist and Audience, (London) 1996, Dreams 1900-2000, NY Sun, 2003, CAA News, 2003: Sci., Art and the Unconscious Mind (book), 1999, Wilson Quarterly, 1998, Rev. Mag., 1999, Dreamworks: Twentieth-Century Artistic and Psychological Perspectives, 1999; works presented and discussed in TV documentaries, including Welcome to Nocturnia, 1993, Women in Art, Time-Warner, Manhattan Cable, NYC, 1993-94; in books accompanying TV show Bill Moyers Genesis, A Living Tradition, PBS, 1996, Healing and the Mind, 1993. Named Alumna of Yr., Cuesta Coll., 1992; pres.'s scholar San Jose State U., 1986, Johanna Rietz scholar Art Assn. of Morro Bay, Calif., 1981; recipient honorable mention Western States Arts Fedn., Santa Fe, 1994. Mem. Coll. Art Assn. (scholarship 1981). Avocations: nature walks, contemplation, reading. Home: 182 Brian Ln Santa Clara CA 95051-6704 Address: care Forum Gallery 745 Fifth Ave 5th Fl New York NY 10151 E-mail: hlane42@earthlink.net.

LANE, KAREN GALE, operations research analyst; d. Allen and Ruth Lane. BA in French, BS in Math., Salisbury (Md.) U., 1993; MS in Info. Systems Tech., George Washington U., 2002. Ops. rsch. analyst Hdqs., Mil. Traffic Mgmt. Command, Alexandria, 2000, Ctr. for Army Analysis, Fort Belvoir, Va., 2000—. V.p. Chancery Condo Owners Assn., Alexandria, Va., 2001—03. Mem.: Mensa (life). Office: Ctr Army Analysis 6001 Goethals Rd Fort Belvoir VA 22060

LANE, KATHLEEN MARGARET, refrigeration company official; b. Mpls., Oct. 25, 1946; d. Bernard Melvin and Margaret (Beck) Aanerud; m. Kenneth LeRoy Lane, Sept. 1, 1979; 1 child, Dennis Leon. Cost acct. Honeywell, Mpls., 1964-66; bookkeeper Columbia Heights State Bank, Minn., 1968-71; mgr. inventory control Hodes Optical Inc., Torrance, Calif., 1972-75, office mgr., 1975-79; lens supr. Coburn Optical Industries, inc., Carson, Calif., 1979-85, br. mgr. St. Paul, 1985-93; office mgr. J.M. Refrigeration, St. Croix Falls, Wis., 1993—99; owner, mgr. Lanes Portable Bandsaw Mill, 2000—. With customer rels. dept. Opti Fair, Aneheim, Calif., 1978-83. Mem. Am. Inst. Banking, NAFE. Avocations: restoring old furniture, camping, knitting. Office: JM Refrigeration PO Box 478 Saint Croix Falls WI 54024-0478 E-mail: kklane@tds.net.

LANE, KATHY S. information technology executive, consumer products company executive; Dir. tech. svcs. Pepsi Cola Internat., 1997—98; mgr. corp. initiatives group Gen. Electric Co., 1998—99, sr. v.p. and chief info. officer, vendor fin. svcs., 1999—2000; gen. mgr. e- bus. and info. tech. Gen. Electric Oil & Gas, 2000—02; sr. v.p. corp. info. tech. and applications Gillette Co., Boston, 2002—, chief info. officer, 2002—. Office: The Gillette Co Prudential Tower Boston MA 02199-8004*

LANE, LAURA ALICE, librarian; b. N.Y.C. d. Cedric R. and Alice J. (Lay) Lane; m. David R. DeVoe; 1 child, Charles. AB, Lake Erie Coll., Painesville, Ohio, 1963; MLS, U. Calif., Berkeley, 1964. Fine arts libr. acquisitions dept. Fogg Art Mus./Harvard U., Cambridge, Mass., 1964-67; humanities cataloger U. Minn., Mpls., 1967-69; head libr. Am. Heritage Pub. Co., N.Y.C., 1969-82; ref. libr. Mt. Sinai Sch. Medicine, N.Y.C., 1983-87; bibliographer Temple U., Phila., 1991—2000, sci. libr., 2000—. Mem. ALA. Office: Temple U Paley Library Philadelphia PA 19122

LANE, MARGARET BEYNON TAYLOR, librarian; b. St. Louis, Feb. 6, 1919; d. Archer and Alice (Jones) Taylor; m. Horace C. Lane, Jan. 6, 1945; children: Margaret Elizabeth, Thomas Archer. BA, La. State U., 1939, JD, 1942; BS in Libr. Sci., Columbia U., 1941. Reference and circulation asst. Columbia Law Libr., N.Y.C., 1942-44; law libr., asst. prof. U. Conn. Sch. Law, Hartford, 1944-46; law libr. La. State U. Law Sch., Baton Rouge, 1946-48; recorder documents La. Sec. of State's Office, Baton Rouge, 1949-75; law libr. Lane Fertitta, Lane Janney & Thomas, 1976-96. Mem. depository libr. coun. to Pub. Printer, 1972-77; mem. plan devel. com. La. Fed. Depository Libr., 1982-83. Author: State Publications and Depository Libraries, 1981, Selecting and Organizing State Government Publications, 1987. Treas. Delta Iota House Bd. of Kappa Kappa Gamma, 1965-68; mem. La. Adv. Coun. State Documents Depository Program, 1991—. Inductee La. State U. Law Ctr. Hall of Fame, 1987. Mem.: ALA (interdivisional com. pub. documents 1967—74, chmn. 1967—70, govt. documents round table, state and local documents task force 1972—, coord. 1980—82, James Bennett Childs award 1981, anniversary honor roll 1996, Hoduski Founders award 1997), Baton Rouge Bar Assn., La. Bar Assn., La. Libr. Assn. (Essae M. Culver Disting. Svc. award 1976, Lucy B. Foote award 1986, Margaret T. Lane award named in her honor 1994), Mortar Bd., Baton Rouge Libr. Club, Kappa Kappa Gamma, Phi Delta Delta. Home: 333 Lee Dr Apt 274 Baton Rouge LA 70808 Office: 435 Louisiana Ave Baton Rouge LA 70802-5820 E-mail: mtlane@cox.net.

LANE, MARSHA K. medical/surgical nurse; b. Glendale, Calif., Mar. 22, 1942; m. Albert Lane, Sept. 16, 1961; children: Alan, Mike, Shawn, Eric. LVN, Mira Costa Coll., 1971; ADN, San Diego City Coll., 1975; BS in Health Scis., Chapman Coll., 1986, postgrad., 1991. Head RN CCU Humana Hosp., Huntington Beach, Calif.; supr. ICU/CCU, TELE Tri City Med. Ctr., Oceanside, Calif., asst. unit mgr. ICU/CCU, staffnurse, dir. med./surg. svcs., developer patient diabetes tchg. program; DON LifeCare Ctr. Vista SNF. Home: 1431 Genoa Dr Vista CA 92083-5383

LANE, MEREDITH ANNE, botany educator, museum curator; b. Mesa, Ariz., Aug. 4, 1951; d. Robert Ernest and Elva Jewell (Shilling) L.; m. Donald W. Longstreth, Apr. 6, 1974 (div. Feb. 1985). BS, Ariz. State U., 1974, MS, 1976; PhD, U. Tex., 1980. Asst. prof. U. Colo., Boulder, 1980-88, assoc. prof., 1988-89; assoc. prof., curator div. botany Natural History Mus., U. Kans., Lawrence, 1989-96, prof., 1997—. Vis. asst. prof. U. Wyo., Laramie, 1985-86; vis. scholar U. Conn., Storrs, 1989; cons. editor McGraw-Hill Ency. of Sci. and Tech., N.Y.C., 1985-92; program dir. Nat. Sci. Found., 1995-97; rsch. assoc. Smithsonian Inst., 1995—; agy. rep. Nat. Sci. and Tech. Coun., 1997. Editor Bull., 1990-94; contbr. over 25 articles to profl. jours. Mem. Am. Soc. Plant Taxonomists (sec. 1986-88, program dir. 1986-90, councillor 1993-96, Cooley award 1982), Bot. Soc. Am. (sect. chmn. 1984-86, sect. sec. 1986-90), Internat. Orgn. for Plant Biosystematics (councillor 1989-92), Internat. Assn. Plant Taxonomists, Calif. Bot. Soc. Avocations: reading, conversation, country dance, hiking, furniture refinishing. Office: R L McGregor Herbarium 2045 Constant Ave Lawrence KS 66047-3729

LANE, NANCY, editor, human rights activist; b. N.Y.C., Dec. 20, 1938; d. Morton and Lillian (Gelb) L. AB in Am. Civilization, Barnard Coll., 1960. Mem. staff N.Y. Times, 1959-61; from asst. to assoc. editor Polit. Sci. Quar. and Procs. Acad. Polit. Sci., Columbia U., N.Y.C., 1962-70; from assoc. editor to mng. editor Am. Hist. Rev. Am. Hist. Assn., 1970-74; from sr. editor to exec. editor Oxford U. Press, N.Y.C., 1974-97; cons., 1997—99. Vol. Bellevue-NYU Program for Survivors of Torture, 1998-99; coord. Turkey REgional Action Network; mem. Aegean co-group Amnest Internat. USA, 2002—. Mem.: ACLU, Ams. United for Separation of Ch. and State, Amnesty Internat. U.S.A. Home: 45 W 10th St New York NY 10011-8731

LANE, PATRICIA PEYTON, retired nursing consultant; b. Danville, Ill., Oct. 5, 1929; d. Louis Weldon Sr. and Ruth Jeanette (Meyer) Peyton; m. H.J. Lane, Dec. 23, 1950 (div.); children: Jennifer Lane-Carr, Peter Lane, Amelia Ozog. Diploma, St. Elizabeth Hosp., 1950; BA in Psychology magna cum laude, Rosary Coll., 1974; postgrad., Lakeview Coll. of Nursing, Danville, Ill., 1987-88; student, Triton Jr. Coll., River Grove, Ill., 1969-72. Staff nurse St. Elizabeth Hosp., Danville, Ill., 1950; staff nurse nursery Ill. Rsch. and Ednl. Hosp., Chgo., 1951, charge nurse tumor clinic, 1951-54; res. sch. nurse elem. schs., Oak Park, Ill., 1969-78; sta. mgr. Oak Park-River Infant Welfare, Oak Park, Ill., 1972-76; vision and hearing screener suburban elem. schs., Ill., 1980-82; sch. nurse West Subrban Assn. Spl. Edn., Cicero, 1978-80; caseworker, counselor Vermilion County Mental Health and Devel. Disabilities, Inc., Danville, 1983-86; case coord., nurse cons. Crosspoint Human Svcs., Danville, 1986-88; staff nurse psychiat. acute care unit Community Hosp. of Ottawa, Ill., 1988-89; dir. social svcs. Pleasant View Luther Home, Ottawa, 1989-93; clin. case coord. Access Svcs., Inc., Mendota, Ill., 1993-97; cmty. ombudsman LaSalle County Alternatives for the Older Adult, Peru, Ill., 1993-97; ret., 1997. Cons. in field. Recipient Ill. Gov.'s award for exceptional achievement in cmty. svc. and svc. to elderly, 1997, Vol. of Yr. award Residence at Oak Ridge, 2002. E-mail: PatLane456@msn.com.

LANE, ROSALIE MIDDLETON, extension specialist; b. Savannah, Ga. d. Freddie and Willie Blanche (Jones) Middleton; m. Martin Luther Jones, Apr. 24, 1964 (div. July 1977); children: Regina Veronica, Sharon Yolanda; m. Woodie Lane, Sr., Dec. 6, 1985; 1 stepchild, Woodie M., Jr. BA, Western Mich. U., 1989; M in Urban and Regional Planning, Ala. A&M U., 1995. Exec. sec. Curtis Brown, Ltd., N.Y.C., 1959-64; adminstrv. sec. Bronx (N.Y.)-Lebanon Hosp. Ctr., 1971-76; adminstr. IBM Corp., Savannah, Ga. and Huntsville, Ala., 1980-95; ext. specialist, rschr., educator Coop. Ext. Sys., Ala. A&M U., Normal, 1995—. Past mem. customer interface task force USDA, Washington. Author: (with others) A Directory of Resource for Low Income, Elderly, and Homeless Citizens in North Ala., 1995; author poems. Vol. Coalition/On- At-Risk Minority Males, Huntsville, Ala., 1992; bd. dirs. ARC Minority Initiatives Com., Huntsville, 1994. Mem. NEA, Am. Planning Assn., Com. Minorities in Pub. Transp. Orgn., Alpha Zeta. Presbyterian. Avocations: creative writing, song writing. Office: Ala Cooperative Extension Sys Meridian St Normal AL 35762

LANE, SARAH MARIE CLARK, elementary school educator; b. Conneaut, Ohio, July 27, 1946; d. Robert George and Julia Ellen (Sanford) Clark; m. Ralph Donaldson Lane, May 28, 1977; children: Richard, Laura. BS in Edn., Kent State U., 1977; MS in Edn., Coll. Mt. St. Joseph, 1988. Cert. tchr., Ohio. Coord. newspaper in edn. Tribune Chronicle, Warren, Ohio, 1986-89; tutor MacArthur Found. Project, Warren, Ohio, 1988-89; tchr. chpt. I Lakeview Local Schs., Cortland, Ohio, 1989—. Freelance writer newspaper Conn. News Herald, 1963-64, Tribune Chronicle, 1980-89; contbr. articles to profl. jours.; author: A Walk Through Historic Cortland, 1994. V.p. Bazetta Cortland Hist. Soc., 1983-85; chmn. com. local history project Lakeview Schs., Cortland, 1992—; mem. Trumbull County Bicentennial Commn., 1996—. George Record Found. scholar, 1964-66. Mem. Internat. Reading Assn. (Ohio coun.), Cortland Community Concert Band (pres. 1991-92), Mem. Christian Ch. (Disciples Of Christ). Avocations: writing, historical research, genealogy, reading. Home: 298 Corriedale Dr Cortland OH 44410-1622 Office: Cortland Elem Sch 264 Park Ave Cortland OH 44410-1098

LANE, SYLVIA, economist, educator; b. N.Y.C. m. Benjamin Lane, Sept. 2, 1939; children: Leonard, Reese, Nancy. AB, U. Calif., Berkeley, 1934, MA, 1936; postgrad., Columbia U., 1937; PhD, U. So. Calif., 1957. Lectr., asst. prof. U. So. Calif., 1947—60; assoc. prof. econs. San Diego State U., 1961-65; assoc. prof. finance, assoc. dir. Ctr. for Econ. Edn. Calif. State U., Fullerton, 1965-69, chmn. dept. fin., 1967-69; prof. agrl. econs. U. Calif., Davis, 1969-82, prof. emerita, 1982—; prof. emerita and economist Giannini Found., U. Calif.-Berkeley, 1982—; vis. scholar Stanford U., 1975-76. Cons. Calif. Adv. Commn. Tax Reform, 1963, Adv. Office Consumer Affairs, Exec. Office of Pres., 1972-77, FAO, UN, 1983. Author: (with E. Bryant Phillips) Personal Finance, 1963, rev. edit., 1979, The Insurance Tax, 1965, California's Income Tax Conformity and Withholding, 1968, (with Irma Adelman) The Balance Between Industry and Agriculture in Economic Development, 1989; editl. bd. Agrl. Econs., 1986-92; also articles, reports in field. Project economist Los Angeles County Welfare Planning Coun., 1956-59; del. White House Conf. on Food and Nutrition, 1969, Pres.'s Summit Con. on Inflation, 1974; mem. adv. com. Ctr. for Bldg. Tech., Nat. Bur. Stds., 1975-79; bd. dirs. Am. Coun. Consumer Interests, 1972-74; exec. bd. Am. Agr. Econ. Assn. 1976-79. Ford Found. fellow UCLA, 1963; Ford Found. fellow U. Chgo., 1965; fellow U. Chgo., 1968; fellow Am. Agrl. Econ. Assn., 1984; fellow Sylvia Lane Fellowship Fund, 1993. Mem. Am. Econ. Assn., Am. Coun. Consumer Interests, Omicron Delta Epsilon (pres. 1973-75, trustee 1975-83, chmn. bd. trustees 1982-84). Home and Office: 2231 Caminito Preciosa N La Jolla CA 92037-7231

LANE, TERESA MARIE, language educator; b. Wichita, Kans., Feb. 17, 1957; d. Charles A. and Jean M. Dickenson; m. Michael E. Lane III, Mar. 15, 1975. BA in anthropology and spanish, Wichita State U., 1982; MA in ESL, U. Hawaii, 1990; MA tchg. lang. in Spanish, U. So. Miss., 2000. Instr. Hawaii Pacific U., Honolulu, 1990—. Sec. Hawaii TESOL, Honolulu, 1993—98; acad. coord. modern langs. Hawaii Pacific U., Honolulu, 1995—. Prodr., editor, videos OLELO Pub. Access TV, Honolulu, 1999—; narrator Hawaii Libr. for the Blind, Honolulu, 2001. Mem.: Hawaii Assn. Lang. Tchrs. (sec., v.p. 1999—2002, pres. 2002—03). Avocations: scuba diving, hiking. Office: Hawaii Pacific U 1188 Fort St Mall Honolulu HI 96813

LANE-TRENT, PATRICIA JEAN, information specialist; b. Belleville, Ill., Apr. 3, 1970; d. Lawrence Raymond and Nola Jean (Rosick) Lane; m. Jerry Jackson Trent Jr.; 1 child, Corey Andrew. AA, AS, Belleville Area Coll., 1991; student, So. Ill. U., 1992—, Women's Campaign Sch., 1995. Cert. info. rsch. specialist. Co-owner Jerry's Lawncare and Landscaping, Trent's Quality Constrn., Belleville, Ill., 1993—; youth specialist Mo. Dept. Social Svcs., St. Louis, 1994-95; owner Tracks & Traces Infosource, Belleville, 1997—; social worker Royal Hts. Nursing and Rehab., 1999—. Mem. NOW, NAFE. Democrat. Avocations: fishing, softball, music, singing. Home: 309 S 59th St Belleville IL 62223-4655 Office: Tracks & Traces Infosource 26 Carlyle Plaza Dr Ste 138 Belleville IL 62221-6677

LANEY, MARTI OLSEN, psychoanalyst, researcher, social sciences educator, writer; b. Valparaiso, Ind., May 16, 1945; d. Howard Albert and Julano H. (Oleson) Miller; m. Michael L. Laney, Dec. 31, 1964; children: Tynna Elise DeMillier, Kristen Beth Parks. BA, Calif. State U., Northridge, 1972; MLS, U. So. Calif., L.A., 1977; MA, Azusa Pacific U., Calif., 1980; D of Psychoanalysis, Inst. of Contemporary Psychoanalysis, L.A., 2001. Lic. marriage, family and child therapist Calif., 1982. Children's libr. and head of circulation dept. Inglewood Pub. Libr., 1973—78; therapist Ctr. Individual and Family Counseling, 1978—83; tng. rep. Rockwell Internat., L.A., 1978—83; tng. specialist and mgr. First Interstate Svcs. Co., L.A., 1986—88; faculty mem. Inst. of Contemporary Psychoanalysis, L.A., 1997—, Newport Psychoanalytic Inst., Newport, Calif., 2003—. Exec. dir. Inst. Study of Introverted Temperaments. Author: The Introvert Advantage, 2002 (Books for Better Life award, 2002), How to Thrive in an Extrovert World, 0202; contbr. articles to profl. jours. Mem.: APA (divsn. 39), Internat. Fedn. Psychoanalytic Edn., Am. Assn. Marriage and Family Therapy. Avocations: reading, travel, singing, reflecting, grandmothering. Home: PO Box 8993 Calabasas CA 91372

LANEY, MEREDITH HART, paralegal; d. Mary Converse and Worth Terry Laney; children: Melanie Caitlyn Cawthon, Mackenzie Ryan Kennedy. BA in English, Augusta State U., Augusta, Georgia, 1998—2002. Legal asst./paralegal Law Office of Garrett & Gilliard, P.C., Augusta, Ga., 1999—2003. Co-director (play) The Vagina Monologues (Outstanding Student in Women's Studies, 2002); author: (creative nonfiction - work in progress) Snow on Her Grave, (song lyrics) Free, When I Scream, Woman a capella, These Hands, Good Thing, and Remember (First Pl. in Song Lyric Category at the Sandhills Writers Conf. and the Morgan Fitz Most Promising Student Writer Award, 2001), (poem) Firestorm (Best Poem in Campus Media, 2002), (song lyrics) Cover Myself, What You Take Me For, Come Undone, Hesperides, Less Alone, and Stay (First Pl. in Song Lyric Category at the Sandhills Writers Conf.), (short fiction) The Body Whispers (Read at ASU's Women's Week Symposium 2001), (one act play) Revisions (Performed at ASU's 2003 Summerstock Theatre). Vol. Habitat for Humanity, Cornelius, NC. Personal E-mail: wonderwomanist@yahoo.com.

LANEY, SANDRA EILEEN, service company executive; b. Cin., Sept. 17, 1943; d. Raymond Oliver and Henrietta Rose (Huber) H.; m. Dennis Michael Laney, Sept. 30, 1968; children: Geoffrey Michael, Melissa Ann. AS in Bus. Adminstrn., Thomas More Coll., 1988, BA in Bus. Adminstrn., 1993. Adminstrv. asst. to chief exec. officer Chemed Corp., Cin., 1982, asst. v.p., 1982-84, v.p., 1984-91, v.p., chief adminstrv. officer, 1991-93, sr. v.p., chief adminstrv. officer, 1993-2001, bd. dirs., 1986—, exec. v.p. chief adminstrn. officer, 2001—02; CEO, chmn. Cadre Computer Resources Co., 2001—. Bd. dirs. Omnicare Inc., Covington, Ky. Mem. bd. advisors Sch. Nursing U. Cin., 1992—; bd. overseers Cin. Symphony Orch., 1998; trustee Lower Price Hill Cmty. Sch., Cmty. Land Coop. of Cin. Mem. AAUW, NOW, Internat. Platform Assn., Amnesty Internat., World Affairs Coun., Women's Action Coun. Roman Catholic. Office: Cadre Computer Resources Co. 1200 Chemed Ctr 255 E 5th St Cincinnati OH 45202-4700

LANG, ENID ASHER, psychiatrist; b. LA, Aug. 28, 1944; d. Alvin Melville and Inez (Silverberg) Asher; m. Norton Lang; children: Eugenie, Aaron. BA, Harvard U., 1966; MD, U. So. Calif., 1975; MPH in Pub. Health, Columbia U., N.Y.C., 1975. Intern Beth Israel Hosp., N.Y.C., 1971-72; resident in psychiatry Columbia Psychiat. Inst., N.Y.C., 1972-75; fellow Columbia Health Svc., N.Y.C., 1974-75; asst. clin. prof. psychiatry Mt. Sinai Med. Sch., NYC, 1976—. Lectr. psychiatry and lit. for faculty, Mt Sinai Dept. Psychiatry, NYC, 1983-97. Co-author (Dr. E. Ackerman) Study of Health in Rural France, 1978; (with D. Halperin) Group Psychotherapy, 1983. Bd. govs. Harvard-Radcliffe Club of Westchester County, NY, 1993-98. Milbank fellow Barrio Health Care, LA, 1970-71. Mem.: Am. Psychiat. Assn. Jewish. Avocations: literature, playing cello, judging h.s. debates. Office: 1158 5th Ave New York NY 10029-6917

LANG, K. D. (KATHERINE DAWN LANG), country music singer, composer; b. Consort, Alta., Can., Feb. 11, 1961; d. Adam and Audrey L. Lang. Mem. Tex. swing fiddle band, 1982—; formed band The Reclines. Albums include A Truly Western Experience, 1984, Angel with a Lariat, 1986, Shadowland, 1988, Absolute Torch and Twang, 1990 (Can. Country Music Awards album of the yr.), Ingenue, 1992, Even Cowgirls Get the Blues (soundtrack), 1993, Drag, 1997, Australian Tour, 1997; (with others) All You Can Eat, 1995; actress (film) Salmonberries, 1991; Teresa's Tattoo, 1994, The Last Don, 1997, TV guest appearance Ellen, 1997, Eye of The Beholder, 1999. Recipient Can. Country Music awards, including Entertainer of Yr., 1989, Grammy award, 1990, 1993, Best Pop Female Vocal for Constant Craving, Grammy nomination Best Pop Female Vocal for Miss Chatelaine, 1994, William Harold Moon award Soc. of Composers, Authors and Music Publishers of Can., 1994. Office: Warner Bros Records Inc 3300 Warner Blvd Burbank CA 91505-4694

LANG, LAURIE, entertainment company executive; 1 child. BA in Theater Arts and Polit. Sci., Wash. U.; MBA, Columbia U. V.p., account supr. DDB Needham Advt., N.Y.C.; sr. v.p. strategic mktg. Walt Disney Co., Burbank, Calif., 1988-98, head Learning Initiative, 1998—. Office: Walt Disney Co 500 S Buena Vista St Burbank CA 91521-0006

LANG, LINDA A. food service executive; B in Fin., U. Calif., Berkeley; MBA, San Diego State U. Joined Jack in the Box Inc., 1985, divsn. v.p. new products and promotions, 1994—96, v.p. products, promotions and consumer rsch., 1996—99, v.p. mktg., 1999—2001, sr. v.p. mktg., 2001—02, exec. v.p. mktg. and ops., human resources, restaurant devel., quality assurance and logistics, 2002—03, pres., COO, 2003—, also bd. dirs. Office: Jack in the Box Inc 9330 Balboa Ave San Diego CA 92123

LANG, LISA ANN, music educator; b. Mt. Vernon, Ohio, Dec. 5, 1952; d. Kenneth Richard and June Pauline Auskings; m. Kenneth Ray Lang, Feb. 27, 1951; children: Natalie Ann, Christie Nicole, Matthew Ryan. Student, St. Andrews U., 1971; B of Music Edn., Baldwin-Wallace Conservatory, 1974; MA, Ohio State U., 1987. Cert. k-12 music specialist Ohio Bd. Edn., 1984. Dir,. bands, jr. high and high sch. Pickerington Local Schools, Ohio, 1974—. Asst. dir. high sch. Rep. Rally Performance Pres. George Bush Sr., Columbus, 1988—88, Rep. Rally Performance Pres. Ronald Reagan, 1984—84; asst. dir. high schs. marching band Macy's Thanksgiving Day Parades, N.Y.C., 1990, 2001; asst. dir. high sch. Fiesta Bowl Parades & Nat. Band Championships, Phoenix, 1999, 2003, Orange Bowl Parades & Nat. Band Competitions, Miami, 1995, 2000, 2001, Miss Am. Pageant, Atlantic City, Md., 1994, Cotton Bowl Parade, Dallas, 1989; host chmn. Fairfield All County Music Concerts, Pickerington, 1974—2003; concerts elderly health care facilities Pickerington Jr. High Bands, 1975—2003; curriculum chmn.gifted program Pickerington Schools/Fairfield County, 2000—03. Named Lead Marching Band for Parade, Macy's Thanksgiving Day Parade Com., 2001; recipient Adjudicators Choice award, Music in Parks Competitions, 1999, Outstanding Concert Band Awards, 2000, 2003, Alumni award, Baldwin Wallace Coll. Conservatory, 2003. Mem.: NEA (assoc.), Am. Schools Band Directors Assn. (hon.), Ohio Music Educators Assn. (assoc.; marching band adjudicator 1992—, solo and ensemble adjudicator, concert band adjudicator), Pickerington Edn. Assn. (assoc.; sec. 1986), Ohio Edn. Assn. (assoc.), Music Educators Nat. Conf. (assoc.), Phi Beta Mu (hon.), Phi Mu (assoc.), Tau Beta Sigma (assoc.; sec. 1973—74). Avocations: travel, reading, art. Office: Pickerington Local Schs 130 S Hill Rd Pickerington OH 43147 Office Phone: 614-833-2100. Personal E-mail: langbndldy@aol.com. E-mail: lisa_lang@fc.pickerington.k12.oh.us.

LANG, MABEL LOUISE, classics educator; b. Utica, N.Y., Nov. 12, 1917; d. Louis Bernard and Katherine (Werdge) L. BA, Cornell U., 1939; MA, Bryn Mawr Coll., 1940, PhD, 1943; Litt.D., Coll. Holy Cross, 1975, Colgate U., 1978; L.H.D., Hamilton Coll. Mem. faculty Bryn Mawr Coll., 1943-91, successively instr., asst. prof., 1943-50, assoc. prof., 1950-59, prof. Greek, 1959-88, chmn. dept., 1960-88, acting dean coll. 2d semester, 1958-59, 60-61; chmn. mng. com. Am. Sch. Classical Studies, Athens, 1975-80, chmn. admissions and fellowship com., 1966-72; Blegen disting. rsch. prof. semester I Vassar Coll., 1976-77; Martin classical lectr. Oberlin Coll., 1982. Co-author: Athenian Agora Measures and Tokens; author: Palace of Nestor Frescoes, 1969, Athenian Agora Graffiti and Dipinti, 1976; Herodotean Narrative and Discourse, 1984, Athenian Agor Ostraka, 1990; contbr. articles to profl. jours. Guggenheim fellow, 1953-54; Fulbright fellow Greece, 1959-60 Mem. Am. Philos. Soc., Am. Acad. Arts and Scis., German Archaeol. Inst., Am. Philol. Assn., Soc. Promotion Hellenic Studies (Eng.), Classical Assn. (Eng.). Home: 905 New Gulph Rd Bryn Mawr PA 19010-2941 Office: Dept Greek Bryn Mawr Coll Bryn Mawr PA 19010

LANG, MARGO TERZIAN, artist; b. Fresno, Calif. d. Nishan and Araxie (Kazarosian) Terzian; m. Nov. 29, 1942; children: Sandra J. (Mrs. Ronald L. Carr), Roger Mark, Timothy Scott. Student, Fresno State U., 1939-42, Stanford U., 1948-50, Prado Mus., Madrid, 1957-59, Ariz. State U., 1960-61; workshops with, Dong Kingman, Ed Whitney, Rex Brandt, Millard Sheets, George Post. Maj. exhbns. include, Guadalajara, Mex., Brussels, N.Y.C., San Francisco, Chgo., Phoenix, Corcoran Gallery Art, Washington, internat. watercolor exhbn., Los Angeles, Bicentennial shows, Hammer Galleries, N.Y.C., spl. exhbn. aboard, S.S. France, others, over 80 paintings in various Am. embassies throughout world; represented in permanent collections, Nat. Collection Fine Arts Mus., Smithsonian Instn.; lectr., juror art shows; condr. workshops.; interviews and broadcasts on Radio Liberty, Voice of Am. Bd. dirs. Phoenix Symphony Assn., 1965-69, Phoenix Musical Theater, 1965-69. Recipient award for spl. achievements Symphony Assn., 1966, 67, 68, 72, spl. awards State of Ariz., silver medal of excellence Internat. Platform Assn., 1971; honoree U.S. Dept. State celebration of 25 yrs. of exhbn. of paintings in embassies worldwide, 1989. Mem. Internat. Platform Assn., Ariz. Watercolor Assn., Nat. Soc. Arts and Letters (nat. dir. 1971-72, nat. art chmn. 1974-76), Nat. Soc. Lit. and Arts, Phoenix Art Mus., Friends of Mexican Art, Am. Artists Profl. League, English-Speaking Union, Musical Theater Guild, Ariz. Costume Inst., Phoenix Art Mus., Scottsdale Art Ctr., Ariz. Arts Commn. (fine arts panel 1990-91), Friends of Art and Preservation in Embassies. Home: 6127 E Calle Del Paisano Scottsdale AZ 85251-4212

LANG, NAOMI, ice skater; b. Arcata, Calif., Dec. 18, 1978. Tng. with, Igor Shpilband & Liz Coates, Detroit, 1997—2000, Alexander Zhulin, N.J., 2000—02, Tatiana Tarasova, Conn., 2002, Nikoli Morozov, 2002—. Ice dancer Naomi Lang and Peter Tchernyshev; mem. Team USA Keri Lotion Classic, 1999, Goodwill Games, 2001; U.S. skating team Olympic Winter Games, 2002. Mem. Grand Rapids (Mich.) Ballet Co. Recipient 5th, State Farm U.S. Championships, 1997, 3d, 1998, 1st, 1999, 2000, 2001, 2002, 4th, Goodwill Games, 2001, 2d, Challenge Lysiane Lauret, 1998, 5th, Cup of Russia, 1998, Skate Am., 1998, 3d, 1998, 5th, 2000, 3d, Four Continents Championships, 1999, 1st, 2000, 2d, 2001, 1st, 2002, 3d, 2003, 10th, World Championships, 1999, 8th, 2000, 9th, 2001, 2002, 8th, 2003, 2d, Keri Lotion Classic, 1999, 5th, Trophee Lalique, 1999, 4th, 2000, 1st (team), Hershey's Kisses Challenge, 2002. Office: US Figure Skating Hdqs 20 First St Colorado Springs CO 80906*

LANG, NORMA M. nursing educator; b. Wausau, Wis., Dec. 27, 1939; BSN, Alverno Coll., 1961; MSN, Marquette U., 1963, PhD, 1974. Staff nurse, asst. instr. St. Joseph's Hosp., 1961-62; instr., coord. med.-surg. nursing St. Mary's Sch. Nursing, 1964-65; from instr. to prof. U. Wis. Sch. Nursing, Milw., 1965—92, dean, 1980—92, U. Pa. Sch. Nursing, Phila., 1992—2000, prof., 1992—. Nursing coord. Wis. Regional Med. Program, 1968-73; rsch. assoc. U. Wis., Milw., 1977, ctr. sci. Urban Rsch. Ctr., 1977-79. Contbr. articles to profl. jours. Recipient Ernest A. Codman Award, 2001. Fellow Am. Acad. Nursing; mem. ANA, NAS, AAUP, APHA, Am. Heart Assn. Office: U Pa Sch Nursing 420 Guardian Dr Philadelphia PA 19104-4210

LANG, PEARL, dancer, choreographer; b. Chgo., May 1922; d. Jacob and Frieda (Feder) Lack; m. Joseph Wiseman, Nov. 22, 1963. Student, Wright Jr. Coll., U. Chgo.; DFA (hon.), Juilliard Sch. Music, 1995; PhD (hon.), DFA, Juilliard Sch., 1995. Formed own co., 1953; faculty Yale, 1954-68; tchr., lectr. Juilliard, 1953-69, Jacobs Pillow, Conn. Coll., Neighborhood Playhouse, 1963-68. Soloist, Martha Graham Dance Co., 1944-54; featured roles on Broadway include Carousel, 1945-47, Finian's Rainbow, 1947-48, Danced Martha Graham's roles in Appalachian Spring, 1974-76, El Pentitente, 1954, Primitive Mysteries, 1978-79, Diversion of Angels, 1948-70, Herodiade, 1977-79; role of Solveig opposite John Garfield Broadway include, ANTA Peer Gynt; choreographer: TV shows CBC Folio; co-dir. T.S. Eliot's Murder in the Cathedral, Stratford, Conn., Direction, 1964-66, 67, Lamp Unto Your Feet, 158, Look Up and Live TV, 1957; co-dir., choreographer: full length prodn. Dybbuk for CBC; dir. numerous Israel Bond programs; assumed roles Emily Dickinson: Letter to the World, 1970; Clytemnestra, 1973; Jocasta in: Night Journey, 1974, for Martha Graham Dance Co.; choreographer: dance works Song of Deborah, 1952, Moonsung and Windsung, 1952, Legend, 1953, Rites, 1953, And Joy Is My Witness, 1954, Nightflight, 1954, Sky Chant, 1957, Persephone, 1958, Black Marigolds, 1959, Shirah, 1960, Apasionada, 1961, Broken Dialogues, 1962, Shore Bourne, 1964, Dismembered Fable, 1965, Pray for Dark Birds, 1966, Tongues of Fire, 1967, Piece for Brass, 1969, Moonways and Dark Tides, 1970, Sharjuhm, 1971, At That Point in Place and Time, 1973, The Possessed, 1995, Prairie Steps, 1975, Bach Rondelays, 1977, I Never Saw Another Butterfly, 1977, A Seder Night, 1977, Kaddish, 1977, Icarus, 1978, Cantigas Ladino, (10 sephardic songs), 1978, Notturno, 1980, Gypsy Ballad, 1981, Hanele The Orphan, 1981, The Tailor's Megilleh, 1981, Bridal Veil, 1982, Stravinsky's opera Oedipus Rex, 1982, Song of Songs, 1983, Shiru L'adonay, 1983, Tehillim, 1983, Sephardic Romance and Tfila, 1989, Koros, 1990, Eyn Keloheynu, 1991, Schubert Quartetsatz No. 12, 1993, Schubert Quartet 15 1st Mov., 1994, And Again a Begining, 1994, Dream Voyages, 1996, Memories and Dreams of Isaac the Blind, 1997, A Bouquet of Love Song Waltzes, 1998. Founder Pearl Lang Dance Found.; mem. Boston Symphony, Tanglewood Fest. Recipient 2 Guggenheim fellowships; recipient Goldfadden award Congress for Jewish Culture, Achievement award Artists and Writers for Peace in the Middle East, Cultural award Workmen's Circle, Queens Coll. award, 1991, Jewish Cultural achievement award Nat. Found. for Jewish Culture, 1992; named to Hall of Fame, Internat. Com. for the Dance Libr. of Israel, 1997. Mem. Am. Guild Mus. Artists. Home: 382 Central Park W New York NY 10025-6054

LANG, SHERRIE, director; d. Edmon and Iris June Lang. BS in Edn., U. North Tex., 1979, EdM in Counseling, 1980; EdD in Ednl. Adminstrn., Baylor U., 2000. Cert. profl. counselor Tex. Edn. Agy., tchr. English Tex. Edn. Agy., vocat. counselor Tex. Edn. Agy. Counselor Odessa (Tex.) Coll., 1983—89, supr. evening ext. program, 1986—88, dir. student activities, 1989—95, dir. testing and student retention, 1995—2000, dir. student devel. /Title V, 2000—. Mem. Jr. League, Odessa, 1994; bd. dirs. St. James Bapt. Ch. Scholarship Com., Odessa, 2002; past v.p. Delta Sigma Theta, Odessa, 1977. Finalist Black Women Cmty. Leaders of Tex., Quaker Oats, 1999; named Woman of Distinction, Permian Basin Girl Scouts Am., 2002. Mem.: Tex. C.C. Tchrs.' Assn., Jr./C.C. Student Pers. Assn. Tex. (bd. dirs. 1992—94), Nat. Acad. Advising Assn. Baptist. Avocations: travel, reading, sports. Office: Odessa Coll 201 W University Odessa TX 79764 E-mail: slang@odessa.edu.

LANG, WILMA JEAN, special education educator; b. Bedford, Ohio, Nov. 11, 1935; d. Carl Robert and Jean Marie Walek; m. Ted J. Lang, July 31, 1962; children: Janet Ruth, J. Paul. BS in Edn., Bowling Green State U., Ohio, 1960; MEd, Ashland U., Ohio, 1993. Cert. Levels I and II, Wilson Reading Sys. Tchr. Western Res. Dist., Wakeman, Ohio, 1956—59; spl. edn. tchr. Sandusky City Schs., Ohio, 1960—61; tchr. Berlin Local Schs., Berlin Heights, Ohio, 1961—63; sub. tchr. Norwalk City Schs., Ohio, 1984—86, spl. edn. tutor, 1986—93, resource tchr. learning disabilities, 1993—; pvt. practice reading tutor Norwalk, Ohio, 2000—. Sunday sch. tchr., choir mem. St. Peter Luth. Ch., Norwalk, Ohio. Grantee, Jennings Found., 1999, 2001. Mem.: Coun. Exceptional Children, Internat. Dyslexia Assn. (No. Ohio br. bd. dirs. 2002—), Gideon's Aux. (sec.-treas.). Luthern. Avocations: reading, music, home and family. Home: 169 St Marys St Norwalk OH 44857

LANGBORT, POLLY, retired advertising executive; b. N.Y.C. d. Julius and Nettie (Berman) L. BA, Adelphi U. Sec. Young & Rubicam, Inc., N.Y.C., media buyer, media planner, 1960-65, planning supr., 1965-70, v.p. group supr., 1970-75, v.p. dir. planning devel., 1975-80, sr. v.p., dir. planning, 1980-85, sr. v.p. direct mktg. and media services Wunderman, Worldwide div., 1985-86, exec. v.p. dir. mktg. & media services, 1986-90; assoc. pub. Lear's Mag., N.Y.C., 1990-91; ret., 1991. Author: DMA Factbook, 1986; contbr. articles to profl. jours. Spl. gifts chairperson Am. Cancer Soc., N.Y.C., 1985-90. Mem. Boca Raton Resort and Club, Boca Pointe Country Club. Avocations: classical music, outdoor activities. Home: 7614 La Corniche Cir Boca Raton FL 33433-6055 E-mail: pollylang@aol.com.

LANGE, BILLIE CAROLA, video specialist; b. Cullman, Ala. d. John George and Josephine (Richard) Luyben; m. Harry E. Lange (dec.); children: JoAnne Lange Graham, Linda Jean Lange Reeve; m. Melvin A. Coble (dec.). Grad., Long Beach City (Calif.) Coll.; BMus, U. So. Calif. Chief piano accompanist Long Beach Civic Opera Assn.; tchr./creator aquatic exercise program U. Ala., Huntsville, 1984-87; advisor Aquatic Exercise Assn., Port Washington, Wis., 1988—; creator, prodr. aquatic video exercise tapes Billie C. Lange's Aquatics, Palm Beach, Fla., 1979—. Creator: (aquatic exercise video tapes) Slim and Trim Yoga with Billie In and Out of Pool, 1979, Slim and Trim with Billie In Pool, 1994 (televised on Today Show, NBC 1995); pianist Organ-Piano Duo and various audio tapes; instrumental, audio Tranquility, 1992. Mem. Nat. Acad. Recording Arts and Scis. Avocations: classical pianist, politics. Office: 1920 Compass Cove Dr Vero Beach FL 32963-2820

LANGE, JESSICA, actress; b. Minn., Apr. 20, 1949; d. Al and Dorothy Lange; m. Paco Grande, 1970 (div. 1982); 1 child with Mikhail Baryshnikov, Alexandra; children with Sam Shepard: Hannah Jane, Samuel Walker Student, U. Minn.; student mime, with Etienne DeCroux, Paris. Dancer Opera Comique, Paris; model Wilhelmina Agy., N.Y.C. Film appearances include King Kong, 1976, All That Jazz, 1979, How to Beat the High Cost of Living, 1980, The Postman Always Rings Twice, 1981, Frances, 1982 (Acad. award nominee 1982), Tootsie, 1982 (Acad. award 1983), Country, 1984, Sweet Dreams, 1985, Crimes of the Heart, 1986 (Acad. award nominee 1987), Everybody's All American, 1988, Far North, 1988, Music Box, 1989 (Acad. award nominee 1990), Men Don't Leave, 1990, Cape Fear, 1991, Night and the City, 1992, Blue Sky, 1994 (Golden Globe award Best Actress in a Drama 1995, Acad. award for Best Actress 1995), Losing Isaiah, 1995, Rob Roy, 1995, A Thousand Acres, 1997, Hush, 1998, Cousin Bette, 1998, Titus, 1999, Big Fish, 2003; TV movies: Cat on a Hot Tin Roof, 1984, O' Pioneers!, 1992, A Streetcar Named Desire, 1995 (Golden Globe award 1996), Prozac Nation, 2001; in summer stock prodn. Angel on My Shoulder, N.C., 1980, A Streetcar Named Desire, 1992; prodr. Country, 1984; TV guest appearance Inside the Actors Studio, 1994. Office: ICM rep Toni Howard 8942 Wilshire Blvd Beverly Hills CA 90211-1934

LANGE, KATHERINE J. writer; b. Wyandotte, Mich., Feb. 8, 1957; d. James DiDi and Margaret Ann (Kirk) Putman. Student, Normandale Coll., 1980-82. V.p., artist mgr. T.S.J. Prodns., Richfield, Minn., 1975—99; v.p. T.S.J. Literary Agy., Richfield, 1973—96; mgr., agt. The T.S.J. Booking Agy., Richfield, 1980—96; asst. editor, author Songwriter U.S.A. mag., Atlanta, 1986—87; staff writer Music Mgmt. and Internat. Promotion mag., Copenhagen, 1983—2001; pres. Katherine's Greetings, 1994—, Internat. Literary Concepts, Mpls., 1996—. Contbr. articles to Sun Newspapers, Songwriter Connection, Woman's Press. Mem. ASCAP, NAFE, Am. Fedn. Musicians. Democrat. Lutheran. Avocations: building model ships, painting. Home and Office: International Literary Concepts 422 Pierce St NE Minneapolis MN 55413-2514

LANGE, LIZ STEINBERG, apparel designer and executive; b. N.Y. m. Jeffrey Lange; 2 children. BA in Comparative Lit., Brown U., 1988. Asst. editor Vogue; fashion designer Stephen DiGeronimo; founder Liz Lange Maternity Clothing Line, N.Y.C., 1997—. Office: Liz Lange Maternity Corp Office 1065 Madison Ave New York NY 10028*

LANGE, MARILYN, social worker; b. Milw., Dec. 6, 1936; d. Edward F. and Erna E. (Karstaedt) L.; divorced; children: Lara Cash, Gregory Cash. B of Social Work, U. Wis., Milw., 1962, MSW, 1974. Cert. ind. clin. social worker. Recreation specialist Dept. Army, Europe, 1962-63; social worker Family Svc. Milw., 1967-75, dir. homecare divsn., 1975-85, nat. field rep. Alzheimers Assn., Chgo., 1986-90; exec. dir. Village Adult Svcs., Milw., 1991—. Mem. Nat. Coun. Aging, Wis. Adult Daysvcs. Assn. (past pres.), Dementia Care Network, Older Adult Svc. Providers Consortium, U. Wis.-Milw. Alumni Assn. Home: 8959 Woodbridge Dr Greendale WI 53129 Office: Village Adult Svcs 336 W Walnut St Milwaukee WI 53212-3811 E-mail: marilyn_lange@aurora.org.

LANGE, STEPHANIE ANN, music educator; b. Springfield, Ohio, Mar. 2, 1975; d. David Ronald and Marilyn Kay Hall; m. Lawrence Timothy Lange, Jr., June 21, 1997; 1 child, Joshua Lawrence. B in music edn., Ohio State U., 1994—97. Cert. Teacher Dept. of Edn., Ohio, 1997. Music tchr. Springfield City Schools, Springfield, Ohio, 1998—. Mem.: Ohio Music Educators Assn., Music Educators Nat. Conf. Avocation: camping. Personal E-mail: lslange@erinet.com.

LANGE-CONNELLY, PHYLLIS, musician, music educator; b. Elgin, Ill., Oct. 14, 1935; d. William Carl and Freide Ricka Helena (Reimer) Werneke; children: Catherine Mary Gathman, Debra, Mark William. AA, Elgin (Ill.) C.C., 1985; BA, Nat. Lewis U., 1988; MM, No. Ill. U., 1995. Dir. music, organist Bethlehem Luth. Ch., Dundee, Ill., 1961-79, St. John's Luth. Ch., Algonquin, Ill., 1979-89, Trinity Luth. Ch., Huntley, Ill., 1990-92, St. Paul U.C.C. Ch., Barrington, Ill., 1992-94, St. James Episcopal Ch., Dundee, 1994—; assoc. organist, handbell dir. Holy Trinity Luth. Ch., Elgin, 1995-98; dir. worship and music, 1998-99. Para-profl. tutor Sch. Dist. 300, Dundee, Ill., 1979-85; music educator; mem. AGO del. to Ea. Europe through People-to-People Internat., 1998. Mem. United Way Dundee Twp., 1999, Dundee Main St. Orgn. Mem. Am. Guild Organists (dean N.W. chpt. 1999, Fox Valley chpt.), Am. Guild English Handbell Ringers, Music Tchrs. Nat. Assn., Elgin Choral Union (mem. edn./outreach com. 1999), Pi Kappa Lambda Music Soc. Democrat. Episcopalian. Avocations: reading, golf. Home: 4154 Whatehall Ln Algonquin IL 60102

LANGELAN, MARTHA JANE (MARTY), sexual harassment expert; b. Toledo, May 16, 1949; d. Harry C. and Severina (Gurzynski) L.; m. William M. LeoGrande, July 20, 1985. BA in Econs. and Polit. Sci., Syracuse U., 1973. Economist U.S. Civil Aeronautics Bd., Washington, 1976-84; sr. economist U.S. Dept. Transp., Washington, 1985-94; self-def. instr. D.C. Rape Crisis Ctr., Washington, 1980—, sexual harassment prevention, 1981—; pres. Langelan & Assocs., LLC, Chevy Chase, Md., 1994—; prof. justice and law Am. U., Washington, 1995—. Nonviolence instr. Washington Peace Ctr., 1983-93; assoc. Nat. Coun. for Rsch. on Women, N.Y.C., 1993—; judge expert panel Puget Sound Regional Coun., Seattle, Wash., 1994-96; sexual harassment expert Am. Friends Svc. Com., Budapest, Hungary, 1995; anti-violence expert Freedom House, India, Sri Lanka, 1997; spkr. in field. Author: Back Off! How to Confront and Stop Sexual Harassment and Harassers, 1993; contbr. articles to profl. jours. Pres. D.C. Rape Crisis Ctr., Washington, 1982-86; v.p. Nat. Woman's Party, Washington, 1997-98, pres. Nat. Women's Party, 1999-2004; keynote spkr. ALA Nat. Conf., Miami, Fla., 1995, Women's Leadership Conf., Fairfax, Va., 1996, Statewide Campaign Sexual Assault Conf., Richmond, 1997, Women's Commn. Conf., Raleigh, NC, 2001, NOW Women's Conf., Baltimore, Md., 2002, Women's Leadership Conf., Charlottesville, Va., 2004. Recipient Lifetime Achievement award D.C. Rape Crisis Ctr., Washington, 1994. Fellow Coun. Excellence in Govt.; mem. NAFE, NOW (spkr.), AAUW (spkr.), Women's Transp. Seminar (spkr.), Internat. Assn. for Feminist Econs., Com. on the Status of Women in the Econs. Profession. Office: Langelan & Assocs LLC 7215 Chestnut St Chevy Chase MD 20815-4051 Office Phone: 301-654-0176. E-mail: langelan-assoc@starpower.net.

LANGENHEIM, JEAN HARMON, biologist, educator; b. Homer, La., Sept. 5, 1925; d. Vergil Wilson and Jeanette (Smith) Harmon; m. Ralph Louis Langenheim, Dec. 1946 (div. Mar. 1962). BS, U. Tulsa, 1946; MS, U. Minn., 1949, PhD, 1953. Rsch. assoc. botany U. Calif., Berkeley, 1954-59, U. Ill., Urbana, 1959-61; rsch. fellow biology Harvard U., Cambridge, Mass., 1962-66; asst. prof. biology U. Calif., Santa Cruz, 1966-68, assoc. prof. biology, 1968-73, prof. biology, 1973-93, prof. biology emerita, 1993—, rsch. prof. ecol. and evolution biology, 2001—. Acad. v.p. Orgn. Tropical Studies, San Jose, Costa Rica, 1975—78; chmn. com. humid tropics U.S. Nat. Acad. Nat. Rsch. Coun., 1975—77; mem. com. floral inventory Amazon NSF, Washington, 1975—87; mem. sci. adv. bd. EPA, Washington, 1977—81. Author: (Book) Botany-Plant-Biology in Relation to Human Affairs, Plant Resins: Chemistry, Evolution, Ecology and Ethnobotany, 2003; contbr. articles to profl. jours. Recipient Disting. Alumni award, U. Tulsa, 1979; grantee, NSF, 1966—88. Fellow: AAUW, AAAS, Bunting Inst., Calif. Acad. Scis.; mem.: Soc. Econ. Botany (pres. 1993—94), Assn. Tropical Biology (pres. 1985—86), Internat. Soc. Chem. Ecology (pres. 1986—87), Ecol. Soc. Am. (pres. 1986—87), Bot. Soc. Am. Home: 191 Palo Verde Ter Santa Cruz CA 95060-3214 Office: U Calif Sinsheimer Labs Dept Biol Santa Cruz CA 95064 Office Phone: 831-459-2918. Business E-Mail: lang@darwin.ucsc.edu.

LANGENKAMP, MARY ALICE (M.A. LANGENKAMP), artist, educator; b. N.Y.C., Feb. 19, 1939; d. Horace Ralph and Pattie Lera (Turner) Myers; m. Robert Dobie Langenkamp; children: Heather, Matthew, Daniel, Lucinda. BA, George Washington U., 1962, MFA, 1985. Prof. art George Washington U., Washington, 1992-96. Exhbn. juror Arts Club Washington, 1996, George Washington U. Gallery, 2002; lectr. art law seminar Harvard Law Sch., 2002; rsch. archivist Smithsonian Mus. Hist. and Tech.; docent Philbrook Mus. Exhibited paintings and prints at U.S. Capitol, State Capitol of Okla., U.S. Embassy to Vatican, Galerie Schneider, Rome, Grand Palais, Paris, Hotel de Ville of Malaucene, France, Citibank, Washington; pvt. collections. in U.S. and Europe; work pub. in Nimrod Mag., Joyce Quar., Tulsa Tribune, Washington Post, others. Founding mem. Friends Brady Gallery, George Washington U.; mem. Tulsa County Libr. Book Review Bd., Martin Luther King's March on Washington, 1963; staff U.S. Congress; chmn. Dem. Precinct. Recipient Alfandre prize George Washington U., 1982, Gov.'s award Gov. of Okla., 1989, Air France prize, 1981, M.A. Langenkamp Prize in Abstract Painting, George Washington U. Mem. ACLU, LWV, Coll. Art Assn., F St. Hist. Soc., U.S. Capital Hist. Soc., Tulsa Shakespeare Soc. Democrat. Roman Catholic. Avocations: travel, film, theatre, history, politics. Office: Fontalys Malaucene Vaucluse 84340 France E-mail: malartist@yahoo.com.

LANGENKAMP, SANDRA CARROLL, retired human services administrator; b. St. Joseph, Mo., Feb. 10, 1939; d. William Harry Minger and Beverly (Carroll) Lee; m. R. Hayden Downie, June 1, 1963 (div. Feb. 1979); children: Whitney Downie, Timothy Downie, Allyson Downie; m. R. Dobie Langenkamp, Aug. 1993. BS, Tex. Women's U., 1960. Adjunctive therapist Menninger Meml. Hosp., Topeka, 1960-66; asst. adminstr. Hillcrest Med. Ctr., Tulsa, 1977-82; dir. Vol. Action Agy., Tulsa, 1982-83; exec. dir. Tulsa Bus. Health Group, 1983-95; v.p. Met. Tulsa C. of C., 1985-95; exec. dir. Tulsa Program Affordable Health Care, 1986-96; ret., 1996. Cons. mem. Okla. Employment Security Commn., Oklahoma City, 1988—; exec. dir. Tulsa Cmty. Found. Indigient Health Care, 1986—96, Long-Term Car Authority, 1999—; officer State of Okla. Basic Health Benefits Bd., 1985—96, chmn., 1992—93; mem. health benefit com. Okla. Ins. Commn., 1994—; mem. Gov.'s Com. Health Care, 1993; bd. dirs. Exec. Svc. Corps Tulsa, Associated Ctrs. Therapy. Editl. columnist: Point of View, 1985—, Tulsa Mag., 1985—. Count commn. appointee Tulsa Met. Area Planning Commn., 1973—81; mayor's appointee Tulsa Housing Authority, 1985—88; vol. Police Svc. Homicide Divsn., Police Svc. Detective Divsn., 1999—; exec. dir. Tulsa Met. Literacy Coalition, 1998—; pres. Tulsa Met. Ministry, 1980—83; bd. dirs. ARC, Tulsa, 1971—73, 1984—85, Okla. Arts Inst., 1995—, Simon Estes Found., 2000—, Tylsa Philharm., Inc., 2000—, City of Tulsa Arts Commn., 2003—. Mem.: Met. Tulsa C. of C. (v.p. 1983—95), Am. C. of C. (exec. dir. Okla. chpt.), Tulsa Tennis Club. Democrat. Roman Catholic. Avocations: reading, gardening, knitting, drawing, pottery.

LANGER, ELLEN JANE, psychologist, educator, writer, artist; b. N.Y.C., Mar. 25, 1947; d. Norman and Sylvia (Tobias) L. BA, NYU, 1970; PhD, Yale U., 1974. Cert. clin. psychologist. Asst. prof. psychology The Grad. Ctr. CUNY, 1974-77; assoc. prof. psychology Harvard U., Cambridge, Mass., 1977-81, prof., 1981—. Cons. NAS, 1979-81, NASA; mem. div. on aging Harvard U. Med. Sch., 1979—, mem. psychiat. epidemiology steering com., 1982-90; chair social psychology program Harvard U., 1982-94, chair Faculty Arts and Scis. Com. of Women, 1984-88. Author: Personal Politics, 1973, Psychology of Control, 1983, Mindfulness, 1989, The Power of Mindful Learning, 1997; editor: (with Charles Alexander) Higher Stages of Human Development, 1990, (with Roger Schank) Beliefs, Reasoning and Decision-Making, 1994; contbr. articles to profl. and scholarly jours.; exhibited art at Julie Hellery Gallery, Provincetown, Mass., J&W Gallery, New Hope, Pa. Guggenheim fellow; grantee NIMH, NSF, Soc. for Psychol. Study of Social Issues, Milton Fund, Sloan Found., 1982; recipient Disting. Contbn. of Basic to Applied Psychology award APS, 1995. Fellow Computers and Soc. Inst., Am. Psychol. Assn. (Disting. Contributions to Psychology in Public Interest award 1988, Disting. Contributions of Basic Sci. to Applied Psychology 1995); mem. Soc. Exptl. Social Psychology, Phi Beta Kappa, Sigma Xi. Democrat. Jewish. Avocations: theater, horseback riding, tennis. Office: Harvard U Dept Psychology 33 Kirkland St Cambridge MA 02138-2044

LANGER, EVA MARIE, video specialist; b. Oceanside, Calif., Sept. 23, 1958; d. William Frank and Clotilde (Gonzalo) L. BS, San Diego State U., 1980. Audio engr. Peters Prodns., San Diego, 1980-83; news writer Sta. KSDO, San Diego, 1981-82; audio prodn. engr. Tuesday Prodns., San Diego, 1983-85; video technician Voice & Video, San Diego, 1983-84, ednl. sales staff, 1984-85, govt. and ednl. mktg. saleswoman, 1985-86, retail sales mgr., corp. and comml. mktg. saleswoman, 1986-88, med. sales specialist, 1988-93; key account exec. Audio Video Supply, San Diego, 1993-94; regional mgr. Gen. Projection Sys., 1994-95; dist. sales mgr. Hoffman Video Sys., 1995-96; sr. mgr. video svcs. QUALCOMM Inc., San Diego, 1996—. Ind. radio producer, San Diego, 1984—, ind. music searcher, 1984-85. Prodr.: Persons with AIDS Project, 1984-85, (documentary) Joyu, A Zen Priest, 1987. Camera operator Mothers Embracing Nuclear Disarmament, San Diego, 1985, Reiki Therapist II, 1988; co-chmn. L.L.L.A.C., 1991. Recipient Communicator Crystal award, 1999, 2001, 2002, Telly award,

2000, 2002. Mem. NAFE, Am. Women in Radio and TV (dir.-at-large 1985, 1st v.p. 1986, editor newsletter 1985-86). Democrat. Home: 4565 Lucille Dr San Diego CA 92115-1924 Office: QUALCOMM Inc 5775 Morehouse Dr San Diego CA 92121-1714

LANGER, JUDITH ANN, literacy educator; b. N.Y.C. BA, CUNY, 1960, MSEd, 1965; PhD, Hofstra U., 1978. Asst. prof. L.I. U., 1973-78; asst. prof. dept. ednl. psychology NYU, 1978-80; sr. rschr. lang. behavior rsch. lab. U. Calif., Berkeley, 1980-84; assoc. prof. sch. of edn. Stanford U., 1984-87; prof. SUNY, Albany, 1987—, disting. prof., 2001—. Dir. Albany Inst. for Rsch. in Edn., Nat. Rsch. Ctr. on English Learning & Achievement; co-dir. Nat. Rsch. Ctr. Lit. Tchg. and Learning; trustee Rsch. Found.; task force mem. Nat. Commn. on Edn. Stds. and Testing; adv. com. New Stds. in Edn. Project, Literacy Unit, LRDC and Nat. Ctr. on Edn. and the Economy; adv. bd. Nat. Coun. of Chief State Sch. Officers, Nat. Objective in Reading, Nat. Assessment of Ednl. Progress, Reading and Writing Assessments, 1980—; cons. Calif. Assessment Program, N.C. English Lang. Arts Standards, Calif. State Dept. Edn., Ctr. for Lang. Edn. and Rsch., Ctr. for the Study of Writing, Rev. of Rsch. on Reading and Writing Relationships, Mich. State Edn. Dept. Author: Reader Meets Author/Bridging the Gap, 1982, Understanding Reading and Writing Research, 1985, Children Reading and Writing: Structures and Strategies, 1986, Language, Literacy, and Culture, 1987, Issues of Society and Schooling, How Writing Shapes Thinking: Studies of Teaching and Learning, 1987, Literature Instruction: A Focus on Student Response, 1992, Literature Instruction: Practice & Policy, 1994, Envisioning Literature, 1995, Effective Literacy Instruction: Building Successful Reading and Writing Programs, 2002, Getting To Excellent: How to Create Better Schools, 2004; contbr. articles to profl. jours.; editor: Research in the Teaching of English, 1984-92; editl. bd. English Internat., Jour. of Reading Behavior, Newsletter, Lab. of Comparative Human Cognition, Jour. of Reading and Writing, Internat. Jour. of Reading and Writing; reviewer in field. Recipient numerous grants; fellow Rockefeller Found., Benton fellow U. Chgo. Fellow Am. Psychol. Assn., Nat. Conf. on Rsch. in English; mem. MLA, Am. Ednl. Rsch. Assn., Am. Psychol. Soc., Conf. on Coll. Composition and Comm., Internat. Reading Assn., Nat. Reading Conf., Nat. Coun. of Tchrs. of English (trustee), Soc. for Rsch. in Child Devel., Soc. for Text and Discourse, Kappa Delta Pi. Office: Univ at Albany 1400 Washington Ave Albany NY 12222-0100

LANGFORD, CECILIA MOTES, nursing educator; b. Saginaw, Mich., Apr. 15, 1950; d. Robert D. and Jeanette K. (Richardson) Grzegorczyk; children: Larry F., Michael A., Christopher J. ADN, Ariz. Western Coll., 1980; BSN, Sonoma State U., 1985; MS in Health, U. North Fla., 1994, postgrad. Cert. BLS instr. Am. Heart Assn. Staff nurse in psychiatry Yuma (Ariz.) Regional Med. ctr., 1980-81; staff nurse, charge nurse Community Hosp., Santa Rosa, Calif., 1981-85; staff nurse Saddleback Hosp., El Toro, Calif., 1985-86; sch. health nurse Dept. of Def., Iwakuni, Japan, 1986-87; staff nurse intensive and critical care units Humana Hosp., Orange Park, Fla., 1987-89, nurse educator, 1989-95, Columbia/HCA Specialty Hosp., Jacksonville, Fla., 1995-97; mem. staff, patient edn. coord. Shands Jacksonville (formerly Meth. Med. Ctr.), Jacksonville, 1997—. Adj. prof. nursing Fla. Community Coll., Jacksonville, 1990-96. Author ednl. materials. Counselor Suicide Prevention, Santa Rosa, 1984; receptionist Navy Relief Soc., Iwakuni, 1986; vol. Am. Heart Assn., Jacksonville, 1992—, HIV/AIDS Buddy Program, 1997—. Mem. AACN (cert.), Jacksonville Area Nurse Insvc. Educators, Nat. Nursing Staff Devel. Orgn., Assn. Rehabilitation Nurses. Office: Shands Jacksonville 580 W 8th St Jacksonville FL 32209-6599

LANGFORD, LAURA SUE, corporate financial executive, ratings analyst; b. Evansville, Ind., Sept. 28, 1961; d. Lee Denmar Miller and Susan E. (Morton) Reitz; m. John E. Langford, May 15, 1992; 1 child, Rowan Dian. BFA in Drama, U. So. Calif., L.A., 1983; MBA in Fin. & Pub./Non-Profit, Columbia U., 1992. Credit mgr. Super-Freeze Co., Inc., Burbank, Calif., 1984-86; asst. Salomon Bros. Inc., L.A., 1986-87; rsch. analyst Bank of Calif., N.A., L.A., 1987, pub. fin. officer, 1988-90; intern Citizens Budget Commn., N.Y.C., 1991; analyst Standard & Poor's Ratings Group, N.Y.C., 1992-93, assoc., 1993-94, assoc. dir., 1994-95, dir., 1996-98; v.p. Duff & Phelps Credit Rating Co., N.Y.C., 1998—2000; dir. HypoVereinsbank, N.Y.C., 2000—; CFO HVB Global Assests Co., 2003—. Contbr. to periodical Standard & Poor's Credit Week, 1993—98, Duff & Phelps Credit Rating Co. Issues Update, 1998—2000. Fellow Divsn. Rsch. Assn. Student Officer fellow, Columbia U., 1991—92; scholar Pres.'s scholar, U. Evansville, 1979—81. Avocations: skiing, rollercoaster riding, science fiction. Office Phone: 212-672-5614. Business E-Mail: Laura_Langford@HVBAMERICAS.com.

LANGFORD, LINDA KOSMIN, library consultant; b. Phila., Nov. 7, 1939; d. Edward I. and Ruth (Blumfield) K.; m. Jonathan P. Meyerson, Aug. 7, 1960 (div.); m. George Langford, Oct. 31, 2000. BA, U. Pa., 1961; MSLS, Drexel U., 1966, MS in Environ. Sci., 1974. Chemistry instr. U. Md., College Park, 1961-63; libr. sci. instr., engring. libr. Drexel U., Phila., 1963-78; dep. dir. biomed. libr. U. Pa., Phila., 1979-80; sect. supervisor applied physics lab. The Johns Hopkins U., Laurel, Md., 1980-94; sec. mgr. libr./archives/records NASA Jet Propulsion Lab., Pasadena, Calif., 1994—2000; libr. cons., 2001—. Contbg. editor (author): (Quarterly Jour.) IEEE Engring. Mgmt. Rev., 1999—. Nat. sec. Friends of Danilo Dolci, Inc., Phila., 1971-72, bd. dirs., Short Hills, N.J., 1972-73. Recipient Exceptional Achievement medal NASA, 1998. Mem. IEEE (PCS adminstrv. com. 1995-96, EMS bd. govs. 1998-2003), Spl. Librs. Assn. (v.p., pres.-elect Phila. chpt. 1968-69). Avocation: oil painting. Home: 32 Bodine Rd Berwyn PA 19312-1237 E-mail: l.kosmin@ieee.org.

LANGGUTH, MARGARET WITTY, health facility administrator; b. Evanston, Ill., June 21, 1950; d. LeRoy and Catherine Ann (Conrad) Witty; m. Gregory Bryce Bukar, June 5, 1971 (dec. 1989); children: Michael Bryce, Caroline Nicole; m. Franklin James Langguth, Feb. 2, 2002. BS, DePaul U., 1972, MBA, 1981; MS, Finch U. Health Scis., 1996. Staff med. technologist The Evanston Hosp., 1972-75, immunopathology lab. supr., 1975-77, lab. mgr., 1977-84, dir. lab. adminstrn., 1984-85; bookkeeper Ronald Knox Montessori Sch., Wilmette, Ill., 1986-87; beauty cons. Mary Kay Cosmetics, 1990-96; sec. Northwestern U., Evanston, 1991-94; physician asst. Women's Med. Group, P.C., Skokie, Evanston, Ill., 1996-98; ind. sales assoc. Mannatech, Inc., 1998—2001; adminstrv. dir. clin. lab. Rush North Shore Med. Ctr., Skokie, Ill., 1999—. Den leader Cub Scouts, Boy Scouts Am., Wilmette, 1985—87, den leader coach, 1987—88; active PTA of St. Francis Xavier Sch., 1985—94, chair rummage sale, 1987—88, scouting coord., 1991—92, sch. bd., 1986—90, sec., 1988—89, vice chmn., 1989—90; troop co-leader, song leader Girl Scouts Am., 1992—98; mem. women's bd. Rush North Shore Med. Ctr., 2000—; campaign 2001 com. mem. United Way of Skokie Valley-Rush North Shore, co-chair for campaign 2002; eucharistic min. sick St. Francis Xavier Ch., 1990—93, liturgical song leader, 1993—2002. Recipient Emily Withrow Stebbins award, Evanston Hosp., 1985. Mem.: Clin. Lab. Mgmt. Assn., Am. Soc. Clin. Pathologists, Wilmette Hist. Soc. Avocations: knitting, interior decorating, reading. Office: Rush North Shore Med Ctr Clin Labs 9600 Gross Point Rd Skokie IL 60076 Office Phone: 847-933-6611. Personal E-mail: mlangguth@rsh.net.

LANGHAM, GAIL B. writer; b. Cin., Jan. 25, 1944; 3 children. BA, North Ctrl. Coll., 1989. Columnist Arts Scene, 1988-92; performing arts critic, features writer SUN Press, Naperville, Ill., 1988-92; freelance theatre critic Cin. City Beat, 1994-96; freelance writer Cin., 1993—. Founding mem. Naperville Writers Group, 1986-92. Avocations: travel, reading.

LANGHAM, NORMA E. playwright, educator, poet, composer, inventor; b. California, Pa. d. Alfred Scrivener and Mary Edith (Carter) L. BS, Ohio State U., 1942; B in Theatre Arts, Pasadena Playhouse Coll. Theatre Arts, 1944; MA, Stanford U., 1956; postgrad., Summer Radio-TV Inst., 1960, Pasadena Inst. Radio, 1944-45. Tchr. sci. California High Sch., 1942-43; asst. office pub. info. Denison U., Granville, Ohio, 1955; instr. speech dept. Westminster Coll., New Wilmington, Pa., 1957-58; instr. theatre, California U., Pa., 1955, asst. prof., 1960-62, assoc. prof., 1962-79, prof. emeritus, 1979—, co-founder, sponsor, dir. Children's Theatre, 1962-79. Founder, producer, dir. Food Bank Players, 1985, Patriot Players, 1986, Noel Prodns., 1993. Writer: (plays) Magic in the Sky, 1963, Founding Daughters (Pa., Nat. DAR awards 1991), Women Whisky Rebels (Pa. Nat. DAR awards 1992), John Dough (Freedoms Found. award 1968), Who Am I?, Hippocrates Oath, Gandhi, Clementine of '49, Soul Force, Dutch Painting, Purim, Music in Freedom, The Moon Is Falling, Norma Langham's Job Johnson; composer, lyricist: (plays) Why Me, Lord?, (text) Public Speaking; co-inventor (computer game) Highway Champion. Recipient Exceptional Acad. Svc. award Pa. Dept. Edn., 1975, Appreciation award Bicentennial Commn. Pa., 1976, Gregg award Calif. U. of Pa. Alumni Assn., 1992, Emeriti Faculty award California U. Pa., 2000. Mem. AAUW (co-founder Calif. br., 1st v.p. 1971-72, pres. 1972-73, Outstanding Woman of Yr. 1986, 97), DAR, Internat. Platform Assn. (poetry award 1993, 94, monologue award 1997), California U. Pa. Assn. Women Faculty (founder, pres. 1972-73), California 150, California Hist. Soc., Pa. Assn. Safety Edn., Washington County Hist. Soc., Dramatists Guild, Ctr. in Woods, Mensa, Alpha Psi Omega, Omicron Nu. Presbyterian (elder). Home: 204 Ellsworth St California PA 15419-1206

LANGHINRICHS, RUTH IMLER, playwright, writer; b. Chgo., Oct. 30, 1922; d. Roy Franklin Imler and Susan Martha Smith; m. Richard Alan Langhinrichs, May 31, 1958 (dec. July 31, 1990); children: Julia Marie Lewis-Langhinrichs, Jennifer Florence Langhinrichsen-Rohling. BS cum laude, Northwestern U., Evanston, IL, 1944. Rsch. asst. LOOK Mag., N.Y.C., 1944—46; asst. editor Sci. Illus., N.Y.C., 1946—49; asst. feature editor Scholastic Mag., N.Y.C., 1949—51; assoc. editor Ladies Home Jour., Phila., 1951—58; faculty Purdue U., Fort Wayne, Ind., 1966—76; instr. Channing Sch. for Girls, London, 1974—75; writer Fort Wayne Fine Arts Found., Ind., 1977—79; pub. rels. Pk. Ctr., Fort Wayne, Ind., 1979—84; writing cons. Ind.-Purdue U. a, Fort Wayne, Ind., 1998—. Facilitator: memoir writing workshops Friends of the Libr., Fort Wayne, Ind., 1998—. Playwright (play) Feathers, The Heart of the Limberlost: Gene Stratton-Porter, Mermaids in the Basement; author: (book) Boy Dates Girl, You're Asking Me?, (novel) The Maiden and the Crone; playwright (play) A Night on Walden Pond. Charter mem. Fort Wayne Civic Youtheatre, Ind., 1973—77; bd. mem. Martin Luther King Montessori Sch., Fort Wayne, Ind., 1975—78; founding mem. Cinema Ctr., Fort Wayne, Ind., 1976—80; bd. mem. Citizen's Cable, Fort Wayne, Ind., 1981—84; pres. Aging and In Home Svcs. of N.E. Ind., Fort Wayne, Ind., 1976—2001; bd. mem. Ft. Wayne Women's Bur., Ind., 1991—97, N.E. Ind. Coun. of Tchrs. of English, Fort Wayne, Ind., 1969—73. Recipient Four-year scholarship, Chgo. Women's Ideal Club, 1940, Woman of the Yr. award, Ft. Wayne Women's Bur., 2001, Summit award, Zonta Club Internat., 2003. Mem.: Internat. Assn. of Bus. Communicators (charter mem. 1978—79), Zonta Club Internat. (v.p. 2003), Fortnightly Club, Delta Delta Delta (life). Unitarian Universalist. Avocations: gardener, artist, commissioned clown. Home: 459 Englewood Ct Fort Wayne IN 46807 Personal E-mail: ruthlangx@aol.com.

LANGHOUT-NIX, NELLEKE, artist; b. Utrecht, The Netherlands, Mar. 27, 1939; came to U.S., 1968, naturalized, 1978; d. Louis Wilhelm Frederick and Geertruida Nix; m. Ernst Langhout, July 26, 1958; 1 son, Klaas-Jan Marnix. MFA, The Hague, The Netherlands, 1958. Head art dept. Bush Sch., Seattle, 1969-71; dir. creative projects Project Rsch., Seattle, 1971-72; artist-in-residence Fairhaven Coll., Bellingham, Wash., 1974, Jefferson Cmty. Ct., Seattle, 1978-82, Lennox Sch., N.Y.C., 1982, 2002—03; tchr. summer children's art class Noble Collection, S.I.; dir. NN Gallery, Seattle, 1970—. Guest curator Holland-U.S.A. Bicentennial Show, U. Wash., 1982; project dir. Women in Art Today, Wash., 1989, Wash. State Centennial Celebration; Washington to Washington traveling exhbn., 1989; bd. dirs. Soho 20 Artists Galleries, N.Y.C. Executed wall hanging for King County Courthouse, Seattle, 1974; one-woman shows include Nat. Art Center, 1980, Gail Chase Gallery, Bellevue, Wash., 1979, 80, 83, 84, Original Graphics Gallery, Seattle, 1981, Bon Nat. Gallery, Seattle, 1981, Kathleen Ewing Gallery, Washington, 1986, Ina Broerse Laren, Holland, 1992, Charlotte Daneel Gallery, Holland, 11992, Christopher Gallery, Tucson, 1992, Mercer Island Cmty. Arts Ctr., 1992, Lisa Harris Gallery, Seattle, 1994, Jacques Marchais Mus. Tibetan, S.I., N.Y., 1995, 4th World Conf. on Women, China, 1995, Global Focus, Beijing, 1995, Elite Gallery, Moscow, 1995, Soho 20, N.Y.C., 1998, 99, 2000, 01, 02; exhibited in group shows, including Cheney Cowles Mus., Spokane, 1977, Bellevue Art Mus., 1978, 86, Renwick Gallery, Washington, 1978, Kleinert Gallery, Woodstock, N.Y., 1979, Artcore Meltdown, Sydney Australia, 1979, Tacoma Art Mus., 1979, 83, 86, 87, Ill. State Mus., Springfield, 1979, Plener Sandomierz, Poland, 1980, Western Assn. Art Mus. travel show, 1979-80, Madison Square Garden, N.Y.C., 1981, Exhbn. Space, N.Y.C., 1982, Lisa Harris Gallery (solo exhbns.), 1985, 87, 88, 94, Wash. State Centennial, Tacoma, 1989, Nordic Heritage Mus., Seattle, 1994, Balch Inst. Ethnic Studies, Phila., 1997, Ctr. Contemporary Art, Seattle, 1997, Zaaijer Gallery, Amsterdam, The Netherlands, 1998, Orihon and More, S.I., 2002; solo exhbns. include SoHo20, N.Y.C., 1998, 99, 2003, N.Y.N.Y. Gallery, Plener Collection, Sandomierz, Bell Tel. Co. Collection, Seattle, U. Wash., Seattle, Children's Orthopedic Hosp., Seattle, Nat. Mus. Women in Arts, Washington, Studio D'Ars Gallery, Milan, Italy, 2001, Nat. Mus. Women in Arts, Washington, 2002, Collins Gen. Ctrl. Libr., Portland, Oreg., 2002; installations Tacoma Art Mus; author: (with others) Step Inside the Sacred Circle, 1989, An Artist's Book 1940-45 Remembered, 1991; author: Tsoek: Earthly Writings by a Fourpaw, 1996, Cicada, the Brood of 1996, Zones of Time, Sand and Rain, 2000; writer, designer Papua New Guinea-Where She Invented Bow and Arrow, 1996; pub., editor: (Chelsea Rhodes) A Girl and Her Cat as a Matter of Fact, 2000, (artist's book) Septembereleven o-one, 2002, To Anne Frank, 2002. Bd. dirs. Wing Luke Mus., Seattle, 1978-81, Wash. State Trust Hist. Preservation, 1990-93, Soho 20, 1997-2000; v.p. Denny Regrade Cmty. Coun., 1978-79; mem. Seattle Planning Commn., 1978-84; mem. nat. adv. bd. dirs. Nat. Mus. Women in Arts, Washington, 1996—. Recipient wall hanging award City of Edmonds, Wash., 1974, Renton 83 merit award, 1984; merit award Internat. Platform Assn. Art Exhibit, 1984, silver medal 1st place, 1985, 87, gold medal, 1989; Year 2000 grant Libr. Book Fellows, Nat. Mus. of Women in the Arts, Washington. Mem. Denny Regrade Arts Coun. (co-founder), Internat. Platform Assn., Women in Arts N.Y.C., Nat. Mus. Women in Arts (founding, Libr. fellow, chmn. Wash. State com. 1988-89, mem. nat. adv. bd. 1993—), Seattle-King County Cmty. Arts Network (bd. dirs. 1983-85, chmn. 1984-85), Nat. Artist Equity Assn. Address: PO Box 375 Mercer Island WA 98040-0375 E-mail: nixnelleke@hotmail.com.

LANGLEY, DAWN ELAINE, dean, writer; b. Waltham, Mass., Apr. 15, 1953; d. Donald Earle Brander and Elaine Gordon; m. Robert Gene Reno (div. May 2001); 1 child, Jennifer April Reno ; m. Norris James Langley, Dec. 21, 2002; 1 stepchild, Taylor. AA, Bunker Hill C.C., Boston, 1976; BA summa cum laude, Johnson State Coll., 1990; MFA, Vt. Coll., 1996. Adj. instr. Johnson (Vt.) State Coll., 1990—91, Daytona Beach C.C., Deland, Fla., 1992—97; vis. instr. creative writing U. Ctrl. Fla., Orlando, 1997—99; prof. English Lake City (Fla.) C.C., 1999—2003; dean acad. affairs Keiser Career Coll., Port St. Lucie, Fla., 2003—. Cons. Reno's Lit. Svcs., Vt., 1977—, Fla., 1977—. Author: All That Glitters, 1992 (RT Glitz award, 1993), The Silver Dolphin, 1994, Native American Artists, 2003; contbr. articles to publs. Vol. Big Sisters, Lake City, 2001—02. Fellow, Vt. Ctr. for Creative Arts, 1990, Vt. Studio Colony, 1995. Mem.: Soka Gakkai Internat., Johnson State Coll. Alumni (Outstanding Alumni 1999). Buddhist. Avocations: travel, yoga, mosaics, gardening.

LANGLEY, JANE S. state legislator; b. Norwood, Mass., Aug. 1, 1931; widowed; 2 children. Student, Hesser Bus. Coll. Mem. dist. 24 N.H. Ho. of Reps., precinct rep. to town meeting, mem. constrn. and rev. com. Founder, pres. Concerned Citizens of Seacoast. Mem. Quota Club of Portsmouth, Over 55 Club. Republican. Address: PO Box 115 Rye Beach NH 03871-0115

LANGLEY, LYNNE SPENCER, newspaper editor, columnist; b. West Palm Beach, Fla., June 4, 1947; d. George Hosmer and Elwa June (Harries) Spencer; m. William A. Langley, Oct. 10, 1970 (dec. 2001). Student, Glasgow U., Scotland, 1967-68; BA with honors, Coll. of Wooster, 1969. Feature writer, asst. woman's editor Palm Beach Times, West Palm Beach, 1969-70; asst. editor Brunswick (Maine) Times Record, 1971; investigative reporter Maine Times, Topsham, 1971-75; asst. mng. editor York County Coast Star, Kennebunk, Maine, 1976-78; environ. and med. editor, nature columnist Charleston (S.C.) Post and Courier Newspapers, 1979—. Editor Maine Audubon Soc. News, 1975-76; stringer Newsweek mag., 1971-75; speaker in field; freelance writer. Author: Nature Watch, 1987. Mem. Charleston Mus., S.C. chpt. Nature Conservancy, Charleston Libr. Soc. Recipient Media award S.C. Assn. Mentally Retarded, 1985, Media awards Charleston County Parks and Recreation Commn., 1985, Am. Diabetes Assn., S.C. chpt. 1989, Communicator of Yr. award S.C. Wildlife Fedn., 1983, Writing awards S.C. Press Assn., 1987, First Pl. in column writing S.C. Press. Assn., 1998. Mem. Am. Hort. Soc., Nat. Audubon Soc., Charleston Natural History Soc. (Media award 1985), PEO (sec. chpt. D Maine 1975-76, corr. sec. chpt. J. S.C. 1986-88), Sigma Delta Chi. Home: PO Box 97 Adams Run SC 29426-0097 Office: 134 Columbus St Charleston SC 29403-4806 E-mail: llangley@postandcourier.com.

LANGLEY, PATRICIA ANN, lobbyist; b. Butler, Pa., Feb. 13, 1938; d. F.J. and Ella (Serafine) Piccola; m. Harold D. Langley, June 12, 1965; children: Erika, David. BA, U. Pitts., 1961; postgrad., Georgetown U., 1967, Cath. U. Am., 1985, George Mason U., 1990—. Legis. staff U.S. Congress, Washington, 1961-63; dir. social studies Am. Polit. Sci. Assn., Washington, 1963-65; legis. specialist U.S. Congress, Washington, 1965-67, caseworker, 1967-68; polit. staff Dem. Study Group U.S. Congress, Washington, 1969; Washington rep. Family Services Am., 1975-82, dir. Washington hdqrs., 1989-92, v.p. for govt. rels., 1992; pres. Policy Directions, Arlington, Va., 1992—; vis. lectr. George Mason U., Fairfax, Va., 1994. Vis. lectr. in sociology George Mason U., Fairfax, Va., 1994; bd. dirs. Coalition for Children and Youth, Washington, 1977-78; chmn. steering com. for the Coalition on White House Conf. on Families, 1979-80, Ad Hoc Coalition on A.F.D.C., 1981-82; co-founder Ptnrs. in Change Group, 1996. Mem. Donaldson Run Civic Assn., Arlington, Va., 1980—; bd. mem. Va. Chamber Orch.; vol. guide Hillwood Mus., Washington. Recipient Service Recognition U.S. Dept. Health and Human Services, 1980. Mem. Am. Soc. Assn. Execs., Women in Govt. Rels., Nat. Coun. Family Rels., North Va. Assn. Female Execs., Arnova, Groves Conf. Roman Catholic. Avocations: gardening, reading, old movies, community organizing. Home and Office: 2515 N Utah St Arlington VA 22207-4031

LANGLOIS, ALICIA JEAN, business development planner, small business owner; b. Whittier, Calif., Nov. 15, 1968; d. Fred Albert and Dianne Jean Parrott; m. Ronald Ron Leo Langlois, Nov. 25, 1965; children: Derrick Glenn, Lindsay Jean, Samantha Dianne. BA in Mgmt., N.W. Christian Coll., Eugene, OR, 2003. Cert. nursing asst. Oreg. Nurses Assn., 1986. Ward clk. Sacred Heart Med. Ctr. PeaceHealth, Eugene, Oreg., 1989—90, quality rev. sec., 1990—93, radiation oncology transcriptionist and sec., 1994—97; owner/operator Bon Vivant Catering and Planning, Springfield, Oreg., 1996—; sec. contracting and bus. devel. PeaceHealth, Eugene, 1997, adminstrv. asst. contracting/bus. devel., 1997—99; bus. mgr. Ron Langlois Paints, Springfield, 1999—; bus. devel. coord. PeaceHealth, Eugene, 1999—2000, bus. devel. specialist, 2000—. Dept. rep. PeaceHealth United Way, Eugene, Oreg., 1997—2000, campaign chair PeaceHealth, 2000—02; com. chair pack 339 Boy Scouts of Am., Eugene, 1997—2001; mem. fund distbn. com. PeaceHealth Employee Coun., Eugene, 2001—. Dir. - fellowship ministry Twin Rivers Bapt. Ch., Springfield, Oreg., 2003—03; mem. Health Occupations Students of Am., Springfield, Oreg., 1985—86. Recipient Employee Campaign Leader Award, United Way, 2002. Mem.: Internat. Assn. of Adminstrv. Professionals, Project Mgmt. Inst., Toastmasters (mktg. and advt. dir. 2003, 1st Pl. Speech Evaluator 2001). Baptist. Achievements include development of competitive intelligence Ppogram. Avocations: swimming, reading, children, church activities & ministry, cooking. Office: PeaceHealth Bus Devel 770 East 11th SSB4 Eugene OR 97401 Personal E-mail: alanglois@peacehealth.org. E-mail: alanglois@peacehealth.org.

LANGLOTZ, JENNIFER COOK, music educator; b. Akron, Ohio, Nov. 10, 1973; d. Thomas G. and Karen Jensen Cook. MusB, Westminster Coll., 1996. Cert. tchr. Ohio, Pa. Pvt. instrumental instr., Lodi, Ohio, 1995—; reference libr. Smith Meml. Libr., Chautauqua, NY, 1996—2002; elem. music specialist Cloverleaf Local Schs., Lodi, 1997—. Mem. Right to Read Week com. Lodi Elem., 1997—98, mem. fall harvest com., 1998—99; rep. Medina County fine arts tours com. Medina County Schs. Ednl. Svc. Ctr., Medina, 2000—; mem. staff devel. com. Cloverleaf Local Schs., Lodi, 1998—, mem. levy com., 2003—, dance club instr., 2003—04, math instr., cool club, 2004. Singer: (chorus) Kent Chorus. Recipient Trustee's scholarship, Westminster Coll., 1992—96, Music Activity grant, 1992—96, Ted Billick Meml. scholarship, Cloverleaf Local Schs., 1992, John Phillip Sousa Award, Cloverleaf Local Schools, 1992; scholar Cloverleaf Edn. Assn. Scholarship, Cloverleaf Edn. Assn., 1992. Democrat. Achievements include research in dance and how it affects student performance in music education. Avocations: instrumental and vocal music, travel, astrology, rare book collecting, gardening. Home: 211 Prospect St Lodi OH 44254 Office: Cloverleaf Local Schs 8525 Friendsville Rd Lodi OH 44254 E-mail: cookjena@hotmail.com.

LANGMAN, MADELEINE CHARNA, psychologist; b. Hackensack, N.J., Nov. 20, 1963; d. Eli and Norma Diane Cohen; m. Peter Fabbri Langman; children: Joshua, Anna. BA sum cum laude, Clark Univ., Worchester, Mass., 1985; MA, Leslie Coll., Cambridge, Mass., 1989; PhD, Lehigh Univ., Bethlehem, Pa., 2000. Lic. psychologist Pa., 2000. Staff counselor Worchester Polytechnic Inst., Mass., 1989—92; staff counselor, 1 grade asst. Lehigh Univ., Bethlehem, Pa., 1992—98; staff counselor Lafayette Coll., Easton, Pa., 1999—2003; pvt. practice Allentown, Pa., 2000—. Mem.: APA, Lehigh Valley Psychol. Assn., Psi Chi, Phi Beta Kappa. Office: 825 N Cedar Crest Blvd Allentown PA 18104

LANG-MIERS, ELIZABETH ANN, lawyer; b. Mpls., Nov. 26, 1950; BA, U. Mo., 1972, JD, 1975. Bar: Mo. 1975, Tex. 1977, U.S. Ct. Appeals (5th cir.), U.S. Supreme Ct. Law clk. to presiding justice Mo. Supreme Ct., Jefferson City, 1975-76; ptnr. Locke Liddell & Sapp, LLP, Dallas, 1976—. Bd. dirs. Tex. Bar. Mem. Dallas County Med. Soc. Aux., bd. dirs. Met. YWCA; bd. dirs., chairperson adv. bd. Women's Resource Ctr. Leadership Dallas, Leadership Tex., Leadership Am. Recipient Am. Jurisprudence awards 1973, 74. Mem. ABA (mem. ho. dels), Am. Law Inst., Tex. Bar Found. (trustee), Dallas Bar Assn. (v.p. adminstrn., v.p. activities, sec.-treas., chair, vice chair bd. dirs., pres. 1998), Dallas Found. (bd. govs.), Tex. Young Lawyers Assn. (com. chair), Dallas Assn. Young Lawyers (com. chair), State Bar (bd. dirs., com. chair, Pres.'s citation 1996, 98, Woman of Excellence award, 1998, Louise Raggio award 1998, Judge Sam Williams Leadership award). Office: Locke Liddell & Sapp LLP 2200 Ross Ave Ste 2200 Dallas TX 75201-6776

LANG-PIASECKI, VERA JEAN, financial consultant; b. St. Croix, V.I., Oct. 6, 1965; d. Albert George and Ann Eleanor (Yuengling) Lang; m. Robert John Piasecki. BS summa cum laude, Fairleigh Dickinson U., 1987. CPA N.Y. Mgr. Price Waterhouse, 1987—94; dir. fin. Reed Telepub. Ltd.,

1994—95; U.S. treas. Reed Elsevier, Inc., N.Y.C., 1995—98, treas., v.p. fin. svcs., 1998—2000; CFO Reed Elsevier, New Providence, NJ, 2000—01; pvt. fin. cons., 2001—.

LANGREHR, JOCELYN CLARE, counselor; b. Barton-on-Sea, Eng., Sept. 12, 1963; came to U.S., 1964; BS in Edn., U. Del., 1986; MS Counseling with highest distinction, San Diego State U., 1988. Lic. profl. counselor; lic. elem. tchr., spl. edn. tchr. K-12, guidance counselor K-12, Del.; nationally cert. counselor; cert. case mgr. Spl. edn. tchr. Christina Sch. Dist., New Castle County, Del., 1986; career svcs. advisor U. Calif., San Diego, 1987; counselor San Diego City Schs., 1987; grad. program advisor San Diego State U., 1987-88; vocat. cons. Del. Valley Rehab., Wilmington, Del., 1989-90; vocat. cons. sr. Olsten/Upjohn Inc., Wilmington, 1990-92; dir. vocat. svc. Phoenix Cons. Svc., Chadds Ford, Pa., 1992-97; pvt. practitioner Wilmington, Del., 1997—. Mem. ACA, FSRCA (sec. 1990, pres. 1991, past pres. 1992).

LANGSLEY, PAULINE ROYAL, psychiatrist; b. Lincoln, Nebr., July 2, 1927; d. Paul Ambrose and Dorothy (Sibley) Royal; m. Donald G. Langsley, Sept. 9, 1955; children: Karen Jean, Dorothy Ruth Langsley Runman, Susan Louise. BA, Mills Coll., 1949; MD, U. Nebr., 1953. Cert. psychiatrist, Am. Bd. Psychiatry and Neurology. Intern Mt. Zion Hosp., San Francisco, 1954; resident U. Calif., San Francisco, 1954-57, student health psychiatrist Berkeley, 1957-61, U. Colo., Boulder, 1961-68; assoc. clin. prof. psychiatry U. Calif. Med. Sch., Davis, 1968-76; student health psychiatrist U. Calif., Davis, 1968-76; assoc. clin. prof. psychiatry U. Cin., 1976-82; pvt. practice psychiatry Cin., 1976-82; cons. psychiatrist Federated States of Micronesia, Pohnpei, 1984-87; fellow in geriatric psychiatry Rush-Presbyn./St. Luke Hosp., Chgo., 1989-91. Mem. accreditation rev. com. Accreditation Coun. for Continuing Med. Edn., 1996-98. Trustee Mills Coll., Oakland, 1974-78, 2001—; bd. dirs. Evanston Women's Club. Fellow Am. Psychiat. Assn. (chair continuing med. edn. 1990-96); mem. AMA, Am. Med. Womens Assn., Ohio State Med. Assn., Ill. Psychiat. Assn. (sec. 1993-95, pres.-elect 1995-96, pres. 1996-97, accreditation coun. 1996-98). Home and Office: 9445 Monticello Ave Evanston IL 60203-1117

LANGSTAFF, ELEANOR MARGUERITE, retired library science educator; b. Washington, June 21, 1934; d. William Truman and Bernice Louise (Tharpe-Mccum) De Selms, m. David Knox Langstaff, June 19, 1970 (dec. 1984). BA, Colo. State U., Ft. Collins, 1958; MA, Fordham U., 1961; MS, Cath. U. Am., 1970; MPhil, CUNY, 1994, PhD, 1998; cert. in tropical edn., U. London/Makerere Coll., Uganda. Mem. Tchrs. for East Africa program Columbia U., N.Y.C., 1961-64; fgn. svc. officer USIA, 1965-69, acting country pub. affairs officer, 1967-68, regional books officer, 1968-69; libr. Sch. Libr. and Info. Sci., Pratt Inst., N.Y.C., 1970-72; assoc. prof. libr. sci. Bernard M. Baruch Coll., CUNY, 1973-95, prof., 1996—. Cons. on info. Langstaff-French Assocs., Manchester, Vt., 1982-88; dir. hypermedia devel. project Libr. Svc. and Constrn. Act, U.S. Dept. Edn., 1989-90. Author: Andrew Lang, 1978; (with Thomas V. Atkins) Access to Information: Library Research and Demonstration Methods, 1979, Panama, 1982; co-author: Access Information. Business, 1986, 90, Access Information: Social Sciences and Humanities, 1990; (with others) British Women Writers, 1988. Vol. ARC, Bklyn., 1972—. Recipient excellence in French lit. award French Govt., 1958, Fulbright Lecturing award U. Mauritius, 1992—. Mem. ALA, Libr. Assn. CUNY (v.p. 1974-75, pres. 1975-76), Assn. Coll. and Rsch. Librs., Phi Beta Mu. Episcopalian. Home: 100 Remsen St Brooklyn NY 11201-4256 E-mail: elang2@juno.com.

LANGSTON, NANCY SUE FRIEDRICH, dean; b. Little Rock, Dec. 14, 1944; BSN cum laude, U. Ark., 1966; M in Surg. Nursing, Emory U., 1972; PhD in Edn., Ga. State U., 1977. RN, Va. Staff RN U. Ark. Med. Ctr., Little Rock, 1966-67, Doctor's Hosp., Shreveport, La., 1967; instr. Confederate Meml. Med. Ctr. Sch. Nursing, Shreveport, La., 1967-70, Northwestern State U. Sch. Nursing, Shreveport, La., 1970-71, Emory U. Sch. Nursing, Atlanta, 1972-73; adminstrv. intern U. Tex. Sys. Sch. Nursing, Austin, 1974-75, rsch. assoc., 1975-76; assoc. prof., assoc. dean undergrad. programs U. Nebr. Med. Coll. Nursing, Lincoln, 1976-85; prof., dean U. N.C. at Charlotte Coll. Nursing, 1985-91, Va. Commonwealth U. Sch. of Nursing, Richmond, 1991—. Nurse-cons. Goodwill Industries of Atlanta, Inc., 1973-74; adj. assoc. prof. U. Nebr. at Lincoln Tchrs. Coll., 1983-85 Contbr. articles to profl. jours., chpts. to books; presenter in field. Mem. bd. Fan Free Clinic, strategic planning com., 1994, med. svcs. com, 1994—, chmn. 1995; mem. Richmond Rotary, med. svcs. com. 1993—, chmn. 1994; mem. adv. bd. Here's To Your Health; bd. dirs. Hospice of Charlotte, 1988-91, chair profl. adv. com., 1989-91; mem. Civitan Charlotte, 1989-91, at-large 1991—; bd. dirs. Lincoln Lancaster Commn. on Status of Women, 1983-85, edn. com. 1981-85; bd. dirs. Southeast Nebr. Health Systems Agy., 1981-82; pub. issues com. Nebr. Cancer Soc., 1978-80; adv. bd. geriat. Atlanta Regional Commn., 1973; chair nursing sect., Shreveport chpt. ARC, 1969-71. Recipient award of honor Alumni Assn. Nell Hodgson Woodruff Sch. Nursing, Emory U., 1989; Am. Nurses' Found. scholar 1972, Rockefeller scholar 1962-64. Mem. ANA, Nat. League for Nursing, So. Nursing Rsch. Coun., Phi Kappa Phi, Phi Theta Kappa, Sigma Theta Tau. Office: Va Commonwealth U Sch Nursing PO Box 980567 Richmond VA 23298-0567

LANGWORTHY, AUDREY HANSEN, state legislator; b. Grand Forks, N.D., Apr. 1, 1938; d. Edward H. and Arla (Kuhlman) Hansen; m. Asher C. Langworthy Jr., Sept. 8, 1962; children: Kristin Langworthy McLaughlin, Julia Langworthy Steinberg. BS, U. Kans., 1960, MS, 1962; postgrad., Harvard U., 1989. Tchr. jr. high sch. Shawnee Mission Sch. Dist., Johnson County, Kans., 1963-65; councilperson City of Prairie Village, Kans., 1981-85; mem. Kans. Senate from 7th dist., Topeka, 1985-2001. Alt. del. Nat. Conf. State Legislatures, 1985-87, del., 1987—, nominating com., 1990-92, vice chair fed. budget and taxation com., 1994, chair fed. budget and taxation com., 1995-96, vice chair assembly on federal issues, 1996-97, mem. exec. com., 1997-2000; del. Midwestern Conf. State Legislatures, 1989-98; mem. strategic planning com. Coun. State Govts., 1997-98; bd. dirs. St. Luke's/Shawnee Mission Med. Ctr. Found., 1997—. City co-chmn. Kassebaum for U.S. Senate, Prairie Village, 1978; pres. Jr. League Kansas City, Mo., 1977, Kansas City Eye Bank, 1980-82, chmn., 1983-85, bd. mem., 1977-98; mem. bd. Greater Kansas City ARC, 1975—, pres., 1984, chmn. midwestern adv. coun., 1985-86, nat. bd. govs., 1987-93; mem. Johnson County C.C. Found., 1999—; mem. Leadership Kans., Germany Today Program, 1991; bd. dirs. Kans. Wildlife & Parks Fund; trustee Found. on Aging, 1992-96; hon. co-chair Shawnee Mission Edn. Found. Benefit Showtime 99, 1999; mem. Johnson County adv. com. Met. Orgn. to Counter Sexual Assault, 1999—; bd. dirs. Cmty. Found. of Johnson County, 1999—, Heart of Am. United Way, 2000—; chair Kans. 3rd dist. George W. Bush-Pres., 2000; elected precinct committeewoman, 2000—; del. Rep. Nat. Conv., 2000, mem. platform com. Recipient Outstanding Vol. award Cmty. Svcs. Award Found., 1983, Confidence in Edn. award Friends of Edn., 1984, Pub. Svc. award as Kans. Legislator of Yr., Hallmark Polit. Action Com., 1991, Clara Barton Honor award Greater Kans. City ARC, Intergovtl. Leadership award League Kans. Mcpls., 1994, Disting. Pub. Svc. award United Cmty. Svcs. of Johnson County, 1995, Outstanding Achievement in Hist. Preservation award Alexander Majors Hist. House, 1995, Kansas City Spirit award, 1996, disting. pub. svc. award Prairie Village, 1995, Audrey Langworthy award Univ. Mo-Kansas City Women's Coun. Grad. Asst. Fund, 1997, Audrey Langworthy award Outstanding Youth Vol. Work Greater Kansas City ARC, 1996, Regional Leadership award Mid-Am. Regional Coun., 1999, award of appreciation Kans. Rep. Party, 2000, Cmty. Svc. award Greater Kansas City Women's Polit. Caucus, 2000, Recognition for Leadership and Svc., Greater Kansas City C. of C., 2000; named 1st hon. chair The Genevieve Byrn Series, Greater Kansas City ARC, 2000. Mem. LWV, Women's Pub. Svc. Network, U. Kans. Alumni Assn. Episcopalian. Avocations: hunting, running, family. Home: 6324 Ash St Prairie Village KS 66208-1369 E-mail: alangwo622@aol.com.

LANHAM, SANDRA, conservationist; BA in Social Psychology, We. Mich. U., 1970. Lic. pvt. pilot. Founder, dir. The Desert Sanctuary, Ariz., Environ. Flying Svcs., Tucson, 1991—. Founding bd. mem. Coastal Conservative Found.; bd. dirs. Border Ecology Project. Mem.: Internat. Assn. Natural Resource Pilots. Office: Environ Flying Svcs 250 W Old Ina Rd Tucson AZ 85704

LANICCA ALBANESE, ELLEN, public relations executive; Co-founder, sr. v.p. Patrice Tanaka & Co., N.Y.C., 1990-94, pres., 1994—, head Home, Healthcare and Fin. Svcs. account groups; v.p. Lumin Collaborative. V.p. bd. dirs. League of Women Voters Edn. Found., NY. Mem.: Pub. Rels. Soc. Am. NY (exec. com. bd. dirs.). Office: Patrice Tanaka & Co Inc 320 W 13th St Fl 7 New York NY 10014-1200*

LANIER, JACQUELINE RUTH, curator, artist; b. Boston, Dec. 15, 1947; d. John Stanley and Mary Elizabeth (Porter) L.; 1 child, Raymond Rashad Lanier. BS in Edn., Morgan State U., 1976. Drama specialist Day in Arts Boston Symphony, 1971; drama specialist Balt. City Cultural Arts & Urban Svcs., 1974-78; prodr., host Sta. WEAA-FM, 1985-90; with ACTION, 1987-89; R & D implementer Abell Found., 1988-89; developer, curator Lanier Mus. African-Am. History, 1983—; bus. mgr. League for Handicap-Camp Greentop, 1997; cons., development, program coord. Being Reunited with Opportunity, 1998—. Seminar staff developer dept. edn. Balt. Cith Sch., 1988; lectr., presenter IRS, 1988; R & D implementer Lady Md. Found., 1989; lectr. D.C. Pub. Libr., 1990; asst. devel. coord., collections mgr. Heritage Mus. Art, 1990—, Lanier Enterprises Internat., 1997—; curator, lectr. Benjamin Banner Mus. and Park, 1998—; lectr. in field. Prodr. Call of the Ancestor, 1992; exhbts. include Counciling Ctr., 1992, Internat. Black Women Congress, 1992, Morgan State U., 1992, Busterizing, Inc., Md. Commn. African Am. History & Culture, 1992, City Life Mus., 1992, Encore Theatre Co., 1992, Social Security Adminstrn., 1992, New Shiloh Bapt. Ch., 1992, Enon Bapt. Ch., 1992, St. Peter Clavers Ch., 1992, Immaculate Conception Ch., 1994, Martin Luther King Ch., 1994, Heritage Mus. Art, 1994, Chesapeake Coll., 1994, 97, Native Am. Mus., 1994, Nat. Assn. Black Vets., 1994, Dept. Equal Employment Devel., 1994, Perry Point Vets. Hosp., 1994, UN, 1995, D.C. Country Club, 1995, Howard County C.C., 1995, Cambridge Coll., 1995, Johns Hopkins Rsch. Inst., 1995, Hist. Sharp. St. Ch., 1995, Balt. Aquarium, 1996, Chesapeake Coll., 1996, Allaganey County Arts Coun., 1996, Heritage Mus., 1996, Md. Humanities Coun., 1996, Nat. Aquarium Balt. 1996, Mobil Corp. Hdqrs., 1996, 97, Health Care Fin. Adminstrn., 1996, 97, League Serving People with Disabilities, 1997. Mem. exec. com. Broadway East Cmty. Assn.; bd. dirs., 2d dist. rep. Citizen Plabning & Housing Assn.; chmn. East Balt. Coun. Neighborhoods, Inc.; mem. Empowerment Zone Devel. Bd.; gen. ptnr. Gay St. Housing Partnership Ltd.; bd. dirs., pres. Housing Assistance Corp.; v.p. Mid. East Cmty. Devel. Corp.; vol. Balt. City Commn. Women, Urban Svcs. Agy., Balt. City Youth Fair, WAVR Radio; com. mem. Democratic State Ctrl. Com.; mem. substance abuse prevention coun. Mayor's Coordinating Coun. Criminal Justice, Voices of Electorate; mem. Black Single Parents; mem., pres. Ira Aldridge Players; adv. com. minority bus. tourism Md. Dept. Econ. Employment Devel. Office Tourism; mem. Sankofa exhb. adv. com. Md. Hist. Soc., bd. dirs. Seventh Sons Prodn. Co. Recipient Outstanding Svc. award Campfire, Inc., Fifteen Yr. Svc. award, 100 Hours Vol. Svc. award VA, Outstanding Svc. award Md. House Dels., Citation City of Balt. Citizens, Svcs. Agy. & Citizens Balt. award Urban Svcs. Agy., Svc. to Jazz Cmty. award Gemini Prodns., Inc., Outstanding Cmty. Svc. award African Am. Women's Expo, Outstanding Leadership award AFRAM, 1995; inducted into Black Collectors Hall of Fame, 1992, Wall of Fame, 1994, Health Care Fin. Adminstrn., 1997. Mem. Nat. Assn. Fundraising Execs., Nat. Assn. Black Collectors & Dealers, New Gay St. Improvement Assn. (pres.), Black Ethnic Collectibles Mag. (adv. bd.), Transitional Housing Program (adv. com.). Democrat. Lutheran. Avocations: environmentalist, synchronized swimming, writing, reading, storytelling. Home: 3817 Clifton Ave Baltimore MD 21216-2428

LANIER, MARTHA I. human resources specialist; b. Savannah, Ga., July 12, 1947; d. Ernest Bertram Ike, Jr. and Matt Tuten Ike; m. James McCrary Lanier, Sr., Feb. 17, 1970; children: Elizabeth Lanier Storch, Lauren McCrary, James McCrary Lanier, Jr. AA, Va. Intermont Coll., Bristol. Med. adminstrv. asst. Emory U. Clinic, Atlanta, 1967—71; v.p. relocation and REO svcs. Century 21 Taylor Realty, Framingham, Mass., 1984—93; exec. adminstrv. asst. Riverwood Internat., Atlanta, 1996—99; office mgr./human resources dir. The Shoptaw Group, Atlanta, 1999—2001; pres. Ignite Your Potential, Inc., Atlanta, 2000—. Author: 303 Solutions For Dropping Stress & Finding Balance, 303 Solutions For Accomplishing More in Less Time, 303 Solutions For Developing the Leader in You. Tchr., usher, adv. bd. mem. Peachtree Rd. United Meth. Ch., Atlanta, Ga., 2000—03. Mem.: Ga. Coaches Assn., Internat. Coach Fedn., Ga. Speakers Assn. (v.p. of membership 2003—, Vol. of the Yr. 2001-2002), Nat. Speakers Assn., Toastmasters Internat. - Interstate North Chpt. (v.p. of membership 2001—02, Competent Toastmaster, Advanced Toastmaster (Bronze), Competent Leader, Outstanding Toastmaster, Hervey Ross Outstanding Toastmaster Award 2001-2002). Avocations: skydiving, walking, swimming, boating. Office: Ignite Your Potential Inc PO Box 724075 Atlanta GA 31139 E-mail: martha@marthalanier.com.

LANIER, NANCY MCDANIEL, researcher; b. Hinton, W.Va., Mar. 10, 1944; d. Roy Edward and Mary Elizabeth (Hulme) McDaniel; m. Dawson Edward Watkins III, Aug. 29, 1964 (div. Aug. 1978); children: Patricia Ann, Benjamin Edward; m. Moultrie Shrewsbury Lanier II, May 5, 1989. BA, Lynchburg Coll., 1965; postgrad., Va. Commonwealth U., 1980-83. Adminstrv. asst. to dean of grad. studies Lynchburg (Va.) Coll., 1966-69; sec. engring. dept. AMF Bakery Sys., Richmond, Va., 1977-80; office mgr. behavioral svcs. unit, divsn. youth svcs. Va. Dept. Corrections, Richmond, 1981-83; asst. to the pres. Va. Found. for Ind. Colls., Richmond, 1983-89; dir. devel. rsch. Union Theol. Sem., Richmond, 1989—. Cons. in computer tng. Tenn. Ind. Coll. Fund, Nashville, 1987. Active Jay-C-Ettes, Lynchburg, 1967-69; chmn. fine arts Jr. Women's Club, Staunton, 1970-73; choir mem., tchr. Covenant Presbyn. Ch., Staunton, 1970-77; elder, choir mem. The Gayton Kirk Presbyn. Ch., 1985-99, River Rd. Presbyn. Ch., 2001—; former mem. Richmond Choral Soc., 1988-94; pres. ACCA Temple Chantettes, Richmond, 1989-2001. Mem. Assn. for Profl. Rschrs. for Advancement. Avocations: singing in choral groups, golfing, swimming. Office: Union-PSCE 3401 Brook Rd Richmond VA 23227-4514 Office Phone: 804-278-4251. E-mail: nlanier@union-psce.edu.

LANK, EDITH HANDLEMAN, columnist, educator; b. Boston, Feb. 27, 1926; m. Norman Lank; children: Avrum, David, Anna. BA magna cum laude, Syracuse U. Columnist L.A. Times Syndicate, 1976—2000; TV host Sta. WOKR-TV, Rochester, N.Y., 1983-84; radio host Sta. WBBF-AM, Rochester, 1984-85; columnist Tribune Media Svcs., 2000—02, Creators Syndicate, 2003—. Lectr. St. John Fisher Coll., Rochester, 1977-89; commentator Sta. WXXI-FM, Rochester, 1977—; guest Pub. Radio Internat., St. Paul, 1987—; speaker in field. Author: Home Buying, 1981, Selling Your Home, 1982, Modern Real Estate Practice in New York, 1983, rev. 8th edit., 2001, The Home Seller's Kit, 1988, rev. 4th edit. 1997, The Complete Home Buyer's Kit, 1989, rev. 4th edit., 1997, Dear Edith, 1990, Essentials of New Jersey Real Estate, rev. 5th edit., 2002, 201 Questions Every Homebuyer and Seller Must Ask, 1996, Jane Austen speaks to Women, 2000; co-author: Your Home as a Tax Shelter, 1993; contbr. articles to Time, New Yorker, McCall's, Real Estate Today, Persuasions, Modern Maturity, others. Recipient media award Bar Assn. Monroe County, 1982, Matrix award Women in Ommunications, 1984, Woman of Distinction award Gov. Mario Cumo, N.Y., 1985; named Communicator of Yr., SUNY, Brockport, 1986. Mem. Real Estate Educators Assn. (bd. dirs., Consumer Edn. award 1982, 83, 86, 96, Real Estate Educator of Yr. 1984), Nat. Assn. Real Estate Editors (bd. dirs), Jane Austen Soc. N.Am. (dir.), Phi Beta Kappa. Avocation: scuba diving. Home and Office: 240 Hemingway Dr Rochester NY 14620-3316 E-mail: edithlank@aol.com.

LANNING, YVONNE BRADSHAW, elementary school educator; b. Smithville, Mo., Mar. 12, 1956; d. Arbeth McKinley and Frances Valjean (Whelan) Bradshaw; m. Charles Lanning, Feb. 18, 1977. AA, Kansas City (Kans.) C.C., 1976; BS, St. Mary Coll., Leavenworth, Kans., 1985; MS, Kans. State U., 2002; PhD, St. Regis U., 2003. Cert. tchr., Kans., Kans. Assn. for Edn. Young Children. Paraprofl. St. Peter's Cathedral Sch., Kansas City; elem. and kindergarten tchr. Holy Family Sch., Kansas City; tchr. kindergarten Unified Sch. Dist. 500, Kansas City, Kansas City (Mo.) Sch. Dist. Pres. Mid-County Dem. Club, 1988. Mem. Cath. Edn. Assn., Kans. Edn. Assn. (chmn. polit. action commn. 1988-89), Quill and Scroll.

LANQUETOT, E. ROXANNE, retired special education educator; b. Kansas City, Nov. 29, 1933; d. Myron Lewis and Bonnie (Goldberg) Leiser; m. Guy Alfred Lanquetot, Oct. 3, 1958; 1 child, Serge Normand. Student, Stanford U., 1951-53; cert. in French Pronunciation, Inst. de Phonetique, Sorbonne, Paris, 1954; BS, Columbia U., 1956, MA, 1957, CCNY, 1976; postgrad., CUNY, 1980-83. Asst. tchr. English Lycee Fenelon, Paris, 1960-62; tchr. kindergarten Lycee Francais N.Y., N.Y.C., 1964-65; dir. nursery & kindergarten Lyceum Francais, N.Y.C., 1965-66; tchr. 2d grade Pub. Sch. 113 M, N.Y.C., 1966-69; tchr., jr. guidance counselor Pub. Sch. 87 M, N.Y.C., 1969-71; tchr. emotionally handicapped Pub. Sch. 106, Bellevue Hosp., N.Y.C., 1971-99; ret., 1999. Contbr. articles to profl. publs., Newsday, Wall St. Jour., France-Amerique, others. Fellow Am. Orthophyschiatric Assn.; mem. Nat. Alliance for Rsch. on Schizophrenia and Depression (mem. leadership coun.). Avocations: classical music, theater, creative writing, travel, ballet, classical music, theatre. Home and Office: 315 W 106th St New York NY 10025-3445 E-mail: rglanquetot@yahoo.com.

LANSAW, JUDY W. public utility executive; b. Dayton, Ohio, July 12, 1951; d. Edwin Columbus and Stella Sabra (Roark) Wyatt; m. James L. Schaefer, Oct. 16, 1971 (div. 1975); m. Charles Edward Lansaw, Dec. 30, 1982; 1 child, Eric. BA in Organizational Communications, Wright State U., Dayton, 1988. Legal sec. Robert Abrahamson, atty., Dayton, 1970-78; exec. adminstrv. asst. Dayton Power & Light Co., 1978-81, mktg. rsch. energy specialist, 1981-84, exec. asst. to chief exec. officer, 1984-88, corp. sec., 1988—, v.p., 1989—; corp. sec. DPL Inc., Dayton, 1988—, v.p., 1989—. Trustee Jobs for Grads., Inc., Dayton, 1989-92, Victoria Theatre Assn., Dayton, 1990—. Mem. Am. Soc. Corp. Secs., Dayton Club, Racquet Club. Republican. Avocations: tennis, skiing, golf, sailing. Home: PO Box 750130 Dayton OH 45475-0130 Office: DPL Inc 1065 Woodman Dr Dayton OH 45432-1438

LANSBURY, ANGELA BRIGID, actress; b. London, Oct. 16, 1925; came to U.S., 1940; d. Edgar and Moyna (Macgill) L.; m. Peter Shaw, Aug. 12, 1949 (dec. 2003); children: Anthony, Deirdre. Student, Webber-Douglas Sch. Drama, London, 1939-40, Feagin Sch. Drama, N.Y.C., 1940-42; LHD (hon.), Boston U., 1990. Host 41st-43d Ann. Tony Awards, 45th Ann. Emmy Awards. Actress with Metro-Goldwyn-Mayer, 1943-50; films include: Gaslight, 1944 (Acad. award nomination), National Velvet, 1944, The Picture of Dorian Gray, 1944 (Golden Globe award, Acad. award nomination), The Harvey Girls, 1946, The Hoodlum Saint, 1946, Till the Clouds Roll By, 1946, The Private Affairs of Bel Ami, 1947, If Winter Comes, 1948, Tenth Avenue Angel, 1948, State of the Union, 1948, The Three Musketeers, 1948, The Red Danube, 1949, Samson and Delilah, 1949, Kind Lady, 1951, Mutiny, 1952, Remains to be Seen, 1953, A Life at Stake, 1955, The Purple Mask, 1956, A Lawless Street, 1956, Please Murder Me, 1956, The Court Jester, 1956, The Long Hot Summer, 1958, Reluctant Debutante, 1958, A Breath of Scandal, 1960, Dark at the Top of the Stairs, 1960, Season of Passion, 1961, Blue Hawaii, 1961, All Fall Down, 1962, Manchurian Candidate, 1962 (Golden Globe award, Acad. award nomination), In the Cool of the Day, 1963, Dear Heart, 1964, The World of Henry Orient, 1964, The Greatest Story Ever Told, 1965, Harlow, 1965, The Amorous Adventures of Moll Flanders, 1965, Mister Buddwing, 1966, Something for Everyone, 1970, Bedknobs and Broomsticks, 1971, Death on the Nile, 1978, The Lady Vanishes, 1980, The Mirror Crack'd, 1980, The Pirates of Penzance, 1982, The Company of Wolves, 1983, Beauty and the Beast, 1991, Your Studio and You, 1995, Beauty & the Beast: Enchanted Christmas (vioce), 1997, Anastasia (Voice), 1997; star TV series Murder She Wrote, 1984-96 (Golden Globe awards 1984, 86, 91, 92, 12 Emmy nominations, Lead Actress - Drama), Murder, She Wrote: A Story to Die For, 2000, Murder, She Wrote: The Last Free Man, 2001, Murder, She Wrote: The Celtic Riddle, 2003; appeared in TV mini-series Little Gloria, Happy at Last, 1982, Lace, 1984, Rage of Angels, part II, 1986; other TV movies include: The First Olympics-Athens 1896, A Talent for Murder, Gift of Love, 1982, Shootdown, 1988, The Shell Seekers, 1989, The Love She Sought, 1990, Mrs. 'Arris Goes to Paris, 1992, (musical) Mrs. Santa Claus, 1996; appeared in plays Hotel Paradiso, 1957, A Taste of Honey, 1960, Anyone Can Whistle, 1964, Mame (on Broadway), 1966, 83 (Tony award for Best Mus. Actress 1966), Dear World, 1968 (Tony award for Best Mus. Actress 1969), All Over (London Royal Shakespeare Co.), 1971, Prettybelle, 1971, Gypsy, 1974 (Tony award for Best Mus. Actress 1975, Sarah Siddons award), The King and I, 1978, Sweeney Todd, 1979 (Tony award for Best Mus. Actress 1979, Sarah Siddons award), Hamlet, Nat. Theatre, London, 1976, A Little Family Business, 1983. Named Woman of Yr., Harvard Hasty Pudding Theatricals, 1968, Comdr. of British Empire by Queen Elizabeth II, 1994; named to Theatre Hall of Fame, 1982, TV Hall of Fame, 1996; recipient British Acad. award, 1991, Silver Mask Lifetime Ach. Award, British Acad. Film and TV Arts, 1992, Lifetime Achievement award, Screen Actors' Guild, Hollywood, 1997, 16 Emmy Award Nominations, 8 Golden Globe Nominations; Won 6 Golden Glode Awards; received Nat. medal of the Arts from President Clinton, 1997. Office: c/o William Morris Agy 151 E1 Camino Dr Beverly Hills CA 90212

LANSDOWNE, KAREN MYRTLE, retired English language and literature educator; b. Twin Falls, Idaho, Aug. 11, 1926; d. George and Effie Myrtle (Avotte) Martin; m. Paul L. Lansdowne, Sept. 12, 1948; children: Michele Lynn, Larry Alan. BA in English with honors, U. Oreg., 1948, MEd, 1958, MA with honors, 1960. Tchr. Newfield (N.Y.) H.S., 1948-50, S. Eugene (Oreg.) H.S., 1952; mem. faculty U. Oreg., Eugene, 1958-65; asst. prof. English Lane C.C., Eugene, 1965-82, ret., 1982. Cons. Oreg. Curriculum Study Center. Co-author: The Oregon Curriculum: Language/Rhetoric, I, II, III and IV, 1970; rsch., co-author: Lansdowne Family Genealogy Center Studies, 1995-99. Rep. Calif. Young Neighborhood Assn., 1978—; mem. scholarship com. First Congl. Ch., 1950-70. Mem. MLA, Pacific N.W. Regional Conf. C.C.s, Nat. Coun. Tchrs. English, U. Oreg. Women, AAUW (sec.) Jaycettes, Pi Lambda Theta (pres.), Phi Beta Patronesses (pres.), Delta Kappa Gamma. Home: 2056 Lincoln St Eugene OR 97405-2604

LANSING, JEWEL BECK (JEWEL ANNE BECK), writer, auditor; b. Ronan, Mont., May 13, 1930; d. Lars Martin and Julia Syla Beck; m. Ronald B. Lansing, June 16, 1956; children: Mark, Alyse, Annette. BA in Journalism, U. Mont., 1952; MA in Edn., Stanford U., 1954. CPA, Oreg. Elected auditor Multnomah County, Portland, Oreg., 1975-82, City of Portland, 1983-86; adj. prof. Lewis and Clark Coll., Portland, 1989-92; interim exec. dir. William Temple Ho., Portland, 1994, YWCA, Portland, 1995; interim pres. Oreg. Coll. of Arts and Crafts, Portland, 1996; writer Portland, 1987—. Author: Campaigning for Office, 1991, 101 Campaign Tips, 1991, Deadly Games in City Hall, 1997. Portland: People, Politics, and Power, 1851-2001, 2003. Candidate state treas. Dem. Party, 1976, 80; pres. Oreg. Fedn. of Dem. Women, 1977-78; city-county consolidation task force City of Portland, 1997-98; active Pacific N.W. local govt. rep. Nat.

Intergovtl. Audit Forum, Washington, 1982-85. Recipient Woman of Achievement LWV, 1995, Disting. Leadership award Assn. of Govt. Accts., 1987, Pub. Svc. award Oreg. Soc. of CPAs, 1987, Taxpayers Champion award Oregonians for Cost Effective Govt., 1987. Mem. Womens Investment Network (polit. action com. exec. com., bd. dirs., founder), Oreg. Women's Polit. Caucus (First Woman award 1987), Portland Women's Polit. Caucus (Svc. award 1987), Oreg. Hist. Soc., Oreg. Environtl. Coun., Portland LWV. Unitarian Universalist. Avocations: hiking, playing cards, reading, canoeing, golf.

LANSING, SHERRY LEE (HEIMANN), motion picture executive; b. Chgo., July 31, 1944; d. Norton and Margo L.; m. William Friedkin. BS summa cum laude in Theatre, Northwestern U., 1966. Tchr. math. public high schs., Los Angeles, 1966-69; model TV commls. Max Factor Co., 1969-70, Alberto-Culver Co., 1969-70; story editor Wagner Internat. Prodn. Co., 1972-74, dir. west coast devel., 1974-75; story editor MGM, 1975-77, v.p. creative affairs, 1977; senior v.p. prodn. Columbia Pictures, 1977-80; pres. 20th Century Fox Prodns., 1980-82; founder Jaffee-Lansing Prodns., 1983—92; pres. Paramount Communications, 1990—; chmn. Paramount Motion Pictures Group, L.A., 1992—. Appeared in movies Loving, 1970, Rio Lobo, 1970; ind. producer., Jaffe-Lansing Prodns.; exec. prodr. Racing With the Moon, 1984,Firstborn, 1984; prodr. Fatal Attraction, 1987, The Accused, 1988, Black Rain, 1989, School Ties, 1992, Indecent Proposal, 1993; TV exec. producer When the Time Comes,1987, Mistress, 1992. Recipient Producers Guild of Am. Milestone award, 2000. Office: Paramount Pictures Corp 5555 Melrose Ave Los Angeles CA 90038-3197

LANSKY, ZENA, surgeon; b. Phila., Apr. 18, 1942; d. Jacob and Thelma Lansky. BA summa cum laude, U. Pa., 1963; MD, Allegheny U., 1967. Diplomate Am. Bd. Surgery. Intern Montefiore Hosp., Pitts., 1967-68; resident in surgery Bellevue Hosp., N.Y.C., 1968-72, chief resident in surgery, 1971-72, instr. surgery, 1971-72; teaching asst. NIH, 1970, 71; mem. med. staff Morton F. Plant Hosp.; pres. Metabolic Cons. Inc., infusion co., Clearwater, Fla., 1992—. Staff mem. Largo Med. Ctr., Mease Hosp., Northside Hosp., Bayonet Point Hosp., Healthsouth Rehab. Hosp., New Port Richey Hosp., Vencor Hosp., Columbia Dade City Hosp., Helen Ellis Meml. Hosp., St. Anthony's Hosp., North Bay Med. Ctr., Brooksville Regional Hosp., Bartow Meml. Hosp., Spring Hill Regional Hosp., Transitional Hosp. Tampa, Bayfront Med. Ctr., East Pasco Med. Ctr.; mem. nat. med. adv. bd. New Eng. Critical Care, 1985. Mem. editorial bd. Nutritional Support mag., 1987; contbr. articles to profl. jours.; inventor gastrostomy tube, long term venous catheter repair kit, gastrostomy tube and percutaneous endoscopic kit. Fellow ACS, Southeastern Surg. Congress; mem. Am. Soc. Parenteral and Enteral Nutrition (bd. dirs. 1989), Fla. Med. Assn., Fla. Assn. Nutritional Support (pres. 1986-87), Pinellas County Med. Soc. Office: Metabolic Cons Inc 412 S Missouri Ave Clearwater FL 33756-5836

LANTIS, DONNA LEA, retired banker, art educator, artist; b. Medford, Oreg., Oct. 12, 1931; d. James Warren Fader and Amy Bell (Crump) Fader-Snyder; m. Victor Earl Lantis, July 9, 1950 (div. Apr. 1975); children: Deborah Ann Hayes, Diana Lorraine Keaton. BS, So. Oreg. U., 1966; postgrad., Otis Art Inst., L.A., 1969; 5th yr. cert., U. Oreg., 1974. Art tchr., Oreg., Tenn., Ky.; cert. banker Am. Inst. Banking. Banker First Nat. Bank, Ashland, Oreg., 1951-62; tchr. art, history Klamath County Sch. Dist., Klamath Falls, Oreg., 1966-68; tchr. art Ashland Sch. Dist., 1968-75; banker First Interstate Bank, Medford, Oreg., 1979-92. Supr. student tchrs. So. Oreg. U., Ashland, 1968-75, work with traumatized children, 1968-69. Author illustrated poetry; exhbns. include Oreg. State Fair, So. Oreg. U., Portland, Monmouth Rogue Art Gallery, Medford, Oreg., banks, librs.; dollmaker. Asst. founder lupus support group, Ashland, Oreg., 1977, 78, 79. Elks scholar, 1950, John Dickey Art scholar So. Oreg. U., 1966; recipient Voice of Democracy 1st Place Hon. Mention Broadcasters and Radio Dealers of Am. KWIN, 1949. Mem. AAUW, So. Oreg. Alumni Assn., Libr. of Congress, Women in Arts. Avocations: music, history, writing, gardening, dolls. Home: 617 Catherine St Medford OR 97501-3507

LANTZ, JOANNE BALDWIN, retired academic administrator; b. Defiance, Ohio, Jan. 26, 1932; d. Hiram J. and Ethel A. (Smith) Baldwin; m. Wayne E. Lantz. BS in Physics and Math., U. Indpls., 1953; MS in Counseling and Guidance, Ind. U., 1957; PhD in Counseling and Psychology, Mich. State U., 1969; LittD (hon.), U. Indpls., 1985; LHD (hon.), Purdue U., 1994; LLD (hon.), Manchester Coll., 1994. Tchr. physics and math. Arcola (Ind.) High Sch., 1953-57; guidance dir. New Haven (Ind.) Sr. High Sch., 1957-65; with Ind. U.-Purdue U., Fort Wayne, 1965—, interim chancellor, 1988-89, chancellor, 1989-94, chancellor emeritus, 1994—. Bd. dirs., hon. dir. Ft. Wayne Nat. Corp.; bd. dirs. Foellinger Found. Contbr. articles to profl. jours. Mem. Ft. Wayne Econ. Devel. Adv. Bd. and Task Force, 1988-91, Corp. Coun., 1988-94; bd. advisors Leadership Ft. Wayne, 1988-94; mem. adv. bd. Ind. Sml. Bus. Devel. Ctr., 1988-90; trustee Ancilla System, Inc., 1984-89, chmn. human resources com., 1985-89, exec. com., 1985-89; trustee St. Joseph's Med. Ctr., 1983-84, pers. adv. com. to bd. dirs., 1978-84, chmn., 1980-84; bd. dirs. United Way Allen County, sec., 1979-80; bd. dirs. Anthony Wayne Vocat. Rehab. Ctr., 1969-75. Mem.: AAUW (Am. women fellowship com. 1978—83, program com. 1981—83, chmn. 1981—83, internat. fellowship com. 1986—88, trust rsch. grantee 1980), APA, Southeastern Psychol. Assn. (referee conv. papers 1987, 1988), Ft. Wayne Ind.-Purdue Alumni Soc. (hon. mem. 1987), Ind. Sch. Women's Club (v.p. program chair 1979—81), Delta Kappa Gamma (leadership devel. com. 1978—82, dir. N.E. region 1982—84, adminstrv. bd. 1982—84, exec. bd. 1982—84, gen. chair conv. 1985—86, editl. bd. 1986—88, bd. trustees ednl. found. 1996—2002, nominating com. 2002—), Sigma Xi, Pi Lambda Theta. Avocations: swimming, reading, knitting, boating. E-mail: joalantz@aol.com.

LANZI, BEATRICE A. state legislator; b. Cranston, R.I., Oct. 3, 1966; MA, R.I. Coll., 1989, Emerson Coll., 1991. Mem. spl. legis. com. and joint com. on vet. affairs R.I. Ho. of Dels., Providence; instr. comm., dean jr. coll. Bristol C.C., Cranston, R.I. Mem. Cranston Dem. Com., Save The Bay, R.I. Young Dems.; bd. dirs. Cranston Teen Ctr. Office: 81 Eagle Rd Cranston RI 02920-1203

LANZILLOTTO, ANN RACHELE, performance artist, writer; b. Bronx, NY, June 1, 1963; d. Joseph Rocco and Rachel Claire (Petruzzelli) Lanzillotto. Student, Am. U. Cairo, 1985; BA with honors, Brown U., 1986; MFA, Sarah Lawrence Coll., 1990. Tchr. Sing-Sing, Bedford Hills correctional facilities through Mercy Coll., NY, 1989—92; curator Opera Vindaloo at Dixon Pl., N.Y.C., 1994—96; guest editor Movement Rsch. Performance Jour., N.Y.C., 1995; dir. Opera Stand, Arthur Ave. Retail Market, Bronx, 1996—97; curator The Kitchen, N.Y.C., 1998—2000, guest artist in schs., 2003—. Writing cons. St. John the Divine Interfaith Fellowship for Homeless, N.Y.C., 2003. Dir. : (cmty. art performance) A Schapett!, 1996—97; author, actor, dir. (solo show) Confessions of a Bronx Tomboy, 1993; author, actor, dir How to Wake Up a Marine in a Foxhole, 1998; performance artist at Smithsonian Folklife Festival : A Stickball Memoir, 2001. Cmty. organizer Belmont Small Bus. Assn., Bronx, 2000. Grantee, Franklin Furnace, 1994, Dancing in the Streets, N.Y.C., 1996; prodn. arts prodn. grantee, Rockefeller Found., 1996, multidisciplinary arts fellow, NY State Found. for Arts, 1999, Rockefeller Found. fellow, Next Generation Leadership Program, 2000. Mem.: Italian Am. Writers Assn., Malia Collective of Italian Am. Women. Avocation: flying. Home: 133 7th Ave Brooklyn NY 11215 E-mail: annielanzillotto@earthlink.net.

LAPADOT, SONEE SPINNER, retired automobile manufacturing company official; b. Sidney, Ohio, Apr. 19, 1936; d. Kenneth Lee and Helyn Kathryn (Hobby) Spinner; m. Jan. 13, 1955 (div. Apr. 1970); 1 child, Douglas Cameron Proud; m. Robert Stephen Lapadot, May 4, 1974 (div. Mar. 1994). Student, U. Cin., 1954-56, U. Akron, 1966; BS in Mgmt. Human Resources, Spring Arbor Coll., 1991. Mgr. engring. change implementation Terex divsn. GM, Hudson, Ohio, 1975-77, mgr. prodn. scheduling, 1977-78, gen. adminstr. product purchasing, 1978-79; sr. staff asst. non-ferrous metals GM, Detroit, 1979-80, mgr. tires and wheels, 1980-83, mgr. staff purchasing, 1983-85, mgr. corp. constrn. contracting, 1985-86; mfg. techn. adminstr. Chrysler Motors, Detroit, 1986-87, mgr. mfg. prodn. control adminstrn. and svcs., 1988, mgr. advanced planning and prodn. systems, 1988-89, mgr. advanced planning and control power train, 1989-90, mgr. Mound Rd. engine prodn. control, 1990-95, mgr. corp. project systems, 1995-96, platform exec. material handling engring., 1996-99, platform exec. spl. projects, 2000-01; ret., 2001. Active fundraising Boy Scouts Am., Grosse Pointe, Mich., 1980-82, Detroit, 1985-96, United Fund, Detroit, 1980-99, Jr. Achievement, Detroit, 1984, 90-96. Mem. NAFE, Soc. Automotive Engrs., Am. Soc. Profl. and Exec. Women, Am. Prodn. and Inventory Control Soc., Automotive Industry Action Group (returnable containers and packaging team), Mensa, Women's Econ. Club of Detroit. Home: 1941 Squirrel Rd Bloomfield Hills MI 48304-1162

LAPIDUS, JACQUELINE, poet, editor, educator; b. N.Y.C., Sept. 6, 1941; d. Joseph and Edith Judith (Friedman) L. BA, Swarthmore Coll., 1962; M in Theol. Studies, Harvard U., 1992. Letters corr. Life Mag., N.Y.C., 1962-64; English tchr. Iraklion, 1964-67, Paris, 1977-80; editor, translator Selection du Reader's Digest, Paris, 1981-85; rsch. editor Walking Mag., Boston, 1986-89; sr. editor The Boston Reader, Boston, 1992-93; editl. cons. Boston, 1992—. Tchg. asst. Harvard Ext. Sch., 1996—. Author: Ready to Survive, 1975, Starting Over, 1977, Ultimate Conspiracy, 1987; co-author: Yantras of Womanlove, 1982; contbr. articles to profl. jours.

LAPIERRE, EILEEN MARIE, technical service manager; b. Chgo., June 1, 1966; d. Vernon Francis and Lucille Marie (Hickey) L. AAS in Comml. Art with honors, Harold Washington Coll., 1994; AA in Restaurant Mgmt., Triton Coll., 1987. Cert. photofinishing engr. Soc. Photofinishing Engrs., 2000, A+ cert. computer technician 2003. Sr. photo lab. technician Wolf Camera, Oak Park, Ill., master photo lab. technician Niles, Ill., 2000—. Press photographer Lambda Publs., Chgo., 1996-97. Photographer Garland Ct. Rev., 1993, 94-95. Recipient semi-finalist award N.Am. Open Amateur Photo, 1998, finalist 14th ann. Best of Coll. Photography, 1994, Nat. Deans List 16th ann., Vol. 2, 1992-93, Nat. Deans List 17th ann., Vol. 2, 1993-94, Outstanding Achievement in Photofinishing award Wolfpro Printoff, 1997, 2000. Mem. Internat. Freelance Photographers Assn. (life), Ilfo Pro Photographers Assn., Fuji Film Profl. Pronet, Kodak Viewfinder Forum, Soc. Photofinishing Engrs., Computing Tech. Industry Assn.

LAPIN, SHARON JOYCE VAUGHN, interior designer; b. Lagrange, Mo., July 28, 1938; d. John Nolan and Wilma Emma (Huebotter) Vaughn; m. Byron Richard Lapin, Oct. 14, 1972. BA summa cum laude, U. Wash., Seattle, 1960. Appeared in various Broadway shows, TV commls. and TV shows, 1962-72; mgr. arts and crafts divsn. Convenience Products Clayton Corp., Fenton, Mo. Bd. dirs. St. Louis Conservatory and Schs. for Arts, 1977—92, v.p., 1982—87; chmn. bd. Studio Set, 1978—81, pres., 1975—78, bd. dirs., 1975—83, Friends of Sci. Mus., 1980—90, v.p., 1984—85; pres. assocs. bd. dirs. St. Louis Sci. Ctr., Inc., 1986-87, 1986—87; bd. dirs. Jr. divsn. St. Louis Symphony Women's Assn., 1973—75; bd. dirs. Women's Assn. St. Louis Symphony, 1988—90. Mem. AFTRA, SAG, AEA, ASID, Phi Beta Phi, Mu Phi Epsilon.

LAPOINTE, LUCIE, Canadian government official; b. Valleyfield, Que., Can., Dec. 23, 1954; d. Paul and Jeannette (Gagné) L.; m. Clive Willis, Apr. 13, 1996; 1 child, Lauren Lapointe-Shaw. BSc in Biol. Scis., McGill U., 1977; MBA, U. Ottawa, Ont., Can., 1982. Tech. officer divsn. biol. scis. NRC, Ottawa, 1977-80, program officer program svcs. secretariat, 1982-84, exec. mgr. pub. rels. and info. svcs., 1984-87, dir. mgmt. svcs. br., 1987-89, sec. gen., 1989—2001; v.p. adminstrn., sec.-treas. Pulp and Paper Rsch. Inst. Can., Pointe-Claire, 2001—; exec. mem. Internat. Coun. for Sci. Office: PAPRICAN 570 boul St-Jean Pointe-Claire QC Canada H9R 3J9

LAPOLT, MARGARET, librarian; b. Austin, Pa., June 9, 1931; d. Thomas Wilbur and Frances Leona (Smith) Bennett; m. Sanford Howard LaPolt, Apr. 14, 1957 (dec. Nov. 1996); children: Cheryl Lynn LaPolt Remson, Mark Alan LaPolt. BSEd, Mansfield (Pa.) U., 1953; MSEd, Western Conn. State U., Danbury, 1963; MSLS, So. Conn. State U., New Haven, 1973. Tchr. 5th grade Bd. Edn., Clearfield, Pa., 1953-54; tchr. 6th grade Emporium (Pa.) Bd. Edn., 1954-58; tchr. 5th grade Darien (Conn.) Bd. Edn., 1958-64; tchr. 3d grade Stratford (Conn.) Bd. Edn., 1965-69, libr., 1969-70, Norwalk (Conn.) Bd. Edn., 1973-92, part-time libr., 1993—2002, ret., 2002. Singer, Norwalk Cmty. Chorus, 1961-73; singer Cmty. Bapt. Ch., Norwalk, 1958—, bd. deacons, 1993-99, trustee, 1981-87. Computer grantee, Norwalk Bd. Edn., 1985. Mem. ALA, Kappa Delta Phi, Kappa Pi. Avocations: knitting, embroidery, travel.

LAPORE, JANYCE CATHERINE, writer; b. Beaver Falls, Pa. d. Lawrence and Dorothy Jan Lapore; 1 child, Gary Nicholas Frankowski. MA, Johns Hopkins U., Balt. Author (plays): Ferris Wheel (Internat. Play award Ctr. Theatre, Chgo., Top Ten, Coppola's New Century Writer awards), Derringer (finalist New Century Writer award), Dolored Rain (Fla. Coun. Arts award); author: (screenplays) Screaming My Heart Out (Broadmind Entertainment award, L.A., New Century Writer award), 10 Minutes From Paradise (Best Screenplay, Ohio Ind. Film Festival, Best Screenplay, Hollywood Scriptwriting Inst.), Poppytown. Mem.: Dramatists Guild.

LAPORTE, ADRIENNE AROXIE, nursing administrator; b. Oceanside, N.Y., Sept. 29, 1938; d. Leonide and Grace (Ajamian) LaP. Diploma in nursing, St. John's Episc. Hosp., 1960; BA in Behavioral Scis., Lesley Coll., 1986; MA in Counseling, Liberty U., 1994. RN, N.Y., Fla., Mass., La., Ala.; cert. psychiat./mental health nurse Am. Nurses Credentialing Bd.; cert. legal nurse cons.; lic. alcohol and drug counselor I. Supr. Creedmoor State Hosp., Queens Village, N.Y., 1960-66, Taunton (Mass.) State Hosp., 1985-87, Mental Health Resources, Jacksonville, Fla., 1990-92, Staff Builders Home Health Agy., New Bedford, Mass., 1996-99; supr. psychiat. unit Univ. Hosp. of Jacksonville, 1977-79, Parkwood Hosp., New Bedford, 1980-84; dir. nursing Care Unit of Jacksonville Beach, Fla., 1987-90, Bradford Adult & Adolescent, Pelham, Ala., 1992-93, 94-95; program dir. Bowling Green Hosp., Mandeville, La., 1993; nurse mgr./therapist Ctr. for Health and Human Svcs., Inc., New Bedford, Mass., 1999—. Nurse cons. New Eng. Residential, 1996—. Lt. col. Nurse Corps U.S. Army, 1966-87, Vietnam. Decorated Bronze Star, Legion of Merit, Armed Forces Res. medal, Army Commendation medal, Combat Readiness medal, Meritorious Svc. medal, Presdl. and Unit citation, Republic of Vietnam Campaign medal, Vietnam Svc. medal. Mem. ACA, VFW, Internat. Nurses Soc. on Addictions, Fla. Nurses Assn., Am. Legion, Vietnam Vets. Am., Internat. Soc. Psychiat.-Mental Health Nurses, Internat. Nurses Soc. on Addictions. Home: 47 Little Oak Rd New Bedford MA 02745-2021

LAPP, KATHRYN S. social studies educator; b. Port Clinton, Ohio, July 12, 1941; d. Norton Carl and Emma Katherine (Fisher) Rosentreter; m. Conrad Lee Lapp, Jan. 1, 1969; 1 child, Aaron Carl. BS, U. Colo., 1963; Peace Corps cert. (hon.), Columbia U., 1963; MA, NYU, 1968. Peace Corps vol. Kaduna (Nigeria) Govt. Coll., 1964-66; secondary sch. tchr. N.Y.C. Pub. Schs., 1966-69, Sch. Dist. II, Colorado Springs, Colo., 1969-89, instrnl. specialist, 1989-98, grant coord., 1997-2001; instr. tchg. methods U. Colo., Colorado Springs, 1999—. Tchr. cons. Nat. Geog. Inst., Washington and Colo., 1989-99; cons., instr. for Japan studies Colo. Coll. Summer Program, Colorado Springs, 1991-92; writing task force Colo. Geog. Stds., Colo. Dept. Edn., Denver, 1994-95; S.W. assessment coord. Edn. Goals 2000, Colo. Dept. Edn., Denver, 1997-2000. Contbr. author: Geographic Inquiry into Global Issues, 1992; contbr. articles to profl. jours. Coord. Washington and Colo. Close Up, Colorado Springs, 1990-98; coord. congl. dist. 5, U.S. Congress and Ctr. for Civic Edn., Calabasas, Calif., 1990-2001; mem. steering com. Kids Voting, Colorado Springs, 1995-2001; active Womens Edn. Soc., Colo. Coll., 1999—; mem. Nat. Geog. Soc. adv. com. Colo. Geography Edn. Fund, 2000—. Mem. ASCD, Nat. Coun. for Hist. Edn., Nat. Coun. for Geog. Edn., Nat. Coun. for the Social Studies (ho. of dels. 1980-99), Colo. Coun. for the Social Studies (pres. 1998-99), Colo. and Colorado Springs Assn. Sch. Execs. (Educator of Yr. 1998), Colo. Geog. Alliance (steering com. 1988-99, Contbn. to Geog. Edn. award 1998), Alpha Delta Kappa (pres. 1984-99).

LAPPE, FRANCES MOORE, author, lecturer; b. Pendleton, Oreg., Feb. 10, 1944; d. John and Ina (Skrifvars) Moore; m. Marc Lappe, Nov. 11, 1967 (div. 1977); children: Anthony, Anna; m. J. Baird Callicott, Dec. 1, 1985 (div. 1991); m. Paul Martin DuBois, Aug. 19, 1991 (div. 1999). BA in History, Earlham Coll., 1966; PhD (hon.), St. Mary's Coll., 1983, Lewis and Clark Coll., 1983, Macalester Coll., 1986, Hamline U., 1987, Earlham Coll., 1988, Kenyon Coll., 1989, U. Mich., 1990, Nazareth Coll., 1990, Niagara U., 1993, Ana Maria Coll., 1998, Allegheny Coll., 1999. Co-founder, mem. staff Inst. for Food and Devel. Policy, Oakland, 1975-90; co-founder, co-dir. Ctr. for Living Democracy, Brattleboro, Vt., 1990—; editor-in-chief The Am. News Svc., 1995-2000; vis. scholar MIT, 2000—. Author: Diet for A Small Planet, 1971, 75, 82, 91, Mozambique and Tanzania: Asking the Big Questions, 1979, What To Do After You Turn Off the T.V., 1985, Rediscovering America's Values, 1989; (with Joseph Collins) Food First: Beyond the Myth of Scarcity, 1977, Aid as Obstacle, 1980, Now We Can Speak, 1984, Nicaragua: What Difference Could a Revolution Make?, 1984, World Hunger: Twelve Myths, 1986; (with Rachel Schurman and Kevin Danaher) Betraying the National Interest, 1987, (with Schurman) Taking Population Seriously, 1990, (with Paul Martin Du Bois) The Quickening of America: Rebuilding Our Nation, Remaking Our Lives, 1994. Named to Nutrition Hall of Fame Ctr. for Sci. and Pub. Interest, 1981; recipient Mademoiselle Mag. award, 1977; World Hunger Media award, 1982, Right Livelihood award, 1987. Office: Ctr Living Democracy 289 Fox Farm Rd PO Box 8187 Brattleboro VT 05304-8187

LAPPIN, JOAN E. financial executive; b. Cleve., Nov. 16, 1943; d. Jack W. Berger and Eleanore E. (Bloomfield) Shallant; m. John W. Lappin, Nov. 11, 1972 (div. May 1989); children: Jessica S., Joshua H. BA, U. Wis., 1964; MBA, NYU, 1972. CFA. Sr. analyst Equity Rsch. Assocs., N.Y.C., 1966-69; asst. to pres. FAS Internat., Westport, Conn., 1970-71; sr. rsch. analyst Seidlitz & Co., N.Y.C., 1971-72, Dreyfus Corp., N.Y.C., 1973-80; v.p. Mfrs. Hanover Trust, N.Y.C., 1980-83, Arnhold & S. Bleichroeder, N.Y.C., 1983-86; pres. Gramercy Capital Mgmt. Corp., N.Y.C., 1986—. Active Women's Campaign Fund; bd. dirs. U. Wis. Alumni Assn.; mem. bd. visitors U. Wis. Sch. Bus. Mem. N.Y. Soc. Security Analysts, Media & Entertainment Analysts of N.Y., Am. Women Entrepreneurs, Fin. Women's Assn., N.Y. Yacht Club, Ida Lewis Yacht Club, Nat. Arts Club. Avocations: sailing, photography. Office: Gramercy Capital Mgmt Corp 515 Madison Ave New York NY 10022-5403*

LARA, ADAIR, columnist, writer; b. San Francisco, Jan. 3, 1952; d. Eugene Thomas and Lee Louise (Hanley) Daly; m. James Lee Heig, June 18, 1976 (div. 1989); children: Morgan, Patrick; m. William Murdock LeBlond, Nov. 2, 1991. BA in English, San Francisco State U., 1976. Reader Coll. of Marin, Kentfield, Calif., 1976-83; freelance editor, 1983-86; mng. editor San Francisco Focus mag., 1986-89; exec. editor San Francisco mag., 1988-89; columnist San Francisco Chronicle, 1989—. Author: History of Petaluma: A California River Town, 1982, Welcome to Earth, Mom, 1992, Slowing Down in a Speeded-up World, 1994, At Adair's House, More Columns by America's Funniest Formerly Single Man, 1995; contbr. articles to profl. publs. Recipient Best Calif. Columnist award AP, 1990. Democrat. Avocations: reading, photography, travel, softball, biking. Office: San Francisco Chronicle 901 Mission St San Francisco CA 94103-2905

LARA-CINISOMO, SANDRA LUZ, psychologist; b. Ensenada, Baja California, Mexico, Aug. 9, 1969; d. Bertha Galindo and Jose Heriberto Lara; m. Vincent Edmund Cinisomo, Oct. 22, 1968. BA, Calif. State U., Northridge, 1993; EdM, Harvard U., 1995; PhD, Columbia U., 2002. Bilingual elem. sch. tchr. LA Unified Sch. Dist., Los Angeles, Calif., 1993—94; rsch. cons. La Raza, L.A., Calif., 1995—96; rsch. fellow Columbia U. Teachers Coll., N.Y.C., 1996—2002; assoc. behavioral scientist RAND Corp., Santa Monica, Calif., 2002—. Founder and pres. Latinos Encouraging Graduation Among Latinos, L.A., Calif., 1993—97; child devel. cons. Hispanic Children and Families, N.Y.C., 1996—98; child devel. cons. and trainer Med. and Health Rsch. Assn., N.Y.C., 1998—2001; co-founder, pres. Mexican Ednl. Found. N.Y., Inc. (Mex-Ed), N.Y.C., 1997—; spkr. in field. Contbr. articles to profl. jours.; prodr.: (art exhibitions). Mem.: APA. Avocations: bodybuilding, running, hiking, travel. Office: RAND Corp 1700 Main St Santa Monica CA 90401 Personal E-mail: slara@rand.org. E-mail: slara@rand.org.

LARAYA-CUASAY, LOURDES REDUBLO, pediatric pulmonologist, educator; b. Baguio, Philippines, Dec. 8, 1941; came to U.S., 1966; d. Jose Marquez and Lolita (Redublo) Laraya; m. Ramon Serrano Cuasay, Aug. 7, 1965; children: Raymond Peter, Catherine Anne, Margaret Rose, Joseph Paul. AA, U. Santo Tomas, Manila, Philippines, 1958, MD cum laude, 1963. Diplomate Am. Bd. Pediatrics. Resident in pediatrics U. Santo Tomas Hosp., 1963-65, Children's Hosp. Louisville, 1966-67, Charity Hosp. New Orleans-Tulane U., 1967-68; fellow child growth and devel. Children's Hosp. Phila., 1968-69; fellow pediatric pulmonary and cystic fibrosis programs St. Christopher's Hosp. for Children, Phila., 1969-71, rsch. assoc., 1971-72; clin. instr. Tulane U., New Orleans, 1967-68; asst. prof. pediatrics Temple Health Scis. Ctr., Phila., 1972-77; assoc. prof. pediatrics Thomas Jefferson Med. Sch., Phila., 1977-79, U. Medicine & Dentistry N. J., Robert Wood Johnson Med. Sch., New Brunswick, 1980-85, prof. clin. pediatrics, 1985-98, prof. pediat., 1998—. Dir. pediatric pulmonary medicine and cystic fibrosis ctr. U. Medicine and Dentistry, Robert Wood Johnson Med. Sch., New Brunswick, 1981—. Co-editor: Interstitial Lung Diseases in Children, 1988. Recipient Pediatric Rsch. award Mead Johnson Pharm. Co., Manila, 1965. Fellow Am. Coll. Chest Physicians (steering com., chmn. cardiopulmonary diseases in children 1976—), Airways Network, Am. Acad. Pediatrics (tobacco free generation rep. 1986-92); mem. Am. Ambulatory Pediatric Soc., Am. Thoracic Soc., Am. Sleep Disorder Assn., N.J. Thoracic Soc. (chmn. pediatric pulmonary com. 1986-91, governing coun. mem. 1981-94), European Respiratory Soc. Avocation: pianist. Home: 100 Mercer Ave Spring Lake NJ 07762-1208 Office: UMDNJ Robert Wood Johnson Med Sch One RWJ Place New Brunswick NJ 08903 E-mail: cuasaylr@umdnj.edu.

LARDAKIS, MOIRA GAMBRILL, insurance executive, lawyer; b. Cleve., Sept. 14, 1951; d. Merle LC. and Ellen K. (Moore) Gambrill; m. Tony E. Lardakis, Aug. 31, 1985; children: Christopher E., Michael A. BA, Cleve. State U., 1972; JD, Cleveland Marshall Coll. Law, 1981. Bar: Ohio 1981. Child care supr. Lake County Comprehensive Ctr., Cleve., 1973-75, work adjustment counselor, 1975-78; with Progressive Casualty Ins. Co., Mayfield Village, Ohio, 1978—, gen. mgr., 1985-87, div. pres., 1987—. Mem. Ohio Bar Assn.

LARDIN, JESSICA ELIZABETH, vocalist; b. Pitts., Oct. 11, 1977; d. Jeffrey Lee and Patti Lynne Lardin. BS in Music Edn., Indiana (Pa.) U. of Pa., 1999. Vocal Music Education Pa. and Va., 2000. Music tchr. Langston Hughes Mid. Sch., Reston, Va., 2000—01; dir. of choral activities Westfield H.S., Chantilly, Va., 2001—. Pvt. voice tchr., 1999—; dir. of music Grace United Meth. Ch., Indiana, 1998—2000; profl. vocalist, choir mem.

Basilica of the Nat. Shrine of the Immaculate Conception, Washington, 2002—. Mem.: Music Educators Nat. Conf., Am. Choral Dirs. Assn. Office: Westfield H S Choral Dept 4700 Stonecroft Blvd Chantilly VA 20151

LARDY, SISTER SUSAN MARIE, academic administrator; b. Sentinel Butte, N.D., Nov. 9, 1937; d. Peter Aloysius and Elizabeth Julia (Dietz) L. BS in Edn., U. Mary, Bismarck, N.D., 1965; MEd, U. N.D., 1972. Entered Order of St. Benedict, Bismarck, 1957. Elem. tchr. Cathedral Grade Sch., Bismarck, 1958-67, Christ the King Sch., Mandan, N.D., 1967-68, 70-72, St. Joseph's Sch., Mandan, 1968-70; asst. prof. edn. U. Mary, Bismarck, 1972-80; adminstr., asst. prioress Annunciation Priory, Bismarck, 1980-84, prioress, major superior, 1984-96; dir. U. Mary-Fargo (N.D.) Ctr., 1997—. Dir. Fargo Ctr. U. Mary, 1997—. Mem. Delta Kappa Gamma. Home: 1101 32nd Ave S Fargo ND 58103-6036 Office: U Mary Fargo Ctr 3001 25th St S Fargo ND 58103-5055

LARGENT, MARGIE, retired architect; b. Adrian, Mo., Feb. 28, 1923; d. Arlie Everett Largent and Ruby Lacey Grosshart; m. Creighton A. Anderson, May 10, 1954; children: Michael Creig, Jon William Everett. Student, Capital Bus. Coll., 1942, Art Ctr. Sch. of Design, L.A., 1944, 45, 46, Willamette U., 1946-47; BArch, U. Oreg., 1950. Registered arch., Wash., Oreg., Alaska. Sr. structural draftsman Stone & Webster Engrs., L.A. and Boston, 1950-52; prodn. coord. Jon Konigshofer, Carmel, Calif., 1953-54, Daniel-Mann-Johnson, Archs., L.A., 1954-55, Gordon Cochran, Arch., Portland, Oreg., 1956-57, John Groom, Arch., Salem, Oreg., 1958-60; designer Largent & Anderson, Lake Oswego, Oreg., 1961-63; arch. Margie Largent, Lake Oswego, 1964—. Prin. works include Shon Tay Profl. Ctr., Lake Oswego, 1965-78, Jackson Residence, Warm Springs Reservation, Oreg., 1974, Crosby-Earth Shelter, San Juan Island, Wash., 1975, Anderson Tri-Plex, Cordova, Alaska, 1983. Active Land Use Com., Lake Oswego, 1970—, Park Adv. Bd., Clacksmas County, Oreg., 1975-79, Bldg. Bd. Appeals, Lake Oswego, 1978-98; pres. Associated C. of C., Clackamas County, 1970. Mem.: Constrn. Specifications Inst. (Portland chpt. pres. 1977, 1986, editor 1979, 1984, archivist 1980, Capital chpt. archivist 1995—2003). Office: Margie Largent Arch PO Box 1291 Lake Oswego OR 97035-0528

LARK, M. ANN, management consultant, strategic planner, naturalist; b. Denver, Feb. 28, 1952; d. Carl Eugene and Arlena Elizabeth (Bashor) Epperson; m. Larry S. Lark, Apr. 1, 1972 (div. 1979). Asst. corp. sec., savs. dir. Imperial Corp. dba Silver State Savs. & Loan, Denver, 1972-75; client svcs. mgr. 1st Fin. Mgmt. Corp., Englewood, Colo., 1977-81; regional account mgr. Ericsson Info. Systems, Chatsworth, Calif., 1981-82; ind. cons. Denver, 1982-84; regional account mgr. InnerLine/Am. Banker, Chgo., 1984-85; chief info. officer Security Pacific Credit Corp., San Diego, 1985-88; prin. The Genessee Group, Thousand Oaks, Calif. and Denver, 1988—. Avocations: tennis, gardening, hiking, bicycling, writing, sketching. Home and Office: 6715 Village Rd Parker CO 80134

LARKAM, BEVERLEY MCCOSHAM, clinical social worker, family therapist; b. Vancouver, Can., Mar. 3, 1928; arrived in U.S., 1951; d. William Howard and Marjorie Isobel (Jerome) McCosham; children: Elizabeth, Charles, Daphne, Peter, John. Assoc. Royal Conservatory of Mus., U. Toronto, Toronto, 1948; BA, U. B.C., Can., 1949; BSW, U. B.C., 1950, MSW, 1951. Bd. cert. diplomate in clin. social work; LCSW; lic. marriage and family therapist, Tex. Psychiat. social worker Brackenridge Hosp., 1952-54; chmn. dept. sr. high. sch. Univ. Presbyn. Ch., Austin, Tex., 1952-55, mem. Christian edn. com., 1961-67, bd. dirs. developing and organizing nursery sch., 1967-70; social worker Counseling-Psychol. Svcs. Ctr., U. Tex., 1971-72; psychiat. social worker, chief supr. Adult, Children's Mental Health Human-Devel. Ctr.-South, Austin, Tex., 1972-79; pvt. practice marriage and family therapy, sex therapy and individual and group psychotherapy Austin, Tex., 1975—. Field supr. Sch. Social Work U. Tex.; cons. in field. Mem. cmty. orgn. to establish classes for mentally retarded children, 1966-68; mem. City of Austin Commn. for Women, 1978—, chmn., 1982-84, emeritus, 1985—; organizer Austin Assn. for Marriage and Family Therapy, 1980-82, bd. mem. Tex. Assn. for Marriage and Family Therapy, 1980-82, bd. dirs. Nat. Assn. Commns. for Women, 1985-88, Am. Assn. for Marriage and Family Therapy Com. on Racial, Ethic and Cultural Diversity, 1992-95; vol. usher Austin Symphony Orch. Soc., 1972—; mem. Heritage Soc. Austin, Georgetown Heritage Soc., Women's Symphony League of Austin, Collector's Forum Austin Art Mus.; mem. Dean of Sch. and Social Work, Profl. Linhage Com. Mem. Am. Assn. Marriage and Family Therapy (approved supr.), Am. Group Psychotherapy Assn. (cert. group psychotherapist), Southwestern Group Psychotherapy Soc. (sr. faculty), Austin Group Psychotherapy Soc., Am. Assn. Sex Educators, Counselors and Therapists (cert. sex therapist, supr.), Acad. Cert. Social Workers, Nat. Assn. Social Workers, Register Clin. Social Workers, Diplomate Internat. Conf. Advancement of Pvt. Practice of Clin. Social Work, Tex. Soc. for Clin. Social Work (bd. dirs. 1990—, pres. 1997-99), Clin. Social Work Fedn., PEO Sisterhood, Austin Womans Forum (pres. 2002—). Presbyterian (elder, session of Univ. Presbyterian Ch. 1997—). Home and Office: 2102 Raleigh Ave Austin TX 78703-2128 also: 207 E 9th St Georgetown TX 78626-5908

LARKIN, JOAN, poet, English educator; b. Boston, Apr. 16, 1939; d. George Joseph and Celia Gertrude (Rosenberg) Moffitt; m. James A. Larkin, Dec. 23, 1966 (div. 1969); 1 child, Kate. BA, Swarthmore Coll., 1960; MA, U. Ariz., 1969. Asst. prof. English CUNY-Bklyn. Coll., 1969—94, ret., 1994, adj. faculty MFA program, 1997—98; assoc. faculty MFA program Goddard Coll., 1994—96, 2002. Mem. guest faculty poetry writing Sarah Lawrence Coll., Bronxville, NY, 1984—86, 1988, 1997—; poet-in-residence Writers Cmty., N.Y.C., West Side YMCA; mem. core faculty MFA program New Eng. Coll., 2002—. Author: (poems) Housework, 1975, A Long Sound, 1986, Cold River, 1997, (rec. poetry reading) A Sign I Was Not Alone, 1980, (prose) If You Want What We Have, 1998, Glad Day, 1998; co-editor: Gay and Lesbian Poetry in Our Time: An Anthology, 1988 (Lambda Lit. award 1988), Amazon Poetry, 1975, Lesbian Poetry, 1981; editor: A Woman Like That, 1999; co-translator: Sor Juana's Love Poems, 1997; contbr. poems to periodicals including Am. Poetry Rev., Conditions, Ms., Paris Rev., Sinister Wisdom, The Village Voice, Aphra, Endymion, The Lamp in the Spine, Global City Rev., Am. Rev., Genesis West, Sojourner. NEA fellow in poetry, 1987-88, 96, N.Y. Found. for Arts fellow in poetry, 1987-88; Creative Artists Pub. Svc. Program grantee N.Y. State Coun. Arts, 1976, 80; Mass. Cultural Coun. grantee in playwriting, 1995.

LARKIN, JOAN See JETT, JOAN

LARKIN, MARY SUE, financial planner; b. Kansas City, Kans., Sept. 29, 1948; d. Claude Dewey Jr. and Mildred Elaine (Foster) Wyrick; m. James Donald Larkin, June 5, 1971; children: Michael James, David Kirk. BA in Elem. Edn., Baker U., 1970; MA in Edn., Ariz. State U., 1980. CFP. Tchr. Bonner Springs (Kans.) Unified Sch. Dist., 1970-71, Finney County Unified Sch. Dist., Garden City, Kans., 1971-73, Deer Valley Unified Sch. Dist., Phoenix, 1974-80; fin. planner Larkin & Assocs., Sun City, Ariz., 1980—; co-founder, registered rep. Fin. Network Investment Corp., Torrance, Calif., 1983, co-regional dir., 2000—. Co-author: The Larkin Guide-Enjoying the Riches of Retirement, 1987. Bd. dirs. Mingus Mountain Estate Residential Ctr., Inc., 1993, sec., 1994—. Recipient creative programming award Nat. Univ. Continuing Edn. Assn., 1994, Fin. Network Circle of Achievement award, 1999. Mem.: Fin. Planning Assn. (pres. Greater Phoenix chpt. 1994—95), Atrusa (pres. Sun City 1987—89, svc.chair Dist. 11 2003—05), Phi Theta Kappa, Alpha Delta Sigma, Zeta Tau Alpha. Republican. Roman Catholic. Office: 17220 N Boswell Blvd Ste L200 Sun City AZ 85373-2000

LARKIN, MOSCELYNE, retired artistic director, dancer; b. Miami, Okla., Jan. 14, 1925; d. Reuben Frances and Eva (Matlogova) L.; m. Roman Jasinski, Dec. 24, 1943 (dec. 1991); 1 child, Roman. Studied with Serge Grigorieff, Lubov Tchernicheva, Mikhail Mordkin, Anatole Vilzak, Vincenzo Celli; hon. doctorate of Fine Arts, U. of Tulsa, 1991. With Ballet Russe, 1941-47, Ballet Russe de Monte Carlo, 1948-52; prima ballerina Radio City Music Hall, N.Y.C., 1951-52; with Alexandra's Danilova's Great Moments of Ballet touring co., 1952-54; established Tulsa Sch. Ballet, from 1956; artistic dir. Tulsa Civic Ballet, 1956-76, Tulsa Ballet Theatre, 1976-91, artistic dir. emerita, 1991—. Dance performances include Mikhail Forkine's Paganini and Les Sylphides; Leonid Massine's Le Beau Danube, Symphonie Fantastique, Les Presages; George Balanchine's Concerto Barocco, Night Shadow, Cotillion; Agnes De Mille's Rodeo; David Lichine's Graduation Ball; Michael Maule's The Carib Peddler. Recipient Dance Mag. award, 1988, Gov. Arts award, 1988, Rogers State Coll. Lynn Riggs award, 1989, award of Am.,1992; named to Tulsa Press Club Headliner award, Okla. Hall of Fame, 1979, Tulsa Hall of Fame, 1988, Okla. Womens Hall of Fame, 1993, and numerous others. Mem. Southwestern Regional Ballet Assn. (exec. v.p. 1963-76), Nat. Assn. Regional Ballet. Home: 5414 S Gillette Ave Tulsa OK 74105-6434 Office: Tulsa Ballet Theatre 4512 S Peoria Ave Tulsa OK 74105-4563

LARKIN, NELLE JEAN, retired application developer, systems analyst; b. Ralston, Okla., July 4, 1925; d. Charles Eugene and Jennivea Pearl (Lane) Reed; m. Burr Oakley Larkin, Dec. 28, 1948 (div. Aug. 1969); children: John Timothy, Kenneth James, Donald Jerome, Valerie Jean Larkin Rouse. Student, UCLA, 1944, El Camino Jr. Coll., 1946-49, San Jose (Calif.) City Coll., 1961-62. Engring. technician Northrop Aircraft, Hawthorne, Calif., 1944-49; sr. programmer, analyst III Santa Clara County, San Jose, Calif., 1963-69; sr. analyst, programmer Blue Cross of No. Calif., Oakland, 1971-73; sr. programmer, analyst Optimum Systems, Inc., Santa Clara, Calif., 1973-75, Crocker Bank, San Francisco, 1975-77, Greyhound Fin. Service, San Francisco, 1977-78; analyst, programmer TRW, Mountain View, Calif., 1978-79; sr. programer analyst Memorex, Santa Clara, 1979-80; staff mgmt. cons. Am. Mgmt. System, Foster City, Calif., 1980-82; sr. programmer, analyst, project leader Tymeshare, Cupertino, Calif., 1982-83; sr. programmer, analyst Beckman Instruments, Palo Alto, Calif., 1983-89; analyst, programmer U.S. Postal Svc., San Mateo, Calif., 1989—; ret., 2001. Mem. Calif. Scholarship Fedn. (life mem. 1943), Alpha Sigma Gamma. Avocations: needlework, camping. Office: US Postal Svc 2700 Campus Dr San Mateo CA 94497-0001 Home: 4110 Turner Rd Chesterfield VA 23832-8535

LA ROCCA, ISABELLA, artist, educator; b. El Paso, Apr. 14, 1960; d. Remo and Alicia Estela (Gonzalez) La R. BA, U. Pa., 1984; MFA, Ind. U., 1993. Freelance photographer, N.Y.C., 1986-90; assoc. instr. Ind. U., Bloomington, 1991-93; instr. Herron Sch. Art, Indpls., 1992; vis. asst. prof. Ind. U., 1994—; asst. prof. DePauw U., Greencastle, Ind., 1994-95; vis. asst. prof. Bloomsburg (Pa.) U., 1995-96; freelance photographer, designer, animator San Francisco, 1996—. Instr. art Vista C.C., 1998—, Coll. of Marin, 1999—2000, Calif. State U., Hayward, 1999—2001, City Coll. San Francisco, 2000—. One-woman shows include Haas Gallery, Bloomsburg, 1996, Ctr. Photography Woodstock, N.Y., Moore Coll., Pa., 1994, Emison Art Ctr., Greencastle, 1996, exhibited in group shows at 494 Gallery, N.Y.C., 1993, Kala Art Inst., Berkeley, Calif., 2000; prodr., dir. : (films) Mariana of the Universe, 2004. Ind. U. CIC Minority fellow, 1990-91; Jewish Found. Edn. Women scholar, 1990; recipient Friends of Photography Ferguson award, 1993, Serpent Source Grant for Women Artists, 1998. E-mail: ilarocca@mac.com.

LAROCHE, LINDA, writer; d. Octavio Martinez, Benilde Castro. BA in Sociology and Journalism, Calif. State U., L.A., 1982. Set decorator CBS-TV, L.A., 1988—91; actress films, European/German TV, commls., Berlin, 1991—93; prodr., writer Paris Prodns., N.Y.C., 1994—97; journalist The Write Words, Pasadena, Calif., 1997—2000; columnist San Gabriel Valley Tribune, West Corina, Calif., 2000—02, editor, 2002—03. Editor: Jewish Cmty. News, 2002—. Bd. dirs. Hispanic Women's Coun., L.A., 1985—86. Nominee Children's Fantasy screenplay, Nicholl Found., 1997; recipient Silver Star award, 1990; grantee Media grant, L.A. City Cultural Affairs, 1989, Multi-Cultural grant, Calif. Commn. of Arts, 1989, AFI ind. filmmaker grant, Nat. Endowment Arts, 1989. Mem.: L.A. Opera (spkr.'s bur. 2001—). Jewish.

LAROCHE, LYNDA, artist, educator; Asst. prof. Indiana U. of Pa., 1997—. Exhibitions include include Contemporary Arts Ctr., Cin., 1991, exhibitions include Am. Craft Mus., N.Y.C., 1991, Swidler Gallery, Royal Oak, Mich., 1991—92, Nat. Ornamental Metal Mus., Memphis, 1992, 1993, 1997, Aaron Faber Gallery, N.Y.C., 1993, Artifacts Gallery, Indpls., 1993, Fine Arts Gallery, Bloomington, 1993, Arrowmont Sch. Arts and Crafts, Gatlinburg, Tenn., 1994—96, Renwick Gallery/Mus.. Shop, Washington, 1994, Montgomery Coll. Art Gallery, Rockville, Md., 1996, Shipley Gallery, Gateshead, Eng., 1996, Cleve. Craft Ctr., Middlesborough, Eng., 1997, Seafirst Gallery, Seattle, 1998, numerous others. Fellow Visual Artist fellow, Nat. Endowment Arts, 1988—89, Master Summer fellow, Ind. Arts Com. and Nat. Endowment Arts, 1984, 1987, Visual Artists fellow, S.D. Arts Coun. and Nat. Endowment Arts, 1993. Mem.: Soc. N.A. Goldsmiths, Coll. Arts Assn., Soc. Am. Silversmiths (Disting. mem.). Office: Indiana U Pa Dept Art 324 Sprowls Hall 470 S 11th St Indiana PA 15705-1044

LAROSE, MELBA LEE, performing company executive, actress, playwright, theater director; d. Kenneth Lee and Melba Lauren LaRose; m. Elson Jose de Faria, July 14, 1987. AAS in Bus. Mgmt., SUNY, Cobleskill, 1962; at, HB Studios, N.Y.C., 1963—65, Free U. of L.A., 1972—74; pvt. tng., Acting, Dance, Voice, N.Y.C., 1977—90. Freelance actress, playwright, dir., N.Y.C., 1965—; actress, playwright and dir. Group Repertory Theatre, L.A., 1972—76; adminstrv. asst., fundraiser and actress N.Y. St. Theatre Caravan, N.Y.C., 1990—96; adminstrv. asst. The Actors Studio, N.Y.C., 1992—94; artistic and adminstrv. dir. N.Y. Artists Unlimited, Inc., N.Y.C., 1982—. Panelist A.R.T. New York, Lower Manhattan Cultural Coun., Theatre Resources Unlimited, N.Y.C., 2000—; fulbright sr. specialist roster candidate Coun. for Internat. Exch. of Scholars, Washington, 2002—. Playwright-director : (play) Rime Ice; Who's There?; Song of the Simple Truth - El Canto de Julia de Burgos; actor-playwright-director (3 one-act plays) Cityscapes 3; (plays) Little Red - Girl from the Hood; actor-playwright A Builder of Dreams, based on the poems & life of Myrtle Evelyn Lawrence (1893-1963); Tables I Have Danced On; actor: La Ronde, The Love of Don Perlimplin & Belisa in the Garden, Glamour, Glory & Gold (the Life & Legend of Nola Noonan, Goddess & Star), Blues in Rags, The Grand Inquisitor; (films) Eyes of a Blue Dog (Best Actress - Town Hall's First Run Film Festival, 1994), Dadetown, Working Girl. Recipient Disting. Alumnus award, SUNY, 1987; grantee, N.Y.C. Dept. of Cultural Affairs, 1999—, Nat. Endowment Arts, 1999—, Puffin Found., 1999—, N.Y. Coun. for Humanities, 1999—, Manhattan Cmty. Arts Fund, Lower Manhattan Cultural Coun., 2000, 2001, 2002. Mem.: AFTRA, SAG, Actors' Equity Assn., Dramatists Guild of Am., Drama League, Theatre Resources Unlimited, Alliance of Resident Theatres N.Y., Phi Theta Kappa. Avocation: travel. Office: NY Artists Unlimited Inc Ste #2A 212 W 14 Street New York NY 10011 E-mail: nyartunltd@aol.com.

LARRABEE, BARBARA PRINCELAU, retired intelligence officer; b. Oakland, Calif., Sept. 21, 1923; d. Paul and Mary Emilie (Rueger) Princelau; m. John Joseph Boyle, Oct. 21, 1950 (dec.); m. Donald Richard Larrabee, Nov. 2, 1996. BA, U. Calif., Berkeley, 1948. Intelligence officer CIA, Langley, Va., 1954-82. Bd. dirs. The Thift Shop, Washington, 1988-92; mem. Women's Bd. Columbia Hosp. for Women, Washington, 1986-2001, mem. exec. com., 1989-91, 96-98; mem. com. Washington Antiques Show, 1989—; active Rep. Womens Fed. Forum, Washington, League of Rep. Women of D.C., Inc. Recipient Cert. of Distinction CIA, 1982. Mem.: Assn. Former Intelligence Officers (bd. dirs. 1993—99, v.p. 1997—99, exec. com. 1997—99), Ctrl. Intelligence Retiree Assn., Evergreen Garden Club (v.p. 2001—02), Sulgrave Club, Nat. Press Club, U. Calif. Berkeley Alumni Club of Washington (rec. sec. 1976—77, v.p. 1984—86), Sigma Kappa (v.p. No. Va. alumnae 1992—95, devel. com. Sigma Kappa Found., Inc. 1993—95). Episcopalian. Avocations: aerobics, needlework, travel. Home: 4956 Sentinel Dr Apt 304 Bethesda MD 20816-3562

LARSDOTTER, ANNA-LISA, retired translator, artist; b. Uddevalla, Bohus Län, Sweden, May 12, 1932; d. Lars Helge Svensson and Signe Ingeborg Jacobsson-Svensson; m. Erich S. Weibel, Aug. 17, 1956 (div. 1962). Student, Tchrs. Coll. for Women, Stockholm, 1951—52, Art Student's League, N.Y.C., 1953—55, New Sch. for Social Rsch., 1963—66, Summit Art Ctr., N.J., 1964—68, Academie des Beaux-Arts, Lausanne, Switzerland, 1960—62. Sec., translator internat. program Mus. Modern Art, N.Y.C., 1956; archivist Lawrence-Myden Collection, N.Y.C., 1963—64; archivist, translator Frederick Kiesler Catalogue, N.Y.C., 1979; freelance translator Data Profls. Inc., Ft. Lauderdale, Fla., 1986—97. Mem. exec. com. Summit Art Ctr., 1967—69. Contbr. articles to profl. jours.; performer: (dances) Byrd Hoffman Sch., 1969—75; appeared in : (films) Strong Medicine, 1984; (plays) Life and Times of Sigmund Freud, 1969—74; Life and Times of Joseph Stalin, 1973; Attic Clouds, 1973; A Letter for Queen Victoria, 1974; Festival d'Automne, 1974; Overture in N.Y.C., 1972; actor: (tour) Theatre des Nations, 1973; organizer : (exhbns.) with Summit Art Ctr. and Bell Tel. Labs., 1964—69; preparer: catalogue pvt. collection of composer Jack Lawrence and Walter Myden, 1963. Lutheran. Avocations: art, music, history, genealogy. E-mail: aldotter36684@yahoo.com.

LARSEN, PEG, state legislator; b. Aug. 10, 1949; m. Thomas Larsen; 4 children. BA, U. Slippery Rock. Minn. state rep. Dist. 56B, 1994—. Former ednl. asst. spl. needs. Address: 409 Quixote Ave N Lakeland MN 55043-9645 Also: 100 Constitution Ave Saint Paul MN 55155-1232

LARSEN, SYLVIA B. state legislator; b. Troy, Ohio, July 1949; m. Robert M. Larsen; 2 children. Student, Briarcliff Coll., 1968-69; BA, U. Wis., 1972. Past pres., bd. dirs. Bancroft Products, Concord, N.H., 1984-2000; cons. pub. rels. Concord; mem. Concord City Coun., 1989-98; mem. Dist. 15 N.H. Senate, Concord, 1994—, vice chmn. pub. affairs com., mem. edn. com., intrnal affirs com. Named Servant of Yr. Pineconia Grange, 1992, Legislator of Yr., N.H. Grange, 2001. Democrat. Address: 23 Kensington Rd Concord NH 03301-2528

LARSEN-DENNING, LORIE, critical care nurse, risk management consultant, insurance broker, insurance agent; b. Toledo, Apr. 28, 1960; d. Delmar and Shirley (Wasserman) L. Diploma, St. Vincent Hosp. Sch. Nursing, Toledo, 1981; BS in Health Care Adminstrn. magna cum laude, Concordia Coll., Portland, Oreg., 1988; MBA summa cum laude, City Univ., Tigard, Oreg., 1992. Cert. critical care nurse; chartered property casualty uderwriter; registered profl. liability underwriter. Assoc. head nurse, cardiology Good Samaritan Hosp. and Med. Ctr., Portland, 1989-91; profl. liability rep., profl. liability divsn. mgr. Farmers Ins. Group of Cos., Portland, 1991-97; pres. Larsen-Denning, Inc., Portland, 1997-2000; v.p. Marsh USA, Inc., Portland, 2000—. Fellow Am. Soc. Healthcare Risk Mgmt. (disting.); mem. CPCU Soc., Oreg. Soc. Health Care Risk Mgmt. (past pres.), Oreg. Assn. Hosps., Am. Hosp. Assn., Am. Assn. Legal Nurse Cons. E-mail: lorie.h.larsen-denning@marshmc.com.

LARSGAARD, MARY LYNETTE, librarian, writer; b. Dickinson, N.D., Aug. 4, 1946; d. Martin Vilhelm and Helen Maud (Brooks) L. BA in Geology, Macalester Coll., 1968; MALS, U. Minn., 1969; MA in Geography, U. Oreg., 1978. Asst. documents/maps libr. Ctlr. Wash. State Coll., Ellensburg, 1969-76; map libr. Colo. Sch. Mines, Golden, 1978-86, asst. head spl. collections, 1986-88; asst. head map & imagery lab. U. Calif., Santa Barbara, 1988—. Author: Map LIbrarianship: an Introduction, 1978, 3d edit., 1998, Topographic Mapping of the Americas, Australia and New Zealand, 1984, Topographic Mapping of Africa, Australia & Eurasia, 1992. Recipient SLAGON Honors award, 1995, ALCTS Presdl. Citation, 2002. Mem.: ALA (Magert Honors award 1983, MAGERT Honors award 1983), We. Assn. Map Librs. (pres. 1975—76, SLAG & M Honors award 1995, ALCTS Presdl. citation 2002), Beta Phi Mu., Phi Beta Kappa. Avocations: walking, reading, dance. Office: U Calif Santa Barbara Davidson Libr Map and Imagery Lab Santa Barbara CA 93106 Office Phone: 805-893-8799. E-mail: mary@library.ucsb.edu.

LARSON, DIANE LAVERNE KUSLER, principal; b. Fredonia, N.D., July 28, 1942; d. Raymond Edwin and LaVerne (Mayer) Kusler; m. Donald Floyd Larson, Aug. 14, 1965. BS, Valley City (N.D.) State U., 1964; MS, Mankato (Minn.) State U., 1977; EdS, U. Minn., 1987. Cert. tchr., Minn. Tchr. elem. Cokato (Minn.) Elem. Sch., 1962-64, Lakeview Elem. Sch., Robbinsdale, Minn., 1964-66; vocal tchr. Wheaton (Minn.) High Sch., 1966-67; tchr. Owatonna (Minn.) Elem. Sch., 1967-88, prin., 1988—. V.p. Cannon Valley Uniserv, Mankato, 1981-83; NEA del. World Confederation of Orgns. of the Teaching Professions, Melbourne, 1988. Named Woman of Yr., Owatonna Bus. and Profl. Women, 1990. Mem. NEA (bd. dirs. 1986-88), Minn. Edn. Assn. (bd. dirs. 1983-88, Outstanding Woman in Leadership award 1983), Minn. Reading Assn. (bd. dirs. 1983-97, Pres. award 1984), Internat. Reading Assn. (coord. for Minn. 1990-97, bd. dirs. 1997-2000, Celebrate Literacy award 1998), Minn. Elem. Prins. Assn., Valley City State U. Alumni Assn. (Cert. of Merit 1998), Delta Kappa Gamma (legis. chmn. 1986-88, pres. 1992, Woman of Achievement award 1989, Tau leadership chair, Tau State 1st v.p. 1997-99). Congregationalist. Home: 19654 Bagley Ave Faribault MN 55021-2246 Office: Washington Sch 338 E Main St Owatonna MN 55060-3096 E-mail: pianodl@clear.lakes.com.

LARSON, JO ANN, government agency administrator; Student, Montgomery Coll.; AA, U. Md. From pers. clk. to equal employment specialist NASA, 1970—91, mgr. Minority Univ. Program Dryden Flight Ctr., 1991—. Avocation: travel, watercolor painting, reading. Office: NASA Dryden Flight Rsch Ctr PO Box 273 MS 1023 Edwards CA 93523-0273 E-mail: joann.larson@mail.dfrc.nasa.gov.

LARSON, JUDY L. museum director, curator; b. Glendale, Calif., Mar. 9, 1952; d. John Arthur and Lorraine V. Larson. BA, UCLA, 1974, MA, 1978; postgrad., Emory U. Acting asst. curator Los Angeles County Mus. Art, L.A., 1978; sr. cataloguer Am. Antiquarian Soc., Worcester, Mass., 1978-85; curator High Mus. Art, Atlanta, 1985—98; exec. dir. Art Museum of W. Va., W.Va., 1998—2002; dir. Nat. Museum of Women in the Arts, Washington, 2002—. Author: (catalogue) Am. Illustration 1890-1925, 1986; co-author: (catalogue) Am. Paintings at High Mus. Art, 1994; editor: Graphic Arts and the South, 1993. Office: Nat Museum of Women in the Arts 1250 NY Ave NW Washington DC 20005*

LARSON, MARILYN J. retired elementary music educator; b. Lindstrom, Minn., July 20, 1933; d. Reuben and Dorothy (Holm) L.; m. Harold P. Cohen, Aug. 4, 1957 (div. Dec. 1975); children: Paul, Morrie, Robert. BS with distinction, U. Minn., 1955, MA with honors, 1957. Nat. cert. tchr. music; cert. tchr., Minn.; lic. realtor. Tchr. U. Minn., Mpls., 1955-57, Mpls. Jr. High Sch., 1957-60; piano tchr. pvt. studio, Fridley, Minn.; tchr. Mpls. Pub. Schs., 1976-78, St. Paul Pub. Schs., 1978-97. Designed music curriculum Mpls. Pub. Schs.; mem. INS Roundtable, 2000-03; accompanist Adult Day Care, St. Mary's Home, 2001-03; piano music for vets., 2000-03. Accompanist U. Minn. Chorus, 1953-56, Berkshire Music Ctr. at Tanglewood, Mass., 1953. Mem. Music Tchrs. Nat. Assn., Fedn. for Am.

Immigration Reform, Minnesotans for Immigration Reform (founder, exec. dir. 1999—). Independent. Luth. Avocations: reading, music. Home: 5890 Stinson Blvd Fridley MN 55432-6002 E-mail: marilynmusic@webtv.net.

LARSON, NANCY CELESTE, computer systems manager; b. Chgo., July 17, 1951; d. Melvin Ellsworth and Ruth [illegible] L. BS in Music Ed., U. Ill., 1973, MS in Music Edn., 1976; postgrad., Purdue Univ., 1982-86. Vocal music educator Consol. Sch. Dist., Gilman, Ill., 1975-77; elem. vocal music tchr. Sch. Dist. 161, Flossmoor, Ill., 1977-87; instr. Vander Cook Coll., Chgo., 1980-88; systems programmer analyst Sears, Roebuck & Co., Chgo., 1987-92, tech. instr., 1989-90, project leader, 1990-91, sr. systems analyst, 1991-92, Trans Union LLC, Chgo., 1992-94, mgr., 1994—. Tchr. adult computer edn. Homewood-Flossmoor HS, 1986—90. Chmn. Faith Luth. Ch., 1982-87, pres. bd., 1988-91, vocal soloist and voice-over performer. Mem. Ill. Music Educators Assn., Music Educators Nat. Conf., Ill. Educators Assn., Nat. Educators Assn., Am. ORFF Schulwerk Assn., Flossmoor Edn. Assn. (negotiator 1983-86). Republican. Lutheran. Avocations: swimming, reading, antiques. Home: Apt 904 1960 N Lincoln Park W Chicago IL 60614-5440 Office: Trans Union LLC 555 W Adams St Fl 4 Chicago IL 60661-3696

LARSON, PATRICIA JOAN, clinical therapist; b. Muskegon, Mich., Aug. 29, 1941; d. Charles Gordon and Janet Mavis (Bolthouse) Henricks; children: Jane Elizabeth Grimes, David Jack Larson. BA in Elem. Edn. and Sociology, Mich. State U., 1964, MA in Elem. Edn. and Adminstrn., 1967, postgrad., 1985-87; MSW, Wayne State U., 1990. Tchr. Lansing (Mich.) Pub. Schs., 1964-67; exec. v.p., dir. Mich., clin. individual, group, and family therapist Family Life Today, Inc., Southfield, 1976—, dir. tchrs., 1979—. Platform coord. for confs. FLT, Inc., Farmington Hills, Mich., 1976-90, team tchr. growth study groups, 1980-82; co-anchor TV program FLT Channel 62, Detroit, Missionary World Servants, Ecuador, 1989. Chmn. Christian Women's Club, Lansing, 1968-70, also seminar coord.; former dir. Christian edn. com. St. Thomas Presbyn. Ch., Shelby Twp., Mich., 1995-97; fundraiser libr. fund Jr. Women's Club, Shelby Twp., 1976, 78. Mem. NASW, Am. Psychoanalytic Assn., Am. Assn. Christian Counselors, N.Am. Assn. Christians in Social Work, Christian Assn. Psychol. Studies. Avocations: reading, history, art appreciation, health and exercise. Home: 721 Minneapolis Ave Gladstone MI 49837-1725

LARSON, SANDRA PAULINE, music educator; b. Milw., Jan. 27, 1944; d. Arthur Herman and Pauline Frances (Schneck) Voss; m. Dale Edwin Larson, Jan. 20, 1968; children: Eric Dale, Stephan Harold, Jonathan Arthur. MusB, Cardinal Stritch Coll., 1966; MusM, Southeastern La. U., 1992. Cert. Am. Coll. Musicians. Pvt. piano tchr., Slidell, La., 1974—; adj. faculty Delgado C.C. Slidell Learning Ctr. Piano adjudicator Am. Coll. Musicians Nat. Guild, 1994—. Piano accompanist Slidell Little Theater, 1994, 2002, 2003. Named to Order of St. Louis, Archdiocese of New Orleans, 1989. Mem. Music Tchrs. Nat. Assn. (nat. cert., piano adjudicator 1990—), Nat. Guild of Piano Tchrs. (local chair 1993-2003), La. Music Tchrs. Assn. (state cert., piano adjudicator 1990—, chmn. electronic music 1994-97), North Shore Music Tchrs. Assn. (pres. 1993-96), La. Fedn. of Music Clubs (local co-chmn. 1996-2004). Roman Catholic. Avocations: sewing, crafts, reading. Home and Office: 1130 Rue La Tour Slidell LA 70458-2220

LARSON, VICKI LORD, communication disorders educator; b. Prentice, Wis., Sept. 21, 1944; d. Edward A. and Stella Mae (Hilton) Lord; m. James Roy Larson, Sept. 3, 1966. BSEd, U. Wis., Madison, 1966, MS, 1968, PhD, 1974. Speech-lang. pathologist Coop. Ednl. Svc. Agy. 2, Minoqua, Wis., 1967—69; instr. U. Wis., Whitewater, 1969—71, rsch. asst. Madison, 1971—73, asst. prof. Eau Claire, 1973-77, assoc. prof., 1977—81, prof. communication disorders, 1981—91, dept. chair, 1978—83, asst. dean grad. studies and univ. rsch., 1984—89, assoc. dean grad. studies and univ. rsch., 1989—91, prof. comm. Oshkosh, 1991—2000, dean Grad. Sch. Rsch., 1991—94; provost, vice chancellor acad. affairs, 1994—2000. Acquistions editor Thinking Publs., Eau Claire, 2001—. Author: Adolescents: Communication Development and Disorder, 1983, Communication Assessment and Intervention Strategies for Adolescents, 1987; contbr. Handbook of Speech-Language Pathology and Audiology, 1988, Language Disorders in Older Students, 1995, Working Out With Listening, 2002, Communication Solutions for Older Students, 2003, S-MAPs curriculum-based assessment, 2004. Fellow: Am. Speech, Lang., Hearing Assn. (councilor); mem.: Wis. Speech, Lang., Hearing Assn. (pres. 1976, honors 1991), Phi Kappa Phi, Omicron Delta Kappa. Avocations: traveling, quilting, reading. Office Phone: 800-225-4769. E-mail: larsonvl@northnet.net.

LARSON, WANDA Z. writer, poet; b. Cle Elum, Wash., Aug. 26, 1926; d. Stanley Aloysius and Anele (Valente) Zackovich; m. Glen B. Larson, Nov. 18, 1950 (div. Mar. 1967); children: Karen Holk, Margot Huffman, Lisa Larson Landrey (dec. 1998). BA, U. Wash., 1949. Columnist North Bend Herald, Snoqualmie, Wash., 1955-61, Goldendale (Wash.) Sentinel, 1962-67; news editor West Seattle Herald, 1950-51; editor employee newsletter Alaska Steamship Co., Seattle, 1951; editl. asst. Associated Publs., Portland, Oreg., 1970-72, staff writer, 1974-78; pub. Blue Unicorn Press Inc., Portland, 1990—; poet Sta. KOPB, Portland, 1991—. Author: Portlandia, 1991, Miracle at Blowing Rock, 1992, Elisabeth: A Biography, 1997, Our Flag - Born Through Valor, 1999, Bird Woman/Mojave (Sacajawea), 2001, The Legend of Something More, 2004. Co-recipient 2nd pl. award Poetry Forum Quar., 1990; hon. mention Still Water Press, 1990. Avocations: humanitarian interests, history. Home and Office: PO Box 40300 Portland OR 97240-0300 Office Phone: 277-201-7527. E-mail: blueunicornpress@thelifeline.net.

LARUE, LEA MAYLENE, music educator; b. Gettysburg, Pa., Feb. 2, 1976; d. Michael Charles Chandler, Phyllis Marlene Chandler; m. Sean Edward LaRue; 1 child, Hannah Maye. B in Music Edn., Millersville U., 1998. Music tchr. Somerset County Pub. Schs., Princess Anne, Md., 1998—. Mem.: Nat. Assn. Music Educators, Ma. Mus. Educators Assoc., Mus. Educators Nat. Coalition. Home: 30 Heron Way Crisfield MD 21817 Personal E-mail: seanlarue@aol.com.

LARWOOD, LAURIE, psychologist; b. N.Y., 1941; PhD, Tulane U., 1974. Pres. Davis Instruments Corp., San Leandro, Calif., 1966-71; cons., 1969—; asst. prof. orgnl. behavior SUNY, Binghamton, 1974-76; assoc. prof., chair dept. psychology Claremont (Calif.) McKenna Coll., 1976-83, assoc. prof. bus. adminstrn., 1976-83, Claremont Grad. Sch., 1976-85; prof., head dept. mgmt. U. Ill., Chgo., 1983-87; dean sch. bus. SUNY, Albany, 1987-90; dean Coll. Bus. Adminstrn. U. Nev., Reno, 1990-92, prof., 1990—2003, prof. emeritus, 2003—; dir. Inst. Strategic Bus. Issues, 1992—2003. Mem. western regional advisory coun. SBA, 1976-81; dir. The Mgmt. Team; pres. Mystic Games, Inc.; mng. ptnr. Quail Lane Studios, 2003-. Author: (with M.M. Wood) Women in Management, 1977, Organizational Behavior and Management, 1984, Women's Career Development, 1987, Strategies-Successes-Senior Executives Speak Out, 1988, Women's Careers, 1988, Managing Technological Development, 1988, Impact Analysis, 1999; mem. editl. bd. Sex Roles, 1979-2003, Consultation, 1986-91, Jour. Orgnl. Behavior, 1987-2003, Jour. Vocational Behavior, 1999-2003, Group and Orgn. Mgmt., 1982-84, editor, 1986-91; founding editor Women and Work, 1983, Jour. Mgmt. Case Studies, 1983-87; contbr. numerous articles, papers to profl. jours. Mem. acad. Mgmt. (editl. rev. bd. Rev. 1977-82, past chmn. women in mgmt. divsn., managerial consultation divsn., tech. and innovation mgmt. divsn.), Am. Psychol. Assn., Assn. Women in Psychology. Home: 10225 N Quail Ln Tucson AZ 85742 Office: Box 89789 Tucson AZ 85752

LARZELERE, KATHY LYNN HECKLER, paralegal; b. Sellersville, Pa., Dec. 4, 1955; d. Harold Tyson and Hannah Ruth (Wile) Heckler; m. Lawrence Sollanek, Nov. 1984 (div.); m. Loel Harry Larzelere, Aug. 27, 1992; 1 stepdaughter, Lindsie M. AAS magna cum laude, Columbus State C.C., 1991. From sales person to dept. mgr. Macy's New York, North Wales, Pa., 1977-83, [illegible] Dubuque, Wilmington, Del., Towson, Md., 1983-86; customer svc. person Marshall Fields, Chgo., 1987; word processor Franklin County Children Svcs., Columbus, Ohio, 1988-89; legal sec., paralegal M. Cohen and Assocs., Columbus, 1989-94; paralegal Calig and Handelman LPA, Columbus, 1994-97, Weltman, Weinberg & Reis, Columbus, 1997—. Author: (poetry) American High School Poets, 1973. Ward coord. Amelia Salerno for City Coun., Columbus, 1993; co-chmn. Columbus Christmas in Apr. Home Amb. Com., Columbus Christmas in Apr. Materials and In-Kind Donations Com.; vol. Ohio Bicentennial Commn., Ohio Hist. Soc. Mem. award Phi Theta Kappa. Mem. Paralegal Assn. Ctrl. Ohio (writer newsletter The Citator, co-chair student outreach com. 1994-95, chair 1995-97, 1st v.p. 1995-97, 2000-2001, pres. 1997-99, mem. adv. bd. 1999-2000, chair student outreach com. 1999-2000), Columbus Bar Assn. (assoc.). Lutheran. Avocations: handcrafts, reading, walking, watercolor painting, counted cross-stitch. Home: 2119 Kingsglen Dr Grove City OH 43123-1252 Office: Weltman Weinberg & Reis 175 S 3rd St Ste 900 Columbus OH 43215-5177 E-mail: klarzele@columbus.rr.com., klarzelere@weltman.com.

LASALLE, DIANA MARGARET, company executive, writer, consultant; b. Akron, Nov. 9, 1949; d. Frank Charles and Margaret Audrey (Penzenik) LaSalle; m. William Joseph Sanders, Mar. 25, 1972 (div. 1979); children: Aaron Michael, Phillip Andrew; m. Richard Lee Deterding, Apr. 4, 1981 (div. 2001). AA, U. Akron, 1972. Sec. U. Akron, 1969-72; office mgr. Buckeye Fence Co., Akron, 1979-84; designer/writer Dymar Agy., Akron, 1980-83; pres. Dymar Agy., Inc., Gurnee, Ill., 1984-97, Dymar Group, Gurnee, Ill., 1997—2000, True North Strategies, Savannah, Ga., 2002—. Cons. Smithsonian Nat. Mus. Natural History, Washington, 1989—91. Author: Priceless: Turning Ordinary Products into Extraordinary Experiences, 2002; contbr. articles to profl. jours. Bd. dirs. No. Ill. Coun. for Alcoholism and Substance Abuse, 1994-97, adminstrv. v.p. women's bd., 1994-97. Recipient Design award HOW Mag., 1990; named Woman of the Yr. Wadsworth Jaycee Women, 1979, 83; named to Ohio Jaycee Women Hall of Fame, 1981. Mem. U.S. Equine Mktg. Assn. (pres. chmn. bd. 1989-90), Women's Bus. Exch. (pres. 1988-89), Horse Coun. of Ill. (bd. dirs. 1991-94), Am. Horse Pubs., Am. Horse Coun. Republican. Lutheran. Avocation: writing. Office: True North 221 E Gordon St Savannah GA 31401

LASAROW, MARILYN DORIS, artist, educator; b. Seattle, Oct. 23, 1928; d. Samuel Irving and Molly Pearl Powell; m. William Julius Lasarow, Feb. 4, 1951; children: Richard Michael, Elisabeth Hollins Lasarow Tozzi. BA cum laude in Philosophy, Stanford U., 1950. Pvt. art tchr., L.A., 1968—2003. One-woman shows include Feigen Palmer Gallery, L.A., 1967, exhibited in group shows at Purdue U., Ind., 1965, L.A. County Mus. Art, 1966, Feigen Palmer Gallery, L.A., 1966, Occidental Coll., Eagle Rock, Calif., 1967, Lytton Gallery, L.A., 1968, featured, in L.A. Times, Art Forum and Art in Am., work appeared on cover, Home Sect., L.A. Times, 1967. Mem.: AAUW, Nat. Mus. Women in Arts, L.A. Mus. Contemporary Art, L.A. County Mus. Art (award 1966—67), Cap and Gown, Phi Beta Kappa. Avocations: gardening, tennis, photography, filmmaking. Home: 11623 Canton Pl Studio City CA 91604 E-mail: wlasarow@mindspring.com.

LASCELLES, SUSAN, artist; b. Chgo., Jan. 29, 1958; d. Robert John and Donna Lee (Hjorth) L.; m. David Linn Hekelnkaemper, Apr. 17, 1998; children: Michael Lascelles DiCenzo, Max Lascelles Hekelnkaemper. Student, Ohio State U., 1984-87; BA, Empire State Coll., 1990. Artist, painter, photographer, stained glass, animator (film) Uncut, 1981; group shows include The Little Gallery, Springfield, Ohio, 1981, Millennium, N.Y.C., 1981, Rosenmarkt, Zurich, Switzerland, 1982, Upper Arlington Pub. Libr., Columbus, Ohio, 1987, The Dance Circle, Ithaca, N.Y., 1989, Dodajk Internation, Tucson, 1990, New Doors of the Arts, Tucson, 1993, Orts Theatre of Dance, Tucson, 1995, 96, 97, 98, Urban Picnic and Art Auction, Tucson, 1998, Daturo Studios and Gallery, Tucson, 1999, The 14th, 15th Annual Jerome Beillard Festival for Life for So. Ariz. Aids Found., 2002, 2003, El Pollo De Tucson, The Alamo Gallery, 2003, others; represented in permanent collections Corning Mus. Glass Film Libr., Empire State Coll., Färber Hüsli, Hallau, Switzerland, Fred and Pat Crain, Mechanicsburg, Ohio. Acad. merit scholar Scarlet and Gray, Ohio State U., Columbus, 1985, 87; grantee Changes Inc., N.Y.C., 1993. Avocations: gardening, pets, horses, music, alternative healing. Home: 7151 S Sandpiper Ave Tucson AZ 85746-6531

LASCH, PAT, artist, educator; b. N.Y.C., Nov. 20, 1944; d. Fred and Helen Lasch; 1 child, Melinda. BA, Queens Coll., 1970; FAAR, Am. Acad. in Rome, 1983; MFA, Ga. State U., Atlanta, 1990. Mem. found. faculty Parsons Sch. of Design, N.Y.C., 1979-88; asst. prof. R.I. Sch. of Design, Providence, 1988-89; assoc. prof. U. Mass., Amherst, 1990-97, prof., 1997—. Artist: solo exhibits include A.I.R. Gallery, N.Y.C., 1973, 77, 79, 80, 94, Zabrskie Gallery, N.Y.C., 1975, Galleriet, Lund, Sweden, 1980, Galerie Ahlner, Stockholm, 1980, Kathryn Markel Gallery, N.Y.C., 1981, 84, 85, Albright Knox Gallery, Members' Gallery, Buffalo, 1977-84, Thomas Segal Gallery, Boston, 1988, Sculpture Ctr., N.Y.C., 1993, Herter Gallery, U. Mass., Amherst, 1993; group shows inclde Inst. Contemporary Art, Phila., Street Scenes, 1981, Malmo (Sweden) Konsthall, Food, 1984, San Francisco Internat. Airport, The Right Foot Show, 1987, Thomas Segal Gallery, The Raw and the Cooked, Boston, The New Mus., N.Y.C., Bad Girls, 1994; spl. exhibition The Mus. of Modern Art (50th Anniversary), Homage 1929-79; represented in permanent collections Met. Mus. Art, N.Y.C., Mus. Modern Art, N.Y.C., Nat. Acad. Design, N.Y.C., Woman's Mus., Washington, Oberlin Mus., Queen's Coll. Recipient Yaddo, 1978, 80, 94, 98, Rome prize, 1982-83, Lilly fellowship, 1993-94, NEA-MCC fellowship, 1995-96; grantee: C.A.P.S., 1980, NEA, 1980-81, N.Y. State Coun. for the Arts, 1984-85, Ariana Found., 1987-88, Pollock-Krasner, 1987-88. Fellow Soc. of Fellows Am. Acad. in Rome; mem. Nat. Acad. Design (life). Democrat. Roman Catholic. Home: 463 West St Apt 228 G New York NY 10014-2030 Office: Univ Mass Fine Arts Ctr Amherst MA 01002

LASH, SHARON C. psychologist; b. Akron, Ohio, Jan. 31, 1957; d. James and Thelma Lash. D in Psychology, Indiana U. Pa., 1992. Psychologist Southpark Psychology, Moline, Ill., 1993—. Cons. Housing and Urban Devel., Rock Island, Ill., 1996—97. Mem.: APA. Home: PO Box 1352 Moline IL 61266

LASHER, ESTHER LU, minister; b. Denver, June 1, 1923; d. Lindley Aubrey and Irma Jane (Rust) Pim; m. Donald T. Lasher, Apr. 9, 1950 (dec. Mar. 1982); children: Patricia Sue Becker, Donald T., Keith Alan, Jennifer Luanne Oliver. Assoc. Fine Arts, Colo. Women's Coll., 1943; BA, Denver U., 1945; MA Religious Edn., Ea. Bapt. Sem., 1948; MA, Denver U., 1967; grad. Jerusalem Ctr. for Biblical Studies, 1995. Ordained to ministry Bapt. Ch., 1988. Christian edn. dir. 1st Bapt., Evansville, Ind., 1948-52; min. Perrysburg Bapt. Ch., Macy, Ind., 1988-95; min.-at-large Am. Baptist Conv./USA, 1996—; interim pastor United Bapt. Ch., Lewiston, Maine, 1997-98. Libr. Peru (Ind.) Pub. Schs., 1990—91; sec. Ind. Ministerial Coun., Indpls., 1990—92; chairperson Women in Ministry, Indpls., 1988—93; min. Kairos Ministry to Women in Prison, 2002; chmn. Fellowship Mission Circle, Rochester, Ind., 1988—93; mem. Partnership in Ministry, Indpls., 1990—94; bd. mgrs. Am. Bapts./Ind., 1991—93; asst. dir. Greenwood Pub. Libr., 1978—84; dir. Fulton County Pub. Libr., 1984—90; ch. & cmty. chair ABCOM, 2002—; caregiver Edge Nursing Home, Damariscotta, Maine, 2002—. Mem. Evansville Symphonic Orch., 1948—55, Denver Civic Orch., 1955—65, Augusta Symphony Orch., 1998—, Midcoast Cmty. Orch., 1999—; founder Fulton County Literacy Coalition, Rochester, 1989—90, tutor/trainer Peru Literacy Coalition of Peru Pub. Libr., 1994—95; [illegible] CASA Lincoln Co., Maine, 1996—; vol. libr. Rutherford Libr., South Bristol, Maine, 1996—, So. Bristol Libr., Lincoln Retirement Home; mem. Sea Coast Cmty. Orch., 1999—; chair for ch. and cmty. ABC of Me., 2002—; chmn. diaconate bd. Damariscotta Bapt. Ch., 2004—; sec.-treas. North Miami County Mins. Fellowship, 1993—95; chmn. Christian Edn. Bd. and ch. planter, Denver, 1953—59, Colorado Springs, 1959—68; chaplain vol. Miles Hosp., 1997—; prayer advisor Christian Women's Club Damariscotta Bapt. Ch., 1997—, hostess, 1995—97, exec. bd., 1995—, chair missions com., 1997—; pres. Women's Mission Cir., Damariscotta Bapt. Assn., 1997—; chaplain-on-call Miles Meml. Hosp.; bd. dirs. Manitau Tng. Ctr., Rochester, 1988—90, Peru Civic Ctr., 1995; pres. Toastmasters, Rochester, 1984—90, 1995, edn. v.p., 1992—93; v.p. Mental Health Ctr., Rochester, 1987—90; sec. Northwest Area ABC/IN, 1994—95. Named Outstanding Libr., Biog. Inst., 1989. Mem. Leadership Acad. (bd. dir., sec.), Bus. and Profl. Women (pres. Greenwood, Ind. chpt. 1984-86), Rochester Women's Club (pres. 1989-92), Fulton County Mins. Assn. (treas. 1993-95), Logansport Assn. Bapt. Women, Peru Lit. Club (v.p.-elect 1995), CASA Miami County, Rotary, Sigma Alpha Iota (adv.), Christian Edn. (chmn. 1996-98), Damariscotta Assn. Women (pres. 1998—, mem. small ch. com. 1998—), Christian Women's Club (prayer group 1999—). Republican. Home and Office: 2063 State Route 129 South Bristol ME 04568-4317

LASHER, HARRIET PINSKER, director, educator; b. Bay Shore, N.Y. d. Albert and Irene (Kuchlik) Pinsker; children: Heather Lasher, Todd Lasher. BA, Conn. Coll., 1965; MEd, N.C. State U., 1986. Cert. prin., tchr. N.C. State Dept. Pub. Instrn. Tchr. Yonkers (N.Y.) Bd. Edn., 1966-72; dir. The Raleigh (N.C.) Sch., 1982—2002, head sch., 2002—. Mem. ASCD, Nat. Assn. for Edn. Young Children, Nat. Coun. Tchrs. Math., N.C. Assn. for Edn. Young Children. Office: The Raleigh Sch 1141 Raleigh Sch Dr Raleigh NC 27607

LASHLEY, KAREN HUGGINS, psychologist, educator; b. Muskogee, Okla., Dec. 29, 1947; d. James Clarence Huggins and Wilma Leah Jones; m. Tommy G. Lashley, Aug. 17, 1968 (div. Jan. 15, 1996); children: Ryan Thomas, Nathan James, Jason Andrew. BA in English magna cum laude, Okla. Chrisitan U., 1969; MA in Letters, U. Ctrl. Okla., 1971; PhD in Psychology, Okla. State U., 1989. Lic. psychologist, H.S.P. Okla., Tex., Tenn.; cert. secondary tchr. Okla. Tchr. lang. arts Putnam City Schs., Oklahoma City, 1969—72, McAlester (Okla.) Pub. Schs., 1972—73; asst. prof. Bacone Coll., Muskogee, 1975—82; instr. Tulsa CC, 1982—83; tchg. asst. psychology Okla. State U., Stillwater, 1983—88; resident in clin. child psychology Ctrl. Okla. County, Oklahoma City, 1988—90; pvt. practice Bethany (Okla.) Med. Ctr., 1990—96; staff psychologist Okla. Christian Counseling Ctr., Oklahoma City, 1996—. Adj. faculty Okla. Christian U., 1996—, Okla. State U., 1996—, U. Ctrl. Okla., 1996—; asst. instr. Core Comm. Corp., Evergreen, Colo., 1998—. Vol., spokesperson HOPE Ctr. Cmty. Svcs., Edmond, Okla., 1991—94; bd. dirs. Comprehensive Cmty. Svcs., Oklahoma City, 1994—96; profl. advisor to bd. dirs. Kid's Pl., Edmond, 1995—97; vol. psychologist The Cross & The Crown, Oklahoma City, 2002—. Mem.: APA (cert. HIV trainer), Assn. Am. Indian Psychologists, Am. Assn. Marriage & Family Therapy, Okla. Psychol. Assn., Assn. Am. Indian Affairs, Kappa Delta Phi, Alpha Chi. Democrat. Mem. Ch. Of Christ. Avocations: literature, writing, music, art, history. Home: 1817 Kings Rd Edmond OK 73013 Office: 13301 N Meridian # 100 Oklahoma City OK 73120

LASHLEY, VIRGINIA STEPHENSON HUGHES, retired computer science educator; b. Wichita, Kans., Nov. 12, 1924; d. Herman H. and Edith M. (Wayland) Stephenson; m. Kenneth W. Hughes, June 4, 1946 (dec.); children: Kenneth W. Jr., Linda; m. Richard H. Lashley, Aug. 19, 1954; children: Robert H., Lisa Lashley Van Amberg, Diane Lashley Tan. BA, U. Kans., 1945; MA, Occidental Coll., 1966; PhD, U. So. Calif., 1983. Cert. info. processor, tchr. secondary and community coll., Calif. Tchr. math. La Canada (Calif.) High Sch., 1966-69; from instr. to prof. Glendale (Calif.) Coll., 1970-92, chmn. bus. div., 1977-81, coord. instructional computing, 1974-92, prof. emeritus, 1992—; sec., treas., dir. Victory Montessori Schs., Inc., Pasadena, Calif., 1980—; pres. The Computer Sch., Pasadena, 1983-92, ret., 1992—; real estate investor, 1992—. Pres. San Gabriel Valley Data Processing Mgmt. Assn., 1977-79, San Gabriel Valley Assn. for Systems Mgmt., 1979-80; chmn. Western Ednl. Computing Conf., 1980, 84. Editor Jour. Calif. Ednl. Computing, 1980. NSF grantee, 1967-69, EDUCARE scholar U. So. Calif., 1980-82; John Randolph and Dora Haynes fellow, Occidental Coll., 1964-66; student computer ctr. renamed Dr. Virginia S. Lashley Ctr., 1992. Mem. AAUP, AAUW, DAR (scholarship chair, 1994-2002, vice regent 2002—), Calif. Edn. Computing Consortium (bd. dirs. 1979—, v.p. 1983-84, pres. 1985-87), Orgn. Am. Historians, San Marino Women's Club, Colonial Dames, XVII Century (scholarship chair, 1997-99), Nat. Geneal. Soc., New Eng. Hist. Geneal. Soc. (life mem.), Town Hall, World Affairs Coun., Phi Beta Kappa, Pi Mu Epsilon, Phi Alpha Theta, Phi Delta Kappa, Delta Phi Upsilon, Gamma Phi Beta. Republican. Congregationalist. Home: 1240 S San Marino Ave San Marino CA 91108-1227 E-mail: vslash@aol.com.

LASHOF, CAROL SUZANNE, literature educator; b. Chicago, Aug. 8, 1956; d. Richard Kenneth and Joyce (Cohen) Lashof; m. William Tobin Newton Jr., Aug. 20, 1983; children: Elisabeth, Erica. BA, U. Calif., Santa Barbara, 1976; PhD, Stanford U., 1984. Asst. prof. St. Mary's Coll., Moraga, Calif., 1983—89, assoc. prof., 1989—96, prof. English and drama, 1996—. Author: (plays) The Story, 1981, Fräulein Dora, 1989, Medusa's Tale, 1991, Nora's Daughter, 1994, Persephone Underground, 1999, The Minotaur, 2001, The Melting Pot II, 2002, The Melting Pot (II), 2002. Mem.: Assn. Theater in Higher Edn., Dramatists Guild. Office: St Mary's Coll of Calif Moraga CA 94575 E-mail: clashof@stmarys-ca.edu.

LASHOF, JOYCE COHEN, public health educator; b. Phila. d. Harry and Rose (Brodsky) Cohen; m. Richard K. Lashof, June 11, 1950; children: Judith, Carol, Dan. AB, Duke U., 1946; MD, Women's Med. Coll., 1950; DSc (hon.), Med. Coll. Pa., 1983. Dir. Ill. State Dept. Pub. Health, 1973—77; dep. asst. sec. for health programs and population affairs Dept. Health, Edn., and Welfare, Washington, 1977—78; sr. scholar in residence IOM, Washington, 1978; asst. dir. office of tech. assessment U.S. Congress, Washington, 1978—81; dean sch. pub. health U. Calif., Berkeley, 1981—91; prof. pub. health U. Calif. Sch. Pub. Health, Berkeley, 1981—94, prof. emeritus, 1994—. Co-chair Commn. on Am. after Roe vs. Wade, 1991—92; mem. Sec.'s Coun. Health Promotion and Disease Prevention, 1988—91; chair Pres.'s Adv. Com. on Gulf War Vets. Illnesses, 1995—97. Mem. editl. bd.: Wellness Letter, 1993—, Ann. Rev. of Pub. Health, 1987—90. Recipient Alumni Achievement award, Med. Coll. Pa., 1975, Sedgewick Meml. medal, APHA, 1995. Avocation: hiking. Home: 601 Euclid Ave Berkeley CA 94708-1331 Office: U Calif Sch Pub Health 140 Earl Warren Hl Berkeley CA 94720-7360

LASPADA, CARMELLA, government agency administrator; BS in Psychology and TV Comm., Pa. State U., 1960. Organizer USO tour to S.E. Asia White House Spl. Projects Aid, 1967; founder No Greater Love, 1971—; White House liaison and exec. dir. White House Commn. on the Nat. Moment of Remembrance, 2001—. Initiator Nat. Moment of Remembrance, 2000. Named Washingtonian of the Yr., Unsung Heroine, VFW Women's Aux.; recipient U.S. Spl. Ops. Command medal, Ellis Island Medal of Honor, Dickey Chapelle award, USMC League, Spirit of

Enterprise award, U.S. C. of C., Humanitarian award, Rotary Club, Outstanding Alumni award, Pa. State U., Woman of the Yr. award, Christopher Columbus Assn. Office: No Greater Love 1750 New York Ave NW Washington DC 20006*

LASS, TERESA LEE, secondary school educator, special education educator; b. Atlanta, Aug. 30, 1958; d. Houston Lee and Carolyn (Cowan) L.; m. William Gary Carpenter, Oct. 1, 1983 (div. Sept. 1995). BA in German, Studio Art, Art History, Agnes Scott Coll., 1980; MEd, Ga. State U., 1994. Art gall. dir. TPS/Decor Corp., Atlanta, 1978-88; instr. adult literacy State Ga., Dept. Continuing Edn., Atlanta, 1990—; instr. New Tchr. Inst. Ga. State U., Atlanta, 1990-91; instr. staff devel. Dekalb Schs., Decatur, Ga., 1996—; tchr. prodn. and distbn. Warren Tech. Sch., Chamblee, Ga., 1988—, Ptnr. in Edn. liaison, 1994—, chair human rels., 1996—. Cons. Ga. Learning Resource Svcs., Atlanta, 1993—. Chmn. Peachtree Arts, High Mus. of Art, Atlanta, 1996-97, sec./liaison 1991-95, sec., 1999—, chair-elect, 2000-01, chair, 2001-02, membership chair, 2003—; artistic coord. Habitat for Humanity Artfest, Atlanta, 1996—. Named Tchr. of Yr., 1994-95, Tchr. Support Specialist, 2001—. Mem. Phi Beta Kappa, Kappa Delta Pi. Baptist. Avocations: travel, reading, art collecting, cooking, writing. Home: 2155 Morris Ave Tucker GA 30084-4510 Office: Warren Tech Sch 3075 Alton Rd Chamblee GA 30341-4301

LASSA, JULIE M. state representative; b. Oct. 21, 1970; married. BS, U. Wis., Stevens Point, 1993. Former exec. dir. Plover Area Bus. Assn., Wis.; former legis. aide Wis.; mem. state assembly dist. 71 Wis. State Assembly, Madison, 1998—, mem. child abuse and neglect bd., mem. agr., colls. and univs., econ. devel., and labor and workforce devel. coms., minority caucus sec., 1999. Former chair Portage County Dem. Party, Wis.; mem. town bd. Dewey, Wis., 1993—94. Mem.: Portage County Bus. Coun., Portage County Hist. Soc. Democrat. Office: State Capitol Rm 122N PO Box 8952 Madison WI 53708-8952 E-mail: rep.lassa@legis.state.wi.us.

LASSALETTA, ANTONIA MIR, language educator; b. Arecibo, P.R., Mar. 25, 1936; m. Manuel C. Lasaletta, Oct. 12, 1962; children: Margarita, Maria, Teresa, Manuel, Antonio. BA, U. Del Sagrado Corazión, San Juan, 1958; MA, Middlebury Coll., 1964. Exec. sec., home svc. dir. ARC, Mayaguez, PR, 1958—61; instr. Spanish Kimball Union Acad., Meriden, NH, 1963—64, Roanoke Coll., Salem, Va., 1965, U. Va., Roanoke, 1966, grad. instr. Charlottville, 1969; instr. Spanish Inter-Am. U., Bayamon, PR, 1976—78, Hawthorne Jr. High Sch., Charlotte, NC, 1984—; asst. prof. Johnson C. Smith U., 1984—92; instr. Spanish Indpendence High Sch., 1993—; asst. prof. Ctrl. Va. C.C., Lynchburg, 1993—. Mentor Johnson C. Smith U., 1985—92. Author: Intimo mundo compartido, 1986, short stories, poems; contbr. articles to profl. jours. Recipient frist prize, Sociedad Cultural Hispana, 1979, Santa Teresa medal, Colegio U. del Sagrado Corazon, P.R., 1958, 1st and 2d prizes, Cath. Daus. Am., San Juan, P.R., 1957; fellow Gov.'s fellow, U. Va., Dept. Romance Langs., Charlottesville, 1969—70. Office: Ctrl Va CC Humanities Social Scis Divsn Lynchburg VA 24502

LASSEN, BETTY JANE, gifted and talented educator; b. Topeka, Kans., Apr. 19, 1923; d. Harvey Leroy and Anna Elizabeth (Day) Rose; m. Emil Lassen Jr., June 5, 1944 (dec. Sept. 1989); 1 child, Emil III. Instr., guide YMCA-YWCA, Albuquerque, 1975-84, U. N.Mex. Continuing Edn., Albuquerque, 1979—, Ft. Lewis Coll. Continuing Edn., Durango, Colo., 1992-93. Liaison, asst. coord. San Juan Coll. Elder Hostel, Farmington, N.Mex., 1993-94; owner, pres. Outdoor Adventure Tours, Inc., Albuquerque, 1982—; mem. curriculum com., human svcs. tng. coun. gerontology divsn. continuing edn. U. N.Mex., 1979-82; spkr. in field. Designer ski equipment; contbr. articles, poetry to profl. publs. Vol. instr., guide for disabled Easter Seals Soc., Albuquerque, 1983; vol. campground host Nat. Park Svc., Chaco Canyon Ruins, N.Mex., 1990; campaign vol. Dem. Party, Albuquerque, 1976. Recipient Appreciation award Easter Seals Soc., 1983. Mem. Puerto Del Sol Ladies Golf Assn. (pres. 1976-77), N.Mex. Outfitters/Guides, N.Mex. Cross-Country Ski Club (sec. 1973-76), N.Mex. Mountain Club. Avocations: cross-country skiing, hiking, bicycling, golf, ballroom dancing. Home: Apt 212 13991 E Marina Dr Aurora CO 80014-3787

LASSEN-FELDMAN, WENDY ANNE, sales executive, lawyer; b. Washington, Apr. 17, 1968; d. Allan Norris and Sylvia Judith (Wolf) L.; m. Evan Jay Feldman, Aug. 20, 1994; children: Harley Allyn, Nicholas Ryan. BA, U. Mich., 1990; JD cum laude, U. Balt., 1993. Bar: MD, 1993. Attorney Howell, Gately, Whitney & Carter, Towson, MD, 1993-94; placement coord. Attorneys Per Diem, Balt., 1994-95; applications cons. Lexis-Nexis, Washington, 1995-96, acct. mgr., 1996—. Bd. mem., application cons. adv. bd. Lexis-Nexis, Wash., 1995-96; corr. sec. U. Balt. Law student govt., Balt., 1992-93; mem. U. Balt. Faculty Appointment com.,1992-93. Exec. editor U. Balt. Law Rev., 1992-93, author, 1993; contbr. to legal publs. Pres. Child Study, Balt. chpt., 1999-2001; com. mem. Women's Leadership Coun. of The Associated Jewish Fedn. Balt., 2000-01; precinct chairperson Dem. Party, Md., 1995-96. Recipient Turner Svc. award, U. Balt., 1997, 98. Bd. mem. U. Balt. Law Sch. Alumni (co-chair); mem. ABA, Md. State Bar Assn. Democrat. Jewish. Avocations: art, guitar. Home: 2824 Quarry Heights Way Baltimore MD 21209-1060 Office: LEXIS-NEXIS 1150 18th St NW Washington DC 20036-3816 E-mail: wendy.lassen-feldman@lexis-nexis.com.

LASSER, GAIL MARIA, psychologist, educator; b. Saddle River, N.J., Feb. 29, 1960; d. Dominick A. and Genevieve M. Sanzo; children: Michael, Jason, Jonathan. B.A., Seton Hall U., 1971; postgrad., Seton HaLL u., 1975—77; tchg. cert., William Paterson Coll., 1973; M.A., Montclair State Coll., 1975. Cert. staff psychologist N.J., 1977; lic. real estate agt. N.J., 1977, notary pub. Pub. rel. rep. European Health Spa, 1970—71; med. asst. Sci. Prevention and Rehab. Assn., 1973; grad. tchg. and rsch. asst. Montclair State Coll., 1973—74; clin. asst. Dr. Brower, 1974; instr. psychology Essex County Coll., 1976—77; clin. psychologist intern Cmty. Mental Health Ctr., Mt. Carmel Guild, Newark, 1976—77; lectr. St. Michaels Med. Ctr.-N.J. Coll. Medicine, 1977—80; instr. psychology Bergen Cmty. Coll., Paramus, NJ, 1977—. Asst. to ct. adminstr. Bergen County Cts., 1977—78; cons. telecom., 1994. Vol. Am. Heart Assn. Mem.: Am. Soc. Phy. Rsch., Am. Psychol. Assn., Psi Chi, Pi Lambda Theta. Home: 234 E Saddle River Rd Saddle River NJ 07458-2614

LASSITER, SHERI L. insurance company executive; b. Orange, N.J., Sept. 16, 1968; d. Robert and Joan Dixon; m. James E. Lassiter III, May 18, 1997. MBA, Rutgers U., 1992. Sr. bus. analayst AT&T, Morristown, 1992-95, fin. analyst, project mgr. Pitts., 1995-96, fin. analyst Bridgewater, N.J., 1996-97, sr. bus. analyst Short Hills, N.J., 1997-98; sr. bus. analyst/project mgr. Paragon Computer Profls., Cranford, N.J., 1998-2000; project mgr. Metlife, N.Y.C., 2000, project mgr. web develop., 2001. Mem. devel. program AT&T, Morristown, N.J., 1992-96. Author: (booklet) Order of the Eastern Star, 1999. Mem. choir Black History Celebration, 1995; mem. fundraising team Jr. Achievement, 2003. Mem. Order of the Ea. Star (officer 1998-2000, Outstanding Leadership award 1999), Drew Alumni, Black MBA Assn. Office: Metlife One Madison Ave New York NY 10010 E-mail: shersher68@yahoo.com.

LAST, MARIAN HELEN, social services administrator; b. L.A., July 2, 1953; d. Henry and Renee (Kahan) Last. BA, Pitzer Coll., 1975; postgrad., U. So. Calif., 1975-84; MS, Long Beach State U., 1980. Lic. marriage therapist. Coordinator City of El Monte, Calif., 1975-76, project dir., 1976—; pvt. practice psychotherapist Long Beach, Calif., 1982—; div. mgr. City of El Monte, 1982—. Cons. U. So. Calif. Andrus Ctr., L.A., 1977-78; bd. dirs. Coord. Coun., City of El Monte, 1975—, Sr. Pres.'s Coun., 1982—; Congl. del. White House Conf. on Aging, 1995; chair Nutrition Focus Group, L.A. Co. Area Agy. On Aging, 1993—. Co-author rape survival guide, 1971. Dir., co-founder Rape Response Program, Pomona, San Gabriel Valley, Calif., 1971-80; cons. on sexual assault Pitzer Coll., Claremont, Calif., 1975-78; past pres. El Monte-South El Monte Coord. Coun. Recipient Susan B. Anthony award NOW, Pomona, 1976, Gold award Calif. Emergency Svcs. Assn., 1995, Founders award Project Sister sexual assault ctr., 2002. Mem. Am. Soc. on Aging, Calif. Assn. Sr. Ctr. Dirs. (dist. dir. XIII), Calif. Parks and Recreation Soc. (Profl. Citation award 1993), Calif. Assn. Marriage and Family Therapists, Emergency Resources Assn. (bd. dirs.), Women's Club, Civitan, Chi Kappa Rho Gamma. Democrat. Jewish. Avocations: golf, advocating rights of elderly. Office: City of El Monte 3120 N Tyler Ave El Monte CA 91731-3354

LAST, SUSAN WALKER, training developer; b. Waterbury, Conn., Sept. 26, 1962; d. Harold Alfred and Mary (Alferie) Hull; m. Michael Allen Walker, Feb. 11, 1984 (div. July 1988); 1 child, Cassandra Mary; m. Robert Lee Last, Sept. 26, 1992. BS, Ind. U., 1983. Cert. franchise exec. Internat. Franchise Assn., 2003. Ctr. dir. Sylvan Learning Corp., Arlington, Tex., 1984-88, franchise cons., 1988-89, dist. mgr., 1989-90; coord. of program devel. Sylvan Learning Systems, Arlington, Tex., 1991-96; dir. tng. devel. Am. Fastsigns, Inc., Carrollton, Tex., 1996-97, v.p. tng., 1997—99, sr. v.p. franchise svcs., 1999—. Trainer, cons. Charles R. Hobbs Corp., Salt Lake City, 1989-96; cons. Highpointe, Arlington, 1988-94. Author: (curriculum) Study Skills Program, 1990, Study Power Video, 1991, Basic Math Program (K-8), 1994, Adult Reading Program, 1993, ESL program, 1995. Mem., speaker Parents Without Ptnrs., Arlington, 1991. Mem. ASCD, ASTD, Children and Adults with Attention Deficient Disorder, Nat. Coun. Tchrs. of Math., Nat. Coun. Tchrs. of English, Meeting Planners Internat., Internat. Franchise Assn., Internat. Sign Assn. Avocations: reading, writing, gardening, swimming. Home: 1316 Willow Wood Dr Carrollton TX 75010-1304 Office: FASTSIGNS International Inc 2550 Midway Rd Ste 150 Carrollton TX 75006-2372

LASTER, GAIL W. lawyer; BA, Yale U.; JD, NYU. Law clk. to Judge Mary Johnson Lowe U.S. Dist. Ct. (so. dist.) N.Y., 1983-85; staff atty. Pub. Defender Svc. D.C., 1985-90; counsel com. labor and human resources, subcom. labor U.S. Senate, 1990-92; counsel subcom. antitrust, monopolies and bus. rights U.S. Senate on Judiciary, 1992-94; dir. govtl. rels., counsel Legal Svcs. Corp., 1994—; gen. counsel U.S. Dept. Housing and Urban Devel., Washington, 1997—. Office: Dept Housing and Urban Devel 451 7th St SW Washington DC 20410-0002

LASYS, JOAN, medical nurse, writer, educator, publisher; b. Siauliai, Lithuania, Sept. 1, 1924; arrived in Can., 1948; came to U.S., 1960; d. Joseph-Apolinarius and Elena (Šlapokaite) Barcevičius; m. Bill Lasys, July 31, 1949. RN degree, Lithuanian Red Cross Sch. Nursing, 1945; student, Ariz. State U., 1981—86, Ea. Ariz. Coll., 1981—86. RN, Can., Nebr.; cert. nursing tchr., Ariz.; C.C., occupl. tchg. cert. Ariz. Staff RN St. Mary's Hosp., Montreal, Can., 1949-51, Montreal Gen. Hosp., 1951-53, 1959-60; pvt. duty Nurses Registry, Montreal, 1953-56; Can. civil svc. RN R.H.O. Ctr. Dept. Vets. Affairs, Ottawa, Can., 1956-57, Queen Mary Vets. Hosp., Montreal, 1957-58; staff RN St. Joseph's Hosp., Omaha, 1968-69, Meryvale Hosp., Phoenix, 1969-71, Valley View Hosp., Youngtown, Ariz., 1971-72, Boswell Hosp., Sun City, Ariz., 1972-76; RN Kivel Care Ctr., Phoenix, 1986—93, 2000—02. Past v.p. and officer Pine-Strawberry (Ariz.) Health Svcs.; columnist/reporter Payson (Ariz.) Roundup Pub. (mag.) Small Town U.S.A.; prodr. audio tapes: Time Management, Nursing Communications. Life mem. Pine-Strawberry and Gila County Homemakers, Payson Regional Med. Ctr. Aux. Mem.: AAUW, Libr. Congress, Nat. Mus. Women in the Arts, Payson Libr., Rep. Presidential Task Force, Kivel Geriatric Ctr. Aux. (life), County Attys. and Sheriffs Assn. (hon.), Arbor Day Found., Nature Conservancy, Cooking Club of Am. (charter). Republican. Roman Catholic. Avocations: cooking, writing poetry, public speaking, arts and crafts. Home: 506 N William Tell Cir Payson AZ 85541-4050

LATHAM, DEBORAH L. energy marketing and services company executive; BSBA with honors, U. Tenn. Pres., gen. mgr., an owner Optimum Energy Sources, Inc., Roswell, Ga. Condr. numerous seminars and tng. sessions Petroleum Mktg. Edn. Found., also Petroleum Infotech; former instr. Phillips Petroleum Co. Mktg. and Mgmt. Inst.; guest host Sta. WSN News Talk Radio; featured on CNN. Mem. Energy Svc. Providers Assn. (founding bd. dirs.), Southeastern Oil Marketers Assn. (past mem. bd. dirs.). Office: Optimum Energy Sources Inc Ste 218 1422 W Peachtree St NW Atlanta GA 30309-2940

LATHAM, LAVONNE MARLYS, physical education educator; b. Garrison, Iowa, Mar. 17, 1942; d. Harry August and Vona Irene (Loveless) Hilmer; m. Robert Allen Latham Jr., July 21, 1979. BA, U. Iowa, 1964; postgrad., No. Ill. U., 1985, Western Ill. U., 1970-88, Bemidji State U., 1979. Cert. tchr., Ill. Tchr. phys. edn., elem. computer coord. Erie (Ill.) Community Unit 1, 1964—. Head counselor Camp Lenore Owaissa, Hinsdale, Mass., 1964-78. Mem. NEA, AAHPER, Ill. Assn. Health, Phys. Edn. and Recreation, U. Iowa Alumni Assn., Ill. Edn. Assn., Erie Tchrs. Assn. (pres. 1982-83), Nat. Audubon Soc., Nature Conservancy, Delta Kappa Gamma. Baptist. Avocations: violin, computers, photography, travel, outdoor activities. Home: 1002 6th St Erie IL 61250 Office: Erie Community Unit 1 605 6th Ave Erie IL 61250-9452

LATHAM, TAMARA BERYL, chemist, researcher; b. Brisbane, Australia, July 31, 1944; arrived in U.S., 1946; d. James Samuel and Beryl (Holzheimer) Latham. BS in Chemistry, CUNY, 1979, postgrad., 1980—81. With Novocol Chem. Co., Bklyn., 1980, Sloan Kettering Inst. Cancer Ctr., N.Y.C., 1984; chemist BOC Group, Murray Hill, NJ, 1984—95, Bayer Corp., West Haven, Conn., 1995—99; with Grolier/Scholastic, West Haven, 1999—2001; rsch. recruiter 20/20 Rsch., Nashville, 2002—. Forum moderator metric poetry Moontown Cafe Website, 2001. Author: (poetry chapbook) Mirror Of My Soul, 1999, (poetry book) The Poet, 2003; contbr. articles to profl. jours. With USN, 1963—66. Recipient Amos Alonzo Stagg award, U.S. Navy, 1965, Editors Challenge award for poetry, Internat. Soc. Authors and Artists, 1996. Mem.: Am. Chem. Soc., Am. Legion, The Workshop Poets. Achievements include patents for cancer anti-emetic. Avocations: singing, reading, gardening, chess.

LATHAN, CORINNA ELISABETH, aerospace engineer; b. Nov. 7, 1967; m. David Kubalak. BA in Biopsychology and Math., Swarthmore Coll., 1988; PhD in Neurosci., MIT, 1994, SM in Aeronautics and Astronautics, 1995. Asst. prof. biomed. engring. Cath. U., Washington, 1995—99, assoc. prof. biomed. engring., 1999—2000; adj. prof. aerospace engring. U. Md., 2002—; founder, pres., CEO AnthroTronix, College Park, Md., 1999—. Mem. editl. bd.: Jour. Human Performance in Extreme Environs., 1998—. Founder Keys to Empowering Youth; spl. projects advisor FIRST, Inc. Named Top Innovator of Yr., Md. Daily Record, 2002, Tech. Pioneer, World Econ. Forum, 2004; named one of Top 100 World Innovators Under the Age of 35, Tech. Review-MIT's Mag. of Innovation, Top 100 Women, Md. Daily Record, 2003; recipient Creating a Future of Opportunity award, Dept. Aeronautics and Astronautics, MIT, 2000, Women in Tech. Leadership award for entrepreneurship, 2002. Mem.: Assn. for Advancement of Med. Instrumentation (mem. human engring. stds. com. 1997—). Office: AnthroTronix Inc 387 Technology Dr Ste 1101 College Park MD 20742*

LATHON, SHERAINE, clergyman; b. Chicago Heights, Feb. 20, 1952; d. Roosevelt Willingham and Norma L. Cobb; m. Willie Lathon, Jr., June 11, 1983; children: Eric, Christopher. AAS, Prairie State Jr. Coll., 1972; BS, Friends Internat. U., 1992, MS, 1994, PhD, 1997. Ordained to ministry, 1999. Collection mgr. Donnelley Directory, Chgo., 1973-87; ch. adminstr. Liberty Temple Full Gospel Ch., Chgo., 1987—, sr. pastor, 1999—. Assoc. prof. Logos Ministerial Tng. Inst., Friends Internat. U. Co-author: Recovery, 2000. Sec.-treas. Bushido-Kan Acad.; pres. Sheraine Lathon Evangelistic Ministries. Mem. NAFE. Office: Liberty Temple Full Gospel Ch 2233 W 79th St Chicago IL 60620-5803 E-mail: slathon1063@aol.com.

LATHROP, JENNIFER FARGO, audiologist; b. Corning, N.Y., Oct. 8, 1950; d. Jarvis Jerome and Gloria Mary (Christy) Fargo; m. Steve Cate, 1977 (div. 1983); m. John Walter Lathrop, Jan. 26, 1985; children: Laurel, Ellen. BA, U. Redlands, 1972; MA, Kent State U., 1973. Audiologist Behavioral Scis. Inst., Monterey, Calif., 1973; pvt. practice audiologist, 1973-79; audiologist, owner Pacific Hearing Svc., Los Altos, Calif., 1979—. Mem. adv. bd. Self Help for the Hard of Hearing; sec. Calif. Speech Pathologists and Audiologists in Pvt. Practice, 1989-91. Fellow Am. Acad. Audiology; mem. Am. Speech, Lang. and Hearing Assn. (cert. in audiology), Calif. Speech, Lang. and Hearing Assn., Calif. Acad. Audiology (treas. 1993-96, chair 1995-97), Audiology Assn. Calif. Democrat. Congregationalist. Avocations: horseback riding, painting. Home: 575 Los Altos Ave Los Altos CA 94022-1602 Office: Pacific Hearing Svc 496 1st St Ste 120 Los Altos CA 94022-3677

LATIANO, SISTER OLIVIA MARIA, minister, secondary school educator; b. Elyria, Ohio, Mar. 14, 1949; d. William David Latiano and Rosalind Gottuso. BA, Notre Dame Coll., Cleve., 1972; MusM, Miami U., Oxford, Ohio, 1980. Cert. advanced catechist Diocese of Arlington, 1982, mem. Sisters of Notre Dame 1969; permanent h.s. educator for computer sci., music, English Ohio Dept. of Edn. Tchr. music, religion, English Notre Dame Acad., Chardon, Ohio, 1972—80, chair music dept., English and religion tchr. 9-12 Middleburg, Va., 1980—83; tchr. religion, English, orch., computer sci. Notre Dame - Cathedral Latin, Chardon, 1983—89; dir. music and liturgy St. Joseph Parish, Amherst, Ohio, 1989—2004. Liturgical musician Sisters of Notre Dame, Chardon, 1967—89; Reiki master practicioner; mem. Choral Spectrum. Composer: (vocal composition) Jesus is Lord. Retreat team mem. Sisters of Notre Dame, Chardon, 1980—83; retreat team SACRED Space, Cleve., 2000—03. Mem.: Nat. Pastoral Musicians, Choristers Guild. Roman Catholic. Avocations: water walking, roller skating dancing, painting, ceramics, Jungian analysis. Office Phone: 440-988-2848.

LATIMER, ALLIE B. retired lawyer; b. Coraopolis, Pa. d. Lawnye S. and Bennie Latimer BS, Hampton Inst.; JD, MDiv, DMin, Howard U.; LLM, Cath. U.; postgrad., Am. U., 1960-61. Bar: N.C. bar 1955, D.C. bar 1960. Vol. in projects Am. Friends Service Com., N.J. and, Europe, 1948-49; correctional officer Fed. Reformatory for Women, Alderson, W.Va., 1949-51; personnel clk. NIH, Bethesda, 1953-55; realty officer Mitchell AFB, N.Y., 1955-56; with Office Gen. Counsel, GSA, Washington, 1957-76, chief counsel, after 1966, asst. gen. counsel, 1971-76, gen. counsel, 1977-87; asst. gen. counsel NASA, 1976-77; spl. counsel Gen. Svcs. Adminstrn., Washington, 1987-96. Past chmn. central office com. Fed. Women's Program, GSA; mem. membership and budget com. Health and Welfare Council, 1967-72 Bd. dirs. D.C. Mental Health Assn., pres., 1977-79; bd. dirs. Friendship House, Washington; elder Presbyn. Ch.; mem. com. on office of Gen. Assembly, Presbyn. Ch. USA; pres. Interacial Council, 1964-75; chmn. Presbyn. Econ. Devel. Corp., 1975-81; mem. governing bd. Nat. Council Chs. of Christ in U.S.A.; bd. trustees Johnson C. Smith Theol. Sem. Recipient GSA Sustained Superior Service award, 1959, Meritorious Service award, 1964, Commendable Service award, 1964, Pub. Service award, 1971, Outstanding Performance award, 1971, Presdl. Rank award, 1983, Disting. Service award, 1984. Mem. ABA, Nat. Bar Assn. (sec. 1966-74, Hall of Fame award 1999), Fed. Bar Assn., Washington Bar Assn. (Ollie M. Cooper award 1998), N.C. Bar Assn., Nat. Bar Found. (dir. 1970-71, pres. 1974-75), Hampton Alumni Assn. (pres. Washington chpt. 1970-71), Howard Law Alumni Assn. (v.p. 1962-63) alumni assns), Links (pres. Washington chpt. 1971-74, nat. v.p. 1976-80), Federally Employed Women (founder, 1st pres.) Home: 3050 Military Rd NW #520 Washington DC 20015-1364

LATIMER, HELEN, information resource manager, writer, researcher; b. Elizabeth, N.J. d. Raymond O. and Minna A. Mercner; divorced; children: Alexander, Victoria. AB, Duke U.; MS in Journalism, Columbia U.; cert. in bus. adminstrn., Harvard-Radcliffe, MBA in Mktg., Am. U., attended, U. Calif., Berkeley, Rutgers U.; cert. in MBA Upgrade, Syracuse U., 1995. Instr. mktg. Am. U., Washington; mgr. info. resources Burdeshaw Assocs., Ltd., Bethesda, Md., 1985-94, assoc., 1994—; commr. Mayor's Commn. on Violence Against Women, Washington, 1996—2001, D.C. Commn. Women, 1996-99. Initiated publ. specialists program George Washington U., Washington; officer alumni bds. Harvard-Radcliffe Program in Adminstrn., Am. U.; comm., info. resource mgmt. cons., tech. editor MIT Servomechanisms Lab.; AA to editor Reinhold Pub. (former subs. McGraw-Hill); facilitator, subgroup on mktg. The White House Conf. on Libr. and Info. Svcs., 1991. Contbr. articles to newspapers and mags. Past leader Troop 1907, Girl Scouts Am.; mem. Troop 100 com. Boy Scouts Am.; pres. D.C. Unit Ch. Women United, 2003--. Mem. Spl. Librs. Assn., Harvard Bus. Sch. Club D.C. (past v.p., bd. dirs.).

LA TORRE, CARISSA DANITZA, counselor; d. Luis Francisco and Elia Danitza La Torre. AA in Spanish, AA in Psychology, Saddleback C.C., Mission Viejo, Calif., 1995, AA in Bus. Adminstrn., 2002; BA in Spanish, BA in Psychology, Calif. State U., Fullerton, 1998, MS in Edn., 2000. Lic. Behavior Modification Case Mgr./Specialist Calif., 1999, cert. Specialist Mild/Moderate/Severe Disabilities Calif., 1999, Multiple Subject Calif., 1999, Single Subject Calif., 1999. Educator Capistrano Unified Sch. Dist., San Juan Capistrano, Calif., 1997—99; bilingual grad. rschr. UCLA/Calif. State U., L.A., Calif., 1998—; office/human resource mgr. GlobalStar Electronics, Inc., Aliso Viejo, Calif., 2002—03; birth mother counselor Adoption Network Law Ctr., Inc., Laguna Beach, Calif., 2003—. Presenter in field of infant devel. Rep. and spkr. MADD, Tustin, Calif., 1996; youth group ministry leader Mission San Juan Capistrano, San Juan Capistrano, Calif., 2001. Recipient Dedication and Svc. in Counseling award, Outreach Concern, Inc., 1997, 1998. Mem.: Coun. for Children with Behavioral Disorders (assoc. presenter internat. conf. 2001), Divsn. for Early Childhood (assoc. presenter internat. confs. 2000—01), Phi Kappa Phi (life), Zeta Tau Alpha (life; pres. and v.p. 1995—97). Personal E-mail: xclatorre@collegeclub.com.

LATOURRETTE, KATHRYN, family therapist, counselor, artist; b. Camp Atterbury, Ind., Nov. 16, 1942; d. Herbert Cecil and Goldie Ann (Wright) Little; m. Robert William LaTourrette, Dec. 22, 1964; children: Robert Scott, Bradley Talon, Todd Lawson. BS in Elem. Edn. and Psychology, N.Mex. State U., 1964; MS in Counseling, Troy State U., 1985. Lic. marriage and family therapist, N.Mex. Counseling and Therapy Practice Bd. Elem. tchr. Univ. Hills Elem., Las Cruces, N.Mex., 1964-65; substitute tchr. Mesa (Ariz.) Sch. Sys., 1974-75; counselor Las Vegas (Nev.) Rape Crisis Ctr., 1985-86; group facilitator Nev. State Dept. Corrections, Las Vegas, 1985-86; counselor and family therapist Drug Abuse Comprehensive Coordinating Office, Tampa, Fla., 1989-91, Pinon Hills Hosp., Santa Fe, 1991-99; pvt. practice Jefferson Davis, MD, Santa Fe, 1999—2003. Instr. Abuse Shelter, Okinawa, Japan, 1987-89. Works exhibited Albuquerque Art Soc., 1968-71, Old Town Gallery, Alexandria, Va., 1977-78 (Best in Show award 1977), Conquistador Gallery, Taos, N.Mex., 1982-84. Cub Scout leader, Hahn, Germany, 1965-66; hon. chmn. ARC, Okinawa, 1986-88; advisor Kadina Officers Wives Club, Okinawa, 1986-89. Mem. Am. Assn. Marriage and Family Counselors, Gamma Beta Phi. Presbyterian. Avocations: art, hiking, brass rubbing, gardening. Home: 10648 Weybridge Dr Tampa FL 33626-1824

LATSIOS, BARBARA LYNN, government official; b. Phila., Jan. 25, 1954; d. Stephen and Helen Valentina (Matweychuk) Sameruck; m. George Latsios, Aug. 29, 1976; 1 child, Cassandra. Clk., stenographer Nat. Park Svc., Phila., 1971-72, park ranger, 1972-79, supervisory park ranger, 1979-85, purchasing agt., 1985-87; contract specialist EPA, Phila., 1987-90, program analyst, 1990—. Mem. Nat. Contract Mgmt. Assn., AFL-CIO (sec. Local 2058 Phila. 1973-75, 2d v.p. 1976-79). Republican. Russian Orthodox. Office: EPA Region III 1650 Arch St Philadelphia PA 19103-2029 E-mail: latsios.barbara@epamail.epa.gov.

LATTIMORE, BARBARA, healthcare administrator, consultant; b. Birmingham, Ala., June 11, 1961; d. Butler and Alfreda (Kelley) Jackson; m. Ernest Eugene Lattimore, June 7, 1980; children: Kendra, Kimberly, Kandis. BS in Psychology, U. Md., 1988; MEd in Counseling, Boston U., 1990; MSA in Health Svcs., Ctrl. Mich. U., 1998. Lic. profl. counselor; nat. cert. counselor. Sta. mgr. ARC, Hanau, GErmany, 1986-89; program mgr. Sci. Applications Internat., Hanau, 1989-93; behavioral health clinician South Fulton Mental Health, East Point, Ga., 1993-96; program mgr. Child and Adolescent Program, Atlanta, 1996-98; dir. substance abuse Alcohol and Drug Treatment Ct., Atlanta, 1998—. Founder, CEO, Alternative R&D, Decatur/Stone Mountain, Ga., 1993-99; CEO, Therapeutic Managed Care, Decatur/Stone Mountain, 1999—; cons. Gwinnett County Juvenile Ct., Lawrenceville, Ga., 1998—, Daus. Endowed With Wisdom, Decatur, 1998—, ACE Check Casing, Inc., Atlanta, 1999—, Social Work Svcs., Frankfurt, Germany, 1991-93. Treas., NAACP, Hanau, 1990, v.p., 1991, pres., 1992; troup leader Girl Scouts U.S., Mannheim, Germany, 1989-92; Sunday sch. tchr. Christ Temple Fellowship, 1980—. Recipient Comdr.'s award for cmty. svc. U.S. Army, 1990. Mem. Am. Coll. Healthcare Execs., Sigma Iota Epsilon, Delta Sigma Theta. Home: 7052 Shore Rd Lithonia GA 30058-8214 Office: Fulton County Alcohol and Drug Treatment Ctr 265 Boulevard NE Atlanta GA 30312-1284

LATTIMORE, PATRICIA, administration and management administrator; Grad., Southeastern U.; postgrad., Harvard U., Am. U., Washington. Clerical employee Post Office Dept., Washington, 1964-68; legis. and press aide Ho. of Reps., Washington, 1968-71; personnel mgmt. evaluator Office of Personnel Mgmt., Phila., Washington, 1972-77; various positions Dept. of Labor, Phila., Washington, 1978-90; dep. assoc. dir. Career Entry and Employee Devel. Group, Office of Personnel Mgmt., 1990-91, assoc. dir. adminstr., 1991-93, dir., 1993, assoc. dir. investigations, 1993-95, asst. sec. adminstrn. and mgmt., 1997—. Mem. Macedonia Bapt. Ch., Arlington, Va.; organizer ann. auction fundraiser Banneker Acad. H.S.; vol. Stuart-Hobson Mid. Sch. Mem. Nat. Coun. Negro Women, Nat. Forum Black Pub. Adminstrs., Delta Sigma Theta. Office: Dept of Labor Asst Sec Adminstrn Mgmt 200 Constitution Ave NW Washington DC 20210-0002

LATZA, BEVERLY ANN, accountant; b. Pompton Plains, N.J., June 10, 1960; d. George and Helen Mae (Ryan) L. BA in Acctg., Bus. Adminstrn., Thiel Coll., 1982. Internal auditor Monroe Systems for Bus., Morris Plains, N.J., 1983-85; acct. Am. Airlines, Tulsa, 1985-86, Accountemps, Tulsa, 1986-87; credit investigator Denrich Leasing, Inc., Kansas City, Mo., 1987-89; with accounts receivable dept. Coca Cola Bottling Co. Am., Lenexa, Kans., 1989; with acctg. and accounts payable depts. Wolferman's Fine Breads, Lenexa, Kans., 1992-93; tax examining asst. IRS, Kansas City, Mo., 1989-98, customer svc. rep., 1998—2001, collection due process/collection appeals case worker, 2001—. Vol., disaster action team mem. ARC, 1996-97; reading tutor Literacy of Kansas City, 2001—02. Lutheran. Avocations: reading, movies, singing, counted cross stitch. Home: 8323 W 108th St Apt C Overland Park KS 66210-1625 Office: IRS 2306 E Bannister Rd Kansas City MO 64131-3011

LATZEL, GRETA, marketing professional, director; b. Pa. MBA, Temple U., 1994. Cons. McCann Assocs., Inc., Langhorne, Pa., 1990—94, dir. of mktg. & ops., 1994—97, v.p., 1997—2003; mktg. comm. mgr. Vantage, Newtown, Pa., 2003—. Contbr. articles to mags. Vol. Hist. Fallsington, Fallsington, Pa. Office: Vantage 110 Terry Dr Newtown PA 18940

LAU, JOANNA T. information technology executive; BS in Computer Sci. and Applied Math., SUNY, Stony Brook; MS in Computer Engring., Old Dominion U., 1985; MBA in Bus. and Ops., Boston U., 1991; PhD (hon.), Suffolk U., 1999, Bentley Coll., 1998, Bryant Coll., 1997. Software engr. aerospace control systems dept. GE, 1981—83, consumer electronics ops. systems engr., 1983—85, CIM project mgr. aircraft engine bus. group, 1986—89; supr. mfg. engring. Digital Equipment Corp., 1989—90; pres., chmn. bd. LAU Acquisition Corp./LAU Technologies, Littleton, Mass., 1990—. Mem. Army Sci. Bd. Mem. Kennedy Libr. Found., Com. of 200. Named Nat. Turnaround Entrepreneur of the Yr., 1995, 8(a) Small Bus. Person of the Yr. for Mass., 1995; recipient Pinnacle award, Greater Boston C. of C., 1997, Leadership award to Women in Bus., New Eng. Coun., Young Engring. award, GE Aircraft Engine Group. Mem.: Young Pres.'s Orgn., Internat. Women's Forum, Assn. of U.S. Army, Nat. Def. Indsl. Assn. Office: Lau Technologies 30 Porter Rd Littleton MA 01460

LAU, PAULINE YOUNG, chemist; b. Harbin, China, June 18, 1943; d. Ching-ju and Chuan-erh (Fu) Young; m. Roland Lau, Sept. 16, 1967 (div. 1990); 1 child, Joan Mann. BS in Med. Tech., Nat. Taiwan U., 1964; MS in Chemistry, Wayne State U., Detroit, 1967; PhD in Chemistry, 1984. Med. technologist Detroit Gen. Hosp., 1967-68; adminstrv. asst. in rsch. Purdue U., W. Lafayette, Ind., 1970-72; supr. chemistry dept. Raritan Valley Hosp., Greenbrook, N.J., 1973-75; head chemistry dept. Princeton (N.J.) Med. Ctr., 1975-80; mgr. S.E. region RIA Ctr., Columbia, S.C., 1980-82; rsch. chemist Med. Product dept. DuPont Co., Wilmington, Del., 1984-88; mgr. rsch./devel. Boehringer Mannheim Diagnostics, Indpls., 1988—. Com. mem. Nat. Com. on Clin. Lab. Stds., 1989—. Author: Clinical Chemistry Laboratory Procedures, 1977. Recipient Outstanding Product Devel. award, Boehringer Mannheim Co., 1990. Mem. Chinese Acad. and Profl. Assn. in Mid-Am. (bd. dirs. 1990—), Ind. Assn. Chinese Ams. (pres. 1993), Mt. Jade Assn. (chmn. biomed. div. 1990—), Ctrl. Ind. Clin. Biochemistry Forum (pres. 1993—), Am. Assn. Clin. Chemistry (chpt. treas. 1989-92, divsn. sec. 1992-93), Am. Chem. Soc. (chpt. bd. dirs. 1990-91), Ind. Chinese Profl. Assn. (v.p. 1990-91, pres. 1992-93), N.Am. Chinese Clin. Chemists Assn. (bd. dirs. 1988-91, pres. 1992—). Office: Roche Diagnostic Corp 9115 Hague Rd Indianapolis IN 46256-1025

LAUBER, KELLI KATHERINE MARGARET, criminal justice instructor; b. Pasadena, Calif., July 31, 1968; d. Dianne Kathleen Johnson. BS in Psychology, Boise State U., 1993, BA in Anthropology, 1995; M in Forensic Sci., Nat. U., San Diego, 1998. Cert. peace officer, Calif. Dep. sheriff Ada County Sheriff's Dept., Boise, Idaho, 1991-96; probation officer juvenile and adult field svcs. San Diego County Probation Dept., 1998-2001; intensive probation officer Maricopa County Probation Dept., Mesa, Ariz., 2001—; criminal justice instr. Education America, Tempe, Ariz. Mem. San Diego County Juvenile Firesetter's Adv. Coun., San Diego County Sex Offender Mgmt. Program. Mem. Am. Acad. Forensic Scis., Am. Coll. Forensic Examiners. Avocations: seminars, animal rights activist, camping/hiking/outdoor activities, photography. Home: 1325 W Musket Way Chandler AZ 85248 E-mail: kellik31@yahoo.com.

LAUBER, PATRICIA GRACE, writer; b. N.Y.C., Feb. 5, 1924; d. Hubert Crow and Florence (Walker) Lauber. BA, Wellesley Coll., 1945. Rsch., writer Look Mag. Book Dept., N.Y.C., 1945-46; staff writer Scholastic Mags., N.Y.C., 1946-48, editor, 1948-54, freelance editor, 1954-56, Challenge Books, Coward-McCann, N.Y.C., 1955-59; founding editor, editor-in-chief Science World, Street & Smith, N.Y.C., 1956-59; chief editor Science and Mathematics, The New Book of Knowledge, Grolier, N.Y.C., 1961-67; freelance editor Good Earth Books, Garrard, Scarsdale, N.Y., 1973-79. Cons. editor Sci. Am. Books, N.Y.C., 1977—80; cons. Nat. Sci. Resources Ctr., NAS-Smithsonian Instn., 1992—94. Author: (children's book) Volcano: The Eruption and Healing of Mount St. Helens, 1986 (Newbery Honor Book, 1987, N.Y. Acad. Scis. Hon. Mention, 1987), From Flower to Flower: Animals and Pollination, 1986 (N.Y. Acad. Scis. Hon. Mention, 1988), Dinosaurs Walked Here and Other Stories Fossils Tell, 1987, Snakes are Hunters, 1988, Lost Star, the Story of Amelia Earhart, 1988, Meteors and Meteorites: Voyagers from Space, 1989, The News About Dinosaurs, 1989 (N.Y. Acad. Scis. Hon. Mention, 1990), Living with Dinosaurs, 1989 (Orbis Pictus Hon. Mention Nat. Coun. Tchrs. English, 1990), Seeing Earth from Space, 1990 (Orbis Pictus Hon. Mention Nat. Coun. Tchrs. English, 1991), Summer of Fire, 1991, Fur, Feathers, and Flippers, 1994, How Dinosaurs Came To Be, 1996, Hurricanes, 1996, Flood: Wrestling with the Mississippi, 1996, Painters of the Caves, 1998, Purrfectly Purrfect, 2000, Tubs, Toilets and Showers, 2001, Who Came First? New Clues to Prehistoric Americans, 2003. Recipient award for Overall Contbn. to Children's Lit., Washington Post/Children's Book Guild, 1983, Eva L. Gordon award, Am. Nature Study Soc., 1988, Lit. award, Ctrl. Mo. State U., 1989, Lifetime Achievement commendation, Nat. Forum Children's Sci. Books, Carnegie-Mellon U., 1992, Alumnae Achievement award, Wellesley Coll., 1998, Kerlan award, 2000. Mem.: PEN, Soc. Children's Book Writers, Authors Guild. Democrat. Congregationalist. Avocations: reading, music, hiking, travel, sailing. Office: care Scholastic Press 555 Broadway New York NY 10012-3919

LAUCK, DONNA L. mental health nurse; b. Berwick, Pa. d. Earl Andrew and Catherine Arlene Kreiser; m. Ronald Joseph Lauck, Oct. 21, 1966; 1 child, Ronald Joseph Jr. BSN, U. Pa., 1973, MSN, 1982, DNSc, 1991. Diplomate Am. Bd. Forensic Examiners; RN Pa., cert. cert. clin. nurse specialist, ANA, adult psychiat. and mental health nursing, 94, founding certificant, Nat. Registry of Certified Group Psychotherapists, 95, BLS instr., Am. Heart Assn., sexual assault nurse examiner, 96, cognitive behavioral therapist, 01. Oper. room staff nurse Lower Bucks County Hosp., Pa., 1959-60; charge nurse Boron (Pa.) Cmty. Hosp., 1960; part-time staff nurse Barstow (Calif.) Cmty. Hosp., 1960-65; office nurse S.W. French, III, M.D., Barstow, 1960-65; IV team nurse Jefferson Hosp., Pa., 1966; staff nurse critical care unit Presbyn. Hosp., Pa., 1966; head nurse ICU/CCU Meth. Hosp., Pa., 1966-69; head nurse ICU Frankford (Pa.) Hosp., 1970-76; dir. nursing Geriat. and Med. Ctrs., Inc., 1977-79; staff nurse, asst. sr. nurse, charge nurse Friend's Hosp., Phila., 1971-86, relief 11-7 supr., 1971-86; nursing staff devel. specialist Inst. of Pa. Hosp., Phila., 1986-92, clin. nurse specialist, 1992-96; dir. clin. svc. Kirkbride Ctr., Phila., 1997; clin. nurse specialist, sr. nurse in-charge admissions Friend's Hosp., Phila., 1998-2000, sr. nurse therapist Cognitive Behavioral Unit, 2000, clin. nurse specialist, therapist Adult Svcs., 2000—03, advanced practice nurse Adult Svcs., 2000—03, unit mgr. women's unit, 2002—03; therapist Collaborative Care Abington, Phila., 2002—. Spkr. in field. Chmn. fundraising telethon U. Pa. Sch. Nursing, 1981, 1982, active mem.; mem. adv. bd. West Phila. Coalition Neighborhoods and Bus., Advanced Practices Nurses Coun., Pa. Hosp., 1994—96; active mem. liaison program for undergrad. freshman students U. Pa., 1990—, facilitator comm. workshop sr. student nurses, 1999—. Mem.: Am. Coll. Forensic Examiners, Internat. Soc. Hypnosis, Eastern Pa. Assn. Nurses Diagnosis (mem. psychiat.-mental health spl. interest group), Psychiat. Advanced Practice Nurses Pa., Internat. Assn. Study Dissociative Disorders, Am. Soc. Clin. Hypnosis, Presbyn. Hosp. Alumni Orgn. Office: 1369 Old York Rd Abington PA 19001

LAUDER, AERIN, cosmetics executive; 2 children. Degree, U. Pa. From dir. mktg. Prescriptives to v.p. global adv. Estée Lauder Inc., N.Y., 1992—2001, v.p. global adv., 2001—. Office: Estée Lauder Inc Corp HQ 767 Fifth Ave New York NY 10153*

LAUDER, EVELYN H. cosmetics executive; b. Vienna; arrived in U.S., 1940; m. Leonard A. Lauder, 1959; children: William, Gary. BA, Hunter Coll.; hon. degree, Muhlenberg Coll., 1996. Joined as edn. dir. Estée Lauder Cos., N.Y.C., 1959, v.p., sr. corp. v.p., 1989—. Photographer: (book) The Seasons Observed, 1994, An Eye For Beauty, 2002. Founder, chmn. Breast Cancer Rsch. Found., 1993—; mem. bd. overseers Meml. Sloan-Kettering Cancer Ctr.; trustee Ctrl. Pk. Conservancy Inc.; trustee emirata The Trinity Sch., N.Y.C.; bd. dirs. New Yorkers for Parks. Named Disting. Fgn. Born Citizen, Internat. Ctr., 1987; named one of 75 Most Influential Bus. Women, Crain's Newspaper, 1996, Women of Yr., Glamour mag., 1999; recipient Spirit Achievement award, Albert Einstein Coll. Medicine, 1991, Mary Waterman award, Breast Cancer Alliance, 1998, Humanitarian award, Coun. Fashion Designers Am., 2001, award for excellence in philanthropy, Soc. Meml. Sloan-Kettering, 2001, Ellis Island Medal of Honor, Nat. Ethnic Coalition Orgns., 2001. Achievements include founder of The Breast Cancer Research Foundation, the largest national organization dedicated solely to breast cancer research; implementing breast cancer awareness programs from Pink Ribbon campaigns to illuminating world landmarks in a pink glow for Breast Cancer Awareness Month. Office: Estée Lauder Cos 767 5th Ave New York NY 10153-0023*

LAUDER, VALARIE ANNE, editor, educator; b. Detroit, Mar. 01; d. William J. and Murza Valerie (Mann) L. AA, Stephens Coll., Columbia, Mo., 1944; postgrad., Northwestern U. With Chgo. Daily News, 1944-52, columnist, 1946-52; lectr. Sch. Assembly Svc., also Redpath lectr., 1952-55; freelance writer for mags. and newspapers including New York Times, Yankee, Ford Times, Travel & Leisure, Am. Heritage, 1955—; editor-in-chief Scholastic Roto, 1962; editor U. N.C., 1975-80, lectr. Sch. Journalism, 1980—. Gen. sec. World Assn. for Pub. Opinion Rsch., 1988-95; nat. chmn. student writing project Ford Times, 1981-86; pub. rels. dir. Am. Dance Festival Duke U., 1982-83, lectr., instr. continuing edn. program, 1984. Contbg. editor So. Accents mag., 1982-86. Mem. nat. fundraising bd. Kennedy Ctr., 1962-63; bd. dirs. Chapel Hill Mus., Inc., 1996-98. Recipient 1st place award Nat. Fedn. Press Women, 1981, 1st place awards Ill. Women's Press Assn., 1950, 51. Mem. Pub. Rels. Soc. Am. (treas. N.C. chpt. 1982, sec. 1983, v.p. 1984, pres.-elect 1985, pres. 1986, chmn. coun. of past pres., chmn. 25th Ann. event 1987, del. Nat. Assembly 1988-94, S.E. dist. officer, nat. nominating com. 1991, 1st pres.'s award 1993), Women in Comms. (v.p. matrix N.C. Triangle chpt. 1984-85), N.C. Pub. Rels. (mem. Hall of Fame com.), DAR, Soc. Mayflower Desc. (bd. dirs. Ill. Soc. 1946-52), Chapel Hill Hist. Soc. (bd. dirs. 1981-85, 94-2001, chmn. pub. com. 1980-85, pres. 1996-2001), Chapel Hill Preservation Soc. (bd. trustees 1993-96, nominating com. 1994), N.C. Press Club (3d v.p. 1981-83, 2d v.p. 1983-85, pres. 1985, 1st pl. awards 1981, 82, 83, 84), Univ. Women's Club (2nd v.p. 1988), The Carolina Club, The Nat. Press Club. Office: U NC Sch Journalism and Mass Comm CB 3365 Chapel Hill NC 27599-0001

LAUDERDALE, KATHERINE SUE, lawyer; b. Wright-Patterson AFB, Ohio, May 30, 1954; d. Azo and Helen Ceola (Davis) L. BS in Polit. Sci., Ohio State U., 1975; JD, NYU, 1978. Bar: Ill. 1978, U.S. Dist. Ct. (no. dist.) Ill. 1978, Calif. 1987. Assoc. Schiff, Hardin & Waite, Chgo., 1978-82; from dir. bus. and legal affairs to sr. v.p. Sta. WTTW-TV, Chgo., 1982—2000, sr. v.p. strategic partnerships and gen. counsel, 2000—02; sr. v.p. and gen. counsel PBS, Alexandria, Va., 2002—. Mem. Lawyers Com. for Harold Washington, Chgo. 1983; bd. dirs. Midwest Women's Ctr., Chgo., 1985-94; active Chgo. Coun. Fgn. Rels., 1981—, mem. fgn. affairs com., 1985—; mem. adv. bd. Malcolm X Coll. Sch. Bus., 1996-99. Mem. ABA, Chgo. Bar Assn. (bd. dirs. TV Prodns., Inc. 1986—2002), Lawyers for Creative Arts (bd. dir. 1984—2002, v.p. 1998—2002), ACLU (bd. dirs. 1987-94), Nat. Acad. TV Arts and Scis., NYU Law Alumni Assn. Midwest (mem. exec. bd. 1982—86), The Ohio State U. Pres.'s Nat. Adv. Coun. on Pub. Affairs (Chgo. com., 1994—), The U. Chicago Women's Bd., 1996—2002. Democrat. Office: PBS 1320 Braddock Place Alexandria VA 22315

LAUDONE, ANITA HELENE, lawyer; b. Boston, Sept. 14, 1948; m. Colin E. Harley, May 20, 1978. AB, Conn. Coll., 1970; JD, Columbia U., 1973. Bar: N.Y. 1974. Law clk. to judge Fed. Dist. Ct., N.Y.C., 1973-74; asso. Davis Polk & Wardwell, N.Y.C., 1974-78; assoc. Shearman & Sterling, N.Y.C., 1978-79; with Phelps Dodge Corp., N.Y.C., 1979-85, corp. sec., 1980 85, v.p., corp. sec., 1984-85. Editor: Columbia Law Rev., 1973.

LAUENSTEIN, ANN GAIL, librarian; b. Milw., Nov. 8, 1949; d. Elmer Lester Herbert and Elizabeth Renatta (Bovee) Zaeske; m. Mark Lauenstein, Aug. 16, 1986; 1 child, Maria. MA, U. Wis., 1972. Asst. libr. U. Wis., Wausau, 1972-73; cataloger, libr. MacMurray Coll., Jacksonville, Ill., 1973-76; corp. libr. Anheuser-Busch Cos. Inc., St. Louis, 1976—. Facilitator Anheuser-Busch Quality Circle, St. Louis, 1984—. Treas. Friends of Kirkwood Libr., 1986-98; mem. adv. coun. Sch. Info. Sci. U. Mo., 1987-95. Mem. AAUW (editor jour. 1981-84, publicity chmn. 1985-87, scholar 1984), Spl. Librs. Assn. (network liaison 1981-83, chmn. employment com. 1983-84, chmn. hospitality com. 1984-85, membership chmn. 1988-89, newsletter editor 1992-94, advt. editor 1995-97, bus. mgr. 1999—), St. Louis Regional Libr. Network (coun. 1981-83), St. Louis Online Users Group, Women in Bus. Network (adv. panel 1980-82, 86-87, programs planner 1987-88, asst. coord. 1988-89), Ohio Coll. Libr. Consortium Acquisitions Users Coun. Avocations: stamp collecting, cooking, cookbook collecting. Office: Anheuser-Busch Co Inc 1 Busch Pl Saint Louis MO 63118-1852

LAUER, JEANETTE CAROL, college dean, history educator, writer; b. St. Louis, July 14, 1935; d. Clinton Jones and Blanche Aldine (Gideon) Pentecost; m. Robert Harold Lauer, July 2, 1954; children: Jon, Julie, Jeffrey. BS, U. Mo., St. Louis, 1970; MA, Washington U., St. Louis, 1973, PhD, 1975. Assoc. prof. history St. Louis C.C., 1974-82, U.S. Internat. U., San Diego, 1982-90, prof., 1990-94, dean Coll. Arts and Scis., 1990-94, rsch. prof., 1997—. Author: Fashion Power, 1981, The Spirit and the Flesh, 1983, Til Death Do Us Part, 1986, Watersheds, 1988, The Quest for Intimacy, 5th edit., 2002, No Secrets, 1993, The Joy Ride, 1993, For Better of Better, 1995, True Intimacy, 1996, Intimacy on the Run, 1996, How to Build a Happy Marriage, 1996, Sociology: Contours of Society, 1997, Windows on Society, 1999; Becoming Family: How to Build a Stepfamily that Works, 1999, How to Survive and Thrive in an Empty Nest, 1999, Troubled Times: Readings in Social Problems, 1999, Love Never Ends, 2002, The Play Solution: How to Put the Fun Back into your Relationship, 2002. Woodrow Wilson fellow, 1970, Washington U. fellow, 1971-75. Mem. Am. Hist. Assn., Orgn. Am. Historians. Democrat. Presbyterian.

LAUFF, JENNIFER, corporate financial executive; b. Sterling, Ill., May 27, 1975; d. Gary and Carol Lauff; m. Steven Stavropoulos, Sept. 7, 2002. BS in Fin., Ill. State U., 1997; postgrad., DePaul U., 2002—. Staff acct. Motorola, Libertyville, Ill., 1997—99, cost acct. Boynton Beach, Fla., 1999—2000, sr. fin. analyst Arlington Heights, Ill., 2000—01; fin. mgr. Baxter Healthcare, Round Lake, Ill., 2001—. Children's vol. Elgin (Ill.) Cmty. Crisis Ctr., 2000—03.

LAUFMAN, LESLIE RODGERS, hematologist, oncologist; b. Pitts., Dec. 13, 1946; d. Marshall Charles and Ruth Rodgers; m. Harry B. Laufman, Apr. 25, 1970 (div. Apr. 1984); children: Hal, Holly; m. Rodger Mitchell, Oct. 9, 1987. BA in Chemistry, Ohio Wesleyan U., 1968; MD, U. Pitts., 1972. Diplomate Am. Bd. Internal Medicine and Hematology. Intern Montefiore Hosp., Pitts., 1972-73, resident in internal medicine, 1973-74; fellow in hemotology and oncology Ohio State Hosp., Columbus, 1974-76; dir. med. oncology Grant Med. Ctr., Columbus, 1977-92; practice medicine specializing in hematology and oncology Columbus, 1977—. Bd. dirs. Columbus Cancer Clinic; prin. investigator Columbus Cmty. Clin. Oncology Program, 1989-98. Contbr. articles to profl. jours. Mem. AMA, Am. Women Med. Assn. (sec./treas. 1985-86, pres. 1986-87), Am. Soc. Clin. Oncology, Southwest Oncology Group, Nat. Surg. Adjuvant Project for Breast and Bowel Cancers. Avocations: tennis, piano, sailing, hiking, travel. also: 8100 Ravines Edge Ct Columbus OH 43235-5426 Office: 8100 Ravines Edge Ct Columbus OH 43235-5426

LAUGHLIN, CHRISTEL RENATE, translator, consultant; b. Berlin, Dec. 18, 1940; came to U.S., 1966; d. Werner Wilhelm and Rosa Ida (Conrad) Friedrich; m. Phillip Edward Laughlin, July 1, 1966; 1 child, Christina Rosa. Cambridge proficiency diploma, Davies's Sch., London, 1960; French lang. diploma, U. Paris, 1961; Italian lang. diploma, Centri Europei Lingua, Florence, Italy, 1961; BA in Translating, U. Geneva, 1964; accredited travel agt., N.Am. Sch. Travel, Newport, Calif., 1976. Mem. touring svc. Swiss Touring Club, Geneva, 1962-63; hostess, interpreter Intercontinental Hotel, Geneva, 1964, Swiss Nat. Exhbn., Lausanne, 1964; exec. sec. Intercom S.A., Geneva, 1964-65, Soc. Luchard, Paris, 1965-66; outside saleswoman Hunnicutt Travel, Ft. Worth, 1974-76; pres. Simon Stevens Laughlin Travel, Ft. Worth, 1976-81; cons., translator K.T. Lendt & Co., N.Y.C., 1969-96; tax acct. Tarrant Operators, Inc., Ft. Worth, 1996-98. Market rsch. analyst Power Base, Denver, 1997; cons. Schwartzkopf Cosmetics, Duesseldorf, Germany, 1997; traffic cons. ADAC-Automobil Club Germany, Munich, 1997. Pres. Symphony League Ft. Worth, 1972-74; juror host family, interpreter Van Cliburn Internat. Piano Competition, Ft. Worth, 1973-97; host family interpreter XX World Gymnastics Championships, Ft. Worth, 1979, U.S. Gymnastics Internat., Ft. Worth, 1982. Mem. AAUW, Nat. Assn. Market Rsch. Analysts, Bot. Rsch. Inst. Tex. (sponsor), Arts Coun. Ft. Worth, Modern Art Mus. Fort Worth. Avocations: tennis, skiing, classical music, opera, travel. Home: 6212 Indian Creek Dr Fort Worth TX 76107-3526 E-mail: texasmanlaughlin@hotmail.com.

LAUGHLIN, NANCY, newspaper editor; Nation/world editor Detroit Free Press, 1992—. Office: Detroit Free Press Inc 600 W Fort St Detroit MI 48226-2706

LAUGHLIN, NAOMI MYERS, realtor; b. Oliver, Ill., Mar. 11, 1913; d. Jesse and Mary Grace (Macke) Myers; m. Otis Alton Worthington, July 24, 1936 (dec. Apr. 1948); m. Cyril James Laughlin, Feb. 19, 1955. BA, George Washington U., 1934. Cert. assn. exec. Realtor, Silver Spring, Md., 1943-50, 70—. Recipient 1st A.V. Pisani Lifetime Achievement award, Capital Area Realtors Assn. Mem. AAUW (hon., past pres.), Realtors Land Inst. (hon., pres. 1976-77, ind. land specialist), Montgomery County (Md.) Bd. Realtors (exec. v.p. 1950-70, pres. fed. credit union 1981-84, Lifetime Achievement award, 2003), Manor Country Club (hon.). Democrat. Roman Catholic. Home: 13716 New Hampshire Ave Silver Spring MD 20904-6215

LAUGHLIN, SUSAN, state legislator; b. Sewickley, Pa., Mar. 16, 1932; widowed. Grad., Ambridge H.S. Pa. state rep. Pa. Ho. of Reps., Harrisburg, 1989—. Home: 1305 Sampson St Conway PA 15027-1130 Office: Pa Ho of Reps 401 S Pffoce Hpise Box 202020 Harrisburg PA 17120-2020 also: Rm 120 South Office Bldg Harrisburg PA 17120

LAUGHREY, NANETTE KAY, judge, federal; b. Cheyenne, Wyo., Feb. 11, 1946; m. Christopher Sexton Kelly; children: Hugh, Jessica Katherine. BA, UCLA, 1967; JD, U. Mo. Columbia, 1975. Bar: Mo. 1975, U.S. Dist. Ct. (we. dist.) Mo. 1975, U.S. Ct. Appeals (8th cir.) 1976, U.S. Supreme Ct. 1978. Asst. atty. gen. Mo. Atty. Gen.'s Office, Kansas City, 1975-79; assoc. Craig Van Matre, P.C., Columbia, 1980-83; assoc. prof. law U. Mo. Columbia, 1983-87, prof. law, 1987-89, William H. Pittman prof. law, 1989-96; judge U.S. Dist. Ct. (we. dist.) Mo., Kansas City, 1996—. Mcpl. judge City of Columbia, 1979-83; vis. prof. law U. Iowa, 1990; dep. atty. gen. Mo. Atty. Gen.'s Office, 1992-93. Contbr. articles to profl. jours. Bd. dirs. Columbia Housing Authority. Mem.: ABA, Mo. Bar Assn., Am. Law Inst., U. Mo. Alumni Assn., Am. Whitewater Assn., Mo. Whitewater Assn. Office: US Dist Ct 400 E 9th St Ste 7452 Kansas City MO 64106-2670

LAUPER, CYNDI, musician; b. Queens, N.Y., June 20, 1953; Studied with Katie Agresta, N.Y., 1974. Toured with Doc West's Disco Band Flyer; mem. musical group Blue Angel, N.Y.C., 1980. Featured in German TV music program; rec. artist: (album) She's So Unusual, 1983, A Night To Remember, 1989, Hat Full of Stars, 1993, Twelve Deadly Cyns...and Then Some, 1995, Sisters of Avalon, 1997, Merry Christmas...Have a Nice Life, 1998, Feels Like Christmas, 2001, The Essential Cyndi Lauper, 2003, At Last, 2003; co-writer: (songs) Girls Just Want to Have Fun, She Bop, Money Changes Everything, Time After Time, Goonies R Good Enough, 1985, True Colors, 1986, A Night to Remember, 1989; contbr. A Very Special Christmas, 1992, vol. 2, 1993; star: (videos) Girls Just Want to Have Fun, Time After Time, others; appearance (film) Vibes, 1988, Off and Running, 1991, Life with Mikey, 1993; (TV movie) Mother Goose Rock n' Rhyme, 1990; TV appearances include The Tonight Show, The David Letterman Show, Mad About You (Emmy award, Guest Actress - Comedy Series, 1995); concert tours in Japan, Australia, Hawaii and Eng. Named one of Women of Yr., 1984, Best Female Video Performer, MTV Video Music Awards, 1984, Best Female Performer, Am. Video Awards, 1985; recipient 6 Grammy awards, 1985, 2 Am. Video awards, 1985. Office: Epic Records care Sony Music Entertainment 550 Madison Ave New York NY 10022-3211

LAURENT, J(ERRY) SUZANNA, technical communications specialist; b. Oklahoma City, Okla., Dec. 28, 1942; d. Harry Austin and M. LaVerne (Barker) Minick; m. Leroy E. Laurent, July 2, 1960; children: Steven, Sandra, David, Debra. AS in Engr. Tech., Okla. State U., 1986. Owner, CEO Technically Write, Mustang, Okla., 1989-95; sr. tech. comms. specialist Applied Intelligence Group, Edmond, Okla., 1995-98, DCA Svcs., Oklahoma City, 1998—2003; owner, CEO Comm. Design Group, Mustang, 2003—, pres. Oklahoma City, 2003—. Named One of The Top Ten Business Women in Nation Am. Bus. Women's Assn., 1997. Fellow: Soc. Tech. Comm. (assoc.; Superscript editor 1985, v.p. 1985, feature editor 1986, student chpt. pres. 1986, program coord. Okla. chpt. 1992—93, sec. 1993—94, v.p. 1994—95, state pres. 1995—96, state treas. Okla. chpt. 1998—99, dir./sponsor region 5 1999—2002, bylaws com. mgr. 2001—02, Region 5 conf. mgr. 2002, 2nd v.p. 2003—04, 1st v.p. 2004—, Disting. Chpt. Svc. award 1997, Outstanding Achievement award 2001); mem.: Am. Bus. Women's Assn. (area coun. pres. 1987—89, v.p. dist. III 1988—89, sec. 1990—91, conf. gen. chair 1992, chmn. bd. dirs. Help Us Grow Spiritually 1993—95, editor Smoke Signals, Bull. award 1977, Woman of Yr. 1978, Bull. award 1981, 1983, Bus. Assoc. of Yr. 1983—84, Bull. award 1984, 1993, 1995, Woman of Yr. 1996, 1997, Bull. award 1997—99, Nat. Newsletter award 1999, Bull. award 2003—04). Democrat. Baptist. Avocations: reading, public speaking, motivating people, volunteer activities. Home and Office: Comm Design Group 347 W Forest Dr Mustang OK 73064-3430

LAURIE, MARGARET SANDERS, retired English educator; b. Phila., Oct. 11, 1926; d. Joseph A. and Elizabeth Esther (Simmons) Sanders; m. Dominic Laurie, Jan. 30, 1945 (dec. Sept. 1995); children: Lucille M., Donald J. AB, Alfred U., 1948; MA, Niagara U., 1967. Engr. Remington div. I.E. DuPont, Ilion, N.Y., 1943-47; English tchr. Lewiston (N.Y.)-Porter H.S., 1961-63; English prof. Niagara County C.C., Sanborn, N.Y., 1966-87. Author: Centering: Your Guide to Inner Growth, 1978—2004, Lewiston, Crown Jewel of the Niagara, 2001—, Building Blocks of Light, 2004; author of numerous hist. dramas about Niagara River region. Pres. YWCA Niagara Falls, 1972—78; chmn. Lewiston Hist. Preservation Commn., 1988—92; mem. Lewiston sch. bd., 1999—2003; vol. NACC, 2003—; bd. dirs. Niagara Arts and Cultural Ctr., 2000—, sec., 2003—. Named Woman of Yr. Niagara Falls Assn., 1972, Woman of Week WHLD Radio Sta., Niagara Falls, 1973, Vol. of Yr. Niagara Falls YWCA. Mem.: Western Door Playhouse (pres. 1988—), Assn. Profl. Women Writers (pres. 1986—94, v.p. 1988, state v.p.). Republican. Roman Catholic. Avocations: reading, travel, golf, drama, gourmet cooking. Home: 310 N 4th St Lewiston NY 14092-1242

LAUTENSCHLAGER, PEGGY A. state attorney general; b. Fond du Lac, Wis., Nov. 22, 1955; d. Milton A. and Patsy R. (Oleson) L.; m. Rajiv M. Kaul, Dec. 29, 1979 (div. Dec. 1986); children: Joshua Lautenschlager Kaul, Ryan Lautenschlager Kaul; m. William P. Rippl, May 26, 1989; 1 child, Rebecca Lautenschlager Rippl. BA, Lake Forest Coll., 1977; JD, U. Wis., 1980. Bar: Wis., U.S. Dist. Ct. (we. dist.). Pvt. practice atty., Oshkosh, Wis., 1981-85; dist. atty. Winnebago County Wis., Oshkosh, 1985-88; rep. Wis. Assembly, Fond du Lac, 1988-92; U.S. atty. U.S. Dept. of Justice, Madison, Wis., 1992—2000; atty. gen. State of Wis., 2003—. Apptd. mem. Govs. Coun. on Domestic Violence, Madison, State Elections Bd., Madison; bd. dirs. Blandine House, Inc. Active Dem. Nat. Com., Washington, 1992-93; com. Wis., 1989-92. Named Legislator of Yr., Wis. Sch. Counselors, 1992, Legislator of Yr., Wis. Corrections Coalition, 1992. Mem. Wis. Bar Assn., Dane County Bar Assn., Western Dist. Bar Assn., Fond du lac County Bar Assn., Phi Beta Kappa. Avocations: gardening, house renovation, sports, cooking. Office: State Capitol Ste 114 E PO Box 7857 Madison WI 53707

LAUTENSCHLAGER, YETTA ELIZABETH, clinical social worker; b. New Haven, Jan. 23, 1942; d. Theodore Mikolinski and Yetta Christina (Zdanovich) Meehan; m. Charles M. Lautenschlager, Dec. 11, 1982 (div.); children: Yetta Ann Auger, Kristin M. Wetmore. BS, So. Conn. State U., 1964, MS, 1973; MSW, U. Conn., West Hartford, 1983. LCSW; cert. co-active coaching, employee assistance profl. Educator Bd. Edn., Hamden, Conn., 1964-81; cmty. educator Lower Naugatuck Valley Coun. Alcohol and Drug Abuse, Ansonia, Conn., 1983-84; outpatient clinician Shirley Frank Found., New Haven, 1984-85; dir., clinician Personal Growth Ctr., Hamden, 1984—; employment assistance program cons. Johnson & Johnson Med., Southington, Conn., 1995—, Midstate Med. Ctr., Meriden, Conn., 1998—. Cons. Village for Families and Children, Hartford, Conn., 1992—. Participant Mary Mashinsky campaign, Wallingford, Conn., 1984. Mem.: ASTD, NASW, Network Inc. (pres.), Internat. Fedn. Coaches, NY Women in Comm. Inc., Conn. Soc. Clin. Social Workers, Acad. Lic. Social Workers, Internat. Soc. for New Identity Process (tchg. fellow, pres.), Menninger Found. Avocations: hiking, cross country skiing, biking, reading, attending the theater.

LAUTRUP, GREER OLSEN, lawyer; BS with merit, U.S. Naval Acad., 1985; JD, U. Va., 1996. Bar: Va. 1996, D.C. 1998. Commd. ensign USN, 1985, naval intelligence officer, 1985-94; resigned, 1994; clk. to Hon. Samuel G. Wilson, chief judge U.S. Dist. Ct. for Western Dist. Va., 1996-97; assoc. Sidley & Austin, Washington, 1997—. Office: Sidley & Austin 1722 I St NW Fl 7 Washington DC 20006-3705 Fax: 202-736-8711. E-mail: glautrup@sidley.com.

LAUTTENBACH, CAROL, artist; b. New Haven, Nov. 26, 1934; d. Gustav Fredrick and Wanda M. (Eshner) Stolze; m. Francis John Lauttenbach; children: Daniel M., William J. Grad. with honors, Washington Sch. Art, Chgo., 1967. One-woman shows include Greene Art Gallery, Guilford, Conn., Carriage House Gallery Ltd., Guilford, Gallery 53, Meriden, Conn., John Slade Ely House Gallery, New Haven. Recipient Prix de Paris award, Musee Des Raymon Duncan, France, 1972, 1976, 1980, award, Salon DEs Surindependants, 1981, Gabriel D. Luchetti award, Conn. Classics Arts, 1984, 1986, 1st prize, Conn. Classic Arts, 1987, 1993, 3d prize, 1994, Rosemary Landino Meml. award, 1995, 2d prize in acrylic and oils, 1998, Guilford Savs. Bank award, Guilford Art League, 1985, Best in Show award, Mt. Carmel Art Assn., Inc., 1986, Elizabeth Greeley Meml. award, 1987, Donald L. Perlroth, Inc. award, 1988, Marc D. Rosenberg Meml. award, 1990, New Haven Savs. Bank award, 1998, Beazley Realtors award, 2000, Jean Cowels award, Shoreline Alliance Arts, 1987, Koenig Art Emporium prize, New Haven Brush & Palette Club, 1990, Henry T. & Stella King Meml. award, Arts & Crafts Assn. Meriden, 1990, Merriam Motors award, 1995, Stella King Meml. award, 1997, Jerry's Artarama cert. award, 1998, 3d prize, Nat. League Am. Pen Women, 1992, others. Mem.: Arts and Crafts Assn. Meriden (Grumbacher Silver medal 1983—84, Gold medal 1993), Conn. Classic Arts, Inc., Internat. Soc. Artists, Provincetown Art Assn., New Haven Paint and Clay Club, Conn. Acad. Fine Arts, Wallingford Hist. Soc. (life). Home: 39 Ridgewood Rd Wallingford CT 06492-2116

LAUTZENHEISER, BARBARA JEAN, insurance company executive; b. LaFeria, Tex., Nov. 15, 1938; d. Fred E. and Verna V. L. BA with high distinction, Nebr. Wesleyan U., 1960. Actuarial trainee Bankers Life Ins. Co. Nebr., Lincoln, 1960-64, programmer and systems analyst, 1964-65, asst. actuary, 1965-69, assoc. actuary, 1969-70, 2d v.p., actuary, 1970-72, v.p., actuary, 1972-80; sr. v.p. Phoenix Mut. Life Ins. Co., Hartford, Conn., 1980-84; pres. Montgomery Ward Life Ins. Co., Montgomery Ward Ins. Co., Forum Ins. Co., Schaumberg, Ill., 1984-85; prin., CEO Lautzenheiser & Assocs., Hartford, 1986—. Spokesperson for ins. industry, witness U.S. Senate and Ho. of Reps. coms., commns. and state legislatures; featured on TV, nat. mags. and newspaper articles; mem. Interim Actuarial Std. Bd., 1986-88, Actuarial Std. Bd., 1989-90; chmn. Com. for Fair Ins. Rates, 1983-86; mem. adv. com. Nat. Assn. Ins. Commrs. Life Disclosure (A) Com. working group, 1993; bd. dirs. LifeUSA Holding Co. Contbr. articles to profl. jours. Mem. Lincoln Electric Sys. Adminstrv. Bd., 1977-79; bd. dirs. Nebr. Wesleyan U., 1977-82, 89-93, Am. Coll., 1987-97. Recipient Young Alumni svc. award Nebr. Wesleyan U., 1971, Corp. Woman award Women Bus. Owners of N.Y., 1983, C.H. Poindexter award for disting. achievement and exceptional svc. to the assn. and ins. industry Nat. Assn. Life Cos., 1989. Fellow: Conf. Cons. Actuaries (dir. 1997—98), Soc. Actuaries (dir. 1975—80, exec. com. 1978—80, chmn. adminstrn. and fin. com. 1981—82, exec. com. 1981—84, dir. 1981—85, pres. 1982—83, assoc. editor The Actuary 1992—93, life nonforfeiture task force 1995—96); mem.: Am. Coun. Life Ins. (risk classification com. 1973—81), Life Office Mgmt. Assn. (corp. fin. planning com. 1974—81, chmn. 1976—78), Nat. Alliance Life Companies (bd. dirs. 1992—95), Soc. of Actuaries Found. (founding trustee 1994—98, trustee emeritus Actuarial Found. 1998—), Am. Acad. Actuaries (dir. 1974—77, chmn. com. on publs. 1980—81, disclosure working group 1994—2001, nonforfeiture working group 1994—, com. on life ins. 1995—98, life practice coun. vice chair 1998, co-chair 1998—, v.p. life 1999—2001, editl. adv. bd. mem. Contingencies mag. 2002—, pres.-elect 2002—03, pres. 2003—), Greater Hartford C. of C. (nat. policies panel 1980—84), Nebr. Actuaries Club (dir. 1969—70, 1971—74, 1992—94, chmn. 1973—74, pres. 1972—73, sec.-treas. 1971—72). Home: 17 Huntingridge Dr South Glastonbury CT 06073-3614 Office: Lautzenheiser & Assocs City Place II 185 Asylum St Fl 11 Hartford CT 06103-3611

LAUZIER, MARIJEAN, public relations executive; Grad., Rutgers U.; postgrad., Columbia U. Founder Neva Group, 1993-97, pres., CEO The Weber Group, Cambridge, 1997—. Office: The Weber Group Inc 101 Main St Ste 8 Cambridge MA 02142-1514

LAUZON, MARCIA LOUISE, performing company executive; b. Evanston, Ill., July 17, 1948; d. Charles William and Marguerite Agnes (Postill) L.; m. Edward Anthony Schalk, Oct. 24, 1970 (div. Aug. 1992); children: Kenneth Charles Schalk, Elizabeth Margaret Schalk; m. Henry Paul Boyle, Nov. 28, 1997. BA in Theatre, Western Ill. U., 1970; MA, Columbia Coll., 1992. Sec. Arthur Andersen & Co., St. Charles, Ill., 1984-88; gen. mgr. Elgin (Ill.) Choral Union, 1988-90; adminstrv. asst., concert mgr. Glen Ellyn (Ill.) Childrens Chorus, 1990-91; exec. dir. Mont. Chorale, Great Falls, 1997; founder, bd. dirs. First Night Great Falls, 2000—03. Bus. mgr. Elgin Childrens Chorus, 1989-91; adv. bd. Fox Valley Arts Coun., St. Charles, 1991-92. Bd. dirs. Elgin Choral Union, 1979-88; active People for the Am. Way, 1985—; chalice bearer, lector Episcopal Ch. of the Incarnation, Great Falls, 1994—. Follett fellow Columbia Coll., 1988. Mem. NOW, l'Association des familles Lauzon d'Amerique (chief regional del. 1997-2000). Episcopalian. Avocations: reading, organic gardening, camping, church activities, symphony choir. Home: 1600 4th Ave N Great Falls MT 59401-2726

LAVALLE, JENNIFER SUZETTE, marketing communications specialist, consultant; b. Texas City, Tex., Apr. 15, 1964; d. Peter Joseph and Billie Jo LaValle; m. Kenneth Michael Landgren, May 3, 1997. BS in Human Scis., Tex. Tech. U., 1986; MA in Comm., U. Houston, 1999. Lic. social worker, Tex. Camp/spl. projects coord. U. Tex., M.D. Anderson Cancer Ctr., Houston, 1989-90; child care placement specialist Neighborhood Ctrs., Inc., Houston, 1990-91; case mgr. II Tex. Dept. Human Svcs., Houston, 1991-94; pub. rels. intern Out There Pub. Rels., Houston, 1994-95; advt. and promotions coord. RE/MAX of Tex., Inc., Houston, 1994-95; dir. mktg. Williams, Birnberg & Andersen, LLP, Houston, 1995-96; pub. rels. cons. Houston, 1996-99; mktg. comm. mgr. Compaq Computer Corp., Houston, 1999—; now comms. specialist Honeywell IAC, Phoenix. Cons. La Trattoria, Houston; writer Wynn Solutions, Houston. Mem. Internat. Assn. Bus. Communicators, Tex. Assn. Social Workers, Tex. Tech. U. Alumni, U. Houston Alumni. Avocations: jogging, rollerblading, scuba diving. Office: Honeywell IAC 16404 N Black Canhon Hwy Phoenix AZ 85053 Home: 7613 E Phantom Way Scottsdale AZ 85255-4626 E-mail: jlavalle@hypercon.com., jennifer.lavalle@honeywell.com.

LAVALLEE, DEIRDRE JUSTINE, marketing professional; b. Woonsocket, R.I., June 14, 1962; d. Albert Paul and Margaret Justine (O'Brien) L. BS in Chem. Engring., U. R.I., 1984; MBA, U. Denver, 1995. Sales engr. NGS Assocs. Inc., Canton, Mass., 1985-87; mgr. dist. sales MKS Instruments Inc., Balt., also Boulder, Colo., 1987-96, sales and mktg. mgr. API divsn. Phoenix, 1996, product mktg. mgr. Methuen, Mass., 1996-98, cons., 1998-99; sales mgr. ea. region Applied Sci. and Tech., Inc., Woburn, Mass., 1999-2000; staff product mgr. Am. Power Conversion, 2000—01; with MSGI (Boston Ballet), 2001—. Fundraiser MSGI (Boston Ballet), 2001-; v.p., bd. dirs. Nat. Conf. Standards Labs.; mem. adv. bd. Tex. State Tech. Coll.; vol. SCORE, 1999—. Mem. AIChE (sec. (chpt.), Am. Soc. Materials, Am. Inst. Physics, Am. Vacuum Soc., Svc. Corps. Ret. Execs. Avocations: piano, sailing, skiing, choir.

LAVALLY, REBECCA JEAN, research editor, journalist; b. Danville, Ill., Dec. 9, 1949; d. Nelson Charles and Mary (Hayes) L.; m. William Warner Kirby, June 7, 1975 (div. 1988); 1 child, Sarah Jean; m. Jeffery Manuel Raimundo, Nov. 16, 1991; stepchildren: Scott, Amy, Todd. BA in Journalism, Calif. State U., 1971. Reporter Lorain (Ohio) Jour., 1972-73; reporter, copy editor Cleve. Plain Dealer, 1973-75; reporter San Jose (Calif.) Mercury News, 1975-77, UPI, Sacto., 1977-85, bur. mgr., 1985-89, Gannett News Svc., Sacto., 1989-90; editor State of Calif., Senate Office of Rsch., Sacto., 1990—. Co-author newspaper column Stepfamily Tips. Mem.: Am. River Natural History Assn. (bd. dirs. 1998—2001). Avocations: running, writing, travel. Office: Calif Senate Office of Rsch 1020 N St # 200 Sacramento CA 95814-5624

LAVE, JUDITH RICE, economics educator; b. New Brunswick, Can. came to U.S., 1961; d. J.H. Melville and G.A. Pauline (Lister) Rice; m. Lester Bernard Lave, June 21, 1965; children: Tamara Rice, Jonathan Melville. BA in Econs., Queen's U., Kingston, Ont., Can., 1957-61; MA in Econs., Harvard U., 1964, PhD, 1967; LLD, Queen's U., 1994. Lectr., asst. prof. econ. Carnegie Mellon U., Pitts., 1966-73, assoc. prof., 1973-78; dir. econ. analysis Office of Sec., Dep. of Asst. Sec. Planning and Evaluation, Washington, 1978-79; dir. office of rsch. Health Care Fin. Adminstrn., Washington, 1980-82; prof. health econ. U. Pitts., 1982—, co-dir. Ctr. for Rsch. on Health Care, 1996—, chair dept. health policy and mgmt., 2003—. Cons. Nat. Study Internal Medicine Manpower, Chgo., 1976, Wash. State Hosp. Assn., 1984, Horty, Springer & Mattern, Pitts., 1984, Hogan and Hartson, Washington, 1989, Ont. Hosp. Assn., Conn. Hosp. Assn., 1991; cons. various agys. U.S. HHS (formerly U.S. HEW), 1971-89; mem. adv. panel Robert Wood Johnson Found., Princeton, N.J., 1983-84, 96—, Leonard Davis Inst., Phila., 1984, U.S. Congress, 1977, 82, 83—; com. mem. Inst. Medicine Coms., Washington, 1975-91, Project 2000 Commn. on Future of Podiatry, Washington, 1985-86. Editl. bd. Wiley Series in Health Svcs., 1989-90, Health Svcs. Rsch., 1970-74, Inquiry, 1979-82, AUPHA Press, 1986, Jour. of Health Policy Politics and Law, Health Affairs, 1998—; co-author: Hospital Construction Act - An Evaluation of the Hill Burton Program, 1948-73, 74, Health Status, Medical Care Utilization and Outcome: A Bibliography of Empirical Studies (4 vols.) 1989, Providing Hospital Services, 1989; contbr. numerous articles to profl. jours. Mem. Prospective Payment Assessment Commn., 1993—97, Medicare Payment Adv. Commn., 1997—2000; mem. planning com. ARC, Pitts., 1986—; mem. rev. com. United Way, Pitts., 1988—90; bd. dirs. Craig House, Pitts., 1976—77, Presbyn. Sr. Care, Pitts., Jewish Health Care Found., 2002—. Woodrow Wilson fellow, 1961-62. Fellow Assn. Health Svcs. Rsch. (disting., pres. 1977-88, bd. dirs. 1983-93); mem. Found. for Health Svcs. Rsch. (pres. 1988-89, bd. dirs. 1983—), Am. Pub. Health Soc., Am. Econ. Soc. (com. mem.), Inst. Medicine, Nat. Acad. Social Ins., Robert wood Johnson Found. (coun. on econ. impact of health sys. change 1996—). Democrat. Home: 1008 Devonshire Rd Pittsburgh PA 15213-2914 Office: U Pitts A649 Pub Health Pittsburgh PA 15213

LAVECCHIA, JAYNEE, state supreme court justice; b. Paterson, N.J. m. Michael R. Cole. Grad., Douglass Coll., 1976, Rutgers U., 1979. Bar: N.J. 1980. Pvt. law practice; dep. atty. gen. divsn. of law State of N.J., dir. divsn. of law dept. law anf pub. safety, 1984-98, commr. banking and ins., 1998-99; asst. counsel to Gov. Thomas H. Kean Office of Counsel, dep. chief counsel to Gov. Thomas H. Kean; dir., chief adminstrv. law judge Office of Adminstrv. Law, 1989-94; assoc. justice N.J. Supreme Ct., Trenton, 2000—. Chair various N.J. Supreme Ct. Coms. Fellow ABA; mem. Douglss Coll. Alumnae Assn. Office: North Tower 158 Headquarters Pla Morristown NJ 07960

LAVELLE, DANIELLE M. school psychologist; b. Englewood, N.J., Dec. 15, 1967; d. Joseph William and Carol Lou LaVelle. MA, Hunter Coll., 1993; MEd, Temple U., 1996, PhD, 2002. Cert. sch. psychologist Pa., N.J. Clinician UMDNJ, Newark, 1993—97; rsch. asst. UMDNJ-Rutgers, Piscataway, NJ, 1997—2000; sch. psychologist Newark Pub. Schs., 1999—2000, Toms River (N.J.) Regional Schs., 2000—03; pvt. practice sch. psychologist Associated Psychol. Svcs., Holmdel, NJ, 2003—. Adj. prof. psychology Georgian Ct. Univ., Lakewood, NJ, 2003—. Mem.: APA, N.J. Psychol. Assn. Avocations: fitness, cooking, baking, interior decorating.

LAVENSON, SUSAN BARKER, hotel corporate executive, consultant; b. L.A., July 26, 1936; d. Percy Morton and Rosalie Laura (Donner) Barker; m. James H. Lavenson, Apr. 22, 1973 (dec. Sept. 1998); 1 child, Ellen Ruth Stanclift. BA, Stanford U., 1958, MA, 1959; PhD (hon.), Thomas Coll., 1994. Cert. gen. secondary credential tchr., Calif. Tchr. Benjamin Franklin Jr. H.S., San Francisco, 1960; tchr. French dept. Lowell H.S., San Francisco, 1960 61; v.p. Monogram Co., San Francisco, 1961-62, creative dir. N.Y.C., 1973-86; pres. SYR Corp., Santa Barbara, Calif., 1976-89; mng. ptnr. Lavenson Ptnrs., Camden, Maine, 1989—. Mem. commn. on co-edn. Wheaton Coll., Norton, Mass., 1985-87; mem. Relais et Chateaux, Paris, 1978-89, cons. World Bank Recruit Divsn., 1993. Author: Greening of San Ysidro, 1977 (Conf. award 1977). Trustee Camden Pub. Libr., 1989—95, v.p., 1991—93; vice chair bd. trustees Thomas Coll., Waterville, Maine, 1990—2001, trustee emerita, 2001—; trustee Atlantic Ave. Trust, 1989—91; founding pres. Maine chpt. Internat. Women's Forum, 1991—; mem. Coun. of Advisors Coll. of the Atlantic, Bar Harbor, Maine, 1996—2001, Ariz. Women's Forum; chair dean's adv. coun. Ariz. State U., 2002, chair coun. advisors Virginia Piper Creative Writing Ctr., 2004—. Recipient Piper award for entrepreneurial excellence, 2002. Mem. Advice Inc., Camden Yacht Club, Stanford Alumni Assn., Com. of 200 (treas. 1985-86), Women's Entrepreneur Corps, Phi Delta Kappa (Stanford U. chpt., founding mem.). Home and Office: 7841 E Shooting Star Way Scottsdale AZ 85262 E-mail: sbl1@cox.net.

LAVERTU, MONIQUE THERESE, music educator; b. Berlin, NH, Sept. 20, 1964; d. J. Paul Cusson and Lucille Regina LeClerc; m. Robin Lee Lavertu, Aug. 9, 1986; children: Monica Lea, Ryan Alan, Brandon Patrick. BS in Music Edn., 1986. Cert. Cert. tchr. N.H., 1986. Suppy and fiscal date entry profl. Rodman Naval Sta., Panama, 1987—88; music tchr. Valent Recreation Ctr., Ft. Clayton, Panama, 1986—88; presch. music tchr. Air Force Preschs., APO, Panama, 1986—87; tng. dept. sec. James River Corp., Berlin, NH, 1988—90; gen. music tchr. Berlin Jr. H.S., Berlin, NH, 1990—96; Title 1 Reading tutor Brown Elem. Sch., Berlin, 1998—2000; vis. instrumental tchr. St. Michael Sch., Berlin, 1997—; music educator Gorham (N.H.) Sch. Dist., 2000—. Trombonist Berlin Jazz, Berlin, 1988—; guest condr. Balboa Honors Band, Balboa, Panama, 1986; bell ringer St. Paul Luth. Ch., Berlin, 1994—96; flutist area churches, Berlin, 1988—. Mem.: Gorham Tchrs. Assn., N.H. Music Educators Assn., Music Educators Nat. Conf. Republican. Roman Catholic. Avocation: jazz band, bell choir, snow mobiling, golf. Home: 113 Shepard St Berlin NH 03570 Office: Gorham High Sch 120 Main St Gorham NH 03581

LAVEY, MARTHA, theater director; b. Lawrence, Kans. BA in Comms., Northwestern U., 1979, PhD in Performance Studies, 1994. Mem. ensemble Steppenwolf Theatre Co., Chgo., 1993—, artistic assoc., 1994—95, artistic dir., 1995—. Recipient Sarah Siddons award. Office: Steppenwolf Theatre Company 758 W North Ave 4th Fl Chicago IL 60610*

LAVIGNE, AVRIL, musician; b. Napanee, Ont., Can. Performer: (albums) Let Go, 2002 (nominee Grammy award Best New Artist, 2002, nominee Grammy award Best Pop Vocal Album, 2002, nominee Grammy award for Song of Year for Complicated, 2002, nominee Grammy award for Best Female Pop Vocal Performance for song Complicated, 2002, nominee Grammy award for Best Female Rock Vocal Performance for song Sk8er Boi, 2002), Under My Skin, 2004. Achievements include signed with L.A. Reid of Arista Records at age 16. Avocations: hockey, basketball, skateboarding. Office: Network Mgmt 1650 W 2nd Ave Vancouver BC Canada V6J 4R3*

LAVIN, BERNICE E. cosmetics executive; b. 1925; m. Leonard H. Lavin, Oct. 30, 1947; children: Scott Jay (dec.), Carol Marie, Karen Sue. Student, Northwestern U. Vice chairperson of bd., sec.- treas. Alberto-Culver Co.; dir., v.p., sec.- treas. Alberto-Culver U.S.A., Inc. Sec.-treas., dir. Alberto-Culver Internat., Inc.; sec.-treas. Sally Beauty Co., Inc. Office: Alberto-Culver Co 2525 Armitage Ave Melrose Park IL 60160-1163 E-mail: blavin@alberto.com.

LAVIN, LINDA, actress; b. Portland, Maine, Oct. 15, 1937; d. David J. and Lucille (Potter) L. BA, Coll. William and Mary, Williamsburg, Va., 1959. Debut: (Off-Broadway) Oh, Kay!, 1960, (Broadway) A Family Affair, 1962; appearances in revues Wet Paint, 1965, The Game Is Up, 1965, The Mad Show, 1966; with nat. touring company On a Clear Day You Can See Forever, 1966-67; mem. acting company Eugene O'Neil Playwrights' Unit, 1968; other stage appearances include It's a Bird... It's a Plane... It's Superman, 1966, Something Different, 1967, Little Murders, 1969, Cop-Out, 1969, The Last of the Red Hot Lovers, 1969 (Tony nominee), Story Theatre, 1970, The Enemy is Dead, 1973, Love Two, 1974, The Comedy of Errors, 1975, Dynamite Tonite!, 1975, Six Characters in Search of an Author, Am. Repertory Theatre, Cambridge, Mass., 1983-84 season, Broadway Bound, 1986 (Tony award 1987), Gypsy, 1990, The Sisters Rosensweig, 1993, Death Defying Acts, 1995; film appearances: See You In The Morning, 1989, I Want to Go Back Home, 1989; star: (TV series) Alice, 1976-85 (Golden Globe award 1979); star and prodr.: (TV series) Room for Two, 1992 ; prodr.: (PBS TV miniseries) The Sunset Gang, 1991; (TV mini-series) The Ring, 1996, other TV appearances on Phyllis, Family, Rhoda, Harry O; TV movies include: The Morning After, 1974, Like Mom, Like Me, 1978, A Matter of Life and Death, 1981, Another Woman's Child, 1983, A Place To Call Home, Lena: My One Hundred Children, A Dream is a Wish Your Heart Makes: The Annette Funicello Story, 1995, Best of Friends for Life, 1996, The Ring, 1996, For the Children: The Irvine Fertility Scandal, 1996, Conrad Bloom, 1998 (series); prodr., actress (TV movie) Stolen Memories: Secrets from the Rose Garden, 1995. Recipient Sat. Rev., Outer Critics Circle awards for Little Murders, Theater World award for Wet Paint. Office: 411 S Front St Wilmington NC 28401

LAVINE, THELMA ZENO, philosophy educator; b. Boston; d. Samuel Alexander and Augusta Ann (Pearlman) L.; m. Jerome J. Sachs, Mar. 31, 1944; 1 child, Margaret Vera. AB, Radcliffe Coll., 1936; A.M., Harvard U., 1937, PhD, 1939. Instr. Wells Coll., 1941-43, asst. prof., 1945-46; asst. prof. philosophy Bklyn. Coll., 1946-51; asst. prof. U. Md., 1955-57, assoc. prof., 1957-62, prof., 1962-65; Elton prof. George Washington U., 1965-85, chmn. dept., 1969-77; Clarence J.Robinson Univ. prof. George Mason U., Fairfax, Va., 1985—. Lectr., seminar cons. Inter-Am. Def. Coll., 1975—; exec. bd. Jour. of Speculative Philosophy, 2000—. Author: From Socrates to Sartre, 1980, From Socrates to Sartre: The Philosophic Quest, 1984; co-author: introduction to Collected Works of John Dewey, Vol. 16, 1990, contbg. author: Rorty and Pragmatism, 1996, contbg. author: Perspectives on Habermas, 2000, contbg. editor: Free Inquiry, 1980—, exec. bd.: Jour. of Speculative Philosophy, 2000—; contbr. articles to profl. jours., chpts. to books; author: (TV course) From Socrates to Sartre: The Philosophic Quest, 1984; co-author: introduction to Collected Works of John Dewey, Vol. 16, 1990, contbg. author: Rorty and Pragmatism, 1996, contbg. author: Perspectives on Habermas, 2000, mem. exec. bd.: Jour. Speculative Philosophy, 2000—; contbr. articles to profl. jours., revs., chpts. to books. Recipient Outstanding Faculty award U. Md., 1965, Outstanding Faculty award George Washington U., 1968, Alumnae Achievement award Radcliffe Coll., 1991; NEH sr. rsch fellow, 1980; Am. Enterprise Inst. Public Policy Research fellow, 1980-81, Va. Found. Humanities fellow, 1990; Herbert W. Schneider award contbns. to Am. Philosophy, 2000. Mem. Am. Philos. Assn. (5th Ann. Romanell lectr. 1991), Soc. Advancement Am. Philosophy (exec. com. 1979-82, pres. 1992-94), Internat. Soc. Sociology Knowledge, Internat. Soc. Polit. Psychology, Metaphys. Soc. Am., Washington Philosophy Club (pres. 1967-68), Washington Sch. Psychiatry, Forum Psychiatry and Humanities (exec. bd.), Cosmos Club, Harvard Club, SOPHIA, Phi Beta Kappa (pres. chpt. 1978-80). Home: 1625 35th St NW Washington DC 20007-2316 Office: George Mason U Robinsons Profs E 207 Fairfax VA 22030 E-mail: tzlavine@erols.com.

LAVIN-PENNYFEATHER, ROSE, artist; b. Perth Amboy, N.J., Oct. 16, 1952; d. James V.P. and Emma (Kiblosh) Lavin; m. Franco Casentini, Feb. 14, 1974 (div. 1978); 1 child, Franco K. Casentini; m. Stefano Corti, Oct. 24, 1984 (div. 1997); 1 child, Sandro J. Corti; m. Wayne Pennyfeather, May 8, 1999. Student, Georgian Ct., 1970-72, U. Florence (Italy), 1972-73. Saleswoman Correges, Rome, 1977-78; sec. McDonnell-Douglas, Rome, 1978-80, McCann-Erickson, Rome, 1980-82, RAI TV and Radio Corp., N.Y.C., 1983-84; mgr. Benetton, Woodbridge, N.J., 1984-85; sole proprietor Art Studio LC, Woodbridge, 1990-99; art tchr. Perth Amboy Cath. Schs. K-8, 1999—. Artist drawing logo contest, Tarquinia, Italy (Silver medal 1978). Directress St. Peter's Altar Guild, Perth Amboy, 1991-2002. Mem. NOW, Nat. Mus. of Women in the Arts. Democrat. Episcopalian. Avocations: karate (brown belt), swimming, cooking. Home: 677 Parker St Perth Amboy NJ 08861-2913 Office: Perth Amboy Cath Schs 680 Catherine St Perth Amboy NJ 08861-2802

LAVIZZO-MOUREY, RISA JUANITA, academic administrator, medical association administrator; MD, Harvard U., 1979; MBA, U. Pa., 1986. Sylvan Eismann prof. of medicine U. Pa., Phila., dir. Inst. of Aging, 1995; dep. adminstr. Agy. Healthcare Policy and Rsch., U.S. Dept. Health and Human Svcs., 1991; sr. v.p., dir., Health Care Group Robert Wood Johnson Found., Princeton, NJ, 2001—02, pres., CEO, 2003—. Mem. Pres.'s Commn. on Consumer Rights and Quality in the Healthcare Industry, 1997-98. Office: The Robert Wood Johnson Foundation PO Box 2316 College Road East and Route 1 Princeton NJ 08543-2316

LAVOIE, KATHY L. state representative; b. Burlington, Vt., Aug. 5, 1963; BS in Bus., Trinity Coll. Past program material planner Gen. Electric/Martin Marietta; mgr. info. sys. and tech. St. Albans Coop. Creamery; state rep. State of Vt., 2001—. Past mem. Swanton Planning Commn., Swanton Sch. Bd. Dirs.; co-pres. Swanton PTO; mem. Swanton Downtown Vitality Task Force, Holy Angels. Republican. Address: 99 Beebe Rd Swanton VT 05488 E-mail: klavoie@together.net.

LAVORI, NORA, real estate executive, lawyer; b. S.I., N.Y., Aug. 11, 1950; d. William P. and Mary E. Lavori; div. 1990; children: Liana Sterling, Alexander O. Sterling. BA, Bryn Mawr Coll., 1971; JD, Bklyn. Law Sch., 1976. Bar: N.Y. 1977. Atty., N.Y.C., 1977—; ptnr. Orleans Realty, N.Y.C., 1978—; officer The Culture Ctr., N.Y.C., 1990—. Author: Living Together, Married or Single: Your Legal Rights, 1976. Mem. real estate coun. Metro. Mus. Art, N.Y.C., 1998—; trustee Bryn Mawr (Pa.) Coll., 1999—; vice-chair Columbus Ave. Bus. Improvement Dist., N.Y.C., 2000. Mem. Women's City Club N.Y. (pres. 1995-96; hon. dir.). Home: 100 W 80th St New York NY 10024

LAW, CARLENE, state agency administrator; CEO Elk Country Motels, Inc.; mem. Ho. of Reps., 1962—, chair house travel, recreation, wildlife and cultural resources com. Bd. dirs. Jackson State U., Snow King Resort. Mem. steering com. Heritage Soc.; chmn. bd. dirs. Teton County Schs. Named Jackson Hole Citizen of the Yr., 1976, Wyo. Small Bus. Person, 1977, Bus. Person of the Yr., 1987. Mem.: Wyo. Lodging and Restaurant Assn. (past chmn., Big Wyoming award 1987), Internat. Leisure Hosts (bd. dirs.), Jackson Hole Resort Assn. (bd. dirs.). Office: Wyoming Business Council 214 W 15th St Cheyenne WY 82002

LAW, CAROL JUDITH, medical psychotherapist; b. N.Y.C., May 1, 1940; d. Aldo and Jennie (Feldman) Settimo; m. Perry J. Koll, Dec. 26, 1967 (div. Nov. 1974); 1 son, Perry J.; m. Edwin B. Law, June 1, 1979. BA, Upsala Coll., 1962; postgrad., Rutgers U., 1964-66; MA, Columbia Pacific U., 1982, PhD, 1984. Diplomate Am. Bd. Med. Psychotherapy. Pers. dir. Hotel Manhattan, N.Y.C., 1961; supr. social work Essex County, Newark, 1962-67; exec. dir. USO, Vung Tau, South Vietnam, 1967-68; dir. Dept. Health and Rehab. Svcs., Pensacola, Fla., 1968-79; therapist, tchr. Franciscan Renewal Ctr., Scottsdale, Ariz., 1982-92; pvt. practice Scottsdale, 1982-92; drug free workforce cons. Pensacola C. of C., Fla., 1992—; pres. Drug Free Workplaces, Inc., 1993—. Mem. Healthy Start of N.W. Fla.; dist 1 chmn. Alcohol, Drug Abuse and Mental Health Planning Coun. Mem. state adv. bd. Parents Anonymous, Phoenix, 1982; chmn. Gov.'s Adv. Commn. Drugs and the Elderly, Tallahassee, 1978; pres. Jaycettes, Pensacola, 1969; chmn. social com. United Way Fund, Pensacola, 1977; mem. adv. bd. USO, Pensacola, 1973, H.R.S. Dist. 1 Community Collaboration Project; trustee ORME Sch. Fellow Am. Acad. Polit. and Social Sci.; mem. Am. Assn. Pub. Adminstrs., Pensacola Country Club, Escambia County Drug Court Coalition, Fla. State C. of C. (drug issues com.,), Nat. Drugs Free Workplace Alliance (bd. dirs.), Partnership for a Drug Free Fla. (bd. dirs.), Pensacola Downtown Rotary, ESCA Rosa Work Force Bd. (chmn. personnel comm.). Roman Catholic. Home: 27 Mar Vista Cir Pensacola FL 32507-3486

LAW, CLARENE ALTA, small business owner, state legislator; b. Thornton, Idaho, July 22, 1933; d. Clarence Riley and Alta (Simmons) Webb; m. Franklin Kelso Meadows, Dec. 2, 1953 (div.); children: Teresa Lin Meadows, Charisse Meadows Haws, Steven Riley; m. Creed Law, 1973. Student, Idaho State Coll., 1950. Sec., sub. tchr. Grand County Schs., Cedar City, Utah, 1954-57; UPI rep. newspaper agy. Moab, Utah Regional Papers, Salt Lake City and Denver; auditor Wort Hotel, Jackson, Wyo., 1960-62; innkeeper, CEO Elk Country Motels, Inc., Jackson, Wyo., 1962—; rep. Wyo. Ho. of Reps., Cheyenne, 1991—. Bd. dirs. Jackson State Bank, Snow King Resort; mem. bank bd. Wyo. State Ho. Reps., 1991-98, chmn. travel com., 1993-2000, chmn. minerals and econ. devel. com., 2001-04. Chmn. sch. bd. dirs. Teton County Schs., Jackson, 1983-86; bd. dirs. Wyo. Taxpayers Assn., Bus. Coun., 1998—. Named Citizen of Yr. Jackson C. of C., 1976, 99, Bus. Person of Yr. Jackson Hole Realtors, 1987, Wyo. Small Bus. Person SBA, 1977. Mem. Wyo. Lodging and Restaurant Assn. (pres., chmn. bd. dirs. 1988-89, Big Wyo. award 1987), Soroptimists (charter), Bus. Profl. Womens Orgn. (Woman of Yr. 1975, mem. Heritage steering com. 1996—), Gov.'s 15-Mem. Bus. Coun. Republican. Avocations: grandchildren, travel, study, old cars. Address: PO Box 575 Jackson WY 83001-0575 Office: Elk County Motels Inc Box 575 43 W Pearl Jackson WY 83001

LAW, MARCIA ELIZABETH, aide; b. Spokane, Wash., Oct. 9, 1950; d. John Glen and Jean Carolyn (Lines) L.; 1 child, Michael Sean. AA, Spokane C.C., 1973. Notary public. Data entry operator, controller CyCare Sys., Spokane, Wash., 1974-78, tape libr., 1978-79; data entry operator Wash. state Dept. Employment Security, Spokane, 1986-87, Cath. Charities, Spokane, 1987, Cath. Diocese Spokane, 1987-90, Divsn. Vocat. Rehab. Dept. Health & Social Svcs., Seattle, 1990-95, sec. sr., 1994-99, counselor aide, 1999—, regional adv. com.; state internal adv. com. Stakeholders Commn. Avocations: reading, movies, cross stitch, swimming. Home: 3002 S 208th St Apt P3 Seatac WA 98198-5933 Office: 18000 International Blvd Ste 1000 Seattle WA 98188-4251 Fax: 206-439-3753. E-mail: lawm@dshs.wa.gov.

LAWER, BETSY, banker; b. Anchorage, July 27, 1949; d. Daniel H. and Betti Jane Cuddy; m. David A. Lawer, June 9, 1972; 1 child. Vice chair bd., COO 1st Nat. Bank Alaska, 1974—. Emeritus bd. dirs. Providence Health Care Found., 2001; shareholder Folie Deux Winery, 1997; bd. dirs. Commonwealth North. Co-chmn. United Way, 2000; pres. cmty. panel mem. Alyeska Pipeline Svc. Co., 2001—03. Selected as one of the Top 25 Most Powerful Alaskans Alaska Jour. of Commerce, 1999-2003; named One of 25 Women to Watch U.S. Banker, 2003. Mem.: Anchorage Athena Soc. (Athena award 2001).

LAWHON, CHARLA, editor; Grad., Duke U. With Apt. Life Mag., Des Moines; dir. editl. svcs. Meredith Design Group, 1990; editor Met. Home; dep. editor InStyle Mag., N.Y.C., 1994—98, exec. editor, 1998—2002, mng. editor, 2002—. Office: InStyle Mag 1271 Ave of the Ams New York NY 10020

LAWHON, TOMMIE COLLINS MONTGOMERY, child development and family living educator; b. Shelby County, Tex., Mar. 15; d. Marland Walker and Lillian (Tinsley) Collins; m. David Baldwin Montgomery, Mar. 31, 1962 (dec. Aug. 1964); m. John Lawhon, Aug. 27, 1967; 1 child, David Collins. BS, Baylor U., 1954; M in Home Mgmt. Edn., M in Home Econs., Tex. Woman's U., 1964, PhD, 1966, M in Child Devel. and Family Studies. Cert. tchr., Tex.; cert. family and consumer scis.; cert. family life educator. Tchr. Victoria (Tex.) Pub. Schs., 1954-55; stewardess, supr. Am. Airlines, Dallas/Ft. Worth, 1955-62; assoc. prof. home econs. Ea. Ky. U., Richmond, 1966-67, U. North Tex., Denton, 1968—, head divsn. child devel. and family studies, 1974—77, program head, 1993-94, mem. faculty senate, 1984-90, chmn. com. on coms., 1987-88, mem. com. status on women, 1984-87, mem. faculty salary student com., 1989-95, chmn., 1989-91, mem. tradition com., 1989-95, recorder, 1989-91. Bd. dirs. U. North Tex., Univ. Union, 1985-88, mem. status of women com., 1984-87, mem. student mentor com., 1990-00, mem. benefits com., 1994-00, vice chair, 1994-95, chair, 1997-98, mem. faculty sen. Faculty Handbook com., 1998—, mem. faculty sen. mentor com., 1990-96; presenter in field. Co-author: Children are Artists, 1971, Hidden Hazards for Children and Families, 1982; editor: What to Do with Children, 1974, Field Trips for Children, 1984; contbr. more than 120 articles to profl. jours. Chmn. United Way North Tex. State U., 1980-81; chmn. crusade Am. Cancer Soc., Denton County, 1982-83; chmn. nominating com. First Bapt. Ch., Denton, 1983-84, 84-85; active Girls Inc. of Met. Dallas; mem. adv. com. Career Action Ctr., 1999, chair, 2000-01; advisor North Tex. Student Coun. on Family Rels., 1994—. Recipient Presdl. award Tex. Coun. on Family Rels., 1979, Fessor Graham award North Tex. State U., 1980, Svc. award Am. Cancer Soc., 1983, Outstanding Home Economists Alumni award Baylor U., 1985; named Hon. Prof. North Tex. State U., 1975. Mem. Tex. Coun. on Family Rels. (pres. 1977-79, chmn. policy advisor com. 1986-88, nominating com. 1986-88, 94-96, chair 1994-96, family life edn. com. 1994-97, Moore-Bowman award 1994), Denton Assn. for Edn. Young Children (pres. 1970-72, 84-85, 85-86, v.p. 1986-87), Tex. Assn. Coll. Tchrs. (nominating com. 1988-89, 89-90, v.p. 1990-92, v.p. U. North Tex. chpt. 1987-88, pres. 1988-89, 89-90), Tex. Home Econs. Assn. (chmn. FLCD nominating com. 1983-84, chmn. child devel. and family rels. sect. 1988-90, sec. rep. bd. 1989-90), Nat. Coun. Family Rels. (com. 1982-83, cert. family life's continuing edn. com. 1996-99, chair elect cert. family life continuing edn. com. 1996, chair 1997-98, cert. family life edn. focus group and regional-state coord., chair 1996-97, coord. of all student asst. annual conf., 2001-02), Nat. Assn. Early Childhood Tchr. Educators (membership com. 1995-97), North Tex. Home Econs. Inter-orgnl. Coun. (adviser 1983-85), Phi Delta Kappa (pres. local chpt. 1991-92), Alpha Iota/Phi Upsilon Omicron (advisor 1970-82, chmn. nat. com. 1984-87, nat. bd. dirs. edn. found. 1990-94, com. pubs. 1991-92, vice chair ednl. found. 1992-94), Tri D Club (v.p. Baylor U. chpt. 1953-54), Univ. Grad. Club (pres. Tex. Woman's U. chpt. 1965-66). Democrat. Office: U North Tex Coll Edn Denton TX 76203

LAWLAH, GLORIA GARY, state legislator, educator; b. Newberry, S.C., Mar. 12, 1939; d. Eugene Calvin and Erline (Guess) Gary; m. John Wesley Lawlah III, 1960; children: John Wesley IV, Gloria Gene, Gary McCarrell. BS, Hampton U., 1960; MA, Trinity Coll., Washington, 1970; postgrad., George Washington U., 1968-81. Mem. Md. Ho. of Dels., 1987-90, Md. Senate, Annapolis, 1991—. Mem. Dem. State Cen. Com., 1982-86; mem. coordinating com. 26th Legis. Dist., Prince Georges, Md., 1982-87; mem. Black Dem. Council, Md. Bd. dirs. Nat. Polit. Congress Black Women, 1984-87, Coalition on Black Affairs, 1980-82, Pub. Access Cable Corp., Prince Georges City, 1980-85, Hillcrest-Marlow Planning Bd., Prince Georges City, 1982-87, Family Crisis Ctr., Prince Georges City, 1982-84; co-chair Rev. Task Force for Pub. Safety, Prince Georges City, 1982; del. Dem. Nat. Conv.; co-chair Prince Georges City Exec. 7th Councilmanic Dist. Campaign, 1982; mem. Ctr. for Aging Greater S.E. Community Found. Mem. Nat. Council Negro Women (life), NAACP (3d v.p. Prince Georges City chpt. 1980-82), Alpha Kappa Alpha, Black Dem. Council. Clubs: Links. Home: 3801 24th Ave Temple Hills MD 20748-3003 Address: State House 110 College Ave Annapolis MD 21401-8012

LAWLER, DAISY, state senator, elementary school educator, farmer, rancher; b. Walters, Okla., Dec. 24, 1942; m. Larry Lawler; 2 children. BS in Elem. Edn.; grad., Cameron U., 1974. Tchr. elem. edn., 1st grade, pre-1st, 6th grade Empire Pub. Sch., Duncan Pub. Sch.; farmer, rancher; mem. Okla. Senate, 2003—. Mem. nominating com. Girl Scouts. Mem.: AARP, AAUW, Ret. Tchrs. Assn., Beta Zeta. Democrat. Baptist. Office: State Capitol 2300 N Lincoln Blvd Rm 513 A Oklahoma City OK 73105-4808 Office Phone: 580-521-5569.

LAWLER, LINDA, disability examiner; b. Boston, Mass., Dec. 16, 1948; d. Edward Joseph Augustine and Angelina Ann (Bianculli) Lawler. BS, U. Mass., 1971. Cert. disability examiner. Junson clerk typist M.R.C. DDS, Boston, 1971—73, sonson qa tech. specialist, 1973—75, initial vocat. pss examiner, 1975—79, sonson vocat. examiner, 1979—86, acting chief vocat. disability examiner, 1994—98, asst. chief vocat. disability examiner, 1986—2003. Bd. mem. Tan Health Fox Hunting Club, 1984—86. Mem. ACLU, Boston, 1999—; contbr. Habitat for Humanity, 1999—. Recipient Commissioners Outstanding Performance award, Mass. Rehab Commn. DDS, 1996. Mem.: Nat. Assn. Disability Examiners. Avocations: physical fitness, dance, horseback riding, reading. Home: 104 Russell St Quincy MA 02171

LAWLESS, JANINE A. lawyer; m. Greg Lawless. Cert.: Nat. Elder Law Found. (elder law atty.). Ptnr. Lawless Partnership, Seattle. Fellow: Nat. Acad. Elder Law Attys. (bd. dirs., pres.-elect Wash. chpt.); mem.: Wash. State Bar Assn. (chair elder law sect.). Office: Lawless Partnership 6018 Seaview Ave NW Seattle WA 98107-2657 Business E-Mail: jlawless@lawless2.com.

LAWLEY, DEENA C. BUTTERFIELD, music educator, legal assistant; b. Valparaiso, Ind., July 27, 1974; d. David Allen Butterfield and Katherine Dena Adams Butterfield; m. Jeffrey L. Lawley, Jr., May 6, 2000. MusB in Edn., student in Edn., Valparaiso (Ind.) U., 1996—. Legal sec. Butterfield Law Office, Valparaiso, 1985—; music educator Union Twp. Schs., Valparaiso, 1998—2001, Duneland Sch. Corp., Chesterton, Ind., 2001—. Ind. sales cons. Tastefully Simple, Chesterton, 2002—. Recipient Vol. of Yr. award, United Way, 1993; grantee, Duneland (Ind.) Sch. Found., 1993, Safe Haven, 1993. Mem.: Ind. Music Educators Assn. (recording sec. 1999—, exhibits chmn. 1999—), Valpo Area Dem. Club, Alpha Xi Epsilon Alumnae Assn. (v.p. 2001—). Greek Orthodox. Home: 1504 N Campbell Valparaiso IN 46385

LAWLIS, PATRICIA KITE, air force officer, computer consultant; b. Greensburg, Pa., May 5, 1945; d. Joseph Powell Jr. and Dorothy Theresa (Allshouse) Kite; m. John Charles Ryan, Feb. 6, 1965 (div. 1973); m. Mark Craig Lawlis, Sept. 17, 1976 (div. 1983); 1 child, Elizabeth Marie. BS in Math., East Carolina U., 1967; MS in Computer Sci., Air Force Inst. Tech., 1982; PhD in Computer Sci., Ariz. State U., 1989. Cert. secondary math. tchr. Employment counselor Pa. State Employment Svc., Washington, Pa., 1967-69; math. tchr. Fort Cherry Sch. Dist., McDonald, Pa., 1969-74; commd. 2d lt. USAF, 1974, advanced through grades to lt. col., 1994; data base mgr. Air Force Space Command, Colorado Springs, Colo., 1974-77; computer sys. analyst USAF in Europe, Birkenfeld, Germany, 1977-80; prof. computer sci. Air Force Inst. Tech., Wright-Patterson AFB, Ohio, 1982-86, 89-94; ret. USAF, 1994; computer cons., pres. C.J. Kemp Systems, Inc., Fairborn, Ohio, 1983—2003; women's dir. Sr. Softball USA, Sacramento, 2002—; pres. 2nd Chance Sports, Inc., Phoenix, 2002—; engring. specialist Jacobs Sverdrup, 2003—. Ada cons., Ada Joint Program Office, Washington, 1984-94. State treas. NOW, Pa., 1973-74; chair women's adv. coun. Nat. Sr. Softball Summit, Sacramento, 2003--. Recipient Mervin E. Gross award Air Force Inst. Tech., 1982, Prof. Ezra Kotcher award, 1985. Mem. Computer Soc. of IEEE, Assn. Computing Machinery, Tau Beta Pi (v.p. chpt. 1981-82), Upsilon Pi Epsilon. Office: 2nd Chance Sports Inc PO Box 93514 Phoenix AZ 85070-3514 also: Jacobs Sverdrup 4414 Centerview Dr Ste 264 San Antonio TX 78228 E-mail: lawlis@aol.com.

LAWRENCE, ANNETTE, artist; b. N.Y.C., 1965; BFA, U. Hartford, 1986; MFA, Md. Inst., 1990. Mem. artist com. Lawndale Art and Performance Ctr., 1991—95; mem. cmty. arts panel Tex. Commn. on Arts, 1995—96; artist-in-residence Cmty. Artist's Collective, Houston, 1990—91, Housing Authority City of Houston, 1992—93, Glassell Sch. Art, Houston, 1993; guest artist Tex. So. U., Houston, 1992; cons. HSPVA, Houston, 1993—94; affiliate artist U. Houston, 1995; adj. faculty U. Houston-Downtown, 1993—96, U. North Tex., Denton, 1996—. One-woman shows include ArtPace, San Antonio, 1995, Art League of Houston, 1996, Gerald Peters Gallery, Dallas, 1996, one-man shows include, 1998, one-woman shows include Women and Their Work, Austin, 1996, African Am. Mus., Dallas, 1998, exhibited in group shows at Minor Injury Gallery, Bklyn., 1986, Bronx River Art Gallery, N.Y., 1987, Manhattan Cable, N.Y.C., 1988, Meyerhoff Gallery, Balt., 1990, Laguna Gloria Mus. Art, Austin, Tex., 1992, Inman Gallery, Houston, 1993, Tex. Gallery, 1994, Gerald Peters Gallery, Dallas, 1995, 1996, 1997—98, U. Houston, Clear-lake, Tex., 1998, numerous others, Represented in permanent collections Dallas Mus. Art, ArtPace, San Antonio, Mus. Fine Arts, performances include, Sangoma, 1990, Square One, 1990, Amazon Papers, 1991, Parachute Project, 1995. Recipient Artist award, Cultural Arts Coun., Houston, 1994, Arch and Anne Giles Kimbrough award, Dallas Mus. Art, 1994; fellow W.E.B. Dubois fellow, W.Va. U., 1987—88. Patricia Robert Harris fellow, Md. Inst., 1988—90, Skowhegan Camille Hanks Cosby fellow, African-Am. Artists, 1996; Art Matters grantee, 1994. Office: care Gerald Peters Gallery 2913 Fairmount St Dallas TX 75201-1455

LAWRENCE, DEBORAH JEAN, quality assurance professional; b. San Jose, Calif., June 25, 1960; BA in Math., San Jose State U., 1982; MS in Stats., Stanford U., 1985. Math. aide Info. Mgmt. Internat., Moffet Field, Calif., 1980-82; group engr. Lockheed Missiles and Space Co., Sunnyvale, Calif., 1982-89; mgr. quality assurance Analog Devices, Inc., Santa Clara, Calif., 1989—. Reengring. spl. interest group leader Coun. for Continuous Improvement, 1994-96, QS 9000 spl. interest group leader, 1995-97. Author tech. papers. Mem. Am. Soc. for Quality Control (sr. mem., cert. engr.), Am. Statis. Assn. Office: Analog Devices Inc 1500 Space Park Dr Santa Clara CA 95054-3434

LAWRENCE, ESTELENE YVONNE, musician, transportation executive; b. Lynch, Ky., Aug. 10, 1933; d. Samuel Coleridge and Florence Estelle (Gardner) Taylor; m. Otto Lee Lawrence, Sept. 14, 1957; children: Stuart, Neil, Adelbert. Student Fenn Coll., 1953-60, Cleve. Inst. Music, 1955-56, John Carroll U., 1977-78, Northeastern U., 1979-80; BA Cleve. State U., 1993. Stenographer Cleve. Transit System/Regional Transit Authority, 1951-76, tng. asst., 1976-78, pers. devel. asst., 1978-82, dist. adminstr., 1983-86; supr./mgmt. skills instr. RTA, 1976-86, dir. tng. and career devel., 1986-88. Dir. music Friendly United Baptist Ch., 1947-95; piano tchr., 1953-73; minister of music Mt. Nebo Baptist Ch., 1995—; pianist/organist Nat. Bapt. Conv., 1971, 80. Publicity chmn. Moses Cleve. Sch. PTA, 1965-75; audit chmn. RTA Main Office Credit Union, 1980-83; dist. sec. Boy Scouts Am., 1982-83; chmn. adv. bd. Baldwin Wallace Coll., 1984-88; mem. adv. bd. Cleve. Mgmt. Devel. Consortium, 1985-88; chief musician RTA Choir; mem. Cleve. Choral Union, 1992-96. Mem. Am. Choral Dirs. Assn., Cleve. Mgmt. Seminars (treas. 1979-81, pres. 1981-83), Conf. Minority Transp. Ofcls., Phi Kappa Gamma (pres. 1966-69), Mu Phi Epsilon (historian 1990-91, chorister 1991-92, pres. 1992-93), Alpha Kappa Alpha. Mem. A.M.E. Ch. Clubs: East 153d St. (v.p. 1980—), East Ky. Social. Home: 4066 E 153rd St Cleveland OH 44128-1926

LAWRENCE, GWYNN LEWIS, language educator; b. Hollywood, Calif., Sept. 7, 1953; d. Robert Eli and Catherine Louise Lewis; m. Mark Frazer Lawrence, June 1, 1998; 1 child, Robert Eli ; m. Mohammad Reza Sadeghian, Jan. 21, 1980 (div.); children: Roya Lewis, Madalynn Rose, Hannah Kay. BA, U. Calif., LA, 1975, cert. in ESL, 1977, MA, 1978, PhD, 1998. Tchr. LA (Calif.) Unified Sch. Dist., 1977—78; tchr. ESL U. Cmty. Adult Sch., LA, 1979—; writer and rschr. Law Office Leo Terrel, Beverly Hills, Calif., 1991—92; tchr. Beverly Hills (Calif.) Adult Sch., 1994—98; curriculum writer LA (Calif.) Unified Sch. Dist., 1998; adj. prof. Santa Monica (Calif.) Coll., 2000—02. Mem. Calif. Coun. Adult Edn., 1995—. Editor: History Standards K-12, 1991. Mem.: U. Calif. L.A. Alumni Assn.

Avocations: swimming, piano, tango. Home: 249 South Clark Drive Beverly Hills CA 90211 Office: U HS 11800 Texas Ave Los Angeles CA 90025

LAWRENCE, JOAN WIPF, former state legislator; m. Wayman; children: Wayman, Anne, David. RN, L.I. Coll. Hosp. Sch. Nursing, 1952; student, Douglass Coll., 1952-53, Rutgers U., 1953, Ohio State U., 1968-70. Rep. Dist. 87 Ohio Ho. Dist., 1983-92, rep. Dist. 80, 1993-99; dir. Ohio Dept. Aging, 1999—. Mem. Big Walnut Bd. Edn., 1970-73. Mem. LWV (Ohio pres. 1975-77), YWCA, Women's Polit. Caucus, Ohio Reps. for Choice, Farm Bur. Office: Ohio Dept Aging 9th Fl 50 W Broad St Fl 9 Columbus OH 43215-3301

LAWRENCE, JOANIE See **MCEWEN, JOAN GRACE**

LAWRENCE, KATHERINE MICHELE, government affairs consultant; b. Davenport, Iowa, Apr. 18, 1970; d. Michael Joseph and Marianne Lawrence. BA, Ea. Ill. U., 1992. Asst. legis. liaison Ill. EPA, Springfield, 1993—94; dir. govt. affairs Ill. Mfrs. Assn., Springfield, 1994—2002; pres. KML Consulting, Springfield, 2002—. Sec. Sojourn Shelter and Svc., Springfield, 2001. Mem.: NAFE. Avocations: golf, travel. Office: KML Consulting 421 W Edwards Springfield IL 62704

LAWRENCE, LAUREN, author, dreams expert, psychoanalytical theorist, psychoanalyst; b. N.Y.C., June 26, 1950; d. Jack and Elaine (Gaumont) Soefer; m. D. Henry Lawrence, June 24, 1972; 1 child, Graham. MA in Psychology, New Sch. for Social Rsch., 1993. Psychoanalyst, N.Y.C., 1992—. Author: Dream Keys: Unlocking the Power of Your Unconscious Mind, 1999, Dream Keys for Love, 1999, Dream Keys for the Future: Unlocking the Secrets of Your Destiny, 2000, La Llave De Los Suenos, 2001, A Quoi Revent Les Stars, 2002, Private Dreams of Public People, 2002; columnist: N.Y. Daily News, Newport This Week, Swing Mag., George Mag.; contbr. sci. papers and articles to profl. jours. and mags.; performer: (TV series) The Dream Zone; appeared on numerous TV and radio shows. Friend N.Y. Psychoanalytic Soc. Achievements include founding of a third person analysis, a new method of analysis in clinical practice, which provides the analysand a narrational objectivity; the covert seduction theory, which expounds the dangers of a non-physical parental seduction, the Actualized Dream, a conscious behavioral manifestation of symbolic material-unconscious desires that manifest themselves during consciousness through extreme behavioral acts, the undisclosed visual cliche, as an attribute or assessment drawn from a visual that leads to a cliche, and the externalized dream as a manifestation of a vision. Home and Office: 31 E 72d St New York NY 10021-4146 Office Phone: 212-737-3911. E-mail: LaurenLawrence@aol.com.

LAWRENCE, MARILYN EDITH (MARILYN GUTHRIE), association executive; b. Oct. 5, 1946; d. George Nelson and Marjorie Estelle (Field) G.. AAS, SUNY, Morrisville, 1966. Various secretarial positions, 1966—75; exec. asst. Northeastern Retail Lumbermens Assn., Rochester, NY, 1975—79, sr. v.p. Wellesley, Mass. and Rochester, 1979—86; placement specialist Renda Pers. Cons., Rochester, 1986—89; exec. dir. Oil Heat Inst. Upstate N.Y., Rochester, 1989—92; owner Profl. Bus. Svcs., Newark, NY, 1992—94; program dir. Assn. Mgmt. Svc., Rochester, 1992—94; exec. dir. Internat. Mcpl. Signal Assn., 1994—. Mem.: Am. Soc. Assn. Execs. Republican.

LAWRENCE, MARY JOSEPHINE (JOSIE LAWRENCE), artist, retired library official, retired library director; b. Carbondale, Pa., Mar. 9, 1932; d. Domenick Anthony and Teresa Rose (Zaccone) Gentile; m. John Paul Lawrence, Apr. 25, 1953 (dec. June 1977); children: Mary Josephine, Jane Therese, Susan Michele. BFA, Mass. Coll. Art, 1989; postgrad., Chelsea (Eng.) Sch. Art, 1989, San Pancrazio Art Sch., Tuscany, Italy, 1990, 91, 92; cert. in grad. studies, Guangzhou Acad. Fine Arts, China, 1993; postgrad., Md. Inst. Fine Art, Sorrento, Italy, 1994, Ctrl. Acad. Arts and Design, Beijing, 1997, Skopelos, Greece, 1998, N.Y. Sch. Visual Arts, Barcelona, Spain, 1999, Internat. Sch. Art, Umbria, Italy, 2000. Sales clk. Gorins, 5&10, Jordan Marsh, Boston, 1946-49; clk.-typist, sec. John Hancock Ins. Co., Boston, 1950-53; machine operator, quality control supr. Rust Craft Greeting Cards, Dedham, Mass., 1961-69; restaurant hostess Tony's Villa, Waltham, Mass., 1972-73; mus. sales clk., artist John F. Kennedy Libr., Boston, 1979-87, mgr. mus. store, supr., 1988-2000; freelance artist, 2000—. Tchr.'s asst. San Pancrazio Art Sch., 1992; guest appearance TAKE TWO cable TV, Channel 11, 1996, Walpole Cmty. TV, 2001, WEZE Family 590 Talk Show, 2001. One woman shows include de Havilland Fine Art Gallery, Boston, 1997, Dr. James McDermott Gallery, Boston, 1996, Cranberry Cafe, Boston, 1997; exhibited in group shows at South Shore Arts Ctr., Cohasset, Mass., 1991, N. River Arts Soc., Marshfield Hills, Mass., 1994 (Best of Show), Boston Visual Artists Union, 1996, de Havilland Fine Art Gallery, Boston, 1997, United South End Open Studios, 1998, Artana Gallery, Framingham, Mass., 2000. Juror Quincy Art Assn., 1996, 98, 2002, Weymouth Art Assn., 1995, 97, Arts Affair, 1999. Recipient Outstanding Achievement award, Nat. Archives and Rsch. Adminstrn., 1989, 1994, 1996—97, Svc. award, 1990, Hon. mention award, South Shore Arts Ctr., 1991, Blue Ribbon Mems. award, 2003, Best of show award, De Havilland Fine Arts Gallery, 1992, honorium, Weymouth Art Assn., 1995, 1997, Quincy Art Assn., 1996, 1998, 2002; grantee Vt. Studio Ctr., 2002, 2004. Mem. Boston Visual Artist Union, de Havilland Fine Art Gallery, South Shore Art Ctr., North River Arts Soc., Nat. Mus. Women in Arts (charter), Milton Art Mus. (Hon. Mention award 1998), United S. End Artists, Fuller Mus. Art., South Boston Arts Assn. Democrat. Roman Catholic. Personal E-mail: josielawrence@comcast.net.

LAWRENCE, MERLOYD LUDINGTON, editor; b. Pasadena, Calif., Aug. 1, 1932; d. Nicholas Saltus and Mary Lloyd (Macy) Ludington; m. Seymour Lawrence, June 21, 1952 (div. 1984); children: Macy, Nicholas; m. John M. Myers, 1985 AB, Radcliffe Coll., 1954, MA, 1957. With Houghton Mifflin Co., 1955-57; free lance translator, 1957-65; editor, treas., v.p. Seymour Lawrence Inc., Boston, 1965-83; pres. Merloyd Lawrence, Inc., Boston, 1983—. Translator works of Flaubert and Balzac, modern French fiction, German and Swedish children's books. Treas., v.p. Milford House Properties, Ltd., N.S., Can., 1975-80; trustee Milton (Mass.) Acad., 1974-82; mem. com. clin. investigations Beth Israel/Deaconess Hosp.; bd. dirs. Northeast Wilderness Trust, 2002—. Mem. Am. Translators Assn., New Eng. Forestry Found. (exec. bd. officer 1989—), Mass. Audubon Soc. (dir. 1974-2001, exec. com. 1992-2001, hon. dir. 2001—), Tavern Club, Phi Beta Kappa. Home: 102 Chestnut St Boston MA 02108-1120 Office: 102A Chestnut St Boston MA 02108-1120

LAWRENCE, NINA, publishing executive; Assoc. pub. Mademoiselle mag. Conde Nast Pubs., N.Y.C., 1994-96; pub. Modern Bride mag. Primedia Inc., N.Y.C., 1996-98; pub. Bride's mag. Conde Nast Pubs., N.Y.C., 1999—.

LAWRENCE, PAULA DENISE, physical therapist; b. Ft. Worth, May 21, 1959; d. Roddy Paul and Kay Frances (Spivey) Gillis; m. Mark Jayson Lawrence, Apr. 20, 1985 (div. 1998). BS, Tex. Women's U., 1982. Lic. phys. therapist, Tex., Calif. Sales mgr. R. and K Camping Ctr., Garland, Tex., 1977-82; staff phys. therapist Longview (Tex.) Regional Hosp., 1982-83, dir. phys. therapy, 1983-87, dir. rehab. svcs., 1987-88; staff phys. therapist MPH Home Health, Longview, Tex., 1983-84; owner, pres. Phys. Rehab. Ctr., Hemet, Calif., 1988—. Mem. adv. com. div. health occupations Kilgore (Tex.) Coll., 1985-88; mem. profl. adv. bd. Hospice Longview, 1985-88. Bd. dirs. V.I.P. Tots; active Valle Vista PTA, sec. 1998-2000, 01-03; v.p. 2000-2001; v.p. Dartmouth Mid. Sch. PTSA, 2002-03, sec., 2003—. Mem. NAFE, Am. Phys. Therapy Assn., Calif. Phys. Therapy Assn., Am. Bus. Women's Assn. (v.p. 1987, 89, pres. 1990, Woman of Yr. 1988, 91), Assistance League Aux., Soroptomist (corr. sec. 1992, dir. 1993-95, 97-98, sec. 1995-97, v.p. 1998-2000, pres. 2000-2001, bd. dirs. 2001-02), Hemet C. of C. (sec. 1998-99, bd. dirs. 1996-99), Psi Chi, Omega Rho Alpha. Avocation: travel. Home: 43725 Mandarin Dr Hemet CA 92544-8529 Office: 901 S State St Ste 500 Hemet CA 92543-7185 E-mail: prch@linkline.com.

LAWRENCE, RUTH, writer, illustrator; b. Bklyn., Aug. 1, 1926; d. Joseph Katz and Sara Rachel Leibick; m. Martin Robert Lawrence, June 4, 1950 (div. June 1975); children: Sandra, Audrey. AA, Nassau C.C., 1968; BA, C.W. Post Coll., 1975. Artist Merrick (N.Y.) Libr., 1973—75; worker U.S. Govt., 1980—95; artist, poet, tchr., lectr., children's book illustrator, 1995—. Cons. Merrick Art Gallery, 1976. Author: My Famous Grandma, 1996, Mostly Limericks for the Millennium, 1998, Columbus, 1999, Barbara Bubbles, 2000. Recipient 1st in oil award, Nassau C.C., Garden City, N.Y., 1975, Best in Show award, 1975. Mem.: Suburban Art League.

LAWRENCE, RUTH ANDERSON, pediatrician, clinical toxicologist; b. N.Y.C. d. Stephen Hayes and Loretta (Harvey) A.; m. Robert Marshall Lawrence, July 4, 1950; children, Robert Michael, Barbara Asselin, Timothy Lee, Kathleen Ann, David McDonald, Mary Khalil, Joan Margaret, John Charles, Stephen Harvey. BS in Biology summa cum laude, Antioch Coll., 1945; MD, U. Rochester, 1949. Internship and residency in pediatrics Yale New Haven (Conn.) Hosp., 1949-50; asst. resident in Medicine Yale New Haven (Conn.) Community Hosp., 1950-51; postdoctoral fellow Yale New Haven Hosp., 1951, chief resident newborn svc., 1951; cons. in medicine U.S. Army, Ft. Dix, N.J., 1952; from clin. instr. to sr. instr. in pediatrics U. Rochester, N.Y., 1952-64, assoc. resident, 1957-58, asst. prof., 1964-70, assoc. prof., 1970-85, prof. pediatrics, ob.-gyn., 1985—. Rsch. pediatrician, Monroe County Health Dept., Rochester, 1952-58; dir. Finger Lakes Regional Poison Control Ctr., 1958—; chief nursery svc. Strong Meml. Hosp., Rochester, 1960-73, chief dept. pediatrics, The Highland Hosp., Rochester, 1960-91; adj. prof. Sch. Pub. Health, SUNY, Albany, 1996-99; rsch. in field. Author: Breastfeeding: A Guide for the Medical Profession, 5th edit., 1999; editor: various periodicals; contbr. numerous articles to profl. publs. Mem. Safety Coun. Rochester and Monroe County, also past pres.; bd. dirs., past pres. Life Line. Recipient Gold Medal award U. Rochester Alumni Assn., 1979, William Keeler award Rochester Safety Coun., 1982, Civic Contribution citation Rochester Safety Coun., 1984, Career Achievement award Girl Scouts U.S. of Genesee Valley, 1987, Rochester Diocesan award for women, St. Bernard's Inst., 1989, Albert David Kaiser medal, 1991, Chamber Civic Health Care award, 1996, Humanism in Medicine award Am. Assn. Med. Colls., 1999, Edward Mott Moore award, Monroe County Med. Soc., 2001, Nat. Best Physician award, 2002-03, Lifetime Achievement award Healthy Children, 2003, 1st Annual Leading Lady award Leading Lady Cos., Beachwood, Ohio, 2003, numerous svc. awards; named Woman of Yr. Girl Scouts U.S. of Monroe County, 1968; hon. fellow Am. Sch. Health Assn., 1960, rsch. fellow Jackson Meml. Rsch. Labs., 1945. Fellow Am. Pediatric Soc., Am. Acad. Clin. Toxicology (past trustee, Lifetime Achievement award 2002); mem. Internat. Soc. for Rsch. in Human Milk and Lactation (exec. com. 1995-98), Human Milk Banking Assn. N.Am. (adv. bd.), NAS (subcom. on nutrition during lactation), Acad. Breastfeeding Medicine (founding bd. dirs. 1994—, pres. 1997-98), Alpha Omega Alpha. Roman Catholic. Office: U Rochester Sch Medicine 601 Elmwood Ave Rochester NY 14620-2945 E-mail: ruth_lawrence@urmc.rochester.edu.

LAWRENCE, SALLY CLARK, retired academic administrator; b. San Francisco, Dec. 29, 1930; d. George Dickson and Martha Marie Alice (Smith) Clark; m. Henry Clay Judd Jr., July 1, 1950 (div. Dec. 1972); children: Rebecca, David, Nancy; m. John I. Lawrence, Aug. 12, 1976; stepchildren: Maia, Dylan. Docent Portland Art Mus., Portland, Oreg., 1958-68; gallery owner, dir. Sally Judd Gallery, Portland, Oreg., 1968-75; art ins. appraiser, cons. Portland, Oreg., 1975-81; interim dir. Mus. Art Sch. Pacific NW Coll. Art, Portland, Oreg., 1981—82, asst. dir., 1982—83, acting dir., 1983—84, dir., 1984—94, pres., 1994—2003, pres. emerita, 2003—, prof. emerita, 2003—. Bd. dir. Art Coll. Exch. Nat. Consortium, 1982-91, pres., 1983-84. Bd. dir. Portland Arts Alliance, Portland, Oreg., 1987—2003, Assn. Ind. Coll. of Art and Design, 1991—2003, pres., 1995—96, sec., 1996—2001. Fellow: Nat. Assn. Sch. Art and Design (life; bd. dirs. 1984—91, 1994—2002, pres. 1996—99); mem.: Oreg. Ind. Coll. Assn. (bd. dirs. 1981—2003, exec. com. 1989—94, pres. 1992—93, v.p. 2001—03), Pearl Arts Found. (chair bd. dirs. 2000—03).

LAWRENCE, STAR, marketing executive, film company executive; b. Waukegan, Ill., Mar. 5, 1944; d. George Herbert and Hope Delinda (Warren) L.; 1 child, Kelsey Hope. BA, George Washington U., 1966. Tchr. editor Am. Chem. Soc., Washington, 1966; proposal writer Krohn-Rhodes Inst., Washington, 1966-67; legis. counsel Aerospace Industries Assn., Washington, 1967-82; v.p., co-owner Data Specific, Washington, 1985-86; pres. Angel Watch Prodn., Washington, 1992, Success Stories, Washington, 1996—. Contbg. editor: Comm. Concepts, 1983—86; editor, pub., creator: newsletters Get It Done!, 1987—88, Cheap Relief, 1988—2004; prodr.: (films) OMNIFAX, 1994. Recipient Winner Bronze Telly award Telly Awards, Inc., 1995. Mem. Women in Film. Democrat. Methodist. Avocation: essayist. Address: 734 W El Alba Way Chandler AZ 85225-2620

LAWRENCE, SUSAN, art dealer; b. N.Y.C., Dec. 10, 1939; d. Sidney and Anne (Marom) L.; m. Charles David Nicol, July 1, 1962 (div. Sept. 1973); 1 child, David Lawrence. BA in English, U. Kans., 1961; student art history, U. Mo., 1974-76. Art dealer Lawrence Gallery, Kansas City, Mo., 1976-84, Batz/Lawrence Gallery, Kansas City, Mo., 1984-88, Susan Lawrence Fine Arts, Kansas City, Mo., 1988—. Coord. film prodn., Kansas City, 1988-90; coord. med. edn. Trinity Luth. Hosp., Kansas City, 1990-2001; edn. coord. Vis. Nurse Assn., Kans. City, Mo., 2001—; bd.dirs. Ko-ARTS. Mem. Kansas City Film Soc. (founder, bd. dirs., dir. membership 1990—), Contemporary Art Soc., Kansas City Artists Coalition, Nelson-Atkins Mus. Friends Art. Avocations: movies, theatre, antiques and collectibles, ballroom dancing, gourmet cooking. Home and Office: Susan Lawrence Fine Art 804 W 48th St Apt 305 Kansas City MO 64112-1817

LAWRENCE, TRUDY KAY, art educator; b. Belleville, Ill., Aug. 29, 1942; d. William G. and Gertrude M. Kulessa; m. Gordon L. Lawrence, July 25, 1971. BA, So. Ill. U., Carbondale, 1965; MA in Tchg., Webster U., Mo., 1989, postgrad., 1989—90. Cert. art tchr. Ill., tchr. Mo. Art tchr. Harmony-Emge-Ellis Sch. Dist., Belleville, Ill., 1965—68, Ferguson-Florissant Schs., Mo., 1968—2003. Chair dept. art Ferguson Mid. Sch., Mo., 1970—2003, mem. bldg. improvement com., 1990—92. Mem.: NEA, Mo. Edn. Assn., Sigma Kappa. Avocations: lake house, painting, hiking, bicycling, bird-watching. Office: Ferguson Mid Sch 701 January Ave Ferguson MO 63135

LAWRENCE, WENDY B. astronaut; b. Jacksonville, Fla., July 2, 1959; d. William P. Lawrence and Anne Haynes. BS in Ocean Engring., U.S. Naval Acad., 1981; MS in Ocean Engring., MIT, 1988. Naval aviator USN, 1982; with Helicopter Combat Support Squadron HC-6; officer in charge of detachment ALFA Helicopter Anti-Submarine Squadron Light THIRTY HSL-30; physics instr., novice women's crew coach U.S. Naval Acad., 1990-92; mission specialist, astronaut NASA, 1992—, flight software verifier Shuttle Avionics Integration Lab., astronaut office asst. tng. officer, ascent/entry flight engr., blue shift orbit pilot on STS-67, 1995, dir. ops. Gagarin Cosmonaut Tng. Ctr., with crew on STS-86 on space shuttle Atlantis, 1997, with crew on STS-91 on space shuttle Discovery, 1998. Recipient Capt. Winifred Collins award for inspirational leadership Nat. Navy League, 1986. Mem. Assn. Naval Aviation, Women Mil. Aviators, Naval Helicopter Assn., Phi Kappa Phi. Office: NASA Lyndon B Johnson Space Ctr Houston TX 77058

LAWRENCE-COX, NANCY NELL, artist, retired executive secretary; b. Columbus, Miss., Mar. 4, 1934; d. James Edward and Elizabeth Caplinger (Land) Lawrence. BFA, U. Ark., Little Rock, 1983, postgrad., 1983-84. Office boy Miss. State Hwy. Dept., Columbus, 1952-53; clk.-typist FBI, Washington, 1953-54; sec.-automation Little Rock AFB, Ark., 1984-2000; ret., 2000. Exhibited sculptures at U. Ark., 1982 (Best of Show 1981-82), Centre International D'Art Contemporain, 1984, photography at Les Editions Arts et Images du Monde, 1990, Who's Who Internat. Art, Lausanne, Switzerland, 1993. Civic vol. Yes We Can Team 314th Supply Squadron Care Team, 1989-94. Recipient Cert. of Recognition, Jacksonville C. of C., 1991, other awards. Home: 13 Phyllis Cir Jacksonville AR 72076-2403

LAWS, ANGELA KAY, gifted and talented educator; b. Columbia, Tenn., Feb. 6, 1976; d. Michael Ray and Jewel Dean Johnson; m. Eric Dan Laws, July 11, 1998. B in Elem. Edn., U. Tenn., Martin, 1998; M in Ednl. Leadership, Harding U., 2003. Cert. 1st - 6th grade elem. tchr. Ark., 5th - 8th grade sci. tchr. Ark., K-12 gifted and talented tchr. Ark., Pathwise mentor tng. Ark., Pre-K - 12 adminstr. Ark. 6th grade sci. tchr. Humphreys County Sch. Dist., McEwen, Tenn., 1998—2000; k-12 gifted and talented coord. Pangburn (Ark.) Pub. Sch. Dist., 2000—. Gifted and talented adv. bd. Wilbur D. Mills Coop., Beebe, Ark., 2000—; tchr. kids coll. Harding U., Searcy, Ark., 2001—; bd. dirs. AGATE. Named Tchr. of the Yr., Wal-Mart, 2003; recipient Barnabas award, Ch. of Christ, 1997, Outstanding Dedication and Profl. Leadership in Edn., U. Tenn., 1998, Outstanding Dedication to Edn., Harding U., 2003; grantee, Ark. Cmty. Found., 2002. Mem.: Ark. Assn. Gifted Edn. Administrs., Ark. Gifted and Talented Edn. Assn. (bd. dirs. 2003), Women's Found. Ark. Church Of Christ. Avocations: travel, camping, shopping for unusual finds. Office: Pangburn Pub Schs 1100 Short St Pangburn AR 72121 Office Phone: 501-728-4912. Personal E-mail: angielaws@hotmail.com.

LAWSON, BETH ANN REID, strategic planner; b. N.Y.C., Jan. 9, 1954; d. Raymond Theodore and Jean Elizabeth (Frinks) Reid; m. Michael Berry Lawson, Jan. 29, 1983; children: Rayna, Sydney. BA, Va. Tech., 1976; MPA, Golden Gate U., 1983; JD, Regent U. Law, 2004. From systems analyst I to support ops. asst. City of Virginia Beach, Va., 1977-93, water conservation coord., 1993-94; owner Strategic Planning and Teamwork, Virginia Beach, 1993—; cons. Resort Leadership Coun., 1998-99. Cons., 1996-2000, Lifesaving Mus. Va., 1994, 98, Virginia Beach C.A.R.E. Com., 1995, Virginia Beach Rescue Squad, 1992—, Virginia Beach Mcpl. Employees Fed. Credit Union, 1992—, Virginia Beach Resort Area Adv. Commn., 1993, Virginia Beach Conv. and Visitors Devel. Bur., 1991-93, 98—; customer svc. trainer Virginia Beach Hotel/Motel Superhost, 1995—. Sunday sch. tchr. Wycliffe Presbyn. Ch., Virginia Beach, 1996—, softball coach, 1997. Mem. Virginia Beach Rescue Squad (hon., life), Va. Tech. Alumni Assn. (pres. 1982-83), Rotary (Outstanding Employee award 1993). Avocations: tennis, movies, planning, writing. Home: 701 Earl Of Warwick Ct Virginia Beach VA 23454-2910 Office: Strategic Planning and Teamwork 701 Earl Of Warwick Ct Virginia Beach VA 23454-2910

LAWSON, CAROLE JEAN, religious educator, author, poet; b. San Antonio, June 18, 1944; d. Albert Joseph and Pearl Nettie (Garner) Fuller; m. James Ray Lawson, Sept. 7, 1962; children: Regina Anne (Lawson) Kacho, Clinton Ray. Founder Love Makes the World Go Around in Peace, Ft. Worth, 1988—; founder, dir. Healing Thru Love Seminars, Ft. Worth, 1988—; founder Sunshine 'n Rainbows Stress Overcomers, Ft. Worth, 1985-87; founder, head Omni-Vision Pub. and Prodns., Ft. Worth, 1990—93, 2002—. Life mgmt. cons., 2003—. Pub. editor Omni Vision newsletter, 1985-93, 2002-; author: To God Be the Glory, poetry collection, 1988-90, My Rocky Mountain High, 1989, The Reflection of God's Smile, 1991. Sec. Lightly Speaking Forum, Ft. Worth, 1987—89; supporter publicity Campaign for the Earth, 1990—91; founder Omni Vision Ministries, 1993—99, 2002—; dir. Chapel of Light Conf. Ctr., Lake Whitney, 2001—02; founder Universal World Investments, Chi Energy Wholeness Ctr., Lake Whitney, Tex., 2001—02, life mgmt. cons., 2003. Named Honorary Mayan Centurian. Mem. Internat. Platform Assn. Home and Office: 1112Edney St Fort Worth TX 76115-4317

LAWSON, CONNIE, state legislator; b. Indpls., Apr. 20, 1949; m. Jack Lawson; 2 children: Brandon, Kylie. Diploma, Assn. Ind. Counties, 1996. Owner Lawson Bros. Auctioneers, Jack Lawson Realtors; mem. Ind. Senate from 24th dist., Indpls., 1996—; mem. agr. and small bus. com., mem. elections com. Ind. Senate, Indpls. Mem. liaison com. Nat. Election Ctr. Recipient Outstanding Election Adminstr. award Ind. State Election Bd., 1994, Cir. Ct. Clk. of Yr., 1993, Cert. Appreciation Hendricks County Bar Assn., 1996. Mem. Assn. Cir. Ct. Clks. Ind. (pres.), Ind. Supreme Ct. Records (mgmt. com.), Assn. Ind. Counties (legis. com., bd. dirs., Clk. of Yr. 1996). Republican. Office: 200 W Washington St Indianapolis IN 46204-2728

LAWSON, DIANE MARIE, counselor; b. Dallas, July 21, 1947; d. Michael and Clara Mae (McGuire) Maida; m. Howard Lynn Lawson, July 22, 1966; children: Scott M., Stephen L. BA, North Tex. State U., 1971, MEd. Cert. secondary English, history, learning disabilities tchr., secondary sch. counselor, vocational counselor, spl. edn. counselor, mid-mgmt. adminstr., Tex. Tchr. Italy (Tex.) Ind. Sch. Dist., 1972-80, instrnl. leader, 1984-89, elem. prin., 1989-91, h.s. counselor, 1992—; tchr. Red Oak (Tex.) Ind. Sch. Dist., 1980-81; instrnl. leader ESC Region 10, Richardson, Tex., 1981-84; GED instr. Navarro Coll., Coriscana, Tex., 1991-92. City election judge, City of Italy, 1993-95, sch. election judge, Italy, 1992; primary election clk., Ellis County, Italy, 1991. Mem. Am. Counseling Assn., Assn. Tex. Profl. Educators. Avocations: reading, gardening, musicals. Office: Italy ISD 300 S College Italy TX 76651

LAWSON, EVE KENNEDY, dancer; b. Washington, Mar. 28, 1964; d. John and Elizabeth Lawson. Student, Sch. Am. Ballet, N.Y.C., 1972-83. Prin. dancer State Ballet Mo., Kansas City, 1983-87; dancer Miami City Ballet, Miami Beach, Fla., 1988-94, coord. edn., 1993-94, ballet mistress, 1994—. Created prin. roles in ballet Voyager (Bolender), 1984, Miniatures (Gamonet), 1990, Tango Tonto (Gamonet), 1991. Office: Miami City Ballet 2200 Liberty Ave Miami Beach FL 33139-1641

LAWSON, JANE ELIZABETH, bank executive; b. Cornwall, Ont., Can. d. Leonard J. and Margaret Lawson. BA, U. N.B., Can., LLB, 1971. With law dept. Royal Bank Can., Montreal, 1974-78, sr. counsel, 1978-84, v.p., corp. sec., 1988-92, sr. v.p., sec., 1992—. Mem.: Am. Soc. Corp. Secs., Inst. Corp. Dirs., Inst. Chartered Secs. and Adminstrs., Que. Bar Assn., N.B. Bar Assn., Can. Bar Assn., Royal Can. Yacht Club, Mt. Royal Tennis Club. Office: Royal Bank Plz PO Box 1 Toronto ON Canada M5J 2J15

LAWSON, JENNIFER, broadcast executive; b. Birmingham, Ala., June 8, 1946; d. Willie DeLeon and Velma Theresa (Foster) L.; m. Elbert Sampson, June 1, 1979 (div. Sept. 1980); m. Anthony Gittens, May 29, 1982: children: Kai, Zachary. Student, Tuskegee U., 1963—65; MFA, Columbia U., 1974; LHD (hon.), Teikyo Post U., Hartford, Conn., 1991. Assoc. producer William Greaves Prodns., N.Y.C., 1974-75; asst. prof. film studies Bklyn. Coll., 1975-77; exec. dir. The Film Fund, N.Y.C., 1977-80; TV coord. Program Fund Corp. for Pub. Broadcasting, Washington, 1980-83, assoc. dir. TV Program Fund, 1983-89, dir. TV Program Fund, 1989; exec. v.p. programming PBS, Alexandria, Va., 1989-95; broadcast cons. Md. Pub. TV, 1995—98, exec. cons., 1996—, exec. prodr. Africa, 1998-2001; pres. Magic Box Mediaworks, 1996—. V.p. Internat. Pub. TV, Washington, 1984-88; panelist Fulbright Fellowships, Washington, 1988-90. Author, illustrator: Children of Africa, 1970; illustrator: Our Folktales, 1968, African Folktales:

A Calabash of Wisdom, 1973. Coord. Nat. Coun. Negro Women, Washington, 1969. Avocations: painting, reading. Office: 1838 Ontario Pl NW Washington DC 20009-2109 Office Phone: 202-232-7327. Business E-Mail: magicboxmedia@aol.com.

LAWSON, LINDA, state senator; Grad., Gavit H.S., 1966. Ret. police Capt.; state rep. dist. 1 Ind. Ho. of Reps., Indpls., 1998—, chair judiciary com., vice chair cts. and criminal code com., mem. labor and employment com. Mem. Hammond Sch. Bd., 12 yrs. Democrat. Office: Ind Ho of Reps 200 W Washington St Indianapolis IN 46204-2786

LAWSON, LINDA JEAN, elementary school educator; b. Elizabethtown, Ky., Sept. 15, 1959; d. Billy Gene Lawson and Geneva Ruth Thomas; m. Jimmy Frank McGouyrk, Aug. 24, 1985 (div. July 1994); 1 child, Kyndra Lynn. B in Music Edn., Morehead State U., 1981; MA in Edn., Western Ky. U., 1986. Band dir., gen. music tchr. Monroe County Schs., 1981—86; band dir. Gadsden City Schs., 1986—87; gen. music tchr., band and choral dir. Cloverport Ind. Schs., 1987—88; band dir. Ctrl. Ala. C.C., 1992—93; gen. music tchr., beginning and advanced band dir. Nelson County Schs., 1993—95; tchr. music, practical living and arts and humanities Hardin County Schs., 1995—. Mem. content adv. com. Ky. Dept. Edn., Frankfort, 2001—03; arts and humanities profl. devel. trainer Holiday Elem., Hopkinsville, Ky., 2003. Author: Arts and Humanities: What to Know Before You Go to Middle School, 2000. Pres. Jaycee Women Jr. C. of C., Tompkinsville, Ky., 1986; bd. govs. Ky. Cols., Elizabethtown, 1995—2003; vol. Hardin County Schs., Elizabethtown, 1998—2003. Mem.: NEA, 4th Dist. Music Educators Assn. (chairperson 4th Dist. All-treble Chorus 2002—03), Ky. Music Educators Assn. (4th Dist. Music Tchr. of Year), Kappa Delta Pi. Avocations: singing, dance, playing flute, travel, sightseeing. Office: Upton Elem Sch 304 College St Upton KY 42784

LAWSON, NANCY LOUISE, computer scientist, educator; b. Boston, Sept. 22, 1943; d. James Llewellyn and Jane Hancock (Kraft) L.; m. Michael Douglass Marvin, June 14, 1965 (div. Oct., 1985); children: Heidi Jo Newburg, Russel Hugh Marvin, Daryl James Marvin; m. Peter William Henner, June 6, 1992. BA, Oberlin Coll., 1965; MS in Math. Edn., U. Pa., 1973; MS in Computer Sci., Rensselaer Poly. Inst., 1986; PhD in Computer Sci., Rensselaer Polytech. Inst., 1996. Cert. tchr. math., gen. sci., chemistry, N.Y. Math. tchr. various schs., N.Y., 1973-79; farmer, 1976-84; software engr. GE & Rensselaer Poly. Inst., 1984-92; teaching asst., lectr. Rensselaer Poly. Inst., Troy, N.Y., 1992-95; prof. Coll. St. Rose, Albany, N.Y., 1996—. Mem. Emergency Med. Tech. Scho-Wright Ambulance Corps, Schoharie, N.Y., 1979-81. Mem. Alliance for Environ. Renewal (bd. dirs., v.p.), Adirondack 46ers, Schoharie Valley Concert Band, Pi Mu Epsilon. Avocations: rock climbing, back country skiing, French horn. Home: 60 Scutt Rd Feura Bush NY 12067-2332

LAWSON, NANCY P. retired county official; b. Manassas, Va., Apr. 23, 1926; d. Edgar goodloe and Alverda Reita (Jennings) Parrish; m. Richard Challice Haydon, Jr., June 19, 1948 (dec. Oct. 1964); children: Victoria Lucille Haydon Bonifant, Richard Challice III, Geoffrey Jennings; m. Garland Loyd Lawson, Sept. 15, 1979 (dec. June 29, 2002). BA in Edn., Longwood Coll., 1947. Gen. registrar Prince William County, Manassas, 1965-91; organizer Voter Registrars Assn. Va., 1971, pres., 1972, 73, 74, parliamentarian, 1975-99. Bd. dirs., sec. Commonwealth Savs. and Loan Assn., 1980-91. Active Manassas Jr. Womans Club, 1953-61, pres., 1956; membership chmn., parliamentarian Aux. to Prince William Hosp., 1962-; bd. dirs. Manassas Cmty. Concert Assn., 1985-; trustee Manassas United Meth. Ch., 1986-. Mem. Evergreen Country Club (bd. dirs. 1995-), Sudley Swim and Tennis Club (pres., bd. dirs.). Avocations: tennis, golf, piano, bridge. Home: 9007 Longstreet Dr Manassas VA 20110-4904

LAWSON, PAMELA ANN, musician, educator; b. Wichita, Kans., Nov. 6, 1964; d. James Edward and Claudette Madell Lawson. BS, B of Mus. Edn., Friends U., Wichita, 1993. Tchr., orch. dir. Cumberland County Schs., Fayetteville, NC, 1993—94, Robeson County Schs., Lumberton, NC, 1994—99, dir. youth orch., 1994—99; tchr., orch. dir. New Hanover County Schs., Wilmington, NC, 1999—; prin. concert violinist Long Bay Symphony, Myrtle Beach, SC, 1999—; orch. adjudicator S.C. Music Edn. Assn., Myrtle Beach, 2002. Concert violinist Downtown String Ensemble, Raleigh, 1995—; pvt. tchr. violin, viola Wilmington Acad. Music, 2002—. Mem.: N.C. Assn. Educators, N.C. Music Educators Assn., Music Educators Nat. Conf. Avocations: travel, reading, archaeological findings, family gatherings, performing. Home: # 101 389 Darlington Ave Wilmington NC 28403 Office: Williston Mid Sch 401 S 10th St Wilmington NC 28403 E-mail: plwson4@aol.com.

LAWSON, PATRICIA LYNN, technologist; b. Council Bluffs, Iowa, June 3, 1953; d. Lawrence Jr. McDaniel and Sarah Harriet Watkins; m. Lawrence Dwayne Moore, Nov. 15, 1968 (div. Sept. 15, 1972); 1 child, Larry Dean Moore ; m. Terrance John Lawson, Aug. 21, 1980. Cert. oper. rm. technician, Iowa Western C.C., 1975. Mem. adv. com. surg. technologist program Iowa Western C.C.i. Sec. Equal Access for Disabled, Council Bluffs; mem. Mayor's Commn. for the Disabled; contact person Edn. of Latex Allergy/Support Team/ Info. Coalition, Iowa, 1996—2003; dir. Iowa Latex Allergy Resource Network, 2003. Mem.: Assn. Surg. Technologists (chpt. pres. 1983—84, 1987—88, tellers com. 1990, chpt. pres. 1990—91, nat. membership rep. 1991—97, nat. membership chmn. 1993—95, chpt. sec. 1994—96, mem. mil. ad hoc com. 1995—96, mem. stds. of practice com. 1996—98, chmn. stds. of practice com. 1997—98, nat. bd. dirs. 1998—2002, chpt. pres. 1998—, mem. policy and procedure com. 1999—2002, mem. credential com. 2001). Home: 18703 Hanover Ln Council Bluffs IA 51503-8183

LAWTON, BARBARA, lieutenant governor; b. Wis. m. Cal Lawton; children: Joseph, Amanda Krupp. BA summa cum laude, Lawrence U., 1987; MA, U. Wis., 1991. Lt. gov. State of Wis., Madison, 2003—. Founding mem. Ednl. Resource Found.; founding trustee Cmty. Found.; founding mem. Latinos Unidos; mem. adv. bd. Green Bay Multicultural Ctr., Women's Polit. Voice; mem. bus. planning and resource team Entrepreneurs of Color; bd. mem. Planned Parenthood Advs. Wis., Northeastern Wis. Tech. Coll. Edn. Found. Named Feminist of the Yr., Wis. Chpt. NOW, 1999; recipient Ft. Howard Founds. Humanitarian award. Mem.: AAUW, LWV, Nat. Women's Polit. Caucus. Office: Rm 19 East State Capitol Madison WI 53701*

LAWTON, DEBORAH SIMMONS, library director, educational media specialist; b. Dover, N.J., Sept. 14, 1950; d. Coryden Jerome Simmons and Marjorie Lynd (Jewell) Weber; children: Catherine Randall, Christopher James. BA, Lebanon Valley Coll., 1972; tchr. cert., Coll. St. Elizabeth, 1974; MLS, Rutgers-The State U., 1994. Cert. ednl. media specialist, profl. libr., supr. Confidential ratings analyst Martindale-Hubbell, Summit, N.J., 1972-74; tchr. St. Rose Sch., East Hanover, N.J., 1975-77, St. Paul Sch., Princeton, N.J., 1977-78; libr. Mary Jacobs Libr., Rocky Hill, N.J., 1988-92, South Brunswick H.S., Monmouth Junction, N.J., 1994—. Reviewer Infolink, 1995—; chair press rev. com. Am. Assn. Univs. Author: Knowledge Quest, Book Report; co-author: Authentic Assessment in South Brunswick, Partnerships at Work in the Library. Chair Montgomery jointure com., Montgomery Twp., N.J., 1985; coach/dir. Montgomery Girls Softball, 1988-91; v.p., exec. bd. Montgomery Twp. PTSA, 1986-90; pres., treas. Lawrenceville (N.J.) Presbyn. Coop. Nursery Sch., 1981-84; ranking chair jrs. N.J. Tennis Dist.; mem. INFOLINK Book Evaluation Criteria Com., KidsConnect, INFOLINK Youth Svcs. Com.; deacon Blawenburg Reformed Ch., elder. Internet grantee N.J. State Libr., 1994, Instrnl. Coun. grantee South Brunswick Instrnl. Coun., 1995, 96, 97; recipient Pres.'s award N.J. Tennis. Mem. ALA, Am. Assn. Sch. Librs. (assn. am. univ. presses com. 1996—, legis. com., chair youth svcs. com., intellectual freedom com., bd. tristees), Assn. for Libr. Svc. to Children, Young Adult Libr. Svcs. Assn., Intellectual Freedom Round Table, Ednl. Media Assn. N.J. (legis. chair, intellectual freedom chair), Assn. of Am. Univ. Presses (rev. com.), N.J. Libr. Assn., Beta Phi Mu, Pi Gamma Mu. Avocations: water sports, quilting. Office: South Brunswick HS 750 Ridge Rd Monmouth Junction NJ 08852-0183 E-mail: dlawton@sbschools.org.

LAWTON, NANCY, artist; b. Gilroy, Calif., Feb. 28, 1950; d. Edward Henry and Marilyn Kelly (Boyd) L.; m. Richard Enemark, Aug. 4, 1984; children: Faith Lawton, Forrest Lawton. BA in Fine Art, Calif. State U., San Jose, 1971; MFA, Mass. Coll. Art, 1980. Artist-in-residence Villa Montalvo Ctr. Arts, Los Gatos, Calif., 1971, Noble & Greenough Sch., Dedham, Mass., 1990. One-woman shows include The Bklyn. Mus., 1983, Victoria Munroe Gallery, N.Y.C., 1993, Hirschl & Adler Galleries, N.Y.C., 2002; group shows include San Francisco Mus. Modern Art, 1973, The Bklyn. Mus., 1980, 83, Staempfli Gallery, N.Y.C., 1984, The Ark. Art Ctr. Mus., Little Rock, 1984, 88, 92, 93, Victoria Munroe Gallery, 1985, 87, 88, 92, Butler Inst. Am. Art, Ohio, 1988, Smith Coll. Mus. Art, 1988, NAD, N.Y.C., 1988, Reynolds Gallery, Richmond, 1994, Nancy Solomon Gallery, Atlanta, 1995, Arnot Art Mus., Elmira, N.Y., 2001-03, Hunt Inst. for Bot. Documentation, Carnegie Mellon U., Pitts., 2001-02, Hirsch and Adler Galleries, N.Y.C., 2002-04, John Pence Galleries, San Francisco, 2004, Vose Galleries, Boston, 2004; pub. collections include The Ark. Art Ctr. Mus., Art Inst. Chgo., Bklyn. Mus., Smithsonian Am. Art Mus., Washington. Scholar Mellon Found., 1982; N.Y. State Creative Artists grantee, 1983, N.Y. State Arts Devel. Fund grantee, 1989. Home and Office: 78 Willett St Albany NY 12210-1001 Office Phone: 518-449-7022. E-mail: nancydraws@aol.com.

LAWTON, VIOLET, writer; b. Cumberland, R.I., Oct. 11, 1925; d. John Arthur and Emma (Butterworth) Grayson; m. Donald Morrison, Aug. 6, 1950 (div. Feb. 1952); 1 child, Darcy Louise; m. Charles Dean Lawton, Nov. 30, 1968 (dec.); stepchildren: Peter E., Mark D. Student, Tabbot-Hubbard Bus. Sch., 1944. Bookkeeper Lonsdale Co. Berkeley Mill, Cumberland, R.I., 1943-45; purchasing sales, house newsletter advt. The Fram Corp., East Providence, R.I., 1945-50; accts. receivable, sr. credit adminstrn. The Foxboro (Mass.) Co., 1952-85; corr. The Alameda (Calif.) Jour., 1999—. Contbr. articles to mags. Mem. Writers West Alameda, Inc. (pres. 1999, sec. 1995-97). Episcopalian. Avocations: swimming, walking, dance, gardening, group singing.

LAX, KATHLEEN THOMPSON, judge; b. 1945; BA, U. Kans., 1967; JD, U. Calif., L.A., 1980. Law clk. U.S. Bankruptcy Ct., L.A., 1980-82; assoc. Gibson, Dunn & Crutcher, L.A., 1982-88; judge ctrl. dist. U.S. Bankruptcy Ct., L.A., 1988—. Bd. dirs. L.A. Bankruptcy Forum; bd. govs. Fin. Lawyers Conf., Los Angeles, Calif., 1991—92, Los Angeles, 1994—2000. Bd. editors: Calif. Bankruptcy Jour., 1988—. Office: US Bankruptcy Court 21041 Burbank Blvd Woodland Hills CA 91367-6606

LAXTON, PATRICIA M. technologist; b. Harriman, Tenn., Mar. 16, 1956; d. Elmer Don King and Patsy Lee; m. Charles David Laxton, June 10, 1977 (div. Nov. 2000); children: David Michael, Misty Lachelle. AS in Radiology, Roane State C.C., Harriman, 1981. Registered radiographer, ultrasonographer. Lead sonographer Roane Med. Ctr., Harriman, 1981—87, Ft. Sanders Regional, Knoxville, Tenn., 1981—86; ultrasound-x-ray technician Harriman City Hosp., 1988—91; dir. radiology Chamberlain Meml. Hosp., Rockwood, Tenn., 1991; asst. dir. radiology Harriman City Hosp., 1991—. Tech. dir., vascular lab. Roane Med. Ctr., Harriman. Pres. Harriman H.S. PTO, 1980—81, v.p., 1979—80; treas. Harriman H.S. Parents' Assn., 2000—. Mem.: East Tenn. Ultrasound Soc. (treas.). Avocations: counted cross stitch, music. Home: 324 Washington Ave Rockwood TN 37854 Office: Roane Med Ctr 412 Devonia St Harriman TN 37748

LAY, MARION, sports association executive; M of Sociology, Calif. State U., Hayward. Mem. exec. com. Can. Olympic Assn.; founder, chair Nat. Sport Ctr., Greater Vancouver; chair PacificSport Group; co-chair BC Games com.; mem. WomenSport Internat. Former Can. Olympic swimmer; founding mem. Can. Assn. for Advancement of Women in Sport & Phys. Activity; pres. 2010 LegaciesNow Society (Vancouver Olympic bid), 1998—. Recipient Women of Distinction award Recreation and Sport, YWCA, 1991, Herstorical award, CAAWS, 1994, Bryce Taylor Meml. award Outstanding Contbn. Amateur Sport, 1995, Can. Citizenship award, 1996, Bobbie Steen award Excellence Leadership Sport Cmty., 1998, Bronze medal 4x100 metre relay, Olympics, Mexico City, 1968, Internat. Olympic Com.'s Women and Sport Trophy, 2001, Leadership in Sports award, Can., 2001, Carole Anne Letheren Internat Sport Leadership award, COC & CAAWS, 2002, History Breakthrough award award, CAAWS, 2002. Office: Can Assn Adv Women & Sport & Phys Act N202 801 King Edward Ave Ottawa ON K1N 6N5 Canada*

LAY, ROBIN RENEE, small business owner; b. Chgo., Dec. 19, 1959; d. Clarence and Judith Lay. BS with honors in Bus. Adminstrn., Roosevelt U., 2001; postgrad., Keller Grad. Sch. Mgmt., Chgo. Lic. real estate salesperson Ill., 1993, registered coop. mgr. Ill., 01. Customer svc. mgr. Wieboldts Dept. Store, Chgo., 1978—86; res. force banker Harris Bank, Chgo., 1987—90; from receptionist to property mgr. The Habitat Co., Chgo., 1990—. Mem. deacon bd. New Heritage Cathedral, Chgo., 2003, mem. womans ministry leadership team, 2003—. Office Phone: 773-285-8600.

LAYBOURNE, GERALDINE B. broadcast executive; b. Plainfield, N.J., 1947; m. Kit Laybourne; children: Emily, Sam. BA art history, Vassar Coll., 1969; MS elem. ed., U. Pa., 1971. Former high sch. tchr.; joined Nickelodeon as program manager, 1980; created Nick at Nite, 1985; exec. v.p./gen. mgr. Nickelodeon/Nick at Nite, 1986—89, pres., 1989—96; vice chmn. MTV Networks, 1993—96; pres. Disney/ABC Cable Networks, N.Y.C., 1996—98; co-founder and CEO Oxygen Media, N.Y.C., 1998—. Bd. dirs. Insight Comm. Co., The YES Network, Nat. Coun. Families and TV. Bd. dirs. Nat. Coun. Families and TV, Children Affected by AIDS Found., Nat. Ctr. Children's TV, The Nat. Cable TV Assn., Vassar Coll. Named one of 25 Most Influential People in Am., Time mag., 1996; named to, Broadcasting Hall of Fame, 1995, Broadcasting and Cable Hall of Fame, 1995; recipient Idell Kaitz award, Nat. Cable and Telecom. Assn. Vanguard Awards, 1990, Film Muse award, N.Y. Women, 1991, Entrepreneur of Yr. award, U. Mo., Kansas City, 1991, Women in Cable award, 1992, Genii award, Am. Women in Radio and TV, 1992, Govs. award, Nat. Acad. Cable Programming, 1993, Grand Tam award, Cable TV Adminstrn. and Mktg. Com., 1994, Spotlight award, Creative Coalition, 1995, Matrix award for broadcasting, N.Y. Women in Comm., 1996, award for disting. lifetime contbn. to children and TV, Annenberg Pub. Policy Ctr., 1997, Crystal Apple award, Mayor Rudy Giuliani, 2001, award for disting. lifetime contbn. to children and TV, Annenberg Pub. Policy Ctr., Matrix award for broadcasting, N.Y. Women in Comm., Spotlight award, Creative Coalition. Mem.: Nat. Cable TV Assn. (bd. dirs.), Cable Positive (hon. chair), N.Y. Women in Film and TV (adv. bd.). Office: Oxygen Media 75 9th Ave Fl 7 New York NY 10011-7006*

LAYCOCK, MARY CHAPPELL, gifted and talented education educator, consultant; b. Jefferson City, Mo., Jan. 11, 1915; d. Alvin E. and Ollie (Harris) Chappell; m. James Charles Laycock, June 22, 1937; children: Charles, Ann, Donald E., Jane. AB, Judson Coll., 1937; MA in Math. Edn., U. Tenn., 1961. Math. tchr. various, 1938-41; math. tchr. Kingsport (Tenn.) Jr. High Sch., 1942; math. coord. Oak Ridge (Tenn.) City Schs., 1956-68, high sch. math. tchr., 1945-68; math. specialist Nueva Ctr. for Learning, Hillsborough, Calif., 1968-98; cons. Hayward, Calif., 1990-97. Author many books including Mathematics for Meaning, The Fabric of Mathematics, Algebra in Concrete, Focus on Geometry, Hands On Mathematics for Secondary Teachers, Weaving Your Way from Arithmetic to Mathematics, 1993, The Magician's Castle Fantasy, 1995; developed documentary Don't Bother Me, I'm Learning, 12 videotapes on teaching manipulatives; contbr. articles to profl. jours. Recipient Calif. Educator award, 1989, Elem. Math. Tchr. award Calif. Math. Coun. and State of Calif., 1989, Award of Recognition Calif. Assn. for the Gifted. 1984, Glenn Gilbert Nat. Leadership award for outstanding contbns. to math. edn. Nat. Coun. Suprs. Math., 2003. Mem. NEA, Nat. Coun. Tchrs. Math., Oreg. Math. Coun., Calif. Math. Coun. (life), Fla. Math. Coun., Greater San Diego Math. Coun., San Mateo County Math. Coun., Calif. Assn. for the Gifted. Avocation: geometric art. Home and Office: 20655 Hathaway Ave Hayward CA 94541-3740 E-mail: info@activityresources.com.

LAZANO, MONICA, publishing executive; Assoc. pub. La Opinion, 1989-91, editor, 1991—; pres., CIO Lozano Comms. (parent co.). Mem. N.Y. Stock Exch. Individual Investors Adv. Com. Pub. spl. tabloid on AIDS (Advocacy award Hispanic Coalition on AIDS 1988, Best Pub. Svc. Publ., Inter-Am. Press Assn.). Trustee U. So. Calif., chair pub. affairs com.; vice-chmn. L.A. Annenberg Met. Project; mem. Calif. Citizens Commn. on Higher Edn.; bd. dirs. Venice Family Clinic, U.S., YMCA of Met. L.A., Nat. Coun. of La Raza; mem. adv. bd. Pub. Policy Inst. of Calif.; mem. Inter-Am. Dialogue and the Pacific Coun. on Internat. Policy. Recipient Distinction in Media Excellence award March of Dimes, 1991, Pub. Svc. Recognition award State Bar of Calif., 1992; named to 100 Most Influential Hispanic Women, Hispanic Bus. mag., 1987, 92, 96. Mem. Nat. Assn. of Women Bus. Owners, Nat. Assn. Hispanic Journalists, Calif. Chicano News Media Assn., Am. Soc. Newspaper Editors. Office: La Opinion 411 W 5th St Ste 1200 Los Angeles CA 90013-1028

LAZAR, JILL SUE, home healthcare company executive; b. Oak Park, Ill., June 15, 1954; d. Norton David and Carol Ellen (Kaufmann) Freyer; m. Bruce Horwich, Aug. 21, 1976 (div. Sept. 1982); 1 child, Mathew Freyer Horwich; m. Neil Lazar, Nov. 23, 1986. BS in Mktg., No. Ill. U., 1975. Mktg. rsch. assoc. McDonald's Corp., Oak Brook, Ill., 1976-80; renewal coord. Time, Inc., Chgo., 1984-87; product mgr. Macmillan Directory Div., Wilmette, Ill., 1987-92; with DependiCare, Broadview, Ill., 1992—. Mem. provider adv. panels Chad Therapeutics, Aradigm Corp., others. Mem. Chgo. Health Execs. Forum. Avocations: swimming, reading. Office phone: (708) 345-7599 ext. 202. Office: DependiCare 1815 Gardner Rd Broadview IL 60155-4401

LAZAR, KATHY PITTAK, lawyer; b. Lorain, Ohio, Nov. 12, 1955; BA summa cum laude, Kent State U., 1978; JD, Case Western Res. U., 1982. Bar: Ohio 1982. Sr. counsel TRW Inc. Rsch. editor Case Western Res. U. Law Rev., 1981-82. Mem. ABA, Ohio State Bar Assn., Cleve. Bar Assn., Order of Coif, Phi Beta Kappa. Office: TRW Inc 1900 Richmond Rd Cleveland OH 44124-3760

LAZAR, LUDMILA, concert pianist, music educator, pedagogue; b. Celje, Slovenia; married; two children. MusB, Roosevelt U., 1963, MusM, 1964; D of Musical Arts, Northwestern U., 1987. Faculty Roosevelt U., Chgo., 1967—, prof. piano Chgo. Musical Coll., 1988—, prof. emerita, 2003—, chmn. keyboard dept., 1983—2003. Lectr., demonstrator in field. Roosevelt U. rsch. grantee, 1988, 96; recipient Goethe Inst. award, 1987, Outstanding Coll. Tchr. award Roosevelt U., 1981; named to All Star Profs. Team Chgo. Tribune, 1993. Mem. AAUP, Music Tchrs. Nat. Assn. (master tchr. cert. 1991), European Piano Tchrs. Assn., Ill. State Music Tchrs. Assn., Soc. Am. Musicians (pres., v.p.), Coll. Music Soc., Mu Phi Epsilon (pres., v.p.). Office: Roosevelt U 430 S Michigan Ave Chicago IL 60605-1394 Office Phone: 312-341-3779.

LAZARIS, PAMELA ADRIANE, community planning and development consultant; b. Dixon, Ill., Oct. 13, 1956; d. Michael Christ and Ellen Euridice (Eftax) L.; m. Eugene Dale Monson, Oct. 17, 1987; children: Anthony Edward, Anna Adriane. BFA in Fine Arts, U. Wis., Milw., 1978; MS in Urban and Regional Planning, U. Wis., 1982; MBA, U. St. Thomas, 1992. Analyst planning Wis. Dept. Natural Resources, Madison, 1979-82; asst. city planner City of Albert Lea, Minn., 1982-83; specialist community devel. City of Winona, Minn., 1983-85; dir. community devel. City of Waseca, Minn., 1985-98; assoc. Real Estate Dynamics, Inc., Madison, Wis., 1998-99; prin. Planning Svc. and Solutions, Lake Mills, Wis., 1999—. Vol. spl. events Farmam-Minn. Agrl. Interpretive Ctr., Waseca, 1985-86; mem. Waseca County Econ. Devel. Commn., 1989-98; com. dir. Waseca Area Found., 1989-98; mem. dist. 2 city coun. City of Lake Mills, Wis., 1999—, city plan commn., 1999—; troop 148 advancement coord. Boy Scouts Am., 2002-. Named one of Outstanding Young Women of Am., 1986. Mem. Am. Inst. Cert. Planners (cert.), Am. Planning Assn. (chpt. bd. dirs. 1986-89), Minn. Planning Assn. (v.p. 1989-90, dist. bd. dirs. 1985-89), Toastmasters (chpt. sgt.-at-arms 1987, edl. v.p. 1988, 91-98), Lake Mills Area C. of C. Avocations: public speaking, travel, art. Home: PO Box 17 Lake Mills WI 53551-0017 Office: 110 E Madison St Lake Mills WI 53551-1644 E-mail: pal@gdinet.com.

LAZARUS, ARLEEN, lawyer; b. Manhattan, N.Y., Jan. 7, 1965; d. Joseph Anthony and Flor Maria Cabutto; m. Gary Thomas Lazarus, May 1, 1993; 1 child, Lisette. BS, St. John's U., Jamaica, N.Y., 1987; JD, U. Miami, 1990. Bar: Fla. 1990. Assoc. Markowitz, Davis, Ringel & Trusty, Miami, Fla., 1990—95; ptnr. Lazarus & Lazarus, P.A., Ft. Lauderdale, Fla., 1997—. Sponsor Adopt a Hwy. Program, Broward County, Fla., 2001—, Boys and Girls Club, Ft. Lauderdale, 2002—. Avocations: painting, cooking, dance. Office: Lazarus & Lazarus PA 401 E Las Olas Blvd Ste 1400 Fort Lauderdale FL 33301 Home: 15322 SW 33rd St Davie FL 33331-2706 E-mail: alazaru@aol.com.

LAZARUS, ROCHELLE BRAFF (SHELLY LAZARUS), advertising executive; b. N.Y.C., Sept. 1, 1947; d. Lewis L. and Sylvia Ruth (Eisenberg) Braff; m. George M. Lazarus, Mar. 22, 1970; children: Theodore, Samantha, Benjamin. AB, Smith Coll., 1968; MBA, Columbia U., 1970. Product mgr. Clairol, N.Y.C., 1970-71; account exec. Ogilvy & Mather, N.Y.C., 1971-73, account supr., 1973-77, mgmt. supr., 1977-84, sr. v.p., 1981—, account group dir., 1984-87; gen. mgr. Ogilvy & Mather Direct, N.Y.C., 1987-88, mng. dir., 1988-89, pres., 1989-91, Ogilvy & Mather, N.Y.C., 1991-94, pres. N. Am., 1991-94; pres., COO Ogilvy & Mather Worldwide, N.Y.C., 1995-96, CEO, 1996—, chmn., 1997—. Bd. dirs. Ann Taylor, GE, 2000—. Mem. Women's Forum, Com. to Encourage Corp. Philanthropy, Deloitte & Touche Coun. for Advancement of Women; mem. adv. coun. 4A; mem. bd. overseers Columbus Bus. Sch.; mem. Yale Pres.'s Coun. on Internat. Activities; bd. dirs. Advt. Edn. Found., N.Y. Presbyn. Hosp., Am. Mus. Natural History, World Wildlife Fund. Recipient YWCA Women Achievers award, 1985, Matrix award, 1995; named Businesswoman of Yr. N.Y.C. Partnership and C. of C., 1996. Mem.: Am. Assn. Advt. Agys. (vice chmn. 1998—99, chmn. 1999—2000, bd. dirs.), The Bus. Coun., Coun. on Fgn. Rels., Com. of 200, Advt. Women of NY (coun. fgn. rels. com. to encourage corp. philanthropy, Woman of Yr 1994). Home: 106 E 78th St New York NY 10021-0302 Office: Ogilvy & Mather Worldwide 309 W 49th St New York NY 10019-7316

LAZO, CAROLINE EVENSEN, writer; b. Mpls. children: Stephanie, Peter, Mark (Chip). AA, Pine Manor Jr. Coll., Wellesley, Mass.; cert., U. Oslo; BA, U. Minn. Author: Jimmy Carter: On the Road to Peace, Gloria Steinem: Feminist Extraordinaire, Wilma Mankiller, 1994 (Tchr.'s choice award, 1995), Arthur Ashe, 1999 (Notable Social Studies Trade Book for Young People, 1999), Alice Walker: Freedom Writer, 2000 (Soc. Sch. Librs. Internat. Honor Book award, 2001), Society of School Librarians International Honor Book, 2001, Leonard Bernstein: In Love with Music, 2003, F. Scott Fitzgerald: Voice of the Jazz Age, 2003.

LAZOR, PATRICIA ANN, interior designer; d. Charles A. and Grace E. (Siegrist) LaGattuta; m. E. Alexander Lazor; children: Pamela A., Carolyn L., Charles L., Peter A. BA, Chestnut Hill Coll., 1957; MEd, Rutgers Coll., 1962; cert., N.Y. Sch. Interior Design, 1972. Tchr. Bridgewater (N.J.) Raritan Schs., 1958-60; designer Patricia A. Lazor Interior Design, Bernardsville, N.J., 1975-85; pres. Alexander Abry, Inc., Washington, 1985-87; owner, designer Patricia A. Lazor Interior Design Antiques, Inc., Bernardsville, 1985—. Designer numerous residential interior design projects throughout the U.S.; featured in 100 Designers Favorite Rooms. Rep. com. woman, Somerset County, N.J., 1978; chmn. Family Counseling Svc. Somerset County, 1972-78. Mem. Garden Club Morristown, Morristown Club, Kappa Delta Phi. Office: Patricia A Lazor Inc Roebling Rd Bernardsville NJ 07924

LAZZARA, BERNADETTE See PETERS, BERNADETTE

LAZZO, JANELLE, humanities educator, writer; b. Clarksville, Ark., Mar. 5, 1935; d. Frank Karl and Clara Spanke Knoedel; m. Leo Eugene Lazzo, Aug. 8, 1959; children: Mike, Mark, Tom, Susan, John, David. BA, Mt. St. Scholastica Coll., 1957; MA, U. Mo., Kansas City, 1977. Writer Ea. Kans. Register, Kansas City, Kans., 1957—59; tchr. English and religion Bishop Miege H.S., Roeland Pk., Kans., 1976—98. Tchr. English Penn Valley C.C., Kansas City, Mo., 1985—. Essayist: mag. Celebration, 1995—; contbr. articles to local newspaper. Active Common Cause, Amnesty Internat., Call To Action, LWV. Named Outstanding Alumna, Benedictine Coll., 1982, Outstanding Tchr., Archdiocese Kansas City, Kans., 1997. Mem.: Am. Assn. Ret. People. Democrat. Roman Catholic. Avocations: reading, water aerobics. Home: 5116 Reinhardt Dr Shawnee Mission KS 66205

LÊ, AN-MY, photographer, educator; BA with honors in Biology and French, Stanford U., 1982, MS in Biology, 1985; MFA in Photography, Yale U., 1993. Rsch. asst. in immunology Blood Ctr., Med. Ch. Stanford (Calif.) U., 1981—86, lectr. photography art dept., 1996—97, lectr. photography continuing studies dept., 1997; tchg. asst. photography dept. Yale U. Sch. Art, New Haven, 1992; lectr. photography Fordham U., NYU, Bard Coll., N.Y.C., 1998; free-lance photographer, 1993—. Staff photographer Compagnons du Devoir, France, 1986—91; vis. asst. prof. Bard Coll., 1999. Author: Dirs. Guild Am., 1993; Exhibited in group shows at Canton (China) Cultural Ctr., 1993, Lowinski Gallery, N.Y.., 1994, Houston Ctr. for Photography (traveled to Webster U., St. Louis and Silver Eye Ctr. for Photography, Pitts.), 1994—96, 1997, Mus. Modern Art, N.Y.C., 1997, Fotofest, Houston, 1998, Scott Nicols Gallery, San Francisco, 1999, Represented in permanent collections Mus. Fine Arts, Houston, Mus. Modern Art, N.Y.C., San Francisco, Met. Mus., N.Y.C., Bibliotéque Nationale, Paris. Fellow Photography fellow, N.Y. Found. for Arts, 1996; CameraWorks Inc. grantee, 1995, Guggenheim fellow, 1997.

LE, DUY-LOAN, electrical engineer; b. Vietnam; arrived in U.S., 1975; BSEE magna cum laude, U. Tex., 1982; MBA, U. Houston. With Tex. Instruments, Dallas, 1982—, sr. fellow. Contbr. articles to profl. publs. Named One of Houston's Women on the Move, Tex. Exec. Women, Nat. Technologist of Yr., Women of Color; named to Internat. Hall of Fame, WITI. Achievements include patents in field. Office: MS 722 12203 SW Freeway Stafford TX 77477 Office Phone: 281-274-3714. E-mail: dlon@Ti.com

LEA, FILOMENA, English language educator, writer; b. Milw., Sept. 14, 1929; d. Peter and Noemi Volpintesta; m. Merlyn Bud Lea, Dec. 6, 1928; children: Dean, Perry. BA in Interior Design, Mount Mary Coll., 1986, postgrad.; PhB in Journalism, Marquette U., 1951. Women's feature writer Milw. Sentinel, 1952—54, home furnishing editor, 1956—64; interior designer Designed Interiors, Milw., 1964—90; writing instr. Milw. Area Tech. Coll., 1958—; instr. interior design Waukesha (Wis.) County Tech. Coll., 1989—99; feature writer 50 Plus Mag., Hartland, Wis., 1996—, Wis. Woman Mag., Hartland, 1998—. Author: (personality features) Milw. Ethnic Coun. Vol., 2002—. Mem.: Milw. Area Acad. Alliance in English, Future Milw. Home and Office: 6700 N Range Line Rd Milwaukee WI 53209

LEACH, CYNTHIA ELIZABETH, social worker, communications executive; d. Ralph Wilson Leach Jr. and Cynthia Weisheit Leach; m. Gregory Nicholas Piro, May 9, 1999. BA in Religious Studies, Brown U., 1987; MSW, NYU, 1995. LCSW Fla., cert. social worker N.Y. Sr. counselor then program asst. Victim Svcs. Agy./Travelers Aid Svcs., N.Y.C., 1987—89; mgmt. trainee then project coord. AVMD Group/Triclinaca Comm., N.Y.C., 1989—92; dir. cmty. rels. United Seamen's Svc., N.Y.C., 1992—96; staff psychotherapist Samaritan Counseling Ctr., Scotia, NY, 1996—99, Boca Raton, Fla., 1996—99; dir. cmty. outreach The Wellness Cmty., Boca Raton, 2000—01; project mgr. Parexel MMS, Hackensack, NJ, 2001—03; dir. corp. comm. Jordan Anderson Inc./Corp. Healers Inc., N.Y.C., 2003—04. Mem.: NAFE, NASW, Nat. Network Social Work Mgrs. Avocations: piano, gardening, reading, equestrian, cross training.

LEACH, JANET C. publishing executive; b. 1956; m. John Leach; 3 children. Degree in Journalism, Bowling Green State U. Mng. editor The Cin. Enquirer, until 1998; editor Akron Beacon Jour., 1998—2003; profl. in residence Sch. Journalism and Mass Comm. Kent State U., 2003—; police reporter The Rev. Times, Fostoria. Mem. staff Ariz. Republic, Phoenix (Ariz.) Gazette; instr. journalism No. Ky. U., U. Cin. Mem. Knight Found. Recipient 4 Pulitzer prizes, Golden medal Meritorious Svc., 1994. Mem.: Am. Soc. Newspaper Editors, Akron Press Club, Soc. Profl. Journalists.*

LEACH, MARY JANE, composer; b. St. Johnsbury, Vt., June 12, 1949; d. Benjamin George Leach and Juliet Anne (Cooke Barton). BA, U. Vt., 1972; postgrad., Columbia U., 1977-78. Composer, 1978—. Co-dir. Re:Soundings, N.Y.C., 1993—. Composer (choral works) Ariadne's Lament, 1993, Song of Sorrows, 1995, Bruckstück, 1989, O Magna Vasti Creta, 1997, Call of the Dance, 1997, Ceremony of the Ball, 1998, (piano) By'n Bye, 2001, (piece for oboe) Xantippe's Rebuke, 1994, (wind trio) Windjammer, 1995, (piece for countertenor) Tricky Pan, 1995; recordings include Celestial Fires, 1993, Ariadne's Lament, 1998. Recipient comm. Mary Flagler Cary Charitable Trust, 1994, 96, Mirieam Gideon prize Internat. Alliance Women in Music, 2002; Found. for Contemporary Performing Arts career grantee, 1995-96; Composers fellowNat. Endowment for Arts, 1995, Artists fellow NY Found. for Arts, 2002. Mem. Am. Music Ctr., Am. Composers Forum. Home: 90 La Salle St Apt 13H New York NY 10027-4722

LEAGUE, CHARLE ALLPORT (CHARLENE LEAGUE), federal official, minister; b. Washington, D.C., Jan. 4, 1954; d. Charles Lester Allport, Sr. and Lois Wilson Allport Robey, James Everett Robey, Sr. (Stepfather); children: William Francis League, IV, Charles Brandt. Reverend The Brigade of Light Mountain Mystery Sch., N.C., 1998. Sec. optometrist office, Springfield, Va., 1970—71; clk. US Hdqs. Marine Corps, Washington, 1971—73; sec. US Air Force, Wright-Patterson Air Force Base, Ohio, 1973—75, US Army Rsch. Office, Rsch. Triangle Pk., 1975—76, NIH, 1976—81; self-employed child care provider Raleigh, 1981—83; sec. NIH, Rsch. Triangle Pk., 1983—86; adminstrv. Unity Ctr. of the Triangle, Raleigh, 1986—88; clk. US Fed. Crop Ins., Raleigh, 1988—89; sec. adminstrn. NIH, Rsch. Triangle Pk., NC, 1989—96, adminstrn./mgmt., 1996—. Vol. The Brigade of Light at Terra Nova Ctr., Cedar Mountain, NC, 1998—; music program coord. Religious Sci. Ctr. for Conscious Living, Raleigh, NC, 2003—. Vol. Habitat for Humanity, Raleigh, 2001—03; chmn. & vice chmn. SOAR 8, Inc., Southeastern US, Bermuda, 1989—93; v.p. Shamrock/Northshore Exchangette Club, Raleigh, NC, 1980—82. Recipient Exchangette of Yr., Shamrock/Northshore Exchangette Club, 1981-82. Avocations: spirituality, reading, gardening, people-watching, raising consciousness. Office: Nat Inst Environ Health Scis/NIH/DHHS PO Box 12233 Research Triangle Park NC 27709-2233

LEAHEY, LYNN, editor-in-chief; From mem. staff to editor-in-chief Soap Opera Digest, N.Y.C., 1984—91, editor-in-chief, 1991—; editl. dir. Soap Opera Weekly, N.Y.C., 2001—. Office: Soap Opera Digest 261 Madison Ave Fl 10 New York NY 10016-2303

LEAHY, CHRISTINE A. information technology executive; b. 1964; Degree, Brown U.; JD, Boston Coll. Former ptnr. Sidley Austin Brown & Wood, Chgo.; pres., gen. counsel, corp. sec. CDW Computer Ctrs., Vernon Hills, Ill., 2002—. Office: CDW 200 N Milwaukee Ave Vernon Hills IL 60061

LEAK, MARGARET ELIZABETH, insurance company executive; b. Atlanta, Sept. 9, 1946; d. William Whitehurst and Margaret Elizabeth (Whitsitt) L. BS in Psychology, Okla. State U., 1968; postgrad., U. Okla., 1968-69, Cornell U., 1976-78; grad. advanced mgmt. program, Harvard U., 1983-84. Editor comm. Ea. State Bankcard Assn., N.Y.C., 1969-71; sr. edn. specialist Citibank, N.Y.C., 1971-73; adminstr. orgn. devel. NBC, N.Y.C., 1973-74; mgr. tng. and devel. Atlantic Mut. Cos., Property/Casualty Ins., N.Y.C., 1974-76, sec. human resources, 1976-78, v.p. human resources, 1978-84, v.p. human resources and corp. comm., 1984-86, sr. v.p. adminstrv. svcs., 1987-97, sr. v.p. adminstrn., corp. sec., 1998—. Office: Atlantic Mut Cos 3 Giralda Farms Madison NJ 07940-1027

LEAK, NANCY MARIE, artist; b. Takoma Park, Md., Nov. 24, 1931; d. George Morton and Ella (Oberholtzer) Hinkson; m. Thomas Clayton Leak Jr., Dec. 30, 1950; children: Suzanne M. Street, Sharon Leak-Hayden, Stephen, Scott. Grad. h.s., Washington. Co-illustrator: The Kissing Hand, 1993; exhbns. include Olney Art Assn., Internat. Exhbn. of the Miniature, Fla., Ga., Washington, N.J., Nev., Wash., Oreg., N.H., Mont. and Wyo., W.Va. and Pa., Cider Painters Am. Nat. Exhbn., Hunterdon Art Ctr., N.J., Sumner Mus., Washington, Gurmukhs Gallery, Aspen Hill, Md., Worldwide Miniature Exhbn., London, 1996, Australia, 2000, Hoffberger Gallery, Balt., Ocean City (Md.) Art League, Rockville (Md.) Art League, Md. Printmakers, Md. Ho. of Dels., Annapolis, NIH, Bethesda, Md., Johns Hopkins Space Telescope Sci. Inst., Balt., Del Bello Gallery, Ont., Can., Rockville Art League, Pinneberg, Germany, Gov's. Mansion, Annapolis, 1999, George Mason U. Art Gallery, Arlington, Va., 2000, The Women's Nat. Dem. Club, Washington, D.C., 2003, Sandyspring Mus., Md., 2003, Smithsonian Mus., Wash., 2004; participated in numerous juried or invitational exhbns. Recipient numerous awards for art. Mem.: Strathmore Arts Ctr. of Bethesda, Sr. Artists Alliance, Am. Art League, Rockville Arts Place, Cider Painters Am., Olney Art Assn., Rockville Art League, Miniature Art Soc. Fla., Miniature Painters, Sculptors and Gravers Assn. Washington, Md. Printmakers Assn., Nat. League Am. Pen Women. Democrat. Methodist. Avocations: crafts, reading, designing notecards, genealogy, photography.

LEAMY, NANCY M. professional athletics coach; b. Phila., Dec. 3, 1938; d. John E. and Anna Cecilia Madden; children: Anne Marie-Elizabeth Frances, Charles John, Catherine. BA, Boston Coll.; postgrad., Fairfield U. Dir. Greenwich Skating Sch. Dorothy Hamill Rink, Conn., 1971—; dir. Skating Greenwich Skating Club, Conn., 1971—95; internat., nat., regional, sectional figure skating coach, 1973—; head skating dir. Darien (Conn.) Ice Pk., 1997—2001, coach U.S. internat. team, Milan, 1997; U.S. nat. coach 2000 N. Am. Cup Challenge, 2000—01. Powerskating coach N.Y. Rangers Orgn., 1996—98; coach gold medalist Spl. Olympics, 1996; jr. olympic coach, 95, 97, 98. Mem.: Profl. Skaters Assn., U.S. Figure Skating Assn., Williams Club. Republican. Roman Catholic. Avocation: horseback riding. Home: 15 Mead Ave Cos Cob CT 06807

LEAN, JUDITH, physicist, researcher; BSc in Physics with honors, Australian Nat. U., 1974; PhD in Atmospheric Physics, U. Adelaide, Australia, 1980. Rschr. space sci. div. Naval Rsch. Lab., 1986—. Expert on sun's role in global climate change; mem. panels and adv. groups NASA; mem. adv. com. geosciences NSF; mem. panels and adv. groups NRC. Fellow: Am. Geophysical Union; mem.: NAS, Am. Meterol. Soc., Am. Astron. Soc. (mem. solar physics div.), Internat. Assn. Geomagnetism and Aeronomy. Office: Ballston Twr 800 N Quincy St Arlington VA 22217-5660

LEARY, CAROL ANN, academic administrator; b. Niagara Falls, N.Y., Mar. 29, 1947; d. Angelo Andrew and Mary Josephine (Pullano) Gigliotti; m. Noel Robert Leary, Dec. 30, 1972. BA, Boston U., 1969; MS, SUNY, Albany, 1970; PhD, Am. Univ., 1988. Asst. to v.p. for student affairs, dir. women's programs Siena Coll., Loudonville, N.Y., 1970-72; asst. dir. housing Boston U., 1972-78; dir. residence Simmons Coll., Boston, 1978-84, assoc. dean, 1984-85; assoc. dir. The Washington Campus, Washington, 1985-86; adminstrv. v.p., asst. to pres. Simmons Coll., Boston, 1988-94; pres. Bay Path Coll., Longmeadow, Mass., 1995—. Past pres., bd. govs. Colony Club; past pres. Cooperating Colls. of Greater Springfield; exec. com., vice-chair Cmty. Found. Western Mass; past pres. WGBY; bd. dirs. United Coop. Bank, Women's Coll. Coalition; dir. Frank Stanley Beveridge Found. Mem.: Assn. Ind. Colls. and Univs. Mass. (chair). Avocations: art, traveling overseas, hiking. Office: Bay Path Coll Office of the President 588 Longmeadow St Longmeadow MA 01106-2212 Office Phone: 413-565-1241.

LEARY, MARGARET, law librarian, library director; Dir. Law Libr. U. Mich., Ann Arbor. Office: U Mich Law Sch S180A Legal Rsch Bdlg S State St Ann Arbor MI 48109-1215 Business E-Mail: mleary@umich.edu.

LEARY, MARY LOU, prosecutor; Interim U.S. atty., Washington; acting dir. cmty. oriented policing svcs. U.S. Dept. Justice. Office: US Dept Justice Cmty Oriented Policing Svcs 1100 Vermont Ave NW Washington DC 20530-0001

LEASON, JODY JACOBS, newspaper columnist; b. Margarita, Venezuela, June 8, 1926; came to U.S., 1928; d. Jose Cruz Caceres and Graciela Rodriguez; m. Russell L. Jacobs (div.); 1 child, Jessica Jacobs Salet; m. Barney Leason, Dec. 29, 1976. BA, Hunter Coll.-CUNY, 1940's. Assoc. fashion editor Women's Wear Daily, N.Y.C., 1969-70, West Coast fashion editor L.A., 1957-69, London fashion editor, 1970-72; soc. editor L.A. Times, 1972-86. Author: (novel) The Right Circles, 1988. Avocations: needlework, gardening. E-mail: jaclea@lcan.net., jaclea@tcsn.net.

LEASOR, JANE, religion and philosophy educator, musician; b. Portsmouth, Ohio, Aug. 10, 1922; d. Paul Raymond Leasor and Rana Kathryn (Bayer) Leasor-McDonald. BA, Wheaton Coll., 1944; MRE, N.Y. Theol. Sem., 1952; PhD, NYU, 1969. Asst. prof. Belhaven Coll., Jackson, Miss., 1952-54; dept. chmn. Beirut Coll. for Women, 1954-59; asst. to pres. Wheaton (Ill.) Coll., 1961-63; dean of women N.Y. Theol. Sem., N.Y.C., 1963-67; counselor CUNY, Bklyn., 1967-74; assoc. prof. Beirut U. Coll., 1978-80; tchr. internat. sch., Les Cayes, Haiti, 1984-85; pvt. tutor, 1985—; tchr. Fayette County (W.Va.) Schs., 1993—; prof. religion dept. U. Charleston, W.Va., 1999—. Author religious text for use in Syria and Lebanon, 1960; editor books by V.R. Edman, 1961-63, Time and Life mags. Mem. Am. Assn. Counselors, Am. Guild Organists. Episcopalian. Avocations: reading, gardening, golf, travel, history Islam religion. Home and Office: 1429 1/2 Quarrier St Charleston WV 25301-3009

LEATHER, VICTORIA POTTS, college librarian; b. Chattanooga, June 12, 1947; d. James Elmer Potts and Ruby Lea (Bettis) Potts Wilmoth; m. Jack Edward Leather; children: Stephen, Sean. BA cum laude, U. Chattanooga, 1968; MSLS, U. Tenn., 1978. Libr. asst. East New Orleans Regional Libr., 1969-71; libr. Erlanger Nursing Sch., Chattanooga, 1971-75; chief libr. Erlanger Hosp., Chattanooga, 1975-77; dir. Eastgate Br. Libr., Chattanooga, 1977-81; dir. libr. svcs. Chattanooga State Tech. C.C., 1981-95, dean libr. svcs., 1996—. Mem. Allied Arts, Hunter Mus., High Mus. Art. Mem. ALA, Southeastern Libr. Assn., Tenn. Libr. Assn. (past chair legis. com.), Chattanooga Area Libr. Assn. (pres. 1978-79), Tenn. Bd. Regents Media Consortium (chair 1994-95), Phi Delta Kappa. Episcopalian. Avocations: reading, needlework, traveling. Office Phone: 615-697-2576. E-mail: vicky.leather@chattanoogastate.edu.

LEATHERBERRY, ANNE KNOX CLARK, architect; b. Geneva, Ill., Jan. 19, 1953; d. Donald William and Margaret Lorraine (Johnson) Clark; m. David Boyd Leatherberry, Aug. 5, 1978; children: Elizabeth Anne, Laura Knox. BS in Bus., Miami U., Oxford, Ohio, 1975. With Carson, Pirie, Scott & Co., Chgo., 1975-77; health care sales specialist Gen. Foods Corp., Northlake, Ill., 1977-78; account mgr. Cin., 1978-79; pres., owner Annie's Originals/Kids Collectables, Ltd., Waukesha, Wis., 1979—; mktg. rep./demonstrator mktg. Waukesha, 1988-91; owner Dreamhouse Designs, Waukesha, 1990—, Creative Enterprises Inc., 1990—. Cons. Lamb's Quarters, Hartford, Wis., 1982-83, Ungerwear, West Alexandria, Ohio, 1982-84, Little Bits, Waukeshaw, 1984-90, Evelyn's Creations, East Troy, Wis., 1986-90, The Queen's Empire, Inc., Pitts., 1989-90, DRC Co., Mukwonago, Wis., 1990—, Don Belman Builders, 1991-92, Millikin Homes, 1992—, Opportunity Homes, 1993—, Affordable Homes, 1993—, Gemini Homes, 1993, Nelson Remodeling, 1993. Active Waukesha Area Symphonic Band, 1979—, 98, 99, sec. bd. dirs., 1987-89, 99-02, v.p.; active Carroll Coll. Cmty. Orch., 1985-86; vol. tchr.'s aide Clarend on Avenue Sch., Mukwonago, 1988-89; asst. leader Girl Scouts U.S.A., 1988, leader, 1988-89; vol. staff aide Jim Thompson for Gov. Campaign, 1975-76; dir. Children's Choir, 1986; summer music dir. Luth. Ch., 1986, 88; events chmn. Edgewood Golf League, 1988-92; vol. Rose Glen Reading Rams, Waukesha, 1990-92, Health Room, 1990-91, tchr.'s aid, 1991-92; pres. archtl. rev. bd. Red Wing Hills Assn., 1993-96; instr. architecture mentor program Waukesha Sch. Dist., 1995—; spirit wear sales chmn., 1998-2002, Waukesha West H.S. Band Boosters, 1997—, bd. dirs., 1999-2002. Recipient Ptnrs. for Edn. award, 1998; named Parent Vol. of Yr. Waukesha C. of C., 1998. Mem. NAFE, PEO (officer 1980-82), Direct Mktg. Assn., Soc. Craft Designers, Met. Builders Assn., Nat. Assn. of Remodeling Industry, Kappa Kappa Gamma. Republican. Lutheran. Avocations: painting, sewing, reading, golf, gardening. E-mail address. Home and Office: W241s5910 Autumn Haze Ct Waukesha WI 53189-9512 Office Phone: 262-542-1498. E-mail: dreamhouse53@cs.com., dreamhouse53@cs.com.

LEATHERS, SUSAN LYNN, music educator; d. Richard Dean and Norma Ann (Whitemeyer) Young; m. Ronald Keith Leathers; children: Melissa Miller, Kyle. B. in Music Edn., Mount Union Coll., Alliance, Ohio, 1973; MusM, Ariz. State U., Tempe, 1980. Cert. Music Edn. K-12, Ariz. 1973. Music Educator, K-8 Creighton School District, Phoenix, 1973—85; Group Piano Instructor City of Phoenix, Phoenix, 1989—93; Assistant Program Director Girl Scouts of America, Cactus Pine Council, Phoenix, 1989—90; Private Music Teacher The PLACe Music Academy, Phoenix, 1991—2001; Music, Band and Strings Educator Washington School District, Phoenix, 1990—now. Volunteer Organist Faith United Methodist Church, Phoenix, 1981—95; musician Fiesta Bowl Play It Again Band, Phoenix, 1990—96, Ariz. Winds Concert Band, Glendale, 1990—; substance abuse coord. for Sunburst Sch. Washington Sch. Dist., Phoenix, 1995—00, mem. site coun., 1996—98. Mem.: Music Educators Nat. Conf. Methodist. Avocations: genealogy, needlecrafts, photography. Home: 11437 N 61st Drive Glendale AZ 85304 Office: Sunburst School 14218 N 47th Ave Phoenix AZ 85006 Personal E-mail: leatherssl@aol.com. Business E-Mail: sleathers1@cox.net.

LEAVITT, JUDITH WALZER, history of medicine educator; b. N.Y.C., July 22, 1940; d. Joseph Phillip and Sally (Hochman) Walzer; m. Lewis Arger Leavitt, July 2, 1966; children: Sarah Abigail, David Isaac. BA, Antioch Coll., 1963; MA, U. Chgo., 1966, PhD, 1975. Asst. prof. history of medicine U. Wis., Madison, 1975-81, assoc. prof., 1981-86, prof., 1986—, Evjue-Bascom prof., 1990-95, chmn. dept., 1981-93, assoc. dean for faculty, 1996-99, Ruth Bleier prof., 1997—. Author: The Healthiest City, 1982, Brought to Bed, 1986, Typhoid Mary, 1996; editor: Women and Health, 1984, 2d edit., 1999, Sickness and Health in America, 1985, 3d edit., 1998. Office: U Wis Dept History Medicine 1300 University Ave Madison WI 53706-1510

LEAVITT, MARY JANICE DEIMEL, special education educator, civic worker; b. Washington, Aug. 21, 1924; d. Henry L. and Ruth (Grady) Deimel; m. Robert Walker Leavitt, Mar. 30, 1945; children: Michael Deimel, Robert Walker, Caroline Ann Leavitt Snyder. BA, Am. U., 1946; postgrad., U. Md., 1963-65, U. Va., 1965-67, 72-73, 78-79, George Washington U., 1966-67. cert. spl. edn. tchr. 1968. Tchr. Rothery Sch., Arlington, Va., 1947; dir. Sunnyside Children's House, Washington, 1949; asst. dir. Coop Sch. for Handicapped Children, Arlington, 1962; dir. Arlington and Springfield, Va., 1963-66; tchr. mentally retarded children Fairfax (Va.) County Pub. Schs., 1966-68; asst. dir. Burgundy Farm Country Day Sch., Alexandria, Va., 1968-69; tchr., substitute tchr. specific learning problem children Accotink Acad., Springfield, Va., 1970-80; substitute tchr. learning disabilities Children's Achievement Ctr., McLean, Va., 1973-82, Psychiat. Inst., Washington and Rockville, Md., 1976-82, Home-Bound and Substitute Program, Fairfax, Va., 1978-84. Asst. info. splst. Ednl. Rsch. Svc., Inc., Rosslyn, Va., 1974-76; docent Sully Plantation, Fairfax County (Va.) Park Authority, 1981-87, 88-94, Children's Learning Ctrs. Vol. Honor Roll, 1987, Walney-Collections Fairfax County (Va.) Park Authority, 1989-97; sec. Widowed PersonsSvc., 1983-85, mem., 1985-90; mem. ednl. subcom. Va. Commn. Children and Youth, 1973-74; den mother Nat. Capital Area Cub Scouts, Boy Scouts Am., 1962; troop and fundraising chmn. Nat. Capitol coun. Girl Scouts U.S.A., 1968-69; capt. amblyopia team No. va. chpt. Delta Gamma Alumnae, 1969; vol. Prevention of Blindness, 1980-95; fund raiser Martha Movement, 1977-78; mem. St. John's Mus. Art, Wilmington, N.C., 1989—, Corcoran Gallery Art, Washington, 1989-90, 94—, Brunswick County Literacy Coun., N.C., 1989—; Sunday sch. tchr. St. Andrews Episcopal Ch., Burke, Va., 1995-99, mem. search com., 1996, libr. project, 1999; mem. World Affairs Coun. Washington DC, 1998—. Recipient award Nat. Assn. Retarded Citizens, 1975, Sully Recognition gift, 1989, Ten Yr. recognition pin Honor Roll, 1990. Mem. AAUW (co-chmn. met area mass media com. DC chpt. 1973-75, v.p. Alexandria br. 1974-76, fellowship co-chmn., historian Springfield-Annandale br. 1979-80, 89-94, 94-95, name grantee ednl. found., 1980, cultural co-chmn. 1983-84), Assn. Part-Time Profls. (co-chmn. Va. local groups, job devel. and membership asst. 1981), Older Women's League, Nat. Mus. Women in the Arts (charter), Libr. Congress Assocs. (nat.), Mil. Dist. Washington Officer's Clubs (McNair, Ft. Myer), Delta Gamma (treas. No. Va. alumnae chpt. 1973-75, pres. 1977-79, found. chmn. 1979-81, Katie Hale award 1989, treas. House Corp. Am. U. Beta Epsilon chpt. 1994-97). Episcopalian. Home: 7129 Rolling Forest Ave Springfield VA 22152-3622 also: 325A Brunswick Ave W Holden Beach NC 28462-1903

LEAVITT, SANDRA B. editor; b. Chgo., Nov. 27, 1933; d. Sidney S. and Jean (Goldberg) Bloch; m. Arnold Keith Leavitt, July 5, 1953; children: Debbie Leavitt Castleberry, Gail Leavitt Culberson. BA, Northeastern Ill. U., 1974, MA, 1978. Asst. editor Irving-Cloud Pub., Lincolnwood, Ill., 1979-82; assoc. editor Cahners Pub., Des Plaines, Ill., 1982-85; mng. editor Vance Pub., Lincolnshire, Ill., 1985-86; ret. Freelance feature writer in the field. Editor, newsletter Brandeis U. Nat. Women's Com., North Shore, Ill., 1994—. Mem. Am. Contract Bridge League (Master bridge player, winner nat. women's knock-out team, 1981), Brandeis U. Nat. Women's Com. (bd. dirs. 1993—). Avocations: frequent travel, walking, alumni courses at Northwestern, reading, stock and option trading. Home: 195 Linden Park Pl Highland Park IL 60035-2517

LEBEDOFF, RANDY MILLER, lawyer; b. Washington, Oct. 16, 1949, m. David Lebedoff; children: Caroline, Jonathan, Nicholas. BA, Smith Coll., 1971; JD magna cum laude, Ind. U., 1975. Assoc. Faegre & Benson, Mpls., 1975-82, ptnr., 1983-86; v.p., gen. counsel Star Tribune, Mpls., 1989—2001; asst. sec. Star Tribune Cowles Media Co., Mpls., 1990—98; pvt. practice Mpls., 2001—02; v.p., gen. counsel Twin Cities Public Television, 2002—. Bd. dirs. Milkweed Editions, 1989-96. Bd. dirs. Minn. Opera, 1986-90, YWCA, 1984-90, Planned Parenthood Minn., 1985-90, Fund for Legal Aid Soc., 1988-96, Abbott-Northwestern Hosp., 1990-94. Mem. Newspaper Assn. Am. (legal affairs com. 1991-2002), Minn. Newspapers Assn. (bd. dirs. 1995-2002, pres. 2002). Home: 1738 Oliver Ave S Minneapolis MN 55405-2222 Office: 172 E Fourth St Saint Paul MN 55101

LEBENTHAL, ALEXANDRA, investment firm executive; d. James and Jacqueline Beymer Lebenthal; m. Jeremy Diamond, 1991; children: Benjamin, Charlotte. AB history, Princeton U., 1986. Municipal bond dept. Kidder Peabody & Co., 1986—88; joined sales department Lebenthal & Co., N.Y.C., 1988, bd. dirs., 1992—, v.p., dir. mut. fund dept., 1993—94, v.p., dir. sales, 1994—95, pres., CEO, 1995—; chmn. Lebenthal Funds Inc., N.Y.C.; bd. dirs. Advest Inc., N.Y.C. Mem. adv. bd. Barbara K. Enterprises. Trustee Nightingale Bamford Sch., Citizen's Budget Commn.; co-founder, bd. dirs. The Women's Exec. Cir.; bd. dirs. United Jewish Appeal Fedn. N.Y. Named one of New York's 100 most influential women, Crain's N.Y. Bus., 1999. Mem.: Bond Market Assn. (bd. dirs. 2004), The Com. of 200, The Young Pres. Orgn. Office: Lebenthal & Co 120 Broadway Fl 12 New York NY 10271-0005*

LEBLANC, ADRIAN NICOLE, writer; b. Dec. 1963; BA, Smith Coll.; MA in philosophy and modern lit., Oxford; M in law studies, Yale U. Fiction editor, sr. editor Seventeen. Vis. scholar NYU Sch. Journalism. Author: Random Family: Love, Drugs, Trouble, and Coming of Age in the Bronx, 2003; contbr. The New York Times Magazine, The New Yorker, Esquire, Elle, Spin, The Source, The Village Voice; author: (stories and features) Gang Girl: When Manny's Locked-Up, 1994 (nominated George Polk Journalism Award), Landing From the Sky, 2000, When the Man of the House is in the Big House, 2003. Fellow: Mary Ingraham Bunting Inst., Open Soc. Inst. (media fellowship, Ctr. Crime, Cmty., and Culture 2001), Knight Assn.*

LE BLANC, ALICE ISABELLE, public health program, academic program administrator; b. New Orleans, Dec. 23, 1949; d. Joseph and Mary Elizabeth (Welsh) Le B.; divorced; 1 child, Matthew. BA in Drama & Comm., U. New Orleans, 1971; MPH, Tulane U., 1996. Sect. editor, feature writer Las Vegas Rev.- Jour., 1972-74; asst. dir. pub. rels. Touro Infirmary, New Orleans, 1980-82; dir. cmty. rels. AMI Riverside Hosp., Corpus Christi, Tex., 1982-84; dir. comm. United Way of the Coastal Bend, Corpus Christi, 1984-86; dir. pub. rels. & devel. Ada Wilson Hosp. Phys. Medicine and Rehab., Corpus Christi, 1986-89; mktg. mgr. nat. sexual trauma program River Oaks Psychiat. Hosp., New Orleans, 1989-90; mktg. cons./physician recruitment contract Eye, Ear, Nose & Throat Hosp., New Orleans, 1990; mgr. prog. svcs./exec. MHA recruitment, dept. health sys. Tulane U. Sch. Pub. Health and Tropical Mediicne, New Orleans, 1990-96; dir. admissions and student affairs Sch. Pub. Health, La. State U. Health Scis. Ctr., New Orleans, 1996—. Bd. dirs., bd. exec. com., chmn. standing com. United Way of the Coastal Bend, Corpus Christi, 1986, 87; bd. dirs. Early Childhood Devel. Ctr., Corpus Christi, 1988. Recipient Cert. of Appreciation, Gov. of Nev., 1974, Mayor of New Orleans, 1981, First Pl. award La. Hosp. Assn., 1982, Addy award of Excellence, Corpus Christi Advt. Fedn., 1986, 87, Addy First Place awards, 1988, Cert. of Recognition, United Way of the Coastal Bend, 1986, Cert. of Appreciation, Corpus Christi Jr. League, 1987. Avocations: gardening, carpentry, writing. Office: La State U Med Ctr Health Sci Ctr 1600 Canal St Ste 800 New Orleans LA 70112-2854

LEBLANC, EUGENIA TALBERT, counselor, educator; b. Gainesville, Fla., July 17, 1947; d. Samuel Stubbs and Francis Eleandor (Selzer) T.; m. Randall Joseph LeBlanc, children: Samuel Joseph, Joshua Randall, Virginia Adeline. BA in Edn., U. Miss., 1969, MEd in Guidance & Counseling, 1972; postgrad., Memphis State U., 1972-74. Cert. counselor; type "A" La. tchg. cert.; nat. cert. counselor; lic. profl. counselor, La. Liaison-tchr. counselor Western State Psych. Hosp., 1972-74; educator St. Charles Sch. Dist., Luling, La., 1986-93; counselor Nicholls State U., Thibodaux, La., 1993—. Coach various recreational youth soccer teams, Luling, La., 1987—, Youth Softball, Baseball & Track, Luling, La., 1987-91. Mem. ACA, Am. Coll. Counseling Assn., La. Counseling Assn., La. Career Devel. Assn., La. Sch. Counselors Assn., Southwest Assn. Student Assistance Program, La. Assn. Student Assistance Program. Avocations: tennis, camping, reading, gardening.

LEBLANC, JEAN EVA, writer, poet, educator; b. Leominster, Mass., Apr. 16, 1961; d. J. Camille and Sydne Grace (Lloyd) LeB. BS in Biology summa cum laude, Fitchburg State Coll., 1986; MA in English, Middlebury Coll., 1993. Adj. instr. English Sussex County C.C., Newton, NJ, 1999—. Contbr. poetry, book revs., and essays to various periodicals, mus. revs. to Classical disCDigest; contbr. natural history articles to Appalachian Trailway News, Gen. Store Mag. Avocations: hiking, visiting museums, reading, art.

LEBLANC, JEANNE MARIE, psychologist, educator; b. Tallahassee, Fla., May 19, 1965; d. Joseph Wilfred Jr. and Annalois (Jackson) LeB.; m. William Robert Hitch, Dec. 17, 1983 (div. Mar. 1992); 1 child, Jessica Elaine; m. Patrick Henry Bogan III, Oct. 8, 1994. AA, Richland Coll., 1987; BA summa cum laude, U. Tex., Dallas, 1989; PhD, U. Tex. Southwestern Med. Ctr., 1997. Lic. psychologist, Tex. Clin. psychology intern Parkland Meml. Hosp., Dallas, 1990-93, Terrell (Tex.) State Hosp., 1990-91, Scottish Rite Hosp., Dallas, 1991-92, So. Meth. U., Dallas, 1992-93; assessment specialist, neurocognitive therapist Pate Rehab., Dallas, 1993-99, neuropsychol. resident, 1997-99; asst. prof. counseling and human behavior Amber U., Garland, Tex., 1998—; program mgr. Marshall (Tex.) Youth Svcs. Sabine Valley Ctr., 1999—. Test examiner The Psychol. Corp., San Antonio, 1999—. Presenter (symposium) Ecologically Valid Treatment, 1998. Vol. crisis worker The Family Place, Dallas, 1986-88; vol. family facilitator Divert Ct.—Dallas County, 1999. Mem. APA, Tex. Psychol. Assn., MENSA. Avocations: playing clarinet, traveling, attending cultural events, literary discussions. Office: Sabine Valley Ctr 2615 E End Blvd S Marshall TX 75672-7403

LE BLANC, SUZANNE, museum director; Exec. dir. Lied Discovery Children's Mus., Las Vegas, Nev., 1990—. Office: Lied Discovery Childrens Mus 833 Las Vegas Blvd N Las Vegas NV 89101-2059

LEBLANC, TINA, dancer; b. Erie, Pa. m. Marco Jerkunica, May 1988; children: Marinko James, Sasha Johan. Trained, Carlisle, Pa. Dancer Joffrey II Dancers, N.Y.C., 1982-83, The Joffrey Ballet, N.Y.C., 1984-92; prin. dancer San Francisco Ballet, 1992—. Guest tchr. Ctrl. Pa. Youth Ballet, 1992, 94—. Work includes roles in (with San Francisco Ballet) Con Brio, Bizet Pas de Deux, Swan Lake, Nanna's Lied, Handel--A Celebration, La fille mal gardée, Rubies, Tchaikovsky Pas de Deux, Seeing Stars, The Nutcracker, La Pavane Rouge, Company B, Romeo and Juliet, Sleeping Beauty, The Dance House, Terra Firma, Lambarena, Fly by Night, In the Night, Ballo della Regina, The Lesson, The Tuning Game, Quartette, Etudes, Western Symphony, Maelstrom, Pacific, Criss-Cross, Giselle, Theme and Variations, Gala Performance, The Vertiginous Thrill of Exactitude, Taiko, Sandpaper Ballet, La Bayadere, Night, Serenade, Celts, Stars & Stripes, Tarantella, Symphony in C, Dances at a Gathering, Don Quixote (full length), Square Dance, Apollo, Rush, Paquita, Who Cares, Study in Motion, 7 for Eight, Symphonic Variations, Sea Pictures; (with other companies) The Green Table, Les Presages, Le sacre du printemps, Les Noces, Light Rain, Romeo and Juliet, Runaway Train, Empyrean Dances, La Vivandière, L'air D'esprit, Corsaire Pas de deux, Don Quixote pas de deux, Lacrymosa, Confetti, Kettentanz Le Beau Danube, Offenbach in the Underworld, Suite Saint Saens, Forgotten Land, Dream Dances, Postcards, Coppelia, Remembrances, Reflections, Cotillion. Recipient Princess Grace Found. award, 1988, Princess Grace Statuette award, 1995, Isadora Duncan award, 1998-99, 2000-01. Office: San Francisco Ballet Assn 455 Franklin St San Francisco CA 94102-4471

LEBLANC, VICTORIA ANNE, elementary school educator; b. Port Arthur, Tex., May 17, 1952; d. Carl Nelson and Vera Adoree (Langworthy) LeB. BS in Theatre/speech, Lamar U., 1974; MA in Theatre/speech, U. Ala., 1977. Voice and diction tchr. asst. U. Ala., Tscaloosa, 1974-76; theatre, speech instr. Lamar U., Beaumont, Tex., 1976-78, 82-83, 93-94, Port Arthur, Tex., 1978-81, 94-95; 1st grade tchr. L.A. Unified, 1985-86; tchr. theatre and reading Groves Mid. Sch., 1997—. Performer My Fair Lady, 1973, 81, The Belle of Amherst, 1982, Little Broadway, L.A., 1986-88, Rock Salt Co., L.A., 1989-91, Imagination Co., L.A., 1991-92, Am. Family Theatre, 1994, Man of La Mancha, 1995. Mem. Mensa, Lions, Alpha Psi Omega. Avocations: music, singing, chinese painting, reading, yoga.

LEBO, LENORE B. counselor; b. West Newbury, Mass., Oct. 16, 1938; d. Francis Alfonso Bartlett and Margaret Gordon McKay Bartlett; m. Burton C. Lebo, June 20, 1959; children: Peggy, Martin, Karen, Edward. BS in English, Springfield Coll., 1960; EdM in Early Childhood, R.I. Coll., 1976, MA in Agy. Counseling, 1977; postgrad., Gordon-Cornwell Sem., 1980—82. LCSW; lic. tchr. Owner preschools various locations, 1968—2000, pvt. grant writer, 1979—89; Head Start dir. Cape Ann Child Devel. Project, Gloucester, Mass., 1979—86; Christian edn. min. 1st Congl. Ch., South Hamilton, Mass., 1980—83; Child Devel. Assoc. trainer Wheelock Coll., 1982—85; vol. counselor, grant writer Advent Christian Village, Fla., 2002—. Author: (children's book) Andy's Red Wagon, 1997; contbr. poetry to anthologies. Republican. Avocations: crafts, quilting, knitting, travel, doll collecting. Home and Office: PO Box 4788 23310 River Birch Ln Dowling Park FL 32064

LEBOUTILLIER, MEGAN, writer; b. N.Y.C., Apr. 5, 1955; d. Charles and Deirdre Jones (Johnson) LeB. BA, Vt. Coll., 1985; PhD, Union Inst., Cin., 1998. Health educator Planned Parenthood, Missoula, Mont., 1977-80, dir. cmty. edn. Atlanta, 1980-85; pres. Seaglass Publs., Atlanta, 1985-88, pres., writer Pawleys Island, S.C., 1988-88; facilitator The Courage to Teach, Free Union, Va., 1998—; freelance writer, Free Union, 1998—. Vis. author, lectr. Emory U., Atlanta, 1987, 91, Waccamaw Libr., Pawleys Island, 1996, 2000, Coastal Carolina U., Conway, S.C., 1999, 2000; facilitator Leadership Acad., Conway, 1993, 94. Author: Little Miss Perfect, 1990, "No" Is a Complete Sentence, 1995; co-author: Birth Control, The Movie, 1986. Bd. dirs. LWV, Georgetown, S.C., 1989-98, pres., 1993-95; bd. dirs., eductor AIDS Task Force, Georgetown, 1991-96. Avocations: bicycling, hiking, cooking, gardening, weaving. Office: PO Box 325 Free Union VA 22940 E-mail: mimileb@mindspring.com.

LEBOWITZ, CATHARINE KOCH, state legislator; b. Winchester, Mass., June 30, 1915; d. William John and Carolyn Sophia (Kistinger) Koch; m. Murray Lebowitz, Sept. 21, 1971 (dec. Oct. 1978). Student, Northwestern U., 1948-49, Boston Coll., 1949-52; degree (hon.), Ea. Main Tech. Coll., 2003. Sec. ERA, Bangor, Augusta, Maine, 1935-38, WPA, Portland, Maine, 1938-42; pers. officer, exec. sec. USN, Portland, 1942-47; exec. sec. Clark Babbitt, Boston, 1947-48; adminstrv. asst. Moore Bus. Forms, Boston, 1948-52; apt. mgr., wholesale appliance divsn. Coffin-Wimple Inc., 1952-62; clk. U.S. Dist. Ct. Bangor (no. dist.), 1962-79; sec. Portland Credit Bur., 1980-86; mem. Bangor City Coun., 1985-87, Maine State Legislature, 1982-92. Bd. dirs. Eastern Transp., 1989—94; mem. Bus. Adv. Coun., 1991—; active Program Rev. Subcom., 1991—; mem. adv. coun. Ea. Maine Tech. Coll., 1992—; bd. dirs. Rural Health Ctrs. Maine, Inc., 1992—99; chair, adv. bd., Gala decorating com. Maine Ctr. for Arts, U. Maine, 1992—2003. Sec. Symphony Women, Bangor, 1964—84; bd. dirs. Opera House Com., 1978—94; legis. com. United Way of Penobscot Valley, 1988—93, bd. dirs., 1993—99; adv. com. Maine Devel. Found., 1988—90; adv. bd. Aftercare, Cmty. Health & Counseling Svc., 1992; planning bd. St. Joseph Hosp., 1987—92; dir., v.p. St. Joseph Hosp. Aux., 1994—99, Maine Ctr. Arts Adv. Bd., 1994—; apptr. by gov. Maine Commn. Cmty. Svc., 1996—2002; mem. Bangor City Hosp. Aux., 1988—; bd. dirs. Penobscot Theatre, 1990; accredited Beauty Pageant judge, 1986—; mem. Eastern Main Commn. Cmty Svc., 1996; del. Rep. Nat. Conv., 1984, 1988. Recipient Civilian Meritorious Svc. award USN, Portland, Maine, 1946, Paul Bunyan award, C. of C., 1997, Cmty. Spirit award Sr. Star recognition Merrill Merchants Bank Bangor, 1999; named Hon. Alumnus Secretarial Sci., Husson Coll., 1980, Ea. Main Tech. Coll. Champion award, 2002. Mem.: Ea. Maine Med. Ctr. Aux., Ret. Fed. Employees (v.p. 1994—, pres. 1996), Newcomb Soc., Penobscot County Reps., Bangor C. of C. (mem. comsumer rels. coun., 1981-90, gov. affairs com. 1996—, coord. 150th ann. prodn. Music Man 1984), Bangor Dist. Nursing Assn. (corp. mem. at large), Credit Women Bangor (sec. 1965—67), Nat. Assn. Ret. Fed. Employees (v.p. bd. dirs. 1993—, sec. 1994), Credit Profls. Bangor Cmty. Theater (treas. 1973—98), Credit Women Internat. (treas. 1975—77), Penobscot County Ext. Svc. (hon.; bd. dirs. 1995—), Main Art N.G. (hon.), Maine N.G. Assn. (hon.), Bangor Hist. Soc. (bd. dirs. 1993—, exec. bd. sec. 1994—99, pres. 1999—2002), U. Maine Maine Masque Theater (judge 1983—90), Mgmt. Club, Bangor City Rep. Club (bd. dirs., treas. 1993—97), Penobscot County Rep. Women's Club (sec. 1979), Zonta Club (pres. Bangor 1962—64, 1980—82, v.p. 1994, adv. bd. Maine migrant health program 2001—, cooperator cmty. health and counseling svcs. 2001—, Outstanding Leader 1991).

LEBOWITZ, CHARLOTTE MEYERSOHN, social worker; b. Germany, Dec. 22, 1924; arrived in U.S., 1938, naturalized, 1943; d. Franz and Magda (Wellisch) Meyersohn; m. Marshall Lebowitz, Aug. 7, 1949; children: Wendy, Marian, Mark (dec.). BA, Brown U., 1946; MSW, Simmons Coll., 1948. Psychiat. social worker Jewish Family and Children's Svc., Boston, 1948-49, ARC Home Svc. Dept., Boston, 1949-53, Youth Guidance Ctr., Framingham, Mass., 1962-69, Brandon Sch., Natick, Mass., 1969-74, Natick Pub. Schs., 1975-92. Adj. clin. instr. Boston Coll. Sch. Social Work, 1981-82; mem. exec. bd. Natick Svc. Coun., 1982-95; cons. YWCA, 1970-71. Mem. exec. bd. PTA, 1955-71, chmn. pre-sch. unit, 1955-56, mem. coun., 1956-70; trustee coun. Leonard Morse Hosp., 1976-91. Fellow: Am. Orthopsychiat. Assn.; mem.: NASW, Boston Inst. Devel. Infants and Parents, Social Workers Employed Less than Full Time, Sch. Adjustment Counselors Assn., Acad. Cert. Social Workers, Sisterhood of Temple Israel of Natick, Nonesuch Pond Improvement Assn., Brown U. Alumni Assn., Simmons Coll. Sch. Social Work Alumni Assn. Home: 2 Abbott Rd Natick MA 01760-1913

LEBRETON, MARJORY, senator; b. City View, ON, Can., July 4, 1940; m. Douglas LeBreton; children: Linda Marlene(dec.), Michael Bruce. Student, Ottawa Bus. Coll. Campaign worker Progressive Conservative Nat. Hdqrs., 1962—63, Office of Rt. Hon. John G. Diefenbaker, 1963—67; office supr. Hon. Robert L. Stanfield, 1967—75; tour coord. Office of Rt. Hon. Joe Clark, 1976—79; dir. scheduling Office of Prime Min. Clark, 1979—80; dir. leader's tour and spkrs. bur. Progressive Conservative Nat. Hdqrs., 1981—83; tour coord., co-dir. nat. campaign tour Rt. Hon. Brian Mulroney, 1983—84; gen. mgr., dir. ops. Ottawa office Progressive Conservative Party, 1985; spl. asst. Office of Prime Min., 1986—87, dep. chief staff, spl. asst., 1987—93; senator The Senate of Can., Ottawa, 1993—. Bd. dirs. Manotick Watsons Mill Millenium Fund. Mem.: MADD (nat. bd. dirs., chair pub. policy com.), Nepean Carleton Riding Assn., Nat. Press Club, Albany Club. Progressive. Avocation: gardening. Office: 802 Victoria Bldg The Senate of Canada Ottawa ON Canada K1A 0A4

LECHER, BELVADINE (BELVADINE REEVES), museum curator; b. Plainview, Nebr., Nov. 14, 1921; d. Robert Ancil and Myrtle Ivian (Rodgers) Reeves; m. Raymond Ralph Lecher, June 6, 1943; children: Krissa R. Lecher Randall, Pamela G. Lecher Hersh, Kim N. Lecher. Cert. in Hosp. Adminstrn., St. Louis U., 1967. Sec. Baird Law Office, Gordon, Nebr., 1938-39; cashier, bookkeeper, receptionist Western Pub. Svc. Co., Gordon, 1939-41, Consumers Pub. Power Co., Chadron, Nebr., 1941-45; cashier, bookkeeper, med. records Luth. Hosp. Homes Soc., Crawford, Nebr., 1952-62, adminstr., 1962-70; rate auditor, acct. Ross Transfer, Inc., Chadron, 1970-90; curator, dir. Dawes County Hist. Soc. Mus., Chadron, 1992—. Editor: (newspaper) Golden Age Courier, 1994—, (newsletter) Dawes County Hist. Soc., 1981—; co-editor: (book) Man of Many Frontiers - The Diaries of Billy the Bear Iaeger, 1994. Active Am. Cancer Soc., Dawes County, 1981—2003; tutor adult basic edn., Chadron, 1990—95; bd. dirs. Habitat for Humanity, Chadron, 1993—95. Recipient Cmty. Svc. award Rotary, Chadron, 1985, Good Neighbor award Ak-Sar-Ben/Omaha World Herald, Omaha, 1994, Woman of the Yr. award Chadron Bus. and Profl. Women's Club, Chadron, 1996, Recognition of Vol. Svc. award Am. Legion Aux., Chadron, 1994. Mem. Nebr. Mus. Assn., Nebr. State Genealogy Soc. (query editor 1982-84), Northwest Genealogy Soc. (county dir. 1992-94), Dawes County Hist. Soc. (pres. 1981-92, mus. curator 1992—), DAR (regent 1978, 80, 2000-02, registrar, 1982-95, treas. 1972-82), Area C. of C. (vis. com. 1996—). Republican. Methodist. Avocations: historic and lineage research, reading, writing, handcrafts, hiking. Office: Dawes County Hist Soc PO Box 1319 Chadron NE 69337-7329

LECHEVALIER, MARY PFEIL, retired microbiologist, educator; b. Cleve., Jan. 27, 1928; d. Alfred Leslie Pfeil and Mary Edith Martin; m. Hubert Arthur Lechevalier, Apr. 7, 1950; children: Marc E.M., Paul R. BA in Physiology-Biochemistry, Mt. Holyoke Coll., 1949; MS in Microbiology, Rutgers U., 1951. Rsch. fellow Rutgers U., New Brunswick, N.J., 1949-51, rsch. assoc. inst. microbiology, 1962-74, from asst. to assoc. rsch. prof., 1974-85, rsch. prof. Waksman inst. microbiology, 1985-91, prof. emerita, 1991—; ind. rschr., 1955-59; microbiologist steroid preparative lab. E.R. Squibb and Sons, New Brunswick, 1960-61; vis. investigator Inst. Biology Czechoslovak Acad. Scis., Svc. de Mycologie Pasteur Inst., Prague, Paris, 1961-62. Cons. in field. Contbr. over 100 chpts. to books and articles to rsch. jours.; mem. adv. com. actinomycetes Bergey's Manual of Determinative Bacteriology, 8th edit.; chair adv. com. muriform actinomycetes Bergey's Manual, 9th edit. Assoc. mem. Bergey's Trust, 1989-92. Recipient Charles Thom award Soc. Indsl. Microbiology, 1982, Waksman award Theobald Smith Soc., 1991. Mem. AAAS, Am. Soc. Microbiology (former mem. com. actinomycetales), U.S. Fedn. Culture Collections (exec. com. 1982-85, J. Roger Porter award nominating com. 1983-84, 87-88, chair 1989-90, J. Roger Porter award 1992), N.Am. Mycol. Assn., Soc. for Actinomycetes Japan, Sigma Xi (pres. Rutgers U. chpt. 1977-78). Achievements include patents for immunological adjuvant and process for preparing same, pharmaceutical composition and process, restriction endonuclease Fse I, antibiotic LL-14E605B and O-Methyl LL-14E605B. Home: 131 Goddard-Nisbet Rd Morrisville VT 05661-8041

LECHOWICZ, LISA MARIE, retired insurance company executive; b. Chgo., Feb. 11, 1954; d. Edmund Lawrence and Gloria Marie (Radtke) L.; m. John F. Hession, Jr. May 26, 1983. BS, MS, Purdue U., 1977. CLU, ChFC; cert. employee benefits specialist, health ins. assoc. Cons. Accenture, Chgo., 1978-79, sr. cons. Omaha, 1979-81; systems analyst Mutual of Omaha, 1981-82, mgr., 1982-87, asst. v.p., mgr., 1987-89, 2nd v.p., dir., 1989-92, v.p., dir., 1992-95, sr. v.p., 1995-96; pres. Health Data Mgmt. Corp., Omaha, 1996—. Part-time instr. Met. C.C., Omaha, 1988-91, adv. bd., 1989-90, Coll. of St. Mary's, 1990-94. Campaign com. various local candidates, Omaha, 1988—; hon. chair A Taste for Independence Easter Seals, 2003. Mem. CLU Soc., WEDI, Omaha Jaycees (bd. dirs. 1988-89, Bronze Key award 1989), Nebr. Choral Arts Soc. (voce chair event 2002, voce silent auction chair 2002-2003). Home: 15611 Burt St Omaha NE 68118-2219 Office: HDM Corp 720 N 129th St Omaha NE 68154-6109 E-mail: ll@hdmcorp.com.

LECHTANSKI, CHERYL LEE, chiropractor; b. Elizabeth, N.J., Dec. 27, 1961; d. Leo Joseph and Barbara Frances (Sullivan) Lechtanski. BA in Biology and Journalism, NYU, 1985; DC, N.Y. Chiropractic Coll., 1989; AAS in Acctg., Brookdale CC, 1998; MBA, Monmouth U., 2002. Lic. chiropractor N.J., N.Y., Pa., Del., Mich. Chiropractic assoc. Chiropractic Arts Ctr., Downingtown, Pa., 1990—91; pvt. practice Newark, 1992-93; with Morganville (N.J.) Family Chiropractic Office, 1993—. Mem.: Marine Mammal Stranding Ctr., Save the Manatee Club, Pa. Chiropractic Assn., Ocean Conservancy, Box Turtle Coalition N.E. (founder), Beta Gamma Sigma, Phi Chi Omega. Buddhist. Avocations: horseback riding, hiking, herpetology, softball, swimming. Home: 1 Kennedy Ct Middletown NJ 07748-3531 Office: Morganville Family Chiropractic Office 52 Tennent Rd Morganville NJ 07751-4153 Office Phone: 732-591-1223. E-mail: paboxies@hotmail.com.

LECKEY, DOLORES R. religious organization administrator, writer; b. N.Y.C., Apr. 12, 1933; d. Joseph Francis and Florence Marie Conklin; m. Thomas Philip Leckey, June 22, 1957; children: Mary Kate Marcellus, Celia E., Thomas Joseph, Colum. BA, St. John's U., Bklyn., 1954; MA, George Washington U., 1971; 12 hon. degrees. English tchr. Delahanty H.S., N.Y.C., 1954-56; elem. tchr. Oliver Sch., South Bend, Ind., 1957-58; sem. prof., adminstr DeSales Sch. Theology, Washington, 1971-77; TV prodr. Pub. TV/WNVT, Annandale, Va., 1974-76; ch. exec. Nat. Conf. Cath. Bishops, Washington, 1977-97; sr. fellow WTC, Georgetown U., Washington, 1998—. Author: The Ordinary Way, 1982 (Critic's Choice, Commonweal 1982), Laity Stirring the Church, 1987, Practical Spirituality, 1987, Women and Creativity, 1991, Winter Music, 1992, 7 Essentials for the Spiritual Journey, 1999, Blessings All Around, 1999, Co-Author: Facing Fear with Faith, 2002, exec. prodr. videos. Founder Arlington Partnership for Affordable Housing, 1989—; mem. Arlington Com. of 100, 1976—; mem. adv. bd. Arlington Street People Assistance, 1998—; trustee U. Dayton, 1991-2001, St. Mary's U. and Sem., Balt., 1989-95; bd. dirs. Arlington Symphony. Recipient Recognition award Nat. Assn. Cath. Family Life Mins., 1998, Disting. Svc. award Washington Theol. Union, 1988; Louisville Inst. grantee, 1998. Mem. Assn. for Religion and Intellectual Life. Democrat. Roman Catholic. Avocations: piano, theater and opera, hiking, reading. Office: Georgetown U Woodstock Theol Ctr Washington DC 20052-0001 Home: Apt 601W 3835 9th St N Arlington VA 22203-4083

LECKIE, CAROL MAVIS, retired state government administrator; b. Watertown, Wis., Feb. 25, 1929; d. Arthur Walter Bessel and Effie Vada (Squires) Downs; m. Ralph Junior Judd, Sept. 27, 1947 (div. Dec. 1952); Children: Russell Howard, Barbara Rae; m. Leonard John Leckie, Sept. 30, 1977 (dec. May 1990); stepchildren: Leonard John, Gordon Armstrong, Lorna Jean. Grad. h.s., Madison, Wis. Mgr. data processing Dept. Justice, State of Wis., Madison, 1971-79, mgr. Records Mgmt. Program, 1979-83, mgr. Typography Sect., 1983-90; ret. Mem. com. State of Wis. Employees Combined Campaign, Madison, 1986, 88-91, co-chair, 1987; co-chair East 1946 Class Reunion Com. Mem. Assn. Records Mgrs. and Adminstrs. (pres. 1983-84), Assn. Career Employees, Bus. Forms Mgmt. Assn. Lutheran. Avocations: travel, church work. Home: 5555 Tancho Dr Apt 106 Madison WI 53718-1929 E-mail: cmjl106@chorus.net.

LECKLE, CHERYL ANN, special education educator; d. James Francis and Edene Frances Barbour; m. Joseph Michael Leckle, June 11, 1983; children: Shalah Renee, Brianna Colleen. AA, Linn-Benton C.C., 1980; BS in Music Edn., Oreg. State U., 1983; student program in music edn., Western Oreg. U., 1987, Oreg. State U., 2004. Lic. in tchg. music edn. K-12, spl. edn. Tchr. music Philomath H.S., Ohio, 1983—99, tchr. spl. edn., 1999—, Philomath Mid. Sch., 2003—. Transition coord. Philomath H.S., 1999—2003. Mem. Music Educators Nat. Conf., 1983—, McDonald's Nat. Marching Band, 1983, State Band Competition, 1987. Mem.: Coun. Exceptional Children. Democrat. Avocations: tuba, bass, saxophone, theater. Office: Philomath HS 2054 Applegate St Philomath OR 97370

LECLAIR, SUSAN JEAN, hematologist, clinical laboratory scientist, educator; b. New Bedford, Mass., Feb. 17, 1947; d. Joseph A. and Beatrice (Perry) L.; m. James T. Griffith; 1 child, Kimberly A. BS in Med. Tech., Stonehill Coll., 1968; MS in Med. Lab. Sci., U. Mass., Dartmouth, 1977; PhD in Clin. Hematology, Walden U., 2001. Cert. clin. lab. scientist; cert. med. technologist. Med. technologist Union Hosp., New Bedford, Mass., 1968-70; supr. hematology Morton Hosp., Taunton, Mass., 1970-72; edn. coord., program dir. Sch. Med. Tech. Miriam Hosp., Providence, 1972-79; hematology technologist R.I. Hosp., Providence, 1979-80; asst. prof. med. lab. sci. U. Mass., Dartmouth, 1980-84, assoc. prof. med. lab. sci., 1984-92, prof. med. lab. sci., 1992—. Instr. hematology courses Brown U., Providence, 1978-80; cons. bd. Div. Clin. Hematology, Charlton Meml. Hosp., St. Luke's Hosp., 1984-2000, Nemasket Group, Inc., 1984-87, Gateway Health Alliance, 1985-87, Pawtucket Meml. Hosp., 1999-2001; chair hematology/hemostasis com. Nat. Cert. Agy. for Med. Lab. Pers. Exam. Coun., 1994-98. Editor-in-chief, Clin. Lab. Sci., 2000; contbr. articles to profl. jours.; contbr. articles to jours and chpts. to books; author computer software in hematology; creator, dir. consumer info. web page, 2000-. Reviewer Nat. Commn. Clin. Lab. Scis., 1986-89; chairperson Mass. Assn. Health Planning Agys., 1986-87; bd. dirs. Southeastern Mass. Health Planning Devel. Inc., (1975-88, numerous other offices and coms.); planning subcom. AIDS Edn. (presentor Info Series). Mem. Am. Soc. Clin. Lab. Sci. (editor clin. practice sect. CLS jour. 1996-2000, editor-in-chief CLS jour. 2001—, creator and dir. Consumer INfo. Web Page), Am. Soc. Med. Tech. Edn. and Rsch. Fund, Inc. (chair 1983-85), Mass. Assn. for Med. Tech. (pres. 1977-78), Southeastern Mass. Soc. Med. Tech. (pres. 1975-76), Alpha Mu Tau (pres. 1993-94). Avocations: choral singing, cooking, reading. Office: U Mass Dept Med Lab Sci Dartmouth MA 02747 E-mail: sleclair@umassd.edu.

LECOCQ, KAREN ELIZABETH, artist; b. Santa Rosa, Calif., Nov. 4, 1949; d. Maynard Rodney and Lois May (Lessard) LeC.; m. David Lawrence Medley, Sept. 7, 1995. BA, Calif. State U., Fresno, 1971, MA, 1975; postgrad., Calif. Inst. of the Arts, L.A., 1971-72. Founding mem. Feminist Art Program, Fresno, Calif., 1971, Calif. Inst. of the Arts, L.A., 1972. Vis. artist Merced County Schs., 1977-82, 88-91; grad. instr. Calif. State U., Fresno, 1976-78. One-woman shows include Calif. State U. Art Gallery, Fresno, 1970, 76, Merced (Calif.) Coll., 1969, 77, 91, Calif. Inst. of the Arts, L.A., 1972, Womanart Gallery, N.Y.C., 1980, Amos Eno Gallery, N.Y.C., 1994, 97, 750 Gallery, Sacramento, 1995, Meridian Gallery, San Francisco, 1993, Wild Gallery, Sacramento, 1999; group shows include Womanhouse, L.A., 1972, Off Centre Centre, Calgary, Alta., Can., 1985, 86, Ryosuke Gallery, Osaka, Japan, 1986, Gallery Six Oh One, San Francisco, 1989, Fresno Art Mus., 1989, Pro arts Gallery, Oakland, Calif., 1991, Calif. Mus. Art, Santa Rosa, 1991, Harbs Gallery, Lexington, Va., 1992, Russell Sage Gallery, Troy, N.Y., 1992, Amos Eno Gallery, 1994, 97, ARC Gallery, Chgo., 1993, 96, Lengyel Gallery, San Francisco, 1995, 750 Gallery, Sacramento, 1994-96, L.A. Mus. Contemporary Art, 1995, Armand Hammer Mus., L.A., 1996, Whitney Mus. Am. Art, N.Y.C., 1999, numerous others; commns. include Absolut Vodka, 1993. Docent Gallery Guide Art Train, Merced, 1983; artistic dir. Black and White Ball, Merced Regional Arts Coun., 1989-99. Democrat. Home and Office: PO Box 2204 Merced CA 95344-0204 E-mail: sales@karenlecocq.com.

LECOMPTE, ELIZABETH, theater director; b. Summit, N.J., Apr. 28, 1944; BS, Skidmore COll., 1967. Founder, dir. Wooster Group, N.Y.C., 1980—. Director: Frank Dell's The Temptation of Saint Antony, 1987, Brace Up!, 1991, Fish Story, 1993, The Emperor Jones, 1994, The Hairy Ape, 1995. Recipient Obie award for Point Judith; MacArthur fellow, 1995, NEA Disting. Artists fellow for lifetime achievement in Am. theater. Office: The Wooster Group PO Box 654 Canal St New York NY 10013

LECORGNE, LISETTE MARY, family practice nurse practitioner; b. New Orleans, La., Aug. 11, 1955; d. Louis Constant and Nodileen LeCompte LeCorgne. RN, No. Ariz. U., 1978; nurse practitioner, U. of Colo., 1980—82; BS in Health Arts, U. St. Francis, 1982, MS in Healthcare Adminstrn., 2004. NP, Ariz., ANCC, 1983. Med. coord. Hozhoni Found., Flagstaff, Ariz., 1979—83; nurse practitioner U. of Ariz. Campus Health, Tucson, 1983—, coord. urgent care, triage/radiology. Past pres., bd. mem. Flying Samaritans, Tucson, 1996—. Delivery of health care to indigent, Tucson, 1996—2003. Recipient Appreciation award, Associated Students with Disabilities, 1998. Mem.: ANA (assoc.). Episcopal. Avocations: woodworking, travel. Home: 5133 E Adams St Tucson AZ 85713-4105 Office: University of Arizona Campus Health PO Box 210063 Tucson AZ 85721-0063 Office Phone: 520-621-6490. Personal E-mail: lisettelecorgne@hotmail.com. E-mail: lecorgne@health.arizona.edu.

LE COUNT, VIRGINIA G. communications company executive; b. Long Island City, N.Y., Nov. 22, 1917; d. Clifford R. and Luella (Meier) LeCount. BA, Barnard Coll., 1937; MA, Columbia U., 1940. Tchr. pub. schs., P.R., 1937-38; supr. HOLC, N.Y.C., 1938-40; translator Guildhall Publs., N.Y.C., 1940-41; office mgr. Sperry Gyroscope Co., Garden City, Lake Success, Bklyn. (all N.Y.), 1941-45; billing mgr. McCann Erickson, Inc., N.Y.C., 1945-56; v.p., bus. mgr., bd. dirs. Infoplan Internat, Inc., N.Y.C., 1956-69; v.p., bus. mgr. Communications Affiliates Ltd., Communications Affiliates (Bahamas) Ltd., N.Y.C., 1964-69; bus. mgr. Jack Tinker & Ptnrs., Inc., N.Y.C., 1969-70; mgr. office services Interpublic Group of Cos., Inc., N.Y.C., 1971-72, corp. records mgr., 1972-83, mktg. intelligence data mgr., 1975-83. Mem. Alumnae Barnard Coll., N.Y. Health and Racquet Club Spa. Mem. Marble Collegiate Ch. Home: 136 E 55th St Apt 10Q New York NY 10022-4523

LEDBETTER, SHARON FAYE WELCH, retired educational consultant; b. L.A., Jan. 14, 1941; d. James Herbert and Verdie V. (Mattox) Welch; m. Robert A. Ledbetter, Feb. 15, 1964; children: Kimberly Ann, Scott Allen. BA, U. Tex., Austin, 1963; learning disabilities cert., Southwestern U., Tex., 1974; MEd, Southwest Tex. State U., 1979, prin. cert., 1980, supt. cert., 1984. Speech pathologist Midland (Tex.) Ind. Sch. Dist., Tex., 1963, Austin (Tex.) Ind. Sch. Dist., Tex., 1964-72; speech pathologist, asst. prin. Round Rock Ind. Sch. Dist., Tex., 1972-84; prin. Hutto Ind. Sch. Dist., 1984-88; asst. dir. divsn. med. sch. edn. Tex. Edn. Agy., 1989-94. Pres. Berkman PTA, 1983-84; v.p. Round Rock Women's Club, 1977, pres., 1978-79; sponsor Jr. Woman's Club, 1980-82; vol. Round Rock Ind. Sch. Dist., 1984; mistress ceremonies Hutto Beauty Pageant, 1986-87. Recipient Meritorious Svc. award Round Rock Ind. Sch. Dist., 1984, St. Judes Children's Rsch. Hosp., 1985, Soc. Disting. Am. H.S. Students, 1984, Disting. Svc. award Tex. Edn. Agy., 1994. Mem. ASCD, Phi Delta Kappa. Home: 43 Woodland Loop Round Rock TX 78664-9776 E-mail: sledbet338@aol.com.

LEDDY, SUSAN, nursing educator; b. N.J., Feb. 23, 1939; d. Bert B. and Helen (Neumann) Kun; children: Deborah, Erin. BS, Skidmore Coll., 1960; MS, Boston U., 1965; PhD, NYU, 1973; cert., Harvard U., 1985. Chair dept. nursing Mercy Coll., Debbs Ferry, N.Y.; dean sch. nursing U. Wyo., Laramie, dean coll. health scis.; prof. Widener U. Sch. Nursing, Chester, Pa., 1988—, dean, 1988-93. Author: (with M. Pepper) Conceptual Bases of Professional Nursing, 1985, 4th edit., 1998, (with L. Hood), Leddy and Pepper's Conceptual Bases of Professional Nursing, 2003, Integrative Hearth Promotion, 2003. Bd. dirs. Springfield Hosp., 1992-94. Postdoctoral fellow U. Pa., 1994-96. Mem. NLN (bd. dirs. and 1st v.p. 1985-87), Soc. Rogerian Scholars (bd. dirs. 2001-03).

LEDER, MIMI, television director, film director, film producer; b. N.Y.C., Jan. 26, 1952; d. Paul and Etyl Leder; m. Gary Werntz, Feb. 6, 1986; 1 child, Hannah. Student, Los Angeles City College, Am. Film Inst. Dir. TV movies A Little Piece of Heaven (also known as Honor Bright), 1991, Woman with a Past, 1992, Rio Shannon, 1992, Marked for Murder, 1992, There Was a Little Boy, 1993, House of Secrets, 1993, The Sandman, 1993, The Innocent, 1994, John Doe, 2002; dir. TV series L.A. Law, 1986, Midnight Caller, 1988, A Year in the Life, 1988, Buck James, 1988, Just in Time, 1988, Crime Story, 1988, ER, 1994- (Emmy award 1995, 96), John Doe, 2002, China Beach (also prodr.), The Beast (also exec. prodr.), 2001; dir. movies, The Peacemaker, 1997, Deep Impact, 1998, Sentimental Journey, 1999, Pay it Forward, 2000; supervising prodr. China Beach, 1988-91 (Emmy nominations for outstanding drama series 1989, 90, and outstanding directing in drama series 1990, 91), Nightingales, 1989 Mem. Dirs. Guild Am. Office: c/o CAA 9830 Wilshire Blvd Beverly Hills CA 90212-1804 also: United Talent Agy 9560 Wilshire Blvd Beverly Hills CA 90212

LEDERER, KATHERINE GAY, English language educator; b. Trinity, Tex., Mar. 19, 1932; d. Leon MacRae and Katherine Waties (Lipscomb) Gay; divorced; children: Susan, Geoffrey. BA in English, Sam Houston State U., 1952; MA in English, U. Ark., 1958, PhD in English, 1967. Pub. sch. tchr., Houston, 1953-55; grad. asst. U. Ark., Fayetteville, 1956-59, instr., 1959-60; prof. S.W. Mo. State U., Springfield, 1968—. Author: (book) Lillian Hellman, 1979, Many Thousand Gone: Springfield's Lost Black History, 1986; guest editor: Ozarkswatch: African Americans in the Ozarks jour., 1999; prodr. media show on black history, 1983. Bd. dirs. Springfield Little Theater, 1970s; founder, bd. dirs. Springfield Jazz Soc., 1973-79. Recipient Gov.'s Humanities award Mo. Humanities Coun., 1999, award for tchg. S.W. Mo. State U., 1999, Excellence in Cmty. Svc. award, 1999, others; named to Mo. Writers Hall of Fame, 2001. Mem. Midwest Orgn. for Recognition and Recovery of Ethnic History (v.p., exec. com. St. Louis 1997—), Toni Morrison Soc. (charter mem., mem. adv. coun.), Coll. Lang. Assn., MLA, Mo. Folklore Soc. (bd. dirs. 1980s). Democrat. Avocations: reading, writing, Black history rsch., jazz. E-mail: katherinelederer@smsu.edu.

LEDERER, LAURA J. educational program administrator; b. Detroit, Dec. 12, 1951; d. Creighton C. and Natalie Irene (Mattson) L. Student, U. Mich., 1975. Asst. to dir. program on studies in religion U. Mich., Ann Arbor, 1971-75; exec. dir. Women Against Pornography, San Francisco, 1976-80; program dir. The L.J. and Mary C. Skaggs Found., Oakland, Calif., 1980-91; dir. protection project Kennedy Sch. Govt. Harvard U., 1993—. Editor: Take Back the Night: Women on Pornography, 1980. Bd. dirs. Global Fund for Women, Los Altos, Calif., 1987-95; mem. adv. bd. The Women's Found., San Francisco, 1980-95. Office: Kennedy Sch Govt Harvard U 1779 Massachusetts Ave #515 Washington DC 20036

LEDERER, MARIE A. state legislator; b. state legislator, Phila., Oct. 24, 1927; d. Donato and Edith (Vitacolonna) Panosetti; m. William J. Lederer, June 17, 1950; children: Donada M. Lederer Guyon, William M., Regina M. Ed., Phila. Pub. Rels. Inst., 1966-67, Temple U., 1973-76. Instr. polit. sci. Temple U., Phila., 1976-77; exec. dir. Jackson for Pres. Com., 1976; del. Dem. Nat. Conv., 1976, 84; chmn. voter registration Dem. Nat. Com., 1978-79; adminstrv. asst. to Congressman Joseph F. Smith of Pa., U.S. Ho. of Reps., 1981-82; asst. to dep. auditor gen State of Pa., Harrisburg, 1985; now mem. Pa. Ho. of Reps., Harrisburg. Bd. dirs. Southeastern Pa. Heart Assn., 1966-71, Balch Inst., ARC, USS Cruiser Olympia; me. Phila. Art Alliance. Mem. Hist. Ships Assn., Mexican Soc., Am. Legion Ladies Aux. Roman Catholic. Home: 1237 Shackamaxon St Philadelphia PA 19125-3913 Office: Pa Ho of Reps 224 South St Office Harrisburg PA 17101-1356

LEDERER, MARION IRVINE, cultural administrator; b. Brampton, Ont., Can., Feb. 10, 1920; d. Oliver Bateman and Eva Jane (MacMurdo) L.; m. Francis Lederer, July 10, 1941. Student, U. Toronto, 1938, UCLA, 1942-45. Owner Canoga Mission Gallery, Canoga Park, Calif., 1967—, cultural heritage monument, 1974—. V.p. Screen Smart Set women's aux. Motion Picture and TV Fund, 1973, pres., 2002—03; founder sister city program Canoga Park-Taxco, Mex., 1963. Mem. Mayor's Cultural Task Force San Fernando Valley, 1973—, L.A. Cultural Affairs Commn., 1980—85; pres. Women's Aux. of Motionn Pictures, TV Fund. Recipient numerous pub. service awards from mayor, city council, C. of C. Mem. Canoga Park C. of C. (cultural chmn. 1973-75, dir. 1973-75) Presbyterian. Home: PO Box 32 Canoga Park CA 91305-0032 Office: Canoga Mission Gallery 23130 Sherman Way Canoga Park CA 91307-1402

LEDERMAN, SALLY ANN, nutrition researcher; b. N.Y.C., July 8, 1937; d. Joseph Edward and Leanora Rossi; m. Lawrence Lederman, Jan. 26, 1958 (div. Feb. 1991); children: Leandra, Evin. BS in Chemistry, Bklyn. Coll., 1957; MS in Nutrition, Columbia U., 1976, PhD, 1980. Analytical chemist U.S. FDA, N.Y.C., 1957—62; lectr. dept. chemistry Bklyn. Coll., 1962-66, 74; postdoctoral fellow Inst. Human Nutrition Columbia U., N.Y.C., 1980—82, postdoctoral fellow obstetrics and biochemistry, 1983, asst. prof. Sch. Pub. Health, 1983—90, assoc. prof. Sch. Pub. Health, 1990—94, prof. Tchrs. Coll., 1994—97, rschr. Tchrs. Coll., 1997—99; rsch. assoc. divsn. endocrinology, diabetes, nutrition St. Luke's-Roosevelt Hosp. Ctr., N.Y.C., 1998—. Spl. lectr. Mailman Sch. Pub. Health, Inst. of Human Nutrition, Columbia U., 2000—. Editor: Controversial Issues in Public Health Nutrition, 1983; contbr. articles to profl. jours. Mem. APHA, AAAS, Am. Soc. Nutrition Sci., Am. Women in Sci., N.Y. Acad. Scis. Office: St Luke's Hosp Ctr Obesity Rsch Ctr 1090 Amsterdam Ave # 14H New York NY 10025-1737 E-mail: sal1@columbia.edu.

LEDERMAN, SUSAN STURC, public administration educator; b. Bratislava, Slovakia, May 28, 1937; came to U.S., 1948; d. Ludovit and Helen Sturc; m. Peter Bernd Lederman, Aug. 25, 1957; children: Stuart, Ellen. AB in Polit. Sci., U. Mich., 1958; MA in Polit. Sci., Rutgers U., 1970, PhD in Polit. Sci., 1978. Vis. instr. Fairleigh Dickinson U., Madison, N.J., 1973-74, Drew U., Madison, 1975-76; from asst. prof. to assoc. prof. pub. adminstrn. Kean U., Union, N.J., 1977-89, prof., dir. MPA program, 1989-97; exec. dir. Gateway Inst. Regional Devel. Kean U., Union, N.J., 1997-2000; prof. Kean U., Union, N.J., 1990—. Vis. fellow Woodrow Wilson Sch., Princeton (N.J.) U., 1988-89. Co-author: (book) Elections in America—Control and Influence in Democratic Politics, 1980, (monograph) Campaign Watch: A Report on the 1992 Campaign Watch Project, 1993; editor: (book) The SLERP Reforms and Their Impact, 1989; contbr. articles to profl. jours. Mem. nat. gov. bd. Common Cause, Washington, 1994-2000; bd. dirs., sec.-treas. The Jefferson Ctr., Mpls., 1992-2002; dir. Regional Plan Assn., N.Y.C., 1991—; pres. LWV of N.J., 1985-89, program v.p., 1983-85, sec., fiscal policy dir., 1981-83, fiscal policy dir., 1979-81, adminstrn. of justice dir., 1976-79; pres. LWV of U.S., 1990-92, chair edn. fund., 1990-92; mem. bd. trustees exec. com., sec. N.J. Future, 1993—; pub. mem. Supreme Ct. of N.J. Disciplinary Oversight Com., 1994-98, Coun. of Engring. and Sci. Splty. Bds., 1996-2002; mem. Property Tax Commn., 1998; mem. N.J. Legis. Coun. of Acad. Advisors; commr. N.J. State and Local Expenditure Revenue Policy Commn., 1985-88, N.J. Election Law Enforcement Commn., 2000—; pres. Northeastern Polit. Sci. Assn., 1984-85. Recipient Disting. Svc. award N.J. Polit. Sci. Assn., 1984, Pub. Svc. award ASPA, 1993, Eric Neisser Pub. Svc. award Pub. Interest Law Ctr., 2001; rsch. grantee Fund for N.J., 1981, Florence and John Schumann Found., 1988-89. Mem. Internat. Women's Forum (N.J. Forum bd. dirs. 1998—), Phi Kappa Phi, Pi Sigma Alpha, Pi Alpha Alpha. Home: 17 Pittsford Way New Providence NJ 07974-2428 Office: Kean U 1000 Morris Ave Union NJ 07083-7131 E-mail: slederma@kean.edu.

LEDESMA-NICHOLSON, CHARMAINE, psychotherapist; b. L.A., Aug. 29, 1943; d. Louis Edgar Dern and Reba Marie Willis; m. Raymond Cano Ledesma, May 4, 1968 (div. June 1992); 1 child, Michael; m. Steven Nicholson, Aug. 7, 1993. BA, Calif. State U., 1966; MA, Pepperdine U., 1982. Lic. marriage, family, child counselor, Calif.; lic. clin. profl. counselor, Mont. Social worker Dept. Pub. Social Svcs., L.A., 1967-70; child protection svcs. social worker County of Orange (Calif.) Pub. Social Svcs., 1970-88; supr. child protection svcs. Riverside (Calif.) County Pub. Social Svc., 1988-92; psychotherapist for sex offenders Parents United, Beaumont, Calif., 1988-92, Mont. State Prison, Deer Lodge, 1992-96, Crossroads Correctional Ctr., Shelby, Mont., 1999—2002; pvt. practice Great Falls, Mont., 1999—. Self-employed cons., supr., Great Falls, 1999—. 1st responder Avon (Mont.) Quick Response Unit, 1992-99; mem. Lewis & Clark Search & Rescue, Helena, Mont., 1994-99; vol. Eaglemount, Great Falls, 1999— (profl. ski instr. of Am.), ARC, Great Falls, 1990—. Mem. Am. Assn. of Marriage Family Therapists (clin. mem.), Assn. for Treatment of Sex Abusers (clin. mem.), Mont. Sex Offender Treatment Assn. (clin. mem.), Profl. Ski Instrs. Am. Democrat. Roman Catholic. Avocations: horseback riding, sewing, skiing, mountain climbing, canoeing. Home: 5705 62d Ave SW Great Falls MT 59404 Office Phone: 406-788-1977. E-mail: stevecharm1@juno.com.

LEDET, PHYLLIS L. educational administrator; b. Delcambre, La., Apr. 10, 1942; d. John and Claire (Landry) LeBlanc; children: Lonny Ledet, Leah Ledet Terro, Elizabeth Ledet Romero, Laurie. BA in Elem. Edn., U. Southwestern LA, 1963, MEd in Ednl. Counseling, 1989, EdS in Ednl. Adminstrn. and Supervision, 1992. Asst. prin. L. J. Alleman Mid. and Arts Acad., Lafayette, La., 1993—2002, Scott Mid. Sch., 2002—. Bd. dirs. Jr. League Lafayette; mem. Am. Cancer Soc. (Spring Family Fair Chmn.), Govs. Commn. Goals 2000, La. State Dept. Edn. Panel VIII Com., United Way of Acadiana; leader Girl Scouts Am.; pres. Edgar Martin PTC; religious tchr. Holy Cross Cath. Ch. Mem. Assn. Profs. Edn. of La. (state pres. 1996-97), Leadership Lafayette C. of C. (class XI), Univ. La. Coll. Edn. Alumni Assn. (charter). E-mail: pledet@lft.k12.la.us.

LEDFORD, BRENDA KAY, writer; b. Young Harris, Ga., Apr. 9, 1952; d. James Ronda and Blanche Willie (Lee) L.. BS in Edn., We. Carolina U., Cullowhee, N.C., 1976, MA in Edn., 1979. Cert. tchr. N.C. Clerk, typist FBI, Washington, 1970—71; tchr. Cherokee County Bd. Edn., Murphy, NC, 1976—90; freelance writer Smoky Mountain Sentinel, Hayesville, NC, 1990—2001. Writing instr. John Campbell Folk Sch., Brasstown, NC, 2000; storyteller Clay Revitalization Assn., Hayesville, 1999—2001. Author: poems; editor: Tri-County C.C. newspaper, 1996; contbr. articles Our State mag., 2000. Named winner photo contest, Writers' Jour., 1998; recipient award journalism contest, N.C. Press Assn., 2000. Mem.: DAR, Clay County C. C., Clay County Arts Coun. (bd. dirs. 1999, sec. 1999, poetry contest judge 2000), N.C. Storytelling Guild, N.C. Writer's Network, Order Ea. Star (Clay chpt., Angels Among Us award 1999). Democrat. Baptist. Avocations: travel, piano, drawing, reading, photography.

LEDIN, PATRICIA ANN, nurse, nurse legal consultant; b. Downey, Calif., May 6, 1959; d. Clyde Burdette and Estelle Angelina (Acceturo) Bornhurst; m. Scott Richard Ledin, Sept. 9, 1989. BSN, U. Ariz., 1981; postgrad., U. Phoenix, 2000. Cert. electronic fetal monitoring, inpatient obstetrics, ACLS, PALS, NRP; RN Ariz., cert. instr. PALS. Labor and delivery nurse Tucson Med. Ctr., 1981-86, childbirth instr., 1983-95, nurse, mother-baby unit, 1995-97, clin. educator obstetrics, 1986—95, CPR instr., 1986—, learning and devel. specialist, 2001—, clin. nurse specialist, 2001, clin. educator obstetrics, 1997—2001, nurse recruiting, 2002—. Adj. faculty preceptor U. Ariz., Tucson, 1988—; expert witness for legal cases, 1992—; expert reviewer Lifelines mag., 2002-; faculty, Az. Perinatal Edn. Coalition, 2000—. Contbr. articles to profl. jours. Mem. adv. com. March of Dimes, 1991—95; mentor Nat. Cert. Corp., 2001. Bristol-Meyers fellow, 1994. Mem.: Nat. Nursing Staff Devel. Orgn., Assn. Women's Health, Obstet. and Neonatal Nursing (edn. coord. 1991—98, sec.-treas. 1999—2002, Recognition award for fin. budget submission 2001, 2002, award for outstanding performance in fin. responsibility 2001), Beta mu, Omicron Delta, Sigma Theta Tau (chair nominations 2002—). Avocations: water skiing, nascar races, boating, travel, aerobics. Office: Tucson Med Ctr 5301 E Grant Rd Tucson AZ 85712-2805

LEDLEY, TAMARA SHAPIRO, earth system scientist, climatologist; b. Washington, May 18, 1954; d. Murray Daniel and Ina Harriet (Gordon) Shapiro; m. Fred David Ledley, June 6, 1976; children: Miriam Esther, Johanna Sharon. BS, U. Md., 1976; PhD, MIT, 1983. Rsch. assoc. Rice U., Houston, 1983-85, asst. rsch. scientist, 1985-90, sr. faculty fellow, 1990-98; assoc. rsch. scientist Tex. A&M U., College Station, 1995-96; sr. scientist TERC, Cambridge, Mass., 1997—; vis. scientist MIT, 1997-98. Alaska SAR facility archive working team NASA, Pasadena, Calif., 1988, McMurdo SAR faculty sci. working team, 1990; participant workshop of Arctic leads initiative Office Naval Rsch., Seattle, 1988, 1st DeLange Conf. on Human Impact on Environ., Houston, 1991; cons. Houston Mus. Natural Sci., 1989—90, Broader Perspectives, Houston, 1989; dir. weather project for tchr. tng. program George Obs., Rice U., 1990—92; co-dir. Rice Houston Mus. Natural Sci. Summer Solar Inst., 1993; mem. Mus. Tchg. Planet Earth Project, 1998—2003, GLOBE Program, 1998—; vice chmn. standing com. on cmty. engagement Fedn. Earth Sci. Info. Ptnrs., 2000—02, leader edn. cluster, chair standing com. for edn., 2002—; use case expert exploring tchg. methods Digital Libr. Earth Sys. Edn., 2000—01, program chair 3d ann. meeting, 2001—02, chair 4th ann. meeting, 2002—03, mem. mgmt. coun., 2003—, PI data svcs., 2003—; mem. rev. panels NSF, 1993, 95, NASA, 2002. Contbr. articles to profl. jours. Spl. judge Houston Area Sci. and Engring. Fair, 1985; judge S.W. Tex. Region H.S. Debates, 1986, Houston Area Sci. and Engring. Fair, 1990-92, 95; guest expert Great Decisions '88 Polit. Discussion Group, 1988; participant U.S. Global Change Rsch. Program's Climate Modeling Forum, 1994. Fellow sci. computing Nat. Ctr. for Atmospheric Rsch., 1978, Fed. Jr. fellow, 1972-74; senatorial scholar State of Md., 1972-76; grantee NSF, 1985-87, 89—, Tex. Higher Edn. Coordinating Bd., 1988-92, Univ. Space Rsch. Assn., NASA, 1991-94. Mem. AAAS (electorate nominating com. 1995-98), Am. Geophys. Union (com. global environ. change 1993-2000, chmn., 1996-2000, chair panel on climate change and greenhouse gases, pub. info. com. 2000, assoc. editor Jour. Geophys. Rsch.-Atmospheres 1993-96), Am. Meteorol. Soc., Oceanography Soc., Sigma Xi, Phi Beta Kappa, Phi Kappa Phi, Alpha Lambda Delta. Avocations: reading, running, aerobics, hiking. E-mail: tamara_ledley@terc.edu.

LEE, AMY, singer; b. Riverside, Calif., Dec. 13, 1981; d. John and Sara Lee. Lead singer Evanescence. Musician: (albums) Origin, 2002, Fallen, 2003 (album went Double Platinum, Grammy award best new artist, 2003); musician: (guest vocalist) (songs) "Broken" by Seether; musician: (breakout single) "Bring Me To Life" (Grammy award best hard rock performance, 2003). Office: Wind-Up Records 72 Madison Ave New York NY 10016 Office Phone: 212-895-3100.*

LEE, ANDREA JANE, academic administrator, nun; 1 adopted child, Lahens. AA in Italian, Villa Walsh Coll.; BA in music and elem. edn., Northeastern Ill. U.; MEd, PhD in edn. adminstrn., Pa. State U. Instr. tchr. edn. Pa. State U.; dean continuing edn. and cmty. svcs. Marygrove Coll., 1981—84, exec. v.p. and COO, 1984—97, interim pres., 1998; pres. Coll. of St. Catherine, St. Paul, 1999—. Office: Coll of St Catherine 2004 Randolph Ave Saint Paul MN 55105*

LEE, ANGIE, basketball coach; d. John and Jean Lee. BS, U. Iowa, 1984, MS in Athletic Adminstrn., 1987. Asst. women's basketball coach U. Iowa, Iowa City, grad. asst. coach, 1985-87, asst. coach, 1989-96, head women's basketball coach, 1996—; asst. basketball coach Western Ill. U., 1987-89 Named Big Ten Conf. Coach of the Yr. 1996, Assoc. Press Nat. Coach of the Yr., 1996, Dist. IV WBCA Coach of the Yr. 1996, Coll. Sports Mag. Coach of the Yr. Mem. Women's Baksetball Coaches Assn. (rep. to dist. IV asst. coaches 1993-94). Office: University of Iowa 252 Carver Hawkeye Arena Iowa City IA 52242-1020

LEE, ANN MCKEIGHAN, curriculum specialist; b. Harlan, Iowa, Nov. 18, 1939; d. Earl Edward and Dorothy Elizabeth (Kaufman) McK.; m. Duane Edward Compton, Aug. 13, 1960 (div. 1985); children: Kathleen, David, Anne-Marie, John. Cert. in med. tech., Creighton U., 1960; BA in Art History, Ind. U., 1984; MA, U. South Fla., 1992, PhD, 2002. Cert. secondary tchr., Fla.; cert. med. technologist. Realtor Savage/Landrian Realty, Indpls., 1978-84; lectr. Marian Coll., Indpls., 1987-88; tchr. Sarasota (Fla.) County Schs., 1989-92, rep. faculty coun., 1991-92; lectr. curriculum & instrn. U. South Fla., 1993—2000. Vis. prof. U. South Fla., 2001—03; docent Historic Spanish Point, Osprey, Fla., 1989—93, Ringling Mus. Art, 1993—; presenter panel Bibliographic Instrn. Art History. Contbr. articles to profl. jours. V.p. fin. LWV, Indpls., 1971-73; v.p. dist. IV aux. ADA, 1976-78, comptroller, 1978-89; coord. Gold Coun. and Ambs. U. South Fla., 1990-92. Recipient Silver Svc. award Crossroads Guild, 1981. Mem.: Sarasota Arts Coun., Gulf Coast Heritage Assn. (ch-chmn. pub. rels.), Soc. Archtl. Historians (tchr. rep. 1990), Coll. Art Assn., Phi Delta Kappa, Phi Kappa Phi. Roman Catholic. Avocations: photography, tennis, landscape architecture, swimming. Home and Office: 3617 Shady Brook Ln Sarasota FL 34243-4840

LEE, ANNE, music educator; b. Taipei, Taiwan, July 19, 1951; d. William Chiang and Su-Chen Wu; married, Jan. 20, 1979; children: Joseph, Matthew. Degree, Shih Chien Univ., 1972. Tchr. Yamaha Music Found., Taipei, Taiwan, 1974—81; co-founder Polyphony Chamber Orch., Cupertino, Calif., 1998—. Music judge Taiwan TV music program, Taipei, 1978, Cupertino Sch. Dist., 1998—99. Ch. organist. Recipient 1st prize Composition, Shih Chien U., 1972. Mem.: Nat. Guild Piano Tchrs. (tchr. divsn. am. coll. musicians, Nat. Honor Roll Piano Tchr. 1999, 2000, 2001), Music Tchr. Nat. Assn., Music Tchr. Assn. Calif., Chinese Music Tchr. Assn. Calif. (music judge internat. music competition 1999, chmn. bd. dir. 1997—99, pres. 1996—97), Calif. Assn. Profl. Music Tchr. Avocations: chamber music, shopping, movies, church choir.

LEE, BARBARA, congresswoman; b. El Paso, Tex., July 16, 1946; m. Michael Millben (div.); children: Tony, Craig. BA, Mills Coll., 1973; M in Social Welfare, U. Calif. Berkeley, 1976. Chief of staff U.S. Rep. Ron Dellums, 1975—87; rep. Calif. State Assembly, 1990-96; mem. Calif. State Sen., 1996-98, U.S. Congress from 9th Calif. dist., Washington, 1998—; mem. fin. svcs. com., internat. rels. com. Co-chmn. Progressive Caucus; chmn. Congl. Black Caucus Task Force HIV/AIDS; whip Congl. Black Caucus, mem. Minority Bus. Task Force; mem. adv. bd. Alameda Boys Club; bd. dirs. Bay Area Black United Fund; with Black Women Organized Polit. Action; founder Calif. Commn. Status African Am. Male; mem. Calif. Commn. Status Women; mem. bd. Calif. Coastal Conservancy/Dist. Export Coun. Democrat. Office: US Ho Reps 1724 Longworth Ho Office Bldg Washington DC 20515-0509*

LEE, BARBARA A. retired federal magistrate judge; b. Conn. AB, Boston U., 1959; LLB, Harvard Law Sch., 1962. Bar: Conn. 1962, N.Y. 1966. Atty. Poletti Freidin Prashker Feldman & Gartner, 1968-74, ptnr., 1974-82; pvt. practice N.Y.C., 1983-87; U.S. magistrate judge U.S. Dist. Ct. (so. dist.), N.Y., 1988-96; ret., 1996. Adj. prof. law Seton Hall U., Newark, 1984—87. Mem. com. on ecumenical and inter-religious affairs of Roman Cath. Archdiocese of N.Y., 1983—. Mem. Fed. Magistrate Judges Assn. (chair, ret. magistrate judges' com. 1998-99), Assn. of Bar of City of N.Y. (adminstrv. law com. 1973-74, fed. cts. com. 1981-84, com. on state cts. of superior jurisdiction 1984-87, libr. com. 1989-92, Books at the Bar com. 1997-99), N.Y. County Lawyers' Assn. (fed. cts. com. 1995—).

LEE, BARBARA ANNE, law educator, dean; b. Newton, N.J., Apr. 9, 1949; d. Robert hanna and Keren (Dalrymple) L.; m. James Paul Begin, Aug. 14, 1982; 1 child, Robert James. BA, U. Vt., 1971; MA, Ohio State U., 1972; JD, Georgetown U., 1982; PhD, Ohio State U., 1977. Bar: N.J. 1983, U.S. Dist. Ct. N.J. 1983. Instr. Franklin U., Columbus, Ohio, 1974-75; rsch. asst. Ohio State U., Columbus, 1975-77; policy analyst U.S. Dept. Edn., Washington, 1978-80; dir. data trands Carnegie Found., Princeton, N.J., 1980-82; asst. prof. Grad. Sch. Edn. Rutgers U., Brunswick, N.J., 1982-84, asst. prof. Sch. Mgmt. and Labor Rels., 1984-88, assoc. prof., 1988-94, prof., 1994—, assoc. provost, 1995-96, dean, 2000—. Mem. Study Group on Excellence in Higher Edn., Nat. Inst. Edn., 1983-84; project dir. Carnegie Corp., N.Y.C., 1982-84. Author: Academics in Court, 1987; co-author: The Law of Higher Education, 3d edit., 1995; contbr. numerous articles to profl. jours. Corse fellow U. Vt., 1971; recipient John F. Kennedy Labor Law award Georgetown U., 1982; grantee Bur. Labor-Mgmt. Rels. and Coop. Programs, 1985-86. Mem. ABA, N.J. Bar Assn. (mem. exec. com. labor and employment law sect. 1987—, women's rights sect.), Am. Ednl. Rsch. Assn., Indsl. Rels. Rsch. Assn., Acad. Mgmt., Assn. Study Higher Edn. (legal counsel 1982-88), Nat. Assn. Coll. and Univ. Attys. (vice chair editl. bd. 1986-89, chair 1995-96, chair publs. com. 1988-91, bd. dirs. 1990-93). Office: Rutgers U Office of Dean Sch Mgmt and Labor Rels 94 Rockafeller Rd Piscataway NJ 08854-8054

LEE, BARBARA CATHERINE, career counselor; b. Augusta, Ga., Apr. 30, 1931; d. Walter Charles and Dorothy Fulgum (Sasser) L.; married, Dec. 23, 1951 (div. Feb. 1959); 1 child, William Lee Hooton. BS in Vocat. Hom Econs., Winthrop Coll., 1952; MEd, U. Ga., 1960, MS in Family and Child Devel., 1968; EdS in Counselor Edn., Ga. Southern U., 1991. Nat. bd. cert. counselor, 1994; nat. bd. cert. career counselor, 1997. Vocat. hom econs. tchr. Evans (Ga.) High Sch., 1955-56; vocat. home econs. tchr. Murphey Jr. High Sch., Augusta, Ga., 1956-63; vocat. consumer home econs. tchr. Butler High Sch., Augusta, 1963-75, Josey High Sch., Augusta, 1975-81; vocat. child devel. tchr. Hephzibah High Sch., Augusta, 1981-85; elem. and middle sch. counselor Ridge Spring-Monetta Elem. and Middle schs., 1986-87; part-time grad. rsch. asst. Ga. Southern U., Statesboro, 1990; career counselor St. John's High Sch., Charleston, S.C., 1991-96. Part-time tchr. Augusta Coll., 1972-73; part-time child devel. tchr. Augusta Tech. Sch., 1985-86; part-time edl. dir. adolescent program Human Hosp., 1988-89. Recipient Ga. Six-Yr. Study scholarhips Richmond County Bd. Edn., 1958; recipient Augusta Woman's Club scholarship, 1990. Mem. AAUW (scholarship chmn. Ga. chpt. 1983), Am. Counseling Assn., Nat. Career Devel. Assn., Ga. Career Devel. Assn., Kappa Delta Pi, Phi Upsilon Omicron, Phi Kappa Phi. Avocations: reading, swimming, painting, riding, remodeling and redecorating homes and offices occupied.

LEE, BARBARA MAHONEY, career officer, educator; b. Roanoke, Va., July 25, 1942; d. Archer W. and Marie Adeline (Gray) Mahoney; m. Walter Kenneth Lee, Aug. 5, 1956 (div. 1969); children: Kenneth Michael, Alan David. AS, Va. Western C.C., Roanoke, 1970; BA, Hollins (Va.) Coll., 1972; MS, Va. Commonwealth U., Richmond, 1979; postgrad., Am. U. Commd. ed lt. U.S. Army, 1973, advanced through grades to col., 1995; asst. prof. U.S. Mil. Acad., West Point, N.Y., 1979-83; orgnl. effectiveness staff officer Army Materiel Command, Alexandria, Va., 1983-88, Cong. liaison officer, 1988-90; v.p. human resources INTEGRATEC, Inc., Atlanta, 1990-92; orgnl. devel. cons. in pvt. practice, Atlanta, 1992-93; mil. asst. U.S. Army, Pentagon, Washington, 1993—2002; ret. USAR. Decorated Legion of Merit. Mem.: Alliance for Nat. Def., Am. Sociol. Assn., Women in Internat. Security (exec. bd. 1999—), Alpha Kappa Delta. Episcopalian. Home: 11957 Holly View Dr Woodbridge VA 22192-1040

LEE, BARBARA S. elementary school educator; b. Long Beach, Calif. Oct. 25, 1942; d. George Hubert Staley and Doris Emma Geer/Staley; m. Stanley Yau Ning Lee, Sept. 7, 1963; children: Tracey Golden, Linda Samuels, Tanya Prucher. BS in Phys. Sci., U. N.D., 1964; tchg. cert., Nat. U., Irvine, Calif., 1988. Cert. tchr. Ariz. Tchrs. aide Fountain Valley (Calif.) Sch. Dist., 1979—89; tchr. Pk. Pvt. Day Sch., Costa Mesa, Calif., 1990—96, Laveen (Ariz.) Sch. Dist., 1997—2000; tchr. ADJC Ariz. Dept. Corrections, Phoenix, 2000—. Mem. curriculum com. Adobe Mountain Sch., Phoenix. Life mem. PTO-Moiola Sch., Fountain Valley, 1985. Mem.: ASCD, Ariz. Pub. Employees Assn., Assn. for Rsch. and Enlightment. Avocations: dance, hiking, camping, reading, quilting. Home: 10251 W Snead Cir N Sun City AZ 85351 Office: Adobe Mountain Sch 2800 W Pinnacle Peak Phoenix AZ 85027

LEE, BETTY REDDING, architect; d. Joseph Alsop and Mary (Byrd) Redding; m. Frank Cayce Lee, Nov. 22, 1940 (dec. Aug. 1978); children: Cayce Redding, Clifton Monroe, Mary Byrd (Mrs. Kent Ray). Student La. State U., 1936-37, 37-38, U. Calif. War Extension Coll., San Diego, 1942-43; sudent Centernary Coll., 1937; attended Roofing Industry Ednl. Inst., 1980-82, 84, 86-88, 89-90, 93, Better Understanding Roofing Sys. Inst., 1989. Sheetmetal worker Consol. Vultee, San Diego, 1942; engring. draftsman, 1943-45; jr. to sr. archtl. draftsman Bodman & Murrell, Baton Rouge, 1954-55; sr. archtl. draftsman to architect Post & Harelson, Baton Rouge, 1955-58; assoc. arch. G. Ross Murrell, Jr., Baton Rouge, 1960-66; staff arch. Charles E. Schwing & Assocs., Baton Rouge, 1966-71, Kenneth C. Landry, Baton Rouge, 1971, 73-74; engring., design draftsman Rayner & McKenzie, Baton Rouge, 1972-73; cons. arch. and planner Office Engring. and Cons. Svcs., La. Dept. Health and Human Resources, Baton Rouge, 1974-82; sr. arch. roofing and waterproofing sect. La. Dept. Facility Planning and Control, 1982-96; pvt. consulting practice, Baton Rouge, 1996—; Betty Redding Lee, Architect, 1996; Author Instructions to Designers for Roofing Systems for Louisiana Public Buildings: co-author: Building Owners Guide for Protecting and Maintaining Built-up Roofing Systems, 1981; designed typical La. country store for La. Arts and Sci. Ctr. Mus. Recipient Honor award Schuller/Johns Manville BURSI Group, 1989, 90, 91, 92, 93. Mem. La. Assn. Children with Learning Disabilities, 1967-69, Multiple Sclerosis Soc., 1963—, CPA Aux., 1960-69, PTA, 1953-66; troop leader Brownies and Girl Scouts U.S.A., 1959-60; asst. den mother Cub Scouts, 1955-57. Licensed architect. Mem. ASTM, Nat. AIA, AIA La., AIA Baton Rouge (first Shreveport & Baton Rouge, La. woman architect), DAR, Roofing Industry Ednl. Inst. Alumni Assn. (charter mem.), Constrn. Specifications Inst.(charter mem. Baton Rouge chpt.), Roof Cons. Inst. (profl. mem.), Roof Cons. Inst. (profl. mem.), Jr. League Baton Rouge, Kappa Delta. Republican. Episcopalian. E-mail: brlee@worldnet.att.net. Home: 881 Kenmore Ave Baton Rouge LA 70806-5521 Office: 225 Kenmore Ave Baton Rouge LA 70806

LEE, BOK SIN See POWELL GEBHARD, JOY

LEE, BRENDA, state representative; d. James N. and Costella (Coln) Foster. Student, U. SC. Mem. SC Ho. of Reps., 1995—. Dist. mgr. US Census, Spartanburg, SC, 1980; mem. Spartanburg Devel. Coun.; pres.'s adv. com. Wofford Coll.; bd. dirs. Spartanburg Meml. Com. Recipient E. Lewis Miller Leadership award, 1998. Mem.: Urban League Upsate. Democrat. Office: State Capitol 414 D Blatt Bldg Columbia SC 29211

LEE, CAROL, artist, songwriter; b. Quanah, Tex., Oct. 20, 1946; d. Luther Benjamen and Elsie Ethel (Roman) Atwood; m. Cecil Ross Lee, Jr., Feb. 4, 1966 (div. Feb. 1994); children: Kevin Shawn, Dayna Michelle. Grad. h.s. Staff songwriter Purple Haze Music, Beckley West, Va., 1990—, artist, repertoire, 1991—. Co-writer (with Jimmie Crane) 5 songs; writer for Elvis, Doris Day, Bobby Vinton. Recipient award for short stories Robert W. Shields Editor, Washington, 1985, Semi Finalist Song, Starquest Contest, Tyler, Tex., 1993. Mem. Beckley Art Group. Avocations: flea marketing, collecting. Home: 606 N Oakwood Ave Beckley WV 25801-4435

LEE, CATHERINE, sculptor, painter; b. Pampa, Tex., Apr. 11, 1950; d. Paul Albert and Alice (Fleming) Porter; m. B. R. Mangham, 1967 (div. 1976); 1 child, Monk Parker; m. Sean Scully, 1977 (div. 2004). BA, San Jose State U., 1975. Asst. prof. sculpture U. Tex., San Antonio, 2000. Artist-in-residence Mpls. Coll. Art and Design, Minn. Inst. Art, 1982; vis. asst. prof. painting U. Tex., San Antonio, 1983, vis. asst. prof. sculpture, 2001; adj. asst. prof. Columbia U., N.Y.C., 1986-87. Group exhbns. include Albright-Knox Mus., Buffalo, 1987, Mus. Art, Carnegie Inst., Pitts., 1988, Am. Acad. & Inst. Arts & Letters, N.Y.C., 1988, Mus. Folkwang, Essen, Germany, 1992, Stadtische Galerie im Lenbachhaus, Munich, 1992, Neue Galerie Der Stadt Linz, Austria, 1992, Cleve. Mus. of Art, 1993, Galleria Nazionale d'Arte Moderna, San Marino, Italy, 1996, The Tate Gallery, 1994, U. R.I. Art Gallery, 1996, Sonoma State U. Art Gallery, 1997, Bemis Ctr. for Contemporary Art, 1998, Städtische Gallery, Lenbachhaus, Munich, 1999, Lafayette Coll. Art Ctr., Easton, Pa., 1999, San Diego State U. Art Gallery, San Diego, 1999, Grounds for Sculpture, The Johnson Atelier, 2002, S.W. Schy. Arts and Crafts Gallery, 2004. Creative Artists Pub. Svc. fellow, 1978; NEA grantee, 1989. Office: 106 Spring St New York NY 10012-3814 also: Galerie Karsten Greve Wallrafplatz 3 5000 Koln Germany also: Galerie Lelong 528 W 26th St New York NY 10001 E-mail: catherlee@aol.com.

LEE, CATHERINE M. business owner, educator; b. Grand Rapids, Mich., Aug. 21, 1941; m. Gordon Timothy Lee; 4 children. BA, Aquinas Coll., 1963; MA, U. Mich., 1964; postgrad., Wayne State U., 1965-67. Pres. CDL & Assocs., Barrington, Ill., 1988—. Mem. Unit Dist. 220 Bd. Edn., 1984-93; Dem. candidate Ill. Ho. of Reps., 1992; Dem. candidate 16th dist. Ill. U.S. Ho. of Reps., 1996. Roman Catholic. Office: CDL & Assocs 445 Shady Ln Barrington IL 60010-4141

LEE, CORINNE ADAMS, retired English teacher; b. Cuba, N.Y., Mar. 18, 1910; d. Duston Emery and Florence Eugenia (Butts) Adams; m. Glenn Max Lee, Oct. 30, 1936 (dec.). BA, Alfred U., 1931. Cert. tchr. N.Y. Tchr. English Lodi (N.Y.) H.S., 1931—36, Ovid (N.Y.) Ctrl. Sch., 1936—67. Author: (light verse) A Little Leeway, 1983, (anecdotes, light verse, quips) A Little More Leeway, 1984, (essays, short stories, poems) Still More Leeway, 1986. Trustee Montour Falls Meml. Libr. Mem.: LWV, Elmira and Area Ret. Tchrs. Assn., Schuyler County Ret. Tchrs. Assn., N.Y. State Ret. Tchrs. Assn., Nat. Ret. Tchrs. Assn., PTA (life). Avocations: reading, travel, writing.

LEE, DEANN, secondary school educator; b. Pascagoula, Miss., May 15, 1967; d. Dan and Donna Hamiter(Stepmother), Ann Hamiter; m. Jimmy Lee, Dec. 15, 1990; 1 child, Travis. BS, So. Nazarene U., 1988; MA, Tex. Woman's U., 1991. Cert. edn. administr. State Bd. for Edn. Certification, 1997, tchr. Tex. State Bd. for Edn. Certification, 1988. Tchr. Arlington (Tex.) Ind. Sch. Dist., 1988—91; tchr., chmn. dept. Paris (Tex.) Ind. Sch. Dist., 1991—. Cons. critical reader Holt, Rinehart and Winston, 2002; grant reviewer U.S. Dept. of Edn., Washington, 2002—; certification reviewer Nat. Evaluations Sys., Austin, Tex., 2003—; mentor dir. Paris (Tex.) Edn. Found., 1996—2002; presenter in field. Sunday sch. tchr. First Bapt. Ch., Paris, 1994—, choir mem., 1994—. Recipient Outstanding Yex. History Tchr. award, Daus. of Rep. of Tex., 1997—2001, Linden Heck Howell Outstanding Teaching of Texas History award, NEH, 2003. Mem.: Tex. Assn. Secondary Sch. Prins. (licentiate), Assn. Supervision and Curriculum Devel. (licentiate), Assn. of Tex. Profl. Educators (licentiate; sec., v.p., pres. local and region level 1996, chmn. state edn., policy and curriculum com. 2001—02, mem. legis. com. 2002—, treas. 1996—, State Tchr. of Yr. finalist 1999—2000), Kappa Delta Pi (life), Independent. Baptist. Avocations: gardening, golf, singing, aerobics. Office: Paris Ind Sch Dist 655 S Collegiate Paris TX 75460 [illegible]

LEE, DEBRA L. broadcast executive; m. Randall Coleman; 2 children. B in Polit. Sci., Brown U., 1976; M in Pub. Policy, JD, Harvard U., 1980. Law clk. hon. Barrington Parker U.S. Dist. Ct. D.C., 1980—81; atty. Steptoe & Johnson, Washington, 1985—86; v.p., gen. counsel BET, 1986, network exec. v.p. strategic bus. devel., exec. v.p. legal affairs dept., gen. counsel, corp. sec., pres., pub. pub. divsn.; pres., COO BET Holdings, Inc., 1996—. Bd. dirs. BET Holdings, Inc., Eastman Kodak Co. Bd. dirs. Kennedy Ctrs. Comty. Bd., Women in Cable, Telecom Devel. Fund, Nat. Symphony Orch. Bd. Named Woman of Yr., Women in Cable and Telecom., 2001; named one of Hundred Heavy Hitters, Cable Fax Mag., 100 Most Powerful Women in Washington, Washingtonian Mag.; recipient Tower of Power Trumpet award, Turner Broadcasting Sys., 2000, Silver Star award, Am. Women in Radio and TV, Par Excellence award, Dollars and $ense Mag., Wonder Woman award, Cablevision Mag. Office: BET Holdings Inc One BET Plaza 1235 W St NE Washington DC 20018-1211

LEE, DONNA JEAN, retired hospice and respite nurse; b. Huntington Park, Nov. 12, 1931; d. Louis Frederick and Lena Adelaide (Hinson) Munyon; m. Frank Bernard Lee, July 16, 1949; children: Frank, Robert, John. AA in Nursing, Fullerton (Calif.) Jr. Coll., 1966; extension student, U. Calif., Irvine, 1966-74; student, U. N.Mex., 1982. RN, Calif.; cert. Intraventous Therapy Assn. U.S.A. Staff nurse Orange (Calif.) County Med. Ctr., 1966-71, staff and charge nurse relief ICU, CCU, Burn Unit, ER, Communicable Disease, Neo-Natal Care Unit, 1969-71, charge nurse communicable disease unit, 1969-70; staff and charge nurse ICU, emergency rm., CCU, med./surg. units Anaheim (Calif.) Meml. Hosp., 1971-74; charge and staff nurse, relief Staff Builders, Orange, 1974-82; agy. nurse Nursing Svcs. Internat., 1978-89; asst. DON Chapman Convalescent SNF, Orange, 1982; geriat. and pediat. nurse VNASS, 1985-93; hospice/respite nurse VIA Upjohn Home Healthcare Svcs and VNA Support Svcs. of Orange, 1985-93; ret. Staff relief nurse ICU/CCU various hosps. and labs, including plasmapheresis nurse Med. Lab. of Orange, 1978. Life mem. in honor of spouse Republican. Presdl. Task Force, 1982—, Nat. Rep. Com. Ocean Conservancy, Natl. Park Trust, Wildlife Land Trust, Sierra Club. Mem. AACN, Harvard Med. Sch. Nurses, Am. Lung Assn., Am. Heart Assn., Arthritis Found., Life Extension Found. Baptist. Home: 924 S Hampstead St Anaheim CA 92802-1740

LEE, ELLA LOUISE, librarian, educator; b. Pitts., Aug. 15, 1929; d. Louis C. and Ida Lily (Ward) Lee; 1 child, Lily I. Lee-Braithwaite. BA in French and Libr., U. San Francisco Jesuit U., 1971, MA in History, 1978; MLS, San Jose State U., 1993. Cert. tchg. K-12 Calif., tchg. 13-14 Calif. Clk. Bus. Coll. Fgn. Svc., 1951—61; adult ednl. profl. UN - UNESCO, Paris, 1961—67; tchr. French and history San Francisco Unified Sch., 1972—80; instr. San Francisco C.C., 1994—98; assoc. libr. U. San Francisco Jesuit U., 2000—. Home: # 3 415 MacArthur Blvd Oakland CA 94610 Office: U San Francisco 2808 Lakeshore Blvd Oakland CA 94610 E-mail: leee@usfca.edu.

LEE, EVA, medical educator; b. Kaohsiung, Taiwan; B, M, Nat. Taiwan Normal U.; D in Cell Biology, U. Calif., Berkeley, 1984. Mem. faculty U. Calif., San Diego, 1984—91, rsch. positions, 1984—91; prof. molecular medicine Inst. Biotech. U. Tex.; prof. dept. developmental and cell biology Sch. Biol. Scis. and dept. biol. chemistry Coll. Medicine U. Calif., Irvine, 2001—. Program dir. two nat. programs for rsch. on tumor-suppressor genes Nat. Cancer Inst.; mem. Cancer Rsch. Inst. U.Calif., mem. Chao Family Comprehensive Cancer Ctr. Recipient Presdl. Outstanding Scientist award, Soc. Chinese Bioscientists in Am., Merit award, Nat. Cancer Inst. Office: U Calif Irvine Coll Medicine Irvine CA 92697

LEE, EVELYN MARIE, elementary school educator, secondary school educator; b. Germantown, Ohio, Dec. 17, 1931; d. Robert Orlandus and Edna Cathern (Durr) Stump; m. John Henry Lee, Dec. 16, 1956; children: Mark Douglas, David Matthew, Lori Ann Lee Delehoy. BS in Edn., Otterbein Coll., 1954; EdM with emphasis in reading, U. Alaska, 1979. Dept. store tng. supr., asst. mdse. mgr. The Home Store, Dayton, Ohio, 1954-55; tchr. Parma Pub. Sch., Ohio, 1955-56; math aide civil svc. Nat. Adv. Com. for Aeros. Ames Lab., Moffett Field, Calif., 1956-57; substitute tchr. Warren Pub. Sch., Ohio, 1957-59, tchr., 1959-60, Gwinn Pub. Sch., Mich., 1960-64, Anchorage Sch. Dist., 1964-65, 68-87, substitute tchr., 1987-96. Hon. life mem. Alaska PTA; vol. City of Loveland, The Lincoln Ctr., Fort Collins Mem. NEA (ret.; life), NEA-Alaska (ret.; life), Alaska Hist. Soc. (life), Tulpehocken Settlement Hist. Soc., Hist. Soc. Germantown, The Alaskans, Queen Mother of the Loveland Red Hattitudes (Red Hat Soc.), Loveland New Friendship Club, Order Eastern Star. United Methodist. Avocations: travel, reading, arts and crafts, genealogy. Home: 1521 Park Dr Loveland CO 80538-4285

LEE, FRANCES HELEN, editor; b. NYC, Jan. 6, 1936; d. Murray and Rose (Rothman) Lee. BA, Queens Coll., 1957; MA, NYU, 1962. Editl. asst. Christian Herald Family Bookshelf, N.Y.C., 1957-62; with Gordon and Breach Sci. Pubs., Inc., N.Y.C., 1964-66, Am. Electric Power Svc. Corp. AEP Operating Ideas, N.Y.C., 1966-69, Indsl. Water Engring. Mag., N.Y.C., 1969-71; directory editor photographic divsn. United Bus. Publs., N.Y.C., 1971-80; editor Am. Druggist Blue Book Hearst Books/Bus. Publs. Group, 1980-81; spl. projects coord. motor manuals Hearst Book Divsn., 1981-82; editor New Price Report, 1982-84, Am. Druggist Blue Book, 1982-88; freelance editor, cons., 1988—. Supr. Bronx divsn. N.Y. State Civil Defense, 1953-59; mem. com. on N.Y.C. charter revision, Citizens Union, 1975, com. on city mgmt., 1977-92, bd. dirs., co-chmn. com. on N.Y.C. cultural concerns, 1979-97, chmn., 1997-98; vol. N.Y.C. Opera, 1988—, info. project mgr., 2001—. Recipient cert. of honor NYU Alumni Fedn., 1985, Meritorious Svc. award, 1986. Mem. N.Y. Bus. Press Editors (bd. dirs. 1988-90, sec. 1990-91), Women's Equity Action League (chmn. rsch. com.), NYU Alumnae Club (dir. 1976-78, rec. sec. 1978-80, v.p. 1980-82, pres. 1982-84, rep. to bd. dirs. fedn. 1984-86), NYU Alumni Fedn. (dir.-at-large 1986—), Villa-Lobos Music Soc. (sec. 1989-91, treas. 1992-95), NYU Club (bd. govs. 1987-89). Home: 170 2nd Ave New York NY 10003-5754

LEE, GLENDA DIANNE, accountant; b. Anniston, Ala., Dec. 10, 1953; d. Viola (Williams) Walker; children: Tashira Johnson, Bobby Lee II. BS in Acctg., Ala. State U., 1980. Acct. Robins Air Force Base, 1981—87; co-pub. Metro Forum, Jackson, Tenn., 1989-93; acct. Housing Dept., Fort Worth, 1995—97; dir. of roster advt. Inst. of Mgmt. Accts., 1996—; acct. Lee's Accounting Service, Macon, Ga., 1999—2001. Instr. acctg. Dyersburg State C.C., 1989-90, Lee's Acctg. Svc., Macon, Ga., 1999-2001; v.p. pub. affairs Speak n Eat Toastmasters, Fort Worth, 1995; tchr. Hancock Cty. Schools, 2001-2003. Grantee Poynter Inst., 1991. Avocations: reading, singing, tennis. Home: PO Box 6003 Warner Robins GA 31095-6003

LEE, GLORIA DEANE, artist, educator; b. Council Bluffs, Iowa, Feb. 10, 1937; d. Carroll and Margaret Kathleen (Morse) Hamilton; m. Robert Dean Lee, June 29, 1962. BFA, U. Iowa, 1959; postgrad., Long Beach State U., 1964-68. Tchr. Garden Grove (Calif.) Unified Sch. Dist., 1959-64, Las Vegas (Nev.) Unified Sch. Dist., 1964, Compton Unified Sch. Dist., 1964-72, Manhattan Beach (Calif.) Unified Sch. Dist., 1984-95, L.A. Unified Adult Sch., 1993—; pvt. tutor academics and Positive Parenting, Manhattan Beach, 1978—; tutor Keys to Learning, Redondo Beach, Calif., 1984-96. Tchr. painting Beverly Hills (Calif.) Recreation, 1995-98, Palos

Verdes (Calif.) rt Ctr., 1990—, El Segundo (Calif.) Recreation Sr. Ctr., 1996-98; dir. Palos Vedes (Calif.) Artists, 1985-89; mem. edn. com. Palos Verdes Art Ctr., 1986-90; represented by Artist's Studio Galleries, Palos Verdes Peninsula, 1987-99, Gail's Frames Gallery; juried assoc. Watercolor West, 1992, 96—, Women Artists of the West, 1992—, Women Painters West, 1992—, Fine Arts Inst., San Bernardino, Calif., 1995—. One woman shows at Collectors Gallery, Palos Verdes Art Ctr., 1995, Norris Theater, Rolling Hills Estates, Calif., 1995; exhibited in group shows at Malaga Cove Libr., Palos Verdes Estates, 1993, Beckstrand Gallery, Rancho Palos Verdes, 1993, 94, 95, 96, Artists' Studio, Rolling Hills Estates, 1993, 94, 96, Taos (N.Mex.) Convention Ctr., 1993, Stewart Gallery, Rancho Palos Verdes, 1993, 94, 96, 97, Petropavlovsk (Russia) Mus./Gallery, 1993, Gate Gallery, San Pedro, Calif., 1993, Palos Verdes Art Ctr., 1994, 95, 96, 97, 98, Lancaster (Calif.) Art Mus., 1994, Millennium Show, Montrose, CA, 2000, Square One Finegood Gall., West Hills, CA, Village Square Gall., Riverside (Calif.) Art Mus., 1995, 96, Long Beach (Calif.) Arts, 1995, 97, Joslyn Fine Arts Gallery, Torrance, Calif., 1995, 96, 97, 98, San Bernardino County Mus., 1996, Janet Turner Print Gallery, Chico, Calif., 1997, Brand Libr., 1997, Royal Birmingham (Eng.) Soc. Artists Gallery, 1997, Women Artists West, Biloxi, Miss., 1997, Lankersham Art Ctr. Gallery, Calif., 1997, Printmaking Coun. N.J., Cerritos Art Gallery/Cerritos Coll., Calif., 1998, Met. Life, Bridgewater, N.J., 1998, Monoprints and Books, Rancho Palos Verdes, 1998, Gallery 825, L.A., Lankersham Art Gallery, L.A., 1998, 99, NAPA 3d Ann. Exhbn., Covington, La., 1998, 99, Brand XXVIII Works on Paper, Glendale, Calif., 1998, 99, Brand XXIX Works on Paper, 1999-00, WAOW Membership Exhbn., Rancho Capistrano, Calif., 1998, 99, UCLA Med. Ctr., 1998, Lancaster (Calif.) Art Mus., 1999, Finegood Gallery, West Hills, Calif., 2000, Charles Borman Gallery, Montrose, Calif., 2000, Soleil, Manhattan Beach, 2000, others; represented in various pvt. collections; watercolors added to UCLA Med. Ctr. collection, 1998. Mem. South Bay Watercolor Soc. (bd. dirs. 1995-97, pres.), Nat. Acrylic Painters Assn., L.A. Printmaking Soc., Calif. Watercolor Assn., Pacific Art Guild (past officer), Paletteers, Women Artists of the West, Women Painters West. Avocations: singing, playing musical instruments, writing poetry, sailing, gardening. Home: 461 28th St Manhattan Beach CA 90266-2126

LEE, IARA, filmmaker; Co-founder, acting pres. Calpirinha Prodns., N.Y.C. Filmmaker : Prufrock, 1991; Neighbors, 1992 (Best of Festival, Dysfunctional Family Film Festival Chgo., 1993, Jury prize Rochester Internat. Film Festival, 1993, Silver award Houston Internat. Film Festival, 1993, Bronze award Festival Der Nationen-Ebensee, Germany, 1993); An Autumn Wind, 1993; Synthetic Pleasures, Modulations--cinema for the ear, 1998; participant numerous festival screenings including :, 1992, 1992; Karlsruhe Film Festival, 1992; Hawaii Internat. Film Festival, 1992; Film Front Film Festival, 1992; Ind. Feature Film Market, 1992, 1993; Mill Valley Film Festival, 1993; Internat. Film Festival Dhaka, 1993; Worldfest Houston, 1993; New Orleans Film and Video Festival, 1993; St. Petersburg Internat. Film Festival, 1994; Social Outcast Film and Video Festival, 1994; others. Office: C/O The Presidio 39 Mesa St Ste 300 San Francisco CA 94129-1019

LEE, JAMIE LEE, video specialist; b. Rapid City, S.D., June 24, 1959; d. Arzean Nellie (Lee) Fiedler. BS, Black Hills State Coll., Spearfish, S.D., 1981; postgrad., Sony Inst. Video, 1993. News reporter Sta. KEVN-TV, Rapid City, 1981-82; prodn. mgr. Sta. KSNK-TV, Oberlin, Kans., 1982-84; film and promotion and news dir. Sta. KLBY-TV, Colby, Kans., 1984-86; owner, mgr. Balloons in Motion, advt., Spearfish, 1986-88; audio video technician II, Rapid City Police Dept., 1988—. Prodr., videographer Behind the Badge, 1996, also others. Vol. United Way, Rapid City, 1988—; co-chmn. Indian-White Rels., Rapid City, 1991-93; organizer Parent Cruiser Night, Rapid City, 1991—. Recipient award for extraordinary svc. Sa. KBHU-FM, Spearfish, 1981, media promotion award Victims Assistance Office, Rapid City, 1991. Mem. Law Enforcement Video Assn., Assn. Profl. Videographers, Black Hills Advt. Fedn. (assoc.). Avocations: reading, camping, animals, motorcycles. Office: Rapid City Police Dept 300 Kansas City St Rapid City SD 57701-2821

LEE, JANET MENTORE, psychologist, educator; b. N.Y.C., July 21, 1972; d. Percy Edward and Celina Mentore(Stepmother); m. Ryan Todd Lee, Aug. 5, 2000; 1 child, Jordyn Olivia. BA, Ithaca Coll., 1994; MS in Edn., Fordham U., 1997, PhD, 1999. Lic. psychologist Conn., 2001, N.Y., 2001, cert. sch. psychologist Conn., 2000, N.Y., 1999. Psychologist Westport (Conn.) Pub. Schs., 2000—. Psychologist Hawthorne (N.Y.) Union Free Sch. Dist., 1999—2000; adj. asst. prof. Fordham U., N.Y.C., 2000—03, Fairfield (Conn.) U., 2002—03; presenter in field. Advisory editor: The School Psychologist-APA; contbr. articles to profl. jours. Bd. mem. Cmty. Free Dems., N.Y.C., 1997—99. Grad. Assistantship, Fordham U., 1995—99, Internat. Congress on Obesity scholar, Pfizer Pharmaceuticals, 1998. Mem.: NASP, APA (Hon. Mention Outstanding Dissertation award Divsn. 16 2000), Conn. Assn. Sch. Psychologists, Conn. Psychol. Assn., N.Y. Assn. Sch. Psychologists (Ted Bernstein Outstanding Student award 1999), N.Y. State Psychol. Assn. (future psychologists sect. chair 1997—99, Conv. scholar 1998, Spl. Citation award 1999). Democrat. Achievements include co-investigator baseline levels of obesity and weight gain among patients taking antipsychotic medications. Home: Unit #10 1611 Washington Blvd Stamford CT 06902 Office: Westport Public Schs/Long Lots Elem 13 Hyde Ln Westport CT 06880 Personal E-mail: jmentore@yahoo.com. E-mail: jmlee@westport.k12.ct.us.

LEE, JANIE C. curator; b. Shreveport, La., Apr. 22, 1937; d. Birch Lee and Joanna (Glassell) Wood; m. David B. Warren, Jan. 2, 1980. Student, Nat. Cathedral Sch., 1951-55; BA, Sarah Lawrence Coll., 1959. Asst. to Cheryl Crawford, Actors Studi o, N.Y.C., 1962-63; co-prodr. Off Broadway Theatre Co., N.Y.C., 1963-65; owner, pres. Janie C. Lee Gallery, Dallas, 1967-74, Houston, 1973-96, Janie C. Lee Master Drawings, N.Y.C., 1983-96; curator of drawings Whitney Mus. Am. Art, 1997—. Mem. art appraisal panel IRS, Washington, 1987-94; trustee Menil Found., Inc., 2000—. Prodr. ann. catalogue on 20th Century drawings, 1979-93. Mem. Alumnae Bd. Sarah Lawrence Coll. (1972-74); pres. Nancy Graves Found., 1996—. Mem. Art Dealers Assn. Am. (bd. dirs. 1980-88, 92-94, v.p. 1984-88). Office: 1209 Berthea St Houston TX 77006-6411

LEE, JANIS K. state legislator; b. Kensington, Kans., July 11, 1945; m. Lyn Lee; children: David, Brian, Daniel. BA, Kans. State U., 1970. Mem. from dist. 36 Kans. State Senate, 1988—. Mem. Kappa Delta Pi, Phi Kappa Phi. Democrat. Home: RR 1 Box 145 Kensington KS 66951-9801 Office: Kansas Senate State Capitol Rm 402-S Topeka KS 66612

LEE, JEANNE ANN, music educator, consultant; b. Harlan, Ky., Apr. 6, 1957; d. Gurney Clay and Carolyn Perkey Luttrell; life ptnr. Larry Clark Lee; children: Jeremy Thomas, Jonathon Clay, Jared David. MA in Edn. rank 1, Union Coll., Barbourville, Ky. Cert. elem. edn. Ky. Dept. of Edn., 1989, music edn. k-12 Ky. Dept. of Edn., gifted edn. k-12 Ky. Dept. of Edn., mid. level prin. Ky. Dept. of Edn. Tchr. Woodland Hills Christian Sch., Harlan, Ky., 1984—90, Harlan Ind. Schools; dist. arts and humanities resource tchr. Harlan County Bd. of Edn. Std. setting com. Ky. Dept. of Edn., Frankfort, ctb bookmark com.; core content adv. com. KDE and West Ednl. Cons., L.A.; founding mem. Ea. Ky. U. Arts Collaborative, Richmond, Ky.; assoc. dir. Harlan Boys Choir, Inc., Harlan, Ky.; accompanist Harlan Musettes; dir. Harlan Elem. Choir, Harlan County Children's Choir. Composer: (2 part choral anthem) Simply Amazing. Arts and humanities week in Harlan county Harlan County Fiscal Ct.; dir. choir and children's music dir. Harlan Bapt. Ch.; mem. sch. bd. Woodland Hills Christian Sch., Harlan, 1982—84. Nominee Tchr. of the Yr., Walt Disney Corp.; recipient Golden Apple Tchg. award, Ashland Oil, Excellence in Tchg. award, U. of Ky. Mem.: Ky. Arts Edn. Assn., Ky. Assn. for Suprs. and Adminstrs., Am. Choral Dirs. Assn., Ky. Music Educators Assn., Ky. Assn. of Gifted Edn., Ky. Leadership Acad. Baptist. Avocations: reading, travel, music. Office: 251 Ball Park Rd Harlan KY 40831 E-mail: jlee@harlan.k12.ky.us.

LEE, JEANNE KIT YEW, administrative officer; b. N.Y.C., July 31, 1959; d. Tat Yuen and Yow Seum (Chu) Lee. BBA, Baruch Coll., 1982. Clk. typist U.S. Dept. Health and Human Svcs., N.Y.C., 1980-83, U.S. Consumer Product Safety Commn., N.Y.C., 1983-85, adminstrv. asst., 1985-90, sys. adminstr., 1986-93, adminstrv. officer, 1990—. Mem. NAFE, Humane Soc., Nat. Wildlife Fedn. (assoc.), Am. Humane, DAV (Commanders Club 1988—). Business E-Mail: jklee@cpsc.gov.

LEE, JENNIFER MORITA, secondary school educator; b. Fairfield, Calif., Aug. 30, 1949; d. Harry Hideo and Takako M.; children: Jessica Mayumi, Jordan Minoru. BA, UCLA, 1971. Tchr. L.A. Unified Sch. Dist., 1973—. Mentor tchr., facilitator Nat. Bd. Cert.; lectr. UCLA. Vol. Boy Scouts Am., Hacienda Heights, Calif., 1987-91, Girl Scouts U.S., Hacienda Heights, 1989-91. Grant Ahmanson Found. Mem. United Tchrs. L.A., So. Calif. Paleontol. Soc. (sec.). Democrat. Avocations: archaeology, anthropology, antiques. Office: 725 S Indiana St Los Angeles CA 90023-1840

LEE, JOSELYN C.R. physician, researcher; b. Hong Kong, June 7, 1961; came to U.S., 1979; d. Joseph Mui Hok and Myra Jeannon (Yip) L. BS in Chemistry, Stanford (Calif) U., 1983, MS in Biology, 1984; MD, U. Chgo., 1990. Diplomate Am. Bd. Pediatrics; lic. physician, Calif., S.C. Tchr. asst. dept. chemistry Stanford U., 1983-84; rsch. asst. pharmacology and physiology U. Chgo., 1987-89; intern dept pediatrics Harbor UCLA Hosp., Torrance, Calif., 1990-91, resident in pediatrics, 1991-93; temporary clin. lectr. pediatrics Hong Kong U. Sch. Medicine, 1993-94; pediatric cardiology fellow Med. U. S.C., Charleston, 1994—; asst. prof., pediatric cardiac electrophysiology Tulane U. Med. Sch.; dir. Children's Heart Rhythm Inst., L.A. Recipient Bristol-Myers Squibb Affiliate Travel award Am. Coll. Cardiology, 1997, Young Investigator award Am. Acad. Pediatrics, 1995, Nat. Rsch. Svc. award NIH, 1995, 97; Grantham scholar, Dr. and Mrs. Charles Yau scholar, Hong Kong Govt. scholar. Mem. AAAS, Am. Acad. Pediatrics, Am. Coll. Cardiology, N.Y. Acad. Sci., Phi Beta Kappa, No. Am. Soc. of Pacing and Electrophysiology, Phi Lambda Upsilon. Avocations: piano, singing. Office: Children's Heart Rythum Inst POBox 24854 Los Angeles CA 90024

LEE, JOYCE ANN, computer educator; b. Safford, Ariz., Sept. 18, 1942; d. Roy and Minnie R. (Mobley) Brewer; m. Eugene W. Gaddy Jr., Mar. 16, 1970 (div. 1985); children: Carol, Kevin, Aaron; m. Glenn A. Lee, Oct. 16, 1992. AA, Ea. Ariz. Coll., 1980, AAS, 1993; BA in Mgmt., U. Phoenix, 1995, MS in Computer Info. Sci., 2001. Dispatcher Mohave County Sheriff's Office, Kingman, Ariz., 1969-74; sec. Globe (Ariz.) Mobile Home Sales, 1975-83; data entry supr. SMC & Assocs., Globe, 1985-88; tax preparer H&R Block Co., Globe, 1992; adminstrv. asst. Am. Pub. Co., Globe, 1994—. Instr. computer, bus. classes Ea. Ariz. Coll. Gila Pueblo campus, Globe, 1996-2001, instr. computers Pima Cmty. Coll., 2002. Girls camp dir. LDS Ch., Globe, 1985-90; mem. com. Boy Scouts Am., Globe. Mem. NAFE, Phi Theta Kappa. Democrat. Avocations: hunting, fishing, hiking, archery, camping. Home: 5201 W Bobwhite Way Tucson AZ 85742 Office: Pima Cmty Coll Tucson AZ 85742- E-mail: azgirl1942@yahoo.com.

LEE, JUNE WARREN, dentist; b. Boston, Feb. 24, 1952; d. Earl Arnold and Rosemary Regina (Leary) Warren; m. William Lee, July 25, 1976; children: Jaime Michelle, Daniel William. BA, Brandeis U., 1973; DDS, Georgetown U., 1977; student, U.S. Dental Inst., 1985-87. Pvt. practice, Boston, 1977—. Mem. Dorchester Bd. of Trade, 2000—. Active Pierce Mid. Sch. PTO, 1997-2000, Cunningham Sch. PTO, Milton, Mass., 1987-97, Parent-Adv. Coun., Collicot Elem. Sch., Milton, 1986-87; dental instr. Cunningham Sch., 1987-97; dental screening Healthworks, Neponset Health Ctr., Boston, 1981-84; bd. dirs. Delta Dental Plan Mass., 1995-2001, Delta Dental Found. Mass., 1995-2001; vol. Dentist for SmileLine On-Line, 2001-02, Masons Child Identification Program, 2000—. Master Acad. Gen. Dentistry (coun. am. meetings and internat. confs. 1993-98, 2002-, chmn. 1998 local arrangements com., past pres. New Eng. Mastertrack program, pres. Mass. chpt. 1998-2001, past chmn. editl. rev. bd. Audiodent, coun. constn. and bylaws and jud. procedures 2001-02, region one dir. 2003--); fellow Am. Coll. Dentists, Internat. Coll. Dentists, Acad. Dentistry Internat.; mem. ADA, Mass. Dental Soc. (allied profl. liaison com. 1998-99, 2000-, amb. 2000), Yankee Dental Congress (steering com. 1997-2000, 00-, gen. chmn. 2003-04, co-chmn. social and cultural com., 2001, co-chmn. sci. com., 1998, co-chmn. gen. arrangements, 1996, allied sci. co-chmn. 1994), South Shore Dist. Dental Soc. (chmn.-elect 1991, chmn. 1992, chmn. program com. 1995-96), Am. Orthodontic Soc., Am. Assn. for Functional Orthodontics, Am. Assn. Women Dentists (sec. 1987, v.p. 1988, pres.-elect 1989, pres. 1990, A.T. Cross Co. Women of Achievement award 1985, bd. dirs., treas. Gillette Hayden Meml. Found. 1996-2000), Women's Dental Soc. Mass. (sec. 1978, v.p. 1979-81, pres. 1981-83), Mass. Dentists Interested in Legislation, Chestnut Hill Rsch. Study Club. Roman Catholic. Avocations: travel, geneology, reading, writing, celtic music. Office: 383 Neponset Ave Dorchester MA 02122-3104 Office Phone: 617-288-2680. E-mail: drsinelee@hotmail.com.

LEE, KAREN, art appraiser; b. B Polit. Sci., Tung-hai U., Taiwan; JD, Washburn U., 1983. Ind. art dealer, Topeka. Bd. regents Washburn U., 1999—. Home and Office: 132 SW Fairlawn Rd Topeka KS 66606

LEE, KRISTI, broadcast executive, reporter; b. Indpls., July 17, 1960; d. Sammy Cecil Gibson and Mary Scott (Pounds) Crawley. Student, Ind. U., 1978—. T.v. engr. WRTV-Channel 6, Indpls., 1980-86; t.v. engr., dir. KOAT-TV, Albuquerque, 1986-88; radio news dir. Bob and Tom Show WFBQ-095, Indpls., 1988—; sports reporter ESPN, ESPN 2, 1993—. Dir. Musicians Against Child Abuse, Indpls., 1995—; fundraiser, vol. Hope Lodge. Mem. Am. Women in Radio and TV (95 Radio Personality of the Yr. award). Avocations: movies, golf, sports events, gardening, travel. Office: WFBQ-Q95 6161 Fall Creek Rd Indianapolis IN 46220-5032

LEE, LEILA, interior designer, artist; b. Chgo., Aug. 06; d. George Mitchell and Jen (Klein) Gollin; children: Boni Joy Weinstein, David Steven Slack. Student, Chgo. Art Inst., Inst. Design, Loyola U. Chair interior design seminar U. Wis., 1993; design cons. Mdse. Mart, 1990-95. Exhbns. include Unique Accent, Chgo., 1995, Mead Gallery, Oak Park, Ill., 1995, Warner Showroom, Chgo., 1995, Acad. Fine Arts, Beijing, Textile Mus. & Inst., Moscow, Russia Ethnographic Mus., St. Petersburg, various juried art fairs; contbr. to publs. including Parade Mag., Chgo. Sun-Times, HFD Fairchild Publ., Chgo., Profile News, Chgo., Interior Design Mag., River North News, Oak Park News, The Skyline; editor: (newsletter) Hi There, This is Lee; on radio show No Space Like Home; represented in pvt. collections. Mem. Internat. Interior Design Assn., Nat. Assn. Women Bus. Owners, Chgo. Artists Coalition, Am. Soc. Artists. Avocations: theater, travel, reading, art, music. Home and Office: 21 W Goethe St Apt 15L Chicago IL 60610-7403

LEE, LINDA M. technical recruiter; b. L.A., Dec. 28, 1972; d. Jack K. C. and Grace K. C. Lee. BA, U. Calif., Berkeley, 1995; cert. in human resource mgmt., cert. in tng. and human resource devel. Tech. recruiter Microsoft Corp., Mountain View, Calif. Vol. Asian Women Shelter, 1998—; mentor Chinatown Leo Club, San Francisco, 1998—, Children and Family Social Svcs., 1999—. E-mail: lindalee00@msn.com.

LEE, MARGARET ANNE, psychotherapist, social worker; b. Scribner, Nebr., Nov. 23, 1930; d. William Christian and Caroline Bertha (Benner) Joens; m. Robert Kelly Lee, May 21, 1950 (div. 1972); children: Lawrence Robert, James Kelly, Daniel Richard. AA, Napa Coll., 1949; student, U. Calif., Berkeley, 1949-50; BA, Calif. State Coll., Sonoma, 1975; MSW, Calif. State U., Sacramento, 1977. Diplomate clin. social worker; lic. clin. social worker, Calif.; lic. marriage and family counselor, Calif.; tchr. Columnist, stringer Napa (Calif.) Register, 1946-50; eligibility worker, supr. Napa County Dept. Social Services, 1968-75; instr. Napa Valley Community Coll., 1978-83; practice psychotherapy Napa, 1977—; oral commr. Calif. Dept. Consumer Affairs, Bd. Behavioral Sci., 1984-90. Pres. bd. Napa Valley C.C., 1995, trustee, 1983—, v.p. bd., 1984—85, 2003—, pres. bd., 1986, 1990, 2004, clk., 1988—89, 2002—03; bd. dirs. Napa County Coun. Econ. Opportunity, 1984—85, Napa chpt. March of Dimes, 1957—71, Mental Health Assn. Napa County, 1983—87; vice chmn. edn. com. Calif. C.C. Trustees, 1987—88, chmn. edn. com., 1988—89, legis. com., 1985—87, bd. dirs., 1989—99, 2nd v.p., 1991, 1st v.p., 1992, pres., 1993; student equity rev. group Calif. C.C. Chancellors, 1992; bd. dirs. C.C. League Calif., 1992—95, 1st v.p., 1992; appointed mem. Napa County Paratransit Coord. Coun., 1999—, coun. chairperson, 2002—; bd. dirs. Napa County Transp. Planning Agy., 2002—. Recipient Fresh Start award Self mag., award Congl. Caucus on Women's Issues, 1984; named Woman of distinction, Soroptimist Internat. and Sunrise Clubs of Napa, 1997. Mem. NASW, Calif. Elected Women's Assn. Edn. and Rsch. Democrat. Lutheran. Office: 1100 Trancas St Napa CA 94558-2908 Office Phone: 707-224-8661.

LEE, MARGARET BURKE, college president, English educator; b. San Diego, Dec. 28, 1943; d. Peter John and Margaret Mary (Brown) Burke; m. Donald Harry Lee, June 30, 1973; children: Katherine Louise, Kristopher Donald. BA summa cum laude, Regis Coll., 1966; MA with honors, U. Chgo., 1970, PhD, 1978; IEM Cert., Harvard U., 1992, Seminar for New Pres., 1996. Asst. to humanities MIT, Cambridge, 1969; instr. Dover-Sherborn H.S., Dover, 1973-75, Alpena (Mich.) C.C., 1975-80, dean liberal arts, 1980-82; dean instrn. Kalamazoo Valley C.C., 1982-85; v.p. Oakton C.C., Des Plaines, Ill., 1985-95, pres., 1995—. Cons. evaluator North Ctrl. Assn., Chgo., 1982—, commr.-at-large, 1988-92, commn. on inst. of higher edn. bd. dirs., 1992—, vice chair, 1996-98, chair, 1998, now v.p.; vice chair Am. Coun. on Internat. Intercultural Edn.; cons., field faculty Vt. Coll., Montpelier, 1982-85; mem. admissions com. Ill. Math and Sci. Acad., 1988—; bd. govs. North Cook Ednl. Svc. Ctr., 1988—, bd. dirs., 1989—, vice chair, 1990-91, chair, 1992-94. Mem. Bd. Edn. Dist. 39, Wilmette, Ill., 1990-92, Des Plaines Sister Cities, 1995—; bd. dirs. Ill. C.C. Atty.'s Assn., 1994—; mem. Career Edn. Planning Dist., Kalamazoo, 1982, Kalamazoo Forum/Kalamazoo Network, 1982, Needs Assessment Task Force, 1984. Ford Found. fellow, 1969-73, Woodrow Wilson Found. fellow, 1975; fed. grantee, 1978-84. Mem. Am. Assn. of C.C.'s (bd. dirs.), Am. Assn. Cmty. and Jr. Colls., Mich. Assn. C.C. Instrnl. Adminstrs. (pres. 1983-85), Mich. Occupl. Deans Adminstrs. Coun. (exec. bd. 1983-85), Mich. Women's Studies Assn. (hons. selection com. 1984), North Ctrl. Assn. Acad. Deans (pres. 1988-90), Kalamazoo Consortium Higher Edn. (pres.'s coun. coord. com. 1982-85), Kalamazoo C. of C. (vocat. edn. subcom. indsl. coun. 1982), North Ctrl. Assn. Acad. Deans (v.p., pres. 1985-87), Des Plaines C. of C. (mem. bd. dirs. 1995—). Democrat. Lutheran. Avocations: quilt collecting, reading, listening to classical music, sports spectating, theatre-going. Home: 2247 Lake Ave Wilmette IL 60091-1410 Office: Oakton CC 1600 E Golf Rd Des Plaines IL 60016-1234

LEE, MARGARET NORMA, artist; b. Kansas City, Mo., July 7, 1928; d. James W. and Margaret W. (Farin) Lee; PhB, U. Chgo., 1948; MA, Art Inst. Chgo., 1952. Lectr., U. Kansas City, 1957-61; cons. Kansas City Bd. Edn., Kansas City, Mo., 1968-86; guest lectr. U.Mo.-Columbia, 1983, 85, 87, 89, 91, 93-95, 97; one-woman shows Univ. Women's Club, Kansas City, 1966, Friends of Art, Kansas City, 1969, Fine Arts Gallery U. Mo. at Columbia, 1972, All Souls Unitarian Ch. Kansas City, Mo., 1978; two-Woman show Rockhurst Coll., Kansas City, Mo., 1981 exhibited in group shows U. Kans., Lawrence, 1958, Chgo. Art Inst., 1963, Nelson Art Gallery, Kansas City, Mo., 1968, 74, Mo. Art Show, 1976, Fine Arts Gallery, Davenport, Iowa, 1977; represented in permanent collections Amarillo (Tex.) Art Center, Kansas City (Mo.) Pub. Library, Park Coll., Parkville, Mo. Mem. Coll. Art Assn. Roman Catholic. Contbr. art to profl. jours.; author booklet. Home: 4109 Holmes St Kansas City MO 64110-1127

LEE, MARILYN B. state representative; b. Schenectady, N.Y., Jan. 15, 1940; m. Samuel S.H. Lee; children: Mary, John, Thomas, Andrew. BS, Syracuse U., 1962. Full lt., nurse USN, 1960—66; RN, 1962—. Chair Mililani Waipio Melemanu Neighborhood Bd., 1992—96. Moderator (on legis. issues TV series) The Kukui Connection. Flemming Fellow, 1999, Eleanor Roosevelt Fellow, 2002. Mem.: Am. Cancer Soc., AAUW. Democrat. Office: State Capitol Rm 421 415 S Beretania St Honolulu HI 96813 E-mail: replee@capitol.hawaii.gov., sshlee@pixi.com.

LEE, MARTHA, artist, writer; b. Chehalis, Wash., Aug. 23, 1946; d. William Robert and Phyllis Ann (Herzog) L.; m. Peter Reynolds Lockwood, Jan. 25, 1974 (div. 1982). BA in English Lit., U. Wash., 1968; student, Factory of Visual Art, 1980-82. Reporter Seattle Post-Intelligencer, 1970; personnel counselor Theresa Snow Employment, 1971-72; receptionist Northwest Kidney Ctr., 1972-73; proprietress The Reliquary, 1974-77; travel agt. Cathay Express, 1977-79; artist, 1980—; represented by Mahler Fine Arts, Seattle, Pacific Rim Gallery, Astoria, Oreg. Painter various oil paintings; exhibited in numerous one-woman and group shows throughout Oreg. and Washington; author: To The Beach and Other Poems, 1998. Avocations: horseback riding, beachcombing, reading, music. Home: PO Box 1157 Ocean Park WA 98640-1157

LEE, MICHELE CHERRY, counseling administrator; b. Dublin, Ga., Apr. 2, 1971; d. William Morris Cherry and Carolyn Sue Burgamy, Becky Haynes Cherry (Stepmother); m. Lyman V. Lee, July 25, 1998; children: Peyton Parker, Cage Alexander. AA in Spl. Edn., Mid. Ga. Coll., Dublin, 1992; BS in Sociology, Ga. Coll., Milledgeville, 1994; MA in Mental Health Counseling, Fort Valley State U., 1998. Cert. spl. edn. tchr. 2000. Spl. instr. early intervention Ft. Valley State U., Ga., 1994; svc. coord. Babie's Can't Wait, Dublin, Ga., 1999—2002; child specialist All God's Children, Bogart, Ga., 2001—; regional site coord. ATEAM, Dublin, Ga., 2002—; svc. coord. Profl. Counseling Svcs. of Am., Americus, Ga., 2002—; youth svcs. specialist Heart Of Ga. RESA, Eastman, Ga., 2003—. Mem.: Devel. Disabilities Orgn., The Assn. for Gifted, Coun. for Exceptional Children (assoc.), Gamma Beta Phi. Home: PO Box 807 Dublin GA 31040 Personal E-mail: shellielee@bellsouth.net.

LEE, NANCY RANCK, management consultant; b. Yonkers, N.Y., Oct. 31, 1932; d. William Edward and Marion Edna Ranck; children: John Gregory, Paul Edward. BS, Cornell U., 1953; postgrad., Boston U., 1974-75. Social worker Tompkins County, Ithaca, N.Y., 1953-54; pers. adminstr. GE Advanced Electronics Ctr., Ithaca, 1954-55; fashion publicist Macy's, N.Y.C., 1956-59; mgr. advt. and pub. rels. Josiah Wedgwood & Co., N.Y.C., 1959-65; dir. comms. Gregory Fosella Assocs., Boston, 1969-71; dir. mktg. Kuras & Co., Boston, 1971-73; internat. sales mgr. Laser Focus Mag., Boston, 1973-75; pres. Lee Assocs., Boston, 1975-82; exec. v.p. Infotech, Boston, 1982-92; pres. Requisite Orgn. Assoc., Sarasota, Fla., 1992—. Lectr. Simmons Coll. Author: Targeting the Top: Everything a Woman Needs to Know to Succeed in Business, 1980. Mem. Cornell Cb, Ivy League Club, Phi Kappa Phi. Avocation: skiing. Home: PO Box 48818 Sarasota FL 34230-5818

LEE, PALI JAE (POLLY JAE STEAD LEE), retired librarian, writer; b. Nov. 26, 1925; d. Jonathan Everett Wheeler and Ona Katherine (Grunder) Stead; m. Richard H.W. Lee, Apr. 7, 1945 (div. 1978); children: Catherine

Lani Honcoop, Karin Elizabeth Robinson, Ona G., Laurie Brett, Robin Louise Halbert; m. John K. Willis, 1979 (dec. 1994). Student, U. Hawaii, 1944-46, Mich. State, 1961-64. Cataloguer and processor U.S. Army Air Force, 1945-46; with U.S. Weather Bur. Film Library, New Orleans, 1948-50, FBI, Wright-Patterson AFB, Dayton, Ohio, 1952, Ohio Wholesale Winedealers, Columbus, Ohio, 1956-58, Coll. Engring., Ohio State U., Columbus, 1959, writer tech. manual Annie Wittenmyer Home, Davenport, Iowa, 1960; with Grand Rapids (Mich.) Pub. Library, 1961-62; dir. Waterford (Mich.) Twp. Libraries, 1962-64; acquisition librarian Pontiac (Mich.) Pub. Libraries, 1965-71, dir. East Side br., 1971-73; rsch. asst. dept. anthropology Bishop Mus., Honolulu, 1975-83; pub. Night Rainbow Pub., Honolulu, 1984—. Author: HIstory of Wine Growing in America, 1952, House Parenting at its Best, 1960, Mary Dyer, Child of Light, 1973, Giant: Pictorial History of the Human Colossus, 1973, History of Change: Kaneohe Bay Area, 1976, English edit., 1983, Na Po Makole-Tales of the Night Rainbow, 1981, rev. edit., 1988, Mo'olelo O Na Pohukaina, 1983, Ka Ipu Kukui, 1994, Ho'opono, 1999, Remembrance: The History of a Family, 2003; contbr. articles to profl. jours. Chmn. Oakland County br. Multiple Sclerosis Soc., 1972-73, co-chmn. Pontiac com. of Mich. area bd., 1972-73; sec. Ohana o Kokua, 1979-83, Paia-Willis Ohana, 1982-91, Ohana Kame'ekua, 1988-91; bd. dirs. Detroit Multiple Sclerosis Soc., 1971; mem. Mich. area bd. Am. Friends Svc. com., 1961-69; mem. consumer adv. bd. Libr. for Blind and Physically Handicapped, Honolulu, 1991-96, mem. adv. bd., 1997-98, bd. dirs. 1999; pres. consumer 55 plus Hawaii Ctr. for Ind. Living, 1990-94, pres., 1995-96; pres. Honolulu chpt. Nat. Fedn. of Blind, 1991-93, 1st v.p. #93 state affiliate, 1991-93, editor Na Na Maka Aloha newsletter, 1990-94; 1st v.p. Hawaii chpt. Talking Book Readers Club, 1994-95, pres., 1996. Recipient Mother of the Yr. award Quad City Bus. Men, 1960, Bowl of Light award Hawaiian Community of Hawaii, 1989. Mem. Soc. Friends. Office: PO Box 10706 Honolulu HI 96816-0706 E-mail: palijae@hawii.rr.com.

LEE, PAMELA ANNE, bank executive, accountant, business analyst; b. San Francisco, May 30, 1960; d. Larry D. and Alice Mary (Reece) L. BBA, San Francisco State U., 1981. CPA, Calif. Typist, bookkeeper, tax acct. James G. Woo, CPA, San Francisco, 1979-85; tutor bus. math. and stats. San Francisco State U., 1979-80; from teller to ops. officer Gibraltar Savs. and Loan, San Francisco, 1978-81; sr. acct. Price Waterhouse, San Francisco, 1981-86; corp. acctg. mgr. First Nationwide Bank, Daly City, Calif., 1986-89, v.p., 1989-91, v.p., project mgr., 1991-92, sr. conversion and bus. analyst, 1992-93; sr. bus. analyst, asst. v.p. Bank of Am., 1996-98, mktg. cons., v.p., 1998-99, sr. cons. bus. automation, v.p., 1999-2001, sr. v.p., 2001—. Acctg. cons. New Performance Gallery, San Francisco, 1985, San Francisco Chamber Orch., 1986; treas. Golden Gate chpt. Team Bank of Am., 2000-02, co-chmn., 2003--. Founding mem., chair bd. trustees Asian Acctg. Students Career Day, 1988-89; vol. Mickaboo Cockatiel Rescue, 1998—, CFO, 2002--. Mem.: AICPA, Calif. Soc. CPAs, Toastmasters Internat. (co-v.p. membereship Tower of Talk chpt. 2000—01, co-v.p. edn. 2001, v.p. membership 2002, competetent toastmaster status 2001, competent leader status 2002). Republican. Avocations: reading, music, travel, personal computing, crafting. Office: 1455 Market St 13th Fl San Francisco CA 94103

LEE, PATRICIA Y. lawyer; BS, U. Hawaii; MS, Columbia U.; PhD, Northwestern U.; JD, William S. Richardson Sch. Law; Cert. with Hon. Mention (hon.), U. Paris. Faculty Rockhurst Coll., Mo.; asst. prof. Northeastern Ill. U.; asst. prof. French U. Hawaii, Honolulu; trusts and estates atty. Goodsill Anderson Quinn & Stifel, Honolulu, 1979—, ptnr., 1985—; mem. U. Hawaii Bd. Regents, Honolulu, 2001—. Dir. French Festival of Hawaii, Jean Charlot Found.; hon. consul of France State of Hawaii. Office: 1099 Alakea St Ste 1099 Honolulu HI 96813

LEE, REBECCA, literature educator, writer; b. Copperhill, Tenn., June 19, 1943; d. Avery Lee and Virginia Quinn Smith. BA in English, Conn. Coll., 1964; MA in English, U. Mont., 1972; PhD, U. Ariz., 1981. Secondary sch. tchr. U.S. Peace Corps, Tabora, Tanzania, 1964—66; newspaper reporter W.Va. Pub. Co., Morgantown, 1966—68; moderator of radio show Missoula, Mont., 1968—69; lectr. Humboldt State U., Arcata, Calif., 1981—84; asst. prof. English U. Hawaii, Honolulu, 1984—91, Pearl City, 1992—97, dir. writing program, 1993—2003, assoc. prof. lit., 1997—2003, coord. distributed learning, 2002, prof. lit., 2003—. Freelance editor/writer, Calif., 1968—81. Editor: various books; contbr. poems, stories, and articles to mags. and newspapers. V.p. U. Hawaii Profl. Assembly, Honolulu, 1998—99, mem., 1996—2000; chair faculty senate U. Hawaii, 1993—95; v.p. Hawaii Lit. Arts Coun., Honolulu, 1988—89. Grantee, NEH, 1997-1998. Mem.: NEA. Avocations: swimming, yoga, walking, bridge, photography. Office: U Hawaii West Oahu 96-129 Ala Ike Pearl City HI 96782 Office Fax: (808) 453-6176. Personal E-mail: rebecca@hawaii.edu. Business E-Mail: rebecca@hawaii.edu.

LEE, SALLY A. editor-in-chief; m. Rob Niosi. Grad., Durham U., Eng.; MA, Clark U., Mass. Tchr. writing and lit. Clark U.; reporter Worcester (Mass.) Telegram; mng. editor Worcester (Mass.) Monthly; spl. features editor Woman's World mag., N.Y.C.; articles editor Woman's Day mag., N.Y.C.; sr. editor Redbook mag., N.Y.C.; editor-in-chief YM, N.Y.C., 1994—96, Fitness Mag., N.Y.C., 1996—98, Parents Mag., N.Y.C., 1998—; editl. dir. YM mag., N.Y.C., 2004. Corr. E! Entertainment Network. Author: The Best Advice I Ever Got, 2001. Bd. dirs. Room to Grow, Women for Women Internat. Mem.: Parenting Network. Office: Parents Mag 375 Lexington Ave Fl 10 New York NY 10017-5514

LEE, SUN MYUNG, physician; b. Seoul, Korea, July 9, 1940; d. Jong Suk and Soo Nam Lee; m. Hi Young; children: Sandra Shon, Grace, David. BS, Yonsei U., Seoul, 1961, MD, 1965; cert. in lay ministry, Whitworth Coll., 2001. Diplomate Am. Acad. Family Practice; ordained elder Korean Presbyn. Ch., 1999. Intern Riverside Methodist Hosp., Columbus, Oh., 1967-68; resident Veteran's Adminstrn. Hosp., Dayton, Oh., 1968-69; intern Riverside Meth. Hosp., Columbus, Ohio, 1966-67; resident Ohio State VA Hosp., Dayton, 1967-70; pvt. practice family medicine Drs. Lee & Lee PS, Spokane, Wash., 1974—. Mem. med. staff Ea. State Hosp., Medical Lake, Wash., 1972-74; pres. Drs. Lee & Lee P.S., 1974—. Author: Best Poetry of 1997, 1997; columnist Rainier Forum, Korea Post, 1995-96. Pres. Korean Lang. Sch., Spokane, 1974; Guwonsa, Korean Presbyn. Ch. Spokane, 1989-99; trustee Korean Assn. Inland Empire, Spokane, 1995; elder Korean Presbyn. Ch., Spokane, 1999, chair music ministry team, 2001. Recipient Editors Choice award Nat. Libr. Poetry, 1996. Fellow Am. Acad. Family Physicians. Avocations: choral music, poetry, gardening. Office: Drs Lee and Lee PS 17 E Empire Ave Spokane WA 99207-1707 E-mail: drsunleemd@yahoo.com.

LEE, THAI THERESA, information technology executive; BA in Econs. and Biology, Amherst Coll., 1980; MBA, Harvard U., 1985. Assoc. brand mgr. Procter & Gamble Co., Cin., 1985—87; mktg. mgr., TRS Divsn. Am. Express, N.Y.C., 1987—89; CEO, pres. Software House Internat. (SHI), Somerset, NJ, 1989—; pres. SHI-GS, Inc., Austin, Tex., 1999—. Bd. trustees Amherst (Mass.) Coll., 1992—99. Office: Software House Internat 2 Riverview Dr Somerset NJ 08873

LEE, THERESA K. chemicals executive; b. Gary, W.Va., Nov. 21, 1952; BS in Polit. Sci. and History, East Tenn. State U., 1974; JD, U. Tenn., 1977; postgrad., Harvard U., 1999. Staff atty. Legal Svcs. Upper East Tenn., 1977—79; sr. law clk. to Judge H. Emory Widener, Jr. U.S. Ct. Appeals (4th cir.), 1979—87; atty. Eastman Chem., 1987—91, asst. to pres., 1991—92, asst. sec., sr. counsel Tex. Eastman divsn., 1992—93, asst. sec., asst. gen. counsel legal dept. health safety and environ. group, 1993—95, asst. sec., asst. gen. counsel legal dept., corp. group, 1995—97, v.p., sec., assoc. gen. counsel, 1997—2000, sec., 1997—, chief legal officer, 2000—, sr. v.p., 2002—. Recipient Outstanding Alumna award, East Tenn. State U. Nat. Alumni Assn., 2002. Mem.: ABA (gen. counsel com.), Kingsport Bar Assn., Tenn. Bar Assn. (ho. of dels.), Am. Soc. Corp. Secs., Am. Corp. Counsel Assn. (bd. dirs.). Office: Eastman Chem PO Box 2198 Memphis TN 38101 9812 Address: Eastman Chem PO Box 1975 Kingsport TN 37662-5075

LEE, TRACY D. speech pathology/audiology services professional; b. Okla., June 2, 1971; d. Donald Robert and Jacqueline Dene DePriest; m. Kevin Alan Lee, Sept. 23, 2000. BS in Communicative Disorders, U. Kans., 1994, MA in Speech-Lang. Pathology, 1998. Lic. speech-lang. pathogoist 1999. Speech-lang. pathologist AMW Edn. Coop., Humboldt, Kans., 1998—, Aegis Therapies, Iola, Kans., 2000—. Mem.: Kans. Speech-Lang. Hearing Assn., Kans. Nat. Edn. Assn., Am. Speech-Lang.-Hearing Assn. Republican. Avocations: gardening, reading, cooking, walking, running. Home: PO Box 722 Iola KS 66749 Office: ANW Edn Coop PO Box 207 Humboldt KS E-mail: TLee-Speech@Hotmail.com.

LEE, VIRGINIA M. Y. medical educator, health science association administrator; PhD, U. Calif., San Francisco, 1973; MBA, U. Pa., 1984. Prof. dept. pathology and lab. medicine U. Pa. Sch. Medicine, co-dir. neurodegenerative disease rsch., 1992—2002, dir. neurodegenerative disease rsch., 2002—. Mem. grant rev. com. NIH Study Sect., others; mem. med./sci. adv. com. Alzheimer's Assn., S.E. Pa. Contbr. papers to profl. jours. Recipient John H. Ware 3d Chair for Alzheimer's Disease Rsch., Stanley N. Cohen Biomed. Rsch. award, 2000. Mem.: Soc. for Neurosci. (elected councilor). Achievements include research in Alzheimer's disease; neuronal cytoskeleton. Office: Ctr for Neurodegenerative Disease Rsch 3d Fl Maloney Bldg 4283 3600 Spruce St Philadelphia PA 19104-4283

LEE, YEU-TSU MARGARET, surgeon, educator; b. Xian, Shensi, China, Mar. 18, 1936; m. Thomas V. Lee, Dec. 29, 1962 (div. 1987); 1 child, Maxwell M. AB in Microbiology, U. S.D., 1957; MD, Harvard U., 1961. Diplomate Am. Bd. Surgery. Assoc. prof. surgery Med. Sch., U. So. Calif., L.A., 1973-83; commd. lt. col. U.S. Army Med. Corps, 1983, advanced through grades to col., 1989; chief surg. oncology Tripler Army Med. Ctr., Honolulu, 1983-98; ret. U.S. Army, 1999; assoc. clin. prof. surgery Med. Sch., U. Hawaii, Honolulu, 1984-92, clin. prof. surgery, 1992—. Author: Malignant Lymphoma, 1974; author chpts to books; contbr. articles to profl. jours. Pres. Orgn. Chinese-Am. Women, L.A., 1981, Hawaii chpt., 1988; active U.S.-China Friendship Assn., 1991—. Decorated Nat. Def. Svc. medal, Army Commendation medal, Army Meritorious Svc. medal, Army Humanitarian Svc. medal; recipient Chinese-Am. Engrs. and Scis. Assn., 1987; named Sci. Woman Warrior, Asian-Pacific Womens Network, 1983. Mem. ACS, Soc. Surg. Oncology, Assn. Women Surgeons. Avocations: classical music, movies, hiking, ballroom dancing. Address: PO Box 6486 Honolulu HI 96818-0486 E-mail: ytm_lee@hotmail.com.

LEECH, MARLA RENÉE, media specialist, educator; b. San Diego, Calif., Apr. 6, 1961; d. Thomas Franklin Leech and Margaret Vernon Blaisdel-Johnson. BA in Psychology, U. Calif., Davis, Calif., 1983; cert. in Film, U. Calif., Santa Cruz, Calif., 1987; MA in Broadcasting, U. Calif., San Francisco, Calif., 1993; B in Tchg., New Coll., 1996. Prof. broadcasting City Coll., San Francisco, 1996—. Self employed video prodr., editor, San Francisco, 1993—; prof. media Laney Coll., Oakland, Calif., 2003—; instr. online Nat. Acad. TV Arts and Scis., San Francisco, 1999; prodn. mgr. Mission Movie, San Francisco, 2003; bd. dirs. Women in Film and TV, 2004. Prodr.: (films) Breakin' The Glass, 1999, It's A Boy! Journeys From Female to Male, 2000; editor: (films) Love Makes a Family, 1993, 2004, Strings Attached, 1998, Radical Harmonies, 2002 (Best Documentary award Frameline Fest, 2002). Outdoor educator Environ. Travel Companions, San Francisco, 1999—; vol. Film Arts Found., San Francisco, 1993—95. Named Woman of Vision, Coll. San Mateo, 1999; grantee Sheldon Fay grant, Nat. Acad. TV Arts and Scis., 1993. Democrat. Avocations: drums, kayaking, guitar, politics, meeting people. Home: PO Box 460542 San Francisco CA 94146

LEEDER, ELAINE, sociologist, educator, writer; b. Lynn, Mass., July 7, 1944; d. Samuel and Ida (Rosenfield) Sneierson; m. David Leeder, July 15, 1971 (div. 1999); 1 child, Abigail. BA, Northeastern U., Boston, 1967; MSW, Yeshiva U., 1969; MPH, U. Calif., Berkeley, 1975; PhD, Cornell U., 1985. Cert. social worker. Psychiat. soc. worker Elmira (N.Y.) Psychiat. Ctr., 1971-72; clin. psychiat. soc. worker Elmira, 1972-80; assoc. prof. Ithaca (NY) Coll., 1977—97, prof., 1997—2001; pvt. practice Ithaca, 1980—92; dean Sch. Social Scis. Sonoma State U., Rohnert Pk., Calif., 2001—. Dept. chair Ithaca Coll., 1992-95. Author: The Gentle General: Rose Pesotta, Anarchist & Labor Organizer, 1993, Treating Abuse in Families: A Feminist & Community Approach, 1994, the Family in Global Perspective: A Gendered Journey, 2004; contbr. articles to profl. jours. Feminist Therapy Inst. (steering com. 1990-97). Jewish. Avocations: travel, swimming. Office: Sonoma State U 2078 Stevenson Rohnert Park CA 94928 Home: 5299 Lone Pine Rd Sebastopol CA 95472-5737 Office Phone: 707-664-2112. Business E-Mail: leeder@sonoma.edu.

LEEDS, ELIZABETH LOUISE, miniature collectibles executive; b. L.A., July 24, 1925; d. Charles Furnival and Etta Louise (Jackson) Mayes; m. Walter Albert Leeds, Jan. 20, 1973 (dec.); children: Pam Ravey Lewis, Linda Ravey McCallam, Diane Ravey Lathrop, Tom Ravey. Student pub. sch., Prescott, Ariz. Lic. real estate agt., Ariz., cert. motel mgr. Real estate agt., Prescott, Ariz., 1962-64; sec. to mgr. Kon Tiki Hotel, Phoenix, 1964-65; draftsman Goleta Water Dist., Calif., 1965-68; asst. to v.p. rsch. and design House of Mosaics, Santa Barbara, Calif., 1968-69; exec. chmn. poster design, dept. music U. Calif.-Santa Barbara, 1969-74; v.p. Colorform West, Inc., Santa Barbara, 1974-75; pres. Leeds Miniatures, Inc., Lincoln City, Oreg., 1975-86, Leed's Co., Inc., 1989—; cert. instr. Technologies for Creating, DMA, Inc., 1986—; lamp and silk screen designer Colorform West, Inc.; ind. assoc. The Environ. Network. Illustrator: Just A Story by Gustav Coenod, 1964. Active Global Vols., 1993, Oceanic Soc. Expeditions, 1993. Mem. Hobby Industry Am., Miniatures Industry Assn. Am., Nat. Assn. Female Execs., Eugene C. of C., Eugene Bus. and Profl. Women (cert. practitioner neuro-linguistic programming, trainer values realization). Clubs: Assn. Humanistic Psychology, Internat. New Thought Alliance, Assn. Transpersonal Psychology. Home: 2290 Arthur Ct Eugene OR 97405-1525

LEEDS, NANCY BRECKER, sculptor, lyricist; b. N.Y.C., Dec. 22, 1924; d. Louis Julius and Dorothy (Faggen) Brecker; m. Richard Henry Leeds, May 9, 1945; children: Douglas Brecker, Constance Leeds Bennett. BA, Pine Manor Coll., 1944. Pres. Roseland Ballroom, N.Y.C., 1977-81. One-woman shows include Andrew Crispo Gallery, N.Y.C., 1979, Jeannette McIntyre Gallery Fine Arts, Palm Springs, Calif., 1987-88; exhibited in group shows at Bond St. Gallery, Great Neck, N.Y., Gallery Ranieri, N.Y.C., 1978, Country Art Gallery, 1984, Nature Conservatory Show, Country Art Gallery, 1985, Bonwit Teller, Manhasset, N.Y., 1985, Jeanette C. McIntyre Gallery, Palm Springs, Calif., 1987, The Empire Collection, N.Y.C., 1988, 89, Nassau County Mus. of Art, 1992, Chrysalis, East Hampton, 1998, Christmas Miniature Art Show at Chelsea, Nassau County Mus. of Art "Dance Dance", 2000; represented in permanent collections at New Orleans Mus. Art; writer lyrics for musical Great Scot, 1965, score for Scrooge Musical Theatre of Ariz., 1989; lyricist for popular music. Trustee Floating Hosp., N.Y.C., 1975—, v.p.; mem. Upper Brookville (L.I., N.Y.) Planning Bd., 2000-01. Mem. ASCAP, Dramatist Guild, Songwriters Guild.

LEEDS, SUSANNE, special education educator, writer; d. Joel and Hilda (Reiss) Leibowitz. BA, Queens Coll. of CUNY, 1972; MA, NYU, 1978. Cert. spl. edn. tchr. N.Y., 1978. Spl. edn. tchr. N.Y.C. Bd. Edn., 1972—82; tchr. Palm Beach County Sch. Bd., Boca Raton, Fla., 1994—. Author: (poem) Illumination (In Honor of Ethiopian Jews), 1999, At The U.S. Holocaust Meml. Mus., 2002, Gone (In Memory of Victims of 9/11), 2001; contbr. numerous poems publ. in jours. and mags.; singer: (performed with Barry Harris Jazz Ensemble) Beacon Theater, N.Y.C., 1984. Recipient 3rd prize Yi Bagliore Mem. award, Nat. League Am. Pen Women, 2000, 1st prize, 11th Ann. Sylvia Wolens Jewish Heritage Writing Competition, 2002, finalist, 15th Ann. Robert Penn Warren Poetry awards, 2002, 1st prize Grandmother Earth Nat. Writing awards (Haiku category), 2002. Mem.: Nat. Fedn. State Poetry Socs., Fla. State Poetry Assn., Nat. League of Am. Pen Women. Avocations: music, singing, opera, piano. Home: 6507 Royal Manor Cir Delray Beach FL 33484-2411

LEEDS, VALERIE ANN, art historian, curator, writer; b. Summit, N.J., Jan. 22, 1958; d. Morton W. and Norma Sterne Leeds. BA in Art History, U. Rochester, 1979; MA in Art History, Syracuse U., 1981; PhD in Am. Art, CUNY, 2000. Curatorial asst. Whitney Mus. Am. Art, N.Y.C., 1982—84; rschr., gallery asst. Spanierman Gallery, N.Y.C., 1984—86; curator exhbns. Tampa (Fla.) Mus. Art, 1987—90; cur. 19th and 20th century Am. art Orlando (Fla.) Mus. Art, 1990—96; curatorial cons., 1996—. Adj. curator Am. Art Flint (Mich.) Inst. Arts, 2000; adj. prof. Eckerd Coll., St. Petersburg, Ill., 2000. Author (curator): (exhbn. and book) My People: The Portraits of Robert Henri, 1994; author: (exhbn. catalogues) Robert Henri and Santa Fe, 1998, Leon Kroll Revisited, 1998; author: (co-curator) (exhbn.) In The American Spirit: Realism and Impressionism from the Lawrence Collection, 1999; author: Ernest Lawson, 2000, Works from the John and Dolores Beck Collection, 2000, The Eight, 2002, Martha Simkins Rediscovers, 2002, William Glackens, 2003, Dreams and Dramas: Moonlight and Twilight in American Art, 2003; author: (curator) Ray Ellis In Retrospect: A Painter's Journey, 2004; Am. Art at the Flint Inst. of Arts, 2003. Grantee, NEA, 1994; Douglass fellow in Am. Art, CUNY Grad. Ctr., 1999—2000. Home: 728 Sergeantsville Rd Stockton NJ 08559 Office: Flint Inst Arts 1120 E Kearsley St Flint MI

LEEK, DIANE WEBB, nurse; b. St. Louis, Dec. 19, 1956; d. Paul Benedict and Bessie Marie (Brenneison) Webb; m. Gregory Leek, Apr. 4, 1992; children: Jon, Cliff. AS in Nursing, Maryville Coll., 1978; BSN, St. Louis U., 1982, MSN, 1994. RN, Mo.; cert. case mgr.; cert. legal nurse cons. Staff nurse Jewish Hosp., St. Louis, 1978-82; critical care staff nurse St. Luke's Episcopal Hosp., Houston, 1983-84; staff nurse, emergency room Meml. Hosp., South Bend, Ind., 1984; staff nurse, trauma emergency rm. Med. Ctr. Hosp., San Antonio, 1985-88; tchr. asst. U. Tex. Health Sci. Ctr., San Antonio, 1988; utiliation rev. coord. Group Health Plan, St. Louis, 1988-90; trauma staff nurse emergency rm. Barnes/Jewish Hosp., St. Louis, 1988-97; nurse cons. Aetna Life & Casualty, 1991-93; case mgr. cons. St. Paul Fire & Marine Ins., 1993-97; mgr. health care cons. Ernst & Young, 1997-98; mgr. legal nurse cons. RGL Forensic Accts. and Consultants, St. Louis, 1998—. Contbg. author: Case Management Practice Guidelines, 1996. Vol. RN supr. ARC, San Antonio, 1987. Recipient Pres. award for Excellence and Achievement Group Health Plan, 1990. Mem. Case Mgmt. Soc. St. Louis (sec., bd. dirs. 1994, pres. 1997), Am. Assn. Legal Nurse Cons. (newsletter editor 1999, bd. dirs. 1999), Sigma Theta Tau (award for Acad. Excellence 1994). Republican. Roman Catholic. Avocations: classical music, piano, needlepoint, crafts, photography. Home: 1209 Crested View Dr Saint Louis MO 63146-5518

LEEKLEY, MARIE VALPOON, secondary school educator; b. Honolulu, Mar. 28, 1941; d. Amil Richard and Florence Haruko (Soken) V.; m. John Darwin Leekley, Jr., June 26, 1965; children: Katherine Joan, Tracy Ann Kehaunani. BS, Carroll Coll., Waukesha, Wis., 1963; MEd, Nat. Coll. Edn., Evanston, Ill., 1990; PhD, Marquette U., 2002. Dir. Christian edn. Kamehameha Sch. for Girls, Honolulu, 1963-64; elem. tchr. Milw. Pub. Schs., 1965-67; vol. Marianas Edn. Dept. Peace Corps, Saipan, Mariana Islands, 1967-69, dist. coord. tchr. edn., 1969-71; tchr. Ethan Allen Sch. for Boys, Wales, Wis., 1977-96. Tchr. adult basic edn. Waukesha County Tech. Coll., Pewaukee, Wis., 1977—. Mem. Menomonee Falls (Wis.) Pub. Schs. Bd. Edn., 1990—; bd. dirs. Comprehensive Ednl. Svcs. Agys., West Allis, Wis., 1991-96. Recipient vol. appreciation award Greater Menomonee Falls Com., 1991, Boardmanship award Wis. Assn. Sch. Bds., 1991, 92, 93; named Edn. Leader of Yr. AAUW, 1996. Mem. ASCD, Correctional Edn. Asn., Nat. Sch. Bd. Assn., Wis. Assn. Adult and Continuing Edn., Wis. Vocat. Assn., Wis. Edn. Assn. Methodist. Home: W148N7590 Woodland Dr Menomonee Falls WI 53051-4522 Office: Waukesha County Tech Coll 327 E Broadway Waukesha WI 53186-5008

LEEMAN, SUSAN EPSTEIN, neuroscientist, educator; b. Chgo., May 9, 1930; d. Samuel and Dora (Gubernikoff) Epstein; m. Cavin Leeman (div.); children: Eve, Raphael, Jennifer. BA, Goucher Coll., 1951; MA, Radcliffe Coll., 1954, PhD, 1958; DS (hon.), SUNY, Utica, 1992; hon. degree, Goucher Coll., 1993. Instr. Harvard Med. Sch., Boston, 1958-59; postdoctoral fellow Brandeis U., Waltham, Mass., 1959-62, 62-66; rsch. assoc., adj. ast. prof., asst. rsch. prof. Brandieis U., Waltham, Mass., 1966-68, 68-71; asst. prof. Harvard Med. Sch., 1972-73, assoc. prof., 1973-80; prof. U. Mass. Med. Ctr., Worcester, 1980-92, dir. interdept. neurosci. program, 1984-92; prof. dept. pharmacology Boston U. Sch. Medicine, 1992—. Burroughs Wellcome vis. prof. U.Ky., 1992. Fogarty scholar NAS, 1994; recipient Women in Sci. award N.Y. Acad., 1995. Mem. NAS (17th Lilly lectr. 1994, Fred Conrad Koch award 1994, Women in Sci. award 1995), Am. Acad. Arts and Scis. (Isadore Rosenberg lectr. 1999). Office: Boston U Sch Medicine Dept Pharmacology 715 Albany St # R-616 Boston MA 02118-2526 Office Phone: 617-638-4364. E-mail: sleeman@bu.edu.

LEES, MARJORIE BERMAN, biochemist, neuroscientist; b. N.Y.C., Mar. 17, 1923; d. Isadore I. and Ruth (Rogalsky) Berman; m. Sidney Lees, Sept. 17, 1946; children: David E., Andrew, Eliot. BA, Hunter Coll., 1943; MS, U. Chgo., 1945; PhD, Harvard U., Radcliffe Coll., 1951. Assoc. biochemist, asst. biochemist McLean Hosp., Belmont, Mass., 1953-62; rsch. assoc. Dartmouth Med. Sch., Hanover, 1962-66; assoc. biochemist McLean Hosp., Belmont, 1966-76; prin. and sr. rsch. assoc. Harvard Med. Sch., Boston, 1966-85; biomed. scientist E.K. Shriver Ctr., Waltham, Mass., 1976-98; prof. biochemistry (neurology) Harvard Med. Sch., Boston, 1985-94, prof. emerita, 1994—; biochemist Mass. Gen. Hosp., Boston, 1976-98; assoc. dir. biochemistry E.K. Shriver Ctr., Waltham, 1982-90, dir. biochemistry, 1990-93, assoc. dir. mental retardation rsch. ctr., 1994-97, sr. biomed. sci., 1998—; prof. emerita U. Mass. Med. Sch., 1999—. Mem. adv. com. biomed. and behavioral rsch. NASA/NIH, 1993—; mem. sci. adv. com. Nat. Multiple Sclerosis Soc., 1988-93. Chief editor Jour. of Neurochemistry, 1986-90; author (with others) books; contbr. articles to profl. jours. Mem. adv. coun. Nat. Inst. Neurological Disorders, Bethesda, Md., 1979-82; chmn. Radcliffe Grad. Soc., Cambridge, Mass., 1978-80. Predoctoral fellow USPHS, 1947-50, postdoctoral fellow Am. Cancer Soc., 1951-53; Javits Neurosci. grantee NIH, 1983-90, 91-97, prin. grantee NIH, 1962-98; named to Hunter Coll. Hall of Fame, 1982. Mem. Am. Soc. Biochemistry and Molecular Biology, Internat. Soc. Neurochemistry, Am. Soc. Neurochemistry (treas. 1975-81, pres. 1983-85), Soc. for Neurosci., Am. Assn. Neuropathology (assoc.), Phi Beta Kappa. Office: Shriver Ctr U Mass Med Sch Neurobiology Program 200 Trapelo Rd Waltham MA 02452-6332 E-mail: marjorie.lees@umassmed.edu.

LEESMAN, BEVERLY JEAN, artist, art critic, art educator; b. Lincoln, Ill., Apr. 22, 1953; d. Robert Eugene and Jean (Bruner) L.; m. Paul A. Martin, Nov. 28, 1987; children: Danielle, Stewart Martin. AS in Fine Art, Springfield Coll., 1973; BS in Art History, Graphics Design, Painting, Ill. State U., 1976; postgrad., U. Grenoble, France, 1980, L'Ecole de Louvre, Paris, 1980, U. Ill., 1986. Dept. mgr. J.C. Penney, Springfield, Ill., 1979; head asst. to curator Slide Libr. Ill. State U., Normal, 1981-82; teaching asst. U. Ill., Urbana-Champaign, 1983-84, instr., 1984-85; art instr. North

Syracuse Adult Edn. Program, 1992-94. Guest lectr. U. Ill., 1981-85; layout, past-up artist Dynamic Graphics, Inc., Peoria, Ill., 1976-78; tech. illustrator I-270 Project, St. Louis, 1984-85; freelance artist, 1986—; juried national and regional art shows. One-woman shows include Paine Br. Libr., Syracuse, N.Y., 1993, Liverpool Pub. Libr., 1994, Manlius (N.Y.) Libr., 1995, Roaster's Corner Cafe, Fayetteville, N.Y., 1995, JCC Gallery, Albuquerque, N.Mex., 2003; group shows include SUNY Inst. Tech., Utica, Rome, N.Y., 1990, 92-94, Skaneateles (N.Y.) Arts Expn., 1990, 93, Everson Mus., Syracuse, 1994-95, Canastota (N.Y.) Canal Town Mus., 1991-95, Cooperstown (N.Y.) Art Assn., 1992, 94-95, Rome Art & Cmty. Ctr., 1994, Great N.Y. State Fair, Syracuse, 1994-95, CNY Art Open, DeWitt, N.Y., 1995, North East Watercolor Soc., Goshen, N.Y., 1994, Pitts. Watercolor Soc., 1995, 16th Ann. Internat. Exhbn. La. State U., Baton Rouge, 2003, 26th Internat. Exhbn., Houston, N.Mex. State Fair, Albuquerque, 2002, 2003, Watercolor Soc., Pitts., 2002, River Road Show, Baton Rouge (2nd Pl.), 2002, Hilton Head Art League's Nat. Juried Art Exhbn., Hilton Head Island, S.C., 2003, Farnsworth Taos (N.Mex.) Gallery, 2003, 26th Ann. Non-mem. Juried Exhbn., N.Y.C., 2003, Barnsite Gallery, Kewaunee, Wis., 2003, TGA Stables, Taos, 2003, Masterworks, Albuquerque, 2003, Salmugundi Club, N.Y.C., N.Y., 2003, Barns & Farms, Kewaunee, Wis., 2003, Wolfe Art Club, N.Y.C., N.Y., 2003, N.Mex. Watercolor Soc., 2003 (M. Graham & Co. Merchandise award 2002); painter (dinosaur mural) Gold Cup Gymnastics, Albuquerque. N.Mex., 2002-2003. Recipient Cooperstown Vet. Clinic prize, 1995, Dick Blick award Pitts. Watercolor Soc., 1995. Mem. Nat. League Am. Pen Women, City N.Y. Art Guild, Inc. (founding pres. 1994-95, 2d v.p. 1995-96), Am. Artists Profl. League, Nat. Assn. Women Artists, N.Mex. Watercolor Soc. (Fall Exhibit Bd. Dirs. award 2002, M. Graham and Co. Merchandise award 2003). Home: 12214 Camelot Pl NE Albuquerque NM 87122

LEESON, SUSAN M. former state supreme court judge; Law clerk U.S. 9th Cir. Ct. of Appeals, Tom. C. Clark judicial fellow U.S. Supreme Ct.; prof. polit. sci., assoc. prof. law Willamette U., Salem, Oreg.; judge Oreg. Ct. Appeals, 1993—98; justice Oreg. Supreme Ct., 1998—2003. Former mem. Oreg. Criminal Justice Coun., Marion-Polk Local Govt. Boundary Commn.

LEET, MILDRED ROBBINS, corporate executive, consultant; b. NYC, Aug. 9, 1922; d. Samuel Milton and Isabella (Zeitz) Elowsky; m. Louis J. Robbins, Feb. 23, 1941 (dec. 1970); children: Jane, Aileen; m. Glen Leet, Aug. 9, 1974 (dec. 1998). BA, NYU, 1942; LHD (hon.), Coll. Human Svcs., 1988; LLD honoris causa, Marymount Coll., Tarrytown, N.Y., 1991; HHD, Lynn U., 1993; D Humanitarian Svc. (hon.), Norwich U., 1994; DHL, Conn. Coll., 1996, Wilson Coll., 2003. Pres. women's div. United Cerebral Palsy, N.Y.C., 1951-52, bd. dirs., 1953-55; rep. Nat. Coun. Women U.S. at UN, 1957-64, 1st v.p., 1959-64, pres., 1964-68, hon. pres., 1968-70; sec., v.p. conf. group U.S. Nat. Orgns. at UN, 1961-64, 76-78, vice chmn., sec., 1962-64, mem. exec. com., 1961-65, chmn. hospitality info. svc., 1960-66; vice chmn. exec. com. NGO's UN Office Public Info., 1976-78, chmn. ann. conf., 1977; chmn. com. on water, desertification, habitat and environment Conf. NGO's with consultative status with UN/ECOSOC, 1976-77; mem. exec. com. Internat. Coun. Women, 1960-73, v.p., 1970-73; chmn. program planning com., women's com. OEO, 1967-72; chmn. com. on natural disasters N.Am. Com. on Environment, 1973-77; N.Y. State chmn. UN Day, 1975; ptnr. Leet & Leet (cons. women in devel.), 1979—98. Co-founder Trickle Up Program, 1979—, pres., 1991—2000, chair, 2001—; mem. task force on Africa UN, 1995—. Contbr. articles to profl. jours.; editor UN Calendar & Digest, 1959-64, Measure of Mankind, 1963; editorial bd.: Peace & Change. Co-chmn. Vols. for Stevenson, N.Y.C., 1956; vice chmn. task force Nat. Dem. Com., 1969-72; commr. N.Y. State Commn. on Powers Local Govt., 1970-73, chmn. Coll. for Human Svcs. Audrey Cohen Coll., 1985-2000; former mem. bd. dirs. Am. Arbitration Assn., New Directions, Inst. for Mediation and Conflict Resolution, Spirit of Stockholm; bd. dirs. Hotline Internat.; v.p. Save the Children Fedn., 1986-93 rep. Internat. Peace Acad. at UN, 1974-77, Internat. Soc. Cmty. Devel., 1977-98, del. at large 1st Nat. Women's Conf., Houston, 1977; chmn. task force on internat. interdependence N.Y. State Women's Meeting, 1977; mem. Task Force on Poverty, 1977; chmn. Task Force on Women, Sci. and Tech. for Devel., 1978; U.S. del. UN Status of Women Commn., 1978, UN Conf. Sci. and Tech. for Devel., 1979, Brazzaville Centennial Celebration, 1980; mem. global adv. bd. Internat. Expn. Rural Devel., 1981—; mem. Coun. Internat. Fellows U. Bridgeport, 1982-88; trustee overseas edn. fund LWV, 1983-91; v.p. U.S. Com. UN Devel. Fund for Women, 1983-94, trustee, 1998-2000; mem. Nat. Consultative Com. Planning for Nairobi, 1984-85; co-chmn. women in devel. com. Interaction, 1985-91; mem. com. of cooperation Interam. Commn. of Women, 1986; bd. dirs. Internat. Devel. Conf., 1991-2001; mem. UN task force informal sector devel. Africa, 1995—. Recipient Crystal award Coll. Human Svcs., 1983, Ann. award Inst. Mediation and Conflict Resloution, 1985, Woman of Conscience award Nat. Coun. Women, 1996, Temple award Inst. Noetic Scis., 1987, Presdl. End Hunger award, 1987, Giraffe award Giraffe Project, 1987, Woman of the World award Eng.'s Women Aid, 1989, Mildred Robbins Leet award Interaction, 1995; co-recipient Rose award World Media Inst., 1987, Human Rights award UN Devel. Fund for Women, 1987, Leadership award U.S. Peace Corps, Woman of Vision award N.Y.C. NOW, 1990, Matrix award Women in Comm., Inc., Spirit of Enterprise award Rolex Industries, 1990, Ann. Bush's Ann. Points of Light award, 1992, Internat. Humanity award ARC Overseas Assn., 1992, Excellence award U.S. Com. for UNIFEM, 1992, Champion of Enterprise award Avon, 1994, Achievement award NYU-Washington Sq. Coll. Alumni. Assn., 1995, Lizette H. Sarnoff Vol. Svc. award Yeshiva U., 1996, Disting. Svc. award N.Y. African Studies Assn., 1996, Disting. Svc. award 50th Anniversary United Cerebral Palsy, 1997, Eleanor Schnurr award UN Assn./USA, Women of Distinction honoree Birmingham So. Coll., Spirit award Nat. Assn. Women Bus. Owners, 1998, Nat. Caring Inst. award, 2001, Nat. Women's Hall of Fame, 2003. Mem. AAAS, Women's Forum, Coun. on Fgn. Rels., Cosmopolitan Club, Princeton Club. Home and Office: 54 Riverside Dr New York NY 10024-6509 E-mail: info@trickleup.org.

LEETCH, NANCY WIKOFF, artist; b. Muncie, Ind., Apr. 11, 1934; d. Charles Henry and Hazel Annetta (Bidlack) Wikoff; m. James Frederick Leetch, Sept. 6, 1958; children: Alice Annette, Elaine Marie. BS in Home Econs., Ohio State U., 1955; MA in Painting, Bowling Green State U., 1986. Home svc. advisor Cols. & S. Ohio Electric Co., Columbus, 1955-59; presch. head tchr. North Broadway Meth. Ch., Columbus, 1959-61; artist, poet Bowling Green, Ohio, 1984-95. Tchr. gifted students Bowling Green Schs., 1991-93. One woman exhibits include Ohio Citizens Bank, Toledo, 1987, Obetz Gallery, Columbus, 1987, Currents Gallery, 1988, Images Gallery, 1990, 92, Cable Gallery, 1992, Millikin Hotel Lobby, Bowling Green, 1994, Court House Gallery, 1995, Wile-Kovach Gallery, Columbus, Ohio, 1996, Croswell Opera House, Adrian, Mich., 1997, Cosmos, Bowling Green, 2001, Dublin (Ohio) Arts Coun., 2001, Toledo Pub. Libr., 2001, Cable Gallery, San Diego, 1992; two-woman show at Angelwood Gallery, 1998; group shows include Owens Ill., 1983, 86, Toledo Mus. Art, 1983, Gallery 200, Columbus, Obetz Gallery, 1987-89, Images Gallery, Toledo, 1985-94, Currents Gallery, 1990, And Beautiful Baskets Gallery, Lyme Regis, Eng., 1990, Medici Gallery, London, 1991, Art Moves Gallery, 1993, Toledo Mus. Art, 1993-03, Angelwood Gallery, 1994-2002, Studio 129, 1995, Lafayette Gallery, Adrian, Mich., 1995, Main Street Gallery, 1995, American Gallery, Sylvania, 1995, Olive Rose Gallery 4 Women Artists, 2001-02; represented in permanent collections Gt. Bidlake Manor, Okehampton, Eng., Alexandra Hotel, Lyme Regis, Dorset, Eng., Coll. Human Ecology, Ohio State U., Colonial Hotel, Puebla, Mex., Bowling Green State U. Recipient Purchase award Toledo Mus. Art, 1983, Black Swamp Arts Festival, 1995-97, Best of Show, Wood County Fair. Avocations: antiques, swimming, knitting, sewing, traveling. Studio: #212 Huntington Bank Bldg Bowling Green OH 43402

LEEVES, JANE, actress; b. Essex, England, Apr. 18, 1961; m. Marshall Coben, 1996; 2 children. Actress (TV series) The Benny Hill Show, 1983-84, Double Trouble, 1984, Throb, 1986-88, Murphy Brown, 1989-1993, Just Deserts, 1992, Frasier 1993-2004 (Emmy award nom. sup. actress, 1998, SAG award outstanding performance ensemble, 2000); (TV movies) Red Dwarf, 1992, Pandora's Clock, 1996, Just Deserts, 1999; (films) The Hunger, 1983, To Live and Die in L.A., 1985, Miracle on 34th Street, 1994, The Meaning of Life, 1983, Mr. Write, 1994, James and the Giant Peach (voice), 1996, Don't Go Breaking My Heart, 1999, Music of the Heart, 1999, Adventures of Tom Thumb and Thumbelina (voice), 2002, The Event, 2003; (TV guest appearances) Murder, She Wrote, 1987, It's a Living, 1989, Hooperman, 1989, Mr. Belvedere, 1989, My Two Dads, 1990, Who's the Boss?, 1990, Blossom, 1991, Seinfeld, 1992-93, 98, Caroline in the City, 1995, Hercules (voice), 1998, The Simpsons, 2003; (Broadway show) Cabaret, 2002. Avocations: reading, cooking, sports, dance. Office: Talent Group Inc 5670 Wilshire Blvd #820 Los Angeles CA 90036-5679*

LEFAVRE, HADIA, human resources executive; Various human resources positions Bull, Paris, Compaq Computer, Regie Renault, France; sr. v.p. human resources worldwide Rhône-Poulenc Rorer, Inc., The Scott Co., 1999—. Office: 41 S High St Ste 3500 Columbus OH 43215-6110

LEFCO, KATHY NAN, law librarian; b. Bethesda, Md., Feb. 24, 1949; d. Ted Lefco and Dorothy Rose (Fox) Harris; m. Stephen Gary Katz, Sept. 2, 1973 (div. May 1984); m. John Alfred Price, Nov. 24, 1984 (dec. Jan. 1989); m. Richard Louis Edmonds, Apr. 12, 2002. BA, U. Wis., 1971; MLS, U. Wis., Milw., 1975. Rsch. asst. Ctr. Auto Safety, Washington, 1971-73; asst. to dir. Ctr. Consumer Affairs, Milw., 1973-74; legis. libr. Morgan, Lewis & Bockius, Washington, 1976-78; dir. library Mulcahy & Wherry, Milw., 1978; paralegal Land of Lincoln Legal Assistance, Springfield, Ill., 1979-80; reference and interlibrary loan libr. So. Ill. U. Sch. Medicine, Springfield, 1980; reader svcs. libr. Wis. State Law Library, Madison, 1981-83; ref. libr. Mudge Rose Guthrie Alexander & Ferdon, N.Y.C., 1983-85; sr. legal info. specialist Cravath, Swaine & Moore, N.Y.C., 1985-86; asst. libr. Kaye, Scholer, Fierman, Hays & Handler, N.Y.C., 1986-89; head libr. Parker Chapin Flattau & Klimpl, N.Y.C., 1989-94; dir. libr. svcs. Winston & Strawn, Chgo., 1994—. Author: (with others) Mobile Homes: The Low-Cost Housing Hoax, 1973. Mem. Chgo. Assn. Law Librs., Am. Assn. Law Librs. Democrat. Jewish. Avocations: biking, backgammon, politics. Home: 543 Oakdale Ave Glencoe IL 60022 Office: Winston & Strawn 35 W Wacker Dr Ste 4200 Chicago IL 60601-1695 Office Phone: 312-558-5813. E-mail: klefco@winston.com.

LEFEBVRE, SHARON ELAINE, psychiatric nurse practitioner; d. James Paul McLaughlin and Madalyn Ann Powers; children: Erin, Kevin. AS in Nursing with honors, Middlesex C.C., Lowell, Mass., 1993; BSN summa cum laude, Salem (Mass.) State Coll., 2002. RN Mass., cert. ANCC. Staff nurse Tewksbury (Mass.) State Hosp., 1993—97, charge nurse, 1997—. Mem. ethics com. Tewksbury State Hosp., 1999—. Mem.: Mass. Nurses Assn. (co-chair Unit 7 2002—), Phi Kappa Phi, Sigma Theta Tau. Office: Tewksbury State Hosp 365 East St Tewksbury MA 01876 E-mail: rnc593@aol.com.

LEFEVER, MAXINE LANE, music educator; b. Elmhurst, Ill., May 30, 1931; d. Thomas Clinton and Georgia Marie (Hampton) Lane; m. Orville Joseph Lefever, Aug. 18, 1951 (div.); m. Geoffrey Ashe, Dec. 8, 1992. Student, Ill. Wesleyan U., 1949-51; BA, Western State Coll., 1958, MS, Purdue U., 1964, postgrad., 1965. Elem. sch. tchr. Leaf River (Ill.) Pub. Schs., 1953-54, Mancos (Colo.) Pub. Schs., 1954-56; elem./jr. hs tchr. Cortez (Colo.) Pub. Schs., 1956-60; instr. bands Purdue U., Lafayette, Ind., 1965-79, asst. prof., 1980-88, prof. emerita, 1989. Cons. numerous festivals and contests; pres., dir. Am. Mus. Ambs., 1967—. Contbr. articles to profl. jours.; composer: percussion ensembles. Hon. mem. USN Band, 1970—. Recipient Disting. Pinnacle award, Purdue U., 2003, Excellence citation, NBA, 1976, award, John Philip Sousa Found., 1984. Mem.: Big Ten Band Dirs. Assn., Percussion Ats Soc., Coll. Band Dirs. Nat. Assn., Nat. Band Assn. (exec. sec., citation of excellence), Music Educators Nat. Conf., Inc. Music Educators Assn., John Philip Sousa Found. (v.p., exec. sec., Star of Order of Merit), Tau Beta Sigma, Delta Omicron, Alpha Lambda Delta, Phi Sigma Kappa (hon.), Kappa Kappa Psi (hon.). Office: 225 Tamiami Trl West Lafayette IN 47906-1207 E-mail: mlefever@verizon.net.

LEFF, DEBORAH, government executive; b. Washington, Oct. 25, 1951; d. Sam and Melitta Leff. AB, Princeton (N.J.) U., 1973; JD, U. Chgo., 1977. Trial atty. Civil Rights divsn. U.S. Dept. Justice, Washington, 1977-79; dir. office of pub. affairs Fed. Trade Commn., Washington, 1980-81; sr. producer Nightline-ABC News, Washington and London, 1983-89, World News Tonight-ABC News, N.Y.C., 1990-91; pres. The Joyce Found., Chgo., 1992-99, also bd. dirs.; pres., CEO Am.'s Second Harvest, Chgo., 1999-2001; dir. John F. Kennedy Presdl. Libr., Boston, 2001—. Bd. dirs. CARE, Inc., Sound Portraits; chmn. Midwest Rhodes Scholars Selection Com., Chgo., 1992. Office: John F Kennedy Libr Columbia Point Boston MA 02125

LEFF, ILENE J(AFNEL), management consultant, corporate and government executive; b. N.Y.C., Mar. 29; d. Abraham and Rose (Levy) L. BA cum laude, U. Pa., 1964; MA with honors, Columbia U., 1969. Statis. and computer analyst McKinsey & Co., N.Y.C., 1969-70, rsch. cons., 1971-74; mgmt. cons. N.Y.C. and Europe, 1974-78; dir. exec. resources Revlon, Inc., N.Y.C., 1978-81, dir. human resources, 1981-83, dir. pers., 1983-86; cons. APM Inc., 1986-88; mgmt. cons. The Estee Lauder Cos., 1988-92; dep. asst. sec. for mgmt. HUD, Washington, 1993-94; pres. Leff Mgmt. Cons., N.Y.C., 1995-97; mng. dir. Eisner LLP, N.Y.C., 1997-2000; pres. Leff Mgmt., 2000—. Rsch. asst. U. Pa., Phila., 1964-65; employment counselor State of N.J., Newark, 1965-66; tchr., Newark, 1966-69; lectr. Grad. Program in Pub. Policy, New Sch. for Social Rsch., Wharton Sch., Duke U.; chmn. com. on employment and unemployment, mem. exec. com. Bus. Rsch. Adv. Coun., U.S. Bur. Labor Stats., 1980; sr. del. econ. rels. and trade Sino-U.S. Conf., 1986; mem. nat. adv. bd. First Book. Contbr. issues papers and program recommendations to candidates for U.S. Pres., U.S. Senate and Congress, N.Y. State gov., mayor N.Y.C. Mem. ops. coun. Jr. Achievement Greater N.Y., 1975-78; cons. Com. for Econ. Devel., N.Y. Hosp., Regional Plan Assn., Am. Cancer Soc.; mem. adv. bd. First Book; vol. for dep. mayor for ops. N.Y.C., 1977-78. Mem. N.Y. Human Resource Planners (treas. 1984), Fin. Women's Assn. N.Y. (exec. bd. 1977-78, 83-84), Fashion Group (treas. 1989). Office: 767 Fifth Ave New York NY 10153-0023 Office Phone: 212-674-1140. E-mail: ileneleff@aol.com.

LEFF, SANDRA H. gallery director, consultant; b. N.Y.C., Dec. 24, 1939; d. I. Bernard and Rose (Kupfer) L. BA, Cornell U., 1960; MA, Inst. Fine Arts, N.Y.C., 1969. Editorial asst. Indsl. Design Mag., N.Y.C., 1960-61; instr., asst. Mus. of City of N.Y., 1962-65; assoc. print dept. Sotheby Parke Bernet, N.Y.C., 1969-73; rsch. asst. Daniel Chester French Exhibit, Washington, 1975-77; dir. Am. painting Graham Gallery, N.Y.C., 1977-93. Author: (exhbn. catalogs) Thomas Anshutz: Paintings, Watercolors and Pastels, 1979, Guy Pène du Bois: Painter, Draftsman and Critic, 1979, Helen Torr, 1980, John White Alexander: Fin-de-Siècle American, 1980, Jan Matulka & Vaclav Vytlacil, 1992. Ford Found. fellow, 1967. Mem. Phi Beta Kappa. Avocations: reading, traveling, jogging, film, photography. Office: 11 W 17th St Apt 10 New York NY 10011-5500 E-mail: sanmichkan@earthlink.net.

LEFFINGWELL, DENISE C. social worker; b. Pasadena, Calif., Dec. 8, 1975; d. Richard and Sharon Rice; m. Ryan Leffingwell, Nov. 18, 2001. MSW, Calif. State U. San Bernardino, 2001; B in Sociology, U. La Verne, 1997. Lic. social worker. Sr. child care worker Family Solutions, Santa Ana, Calif., 1997—98, social work asst., 1998—99; in-home counselor Cmty. Svc. Programs, Santa Ana, 1999—2000, counselor, 2000—02; med. social worker St Mary Corwin Med. Ctr., Pueblo, Colo., 2002—03; cmty. connector Resource Exch., Colorado Springs, Colo., 2003—; caseworker Kids Crossing, Colorado Springs, 2003—. Mem.: NASW. Office: Kids Crossing 1440 E Fountain Blvd Colorado Springs CO 80910 Personal E-mail: deniserice@hotmail.com. E-mail: dleffingwell@kidscrossing.tv.

LEFFLER, CAROLE ELIZABETH, mental health nurse, women's health nurse; b. Sidney, Ohio, Feb. 18, 1942; d. August B. and Delores K. Aselage; children: Veronica, Christopher. ADN, Sinclair Community Coll., Dayton, Ohio, 1975. Cert. psychiat. nurse supr. Nurse Grandview Hosp, Dayton, 1961-76; substitute sch. nurse Fairborn (Ohio) City Schs., 1981-82; dir. nursing Fairborn Nursing Home, 1983; psychiat. nurse supr. Twin Valley Behavioral Health Ctr., 1984—. Mem. exec. bd. 1199; chmn. disaster mental health com. ARC Ohio. Vol., instr., disaster health nurse ARC, chmn. State of Ohio disaster mental health com.; officer, leader, camp nurse for Girl Scouts, Boy Scouts; Ch. Parish Coun. Recipient Fleur de Lis award Girl and Boy Scouts, Svc. award ARC, Fairborn Mayor's Cert. of Merit for Civic Pride, State of Ohio Govs. award Innovation Ohio. Mem. ANA, Ohio Nurses Assn. Home: 3020 N Dayton Lakeview Rd New Carlisle OH 45344-8505

LEFKOWITZ, MARY ROSENTHAL, Greek literature educator; b. N.Y.C., Apr. 30, 1935; d. Harold L. and Mena (Weil) Rosenthal; m. Alan L. Lefkowitz, July 1, 1956 (div.); children: Rachel, Hannah; m. Hugh Lloyd-Jones, Mar. 26, 1982. BA, Wellesley Coll., 1957; AM, Radcliffe Coll., 1959, PhD, 1961; LHD (hon.), Trinity Coll., Hartford, Conn., 1996, Grinnell Coll., 2000; PhD (hon.), U. Patras, Greece, 1999. Instr. Greek Wellesley (Mass.) Coll., 1960-63, asst. prof. Greek and Latin, 1964-69, assoc. prof. Greek and Latin, 1969-75, prof. Greek and Latin, 1975-79; Andrew W. Mellon prof. in the humanities Wellesley (Mass.) Coll, 1979—. Vis. prof. U. Calif., Berkeley, 1978; vis. fellow St. Hilda's Coll., 1979-80, Corpus Christi Coll., 1991. Author: Heroines and Hysterics, 1981, Lives of the Greek Poets, 1981, Women in Greek Myth, 1986, First Person Fictions, 1991, Not Out of Africa, 1996, 2d edit., 1997, Greek Gods, Human Lives, 2003; co-editor: Women's Life in Greece and Rome, 1982, 2d edit., 1992, Black Athena Revisited, 1996. Fellow NEH, 1979-80, 91, ACLS, 1972-73, Hon. fellow St. Hilda's Coll., Oxford, 1994—. Mem. Am. Philol. Assn. (bd. dirs. 1974-77), Class Assn. New Eng. (pres. 1972-73). Home: 15 W Riding St Wellesley MA 02482-6914 Office: Wellesley Coll 106 Central St Wellesley MA 02481-8203 E-mail: mlefkowitz@wellesley.edu.

LEFLY, DIANNE LOUISE, research psychologist; b. Denver, July 17, 1946; d. Gordon Eugene Boen and Elizabeth (Welsh) Tuveson. AB, U. No. Colo., 1968; MA, U. Colo., 1980; PhD, U. Denver, 1994. Classroom tchr. Adam County Sch. Dist. 12, Thornton, Colo., 1968-77; rschr. John F. Kennedy Child Devel. Ctr., Denver, 1979-81, U. Colo. Health Scis. Ctr., 1981-89, U. Denver, 1989-98; rschr. mgr. Denver Pub Schs., 1998—2003; supr. of measurement Colo. Dept. Edn., Denver, 2003—. Cons. Colo. Dept. Edn., 1997—, Colo. Dept. Pub. Health and Environ., 1997—, Piton Found., 2002—. Contbr. articles to profl. jours. Mem. Colo. Rep. Party, Denver, 1968—. Scholarship U. No. Colo., 1964-68; fellowship U. Denver, 1989. Mem. Mensa, Am. Ednl. Rsch. Assn., Nat. Coun. on Measurement in Edn. Republican. Avocations: computer activities, dance, hiking, reading. Home: 6213 Secrest St Arvada CO 80403 Office: Colo Dept Edn 201 E Colfax Ave Denver CO 80203 E-mail: dlefly@earthlink.net., Lefly_D@CDE.State.co.us.

LÉGER, VIOLA, Canadian senator; b. June 29, 1930; BA, BEd, U. Moncton; MFA, Boston U. Tchr. drama; star of theatre, films, tv; senator The Senate of Can., Ottawa, 2001—. Founder La Compagnie Viola Léger Inc., 1985—. Named Officer of Order of Can., 1989; recipient Chevalier de l'Ordre de la Pléiade, 1978, Dora Mavor Moore award, 1981, Médaille du Conseil de la vie française en Amérique, 1987, Chevalier de l'Order française des Arts et des Lettres, 1991, Masque de l'interprétation féminine de l'Academie québécoise du théâtre. Liberal. Office: 204 Victoria Bldg The Senate of Canada Ottawa ON Canada K1A 0A4

LEGG, HILDA GAY, federal agency administrator; BS in Sociology, Campbellville Coll.; MEd, We. Ky. U. Tchr. social sci. jr. and sr. hs, Adair County, Ky., 1974—81; acting exec. dir. nat. coun. on handicapped U.D. Dept. of Edn., Washington, 1981—83; field rep. Senator Mitch McConnell, Bowling Green, Ky., 1985—87; dir. admissions Lindsey Wilson Coll., Columbia, Ky., 1987—90; alt. fed. co-chmn. Appalachian Regional Commn., Washington, 1990—93; exec. dir., CEO Ctr. for Rural Develop., Somerset, Ky., 1994—2001; adminstr. rural utilities svcs. USDA, Washington, 2001—. Republican. Office: USDA Rural Utilities Svcs 1400 Independence Ave SW Washington DC 20250

LEGGE KEMP, DIANE, architect, landscape architect; b. Englewood, N.J., Dec. 4, 1949; d. Richard Claude and Patricia (Roney) L.; m. Kevin A. Kemp; children: Alloy Hudson, McClelland Beebe, Logan Roney. BA, Stanford U., 1972; M in Architecture, Princeton U., 1975. Architect Northrop, Kaelber & Kopf, Rochester, N.Y., 1971, Michael Graves, Architect, Princeton, 1972-75, The Ehrenkrantz Group, N.Y.C., 1975-77; ptnr. Skidmore Owings & Merrill, Chgo., 1977-89; prin. Diane Legge Kemp Architecture and Landscape Consulting, Riverside, Ill., 1989-93, pres., 1993—, DLK Architecture, 1993—. Chair Princeton U. adv. bd. Sch. Architecture, 1991—; dir. Newhouse Archtl. Found., Chgo., 1991—. Designer, architect: Boston Globe Satellite Printing Plant, 1984, Mfrs. Hanover Plaza, Wilmington, 1987, Herman Miller Showroom, Chgo., 1988, Arlington Internat. Racecourse, 1989, Phila. Newspapers Espansion and Retrofit, 1989, Navy Pier R constrn., 1990, McCormick Place Retrofit and Exapansion, 1991, L.A. Times Master Plan, 1992, CRSS capital project mgmt. Chgo. Park Dist., 1993, Chgo. Hist. Blvds. Restoration, 1993, Roosevelt Rd. Reconstruction, Chgo., 1993, Field, Shedd, Adler Mus. Campus, Goodman Theater, Chgo., 1995, Job Corps Tng. Campus, 1995, Chgo. area Circulator Urban Design, 1995, Cook County Hosp., 1996, Ft. Sherman Base, 1997, Girl Scouts Svc. Ctr., 1997, Michigan Ave. Renovation, 1997. Mem. bd. govs. Sch. of Art Inst., Chgo., 1991—; dir., past pres. Soc. for Contemporary Art, Chgo., 1991—. Recipient 40 under 40 award N.Y. Archtl. League, 1986; Urban Design award Progressive Architecture, 1984; named one of 100 Most Influential Women in Chgo., Crain's, 1996. Fellow AIA (Disting. Bldg. award 1983, Interiors award 1988, Nat. Urban Design award 1996); mem. NCARB, Am. Soc. Landscape Architects, Urban Land. Inst. Avocations: piano, flute, skiing, sailing, gardens. Office: DLK Architecture 410 S Michigan Ave Chicago IL 60605-1308

LEGGETT, ROBERTA JEAN (BOBBI LEGGETT), retired social services administrator; b. Kankakee, Ill., Nov. 30, 1926; d. Clyde H. and Sybil D. (Billings) Karns; m. George T. Leggett, Aug. 25, 1956. Sec. Cardov div. Chemetron Corp., Chgo., 1951-60; sec., asst. mgr. Ravisloe Country Club, Homewood, Ill., 1961-65; sec. Nationwide Paper Co., Chgo., 1966-68; exec. dir. Am. Bd. Oral and Maxillofacial Surgery, Chgo., 1969-87. Mem. Chgo. Sec. Assn. Execs., Conf. Med. Soc. Execs. of Greater Chgo., Profl. Secs. Internat. Methodist.

LEGRO, PATRICE, museum director; b. Dec. 1953; m. Alan Legro. BA in Art History, Old Dominion U., 1977; MA in internat. transaction, George Mason U., 1996. Program officer Office Internat. Affairs Nat. Acad., Wash., DC, 1987—93, mgr. Nat. Sci. Edn. Standards Project, co-study dir. Tchg. About Evolution and Nature of Sci., 1998, dir. Divsn. Comm. and Special

Projects Ctr. Sci., Math., and Engring. Edn., 1998, dir. Philanthropy Svcs., 1998—2002; dir. Marian Koshland Sci. Mus. Nat. Acad. Scis., Wash., DC, 2002—. Office: Marian Koshland Sci Mus Nat Acad 500 Fifth St NW Washington DC 20001*

LE GUIN, URSULA KROEBER, writer; b. Berkeley, Calif., Oct. 21, 1929; d. Alfred Louis and Theodora (Kracaw) Kroeber; m. Charles A. Le Guin, Dec. 22, 1953; children: Elisabeth, Caroline, Theodore. BA, Radcliffe Coll., 1951; MA, Columbia, 1952; 9 hon. degrees. Vis. lectr. or writer in residence numerous workshops and univs., U.S. and abroad. Author: Rocannon's World, 1966, Planet of Exile, 1966, City of Illusion, 1967, A Wizard of Earthsea, 1968, The Left Hand of Darkness, 1969, The Tombs of Atuan, 1970, The Lathe of Heaven, 1971, The Farthest Shore, 1972, The Dispossessed, 1974, The Wind's Twelve Quarters, 1975, A Very Long Way from Anywhere Else, 1976, Orsinian Tales, 1976, The Word For World is Forest, 1976, The Language of the Night, 1979, rev. edit., 1992, Leese Webster, 1979, Malafrena, 1979, The Beginning Place, 1980, Hard Words, 1981, The Eye of the Heron, 1983, The Compass Rose, 1982, King Dog, 1985, Always Coming Home, 1985, Buffalo Gals, 1987, Wild Oats and Fireweed, 1988, A Visit from Dr. Katz, 1988, Catwings, 1988, Solomon Leviathan, 1988, Fire and Stone, 1989, Catwings Return, 1989, Dancing at the Edge of the World, 1989, Tehanu, 1990, Searoad, 1991, Fish Soup, 1992, A Ride on the Red Mare's Back, 1992, Blue Moon Over Thurman Street, 1993, Wonderful Alexander and the Catwings, 1994, Going Out With Peacocks, 1994, A Fisherman of the Inland Sea, 1994, Four Ways to Forgiveness, 1995, Unlocking the Air, 1996, (with Diana Bellessi) The Twins, The Dream, 1997, Lao Tzu: Tao Te Ching: A Book About the Way and the Power of the Way, 1997, Steering the Craft, 1998, Jane on Her Own, 1999, Sixty Odd, 1999, The Telling, 2000, The Other Wind, 2001, Tales From Earthsea, 2001, The Birthday of the World, 2002, Tom Mouse, 2002, Kalpa Imperial, 2003, Selected Poems of Gabriela Mistral, 2003, Changing Planes, 2003, The Wave in the Mind, 2004, also numerous short stories, poems, criticism, screenplays. Recipient Jupiter award 1975, 76, Lewis Caroll Shelf award 1979, Internat. Fantasy award 1988, Howard D. Vursell award Am. Acad. Arts and Letters, 1991, Pushcart prize, 1991, Boston Globe-Hornbook award for excellence in juvenile fiction, 1968, Newbery Honor medal, 1972, Nebula award (novel) 1969, 75, 90, (story) 1975, 96, Hugo award (novel) 1969, 75, (story) 1974, 88, Gandalf award, 1979, Kafka award, 1986, Nat. Book award, 1972, H.L. Davis award Oreg. Inst. Literary Arts, 1992, Hubbub annual poetry award, 1995, Asimov's Reader's award, 1995, 2003, James Tiptree Jr. award, 1995, 97, Retrospective award, 1996, Theodore Sturgeon award (story), 1995, Locus Readers award (novel), 1973, (story) 1984, 95, 2003, (collection) 1996, (novel and story) 2001, 2002, Prix Lectures-Jeunesse award, 1987, Bumbershoot Arts award, Seattle, 1998, Lifetime Achievement award Robert Kirsch/L.A. Times, 2000, Lifetime Achievement award Pacific NW Booksellers Assn., 2001, Endeavor award, 2001, 2003, Willamette Writers Lifetime Achievement award, 2002, World Fantasy award (novel), 2002, PEN/Malamud award for short fiction, 2002, Grandmaster SWFA, 2003, Arbuthnot lectr. Am. Libr. Assn., 2004, Margaret A. Edwards Award for lifetime contbn. in writing for young adults, 2004. Mem. NARAL, Amnesty Internet. USA, Environ. Def. Fund, Nat. Resources Def. CTEE, Planned Parenthood Fedn. of Amer., Oreg. Nature Conservancy, Sci. Fiction Research Assn., Sci. Fiction Writers Assn., Authors League, PEN, Writers Guild West, Phi Beta Kappa. Office: care Virginia Kidd Lit Agy PO Box 278 Milford PA 18337-0278 also: care Eric Zohn William Morris Agy 1350 Avenue Of The Americas New York NY 10019-4702

LEHMAN, ALICE, bank executive; BA, U. Calif., Davis, 1969, MEd, 1970; MBA, U. Calif., Berkeley, 1978. V.p. fin. instns. group Bank Am., N.Y.C., N.C., 1978-84, v.p., mgr. Charlotte, N.C.; v.p., mgr. fin. instns. group First Union Corp., Charlotte, 1986-90, sr. credit officer capital markets, 1990-93, sr. v.p., mng. dir. loan sydications, 1993-96; sr. v.p. investor rels., corp. comm. & cmty. devel. First Union Corp. (merged with Wachovia), Charlotte, 1996—. Office: Wachovia 301 S College St Ste 4000 Charlotte NC 28288-0013

LEHMAN, CASSANDRA, psychologist; b. Lancaster, Pa., Oct. 27, 1968; d. Charles and Katherine Lehman. PhD, Boston U., 1994—2000. Lic. Psychologist CA, 2000. Behavioral medicine fellow VA Palo Alto Health Care Sys., Palo Alto, Calif., 2000—01; behavioral medicine specialist Kaiser Permanente, Santa Clara, Calif., 2001—03, behavioral medicine subchief, 2003—. Contbr. articles to jours. Ch. bd. mem. Clara Mayo fellowship, Boston U., 1999—2000. Mem.: APA, Divsn. of Health Psychology of the APA, Assn. for Advancement of Behavior Therapy. Avocations: ballroom dancing, hiking, flute. Office: Kaiser Permanente 900 Kiely Blvd Santa Clara CA 94301 Personal E-mail: cassandra_lehman@hotmail.com.

LEHMANN, DORIS ELIZABETH, elementary school educator; b. Ramsey, N.J., Aug. 17, 1933; d. Alfred Harrison and Anna Elizabeth (Gerhold) Rockefeller; m. Victor S. Lehmann, June 25, 1955; children: Joanne E. Cathy Lynn, Victor A., Kristie Sue. BS in Edn. magna cum laude, Wagner Coll., 1955; student in edn., Columbia U., summers 1988-91, Jersey City State, 1990—, William Paterson, 1971. Elem. tchr. Sch. St. Sch., Ramsey, 1955-56; bedside instr. N. Bergen County schs., N.J., 1966-71; elem. tchr. Edith A. Bogert Sch., Upper Saddle River, N.J., 1971-2000. Author numerous poems; author: (with others) Curriculum for Values Education in New Jersey, 1991. Indian cons. Bergen County Mus. of Art and Sci., Paramus, N.J., 1983—. Recipient Fellowship of Life award Luth. Layman's Movement, 1955. Fellow Upper Saddle River Edn. Assn. (social sec. 1972-73, v.p. 1974-75, 84-85, liaison to USR hist. soc. 1986—) N.J. Edn. Assn., N.J. North Edn. Assn., Alpha Omicron Pi (life, treas. 1954, v.p. 1955). Republican. Lutheran. Office: Edith A Bogert Sch 395 W Saddle River Rd Saddle River NJ 07458-1622 E-mail: vlcco@aol.com.

LEHMANN, ESTHER STRAUSS, investment company executive; b. Binghamton, N.Y., Apr. 19, 1944; d. Julius and Betty (Lind) Strauss; m. Aaron Lehmann, Feb. 27, 1966; children: Shanna, Shira, Marc, David. BS, Cornell U., 1966; cert. in vol. and non-profit orgn. mgmt., U. Conn., 1976; cert. employee benefits specialist, U. Pa., 1983. V.p. Fairway Mgmt., West Hartford, Conn., 1976-80; investment exec. Herzfeld & Stern, Paramus, N.J., 1980-86; assoc. v.p. Ryan Beck, Inc., Ft. Lee, 1988—. Home: 1632 Dover Ct Teaneck NJ 07666-2965 Office Fax: 201-461-9121.

LEHMANN, PHYLLIS WILLIAMS, archaeologist, educator; b. Bklyn., Nov. 30, 1912; d. James Barnes and Florence Lourene (Richmond) Williams; m. Karl Lehmann, Sept. 14, 1944 (dec. Dec. 1960). BA, Wellesley Coll., 1934, L.H.D., 1976; PhD, NYU, 1943; Litt.D., Mt. Holyoke Coll., 1971; D.F.A., Coll. Holy Cross, 1973. Asst. charge classical collection Bklyn. Museum, 1934-36; part-time instr. history art Bennett Jr. Coll., 1936-39; mem. faculty Smith Coll., 1946—, prof. art, 1955-67, Jessie Wells Post prof. art, 1967-72, William R. Kenan, Jr. prof. art, 1972-78, prof. emeritus, 1978—, dean, 1965-70; asst. field dir. excavations conducted by Archaeol. Research Fund of NYU at Samothrace, 1948-60, acting dir., 1960-62, adv. dir., 1962—; research prof. Inst. Fine Arts, NYU, 1961-62; adj. prof. Inst. Fine Arts, N.Y. U., 1965—. Flexner lectr. Bryn Mawr Coll., 1977; Baldwin lectr. Oberlin Coll., 1982 Author: Statues on Coins of Southern Italy and Sicily in the Classical Period, 1946, Roman Wall Paintings from Boscoreale in the Metropolitan Museum of Art, 1953, The Pedimental Sculptures of the Hieron in Samothrace, 1962, Samothrace, vol. 3, 1969, (with Karl Lehmann) Samothracian Reflections. Aspects of the Revival of the Antique, 1973, Skopas in Samothrace, 1973, Cyriacus of Ancona's Egyptian Visit and Its Reflections in Gentile Bellini and Hieronymus Bosch, 1977, Samothrace, Vol. 5, 1982, contbr. Vol. 7, 1992; also articles in profl. jours.; Editor: (with Karl Lehmann) Samothrace, 1961—; asst. editor: Art Bull., 1945-47; book rev. editor, 1949-52. Named hon. citizen of Samothrace, 1968; recipient Wellesley Coll. Alumnae Assn. Achievement award, 1976; Gold medal Pan Samothracian Hearth of Athens, 1981; hon. mem. Pan Samothracian Hearth of Athens, 1979; Fulbright research grantee Italy, 1952-53; Guggenheim fellow, 1952-53; Bollingen fellow, 1960 Fellow Am. Acad. Arts and Scis.; mem. Archaeol. Inst. Am. (trustee 1970-73), Coll. Art Assn. Am., Am. Numis. Soc., Soc. Archtl. Historians (Alice D. Hitchcock award 1969), AAUW, Renaissance Soc. Am., Am. Sch. Classical Studies in Athens (research fellow fall 1970, 76, exec. com. 1970-75, publ. com. 1975-80, chmn. 1977-80), Williamsburg Hist. Soc., Phi Beta Kappa. Office: Smith Coll Hillyer Hall Northampton MA 01063

LEHMANN-CARSSOW, NANCY BETH, secondary school educator, coach; b. Kingsville, Tex., Sept. 9, 1949; d. Valgene William and Ella Mae (Zajicek) Lehmann; m. William Benton Carssow, Jr., Aug. 1, 1981. BS, U. Tex., 1971, MA, 1979. Freelance photographer, Austin, Tex., 1971-99; geography tchr., tennis coach Austin Ind. Sch. Dist., 1974-98, geography tchr., instrnl. specialist, girls' wrestling coach, 1999—. Founder Custom Pet Wheels, 1997; salesperson, mgr. What's Going On-Clothing, Austin, 1972-78; area adminstr. Am. Inst. Fgn. Study, Austin, 1974-81; area rep. World Encounters, Austin, 1981—, tour guide, Egypt, Kenya, 1977, 79, 81, 87, 92, 97, 98, 99, 2000; participant 1st summer inst. Nat. Geog. Soc., Washington, 1986; tchr., cons. Nat. Geog., 1986—; tchr. Leader for People in Soviet Union, 1989, 90; vol. First Internat. Environ. Expedition to Antarctica, 1995; presenter Populaton Education, 1995—. Author curriculum materials; photographer (book) Bobwhites, 1984. Co-chair Peace-Works. Recipient Merit award Nat. Coun. Geog. Edn., 1975, Creative Tchg. award Austin Assn. Tchrs., 1978, study grant to Malaysia and Indonesia, 1990, Excellence award for outstanding H.S. tchr. U. Tex., 1997, Edn.'s Unsung Hereos award No. Life, 1998, Outstanding Tchg. of the Humanities award, 1998, Excellence award Tex. State Bd. Edn., 1995, Peacemaker award Austin Dispute Resolution Ctr., 1998; Fulbright scholar, Israel, 1983. Mem. NEA, Nat. Coun. Geog. Edn., Earthwatch (participant archaeol. dig in Swaziland 1984, Romania 2003), World Wildlife Fund, Rotary, Delta Kappa Gamma (pres. 1986-88), Phi Kappa Phi. Democrat. Roman Catholic. Avocations: stained glass, photography, tennis, gardening, needlepoint. Home: 1025 Quail Park Dr Austin TX 78758-6749 Office: Lanier High Sch 1201 Payton Gin Rd Austin TX 78758-6699 E-mail: nlehmann@ev1.net.

LEHMKUHL, LYNN, publishing executive; Pub. Disney Adventures mag., 1990—93, Nickelodeon mag. Nickelodeon Online, 1993—96; group pub. Kids Mag. Divsn. The Walt Disney Co., 1996—98; pres., Youth Pub. Peterson's Pub., 1998—2002; pres. Teen Magazine, L.A., 1998—2002; v.p. corp. sponsorship Sesame Workshop, N.Y.C., 2002; pub. Ladies Home Jour., 2002—. Office: Ladies Home Journal 125 Park Ave New York NY 10017-5529 E-mail: lynn.lehmkuhl@meredith.com.

LEHMKUHLER, ELAINE LOUISE, speech pathology/audiology services professional; b. North Platte, Nebr., Nov. 14, 1956; d. James Francis and Jacqueline Cecilia Ryan; m. Paul Eugene Lehmkuhler, Aug. 4, 1979; children: Jennifer Cecilia, Ryan Paul. BS in Speech Pathology and Audiology, U. Nebr., Lincoln, 1979, MA in Speech Pathology, 1980. Cert. Clinical Competence (CCC) in Speech Pathology Am. Speech-Lang.-Hearing Assn., 1981. Speech/lang. pathologist Scottish Rite Clinic/U. Nebr., Hastings, Nebr., 1981—83, St. Mary's Hosp./Pierre (S.D.) Schs., 1983—84, SW Kans. Dist. #613, Dodge City, Kans., 1984—94, 1996—, Western Plains Regional Hosp., Dodge City, Kans., 1994—96. Vol. Kan-Read Program, Dodge City, Kans., 1991—96; mem. Traumatic Brain Injury Team, Kans., 2001—. Recipient Therapist of Yr. award, Nat. Assn. Am. Bus. Clubs, 1992. Mem.: Am. Speech-Lang.-Hearing Assn., Kans. Speech-Lang.-Hearing Assn. Republican. Roman Catholic. Avocations: swimming, spectator sports, reading.

LEHNE, KATHY PRASNICKI, gas industry executive; Pres. Sun Coast Resources, Houston. Office: Sun Coast Resources 6922 Cavalcade St Houston TX 77028-5802

LEHNER, REMY D. publishing executive; b. N.Y.C., 1956; Pres., CEO Inflight Newspapers & Mags., Inc., Valley Stream, NY, 1997—. Bd. trustees Franklin Hosp. Med. Ctr.; mem. Long Island Hispanic C. of C.; various other charity and cmty. orgns.; fundraiser for over 40 local and nat. charities; established TALI Edn. Program, Alona Pub. Sch., Israel; mem. U.S. Hispanic C. of C., Long Island Breast Cancer Coalition, Lawrence Spl. Edn. PTA; mem. nat. com. Furtherance Jewish Edn. Named a sch. after her, TALI Edn. Fund & Sem. Judaic Studies, Israel, 1996. Mem.: NAACP (life). Office: Inflight Newspapers Inc 125 S Cottage St Valley Stream NY 11580

LEHNER-QUAM, ALISON LYNN, library administrator; b. Oak Harbor, Wash., Apr. 25, 1960; d. Paul Elias and Johanna Marie (Vinson) Q.; m. Matthias Karl-Eugen Lehner, Oct. 3, 1997; 1 child, Peter Elias Bernhard Lehner. BA, U. Wash., 1983; cert. tech. theater, Yale U., 1985; MS in Libr. Sci., Columbia U., 1991. Freelance costumer various prodns., N.Y.C., 1984-90; cataloging asst. Fashion Inst. of Tech., N.Y.C., 1986-91; intern Bank St. Sch., N.Y.C., 1991; asst. dir. Columbia Children's Lit. Inst., N.Y.C., 1990; libr. dir. Lincoln Ctr. Inst., N.Y.C., 1991—, mgr. website, 2000—. Project dir. Arts Edn. Reference Window on the Work, 1992—. Pub. mgr.: (periodical) The Institute View, 1996—, Lincoln Ctr. Inst., 1999, website mgr., 2000—. Vol. mgr. Lincon Ctr. Inst., N.Y.C., 1995—. Recipient Dirs.' Emeriti award Lincoln Ctr. for Performing Arts, 1997; scholar Sch. Libr. Svcs., Columbia U., 1989, 90. Mem. ALA, N.Y. Arts in Edn. Roundtable (steering com. 1995-98), Theater Libr. Assn., Beta Phi Mu (bd. dirs. Theta chpt. 1997—, v.p. 1994-96). Avocations: reading, the arts. Home: 231 garfield pl apt 3 Brooklyn NY 11215-2263 E-mail: alquam@lincolncenter.org.

LEHRMAN, MARCELINE BARBARA, psychotherapist; b. N.Y.C., Oct. 17, 1930; d. Samuel Rockower and Hattie; m. Theodore Howard Lehrman, Jan. 15, 1950; children: Russ, Laurie. BS in edn., Bklyn. Coll., 1958; M in guidance, Queens Coll., 1965; MSW, Adelphi U., 1979. Cert. Marriage and Family Alfred Adler Inst., 1975. Tchr. N.Y.C. BOE, 1958—65, guidance counselor, 1965—75, clin. liaison, 1975—90; psychotherapist Pvt. Practice, N.Y.C., 1990—. Assembly del. UFT-NYC, N.Y.C., 1965—70. Mem.: Nat. Assn. Social Workers, Assn. Marriage Family Therapists (pres. 2001—03). Avocations: tennis, bridge, theater, lic. N.Y.C. tour guide. Home: 160 E 38th St Apt 5D New York NY 10016 E-mail: the4149818@aol.com.

LEHRMAN, MARGARET MCBRIDE, television news executive, producer; b. Spokane, Wash., Sept. 25, 1944; d. John P. and Ruth A. McBride; m. Michael L. Lehrman, June 27, 1970. BA, U. Oreg., 1966; MS, Columbia U., 1970. Staff Peace Corps, Washington, 1966-69; with The Morning News Co., Washington, 1970-72; radio and newspaper reporter Albright Comms., Washington, 1973-74; tv assignment editor ABC News, Washington, 1974; press asst. Senator Robert P. Griffin, Washington, 1975-79; rschr. Today Show, NBC News, Washington, 1979, assoc. prodr., 1979—83, Washington prodr., 1983-89, dep. bur. chief, 1989-95, sr. Washington prodr. spl. coverage and events, 1995—. Trustee U. Oreg. Found., 1990-2000. Recipient Edwin M. Hood award for diplomatic reporting (China), adv. bd. Internat. Women's Media Found., Women's Fgn. Policy Group, World Affairs Coun. Office: NBC News 4001 Nebraska Ave NW Washington DC 20016-2733 E-mail: margaret.lehrman@nbc.com.

LEHRMANN, RUBY JEAN, protective services official; b. Riesel, Tex., June 14, 1947; d. Ruby Mullins Lehrmann. BS in Health Edn. and Geography, Sam Houston State U., 1969, MA in Health Edn. and Sociology, 1972; postgrad., Tex. A&M U., 1981—84. Pharmacist asst., recreation officer; health edn. tchr., edn. and recreation dir., asst. warden Tex. Dept. Corrections, Huntsville, 1969—75; chief U.S. probation officer U.S. Probation Office, San Antonio, 1975—. Faculty Fed. Jud. Ctr., Washington, 1976—2003. Teaching fellow, Sam Houston State U., 1969—71. Mem.: Am. Probation and Parole Assn., Am. Corrections Assn., Am. Assn Probation and Parole, Fed. Probation and Pretrial Svcs. Officers Assn. (Richard F. Doyle award 1996), Tex. State Teachers Assn., San Antonio Conservation Soc. Home: 608 Kendall Pky Boerne TX 78015 Office: US Probation Office 727 E Durango Rm A-405 San Antonio TX 78206-1203 E-mail: ruby_lehrmann@txwp.uscourts.gov.

LEIBER, JUDITH MARIA, designer, manufacturer; b. Budapest, Hungary, Jan. 11, 1921; came to U.S., 1947, naturalized, 1949; d. Emil and Helen (Spitzer) Peto; m. Gerson Leiber, Feb. 6, 1946. Student pvt. schs., Hungary and Eng.; DFA (hon.), Internat. Fine Arts Coll., 1993; PhD (hon.), Bar Ilan U., Israel, 1993, Internat. Fine Arts Coll., Miami, Fla., 1993. Master handbag maker, Hungary, 1942; pattern maker, designer Nettie Rosenstein, N.Y.C., 1947-60, Koret, N.Y.C., 1960-61; owner, mgr. Judith Leiber, Inc., N.Y.C., 1963—. Author: (Book) Judith Leiber, The Artful Handbag; (Designer) Retrospective exhbn. 30 yrs. F.I.T. Mus., N.Y.C., 1993—94, Retrospective exhbn. Corcoran Mus., Washington, 2002. Recipient Swarovski award and Am. Handbag Designer award, Leather Industries Am., 1970, Hall of Fame award, Accessory Coun., 2001, George Washington award, Am. Hungarian Found., 2001, Coty award, Am. Fashion Critics, 1973, Neiman-Marcus award, 1980, Women Who Made a Difference award Fashion Group, 1986, Lifetime Achievement award, Dallas Mart, 1991, Am. Acad. Achievement award, 1992, FAAB Lifetime Achievement award, 1992, Ellis Island Medal Honor, 1993, Lifetime Achievement award, Coun. Fashion Designers Am., 1993, Fashion Hall of Fame award, Shannon Rodgers & Jerry Silverman Sch. Fashion Design and Merchandising, Kent State U., 1995, featured Retrospective of Work New Orleans Mus. Mem. Nat. Handbag Authority (dir. 1972—) Achievements include pioneering woman master handbag maker, Hungary; first woman patternmaker Am. handbag industry.

LEIBOVITZ, ANNIE, photographer; b. Conn., Oct. 2, 1949; Student, San Francisco Art Inst. Photographer Rolling Stone, 1970-83, chief photographer, 1973-83; photographer for advertisements Vanity Fair, 1980—, photographer, 1983—; proprietor Annie Leibovitz Studio, N.Y.C. Works exhibited in various galleries and mus. including the National Portrait Gallery, Washington DC, 1991, The Corcoran Gallery, 1999; author: Photographs: Annie Leibovitz 1970-1990, 1992, Olympic Portraits: Annie Leibovitz, 1996, Annie Leibovitz: Women,(with essay by Susan Sontag) 1999, American Music, 2003; creator offcl. portfolio for 26th Olympic Games, Atlanta, 1995. Recipient Innovation in Photography award Am. Soc. Mag. Photographers, 1987. Achievements include first woman and second photographer to have a solo exhibit at The National Portrait Gallery. Office: Annie Leibovitz Studio 547 W 26th St New York NY 10001-5503 also: Art & Commerce Care Jim Moffat 755 Washington St New York NY 10014-1746 E-mail: als@leibovitzstudio.com.

LEIBOWITZ, FLORA LYNN, philosophy educator; b. Bklyn., Jan. 22, 1951; d. Joseph and Shirley (Ellenbogen) L.; m. Loren Kenneth Russell. BA, SUNY, Stony Brook, 1973; MA, Johns Hopkins U., 1975, PhD, 1979. Asst. prof. philosophy Oreg. State U., Corvallis, 1977-84, assoc. prof., 1984-93, prof., 1993—, dir. grad. studies dept. philosophy, 1994—99. Vis. rsch. fellow Ctr. philosophy and lit. U. Warwick, Eng., 1993. Contbr. articles to profl. jours. Publicity dir. Friends of Chamber Music, Corvallis, 1994-2003. Mem. Am. Soc. Aesthetics, Brit. Soc. Aesthetics (divsn. program chmn., 2000), Am. Philos. Assn. (program com. pacific divsn. 1996-99). Office: Philosophy Dept Oreg State U 208B Hovland Hall Corvallis OR 97331-8543 Office Phone: 541-737-5647. Business E-Mail: fleibowitz@oregon-state.edu. E-mail: fleibowitz@orst.edu.

LEICHTMAN, MARIA LUISA, mental health services professional; b. Philippines; B, Assumption Coll.; D of Clin. Psychology, U. Kans. With Irving Schwartz Inst. Children, Phila. Psychiat. Ctr., until 1979, Menninger, Topeka, 1979—, dir. child & adolscent residential treatment program, 1999—. Fulbright scholar. Office: Menningers PO Box 809045 Houston TX 77280

LEICK, CAROL LYNN, special education educator; b. Belleville, Ill., May 9, 1950; d. Wilbur Glenn and Jeannene Elosise Fritz; m. John Kenneth Leick, Nov. 7, 1992; children: Terry Glenn, Patrick Ryan. BS in Edn., S.W. Mo. State U., 1975; cert., Drury Coll., 1976. Lic. tchr. Mo., N.J. Tchr., Springfield, Mo., 1971—77, Mansfield Twp., Port Murray, NJ, 1977—79, Vigo County Sch. Corp., Terre Haute, Ind., 1979—80; tutor, daycare provider Terre Haute, 1981—85; tchr. Park Ctrl. Hosp., Springfield, Mo., 1986, Springfield R-12 Sch., 1986—90, Gasconade R-12 Sch., Owensville, Mo., 1990—; family educator for 1st Steps Franklin County Bd. for Handicapped, Union, Mo., 1991—92. Recorder for pilot behavioral modification program, Springfield, 1969; mentor York Elem. and Owensville H.S., 1989, 1994—. Vol. tchr. Delaware Elem. Class for Deaf/Blind, Springfield, 1968; sponsor, leader Say No to Drugs Club, Springfield, 1989—90; mem. adv. team, discipline com., at-risk com. York Elem., Springfield, 1988—90; mem. adv. com. Owensville H.S., 1994—; leader Boy Scouts Am.; mem. cert. team Support Dogs, Inc.; tchr. Sunday Bible Sch., 1963—89; bd. dirs. Learning Disabilities Assn., Springfield, 1989—90. Recipient Top 100 Curriculum Ideas award, Am. Sch. Bd. Jour./The Exec. Educator, 1989. Mem.: Cmty. Tchr. Assn. Avocations: reading, canoeing, travel. Office: Owensville HS Gasconade County R-2 Box 536 Owensville MO 65066

LEIDIG, MARGOT HELENE, retired elementary and secondary education educator; b. Fresno, Calif., May 31, 1945; d. Euvelle R. and Anita S. Enderlin; m. Leigh Arthur Leidig, June 11, 1972; children: Bonnie Ann, Kimberly Minnick. BA, Chico State U., 1967, MA, 1970. 3/5 faculty appt. phys. sci. dept. Chico (Calif.) State Coll., 1967-68; tchr. math., sci. Oak Grove Intermediate Sch. Mt. Diablo Unified Sch. Dist., Concord, Calif., 1968-73; tchr. resource maths. John Still Jr. High Sch. Sacramento City Unified Sch. Dist., 1973-80, tchr., maths. Kit Carson Middle Sch., 1980-86, tchr. maths. John F. Kennedy High Sch., 1986-96; tchr. maths., sci. Capital City Schs., 1996—; ret., 2002. Presenter No. Calif. Maths. Conf., Asilomar; chair No. Calif. Math Project U. Calif., Davis, 1985. Author: 5 math books. Mem. AAUW, Calif. Math Coun., Order of Ea. Star (# 150, 25 Yr. Pin), Daus. of the Nile, Phi Delta Kappa. Avocations: golfing, gardening, travel, reading, bridge.

LEIFER, ERICA HAFT, speech therapist; b. N.Y.C., Aug. 5, 1955; d. Alfred Haskel and Julie Ann Haft; m. Kevin Leifer, Mar. 6, 1976; children: Ethan Jay, Katie, Sara, Megan. BA in Speech Pathology, Adelphi U., 1977, MS in Speech Pathology, 1978. Cert. speech lang. pathologist Dept Edn., N.Y. Speech and lang. clinician N.Y.C. Dept. Edn., Bronx, 1993—. Camp mother Camp Lavi, Pa.; sisterhood pres. Young Israel of Hillcrest, NY, 1988—90. Mem.: N.Y. State Speech Hearing Lang. Assn., Am. Speech Hearing Assn. (cert. clin. competence, award for continuing edn. 2003). Avocations: swimming, hiking, reading, yoga. Office: NYC Dept Edn 850 Baychester Ave Bronx NY 11365 Personal E-mail: ehl@nyc.rr.com.

LEIGH, CHERI J. engineering consulting executive; BS Civil Eng., Southern Methodist U.; MS Eng. Mgmt., Kansas U. Positions with GM, Norfolk & Western Railway; founder and principle partner Leigh & O'Kane LLC, 1983—. Volunteer Reach to Recovery. Fellow: Soc. Women Engineers (Entrepreneur award 2003); mem.: Missouri Soc. Profl. Engineers.

Achievements include being the first woman engineer to be appointed to the Missouri Board for Architects, Professional Engineers, and Land Surveyors. Office: Leigh & O'Kane LLC 9201 Ward Pkwy Kansas City MO 64114-3339*

LEIGH, JENNIFER JASON (JENNIFER LEIGH MORROW), actress; b. L.A., Feb. 5, 1962; d. Barbara Turner and Vic Morrow. Student, Lee Strasberg Inst. Appearances include (films) Eyes of a Stranger, 1980, Fast Times at Ridgemont High, 1982, Wrong is Right, 1982, Easy Money, 1983, Grandview U.S.A., 1984, Flesh + Blood, 1985, The Hitcher, 1986, The Men's Club, 1986, Sister, Sister, 1987, Under Cover, 1987, Heart of Midnight, 1988, The Big Picture, 1989, Last Exit to Brooklyn, 1989, Miami Blues, 1990, Crooked Hearts, 1991, Backdraft, 1991, Rush, 1992, Single White Female, 1992, Short Cuts, 1993, The Hudsucker Proxy, 1994, Mrs. Parker and the Vicious Circle, 1994, Dolores Claiborne, 1994, Kansas City, 1996, Bastard Out of Carolina, 1996, A Thousand Acres, 1997, Washington Square, 1997, eXistenZ, 1998, The King is Alive, 2000, Skipped Parts, 2000, Beautiful View, 2000, The Quickie, 2001, Hey Arnold! The Movie, (voice) 2002 Road to Perdition, 2002, In the Cut, 2003, The Machinist, 2004; (TV movies) Angel City, 1980, The Killing of Randy Webster, 1981, The Best Little Girl in the World, 1981, The First Time, 1982, Girls of the White Orchid, 1983, Buried Alive, 1990, The Love Letter, 1998, Crossed Over, 2002 (mini series) Thanks of a Grateful Nation, 1998; prodr., actress Georgia, 1995; writer, dir., prodr., actor The Anniversary Party, 2001; TV guest appearances include The Waltons, 1972, Tracey Takes On..., 1996, King of the Hill, 1997; (TV series) Hercules (voice), 1998. Office: ICM c/o Tracey Jacobs 8942 Wilshire Blvd Beverly Hills CA 90211-1934 also: care Elaine Rich 2400 Whitman Pl Los Angeles CA 90068-2464

LEIGH, SHERREN, communications executive, editor, publisher; b. Cleve., Dec. 22, 1942; d. Walter Carl Maurushat and Treva Eldora (Burke) Morris; m. Norman J. Hickey Jr., Aug. 23, 1969 (div. 1985). BS, Ohio U., 1965. Communications dir. Metal Lath Assn., Cleve., 1965-67; creative dir. O'Toole Inc., Chgo., 1967-69; sr. v.p. RLC Inc., Chgo., 1969-77; pres. Leigh Communications Inc., Chgo., 1978—; chmn. Today's Chgo. Woman mag., 1982—. Pres. Ill. Ambassadors, Chgo., 1985-86; bd. dirs. Chgo. Fin. Exchange, 1985-87. Author: How to Write a Winning Resume, How to Negotiate for Top Dollar, How to Find, Get and Keep the Job You Want. Bd. dirs. Midwest Women's Ctr., Chgo., 1984-86, Girl Scouts Chgo., 1985-87, Black Women's Hall of Fame Found., Chgo., 1986—, Apparel Industry Bd., Chgo., 1988, Auditorium Theater of Roosevelt U.; pres. Today's Chgo. Woman Found., 1998; mem. adv. bd. Salvation Army, 1998. Recipient Corp. Leadership award YWCA Met. Chgo., 1979, Entrepreneurship award, 1988, Media Advocate of Yr. award U.S. SBA, 1994, Achievement award Network of Women Entrepreneurs, 1998, Golden Heart award Ill Assn. Non-Profit Orgns., 1998, Women with A Vision award Women's Bar Assn. Ill., 1998; named one of 10 Women of Achievement Midwest Women's Ctr., Chgo., 1987, Advt. Woman of Yr. Women's Advt. Club, Chgo., 1988; inducted City of Chgo. Women's Hall of Fame, 1988. Mem. Chgo. Network, Econ. Club Chgo., Execs. Club Chgo., Com. of 200 (founding mem.). Office: Leigh Communications Inc 150 E Huron St Ste 1225 Chicago IL 60611-2872 E-mail: sleigh@todayschicagowomen.com.

LEIGHTON, ANNE RENITA, writer, educator; b. Queens, N.Y., Oct. 15, 1957; d. Richard Eli Leighton and Halin Pryves. Student, Fredonia State U., 1976—80, Lehman Coll., 2002—. Radio personality WBUZ, Fredonia, NY, 1976—80, WZIR, Buffalo, 1980—81, WRNW, Briarcliff Manor, NY, 1981—82; editor Hit Pardder, N.Y.C., 1986—94; publicist Leighton Media-Motivation-Mktg., Bronx, NY, 1993—; tchr. Baruch Coll., N.Y.C., 1996—. Mentor Just Plainfolks, 1998—2003. Author: (plays) Reach for the Sun, 1976; contbr. articles to jours. Writer, event planner City Critters, N.Y.C., 1998, 2003; writer Poor Friends St. Francis, Bronx, 2003. Democrat. Avocations: animal rescue, art, films, music. Home: 3050 Decatur Ave #1D Bronx NY 10467

LEIGHTON, CAROL, retired educator; b. Kansas City, Mo., Mar. 6, 1944; d. Verl Leon and Josephine Ruth Clemans; m. Wallace Ralph Leighton, Aug. 10, 1968. AA, Neosho County C.C., Chanute, Kans., 1963; BA, U. Kans., 1966; postgrad., London U., 1978; MLA, Baker U., 1985. Paralegal, dep. pub. adminstr. Ralph Martin Pub. Adminstr., Kansas City, Mo., 1972—74, Jackson County Mo. Pub. Adminstr., Kansas City, 1974—76; paralegal probate Barr, Glynn & Morris, Kansas City, 1976—77; paralegal, asst. mgr. Devinki Developers, Kansas City, 1977—80; adminstrv. asst. Program for Adult Coll. Edn. Longview C.C., Lee's Summit, Mo., 1980—82; dir., adj. faculty Program for Adult Coll. Edn. Kansas City (Kans.) C.C., 1982—2001, equivalency specialist, 2001—02; ret., 2002. Sec. bd. dirs. Gorilla Theatre Prodns., Kansas City, Mo., 1991—2004. Election supr. judge Kansas City Mo. Bd. Elections Commn., 2002—. Mem.: Bat Conservation Internat. Democrat. Roman Catholic. Avocations: playing fiddle and guitar, wildlife photography, bluegrass, country and folk music, environmental protection, civil and human rights promoting. Home: 3820 Campbell Kansas City MO 64109

LEIGHTON, CAROLYN, foundation administrator; b. Providence, R.I. BS in Human Devel., Pacific Oaks Coll. Founder Leighton Corp., 1978—82, Legal Talent Directory, 1982—; chmn. Core Competency Database Project Stanford (Conn.) U., 1982—84; founder Criterion Rsch., Sherman Oaks, Calif., 1984—89, Women in Tech. Internat., Sherman Oaks, 1989—. Office: Women in Tech Internat 13351 0 Riverside Dr 441 Sherman Oaks CA 91423*

LEIGHTON, FRANCES SPATZ, writer, journalist; b. Geauga County, Ohio; m. Kendall King Hoyt, Feb. 1, 1984 (dec. Aug. 2001). Student, Ohio State U. Washington corr. Am. Weekly, Internat. News Svc.; corr. and Washington editor This Week Mag.; Washington corr. Met. Group Sunday Mags.; contbg. editor Family Weekly; free-lance journalist Metro Sunday Group, Washington. Lectr. summer confs. Dellbrook-Shenandoah Coll., Georgetown U., Washington Author over 30 books on hist. figures, celebrities, Hollywood, psychiatry, the White House and Capitol Hill, 1957—; (with Louise Pfister) I Married a Psychiatrist, 1961, (with Francois Rysovy) A Treasury of White House Cooking, 1968, (with Frank S. Caprio) How to Avoid a Nervous Breakdown, 1969, (with Mary B. Gallagher) My Life with Jacqueline Kennedy, 1969, (with Traphes Bryant) Dog Days at the White House, 1975, (with William Fishbait Miller) Fishbait— the Memoirs of the Congressional Doorkeeper, 1977, (with Lillian Rogers Parks) My 30 Years Backstairs at the White House (made into TV mini-series), 1979, (with Hugh Carter) Cousin Beedie, Cousin Hot--, My Life with the Carter Family of Plains, Georgia, 1978, (with Jerry Cammarata) The Fun Book of Fatherhood-or How the Animal Kingdom is Helping to Raise the Wild Kids at Our House, 1978, (with Natalie Golos) Coping with Your Allergies, 1979, (with Ken Hoyt) Drunk Before Noon— The Behind the Scenes Story of the Washington Press Corps, 1979, (with Louis Hurst) The Sweetest Little Club in the World, The Memoirs of the Senate Restaurateur, 1980, (with John M. Szostak) In the Footsteps of Pope John Paul II, 1980, (with Lillian Rogers Parks) The Roosevelts, a Family in Turmoil, 1981, (with June Allyson) June Allyson, 1982, (with Beverly Slater) Stranger in My Bed, 1985 (made into TV movie, 1987), The Search for the Real Nancy Reagan, 1987, (with Oscar Collier) How To Write and Sell Your First Nonfiction Book, 1990, How to Write and Sell Your First Novel, 1986, rev. edit., 1998, (with Stephen M. Bauer) At Ease at the White House, 1991; contbg. author: Katherine Graham's Washington, 2002; contbr. numerous feature stories on polit., social and govtl. personalities to various publs. Bd. dirs. Nat. Found., from 1963. Recipient Edgar award, 1961 Mem. AAUW, Senate Periodical Corr. Assn., White House Corr. Assn., Am. News Women's Club, The Writers Club, Nat. Press Club, Writers League of Washington (pres.), Washington League Am. Pen Women (pres.), Washington Ind. Writers, Smithsonian Assocs., Nat. Trust Historic Preservation, Lake Barcroft Women's Club, Delta Phi Delta, Sigma Delta Chi. Unitarian Universalist. Office: Lake Barcroft 6336 Lakeview Dr Falls Church VA 22041-1331

LEIH, GRACE JANET See FORELLE, HELEN

LEIMAN, JOAN MAISEL, hospital and university administrator, hospital administrator; b. Rochester, Minn., Apr. 26, 1934; d. John Josiah and Ida (Rubenstein)Maisel; m. Leonard M. Leiman June 26, 1955; children: Elizabeth, Alan. BA, Wellesley (Mass.) Coll., 1955; MA, Columbia U., 1958, MPhil, 1976, PhD, 1977. Prog. analyst N.Y.C. Bur. Budget, 1966-68, sr. budget examiner, 1968-69, asst. budget dir., 1969-71; advisor to Mayor N.Y.C. Govt., Office of Mayor, 1972-74; v.p. prog. devel. and budget Manpower Demonstration Research Corp., N.Y.C., 1977-81; v.p. planning Interfaith Med. Ctr., N.Y.C., 1982-84; exec. dep. v.p. Columbia U. Health Scis., N.Y.C., 1984-2001; chief of staff to the pres. and CEO, N.Y. Presbyn. Hosp. and Healthcare Sys., 2001—. Clin. prof. pub. health Columbia U., 1991—; pres. past. pres. Grad. Facules, Alumni of Columbia U., 1985-91; dir., vice chair N.Y. Found., 1985-93; del. White House Conf. on Aging, 1995; exec. dir. Commonwealth Fund Commn. on Women's Health, 1993-99; cons. in field. Durant scholar, 1954-55. Fellow: N.Y. Acad. Medicine (chair sect. health care delivery); mem.: Women's Health Forum, Am. Med. Women's Assn. Found. (bd. dirs. 1999—2001), Am. Assn. Med. Colls., Health Care Exec. Forum (v.p. 1986—87), YMCA Acad. Women Achievers, Women's City Club, Phi Beta Kappa. Office: NY Presbyn Hosp AP-1466 161 Ft Washington Ave New York NY 10032-3795

LEIN, HEBE BEATRIZ, psychologist; b. Rosario, Argentina, Mar. 18, 1945; came to U.S., 1979; d. Adolfo and Debora (Slepoy) L.; m. Leonardo Berezovsky, Nov. 13, 1968 (div. Nov. 1987); children: Karen, Sonia. M in Psychology, U. Rosario, 1967; PhD in Psychology, U.S. Internat. U., San Diego, 1982. Lic. psychologist, Calif. Cons. psychologist Regional Ctrs., L.A., 1985-87; mem. panel of experts L.A. Superior Ct., Calif., 1986—; pvt. practice psychologist L.A., 1986—; cons. psychologist Mc Laren Hall, El Monte, Calif., 1990—. Mem. Am. Psychol. Assn. Office: 3407 W 6th St Ste 803 Los Angeles CA 90020-2555

LEINEN, MARGARET SANDRA, oceanographic researcher; b. Chgo., Sept. 20, 1946; d. Earl John and Ester (Louis) Leinen; 1 child, Daniel Glenn Whaley. BS, U. Ill., 1969; MS, Oreg. State U., 1975; PhD, U. R.I., Kingston, 1980. Marine scientist U. R.I., Kingston, 1980-82, asst. rsch. prof., 1982-86, assoc. prof., 1986-88, prof., 1988—, assoc. dean, 1988-92, dean and vice provost, 1992—; asst. dir. geoscis. NSF, Alexandria, Va. Office: NSF 4201 Wilson Blvd Rm 705N Arlington VA 22230-0001 E-mail: mleinen@nsf.gov.

LEININGER, MADELEINE MONICA, nursing educator, consultant, anthropologist, therorist, editor, writer; b. Sutton, Nebr., July 13, 1925; d. George M. S. and D. Irene (Sheedy) L. BS in Biology, Scholastic Coll., 1950, LHD, 1976; MS in Nursing, Cath. U. Am., 1953; PhD in Anthropology, U. Wash., 1965; DSc (hon.), U. Indpls., 1990; PhDN (hon.), 1990, U. Kuopio, Finland, 1991. RN; cert. transcultural nurse FAAN/Am. Acad. Nursing. Instr., mem. staff, head nurse med.-surg. unit, supr. psychiat. unit St. Joseph's Hosp., Omaha, 1950-54; assoc. prof. nursing, dir. grad. program in psychiat. nursing U. Cin. Coll. Nursing, 1954-60; research fellow Nat. League Nursing, Papua New Guinea, 1960—62, 1978, 1992, 1994; research assoc. U. Wash. Dept. Anthropology, Seattle, 1964-65; prof. nursing and anthropology, dir. nurse-scientist PhD program U. Colo., Boulder and Denver, 1966-69; dean sch. nursing, prof. nursing, lectr. anthropology U. Wash., Seattle, 1969-74; dean coll. nursing, prof. nursing and anthropology U. Utah, Salt Lake City, 1974-80; Anise J. Sorell prof. nursing Troy (Ala.) State U., 1981; prof. nursing, adj. prof. anthropology, dir. Ctr. for Health Research, dir. transcultural nursing offerings Wayne State U., Detroit, 1981-95, prof. emeritus, 1995—; prof. Coll. Nursing U. Nebr. Med. Ctr., 1997—2001; ret., 2001—. Adj. prof. anthropology U. Utah, 1974-81; adj. prof. nursing U. Nebr., 1997—; disting. vis. prof. over 120 univs., U.S. and overseas, 1970—; docent Boys and Girls Town of Am., Omaha Father Flanaghan Ctr., 1996; cons. and lectr. in field. Author: 30 books including Nursing and Anthropology: Two Worlds to Blend, 1970, Contemporary Issues in Mental Health Nursing, 1973, Caring: An Essential Human Need, 1981, Reference Sources for Transcultural Health and Nursing, 1984, Basic Psychiatric Concepts in Nursing, 1960, Care: The Essence of Nursing and Health, 1984, Qualitative Research Methods in Nursing, 1985, Care: Discovery and Clinical-Community Uses, 1988, Ethical and Moral Dimensions of Caring, 1990, Culture Care, Diversity and Universality: A Theory of Nursing, 1991, 2002, 2d edit. 2003, Care: The Compassionate Healer, 1991, Caring Imperative for Nursing Education, 1991, Transcultural Nursing, 2d edit., 1995, (with M. McFarland) Transcultural Nursing Concepts, Theories, Research and Practice, 3d edit., 2002; editor, founder Jour. Transcultural Nursing, 1988-2000 (AJN award 2003); contbr. over 250 articles to profl. jours., chpts. to books. Recipient Outstanding Alumni award Cath. U. Am., 1969, Hon. award Am. Assn. Colls. Nursing, 1976, 96, Nurse of Yr. award Dist. 1 Utah Nurses Assn., 1976, Lit. award Utah Nurses Assn., 1978, Trotter Disting. Pub. Lectr. award U. Tex., 1985, Disting. Faculty Tchg. Recognition award Wayne State U., 1985, Outstanding Faculty Rsch. scholar award Wayne State U. and Gerontology Inst., 1985, Gershenson Rsch. award Wayne State U., 1985, Pace Inst. Rsch. award, 1992, Hewlett Packard Rsch. award, 1992, award for Acad. Excellence AAUW-Detroit, 1986, Disting. award Bd. Govs., 1987, Pres. Excellence in Tchg. award, 1988, Women of Sci. award U. Calif., Fullerton, 1990, Outstanding U. Grad. Mentor award Wayne State U., 1995, 97, Nightingale Rsch. award Oakland U., 1995, Outstanding Nursing Leader Russell Sage Coll, Sigma Theta Tau Intl. Disting. scholar award Russell Sage Coll., 1995, Nobel prize nominee, 1999, Can. Outstanding Rsch. award Can. Nurses Assn., 2003; Womens Hall of Fame, 2004, Leininger Learning and Transcultural Nursing Collection libr. and reading sects. at Madonna U., Livonia, Mich. named in her honor, 1996; Leininger Archival Room at Trinity Coll., Moline, Ill. named in her honor, 2002; Mary Boynton Disting. lectr., 1998; Disting. vis. scholar Jimmy Crockett Lectr. Series, Disting. Vis. scholar U. Nebr., 1999; named Disting. scholar U. Wis., 2001-02; Worldwide Transcultural Nursing Ctr. named in her honor, 2001; Dist. honoree Worldwide Transcultural Nursing Soc., 2003; Nominee Women's Hall of Fame, 2003. Fellow ANA, Am. Anthropol. Soc. for Applied Anthropology (exec. com. 1980-84), Am. Acad. Nursing (Living Legend award 1998), Royal Coll. Nursing Australia (First Internat. Achievement award 2000, First Qualitative Achievement award 2003); mem. Am. Assn. Humanities, Am. Applied Anthropol. Soc., Royal Coll. Nursing Australia, Mich. Nurses Assn. (Bertha Culp Human Rights award 1994), Ctrl. States Anthropology, Amnesty Internat., Transcultural Nursing Soc. (founder, bd. dirs., pres. 1974-80), Cultural Cmty. Group Assn. (ethics, humanities heritage study group), Australian Nat. Rsch. Care Confs. (leader human care rsch.), Internat. Assn. Human Caring (founder, pres., bd. dirs.), Nordic Caring Soc. Sweden (hon.), Sigma Xi, Pi Gamma Mu, Sigma Theta Tau (Lectr. of Yr. 1987—), Delta Kappa Gamma, Alpha Tau Delta. Office: 11211 Woolworth Plz Omaha NE 68144-1875

LEINO, DEANNA ROSE, business educator; b. Leadville, Colo., Dec. 15, 1937; d. Arvo Ensio Leino and Edith Mary (Bonan) Leino Malenck; 1 adopted child, Michael Charles Bonan. BSBA, U. Denver, 1959, MS in Bus. Adminstrn., 1967; postgrad., C.C. Denver, U. No. Colo., Colo. State U., U. Colo., Met. State Coll. Cert. tchr., vocat. tchr., Colo. Tchr. Jefferson County Adult Edn., Lakewood, Colo., 1963-67; tchr. bus., coord. coop. office edn. Jefferson HS, Edgewater, Colo., 1959-93, ret., 1993; sales assoc. Joslins Dept. Store, Denver, 1978—89; mem. ea. team. clk. office automation Denver Svc. Ctr., Nat. Pk. Svc., 1993-94; wage hour tech. US Dept. Labor, 1994—. Instr. C.C. Denver, Red Rocks, 1967-81, U. Colo., Denver, 1976-79, Parks Coll. Bus. (now Parks Coll.), 1983—, Front Range C.C., 1998-2000; dist. advisor Future Bus. Leaders Am. Author short story. Active City of Edgewater Sister City Project Student Exch. Com., Opera Colo. Assocs. and Guild, I Pagliacci; pres. Career Women's Symphony Guild; treas. Phantoms of Opera, 1982—; ex-officio trustee Denver Symphony Assn., 1980-82. Recipient Disting. Svc. award Jefferson County Sch. Bd., 1980, Tchr. Who Makes a Difference award Sta. KCNC/Rocky Mountain News, 1990, Youth Leader award Lakewood Optimist Club, 1993; named to Jefferson HS Wall of Fame, 1981, Jefferson County Hist. Commn. Hall of Fame, 2000, countess of the Wheat Ridge Carnation Festival, 2001. Mem. NEA (life), Colo. Edn. Assn., Jefferson County Edn. Assn., Colo. Vocat. Assn., Am. Vocat. Assn., Colo. Educators for and about Bus., Profl. Sec. Internat., Career Women's Symphony Guild, Profl. Panhellenic Assn., Colo. Congress Fgn. Lang. Tchr., Wheat Ridge C. of C. (edn. and scholarship com.), Federally Employed Women, Tyrolean Soc. Denver, Delta Pi Epsilon, Phi Chi Theta, Beta Gamma Sigma, Alpha Lambda Delta. Republican. Roman Catholic. Avocations: decorating wedding cakes, crocheting, sewing, music, world travel. Home: 3712 Allison St Wheat Ridge CO 80033-6124 E-mail: Leino.Deanna@dol.gov.

LEINS, CYNTHIA MARIE, school nurse practitioner; b. Attleboro, Mass., Apr. 5, 1951; d. George Vincent and Eleanor Isabelle Conley; m. Gregory Richard Leins, June 8, 1973; children: Michael Gregory, Jeffrey David, Kristen Michelle. BSN, Salve Regina Coll., Newport, RI, 1973. RN, Tex., 1973. Clinic nurse Blvd. Med. Clinic, Key West, Fla., 1973—74; staff nurse Hillcrest Med. Ctr., Tulsa, Okla., 1976—77, Meth. Hosp., Houston, 1977—78, St. David's Hosp., Austin, Tex., 1974—76, Meml. Hosp. SW, Houston, 1979—82; sch. nurse Hairgrove Elem. Sch., Houston, 1994—. Vol. Ronald McDonald Ho., Houston, Tex., 1983—84. Recipient Excellence in Sch. Health, Tex. Dept. of Health, 2001, Recognition at All Well Inst., Tex. Health Commr., 2002; grantee Instrnl. Excellence Grant, Cypress Fairbanks Ind. Sch. Dist., 2000-2001, Worksite Wellness Grant, Tex. Dept. of Health, 2002-2003. Mem.: Tex. Assn. Sch. Nurses Region IV (assoc.), Tex. Assn. Sch. Nurses (assoc.), Nat. Assn. Sch. Nurses (assoc.). Roman Catholic. Avocation: knitting prayer shawls. Office: Hairgrove Elementary 7120 North Eldridge Pky Houston TX 77041 E-mail: cynthia.leins@cfisd.net.

LEINWAND, DONNA CLAIRE, journalist; d. Michael H. and Judith I. Leinwand. BA in Journalism, U. N.C., 1989. Reporter The Miami (Fla.) Herald, 1989—97; fellow Casey Sch. Journalism U. Md., College Park, 1996; Washington corr. Knight-Ridder, Washington, 1997—99, Gannett News Svc., Washington, 1999; nat. reporter USA Today, Washington, 2000—. Instr. U. Md. Sch. Journalism, College Park, 2001. Mem.: Nat. Press Club (gov. 2002—, Vivian award for svc. 2001), Zeta Tau Alpha. Office: USA Today 7950 Jones Branch Dr Mc Lean VA 22108 E-mail: dleinwand@usatoday.com.

LEISETH, PATRICIA SCHUTZ, educational technology specialist; b. Menomonie, Wis., Dec. 13, 1942; d. Herb D. and Dorothy F. (Husby) Schutz; m. Keith M. Leiseth, June 12, 1964; children: Kirsten Leiseth Bobb, Jon. BA, Macalester Coll., 1964, MEd, 1972; MS, St. Cloud State U., 1994. Elem. music coord. Hopkins (Minn.) Pub. Schs., 1964-65; English instr. Bloomington (Minn.) Pub. Schs., 1965-67, Maple Lake (Minn.) Pub. Schs., 1974-90, vocal music tchr., 1990-93, K-12 technology coord., 1993-98; info. tech. specialist Dist. 279 Osseo (Minn.) Pub. Schs, Buffalo, 1998—. Vol., Buffalo (Minn.) Pub. Libr., 1993-94, Nat. Forest Svc., 1991, Okla. State Parks, 1997. Mem. NEA, Minn. Ednl. Media Orgn., Phi Kappa Phi. Avocations: reading, cross-country skiing. Home: 6051 Laurel Ave Golden Valley MN 55416 Office: Osseo Public Schs Dist 279 15900 Weaver Lake Rd Maple Grove MN 55311-1432 E-mail: Kpleiseth@aol.com.

LEISSNER, JANET, television news bureau chief; b. NY; Prodr. Can. Broadcasting Corp.; joined CBS, 1984—; prodr. Wash. bureau, CBS, 1984—96, sr. prodr., 1984—96, CBS Evening News, NY, 1996—99; v.p., bureau chief CBS News, Wash., 1998—. Bd. mem. Nat. Press Found. Named one of 100 Most Powerful Women in Wash., Washingtonian mag., 2001. Office: CBS News 2020 M St NW Washington DC 20036 Office Phone: 202-457-4321., 202-457-4401. Office Fax: 202-659-2586.*

LEITENBERGER, MAUREEN DORIS, art educator; b. Mineola, N.Y., Oct. 10, 1961; d. James Patrick and Joan Cullen Doris; m. Richard Vincent Leitenberger, Jr, Nov. 10, 1996; children: Kristi Badolato, Keri, Brandon. A in Liberal Arts, magna cum laude, Nassau C.C., Garden City, N.Y., 1990; BFA cum laude, N.Y. Inst. Tech., 1992; MS in Integrating Tech. in classroom, Walden U., Chgo., 2005. Collegiate profl. lic. State Bd. Edn./Commonwealth Va., 2001, cert. pub. sch. tchr. N.Y. Edn. Dept., 1993. Dental technician Denco Labs, Rockville Centre, NY, 1980—88; waitress J.T. Bullitt, Port Washington, NY, 1988—96; substitute tchr. Hicksville (N.Y.) Pub. Schs., 1992—94; art tchr. Edn. and Assistance Corp., Devel. Learning Program, Port Washington, 1994—97, The Lowell Sch., Flushing, NY, 1997—2000, Franklin County Pub. Schs., Rocky Mount, Va., 2000—. Mem.: Va. Art Edn. Assn. (assoc.), Nat. Art Edn. Assn. (assoc.). Home: 1656 Farm View Rd Glade Hill VA 24092

LEITER, BARBARA F. music educator; b. Phila., Sept. 14, 1948; d. Robert Frank and Betty VanBaalen Field; m. Robert Alan Leiter, May 6, 1973; children: Lauren, James, Rebecca. B.Mus.Edn., Temple U., 1970; postgrad., Pa. State U., U. of the Arts, Phila. Music tchr., dir. Sch. Dist. of Phila., 1970—73, Mitchell Main Line Day Sch., Haverford, Pa., 1973—75, Forman Ctr., Elkins Park, Pa., 1975—80; tchr. music Perelman Day Sch., Melrose Park, Pa., 1980—, Jenkintown Elem. Sch., Pa., 1980—. Swim dir. Pine Forest Camp, Greeley, Pa., 1980—94; dir. Broadway Style Prodns., 1982—; camp dir. Pine Forest Camp, 1994—96. Vol. USO, Phila., 2001—, Children's Hosp., Phila., 1995—96. Mem.: Am. Choral Dirs. Assn., Pa. Music Educators Assn. Avocations: needlecrafts, exercise. Home: 1002 Prospect Ave Melrose Park PA 19027 Office: Jenkintown Sch Dist West and Highland Jenkintown PA 19046

LEITER, ELAINE CAROL, technical writer; b. Pitts., Jan. 12, 1942; d. Joseph and Ruth Grumer; m. Kenneth C.W. Leiter, May 20, 1984. BS in English and Tech. Writing & Editing, Carnegie-Mellon U., 1963. Tech. pubs. editor U.S. Geol. Survey, Silver Spring, Md., 1963-72; tech. writer Otis Engrng. Corp., Carrollton, Tex., 1979-82, Syntech Internat., Inc., Richardson, Tex., 1982-87; cons. Dallas, 1987-96; tech. writer EDS, Plano, Tex., 1996—2001. Del. Senatorial Dist. Conv., Dallas, 1992, 96. Frances Camp Parry Meml. Book grantee, 1959-63; Carnegie scholar, 1959-63, C.S. May scholar, 1959-63. Mem. Soc. Tech. Comm., Bus. & Profl. Women, Hadassah. Jewish.

LEITES, BARBARA L. (ARA LEITES), artist, educator; b. Hamilton, Ohio, June 3, 1942; d. Wilbur Frank and Alice Marie (Butts) Mayer; m. William Michael Whitley, Oct. 29, 1972 (div. Nov. 1977); 1 child, Rachel; m. Andre Leo Leites, Dec. 15, 1981 (div. Mar. 2000); chldren: David, Bevin; 1 stepchild, Daniella. BFA, Miami U., Oxford, Ohio, 1964, MFA, 1967. Tchr. Madison Elem. Sch., Hamilton, 1964-65; tchr. art and humanities Key West (Fla.) H.S., 1967-70, tchr. adult edn. in art, 1968-70; instr. Fla. Keys Jr. Coll., Key West, 1969-70; co-dir. Kleinert Gallery, Woodstock, N.Y., 1977-80; self employed artist under the name Ara Leites, 1981—. Bd. dirs. Woodstock Guild of Craftsmen, 1978—79; instr. drawing and painting, divsn. head visual arts Georgiana Bruce Kirby Preparatory Sch., Santa Cruz, Calif., 1998—2001, ret., 2001; owner Ara Fine Art Giclee Studio; workshop instr. painting, Tuscany, 2001, ARA Fine Art Studio, Tuscany, 2002. Exhibited at Gallery El Ciruello, Tepoztlan, Mex., Club 209 Gallery, Cuernavaca, Mex., Black Sheep Art Gallery, Eng., Westminster Gallery, London, Cin. Art Mus., Dayton Art Inst., Springfield (Mo.) Art Mus., Miami U.; U.S. nat. exhbns. of over 200 shows and 70 awards including Rocky

Mountain Nat., Watercolor USA, Adirondacks Nat., Nat. Watercolor Soc., Am. Watercolor Soc., Audubon Artists, Phila. Watercolor Club, Allied Artists, N.Y.C., Calif. Nat. Watercolor Soc.; subject of articles in publs. Mem. AAUW, Internat. Soc. Exptl. Artists (signature), Am. Artists Profl. League (signature), Nat. Watercolor Soc. (signature), Nat. Soc. Painters in Casein and Acrylic (signature), Nat. Acrylic Painters Assn. (signature), Watercolor USA Honor Soc. (signature), Ky. Watercolor Soc. (signature), Tex. Watercolor Soc. (signature), Ga. Watercolor Soc. (signature), Mo. Watercolor Soc. (signature), Miss. Watercolor Soc. (signature), Phila. Watercolor Club Soc. (signature), Audubon Artists (signature), Mont. Watercolor Soc. (signature), Rocky Mountain Nat. Watercolor Soc. (signature), Fedn. of Can. Artists (signature), Soc. Layerists in Mixed Media (signature), Watercolor Soc. Ala. (signature), Pa. Watercolor Soc. (signature), Taos Nat. Watercolor Soc. (signature), Ea. Washington Watercolor Soc., Delta Delta Delta Alumnae Assn. Democrat. Avocations: gardening, carpentry, skiing, snowboarding, surfing. Home: 168 Oxford Way Santa Cruz CA 95060-6447 E-mail: araleites@sbcglobal.net.

LEITH, KAREN PEZZA, psychologist, educator; b. Providence, Sept. 27, 1948; d. Henry and Lucy Maria (Bevilacqua) P.; m. James Robert Leith, June 6, 1970; children: Douglas Clay, Cara Beth. BA, Brown U., 1970; MA in Religious Studies, John Carroll U., 1988; MA in Psychology, Case Western Res. U., 1995, PhD, 1997. Substitute elem. tchr. City of Chgo., 1970; math. tchr. Lane Tech. HS, Chgo., 1971; instr. preschool art and coordination programs Pk. Dist. Deerfield, Ill., 1973-75, coord. preschool day camp, 1975-80; jr. high religious edn. coord., catechist trainer Holy Cross, Deerfield, 1975-80; H.S. religious edn. coord. St. Mary parish, Hudson, Ohio, 1981-85, youth min., dir. religious edn., 1985-88, pastoral assoc., 1988-91; pvt. math. tutor Hudson, Aurora sch., Ohio, 1980-88; cons. for ministry devel. Diocese of Cleve., 1989—, steering com., instr., Faith and Justice Leadership Inst., 1995—; adj. faculty John Carroll U., 1988—97, 1998—99; rsch. asst. Case Western Res. U., 1993-97; adj. faculty Baldwin Wallace Coll., 1997—. Editor and contbr., chair com. manual on parish and sch. partnerships, Diocese of Cleve., 1997; adv. bd. Office on Women in Ch. and Soc., Diocese of Cleve., chair 1993-97; steering com. Cath. Diocese of Cleve. Social Justice Leadership Inst., 1995-98; coord. tng. Justice Tng. Diocese of Cleve., 2000—; exec. dir. Call to Renewal of Summit County, 2001--; presenter in field. Contbr. articles to profl. jours. Recipient Bishop Anthony M. Pilla Leadership award Roman Cath. Diocese Cleve., 1998, 2002; faculty rsch. grantee Baldwin Wallace Coll., 1997, grad. alumni travel grantee Case West Res. U., 1993-95. Mem. APA (grad. student travel award 1994), Am. Psychol. Soc., Midwestern Psychol. Assn., Soc. for Personality and Social Psychology, Cath. Commn. (bd. dir. 1984-2001, chair 1997-2001), Hudson LWV (bd. dir. 1980-92, v.p., treas.), Holy Ground (founder, spiritual dir.), mem., FutureChurch Leadership Coun., 2000-. Avocations: reading, needlework.

LEITZEL, JOAN RUTH, university president emerita; BA in Math., Hanover Coll., 1958; MA in Math., Brown U., 1961; PhD in Math., Ind. U., 1965. Instr. math. Oberlin (Ohio) Coll., 1961-62; asst. prof. math. Ohio State U., Columbus, 1965-70, assoc. prof., 1970-84, prof., 1984-92, vice-chmn. dept., 1973-79, acting chmn., 1978, assoc. provost, 1985-90; prof. dept. math. and stats. U. Nebr., Lincoln, 1992-96, sr. vice chancellor for acad. affairs, 1992-96, interim chancellor, 1995-96; pres. U. N.H., Durham, 1996—2002, pres. emerita, 2002—. Adv. com. Griffith Ins. Found., 1979-82; cons. Ohio Dept. Edn., 1980-83; participant Am. Coun. on Edn., 1980, 82; cons. Nat. Commn. on Excellence in Edn., U.S. Dept. Edn., 1982; univ. math. edn. del. to China, 1983; dir. divsn. materials devel., rsch. and info. sci. edn. NSF, 1990-92; presenter in field, 1980—; bd. dirs. Am. Assn. Higher Edn., chmn.-elect, 1996-97, chmn., 1997-98; mem. interpretive reports adv. bd. Nat. ssessment Ednl. Progress, 1995-98; trustee Consortium on Math. and Its Applications, 1994-95; mem. exec. coun. com. on acad. affairs Nat. Assn. State Univs. and Land-Grant Colls., 1994-96, bd. dirs., 1997-99, chmn. com. on faculty, 1994-96; coord. coun. for edn. NRC, 1993-95, mem. bd. on math. scis. edn., 1985-87, math. scis. edn. bd., chmn. 2000—. Bd. dirs. United Way Lincoln, 1995-96, 1st Plymouth Ch., 1996, Lincoln Partnership for Econ. Devel., 1996, N.H. Charitable Found., 1998-02, Durham Cmty. Ch., 1996-02. Recipient Disting. Alumni award Hanover Coll., 1986, dir.'s award for mgmt. excellence NSF, 1991; Disting. Tchg. award Ohio State U., 1982, Disting. Svc. award Ohio State U., 2002, Pettee medal U. N.H., 2002; grantee NSF, 1976-798, 84-88, Battelle Found., 1981-83, SOHIO, 1983-85. Mem. AAAS (edn. com. 1981-84), Am. Math. Soc. (com. on excellence in scholarship 1993-95), Assn. for Women in Math., Math. Assn. Am. (nominatinig com. 1978-79, com. on tchr. tng. and accreditation Ohio sect. 1976-79, nat. com. on undergrad programs 1982-85, chmn. joint task force on curriculum for grades 11-13 with Nat. Coun. Tchrs. Math. 1986-88), Nat. Coun. Tchrs. Math., Mortar Bd., Sigma Xi, Phi Kappa Phi. Home: 912 Linworth Village Dr Columbus OH 43235

LEIVE, CINDI, editor-in-chief; m. Howard Bernstein. With The Paris Rev, The Saturday Rev.; editl. asst., then dep. editor Glamour Mag., 1988—99; editor-in-chief Self Mag., 1999—2001, Glamour Mag., 2001—. Office: Glamour Mag 350 Madison Ave New York NY 10017-3704

LEKAS, MARY DESPINA, retired otolaryngologist; b. Worcester, Mass., May 13, 1928; d. Spyridon Peter and Merciny S. (Manoliou) L.; m. Harold William Picozzi. Student, Boston U.; BA, Clark U., 1949, DSc, ScD, Clark U., 1997; MD, Athens (Greece) U., 1957; MA, Brown U., 1986. Diplomate Am. Bd. Otolaryngology. Sci. instr. Hahnemann Hosp. Sch. Nursing; rotating intern Meml. Hosp., Worcester, 1957-58; resident in otolaryngology R.I. Hosp., Providence, 1958-62; resident in otolaryngology and otorhinolaryngology U. Pa. Grad. Sch. Medicine, 1960; surgeon in chief, dept. otolaryngology R.I. Hosp., 1984-96, surgeon-in-chief emerita; pvt. practice Providence, 1962—. Chmn. dept. otolaryngology Brown U., Providnce, 1984, clin. prof. emerita surgery divsn. otolaryngology, head and neck; cons. Cleft Palate Clin. and Craniofacial of R.I. Hosp., 1964—, VA Hosp., Providence, 1967—, St. Joseph Hosp., Providence, 1983—, Miriam Hosp., Providence, 1984—; lectr. profl. orgns.; mem. Project Hope in Columbia, Ceylon/Sri Lanka, SS Hope Hosp. Ship, People-to-People, Inc., Washington, 1968-69. Mem. editl. bd. Am. Jour. Rhinology, 1987—; contbr. articles to profl. jours. Mem. alumni coun. Clark U.; pres. Providence Med. Assn., 1987-88. Named R.I. Woman Physician of Yr., 1992; recipient Disting. Svc. award, Providence Med. Assn., 1996, Emeriti award, Brown U., 1999, Outstanding Svc. award, Brown Med. Alumni Assn., 1999, cert. of recognition, People-to-People, Inc.; fellow Jonas Clark fellow. Fellow ACS, Soc. Univ. Otolaryngologists-Head and Neck Surgeons, Triological Soc. (ea. sect. sec., Presdl. Citation 1993), Am. Acad. Otolaryngology-Head and Neck Surgeons (gov. R.I. chpt. bd. of govs. 1985-), Am. Acad. Facial Plastic and Reconstructive Surgeons, Am. Acad. Broncho-Escophalogy (treas., v.p. 1990); mem. AMA, Assn. Acad. Dept. Otolaryngology-Head and Neck Surgery, Deafness Rsch. Found., Am. Cleft Palate Assn., Am. Med. Women's Assn. (R.I. Woman Physician of Yr. 1992), Am. Broncho-Esophagological Assn. (hon.), New Eng. Otolaryng. Soc. (pres. 1987-88, Cert. of Recognition 1980-81), Centurion Club. Greek Orthodox. Avocations: cycling, swimming, church choir. Home: 129 Terrace Ave Riverside RI 02915-4726

LELAND, DIANA JEAN, music educator; d. Orvis and Althea Leland. MusB in Edn., Valparaiso U., 1969; MS in Tchg., U. Wis., Platteville, 1971. Choral dir. Janesville (Wis.) Pub. Schs., 1969—70; jr. high choral dir. Manitowoc (Wis.) Pub. Schs., 1971—74; choral dir. Edina (Minn.) Pub. Schs., 1974—80; gen. mgr. The Dale Warland Singers, St. Paul, 1980—83; choral dir./tchr. on spl. assignment Edina Pub. Schools, 1983—. Bd. mem. Sixth World Symposium on Choral Music, Mpls., 1998—2002. Contbr. articles to profl. jours. Recipient Arts Advocacy Leadership: Arts Coord. award, Minn. Alliance Arts in Edn., 2004. Mem.: NEA, ASCD, Edn. Edina Assn., Edn. Minn. Assn., Music Educators Nat. Conf., Internat. Fedn. for Choral Music (bd. dirs. 1996—2002), Chorus Am., Am. Choral Directors Assn. (life; state pres. 1979—81, north ctrl. divsn. pres. 1984—86, nat. pres. 1989—91, F. Melius Christiansen Lifetime Achievement award 2003).

LELAND, JANET K, social work therapist; b. Saginaw, Mich., Dec. 6, 1954; d. Ward Coville and Betty Jane (Brown) Leland; m. Loren Jeremy Young, June 5, 1982 (div. Apr. 1994); 1 child, Amanda R. Leland-Young. BA, Mich. State U., 1977, MSW, 1981. Cert. social worker, Mich. Instr. Lansing (Mich.) C.C., 1979-93; instr. social work Mich. State U., East Lansing, 1979-81; therapist Sanctuary for Runaways, Royal Oak, Mich., 1981-83; residential dir. Haven Battered Women's Shelter, Pontiac, Mich., 1983-84; family therapist, instr. Cath. Social Svcs. of Oakland County, Royal Oak, Mich., 1983-2000; with Oakland Family Svcs., Berkeley, Mich., 2000—. Bd. dirs. Listening Ear Crisis Ctr., East Lansing, 1979-80; cons. Ingham County Women's Commn., Lansing, 1980-81, Ingham County Prosecutors Office, Lansing, 1981-82; founder REACT-Rape Edn. and Counseling Team, East Lansing, 1981-82. Contbg. author: Women, Power and Therapy, 1988; author articles. Founding mem. Coun. Against Domestic Assault, Lansing, 1979; cmty. organizer Mich. State U. Rape Crisis Ctr., 1980. Recipient Cert. of Appreciation, Cooley Law Sch./Ingham County Women's Commn., 1994, NOW, 1981, others. Mem. Acad. Cert. Social Workers. Democrat. Avocations: garage sales, furniture painting, cooking. Office: Oakland Family Svcs 2351 W 12 Mile Rd Berkley MI 48072-1826 Home: 582 Liberty Pointe Dr Ann Arbor MI 48103-6806

LELAND, JOY HANSON, anthropologist, alcohol research specialist; b. Glendale, Calif., July 29, 1927; d. David Emmett and Florence (Sockerson) Hanson; m. David A. Riegert, Nov. 14, 1993. BA in English Lit., Pomona Coll., Claremont, Calif., 1949; MBA, Stanford U., 1960; MA in Anthropology, U. Nev., 1972; PhD in Anthropology, U. Calif., Irvine, 1975. With Desert Research Inst., U. Nev., 1961—, asst. research prof., 1975-77, assoc. research prof., 1977-79, rsch. prof., 1979-89, rsch. prof. emerita, 1990—. Author: monograph Firewater Myths, Frederick West Lander-A Biographical Sketch; contbg. author: Smithsonian Handbook of North American Indians; also articles, book chpts. Trustee Robert and Joy Leland Charitable Trust, 1992—. NIMH grantee, 1972-73; Nat. Inst. Alcohol Abuse and Alcoholism grantee, 1974-75, 79-81 Mem. Am. Anthrop. Assn., Southwestern Anthrop. Assn., Soc. Applied Anthropology, Soc. Med. Anthropology, Gt. Basin Anthrop. Conf., Phi Kappa Phi. Address: 6126 Carriage House Way Reno NV 89509-7326

LELE, AMOL SHASHIKANT, obstetrician and gynecologist; b. Chhindnara, India, May 23, 1944; came to U.S., 1970; d. Gajanan S. and Sarala S. (Manjrekar) Karande; m. Shashikant Lele, Feb. 28, 1970; children: Kedar, Rajal. MBBS, Bombay U., 1967, MD, 1970; D Ob-Gyn., Coll. Physicians, Bombay, 1969. Diplomate Am. Bd. Ob-Gyn. Clinician ob-gyn. clinic St. Luke's Hosp., Cleve., 1974; instr. SUNY, Buffalo, 1974-76, asst. prof., 1978-84, clin. assoc. prof., 1984—; fellow Children's Hosp., Buffalo, 1976-78, dir. women's svcs., 1976—, dir. outreach program, 1991-97; dir. prenatal care Erie County Med. Ctr., Buffalo, 1979-97; clin. chief ob-gyn. CHOB Kaleida Health Sys., 1999—. Mem. health com. Planned Parenthood, Buffalo, 1992-97; mem. infant mortality task force Health Systems Agy., Buffalo, 1994—. Avocations: reading, theater, light music. Home: 75 Nottingham Ter Buffalo NY 14216-3620 Office: 1275 Delaware Ave Ste 500 Buffalo NY 14209-2408

LELEWICZ, DEBORAH GATLIN (DEBBI LELEWICZ), artist; b. Dallas, Dec. 22, 1951; d. Herman Maurice and Irene (Evans) Gatlin; m. Kenneth Frank Lelewicz, May 17, 1975; 1 child, Veronica Sarah. AA in Edn., Tyler (Tex.) Jr. Coll., 1971; student, So. Meth. U., Dallas, 1971-74. Educator Richardson (Tex.) Montessori Sch., 1975-78; owner, operator Gold Mine Gallery, Plano, Tex., 1979-87; instr. art Heights Recreation Ctr., Richardson, 1987—. Cons Wildflower Festival, Richardson, 1993-95, Dallas Christmas Parade, 1993. Troop leader, recruiter Girl Scouts, Richardson, 1988-93, mem. adv. bd. Tex. coun., 1989-91; docent The Sixth Fl. Mus., Dallas, 1995—; treas. Greenwood Hills Neighborhood Assn., 2001, pres., 2002; sec. lecture series Friends of Richardson Pub. Libr., 2003—. Named Outstanding Leader Tex. Girl Scout Coun., Dallas, 1990, Green Angel award, 1991. Mem. Richardson Civic Art Soc., Vinyl Goddess Club Dallas (pres. bd. dirs. 1994—). Democrat. Methodist. Avocations: barbie doll collecting, tennis, gardening, reading. Home: 911 Wayside Way Richardson TX 75080-4018

LELYVELD, GAIL ANNICK, actress; b. Boston, May 22, 1948; d. Edward I. and Beatrice Elizabeth (Hewitt) L. BA in Polit. Sci., Boston U., 1970; MA in Polit. Sci., Goddard Coll., 1974; studies with Paul Barry, Peter Donat, Ray Reinhardt, Darrell Lauer, others. Actress, 1970—; tech. staff USA Prodns. and Midseason, Hempstead, N.Y., 1986-87, prodn. stage mgr., 1987—. Tech. staff Gray Wig, Hempstead, 1986, 87; cons. Talking With prodn. M.A., C.W. Post. Appeared in numerous films including Frances, Halloween III, Children On Their Birthdays, Project 1917, Rocky II, Happy Endings, Seeds of Innocence, Bonfire of the Vanities, The Music of the Heart, The Bird's Eye View, Insomnia, Monster Math, The Lesson, I'm Not Rappaport, City Hall, The House of the Venus Flytrap (ind. film), Believe for Hofstra University (film), Baby Buyer (NYU short film); (TV shows): Archie Bunker's Place, Mister Clown Says, White Noise, The Gentle Creature, (ABC Afterschool Spl.) Summer Stories: The Mall, Mathnet, Bill Cosby Murder Mystery, Cosby: You're OK, I'm Hilton, Upright Citizen Brigade; actor: Alice in Wonderland, Not So Grimm Fairytale Players; actress (Littletop Theater Co.) Toby Tyler, Marmalade Gumdrops, Bohemian Lights, King Lear - Tenant, Doctor & Knight Plainedge Playhouse, The Hostage, USA Prodns., The Cherry Orchard, Broadhollow Theater Bay Way Art Ctr., The House of Blue Leaves, The Lady of Larkspur Lotion, Broadhollow Theatre Bay Way Arts Ctr., Sarah Good and the Voice of Martha Corey, BDR Repertory Co., also The Worst Play in the World, Women's Theatrical Collective, The Man Who Came to Dinner, U.S.A. Prodns., Holocaust Survivor-Columbia Univ.; reader Yom Kippur Svcs., Temple Emanuel San Francisco; Singer: Gospel Oedipus at Colonus evangelist, townsperson, choir, Musicum Collegium Hofstra U., Pala Opera Assn., St. Patrick's Cathedral Choir, Temple Emanuel New Hyde Park Choir; singer and leader Christmas Carols Garden City Group Christmas Party, Garden City Group Chorus Holiday Songs and Soloist; soloist piano recital, solo singer Ecumenical Thanksgiving Svc.; one-person performance, Dona Gracia Nasi, Memoirs of Glüchel of Hameln, Temple Emanuel of New Hyde Park, Karen Finley Workshop Performance Arts; theater tech. involvement includes stage mgr., sound asst. Wings; sound asst. Danton's Death; asst. stage mgr. props, fx, dresser Accomplice; cons. on reading The Sisters Rosenweig. Mem. AFTRA Jewish. Avocations: reading, knitting, walking. Home: 291 Saville Rd Mineola NY 11501-1345 E-mail: Gail_Lelyveld@gardencitygroup.com.

LEMASTER, SHERRY RENEE, fundraising administrator, foundation administrator, consultant; b. June 25, 1953; d. William and Mary Charles (Thompson) LeMaster. BS, U. Ky., 1975; MS in Higher Edn. Adminstrn., Bryn Mawr Coll. Inst. for Women, 1984. Cert. fund raising exec. Lab. technician Cen. Ky. Animal Disease Diagnostic Lab., Lexington, 1975—76; grant coord., environ. specialist Commonwealth Ky. Dept. for Natural Resources and Environ. Protection, Frankfurt, 1976—78; coord. residence hall program Murray (Ky.) State U., 1978—80; dean students Midway (Ky.) Coll., 1980—81, v.p. devel. alumnae affairs, 1981—86; dir. devel. Wilderness Road Coun. Girl Scouts U.S., Lexington, 1986—88, Coll. of Agr. and Life Scis. Va. Tech., Blacksburg, Va., 1988—94; sr. major gifts officer Sch. Medicine Wake Forst U.; sr. major gifts officer NC Bapt. Hosp., Inc., Winston-Salem, 1994—98; exec. dir. devel. and alumni affairs U. Oklahoma City Health Scis. Ctr., 1998—2000; owner, cons. LeMaitre Fundraising and Found. Mgmt., 2001—. Amb. U. Ky. Coll. Agr.; cons. U.S. Dept. Edn., 1987—. Charter mem. planning com. Nat. Disciples Devel. Execs. Conf., 1984; chmn. Midway chpt. Am. Heart Assn., 1981; mem. Coun. for Advancement and Support Edn., 1981—, chmn. Ky. conf., 1982; mem. East Ky. First Quality of Life Coun., 1987—88; mem. adminstrv. bd. First United Meth. Ch., Lexington, 1982—84, 1987. Named hon. sec. state, 1984; named to Hon. Order of Ky. Cols., 1977, recipient Young Career Woman award, Bus. and Profl. Women's Club, Frankfurt, 1981. Mem.: Advancement Women in Higher Edn. Adminstrn. (former mem. state planning com. Ky.), Assn. Fundraising Profls. (bd. dirs. Lexington chpg. 1986), Jr. League, P.E.O. (charter mem., sec. chpt. AU-Va. 1991—93, Va. state chpt. amendments and accommendation com. 1990—92), U. Ky. Alumni Assn. (life), Ninety-Nines Internat. Assn. Women Pilots (vice chmn. Ky. Bluegrass chpt. 1986—87, chmn. bd. dirs. 1987—88, dir. South Ctrl. sect. 2000—02), Pi Beta Phi Nat. Alumnae Assn. (alumnae province pres. 1980—81, sec. bd. dirs. Ky. Beta chpt. 1982—84, pres. Va. Zeta chpt. house corp. 1991—94). Avocations: needlepoint, swimming, equitation. Office: 396 Hwy DD Defiance MO 63341

LEMASTER, SUSAN M. marketing executive, writer; b. Cody, Wyo., May 9, 1953; d. Floyd Morris and Virginia Kristena (Renner) LeM. AA, Casper Coll., 1977; BA, U. Wyo., Casper, 1979. Reporter, night editor Casper Star Tribune, 1972-76; copy editor, editor In Wyo. mag., Casper, 1979; info. dir. Wyo. Rural Electric Assn., Casper, 1980-81; story editor Wyo. Horizons mag., Casper, 1981-82; asst., instr. English lab. Casper Coll., 1982-84; mktg. mgr. Chen & Assocs., Inc., 1984-87; mktg. cons., 1987-90; dir. mktg. KaWES and Assocs., Inc., 1990-91, pub. rels. and mktg. cons., 1992-95; comm. mgr. Arthur Andersen, L.A., 1995-97, assoc. dir. sales and mktg., 1997-99, mktg. dir., 1999-2000, Pacific Region Bus. Consulting, 2000—01, mktg. mgr. healthcare, 2001—02; mktg. dir. PacifiCare Dental & Vision, Santa Ana, Calif., 2002—03; west unit mktg. leader Mercer HR Consulting, L.A., 2003—. Freelance writer and editor, 1982—; night sch. instr. Casper Coll., 1983-84, summer sch. instr., 1984. Editor Casper Jour., 1983-84. Recipient 1st Place News Story award Wyo. Press Assn., 1973, 1st Place Editing award Wyo. Press Women, 1980. Mem. L.A. Press Club, Phi Theta Kappa, Phi Kappa Phi, Alpha Mu Gamma. Democrat. Home: 1059 E Cypress Ave Burbank CA 91501-1309 Office: Mercer HR Consulting 777 S Figueroa St Los Angeles CA 90017

LEMAY, NANCY, graphic designer, painter; b. N.Y.C., Sept. 7, 1956; d. Michael and Mary Potenzano; m. Harry Adrian LeMay, Jan. 24, 1986. BFA with honors, Sch. Visual Arts, 1978; postgrad., NYU, 1981-84. Admissions counselor Sch. Visual Arts, N.Y.C., 1979-81, acad. advisor, 1981-84; asst. art dir. NYU, N.Y.C., 1984-87; graphic designer J. C. Penney, N.Y.C., 1987-89; art dir. Catch A Rising Star, N.Y.C., 1989; graphic designer WNBC TV News Graphics, N.Y.C., 1989-90; graphics engr. NBC Network News Graphics, N.Y.C., 1990-91, KCOP TV News, L.A., 1991-94, supervising graphic designer, 1994—2000; graphic designer KNBC-TV, 2000—01. Exhibited in group show Wings N Water Festival (poster winner), 1990; designer: (logotype design) Art Direction Mag. (Award of Merit), 1985; contbr. MacWeek Mag., 1989. Recipient 5 L.A. Area Emmy awards, 1996-99. Mem. AIGA, Acd. TV Arts and Scis. Avocations: painting, bird watching, sculpture, photography. Office: KCOP TV 915 N La Brea Ave Los Angeles CA 90038-2321

LEMBARK, CONNIE WERTHEIMER, art consultant; b. Omaha, Mar. 8, 1934; d. Sam Wertheimer and Elinor (Livingston) Wertheimer-Dombrowsky; m. Daniel Lembark, July 10, 1955; 1 child, Steven. Student, U. Ariz. Docent UCLA, 1964-71; owner, art cons. Connie W. Lembark, Nashville, 1992—2000, L.A.; owner, founding ptnr. Art Posters Ltd., L.A., 1971-82; art cons., 1983—. Lectr. L.A. County Mus. Art, 1994; founder Mus. Contemporary Art L.A. Author: The Prints of Sam Francis, 1992; Exhibited in group shows at Tenn. State Mus. Recipient Herb Alpert honoree, Lincoln Ctr., N.Y., 2001. E-mail: clembark@earthlink.net.

LEMBERGER, PHYLLIS, language educator, elementary school educator; b. N.Y.C., May 20, 1947; d. Morton Daniel Friedman and Elvera Soustiel; m. Kenneth Lemberger, June 22, 1968; children: Beth Lisa, Jeffrey Scott. BA, CUNY, Queens, 1967, MS in Edn., 1970. Cert. secondary fgn. lang. tchr. N.Y., 1967. Fgn. lang. tchr. Oceanside (N.Y.) Pub. Schs., 1967—73, Montclair Coll. Prep. Sch., Van Nuys, Calif., 1985—. Avocations: travel, opera. Office: Montclair Coll Prep Sch 8071 Sepulveds Blvd Van Nuys CA 91402

LE MENAGER, LOIS M. incentive merchandise and travel company executive; b. Cleve., Apr. 25, 1934; d. Lawrence M. and Lillian C. (Simicek) Stanek; m. Charles J. Blabolil (dec. 1982); children: Sherry L., Richard A.; m. Spencer H. Le Menager, Mar. 23, 1984. Grad. high sch. Travel counselor Mktg. Innovators, Rosemont, Ill., 1978-80, mktg. dir., 1980-82, chmn., CEO, owner, 1982—. Dir. Northwest Commerce Bank, Rosemont. Recipient Entrepreneurial Success award U.S. Small Bus. Adminstrn., 1999; named Supplier of Yr., J.C. Penney Co., Inc. Mem. NAFE, Am. Inst. Entrepreneurs (Entrepreneur of Yr. 1988), Am. Mktg. Assn., Internat. Soc. Mktg. Planners, Soc. Incentive Travel Execs., Am. Soc. Travel Agts., Nat. Fedn. Ind. Bus., Nat. Assn. Women Bus. Owners, Des Plaines C. of C., Rosemont C. of C., Chicagoland C. of C. (dir.), The Chgo. Network, Exec. Club (Chgo.). Congregationalist. Office: Mktg Innovators Internat Inc 9701 W Higgins Rd Des Plaines IL 60018-4703

LEMIEUX, LINDA DAILEY, museum director; b. Cleve., Sept. 6, 1953; d. Leslie Leo LeMieux Jr. and Mildred Edna (Dailey) Tutt. BA, Beloit Coll., 1975; MA, U. Mich., 1979; assoc. cert., Mus. Mgmt. Program, Boulder, Colo., 1987. Asst. curator Old Salem, Inc., Winston-Salem, NC, 1979-82; curator Clarke House, Chgo., 1982-84, Western Mus. Mining and Industry, Colorado Springs, Colo., 1985-86, dir., 1987—. Author: Prairie Avenue Guidebook, 1985; editor: The Golden Years--Mines in the Cripple Creek District, 1987; contbr. articles to mags. and newspapers. Fellow Hist. Deerfield, Mass., 1974—. Rsch. grantee Early Am. Industries Assn., 1978. Mem. Am. Assn. Mus., Am. Assn. State and Local History, Colo.-Wyo. Mus. Assn., Colo. Mining Assn., Mountain Plains Assn. Mus., Women in Mining, Colo. Mont. Wyo. State Conf. Edn. Com. NAACP. Mem. First Congl. Ch. Home: 1337 Hermosa Way Colorado Springs CO 80906-3050 Office: Western Mus Mining & Industry 1025 N Gate Rd Colorado Springs CO 80921-3018 E-mail: director@wmmi.org., lindalemieux1@aol.com.

LEMKE, JILL, city planner; b. Buffalo, Jan. 17, 1967; d. James Paul and Lynne Marie Lemke. BS in Comm., SUNY, Brockport, 1989; M of Regional Planning, Cornell U., 1997. Legis. intern Monroe County Legislature, Rochester, N.Y., 1989-90; comm. coord. N.Y. State Asembly, Rochester, 1991-94; rsch. and tchg. asst. Cornell U., Ithaca, N.Y., 1994-96; govt. rels. officer Greater Buffalo Partnership, 1997; planning specialist Buffalo Gen. Health Sys., 1997-98; outreach coord. Heart of the City Neighborhoods, Buffalo, 1998-99; dir. cmty. planning City of Buffalo, 2001—. Rsch. asst. Neighborhood Reinvestment Corp., Buffalo, 1996. Contbr. chpt. to book. Sec. 23d Legislature Dem. Com., Rochester, 1993-94; polit. organizer Dem. Com. and campaigns, Rochester and Buffalo, 1989—; mem., vol. Western N.Y. Hispanics and Friends Civic Assn., Buffalo, 1997—; vol. Habitat for Humanity, 1992-96; mem. housing com. Allentown Assn., Buffalo, 1996-99. Acad. All-Am. scholar, 1985-86; Dem. Women of the Legislature grantee, 1994. Mem. Am. Planning Assn., Am. Inst. Cert. Planners. Avocations: music, politics, painting, rollerblading. Office: City of Buffalo Mayors Office Planning Rm 920 City Hall Buffalo NY 14202 E-mail: jlemke@ch.ci.buffalo.ny.us.

LEMKE, JUDITH A. lawyer; b. New Rochelle, N.Y., Sept. 28, 1952; d. Thomas Francis and Sara Jane (Blish) Fanelli; m. W. Frederick Lemke, Apr. 1, 1980; 1 child, Morgan Frederick. Student, Manhattanville Coll., Purchase, N.Y., 1970-72; BA, Case Western Res. U., Cleve., 1974, MA, 1975,

JD, 1978. Sr. cert. pub. acct. Price Waterhouse, Cleve., 1978-81; assoc. Benesch Friedlander Coplan & Aronoff, Cleve., 1981-85; adjunct faculty Cleve. Marshall Coll. Law, 1982-86; ptnr. Benesch Friedlander Coplan & Aronoff, Cleve., 1986-94; prin. Kahn Kleinman Yanowitz & Arnson Co., Cleve., 1994-95; tax mgr. N.Am./L.Am. tax planning and compliance Chiquita Brands Internat., Cin., 1995-97, tax mgr. Europe, Colombia, Panama, 1998—, asst. v.p. taxation, 1998-99; v.p. tax Pepsi Bottling Group, Somers, N.Y., 1999—. Adj. faculty Case Western Res. U. Sch. of Law, 1993-95. Recipient Elijah Watt Sells award for highest distinction AICPA, N.Y.C. 1979. Mem. ABA, Ohio State Bar Assn., Internat. Fiscal Assn., Case Western Res. U. Undergrad. Alumni Assn. (exec. com. 1987-95, trustee 1987-95, chmn. spl. events com. 1989-90, pres. 1990-92, v.p. 1993-94). Avocations: wilderness canoe camping, guitar. Home: 39 Brundige Dr Goldens Bridge NY 10526-1413 Office: Pepsi Bottling Group 1 Pepsi Way Somers NY 10589-2204

LEMMON, JEAN MARIE, editor-in-chief; b. Duluth, Minn., Nov. 11, 1932; d. Lawrence and Marie Julien (Gunderson) Howard; m. Richard LuVerne LemMon, Apr. 17, 1965 (div. 1976); 1 child, Rebecca Jean. BA, U. Minn., 1954. Editor Better Homes and Gardens Mag., Des Moines, 1961—63, dept. head crafts, 1985—86, v.p., editor-in-chief, 1993—2001; women's editor Successful Farming, Des Moines, 1963—68; pres. Jean LemMon & Assocs., Des Moines, 1968—84; project editor Meredith Pub. Svcs., Des Moines, 1984—85; editor-in-chief Country Home Mag., Des Moines, 1986—93; adv. bd. Drake U. Journalism Sch., 1991—. Author: (book) Putting the Heart in Your Home, 2004. Mem.: Am. Soc. Interior Designers, MENSA Internat., ASCAP.*

LEMMON, NICOLETTE, small business owner, marketing professional; b. Phoenix, Sept. 23, 1956; d. Stanley Vaughn and Emma Lou (Nims) L.; m. Dennis Koepke, Dec. 31, 1996; 1 child, Amanda. BS, Ariz. State U., 1978, MBA, 1983. Sales rep. Cort Furniture Rental, Phoenix, 1978-79; advt. dir. Sun Lakes (Ariz.) Mktg., 1979-80; mktg. dir. Ariz. Telco FCU, Phoenix, 1980-84; pres. LemmonTree Enterprises, Tempe, Ariz., 1984—. Author: Successful Product Development: From Research to Results, 1995, Almost Famous: How to Market Yourself for Success, 1996. Bd. dirs., past pres. MBA Coun., Coll. of Bus., Ariz. State U., Tempe, 1992-96; bd. dirs. WalkAmerica chair, March of Dimes, Phoenix, Tempe Impact Edn. Found., 1992-94. Nominee Entrepreneur of Yr., Inc. Mag., Ariz., 1996; named one of Top 50 Women Bus. Owners in Ariz., Today's Ariz. Woman Success Mag., 1995. Mem. Am. Mktg. Assn. (bd. dirs. 1989—, pres. 1996-97), Nat. Spkrs. Bur., Credit Union Exec. Soc. Suppliers Forum, Ariz. State U. Alumni Assn. (bd. dirs. 1993—, chair 2001—02, Young Alumni Achievement award 1994). Republican. Presbyterian. Office: LemmonTree Enterprises Ste 103 1515 W University Dr Tempe AZ 85281-3279

LEMONCELLI, LORINE BARBARA, counselor, elementary school educator; b. Pittston, Pa., Sept. 28, 1958; d. Lawrence and Valerie (Mislevy) Dalessandro; m. Peter Jerome Lemoncelli, Oct. 24, 1987; 1 child, Violetta Enrica. BA in Tchg., Coll. Misiercordia, 1981; MA in Counseling, Marywood Coll., 1996; phlebotomy cert., Allied Med. Career, Scranton, Pa., 1986. Elem. tchr. Montessori Sch./ Scranton Sch. Dist., Scranton, 1990-92; counselor Act 1, Wilkes-Barre, Pa., 1995, Friendship House, Scranton, 1995, Keystone City Residence, Scranton, 1996-97, Scranton Counseling, 1997-2000, Cath. Social Svcs., 2000—02; tchr. Little People, 2003—04; retail bus. owner, 2004—. Mem. PTA Riverside H.S., Taylor, Pa., 1995—; religious studies tchr. St. Ann, 1997—. Mem. Am. Counseling Assn., Marywood Counseling Assn. (pres. 1995-96), Wyoming Valley Mental Health Assn., Chi Sigma Iota. Democrat. Roman Catholic. Avocations: walking, music, travel, reading. Home: PO Box 3061 Scranton PA 18505-0061

LEMONE, MARGARET ANNE, atmospheric scientist; b. Columbia, Mo., Feb. 21, 1946; d. David Vandenberg and Margaret Ann (Meyer) LeMone; m. Peter Augustus Gilman; children: Patrick Cyrus, Sarah Margaret. BA in Math., U. Mo., 1967; PhD in Atmospheric Scis., U. Wash., 1972. Postdoctoral fellow Nat. Ctr. for Atmospheric Rsch., Boulder, Colo., 1972-73, scientist, 1973-92, sr. scientist, 1992—; chief scientist Globe, 2003—. Mem. bd. on atmospheric sci. and climate NRC, 1993-97, 2001—; mem. sci. adv. com. U.S. Weather Rsch. Program, 1997-99. Contbr. articles to profl. jours.; contbg. author: D.C. Heath Earth Science, 1983-93; editor Jour. Atmospheric Scis., 1991-95. Woodrow Wilson fellow, NSF fellow, NDEA fellow, 1967. Fellow AAAS, Am. Meteorol. Soc. (councillor, mem. exec. com. 1992-96, Editor's award); mem. Am. Geophys. Union, Nat. Acad. Engring. Achievements include research in dynamics of linear convection (roll vortices) in daytime atmospheric boundary layer and its relationship to clouds; demonstrating that bands of deep convection (like squall lines) can increase the vertical shear of horizontal wind (contrary to conventional wisdom at that time); developing technique to estimate small fluctuations in air pressure from aircraft flying over land, used to estimate pressure field around clouds and storms. Home: 2048 Balsam Dr Boulder CO 80304-3618 Office: Nat Ctr Atmospheric Rsch PO Box 3000 Boulder CO 80307-3000 E-mail: lemone@ucar.edu.

LEMONNIER, SHARI SMITH, artist; b. Moses Lake, Wash., Jan. 22, 1958; d. Jerald E. and Darlene Wilhelmi Smith; m. Daniel Brian LeMonnier, May 27, 1995; children: Flynn, Claire. BFA, So. Meth. U.; MFA, Sch. Art Inst. Chgo. Sr. toy designer Breslow, Morrison, Terzian & Assocs., Chgo.; owner Wax Tadpole Gallery, Chgo.; owner, pres. Braindance, Inc., Munster, Ind.; owner Gallery Ex. 31, Munster. Juror Calumet Coll. Art Show, East Chicago, Ill.; artist in residence Epgostipi Kepamikh, Crete, Greece. Author: (lecture series video) Visualizing the Text Contemporary Christian Art, 2002, (video) Fresco Techniques, 2003. Active Towers of Angels Charity Print Fund Gallery Ex. 31, Munster, 2001—03. John Quincy Adams fellow, Art Inst. Chgo., 1982, Artist grant, Ind. Arts Coun., 2003, Profl. Artist resident, Sch. Art Inst. Chgo., 2003. Mem.: Illiana Artists, Christians in the Visual Arts, No. Ind. Arts Assn. (Jurors award 2000). Achievements include patents for hand held electronic game housing; research in Minoan Fresco techniques and pigment analysis. Avocations: polygot, winemaking, gardening, bicycling, travel. Home: 8540 Hawthorne Dr Munster IN 46321

LEMONS ODELL, LAUREN SHARNELLE, secondary school educator; b. Riverside, Calif., June 25, 1974; d. Powell Harmon and Virginia Darnelle Lemons, Martha Granados Lemons (Stepmother); m. Ryan Spencer Odell, June 9, 2001. BA in History and Polit. Sci., Vanguard U., 1996; MA in Theology, Fuller Theol. Sem., Pasadena, Calif., 1999. Student mentor, tutor Vanguard U., Costa Mesa, Calif., 1994—96; editor and asst. Artist Phyllis Neufeld, Fresno, Calif., 1997—98; distance learning asst. Fuller Theol. Sem., 1998—99; editor Barnabus Pub. Co., Pasadena, 1999; educator Fresno Unified Sch. Dist., 1999—. Newspaper advisor Roosevelt H.S., 1999—2001, yearbook advisor, 2000—, chair lang. arts, chair comm. com., participating mem. Raise the Bar com., 2002—; participating mem., grant participant Roosevelt Sch. of the Arts, Fresno. Coll. and career pastor, mem. women's bd. Bethel Christian Ctr., Fresno, 1997—98, young marrieds pastor, mem. welcome com., 2002—03. Named Student Body Favorite Tchr., Roosvelt H.S. Students, 2000. Mem.: ASCD, Calif. Assn. Bilingual Educators. Mem. Assemblies Of God. Home: 5746 E Erin Fresno CA 97327 Office: Fresno Unified Sch Dist 4250 E Tulare Fresno CA 93702 Personal E-mail: llemongirl@aol.com. E-mail: mrs_lemons_rhs@yahoo.com.

LENARD, MARY JANE, accounting and information systems educator; b. York, Pa., July 8, 1955; d. Martin and Anne Ruth (Zimmerman) Kondor; m. Robert Louis Lenard, July 9, 1977; children: Kevin, Kelsey. BS in Econ. and Adminstrv. Sci., Carnegie Mellon U., 1977; MBA in Fin., U. Akron, 1982; PhD in Bus. Adminstrn., Kent State U., 1995. Cert. mgmt. acct. Mgmt. trainee Equibank, NA, Pitts., 1977-78; acct., auditor Goodyear Tire and Rubber Co., Akron, Ohio, 1978-86; instr. U. Akron, 1986-93; mem. adj. faculty Cleve. State U., 1994-97; assoc. prof. Barton Coll., Wilson, NC, 1997—2001; asst. prof. U. N.C., Greensboro, 2001—. Author procs.; contbr. articles to profl. jours. Pres. Hillcrest Elem. PTA, Richfield, Ohio, 1992—93; v.p. Summit County PTA, Akron, 1994—96; mem., newsletter dir. Wakefield Mid. Sch. PTSA, 2000—02; coord. Vol. Income Tax Assistance, Barton Coll., Wilson, 1998—2001; active Revere Schs. Computer Curriculum Com., 1994—95; mem. Wakefield H.S. PTSA, 2002—; mem. and chair IT Com. for Acctg. Dept. at UNC, 2001—; mem. Bryan Sch., UNC Greensboro Planning Com., 2002—, Bryan Sch., UNC Greensboro Faculty Develop. Com., 2002—. Grantee Faculty Devel. grant, Barton Coll., 1997, 1999. Mem.: Decision Scis. Inst., Akron Women's Network, Assn. for Info. Systems, Inst. Mgmt. Accts. (dir. mem. retention 1994—96), Am. Acctg. Assn. (Best Paper award 1998), Beta Gamma Sigma. Office: U NC Bryan Sch Bus & Econ Greensboro NC 26165 Home: 3049 Imperial Oaks Dr Raleigh NC 27614-7001 E-mail: mjlenard@uncg.edu.

LENDERMAN, JOANIE, elementary school educator; b. Medford, Oreg., Jan. 20, 1946; d. Jay Lenderman and Vivian Spencer. BS in Edn., So. Oreg. Coll., Ashland, 1969; MS in Edn., Portland State U., 1972; postgrad., U. Va., 1985. Elem. tchr. Beaverton (Oreg.) Schs., 1972-76, Internat. Sch. Svcs., Isfahan, Iran, 1976-78; ESL instr. Lang. Svcs., Tucker, Ga., 1983-84; tchr. Fairfax (Va.) Schs., 1985-86; elem. tchr. Beaverton (Oreg.) Schs., 1990-96, Smithsonian Instn., 1996—. Mem. Smithsonian Instn. Home: 4105 Jefferson Pkwy Lake Oswego OR 97035-1479

LENDSEY, JACQUELYN L. foundation administrator; BS, Adelphi U.; MEd, Howard U. With pub. sch. sys., Prince George County, Md.; v.p. corp. and cmty. devel. Greater S.E. Healthcare; v.p. pub. policy Planned Parenthood Fedn. Am., N.Y.C., 1998—2001; pres., CEO Women in Cmty. Svc., Alexandria, Va., 2001—. Bd. dirs. Nat. Assembly Health and Human Svcs. Orgns., Reproductive Health Tech. Project. Mem.: Leadership Washington. Office: 1900 Beauregard St Ste 103 Alexandria VA 22311*

LENG, MARGUERITE LAMBERT, biochemist; b. Edmonton, Alta., Can., Sept. 25, 1926; came to the U.S., 1950; d. Joseph Edouard and Marie (Kiwit) Lambert; m. Douglas Ellis Leng, June 18, 1955; children: Ronald Bruce, Janet Leng Dumas, Douglas Lambert. BSc in Honours Chemistry, U. Alta., 1947; MSc, U. Sask., 1950; PhD, Purdue U., 1956. Rsch. asst. U. Mich. Med. Rsch. Inst., Ann Arbor, 1950-53; with agrl. dept. Dow Chem. Co., Midland, Mich., 1956-59, 66-76, with health and environ. scis. dept., 1976-86, mgr. internat. regulatory affairs, 1986-90; ret., 2002. Editor: Pesticide Chemist and Modern Toxicology, 1981, Agrochemical Environmental Fate Studies: State of the Art, 1995; contbr. articles to profl. jours., chpts. in books and encys. Life ins. med. rsch. fellow Equitable Life Assurance Co., 1949-50. Fellow: Am. Inst. Chemists (bd. dirs. 1991—97); mem.: Internat. Soc. for Study Xenobiotics, Am. Chem. Soc. (agrochem. divsn. fellow 1976, chmn. 1981, program chmn. 1980). Avocations: international travel, family activities, foreign languages, sailing. Home: 1714 Sylvan Ln Midland MI 48640-2538 E-mail: mlleng1@chartermi.net.

L'ENGLE, MADELEINE (MRS. HUGH FRANKLIN), writer; b. N.Y.C., Nov. 29, 1918; d. Charles Wadsworth and Madeleine (Barnett) Camp; m. Hugh Franklin, Jan. 26, 1946 (dec., 1986); children: Josephine Franklin Jones, Maria Franklin Rooney, Bion. AB, Smith Coll., 1941; postgrad., New Sch., 1941-42, Columbia U., 1960-61; holder 19 hon. degrees. Tchr. St. Hilda's and St. Hugh's Sch., 1960—; mem. faculty U. Ind., 1965-66, 71; writer-in-residence Ohio State U., 1970, U. Rochester, 1972, Wheaton Coll., 1976—, Cathedral St. John the Divine, N.Y.C., 1965— Author: The Small Rain, 1945, Ilsa, 1946, Camilla Dickinson, 1951, A Winter's Love, 1957, And Both Were Young, 1949, Meet the Austins, 1960, A Wrinkle in Time, 1962, The Moon by Night, 1963, The 24 Days Before Christmas, 1964, The Arm of the Starfish, 1965, The Love Letters, 1966, The Journey with Jonah, 1968, The Young Unicorns, 1968, Dance in the Desert, 1969, Lines Scribbled on an Envelope, 1969, The Other Side of the Sun, 1971, A Circle of Quiet, 1972, A Wind in the Door, 1973, The Summer of the Great-Grandmother, 1974, Dragons in the Waters, 1976, The Irrational Season, 1977, A Swiftly Tilting Planet, 1978, The Weather of the Heart, 1978, Ladder of Angels, 1980, A Ring of Endless Light, 1980, Walking on Water, 1980, A Severed Wasp, 1982, And It Was Good, 1983, A House Like a Lotus, 1984, Trailing Clouds of Glory, 1985, A Stone for a Pillow, 1986, Many Waters, 1986, Two-Part Invention, 1988, A Cry Like a Bell, 1987, Sole Into Egypt, 1989, From This Day Forward, 1988, An Acceptable Time, 1989, The Glorious Impossible, 1990, Certain Women, 1992, The Rock That Is Higher: Story As Truth, 1993, Anytime Prayers, 1994, Troubling a Star, 1994, Penguins and Golden Calves, 1996, A Live Coal in the Sea, 1996, Glimpses of Grace, 1996, Wintersong, 1996, Mothers and Daughters, 1997, Friends for the Journey, 1997, Bright Evening Star: Mystery of the Incarnation, 1997, The Other Dog, 2001. Pres. Crosswicks Found. Recipient Newbery medal, 1963, Sequoyah award, 1965, runner-up Hans Christian Andersen Internat. award, 1964, Lewis Carroll Shelf award, 1965, Austrian State Lit. award, 1969, Bishop's Cross, 1970, U. South Miss. medal, 1978, Regina medal, 1985, Alan award Nat. Coun. Tchrs. English, 1986, Kerlan award, 1990, Margaret Edwards award, 1998; collection of papers at Wheaton Coll. Mem. Authors Guild (mem. council), Authors League (mem. council), Writers Guild Am. Episcopalian. Office: Cathedral Libr St John the Divine 1047 Amsterdam Ave New York NY 10025-1747 also: care Random House Children's Media 1540 Broadway New York NY 10036-4039*

LENHART, CYNTHIA RAE, conservation organization executive; b. Cheverly, Md., Nov. 3, 1957; d. Donald Edward and Vesta Jean (Morris) L. BS in Environ. Studies, Coll. William & Mary, 1979; MS in Environ. Sci., SUNY, Syracuse, 1983. Asst. to pres. Environ. Policy Inst., Washington, 1979-81; wildlife policy analyst Nat. Audubon Soc., Washington, 1984-90; exec. dir. Hawk Mountain Sanctuary, Kempton, Pa., 1990—. Bd. dirs. Am. Bird Conservancy, Washington, Pa. Environ. Coun., Phila. Contbr. chpts. to Audubon Wildlife Report, 1985, 87, 88, 89. Chair Everglades Coalition, Washington, 1986-88. Office: Hawk Mountain Sanctuary 1700 Hawk Mountain Rd Kempton PA 19529-9379 E-mail: lenhart@hawkmountain.org.

LENHART, LORRAINE MARGARET, county official; b. Schuylkill County, Pa., Nov. 18, 1944; d. Thomas Edward and Margaret Elizabeth (Klinger) Kimmel; m. William Charles Reber II, May 10, 1964 (div. 1968); 1 child, William Charles II; m. Kenneth Edward Lenhart, June 30, 1972; children: Vickie Elaine Lenhart Marino, Sonya Lynn Lenhart Yost. Grad. H.S., Mifflinburg, Pa., 1962; Cert. sect. I, II, III, Pa. Land Title Inst., 1988; instrn. course cert., Pa. State Mcpl. Ofcl. Instrn., 1992; Newly Elected Officials Tng. I, II Cert., Commonwealth of Pa., 1994, Mcpl. Fin. Elected Officials, 1995; genealogy cert., Williamsport Area C.C.; estate planning course cert., Pa. State Co-op Ext. Leadership Susquehanna Valley Program cert. Various positions; deputy register and recorder Union County Pa., Lewisburg, 1978-95, register of wills, recorder of deeds, 1996—. Mem. Preservation Mifflinburg Inc.; former dir. Am. Cancer Soc., Susquehanna Valley, Lewisburg, Pa.; past coun. mem. Postal Customer Adv. Coun., Mifflinburg; mem. Union County Hist. Soc., Lewisburg; past mem. Bald Eagle State Forest Roundtable, Mifflinburg, OUE, Allenwood, Pa.; vol. Union County Emergency Svcs., Lewisburg; past dir. Ctrl. Susquehanna unit Am. Cancer Soc., Union County Found., Lewisburg, 1997—2003; former councillor and v.p. Mifflinburg Borough Coun.; cert. Leadership Susquehanna Valley; past treas. Mifflinburg Hist. Soc.; past dir. Buffalo Creek Watershed Alliance; mem. Union County Coun. of Rep. Women, Pa. Coun. Rep. Women; committeeperson Union County Rep. Com., East Ward, Mifflinburg; past bd. dirs. Mifflinburg Hist. Soc. Mem.: Register of Wills and Clk. of Orphan's Ct. Assn. Pa., Pa. Recorder of Deeds Assn., Internat. Assn. Clks., Recorders, Election Ofcls. and Treas., Kiwanis Club of Buffalo Valley A.M. of Lewisburg (past sec.). Republican. Lutheran. Avocations: reading, needlework, gardening. Office: Union County Court House 103 S 2d St Lewisburg PA 17837-1996 Office Phone: 570-524-8761.

LENIHAN, BARBARA DESCH, neonatal clinical nurse specialist; b. Jamaica, N.Y., Aug. 7, 1952; d. Carl William and Katharine (Woerner) Desch; m. Michael Daniel Lenihan, Oct. 5, 1974; children: Kathryn, Laura, Michael. BSN, Columbia U., 1974; MS in Parent/Child Nursing, Adelphi U., 1987. RN, Mass.; IBCL,; N.Y. Staff nurse pediatrics L.I. Jewish Med. Ctr., New Hyde Park, N.Y., 1974-77, staff nurse newborn nursing, 1977-81, advanced practice nurse, 1981-85, clin. nurse specialist, 1986-96. Apnea infant/SIDS program Schneider Children's Hosp., neonatal, lactation cons.; instr. BLS Am. Heart Assn., Mineola, N.Y., 1991—. Co-author: Our Baby is Coming Home, 1992. Mem. Columbia U. Nursing Alumni, Nat. Assn. of Neonatal Nurses, Internat. Lactation Cons. Assn., Sigma Theta Tau. Avocations: jogging, golf, needlework. Home: 58 Osgood St North Andover MA 01845-4528

LENKE, JOANNE MARIE, publishing executive; b. Chgo., Aug. 27, 1938; d. August Julian and Dorothy Anna (Gold) L. BS, Purdue U., 1960; MS, Syracuse U., 1964, PhD, 1968. Tchr. pub. schs., Evanston, Ill., 1960-63; editor Test Dept. Harcourt, Brace & World, Inc., N.Y.C., 1967-70; rsch. psychologist Harcourt Brace Jovanovich, Inc., N.Y.C., 1970-73, exec. editor, 1973-75; asst. dir. ednl. measurment divsn. The Psychol. Corp., N.Y.C., 1975-83, dir. ednl. measurement and psychometrics Cleve., 1983-85, San Antonio, 1986, v.p. dir. measurement divsn., 1986-88, sr. v.p., 1988-91, exec. v.p., 1991-97, pres., 1997-99; cons., 1999—2002; assoc. v.p. Ednl. Testing Svc., 2002—. Field reader U.S. Office Edn., 1972. Adv. editor Jour. Ednl. Measurement, 1974-78. NSF grantee, 1963-64. Mem. APA, Nat. Coun. Measurement in Edn., Am. Ednl. Rsch. Assn. Home: 1311 Vista Del Monte San Antonio TX 78216-2229 E-mail: jlenke@usa.net.

LENN, MARJORIE PEACE, education association administrator, consultant; b. Bowling Green, Ohio, Jan. 17, 1946; d. Frederick Elwynn and Nelvia P. Peace; m. D. Jeffrey Lenn; 1 child, Rebecca. BA, Transylvania Coll., 1968; M in Arts and Religion, Yale U., 1970; MEd, U. Mass., 1973, EdD, 1978. Dir. student svcs. U. Mass., Amherst, 1970-79, dir. residential life, 1979-82; dir. profl. svcs. Coun. on Postsecondary Accreditation, Washington, 1982-89, v.p., 1989-92, exec. dir. Ctr. for Quality Assurance in Internat. Edn., Washington, 1992—, Global Alliance for Transnat. Edn., Washington, 1996—2000. Cons. govts. China, India, Indonesia, South Africa, Mex., Belize, Argentina, Chile, Mauritius, Romania, Hungary and others in higher edn. reform, 1991—; spl. adviser on trade in edn. svcs. U.S. Govt., 2000—. Author: International Developments in Assuring Quality in Higher Education, 1994, Ambassadors of U.S. Higher Education: Quality Credit Bearing Programs Abroad, 1997, Globalization of the Professions and the Quality Imperative, 1997, Multinational Discourse on Professional Accreditation, Certification, and Licensure: Bridges for the Globalizing Professions, 1998, The Foundations of Globalization of Higher Education and the Professions, 1999, The Globalization of the Professions in the United States and Canada: A Survey and Analysis, 2000, Higher Education and Training in the Global Marketplace: Exporting Issues and the Trade Agreements, 2002; author: (with others) Ethics in Higher Education, 1990; editor: New England Consultation Network, 1978, Site Visitors in the Accreditation Process: A Guide to Issues and Practical Concerns, 1988, International Education and Accreditation: Uncharted Waters, 1990, Conflicts of Interest in the Accreditation Process, 1991, Distance Learning and Accreditation, 1991, Diversity, Accessibility, and Quality: An Introduction to Education in the United States for Educators for Other Countries, 1995; editor, contbr. Globalization of Higher Education and the Professions: The Mobility of Students, Scholars, and Professionals, 1993, Globalization of Education and the Professions: The Case of North America, 1994, (series) Studying in the United States, 1994; contbr. articles to profl. jours. Bd. dirs. Regents Coll., 1996-98, Hong Kong Coun. Acad. Accreditation, 1989-92; v.p. adminstrv. Women's Nat. Dem. Club, Washington, 1990-91; elder Old Presbyn. Meeting House, Alexandria, Va., 1983—. Recipient Outstanding Alumni award Transylvania U., 1998, Outstanding Contbn. to Global Higher Edn. award Assn. Christian Colls. and Univs., Internat. Ecumenical Forum, 1998. Fellow Soc. for Values in Higher Edn. (bd. dirs. 1994-95); mem. Women Adminstrs. in Higher Edn. (bd. dirs. 1984-90), Internat. Network Quality Assurance Agys. in Higher Edn. (bd. dirs. 1994—), Sigma Kappa (Colby award for outstanding svc. 2000). Democrat. Presbyterian. Avocations: choral music, travel. Office: Ctr for Quality Assurance in Int Edn Nat Ctr for Higher Edn 1 Dupont Cir NW Ste 515 Washington DC 20036-1135 E-mail: cqaie@aacrao.org.

LENNON, AMY JO, elementary school educator, principal; b. Watertown, N.Y., Feb. 28, 1958; d. William Arnold and Evelyn Louise (Timerman) L. A in Edn., Cazenovia (N.Y.) Coll., 1978; BS in Edn., SUNY, Cortland, 1980; MS in Edn., U. N.Mex., 1982. Cert. tchr., N.Y. Lifeguard Gloversville (N.Y.) City Dept. Recreation, 1977-83; tchr. phys. edn. Middleburgh (N.Y.) Ctrl. Sch., 1983—. Curriculum coord. Middleburgh Ctrl. Sch., 1990—, citizen mgrs. cons., 1993—, mem. discipline task force, 1995—. Mem. ARC, 1976—; fund raiser Cmty. Playground Project, Middleburgh, 1990-91; co-organizer Cmty. Girls Basketball Camp, Middleburgh, 1990—. Recipient award for 300 hours of svc. ARC, 1984. Mem. AAHPERD (profl.), Nat. Assn. Girls and Women's Sports (profl.), N.Y. State Alliance Health, Phys. Edn., Recreation and Dance (profl.). Office: Middleburgh Ctrl Sch PO Box 850 Middleburgh NY 12122

LENNON, ELIZABETH MARIE, retired educator; b. Chgo., Apr. 29; d. John Joseph and Johanna Amelia (Pfaff) L. AB, Ind. U., 1941; postgrad., Butler U., 1946, N.C. State U., 1956, San Francisco State U., 1960; MA in Edn. of Physically Handicapped, Columbia U., 1947. Elem. tchr., typing tchr. Ind. Sch. for the Blind, 1941-51; lower sch. tchr. Perkins Sch. for the Blind, 1951-53; tchr., insvc. coord. Gov. Morehead Sch., Raleigh, N.C., 1953-64; staff devel. specialist N.C. Commn. for the Blind, 1964-67; asst. prof. blind rehab. Western Mich. State U., Kalamazoo, 1967-78, part-time asst. prof. blind rehab., 1978-81, 88. Author publs. in field. Bd. dirs. Nat. Accreditation Coun. for Agys. Serving the Blind and Visually Impaired, 1976-83; vice chair Mich. Commn. for the Blind, 1978-84; vice chair bd. dirs Shepherd's Ctr. of Greater Kalamazoo, 1989-90, chmn., 1990—; sec. Affiliated Leadership League of and for the Blind of Am., 1978-91; bd. dirs. Southcentral Mich. Commn. on Aging, 1978-91, sec., 1986-88; sec. Am. Coun. of the Blind, 1988-90; bd. dirs. Voluntary Action Ctr. of Greater Kalamazoo, 1986—; bd. dirs., mem. com., founder Kalamazoo Ctr. for Ind. Living, 1980—; pres. Coun. of Citizens with Low Vision, 1985-88. Recipient Robert D. Mahoney award for Outstanding Svc. to Visually Impaired of Mich., Mich. Assn. of Blind and Visually Impaired, 1978, Clare Lynch award Kalamazoo Coun. of the Blind, 1981, George Card award for Outstanding Svc. to Visually Imparied Nationwide, Am. Coun. of the Blind, 1983, Spl. Tribute, State of Mich., 1984, Lifetime Achievement award Kalamazoo Ctr. for Ind. Living, 1987, Outstanding Svc. to the Older Citizens of S.W. Mich., Mich. Legislature, 1990, Jim Neubacher Lifetime Achievement award Kalamazoo Ctr. for Ind. Living, 1991, Golden Bell award J.C. Penney, 1992. STAR award, Volutary Action Ctr. of Kolonozoo for Cmty. svc., 2002. Mem. Assn. for Edn. and Rehab. of the Blind and Visually Impaired (mem. various coms. on state and nat. levels), Coun. for Exceptional Children, Mich. Assn. of Transcribers for the Visually Impaired (past pres., editor newletter, bd. dirs., founding mem.). Avocations: reading, music, travel. Home: 1400 N Drake Rd Apt 218 Kalamazoo MI 49006-3951

LENNOX, HEATHER, lawyer; b. Cleve., Sept. 22, 1967; d. Rand Tru and Leilani Marie (Petrovich) L.; m. Douglas Robert Krause, Sept. 17, 1994. BA summa cum laude, John Carroll U., 1989; JD cum laude, Georgetown U., 1992. Bar: Ohio 1992, U.S. Dist. Ct. (no. dist.) Ohio 1992. Ptnr. Jones

Day, Cleve., 1992—. Contbr. articles to law jours. Mem. Ohio Bar Assn., Cleve. Bar Assn. Avocations: reading, music, cooking, outdoor activities, theater. Office: Jones Day North Point 901 Lakeside Ave E Cleveland OH 44114-1190

LENOIR, GLORIA CISNEROS, consultant, educator; b. Monterrey, Nuevo León, Mex., Aug. 18, 1951; came to U.S., 1956, naturalized; d. Juan Antonio and Maria Gloria (Flores) Cisneros; m. Walter Frank Lenoir, June 6, 1975; children: Lucy Gloria, Katherine Judith, Walter Frank IV. Student, Inst. Am. Univs., 1971-72; BA in French Art, Austin Coll., 1973, MA in French Art, 1974; MBA in Fin., U. Tex., 1979, postgrad. in Ednl. Policy and Planning, 2001—03. French tchr. Sherman (Tex.) H.S., 1973-74; French/Spanish tchr, dept. chmn. Lyndon Baines Johnson H.S., Austin, 1974-77; legis. aide Tex. State Capitol, Austin, Tex., 1977-81; stock broker Merrill Lynch, Austin, 1981-83, Schneider, Bernet and Hickman, Austin, 1983-84; bus. mgr. Holleman Photographic Labs., Inc., Austin, 1984-87, 88-90; account exec., stock broker Eppler, Guerin & Turner, 1987-88; ind. distbr. Austin, 1990-93; owner, cons. Profl. Cons. Svcs., Austin, 1991—2001; adj. faculty Spanish for internat. trade St. Edwards U., 1991-99; bilingual interviewer The Gallup Orgn., 1997-98; Spanish tchr., club sponsor Hyde Park Bapt. Schs., 1997-99; tchr. computer applications Travis H.S. Comm. Acad., 1999-2000, 9th grade coord., 2000—01; tchr. langs. Travis HS Comm. Acad., 2001—. Group counselor, organizer Inst. Fgn. Studies, U. Strasbourg, France, 1976; mktg. intern IBM, Austin, 1978; mktg. cons. Creative Ednl. Enterprises, Austin, 1980-81; hon. speaker Mex.-Am. U. Tex., Austin, 1984; coord. small bus. workshops, 1985; group sponsor, advisor Travel Selections, 1997-2003, Explorica, Inc., 2003—; mem. campus adv. coun. Travis H.S., 1999-2002; Southwest area rep. Travel Selections from Campbell, Calif., 2000—03; spkr. in field. Photographs pub. in Women in Space, 1979, Review, 1988; exhibited in group shows, Tex., 1979, 88-89, 99. Neighborhood capt. Am. Cancer Soc., Austin, 1982-86, 90, Am. Heart Assn., 1989; active PTA, 1989—, Advantage Austin, 1988; mem. Bryker Woods Elem. PTA Bd., 1990-92, pres., 1990-91, mem. Austin City coun. PTA Bd., 1991-96, Kealing Jr. H.S. PTA Bd., 1992-94, chair 50th anniversary celebration com., 1990, hospitality chmn., 1st grade coord., Austin, 1986, legis. com. Tex. State, 1990-92; vol. liaison leads program Austin Coll., 1983-2000; peer panelist Maj. Art Insts., Austin; elder Ctrl. Presbyn. Ch., 1988-90, 2000-02, mem. ch. choir, 1975-78, 2003—, renovation and implementation com., 2002—, H.S. Sunday sch. tchr., 2002-03; Megaskills leader Austin Ind. Sch. Dist., 1991-96; bd. dirs. Magnet Parents Coalition, 1995-98; cultural arts chair Dist. 13 PTA Bd., 1996-97; participant NASA Urban and Rural Cmty. Enrichment Program, 2002; mem. smaller learning communities com. Travis H.S., Austin, Tex., 2002—, mem. partnership for behavioral success com., 2003—. Recipient Night on the Town award IBM, 1978. Mem.: NEA, Edn. Austin, Tex. Fgn. Lang. Assn., Am. Assn. French Tchrs. Republican. Home and Office: 1801 Lavaca St Apt 11E Austin TX 78701-1331 E-mail: mrs_lenoir@hotmail.com.

LENOX, ANGELA COUSINEAU, healthcare consultant; b. Vergennes, Vt, Dec. 12, 1946; d. Romeo Joseph and Colombe Mary (Gevry) C.; m. Donald Allen Lenox, Oct. 5, 1969 (div.); 1 child, Tiffanie Jae. RN diploma, Albany Med. Ctr. Sch. Nursing, 1969; BS, Barry U., 1982; M of Health Mgmt., St. Thomas U., 1990. Cert. in profl. healthcare quality. Intravenous therapist Holy Cross Hosp., Ft. Lauderdale, Fla., 1979-91; utilization review coord. North Broward Hosp., Pompano Beach, Fla., 1984-89; med. staff quality mgr. Humana Bennett, Plantation, Fla., 1990-91; med. resource analyst Hermann Hosp., Houston, 1991-93; assoc. mgr. quality improvement The Prudential, Sugar Land, Tex., 1993-95; quality dir. United Healthcare of Tex., 1999—. Contbr. articles to profl. jour. Capt. US Army res., 1991—. Mem. Tex. Gold Coast Assn. Healthcare Quality, Tex. Soc. Quality Assurance, Nat. Assn. Healthcare Quality. Avocations: skiing, running, reading, writing. Home: 8523 Dawnridge Dr Houston TX 77071-2441 E-mail: angeler.lenox@sbcglobal.net.

LENOX, CATHERINE CORNEAU, volunteer; b. Evanston, Ill., Sept. 16, 1920; d. Joseph Addison and Catherine Roberts Corneau; m. Lionel R. Lenox II, Dec. 9, 1945 (dec. Jan. 1994); children: Ruth Lenox Jones, Nancy, Catherine L., Elizabeth L. Howey. BA in English, Wellesley Coll., 1941; BA in Early Childhood Edn., Mills Coll., 1946; cert. in applied social gerontology, San Jose State U., 1983. Adult edn. credential San Jose State U. Tchrs. asst. Rivers Country Day Sch., Boston, 1941—42, Chestnut Hill Country Day Sch., Bethesda, Md., 1942—48; dir. Day Care Ctr., Springfield, Ill., 1943—44; tchr. Mills Coll. Childrens Sch., Oakland, Calif., 1944—45. Mem.: Sisters of Hiram (past pres., mem. sunshine com.). Republican. Baptist. Avocations: music, reading. Home: 210 Old Graham Hill Rd Santa Cruz CA 95060-1427

LENSING, VICKI, state representative, funeral home business owner; b. Iowa City, June 1957; m. Rich Templeton; children: Amanda, Alex, Nick. BA, U. Iowa, 1979. Co-owner Lensing Funeral and Cremation Svc.; state rep. dist. 78 Iowa Ho. of Reps., 2001—; mem. econ. growth com.; mem. judiciary com.; mem. local govt. com.; ranking mem. govt. oversight com. Facilitator adult bereavement support groups, 1985—, S.E. Jr. High bereavement support group, 1998—2001, ICARE AIDS bereavement support group, 1995—97. Mem. econ. well-being task force City of Iowa City, 1994, mem. citysteps task force, 1994; pres. Johnson County Women's Network, 1997—98; co-pres. Dist. Parent Orgn., 1998—99; parent rep. site-based decision-making team City H.S., 1995—99; site coun. facilitator Weber Elem. Sch., 1998—2000; mem. Old Brick Adv. Coun., 1999—2000; bd. dirs. Iowa City Cmty. Sch. Dist. Found., 1998—2000; co-chair women's leadership cir. United Way, 1999. Named Disting. Alumni, Iowa City W. High, 1992; recipient Gov.'s Vol. award in edn., 1998. Mem.: Preferred Funeral Dirs. Internat. (pres.), Iowa City Area C. of C. (bd. dirs. 1991, 1994—96, 1998—2000, chair 2000, 2000). Democrat. Office: State Capitol East 12th and Grand Des Moines IA 50319

LENTI PONSETTO, JEAN, athletic director; Grad, DePaul U., 1978. Asst. basketball coach DePaul U., 1978—81, asst. athletic dir., 1981—83, assoc. athletic dir., 1983—90, sr. assoc. athletic dir., 1990—2002, athletic dir., 2002—. Mem. Div. I Women's Basketball Com., 0992—1998, chmn., 1996—98. Named Adminstr. of Yr., Women's Basketball Coaches Assoc. & Nat. Assn. of Collegiate Women's Athletic Adminstrs., 1998. Office: DePaul Athletic Ctr 2323 N Sheffield Ave Chicago IL 60614*

LENTZ, SANDRA M. family practice nurse practitioner; b. Williamsport, Pa., May 11, 1962; d. Wesley Bruce and Marian Elizabeth (Avery) Lentz; m. Steven F. Kuni, Feb. 14, 1987 (div. Feb. 1988); 1 child, Avery Christopher ; m. Roderick C. Strother, June 19, 1999; 1 child, Ethan Campbell Lentz Strother. AA magna cum laude, Williamsport Area C.C., 1982; BS, York Coll. Pa., 1985; MS, U. S.C., 1993. RN; cert. family nurse practitioner. Nurse Humana Hosp., Augusta, Ga., 1990-93; family nurse practitioner Pee Dee Cmty. Health. Svcs., Society Hill, S.C., 1993-94; dir. Chambersburg (Pa.) Hosp. Maternity Clinic, 1994-96; family nurse practitioner Rappahannock Family Physicians, Fredericksburg, Va., 1996-98, Pa. State U. Health Svcs., 1999—2000; nurse practitioner Women's Health Care Assocs., 2000—. Bd. dirs. March of Dimes, 1994—96. With Nurse Corps U.S. Army, 1986—91. Decorated Army Commendation medal. Mem.: Am. Coll. Nurse Practitioners, Am. Acad. Nurse Practitioners. Independent. Lutheran. Avocations: outdoor activities, jazz, tennis, walking, sewing.

LENZ, DEBRA LYNN, financial analyst; b. Watertown, Wis., June 8, 1973; d. Ron Floyd and Sandy Jean Lenz. BS in Acctg., Marquette U., Milw., 1996, postgrad. CPA, Wis. Sr. auditor Deloitte & Touche LLP, Milw., 1996-99; sr. fin. analyst Rockwell Automation, Milw., 1999-2000, Harley-Davidson, Milw., 2000—. Mem. AICPA, Bus. Profl. Women, Wis. Inst. CPAs, Alpha Sigma Nu, Beta Gamma Sigma. Home: 8472 Northview Dr Pleasant Prairie WI 53158 Office: Harley-Davidson 3700 W Juneau Ave Milwaukee WI 53208 E-mail: debra.lenz@harley-davidson.com.

LEO, JACQUELINE M. editor in chief; Feature writer AP, sr. editor Modern Bride, co founder Child, N.Y.C., 1986, editor-in-chief, 1987-88, Family Circle, N.Y.C., 1988-94; editl. dir. women's mags. group N.Y. Times Co., N.Y.C., 1994, dir. mag. and media devel., 1994-95; editorial dir. Good Morning America ABC-TV News, N.Y.C., 1994-97; editl. dir. Consumer Reports, 1997-99; v.p., editl. dir. Interactive Media/Meredith Corp., 1999—2001; editor-in-chief Reader's Digest, Pleasantville, NY, 2000—. Author: New Woman's Guide To Getting Married. Recipient Matrix award Women in Comm., 1993. Mem. Am. Soc. Mag. Editors (bd. dirs., pres.), N.Y. Acad. Scis. (bd. govs.). Office: Reader's Digest Rd Pleasantville NY 10570 E-mail: jleo@rd.com.

LEON, JEANNETTE CARIDAD, mental health services professional, consultant; b. Hollywood, Fla., Sept. 8, 1972; d. Linda Carol Rodriguez, Gregorio Fransico Rodriguez; m. Noel Leon; 1 child, Jeanel-Angelle. AA in Med. Sci., Miami Dade C.C., 1993; BA in Psychology, St. Thomas U., 1995, MS in Mental Health Counseling, 1997, MBA, 2001. Cert. cognitive behavioral therapist 99, addiction specialist. Receptionist, med. asst., billing clk. Gerardo C. Perez, DO, Miami, 1989—96; program therapist Greater Miami Mental Health, Fla., 1996—97; pres. JNL Assoc., Inc., Plantation, Fla., 1997—2000; health care adminstr. Ctr. for Prog. Medicine, Ft. Lauderdale, Fla., 2001—. Dir. accts. receivable, collections, billing Carlos Rodriguez MD, Aventura, Fla., 1996—99; cons. JNL Assoc., Inc., Plantation, 1997—2000; adminstr., program dir. Southeastern Health Mgmt., Hialeah, Fla., 1997—2000. Bd. dirs. Ventana, Plantation, 2001; vol. Palmetto Hosp., Miami, 1988—89. Recipient Cert. of Recognition, Bd. Trustees, Internat. Thespian Soc. 1987. Mem.: Nat. Soc. Hispanic MBA's, Am. Counseling Assn., Fla. Mental Health Counseling Assn., Sigma Tau. Baptist. Avocations: designing albums, reading, running, bicycling. Personal E-mail: jclcpm@bellsouth.com. Business E-mail: jcleon@aol.com.

LEONARD, ANGELA MICHELE, librarian, educator; b. Washington, June 26, 1954; d. Walter Jewell and Betty (Singleton) L. AB, Harvard U., 1976; MLS, Vanderbilt U., 1982; MPhil, George Washington U., 1987, PhD, 1994; postgrad., Dartmouth Sch. Criticism and Theory, 1996, NEH Inst., 1998, Chesapeake Regional Scholars Inst., 1999, Gilder Lehman Inst. Am. History, 2003. Cons. Seigenthaler Assocs., Nashville, 1979-81; instr. Trevecca Nazarene Coll., 1979, Nashville State Tech. Inst., 1980-81; rschr., learning libr. program Fisk U. Libr., 1981-82; cataloguer Howard U. Librs., 1983; reference libr. Founders Grad. Libr., 1983-89; tchg. asst. George Washington U., 1986-90; lectr. Bowdoin Coll., 1990-91; instr. St. Cloud State U., 1991; asst. prof. Dickinson Coll., 1992-94, Bucknell U., 1994-95; lectr. UMCP, 1995; asst. prof. Loyola Coll., Md., 1996—. Vis. prof. Johns Hopkins U., 1998; corp. and spl. ref. libr., 1988-90, 95-97. Copy editor Am. Quarterly, 1988-90; editor: Boorstin Bibliography, Antislavery Materials; contbr. articles to books, profl. jours. Scholar Coolidge scholarship, 2003. Mem. ALA, NAACP, AAUW, Am. Hist. Assn., Orgn. Am. History, Semiotics Soc. Am., Nat. Soc. Exptl. Edn., Nat. Urban League, Ga. Hist. Soc., Mo. Hist. Soc., Assn. Black Women Historians (Eastern Area dir.), Assn. Study African Am. Life and History, Links, Inc., Alpha Kappa Alpha, Beta Phi Mu. Roman Catholic. Office: Loyola Coll Dept Hist 4501 N Charles St Baltimore MD 21210-2601 E-mail: aleonard@loyola.edu.

LEONARD, SISTER ANNE C. superintendent, education director; b. N.Y.C., Dec. 22, 1936; d. Patrick A. and Mary T. (McAlpin) L. BS in Edn. and Social Sci., Fordham U., 1962, MA, 1965; CAGS, Boston U., 1972; postgrad., Hunter Coll., U. San Francisco, U. Northern Ill., Notre Dame U. Cert. tchr. K-12, adminstr. N.Y. Tchr., asst. prin., prin. Notre Dame Acad., Staten Island, N.Y., 1957-68; prin. Maternity B.V.M. Sch., Bourbonnais, Ill., 1968-69, St. Jude the Apostle Sch., South Holland, Ill., 1969-78; dir. Cath. Elem. Schs. Archdiocese of Chgo., 1978-83, dir. ednl. svcs., mem. Cardinal Bernadin's cabinet, 1983-90, exec. officer commn. ednl. svcs., 1983-90; supt. schs., dir. edn. Archdiocese of Okla. City, 1990-96; U.S. province leader Congregation of Notre Dame, Ridgefield, Conn., 1996—. Chair edn. divisn. Cath. Conf. Ill., 1988-90; del. gen. chpt. Congregation Notre Dame, mem. provincial coun.; mem. edn. com. U.S. Cath. Conf. Bishops, Washington, 1985-88; mem. Nat. Cath. Bishops' Millennium Com.; speaker in field; lectr., presenter workshops; mem. Fortune 500 panel edn. and bus.; devel. mission statement, just principles compensation, new models compensation for prins., 1987-91; initiated, organized Dirs. Edn. Wis., Ill., Ind., Ohio, Mich.; attended symposia in field; mem. com. prep. Office of Cath. Edn. Conciliation Process; exec. officer local sch. bds.; initiated individually guided edn. program St. Jude Sch. Cons. textbooks William H. Sadlier, Inc.; contbr. articles to profl. jours. Trustee DePaul U., 1986—; trustee Midwestern U., 1999—, bd. dirs., vice chair acad. affairs com.; bd. dirs. Jr. Achievement, Chgo., 1984-90, Oklahoma City, 1991-96; mem. NCCJ, 1992-96, Gov. Ill. adv. com. on non-pub. schs., Springfield, 1978-82, planning com. Big Shoulders Project, officer Leadership Conf. of Women Religious (Region I), 1997—; active Congregation of Notre Dame Mem. ASCD, Nat. Cath. Ednl. Assn. (pres. chief adminstrs. Cath. edn. 1991-94, v.p. 1989-91, vice chair bd. 1991-94, task force 1990-91, centennial com. 1997—, supervision, pers., curriculum, Educator of Yr. award 1990), Archdiocesan Prins. Assn. (pres. 1973-78), Nat. Religious Retirement Bd. (grant com.), Chgo. Coun. Fgn. Rels., Phi Delta Kappa (Educator of Yr. 1984). Avocations: reading, swimming, travel. Home and Office: 223 W Mountain Rd Ridgefield CT 06877-3627 E-mail: provsec@juno.com.

LEONARD, CAROLYN BRANCH, publisher, editor, writer; b. Buffalo, Okla., Aug. 21, 1937; d. Ernest S. and Imogene (Parsons) Branch; m. John C. Leonard, Apr. 15, 1956 (div. June 1984); children: Judith G., James C.; m. Jon Heavener, Feb. 14, 1993. BA, Oklahoma City U., 1991. Pub. SAGEst PRESS, Oklahoma City, 1990—. Pub. affairs asst. U.S. Treas., Oklahoma City, 1988-94. Asst. editor: Woodward County Jour. Newspaper, 1982-83; editor: Harper Co. Jour., Buffalo, Okla., 1983-88, News U Can Use, Nat. Treas. Employees Union, Oklahoma City, 1994-96. Senate encoder Okla. State Capitol, 1996-99; area rep., bd. dirs. Briarcreek Neighborhood Assn.; treas. Profit Ptnrs. Investment Club, 1997-2002; mem. Meth. Ch. of the Servant, Okla. Hist. Soc. Recipient numerous awards. Mem. DAR, Writers of the Purple Sage (past pres.), Oklahoma City Writers (past pres.), Okla. Writers Fedn., Mayflower Descs. Soc., Okla. Hist. Soc., Okla. Geneal. Soc., Mo. Hist. Soc., Ohio Hist. Soc., Ill. Hist. Soc., Bentonville Anti-Horse Thief Soc., Friends of the Libr., Servants Dinner Club.

LEONARD, JACQUELYN ANN, retired elementary school educator; b. Hollister, Okla., Apr. 2, 1931; d. Alex and Dolly M. (McCurty) McKinney; m. Malvin Paul Leonard, Feb. 6, 1952 (div. Apr. 1993); children: Diana, Andrea. BA in Art Edn. and Pub. Sch. Music, Ctrl. State U., 1955; postgrad., U. Mich., 1955—62, Mich. State U., 1955—62. Pres. Jacquelyn-Jackie Leonard Corp., Lake Orion, Mich., 1994—. Contbr. articles to profl. jours. Mem.: AAUW, Nat. Trust. Avocations: reading, singing, piano, swimming. Home: 3091 Oakridge Lake Orion MI 48360

LEONARD, JUDITH PRICE, educational advisor; b. Milw., July 10, 1941; d. Ralph H. and Sylvia (Shames) Price; m. Richard Black Leonard Jr., Dec. 15, 1962 (dec. Dec. 1978); m. Norman Crasilneck, Aug. 31, 1991. BS in Math., Antioch U., 1963; MS in Math., St. Louis U., 1970. Tchr. math. Ferguson Florissant (Mo.) Schs., 1963-94, coord., 1971-73; mentor, co-dir., faculty advisor Engelmann Math. & Sci. Inst., U. Mo., St. Louis, 1988-96; supr. student tchrs. U. Mo., St. Louis, 1995, 96; coord. Regional Inst. Sci. Edn., St. Louis, 1996-2000; evaluator and cons. math. programs St. Louis Pub. Schs., 1994—2004; faculty advisor NSF Young Scholars, U. Mo., St. Louis, 1997, NSF Students & Tchrs. as Rsch. Scientists, U. Mo., St. Louis, 1998—99. Co-dir. Post Dispatch and Monsanto Greater St. Louis Sci. Fair, 1998—99; adv. bd. Post Dispatch and Monsanto Greater St. Louis Sci. Fair, 1997—2004, Intel Internat. Sci. and Edn. Fair, 1996—99, adults in charge, 1997—99, fair dir., 1999; chair Discovery Young Scientist Challenge, St. Louis, 1999—2004; sec. exec. bd. Math Educators Greater St. Louis, 2001—04; mem. Math. Sci. Network of Greater St. Louis (Expanding Your Horizons), 1995—2004; math. cons. U. Mo., St. Louis, 2002—03; presenter, judge, chmn. judges for math. computer sci., physics and engring. Jr. Sci., Engring. and Humanities Symposium, 1995—2001, 2003—04. Author: Word Problems, Basic Skills Instructional Fair, 1996; author, editor: (brochure) Teacher Linking Collaborative, 1997, 2002; editor 3 Math Books, 2002, 5th and 6th Pre Algebra, 2002. Hon. Engelmann scholar Engelmann Math. and Sci. Inst., St. Louis, 1993, NSF Young scholar U. Mo., St. Louis, 1997; recipient Math. Edn. award Math. Educators Greater St. Louis, 1994, NSF STARS award U. Mo., St. Louis, 2000. Mem. NEA, Nat. Coun. Tchrs. Math., Mo. Coun. Tchrs. Math. (life), Ferguson Florissant NEA (life). Avocations: tennis, biking, walking. Home: 22 Bellerive Acres Saint Louis MO 63121-4321 Personal E-mail: judy@judyleonard.net.

LEONARD, KANDI, English language educator; b. Oxnard, Calif., Jan. 13, 1959; d. Ron and Bobbie Jo Seaman; m. Ralph Hanna; 1 child, McGee Jeordi. BA, San Francisco State U., 1984, MA, 1986; PhD, U. Calif., Riverside, 1993. Cert. secondary sch. English tchr., Calif. Assoc. prof. Nat. U., L.A., 1996-98; English tchr. Ontario (Calif.) H.S., 1997—. Exec. v.p. YWCA, San Bernardino, Calif., 1993-94; fundraiser Dem. Party, Riverside, Calif., 1994. Mem. Nat. Assn. Tchrs., Sisters in Crime. Home: 932 N Crescent Heights Blvd Los Angeles CA 90046-6916

LEONARD, LAURA L. L. lawyer; b. 1956; AB, U. Calif., Davis, 1978; JD, Loyola U., Chgo., 1983. Bar: Ill. 1983. With Sidley & Austin, Chgo., 1983—, ptnr., 1991—. Lectr. on environ. aspects of bus. trans., including Northwestern U. Kellogg Grad. Sch. Mgmt.; mem. adv. bd. BNA's Environ. Due Digigence Guide. Office: Sidley & Austin Bank One Plz 10 S Dearborn St Chicago IL 60603 Fax: 323-853-7620. E-mail: lleonard@sidley.com.*

LEONARD, MONA FREEMAN, adult education educator; d. Jack Robinson and Ruth Olivia Freeman; m. Jeffrey Allen Leonard, Oct. 27, 1989; 1 child, Jared Alexander. BA, Howard U., Washington, 1986, MA, 1989; postgrad., U. Ky., Lexington, 1994—97. Adj. prof. U. Louisville, 1991—2002; assoc. prof. Jefferson C.C., Louisville, 1993—. Author (chpt.): Our Voices: Essays in Culture, Ethnicity and Communication, 2004. Mem.: Nat. Comm. Assn. Office: Jefferson CC 109 E Broadway Louisville KY 40202

LEONARD, NEDRA V. music educator; b. Quanah, Tex., Nov. 27, 1942; d. Edward P. and Arliss Laverne Hurst; m. Doyle Ray Leonard, July 20, 1958; children: Cheri, Debbie, Toni, Rob, Dave. AA in Music, Gardin City C.C., Kans., 1971; BA in Music, Cameron U., 1992. Ins. underwriter Dempsey Ins., Altus, Okla., 1963—66; purchasing mgr. Kelwood Mfg., Altus, Okla., 1967—69; pvt. music tchr. Gardin City, 1970—85; tchr. music Cache (Okla.) Pub. Schs., 1992—. Student tchr. mentor Cameron U., Lawton, 2000—01. Sunday sch. tchr. Mem.: Am. Choral Dir. Assn., Okla. Music Educators Assn. Mem. Ch. Of Christ. Avocations: camping, travel, reading, musical theater. Mailing: RR 1 Box 990 Elgin OK 73538-9801

LEONARD, PAMELA DIAN, architect, artist; b. Corpus Christi, Tex., Mar. 25, 1968; d. John David and Loretta Kay Leonard. BArch, Miss. State U., 1991. Cert. Nat. Coun. Arch. Registration Bds., 1997, registered architect, Miss., 1996. Intern architect BSW Internat., Tulsa, Okla., 1991—93, Canizaro Trigiani Architects, Jackson, Miss., 1993—96; architect Canizaro Cawthon Davis, Jackson, Miss., 1993—. Accreditation rev. team Nat. Coun. Accreditation Bd., 1989—90. Watercolor painting, St. Mark's, 1987, The Girl, 1990. Mentor Jackson Pub. Schs. VAST Mentor Program, Jackson, 1999—2000; big sister Big Brothers / Big Sisters of Green Country, Tulsa, 1992—93; catechumenate adminstr. St. Andrew's Episcopal Cathedral, Jackson, 1999—, facilities study com., 2001—, adult formation com., 2000—01, Christmas alternate giving program chair, 1999—; mem. Episcopal Diocese Miss. Young Adults Task Force; bd. dirs. Miss. Children's Mus., Jackson, 1997—99, pres. bd. dirs., 1998—99, founding sec., pres. elect bd. dirs., 1997—99, bldg. com. chair, 1997—99, jubilee jam com. chair, 1999, founding com., 1995—97. Mem.: AIA (cmty. enhancement program design competition team leader 1993, cont. edn. com. 1997—98), Angel Flight Alumni Assn., Mortar Bd. Alumni Assn. Episcopalian. Avocations: painting, drawing, writing, cooking, walking. Office: Canizaro Cawthon Davis 129 S President St Jackson MS 39201

LEONARD, PENNY SUE EVANS, nurse; b. Monroe, La., Apr. 26, 1945; d. John Lewis Evans and Jeanette Armeda (Cross) Swartz; m. Peter Allen Wright, Feb. 14, 1974 (div. Aug. 1984); m. James Brian Leonard, July 4, 1987. Student, U. Cen. Fla., 1973-74, Edison Community Coll., Ft. Myers, Fla., 1974-75; AS in Nursing, Seminole Community Coll., Fla., 1982; BA, U. State of N.Y., 1996. RN, Fla. RN, night supr., psychiatry and detox. Lake Sumter Community Mental Health Ctr., Eustis, Fla., 1982-83; RN, dir. nurses and dir. detox. White Deer Poly Addiction Treatment Ctr., Bushnell, Fla., 1983; RN, specialist, outpatient nursing and verbal therapist Mental Health Svcs. of Orange County, Orlando, Fla., 1984-87, 89-90; RN, charge nurse psychiatry De Poo Hosp., Key West, Fla., 1988—; pvt. practice, cons. Orlando. Drug and alcohol cons. Care Unit, Orlando, 1987; group leader REACH, Orlando, 1984-87, 89—; sr. case supr. med. and psychiatr. Olsten Healthcare, 1991-93; dir. Home Health Agy., Orlando Luth. Towers, 1993-94; wound care specialist, instr., cons. Wound Mgmt. Svcs., Longwood, Fla., 1994—; ind. wound care cons., 1996—; tchr. wound care, Belize, 1996. Mem. Am. Nurses Assn., Fla. Nurses Assn. Democrat. Avocations: writing, sailing, baking, fiber artist, reading. Home and Office: 3208C E Colonial Dr Apt 221 Orlando FL 32803-5127

LEONARD, SUZANNE LOUISE, artist, photographer; b. San Francisco, Feb. 27, 1951; d. Randall Clarence and Elizabeth Louise (Humphrey) L.; m. Lloyd Bernerd Dykes, June 1, 1980. BA in Psychology, St. Mary's Coll., Moraga, Calif., 1973; acctg. cert., Heald Bus. Coll., 1977. Owner Purple Pony, Vacaville, Calif., 1992—. Mem. Calif. Dressage Soc. Avocations: horseback riding, reading, aviculture, martial arts. Office: Purple Pony PO Box 398 Vacaville CA 95696-0398 E-mail: sleonard@cwnet.com.

LEONARD, VIRGINIA WAUGH, history educator, writer, researcher; b. Willimantic, Conn., Dec. 9, 1941; d. William Norris and Elizabeth Flora (Waugh) L.; m. James Madison Ewing, May 14, 1978. BA in Internal. Rels., U. Calif., Berkeley, 1963; MA in Social Scis., Hofstra U., 1967; PhD in History, U. Fla., 1975. Cert. social studies tchr., N.Y.; cert. bilingual social studies tchr., N.Y.; lic. pvt. pilot. Civilian recreation officer U.S. Army Spl. Svcs., Nuremburg, West Germany, 1963-64; tchr. social studies Colegio Lincoln, La Lucila, Argentina, 1970, Seward Park H.S., N.Y.C., 1975-77; asst. prof. history Western Ill. U., Macomb, 1977-83, assoc. prof. history, 1983-90, prof. history, 1990—. Sr. program mgr. Nat. Faculty Exchange-Dept. of Edn., Washington, 1986-87; chairperson Univ. Personnel Commn., Western Ill. U., 1990-91; mem. internat. adv. bd. 5th Internat. Interdisciplinary Congress on Women, San Jose, 1992-93; mem. nat. screening com. U.S. Grad. Student Fulbright Program, 1999, 2002-03. Author: Politicians, Pupils and Priests: Argentine Education since 1943, 1989; author: (chpt.) Los Ensayistas, 1989, (chpt.) Women in the Thrd World: An Encyclopedia of Contemporary Issues, 1998; contbr. articles to profl. jours. Treas. Bus. and Profl. Women, Macomb, 1994-95; seminar leader Project Democracy, LWV, Dubna, Russia, summer 1995; coord. Grassroots, LWV, McDonough County, Ill., 1995. Recipient grant Orgn. Am. States, 1971-72, Fulbright Rsch. award Fulbright Office-Argentina, 1983, Grassroots Democracy grant

LWV/USAID, 1995, NEH Summer Inst., Mystic Seaport, Conn., 1996. Mem. Am. Hist. Assn., Midwest Assn. for Latin Am. Studies (pres. 1984-85, Tchg. award 1997), North Ctrl. Coun. Latin Am. (chair nominating com. 1990-91, Tchg. award 1990), Berkshire Conf. of Women Historians (book prize com. 1990-95), Charlevoix Hist. Soc., Phi Kappa Phi, Delta Kappa Gamma (legis. com. 1993-94, 2002--), Nat. Screening Com. for the U.S Grad. Student Fulbright Program, 1999, 2002-03. Unitarian Universalist. Avocations: skiing, swimming, tennis, reading, travel. Office: Western Ill Univ Dept History Macomb IL 61455 Business E-Mail: V_Leonard@wiu.edu.

LEONARD, ZOE, artist; b. Liberty, N.Y., 1961; One-woman shows include Fourth St. Photo Gallery, N.Y.C., 1979, Hogarth Gallery, Sydney, Australia, 1983, Greathouse, N.Y.C., 1985, Galerie Gisela Capitain, Cologne, Germany, 1990, 1991, 1998, Richard Foncke Gallery, Ghent,Belgium, 1991, Trans Avant-Garde Gallery, Sanb Francisco, 1991, U. Art Mus./Pacific Film Archives U. Calif., Berkeley, 1991, Luhring Augustine Hetzler, L.A., 1991, Paula Cooper Gallery, N.Y.C., 1992, 1997, 1999, The Renaissance Soc. U. Chgo., 1993, Galerija Dante Marino Cettina, Umago, Croatia, 1995, 1997, Galerie Jennifer Flay, Paris, 1995, 1997, La Case d'Arte, Milan, 1995, Mus. Contemporary Art, North Miami, Fla., 1997, Kunsthaus Glarus, Switzerland, 1997, Kunsthalle Basel, 1997, Vienna Secession, Vienna, 1997, Jan Weiner Gallery, Kansas City, Mo., 1998, Phila. Mus. Art, 1998, Ctr. Nat. Photographie, Paris, 1998, exhibited in group shows at Inst. Contemporary Art, Boston, 1997, Nassau County Mus. Art, Roslyn Harbor, N.Y., 1997, Jennifer Flay Gallery, Paris, 1997, Annika Sundvik Gallery, N.Y.C., 1997, Whitney Mus. Am. Art, 1997, Galerija Dante Marino Cettina, Umag, Croatia, 1997, The Art Gallery NSW, Australia, 1997, Mitxelena Kulturunea Exhbn. Gallery, Donostia-St. Sebastian, Spain, 1997, Deutsche Arbeitsschutz und Arbeitsmedizin, Dortmund, Germany, 1997, Bowdoin Coll. Mus. Art, Brunswick, Maine, 1998, U. Art Gallery, Montclair State U., N.J., 1998, Upper Austrian Regional Gallery, Linz, 1998, Paula Cooper Gallery, N.Y.C., 1998, Thomas Healy Gallery, 1998, Linda Kirkland Gallery, 1998, Kunstverein Hamburg, Germany, 1998, Patricia Faure Gallery, Santa Monica, Calif., 1998, Groninger (The Netherlands) Mus., 1998, Ctr. Curatorial Studies Bard Coll., Annandale-on-Hudson, N.Y., 1999, Israeli Mus., Jerusalem, 1999, Mus. Modern Art, N.Y.C., 1999, Photographic Resource Ctr., Boston, 1999, Boulder (Colo.) Mus. Contemporary Art, 1999, many others. Office: c/o Paula Cooper Gallery 534 W 21st St New York NY 10011-2812

LEONARDO, ANN ADAMSON, marketing and sales consultant; b. Hamilton, Lanark, Scotland, Jan. 4, 1944; d. James Walker and Margaret Patterson (Burnside) Adamson; m. John Constantine Leonardo, Jr., Mar. 29, 1975; 1 child, Elizabeth Margaret. BA in Bus., McGill U., Montreal, Que., Can., 1970. Market rsch. mgr. MacLaren Advt., Toronto, Ont., Can., 1965-70; group product mgr. Menley & James, Montreal, 1970-74; mktg. mgr. Maybelline divsn. Plough, Toronto, 1074-75; v.p. mktg. Van De Kamp's Bakery, Glendale, Calif., 1976-80; v.p. mktg. and sales Cal West Periodicals, Oakland, 1980-84; mktg. cons., San Francisco, 1984-87; pes., owner MicroCosmic Rsch., Ketchum, Idaho, 1988—. Bd. dirs. Family House Inc., San Francisco. Home: 77 6516 Alii Drive Kailua Kona HI 96740 Office: PO Box 956 Ketchum ID 83340-0956

LEONARD-ZABEL, ANN MARIE T. psychologist, educator; d. Thomas M. Leonard, Sr. and Gertrude A. Leonard; m. Raymond G. Zabel, Sept. 16, 1979; children: Jessica Zabel, Steve Zabel. BA, U. Mass., Boston, 1979, CAGS in Sch. Psychology, 1991; EdM in Counseling, Bridgewater State Coll., 1981; EdD in Child and Youth Studies-Exceptional Svcs., Nova Southeastern U., 1996. Lic. ednl. psychologist Mass., mental health counselor Mass., cert. sch. psychologist Mass., Nat., diplomate Am. Psychotherapy Assn.; lic. social worker Mass., cert. sch. social worker/sch. adjustment counselor, internat. cert. alcohol and drug counselor, nat. cert. masters addictions counselor, nat. cert. criminal justice specialist, nat. cert. counselor, nat. cert. cognitive behavioral therapist, nat. cert. cognitive forensic therapist; cert. alcohol and drug abuse counselor Mass. Asst. dir., counselor Project Friend, Inc., Plymouth, Mass., 1982; counselor, dir. Alcoholic Family Rehab., Plymouth, 1983; psychologist Middleboro (Mass.) Pub. Schs., 1991; owner, dir. New Eng. Attentional Clinic, Plymouth, 1996; prof. Bridgewater (Mass.) State Coll., 1996; lead psychologist Foxboro (Mass.) Pub. Schs., 1999; prof. Curry Coll., Milton and Plymouth, 2002. Mem.: Am. Psychotherapy Assn. (bd. dirs., membership com.), Coun. for Exceptional Children, Nat. Assn. Sch. Psychologists, Mass. Sch. Psychologist Assn. (bd. dirs. 1997—, co-chairperson Cape and Islands Sch. Psychologist Chpt. 1994—98). Office: New Eng Attentional Clinic Park Ave Trust Bldg 7 S Park Ave 2nd Fl Plymouth MA 02360 Office Phone: 508-746-5666. E-mail: dramlz@yahoo.com.

LEONDAKIS, NIKI ANNA, food service executive; b. West Springfield, Mass., Nov. 28, 1960; B in Hotel and Restaurant Mgmt., U. Mass. Restaurant and beverage mgr. Marriott, Nashville; dir. catering Ritz Carlton Hotels, Atlanta, dir. food and beverage Marina Del Rey, Calif., San Francisco; joined Klimpton Hotel and Restaurant Group, Inc., San Francisco, 1993, regional mgr. N.W., 1993-95, v.p. restaurant ops., 1995—. Named Rising Star, Restaurant Hospitality Mag. Avocations: snow skiing, running, painting, family activities. Office: Kimpton Hotel & Restaurant Group Inc 222 Kearny St Ste 200 San Francisco CA 94108

LEONE, GILDA C. adult education educator; b. Albany, N.Y., Oct. 1, 1955; d. Frank and Agatena Leone; m. Keith B. Gresens, May 21, 1987; children: Regina Gresens, Keith K. Gresens. AA in Liberal Arts, Hudson Valley C.C., Troy, N.Y., 1975; BA in Edn., Italian and Spanish magna cum laude, SUNY, Albany, 1977, MS in TESOL, 1983. Cert. tchr. ESL, Italian and Spanish N.Y. Italian tchr. evening divsn. Albany H.S., 1979—89, tchr. ESL, 1996—2000, Adult Learning Ctr., Albany, 1984—, Albany Pub. Libr., 1984—85, Chinese Sch. Cmty. Ctr., Latham, NY, 1987—89, Colonie (N.Y.) Town Libr., 1992—93; tchr. ESL, cons. Albany Med. Coll., 1992—93. GED proctor N.Y. State Edn. Dept., 1995—, ESOL cons., 1988—2000, ESOL assessor and tester, 1988—89; ESOL coord. ALC, Albany, 1990—98; advisor, developer, writer N.Y. State Edn. Dept. and Hudson River Ctr. ESOL Literacy Curriculum, 1994; Upstate trainer facilitator Communicative ESOL Practitioner's Consortium; Upstate trainer Adult Edn. Resource Guide and Learning Stds. Capital Dist. Adult Edn. Profl. Devel. Consortium. Co-author: Amnesty Act Curriculum, 1988. Mem. comprehensive dist. edn. plan team Albany Schs., 2000—, mem. shared decision making com., 1994—2000, mem. interview com. Adult Learning Ctr., 1996. Mem.: CDACCE, Albany Network Hispanic Svc. Providers, N.Y. State TESOL. Democrat. Avocations: cooking, dance, gardening. Office: Adult Learning Ctr 27 Western Ave Albany NY 12203

LEONE, JEANNE, artist; b. Revere, Mass., June 8, 1946; d. Gerard Leone and Jeanne Irene DeSimone. BA Polit. Sci. with highest honors, Adelphi U., 1968. Lic. real estate broker, Mass. Dir. advt., mktg., publ. rels. Keydata Corp., Watertown, MA, 1970-74; founding and managing editor The Jour. Technol. Horizons in Edn., Acton, MA, 1974-76; pres. M & M Constrn., Chestnut Hill, MA, 1978-82; cons. F.L. Putnam Brokerage Ho., Boston, 1981; dir. advtg., mktg., publ. rels. Gould Computer Sys., Plantation, FL, 1983; cons. Northern Telecom, Toronto, Canada, 1984-85; closing and title officer Malibu Escrow Corp., Malibu, CA, 1986-87; cons. Wespac Investors Trusts, Santa Monica, CA, 1988-90, The Marquardt Co., Van Nuys, CA, 1990-95, Philip R. Gustlin, Esq., 1994-95, Technol. Renaissance Corp., Atlanta, 1996, Microtrends, Inc., Pasadena, CA, 1996-97, Bklyn., 1999. Founder Greenpoint Riverfront Artists, 1999. One-woman shows include Univ. Pl. Gallery, Harvard U., Cambridge, Mass., 1991, Wilshire Landmark Bldg,. L.A., 1993-94, Margaret Crow Gallery, Pasadena, Calif., 1995-96; commn. to create art book on the Earl Gales Jr. Collection of West African Art, Art on the Loose, 1998. Bd. dirs. Cmty. Champions, San Francisco. Mem. MENSA. Fax: 718-383-9658. E-mail: leonejean@aol.com.

LEONE, JUDITH GIBSON, educational media specialist, video production company executive; b. Toms River, N.J., Sept. 27, 1945; d. James Delaney and Louise Gertrude (Eberhardt) Gibson; m. Stephan Robert Leone, Nov. 27, 1971; stepchildren: Cheryl, Debra. BA, Kean Coll., 1970; MLS, Rutgers U., 1980. Cert. edn. media specialist. Tchr. Toms River Schs., 1970-84, media specialist, 1984-89; v.p., owner Prodn. House, Toms River, 1985-94; libr. coord. Amb. Christian Acad., Toms River, 1989-95; exec. dir. Designer Showcase, 1995-96. Mem. region 5 book evaluation com. N.J. State Libr. System, 1986-90. Sec., bd. dirs. The Shelter, Inc., Bricktown, N.J., 1979—; past pres. Open Arms, Inc.; past pres., bd. dirs. Harbor House; v.p., bd. dirs. Ocean County chpt. United Way, 1992-2000; pres. Garden State Philharm.; bd. dirs., past pres. Italian-Am. Cultural and Heritage Soc.; candidate N.J. State Senate, 1997; co-founder Dem. POWER, 1999; mem. WWFM Adv. Commn., 1999—; chmn. Ocean's Harbor House Found., 2002-; trustee, Nat. Conf. Cmty. and Justice; mem. Ocean County Dem. Fin. Com., 2001-, bd. dirs. Nat. Conf. Christians and Jews., 2003, mem. N.J. State Coun. Arts, 2004—. Honoree for cmty. svc. Italian Am. Cultural Soc., 1995; named Vol. of Yr., United Way of Ocean County, 1996, Humanitarian of Yr., Nat. Conf. Christians Jews, 1998; recipient Garden State Philharm. Disting. Svc. award, 2003, ADACO Disting. Service award, 2004. Mem.: Toms River Country Club. Democrat. Avocations: sailing, skiing, handbell choir, golf. Home: 143 Cranmoor Dr Toms River NJ 08753-6805

LEONG, ANTOINETTE MARIE, musician, director; b. Honolulu, Dec. 29, 1952; d. Albert Paul and Irma Kuulei Leong. B of Music Edn., U. Hawaii, Honolulu, 1975. Tchr. Holy Nativity Sch., Honolulu, 1977—; dir. Holy Nativity Christmas Program, Honolulu, 1977—, Holy Nativity Lei Day Pageant, Honolulu, 1985—, Holy Nativity Sch. Choir, Honolulu, 1997—. Composer (children's songs): Go!, 1998, Charity, 1999, And There is Peace, 2000. Mem.: Music Educators Nat. Conf. Avocations: Hawaii history, musical theatre. Office: Holy Nativity Sch 5286 Kalanianaole Hwy Honolulu HI 96821

LEONG, BERTHA F.K. state representative; b. Honolulu, Oct. 21, 1937; married. BA in govt. and edn., U. of Hawaii, 1957. Realtor Prudential Locations, CRS, GRI; ptnr. with COE in tng. future tchrs. U. of Hawaii Coll. of Edn.; tchr. Holulaini and Aina Haina Elem. Schs. Dir. Straub Found., 1999; chair Kuliouou-Kalani Iki Neighborhood Bd. #2, 1989—98; bd. dirs. Aina Haina Cmty. Assn.; medication chair Honolulu Bd. of Realtors, 1995—97; chair negotiations bd. Honalulu; mediator Neighborhood Justice Ctr. Mem.: Daughters of Hawaii (life), Elks Club. Republican. Roman Catholic. Office: State Capitol Rm 327 415 S Beretania St Honolulu HI 96813 E-mail: repleong@capitol.hawaii.gov.

LEONG, MARGARET, construction executive; CFO Shapell Industries, Beverly Hills, Calif., 1993—. Office: Shapell Industries 8383 Wilshire Blvd Ste 700 Beverly Hills CA 90211-2472

LEONHART, MICHELE MARIE, government agency administrator; BS in Criminal Justice, Lakewood C.C., Minn., 1978. Police officer Balt. Police Dept., Md.; spl. agt. Drug Enforcement Adminstrn., Mpls., 1980—85, spl. agt. recruiter St. Louis, 1986—88, group supr., intelligence supr. San Diego, 1988—93, OPR (internal affairs) inspector Arlington, Va., 1993—94, bd., 1994—95, asst. spl. agt. in charge of field divsn., 1995—96, sr. exec. svc. mem. spl. agt. recruitment program, 1996—97, spl. agt. in charge field divsn., 1997—98, L.A., 1998—2003, acting dep. adminstr. Alexandria, 2003—04, dep. adminstr., 2004—. Office: Drug Enforcement Adminstrn Mailstop AXS 2401 Jefferson Davis Hwy Alexandria VA 22301*

LEONI, TEA (ELIZABETH TEA PANTALEONI), actress; b. N.Y.C, Feb. 25, 1966; m. David Duchovny, 1997, 2 children Actress Television: Santa Barbara, 1984, Flying Blind, 1992, The Counterfeit Contessa, 1994, The Naked Truth, 1995; Films: Switch, 1991, A League of Their Own, 1992, Wyatt Earp, 1994, Bad Boys, 1995, Flirting with Disaster, 1996, Deep Impact, 1998, There's No Fish Food in Heaven, 1999, The Family Man, 2000, Jurassic Park 3, 2001, Hollywood Ending, 200, People I Know, 2002 Recipient Saturn Award, best actress for "The Family Man", 2001.

LEPAGE, EILEEN MCCULLOUGH See MCCULLOUGH, EILEEN

LEPKE, CHARMA DAVIES, musician, educator; b. Delavan, Wis., Oct. 1, 1919; d. Ithel B. and Florence Mary (Jones) Davies; m. John Richard Lepke, Dec. 22, 1949 (div. July 1974). BA, Wellesley Coll., 1941, MA, 1942; MMusic, Am. Conservatory of Music, Chgo., 1946. Piano tchr., organist Fairfax Hall Jr. Coll., Waynesboro, Va., 1942-44; piano tchr. U. Nebr., Lincoln, 1946-50; ch. organist Trinity Methodist, Unitarian, Lincoln, 1946-50; missionary Am. Bd. Congl. Ch., Durban, Johannesburg, South Africa, 1950-56; ch. organist, choir dir. Congl. United Ch. of Christ, Oconomowoc/Sheboygan, Wis., 1957-70; organist Coloma, Mich., 1970-73; ch. organist Brick Bapt. Ch., Walworth, Wis., 1974, United Meth. Ch., Delavan, 1974-77, Congl. United Ch. of Christ, Delavan, 1977—. Music editor revised Zulu hymnal Amagama Okuhlabalela, South Africa, 1951-56; composer preludes for organ, piano pieces, song and anthem. Recipient 1st prize for song Wis. Fedn. Music Clubs, 1960, others. Mem. Am. Guild of Organists, Music Tchrs. Nat. Assn., Wis. Alliance for Composers, Delavan Musical Arts Soc. (founder, pres.), Phi Beta Kappa. Congregationalist. Home: 223 W Geneva St Delavan WI 53115-1626

LEPOME, PENELOPE MARIE, rehabilitation counselor, educator; b. Buffalo, Dec. 17, 1945; d. Raymond Arthur and Mildred Evelyn Kramer; m. Robert Charles LePome, May 26, 1966 (div. Jan. 1982); children: Lisa Anne, Kathryn Jane, Robert Charles II. BA in Biology, SUNY, Buffalo, 1967; MS in Vocat. Rehab., U. Nev., Las Vegas, 1984; postgrad., U. Nev., Reno, 1993-2000, Calif. State U., Bakersfield, 2002—. Cert. rehab. counselor, substance abuse counselor, disability mgmt. specialist; lic. substitute tchr. and sch. counselor, Nev.; lic. alcohol and drug abuse counselor, Nev.; pupil personnel credential (sch. counselor), Calif. Co-owner, salesman Flamingo Realty, Las Vegas, Nev., 1974-76; substitute tchr. Clark County Sch. Dist., Las Vegas, 1969-74, 82-84; adj. faculty Clark County C.C., Las Vegas, 1984-86, Truckee Meadows C.C., Reno, 1987; bus. and industry field specialist Tng. Inst. Clark County C.C., 1985-86; probation officer on call Clark County Juvenile Svcs., Las Vegas, 1984; counselor Nike House, Las Vegas, 1984; mental health technician III State of Nev., 1984-86; rehab. coord. I Nev. Bur. Vocat. Rehab., Reno, 1986-92; pvt. practice rehab. counseling, 1984-86; rehab. counselor GENEX Svcs. Inc., Reno, 1992-95; quality assurance specialist Divsn. Mental Health & Mental Hygiene, State of Nev., 1995-96; substance abuse counselor Divsn. Parole & Probation, 1996-2000; spl. svcs. coord., counselor Cerro Coso C.C., Ridgecrest, Calif., 2000—01; social worker Aspira Foster Family Agy., 2001—02; spl. edn. tchr., sch. counselor Total Edn. Solutions, Inc., 2002; social svcs. worker I Kern County Dept. Human Svcs., 2003—. Active Nev. Womens Polit. Caucus, Las Vegas, 1983-85; carnival chmn. Rex Bell PTA, Las Vegas, 1974-75, treas., 1975-76; leader Frontier Area Girl Scouts U.S., Las Vegas, 1975-76, cookie sale chmn., 1980; treas., bd. dirs. Young Audiences, Las Vegas, 1979-80; mem. Reno City Coun. Adv. Com. Persons With Disabilities, 1991-93. N.Y. State Regents scholar, 1963. Mem.: AAUW (life; v.p. membership 1980—81, v.p. programming 1981—82, pres. 1982—83, divsn. officer Nev. 1983—85, pres.-elect/programming 2002—03, branch pres. 2003—), Assn. Part-time Profls. (bd. dirs.), Am. Counseling Assn.

LEPORE, LISA, principal; d. Ann Nancy and Anthony Nicholas Lepore. BA, R.I. U., Providence, 1981, MA, 1987. Cert. tchr. R.I., 2000. Tchr. St. Leo the Gt. Sch., Pawtucket, RI, 1985—2001, prin., 1985—. Substance abuse coord. St. Leo the Gt. Sch., Pawtucket, RI, 1987—. Pres. Girls Softball League; appeals com. chairperson Cath. Athletic League, Providence, 2003. Named Coach of Yr., CYO League, 1995. Mem.: NCEA. Home: 534 Charles St Providence RI 02904 Office: St Leo the Great Sch 723 Central Ave Pawtucket RI 02861 Personal E-mail: boggs534@aol.com. E-mail: rid04179@ride.ri.net.

LEPPIK, MARGARET WHITE, municipal official; b. Newark, June 5, 1943; d. John Underhill and Laura (Schaefer) White; m. Ilo Elmar Leppik, June 18, 1967; children: Peter, David, Karina. BA, Smith Coll., 1965. Rsch. asst. Wistar Inst., U. Pa., Phila., 1967-68, U. Wis., Madison, 1968-69; mem. Minn. Ho. Reps., St. Paul, 1991—2003, chair higher edn. fin. com.; mem. Met. Coun., 2003—. Active Golden Valley (Minn.) Planning Commn., 1982—90, Golden Valley Bd. Zoning Appeals, 1985—87; commr. Midwest Higher Edn. Commn., 1999—2003; bd. dirs. Minn. Partnership Action Against Tobacco, 1998—2003. Named Citizen of Distinction, Hennepin County Human Svcs. Planning Bd., 1992, Legislator of Yr., U. Minn. Alumni Assn., 1995, 1998—2001, Minn. State U. Student Assn., 1999; recipient Presdl. medallion, North Hennepin CC, 2003. Mem.: LWV (v.p., dir. 1984—90), Hubert H. Humphrey Inst. (adv. coun. 2003—), Nature Conservancy (bd. trustees 2003—), Minn. Opera Assn. (pres. 1986—88), Optimists, Rotary. Republican. Avocations: gardening, bicycling, canoeing. Home: 7500 Western Ave Golden Valley MN 55427-4849 E-mail: peggy@leppik.net.

LERCH, CAROL M. mathematics educator; b. Revere, Mass., Dec. 18, 1947; d. John P Hennessey and Olive F (Swain) Hennessey; m. Bruce F Lerch, Feb. 14, 1971; children: Bruce F Lerch, II, Kelly A, Jamie. Ph. D., Boston Coll., Chestnut Hill, MA, 2000; MA in Tchg., Bridgewater State Coll., Bridgewater, MA, 1991; BA, Regis Coll., Weston, MA, 1970. Instr. Newbury Coll., Brookline, Mass., 1991—2000; assoc. prof. math. Daniel Webster Coll., Nashua, NH, 2000—. Contbr. articles and papers to jours. Vol. Womens Golf Assn. of Mass., Norton, Mass., 2001—03. Recipient Student Life Award, Newvury Coll., 1996, Athletic Director's Award, Newbury Coll., 1996, Outstanding Contributions to Newbury Coll. Men's Basketball, 1996; fellow Presdl. Fellowship, 1999. Mem.: Internat. Soc. For Cultural and Activity Rsch., Nat. Coun. of Teachers of Math., Am. Edn. Rsch. Assn., Am. Math. Assn. of Two Yr. Colleges. Avocations: golf, travel. Office: Daniel Webster College 20 University Drive Nashua NH 03063 Office Phone: 603-577-6642. E-mail: lerch@dwc.edu.

LERNER, BARBARA, think-tank executive, researcher; b. Chgo., Mar. 31, 1935; d. Jacob Israel and Mary (Turen) Lerner. BA with honors, U. Ill., 1956; MA, U. Chgo., 1961, PhD, 1965, JD, 1977. Bar: Ill. 1977. Intern U. Chgo. Hosp. and Clinic, 1962-63; instr. Coll. Medicine U. Ill., 1963-64; clin. psychologist Ill. Mental Health Ctr., Chgo., 1965-68; assoc. prof. Ohio U., Athens, 1968-70; pvt. practice clin. psychologist Chgo., 1970-78; assoc. prof. Roosevelt U., Chgo., 1972-74; study dir. Nat. Acad. Scis., Washington, 1977-78; pres. Lerner Assocs., Princeton, N.J., 1981-96, Chgo., 1997—. Vis. scholar Ednl. Testing Svc., Princeton, 1978—79, sr. rsch. scientist, 1980—81; expert witness fed. cts. Debra P. vs. Turlington, Tampa, Fla., Marshall vs. Ga., 1983; vis. prof. U. Tex., Austin, 1989. Author: Therapy in the Ghetto, 1972, Minimum Competence, Maximum Choice, 1980; assoc. editor: U. Chgo. Law Rev., 1975—77, columnist: Phila. Inquirer, 1992—93; contbr. articles to profl. jours., newspapers and mags. Mem. U.S. Commn. Civil Rights, NJ, 1985—87; Pres. nominee U.S. Dept. of Edn., Washington, 1986. Recipient Cert. of Appreciation award for outstanding svc., U.S. Dept. of Edn., 1985. Mem.: Sigma Xi, Phi Beta Kappa. Avocation: gardening. Office: 5050 S East End Ave Chicago IL 60615-5901 E-mail: xlerner@ameritech.net.

LERNER, LINDA JOYCE, human resources executive; b. N.Y.C., Aug. 19, 1944; d. Morris and Victoria (Mizrahi) L. BS in Bus., U. Bridgeport, 1966. Asst. dir. pers. Bridgeport (Conn.) Hosp., 1969-73; dir. pers. Tufts U., Boston, 1973-80; sr. v.p. human resources Provident Instn. Savs., Boston, 1981-88; sr. v.p. UST Corp. Bank Holding Co., Boston, 1988—. Mem. allocations com. Combined Jewish Philanthropies; v.p. bd. dirs. Horizons for Youth, Boston, 1991—; bd. dirs. Operation A.B.L.E. Fellow Internat. Mktg. Inst., Boston, 1978. Mem. ASTD, N.E. Human Resources Assn., Am. Bankers Assn. (human resources exec. com. 1991—), Mass. Bankers Assn. (human resources com. 1989—, chmn. human resources com. 1993-94), Fin. Women Internat., Boston Human Resources Assn. (chmn. sr. practitioners, bd. dirs.), The Boston Club. Avocations: photography, international travel. Office: UST Corp 40 Court St Boston MA 02108-2202

LERNER, RENÉE, artist; b. N.Y.C., Mar. 30, 1936; d. Joseph and Helen (Kahn) Orlan; m. Henry R. Lerner, Mar. 15, 1959; children: Stephen, Claire, Alan. BA, Vassar Coll., 1957; postgrad., Art Ctr. Northern N.J., 1981-85, Art Students League, N.Y.C., 1981-82, Sch. Visual Arts, 1983-84, New Sch. Social Rsch., 1984-85. One woman shows include William Carlos Williams Ctr. Gallery, Rutherford, N.J., 1987, Maurice M. Pine Free Pub. Libr., Fair Lawn, N.J., 1993, Ceres, Soho, 1995, 98; exhibited in group shows at Pindar Gallery, N.Y.C., 1989, White Gallery, Franklin Lakes, N.J., 1989, Silvermine Galleries, New Canaan, Conn., 1989, 91, Butler Inst. Am. Art, Youngstown, Ohio, 1989, 94, Paterson Mus., N.J., 1991, William Paterson Coll., Wayne, N.J., 1992, City Without Walls, Newark, 1993, Lever House, N.Y.C., 1993, Stedman Gallery Rutgers U., Camden, N.J., 1993, Ceres, Soho, 1994, 96, 97, Lobby Gallery, N.Y.C., 1995, Viridian Gallery, N.Y.C., 1995, 96, John Harms Intermission Gallery, Englewood, N.J., 1997, Frauen Mus., Bonn, Germany, 1998; numerous pvt. collections. Past pres., past acting dir. Art Ctr. No. N.J., New Milford, trustee, 1987—. Fellow N.J. State Coun. on Arts/Dept. State, 1991-92; recipient Outstanding Achievement award Long Beach Island Found., 1993. Mem. Painting Affiliates of Art Ctr. of Northern N.J., Salute to Women in the Arts. Democrat. Jewish. Home: 25 Stephen Dr Englewood Cliffs NJ 07632-2230 Studio: 40 W Palisade Ave Englewood NJ 07631-2700

LERNER, SANDY, cosmetics executive; b. Phoenix, 1955; BA, Calif. State U.; student, Claremont Coll., Stanford U. Co-founder Cisco Sys., 1984-90, Ampersand Capital, 1990—; CEO Urban Decay, Mountain View, Calif., 1996—. Office: Urban Decay 729 Farad St Costa Mesa CA 92627-4304

LEROY, BETH SEPERACK, jazz musician, piano teacher; b. Bridgeport, Conn., Feb. 18, 1964; d. Reinhold Joseph and Marjorie Louise (Lundahl) Seperack; m. Jonathan Paul LeRoy, Feb. 8, 1994; children: Jessica Michelle, Jonathan Paul Jr. BMusic in Jazz Studies, Ind. U., 1989. Lic. kindermusik educator. Piano instr. DeSantis Music Schoolhouse, Syracuse, N.Y., 1986-91, Carondelet Music Ctr., Latham, N.Y., 1994-96; pianist Nelson Riddle Orch., Watertown, N.Y., 1999; keyboardist Nat. Touring Co. of Annie, Schenectady, N.Y., 1997; owner, instr. Creative Keyboard Studio, Latham, 1996—; owner, artist Keyboard Occasions, Latham, 1996—. Piano accompanist Syracuse Opera Co., 1989. Mem.: Albany Music Tchrs. Assn., Music Tchrs. Nat. Assn. (auditions asst. 1999, chmn. fall recital 1999, 2000, 2001), Am. Fedn. Musicians. Avocations: running, making hand-hooked rugs, baking, weight training. Office: Keyboard Occasions PO Box 962 Latham NY 12110-0962

LEROY, MISS JOY, model, apparel designer; b. Riverdale, Ill., Sept. 8, 1927; d. Gerald and Dorothea (Wingebach) Reasor. BS, Purdue U., 1949. Model, sales rep. Jacques, Lafayette, Ind., 1950; book dept. sales rep. Loebs, Lafayette, 1951-52; window trimmer Marshall Field's and Co., Evanston, Ill., 1952-53; sales and display rep. Emerald Ho., Evanston,

1954-55. Model, narrator, designer J. L. Hudson Co., GM Corp., Coca Cola Co., Hoover Vacuum Co., Jam Handy Orgn., Rambler and Kelvinator divsn. Am. Motors Corp., Speedway Petroleum Corp., Ford Motor Co., auto, tractor & implement divsn., Sykes Co., Detroit, 1956—61; tour guide, model, freelance writer Christian Sci. Publ. Soc. and Monitor, spl. events coord. Prudential Ins. Co.; model Copley 7, Boston, 1962—70; dep. dir., vice consul Internat. Biog. Inst. Author: Puzz-its, 1986—2002. Founding angel Asolo Theatre, Sarasota, 1960; mem. Ft. Lauderdale Internat. Film Festival, 1990, Mus. of Art, 1978, Fla. Conservation Assn., Rep. Senatorial Com. Inner Cir., 1990, Rep. Nat. Hall of Honor, 1992, Congl. Com., 1990, Nat. Trust for Hist. Preservation, 1986, Fla. Trust for Hist. Preservation, 1987; one of founding friends 1000 Friends of Fla., 1991; sec. gen. World Cultural Conv.-Noble Prize and Internat. Peace Prize; life mem. Rep. Presdl. Task Force, 1993; mem. Grand Club Rep. Party Fla., 1996. Recipient Rep. Presdl. Legion Honor medal, 1993, Rep. medal of Freedom and Wall of Honor, 1994, Disting. 20th Century Rep. Leader, 1994, 1998, Founder's Wall award, 1995, Hallmark medal of honor, Rep. Presdl. Roundtable, 2000, Internat. Order of Merit, Am. Order of Excellence, 2000, Order of Internat. Ambs., 2000, World Laureate of Eng., 1999, Rep. Senatorial Millennium medal of freedom, Congl. medal of excellence, 2002, Am. medal of honor, 2003. Mem.: Am. Rivers, Stratford Shakespearean Festival of Can., USS Constn. Mus. (charter mem. 1993), Am. Queen Inaugural Soc., Libr. of Congress (nat. mem.), Wilderness Soc., Heritage Found., The Crystal Soc., Nat. Parks and Conservation Assn., Internat. Honour Soc. (charter mem.), Ellis Island Found. (charter), Cousteau Soc., Heralds of Nature Soc., Purdue U. Alumni Assn. (pres.'s coun.), Paddlewheel Steamboatin' Soc. Am., Nat. Corvette Owners Assn., Soc. Honorary Mariners, INTRAV-Pinnacle-Elite Explorer Club, Internat. Gov.'s Club (continental gov.), Maupin Travelers Club, Captain's Cir., Ducks Unltd., Skald Club, Seabourn Club, Cunard World Club, Magic Kingdom Entertainment Club, Order Internat. Fellowship (charter mem., Internat. Woman of Yr. 1996—99, Woman of Yr. 1998—99, 2001—03), Zeta Tau Alpha. Avocations: travel, art, education, design, photography. Home: 2100 S Ocean Ln Apt 2104 Fort Lauderdale FL 33316-3827

LESACK, BEATRIZ DIAZ, secondary school educator; b. Arequipa, Peru, Dec. 2, 1948; came to U.S., 1977; d. Jésus Heradio Díaz Vargas and Elisa (Huamán) Díaz Peralta; m. Federico Vera Ponce de León, May 22, 1965 (div. 1977); 1 child, Edson Giovanni; m. Leo Pap Dorn, Oct. 27, 1977. BS in Spanish, San Agustin U., 1974; MS in Gen. Edn., SUNY, New Paltz, 1978-81, postgrad. Cert. elementary and secontary tchr., French and Spanish lang. tchr., N.Y. Tchr. Spanish Huguenot Nursery Sch., New Paltz, N.Y., 1983; tchr. elem. bilingual Ellenville (N.Y.) Sch. Dist., 1984-85; tchr. Spanish Poughkeepsie (N.Y.) Sch. Dist., 1985-86, Liberty (N.Y.) Sch. Dist., 1986-88, Fla. Unified Sch. Dist., Fla., N.Y., 1988-89; tchr. Spanish-French Hyde Park (N.Y.) Sch. Dist., 1989-91; tchr. Spanish Greenburgh Eleven Unified Sch. Dist., Dobbs Ferry, N.Y., 1991—, Copake-Taconic Hills Sch., Hillsdale, N.Y., 1995-96, FDR Sch., Bristol Twp., Pa., 1996-97; tax examiner U.S. Treasury, 1998-99, rschr., 1999—. Substitute tchr. Newburgh, Wallkill, Onteora Sch. Dists., Poughkeepsie, N.Y., 1982-83; exec. sec. Hotels and Restaurants Assn., Arequipa, 1972-73; mem. asst. Radio Club Dr. Oscar Guillen, Arequipa, 1971; tax examiner U.S. Treasury, 1998-99, rsch., 1999-2000. Fund chairman Dem. Com., New Paltz, 1991-92; mem. fundraising com. Multicultural Edn., New Paltz, 1992; mem. Mid. Sch. Steering Com., 1989-91, Multicultural Edn. Com., 1991—, steering com. Maurice Hinchey Nat. Bilingual Edn., 1980—; candidate for Phila. Bd. Edn., 2000. Fulbright Hays fellow to Dominican Rep., 1991; faculty grantee SUNY, 1978, 83-84. Mem. NAFE, Am. Assn. Tchrs. Spanish, N.Y. Fgn. Lang. Tchrs. Assn. (pres.), N.Y. Union Tchrs., Faculty Wives and Women (pres. 1989-92). Avocations: photography, video production, handicrafts, reading, golf. Home: 5411 Vicaris St Philadelphia PA 19128-2823 Office: Greenburgh Eleven Unified Sch Dist PO Box 501 Dobbs Ferry NY 10522-0501

LESAK, ALICE ELAINE, psychotherapist, minister; b. Allentown, Pa., May 7, 1955; d. Joseph Michael Lesak and Charlotte Anna Lesak ne Rockel. BA magna cum laude, Moravian Coll., 1974—78; MDiv, Pacific Sch. of Religion, 1978—81; M in profl. writing, U. of So. Calif., 1985—87; MEd, Springfield Coll., 1998. Cert. Operating Room Technician Pa., 1974; Ordained Minister United Ch. of Christ, 1981; lic. Marriage and Family Therapist Mass., 2000. Min. Madison Congl. United Ch. of Christ, Minn., 1981—85, Marietta Congl. United Ch. of Christ, Minn., 1981—85; arbitration assignment coord. LA County Bar Assn., Atty.-Client Rels. Office, Los Angeles, 1985—92; min. Tri-Parish Cmty. Ch., New Braintree, Mass., 1992—; psychotherapist Worcester Pastoral Counseling Ctr., Mass., 1998—. Psychotherapist, anger mgmt. instr., and cons. Jeremiah's Inn, Worcester, Mass., 1999—. Editor: (textbook) Hazardous Materials Strategies and Tactics. Recipient Young Career Woman of the Yr., Madison, Minn. Bus. and Profl. Women's Club, 1982. Mem.: Eye Movement Desensitization and Reprocessing Internat. Assn. United Church Of Christ. Avocations: cooking, gardening, animal rescue. Office: Tri-Parish Community Church PO Box 202 New Braintree MA 01531 Office Phone: 508-867-3306. Personal E-mail: aelesak@aol.com.

LESAR, MICHELLE DANIT, epidemiologist, researcher; b. Santa Cruz, Calif., Apr. 20, 1974; d. Albert Keith and Florence Ruth (Yellin) Lesar; m. James Michael Halderman, Aug. 16, 2003. AB in Human Biology with honors, Stanford U., 1997; MPH in Epidemiology and Biostats., postgrad. in epidemiology, U. Calif., Berkeley, 2003—. Rsch. health sci. specialist Ctr. for Health Care Evaluation Vets. Affairs Alto Healthcare Sys., Menlo Park, Calif., 1997—2001; grad. student rschr. Ctr. for the Health Assessment of Mothers and Children of Salinas, Berkeley, 2002—. Rschr. behavioral medicine Eating Disorder Pathology Lab. Stanford (Calif.) U., 1997—98. Contbr. articles to profl. jours. Tutor/mentor Upward Bound Stanford U., 1993—95, peer health counselor Cowell Student Health Ctr., 1995—96, health edn. instr. Health Corps, 1995—97; tutor, mentor pub. health Health Professions Partnership Initiative, 2001, 2004. Mem.: Spanish for Pub. Health (coord. 2002—). Avocation: tap dancing.

LESCH, ANN MOSELY, political scientist, educator; b. Washington, Feb. 1, 1944; d. Philip Edward and Ruth (Bissell) Mosely. BA, Swarthmore Coll., 1966; PhD, Columbia U., 1973. Rsch. assoc. Fgn. Policy Rsch. Inst., Phila., 1972-74; assoc. Middle East rep. Am. Friends Svc. Com., Jerusalem, 1974-77; Middle East program officer Ford Found., N.Y.C., 1977-80, program officer Cairo, 1980-84; assoc. Univs. Field Staff Internat., 1984-87; prof. Villanova U., 1987—, assoc. dir. ctr. Arab and Islamic studies, 1992-95. Author: The Politics of Palestinian Nationalism, 1973, Arab Politics in Palestine, 1979, Political perceptions of the Palestinians on the West Bank and Gaza, 1980, (with Mark Tessler) Israel, Egypt and the Palestinians, 1989, Transition to Palestinian Self-Government, 1992, (with D. Tschirgi) Origins and Development of the Arab-Israeli Conflict, 1998, The Sudan: Contested National Identities, 1998, (with Steven Wondu) Battle for Peace in Sudan, 200, (with Osman Fadl) Coping with Torture: Images from Sudan, 2004; contbr. articles to profl. jours. Co-chair Middle East Program Com., Am. Friends Svc. Com., 1989—94; mem. Quaker UN Com., 1979—80; U.S. adv. com. Interns for Peace, 1978—82; bd. dirs. Am. Near East Refugee Aid, 1980—86, Middle East Report, 1989—93, Human Rights Watch/Middle East, 1989—. Fellow Catherwood Found., 1965; NDFL, 1967-71; Am. Rsch. Ctr. grant Egypt, 1988, U.S. Inst. of Peace Rsch. grants, 1990-91, 97, 2002-03, Wilson Ctr. Guest scholar Smithsonian, 1990, Rockefeller Fdn. Bellagio Ctr., 1996, Fulbright scholar, Cairo, 1999-2000, Beirut, 2003. Mem.: Palestinian Am. Rsch. Ctr. (co-chair 1998—2001, U.S. dir. 2001—), Coun. on Fgn. Rels., Sudan Studies Assn. (sec. 1993—96, pres. 1998—2000), Am. Polit. Sci. Assn., Mid. East Inst., Mid. East Studies Assn. (bd. dirs. 1988—91, pres. 1993—96, bull. editor 1997—99). Unitarian Universalist. Office: Villanova U Dept Polit Sci Villanova PA 19085

LESCINSKI, JOAN, higher education administrator, English educator; b. Albany, N.Y., June 27, 1947; BA, Coll. St. Rose, 1970, MA, 1974; PhD, Brown U., 1981. Cert. secondary tchr., N.Y. Prof. Coll. St. Rose, Albany, N.Y., 1974-91; assoc. academic dean Avila Coll., Kansas City, Mo., 1991-93; v.p., dean Fontbonne Coll., St. Louis, 1993-98; pres. St. Mary-of-the-Woods (Ind.) Coll., 1998—. Avocation: organic vegetable gardening. Office: Pres Office St-Mary-of-the-Woods Coll Saint Mary Of The Woods IN 47876 E-mail: presofc@smwc.edu.

LESER, ANNE ELIZABETH, education educator; d. Stark William and Ann Moloney Leser. BA, Ohio No. U., 1972; MA, Ohio State U., 1984, PhD, 1989. Cert. elem. and secondary tchr. Tchr. Gallipolis (Ohio) City Schs., 1973—74, Hancock Hardin Wyandot Putman Head Start, Findlay, Ohio, 1974—76, edn. dir., 1976—81; cons. Upper Sandusky, Ohio, 1981—83; grad. asst. Ohio State U., Columbus, 1984—88; asst. prof. U. Fla., Gainesville, 1988—89; faculty devel. Ohio State U., Columbus, Ohio, 1989—90, U. Ill., Champaign, 1990—92; from asst. to assoc. prof. Maryville U., St. Louis, 1992—2003; assoc. prof., dir. Early Childhood Studies Bowling Green State U.-Firelands, Huron, Ohio, 2003—. Condr. workshop for tchrs. Amy Biehl Found., Cape Town, South Africa, 1999; cons. pub. schs., Cape Town, South Africa, 2000; presenter nat. confs., 1994—. Co-author: (handbook) Handbook for Clinical Instructors, 1990. Mem. ACLU, So. Poverty Law Ctr., Birmingham, Ala.; vol. Rape Crisis Ctr., St. Louis, 1995—98. Mem.: Nat. Assn. Early Childhood Tchr. Edn., Nat. Assn. Edn. Young Children, Ohio State Alumni Club (pres. 2001, sec. 2002), Phi Delta Kappa. Avocations: travel, social justice activities, reading. Office: Bowling Green State U-Firelands 1 University Dr Huron OH 44839 Business E-Mail: aleser@bgnet.bgsu.edu.

LESEWSKI, ARLENE, state legislator, insurance agent; b. Apr. 12, 1936; m. Thomas Lesewski; three children. Student, Southwest State U., Minn. Ins. agent; mem. Minn. Senate from 21st dist., St. Paul, 1993—. Home: PO Box 341-b Marshall MN 56258-0690 Office: Minn State Senate State Capital Building Saint Paul MN 55155-0001 Also: 807 Columbine Dr Marshall MN 56258-2406

LESH, KATHRYN ANN, nursing researcher; b. Harrisburg, Pa., Nov. 26, 1955; d. Roy Layton and Dorothy Jean (Jones) L.; m. Charles LaVerne Wilkerson, Nov. 17, 1981 (div. Feb. 1993); children: Nicholas Ryan, Alexandra Lynn. BS, Wilkes Coll., 1978; MEd, Boston U., 1986; MS, U. Ill., 1992; postgrad., Johns Hopkins U., 1993—99, Kennedy-Western U., 2000—. RN, Md. Program coord., instr. City Colls. Chgo., Wiesbaden, Germany, 1984-86; vol. safety instr. ARC, Wiesbaden, Germany, 1984-88, asst. sta. mgr., 1987-88; head nurse St. John's Hosp., San Angelo, Tex., 1988-89; nursing instr. Crouse Irving Meml. Hosp., Syracuse, N.Y., 1989-90; staff devel. coord. Elmhurst (Ill.) Meml. Hosp., 1990-92; rsch. nurse, program coord. Johns Hopkins U., Balt., 1992-96; sci. editor Kevric Co., Nat. Libr. Medicine, Silver Spring, Md., 1996—; health informaticist Kevric Co., 1999—. Nurse cons. County North Children's Ctr., Syracuse, 1989-90. Vol. firefighter, vol. ambulance Chinchilla Vol. Fire Dept., Pa., 1972-78; vol. instr., chair, ARC, Wiesbaden, 1984-88; vol. instr. Am. Heart Assn., 1985-95; mem. Lipid Nurse Task Force, 1995-99. Capt. USAF, 1979-84. Mem. ANA, Sigma Theta Tau. Democrat. Home: 2244 Prince Of Wales Ct Bowie MD 20716-1476

LESH-LAURIE, GEORGIA ELIZABETH, university administrator, biology educator, researcher; b. Cleve., July 28, 1938; d. Howard Frees and Josephine Elizabeth (Taylor) Lesh; m. William Francis Laurie, Aug. 16, 1969. BS, Marietta Coll., 1960; MS, U. Wis., 1961; PhD, Case Western Reserve U., 1966. Asst. prof. SUNY, Albany, 1966-69; asst., then assoc. prof. Case Western Reserve U., 1969-77, asst. dean, 1973-76; interim dir. Cleve. State U., Ohio, 1980, prof., chairperson, 1977-81, dean grad. studies, 1981-86, dean arts and scis., 1986-91, interim provost, v.p. academic and student affairs, 1989-90; vice chancellor acad. and student affairs U. Colo., Denver, 1991-95, interim chancellor, 1995-97, chancellor, 1997—2003, chancellor emerita, 2003—. Cons. in field; reviewer numerous granting agencies, profl. jours., 1968—; advanced placement exam. Edn. Testing Service, Princeton, N.J., 1982-83. Contbr. sci. articles to profl. pubs. Trustee Marietta Coll., Ohio, 1980-84, 85-95; mem. city/univ. interchange com., Cleve., 1983-91; chmn. commn. on women Am. Coun. Edn., 2002—. Fellow NSF, NIH; grantee NIH, Am. Cancer Soc., Am. Heart Assn., Research Corp., 1968—; recipient Wright fellowship Bermuda Biol. Station; named among AAUW Women of Distinction; named to Girl Scouts Women's Leadership Cir. Fellow AAAS; mem. Am. Soc. Zoologists, Soc. Devel. Biology, Am. Soc. Cell Biology, Phi Beta Kappa. Home: 1761 E Phillips Ave Littleton CO 80122-3260 E-mail: georgia.lesh-laurie@cudenver.edu.

LESK, ANN BERGER, lawyer; b. N.Y.C., Feb. 7, 1947; d. Alexander and Eleanor A. (Dickinson) Berger; m. Michael E. Lesk, June 30, 1968. AB cum laude, Radcliffe Coll., 1968; JD with high honors, Rutgers U., 1977. Bar: N.Y. 1979. Law clk. to justice N.J. Supreme Ct., Mountain, 1977-78; assoc. Fried, Frank, Harris, Shriver & Jacobson, N.Y.C., 1978-84, ptnr., 1984—. Editor-in-chief Rutgers Law Rev., 1976-77. Mem.: ABA, Assn. of the Bar of City of N.Y. (com. trusts, estates and surrogates cts. 1992—95, com. estate and gift taxation 1997—2003, com. trusts, estates and surrogates cts. 2000—03), N.Y. State Bar Assn. (mem. ho. of dels. 2003—), New York County Lawyers Assn. (co-chair com. trusts and estates legislation and govtl. affairs 1995—98, co-chair com. trusts and estates sect. 1998—2001, bd. dirs. 2001—04, sec. 2004—). Office: Fried Frank Harris Shriver & Jacobson LLP 1 New York Plz Fl 22 New York NY 10004-1980 Office Phone: 212-859-8113.

LESKE, M. CRISTINA, medical educator, medical researcher; MD with highest honors, U. Chile, 1964; MPH, Harvard U., 1966. Resident preventive medicine Harvard Sch. Pub. Health, Boston, 1966; resident pub. health Mass. Dept. Pub. Health, Boston, 1966—67, asst. dir. divsn. local health svcs., 1967—68; resident preventive medicine U. Rochester, NY, 1974, asst. prof. preventive medicine, 1975; asst. clin. prof. epidemiology and biostats. SUNY Coll. Optometry, N.Y.C., 1976—77, assoc. clin. prof., 1977—79; asst. prof. preventive medicine SUNY Sch. Medicine, Stony Brook, 1979—82, assoc. prof., 1982—89, prof. preventive medicine and ophthalmology, 1989—97, disting. svc. prof., 1997—, disting. prof., 2001—, head divsn. epidemiology, 1986—2002, chair dept. preventive medicine, 1991—2002; med. staff Univ. Hosp., Stony Brook, 1981—. Nat. adv. eye coun. NIH, 1987—91. Contbr. over 200 articles to profl. jours. Named Woman of the Yr. in Health, Three Village Times, N.Y., 1996, Outstanding Woman of Yr. in Sci., Town of Brookhaven, N.Y., 1998, Local Legend, Am. Med. Women Assn.; recipient Bicentennial medal, U. Cath. Chile, 1988, Disting. Achievement award in rsch., N.Y. Optometric Assn., 2000, Alumni Merit award, Harvard Sch. Pub. Health; Pub. Health fellow, Orgn. Am. States, 1965—67. Fellow: Am. Coll. Epidemiology, Am. Coll. Preventive Medicine; mem.: Inst. of Medicine of NAS. Achievements include research in in breast cancer; epidemiology of eye diseases, especially open-angle glaucoma and cataract. Office: 086L3 Health Sciences Ctr Stony Brook NY 11794-8036

LESLIE, LISA DESHAUN, professional basketball player; b. Gardena, Calif., July 7, 1972; Grad., U. So. Calif., 1994. Basketball player USA Women's Nat. Team, 1996, L.A. Sparks WNBA, 1997—. Mem. gold medal winning 1994 Goodwill Games Team; color commentary USC Basketball Games; guest corr. NBA Inside Stuff. Named 1993 USA Basketball Female Athlete of Yr.; recipient gold medal Atlanta Olympics, 1996, Sydney Olympics 2000; named MVP 1st WNBA All-Star Game, 1999; named MVP of season, WNBA Championship & All-Star Game, 2001, MVP WNBA Championship and All-Star Game, 2002; named 2003 Sportswoman of the Year for a team sport, Women's Sports Foundation; named to All-WNBA First Team, 1997, 2000, 01, 02. Office: Los Angeles Sparks 555 N Nash St El Segundo CA 90245

LESLIE, MAE SUE, writer; b. Forrester, Ark., Dec. 22, 1940; d. Doyle Joseph and Ruby Estelle (Stewart) Davis; m. Gerald Robert Leslie, Sept. 2, 1967; children: Neal R., Denise. Student, Instituto Allende, San Miguel Allende, Mex., 1960-61; BA in Journalism, Sam Houston State U., 1966. Cert. nursing home social worker, Tex. Sec. Am. Gen. Ins. Co., Houston, 1966-67; social worker Harris County, Houston, 1968; sec. temp. agys.. Houston, 1977-81; freelance writer, 1981—. Author: (novel) Canadian Capers, 1998; author of three childrens books and screenplay; freelance cartoonist. Pianist, Sunday sch. tchr. Riverside (Tex.) Bapt. Ch., 1963-65. Recipient 3d pl. for article Fla. State Writing Competition, 1994, 2d pl. for short story Manuscripts Guild, 1994, 3d pl. for nonfiction, 1994. Mem. Nat. Writer's Union, Houston Screenwriters, Nat. Honor Soc. for Journalism Students. Democrat. Baptist. Home: 5326 De Lange Ln Houston TX 77092-4208

LESLIE, MAUREEN HEELAN, university director; b. Bronx, N.Y. d. James Joseph, Sr. and Evelyn (McDonald) H.; m. Bruce Allan Leslie; children: James Christopher, Michael Patrick. BA in Bus. Mgmt. cum laude, Molloy Coll., 1997. Adminstrv. asst., A placement dir., counselor Berkeley Coll., N.Y.C., 1965—71; entrepreneur The Silk Floral Gallery, Huntington, 1984-86; gen. orgn. treas. South Huntington Sch. Dist., 1984-98; devel. assoc. Molloy Coll., Rockville Ctr., 1998-99; dir. alumni rels., 1999—. Mem. industry adv. bd. South Huntington Sch. Dist., 1998—, Mt. Sinai (N.Y.) Sch. Dist., 1999—. V.p. St. Hugh of Lincoln Sch. Bd., Huntington Sta., N.Y., 1983; mem. LIA/Long Isalnd Works Coalition, Commack and Melville, N.Y., 1998—. Mem. AAUW, Exec. Women's Golf Assn., Long Island Women's Agenda, Long Island Ctr. Bus. and Profl. Women, L.I. Regional C. of C. (mem. industry adv. bd. 2001—), Young Profls. C. of C. (mem. industry adv. bd. 1998—), Delta Epsilon Sigma, Delta Epsilon Pi, Lambda Pi Eta. Roman Catholic. Avocations: tennis, golf, swimming, dance, reading.

LESNER, SHARON A. audiologist, educator; b. Lorain, Ohio, Apr. 1, 1951; d. Donald A. and Sylvia A. Lesner. BA, Hiram Coll., 1975; MA, Kent State U., 1975, Wayne State U., 1976; PhD, Ohio State U., 1979. Cert. clin. competency Am. Speech, Lang. and Hearing Assn., lic. audiologist Ohio. Prof. U. Akron, Ohio, 1979—, fellow Inst. Life Span Learning and Gerontology, 1985—; coord. N.E. Ohio Dr. Audiology Consortium, 2002—. Co-author: Hearing Care for Older Adults, 1995. Bd. dirs. Quota Club, Akron, 1983—89. Recipient Ace award, Am. Speech and Hearing Assn., 1989, 1993, 1995, Golden Apple award, 1995. Fellow: Am. Acad. Audiology; mem.: Ohio Acad. Audiology (pres. 1996), Acad. Rehabilitative Audiology (pres. 1973). Office: Sch Speech Pathology and Audiology Univ Akron Akron OH 44325-3001

LESO, CYNTHIA J. social services administrator; b. Escondido, Calif., Jan. 6, 1956; d. Bill and Norma Jean Birdsell; m. Robert V. Leso, Oct. 5, 1985; children: Kara Marie Howard, Timothy K. AA in Child Devel., Palomar Jr. Coll., San Marcos, Calif., 1978; BA in Psychology, San Diego State U., 1991; MA in Edn., Concordia U., St. Paul, 2003. Child devel. staff Buena Vista Bapt. Ch., Vista, Calif., 1974—78; lead tchr. YMCA, Escondido, 1980—83; dir. Risk on Cmty. Child Devel. Ctr. SCCC, Valley Center, Calif., 1983—85; dir. child devel. YMCA of San Diego County, Escondido, 1985—. Pres. Program Quality Consortia, State of Calif. Program Quality, Escondido, 1994—98; chair YMCA of San Diego County Child Devel. Cluster, 2000—02; program quality reviewer Nat. Sch. Age Child Care Alliance, Boston, 1999—. Avocation: reading. Home: 1366 Chisholm Trail San Marcos CA 92069 Office: YMCA of San Diego County 1050 N Broadway Escondido CA 92026

LESONSKY, RIEVA, editor; b. N.Y.C., June 20, 1952; d. Gerald and Muriel (Cash) L. BJ, U. Mo., 1974. Rschr. Doubleday & Co., N.Y.C., 1975-78, Entrepreneur Mag., L.A., 1978-80, rsch. dir., 1983-84, mng. editor, 1985-86, exec. editor, 1986-87, editor Irvine, Calif., 1987-90; sr. v.p., editor dir. Entrepreneur Media, Inc., Irvine, 1990—; rsch. dir. LFP Inc., L.A., 1980-82; editor-in-chief Entrepreneur Mag., Irvine. Spkr., lectr. in field. Author: Start Your Own Business, 1998, 3d edit., 2004, Young Millionaires, 1998, Get Smart!, 1999, 303 Marketing Tips, 1999, Ultimate Guide to Franchises, 2004; editor: Complete Guide to Owning a Home-based Business, 1990, 168 More Businesses Anyone Can Start, 1991, 111 Businesses You Can Start for Under $10,000, 1991; contbr. articles to mags. Bd. disting. counselors Johnson & Wales U.; mem. nat. adv. coun. SBA, 1994—96, 1996—2000; bd. dirs. Students in Free Enterprise, Johnson & Wales U., Jr. Achievement, Orange County. Named Dist. Media Adv. of Yr., SBA, 1993, Dist. Women in Bus. Adv., SBA, 1995; Bus. Luminaries award. Mem. Women's Network for Entrepreneurial Tng. (bd. dirs., advisor, nat. steering com.). Avocations: books, magazines, baseball. Office: Entrepreneur Media Inc 2445 Mccabe Way Irvine CA 92614-6244 E-mail: rieva@entrepreneur.com.

LESOURD, NANCY SUSAN OLIVER, lawyer, writer; b. Atlanta, Aug. 22, 1953; d. Carl Samuel and Jane (Meadows) Oliver; m. Jeffrey Alan LeSourd, Oct. 18, 1986; children: Jeffrey Luke, Catherine Victoria. BA in Polit. Sci., Agnes Scott Coll., 1975; MA in History, Edn., Tufts U., 1977; JD, Georgetown U., 1984. Bar: Pa. 1985, D.C. 1986, Va. 1992, Fed. Cir. Ct. Appeals., 1988, U.S. Claims Ct., 1988, U.S. Supreme Ct. Instr. Newton (Mass.) High Sch., 1976-78, The Stony Brook (N.Y.) Sch., 1978-81; assoc. Gammon and Grange, Washington, 1984-88; shareholder Gammon and Grange, P.C., 1988—; mgr. Marshall-LeSourd L.L.C., 1996—. Legal commentator (radio shows) UPI News, Washington, 1985-91, Focus on the Family (Washington corr.), Colorado Springs, Colo., 1987-94; legal columnist Christian Mgmt. Rev., Downers Grove, Ill., 1987-90; spkr. in field. Author: No Longer The Hero, 1992, Liberty Letters: Underground Railroad, 2003, Liberty Letters: The Story of Pocahontas, 2003, Liberty Letters: Civil War Spies, 2004, Liberty Letters: Pearl Harbor, 2004, Christy: Christmastime in Cutter Gap, 2003; editor: Georgetown Law Jour., 1982-84; contbr. articles to profl. jours.; cons., prodr. three TV movies based on Christy, 2000—. Founder, vice-chmn. bd. trustees Ambleside Sch., 1998—2001; Bd. dirs. Arlington County Equal Employment Opportunity Commn., 1985. William Robertson Coe fellow SUNY, Stony Brook, 1978. Mem. D.C. Bar Assn., Va. Bar Assn., Christian Legal Society (bd. dirs. 1990-93). Republican. Home: 2624 New Banner Ln Herndon VA 20171-2659 Office: Gammon and Grange PC 8280 Greensboro Dr Fl 7 Mc Lean VA 22102-3807 E-mail: nol@gandglaw.com.

LESSARD, LISA KATHLEEN HAMLIN, spiritual counselor; b. Nashville, Mar. 8, 1962; d. James William Hamlin and Margaret Louise (Reid) Cox; m. Ronald Edward Lessard, May 19, 2001. BS, Belmont U., 1983; MLS, Vanderbilt U., 1985; PhD in Metaphys. Sci., Progressive Universal Life Ch., 1995; PhD in Parapsychology, DD, P.U.L.C., 1995; BMSc., U. Metaphysics, 1995, MMSc, 1996. Ordained metaphysical min. Internat. Metaphysical Ministry, 1995; cert. holistic life coach U. Metaphysics, Reiki master. Grad. asst. to dir. edn. libr. Vanderbilt U., Nashville, 1984-85; cataloging libr. Shiloh Regional Libr., Jackson, Tenn., 1985-86; various temp. positions Nashville, 1986; sch. libr. Mt. Juliet (Tenn.) Elem. Sch., 1987-89; tech. svcs. divsn. mgr. Brentwood (Tenn.) Libr., 1990—2003. Co-author: (poems) At Water's Edge, 1995 (Editor's Choice award), The Best Poems of 1996, 1996, Poetic Voices of America, 1996. Ch. pianist, asst. choir dir., Sunday sch. tchr. Nashville Bapt. Temple, 1977—84; mem. Inst. Noetic Scis. Mem.: ALA (audiovisual roundtable 1985—86), Interstitial Cystitis Assn., Chronic Fatigue and Immune Dysfunction Syndrome Soc., Tenn. Libr. Assn., Care2.com, Assn. Rsch. and Enlightenment. Avocations: music, art, writing. Home and Office: PO Box 757 Nolensville TN 37135-0757

LESSER, WENDY, editor, writer, consultant; b. Santa Monica, Calif., Mar. 20, 1952; d. Murray Leon Lesser and Millicent (Gerson) Dillon; m. Richard Rizzo, Jan. 18, 1985; 1 child, Nicholas 1 stepchild, Dov Antonio. BA, Harvard U., 1973; MA, Cambridge (Eng.) U., 1975; PhD, U. Calif., Berkeley, 1982. Founding ptnr. Lesser & Ogden Assocs., Berkeley, 1977-81; founding editor Threepenny Rev., Berkeley, 1980—. Bellagio resident Rockefeller Found., Italy, 1984. Author: (novels) The Life Below the Ground, 1987, His Other Half, 1991, Pictures at an Execution, 1994, A Director Calls, 1997, The Amateur, 1999, Nothing Remains the Same, 2002; editor Hiding in Plain Sight, 1993; author: The Genius of Language, 2004. Fellow, NEH, 1983, 1992, ACLS, 1996, Am. Acad. Berlin, 2003—; Guggenheim fellow, 1988, Open Soc. Inst. fellow, 1998, Nat. Arts Journalism Program Sr. fellow, Columbia U., 2000—01. Democrat. Office: The Threepenny Rev PO Box 9131 Berkeley CA 94709-0131

LESSICK, MIRA LEE, nursing educator; b. Hazleton, Pa., Jan. 25, 1949; d. Jack H. and Shirley E. (Frumkin) Lessick. Diploma in Nursing, Albany (N.Y.) Med. Ctr., 1969; BSN, Boston U., 1972; MS, U. Colo., 1973; PhD, U. Tex., 1986. Staff nurse Boston City Hosp. and Mass. Gen. Hosp., 1969-72; instr. to asst. prof. nursing, genetics clinician U. Rochester, NY, 1973-79; asst. prof. nursing, practitioner Rush U. Coll. Nursing, Chgo., 1986-91, assoc. prof. nursing, 1992—2001, project dir. genetic health nursing program, 1993—2001; assoc. prof. U. Toledo, 2001—. Mem. human genome rsch. initial rev. group, ethical, legal, and social implications subcom. Nat. Human Genome Rsch. Inst., NIH, 1996-99; peer reviewer Bur. Health Professions, HHS, 2001-02. Mem. editl. adv. bd. AWHONN Lifelines, 1999—, Manuscript Rev. Panel, Rsch. in Nursing and Health Jour.; genetics column editor Medsurg Nursing: The Jour. of Adult Health, 2001—; contbr. articles to profl. jours. and textbooks. Recipient Bd. of Govs. award, Excellence in Pediatric Nursing award Albany Med. Ctr., 1969, Outstanding Nurse Recognition award March of Dimes Birth Defects Found., 1991, Recognition award for Individual Contbn. to Maternal-Child Health Nat. Perinatal Assn., 1993, Founders Award in Edn., Internat. Soc. Nurses in Genetics, 1997. Mem. AAAS, ANA, APHA, Internat. Soc. Nurses in Genetics (chair rsch. com. 1993-2002, co-chair rsch. com. 2003—, mem. Genetic Nursing Credentialing Commn., 2001—, mem. web site editl. bd., 2001—, hon. mention Genetic Nursing Writer's award, 2002), Assn. Women's Health, Obstetric, and Neonatal Nurses, Am. Soc. Human Genetics, Chgo. Nurses Assn. (legis. com. 1990-91), N.Y. Acad. Scis., Midwest Nursing Rsch. Soc., Sigma Theta Tau (Luther Christman award for excellence in published writing 1993, Luther Christman award Excellence Pub. Writing, 1998), Phi Kappa Phi. Achievements include development of a genetic health area of concentration within a graduate level nursing program. Office: U Toledo Coll Health and Human Svcs Scott Park Campus Toledo OH 43606-3390 E-mail: mlessic@utnet.utoledo.edu.

LESTER, ALICIA LOUISE, financial analyst; b. Niagara Falls, N.Y., Aug. 28, 1955; d. Belmira Hinto Harris and James Lester; children: Deláno Thompson, Michael, Jr. Thompson. BS in Commerce, Niagara U., 1977. Underwriting cert. Robert Morris Assn., 1997. Mktg., acctg. analyst Carborundum Abrasives Co., Niagara Falls, NY, 1978—87; self employed contractor - analytical various corps., Buffalo, 1990—96; comml. fin. analyst Fleet Boston Financial Corp. Banking, Buffalo, 1996—2000; fin. analyst Motorola Inc., Elma, NY, 2000—02; fin. analyst II, banking officer M & T Bank, Buffalo, 2002—. Owner Thunder Solutions Programming and Mktg., Buffalo, 1997—. Chmn. arts facet The Links Inc., Niagra Falls, NY, 1997—2002, co-chmn. tech., 1997—2002, fin. sec., 2003—; chair Clark Acad. Performing Arts, 1990—2002. Mem.: Inst. Mgmt. Accts., Harriet Tubman 300, Inc., Fin. Women Internat. (comm. chair 1997—99), The Links, Inc. (Niagara Falls chp., co-chair tech. 1997—2002, chair arts facet 1997—2002, fin. sec. 2003—). Personal E-mail: A.Lester@Verizon.net.

LESTER, JOAN STADELMAN, music educator; b. Hopkinsville, Ky., July 4, 1937; d. Roy Albert Stadelman and Maurine Miriam Blythe; m. Robert Worth Lester, Sept. 10, 1960; children: Katherine, Evelyn, Jennifer. MusB, U. Ky., 1959; MusM, Ithaca Coll., 1969; D in Musical Arts, U. Tex., 1991. Cert. supt. schs. Ky., Tex., mid-mgmt. Tex., music tchr. Ky., Tex. Music supr. and tchr. Hopkinsville Pub. Schs., 1959—66; coord. music in schs. Elmira (N.Y.) Symphony and Choral Soc., 1972—75; tchg. asst. in music edn. dept. music U. Tex., Austin, 1975—78; dir. choral music O. Henry Jr. High/Middle Sch., Austin, 1979—95; prin. Pennyrile Accelerated Learning Sch., Elkton, Ky., 1995—97; owner, cons. The Thinking Place, Hopkinsville, 1997—. Vis. instr. voice, dir. choral activities Elmira Coll., 1973—75; instr. music and edn. Hopkinsville C.C., Ft. Campbell, Ky., 2001—; founder, dir. Town & Gown Chorale, Hopkinsville, 1998—. Bd. mem. Pennyroyal Arts Coun., Hopkinsville, 1998—. Programming grant for open program, Pennyroyal Arts Coun., 2002. Mem.: Coll. Music Soc., Music Educators Nat. Conf., Am. Choral Dirs. Assn., Christian County Dem. Womens Club. Presbyterian. Home: 210 Jim Green Rd Trenton KY 42286 Office: The Thinking Place 1720 Lovers Ln Hopkinsville KY 42240

LESTER, JUNE, library information studies educator; b. Sandersville, Ga., Aug. 25, 1942; d. Charles DuBose and Frances Irene (Cheney) L.; 1 child, Anna Elisabeth Engle. BA, Emory U., 1963, M in Librarianship, 1971; D in Libr. Sci., Columbia U., 1987, cert. in advanced librarianship, 1982. Asst. prof., cataloger U. Tenn. Libr., Knoxville, 1971-73; libr. divsn. libr. and info. mgmt. Emory U., Atlanta, 1973-81, asst. prof. div. libr. and info. mgmt., 1976-80, assoc. prof., 1980-87; accreditation officer Am. Libr. Assn., 1987-91; assoc. dean, assoc. prof. Sch. Libr. and Info. Scis. U. North Tex., Denton, 1991—93; prof. U. Okla., Norman, 1993—, dir. Sch. Libr and Info. Studies, 1993—2000. UCLA sr. fellow, 1987. Mem. ALA (coun. mem. 1987), Assn. for Libr. and Info. Sci. Edn. (bd. dirs. 1985-87, 94-97, pres. 1995-96), Am. Soc. Info. Sci. and Tech., Okla. Libr. Assn., Phi Beta Kappa, Beta Phi Mu. Unitarian Universalist. Home: 2006 Trailview Ct Norman OK 73072-6654 Office: U Okla Sch Libr and Info Studies 401 W Brooks St Norman OK 73019-6030 Office Phone: 405-325-3921. E-mail: jlester@ou.edu.

LESTER, PAMELA ROBIN, lawyer; b. N.Y.C., Aug. 5, 1958; d. Howard M. and Patricia Barbara (Briger) L. Student, Princeton U., 1978-79; BA cum laude, Amherst Coll., 1980; JD, Fordham U., 1983. Bar: N.Y. 1984, D.C. 1985. With Advantage Internat., Inc., Washington, 1984-89, gen. counsel, 1987-89; assoc. Akin, Gump, Strauss, Hauer & Feld, Washington, 1989-90; sr. v.p. bus. affairs and gen. counsel Time Warner Sports, N.Y.C., 1991-99; COO HBO Properties, 1998—. Adj. lectr. sports law Am. U. Law Sch., 1989-91; adj. faculty sports law Fordham U. Law Sch., 1992-96; bd. advisors Ctr. for Protection of Athletes Rights, 1994-97. Contbr. chpt. to: The Law of Professional and Amateur Sports, 1989, 95. Mem. ABA (program and sports divsn. chair forum entertainment and sports industries' governing com. 1992-96, chair elect 1996, chair 1997-99, immediate past chair 1999—, governing com. standing com. on forum-coms. 1994), Assn. Bar City N.Y. (sports law com. 1991-95), Sports Lawyers Assn. (bd. dirs., pres.-elect 2000—), N.Y. State Bar Assn., Women's Sports Found. (mem. bd. adv. 1991-99), Va. Commonwealth U. Sportscenter (adv. bd. 1999—). Office: HBO Properties 1100 Avenue Of The Americas New York NY 10036-6740

LESTER, SUSAN E. bank executive; CFO U.S. Bancorp, Mpls., to 2000; exec. v.p., CFO HomeSide Lending. Bd. dirs. VisionShare, Inc., First Community Bancorp, Rancho Sante Fe, Calif., Derma, Inc., Edinda, Minn.; strategic advisor thedatabank, Inc. Trustee Coll. Saint Benedict. Mem.: Hazeltine Nat. Golf Club (bd. govs.). Office: 1500 S Hwy 100 Suite 200 Golden Valley MN 55416

LESTER, VIRGINIA LAUDANO, education administrator; b. Phila., Jan. 5, 1931; d. Edmund Francis and Emily Beatrice (Downes) Laudano; children: Pamela Lester Golde, Valerie Lester. BA, Pa. State U., 1952; MEd, Temple U., 1955; PhD, Union Grad. Sch., 1972; JD, Stanford U. Law Sch., 1988. Tchr. pub. schs., Abington, Pa., 1952-55, Greenfield Center, N.Y., 1956; instr. edn. dept. Skidmore Coll., Saratoga Springs, N.Y., 1962-64, dir. ednl. research, 1967-72, asst. to the pres., 1968-72; asst. dir. Capitol Dist. Regional Supplementary Edn. Ctr., Albany, NY, 1966-67; assoc. dean, asst. prof. state-wide programs Empire State Coll., State U. N.Y., Saratoga Springs, 1973-75, sr. assoc. dean, assoc. prof., 1975-76, acting dean state-wide programs, 1976; pres., prof. interdisciplinary studies Mary Baldwin Coll., Staunton, Va., 1976-85, cons. to bd. trustees, 1985-88; assoc. Hunton & Williams, Richmond, Va., 1988-90; interim pres. Friends World Coll., Huntington, N.Y., 1990-91; dir. presdl. search consultation svc. Assn. of Governing Bds. of Univs. and Colls., 1991-94; of counsel spl. projects office of exec. dir. Am. Assn. Retired Persons, 1994—2001. Mem. cons. core faculty Union Grad. Sch., Union for Experimenting Colls. and Univs., Cin., 1975—82; vis. faculty fellow Harvard U. Grad. Sch. Edn., 1976; bd. dirs. So. Bankshares, So. Bank, Coun. Advancement of Small Colls., 1977—81, Am. Council Edn., 1983-85; adj. faculty mem. Grad. Sch. George Washington U., 1996, 2002—; cons. Nat. Exec. Svc. Corp., 1991—. Mem. com. on criminal sexual assault Va. State Crime Commn., 1976; v.p. Costume Collection, Inc., 1971-73; v.p. Warren, Washington, Saratoga Counties Planned Parenthood, 1972-74, bd. dirs., 1970-74; mem. Saratoga Springs Housing Bd. Appeals, 1966-76, Commn. on Future of Va., 1982-84; bd. dirs. Nat. Urban League, 1979-86; pres. commn. NCAA, 1984-85. Mem. Am. Acad. Polit. and Social Scis., Va. Found. Ind. Colls. (trustee, exec. com.), Va. Council Ind. Colls., Am. Council on Edn. (commn. on women in higher edn. 1977-80, bd. dirs. 1981-85), Nat. Assn. Ind. Colls. and Univs. (dir.), Assn. Va. Colls. (sec.-treas. 1978-79, pres. 1980-81, dir.), Assn. Ch. Related Colls. and Univs. of South (pres. 1983), Pi Lambda Theta, Pi Gamma Mu, Chimes. Mem. Soc. Of Friends. E-mail: vlester55@msn.com.

LETCHER, NAOMI JEWELL, quality engineer, educator, counselor; b. Belle Point, W. Va., Dec. 29, 1924; d. Andrew Glen and Ollie Pearl (Meadows) Presley; m. Frank Philip Johnson, Oct. 5, 1945 (div. Dec. 1953); m. Paul Arthur Letcher, Mar. 6, 1954; children: Frank, Edwin, Richard, David. AA, El Camino Jr. Coll., 1964; BA, Calif. State U., 1971. Inspector N. Am. Aviation, Downey, Calif., 1964-71; substitute tchr. ABC Unified Sch. Dist., Artesia, Calif., 1971-72; recurrence control rep. Rockwell Internat., Downey, Calif., 1972-80, quality engr., 1981-86; counselor Forest Lawn Cemeteries, Cerritos, Calif., 1980-81; tech. analyst Northrop, Pico Rivera, Calif., 1986-89. Gov. divsn. D-2 area T.M. Internat., Downey, Calif., 1978-79. Author: History of the Letcher Family, 1995. Docent Temecula (Calif.) Valley Mus., 1994—. Mem. AAUW, Nat. Mgmt. Assn., NOW, Srs. Golden Yrs. Club, Alpha Gamma Sigma. Democrat. Baptist. Avocations: genealogy, needlework, stamp collecting, dance, bowling. E-mail: OMIE8@aol.com.

LETIZI, SUNNY SELMA, social worker; b. N.Y.C., Oct. 11, 1930; d. Nathan Feferblum and Rebecca Kleinberg; m. Richard A. Letizi; children: Dana, Victor, Ann. BA, Hunter Coll., 1952. With N.Y.C. Dept. Welfare, 1953—56; group worker Neighborhood Ctr., Phila., 1958—59; with Cornucopia Health Food Store, Rockledge; social worker Bucks County Housing Group, Wrightstown, Pa., 1989—. Vol. Women's Ctr., Abington, Pa., 1975—2001. Mem.: LWV (legis. chmn. 1960—76), AAUW (dir. 1970—2001, chmn. various coms.). Avocations: music, dance, travel, swimming, art. Home: 792 Dale Rd Jenkintown PA 19046 Office: Bucks County Housing Group 2324 Second St Pike Newtown PA 18940

LETT, CYNTHIA ELLEN WEIN, speaker, trainer, coach; b. Takoma Park, Md., Dec. 24, 1957; d. Arthur Benjamin and Mary Louise (Barker) Wein; m. Gerald Lee Lett, June 1, 1991; 1 child, Cameron Barker Wein Lett. BS, Purdue U., 1979; M, Antioch Sch. Law, 1982-83. Mktg. researcher Sheraton, Washington, 1979-80; sales mgr. Sea Pines Plantation Co., Hilton Head Island, SC, 1980-81; dir. sales Sheraton Potomac Hotel, Rockville, Md., 1981-82, Ritz Carlton Hotel, Washington, 1982-83; pres. Creative Planning Internat., Washington, 1983—; dir. The Lett Group, 1983—. Dir. mem. Great Inns Am., Annapolis, 1987-89; etiquette cons., 1989—; dir. meetings Am. Healthcare Inst., 1991-92; corp. affairs mgr. MCI Telecom Corp., 1992-95; pres. The Lett Group, 1996—. Author: Getaway Innstyle, America's Fifty Best Inns, 1990; editor Travel Inn Style Newsletter, 1990-91, Apropos!, 1996—. Mem. ASTD, Profl. Conv. Mgmt. Assn., Found. for Internat. Meetings (bd. govs. 1985-86), Nat. Spkrs. Assn., Washington Conv. Visitors Assn., Purdue Club, Univ. Club, Internat. Soc. of Protocal & Etiquette Profls. (ISPEP) Exec. Dir. 2002-. Avocations: classical music, amateur photography, country inns, foreign travel, gardening. Office: Lett Group 13116 Hutchinson Way Ste 100 Silver Spring MD 20906-5947 Office Phone: 301-946-8208. E-mail: clett@lettgroup.com.

LETTERIE, KATHLEEN, broadcast executive; Head, talent WB Network, 1994—97, sr. v.p. talent and casting, 1997—2001, exec. v.p. talent and casting, 2001—. Office: WB TV Network 4000 Warner Blvd Bldg 34R Burbank CA 91522-0001

LETZIG, BETTY JEAN, financial consultant; b. Feb. 18, 1926; d. Robert H. and Alina Violet (Mayes) L. BA, Scarritt Coll., 1950, MA, 1968. Ednl. staff The Meth. Ch. Ark., Okla., Tex., 1953-60; with Internat. Deaconess Exch. Program, London, 1961-62; staff exec. nat. divsn. United Meth. Ch., N.Y.C., 1962-95, ret., 1995, cons. current and deferred giving, 1995—. Coord. Mission Pers. Support Svcs., 1984-88; exec. sec. Deaconess Program Office, 1989-95. Contbr. articles to profl. jours. Bd. dirs. Global Health Action, Atlanta, 1974-88, Vellore Christian Med. Coll., N.Y.C., 1984-94; mem. U.S. com. Internat. Coun. Social Welfare, Washington, 1983-89; active Nat. Interfaith Coalition on Aging, Athens, Ga. and Washington, 1972—, pres., 1981-85. Mem.: LWV, AAUW, Older Women's League, Nat. Coun. Social Welfare, Nat. Voluntary Orgns. Ind. Living for Aging, Nat. Coun. Aging. Avocations: travel, beachcombing, photography, needlework. Home: 266 Merrimon Ave Asheville NC 28801 Office: St Paul's United Meth Ch 223 Hillside St Asheville NC 28801

LEUCHOVIUS, DEBORAH, advocate, special education services professional, consultant; b. Litchfield, Minn., Dec. 22, 1954; d. David Robert Leslie and Corinne Ardell Shiell; m. James Raphael Poole, Aug. 18, 1979; 1 child, Frederick Winston Leuchovius Poole. BA, Hamline U., 1978; MA, Rutgers U., 1981. Americans with Disabilities Act specialist PACER Ctr., Inc., Mpls, tech. assistance specialist Mpls., 1994—96, project dir., tatra project, 1996—, nat. coord., transition tech. assistance programs, 2001—. Cons. Change Agy., St. Paul, 1990—. Editor: (newsletter) Point of Departure, (book) The Americans with Disabilities Act: A Guide for People with Disabilities, Their Families and Advocates. Advisor to nat. leadership team Assn. Sci. and Tech. Ctrs., Mus. and Access; mem. Spina Bifida Assn. Minn., 1994—, sec., 2000; advisor VSA Arts Minn., Mpls., 1995—99; advisor to access com. Walker Art Ctr.; bd. dirs. ADA Minn., St. Paul, 1992—95; founding mem. Minn. Ind. Scholars Forum, 1981—89. Mem.: Nat. Rehab. Assn., Coun. Exceptional Children (parents rep. divsn. career devel. 1997—99). Office: PACER Ctr 8161 Normandale Blvd Minneapolis MN 55437

LEUCK, CLAIRE M. state legislator; m. Richard Leuck. Student, Ind. Vo-Tech. Coll., Ind. State U. Clk. Benton County Cir. Ct., Ind., 1974-82, bailiff, sec., 1984-86; state rep. Dist. 25 Ind. Ho. of Reps., 1986—, chmn. agr. com., mem. natural resources, rds. and transp. com., mem. county and twp. elec., agr. and rural devel. com., ranking minority mem. Farmer. Bd. dirs. Coun. for Acad. Excellence-Dollars for Scholars; mem. St. Anne Soc.; mem. dean's adv. coun. Purdue U. Agr. Mem. Am. Legion Aux., No. Dist. Cir. Ct. Clks., Kappa Kappa Kappa. Home: RR 1 Box 203 Fowler IN 47944-9772 Office: Ind Ho of Reps State Capitol Indianapolis IN 46204 Also: 2816 N 400 E Fowler IN 47944-8081

LEUKART, BARBARA J. J. lawyer; b. N.Y.C., Nov. 24, 1948; BA, Barnard Coll., 1971; JD, Case Western Reserve U., 1975. Bar: Ohio 1975. Mem. Jones, Day, Reavis & Pogue, Cleve. Mem. Order Coif. Office: Jones Day Reavis & Pogue North Point 901 Lakeside Ave E Cleveland OH 44114-1190 also: Jones Day Reavis & Pogue 901 Lakeside Ave E Cleveland OH 44114-1116

LEUNER, JEAN D'MEZA, nursing administrator; d. Jay and Marilyn Sprigg D'Meza; m. Richard Joseph Leuner; children: Kirstyn Jean, Kyle Joseph. Diploma in nursing, St. Lukes Hosp., 1972; BSN, Seton Hall U., 1975; MSN, Boston Coll., 1979, PhD, 1994. Staff nurse Nyack (N.Y.) Hosp., 1972—75; instr. St. Anselm's Coll., Manchester, NH, 1976—78; assoc. prof., interim dir. MGH Inst. Health Prof., Boston, 1980—95; assoc. dean Med. U. S.C. Coll. Nursing, Charleston, 1995—2003; dir. Sch. Nursing U. Cen. Fla., Orlando, 2003—. Chair adv. com. S.C. Bd. Nursing, Columbia, 2002—03; chair Deans and Dirs. Coun. Nursing Programs in S.C., 1999—2001. Author: (book) Mastering the Nursing Process: Case Method Approach, 1990. Mem. Def. Adv. Com. on Women in the Svcs., 2000—02. Recipient Palmetto award, S.C. Nurses Found., Twin award, Charleston S.C. YWCA. Mem.: ANA, Phi Delta Kappa, Sigma Theta Tau. Avocations: tennis, golf, reading. Office: U Cen Fla Orlando FL 32816

LEUPP, EDYTHE PETERSON, retired education educator; b. Mpls., Nov. 27, 1921; d. Reynold H. and Lillian (Aldridge) Peterson; m. Thomas A. Leupp, Jan. 29, 1944 (dec.); children: DeEtte(dec.), Patrice, Stacia, Roderick, Braden. BS, U. Oreg., 1947, MS, 1951, EdD, 1972. Tchr. various pub. schs., Idaho, 1941-45, 1945-55; dir. tchr. edn. N.W. Nazarene Coll., Nampa, Idaho, 1955-61; sch. adminstr. Portland Pub. Schs., 1963-84; dir. tchr. edn. George Fox Coll., Newberg, Oreg., 1984-87; ret., 1987. Vis. prof. So. Nazarene U., Bethany, Okla., 1988—95, Asia Pacific Nazarene Theol. Sem., 1996, prof., 2000; adj. prof. Warner Pacific Coll., Portland, 1996—97; pres. Portland Assn. Pub. Sch. Adminstrs., 1973—75; dir.-at-large Nat. Coun. Adminstv. Women Edn., Washington, 1973—76; state chmn. Oreg. Sch. Prins. Spl. Project, 1978—79; chair Confdn. Oreg. Sch. Adminstrs. Ann. Conf.; rschr. 40 tchr. edn. programs in colls. and univs.; designer tchr. edn. program George Fox Coll. Author: tchr. edn. materials. Pres. Nampa PTA, 1958, Idaho State Aux. Mcpl. League, 1957. Named Honored Tchr. of Okla., 1993; recipient Golden Gift award, 1982; fellow, Charles Kettering Found., 1978, 1980, 1987, 1991, 1992, 1993, 1994; scholar Hazel Fishwood, 1970. Mem.: Am. Assn. Colls. Tchr. Edn., Pi Lambda Theta, Phi Delta Kappa, Delta Kappa Gamma (pres. Alpha Rho State 1986—88). Republican. Nazarene. Avocations: travel, crafts, photography. Home: 8100 SW 2nd Ave Portland OR 97219-4602

LEUZZI, LINDA, writer; b. N.Y.C., Aug. 1, 1947; d. Benjamin DeClara, Fanna DeClara; m. Vincent Leuzzi, Oct. 31, 1970. BS in Journalism, St. John's U., 1986. Coord. pub. rels., mgr. pub. rels. Avon Products Inc., N.Y.C., 1979—83; freelance corr. N.Y. Newsday, Rego Park, 1985—87; assoc. copy editor King Features Syndicate, N.Y.C., 1987—88; freelance journalist, author numerous mags., Sayville, NY, 1988—; editor The Suffolk County News and Islip (N.Y.) Bull., 2003—. Author: To the Young Environmentalist, 1997, A Creative Life: The Young Person's Guide, 1997; author: (series) Life in America: 100 Years Ago-Vol. on Transportation, 1995, Life in America: 100 Years Ago-Vol. on Urban Life, 1995, Life in America: 100 Years Ago-Vol. on Industry, 1997, Life in America: 100 Years Ago-Vol. on Education, 1997; author: The Portuguese Boy, 2001, A Matter of Style: Women in the Fashion Industry, 1997 (Books for the Teenage List, 1997), Life Connections: Pioneers in Ecology (Books for the Teenage List, 2001); contbr. chapters to books. Former trustee Sci. Mus. L.I., Plandome, NY, 1996—2001; trustee Splashes of Hope, Huntington, NY, 2001—; bus. adv. bd. mem. Sayville Sch., 1999—2002. Recipient 2d place and 3d place awards, N.Y. Press Assn., 2002. Mem.: Am. Soc. Journalists and Authors, Rotary (host Rotary exchange students). Avocations: hiking, jogging, travel, music. Home and Office: 131 Gillette Ave Sayville NY 11782 E-mail: lindaleuzzi@aol.com.

LEV, DARLEEN KATHERINE, interior designer, writer; b. Evanston, Ill., Aug. 3, 1961; d. Charles Rudolph and Lenore Houck Lev. BA in English and Creative Writing, San Francisco State U., 1992; MFA in Fiction, U. Iowa, 1994. Instr. fiction Gotham Writers Workshop, N.Y.C., 1999—; interior decorator and pres. Funky Chic Decorating, Bklyn., 2000—. Author: (short stories) Bad Wind, Good Wind, 2001. Office: Funky Chic Decorating 151 Ainslie St Brooklyn NY 11211

LEVALLEY, JOAN CATHERINE, accountant; b. Decatur, Ill., Nov. 27, 1931; d. Clarence and Pearl Mae (McClure) Krall; m. Charles R. LeValley, Apr. 13, 1958 (div.); children: Curtis Ray, Cara Marie. BA in Bus., Manchester Coll., 1957. Accredited tax advisor, Ill. Acct. with various firms, 1960-76; pvt. practice acctg., Park Ridge, Ill., 1964-79; pres., dir. LeValley & Assocs., Inc., Park Ridge, 1979—; mem. tax adv. com. Chgo. IRS Dirs.; mem. com. United Way of Park Ridge, 1991, co-chmn., 1992. Mem. Nat. Assn. Pub. Accts., Ind. Acct. Assn. Ill. (2d woman pres. 1987-88, Person of Yr. award 1990), Bus. and Profl. Women Park Ridge (pres. 1974-75, Bus. Woman of Yr. 1983), Park Ridge C. of C. (treas. 1985-87). Baptist. Avocations: baking; sewing; gardening. Home: 2200 Bouterse St Apt 101 Park Ridge IL 60068-2367 Office: LeValley & Assocs Inc 6215 S 44th St Lincoln NE 68516-5506

LEVANDOWSKI, BARBARA SUE, educational administrator; b. Mar. 16, 1948; d. Earl F. and Ann (Klee) L. BA in Edn. and Spanish, North Park Coll., 1970; MS in Elem. Edn., No. Ill. U., 1975, degree in curriculum and supervision/, 1977, EdD, 1979. cert. elem. tchr.; cert. secondary tchr.; cert. in administrv. with supt. endorsement; cert. sr. reviewer, Ill. Tchr. Round Lake (Ill.) Sch. Dist., 1970-75, Schaumburg (Ill.) Sch. Dist., 1975-87, asst. prin., 1977-87; prin., staff devel. dir. Dist. 200 Northwood Elem. Sch., Woodstock, Ill., 1987-94, dir. curriculum and instrn., 1994—; developer, dir. Woodstock Mentor-Instrn. for Tchrs., 1998—. Curriculum cons. Spring Grove (Ill.) Sch. Dist., 1980-81; instr. various courses, Schaumburg, 1984-86; dir. Einstein Sch. Writing Project, 1986-87; dir. Dist. 200 Thinking Thinking Skills, 1988—; co-instr. Dist. 200 Tchg. Thinking Skills Across the Curriculum, 1992—, dir. curriculum and instrn.; chair north ctrl. assn. visitation team Huntley Sch. Dist, 1989; co-developer 4 yr. tchr. mentor program, 1994—. Mem. editorial bd. Ill. Sch. R & D Jour., 1981—; contbr. articles to profl. jours. Chair Computer/Tech. Strategic Action Team, Woodstock, 1988-89. Recipient numerous awards for excellence in teaching, Those Who Excel award State of Ill., 1979; fed. grantee. Mem. NAESP, NAFE, ASCD (insvc. presenter 1984—, presenter state and nat. conv. 1989—), Am. Biog. Rsch. Assn. (bd. dirs. 1985—, publs. com. 1983), Nat. Staff Devel. Coun., Nat. Coun. of States for Insvc., Ill. Staff Devel. Coun., Ill. Assn. for Supervision and Curriculum Devel. (chair rsch. com. 1982), Ill. Computer Educators, Inst. Ednl. Rsch. (editorial bd. advisors, co-chair effective teaching characteristics observation 1990—, Omega award), Ill. Prin. Assn. Phi Delta Kappa, Delta Kappa Gamma. Home: 426 Normandie Ln Round Lake IL 60073-3711 Office: Woodstock Sch Dist 200 227 W Judd St Woodstock IL 60098-3126 E-mail: levandbs@netscape.net.

LEVEN, ANN RUTH, museum financial officer; b. Canton, Ohio, Nov. 1, 1940; d. Joseph J. and Bessie (Scharff) L. AB, Brown U., 1962; cert. with distinction in program in bus. adminstrn., Harvard-Radcliffe Univs., 1963; MBA, Harvard U., 1964. Product mgr. household products div. Colgate-Palmolive, N.Y.C., 1964-66, account exec. Grey Advt., N.Y.C., 1966-67; fin. asst. Met. Mus. Art, N.Y.C., 1967-69, asst. treas., 1970-72, treas., 1972-79, v.p., sr. corp. planning officer Chase Manhattan Bank, N.Y.C., 1979-83; pres. ARL Assocs., N.Y.C., 1983—; treas. Smithsonian Instn., 1984-90; dep. treas. Nat. Gallery Art, Washington, 1990-94, treas. and CFO, 1994-99. Adj. asst. prof. Grad. Sch. Bus., Columbia U., 1975—77, adj. assoc. prof., 1977—79, adj. prof., 1980—93; exec.-in-residence Amos Tuck Sch., Dartmouth Coll., 1976, 84; bd. dirs. Del. Group Family of Funds, Systemax; bd. govs. Investment Co. Inst., 1997—2004. Artist (awarded prizes for painting and graphic arts); contbr. articles to profl. jours. Exec. bd. new leadership divsn. Fedn. Jewish Philanthropies, 1968-70; coun. mem. N.Y. Public Libr., exec. com., 1976-79; mus. adv. panel N.Y. State Council on Arts, 1977-79; bd. dirs. Camp Rainbow, 1970-84, v.p., 1976-78, treas., 1982-84; bd. overseers Amos Tuck Sch., 1978-84, chmn. ednl. affairs com., 1979-84; trustee Brown U., 1976—, fin. and budget com., student life com., devel. com., adv. and exec. coms.; bd. dirs. Ctr. for Fgn. Policy Devel., 1989-94, 2002-, Am. Arts Alliance, 1990-92; bd. dirs. Twyla Tharp Dance Found., 1982-87, Reading Is Fundamental, 1987-91, adv. coun., 1991-94; trustee Artists' Choice Mus., 1979-87; vis. com. Harvard U. Bus. Sch., 1979-84; bd. overseers Hood Mus.-Hopkins Ctr. Dartmouth Coll., 1984-91, chmn., 1988-91; trustee ARC Endowment Fund, 1985-90, N.Y. Sch. Interior Design, 1996—, Andy Warhol Found., 1999—; staff Presdl. Task Force on Arts and Humanities, 1981. Recipient Young Leadership award Council Jewish Fedns. and Welfare Funds, 1968; named N.Y. State's Outstanding Young Woman, 1976. Mem. Harvard Bus. Sch. Alumni Assn. (exec. coun. 1976-79, v.p 1978-79), Women's Fin. Assn., Women's Forum, Econ. Club of N.Y., Cosmopolitan Club, Harvard Bus. Sch. Club, Radcliffe Club, Brown Club, Art Table, Century Assn. Home: 785 Park Ave New York NY 10021-3552

LEVENSON, LAURIE L. law educator; b. Inglewood, Calif., Dec. 7, 1956; d. Daniel and Irene (Moses) L.; m. Douglas E. Mirell, Sept. 3, 1984; children: Solomon, Hava. AB, Stanford U., 1977; JD, UCLA, 1980. Bar: Calif. 1981, U.S. Dist. Ct. (cen. dist.) Calif. 1981, U.S. Ct. Appeals (9th cir.) 1981. Jud. law clk. to hon. judge James Hunter III, L.A., 1980-81; asst. U.S. atty., criminal sect. U.S. Dept. of Justice, 1981-89; adj. prof. Southwestern U., 1982—89; prof. law Loyola U., 1989—, assoc. dean, acad. affairs, 1996—99. Mem. Calif. Bar Assn. (sec., treas. exec. com. criminal law sect. 1988—). Democrat. Jewish. Office: Loyola Law Sch 919 Albany St Los Angeles CA 90015-1211 E-mail: laurie.levenson@lls.edu.*

LEVENTHAL, ANN Z. writer, educator; d. Samuel and Sadie K. Zinman; children: Amy, Adam, Max, Seth. BS, St. Joseph Coll., 1957; MFA, Goddard Coll., 1979. Tchr. Greater Hartford (Conn.) C.C., 1990, Hartford (Conn.) Coll. Women, 1999—2000, AIDS Project Hartford, 1995—. Author: Life-Lives, 1987. Mem. permanent commn. The Status of Hartford, 1999—. Recipient Crahre Nonfiction award, Hywall, 1998. Democrat. Jewish. Avocations: music, gardening.

LEVENTHAL, ELAINE A. internist; MD, U. Wis., 1974; PhD. Diplomate Am. Bd. Internal Medicine. Intern U. Hosps., Madison, Wis., 1974—77; resident in internal medicine Mt. Sinai Med. Ctr., Milw., 1977—79; fellow in geriat. Williams S. Middleton Vets. Meml., Madison, 1979—81; physician divsn. gen. internal medicine Robert Wood Johnson U. Med. Group, New Brunswick, NJ. Office: Robert Wood Johnson U Med Group Clinical Acad Bldg 125 Paterson St Ste 5100A New Brunswick NJ 08901-1977

LEVENTHAL, RUTH, retired parasitology educator, university official; b. Phila., May 23, 1940; d. Harry Louis Mongin and Bertha (Rosenberg) Mongin Blai; children: Sheryl Anne, David Alan. BS, U. Pa., 1961, PhD, 1973, MBA, 1981; HHD (hon.), Thomas Jefferson U., 1995; student, Pa. Acad. Fine Arts, 2000—03. Cert. med. technologist, clin. lab. scientist. Trainee NSF, 1971, USPHS, 1969-70, 73; asst. prof. med. tech. U. Pa., Phila., 1974-77, acting dean, 1977-81; dean Hunter Coll., CUNY, 1981-84; provost, dean, prof. biology Capital Coll., Pa. State U., Middletown, 1984-95; prof. biology Pa. State U. Hershey Med. Ctr., 1996—2002; ret., 2002. Site visitor Mid. State Assn. Colls. and Secondary Schs., Phila., 1983—98. Author (with Creadle): Medical Parasitology: A Self Instructional Text, 1979; author: 5th edit., 2002. Chmn. founds. Tri-County United Way, South Central Pa., 1996, 97; mem. health found. bd. Harrisburg Hosp., Pa., 1984-92; pres. bd. dirs. Open Stage Harrisburg, 1996-97, bd. dirs. 1996-2000; bd. dirs. Tri-County Planned Parenthood, 1984-87, Harrisburg Acad., Wormleysburg, Pa., 1984-88, Metro Arts of Harrisburg, 1984-87, Tech. Coun. Ctrl. Pa., 1996-99; founding chmn. Coun. Pub. Edn., 1984-99. Recipient Alice Paul award Women's Faculty Club, U. Pa., 1981; Recognition award NE Deans of Schs. of Allied Health, 1984, Athena award Capital Region C. of C., 1992, John Baum Humanitarian award Am. Cancer Soc., 1992, Lifetime Achievement award Family and Children's Svcs., 1996, Coll. and Cmty. Svc. award Harrisburg Area C.C., 1993; named Disting. Dau. Pa. by Gov. of Pa., 1995. Avocations: painting, sculpture.

LEVESON, NANCY G. aeronautical engineer; PhD, UCLA, 1980. Prof. computer sci. U. Calif., Irvine; Boeing prof. computer sci. and engring. U. Wash.; prof. aeronautics and astronautics MIT, Cambridge. Author: Safeware: System Safety and Computers, 1995; contbr. articles to profl. jours.; past editor-in-chief IEEE Transactions on Software Engring. Recipient Info. Sys. award AIAA, 1995. Fellow ACM (mem. com. on computers and pub. policy, Allen Newell award 1999); mem. IEEE, NAE, Internat. Coun. on Sys. Engring. (past bd. dirs.), Computing Rsch. Assn., NRC (commn. on engring. and tech. sys., liaison to aeronautics and space engring. bd.), NASA Langley Adv. Subcom. on Air Frame Sys. Rsch. Achievements include research in software safety, which is concerned with the problems of building software for real-time systems where failures can result in loss of life or property. Office: Dept Aeronautics and Astronautics Rm 33-406 MIT 77 Mass Ave Cambridge MA 02139 E-mail: leveson@mit.edu.

LEVESQUE, CHANTAL, psychologist, researcher; b. Ottawa, Ontario, Canada, Mar. 5, 1973; d. Michel and Paulyne Seguin; m. Marc Levesque, May 20, 1995; children: Dustin, Dylan. BA, U. Ottawa, 1995, PhD in psychology, 2000. Vis. asst. prof. U. Rochester, NY, 1999—2002; asst. prof. SW Mo. State U., Springfield, Mo., 2002—. Rsch. project mgr. U. Rochester, NY, 2000—02. Contbr. chapters to books Emotional Displays and Social Identity: Emotional Investment in Organizations, articles to sci. jours. Rsch. cons. Various Non-profit Orgns., Springfield, Mo., 2002. Recipient Silver Medal Academic Performance, U. Ottawa, 1995; grantee Social Scis. Humanities Rsch. Coun. scholar, Rsch. Coun. Can., 1996—2000, Rsch. grant, Positive Psychology Inst., 2000; Faculty Summer fellow, S.W. Mo. State U., 2003. Mem.: APA, Am. Psychol. Soc. Office: Psych Dept SW Mo State U 901 South National Ave Springfield MO 65804 Personal E-mail: chl131f@smsu.edu. E-mail: chl131f@smsu.edu.

LEVEY, JUDITH S. editor, publishing executive; b. New Haven, Oct. 2, 1936; d. Morris and Betty Sweetkind; m. Lawrence Levey, Sept. 9, 1961. BA, Mt. Holyoke Coll., 1958; MA, Adelphi U., 1968. Copy editor, publications Am. Heart Assn., N.Y.C., 1958-62; sr. editor and copy chief, special projects Macmillan Pub. Co., N.Y.C., 1962-68, exec. editor, lexicographer, 1968-72; editor, encyclopedias Columbia U. Press, N.Y.C., 1972-83, editor-in-chief, reference books, 1983-85; editor-in-chief, dictionaries Macmillan Pub. Co., N.Y.C., 1985-92; editorial dir. Chambers Pub./CKG, N.Y.C., 1992-93; book developer, pub. cons. Montclair, NJ, 1993—. Exec. editor Macmillan Dictionary for Students, 1973; mng. editor The New Columbia Encyclopedia, 4th edit., 1975, The New Illustrated Columbia Encyclopedia, 1978; co-editor The Concise Columbia Encyclopedia, 1st edit.; editor-in-chief Macmillan School Dictionary 2, 1989, Macmillan Dictionary for Children, 2d edit., School Dictionary 1, 1989, Macmillan First Dictionary, 1990, Macmillan Picture Word Book, 1990, Macmillan/McGraw-Hill School Dictionary 3, 1993, Scholastic First Dictionary, 1998; editor: The 1996 World Almanac for Kids, 1995, The 1997 World Almanac for Kids, 1996, The 1998 World Almanac for Kids, 1997. Mem.: Soc. Children's Book Writers and Illustrators, Dictionary Soc. N.Am.

LEVI, BARBARA GOSS, physicist, editor; b. Washington, May 5, 1943; d. Wilbur H. and Mildred C. (Wallin) Goss; m. Ilan M. Levi, Sept. 10, 1966; children: Daniel S., Sharon R. BA, Carleton Coll., 1965; MS, Stanford U., 1967, PhD, 1971. Assoc. editor Physics Today Am. Inst. Physics, N.Y.C., 1969-70, cons. editor Physics Today, 1970-89, assoc. editor Physics Today, 1987-88; sr. assoc. editor Physics Today, N.Y.C., 1989-93, sr. editor, 1993—2003, cons. editor, 2003—; mem. tech. staff Bell Labs, Holmdel, N.J., 1982-83; mem. rsch. staff Ctr. for Energy and Environ. Studies Princeton (N.J.) U., 1981-82, 83-87. Lectr. Fairleigh Dickinson U., Madison, NJ, 1970—75, Ga. Tech., Atlanta, 1976—80; cons. U.S. Office Tech. Assessment, Washington, 1976—93; vis. prof. Rutgers U., Piscataway, NJ, 1988—89; adj. assoc. prof. physics U. Calif., Santa Barbara, 1998—. Editor (with others): (book) Energy Sources: Conservation and Renewables, 1985, The Future of Land-Based Strategic Missiles, 1989, Global Warming: Physics and Facts, 1992. Treas. LWV, Holmdel and Colts Neck, NJ, 1983—94. Fellow: AAAS (mem. steering com. physics group 1997—), Am. Phys. Soc. (edn. com. 1989—91, chmn. forum on physics and soc. 1988—89, forum councilor 1992—95, mem. exec. bd. 1994—95, Lilienfedl prize com. 1993—95, chair 1995, com. on coms. 1994—96, chair 1996, mem. exec. com. forum edn. 1997—98, mem. Nicholson medal com. 1998—99, chair 1999); mem.: AAUW (mem. nuc. energy task force 1975—77), Am. Assn. Physics Tchrs., Fedn. Am. Scientists (gov. bd. 1985—89). Avocations: tennis, travel, hiking, skiing.

LEVI, JANICE LAWAN, counselor; b. Refugio, Tex., July 4, 1946; d. Guy Nolen and Lillian Lorene (Whitten) Weeks; m. Thomas Jack Levi, Jan. 18, 1968; children: Kimberly D., Marcel N. BS, Tex. A&I U., 1964; MS, U. Houston, 1988. Lic. profl. counselor Tex., chem. dependency counselor Tex. Journalism tchr. Sinton (Tex.) Ind. Sch. Dist., 1968—70; drama tchr. Pasadena (Tex.) Ind. Sch. Dist., 1970—88; lead counselor Pasadena (Tex.) Ind. Sch. Dist. Alternative Sch., 1988—96; sch. coord. Clear Creek Ind. Sch. Dist. Harris County Youth Village, Houston, 1996—97; counselor LaPorte (Tex.) Ind. Sch. Dist. Alternative Sch., 1997—. Facilitator family support groups Pasadena Ind. Sch. Dist., 1989—94. Active C. of C. Leadership Pasadena Group, 1994—95. Grantee Alcoa Found. grantee, Alcoa Aluminum, Pasadena, 1995, Edn. Found. grantee, LaPorte Edn. Found., 2001. Mem.: ACA, Tex. Counseling Assn. Methodist. Avocations: woodturning, motorcycle riding, stained glass, sewing, arts and crafts. Office: DeWalt Alternative Sch 301 E Fairmont Pkwy La Porte TX 77571

LEVI, MARGARET, humanities educator; b. Balt., Mar. 5, 1947; d. Beatrice Looban and Joseph Meyer Levi; m. Robert David Kaplan. BA, Bryn Mawr Coll., 1968; PhD, Harvard U., 1974. Harry Bridges chair in labor studies U. Wash., 1996—2000, Jere I. Bacharach prof. internat. studies, 2000—. Dir., WTO history project U. Wash. Author: Of Rule and Revenue, 1988, Consent, Dissent and Patriotism, 1997; editor: Trust and Governance, 1998, Competition and Cooperation, 1998; gen. editor: Cambridge Studies in Comparative Politics; co-author: Analytic Narratives, 1997. Lender (with Robert D. Kaplan) Seattle Art Mus., 1995; trustee Ctr. for Advanced Study in Behavioral Sci., 2002—; mem. nat. exec. coun. Students for a Dem. Soc., 1964—66. Recipient Allan Sharlin Meml. prize hon. mention, Social Sci. History Assn., 1998; John Simon Guggenheim fellow, 2002—03. Mem.: Am. Acad. Arts and Scis., Am. Polit. Sci. Assn. (pres.-elect 2003—04, pres. 2004—). Democrat. Jewish. Avocation: collecting Australian Aboriginal art. Office: U Wash Dept Polit Sci Box 353530 Seattle WA 98195

LEVIN, CAROL ARLENE, language educator; b. L.A., Apr. 4, 1945; d. Harold Allen and Sally (Salter) L. AA, Santa Monica Coll., 1965; BA, UCLA, 1967; MS, Pepperdine U., 1990. Cert. tchr., 1969, bilingual tchr., 1977. Tchr. L.A. Unified Sch. Dist., 1969-89, asst. prin., 1998—2001; master tchr. UCLA, 1985-89; tchr., adviser bilingual editor newspaper D.A.R.E. to Read, 1989-94; adviser drug, alcohol and tobacco edn., 1994—98; learning support faculty Calif. State TEACH, 2001—. Pres., v.p. Calif. Assn. Childhood Edn., Los Angeles, 1977-81; chmn. workshop Calif. State Assn. for Childhood Edn. Internat. Conf., Universal City, 1979; invited observer Assn. for Childhood Edn. Internat. White House Conf.-Families, Los Angeles, 1980; tchr., adviser elem. news Sta. KTTV, Los Angeles, 1980-82. Editor: (with others) Our Los Angeles, 1976; contbr. articles to profl. jours. Treas. Dickens Towers Homeowners Assn., Sherman Oaks, Calif., 1978-80; sec. Sherman Villas Homeowners Assn, Sherman Oaks, 1981-83; mem. Sherman Oaks Homeowners Assn., 1986—, Palm Springs (Calif.) Tennis Club Owners Assn., 1981—; mem. Los Angeles Music Ctr. Theatre Group Vols., 1987-88. Recipient P.I.E. award Los Angeles Schs., 1978, 79, 80, 81. Mem. NEA, Calif. Tchrs. Assn., Women in Ednl. Leadership, Delta Kappa Gamma (sec. Epsilon chpt.), Unihi Edn. Found. (bd. dirs., sec.). Avocations: swimming, boating, reading, rug hooking, piano. Office: Calif State U 5151 State University Dr Los Angeles CA 90032

LEVIN, CAROLE, history educator; b. Chgo. d. Frank Kern and Charlotte (Goodman) L. BA, So. Ill. U., Edwardsville, 1970; MA, Tufts U., 1972, PhD, 1976. Vis. asst. prof. Ariz. State U., Tempe, 1979-80, U. Iowa, Iowa City, 1982-84; coord. women's studies U. Wis., La Crosse, 1980-82; mem. faculty dept. history SUNY, New Paltz, 1984-98, prof., 1993-98; prof. dept. history U. Nebr., Lincoln, 1998—2002, Willa Cather Prof., prof. history, 2002—. Author: Propaganda in the English Reformation, 1988, The Heart and Stomach of a King, 1994; author: (with others) Extraordinary Women of the Medieval and Renaissance World, 2000, The Reign of Elizabeth I, 2002; editor: Ambiguous Realities, 1987, Sexuality and Politics in Renaissance Drama, 1991, Political Rhetoric, Power, and Renaissance Women, 1995. Office: U Nebr Dept History 612 Old Father Hall Lincoln NE 68588-0327

LEVIN, CAROLYN BIBLE, volunteer; b. Dayton, Ohio, Aug. 31, 1948; children: Jennifer Levin Atocha, Brittany Levin Vogel. AS, Monticello, 1968; AB, Inst. of Merchandising., 1969. Spl. events mgr. Nat. Multiple Sclerosis Soc., 1988—89; freelance fashio coord. self-employed, 1979—90; publ. rep. freelance, Bloomfield Hills, Mich., 1989—2001; exec. dir. gifts Jules R. Schubot Jewelers, 2001—. Vol. coun. Hospice of Mich.; mem. women's com. Hospice Care, Cranbrook Acad. Art and Art Mus.; entertainment chair Oakland Family Svcs., 2003; mem. vol. coun. Detroit Symphony Orch., chmn. auction, 2003; vol. ArtServe Mich.; bd. dirs. Founders Jr. Coun., Detroit. Home: 6028 Hickory Tree Trl Bloomfield Hills MI 48301

LEVIN, DEBBE ANN, lawyer; b. Cin., Mar. 11, 1954; d. Abram Asher and Selma Ruth (Herlands) Levin. BA, Washington U., St. Louis, 1976; JD, U. Cin., 1979; LLM, NYU, 1983. Bar: Ohio 1979. Staff atty. US Ct. Appeals (6th cir.), Cin., 1979—82; shareholder Schwartz, Manes & Ruby, Cin., 1983—2002; of counsel Drew & Ward Co., LPA, Cin., 2002—04; shareholder Graf, Stiebel & Moyers Co., LPA, Cin., 2004—. Editor: U. Cin. Law Rev., 1972—79. Active Cin. Estate Planning Coun. Mem.: ABA, Nat. Acad. Elder Law Attys., Cin. Bar Assn. (chair advanced estate planning inst. 2001), Ohio Bar Assn., Greater Cin. Planned Giving Coun., Order of Coif. Jewish. Office: Graf Stiebel & Moyers Co LPA 625 Walnut St Ste 2400 Cincinnati OH 45202-3954 E-mail: dlevin@grafstiebel.com.

LEVIN, SUSAN BASS, lawyer; b. Wilmington, Del., July 18, 1952; d. Max S. and Harriet C. (Rubin) Bass; children: Lisa, Amy. BA, U. of Rochester, 1972; JD, George Washington U., 1975. Bar: D.C. 1975, U.S. Ct. Claims 1976, N.J. 1976, Pa. 1981, U.S. Ct. Appeals (3rd cir.) 1983, U.S. Supreme Ct. 1984. Law clk. to assoc. justice U.S. Ct. Claims, Washington, 1975-76, assoc. Covington & Burling, Washington, 1976-79; pvt. practice Cherry Hill, N.J., 1979-87; counsel Ballard, Spahr, Andrews & Ingersoll, Phila., Camden (N.J.), 1993-96, Pepper Hamilton LLP, Phila. and Cherry Hill, Pa., 1996-2000; spl. counsel Fox Rothschild OBrien Frankel, 2001—02; commr. NJ Dept. Cmty. Affairs, 2002—. Pres. Cherry Hill (N.J.) Twp. Coun., 1986—88; mayor City of Cherry Hill, 1988—2002; trustee N.J. Coalition of Small Bus. Orgns., 1985—87; del. to President's Summit on Am.'s Future, chair Pam's List; commr. N.J. Dept. Cmty. Affairs, 2002—; del. Dem. Presdl. Conv., 1992, 1996; bd. dirs. N.J. Alliance for Action, South Jersey Devel. Coun., U.S. Holocaust Coun., Big Bros./Big Sisters, Boys and Girls Club, trustee; bd. dirs. N.J. League Municipalities. Recipient Woman of Achievement award Camden County Girl Scouts, 1986, Barbara Boggs Sigmuno award N.J. Women Polit. Caucus, 1996, Gov.'s award on volunteerism, 1998. Mem. Tri County Women Lawyers (pres. 1984-85), N.J. Assn. Women Bus. Owners (state pres. 1984-85 named Woman of Yr. 1985), Phi Beta Kappa, Order of Coif. Office: 1001 Broad St Trenton NJ 08002 Office Phone: 609-292-6420. E-mail: brook@voicenet.com.

LEVINA, ANNA, computer scientist; b. St. Petersburg, Russia, Apr. 29, 1947; arrived in U.S., 1987; d. Lasar and Leah Sverdlov; m. Aleksandr Sadkin, May 4, 1998; m. Igor Arshansky, Apr. 28, 1972 (div. May 4, 1974); m. Grerory Levin, Aug. 25, 1979 (div. Apr. 7, 1984); 1 child, Yana. MS, LEIS Bonch-Bruevicha, St. Petersburg, 1965. Comms. engr. Ctrl. Telephone Dept., St. Petersburg, Russia, 1965—87; computer programmer Empire Blue Cross and Blue Shield, N.Y.C., NY, 1990—98, AMS, Bklyn., 1998—. Author (in Russian): Make Me a Match, 1994 (Gold Ostap, 2003), Marriage, Emigre Style, 1995 (Gold Ostap, 2003), Oh, Little Apple!, 1996. Avocations: writing, acting, singing, dance, aerobics.

LEVINE, AUDREY PEARLSTEIN, foundation administrator; b. N.Y.C., July 6, 1934; d. Irving and Flora Malkin Pearlstein; m. Arthur Levine, Mar. 15, 1958; children: Michael S., Charles T., Andrew S. Student, Hofstra U., 1952, student, 1957. Sec., treas. Pearlstein Found., 1976—; gen. ptnr. Adams County Realty LLP, McSherrystown, Pa., 2003—. Specialist trade shows Stone Care Internat. Inc., Owings Mills, Md., 1991—; adminstr. Pearlstein Partnership, Palm Beach, Fla., 1998—. V.p. PTA Ft. Garrison Sch., Pikesville, Md., 1968—69; chmn. Hadassah Ho. & Garden Tour, Balt., Palm Beach, 1969, 1970, 1999, Booster Club Pikesville H.S., Pikesville, 1970, 1971, 1975—76, 1980—82; v.p. PTA Pikesville Sr. H.S., Pikesville, 1970, 1976, 1980—82; v.p. parents-student bd. Am. U., Washington, 1978—79, 1984—86; chmn. Save Ft. Garrison, Pikesville, 1965—66, 2001; mem. com. Senator Henry Jackson Save Soviet Jews, Washington, 1972—73; v.p. Jewish Nat. Fund Women, Balt., 1973—75; pres. Balt. (Md.) Suburban Hadassah, 1963—64; bd. dirs. Women's Aux. Sinai Hosp., Balt., 1985—88, Nat. Coun. Johns Hopkins, Balt., 1990—92, Pikesville Recreation Coun., Pikesville, 1968—71; chmn. Rededication of Fort Garrison, Pikesville, Md. Republican. Jewish. Avocations: sculpting, painting, flower arranging, boating, tennis. Home (Summer): 3421 Garrison Farms Rd Baltimore MD 21208 Home: 3421 Garrison Farms Rd Pikesville MD 21208-1852

LEVINE, ELAINE PRADO, school psychologist, musician, artist; b. Inglewood, California, Feb. 16, 1962; d. John Franklin, Jr. and Carolyn Mae (Cable) Watler; m. Paul David Prado, Mar. 2, 1985 (div. 1994); children: Paul David and Lauren Mae; m. Leonard Ralph Levine, Jan. 8, 2000 (dec. May 2001). BA in Music Composition and Theory, Flute, Univ. Calif. at Los Angeles, 1986; MA in Edn. counseling, Calif. State U., 1999. Tchr. multiple subjects Torrance Unified Sch. Dist., Calif., 1994-96, tchr. music, dir. band and choir, 1996-99, counselor, 1999-00; sch. psychologist Hemet Unified Sch. Dist., Hemet, Calif., 2000—02, Palm Springs Unified Sch. Dist., 2002—. Part time asst. prof. Calif. State U., Dominguez Hills, 1999-00; prodr., dir., pub. Prado Prodn. and Publ., Hemet, 2000—. Author: He Always Goes First!, 1998; prodr., dir. CD, Dreams of the Jaguar, 1999. Sec., faculty rep. Jefferson Sch. Site Coun., Torrance, Calif. 1998-99. Mem. Nat. Assn. Sch. Psychologists; Calif. Assn. Sch. Psychologists; Calif. Tchrs. Assn.; So. Calif. Vocal Assn.; Screen Actors Guil;, Wiseburn Faculty Assn. (scholarship 1985); UCLA Alumni Assn.; Phi Kappa Phi. Avocations: tennis, snow skiing, swimming, travel, gardening. Home and Office: Prado Prodn and Pub 26208 Avenida Hortensia Hemet CA 92544-6548 E-mail: musesmaker@aol.com.

LEVINE, ELLEN R. editor; b. NYC, Feb. 19, 1943; d. Eugene Jack and Jean (Zuckman) Jacobson; m. Richard U. Levine, Dec. 21, 1964; children: Daniel, Peter. Student, Wellesley Coll. Reporter The Record, Hackensack, NJ, 1964—70; editor Cosmopolitan mag., N.Y.C., 1976—82; editor in chief Cosmopolitan Living mag., N.Y.C., 1980—81, Woman's Day mag., N.Y.C., 1982—91, Redbook mag., N.Y.C., 1991—94, Good Housekeeping, N.Y.C., 1994—; editorial cons. O, The Oprah Mag., 2000—. Commr. U.S. Atty. Gen.'s Commn. on Pornography, 1985—86; bd. dirs. NY Restoration Project, Lifetime TV; bd. adv. NY Women in Comm. Author: Planning Your Wedding, Waiting for Baby, Rooms That Grow With Your Child; mem. editl. bd. O mag.; contbr. articles to profl. jours. Bd. dirs. Lifetime TV, Christopher Reeve Paralysis Found., N.Y. Restoration Project. Named to Writers Hall of Fame, 1981; recipient Acad. Women Achievers, YWCA, 1982, Outstanding Profl. Achievement award, N.J. Fedn. Women's Clubs, 1984, Matrix award, N.Y. Women in Comm., 1989, Am. Health Found., 1996, 2d Century award, Columbia U. Sch. Nursing, 1997, Nat. Mag. award for personal svc., 1999. Office: Good Housekeeping 250 W 55th St New York NY 10019

LEVINE, FELICE, educational association administrator; AB in Sociology and Psychology, AM in Sociology and Psychology, PhD in Sociology and Psychology, U. Chgo. Sr. rsch. social scientist Am. Bar Found., 1974—79; program dir. NSF, 1979—91; exec. officer Am. Sociol. Assn., Washington, 1991—2002; exec. dir. Am. Ednl. Rsch. Assn., Washington, 2002—. Mem. nat. human rsch. protections adv. com. U.S. Dept. Health and Human Svcs., co-chair social and behavioral sci. working group; exec. com. Consortium of Social Sci. Assns., chair, 1997—2000; mem. adv. com. Decennial Census; bd. mem. Nat. Humanities Alliance; mem. adv. com. Nat. Consortium of Violence Rsch. Fellow: AAAS, Am. Psychol. Soc. Office: Am Ednl Rsch Assn 1230 Seventeenth St NW Washington DC 20036

LEVINE, MADELINE GELTMAN, Slavic literatures educator, translator; b. N.Y.C., Feb. 23, 1942; d. Herman and Nettie (Kritman) Geltman; m. Steven I. Levine; children: Elaine, Daniel. BA, Brandeis U., 1962; MA, Harvard U., 1964, PhD, 1971. Asst. prof. Grad Sch. CUNY, N.Y.C., 1971-74; assoc. prof. U. N.C., Chapel Hill, 1974-80, prof., 1980-94, Kenan prof. Slavic lits., 1994—, chmn. dept. Slavic langs., 1979-87, 94-99. Chmn. joint com. on Ea. Europe, Am. Coun. Learned Socs.-Social Sci. Rsch. Coun., 1989-92; chmn. bd. govs. U. N.C. Press, 1999-. Translator: A Memoir of the Warsaw Uprising (Miron Bialoszewski), 1977, 2d edit. 1991, The Poetry of Osip Mandelstam: God's Grateful Guest (Ryszard Przybylski), 1987, Beginning With My Streets: Essays and Recollections (Czeslaw Milosz), 1992, A Year of the Hunter (Czeslaw Milosz), 1994, Bread for the Departed (Bogdan Wojdowski), 1997, Lost Landscapes: In Search of Isaac Bashevis Singer and the Jews of Poland (Agata Tuszynska), 1998, Milosz's ABCs (Czeslaw Milosz), 2001; translator with Francine Prose: A Scrap of Time and Other Stories (Ida Fink), 1986, 2d edit., 1995; author: Contemporary Polish Poetry, 1925-75, 1981; co-editor (with Bogdana Carpenter): To Begin Where I Am: Selected Essays (Czeslaw Milosz), 2001. NEH fellow, 1984, 2000; recipient (with Francine Prose) award for lit. translation PEN-America, 1988. Mem. Am. Assn. for Advancement of Slavic Studies, Polish Inst. of Arts and Scis. Am., Am. Assn. Tchrs. of Slavic and East European Langs., Am. Literary Translators Assn., Pen-Am. Home: 5001 Whitehorse Rd Hillsborough NC 27278-9399 Office: U NC CB # 3165 425 Dey Hall Chapel Hill NC 27599-3165 E-mail: mglevine@email.unc.edu.

LEVINE, MARILYN MARKOVICH, lawyer, arbitrator; b. Bklyn., Aug. 9, 1930; d. Harry P and Fannie L (Hymowitz) Markovich; m. Louis L Levine, June 24, 1950; children: Steven R, Ronald J, Linda J Morgenstern. BS summa cum laude, Columbia U., 1950; MA, Adelphi U., 1967; JD, Hofstra U., 1977. Bar: NY 1978, US Dist Ct (no and ea dists) NY 1978, DC 1979, US Supreme Ct 1982. Sole practice, Valley Stream, N.Y., 1978—. Panel arbitrator retail food indust, New York, NY, 1980—; arbitrator NY Dist Cts, Nassau County, 1981—; contract arbitrator bldg serv indust, New York, NY, 1982—; mem Nat Acad Arbitrators, 1992—. Panel arbitrator Suffolk County Pub Employee Relations Bd, 1979—, Nassau County Pub Employee Relations Bd, 1980—, Nat Mediation Bd, 1986—; mem adv coun Ctr Labor and Indust Relationa, NY Inst Technology, 1985—; counsel Nassau Civic Club, 1978—. Mem.: ABA, Fed Mediation Bd (arbitrator 1980—), Am Arbit Asn (arbitrator 1979—), NJ Bd Mediation (panel arbitrator), Nassau County Bar Asn, DC Bar Asn, NY State Bar Asn. Home and Office: 1057 Linden St Valley Stream NY 11580-2135 E-mail: mmllevine@yahoo.com., ml-levine@worldnet.att.net.

LEVINE, NAOMI BRONHEIM, academic administrator; b. N.Y.C., Apr. 15, 1923; d. Nathan and Malvina (Mermelstein) Bronheim; m. Leonard Levine, Apr. 11, 1948; 1 child, Joan. BA, Hunter Coll., 1944; LLB, Columbia, 1946, JD, 1970. Bar: N.Y. 1946. With Scaadrett, Tuttle & Chalaire, N.Y.C., 1946-48, Charles Gottleib, N.Y.C., 1948-50, Am. Jewish Congress, 1950-78, exec. dir., 1972-78; v.p. to sr. v.p. external affairs NYU, N.Y.C., 1978—2002, spl. advisor to pres., 2002—; chmn., dir. Heyman Ctr. for Philanthropy and Fund Raising, 2002—. Asst. prof. law and police sci. John Jay Coll., N.Y.C., 1969—73, L.I. U., 1965—69. Author: (book) Schools in Crisis, 1969, The Jewish Poor-an American Awakening, 1974, Politics, Religion and Love, 1990; mem. editl. bd. Columbia Law Rev., 1945—46. Chmn. N.Y.U. Bronfman Ctr., N.Y.U. Ctr. for Israeli Studies; bd. dirs. Jewish Cmty. Rels. Coun., N.Y. Ctr. Philanthropy and Fund Raising. Named to Hunter Coll. Hall of Fame, 1972. Office: NYU 29 Washington Square West New York NY 10011 Office Phone: 212-998-2380.

LEVINE, RUTH HANNAH, retired sculptor; b. Bronx, N.Y., Feb. 5, 1915; d. Harry and Tillie Blum; m. Philip Levine; children: Howard A., Michael, Maxine Franklin. Student, Lowell Tech. Inst., Mus. Sch., Boston, Internat. Barckhardt Akademia, Italy; studied with George Aarons, Peter Abate, Arthur Roberts. Sculptor, Rome, 1965; tchr. sculpture Whistler House, Lowell, 1964-68. One man shows include Lexington Arts and Crafts Soc., 1968, Lowell City Libr., Showcase Cinemas, 1968—; group exhbns. include Lowell Art Assn. (1st prize 1962, 64, 68), Weeden Gallery, Prudential, Boston, MIT, Loeb Drama, Harvard Coop., Concord Art Assn., 1966-68, So. Vt. Arts Ctr., Cape Cod Art Assn. (honorable mention 1967), Addison Gallery, Springfield Mus., Winterfest, Boston, Pittsfield Mus., Candle Art Gallery, Nantucket, Marblehead Art Assn., Wayside Inn, Newport Art Assn., New Bedford Festival, Nat. Iron and Steel, Washington, 1966, Chapman Gallery, N.Y.C. Mem. New England Sculptors Assn. (pub. chmn. 1968, 1st prize 1997), Lowell Art Assn. (bd. dirs., festival chmn. 1966), Cambridge Art Assn., Lexington Arts and Crafts Soc., Concord Art Assn., So. Vt. Arts Ctr., Cape Cod Art Assn. Avocations: flower arranging, golf, aerobics. Home: 821 Cypress Blvd #99-204 Pompano Beach FL 33069-7060

LEVINE, TOBY KLEBAN, communications executive, educational media developer; b. N.Y.C., Apr. 12, 1944; d. Julian Milton and Sylvia (Kandel) Kleban; m. Andrew Seth Levine, Feb. 4, 1964; children: Caren Beth Pelletier, Amy Ruth. BS, Cornell U., 1964; MEd, Boston U., 1965. Rsch. asst. Synetics, Inc., Cambridge, Mass., 1964-66; project dir. The Children's Mus., Boston, 1965-66; rsch. assoc. Creative Studies, Inc., Boston, 1968-69, curriculum coord., 1969-71, v.p. ednl. devel., 1971-73; founder, pres. Levine Rsch. Assocs., Brookline, Mass., 1973-78; curriculum dir. WETA-TV, Washington, 1978-81, dir. ednl. activities, 1981-84; founder, pres. Toby Levine Comm., Inc., Bethesda, Md., 1984—. Author: (handbook) Telecourses: Opportunities and Options, Everyone Wins! Quality Care Without Restraints, The World of Abnormal Psychology, Chicano: History of the Mexican American Civil Rights Movement, The Africans. Trustee, sch. com. chair Temple Israel, Boston; founding bds. dirs. 2 after-school day care ctrs.; bd. mem. Cornell/Found. House Expts. in Distance Learning, Inc., 1997-99. Recipient Gold plaque Chgo. Internat. Film Festival, 1992, Mental Health Media award Nat. Mental Health Assn., 1993, Gold award Washington Ednl. Press, 1993, Spl. Achievement OWL award Retirement Rsch. Found., 1996. Mem. Assn. Ednl. Comm. and Tech., Pres.'s Coun. Cornell Women (chair 1999-2001), Cornell Univ. Coun. Avocations: fitness, cooking, reading, crafts. Home: 2 Hill Rd West Stockbridge MA 01266-9734 Office: Toby Levine Comm, Inc 2 Hill Rd West Stockbridge MA 01266-9734

LEVINGS, THERESA LAWRENCE, lawyer; b. Kansas City, Mo., Oct. 24, 1952; d. William Youngs and Dorothy (Neer) Frick; m. Darryl Wayne Levings, May 25, 1974; children: Leslie Page, Kerry Dillon. BJ, U. Mo., 1973; JD, U. Mo., Kansas City, 1979. Bar: Mo. 1979, U.S. Dist. Ct. (we. dist.) Mo. 1979, U.S. Ct. Appeals (8th cir.) 1982, U.S. Ct. Appeals (10th cir.) 1986, U.S. Dist. Ct. (ea. dist.) Mo. 1989. Copy editor Kansas City Star, 1975-78; law clk. to judge Mo. Supreme Ct., Jefferson City, 1979-80; from assoc. to ptnr. Morrison & Hecker, Kansas City, 1980-94; founding ptnr. Badger & Levings, L.C., Kansas City, 1994—2004. Mem. fed. practice com. U.S. Dist. Ct. (we. dist.), 1990-95; mem. fed. adv. com. U.S. Ct. Appeals (8th cir.), 1994-97. Mem. Mo. Bar (bd. govs. 1990—03, pres. 2001-02, young lawyers coun. 1982-89, chair 1988-89, Pres. award 1989, Outstanding Svc. award young lawyers coun. 1985, 86), Assn. Women Lawyers Greater Kansas City (pres. 1986-87, Woman of Yr. 1993), Lawyers Assn. Greater Kansas City (bd. dirs. young lawyers sect. 1982-83), Kansas City Met. Bar Assn. (chair civil practice and procedure com. 1988-89, chair fed. practice com. 1990-91). Office: Badger & Levings LC 1101 Walnut St Kansas City MO 64106-2134

LEVINSON, KATHY, former investment company executive, philanthropist; 2 children. BA in Econs., Stanford U., 1977. With Charles Schwab, 1981-94, sr. v.p. credit svc., 1989-94; cons. E*TRADE Securities, Inc., E*TRADE Group, Palo Alto, Calif., 1995, pres., COO, 1996—2000, corp. sr. v.p., 1996—2000, dir., 1996—2000, corp. exec. v.p. ops., 1996; pres., COO E*Trade Group, 1999—2000. Founder Mishkan HaLev. Recipient Davidson/Valenti award, Gay & Lesbian Alliance Against Defamation, 2000.

LEVINSON, MARINA, information technology executive; arrived in US, 1980; BS in computer sci., Leningrad Inst. Precision Mechanics and Optics. Various positions with TRW, San Jose, Calif., Tandem Computers (now part of HewlettPackard), SpectralPhysics; sr. dir. global integration 3Com Corp., Mass.; v.p., CIO PalmOne Inc., Milpitas, Calif., 1999—. Named one of Premier 100 IT Leaders, Computerworld mag., 2004. Office: PalmOne Inc 400 N McCarthy Blvd Milpitas CA 95035 Office Phone: 408-503-7000.*

LEVINSON, NANETTE SEGAL, international relations educator, administrator; b. Boston, Nov. 8, 1946; d. Oscar and Rose (Menicks) Segal; m. Peter Joseph Levinson, Mar. 30, 1968; children: Sharman Risa, Justin David. AB cum laude, Harvard U., 1968, EdM, 1969, EdD, 1979. Asst. prof. Am. U., Washington, 1980-86, dir. advanced tech. mgmt. program, 1983-88, assoc. prof., 1986—, assoc. dean sch. internat. svc., 1988—; visiting prof. Inst. Etudes Politiques, Paris, 2001. Cons. David Taylor Naval Ship Rsch. and Devel. Ctr., 1984-86, Xerox Corp., Leesburg, Va., 1986-91; chair bd. dirs. Nat. Conf. on Advancement of Rsch., 1992-93, bd. dirs., 1996-2000; bd. dirs. Women's Fgn. Policy Group, 1997-2000, mem. adv. cou., 2000-2003; bd. dirs. Transatlantic Info. Exch. Svcs., sec.-gen., 1997-99; vis. scholar Ritsumeikan U., Kyoto, Japan, 1993; bd. dirs. Internat. Adv. Bd. Transatlantic Internet Seminars, 2000—; vis. prof. Fondation Nationale des Sciences Politiques/Inst. d'Etudes Politiques de Paris, 2001. Contbr. numerous articles to profl. jours. Bd. dirs. Joint Bd. on Sci. and Engring. Edn., Washington, 1982-85; co-chair The Rsch. Project on Women Leaders in Internat. Affairs, 1995-99. Mem. Internat. Studies Assn., Am. Polit. Sci. Assn., Internat. Assn. for Media and Comm. Rsch. Office: Am U Office of Dean 4400 Massachusetts Ave NW Washington DC 20016-8071 E-mail: nlevins@american.edu.

LEVINTHAL, JEANA DAVISON, pediatrician; b. Balt., Mar. 9, 1923; d. Wilburt Cornell Davison and Atala Townsend Scudder; m. Cyrus Levinthal, Apr. 12, 1944 (div. Jan. 1962); children: Sarah, David, Adam. BA, Swarthmore Coll., 1943; MD, Duke U., 1950. Diplomate Am. Bd. Pediat., 1958. Intern in pediat. U. Mich. Hosp., Ann Arbor, Mich., 1950—57, resident, 1950—57, instr., 1950—57; rsch. fellow dept. pathology Children's Cancer Rsch. Found., Brookline, Mass., 1957—59; rsch. fellow, assoc. bacteriology and immunology Harvard Med. Sch., Brookline, Mass., 1959—65; rsch. fellow Nat. Ctr. for Rsch. on Cancer, Villejuif, France, 1965—66; rsch. asst. prof. U. Calif., Berkeley, Calif., 1966—70; pvt. practice in pediat. Petaluma, Calif., 1970—. Co-author: The Compleat Pediatrician, 7th edit., 1961; contbr. articles over 25 to profl. jours. Democrat. Avocations: sailing, reading, gardening, travel. Office: 104 Lynch Creek Way Ste 11 Petaluma CA 94954

LEVISAY, LEESA DAWN, music educator, composer; b. Fort Worth, Tex., Mar. 30, 1959; d. Earl Lee and Dawn Estelle (Langley) Hall; m. Charles Glen Levisay, Apr. 14, 1984; children: Laura, Leah, Chad. MusB, Tarleton State U., 1982, MBA, 1983. Grad. asst. dept. fine arts and speech, asst. condr. choirs Tarleton State U., Stephenville, 1982-83, piano tchr., 1983; ins. underwriter Carter, Metsger, & Jones, Inc., Stephenville, 1984-85; piano, vocal instr. Stephenville, 1985—; co-owner A Musical Spectrum - Sch Music, Stephenville, 1999—. Mem. Cross Timbers Fine Arts Coun. Bd. Dirs., Stephensville, 1989-90; adjuctor piano competition Music Tchrs. Assn., Weatherford, Tex., 1990-96, Ft. Worth, 1991-92, Abilene, Tex., 1992-93; composer Concert Master Pub. Co., Dallas, 1993—; condr., composer Nat. Group Piano Tchrs. Assn., 1994; guest condr. The Keynote Studio, Dallas, 1996-97; guest composer, condr. Nat. Piano Tchrs. Inst., So. Meth. U., Dallas, 1997; adjudicator vocal judge Tarleton State U., 1998. Composer, arranger Christmas Collection, 1993, Canon in D-Pachelbel, 1996; composer Laura's Song, 1994. Singer Cross Timbers Civic Chorale, Stephenville, 1982-99; com. mem. Cross Timbers Habitat for Humanity, Stephenville, 1997-99. Mem. Nat. Piano Tchrs. Guild, Music Tchrs. Nat. Assn. (cert. profl. music tchr.), Tex. Music Tchrs. Assn., Cross Timbers Music Tchrs. Assn. (ensemble dir. 1985-97), Early Childhood Music and Movement Assn. (cert. early childhood music level 1), Stephenville C. of C. Presbyterian. Avocations: crafts, church work, gardening, reading. Office: A Musical Spectrum - Sch Music 495 N Harbin Dr Stephenville TX 76401-2861

LEVIT, EDITHE JUDITH, physician; b. Wilkes-Barre, Pa., Nov. 29, 1926; m. Samuel M. Levit, Mar. 2, 1952; children: Harry M., David B. BS in Biology, Bucknell U., 1946; MD, Med. Coll. Pa., 1951, DMS (hon.), 1978; DSc (hon.), Wilkes U., 1990. Grad. asst. in psychology Bucknell U., 1946—47; intern Phila. Gen. Hosp., 1951—52, fellow in endocrinology, 1952—53, clin. instr., assoc. in endocrinology, 1953—57, dir. med. edn., 1957—61, cons. med. edn., 1961—65; asst. dir. Nat. Bd. Med. Examiners, Phila., 1961-67, assoc. dir., sec. bd., 1967—75, v.p., sec. bd., 1975—77, pres., CEO, 1977—86, pres. emeritus, life mem., bd. dirs., 1987—. Adv. coun. Inst. for Nuclear Power Ops., Atlanta, 1988—93; cons. in field. Contbr. articles to profl. jours. Bd. sci. counselors Nat. Libr. Medicine, 1981—85; bd. dirs. Phila. Gen. Hosp. Found., 1964—70, Phila. Council for Internat. Visitors, 1966—72. Recipient award for outstanding contbns. in field of med. edn., Commonwealth Com. of Woman's Med. Coll., 1970, Alumni award, Bucknell U., 1978, Disting. Dau. of Pa. award, 1981, Spl. Recognition award, Assn. Am. Med. Colls., 1986, Disting. Svc. award, Fedn. State Med. Bds., 1987. Master: ACP; fellow: Coll. Physicians of Phila.; mem.: AMA, Phila. County Med. Soc., Pa. Med. Soc., Inst. Medicine Nat. Acad. Scis., Phi Sigma, Alpha Omega Alpha, Phi Beta Kappa. Home: The Rittenhouse #2305 210 W Rittenhouse Sq Philadelphia PA 19103-5726

LEVIT, HÉLOÏSE B. (GINGER LEVIT), art historian, art dealer, art consultant, journalist; b. Phila., Apr. 2, 1937; d. Elmer and Claire Frances (Schwartz) Bertman; m. Jay Joseph Levit, July 14, 1962; children: Richard Bertman, Robert Edward, Darcy Francine Honker. BA in French Literature, U. Pa., 1959; MA in French Literature, U. Richmond, 1975; MA Art History, Va. Commonwealth U., Richmond, 1998; Cert., Alliance Française, Paris, 1991, Chambre de Commerce et d'Industrie de Paris, 1991, La Sorbonne, Paris, 1994, Istituto Lorenzo di Medici Firenze, Italy, 1996, Ecole du Louvre, 1998. Arts broadcaster, Richmond, Va., 1976-82; dir. Fine Arts Am., Inc., Richmond, 1982-84; tchr. Henrico County Pub. Schs., Richmond, 1984-88; dir. devel. Sta. WVST-FM Va. State U., Petersburg, 1987-88; mgr., dir. devel. Richmond Philharm. Orch., 1988-99; fine arts and media cons. Art-I-Facts, Richmond, 1988—; cons., 1997-98. Author: Moments, Monuments & Monarchs, 1986 (Star award, 1986); arts writer: Richmond Rev., 1989—90, Mid Atlantic Antiques mag., Mid-Atlantic Antiques News, Washington Jewish Week, Tidewater Women Richmond Jewish News; anchor, prodr. (syndicated radio series) Va. Arts Report, 1978—83, Va. Women, 1984. V.p. Va. Mus. Collector's Cir., Richmond, 1986-91, mem. steering com.; pres. Richmond Area Dem. Women's Club, 1992-93; mem. Va. Mus. Coun., Richmond; rec. sec. Richmond Symphony Orch. League, 1998-2000, dir. pub. rels., 2000—, guest condr., 2000. Mem. Va. Press Women (2d pl. award 2001, 02, 03), U. Pa. Alumni Club (v.p. 1980-90, Ben Franklin award 1990), Am. Symphony Orch. League, L'Accueil Francais, Alliance Francaise, La Table Francaise (chmn. 1996—). Avocations: tennis, art collecting, classical music, foreign travel. Home and Office: Art-I-Facts 419 Dellbrooks Pl Richmond VA 23233-5559

LEVITAS, MIRIAM C. STRICKMAN, documentary filmmaker, designer, consultant intergenerational relationships; b. Aug. 3, 1936; d. Morris and Bella (Barsky) Cherrin; m. Bernard Strickman, June 3, 1956 (dec. Jan. 1975); children: Andrew, Brian, Craig, Deron; m. Theodore Clinton Levitas, Apr. 25, 1976; children: Steven, Leslie, Anthony. Student, Temple U., 1953-56; accelerated student interior design, LaSalle U., Chgo., 1968; cert. in gerontology/cmty. svc., Ga. State U., 1988. Intergenerational Connections Contact State of Ga., 1989—. V.p. programming interior design Nat. Home Fashions League, Atlanta, 1974—75, Ga. Bd. Realtors, 1971—; founding adminstr. Stanley H. Kaplan Ednl. Ctr., Atlanta, 1974—84; owner, pres. Levitas Svcs. Inc. (Internat. Destinations), Atlanta, 1984—85; owner, v.p. Nat. Travel Svcs. and Internat. Destinations, Atlanta, 1984—85; realtor Philip White Properties Inc./Sotheby's Internat. Realty, 1985—91, Coldwell Banker Previews, 1991—; intergenerational programs and events cons.; interior designer for loft living. Prodr.(host cmty. svc. videos TV cable broadcast):, 1988—91. Pres. Ahavath Achim Sisterhood, Atlanta, 1977—79, 1996—98; bd. dirs. Jewish Family Svcs., 1993—96; bd. dirs. Atlanta chpt. Nat. Osteoporosis Found., 1990—91, Outings in the Park, 1989—91; chmn., coord. Tea at the Ritz Scottish Rite Children's Med. Ctr., 1987—90; chmn. women's divsn. Israel Bond, Atlanta, 1987, 1988, 1989, mem. auc.; chmn., coord. Who's Bringing in the Great Chefs Scottish Rige Children's Med. Ctr., 1990, 1991, 1992; mem. Atlanta Symphony, High Mus. Art, Nat. Mus. of Women in Arts, William Bremen Jewish Heritage Mus., Alliance Theater Atlanta, Atlanta Hist. Ctr.-Atlanta Hist. Soc., Alliance No. Dist. Dental Soc.; charter mem. U.S. Holocaust Mus.; bd. dirs. Jewish Ednl. Loan Fund; nat. bd. advisors Brevard Mus. Ctr., 1993—. Named Woman of Achievement, Atlanta Jewish Fedn., 1993; scholar, Phila. Bd. Edn. Music, 1952. Mem.: NAFE, Image Film and Video Ctr., Am. Women in Radio and TV, Women in Film (Atlanta chpt.), Internat. Furnishings and Design Assn., Spl. Children of the South (chmn. 1991—93), Atlanta Bd. Realtors, Ga. Gerontology Soc., Scots (life), B'nai Brith (life), Nat. Coun. Jewish Women (life), Hadassah (life), Brandeis Nat. Women (life), Ga. Dental Assn. Aux., Children's Med. Ctr. Aux. Office Phone: 404-431-9846. E-mail: mslprod1@biltmorecomm.com.

LEVITEN, RIVA SHAMRAY, artist; b. L.A., Oct. 26, 1928; d. Peter Leo and Edythe (Smith) Shamray; m. Paul Leviten, Oct. 15, 1950 (dec. Oct. 19, 1988); children: Priscilla Leviten Warner, Marcia Leviten, Peter Leviten. BS in Apparel Design, UCLA, 1950; postgrad., Cal Arts, L.A., 1949-50, Exptl. Etching Studio, Boston, 1980-90. 1st v.p. R.I. chpt. Nat. Mus. Women in the Arts, 1997-99. Visual Rev. Bd. Newport Rev., 1997-98, R.I. Women Speak, Nat. Mus. Women in the Arts, Crone elderwoman, 1997, Monotype Printmaking and Painting Travel Show, 1998—; represented in collections at R.I. Sch. Design Mus., Danforth Mus., Slater Mus., El Paso Mus., Midwest Mus. Am. Art, Mass. Coll. Art, R.I. Coll., Tougaloo Coll., U. Ark., Marist Coll., Muscatine Art Ctr., Laura Musser Mus. Dickenson State U., Art in Embassies U.S. Dept. State, Saginaw Art Mus.; exhibited Russia, Australia, Mex., Can. Founding mem. Gallery of Social and Polit. Justice, Boston, 1996—. Recipient Herbert Cross prize South County Art Assn., Kingston, R.I., 1979. Founding mem. Showcase for Collage; elected artist mem. Mystic Art Assn.; mem. Providence Art Club, Monotype Guild of New Eng., Providence Art Club (Providence Art Club award 1998, J. Bannigan Sullivan award 1995, Bradford Swan award 1987), Nat. Assn. Women Artists (Martha Reed award 1994). Avocations: urban gardening, interior design, writing poetry, innkeeping, public speaking at art symposiums. Home and Office: 425 Benefit St Providence RI 02903-2933

LEVITIN, VALERIA OSKAR, family physician; b. Simferopol, Russia, Mar. 16, 1939; came to U.S., 1987; d. Oskar Yakov and Mirra Boris (Urovitskaya) Miretsky; m. Anatoly Levitin, Dec. 31, 1967; 1 child, Yelena. MD, Crimean State Med. Sch., Simferopol, Ukraine, 1961; PhD, Kharkov Sci. Rsch. Inst., 1979. Diplomate Am. Bd. Family Practice. Resident physician Mt. Sinai Hosp. Med. UHS/Chgo. Med. Sch., 1990-91, St. Elizabeth's Hosp., Chgo., 1991-94; attending physician N.W. Cmty. Hosp., Arlington Hgts., Ill., 1994—, Holy Family Hosp., DesPlaines, Ill., 1994—, Luth. Gen. Hosp., Park Ridge, Ill., 1995—; physician Clin. Assocs., S.C., DesPlaines, 1994—. Attending physician Kharkov (Ukraine) Dist. Hosp., 1964-79, Regional Clin. Hosp., Kharkov, 1980-87. Author: Cumulative Index Medicus1979, Volume 20, 1979; contbr. 12 articles to profl. med. jours. Mem. Holy Family Med. Ctr. Women's Bd., Des Plaines, 1995. Mem. AMA, Am. Acad. Family Practice, Ill. Med. Soc., Chgo. Med. Soc. Avocations: travel, swimming. Office: Clin Assocs Sc 1455 E Golf Rd Ste 100 Des Plaines IL 60016-1253

LEVITT, MIRIAM, pediatrician; b. Lampertheim, Germany, June 10, 1946; came to U.S., 1948; d. Eli and Esther (Kingston) L.; m. Harvey Flisser, June 25, 1967; children: Adam, Elizabeth, Eric. AB, NYU, 1967; MD, Yeshiva U., 1971. Diplomate Am. Bd. Pediatrics. Intern Montefiore Med. Ctr., Bronx, N.Y., 1970-71, resident in pediatrics, 1971-73, attending pediatrician, 1975—; instr. pediatrics Albert Einstein Coll. Medicine, N.Y.C., 1973-76, asst. prof. clin., 1976—; med. staff Lawrence Hosp., Bronxville, NY, 1978—, dir. pediatrics, 1988—, pres. med. staff, 2002—, mem. bd. govs., 2002—. Sch. physician Bronxville Bd. Edn., 1983—; mem. faculty coun. faculty of medicine health scis. divsn. Columbia U., 2002—. Expert office profl. med. conduct N.Y. State Dept. Health, 1996—. Named Hon. Founder, Albert Einstein Coll. Medicine, 1995, hon. founder, 1995—. Fellow Am. Acad. Pediatrics; mem. Westchester County Med. Soc., Albert Einstein Coll. Medicine Alumni Assn. (nat. bd. govs. 1999—). Office: 1 Pondfield Rd Bronxville NY 10708-3706

LEVY, BARBARA ELLEN, music educator; b. Marion, Ohio, Feb. 23, 1951; d. Harold Joseph and Carolyn Selina Wade; m. Sheldon David Levy, Aug. 7, 1976. MusB, Cinn. Coll, Conservatory of Music, 1973. Musician US Navy, 1973—93; tchr. self employed, Orlando, Fla., 1993—. Pres. Orlando Concert Band, 2000—; prin. Oboe Space Coast Pops Orch., Cocoa, Fla., 1994—. With USN, 1973—93. Decorated Nat. Def. medal US Navy, Good Conduct Joint Svc. Commendation. Mem.: Internat. Clarinet Assn., Nat. Flute Assn., Internat. Double Reed Soc. Avocations: sewing, computers, collecting. Home: 3773 Peaceful Pl Orlando FL 32810 E-mail: barb073@msn.com.

LEVY, BETH ANN, music educator; b. Pittsburgh, Pa., Jan. 29, 1974; d. Jane Ann and Gregory John Levy. MusB edn., Kent State Univ., Kent, Ohio, 1992—96. Assoc. band dir. Nordonia Hills City Schools, Northfield, Ohio, 1998—. Mem.: Ohio Music Educators Assn. Home: 2455 1/2 State Rd Cuyahoga Falls OH 44223 Office: Nordonia High School 8006 S Bedford Rd Macedonia OH 44056 Personal E-mail: bethlevy10@hotmail.com. E-mail: beth.levy@nordoniaschools.org.

LEVY, DALE PENNEYS, lawyer; b. Phila., Sept. 10, 1940; d. Harry M. and Rosalind (Fried) Penneys; m. Richard D. Levy, Dec. 20, 1970; children: Jonathan D., Michael Z. BA, Wellesley Coll., 1962; JD, U. Pa., 1967. Bar: Pa. 1967, U.S. Ct. Appeals (3rd cir.) 1971. Assoc. Blank, Rome, Comisky & McCauley, LLP, Phila., 1967-76; ptnr. Blank, Rome, Comisky & McCauley, Phila., 1976—. Bd. dirs. Phila. Sch., Phila. Indsl. Devel. Corp. Contbr. articles to profl. jours. Bd. dirs., chair Women in Transition, 1983-85, active adv. bd., 1985—; chair Women's Rights Com., 1978; bd. dirs. Phila. Sr. Ctr., 1994—, Phila. Theatre. Co., 1995—. Mem. ABA (real property, probate and trust law sect., chairperson com. on pub.-pvt. ventures/privatization), Phila. Bar Assn. (real estate, corp., banking and bus. law sect., mem. women's rights com.). Office: Blank Rome Comisky & McCauley LLP One Logan Sq Philadelphia PA 19103-6998

LEVY, DEBORAH, security company executive; m. Barry W. Levy (dec.). Student, So. Ill. U. Exec. v.p., sec., officer, dir. Levy Security Corp., Chgo., until 1994, chair, CEO, 1994—. Mem. Women Bus. Enterprise Initiative (Mem. of Yr. award 1997), Nat. Assn. Women Bus. Owners, Am. Soc. Indsl. Security. Office: Levy Security Corp 230 E Ohio St Ste 700 Chicago IL 60611-3258

LEVY, ELLEN J. writer, educator; d. Seymour and Virginia Mae (Riggs) Levy. BA magna cum laude, Yale U., 1986; MFA, Ohio State U., 2002. Editor, founder Common Lang. Newspaper, Taos, N.Mex., 1988—90; mng. editor Ind. Film and Video Mag., NYC, 1991—93; outreach dir. Amigos Bravos: Friends of Rivers, Taos, 1997—99; asst. prof. Am. U., Washington, 2003—. Vis. asst. prof. Colo. Coll., Colorado Springs, 2002. Editor: Tasting Life Twice, 1995 (Lambda Lit. award, 1995); author: Another Chgo. Mag., 2001 (Chgo. Lit. award Writer's Digest, 2001); contbr. articles to popular mags. Media co-coord. Lesbian Avengers, NYC, 1992—93. Recipient Loft-McKnight Found. award, 1995—96, Nelson Algren award, Chgo. Tribune, 2002; Presdl. fellow, Ohio State U., 2001—02. Mem.: ACLU, MLA, Associated Writing Programs. Democrat. Jewish. Office: Dept Lit Am Univ 4400 Mass Ave NW Washington DC 20016

LEVY, JULIA, immunology educator, researcher; b. Singapore, May 15, 1935; came to Can. 1940; d. Guillaume Albert and Dorothy Frances (Brown) Coppens; m. Howard Bernard Gerwing, Oct. 8, 1955 (div. 1962); children— Nicholas, Benjamin; m. Edwin Levy, June 13, 1969; 1 child, Jennifer BA with honors, U. B.C., 1955; PhD, U. London, 1958; Dr. of

Univ. (hon.), U. Ottawa, 1993; DLitt (hon.), Mt. St. Vincent's U., 1994; DSc (hon.), U. Western Ont., 1997; LLD (hon.), Simon Fraser U., 1999; DSc honoris causa (hon.), U. B.C., 2001; DSc (hon.), U. Victoria, 2002; LLD (hon.), Concordia U., 2002; D of Tech. (hon.), B.C. Inst. Tech., 2002. Asst. prof. U. B.C., Vancouver, 1959-65, assoc. prof., 1965-72, prof. immunology, 1972—99, prof. emeritus, 1999—; pres. CEO QLT Inc., Vancouver, 1996—2002, exec. chmn. sci. adv. bd., 2002—. Dir. v.p. rsch. and devel. Quadra Logic Techs., Vancouver, 1980—2002; cons. Monsanto Chems., Mo., 1978—80; mem. Prime Minister's Nat. Adv. Bd. on Sci. and Tech., 1987—; exec. chmn. sci. adv. bd. QLT, Inc., 2002—. Decorated Officer of Order of Can.; named Pacific Can. Entrepreneur of Yr., 2000, Pioneer of Innovation, Bd. of Trade, 2001, Person of Yr., B.C. Tech. Industries Assn., 2001; recipient award, Can. Women Entrepreneur in Internat. Bus., 1998, Vision and Leadership award, BCBA, 1999, Amb.'s award for outstanding achievement of Can. women entrepreneurs, 1999, Nat. Merit award, Ottawa Life Scis. Coun., 1999, Future of Vision award, Found. Fighting Blindness, 2001, Women of Distinction award, YWCA, 2001, Friesen-Rygiel prize, 2002, Prix Galien Can. 2002 Rsch., 2002, award of leadership in Can. pharm. rsch. and devel., Can. Soc. Pharm. Scis., 2002, Helen Keller award, The Helen Keller Found. Rsch. and Edn., 2003. Fellow Royal Soc. Can.; mem. Am. Soc. Immunology, Can. Soc. Immunology (pres. 1983-85), Can. Fedn. Biol. Sci. (pres. 1983-84) Office: QLT Inc 887 Great Northern Way Vancouver BC Canada V5T 4T5

LEVY, LEAH GARRIGAN, federal official; b. Miami, Fla., Apr. 29, 1947; d. Thomas Leo and Mary (Flaherty) Garrigan; m. Roger N. Levy, May 2, 1977; children: Philip, Aaron. BA in Polit. Sci., George Mason U., 1998, postgrad., 2001—. Mem. legis. staff U.S. Ho. Reps., 1973-75; mem. scheduling staff U.S. Senate, 1975-77, mem. administrv. scheduling staff, 1977-81; staff asst. pub. liaison The White House, 1982-84; spl. asst. U.S Dept. Transport, Washington, 1984-89, U.S. Dept. Housing, Washington, 1989—; scheduling asst. Empower Am., Washington, 1993-94; scheduler majority leader Dick Armey U.S. Ho. of Reps., Washington, 1995-2001; dir. scheduling and advance Sec. of Labor, Washington, 2001—02, spl. asst. Office of the Sec., 2002—03; dir. scheduling U.S. Senator Elizabeth Dole, Washington, 2003—; v.p. devel. Empower Am., Wash., 2003—. Contbr. to Rep. Nat. Com., Washington. Contbr. Rep. Nat. Conv. Va. Rep. Party, Washington; del. Va. State GOP Conv., Richmond, 1994. Mem. Alpha Chi. Roman Catholic. Avocations: tennis, golf, reading (non-fiction). Office: Empower Am Washington DC 20006 E-mail: thelevys@aol.com., levy@empower.org.

LEVY, LESLIE ANN, application developer; b. N.Y.C., Dec. 25, 1941; d. Paul and Ruth Candace (Tachna) Bauman; m. Marc Gersan Gerard Levy, Oct. 1962 (div.); children: Benjamin Gerard, Remy Marcel Gerard. BA summa cum laude in philosophy and history, Smith Coll., 1962; MBA, Harvard U., Boston, 1976, DBA, 1980. Cert. French Fashion Acad., 1964. Tchg. asst. in philosophy UCLA, 1962-63; pres. Commonwealth Collaborative, Inc., Cambridge and Sarasota, Fla., 1976—99; sr. rsch. assoc. Harvard Sch. Bus. Adminstrn., Boston, 1979-81; asst. prof. mgmt. policy, industry analysis Case Western Res. U., Cleve., 1981-84; pres., CEO Acad. for Corp. Governance, Fordham U. Grad. Sch. Bus., 1990-91; pres., dir., treas., sec. Directors, Data, Inc., 1999—; pres., sec. Life Choices and Death Wishes, 2000—. Sr. advisor, pres., dir. Inst. Rsch. on Bd. Dirs., 1998-; with Honeywell Info. Sys., Boston, 1971-75; former cons. and lectr. in field. Author: Director Motivation: Incentives and Disincentives to Board Service, 1996, Separate Chairmen of the Board: Their Roles, Legal Liabilities, and Compensation; editor, co-author: Boards of Directors Part II; columnist: Directors and Boards, 1996-97; contbr. aricles to profl. jours. Mem. Boston and Tampa Bay Com. on Fgn. Rels. Acad. Corp. Governance rsch. fellow; Fulbright scholar. Mem. Am. Soc. Corp. Secs., Nat. Assn. Corp. Dirs., Acad. Mgmt. (article reviewer), Nat. Investor Rels. Inst., Inst. of Dirs., Federalist Soc., Women in Pensions, So. Fin. Assn., Harvard Club of Sarasota, Am. Jewish Com., Am. Jewish Congress, Nat. Coun. Jewish Women. Avocations: hiking, art history, construction, whitewater canoeing. E-mail: dirsdata@drleslielevy.com., irbd@drleslielevy.com.

LEVY, ROCHELLE FELDMAN, artist; b. NYC, Aug. 4, 1937; d. Harry and Eva (Krause) Feldman. m. Robert Paley Levy, June 4, 1955; children: Kathryn Tracey, Wendy Paige, Robert Paley, Angela Brooke, Michael Tyler. Student, Barnard Coll., 1954-55, U. Pa., 1955-56; BFA, Moore Coll. Art, 1979, HHD (hon.), 1998. Mgmt. cons. Woodlyn Sch., Rosemont, Pa., 1983—2003; sr. ptnr. DRT Interiors, Phila., 1983—2003; ptnr. Phila. Phillies, 1981-94. One-woman shows include Watson Gallery Wheaton Coll. Norton, Mass., 1977, U. Pa., 1977, Med. Coll. Pa. Phila., 1982, Aquaduct Race Track, 1982, Phila. Art Alliance, 1983, Paley Gallery, Moore Coll. Art and Design, 1984, 2003, Art Alliance, 1994, Frost & Reed Gallery, Saratoga, NY, 2000-2004. Pres. League of Children's Hosp. Phila., 1969-70; bd. overseers Ctr. for Judaic Studies U. Pa., 1993-96; bd. mgrs. Moore Coll. Art and Design, 1970—, chmn. exec. com., 1982-99, trustees 1979-99, chmn. emerita bd. trustees, 1999-2003. Recipient G. Allen Smith Prize Woodmere Art Gallery, Chestnut Hill, Pa., 1979; woman honoree Samuel Paley Day Care Ctr., Phila., 1990; Jefferson Bank Declaration award, 1991, Nat. Philanthropy honoree Nat. Soc. Fund Raising Execs. Greater Phila. chpt., 1994. Mem. Pa. Acad. Fine Arts (selections and acquisitions com. 1970—, bd. mgrs. 1975—, chmn. exec. com. 1982—, trustee 1990—), Artist's Equity, Phila. Art Alliance, Phila. Mus. Art (assoc), Phila. Print Club. Office: 2 Logan Sq Ste 2450 Philadelphia PA 19103-2724

LEVY, WENDY, psychologist; b. Sao Paulo, Brazil, Sept. 21, 1956; d. Merwin Ronald and Edith (Pressburger) L.; m. Leo Massarani, Sept. 4, 1993; childre: Julian, Marcel. BA, Coll. William and Mary, 1978; MA, MEd, Columbia U., 1985; D of Psychology, Yeshiva U., 1995. Lic. psychologist, Conn. Dual diagnosis therapist Gracie Square Hosp., N.Y.C., 1991-94; psychologist Karen Horney Clinic, N.Y.C., 1992-94; intern Yale Sch. Medicine, New Haven, Conn., 1994-95; coord. domestic violence program Hill Health Ctr., New Haven, Conn., 1995-96; clin. instr., clin. supr. Yale Sch. Medicine, 1997—; pvt. practice pvt. practice, Westport, Conn., 1998—. Mem. APA, Conn. Psychol. Assn. Avocations: choral singing, biking, hiking. Office: 31 Imperial Ave Westport CT 06880-4303

LEWALLEN REYNOLDS, CYNTHIA MAIRE, city administrator, small business owner; b. Oneida, Tenn., Feb. 13, 1955; d. Reason Henderson and Dorothy D. Cross; m. Ray Lewallen; children: Bradley Shane, Keisha Rae; m. Jeffrey D. Reynolds; 1 child, Akeia Grace. Student, Roane State C.C., Harriman, Tenn.; cert. pub. supervision, cert. mcpl. ofcl., U. Tenn.; cert. clk., Mid. Tenn. State U.; diploma in bus. adminstrn., Tenn. Tech., 1991. Salesclk., buyer Conastsers Dept. Store, Oneida, Tenn., 1977-97; owner day care ctr., Huntsville, Tenn., 1979-84; city recorder, adminstr. Town of Huntsville, 1984—; co-owner Tri-Tech. Environ., Huntsville, 1996—. Mem. adv. bd. Plateau Electric Coop., Oneida, 1990-91; promoter, recruiter Appalachian Ednl. Ctr., Tazewell, tenn., 1986-90. Mem. Huntsville Planning Commn., 1996—; cmty. devel. dir. Town of Huntsville, 1986-88; chmn. Tenn. Bicentennial; mem. Scott Leadership Class of 2000, 1999—; co-founder Scott County Jr. Pro Youth Program, 1986; mem. festival com. Firemen 4th Celebration, Huntsville; cheerleader coach Huntsville Jr. Pro League, 1986-96; mem. New River (Tenn.) Bapt. Ch. Mem. Tenn. Assn. Mcpl. Clks., Internat. Inst. Mcpl. Clks., Advanced Acad. Recorders, Scott County C. of C. (bd. dirs. 1998-99). Democrat. Baptist. Avocations: hiking, spending time with family, bowling, working with children. Office: Town of Huntsville PO Box 150 3053 Baker Hwy Huntsville TN 37756-4014

LEWENT, JUDY CAROL, pharmaceutical executive; b. Jan. 13, 1949; BA, Goucher Coll., 1970; MS in Mgmt., MIT, 1972. With corp. fin. dept. E.F. Hutton & Co., Inc., 1972—74; asst. v.p. for strategic planning Bankers Trust Co., 1974—75; sr. fin. analyst corp. planning Norton Simon, 1975—76; divsn. contr. Pfizer, Inc., 1976—80; dir. acquisitions and capital analysis Merck & Co., Inc., Whitehouse Station, NJ, 1980—83, asst. contr., 1983—85, exec. dir. fin. evaluation and analysis, 1985—87, v.p., treas., 1987—90, v.p. fin., CFO, 1990—92, sr. v.p., CFO, 1993—2001, exec. v.p., CFO, 2001—02, exec. v.p., CFO, pres. human health Asia, 2003—. Bd. dirs. Dell Inc., Motorola Inc., Nat. Bur. Econ. Rsch., life mem. MIT Corp., trustee Rockefeller Family Trust. Mem. exec. com. Penn Medicine. Mem.: Am. Acad. Arts and Scis. Office: Merck & Co Inc PO Box 100 One Merck Dr Whitehouse Station NJ 08889-0100

LEWIE, REVA GOODWIN, artist, educator; b. Balt., Feb. 14, 1930; d. William Milton Goodwin Sr. and Edith Elizabeth (Koon) Goodwin; m. Lemuel Arthur Lewie Jr., Aug. 28, 1948; 1 child, Reva Marcia Lewie-Thompson. BS, Morgan State U., 1956; MA, NYU, 1961; postgrad., U. Md., Towson State U. Tchr. art and geography Balt. City Pub. Schs., 1956, coord. art, 1966; instr. art Morgan State U., 1968; tchr. art resource Balt. City Pub. Schs., 1959—67, chair art dept., 1967—71, head art dept., 1971—87; v.p. Lewie Consol. Enterprises, 1990—. Docent Walters Art Mus., Balt., 1993—, mem. adv. bd. African Am. steering com., 1990—98; commr. Balt. County Commn. Arts & Scis., 1990—. Represented in permanent collections James E. Lewis Collection, Morgan State Univ., Balt., Md., exhibitions include Loeb Ctr., N.Y.C., Washington County Mus., Hagerstown (Artists Equity Shows), State Capital, Annapolis, Md, James E. Lewis Mus. Morgan State Univ., Balt., MD, Walters Art Mus., commn., Madison Med. Ctr., Balt., Md, DHIS Inst., Lanham, Md., Commn., Garwyn Med. Ctr., Balt., Md, commn., Mercy Med. Ctr., Balt.,Md. Mem. WAM Womens Com., 1993. Named Woman of Yr. Cmty. Svc. award, U.S. Senator Barbara Mikulski, 2003; recipient Tchr. of the Yr. award, Nat. Art Edn. Assn., 1985, Md. Art Edn. Assn. award, 1986, Walters Art Gallery award, 1996, NAACP ACTSO award, 1992, Mary Fritzpatrick award, Federated Garden Clubs of Marland Inc., 1998, 2001, Patapsco River Links Art award, 1999, Woman of the Yr. in Cultural Arts, Balt. City's Mayoral award, City Coun. awards, Md. State awards, 1998—2003. Mem.: Les Grandes Dames (pres. 1999—), Nat. Coalition of 100 Women, Inc., The Pierians, Inc., Beautiful Balt. (bd. dirs.), For-Win-Ash Garden Club (pres. 2000—), Federated Garden Clubs Md. (sec. 2000), The Links (charter), Zeta Phi Beta. Avocations: travel, floral design, art.

LEWIN, MARION EIN, consultant, physician, former medical association administrator; grad., MD, Columbia U. Dir. Ctr. for Health Policy Rsch. Am. Enterprise Inst. for Pub. Policy Rsch.; dep. dir. Nat. Health Policy Forum; sr. staff officer, dir. Office Health Policy Programs Inst. of Medicine, Washington. Sr. cons. Grantmakers in Health; dir. project Assn. for Health Svcs. Rsch. Co-editor: Information Trading: How Information Influences the Health Policy Process; contbr. Jour. Med. Practice Mgmt., JAMA, among others. Bd. dirs. Providence Hosp., Washington, chair planning com.

LEWIN, NANCY S. actress; d. Derek Jonathan Lewin and Harriet Ria Lihs. BA in Humanities, U. Calif., Berkeley, 1988, MA in History, 1989; voice cert., John Ford Sch. Voice, 1992. Musician various bands, San Francisco, 1986—94; cons. Fore-1, San Francisco, 1992—2002; actress, model Wilhelmina Scouting Network, Houston, 2003. Contbr. poetry to anthologies; composer: (songs) Music Folios I and II, 2000; musician, performer: benefits Amnesty Internat., 2000, musician, performer: S.E. Texans Organized for Peace. Mem. ACLU, Beaumont, 2003—. Mem.: Inst. Noetic Sci., Nat. Mus. Women in Arts, The Art Studio, Inc., Beaumont Art League. Achievements include discovery of answer to Einstein's theory of relativity; invention of Synopses. Avocations: exhibiting art, poetry, bicycling, metaphysics. Office: Starseed Rear Apt 612 Elgie St Beaumont TX 77705 E-mail: nlewin@gt.rr.com.

LEWIN, PEARL GOLDMAN, psychologist; b. Bklyn., Apr. 25, 1923; d. Frank and Anna Goldman; m. Seymour Z. Lewin, Oct. 17, 1943; children: David, Jonathan. BA, Hunter Coll., 1943; MS, U. Mich., 1947; PhD, NYU, 1980. Lic. psychologist, N.Y. Insp. chemist quarter master corps U.S. Army, 1943-45, chemist chem. warfare, 1945; asst. psychologist Bur. Psychol. Svcs., U. Mich., Ann Arbor, 1947-48; freelance rsch. asst. chemistry N.Y.C., 1955-71; adj. lectr. CUNY, Bklyn., 1973-74, instr., 1974-79, asst. prof., 1979-80; psychologist Creedmore Psychiat. Ctr., N.Y.C., 1980-82; sr. psychologist Manhattan Family Ct., N.Y.C., 1982-87; cons., 1987—. Mentor Peer Counseling Orgn., Bklyn. Coll., 1976-80, coord. student svcs. New Sch. Liberal Arts, 1974-76, adminstr. acad. regulations, 1974-76. Author: Sexist Humor, 1979. Mem. APA, Pi Lambda Theta, Phi Kappa Phi. Avocations: management, reading, woodworking. Home and Office: 4231 N Walnut Ave Arlington Heights IL 60004-1302

LEWIS, AMY BETH, newswriter, reporter, writer, photographer; b. Silver Creek, N.Y., Dec. 12, 1964; d. Jon Michael Lewis and Elizabeth Jean Chodacki-Berns, Mary Lewis (Stepmother) and Charles Johnson(Stepfather); life ptnr. Michael Ohl. Degree in Comm. and Media Arts, Erie C.C. South, 2000. Supr. sheltered workshop Suburban Adult Services, Inc., Sardina, NY, 1996—98; sec., receptionist William Shoemaker Associates, Inc., Hamburg, 1996—98. Reading tutor Erie C.C., Boston, 1999—2001; writer-reporter, freelance photographer Dunkirk Observer, 2000—03. Author of poems. Orgnl. mem. Bus. and Profl. Women, Silver Creek, NY, 2001—02. Recipient Outstanding News Writing, Irving-Chautauqua County C. of C., 2002. Avocations: horseback riding, gardening, creative writing, travel, movies. Office: Dunkirk Observer 10 East Second St Dunkirk NY 14048-1602

LEWIS, AMY C. finance educator, researcher; d. William E. and Mary Frances Lewis. BS, Ariz. State U., 1994; PhD, Ind. U., 2000. Postdoctoral rsch. assoc. David Eccles Sch. of Bus., Salt Lake City, 2000—02, vis. asst. prof., 2002—. Contbr. articles to profl. jours. Recipient Hon. Mention, Grad. Fellowship Competition, NSF, 1995. Mem.: Soc. for Personality and Social Psychology, APA, Acad. of Mgmt. Office: U Utah #106 1645 E Campus Center Dr Salt Lake City UT 84112

LEWIS, ANN FRANK, former government official; b. Jersey City, Dec. 19, 1937; d. Samuel and Elsie (Golush) Frank; m. Myron Sponder, 1989; children from previous marriage: Patricia Fay, Beth Ellen Susan Jane. Student, Radclffe Coll., 1954-55. Asst. to mayor City of Boston, 1968-75; dep. campaign mgr. Bayh for Pres., 1975-76; adminstrv. asst. to Congressman Stan Lundine, U.S. Ho. of Reps., Washington, 1976-81, adminstrv. asst. to Congresswoman Barbara Mikulski, 1978-81; polit. dir. Dem. Nat. Com., Washington, 1981-85; nat. dir. Ams. for Dem. Action, Washington, 1985-87; nat. affairs columnist MS mag., 1988-92; analyst Monitor Radio and Sta. WHDH-TV, 1992; v.p. for pub. policy Planned Parenthood Fedn. Am.; pres. Politics, Inc.; co-chmn. Back to Bus. Com., 1994; dep. campaign mgr. Clinton-Gore, 1996; dep. dir. comm. and strategic planning The White House, Washington, 1997, counselor to Pres., dir. comm. and strategic planning, 1997-2000. Inst. Politics of Kennedy Sch. Govt. fellow Harvard U., 1989. Office: Office of the President Rm GLF, West Wing White House Washington DC 20500

LEWIS, ANNE MCCUTCHEON, architect; b. New Orleans, Oct. 15, 1943; d. John Tinney and Susan (Dart) McCutcheon; m. Ronald Burton Lewis, Oct. 2, 1971; children: Matthew, Oliver. BA magna cum laude, Radcliffe Coll., 1965; MArch, Harvard U., 1970. Registered architect, D.C., Md., Va., Pa. Architect Skidmore, Owings & Merrill, Washington, 1969—72, Keyes, Lethbridge & Condon, Washington, 1972—75; ptnr. McCartney Lewis Architects, Washington, 1981—98; prin. Anne McCutcheon Lewis AIA, Washington, 1976—81, 1999—. Mem. Harvard U. Grad. Sch. Design Alumni Coun., Cambridge, Mass., 1979-82; bd. dirs. Friends Non-Profit Housing, Washington, 1981-98, Washington Humane Soc., 1990—, D.C. Hist. Preservation Rev. Bd., 2003—. Fellow: AIA (dir.-at-large Washington chpt. 1982—84, Design awards 1979, 1983, 1989, 1990, 1991, 1992, 1993, 1996, 1998, 2000, 2001). Office: Anne McCutcheon Lewis FAIA 2400 Reservoir Rd NW Washington DC 20007-2328

LEWIS, AUDREY GERSH, financial marketing, public relations, strategic communications consultant; b. Phila., Dec. 1, 1933; d. Benjamin and Augusta (Fine) Gersh; divorced; children: Jamie Lewis Keith, Ruth-Ellen Lewis. Student, Temple U., 1951—53. Asst. mgr. accounts payable/receivable Turner Constrn. Co., Louisville, 1953—55; rep. sales, mktg., fin. depts. Benjamin Gersh Wholesaler Jeweler, Wyncote, Pa., 1955—69; registered rep. Seaboard Planning Corp. (formerly B.C. Morton Broker Del.), Greenwich, Conn. and Wyncote, 1969—72; placement counselor sales and mktg. dept. Greyhound Permanent Pers. subs. Greyhound Corp., Stamford, Conn., 1974—77; asst. v.p., mgr. investor rels.l, mktg. Am. Investors Corp., Greenwich, 1977—85; founder, pres. Audrey Gersh Lewis Cons. Ltd., Greenwich, 1985—, Corp. Exec. Coach, LLC, Greenwich, 2002—, Strategic Comm. Planning. Chair Cancer Fund, Wyncote, United Fund Leadership Award, Wyncote, 1963-68; asst. treas. Rep. Town Com., Greenwich, 1981-82; mem. Greenwich rep. Town Meeting, 1981, 82; mem. Greenwich Town Alarm Appeals Bd., 1985-98. Mem. Assn. Corp. Growth (bd. dirs., v.p. mktg. and pub. rels. N.Y. chpt. 1989-92, mem. nat. ann. meeting planning com. 1992, 93, 94), Assn. Corp. Growth (N.Y. chpt.), Forum Club. Avocations: antiquing, walking, reading. Office: Audrey Gersh Lewis Cons Ltd Corp Exec Coach LLC PO Box 4644 Greenwich CT 06831-8644

LEWIS, CAROL E. academic administrator, management consultant; d. Otto A. and Edna M. Zunker(Stepmother); m. John S. Lewis. BS, U. Fla., 1962, MS, 1966; PhD, Georgetown U., 1970; MBA, U. Alaska, 1978. Interim dean Sch. Agr. and Land Resources Mgmt. U. Alaska, Fairbanks, 2000—02, dean, dir. Sch. Nat. Resources and Agr. Scis. Agr. and Forestry Expt. Sta., 2002—. From asst. to assoc. to prof. resources mgmt. U. Alaska, Fairbanks, 1973—, head dept. resources mgmt., 1989—98; rsch. physicist Dahlgren (Va.) Naval Weapons Lab., 1969—72; asst. prof. Clinch Valley Coll., U. of Va., Wise, Va., 1967—68. Mem.: Internat. 99s (pres. Midnight Sun chpt. 1993—97), Rotary Internat. (pres. College Rotary 1996—97), Phi Kappa Phi (pres. 1996—2002), Sigma Xi. Achievements include patents for ultrasonic imaging device /detection of tree disease and lumber/timber imperfections. Office: U Alaska 172 AHRB Box 757140 Fairbanks AK 99775-7140 E-mail: ffcel@uaf.edu.

LEWIS, CORINNE HEMETER, psychotherapist, educator; b. N.Y.C., Nov. 28, 1925; d. Leslie Hall and Frances Pope Hemeter, m. Aug. 22, 1947 (div. 1984); children: Anne Marie, Richard Allyn, Timothy Hall; m. Ceylon S. Lewis Jr., Aug. 6, 1999. BSN, U. Pitts., 1947; MSW, U. Okla., 1978. Diplomate in clin. social work. Staff nurse St. Joseph's Hosp., Buckhannon, W.Va., 1947; head nurse Myer's Clinic, Phillipi, W.Va., 1948; clin. instr., supr. Allegheny Valley Hosp., Tarentum, Pa., 1949; coord. psychiat. nursing edn. Hillcrest Med. Ctr., Tulsa, 1966-67; clin. staff mem. Tulsa Psychiat. Ctr., Tulsa, 1968-77; tchr. principles personality devel. Hillcrest Med. Ctr., Tulsa, 1966-75; supr., interns in psychotherapy Tulsa Psychiat. Ctr., 1971-77; pvt. practice psychotherapist Tulsa, 1978—. Dir. Drug Day Hosp., Tulsa Psychiat. Ctr., 1969, dir. nursing, 1970-71; adminstrv. cons. Family and Children's Svcs., Tulsa, 1978; renal dialysis unit cons. Hillcrest Med. Ctr., 1978; dir. Am. Cancer Soc. funded program Tulsa Psychiat. Ctr., 1977-79, cons. to dept. internal medicine, Tulsa Med. Coll., 1977-98. Jr. bd. mem. Women's Assn., Tulsa Boys Home, 1957-59; mem. Mental Health Assn. Tulsa, 1968-83, bd. dirs., 1982-83; vol. Jr. Assn., Tulsa Boys Home, 1958-59, Children's Med. Ctr., 1953-56; bd. dirs. Nursing Svc. Inc., Tulsa, 1982-83. Mem. Nat. Assn. Social Workers, Acad. Cert. Social Workers, Sigma Theta Tau. Democrat. Presbyterian. Avocations: classical music, reading. Home: 2300 Riverside Dr Apt 8F Tulsa OK 74114-2403

LEWIS, DEBORAH ALICE, tax company executive, writer; b. Griffin, Ga., Mar. 26, 1947; d. Durward and Imogene Hinds L. AA, Miss. Gulf Coast Jr. Coll., Gulfport, 1973; student, William Carey Coll., 1973; BA in English cum laude, U. So. Miss., 1978. Vets. counselor Miss. Gulf Coast Jr. Coll., Gulfport, 1973-76; spl. agt. Dept of Def., 1976-84; instr., adj. faculty Phillips Coll., Gulfport, 1979-81; mgr. H&R Block Inc., Jacksonville, 1984—, tax edn. specialist Anniston, Ala., 1986—. Author: Duty, 1992, (poetry) Dan River Anthology, 1988; regional editor Feminist Lit., 1984. With USMC, 1965—68, with USMCR, 1968—75. Recipient Outstanding Young Women of Am. award, 1980. Mem. Nat. Tax Preparers Assn., Women Marines Assn., League for Animal Welfare (life mem.), Lambda Iota Tau. Avocation: historian. Office: H&R Block Inc 500 Pelham Rd Jacksonville AL 36265 Fax: 256-435-4189. E-mail: dlewis2233@aol.com.

LEWIS, ELEANOR ROBERTS, lawyer; b. Detroit, Jan. 5, 1944; m. Roger Kutnow Lewis, June 24, 1967; 1 child, Kevin Michael. BA, Wellesley Coll., 1965; MA, Harvard U., 1966; JD, Georgetown U., 1974. Bar: DC 1975. Atty. HUD, Washington, 1974-76, asst. gen. counsel, 1979-82; atty. Brownstein Zeidman & Schomer, Washington, 1976-79; chief counsel internat. commerce U.S. Dept. Commerce, Washington, 1982—. Author, editor (with others): book Street Law, 1975; contbr. chapters to books, articles to legal and fin. jours. Bd. dirs. Dana Pl. Condominium, Washington. Mem.: ABA (U.S. govt. liaison to internat. sect.), Sr. Execs. Assn. (nat. bd. dirs.), DC Bar Assn. Home: 5034 1/2 Dana Pl NW Washington DC 20016-3441 Office: US Dept Commerce 14th & Constitution Ave NW Washington DC 20230-0001

LEWIS, EVELYN, management consultant; b. Goslar, Germany, Sept. 19, 1946; came to U.S., 1952, naturalized, 1957; d. Gerson Emanuel and Sala (Mendlowicz) L. BA, U. Ill., Chgo., 1968; MA, Ball State U., 1973, PhD, 1976. Rsch. analyst Office Comptr., State of Ill., Chgo., 1977-78; lectr. polit. sci. dept. Loyola U., Chgo., 1977; asst. to commr. Dept. Human Svcs., Chgo., 1978-81; group mgr. comm. Arthur Andersen & Co., Chgo., 1981-84; dir. comm. and pub. rels. Heidrick and Struggles, Inc., Chgo., 1984-88; assoc. ptnr. organization and human performance Accenture, Chgo., 1989—. Mem. adj. faculty Sch. Bus. Adminstrn., Roosevelt U., 1988. Mem. Children of Holocaust, Chgo., 1982; bd. dirs. Internat. Children's Benefit Fund. Mem. B'nai B'rith. Jewish. Avocations: writing, poetry, bicycling, hiking. Office: Accenture 161 N Clark Chicago IL 60601 E-mail: evelyn.lweis@accenture.com.

LEWIS, GOLDY SARAH, real estate developer, corporation executive; b. West Selkirk, Man., Can., June 15, 1921; d. David and Rose (Dwor) Kimmel; m. Ralph Milton Lewis, June 12, 1941; children: Richard Alan, Robert Edward, Roger Gordon, Randall Wayne. BS, UCLA, 1943; postgrad., U. So. Calif., 1944-45. Pvt. practice acctg., L.A., 1945-57; law office mgr., 1953-55; dir., exec. v.p. Lewis Homes, Upland, Calif., 1955—, Lewis Construction Co. Inc., Upland, 1959—, Lewis Bldg. Co., Inc., Las Vegas, 1960—, Republic Sales Co., Inc., 1956—, Kimmel Enterprises, Inc., 1959—; mng. partner Lewis Homes of Calif., 1973—; mng. ptnr. Lewis Homes of Nev., 1972—. Western Properties, 1972—, Foothill Investment Co., 1971—, Republic Mgmt. Co., 1978—. Contbr. articles to mags., jours. Mem. Dean's Coun. UCLA Grad. Sch. Architecture and Urban Planning; mem. UCLA Found., Chancellor's Assocs.; endowed Ralph and Goldy Lewis Ctr. for Regional Policy at UCLA, 1989, Ralph and Goldy Lewis Hall of Planning and Devel. at U. S.C., 1989, others. Co-recipient Builder of Yr. award, Profl. Builder Mag., 1988, Housing Person of Yr. award, Nat. Housing Conf., 1990, Entrepreneur of Yr. award, Inland Empire, 1990; named Ralph and Goldy Lewis Sports Ctr. in their honor, City of Rancho Cucamonga, 1988, also several other parks and sports fields including Lewis Park in Claremont; named one of Women of Yr., Calif. 25th Senate Dist., 1989, (with husband Ralph M. Lewis) Disting. CEO, Calif. State U., San Bernadino, 1991, Mgmt. Leaders of the Yr., Univ. Calif., Riverside,

1993; recipient 1st award of distinction, Am. Builder mag., 1963, Homer Briggs Svc. to Youth award, West End YMCA, 1990, Spirit of Life award, City of Hope, 1993, Builder of Century award, Bldg. Industry Assn., Baldy View chpt., 1999. Mem. Nat. Assn. Home Builders, Bldg. Industry Assn. So. Calif. (Builder of Yr. award Baldy View chpt. 1988), Internat. Coun. Shopping Ctrs., Urban Land Inst. Office: Lewis Homes PO Box 670 Upland CA 91785-0670

LEWIS, JENNIFER L. internist, educator; b. Pitts., Nov. 26, 1971; d. Thomas J. Lewis, Sr. and Bonnie L. Lewis; m. Robert F. Liberatore, Jr.; 1 child, Matthew Robert Liberatore. BS, U. Pitts., 1993, MD, 1997. Internal medicine resident Allegheny Gen. Hosp., Pitts., 1997—2000, chief resident internal medicine; physician internal medicine Pitts. Gen. Medicine Assocs., Pitts. Intern selection com. internal medicine residency Allegheny Gen. Hosp., Pitts., 2000—, mem. clin. competency com.; asst. prof. medicine coll. medicine Drexel U., Pitts., 2001—, third yr. medicine clerkship dir. Sch. Medicine, 2001—. Scholar, U. Pitts., 1989—93. Mem.: AMA, Pa. Med. Soc., Allegheny County Med. Soc. Avocations: horses, horseback riding, fitness. Office: Pitts Gen Medicine Assocs Ste 107 490 E North Ave Pittsburgh PA 15212 Office Phone: 412-359-3682. Office Fax: 412-359-8541.

LEWIS, JOSEPHINE VICTORIA, retired marketing executive; b. Chgo., Dec. 3, 1936; d. Wincenty and Helena (Francysczak) Gurbacki; m. Laurence Warren Lewis, Jan. 8, 1955; children: Laurence Michael, Michaleen Kay, Gregory Michael. AS in Mktg., Triton Coll., 1979; BA in Psychology, Benedictine U., 2001. Sec. Marsh & McLennan, Chgo., 1953-57; with factory prodn. Motorola, Franklin Park, Ill., 1969-70; with inventory control Reflector Hardware, Melrose Park, Ill., 1970-71; distbn./inventory supr. Jewel Imports (Osco Drug, Inc.), Oakbrook, Ill., 1971-83; Midwest regional mgr. Port of Seattle, 1983-96. Leader Dupage County coun. Girl Scouts U.S.A., 1968-71; den mother Woods Coun. Boy Scouts Am., 1974-75; fundraiser United Way, Northlake, Ill., 1972-74; active Christian Family Movement, Marriage Encounter; vol. and mentor on transitional housing Cath. Charities, 1996—2003; vol. St. Margaret Mary Roman Cath. Ch., Naperville, 1992—, Morton Arboretum, 1999—2003. Mem. Women in Internat. Trade, Internat. Trade Assn. Greater Chgo., Customs Brokers and Fgn. Freight Forwarders Assn., Ocean Freight Agts. (sec. 1993, treas. 1994, v.p. 1995, pres. 1996, chmn. bd. 1997), Piggyback Assn. Chgo., Midwest Fgn. Commerce Club (bd. govs. 1996-97), Chgo. Transp. Club. Avocations: gardening, golf, tap dancing.

LEWIS, JULIETTE, actress; b. San Fernando Valley, Calif., June 21, 1975; d. Geoffrey L. and Glenis Batley; m. Stephen Berra, 1999. TV appearances include The Wonder Years, 1987, The Facts of Life, 1988, Dharma & Greg, 2001; TV Movies include Homefires, 1987, I Married Dora, 1988, Too Young To Die, 1989, A Family For Joe, 1990, My Louisiana Sky (Emmy nominee), Hysterical Blindness, 2002, Chasing Freedom, 2004; films include My Stepmother is an Alien, 1988, Runnin' Kind, 1989, Meet the Hollowheads, 1989, National Lampoons Christmas Vacation, 1989, Cape Fear, 1991 (Academy Award and Golden Globe nomination best supporting actress 1991), Crooked Hearts, 1991, Husbands and Wives, 1992, Kalifornia, 1993, That Night, 1993, What's Eating Gilbert Grape, 1993, Romeo is Bleeding, 1994, Natural Born Killers, 1994, Mixed Nuts, 1994, Strange Days, 1995, The Basketball Diaries, 1995, Audition, 1996, From Dusk Till Dawn, 1996, The Evening Star, 1996, Full Tilt Boogie, 1997, Somegirl, 1998, The 4th Floor, 1999, The Other Sister, 1999, Way of the Gun, 2000, Room to Rent, 2000, Picture Claire, 2001, Gaudi Afternoon, 2001, Armitage: Dual Matrix, 2001, Enough, 2002, Old School, 2003, Cold Creek Manor, 2003, Blueberry, 2004, Starsky & Hutch, 2004; singer, Juliette Lewis and the Licks. Office: William Morris Agy care Norman Brokaw 151 S El Camino Dr Beverly Hills CA 90212-2775 also: care Michelle Bega Rogers & Cowan PR 1888 Century Pk E Ste 500 Los Angeles CA 90006*

LEWIS, KAREN MARIE, writer, human services professional; b. Syracuse, N.Y., Oct. 29, 1965; d. Stephan Joseph and Mary Josephine (Scully) L. Student, Simon's Rock of Bard Coll., 1982-83; BA in Linguistics cum laude, Barnard Coll., 1986; MA in Psychology, Brandeis U., 1989; Cert. in Human Svcs. with honors, Berkshire C.C., 2003. Prodn. asst. Claremont Rsch. and Pub., N.Y.C., 1984-86; tchg. asst. Barnard Coll., N.Y.C., 1984-86, Brandeis U., Waltham, Mass., 1988; freelance writer Great Barrington, Mass., 1989—; editl. asst. o.blek, Great Barrington, 1992-93; ESL algebra tutor Lenox (Mass.) Meml. High, 1995; editor Construct, Inc., Great Barrington, 1994-97, tutor adult edn., 1996-98; intern The Artful Mind, Great Barrington, 1996, office mgr., contbg. writer, editor, 1997—98; calendar prodr., 1999—2002; resident advisor Construct Inc., 1999—2002, head resident advisor, 2002—. Intern College Internship Program, Lee, Mass., 2003. Contbr. articles to anthologies, newspapers and poetry jours. Roman Catholic. Home: 309 Main St Apt D Great Barrington MA 01230-1616 Office Phone: 413-528-1985.

LEWIS, KAREN DEWITT, English language educator; b. N.Y.C., June 1, 1942; d. William DeWitt and Rosalind (Walter) Smith; m. Tom J. Lewis, Jan. 30, 1965 (div. Apr. 1992); 1 child, Gregory William. BA in English, U. Ill., 1964, MA in Tchg. of English, 1966. Tchr. English Crispus Attucks H.S., Indpls., 1968-70; instr. ESL English Lang. Svcs. Lang. Ctr., Norman, Okla., 1975; instr. adult edn. and ESL Lincoln Parish Sch., Ruston, La., 1975-77; instr. ESL La. Tech. U., Ruston, 1977-92, instr. English, 1992—. Vol. Peace Corps, Guatemala, 1966-68. Mem. La. TESOL (pres. 1991-92), South Cen. MLA, Conf. on Coll. Composition and Comm. Office: La Tech U English Dept PO Box 3162 Ruston LA 71272-0001 Office Phone: 318-257-2390. Business E-Mail: klewis@garts.latech.edu.

LEWIS, LISA, psychologist, administrator; B of Psychology and Biology, Pa. State U.; M of Clin. Psychology, Conn. Coll.; D of Clin. Psychology, Miami U., Oxford, Ohio. Intern Fla. Med. Sch.; dir. clin. psychology Menninger, Topeka. Presenter in field. Contbr. articles to profl. jours. Recipient David Rappaport Excellence in Teaching award; postdoctoral fellow Menninger. Address: Menningers PO Box 809045 Houston TX 77280

LEWIS, LOIDA NICOLAS, food products holding company executive; b. The Philippines, Dec. 23, 1942; m. Reginald Lewis, 1969 (dec. 1993). BA, St. Theresa's Coll., 1963; LLB, U. Philippines, 1967. Immigration atty., N.Y.C.; with Immigration and Naturalization Svc.; chmn., CEO TLC Beatrice Internat., N.Y.C., 1994—. Chmn. Nat. Federation of Filipino Americans Assoc. Author: How the Filipino Veteran of World War II Can Become a U.S. Citizen (According to the Immigration Act of 1990), 1991, How to Get a Green Card According to the Immigration Act of 1990, 1992, How to Get a Green Card: Legal Ways to Stay in the U.S.A., 1993. Office: TLC Beatrice Internat 115 E 57th St Ste 1430 New York NY 10022-2110

LEWIS, LOUISE MILLER, gallery director, art history educator; b. St. Louis, Dec. 4, 1940; d. Hugh Milton and Jeanne (Vical) Miller; m. Guy R. Lewis, Nov. 26, 1966; 1 child, Kevin. BA with distinction, 1963; cert. practique de la langue Francaise, U. Paris, 1963; MA in French, U. N.Mex., 1966, MA in Art History, 1972. Curator Art Mus. U. N.Mex., Albuquerque, 1966-70, asst. dir., 1970-72, acctg. dir., 1970, 71-72; assoc. dir. Art Gallery Calif. State U., Northridge, 1972-80, dir., 1980—; asst. prof. art history/recent art of internat. origins Calif. State U., 1972-79, assoc. prof., 1979-83, prof., 1983—, v.p. faculty, 1990-92, pres. faculty, 1992-94. Mem. Phi Beta Kappa. Office: Calif State U 18111 Nordhoff St Northridge CA 91330-8299 E-mail: louise.lewis@csun.edu.

LEWIS, MARCIA, actress; b. Melrose, Mass., Aug. 18, 1938; d. Edwin Parker and Bernice (Lamb) Lewis; m. Richard Alan Woody, Nov. 19, 1966 (div. 1990). RN, Jewish Hosp. Sch. Nursing, Cin., 1959; student, U. Cin., 1961-64. Actress with roles as Golde in Fiddler on the Roof, Nurse Porter in Orpheus Descending, Fraulein Schneider in Cabaret, Madam Katz in Roza, Rachel Halpern in Rags, Miss Hannigan in Annie, Ernestina Money in Hello Dolley, Mary desti in When She Danced, Lorene in The Time of Your Life, Ellen Emerson in Romance Language, Kitty Katz in Miami; stock roles include Mae in Bye Bye Birdie, Clairee in Steel Magnolias, Sister Mary Hubert in Nunsense, Jan in Woman of the Year, Rose in Gypsy, others. Feature films include Curtain Call (Japanese prodn.), Ice Pirates (cameo/co-star), Night Warning; TV films include Orpheus Descending, Legs, The Night They Took Miss Beautiful, When She was Bad..., How to Survive a Happy Divorce, Bobby and Sarah; guest appearances on All My Children, Ryan's Hope, One Life to Live, Loving; guest star in Kate and Allie, Mr. Belvedere, Happy Days, The Bob Newhart Show, The Bionic Woman, others. Office: The Gage Group Inc 315 W 57th St Frnt 4H New York NY 10019-3158

LEWIS, MARGARET MARY, marketing professional; b. Bridgeport, Conn., Sept. 27, 1959; d. Raymond Phillip and Catherine Helen (Gayda) Palovchak; m. William A. Lewis Jr., Oct. 4, 1980. BS summa cum laude, Sacred Heart U., 1986; postgrad., U. Bridgeport; AS, Katherine Gibbs Sch., 1980. Program mgr. sales svc. group Newspaper Coop. Couponing, Inc., Westport, Conn., 1985-87; sales adminstr. Supermarket Communication Systems, Inc., Norwalk, Conn., 1987-88, mgr. mktg. support, 1988-89; asst. project mgr. sales promotion Mktg. Corp. Am., Westport, 1989-91, account exec., 1991-92; mgr. program svcs. Ryan Partnership, Westport, 1992-93, sr. program mgr., 1993-95, mng. dir., 1995-96; account dir. Creative Alliance, Westport, Conn., 1996-97; promotion mktg. cons. CSC Weston Group, Wilton, Conn., 1997-98; account dir. TLP Inc., Wilton, Conn., 1998-2000, group account dir., 2000-01; sr. dir. Source Mktg., Westport, 2001—02; mng. dir. Ryan Partnership, Wilton, 2002—. Democrat. Roman Catholic. Home: 16 Nickel Pl Monroe CT 06468-3010 Office: Ryan Partnership 50 Danbury Rd Wilton CT 06897-4411

LEWIS, MARTHA NELL, Christian educator, minister, expressive arts therapist; b. Atlanta, Mar. 4, 1944; d. Clifford Edward and Nell (Shropshire) Wilkie; m. Jeffrey Clark Lewis, Aug. 20, 1966 (div. Aug. 1986); children: John Martin, Janet Michelle Teal. BA, Tex. Tech. U., 1966; massage therapy, The Winters Sch., 1991; MA, Norwich U., 1994; MTS, Ch. Divinity Sch. Pacific, 2000. Cert. music practitioner, expressive therapist, massage therapist, music instr. Geophys. analyst Shell Oil Co., Houston, 1966-68; photogravity specialist Photogravity, Inc., Houston, 1972-80; tchr. music Little Red Sch. House, Houston, 1974-75; sec., treas. Lewis Enterprises, Inc., Houston, 1976-83; regulatory supr. Transco Energy Co., Houston, 1983-92; expressive arts therapist Shalom Renewal Ctr., Splendora, Tex., 1995—, River Oaks Health Alliance, Houston, 1995-96; co-founder, past nat. exec. dir., pres., tchr. Music for Healing and Transition Program, 1994—. Massage therapist, expressive therapist, Houston, 1991-2000, Calif., 1996-2000; adj. prof. Holy Names Coll., Oakland, Calif., 1998-99; Sunday sch. coord. St. Stephen's Episc. Ch., Belvedere, Calif., 2000; min. Christian edn. St. Paul's Episc. Ch., Waco, Tex., 2000—. Advisor youth Corpus Christi Ch., Houston, 1970-80; vocalist, instrumentalist Sounds of Faith Folk Group, Houston, 1978—; harpist Houston Harpers Harp Ensemble, 1990-92; liturgical dancer Random Dance, Berkeley, Calif., 1997-2000; instr. exercise, body awareness Transco Energy Co. Fitness Ctr., Houston, 1990-92; vol. The Inst. for Rehab. and Rsch., Houston, 1989-90, Houston Hospice, 1992-96, Houston Healing Healthcare Project, 1993-96; vol. Healing Environ. Coun. St. Luke's Episc. Hosp., 1993-96; lay chaplain Cmty. of Hope, 1994—; founder The Winters Sch. Massage Therapy Care Team, Houston, 1991-96; vol. Ctr. for AIDS Svcs., Oakland, 1996-2000, Hillcrest Hospice, 2003—. Mem.: Nat. Assn. for Episcopal Edn. Dirs., Nat. Network Lay Profls., Christian Dance Fellowship USA, Nat. Sacred Dance Guild, Am. Massage Therapy Assn., Internat. Folk Harp Assn., Internat. Expressive Arts Therapy Assn., Sigma Kappa Alumnae Sorority (pres. Houston chpt. 1974—76, nat. collegiate province officer 1981—85, Houston Alumnae of Yr. 1981, Tex. Alumnae of Yr. 1980, Pearl Ct. award 1991), Houston Sigma Kappa Found. (bd. dirs.), Space City Ski Club (asst. trip coord. 1991—92). Roman Catholic. Episcopalian. Avocations: harp, piano, voice, dance, travel. Home: 1625 Wooded Acres #115 Waco TX 76710 Personal E-mail: mlewis3444@aol.com. Business E-Mail: marthal@stpaulswaco.org.

LEWIS, MARY ETTA, special education educator; b. Ontario, Calif., Oct. 23, 1928; d. Franklin Carr and Marguerite Mae (Wood) McMakin; m. Charles Jesse Lewis, Dec. 15, 1946; children: Kenneth Arnold, Linda Marie. AA, Chaffey Coll., Alta Loma, Calif., 1963; BA, LaVerne Coll., 1965; MA, Calif. State U., L.A., 1979. Cert. elem. tchr., learning handicapped specialist. Tchr. Chino (Calif.) Unified Sch. Dist., 1965-67, Ontario-Montclair Sch. Dist., 1967-79, spl. edn. tchr., 1979-80, resource specialist, 1980-88; resource specialist, math cadre Morongo Unified Sch. Dist., Yucca Valley, Calif., 1988—2003; ret., 2003. Tchr. Presby. Ch., Upland, CAlif., 1956-78, deacon 1976-79, Alta Loma, Calif., 1980-85. Recipient Delta Kappa Gamma award Teaching Colleagues, 1982-88. Mem. AAUW (sec. 1967-69), NEA, Pilot's Internat. Assn., Calif. Tchrs. Assn., Coun. for Exceptional Children, ZONTA, Calif. Assn. Resource Specialists (co-chmn. Hi-Desert chpt.), 99er's Club, Assistance League Club. Republican. Avocations: weaving, writing, flying, hiking, camping. Home: PO Box 2349 Yucca Valley CA 92286-2349 Personal E-mail: clewis2349@earthlink.net.

LEWIS, MARY JANE, film producer, director, scriptwriter; b. Kansas City, Mo., July 22, 1950; d. J.W. Jr. and Hilda (Miller) L. BA, Stephens Coll., Columbia, Mo., 1971; MA, NYU, 1984, PhD, 1996. Office mgr. Crazy Shirts, Inc., Honolulu, 1974-79; creator Exotic Exports, Honolulu, 1979-80; asst. buyer Bloomingdale's, N.Y.C., 1980-82; office mgr., media dir. Andiamo, Inc., N.Y.C., 1982-85; freelance stylist Condé Nast, Inc., N.Y.C., 1985-86; tchg. fellow NYU, 1988-90, adj. prof., 1990-92. Adj. faculty Fashion Inst. Tech., N.Y.C., 1983; lectr. U. Hawaii, creator adult edn. programs and credit classes, 1986—97; lectr. NYU Sch. Cont. Edn., 1991—94; freelance video stylist, asst. prodr. State of Hawaii, Honolulu, 1994—2003; TV prodr. Office of the Mayor, City and County of Honolulu, 1998; video prodr. Olelo Cmty. TV, Honolulu. Author: Careers in Fashion Manual, 1992, (screenplays) The Last Rose of Summer, 1992, (TV movie scripts) The Mustard Seed, 1992 (Maui Writers Conf. Screenwriting Competition award, 1998); prodr., dir., writer, narrator (video) Learning Through Community Service, 1998 (Communicator award, 1998, Videographer award, 1999); prodr.: (live TV show) City Lights, Honolulu City Lights, 1998; prodr., dir., writer (documentary) Sarah Josepha Hale and The Godey Girls, 2002—. Mem. Friends of the Richards Free Libr., Newport, NH, Friends Libr. Co. Phila.; sponsor Women Make Movies. Mem. AAUW, The Fashion Group Internat., Inc., NYU Alumni Assn., Nat. Trust for Historic Preservation, Nat. Women's History Project, Kappa Alpha Theta Alumni (pres. pledge class 1968), Elks Club. Avocations: psychic tarot readings, harpsicord, sailing, gardening, cats. Home: 91-513 B Hapalua St Ewa Beach HI 96706-2929 Office Phone: 808-689-4225. E-mail: godeygirls@yahoo.com.

LEWIS, MARY MAY SMITH, retired family practice nurse practitioner; b. Curtis, Okla., May 18, 1919; d. James Thomas and Maggie May (Patten) Smith; m. Leo Burch Lewis, July 11, 1993; m. Leslie Wilson Enis, Nov. 8, 1965 (dec. Oct. 11, 1991); 1 child, Mary Corliss Enis. RN, Okla. City Gen. Hosp. Sch. Nursing, 1945. RN, Okla., 1945—50, 1993—, 1950—54, 1958—92, 1948. Author poetry. Second lt. U.S. Army, 1945—46, South Pacific. Mem.: VFW Ladies Aux. (life), Am. Legion (life). Republican. Christian. Avocations: genealogy, gardening, flower arranging, cooking, research. Mailing: PO Box 932 Perkins OK 74059

LEWIS, MARY SALS, social services administrator, educator; b. Detroit, Dec. 6, 1942; d. Robert James and Charlotte Christine (Brasch) Sals; m. James Allen Lewis, Sept. 9, 1964; children: Robert Blacklock, Christine Rozelle, Laura Marie. BS, Tex. Ea. U., 1976; MA, U. Tex., 1979. Exec. dir. Smith County ARC, Tyler, Tex., 1976-78; drug abuse planner NETHSA, Marshall, Tex., 1979; legal asst. Tyler, 1980-87; contr. Western Map & Pub. Co., Bullard, Tex., 1988-92, Burchfield Pipe, Tyler, 1992-94; owner, ptnr. Theatre on Tour, Tyler, 1994—; instr. Tyler Jr. Coll., 1988—; exec. dir. Family Violence & Sexual Assault Inst., Tyler, 1994-96; chair dept. social sci. Jacksonville Coll., 2000—. Conf. coord. on children exposed to domestic violence, Austin, Tex., 1996., 6th nat. conf. on trauma, abuse and dissociation, Austin, 1995. Editor: Trauma, Amnesia and Denial of Abuse, 1995; editor EGuide Mag.; mng. editor Family Violence and Sexual Assault Bulletin, 1994-96. Cmty. rels. com. Tyler United Way, 1996; prodn. dir. summer musicals Lake County Playhouse, Mineola, Tex., 1995-96; pres. Tyler Interagency Projects, 1979; participant Synergy 95, Chgo., 1995. Recipient History honors Phi Alpha Theta, 1977, Acad. honors Alpha Chi, 1977, Theatre honors Alpha Psi Omega, 1994. Mem. Brickstreet Playhouse (adminstrv. v.p. 1991-93), East Tex. Hist. Asn., Tex. C.C. Tchrs. Assn., Tyler Civic Chorale Assn. (bd. dirs. 1979-99, pres.), Tyler Music Coterie/Nat. Fedn. Music Clubs. Democrat. Methodist. Avocations: theatre, music, history, govt. Home: 3024 Terilinga Dr Tyler TX 75701-6314 Office: Jacksonville Coll 105 BJ Albritton Jacksonville TX 75766 E-mail: mlewis@jacksonville-college.edu.

LEWIS, MOKSHA, chemist; b. Atlanta, Nov. 28, 1976; d. Michele R. Lewis. BS in Chemistry, Clark Atlanta U., 2001. Chemist Ga. Pacific Resins, Inc., Decatur, 2001—. Troop leader Girl Scouts Am., Decatur, 2002—03. Mem.: Am. Chem. Soc.

LEWIS, NINA, social worker; b. Cleve., July 21, 1953; d. William Paul and Gloria Louise (Pearch) L. BA in Sociology, Ohio State U., 1976, MSW, 1988. Lic. ind. social worker, Ohio. ACSW, rsch. asst. Disaster Rsch. Ctr. Ohio State U., Columbus, 1974-75; social worker Huckleberry House, Columbus, 1976-78, North Cen. Community Mental Health Ctr., Columbus, 1979-80, CHOICES for Victims Domestic Violence, Columbus, 1980-90; social worker state HIV case, mgmt, cons. AIDS unit Ohio Dept. Health, Columbus, 1990-93; dir. supportive housing dept. Lutheran Social Svcs. Central Ohio, 1992-97; HIV housing coord. Columbus Health Dept., 1997—. Adj. faculty Capital U., Ohio State U., Dominican Coll., Columbus State, Wright State. Coord. operation feed campaign Legal Aid Soc., Columbus, 1987. John H. Smith scholar, 1986-88, Anna Marie Mills scholar, 1986-88; recipient Walter and Marian English award, 1986-88, Social Worker of Yr. award Region V., 1996, Bob Fay award Franklin County ADMH Bd., 2000, Exec. Com. award Columbus Coalition for the Homeless, 2002. Mem. NASW, Ohio State Coll. Social Work Alumni Assn. Office: Columbus Health Dept 240 Parsons Ave Columbus OH 43215-5331

LEWIS, OLI PAREPA, curator; b. Cleve., Dec. 14, 1958; d. Raymond Joseph and Yarmila Manlet; m. Fred Lewis. BA, U. Las Vegas. Gen. mgr., curator Guinness World Records Mus., Las Vegas, Nev., 1990—. Pres. Mus. and Attractions in Nev. Recipient Voluntourism award Nev. Commn. Tourism, 1994. Office: Guinness World Records Mus 2780 Las Vegas Blvd S Las Vegas NV 89109-1102

LEWIS, REBA JOLENE, secondary school educator, consultant; b. Duncan, Okla., July 18, 1949; d. Rube Ira and Loretha Corene Rose; m. Donald Lawrence Lewis, Aug. 29, 1969; children: Don, Joni, Thomas, Sunnie, Tyler. BS, Tex. A&M U., 1971; MEd, E. Ctrl. U., Ada, Okla., 1985. Cert. Nat. Bd. Tchg. Stds., secondary tchr. Okla., Tex. Tchr. English and speech Port Arthur (Tex.) Ind. Sch. Dist., 1972—75; tchr. Healdton (Okla.) HS, 1976—89, 1995—, Pampa (Tex.) HS, 1990—94; realtor Walker Realty, Healdton, 1995—98; instr. Murray State Coll., Ardmore, Okla., 1995—99. Cons. tchr. testing Okla. Dept. Edn., Oklahoma City, 1999. Del. to state conv. Tex. Rep. Com., Pampa, 1994. Mem.: NEA, Healdton Assn. Classroom Tchrs. (pres., treas., named one of Outstanding Young Women of Am. 1986, Tchr. of Yr. 1986), Okla. Edn. Assn. (del. 1975—89, Zone Tchr. of Yr. 1986). Republican. Baptist. Avocations: reading, writing, horses. Home: 320 Lamar Healdton OK 73438 Office: Healdton HS 432 W Texas Healdton OK 73438

LEWIS, RITA HOFFMAN, plastic products manufacturing company executive; b. Phila., Aug. 6, 1947; d. Robert John and Helen Anna (Dugan) Hoffman; 1 child, Stephanie Blake. Student, Jefferson Med. Coll. Sch. Nursing, 1965—67, Gloucester County Coll., 1993—. Gen. mgr. Sheets & Co., Inc. (now Flower World, Inc.), Woodbury, NJ, 1968—72; dir., exec. v.p., treas. Hoffman Precision Plastics, Inc., Blackwood, 1973—. Ptnr. Timber Assocs. Author: The Part of Me I Never Really Meant to Share, 1979, In Retrospect: Caught Between Running and Loving; editor (poetry): (singles mag.) SPOTLIGHTER; author: (columnist) Innovative Singles Mag., 1989—. Commn. N.J. Expressway Authority, 1990—, sec. 1990—91, treas., 1991—, chmn. pers., 1991—; apptd. mem. N.J. Senate Forum on Budget and Revenue Alternatives, 1991; guest spkr. various civic groups, 1974; mem. Coun. for Citizens of Glen Oaks, NJ, 1979—, Cloucester Twp. Econ. Devel. Com., 1981—, Cloucester Twp. Day Scholar Com., 1984—; mem. adv. coun. Gloucester Twp. Econ. Adv. Coun., 1985—; chairperson Gloucester Twp. Day Scholar Found., 1985—96; bd. dirs. Diane Hull Dance Co. Recipient Winning Eagle award, 1982, Mayor's award for Womens' Achievement, 1987, Outstanding Cmty. Svc. award Mayor, Coun. and Com., 1987, Don L. Stackhouse Achievement award, 1996. Mem.: NAFE, Soc. Plastic Engrs., Blackwood Businessmen's Assn., Sales Assn. Chem. Industry, Stratford-Lindenwold Rotary (sargent-at-arms 2003, sec. 2004). Roman Catholic.

LEWIS, SANDRA COMBS, research psychologist, writer; b. Troup County, Ga., Oct. 8, 1939; d. Robert Milton and Imogene (Richardson) Combs; children: Virginia Susan Lewis, Charles James III. AB, Wesleyan Coll., 1961; MEd, Mercer U., 1972, Ga. State U., 1976; PhD, U. Ga., 1980. Personnel asst. Sears Roebuck & Co., Atlanta, 1961—62; rsch. asst. bd. regents U. Sys. Ga., 1962—63; asst. psychol. svcs. Bibb County Bd. Edn., Macon, 1972—73; instr. Macon Jr. Coll., 1973, 1982, Wesleyan Coll., 1973—75, 1981; psychometrist Middle Ga. Psychoednl. Ctr., 1975—76; instr. Mercer U., 1980—82. Presenter at profl. confs. Co-author: Christian Love and Problems of Living, 1992, God and Positive Christianity, 1998, Psychology for Life, 2000, A Revolutionary View of Education and Teaching for the Third Millennium, 2002; assoc. editor Truth Seekers Newsletter, 1998—. Pres. Macon Wesleyan Alumnae Club, 1973-74; bd. dirs. Family Counseling Ctr., Macon, 1975-76; ruling elder, clk. of session Northminster Presbyn. Ch., Macon, 1988-90, 94-96, vice moderator Presbyn. Women, 1989-90, 2002, moderator Presbyn. Women, 1990-91, 2003; v.p. Fore(In)Sight Found., 1991—. Mem.: APA, Mid. Ga. Psychol. Assn., Ga. Psychol. Assn. Avocations: gardening, photography. Home and Office: 4976 Oxford Rd Macon GA 31210-3059

LEWIS, SANDRA JEAN, cardiologist; b. Portland, Oreg., Apr. 11, 1949; d. Stanley Bernard and Susanne Laurel (White) L.; m. James Todd Rosenbaum, June 27, 1970; children: Lisa Rosenbaum, Jennifer Rosenbaum. BA, Stanford U., 1971, MD, 1977. Diplomate Am. Bd. Cardiology. Intern Stanford (Calif.) Univ. Hosp., 1977-78, resident, 1978-80, fellow cardiology, 1980-83; cardiologist Kaiser Permanente, San Francisco, 1983-85, The Heart Clinic, Portland, 1985-94; clin. asst. prof. medicine Oreg. Health Scis. U., 1986—; cardiologist Portland Cardiovascular Inst., 1995—. Chief cardiology Good Samaritan Hosp., Portland, 1990-93. Fellow Am. Coll. Cardiology; mem. AMA, Am. Med. Womens Assn., Am. Heart Assn.

LEWIS, SHIRLEY ANN REDD, college president; b. Winding Gulf, W.Va., June 11, 1937; d. Robert Fountain and Thelma Danese (Biggers) Redd; m. Ronal McGhee Lewis, Aug. 17, 1963; 1 child, Mendi Dessalines Shirley. BA, U. Calif., Berkeley, 1960, MSW, 1970; PhD, Stanford U., 1979, cert., U. London, U. Ghana, 1971. Tchr. Ravenswood City Schs., East Palo Alto, Calif., 1962-63, N.Y.C. Schs., 1964-65; counselor coordinator U. Calif., Berkeley, 1967-71; college instr. Los Altos (Calif.) Community Coll., 1970-72; researcher Stanford (Calif.) Sch. Edn., 1972-79; prof. Peabody Coll., Vanderbilt U., Nashville, Tenn., 1980-81; prof., assoc. dean Meharry Med. Coll., Nashville, 1982-85; asst. gen. sec. The Black Coll. Fund, Nashville, 1986-94; pres. Paine Coll., Augusta, Ga., 1994—. Co-author: The Nairobi Method, 1972, The 1-2-3 Method, 1985. Bd. dirs. United Negro Coll. Fund, Ga. Bank & Trust, Morris Mus., United Way. Recipient Carnegie fellow, 1968-70; named Outstanding Contributor, Meharry Med. Coll. Pre Alumni Assn., 1986. Mem. Nat. Assn. of Ind. Colls. & Univs., Coun. Pres. (bd. dirs.), Alpha Kappa Al pha, The Links. Democrat. United Methodist. Avocations: reading, public speaking. Office: Paine Coll 1235 15th St Augusta GA 30901-3105

LEWIS, SYLVIA DAVIDSON, foundation executive; b. Akron, Ohio, Apr. 28, 1927; d. Harry I. and Helen E. (Stein) Davidson; m. Allen D. Lewis, Oct. 12, 1947; children: Pamela Lewis Kanfer, Randy, Daniel, Cynthia Lewis Lagdameo. Student, U. Mich., 1945—47, U. Akron, 1961—62. Editor Akron Jewish News, 1948-50; tchr. Revere Rd. Congregation, Akron, 1964-70; office mgr. Acme Lumber & Fence Co., Akron, 1970-85; nat. pres. NA'AMAT USA (Movement of Working Women & Vols.), N.Y.C., 1993-97. Pres. Planned Parenthood Summit Portage and Medina Counties, 1999-2001; founding mem. Govt. Affairs Com., Columbus, Ohio, 1981—, exec. com., 1988-89; v.p. Akron Jewish Cmty. Fedn., 1988-94, pres. women's divsn., 1987-90; elect mem. Akron Jewish Cmty. Bd., 1999—. Named Woman of Distinction, YWCA Summit County, 2001; named one of No. Ohio's Top Women Profls., No. Ohio Live mag., 1997; named to Ohio Women's Hall of Fame, 1995; recipient Golden Rule award, J.C. Penney, 1994, Vol. of Yr. award, Lippman Cmty. Day Sch., 1992, Commendation of Honor award, Ohio Gen. Assembly, 1993, Women of Achievement award, YWCA of Summit County, 1999. Democrat. Jewish. Avocations: reading, writing, travel, grandchildren. Home: 4389 Everett Rd Richfield OH 44286 E-mail: syllewis1@aol.com.

LEWIS, THOMASINE ELIZABETH, magazine editor-in-chief; b. Manila, Phillipines, Sept. 20; d. Thomas Donald and Elizabeth Jane (Munson) L. Student, Broward C.C., 1976, Universidad de las Americas, Mexico City, 1979, U. Fla., L.A. Valley Coll., 1981, UCLA, 1984. Copy editor, reporter Mexico City News, 1979-81; mng. editor, editor-in-chief Playgirl Mag., Santa Monica, Calif., 1984-86; exec. editor mag. devel. Petersen Pub., Hollywood, Calif., 1986-87; exec. editor Japan Jour. Mag., Marina del Rey, Calif., 1987-88; assoc. pub., dir. Radio Guide Mag., L.A., 1988-90; editor-in-chief Disney Adventures Mag., Burbank, Calif., 1991-95, Sassy Mag., L.A., 1995; exec. dir. Live! Mag., L.A., 1995-98; editor, chief Teen Mag., 1998—. Bd. dirs. Santa Monica Red Cross; mem. League of Women Voters, NOW, People for the Am. Way. Avocations: traveling, writing, running.

LEWIS, TINA, music educator, writer; b. Lansing, Mich., Feb. 16, 1940; d. John Bozanis and Georgia Papadopoulos Lewis. MS, Mich. State Univ., 1962, MusM, 1964; cert. in Kodaly Methods, Silver Lake Coll., 1982. Alumna and fundraiser Interlochen Music Camp, 1953—60; elem. music tchr. Haslett (Mich.) Schs., 1962—2002; violinist Lansing (Mich.) Symphony Orch., 1962—82; piano tchr. pvt. practice, Haslett, Mich., 2002—. Historian Midwest Kodaly Music Educators, 1982—86, Lansing Women's Symphony Assn., 1982—84. Author: (book) Favorite Mich. Folk Songs, 1987, Songs For Very Young Children, 1984; contbr. articles to jours. in field. Mem. Haslett Women's Club, 2002—; Lansing Rose Soc., 2002—; mem. Grosse Pointe Garden Ctr., 1995—. Recipient Mich. Music Educator of the Yr. award, Mich. Music Educators Assn., 2000, Gov. Minuteman award, Mich. Found., 1987; grantee Post Grad. Grant, Delta Omicron, Haslett Education Found. Mem.: Haslett Education Assn. (v.p.), Lansing Matinee Musicale, Mich. Music Educators Assn. (exec. bd. mem.), Delta Omicron Music Honrary. Greek Orthodox. Avocations: rose gardening, reading biographies, hiking, travel. Home: 731 Touraine East Lansing MI 48823

LEWIS, TOMMI, magazine editor; Editor-in-chief Disney Adventures Walt Disney Pub. Co.; editl. dir. Radio Guide Magazine; exec. editor Japan. Journal Magazine; exec. editor mag. devel. Petersen Pub.; editor-in-chief Sassy Magazine; exec. editor LIVE! Magazine; editor-at-large Teen Magazine, 1998-2000, editor-in-chief, 2000—. Office: EMAP USA 6420 Wilshire Blvd Los Angeles CA 90048-5502

LEWIS, WILMA ANTOINETTE, lawyer, former prosecutor and federal agency admin; b. Santurce, P.R. BA with distinction, Swarthmore Coll., 1978; JD, Harvard U., 1981. Assoc. Steptoe & Johnson, Washington, 1981-1986; asst. U.S. atty. civil divsn. U.S. Atty.'s Office, Washington, 1986-1993; assoc. solicitor divsn. gen. law U.S. Dept. Interior, 1993-95, inspector gen., 1995-98; U.S. atty. Washington, 1998-2001; ptnr. Crowell & Moring LLP, Washington, 2001—. Mem. civil justice reform act adv. group U.S. Dist. Ct. D.C., mem. adv. com. on local rules; adj. faculty mem. George Washington U. Nat. Law Ctr. Mem. Phi Beta Kappa. Office: Crowell & Moring 1001 Pennsylvania Ave NW Washington DC 20004-2595 E-mail: wlewis@crowell.com.

LEWIS, YVONNE ANTIONETTE FLUKER, secondary school educator; d. Clyde and Eloise Byner Fluker; m. Henry Allen Lewis, June 22, 1991. BA in Math., Miles Coll., 1969; Master's in Math. Edn., U. Ala., Birmingham, 1977. Class II tchg. cert. Ala. Tchr. math. grade 8 Sylacauga H.S., Ala., 1969—70; tchr. math. grades 7 and 8 E. Highland H.S., Sylacauga, 1970—79; tchr. math. grades 9 and 11 Banks H.S., Birmingham, 1979—89; tchr. math. grade 8 Banks Mid. Sch., Birmingham, 1989—94; tchr. math. grade 9 and 11 Woodlawn H.S., Birmingham, 1994—2003. Active 4th Ave. Bapt. Ch., Birmingham, 1963—; chaplain Greater Birmingham Inter-Alumni chpt. United Negro. Coll. Fund, 1989—. Recipient Leadership Plaque award, Greater Birmingham Inter-Alumni Coun. of United Negro Coll. Fund, 1985, 1992, Dedicated Svc. and Leadership award, 4th Bapt. Ch., 1987, 1997, 1999, 2001. Mem.: NEA, Ala. Coun. Teachers Math., Ala. Edn. Assn., Coll. Hills Neighborhood Assn. (chaplain 7th St. Block Club 1998—2002), Birmingham Edn. Assn. (faculty rep. 1981—2003), Gamma Phi Delta (fin. sec. 2000—, sec. 2003—). Democrat. Avocations: sewing, singing, poetry, reading. Home: 717 Lamplighter Cir Birmingham AL 35214

LEWITZKY, BELLA, choreographer; b. Los Angeles, Jan. 13, 1916; d. Joseph and Nina (Ossman) L.; m. Newell Taylor Reynolds, June 22, 1940; 1 child, Nora Elizabeth. Student, San Bernardino Valley (Calif.) Jr. Coll., 1933-34; hon. doctorate, Calif. Inst. Arts, 1981; PhD (hon.), Occidental Coll., 1984, Otis Parsons Coll., 1989, Juilliard Sch., 1993; DFA, Santa Clara U., 1995; DFA (hon.), Calif. State U., Long Beach, 1997. Chmn. dance dept., chmn. adv. panel U. So. Calif., Idyllwild, 1956-74; founder Sch. Dance, Calif. Inst. Arts, 1969, dean, 1969-74; vice chmn. dance adv. panel Nat. Endowment Arts, 1974-77, mem. artists-in-schs. adv. panel, 1974-75; mem. Nat. Adv. Bd. Young Audiences, 1974—, Joint Commn. Dance and Theater Accreditation, 1979. Com. mem. Am. chpt. Internat. Dance Coun. of UNESCO, 1974—; trustee Calif. Assn. Dance Cos., 1976—, Idyllwild Sch. Music and Arts, 1986-95, Dance/USA, 1988-95, Calif. State Summer Sch. of Arts, 1988—; cons. the dance project WNET, 1987—. Co-founder, co-dir. Dance Dance Assocs., L.A., 1951-55; founder, 1966; artistic dir. Lewitzky Dance Co., L.A.; choreographer, 1948-97; founder, former artistic dir. The Dance Gallery, L.A.; contbr. articles in field; choreographed works include Trio for Saki, 1967, Orrenda, 1969, Kinaesonata, 1971, Pietas, 1971, Ceremony for Three, 1972, Game Plan, 1973, Five, 1974, Spaces Between, 1975, Jigsaw, 1975, Inscape, 1976, Pas de Bach, 1977, Suite Satie, 1980, Changes and Choices, 1981, Confines, 1982, Continuum, 1982, The Song of the Woman, 1983, Nos Duratori, 1984, 8 Dancers/8 Lights, 1985, Facets, 1986, Impressions #1, 1987, Impressions #3, 1988, Agitime, 1989, Impressions #3, 1989, Episode #1, 1990, Glass Canyons, 1991, Episode #2, 1992, Episode #3, 1992, Episode #4, 1993, Meta 4, 1994, Four Women in Time, 1996. Mem. adv. com. Actors' Fund of Am., 1986—, Women's Bldg. Adv. Council, 1985-91, Calif. Arts Council, 1983-86, City of Los Angeles Task Force on the Arts, 1986—; mem. artistic adv. bd. Interlochen Ctr. for Arts, 1988—. Recipient Mayoral Proclamation, City of L.A., 1976, 1982, ann. award Dance mag., 1978, Dir.'s award Calif. Dance Educators Assn., 1978, Plaudit Award, Nat. Dance Assn., 1979, Labor's Award of Honor for Community Svc., L.A. County AFL-CIO, 1979, L.A. Area Dance Alliance and L.A. Junior C. of C. Honoree, 1980, City of L.A. Resolution, 1980, Distguished Artist Award, City of L.A. and Music Ctr., 1982, Silver Achievement award YWCA, 1982, California State Senate Resolution, 1982, 1984, Award of Recognition, Olympic Black Dance Festival, 1984, Distinguished Women's Award, Northwood Inst., 1984, California State U. Distinguished Artist, 1984, Vesta Award, Woman's Bldg, L.A., 1985, L.A. City Council Honors for Outstanding Contributions, 1985, Woman of the Year, Palm Springs Desert Museum, Women's Committee, 1986, Disting. Svc. award Western Alliance Arts Adminstrs., 1987, Woman of Achievement award, 1988, Am. Dance Guild Ann. award, 1989, So. Calif. Libr. for Social Studies & Rsch. award, 1990, Am. Soc. Journalists & Authors Open Book award, 1990, Internat. Soc. Performing Arts Adminstrs. Tiffany award, 1990, Burning Bush award U. of Judaism, 1991, 1st recipient Calif. Gov.'s award in arts for individual lifetime achievement, 1989; honoree L.A. Arts Coun., 1989, Heritage honoree, Nat. Dance Assn., 1991, Vaslav Nijinsky award, 1991, Hugh M. Hefner First Amendment award, 1991, Artistic Excellence award Ctr. Performing Arts U. Calif., 1992, Lester Horton Lifetime Achievement award Dance Resource Ctr. of L.A., 1992, Occidental Coll. Founders' award, 1992, Dance/USA honor, 1992, Visual Arts Freedom of Expression award Andy Warhol Found., 1993, Artist of Yr. award L.A. County High Sch. Arts, 1993, Freedom of Expression honor Andy Warhol Found. Visual Arts, 1993, Calif. Alliance Edn. award, 1994, Lester Horton Sustained Achievement award, 1995 Dance Resource Ctr. of L.A., Lester Horton award for Restaging and Revival, Dance Resource Ctr. of L.A., 1996, 97, Disting. Artists of 1996, High Sch. of Performing Arts, Houston Tex., Bill of Rights award, Am. Civil Liberties Union of So. Calif., Nat. Medal of Arts, 1996, Gypsy award Profl. Dancers Soc., 1997, We. Arts Alliance Emeritus Mem. award, 1999, Capezio ann. Dance award for Significant Conbns. to Dance in U.S., 1999, Lifetime Achievement award Calif. Arts Coun., 2001; grantee Mellon Found., 1975, 81, 86, Guggenheim Found., 1977-78, NEA, 1969-94; honoree Women's Internat. League Peace and Freedom, 1995; presented with Key to the City, Cin., 1997. Mem. Am. Arts Alliance (bd. dirs. 1977), Internat. Dance Alliance (adv. council 1984—), Dance/USA (bd. dirs. 1988), Phi Beta (hon.). Fax: 505-897-9259.

LEWTER, HELEN CLARK, elementary education educator, retired; b. Millis, Mass., Jan. 14, 1936; d. Waldimar Kenville and Ida Mills (Currier) Clark; m. Alvin Council Lewter, June 18, 1966; children: Lois Ida, David Paul, Jonathan Clark. BA, U. Mass., 1958; MS, Old Dominion U., 1978. Tchr. Juniper Hill Sch., Framingham, Mass., 1960-63, Aragona Elem. Sch., Virginia Beach, Va., 1963-65, Park Elem., Chesapeake, Va., 1965-67; edn. specialist Riverview Sch., Portsmouth, Va., 1977-78; reading tchr. Truitt Jr. H.S., Chesapeake, 1979-83; reading resource tchr. Southeastern Elem., Chesapeake, 1983-86; tchr. Deep Creek Elem. Sch., Chesapeake, 1986-99, ret., 1999. Pers. task force, textbook adoption com. Chesapeake Pub. Schs., Va., 1984—85, employee handbook com., Va., 1986—87, K-6 writing curriculum com., Va., 1988—89. Active PTA, 1979—99; mem. mayor's adv. coun. City of Chesapeake, Va., 1988—89; tchr., workshop leader, dir., mem. various coms. Fairview Heights Bapt. Ch., Deep Creek Bapt. Ch., Va. So. Bapt. Retreats, 1968—; mem. summer missionary Va. So. Bapts., 1993. Mem.: NEA, Va. Reading Assn., Internat. Reading Assn., Chesapeake Reading Assn. (v.p., pres., honor and merit coun., chmn. various coms.), Chesapeake Edn. Assn., Va. Edn. Assn., Phi Kappa Phi, Kappa Delta Pi, Delta Kappa Gamma (legis. chmn.). Republican. Avocations: church related activities, reading. Home: 428 Plummer Dr Chesapeake VA 23323-3116

LEWY, HELEN CROSBY, artist, writer, translator, painter; d. Hewitt Crosby and Helen Louise Pratt; m. Hans Lewy (dec.); 1 child, Michael Robert. Studied with Edward Shenton, Swarthmore Coll., 1936—39; AB in Cinematography, U. So. Calif., 1947; studied with Fred Reichman, San Francisco, 1967—69; student, Nat. Art Sch. Analyst strategic svcs. OSS, Wash., N.Y.; polit. cons. Allied Election Mission to Greece; editor Portfolio, Phila., 1937—40; editor polit. intelligence Office Strategic Svcs., London, 1942—44, Naples, Italy, 1944—45; translator German Stories, N.Y.C., 1953—54, Christian Morgenstern Poems, N.Y.C., 1955—60. Contbr. articles to publs.; Exhibited in group shows at U. Calif. Ext., San Francisco, 1969, Richmond Art Ctr., 1972, Brickwall Gallery, Berkeley, 1972, Vacaville Art League Open Competition, 1973 (Blue Ribbon, 1973), ACCI Gallery, Berkeley, 1973, Crown Zellerbach Gallery, San Francisco, 1973, 1st winter ann. art co-op, 1974, Camelia Capital Art Exhbn., Sacramento, 1974; artist (invitational show) Hayward Area Art Festival, 1974; one-woman shows include Mezzanine Gallery, Bank of Calif., Berkeley, 1971, Athena Gallery, Oakland, 1974, Retrospective, Galerie de la cité, Lausanne, Switzerland, 1996, Represented in permanent collections, Italy, Israel, Germany, Switzerland, U.S., Oreg., Calif.; featured in (Italian mag. written by Adriano Sofri) Panorama. Mem.: Berkeley Art Co-op, Oakland Art Assn., Marin Soc. Artists, Artists Equity Assn., San Francisco Women Artists. Avocations: languages, art, dogs.

LEWYN, ANN SALFELD, retired English as a second language educator; b. N.Y.C., Dec. 1, 1935; d. Henry and Betty (Ahrens) Salfeld; m. Thomas Mark Lewyn, July 15, 1955; children: Alfred Thomas, Mark Henry. BA, Hunter Coll., 1967, MA, 1982. Mem. faculty UN Hospitality Extension Lang. Program, N.Y.C., 1974-86; adj. instr. ESL NYU, 1986-90, adj. asst. prof., 1990-95, adj. assoc. prof., 1995-2000, adj. prof., 2001—02; ret., 2003—. Editor-in-chief (Newsletter) UN Hospitality Com., 1967-86. Mem. exec. bd. Small Press Ctr., N.Y.C., 1990-98; mem. adv. coun. Hospitality Com. for UN Dels. Inc., 1991-98; bd. dirs. Hunter Coll. Scholarship and Welfare Fund, N.Y.C., 1992—, sec., 1998-2000, 3d v.p., 2000-2001, 2d v.p., 2001—. Mem. Teachers of English as Second Lang. (author in Aug. 1990 newsletter), N.Y. State Tchrs. of English as Second Lang., Pi Sigma Alpha, Kappa Delta Pi. Avocations: travel, tennis, needlepoint, photography, golf. Home: 911 Park Ave New York NY 10021-0337

LEYDON, DEBRA JEAN, food products executive; b. Bridgeport, Conn., Mar. 24, 1954; d. Thomas George and Joan Marie L. Materials specialist, receiving mgr. StorageTek Corp., Louisville, Colo., 1979-85; warehouse mgr. McData Corp., Broomfield, Colo., 1985-87; warehouse supr. Melco Industries, Westminster, Colo., 1987-92; master scheduler SPM/Denver, 1993-94; corp. warehouse mgr. Walker Component Group, Denver, 1994-95; materials mgr. DTM Products, Niwot, Colo., 1995-97; ops. mgr. Avalon Imaging, Boulder, 1997-99; pres., CEO Rocky Mountain Land & Sea Food Co., 1999—. Victim's adv. State of Colo., 2001—. Mem. Big Sisters, Denver, 1985-90. Mem. Am. Prodn. Inventory Control Soc. Home: 676 Monroe St Denver CO 80206-4451

LEYVA, ELLEN, newscaster; m. Mark Leyva; 2 children. BA in broadcast journalism, Ariz. State U. Reporter KCBS 2, Los Angeles; anchor, reporter KABC 7, Los Angeles, 1995—, co-anchor, Eyewitness News at 5pm, 2002—. Office: ABC 7 Broadcast Ctr 500 Circle Seven Dr Glendale CA 91201*

L'HEUREUX-DUBÉ, CLAIRE, judge; b. Quebec City, Can., Sept. 7, 1927; d. Paul H. and Marguerite (Dion) L'H.; m. Arthur Dubé (dec. 1978); children: Louise, Pierre (dec. 1994). BA magna cum laude, Coll. Notre-Dame de Bellevue, Que., 1946; LLL cum laude, U. Laval Law Faculty, Que., 1951; LLD (hon.), Dalhousie U., 1981, U. Montreal, 1983, Laval U., Que., 1984, Ottawa U., 1988, U. Que., 1989, U. Toronto, 1994, Queen's U., 1995, Gonzaga U., 1996. Bar: Que. 1952. Ptnr. Bard, L'Heureux & Philippon, 1969; sr. ptnr. L'Heureux, Philippon, Garneau, Tourigny, St. Arnaud & Assocs., 1952-73; Puisne judge Superior Ct. Que., 1973-79, Ct. Appeal of Que., 1979-87, Supreme Ct. Can., Ottawa, 1987—. Commr. Part II Inquiries Act Dept. Manpower and Immigration, Montreal, 1973-76; del. Gen. Coun. Bar of Que., 1968-70, com. on adminstrn. justice, 1968-73, others; pres. family law com. Family Ct. com. Que Civil Code Rev. Office, 1972-76; pres. Can. sect. Internat. Commn. Jurists, 1981-83, v.p., 1992-98, pres., 1998-2002; lectr. in field. Editor: (with Rosalie S. Abella) Family Law - Dimensions of Justice, 1983; chmn. editorial bd. Can. Bar Rev., 1985; contbr. articles to profl. jours., book chpt. Bd. dirs. YWCA, Que., 1969-73, Ctr. des Loisirs St. Sacrement, 1969-73, Ctr. Jeunesse de Tilly-Ctr. des Jeunes, 1971-77; v.p. Can. Consumers Coun., 1970-73; v.p. Vanier Inst. of the Family, 1972-73; lifetime gov. Found. Univ. Laval, 1980, bd. dirs., 1984-85; com. des grandes orientations l'Univ. Laval, 1971-72; nat. coun. Can. Human Rights Found., 1980-82, 82-84; mem. Can. del. to Peoples Republic China on Status of Women, 1981; mem. Nat. Coun. Can. Human Rights Found., 1980-84; v.p. Vanier Inst. of Family, 1972-73. Apptd. Queen's Counsel, 1969; recipient Medal of the Alumni, U. Laval, 1986, Médaille du Barreau de Que., 1987, Montreal Bar, 1994, Barrecece dee Quebec, 1995, Medal Internat. Yr. of the Famig, Que., 1994, Can. award Can. Hadassah-WIZO, 1996, Prix de la Justice, Can. Inst. Adminstrn. Justice, 1997, Margaret Brent Women Lawyers Achievement award ABA Commn. Women in the Profession, 1998, Yves Pelicier award Internat. Acad. Law and Mental Health, 2002. Mem. Can. Bar Assn., Can. Inst. Adminstrn. Justice, Internat. Soc. Family Law (hon., bd. dirs. 1977, v.p. 1982-88), Fedn. Internat. des Femmes Juristes, L'Assn. des Femmes Diplômées d'Univ., Assn. Québécoise pour l'Étude Comparative du Droit (pres. 1984-90), Am. Coll. Trial Lawyers (hon.), Am. Law Inst., Phi Delta Phi. Roman Catholic. Office: Univ Laval rue des Sci Humaines Pavillon de Koninck Bur 3107 Quebec QC Canada G1K 7P4

LI, JOANNE, finance educator; b. Hong Kong; d. Ming and Oi Yung Li; m. Scott Krolak, Nov. 3, 2001. PhD. in Fin., Fla. State U., 1992. CFA 2001. Office: Loyola Coll in Maryland 4501 N Charles St Baltimore MD 21210

LI, LIJUAN, chemistry educator; b. Jilin, China, Mar. 12, 1962; came to U.S., 1998; d. Sheng Li and Shufang; m. Kai Li, May 1, 1987; children: Christopher, Jessica. BSc, Jilin U., 1983, MSc, 1987; PhD, McMaster U., Hamilton, Ont., Can., 1992. Vis. scholar McMaster U., 1987-88, postdoctoral fellow, 1992, asst. prof., 1995-98; rsch. assoc. Nat. Rsch. Coun. Can., Ottawa, Ont., 1993-95; asst. prof. chemistry Calif. State U., Long Beach, 1998-2001, assoc. prof. chemistry, 2001—. Mem. exec. com. Chem. Inst. Can., Hamilton, 1995-98; organizer Ont. Undergrad. Student Conf., Hamilton, 1996; rschr. in inorganic chemistry; guest prof. Jilin U., 1998—. Contbr. numerous articles to profl. jours. J.R. Longstaffe scholar, 1989-90, Yates Fund scholar, 1992, McMaster U. Centennial scholar, 1988-92, Ont. Grad. scholar, 1990-92; recipient Women's Faculty award NSERC, 1995-98, travel award Internat. Union for Pure and Applied Chemistry, 1999-2001; grantee McMaster U., 1995-97, Nat. Scis. and Engring. Rsch. Coun. of Can., 1995-99, Materials Mfg. Ont., 1998-99, Calif. State U., 1998-2000, Nat. Inst. Health, 2001—, Rsch. Corp., 2001—, Am. Chem. Soc.-Petroleum Rsch. Fund, 2001—. Mem. Am. Chem. Soc., Can. Chem. Soc., Internat. Union for Pure and Applied Chemistry. Avocations: travel, reading, swimming, dance, photography. Office: Calif State U Long Beach 1250 N Bellflower Blvd Long Beach CA 90840-3903 E-mail: lli@csulb.edu.

LI, LILIA HUIYING, journalist; b. Hunan, China, June 14, 1932; d. Chun-chu and Sol-ran (Chang) L.; m. Ma Luk Son, May 18, 1953 (dec. Feb. 1963); 1 child, Blanche; m. George Oakley Totten III, July 1, 1976; children: Vicken Yuriko, Linnea Catherine. MA (equivalent grad. study), Hong Kong U., 1955. Mng. dir. Oriental Evening News, Hong Kong, Midday News, Hong Kong, Tsuwan Daily News, Hong Kong; gen. mgr. Ch. Guest House, Hong Kong, 1962-68; spl. corr. UN, N.Y.C., 1975; dir. L.A. br. The Mirror Monthly, Hong Kong, 1988—, The Depingxian Montly, Hong Kong, 1998—. Vis. lectr. East Asian Studies Ctr. U. So. Calif., L.A., 1976, fellow, 1976—; leader delegation of Hong Kong Businesswomen to Conf. on Commerce, Beijing, 1956; speaker First Internat. Women's Conf., Mexico City, 1975; organizer Internat. Women's Year Arts Festival, N.Y.C., 1975-77; invited participant Soc. for the Promotion of Chinese Cultural Unity, Taiwan, 1995, Kunming, China, 1999, ceremonies at Hand Over of Hong Kong to People's Republic of China, 1997; founder, pres. China Seminar-forum for peace across the Taiwan straits, 1985—, a forum for good rels. across the Taiwan straits, 1991—. Author: Unforgettable Journey, 1957, Nine Women and Other Writings, 1959, Li Huiying's Writings, 1979, Sidelights on World Affairs, 1985, Expanded Edition of Collected Writings, 1988, Farewell 20th Century!, 2001, revised edit. 2004; contbr. numerous articles to periodicals. Mem. China Soc. People's Friendship Studies, Beijing, Chinese Am. Alliance in Am. for China's Peaceful Reunification, Chgo., 2002, (pres.); mem. St. John's Episcopal Ch., L.A., L.A.-Guangzhou Sister City Assn. Designated Outstanding Bus. Woman in Hong Kong by South China Morning Post, 1962, Peace ambassador St. John's Episcopal Ch., L.A., 2003; recipient of award. from US China People's Friendship Assn., 1981; award. from The L.A. Guangzhous Sister City Assn., 1984; made First Hon. Reporter, Xinmin Evening News, Shanghai, 1999. Mem. Asian-Am. Journalists Assn., Assn. for Asian Studies. Avocations: photography, calligraphy, gardening, flower arrangement, interior decorating. Home and Office: 5129 Village Grn Los Angeles CA 90016-5205

LI, MARY J. scientist, educator; b. Jinan, China; came to U.S., 1986; d. Jiawen and Changxian (Liu) Li; m. Liqin Len Wang; 1 child, Stefany C. Wang. BS, Ctrl.-South Inst. Tech., Changsha, China, 1982; MS, U. Md., 1989, PhD, 1992. Engr., instr. Xian (China) Mining Inst., 1982-86; tchg. asst. U. Md., College Park, 1986-92, rsch. scientist, 1992-98, assoc. dir., 1996-98, adj. prof., 1998-2001; prin. scientist Raytheon STX/NASA Goddard Space Flight Ctr., Greenbelt, Md., 1998-2001, chief scientist, 2000—. Panel reviewer NSF, Arlington, Va., 1995, 98. Contbr. chpt. to book, articles to profl. jours. Bd. dirs. Hope Chinese Sch., Md., 1996-98. Recipient Engring. Rsch. award NSF, 1995, Materials Rsch. award Army-DURIP, 1997, others. Mem. IEEE, Soc. Photo-Optical Instrumentation Engrs., Microscopy and Microanalysis Soc., Chinese-Am. Sci. and Tech. Assn. (bd. dirs. 1997—). Avocations: gardening, reading, water skiing, skiing. Office: Raytheon/NASA Goddard Space Flight Ctr Detector Sys Br Greenbelt MD 20771-0001

LI, PEARL NEI-CHIEN CHU, technology company executive; b. Jiangsu, China, June 17, 1946; came to U.S., 1968; d. Ping-Yung and Yao-Hwa (Li) Chu; m. Terry Teng-Fang Li, Sept. 20, 1969; children: Ina Ying, Ping Li. BA, Nat. Taiwan U., Taipei, 1968; MA, W.Va. U., 1971; cert. advanced study in info. studies, Drexel U., 1983. Cert. sr. libr., N.J. Instr. Nat. Tchr.'s Coll., Chang-Hua, Taiwan, 1977-78; reference libr. Camden County Libr., Voorhees, NJ, 1981-82; libr. Kulzer and Dipadova, P.A., Haddonfield, NJ, 1982-87; libr. dir. Am. Law Inst., Phila., 1987-92; gen. mgr., info. specialist Unitek Internat. Corp. (Am.), Mt. Laurel, NJ, 1992-96; owner Universal Tech. Inc., Mt. Laurel, 1997—. Tchr. South Jersey Chinese Sch., Cherry Hill, N.J., 1978-82. Editor: CLE Around the Country (annually), 1988-92; contbr. articles to profl. jours. Bus. mgr. Chinese Cmty. Ctr., Voorhees, 1981; mem. N.J. Dept. Commerce and Econ. Devel. for Small and Women and Minority Businesses, City of Phila. Minority/Women and Disadvantaged Bus. Enterprise, Md./D.C. Minority Supplier Devel. Coun., N.Y./N.J. Minority Purchasing Coun., N.Y./N.J. Port Authority Minority

Bus. Enterprise. Home: 1132 Sea Gull Ln Cherry Hill NJ 08003-3113 Office: Universal Technology Inc 125 Gaither Dr Ste E Mount Laurel NJ 08054-1706 Fax: 856-235-0590. E-mail: ask@uti8.com.

LI, QIN, television anchor, reporter, director, producer; came to U.S., 1999:; d. Jinkui and Hong Li. BA in Law, Chinese Youth Coll. Polit. Sc., Beijing, 1992; MS in Econs., Chinese Acad. Social Sci., Beijing, 1998; MS in Journalism, Columbia U., 2000. Cert. in pub. affairs. Reporter People's Daily, Beijing, 1992-94, editor, reporter Shanghai, 1994-99; TV anchor, prodr., news reporter Sino TV, Inc., N.Y.C., 2001—. Dep. editor-in-chief New Asia Culture Found. and Pub. House, Hong Kong, 1999—. Prodr.: (TV news documentary) Blue Sky Station: 8th Avenue-New York's 3d Chinatown, 2000 (Emmy award NATAS, 2000); dir., prodr. (TV documentary) A Hole in Chinatown's Heart, 2003; contbg. author: First-Hand Experience with China's Hope Project in One Hundred Counties, 1991; co-author: Japan: Another Miracle in the 21st Century?, 1993; contbr. feature stories to internat. publs. Mem. selection com. Internat. Fanzhian Scholarship, Hong Kong, 1998-2001 Recipient Best News award Chinese Nat. Journalists Assn. and Chinese Disability Assn., 1994, Best News award Chinese People's Polit. Consultative Conf., 1993; featured in Selected Works of Outstanding Chinese Editors and Reporters, 1996. Mem. Soc. Profl. Journalists. Home: Apt 4EE 4125 Kissena Blvd Flushing NY 11355-3160 Office Fax: 212-965-8917. E-mail: ql20@columbia.edu.

LI, YING, dancer; b. China; Student, Beijing Dance Sch. Prin. dancer Ctrl. Ballet China, BalletMet, Columbus, Ohio, Pitts. Ballet Theatre, 1994—. Dancer Giselle, Romeo and Juliet, Don Quixote, Swan Lake, Sleeping Beauty, The Nutcracker, Rubies. Recipient Prix de Lausanne, Osaka, Varna. Office: Pitts Ballet Theatre 2900 Liberty Ave Pittsburgh PA 15201-1511

LIANG, CHRISTINE, import company executive; m. Marcel Liang; 2 children. Grad. Tang Ming Coll., Taiwan, 1979. Pres., founder ASI Corp., Fremont, Calif., 1987—. Recipient 17th Top Women Owned Bus., Working Women mag., 1996, 12th Top Women Owned Business, 1997, Number 1 Woman Owned Business, Silicon Valley Bus. Journal, 2002. Office: ASI Corp 48289 Fremont Blvd Fremont CA 94538-6510

LIAO, MEI-JUNE, biopharmaceutical company executive; came to U.S., 1974; BS, Nat. Tsing-Hua U. Taiwan, 1973; MPh, Yale U., 1977, PhD, 1980. Tchg. asst. Nat. Taiwan U., 1973-74, Temple U., Phila., 1974-75, Yale U., New Haven, 1975-76, rsch. asst., 1976-79; postdoctoral assoc. MIT, Cambridge, 1980-83; sr. scientist Interferon Scis., Inc., New Brunswick, N.J., 1983-84; group leader Interferon Scis. Inc., New Brunswick, N.J., 1984-85, dir. cell biology, 1985-87; dir., rsch. & devel. Interferon Scis., Inc., New Brunswick, NJ, 1987—94, v.p., rsch. & devel., 1995—2003; v.p., regulatory affairs and quality Hemispherx Biopharma, Inc., New Brunswick, 2003—. Contbr. articles to profl. jours.; inventor in field. Mem. Am. Soc. Biochemistry and Molecular Biology, Internat. Soc. Interferon and Cytokine Rsch., Internat. Cytokine Soc., Soc. Chinese Bioscientists in Am., N.Y. Acad. Sci. Office: Interferon Sci Inc 783 Jersey Ave New Brunswick NJ 08901-3660 E-mail: meijuneliao@yahoo.com.

LIBBIN, ANNE EDNA, lawyer; b. Phila., Aug. 25, 1950; d. Edwin M. and Marianne (Herz) L.; m. Christopher J. Cannon, July 20, 1985; children: Abigail Libbin Cannon, Rebecca Libbin Cannon. AB, Radcliffe Coll., 1971; JD, Harvard U., 1975. Bar: Calif. 1975, U.S. Dist. Ct. (cen. dist.) Calif. 1977, U.S. Dist. Ct. (no. dist.) Calif. 1979, U.S. Dist. Ct. (ea. dist.) Calif. 1985, U.S. Ct. Appeals (2d cir.) 1977, U.S. Ct. Appeals (5th cir.) 1982, U.S. Ct. Appeals (7th cir.) 1976, U.S. Ct. Appeals (9th cir.) 1976, U.S. Ct. Appeals (D.C. cir.) 1978, U.S. Supreme Ct. 2001. Appellate atty. NLRB, Washington, 1975-78; assoc. Pillsbury Madison & Sutro LLP, San Francisco, 1978-83, ptnr., 1984-99; sr. counsel SBC Pacific Telesis Group, San Francisco, 1999—; dir. Jewish Vocat. Svcs., San Francisco, 2002—. Three Guineas fellow Harvard Law Sch., 1997; dir. Alumnae Resources, San Francisco, 1991-97. Mem. ABA (labor and employment sect.), State Bar Calif. (labor law sect.), Bar Assn. San Francisco (labor law sect.), Radcliffe Club (San Francisco). Office: SBC Pacific Telesis Group 140 New Montgomery St San Francisco CA 94105-3705

LIBBY, JANE ELLIOTT, retired dietitian; b. Long Beach, Calif., Apr. 16, 1935; d. Edwin Windsor Jr. and Marion Virginia (Applegate) Elliott; m. J. Donald Libby, July 18, 1959 (dec. Jan. 1981); children: Therissa Anne, Peter Francis. BA in Home Econ., U. Calif., Santa Barbara, 1957; MA in Psychology, Washington Coll., 1977. Registered dietitian. Sewing tchr. Beverly Hills (Calif.) H.S., 1957; asst. dietitian Yale New Haven Med. Ctr., 1958-59; from dir. food svc. tng. to food svc. dir. Md. State Dept. Health and Mental Hygiene, 1971-96, dir. dietetic internship, 1980-96. Author: Twelvemonth, 1992. Mem. Am. Dietetic Assn. (site visitor commn. on accreditation of dietetics edn., Outstanding Dietetic Educator 1997, deleg. for ret. mems., 2001-03), Dietetic Educators of Practitioners (area rep., sec. bylaws chair Md.), Md. Dietetic Assn. (past. pres., del., sec., treas., com. chair, Outstanding Dietitian in Md. 1999). Episcopalian. Avocations: travel, reading, theater. Home: 601 Burtons Cove Way Apt 2 Annapolis MD 21401-8811

LIBBY, WENDY B. academic administrator; m. Richard Libby; children: Glenn, Gregg. BS in Biology, Cornell U., Ithica, N.Y., 1972; MBA, Johnson Grad. Sch. of Mgmt. at Cornell U., Ithaca, N.Y., 1977; PhD in Ednl. Adminstrn., U. Conn., 1994. Dir. adminstrv. ops. Coll. of Architecture, Art and Planning, Ithaca, NY, 1979—84; dir. adminstrn. pub. mgmt. program Johnson Grad. Sch. of Mgmt. at Cornell U., Ithaca, NY, 1979—84; adminstrv. mgr. Coll. Edn. Ohio State U., Columbus, 1984—85, adminstrv. assoc. Office of Fin., 1984—85; asst. dir. U. Conn. Med. Ctr. John Dempsey Hosp., Farmington, Conn., 1985—87, asst. to assoc. exec. dir., 1985—87; spl. asst. to pres. and sr. human resources officer U. Hartford, Conn., 1987—89; chief fin. and bus. officer Westbrook Coll., Portland, Maine, 1989—95; v.p. bus. affairs and CFO Furman U., Greenville, SC, 1995—2003; pres. Stephens Coll., Columbia, Mo., 2003—. Founding bd. mem. Tuition Plan Consortium, Caribbean Inst. of Tech. Bd. mem. Greenville Literacy Assn., mem. fund raising com. Mem.: Soc. Coll. and U. Planning, So. Assn. of Coll. and U. Bus. Officers, Ea. Assn. of Coll. and U. Bus. Officers (bd. dirs.), Nat. Assn. of Coll. and U. Bus. Officers. Office: Stephens Coll 1200 E Broadway Columbia MO 65215*

LIBERATI, MARIA THERESA, fashion production company executive; b. Phila., July 16, 1965; d. Edward Michael and Anna Maria Liberati. Student, Laval U., Que., Can., 1984; BS in Fgn. Lang. Edn., Temple U., 1986. Pres., bd. dirs. Sierra Ctr., Feasterville, Pa., 1988—; pres. M.T.L. Prodns., Phila., 1989—. Spokesperson Compassion for Animals, Phila., 1988—. Author: Fashion, Fun and Fitness, 1989, The Model's Guide, 1998; editor mag. Better Nutrition for Today's Living, 1990—. Named Miss Pa., 1985, Miss World, 1986; recipient Merit award Actors and Artists Assn., Rome. Mem. AFTRA, NAFE (adv. bd. 1988—). Avocations: reading, cooking. Office: MTL Prod PO Box 52457 Philadelphia PA 19115-7457 E-mail: marialib@hotmail.com.

LIBERMAN, GAIL JEANNE, editor; b. Neptune, N.J., Feb. 26, 1951; d. Si and Dorothy (Gold) L.; m. Alan Lavine, Dec. 20, 1991. BA, Rutgers U., 1972. Youth editor AP, N.Y.C., 1972-73; writer United Feature Syndicate, N.Y.C., 1973; reporter, broadcast editor UPI, Phila. and Hartford, Conn., 1973-75; reporter Courier-Post, Camden, N.J., 1976-80, Bank Advt. News, North Palm Beach, Fla., 1981-82; editor Bank Rate Monitor, North Palm Beach, 1982-97. Author: Improving Your Credit and Reducing Your Debt, 1994 (endorsed Inst. CFPs), The Complete Idiot's Guide to Making Money With Mutual Funds, 1996, Love, Marriage and Money, 1998, Rags to Riches: Motivating Stories of How Ordinary People Achieved Extraordinary Wealth, 2000, Short and Simple Guide to Life Insurance, 2000, More Rags to Riches: All New Stories of How Ordinary People Achieved Extraordinary Wealth, 2002, Rags to Retirement, 2003; columnist: Boston Herald, 1994—, America Online, 1996—, Investor Square, 1996—, Mutual Funds Interactive, 1996—, Quicken, 1998—, Palm Beach Daily News, 1998—, CNBC.com, 2000, Fasttrack mag., 2001, Pitts. Post-Gazette, 2001-; contbr. articles to profl. jours. Mem. Soc. Am. Bus. Editors and Writers.

LIBKIND, JEAN SUE JOHNSON (JEAN SUE JOHNSON-LIBKIND), publishing executive; b. Racine, Wis., Apr. 4, 1944; d. John Bert and Loretta Laura (Richards) Johnson; m. D.M. Spradling, June 5, 1966 (div. Nov. 1971); 1 child, Eric David (dec.); m. Robert Lawrence Libkind, Oct. 13, 1991. Student, U. Oslo, Norway, 1965; BA in Journalism, U. Wis., 1966. Libr. asst. Racine (Wis.) Pub. Libr., 1962-64; mng. editor Daily Cardinal, Madison, 1965-66; project assoc. U. Wis.-Ctr. Sys., Madison, 1966-68; office mgr. Senrac Enterprises, Madison, 1968-71; prodn. jours. mgr. U. Wis. Press, Madison, 1971-72, asst. jours. mgr., 1972-77, asst. mktg. mgr., 1977-80; mktg. mgr. U. Ga. Press, Athens, 1980-84; sales, mktg. mgr. U. Penn Press, Phila., 1984-88; mktg. dir. Jewish Publ. Soc., Phila., 1988-91, dir. pub. ops., 1991-94; owner Johnson Libkind Pubs.' Agy., 1994-98; dir. Worldwide Books, Ithaca, NY, 1998—2001; owner Bookschlepper, 2001—. Spke. and cons. in field. Pres. Friends of Ea. State Penitentiary Park, 1996—98; treas. Commonland Cmty. Resident's Assn., 2000—01; program chair Unitarian Universalist Fellowship, Athens, 1982—84. Recipient Svc. award USMC, 1966, Svc. award After Sch. Day Care Assn., 1976; named Hon. Lt. Col., Ga. Militia, 1985. Mem. Women in Comms. (treas. 1990-91, sec. 1989-90, pres. 1970-71), Phila. Pub. Group (pres. 1990-92), Women in Scholarly Pub. (newsletter editor 1981-83, mentoring co-chair 1993-94, pres. 1998-99). Home: 837 N Woodstock St Philadelphia PA 19130-1408

LICARY, CHERYL ANN, music educator, church musician; b. Beloit, Wis., Mar. 15, 1951; d. Wilbur John and Verna Elise Dietzman; m. Nicholas J. Licary, Mar. 25, 1972 (div. June 15, 1985); children: Nunzio, Chiara. BA, Luther Coll., 1972; MST, U. Wis., Whitewater, 1976. Vocal music instr., dept. chmn. Sch. Dist. Beloit, 1973—; ch. musician, 1973—. Clinician, adjudicator, 1975—. Vol. Red Cross, Beloit, 1983—. Recipient Silver Star award, Wis. Dept. Recreation, 1995, Tchr. Recognition award, Beloit Rotary, 2001, Contbr. award, Zonta Commn., 2001, award for Excellence in Tchg. Music, State of Wis. Mem.: Am. Guild of Organists, Assn. for Supr. and Curriculum Devel., Wis. Alliance for Arts Edn., Beloit Edn. Assn., Wis. Choral Dir.'s Assn., Wis. Music Educator's Assn. (Wis. award 2003, Gt. Minds 21st Century 2003), Nat. Edn. Assn., Music Educator's Nat. Conf., Am. Choral Dirs. Assn. Lutheran. Avocation: organist, choir director. Home: 1305 11th St Beloit WI 53511

LICHTENBERG, MARGARET KLEE, publishing company executive; b. N.Y.C., Nov. 19, 1941; d. Lawrence and Shirley Jane (Wicksman) Klee; m. James Lester Lichtenberg, Mar. 31, 1963 (div. 1982); m. William Shaw Jones, July 2, 2000; children: Gregory Lawrence, Amanda Zoe. BA, U. Mich., 1963; postgrad., Harvard U., 1963. Book rev. editor New Woman mag., 1972-73; assoc. editor children's books Parents Mag. Press, 1974, editor, rights dir. Books for Young People, Frederick Warne & Co., N.Y.C., 1975-78; sr. editor Simon & Schuster, N.Y.C., 1979-80; dir. sales promotion Grosset & Dunlap, N.Y.C., 1980-81; ednl. sales mgr. Bantam Books, N.Y.C., 1982-84; dir. mktg. and sales Grove Press, N.Y.C., 1984-86, dir. of sales, 1986-87; dir. sales Weidenfeld & Nicolson, N.Y.C., 1986-87; mktg. dir. Beacon Press, Boston, 1988-95; bus. and pub. coach, 1993—. Writer, freelance critic, 1961—. Contbr. articles, essays, stories, poetry, revs. to mags., newspapers and anthologies. Bd. dirs. Children's Book Council, 1978. Recipient 2 Avery Hopwood awards in drama and fiction, 1962, 2 in drama and poetry, 1963; coll. fiction contest award Mademoiselle mag., 1963; Woodrow Wilson fellow, 1963. Mem. Women's Nat. Book Assn. (past pres. N.Y. chpt.), Internat. Coach Fedn. (cert.), The Coaching Collective, Pubs. Mktg. Assn., N.Mex. Book Assn., SW Writers Workshop, PEN N.Mex Home and Office: 4 Cosmos Ct Santa Fe NM 87508-2285 E-mail: maggie@maggielichtenberg.com.

LICHTENSTEIN, ELISSA CHARLENE, legal association executive; b. Oct. 23, 1954; d. Mark and Rita (Field) L. AB cum laude, Smith Coll., Northampton, Mass., 1976; JD, George Washington U., 1979. Bar: D.C. 1980, U.S. Dist. Ct. (D.C. dist.) 1980, U.S. Ct. Appeals (D.C. cir.) 1980. Law clk. U.S. EPA, Washington, 1978-79; staff dir. ABA, Washington, 1979—, assoc. dir. pub. svcs. divsn., 1981-85, dir., 1985—. Editor, contbr.: Common Boundary/Common Problems: The Environmental Consequences of Energy Production, 1982, Exit Polls and Early Election Projections, 1984, The Global Environment: Challenges, Choices and Will, 1986, (newsletter) Environ. Law; co-editor, contbr. The Environ. Network; co-editor: Determining Competency in Guardianship Proceedings, 1990, Due Process Protections for Juveniles in Civil Commitment Proceedings, 1991, Environmental Regulation in Pacific Rim Nations, 1993, The Role of Law in the 1992 UN Conference on Environment and Development, 1992, Trade and the Environment in Pacific Rim Nations, 1994, Public Participation in Environmental Decisionmaking, 1995, Endangered Species Act Reauthorization: A Biocentric Approach, 1996, Sustainable Development in the Americas: The Emerging Role of the Private Sector, 1996, Environmental Priorities in Southeast Asian Nations, 1997, Law School Public Interest Law Programs, 1995, 99, numerous others. Named Outstanding Young Woman of Am., 1982. Mem.: NAFE, ABA, Greater Washington Soc. Assn. Execs., D.C. Bar Assn., Met. Washington Environ. Profls. (pres. 1986—96), Assn. Women in Comms., Am. Soc. Assn. Execs., Environ. Law Inst. (assoc.). Democrat. Jewish. Office: ABA Div Pub Svcs 740 15th St NW 9th Fl Washington DC 20005-1019

LICHTENSTEIN, SARAH CAROL, lawyer; b. East Orange, N.J., May 25, 1953; d. Carl and Hilda Ruth (Warshaw) L. BA, Wellesley Coll., 1975; JD, Columbia U., 1978. Bar: N.Y. 1979, U.S. Dist. Ct. (ea. and so. dists.) N.Y. 1979, U.S. Ct. Appeals (2d cir.) 1981. Assoc. Milbank, Tweed, Hadley & McCloy, N.Y.C., 1978-84, Dreyer and Traub, N.Y.C., 1984-87, ptnr., 1987-93, Shea & Gould, N.Y.C., 1993-94; arbitrator small claims ct. Civ. Ct. of the City of New York, 1988-93; ptnr. Morrison Cohen Singer & Weinstein LLP, N.Y.C., 1994-2000; counsel Lamb & Barnosky, LLP, Melville, N.Y., 2000—. Dir. Eleven Riverside Dr. Corp., 1986-89, 98-2000, pres., 1988-89; mem. panel of chpt. 7 trustees So. Dist. of N.Y., 1993-97; mem. mediation panel U.S. Dist. Ct. So. Dist. N.Y., Bankruptcy Ct. So. Dist. N.Y.; mem. faculty N.E. Deposition Program, Nat. Inst. Trial Advocacy. Contbr. articles to profl. jours. Trustee Stephen Wise Free Synagogue, 1987-90, officer, 1990-98. Wellesley scholar, 1975, Stone scholar Columbia U., 1977-78. Mem. ABA, Suffolk County Bar Assn. E-mail: scl@lambbamosky.com.

LICHTENSTEIN, THERESE ELLEN, art educator; d. Hyman Saul and Sylvia Lily Feiertag; m. David Charles Lichtenstein, Aug. 22, 1967 (div. 1977); m. Stanley Simon Gans, Sept. 21, 1997. BA in English Lit., SUNY, Stony Brook, 1976, MA in English Lit., 1977; PhD in Art History, CUNY, 1991. Tchr. Navajo Tribe, Crownpoint, N.Mex., 1970—71; tutor King and Queen Sikkim, 1971—72; prof. NYU, N.Y.C., 1985—2000; tchr., curriculum writer Ross Sch., Easthampton, NY, 2000—. Prof. MIT, Cambridge, Mass., 1990, Rice U., Houston, 1991, Mt. Holyoke, Hadley, Mass., 1992; art critic Art in Am., Art Forum, Arts Mag. Author: Ansel Adams: Master of Light, 2000, Behind Closed Doors: The Art of Hans Bellmer, 2001. Named Best Photography Show of Yr., Internat. Art Critics Assn., 2001. Mem.: Coll. Art Assn. Avocations: writing, poetry, swimming, reading, tennis. Office: Ross Sch 18 Goodfriend Dr East Hampton NY 11937

LICHTMAN, JUDITH L. lawyer, organization administrator; m. Elliott Lichtman; children: Sarah, Julia. Bachelor's degree, U. Wisconsin, Madison, 1962, LLB, 1965. Worked on sch. desegregation in South US Dept Health, Edn., and Welfare; teacher Jackson State Coll.; with Urban Coalition, US Commn. Civil Rights; worked on George McGovern's presdl. campaign, 1972; legal advisor Commonwealth of Puerto Rico; pres. Women's Legal Def. Fund (National Partnership for Women & Families since 1998), Washington, 1974—. Bd. mem. Women's Law and Pub. Policy Fellowship Program. Recipient Hubert H. Humphrey award, Leadership Conf. on Civil Rights, 2000. Office: Women's Legal Def Fund 2000 P St NW Washington DC 20036-5915*

LICHTMAN, SUSAN LORRAINE, psychologist, consultant; b. N.Y.C., Sept. 11, 1958; d. Bernard and B. Hope (Cummings) L. BA in Psychology with honors, Wheaton Coll., 1980; postgrad., U. Minn., 1980-81; MA in Theology, PhD in Clin. Psychology, Fuller Theol. Sem., 1989. Lic. psychologist, Maine. Program dir. Casa Maria Guest Home, Montebello, Calif., 1984-87; dir. Ctr. for Aging Resources, Pasadena, Calif., 1988-92; asst. prof. Fuller Theol. Sem., Pasadena, 1990-92; pvt. practice Bangor, Maine, 1992—. Cons. The Acadia Hosp., Bangor, 1993—, N.E. Crisis Svcs., Bangor, 1997-98; mem. mental health adv. com. The AIDS Svc. Ctr., Pasadena, 1988-93; chair West San Gabriel Valley Elder Abuse Task Force, Pasadena, 1992-93, Living at Home Task Force, Pasadena, 1992-93; presenter in field. Contbr. articles to profl. jours. Vol. Penobscot Theater Co., Bangor, 1997—; mem. Bangor Cmty. Chorus, 1997-98, Bangor Oratorio Soc., 1998—. Mem. APA (cert. trainer HIV office of profl. edn.), Maine Psychol. Assn. (sec.-treas. 1994-96, pres.-elect 1996-97, 97-98, pres. 1998-99, Svc. Appreciation award 1996). Democrat. Episcopalian. Avocations: theater, traveling, music, gourmet cooking. Office: 67 Pine St Ste 1 Bangor ME 04401-6556

LIDDELL, JANE HAWLEY HAWKES, civic worker; b. Newark, Dec. 8, 1907; d. Edward Zeh and Mary Everett (Hawley) Hawkes; AB, Smith Coll., 1931; postgrad. in art history, Harvard U., 1933-35; MA, Columbia U., 1940; Carnegie fellow Sorbonne, Paris, 1937; m. Donald M. Liddell, Jr., Mar. 30, 1940; children: Jane Boyer, D. Roger Brooke. Pres., Planned Parenthood Essex County (N.J.), 1947-50; trustee Prospect Hill Sch. Girls, Newark, 1946-50; mem. adv. bd., publicity and public relations chmn. N.J. State Mus., Trenton, 1952-60; sec., then v.p. women's br. N.J. Hist. Soc.; women's aux. prodn. chmn. Englewood (N.J.) Hosp., 1959-61; pres. Dwight Sch. Girls Parents Assn., 1955-57; v.p. Englewood Sch. Boys Parents Assn., 1958-60; mem. Altar Guild, women's aux. bd., rector's adv. council St. Paul's Episcopal Ch., Englewood, 1954-59; bd. dir. N.Y. State Soc. of Nat. Soc. Colonial Dames, 1961-67, rep. conf. Patriotic and Hist. Socs., 1964—; bd. dirs. Huguenot Soc. Am., 1979-86, regional v.p., 1979-82, historian, 1983-84, co-chmn. Tercentennial Book, 1983-85; bd. dirs. Soc. Daus. Holland Dames, 1965-82; nat. jr. v.p. Dames of Loyal Legion, USA; bd. dirs., mem. publs. com. Daus. Cin., 1966-72; bd. dirs. Ch. Women's League Patriotic Service, 1962—, pres., 1968-70, 72-74; bd. dirs., chmn. grants com. Youth Found., N.Y.C., 1974—; chmn. for Newark, Smith Coll. 75th Ann. Fund, 1948-50; pres. North N.J. Smith Club, 1956-58; pres. Smith Coll. Class 1931, 1946-51, 76-81, editor 50th anniversary book, 1980-81. Author: (with others) Huguenot Refugees in the Settling of Colonial America, 1982-85; contbr. The Dutch Contribution to the Development of Early Manhattan, 1969. Recipient various commendation awards. Republican. Mem. Colonial Dames Am. (N.Y.C. chpt.). Clubs: Colony, City Gardens, Church (N.Y.C.); Jr. League N.Y.; N.Y. Jr. League; Needle and Bobbin, Nat. Farm and Garden . Editor: Maine Echoes, 1961; research and editor asst., Wartime Writings of American Revolution Officers, 1972-75; co-chmn., rschr. Hughenot Refugees in the Settling of Colonial Am., 1985.

LIDSKY, ELLA, retired law librarian; b. Wilno, Poland; came to U.S., 1962; d. Leib and Sheina (Izygzon) Cwik; m. Alexander Lidsky, Feb. 20, 1963 (dec. Mar., 1996); 1 son, David Abraham. BA, Pedagogical Inst. Odessa, USSR; MS, Columbia U., 1966, MA, 1973. Cert. Russian and Hebrew lang. tchr. Tchr. high sch., Poland, 1948-51; elem. sch., 1961-62; asst. cataloger Tchrs. Coll. Columbia U., N.Y.C., 1966-68; cataloger Fairleigh Dickinson U., Teaneck, N.J., 1968-69, asst. dir. tech. services Madison, N.J., 1973-84; head cataloger Ramapo Coll., Mahwah, N.J., 1971-73; asst. libr. U.S. Ct. Internat. Trade Law Libr., N.Y.C., 1985-2000. Mem. Am. Assn. Law Libraries, Law Librarians of Greater N.Y., N.Y. Tech. Services Librarians, N.J. Law Librarians Assn. Democrat. Jewish. Avocations: music, travel. E-mail: ella64@rcn.com.

LIDTKE, DORIS KEEFE, retired computer science educator; b. Bottineau County, N.D., Dec. 6, 1929; d. Michael J and Josephine (McDaniels) Keefe; m. Vernon L Lidtke, Apr. 21, 1951. BS, U. Oreg., 1952, PhD, 1979; EdM cum laude, Johns Hopkins U., 1974. Programmer analyst Shell Devel. Co., Emeryville, Calif., 1955-59, U. Calif., Berkeley, 1960-62; asst. prof. Lansing (Mich.) C.C., 1963-68; ednl. specialist Johns Hopkins U., Balt., 1968; assoc. program mgr. NSF, Washington, 1984-85, program dir., 1992-93; sr. mem. tech. staff Software Productivity Consortium, Reston, Va., 1987-88; asst. prof. computer sci. Towson U., Balt., 1968-80, assoc. prof., 1980-90, prof., 1990—2002, prof. emerita, 2002—. V.p. Computing Scis. Accreditation Bd., 1993—98, pres., 1995—97. Named Outstanding Educator, Assn. Edn. Data Sys., 1986. Mem.: Nat. Edn. Computer Conf. (steering com., vice-chmn. 1983—85, chmn. 1985—89, Outstanding Svc. award 1999, Outstanding Leadership award 1999), Computer Soc. of IEEE (Outstanding Contbn. award 1986, 1992, Golden Core), Assn. Computing Machinery (edn. bd. 1980—98, coun. 1984—86, spl. interest group bd. 1985—99, chmn. 1994—98, coun. 1994—98, Recognition Svc. award 1978, 1983, 1985, 1986, 1990, 1991, Outstanding Contbn. award 1995). Home: 4806 Wilmslow Rd Baltimore MD 21210-2328 Office: Towson U Computer and Info Scis Baltimore MD 21252-0001 also: ABET 111 Market Pl Baltimore MD 21202 E-mail: lidtke@acm.org.

LIEB, SUSAN M. elementary school educator; b. Barnesboro, Pa., Jan. 20, 1954; d. Daniel W. and Ethel M. Miller; m. Benedict A. Lieb, Aug. 3, 1974; children: Natalie Lynn, Caroline Bridget, Audrey Sue, Angela Dawn. MEd, Ind. U. Pa., 1978. Tchr. Purchase Line Sch. Dist., Commodore, Pa., 1976—91; dir. day care Ind. County Day Care, Indiana, Pa., 1991—93; tchr. Purchase Line Sch. Dist., Commodore, 1993—. Mem.: Purchase Line Edn. Assn. (life). Home: 2755 Valley Road Cherry Tree PA 15724 Office: Purchase Line School District 5995 Fire Tower Road Mahaffey PA 15757 Personal E-mail: lieblady@pennswoods.net.

LIEBELER, SUSAN WITTENBERG, lawyer; b. July 3, 1942; d. Sherman K. and Eleanor (Klivans) Levine; m. Wesley J. Liebeler, Oct. 21, 1971; 1 child, Jennifer. BA, U. Mich., 1963, postgrad., 1963-64; LLB, UCLA, 1966. Bar: Calif. 1967, Vt. 2002, D.C. 2002. Law clk. Calif. Ct. of Appeals, 1966-67; assoc. Gang, Tyre & Brown, 1967-68, Greenberg, Bernhard, Weiss & Karma, L.A., 1968-70; assoc. gen. counsel Rep. Corp., 1970-72; gen. counsel Verit Industries, 1972-73; prof. Loyola Law Sch., L.A., 1973—85; spl. counsel, chmn. John S. R. Shad, SEC, Washington, 1981-82; commr. U.S. Internat. Trade Commn., Washington, 1984-88, vice-chmn., 1984-86, chmn., 1986-88; ptnr. Irell & Manella, L.A., 1988-94; pres. Lexpert Rsch. Svcs., L.A., 1995—. Vis. prof. U. Tex., summer 1982; cons. Office of Policy Coordination, Office of Pres.-elect, 1981-82; cons. U.S. Ry. Assn., 1975, U.S. EPA, 1974, U.S. Price Commn., 1972; mem. Adminstrv. Conf. U.S., 1986-88. Mem. editl. adv. bd. Regulation mag. CATO Inst.; sr. editor UCLA Law Rev., 1965-66; contbr. articles to profl. jours. Mem. adv. bd. U. Calif. Orientation in USA Law; bd. govs. Century City Hosp., 1992—2002, vice chair, 1997—99, chair, 1999—2001. Stein scholar UCLA, 1966. Mem. State Bar Calif. (treas., vice chair, chair exec. com. internat. law sect.), Practicing Law Inst. (Calif. adv. com.), Washington Legal Found. (acad. adv. bd.), Order of Coif. Jewish. E-mail: lexpert@lexpertresearch.com.

LIEBER, CAROLE MARGUERITE RENEE, human resources specialist, consultant; b. Paris, Feb. 27, 1956; came to U.S., 1957; d. Edward John and Alice Lucie (Barro) L. BSBA, U. Md., 1988; BA in Psychology summa cum laude, Stonehill Coll., 1977; MEd, Boston U., 1978. Lic. cert. social worker, Mass. Program counselor CETA, Chelsea, Mass., 1979-81; asst. dir. Camp Hanson USO, Okinawa, Japan, 1982-84, asst. dir. Camp Foster, 1984-86; pers. mgr. specialist Dept. Navy, Arlington, Va., 1987-91, Dept. Def., Arlington, Va., 1991-98; pers. policy specialist Office Pers. Policy Dept. Treas., Washington, 1998-2001; supr., HR specialist Defense Information Systems Agency, 2001—. Tng. officer Human Resources Devel. Coun., Washington, 1985—; mem. Pres.'s taskforcefor Fed. Tng. Tech. Vol. White House, Washington, 1996—, Arlington Dem. Com., 1997—; mem. Arlington Heights Civic Assn., 1998—. Named Outstanding Young Virginian Virginia Jaycees, 1993, Sec. of the Treasury awd. for Excellence, 2001. Mem. ASTD, Internat. Personnel Mgmt. Assn., Nat. Conf. State Soc.s (sec. 1995-96), Mass. Soc. (pres. 1996-98), Jr. C. of C. (dist. dir., regional dir. Internat. Affairs Commn., program dir. 1992-93, award 1995), Toastmasters Internat. (divsn. gov. 1987-88). Democrat. Avocations: community volunteering, art, photography, travel. Home: 404 S Fenwick St Arlington VA 22204-2082 Office: Defense Information Systems Agency 701 S Courthouse Rd Arlington VA 22204-2199 E-mail: lieberc@ncr.disa.mil.

LIEBER, SALLY J. state representative; b. Detroit; m. Dave Phillips. Student, Stanford U., Foothill Coll., City Coll. San Francisco. Mem. Calif. Assembly, 2002—. Chair Santa Clara Valley Water Commn., Santa Clara County Social Svcs. Commn.; chair adv. com. Santa Clara County Children's Shelter; mem. Com. Green Foothills, Healthy Ventures Collaborative; policy com. Million Mom March; mayor City of Mountain View, Calif., councilmember; bd. dirs. Valley Transp. Authority. Mem.: YWCA (bd. dirs.), NAACP, LWV (naturalizations coord.), Nat. Women's Polit. Caucus, Calif. Elected Women's Assn. Edn. Rsch., Sierra Club. Democrat. Office: PO Box 942849 Rm 4162 Sacramento CA 94249 Address: 100 Paseo San Antonio Rm 300 San Jose CA 95113

LIEBERGOTT, JACQUELINE W. academic administrator; b. Balt., Mar. 17, 1942; d. Mendel Stiebel and Jeane (Levin) Weis; m. Harvey Liebergott, June 20, 1965; children: Jessica Liebergott Hamblen, Cory. BA in Hearing and Speech Sci., U. Md., 1963; MS in Speech-Lang. Pathology, U. Pitts., 1966, PhD in Speech-Lang. Pathology, 1973. Lic. in speech-lang. pathology Commonwealth of Mass. Lectr. dept. speech and hearing U. Md., College Park, 1969-70; asst. prof. dept. comm. disorders Emerson Coll., Boston, 1970-73, assoc. prof. divsn. comm. disorders, 1973-79, prof. divsn. comm. disorders, 1979—, dean grad. studies, 1984-87, v.p., acad. dean, 1987-92, interim pres., 1992-93, pres., 1993—. Manuscript reviewer in speech and hearing Grune and Stratton Pub. Co., 1972-73; manuscript reviewer in lang. Little Brown and Co., 1977; vis. assoc. prof. dept. comm. disorders Memphis (Tenn.) State U., summer 1974; co-chairperson conv. program com. Mass. Speech and Hearing Assn., 1978; cons. to ABT Assocs., Evaluating the Health Impact of Head Start, 1978-80; proposal reviewer Boston Univ. Lang. Conf., 1978, 84, 86; cons. on spl. edn. tng. in P.R., U.S. Office of Edn., Bur. Edn. of the Handicapped, 1979, cons. and proposal reviewer divsn. pers. preparation, 1978, 79, 80, 84-88; study sect. reviewer Divsn. Communicative Diseases and Stroke, NIH, 1979, 80, 83, 84, 85; cons. in lang. Brookline Early Edn. Project, 1979-83; project cons. TADS, Chapel Hill, N.C., 1980; program evaluator Pre-Sch. Program, Chepecket, R.I., 1980; editl. advisor in speech and lang. Little Brown and Co., 1980-88; associated sci. staff Children's Hosp. Med. Ctr., Harvard Med. Sch., 1984—; program chairperson and responder Session on Lang. Disabilities, Boston U. Lang. Conf., 1984-85; proposal reviewer minority participation in higher edn. U.S. Dept. Edn., Office of Post-Secondary Edn., 1990-92; accreditation vis. team New Eng. Assn. Schs. and Colls., 1992; presenter and cons. in field. Mem. editl. bd. ACTA Symbolica, 1973-80, Applied Health and Behavioral Scis. Jour., 1977-80, Jour. Speech and Hearing Disorders, 1977-81, Jour. Speech and Hearing Rsch., 1981-85, Am. Speech and Hearing Assn., 1985-90; contbr. articles to profl. jours. Chair staff com. Children's Ctr. Brookline, 1970-75; founding parent, mem. staff com. Newton After-Sch. Program, 1978-81; v.p., trustee Autism Soc., 1984—; trustee, mem. programming com. Boston Cable Access Bd., 1991—; trustee New Eng. Bus. Coun., 1992—, bd. mem., 1993—; bd. mem. Downtown Crossing Assn., 1994—, The Cambridge Partnership for Pub. Edn., 1994—; active Friends of the Pub. Garden and Boston Common, 1994—. Fellow Am. Coun. Edn. (fellowship selection com. 1991-92); mem. Am. Speech-Lang. and Hearing Assn. (com. on lang., subcom. on speech-lang. pathology svc. delivery with infants and toddlers 1987-90), Am. Assn. Higher Edn., Assn. Ind. Colls. and Univs. Mass., Mass. ACE/NIP, New Eng. Assn. Schs. and Coll. Inc. (liaison), New Eng. Coun., Mass. Women's Forum, Boston C. of C. Office: Emerson Coll Office of the Pres 120 Boylston St Boston MA 02116-4624

LIEBERMAN, EVELYN S. diplomat; b. N.Y.C., 1944; m. Edward H. Lieberman. BS in English, SUNY, Buffalo, 1966; graduate in English Lit., St. John's U. Press sec. U.S. Senator Joseph R. Biden, Jr. (D-DE), 1988-93; asst. to chief of staff Office of First Lady The White House, 1993-94, dep. asst. to Pres., dep. press sec. for ops., 1994-95, asst. to Pres. and dep. chief of staff, 1996-97; dir. Voice of Am., Washington, 1997-99; under sec. of state for public diplomacy and public affairs Dept. of State, Washington, 1999—. Dir. pub. affairs, comms. dir. Children's Def. Fund, Nat. Urgan Coalition. Dir. public affairs Children's Defense Fund; comms. dir. Nat. Urban Coalition. Home: 3216 Newark St NW Washington DC 20008-3345 Office: Us Dept State Washington DC 20520-0001

LIEBERMAN, GAIL FORMAN, investment company executive; b. Phila., May 26, 1943; d. Joseph and Rita Forman. BA in Physics and Math., Temple U., 1964, MBA in Fin., 1977. Dir. internat. fin. Std. Brands Inc., N.Y.C., 1977-79; staff v.p. fin. and capital planning RCA Corp., 1979-82; CFO, exec. v.p. Scali McCabe Sloves, Inc., 1982-93; v.p. fin., CFO, mng. dir. Moody's Investors Svc., N.Y.C., 1994-96; CFO TFPPG Thomson Corp., Boston, 1996-99; CEO Liquid Alternatives Inc., 2000; mng. ptnr. Rudder Capital LLC, 2001—. Bd. dirs. Allied Devices, Inc. Mem. Fin. Execs. Inst. Office Phone: 917-207-4969. E-mail: liebermang@earthlink.net.

LIEBERMAN, ILENE D. art history and humanities educator; b. L.A., Aug. 18, 1954; BA, U. Calif., Berkeley, 1976; PhD, Princeton U., 1983. Lectr. Princeton (N.J.) U., 1983, Villanova (Pa.) U., 1983-84; prof. Gabriel Lukas Chair Fine Arts Widener U., Chester, Pa., 1985—, dir. hon. program in gen. edn., 1995—. Contbg. author: The Memorial Redefined: New Dimensions of Public Memory, 1989; contbr. articles to profl. jours. Grantee Am. Coun. Learned Socs., 1984-86, NEH, 1985. Mem. Coll. Art Assn., Historians Brit. Art, Assn. Historians 19th Century Art, Walpole Soc., Womens Caucus for Art, Phi Kappa Phi. Office: Widener U Humanities Div One Univesity Pl Chester PA 19013

LIEBERMAN, JANET ELAINE, academic administrator; b. N.Y.C., Oct. 21, 1921; d. Samuel and Ida (Schubert) Rubensohn; m. Allen L. Chase, July 9, 1940 (div. 1954); children: Gary Andrew, Randolph H.; m. Jerrold S. Lieberman, June 30, 1957. Student, Vassar Coll., 1939-40; BA, Barnard Coll., N.Y.C., 1943; MA, City Coll., N.Y.C., 1946; PhD, NYU, N.Y.C., 1965. Asst. prof. Hunter Coll., N.Y.C., 1965-70; prof. LaGuardia C.C., Long Island City, N.Y., 1970-72, asst. dean faculty, 1972-74, prof. psychology, 1974-86, asst. to pres., 1986—. Recipient Innovation in Higher Edn. award Charles A. Dana Found., N.Y.C., 1989, Break the Mold award U.S. Dept. Edn., Washington, 1992, LaGuardia medal of honor, 2002, Disting. Alumni award NYU, 2003. Mem. Am. Assn. Higher Edn. Avocation: tennis. Office: LaGuardia CC 31-10 Thomson Ave Long Island City NY 11101-3071

LIEBERMAN, JOSEFA NINA, psychologist, educator, writer; b. Jaroslaw, Poland, May 16, 1921; came to U.S., 1946; d. David Samuel and Rosa Zerline (Leinwand) Margules; m. Meyer Frank Lieberman, Feb. 12, 1956. BS, Columbia U., 1957, MA, 1959, PhD in Ednl. Psychology, 1964. Lic. psychologist, N.Y. Lectr. Bklyn. Coll., 1964-65, asst. prof., 1965-71, assoc. prof., 1972-79, prof., 1979-83, prof. emerita, 1983—. Spkr. in field. Author: Playfulness: Its Relationship to Imagination and Creativity, 1977, Japanese translation, 1981, He Came to Cambridge, 1982, (chpt.) I Came Alone, 1990, The Salzburg Connection: An Adolescence Remembered, 2004; contbr. articles to profl. jours. Mem., chair Hillel Found., Bklyn., 1964—83; founding mem. Solomon Schechter H.S.l, Bklyn., 1971; mem. Sr. Recreation, Woodstock, NY, 1984—. Recipient fellowships and rsch. grants NIMH, 1958-78. Mem. APA, Phi Beta Kappa, Sigma Xi. Democrat. Avocations: languages, music, swimming, chess. Home: 648 Zena Rd Woodstock NY 12498 E-mail: Jnina@aol.com.

LIEBERMAN, NANCY ANN, lawyer; b. N.Y.C., Dec. 30, 1956; d. Elias and Elayne Hildegarde (Fox) L.; m. Mark Ellman, Sept. 6, 1997. BA summa cum laude, U. Rochester, 1977; JD, U. Chgo., 1979; LLM in Taxation, NYU, 1981. Bar: N.Y. 1980. Intern White House, Washington, 1975; law clk. Hon. Henry A. Politz U.S. Ct. Appeals (5th cir.), Shreveport, La., 1979-80; assoc. Skadden Arps Slate Meagher & Flom LLP, N.Y.C., 1981-87; ptnr. Skadden Arps Slate Meagher & Flom LLC, N.Y.C., 1987—. Bd. trustees U. Rochester, 1994—; bd. dirs. Pacific Coun. Internat. Policy. Mem. ABA, Assn. Bar City N.Y., Coun. Fgn. Rels., Phi Beta Kappa. Republican. Jewish. Home: 935 Park Ave New York NY 10028-0212 Office: Skadden Arps Slate Meagher & Flom LLP 4 Times Sq New York NY 10036-6595 E-mail: nlieberm@skadden.com.

LIEBERMAN, PAMELA FORBES, consumer products company executive; MBA. With Price Waterhouse, 1975—88; v.p. fin. Bunzl Bldg. Supply, 1988—92; v.p., CFO Fel-Pro Inc., 1993—98; CFO Shoptalk, Inc., 1998—2001, TruServ Corp., Chgo., 2001—, COO, 2001—, CEO, 2001—. Office: TruServ Corp 8600 W Bryn Mawr Ave Chicago IL 60631-3505

LIEBERMAN, RITA LEAH, psychologist; b. Poland, Aug. 16, 1945; came to U.S., 1950; d. Isaac and Dora (Apfelbaum) L.; m. Martin Ira Becker, Dec. 18, 1994; children: Adam Seth Ziffer, Matthew Jed Ziffer. BS, Fairleigh Dickinson U., 1967; cert. in journalism, Sarah Lawrence Coll., 1978; MS, L.I. U., 1984; PhD in Psychoanalysis and Psychotherapy, NYU, 2003. Lic. psychologist Nat. Register Health Svc. Providers in Psychology; cert. English tchr., N.Y., N.J.; cert. Assn. State and Provincial Psychology Bds. Tchr. secondary and alternative schs. N.Y.C. Bd. Edn., 1967-76; freelance writer, 1976-80; adminstr., clinician ROPEC, Spring Valley, N.Y., 1980-84; asst. coord. Adult Ctr. Orange-Ulster Bd. Coop. Ednl. Svcs., N.Y., 1985-87; psychologist Edwin Gould Acad., Chestnut Ridge, N.Y., 1990-92; pvt. practice, Nyack, 1991—; dir. Rockland County Guidance Ctr., Nyack, N.Y., 1992—. Adj. prof. NYU, N.Y.C., 1990-91, mem. adult edn. adv. bd. BOCES, Nyack, N.Y.; mem. exec. bd. Nyack Literacy Coop., 1992-94, Westchester-Rockland Assn. for Adult and Continuing Edn., 1994; cons. N.J. Unemployment Coalition, 1993-94; presenter in field. Contbr. articles to profl. jours. and newspapers. Chmn. Pomona (N.Y.) Parks and Recreation Commn., 19776-79; mem. Rockland County women's com. Rockland Legislature, 1992. Mem. APA, N.Y. State Psychol. Assn., Rockland County Psychol. Assn., NOW, Rockland County Women's Network (columnist), Women Entrepreneurs. Avocations: cooking, dance, reading. also: Rockland County Guidance Ctr 17 S Broadway Nyack NY 10960-3120 Office: 20 N Broadway Nyack NY 10960-2636

LIEBERMAN-CLINE, NANCY, sports commentator, former professional basketball coach, former player; b. July 1, 1958; m. Tim Cline, 1988; 1 child, Timothy Joseph. Grad., Old Dominion U., 1981. Guard WBL's Dallas Diamonds, 1980-86, USBL's L.I. Knights, 1986-87, Washington Generals, 1987-88, Athletes in Action, 1996-97, WNBA - Phoenix Mercury, 1997; head coach, gen. mgr. WNBA - Detroit Shock, 1998—2000; now sports commentator. Women's basketball analyst NBA Broadcasting, ESPN, ABC, ESPN 2, Fox Sports Network, NBC. Recipient Broderick Cup, 1979, 80, Wade Trophy (2), U.S. Olympic Silver medal, 1976; named All-Am., 1978-80, ODU Outstanding Female Athlete of Yr., 1977-80; mem. Women's Am. Basketball Championship team, 1985; Named to Basketball Hall of Fame, 1996.*

LIEBES, RAQUEL, retired import/export company executive; b. San Salvador, El Salvador, Aug. 28, 1938; arrived in U.S., 1952, naturalized, 1964; d. Ernesto Martin and Alice (Philip) Liebes; m. Richard Paisley Kinkade, June 2, 1962 (div. 1977); children: Kathleen Paisley Kinkade, Richard Paisley Kinkade Jr., Scott Philip Kinkade. BA, Sarah Lawrence Coll., 1960; MEd, Harvard U., 1961; MA, Yale U., 1963, postgrad., 1963-65; D (hon.), Oxford U., 1994. Tchg. fellow in Spanish Sarah Lawrence Coll., Bronxville, NY, 1958-60; econ. tchg. fellow Yale U., New Haven, 1964-65, instr. Spanish dept., 1964-66; exec. stockholder Import Export Co., San Salvador, 1968-89, also bd. dirs.; ret., 1989. Adj. prof. Am. U., Washington, 1989—91, Georgetown U., Washington, 1989—93; lectr., conf. participant L.Am. art. Contbr. glossary of Spanish med. terms. Hon. consul Govt. of El Salvador, 1977—80; mem. outreach group L.Am. The White Ho., Washington, 1982—86; vol. Grady Hosp., Atlanta, 1966—71; chmn. Atlanta Coun. Internat. Visitors, 1966—71; docent High Mus. Art, Atlanta, 1972—77; founding mem. John Kennedy Ctr. Peforming Arts, 1980—, Agape, El Salvador, 1981—, Concultura, El Salvador, 1999—, Libr. of Congress, Wahington; mem. Folger/Shakespeare Libr., Smithsonian Inst. Econ. fellow, Yale U., 1964—65, Smithsonian Mus. grantee, 1981—96, Corcoran Mus. Art fellow, 1984—85. Mem.: AAUW, MLA, Rsch. Assn., Am. Biog. Inst., Jr. League of Washington, Concultura El Salvador, Yale Club, Harvard Club. Republican. Avocations: comparative literature, languages, international business, english literature, shakespeare. Office: V I P Sal # 148 PO Box 52-5364 Miami FL 33152-5364

LIEBICH, MARCIA TRATHEN, community volunteer; b. Troy, N.Y., Mar. 10, 1942; d. Roland Henry and Ida Mae (Horsfall) Trathen; m. Donald Herbert Liebich, May 13, 1941; children: Kurt Roland, Mark Christian. BA, Elmira Coll., 1964. With Sunnyview Hosp. and Rehab. Ctr., Schenectady, 1982-96, dir. devel., 1992-94; CEO Sunnyview Hosp. Found., 1994-96. Co-founder Parent Anonymous Lay Therapy, Schenectady, 1974-80; trustee Elmira (N.Y.) Coll., 1978-94; bd. dirs. United Way, Schenctady, 1980-81, pres. 1985, bd. dirs. United Way, N.Y., 1991—, Sunnyview Rehab. Hosp., Schenectady, 1982, pres. 1988-91; social svcs. Women's Legis. Forum, Albany, 1984-91; bd. dirs. Leadership Schenectady, 1987-92, Schenectady C. of C., 1987-90, YMCA Capital Dist., 1991-94, WMHT Pub. Radio and TV, 1991-96; pres. Samaritan Counseling Ctr., Schenectady, 1988-91; bd. dirs., treas. Bridge Ctr. Drug Treatment, Schenectady, 1988-91; bd. dirs. Backstage Theater, 1999-2002; mem. Wood River Med. Ctr. Aux., 2002—, Croy Canyon Ranch Found., Inc., 2004—. Recipient YWCA Community Vol. award, 1986, K.S. Rozendaal award Community Svc. Schenectady, 1987, Liberty Bell award Schenectady Bar Assn., 1990, Women of Vision Betty Bean award YWCA, 1990. Mem. AAUW (pres. 1978), PEO, Jr. League Schenectady (Vol. of Yr. award 1981), Summit Pub. Radio (treas. 1998-2002), Applause (sec. 1998-2002), Breckeridge Resort Chamber (amb. 1998-2002), Phi Beta Kappa. Republican. Lutheran. Avocations: tennis, reading, knitting, skiing, watching hockey. Home: 196 Nez Perce Cir Hailey ID 83333-8573

LIEBMAN, JUDITH RAE STENZEL, operations research educator; b. Denver, July 2, 1936; d. Raymond Oscar and Mary Madelyn (Galloup) Stenzel; m. Jon Charles Liebman, Dec. 27, 1958; children: Christopher Brian, Rebecca Anne, Michael Jon. BA in Physics, U. Colo., Boulder, 1958; PhD in Ops. Rsch., Johns Hopkins U., 1971. Successively asst. prof., head indsl. systems, assoc. prof. U. Ill., Urbana, 1972-84, prof., 1984-96, prof. emerita, 1996—, acting vice chancellor for rsch., 1986-87, vice chancellor for rsch., 1987-92, acting dean Grad. Coll., 1987-92, dean, 1987-92. Vis. prof. Tianjin (China) U., 1985; charter mem. Ill. Gov.'s Sci. Adv. Com., Ill. Engrng. Com., 1989-92, mem. adv. com. for engring. NSF, 1988-92, chmn., 1991-92; mem. NRC Bd. Engring. Edn., 1997-2001, Army Sci. Bd., 1997-99. Author: Modeling and Optimization with GINO, 1986; author numerous articles in field. Bd. dirs. United Way, Champaign, Ill., 1986-91, U. Colo. Found., 1999-2003; bd. dirs. East Cen. Ill. Health Systems Agy., Champaign, 1977-82, pres., 1980-82. Mem. Ops. Rsch. Soc. Am. (pres. 1987-88), Nat. Assn. State Univs. and Land Grant Colls. (exec. bd. 1990-92), Rotary, Sigma Xi, Sigma Pi Sigma, Alpha Pi Mu, Phi Kappa Phi. Home: 110 W Whitehall Ct Urbana IL 61801-6664

LIEBMAN, NINA R. economic developer; b. Toledo, Ohio, May 27, 1941; d. Jules Jay and Phyllis Gertrude (Kasle) Roskin; m. Theodore Liebman, Oct. 27, 1968; children: Sophie, Hanna, Tessa. Student, U. Marseilles, Aix-en-Provence, France, 1959-60, Skidmore Coll., 1960-61, NYU, 1961-63; cert. labor negotiator, Cornell U., 1993. Pub. info. officer Young Adult Inst., N.Y.C., 1978-81; U.S.A. dir. Rhone-Alps Econ. Devel. Assn., N.Y.C. and Lyon, France, 1981-85; internat. mktg. specialist N.Y. State Dept. Econ. Devel., N.Y.C., 1985-89, chief internat. programs, 1989-95; cons. Russian Fedn. Housing project The World Bank, 1995, cons. Russian Cmty. Social Infrastructure project, 1997. Exec. dir. Nat. Assn. Export Cos., 1997—99; assoc. dir. Architecture Rsch. Inst., 2000—02; assoc. The Corcoran Group, 2002—. Co-author: Biz Speak: A Dictionary of Business Terms, Slang and Jargon, 1986. Vol., trained mediator Bklyn. Mediation Ctr.; former mem. internat. adv. coun. Eisenhower Found.; mem. internat. adv. bd. Nat. Minority Bus. Coun., Bklyn. Philharmonic Chorus; bd. dirs. Murray Hill Neighborhood Assn.. Fellow Eisenhower Exch. Fellowship Program, 1993. Mem. UN Assn., Alliance Am. and Russian Women, U.S. Com. for UN, Devel. Fund for Women, Mcpl. Arts Soc. Democrat. Jewish. Avocation: choral singing. E-mail: nina.liebman@prodigy.net.

LIEBMAN, WILMA B. government agency administrator; b. Phila. BA, Barnard Coll., N.Y.C.; JD, George Washington U., Washington. Staff atty. NLRB, 1974—80; legal counsel Internat. Brotherhood of Teamsters, 1980—89; labor counsel Bricklayers and Allied Craftsmen, 1990—93; asst. to dir. Fed. Mediation and Conciliation Svc., 1994—96, dep. dir.; mem. NLRB, Washington, 1997—. Mem.: Coll. of Labor and Employment Lawyers, Inc. (exec. bd.), Indsl. Rels. Rsch. Assn. (exec. bd.). Office: NLRB 1099 14th St NW Washington DC 20570-0001*

LIEBOW, JOANNE ELISABETH, poet and freelance publicist; b. Cleve., May 15, 1926; d. Arnold S. and Rhea Eunice (Levy) King; m. Irving M. Liebow, June 30, 1947 (div. Jan. 1972); children: Katherine Ann Liebow Frank, Peter. Student, Smith Coll., 1944-47; BA, Case Western Res. U., 1948. Cleve. reporter Fairchild Publs., N.Y.C., 1950-51; pub. info. specialist, mktg. comms. coord. Cuyahoga C.C., Cleve., 1979-99. Founder, pres. Mt. Sinai Jr. Women's Aux., Cleve., 1948-50; pres. PTA, Bryden Elem. Sch., Beachwood, Ohio, 1964; bd. dirs., pres. Beachwood Bd. Edn., 1968-76. Recipient Exceptional Achievement award Coun. for Advancement of Edn., 1982, Citation award, 1982, Grand prize, 1983, Cleve. Communicator's award Women in Comms. Inc., 1982; Sophia Smith scholar Smith Coll., 1946. Home: Apt 201 23511 Chagrin Blvd Beachwood OH 44122-5538

LIEBSON, ALICE RUTH, political scientist, advocate; b. Washington, Oct. 2, 1950; d. Sidney Harold and Jeannette Burman Liebson. BA, Western Conn. State U., 1974. Chief aide Ella Grasso for Gov. Re-Election, 1978; exec. asst. State Dept. Housing, 1979—88; chair Conn. Permanent Commn. on the Status of Women, 1989—92; dep. coord. Labor for Dodd-Clinton/Gore, 1992; staff mem. Presdl. Debate, 1996; staff Conn. State Legis., 1999. Active Capitol Region Coun. Govts. Citizens Forum, 1979—83; mem. allocations com. United Way of the Capitol Area, 1981—84, mem. strategic planning com., 1988—90; corporator YMCA Met. Hartford, Inc., 1995; trustee Nat. Multiple Sclerosis Soc.-Conn. chpt., 1995—96; chair Food for All-Conn. Coun., 1996—98; mem. adv. bd. Conn. Pub. TV and Radio, 1999—; dir. Nutmeg Big Bros./Big Sisters, Inc., 1985—90, Combined Health Appeal (of Conn.) for Bus. and Industry, Cmty. Health Charities Conn., 1985—89, Cystic Fibrosis Found. Conn., Inc., 1985—90, Constn. Coun. Campfire Boys and Girls Conn., 1986—87. Named one of Ten Outstanding Young Citizens Conn., Conn. Jaycees and WFSB TV Ch. 3, 1985; recipient GE award for outstanding cmty. svc., 1977, Outstanding Young Woman Am. award, 1980, Women in Leadership Recognition award, YWCA, 1983, The Hartford Courant award for social and human svcs., 1986, Vol. in Pediat. award, Conn. Children's Med. Ctr., 1998, Easter Seals Conn. Galaxy Awards Star, 1999, Amb. Jean Kennedy Smith Founder's award, VSAarts, 1999, Spl. Congl. Recognition cert., 2003.

LIEF, BETH, educational association administrator; b. Huntington, Ill. married; 2 children. BA in Urban Studies, Barnard Coll.; JD, NYU. Counsel Legal Def. and Ednl. Fund NAACP; spl. asst. to Richard Beattie N.Y. Bd. Edn.; staff counsel Pub. Edn. Assn.; exec. dir. Mayor's Commn. on Spl. Edn., 1984—86; dir. Program for Homeless Families and Spl. Projects Edna McConnell Clark Found.; founding pres. New Visions for Pub. Schs., 1989—2000; sr. v.p. strategic rels. Teachscape, 2000—03; cons. N.Y.C. Dept. Edn. Children First Strategic Planning Initiative; nat. fellow Inst. for Learning, Learning R&D Ctr., Pitts., 2003—. Bd. dirs., sec. Pub. Edn. Network, Washington; bd. dirs. New Visions for Pub. Schs.; sr. fellow edn. New Democracy Project. Bd. dirs. Bank St. Coll. Edn., United Cerebral Palsy N.Y.C.; Parent Resource Ctr. Scholar Root-Tilden scholar 2nd cir. Office: Pub Edn Network 601 13th St NW Washington DC 20005*

LIEGLER, ROSEMARY MENKE, dean; b. Fairfield, Iowa, Aug. 21, 1939; d. Vincent Thomas and Catherine Lucille Menke; m. Donald G. Liegler, June 8, 1963; children: Katherine, Jerry. BSN, St. Ambrose Coll., 1961; MS in Nursing, Marquette U., 1962; PhD, Claremont Grad. Sch., 1994. Asst. prof. Miami (Fla.)-Dade Jr. Coll., Georgetown U., Washington, U. Miami; prof., dean Sch. Nursing Azusa (Calif.) Pacific U. Bd. dirs. Huntington East Valley Hosp. Mem. ANA, Calif. Assn. Colls. Nursing, East San Gabriel Valley Vis. Nurses' Assn. (cmty. bd. 1995), Sigma Theta Tau. Home: 3226 E Whitebirch Dr West Covina CA 91791-3037 Office: Azusa Pacific U Sch Nursing 901 E Alosta Ave Azusa CA 91702-2769

LIEM, ANNIE, pediatrician; b. Kluang, Johore, Malaysia, May 26, 1941; d. Daniel and Ellen (Phuah) L. BA, Union Coll., 1966; MD, Loma Linda U., 1970. Diplomate Am. Bd. Pediatrics. Intern Glendale (Calif.) Adventist Hosp., 1970-71; resident in pediatrics Children's Hosp. of Los Angeles, 1971-73; pediatrician Children's Med. Group, Anaheim, Calif., 1973-75, Anaheim Pediatric Med. Group, 1975-79; practice medicine specializing in pediatrics Anaheim, 1979-96, Camas, Wash., 1996—. Fellow Am. Acad. Pediatrics; mem. Los Angeles Pediatric Soc., Orange County Pediatric Soc., Adventist Internat. Med. Soc., Chinese Adventist Physicians' Assn. Avocations: music, reading, gardening. Office: 713 NE 4th Ave Camas WA 98607-2037 Office Phone: 360-833-4519. E-mail: all526@aol.com.

LIETCH, MARGIE, insurance company administrator; b. Macon, Ga., May 31, 1953; d. James Milton Scarbary and Samantha Lou Mercer; m. Gary Tye Riddle, July 11, 1970 (div. July 1981); chldren; Gary Kenneth Riddle, Richard Drake Riddle; m. Larry Joe Lietch, Aug. 2, 1991. Student, Ins. Inst. Am., Atlanta, 1989, 98. Cert. profl. ins. woman; cert. assoc. in ins. svcs. Rate and code clk. Ctrl. Mut. Ins. Co., Atlanta, 1972-75; underwriter Byrd & Lancaster Ins. Agy., Atlanta, 1975-77, Vickery & Christopher Ins. Agy., Stone Mountain, Ga., 1978-80; underwriting office mgr. Klepac and Assocs. Ins. Agy., Lilburn, Ga., 1980-92; policy svcs. supr. Atlanta Casualty

Ins. Co., Norcross, Ga., 1992-98; underwriting/ops. mgr. Sun States Ins. Group, Decatur, Ga., 1998—2000; ops. mgr. Regulatory Techs., Inc., Roswell, Ga., 2001—. Named Woman of Yr. Gwinnett Assn. Ins. Women, 1983, 87. Mem. Nat. Assn. Ins. Women (pres.N.E. Atlanta chpt. 1990-91, Ga. state dir. 1995-96, Ga. state treas. 1996-97, Woman of Yr. N.E. Atlanta chpt. 1990, 97). Republican. Baptist. Avocations: travel, water sports, flower gardening, arts and crafts. Home: 245 Forest Way Lawrenceville GA 30043-4494 Office: Regulatory Techs Inc 645 Hembree Pkwy S # A Roswell GA 30076-3868 E-mail: Lietch@MCCON.com.

LIFKA, MARY LAURANNE, history educator; b. Oak Park, Ill., Oct. 31, 1937; d. Aloysius William and Loretta Catherine (Juric) L. B.A., Mundelein Coll., 1960; M.A., Loyola U., Los Angeles, 1965; Ph.D., U. Mich., 1974; postdoctoral student London U., 1975. Life teaching cert. Prof. history Mundelein Coll., Chgo., 1976-84, coordinator acad. computer, 1983-84, prof. history Coll. St. Teresa, Winona, Minn., 1984-89, Lewis U., Romeoville, Ill., 1989—; chief reader in history Ednl. Testing Service, Princeton, N.J., 1980-84; cons. world history project Longman, Inc., 1983— ; cons. in European history Coll. Bd., Evanston, Ill., 1983— ; mem. Com. on History in the Classroom. Author: Instructor's Guide to European History, 1983; contbr. articles to publs. Recipient Br. Miguel Febres Cordero award for scholarship, 1998. Mem. Am. Hist. Assn., Ednl. Testing Service Devel. Com. of History. Democrat. Roman Catholic. Office: Lewis U RR 53 Romeoville IL 60446

LIFSHUTZ, MELANIE JANET BELL, patient education, medical, and surgical nurse; b. Dallas; d. Trigg Alvin Ralph and Shirley Theo (Templeton) Bell; m. David Martin Lifshutz. BS, Tex. Woman's U., 1971. Cert. Vol., Chaplain in the Chaplaincy Ministry. Nurse practice coord. La. State U., Shreveport; RN intensive care unit Presbyn. Hosp. Dallas; charge RN surgery Parkland Meml. Hosp., Dallas; patient edn. coord. Parker County Surg. Clinic, Weatherford, Tex. Mem. Am. Assn. Critical Care Nurses, Am. Heart Assn., ANA, Am. Soc. for Health Edn. and Tng., Am. Cancer Assn. (pub. edn. chmn.). Home: RR 1 Box 1978 Shelbyville TX 75973-9801

LIFTON, BARBARA, state legislator, secondary school educator; m. Don Lifton; children: Christine Brouwer, Paul Sylvester 1 stepchild, Rebecca. English tchr. Geneseo Ctrl. Sch., 1976—82, Ithaca Schs., 1985—88. Chief of staff Assemblyman marty Luster; mem. Tompkins Co. Dem. Com.; treas 3rd Ward Dem. Com. Mem. Justice for All; founder Coalition for Cmty. Unity, 1988, Democratic Response Group. Democrat. Office: 106 E Court St Ithaca NY 14850

LIGGETT, TWILA MARIE CHRISTENSEN, academic administrator, public television executive; b. Pipestone, Minn., Mar. 25, 1944; d. Donald L. Christensen and Irene E. (Zweigle) Christensen Flesher. BS, Union Coll., Lincoln, Nebr., 1966; MA, U. Nebr., 1971; PhD, 1977; DHL (hon.), Marymount Manhattan Coll., 2000. Dir. vocal and instrumental music Sprague (Nebr.)-Martell Pub. Sch., 1966-67; tchr. vocal music pub. schs., Syracuse, Nebr., 1967-69; tchr. Norris Pub. Sch., Firth, Nebr., 1969-71; cons. fed. reading project pub. schs., Lincoln, Nebr., 1971-72; curriculum coord. Westside Cmty. Schs., Omaha, 1972-74; dir. state program Right-to-Read Nebr. Dept. Edn., 1974-76; asst. dir. Nebr. Commn. on Status of Women, 1976-80; asst. dir. project adminstrn./devel. Great Plains Nat. Instructional TV Libr. U. Nebr., Lincoln, 1980-97; sr. v.p. for edn. Lancit Media Ent., Ltd. a Junior Net Co., N.Y., 1998-2001. Exec. prodr. Nebr. ETV Network/GPN a nat. PBS children's series Reading Rainbow, 1980—; cons. U.S. Dept. Edn., 1981; cons. Far West Regional Lab. Nebr. Edn. TV Network, San Francisco, 1978—79; panelist, presenter in field, Blue Ribbon panelist NATAS, 1991—2004; final judge Nat. Cable Ace Awards, 1991—92, 1997. Author: Reading Rainbow's Guide to Children's Books: The 101 Best Titles, 1994, rev. edit., 1996. Bd. dirs. Planned Parenthood, Lincoln, 1979-81. Recipient Grand award, N.Y., 1993, Gold medal, Internat. Film and TV Festival, 1996, 1999, World Gold medal, N.Y. Internat. Film and TV, 1995, Golden Eagle award, Coun. on Non-theatrical Events, 1995, Image award, NAACP, 1994, 1996, 1999, 2002, 20 Nat. Emmy awards, 8 for Outstanding Children's Series, 1985—2003. Mem. NATAS, Internat. Reading Assn. (panelist, presenter, Spl. award Contbns. Worldwide Literacy 1992), Am. Women in Film and TV, Phi Delta Kappa. Presbyterian. Home: 37 Crescent Pl Matawan NJ 07747 Personal E-mail: tcliggett@aol.com.

LIGGIO, JEAN VINCENZA, adult education educator, artist; b. NYC, Nov. 5, 1927; d. Vincenzo and Bernada (Terrusa) Verro; m. John Liggio, June 6, 1948; children: Jean Constance, Joan Bernadette. Student, N.Y. Inst. Photography, 1965, Elizabeth Seton Coll., 1984, Parsons Sch. of Design, 1985. Hairdresser Beauty Shoppe, N.Y.C., 1947-65; instr. watercolor N.Y. Dept. Pks., Recreation and Conservation, Yonkers, 1985-89, Bronxville (N.Y.) Adult Sch., 1989—. Substitute tchr. cosmetology Yonkers Bd. Edn., 1988-89; tchr. watercolor painting J.V.L. Watercolor Workshop of Fine Arts, Jakes Art Ctr., Mt. Vernon, N.Y. Paintings pub. by Donald Art Co., C.R. Gibson Greeting Card Co., Enesco Corp., 1996; paintings for Avon Calendar, Avon Cosmetics Co., 1994, 96, Avon-Can. Publ., 1996-97; greeting cards published by C.R. Gibson Co. Publ., 1996-1997, boxed notecards by C.R. Gibson; painting on cover of C.R. Gibson Jour., 2000, C.R. Gibson Inspirational Jour.; pub. Friends Jour. Mag., Phila. Mem.: Art Soc. Old Greenwich, Hudson Valley Art Assn., New Rochelle Art Assn., Scarsdale Art Assn. (publicity chmn. 1984—89), Mt. Vernon Art Assn. (pres. membership com. 1983—). Avocation: antiques. Home and Office: 166 Helena Ave Yonkers NY 10710-2524 Office Phone: 914-779-3882.

LIGGON, PRISCILLA MURPHY, radiology educator, x-ray technologist; b. Lynchburg, Va., Sept. 27, 1956; d. Henry Clay and Mary Jean Murphy; m. Gary Sharone Liggon, Sr., Nov. 27, 1977; children: Cotrena Denea, Gary S. Jr., Regina Lynn. AAS, Ctrl. Va. C.C., Lynchburg, 1977. Registered radiologic technologist. Office x-ray technologist R. Robert Bowen, M.D., Lynchburg, 1977—80; staff x-ray technologist Lynchburg Gen. Hosp., 1980; clin. coord. Ctrl. Va. C.C., 1989—. Mem. radiology adv. bd. Ctrl. Va. C.C., 1989; sec. Ctrl. Va. Dist. Radiologic Technologists, 2003—. Mem. Amherst County Sch. Bd., Amherst, Va., 1997—; v.p. Amherst County Dixie Softball, 1980—2002; mem. South Ctrl. Area Health Edn. Ctr., Altavista, Va., 2002—. Democrat. Bapt. Avocations: reading, talking, religious functions, sports. Home: 931 Amelon Rd Madison Heights VA 24572 Office: Ctrl Va Cmty Coll 3506 Wards Rd Lynchburg VA 24501 Office Phone: 434-832-7694. E-mail: liggonp@cvcc.vccs.edu.

LIGHT, BETTY JENSEN PRITCHETT, former college dean; b. Omaha, Sept. 14, 1924; d. Lars Peter and Ruth (Norby) Jensen; m. Morgan S. Pritchett, June 27, 1944 (dec. 1982); children: Randall Wayne, Robin Kay Pritchett Church, Royce Marie Pritchett Bishop; m. Kenneth F. Light, Nov. 23, 1985 (dec. 2003). BS, Portland State U., 1965; MBA, U. Oreg., 1966; Ed.D., Oreg. State U., 1973. Buyer Rodgers Stores, Inc., Portland, Oreg., 1947-62; chmn. bus. div. Mt. Hood Community Coll., Gresham, Oreg., 1966-70, dir. evening coll., 1970-71, assoc. dean instn., 1972-77, dean humanities and behavioral scis., 1977-79, dean devel. and spl. programs, 1979-83, dean communication arts, humanities and social scis., 1983-86. State com. for articulation between cmty. colls. and higher edn., 1976-78; mem. Gov.'s Coun. on Career and Vocat. Edn., 1977-86; owner Effective Real Estate Mgmt., 1982-2002. Author: Values and Perceptions of Community College Professional Staff in Oregon, 1973; contbg. author: The Pritchett Study in Retailing, An Economic View, 1969. Mem. Gresham City Council, 1983-86. Mem.: Oreg. Vocat. Assn., Am. Vocat. Assn., Am. Assn. Higher Edn., Oreg. Bus. Edn. Assn., Danish Brotherhood, N.W. Danish Found., Danish Heritage Soc. Home: 1635 NE Country Club Ave Gresham OR 97030-4432

LIGHT, JO KNIGHT, stockbroker; b. DeQueen, Ark., Mar. 15, 1936; d. Donald R. and Auda (Waltrip) Knight; m. Jerry T. Light, June 21, 1958 (dec. 1979); m. Victor E. Menefee Jr., Nov. 18, 1981; 1 child, Jerry T. Jr. BA cum laude, U. Ark., 1958. CFP. Travel cons. Comml. Nat. Bank, Little Rock, 1971-76; dist. mgr. Am. Express Co., N.Y.C., 1976-82; fin. advisor and retirement planning specialist Morgan Stanley, N.Y.C., 1982—, registered investment advisor, 1996—, sr. v.p. investments, 1999—. Mem. Jr. League of Little Rock Sustainers; vol. Happiness Singers. Mem. Fin. Planning Assn., Internat. Assn. Fin. Planners (bd. dirs. 1992-98, pres. bd. 1995-96), U. Ark. Alumni Assn. (bd. dirs. 1974-77), Morgan Stanley Pres.'s Club, Morgan Stanley Dir.'s Club, Phi Beta Kappa, Kappa Kappa Gamma. Avocations: music, tennis, sailing, snow skiing. Office: Morgan Stanley 425 W Capitol Ave Ste 200 Little Rock AR 72201-3440 E-mail: jo.light@morganstanley.com.

LIGHT, MARION JESSEL, retired elementary education educator; b. San Antonio, Dec. 5, 1915; d. Marion Jackson and Kate Jessel (Cox) Parr; m. Marion Russell Light, Nov. 8, 1958 (dec. July 1983); children: Russell Jeffers, Paul Love. BA, So. Meth. U., 1936; MA, U. Tex., 1947. Cert. elem. and secondary sch. tchr., Tex. Elem. tchr. Dallas Ind. Sch. Dist., 1936-72. 1st v.p. The Cosmos Rev. Class, 1991-92, 97-98. Del. to 16th Senatorial Dist. Dem. Conv., 1988; moderator Presbyn. Women, 1st Ch., Dallas, 1989-90, co-moderator, 1994-95. Mem. AAUW (chmn. hobbies and crafts Dallas br. 1970s), Dallas Ret. Tchrs. Assn. (corr. sec. 1984-90), Dallas Women's Forum (rec. sec. Friday study 1987-89), Bay View Century Club (corr. sec. 1988-89, pres. 1993-95), Dallas Symphony Orch. League, Delta Kappa Gamma (pres. Delta Sigma chpt. 1956-58, Chpt. Achievement award 1979, Marion Parr Light Recruitment grantee named in her honor Delta Sigma chpt. 1958). Avocations: photography, reading.

LIGHT, SALLY G. cultural organization administrator; b. Denver, Aug. 14, 1942; d. Horace M. and Nancy Smith Gaims; m. William John Light, Mar. 1965 (div. May 1968); 1 child, Rebecca. BA in Anthropology, U. Calif., Berkeley, 1965; JD, New Coll. Calif. Sch. Law, 1996. Social worker L.A. County, 1968—78; opera singer various operas in Europe and the U.S., 1976—90; law clk., summer intern Calif. Rural Legal Assistance, San Francisco, 1995, 1st Dist. Ct. Appellate Project, San Francisco, 1996; project coord. Prisoners Rights Program Nat. Lawyers Guild, San Francisco, 1996; nuc. weapons program analyst Tri-Valley CARE (Communities Against a Radioactive Environment), Livermore, Calif., 1997—2000; exec. dir. Nev. Desert Experience, Berkeley, 2000—, Las Vegas, Nev., 2000—. Mem. coordinating com. U.S. Network to Abolish Nuc. Weapons, Oakland, Calif., 1998—; mem. global coun. Abolition 2000-Global Network to Eliminate Nuc. Weapons, Santa Barbara, Calif., 2001—; bd. mem. Global Network Against Weapons and Nuc. Power in Space, Gainesville, Fla., 2001—; lectr. Journees Desarmaments Nucleaire, Lyon, France, 2003. Contbr. articles to profl. jours. Spkr. U.S. Nuc. Program The Hague (The Netherlands) Appeal for Peace, 1998, rep. U.S. Nuc. Abolition Movement Mouvement de la Paix, Saintes, France, 2001. Recipient honorarium, Ritsumeikan U., Kyoto, Japan, 2001. Mem.: Free Speech Movement Meml. Orgn. Green Party. Avocations: singing, translation, horticulture. Office: Nev Desert Experience PO Box 7849 Oakland CA 94601

LIGHT, SYBIL ELIZABETH, executive secretary; Student, Berkeley Coll., 1978—79, Marist Coll., 1994—2001. Cert. pub. rels., profl. sec. Sec. Peale Ctr. for Christian Living, Pawling, NY, 1979—86, exec. sec. to Norman Vincent Peale, 1986—91; exec. sec. to Ruth Stafford Peale Guideposts, Pawling, NY, 1991—2002, outreach comms. assoc., 2002—. Editor: (book) My Favorite Bible Passages, 1995. Sec.-treas. 2d Kent Bapt. Ch., Carmel, NY, 1990—2001; Organist 2d Kent Bapt.-Faith Bible Fellowship Ch., Holmes, NY, 1976—. Mem.: Internat. Assn. Adminstrv. Profls. (pres. Mid-Hudson chpt. 1997—99). Home: PO Box 439 Pawling NY 12564 Office: Guideposts - Peale Ctr 66 E Main St Pawling NY 12564 Business E-Mail: slight@guideposts.org.

LIGHTBOURNE, ALESA M. writer; b. Carmel, Calif., July 29, 1952; d. Hugh Everett and Gyla M. (Marmont) Smith; children: Marc, Neil, Joel. BA with honors, U. Calif.-Santa Cruz, 1974; MA, U. Wash., 1985, PhD in Comms., 1996. Pres. Lightworks Corp. Comms., 1989—; speechwriter to CEOs; freelance writer for bus., acad., trade, travel, women's, and children's publs. Author numerous books; website writer for Microsoft and Weyerhaeusen. Mem. Zones of Peace Internat. Avocations: anthropology, innovative travel, harp. Home: 1499 SE 9th Ave #302 Oak Harbor WA 98277

LIGHTBURN, ANITA LOUISE, dean, social work educator; b. San Diego, Jan. 2, 1946; d. Kenneth E. and Ann Lorraine (Rosepiler) Schimp; m. Kenneth Dale Lightburn, Aug. 25, 1973; children: Tiffany, Kara. BA, Wheaton Coll., 1968; MS, Columbia U., 1972, MEd, 1988, EdD, 1989. Social worker Mass. Divsn. Child Guardianship, Boston, 1968-70; supr. psychiat. social work McMahon Meml. Shelter, N.Y.C., 1972-73; lectr. Flinders U., Adelaide, Australia, 1973-85; asst., then assoc. prof. Columbia U., N.Y.C., 1989-94; dean, prof. Sch. Social Work Smith Coll., Northampton, Mass., 1994—. Vis. prof. U. Conn., West Hartford, 1985, Columbia U., N.Y.C., 1986-88; cons., clinician, therapist in field. Author chpts. to books; contbr. articles to profl. jours. Mem. NASW. Home: 22 Main St Hatfield MA 01038-9784 Office: Smith Coll Sch Social Work Lilly Hl Northampton MA 01063-0001

LIGHTBURN, CHRISTA PIERPONT, agricultural business manager; b. Marietta, Ohio, July 11, 1947; d. Howard Clemeth and Mary Irene Pierpont; m. John James Thomasson (div.); m. Robert Cole Lightburn, Aug. 20, 1995; children: David, Benjamin, Matthew, Robert, Ashley, Kelby. BS, Radford U., 1969; M in Edn., Curry Sch. Edn./U. Va., 1977. lic. tchr. Tchr. Mercer Co. Schs., Bluefield, W. Va., 1969-71, Fayette Co. Schs., Fayetteville, W. Va., 1971-75, Albemarle Co. Schs., Charlottesville, Va., 1975-97; asst. owner GameBit, Inc., Rochelle, Charlottesville, Va., 1995—; projects coord. Lightburn Farms, Va., 1997—. Assoc. dir. Culpeper Soil and Water Conservation Dist. Recipient Cheatham Leadership award, Thomsa Jefferson Meml. Ch., 1994. Mem. Nat. Edn. Assn., Va. Edn. Assn., Coun. Exceptional Children, Conflict Resolution Ednl. Network, U. Va. Alumni Assn. Avocations: caving, outdoor activities.

LIGHTFOOT, MARJORIE JEAN, English educator; b. Oak Park, Ill., Apr. 24, 1933; d. Cecil Dane and Maybelle June (Doyle) L. BA, Brown U., 1955; MA, Northwestern U., 1956, PhD, 1964. Tchg. asst. Northwestern U., Evanston, Ill., 1957-60; instr. U. Ariz., Tucson, 1960-63; asst. prof. English Ariz. State U., Tempe, 1964-69, assoc. prof. English, 1969-74, prof. English, 1974—. Author: Glimpses of the Brontes: A Biography on Stage, 1980; dramatist: (Chaucer) Troilus and Criseyde, 1978, (Edgeworth) Belinda: Oh, What a Fine Confusion, 1995. Mem. Am. Soc. for 18th Century Studies, Rocky Mountain Modern Lang. Assn. Avocations: acting, directing, singing, traveling, reading. Office: Ariz State U English Dept Tempe AZ 85287

LIGHTFORD, KIMBERLY A. state legislator; BA in Pub. Comm., Western Ill. U.; MPA, U. Ill., Springfield. Mem. Ill. Senate, Springfield, 1998—. Elected chair Ill. Senate Black Caucus, chair fin. instns., vice-chair edn.; former trustee Village of Maywood. Democrat. Office: State Capitol 218 Capitol Bldg Springfield IL 62706-0001 also: 1127 S Mannheim Rd Ste 114 Westchester IL 60154

LIGHTMAN, MARJORIE, historian; b. NYC, Aug. 6, 1940; d. Earl Rivkin and Ida Ola Friedman; m. Benjamin Lightman, Sept. 6, 1959; children: Andrew, Timothy, Suzanne. BA, CUNY, 1961, MA, 1969; PhD, Rutgers U., 1980. Exec. dir. Inst. Rsch. in History, NYC, 1975—88; founding ptnr. QED Assocs., Teaneck, NJ, 1988—; co-founder Women's Working Group Internat. Human Rights, Washington, 1994—95; leader del. Internat. League Human Rights, Vienna, 1994, Beijing, 1995, Geneva, 1996, 2002, rep. to UN commn. NYC, 1995—97. Treas. Nat. Coun. Rsch. Women, NYC, 1983—85; commr. Nat. Commn. Women Higher Edn., NYC, 1983—85; cons. Network East/West Women, 1992—94; organizer book exhibit Inst. Rsch. History, 1985. Co-author: Ellis Island and the Peopling of America, 1997 (Official Guide to the Ellis Island Mus., 1997); co-editor: Outside Academe: New Ways of Working in the Humanities, 1979; co-author: A Biographical Dictionary of Ancient Greek and Roman Women, 1999; co-editor: Without Precedent: The Life and Career of Eleanor Roosevelt, 1985. Tester Fair Housing, Bergen County, 1967; co-founder Feminist Action Coalition of Teaneck, NJ, 1973—76; founding bd. advisors Lang Coll., NYC, 1984—86; chair panel scholars Sewall-Belmont House Mus., Washington, 2000—02; bd. dirs. Women's Interart Ctr., NYC, 1985—88, Ctr. Ethics and Action, U. New Eng., Maine, 2001—, Feminist Press, CUNY, NYC, 2003—. Ford Found. grantee, Inst. Rsch. History, 1979, 1982, Nat. Endowment Humanities grantee, 1982, Rockefeller Found. grantee, 1985, 2002, Sr. fellow, Women's Rsch. Edn. Inst., 2002—. Home: 2737 Devonshire Pl NW Washington DC 20008 Office: QED Assocs PO Box 899 Teaneck NJ 07666 also: WREI 1750 New York Ave Washington DC 20006

LIGHTNER, CANDACE LYNNE, nonprofit management consultant, advocate; b. Pasadena, Calif., May 30, 1946; d. Dykes Charles and Kathryn Josephine Doddridge; children: Serena, Travis. D (hon.), St. Francis Coll., Pa., 1984, Kutztown (Pa.) U., 1987, Marymount U., N.Y., 1987. With various pvt. offices, 1964-70; real estate salesperson, 1972-80; govt. rels. cons., 1993-94; owner Candace Lightner & Assocs., Alexandria, Va. Spkr., condr. tng. sessions various orgns. Author: Giving Sorrow Words: How to Cope With Grief and Get On With Your Life, 1990; guest nat. talk shows including Good Morning America, Today, 60 Minutes, MacNeil-Lehrer, Phil Donahue, Nightline, Turning Point. Founder MADD, 1980, chief exec. officer, pres., chmn., 1980-85; mem. adv. bd. Mothers Against Sexual Abuse; bd. dirs. Air Crash Support Network; active Sacramento County Task Force on Drunk Driving, Presdl. Commn. on Drunk and Drugged Driving; bd. dirs. Nat. Commn. on Drunk Driving, 1984-86, Nat. Partnership for Drug Free Use, Nat. Hwy. Safety Adv. Com., Love is Feeding Everyone, 1988-89, others; judge Gleitsman Found.; bd. advisors Bhopal Justice Campaign. Recipient Jefferson award Am. Inst. Pub. Svc., Pres. Vol. Action award, Woman of Yr. award YWCA, Woman of Yr. award Women's Internat. Ctr., award for excellence Film Adv. Bd., Testimonial award Civitan Internat., 1984, Epilepsy Found award, 1984, Woman of Year award Mortar Bd. Soc., Baylor U., 1985, Anti-discriminationaward Am. Anti descrimination Com., 1985, YWCA Woman of Year award, 1986, Commonwealth award U. Del., 1986, Black and Blue award Thomas Jefferson U. Hosp. Emergency Medicine Soc., Human Dignity award Kessler Inst. for Rehab., Woman of Distinction award Third Nat. Congress Coll. Women Student Leaders and Woman of Achievement, 1987, Disting. Leadership award World Congress of Victimology, 1987, Living Legacy award Women's Internat. Ctr., 1988, Friends of Children award Assn. Childhood Edn. Internat., 1988; Named to Good Housekeeping's Most Admired Woman's Poll, 1986; ranked in Top 25 of Am. most influential people World Almanac and Book of Facts, 1986, one of the original thinkers of the eighties, Life mag., 1990; selected by Johns Hopkins U. to participate in Anglo-Am. Successor Generation program, 1985; honored as one of Seven Who Succeeded, Time Mag., 1985; honored by Edquire mag. as mem. Am.'s New Leadership Class, 1985, others. Mem. Nat. Soc. Fund Raising Execs., Women in Arts, Nat. Bd. Realtors. Avocations: gardening, reading, swimming, traveling. Office: 1216 Portner Rd Alexandria VA 22314-1317 E-mail: cd_light2003@yahoo.com.

LIGHTNER, JANET (JAN) ANDERSON, information technology manager, consultant, writer; b. Wilsonville, Nebr., Mar. 2, 1939; d. Arlo Albert Anderson and Lilia Leahnora Critchfield-Anderson; m. Gene E. Lightner, July 2, 1966; children: Robert Bruce, Jill Ann. BSc, U. Nebr., 1961, MA, 1965. MCSE. Tng. coord. Lightner Assocs., Federal Way, Wash., 1985—90, Lane Powell Spears Lubersky, Seattle, 1995—98; exec. dir. Eton Tech. Inst., Federal Way, 1990—95; trainer, writer, project mgr. Payne Consulting Group, Seattle, 1998—2001; sr. tech. trainer Perkins Coie LLP, Seattle, 2001—. Scholarship chair, bd. dirs. Wash. Cornhuskers, Seattle, 2000—. Bd. dirs. Atlantic St. Ctr., Seattle, 1985—88; pres. bd. dirs. Federal Way Libr., 1990—92; South King County coord. Perot for Pres., Wash., 1996; mem. Com. to Reelect Jeanne Burbidge, Federal Way. Nebr. Regents scholar, U. Nebr., 1957—61. Mem.: Alpha Xi Delta (life; nat. membership v.p. 1980—82, sec. Alpha Xi Delta Found. 1978—80, Edna Epperson Brinkman award 1975). Independent. Avocations: travel, cross country skiing, Cornhusker football/volleyball/softball, reading, digital photography. Home: 706 SW 296th St Federal Way WA 98023-3549 Office: Perkins Coie LLP 1201 Third Ave Seattle WA 98101-3099 Business E-Mail: jlightner@perkinscoie.com.

LIGOCKI, KATHLEEN A. auto parts company executive; Dir. bus. strategy Ford Motor Co., 1998—2000, pres., 2000—01, corp. v.p. Can., Mex. and N.Am. strategy, 2001—02; corp. officer, v.p. Ford Customer Svc. Divsn., 2002—03; v.p. N.Am. mktg. Ford Moror Co., 2002; dir. Tower Automotive, Inc., Haggerty, Mich., 2003—, pres., CEO, 2003—. Office: Tower Automotive Inc 27175 Haggerty Rd Novi MI 48377

LIGONDE-MINOR, GINA, social worker, consultant; d. Edner B. and Gisele Ligonde; m. Aaron E.D. Minor, Feb. 7, 2003. BA, W.Va. U., Morgantown, 1991—95; MSW, U. Pitts., 1997—99. LCSW N.Y. Dept. Edn., 2002, lic. Nat. Assn. Social Workers; cert. Notary Public N.Y. Dept. State, 2003. Sr. social worker, cons. Spring Valley Ch. of God, NY, 1999—, notary pub., 2003—. Mem. United Odd Fellow & Rebekah Lodge, Bronx, NY. Adminstrv. asst. Spring Valley Ch. of God, NY, 1999. Mem.: NAFE, NASW, Zeta Phi Beta. Democrat. Pentecostal. Avocations: travel, music, art. Home: 13 E Church St Spring Valley NY 10977 Office: Spring Valley Church of God 13 E Church St Spring Valley NY 10977 E-mail: gligonde@yahoo.com.

LIHS, MARILYN LOUISE, retired accountant; b. Burlington, Iowa, May 5, 1941; d. Omer C. and Geraldine E. (Berges) Wickerham; m. Craig E. Lihs, Mar. 26, 1961; children: Jeffrey A., Michael S. AA, S.E. Iowa C.C., Burlington, 1961; BBA, U. Iowa, 1986, MBA, 1991. Ch. organist Mil. Chapel, Bremerhaven, Germany, 1966-68; accts. payable clk. City of Burlington, 1968-71; accts. recieveable clk. Economy Advt., Iowa City, 1971-74; office mgr. Shay Electric, Iowa City, 1974-76; contr. Midwest Elect. Cont., Iowa City, 1976-82; from adminstrv. asst. to fin. analyst U. Iowa, Iowa City, 1982-86, adminstrv. acct., 1986-98, ret., 1998. Contbr. articles to Iowa Bus. Woman Mag. Pres. Bus. and Profl. Women Iowa Found., Des Moines, 1995—96; program facilitator Iowa City Cable TV, 1997; rep., com. chair U. Iowa Staff Coun., 1991—97; v.p. Village United Meth. Women, 2000—02, pres., 2002—03. Mem. AAUW, Bus. and Profl. Women (Iowa pres. 1995-96, Iowa City pres. 1997-98, newsletter editor 1997-99, Woman of Yr. 1995-96, 98-99, Spa Area Woman of Yr. 2001-2002), U. Iowa Alumni Assn. (life), Village Quilt Guild (pres. 2000-01). Democrat. Methodist. Avocations: travel, quilting, writing, genealogy. Home: 62 Promesa Dr Hot Springs Village AR 71909-7757 E-mail: MarilynLihs@netscape.net.

LIKINS, ROSE MARIE, foreign service officer; b. Andrews AFB, Md., Jan. 22, 1959; d. Eugene Aloysius and Merlyn (Houghland) McCartney; m. John Foster Likins, MAy 30, 1981; children: James, Kevin. BA in Internat. Affairs, BA in Spanish, Mary Washington Coll., Fredericksburg, Va., 1981. Joined Fgn. Svc., U.S. Dept. State, Washington, 1981—, previous fgn. svc. assignments, U.S. amb. to El Salvador, 2000—03. Rm. mother Tuckahoe

Elem. Sch., Arlington, Va., 1993-94. Mem. Am. Fgn. Svc. Assn., Mortar Board (pres. chpt. 1980-81), Phi Beta Kappa. Roman Catholic. Achievements include fluent in Spanish and Bulgarian.*

LILLESTOL, JANE BRUSH, development consultant; b. Jamestown, N.D., July 20, 1926; d. Harper J. and Doris (Mikkelson) Brush; m. Harvey Lillestol, Sept. 29, 1956; children: Kim, Kevin, Erik. BS, U. Minn., 1969, MS, 1973, PhD, 1977; grad. Inst. Ednl. Mgmt., Harvard U., 1984. Dir. placement, asst. to dean U. Minn., St. Paul, 1975-77; assoc. dean, dir. student acad. affairs N.D. State U., Fargo, 1977-80; dean Coll. Human Devel. Syracuse (N.Y.) U., 1980-89, v.p. for alumni rels., 1989-95, project dir. IBM Computer Aided Design Lab., 1989—92; prin. Lillestol Assocs.; emeritus faculty Syracuse (N.Y.) U., 1995—; faculty U. Phoenix, 2002—. Charter mem. Mayor's Commn. on Women, 1986-90; NAFTA White House Conf. for Women Leaders, 1993; faculty, U. Phoenix Online, 2002—, curriculum devel. specialist, 2003. Bd. dirs. Univ. Hill Corp. Syracuse, 1983-93; mem. steering com. Consortium for Cultural Founds. of Medicine, 1980-89; trustee Manlius Pebble Hill Sch., 1990-94, Archbold Theatre, 1990-95, N.D. State U., 1992—. Recipient award U.S. Consumer Product Safety Commn., 1983, Woman of Yr. award AAUW, 1984, svc. award Syracuse U., 1992; named among 100 Outstanding Alumni Over Past 100 Yrs., U. Minn. Coll. Human Ecology, 2001. Office: 8046 E Via De Los Libros Scottsdale AZ 85258-3056 E-mail: jane@lillestol.com.

LILLEY, MILI DELLA, insurance company executive, entertainment management consultant; b. Valley Forge, Pa., Aug. 29; d. Leon Hanover and Della Beaver (Jones) L. MBA, Tex. Christian U., 1957, PhD, 1959. Various positions G & G Cons. Inc., Ft. Lauderdale, Fla., 1971-75; v.p. AMEX, Inc., Beverly Hills, Calif. and Acapulco, Mex., 1976-80; pres. The Hanover Group, Ft. Lauderdale, 1981—; personal and bus. mgr. entertainers including Ink Spots, Ft. Lauderdale, 1984—, Lanny Poffo, Ft. Lauderdale, 1990—. Dist. agt. ITT Life Ins. Corp., also other leading cos. Named to All Stars Honor Roll Nat. Ins. Sales Mag., 1989. Mem. Fla. Assn. Theatrical Agents, Fla. Guild of Talent Agts., Mgrs., Producers and Orchestras. Office: The Hanover Group PO Box 70218 Fort Lauderdale FL 33307-0218 Office Phone: 954-491-1101.

LILLIE, CHARISSE RANIELLE, lawyer, educator; b. Houston, Apr. 7, 1952; d. Richard Lysander and Vernell Audrey (Watson) Lillie; m. Thomas L. McGill Jr., Dec. 4, 1982. BA cum laude, Conn. Wesleyan U., 1973; JD, Temple U., 1976; LLM, Yale U., 1982. Bar: Pa. 1976, U.S. Dt. Ct. (ea. dist.) Pa. 1977, U.S. Ct. Appeals (3d cir.) 1980. Law clk. U.S. Dist. Ct. (ea. dist.) Pa., Phila., 1976-78; trial atty., honors program, civil rights divsn. Dept. Justice, Washington, 1978-80; dep. dir. Cmty. Legal Svcs., Phila., 1980-81; asst. prof. law Villanova U. Law Sch., Pa., 1982-83, assoc. prof., 1983-84, prof., 1984-85; asst. U.S. atty. U.S. Dist. Ct. (ea. dist.) Pa., Phila., 1985-88; with Redevel. Authority of Phila., 1988-90; city solicitor law dept. City of Phila., 1990-92; chair litigation dept. Ballard, Spahr, Andrew & Ingersoll LLP, Phila., 2002—, also. bd. dirs. Mem. 3d Cir. Lawyers Adv. Com., 1982—85; legal counsel Pa. Coalition of 100 Black Women, Phila., 1983—88; bd. dirs. Juvenile Law Ctr., Phila., Pa. Intergovtl. Coop. Authority, Fed. Res. Bank Phila., dep. chmn. bd. dirs., 1998—2000, chmn. bd. dirs., 2001—02; commr. Phila. Ind. City Charter Commn., 1991—94; trustee Women's Law Project, Phila., 1984—90; mem. Mayor's Commn. on May 13 MOVE Incident, 1985—86; mem. com. on racial and gender bias in the justice sys. Supreme Ct. Pa., 1999—. Bd. dirs. Leadership Inc.; mem. adv. com. Women's Way, Phila., 1986—. Named One of Phila.'s Most Influential African Americans, Phila. Tribune, 2002, 2003, One of Top Three Phila. Labor Mgmt. Attys., Phila. Mag., 1994, 1999; named to the Women's Hall of Fame, Southwest Belmont Cmty. Assn., 2002; recipient Equal Justice award, Cmty. Legal Svcs., Inc., 1991, Outstanding Alumna award, Wesleyan U., 1993, Elizabeth Dole Glass Ceiling award, ARC, Phila. chpt., 1994, Whitney Young Leadership award, Phila. Urban League, 1996, Take the Lead award, U.S. Girl Scouts, 2002, Women of Distinction award, Phila. Bus. Jour., 2002, Penn Towne Links Svc. award, 2002, Image award, Black Women in Sport Found., 2002, J. Michael Brown award, DuPont Minority Counsel Conf., 2002, Bd. Dirs. Hall of Fame award, Teenshop, 2002, Mother of Yr., Mary Mason Cmty. Found., 2002, Women of Achievement award, The Barristers' Assn., 2002, Awards of Excellence, The Thurgood Marshall Scholarship Fund, Inc., 2003; fellow Davenport fellow, 1973, Yale Sch. fellow, 1981. Mem.: ABA (vice chmn. commn. on ethnic diversity in the professio 1997—99, chmn. commn. on ethnic diversity in the professio 1999—2002, mem. standing com. on fed. jud. 2002—), Hist. Soc. U.S. Dist. Ct. (ea. dist.) Pa. (dir. 1983—87), Phila. Bar Assn. (vice chair bd. govs. 1994, chair bd. govs. 1995—96), Barristers Assn. (J. Austin Norris award 1983—87), Am. Law Inst., Nat. Conf. Black Lawyers (pres. 1970), Fed. Bar Assn. (1st v.p. Phila. chpt. 1982—84, pres. Phila. chpt. 1984—86, 3d cir. rep. 1991—), Nat. Bar Assn. Home: 7000 Emlen St Philadelphia PA 19119-2556 Office: Ballard Spahr Andrews Ingersoll 1735 Market St Fl 51 Philadelphia PA 19103-7599

LILLY, ELIZABETH GILES, small business owner; b. Bozeman, Mont., Aug. 5, 1916; d. Samuel John and Luella Elizabeth (Reed) Abegg; m. William Lilly, July 1, 1976; children: Samuel Colborn Giles, Elizabeth Giles. RN, Good Samaritan Hosp., Portland, Oreg., 1941; student, Walla Walla Coll., Lewis and Clark Coll. Bus., Portland. ARC nurse, tchr. area high schs., Portland; owner Welton Studio Interior Design, Portland; in pub. rels. Chas. Eckelman, Portland, Fairview Farms-Dairy Industry; owner, builder Mobile Park Plaza, Inc., Portland. Del. platform planning com. Rep. Party; mem. Sunnyside Seventh Day Adventist Ch., deaconess. Recipient Svc. award Multnomah County Commrs., 1984. Mem. Soroptimist Internat. (local bd. dirs., bd. dirs. Women in Transition), Rep. Women's Club (pres.), C. of C., World Affairs Coun., Toastmistress (pres.), Oreg. Lodging Assn. (pres. bd. dirs.), Rep. Inner Circle (life). Address: 19825 SE Stark St Portland OR 97233-6039

LILLY, KRISTINE MARIE, professional soccer player; b. Wilton, Conn., July 27, 1971; BA in Comm., U. N.C., 1993. Midfielder U.S. Women's Nat. Soccer Team, Chgo., 1987—; profl. soccer player Boston Breakers, 2001—03. Named Most Valuable Offensive Player, NCAA Championship, 1989, 1991, MVP, U.S. Women's World Cup, 1991, U.S. Soccer's Female Athlete of Yr., 1993, MVP, U.S. Women's World Cup, 1999, U.S. Nat. Team All-Time Appearance Leader (more than 90 games); named to, World Cup Championship Team, 1999; recipient Hemann Trophy, 1991, Gold medal, Centennial Olympic Games, 1996, Silver medal, Sydney Olympic Games, 2000. Achievements include member FIFA Women's World Championship Team, 1991; member World Cup Team, 1999; member U. N.C. NCAA National Championship Teams, 1989-92. Office: US Soccer Fedn 1801 S Prairie Ave Chicago IL 60616-1319

LILLY, LUELLA JEAN, academic administrator; b. Newberg, Oreg., Aug. 23, 1937; d. David Hardy and Edith (Coleman) L. BS, Lewis and Clark Coll., 1959; postgrad., Portland State U., 1959-61; MS, U. Oreg., 1961; PhD, Tex. Woman's U., 1971; postgrad., various univs., 1959-72. Tchr. phys. edn. and health, dean girls Cen. Linn Jr.-Sr. High Sch., Halsey, Oreg., 1959-60; tchr. phys. edn. and health, swimming, tennis, golf coach Lake Oswego (Oreg.) High Sch., 1960-63; instr., intramural dir., coach Oreg. State U., Corvallis, 1963-64; instr., intercollegiate coach Am. River Coll., Sacramento, 1964-69; dir. women's phys. edn., athletics U. Nev., Reno, 1969-73, assoc. prof. phys. edn., 1971-76, dir. women's athletics, 1973-75, assoc. dir. athletics, 1975-76; dir. women's intercollegiate athletics U. Calif., Berkeley, 1976-97. Organizer, coach Lue's Aquatic Club, 1962-64; v.p. PAC-10 Conf., 1990-91. Author: An Overview of Body Mechanics, 1966, 3d rev. edit., 1969. Vol. instr. ARC, 1951; vol. Heart Fund and Easter Seal, 1974-76, Am. Heart Assn., 1991-95, ofcl. Spl. Olympics, 1975; mem. L.A. Citizens Olympic Com., 1984; bd. dirs. Las Trampas, 1993-98, sec. 1996-98; v.p. Multiple Sclerosis Soc., 1999-2003. Recipient Mayor Anne Rudin award Nat. Girls' and Women's Sports, 1993, Lifetime Sports award Bay Area Women's Sports Found., 1994, Golden Bear award Vol. of Yr., 1995; inducted Lewis and Clark Coll. Athletic Hall of Fame, 1988; named to U. Calif. First 125 Yrs. Women of Honor, 1995 Mem. AAHPER (life), AAUW, Nat. Soc. Profs., Women's Sports Found. (awards com. 1994-2000), Nat. Assn. Coll. Women Athletic Adminstrs. (divsn. I-A women's steering com. 1991-92, Lifetime Achievement award 1999), Women's Athletic Caucus, Coun. Collegiate Women Athletics Adminstrs. (membership com. 1989-92), Western Soc. Phys. Edn. Coll. Women (membership com. 1971-74, program adv. com. 1972, exec. bd. 1972-75), Western Assn. Intercollegiate Athletics for Women (exec. bd. dirs. 1973-75, 79-82), Oreg. Girls' Swimming Coaches Assn. (pres. 1960, 63), Ctrl. Calif. Bd. Women Ofcls. (basketball chmn. 1968-69), Calif. Assn. Health, Phys. Edn. and Recreation (chmn.-elect jr. coll. sect. 1970), Nev. Bd. Women Ofcls. (chmn. bd., chmn. volleyball sect., chmn. basketball sect. 1969), No. Calif. Women's Intercollegiate Conf. (sec. 1970-71, basketball coord. 1970-71), No. Calif. Intercollegiate Athletic Conf. (volleyball coord. 1971-72), Nev. Assn. Health Phys. Edn. and Recreation (state chmn. 1974), No. Calif. Athletic Conf. (pres. 1979-82, sec. 1984-85), Soroptimists Club (bd. dirs. 1988-02, 2000-2003, v.p. 1989, 92-93, sec. 1993-95, 2001-02, 1st v.p. 1996-97, corr. sec. 1997-98, pres. 1998-2000, Women Helping Women award 1991, Women of Distinction award 2002), Phi Kappa Phi, Theta Kappa. Avocation: Held Am. records in swimming, 1950's. Home and Office: 60 Margrave Ct Walnut Creek CA 94597-2511 Office Phone: 925-934-3868.

LILYQUIST, CANDACE LOUISE, labor union administrator; b. Longville, Minn., Mar. 21, 1968; d. Clinton Russell and Marilyn Louise Lilyquist. BA, Concordia Coll., 1990. Tchr. Cameron Elem. Sch., Odessa, Tex., 1990—92, Cass Lake (Minn.)-Bena Pub. Schs., 1992—98; union rep. Edn. Minn., St. Paul, 1998—. Dir. 5th Senate Dist. DFL, Hibbing, Minn., 1999—2001. Mem.: TEMPO Union (v.p. 1998—), LWV, AAUW (pub. policy chair 2002—03). Lutheran. Avocations: reading, yoga, gardening, hunting. Office: Edn Minn 1711 13th St E Hibbing MN 55746

LIM, JEANETTE J. federal agency administrator; b. July 23, 1940; BS in chem., U. Mich., 1962; M in med. genetics, U. Wis. Med. Sch., 1965; JD, Temple U. Law Sch., 1978. Dep. asst. sec. US Dept Edn., Mgmt. and operations, Wash., 2002—; atty. US Dept. Edn., Off. Civil Rights, Wash., acting asst. sec, 1992—93, 2000—01; spec. asst. to pres. Wes Chester State U., Pa., 1976—79; med. geneticist; rschr. and bench scientist. Office: US Dept Edn Mgmt and Operations 400 Maryland Ave SW FOB-6 Rm 3W314 Washington DC 20202 E-mail: jeanette.lim@ed.gov.

LIMA, CHARLENE, state legislator; b. Providence, Aug. 18, 1953; BA, U. R.I., 1975; student, R.I. Coll., 1979. Tchr. Providence Pub. Schs.; rep. dist. 14 R.I. Ho. of Reps., Providence, 1992—. Mem. health, edn. and welfare coms. R.I. Ho. of Reps., mem. separation of powers com., mem. dist. 14 coms., and women's legis. caucus. Office: State House Providence RI 02903

LIMACHER, MARIAN CECILE, cardiologist; b. Joliet, Ill., May 4, 1952; d. Joseph John and Shirley A. (Smith) L.; m. Timothy C. Flynn, May 17, 1980; children: Mary Katherine Flynn, Brian Patrick Flynn. AB in Chemistry, St. Louis U., 1973, MD, 1977. Diplomate Am. Bd. Internal Medicine, Am. Bd. Cardiovascular Diseases. Resident in internal medicine Baylor Coll. Medicine, Houston, 1977-80, cardiology fellow, 1980-83, instr. medicine, 1983-84; dir. cardiology non-invasive labs. Ben Taub Hosp., Houston, 1983-84; asst. prof. medicine U. Fla., Gainesville, 1984-91, assoc. prof., 1991-97, prof., 1997—; dir. non-invasive labs. Gainesville VA Med. Ctr., 1984-99, chief cardiology, 1995-99. Dir. preventive cardiology program U. Fla., 1987—. Author (with others): Cardiac Transplantation: A Manual for Health Care Professionals, 1990, Geriatric Cardiology, 1992, The Role of Food in Sickness and in Health, 1993, Clinical Anesthesia Practice, 1994, Primary Care, 1994; mem. editl. bd.: Clin. Cardiology, 1990—, Preventive Cardiology, 1997—, assoc. editor: Jour. Watch Women's Health, 2001—, Clin. Jour. Women's Health, 2001; contbr. articles to profl. jours. Mem. bioethics commn. Diocese of St. Augustine, Jacksonville, Fla., 1990-94. Recipient Preventive Cardiology Acad. award NIH, 1987-92; grantee for Women's Health Initiative, NIH, 1994—. Fellow: ACP, Soc. Geriatric Cardiology (bd. dirs. 1997—, pres. 2002), Am. Coll. Cardiology (chair com. women cardiology 1998—2002, trustee 1999—2004); mem.: Am. Heart Assn. (pres. Alachua County divsn. 1986—89, fellow coun. clin. cardiology, bd. dirs.), Am. Soc. Preventive Cardiology (pres. 1998). Roman Catholic. Avocations: tennis, jogging, snow skiing, playing piano. Office: U Fla Coll Medicine PO Box 100277 Gainesville FL 32610-0277

LIMAN, JOAN PAMELA, university dean; BA in Psychology magna cum laude, SUNY, Buffalo, 1970; student, Columbia U., 1977-79, Hunter Coll., 1974-76; MD, N.Y. Med Coll., 1983, MPH, 1993. Resident in pathology Lenox Hill Hosp., N.Y.C., 1983; instr. cmty. and preventive medicine N.Y. Med. Coll., Valhalla, 1987-92, assoc. dean for med. edn., 1989-92; instr. preventive medicine and cmty. health UMDNJ-N.J. Med. Sch., 1994-97, assoc. dean for student affairs, 1993—, adj. instr. preventive medicine and cmty. health, 1997—. Chair grad. edn. com. N.E. group on student affairs Am. Assn. Med. Colls., 1998—. Contbr. articles to profl. jours. Bd. dirs. YM-YWHA of Bergen County, N.J., 1988-91. Named hon. alumnae N.J. Med. Sch. Alumni Assn., 1999—. Mem. AMA, Women's Med. Assn. N.Y., Phi Beta Kappa, Sigma Xi, Alpha Omega Alpha. Office: UMDNJ-NJ Med Sch Office of Student Affairs 185 S Orange Ave Rm C-642 Newark NJ 07103-2757 E-mail: liman@umdnj.edu.

LIMBACH, BARBARA JUNE, management educator; b. Crawford, Nebr., June 29, 1958; d. William Bruce and Joann (Whipple) Corbin; m. Robert S. Limbach, Aug. 6, 1977; children: Zachary, Zane, Zalie. B, Chadron State Coll., 1979, M, 1985, specialist, 1992; PhD, U. Wyo., 1994. Loan officer Occidental Nebr. Fed. Sav. Bank, Crawford, 1981-86; instr., registrar Chadron (Nebr.) State Coll., 1987-92, prof., 2004. Chair self-study com. North Ctrl. Accreditation, Chadron, 1995—. Mem. editl. bd. Collegiate Press, 1994. Mem. parish coun. St. John's Cath. Ch., Crawford, 1992—; sec.-treas. Music Boosters, Crawford, 1995—. Mem. NEA, AAUW, Nat. Bus. Edn. Assn. (presenter 1995), Nebr. State Edn. Assn. (treas. 1996—), Chadron State Edn. Assn. (treas. 1992-96, pres. 1997-98), Phi Delta Kappa (sec. 1998—). Avocations: sports spectator, tole painting, reading, exercising. Office: Chadron State Coll 1000 Main St Chadron NE 69337-2667 Home: 1016 2nd St Crawford NE 69339-1228

LIMBACK, E(DNA) REBECCA, vocational education educator; b. Higginsville, Mo., Mar. 23, 1945; d. Henry Shobe and Martha Pauline Rebecca (Willard) Ernstmeyer; m. Duane Paul Limback, Nov. 9, 1963; children: Lisa Christine, Derek Duane. BE, Cen. Mo. State U., 1968, MEd, 1969, EdS, 1976; EdD, U. Mo., 1981. Cert. bus., English and vocat. tchr. Supervising tchr. Lab. Sch. Ctrl. Mo. State U., Warrensburg, 1969-76, asst. to grad. dean, 1977-79, asst. prof., asst. to bus. dean, 1981-83, assoc. prof. computer and office info. systems, 1984-95, 1986-95, prof. computer and office info. sys., 1996—2003, prof. emeritus, 2003—. Mem. manual editing/revision staff State of Mo., Jefferson City, 1989-90; textbook reviewer Prentice-Hall, Englewood Cliffs, N.J., 1990-91. Author various curriculum guides; mem. editl. bd. Cen. Mo. State U. Rsch., 1982-92. Recipient Mo. Gov.'s Excellence in Tchg. award, 2001; grantee, RightSoft Corp., 1988. Mem. DAR, Nat. Bus. Edn. Assn. (conf. profl. opportunities com. 1989-99, info. processing editor Bus. Edn. Forum 1991), Assn. Career and Tech. Edn., North Cen. Bus. Edn. Assn. (Mo. rep., Collegiate Disting. Svc. award 1993), Mo. Bus. Edn. Assn. (all-chpt. pres. 1988-89, chair strategic planning com. 1999—, Postsecondary Tchr. of Yr. 1992), Assn. Bus. Comms., Mid-Mo. Artists, Phi Delta Kappa (all-chpt. pres. 1985), Delta Pi Epsilon (rsch. rep. 1989-92, nat. publs. com. 1993—). Lutheran. Avocations: archaeology, painting, photography, fishing. Home: 1102 Tyler Ave Warrensburg MO 64093-2040 Office: Dockery 200 D/COIS Dept Cent Mo State U Warrensburg MO 64093 E-mail: rlimback@iland.net.

LIMERICK, PATRICIA NELSON, history educator; b. Banning, Calif., May 17, 1951; BA, U. Calif., Santa Cruz, 1972; PhD, Yale, 1980. Prof. history dept. U. Colo., Boulder. Chmn. bd. dirs. Ctr. Am. West. Author: (books) Desert Passages: Encounters With the American Deserts, 1985, The Legacy of Conquest: The Unbroken Past of the American West, 1987, Something in the Soil: Legacies and Reckonings in the New West, 2000. MacArthur fellow, 1995. Office: U Colo Ctr Am West MAcky 229 282 UCB Boulder CO 80309 E-mail: patricia.limerick@colorado.edu.

LIMMROTH, KARIN LEIGH, international producer, television correspondent; b. New Orleans, Tex., Oct. 4, 1949; d. Weldon Eugene and Cora Elizabeth (Graby) L. BA, So. Meth. U., 1969; BFA, Sch. Visual Arts, N.Y.C., 1970. Designer, assoc. art dir. Essence mag., N.Y.C., 1973-74; designer RCA Records, N.Y.C., 1970-72; asst. art dir. Seventeen mag., N.Y.C., 1970-72; designer CBS Records, N.Y.C., 1974-75, Fantasy Records & Filmworks, Berkeley, Calif., 1975-76; asst. art dir., set designer CBS TV, L.A., 1979-81; art dir. CBS News, N.Y.C., 1981-83, CBS Entertainment, L.A., 1981-83; art dir., design cons. Ogilvy & Mather, N.Y.C., L.A., 1983-87; assoc. creative dir. E&J Gallo Winery, Modesto, Calif., 1987-89; dir. Image Assocs., Paris and N.Y.C., 1989—; mktg. cons. U.S. Embassy, Paris, 1991—. Design cons. San Francisco Opera, 1975-76, U.S. Olympic Com., Boulder, Colo., 1978-79, Internat. Olympic Com., Barcelona, Spain, 1989—; art dir., design cons. Ogilvy & Mather, N.Y.C. and L.A., Young & Rubicom, L.A., Saatchi & Saatchi/Compton, N.Y.C., Scali McCabe Sloves, N.Y.C., 1983-87; field prodr.-dir. VOX-TV, Germany, 1993—. Co-star talk show La 5 TV, Paris, 1990-92; European corr./prodr. City-TV show MediaTV (seen in 68 countries), 1992—; European music corr. BET Network (USA), 1993-95; French corr. NBC Super Channel, 1993-94, RTL-TV Germany, 1994—, Worldwide TV News, 1995-98; field prodr./dir. Nat. Geog. TV Explorer; field prodr. NBC Access Hollywood, 1996—, CNN, 1998—; dir. Euroshoots, Internat. TV Prod. Co., 1999—. Fundraiser Martha Graham Dance Co., N.Y.C., 1985, Amnesty Internat., Paris, 1989. Recipient award N.Y. Art Dirs. Club, 1977-78; nomination Internat. Emmy, 1993, N.Y. Festival, 1993. Mem. NARAS (bd. dirs. 1976-78, Grammy nomination 1973, Internat. Emmy nomination 1993, N.Y. Festival nomination 1993), Am. Film Inst. (art direction fellow 1976, 77), Am. Inst. Graphics Arts, La Maison des Artists (France), Women in Film), Anglo-am. Press Assoc. (Paris). Avocation: skiing. Home: 29 King St New York NY 10014-4966 Office Phone: 212-243-1180. E-mail: karin@euroshoots.com.

LIMON, LAVINIA, social services administrator; b. Compton, Calif., Mar. 5, 1950; d. Peter T. and Marie W. Limon; m. Mohamad Hanon. BA in Sociology, U. Calif., Berkeley, 1972. Asst. dir., office mgr. Ch. World Svc., Camp Pendleton, Calif., 1975-77; chief Vietnamese refugee sect. Internat. Rescue Com., Bangkok, 1977-79, dir. L.A., 1983-86, 1983-86; asst. dir. ops. Am. Coun. for Nationalities Svcs., L.A., 1979-83; exec. dir. Internat. Inst., L.A., 1986-93; dir. office refugee resettlement and office family assistance Adminstrn. for Children and Families Dept. HHS, Washington, 1993-98, dir. office refugee resettlement, 1998—. Bd. dirs. Am. Coun. for Nationalities Svc., 1992, chair standing com. of profl. coun., 1992; organizer U.S. refugee conf. Am. Coun. Vol. Agys., Manila, 1982; cons. Dept. of State, 1979, 80. Mem. bd. human rels. hate violence response alliance City of L.A., 1992; chair corp. coun. execs. United Way of L.A., 1992, mem. task force fund on devel., 1990; mem. citizen's adv. com. Eastside Neighborhoods Revitilazation Study, 1992; mem. steering com. Coalition for Humane Immigration Rights of L.A., 1992; mem. steering com. Jerusalem Coop. Cities Project, 1991; chair Refugee Forum L.A. County, 1984-85, chair vol. agy. com., 1983-84; treas. Calif. Refugee Forum, 1985-86. Democrat. Home: 309 Yoakum Pkwy Apt 608 Alexandria VA 22304-3931 Office: Refugee Resettlement Office 370 Lenfant Plz SW Washington DC 20447-0001

LIN, ALICE LEE LAN, physicist, researcher, educator; b. Shanghai, Oct. 28, 1937; came to U.S., 1960, naturalized, 1974; m. A. Marcus, Dec. 19, 1962 (div. Feb. 1972); 1 child, Peter A. AB in Physics, U. Calif., Berkeley, 1963; MA in Physics, George Washington U., 1974. Statis. asst. dept. math. U. Calif., Berkeley, Calif., 1961-63; rsch. asst. in radiation damage Cavendish Lab. Cambridge U., England, 1965-66; info. analysis specialist Nat. Acad. Sci., Washington, 1970-71; tchng. fellow, rsch. asst. George Washington U., Cath. U. Am., Washington, 1971-75; physicist NASA /Goddard Space Flight Ctr., Greenbelt, Md., 1975-80, Army Materials Tech. Lab., Watertown, Mass., 1980—. Contbr. articles to profl. jours. Mencius Ednl. Found. grantee, 1959-60. Mem. AAAS, N.Y. Acad. Scis., Am. Phys. Soc., Am. Ceramics Soc., Am. Acoustical Soc., Am. Men and Women of Sci., Optical Soc. Am. Democrat. Avocations: rare stamp and coin collecting, art collectibles, home computers, opera, ballet. Home: 28 Hallett Hill Rd Weston MA 02493-1753 Office Phone: 781-899-6751.

LIN, AMY YUH-MEI, industrial engineer, real estate investor; b. Chuang-Hua, Taiwan, Jan. 22, 1948; Came to U.S., 1973; d. Tu-To and Show-Lan (Wu) Tsai; m. Edward Yih-Ling Lin, Dec. 24, 1975; children: Shirley, Kenneth. BSBA, Cheng Kung U., Taiwan, 1971; MS in Indsl. Engring., W.Va. U., 1975. Supr. Yellow Springs (Ohio) Instrument Corp., 1977-78; indsl. engr. MSI Data Corp., Costa Mesa, Calif., 1978-79; sr. programmer, analyst MAI Basic Four Corp., Tustin, Calif., 1979-81; supr., sr. indsl. engr. LH Rsch., Inc., Tustin, 1981-85; sr. indsl. engr. Rockwell Internat., Anaheim, Calif., 1985-90; pres., gen. mgr. Maylyne Creations, Irvine, Calif., 1990—. Fortune Investment & Mgmt., Irvine, 1989—. Sec. Cheng Kung U. Found., 1992, treas. 1994—; v.p., treas. Woodbridge High Sch. Chinese Parent Assn., Irvine, Calif., 1993—. Mem. Cheng Kung U. Alumni Assn. (treas. 1992, v.p. 1994—), Apt. Owners Assn. So. Calif., Internat. Inst. Indsl. Engring. Avocations: tennis, writing, reading, ping pong/table tennis. Office: PO Box 18404 Irvine CA 92623-8404

LIN, FOONG-YI, physician; d. See Yan and Emily Lin. BA, Columbia U., N.Y.C., 1989; MD, Dartmouth Med. Sch., Hanover, N.H., 1992. Lic. R.I., bd. eligible in pediats., U.S. Med. Lic. Exam. Level II nursery, pediat. cons. dept. Neonatology Kent County Hosp., Warwick, RI, 1995—97; dept. pediats. The Westerly (R.I.) Hosp., 1997—. Pharmacy and therapeutics com. The Westerly (R.I.) Hosp., 1998—. Grantee Scholarship, Lee Found., Malaysia, 1984—89, 1990. Mem.: R.I. Med. Soc., AMA, Am. Acad. Pediats. Office: Westerly Pediats 45 Wells St Ste 201 Westerly RI 02891

LIN, MARIA C. H. lawyer; b. Kunming, Yunnan, China, Jan. 27, 1942; BSc, Coll. Mount St. Vincent, 1966; MSc, U. Kans., 1970; JD, Fordham U., 1978. Bar: N.Y. 1979, U.S. Dist. Ct. (so. and ea. dists.) N.Y. 1979, U.S. Ct. Appeals (Fed. cir.) 1982, U.S. Patent and Trademark Office, 1979, U.S Supreme Ct. 1985. Atty. Morgan & Finnegan, N.Y.C. Mem. ABA, N.Y. State Bar Assn., World Intellectual Property Orgn. (domain name dispute panelist), N.Y. Intellectual Property Law Assn. (bd. dirs. 1979-88, internat. law and practice China com. 1979-85, fgn. patent law and practice 1986—, chmn. 1990-91), Am. Intellectual Property Law Assn. (Chinese rels. com. 1983-87, internat. patent law and practice 1988—, chmn. 1995-96, co-chmn., China study group, 1997-2000), Internat. Intellectual Property Soc. (chair 2000—02). Office: Morgan & Finnegan LLP 345 Park Ave New York NY 10154-0053 Office Phone: 212-758-4800. E-mail: mclin@morganfinnegan.com.

LIN, MAYA, architect, sculptor; b. Athens, Ohio, Oct. 5, 1959; d. Henry H. and Julia (Chang) L. BA, Yale U., 1981, MA, 1986, PhD in Fine Arts, 1987. Architectural designer Peter Forbes & Assocs., N.Y.C., 1986-87; pvt.

practice N.Y.C., 1987—. Mem. Batey & Mack, San Francisco, 1983, Fumihiko Maki Assoc., Tokyo, 1985. Prin. work include Vietnam Veterans Meml., Washington, 1981, Civil Rights Meml., Montgomery, Ala., 1986. Author: Boundries, 2000. Achievements include submitting the winning design for the Vietnam Veterans Memorial at the age of 21.

LIN, YING-CHU See WU, SUSAN YING CHU LIN

LIN, YVONNE Y. foreign language teacher; b. Taipei, Taiwan; d. Munetake and Eiko Hayashi; children from previous marriage: Eric T. Manzoku, J. Yumi Manzoku. BA Gakushuin U., Tokyo; BS, U. Calif., Davis; MS, Purdue U. Japanese drillmaster Mililani H.S., Mililani, Hawaii, 1990—91; Japanese conversational instr. Wahiawa Cmty. Sch. for Adults, Wahiawa, Hawaii, 1996—97; Japanese drillmaster McKinley H.S., Honolulu, 1997—98; sub. tchr. Punahou Sch., Honolulu, 1996—98; Japanese lang. tchr. St. Francis Sch., Honolulu, 1998—. Mem.: Nat. Coun. of Japanese Lang. Tchrs., Hawaii Assn. of Tchrs. of Japanese (bd. dirs. 1997—2000), Hawaii Assn. of Lang. Tchrs. Office: St Francis School 2707 Pamoa Rd Honolulu HI 96822-1886

LINCOLN, ANNA, publishing executive; b. Warsaw, Dec. 13, 1932; came to U.S., 1948; d. Wigdor Aron and Genia (Zalkind) Szpiro; m. Adrian Courtney Lincoln Jr., Sept. 22, 1951; children: Irene Anne, Sally Linda, Allen, Kirk. Student, U. Calif., Berkeley, 1949-50; BA in French and Russian with honors, NYU, 1965; student, Columbia Tchrs. Coll., 1966-67. Tchr. Waldwick (N.J.) H.S., 1966-69; chmn. Tuxedo Park (N.Y.) Red Cross, 1969-71; pres. Red Cross divsn. Vets. Hosp.; pres. China Pictures U.S.A. Inc., Princeton, N.J., 1994—; prof. fgn. rels. Fudan U., Shanghai, 1994—, prof. English and humanitarian studies, 1996—. Adv. bd. guidance dept. Waldwick (N.J.) H.S., 1966-69; hon. bd. dirs. Shanghai Fgn. Lang. Assn., 1994, hon. prof. Fudan U., Shanghai, 1994; leader seminars, China at top univs., 1996—; pub. spkr., human rels., China, 2003—. Author: Escape to China, 1940-48, 1985, Chinese transl., 1985, The Art of Peace, 1995, Anna Lincoln Views China, 2000; publ.: China Beyond the Year 2000 and the Nature of Love, 1997, Anna Lincoln Views China, 1999; co-dir. (TV docudrama) Escape to China 1941-48, 1998. Hon. U.S. Goodwill amb. for peace and friendship, China, 1984, 85, 86, 88; founder Princeton-Lincoln Found., Inc., 1985—. Named Woman of Yr. Am. Biog. Soc., 1993; recipient Peace Through the Arts prize Assn. Internat. Mujeres en las Artes, Madrid, 1993. Mem. AAUW, Women's Coll. Club (publicity chmn. 1991-96), Lit. Coll. Princeton, Present Day Club. Avocations: reading, swimming, bridge, seminars, ballroom dancing. Home and Office: China Pictures USA Inc 550 Rosedale Rd Princeton NJ 08540-2315

LINCOLN, BLANCHE LAMBERT, senator; b. Helena, Ark., Sept. 30, 1960; BA, Randolph-Macon Woman's Coll., 1982. Sr. assoc. The Pagonis & Donnelly Group, Inc., 1989-91; mem. U.S. Congress from 1st Ark. dist., 1992-96; U.S. senator from Ark., 1999—. Mem. agr. com., energy and natural resources com., spl. com. on aging; mem. Senate Social Security Task Force. Democrat. Office: US Senate 355 Dirksen Senate Office Bldg Washington DC 20510-0001 also: 912 W Fourth St Little Rock AR 72201*

LINCOLN, GEORGIANNA, state legislator; b. Fairbanks, Alaska, Feb. 22, 1943; children: Gidget, Sean. Student, U. Alaska. Mem. Alaska Ho. of Reps., 1990-92, Alaska Senate, Dist. R, Juneau, 1992—; mem. resources, transp. and adminstrv. regulation rev. coms. Bd. dirs. Doyon Ltd., Doyon Drilling, Inc. Commr. Alaska Commn. on Jud. Conduct, 1984-90; U.S. del. East Asia and Pacific Parliamentarian's Conf. on Environment and Devel., 1993; mem. Local-State Tribal Rels. Task Force, 1994; vice-chair NCSL. Democrat. Avocation: working with children and people. Office: State Capitol 120 4th St Rm 11 Juneau AK 99801-1142 Fax: 907-465-2652. E-mail: georgiannalincoln@legis.state.ak.us.

LINCOLN, MARGARET, library media specialist; b. NYC, May 22, 1949; d. Irving Herman and Ann Ruth (Silver) Goldin; m. Gary Samuel Lincoln, June 5, 1971; children: Geoffrey, Benjamin, Ruth. AB in French, U. Mich., 1970, AMLS, 1973; Edn. Tech. Specialist, Mich. State U., 1996. Libr. media specialist Lakeview HS, Battle Creek, Mich., 1973—. Computer skills, internet rsch. tchr. Battle Creek Area Pub. Schs., 1997—; chair, sec. REMC 12 Media Coun., Marshall, Mich., 1996—. Contbr. articles to profl. jours. Vol. libr. Temple Beth El, Battle Creek, 1984—, Sunday sch. tchr., 1984—. Grantee Excellence in Edn., Kellogg Found., 1994, 1999; Am. Memory fellow, Libr. of Congress, 2000, Mandel fellow, US Holocaust Meml. Mus., 2002. Mem.: Phi Beta Kappa, Beta Phi Mu. Home: 13166 11 Mile Rd Ceresco MI 49033-9769 Office: Lakeview HS 300 S 28th St Battle Creek MI 49015-2854

LINCOLN, PATRICIA J. auditor; b. Connellsville, Pa., Apr. 30, 1952; d. Carl Clifford Lincoln and Clara Mae Collins; m. Robin Keith Goodin, May 24, 1975 (div. Apr. 1988); 1 child, Jessica Marie. BA in Acctg. and Info. Systems, Queens Coll., Charlotte, N.C., 1997. Cert. internal auditor Inst. Internal Auditors, 2001, fraud examiner Assn. Cert. Fraud Examiners, 2003. Paralegal Parshall & Lewellan Atty. at Law, Uniontown, Pa., 1971—74; operator BellSouth Corp., Charlotte, 1974, stenographic clk., 1974—77, sec.-stenographer, 1977—80, acctg. asst., 1980—93, electronic technician, 1993—98, internal auditor Atlanta, 1998—2000, mgr. audits, 2000—. Advisor Jr. Achievement, Charlotte, 1977—97, advisor/fundraising, 1998—99; v.p. BellSouth Tel. Pioneers, Atlanta, 1998—99. Mem.: BellSouth Fin. Soc. (seminar com.), Inst. Internal Auditors (newspaper editor 1997—98). Republican. Lutheran. Avocation: gardening. Home: 14 Inland Ct Newnan GA 30263 Office: BellSouth Corp 1155 Peachtree St NE Atlanta GA 30309

LINCOLN, ROSAMOND HADLEY, modern painter, photographer; b. Worcester, Mass., June 27, 1924; d. Ralph Gorham and Grace (Wardwell) Hadley; m. Brayton Lincoln, Jan. 15, 1949; children: Rosamond, Christopher, Daniel, Dorothy. BA, Radcliffe Coll., 1946; postgrad., Assumption Coll., 1975-76. Interior display trainee G. Fox & Co. Dept. Store, Hartford, Conn., 1944; advt. mgr. So. New Eng. Ice and Oil Co., Hartford, Conn., 1945-46; head instr. Worcester (Mass.) Art Mus., 1946-48, 70-76; dir. continuing edn. Swain Sch. Design, New Bedford, Mass., 1980-83; artist self-employed South Dartmouth, Mass., 1983—. Bd. dirs. The Arts Ctr., New Bedford, 1977-80; pres. The Bierstadt Art Soc., New Bedford, 1982-84; chmn. Dartmouth Arts Lottery Coun., 1984-86. Mem. League of Women Voters, New Bedford, 1980-86. Recipient Four First prize awards, Bierstadt Art Gallery, 1989. Mem. AAUW, Westport Art Group, Waterfront Hist. Area League, Rotch-Jones-Duff House and Garden Mus., The Whaling Mus., ARTWORKS! at Dover St., New Bedford Art Mus., Gallery X. Unitarian Universalist. Home: 114 Riverside Ave Apt 259 New Bedford MA 02746-2481

LINCOLN, SHARON ANN, retired county official; b. Forsyth, Mont., Oct. 3, 1939; d. Francis Xavier and Catherine Minerva (McRae) Faust; m. Cecil Wilbur Lincoln, Aug. 6, 1957 (dec. May 1992); children: Michael David, Mark Daniel, Teresa Marie. Grad. high sch., Forsyth, Mont. Bookkeeper 1st State Bank, Forsyth, Mont., 1967-69; clk. to county supt. schs. Rosebud County, Forsyth, Mont., 1969-73, deputy county treas., 1973-86, county treas., 1987-98. Chair bd. dirs. Bd. Sch. Trustees, Forsyth, 1982, mem., 1979-82; mem. edn. com. Gov.'s Task Force to Renew Mont. Govt., 1994; bd. dirs. Rosebud Health Care Found., 1998-99. Mem. Mont. County Treas. Assn. (pres. 1989), Forsyth C. of C. (treas. 1989-97, Profl. Person of Yr. 1996), Forsyth Country Club (pres. bd. dirs. 1996-99). Republican. Avocations: stained glass art, oil painting, gardening, golf, sewing. Home: 2315 Brentwood Ln Billings MT 59102-2105 Office: Rosebud County Courthouse 1200 Main St Forsyth MT 59327

LINCOLN-SMITH, DOROTHY, vocalist, music educator; b. Lansing, Iowa, May 3, 1936; d. Harold J. Ashbacher and Louise Scharping; m. Joseph C. Lincoln, July 25, 1970 (dec. May 1975); children: Kerstan Louise Lincoln, Lisa Marianne Lincoln; m. Harvey K. Smith, Mar. 5, 1976. Bachelor of Music Edn., Cornell Coll., 1958; Master of Music, Ariz. State U., 1964, EdD, 1973. Singer/soloist Ariz. Opera and Bach Soc., Phoenix, 1959—67, Roger Wagner Chorale, L.A., 1966—69; tchr. and singer Maryvale H.S., Ariz., 1964—68; prof. and singer Glendale C.C., Ariz., 1968—70, Phoenix Coll., 1973—2003; tour coord., vocal coach, and soloist Phoenix Boys Choir, 1976—99; soloist First Ch. of Christ Scientist, Phoenix, 1994—. Mem. adv. bd. Phoenix Boys Choir, 1999—2003; trustee San Francisco Theol. Sch., San Anselmo, Calif., 1985—95. Co-author: (videos) Singing and Growing, 1981, 1984. Episc. lay eucharistic min. Recipient Rose of Honor, Sigma Alpha Iota, 2000. Mem.: Nat. Soc. Arts and Letters (mem. exec. bd. 1973—, 1st v.p. 2002—), Nat. Assn. Tchrs. Singing (auditions chair 1976—2003). Republican. Avocations: scuba diving, tennis.

LINDBLAD, CYNTHIA MERRILL, music educator; b. Gowanda, N.Y., Mar. 8, 1958; d. Barbara Jean and Melvin Ralph Van Note; m. Rickie Lane Lindblad, Oct. 30, 1981; children: Nicholas Arthur, Nathan Merrill, Sean Michael. B in Music Edn., SUNY Fredonia, 1980. K-12 music educator Diller Cmty. Sch., Nebr., 1980—2000; educator 5-12 instrumental, 7-12 vocal music Diller Odell Cmty. Schs., Odell, Nebr., 2000—. Dir. Class D All State Bands, Odell, 1999—2000. Home: 4274 W State Hwy 4 Beatrice NE 68310 Office: Diller Odell High School 506 Perry St Odell NE 68415 Personal E-mail: clindblad.bie@beatricene.com.

LINDBOE, BERIT ROBERG, language educator, literature educator; b. Stavanger, Norway, July 28, 1944; arrived in U.S., 1947; d. Odd and Ingbjorg Roberg. BA, Wellesley Coll., 1966; MA, Yale U., 1967. English tchr. Daniel Hand H.S., Madison, Conn., 1967—69; tchg. asst. U. Va., Charlottesville, 1971—73; asst. prof. English Humboldt State U., Arcata, Calif., 1973—77; grad. instr. U. Va., 1979—83; English tchr. Barstow Sch., Kansas City, Mo., 1983—. Cons. Ednl. Testing Svc., Princeton, NJ, 1991—2002; panelist NEH, Washington, 1991. Contbr. articles to profl. jours. Grantee, NEH, London and Oxford, Eng., English-Speaking Union, Mo. Humanities Coun. Mem.: Lychnos Honor Soc., Cum Laude Soc., Mensa.

LINDE, LUCILLE MAE (LUCILLE JACOBSON), motor-perceptual specialist; b. Greeley, Colo., May 5, 1919; d. John Alfred and Anna Julia (Anderson) Jacobson; m. Ernest Emil Linde, July 5, 1946 (dec. Jan. 27, 1959). BA, Colo. State Coll. of Edn., 1941, MA, 1947; EdD, U. No. Colo., 1974. Cert. tchr. Calif., Colo., Iowa, N.Y.; cert. ednl. psychologist; guidance counselor. Dean of women, dir. residence C.W. Post Coll. of L.I. Univ., 1965-66; asst. dean of students SUNY, Farmingdale, 1966-67; counselor, tchr. West High Sch., Davenport, Iowa, 1967-68; instr. grad. tchrs. and counselors, univ. counselor, researcher No. Ariz. U., Flagstaff, 1968-69; vocat. edn. and counseling coord. Fed. Exemplary Project, Council Bluffs, Iowa, 1970-71; sch. psychologist, counselor Oakdale Sch. Dist., Calif., 1971-73; sch. psychologist, intern Learning and Counseling Ctr., Stockton, Calif., 1972-74; pvt. practice rsch. in motor-perceptual tng. Greeley, 1975—. Rschr. ocumeter survey Lincoln Unified Sch. Dist., Stockton, 1980, 81, 82, Manteca (Calif.) H.S., 1981; spkr. Social Sci. Edn. Consortium, U. Colo., Boulder, 1993; mem. Monday Morning steering com. House Spkr. Newt Gingrich, 1997-98; mem. Attention Disorder Advocacy Group, 1997-2001; instr. seminars for ADD and ADHD, alleviating lag/dysfunction in neural system noted, 1997-98, 1998-99, presenter seminars in field. Author: Psychological Services and Motor Perceptual Training, 1974, Guidebook for Psychological Services and Motor Perceptual Training (How One May Improve in Ten Easy Lessons!), 1992, Manual for the Lucille Linde Ocumeter: Ocular Pursuit Measuring Instrument, 1992, Motor-Perceptual Training and Visual Perceptual Research (How Students Improved in Seven Lessons!), 1992, Effects of Motor Perceptual Training on Academic Achievement and Ocular Pursuit Ability, 1992, Teaching University of Northern Colorado Laboratory Students and Greeley District 6 Students Motor-Perceptual Training Seminar, 2001; inventor ocumeter, instrument for measuring ocular tracking ability, 1989, ocutarget for use, 1991, cure for oculomotor dysfunction noted; patentee in field. Mem. Rep. Presdl. Task Force, 1989-96, trustee, 1991-92, charter mem., 1994—, life mem., 1994-95; mem. Rep. Nat. Com., 1990, 93-2003, Rep. Nat. Com. on Am. Agenda, 1993, Nat. Rep. Congl. Com., 1990, 92, 93, 95-2003, Nat. Fedn. Rep. Women, Greeley Rep. Women, 1996-2003; advisor Senator Bob Dole for Pres.; charter mem. Rep. Newt Gingrich's Speaker's Task Force, Senator Phil Gramm's Presdl. Steering Com.; at-large del. Rep. Platform Planning Com.; team leader Nat. Rep. Rapid Response Network, Campaign America, 1996; active Heritage Found. (certificate as honored mem. leadership adv. bd., 1998-2000), Christian Bus. Men's Assn., Friends U. N.C. Librs., Citizens Against Govt. Waste, 1996-2003, Concerns of Police Survivors, 1996-98, Nat. Assn. of Police Orgn., elected to Libr. of Congress Nat. membership, 1997-2001; mem. WW II Vets. Com., 2000-03, Rep. Gov.'s Assn., 2001; mem. Rep. Gov.'s Policy Commn. Recipient Presdl. medal of merit and lapel insignia, 1990, Nat. Rep. Senatorial Com., 1991-2003, cert. of appreciation Nat. Rep. Congl. Com., 1992, 95, lapel pin Rep. Senatorial Inner Circle, 1990-96, Rep. Presdl. commemorative honor roll, 1993, Rep. Senatorial Freedom medal, 1994, Rep. Legion of Merit award, 1994, 96, Rep. Congl. Order of Freedom award, 1995, Senatorial Inner Cir. Lapel Pin, 1998, Lapel Pin award RNC, 1996, Leadership citation Rep. Senatorial Inner Cir./ Rep. Nat. Conv., 1996, Legion of Merit Rep. Presdl. exec. com., 1996, Honor cert. House Spkr. Newt Gingrich, 1996, Rep. Presdl. Legion of Merit medallion and matching lapel pin, 1994, Order of Merit, 1996, Conservative Leadership award Young Am.'s Found., 1999, Nat. Rep. Congl. Com. Rep. of the Yr. from Colo. award, 2000, Majority Leader's Commn. Cert., 2001, 2001 Conservative Patriot award The Pres., Ron Robinson and Bd. of Dirs. of The Young America's Found.; named to Rep. Nat. Hall of Honor, 1992. Mem. AAUP, NAFE, Nat. Assn. Sch. Psychologists and Psychometrists (spkr. conf. 1976), Rep. Senatorial Inner Cir. (name engraved on Ronald Wilson Reagan Eternal Flame of Freedom, 1995, on the Nat. Rep. Victory Monument, Washington, 1996, Rep. Sen. Inner Cir. (Conv. Medallion 1996, RNC Mems. Only pin 1996), 20th Century Rep. Leader, Rep. Sen. Inner Cir., 1998, The Smithsonian Assocs., Ronald Reagan Presdl. Libr. and Mus., Bush Presdl. Libr. and Mus., Nat. Trust for Hist. Preservation, Internat. Platform Assn., Friends of Newt Gingrich, 1998-99, Independence Inst., Assn. Children Learning Disabilities (spkr. internat. conv. 1976), Libr. of Congress Assn., 1999, Children and Adults with Attention Deficit Disorder, Learning Disabilities Assn. Colo., Nat. Fragile X Found., Fraxa Rsch. Found., Pi Omega Pi, Pi Lambda Theta. Avocations: music, architecture. Home: 1954 18th Ave Greeley CO 80631-5208

LINDE, MAXINE HELEN, lawyer, business executive, private investor; b. Chgo., Sept. 2, 1939; d. Jack and Lottie (Kroll) Stern; m. Ronald K. Linde, June 12, 1960. BA summa cum laude, UCLA, 1961; JD, Stanford U., 1967. Bar: Calif. 1968. Applied mathematician, rsch. engr Jet Propulsion Lab., Pasadena, Calif., 1961—64; law clk. U.S. Dist. Ct. No. Calif., 1967—68; mem. firm Long & Levit, San Francisco, 1968—69, Swerdlow, Glikbarg & Shimer, Beverly Hills, Calif., 1969—72; sec., gen. counsel Envirodyne Industries, Inc., Chgo., 1972—89; pres. The Ronald and Maxine Linde Found., 1989—; vice chmn. bd., gen. counsel Titan Fin. Group, LLC, Chgo., 1994—98. Mem. bd. visitors Stanford Law Sch., 1989—92, law and bus. adv. coun., 1991—94, dean's adv. coun., 1992—94. Mem.: Alpha Lambda Delta, Pi Mu Epsilon, Phi Beta Kappa, Order of Coif.

LINDELL, ANDREA REGINA, dean, nurse; b. Warren, Pa., Aug., 21, 1943; d. Andrew D. and Irene M. (Fabry) Lefik; m. Warner E. Lindell, May 7, 1966; children: Jennifer I., Jason M. B.S., Villa Maria Coll., 1970; M.S.N. Catholic U., 1975, D.N.Sc., 1976; diploma R.N., St. Vincent's Hosp., Erie, Pa. Instr. St. Vincent Hosp. Sch. Nursing, 1964-66; dir. Rouse Hosp., Youngsville, Pa., 1966-69; supr. Vis. Nurses Assn., Warren, Pa., 1969-70; dir. grad. program Cath. U., Washington, 1975-77; chmn., assoc. dean U. N.H., Durham, 1977-81; dean, prof. Oakland U., Rochester, Mich., 1981-90, dean, Schmidlapp prof. nursing U. Cin., 1990—; bd. dirs. CHEMED Corp.; cons. Moorehead U., Ky., 1983. Editor; Jour. Profl. Nursing, 1985; contbr. articles to profl. jours. Mem. sch. bd. Strafford Sch. Dist., N.H., 1977-80; Gov.'s Blue Ribbon Commn. Direct Health Policies, Concord, N.H., 1979-81; vice chmn. New England Commn. Higher Edn. in Nursing, 1977-81; mem. Mich. Assn. Colls. Nursing, 1981— . Named Outstanding Young Woman Am., 1980. Mem. Nat. League Nursing, Am. Assn. Colls. Nursing (pres. 1996—), Sigma Theta Tau. Democrat. Roman Catholic. Avocations: water skiing, roller skating, reading, fishing, camping. Office: College of Nursing & Health 3110 Vine St Cincinnati OH 45221-0001

LINDEN, BLANCHE MARIE GEMROSE, history educator; b. Battle Creek, Mich., July 4, 1946; d. George and Lauretta (Cate) Gemrose; m. Thomas Elwood Lindow, Aug. 2, 1968 (div. 1976); children: Julia C. Lindow, Marc T. Lindow; m. Alan Lester Ward, June 26, 1982. BA, U. Mich., 1968; MA, U. Cin., 1976; PhD, Harvard U., 1981. Teaching asst. U. Cin., 1974-76; teaching fellow Harvard U., Cambridge, Mass., 1977-79; instr. Brandeis U., Waltham, Mass., 1979-81; vis. asst. prof. Middlebury (Vt.) Coll., 1981-82; asst. prof. history Brandeis U., Waltham, 1982-85, assoc. prof., 1993-94; asst. prof. history Emerson Coll., Boston, 1985-90, assoc. prof., 1990-93, U. N.H., Durham, 1993—. Hist. cons. Mt. Auburn Cemetery, Cambridge, 1981—, Soc. Preservation of New Eng. Antiquities, African Meetinghouse, Arnold Arboretum, all Boston, 1991-93. Author: Silent City on a Hill: Landscapes of Memory, 1989; co-author: American Women in the 1960's: Changing the Future, 1993; assoc. editor: Encyclopedia New Eng. Culture, 1993—; contbr. articles to profl. jours. Mem. Am. Studies Assn., New Eng. Am. Studies Assn. (pres. 1985-87, sec., newsletter editor 1989—), Am. Hist. Assn., Orgn. Am. Historians, Am. Culture/Popular Culture Assn., New Eng. Hist. Assn. (chair exec. com. 1992-94). Democrat. Avocations: photography, travel in france. Home: 3019 NE 20th Ct Fort Lauderdale FL 33305-1807 Office: U NH Ctr Humanities Murkland Durham NH 03824-3596

LINDEN, CAROL MARIE, special education educator; b. Pitts., Dec. 24, 1953; d. Enio P. and Mary C. (Santillo) Cardone; m. Frank J. Miller Jr., Dec. 21, 1974 (div. 1989); children: Emily, Karl, Richard; m. James Anthony Linden, Dec. 9, 1989; children: Shiloh, Shane, Shasta, Shelby (dec.). BS, California (Pa.) State U., 1974; MS, Youngstown State U., 1981. Cert. moderate, severe, profoundly retarded, educable mentally retarded, learning disabled/behavior disordered, speech and hearing. Tchr. multi-handicapped Youngstown (Ohio) City Schs., 1987—; tchr. multihandicapped Trumbull County Bd. Edn., Lordstown, Ohio, 1986-87; spl. vocat. edn. coord. Trumbull County Joint Vocat. Sch., Warren, Ohio, 1985-86; lang. devel. specialist Fairhaven Sheltered Workshop, Niles and Champion, Ohio, 1976-85. Grantee N.E. Ohio Spl. Edn. Resource Ctr., 1989-92, Ohio Bell and Ameritech Impact II, 1991-92, 95, Consumer/Econ. grantee, 1989-95; Wolves Club Carapolis scholar, 1971. Mem. Ohio Speech and Hearing Assn., Coun. for Exceptional Children, Nat. Soc. for Autistic Citizens (sec. 1986-87). Roman Catholic/Baptist. Avocations: reading, crafts, camping. Home: 432 Hunter Ave Niles OH 44446-1625

LINDEN, PEPPY G. museum director; b. Louisville, Dec. 19, 1949; d. Bernard Sylvan and Helen Novitsky Goldstein; m. Russell Mathew Linden, May 9, 1971 (div. May 1979). BEd, U. Mich., 1971. Cert. elem. tchr. Va. Program coord. Project Cmty., Ann Arbor, Mich., 1971-72; sr. rsch. asst. Inst. for Social Rsch., Ann Arbor, 1972-74; infant educator dept. pediats. U. Va., Charlottesville, 1975-76; pediat. admissions and adolescent coord. Kluge Children's Rehab. Ctr., U. Va. Med. Ctr., Charlottesville, 1976-89; exec. dir. Va. Discovery Mus., Charlottesville, 1990—. Mem. Cable TV Citizens' Adv. Com., Charlottesville, 1992-98; mem. Social Svcs. Adv. Bd., Charlottesville, 1996—. Judge Nat. History Day, Charlottesville, 1993-96; bd. dirs. Piedmont Coun. of Arts, Charlottesville, 1989-92, Charlottesville Regional Tourism Coun., 2001—; regional bd. dirs. Sorensen Inst. for Polit. Leadership, 2001—; sec., chair Charlottesville Electoral Bd., 1993-96; election ofcl. City of Charlottesville, 1991-93; pres., v.p. North Downtown Residents' Assn., Charlottesville, 1986-89; treas. Nat. Host Program, Charlottesville, 1993-94; mem. adv. bd. Piedmont Va. C.C. Dickinson Theater; mem. program com. Paramount Theatre, 2002—. Named Woman of Distinction, Va. Skyline coun., Girl Scouts U.S., 1993, Artist of Yr., Piedmont Coun. of Arts, 2001. Fellow Sorensen Inst. Polit. Leadership; mem. Leadership Charlottesville Alumni Assn., Nat. Soc. Arts and Letters (founding bd. mem. Va./NC chpt.). Jewish. Avocations: theater, water sports, politics, film. Office: Va Discovery Mus 524 E Main St Charlottesville VA 22902-5336

LINDEN, SUSAN PYLES, marketing executive; b. Mt. Clemens, Mich., Apr. 29, 1954; d. Paul James Pyles and Charlotte Ettalene Snowden. BA cum laude, U. South Fla., 1976. Copywriter, account exec. Denton & French, Tampa, Fla., 1977-81, account exec., 1979-81; account rep. J. Walter Thompson, Atlanta, 1981-82; account exec. Liller Neal, Atlanta, 1982-83, The Bloom Agy., Dallas, 1983-85, sr. account exec., 1985-86, v.p., account supr., 1986-89; sales and mktg. dir. Sta. KSPN-FM, Aspen, Colo., 1989-91, World Wide Ski Corp., Aspen, 1991-93; owner Susan Pyles Mktg., 1993-98; mktg. dir. Aspen Glen, 1999—2003; owner Linden Mktg., 2003—. Mem. Women's Forum, Aspen. Avocations: skiing, photography, hiking, cycling. Office: PO Box 1800 Carbondale CO 81623 Office Phone: 970-704-1747. Business E-Mail: susan@lindenmarketing.net.

LINDENBAUM, SHARON, publishing executive; b. Johannesburg; B., U. Kans.; M. in acctg., Wichita State U. Sr. acct. Main Hurdman, Wichita, Kans.; mng. partner Lindenbaum & O'Sullivan, Wichita, Kans.; controller Pennypower Shopping News Inc., Wichita, Kans.; v.p. fin. Kansas City (Mo.) Star, 1995—. Office: Kansas City Star 1729 Grand Blvd Kansas City MO 64108-1458

LINDENFELD, NAOMI, ceramic artist; b. Princeton, N.J., May 14, 1958; d. Peter and Lore (Kadden) L. BA, Boston U., 1980. Apprentice Fred Tregaskis, Kent, Conn., 1980, Elizabeth McDonald, Bridgewater, Conn., 1981, Carol Sevick, Westminster W., Vt., 1981; baker Innisfree Farms Bakery, Brattleboro, Vt., 1982; potter Brattleboro Clayworks, 1983; tchr. ceramics The Putney Sch., 1997. Pres. Brattleboro Clayworks, 1988—; ceramics tchr. Putney (Vt.) Sch., 1997—; workshop instr. in field. Bd. dirs. Windham Citizens for Responsible Growth, Brattleboro, 1993-94. Mem. League N.H. Craftmen, Vt. Craftsmen., N.H. Potter's Guild, Am. Crafts Coun. Avocations: dance, hiking, skiing. Office Phone: 802-254-9174.

LINDER, BEVERLY L. elementary school educator; b. Kansas City, Mo., Mar. 12, 1951; d. William B. and Una M. (Dishman) Reese; m. John H. Linder, Feb. 24, 1979; 1 child, Elaine M. BSEd, Cen. Mo. State U., 1972; MA in Reading, U. Mo., Kansas City, 1975. Cert. elem. edn., reading. Elem. tchr. Ft. Osage Sch. Dist., Independence, Mo., tchr. 4th grade chpt. I reading. Mem. Internat. Reading Assn., Nat. Coun. Tchrs. Math. Home: 1317 NE Buttonwood Ave Lees Summit MO 64086-8438

LINDER, IRIS KAY, lawyer; b. Davenport, Iowa, May 3, 1952; d. Forrest Wesley and Josephine Jeanette (Barnett) Shaffer; 1 son, Eric Scott Socolofsky. m. Stephen J. Linder. BS, Mich. State U., 1976; JD, U. Mich., 1980. Bar: Mich. 1980, U.S. Dist. Ct. (we. and ea. dists.) Mich. 1980. Ptnr. Fraser, Trebilcock, Davis & Dunlap, P.C., Lansing., Mich., 1980—. Adj. faculty Cooley Law Sci., 1999—; mem. Office Fin. and Ins. Svcs. Securities Coun.

Mich., 1991—. Co-author: Michigan Usury Manual, 1982; contbr. chpt. to Litigation of the Commercial Case, 1992. Mem. planning bd. Ingham County Office for Young Children, 1986—87; mem. Mayor's Parking Adv. Com., 1990—93; chair group com. Shared Vision Sys. and Rsch., 1994—96, bd. dirs. Capitol Area Girl Scouts USA, 1986—88, Capitol Area Polit. Action Com., 1990—96, chair, 1995; bd. dirs. Capitol Enterprise Forum, 1989—95, pres., 1993; bd. dirs. Capitol Area United Way, 1994—2001, Infoguys, Inc., 1996—99, Congregation Kehillet Israel, Venture Ctr., Inc., 1996—2001, chair, 1999—2001. Recipient Book award U. Mich. Law Sch., 1980. Mem. ABA, Ingham County Bar Assn., State Bar Assn. Mich., Lansing Regional C. of C. (bus. women's coun. 1984-87, bd. dirs. 1987-92, dir. govt. affairs 1991-92, Tireless award 1992, Small Bus. Advocate of Yr. award 1993), Lansing Assn. Career Women (bd. dirs. 1985-87), Athena Found. (bd. dirs. 1986-87). Home: 2550 Dustin Rd Okemos MI 48864-2073 Office: Fraser Trebilcock Davis & Dunlap 1000 Michigan Nat Towers Lansing MI 48933 E-mail: ilinder@fraserlawfirm.com.

LINDERMAN, JEANNE HERRON, priest; b. Erie, Pa., Nov. 14, 1931; d. Robert Leslie and Ella Marie (Stearns) Herron; m. James Stephens Linderman; children: Mary Susan, John Randolph, Richard Webster, Craig Stephens, Mark Herron, Elizabeth Stewart. BS in Indsl. and Labor Rels., Cornell U., 1953; MDiv magna cum laude, Lancaster Theol. Sem., 1981; postgrad., clin. pastoral edn., Del. State Hosp., New Castle, 1981. Ordained priest, Episcopal Ch. Mem. pers. staff Hengerer Co., Buffalo, 1953-55; chaplain Cathedral Ch. St. John, Wilmington, Del., 1981-82; priest-in-charge Christ Episcopal Ch., Delaware City, Del., 1982-87, vicar, 1987-91; assoc. rector St. Andrew's Episcopal Ch., Wilmington, 1992—94, priest in charge, 1995-96; assoc. priest for pastoral care The Episc. Ch. of Sts. Andrew and Matthew, 1998—. Chair human sexuality task force, Diocese of Del., 1981-82, mem. clergy compensation com. and diocesan coun., 1982-86, pres. standing com., 1991—, com. on constitution and canons, 1989, designer and leader religious/spiritual retreats, mem. diocesan ret. clergy com., 1999—, chmn., 2004. Author, editor hist. study papers. Bd. dirs. St. Michael's Day Nursery, Wilmington, 1985-88; mem. secondary schs. com. Cornell U., bd. dirs., chmn. pers. com. Geriatric Svcs. of Del., 1989-96, sec. bd., 1993-96. Mem. Episcopal Women's Caucus, Del. Episcopal Clergy Assn., Nat. Assn. Episcopal Clergy, DAR (v.-regent Caesar Rodney chpt. 1996—), Mayflower Soc. (elder 2000—, surgeon 1983-95), Nat. Soc. Colonial Dames Am. Del., Dutch Colonial Soc. Del., Stoney Run Questers (pres.), Cornell Women's Club Del. (pres. 1966), Women of St. James the Less (pres. 1972-73), Women's Witnessing Cmty. at Lambeth, Patriotic Soc. in Del. (sec.-treas. conv. 1965-68), Chi Omega. Republican. Avocations: history, genealogy, travel. Home: 307 Springhouse Ln Hockessin DE 19707-9691 Office: The Episcopal Ch of Sts Andrew and Matthews Eighth And Shipley St Wilmington DE 19801 E-mail: linderjs@bellatlantic.net.

LINDH, PATRICIA SULLIVAN, banker, former government official; b. Toledo, Oct. 2, 1928; d. Lawrence Walsh and Lillian Winifred (Devlin) Sullivan; m. H. Robert Lindh, Jr., Nov. 12, 1955; children: Sheila, Deborah, Robert. BA, Trinity Coll., Washington, 1950, LL.D., 1975, Walsh Coll., Canton, Ohio, 1975, U. Jacksonville, 1975. Editor Singapore Am. Newspaper, 1957-62; spl. asst. to counsellor to Pres., 1974; spl. asst. to Pres., 1975-76; dep. asst. sec. state for ednl. and cultural affairs Dept. State, 1976-77; v.p., dir. corp. comms. Bank Am., L.A., 1978-84, corp. pub. rels. San Francisco, 1985-93. Trustee La. Arts and Sci. Center, 1970-73, Calif. Hosp. Med. Ctr., 1979-84; bd. dirs. Jr. League of Baton Rouge, 1969, Children's Bur. Los Angeles, 1979, 84, USO Northern Calif.; Rep. state vice chairwoman La., 1970-74; Rep. nat. committeewoman, La., 1974; mem. pub. affairs com. San Francisco World Affairs Coun., 1985; adv. bd. Jr. League Los Angeles, 1980-84; bd. visitors Southwestern U. Sch. Law. Roman Catholic. Home: 12380 Grandee Ct San Diego CA 92128-2120

LINDLEY, JOYCE E. health facility administrator, real estate appraiser; b. Clinton, Ind., May 29, 1953; d. Clyde M. and Juanita M. Delp; m. James A. Lindley; children: Brian, Richard Neil; m. William R. Travis, July 22, 1972 (div. 1983). Cosmetologist, Harolds Sch. Beauty, Terre Haute, Ind., 1975; real estate profl., Ind. State U., Terre Haute, 1989; real estate appraiser, Ind. U.-Purdue U., Indpls., 1993. Cert. assisted living adminstr. Assisted Living Fedn. Am., 2001. Hairstylist, owner, mgr. Hairbarn I, II and You're Special, Wabash Valley area, 1976—89; real estate appraiser Mike Ofsansky and Assoc., Terre Haute, 1993—98; comml. real estate sales dir. Century 21, Terre Haute, 1989—93; mktg. dir. Lakeview Nursing & Rehab., Terre Haute, 1995—99; exec. dir. Morningside Assisted Living, Terre Haute, 1999—2001; pres. Lindley McVeigh and Assocs., Terre Haute, 2001—; adminstr. Bethesda Gardens, Terre Haute, 2001—. Cons. Lindley Advt., Terre Haute, 1994—99; adv. bd. mem. Vencare Hospice, Terre Haute, 1998—99; chairperson adv. bd. Lakeview Golden Health Unit, Terre Haute, 1997—99. Chairperson United Way, Clark County, Ill., 1999—2000; bd. dirs. ARC, Terre Haute, 2002—, Big Brother / Big Sister, Terre Haute, 1999—. Recipient Above and Beyond award, Bethesda Living Ctrs., 2002. Mem.: C. of C. Greater Terre Haute (amb. 1995—, chairperson 2000—02), Appraisor Assn. (developer mktg. / tng. manuals and classes), Terre Haute Bd. Realtors, Wabash Valley Healthcare Mktg. Group (pres. 1998—99, Outstanding Pres. 1999), Am. Mktg. Assn., Exch. Club Terre Haute (pres. 1999—2001, dist. dir. 2002—03, Outstanding Membership Drive award 2001, Outstanding Pres. 2003). Avocations: professional singing, golf, horticulturist, speaking, songwriting. Home: 7 Lakeview Marshall IL 62441 Office: Bethesda Gardens 1450 E Crossing Blvd Terre Haute IN 47802 Business E-Mail: jlindley@blcmail.com.

LINDLEY, MARALEE IRWIN, county official, consultant, speaker; b. Springfield, Ill., June 30, 1925; d. Oramel Blackstone and Rachel Virginia (Elliott) Irwin; m. Joseph Perry Lindley, Sept. 18, 1948; children: Joseph Perry, Richard Fleetwood. BS Psychology, Northwestern U., 1947; MA in Counseling, U. Ill., Springfield, 1973, MA in Comm., 1979. Cert. tchr., Ill. Bookkeeper, acct. Ill. State Bar Assn., Springfield, 1947-48; curriculum coord., tchr. Sch. Dist. 186, Springfield, 1966-80; auditor, trustee Woodside Twp., Springfield, 1977-81; county auditor Sangamon County, Ill., 1980-86, county clk., 1986—. Dir. Ill. Dept. on Aging, Springfield, 1992-99; co-author/developer Ill. Elem. Gifted Program, 1977-80 (exemplary citation 1978); rep. Internat. Fedn. on Aging of UN; vice chair U.S. Com. for Celebration of UN Internat. Yr. of Older Persons, 1999; chair Nat. Effort for Global Embrace Walk, 1999; adv. com. Nat. Silver Haired Congress; charter mem. Internat. Conf. Intergenerational Programs to Promote Social Change. Mem. Mayor's Commn. on Internat. Visitors, Springfield, 1964—; sec. Sangamon State U. Found., 1984-86, Symphony Guild, Springfield, 1983-86; treas. Springfield Women's Polit. Caucus, 1983-85; pres. Capitol City Rep. Women's Club, Springfield, 1985-87. Recipient hon. Thanks award Land of Lincoln coun. Girl Scouts U.S., 1958, Appreciation award City of Springfield, 1964, Disting. Citizen award Sch. Dist. 1986, Elizabeth Cady Stanton award Springfield Women's Polit. Caucus, 1987; named to Women of Achievement in Govt., Sangamon State U., 1985, One of 5 Rep. County Ofciles. of Yr., 1985. Mem. Ill. Assn. County Auditors (sec. 1982-84, treas. 1984-86, v.p. 1986), Assn. Govt. Accts. (pres. 1984-85), Am. Soc. Pub. Adminstrn., Nat. Assn. Govt. Accts. (regional v.p.), Ill. Women in Govt. (treas.), Women in Mgmt. (Woman of Achievement award 1985), LWV. Lodges: Zonta. Avocations: dulcimer, folk singing, sports, reading, public speaking. Home: 2332 S Noble Ave Springfield IL 62704-4344

LINDQUIST, KIRSTEN MARY, critical care nurse; d. Kenneth and Jean Lindquist. BS in Nursing, Auburn U., 2000; postgrad., Seton Hall U. RN N.J., cert. BLS, ACLS. Info. aid U.S. Dept. Agr., Auburn, Ala., 1999—2000; staff nurse JFK Med. Ctr., Edison, NJ, 2000—02, charge nurse, 2002—. Cert. HHA supr. Preferred Nursing and Staffing, N. Brunswick, NJ, 2002—; mem. Solaris Svc. Excellence Acad., Edison, 2002—. Vol. The Sharing Network, NJ, 2001—. Mem.: Phi Eta Sigma, Golden Key, Sigma Theta Tau Internat. Soc. Avocations: painting, reading.

LINDQUIST, SUSAN LEE, biology and microbiology educator; b. June 6, 1949; BA in Microbiology with honors, U. Ill., 1971; PhD in Biology, Harvard U., 1976. Asst. prof. dept. biology U. Chgo., 1978-84, assoc. prof., 1984-88, prof. dept. molecular genetics & cell biology, 1988—, investigator Howard Hughes Med. Inst., 1988—. Mem. com. genetics, com. devel. biology U. Chgo., 1999—; cons. Mus. Sci. & Industry, Chgo., 1983-87; vis. scholar Cambridge U., 1983; cons., prin. in film Lights Breaking, 1985; mem. sci. adv. com. Helen Hay Whitney Found., 1997—; lectr. in field. Co-editor: The Stress Induced Proteins, 1988, Heat Shock, 1990; assoc. editor The New Biologist, 1991-93; mem. editl. bd. Cell Regulation, 1989—, Molecular and Cell Biology, 1984—, Gene Expression, 1994-95, Cell Stress and Chaperones, 1995—, Current Biology, 1996—, Molecular Biology of the Cell, 1996—; monitoring editor Jour. Cell Biology, 1993—; contbr. articles to profl. jours. Teaching fellow Harvard U., 1973-74, Postdoctoral fellow Am. Cancer Soc., 1976-78. Fellow Am. Acad. Microbiology, AAAS, NAS, Am. Acad. Arts and Sci.; mem. Am. Soc. Cell Biology, Am. Soc. Microbiology, Fedn. Am. Scientists for Exptl. Biology, Genetics Soc. Am. (elected sec. 1998—), Molecular Medicine Soc. Home: 1200 E Madison Park Chicago IL 60615-2961 Office: U Chgo 5841 S Maryland Ave Chicago IL 60637-1463

LINDROTH, LINDA (LINDA HAMMER), artist, curator, writer; b. Miami, Sept. 4, 1946; d. Mark Roger and Mae Lang Hammer; m. David George Lindroth, May 26, 1968 (div. Mar. 1985); m. Craig David Newick, June 6, 1987; 1 child, Zachary Eran Newick. BA in Art, Douglass Coll., 1968; studied with Gordon Matta-Clark, Rutgers U., 1975; studied with Garry Winogrand, N.Y., 1976; MFA in Art, Rutgers U., 1979; master class in non-fiction writing, Yale U., 1997. Adj. asst. prof. art Quinnipiac Coll., Hamden, Conn., 1998—. editor: Co-author, Virtual Vintage: The Insider's Guide to Buyin and Selling Fashion Online. Exhibitions include Aetna Gallery, 1987, 1989, 1991, Franklin Furnace, N.Y.C., 1977, Conn. Commn. Arts, Hartford, 1985, 1996, Aldrich Mus. Contemporary Art, Ridgefield, Conn., 1987, 1987, Downey Mus. Art, Calif., 1989, Zimmerlo Art Mus. Rutgers U., 1989, Wesleyan U. Ctr. for Arts, 1990, Boston Pub. Libr., 1991, John Michael Kohler Art Ctr., Sheboygan, Wis., 1992, Joseloff Gallery U., Hartford, 1994, Artspace, New Haven, 1991, 1992, 1993, 1994, 1995, DeCordova Mus., Lincoln, Mass., 1995, Urban Glass, Bklyn., 1996, U. Conn. Atrium Gallery, 1999, Creative Arts Workship, 1999, New Haven Hist. Soc., 1999, Stedman Gallery, 1999, Rutgers U., 1999, others, Represented in permanent collections The Mus. Modern Art, N.Y.C., The Met. Mus. Art, The Mus. City of N.Y., Internat. Polaroid Collection/Artist Program, N.J. State Mus., Trenton, The Bibliotheque Nationale, Paris, Ctr. Creative Photography, Tucson, The Newark Mus., The Jane Voorhees Zimmerli Art Mus., New Brunswick, N.J., High Mus. Art, Atlanta, Yale U., Mus. d'art et d'histoire, Fribourg, Switzerland; co-author: Out of Bounds, 1994 (1st prize), Virtual Vintage, 2002. Dir. Artspace, Inc., New Haven; mem. Mayor's Task Force on Pub. Art, New Haven. Recipient Ann. Design Rev. award ID Mag., 1990, 91, 93, Honorable Mention, Nat. Peace Garden Design Competition, 1989, Pitts. Corning Archtl. Design Competition, 1988, Individual Artist fellow N.J. State Coun. on Arts, 1974-75, 83-84, Wilmer Shields Rich award Coun. Founds., 1995, Printing Industry Am. award, 1995; grantee Found. for Contemporary Performance Arts, Inc., 1989, 90, Fission Fusion NEA InterArts, 1989, New Eng. Found. for Arts, 1992, Fairfield U., 1995, Ruth Chenven Found., N.Y.C., 1997, Ruth Chevnen Found., 1997; Conn. Commn. Arts fellow, 1995, New Eng. Found. Arts/NEA Regional Photography fellow, 1995-96; Emerging Voices lectr. Arch. League of N.Y., 1996; fellowship grantee in sculpture Conn. Commn. on the Arts, 2000, Te Found. Grant, 2002. Studio: Lindroth & Newick 219 Livingston St New Haven CT 06511-2209

LINDSAY, COSIMANO, marketing professional; d. Betty Willis; m. Cory Cosimano, Feb. 3, 2001. BS in Journalism, U. Kans., 1998; MBA, U. Nebr., 2001—. Writer, editor U. Nebr. Med. Ctr., Omaha, 1998—2000; mktg. dir. Cassling Diagnostic Imaging, Omaha, 2000—. Bd. dirs. Am. Nebr. chpt. Pub. Rels. Soc., Omaha, 2000—. Pub. rels. adv. com. Alzheimer's Assn., Omaha, 1998—2003, Am. Heart Assn., Omaha, 2002—03. Recipient Bronze Quill award, IABC, 2001. Mem.: Am. Mktg. Assn. (Pinnacle award 2001), Pub. Rels. Soc. of Am. (assoc.; dir. programs Nebr. chpt. 1999—2003, James Leuschen fellow 2001, Paper Anvil award 2000, 2001, 2002, Newcomer of Yr. 1999). Office: Cassling Diagnostic Imaging 13808 F St Omaha NE 68137 E-mail: lcosimano@cassling.com.

LINDSAY, DIANNA MARIE, educational administrator; b. Boston, Dec. 7, 1948; d. Albert Joseph and June Hazelton Raggi; m. James William Lindsay III, Feb. 14, 1981. BA in Anthropology, Ea. Nazarene Coll., 1971; MEd in Curriculum and Instrn., Wright State U., 1973, MA in Social Studies Edn., 1974, MEd in Edn. Adminstrn., 1977; EdD in Urban History, Ball State U., 1976; MA in Counseling, U. Dayton, 2000. Supr. social edn. Ohio Dept. Edn., Columbus, 1976-77; asst. prin. Orange City Schs., Pepper Pike, Ohio, 1977-79; prin. North Olmsted (Ohio) Jr. High Sch., 1979-81; dir. secondary edn. North Olmsted City Schs., 1981-82; supt. Copley (Ohio)-Fairlawn City Schs., 1982-85; prin. North Olmsted High Sch., 1985-89, New Trier High Sch., Winnetka, Ill., 1989-96, Worthington Kilbourne H.S., Columbus, Ohio, 1996-2001; headmaster Columbus Jewish Day Sch., New Albany, Ohio, 2001—03; prin. Ridgefield H.S., Ridgefield, Conn., 2003—. Bd. dirs. Harvard Prins. Ctr., Cambridge, Mass., adj. prof. ednl. adminstrn., Grad. Sch. Edn., U. Dayton, Bexley, OH Contbr. articles to profl. jours. Bd. dirs. Nat. PTA, Chgo., 1987-89 (Educator of Yr. 1989), Found. Human Potential, Chgo.,; bd. trustee Columbus Jewish Country Day Sch. Named Prin. of Yr. Ohio Art Tchrs., 1989, one of 100 Up and Coming Educators, Exec. Educator Mag., 1988, Milken Educator of the Yr. Ohio, 1999; recipient John Vaughn Achievements in Edn. North Cen. Assn., 1988; named Ohio Prin. of Yr, 2000. Mem. AAUW, Ill. Tchrs. Fgn. Lang., Rotary Internat., Phi Delta Kappa. Methodist. Avocations: stained glass, reading, travel, biking, harpist. Office: Ridgefield HS 700 N Salem Rd Ridgefield CT 06877*

LINDSAY, JANICE CAMPBELL, communications executive, writer; b. Providence, R.I., Apr. 11, 1943; d. Everett William and Eleanor Paine (Battey) Inman; m. Richard Paul Lindsay, July 20, 1968; 1 child, Christopher Joseph. BA, Northeastern U., 1965; BDiv, Harvard U., 1968. Pub. rels. profl. Norton Co., Worcester, Mass., 1977—90; dir. internal comms., exec. speechwriter Saint-Gobain Corp., Worcester, 1990—93; pres. Janic Lindsay Comms., Marlborough, Mass., 1993—. Author: (book) The Milly Stories, 1998; contbr. newspaper column to local newspapers, short fiction and articles to various pubIs. Trustee Marlborough Pub. Libr., 2003—. Mem.: Marlborough C. of C. (Mar Comm com. 1993—), Soc. Children's Book Writers and Illustrators, Soc. Profl. Comms. (pres. 2002—, Communicator of Yr. 2001). Office: Janice Lindsay Comms 126 Crosby Rd Marlborough MA 01752 E-mail: janice@janice-lindsay.com.

LINDSAY, JUNE CAMPBELL MCKEE, communications executive; b. Detroit, Nov. 14, 1920; d. Maitland Everett and Josephine Belle (Campbell) McKee; m. Powell Lindsay, Nov. 25, 1967; 1 child, Kristi Costa-McKee. BA in Speech with honors (McGregor Fund Mich. grantee), U. Mich., 1943; cert. in electronics engring., Signal Corps Ground Signal Svc., 1943; postgrad. (Inst. Gen. Semantics grantee), U. Chgo., 1944-45; postgrad. (Armour grantee), NYU, 1945-46; postgrad., Columbia U., 1946-47, Wayne State U., 1960-64, U. Mich., 1964-70, 78—; MA, Specialist-in-Aging Cert., Inst. of Gerontology, 1982. Coord., activator McKee Prodns., Detroit, 1943-56, Being Unltd., Detroit, 1957—, InterBeing Inc., Detroit, 1979—, M.U.T.U.A.L.A.I.D., 1981—. Info. dir. Suitcase Theatre Inc., Lansing and Ann Arbor; cons. Cornelian Corner Detroit Inc., 1957-63, Islamic Ctr. Found. Soc., Detroit, 1959-62, city Ann Arbor Human Rels. Commn., 1966-68, Urban Adult Edn. Inst., Detroit, 1968-69, Mich. Bell Tel. Co., Detroit, 1969, African Art Gallery Founders, Detroit Inst. Arts, 1964, WKAR-TV, Mich. State U., 1971—. Mem. Nat. Caucus, Ctr. for Black Aged; bd. dirs. Mus. Youth Internat., Saline, Mich., Ann Arbor Cmty. Devel. Corp.; chaplain's asst. U. Hosp., Ann Arbor, 1971-72; program dir. People-to-People, Ann Arbor, 1971-72; Suitcase Theatre tour coord. Brit. Empire's Leprosy Relief Assn., 1972—; assembly cons. Baha'i Faith, 1960—; mem. Comprehensive Health Planning Coun. S.E. Mich., Baha'i Internat. Health Agy., Inst. for Advancement of Health, Mission Helath, Catherne McAuley Health Ctr. Share and Care Support Group. Recipient Award for Excellence Mich. Ednl. Assn.,1971, Mich. Assn. Classroom Tchrs., 1972; exec. dir. Powell Lindsay Meml. Program in Theatre and Comm., Louhelen Baha'i Sch. and Residential Coll., U. Mich., Flint, Mott Cmty. Coll., 1988—. Mem. ACLU, Soc. for Individual Responsibility, Am. Women in Radio and TV, Broadcast Pioneers, Am. Fedn. Advt., Internat. Platform Assn., Gray Panthers, Planetary Citizens, Am. Assn. Adult and Continuing Edn., Am. Pub. Health Assn., Wellness Assocs., Mich. Assn. Holistic Helath, Internat. Health Found., Inst. Study Conscious Evolution, Am. Soc. on Aging, Mich. Health Coun., Nat. Coun. on Aging, U.S. Assn. Humanistic Psychology, Assn. Holistic Health, Internat. Soc. for Study of Subtle Energies and Energy Medicine, Nat. Inst. for Clin. Application of Behavioral Medicine, Assn. Baha'i Studies, Interfaith Coun. Peace and Justice, Mental Health Assn. in Mich., Mich. League Human Svcs., Mich. Soc. Gerontology, Comprehensive Health Planning Coun. Southeastern Mich., Subarea Adv. Coun., Washtenaw County Coun. on Aging, Nat. Coun. Sr. Citizens, Am. Assn. Ret. Persons, Nat. Assn. Pub. Health Policy, People's Med. Soc., Alliance for Democracy and Diversity, Giraffe Soc., Living Tao Found., World Future Soc., Nat. Trust for Historic Preservation, Orgn. Devel. Inst. (registered orgn. devel. profl.), UN Assn of U.S., Age-Groups United Relating On-site Respecting Autonomy (activator, troupe leader, prodr., developer of videotape vignettes and revues). Home: 2339 S Circle Dr Ann Arbor MI 48103-3442

LINDSAY, LESLIE, packaging engineer; b. Amsterdam, N.Y., Oct. 30, 1960; d. R. Gardner and Dorothy (Loucks) L. BA in Advt., Mich. State U., 1981, BS in Package Engring., 1982. Cert. profl. engr. in packaging. Constrn. inspector N.Y. State Dept. Transp., Albany, 1983; sr. package design engr. Wang Labs., Inc., Lowell, Mass., 1983-90; sr. packaging engr. Apple Computer, Inc., Cupertino, Calif., 1990-97, Bose Corp., Framingham, Mass., 1997—2002, Syratech Corp., East Boston, Mass., 2003—. Conf. speaker Internat. Safe Transit Assn., 1994; AmeriStar judge, 1999, 2000. Staff editor Packaging Horizons Mag. N.Y. State Regents scholar, 1977; recipient Silver Ameristar award for electronics packaging, 1993, 2000, ID mag. packaging award, 1993, Ameristar judges award for merit, 1995, Mem. Women in Packaging, Inst. Packaging Profls. (cert., mem. reduction, reuse, and recycling of protective packaging task group), Molded Pulp Environ. Pkg. Assn. (founding bd. mem., seminar spkr. 1997), Am. Contract Bridge League, Boston Women's Rugby Club (tour chmn. 1985), Wang Ultimate Frisbee (social chmn. 1986-89). Home: 193 Winter St Framingham MA 01702-2435

LINDSAY, TWYLA LYNN, music educator; b. Chillicothe, Mo., June 22, 1964; d. Jesse Earl and Linda Louise Dodd; m. Ronald Retar Lindsay, Aug. 2, 1986; children: Jesalynn Delores, Ronald Micah. B in Edn. Music, Mo. Western State Coll., 1987; EdM, Lesle Coll., 1998. Music educator Kans. City (Mo.) Sch. Dist., 1987—, program dir., coord. career ladder program, 1999—2003. Sunday sch. tchr., youth worker Concord Bapt. Ch., Kansas City, 1986—2003, dir., musician, 1986—2000. Mem.: Mo. Music Educators Assn. Baptist. Avocations: travel, reading, bowling, singing, piano. Office: Kansas City Mo Sch Dist 1211 McGee Kansas City MO 64109 Office Phone: 816-418-7700.

LINDSEY, ADA MARIE, dean, nursing educator; b. Dayton, Ohio, May 8, 1937; m. George T. Lindsey. BS in Nursing, Ohio State U., 1959, MS, 1960; PhD, U. Md., 1977. RN. Staff nurse Ohio State U. Hosp., Columbus, 1960; instr. Mt. Carmel Sch. Nursing., Columbus, 1960-65, asst. dir., 1965-68; asst. prof. U. Md., Balt., 1968-77, assoc. prof., asst. dean, 1977-78; assoc. prof. U. Calif., San Francisco, 1979-83, chmn., 1979-86, prof., 1983-86; prof., dean Sch. Nursing UCLA, 1986-95; dean coll. nursing U. Nebr. Med. Ctr., 1995—. Co-editor: Pathophysiological Phenomena in Nursing, 1993 (Book of Yr. award 1986); contbr. articles to profl. jours. Fellow Am. Acad. Nursing; mem. Am. Nurses Assn., Nebr. Nurses Assn., Oncology Nursing Soc., Sigma Theta Tau. Office: U Nebraska Med Ctr 98-5330 Coll Nursing Omaha NE 68198-0001

LINDSEY, CAROL ANNETTE, nursing administrator, educator; d. Carl Victor and Ernestine Roberts; m. Ruben Amaro LIndsey, Apr. 6, 1991; children: Dominique, Brandon. BS Howard U., Washington, 1982. RN. Supervising staff nurse one Martin Luther King Jr. Hosp., LA, 1982—85; staff nursing Columbia Hosp. Women, Washington, 1985—86; utilization rev. nurse Calif. Med. Rev. Inc., Torrance, Calif., 1986—88; asst. DON Pacific Coast Coll., LA, 1988—91; nursing instr. SW Jr. Coll., LA, 1991—98, LA Trade Tech. Coll., 1992—99; DON Maxine Waters Employment Preparation Ctr., LA, 1992—. Ednl. cons. Springfield Coll., LA, 2003—. Recipient Outstanding Health Care Svcs. award, County LA, 1998. Office: Maxine Waters Employment Preparation Ctr 10925 Ctrl Ave Los Angeles CA 90059

LINDSEY, GINA MARIE, airport executive; Dir. Anchorage Internat. Airport, Alaska Airport System; gen. mgr. Seattle-Tacoma Internat. Airport, now mng. dir. aviation divsn. Office: Seattle Tacoma Internat Airport PO Box 68727 Seattle WA 98168-0727

LINDSEY, JACQUELYN MARIA, editor; b. Buffalo, June 6, 1952; d. George Henry and Patricia Ann (Rott) Bilkey; m. Timothy Paul Murphy, Jan. 29, 1970 (div. May 1981); children: Paul Jeffrey, Jeremy Michael; m. Warren Lee Eckert, Dec. 5, 1987 (div. June 1992); m. Donald J. Lindsey, Nov. 5, 1994. Student, Ind. U., 1984. Adminstrv. asst. Western N.Y. Cath. Visitor, Buffalo, 1979-81; sec. religious edn. Our Sunday Visitor, Huntington, Ind., 1981-84, editl. asst. periodicals dept., 1985, staff editor periodicals and books, editor My Daily Visitor, 1985-91, coord. Diocesan edits., 1986-88, assoc. editor books, 1987-90, editor trade books, 1990-93, acquisitions editor trade books, 1991—, acquisitions editor religious edn., 1991-2001, editl. devel. mgr., 2001—. Co-founder, co-owner Specialty Tool & Engring., LLC, 1995—; bd. dirs. STE, Inc. Editor, compiler: Photo Directory of U.S. Catholic Hierarchy, 1987, 90, 93; editor Leaves Marianhill Missionaries, 1991—, Catholic Family Prayer Book, 2001, Catholic Pocket Prayer Book, 2002, Catholic Prayer Book, 2003. Candidate for rep. Ind. Gen. Assembly 21st Dist., 1984; mem. LaFontaine Arts Coun., Huntington County, 1985-88; mem. Huntington County Dems., 1986-88. Mem. Cath. Press Assn. Office: Our Sunday Visitor Pub 200 Noll Plz Huntington IN 46750-4304

LINDSEY, JANE WILLANN, minister; b. Spencer, Tenn., Oct. 13, 1936; d. William Ezra Keyt and Martha Jane Anderson; m. Jack Lee Lindsey; children: Michael, Deborah Boggs. Cert. pastor. Fl. mgr. Nationwide Jewelry Co., N.Y.C., 1965—69; office mgr. Davicon Jewelers,Inc., N.Y.C., 1969—72. Bookkeeper Ctrl. Fla. Aluminum, Winter Haven, Fla., 1973—76; race rels. adv. Nationwide Jewelry Co., 1965—69. Author: Fantasy Come True (Best of Poets award The Internat. Libr. of Poetry, 2002), From Hell to Glory, 2004. Founder of mission for the needy Trinity Ho. Of Prayer, Winter Haven, Fla., 1979—85. Nominee Poet of the Yr., Internat. Soc. of Poets, 2002; recipient editor's choice award, 2002. Democrat. Pentecostal. Avocations: songwriting, painting, singing, poetry, gardening. Home: 519 Avenue K Northeast Winter Haven FL 33881-4154 Personal E-mail: jjandjlin@aol.com.

LINDSEY, JOANNE M. flight attendant, poet; b. Peoria, Ill., Aug. 27, 1936; d. George Edward and Elsie Rosetta (Mann) Lindsey; AA, El Camino Coll., Torrance, Calif., 1958. Exec. adminstrv. sec. Space Tech. Labs. (formerly Ramo-Woolridge), Hawthorne, Calif., 1958-64; flight attendant Am. Airlines, L.A., 1964—, Civil Res. Air Fleet Mil. Missions, 2003. Mem. acad. coun. Diplomatic Acad., London; vice consul Internat. Biog. Ctr.; with Airlift Svcs. Solicitation, 2003—. Contbr. poems to anthologies. Attended People to People Amb. Program's S. African Tour of Women Writers, 1998; active Civil Res. Air Fleet Mil. Missions, 2003; with Airlift Svcs. Solicitation, 2003—. Named to Internat. Libr. Poetry, 1996, 1997, 1998, 2002; recipient 7 Poetry Editor's Choice awards in anthologies. Mem.: Friends of Poets and Writers, L.A. World Affairs Coun., Internat. Soc. Poets, Audie Murphy Rsch. Found., Acad. Am. Poets. Avocations: gardening, writing, skiing, mountain biking, home refurbishing. Home: 846 American Oaks Ave Newbury Park CA 91320-5572

LINDSEY, LINDA LEE, sociology educator; b. St. Louis, Aug. 16, 1947; d. Robert Houston and Ruth Margaret (Weimert) L. BA in Sociology and Edn., U. Mo., 1969; MA, Case Western Res. U., 1972, PhD in Sociology, 1974; MA in Counseling, St. Louis U., 1983. Cert. secondary social sci. tchr., Mo. Asst. prof. sociology John Carroll U., Cleve., 1973-78; mktg. rsch. supr. Southwestern Bell, St. Louis, 1978-79; assoc. prof. St. Louis Coll. Pharmacy, 1979-86; prof. social thought and analysis Washington U., St. Louis, 1981—; prof. sociology Maryville U., St. Louis, 1986—. Cons. Fact Finders Mktg. Rsch., 1982-2002; rep., co-chair Women's Program Coun. St. Louis, 1983—; rschr. Women in the Developing World, Washington U. and Maryville U., 1990—; spokesperson Tobacco-Free Mo., St. Louis, 1996—; presenter World Congress Sociology, 1978, UN Conf. on Women, Beijing, 1995; program evaluator Asian Studies devel. program East-West Ctr., 1999-2002; fellowship coord. Asian Studies Devel. Program, Pearl River Delta, Hong Kong, 2001, Hong King-Shanghai, 2004. Author: Gender Roles: A Sociological Perspective, 1997; contbr. articles to profl. jours. Trustee Children's Survival Fund, Carbondale, Ill., 1985-96; chair advocacy com., bd. dirs. Luth. Family and Children's Svcs., St. Louis, 1992—; feedback supr. health focus group Med. Sch. St. Louis U., 1986—. Japanese Culture fellow NEH, 1995, fellow Keizai Koho Ctr., Tokyo, 1990, NSF fellow Harvard U., 1989, Malone fellow Nat. Coun. U.S.-Arab Rels., Jordan, 1988, Fulbright fellow, India, 1981, Pakistan, 1986, India Inst., 1999, S.E. Asia Inst., 2002; grantee Freeman Inst./Japan Studies Assn., 2003; NEH summer Seminar awardee, Asian Studies Devel. Program summer Inst. award to Korea, 2000. Mem. Am. Sociol. Assn., Global Health Coun., Japan Studies Assn. (freeman fellow 2003), Sociologists for Women in Soc., Midwest Sociol. Soc. (presenter 1979—), Mo. State Sociol. Soc. (pres. 1994-95, conf. presenter 1997-99), Fulbright Assn. Democrat. Lutheran. Avocations: international travel, swimming, speaking, writing. Home: 29 Algonquin Wood Pl Saint Louis MO 63122-2013 Office: Maryville Univ 13550 Conway Rd Saint Louis MO 63141-7299 Office Phone: 314-529-9456. E-mail: lindsey@maryville.edu.

LINDSEY, ROBERTA LEWISE, music researcher, historian; b. Munich, Apr. 23, 1958; d. Fred S. and Elsie E. (White) L. BMus, Butler U., 1980, MMus, 1987; PhD, Ohio State U., 1996. Pres., owner Profl. Typing Svcs., Indpls., 1980-84; mktg. specialist Merchants Mortgage Corp., Indpls., 1985-87; exec. asst. Ind. Arts Commn., Indpls., 1988-90; GTA Ohio State U., Columbus, 1990-94, music libr. asst., 1991-93, student coord. music in Ohio festival, 1993, vol. tutor coord., 1994-95, lectr. Marion, 1995; rsch. editor Ind. High Tech. Directory, 1995-97; lectr. Ind. U. Sch. Music, 1999, vis. asst. prof., 1999—2001, asst. prof. Indpls., 2001—. Rep. Susan Porter Meml. symposium Ohio State U., Columbus, 1995; program com. AMS Midwest, 2001—02; vis. rsch. fellow Am. Music Rsch. Ctr., 1997; tchr. of record Digital Music Libr. Grant project Ind. U., 2000—; presenter, spkr. in field. Book reviewer Ohioana Jour., 1997—2002, contbg. editor Lenten Devotional, 2000—01; contbr. articles to profl. jours. Reader Ctrl. Ind. Radio Reading, Inc., Indpls., 1985-90; co-founder, mem. Grad. Music Students Assn., Ohio State U., Columbus; mem. multicultural diversity com. Coun. of Grad. Students, Columbus, 1992, mem. orgns. and elections com., 1992, co-chair orientation com., 1993; pre-concert lectr. Carmel Symphony Orch., 1998; mem. Inst. Rep. for the Arts, 1999—; mem. IUPUI/Eiteljorg, adv. bd. Eiteljorg Mus., 1999—. Recipient Grad. Student Alumni Rsch. award, Ohio State U., 1993, Innovative Teaching Recognition award, Ind. U. Sch. Music, 2002; grantee Dena Epstein grantee, 2001, Ind. U. Purdue U. Indpls., 2001. Mem. Soc. Am. Music, Am. Musicol. Soc. (prof. com. 2001—, program com. midwest chpt. 2001-02), Coll. Music Soc. (Gt. Lakes chpt. conv. 2001, 02), Soc. Ethnomusicology, Am. Music Rsch. Ctr., Classic Ragtime Soc. Presbyterian.

LINDSEY, SUSAN LYNDAKER, zoologist; b. Valley Forge, Pa., Aug. 23, 1956; d. Howard Paul and Lillian Irene (Whitman) Lyndaker; m. Kevin Arthur Lindsey, July 17, 1982; children: Ryan Howard, Shannon Marie. BS in Biology, St. Lawrence U., 1978; MA in Zoology, So. Ill. U., Carbondale, 1980; PhD in Zoology, Colo. State U., 1987. Rschr. St. Lawrence U., Kenya, East Africa, 1978; tchr. Beth Jacob H.S., Denver, 1986-87; rschr. mammal dept. Dallas Zoo, 1988-93; exec. dir. Wild Canid Survival and Rsch. Ctr., Eureka, Mo., 1993—. Adj. prof. Cedar Valley Coll., 1992-93, So. Ill. U., Carbondale, 1996—; mgmt. group mem. Red Wolf Species Survival Plan, Tacoma, Wash., 1994—, Mexican Gray Wolf Species Survival Plan, Albuquerque, 1993—, Maned Wolf Species Survival Plan, Washington, 1999—. Author: (with others) The Okapi: Mysterious Animal of Congo-Zaire, 1999; contbr. articles to profl. jours. Docent Denver Zool. Found., Denver Zoo, 1985-88. Recipient Disting. Alumni citation, St. Lawrence U., 2003. Mem. Acad. Sci. St. Louis, Am. Zoo and Aquarium Assn., Am. Behavior Soc., Am. Soc. of Mammalogists, Beta Beta Beta, Phi Beta Kappa, Psi Chi. Avocations: horseback riding, canoeing, gardening, photography, travel. Office: Wild Canid Survival Rsch Ctr Wash U PO Box 760 Eureka MO 63025-0760 Office Phone: 636-938-5900.

LINDSLEY, MICHELLE A. theater educator; MS in Edn., Hofstra U., 1991. Cert. tchr. N.Y. Dir. of drama workshop Valley Stream (N.Y.) Cen. H.S., 1990—; dir. of choral activities Farmingdale (N.Y.) H.S., 1992—. Vocal coach/tchr. ML Studios, North Babylon, NY, 1986—; mus. dir. Farmingdale H.S., 1993—; drama dir. Weldon E. Howitt Mid. Sch., Farmingdale, 1992—2002. Dir., singer: choral performance Carnegie Hall Debut. Recipient Grammy Signature Sch. grant, Grammy Found., 1997, 2003. Master: Tri M Music Honor Soc. (chpt. sponsor 1992—2003); mem.: Am. Choral Directors Assn. (advocacy chair 2003—), Nassau Music Educators Assn. (pub. rels. dir. 1995—96), N.Y. State Sch. Music Assn., Music Educators Nat. Conf. Liberal. Roman Catholic. Avocations: music, travel, reading, photography. Office: Farmingdale H S 150 Lincoln St Farmingdale NY 11735 E-mail: fhschorus@hotmail.com.

LINEBERRY, BETTY O. hotel executive; b. Galax, Va. d. Claude Lester and Rose Gladys (Diamond) Osborne. BS, Radford U., 1985, MBA, 1988. Adminstrv. asst. J.C. Wheat & Co., Inc., Richmond, Va., 1960—62; customer svc., loan officer Blue Ridge Bank, Floyd, Va., 1979—88; asst. v.p., loan rev. officer Bank Svcs. of Va., Inc., Bassett, 1988—2001; ret., 2001; owner, mgr. Eagles' Wings Bed & Breakfast, Floyd, 1994—. Trustee, past pres. Jessie Peterman Libr. Endowment Fund, 1990—; pianist Floyd United Meth. Ch., past pres. Mem.: Floyd County Women's Club, Inc. Methodist. Avocations: golf, bridge, travel. Home and Office: PO Box 410 Floyd VA 24091

LINEBERRY, LAURIE LAWHORN, urban planner; d. Jarrett Lee and Mary Lou Lawhorn; m. Richard Paul Lineberry, Sept. 2, 2002; children: Caitlin Dale Grimes, Molly Louise Grimes. BS in Urban Planning, Calif. State Poly. U., 1981; MPA, Calif. State U., Northridge, 1990. Asst. dir. advanced planning City of Fontana, Calif., 1985—87; sr. planner City of Chino, Calif., 1987—91; asst. dir. planning and devel. Okanogan County, Wash., 1992—94, dir. planning and devel., 1994—96; asst. dir. Spokane County, Wash., 1996—99; asst. dir. cmty. planning City of Yuma, Ariz., 1999—. Pres. Yuma Fire Dept. Ladies' Aux., 2002—04; sec. Cibola Dance Team Booster Club, 2003—04; mem. handbell choir Trinity United Meth. Ch., 2000—, leader adult Sun. sch. class, 2001, chair Christian Edn. Com., 2002—04, sr. high youth leader, 2003—04. Mem.: Am. Inst. Cert. Planners. Methodist. Office: City of Yuma P O Box 13013 Yuma AZ 85366 Personal E-mail: lginyuma@digitaldune.net. E-mail: laurie.lineberry@ci.yuma.az.us.

LINEBERRY, REBECCA J. municipal official, treasurer; b. Pulaski, Va., Feb. 12, 1963; d. Leroy Martin Sr. and Virginia Lineberry; div. Jan. 25, 2002. AAS in Acctg., New River C.C., Dublin, Va., 1983. Cert. govt. treas. U. Va.; notary public Commonwealth of Va. Bookkeeper Bell Realty, Dublin, Va., 1983; clk., sec. Town of Dublin, 1983-87, asst. treas., 1987-90, treas., 1990—. Mem. Va. Govt. Fin. Officers Assn., Treas.' Assn. Va., S.W. Va. Treas.' Assn. (vice chair 1997-99, chmn. 1999-2001), Assn. Govt. Accts. mem. Am. Registry of Outstanding Profl. Avocations: archery, tennis, cross-stitch, travel, hot air ballooning. Office: Town of Dublin PO Box 1066 Dublin VA 24084-1066 E-mail: rlineberry@dublintown.org.

LINES, CHERYL ELAINE, music educator; b. Marshall, Mo., Dec. 24, 1964; d. W. Maurice Eckhoff; m. Kevin Lee Lines, July 25, 1987; children: Dalton Keith, Charlotte Faith. MusB in Edn., Ctrl. Meth. Coll., 1987; MA in Music Edn., Ctrl. Mo. State U., 1995. Band instr. Shelby (Mo.) County Sch., Shelbina, Mo., 1988—90; vocal music instr. Marshall (Mo.) Pub. Schs., 1990—. Chmn. Dept. Fine Arts Bueker Mid. Sch., Marshall, 1997—. Prin. clarinetest Marshall (Mo.) Philharm. Orch., 2001—; clarinetist Marshall (Mo.) Mcpl. Band, 1990—; dir. vocal choir Our Redeemer Luth. Ch., Marshall, 1993—; bd. dir. Marshall (Mo.) Philharm. Orch., 2000—. Mem.: Am. Choral Dir. Assn., West Ctrl. Mo. Music Educators Assn. (sec., treas. 1998—2003, v.p. jr. high choral), Mo. State Tchrs. Assn. (sec., pres. local cta 1990—96), Music Educators Nat. Conf., Pi Kappa Lambda. Lutheran. Home: 910 S Ann Drive Marshall MO 65340 Office: Bueker Middle School 565 S Odell Avenue Marshall MO 65340

LING, CHIEW SING, investment company executive; b. Bintulu, Malaysia, Dec. 5, 1964; came to U.S., 1996; d. Kong Gui Li. BE, Monash U., Melbourne, Victoria, Australia, 1986; M of Engring., U. NSW, Sydney, 1990. Mem. tech. staff Info. Tech. Inst., Singapore, 1990-93; asst. v.p. Bank of Am., Singapore, 1994-95; internat. rsch. & portfolio strategist Advanced Investment Tech., Clearwater, Fla., 1996-98; prin. State St. Global Advisors, Boston, 1998—. Mem. Boston Security Analyst Soc. Office: State St Global Advisors 2 Internat Pl Boston MA 02110

LING, KATHRYN WROLSTAD, health association administrator, minister; b. Watertown, Wis., Aug. 3, 1943; d. Jeffrey Harold and Constance Devina (Egre) Wrolstad; stepchildren: Renee Rainey, Roz Harper. BS in History and Polit. Sci., U. Wis., 1965; MDiv, Garrett-Evangelical Sem., 2001. Supr. recreation ARC, DaNang, Cam Ran Bay, VietNam, 1968; assoc. exec. dir. Am. Cancer Soc., Evanston, Ill., 1968-71, exec. dir., 1971-73, exec. dir. Montgomery County Unit, 1973-76, cons. income devel., 1976, dir., profl. edn. cancer incidence and end results, 1976-78, dir. income devel., 1978-82, exec. dir., 1982-84; assoc. exec. dir. Alzheimer's Disease and Related Disorders Assn., Chgo., 1986-87, v.p. community svcs., 1988-91, sr. v.p. chpt. Family Svcs. and Edn. divsn., 1991-93. Cons. Nat. Aphasia Assn.; pres. The Leadership Edge, Chgo.; chmn. bd. dirs. Kaleidoscope. Past chair Kaleidoscope; bd. mem. ROTARY/One; founding bd. Ill. Victnam Women's Project; Pastor, Lanark United Meth. Ch. Mem. Soc. Non-Profit Orgn. (chmn. bd. dirs., exec. v.p.). Home: 405 E Locust Lanark IL 61046-3467 Office Phone: 815-493-6400. Business E-Mail: pastorkate@internetni.com.

LINGÉ, VIRGINIA ANN, elementary school educator; b. North Little Rock, Ark., Dec. 28, 1952; d. Norman and Bernice Lucille (Austin) Johnson; m. Michael Douglas Lingé, June 17, 1987 (div. Oct. 2000); 1 child, Eric Michael. BA in English, U. Colo. Denver, 1995; MEd, U. Denver, 1998, postgrad. Lic. tchr. Colo., 1997. Tchr. elem. Denver Pub. Schs., 1997—. Mem.: Denver Classroom Tchr. Assn. (Minority Leadership Coun. 2003—). Democrat. Avocations: hiking, reading, gardening. Home: 3025 Zion St Aurora CO 80011 Office: Whittier Elem Sch 2480 Downing St Denver CO 80205*

LINGLE, KATHLEEN MCCALL, human resources specialist, consultant, marketing executive, entrepreneur; b. Berea, Ohio, Aug. 24, 1944; d. Arthur Vivian McCall and Mary M. (Maxwell) Miller; m. John Hunter Lingle, Sept. 3, 1968 (div. 1991); 1 child, Michael Cameron; m. Sam F. Serrapede, Aug. 15, 1993. BA, Occidental Coll., 1966; MS, Ohio State U., 1977. Vol. Peace Corps, Chile and Venezuela, 1966, 69-72; project dir. Ohio State U. Hosp., Columbus, 1977-78; rsch. assoc. Ednl. Testing Svc., Princeton, NJ, 1978-82; mgr. mktg. svcs. Gulton Industries, Princeton, 1982-84; rsch. dir. Rsch. 100, Princeton, 1984-85; dir. mktg. planning and rsch. Applied Data Rsch., Princeton, 1985-88; Western European sales mgr. Heuristics Software, Inc., Sacramento, 1988-89; pres., CEO Princeton Leadership Dynamics, 1989-90; rsch. dir. Families & Work Inst., N.Y.C., 1990-91, dir. tng., 1991-93; cons. Wyatt Co., N.Y.C., 1994-96; mgr. world class HR KPMG LLP, Princeton, 1996-97; sr. cons. Stromberg Cons., Purchase, NY, 1997-98; nat. work/life dir. KPMG LLP, Montvale, NJ, 1998—2003; exec. dir. Alliance for Work-Life Progress, Scottsdale, Ariz., 2003—. Co-chair work-life leadership coun. Conf. Bd., 2001, chair, 2002. Vice pres. ops. Unitarian Ch. of New Brunswick (N.J.), 1983-84; mem. adv. com. Boston Coll. Ctr. Work Family Standards of Excellence. Mem. NAFE, Am. Mktg. Assn., Am. Mgmt. Assn., Bus. and Profl. Women (chmn. membership com., 1990-91), N.J. Assn. Women Bus. Owners, Princeton Network Profl. Women, Princeton Area C. of C. (membership com.), Am. Field Svc., Wharton Work/Life Roundtable, Boston Coll. Work/Life Roundtable (steering com. 2002), Conf. Bd. Work/Life Leadership Coun. (bd. dirs. 2002), Alliance for Work/Life Progress. Democrat. Avocations: skiing, jogging, collecting modern art. Home: 16792 N 108th Way Scottsdale AZ 85255

LINGLE, LINDA, governor; b. St. Louis, June 4, 1953; Mayor County of Maui, Hawaii; chair. Democratic Party of Hawaii; mem. Maui County Coun., 1980—90; mayor Maui County, 1990—98; chmn. Hawaii Republican Party, 1999—2001; gubernatorial candidate for gov., 2002; gov. State of Hawaii, Honolulu, 2003—. Recipient Evelyn McPhail award, 2000. Office: Off of the Gov State Capitol Executive Chambers Honolulu HI 96813 Address: PO Box 25111 Honolulu HI 96825*

LINGLE, MARILYN FELKEL, freelance writer, columnist, author; b. Hillsboro, Ill., Aug. 16, 1932; d. Clarence Frederick and Anna Cecelia (Stank) Felkel; m. Ivan L. Lingle, Oct. 4, 1950 (dec. Aug. 2001); children: Ivan Dale, Aimee Lee Lingle Galligan, Clarence Lingle. Sec. Ill. State Police, 1950; with welfare dept. Ill. Pub. Aid, Hillsboro, 1951-52; rschr. Small Homes Coun., Champaign, 1952-53; sec. Hillsboro Schs., 1954; office, payroll clk. Eagle Picher Zinc, Hillsboro, 1955-56; continuity dir. Sta. WSMI, Litchfield, Hillsboro, 1966-87. Adv. bd. Am. Savs. Bank/Citizens Savs. Bank, vice chmn., 1986-93. Contbr. poetry to profl. jours. Cmty. edn. bridge instr. Lincoln Land C.C.; fin. chmn. Hillsboro Hosp. Aux., 1972; lit. vol. Graham Correctional Ctr., Hillsboro, 1986-97; pres., bd. dirs. Montgomery Players and Encore Play Theatre, 1954-70. Recipient Vol. of Yr. award Graham Correction Ctr., 1995, award of Merit Ill. State Bd. Edn., 1994-95. Mem. Cousteau Soc., Internat. Wildlife Fedn., Nat. Wildlife Fedn., Natural Resources Def. Coun., Phi Theta Kappa Internat., Hillsboro Country Club, Hillsboro Book Club, Hillsboro Study Club, Red Hat Soc. Democrat. Lutheran. Avocations: bridge, golf, gardening, travel, reading.

LINGLE, SARAH ELIZABETH, research scientist; b. Woodland, Calif., July 22, 1955; d. John Clayton and Dorothy Adelaide (Dubois) L.; m. Thomas Pratt Washington IV, May 20, 1989. BS, U. Calif., Davis, 1977; MS, U. Nebr., 1978; PhD, Wash. State U., 1982. Lab. asst. U. Calif., Davis, 1975-77; rsch. asst. U. Nebr., Lincoln, 1977-78; rsch., teaching asst. Wash. State U., Pullman, 1979-82; rsch. assoc. Agrl. Rsch. Svc., USDA, Fargo, N.D., 1982-84, supr. plant physiologist Weslaco, Tex., 1984-97, acting rsch. leader, 1991-92, plant physiologist New Orleans, 1997—. Assoc. editor Crop Sci., 1991-97; contbr. articles to profl. jours., chpts. to 2 books. Fellow Am. Soc. Agronomy; mem. AAAS, Am. Soc. Plant Physiologists, Crop Sci. Soc. Am., Sigma Xi. Episcopalian. Achievements include research in biochemistry and physiology of sugar deposition in sucrose-storing plant tissues. Office: USDA Agrl Rsch Svc 1100 Robert E Lee Blvd PO Box 19687 New Orleans LA 70179-0687 E-mail: slingle@srrc.ars.usda.gov.

LINHARES, JUDITH YVONNE, artist, educator; b. Pasadena, Calif., Nov. 21, 1940; m. Philip E. Linhares June 15, 1961 (div. July, 1971); 1 child, Amanda Linhares Mason. Student, LA Otis Art Inst., 1960, San Francisco Art Inst., 1963; BFA, Calif. Coll. Arts & Crafts, 1964, MFA, 1970. Art tchr. San Francisco State Coll., 1969-71, San Jose City Coll., 1971-72, U. Calif., Davis, Berkeley, 1979, U. San Francisco, San Francisco Art Inst. other univs., Calif., N.Y., La., 1978—, Sch. of Visual Arts, N.Y.C., 1981—, NYU, 1990—. Lectr. at univs. and art insts. nationwide, 1974— One-woman shows include include Berkeley Gallery, San Francisco, 1972, one-woman shows include San Francisco Art Mus., 1976, Paule Anglim Gallery, San Francisco, 1978, 1980, 1982, 1984, 1988, 1989, 1994, 2003, Nancy Lurie Gallery, Chgo., 1981, 1989, 1990, Concord Gallery, N.Y.C., 1982, 1983, Ruth Siegel Gallery, 1985, Mo David Gallery, 1985, L.A. Louver Gallery, Venice, Calif., 1988, Julie Sylvester Edition, N.Y.C., 1989, The Gaibreath Gallery, Lexington, Ky., 1993, Greenville (S.C.) County Mus. of Art, 1994 (survey exhibition 1971-93), Sonoma (Calif.) State U., 1994, Edward Thorp Gallery, N.Y.C., 1997, 2001, exhibited in group shows at San Francisco Art Inst., 1973, Indpls. Mus. Art, 1984, Peninsula Mus., Monterey, Calif., 1987, Michael Walls Gallery, N.Y., 1987, Rosenberg Gallery, N.Y.C., 1992, pub. collections including Greenville (S.C.) County Mus. Art, pub. collections, Oakland (Calif.) Mus., Butler Inst. Am. Art, Youngstown, Ohio, Crocker Art Mus., Sacramento, Calif., San Francisco Mus. Modern Art, San Francisco Airport Commn. Recipient Adeline Kent award San Francisco Art Inst., 1976; grantee Nat Endowment for Arts, 1979, 87, 93-94, Gottlieb grantee, 1993; Guggenheim fellow, 1997, Anonymous Was a Woman Found. grantee, 1999-2000. E-mail: judithlinhares@aol.com.

LINHART, LETTY LEMON, editor; b. Pittsburg, Kans., Sept. 22, 1933; d. Robert Sheldon and Lois (Wise) Lemon; m. Robert Spayde Kennedy, June 8, 1955 (div. 1978); children: Carole Shea, Nancy Schrimpf, Nina Kennedy; m. Daniel Julian Linhart, June 9, 1986. BS, BA in English and Journalism, U.Kans., 1955; MS in Journalism, Boston U., 1975. Reporter Leavenworth (Kans.) Times, 1954; editor Human Resources Rsch. Office George Washington U., Washington, 1955-56; editor Behavior Rsch. Lab. Harvard Med. Sch., Boston, 1956-58; instr. Boston YMCA, 1960-64; freelance writer and columnist, 1975—; editor Somerville (Mass.) Times, 1975-77; pub. rels. dir. Lettermen of Lexington, Mass., 1978, instr. English Rollins Coll., Winter Park, Fla., 1978-79, Valencia Community Coll., Orlando, Fla., 1978-82, U. Cen. Fla., Orlando, 1979-82; tech. writer Kirschman Software, Altamonto Springs, Mass., 1980-81, Dynamic Control Software, Winter Park, Fla., 1981-82; editor Fla. Specifier, Winter Park, 1982-85, Mobile Home News, Maitland, Fla., 1985-86; instr. English, Seminole C.C., Sanford, Fla., 1986-94; Elderhostel instr. Canterbury Rsch. Ctr., 1994—; editor Oviedo (Fla.) Voice, 1994-95, 96, Tuscawilla Today Monthly Mag., 2000—01; columnist Oviedo Voice, Oviedo, Fla., 2001; reporter North County Times, Vista, Calif., 2001—. Resource person Am. on Line, 1996—. Author: Are These Extravagant Promises, 1989, Clues for the Clueless, 1996, Bits and Bytes of Recovery, 1998, Turn Your Eyes, 2002, In The End it's Faith, 2003, The Minister Made Macramé, 2004; contbr. articles to profl. jours. Pres. MIT Dames Boston, 1958-59, Boston Alumnae of Delta Delta Delta, 1959-62; dist. pres Delta Delta Delta, Tex., 1962-65; svc. provider, content provider, cmty. leader Am. On Line Careers and Work Forum, 1996-2000; cmty. leader media & journalism, AOL, 2000-. Named Outstanding Collegiate Delta Delta Delta, 1955. Mem. NAFE, Ctrl. Fla. Jazz Soc. (bd. dirs. 1983-93), Internat. Platform Soc., Soc. Women Execs., Altrusa Club (publicity com. 1980-83), Orlando Press Club (bd. dirs.), Mortar Bd., Phi Beta Kappa (Belmont, Mass. pres. 1965-78), Theta Sigma Phi, Sigma Delta Chi, Delta Sigma Rho. Avocations: swimming, singing, jazz. Home and Office: 1600 E Vista Way # 5 Vista CA 92084-1020 E-mail: oviedoletty@aol.com.

LINK, PHOEBE FORREST, educator, poet, author; b. Palmerton, Pa., Feb. 20, 1926; d. Phoebe Eleanor (Lewis) Forrest and John Nevins Forrest; m. Robert H. Link, July 13, 1962; children: David Forrest, Anne Harris. BA in Psychology, Pa. State U., 1947, MS in Child Devel. and Family Relationships, 1952; postgrad. U. Rochester, 1957-59, Harvard U., 1958. Dir. teen age program YWCA, Lansing, Mich., 1947-50, Rochester, N.Y., 1952-56; research asst. Pa. State U., State College, 1950-52; tchr. Rochester, 1956-60; demonstration tchr. William Antheil Sch., Trenton, N.J., 1960-63; mem. faculty Trenton State Coll., 1960-63; tchr. State College area schs., 1971-1993; lectr. Am. Home Econs. Assn. Conv.; cons. family studies, leader continuing edn. workshops Pa. State U., 1977, others; mem. staff dean women Harvard U., Cambridge, Mass., summer 1958; dir. Children's Program for Pa. Dist. Attys. Author: Small? Tall? Not At All, 1973, Passionate Realist, 1994; staff writer Horizon, 1985-87; author, creator Hearthrob series, Pa. State U., 1987; contbr. articles to profl. jours. Trustee Schlow Pub. Library, State College, Pa., 1980-83; founder, first chmn. poetry com. Cen. Pa. Festival Arts; founder Children's Link, Bar Harbor, Maine. AAUW Simmons grantee, 1984; recipient Excellence in Edn. award Pa. State Univ., 1993; featured author on TV series The Writing Life, featured speaker at 50th class reunion P.S.U., reader-editor for WPSX-TV, Mem. AAUW, NEA, Pa. Edn. Assn., State Coll. Area Edn. Assn.(scholarship com.), Mortar Board Alumni (founder, 1st pres., pres.), Pa. State U. Coll. Human Devel. Alumni (bd. dirs.). Phi Delta Kappa, Omicron Nu Alumni, Tau Phi Sigma, Peterson Society P.S.U. Home: 22 Cricklewood Cir State College PA 16803-2105

LINKE, ERIKA C. school librarian; d. Heinz G. and Martha Linke; m. Henry A. Pisciotta, Feb. 22, 1979; 1 child, Rachel N. L. Pisciotta. BA, Miami U., 1970; MLS, U. Minn., Mpls., 1978; cert., ACRL Harvard Leadership Inst., 2000. Assoc. libr. Carnegie Mellon U., Pitts., 1985—. Bd. dirs. Oakland Libr. Consortium, Pitts., 1991—98. Treas. Carnegie Mellon U. Fed. Credit Union, Pitts., 1993—2003; adv. coun. Pitts. Bibliophiles, Pitts., 2001—. Recipient award, Mortar Bd., 1969, Sr. Fellow, UCLA, 2003. Mem.: Libr. Adminstrn. & Mgmt. Assn. (exec. com. stats. sect. 1999—2001), We. Pa./W.Va. Assn. Coll. & Rsch. Libr. (v.p./pres.-elect 2002—), Assn. Coll. & Rsch. Libr. (chair copyright con. 1995—97, exec. bd. 2001—, chair budget & fin. com. 2001—). Office: Carnegie Mellon Univ 5000 Forbes Ave Pittsburgh PA 15213

LINKLATER, ISABELLE STANISLAWA YAROSH-GALAZKA (LEE LINKLATER), foundation administrator; b. Chgo., Sept. 15, 1939; d. Baron Stanislaw and Isabelle Lydia (Yarosh) Galazka. BE, Chgo. State U., 1959. Cert. tchr., Ill. Pub. rels. coord. Kelling Co., Chgo., 1955-57; tchr. Chg. Bd. Edn., 1957-89, coord. computer lab., 1989—; founder, pres., exec. dir. Assisi Animal Found. Edn. writer, coord. Elsa Internat. Wild Animal

Appeal, Ill., 1985—; writer Lakeland Press, 1992. Bd. dirs. Townsquare Players, Woodstock (Ill.) Opera House, 1989-91. Recipient Outstanding Citizen award CBS Broadcasting, 1992. Mem. McHenry County Defenders (bd. dirs. 1989-91), East African Wildlife Soc. (U.S. rep.). Avocations: travel, music, theater. Office: Assisi Animal Found PO Box 143 Crystal Lake IL 60039-0143

LINKONIS, SUZANNE NEWBOLD, probation officer, counselor; b. Phila., Aug. 24, 1945; d. William Bartram and Kathryn (Taylor) Newbold; m. Bertram Lawrence Linkonis, May 29, 1966; children: Robert William, Deborah Anne, Richard Anthony. AA in Psychology, Albany (Ga.) Jr. Coll., 1979; BA in Psychology, Albany (Ga.) State U., 1981; MS in Indsl. Psychology, Va. Commonwealth U., 1986. Office mgr., media buyer Long Advt. Agy., Richmond, Va., 1981-84; media mgr. Clarke & Assocs., Richmond, 1984-85; human resources asst. Continental Ins., Richmond, 1985; rsch. assoc. Signet Bank, N.A., Richmond, 1986-87; program coord. Med. Coll. Va., Richmond, 1988; personnel mgr. Bur. Microbiology, Richmond, 1988-89; pers. specialist Va. State Dept. Corrections, Richmond, 1989-90; human rights adv. Va. State Dept. Youth and Family Svcs., Richmond, 1990-92, rehab. counselor, 1992-94, sr. rehab. counselor, 1994; pre-trial case mgr./counselor Henrico County Govt., Richmond, 1994-97, cmty. corrections case mgr., counselor, 1997-2000, sr. county probation officer, counselor, 2001—. Future dir., cons. Mary Kay Cosmetics, Springfield, Va., 1975-77. Republican. Roman Catholic. Avocations: networking, walking, reading. Home: 401 Saybrook Dr Richmond VA 23236-3621 Office: 8600 Dixon Powers Dr Richmond VA 23273-7032 E-mail: blinkonis@cs.com.

LINN, CAROLE ANNE, dietician; b. Portland, Oreg., Mar. 3, 1945; d. James Leslie and Alice Mae (Thorburn) L. Intern, U. Minn., 1967-68; BS, Oreg. State U., 1963-67. Nutrition cons. licensing and cert. sect. Oreg. State Bd. Health, Portland, 1968-70; chief clin. dietitian Rogue Valley Med. Ctr., Medford, Oreg., 1970—; clin. faculty, dietetic internship program Oreg. Health Scis. U., Portland, 2000—. Cons. Hillhaven Health Care Ctr., Medford, 1971-83; lectr. Local Speakers Bur., Medford. Mem. ASPEN, Am. Dietetic Assn., Am. Diabetic Assn., Oreg. Dietetic Assn. (sec. 1973-75, nominating com. 1974-75, Young Dietitian of Yr. 1976), So. Oreg. Dietetic Assn., Alpha Lambda Delta, Omicron Nu. Democrat. Mem. Christ Unity Ch. Avocations: sewing, needlecrafts, cooking, swimming, skiing. Office: Rogue Valley Med Ctr 2825 E Barnett Rd Medford OR 97504-8332

LINN, MARCIA CYROG, education educator; b. Milw., May 27, 1943; d. George W. and Frances (Vanderhoof) Cyrog; m. Stuart Michael Linn, 1967 (div. 1979); children: Matthew, Allison; m. Curtis Bruce Tarter, 1987. BA in Psychology and Stats., Stanford U., 1965, MA in Ednl. Psychology, 1967, PhD in Ednl. Psychology, 1970. Prin. investigator Lawrence Hall Sci. U. Calif., 1970-87, prin. investigator Sch. Edn., 1985—, asst. dean Sch. Edn., 1983-85, prof., 1989—; prin. investigator NSF Funded Ctr.- Tech.-Enhanced Learning in Sci. (TELS), 2003—08; chancellor's prof., 2003—. Fulbright prof. Weizmann Inst., Israel, 1983; exec. dir. seminars U. Calif., 1985-86, dir. instnl. tech. program, 1988-96, chair cognition and devel., 1996—98; cons. Apple Computer, 1983—; mem. adv. com. on sci. edn. NSF, 1978—85, Ednl. Testing Svc., 1986—, Smithsonian Instn., 1986—, Fulbright Program, 1983-86, Grad. Record Exam. Bd., 1990-94, adv. com. edn. and human resources directorate, NSF; chair Cognitive Studes Bd. McDonell Found., 1994-97; mem. computing svcs. adv. bd. Carnegie Mellon U., 1991-99; mem. steering com. 3d Internat. Math. and Sci. Study, U.S., 1991-2002. Author: Education and the Challenge of Technology, 1987; co-author: The Psychology of Gender--Advances Through Meta Analysis, 1986—, Designing Pascal Solutions, 1992—, Designing Pascal Solutions with Data Structures, 1996, Computers, Teachers, Peers-Science Learning Partners, 2000, Internet Environments for Science Education, 2003; contbr. articles to profl. jours. Sci. advisor Parents Club, Lafayette, Calif., 1984-87; mem. Internat. Women's Forum, Women's Forum West, 1992—, membership com., 1995-98; bd. dirs. Nat. Ctr. for Sci. Edn., 1997—, GIS and edn. com., 2000—; mem. bd. on behavioral, cognitive and sensory scis. Nat. Rsch. Coun., 1997—, mem. com. on info. tech. literacy, computer sci. and telecomms., 1997-2000; mem. nat. adv. bd. Nat. Ctr. for Improving Studnet Learning and Achievement in Math. and Sci., 1997—. Recipient fellow Ctr. for Adv. Study in Behavior. Scis. 1995-96, 2001-02, Excellence Ednl. Rsch. award Coun. Sci. Soc. Pres., 1998. Fellow AAAS (bd. dirs. 1996-2001), APA, AAUW (mem. commn. tech. and gender 1998-2001), Am. Psychol. Soc.; mem. Nat. Assn. Rsch. in Sci. and Teaching (bd. dirs. 1983-86, assoc. editor jour., Outstanding Paper award 1978, Outstanding Jour. Article award 1975, 83, Disting. Contbns. to Sci. Edn. Through Rsch. award 1994), Am. Ednl. Rsch. Assn. (chmn. rsch. on women and edn. 1983-85, Women Educators Rsch. award 1982, 88, edn. in sci. and tech. 1989-90, ann. mtg. program com. 1996, Willystine Goodsell award 1991), Nat. Sci. Tchrs. Assn. (mem. rsch. agenda com. 1987-90, task force 1993-94), Soc. for Rsch. in Child Devel. (editl. bd. 1984-89), Soc. Rsch. Adolescence, Sierra Club. Avocations: swimming, hiking. Office: U Calif Grad Sch Edn 4611 Tolman Hl Berkeley CA 94720-0001

LINNANSALO, VERA, engineer; b. Helsinki, Finland, Oct. 9, 1950; came to U.S., 1960, naturalized, 1969; d. Boris and Vera (Schkurat-Schkuropatsky) L. BS in Computer and Info. Sci., BME, Cleve. State U., 1974; MBA, U. Akron, 1983. Engring. assoc. B.F. Goodrich Co., Akron, Ohio, 1974-75, assoc. product engr., 1975-77, tire devel. engr., 1977-79, advanced tire devel. engr., 1979-84, quality devel. engr., 1984-85, sr. quality devel. engr., 1985-86; coord. GM-10 Uniroyal Goodrich Tire Co., Akron, 1986-88, sr. tire devel. scientist, 1988-89; mgr. design and product quality Pirelli Armstrong Tire Corp., New Haven, 1989-90; product design engr. truck ops. Ford Motor Co., Dearborn, 1990-93, vehicle quality and process specialist, corp. quality office, 1993-94, supr. econoline quality and reliability comml. truck, 1995-96, supr. ranger quality and reliablity light truck vehicle ctr., 1996-98, supr. explorer quality and reliability truck vehicle ctr., 1998-99, supr. tech. strategy, rsch. and advanced tech., 2000—02, performance cons. global core engring., 2002—. Mem. Am. Soc. Quality (sr., cert. quality engr.), Soc. Automotive Engrs., Mensa. Home: 9234 Mayflower Plymouth MI 48170 Office: WHQ The American Rd Dearborn MI 48124-3958 E-mail: vlinnans@ford.com.

LINNÉA, SHARON, writer, playwright; d. William Diderichsen and Marilynn Joyce Webber; m. Robert Owens Scott; children: Jonathan Brendan Scott, Linnéa Juliet Scott. Student, Wheaton Coll., 1974-76; BA, NYU, 1978. With editl. dept. various titles William Morrow and Co., N.Y.C., 1977-78, Taplinger and Assocs., N.Y.C., 1978-80, Flying Magazine, N.Y.C., 1982-83; features editor Scholastic Voice, N.Y.C., 1983-85; staff writer Guideposts Mag., N.Y.C., 1985-91, contbg. editor, 1991—99, Angels on Earth, 1995—99; prodr. Inspiration Beliefnet.com, 1999—2002; head writer New Morning Show Hallmark Network, 2002. V.p. Imagining Things Enterprises, N.Y.C.; spkr. in field. Producer (film) Knowing Lisa, 1991 (Silver award Worldfest/Houston film festival); author: (study guide) Romeo and Juliet by William Shakespeare, 1984, Hedda Gabbler and A Doll's House by Henrik Ibsen, 1985, (book) Raoul Wallenberg: The Man Who Stopped Death, 1993 (Best Book of 1993 Jewish World, Dayton Jewish Chronicle, The Speaker), Princess Ka'iulani: Hope of A Nation, Heart of A People, 1999 (Carter G. Woodson award), (with Jeff Meyer) America's Famous and Historic Trees, 2001, (plays), Clown of God, 1977, The Singer, 1978, A Matter of Time, 1981, Tales from the Vermont Woods, 1982, (screenplays) Missouri, Ma Cheri, Tomorrow Is My Dancing Day; co-author: Chicken Soup from the Soul of Hawaii, 2003; ghostwriter articles in Reader's Digest and Guideposts Mag.; profile biographer World of Heroes Sch. Curriculum; psychology columnist Beliefnet.com; freelancer Marvel Comics, Children's TV Workship, Hallmark Hall of Fame; freelance editor Chicken Soup for the Soul; contbr. to book pubs. including From the Ashes, 2001, Big Book of Angels, 2002; contbr. articles to popular publs. Recipient Storytelling World award, 2004. Mem.: Authors Guild. Avocations: latching rugs, public speaking. Office: Imagining Things Enterprises 36 Crystal Farm Rd Warwick NY 10990-2862

LINNEY, BEVERLY See HALLAM, BEVERLY

LINNEY, LAURA, actress; b. N.Y.C., Feb. 5, 1964; d. Romulus Linney and Ann Leggett Perse; m. David Adkins, 1995 (div. 2000). BFA, Brown U., 1986; grad., Juilliard Sch., 1989. Motion picture and T.V. actress. Films include Lonrenzo's Oil, 1992, Searching for Bobby Fischer, 1993, Blind Spot, 1993, Dave, 1993, A Simple Twist of Fate, 1994, Congo, 1995, Primal Fear, 1996, The Truman Show, 1998, Absolute Power, 1998, Lush, 1999, You Can Count on Me, 2000, The House of Mirth, 2000, Running Mates, 2000, Maze, 2000, The Laramie Project, 2002, The Mothman Prophecies, 2002, The Life of David Gale, 2003, Mystic River, 2003, Love Actually, 2003 (T.V. films) Tales of the City, 1993, More Tales of the City, 1998, Love Letters, 1999, Wild Iris, 2001; theatre prodn.: The Crucible, 2002 (Tony nominee). Office: c/o CAA 9830 Wilshire Blvd Beverly Hills CA 90212-1804

LINO, MARISA ROSE, diplomat; d. Luigi and Vida (Bego) L. BA in Polit. Sci., Portland State U., 1971; MA in Internat. Affairs, George Washington U., 1972; postgrad., U. Zagreb, Yugoslavia, 1972-73; cert. in advanced engrng. studies, MIT, 1982. Rotational officer Dept. State, Lima, Peru, 1975-77, watch officer ops. ctr. Washington, 1977-78, staff asst. policy planning staff, 1978-79, econ./comml. officer Baghdad, Iraq, 1979-81, info. systems officer, 1982-83, adminstrv. officer, 1983-85, econ. counselor Damascus, Syria, 1986-88, refugee coord. Islamabad, Pakistan, 1988-90, consul gen. Florence, Italy, 1990-93, mem. sr. exec. seminar, 1993-94, dep. exec. sec. of state, 1994-96; U.S. amb. Republic of Albania, 1996-99; sr. inspector Office Inspector Gen., Washington, 1999-2000; sr. negotiator for base access and burden sharing Polit. Mil. Affairs Bur., Washington, 2000—. Exhibited in group show of watercolor monotypes, Province of Florence, 1993. Mem. Am. Fgn. Svc. Assn. Avocations: tennis, sailing, hiking. Office: Polit Mil Affairs Bur Washington DC 20520-0001

LINS, DEBRA, bank executive; BA, Lakeland Coll.; MBA, U. Wis. Pres., CEO, dir. Cmty. Bus. Bank, Sauk City, Wis., 1994—. Bd.dir. Badger Chpt. ARC; bd. dirs. Sauk Prairie Area C. of C.; bd. dir. Sauk Prairie Meml. Hosp., 1992—98, Sauk Prairie United Way, Inc., 1996—2001, benedictine Life Found. Wis., Inc., 2000—02. Named Disting. Woman in Banking, N.W. Fin. Rev., 1994, Outstanding Entrepreneurial Woman in Dane County, The Bus. Forum, 1997, Outstanding Woman in Agr., Assn. Women in Agr., 1998, Wis. Woman of Century, Wis. Woman Mag., 2000, One of 25 Most Powerful Women in Banking, U.S. Banker Mag., 2003. Mem.: Am. Banker's Assn. (mem. cmty. bankers Coun.). Office: Community Business Bank 1111 Sycamore St PO Box 636 Sauk City WI 53583-0636*

LINSE, MARION MARILYN, art educator; b. Janesville, Wis., Feb. 27, 1957; d. Charles John and Marilyn Marion Swanson; m. James Thomas Linse, Sept. 2, 1979; children: Melissa, Joshua, Katrina, Anna. AA, Concordia U., St. Paul, Minn., 1977, BA, 1979. Lic. tchr. Wis. Tchr. grades 5, 6 St. John's Luth., Chaska, 1979—90; subst. tchr. Chaska (Minn.) Schs., 1980—81; with Sears, Eden Prairie, Minn., 1980—81; tchr. day care, Chanhassen, Minn., 1981—82; tchr. grade 5 Bethlehem Luth., Sheboygan, Wis., 1982—90; migrant tchr. Cedar Grove(Wis.) Belgium, 1990—92, art tchr. grades 1-8, 1992—; vol. art tchr. Trinity Luth. Sch., Sheboygan, 1991—. Author: poems. Mem.: Nat. Arts Edn. Assn., Wis. Arts Edn. Assn. Republican. Lutheran. Avocations: photography, sewing, crafts, hiking, skiing. Home: 1609 N 3rd St Sheboygan WI 53081

LINSENMEIER, CAROL VINCENT, music educator; b. Manchester, Conn., Feb. 5, 1952; d. Donald Scott and Alyss (Campbell) Vincent; m. John Andrew Linsenmeier, Dec. 28, 1979; children: Andrew, Thomas. B Music Edn., Coll. of Wooster, Ohio, 1974; M Music Edn., U. Ga., Athens, 1978; grad. student, Kent U., 1996—. Strings specialist Greenville (S.C.) County Schs., 1974—76; Suzuki coord. U. Ga., Athens, 1977—80; violin/viola tchr. The Sch. of Fine Arts, Willoughby, Ohio, 1980—, chair music dept., 1988—. Arranger: children's musical How Big Is Your Circle, 2000. Rschr., bd. trustees No. Ireland Comty. Cooperation Initiative, Mentor, Ohio, 1999—; sec., bd. trustees Svcs. for Ind. Living, Cleve., 1998—; treas., bd, trustees SANO/IMF, Stow, Ohio, 2001—. Mem.: Suzuki Assn. of the Americas, Music Educators Nat. Conf., Am. String Tchrs. Assn., Kappa Lambda, Kappa Delta Pi, Phi Kappa Phi. Avocations: Irish fiddling, Traditional Am. fiddling, needlepoint. Office: The Fine Arts Assn 38660 Mentor Ave Willoughby OH 44094

LINTNER, KAREN LOUISE, art educator; d. Frederic Paul and Margaret Elizabeth Anthony; m. John Gilbert Lintner, June 19, 1965; children: Colby James, Kevin John. BS, Kutztown State U., Pa., 1966. Art tchr. Henrico County Sch. Dist., Richmond, Va., 1965—66, Fairfax County Sch. Dist., Fairfax, Va., 1966—70; art tchr, coord. Fairfax County Adult Edn., Fairfax, Va., 1968—76; art tchr. State Coll. Area Sch. Dist., State College, Pa., 1978—. Regional chair Scholastic Art Awards of Ctrl. Pa, Harrisburg, Pa., 1987—98. Banner design, Animal Stack (first prize, 1979), Landscape (first prize, 1980), Two Moons (hon. mention, 1981), exhibitions include Geneva (hon. mention, 1982). Vol. - juror; art demonstrations Ctrl. Pa. Festival of the Arts, State College, 1980—2001; parade com. CPFA First Night, State College, Pa., 1994—96. Recipient Marie Walsh Sharpe Tchrs. as Artists award, Marie Walsh Sharpe Found., 1989, Outstanding k-12 Art Tchr. award in Sculpture, Internat. Sculpture Ctr., 2001. Mem.: Nat. Art Edn. Assn. (assoc.; ea. region divsn. dir. 1996—98, Mid-Level Art Educator of the Yr. 2001, Ea. Region Mid-Level Art Educator of the Yr. 2000), Pa, Art Edn. Assn. (assoc.; regional rep., Mid-Level Art Educator of the Yr. 1999), Potter's Guild of Ctrl. Pa, (assoc.; pres. 1985—91). Avocations: painting, ceramics, reading, travel, gardening. Office: State College Area Sch Dist 131 West Nittany Ave State College PA 16801 E-mail: kll11@scasd.k12.pa.us.

LINTON, KRISTY ANN, primary school educator; b. Dothan, Ala., Oct. 11, 1975; d. William Kenneth and Peggy Cobb Linton. BS, Troy State U., 1998; post grad., Fla. State U., U. West Fla. Cert. Early Childhood Edn. Ala., Fla., ESOL. From 2nd grade tchr. to kindergarten tchr. Jackson County Sch., Marianna, Fla., 1998—2001, kindergarten tchr., 2001—03, Alachua County Sch., Gainesville, 2003—. Summer kid's coll. tchr. Chipolia Jr. Coll., Marianna, 2000—01. Vol. Am. Heart Assn.; team capt. relay for life Am. Cancer Soc., Marianna, 1999—2002; vol. cheerleader coach Grand Ridge H.S.; cheerleader judge Jackson County H.S.'s; after sch. tutor; vol. Eastside Bapt. Ch., 2001—. Recipient Internat. Educator Yr. award, Who's Who of Am. Educators, 2004. Republican. Baptist. Avocations: teaching cheerleading, volunteering, tennis, reading. Home: #G302 5133 SW 91st Ct Gainesville FL 32608 Office: Kimball Wiles Elem Sch Gainesville FL 32608 Office Phone: 352-955-6955. E-mail: kristylinton594@hotmail.com.

LINTULA, MARGARET M. elementary and secondary school educator; b. Duluth, Minn., June 19, 1941; d. Yule Porter Eaton and Catherine Gurine Fleming Eaton Berg; m. John Elias Lintula, Aug. 17, 1963; 1 child, Maija Gurine Lintula Alexandrou. BS, U. Minn., 1963; MS, U. Wis., Superior, 1975. Lic. elem. tchr., K-12 reading specialist, Wis. Tchr. grade 4 Lakeside Elem. Sch., Duluth, 1963-66; tchr. grades 3-4 Boze Elem., Tacoma, 1967-71; tchr. English grades 7-8 Drummond (Wis.) Sch., 1971—2002, K-12 dist. reading specialist, 1976—2002; ret., 2002. Del. Dem. Nat. Conv., N.Y.C., 1992, state convs., 1988-97, vice-chmn. Dem. party, Bayfield County, 1986—. Named Secondary Tchr. of Yr., Wis. Congress Parents & Tchrs. Inc., 1989—90. Mem. NEA (bd. dirs. 1991-98, mem. women's issues com. 1998—), Wis. Edn. Assn. Coun. (bd. dirs. 1976-82, 88-98), Drummond Edn. Assn. (pres., chief negotiator 1980—), Wis. State Reading Assn., Internat. Reading Assn., Lions Club (Cable, Wis. chpt.). Democrat. Avocations: poetry, biking, painting, reading, travel. Home: PO Box 136 Drummond WI 54832-0136

LINZEY, VERNA MAY, minister, writer; b. Coffeyville, Kans., May 17, 1919; d. Carey Franklin Hall Jr. and Alice May (Hart) Hall-Doyle; m. Stanford Eugene Linzey Jr., July 13, 1941; children: Gena May English, Janice Ellen Schreuder, Stanford Eugene III, Virginia Darnelle Lemons-(dec.), Sharon Faye, George William, Vera Evelyn Clark, Paul Edward, David Leon, James Franklin. Student, Southwestern Assembly of God U., Waxahachie, Tex., 1938—39, Fuller Theol. Sem., Pasadena, Calif., 1980—. Lic. Minister Assembly of God, 1945. Asst. minister First Assembly of God, Baldwin Park, Calif., 1953—54; co-founder Holy Spirit Evangelism, Escondido, Calif., 1976—. Consultant Holy Spirit Evangelism, Escondido, Calif., 1976—; leader Pentecostal Movement Worldwide, 1976. Songwriter: O Blessed Jesus, 1971; author: The Baptism with the Holy Spirit, 2004; contbr. articles to religious publs., 2001—02. Mem. nat. com. Dem. orgn., 1943—45; mem. nat. com. Republican Orgn., 1946—. Recipient Cert. of Recognition, Mayor of Escondido, Calif., 2001, Congressional Proclamation Rev. Dr. Verna May Linzey Day April 29th, 2001. Avocations: gardening, piano, photography, genealogy, singing. Home: 1641 Kenora Dr Escondido CA 92027 Office: Verna M Linzey 354 E Washington Ave Ste A Escondido CA 92025 Office Phone: 760-743-3913.

LION, JILL ALTSCHUL, sculptor; b. Norfolk, Va., June 15, 1941; d. Herbert Bernard and Rashelle Goldberg Altschul; m. John R. Lion, Dec. 29, 1963; children: David, Trina. BA in Russian, George Washington U., 1963; MA in Polit. Sci., SUNY, Albany, 1965; postgrad., Notre Dame Coll., 1978—79. Transp. planner Balt. Govt. Older Citizens, 1975—77; dir. energy savs. State DNR, Balt., 1977; pvt. stone sculptor Balt., 1980—. Prin. works include included in 3 books and 1 mag. Vol. Libr. #31, Balt., Our Daily Bread Soup Kitchen, Balt. Mem.: Sculptors Inc. Studio: Studio 342 Mill Ctr 3000 Chestnut St Baltimore MD 21211

LION, LINDA N. retired federal agency administrator; b. Brookline, Mass., Feb. 18, 1949; m. Donor M. Lion, Sept. 29, 1978; 2 children. BA in Biology, Wheaton Coll., 1970; PhD, MIT, 1975; grad., Nat. Def. U., Ft. Lesley J. McNair, Washington, 1990. Instr. human nutrition MIT, Cambridge, 1975-76; ind. nutrition cons. Haiti, Dominican Republic, Ghana, Bolivia, 1976-77; regional health and nutrition adviser Health & Nutrition Divsn. Office Devel. Resources Bur. Latin Am. and Caribbean USAID, Washington, 1977-78; dir. Office Health, Population & Nutrition USAID, Jamaica, 1978-79; health devel. officer, officer policy devel. & program rev. Bur. Policy and Program Coord. USAID, Washington, 1979; dir. Office Health Population & Nutrition USAID, Guyana, 1979-81, dir. Office Project Devel. & Monitoring, 1981-85; chief Mid. East Divsn. Office Project Devel. Bur. Asia and Near East USAID, Washington, 1985-86; chief Capital Devel. Project Divsn. USAID, Peru, 1986-87, dir. Office Human Resources, 1987-89, dep. dir. Office Info. Resources Mgmt. Bur. Mgmt., 1990-94, mission dir. regional support mission for East Asia Bangkok, 1994-96, dep. asst. adminstr. human resources Bur. Mgmt. Washington, 1996—2000, dep. asst. adminstr. global programs, 2000—02. Avocations: golf, bridge. Office: 6600 Baymeadow Ct Mc Lean VA 22101

LIONE, SUSAN GARRETT, consultant; b. Boston, May 23, 1945; d. Charles Gerard and Josephine (Galgano) Garrett; m. Gerald Frederick Lione, Nov. 9, 1968; children: Mark Garrett, Christina Marie. BA in Econs., Immaculata Coll., 1966. Investment asst. Morgan Guaranty Trust, N.Y.C., 1966-69; portfolio mgr. Union Trust Co., Stamford, Conn., 1969-72; sales coord. Japan Air Lines, Hong Kong, 1977-84; mktg. coord. Hong Kong Tennis Patron Assn., 1982-84; ind. study on schs. Cen. Pk. Task Force, N.Y.C., 1990; sales assoc. Preferred Properties, New Canaan, Conn., 1991-96; assoc. HTG Investment Advisors, Inc., New Canaan, 1997—. Pres. Am. Women's Assn., Hong Kong, 1977-78; sec. New Canaan CARES, 1989-90, v.p., 1990-91, pres., 1991-93, mem. adv. bd., 1998—. Bd. dirs. United Way New Canaan, 1994-2000, bd. sec., 1996-98, mem. allocations com., 1994—, allocations chmn., 1995-96, bd. chmn., 98-2000; bd. dirs. Vol. Ctr. Lower Fairfield County, 1996-99, sec., 1997-98, mem. adv. bd., 1999—; mem. lay adv. bd. St. Aloysius Ch., New Canaan, 1994, 95-98, 2003—. Avocation: tennis. Office: HTG Investment Advisors 112 Main St New Canaan CT 06840-4730 Office Phone: 203-972-8262.

LIONNET, FRANCOISE, French and comparative literature educator; b. Mauritius, July 28, 1948; came to U.S., 1969; d. Joseph Louis L. and Madeleine Berenger; m. John A McCumber, May 8, 1972; children: Jonathan, Danielle. PhD in Comparative Lit., U. Mich., 1986. Prof. French & comparative lit. Northwestern U., Evanston, Ill., 1986-98; prof., chair French UCLA, L.A., 1998—. Vis. prof. Duke U., Durham, N.C., 1996. Author: Autobiographical Voices, 1989, Postcolonial Representations, 1995. Fellow Soc.Humanities, Cornell U., 1988-89, U. Calif. Humanities Rsch. Studies Inst., 1992, Rockefeller Found., 1991-92, Social Sci. Rsch. Coun., Mauritius, 1996, Fulbright fellow U.Mauritius, 1996-97. Mem. MLA (mem. exec. com. 1999—), Am. Philos. Soc., Am. Coun. Learned Socs., Am. Comparative Lit. Assn. Avocations: hiking, swimming, music. Office: UCLA 212 Royce Hl Los Angeles CA 90095-0001

LIOTUS, SANDRA MARY, lighting designer, small business owner, consultant; b. Pitts., Aug. 23, 1959; d. George A. Liotus and Marlene A. Rouse. BFA in Design, Carnegie Mellon U., 1984. Designer George Kovacs Lighting, Inc., N.Y.C., 1985-89; lighting designer with LeMar Terry N.Y.C. and Hoboken, N.J., 1993-95; lighting design cons. Sandra Liotus Lighting Design, N.Y.C. and Newport, R.I., 1995—. Spl. exhibits designer Redwood Libr. and Athenaeum, Newport, 1999—; lighting consulting design svcs. Preservation Soc. of Newport County, Newport, 1997—, Harvard U., Cambridge, Mass., 1995—, Ctr. Art Studio, N.Y.C., 1995—, Robin Symes Ltd., London, 1999—, Mus. of City of N.Y., 2000—, City of Boston Firemen-Vendome Meml., 2001—, Hist. Soc. Greenwich, Conn., 2002—, N.Y. Yacht Club, 2002—, David Rockefeller Residence, N.Y.C., 2003—, pvt. clients. David Rockefeller Coll., 2003—. Avocation: artist. Office: Sandra Liotus Lighting Design LLC 68 William St Newport RI 02840-3309 Fax: 401-845-8949. Office Phone: 401-845-9236. E-mail: s.liotus@worldnet.att.net.

LIPAN, PETRUTA E. semiotician, curator, artist; b. Braila, Romania, Oct. 18, 1957; d. Ene and Maria C. L. BFA, Washington Univ., 1991; MFA, PhD in Semiotic Studies, Ind. Univ., 1995. Instr. sculpture Ind. U., Bloomington, 1993-94, instr. 3-dimensional design, 1994-95; instr. sculpture Laumeyer Sculpture Mus., St. Louis, 1995-96; prof. art appreciation St. Louis U., 1996, assoc. curator S. Cuples House and McNamee Gallery, 1996—; mem. faculty Washington U., St. Louis, 1996-99; prof. art history St. Louis U., 1999-2000. Vis. artist Laumeier Sculpture Park, 1997, 1996, artist in residence, 1996; assisted in curating, organization and mktg. of shows including Edward Boccia: The Eye of the Painter, 1996, Ads With A Conscience, 1997, A Voice of Their Own, 1997, Mev Puelo: Witness to Life, 1997, Iridescence, 1998; curator Enduring Light: Fragility and Persistence, 1998, Passion for Color: Frederick Carder at Steuben Glass Works, 1999; presenter 5th Argentinian congress on Color, APHRA Behn Soc., Phila., 1999, Can. Semiotic Assn. Conf., Que., 1999, 7th Congress of IASS-AIS, Dresden, Germany, 1999, Math. Connections in Art, Music, and Sci., Winfield, Kans., 1999. Group exhibitions include Sioux City Art Ctr., 1997, Ind. Univ., 1996, Centre Interculturel Strathearn, 1996, The Editions Limited Gallery of Art, 1995, The Carver Cultural Ctr., 1995, Ind. Univ. Art Mus., 1995, Ind. Univ., 1993, 94, 95, San Diego Art Inst., 1993, Steinberg Gallery, 1991, Bixby Gallery, 1991, South Grand Gallery, 1986, numerous others. Mem. Nat. Sculpture Soc., Internat. Assn. for Semiotic Studies (presenter at confs.), Semiotic Soc. Am., Am. Assn. Mus., Assn. for Art

History, Internat. Assn. for Visual Semiotics, Midwest Art History Soc. Home: 1129 Olivaire Ln Saint Louis MO 63132-3010 E-mail: lipanp@yahoo.com.

LIPIN, JOAN CAROL, healthcare executive, consultant; b. Denver, Aug. 25, 1947; d. Theodore and Kathe (Pardo) Lipin. BA, NYU, 1969; postgrad., MIT, 1973-74; MBA, Boston U., 1977; postgrad., N.Y. Law Sch., 2000—. Adminstrv. staff MIT, Boston, 1969, tech. asst., 1977; adminstr. Mass. Gen. Hosp., Boston, 1975-76, mgmt. cons., 1976; dept. head N.Y. Hosp., N.Y.C., 1977-80; exec. v.p. Gordon-Keeble, N.Y.C., 1980-83; owner, pres. Thor Sci., N.Y.C., 1983-86; sr. mgr. health svcs. ARC in Greater N.Y., 1986-88; cons. to pres. Nat. Inst. Life Threatening Illness and Loss, 1988-91; owner, pres. Thor Rsch., N.Y.C., 1989—; asst. to sr. atty. Wisehart & Koch, N.Y.C., 1990—. Cons., mem. rev. bd. Ind. Testing Lab., N.Y.C., 1981-85, Forum Corp. Responsibility, 1981-82. Pub. poet; Libr. of Congress/Poetry Guild. Exec. mem., officer Lexington Dem. Club, 1993-2003; judicial del.-alt., 1995-2003; mem. county com. Dem. Party County of N.Y., 1994—; mem. Nat. Def. Counsel, Drs. Without Borders, Physicians for Social Responsibility; charter mem. So. Law Poverty Ctr., 2000; founding mem. Nat. Campaign for Tolerance, Earth Justice Legal Def. Fund.; mem. Women's Action Coun., 2001—; charter mem. women's action coun., Amnesty Internat., 2001—. Student mem. ABA, N.Y. State Bar Assn. (com. on atty. professionalism 2002—, com. profl. responsibility of ins.), Am. Trial Lawyers Assn., N.Y. Acad. Sci., Am. Soc. Zoologists, Union Concerned Scientists, Amnesty Internat., Audubon Soc., World Wildlife Fund, Thanantology Found. (steering com., spl. asst. to pres. 1988-91), Amnesty Internat. (charter), Nat. Inst. Life (co-chair Threatening Illness and Loss symposium 1991), Pre-Hosp. Care Providers, Sierra Club. Home: 45 E 89th St Apt 14G New York NY 10128-1229 Office: Thor Rsch PO Box 1257 New York NY 10028-0009 E-mail: wisehartAM@aol.com.

LIPINSKI, ANN MARIE, newspaper editor; b. Trenton, Mich. Assoc. mng. editor for met. news. Chgo. Tribune, 1991—93, dep. mng. editor, 1994—95, mng. editor, 1995—2000, VP & exec. editor, 2000—01, Senior VP & exec. editor, 2001—. Recipient Pulitzer prize for series on politics and conflicts of interest Chgo. City Coun., 1988; grand prize, Robert F. Kennedy journ. award, 1993. Office: Chgo Tribune 435 N Michigan Ave Chicago IL 60611-4066*

LIPINSKI, BARBARA JANINA, psychologist, psychotherapist, educator, writer; b. Chgo., Feb. 29, 1956; d. Janek and Alicja (Brzozkiewicz) L. (dec.); m. Bernard Joseph Burns, Feb. 14, 1976 (div. 1985). B of Social Work, U. Ill., Chgo., 1978; MFCC, MA, U. Calif., Santa Barbara, 1982; PhD, U. So. Calif., 1992. Diplomate Am. Bd. Forensic Medicine; cert. tchr., Calif., psychology tchr., Calif.; cert. adminstr., non-pub. agent; lic. marriage, family and child therapist; bd. cert. forensic examiner; lic. psychologist. Police svc. officer Santa Barbara (Calif.) Police Dept., 1978-79, peace officer Airport Police, Santa Barbara, 1979-80; emergency comms. Univ. Police, Santa Barbara, 1980-82; facilitator, instr. Nat. Traffic Safety Inst., San Jose, Calif., 1981-87; assoc. dir. Community Health Task Force on Alcohol and Drug Abuse, Santa Barbara, 1982-86; instr. Santa Barbara C.C., 1987-88; patients' rights adv. Santa Barbara County Calif. Mental Health Adminstrn., 1986-89; pvt. practice psychotherapist Santa Barbara, 1985—; faculty mem., chair Pacifica Grad. Inst., Carpinteria, Calif., 1989-2000; police psychologist L.A. Police Dept., 2000; evaluator mentally ill offender crime reduction grant Bd. Corrections, Ventura, 2002—03. Intern clin. psychology L.A. County Sheriff's Dept., 1991-92, cons. Devereaux Found., Santa Barbara, 1993-95, Ctr. for Law Related Edn., Santa Barbara, 1986; cons., trainer Univ. Police Dept., Santa Barbara, 1982, 89. Author: In The Best Interest of the Patient: Ethical and Legal Issues in the Practice of Psychotherapy, 1999, Wisdom of the Oracle, 2000m, Feng Shui Wisdom, 2001, Heed the Call: Psychological Perspectives on Child Abuse, 2001, The Tao of Integrity: Legal, Ethical and Professional Issues in Psychology, 2002. Vol. crisis work Nat. Assn. Children of Alcoholics, L.A., 1987; crisis intervention worker Women in Crisis Can Act, Chgo., 1975-76; vol. counselor Santa Barbara Child Sexual Assault Treatment Ctr.-PACT, Santa Barbara, 1981-82. Recipient Grad. Teaching assistanship U. So. Calif., 1990-92. Mem. APA, Am. Profl. Soc. on Abuse of Children, Am. Coll. Forensic Examiners, Calif. Assn. Marriage and Family Therapists, Am. Psychotherapy Assn. (exec. adv. bd. 1997-99). Avocations: horticulture, aviculture, ecology. Office: Pacific Meridian 301 Los Cabos Ln Ventura CA 93001-1183 E-mail: pacificmeridian@aol.com.

LIPINSKI, TARA KRISTEN, retired professional figure skater; b. Phila., June 10, 1982; Prof. figure skater Stars On Ice, 1998—. Nat. spokesperson Campaign for Tobacco-Free Kids. Tara Lipinski's A Night of Skating Champions, Houston, 2003; actor(TV appearance): 7th Heaven, 2003, The Wayne Brady Show, 2003. Recipient Mary Lou Retton award, U.S. Olympic Festival, 1994, 2nd Place, Skate Can., 1996, 1st (team), Postal Svc. Challenge, 1996, 2nd Place, Nations Cup, 1996, 3rd Place, Trophy Lalique, 1996, 1st Place, Hershey's Kisses Challenge, 1997, World Championships, 1997, Champion Series Final, 1997, 1998, 1st Nat. Sr., 1997, 2nd Place, Nat. Championship, 1998, 1st Place, Rattle and Roll, 1998, Gold Medal, Winter Olympic Games, 1998. Achievements include youngest Olympic Festival gold medalist at age 12. Avocations: reading, cooking, tennis.*

LIPITZ, ELAINE KAPPEL, secondary education fine arts educator; b. N.Y.C., Oct. 5, 1924; d. Herman Kappel and Ceil (Friedson) Ferester; m. Elliott Alan Lipitz, Mar. 20, 1945; children: Linda Marsha Schreiber, Alice Lynn Lindholm. BFA, Pratt Coll., 1946; MA, Columbia U., 1955; MA in Adminstrn., St. Johns U., 1974. Fine art tchr. Art & Design High Sch., N.Y.C., 1946-47, Jamaica High Sch., Queens, N.Y., 1949-70, fin art supr., 1970-75; coord. student affairs John Bowne High Sch., Queens, 1979-90, dir. community rels., 1990-93. Interior design cons., 1950-80; jewelry designer, 1950-62. One woman shows include Gallery of Manhasset, 1968, Booth Meml. Art Gallery, Queens, 1989; exhibited in group shows at Ctr. Kew Gardens Hills, 1966, Bklyn. Mus. Art, 1969, Park Ave. Christian Ch., 1969, N.Y. Regional Exhbn. Painting and Sculpture, 1969, Newsday Fed. Art Show, 1969 (1st Prize), 70 (2d Place award), Norfolk Mus., 1970, Gallery North, Setauket, N.Y., 1994, 95, Art Guild of Coconut Creek, 1995, 96, Schacknow Mus., 1997 (Spl. award), Coral Springs Artist Guild, 1997, Bailey Hall Gallery, 1998 (hon. mention), Schaknow Mus., 1998, Coral Springs Museum, 1999, 2000, 01, Serve Gallery (3d place spl. mention), 2000, 01, Coral Spring Mus., 2002, Courtyard Gallery, Boca Raton, 2003 (Merit award), Port Jefferson Libr. Gallery, 2003. Recipient Mayor's Honor award for Cmty. Svc., 1989, 1st prize sculpture Govt. Ctr. Art Guild of Coconut Creek, Fla., 1994. Avocations: swimming, walking, traveling, concerts, theatre. Home: 3 Princess Tree Ct Port Jefferson NY 11777-1742

LIPKE, KATHRYN, artist, educator; b. Cooperstown, N.D., Dec. 16, 1939; d. Herluf O. Vigesaa and Ruth E. Vigessa; children: Tanya, Shannon. BS, N.D. State U., Fargo, 1962; MA, U. Calif., Berkeley, 1969. Prof. faculty fine arts Concordia U., Montreal, 1977—96, founder fibres, dept. sculpture, ceramic and fibres, 1977—96, assoc. dean rsch. faculty fine arts, 1992—96, prof. emeritus, 1997; docent prof. sculpture U. Lapland, Rovaniemi, Finland, 1997—. Vis. artist and prof. Goldsmiths Coll., U. London, Acad. Art and Design, Lodz, Poland, U. Calif., Davis, Emily Carr Coll. Art, Vancouver, B.C., Canada,, Ont. Coll. Art and Harborfront, Toronto, Form Design Ctr., Malmo, Sweden; lectr. textiles Coll. of Marin, Kentfield, Calif., 1972-1974, Ind. U., Bloomington, 1973; lectr. Hartford Arts Sch., U. Hartford, 1977; sculptor, with works in U.S., Cordoba, Argentina, Kemijarvi and Levi Tunturi, Finland, Germany; numerous corp. commns.; solo and group art exhbns. in U.S., Can., Europe; prodr., dir. videos. Vol. art orgns., women's groups, environ. groups, 1969—. Recipient Outstanding Documentary Video Prodn. award Maya Women of Guatemala, 1993, 97, Seagram Fund Acad. Innovation, Re-presenting Women, 1995-97; fellow NEA, 1977-78; grantee Vt. Arts Coun. and NEA, 2004. Mem.: RAVA (Assoc. Visual Arts), Textile Soc. Am., Assoc. Ind. Video and Filmmakers, USA. Home and Office: Dakota Prodns 6559 Vt Route 109 Belvidere Center VT 05442-9699

LIPNIC, VICTORIA A. federal agency administrator; Grad., Allegheny Coll., George Mason U. Spl. asst. to dir. bus. liaison, spl. asst. asst. sec. trade devel. Dept. Commerce, 1984—89; atty. pvt. practice; atty. employment and labor law dept. U.S. Postal Svc., 1994—2000; profl. staff mem., counsel U.S. Ho. Rels. Com. Edn. and the Workforce, 2000—02; asst. sec. employment stds. adminstrn. U.S. Dept. Labor, Washington, 2002—. Office: US Dept Labor FPB 200 Constitition Ave NW Washington DC 20210-0001

LIPNICK, ANNE RUTH, advocate; b. Cambridge, Mass., Aug. 9, 1943; d. Henry and Celia Florence (Weinberg) Goldberg; m. Robert Louis Lipnick, June 11, 1967; children: Deborah Ellen Lipnick Bort, David Henry. BA, Brandeis U., 1965; MSW, U. Minn., 1972. Academy of Certified Social Workers NASW, 2003. Rsch. asst. Brandeis U., Waltham, Mass., 1965—66; social worker Divsn. Child Guardianship, Boston, 1966—68, Jewish Family Svc., St. Paul, 1968—70, Family and Children's Svcs., Stamford, Conn., 1974—78; coord. spl. edn. parent resource ctr. Alexandria (Va.) City Pub. Schs., 1989—. Study group chair Children Together, Alexandria, 1999—; mem. Early Intervention Interagency Coordinating Coun., Alexandria. Exec. com. Brookville-Seminary Valley Civic Assn., Alexandria; v.p. for youth svcs. Agudas Achim Congregation, Alexandria, 1999—2001. Recipient Riggs-ARC Ednl. Leadership award, Assn. for Retarded Citizens No. Va., 1991, John Duty Collins III Outstanding Adv. for Persons with Disabilities award, Alexandria Commn. on Persons with Disabilities, 1996. Mem.: NASW. Home: 5308 Pender Ct Alexandria VA 22304 E-mail: alipnick@acps.k12.va.us.

LIPOWSKI, EARLENE E, pharmacist, education educator; b. Merrill, Wis., May 2, 1949; d. Earl E and Mardell R Koehler; m. Gary E Lipowski, June 4, 1972; children: Catherine Bernards, Steven P. BS, U. of Wis.-Madison, 1967—72, MS, 1983—86, PhD, 1986—90. Registered Pharmacist Wis., 1973, Fla., 1990. Pharmacist Beaver Dam Cmty. Hospitals, Beaver Dam, Wis., 1975—83; tchg./rsch. asst. U. of Wis.-Madison, Madison, Wis., 1983—90; assoc. prof. U. of Fla., 1990—. Aaas congl. fellow US Senate, Washington, 1996—97; vis. faculty Chiang Mai U., Thailand, 2002. Mem. Fla. Medicaid Drug Use Rev. Adv. Bd., 1993, Wis. Medicaid Drug Use Rev. Bd., 1984—94. Fellow: Am. Pharmacists Assn. (pres. acad. of pharm. rsch. and sci. 2003—); mem.: Am. Assn. of Colleges of Pharmacy, Am. Soc. of Health-System Pharmacists, Am. Soc. of Cons. Pharmacists, Phi Lambda Sigma, Ro Chi Nat. Pharmacy Honor Soc., Phi Kappa Phi. Office: University of Florida PO Box 100496 Gainesville FL 32610-0496 E-mail: lipowski@cop.ufl.edu.

LIPPARD, LUCY ROWLAND, writer, lecturer; b. NYC, Apr. 14, 1937; d. Vernon William and Margaret Isham (Cross) L.; m. Robert Tracy Ryman, Aug. 19, 1961 (div. 1968); 1 child, Ethan Isham Ryman. BA, Smith Coll., 1958; MA in Art History, NYU, 1962; DFA (hon.), Moore Coll. Art, 1972, San Francisco Art Inst., 1984, Maine Coll. Art, 1994, Mass. Coll. Art, 1998, Art Institute of Chgo., 2003. Freelance writer, lectr., curator, 1964—. Prof. Sch. Visual Arts, N.Y.C., Williams Coll., Queensland U., Brisbane, Australia, U. Colo., Boulder; mem. adv. bd. Franklin Furnace, N.Y.C., 1979—; bd. dirs. Printed Matter, N.Y.C., Ctr. Study Polit. Graphics, L.A., Time & Space Ltd., Hudson, NY, Sustainable Settings, Woody Creek, Colo., Earthworks Inst., Santa Fe; co-founder W.E.B., Ad Hoc Women Artist's Com., Artists Meeting for Cultural Change, Heresies Collective and Jour., Artists Call Against US Intervention in Ctrl. Am., Polit. Art Documentation/Distbn. Author: Overlay: Contemporary Art and the Art of Prehistory, 1983, Mixed Blessings: New Art in a Multicultural America, 1990, Pop Art, 1966, The Graphic work of Philip Evergood, 1966, Changing: Essays in Art Criticism, 1971, Tony Smith, 1972, Six Years: The Dematerialization of the Art Object, 1973, From the Center: Feminist Essays on Women's Art, 1976, Eva Hesse, 1976, (with Charles Simonds) Cracking (Brüchig Werden), 1979, Ad Reinhardt, 1981, Get the Message? A Decade of Art for Social Change, 1984, A Different War: Vietnam in Art, 1988, The Pink Glass Swan: Selected Feminist Essays on Art, 1995, The Lure of the Local: Senses of Place in a Multicentered Society, 1997, Florence Pierce: In Touch With Light, 1998, On the Beaten Track: Tourism, Art and Place, 1999, (with Alfred Barr and James Thrall Soby) The School of Paris, 1965, (novel) I See/You Mean, 1979; author, editor: Partial Recall: Photographs of Native North Americans, 1992; editor: Surrealists on Art, 1970, Dadas on Art, 1971; contbg. editor: Art in Am.; editor El Puente de Galisteo, 1997—; contbr. monthly columns Village Voice, 1981-85, In These Times, Z Mag., also numerous articles to mag., anthologies, and mus. catalogs, 1964—. Mem. planning and adv. com. Santa Fe County Open Land and Trails, 1999. Recipient Frederick Douglass award North Star Fund, 1994, Frank Jewett Mather award for criticism Coll. Art Assn., 1974, Claude Fuess award for pub. svc. Phillips Andover Acad., 1975, curating award Penny McCall Found., 1989, citation NYC mayor David Dinkins, 1990, Smith Coll. medal, 1992, Guggenheim fellow, 1968, ArtTable award, 1999; grantee Lannan Found., 2000. Avocations: hiking, rock art, local history. Home and Office: 14 Avenida Vieja Galisteo NM 87540-9783

LIPPE, HARRIET ROTHFEDER, retired elementary school educator; b. Harrison, N.J., Dec. 31, 1922; d. Max and Mary Fiks Rothfeder; Student, Mills Coll., 1940—41; BS, N.J. State Tchrs. Coll., Newark, 1944, postgrad., 1949, Columbia U. Tchrs. Coll., 1944—46. Cert. driver's edn. tchr. Tchr. kindergarten, Title I remedial classes in reading, lang., and math., Head Start, registration Newark Bd. Edn., 1950—88. Acting pres. social com., chmn. LaMer Condominium, 1998—2000; founder-mem. Jewish Home for Agedat Douglas Gardens, 1998; mem. Shaare Zedek Hosp., 2000—; pres., cemetery chair Klausner Lodge Bnai Zion, 1987. Mem.: LWV (mem. fundraising com. 1950), Chopin Soc., Friends of Music. Avocations: walking, golf, ping pong/table tennis, theater, concerts. Home: Apt 508 W 1880 S Ocean Dr Hallandale FL 33009

LIPPENS, NANCY COBB, music educator; b. Albuquerque, Nov. 15, 1951; d. Ernest Oscar and Mona Faye Hill; m. Larry W. Cobb, July 2, 1977 (div. Mar. 1992); children: Cary Andrew, Allison Elizabeth; m. Stephen Frank, Jan. 8, 2000. BM, Okla. Bapt. U., 1973; MM, Mich. State U., 1975; DMA, U. Okla., 1987. Instr. music Mercer U., Macon, Ga., 1975—76, Okla. Bapt. U., Shawnee, Okla., 1976—2002; prof. music Dallas Bapt. U., 2002—. Reader and table leader AP music theory ETS, Princeton, NJ, 2000—. Composer: Threnody for chorus and orch., 1998 (ASCAP Spl. Distinction award in Rudolph Nissim competition, 1998), The Seven Last Words. Com. chair Habitat for Humanity, Shawnee, 1999—2000; pres. Shawnee Band Boosters, 1999—2000; bd. dirs. Shawnee Little Theater, 2001—02. Mem.: Am. Choral Dirs. Assn. (Okla. Dir. of Distinction 1995), Pi Kappa Lambda, Sigma Alpha Iota (Nat. Leadership award 1973). Avocations: tennis, reading. Office: Dallas Baptist U 3000 Mountain Creek Pky Dallas TX 75211

LIPPINCOTT, JANET, artist, art educator; b. N.Y.C., May 16, 1918. Student Emil Bisttram, Taos., N.Mex., Colorado Springs Fine Art Ctr., Art Students League N.Y.C., San Francisco Art Inst. Artist in residence, Durango, Colo., 1968; guest artist Tamarind Inst., Albuquerque, 1973; participant TV ednl. programs, Denver, Albuquerque; art instr. Santa Fe Community Coll., N.Mex., 1984— . Participant juried exhbns. including: Denver Mus., 1968, N.Mex. Arts Commn. traveling shows, 1967, Chautauqua Exhbn. Am. Art, N.Y., 1967, High Mus., Atlanta, Butler Inst. Am. Art, Springfield, Ohio, Dallas Mus. Fine Art, Mid Am. Exhbn., Nelson Atkins Mus., Kansas City, Kans., Mus. Fine Arts, Houston, Denver Art Mus., U. N.Mex. Art Gallery, Albuquerque, Ball State Tchrs. Coll., Muncie, Ind., N.Mex. Painting Invitational, 1968, Colorado Springs Fine Art Ctr., 1968, N.Mex. Biennial, Santa Fe, 1969, 72, 73 (award 1962), Tyler Mus. Art, Tex, 1977, Santa Fe Arts Festival, 1978, 79, 80, Enthios Gallery, Santa Fe, 1987; participant invitation exhbns. including: Albuquerque Mus. Art, 1977, Bethune & Moore, Denver, 1969, Yellowstone Art Ctr., Billings, Mont., 1967, Tucson Fine Art Ctr., 1965, Hockaday Sch., Dallas, 1965, Hayden Calhoun Galleries, Dallas, 1966, Leone Kahl Gallery, Dallas, 1965, U. Utah, Salt Lake City, 1966, Roswell Mus. and Art Ctr., N.Mex., 1963, Lucien Labaudt Gallery, San Francisco, 1963, Denver U.S. Nat. Ctr., 1963, Muse d'Art Moderne, Paris, 1962, Instituto Cultural, Mexico City, 1957, Colo. State Coll., Greeley, 1961, Highland U., Las Vegas, N.Mex., 1960-70, St. John's Coll., Santa Fe, 1965, 75, 80, Coll. Santa Fe, 1968, 81, 4748 Galleries, Oklahoma City, 1965, Owen Gallery, Denver, 1970, New West Gallery, Albuquerque, 1970, 71, 72, 73, 74, Columbia Fine Arts Mus., S.C., 1972, Arts and Crafts Mus., Columbus, Ga., 1972, Dubose Gallery, Houston, 1972, Jamison Gallery, Santa Fe, 1972, Tex. Tech U., Lubbock, 1973 (award), Triangle Gallery, Tulsa, 1973, Gallery 26, Tulsa, 1974, West Tex. Mus., Lubbock, 1976, Britton Gallery, Denver, 1975, 77, 78, 79, 80, Osborne Gallery, Winnipeg, Ont., Can., 1979, Blair Gallery, Santa Fe, 1979, 80; works represented in pvt. and mus. collections; represented by Fletcher Gallery, Santa Fe, 1989-90; Day Star Internat. Galleries, Albuquerque, 1990; New Directions Gallery, Taos, N.Mex., 1995—; Laurel Seth Gallery, Santa Fe, N.Mex., 1995—; Tartan Pony Gallery, 1995—; New Directions Gallery, Taos N. Mex., 1996, Karen Ruhen Gallery, Santa Fe, 1996. With WAC, 1943-45, ETO. Purchase awards and prizes include: Southwestern Biennial, Santa Fe, 1966, N.Mex. Mus. Fine Arts, 1957, Roswell Mus., 1958, Okla. Art Ctr., Oklahoma City, 1962, Atwater Kent award, Palm Beach, Fla., 1963, Chautauqua Art Award Assn. prize, 1963, El Paso Mus. prize, 1962, 76. Home and Office: 1270 Upper Canyon Rd Santa Fe NM 87501-6189

LIPPINCOTT, SARAH LEE, astronomer, graphologist; b. Phila., Oct. 26, 1920; d. George E. and Sarah (Evans) L.; m. Dave Garroway (dec.); m. Christian Zimmerman (dec.). Student, Swarthmore Coll., 1938-39, MA, 1950; BA, U. Pa., 1942; DSc (hon.), Villanova U., 1973. Research asst. Sproul Obs., Swarthmore (Pa.) Coll., 1941-50, research asso., 1951-72, dir., 1972-81, prof., 1977-81, prof. and dir. emeritus, 1981—, research astronomer, 1981—. Vis. assoc. in astronomy Calif. Inst. Tech., 1977. Author: (with Joseph M. Joseph) Point to the Stars, 1963, 3d edit., 1977, (with Laurence Lafore) Philadelphia, the Unexpected City, 1965; contbr. articles to profl. jours. Mem. Savoy Opera Co., Phila., 1947— ; bd. mgrs. Societe de Bienfaisance de Philadelphie, 1966-69. Recipient achievement award Kappa Kappa Gamma, 1966; Disting. Daus. of Pa. award, 1976; Fulbright fellow Paris, 1953-54; Jessie Kovalenko scholar, 1953-54. Mem. Am. Soc. Profl. Graphologists (treas. 1988-93), Rittenhouse Astron. Soc. (sec. 1946-48), Am. Astron. Soc. (lectr. 1961-84), Internat. Astron. Union (v.p. commn. 26, 1970-73, pres. 1973-75), Disting. Daus. Pa. (sec. 1988-99), Sigma Xi (pres. chpt. 1959-60). Home: 29 Kendal Dr Kennett Square PA 19348-2323 E-mail: zimlip@swarthmore.edu.

LIPPMAN, DONNA ROBIN, psychotherapist; b. N.Y.C., Jan. 26, 1950; 1 child, Benjamin Aaron Steinberger Lippman. BA, U. Wis., 1971; MS, CCNY, 1977. Cert. Rubenfeld synergy method. Dir., clinician Incest/Rape Recovery Ctr., N.Y.C., 1989—; exec. dir. Incest Awareness Found., N.Y.C. Cons. N.Y.C. Creator To Tell the Truth: Am. Speaks Out Against Incest and Sexual Abuse, N.Y.C., 1993, 1994, 1999—2002. Office: Incest Recovery Ctr 853 Broadway Ste 2022 New York NY 10003-4703 E-mail: donnarobin@incestrecovery.org.

LIPPMAN, SHARON ROCHELLE, art historian, art therapist, filmmaker; b. NYC, Apr. 9, 1950; d. Emanuel and Sara (Goldberg) L. Student, Mills Coll., Columbia U., 1968; BFA, New Sch. Social Rsch., 1970, CCNY, 1972; MA in Cinema Studies, NYU, 1976, postgrad., 1987. Cert. secondary tchr., N.Y.; cert. in nonprofit orgn. mgmt. Instr., dir., founder Sara Sch. of Creative Art, Sayville, N.Y., 1976-85; founder, exec. dir., tchr. Art Without Walls, Inc., Sayville and N.Y.C., 1985—; curator art exhbn. Mus. Without Walls Heckscher State Park, East Islip, NY, 1985-87; exec. dir., curator Profl. Artist Network for Artists Internationally, 1991—; founder Art Without Walls, Inc., 1985—. Organizer Profl. Artist Network for Nat./Internat. Artists, 1994; curator Pub. Art in Pub. Spaces. Author: Patterns, 1968, College Poetry Press Anthology, 1970, America at the Millennium, 2000; exhibited in group shows at L.I. Children's Mus., Garden City, N.Y., 1995-97, Suffolk County Legislature, Hauppauge, N.Y., 1997, Bayport-Bluepoint Libr., 1997, East Islip Libr., 1997-98, U.S. Dept. Interior, Ft. Wadsworth, N.Y., 2001, Ellis Island Immigration Mus., N.Y., 2002, West Islip Libr., 2000-01, Battery Park, N.Y.C., 2002, Central Park, N.Y.C., 2003, Spirit Walk Gallery, Sayville, N.Y., 2003, Within These Walls, Nassau County Detetion Ctr., Westbury, N.Y., 2003, By Land or By Sea, South St. Seaport, N.Y.C., 2004, others; pub. art mural History of L.I. Baymen, 1987, Immigration on the NYS Waterways, 2001, Art Therapy Program and Exhbn. at Leadership Tng. Inst., Hempstead, N.Y., 2003, Nassau County Detension Ctr., 2003; represented in permanent collection Devel. Disabilities Inst., Suffolk County Legis. Bldg., Polish Consulate, N.Y., West Islip Pub. Libr., East Islip Pub. Libr., Ctrl. Park Zoo, Coll. Art Assn. Bull. Conv. N.Y., Robert Moses State Park, N.Y., Smith Haven Mall Lake Grove, Garden City Mall, N.Y., Southside Hosp., Bayshore, N.Y.; art therapy program and exhbn. Leadership Tng. Inst., 2003, Suffolk Outreach Project, Art Therapy Wellness Program, 2003. Vol. Good Samaritan Hosp., 1984, Southside Hosp., 1983, U. Stony Brook Hosp., 1985, Schneider Children's Hosp., New Hyde Park, N.Y., 1992, New Light-AIDS Patients, Smithtown, N.Y., 1993, Helen Keller Svcs. for the Blind, Hempstead, N.Y., 1993-94, St. Charles Hosp. and Rehab. Ctr., 1996, Nat. Health Bill Pub. Forum, Sayville Mid. Sch., 1996, Art Puzzles-Art Therapy Geriatrics Ward, Brookhaven (N.Y.) Meml. Hosp., 1990, Art Therapy Program Original Dept. Disabilities, Suffolk County, N.Y., 1988, Din-o-Soar Art Therapy Southside Hosp.-Pediatrics Ward, Bayshore, N.Y., 1999, Art Box-Art Therapy, Pediat. Ward Southside Hosp., Bayshore, 2000, It Takes Two Art Therapy, St. Charles Hosp., Port Jefferson, N.Y., 2000; mem. Whitney Mus., Guggenheim Mus., Mus. Modern Art, Met. Mus. Art, Jewish Mus., Mus. of the City of N.Y., Art in Am., Art News, Am. Artist; trustee Sayville Libr. Bd., 1996; bd. dirs. Friends of the Arts St. Joseph's Coll., N.Y., 1997. Recipient Suffolk County New Inspiration award, 1990, Am. Artist Art Svc. award Am. Artists mag., 1993, Suffolk County Legis. proclamation, 1993, Newsday Leadership Vol. award Newsday newspaper, 1994, Nat. Women's Month award Town of Islip, 1996, Disting. Women's award Town of Islip, 1996, Nat. Poetry Press award, 1996, Cmty. Action award Suffolk County Ret./Sr. Vol. Program, 2002. Mem. Orgn. Through Rehab. and Tng., Coll. Art Assn., Met. Mus. Art, Mus. Modern Art Univ. Film Assn., Sayville C. of C. Avocations: fine art, books, cinema, political science, inventions. Office: Art Without Walls Inc PO Box 341 Sayville NY 11782-0341 E-mail: artwithoutwalls@webtv.net.

LIPPMAN SALOVESH, DOROTHY, nurse practitioner; b. Long Beach, Calif., Feb. 10, 1950; d. Emile Ferrer and Virginia Frances Lippman; children: Launa, Benjamin, Diana. ADN, Chaffey Coll., 1982; BSN, Calif. State U., Fullerton, 1995; MSN, UCLA, 1999; postgrad., U. Calif., Irvine, 2003. RN, Calif.; family nurse practitioner. Staff nurse St. Jude Med. Ctr., Fullerton, 1982—2002; nurse practitioner with Christopher Lundquist, 2002—04, Palliative Care APN, 2004. Mem.: Am. Coll. Nurse Practioners, Calif. Assn. Nurse Practioners, Nat. Conf. Gerontol. Nurse Practioners, Nat Gerontol. Nurse Assn., Am. Acad. Nurse Practitioners, Sigma Theta Tau.

LIPPOLD, JUDITH ROSENTHAL, retired occupational therapist; b. Chgo., Feb. 27, 1931; d. Irving and Shulamite Hurwitz Rosenthal; m. Henry William Lippold, May 4, 1952; children: Luanne Joy, Laura Beth. BS in occupational therapy, U. Wisc., 1951. Occupational therapist Holladay Park Hosp., Portland, Oreg., 1952-53, Ruth Lodge Residential Tng. Ctr. for C.P.

Children, Chgo., 1953-54, The Threshold, Champaign, Ill., 1968-72, Sacred Heart Hosp., Eau Claire, Wis., 1972-96, Next Step, Brotoloc Corp., Eau Claire, 1996-97; facilitator Renewing Life program Sacred Heart Hosp., Eau Claire, 1997—. Leadership roles PTA and Girl Scout Am., Champaign, Ill., 1962-72; newsletter editor Chippewa Valley Ostomy Assn., 1992—. Avocations: reading, drawing, painting, writing. Home: 1304 Bradley Ave Eau Claire WI 54701 6523

LIPSCOMB, ANNA ROSE FEENY, entrepreneur, arts organizer, fund-raiser; b. Greensboro, N.C., Oct. 29, 1945; d. Nathan and Matilda (Carotenuto) L. Student langs, Alliance Francaise, Paris, 1967-68; BA in English and French summa cum laude, Queens Coll., 1977; diploma advanced Spanish, Forester Instituto Internat., San Jose, Costa Rica, 1990; postgrad., Inst. Allende San Miguel, Mex., 1991. Reservations agt. Am. Airlines, St. Louis, 1968-69, ticket agt., 1969-71; coll. rep. CBS, Holt Reinhart Winston, Providence, 1977-79; sr. aquisitions editor Dryden Press, Chgo., 1979-81; owner, mgr. Historic Taos (N.Mex.) In, 1981-89, Southwest Moccasin and Drum, Taos; pres., co-owner Southwest Products, Ltd., 1991—; owner, pres. All One Tribe, Inc., 1996—. Fundraiser Taos Arts Celebrations, 1989—; bd. dirs. N.Mex. Hotel and Motel Assn., 1986—; sem. leader Taos Women Together, 1989; founder All One Tribe Found., 1994, all One Tribe Drumming Festival, 1991—; mem. adv. bd. Drum Bus. Mag., 1996—; presenter workshop in field. Editor: Intermediate Accounting, 1980, Business Law, 1981; contbr. articles to profl. jours.; patentee in field. Bd. dirs., 1st v.p. Taos Arts Assn., 1982-85; founder, bd. dirs. Taos Spring Arts Celebration, 1983—; founder, dir. Meet-the-Artist Series, 1983—; bd. dirs., co-founder Spring Arts N.Mex., 1986; founder Yuletide in Taos, 1988, A Taste of Taos, 1988; bd. dirs. Music From Angel Fire, 1988—; founding mem. Assn. Hist. Hotels, Boulder, 1983—; organizer Internat. Symposium on Arts, 1985; bd. dirs. Arts in Taos, 1983, Taoschool, Inc., 1985-99, Roadrunner Recyclers, 1995—, TALKBACK, Taos, 1997-98; mem. adv. bd. Chamisa Mesa Ednl. Ctr., Taos, 1990—; organizer Drumming the Year 2000, 1996—. Recipient Outstanding English Student of Yr. award Queens Coll., 1977; named Single Outstanding Contbr. to the Arts in Taos, 1986. Mem. Millicent Rogers Mus. Assn., Taos Lodgers Assn. (mktd. task force 1989), Taos County C. of C. (1st v.p. 1988-89, bd. dirs. 1987-89, advt. com. 1986-89, chmn. nominating com. 1989), Taos Women Bus. Owners, Phi Beta Kappa. Home: Talpa Rte Taos NM 87571 Office: PO Drawer N Taos NM 87571

LIPSHUTZ, LAUREL SPRUNG, psychiatrist; b. Easton, Pa., Dec. 11, 1946; d. Joseph A. and Helen A. (Rochlin) S.; m. Robert M. Lipshutz, June 15, 1975; 1 child, Jonathan. BA, U. Pa., 1968; MD, Albany Med. Coll. of Union U., 1972. Diplomate Am. Bd. Psychiatry and Neurology. Resident in psychiatry Johns Hopkins Hosp., Balt., 1972-75; unit chief psychiat. inpatient unit Phila. Gen. Hosp., 1975-77; dir. psychiat. inpatient svc. Pa. Hosp., Phila., 1977-96; assoc. dir. residency tng. Inst. of Pa. Hosp., Phila., 1983-96; coord. psychiat. clerkship for U. Pa. med. students Pa. Hosp., Phila., 1982-95. Sr. examiner Am. Bd. Psychiatry and Neurology, 1979—; sr. attending psychiatrist Inst. Pa. Hosp., Phila., 1989-97, psychiatrist, 1984—; clin. assoc. prof. psychiatry U. Pa. Sch. Medicine, Phila., 1997—, Thomas Jefferson Med. Coll., Phila. 1994-97. Fellow Am. Psychiat. Assn. (disting.); mem. Am. Soc. Psychoanalytic Physicians, Pa. Psychiat. Assn. (com. on women), Phila. Psychiatry Soc., Assn. Acad. Psychiatry (region III Excellence in Tchg. award 1995). Office: 210 W Washington Sq Ste 750 Philadelphia PA 19106-3514 Fax: 215-829-7887. Office Phone: 215-829-7851.

LIPSKY, LINDA ETHEL, business executive; b. Bklyn., June 2, 1939; d. Irving Julius and Florence (Stern) Ellman; m. Warren Lipsky, June 12, 1960 (div. Sept. 1968); 1 child, Phillip Bruce; m. Jerome Friedman, Jan. 17, 1988. BA in Psychology, Hofstra U., 1960; MPS with hon. in Health Care Adminstrn., Long Island U., 1979. Child welfare social worker Nassau County Dept. Social Service, N.Y., 1960-64; adminstr. La Guardia Med. Group of Health Ins. Plan of Greater N.Y., Queens, 1969-72; cons. Neighborhood Svc. Ctr., Bronx, N.Y., 1973-78; dir. ODA Health Ctr., Bklyn., 1978-82; pres. Millin Assocs., Inc., Nassau, N.Y., 1982—. Mem. Health Care Fin. Mgmt. Assn., Nat. Assn. Community Health Ctrs., Nat. Assn. Female Execs., Cmty. Health Ctrs., Assoc. of N.Y., Hofstra U. Alumni Assn. (mem. senate 1984—, chairperson membership com. 1985—), Pi Alpha Alpha. Republican. Jewish. Avocations: cooking, writing, reading. E-mail: millin521@aol.com. Office: Millin Assocs Inc 521 Chestnut St Cedarhurst NY 11516-2244

LIPSKY, S. KATE, retired social worker; b. Wash., DC, July 31, 1946; d. John Alexander Tipton and Susan Jane Smith; m. Bruce Jay Lipsky, Aug. 2, 1969; children: Jessica, Rachel, Alanna. BS in Social Work and Sociology, Syracuse (N.Y.) U., 1968; MS in cmty. svc. (hon.), U. Rochester (N.Y.), 1980. Social worker Dept. Social Svcs., Rochester, NY, 1970—74; counselor Alexander Women's Group, Rochester, NY, 1980—86; owner children's clothing shop Tickled Pink, Rochester, NY, 1987—93; ret., 1993. Bd. dirs. Rochester City Ballet, 1997—2002, sec., 2000—01, hon. bd. dirs., 2003—. Cast mem. (ballets) Nutcracker, 1996—2000. Avocations: photography, painting, drawing, gardening, poetry. Home: 80 Douglas Rd Rochester NY 14610

LIPSON, PAMELA, information scientist; m. Pawan Sinha. BA, Harvard U., 1989; MS, MIT, 1993, PhD, 1996. Postdoctoral rschr. Artificial Intelligence Lab., MIT, 1996—97; co-founder, pres., CEO, Imagen, Inc., 1997—. Achievements include development of technology for encoding alphanumeric and graphical information with high density on crystalline substrates. Office: Imagen Inc 955 Massachusetts Ave # 351 Cambridge MA 02139*

LIPTON, BRONNA JANE, marketing communications executive; b. Newark, May 10, 1951; d. Julius and Arlene (Davis) L.; m. Sheldon Robert Lipton, Sept. 23, 1984. BA in Spanish, Northwestern U., 1973. Tchr. Spanish Livingston (N.J.) H.S., 1973-78; profl. dancer Broadway theater, film, TV, N.Y.C., 1978-82; v.p., mgr. Hispanic mktg. svcs. Burson-Marsteller Pub. Rels., N.Y.C., 1982-89; exec. v.p. Lipton Comms. Group, Inc., N.Y.C., 1989-99, Latin Reports, 1996-99; v.p. Bienestar LCG Comms., Inc., 1999—2003; prin. Cmty. Direct, N.Y.C., NY, 2003—. Mem. minority initiatives task force Am. Diabetes Assn., Alexandria, Va., 1987-90, mem. pub. rels. com., 1990-91, mem. visibility and image task force, 1991-92, bd. dirs. N.Y. Downstate affiliate, chmn. visibility and image com., 1992-93. Mem. rev. panel Hispanic Designers, Inc. Recipient Pinnacle award Am. Women in Radio and TV (N.Y. Chpt.), 1984, Value Added awards Burson-Marsteller, N.Y.C., 1982, 83, 84. Mem. Hispanic Pub. Rels. Assn. Avocations: ballet, jazz dance, tennis, fgn. travel, birding. Home: 1402 Chapel Hill Rd Mountainside NJ 07092-1405 E-mail: blipton@gocommunitydirect.com.

LIPTON, JOAN ELAINE, advertising executive; b. N.Y.C., July 12, 1927; 1 child, David Dean. BA, Barnard Coll., 1948. With Young & Rubicam, Inc., N.Y.C., 1948-52, Robert W. Orr & Assocs., N.Y.C., 1952-57, Benton & Bowles, Inc., N.Y.C., 1957-64; asso. dir. Benton & Bowles, Ltd., London, Eng., 1964-68; with McCann-Erickson, Inc. (advt. agy.), N.Y.C., 1968-85, v.p., 1970-79, sr. v.p., creative dir., 1979-85; pres. Martin & Lipton Advt. Inc., 1985—. Mem. Bus. Coun. for the UN Decade for Women, 1977-78; bd. vis. PhD program in bus. CUNY, 1986—. Recipient Honors award Ohio U. Sch. Journalism, 1976, Matrix award, 1979, YWCA award for women achievers, 1979, Clio Classic award; named Woman of Yr., Am. Advt. Fedn., 1974, Advt. Woman of Yr., 1984; named to Matrix Hall of Fame, 1998. Mem. Advt. Women N.Y. (1st v.p. 1975-76, v.p. Found. 1977-78), Women's Forum (bd. dirs. 1988-90), Women in Communications (pres. N.Y. chpt. 1974-76, named Nat. Headliner 1976). Office: 163 E 62nd St New York NY 10021-7613 Office Phone: 212-832-3049.

LIPTON, LEAH, art historian, educator, museum curator; b. Kearny, N.J., Mar. 22, 1928; d. Abraham and Rose (Berman) Shneyer; m. Herbert Lipton, Sep. 19, 1951 (dec. 1979); children: David, Ivan, Rachel. BA, Douglass Coll. Rutgers U., New Brunswick, N.J., 1949; MA, Harvard U., Cambridge, Mass., 1950; postgrad., Harvard U., 1970-73, Wellesley Coll., 1970-73. Photo. library researcher Mus. Fine Arts, Boston, 1950-53, lectr., division edn., 1965-70; instr. Boston Coll., 1968-69; faculty, full prof. Framingham State Coll., Mass., 1969-94; ret., 1994. Guest curator Nat. Portrait Gallery, Washington, 1985. Author: Book, 1985, Exhibition Catalogues, 1988-01 contbr. articles to profl. jours., 1981—. Co-founder Danforth Mus. Art., Framingham, Mass. 1973-75, interim dir., 1994-95, 98-99, trustee, 1975-2002, curator Am. art, 1994-99, mem. collections com., 1988-2002. Recipient Disting. Svc. award Framingham State Coll., 1978, 87. Mem. Coll. Art Assn., Am. Studies Assn. Office: Danforth Mus of Art 123 Union Ave Framingham MA 01702-8223

LIPTON, LOIS JEAN, lawyer; b. Chgo., Jan. 14, 1946; d. Harold and Bernice (Reiter) Farber L.; m. Peter Carey, May 30, 1978; children: Rachel, Sara. BA, U. Mich., 1966; JD summa cum laude, DePaul Coll. Law, Chgo., 1974; postgrad., Sheffield (Eng.) U., 1966. Bar: Ky. 1974, U.S. Dist. Ct. (we. dist.) Ky. 1974, U.S. Ct. Appeals (6th cir.) 1974, Ill. 1975, U.S. Dist. Ct. (no. dist.) Ill. 1975, U.S. Ct. Appeals (7th cir.) 1976. Staff counsel Roger Baldwin Found. of ACLU, Inc., Chgo., 1975-79, dir. reproductive rights project, 1979-83; atty. McDermott, Will & Emergy, Chgo., 1984-86, G.D. Searle, Skokie, Ill., 1988-90; sr. atty. AT&T, Chgo., 1990—. Del. White House Conf. on Families, Mpls., 1980; bd. dirs. Chgo. Found. for Women. Recipient Durfee award, 1984. Mem. ACLU (v.p.), ABA, Chgo. Coun. Lawyers. Office: AT&T # R15 222 W Adams St Chicago IL 60606-5017 E-mail: llipton@att.com.

LIPTON, NINA ANNE, healthcare executive; b. N.Y.C., Oct. 6, 1959; d. Robert and Rita Kay (Wolfman) L. BA in Econs., Wellesley Coll., 1981; postgrad., London Sch. Econs., 1981-82. Rsch. asst. Nat. Econ. Rsch. Assocs., White Plains, N.Y., 1983-84; cons. A.T. Hudson and Co., Paramus, N.J., 1984; asst. economist Dean Witter Reynolds, N.Y.C., 1984-89; dir. market rsch. Platinum Guild Internat., N.Y.C., 1989-94; v.p., exec. dir. Ctr. for Alternative Healthcare, Inc., Miami, Fla., 1995-98; exec. dir. Summit Med. Group, Conn., Ga., Ala., Mich., 1995—2001; prin. Lipton Cons., 2003—. Exec. dir., v.p. Aztec Mgmt. Co., 1995-2001. Writer This Week in Platinum weekly, 1989-94; contbr. articles to profl. jours. Recruiter, fundraiser, reunion com. chair Wellesley (Mass.) Coll. Alumnae Assn.,1982—, mem. spl. gifts com., 1991, co-chair 20th reunion 2000-2001, ann. giving rep. '81, 2001—, ann. giving com., 2002—; dir. Women's Outreach, Erskine Bowles for U.S. Senate, N.C., 2002, cons. N-Squared. Office Phone: 704-372-1194. E-mail: nlsmt@aol.com.

LIRETTE, DOROTHY LOU, artist, educator; b. Denver, Nov. 19, 1946; d. Jewel Robert Myers and Dorothy Katherine Higdon; m. Richard Paul Lirette, Dec. 13, 1968; children: Michael, Anne. BA, Colo. State U., 1969. Art tchr. The Colorado Springs Sch., Colorado Springs, 1970—92, Acad. Dist. #20, 1992—99, Colorado Springs Sch. Dist. #11, 1999—. Named Master Tchr., Arts, Bus. and Edn. Consortium, Colo. Springs, Colo., 1996, Outstanding Elem. Art Tchr. in Colo., Denver Art Mus., 1999. Home: 1301 La Veta Way Colorado Springs CO 80906

LISANDRELLI, ELAINE SLIVINSKI, secondary school educator; b. Pittston, Pa., July 11, 1951; d. Leo Joseph and Gabriella Alexandra (Sharek) Slivinski; m. Carl A. Lisandrelli, June 20, 1980. BA, Marywood U., Scranton, Pa., 1973, MS, 1976. Cert. secondary tchr. English and counselor, Pa. Tchr. English, North Pocono Mid. Sch., Moscow, Pa., 1973—. Part-time instr. Marywood U., 1986—; ednl. cons., Pa., 1988--93. Author: Maya Angelou: More Than a Poet, 1996 (Carter G. Woodson honor), Bob Dole: Legendary Senator, 1997, Ida B. Wells-Barnett: Crusader Against Lynching, 1998, Ignacy Jan Paderewski: Polish Pianist and Patriot, 1999, Jack London: A Writer's Adventurous Life, 1999; contbr. articles to lit. mags. Named to the Young Adult's Choice List, 1998. Mem. Nat. Coun. Tchrs. English, Soc. Children's Book Writers and Illustrators, Pa. Edn., Assn., Kosciuszko Found., Polish Arts and Cultural Found. Avocations: aerobics, reading, researching, movies. Home: 3501 Lawrence Ave Moosic PA 18507-1729 Office: North Pocono Mid Sch Church St Moscow PA 18507

LISBOA-FARROW, ELIZABETH OLIVER, public and government relations consultant; b. N.Y.C., Nov. 25, 1947; d. Eleuterio and Esperanza Oliver; m. Jeffrey Lloyd Farrow, Dec. 31, 1980; 1 child, Hamilton Oliver Farrow; 1 stepchild, Maximillian Robbins Farrow. Student pvt. schs., N.Y.C. With Harold Rand & Co. and various other pub. rels. firms, N.Y.C., 1966-75; dir. pub. rels. N.Y. Playboy Club and Playboy Clubs Internat., 1975-79; pres., CEO Lisboa Assocs., Inc., N.Y.C., 1979—; founder, pres. Lisboa Prodns., Inc., Washington, 1994—. Counselor Am. Woman's Devel. Corp. Sec. Nat. Acad. Concert and Cabaret Arts; mem. nat. adv. coun. SBA, 1980-81, apptd., 1994—; exec. dir. Variety Club of Greater Washington Children's Charity, Inc., 1985-90; bd. dirs. Variety Myoelectric Limb Bank Found., 1990-91, Comcast, 2001, Hispanic Radio Network, 2001; trustee Hispanic Coll. Fund, 1995—, vice chair, 1996—; chair bd. trustees Southeastern U., 1997—; mem. adv. bd. Indsl. Bank, N.A., 1996; bd. dirs. Bell Multicultural H.S. Named Pub. Rels. Woman of Yr., Women in Pub. Rels., 1992, Empresaria del Milenio, Duodecimo Encuentro Empresarian, P.R., 2001, Hispanic Bus. Woman of Yr., Nat. Hispanic Bus. Coun., 1996, Hispanic of Yr. in Bus., La Nacion Newspaper, 1997, Entrepreneur of Yr., Hispanic Mag., 1999, Bus Woman of Yr., N.Y. State Hispanic Chambers Commerce; recipient Disting. award of Excellence, SBA, 1992, Women Bus. Enterprise award, U.S. Transp. Nat. Hwy. Transp. Safety Adminstrn., 1994, Civic Cmty. Achievement, Black Bus. and Profls. Network, 1999, Excellence in Entrepreneurship award, Dialogue on Diversity, Inc., 1995, Women of Distinction award, Nat. Conf. Coll. Women Student Leaders, 2000, Applause award, Women's Bus. Enterprise Nat. Coun., 2000, Imagen award, San Juan, P.R., 2001, Presdl. medal, Sistema U. Ana G. Mendez, U. Metropolitana, San Juan, 1999, Internat. Leadership award, Mex. Am. C. of C., 2001. Mem. U.S. Hispanic C. of C. (bd. dirs. 1998, Nat. Hispanic Businesswoman of Yr. 1996, vice chair 1999, chair 2000—), D.C. C. of C. (pres. 2000), Small Bus. Adv. Coun., U.S. C. of C. (Blue Chip Enterprise award 1993), Advt. Coun., Am. Heart Assn., Hispanic Bus. and Profl. Women's Assn., Ibero-Am. C. of C. (bd. dirs. 1993, v.p. 1995, pres. 1997, pres. 1998, adv. chair 1999, Small Bus. award 1993, corp. of yr. award 2000), City Club Washington., bd. dirs. Nat. Edn. Assn. Found., 2004, mem. Internat. Womens Forum, 2004. Office: 1112 16th St NW Washington DC 20036

LISCHER, TRACY KENYON, lawyer; b. St. Louis, Oct. 3, 1944; d. Robert C. and Nina N. Kenyon; m. Richard A. Lischer, June 4, 1966; children: Sarah Kenyon, Richard Adam. BA with honors, Mo. U., 1965; MA, St. Louis U., 1967, PhD, 1977; JD with honors, U. NC, Chapel Hill, 1984. Bar: NC 1984, US Dist. Ct. (ea., mid., we.) NC 1985, US Supreme Ct. 1995. H.S. tchr., St. Louis, 1966—69; instr. Tidewater CC/Va. Wesleyan Coll., 1977—79, Duke U., Durham, NC, 1979—80; clk. NC Ct. Appeals, Raleigh, 1984—85; assoc. atty. Pulley, Watson, King & Hofler, Durham, 1985—88; ptnr. Pulley, Watson, King & Lischer, Durham, 1988—. Spkr. in field. Contbr. articles to profl. jours. Mem.: ABA, ATLA, Million Dollar Advocates Forum, Durham County Bar Assn. (bd. dirs. 1995—96), NC Assn. Women Attys. (chair govt. action com., lobbyist 1989—92, bd. dirs. 1989—93, bd. dirs.-at-large 1992—93, pres. 1995—96), NC State Bar Assn. (com. on lawyer advt. 1992—94, medicolegal com. 1993—94, quality of life bar com. 2001—), NC Acad. Trial Lawyers (legis. com., chair legis. subcom. family law sect. 1991—93, chair-elect family law sect. 1992—93, chair family law sect., ex-officio mem. bd. govs. 1993—94, mem. editl. bd. 2001—, Kellie Crabtree award 2003), Phi Beta Kappa. Office: Pulley Watson King & Lischer PA 905 W Main St Ste 21-F Durham NC 27701 Office Phone: 919-682-9691. Business E-Mail: tkl@pwkl.com.

LISENBY, DORRECE EDENFIELD, realtor; b. Sneads, Fla., Dec. 3, 1942; d. Neal McLendon and Linnie (McCroan) Edenfield; m. Wallace Lamar Lisenby, Nov. 18, 1961; children: Pamela Ann, Wallace Neal. BS in Tech. Bus. magna cum laude, Athens (Ala.) State Coll., 1991. Stenographer State of Fla., Tallahassee and Miami, Fla., 1960-62, Gulf Oil Corp., Coral Gables, Fla., 1962-64, Gulf Power Co., Pensacola, Fla., 1965-68; loan svc. asst. First Fed. Savs. and Loan Assn., Greenville, S.C., 1969-70; various real estate positions Greenville, 1978-85; adminstrv. asst. Charter Retreat Hosp., Decatur, Ala., 1986-91; broker/salesperson Ferrell Realty Plus, Inc., Tallahassee, Fla., 1995-2001; broker, owner Lisenby Realty, Inc., 2001—. Mem.: P.E.O. Sisterhood, Tallahassee C. of C., Econ. Club Fla., Tallahassee Symphony Soc., Killearn Ladies Club (pres.), Taylor's Garden Club (pres. Taylor's chpt. 1975—76), Avondale Forest Cmty. Club (pres. Taylors, S.C. chpt. 1969), Am. Legion (Citizenship award 1957). Republican. Baptist. Avocations: reading, music, bridge, gardening. Home: 2925 Shamrock St S Tallahassee FL 32309-3226 E-mail: lisenby@lisenbyrealty.com.

LISH, DONNA LEE, art educator; m. Richard J. Lish, Nov. 21, 1978; children: Helena, Jessie, André. BA in Art Edn., Montclair (N.J.) State U., 1970, MA, 1978; EdD, Rutgers U., 1997. Cert. tchr. N.J., 1970. Tchr. Bridgewater (N.J.) Raritan Schs., 1970—2003. Vis. specialist Montclair (N.J.) State U., 1993; educator Hunterdon Mus. Art, Clinton, NJ, 1985—90, Clinton, 2003—. Co-author: Inspiration for Artmaking, 1994; one-woman shows include Hunterdon Mus. Art, 2001, Represented in permanent collections Johnson & Johnson Co., Noyes Mus. Fellow, N.J. State Coun. on Arts, 1999; grantee, N.J., 1971, Bridgewater Edn. Found., 1998, 2001. Mem.: Surface Design Assn., Artemision, Nat. Art Edn. Assn. Avocations: textile and beaded scupture, crafts, research relating to art making. Home and Studio: 129 Center St Clinton NJ 08809

LISH, JENNIFER D. psychologist; b. Tucson, Ariz., Oct. 5, 1957; d. Gordon Jay and Frances (Fokes) L. AB, Brown U., 1979; PhD, NYU, 1986. Lic. psychologist, N.Y., Pa., Mass. Postdoctoral fellow Columbia U., 1986-88, asst. prof., 1988-91, U. Pa., Phila., 1991-93, Med. Coll. of Pa. and Hahnemann U., 1993—96; rsch. scientist Compass Info. Svcs., King of Prussia, Pa., 1995—96; pvt. practice psychology Worcester, Mass., 2003—. With Unum Provident Ins., 1999—2002. Contbr. articles to profl. jours. Recipient Lebensohn award Am. Assn. Gen. Hosp. Psychiatrists, 1994, Best Poster award Acad. Psychosomatic Medicine, 1994. Mem. APA. Democrat. Jewish. Avocations: hiking, biking. Home: 15 Avery Rd Holden MA 01520-1235 Office: 23 Fruit St Worcester MA 01609

LISI, LORI A. (LORI FREDEKING), freelance/self-employed editor, writer; b. Ft. Worth, July 28; d. Nelsie Ann Austin; m. James Lisi, Apr. 20, 2001. Student, U. Tex., Arlington, 1991—96. Freelance editor, writer, Burleson, Tex., 1991—. Mem.: Nat. Writer's Union, Editl. Freelancers Assn. Home: PO Box 1111 Burleson TX 76097 Personal E-mail: lorifredeking@aol.com.

LISI, MARY M. federal judge; BA, U. R.I., 1972; JD, Temple U., 1977. Tchr. history Prout Meml. High Sch., Wakefield, R.I., 1975-76; law clk. U.S. Atty., Providence, R.I., 1976, Phila., 1976-77; asst. pub. defender R.I. Office Pub. Defender, 1977-81; asst. child advocate Office Child Advocate, 1981-82; also. pvt. practice atty. Providence, 1981-82; dir. office ct. appointed spl. advocate R.I. Family Ct., 1982-87; dep. disciplinary counsel office disciplinary counsel R.I. Supreme Ct., 1988-90, chief disciplinary counsel, 1990-94; U.S. Dist. judge Dist. Ct., Providence, Dist. R.I. (1st cir.), Providence, 1994—. Mem. Select Com. to Investigate Failure of R.I. Share and Deposit Indemnity Corp., 1991-92. Recipient Providence 350 award, 1986, Meritorious Svc. to Children of Am. award, 1987. Office: Fed Bldg and US Courthouse 1 Exchange Ter Providence RI 02903-1744

LISK, MARTHA ANN, vocational rehabilitation counselor; b. Manchester, Conn., Jan. 20, 1956; d. Burton Roy and Ruth Elizabeth (Coe) L. BA, Colo. State U., 1978; MA, U. No. Colo., 1983. Rehab. counselor State of Colo. Rehab. Ins. Svcs. for Employment, Loveland, 1984-86; owner, mgr. Pro-Three One Wear, Loveland, 1986-89; coord. employment and tng. Epilepsy Found. Am., Denver, 1989-93; vocat. rehab. counselor II Kans. Rehab. Svcs., Garden City, 1993—. Summer youth counselor Colo. Job Svc., Aurora, 1984; adv. Colo. Rehab. Svcs. Adv. Bd., Denver, 1991-93; pres. Job Developers Network, Denver, 1992. Contbr. articles to popular mags. Vol. Friends the Nat. Parks at Gettysburg. Mem. Nat. Trust for Hist. Preservation. Avocations: reading, civil war living history, historical research. Home: 2103 Commanche Dr Garden City KS 67846-3827 E-mail: mlisk0120@aol.com.

LISOVICZ, SUSAN, anchor, correspondent; Degree in comm., William Paterson Coll. Prodr., writer Sta. WABC-TV, N.Y.C.; anchor, corr. CNBC, Ft. Summit, N.J., 1991-97, CNN Fin. News, N.Y.C., corr. The Moneyline Newshour with Lou Dobbs. Mem. N.Y. Fin. Writers Assn. (pres.). Office: CNN 5 Penn Plz Fl 20 New York NY 10001-1810

LISSAKERS, KARIN MARGARETA, former federal agency administrator; b. Aug. 16, 1944; married; 2 children. BA in Internat. Affairs, Ohio State U., 1967; MA in Internat. Affairs, Johns Hopkins U., 1969. Mem. staff com. fgn. rels. U.S. Senate, Washington, 1972-78, mem. staff subcom. multinat. corps., 1972, staff dir. subcom. fgn. econ. policy, 1977; dep. dir. econ. policy planning staff U.S. Dept. State, Washington, 1978-80; sr. assoc. Carnegie Endowment for Internat. Peace, N.Y.C., 1981-83; rsch. with nobel prize winning economist Gunnar Myrdal Stockholm Internat. Peace Rsch. Inst.; lectr. internat. banking, dir. internat. bus. and banking program Sch. Internat. Pub. Affairs Columbia U., N.Y.C., 1985-93; U.S. exec. dir. Internat. Monetary Fund, Washington, 1993-2001; sr. adv. Soros Fund Mgmt., 2001—. Author: Banks, Borrowers and the Establishment, 1991; contbr. articles to profl. jours.

LIST, ANNITA, social worker, educator; b. Guayaquil, Ecuador, Apr. 5, 1945; arrived in U.S., 1962, naturalized, 1967; d. Joachim Walther and Lola Verdesoto (Oyague) List; m. List Wheeler, Aug. 4, 1985; 1 child, Debiana ; children from previous marriage: Annamaria, Rob. AA, Monroe (Mich.) C.C., 1975; BS in Social Work, Ea. Mich. U., 1980; MSW, U. Mich., 1988. Diplomate clin. forensics counseling; cert. social worker Mich., acad. cert. social worker Mich., cert. family therapist Mich.; addictions counselor I. Asst. to exec. dir. Am. Cancer Soc., Ann Arbor, Mich.; addictions counselor Solutions, Grand Rapids, Mich.; clin. bilingual social worker Cath. Social Svcs., Grand Rapids, Family Outreach Ctr., Grand Rapids; owner, operator Diversity Counseling and Therapy Ctr., PLLC, Grand Rapids; affiliate prof. sch. social work Grand Valley State U., Grand Rapids. Cons., trainer, El Salvador, United States. Chair bd. dirs. AIDS Resource Ctr., Grand Rapids, 1993—97. Mem.: ACLU, NASW (nat. com. chair 1992—95, bd. dirs. Mich. chpt. 1998, Social Worker of Yr., Mich. chpt. 1993), Batterer Svc. Coalition of Mich., El Salvador Assn. Social Workers (hon.), Phi Theta Kappa. Avocations: providing therapy in Spanish, camping, gardening, reading, writing. Office: Diversity Counseling and Therapy Ctr 820 Monroe NW Ste 315 Grand Rapids MI 49503 also: Grand Valley State U Sch Social Work De Vos Ctr 3d Fl W Fulton Grand Rapids MI 49503 E-mail: alist85886@aol.com.

LISTER, LINDA JOANNE, music educator, composer, vocalist; b. Tarrytown, N.Y., June 30, 1969; d. Gordon Frank and Judith Smith Lister. AB in Voice, Vassar Coll., 1991; MMus in Voice, Eastman Sch. of Music, 1993; D Musical Arts in Voice, U. N.C., Greensboro, 1998. Instr. Sch. of

Choral Studies, Saratoga Springs, NY, 1994, Hochstein Sch., Rochester, NY, 1994—95; lectr. SUNY, Fredonia, 1993—95; dept. chair, instr. Music Acad. of N.C., Greensboro, 1997—2002; instr. Greensboro Coll., 1997—2000; asst. prof. Elon (N.C.) U., 2000—02, Shorter Coll., 2002—. Composer: (mini-operas) Tryst & Thereafter, 1989, How Clear She Shines, 2001, Love Theories, 2004, (musical) The Little Match Girl, 1984, (song cycles) Dependencies, 1995, Deep Dreams & Delicacies, 1996, The Landscape of Love, 2000; contbr. articles to profl. jours. Recipient Dissertation prize, Nat. Opera Assn., Washington, 1998, Jane Dillard award, Met. Opera Dist. Auditions, Charlotte, N.C., 2001. Mem.: Nat. Assn. Tchrs. of Singing, Phi Beta Kappa, Pi Kappa Lambda. Avocations: yoga, tennis, poetry, beading. Office Phone: 706-233-7362.

LISTON, HELEN J. minister; b. Joplin, Mo., Nov. 2, 1932; d. Kenneth Harold Latta and Erma Nadine Latta - Pieffer; children from previous marriage: Diane, Dan, Del, Darin, Darci. BA, Kans. U., Lawrence, 1981; MDiv, St. Paul Sch. Theology, Kans. City, Mo., 1991. Kalaidescope staff Hallmark Cards, Kansas City, Mo., 1987—91; min. Asbury United Meth. Ch., Prairie Village, Kans., 1990—93, Leawood United Meth. Ch., Kans., 1995—2003; chaplain Heartland Hospice, Kansas City, Mo., 1998—. Author: (book) The Dime Store, 2002; presenter Kans. City Hist. Soc., 1998—, Women's Wisdom Week, Crete, Greece; contbr. articles to periodicals. Home: 8731 Walmer Overland Park KS 66212 E-mail: hliston@kc.rr.com.

LISTON, MARY FRANCES, retired nursing educator; b. N.Y.C., Dec. 17, 1920; d. Michael Joseph and Ellen Theresa (Shaughnessy) L. BS, Coll. Mt. St. Vincent, 1944; MS, Catholic U. Am., 1945; EdD, Columbia, 1962; HHD (hon.), Allentown Coll., 1987. Dir. psychiat. nursing and edn. Nat. League for Nursing, N.Y.C., 1958-66; prof. Sch. Nursing, Cath. U. Am., Washington, 1966-78, dean, 1966-73; prof. Marywood Coll., 1984-87. Spl. assignment Imperial Med. Center, Tehran, Iran, 1975-78; dep. dir. for program affairs Nat. League for Nursing, N.Y.C., 1978-84 Mem. Sigma Theta Tau. Home: 182 Garth Rd Scarsdale NY 10583-3863

L'ITALIEN, BARBARA A. state legislator, social worker; Diploma, Merimack Coll. State rep. Mass. House, 2003—. Mem. Andover League of Women Voters, YMCA, Andona Soc., Andover Svc. Club, Andover Dem. Town Com., Merrimack Valley C. of C., Mass. Womens Political Caucus. Democrat. Office: Rm 437 State House Boston MA 02133

LITCHFIELD, JEAN ANNE, nurse; b. Gary, Ind., Oct. 6, 1942; d. Donald Kleine and Helen Louise (Sweet) Eller; m. Norman E. Stone, Dec. 27, 1965 (div. Aug. 1973); children: Diana, David, Julie; m. Frank Litchfield, Jan. 26, 1974. Lic. practical nurse, Ind. U. Vocat. Tech. Coll., 1973; AS in Biology, Richland C.C., 1991; BSN, Millikin U., 1993; MSN, Ind. State U., 1995. RN, Ind., Ill. Nurse asst. St. Anthony Hosp., Terre Haute, Ind., 1960-73, nurse, 1973-93; charge nurse psychiatric ward St. Mary's Hosp., Decatur, Ill., 1993-99; asst. prof. AD Nursing program Richland C.C., Decatur, 1995—. Mem. student welfare com. Millikin U., Decatur, 1991-92. Recipient 1st place art award 1984, 85, 86, 2d place art award 1984, 85, 2d place County Fair, 1985, Gold Poet award World of Poetry, 1989, Silver Poet award, 1990, Outstanding Innovations in Tchg. and Learning award Richland C.C., 1997, 98, Excellence in Nursing Edn. award Decatur Area Task Force Nursing Edn., 2000; named Most Caring Nurse St. Mary's Hosp. 1990, Clara Compton scholar, St. Mary's Hosp., 1990, 91, scholar Am. Legion, 1992. Mem. Internat. Platform Assn., Burn Colony Artists (treas. 1986-88), Phi Theta Kappa, Beta Sigma Phi (treas. 1976-78), Alpha Tau Delta (treas. 1991-92, pres. 1992-93), Sigma Theta Tau Internat. Home: 1680 N 30th St Decatur IL 62526-5416

LITHERLAND, DONNA JOYCE, counselor; b. Moorhead, Minn., Oct. 15, 1927; d. Hobart Marion and Mildred (Carlson) L. BS, N.D. State U., 1949; MA, Fresno State U., 1967. Tchr. high sch. English Page (N.D.) Pub. Schs., 1950-51; tchr. jr. high sch. English Bakersfield (Calif.) Pub. Schs., 1951-65; counselor Bakersfield Jr. Coll., 1968-91; writer Barney Press, Bakersfield, 1991—. Presenter seminars in speed reading. Author: Speed Reading for Executives, 1981, The Yellow Verandah, 1984, Dancing on the Sun, 1986, Speed Reading for Progressive Adults, 1995, Walker Pass Lodge, 1996, Speed Your Read, 1999, The Next Great Flood of California. Bd. dirs. Cayucos Beach Condominium Assn.; v.p. Golden Empire 270. Mem. Toastmasters Internat. (officer). Democrat. Avocation: writing. Home: 3807 Noel Pl Bakersfield CA 93306-1448 Office: 3807 Noel Pl Bakersfield CA 93306-1448

LITMAN, ROSLYN MARGOLIS, lawyer; b. N.Y.C., Sept. 30, 1928; d. Harry and Dorothy (Perlow) Margolis; m. S. David Litman, Nov. 22, 1950; children: Jessica, Hannah, Harry. BA, U. Pitts., 1949, JD, 1952. Bar: Pa. 1952; approved arbitrator for complex comml. litigation and employment law. Practiced in Pitts., 1952—; ptnr. firm Litman Law Firm, 1952—; adj. prof. U. Pitts. Law Sch., 1958—. Permanent del. Conf. U.S. Circuit Ct. Appeals for 3d Circuit; past chair dist. adv. group U.S. Dist. Ct. (we. dist.) Pa., 1991-94, mem. steering com. for dist. adv. group, 1991—; chmn. Pitts. Pub. Parking Authority, 1970-74; mem. curriculum com. Pa. Bar Inst., 1986—, bd. dirs., 1972-82. Bd. dirs. United Jewish Fedn., 1999—, cmty. rels. com., co-chair ch./state com.; bd. dirs. City Theatre, 1999—. Recipient Roscoe Pound Found. award for Excellence in Tchg. Trial Advocacy, 1996, Disting. Alumnus award U. Pitts. Sch. Law, 1996; named Fed. Lawyer of Yr., We. Pa. Chpt. FBA, 1999. Mem. ABA (del., litigation sect., anti-trust health care com.), ACLU (nat. bd. dirs., Marjorie H. Matson Civil Libertarian award Greater Pitts. chpt. 1999), Pa. Bar Assn. (bd. govs. 1976-79), Allegheny County Bar Assn. (bd. govs. 1972-74, pres. 1975, Woman of Yr. 2001), Allegheny County Acad. Trial Lawyers (charter), Order of Coif. Home: 5023 Frew St Pittsburgh PA 15213-3829 Office: One Oxford Centre 34th Fl Pittsburgh PA 15219

LITRENTA, FRANCES MARIE, psychiatrist; b. Balt., June 25, 1928; d. Frank P. and Josephine (DeLuca) L. AB, Coll. Notre Dame Md., 1950; MD, Georgetown U., 1954. Diplomate Am. Bd. Psychiatry and Neurology. Intern St. Agnes Hosp., Balt., 1954-55, asst. resident in psychiatry, 1955-56; fellow psychiatry Univ. Hosp., Balt., 1956-57; fellow child psychiatry Georgetown U. Hosp., Washington, Washington, 1957-59; clin. instr. psychiatry Med. Ctr. Georgetown U., Washington, 1959-63, clin. asst. prof. Med. Ctr., 1963-72, clin. assoc. prof. psychiatry Med. Ctr., 1972-87; pvt. practice Balt., 1959—. Cons. St. Vincent's Infant Home, Balt., 1965-75; mem. coun. to dean Georgetown U. Sch. Medicine, 1977-93. Recipient Georgetown U. Alumni Assn. John Carroll award, 1998. Fellow Am. Acad. Child and Adolescent Psychiatry, Am. Orthopsychiat. Assn. (life); mem. Am. Psychiat. Assn. (life), Md. Psychiat. Soc. (life), Georgetown Med. Alumni Assn. (nat. comm. chair 1987-90, class co-chair 1974-87, class comm. chair 1987—, bd. dirs. 1989—, gov. 1989-95, senator 1995—), Georgetown U. Alumni Assn. (Founder's award 1994, John Carroll award 1998). Office: 6110 York Rd Baltimore MD 21212-2697 Office Phone: 410-435-6340.

LITSKY, BERTHA YANIS, microbiologist, artist; b. Chester, Pa., Jan. 2, 1920; d. Edward Bernard and Hattie (Howell) Meade; m. Martin Yanis, June 27, 1942 (dec.); children: Libby Nesvold, Rosalind Yanishevsky; m. Warren Litsky, July 27, 1965 (dec. July 1994). BSc, Phila. Coll. Pharmacy, 1942; MPA, NYU, 1964; PhD, Walden U., 1974. Lic. med. technologist. Head dept. bacteriology Assoc. Labs., Phila., 1942-44; asst. supr. prodn. Nat. Drug Co., Swiftwater, Pa., 1944-45; rsch. bacteriologist U. Pa., Phila., 1945-50; cons. microbiologist Phila., 1950-56; head dept. bacteriology S.I. Hosp., N.Y.C., 1956-65; rsch. assoc. U. Mass., Amherst, 1965—. Nurse cons. Bingham Assocs. Fund New Eng. Med. Ctr. Hosp., Boston, 1965-85 Author: An Administrative Program for Hospital Sanitation, 1966, Food Service Sanitation, 1973; contbr. chpts. to books; contbr. more than 115 articles to profl. jours. Troop mother Girl Scouts USA, S.I., 1953-60; judge Acad. Sci., N.Y.C., 1953-60; aided students in project for Sci. Fair, N.Y.C., 1953-62; mem. animal control com. Town of Amherst, 1978-80; sanitation cons. Town Hall, Amherst, 1994—; v.p. Friends of Amherst Stray Animals, 1980—; mem. fundraising com. MSPCA, Boston, 1995. Recipient scholarship NYU, 1964, Editl. award, Hosp. Mgmt., 1964, 65, 68, Annual Alumni award Phila. Coll. Pharmacy and Sci., 1979, Leonard A. Leipus award Am. Soc. for Hosp. Ctrl. Svc. Pers., 1982, 9th Annual Dr. John J. Perkins Meml. award Surgicot, Inc., 1983, Pub. Svc. award Assn. Surg. Technologists, 1983, 85, Appreciation award N.C. Assn. for Hosp. Ctrl. Svc. Pers., 1987, Pioneer in Infection Control award Smith Bros. Whitehaven, Ltd., 1992, among others. Mem. APHA, Am. Hosp. Assn., Am. Soc. Microbiology, Internat. Assn. for Hosp. Ctrl. Svc. Material Mgmt. (Pres.'s award 1992), Amherst Club. Avocations: painting, working with homeless animals, playing the violin, teaching art history, international hospital work. Home: 21 Lowery Ln Mendham NJ 07945-3403 Office: U Mass Amherst MA 01003

LITT, IRIS FIGARSKY, pediatrics educator; b. N.Y.C., Dec. 25, 1940; d. Jacob and Bertha (Berson) Figarsky; m. Victor C. Vaughan, June 14, 1987; children from previous marriage: William M., Robert B. AB, Cornell U., 1961; MD, SUNY, Bklyn., 1965. Diplomate Am. Bd. Pediatrics (bd. dirs. 1989-94), sub-specialty bd. cert. in adolescent medicine. Intern, then resident in pediat. N.Y. Hosp., N.Y.C., 1965-68; assoc. prof. pediat. Stanford U. Sch. Medicine, Palo Alto, Calif., 1982-87, prof., 1987—, dir. divsn. adolescent medicine, 1976—, dir. Inst. for Rsch. on Women and Gender, 1990-97. Editor Jour. Adolescent Health; contbr. articles to profl. jours including Jour. Am. Med. Assn., Pediatrics. Mem. Soc. for Adolescent Medicine (charter), Am. Acad. Pediatrics (award sect. on adolescent health), Western Soc. Pediatric Rsch., Soc. Pediatric Rsch., Am. Pediatric Soc., Inst. of Medicine/NAS. Office: 750 Welch Rd Ste 325 Palo Alto CA 94304-1510 E-mail: iris.litt@stanford.edu.

LITTLE, ANGELA CAPOBIANCO, nutritional science educator; b. San Francisco, Jan. 12, 1920; d. Alfredo Agosto and Elizabeth (Kruse) Capobianco; m. George Gordon Little, Nov. 8, 1947; 1 child, Judith Kristine. BA, U. Calif., Berkeley, 1940, MS, 1954, PhD, 1969. Specialist jr. to asst. to assoc. U. Calif., Berkeley, 1958-69, food scientist, 1969-85, assoc. prof. to prof, 1977-85, prof. emeritus, 1985—, acad. ombudsman, 1985-87, 89-91. Cons. in field; v.p., bd. dirs. Math/Sci. Network, Berkeley; vis. scholar U. Wash., Seattle, 1976-77, Kans. State U., Manhattan, 1972; mem. faculty Fromm Inst., U. San Francisco, 1992-96; pres. bd. dirs. Laguna Heights Co-op Corp., 1999-2001. Author: Color of Foods, 1962. Nutritional adv. bd. Project Open Hand, San Francisco, 1989—91, vol., 1988—91, UNICEF, San Francisco, 1986—89, Saint Francis Hosp., 1992—; mem. San Francisco Museum of Modern Art, Calif. Palace of the Legion of Honor, Asian Art Museum, Yerba Buena Ctr. of the Arts, Museo Italo-Am. Rsch. grantee Robert Woods Johnson Found., 1989-90, others 1960-85. Mem. AAUW, San Francisco Acad. Sci., San Francisco Mus. Soc., U. Calif. Berkeley Emeritii Assn. (pres. 1991-93), Am. Assn. for History of Medicine, Exploratorium, Bay Area History of Medicine Club (pres. 1995-97), Laguna Heights Co-op Corp. (pres., bd. dirs. 1999-2001), Sigma Xi. Avocations: music, books, travel, exercising, walking. Home: 85 Cleary Ct Apt 3 San Francisco CA 94109-6518 Office: U Calif Dept Nutritional Scis Berkeley CA 94720-0001 E-mail: aclittle@uclink.berkeley.edu.

LITTLE, CAROLE, women's apparel company executive; Co-founder CL Cinema Line Films Corp., L.A.; co-founder, co-chmn. Calif. Fashion Industries, Inc., L.A. Guest design tchr. Parson's Sch. Design, N.Y.C., L.A.; contbg. designer Divine Design, sponsor many benefit fashion shows; guest designer Acad. Awards; costume designer feature film. Co-prodr. Anaconda, 1997. Mem. bds. Calif. Am. Women's Econ. Devel., Women Inc., The Trusteeship; hon. co-chair mus. Fashion Designers and Creators; mem. Pres. Circle, L.A. County Mus. Art; found. mem. Internat. House of Blues Found. Named One of Leading Women Entrepreneurs of World, Nat. Found. Women Bus. Owners, Paris, 1997. Office: CL Fashions Corp # 9 15233 Ventura Blvd Sherman Oaks CA 91403-2201

LITTLE, CLAIRE LONG, education educator, humanities educator; b. Caswell County, N.C. d. William McKinley and Rachel (Garland) Long; m. Clarence Little, June 19, 1965; children: Cedric Ty, Cerise Jeanyne. BS, Barber-Scotia Coll., 1964; MS, Hofstra U., 1973, CAS in Edn. Adminstrn., 1983, EdD in Reading, Lang. and Cognition, 1993; postgrad., CUNY. Cert. tchr., English, reading, sch. dist. adminstrn., N.Y., sch. adminstr./supr. Lang. arts tchr. Levittown (N.Y.) Pub. Schs., 1967-70; adj. instr. SUNY, Westbury, 1975-77, lectr. Jamaica; reading and lang. specialist Hicksville (N.Y.) Sch. Dist., 1973—. Advisor, organizer to numerous civic and charitable orgns. Mem. NEA, ASCD.

LITTLE, ELIZABETH O'CONNOR, state legislator; b. Glens Falls, N.Y. children: Elizabeth, David, Robert, Thomas, Carolyn, Luke. BS in Edn., Coll. Saint Rose. Lic. realtor, N.Y. Mem. N.Y. State Assembly, Albany, 1995—, mem. edn., tourism, arts and sports devel. coms., ranking Rep. mem. children and families com., mem. social svcs. com., apptd. N.Y.C. Commn. on Restoration of Capitol, 1997. Mem. regional adv. bd. Glens Falls Nat. Bank. At-large supr. Warren County, Town of Queensbury, 1986, county budget officer, 1990, 91, mem. recycling adv. com.; bd. dirs. St. Mary's Parish, Glens Falls. Recipient Liberty Bell award for Cmty. Svcs., 1992, Adirondack Girl Scouts USA Woman of Distinction award, 1997. Mem. Adirondack C. of C., Zonta. Office: 21 Bay St Glens Falls NY 12801-3049

LITTLE, EMILY BROWNING, architect; b. Austin, Tex., June 4, 1951; d. Betty (Browning) L. BA in Cultural Anthropology, U. Tex., 1973, MArch, 1979. Registered architect, Tex. Archtl. apprentice Austin Design Assocs., 1980-81; project mgr. Nutt, Wolters & Assocs., Austin, 1981-84; prin. Emily Little Architects, Inc., Austin, 1984—. Prin. works include numerous residences, hist. restorations and comml. bldgs. Mem. citizens adv. com. Travis County Juvenile Ct., Austin, 1984-86; mem. adv. bd. Deborah Hay Dance Co., Austin, 1984—; chmn. Austin Design Commn., 1987-89. Recipient Archtl. Merit award Austin Bd. Realtors, 1989. Mem. AIA (commr. Austin chpt. 1987-88, Outstanding Young Arch. of Tex. 1993), Tex. Soc. Archs. (honors com. 1992, Design award 1996), Austin Women in Arch. (pres. 1985-86), Nat. Trust for Hist. Preservation, Tex. Fine Arts Assn. (pres. 1990-92), Heritage Soc. Austin (bd. dirs. 1989-98, pres. 1995, Bldg. award 1988, 90, 92, 93). Democrat. Avocations: travel, swimming. Office: 1001 E 8th St Austin TX 78702-3248

LITTLE, GRACE RUIZ, computer services administrator; b. Habana, Cuba, Aug. 16, 1956; d. Abelardo A. and Marta E. (Nodarse) Ruiz; m. Michael S. Little, Mar. 1, 1980; children: Kristina, Christopher. BS, Coll. William & Mary, 1978. Programmer Old Dominion U., Norfolk, Va., 1978-79, programmer, analyst, 1979-80, sr. programmer, analyst, 1980-82, systems analyst, 1982-84, asst. dir., 1984—. Coord. Great Computer Challenge, Norfolk, 1982—; mem. Help Desk Inst., 1995—. Sec. St. Gregory PTG, Virginia Beach, 1992-95; tchr. St. Gregory Ch., Virginia Beach, 1989—, asst. soccer coach, 1996-98, coord. children's liturgy. Roman Catholic. Office: Old Dominion U 128 Hughes Hall Norfolk VA 23529

LITTLE, JUDITH, cultural organization administrator; BS, U. Santa Clara, Calif.; AM, MA in drama, Stanford U.; PhD, Cornell U. Asst. dean grad. studies Stanford U., 1983-95, dir. office multicultural devel., 1983-95, dir. development, 1983-95, adv. panel investment, 1991-94, assoc. dir. found./corp. relations, 1991-94; dir. found. fundraising Nat. Urban League; v.p. external affairs Africian Am. Inst., New York, 1999—. Recipient St. Clare medal, Stanford U. Office: The Africa-Am Inst Chanin Bldg 380 Lexington Ave New York NY 10168-0002 Fax: 212-682-6174. E-mail: aainy@aaionline.org.

LITTLE, KAREN ANN, marriage and family therapist, psychotherapist; b. Columbus, Ohio, Aug. 13, 1967; d. Randolph Scott and Jo-Ann Marie Little. BS in Clin. Nutrition, Cornell U., Ithaca, NY, 1989; MA in Counseling Psychology, Rosemont (Pa.) Coll., 2000. Lic. profl. counselor Nat. Bd. of Cert. Counselors, 2003; cert. CPR ARC, SFA ARC. Dir. of fitness The Cornell Club, N.Y.C., 1989—91; asst. coord.- employee health & wellness Prudential Ins. Co., Roseland, NJ, 1991—93; dir. aquatic therapy Melmark Home, Berwyn, Pa., 1993—95; dir. fitness The Fitness Company - Franklin Plz., Phila., 1995—98; dir. of spl. projects Nutrition Mgmt. Svcs., Kimberton, 1998—2000; rsch. asst. The Beck Inst., Bala Cynwydd, 1998—2000; clin. coord. Mentor, Norristown, Pa., 2000—02; family therapist Young People's Unit Friends Hosp., Phila., 2002—. Mobile therapist Devereux, Paoli, Pa., 2001—03; vol. IAPT Conf. Contbr. chapters to books Efficacy of Cognitive Therapy with Suicide Attemptors. Mem. class coun. Cornell U., class coun. rep., 1999—2003. Mem.: ACA, APA (assoc.), Pa. Counseling Assn., Internat. Assn. for Play Therapy, Cornell Coll. Human Ecology Alumni Assn. (chairperson membership com. 1996—2000, sec. 1998—2000). Roman Catholic. Avocation: ARC vol.. Home: 401 Llanerch Ave Havertown PA 19083 Office: Friends Hospital 4641 Roosevelt Blvd Philadelphia PA 19141 Personal E-mail: kal36@cornell.edu.

LITTLE, TERESA CLINTON, special education educator; b. High Point, N.C., Aug. 20, 1962; d. Ulysses and Betty Jane Clinton; m. Marcel Alexander Little, June 20, 1992; 1 child, Selena. BS, Greensboro Coll., 1984; MA, Appalachian State U., 1988; postgrad., U. N.C., Greensboro, 1996—. Cert. spl. edn. (learning disabilities, mental disabilities-behavioral-emotional disabilities N.C. Spl. educator Halifax County Schs., South Boston, Va., 1984—85, Stokes County Schs., Walnut Cove, NC, 1985—88, Winston-Salem (N.C.)/Forsythe Co., 1988—93, 1996—; instr. Winston-Salem State U., 1993—96. Sch. sys. rep. Cmty. Transition Adv. Coun., Winston-Salem, 2000—; mem. N.C. State Transition Coun., Winston-Salem, 2000—, Greensboro Coll. Alumni Univ. Bd., 2000—; instr. Greensboro Coll., 2003. Mem.: Coun. for Exceptional Children.

LITTLE, WANDA VICKERY, school system administrator; d. Thomas Ray and Clara Crook Vickery; m. Lanny Alexander Little, Dec. 14, 1974; children: Kerri Leigh, Ashley Little Wright. B in Child Devel., U. of NC, Charlotte, NC, 1983—85, M math edn., 1987—91, M in Sch. Adminstrn., 2001—03. Cert. Sch. Adminstrn. State of NC, 2003. Asst. prin. Union County Pub. Schools, Monroe, NC, 2001—, tchr., 1985—2001. Mem.: ASCD (assoc.), Kappa Delta Pi (assoc.). Democrat-Npl. Southern Baptist. Avocations: cross-stitch, knitting, reading. Home: 6408 Little Road Monroe NC 28110 Office: Union County Public Schools 500 North Main Street Monroe NC 28110 Personal E-mail: wlittle@trellis.net.

LITTLEFIELD, VIVIAN MOORE, nursing educator, administrator; b. Princeton, Ky., Jan. 24, 1938; children: Darrell, Virginia. BS magna cum laude, Tex. Christian U., 1960; MS, U. Colo., 1964; PhD, U. Denver, 1979. Staff nurse USPHS Hosp., Ft. Worth, 1960-61; instr. nursing Tex. Christian U., Ft. Worth, 1961-62; nursing supr. Colo. Gen. Hosp., Denver, 1964-65; pvt. patient practitioner, 1974-78; asst. prof. nursing U. Colo., Denver, 1965-69, asst. prof., clin. instr., 1974-76, acting asst. dean, assoc. prof. continuing edn. regional perinatal project, 1976-78; assoc. prof., chair dept. women's health care nursing U. Rochester Sch. Nursing, N.Y., 1979-84; clin. chief ob-gyn., nursing U. Rochester Strong Meml. Hosp., N.Y., 1979-84; prof., dean U. Wis. Sch. Nursing, Madison, 1984-99, prof., 2000—. Cons. and lectr. in field. Author: Maternity Nursing Today, 1973, 76, Health Education for Women: A Guide for Nurses and Other Health Professionals, 1986; mem. editl. bd. Jour. Profl. Nursing; contbr. articles to profl. jours. Bur. Health Professions Fed. trainee, 1963-64. Recipient Nat. Sci. Service award, 1976-79. Mem. MAIN, AACN (bd. dirs.), NLN (bd. dirs.), Am. Acad. Nursing, Am. Nurses Assn., Consortium Prime Care Wis. (chair), Health Care for Women Internat., Midwest Nursing Research Soc., Sigma Theta Tau (pres. Beta Eta chpt., co-chair coun. nursing practice and edn. 1995). Avocations: golf, biking. Office: U Wis Sch Nursing 600 Highland Ave # H6150 Madison WI 53792-3284

LITTLETON, NAN ELIZABETH FELDKAMP, psychologist, educator; b. Covington, Ky., Oct. 23, 1942; d. William Albert and Norma Elizabeth (Smith) Feldkamp; m. O.W. Littleton, Oct. 4, 1969 (div. 1979). AAS, No. Ky. U., 1976, BS, 1978; MACE, Morehead State U., 1981; MA, U. Cin., 1986, PhD, 1995. Prof. No. Ky. U., Highland Heights, 1976—, dir. mental health and human svcs. program, 1989—. Officer, pres. Holly Hill Children's Home, Cold Spring, Ky., 1980-86; cons. Attituding Healing Ctr., Cin., 1990-94. Treas., editor So. Orgn. Human Svcs. Edn. Link, 1997-2002. Bd. dirs. Coun. for Stds. in Human Svc. Edn., Chgo., 1990-98—, Cancer Family Care, Cin., 1992-96. Mem. APA, Am. Psychol. Soc., Nat. Orgn. Human Svc. Edn., Am. Coun. Assn., So. Orgn. Human Svc. Edn. (state rep. 1991—, treas., 1999-2002), Nat. Women's Studies Assn., Assn. Humanistic Psychologists. Home: 333 W 17th St Covington KY 41014-1007 Office Phone: 859-572-5788.

LITTMAN, MARLYN KEMPER, information scientist, educator; b. Mar. 26, 1943; d. Louis and Augusta (Jacobs) Janofsky; m. Bennett I. Kemper, Aug. 1, 1965 (dec. June 1987); children: Alex Randall, Gari Hament, Jason Myles; m. Lewis Littman, Apr. 22, 1990. BA, Finch Coll., 1964; MA in Anthropology, Temple U., 1970; MA in Info. Sci., U. South Fla., 1983; PhD in Info. Sci., Nova Southeastern U., 1986. Dir. Hist. Broward County Preservation Bd., Hollywood, Fla., 1979—87; automated systems libr. Broward County Main Libr., Ft. Lauderdale, Fla., 1984—86; assoc. prof. info. sci. Nova U., Ft. Lauderdale, Fla., 1987—94, dir. info. sci. doctoral program, 1987—94; prof. info. sci. Nova Southeastern U., Ft. Lauderdale, Fla., 1995—. Weekly columnist Ft. Lauderdale News, 1975—79; contbg. editor Hyper Nexus-Jour. Hypermedia and Multimedia Studies, 1996—2000; assoc. editor Jour. On-Line Learning, 1997—2002. Author: A Comprehensive Documented History of the City of Pompano Beach, 1982, A Comprehensive History of Dania, 1983, A Comprehensive History of Hallandale, 1984, A Comprehensive History of Deerfield Beach, 1985, A Comprehensive History of Plantation, 1986, A Comprehensive History of Davie, 1987, Networking: Choosing a LAN Path to Interconnection, 1987, Building Broadband Networks, 2002; author: (with others) Mosaics of Meaning, New Ways of Learning, 1996; contbr. articles to profl. jours., chapters to books. Pub. info. officer Broward County Hist. Commn., 1975—79; vice chmn. Broward County Adv. Bd., 1987—92; bd. dirs. Ctrl. Agy. Jewish Edn., 1992—94. Recipient Judge L. Clayton Nance award, 1977, Broward County Hist. Commn. award, 1979. Mem.: IEEE, Assn. Computing Machinery, Internat. Soc. for Tech. in Edn., Phi Kappa Phi, Beta Phi Mu. Home: 2845 NE 35th St Fort Lauderdale FL 33306-2007 Office: Nova Southeastern U Grad Sch Computer and Info Sci 6100 Guffin Rd Fort Lauderdale FL 33314 E-mail: marlyn@nova.edu.

LITTON, NANCY JOAN, education educator; b. Baton Rouge, Mar. 26, 1952; d. Gilbert Dupre and Mell Baynard Litton. BS in Elem. Edn., La. State U., 1973, MEd in Elem. Edn., 1977, MA in History, 1986. Tchr., various grades various sch., Baton Rouge area, Eng. and Switzerland, 1974—94; tchg. assoc., Learning Assistance Ctr. La. State U., Baton Rouge, 1994—96, instr. for Coll. Edn., 1996—. Evaluator for talented drama students East Baton Rouge Parish Pub. Sch. Actor: over 70 plays. Christmas caroler for benefit Gilbert and Sullivan Soc., Baton Rouge, 2000—01; lector Our Lady of Mercy Cath. Ch., Baton Rouge, 1989—. Recipient Best Actress in a Play award, Baton Rouge Little Theater, 1998, Actress of Yr.

award, Baker Little Theatre, 1995, Supporting Actress of Yr. award, 1997. Roman Catholic. Avocations: public speaking, singing, travel, acting. Home: 4900 Claycut Rd Apt 52 Baton Rouge LA 70806 Office: La State U Coll of Edn Baton Rouge LA 70803 E-mail: nlitto@lsu.edu.

LITVIN, INESSA ELIZABETH, piano educator; b. Gorky, Russia, Sept. 13, 1939; came to U.S., 1980; d. Aron J. and Elizabeth I. (Shapiro) Frenkel; m. Edward J. Litvin, Aug. 22, 1975. MA in Piano Performing magna cum laude, Conservatory, Leningrad, Russia, 1965. Prof. music Ctrl. Music Sch., Leningrad, 1965-79; pvt. instr. piano Encinitas, Calif., 1980—. Recipient prize Shostakovich Piano Competition, Leningrad, 1964, recognition for exceptional artistic achievements of students Nat. Found. Advancement in Art, Miami, Fla., 1999. Mem. Calif. Assn. Profl. Music Tchrs., Music Tchrs. Assn. Calif. Home: 1632 Jerrilynn Pl Encinitas CA 92024-4757 E-mail: ielitvin@adelphia.net.

LITWIN, RUTH ANN FORBES, artist; b. Omaha, Apr. 14, 1933; d. Eli Morris and Toby Lena Forbes; m. Martin Louis Litwin, Feb. 10, 1952; children: Brenda, Linda, Bennett, Stuart. Pres. Sculpture Resources, Dallas, 1986; panelist Women in Contemporary Soc., Dallas, 1988; juror Nat. Arts Program, Dallas, 1995. Artist, producing paintings, sculpture, collagraphs; exhibited works at Dallas Women's Caucus for Art, 1997,, Wise Women Speak Exhbn., 1994, Brookhaven Coll., Dallas, 1996. Recipient Rowena Elkin award, 1997, Soc. Internat. Des Beaux-Arts prize Bern Heim De Villers, Paris, 1998, purchase award Northlake Coll., Irving, Tex., 2001. Mem. Tex. Fine Arts Assn. (prse. 1982-84), Dallas Women's Caucus for Art (adv. bd. 1994-96), Dallas Visual Art Ctr., Tex. Sculpture Assn., Tex. Visual Art Assn. Avocations: reading, travel, crossword puzzles, nature walks, yoga. Home: 6813 Wild Ridge Ct Plano TX 75024-7467

LITWIN, SHARON, orchestra executive; Asst. dir. devel. New Orleans Mus. Art, 1988-99; exec. dir. La. Philharm. Orch., New Orleans, 1999—. Staff writer Times-Picayune, New Orleans. Office: La Philharm Orch 305 Baronne St Ste 600 New Orleans LA 70112-1619

LITZENBERGER, LESLEY MARGARET, textiles executive; b. Ramsay, Eng., June 10, 1945; arrived in U.S., 1946; d. Albert Brockney and Margaret Jean Hendricks; m. Robert H. Litzenberger, Jan. 23, 1968 (div. June 18, 1996); children: Kenneth, William. AA, Canal Zone Coll., 1965; postgrad., U. N.C., 1965—66, postgrad., 1967—69. Sec. U.S. Army, Ft. Amador, 1966—67, U. N.C., Chapel Hill, 1968—69; dancer Ballet Panama, 1961—67, Bay Area Dance Theatre, Oakland, Calif., 1970—72; dance instr. Calif., Pa., 1972—86; CFO Robert Litzenberger Assoc., Stanford, Calif. and Haverford, Pa, 1982—94; textile artist Beaufort, S.C. and California, Pa., 1980—. Bd. dirs. Arts Coun. Beaufort County, 1998—2004; artistic dir. Byrne Miller Dance Theatre, Beaufort, 1999—2002; pub. rels. dir., bd. dirs. Panama Canal Mus., Seminole, Fla., 1999—; chairperson City of Beaufort, 2004—.

LIU, ALICE Y. C. biology educator; b. Hunan, China, July 12, 1948; came to U.S., 1970; d. Tin-Kai and Te-Ming (Young) L.; m. Kuang Yu Chen, Aug. 26, 1978; children: Andrew T-H, Winston T-C. BS, Chinese U., Hong Kong, 1969; PhD, Mount Sinai Sch. Med., 1974. Postdoctoral fellow Yale U. Med. Sch., New Haven, Conn., 1974-77; asst. prof. Harvard Med. Sch., Boston, 1977-84; assoc. prof. Rutgers U., Piscataway, N.J., 1984-89, prof., 1989—; dir. grad. program in cell and devel. biology Rutgers U.-U. Medicine-Dentistry N.J.-R.W. Johnson Med. Sch., 1994-99. Mem. pharmacological scis. rev. com. NIH, 1984-88, scientific rev. spl. emphasis panel, 1999, 2000, 2003; mem. cell biology panel NSF, 1989-93, 94-95; mem. basic rsch. adv. group N.J. Commn. on Cancer Rsch., 1989-93, 94—. Author: Receptors Again, 1985; mem. editl. bd. Biol. Signals, 1991—2001. Recipient N.Y.C. Bd. of Higher Edn. award, 1972, Am. Cancer Soc. Scholar award, Boston, 1982-85; NIH postdoctoral fellow, 1974-77, Medical Found. fellow, Boston, 1977-79. Mem.: Am. Soc. Biochemistry and Molecular Biology. Home: 4 Silverthorn Ln Belle Mead NJ 08502-5549 Office: Rutgers Univ Nelson Biology Labs 604 Allison Rd Piscataway NJ 08854-8000

LIU, CAROL, state representative; b. Berkeley, Calif., Sept. 12, 1940; m. Michael Peevey; children: Darcie, Maria, Jared. BA, San Jose State Coll., 1963; student, U. Calif., Berkeley, 1964, student, 1978. Tchr. Richmond Unified Sch. Dist., 1964—77, adminstr., 1978—84; mem. assembly Calif. State Assembly, 2000—. Mem. City Coun., La Canada Flindridge, Calif., 1992—96, 1997—98; pres. La Canada H.S. PTA; coun. pres. Mus. Contemporary Art; co-chair capital campaign Pasadena City Coll., pres. found. bd., co-chair phys. edn. campaign; trustee U. Calif., Berkeley; mayor La Canada Flindridge, Calif., 1996, 1999; bd. dirs. Child Care Info. Svcs., Five Acres. Democrat. Office: PO Box 942849 Rm 4112 Sacramento CA 94249 Address: 215 N Marengo Ave Ste 115 Pasadena CA 91101

LIU, GANG-YU, chemist, educator; b. Zhengzhou, Henan, China, Apr. 19, 1964; came to U.S., 1986; parents Zhen Kun and Quan Xian (Guo) L.; m. Xiaoyuan Li, Dec. 1, 1987. BS, Peking (China) U., 1988; MS, Princeton U., 1990, PhD, 1992. Postdoctoral assoc. U. Calif., Berkeley, 1992-94; asst. prof. chemistry Wayne State U., Detroit, 1994—99. Camille and Henry Dreyfus fellow, 1994-99, Miller Rsch. fellow The Miller Inst. for Basic Rsch. in Sci., 1992-94, Harold W. Dodds Honorific fellow Princeton U., 1991-92, CGP fellow Ministry of Edn., China, 1986-87. Mem. AAAS, Am. Chem. Soc., Am. Phys. Soc., Am. Vacuum Soc. Office: U Cal Dept Chem 1 Shields Ave Davis CA 95616

LIU, HANLI, biomedical engineer, educator; b. Beijing, Mar. 6, 1960; d. Li-ya Wang and Zhongcheng Liu; m. Anqi Wu, July 6, 1957; children: Eric Wu, Rodney Wu. PhD in Physics, Wake Forest U., Winston-Salem, N.C., 1994. Rsch. assoc. U. City Sci. Ctr., Phila., 1992—96; post-doctoral fellow U. of Pa, Phila., 1994—96; asst. prof. of biomed. engring. U. of Tex., Arlington, 1996—2001, assoc. prof. of biomedical engring., 2001—. Adj. faculty mem. joint program in biomed. engring. U. Tex. Southwestern Med. Ctr., Dallas, 1996—. Recipient Outstanding Young Scientist award, Houston Soc. for Engring. in Medicine and Biology, 1998, Outstanding Young Faculty Award, Coll. of Engring., U. of Tex., Arlington, 1999. Mem.: IEEE, Internat. Soc. for Optical Engring., Optical Soc. of Am. Home: 706 Gunnison Ct Arlington TX 76006 Office: Univ Texas at Arlington PO Box 19138 Arlington TX 76019 Business E-Mail: hanli@uta.edu.

LIU, LUCY, actress; b. Queens, N.Y., Dec. 2, 1968; Student, NYU; BA in Chinese Lang. and Culture, U. Mich., 1990. Actor: (TV series) Beverly Hills, 90210, 1991, L.A. Law, 1993, Coach, 1994, Home Improvement, 1995, Hercules: The Legendary Journeys, 1995, ER, 1995, The X-Files, 1996, Nash Bridges, 1996, High Incident, 1996, The Real Adventures of Johnny Quest, 1997, NYPD Blue, 1997, Michael Hayes, 1997, Sex and the City, 2001, (voice only) King of the Hill, 2002, Jackie Chan Adventures, 2004, Pearl, 1996—97, Ally McBeal, 1998—2002, (voice only) Game Over, 2004, : (TV films) Riot, 1997; (films) Ban wo zong heng, 1992, Protozoa, 1993, Bang, 1995, Jerry Maguire, 1996, Gridlock'd, 1997, City of Industry, 1997, Guy, 1997, Flypaper, 1997, Love Kills, 1998, Payback, 1999, True Crime, 1999, Molly, 1999, The Mating Habits of the Earthbound Human, 1999, Play It to the Bone, 1999, Shanghai Noon, 2000, Charlie's Angels, 2001, Hotel, 2001, Ballistics: Ecks vs. Sever, 2002, Cypher, 2002, Chicago, 2002, Charlie's Angels: Full Throttle, 2003, Kill Bill: Vol. 1, 2003, Kill Bill: Vol. 2, 2004. Office: William Morris Agy One William Morris Pl Beverly Hills CA 90212*

LIU, MARGARET C. music educator; b. Canton, China, Aug. 10, 1947; came to the U.S., 1972; d. Man-Hywn Wong and Shau-Chung Ng; m. John Pui-Chee, July 28, 1973; children: Amos Tao-Peng, Deborah Tao-En. BA, Hong Kong Bapt. U., 1970; M in Ch. Music, Southwestern Bapt. Theol. Sem., 1975. Freelance vocal and keyboard performer, various cities, 1972—; pvt. music tchr., 1975; music dir. 1st Chinese Bapt. Ch., Atlanta, 1976-80, 85-89, Chinese Bapt. Ch., College Park, Md., 1980-83; pres., CEO Cambridge Acad. Music and Arts, Atlanta, 1999—. Bd. mem. Alliance Theatre Edn. Adv. Coun., Atlanta, 1996-99; pres. North Dekalb Music Tchrs. Assn., Atlanta, 1997-99; Ga. local rep. Associated Bd. of the Royal Schs. Music, London, 1997—. Deacon Hanley Rd. Bapt. Ch., St. Louis, 1984. Mem. Music Tchrs. Nat. Assn., Music Educators Nat. Conf., Nat. Guild Piano Tchrs., Kindermusik Educators Assn.

LIU, RHONDA LOUISE, librarian; b. Honolulu; d. David Yuk Fong Liu and Shirley May Chong Liu. BA, U. Hawaii at Manoa, Honolulu, 1974, M of Libr. Info. Studies, 1991; grad., FBI Citizens Acad., 1998. Remote regions/homework ctrs. outreach libr. Alu Like Native Hawaiian Libr. Project, Hawaii, 1992; libr. II Hawaii State Libr., Hawaii, 1992; fgn. expert libr. studies in English program Beijing Fgn. Studies U., 1992—93; info. specialist Savs. & Cmty. Bankers of Am., Washington, 1993—94; staff specialist III Md. State Dept. Edn., Md. State Libr. for Blind and Physically Handicapped, Balt., 1995—99; asst. project mgr. Serial Record Holdings Conversion Project/LSSI Libr. of Congress, Washington, 2000; reference libr. George Washington U. at Mt. Vernon Coll., Washington, 2000—01; sr. technician, serial record divsn. Libr. of Congress, Washington, 2001—02, serials control specialist, serial record divsn., 2002—03, sr. technician cataloguing in pub. div., 2003—04, cataloguer, history and lit. cataloguing divsn., children's lit. team, 2004—. Libr. asst. State of Hawaii Legis. Reference Bur. Libr., 1989-90; asst. rschr. State of Hawaii Legis. Info. Sys. Office, 1984-85; ESL tutor Keimei Gakuen, Tokyo, 1979; exhibit facilitator Smithsonian Instn., 1999. Active Friends of the Md. State Libr. for Blind and Physically Handicapped, 1994-99, Md. State Dept. Edn. Employees Adv. Coun., 1998-99; sec. Coalition Opposed to Violence and Extremism, State of Md., 1997-99; v.p., sec. U. Hawaii Sch. Libr. and Info. Studies, 1990-91. Alu Like Native Hawaiian Libr. fellow, 1990-91; Kamehameha Sch./Bishop Estate scholar, 1991. Mem. U. Hawaii Alumni Assn., U. Hawaii Sch. Lib. and Info. Studies Alumni Assn., Kamehameha Schs. Alumni Assn. (East Coast region), Lung Kong Kung Shaw Soc., Libr. Congress Profl. Assn., Libr. Congress Asian Assn., Libr. Congress Cooking Club. E-mail: rliu@loc.gov.

LIVERMORE, ANN M. computer company executive; BA in Econ., U. N.C.; MBA, Stanford U. From mem. staff to pres., corp. v.p. Hewlett-Packard Co., Palo Alto, Calif., 1982-1995, corp. v.p., 1995—, pres., CEO enterprise computing divsn., 1998—, pres. enterprise computing divsn. Bd. dirs. UPS; bd. visitors Kenan-Flagler Bus. Sch. U. N.C., Chapel Hill. Office: Hewlett Packard Enterprise Computing 100 Mayfield Ave Mountain View CA 94043-4158

LIVERMORE, JANE, foundation executive; b. Kansas City, Mo., Feb. 21, 1939; d. George P. and Mary Louise (Luccock) L.; children: Jana, Douglas, George. Student, U. Okla. Owner, pres. Mary L. Livermore Enterprises, Lubbock, Tex.; ptnr. Jermac Co., Levelland, Tex.; pres. Mary L. Livermore Found., Lubbock. Mem. chanceller's coun. Tex. Tech. U.; bd. dirs. Lubbock YWCA; mem. Lubbock Symphony Guild. Address: PO Box 12109 Lubbock TX 79452-2109

LIVESAY, VALORIE ANN, security program analyst; b. Greeley, Colo., Sept. 9, 1959; d. John Albert and Mary Magdalene Yurchak. BA in Edn., U. No. Colo., 1981; M in Computer Info. Sys., U. Denver, 1991; AAS in Fashion Mktg., Colo. Inst. Art, 1996. Drafter Computer Graphics, Denver, 1981, Advanced Cable Sys., Inc., Denver, 1981-82, Am. TV Comm. Corp., Englewood, Colo., 1982-83; janitor Rockwell Internat., Golden, Colo., 1983-84, analytical lab tech., 1984-86, metall. operator, 1986-88; nuclear material coord. EG&G Rocky Flats Inc., Golden, 1988-92, lead security analyst, 1992-95; adminstr., coord. Colo. Inst. Art, Denver, 1996-97. Mem. The Humane Soc. of the U.S., 1998; mem Am. Humane Soc., 1997; mem. Best Friends Sanctuary, 1999. Mem. NAFE, Am. Soc. Insdl. Security Avocations: scuba diving, mountain biking, skiing, reading, boating. Home: 7445 Saratoga Ln Santa Fe NM 87505 Office: U Calif Los Alamos Nat Lab Los Alamos NM 87545

LIVINGS, MELISSA JUNE, music educator, director; d. Bobby Dean Lockwood and Flora Jane Golden; m. Forrest Anthony Livings, June 6, 2002. MusB in edn., U. of Tex. at Arlington, 1996—2000. Cert. Secondary Music Teacher Tex., 2001. Head orch. dir. JJ Pearce H.S., Richardson Ind. Sch. Dist., Richardson, Tex., 2000—. Recipient Orch. award, U. of Tex. Music Dept., 1999, Outstanding Jazz Band Musician, Paris H.S. Band, 1996, Four States Jazz Band, Four States Jazz Band, Tex./Okla./La./Ark., 1994—96; Freshman Honors scholarship, U. of Tex. at Arlington, 1996—2000, Music scholarship, 1996—99. Mem.: Am. String Teachers Assn., Tex. Orch. Directors Assn., Tex. Music Educators Assn., Alpha Chi. Avocations: bicycling, reading. E-mail: jjpearceorchestra@yahoo.com.

LIVINGSTON, JO ELLEN BROOKS, music educator; b. Beckley, W.Va., Dec. 4, 1953; d. Henry Edward and Ramona Ann Brooks; m. James M Livingston, Oct. 3, 1981. BS in music edn., Concord Coll., 1971—77; MusM, U. of So. Miss., 1977—80. Music educator St. Francis de Sales Sch., Beckley, 1980—81; music dir. Theatre W.Va., Beckley, 1981—90, Curtain Callers, Mt. Hope, W.Va., 1981—94; music educator Raleigh County Pub. Schools, Beckley, W.Va., 1981—94, Prince William County Pub. Schools, Manassas, Va., 1995—; music dir. Ctr. for the Arts, Manassas, 1995—, Rooftop Players, Manassas, 2003—. Music curriculum com. Prince William County Pub. Schools, Manassas, 2001; min. of music Meml. Bapt. Ch., Beckley, 1992—94; performer Gary Matheny Trio, Athens, W.Va., 1971—77, Commanders Big Band, Athens, 1972—77; percussionist Hattiesburg Light Opera Co., Hattiesburg, Miss., Opera South, Jackson, Miss., Miss. Ballet Orch., Jackson, Jackson Symphony Orch., Tupelo (Miss.) Symphony Orch., Meridian (Miss.) Symphony Orch., Miss. Opera Co., Jackson; string solo and ensmble chair Prince William County Schools, Manassas, 2002—; percussionist W.Va. Symphony Orch., Charleston; mid. sch. honor choir chair Prince William County, Manassas; Prince William County Mid. Sch. honors orch. chair Prince William County Schools, Manassas; dist. mid. sch. honor choir chair Va. Music Educators Assn., Manassas; dist. 9 honor bands audition chair VBODA, District 9, Va.; region i chair W.Va. Music Educators Assn., Region I, all-state h.s. honors chorus chair, Charleston; auditorium mgr. Woodrow Wilson H.S., Beckley, 1988—90. Mem. Curtain Callers, Mt. Hope, W.Va. Recipient Gilbert award, U. of So. Miss. Theater, Governor's Citation for Musical Contributions, State Of W.Va. Mem.: Nat. Educators Assn. (assoc.; state del. and sch. rep.), Va. Music Educators Assn. (assoc.), Omicron Delta Kappa (assoc.), Mu Phi Epsilon (assoc.; v.p. 1978). Avocation: painting. Home: 9301 Battle St Manassas VA 20110 Office: Parkside Middle School 8602 Mathis Ave Manassas VA 20110 Office Phone: 703-361-3106. Personal E-mail: jbldiva@comcast.net. E-mail: livingjb@pwcs.edu.

LIVINGSTON, JOYCE TORBIC, civilian military employee; b. Lumberton, N.C., Sept. 12, 1953; d. Myles and Rena Mae Torbic; m. Edwin Charles Livingston; 1 child, Kristi. BS in Bus., Troy State U., 1985. Audit clk. IRS, Columbus, Ga., 1976—81; mgmt. analyst Civil Svc., Ft. Benning, Ga., 1981—. Author: (novels) Borrowed Memories, 2000, The Edge of Good-bye, 2001. Vol. Animal Human Soc., Columbus, 2000—02. Methodist. Avocations: physical fitness, reading, gardening. Home: 259 Alexander Ln Fortson GA 31808 Office: Western Hemisphere Inst 7011 Morrison Ave Ridgway Hall Fort Benning GA 31905-2611 Mailing: PO Box 1612 Fortson GA 31808 Business E-Mail: joyce.t.livingston@us.army.mil.

LIVINGSTON, JULIE, publicist; b. Queens, NY; m. Peter Gordan; children: Jacob, Benjamin. Beauty/fashion editor YM mag.; publicist, nat. spokesperson World Gold Coun.; founder, pres. Luxury Mktg. Group, 2001—02; dir. corp. comm. Scholastic Inc., 2002—03; dir. mktg. comm. Toy Industry Assn., 2003—. Adj. Instr. Pace U. Mem.: Fashion Group Internat., NY Women in Comm. Office: Toy Industry Assn 1115 Broadway Ste 400 New York NY 10010 Business E-Mail: jlivingston@toy-tia.org.*

LIVINGSTON, KATHRYN E. writer; b. Schenectady, N.Y., Jan. 11, 1953; d. Abram Fryer Livingston, Virginia Kathryn Swart; m. Mitchell Kriegler, June 5, 1977; 3 children. BA, Kirkland Coll., Clinton, N.Y., 1975; MA, Hunter Coll., N.Y.C., 1979. Freelance writer, 1983—. Text author: Special Effects Photography, 1985, Patrick Demarchelier: Fashion Photographer, 1984, Secrets of Studio Still Life Photography, 1984; co-author: Photographing Your Baby, 1984, Parenting Partners (St. Martins), 1999, The Secret Life of the Dyslexic Child, 2002; contbr. articles to profl. jours. Mailing: 143 Highview Pl Bogota NJ 07603

LIVINGSTON, KRIEMHILDE IRMGARD REINFRIEDE, retired language educator, translator, interpreter; m. Robert R. Livingston, Apr. 27, 1951 (dec. Oct. 1990); 1 child, Douglas Robert. Diploma, U. Munich, 1945, Bavarian State Interpreter/Translator Sch., Regensburg, Germany, 1947. Tchr. pub. sch. sys., Garmisch, Germany, 1945—46; interpreter and translator U.S. Army EUCOM, Sonthofen, Germany, 1947—51; tchr. adult edn. Bd. of Edn., Akron, Ohio, 1965—68; instr. German spl. program U. Akron, 1966—75, lectr. German dept. modern langs., 1968—69, instr. German dept. modern langs., 1969—94; ret., 1994. Contbr. articles to profl. jours. Vol. instr. swimming and water safety ARC, Akron, 1960—86. Mem.: Am. Translator Assn., Delta Phi Alpha. Avocations: reading, swimming, knitting. Home: 357 Sullivan Ave Akron OH 44305-3746

LIVINGSTON, MARGARET GRESHAM, civic leader; b. Birmingham, Ala., Aug. 16, 1924; d. Owen Garside and Katherine (Morrow) Gresham; m. James Archibald Livingston, Jr., July 16, 1947; children: Mary Margaret, James Archibald, Katherine Wiley, Elizabeth Gresham. Grad., The Baldwin Sch., Phila., 1942; AB, Vassar Coll., 1945; MA, U. Ala., 1946. Acting dir. Birmingham Mus. Art, 1978-79, 81, chmn. bd. dirs., 1978-86, mem. exec. bd., 1978—. Bd. dirs. Birmingham Civic Ctr. Authority, 1988-95; bd. dirs. Altamont Sch., Birmingham, 1963—, chmn. bd., 1986. Named Woman of Yr., Birmingham 1986; named to Ala. Tennis Hall of Fame, 1994. Mem. Am. Assn. Mus., Jr. League, Ala. Tennis Assn. Episcopalian.

LIVINGSTON, MARGERY ELSIE, missionary, clinical psychologist; b. Petoskey, Mich., Oct. 29, 1940; d. David Eugene and Beryle Mae (Herrington) L. BS with honors, Taylor U., Upland, Ind., 1962; MA with high honors, Wheaton (Ill.) Coll., 1983; student, U. Paris Sorbonne, 1970. Lic. psychologist, Pa., limited lic. psychologist, Mich. Tchr. Waterford (Mich.) Sch. Sys., 1962-64; ednl. missionary, county dir. BCM Internat., Union County, NJ, 1965-69; ednl. missionary BCM Internat. and AIM Internat., Albertville and Paris, France, 1969-70, ednl. missionary, technician Watsa, Democratic Republic of Congo, 1970-81; counselor, therapist BCM Internat./AIM Internat. Amani Counseling Ctr., Nairobi, Kenya, 1983-84; organizer, dir. counseling dept., counselor, cons. BCM Internat., Upper Darby, Pa., 1985-97, psychol. testing and assessment of mission candidates, 1986—95, organizer, dir. mem. care ministries, 1998—2000, mem. care ministries, cons., 2000—. Guest lectr. Bunia (Dem. Rep. Congo) Theol. Sem., 1984, Adi (Dem. Rep. Congo) Bible Inst., 1978, Aru (Dem. Rep. Congo) Bible Inst., 1978, Todro (Dem. Rep. Congo) Bible Inst., 1980; organizer/facilitator Missions and Mental Health-East, Mt. Bethel, Pa., 1995-97; guest lectr. Communauté Evangelique Ctr. de l'Afrique Chs., Dem. Republic of Congo, 1991; spkr. in field. Editor: Commit Thy Way, 1994; author: (Bible study series) Living in Community, 1980, translator (illustrator) Bible lessons from English to Lingala for use in Congo; contbr. articles to profl. jours. Spkr., adj. staff Rockford (Mich.) Bapt. Ch., 1965—, Haven Reformed Ch., Kalamazoo, 1978—2002, Clinton Hill Bapt. Ch., Union, NJ, 1965—, Silvercrest Bapt. Ch., Waterford, Mich., 1966—, First Congl. Ch., Rockford, Mich., 1985—, North Plainfield (N.J.) Bapt. Ch., 1988—; facilitator Bible Club work Democratic Republic of Congo, 1985—; fundraiser, facilitator printing and distbn. Christian lit., 2001—. Billy Graham Evangelistic Assn. scholar, 1981-83. Mem.: APA (assoc.), Midwest Mem. Care Network (charter), Christian Therapists Bible Study, Assn. N.Am. Missions, Am. Assn. of Christian Counselors (charter, spkr. regional conf. 1999). Baptist. Avocations: writing poetry, clarinet, walking, aerobic weight-lifting, swimming. Office: 309 Colonial Dr Box 249 Akron PA 17501-0249 also: BCMI Western Mich 710 Baldwin St Jenison MI 49428-9706 E-mail: worship@rockfordbaptist.com.

LIVINGSTON, PAMELA A. corporate image and marketing management consultant; b. Richmond Hill, N.Y., Nov. 21, 1930; d. Paul Yount and Anna Margaret (Altland) L. BA, Adelphi U., 1951; postgrad., NYU, 1952, Columbia U., 1959, Am. Acad. Dramatic Art, 1954, IBM Sys. and Mktg. Schs., 1967-70, Brandon Sch. Electronic Data, 1973, Pa. State U., 1993. Pers. and pub. rels. depts. Am. Can Co., N.Y.C., 1951-60; exec. sec. to pres. York (Pa.) divsn. Borg-Warner Corp., 1962-65; freelance writer, 1965-67; mktg. ofcl. IBM Corp., 1967-70; rsch. analyst, dir. new EDP bus. Ins. Co. N.Am., 1971-74; asst. to v.p. corp. affairs IU Internat., Phila., 1974-75; comm. and mktg. mgmt. cons. specializing in corp. identity, 1975—. Corp. image cons., 1984—; freelance writer, spkr. on identity, 1994—. Contbr. articles to tech jours. Recipient various journalism awards, award in mktg. and sales IBM, 1969-70, award for innovative product application, 1969. Mem. AAUW, Sales/Mktg. Execs. Internat., Art Alliance, Pub. Rels. Soc. Am., Econs. Club of York C. of C., Phila. Club Advt. Women, Phila. Acad. Fine Arts, World Affairs Coun., English-Speaking Union, Kappa Kappa Gamma. Home and Office: 108 S Rockburn St York PA 17402-3467

LIVINGSTONE, SUSAN MORRISEY, management consultant, former federal agency administrator; b. Carthage, Mo., Jan. 13, 1946; d. Richard John II and Catherine Newell (Carmean) Morrisey; m. Neil C. Livingstone III, Aug. 30, 1968. AB, Coll. William and Mary, 1968; MA, U. Mont., 1973; postgrad., Tufts U., 1972—73, Fletcher Sch. Law and Diplomacy, 1973—. Rschr. Senator Mark O. Hatfield, Washington, 1969-70; chief legis. and press asst. Congressman Richard H. Ichord, Washington, 1973-75, adminstrv. asst., 1975-81; cons. Congressman Wendell Bailey, Washington, 1981; exec. asst. VA, Washington, 1981-85, assoc. dep. adminstr. logistics and mgmt., 1985-86, sr. procurement exec., 1985-89, assoc. dep. adminstr. logistics, 1985—89; asst. sec. Army U.S. Dept. of Def., Washington, 1989-93; v.p. health and safety svcs. ARC, Washington, 1993-97; cons. mgmt., 1997-2001; under sec. of Navy U.S. Dept. Navy, Washington, 2001—03; mem. return-to-flight task group NASA, 2003—. Mem interagy. com. on women's bus. enterprise The White House, 1985-89; mem. Pres.'s Coun. on Mgmt. Improvement, 1985-86; cons. Def. Sci. Bd., 1998, 2000; mem. adv. bd. Martin Inst. U. Idaho, 2000-01; mem. nat. security studies bd. advs., Maxwell Sch. Syracuse U., 2003—; bd. dirs. The Atlantic Coun. Vice chair White House Commn. on Nat. Moment of Remembrance, 2002—03. Mem. Exec. Women in Govt., Procurement Round Table (bd. dirs. 1994-2001, 2003-), Assn. U.S. Army (bd. dirs. 1994—, coun. trustees 1996-2001, CEO, dep. chmn. 2000-01), Women in Internat. Security (mem. adv. bd. 1994-97), Navy League. Episcopalian.

LIVINGSTONE, TRUDY DOROTHY ZWEIG, dancer, educator; b. N.Y.C., June 9, 1946; d. Joseph and Anna (Feinberg) Zweig; m. John Leslie Livingstone, Aug. 7, 1977; 1 child, Robert Edward. Student, Charles Lowe Studios, N.Y.C., 1950-52, Nina Tinova Studio, 1953-56, Ballet Russe de Monte Carlo, 1956-57, Bklyn. Coll., 1964-66; BA in Psychology cum laude, Boston U., 1968, MEd, 1969; postgrad., Serena Studios, Carnegie Hall Ballet Arts, N.Y.C., 1973-74. Tchr. Millis (Mass.) Pub. Schs., 1969-72, Hebrew Acad. Atlanta, 1974-76, Palm Beach County Pub. Sch., 2002—;

profl. dancer various orgns. including Rivermont Country Club, Jewish Community Ctr., Callanwolde Performing Arts Ctr., Atlanta, 1974-84; founder, owner, instr. dance Sasha Studios, Atlanta, 1974-77; owner Trudy Zweig Livingstone Studios, Wellesley, Needham, Mass., 1987-88, Palm Beach, Fla., 1989—. Judge dance competition Atlanta Council Run-Offs, 1976. Vol. League Sch., Bklyn., 1965, Kennedy Meml. Hosp., Brighton, Mass., 1969, Nat. Affiliation for Literacy Advances, Santa Monica, Calif., 1982. Mem. Am. Alliance for Health, Phys. Edn., Recreation and Dance, Poets of the Palm Beaches, L.A. Athletic Club, Wellesley Coll. Club, Governor's Club (West Palm Beach). Avocation: writing poetry.

LIVINGSTON-MACIRELAN, JOAN PERSILLA, artist; b. Wenatchee, Wash., Oct. 9, 1940; d. Herbert Edgar and Maxine Lucina (Irelan) Macy; m. David Warner Livingston, June 15, 1958 (div. Apr. 1981); children: Dolly Jo, Jennifer Lynn. Student in oil painting, Old Town Gallery, Auburn, Calif., 1966; student, Ft. Mason Art Ctr., San Francisco, 1989. Cert. cosmetologist, Calif., Wash., N.Mex.; nat. cert. massage therapist, 2002. Salon owner TJ's Hair Factory/Hair Today, Auburn, 1969-79; photographer's stylist Ed Young Photography, San Francisco, 1985-86; studio painter Studio Nine, Sausalito, Calif., 1986-90, 94-96; designer sculptor Poupee Millet, San Rafael, Calif., 1990-91; studio painter Studio Nine, San Rafael, 1991-94; wilderness artist Studio Nine Cabin Studio, Stehekin, Wash., 1996-98, Seattle, 1998-99; studio painter, art tchr. Studio Nine, Cashmere, Wash., 1999, studio painter, graphic designer, 2000—03. Exhibited in one-woman and group exhbns. in Zelos Ventures, San Francisco, 1991, Hanson Art GAlleries, Sausalito, 1992, Royal Palm Gallery, Palm Beach, Fla., 1995, The Black Orchid Gallery, Sanibel Island, Fla., 1997, William Vincent Fine Art Gallery, Santa Fe, 1998, Gallery 76, Wenatchee, Wash., 2000—01, Sunburst Gallery, Chelan, Wash., 2001—03, Dartmouth St. Gallery, Albuquerque, 2003, over 30 pvt. collections. Recipient awards for art Placer County Fair, 1957-60, The Artists Mag., 1988, 91, 95, Gallery 76, Wenatchee, 2001. Mem. Nat. Mus. Women in the Arts, Georgia Okeeffe Mus. Avocations: writing children's stories, writing poetry, flamenco dance, hiking. E-mail: josstudio9@msn.com.

LLEWELLYN, LINDA GARRISON, foundation executive; b. Lockport, N.Y., July 25, 1953; d. Robert Groves and Mary Jean Garrison; m. John Frederick Llewellyn, Apr. 15, 1989; 1 step-daughter, Sharon J. BS, Regents Coll., Albany, 1995; D (hon.), Pepperdine U., 1997. V.p. Headline Brokers, Secaucus, N.J., 1976-85; mgr. Forest Lawn Meml. Pks., Glendale, Calif., 1985-89; v.p. Forest Lawn Found., Glendale, 1994-98, pres., 1998—. Dir., officer Goodwill Indistries So. Calif., L.A., 1994-2001; dir., mem. exec. com. ARC, L.A., 1994-2000; dir. Children's Bur. So. Calif., L.A., 1998—. Mem. So. Calif. Assn. Philanthropy (bd. dirs. 2000—). Office: Forest Lawn Found 1712 S Glendale Ave Glendale CA 91205-3320 Home: # 801 13700 Marina Pointe Dr Marina Del Rey CA 90292-9262

LLORENS, MERNA GEE, elementary school educator, music educator; b. Ofahoma, Miss., Oct. 4, 1939; d. Junior McKinley and Birdie Rose Smith; m. Ramon James Llorens Sr., Oct. 1, 1960; children: Regina Llorens Dominguez, Ramon James Llorens Jr. BS, Western Mich. U., 1971. Sec. Follet Pub. Co., Chgo., 1960-62, Mohawk Tablet Co., Chicago Heights, Ill., 1963-65; elem. tchr. St. Basil Cath. Sch., South Haven, Mich., 1965-79, South Haven Pub. Schs., 1979—. Chair Jubilee 100th Ann. St. Basil Ch., Faith and Vision campaign com. Mem.: South Haven Edn. Assn. (chair courtesy com. 1985—2000), Black History Leadership Soc. (charter, treas., publicity/program chair, Spl. Tribute Role Model of Yr. award 2001), St. Basil Altar Rosary Women's Svc. Guild (treas. 2002—, Woman of Yr. 1990), Lions Club (1st v.p.), Delta Sigma Theta (pres. 1999—2001, Benton Harbor/St. Joseph Alumnae chpt., sgt.-at-arms 2002—04). Democrat. Roman Catholic. Avocations: crafts, camping, gardening, Minnie Pearl impersonation. Home: 67556 County Rd 338 South Haven MI 49090-8372 E-mail: mergee@aol.com.

LLOYD, JUNE BURK, librarian, archivist; b. York County, Pa., June 7, 1939; d. Wiley A. Burk and Olive M. Shelley; m. Ronald E. Lloyd, Aug. 14, 1956; children: Lisa A., Linda S. BA summa cum laude, York Coll., Pa., 1995; MA in Am. Studies, Penn State, 1999. Asst. libr. Kaltreider Meml. Libr., Red Lion, Pa., 1980—89; libr. York County Heritage Trust, York, Pa., 1989—. archivist, 1989—. Author: Faith and Family, 2001; curator (exhibitions) Faith and Family in Franktur, 2001. Mem.: Palatines to Am., Pa. German Soc. Lutheran. Avocation: history. Office: York County Heritage Trust 250 E Market St York PA 17403

LLOYD, KIMCHERIE, performing company executive; BA, Ea. Mich. U., 1985, MA, 1987. Asst. condr. Collegium Musicum and Choirs Ea. Mich. U., dir. Symphony Orch.; dir. orchestral studies and opera theatre U. Louisville; dir. music Music Theater Louisville, 1997—, Ky. Opera, Louisville, 1999—. Office: Kentucky Opera 101 S Eighth St Louisville KY 40202*

LLOYD, LILA G. business educator; b. Laurens, S.C., Mar. 10, 1937; d. Shellie and Alberta Barksdale Garrett; m. Clifton H. Lloyd Sr.; children: Clifton H. Jr., William P. BS, Benedict Coll., 1957; MEd, U. N.C., Greensboro, 1971; PhD, Columbia Pacific U., 1999. H.S. tchr., Bath, SC, 1958—59, Siler City, NC, 1963—84; tchr. S.E. H.S., Greensboro, NC, 1984—92; instr. bus. edn. A&T State U., Greensboro, NC, 1992—. Mem. sch. leadership team, Greensboro, 1988—91; chmn. recruiting com. N.C. A&T State U., Greensboro, 1986—91, Greensboro, 1992—. Author: Lloyds: Refresher Course in Computer and Office Skills, 2002. Pres. Friends of McGirt-Horton Libr., Greensboro, 1989—94; v.p. precinct 19 Dem. Party, Greensboro, 1986—90; treas. United Meth. Ch., 1996—; bd. dirs. Claremont Housing Project, 1988, vice chmn. edn. program, 1988. Mem.: AAUW (contbr. newsletter 1997—99, pres. 1997—99, Outstanding Leadership award 1999), N.C. Assn. Educators (Human Rels. award 1990), Young Womens Christian Assn. Methodist. Avocations: amateur photography, reading, viewing old classical movies. Home: 1702 Woodbriar Ave Greensboro NC 27405

LLOYD, MARGARET HARRIS, entrepreneur, educator; b. Washington, Aug. 18, 1947; d. James Arthur Harris and Molly Ida Rains; m. Julian Bernice Lloyd, Jr., Aug. 30, 1973; 1 child, John Barron. BS, East Carolina U., 1969; MA, George Washington U., 1973. Lic. grad. licensure of tchg. N.C., cert. specialist in learning disabilities, mentally disabilities, visually impaired. Elem. tchr. St. Mary's County-Md. Schs., Mechanicsville, Md., 1969—73, Culpeper (Va.) County Sch. Sys., 1973—75; learning disabilities specialist Onslow County Schs., Jacksonville, NC, 1975—88, program specialist, 1988—2001; entrepreneur in wellness Ind. Dist. for Liquidity, Inc., Dallas, 2001—. Ind. tutor, Hubert, NC, 1974—; child advocate to parents, Hubert, 2002—. Contbr. poetry to anthologies. Treas. United Meth. Women, 1985. Methodist. Avocations: genealogy, complementary health research, travel. Home: 107 Kings Pkwy Hubert NC 28539

LLOYD, PRISCILLA ANN, finance educator; b. Defuniak Springs, Fla., June 21, 1946; d. Thomas Sherman and Leona Campbell Brown; m. Leroy Lloyd, Aug. 15, 1969; 1 child, Leroy Erison. BS, U. Okla., 1974, EdM, 1975. Cert. adminstrn. and supervision U. of Ctrl. Fla. Tchr. bus. H.B. Plant H.S., Tampa, Fla., 1975—78, Meadowbrook Jr. H.S., Orlando, Fla., 1978—84, Apopka (Fla.) H.S., 1984—90, Cypress Creek H.S., Orlando, 1990—93; coord. bus. programs Orange County Sch. Dist., Orlando, 1993—96; instr., adminstr. asst. program Mid Fla. Tech, Orlando, 1996—. Pres. Orange County Bus. Edn. Assoc., Orlando, 1991—92, Fla. Bus. Edn. Assn., Orlando, 1992—94; dist. dir. Future Bus. Leaders Am., Orlando, 1992—93. Named Outstanding Tchr., Fla. Bus. Edn. Assn., 1993, Outstanding Educator, Orange County Vocat. Assoc., 1994. Mem.: Fla. Bus. Edn. Assoc. Conf. (chmn. 44th annual conf.), Family Christian Athletic Assn. (bd. mem. 2002—03). Catholic Orthodox. Avocations: reading, writing, photography, travel. Home: 7202 Jonquil Dr5 Orlando FL 32818

LLOYD, SHARON, marketing professional; Mgr. mktg. Raley's Bel Air, West Sacramento, Calif. Office: Raleys Bel Air 500 W Capitol Ave West Sacramento CA 95605-2696

LLOYD, WANDA SMALLS, newspaper editor; b. Columbus, Ohio, July 12, 1949; d. Gloria Walker; m. Willie Burk Lloyd, May 25, 1975; 1 child, Shelby Renee. BA, Spelman Coll., Atlanta, 1971. Copy editor Providence Evening Bull., 1971-73, Miami Herald, Fla., 1973-74, Atlanta Jour., 1974-75, Washington Post, 1975-76; dep. Washington editor Times-Post News Svc., 1976-86; dpt. mng. editor cover stories USA Today, 1986-87, mng. editor/adminstrn., 1987-88, sr. editor, 1988-96; mng. editor The Greenville News, 1996—2000; exec. dir. Freedom Forum Diversity Inst., 2000—04; exec. editor Montgomery Advertiser, Ala., 2004—. Instr. program for minority journalists Columbia U., N.Y.C., summer 1972; cons. So. Regional Press Inst., Savannah State Coll., Ga., 1973-94; mem. adv. bd. urban journalism workshop Howard U., Washington, 1983-96; trustee Spelman Coll., 1988—; bd. dirs. Dow Jones Newspaper Fund, 1992-99. Mem., bd. dirs. Nation's Capital coun. Girl Scouts U.S., Washington, 1985; mem. adv. com. Alfred Friendly Found., 1992-96; active Leadership Greenville, 1999—. Journalism fellow Northwestern U., 1987. Mem. Washington Assn. Black Journalists, Nat. Assn. Black Journalists, Washington Spelman Alumnae Assn. (v.p. 1984-86, named Alumna of Yr. 1985), Am. Soc. Newspaper Editors (bd. dirs. 1997—), Delta Sigma Theta. Baptist. Office: The Greenville News PO Box 1688 Greenville SC 29602-1688

LLOYD-CAMERON, ROSEMARY ANN, music educator; b. Sioux City, Iowa, Sept. 22, 1963; d. Richard Gerard and Marilyn Jane Lloyd; m. Thomas Edward Cameron, Apr. 27, 1996; children: Millicent Rose, Elise Ann, Bridget Mae, Maris Eileen. B in Music Edn., Culver-Stockton Coll., Canton, Mo., 1986; M in Edn., Iowa State U., Ames, 2002. Tchr. music Nodaway-Holt R7, Maitland, Mo., 1986—88, Anita (Iowa) Cmty. Schs., 1988—2003; tchr. music 5th grade band Anita Elem., Iowa, 2003—; tchr. music HS band CAM HS, Iowa, 2003—. Pianist Big Band, 1994—. Dir. choir Meth. Ch., Anita, 1992—. Mem.: Tchr. Edn. Assn. (pres. 1990—), Anita Lit. Club. Home: 209 Rosehill Ave Anita IA 50020 Office: CAM HS/Anita Elem 1000 Victory Park Rd Anita IA 50020

LOAR, PEGGY ANN, foundation administrator, museum administrator; b. Cin., May 14, 1948; d. Jerome Vincent and Elizabeth (Ranz) Wahl. BA in History of Art, U. Cin., 1970, MA in History of Art, 1971; student in Bus., Stanford U., 2003. Summer intern Met. Mus. Art, N.Y.C., 1968; curator edn. Indpls. Mus. Art, 1971-76, asst. to the dir., 1974-75, asst. dir., 1975-77; asst. dir. programs and policy Inst. Mus. Svcs., 1977-80; dir. Smithsonian Inst. Traveling Exhbn. Svc., Washington, 1980-87; founding dir. Wolfsonian Found., Miami, Fla., 1987—96, Genoa, Italy, 1987—96; founding exec. dir. COPIA: The Amer. Ctr. Wine, Food and Arts, Napa, Calif., 1997—. Lectr. art history U. Cin., 1970-71; lectr. art appreciation and criticism Ind. U., Purdue U., 1975-77; mem. women's health adv. com. Stanford U., 2002—; guest lectr. in field. Project dir.: The Art of Cameroon Exhibition and Catalog, 1984, Treasures from the Smithsonian Inst. Exhibition and Catalog, 1984, Paris Style 1900: Art Noveau Bing, 1986, Hollywood: Legend & Reality Exhibition Catalog, 1988. Travel grantee Japan Found., 1984; Swedish Inst. grantee; Aspen Inst. Humanistic Studies fellow, 1986-87, recipient Smithsonian Gold Medal for Disting. Service, 1987. Mem. Am. Assn. Museums (mus. ethics com. 1980-98), Internat. Coun. Museums (pres. U.S. nat. com., 1996-2002), Com. Internat. Musees d'Art Moderne. Avocations: biking, hiking, dogs, gardening, wine. Office: COPIA Am Ctr Wine Food & Arts 500 1st St Napa CA 94559

LOBB, CYNTHIA JEAN HOCKING, lawyer; b. San Francisco, June 12, 1962; d. Thomas Messinger and Diane (Knight) Hocking; m. Jerry Mark Lobb, Dec. 1, 1990; children: Sean Thomas, Kevin Joseph, Braden McMillan, William Ryan. BA in Polit. Sci., UCLA, 1984; JD, Golden Gate U. Law Sch., U. San Diego Law Sch., 1993. Bar: Ca., 1993. Asst. Congressman W. Dannemeyer, Washington, 1987-88; legal sec. Fulbright & Jaworski, Washington, 1988; law clerk MCI Internat. Divsn., Rye Brook, NY, 1990, Kern County Counsel, Bakersfield, Calif., 1991; lawyer Lobb & Cliff, Riverside, Calif., 1997-98, Law Office of Cynthia Hocking, Menifee, Calif., 1995—. Spanish tchr. Good Shepard Lutheran Sch., Menifee, Calif., 1996-99. Mem. Riverside Repub. Women's Federated, Temecula Repub. Women's Federated, Lake Menifee Women's Club, 1998—2002; Assoc. mem. Calif. Repub. Party, 1980—; pub. rels. dir. St. Martha's Ch., 1998—2002, Bible sharing leader, 1994—97; bd. dirs. Mothers and Others, 1999—2002. Mem. Alpha Delta Chi (named Most Outstanding mem. 1984, Outstanding Young Women of Am., 1985). Republican. Roman Catholic. Avocations: fitness training, jazzercize, scrapbooking, Spanish and French, travel. Office: Lobb & Cliff 1650 Spruce St Ste 500 Riverside CA 92507-2436 Home: 32938 Avenida Lestonnac Temecula CA 92591-8000

LOBEL, GRACE, education educator; b. Philadelphia, Pennsylvania, U.S.A., Dec. 18, 1969; d. Harry and Christina Lobel. Ed. M., Temple U., 1995. BA., 1998. English tchr. Sch. District Phila., Pa., 1998—. Accel. Acad., Melrose Park, Pa., 2000—; english. secondary lang. tchr. Wonderland Acad., Seoul, Vietnam, 1995—96. Tutor pvt., Phila., 1999—. Mem. World Affairs Coun., Phila, Pa., 2000—02. Mem.: Phila. Fedn. of Tchrs. Democrat. Avocations: running, writing, travel. Home: 3600 Conshohocken Ave #1714 Philadelphia PA 19131

LOBEL, SHARON, retail executive; Pres., CEO Seal-It, Farmingdale, N.Y. Named to Long Island's 50 Most Influential Bus. Women Hall of Fame, 2003. Office: Seal-It Inc 70 Schmitt Blvd Farmingdale NY 11735-1404 Fax: 516-935-3967. E-mail: sealit@sealitinc.com.

LOBIG, JANIE HOWELL, special education educator; b. Peoria, Ill., June 10, 1945; d. Thomas Edwin and Elizabeth Jane (Higdon) Howell; m. James Frederick Lobig, Aug. 16, 1970 (dec. Dec. 2001); 1 child, Jill Christina. BS in Elem. Edn., So. Ill. U., 1969; MA in Spl. Edn. Severely Handicapped, San Jose State U., 1989. Cert. elem. tchr., Calif., Mo., Ill., handicapped edn., Calif., Mo.; ordained to ministry Presbyn. Ch. as deacon, 1984. Tchr. trainable mentally retarded children Spl. Luth. Sch., St. Louis, 1967-68; tchr. trainable mentally retarded and severly handicapped children Spl. Sch. Dist. St. Louis, 1969-80, head tchr., 1980-83; tchr. severly handicapped children San Jose (calif.) Unifed Sch. Dist., 1983-86; tchr. autistic students Santa Clara County Office Edn., San Jose, 1986—; tchr. Suzanne Dancers, 1991-92. Vol. Am. Cancer Soc., San Jose, 1986—89, 1992, Am. Heart Assn., 1985—, Multiple Sclerosis Soc., 1990—, Wildlife Ctr. Silicon Valley, 1998—; moderator bd. deacons Evergreen Presbyn. Ch., 1986—89. Mem. Council for Exceptional Children, Assn. for Severly Handicapped, Nat. Edn. Assn., Calif. Tchrs. Assn. Avocations: golf, motor home travel, bridge, needlework. Office: James Franklin Smith Elem Sch 2220 Woodbury San Jose CA 95121 Home: 3211 Bracciano Ct San Jose CA 95135 Office Phone: 408-270-6368. Personal E-mail: JanieAngel@aol.com.

LOBINS, CHRISTINE MARIE, accounts sales administrator; b. Erie, Pa., Dec. 19, 1956; d. Ann Marie Lobins. BS, Edinboro (Pa.) Coll., 1978. Salesperson May Co., Cleve., 1989-90, Mace Electronics, Ashtabula, Ohio, 1979-80, sales mgr. Ashtabula, Cleve., 1980-85, dist. mgr. Cleve., 1986-87; asst. mgr. McDonalds, Cleve., 1988, OfficeMax, Cleve., 1988; acct. mgr. Hamburg Bros., Cleve., 1990-94; nat. sales tng. mgr. Whirlpool Corp., Benton Harbor, Mich., 1994-96, nat. acct. sales mgr., 1996-99, nat. sales mgr. contract direct sales network Knoxville, Tenn., 1999—. Mem. adv. bd. Buyers Access, Denver, 1997, 98. Mem. NAFE, Nat. Apt. Assn. (assoc.), Nat. Multi Family Housing Coun., Pi Kappa Delta, Psi Chi. Avocations: golf, gardening. Office: Whirlpool Corp 412 N Peters Rd Knoxville TN 37922-2332

LOBO, REBECCA, professional basketball player; b. Hartford, Conn., Oct. 6, 1973; BA in Polit. Sci., U. Conn., 1995. Basketball player USA Women's Nat. Team, N.Y. Liberty, 1997—2001, Houston Comets, 2001—02, Conn. Sun, Uncasville, 2003—. Mem. U.S. Olympic Festival East Team, 1992, Jr. World Championship Qualifying Team, 1992, USA Jr. World Championship Team, 1993. Co-author: The Home Team, 1996. Founder Ruth Ann & Rebecca Lobo scholarship in allied health U. Conn., 2001. Named Nat. Player of Yr., Naismith, U.S. Basketball Writers Assn., 1995, Big East Conf. Player of Yr., Big East Tournament Most Outstanding Player, 1994, Big East Conf. Women's Basketball Scholar Athlete of Yr., 1995; named to All-Am. 1st team, Kodak, 1994, 1995; recipient Wade trophy. Office: c/o Conn Sun 1 Mohegan Sun Blvd Uncasville CT 06382

LOBRON, BARBARA L. speech educator, writer, editor, photographer; b. Phila., Mar. 19, 1944; d. Martin Aaron and Elizabeth (Gots) L. Student, Pa. State U., 1962-63; BA cum laude, Temple U., Phila., 1966; student art therapy, Erika Steinberger, N.Y.C., 1994—2003; MS, Coll. Mt. St. Vincent, 2001. Reporter, writer Camden (N.J.) Courier-Post, 1966-68; editl. asst. Med. Insight mag., N.Y.C., 1970-71; mng. editor Camera 35 mag., N.Y.C., 1971-75; also assoc. editor photog. anns. U.S. Camera/Camera 35, 1972, 73; freelance editor as Word Woman N.Y.C., 1975-77, 79-99; acct. exec. Bozell & Jacobs, N.Y.C., 1977-79; copy editor Camera Arts mag., N.Y.C., 1981-83; editl. coord. Ctr. mag. Nat. Ctr. Health Edn., 1985; editl. coord. Popular Photography mag., 1986-95; assoc. editor Sony Style, 1995; tchr. speech improvement N.Y.C. Bd. Edn., 1995—. Contbg. editor: Photograph; participant 3M Editor's Conf. (1st woman), 1972; photography group exhbns. include Internat. Women's Art Festival, N.Y.C., 1975, Rockefeller Ctr., N.Y.C., 1976, Photograph Gallery, N.Y.C., 1981; acrylic painting exhbns. Tchrs. Coll., N.Y.C., 1994, Warwick Hotel, N.Y.C., 1995; represented in collection Libr. Calif Inst. Arts, Valencia; copy editor: The Complete Guide to Cibachrome Printing, 1980, The Popular Photography Question and Answer Book, 1979, The Photography Catalog, 1976, Strand: Sixty Years of Photography, 1976, You and Your Lens, 1975; contbr. articles to comml. publs., chpts. to books. Tchr. Sch. Vol. Program, N.Y.C. Recipient 1st pl. honors Dist. 1, Internat. Assn. Bus. Communicators, 1977. Mem. Soka Gakkai Internat. Buddhist. Avocations: dance, reading, photography, origami, walking. Home: 85 Hicks St Apt 7 Brooklyn NY 11201-6825 E-mail: barbaralobron@hotmail.com.

LOBSER, HEATHER A. music educator; b. Douglas B. and Roseanne M. Lobser, Teresa Lobser (Stepmother). BA in Music cum laude, Oral Roberts U., Tulsa, OK, 1994. Cert. tchr. Okla., 2003. Instr. Kirby Kasting & Studios, Tulsa, Okla., 1997—2003; vocal music tchr. Immanuel Christian Acad., Broken Arrow, Okla., 2002—. Asst. dir. Grace Ann Productions, Tulsa, Okla., 1998—2003; mem. chorus Joseph and the Amazing Technicolor Dreamcoat Tulsa (Okla.) Opera, singer Aida. Dir.: (musical prodn.) Meet Me at the Manger; asst. dir. (musical prodn.) Children of Eden, Godspell, Temptations of Mann. Children's ministry vol. Destiny Ch., Broken Arrow, Okla., 2002—03. Mem.: Nat. Assn. for Music Edn. (corr.). Avocations: travel, music, horseback riding, racquetball, orienteering. Office: Immanuel Christian Acad 400 N Aspen Broken Arrow OK 74012 E-mail: hlobser@icaba.org.

LOCHEN, LYNNE CAROL, tourism organization administrator; b. N.Y.C., Feb. 13, 1950; d. Maxwell and Juliette Flower Jurmark; m. Thomas John Lochen, Oct. 27, 1973; 1 child, John Maxwell. BA in History and Classics, Fla. State U., 1972. Hist. interpreter The Colonial Williamsburg Found., Williamsburg, Va., 1975—81; tchr., dir. guidance Ryan Acad. Norfolk, Norfolk, Va., 1988—95; conv. and visitor svcs. Norfolk Conv. and Visitors Bur., 1997—. Exec. bd. Va. Civil War Trails, Richmond. Named Norfolks Downtown Person of the Wk., Downtown Norfolk Coun., 1999. Mem.: NAFE, Va. Hospitality and Travel Assn. (officer), Tidewater Area Concierge Assn., Assn. Conv. Ops. Mgmt., Internat. Assn. Conv. and Visitors Burs., Va. Assn. Conv. and Visitors Burs. (exec. bd.). Avocation: travel. Office: Norfolk Conv and Visitors Bur 232 E Main St Norfolk VA 23510

LOCKE, ELIZABETH HUGHES, foundation executive; b. Norfolk, Va., June 30, 1939; d. George Morris and Sallie Epps (Moss) Hughes; m. John Rae Locke, Jr., Sept. 13, 1958 (div. 1981); children: John Rae III, Sallie Curtis. BA magna cum laude, Duke U., 1964, PhD, 1972; MA, U. N.C., 1966. Instr. English U. N.C., Chapel Hill, 1970-72; dir. univ. pubs. Duke U., Durham, N.C., 1973-79; corp. contbns. officer Bethlehem (Pa.) Steel Corp., 1979-82; dir. edn. divsn. & comm. Duke Endowment, Charlotte, N.C., 1982-96, exec. dir., 1996-97, pres., 1997—. Vis. prof. English Duke U., 1972-73. Editor: Duke Encounters, 1977, prospectus for Change: American Private Higher Education, 1985, (mag) Issues, 1985-96. Pres. Angier B. Duke Meml., Inc., 1997—, The Duke Endowment, 1997—, Nanaline H. Duke Fund, 1997—, Doris Duke Trust, 1998, Jr. League, Durham, 1976, Hist. Preservation Soc., Durham, 1977, Charlotte Area Donors Forum; past pres. Comm. Philanthropy, Washington, Sch. of Arts, Charlotte; mem. legis. com. Coun. on Founds., 1997-, Washington, 1995; trustee Southeastern Coun. of Founds., 1997—, Wing Haven Found.; commr. So. Assn. Colls. & Schs., 1998—; bd. visitors Davidson Coll., Charlotte Country Day Sch., Duke U., Johnson C. Smith U.; trustee Winghaven Found. Recipient Leadership award Charlotte C. of C., 1984; Danforth fellow, 1972. Mem. Nat. Task Force, English Speaking Union, The Most Venerable Order of St. John of Jerusalem (officer sister), Charlotte City Club (bd. govs.), Phi Beta Kappa. Democrat. Epsicopalian. Office: 100 N Tryon St Ste 3500 Charlotte NC 28202-4001 E-mail: elocke@tde.org.

LOCKE, VIRGINIA OTIS, writer; b. Tiffin, Ohio, Sept. 4, 1930; d. Charles Otis and Frances Virginia (Sherer) L. BA, Barnard Coll., 1953; MA in Psychology, Duke U., 1972, postgrad. Program officer, asst. corp. sec. Agrl. Devel. Coun., N.Y.C., 1954-66; staff psychologist St. Luke's-Roosevelt Med. Ctr., N.Y.C., 1973-75; freelance writer and editor N.Y.C., 1976-85; writer-editor Cornell U. Med. Coll./N.Y. Hosp. Med. Ctr., N.Y.C., 1986-89; sr. editor humanities and social scis. coll. divsn. Prentice Hall, Upper Saddle River, N.J., 1989-96; profl. writer behavioral scis., 1996—. Co-author: (coll. textbook) Introduction to Theories of Personality, 1985, (book) The Agricultural Development Council: A History, 1989, (coll. textbook) Child Psychology: A Contemporary Viewpoint, 1999; co-editor: The Life and Work of Arthur T. Mosher, 2001. Founder Help Our Neighbors Eat Yearround (H.O.N.E.Y.), Inc., N.Y.C., chmn., 1983-87, vol., 1987-99, newsletter editor, 1992-97; reader Recording for the Blind, N.Y.C., 1978-84; vol. Reach to Recovery program Am. Cancer Soc., Bergen County, N.J., 1990-96. Recipient Our Town Thanks You award, N.Y.C., 1984, Mayor's Vol. Svc. award, N.Y.C., 1986, Cert. of Appreciation for Community Svc. Manhattan Borough, 1986, Jefferson award Am. Ins. Pub. Svc., Washington, 1986. Home and Office: 9316 Bocina Ln # G Atascadero CA 93422 E-mail: volwriter@mindspring.com.

LOCKETTE, DAPHNEY D. elementary school educator; b. N.Y.C., Sept. 30, 1973; BA, Va. State U., 1995; M in Elem. Edn., Fairleigh Dickinson U., 2001; postgrad. studies in instructional tech., Farleigh Dickinson U., Teaneck, N.J., 2001—; postgrad. in human svcs., 2003—. Technology coord. Americorps/Project First, N.Y.C., 1995—97; substitute tchr. Bergen County Bd. of Edn., Englewood, NJ, 1997; adminstrv. asst. Silver Palate, Cresskill, NJ, 1997; kindergarten tchr. My Friend's Day Sch., Teaneck, NJ, 1997—99; tchr. asst. First Grade Englewood on the Palisades Charter Sch.,

Englewood, NJ, 1999—. Tutor computer tech. and lang. arts Esteem Acad., Englewood. Author: Secrets from the Depths of My Soul, 2000. Treas., Praise Ministries, 2000—. Mem. Alpha Kappa Alpha.

LOCKETT-EGAN, MARIAN WORKMAN, advertising executive; b. Murray, Ky., May 5, 1931; d. Otis H. Workman and Myrtle A. (Jones) Jordan; m. Gene Potts, Jan. 6, 1947 (div. Feb. 1962); children: Reed Nasser, Jennifer Anglin, George M. Potts, Cynthia Klenk; m. Barker Lockett, Oct. 11, 1963 (div. Dec. 1972); 1 child, Stephen R.W.; m. Douglas S. Egan Jr., Feb. 14, 1981 (dec. May 2001). BA, Murray State U., 1962. Asst. media dir. Noble-Dury & Assocs., Nashville, 1963-64; asst. rsch. dir. Triangle Publs., Phila., 1964-66; assoc. media dir. Lewis & Gilman, Phila., 1966-72; v.p. advt. media Scott Paper Co., Phila., 1972-83; pres. DMS Comm. Inc., Ardmore, Pa., 1983—. Exec. dir. The Media Sch., N.Y.C., 1983-85, 87-2003; mem. TV com. Assn. Nat. Advertisers, N.Y.C., 1977-83; guest lectr. Wharton U., Phila., 1981-82, 85, 86, 87; Gannet vis. prof. Sch. Journalism, U. Fla., Gainesville, 1982. Guest editor Media decisions, 1981. Trustee Meth. Hosp. Found., Phila., 1973—87. Mem. Broadcast Pioneers (pres. 1994-96), TV and Radio Advt. Club (pres. 1973). Republican. Episcopalian. Avocation: tennis. Home: 45 Llanfair Cir Ardmore PA 19003-3342

LOCKETT-REYNOLDS, JANAE NIKIA, research psychologist, education educator; b. Cleveland, Ohio, May 5, 1974; d. Mary J. Lockett-Singleton and Tyrone Singleton; m. Cedric Antoine Reynolds, Sept. 21, 2002. BA, Wittenberg U., 1992—96; MA, U. of Toledo, 1996—98, PhD, 1998—2002. Rsch. asst. Wittenberg U., Springfield, Ohio, 1995—96; rsch. assoc. Wright Patterson AFB, Dayton, Ohio, 1997—97; grad. rsch. asst. U. of Toledo, 1996—2000; human factors engr. Ericsson, Inc., Rsch. Triangle Pk., NC, 2000—02; instrnl. accountability analyst Charlotte-Mecklenburg Schools, NC, 2003—; part-time psychology prof. U. of NC, Charlotte, 2003—, rsch. psychologist, 2002—. Human factors/usability cons. Bank Of Am. & Vialogix Comm., Inc., Charlotte, NC, 2002. Contbr. articles to profl. jours. Fellowship, Ohio Bd. of Regents Grad., 1996—98. Mem.: Midwestern Psychol. Assn., Soc. of Automotive Engineers, Human Factors and Ergonomic Soc., Alpha Kappa Alpha Sorority. Achievements include research in Cognition: visual attention & language acquisition. Avocations: reading, travel. Home: 16918 Commons Creek Dr Charlotte NC 28277 Office: University of North Carolina Charlotte 9201 University City Blvd Charlotte NC 28223 Personal E-mail: janae1@msn.com.

LOCKHART, CLAUDIA JO, adult education educator, department chairman; d. Roy Oscar and Helen Mary Eckberg; life ptnr. Charles William Houseman; 1 child, Jennifer Ann Buttram. BFA, U. Long Beach, 1967. Secondary Teaching Degree Dept. Edn. Calif., 1970. Educator, dept. chair Anaheim (Calif.) Sch. Dist., 1968—69, Inglewood (Calif.) Cmty. Adult Sch., 1971—. Grant writing certification L.A. Sch. Grant Writing, 1988—; staff devel. coord. Inglewood Cmty. Adult Sch., 1988—96, mem. chair steering com., 1997—99. Artist, cmty. coord. Art Impacts Day. Recipient Halo awards, Bd. Suprs. L.A., 1982—89. Independent. Achievements include development of principles of alphabet literacy program. Avocations: art, sailing, reading, house design, travel. Office: Inglewood Cmty Adult Sch Ste 350 106 E Manchester Blvd Inglewood CA 90301 Personal E-mail: cjlcwh@aol.com.

LOCKHART, MADGE CLEMENTS, educational organization executive; b. Soddy, Tenn., May 22, 1920; d. James Arlie and Ollie (Sparks) Clements; m. Andre J. Lockhart, Apr. 24, 1942 (div. 1973); children: Jacqueline, Andrew, Janice, Jill. Student, East Tenn. U., 1938-39; BS, U. Tenn., Chattanooga and Knoxville, 1955, MEd, 1962. Elem. tchr. Tenn. and Ga., 1947-60, Brainerd H.S., Chattanooga, 1960-64, Cleveland (Tenn.) City Schs., 1966-88; owner, operator Lockhart's Learning Ctr., Inc., Cleveland and Chattanooga, 1966-2003; co-founder, pres. Hermes, Inc., 1973-79; co-founder Dawn Ctr., Hamilton County, Tenn., 1974; apptd. mem. Tenn. Gov.'s Acad. for Writers. Author poetry, short stories and fiction; contbr. articles to profl. jours. and newspapers. Pres. Cleveland Assn. Retarded Citizens, 1970, state v.p., 1976; pres. Cherokee Easter Seal Soc., 1973-76, Cleveland Creative Arts Guild, 1980; bd. dirs. Tenn. Easter Seal Soc., 1974-77, 80-83; chair Bradley County Internat. Yr. of Child; mem. panel for grants Coun. Govts. S.E. Tenn. Devel. Dist., 1990-92; mem. Internat. Biog. Centre Adv. Coun., Cambridge, Eng., 1991-92; mem. mayor's com. Mus. for Bradley County, Tenn., 1992—. Recipient Service to Mankind award Sertoma, 1978, Gov.'s award for service to handicapped, 1979; mental health home named in her honor, Tenn., 1987. Mem. NEA (life), Tenn. Edn. Assn., Am. Assn. Rehab. Therapy, S.E. Tenn. Arts Coun., Cleveland Edn. Assn. (Service to Humanity award 1987). Mem. Ch. of Christ. Clubs: Byliners, Fantastiks. Home: 3007 Oakland Dr NW Cleveland TN 37312-5281

LOCKHART, PATRICIA ANN, elementary school educator; b. Bklyn., N.Y., Jan. 7, 1961; d. Grace Copp; 1 child, Dana. AAS, Coll. Staten Island, 1988, BA, 1993, MS in Spl. Edn., 1996. Cert. tchr. N.Y. Life skills specialist Cath. Guardian Soc., N.Y.C., 1980; asst. tchr. Soc. Devel. Disabilities & Autism, Staten Island, NY, 1988—94; elem. sch. tchr. PS 57, Staten Island, 1994—. Vol. coord. Staten Island Tough Love, 1997—2001; outreach spkr. United Fedn. Tchrs., 2000—01. Named woman of achievement, Staten Island Advance, 2001; grantee, HUD, 2002. Home: 50 Dongan Hills Ave 2B Staten Island NY 10306

LOCKHART, PATSY MARIE, secondary school educator, consultant; b. San Francisco, Nov. 7, 1949; d. Alfred Jr. and Georgia Anna (Walker) Lax; m. Terence C. Lockhart, Apr. 23, 1977 (div. Apr. 1984); children: Dana Nolley, Therese C., Mishua. BA, San Jose State U., 1975, MA in Adminstrv. Supervision, 1999; M in Edn.-Integrated Studies, Cambridge (Mass.) Coll., 2003. Cert. Nat. Bd. for Profl. Tchr. Standards. Tchr. Ravenswood City Sch. Dist., East Palo Alto, Calif., 1975-79, edn. specialist, 1979-80, tchr., 1980-84; tchr., curriculum leader, social sci. cons. tchr. Barnard White Middle Sch., New Haven Unified Sch. Dist., Union City, Calif., 1984—. Coord. Urban Sites Writing Network, N.Y.C., 1993-94; cons. Bay Area Writing Project, Berkeley, Calif., 1984—; table leader Calif. Learning Assessment Sys.-State of Calif., Sacramento, 1994; writer curriculum devel Calif. Assessment Program Secondary, Sacramento, 1990-92. Mem. choir and Cantateers Pub. Rels., Allen Temple Bapt. Ch.; curriculum leader Barnard White Mid. Sch., 2000-01. Mem. NAACP, Nat. Coun. for Tchrs. of English, Calif. League of Mid. Schs. (adv. bd. 1992—), Calif. Tchr.'s Assn. Minority Caucus. Democrat. Avocations: swimming, sewing, decorating, singing, writing. Home: 4473 Deep Creek Rd Fremont CA 94555-2059 Office: Barnard White Mid Sch 725 Whipple Rd Union City CA 94587-1300 E-mail: patsy_lockhart@nhusdk12.ca.us.

LOCKHART, SHARON, artist; b. Norwood, Mass., 1964; MFA, Art Ctr. Coll. Design, Pasadena, Calif. One-woman shows include Art Ctr., Pasadena, 1994, Neugerriemschneider, Berlin, 1994, 1996, Friedrich Petzel Gallery, N.Y., 1994, 1996, 1998, Kunstlerhaus Stuttgart, Germany, 1995, Blum and Poe, Santa Monica, 1996, 1998, John Spotten Cinema, Toronto, 1997, S.L. Simpson Gallery, 1997, Cinema Paris, Berlin, 1997, Pacific Film Archive, Berkeley Art Mus., 1997, Wako Works Art, Tokyo, 1998, Brit. Coun. Cinema, Daniel Buckholz Gallery, Cologne, 1998, Mus. Contemporary Art, Tokyo, 1998, L.A., 1998, Galerie Yvon Lambert, Paris, 1998, Kemper Mus. Contemporary Art, Kansas City, Mo., 1998, exhibited in group shows at Bliss House, Pasadena, 1992, Merz Acad., Stuttgart, 1993, Margo Leavin Gallery, L.A., 1994, Galerie Paul Andriesse, Amsterdam, 1995, Studio Guenzani, Milan, Italy, 1996, L.A. County Mus. Art, 1996—97, Armand Hammer Mus. Art, L.A., 1997, Le Magasin, Grenoble, 1998, Inst. Contemporary Arts, London, 1998, Mus. Modern Art and the Film Soc. Lincoln Ctr., N.Y., 1998, Stedelijk Van Abbemuseum, Eindhoven, 1999, numerous others, Represented in permanent collections Boijmans van Beuningen Mus., Rotterdam, Eli Broad Family Found., Santa Monica, Calif., L.A. County Mus., Mus. Contemporary Art, L.A., Whitney Mus. Am. Art, N.Y., Albright-Knox Gallery, Buffalo, others. Office: Blom & Poe 2042 Broadway Santa Monica CA 90404-2910 Fax: 212-431-6638.

LOCKLEAR, HEATHER, actress; b. Canoga Park, Calif., Sept. 25, 1961; d. Bill and Diane L.; m. Tommy Lee, 1986 (div. 1994); m. Richie Sambora, 1994, 1 daughter. Student, UCLA. Appeared in (TV series) Dynasty, 1981-89, T.J. Hooker, 1982-87, Going Places, 1990, Melrose Place, 1993-99, Spin City, 1999-2002 (films) Firestarter, 1986, Return of the Swamp Thing, 1990, The Big Slice, 1991, Wayne's World 2, 1993, A Dangerous Woman, 1993, The First Wives Club, 1996, Double Tap, 1997, Money Talks, 1997, Uptown Girls, 2003, Looney Toons: Back in Action, 2003; (TV movies) Twil, 1981, City Killer, 1984, Blood Sport, 1986, Rock 'n' Roll Mom, 1988, Rich Men, Single Women, 1990, Her Wicked Ways, 1991, Dynasty: The Reunion, 1991, Highway Heartbreaker, 1992, Body Language, 1992, Fade to Black, 1993, Texas Justice, 1995, Shattered Mind, 1996, Too Many Lovers, 2003, Once Around the Park, 2003.*

LOCKNER, VERA JOANNE, farmer, rancher, legislator; b. St. Lawrence, S.D., May 19, 1937; d. Leonard and Zona R. (Ford) Verdugt; m. Frank O. Lockner, Aug. 7, 1955; children: Dean M., Clifford A. Grad., St. Lawrence (S.D.) High Sch., 1955. Bank teller/bookkeeper First Nat. Bank, Miller, SD, 1963-66, Bank of Wessington, SD, 1968-74; farmer/rancher Wessington, 1955-2000. Sunday sch. tchr. Trinity Luth. Ch., Miller, 1968-72; treas. PTO, Wessington, 1969-70; treas., vice chmn., chmn., state com. woman Hand County Dems., Miller, 1978-2003; mem. S.D. Dem. Exec. Bd., 1997-2000. Named one of Outstanding Young Women of Am., Women's Study Club, Wessington, 1970. Mem. Order of Ea. Star (warder, marshall, chaplain 1970-2002). Avocations: oil painting, crafts, gardening, photography. Home and Office: 301 3rd St NW Saint Lawrence SD 57373-2324

LOCKWOOD, HELSHI, advertising executive; b. East Orange, NJ, May 18, 1941; d. Warren Sewell and Ann Frances (Gleason) L.; m. Bertram A. Tunnell Jr., Dec. 13, 1969 (div. Oct. 1976); children: Bertram A. III, Tory Lockwood; stepchildren: John, Mark, Tracy, Wendy, Jan, Kate; m. William B. Hewson Jr., May 30, 1981; 1 child, Charles W.; stepchildren: William B. III, Andrew L., Elizabeth S. BA, Pa. State U., 1963. Promotion asst. Vogue Mag., London, 1963-64; advt. sales rep. Brides Mag., London, 1964-65; west coast mgr. Status Mag., L.A., 1965-67, asst. advt. mgr. N.Y.C., 1968-69; advt. sales rep. Eye Mag., N.Y.C., 1967-68; N.Y. mgr. Phil. and Boston Mags., N.Y.C., 1969-76; v.p. Metro Mag., N.Y.C., 1976-78; exec. v.p., ptnr. Catalyst Communications, N.Y.C., 1978-80; account mgr. Dun's Rev., N.Y.C., 1980-82; ea. advt. dir. Dun's Bus. Month, N.Y.C., 1982-84, advt. dir., 1984-85; dir. nat. accounts Chgo. Mag., N.Y.C., 1986; from ea. advt. mgr. to v.p., mng. dir. Mediatex Nat. Sales, N.Y.C., 1987—98; pres. Emmis Pub. Nat. Sales (acquired by Emmis Comm.), NYC, 1998—2003; assoc. mag. pub. Atlanta Mag. Emmis Comm., Atlanta, 2003—, assoc. mag. pub. LA Mag. LA, 2003—. Deacon Brick Ch., N.Y.C., 1983. Mem. Advt. Women N.Y. Republican. Episcopalian. Home: 8 Hanson Rd Darien CT 06820-2502 Office: Emmis Publ Nat Sales 60 E 42d St Ste 1103 New York NY 10165

LOCKWOOD, RHONDA J. mental health services professional; b. Jacksonville, N.C., Apr. 4, 1960; d. George Barton and Sally Lynn (Hassell) L. BA, Newberry Coll., 1982; MS in Edn., Youngstown State U., 1988. nat. cert. counselor. Corrections/tng. officer Geauga County Sheriff's Dept., Chardon, Ohio, 1982-87; forensic counselor Human Svcs. Ctrs., Inc., New Castle, Pa., 1987-89; dir. children & family svcs. Marion Citrus Mental Health Ctrs., Inc., Ocala, Fla., 1989-96; clin. social worker Fla. Dept. Juvenile Justice, Alachua Halfway House, 1996-97; coord. Family Action, Interface Youth & Independent Living programs Corner Drug Store, Inc., Gainesville, Fla., 2000—02. Co-founder Sexual Abuse Intervention Network, Ocala, 1990-96, chair, 1990-92, Family Svcs. Planning Team, 1992-94; cons. Health & Human Svcs. Bd. Dist. 13, 1993-96; mem. Eckerd Youth Comprehensive Treatment Program adv. bd., 1997-99; adj. fculty Webster U., Ocala campus, 1999—. Pol. vol. state campaigns Dem. Party, Warren, Ohio, 1978-85; mem. Sexual Abuse Prevention Edn. Network, New Castle, 1987-88; cons. to gov.'s task force Sex Offenders and Their Victims; cons. Mad Dads Orgn., Ocala, 1993; mem. Juvenile Justice Coun., Ocala, 1993-94; mem. Hamilton, Lafayette, Suwannee and Columbia Counties Juvenile Justice Couns., 1997—; children's svc. rep. Fla. Coun. for Cmty. Mental Health, 1995-96; instr. counselor edn. program, Webster U., Ocala, Fla., 1998—. Recipient Outstanding Teen Vol. award Am. Red Cross, 1977. Fellow N. Eastern Ohio Police Benevolent Assn.; mem. Nat. Mus. for Women in the Arts, Nat. Bd. Cert. Counselors, NGLTF, Ind. Prodr. Womens Music, Human Rights Campaign Fund, Chi Sigma Iota, Phi Kappa Phi. Democrat. Avocations: softball, volleyball, golf, fishing. Home: 201 E Main St Archer FL 32618-5517 Office Phone: 386-758-5780.

LODESKI, LISA, artist, consultant; b. Wilkes-Barre, Pa., Mar. 27, 1960; BA in Art History, Calif. State U., Fullerton, 1991; MA in Art History, San Francisco State U., 1997. Dir., curator Danville (Calif.) Fine Arts Gallery, 1992—97; curator City of Antioch, Calif., 1995—97; ind. curator for Intrepid Women projects Nat. Mus. Women in the Arts, Washington, 1997—2000; prin., owner Lisa Lodeski Fine Arts, Aliso Viejo, Calif., 1997—; founder Salon 6, a divsn. of Lisa Lodeski Fine Arts, Aliso Viejo, Calif., 1999—. Instr. Long Beach (Calif.) City Coll., 1998—, Torrance (Calif.) Cultural Arts Ctr., Irvine (Calif.) Fine Arts Ctr.; lectr. in field. Contbr. articles and papers to profl. confs. Recipient Vol. of Yr. award, City of Danville (Calif.), 1997. Mem.: Art Table, Coll. Art Assn. (mentor, fellowship program 2001—02, portfolio reviewer, conf. 2001—02, presenter 2001—02).

LODGE, PATTI ANNE, state senator; b. Pitts., July 29, 1942; m. Edward J. Lodge; children: Mary Jeanne, Edward, Anne Marie. BA, Maryhurst U., 1964. Edn. media specialist Caldwell Sch. Dist., 1968-99, edn. media coord., 1980-97; pres. Windridge Vineyards, 1987—; mem. 11th dist. Idaho State Senate, Idaho, 2000—. Vice chair. health and welfare com.; mem. jud. and rules com., commerce and human resources com., e-commerce interim com., tech. interim com., drug court coord. interim com.; del. Nat. Rep. Platform Com., 1996; cons. St. Paul's Sch., Our Lady of the Valley, 1999—. Nat. Fedn. GOP Women Resolutions, 1997—99; chair Miss Rodeo Caldwell Com., 1964—80, Canyon County Reps., 1986—88; bd. dirs. Day at the Legislature, 2000; dir. Idaho H.S. Rodeo Dist. 3, 1970—78; precinct chair Canyon County Rep. Com. 22, 1980—2000; pres. Idaho Fedn. Rep. Women, 1991—96; chair Idaho Rep. Gala Celebration, 2000; vol. Latino Voter Registration, 2000; chair bd. dirs. West Valley Med. Ctr., 1986; bd. dirs. Idaho Cath. Found., 1992—. Roman Catholic. Office: Idaho State Senate State Capitol 700 W Jefferson Boise ID 83720-0081 also: PO Box 83720 Boise ID 83720-0003 Fax: 208 459-7199.

LODGE-PETERS, DIANNE SPEED, writer, literature educator, researcher; b. Greenfield, Mass., Nov. 16, 1929; d. Frederick Haigh Speed and Dorris Alice Wood; m. William Riess Peters, Aug. 1, 1953 (div. Sept. 1972); children: Allen Frederick, Benjamin William. BA, U. Mass., 1951; AM, U. Pa., 1953; PhD, U. Mich., 1969. Asst. prof. Tex. Tech. U., Lubbock, 1970—72; assoc. prof. U. Tex., Odessa, 1972—77, dean, 1972—77; assoc. prof. Auburn (Ala.) U., 1977—79; prof. Mont. State U., Bozeman, 1979—89, ret., 1989; writer Evergreen, Ala., 1989—. Mem. editl. bd.: Assn. Study Higher Edn., 1975—77; author: And Pleasantly Ignore My Sex, 1974; contbr. articles to profl. jours. Pres. bd. Globe Theatre, Odessa, 1974—77. Mem.: Magnolia Garden Club (pres. 1991—94). Avocations: reading, travel. Home: Rt 3 Box 620 Evergreen AL 36401

LODISH, SUSAN FISCHER, theater director; b. Cleve., Apr. 8, 1943; d. Joseph L. and Charlotte Woldman Fischer; m. Leonard M. Lodish; children: Max J., Jacob L., Chaim I. BA in Edn., Ohio State U., 1965; MEd, Tufts U., 1968; MA in Theatre, Villanova U., 1983. Tchr. Winchester (Mass.) Sch. Sys., 1965—68; office mgr. Info. Resources, Inc., Phila., 1968—80; founder, chair Soviet emigré outreach com. Jewish Fedn. Greater Phila., 1990—96; founder, co-chair Aviva State of Israel Bonds, Phila., 1992—94; tchr., acting coach, theatrical dir. Theatre Ariel, Temple Beth Hillel-Beth El, Phila., 1982—; internat. v.p., trainer, youth sch. chair Women's League Conservative Judaism, NYC, 1984—. Dir.: (films) Someone is Listening, 1986; co-editor: Passoverama, 1976. Vol. ALS Assn.; Barrymore Awards judge Theatre Alliance Greater Phila., 1997—; chancellor's cabinet, Torah fund cabinet, patron's soc. Jewish Theol. Sem., 1986—; foster parent Jewish Children's and Family Svcs., Phila., 1995—98; chair bd. dirs. Theatre Ariel, Phila., 1994—; bd. dirs. Prince Music Theatre, Phila., 1993—. Recipient Nat. Cmty. Leadership award, Jewish Theol. Sem., 1997. Mem.: Drama League, Assn. Jewish Theatre (v.p., outreach chair 1999—2003). Avocations: theater, bicycling, travel, photography. Office: 301 Kent Rd Wynnewood PA 19096

LODOR, MARCI ANN, dietician; b. Pitts., Pa., Aug. 2, 1965; d. Anthony Nicola Mincucci and Julia Anna Renac; m. John Anthony Lodor Jr., June 1, 2002. BS in Clin. Dietetics, Univ. Pitts., 1988. Registered dietitian Am. Dietetic Assn. Asst. food svc. dir. Morrisons & Wightman, Squirrel Hill, Pa., 1988—91; clin. dietitian Mc Keesport (Pa.) Hosp., 1991—95; cons. dietitian Pvt. Practice, Pitts., 1996—97; food svc. dir. various long term care facilities, Pitts., 1997—2000; regional dietitian Extendicare, We. & Ctrl. Pa., 2000—02; registered dietitian HCR Manorcare, North Hills, Pa., 2003; nutritionist Greater Pitts. Cmty. Food Bank, Duquesne, 2004—. Registered dietitian cons. Three Rivers Family Hosp., White Oak, Pa., 1996—. Bd. dir. White Oak Animal Safe Haven, 2002—. Avocations: skating, dance, flea markets, reading, theater. Home: 3303 Grover St Mc Keesport PA 15132

LODWICK, JUDITH LYNNE, nursing educator; b. New Orleans, Feb. 20, 1954; d. Frank Tillman Jr. and Grace Evelyn (Hilty) L. BSN, La. State U., 1976. RN, La.; cert. CPR, ACLS instr., advanced trauma life support coord., med.-surg. nurse, cert. emergency nurse. Head nurse hemotology-oncology endocrinology Ochsner Found. Hosp., New Orleans, 1978-82, unit instr., head nurse Ochsner emergency dept., 1983-88, staff nurse emergency dept., 1989-91; staff nurse, relief charge nurse, preceptor E. Jefferson Gen. Hosp., Metairie; clin. instr. post ICU East Jefferson Gen. Hosp., Metairie, 1991-96, supr. post ICU, 1996-98. Coord. orientation workshops and preceptorships, affilate faculty Charity Delgado Sch. of Nursing, 1996-97, educator N.A. advancement PCT program; chairperson universal chart order post ICU flowsheet East Jefferson Gen. Hosp. Mem. Nat. Oncology Soc., Emergency Nursing Assn. (sec. emergency dept. quality assurance program com.), Critical Care Nurses Assn. (chmn. post ICU quality assurance com, competency based edn. com.), Nursing Edn. Com., Policy and Procedure Com., ICU flowsheet com. (chmn.). Home: 2056 Lafitte St La Place LA 70068-2029

LOEB, JANE RUPLEY, academic administrator, educator; b. Chgo., Feb. 22, 1938; d. John Edwards and Virginia Pentland (Marthens) Watkins; m. Peter Albert Loeb, June 14, 1958; children: Eric Peter, Gwendolyn Lisl, Aaron John. BA, Rider Coll., 1961; PhD, U. So. Calif., 1969. Clin. psychology intern Univ. Hosp., Seattle, 1966-67; asst. prof. ednl. psychology U. Ill., Urbana, 1968-69, asst. coord. rsch. and testing, 1968-69, coord. rsch. and testing, 1969-72, asst. to vice chancellor acad. affairs, 1971-72, dir. admissions and records, 1972-81, assoc. prof. ednl. psychology, 1973-82, assoc. vice chancellor acad. affairs, 1981-94, prof. edn. psychology, 1982—. Author: College Board Project: the Future of College Admissions, 1989; co-editor: Academic Couples: Problems and Promises, 1997. Chmn. Coll. Bd. Coun. on Entrance Svcs., 1977-82; bd. govs. Alliance for Undergrad. Edn., 1988-93; active charter com. Coll. Bd. Acad. Assembly, 1992-93. HEW grantee, 1975-76. Mem. APA, Am. Ednl. Rsch. Assn., Nat. Coun. Measurement in Edn., Harvard Inst. Ednl. Mgmt. Avocation: the french horn. Home: 1405 N Coler Ave Urbana IL 61801-1625 Office: U Ill 1310 S 6th St Champaign IL 61820-6925

LOEB, SUSANNA, education educator; BSCE, BA in Polit. Sci., Stanford U., 1988; MPP in Pub. Policy Studies, U. Mich., 1994, PhD in Econs., 1998. Rsch. asst. U. Mich. Sch. Edn., 1991—93; rsch. asst. dept. econs. U. Mich., 1993—96; rsch. fellow Population Studies Ctr., U. Mich., 1995—; rsch. asst. U. Mich. Sch. Edn., 1996—; asst. prof. U. Calif., Davis, 1998—99; asst. prof. edn. Stanford (Calif.) U., Calif., 1999—. Rsch. cons. Inst. for Rsch. on Women and Gender, U. Mich., 1997—. Office: Stanford U Sch Edn 485 Lasuen Mall Stanford CA 94305-3096

LOEBL, MARAGARET MARGO, corporate financial executive; b. 1960; BA, Wellesley Coll., 1982; MBA, U. Chgo., 1986. Various fin. positions Gen. Motors Corp., 1987—2000; v.p. corp. fin. NIKE, Inc., 2000—01; group v.p. fin. Archer Daniels Midland Co., Decatur, Ill., 2002—. Office: Archer Daniels Midland Co 4666 Farus Pkway Decatur IL 62526

LOEFFELHOLZ, DIANE, art educator; b. Seward, Alaska, May 11, 1953; d. Robert William and Pauline Elizabeth Foulks; m. Stephen Robert Loeffelholz, June 24, 1972 (dec. Mar. 1990); children: Robert Aaron, Jacob David. BFA, U. Okla., 0975. Art tchr. Moore (Okla.) West Jr. High, 1975—76, Moore Ctrl. Jr. High, 1976—81, Moore West Mid. H.S., 1981—98; head visual art dept. West Moore H.S., Oklahoma City, 1989—. Exhibitions include West Moore H.S., 1999, Moore Pub. Libr., 2002; dir.: (student art exhibit) Moore Pub. Libr., 2001—. Active Cleveland County Dems., Norman, 1995—; vol. various polit. campaigns Norman, 1995—; active St. Josephs Cath. Ch., Norman, 1979—. Recipient Tchr. of Yr. award, Westmore H.S., 2002—03, Western Region Secondary Art Tchr. of Yr., Nat. Art Edn. Assn., 2003—04. Mem.: PTA, NEA, Okla. Art Edn. Assn. (state treas. 1990—, 1999—, young talent in Okla. chmn. 1994), Okla. Edn. Assn. Avocations: reading, travel, movies, painting. Home: 311 Cherry Creek Dr Norman OK 73072

LOEHR, MARLA, spiritual care coordinator; b. Cleve., Oct. 7, 1937; d. Joseph Richard and Eleanore Edith (Rothschuh) L. BS, Notre Dame Coll., South Euclid, Ohio, 1960; MAT, Ind. U., 1969; PhD, Boston Coll., 1988; Degree (hon.), Notre Dame Coll. Ohio, 1995. Cert. high sch. tchr., counselor, Ohio; cert. spiritual dir., pastoral min. Dean students Notre Dame Coll., South Euclid, Ohio, 1972-85, acting acad. dean, 1988, pres., 1988-95; spiritual care coord. Hospice of Western Res., Cleve., 1995—, spiritual dir., 1997—. Author: Mentor Handbook, 1985; co-author: Notre Dame College Model for Student Development, 1980. Hon. mem. Leadership Cleve. Class of 1990; v.p., trustee SJ Wellness Ctr., 1999; mem. leadership coun. Future Ch., Diocese of Cleve. Recipient Career Woman of Achievement award YWCA, 1992; named One of 100 Cleve.'s Most Powerful Women. Mem. Spiritual Dirs. Internat., Nat. Hospice Assn., Alpha Sigma Nu, Kappa Gamma Pi. Avocations: photography, hiking, reading, sports. Office: Hospice Western Res 29101 Health Campus Dr Ste 400 Westlake OH 44145-5268 E-mail: marlajlo@cs.com.

LOEHR, STEPHANIE SCHMAHL, social worker; b. Watertown, N.Y., Dec. 14, 1941; d. John Schmahl and Helene (Mosely) Kay. AB in Elem. Edn., Ripon Coll., 1964; MSW, U. Wis., Milw., 1969, MA in Urban Affairs, 1973; cert. in marriage and family studies, Chgo. Family Inst., 1983. Diplomate Am. Bd. Examiners in Clin. Social Work; cert. ind. clin. social worker, Wis. Clinician Philstan Psychiat. Clinic, Milw., 1977-86; psychotherapist Psychiat. Consultation Assocs., Milw., 1986-89, Charter Behavioral Health Svcs., 1990—2000; sch. social worker Milw. Pub. Schs.,

1989—; case work supr. Milwaukee County Dept. Social Svcs., Milw., 1974-77. Field instr. Sch. Social Welfare, U. Wis., Milw.; presenter workshops; pvt. practice psychotherapy. Mem. Nat. Assn. Social Workers (past state and local chpt. officer), Acad. Cert. Social Workers. Democrat. Unitarian-Universalist. Avocations: piano, singing, photography. Office: Milw Pub Schs Victory 2222 W Henry Ave Milwaukee WI 53221-4920

LOEPKER, PATRICIA M. marketing manager; b. Belleville, IL, Oct. 15, 1962; married. BA, So.Ill. U., Edwardsville, 1983. Analyst A.G. Edwards & Sons, Inc., St. Louis, 1988—94; mgr. portfolio A.G. Edwards & Sons, Inc, St. Louis, 1994—2001, mktg. mgr., 1999—. Mem. sch. bd. Bartelso Elem. Sch., Ill., 1991—99. Mem.: St. Louis Analyst Soc. Office: A G Edwards & Sons Inc 1 North Jefferson Saint Louis MO 63103

LOESCH, KATHARINE TAYLOR (MRS. JOHN GEORGE LOESCH), communication and theatre educator; b. Berkeley, Calif., Apr. 13, 1922; d. Paul Schuster and Katharine (Whiteside) Taylor; m. John George Loesch, Aug. 28, 1948; 1 child, William Ross. Student, Swarthmore Coll., 1939-41, U. Wash., 1942; BS, Columbia U., 1944, MA, 1949; grad., Neighborhood Playhouse Sch., 1946; postgrad., Ind. U., 1953; PhD, Northwestern U., 1961. Instr. speech Wellesley (Mass.) Coll., 1949-52, Loyola U., Chgo., 1956; asst. prof. English and speech Roosevelt U., Chgo., 1957, 62-65; assoc. prof. comm. and theatre U. Ill., Chgo., 1968-87, assoc. prof. emeritus, 1987—. Contbr. articles to profl. jours.; author numerous poems; performer of poetry. Active ERA, Ill., 1975-76. Am. Philos. Soc. grant, 1970, Dylan Thomas scholar. Mem. MLA, Am. Soc. for Aesthetics, Linguistic Soc. Am., Chgo. Linguistic Soc. (co-chmn. 1954-56), Nat. Comm. Assn. (chair interpretation divsn. 1979-80, Golden Ann. award 1969), Celtic Studies Assn. N.Am., Pi Beta Phi. Episcopalian. Home: 2129 N Sedgwick St Chicago IL 60614-4619 Office: U Ill Dept Performing Arts M/C 255 1040 W Harrison St Chicago IL 60607-7130

LOESCH, MABEL LORRAINE, social worker; b. Annandale, Minn., July 1, 1925; d. Rudolph and Hedwig (Zeidler) Treichler; m. Harold Carl Loesch, Oct. 19, 1945; children: Stephen, Gretchen, Jonathan, Frederick. BS, La. State U., 1972, MSW, 1974. Cert. Acad. Cert. Social Worker, bd. cert. diplomate. Tchr. Am. schs., Tegucigalpa, Honduras, 1960-61, Guayaquil, Ecuador, 1962-66, La Ceiba, Honduras, 1966-67; supr. clin. svc. Blundon Home, Baton Rouge, 1974-81; social worker cons. Dhaka, Bangladesh, 1981-85; social worker Manna Food Bank, Pensacola, Fla., 1986—. Adj. instr. social work dept. Southern U., Baton Rouge, 1976-81. Author: Generations in Germany and America, 1995, 300 Years in the Family, 1998, Family Farms, 2001, Exiled to America, 2001, Scattering Immigrant Families, 2003; editor: Making Do, 1989, Making Do II, 1994. Mem. adv. com. Luth. Ministries of Fla., 1993-97. Mem. NASW, Mensa (local sec. 1986-90, chair scholarships com. 1992—), InterTel, Phi Kappa Phi. Democrat. Lutheran. Avocation: genealogy. Home: 2140 E Scott St Pensacola FL 32503-4957 E-mail: mloesch@bellsouth.net.

LOEWENTHAL, NESSA PARKER, intercultural communications consultant; b. Chgo., Oct. 13, 1930; d. Abner and Frances (Ness) Parker; m. Martin Moshe Loewenthal, July 7, 1951 (dec. Aug. 1973); children: Dann Marcus, Ronn Carl, Deena Miriam; m. Gerson B. Selk, Apr. 17, 1982 (dec. June 1987). BA in Edn. and Psychology, Stanford U., 1952. Faculty Stanford Inst. for Intercultural Communication, Palo Alto, Calif., 1973-87; dir. Trans Cultural Svcs., San Francisco, 1981-86, Portland, Oreg., 1986—. Dir. dependent svcs. and internat. edn. Bechtel Group, San Francisco, 1973-81, internat. edn. cons., 1981-84; mem. adv. com. dept. internat. studies Lesley Coll., Cambridge, Mass., 1986—; mem. Oreg. Ethics Commns., 1990—; mem. Bay Area Ethics Consortium, Berkeley, 1985-90; chmn. ethics com. Sietar Internat., Washington, 1987—, mem. governing bd., 1992-95; mem. faculty Summer Inst. for Internat. Comms., Portland, Oreg., 1987-97; core faculty Oreg. Gov.'s Sch. Svc. Leadership, Salem, 1995-97. Author: Professional Integration, 1987, Update: Federal Republic of Germany, 1990, Update: Great Britain, 1987; author, editor book series Your International Assignment, 1973-81; contbr. articles to profl. jours. Mem. equal opportunity and social justice task force Nat. Jewish Coun. on Pub. Affairs; bd. dirs. Kids on the Block, Portland, Portland Jewish Acad., 1996—, Portland Ashkalon Sister City Assn., Portland Jewish Fedn., 1999—, Coalition to Eliminate Bias and Hate Crimes in Oreg., 1999—; bd. dirs., co-chair ethics com. Soc. Humanistic Judaism, 1996-99; task force on Racism and Violence, Portland, Oreg.; mem. Lafayette (Calif.) Traffic Commn., 1974-80; bd. dirs. Ctr. for Ethics and Social Policy, 1988-91; mem. exec. bd. and planning com. Temple Isaiah, Lafayette, 1978-82; bd. dirs. Calif. Symphony, Orinda, 1988-90; mem. exec. com. overseas schs. adv. com. U.S. Dept. State, 1976-82; bd. dirs. Jewish Fedn. Oregon; mem. cmty. rels. com. Portland Jewish Fedn.; mem. Nat. Jewish Cmty. Rels.; mem. Task Force on Racism, Ethnicity and Pub. Policy, 1998—. Named Sr. Interculturalist, Sietar Internat., 1986. Mem. ASTD (exec. bd. internat. profl. performance area 1993-97, 99), Soc. for Intercultural Edn. Tng. and Rsch. (chmn. 1986-87, nomination com. 1984-86, co-chmn. 1989-90, chmn. ethics com. 1989-98, governing bd. 1992-95), World Affairs Coun. Democrat. Avocations: photography, swimming. Office: PO Box 6526 Bend OR 97708-6526 E-mail: nessa@transport.com.

LOFARO, NANETTE, information services administrator; b. Bronx, N.Y., Oct. 25, 1948; d. Anthony Martin and Pia (Gentili) Gentili; m. Anthony Philip Lofaro, Nov. 21, 1970; children: Laura, Gina, Tony. BA, Ladycliff Coll., Highland Falls, N.Y., 1970; MS in LS, Cath. U. Am., 1994. Tchr., ednl. cons. various instns., N.Y., 1970-90, libr. cons., 1991-94; libr. Labat Anderson Inc., Washington, 1995-96; asst. supervisory libr. Garcia Cons. Inc., Washington, 1996-97; dir. info. svcs. Head Start Publs. Mgmt. Ctr., Washington, 1997—. Project leader, select excellence and accountability program N.Y. State Bd. Regents, Clifton Park, 1988; fin. dir. Montessori Sch. of Schenectady, N.Y., 1980-83. Author: Distance Learning: A Resource Guide, 1998, Appreciative Inquiry: A Resource Guide, 1998; co-author: Parent Involvement: A Resource Guide, 1998. Recipient Peg award for meritorious svc. LWV, 1988. Mem. ALA, LWV (pres. Clifton Park 1989-91), Knowledge Mgmt. Consortium Internat., Nat. Assn. for Edn. of Young Children, Coun. for Exceptional Children, Cath. Daus Am. (edn. chair). Roman Catholic. Office: Head Start Publs Mgmt Ctr 1025 Vermont Ave NW Ste 1025 Washington DC 20005-6312 E-mail: nanettel@hskids-tmsc.org.

LOFGREN, ZOE, congresswoman; b. San Mateo, Calif., Dec. 21, 1947; d. Milton R. and Mary Violet Lofgren; m. John Marshall Collins, Oct. 22, 1978; children: Sheila Zoe Lofgren Collins, John Charles Lofgren Collins. BA in Polit. Sci., Stanford U., 1970; JD cum laude, U. Santa Clara, 1975. Bar: Calif. 1975, D.C. Adminstrv. asst. to Congressman Don Edwards, San Jose, Calif., 1970-79; ptnr. Webber and Lofgren, San Jose, 1979-81; mem. Santa Clara County Bd. Suprs., 1981-94, U.S. Congress from 16th Calif. dist., 1995—, Ho. Select Com. on Homeland Security. Mem. com. on stds. of ofcl. conduct, jud. com., sci. com.; part-time prof. law U. Santa Clara, 1978-80. Exec. dir. Cmty. Housing Developers, Inc., 1979-80; trustee San Jose C.C. Dist., 1979-81; bd. dirs. Cmty. Legal Svcs., 1978-81, San Jose Housing Svc. Ctr., 1978-79; mem. steering com. sr. citizens housing referendum, 1978; del. Calif. State Bar Conv., 1979-82, Dem. Nat. Conv., 1976; active Assn. Immigration and Nationality Lawyers, 1976-82, Calif. State Dem. Ctrl. Com., 1975-78, Santa Clara County Dem. Ctrl. Com., 1974-78, Notre Dame H.S. Blue Ribbon Com., 1981-84, Victim-Witness Adv. Bd., 1981-94. Recipient Bancroft-Whitney award for Excellence in Criminal Procedure, 1973. Mem. Santa Clara County Bar Assn. (trustee 1979—), Santa Clara County Women Lawyers Com. (exec. bd. 1979-80), Santa Clara Law Sch. Alumni Assn. (v.p. 1977, pres. 1978), Nat. Women's Polit. Caucus, Assn. of Bay Area Govts. (exec. bd. 1981-86). Democrat. Office: US Ho Reps 102 Cannon Ho Office Bldg Washington DC 20515-0516 also: 635 N 1st St Ste B San Jose CA 95112-5110*

LOFLAND, PATRICIA LOIS, secondary school educator, travel company executive; b. New Orleans, Apr. 18, 1937; d. Willie and Philomene (Foster) Seymore; m. Eugene Joseph LeBeauf, Apr. 24, 1954 (div. 1967); children: Valentino, Renee, Merlin, Tammy, Gina; m. Trusten P. Causey Lofland, Jan. 21, 1974. AA, Long Beach City Coll., 1972; BA in Sociology, Calif. State U., Dominguez Hills, 1972; MA Early Childhood Edn., Calif. State U., 1974. Cert. tchr., Calif. Community/liaison tchr. Long Beach (Calif.) Community Improvement League, 1964-70; dep. probation officer Orange County, Orange, Calif., 1972-74; substitute tchr. Compton (Calif.) Unified Sch. Dist., 1974-76; tchr./pers.commr. Long Beach Unified Sch. Dist., 1976—96; customer service rep. Western/Delta Airlines, L.A., 1978-87; travel agt./sales cons., 1986—. Mem. exec. bd. Westside Neighborhood Assn., Long Beach, 1981, Long Beach Fair Housing Found., 1987—; sec. L.A. County Grand Jury, 1982-83; pres. St. Luke Mission Soc., Long Beach, 1978-88; mem. Christian bd. edn. St. Luke Baptist Ch., Long Beach, 1986-88.,mem., State Calif. Sch. Pers. Commn. Assn., 1999; cmty. development advisor, Long Beach, 1993-2002; Relocation Appeals Bd., 1988-1995, Elected Trustee, Long Beach Cmty. Coll. Bd., 1996-2000, Christ Second Bapt. Ch., mem. Youth Worker Missionary Soc., Fin. Comm., New Members Counselor and Dept. sec., 1995- Recipient cert. of appreciation Westside Neighborhood Assn., 1981, cert. of appreciation Lutheran U., 1996; Long Beach City Coll. recognition for commitment and outstanding svc.to the EOPS and CARE program, 1999, cert. of appreciation for outstanding leadership in the Long Beach Cmty., 1996, 1999, recognition as the first african mem. of the Long Beach City Coll. Bd. of Trustees, 1997, cert. of appreciation, Bd. of Trustees, 2000, cert. of appreciation from the Calif. Senate and Assembly, 1999, State of Calif. Senate and Assembly, 1999, Pearl award Alpha Kappa Alpha, 2000, cert. of appreciation L.A. county Bd. Suprs., 2002. Mem. Calif. Tchrs. Assn., Calif. Personnel Commrs. Assn., Nat. Coun. Negro Women, NAACP, Delta Phi Upsilon (v.p. Nu chpt. 1973-77). Democrat. Avocation: world-wide travel. Home: 1281 W Cameron St Long Beach CA 90810-2209

LOFQUIST, VICKI L. journalist; b. Des Moines, Aug. 2, 1949; d. Edgar William and Gwendolyn Marjorie Lofquist; m. Craig Peter Thiesen, May 23, 1997. Student, St. Andrews (Scotland) U., 1969—70; BA, Grinnell Coll., 1971; MA, U. Minn., 1976. Prodr. Sta. KUOM Radio U. Minn., Mpls., 1974—85, 1989—91; cons., ind. radio prodr. Mpls., 1992—96; devel. dir. Minn. Internat. Ctr., Mpls., 1997—2000, Books for Africa, St. Paul, 2000—; devel. officer Children's Home Soc. and Family Svcs., St. Paul, 2001—. Prodr.(writer): (radio documentaries) Leading to Beijing: Voices of Global Women (Clarion Award, Women In Communication, 1996, Hon. Mention, Internat. Assn. of Women in Radio & T.V., 1997), Science Lives: Women & Minorities in the Sciences. Bd. dirs. St. Paul LWV, 2002—. Grantee Bicentennial Swedish-Am. Exch. Fund, Swedish Inst., Stockholm, Sweden, 1991. Office: Childrens Home Society & Family Service 1605 Eustis St Saint Paul MN 55108 Office Phone: 651-255-2314. Personal E-mail: vlofquist@studio210.com.

LOFSTROM, ARLENE KATHERINE, primary school educator; b. Jersey City, N.J., July 28, 1946; d. Edward and Dorothy Staats McClain; children: Courtney Lynne, Derek Jason. BA, Jersey City State Coll., 1968. Tchr. 4th to 6th grade Jersey City Bd. Edn., 1968—75; tchr. 3d grade Union Beach (N.J.) Bd. Edn., 1989—. Remedial reading tchr. Union Beach Meml. Sch., 1985—89, Latch Key tchr., 1987—88, Gifted and Talented tchr., 1988—89, summer sch. tchr., 1987—; ESL tchr. Union Beach Adult Sch., 2000—01. Mem.: NEA, N.J. Edn. Assn., Highlands Hist. Soc., Highlands Rep. Club. Avocations: golf, travel, book discussion groups. Home: A-12 Oceanview Terr Highlands NJ 07732

LOFTIN, SISTER MARY FRANCES, religious organization administrator; b. Atlanta, Mar. 25, 1928; B, Marquette U., 1955; M, George Washington U., 1970. Various adminstrv. positions, 1955-74; adminstr. St. Thomas Hosp., Nashville, 1974-81; pres. Daus. of Charity Health Sys., Evansville, Ind., 1981-87; pres., CEO Daus. of Charity Nat. Health Sys., St. Louis, 1992-94; chancellor Diocese of Birmingham, Ala., 1995—. Home: St Vincent's Residence 2724 Hanover Cir S Birmingham AL 35205-1706 Office: Chancellor's Office Diocese of Birmingham PO Box 12047 Birmingham AL 35202-2047

LOFTIN, THELMA TEE, writer; b. Kinston, N.C., Jan. 27, 1922; d. Kirby William and Tiffany (Whaley) Loftin; m. Edwin Marion Snell, May 4, 1944 (div.); children: James Loftin Snell, Suzanne Snell Tesh. BJ, U. Mo., 1942; MA in Journalism, Am. U., Washington, 1965. Script/comms. writer KBWD radio, Brownwood, Tex., 1942—43; newscast writer KMOX radio, St. Louis, 1943—44; writer humorous dialogues WRC radio, Washington, 1949; freelance writer quiz show questions WRC-TV, Washington, 1950—52; Washington corr. Kinston Daily Free Press, 1954—64, fgn. corr., 1952, reporter, 1953; ghost writer weekly col. Congressman Charles Jonas, Washington, 1953—54; editor Nat. Acad. Engring., Washington, 1965—66; rschr., book author World Traveler Nat. Geog. Soc. Spl. Pubs., Washington, 1967—87; writer, rschr., pub. Washington and Santa Fe, N.Mex., 1987—. Author: America's Beginnings, the Wild Shores, 1974, Trapper Andy Nault Staying Alive in Alaska's Wild, 1980, Contest for a Capital, 1989, Westward Go! Fremont, Randy and Kit Carson, 2001; contbr. numerous articles to profl. jours., chpts. to books. Chmn. curriculum study com. D.C. Bd. Mgrs., PTA, Washington, 1958—62; bd. dirs. The Santa Fe Playhouse, 2000—. Mem.: N.Mex. Writers Assn., Nat. Congress of Parents and Tchrs. (life). Home and Office: 685 Gonzales Rd Santa Fe NM 87501

LOFTNESS, VIVIAN ELLEN, architecture educator, department chairman; BS, MIT, 1974, MArch, 1975. Instr. MIT, 1976; asst. prof. SUNY, Buffalo, 1977—78; prof., head dept. arch. Carnegie Mellon U., Pitts., 1981—. Bldg. rsch. bd., com. mem. Nat. Acad. Scis., 1986—, bd. applied climatology, 1983—85, adv. bd. for built environment, 1982—84; vis. critic dept. arch. U. Pa., 1985; coun. mem. Nat. Inst. Bldg. Scis., 1983—85; rsch. project mgr. Housing Urban Devel. Office Policy Devel. and Rsch.; spkr. and cons. in field. Author (with others): The Office of the Future: The Japanese Approach to Tomorrows Workplace, 1992; co-author: Evaluating and Predicting Design Performance, 1992; co-author: Occupational Medicine: Building-Associated Illness, 1989, Building Evaluation, 1989, The Handbook of Climatology, 1987, Intelligent Buildings: Applications of IT and Building Automation to High Technology Construction Projects, 1988, The Ergonomic Payoff: Designing the Electronic Office, 1986, The Building Systems Integration Handbook, 1985; contbr. articles to profl. jours. Recipient N.Y. State Passive Solar Residential Design award, 1979; fellow, Rotary, 1975—76, Grunsfeld Found., 1973; grantee, NSF, 1988—, U.S. Army Constrn. Engring. Labs., 1993—94, State Pa. Energy Office, Nat. Endowment for the Arts, 1986—87. Mem.: ASHRAE, ASTM, AIA, Ctr. Internat. Batiment, Am. Solar Energy Soc., Internat. Solar Energy Soc., Internat. Facility Mgmt. Assn., Pa. Soc. Arch. Office: Carnegie Mellon Univ Sch of Architecture Rm 201 Coll Fine Arts Pittsburgh PA 15213-3890

LOFTUS, KAY DOUGLAS COLGAN, social worker; b. Bad Axe, Mich., July 27, 1941; d. James Fletcher and Myrtle Irene (Krueger) Colgan; m. Stephen Deane Loftus, Jan. 2, 1965; children: Amy Loftus Tuitel, Anna. BA, Alma Coll., 1963; MA, Bowling Green State U., 1966; MSW, Western Mich. U., 1983. Cert. social worker; Healthy Families Am. cert. trainer; lic. marriage and family therapist. Clin. social worker Barry County Cmty. Mental Health Svcs., 1983-95; program mgr. Healthy Families Barry County, Hastings, Mich., 1995-98; cons. Children;s Charter of the Cts. of Mich., Lansing, 1999—. Bd. dirs. Barry County Child Abuse Coun., Hastings, 1977. Office: Childrens Charter of Cts Mich 324 N Pine St # 1 Lansing MI 48933-1024 E-mail: loftuskay@comcast.net.

LOGA, SANDA, physicist, researcher; b. Bucharest, Romania, June 13, 1932; came to U.S., 1968; d. Stelian and Georgeta (Popescu) L.; m. Karl Heinz Werther, Mar. 1968 (div. 1970); m. Radu Zaciu, 1996. MS in Physics, U. Bucharest, 1955; PhD in Biophysics, U. Pitts., 1978. Asst. prof. faculty medicine and pharmacy, Bucharest, 1963-67; rsch. asst. Presbyn./St. Luke's Hosp., Chgo., 1968-69; assoc. rsch. scientist Miles Labs., Elkhart, Ind., 1969-70; rsch. asst. U. Pitts., 1971-78; rsch. assoc. Carnegie-Mellon U., Pitts., 1978-80; health physicist VA Med. Ctr., Westside, Chgo., 1980; med. physicist, VA Med. Ctr. N. Chgo., 1980-97. Assoc. prof. Chgo. Med. Sch., N. Chgo., 1985-98. Mem. Am. Assn. Physicists in Medicine, Health Physics Soc. Office: Chgo Med Sch U Health Scis 3333 Green Bay Rd North Chicago IL 60064-3037

LOGAN, ANN D. financial company executive; AB cum laude, Bryn Mawr Coll.; MBA, Columbia U. Staff dir. U.S. Senate Judiciary Com., 1980-81; asst. v.p. mortgage and fin. instns. dept. Standard & Poor's; sr. fin. analyst Fannie Mae, 1985, sr. v.p. northeastern regional office, 1985-93, exec. v.p., chief credit officer Washington, 1993-98, exec. v.p. single-family mortgage bus., 1993—. Office: Fannie Mae 3900 Wisconsin Ave NW Washington DC 20016-2892

LOGAN, BETTY MULHERIN, human services specialist; b. Augusta, Ga., July 14, 1926; d. James B. and Mayclare (Rice) Mulherin; m. Vance Earle Logan, Jr. June 30, 1951; children: James V., Charles E., Mayclare Scherer, Anne Marie Harvey, Vance E III, E. Carson Johnson. Student, Fontbonne Coll. Tchr. St. Mary's and Aquinas Schs., Augusta, Ga., 1960-76; ret. vol., 1998. Organist St. Mary's Ch., Augusta, 1960-76; treas. parish coun. PCCW, Augusta, 1956-57, chmn. various coms., 1957-70; pres. deanery Coun. Cath. Women, Augusta and Savannah, 1970-72, 76-78; founder, dir. Cmty. Clothing Ctr., Augusta, 1967-76; founder Right to Life, 1969—; founder, treas., bd. dirs., trustee Birthright, Augusta, 1971—; chair Am. Cancer Soc. of Augusta, 1960-66; rep. Savannah Diocese Ga. Legis. Forum, 1978-82; pres. Augusta coun. Cath. Savannah Diocesan Coun. Coun. Cath. Women, 1976-78. Mem. Nat. Hist. Soc., Sacred Heart Cultural Ctr. (aux.). Roman Catholic. Avocations: swimming, learning computers, writing memoirs. Home: 2624 Raymond Ave Augusta GA 30904-3379 Office: Birthright Augusta Inc St Joseph Hosp 2260 Wrightsboro Rd Augusta GA 30904-4764

LOGAN, GEORGIANA MARIE, psychotherapist; b. West Palm Beach, Fla., May 6, 1948; parents Georgina Escasena and William D. Logan. MA in sociology, Boston Coll., Chestnut Hill, Mass., 1983, MA in pastoral ministry, 1996; MSW in clin. social work, Boston Coll., Chestnut Hill, Mass., 1996. Tchr. Sacred Heart Sch., San Francisco, 1975—77; ednl. advocate for Hispanic cmty. Alianza Hispana, Inc., Roxbury, Mass., 1977—79; sch. staff Woodlands Acad. Sacred Heart, Lake Forest, Ill., 1984—86; co-dir. Let Nicaragua Live Humanitarian Aid Campaign, Washington, 1986—87; co-coord. Peace Brigades Internat. U.S.A., Cambridge, 1990—91; secretariat staff Soc. Sacred Heart, Casa Generalizia, Rome, 1992—93; psychotherapist Interfaith Counseling Svc. Inc., West Newton, Mass., 1996—; out-patient clinician South End Cmty. Health Ctr., Boston, 1997—; clin. fellow Boston Inst. Psychotherapy, 2000—02. Pastoral psychotherapist Franciscan Counseling Ctr., Inc., Boston, 2002—03. Editor: (book) Conferences: Concepción Camacho, RSCJ, 1993, (booklet) REFLECTIONS: Japanese Spirituality Conference, 1999. Fellow: Am. Assn. Pastoral Counselors; mem.: Soc. Sacred Heart U.S. Province, Nat. Assn. Social Workers. Roman Catholic. Avocations: reading, walking, painting. Office: Interfaith Counseling Svc Inc 60 Highland St West Newton MA 02465 Business E-Mail: gml2003@earthlink.net.

LOGAN, JANET ARTISAM, mental health nurse; b. St. Mary, Jamaica, Feb. 24, 1933; arrived in U.S., 1968; d. James Newton and Edith Eliza Watson; m. Gerold George Logan, Nov. 23, 1974; m. Louis Wilberforce Huffstead, 1966 (div. 1970); 1 child, Ruel. Student, St. Francis Coll. Registered mental nurse Saxondale Hosp., Nottinghamshire, England, 1955—59; state RN Sheffield United Hosp., Sheffield, England, 1960—63; registered mental nurse Middlewood Hosp., Sheffield, 1963—64; RN Baycrest Hosp., Toronto, Canada, 1964—68; RN, head nurse Beekman Downtown, N.Y.C., 1970—74; head nurse Interfaith Med. Ctr., Bklyn., 1974—89; RN SUNY Downstate, Bklyn., 1988—. Chmn. entertainment St. Pauls United Meth., Bklyn., 1975—, co-chmn. youth coun., 1988—96. Recipient Membership award, St. Pauls United Meth., 1998. Mem.: ANA, Critical Care Nurse Assn., N.Y. State Nurses Assn. (Lifetime award 2000), Black Nurse Assn., Am. Nephrology Nurse (legis. rep. 2000—), Bklyn. Coll. Performing Arts, Lions (first v.p. 1999—), Dem. Club (com. mem., Cmty. Svc. award 2000). Avocations: swimming, reading, travel, dance, theater. Home: 760 E 37th St Brooklyn NY 11210 Office: SUNY Downstate Med Ctr 450 Clarkson Ave Brooklyn NY 11203

LOGAN, LYNDA DIANNE, elementary school educator; b. Detroit, June 22, 1952; d. Horatio Bernard and Ruby (Newsom) Graham; m. Keith L. Logan, Aug. 16, 1980 (div); 1 child, Lauren Nicole. BS, Ea. Mich. U., 1974, MA, 1980. Cert. tng. program quality rev., Calif.; cert. tchr., Calif., Miss., Mich.; cert. Lang. Devel. Specialist (CLAD), 1996; lic. guidance counselor basic related edn., Miss.; cert. counselor pupil pers. svc. credential, Mich., Calif. Substitute tchr. Detroit Pub. Schs., 1974-76; mid. sch. tchr. Inkster (Mich.) Pub. Schs., 1976-80; CETA vocat. counselor Golden Triangle Vocat.-Tech. Ctr., Mayhew, Miss., 1980-82, basic related educator, 1980-82; elem. tchr. Inglewood (Calif.) Unified Sch. Dist., 1982-93, reading resource specialist, 1993-96; tchr. Crozier Magnet Mid. Sch., Inglewood, Calif., 1996—. Advisor Assn. Student Body, 2000-2001; tchr.-mentor The Gear-Up Program, 2000—, counselor, 2003; mem. forecast adv. bd. COED Mag., N.Y.C., 1979-80; advisor/founder Newspaper Club Fellrath Mid. Sch., Inkster, 1979-80; mem. interviewing com. Golden Triangle Vocat.-Tech. Ctr., Mayhew, 1980-82, evaluation and follow-up com., 1980-82; pronouncer spelling bee Inglewood Unified Sch. Dist., 1991, 94; organizer student study team meetings Worthington Sch., Inglewood, 1993-96, coord. reading program, 1993-96; mem. interviewing com., 1987-95; co-chair yearbook com., 1993-94, prin. adv. bd., 1987-92, ct.-liaison and child welfare attendance rep. L.A. County Edn., 1995-96, sch. leadership team mem., 1991—, supt. adv. coun., 1995-96, reading is fundamental coord., 1993-96, mem. team earthquake preparedness com., 1994-96, coord. after-sch. tutoring program, 1998-99, curriculum coun. rep. 1998-99, mentor tchr.-gear up program, 2000—, grant proposal writer, 2000-01, mem. sch. site coun.; adult edn. tchr. CBET ESL Program, 2001—; supervising tchr. Calif. State U., Dominguez, 1987, 94, 2002, Nat. U., 1987, 94, 2003, UCLA, 2001-02, mem. bldg. fund com. West Angeles Ch. of God in Christ, 2001—. Youth co-chair March of Dimes, Detroit, 1976-80; com. mem. Nat. Coun. Negro Women, L.A. chpt., 1982-84; com. mem. Cmty. Action Program, Eternal Promise Bapt. Ch., L.A., 1991, pres. choir, 1991, v.p. hospitality com., 1987-88; co-chmn. women's com., 1990; mem. parent adv. com. Knox Presbyn. Ch. Nursery Sch., L.A., 1988-89; co-chair higher learning parent com. West Angeles Ch. of God in Christ, 2003—; v.p., mem. fin. com. Fairview Gardens Homeowner Assn., 2003; mentor, tchr. UCLA. Mem. ASCD, AAUW, NAFE, Black Women's Forum, Ladies Aux. Knights of St. Peter Claver, Ea. Mich. U. Alumni Assn., Phi Gamma Nu. Avocations: bike riding, community organizational activities, travel, movies, theater. Office: Highland Elem Sch 430 Venice Way Inglewood CA 90302 E-mail: pontiaclyn@aol.com.

LOGAN, MARIE-ROSE VAN STYNVOORT, literature educator, publishing executive, writer; b. Brussels, May 26, 1944; d. Jean Stevo and Marie-Rose (Mabille) Van Stynvoort; m. John Frederick Logan, Sept. 7, 1968 (div. 1997); 1 child, Franklin. Licence, U. Brussels, 1966; MA, Yale U., 1970; MPhil, 1972, PhD, 1974. Instr. Yale U., New Haven, 1972-74; asst. prof. Columbia U., N.Y.C., 1974-83; assoc. prof. Rice U., Houston, 1983-93, Goucher Coll., Balt., 1993-96; assoc. prof. dept. English Temple U., Phila., 1996—; vis. prof. Columbia U., 2003—. Gen. editor Annals of Scholarship Quar. in Humanities and Social Scis., 1994—; assoc. editor

Columbia Dictionary in European Lit., N.Y., 1978-81; lectr. in field. Editor: Contending Kingdoms, 1992, Gerard Genette Figures of Literary Discourse, 1981; author: Michel de Ghelderode, 1996; contbr. over 100 articles to profl. jours. Pres. Annals of Scholarship, Inc., 1995—. Recipient Chevalier de l'Ordre des Palmes Academiques Govt. of France, 1980; Nat. Endowment of Humanities fellow, 1981-88, Harvard U. fellow, 1975-76, Inst. for Advanced Study in Humanities fellow U. Edinburgh, 1989. Mem. Soc. Fellows in Humanities Columbia U., Elizabethan Club Yale U. Home: 4041 Ridge Ave # 4-416 Philadelphia PA 19129-1550 Office: Temple U Coll Arts and Scis Dept English Philadelphia PA 19129 E-mail: ml2322@columbia.edu.

LOGAN, NANCY ALLEN, library media specialist; b. Rochester, N.Y., Mar. 27, 1933; d. Warren William and Dorothea Amelia (Pund) Allen; m. Joseph Skinner Logan, Dec. 29, 1952; children: Joseph Skinner Logan Jr., Susan, Annette Logan Miller, Jennifer Logan Haber. Student, Middlebury Coll., 1951-52; BA, Cornell U., 1955; MLS, SUNY, Albany, 1967; cert. legal asst., Marist Coll., 1983. Cert. libr. media specialist, social studies tchr. N.Y. Libr. media specialist Hyde Park (N.Y.) Sch. Dist., 1971-93. Editor: Dear Friends, 1989; editor: (newsletter) Sch. Libr. Media Specialists, 1984—85, Jamestown Hist. Soc., 1997—2001. Arts chmn. Jr. League, Poughkeepsie, NY, 1967—69; dir. Jr. Arts Ctr., 1967—69, edn. chmn., 1970—71; sec. bd. dirs. Poughkeepsie Tennis Club, 1973—79; indexer periodicals Dutchess County Hist. Soc., Poughkeepsie, 1979—93; county rep. Sch. Libr. Media Specialists, 1982, exhibits chmn. ann. meeting, 1983, 1984; indexer Jamestown (R.I.) Press, 1993—; bd. dirs. Friends of Jamestown Philomenian Libr., 1994—97, trustee, 1999—; mem. Jamestown Planning Commn., 1999; stewardship chair Conanicut Island Land Trust, 2002. Mem.: Beavertail Lighthouse Assn. (bd. dirs. 1994—97). Avocation: reading, sailing, swimming, travel, bicycling. Home: 149 Seaside Dr Jamestown RI 02835-3117 Personal E-mail: jslogan@compuserve.com.

LOGAN, NANCY JANE, broadcast sales and marketing executive; b. Buffalo, Oct. 29, 1957; d. Harry Lee and MaryJane (Redinger) Logan. AA, Erie Community Coll., Buffalo, 1977; BS, SUNY, Brockport, 1979. Account exec. Sta. WBUF Radio, Buffalo, 1979-80; account exec. Sta. WBEN Radio, Buffalo, 1980-82; regional mgr. Westwood One Radio Networks, L.A., 1983-84; mktg. rep. TV Guide Mag., L.A., 1984-88, broadcast mktg. supr., 1988-89, western mgr. tune-in advt., 1989—; sr. dir., media licensing BMI, L.A.; pres., foundation chair. AWRT, L.A., 1999-. Mem. NATAS, Am. Women in Radio & TV (pres. so. Calif. chpt. 1988-89), Publicity Club L.A. Democrat. Presbyterian. Avocations: painting, skiing, equestrian, biking, music. Home: 2627 5th St Santa Monica CA 90405-4259 Office: BMI 8730 W Sunset Blvd Fl 3 Los Angeles CA 90069-2210

LOGAN, PAULA M. entertainment company executive, accountant; b. Bklyn., Nov. 23, 1971; d. Charles L. Price and Vyris Logan; 1 child, Tyrone T. BS in Acctg. and Econs., L.I. U., 1999. Account exec. Blanksteen Cos., N.Y.C., 1990-93, property and casualty ins. broker, 1993; account exec. Rude Boy Internat. Sounds, Bklyn., 1989—, Vy's Bake Shop, Bklyn., 1989—, Lady P's Party Cons. Co., Bklyn., 1989-93, v.p., 1993—. Vol. income tax assistance program, IRS, Bklyn., 1997—; youth counselor St. Mary's Ch. of Christ, 1993—. Mem. AICPAs, Lions. Democrat. Pentecostal. Avocations: collecting teddy bears and porcelain dolls, stamps and coins, reading, dance. Office: Lady P's Party Cons 166 St Marks Ave Brooklyn NY 11238 E-mail: PLoganGrant@netscape.net., Lady_P_01@hotmail.com.

LOGAN, SHARON BROOKS, lawyer; b. Nov. 19, 1945; d. Blake Elmer and Esther N. (Statum) Brooks; children: John W. III, Troy Blake. BS in Econs., U. Md., 1967, MBA in Mktg., 1969; JD, U. Fla., 1979. Bar: Fla. 1979. Ptnr. Raymond Wilson, Esq., Ormond Beach, Fla., 1980, Landis, Graham & French, Daytona Beach, Fla., 1981, Watson & Assocs., Daytona Beach, 1982—84; prin. Sharon B. Logan, Esq., Ormond Beach, 1984—. Legal adv. to paralegal program Daytona Beach CC, 1984—. Sponsor Ea. Surfing Assn., Daytona Beach, 1983—, Nat. Scholastic Surfing Assn., 1987—; bd. dir. Ctr. for Visually Impaired, 1991—. Recipient Citizenship award, Rotary Club, 1962—63; fellow Woodrow Wilson, U. md., 1967. Mem.: ABA, Daytona Beach Area Bd. Realtors, Volusia county Estate Planning Coun., Fla. Supreme Ct. Hist. Soc., Volusia County Real Property Coun., Inc. (bd. dirs. 1987—, sec. 1987—88, v.p. 1988—89, pres. 1989—90, sec. 1990—91, 1991—97, pres. 1997—98, 1998—), Volusia County Bar Assn. (bd. dir.), Fla. Bar Assn. (real property and probate sect., cert. real estate atty. 1996), Beech Mountain Country Club, Univ. Ctr. Club (Tallahassee), Daytona Boat Club, Ducks Unlimited, Mus. Arts and Scis., Ormond Beach C. of C., Gator Club, Halifax Club, Tomoka Oaks Country Club, Md. Club, Sigma Alpha Epsilon, Delta Delta Delta (Scholarship award 1964), Omicron Delta Epsilon, Phi Kappa Phi, Alpha Lamba Delta, Beta Gamma Sigma. Democrat. Episcopalian. Avocations: golf, cooking, sewing, tennis, aerobics. Office: Sharon B Logan Esq 180 Vining Ct PO Box 4258 Ormond Beach FL 32175-4258 Office Phone: 386-673-5787.

LOGAN, VERYLE JEAN, retail executive, realtor; b. St. Louis, Oct. 24; d. Benjamim Bishop and Eddie Mae (Williams) Logan. BS, Mo. U., 1968; postgrad., Wayne State U., 1974, 76, U. Mich., Detroit, 1978, 80. Cert. residential specialist. With Hudson Dept. Store, Detroit, 1968-84, Dayton Hudson, Mpls., 1984-86, divsn. mdse. mgr., 1980-84, retail exec. divsn. mdse. mgr. coats and dresses, 1984-86; pres. Ultimate Connection, Inc., Mpls., 1987—. Mem. Golden Valley Black History Month Com., 1987—, co-chair, 1991-92. also bd. dirs., 1993-95; trustee Harry Davis Found., 1988-94, mem. exec. bd., 1991, v.p., 1991-92; chair equal opportunity com. Mpls. Bd. Realtors, also bd. dirs., 1993-96. Named Woman of Yr., Am. Bus. Women, 1984. Mem. Grad. Realtors Inst., Am. Bus. Womens Assn. (v.p. 1983-84, named Woman of Yr. 1984), Minn. Black Networking (exec. bd. 1985-90), Delta Sigma Theta (life, Mpls.-St. Paul alumnae chpt., recording sec. 1985-87, chmn. arts and letters, corr. sec. 1987-88, chmn. heritage and archives 1988-89, 1st v.p. 1991-93, pres. 1993-95, named Delta of the Yr. 1988), M.L. King Tennis Buffs Club. Office: Coldwell Banker Burnet Realty Lakes 3033 Excelsior Blvd Ste 100 Minneapolis MN 55416-4678 Office Phone: 612-925-8428. E-mail: vlogan@cbburnet.com., verylej@aol.com.

LOGAN LAWSON, ANNA, social services administrator; m. Tom Lawson; children: Towles, Blair. PhD Anthropology, U. Va. Chmn. Total Action Against Poverty, Roanoke, Va. Bd. trustees Hollins U. Vice chair, bd. trustees Va. chpt. The Nature Conservancy; co-chair bldg. campaign Planned Parenthood, Blue Ridge; bd. dirs. Ctr. for the Book, The Libr. Va., Art Mus. Western Va., Ctr. Innovative Leadership, Jamestown-Yorktown Found., Inc., Va. LEague Conservation Voters. Office: Total Action Against Poverty 100 Jefferson St NW Roanoke VA 24016

LOGAN-SUTTON, FLORETTA R. elementary school educator; b. Elizabeth City, N.C., Mar. 13, 1930; d. Ivy Hillard and Rosa Lillian (Stewart) Roach; m. Chester C. Sutton, Sept. 19, 1949 (dec. 1988); children: Gwen Omari, Chester Jr., Karen Bailey, Fred, Renee, Verona Dunn; m. Ben L. Logan; stepchildren: Tyrone, Karen Graham, Kathy, Darryl, Victor, Christopher. BA, Elizabeth City State U., 1955; MA, Glassboro (N.J.) State Coll., 1962. Tchr. grades 1-5 Bd. Edn., Atlantic City, N.J., tchr. basic skill improvement program. Contbr. rsch. to profl. jours. Mem. NEA, NAACP, Internat. Assn. Ministers' Wives and Ministers' Widows, Inc., N.J. Ret. Edn. Assn. Atlantic County, N.J. Edn. Assn., Atlantic City Edn. Assn., Phi Delta Kappa, Alpha Bettes. Home: 6025 College Dr #A Suffolk VA 23435-2019

LOGEMANN, JERILYN ANN, speech pathologist, educator; b. Berwyn, Ill., May 21, 1942; d. Warren F. and Natalie M. (Killmer) L. BS, Northwestern U., 1963; MA, 1964, PhD, 1968. Grad. asst. dept. communicative disorders Northwestern U., 1963-68; instr. speech and audiology DePaul U., 1964-65; instr. dept. communicative disorders Mundelein Coll., 1967-71; rsch. assoc. dept. neurology and otolaryngology and maxillo, 1970-74; asst. prof., 1974-78; dir. clin. and rsch. activities of speech and lang., 1975—; assoc. prof. depts. neurology, otolaryngology and comm. scis, 1978-83; prof., 1983; chmn. dept. comm. scis. and disorders, 1982-96; Ralph and Jean Sundin Prof. of Comm. Scis. and Disorders, 1995—; mem. assoc. staff Northwestern meml. Hosp., 1976—; N. Chgo. VA Hosp., 1983—; Evanston (Ill.) Hosp., 1988—. Cons. in field; assoc. dir. cancer control Ill. Comprehensive Cancer Coun., Chgo., 1980-82; mem. rehab. com. Ill. divsn. Am. CAncer Soc., 1975-79, chmn., 1979—; mem. upper aerodigestive tract organ site com. Nat. Cancer Inst., 1986-89; postdoct. fellow Nat. Inst. Neurologic Disease, Communicative Disorders and Stroke,Northwestern U., 1968-70. Author: The Fisher-Logeman Test of Articulation Competence, 1971, Evaluation and Treatment of Swallowing Disorders, 1983, 2nd edit., 1998, Manual for the Videofluorographic Evaluation of Swallowing, 1985, 93; assoc. editor: Jour. Speech and Hearing Disorders, Jour. Head Trauma Rehab., Dysphagia Jour., 1978—. Fellow Inst. Medicine Chgo., 1981—; grantee Nat Cancer Inst., 1975—, Am. Cancer Soc., 1981-82, Nat. Inst. Dental Rsch., 1996—, Nat. Inst. Deafness and Other Comm. Disorders, 1997—; recipient Honors award Conn. Speech Lang. Hearing Assn., 1995, Am. Acad. Otolaryngology-Head Neck Surgery, 1997, Appreciation award Coun. Grad. Prgrams in Comms. Scis. and Disorders, 1995, Cellular One award Vanderbilt U., Am. Special Lang. Hearing Assn., 2003. Fellow Speech, Lang. and Hearing Assn. (pres. 1994, 2000, Honors award 2003), Inst. Medicine; mem. Internat. Assn. Logopedics and Phoniatrics, AAUP, Acoustic Soc. Am. (program com. Chgo. regional chpt.), Linguistic Soc. Am., Speech Comm. Assn., Am. Cleft Palate Assn., Ill. Speech and Hearing Assn. (DiCarlo award 1988), Chgo. Heart Assn., Chgo. Speech Therapy and Auditory Soc. Office: Northwestern U Med Sch 303 E Chicago Ave Chicago IL 60611-3072 also: Northwestern U Dept Comm Sci and Disorder 2240 Campus Dr Evanston IL 60208-0001 Home: 1720 Maple Ave Apt 2251 Evanston IL 60201-3143

LOGGIE, JENNIFER MARY HILDRETH, medical educator, physician; b. Lusaka, Zambia, Feb. 4, 1936; arrived in U.S., 1964, naturalized, 1972; d. John and Jenny (Beattie). M.B., B.Ch., U. Witwatersrand, Johannesburg, South Africa, 1959. Intern Harare Hosp., Salisbury, Rhodesia, 1960-61; gen. practice medicine Lusaka, 1961-62; sr. pediatric house officer Derby Children's Hosp., also St. John's Hosp., Chelmsford, Eng., 1962-64; resident in pediatrics Children's Hosp., Louisville, 1964, Cin., 1964-65; fellow clin. pharmacology Cin. Coll. Medicine, 1965-67; mem. faculty U. Cin. Med. Sch., 1967—, prof. pediatrics, 1975-98, assoc. prof. pharmacology, 1972-77, prof. emeritus pediatrics, 1998—. Contbr. articles to med. publs.; editor Pediatric and Adolescent Hypertension, 1991. Grantee Am. Heart Assn., 1970-72, 89-90 Mem. Am. Pediatric Soc. (Founder's award 1996), Midwest Soc. Pediatric Rsch. Episcopalian. Home: 1133 Herschel Ave Cincinnati OH 45208-3112

LOGSDON, JUDITH KAY LOGSDON, merchandiser, small business owner; b. Tulia, Tex., Dec. 5, 1947; d. Bill and Audrey Lee (Hendrix) Humphrey; m. Muriel Frazier Bussey, Mar. 19, 1965 (div.); children: Jeffrey Eldon Bussey, Shawn DeWitt Bussey; m. Leon Francis Logsdon, Nov. 28, 1980. Attended, South Plains Coll., 1987-88. Lic. cosmetologist. Cosmetologist K-K Beauty Shop, Dimmitt, Tex., 1966-67, The Blue Room, Dimmitt, 1967-68; reporter, interviewer Tex. Crop & Livestock Reporting Svc., Austin, 1972-74; bookkeeper Kearn Machine Shop, Hereford, Tex., 1975-76, Tex. Sesame divsn. ADM, Muleshoe, Tex., 1978-88; merchandiser, owner J&L Fashions, Muleshoe, 1988—. Sec.-treas. Muleshoe Activities Com., 1992-94; vol. Hospice of the Plains, 1996, The Heart Assn., 1985-86. Avocations: painting, needle work, crafts, cooking. Home and Office: J&L Fashions 1911 W Ave G Ste A Muleshoe TX 79347-3854

LOGUE, JUDITH FELTON, psychoanalyst, educator, professional coach; b. Phila., Aug. 21, 1942; d. Martin and Laura (Goldman) Kirshenbaum; m. Stephen Felton, Feb. 8, 1966 (div. Aug. 1989); 1 child, Jane Jennifer; m. A. Douglas Logue, Feb. 14, 1990. AB in Govt., Wheaton (Mass.) Coll., 1963; MSW, Rutgers U., 1966, PhD, 1983; grad., N.Y. Ctr. Psychoanalytic Tng., 1978. Diplomate Am. Bd. Psychotherapy, Am. Bd. Forensic Medicine, Am. Bd. Examiners Clin. Social Worker, Am. Bd. Forensic Examiners, Am. Bd. Psychol. Specialties, cert. profl. coach, mentor coach. Clin. social worker VA, Newark, 1967; psychotherapist Santa Barbara (Calif.) Mental Health Svcs., 1967-69; supr. Santa Barbara Counselling Ctr., 1967-69; pvt. practice psychoanalysis, 1969—. Psychoanalyst, therapist Fifth Ave. Ctr. for Psychotherapy, N.Y.C., 1969-72; instr. Marymount Manhattan Coll., 1971; psychotherapy supr. clin. faculty, dept. psychiatry Rutgers Med. Sch., New Brunswick, N.J., 1972-75, tchg. asst. Grad. Sch. Social Work, 1974-76; vis. lectr. Bryn Mawr Coll. Sch. Social Work and Social Rsch., 1980; mem. faculty N.Y. Ctr. for Psychoanalytic Tng., 1980—, N.J. Inst. Psychoanalysis and Psychotherapy, 1982—; adv. bd. Am. Bd. Forensic Social Workers, 1999; chair adv. bd. Am. Bd. Forensic Social Workers, 2000; pres. Goldilox Co., Inc., ShAIRing, Inc. Mem. editl. bd. jour Current Issues in Psychoanalytic Practice, 1983-93; contbr. articles to profl. jours. Bd. dirs. N.Y. Ctr. for Psychoanalytic Tng., Inst. for Psychoanalysis and Psychotherapy N.J. Faculty, 1982—. Recipient Disting. Faculty award Atlantic County Psychoanalytic Soc., 1987; NIMH fellow, 1965. Fellow N.J. Soc. for Clin. Social Work; mem. AAUP, NASW, APA (div. 39, sect. I), Conf. Psychoanalytic Psychotherapists, Nat. Assn. for Advancement of Psychoanalysis, Groves Conf. on Family, Acad. Cert. Social Workers, Soc. for Psychoanalytic Tng. (bd. dirs. 1983—, dir. social sci. program 1983-86), Am. Coll. Forensic Examiners (mem. editl. bd. jours. 1999—, Outstanding Svc. award 2000), Internat. Coach Fedn.; mem. APA (pres. div. 39 sec. III, 2003-04), Am. Psychoanalytic Assn. (com. on psychotherapist assocs. 2003—), Am. Coll. Forensic Social Workers (chair 2000-01). Home and Office: 159 Valley Rd Princeton NJ 08540-3442 E-mail: judith@judithlogue.com.

LOHAN, LINDSAY, actress; b. Long Island, NY, July 2, 1986; d. Michael and Dina Lohan. Former model. Actor: (TV series) Another World, 1996—97, Bette, 2000; (TV films) Life-Size, 2000, Get A Clue, 2002; (films) The Parent Trap, 1998, Freaky Friday, 2003, Confessions of a Teenage Drama Queen, 2004, Mean Girls, 2004.*

LOHMAN, LORETTA CECELIA, social scientist, consultant; b. Joliet, Ill., Sept. 25, 1944; d. John Thomas and Marjorie Mary (Brennan) L. BA in Polit. Sci., U. Denver, 1966, PhD in Am. History, 1996; MA in Social Sci., U. No. Colo., 1975. Lectr. Ariz. State U., Tempe, 1966-67; survey researcher Merrill-Werthlin Co., Tempe, 1967-68; edn. asst. Am. Humane Assn., Denver, 1969-70; econ. cons. Lohman & Assocs., Littleton, Colo., 1971-75; rsch. assoc. Denver Rsch. Inst., 1976-86; owner, rsch. scientist Lohman & Assocs., Littleton, 1986-99; affiliate Colo. Water Resources Rsch. Inst., Ft. Collins, Colo., 1989-91; Colo. Nonpoint source info./edn. coord. coop. ext. Colo. State U., 1999—. Tech. adv. com. Denver Potable Wastewater Demo Plant, 1986—90; cons. Constrn. Engring. Rsch. Lab., 1984—; peer reviewer NSF, 1985—86, Univs. Coun. Water Resources, 1989; WERC consortium reviewer N.Mex. Univs.-U.S. Dept. Energy, 1989—, Co-Alliance Environ. Edn. Adv. Bd., 2000—; course cons. Regis Coll., Denver, 1992—. Contbr. articles to profl. jours. Vol. Metro Water Conservation Projects, Denver, 1986-90; co-coord. AWARE Colo., 2003--; vol. handicapped fitness So. Suburban Parks and Recreation. Recipient Huffsmith award Denver Rsch. Inst., 1983; Nat. Ctr. for Edn. in Politics grantee, 1964-65. Mem. ASCE (social and environ. objectives com.), Orgn. Am. Historians, Pub. Hist. Assn., Sigma Xi, Pi Gamma Mu, Phi Alpha Theta. Avocations: vegetable and xeriscape gardening, traveling, miniature boxes. Home and Office: 3375 W Aqueduct Ave Littleton CO 80123-2903 E-mail: llohman@juno.com.

LOHR, Mrs. BENJAMIN FRANKLIN See DAVIS, RUTH MARGARET

LOHRLI, ANNE, retired English language educator, writer; b. Bake Oven, Oreg., Feb. 9, 1906; d. Gottfried and Anna (Hüsser) L. BA, Occidental Coll., L.A., 1927, MA, 1928, Columbia U., 1932; PhD, U. So. Calif., 1937. Tchr. L.A. city schs., 1937-45; prof. English N.Mex. Highlands U., Las Vegas, 1945-65. Vis. prof. U. Trieste, 1954. Compiler: Household Words, List of Contributors, etc., 1973; contbr. some 40 articles in Dickensian, Princeton U. Libr. Chronicle, Victorian Studies, Pacific Historian, others, 1963-94. Mem. Phi Beta Kappa, Phi Kappa Phi. Home: 901 Marlene St Apt 3 Ukiah CA 95482-5987

LOHSE, SUSAN FAYE, county official, educator; b. Fergus Falls, Minn., Dec. 23, 1952; d. Philip Irving and Harriet Elinor Arlene (Hanson) Berg; m. Robert Wayne Lohse, July 7, 1973; children: Trevor Robert, Trisha Sue, Thomas Roger, Tana Ruth. BS, Bemidji State U., 1973; cert. sr. accredited assessor, U. Minn., 1993. Tchr. Kensington Pub. Schs., 1973-75; sub. tchr. Elbow Lake (Minn.)-Wendell Pub. Schs., 1975-80, tchr., 1982-83, Ashby Pub. Schs., 1981, Elbow Lake Cmty. Edn., 1976—82, 1990—; assessor's clk. Grant County Assessor's Office, Elbow Lake, 1983, dep. assessor, office mgr., 1985—94, county assessor, 1994—. Instr. U. Minn. Ext. Svcs., Elbow Lake, 1993—99, Elbow Lake, 2000. Mem.: West Ctrl. and Minn. Assessment Pers. (pres. 1990—92), Minn. Assn. Assessing Officers (sec. region 7 1999, treas. 2000, pres. 2001). Lutheran. Avocations: sewing, crocheting, volleyball, camping. Office: Grant County Assessor 10 2d St NE Elbow Lake MN 56531

LOIKKANEN, PIRJO TUULIKKI, music educator; b. Helsinki, Finland; d. Aune Kauhanen; m. Matti Loikkanen. M, Sibelius Acad., Helsinki. Cert. tchr. music. Piano tchr. Tampere (Finland) Music Coll., 1974-78, Savonlinna (Finland) Music Coll., 1981-82, Kapyla Music Coll., Helsinki, 1982-89; pvt. piano tchr. Garden Grove, Calif., 1990-98, Bellevue, Wash., 1998—. Mem. Nat. Guild Piano Tchrs., Music Tchrs. Nat. Assn., Wash. State Music Tchrs. Assn.

LOIS, DOLORES CARMEN, literature educator; b. N.Y., Sept. 15, 1973; d. Francisco and Dolores Lois. BA in English, St. John's U., 1995; MA in Tchg. English as Second Lang., Adelphi U., 2000. Cert. tchr. N.Y. State Dept. of Edn., 2002. English tchr. Jr. HS 189, Flushing, NY, 1996—2000, Valley Stream (N.Y.) Ctrl. HS, 2000—. Journalism, newspaper adviser Valley Stream (N.Y.) Ctrl. HS, 2000—. Mem.: L.I. (N.Y.) Lang. Arts Coun., Nat. Coun. Tchrs. English, Kappa Phi Delta. Avocations: travel, reading, theater, music, art. Home: 34-35 74th Street Jackson Heights NY 11372 Office: Valley Stream Central High School 135 Fletcher Avenue Valley Stream NY 11580 Office Phone: 516-561-4400.

LØJ, ELLEN MARGRETHE, ambassador; b. Gedesby, Denmark, Oct. 17, 1948; Grad. econs., Copenhagen U., 1973. Joined Ministry Fgn. Affairs, 1973; first sec. Permanent Mission to the UN Ministry Fgn. Affairs, N.Y.C., 1977—80, counsellor Permanent Representation of Denmark to the European Cmty. Brussels, 1982—85, head dept., 1986—89; amb. to Israel Ministry Fgn. Affairs, 1989—92; under-sec. multilateral affairs, South Group Ministry Fgn. Affairs, 1992—94, under-sec. bilateral affairs South Group, 1994—96, state sec. South Group, 1996—2001, permanent rep. of Denmark to the UN, amb., 2001—. Mem. supervisory bd. The Investment Fund Ctrl. and Ea. Europe, 1994—96, The Industrialization Fund for Developing Countries, 1994—96, Scandlines AG and Scandlines A/S, 1998—2001; participant Danish dels. to several internat. meetings and U.N. confs. Office: Permanent Rep of Denmark to the UN One Dag Hammarskjöld Plaza 885 Second Ave 18th Fl New York NY 10017-2201

LOK, JOAN MEI-LOK, community affairs specialist, artist; b. Hong Kong, Apr. 2, 1962; d. Chi Hong Stephen Pan and Mui Kan Teresa Chan; m. David Tai-Wai Lok, Jan. 11, 1986; children: Wesley Kevin, Gary Alexander. B in Tourism and Hotel Mgmt., Hong Kong Poly. U., 1983; BBA, Baruch Coll., 1988. Commd. compliance examiner FDIC, 1999. Cmty. affairs specialist FDIC, Balt., 1999—, Chinese money smart transl. mgr., 2002—, compliance examiner Holyoke, Mass., 1997—99, affordable housing specialist Hartford, Conn., 1994—97, bank liquidation specialist South Brunswick, NJ, 1988—94. V.p. Lingnam Art Assn. of Am., NYC, 1992—94; nat. pres. Sumi-e Soc. of Am., Inc., Washington, 2002—; mem. Md. Gov.'s Commn. on Asian Pacific Am. Affairs, 2003—. Recipient Cheng Dia Chien award, Sumi-e Soc. of Am., 1999, Gardens of Edison, Edison Arts Soc., 2002, Best in Watercolors, Audubon Soc. of Conn. in Glastonbury, 1996, Artist of the Yr., Edison Arts Soc., 2000, Grumbacher Gold metal, Sumi-e Soc. of Am., 1998, Artist's Alternative award, Ea. Arts Connection, 1994, First Pl., Glastonbury Art Guild, 1995, Blue Heron award, Sumi-e Soc. of Am., 2002, Benefactors of the Soc. award, 2003, Diana Kan award, 1997, Svc. to Am. medal, Partnership for Pub. Svcs., 2003; Hong Kong Hotel Assn. scholar, 1982, Walt Disney World fellow, 1983—84. Mem.: Edison Arts Soc., Glastonbury Art Guild, Internat. Soc. of Lingnam Artists (dir. of pub. rels. 2003—), Assn. of Chinese Calligraphy in Am. Achievements include initiated the first virtual juried exhibition of sumi-e art in the Sumi-e Society of America's 39 years history; first Chinese-American to be elected national Presdient of the Sumi-e Society of America in its 40 years history; first female executive of a Chinese cultural club in New York Chinatown in 1992. Office: FDIC 8825 Stanford Blvd Ste 210 Columbia MD 21045 Office Phone: 410-953-0451. E-mail: jlok@fdic.gov.

LOKE, JOAN TSO FONG, respiratory therapist; b. Hong Kong, Nov. 29, 1950; d. Choong Shee and Elsie L.C. Loke; m. Fabian Chan, Dec. 2, 1975 (div. July 1993); children: Jeffrey Chan, Jeremy Chan. BS in Biology, U. Puget Sound, 1973, BS in Med. Tech., 1974; AS in Respiratory care, Kapiolani C.C., 1995. Cert. respiratory therapy technician, registered respiratory technologist. Med. technologist Harborview Med. Ctr., Seattle, 1975—76; EKG technologist St. Francis, Honolulu, 1987—94, oxygen technologist, 1994—95, respiratory therapist, 1995, Kapiolani Med. Ctr., Honolulu, 1995—2002, Kaiser Permanente, Honolulu, 1995—, Tripler Med. Ctr., Honolulu, 2002—. Mem.: AARC (pact team mem. 2002—03, pub. rels. chair 2002—03), HSRC (v.p. 2000, bd. dirs. 2000, pres. 2001—03). Avocations: Karate (black belt), swimming, tennis, piano, singing. Home: 965 Prospect St #605 Honolulu HI 96822 Office: Kaiser Permanente 3288 Moanalua Rd Honolulu HI 96819

LOKEN, BARBARA, marketing educator, social psychologist; b. Owatonna, Minn., Aug. 22, 1951; d. Gordon Keith and June Rosaline (Iverson) Anderson; 1 child, Elizabeth Loken Diebel. BA in Psychology magna cum laude, U. Minn., 1973; MA, NYU, 1976; PhD in Social Psychology, U. Ill., 1981. Rsch. and statis. asst. Nat. Soc. Prevention Blindness, N.Y.C., 1974-76; rsch. asst. dept. psychology U. Ill., 1976, 78-80, instr., 1977-78; NIMH trainee in measurement, 1979-80; asst. prof. dept mktg. U. Minn., 1980-86, assoc. prof., 1986-92, prof., 1992—. Co-dir. edn. evaluation Minn. heart health project Sch. Pub. Health, 1982-88, adj. assoc. prof. dept. psychology, 1987-92, adj. prof., 1992—; vis. assoc. prof. mktg. UCLA, 1988. Assoc. editor: Jour. Consumer Rsch., 1996-99; contbr. articles to profl. jours. Rsch. grantee Sch. Mgmt., U. Minn., 1981-84, 86, 88-99. Mem. Am. Psychol. Assn., Am. Mktg. Assn., Assn. Consumer Rsch., Assn. for Consumer Rsch. 2000 (treas.).

LOKER, ELIZABETH ST. JOHN, newspaper executive; b. Leonardtown, Md., Jan. 1, 1948; d. William Meverell and June Whiting (Farner) L.; m. Donald Scott Rice, Sept. 11, 1980 BA, George Washington U., 1969. Analyst Met. Washington Council Govt., 1973-74; analyst, programmer Washington Post, 1974-75, mgr. systems research, 1976, dir. data processing, 1976-78, asst. to pub., 1979, v.p. advanced systems, 1979—, v.p. sys. and engring., 1992—. Contbr. chpt. to book Trustee Greater Washington Research Ctr., also mem. exec. com.; bd. dirs. Copyright Clearance Ctr.; bd. dirs. Washington Chamber Symphony. Mem. Newspaper Systems Group (past pres.), Assn. for Computing Machinery, Soc. Info. Mgmt. Avocations: antiques; gardening; historic preservation. Office: Washington Post Co 1150 15th St NW Washington DC 20071-0002

LOKEY, LINDA H. music educator; b. Buffalo, Sept. 1954; m. Charles G. Lokey; children: Peter, Dawn. A in Fine Arts, St. Petersburg (Fla.) Jr.Coll., 1985; BMus in Piano Performance/Piano Pedagogy, U. South Fla., 1990; postgrad., Calif. State U. Nat. cert. tchr. music. Music tchr. Palm Harbor (Fla.) Montessori Sch., 1986—88; coll. staff accompanist Reinhardt Coll., Waleska, Ga., 1993-95; tchr. pvt. and group piano, 1972—. Music com. Cherokee County (Ga.) Arts Coun., 1994-95; adjudicator for music Music Tchrs. Assn. festivals, Federated Music Clubs; active Cherokee Cmty. Chorale, 1992—, chorale grant com. chair, 2002-. U. South Fla. Talent Grant award, 1985-86, Steinway Educator grant, Steinway Piano Galleries, Atlanta, 2002. Mem.: Blue Ridge Mountain Arts Assn., Cherokee County Arts Coun. (bd. dirs. 2002—, program com. chair 2002—), Am. Coll. Musicians, Cobb Music Tchrs. Assn., Cherokee Music Tchrs. Assn. (pres. 1993—95, fundraising com. 1993—99, v.p. publicity 1995—98, pres. 2003—), Ga. Music Tchrs. Assn. (exec. bd. 2000—02, co-chair state conf. 2003), Music Tchrs. Nat. Assn., Golden Key. Avocations: travel, hiking, sailing, charity work. Home and Office: 866 Valley Dr Canton GA 30114

LOKKEN, CAROLYN GRACE, music educator; b. Lockport, N.Y., Feb. 21, 1954; d. Albert E. and Dolores A. Fiegl; m. Terry W. Lokken; 3 children. BMus, Ithaca Coll., 1976. Vocal music tchr. Rome (N.Y.) City Schs., 1976—77, Dansville (N.Y.) Ctrl. Sch., 1977—85, Clarence (N.Y.) Ctrl. Sch., 1985—87, Grand Island (N.Y.) Sr. HS, 1993—. Mem.: Eric County Music Educators, Music Educators Nat. Conf., Am. Choral Dirs. Assn. Office: Grand Island Sr High Sch 1100 Ransom Rd Grand Island NY 14072

LOKMER, STEPHANIE ANN, international business development consultant; b. Wheeling, W.Va., Nov. 14, 1957; d. Joseph Steven and Mary Ann (Mozney) L. BA in Comm., Bethany Coll., 1980; cert., U. Tübingen, Germany, 1980, Sprach Inst., Tübingen, 1980; MGC in Negotiation, Georgetown U., 2003; degree in nat. security telecom., George Washington U., 2003. V.p. Wheeling Coffee and Spice, W.Va., 1981—; pres. Lokmer & Assocs., Inc., McLean, W.Va., 1986-2000; v.p. strategic devel. Telia Internat. Carrier, Inc., 2000—. Bd. dirs. Am. Found. of Ivory Coast. Mem.: Internat. Assn. Tech. of No. Va., Counselors Acad., World Affairs Coun., Pub. Rels. Soc. Am., Fed. City Club, Zeta Tau Alpha. Republican. Avocations: tennis, reading. Office Phone: 202-744-4740.

LOLLAR, KATHERINE LOUISE, tour director, social worker, therapist; b. Cin., Nov. 1, 1944; d. Robert Miller and Dorothy Marie L.; div.; 2 children. BA, U. Kans., 1966; MSW, Loyola U., 1971. Lic. clin. social worker Oreg., social worker Wash., bd. cert. diplomate clin. social work, cert. local, nat. and internat. tour dir. Internat. Tour Mgmt. Inst., 1998. Head activity therapy dept. Fox Children's Ctr., Dwight, Ill., 1966-68; child care worker Madden Mental Health Ctr., Hines, Ill., 1968-69, social worker, 1971-74; pvt. practice therapy Wheaton and Oakbrook, Ill., 1977-82; intern Monticello Care Unit alcohol and drug treatment program, 1983; cons., residential facility for developmentally disabled adults Battle Ground, Wash., 1983-85; therapist Cath. Community Svcs., Vancouver, Wash., 1983-88; out-sta. mgr. Wash. Div. Devel. Disabilities, Vancouver, 1987-98; pvt. practice therapy Vancouver, 1988-98; mature learning program asst. Clark Coll., 2003—. Troop cons. Columbia River coun. Girl Scouts Am., 1984-86, internat. trip leader, 1993, alt. leader, 1995-96, life mem.; mem. Friends of Sangam Internat. Com., 1994-97; mem. Internat. Field Selection Team, 1994-96; mem. Unity of Vancouver. Mem. NASW (sec. Vancouver chpt. 1982-84, co-chair 1985-87, unit rep. Wash. state unit 1990-92), Recycles Sq. Dance Club (pres. 1995-97). Avocations: travel, reading, camping, dance, hiking, rafting. Office: 104 NE 134th St Vancouver WA 98685-2693

LOMAN, MARY LAVERNE, retired mathematics educator; b. Stratford, Okla., June 10, 1928; d. Thomas D. and Mary Ellen (Goodwin) Glass; m. Coy E. Loman, Dec. 23, 1944; 1 child, Sandra Leigh Loman Easton. BS, U. Okla., 1956, MA, 1957, PhD, 1961. Grad. asst., then instr. U. Okla., Norman, 1956-61; asst. prof. math. U. Ctrl. Okla., Edmond, 1961-62, assoc. prof., 1962-66, prof., 1966-93, prof. emeritus, 1993—. NSF fellow, 1965-67. Mem. Math. Assn. Am., Nat. Coun. Tchrs. Math., Okla. Coun. Tchrs. Math. (v.p. 1972-76), Higher Edn Alumni Coun. Okla., VFW Aux., Delta Kappa Gamma. Home: 2201 Tall Oaks Trl Edmond OK 73003-2325 E-mail: LaVerne@cox.net.

LOMBARD, MARJORIE ANN, financial officer; b. Stoughton, Mass., Feb. 25, 1956; d. John Joseph and Marie Josephine (Hopkins) Lombard; children: Katie Marie Burt, Elizabeth Ann Burt. BSBA with honors, Northeastern U., 1979; MBA, Suffolk U., 2000. Acctg. trainee HEW Audit, Boston, 1976-78; staff acct. Etonic, Inc., Brockton, Mass., 1979-81; ops. acct. Foxboro Co., East Bridgewater, Mass., 1981-82, 86-87; chief acct. New Eng. Structures, Inc., Avon, Mass., 1983-86; bus. mgr. Mutron Corp., Brockton, Mass., 1988-92; contr. Connector Tech. Corp., Warwick, R.I., 1992-94; bus. mgr. Cath. Charities-Laboure Ctr., South Boston, Mass., 1994-97; contr. Cath. Charities, Boston, 1997-98, CFO, 1998-2000; bus. adminstr. Carver (Mass.) Pub. Schs., 2000—. Tchr. confraternity Christian doctrine program St. Thomas Aquinas Ch., Bridgewater, 1988-94; keyperson Old Colony United Way, Brockton, 1988-91, mem. funds allocation com., 1991—; vol. tchr. You and Me drug prevention program, Bridgewater, 1990-92, Parents for Edn., Bridgewater, 1990-97; vol. Am. Electronics Assn.-Brockton Jr. High Sch. Alliance, 1990-92; mem. Bridgewater Parents Collaborative, 1991-97. Mem. Am. Electronics Assn., Small Bus. Assn. New Eng. Roman Catholic. Avocations: reading, writing, crafts, interior decorating, walking.

LOMBARD, REGINA A. elementary school educator; b. Memphis, Jan. 11, 1949; d. Clifton and Geraldine Hester Best; children: Bryan Anthony, Kyle André. BA in Humanities, LeMoyne Coll., Memphis, 1970; MS in Tchg., Drake U., 1972. Cert. tchr. Mo. Adminstrv. asst. Voluntary Action and Info. Ctr., Kansas City, Mo., 1978—80; tchr. pre-sch. U. Mo., Kansas City, 1982—84; tchr. Kansas City Sch. Dist., Kansas City, 1985—. Trainer tchrs. Kansas City Sch. Dist., 1990—2002; career ladder rep. James Sch., Kansas City, 2000—03, profl. devel. com. mem. Democrat. Methodist. Avocations: reading, sewing, travel. Office: James Elem Sch 5810 Scarritt Ave Kansas City MO 64123

LOMBARDI, LINDA CATHERINE, health facility administrator, educator; b. Bronx, N.Y., Apr. 12, 1953; d. Maurice and Catherine (Reidy) L. BA, Herbert H. Lehman Coll., 1975; MA in English, Columbia U., 1976; MA in Psychology, New Sch. for Social Rsch., 1980; MPhil, CUNY, N.Y.C., 1994, PhD, 1995. Assoc. exec. dir. Bellevue Hosp. Ctr., N.Y.C.; assoc. dir. Met. Hosp. Ctr., N.Y.C. Adj. asst. prof. scis. NYU, N.Y.C. Recipient award for tchg. excellence NYU Sch. Continuing Edn., 1995. Mem. AAUW, Nat. Assn. Healthcare Access Mgrs., Crisis Prevention Inst. (cert. instr.), Columbia U. Alumni Assn., New Sch. for Social Rsch. Alumni Assn., Grad. Sch. CUNY Alumni Assn. Office: 462 1st Ave New York NY 10016-9196

LOMBARDI, TRACEY ANNE, financial administrator, medical assistant; b. Teaneck, N.J., Sept. 26, 1965; d. John David and Dianne T. (Regina) Lisch; m. Eugene Nicholas Lombardi, May 20, 1995; children: Aracelis Gianna, Steele Nicholas, Nicolette Cristal. Student in Ophthalmic/Surg. Asst., Bergen C.C./Mercy Coll. and, Manhattan Eye and Ear. Cert. ophthalmic technologist, N.Y. Ophthalmic technologist, fin. adminstr. Cliffside Eye Ctr. Richard E. Levine, MD, Cliffside Park, NJ, 1992—. Office: Cliffside Eye Ctr 663 Palisade Ave Cliffside Park NJ 07010-3012

LOMBARDINI, CAROL ANN, lawyer; b. Framingham, Mass., Dec. 29, 1954; d. Harry and Sarah (Scarano) L. m. William L. Cole, Apr. 23, 1983; children: Kevin Daniel, Kristin Elizabeth. BA, U. Chgo., 1976; JD, Stanford U., 1979. Bar: Calif. 1979. Assoc. Meserve, Mumper & Hughes, L.A., 1979-80, Proskauer Rose Goetz & Mendelsohn, L.A., 1980-82; from counsel to sr. v.p. legal and bus. affairs Alliance of Motion Picture and TV Prodrs., Encino, Calif., 1982—. Trustee Dirs. Guild Contract Adminstrn., Encino, 1982—, Prodr.-Writers Guild Pension & Health Plans, Burbank, Calif., 1983—, SAG-Prodr. Pension & Health Plans, Burbank, 1986—, Dirs. Guild-Prodr. Pension & Health Plans, L.A., 1987—. Avocations: hiking, cooking. Office: Alliance Motion Picture & TV Prodrs 15503 Ventura Blvd Encino CA 91436-3103

LOMBARDO, JANET VOGT, priest; d. Victor Werner and Marie Cecilia Vogt; m. Mark Anthony Lombardo, Aug. 6, 1983; children: Jeffrey Michael, Jennifer Marie. BA, Rutgers U. Douglass Coll., 1981; MEd, Rutgers Grad. Sch. of Edn., New Brunswick, NJ, 1983; MDiv, Epis. Div. Sch., 1997. Rector Trinity Episc. Ch., Tilton, NH, 1998—. Bd. mem. Riverbend Cmty. Mental Health, Concord, NH, 1999—; clergy cons. deployment Diocese of NH., 2002—; mem. Clergy Compensation Com., Diocese, 2002—; dr. ministry student Seabury Inst., Evanston, Ill., 2002—. Mem.: Riverbend Cmty. Mental Health (bd. mem. 1999—), Twin Rivers Interfaith Assn. (pres. 1998—). Episcopalian. Achievements include development of Congregational Development, restoring a struggling congregation to health and vitality. Avocations: painting watercolors, singing, walking, reading. Home: 67 Ridge Rd Concord NH 03301 Office: Trinity Episcl Ch PO Box 225 Tilton NH 03276

LOMBROSO, LINDA ANN, reporter; b. Queens, N.Y., May 17, 1957; d. Stanley and Nina Gottlieb; m. Eytan J. Lombroso, Nov. 24, 1985; children: David, Daria, Daniel. BA magna cum laude, SUNY, Stony Brook, 1979; MS in Elem. Edn., Hunter Coll., 1985. Editl. asst. N.Y. Mag., N.Y.C., 1979—81; asst. editor Rolling Stone, N.Y.C., 1981—83; copy chief US Mag., N.Y.C., 1984—87; staff writer The Jour. News, White Plains, NY, 1997—. Mem.: Phi Beta Kappa.

LONCHYNA-LISOWSKY, MARIA, music educator; b. Munich, Sept. 26, 1945; d. Bohdan Ivan and Irene Lonchyna; m. Bohdan Lisowsky, May 31, 1969; children: Mykola Lisowsky, Danylo Lisowsky, Taras Lisowsky, Petro Lisowsky. Diploma of Artistic Merit, Ukrainian Music Inst. Am., Detroit, 1967; BA, U. Detroit, 1967; MMus, Wayne State U., 1969. Cert. tchr. piano Mich. Music Tchrs. Assn., 2001. Piano soloist various venues, 1960—99; piano tchr. Ukrainian Music Inst. Am., Detroit, 1967—, dir., 2001—. Accompanist Suzuki workshops, Troy, Mich., 1984—98, Mich. Sch. Band and Orch. Assn. Solo and Ensemble Festivals, Troy, 1984—98, Trembita Chorus, Detroit, 1975—77, others; music dir. Luna Ensemble, Warren, Mich., 1977—83; pianist Ukrainian Music Inst. Trio, Detroit, 1965—67; accompanist Immaculate Conception Ukrainian Cath. H.S. Chorus and Orch., Hamtramck, Mich., 1959—63. Musician (accompanist to singer): (ednl. tape) Listen and Sing Along - Ukrainian Christmas Carols, 1981; musician: (stories with piano interludes) (ednl. tape) Ukrainian Stories for Children, 1976; musician: (accompanist to singer) (ednl. tape) Listen and Sing Along, 1979, Immaculate Conception, 1982—98. Librarian Detroit Symphony Civic Orch., Detroit, 1996—98. Recipient Alumna of Yr. award, Parents Club of Immaculate Conception Ukrainian Cath. H.S., 1991. Mem.: Ukrainian Ednl. Assn. (treas. 1985—86, 1992—97, pres. 1986—92), Plast, Inc. (corr. sec. Detroit region 1964—69, subscription chair, sr. divsn. 1984—92, dues, sr. divsn. 1984—92, subscriptions 1992—96, Recognition award 1999), Met. Detroit Musicians League (sec. 2001—), Ukrainian Nat. Women's League of Am. (ednl. com. chair chpt. 53 1976—78, rec. sec. chpt. 53 1978—80, corr. sec. 1980—84, pres. chpt. 53 1995—97, corr. sec. regional coun. 1997—99, press sec. Ukranian lang. 2003—, Recognition award 1998).

LONDON, CHARLOTTE ISABELLA, secondary education educator, reading specialist; b. Guyana, S.Am., June 11, 1946; came to U.S., 1966, naturalized, 1980; d. Samuel Alphonso and Diana Dallett (Daniels) Edwards; m. David Timothy London, May 26, 1968 (div. May 1983); children: David Tshombe, Douglas Tshaka. BS, Fort Hays State U., 1971; MS, Pa. State U., 1974, PhD, 1977. Elem. sch. tchr., Guyana, 1962-66; secondary sch. tchr., 1971-72; instr. lang. arts Pa. State U., University Park, 1973-74; reading specialist/ednl. cons. N.Y.C. C.C., 1975; dir. Skills Acquisition and Devel. Ctr. Stockton (N.J.) State Coll., 1975-77; reading specialist Pleasantville (N.J.) Pub. Schs., 1977—, supr. English dept., supr. gifted and talented program, 1999—, supr. world langs., 2002—. Ind. specialist United Nations Devel. Programme, Guyana, 1988—; v.p. Atlantic County PTA, 1980-82; del. N.J. Gov.'s Conf. Future Edn. N.J., 1981; founder, pres. Guyana Assn. Reading and Lang. Devel., 1987. Sec. Atlantic County Minority Polit. Women's Caucus. Mem. Internat. Reading Assn., Nat. Coun. Tchrs. English, ASCD, AAUW, Pi Lambda Theta, Phi Delta Kappa (sec.). Mem. African Meth. Episcopal Ch. Home: 6319 Crocus St Mays Landing NJ 08330-1107 Office: Pleasantville Pub Schs W Decatur Ave Pleasantville NJ 08232

LONDON, WANDA ELAINE, minister; d. Doris C. London and Archie Lee London (Deceased). BA, George Washington U., Washington, 1981; MDiv, Howard U. Sch. of Div., Washington, 1993. Ordained itinerant elder AME Ch., 1993. Licientiate Campbell AME Ch., Washington, 1988—91, ministerial assoc., 1991—92. Divsn. adminstrv. assoc. The Nat. Academies, Washington, 1989—; spl. asst. to the pastor Campbell AME Ch., Washington, 1992—93; founder and pastor Galilee AME Ch., Washington, 1993—2001; pastor Calvary AME Ch., Mt. Rainier, Md., 2001—. Recipient Rsch. award, Ford Found., 1992. Mem.: Wash. Ann. Conf., AME Ch. (life; rec. sec. 2000—03), AME/Women in Ministry-Washington Ann. Conf. (life; Potomac dist. caucus leader 2001—03, ann. conf. coord. 2003), Ministerial Alliance of Washington, D.C. and Vicinity (life; corr. sec. 2003—03). Methodist. Avocations: collecting recipes, cooking, travel. Office: Calvary AME Ch PO Box 623 Mount Rainier MD 20712

LONEY, MARY ROSE, airport administrator; Planning svcs. mgr. McCarran Internat. Airport, Las Vegas, Nev., 1979-84; asst. aviation dir. Albuquerque Internat. Airport, 1984-86; asst. dir. aviation San Jose (Calif.) Internat. Airport, 1986-89; first dep. commr. aviation Chgo. Airport Sys., 1989-92; dep. exec. dir. fin. and adminstrn. Dallas/Ft. Worth Internat. Airport, 1992-93; dir. aviation Phila. Internat. Airport, 1993-96; commr. avication Chgo. Midway Airport, 1996—. Lectr. in field. Named Santa Clara County Woman of Achievement, 1988, Woman of Yr., Phila. Customs Brokers and Freight Forwarders Assn., 1994, one of State Pa. Honor Roll of Women, 1996; recipient YWCA's Tribute to Women in Industry award, 1989, Bus. Woman of Yr. award Great Valley Regional C. of C., 1994, Transp. award March of Dimes, 1995. Mem. FAA (appointed rsch. engring. and devel. adv. com.), Am. Assn. Airport Execs. (nat. bd. dirs., chmns. award 1994), St. Joseph's U. (bd. trustees). Office: Chgo Midway Airport Mgr's Office 5700 S Cicero Ave Chicago IL 60638-3831

LONG, ANNE T. financial analyst, investment adviser; b. N.Y., June 2, 1923; d. Frederick William and Rose (Haworth) Tenney; m. Richard D. Long, Nov. 11, 1943 (dec. Nov. 1981); children: Mary, Richard. BA in Acctg., Antioch Coll., 1945; MS in Bus., Columbia U. Grad. Sch., 1955. CFA, CPA, CFP. Acct. Barrow, Wade & Gutherie CPA's, N.Y., 1945-47; instr. Davis Bus. Coll., Toledo, 1951-53; security analyst N.J. Bank & Trust, Paterson, 1955-62, asst. treas., 1962-63, asst. v.p., 1963-69; asst. investment officer Bank of N.Y., N.Y., 1969-76, asst. v.p., 1976-85, v.p., 1985-89, registered investment advisor, 2001—. Author: (news column) Womens Fin. World, 1960-70. Mem. Zonta Internat. Women's Svc. Club, Paterson, 1962—, Woman's Club Glen Rock, treas., 1991—, Glen Rock Vol. Ambulance Corps., 1992—. Mem. Am. Soc. Women Accts. (pres. Toledo chpt.). Democrat. Unitarian Universalist. Home and Office: 178 Park Ave Palo Alto CA 94306-1107 E-mail: annetl@aol.com.

LONG, BEVERLY GLENN, retired lawyer; b. Omaha, Mar. 1, 1923; d. Max Edgar and Allise Katherine Dorothea (Nielsen) Glenn; m. Jacob Emery Long, May 6, 1950 AB in Econs., U. Chgo., 1944; LLB, Columbia U., 1947. Bar: N.Y. 1948, R.I. 1951, U.S. Dist. Ct. (so. dist.) N.Y. 1949, U.S. Tax Ct. 1949, U.S. Dist. Ct. R.I. 1951, U.S. Ct. Appeals (2d cir.) 1949, U.S. Ct. Appeals (1st cir.) 1958, U.S. Ct. Claims 1960, U.S. Supreme Ct. 1960. Assoc. Edwards & Angell LLP, Providence, 1950-59, ptnr., 1959-86, of counsel, 1986—. Adv. com. child welfare svcs. R.I. Dept. Social Welfare, 1959-66; pers. com. Big Bros. R.I., 1964-67; mem. Gov.'s Com. on Status of Women, 1965; chmn. R.I. Children's Code Commn., 1967-74; fundraiser Columbia U. Sch. Law, 1947-88, R.I. area for U. Chgo., 1951—; bd. dirs. Child Welfare League of Am., Inc., 1975-80, Children's Friend and Svc., Inc., 1966-75, 77-79, Providence chpt. ARC, 1967-72; bd. dirs. St. Mary's Home for Children, 1966-80, v.p., 1978-80; bd. dirs. R.I. Conf. Social Work, 1961-66, Coun. Cmty. Svcs., Inc., 1957-64; task force evaluation of criminal justice program LEAA, 1974-78; active United Way Southeastern New Eng., Inc., 1951-81, ad hoc adv. com., exec. budget com., 1971-78, bd. dirs., 1973-74, ABA sr. lawyers divsn. coun., 1986-91, sec., 1991-95. Recipient citation for pub. service U. Chgo., 1959 Fellow Am. Bar Found., R.I. Bar Found.; mem. ABA (Outstanding State Membership Chmn. award 1984), R.I. Bar Assn. (ho. dels., exec. com., pres., Merit award 1990), New Eng. Bar Assn. (bd. dirs. 1982-85), Fed. Bar Assn., Am. Law Inst., Am. Judicature Soc. (bd. dirs. 1988-90), U.S. Supreme Ct. Hist. Soc., U. Club R.I. Republican. Home: 200 Elmgrove Ave Providence RI 02906-4233

LONG, BRIDGET TERRY, education educator; married. PhD, Harvard U., 2000. Asst. prof. Harvard Grad. Sch. Edn., Cambridge, Mass., 2000—. Office: Harvard Grad Sch Edn Gutman Library 465 Appian Way Cambridge MA 02138

LONG, DRUCILLA, special education educator; b. Leesville, S.C., Apr. 20, 1940; d. Horace Tillman and Gerlie Ann (Watson) Fallaw; m. Edward Clyde Long, Aug. 3, 1963; 1 child, Rhonda Ann. BS, Winthrop Coll., 1962. Elem. tchr. West Columbia (S.C.) Schs., 1962-64, Aiken County Schs., North Augusta, S.C., 1964-65; tchr. spl. edn. Lexington County # 3, Batesburg-Leesville, S.C., 1965—. Mem., officer Lexingotn County Ext. Svc. Women, 1965-90. Mem. Nat. Edn. Assn., S.C. Carolina Edn. Assn., S.C. Cheerleader Coaches Assn. (Outstanding Svc. award 1999), Lexington County Dist.# 3 Edn. Assn., Delta Kappa Gamam, Alpha Tau (pres. 1994, 95). Republican. Baptist. Avocations: antiques, singing, directing weddings, sports, playing with grandson. Home: 739 N Lee St Leesville SC 29070-9584 Office: Batesburg-Leesville Middle Sch 425 Shealy Rd Batesburg SC 29006-8783

LONG, ELAINE, writer, editor; b. Sterling, Colo., Jan. 12, 1935; d. Guy William and Evelyn Irene (Simpson) Mullenax; m. Thomas John O'Rourke, Aug. 17, 1963 (dec. Feb. 1965); 1 child, Mary Kendall; m. Arthur Warren Long, Oct. 4, 1969 (dec. Jan., 2003). BA, U. Colo., 1955. Tchr. Portland (Oreg.) Pub. Schs., 1955-57, Denver Pub. Schs., 1957-58, U.S. Civil Svc., Upper Heyford, Eng., 1958-59; copywriter KBOL Radio, Boulder, Colo., 1959-61; ranch hand Guy Mullenax, Gillette, Wyo., 1961-62; copy and feature writer, traffic mgr. KKAR Radio, Pomona, Calif., 1962-63; freelance writer Denver, 1966—. Editor Boulder, Buena Vista, Colo., 1974—. Author: Jenny's Mountain, 1987, Bittersweet Country, 1991; cons. editor: Separate Lives: The Story of Mary Rippon, 1999, A Texas Tragedy: Orphaned by Bootleggers, 2001, cons. editor: Dancing with Principle: Hanya Holm in Colorado, 1941-1983, 2001, Behind the Badge: 125 Years of the Boulder Police Department, 2003, author short stories; contbr. articles to profl. jours. Mem. Western Writers Am. (Spur awards chmn. 1993, Svc. award 1994, 95, bd. dirs. 1994-95), Aircraft Owners and Pilots Assn., Women Writing the West, Author's Guild N.Y., Colo. Authors' League (bd. dirs. 1987-88). Avocations: flying, songwriting, singing, hiking, reading. E-mail: elainelong@Chaffee.net.

LONG, ELIZABETH L. state legislator, small business owner; m. Kent Long; children: Amie, Dana, Sarah. Student, Drury Coll. County clk. Laclede County, Mo., 1982-90; owner, mgr. retail gift shop, Lebanon; mem. Mo. Ho. of Reps. Dist. 146, Jefferson City, 1991—. Mem. election fed.-state rels. and vet. affairs, fees and salaries, state parks, recreation and natural resources and tourism, recreation and cultural affairs coms. Mem. Lebanon Area Found. Mem. Lebanon C. of C. Republican. Office: Rm 201E State Capitol Jefferson City MO 65101

LONG, ELIZABETH VALK, former magazine publisher; b. Winston-Salem, N.C., Apr. 29, 1950; d. Henry Lewis and Elizabeth (Fuller) V. BA, Hollins Coll., 1972; MBA, Harvard Bus. Sch., 1979. Clin. adminstr. Mass. Gen. Hosp., Boston, 1973-77; asst. to circulation dir. Time Mag.-Time Inc., N.Y.C., 1979-80, 81-82; circulation dir. Fortune Mag.-Time Inc., N.Y.C., 1982-84, Sports Illustrated-Time Inc., N.Y.C., 1984-85, Time Mag.-Time Inc., N.Y.C., 1985-86; publisher Life Mag.-Time Inc., N.Y.C., 1987-93; pres. Time Mag., 1993-95; exec. v.p. Time Inc., N.Y.C., 1995—2001; bd. dirs. J.M. Smucker Co., 1997—, Jefferson Pilot Corp., 2002—. Trustee Hollins Coll., 1987—; mem. bus. com. Mus. Modern Art, N.Y.C.; mem. bd. visitors Wake Forest U., Winston-Salem, N.C.; bd. dirs. Hanover Direct, Inc., Weehawken, N.J.; mem. Com. of 200. Recipient Matrix award N.Y. Women in Comms., 1992, Silver Medal award Am. Advt. Fedn., 1993. Mem. Phi Beta Kappa. Avocations: golf, gardening.

LONG, HELEN HALTER, writer, educator; b. St. Louis, Nov. 19, 1906; d. Charles C. and Ida (May) Halter; m. Forrest E. Long, June 22, 1944. AB, Washington U., St. Louis, 1927, AM, 1928; PhD, NYU, 1937. Grad. fellow Washington U., 1927-28; tchr. social studies Venice, Ill., 1928-30; asst. prof. social sci. N.Y. State Coll. for Tchrs., Albany, 1930-38; tchr. Mamaroneck, NY, 1938-42; prin. elem. and jr. high schs., 1942-54; asst. supt. schs., 1954-61; dir. Inst. Instructional Improvement, N.Y.C., 1962-88; pres. Books of World, Sweet Springs, Mo., 1962-86; bd. dirs. Roxbury Press, Sweet Springs, 1987—96, emeritus, 1997—. Teaching fellow, instr. Sch. Edn. NYU, 1936-43; assoc. editor Clearing House, 1935-55. Author: Society in Action, 1936, National Safety Council Lesson Units, 1944-52, (with Forrest E. Long) Social Studies Skills, 8th edit, 1976 (with Forrest E. Long). Mem. Phi Beta Kappa, Pi Gamma Mu, Kappa Delta Pi, Alpha Xi Delta (Diamond Jubilee Outstanding Women award 1968) Home: The Gatesworth One McKnight Pl Apt 155 Saint Louis MO 63124 Office: Roxbury Press Inc 601 E Marshall Sweet Springs MO 65351-0295

LONG, JEANINE HUNDLEY, retired state legislator; b. Provo, Utah, Sept. 21, 1928; d. Ralph Conrad and Hazel Laurine (Snow) Hundley; m. McKay W. Christensen, Oct. 28, 1949 (div. 1967); children: Cathy Schuyler, Julie Schulleri, Kelly M. Christensen, C. Brett Christensen, Harold A. Christensen; m. Kenneth D. Long, Sept. 6, 1968. AA, Shoreline C.C., Seattle, 1975; BA in Psychology, U. Wash., 1977. Mem. Wash. Ho. of

Reps., 1983-87, 93-94, mem. Inst. Pub. Policy; mem. Wash. Senate, Dist. 44, Olympia, 1995—2003. Ranking mem. Human Svcs. and Corr. com. Wash. Senate, 1995-96, 99-2002, chair, 1997-98; vice-chair, Rep. Caucus, 1997-98. Mayor protem, mem. city coun. City of Brier, Wash., 1977-80. Republican. Office: PO Box 40482 Olympia WA 98504-0482 E-mail: long_je@leg.wa.gov.

LONG, JODI L. office manager; b. Wilmington, N.C., Sept. 23, 1964; d. Jimmy Ray and Betty Elaine (Teague) L. BA in speech comm., U. N.C. Wilmington, 1986. Cert. Am. Bd. Opticians. Gen. mgr. LensCrafters, Hyattsville, Md., 1991-96; office mgr. Hour Eyes, Reston, Va., 1997—. Mem. Am. Paint Horse Assn. Avocation: horseback riding. Office: Hour Eyes 11130 S Lakes Dr Ste L Reston VA 20191-4395

LONG, JO-NELLE DESMOND, editor, consultant, historian; b. Big Stone Gap, Va., Oct. 20, 1930; d. Daniel Joseph and Mary Pearson Desmond; m. Walter Donald Long, June 12, 1954; children: Donna Long La Tourette, Steven William, Robert Lawrence. Student, Transylvania U., 1948—50; cert., Traphagen Sch. Interior Design, N.Y.C., 1951; BA Fine Arts, Ramapo Coll. N.J., 1976; MA Arts Adminstrn., Costume History and Design, NYU, 1983. Adminstrv. asst. Smyth, Urguhart & Marckwald Interior Design, N.Y.C., 1951—54; intern, rsch. asst., vol. Am. Painting & Sculpture Met. Mus. Art, N.Y.C., 1977—; registrar Hermitage Mus., Ho-Ho-Kus, NJ, 1977—80; rsch. cons. Van Cline & Davenport Appraisers, Franklin Lakes, NJ, 1985—90; owner Long Art Rsch. & Cons., Allendale, NJ, 1985—; editor prodn. Ozer Pub., Englewood, NJ, 1991—. Lectr. in field. Treas. Cub Scout Pack 59; co-chmn. Girl Scout Com.; founder Friends of the Libr., v.p.; vol. Archer Ch. Sunday Nursery Sch. Mem.: Victorian Soc., Nat. Trust, Costume Soc. Am. Avocations: reading, tai chi, yoga, crossword puzzles, travel, decorating. Home and Office: Long Art Rsch & Cons 9 Surrey Ln Allendale NJ 07401 E-mail: larc30@aol.com.

LONG, KATHLEEN ANN, nursing educator, dean, consultant; b. Buffalo, Apr. 2, 1947; d. Edward Del and Rita P. (Arnold) L. BSN, Cath. U., 1968; MSN, Wayne State U., 1970; PhD, Johns Hopkins U., 1980. Head nurse Children's Psychiat. Ctr., West Seneca, N.Y., 1970; nurse chmn., clin. specialist U. Md. Hosp., Balt., 1971-75; instr. nursing program Johns Hopkins U., Balt., 1976-78; clin. asst. prof. Sch. Medicine U. Md., Balt., 1977-78, asst. prof. child psychiat. nursing Sch. Nursing, 1978-80; assoc. prof. psychiat. nursing Mont. State U., Billings, 1980-81; asst. dean, psychiatric nurse clinician Husson Coll./Ea. Maine Med. Ctr., Bangor, 1982-83; asst. dean Coll. Nursing, assoc. prof. Mont. State U., Bozeman, 1984-89, assoc. dean, prof., 1989-90; dean Coll. Nursing, prof. Montana State U., Bozeman, 1990—95; dean Coll. Nursing U. Fla., Gainesville, 1995—. Cons. Monforton Elem. Sch., Bozeman, 1985—, Mont. Gov.'s Office, 1986-87; adv. bd. Rural Health Care Models, Washington, 1989-91, Ctr. Rural Rsch., U. Nebr., Lincoln, 1990—. Contbr. articles to profl. publs. Bd. dirs. Big Bros. and Sisters Gallatin County, Bozeman, 1985-88; rep. Mont. Task Force on Nursing Edn., 1987-88; co-chair Mental Health Task Force Gallatin County, 1988-89; chair Mental Health Adv. Com. Gallatin County, 1989-90. Grantee Alcoholic Beverage Med. Rsch. Found., Balt., 1989-90. Fellow Am. Orthopsychiat. Assn. (bd. dirs. 1989-92), Am. Acad. Nursing; mem. ANA, Nat. League Nursing (nominating com. 1991-92), Western Inst. Nursing (bd. dirs. 1990-92, chair-elect 1992), Western Soc. Rsch. in Nursing, Mont. State Bd. Nursing (chair edn. com. 1988-92), Am. Assn. Colls. of Nursing (bd. dirs. 1992—), Phi Beta Kappa, Sigma Theta Tau, Delta Omega. Avocations: skiing, running, gardening, travel. Home: 9702 NW 63rd Ln Gainesville FL 32653-6808 Office: U Fla Coll Nursing PO Box 100197 Gainesville FL 32610-0197

LONG, LISA VALK, communications company executive; b. Winston-Salem, N.C. Grad., Hollins Coll.; MBA, Harvard Bus. Sch., 1979. Circulation staff Time Mag. TimeInc., N.Y.C., 1979-82, circulation dir. Forbes mag., 1982-84, circulation dir. Sports Illustrated, 1984-85, circulation dir. Time mag., 1985-86, pub. Life mag., 1986-87, v.p., 1987-89, sr. v.p., 1989-95, exec. v.p., 1995—, pub. People mag., 1988-93, pub. Time mag., then pres., 1991-95. Bd. dirs. Hanover Direct, Weehawken, N.J. Bus. com. Mus. Modern Art; bd. dirs. Atlantic Coun.; bd. mgrs. East Side House Settlement, Bronx. Mem. Women in Comms. (Matrix award 1992). Office: Time Inc Rockefeller Ctr TimeLife Bldg New York NY 10020-1393

LONG, MADELEINE J. mathematics and science educator; b. N.Y.C. d. Harry L. and Irma (Silverman) L. BA, Queens Coll., 1960; M.Ed., Harvard U., 1963; Ed.D., Columbia U., 1967. Tchr. Westbury (N.Y.) Sch. System, 1960-61; teaching fellow Harvard U., 1962-63; prof. edn. L.I. U., asst. to dean, 1967-69, chmn. dept., 1969-76, dir. div. edn., dir. grad. programs at Westchester br. campus, 1977-83, dir. Inst. Advancement Math. and Sci., 1983-91; program officer (on leave from L.I. U.) NSF, Washington, 1991-96; v.p. The Implementation Group, 1996-99; program dir. math., sci., tech. and extended day programs AAAS, 1999—. Vis. scientist, spl. asst. comprehensive design planning NSF, 1992-93, sr. program officer Urban Systemic Initiative, 1993-96, reader, 1973, 77, 79, 85, 88, 90, career access panelist and chair, 1988; dir. summer tng. programs N.Y.C. Bd. Edn., 1978, 79, 81; reader Fund for Improvement Postsecondary Edn., 1984, 85, 87, N.J. Bd. Higher Edn., Minority Instns. Sci. Improvement Program; cons. to various univs. and sch. sys.; lectr. in field; apptd. coun. on excellence and equity in math. and sci. edn. N.Y. State, 1986-91; v.p. The Implementation Group, 1996-99; mem. adv. bd. L.A. Collaborative Tchr. Edn., 1997—, Tchrs. Am. Math. & Sci. Programs, 1996—. Mem. editorial bd. Jour. Coll. Sci. Teaching, 1986-89; contbr. articles to profl. jours. Mem. edn. subcom. Mayor's Commn. on Sci. and Tech., 1989-91. Columbia U. fellow, 1963-64, grantee NSF, 1972, 78, 79, 80, 81, 84-87, 87-91, 91-94, Career Edn., 1975, Fund for Improvement Postsecondary Edn., 1983-87, Title II Edn. for Econ. Security Act N.Y. State. Fellow Philosophy of Edn. Soc.; mem. AAAS (chair sect. Q, Sci. Edn., chmn. edn. section, program dir. 1999—), Assn. Supervision and Curriculum Devel., N.Y. Acad. Sci., Nat. Sci. Tchrs. Assn., Nat. Coun. Tchrs. Math., Am. Ednl. Rsch. Assn., Kappa Delta Pi. Office: NSF 4201 Wilson Blvd Arlington VA 22230-0001

LONG, MARSHA TADANO, state official; b. Phoenix, Jan. 14, 1947; d. Tadashi and Michiko (Seki) Tadano; m. Merritt D. Long, Nov. 19, 1976; 1 child, Merisa Tamiko. BA, Pitzer Coll., 1968; MA, Pacific Luth. U., 1976. Vocat. counselor various orgns., 1968-73; vocat. edn. program specialist Wash. State Commn. Vocat. Edn., Olympia, 1973-82; mgr. info. systems Wash. State Dept. Licensing, Olympia, 1982-89, asst. dir., 1989-93; dep. supr. Wash. State Dept. Natural Resources, Olympia, 1993-97; dir. Wash. State Dept. Gen. Adminstrn., Olympia, 1997—. Mem. adv. com. Wing Luke Mus., Seattle, 1997. Mem. Capital High Sch. Site Based Coun., Olympia, 1996-98. Mem. Japanese-Am. Citizen League (past pres., past v.p.). Office: Wash State Dept Gen Adminstrn PO Box 41000 Olympia WA 98504-1000

LONG, MAXINE MASTER, lawyer; b. Pensacola, Fla., Oct. 20, 1943; d. Maxwell L. and Claudine E. (Smith) M.; m. Anthony Byrd Long, Aug. 27, 1966; children: Deborah E., David M. AB, Bryn Mawr Coll., 1965; MS, Georgetown U., 1971; JD, U. Miami, 1979. Bar: Fla. 1979, U.S. Ct. Appeals (5th cir.) 1980, U.S. Dist. Ct. (so. dist.) Fla. 1980, U.S. Ct. Appeals (11th cir.) 1981, U.S. Dist. Ct. (mid. and no. dists.) Fla. 1987. Law clk. to U.S. dist. judge U.S. Dist. Ct. (so. dist.) Fla., Miami, 1979-80; assoc. Shutts & Bowen, Miami, 1980-90, of counsel, 1990-92, ptnr., 1992—. Mem. Fla. Bar Assn. (cert. bus. litigator, mem. bus. litigation cert. com. 1995-99, vice chair, 1996-97, past chair bus. litigation com., chair bus. law sect. 2004—) Dade County Bar Assn. (mem. fed. cts. com., recipient pro bono award/Vol. Lawyers for the Arts 1989). Office: Shutts & Bowen 201 S Biscayne Blvd Ste 1500 Miami FL 33131-4308 E-mail: mlong@shutts-law.com.

LONG, SARAH ANN, librarian; b. Atlanta, May 20, 1943; d. Jones Lloyd and Lelia Maria (Mitchell) Sanders; m. James Allen Long, 1961 (div. 1985); children: Andrew C., James Allen IV; m. Donald J. Sager, May 23, 1987. BA, Oglethorpe U., 1966; M in Librarianship, Emory U., 1967. Asst. libr. Coll. of St. Matthias, Bristol, Eng., 1970-74; cons. State Libr. Ohio, Columbus, 1975-77; coord. Pub. Libr. of Columbus and Franklin County, Columbus, 1977-79; dir. Fairfield County Dist. Libr., Lancaster, Ohio, 1979-82, Dauphin County Libr. Sys., Harrisburg, Pa., 1982-85, Multnomah County Libr., Portland, Oreg., 1985-89; sys. dir. North Suburban Libr. Sys., Wheeling, Ill., 1989—. Chmn. Portland State U. Libr. Adv. Coun., 1987-89, bd. dirs. Am. Libr., Paris, 2000-02. Contbr. to weekly column in Daily Herald; monthly cable show Whats New in Libraries; contbr. articles to profl. jours. Bd. dirs. Dauphin County Hist. Soc., Harrisburg, 1983-85, ARC, Harrisburg, 1984-85; pres. Lancaster-Fairfield County YWCA, Lancaster, 1981-82; vice chmn. govt. and ednl. divsn. Lancaster-Fairfield County United Way, Lancaster, 1981-82; sec. Fairfield County Arts Coun., 1981-82; adv. bd. Portland State U., 1987-89; mentor Ohio Libr. Leadership Inst., 1993, 95. Recipient Dir.'s award Ohio Program in Humanities, Columbus, 1982; Sarah Long Day established in her honor Fairfield County, Lancaster, Bd. Commrs., 1982. Mem. ALA (pres. 1999-2000, elected coun. 1993-97, chair Spectrum fund raising com. 2001-02), Pub. Libr. Assn. (pres. 1989-90, chair legis. com. 1991-95, chair 1998, nat. conf. com. 1995-98), Ill. Libr. Assn. (pub. policy com. 1991-97, Librarian of Yr. award 1999), Ill. Libr. Sys. Dirs. Orgn. (pres. 2000—), Libr. Cmty. Found. (bd. dirs. 1995—). Office: N Suburban Libr Systems 200 W Dundee Rd Wheeling IL 60090-4750 Office Phone: 847-459-1300. E-mail: slong@nsls.info.

LONG, SARAH ELIZABETH BRACKNEY, physician; b. Sidney, Ohio, Dec. 5, 1926; d. Robert LeRoy and Caroline Josephine (Shue) Brackney; m. John Frederick Long, June 15, 1948; children: George Lynas, Helen Lucille Corcoran, Harold Roy, Clara Alice Lawrence, Nancy Carol Sieber. BA, Ohio State U., 1948, MD, 1952. Intern Grant Hosp., Columbus, Ohio, 1952-53; resident internal medicine Mt. Carmel Med. Ctr., Columbus, 1966-69, chief resident internal medicine, 1968-69; med. cons. Ohio Bur. Disability Determination, Columbus, 1970—. Physician student health Ohio State U., Columbus, 1970-73; sch. physician Bexley (Ohio) City Schs., 1973-83; physician advisor to peer rev. Mt. Carmel East Hosp., Columbus, 1979-86, med. dir. employee health, 1981-96; physician cons. Fed. Black Lung program U.S. Dept. Labor, Columbus, 1979-98. Mem. AMA, Gerontol. Soc. Am., Ohio Hist. Soc., Ohio State Med. Assn., Franklin County Acad. Medicine, Alpha Epsilon Delta, Phi Beta Kappa. Home: 2765 Bexley Park Rd Columbus OH 43209-2231

LONG, SARAH SUNDBORG, pediatrician, educator; b. Portland, Oreg., Oct. 31, 1944; MD, Jefferson Med. Coll., 1970. Diplomate Am. Bd. Pediat. Intern St. Christopher Hosp. for Children, Phila., 1970-71, resident, 1971-73, fellow pediat. and infectious diseases, 1973-75, staff, 1975—2002; prof. pediat. Drexel U. Coll. Medicine, 2002—. Chief editor: Principles and Practice of Pediatric Infectious Diseases, 1997; assoc. editor Jour. Pediatrics, 1997—; contbr. over 100 articles to med. jours. Mem. Am. Acad. Pediat., Soc. for Pediat. Rsch., Am. Pediat. Soc., Pediatric Diseases Soc. (pres. 1999-2001). Office: St Christopher Child Hosp Sect Infectious Diseases Erie Ave at Front St Philadelphia PA 19134

LONG, SHARON RUGEL, molecular biologist, plant biology educator; b. Mar. 2, 1951; d. Harold Eugene and Florence Jean (Rugel) Long; m. Harold James McGee, July 7, 1979; 2 children. BS, Calif. Inst. Tech., 1973; PhD, Yale U., 1979. Rsch. fellow Harvard U., Cambridge, Mass., 1979-81; from asst. prof. molecular biology to prof. Stanford U., Palo Alto, Calif., 1982-92, prof. biol. scis., 1992—. Investigator Howard Hughes Med. Inst., 1994—; adv. bd. Jane Coffin Childs Meml. Fund; bd. dirs. Ann. Revs. Inc. Assoc. Editor Jour. Bacteriology; assoc. editor Jour. Plant Physiology, 1992—; mem. editl. bd. Devel. Biology; editl. com. Ann. Review Cell Biology. Recipient award NSF, 1979, NIH, 1980, Shell Rsch. Found. award 1985, Presdl. Young Investigator award NSF, 1984-89; grantee NIH, Dept. Energy, NSF; MacArthur fellow, 1992-97, Georges Morel fellow I.N.R.A., France, 1998; fellow Noble Found. Fellow Assn. Women in Sci.; mem. NAS, Genetics Soc. Am., Am. Soc. Plant Physiology (Charles Albert Shull award 1989), Am. Soc. Microbiology, Soc. Devel. Biology. Office: Stanford U Dept Biol Scis 371 Serra Mall Stanford CA 94305-5008

LONG, SHIRLEY JUNE STAFFORD, artist, educator; b. Herrick, Ill., June 28, 1935; d. Victor Ellis Stafford and Goldie Helen O'Daffer; m. James August Henigman, Dec. 24, 1954 (div. 1983); children: Angela, James, Darin, Kriston, Daniel; m. Wilbur Lester Long, Jr., Aug. 20, 1933. Student, Lincoln Land Coll., Tidewater C.C. Instr. Plan an Hierloom, Macon, Ga., 1989—. Exhibitions include Dante's Gallery, 2002—03, Studio 51, 2002—03. Mem.: Am. Impressionist Soc., Atlanta Portrait Soc. (Peoples Choice award 2002), Am. Portrait Soc., Tubman Mus. Home: 5811 Nature Dr Macon GA 31216

LONG, TERESA C. city health department administrator; m. Tom Denune; 1 child, Katherine. MD, U. Calif., San Francisco; MPH, U. Calif., Berkeley. Med. dir., asst. health commr Columbus Health Dept., Ohio, 1986—2002, commr., 2002—; clin. assoc. prof. Ohio State U., Coll. Medicine and Pub. Health. Chair Ctrl. Ohio Med. Dirs. Coalition, Columbus Area Asthma Coalition; co-chair Healthy Columbus Adv. Bd. Recipient Elizabeth Blackwell award for Pioneering Efforts to Improve Women's and Cmty. Health. Mem.: Columbus Med. Assn. (past pres., past pres., bd. trustees found.). Office: Columbus Health Dept 240 Parsons Ave Columbus OH 43215

LONG, VALERIE JEAN, pastor; b. Dayton, Ohio, June 5, 1949; d. Jason C. and Edna M. Browne; m. James DeWitt Long, July 15, 1972; children: Jamie children: Martha Jean Sonner. MusB, Wright State U., 1972; MDiv, United Theol. Sem., Dayton, 1996. Cert. EMT/paramedic Ohio. Dir. music, dir. Christian edn. Englewood (Ohio) United Meth. Ch., 1972—94; music tchr. Northmont City Schs., Englewood, 1975—78; paramedic Randolph Twp. Fire Dept., Englewood, 1983—96, Montgomery County Sheriff's Office, Dayton, 1988—93; assoc. pastor Cmty. United Meth. Ch., Brookville, Ohio, 1994—96, Sulphur Grove United Meth. Ch., Huber Heights, Ohio, 1996—2001; pastor Ware's Chapel United Meth. Ch., West Manchester, Ohio, 2001—. Bd. ordained ministry Dayton North Dist United Meth. Ch., 1998—2001; spiritual dir. Walk to Emmaus, Ohio, 1995—. Trustee United Meth. Cmty. Care, Dayton, 2002—. Avocations: golf, reading, crafts. Office: Ware's Chapel United Meth Ch 1060 Foos Rd West Manchester OH 45382

LONG, VIRGINIA, state supreme court justice; m. Jonathan D. Weiner; 3 children. Grad., Dunbarton Coll. of Holy Cross; JD, Rutgers U., 1966. Dep. atty. gen. State of N.J.; assoc. Pitney, Hardin, Kipp and Szuch; dir. N.J. Divsn. Consumer Affairs, 1975; commr. N.J. Dept. Banking, 1977-78; judge N.J. Superior Ct., 1978-84, Appellate Divsn. N.J. Superior Ct., 1984-95, presiding judge, 1995-99; assoc. justice Supreme Ct. N.J., 1999—. Office: Supreme Ct NJ PO Box 023 Trenton NJ 08625-0970

LONGABERGER, TAMI, home decor accessories company executive; BBA in Mktg., Ohio State U., 1984. Joined Longaberger Co., Newark, Ohio, 1984, pres., 1994, CEO. Trustee Ohio State U.; bd. dirs. Woodrow Wilson Internat. Ctr. Scholars, John Glenn Inst. for Pub. Svc. and Pub. Policy, Ind. U. Found., 1986—. Named to Ohio Women's Hall of Fame. Mem. Direct Selling Assn. (chmn. bd. dirs.), Ohio Fed. Bus. and Profl. Women, Nat. Audobon Soc. (bd. dirs.)

LONGAN, SUZANNE M. retired elementary school educator; b. San Francisco, June 8, 1936; d. Walter Emerson Murfee and Ferne Inez Nelson; m. George B. Longan III, Aug. 27, 1958 (div. June 7, 1965); 1 child, Nancy Ann. BA with distinction, U. Ariz., 1958; postgrad., Calif. State U., 1987—89. Elem. sch. tchr. Johnson County Sch. Dist., Leawood, Kans., 1958—60; corp. sec., CEO Villa Chartier-Lanai, Inc., San Mateo, Calif., 1965—84. Dir. San Mateo County Hotel and Restaurant Assn., 1971—79. Treas. Pre-Sch. for the Visually Handicapped, Kans. City, Mo., 1961—62, chmn. advisory bd., 1963—65; div. chmn. Heart of Am. United Campaign, Kans. City, 1962; chair sch. solicitation Johnson County (Kans.) United Funds, 1963; mem. adv. bd. Children's Mercy Hosp., Kans. City, 1963—65; treas. Music in the Mountains, Nev. City, Calif., 1986—90; mem. bd. trustees Foothill Theatre Co., Nev. City, Calif., 1990—92; treas. Nev. County Land Trust, Nev. City, 1995—97; mem. Emmanuel Episc. Ch. Choir, Grass Valley, Calif., 1981—91; treas., CFO Emmanuel Episc. Ch., Grass Valley, Calif., 1988—91; mem. bd. dirs. Twin Cities Concert Assn., Grass Valley, 1984—86. Named Vol. Nurse Aide, Am. Red Cross, 1964, Concessionaire Extraordinaire, Foothill Theatre Co., 1986—87, Master Gardener, U. Calif., 1990; recipient Cmty. Svc. award, United Funds Coun., Inc., 1963. Mem.: Jr. League, Gamma Phi Beta. Republican. Episcopalian. Avocations: gardening, wildlife habitat maintenance. Home: 13350 Wildwood Heights Dr Penn Valley CA 95946

LONGDEN, CLAIRE SUZANNE, retired financial planner, investment advisor; b. Sheffield, Yorkshire, Eng., June 2, 1938; came to U.S., 1964; d. John Stewart and Daisy (Heath) L. Diploma in pvt. sec., Coll. Commerce & Tech., Sheffield, 1956; cert. in Fin. Planning, Coll. Fin. Planning, 1979. Sec., Sheffield, 1956-62; G-4 asst. UN/WHO, Geneva, Switzerland, 1962-64; pvt. sec. Arthur Wiesenberger, N.Y.C., 1966-70; v.p. Alex Brown & Sons, N.Y.C., 1970-75; 1st v.p. Butcher & Singer, N.Y.C., 1975-89; pres. Claire Longden Assocs., Rhinebeck, N.Y., 1989-98. Adj. prof. fin. planning NYU, 1981-82. Conf. speaker 1980-86; contbr. articles to profl. jours. Bd. dirs. No. Dutchess Hosp., Rhinebeck, 1989-98, pres., 1995-96; bd. dirs. Cross River Healthcare, 1997-98, No. Dutchess Hosp. Found., 1997-99. Named one of Top Planners Nationwide, Money mag., 1987. Mem. Inst. CFPs (nat. bd. dirs. 1984-86, founder, N.Y.C. chpt. 1982-86, N.E. regional dir. 1985-86, bd. of ethics 1993-95, Cert. Fin. Planner of Yr. 1984), Womens Bond Club N.Y. (pres. 1982-84), Inst. Am. Fin. Planners (bd. dirs. 1983-85), Registry Fin. Planning Practitioners, Rotary (pres. Rhinebeck chpt. 1993-94). Avocations: gardening, swimming, walking, riding, skiing.

LONGENECKER, MARTHA W. museum director; BA in Art, UCLA; MFA, Claremont Grad. Sch.; studied with Millard Sheets, Shoji Hamada, Tatsuzo Shimaoka. Owner ceramics studio, Claremont, Calif.; prof. art, now prof. emeritus San Diego State U.; founder, dir. Mingei Internat. Mus., San Diego. Coord. editing, design and prodn. of exhbn. documentary publs. Mingei Internat. Mus. World Folk Art.; condr. tours. Contbr. chpts. to books; developer videotapes; exhibited at Dalzell Hatfield Galleries. San Diego State U. Found. grantee, 1967, Calif. State U. Rsch. grantee, 1978; recipient Disting. Alumna award Claremont Grad. Sch., 1980, Essence of Life award ElderHelp of San Diego, 1993, Living Legacy award Women's Internat. Ctr., 1994, Women of Distinction award Soroptimist Internat. of La Jolla, 1994. Office: Mingei Internat Mus Balboa Park 1439 El Prado San Diego CA 92101-1617 also: Mingei Internat Mus PO Box 553 La Jolla CA 92038-0553

LONGLEY, MARJORIE WATTERS, newspaper executive; b. Lockport, N.Y., Nov. 2, 1925; d. J. Randolph and Florence Lucille (Craine) Watters; m. Ralph R. Longley, Oct. 1, 1949 (dec.). BA in English with highest honors cum laude, St. Lawrence U., 1947. Sports editor, feature writer Lockport Union Sun and Jour., 1945; with N.Y. Times, N.Y.C., 1948-88, asst. to v.p. consumer mktg., 1975-78, circulation sales mgr., 1978-79, sales dir., 1979-81, dir. pub. affairs, 1981-88; pres. Gramercy Internat., Inc. (mktg. and pub. rels.), N.Y.C., 1988—; assoc. pub. The Earth Times, N.Y.C., 1996—. Dir. pub. affairs and pub. info., N.Y.C. Off-Track Betting Corp., 1990-94; mem. Nat. Newspapers' Readership Coun., 1979-82; mem. adv. coun. API, 1980-85. Author: America's Taste, 1960. Trustee St. Lawrence U., 1969-75, 77—; chmn. bd. dirs. Am. Forum for Global Edn., 1977-98, chmn. emerita, 1999—; pres. N.Y. City Adult Edn. Coun., 1974-77, Grmercy Pk. Lot Owners Assn., Inc., 1995—; mem. N.Y. State Adv. Coun. for Vocat. Edn, 1976-81, postsecondary edn., 1978-81, Mayor's Coun. Environment of N.Y.C., 1983-96; bd. dirs. Nat. Charities Info. Bur., 1983-96, Literacy Ptnrs., Inc., 1996—; chmn. 42d St. Edn., Theatre, Culture, 1984-88, chmn. emeritus, 1988—. Mem. Nat. Inst. Social Scis., Am. Mgmt. Assn. (nat. mktg. coun. 1972-89, bd. dirs. 1986-88), Nat. Arts Club, Overseas Press Club, Phi Beta Kappa. Democrat. Baptist. Office: Gramercy Internat Inc 34 Gramercy Park E New York NY 10003-1731

LONGMAID, KATE JESSAMYN, psychologist; b. Bryn Mawr, Pa., Oct. 7, 1960; d. Deborah Flint and David Dunlop Longmaid; m. Stephen Christopher Baad, Sept. 1, 1985; children: Olivia Longmaid Baad, Alexander Longmaid Baad. BA in Psychology and Art, U. Mich., 1983; MEd in Clin. Psychology, U. Va., Charlottesville, 1988, PhD in Clin. Psychology, 1994. Lic. psychologist Vt., 1994. Dir. of the ctr. for psychol. services St. Michael's Coll., Colchester, Vt., 1994—95, adj. lectr. in psychology, 1995—96; pvt. practice Burlington, Vt., 1995—; clin. asst. prof. U. of Vt. Coll. of Medicine, Dept. of Family Practice, Burlington, Vt., 1999—2003; group therapist, coping together project U. of Vt., Dept. of Psychology, Burlington, Vt., 1999—2002; course co-leader U. of Vt. Coll. of Medicine, Burlington, Vt., 1997—2000; predoctoral fellow in psychology Dartmouth Med. Sch., Dept. of Psychiatry, Lebanon, NH, 1992—93, postdoctoral fellow in psychology, 1993—94, adj. asst. prof. of psychiatry, 1995—98; group therapist, cancer patient support program Fletcher Allen Health Care, Burlington, Vt., 2003—. Contbr. articles to profl. jours. Bd. dirs. Child Care Resource, Williston, Vt., 1996—97. Mem.: APA, Vt. Psychol. Assn., Inc., Vt. Assn. of Sch. Psychologists (assoc.). Office: 92 Adams St Burlington VT 05401

LONG-MAST, PEGGY, state representative; b. Norton, Kans., Aug. 20, 1948; m. John C. Long-Mast; 4 children. Student, Emporia State U., Butler County C.C. Mgr. fin. Mast Engring.; mem. Kans. Ho. of Reps., 1997—. Mem. Greenwood County Econ-Devel.; chmn. platform com. Rep. Party, 1996. Mem.: Am. Bus. Women (vice-chair health and human resources), Greenwood County Rep. Women, Greenwood County Cattlewomen. Office: 446-N State Capitol 300 SW 10th Ave Topeka KS 66612 Home: 765 Rd 110 Emporia KS 66801

LONG-MIDDLETON, ELLEN, family nurse practitioner, educator, researcher; b. Danville, Pa., June 14, 1954; d. Samuel Murray and Dorothy Morgan (Wasley) Long; m. Jeffrey Long-Middleton, Sept. 5, 1981; children: Matthew, Andrew, Douglas, Samuel. BS, U. Vt., 1976; MN, U. Wash., 1982; PhD, Boston Coll., 2001. Cert. family nurse practitioner. Nurse practitioner emergency dept. Hosp. of U. Pa., Phila., 1985—88, nursing dir. admission evaluation ctr., 1988—90; nursing dir. family practice Family Health Svcs., Worcester, Mass., 1990—94; family nurse practitioner U. Mass. Meml. Health Care, 1990—2001; instr. Boston Coll., 1994-98; project co-dir. MassHealth Workforce Devel. Project U. Mass. Med. Sch., 1998—2001; nursing fellow Children's Hosp. of Boston, 1999—2000; asst. prof., coord. family nurse practitioner specialty Mass. Gen. Hosp. Inst. Health Professions, 2001—; family nurse practitioner Family Health Ctr. of Worcester, 2002—. Lectr. U. Pa., 1985-89 Recipient Nat. Rsch. Svc. award Nat. Inst. Nursing Rsch., 1997-2000. Mem. Sigma Theta Tau. E-mail: elongmiddleton@mghihp.edu.

LONGMIRE, VENUS DELOYSE, minister; b. Greenville, Ala., July 21, 1945; d. James Wilbert and Estelle Golson Longmire; m. Melvin Robinson II, July 22, 1966 (div. Nov. 1975); 1 child, Melvin Longmire Robinson III

; m. Amon Olugbala Ra, July 28, 2000. BS, Livingstone Coll., 1965; MSW, Ind. U., 1970; M in Theology, Emory U., 1982; D in Theology (hon.), U. Life Ch. Inst., San Fafael, Calif., 1989; PhD, Columbia Pacific U., 1989; D in Divinty (hon.), New Covenant Inst., 1995. Family svcs. supr. City of Atlanta Housing Authority, 1973—76; v.p. contract develop. Longmire Coal Corp., Knoxville, Tenn., 1976—86; dir. religious develop. Ala. State U., Montgomery, 1987—90; med. social worker State of Ala. Dept. Pub. Health, Hayneville, 1991—92; dir. min. The Sisterhood, Inc., Greenville, 1992—. Grant writer cons., 1965—; cons. energy develop. Del Kijaico Inc., Wilmington, Del., 1990—2002. Author: (prose) As We Are, So Is Our World, 1982; author, editor: Mother's Voice: Lost Writings of Mary, 2003. Mem. Hist. Perservation Soc., Montgomery, 1999—2003; advisor, sponsor Saving Our Cmty. & Kids, Greenville High, Ala. Named Cmty. Advocate, City of Atlanta, 1975; named one of Women in Bus., Knoxville Jour., 1983; recipient Ala. Treasure Forestry award, Forestry Commn., USDA, 2003. Mem.: So. Proverty Law Ctr., Coun. on Aging (lobbyist 1995—), Nat. Assn. Social Workers (lobbyist 1983—). Democrat. Methodist. Avocations: running, chess. Home: 101 N Haardt Dr Montgomery AL 36105 Office: New Covenant Inst Human Svc Ministries 236 W Commerce St Greenville AL 36037 Office Phone: 334-263-1733. E-mail: venuslongmire@aol.com.

LONGO, AMY L. lawyer; BSN, Creighton U., 1970, JD, 1979. Bar: Nebr. 1979. Ptnr. Ellick, Jones, Buelt, Blazek & Longo, Omaha. Mem. moot ct. bd., adj. asst. prof. law Coll. Medicine, U. Nebr., 1987—. Fellow Am. Bar Found.; mem. ABA (del. 1993), Nebr. State Bar Assn. (pres.-elect, ho. dels. 1984—, chair 1996), Omaha Bar Assn. Office: Ellick Jones Buelt Blazek & Longo 8805 Indian Hills Dr Ste 280 Omaha NE 68114-4077

LONGOBARDO, ANNA KAZANJIAN, engineering executive; b. N.Y.C. d. Aram Michael and Zarouhy (Yazejian) Kazanjian; m. Guy S. Longobardo, July 12, 1952; children: Guy A., Alicia. Student, Barnard Coll., 1947; BSME, Columbia U., 1949, MSME, 1952. Sr. systems engr. Am. Bosch Arma Corp., Garden City, N.Y., 1950-65; rsch. sect. head Sperry Rand Corp., Gt. Neck, N.Y., 1965-68, rsch. sect. head systems mgmt., 1968-73; mgr. engring. personnel utilization Sperry Corp., Gt. Neck, 1973-77, mgr. systems mgmt. program planning, 1977-81, mgr. planning systems mgmt. group, 1981-82, dir. tech. svc. sys. devel., 1982-89, dir. field engring., 1989-93; dir. strategic initiatives Unysis Corp., Gt. Neck, 1993-95; bd. dirs. Engring. Found. Gateway Engring. Edn. Coalition, 1998—, also bd. dirs.; vice chmn. Engring. Conf. Found. Bd., 2001—. Chmn. exec. compensation com. Woodward-Clyde Group, Denver, 1989-97. Contbr. articles to profl. publs. Trustee Columbia U., N.Y.C., 1990-96, trustee emerita, 1996—; mem. Columbia Engring. Coun., 1987—, chmn., 1987-91; mem. Bronxville (N.Y.) Planning Bd.; chmn. Bronxville Design Rev. Com., 1993—; pres. Soc. Columbia Grads., 1998-2000. Recipient hon. citation Wilson Coll. Centennial, 1970, Alumni medal for conspicuous svc. Columbia U., 1980, Egleston medal for disting. engring. achievement Columbia U., 1997; named One of 100 N.Y. Women of Influence, New York Woman mag., 1986. Fellow Soc. Women Engrs. (founder, pioneer); mem. AIAA (sr.), ASME (sr.), Columbia U. Engring. Alumni Assn. (pres. 1977-81), Columbia U. Alumni Fedn. (pres. 1981-85), Bronxville Field Club.

LONGSTREET, WILMA S. curriculum and instruction educator; b. N.Y.C., July 3, 1935; d. Hyman Steinberg and Estelle Rosa; widowed; stepchildren: Patricia, Robert, Richard Engle. BA, Hunter Coll., 1956; MS, Ind. U., 1968, PhD, 1970. Cert. tchr., N.Y.C. Asst prof. U. Ill., Champaign/Urbana, 1970-72; from assoc. prof. to prof. edn. U. Mich., Flint and Ann Arbor, 1972-78; dean, prof. edn. DePaul U., Chgo., 1978-82; dean edn. U. New Orleans, 1982-85, prof. curriculum and instrn., 1982—. Mem. Coll. and Univ. Faculty Assembly, 1970—, pres., 1999; cons. to sch. sys., Gary, Ind., Flint, Mich., New Orleans, State of Ind. Author: Aspects of Ethnicity, 1978, The Leaders and the Led, 1979; co-author: A Design for Social Education, 1972, (with Shirley H. Engle) Curriculum for a New Millennium, 1993; contbr. over 70 articles to profl. jours. Mem. Profs. of Curriculum (factotum, chair nominating com. 2001), Phi Delta Kappa. Democrat. Unitarian-Universalist. Home: 49 Gull St New Orleans LA 70148 Office: U New Orleans Coll Edn New Orleans LA 70148 E-mail: wlongstr@uno.edu.

LONGSWORTH, ELLEN LOUISE, art historian, consultant; b. Auburn, Ind., Aug. 21, 1949; d. Robert Smith and Alice Louise (Whitten) L.; m. Frederic Sanderson Stott, Sept. 1, 1973 (div. 1981); m. Joseph Nicholas Teta, June 15, 1991. BA, Mt. Holyoke Coll., 1971; MA, U. Chgo., 1976; PhD, Boston U., 1987. Trainer, designer Polaris Enterprises Corp., Quincy, Mass., 1981-82, asst. v.p., 1982-84, cons., 1989-93; from asst. prof. to assoc. prof. Merrimack Coll., N. Andover, Mass., 1985-95, prof., 1995—, chmn. dept., 1993-2000. Adj. instr. art and art history Bradford Coll., Haverhill, Mass., 1975-80; vis. lectr. art history Lowell (Mass.) U., 1981-82, Boston U., 1982-86, 88, 91, Babson Coll., Wellesley, Mass., 1984-85. Active Merrimack Valley Coun. on the Arts and Humanities, Haverhill, 1975-78, Friends of Kimball Tavern, Bradford Coll., Haverhill, 1975-80, Haverhill Arts Commn., 1996-2002; bd. dirs. Winnekenni Found., Haverhill, 1990— Grantee Faculty Devel., Merrimack Coll., 1989-90, 92-93, 95, 97, 2002, Kress Summer Travel, Boston U., 1980, 86, recipient in-house Ciejek fellowship for humanistic rsch., 1998; Boston U. fellow, 1980-82, 85; recipient internship Isabella Stewart Gardner Mus., Boston, 1979-80. Mem. AAUW, Coll. Art Assn., South-Ctrl. Renaissance Conf. (exec. com. 1998-2002), Italian Art Soc., Renaissance Soc. Am. Republican. Methodist. Avocations: reading, playing the piano, painting and drawing, weight training, swimming. Home: 649 Main St Haverhill MA 01830-2647 Office: Merrimack Coll North Andover MA 01845 E-mail: ellen.Longsworth@merrimack.edu.

LONSTEIN, SHOSHANNA, fashion designer; b. NYC; BA, UCLA, 1997. Fashion designer, NYC, 1998—; contbr. editor Cosmopolitan, 1999. Fashion cons. E! network and WNBC's Today in NY.

LOO, BEVERLY JANE, publishing company executive; b. L.A. d. Richard Y. and Bessie E. Sue Loo. BA, U. Calif., Berkeley. Dir. subs. rights Prentice-Hall, Inc., N.Y.C., 1957-59; fiction editor McCall's mag., 1959-62; exec. editor and dir. subs. rights, gen. books div. McGraw-Hill Book Co., N.Y.C., 1962-82; pres. Beverly Jane Loo Assocs., Inc., N.Y.C., 1982-85; sr. editor, dir. subs. rights World Almanac Pharos Books, N.Y.C., 1985-88; dir. mktg. and subs. rights Paragon House, N.Y.C., 1988-91; dir. mktg. and sales Thomasson-Grant, Charlottesville, Va., 1991-93; dir. pub. and comm. inst. U. Va. Sch. Continuing Edn. & Profl. Studies, Charlottesville, 1993—. Mem.: Arts (London); Overseas Press (N.Y.C.); Va. Writers; U. Va. Faculty. Home: Lewis & Clark Sq # 701 250 W Main St Charlottesville VA 22902-5079 Office: Zehmer Hall 104 Midmont Ln Charlottesville VA 22904-4764

LOO, KATHERINE HAUGHEY, nonprofit organization consultant; b. Concordia, Kans., June 24, 1939; d. James M. and Katherine (Hurd) Haughey; m. Lester B. Loo, June 14, 1961; children: Susan Loo Pattee, James O. BA in Polit. Sci., U. Kans., 1961. Pres. Jr. League, Colorado Springs, Colo., 1974-75, Brockhurst Boy's Ranch, Colorado Springs, Colo., 1975-77; dir. Assn. Jr. Leagues, N.Y.C., 1976-78; pres., founder docent aux., chair capital campaign Cheyenne Mt. Zoo, Colorado Springs, 1969-94; dir. UMB Bank Colo., Colorado Springs, 1994-99. Mem. Colorado Springs Urban Renewal Bd., 1979-85; pres. Colo. Women's Forum, 1990-91; founder, bd. dirs. Colo. Women's Found.; hon. trustee Cheyenne Mt. Zoo, 1994—, Colo. Nature Conservancy, 1998—; bd. dirs., v.p. Pikes Peak Cmty. Found., 1998—; co-chmn. Heart of the West Cap. Campaign. Composer, performer piano music. Councilwoman City of Colorado Springs, 1979-85; vice chair Colo. Commn. on Higher Edn., Denver, 1985-87; trustee, chair music dir. search com. Colorado Springs Symphony, 1994-95; mem. Colorado Springs Leadership Inst., 1997—. Recipient Silver Bell award Assistance League, Colorado Springs, 1975. Mem. Broadmoor Garden Club (civic chair 1992-94), Phi Beta Kappa. Avocations: weaving, piano, hiking, biking, composing. Home: 19 Northgate Rd Colorado Springs CO 80906-4331

LOOBY, EUGENIE JOAN, dean, educator; b. Antigua, Brit. West Indies, Dec. 22, 1956; arrived in Virgin Islands, 1962; d. Herman Donald Looby, Daisybelle Romanita (Samuel) Looby. BA, U. V.I., 1978; MA, U. Ill., 1982; PhD, U. Ga., 1994. Lic. profl. counselor Miss., 1993, nat. cert. counselor. Tchr. English St. Dunstan's Episc. Sch., St. Croix, 1978—80, Charlotte Amalie H.S., St. Thomas, 1982—85; grad. asst., counseling intern U. Ga., Athens, 1985—89; therapist Counseling Ctr. S.C. State U., Orangeburg, 1989—92; prof. counseling Miss. State U., Starkville, 1993—, asst. dean edn., 1999—2002, diversity cons., 1999—. Tchg. fellow Va. Polytech. State U., Blacksburg, 1993. Contbr. articles to profl. jours.; co-author: Multicultural Counseling: Context, Theory and Practice, and Competence, 2002. Edit. bd. Jour. of Humanistic Counseling, Edn., and Devel., Miss. Counseling Jour., Counseling and values. Mem.: Nat. Assn. Multicultural Rehab. Concerns, Assn. Multicultural Counseling and Devel., Assn. Counselor Edn. and Supervision, Assn. for Spiritual, Ethical, and Religious Values in Counseling (bd. dirs.), Mid-South Ednl. Rsch. Assn., Am. Counseling Assn., Chi Sigma Iota. Avocation: Avocations: travel, reading, music, home decorating, cooking. Home: 200 Margaretta Dr Starkville MS 39759 Office: Miss State Univ PO Box 9727 Starkville MS 39762

LOOK, DONA JEAN, artist; b. Port Washington, Wis., Mar. 30, 1948; m. Kenneth W. Loeber. BA, U. Wis., Oshkosh, 1970. Art tchr. Dept. Edn., NSW, Australia, 1976-78; ptnr. Look and Heaney Studio, Byron Bay, NSW, 1978-80; studio artist Algoma, Wis., 1980—. One person shows include Perimeter Gallery, Chgo., 1991; exhibited in group shows Perimeter Gallery, Chgo., 1983, 93, 94, Phila. Mus. Art, 1984, Civic Fine Arts Mus., Sioux Falls, S.D., 1985, Dacotah Prairie Mus., Aberdeen, S.D., 1985, Bergstrom Mahler Mus., Neenah, Wis., 1985, Lawton Gallery, U. Wis.-Green Bay, 1985, J. B. Speed Art Mus., Louisville, 1986, Laguna (Calif.) Art Mus., Am. Craft Mus., N.Y.C., 1985, 86, 87, 89, Ark. Arts Ctr. Decorative Arts Mus., Little Rock, 1987, Cultural Ctr., Chgo., 1988, Erie (Pa.) Art Mus., 1988, Maine Crafts Assn., Colby Coll. Mus. Art, 1989, Ft. Wayne (Ind.) Mus. Art, 1989, The Forum, St. Louis, 1990, Palo Alto (Calif.) Cultural Ctr., 1990, Neville Pub. Mus., Green Bay, Wis., 1992, Waterloo (Iowa) Mus. Art, 1993, Sybaris Gallery, Royal Oak, Mich., 1993, 95, Sun Valley Ctr. for Arts and Humanities, Ketchum, Idaho, 1995, Nat. Mus. Am. Art, Smithsonian Instn., Washington, 1995; represented in permanent collections The White House Collection, Phila. Mus. Art, MCI Telecomms. Corp., Inc., Washington, Am. Craft Mus., N.Y.C., Ark. Arts Ctr., Little Rock, C. A. Wustum Mus. Fine Arts, Racine, Erie Art Mus.; works included in publs. The White House Collection of American Crafts, 1995, Craft Today: Poetry of the Physical, 1986, International Crafts, 1991, FIBERARTS Design Book Four, 1991, The Tactile Vessel, 1989, Creative Ideas for Living, 1988, The Basketmaker's Art: Contemporary Baskets and Their Makers, 1986. Recipient 1st prize award Phila. Craft Show, 1984, 2d prize award, 1985, Design award Am. Craft Mus., 1985, Craftsmen's award Phila. Craft Show, 1986; Nat. Endowment for Arts/Arts Midwest fellow, 1987, Nat. Endowment for Arts Fellowship grantee, 1988. Office: Perimeter Gallery 210 W Superior St Chicago IL 60610-3508

LOOMAN, MARY DALE, psychologist, forensic specialist, consultant; b. Portsmouth, Va., Jan. 16, 1952; d. Charles Dale and Mary Elizabeth (Hanson) Schuman; m. Paul D. Looman, May 14, 1999; children from previous marriage: Calypso Mari Gilstrap, Adrianna Elizabeth Cherry. BA in Corrections, Washburn U., Topeka, Kans., 1977; MA in Adminstrn., Wichita State U., 1979; MS in Counseling, Pitts. (Kans.) State U., 1995; PhD in Clin. Psychology, Fielding Grad. Inst., Santa Barbara, Calif., 2002. Cert. counselor NACC, profl. counselor Okla., clin. forensic counselor ACCFC. Psychologist asst. Kans. Dept. of Corrections, Topeka, 1977—79; dept. mgr. Hallmark Cards, Inc., Kans. City, Mo., 1979—92; dir. Mo. Dept. of Mental Health, Joplin, 1992—95; pvt. practice counselor Grove, Okla., 1995—99; intern forensic psychologist N.E. Okla. Psychology Program, Vinita, Okla., 1999—2000; adj. prof. Kans. City (Kans.) C.C., 2001; forensic psychologist Dept. of Corrections, Okla. City, 2002—. Cons. in leadership skills, 1995—; dissertation adv. to doctoral students, 2003—. Author: Supr. Trainee Relationship, 2002; contbr. articles to profl. jours. Lobbyist Kans. Juvenile Detention Assn., Topeka, 1975—80; vol. hosp. chaplain Grove (Okla.) Gen. Hosp., 1995—98. Recipient Canter Edn. and Tng. award, Am. Psychologists Assn., 2001. Mem.: Am. Corrections Assn., Am. Assn. of Christian Counselors (charter mem.), Am. Coll. of Cert. Forensic Counselors (clin. mem.), Chi Sigma Iota. Achievements include initiation of revision of Kans. Juvenile Code to include treatment protocols; research in effect of supr.- trainee relationship on trainee devel. Avocations: writing, blueberry farm, equestrian activities. Office: JH Correctional Ctr PO Box 548 Lexington OK Business E-Mail: mary.looman@eloc.state.ok.us.

LOOMIS, CAROL J. journalist; b. Marshfield, Mo., June 25, 1929; d. Harold and Mildred (Coco) Junge; m. John R. Loomis, Mar. 19, 1960; children: Barbara, Mark. Student, Drury Coll., 1947-49; B in Journalism, U. Mo., 1951. Editor Maytag News, Maytag Co., Newton, Iowa, 1951-54; rsch. assoc. Fortune mag., N.Y.C., 1954-58, assoc. editor, 1958-68, mem. bd. editors, 1968—. Office: Fortune Mag 1271 Avenue Of The Americas New York NY 10020-1300

LOOMIS, JACQUELINE CHALMERS, photographer; b. Hong Kong, Mar. 9, 1930; parents Am. citizens; d. Earl John and Jennie Bell (Sherwood) Chalmers; m. Charles Judson Williams III, Dec. 2, 1950 (div. Aug. 1973); children: Charles Judson IV, John C., David F., Robert W.; m. Henry Loomis, Jan. 19, 1974; stepchildren: Henry S., Mary Loomis Hankinson, Lucy F., Gordon M. Student, U. Oreg., 1948-50, U. Mo., 1979. Pres. J. Sherwood Chalmers Photographer, Jacksonville, Fla., 1979—, Windward Corp., Washington, 1984—. Contbr. photos to Nat. Geographic books and mag., Fortune mag., Nat. Newspapers, Ducks Unltd., Living Bird Quar., Orvis News, Frontiers Internat., others, also caneldars; one-woman show Woodbury-Blair Mansion, Washington, 1980; rep. in pub. and pvt. collections. Trustee Sta. WJCT-TV, Jacksonville, 1965-73, mem. exec. com., 1965-66; co-chmn. Arts Festival, Jacksonville, 1970, chmn., 1971; bd. dirs., mem. exec. com. Nat. Friends Pub. Broadcasting, N.Y.C., 1970-73; bd. dirs. Washington Opera, 1976-87, Pub. Broadcasting Svcs., Washington, 1972-73, Planned Parenthood of North Fla., 1968-70; bd. dirs. Jacksonville Art Mus., 1968-70, treas., 1968; bd. dirs. Jacksonville Symphony Assn., 1988-94, Children's Home Soc. of Fla., 1988-96. Recipient Cultural Arts award Jacksonville Coun. Arts, 1971, award Easton Waterfowl Festival, 1982, 1st and 2d prizes, 1984. Mem. Profl. Photographers Am. (merit award 1982), Photog. Soc. Am., Am. Soc. Picture Profls., Jr. League Jacksonville Inc., Fla. Yacht Club (Jacksonville), Timuquana Country Club (Fla.), Chattooga Club (N.C.), Republican. Presbyterian. Avocations: travel, golf, sailing, skiing, riding. Home and Office: 4661 Ortega Island Dr Jacksonville FL 32210-7500

LOOMIS, NORMA IRENE, marriage and family therapist; b. Dunlap, Ind., May 6, 1941; d. Edwin Clifford and Lucille DeVere (Hall) Dick; m. Edwin Dale Loomis; children: William Dale, James Vernon. BS in Edn., Western Mich. U., 1973, MA in Edn., 1976; PhD in Christian Counseling, Rocky Mountin Inc., 1990. Cert. marriage and family therapist. Tchr. Cassopolis (Mich.) Schs., 1973—; counseling Christian Counseling Svcs., Goshen, Ind., 1985—. Presenter Elkhart (Ind.) Pub. Schs., 1992—95, Middlebury (Ind.) Pub. Schs., 1992—94, Elkhart Ct., 1995—97; pres. Champion Reality Inc., Elkhart, 1983—; founder, pres. Soaring As Women of Value, 2001. Contbr. articles to profl. publs.; author tchg. materials Hot Shots Prodns. Mem. Cmty. Corrections Adv. Bd., Elkhart County, 1994—; pres. Juniper Beach Assn., Mears, Mich., 1985-96, Women in Action, Elkhart, 1985-94. Mem. ACA, Am. Mental Health Counselors Assn., Ind. Counselors Assn. for Alcohol and Drug Abuse, Am. Assn. Christian Counselors, Christian Assn. Psychol. Studies. Republican. Mem. Bretheran Ch. Avocations: swimming, boating, bowling, crafts. Home: 22650 Lake Shore Dr Elkhart IN 46514-9570 Office: Christian Counseling Svcs 333 E Madison St Goshen IN 46526-3429 E-mail: ml641@juno.com.

LOOMIS, REBECCA C. psychology educator; b. New London, Conn., Nov. 9, 1959; d. Aubrey Kingsley and Marillyn Louise (Dirks) Loomis; m. DeWitt Montgomery Smith, Nov. 24, 1984 (div. Sept. 1997); children: Adrienne Kingsley Smith, Walker Loomis Smith. BA in Sociology and Polit. Sci., Vanderbilt U., 1981; MEd, U. Houston, 1990, postgrad. Group rep. Home Life Ins., Houston, 1981—83; sr. account exec. CNA Ins. Co., Houston, 1983—87; rsch. asst. dept. ednl. psychology U. Houston, 1988—90, 1991—93, tchg. asst., 1993, rsch. asst. Clearwater, Tex., 1993, rsch. assoc., 1999—; acad. advisor Montclair (N.J.) State U., 2001—02; psychology intern Assn. Help of Retarded Children, N.Y.C., 2002—03; prin. investigator Manhattan Ctr. for Pain Mgmt./St. Luke's-Roosevelt Hosp., N.Y.C., NY, 2001—; clinician Assn. for Help of Retarded Children, N.Y.C., 2003—. Group facilitator children div. parents, counselor Houston Child Guidance, 1990; counselor learning support svcs. U. Houston, 1990, counselor counseling and testing svcs., 1994—95; facilitator mentorship program Wildwood Elem. Sch., Mountain Lakes, NJ, 1996. Contbr. articles to various profl. jours. Hospice aid Casa de Ninos Hospice, Houston, 1986—87; vol. Houston Area Women's Ctr., 1992—93, 1994—95; cmty. aid Mountain Lakes, 1999—; vol. organizer grief workshop for September 11, 2001 attacks Cmty. Ch. Mem.: APA, N.J. Psychol. Assn. Democrat. Home and Office: 82 Briarcliff Rd Mountain Lakes NJ 07046 E-mail: beckyloomis@earthlink.net.

LOONEY, CLAUDIA ARLENE, healthcare administrator; b. Fullerton, Calif., June 13, 1946; d. Donald F. and Mildred B. Schneider; m. James K. Looney, Oct. 8, 1967; 1 child, Christopher K. BA, Calif. State U., 1969. Dir. youth YWCA No. Orange County, Fullerton, Calif., 1967-70; dir. dist. Camp Fire Girls, San Francisco, 1971-73, asst. exec. dir. L.A., 1973-77; asst. dir. cmty. resources Childrens Hosp., L.A., 1977-80; dir. cmty. devel. Orthopaedic Hosp., L.A., 1980-82; sr. v.p. Saddleback Meml. Found./Saddleback Meml. Med. Ctr., Laguna Hills, Calif., 1982-92; v.p. planning and advancement Calif. Inst. Arts, Santa Clarita, Calif., 1992-96; pres. Northwestern Meml. Found., Chgo., Ill., 1996-99; sr. v.p. Childrens Hosp., L.A., 1999—. Instr. U. Calif., Irvine, Univ. Irvine; mem. steering com. U. Irvine. Steering com. United Way, L.A., 1984-86. Fellow Assn. Healthcare Philanthropy (nat. chair-elect, chmn. program Nat. Edn. Conf. 1986, regional dir. 1985-89, 98, fin. com. 1988—, pres., com. chn. 1987—, Give To Life com. chmn. 1987-91, mid-west regional conf. chmn. 1998, Orange County Fund Raiser of Yr. 1992, L.A. County fund raiser of yr. 1996), mem. Nat. Soc. Fund Raising Execs. Found. (cert., vice chmn. 1985-90, chair 1993—, mem. Chgo. conf. com. 1997, 98), So. Calif. Assn. Hosp. Devel. (past pres., bd. dirs.), Profl. Ptnrs. (chmn. 1986, instr. 1988—), Philanthropic Ednl. Orgn. (past pres.), Assn. for Healthcare Profls. (regional conf. co-chmn. 2003), Assn. Fundraising Profls. (mem. internat. ethics com. 2004—). Avocations: swimming, sailing, photography. Office: Children's Hosp LA 4650 Sunset Blvd Ste 29 Los Angeles CA 90027

LOOS, ROBERTA ALEXIS, advocate, artist, educator; b. Haddonfield, N.J., Dec. 14, 1943; d. John Thompson Loos and Margaret Gladous Browning; children: James Gray Kane, Alexis Browning Kane. B of Design in Art Edn., U. Fla., 1967. Cert. art edn. K-12 Fla. and Md. State Bds. Edn., 1968. Secondary art and English tchr. Montgomery County Pub. Schs., Silver Spring, Md., 1968—71; pres. Kane Corp. Consultants, Inc., 1982—. Mem. Fla. Arts Coun., 1981—85; mem. panel talent bank Nat. Endowment for the Arts, 1983; mem. Fine Arts Coun. Fla., 1981; mem. adv. coun. Art in Pub. Places, 1989; bd. dirs. Broward County Art in Pub. Places, 1981—83; chair Broward Arts Coun., 1981—83. Mem. publs. com. Broward County Hist. Commn., 1979; mem. pollutiuon control subcom. Broward County Charter Commn., 1974—75; mem. Broward County Pullution Control Bd., 1974—75, City of Ft. Lauderdale Charter Revision Bd., 1990—94; mem. internat. swimming hall of fame subcom. City of Ft. Lauderdale Gen. Obligation Bond Project, 1989—90. Mem.: Order of the Daus. of the King. Home: 2625 NE 26th Ct Fort Lauderdale FL 33306-1701

LOOSER, DEVONEY KAY, English literature educator; b. St. Paul, Apr. 11, 1967; d. LeRoy Joseph and Sharon Lee Ann (Sarslow) Looser; m. George Lewis Justice, 1996; 1 child, Carl Anchor Justice. BA, Augsburg Coll., 1989; PhD, SUNY, Stony Brook, 1993. Instr. English SUNY, Stony Brook, 1989-93; asst. prof. English Ind. State U., Terre Haute, 1993-98, acting dir. women's studies, 1997-98; asst. prof. women's studies U. Wis., Whitewater, 1998-2000; vis. asst. prof. English Ariz. State U., 2000-2001; asst. prof. English La. State U., 2001—02, U. Mo., Columbia, 2002—. Author: British Women Writers and the Writing of History, 1670-1820, 2000 (Choice Outstanding Acad. Title award 2001); editor: Jane Austen and Discourses of Feminism, 1995; co-editor: (with E. Ann Kaplan) Generations: Academic Feminists in Dialogue, 1997; contbr. articles to profl. jours. Fellow, NEH, 1994, Nat. Humanities Ctr. Inst., 2003. Mem. MLA (exec. com. late eighteenth century divsn. 2004—, exec. com. Midwestsect. 2004—), Am. Soc. Eighteenth Century Studies, Jane Austen Soc. N.Am. (bd. dirs. 2000-02), Nat. Women's Studies Assn., N.Am. Soc. Study of Romanticism. Office: U Mo Columbia Dept English Columbia MO 65211 E-mail: looserd@missouri.edu.

LOPAT, ROMALDA REGINA, publisher, editor; b. Bridgeport, Conn., Aug. 2, 1954; d. Francis George and Susan Jane (Hermenze) L.; m. Larry R. Sorensen (div. 1983); m. John Dobyns Drummond, June 11, 1988; children: Danielle Ferree, Leah Michelle. BA, U. Conn., 1976; M Urban Planning & Policy, U. Ill., Chgo., 1979. Dir. programs Ill.-Ind. Bi-State Commn., Chgo., 1979-80, dep. dir., 1981; dir. pub. & cmty. rels. Chgo. Dept. Aviation, 1981-85; prin. R. Lopat Comm., 1985—. Dep. dir. Chgo. Econ. Devel. Commn., 1986-89. Pub. Weedpath Gazette, 1992-2003, Operates Weedpatch.com, 2002-. Recipient Recognition cert. FAA, 1985. Mem. Ill.-Ind. Bi-State Commn. (hon.), Garden Writers Assn. (Best Newsletter 2001). Avocations: gardening, historic preservation, landscape design, land conservation. Office: The Weedpatch Gazette PO Box 339 Richmond IL 60071-0339

LOPER, LINDA SUE, special collections librarian; b. Wakefield, R.I., Jan. 28, 1945; d. Delmas Field and Dora Belle (Hanna) Sneed; children: Matthew Lee Mathany, Amanda Virginia Mathany Van DerHeyden, Morgan Lynnclare Loper. BA, Peabody Coll., Nashville, 1966, MLS, 1979; EdD in Ednl. Adminstrn., Vanderbilt U., Nashville, 1988. Tchr. Parkway Sch., Chesterfield, Mo., 1966-68, Charlotte Mecklenburg Schs., Charlotte, N.C., 1968-71; dir. city libr. Jackson George Regional Libr. System, Pascagoula, Miss., 1979-82; media ctr. specialist Pascagoula Mcpl. Sch. Dist., 1982-83, Moore County Sch. System, Lynchburg, Tenn., 1983-91; ref. libr. Motlow State C.C., Tullahoma, Tenn., 1983-85; dir. learning resource ctr. Columbia (Tenn.) State C.C., 1991-99; CEO Grant Seekers, Inc., 1996-99; CEO Loper Literary Agy., 1999—2001; accounts svcs. mgr. E.B. Stephens Co. (EBSCO), 1999-2001; spl. collections divsn. mgr. Nashville Pub. Libr., 2001—. Presenter TLA Ann. Conv., Knoxville, 1998, Am. Assn. Women in C.C.s Regional Conf., 1997, LEAP State Dept. Edn. Conf. for Libr., Chattanooga; career ladder participant Tenn. Edn. Dept. Level II; TIM trainer Dept. Edn., Nashville; exec. dir. Tenn. Bd. of Regents Media Consortium, 1993-96; chair profl. staff orgn. Columbia State C.C., 1998-99; presenter, judge 6th Ann. Cumberland Writers Conf., Cookeville, Tenn. Author: Bibliography for Tennessee Commission on Status of Women, 1979; contbr. article to profl jour. Pres. Moore County Friends of Libr., Lynchburg, Tenn., 1991; bd. dirs. Moore County Hist. and Geneal. Soc., Lynchburg, 1991; mem. Tenn.

Bicentennial Com., Giles County, 1996; co-dir. So. Tapestry, a Bicentennial oral history project; sec., mem. exec. bd. Hope Ho. Domestic Violence Shelter, 1993—96, mem. adv. bd., 1996—99; mem. steering com. Bus., Industry, Edn. Partnership, 1994—99. Recipient Gov.'s Acad. award State Dept. of Edn., U. Tenn., 1988, Inst. for Writing Tenn. History, U. Tenn., 1990, Gov.'s Conf. on Info. Sci., Nashville, 1990. Mem. ASCD, ALA, S.E. Libr. Assn., Tenn. Libr. Assn. (co-chair strategic planning com. 1996-99), TENNSHARE (chair collection devel. com. 1996-99), Moore County Edn. Assn. (treas., chair tchrs. study coun., chair polit. action commn. 1989-91), Giles County Edn. Found. UDC, DAR (historian), Tenn. Acad. Libr. Collaborative (exec. coun. 1996-99), Phi Delta Kappa, Beta Phi Mu, Delta Kappa Gamma. Democrat. Episcopalian. Avocations: french hand sewing, crosstitch, sewing, reading, gardening. Office: Nashville Pub Libr Spl Collections Divsn 615 Church St Nashville TN 37219 E-mail: sue.loper@nashville.gov.

LOPES, MARIA FERNANDINA, commissioner; b. Ganda, Angola, Portugal, Dec. 12, 1934; came to U.S., 1963; d. Rodrigo do Carmo and Maria Jose Fernandes (Mendes) Marques; m. Fernandes Esteves Lopes, Aug. 11, 1962; children: Lisa Maria Lopes Moss, Mark Esteves Lopes. Student, Lisbon (Portugal) Coml. Inst., 1953, Massasoit Community Coll., Brockton, Mass., 1988. With archives dept. Portuguese Govt., Lisbon, 1958-62; congl. aide Congresswoman Margaret M. Heckler, Fall River, Taunton, Mass., 1972-74; mem. Taunton (Mass.) Sch. Com., 1976-93; commr., chairperson Bristol County, Mass., 1991—. Founder Day of Portugal, 1974. Avocations: traveling, politics, antiques, music. Home: 28 Worcester St Taunton MA 02780-2041 Office: Office County Commissioners Superior Courthouse PO Box 208 Taunton MA 02780-0208

LOPES, MARIA J. state legislator; b. Providence, Aug. 9, 1941; div.; children: Antonio S., Leonard L. Exec. dir. REACH Housing Devel.; rep. dist. 83 R.I. Ho. of Reps., Providence. Chair spl. legis. com., R.I. Ho. of Reps.; chair Nat. and City Tenant Affairs Bd.; mem. Bldg. Code Commn. Mem. R.I. State Women Legislators Assn. (sec.). Home: 100 Hall St East Providence RI 02914-2643 Office: RI House of Reps Office Of House Mems Providence RI 02903

LOPES, MYRA AMELIA, writer; b. Nantucket, Mass., July 9, 1931; d. Leo Joseph and Mary Ellen (Moriarty) Powers; m. Curtis Linwood Lopes, June 25, 1955; children: Dennis, Sherry, Kathy, Curtis, Becky. BS, Bridgewater, 1954; diploma, Inst. Children's Lit., 1982, N.Y. Inst. Journalism, 1984. Cert. elem. educator Mass. Tchr. Fairhaven (Mass.) Sch. Sys., 1954-58; prin. Sheri Ka Kindergarten, Fairhaven, 1960-76; tchr. Oxford Sch., 1977—78, tchr. Title I, 1978—80; writer, 1984—. Author: (novels) Look Around You, 1990, Looking Back, 1991, Seeing It All, 1992, But Then There Was More, 1993, (book) Captain Joshua Slocum: A Centennial Tribute, 1994, Captain Slocum's Life Before and After the Spray, 1997, The Rogers Legacy, 1997, The Castle on the Hill, 1998, My Town, 1999, (documentary) Joshua Slocum: New World Columbus, 2001, Around the Kitchen Table, 2002, Architectural Treasures from the Rogers Mansion: The Michell House, 2002, Pa's Magic Pillow, 2003. Bd. dirs. Fairhaven Improvement Assn., 1986—, chair membership, 1986—96, pres., 1990—93; bd. dirs. YWCA, New Bedford, 1982—88, chair cmty. rels., 1982—83, nominating chair, 1983—84, chair pers. bd., 1984—88; trustee Millicent Libr., 1993—; bd. govs. Am. Biog. Instn., 1997—; bd. dirs. Fairhaven HS Hall of Fame, 1999—. Named Woman of the Yr., New Bedford Std.-Times and cmty., 1999; named to Hall of Fame, Fairhaven H.S., 1997, America's Hall of Fame, 2003. Mem.: Joshua Slocum Soc. Internat. (historian 1997—, bd. dirs.), Rotary (bd. dirs. 1998—99, v.p. 2000—, pres.-elect 2001, pres. Fairhaven chpt. 2002—03, Paul Harris fellow 2000, Internat. Peace prize 2003, Internat. Pres. citation 2003, Dist. 1090 Significant Achievement award 2003, Gt. Women of the 21st Century). Democrat. Roman Catholic. Avocations: gardening, reading, walking, crafts, music. Home: 71 Fort St Fairhaven MA 02719-2811 Personal E-mail: clopes7081@aol.com.

LOPES, ROSALY MUTEL CROCCE, astronomer, planetary geologist; b. Rio de Janeiro, Jan. 8, 1957; came to U.S., 1989; d. Walmir Crocce and Atir (Mutel) Lopes; m. Thomas Nicholas Gautier, III, Nov. 17, 1990 (div.); 1 child, Thomas N. Gautier. BSc in Astronomy, U. London, 1978, PhD in Physics, 1986. Curator Old Royal Obs., Greenwich, Eng., 1985-88; rsch. assoc. Vesuvius Obs., Naples, Italy, 1989; NRC rsch. assoc. Jet Propulsion Lab., Pasadena, Calif., 1989-91, rsch. scientist Galileo Project, 1990—2002, rsch. scientist Cassini Project, 2002—. Mem. Volcanic Eruption Surveillance Team, U.K., 1981; mem. coun. Assn. Astronomy Edn., London, 1988-89. Author numerous works in sci. field. Recipient Latinas in Sci. award Commn. Feminil Mexicana Nat., L.A., 1990; named Woman of the Yr. in Sci., Gems TV, 1997. Fellow Royal Astron. Soc.; mem. Internat. Astron. Union, Am. Astron. Soc., Am. Geophys. Union, Soc. Hispanic Profl. Engrs. Office: Jet Propulsion Lab Mail Stop 183-601 4800 Oak Grove Dr Pasadena CA 91109-8001 Office Phone: 818-393-4584. E-mail: rosaly.m.lopes@jpl.nasa.gov.

LOPEZ, JEAN ENGEBRETSEN, neuroscience nurse, researcher; b. Alliance, Nebr., June 23, 1950; d. John Peter and Helen LaRue (Vyzourek) Engebretsen; m. Samuel Lopez, Dec. 22, 1979. BSN, U. Nebr., 1973; cert. in neuro nursing, Montreal Neurol. Inst., Que., Can., 1978; MSN, Ariz. State U., 1987. RN, Ariz.; cert. clin. rsch. coord. Cert. neuroscience RN U.S. Peace Corps, Kuala Lumpur, Malaysia, 1973-74; staff nurse, charge nurse neuro ICU Barrow Neurolog. Inst. of St. Joseph's Hosp. and Med. Ctr., Phoenix, 1974-89, neuro-oncology and head injury rsch. nurse clinician, 1989-99; clin. rsch. nurse coord. Sun Health Rsch. Inst. Ctr. for Clin. Rsch., Sun City, Ariz., 1999—. Mem. Am. Assn. Neuro Nurses (past. sec. Ariz. chpt., chpt. coun. rep. for S.W.). Office: Sun Health Rsch Inst Ctr for Clin Rsch 10515 W Santa Fe Dr Sun City AZ 85351-3020 E-mail: jean.lopez@sunhealth.org.

LOPEZ, JENNIFER, actress, dancer, singer; b. Bronx, NY, July 24, 1970; d. David and Guadalupe Lopez; m. Cris Judd, 2001 (div. 2002); m. Ojani Noa, 1997 (div. 1998). Appeared in films Money Train, 1995, Jack, 1996, Blood and Wine, 1996, Anaconda, 1997 (ALMA award 1998), Selena, 1997 (ALMA award 1998), My Family, 1995, U-Turn, 1997, Antz (voice), 1998, Out of Sight, 1998 (ALMA award 1999), Thieves, 1999, Pluto Nash, 1999, The Cell, 2000, The Wedding Planner, 2001, Angel Eyes, 2001, Enough, 2002, Maid in Manhattan, 2002, Gigli, 2003, Jersey Girl, 2004; released Latin music albums: On the 6, 1999, J.Lo, 2001, J to Tha L-O!: The Remixes, 2002. Recipient ALMA Female Entertainer Yr. award 2000, Lasting Image award 1998, Lone Star Film and TV award 1998; nominated for Blockbuster Entertainment award, 1998, Golden Globe, 1998, Independent Spirit award 1996, MTV Movie award 1999, ShoWest Female Star Yr., 2002; named one of 50 Most Beautiful People in the World, People mag., 1997; voted #1 in 100 Sexiest Women list, FHM, 2001. Office: Endeavor c/o Patrick Whitesell 9701 Wilshire Blvd, 10th Fl Beverly Hills CA 90212*

LOPEZ, LINDA CAROL, social sciences educator; b. NYC, Dec. 26, 1949; d. Ralph B. and Miriam (Tayor) L. BA, U. Wis., Madison, 1972; MA, Ohio State U., 1974, PhD, 1976. Vis. asst. prof. U. Wis., Eau Claire, 1976-77; instr., asst. prof. SUNY, Oneonta, 1977-83; assoc. prof. Rockford (Ill.) Coll., 1983—89; prof. dept. social scis. Western N.Mex. U., Silver City, 1989—, dir. field experience, 1989-91. Contbr. articles to profl. jours., including Psychol. Reports, Internat. Jour. Addiction, Hispanic Jour. Behavioral Scis., Jour. Genetic Psychology, Jour. Employment Counseling, Perceptual and Motor Skills, Reading Improvement, Counseling and Values, Social Studies Jour. Recipient Best Paper award New Eng. Ednl. Rsch. Orgn., 1979; postdoctoral faculty fellow Northeastern U., Boston, 1980-81. Mem.: Midwestern Ednl. Rsch. Assn., Am. Assn. Behavioral and Social Scis., Phi Delta Kappa. Avocations: walking, reading. Home: PO Box 1479 Bayard NM 88023

LOPEZ, LINDA M. state legislator; BA, MBA, Coll. of Santa Fe. Colls., N.Mex.; mem. N. Mex. Senate, Dist. 11, Santa Fe, 1996—; vice chair edn. com.; mem. jud. com. Democrat. Office: 9132 Suncrest Ave SW Albuquerque NM 87121-8846

LOPEZ, NANCY, former professional golfer; b. Torrance, Calif., Jan. 6, 1957; d. Domingo and Marina (Griego) Lopez; m. Ray Knight, Oct. 25, 1982; children: Ashley Marie Knight, Erinn Shea Knight, Torri Heather Knight. Student, U. Tulsa, 1976-78. Founder and Principal Nancy Lopez Golf Company. Player U.S.A. Solheim Cup, 1990. Author: (book) The Education of a Woman Golfer, 1979. Named first victory winner, Bent Tree Classic, Sarasota, Fla., 1978, AP Athlete, 1978, Rolex Rookie of the Yr., 1978, Rolex Player of the Yr., 1978, 1979, 1985, winner, LPGA Championship, 1978, 1985, Mazda LPGA Championship, 1989, others; named to LPGA Hall of Fame, 1987, PGA World Golf Hall of Fame, 1989; recipient Vare Trophy, 1978. Mem.: LPGA (Player and Rookie of the Yr. 1978). Republican. Achievements include winning 48 LPGA Tour events, 3 maj. championships. Office: care Internat Mgmt Group 1360 E 9th St Ste 100 Cleveland OH 44114-1715*

LOPEZ LYSNE, ROBIN, counselor, writer, artist; b. Rockford, Ill., Nov. 3, 1953; d. Robert Edward and Martha Virginia (Lysne) Heerens; m. Carter Blocksma, Nov. 1, 1976 (div. Jan. 18, 1985); m. Ernesto Lopez-Molina, July 26, 1998; children: Chris Lopez, Matt Lopez, Mari Luna del Sol(dec.). BFA cum laude, U. Wis., Milw., 1975; MA in Spirituality and Psychology, Holy Names Coll., 1988. Art tchr. Battle Creek (Mich.) Art Ctr., 1979—85, Detroit Art House Lectrs., 1979—85, Ella Sharp Mus., Jackson, Mich., 1979—85, curator exhibits and edn., 1980—85; pvt. practice Felton, Calif., 1985—; founding dir. Energy Medicine, 1996—, Ctr. for the Soul, Felton, 2002—. Mem. Somatics Group, Marin County, Calif., 1989—95; presenter, lectr. in energy medicine, spirit guides and divine guidance. Author: (non-fiction and poetry) Dancing Up the Moon, 1995, Living a Sacred Life, 1997, 1999. Exec. bd. Together for Youth-United Way, Santa Cruz, Calif., 1999—; cmty. organizer Mountain Cmty. Resources, Ben Lomond, Calif., 1999—2002. Grantee, Friends of Creation, Oakland, 1988, Flow Fund, N.Y., Calif., 1992, Rockford (Ill.) Arts Coun., 1996, 1997, Santa Cruz Mountain Art Ctr., Ben Lomond, 2000. Mem.: Valley Unity Action Group (dir. 1999—2002).

LOPEZ-MORILLAS, FRANCES M. translator; b. Fulton, Mo., Sept. 3, 1918; d. Erwin Kempton and Laura (Hinkhouse) Mapes; m. Juan Lopez-Morillas, Aug. 12, 1937; children: Martin Morell, Consuelo, Julian. BA, U. Iowa, 1939, MA, 1940. Translator Collins Radio Co., Cedar Rapids, Iowa, 1940-43; tchr. Spanish Lincoln Sch., Providence, 1943-44; tchr. French and Spanish Mary C. Wheeler Sch., Providence, 1951-64; tchr. ESL Internat. Inst., Madrid, 1957-58; freelance translator, 1964—. Co-editor: (with E.K. Mapes) J.J. Fernandez de Lizardi, El periquillo sarniento, 1952; translated more than 25 books and numerous articles including Journey to the Alcarria: Travels through the Spanish Countryside, 1964, Tales of Potosi, 1975, The Krausist Movement and Ideological Change in Spain, 1981, The Medieval Heritage of Mexico, 1992, Castaways: The Narrative of Alvar Nunez Cabeza de Vaca, 1993. Grantee NEH, 1984, NEA, 1986; recipient translation prize Tex. Inst. Letters, 1991. Mem. Internat. Assn. Hispanists, Am. Literary Translators Assn., Phi Beta Kappa. Home: 355 Blackstone Blvd Providence RI 02906-4946*

LOPEZ-MUNOZ, MARIA ROSA P. real estate development company executive; b. Havana, Cuba, Jan. 28, 1938; came to U.S., 1960; d. Eleuterio Perfecto and Bertha (Carmenati Colon) Perez Rodriguez; m. Gustavo Lopez-Munoz, Sept. 9, 1973. Student, Candler Coll., Havana, 1951-53, Sch. Langs., U. Jose Marti, 1954-55. Lic. interior designer, real estate broker. Pres. Fantasy World Acres, Inc., Coral Gables, Fla., 1970-84, pres., dir., 1984—; sec. Sandhills Corp., Coral Gables, 1978-85, dir., 1978—. Treas., Am. Cancer Soc., Miami, Fla., 1981, sec. Hispanic bd., 1987, pres. Hispanic divsn., 1989, bd. dirs., aux. treas.; bd. dirs Am. Heart Assn., Miami, 1985, chmn. Hispanic divsn.; bd. dirs. YMCA, Young Patronesses of Opera, Miami, 1985, Lowe Mus. of U. Miami, 1986—, Linda Ray Infant Ctr.; former pres. Ladies Aux. Little Havana Child Care Ctr.; trustee Ronald McDonald House, sec. exec. bd., 1992; mem. exec. bd., rec. sec. Young Patronesses of the Opera; mem. Fla. Grand Opera; mem. cabinet Children's Cardiac Found., New Horizons Cmty. Devel., Transplant Ctr. Sch., Medicine, U. Miami-Jackson Meml. Hosp., 1992; bd. dirs. Cultura Italiana, Inc.; pres. Messengers of Peace, 2002; amb. 1999 Alpine Ski Championships, Vail, Colo. Recipient Merit award Am. Cancer Soc., 1980, 81, 82, 83, 84, Dynamic Woman award, 1992; Woman with Heart award Am. Heart Assn., 1985, Merit awards, 1980-84, Woman of Yr., 1986, Outstanding Lady award Greater Miami Opera, 1992, Cultural Star of the Millennium award Vizcaya Mus., 1999; named Woman of Yr., Children's Hosp., 1993; named to Great Order José Marti, 1988; named Leading Miami's Beautiful Couples for ACS, 1995. Mem. Real Estate Bd. Realtors, Coral Gables Real Estate Assn., Vail 50 Club, Ocean Reef Club (Key Largo, Fla.), Opera Guild Miami, YPO, Key Biscayle Yacht Club, Regine's Internta. Bath Club (Miami Beach). Republican. Roman Catholic. Avocations: yachting, skiing, scuba diving, guitar, piano.

LOPEZ-SAUNDERS, DELIA ARACELLI, mental health therapist, artist; b. Miami, Fla., May 5, 1960; d. Rufino Lopez; children: Monique Jocette Saunders, Joelle Anjelica Saunders. BFA, U. Miami, 1982; MA, Am. Coll. Metaphys. Theology, 1999. Board Certified Expressive Therapist Bd. Of Examiners, 2000, cert. Master Addictions Counselor Am. Counselor Inc., 2001, Mental Health Counselor Nat. Counselor and Therapist Assn., 2001, clin. therapist Nat. Assn. Drug and Alcohol Intervention, 2001, National Drug and Alcohol Interventionist Nat. Assn. Drug and Alcohol Intervention, 2001, nat. clin. supr. Am. Counselor Inc/NADAI, 2003, Trauma and Addictive Disorders Therapist Inst. of Trauma and Addictive Disorders, 2001, diplomate Nat. Inst. Expressive Therapy, Hawaii and N.Y., 1999. Prodr., adv. asst. GiGi Adv., Miami, 1985—88; life coach web-based, 1994—; pub. New Arts Internat., 1999—2000; therapist Fla., 2000—02; educator Nat. Inst. Expressive Therapy, N.Y.C., NY, 1999—; therapist Cmty. Mental Health and Counseling, Crestview, Fla., 2002—. Cons., Fla., 1999—; attendant care facilitator, Fla., 1997—99; coord. Smart Recovery, Fla., 2002—; animal assisted activities, Fla., 2001—; bd. dirs. Nat. Drug and Alcohol Interventionists, Pa., 2002—. Contbr. articles to profl. jours.; 11th Edit. Ency. of Living Artists, 12th Edit. Ency. of Living Artists. Artist Global Arts Internat., Ariz., 1997; artist/facilitator Very Spl. Arts, Fla., 1998—99. Fellow: Nat. Inst. of Expressive Therapy (life); mem.: Internat. Mus. Women Artists, Fla. Art Edn. Assn., Nat. Assn. Drug and Alcohol Interventions, Fla. Alcohol and Drug Abuse Assn., Nat. Assn. of Expressive Therapists (life). Avocations: art, piano, tennis, swimming, former cross country runner. Personal E-mail: mixedme372@aol.com.

LOPKER, ANITA MAE, psychiatrist, researcher; b. San Diego, May 25, 1955; d. Louis Donald and Betty Jean (Sayman-Campbell) L. BA magna cum laude, U. Calif., San Diego, 1978; MD, U. Rochester, 1982. Diplomate Nat. Bd. Med. Examiners, Am. Bd. Forensic Examiners, Am. Bd. Forensic Medicine. Intern in internal medicine Yale U. Sch. Medicine-Greenwich Hosp., 1982-83; resident in psychiatry Yale U. Sch. of Medicine, 1983-86; postdoctoral fellow Yale U. Sch. Medicine, New Haven, Conn., 1982-86, clin. instr., 1986-88; pvt. practice specializing eating disorders and Lyme disease Westport, Conn., 1987—. Cons. psychiatrist Yale-New Haven Hosp Lyme Disease Study Clinic, 1987-94, Yale U. Lyme Disease Rsch. Project, 1986—, Alcoholism and Drug Dependency Coun., Inc., 1989-90; internat. lectr. on Lyme psychiat. syndrome; nat. lectr. on eating disorders, substance abuse. Contbr. articles to profl. jours. Founding mem. Nat. Mus. for Women in the Arts, Washington, 1986; patron Menninger Found., 1990-94, Met. Opera, 1993-95, bd. dirs. The Fairfield Orch., 1993-96. Recipient Benjamin Rush prize in psychiatry U. Rochester Sch. Medicine, 1982, citation for Scholastic Achievement Am. Med. Women's Assn., 1982. Mem. AAAS, Am. Psychiat. Assn., Conn. Psychiat. Soc., World Fedn. Mental Health (life), N.Y. Acad. Scis., Menninger Found., Alpha Omega Alpha, Phi Beta Kappa. Achievements include discovery of preventable neuropsychiatric disorders associated with Lyme disease and tachyphylaxis as key to rapid reversal of tardive dyskinesia by verapamil, a calcium channel blocker. Home: 101 Regents Park Westport CT 06880-5532 Office: 18 Burr Rd Westport CT 06880-4219 E-mail: alopker@snet.net.

LOPKER, PAMELA, technology industry executive; BS in Math., U. Calif., Santa Barbara, 1976—. Cert. prodn. and inventory mgmt. Sr. sys. analyst Comptek Rsch., 1976-79; founder, chmn., pres. QAD, Carpinteria, Calif., 1979—. Profiled 4 times Forbes Mag. (cover 3 times); named to Women in Tech. Internat. Hall of Fame 1997. Mem. Am. Prodn. and Inventory Control Soc. Office: QAD Inc 6450 Via Real Carpinteria CA 93013-2924

LOPO, DIANA M. lawyer; b. Havana, Cuba, 1957; BS cum laude, U. Miami, 1978; JD, U. Mich., 1981; LLM, NYU, 1982. Bar: N.Y. 1984. Ptnr. Skadden, Arps, Slate, Meagher & Flom, N.Y.C. Office: Skadden Arps Slate Meagher & Flom 4 Times Sq Fl 24 New York NY 10036-6595

LOPRESTO, BIRGITA GUNNEL, b. Stora Levene, Sweden, June 29, 1941; came to U.S., 1971; d. Ivar Antonius and Eva Dagmar (Flink) Anderson; m. Vincent LoPresto, Apr. 24, 1971; 1 child, Catherine. Florist assoc., Stora Levene, 1959-71. Author: (poetry) The Big Darkness, 1994, Anthalagion, 1995. Recipient Pres.'s award of lit. excellence Iliad, 1994, 95. Mem. Nat. Mus. Women in the Arts. Avocations: writing poetry, reading, handicrafts.

LOQUASTO, EILEEN GRACE, sociologist; b. Newark, N.Y., Jan. 9, 1969; d. Lyndon Paul and Brenda Jane (Sargent) Kiesinger; 1 child, Michael. AA, Finger Lakes C.C., Canandaigua, N.Y., 1995; BA, Empire State Coll., 1997. Engr.'s asst. D.J. Bergman & Assocs., Rochester, N.Y., 1991-93; rsch. asst. Cornell U., Geneva, N.Y., 1993-94; asst. dir. Wayne County Rural Ministry, Williamson, N.Y., 1995-98; child psychology specialist dept. psychology Genesee Hosp., Rochester, N.Y., 1998—. Advocate, cons. Wayne County Women's Support Group, Williamson, 1996—; co-founder Stepping Stones Children's Bereavement Support Group, 1997; program develope Come-Unity Ctr., Williamson, 1996—. Mem. AAUW, Nat. Network of Social Work Mgrs., Ms. Found. for Women. Avocations: landscape designing, watercolor, jewelry design, photography. Home: 3243 Shepherd Rd Williamson NY 14589-9553 Office: Genesee Hosp 224 Alexander St Rochester NY 14607-4055

LORBER, BARBARA HEYMAN, communications executive; b. N.Y.C. d. David Benjamin and Gertrude (Meyer) Heyman; divorced. AB in Polit. Sci., Skidmore Coll., 1966; MA, Columbia U., 1973, postgrad., 1973-76. Asst. dir. young citizens divsn. Dem. Party, 1966-68; exec. asst. to dean Albert Einstein Coll. Medicine, Bronx, N.Y., 1968-72; exec. asst. to v.p. devel. Vanderbilt U., Nashville, 1976-77; spl. projects dir. Am. Acad. in Rome, N.Y.C., 1977-78; pub. affairs dir. Met. Opera, N.Y.C., 1978-84; sr. v.p. Hill and Knowlton, N.Y.C., 1985-88; pres. Lorber Group, Ltd., N.Y.C., 1989-95; v.p. comms. and planning N.Y.C. Partnership and C. of C., 1996-98; sr. v.p. major events and promotions NYC & Company, 1998—. Guest lectr. Arts and Bus. Coun., N.Y.C., Internat. Soc. Performing Arts Adminstrs., Columbia U. Tchrs. Coll., N.Y.C., NYU Sch. Continuing Edn., Nat. Media Conf., Nat. Soc. Fund Raising Execs., N.Y.C.; exec. prodr., prodr., writer N.Y. Internat. Festival Arts, N.Y.C., 1988; team leader, 2002 Salt Lake Olympic Torch Relay to N.Y.C., 2004 Athens Olympic Torch Relay in N.Y.C. Contbr. chpts. to book; contbr. articles to profl. jours. Office: NYC & Company/Major Events 810 7th Ave 3d Fl New York NY 10019-5818

LORCH, MARISTELLA DE PANIZZA, writer, educator; b. Bolzano, Italy, Dec. 8, 1919; came to U.S., 1947, naturalized, 1951; d. Gino and Giuseppina (Cristoforetti) de Panizza Inama von Brunnenwald; m. Claude Bové, Feb. 10, 1944 (div. 1955); 1 child, Claudia; m. Edgar R. Lorch, Mar. 25, 1956; children: Lavinia Edgarda, Donatella Livia. Ed., Liceo Classico, Merano, 1929-37; Dott. in Lettere e Filosofia, U. Rome, 1942; DHL (hon.), Lehman Coll., CUNY, 1993. Prof. Latin and Greek Liceo Virgilio, Rome, 1941-44; assoc. prof. Italian and German Coll. St. Elizabeth, Convent Station, N.J., 1947-51; faculty Barnard Coll. and Columbia U., 1951-90; prof. Barnard Coll., 1967—, chmn. dept., 1951-90, co-founder, chmn. medieval and renaissance program, 1972-90. Founder, dir. Ctr. for Internat. Scholarly Exch., Barnard Coll., 1980-90; dir. Casa Italiana, Columbia U., 1969-76, chmn. exec. com. Italian studies, 1980-90, founding dir. Italian Acad. Advanced Studies in Am., 1991-96, founding dir. emerita and dir. external rels., 1996—. Author: Critical edit. L. Valla, De vero falsoque bono, Bari, 1970, (critical edit.) Michaelida (with W. Ludwig), 1976, On Pleasure (with A. K. Hieatt), 1981, A Defense of Life: L. Valla's Theory of Pleasure, 1985, Folly and Insanity in Renaissance Literature, 1986, (with E. Grassi) All' America, 1990, Italy at the Millennium, 2001; editor: Il Teatro Italiano del Renascimento, 1981, Humanism in Rome, 1983, La Scuola, New York, 1987; mem. editorial bd. Italian jour. Romanic Review; also articles on Renaissance lit., philosophy and theater. Chmn. Am. Ariosto Centennial Celebration, 1974; chmn. bd. trustees La Scuola NY, 1986-92; trustee Lycée Française NY, 1986—; adv. bd. Marconi Found., 1998. Decorated cavaliere della Repubblica Italiana, commendatore della Repubblica Italiana, grande ufficiale della Republica Italiana; recipient AMITA award for Woman of Yr. in Italian Lit., 1973, Columbus '92 Countdown prize of excellence in humanities, 1990, Elen Cornaro award Sons of Italy Woman of Yr., 1990, Father Ford award, 1994, hon. mem. Legendary Women, 1997, founding dir. emeritus Italian Acad. in Advance Studies in Am., Columbia U. Mem. Medieval Acad. Am., Renaissance Soc. Am., Am. Assn. Tchrs. Italian, Am. Assn. Italian Studies (hon. pres. 1990-91), Internat. Assn. for Study of Italian Lit. (Am. rep., assoc. pres. 8th Congress 1973), Acad. Polit. Sci. (life), Pirandello Soc. (pres. 1972-78), Arcadia Acad. (Asteria Aretusa 1976). Home: 445 Riverside Dr New York NY 10027-6801 Office: Columbia Univ Italian Acad Adv Study Casa Italiana New York NY 10027 Office Phone: 212-854-8640.

LORD, CARLA, retired art history educator; b. N.Y.C., Oct. 19, 1936; d. Charles Greenhaus and Thelma Nurenberg; m. Jeremy Hugh Baron, Dec. 31, 1990; m. John W. Lord, June 5, 1965 (div. Dec. 29, 1972); 2 stepchildren. BA, Smith Coll., 1958; MA, Columbia U., 1961, PhD, 1968. Preceptor Columbia U., N.Y.C., 1966—68; adj. prof. Queens Coll., N.Y.C., 1969; asst. prof. Rutgers U., New Brunswick, NJ, 1969—70; from asst. prof. to prof. Kean U., Union, NJ, 1970—2002. Author: Royal French Patronage of Art in the Fourteenth Century, 1985; contbr. articles to profl. jours. Recipient Pres.'s fellowship, Columbia U., 1962—63, Summer fellowship, 1963; grantee, Am. Coun. Learned Socs., 1977. Mem.: Am. Friends of Warburg Inst. (treas. 1990—95, v.p. 2000—02). Avocation: travel. Home: 135 W 58th St Apt 6A New York NY 10019-1552

LORD, EVELYN MARLIN, mayor; b. Melrose, Mass., Dec. 8, 1926; d. John Joseph and Mary Janette (Nourse) Marlin; m. Samuel Smith Lord Jr., Feb. 28, 1948; children: Steven Arthur, Jonathan Peter, Nathaniel Edward, Victoria Marlin, William Kenneth. BA, Boston U., 1948; MA, U. Del., 1956; JD, U. Louisville, 1969. Bar: Ky. 1969, U.S. Supreme Ct. 1973. Exec. dir. Block Blight Inc., Wilmington, Del., 1956—60; mem. Del. Senate,

Dover, 1960—62; administrv. asst. county judge Jefferson County, Louisville, 1968—71; corr. No. Ireland News Jour. Co., Wilmington, 1972—74; legal adminstr. Orgain, Bell & Tucker, Beaumont, Tex., 1978—83; v.p. Tex. Commerce Bank, Beaumont, 1983—84; councilman City of Beaumont, 1980—82, mayor pro tem, 1982—84, mayor, 1990—94, 2002—. Tourism chmn. U.S. Conf. Mayors, 1994, adv. bd., chmn. arts, culture and recreation, 1992—94; sr. counselor Ky. Bar, 2002—; adv. bd. U.S. Com. Mayors, 2002—. Trustee United Way, Beaumont, 1990—, pres., 1994, 1997; mem. adv. bd. Boy Scouts Am., Three Rivers, 1978—84, 1989—94, mem. exec. bd., 2000—; mem. (life) Girl Scouts U.S.A., pres. Kentuckiana coun., 1966—70; mem. adv. bd. Lamar U. Found., 1997—99, trustee, 1999—2003; pres. Tex. Energy Mus., 1995—2001; bd. dirs. Symphony Soc. S.E. Tex., 1990—98, 2002—, Evelyn M. Lord Teen Ct., 1993—, Found. S.E. Tex., 1990—, Lincoln Inst., 1994—2001, Beaumont Pub. Schs. Found., 1993—99, Ptnrs. for Children, Child Protective Svcs.; chmn. Spindletop 2001 Com. Named Citizen of Yr., Sales and Mktg. Assn., 1990, Beaumont Man of the Yr., 1993, Woman with Heart, Am. Heart Assn., 2000, Free Ent. Person of the Yr., Assn. Bldg. Contrs., 2000, Newsmaker of the Yr., Press Club Jefferson County, 2001, Hurricane Evelyn, ARC, 2001, Disting. Law Alumni, U. Louisville, 2002, Woman of Yr., Quota Club Internat., 2002, Mrs. S.E. Tex. Dogwood Festival, 2004; recipient Silver Beaver award, Boy Scouts Am., Beaumont, 1979, Disting. Alumni award, Boston U., 1983, Disting. Leadership award, Nat. Assn. Leadership Orgns., Indpls., 1991, Labor-Mgmt. Pub. Sector award, 1991, Disting. Grad. award, Leadership Beaumont, 1993, Rotary Svc. Above Self award, 1994, Excellency award, Tex. State Hist. Commn., 2001, Mrs. S.E. Tex. award, Dogwood Festival, 2004, Cmty. Builder award, Grand Masonic Lodge of Tex., 2003, Athena award, Beaumont C of C, 2003. Mem.: DAR, LWV (Del. state pres. 1960—62, bd. dirs. Tex. 1978—80), Bus. and Profl. Women Assns. (Woman of Yr. 1983), Colonial Dames (Citizenship award 2004), Soc. Mayflower Descs., Rotary, 100 Club (pres. 1995—97). Avocations: writing, reading, african violets, genealogy. Home: 1240 Nottingham Ln Beaumont TX 77706-4316

LORD, HEAVEN, theology studies educator, consultant, minister, translator; b. Paget, Bermuda, May 1, 1963; arrived in U.S., 1975; d. Percival Whaley and Sylvia (Keller) Baynard. BA in Spanish, Coll. of Charleston, 1984, BA in Polit. Sci., 1985, BA in Bus., 1986; MA in Spanish, U. No. Iowa, 1991; MA in Humanistic Psychology, State U. West Ga., 1992; PhD in Consciousness Studies and Theology of Miracles, Union Inst., Cin., 1999. Instr. Spanish State U. West Ga., Carrollton, 1991—92, Duke U., Durham, NC, 1993; rsch. asst. Inst. Parapsychology, Durham, NC, 1993; instr. Spanish U. Mo., Kansas City, 1999; min. of prayer Silent Unity, Unity Village, Mo., 1996—; Spanish translator Traducciones Espirituales, Lee's Summit, Mo., 2000—. Cons. in field, Lee's Summit, 2001—. Avocations: travel, writing, reading, singing, dance. Home: 511 NE Tudor Rd Apt 1 Lees Summit MO 64086

LORD, JACQUELINE WARD, accountant, photographer, artist; b. Andalusia, Ala., May 16, 1936; d. Marron J. and Minnie V. (Owen) Ward; m. Curtis Gaynor, Nov. 23, 1968. Student U. Ala., 1966, Auburn U., 1977, Huntingdon Coll., 1980, Troy State U., 1980; BA in Bus. Adminstrn., Dallas Bapt. U., 1985. News photographer corr. Andalusia (Ala.) Star-News, 1954-59, Sta. WSFA-TV, Montgomery, Ala., 1954-60; acct., bus. mgr. Reihardt Motors, Inc., Montgomery, 1962-69; office mgr., acct. Cen. Ala. Supply, Montgomery, 1969-71; acct. Chambers Constrn. Co., Montgomery, 1972-75; pres. Foxy Lady Apparel, Inc., Montgomery, 1970-76; acct. Rushton, Stakely, Johnston & Garrett, attys., Montgomery, 1975-81; acctg. supr. Arthur Andersen & Co., Dallas, 1981-82; staff acct. Burgess Co., C.P.A.s, Dallas, 1983; owner Lord & Assocs. Acctg. Svc., Dallas, 1983—; tax acct. John Hasse, C.P.A., Dallas, 1984-86; Dallas Bapt. Assn., 1986—. Vol. election law commr. Sec. of State of Ala. Don Siegelman, Montgomery, 1979-80; mem. Montgomery Art Guild, 1964-65, Ala. Art League, 1964-65, Montgomery Little Theatre, 1963-65, Montgomery Choral Soc., 1965. Recipient Outstanding Achievement Bus. Mgmt. award Am. Motors, 1968. Mem. Am. Soc. Women Accts. (pres. Montgomery chpt. 1976-77, area day chmn. 1978, del. ann. meeting 1975-78), Soroptimists Internat. (pres. elect Montgomery chpt. 1975-76), Nat. Assn. Ch. Bus. Adminstrn. Home: 5209 Meadowside Dr Garland TX 75043-2731

LORD, M. G. writer; b. La Jolla, Calif., Nov. 18; d. Charles Carroll and Mary (Pfister) L.; m. Glenn Horowitz, May 19, 1985 BA, Yale U. Editl. artist Chgo. Tribune; editl. cartoonist, columnist Newsday, N.Y.C., 1979-94. Cartoons syndicated L.A. Times Syndicate, 1984-89; column syndicated Copley News Svc., 1989-94; resident humanities fellow U. Mich., 1986-87. Author: Mean Sheets, 1982, Prig Tales, 1990, Forever Barbie: The Unauthorized Biography of a Real Doll, 1994; columnist Preservation, 1996—. Resident humanities fellow U. Mich., 1986-87. Office: care Eric Simonoff Janklow & Nesbit Assoc 445 Park Ave New York NY 10022-2606

LORD, MIA W. advocate; b. N.Y.C., Dec. 2, 1911; m. Robert P. Lord (dec. Nov. 1977); children: Marcia Louise, Alison Jane. BA in Liberal Arts cum laude, Bklyn. Coll., 1935, postgrad., San Francisco State U., 1984—99. Hon. sec. Commonwealth of World Citizens, London; membership sec. Brit. Assn. for World Govt., London; sec. Ams. in Brit. for U.S. Withdrawal from S.E. Asia, Eng.; organizer Vietnam Vigil to End the War, London; pres. Let's Abolish War chpt. World Federalist Assn., San Francisco State U. Appointed hon. sec. Commonwealth of World Citizens, London; officially invited to Vietnam, 1973; organizer Vietnam Vigil to End the War, London. Author: The Practical Way to End Wars and Other World Crises: the case for World Federal Government: listed in World Peace through World Law, 1984, and in Strengthening the United Nations, 1987, War: The Biggest Con Game in the World, 1980. Hon. sec., nat. exec. mem. Assn. of World Federalists-U.K.; founder, bd. dirs. Crusade to Abolish War and Armaments by World Law. Nominated for the Nobel Peace Prize, 1975, 92, 93; recipient four Merit awards Pres. San Francisco State U. Mem. Secretariat of World Citizens USA (life), Assn. of World Federalists USA, Brit. Assn. for World Govt. (membership sec.), Crusade to Abolish War and Armaments by World Law (founder, dir.), World Govt. Orgn. Coord. Com., World Fed. Authority Com., Campaign for UN Reform, Citizens Global Action, World Constitution and Parliament Assn., World Pub. Forum, Internat. Registry of World Citizens. Home: 174 Majestic Ave San Francisco CA 94112-3022

LORD, PAMELA, chemist, educator; d. Ralph and Juanita Lord. BS, U. Wis., Green Bay, 1996; PhD, U. Calif., Davis, 2001. Rsch. asst. U. of Calif., Davis, Calif., 1998—2001; prof. chemistry U. St. Francis, Fort Wayne, Ind., 2002—. Contbr. articles to profl. jours. including Jour. Am. Chem. Soc., Angewante Chemie. Summer Inst. fellow, Project Kaleidoscope, 2000. Mem.: Am. Chem. Soc. Office: U Saint Francis 2701 Spring St Fort Wayne IN 46808 E-mail: plord@sf.edu.

LORD, VICTORIA LYNN, artist; b. Danville, Ill., May 29, 1956; d. Delno and Merlyn LaDonna (Gillis) Gilliland; m. Maurice Powers Lord II, Dec. 1, 1987. Student, Purdue U., 1974-77. Host, instr. painting series PBS, Learning Channel, U.S., Can., Mexico, 1990—; instr. various orgns. Author: Techniques in Acrylics, Alkyds, Oils, 1987, Painting with Alkyds and Oils, 1989, First Steps in Acrylics, 1996. Named one of Top 100 Wildlife Artists, Artist Mag., 1990, Sponsor Artist, Ducks Unltd., Ind., 1991, Featured Ad Artist, Winsor & Newton, 1990-91. Mem. Soc. of Layerists in Multimedia, Soc. Exptl. Artists, Soc. Decorative Painters, Am. Craft Coun., Soc. of Painters in Casein and Acrylic, Tippecanoe Arts Fedn. (bd. dirs. 1992-95). Office: PO Box 2195 West Lafayette IN 47996-2195

LORDI, KATHERINE MARY, lawyer; b. Jersey City, Mar. 24, 1949; d. Peter G. and Hilde E. (Illy) Lordi. AB, Trinity Coll., Washington, 1971; JD, Fordham U., 1975. Bar: N.J. 1975, U.S. Dist. Ct. N.J. 1975, U.S. Supreme Ct. 1983, U.S. Ct. Appeals (3d cir.) 1989. Clk. Friedman & D'Allessandro, East Orange, NJ, 1974-75, assoc., 1975-76; pvt. practice Bloomfield, NJ, 1976—. Adj. instr. Coll. St. Elizabeth, Convent Station, NJ, 1978—86, adj. prof., 1986—; legal adviser Mcpl. Ct. Clks. Assn., 1977—84. Notes editor: Fordham Urban Law Jour., 1974—75. Trustee Cath. Family and Cmty. Svcs., 1980—, v.p., 1986—; mem. adv. bd. Acad. St. Elizabeth, Convent Station, 1980—84; mem. Essex County Adv. Bd. Status Women, 1983—92, chmn., 1985—88, co-chair, 1990—92; trustee New Sch. Arts, 1988—89, Family Svc. League, Inc., 1986—2000, pres., 1991—94; trustee Bloomfield C. of C., 1986—94, v.p. legis., 1990—94. Fellow: Royal Soc. Encouragement Arts, Manufactures and Commerce; mem.: ABA, Essex County Bar Assn., N.J. Bar Assn., Bloomfield Lawyers Club. Roman Catholic. Office: 54 Fremont St Bloomfield NJ 07003-3428 E-mail: k.lordi@worldnet.att.net.

LORE, LINDA, retail executive; b. Calif. With Robinson's Dept. Stores, Calif., 1972-82, fragrance buyer, 1983-86; v.p. sales planning and devel. Giorgio Beverly Hills, Santa Monica, Calif., sr. v.p. mktg.; pres., CEO Giorgio Beverly Hills (acquired by Procter & Gamble Europe), Santa Monica, Calif., 1991-97; corp. v.p., gen. mgr. Giorgio Products-Worldwide Procter & Gamble, 1994-97; pres., CEO Frederick's of Hollywood, Calif., 1999—. Bd. dirs. Inst. Design Merchandising, Coalition to Preserve the Integrity of Am. Trademarks, Fragrance Found. Bd. dirs. L.A. chpt. drop-out prevention prog. Cities in Sch., Inc.; mem. Com. 200, trustee Women's Forum. Recipient Woman Achievement award Beverly Hills Women's Network, 1992, Outstanding Businesswoman award L.A. Advt. Women, 1992, Industry Leadership award So. Calif. Cosmetic Assn., 1993, Beautiful Apple Industry Leadership award Greater N.Y. March of Dimes Birth Defects Found, 1996; named Humanitarian of Year, West Coast Beauty Assn. which funded the Linda LoRe Found. for Pediatric AIDS, 1993. Achievements include winning the exclusive rights to launch the Giorgio fragrance on the West Coast; successful mktg. of Giorgio fragrances RED, RED For Men, WINGS, WINGS For Men, HUGO by Hugo Boss, Giorgio Aire, Ocean Dream, RED 2. Office: Fredericks of Hollywood PO Box 229 Hollywood CA 90078-0229

LOREDO, LINDA S. marketing executive; b. Newark, Mar. 30, 1959; d. Charles Frances and Mary Josephine Loredo. With Dolls by Consolidated Enterprise, Roselle Park, N.J. Office: Dolls by Consolidated 440 E Westfield Ave Roselle Park NJ 07204-2432

LORELL, BEVERLY H. medical products executive; BA with distinction, Stanford U., 1971; MD, Stanford Sch. Medicine, 1975. Intern to resident physician Stanford U. Hosp.; clin. rsch. fellowship, cardiology Mass. Gen. Hosp., Harvard Med. Sch.; dir., program in heart failure Besth Israel Deaconess Med. Ctr.; prof., medicine Harvard U. Med. Sch.; v.p., chief med. tech. officer Guidant, Indpls., 2003—. Mem.: Besth Israel Intervention Cardiology Team, Am. Coll. Cardiology, Heart Failure Soc. of Am., Am. Heart Assn., Guidant Compass Bd. Office: Guidant 111 Monument Cl 2900 Indianapolis IN 46244 Mailing: PO Box 44906 Indianapolis IN 46244

LORENCZ, MARY, public relations executive; BA in English, Mich. State U.; M. in Public Relations, Wayne State U. Various positions to dir. corp. media rels. Kmart Corp., Troy, Mich., 1985—2003; sr. counselor John Bailey & Associates, Inc. Public Relations, 2003—. Mem.: Internat. Assoc. Bus. Communicators, Detroit Chap. (past pres.). Office: Kmart Corp 3100 W Big Beaver Rd Troy MI 48084-3163

LORENS, EMALIE SIGRID, artist, educator, museum staff member; b. Mpls., July 16, 1929; d. William and Viola Anita (Kahn) Shapira; m. Christopher Lorens, Dec. 23, 1952 (div. June 18, 1972); 1 child, Darius ; m. Vincent E. Taylor, Aug. 27, 1949 (div. Oct. 6, 1952); 1 child, Deborah Susan. At, Mpls. Sch. of Art, 1946—47, Walker Art Ctr., Mpls., 1947—49, Skowhegan (Maine) Sch., 1948, Cin. Art Acad., 1948—49; BA, Goddard Coll., Plainfield, Vt., 1977; MA in Expressive Therapy, Lesley U., Cambridge, Mass., 1984. Children's art tchr. Cin. Art Mus., 1949—50; art gallery mgr. Brentano's, Washington, 1971—72, San Francisco, 1978; art therapist Mass. Mental Health Ctr., Boston, 1984—86; activity leader Jewish Sr. Day Ctr., Rockville, Md., 1988; mus. shops staff Smithsonian Inst., Washington, 1990—98; mus. asst. Phillips Collection, Washington, 1998—. One-woman shows include Damien Gallery, 1990, Webster Coll., 1973, exhibited in group shows at Cin. Art Mus., 1948, 1950, 1954, Corcoran Mus., Washington, 1972, Washington Women's Art Ctr., 1981, Gallery 10, Ltd., Washington, 1981, Pallas Athene Gallery, Boston, 1988, George Wash. U., Washington, 1992, 1996, Office of Hon. Eleanor Holmes Norton, U.S. Congress, 1994, Smithsonian Women's Show, 1995, Staff Exhbn. Mus. Am. Art, Smithsonian Inst., 1994, 1996, 1997, Children's Nat. Med. Ctr., Washington, 2001, Millenium Arts Ctr., 2001, Mus. of Contemporary Art, 2001, 2003, Phillips Collection Staff Shows, 1999—2000, 2002, Nat. Mus. of Women in the Arts (benefits), 2001—03, Warehouse Gallery, Washington, 2003, in numerous pvt. and corporate collections. Vol. art tchr. Georgetown Children's Ho., Washington, 1979—81, CMS Homeless Shelter, Washington, 1989. Recipient 2d prize, Sculpture, Duluth (Minn.) Art Inst., 1946, Purchase prize, Painting, Skowhegan Sch., 1948, 3d prize, Painting, Friedman's, Cin., 1955, 2d prize, Painting, Am. Art League, Washington, 1967, Internat. Women's Yr. award, Women's Interarts Ctr., N.Y.C., 1976, 2d prize, Painting, Georgetown U. Hosp., Washington, 1999; Career Advancement Scholarship, Bus. and Profl. Women's Assn., Washington, 1973. Mem.: Internat. Artists Support group. Avocations: journal writing, walking, reading. Home: #403 1401 N St NW Washington DC 20005 Office: Phillips Collection 1600 21st St NW Washington DC 20009

LORENSEN, HILDA S. librarian; b. Flateyri, Iceland, Aug. 1922; arrived in U.S., 1943; d. Snorri Snorrasson and Gudrun Johannesdottir; m. Lyman E. Lorensen, 1950; children: Gudrun, Ingrid, Gilda. BS, Am. U., 1946; MS, Cornell U., 1949; MLS, U. Calif., Berkeley, 1968. Rsch. asst. Icelandic Dept. Edn., Reyjavik, 1949—50; sch. libr. Martinez (Calif.) Sch. Sys.; hon. consul of Iceland Icelandic Govt., Orinda, Calif., 1989—97. Libr. Orinda (Calif.) Cmty. Ch., 1989—99; mem. San Francisco Consular Corps, 1989—97. Mem.: AAUW, Icelandic Soc. No. Calif. (co-founder 1956, pres. 1956—66, v.p. 1999). Democrat. Avocations: gardening, reading, singing. Home: 9 Broadview Terr Orinda CA 94563-3101

LORENTZ, KAREN D. publishing executive, writer; b. Danbury, Conn., Aug. 12, 1946; d. Robert Robert and Ruth Webber Duch; m. John M. Lorentz, June 8, 1968; children: Jason Robert, Jonathan Kurt, James Frederick. BS cum laude, U. Conn., Storrs, 1968; post grad., Rutgers U., New Brunswick, N.J., 1975—76. Cert. secondary tchr. N.J., Conn. Tchr. English Scotch Plains - Fanwood HS, Scotch Plains, NJ, 1968—76; owner - operator Lorenwood Bed and Breakfast, Shrewsbury, Vt., 1979—86; freelance writer, 1980—; dir. Prevention Works, Rutland, Vt., 1992—96; pres. Mountain Pub., Shrewsbury, Vt., 1989—. Student coun. adv. Scotch Plains - Fanwood HS, Scotch Plains, NJ, 1972—74; bd. dirs., newsletter editor Women Bus. Owners of Vt., 1980—82; bd. dirs., treas., editor League of Vt. Writers, 1982—2000; editor newsletters and annual reports Rutland Mental Health, 1992—95; spkr. to groups and orgns. Author: (books) Killington, A Story of Mountains and Men, 1990, Okemo, All Come Home, 1996, Good Vermonters, 2000, Two Harwoods in the House, 2001; author, publisher: A Vt. Parent's Prevention Resource, A Guide to Raising Healthy, Drug-Free Children, 1995; editor: Vermont Voices, An Anthology of Vt. Writing; contbr. articles to periodicals and jours. Mem. Shrewsbury PTO, 1979—86; founder, chair and leader Shrewsbury Pack 8 and Troop 8 Scouts, 1985—2001; chmn. bldg. com. Shrewsbury Elem. Sch., 1987—88; sec. bd. trustees Shrewsbury Cmty. Ch., 1990—2000; bd. dirs. Gaiko Found., Rutland, 1990—92. Mem.: Nat. Assn. of Snowsport Journalists, Ea. Ski Writers Assn., Nat. League of Am. Pen Women (so. Vt. chpt.) (chpt. pres. 1999—, chpt. com. chair). Independent. United Ch. Of Christ. Avocations: skiing, church choir, state history, scout leader. E-mail: KLorentzwriter@aol.com.

LORENZ, KATHERINE MARY, bank executive; b. Barrington, Ill., May 1, 1946; d. David George and Mary (Hogan) L. BA cum laude, Trinity Coll., 1968; MBA, Northwestern U., 1971; grad., Grad. Sch. for Bank Adminstrn., 1977. Ops. analyst Continental Bank, Chgo., 1968-69, supr. ops. analysis, 1969-71, asst. mgr. customer profitability analysis, 1971-73, acctg. officer, mgr. customer profitability analysis, 1973-77, 2d v.p., 1976, asst. gen. mgr. contr.'s dept., 1977-80, v.p., 1980, contr. ops. and mgmt. svcs. dept., 1981-84, v.p., sector contr. retail banking, corp. staff and ops. depts., 1984-88, v.p., sr. sector contr. pvt. banking, centralized ops. and corp. staff, 1988-90, v.p., sr. sector contr. bus. analysis group/mgmt. acctg., 1990-94, mgr. contrs. dept. adminstrn. and tng., 1990-94; v.p., chief of staff to chief adminstrv. officer Bank Am. Ill., Chgo., 1994-96, sr. v.p., mgr. adminstrv. svcs., 1996-97, mng. dir., mgr. adminstrv. svcs., 1998-99; sr. v.p., Chgo. adminstrn. exec. Bank Am., 1999—. Mem. Execs. Club Chgo., Trinity Coll. Alumnae Assn. (bd. dirs.). Office: Bank of Am 231 S La Salle St Rm 1320 Chicago IL 60604-1407

LORENZ, MARIANNE, curator; b. Denver, Nov. 5, 1949; d. Paul Frederick and Celesta (Johnson) Holscher. BA, U. Colo., 1971, MFA, 1981, MBA in Mktg., 1982. Tchr. French/German Adams County #50, Westminster, Colo., 1972-80; coord. pub. programs Colo. State History Mus., Denver, 1984-85, dir. edn., 1985-87; curator edn. Joslyn Art Mus., Omaha, 1987-89; asst. dir. collections and programs Dayton (Ohio) Art Inst., 1989; dir., chief exec. ofcr. Yellowstone Art Museum, Billings, Mont. Author: Theme and Improvisation Kandinsky and the American Avant-Garde, 1912-1950, 1992; contbr. Dictionary of Art, 1993. Fulbright grantee, 1975-76. Mem. Am. Assn. Museums, Coll. Art Assn. Avocations: skiing, running. Office: Yellowstone Art Museum 401 N 27th St Billings MT 59101

LORENZ, NANCY, artist; BFA in Painting and Printmaking, U. Mich., 1985; MFA in Painting, Tyler Sch. Art, Phila. and Rome, 1988. Instr. R.I. Sch. Design, 1996; lectr. in field. One-woman shows include Temple U., Rome, 1988, Willoughby Sharp Gallery, N.Y., 1990, Genovese Gallery, Boston, 1990, 1991, 1994, others, exhibited in group shows at Helander Gallery, N.Y., 1989—93, Palm Beach, 1989—91, N.Y. Pub. Libr., 1994, Austin Ackles Studio, N.Y., 1995, PDX, Portland, 1996, 1998, 2000, Galerie Verneil des Saints-Péres, Paris, Galerie Xippas, numerous others, Represented in permanent collections Senayan Hotel, Jakarta, Yokahama Hotel, Japan, Soho Grand Hotel, N.Y., MIA Ins., Pan Am. Bldg., San Francisco, Muscat Hilton, Oman, David Barton Gym, N.Y. Pub. Libr., Champion Paper, Ohio, Shinwa Med. Inc., Nagoya, Japan, Aero Studios, N.Y., The Boston Co., numerous others. Guggenheim fellow, 1998. Office: c/o PDX Gallery 604 NW 12th Ave Portland OR 97209-3002 E-mail: pdxgallery@aol.com

LORENZEN, JANICE RUTH, physician; b. Chgo., May 29, 1950; d. Andreas Wettring Jr. and Jean Frances (Sinks) L.; ptnr. Margaret E. Johnson. BS, Valparaiso U., 1972; PhD, Albany Med. Coll., 1977; MD, U. Ill., 1986. Diplomate Am. Bd. Endocrinology. Lectr. Northwestern U., Evanston, Ill., 1976-79; rsch. assoc. Coll. Medicine U. Nebr., Omaha, 1979-80, Fla. State U., Tallahasssee, 1980-81; clin. asst. prof. Coll. Medicine U. Ill., Rockford, 1991-97; asst. prof. Western Mich. U., Kalamazoo, 1981-82; fellow U. Wis. Hosps. and Clinics, Madison, 1989-91; physician Rockford (Ill.) Clinic, 1991-97; pvt. practice Beaumont, Tex., 1997-98; pvt. practive Victoria, Tex., 1998—. Contbr. articles to profl. jours. Mem. ACP, Endocrine Soc., Am. Physiol. Soc., Soc. for the Study of Reproduction, Am. Assoc. Clin. Endocrinologists. Avocations: birding, canoeing, golfing, swimming. Office: 2700 Citizens Plz Victoria TX 77901 Home: 106 Evan Cir Victoria TX 77901-2421

LORFANO, PAULINE DAVIS, artist; b. Westbrook, Maine; d. Paul A. and Nellie R. (Robinson) Davis; m. Joseph James Lorfano, Apr. 18, 1952; children: Mary-Jo, Paula, Julie-Ann, Joseph III. Student, Westbrook Coll., 1946-48; Assoc. degree, Maine Coll. Art, 1950; BS, U. Maine, 1951. Tchr. Riggs Sch., Gloucester, Mass., 1951-52; art tchr. Westbriar Elem., Vienna, Va., 1969-76, George Mason U., Fairfax, Va., 1976-80; art tchr., workshop instr. Va., 1980—; juror, lectr. art, 1980—. Illustrator: (book) Visiting Historic Vienna...A Child's Book to Color, 1995; one person shows include Summer Sch. Mus., 1988, Nat. Wildlife Fedn., 1989, Fisher Gallery, Schlesinger Art Ctr., No. Va. C.C., 2002, Dyn Corp. Gallery, Reston, Va., 2003; group shows include Hilton Head Island Exhbn., Va. Watercolor Exhbn., Balt. Watercolor Soc. Mid-Atlantic Regional; works featured for mag. covers. Recipient Heritage Preservation award Historic Vienna, Inc., also awards for art. Mem. Vienna Arts Soc. Inc. (permanent, bd. dirs. 1990-98, pres. 1979-81, 88-90, Stillwell award 1988, Gold medal 1987), Nat. League Am. PEN Women (juried-in mem., cons. art bd. 1994-96, chmn. art bd. 1982-84, 2d Pl. award Biennial Art Exhibit 1992), Va. Watercolor Soc. (co chair 2004, Richmond Region Watercolor award 2002), Potomac Valley Watercolorists (juried, bd. dirs. 1990-98, pres. 1989-90), Washington Watercolor Assn. (juried, exec. bd. chair 1996-97, newsletter editor 1997-2003, Am. Artist award). Home: 402 Old Courthouse Rd NE Vienna VA 22180-3603

LORIMER, LINDA KOCH, university educator; children: Katharine Elizabeth, Peter Brailler. AB, Hollins Coll., 1974; JD, Yale U., 1977; DHL, Green Mountain Coll., 1981, Washington Coll., 1992, Randolph-Macon Coll., 1992. Bar: N.Y. 1978, Conn. 1982. Assoc. Davis Polk and Wardwell, N.Y.C., 1977-78; asst. gen. counsel Yale U., New Haven, 1978-79, assoc. gen. counsel, 1979-84, assoc. provost, 1983-87, acting assoc. v.p. human resources, 1984-85; prof. law, pres. Randolph-Macon Woman's Coll., Lynchburg, Va., 1987-93; v.p., sec. Yale Univ., New Haven, 1993—. Lectr. Yale Coll. Undergrad. Seminars, 1980, 83; bd. dirs. Sprint, McGraw Hill; past pres., mem. exec. com. Women's Coll. Coalition; mem. corp. Yale U., 1990-93, chair Virginia Rhodes scholarship com., 1991-93. Chair editorial bd. Jour. Coll. and Univ. Law, 1983-87. Former trustee Hollins Coll., Berkeley Div. Sch.; mem. com. on responsible conduct rsch. Inst. Medicine, NAS, 1988; bd. dirs. Norfolk Acad.; cabinet mem. United Way of Greater New Haven. Mem. Nat. Assn. Coll. and Univ. Attys. (exec. bd. 1981-84), Nat. Assn. Schs. and Colls. of United Meth. Ch. (1st v.p.), Assn. Am. Colls.,(pres. bd. dirs., chmn. bd.), Am. Assn. Theol. Schs. (bd. dirs.), Mory's Assn., Phi Beta Kappa. Episcopalian. Office: Woodbridge Hall PO Box 208230 Yale Univ New Haven CT 06520-8230

LORING, GLORIA JEAN, vocalist; b. N.Y.C., Dec. 10, 1946; d. Gerald Louis and Dorothy Ann (Tobin) Goff; m. Alan Willis Thicke, Aug. 22, 1970 (div. 1986); children: Brennan Todd, Robin Alan; m. Christopher Beaumont, June 18, 1988 (div. 1993); m. René Lagler, Dec. 20, 1994. Grad. high sch. Owner Glitz Records, L.A., 1984—; pres. Only Silk Prodns., L.A., 1985-90; owner Silk Purse Prodns., 1992—. Began profl. singing, Miami Beach, 1965; appeared in numerous TV shows; featured singer: Bob Hope's Ann. Armed Forces Christmas Tour, 1970; featured several record albums; featured actress: Days of Our Lives, 1980-86; composer: TV themes Facts of Life, 1979, Diff'rent Strokes, 1978; author: Days of Our Lives Celebrity Cookbook, 1981, Vol. II, 1983, Living the Days of Our Lives, 1984, Kids Food and Diabetes, 1986, Parenting a Diabetic Child, 1991, The Kids Food and Diabetes Family Cookbook, 1991, Parenting a Child with Diabetes, 1999. Celebrity chmn. Juvenile Diabetes Rsch. Found. Recipient Humanitarian of Yr. award Juvenile Diabetes Rsch. Found., 1982, 88, Lifetime Commitment award Juvenile Diabetes Rsch. Found., 1999, Woman of Achievement award Miss Am. Orgn., 1999. E-mail: gloria@glorialoring.com.

LORING, HONEY, small business owner; b. Phila. BA in Psychology, U. Md., 1970; MEd, Wash. U., St. Louis, 1971. Lic. psychologist-master Vt.; directress cert. Assn. Montessori Internat. Counselor Gardenville Diagnostic Ctr., St. Louis, 1971-72; tchr. Early Learning Pre-Sch., St. Louis, 1972-74; music dir., cabin counselor Follow Through Day Camp, Brattleboro, Vt., 1972-74; tchr. Montessori Sch., Dublin, 1974-75; ednl. cons. children's books Left Bank Books, St. Louis, 1975-76; program dir. day camp Brattleboro Child Devel., 1975-79; behavioral therapist Behavioral Medicine Unit, Dartmouth Med. Sch., 1979-84; pvt. therapist Brattleboro, Vt., 1984-85; founder, pres. Gone to the Dogs, Inc., Putney, Vt., 1984—. Dog groomer, 1979-92; founder, dir. Camp Gone to the Dogs., 1990—; mfr. dog collars, 1984—; founder Tails Up Inn, 1995-98; took wolves around U.S. to do ednl. environ. programs with the Clem and Jethro Lectr. Svc., 1974-76. Author: (with Jeremy Birch) You're On. . .Teaching Communication Skills, 1984, The Big Good Wolf; contbr. articles to profl. jours. Leader 4-H Dog Club; helper Riding for the Physically Handicapped, St. Louis, 1974. Home and Office: PO Box 600 Putney VT 05346-0600

LORMAN, BARBARA K. former state senator; b. Madison, Wis., July 31, 1932; 3 children. Student, U. Wis., Whitewater and Madison. Pres. Lorman Iron and Metal Recycling Co., Madison, 1979-87; mem. Wis. Senate, Madison, 1980-94. Formerly chair edn. com.; mem. health, human svc. and aging com., mem. fin. insts. and cultural affairs com., mem. select com. on healthcare reform; sec. Legis. Coun., also chmn. spl. com. on farm safety, mem. spl. com. on women offenders in correctional system; mem. spl. com. study sch. aid formula; commr. Edn. Commn. of States. bd. mem. Ft Atkinson Health Svcs., Auril. Bd. dirs. Rainbow Hospice Care, Inc., Ft. Atkinson (Wis.) Devel. Coun., Ft. Atkinson Meml. Hosp., Madison Area Tech. Coll., Wis. Pub. Radio Assn., Ft. Atkinson Hist. Soc., Ft. Atkinson Cmty. Found.; mem. exec. bd. Sinissippi coun. Boy Scouts Am.; mem. Wis. Gov.'s Commn. USS Wisconsin; mem. bd. visitors U. Wis. Extension; active Wis. Rep. Com.; chmn. spl. projects com. City of Ft. Atkinson. Mem. Rotary. Address: 1245 Janette St Fort Atkinson WI 53538-1526

LO RUSSO, DIANE, radiologist; b. N.Y.C., NY, Apr. 22, 1946; MD, SUNY, 1969. Cert. diagnostic radiology 1974. Intern Brookdale Hosp. Med. Ctr., Bklyn., 1969—70; resident Montefiore Med. Ctr., Bronx, 1971—74; radiologist Rye Radiology Assoc., Rye Brook, NY, 1974—. Office: Rye Radiology Assoc 30 Rye Ridge Plz Rye Brook NY 10573-2830

LOSADA-ZARATE, GLORIA, psychologist; b. Havana, Cuba, Apr. 20, 1957; came to U.S., 1962; d. Manuel Benito and Maria del Pilar (Fernandez) Losada; m. Timothy John Henry Paisey, June 4, 1983 (div. June 1989); 1 child, Monica Paisey ; m. Juan S. Zarate, Dec. 31, 2001. BA, Fla. Internat. U., 1980; D Psychology, Nova U., 1984. Lic. psychologist, Conn. Predoctoral pyschology fellow Yale U., New Haven, 1983-84; dir. treatment program for mentally retarded offenders Southbury Tng. Sch., Stat of Conn., 1984—86; clin. psychologist State of Conn. Dept. Mental Retardation New Haven Ctr., New Haven, 1986-88; dir. psychol. svcs. State of Conn. Dept. Mental Retardation Region 6, Waterford, Conn., 1988-92; clin. psychologist State of Conn. Dept. of Mental Health and Addiction Svcs., Middletown, 1997—2002; supervising psychologist Conn. Dept. Children and Families, Middletown, 2002—. Pvt. practice psychology, 1986—. Mem. APA. Democrat. Roman Catholic. Avocations: ballet, classical music, jazz, contemporary dance. Office: 95 E Main St Ste B-15 Meriden CT 06450

LOSCALZO, ANITA BETH, librarian; b. Salem, N.J., Mar. 11, 1950; d. Seymour Sendrow and Pearl Horwitz; m. Joseph Loscalzo, Mar. 10, 1974; children: Julia F., Alexander J. BA cum laude, U. Pa., 1972; MS, Drexel U., Phila., 1974. Ref. libr. Hahnemann Med. Coll., Phila., 1973—75; manuscript libr. Acad. Natural Scis., Phila., 1977—78; rsch. asst. Brigham & Women's Hosp., Boston, 1978—80; med. libr. Glover Meml. Hosp., Needham, Mass., 1982—87; rsch. asst. Brigham & Women's Hosp., Boston, 1990—93; rsch. libr. Whitaker Cardiovascular Inst., Boston, 1994—. Cons. Digital Equip. Corp., Maynard, Mass., 1987—91, Braintree Hosp., Mass., 1988—92; cons. instr. Mass. Med. Soc., Waltham, 1985—86. Contbr. articles to profl. jours. Mem. Dover Dem. Town Com., 1994—; trustee Dover Town Libr., Mass., 1996—; bd. dirs. Friends of the Dover Libr., 1993—2000. Mem.: Acad. Health Info. Profls. (disting. mem.), North Atlantic Health Scis. Librs., Med. Libr. Assn., Mass. Health Scis. Libr. Network (pres. 1999—2000, bd. dirs. 1987—). Avocations: reading, gardening, quilting. Home: 16 Ledgewood Dr Dover MA 02030 Office: Whitaker Cardiovascular Inst 715 Albany St W507 Boston MA 02118

LOSCHIAVO, LINDA BOSCO, library director; b. Rockville Ctr., N.Y., Aug. 31, 1950; d. Joseph and Jennie (DelRegno) Bosco; m. Joseph A. LoSchiavo, Sept. 7, 1974. BA, Fordham U., 1972, MA, 1990; MLS, Pratt Inst., 1974. Picture cataloguer Frick Art Reference Libr., N.Y.C., 1972-75; sr. cataloguer Fordham U. Libr., Bronx, N.Y., 1975-87, head of retrospective conversion, 1987-90, systems libr., 1990-91, dir. libr. at Lincoln Ctr., 1991—. Libr. cons. Mus. Am. Folk Art Libr., N.Y.C., 1985-90; indexer Arco Books, N.Y.C., 1974. Editor: Macbeth, 1990, Julius Caesar, 1990, Romeo and Juliet, 1990. Mng. producer Vineyard Opera, N.Y.C., 1981-88. Mem. ALA, N.Y. Tech. Svcs. Librs., Beta Phi Mu, Alpha Sigma Nu. Home: 317 Collins Ave Mount Vernon NY 10552-1601 Office: Fordham Univ Library 113 W 60th St New York NY 10023-7404

LOSIER-COOL, ROSE MARIE, Canadian senator; b. Tracadie, NB, Can., June 18, 1937; 2 children. BEd, U. Moncton; tchg. cert., École Normale, Fredericton. Tchr. Népisiguit H.S., Bathurst, 1972—93; senator The Senate of Can., Ottawa, 1995—. Co-chmn. Can. Assn. Parliamentarians on Population and Devel. Mem.: Can. Tchrs. Fedn. (Status of Women com., Ednl. Dev. com.). Liberal. Office: 266-N Centre Block The Senate of Canada Ottawa ON Canada K1A 0A4

LOSS, LYNNE FRANKLIN, artist, volunteer; b. Vinita, Okla., July 28, 1943; d. Henry Franklin Davis and Elizabeth Viranda Franklin; m. David Martin Loss, Sept. 3, 1961; children: Scott Martin, Mark Gregory. Degree in Bus. Edn., Draughons Bus. Coll., Albuquerque, 1964. Mem.: DAR (registrar Zia chpt., past vice regent Zia chpt., Cert. of Award for various donations 2001), U.S. Daus. 1812 (organizer and state registrar N.Mex. state chpt.). Baptist. Home: 11401 Claremont NE Albuquerque NM 87112

LOSS, MARGARET RUTH, lawyer; b. Phila., June 17, 1946; d. Louis and Bernice Rose (Segaloff) L.; 1 child, Elizabeth Loss Johnson. BA, Radcliffe Coll., 1967; LLB, Yale U., 1970. Bar: Conn. 1970, N.Y. 1973. Assoc. Sullivan & Cromwell, N.Y.C., 1971-77; with Equitable Life Assurance Soc. U.S., N.Y.C., 1977-88, asst. gen. counsel, 1979-85, v.p. and counsel, 1985-88; counsel LeBoeuf, Lamb, Greene & MacRae, N.Y.C., 1988-98. Mem. com. Yale Law Sch. Fund. Mem. ABA, Am. Law Inst., Conn. Bar Assn., Assn. of Bar of City N.Y. Home and Office: 201 E 80th St # 12A New York NY 10021-0516

LOSSE, CATHERINE ANN, pediatric nurse, critical care nurse, educator, clinical nurse specialist, family nurse practitioner; b. Mount Holly, N.J., Mar. 12, 1959; d. David C. and Bernice (Lewis) Losse; 1 child, Kaitlyn. Diploma, Helene Fuld Sch. Nursing, 1980; BSN magna cum laude, Thomas Jefferson U., 1986; MSN, U. Pa., 1989; Family Nurse Practitioner Cert., Widener U., 1997. RN N.J., Pa. Staff nurse adult med.-surg. Meml. Hosp. Burlington County, Mount Holly, N.J., 1980-81; staff nurse pediatric home care Newborn Nurses, Moorestown, N.J., 1986-87; clin. nurse II surg. intensive care Deborah Heart & Lung Ctr., Browns Mills, N.J., 1986-87, clin. nurse III pediatric cardiology, 1981-86, 87-97; ednl. nurse specialist critical care The Children's Hosp., Phila., 1992-94; instr. nursing of families, maternal-child health, pediat., geriatrics Burlington County Coll., 1994-96; staff nurse pediatric home care Bayada Nurses, Burlington, N.J., 1995; family nurse practitioner Alliance Family Medicine Ctr. Fam. Med. Res. Prog., Mt. Holly, N.J., 1997-99; nurse practitioner long term care The Masonic Home of N.J., Burlington, 1999—. Clin. instr. pediat. Thomas Jefferson U., 1990; clin. instr. adult med. surg. Burlington County Coll., 1991. Rep. Congress on Policy and Practice: Gerongol. Health rep., 2001—03. Mem.: ANA, Congress on Policy and Practice (rep. gerontologic health 2001—03), Am. Geriatrics Soc., N.J. State Nurses Assn. (cabinet on continuing edn. rev. team III 1992—96, advanced practice forum 1994—). Home: 253 Spout Spring Ave Lumberton NJ 08048-2041 Office Phone: 609-239-3954. E-mail: cal@njmasonic.org.

LOTAN, RACHEL, education educator; BA in English Lit. and French Lang., Lit. and Civilization, Tel Aviv U., 1971; MA in Edn., Stanford U., 1981, MA in Sociology, 1983, PhD in Edn., 1985. Assoc. prof. edn. Stanford (Calif.) U., 1999—; tchr. jr. and sr. h.s., 1969—80; rsch. asst. Ctr. for Ednl. Rsch., Stanford U., Calif., 1982—85. Vis. asst./assoc. prof. Inst. for Advancement of Social Integration in Schs., Bar-Ilan U., Israel, 1986—91. Mem. editl. bd.: European Jour. for Intercultural Edn. Office: Stanford U Sch Edn 485 Lasuen Mall Stanford CA 94305-3096

LOTAS, JUDITH PATTON, advertising executive; b. Iowa City, Apr. 23, 1942; d. John Henry and Jane (Vandike) Patton; children: Amanda Bell, Alexandra Vandike. BA, Fla. State U., 1964. Copywriter Liller, Neal, Battle and Lindsey Advt., Atlanta, 1964-67, Grey Advt., N.Y.C., 1967-72; creative group head SSC&B Advt., N.Y.C., 1972-74, assoc. creative dir., 1974-79, v.p., 1975-79, sr. v.p., 1979-82, exec. creative dir., 1982-86; founding ptnr. Lotas Minard Patton McIver, Inc., N.Y.C., 1986—. Fundraiser Nat. Coalition Homeless, N.Y.C., 1986—; mem. creative rev. bd. Partnership Drug-Free Am.; bd. dirs. Samuel Wasman Cancer Rsch. Found., N.Y.C., 1981—88, Women's Venture Fund, 1995—; active scholarship fund raising. Named Woman of Achievement, YWCA; named one of Advt.'s 100 Best Women, Ad Age, 1989; recipient Clio award, Venice Film Festival award, Graphics award, Am. Inst. Graphic Artists, 1970, Effie award, Grad. of Distinction award, Fla. State U., 1993. Mem.: Ad. Coun. (mem. creative rev. bd. 1994—, bd. dirs. 1995—), Advt. Women N.Y. (bd. dirs. 1981—87, 1st v.p. 1984—87, Advt. Woman of the Yr. 1993), Kappa Alpha Theta. Democrat. Home: 45 E 89th St New York NY 10128-1251 E-mail: jlotas@earthlink.net., jlotas@lpny.com.

LOTEMPIO, JULIA MATILD, retired accountant; b. Budapest, Hungary, Oct. 14, 1934; came to U.S., 1958, naturalized 1962; d. Istvan and Irma (Sandor) Fejos; m. Anthony Joseph LoTempio, Mar. 11, 1958. AAS in Lab. Tech. summa cum laude, Niagara County C.C., Sanborn, N.Y., 1967; BS in Tech. and Vocat. Edn. summa cum laude, SUNY, Buffalo, 1970; MEd in Guidance and Counseling, Niagara U., 1973, BBA in Acctg. summa cum laude, 1983, MBA in Mgmt., 1998. Sr. analyst, rschr. Gt. Lakes Carbon Co., Niagara Falls, N.Y., 1967-71; tchr. sci. Niagara Falls Schs., 1973-75; tchr. sci. and English Starpoint Sch. System, Lockport, N.Y., 1975-77; club adminstr., acct. Twinlo Racquetball, Inc., Niagara Falls, 1979-81; bus. cons. Twinlo Beverage, Inc., Niagara Falls, 1981-85; staff acct. J.D. Elliott & Co. PC, CPAs, Buffalo, 1986-87; acct. Lewiston, NY, 1988—2001; instr. applied chemistry Niagara County C.C., Sanborn, NY, 1979, instr. acctg. principles, 1989—2001; ret., 2001. Bd. dirs. Niagara Frontier Meth. Home Inc., Niagara Frontier Nursing Home Inc., The Blocher Homes Inc., Buffalo. Mem. faculty continuing edn., speaker, chairperson fin. and community rels. coms. United Meth. Ch., Dickersonville, N.Y., 1985-90; guest speaker, counselor, tchr. Beechwood Svc. Guild, Buffalo, 1987-91; bd. dirs. Niagara Frontier Meth. Home, Inc., Getzville, N.Y., 1988-2001; bd. dirs., mem. fin., investment, pension, ins., and community rels. coms. Niagara Frontier Nursing Home Co., Inc., Getzville, 1988-2001, Blocher Homes, Inc., Williamsville, N.Y., 1988-2001; asst. sec., bd. dirs., mem. exec., quality and assurance coms., chmn. community rels. com. Beechwood/Blocher Community, Buffalo, 1990-2001; mem. Coop. Parish Coun., Sanborn, N.Y., 1991-94; mem. adminstrv. bd., chmn. outreach com. Pekin (N.Y.) United Meth. Ch., 1992-2000; sec. to bd. dirs. Beechwood/Blocher Found., Amherst, N.Y., 1992-93, asst. treas., 1993-94, treas., 1994, vice chmn., 1994-2001. Mem. NAFE, Nat. Soc. Pub. Accts., Nat. Assn. Accts., Nat. Fedn. Bus. and Profl. Women's Club, Internat. Platform Assn., Niagara U. Alumni Assn., SUNY Coll. Buffalo Alumni Assn., Niagara County C.C. Alumni Assn. Avocations: public speaking, walking, travel, reading, computers. Home and Office: 1026 Ridge Rd Lewiston NY 14092-9704

LOTT, BRENDA LOUISE, insurance company executive; b. Clinton, Ind., July 29, 1955; d. John and Thelma Louise (Anderson) Pastore; m. Robert Ralph Rundle, June 16, 1974 (div. July 1985); children: Danielle Marie Rundle, John Robert Rundle; m. Mark Lee Lott, July 4, 1985. BA in Polit. Sci., Colo. Women's Coll., Denver, 1976; student, Ins. Inst. of Am. Claim adjuster Allstate Ins. Co., Englewood, Colo., 1973-83; field claim adjuster Transamerica Ins. Co., Englewood, 1983-86; claim examiner Colonial Ins. Co., Denver, 1986-87, examiner/supr., 1987-89, regional claim mgr., 1990-92; dir. financial and insurance svcs. Innovative Svcs. Am., Golden, Colo., 1992—. Staff speaker Western Ins. Info. Svc., Denver, 1983-85; participant, invited faculty mem. 5-day lecture series Colonial Univ., Anaheim, Calif., 1990. Sponsor Plan Internat. foster parents program, 1989—. Mem. NAFE, LWV, NAACP (mem.-at-large), Ins. Women of Denver, Internat. Customer Svc. Assn., Colo. Claims Assn. (bd. dirs. 1986-88), Claim Mgrs. Coun., Denver Claims Assn., PGA Tours Ptnrs. Avocations: raquetball, co-ed flag football, basketball, tennis, golf. Office: Innovative Svcs of Am 13922 Denver West Pkwy Ste 200 Golden CO 80401-3142

LOTT, ERIN ELIZABETH, literature educator; b. McAllister, Okla., Sept. 15, 1974; d. Robert Jean and Elizabeth Jean Lott. BA, Denison U., 1996; attended, U. Coll. Galway, Ireland, 1995; MFA, U. Utah, 1998. Engl. tchr. Rowland Hall St. Mark's, Salt Lake City, 1998, Colo. Acad., Denver, 1998—2002, Bentley Sch., Lafayette, Calif., 2002—. Judge Scholastic Press Assn., 2002. Author: (short stories) Cimmaron Review, 1998. Tchr. grant, Nat. Endowment for Humanities, 1999, 2001. Mem.: Amnesty Internat. Democrat.

LOTT, JOYCE GREENBERG, English language educator; b. Atlantic City, Jan. 27, 1938; d. David E. and Florence (Steinig) Feinstein; m. Morton I. Greenberg, June 30, 1956 (div. 1983); m. Gary C. Lott, Sept. 30, 1984; children: Elizabeth Greenberg, Suzanne Greenberg, Larry Greenberg. BA, Douglass Coll., 1976; MA, Rutgers U., 1979. Tchr. English South Brunswick H.S., N.J., 1978-80. Mem. adj. English faculty Somerset County C.C., N.J., 1978-80; leader, cons. in-svc. workshops in pub. schs., N.J., 1992—; spkr. on portfolios, reflective writing, multicultural lit. at nat. convs., Milw., San Diego, Pitts., Seattle, 1990—. Author: When Kids Dare to Question Their Education, 1995, A Teacher's Stories, Reflections on High School Writers, 1994; contbr. stories and articles to mags. and jours. Recipient N.J. Poetry Monthly prize; co-winner Acad. of Am. Poets Contest. Mem. ASCD, Nat. Coun. Tchrs. English, N.J. Edn. Assn. Avocations: tennis, skiing, bicycling. Home: 5 Toth Ln Rocky Hill NJ 08553-1025

LOTT, VERA NAOMI, artist, educator; b. Allentown, Pa., Oct. 26, 1923; d. Russell Edgar and Tivilia Landis (Gerhart) Kemmerer; m. Jack Edward Lott (dec. Nov. 1998); children: Dennis Michael, Jack Andrew(dec.), Gary Randall, Timothy Blair, Bruce Edward. Grad. h.s., Phila. Art tchr., 1960—. YWCA, Ohio. Judge Ohio State Fair for Childrens Art Show; pvt. art tchr., Westerville, Ohio; pvt. dance instr. Singer for 3 ch. choirs; singer for 2 sr. ctrs. With U.S. Coast Guard, 1940—42. Recipient 1st place for pencil portraits of children, Graceland. Mem.: Westerville Art League (past pres., sec.). Lutheran. Home: 7000 Lee Rd Apt3R Westerville OH 43081-9557

LOTZE, BARBARA, retired physicist; b. Jan. 4, 1924; came to U.S., 1961, naturalized, 1967. d. Matyas and Borbala (Toth) Kalo; m. Dieter P. Lotze, Oct. 6, 1958 (dec. Dec. 1987); m. Herbert L. Retcofsky, July 1998. Applied Math. Diploma with honors, Eotvos Lorand U. Scis., Budapest, Hungary, 1956; PhD, Innsbruck (Austria) U., 1961. Mathematician Hungarian Cen. Statis. Bur., Budapest, 1955-56; tchr. math. Iselsberg, Austria, 1959-60; from asst. prof. physics to assoc. prof. to prof. Allegheny Coll., 1963-90, prof. emeritus, 1990—, chmn. dept., 1981-84. Lectr. in history of physics; speaker to civic groups. Editor: Making Contributions: An Historical Overview of Women's Role in Physics, 1984; co-editor: The First War Between Socialist States: The Hungarian Revolution of 1956 and Its Impact, 1984; contbr. articles to profl. jours. Mem. AAUW, Am. Phys. Soc. (mem. com. internat. freedom of scientists 1993-95), Am. Inst. Physics (mem. adv. com. history of physics 1994-97), Am. Assn. Physics Tchrs. (coun., sect. rep. Western Pa. 1978-86, chmn. com. on women in physics 1983-84, com. internat. physics edn. 1991-93, com. history and philosophy of physics 1996-98, Disting. Svc. award 1986, cert. of appreciation 1988), Am. Hungarian Educators Assn. (pres. 1980-82). Home: 2269 Watchfield Dr South Park PA 15129-8977

LOTZE, EVIE DANIEL, psychodramatist; b. Roswell, N.Mex., Mar. 6, 1943; d. Wadsworth Richard and Lee Ora (Norrell) Daniel; m. Christian Dieter Lotze, June 9, 1963; children: Conrad, Monica. BA cum laude, La. State U., 1964; MA, Goddard Coll., 1975; PhD, Union Inst., Cin., 1990. Dir. Casa Alegre, Hogares, Albuquerque, 1979-80; pvt. practice Riyadh, Saudi Arabia, 1980-83, Silver Spring, Md., 1983-85; dir. Gulf States Psychodrama Tng., Houston, 1986-88; founder, dir. Innerstages Psychodrama Tng., Houston and Washington, 1988-99; program devel. cons. in tng. Children's Nat. Med. Ctr., Washington, 1994-96; pvt. practice Paris, 1996-97; mem. sr. profl. staff Pretrial Svcs. Resource Ctr., Washington, 1998-2001; mem. Work Culture Transformation Bd., USAF, 2001; cons. Work Transformation Group, 2001—. Supr. Houston Area psychodramatists, 1988—98; tng. cons. Assn. Applied Psychologists, Moscow, 1992—97; cons. in field. Author: (tng. manual) Clinical Psychodrama Training Manual, 3 vols., 1990, Pretrial Services Reference Book, 1999, From Straw to Gold: Transforming the Work Culture, A Modern Hero's Joruney, 2004. Bd. dirs. Interact Theater, Houston, 1992, Arts & Humanities Alliance, Jefferson County. Recipient Fulbright sr. scholars award for Russia. Democrat. Lutheran. Avocations: cross-country skiing, biking, hiking, camping, reading. Home: 2250 Leetown Pike Kearneysville WV 25430 E-mail: evielotze@citlink.net.

LOU, LIZA, artist; Student, San Francisco Art Inst. One-woman shows include Santa Monica Mus. Art, Bass Mus. Art, Miami, Kemper Mus. Contmporary Art, Kansas City, Ctr. Estudis Art Contemporani, Barcelona, exhibited in group shows at New Mus., NYC, Heinie Onstad Kunstenter, Norway, Victoria and Albert Mus., London, Fondation Cartier, Paris. Fellow MacArthur Found. fellow, 2002. Office: c/o Elizabeth Schwartz/Deitch Projects 76 Grand St New York NY 10013

LOUDERMILK, MARY RUTH, local government volunteer; b. Washington, Ind., Sept. 27, 1944; d. Richard Raymond and Bessie Delores (Collins) Higgins; m. Wilmer Eugene Loudermilk, Sept. 26, 1964; children: Delores, Richard. Operator Bell Phone, Lawrenceville, Ill., 1963-64; coun. person ward 2 Cedar Lake (Ind.) Town Coun., 1984-91, 95-99, pres., 1996. Vol. Boy Scouts Am., Cedar Lake, 1977—; team chmn., life mem. Girl Scouts, 1973-83; mem. Cedar Lake Plan Commn., Ambulance Commn., Derlick Bldg. Commn., 1984-91; vice chmn. Cedar Lake Dem. Orgn., mem. De. Precinct Com.; past mem. Band Boosters, Hanover, Cedar Lake PTA, Cedar Lake Little League, Cedar Lake Girls Softball; past honor queen of Job's Daughters, past Gardine treas. of Jobs, coun. person. Named Woman of Yr. in Govt., Women Jaycees, Cedar Lake, 1984-85. Mem. Cedar Lake Profl. Bus. Women, Order Ea. Star, Job's Daugs. (past honor queen). Democrat. Methodist. Home: PO Box 238 Cedar Lake IN 46303-0238 E-mail: maryruth238@yahoo.com.

LOUGH, SUSAN M. music educator; d. Henry L. and Louise E. Ekstrom; m. Thomas R. Lough, Aug. 11, 1979; children: Ryan T., Jonathan H. BS, Taylor U., 1979; MS, Ind. U., 1982. Jr. high, h.s. choral dir. Churubusco (Ind.) H.S., 1979—82; elem. music specialist Churubusco (Ind.) Elem. Sch., 1982—. Dir. handchimes Ft. Wayne (Ind.) Children's Choir. Bd. mem. Carroll H.S. Cmty. Assn., Fort Wayne, 1998—2003; steering com. mem. Youth For Christ-Campus Life, Fort Wayne, 1997—2003. Recipient Margaret Ann Keegan award, Arts United, Ft. Wayne, 1992, Friend of Rotary award, Churubusco, 2003. Mem.: Ind. Music Educators Assn. (exhibits chair 1994—2000), Music Educators Nat. Conf. Office: Churubusco Elem Sch 3 Eagle Dr Churubusco IN 46723 E-mail: slough@r8esc.k12.in.us.

LOUGHNANE, AUDREY MORAN, town councilor; b. Worcester, Mass., Jan. 2, 1936; d. Samuel J. and Agnes L. (Moran) Donnelly; m. John B. Loughnane, June 11, 1955; children: John B. Jr., Christine M. Diploma, Salter Secretarial, 1954; AA with high honors, Cape Cod C.C., 1973. Sec. Olson Mfg. Co., Worcester, 1954-56; real estate broker Worcester, 1961—; mem. town meeting Town of Barnstable, Mass., 1983-89, town councilor. Pres. West Barnstable Civic Assn., 1989-91; dist. water commr. West Barnstable Fire, 1990-92; treas./sec. Joint Village Assn., Barnstable, 1985-91; gov. Sandy Neck Governing Bd., Town of Barnstable, 1987-89; mem. environ. policy com. Mass. Mcpl. Assn., Boston, 1995—; bd. dirs. Mass. Soc. Prevention Cruelty of Children, Cape Cod, 1991-93; Miracle Kitchen vol. Salvation Army, Hyannis, Mass.; mem. coms. County Barnstable, 1984—. Mem. Barnstable Hist. Soc., Whelden Libr., Barnstable County Selectmen and Councilors Assn. (treas.). Avocation: travel. Home: 26 Point Hill Rd West Barnstable MA 02668-1015 Office: Town of Barnstable 367 Main St Hyannis MA 02601-3907

LOUIS, BARBARA, psychologist, educator; b. Fond du Lac, Wis., Sept. 30, 1950; d. H. J. and Mary Anne (Reichard) Mueller; m. Stanley D. Louis, Jan. 20, 1974 (div. May. 1988); children: Joshua, Justin. M.S./Ph.D., Rutgers U., 1992. Diplomate Am. Bd. Psychol. Spltys.; lic. psychologist. Predoctoral fellow UMDNJ-Robert Wood Johnson Med. Sch., New Brunswick, NJ, 1986—90, instr. pediat., 1990—92, asst. prof. pediat., 1992—2001, assoc. prof. pediat., 2001—; program dir. Gifted Child Clinic, New Brunswick, NJ, 1995—; assoc. prof. Rutgers U., New Brunswick, NJ, 2002—. Admissions cons. Hunter Coll. Campus Schs., N.Y.C., NY, 1994—; guest reviewer Roeper Rev., 1988—89, Early Child Rsch. Quar., 2003; grant rev. panel Ester Katz Rosen Award, 1997—99; grabt rev. panel NJ Assn. for Gifted Children, 1998—2000; mem. editl. bd. Roeper Rev., 2000—. Author: (book/video) Identifying Gifted Preschoolers; contbr. chapters to books, articles to profl. jours. Grad. scholar Rutgers U., 1990. Mem. APA, Nat. Assn. Gifted Children, Internat. Soc. Infant Studies, Soc. Rsch. Child Devel., N.J. Assn. Gifted Children (trustee 1994-2000). Achievements include research in Giftedness in Children; Encouraging Car Seat Use in Inner City Toddlers; Identifying Inner City Minority Gifted Children. Office: UMDNJ-Robert Wood Johnson Medical School 97 Paterson Street New Brunswick NJ 08903 E-mail: louisba@umdnj.edu.

LOUIS-DREYFUS, JULIA, actress; b. N.Y.C., Jan. 13, 1961; d. William and Judith Louis-Dreyfus; m. Brad Hall, 1987; children: Henry, Charles. Attended, Northwestern U. Former mem. Second City and the Practical Theatre Company, Chicago, Ill. TV appearances include Saturday Night Live, 1982-85, Day by Day, 1986-89, The Art of Being Nick, 1986, Seinfeld, 1989-98 (Emmy award supp. actress, 1996, Emmy nom., 1992, 93, 94, 95, 97, 98, Amer. Comedy award best supp. actress, 1993, 94, 95, 97, 98, Golden Globe award supp. actress, 1994, SAG award, 1997, 98), Animal Farm (voice), 1999, Gepetto, 2002; actor, prodr. Watching Ellie, 2002-2003; TV guest appearances include Family Ties, 1988, Dinosaurs, 1991, The Single Guy, 1995, Hey Arnold, 1997, Curb Your Enthusiasm, 2000, 01, The Simpsons (voice), 2001, Arrested Development, 2004; films

Soul Man, 1986, Troll, 1986, Hannah and Her Sisters, 1986, National Lampoon's Christmas Vacation, 1989, Jack the Bear, 1993, North, 1994, Father's Day, 1997, (TV movie) London Suite, 1996, Deconstructing Harry, 1997, A Bug's Life (voice) 1998, Gilligan's Island, 1999, Speak Truth to Power, 2000. Office: Jonas PR 240 26th St Ste 3 Santa Monica CA 90402 also: Hofflund/Polone 9465 Wilshire Blvd Beverly Hills CA 90212*

LOUISON, DEBORAH FINLEY, global public affairs consultant; b. Aberdeen, S.D., Sept. 20, 1951; d. Donald S. and Barbara F. (Lowenstein) Finley; 1 child, Stacey Renee. BA, Nat. Coll. Edn., 1987. Asst. to sec. Dept. Edn. & Cultural Affairs State of S.D., Pierre, 1973-77; program dir. forestry div. State of S.D., Pierre, 1978-81; legisl. dir. Congressman Clint Roberts, Washington, 1981-83, Congresswoman Barbara Vucanovich, Washington, 1983-84; assoc. dir. fed. affairs Nat. Conf. State Legisl., Washington, 1984-89, dir. govt. affairs, 1989; dept. asst. sec. U.S. Dept. of Energy, 1989-93; sr. v.p., dir. global svcs. APCO Assocs. Worldwide, Washington, 1993—2003; v.p. govt. relations Cadbury Schweppes Am. Region, 2004—. Contbr. articles to profl. jours. Planning and devel. com. Pierre C. of C., 1974-76; campaign asst. Clint Roberts for Congress, 1979-80; coordinator for state legisl. Bush/Quayle Campaign, Washington, 1988. Mem. NAFE, Women in Govt. Relations (com. chair), U.S. Energy Assn., Natural Gas Rountable. Republican. Roman Catholic. Avocation: golf. Office: Cadbury Schweppes 1225 I St NW Ste 300 Washington DC 20005 E-mail: deborah.louison@am.csplc.com.

LOUNDMON-CLAY, JUANITA L. academic administrator, educator, dean; b. Charleston, W.Va., Aug. 11; d. Albert D. and Mattie L. (Collins) L.; m. Earl Clay Jr. (dec.); children: Pamela Clay-Mitchell, Kimberly Clay-Clay, Dana Clay-Braddock. BA, W.Va. State Coll.; MSW, W.Va. U.; MA, Ind. U.; PhD, Fla. State U., 1978. Psychologist Navistar Corp., Indpls., 1978-80; pvt. practice psychology, Indpls., 1980-84; clin. psychologist Lakeview Mental Health Ctr., Pensacola, Fla., 1984-85; pvt. practice A Better Way Christian Counseling Ministry, Tallahassee, Fla., 1985-88; prof. Regent U., Virginia Beach, Va., 1988-89; assoc. prof. Am. U. of Les Cayes, Haiti, 1989-91; mental health cons. to Christian Orgns., Ft. Wayne, Ind.; pres., CEO A Better Way Counseling and Cons. Agy., Ft. Wayne; v.p. student affairs, assoc. prof. Bluefield State Coll. Cons. Washington Project, 1989—, Haiti Mins. Conf., Port-Au-Prince, 1989; founder, dir. first group treatment home for adolescent girls in State of Ind.; founder A Better Way Counseling and Diagnostic Agy. Author: New Career Development Strategies For The Black Working Poor, 1977; prodr. Black-on-Black Pub. Svc. TV Program. Precinct chmn. Rep. Exec. Com., Tallahassee, 1987-88; bd. mem. City Coun. EEO Commn., Tallahassee, 1987-89, Bluefield Cmty. Ctr., 2000-01; former pres. Ind. Conf. Social Welfare, Indpls.; bd. dirs. Cmty. Action of N.E. Ind., Ft. Wayne Ballet, Old Fort br. YMCA; life mem. NAACP, mem. cmty. access network TV, Martin Luther King Breakfast Club Inc.; candidate Ind. Legislature, 1996; vol. docent Lincoln Mus.; spkr., motivator Christian Women's Groups, Fla. U. Systems grantee, 1976; named one of Outstanding Young Women Am., 1978; recipient Cmty. Svc. award City of Pensacola, 1974, YMCA, C. of C., Ft. Wayne, Ind., 1970, Ebony in Excellence award, 1997. Mem. Am. Assn. Counseling and Devel., Va. Assn. Counseling and Devel., Ind. Psychology Assn. (life), Kiwanis Internat. Office: 219 Rock St Bluefield WV 24701 Home: 15175 Pratola Ct #B Morgan Hill CA 95037 5836 E-mail: JCandJesus@Juno1.com.

LOVE, APRIL GAYE MCLEAN, librarian; b. San Jose, Calif., Apr. 28, 1947; d. Frederick F. and Geneva A. (Gmelin) McL.; m. Glen Bolinger, 1974 (div. 1984). B.A., U. Oreg., 1969, M.L.S., 1970, M.A. in Biology, 1976; postgrad. U. Calif.-Irvine, 1976-81, 1987—. Research asst. Oreg. State U., Corvallis, 1972-74; sci. illustrator Smithsonian Inst., La Jolla, Calif., 1974; sci. bibliographer U. Calif.-Irvine, 1975—, phys. scis. reference librarian, phys. sci. bibliographer dept. collection and devel., also mem. percussion ensemble, Sch. Fine Arts, U. Calif.-Irvine Symphony Orch., 1986—, co-dir. classical music Sta. KUCI-radio. Mem. ALA (conf. attendant, 1981, 87), Calif. Acad. Research Librarians, Sci. and Engring. Academic Librarians (chair program com., sec. so. br., 1988—), So. Calif. Botanists, Orange County Library Assn; attended confs. in field. Choreographer: Everyone Gets the Blues, 1980; contbr. article to popular mag. Office: Univ Calif Phys Scis Library PO Box 19557 Irvine CA 92623-9557

LOVE, BRENDA ZEJDL, writer; b. Temple, Tex., Dec. 13, 1950; d. Johnnie James Billings and Robbie Erlene (Frazier) Welch; m. Lee James Harwell (div.); 1 child, Clinton Dee; m. Frank Lincoln Leary III, Feb. 14, 1982 (div. 1987); m. Mark K. Zejdl, Oct. 16, 1996. Student, Austin C.C., 1978-80, Foothill Coll., 1984-93; BA, Trinity Coll. and U., 1990; PhD, Hamilton U., 1992—; postgrad., Inst. Advanced Study, San Francisco, 1993—. Emergency med. tech.; lic. pilot. Emergency med. tech. Breckenridge Hosp., Austin, Tex., 1979, Santa Clara Valley (Calif.) Med. Ctr., 1980; outside sales rep. Bus. Equipment Co., San Francisco, 1981-82; counselor Nat. Sexually Transmitted Disease Hotline, Palo Alto, Calif., 1984-86, Nat. AIDS Hotline, Palo Alto, 1986-87, San Francisco Sex Information Switchboard, San Francisco, 1987-88; adminstrv. asst. ALZA Corp., Palo Alto, 1988—2001; adminstrn. Alexza MDC, Palo Alto, Calif., 2002—. Lectr., researcher Inst. for Advanced Study of Human Sexuality; bus. mgr. Frank Leary Racing, 1981-83; adminstrv. asst. to chief adminstrv. law judge Tex. Comptroller Pub. Accounts, 1978-80. Author: Encyclopedia of Unusual Sex Practices, 1992; co-producer: (video) 500 Unusual Sex Practices, 1992; contbr. articles to profl. jours. Mem. Author's Guild, Inst. for Advanced Study of Human Sexuality, Am. Assn. Sex Educators, Counselors and Therapists, Soc. for Sic. Study of Sex, Calif. Writers Club, Mystery Writers Am. Libertarian. Jewish. Avocations: flying, sky diving, skating, photography. Office: Alexza MDC 1001 E Meadow Cir Palo Alto CA 94303 E-mail: lovezejdl@hotmail.com.

LOVE, CAROL, dean; Assoc. dean, educator Simmons Coll. Mem. Commn. Nursing Practice, Mass.; mem. adv. bd. Sch. Pub. Health Ednl. Resource Ctr. Harvard U., mem. faculty Sch. Pub. Health. Contbr. articles to profl. jours. Mem. APHA, Am. Assn. Occupl. Health Nurses, Nat. Orgn. Nurse Practitioner Faculty, Mass. Nurses Assn., Mass. Assn. Colls. Nursing (pres. tri coun. nursing), Sigma Theta Tau. Office: Simmons Coll Grad Sch Health Studies 300 The Fenway Boston MA 02115-5820 Fax: 617-521-3137. E-mail: GSHSADM@simmons.edu.

LOVE, COURTNEY, singer, actress; b. San Francisco, July 9, 1964; d. Hank Harrison and Linda Carroll; m. Kurt Cobain, Feb. 1992 (dec.); 1 child, Frances Bean. Singer, writer, musician Hole, 1989—2002. Albums with Hole include Pretty on the Inside, 1991, Live Through This, 1994, Doll Parts, 1994 (single), My Body, The Hand Grenade, 1997, Celebrity Skin, 1998; Solo album includes America's Sweeteart, 2004; actress (films) Sid and Nancy, 1986, Feeling Minnesota, 1996, The People vs. Larry Flynt, 1996, Not Bad For a Girl, 1996 (also co-prodr.), Basquiate, 1996, Life, 1997, Man on the Moon, 1999, 200 Cigarettes, 1999, Beat, 2000, Julie Johnson, 2001, Trapped, 2002; television appearance on MTV Unplugged, 1995.

LOVE, DIAN, interior architect, educator; b. Bluffton, Ind., Feb. 18, 1940; d. James Edmound and Juaniece (Delight) Morrison L.; 1 child. BS in Interior Design, Purdue U., 1962; postgrad., Lawrence Inst. Tech., 1964-66; MFA, U. Mich., 1970, postgrad. Registered interior designer, Ill. With Benche Assocs. Bus. Interiors, Schenectady, N.Y., 1962; designer, planner interior dept. Giffels and Rossetti Archs., Engrs., Detroit, 1965-66; sr. staff interior designer U. Mich., Ann Arbor, 1966-70, mgr. coord. interior design dept., 1971-73, head interior design Univ. Hosp., 1978-80; head interior design dept. Samborn, Steketee, Otis and Evans, Toledo, 1970; established Design Collective, Ann Arbor, Mich., 1974-88; mgr., coord. interior design Kessler, Zeidler, Giffels Joint Venture, Detroit, 1976-77; mgr., coord. interior design for Detroit Gen. Hosp. Gunnar Birkerts & Assocs., Birmingham, Mich., 1979-80; mgr., coord. interior planning and design Cambridge (Mass.) Seven Assocs., 1984-86; sr. interior designer The Robinson Green Beretta Corp., Providence, 1987; interior designer Dian Love Design Assocs., Providence, 1988-89; sr. staff interior design Payette Assocs., Boston, 1990-94; cons. Perkins & Will, Chgo., 1994-96, Eva Maddox Assocs., Chgo., 1994—2003; owner Dian Love Design Assocs., Ann Arbor, 1996—2003. Coord. grad. studies FIDER-accredited interior environments program, interior design Ea. Mich. U., Ypsilanti, 1977-78; asst. prof. interior design Sch. Art U. Mich., Ann Arbor, 1978-80; head dept. interior arch. RISD, Providence, 1980-84; coord. interior design curriculum Endicott Coll., Beverly, Mass., 1989-90; facilitator Archeworks Design Lab., Chgo., 1995; assoc. prof., head environ. design program Ctr. Creative Studies, Detroit, 1997-98; dir. grad. studies interior design program Eastern Mich. U., 2000-03; spkr., presenter in field. Works include The Children's Hosp., Boston, The New Detroit Gen. Hosp., Edgehill Newport (R.I.) Rehab. Ctr., Good Samaritan Med. Ctr., West Palm Beach, Fla., Greewich (Conn.) Hosp. Assn., Lab. for Atmospheric Rsch. Harvard U., Cambridge, Mass., The Jackson Lab., Bar Harbor, Me., Johns Hopkins Hosp. Outpatient Med. Ctr., Balt., Moffet Lab. Molecular Biology Lab., Princeton (N.J.) U., R.I. Hosp., Providence, Inst. Advanced Scis. and Tech. U. Pa., Phila., New Ctr. Study Human Disease, Yale U., Rehab. Inst. Chgo., 1996, Residential Alzheimer's Faciliteis St. Joseph's Hosp./Mission Health Sys., Ann Arbor and Detroit, 1996, St. Rose Dominican Hsop., Las Veagas, Nev., numerous bldgs. U. Mich.; restorations include: Atlantic City Conv. Ctr. and Exhbn. Hall, Tennis Hall of Fame, Newport, R.I.; featured in Interiors mag. (Health Care Category Design award 1981), Newsweek mag., Interiors & Sources Mag., Interiors Mag., Architecture Mag., others. Avocations: gardening, furniture and textile design, travel, photography, historic architectural sites. Office Phone: 734-340-2662. E-mail: dianlove@aol.com.

LOVE, EDITH HOLMES, theater producer; b. Boston, Oct. 17, 1950; d. Theodore Rufus and Mary (Holmes) L. Student, Denison U., 1968-72; BFA, U. Colo., 1973. Freelance designer various orgns., Atlanta, 1974-75; costumer Atlanta Children's Theatre, 1975-77; prodn. acct. David Gerber Co., L.A., 1980-81; bus. mgr. Alliance Theatre/Atlanta Children's Theatre, 1977-79, adminstrv. dir., 1981-83, gen. mgr., 1983-85, mng. dir., 1985-96, Dallas Theater Ctrn., 1997—. Adv. bd. Stage Hands, Inc., Atlanta, 1983-89; mem. exec. com. Prodn. Valves, Inc., Atlanta, 1985-89; mem. adv. com. arts mgmt. program Carnegie Mellon U.; panelist Nat. Endowment for Arts, 1994-96; vis. prof. Yale Sch. Drama, 1997. Active Cultural Olympiad Task Force, 1996 Summer Olympic Games, 1992-96, Met. Atlanta Arts Fund Bd., 1992-97; bd. dirs. Atlanta Convention and Vistor's Bur., 1993-95, Arts Dist. Friends, Theatre Comm. Group; exec. com. Dallas Theatre League, 1999—. Recipient Deca award for Outstanding Bus. Women in Atlanta, 1992. Mem. League Resident Theatres (treas. 1987-97, v.p. 1997-2000), Atlanta Theatre Coalition (exec. com. 1987-91, pres. 1989), Atlanta C. of C. (bd. dirs. bus. coun. for arts 1988-97), Leadership Atlanta, Charter 100 Dallas, Bd. Arts Dist. Found. Office: Dallas Theater Ctr 3636 Turtle Creek Bvld Dallas TX 75219

LOVE, GAY MCLAWHORN, manufacturing executive; m. J. Erskine Love (dec. 1987); children: Dennis, Jimmy, Bill, Keith, David; 1 child, Carol Anne Love Jennison. Grad., Duke U. Chair PrintPack Inc., Atlanta, 1987—. Co-founder The Gay and Erskine Love Found., 1976. Named an honorary alumnus, Georgia Tech., 1989. Office: PrintPack Inc PO Box 43687 Atlanta GA 30336-0687

LOVE, LAURA, singer, songwriter, Mussician grunge rock bands, performer Carnegie Hall, 1994; rec. artist Z Therapy, 1990, Helvetica Bold, 1990, Pangaea, 1992, Jo MIller and Laura Love Sing Bluegrass and Old-Time Music, 1995, Laura Love Collection, 1995, Octoroon, 1997, Shum Ticky, 1998. Office: Mercury/Polygram Records 825 8th Ave New York NY 10019-7416

LOVE, MARGARET MARKS, business owner; b. Ft. Benning, Ga., June 27, 1948; d. Edwin Hall and Mildred (Ashmore) Marks; m. James Fulford Love, July 18, 1970; children: Halley Margaret, Julia Marks, Benjamin Ashmore. AA, Stephens Coll., 1968; BA, U. S.C., 1970; MA, George Mason U., 1985. Kindergarten tchr. Ft. Benning Children's Schs., 1970-71, West Point (N.Y.) Elem. Sch., 1971-72, Dept. of Def. Schs., Munster, Fed. Republic Germany, 1980-81; pre-sch. tchr. Accotink Acad., Springfield, Va., 1983-84; community liaison officer U.S. Consolate, Hamburg, Germany, 1990-91; owner, founder, CEO, pres. Full Circle Internat. Relocations, Inc., 1994—. Bd. dirs. St. Andrew's Episcopal Day Sch., Burke, Va., 1982-85. Co-chmn. Adopt-A-Sch. program, Killeen, 1985-87; vestry mem., St. Christpoher's Episcopalian Ch. Mem. Jr. League Hampton Roads (bd. dirs. 1986—), Officers Wives Club (bd. dirs. 1986—), Tex. State Tchrs. Assn. (named Friend of Edn. 1986), DAR, Daughters of U.S. Army, Greater Killeen C. of C. (co-chmn. com. 1986-87).

LOVE, SANDRA RAE, information specialist; b. San Francisco, Feb. 20, 1947; d. Benjamin Raymond and Charlotte C. Martin; m. Michael D. Love, Feb. 14, 1971. BA in English, Calif. State U., Hayward, 1968; MS in L.S., U. So. Calif., 1969. Tech. info. specialist Lawrence Livermore (Calif.) Nat. Lab., 1969—. Mem. Beta Sigma Phi. Democrat. Episcopalian. Office: Lawrence Livermore Nat Lab PO Box 808 Livermore CA 94551-0808

LOVE, SARA ELIZABETH, retired elementary school educator; b. Detroit, Nov. 5, 1914; d. Gustav John and Florence Marian (Keller) Scherling; m. Harold O. Love, June 12, 1937 (dec. 1986); children: Robert Evans, Barbara Lynn. AB, U. Mich., 1936. Tchg. cert., Mich. Pres. Tombstone (Ariz.) Historama Corp., 1986—, Tombstone Epitaph, 1986—. Pres. Grosse Pointe (Mich.) Womens Rep. Club, 1952-54, Women's Assn. for the Detroit Symphony Orch., 1956-58; chmn. vol. com. Detroit Mus. Art, 1958-60; founder Detroit Assn. of the Soc. of Contbrs. of the Archives of Am. Art, 1960-62. Recipient Hon. award in French studies French Govt., 1936. Mem. Skytine Country Club. Avocations: golf, travel.

LOVE, SUSAN MARGARET, surgeon, educator, writer; b. N.J., Feb. 9, 1948; d. James Arthur and Margaret Connick (Schwab) L.; life ptnr. Helen Sperry Cooksey, Sept. 8, 1982; 1 child, Katherine Mary Love-Cooksey. BS, Fordham U., 1970; MD, SUNY, N.Y.C., 1974, DSc (hon.), 1998, Northeastern U., 1991; D of Humane Sci. (hon.), Simmons Coll., 1992; LHD (hon.), U. R.I., 1997; MBA, UCLA, 1998; DSc (hon.), Trinity Coll., 1999. Clin. fellow in surgery Harvard Med. Sch., Boston, 1977-78, clin. instr. in surgery, 1980-87; dir. breast clinic Beth Israel Hosp., Boston, 1980-88; clin. assoc. in surg. oncology Dana Farber Cancer Inst., Boston, 1981-92; dir. Faulkner Breast Ctr. Faulkner Hosp., Boston, 1988-92; asst. clin. prof. surgery Harvard Med. Sch., Cambridge, Mass., 1987-92; assoc. prof. clin. surgery UCLA Sch. Medicine, 1992-96; dir. UCLA Breast Ctr., 1992-96; adj. prof. surgery UCLA, 1966—. Adv. coun. Breast and Cervical Cancer Coun., State of Calif., Dept. Human Svcs., 1994—98; mem. NSABP Oversight Com., Pitts., 1994; mem. adv. com. Women's Health Initiative Program, Washington, 1993—95; prin. investigator Nat. Surg. Adjuvant Breast and Bowel Project, 1985—96; mem. Pres.'s Nat. Action Plan on Breast Cancer, DHHS, 1994—2000; co-chair Biol. Resources Working Group, 1994—98, mem. exec. and steering coms., 1995—; mem. Nat. Cancer Adv. Bd., 1998—2004, Susan Love Breast Cancer Rsch. Found., 1996—; founder, sr. ptnr. LLuminari, Inc., 2000—; cons. Cytyc Health Corp., 2002—. Author: Dr. Susan Love's Breast Book, 1990, 3d edit., 2000, Dr. Susan Love's Menopause and Hormone Book, 1997, 2d edit., 2003; Atlas of Techniques in Breast Surgery, 1996; (book chpts.) Breast Disease, 1987, Clinics in Oncology: Breast Cancer, 1989, The Woman's Guide to Good Health, 1991; contbr. articles to profl. jours. Founder, bd. dirs. Nat. Breast Cancer Coalition, 1991—; mem. breast cancer subcom. divsn. cancer treatment Bd. Sci. Counselors, Nat. Cancer Inst., 1992-95; conf. com. co-chair Sec.'s Conf. to Establish Nat. Action Plan on Breast Cancer, 1993; med. dir. Susan Love MD Breast Cancer Found., 1996—. Recipient Rose Kushner award, Am. Med. Writers Assn., 1991, Achievement award, Am. Assn. Physicians for Human Rights, 1992, Women Making History award, U.S. Senator Barbara Boxer, 1993, Woman of Yr. award, YWCA, 1994, Frontrunner award, Sara Lee Corp., 1994, Spirit of Achievement award, Albert Einstein Coll. of Yeshiva U., 1995, Abram L. Sachar medallion, Brandeis U., 1996, Bicentennial honoree, U. Louisville, 1997, Walker prize, Boston Mus. Sci., 1998, Radcliffe medal, 2000, Humanitarian of Yr. award, Western U. Health Sci., Pomona, Calif., 2001, Excellence in Cancer Awareness award, Cancer Rsch. Found. Am., 2002, Dir.'s award, Nat. Cancer Inst., 2004; grantee, Dept. of Def., 1994, 1996. Mem. Am. Med. Women's Assn. (pres. br. 39 1987, Lila Wallis Women's Health award 2004), Soc. for Study of Breast Disease, Am. Soc. Preventive Oncology, Southwestern Oncology Group (women's health and breast com. 1992-96, surg. rep. 1992-96), L.A. Med. Soc., Boston Surg. Soc., N.Am. Menopause Soc., Am. Assn. Cancer Rsch., Am. Coll. Women's Health Physicians, Assn. Women Surgeons. Office: PO Box 846 Pacific Palisades CA 90272-0846 E-mail: connie.long@susanlovemd.org.

LOVEJOY, JEAN HASTINGS, social services counselor; b. Battle Creek, Mich, July 1, 1913; d. William Walter and Elizabeth (Fairbank) H.; m. Allen Perry (dec. 2003); children: Isabel L. Best, Linda L. Ewald, Elizabeth L. Fulton, Margaret L. Baldwin, Helen L. Battad. BA, Mt. Holyoke Coll., So. Hadley, Mass., 1935. Traveling sec. Student Vol. Movement, NYC, 1935; bookkeeper Hartford Consumers Co-op, Conn., 1944; tchr. Pre-School, Congl. Ch., West Hartford, Conn., 1944-45; instr. St. John's U., Shanghai; tchr. Edn., 1st Congl. Ch., Berkeley, Calif., 1958-59; instr. Tunghai U., Taiwan, 1960-63; sec. Pres. Tunghai U., Taichung, Taiwan, 1960-63. Pres. Ecumenical Assn. for Housing, San Rafael, 1971, 78-80; founding mem. Hospice of Havasu, 1982, pres. bd. dir., 1985-87, vol. trainer, 1987-92; bereavement vol. Cmty. Hospice, Tucson, 1993-96; vol. friendly visitor N.W. Interfaith Ctr., Tucson, 1995—; vol. libr. La Rosa Health Ctr., Tucson, 1998-2003. Recipient OACC Sr. Achievement award, 1991; named Vol. of Yr., Marin County, Calif., 1970, 79; street named Lovejoy Way in her honor Novato (Calif.) City Coun., 1980. Mem. LWV (program v.p. Pierce County chpt. 1967, pres. cen. Marin County chpt. 1973-75, legis. analyst land use 1979-80, Calif. chpt.). Mem. United Ch. of Christ (Stephen min.) Home: Apt 8208 7500 N Calle Sin Envidia Tucson AZ 85718-7363

LOVEJOY, JENNIFER CAROLE, medical educator; b. Seattle, Mar. 30, 1961; d. Roland William and Deborah (Daniels) L.; m. Robert M. Straughn, Sept. 24, 1995; 1 child, Teresa S. BS in Zoology magna cum laude, Duke U., 1982; MA in Psychobiology, Emory U., 1986, PhD in Psychobiology, 1988. Rsch. tech. pediatric virology Duke U. Med. Ctr., Durham, N.C., 1982-83; grad. fellow psychobiology dept. psychology Yerkes Primate Rsch. Ctr., Atlanta, 1983-88; rsch. fellow endocrinology and metabolism, dept. medicine Emory U. Sch. Medicine, Atlanta, 1988-89, instr. in medicine dept. medicine, 1989-91; asst. prof. obesity, diabetes and metabolism sect. Pennington Biomed. Rsch. Ctr., La. State U., Baton Rouge, 1991—; clin. asst. prof. rsch. dept. ob-gyn. La. State U., Sch. Medicine, New Orleans, 1993— Lab. specialist glycolipid biochemistry dept. pathology U. Va. Med. Ctr., Charlottesville, 1985; introductory psychology lectr. Oglethorp U., Atlanta, 1990; lectr. and seminar leader in field. Contbr. chpts. to books and articles to profl. jours. Recipient Nat. Rsch. Svc. award NIH-Nat. Inst. Diabetes, Digestive & Kidney Diseases, 1989-91, New Populations award The Obesity Found., 1990. Mem. Am. Diabetes Assn. (coun. mem. nutritional sci. and metabolism, Frances O. Hazzard award 1992, Career Devel. award 1993—, clin. rsch. grantee 1996), Am. Inst. Nutrition, Am. Soc. for Clin. Nutrition, Assn. for Women in Sci., N.Am. Assn. for the Study of Obesity, Internat. Assn. for the Study of Obesity, Soc. for the Study Ingestive Behavior, Sigma Xi. Office: Louisiana State U Pennington Biomed Rsch Ctr 6400 Perkins Rd Baton Rouge LA 70808 4124

LOVEJOY, LYNDA M. state agency administrator; m. Randolph John Lovejoy; 3 children. AA in Elem. Edn., U. N.Mex., Gallup; BSc in Pub. Adminstrn., No. Ariz. U. Exec. staff asst. office of pres. Navajo Nation; case mgr. K'e Project; personnel dir. Pueblo of Zuni Tribe; project dir. adult edn. Crownpoint Inst. Tech.; commr. Pub. Regulation Commn., Santa Fe, 1999—. U.S. del. Guatemala; rep. N.Mex. State House Rep., 1989—98; spkr. in field. Exec. bd. St. Bonaventure Indian Mission, Nat. Order Women Legislatures, Nat. Women's Network. Named one of Yr. 2000 N.Mex. top 100 power brokers, N.Mex. Bus. Weekly ; recipient N.Mex. Woman of Yr. award, Gov. . Office: New Mexico PRC PO Drawer 1269 Santa Fe NM 87504

LOVELACE, JULIANNE, former library director; b. Jackson, Miss., July 30, 1941; d. Benjamin Travis and Julia Elizabeth (Knight) Robinson; m. William Frank Lovelance, July 6, 1963 (div. Mar. 17, 1972); 1 child, Julie Lynn. BA in History, So. Meth. U., 1963; MLS, U. North Tex., 1970. Clk. Dallas Pub. Libr., 1963-64, children's libr. asst., 1964-66, children's libr., 1966-69; libr. Richardson (Tex.) Pub. Libr., 1971-72, supr. pub. svcs., 1972-87, dir., 1987-2001; CFO 4womenShopping, Inc., 2000—. Active Richardson Adult Literacy Ctr., Altrusa Internat., Inc. Richardson, Leadership Richardson Alumni Assn., Friends of the Richardson Pub. Libr., Richardson Regional Med. Ctr. Found.; Women's Adv. Coun., Richardson Regional Med. Ctr.; found. bd. Wildflower Arts & Music Festival. Named one of 21 for the 21st Century, Collin County Bus., 2000. Avocation: blackjack. E-mail: jl3430@swbell.net.

LOVELACE, ROSE MARIE SNIEGON, federal space agency administrator; b. Sweet Hall, Va., Feb. 19, 1937; d. Adolph and Annie (Mickel) Sniegon; m. William Wayne Lovelace, Aug. 11, 1962. Degree in bus., Longwood Coll., 1957. Adminstrv. aide Dept. of Navy, Washington, 1957-60; adminstrv. asst. Joint Blood Coun.-Pvt., Washington, 1960-63; exec. staff NASA, Washington, 1963-73, program analyst-specialist, 1973-80, chief adminstrv. ops. and Congl. affairs br., 1980-92; ret., 1992. Cons. NASA, 1992—. Editor, author: (pamphlet) Space Operations, 1989, (video) Space Communications, 1991. Pres. Jr. Achievement Co., 1953-55, Kettering Recreation Coun., Largo, Md., 1974-76; league coord. U.S. Tennis Assn., Anne Arundel County, Md., 1989-91, team capt., 1984-99, 2001; mem. Hospice Cup Regatta (sponsor 2000-), Hospice Beacon Hope Gala Com. Fundraiser, 2004; active various civic orgns. including LWV, ch., cmty. and county functions, 1957—. Recipient Jr. Achievement Exec. award and Nat. Speakers award, 1954, Gold medal Parks and Planning, Prince Georges County, Md., 1976, Exceptional Svc. award NASA, 1983, Exceptional Svc. medal NASA, 1992. Mem.: Hospice Beacon Hope Com. Gala Fundraiser, Heritage Soc. Anne Arundel Med. Ctr., Historic Annapolis Found., Annapolis Opera, Inc., Am. Heart Assn. (Heart Ball com. fundraiser 2000), Anne Arundel County Tennis Assn., Sportfit Racquet and Fitness Club, Severn Town Club (pres. 1996—98, chair Holly Ball fundraiser 1998—99). Republican. Methodist. Avocations: tennis, gardening, flower arranging, organizing social and tennis events, designing and painting wearable art.

LOVELAND, CHRISTINE FRANCES, psychologist; b. Chester, Pa., Jan. 27, 1953; d. Frank Preston and Elizabeth Theresa (Meehan) L.; 1 child, Catherine Elizabeth Loveland-Jones. BS, Ind. U. of Pa., 1974; MA, West Chester U., 1986; PhD, Temple U., 1993. Lic. psychologist, 1998; cert. elem. and secondary prin.; cert. sch. psychologist. Educator, ESL-Bilingual program dir. Avon Grove Sch. Dist., West Grove, Pa., 1978—; family therapist Counseling Network SCCMC, West Grove, 1989-92; support group facilitator Epilepsy Found. of Phila., 1986-92; pres., psychologist Brandywine Psychol. Svcs., West Grove, 1999—. Adj. prof. Immaculata (Pa.) Coll., 1999; LA curriculum com. Avon Grove Sch. Dist., West Grove, 1998—. Councilwoman Dem. Polit. Party, West Grove, 1998—. Named

Outstanding Young Woman of Yr. Avon Grove Jaycees, 1980. Fellow Pa. Psychol. Assn.; mem. APA, NEA, West Grove Avondale Rotary (pres. 1999—, bd. dirs. 1998), Pa. Edn. Assn., Avon Grove Edn. Assn. Avocations: reading, hiking, piano, spanish, travel. Home: 138 W Evergreen St West Grove PA 19390-1006 Office: Brandywine Psychol Svcs 138 W Evergreen St West Grove PA 19390-1006 E-mail: clovel7778@aol.com.

LOVELESS, KATHY LYNNE, client services executive; b. Corsicana, Tex., Mar. 7, 1961; d. Vernon Ray and Barbara Alice (Brown) L. BA, Baylor U., 1983. Adminstrv. asst. InterFirst Bank, Dallas, 1983-85, Chaparral Steel Co., Midlothian, Tex., 1985-89, audio/visual coord., 1989-93; freelance computer instr. Duncanville, Tex., 1993-94; tng. specialist U. Tex. Southwestern Med. Ctr., Dallas, 1994-95, supr. client svcs. ctr., 1995-97, database coord., 1997-98; tester, trainer Sabre Holdings, Southlake, Tex., 1998-2000, product mgr., 2000—. Bd. dirs. Richardson Theatre Ctr., 1999—; pres., v.p. Midlothian Cmty. Theatre, 1990-93, mem., 1987-94; v.p. Lovers Ln. United Meth. Ch. Choir, Dallas, 1994, 95, Adminstrv. Bd., 1995-96, 1999—, chmn. broadcast com., 2001; chmn. worship and mem. care com. Elmwood United Meth. Ch., 1990, 91; bd. dirs. Trinity River Mission, Dallas, 1994, 95, 96. Mem.: Soc for Theatrical Artists Guidance and Enhancement. Avocations: films, music, reading, sports, theater. Home: 9947 Knoll Krest Dr Dallas TX 75238 E-mail: ilvmovies@aol.com.

LOVELESS, LAUREL PLUMSTEAD, minister; b. N. Plainfield, N.J., May 4, 1951; d. James Albert and Grace Constance Plumstead; m. Scott Edward Loveless, Dec. 29, 1973; children: Marian, Sara, Daniel. BA, Duke U., Durham, N.C., 1973; MDiv, Union Sem. Va., Richmond, 1978. Ordained to ministry Hanover (Va.) Presbytery, 1978. Campus min. Va. Commonwealth U., Richmond, 1978—79; asst. pastor Celtic Cross Presbyn. Ch., Warren, Mich., 1980—82; assoc. pastor Limestone Presbyn. Ch., Wilmington, Del., 1983—94; interim pastor Presbyn. Ch. of the Covenant, Wilmington, 1995—97; pastor Elkton (Md.) Presbyn. Ch., 1997—. Chair com. on preparation ministry Newcastle Presbytery, Wilmington, 1995—2000, chair nominating com., 2002—. Mem. Pacem In Terris, Wilmington, Del., 1986—92; moderator Meeting Ground, Elkton, Md., 2001—03; sec. On Our Own, Md., Elkton, 2002—. Democrat. Avocations: guitar, gardening, travel, walking, tennis. Office: Elkton Presbyn Ch 209 E Main St Elkton MD 21921

LOVELESS, PATTY (PATTY RAMEY), country music singer; b. Pikeville, Ky., Jan. 4, 1957; m. Terry Lovelace (div.); m. Emory Gordy, Jr., Feb. 1989. Recording artist MCA, 1985-93, Sony Music, 1993—. Albums: Patty Loveless, 1987, If My Heart Had Windows, 1988, Honky Tonk Angel, 1988 (gold), On Down the Line, 1990, Up Against My Heart, 1991, Only What I Feel, 1993, Greatest Hits, 1993, When Fallen Angels Fly, 1994, The Trouble With the Truth, Sings Songs of Love, 1996, Long Stretch of Lonesome, 1997, Classics, 1999, Strong Heart, 2000, 20th Century masters: The Millenium Collection, 2000, Mountain Soul, 2001, Bluegrass & White Snow, 2002, On Your Way Home, 2003; # 1 hit singles Timber, I'm Falling in Love, Chains. Named Favorite New Country Artist by Am. Music Awards, 1989, Album of Yr. Country Music Awards, 1995, Top Female Vocalist Acad. Country Music, 1996, Female Vocalist of Yr. Country Music awards, 1996, Vocal Event of Yr., Country Music awards, 1993, 98, 99; recipient TNN Music City News Country Award, Female Artist, 1990, Country Music Awards' Album of the Yr.; co-recipient Grammy award for Best Country Collaboration with Vocals, 1998; inductee Grand Ole Opry, 1988. Office: Sony Music/Epic Records 550 Madison Ave New York NY 10022-3211*

LOVELL, CAROL, museum director; Dir. Kauai Mus., Lihue, Hawaii, 1992—. Mem. Kauai Historical Society. Office: Kauai Mus 4428 Rice St Lihue HI 96766-1338

LOVELL, EMILY KALLED, retired journalist; b. Grand Rapids, Mich., Feb. 25, 1920; d. Abdo Rham and Louise (Claussen) Kalled; m. Robert Edmund Lovell, July 4, 1947. Student, Grand Rapids Jr. Coll., 1937-39; BA, Mich. State U., 1944; MA, U. Ariz., 1971. Copywriter, asst. traffic mgr. Sta. WOOD, Grand Rapids, 1944-46; traffic mgr. KOPO, Tucson, 1946-47; reporter, city editor Alamogordo (N.Mex.) News, 1948-51; Alamogordo corr., feature writer Internat. News Svc., Denver, 1950-54, El Paso Herald-Post, 1954-65; Alamogordo news dir., feature writer Tularosa (N.Mex.) Basin Times, 1957-59; co-founder, editor, pub. Otero County Star, Alamogordo, 1961-65; newscaster KALG, Alamogordo, 1964-65; freelance feature writer Denver Post, N.Mex. Mag., 1949-69; corr. Electronic News, N.Y.C., 1959-63, 65-69; Sierra Vista (Ariz.) corr. Ariz. Republic, 1966; freelance editor N.Mex. Pioneer Interviews, 1967-69; asst. dir. English skills program Ariz. State U., 1976; free-lance editor, writer, 1977—2003; ret., 2003. Part-time tchr., lectr. U. Pacific, 1981-86; part-time interpreter Calif., 1983-91, Interpreters Unlimited, Oakland, 1985-91; sec., dir. Star Pub. Co., Inc., 1961-64, pres., 1964-65, 3d v.p., publicity chmn. Otero County Cmty. Concert Assn., 1950-65; mem. Alamogordo Zoning Commn., 1955-57; mem. founding com. Alamogordo Ctrl. Youth Activities Com., 1957; vice chmn. Otero County chpt. Nat. Found. Infantile Paralysis, 1958-61; charter mem. N.Mex. Citizens Coun. for Traffic Safety, 1959-61; pres. Sierra Vista Hosp. Aux., 1966; pub. rels. chmn. Ft. Huachuca chpt. ARC, 1966; mem. nat. bd. Hospitalized Vets. Writing Project, 1972-99; vol. instr. autobiography and creative writing, 1991-2002. Author: A Personalized History of Otero County, New Mexico, 1963, Weekend Away, 1964, Lebanese Cooking, Streamlined, 1972, A Reference Handbook for Arabic Grammar, 1974, 77; contbg. author: The Muslim Community in North America, 1983. Recipient 1st Pl. awards N.Mex. Press Assn., 1961, 62, Pub. Interest award Nat. Safety Coun., 1962, 1st Pl. award Nat. Fedn. Press Women, 1960, 62; named Woman of Yr. Alamogordo, 1960, Editor of Week Pubs. Aux., 1962, adm. N.Mex. Navy, 1962, col. A.D.C. Staff Gov. N.Mex., 1963, Woman of Yr., Ariz. Press Women, 1973. Mem. N.Mex. Press Women (past sec.), Ariz. Press Women (past pres.), N.Mex. Fedn. Womens Clubs (past dist. pub. rels. chmn., hon. life Alamogordo), N.Mex. Hist. Soc. (life), N.Mex. Fedn. Bus. and Profl. Womens Clubs (past pres., hon. life Alamogordo), Pan Am. Round Table Alamogordo, Theta Sigma Phi (past nat. 3d v.p.), Phi Kappa Phi. Democrat. Moslem. Home: Apt 222 1925 Possum Hollow Rd Slidell LA 70458-8318

LOVENHEIM, BARBARA IRENE, editor; b. Rochester, N.Y., July 19, 1940; d. Clifford Norman and May (Yampolsky) L. BA, Barnard Coll., 1962; MA in Eng. Lit., U. Wis., 1963; PhD in Eng. Lit., U. Rochester, 1970. Lectr. in Eng. Queens Coll., Flushing, N.Y., 1966-70; asst. prof. Eng. Baruch Coll., N.Y.C., 1971-75; account exec. Ruder & Finn, N.Y.C., 1976-78; London arts corr. The Internat. Herald Tribune, Paris, 1979-80; text editor Glamour Mag., N.Y.C., 1980-82; writer, editor, media cons. various pubs., N.Y.C., 1982-95; editor-in-chief, founder NYcitylife, 1995—. Adj. asst. prof. journalism NYU, 1990-95. Author: The Marriage Odds, 1990, Survival in the Shadows: seven Jews Hidden in Hitler's Berlin, 2003; contbr. articles to pubs. Founder, pres. Barnard Columbia Alumni Social Com. Inc., N.Y.C., 1973-83. N.Y. State Regents fellow, 1958-62, U. Rochester Tchg. fellow, 1964-66. Home: 315 E 65th St New York NY 10021-6862

LOVERIDGE-SANBONMATSU, JOAN MEREDITH, communication studies and women's studies educator, poet; b. Hartford, Conn., July 5, 1938; d. Gilbert Thomas and Rosabel Frances (Nowry) Loveridge; m. Akira Sanbonmatsu, Aug. 29, 1964; children: James Michael, Kevin Yosh. BA, U. Vt., 1960; MA, Ohio U., 1963; PhD, Pa. State U., 1971. Writer, programming radio/tv WRUV, WCAX, Burlington, Vt., 1956-60, WOUB, Athens, Ohio, 1962-63, AFKN, Korea, 1960-61; unit head ARC, Japan, Korea, 1960-61; asst. prof. SUNY, Brockport, 1963-77, prof. comm. studies and women's studies Oswego, 1977-98, prof. emerita, 1999—, instr. intensive English summer program, 1993—2001, co-coord. women's studies program, 1978-80, 82, instr. internat. studies infusion program, 1985-91. Vis. prof. Rochester (N.Y.) Inst. Tech., 1971; assoc. adj. prof. Monroe C.C., Rochester, 1972-76; instr. Pa. State, State College, 1966-67; cons. for oral history project ARC Overseas Assn., 1994—; cons. Cazenovia Coll., N.Y., 1988-89; pres. bd. dirs. Woman's Career Ctr. Inc., Rochester, 1975-76, [illegible] 1997. Author: Winged Odyssey: Poems and Stories, 2002; co-author: Feminism and Woman's Life, 1995; contbg. author: Women Public Speakers in the US, 1925-1993, Vol. 2, 1994, Life in a Fishbowl: A Call to Serve, 2003; contbr. poetry to publs., 1986—; poetry editor/editl. bd.: Lake Effect, 1985-92; contbr. articles to profl. jours. including Howard Jour. Comms., Comm. Edn., Phoebe and Feminist Jour. Religious edn. team tchr. May Meml. Unitarian Universalist Soc., Syracuse, 1979-81; mem. adv. parent com., Oswego H.S., 1986-87. Recipient Unsung Heroine award Ctrl. N.Y. NOW, Syracuse, 1987, presdl. citation for social change ARC Overseas Assn., 1998; rsch. grantee Pa. State U., 1970, SUNY, Oswego, 1978, 91, 92, 94, 95, 96, N.Y. State United Univ. Professions Profl. Devel. and Quality of Working Life grantee, 1985, 87, 93, 94, 98, 98 SUNY Oswego Women's Ctr. award, 1996, 98, SEED award for outstanding work with disabled students, 1998, Internat. Awareness and Peace award Coalition for Peace Edn., 2000, Student award ESL, 1995, 96, 98; fellow U. Ill., Chgo., 1983. Mem. N.Y. Asian Studies Assn., Nat. Comm. Assn. (women's caucus job placement dir., exec. bd. 1977-78), Ea. Comm. Assn., N.Y. Nat. Comm. Assn., Soc. for Intercultural Edn., Tng. and Rsch., Nat. Women's Studies Assn., Speech Comm. Assn. P.R., N.Y. State Women's Studies Assn., ARC Overseas Assn. (v.p. 1999-2001), Nat. Assn. Poet and Writers, Inc. Avocations: Spanish, walking. Home: 23 McCracken Dr Oswego NY 13126-6011

LOVETT, CLARA MARIA, university administrator, historian; b. Trieste, Italy, Aug. 4, 1939; came to U.S., 1962; m. Benjamin F. Brown. BA equivalent, U. Trieste, 1962; MA, U. Tex., Austin, 1967; PhD, U. Tex., 1970. Prof. history Baruch Coll. CUNY, N.Y.C., 1971-82, asst. provost, 1980-82; chief European divsn. Libr. of Congress, Washington, 1982-84; provost, v.p. acad. affairs George Mason U., Fairfax, Va., 1988-93; on leave, dir. Forum on Faculty Roles and Rewards Am. Assn. for Higher Edn., 1993-94; pres. No. Ariz. U., Flagstaff, 1994-2001, pres. emerita, 2001—; sr. fellow, dir. Ctr. for Competency-Measured Edn. The Oquirah Inst., 2002—03; pres., CEO, Am. Assn. for Higher Ed., 2003—. Vis. lectr. Fgn. Svc. Inst., Washington, 1979-85. Author: Democratic Movement in Italy 1830-1876, 1982 (H.R. Marraro prize, Soc. Italian Hist. Studies); Giuseppe Ferrari and the Italian Revolution, 1979 (Phi Alpha Theta book award); Carlo Cattaneo and the Politics of Risorgimento, 1972 (Soc. for Italian Hist. Studies Dissertation award), (bibliography) Contemporary Italy, 1985; co-editor: Women, War, and Revolution, 1980, (essays) State of Western European Studies, 1984; contbr. sects. to publs., U.S., Italy. Organizer Dem. clubs Bklyn., 1972-76; mem. exec. com. Palisades Citizens Assn., Washington, 1985-87; vestry mem. St. David's Episc. Ch., Washington, 1986-89; bd. dirs. Blue Cross Blue Shield Ariz., 1995—; trustee Western Govs. U., 1996—; mem. Ariz. State Bd. Edn., 1999-2001. Fellow Guggenheim Found., 1978-79, Woodrow Wilson Internat. Ctr. for Scholars, 1979 (adv. bd. West European program), Am. Coun. Learned Socs., 1976, Bunting Inst. of Radcliffe Coll., 1975-76, others; named Educator of Yr. Va. Fedn. of Bus. and Profl. Women, 1992. Mem. Am. Assn. Higher Edn. (cons. 1979—), Soc. for Italian Hist. Studies, Assn. Am. Coll. and Univs. (bd. dirs. 1990-93). Avocations: choral singing, swimming. Office: One Dupont Cir Ste 360 Washington DC 20036 E-mail: clara.lovett@nau.edu.

LOVETT, KATHERINE VAN EVERY, special education educator; b. St. Petersburg, Fla., Oct. 28, 1960; d. Richard James and Diane Marie Van Every; m. Gregory Alan Lovett. AA, St. Petersburg Jr. Coll., 1989; BS in Elem. Edn., U. S. Fla., 1991; MA in Elem. Edn., Ohio State U., Lima, 2000; MEd in Spl. Edn., Wright State U., 2002. Adminstrv. asst. Home Mortgage Investment Corp., St. Petersburg, 1976—82, R.D. Zande and Assocs., Blue Ash, Ohio, 1996—97; sr. v.p. Fla. Group, Inc., St. Petersburg, 1983—89; v.p. Mortgage Funding Corp. Am., St. Petersburg, 1992—93, Union Am. Mortgage Corp., Tarpon Springs, Fla., 1993—95; prodn. mgr. Crossmann Mortgage Corp., Mason, Ohio, 1997; substitute tchr. numerous sch. dists., Cin., 1997, Lima, 1998; permanent substitute Shawnee Elmwood Primary Sch., Lima, 1998—99; spl. edn. tchr. Lima City Schs., 1999—. Grantee, Martha Holden Jennings Found., 2003—. Avocations: crafts, exercise, computers, photography. Office: Lima City Schs 515 S Calumet Lima OH 45804 Personal E-mail: kvelovett@aol.com. Business E-mail: klovett@limacityschools.org.

LOVEWELL, MARJORIE KLINGENSMITH, secondary school educator; b. Mpls., Aug. 19, 1938; d. Medford Shirley and Margaret Isabel (Jepson) Klingensmith; m. Hubart S. Lovewell Jr., Aug. 6, 1960 (div. Dec. 1981). BS, U. Minn., 1960; MEd, U. Ga., 1974. Cert. secondary edn. tchr., Minn., Ga. Tchr. Ind. Sch. Dist. #281, Robbinsdale, Minn., 1961-69, Dekalb County Bd. Edn., Decatur, Ga., 1969—2002; ret., 2002. Curriculum writer State Dept. Edn., Atlanta, 1989-90; bd. dirs. Ida's Cove, (sec. 2003-). Bd. dirs. Ga. chpt. Myasthenia Gravis Found., 1999—. Mem.: Brain Injury Assn. Ga. (bd. dirs. 2000—03), Ga. Assn. Family and Consumer Sci. (dist. M treas. 1996—), Am. Assn. Family and Consumer Scis. (cert. 1990—), Atlanta Alliance Theater Guild (corr. sec. 2001—02), Alpha Sigma (chpt. pres. 2003—), Delta Kappa Gamma (state scholarship found. com. 2003—), Delta Zeta Found. (sec. 1989—93, treas. 1993—95, v.p. 1995—97, pres. 1997—2001, spl. advisor 2001—), Delta Zeta Sorority (alumnae pres. Atlanta chpt. 1974). Episcopalian. Home: 96 The Prado NE Atlanta GA 30309-3370

LOVING, MARY FRANCES, music educator; b. Dallas, July 10, 1933; d. Jay Luther and Marie Antoinette Branon; m. Donald Ray Loving, Dec. 26, 1955 (dec. Nov. 2000); children: Alice Marie, Cordani, Dee Ann Tackitt, Donald Ray II. BMus Temple U., 1954. Tchr. music edn. Williamstown (N.J.) Pub. Schs., 1954—55; county music tchr. Johnson County Pub. Schs., 1955—56; choral music tchr. Irving (Tex.) Pub. Schs., 1956—58; music dir. St. Luke's Presbyn. Ch., Amarillo, Tex., 1962—68, Grace United Meth. Ch., Corpus Christi, Tex., 1970—80; ind. music tchr. Loving Studio of Music, Corpus Christi, 1970—2003; theory and piano tchr. Del Mar Coll., Corpus Christi, 1968—70. Mem.: Tex. Music Tchrs. Assn. (pres. 1992—94, Tchr. of Yr. 1985). Home: 10734 Timbergrove Corpus Christi TX 78410

LOVING, SUSAN BRIMER, lawyer, former state official; m. Dan Loving; children: Lindsay, Andrew, Kendall. BA with distinction, U. Okla., 1972, JD, 1979. Asst. atty. gen. Office of Atty. Gen., 1983-87, 1st asst. atty. gen., 1987-91; atty. gen. State of Okla., Oklahoma City, 1991-94; ptnr. Lester, Loving & Davies, Edmond, Okla., 1995—. Master Ruth Bader Ginsburg Inn of Ct., 1995-97. Mem. Pardon and Parole Bd., 1995—96, 2003—, vice-chmn., 1995; mem. Gov.'s Commn. on Tobacco and Youth, 1995—97; mem. med. steering com. Partnership for Drug Free Okla., Inst. for Child Advocacy, 1996—97; bd. dirs. Bd. for Freedom of Info., Okla. Inc., 1995—2001, Legal Aid Svcs. of Okla., 2002—03, Legal Aid of West Okla., 1995—2001. Recipient Nat. Red Ribbon Leadership award Nat. Fedn. Parents, Headliner award, By-liner award Okla. City and Tulsa Women in Comm., First Friend of Freedom award, Freedom of Info., Okla., Dir. award Okla. Dist. Attys. Assn. Mem.: Oklahoma County Bar Assn. (bd. dirs. 2001—), Okla. Bar Assn. (mem. ho. dels. 1996—97, 2001—03, past chmn. adminstrv. law sect., chmn. adminstrn. of justice com., chmn. profl. responsibility commn., task force on professionalism and civility 1999—, Spotlight award 1997), Phi Beta Kappa. Office: Lester Loving & Davis PC 1701 S Kelly Ave Edmond OK 73013-3623 E-mail: sloving@lldlaw.com.

LOVINGER, SOPHIE LEHNER, child psychologist; b. N.Y.C., Jan. 15, 1932; d. Nathaniel Harris and Anne (Rosen) Lehner; m. Robert Jay Lovinger, June 18, 1957; children: David Fredrick, Mark Andrew. BA, Bklyn. Coll., 1954; MS, City Coll., N.Y.C., 1959; PhD, NYU, 1967. Diplomate Am. Bd. Profl. Pschology. Sr. clin. psychologist Bklyn. State Hosp., 1960-61; grad. fellow NYU, N.Y.C., 1964—67; psychotherapy trainee Jamaica (N.Y.) Ctr., 1964-67; asst. prof. Hofstra U., Hempstead, N.Y., 1967-70; prof. Cen. Mich. U., Mt. Pleasant, 1970-98; psychotherapist, psychoanalyst Mt. Pleasant, Mich., [illegible]; Charleston, S.C., 1999—. Author: Learning Disabilities and Games, 1978, Language-Learning Disabilities, 1991, Child Treatment from Intake Interview to Termination, 1998; contbr. articles to profl. jours. Fellow: APA, Am. Acad. Clin. Psychology; mem.: Nat. Register Health Svc. Providers. Office: 1744 Sam Pittenberg Blvd Charleston SC 29407 Office Phone: 843-556-0997. Personal E-mail: sllov@earthlink.net.

LOVINS, L. HUNTER, public policy institute executive; b. Middlebury, Vt., Feb. 26, 1950; d. Paul Millard and Farley (Hunter) Sheldon; m. Amory Bloch Lovins, Sept. 6, 1979 (div. 1999). BA in Sociology, BA in Polit. Sci., Pitzer Coll., 1972; JD, Loyola U., L.A., 1975; LHD, U. Maine, 1982. Bar: Calif. 1975. Asst. dir. Calif. Conservation Project, L.A., 1973-79; policy advisor Friends of the Earth, 1979—81; co-CEO, co-founder Rocky Mountain Inst., Snowmass, Colo., 1982—2002; co-chair Natural Capitalism Group, Snowmass, 2000—. Vis. prof. U. Colo., Boulder, 1982; Henry R. Luce vis. prof. Dartmouth Coll., Hanover, N.H., 1982; pres. Nighthawk Horse Co., 1993. Co-author: Brittle Power, 1982, Energy Unbound, 1986, Least-Cost Energy Solving the CO2 Problem, 2d edit., 1989, Factor Four, 1997, Natural Capitalism, 1999. Bd. dirs. Point Found., Basalt and Rural Fire Protection Dist., 1987-2000, Nighthawk Horse Co., Rocky Mountain Inst., 1982-2002, Windstar Land Conservancy, 1996-2002; vol. EMT and firefighter, Engrs. Without Borders, 2003. Recipient Mitchell prize Woodlands Inst., 1982, Right Livelihood Found. award, 1983, Best of the New Generation award Esquire Mag., 1984, Nissan prize, 1995, Lindbergh award, 1999, Bd. Govs.' award Loyola Law Sch., 2000, LOHAS award for svc. to bus., 2001, Shingo Prize for Excellence in Mfg. Rsch., 2001, Leadership in Bus. award, 2001; named Hero of Planet, Time Mag., 2000. Mem. Calif. Bar Assn., Am. Quarter Horse Assn., Am. Polocrosse Assn. Avocations: rodeo, fire rescue, polocrosse. Office: Natural Capitalism Group 5150 St Vrain Rd Longmont CO 80503

LOVIO-RODRIGUEZ, JESSICA BERTHA, accountant; b. Miami, Fla., Apr. 29, 1971; d. Hector Jose and Sonia (Sanchez) L.; m. David Rodriguez. B in Acctg. with honors, Fla. Internat. U., 88-92, MS in Taxation, 93. CPA, Fla. Bookkeeper Internat. Devel. & Investment Corp., Miami, 88-90; mgmt. intern Pan Am. World Airways, Miami, 90; contr. Capital Devel. & Investment Corp., Miami, 91-93; sr. tax acct. Morrison, Brown, Argiz & Co., Miami, 1993-96; internat. tax mgr. Price Waterhouse Coopers LLP, Miami, Fla., 1996—2001; asst. v.p. taxation Visa Internat., Miami, 2001—. Mem. AICPA, Fla. Inst. CPAs, Cuban Am. CPA Assn., Miami Bd. Realtors. Republican. Roman Catholic. Avocations: boating, scuba diving, biking, crafts. Office: Visa International 1004 NW 65 Ave Miami FL 33126

LOW, ANNE DOUGLAS, nurse; b. Balt., Feb. 21, 1947; m. Thomais Aiken Low, 1966; children: Matthew Aiken, Corey Canan. BSN cum laude, U. N.C., Greensboro, 1978; MS, Hood Coll., Frederick, Md., 1988. Utilization rev. evaluator U.S. Dept. Vets. Affaris, Martinsburg, W.Va., 1986-97, quality mgmt. specialist, 1981—. Maj., flight nurse USAF, W.Va. Air N.G. Decorated Air Force Commendation medal and Aerial Achievement medal for hazardous flying duty over Bosnia, 1996-97; recipient nat. fed. award for role in developing a cost recovery program U.S. Dept. Treasury, 1992. Mem. AAUW. Home: 508 Clement Cir Saint Simons Island GA 31522-5801

LOW, LOUISE ANDERSON, consulting company executive; b. Saline, Mich., May 1, 1944; d. Harry Linné and Rose Josephine (Chvala) Anderson; m. James Thomas Low, Dec. 30, 1967; children: James William, Eric Linné, Kari Louise, Antony Anderson. BA in Biology, U. Mich., 1966. Permanent teaching cert., Mich.; cert. master gardener Coop. Ext. Svc. Tchr. secondary sci. Novi (Mich.) Community Schs., 1966-67; rsch. asst. U. Mich. Med. Sch., Ann Arbor, 1967-68; tchr. secondary sci. Livonia (Mich.) Pub. Schs., 1968-72; tax preparer H&R Block, Saline, 1991; sr. exec. asst. Low & Assocs., Saline, 1991—. Mem. Saline H.S. PTO, 1995—2003, Saline Mid. Sch. PTO, 1996; mem. ball com. St. Joseph Hosp., 1994; active Friends of Saline Dist. Libr.; mem. Saline Area Schs. Project, 1997, also mem. bldg. com.; parent advisor; com. mem. Saline H.S. Alumni Assn., 2001—; mem. youth bd. Zion Luth. Ch., Ann Arbor, 1993—98; mem. long-range planning com. Saline Area Schs., 1990—94, mem. gifted and talented com., 1996—2003. Mem. AAUW (life, bd. dirs., com. chairperson), Washtenaw County Alliance for Gifted Edn. (v.p., bd. dirs. 1988-97), U. Mich. Conger Alumnae Group (bd. dirs., mem. exec. bd.), Alumni Assn. U. Mich. (life), Interlochen Ctr. for Arts Alumni Orgn. (life), Ann Arbor Area Panhellenic Alumnae (pres. 1976-77), Saline Sch. Alumni Assn. (bd. dirs.), Wayne State U. Faculty Wives, Jenny Lind Swedish Cultural Club of Mich. (bd. dirs., program chair), U. Mich. Waterman Alumnae Group (bd. dirs., mem. exec. bd.), Travis Pointe Country Club, Huron Valley Swim Club, Sigma Kappa (alumnae pres. 1970-72), Alpha Mu Sigma Kappa (mem. corp. bd., mem. found.). Lutheran. Home and Office: Low & Assocs 3431 Surrey Dr Saline MI 48176-9571

LOW, LOUISE O. volunteer; b. Monroe, Mich., July 6, 1926; d. Peter Orth and Dora M. Grundman; m. Raymond Low, Aug. 16, 1952 (div. Feb. 1986); children: John D., Scott D. (dec.) Student, Southeastern Univ., Washington D.C. Grants specialist fed. govt., 1946-80. Apptd. Fayette County bd. Care and Treatment of Mentally Deficient Persons, 1991—; bd. dirs FayCo Enterprises workshop for devel. disabled adults, 1998-2002; bd. dirs., vol. Operation OUTING, 1987-94; bd. dirs., meml. gift officer Friends and Families of Fayette County Hosp., 1988-99; vol. Fayette County Hosp. Aux., 1995—, scholarship com., 1995—, corr. sec., 1998—, v.p., pres, 2000—; mem. So. Ill. Constituency of Vols. Recipient Abe award, Jan. 1997. Mem. Vandalia Women's Club (exec. bd. 1996—, 2d v.p. 1996-98, pres. 1998-2000, del. state convs. 1998, 99, 2000). Home: 1607 W Fillmore St #24 Vandalia IL 62471-3111

LOW, SETHA MARILYN, anthropology and psychology educator, consultant; b. L.A., Mar. 14, 1948; BA in Psychology and Biology, Pitzer Coll., Claremont, Calif., 1969; MA in Anthropology, U. Calif., Berkeley, 1971, PhD in Anthropology, 1976; MA (hon.), U. Pa., 1983. Instr. anthropology San Francisco State U., 1971; lectr. dept. landscape architecture and regional planning U. Pa., Phila., 1974-76, asst. prof. Sch. Allied Med. Professions, 1976-77, asst. prof. dept. anthropology, 1976-82, assoc. prof. dept. anthropology, 1982-88, mem. grad. group Sch. Social Work, 1977-87; prof. PhD programs in anthropology and environ. psychology CUNY Grad. Sch. and Univ. Ctr., 1987—, dir. pub. space rsch. group Ctr. for Human Environs., 1988—. Hon. prof. U. Costa Rica, 1986-87; cons. Andropogon Assocs., Phila., 1978, Nat. Trust for Hist. Preservation, Washington, 1981-92, U. del Valle Guatemala, 1982-86, Hanna/Olin Assocs., Phila., 1983-89, Carnegie Assocs., Princeton, N.J., 1983-89, Office Tech. Assessment, Washington, 1986, Am. Folklife Ctr., Washington, 1988-90, Central Park Conservancy, N.Y.C., 1992, Columbia U., 1993, State of Pa., Harrisburg, 1994, Nat. Park Svc., 1995-96, N.Y.C. Dept. Parks and Recreation, 1996—; also others; vis. lectr. dept. landscape arch. and regional planning U. Pa., Phila., 1992—; vis. adj. prof. N.Y.U., 1995; cons. Nat. Park Svc., 1994-95; cons. Dept. Parks and Recreation, N.Y.C., 1996-98, Getty Ctr., 1999-00; cons. Granada Television, England, 1999. Corr. editor Med. Anthropology Quar., 1976-82, Practicing Anthropology, 1977-86; editor med. anthropology series SUNY Press, 1983—; editor Cultural Aspects of Design Newsletter, 1985—; assoc. editor Med. Anthropology Jour., 1986—, Advances in Environ., Behavior and Design Series, 1989-91, Gordon and Breach, 1992—, Medical Anthropological Quarterly, 1994—, City and Society, 1995—; contbg. editor unit news Anthropology Newsletter, 1986-89; contbr. articles to profl. jours. Mem. design com. Parks Coun., N.Y.C.,

1992—, Citizens Commn. N.Y.C., 1995-97, Nat. Heritage Coalition, 1993?—, Mcpl. Arts Soc., 1992—; active Phila. Mayor's Commn. on Health in Eighties, 1982-83, Pinelands' Commn. N.J., 1983-84; com. advisor Comprehensive Town Planning. Recipient Robert Textor and Family award for excellence in Anticipatory Anthropology, 2000; grantee Hunter-Grubb Found., El Salvador, 1968-69, U. Calif., Costa Rica, 1973-74, NIMH, 1976-78, Ctr. for Environ. Design and Planning, 1981-82, U. Pa., Guatemala, 1982-83, 85-86, Wenner-Gren Found. for Anthrop. Rsch., 1987-88, 95-96, NSF, Zagreb, Yugoslavia, 1988, Rsch. Found. CUNY, 1989-90, CUNY Caribbean Exch. Program, 1992-93, Wenner-Gren Found. Grant-In-Aid, 1994-96; fellow Ctr. for L.Am. Studies, 1972-74, NIMH, 1972-74, Fulbright rsch. fellow, San Jose, Costa Rica, 1986-87, NEH, John Carter Brown Libr. fellow, 1989-90, John Simon Guggenheim fellow, 1996-97; Getty Conservation Inst. Guest scholar, 2003. Fellow Am. Anthrop. Assn. (exec. bd. 1993-96), Soc. for Gen. Anthropology, Wenner Gren Found., 1997-98, Soc. for Applied Anthropology (exec. bd. 1993-96), Soc. for Cultural Anthropology; mem. Environ. Design Rsch. Assn. (bd. dirs. 1987-90, vice chmn. 1987-88, chmn. 1988-89), Soc. for L.Am. Anthropology (sec. 1986-88), Soc. for Med. Anthropology (exec. bd. 1986-89), Am. Ethnol. Soc., Soc. for Urban Anthropology (exec. bd. 1992—, program editor), Soc. Urban, Nat. and Trnasnat. Anthropology (pres.), Soc. for Psychol. Anthropology, L.Am. Studies Assn., Internat. Assn. People and Their Phys. Surroundings. Office: CUNY The Grad Ctr 365 5th Ave New York NY 10016-4334 E-mail: slow@gc.cuny.edu.

LOWE, DOROTHY ANN, library technician; b. Gibson, N.C., Dec. 20, 1939; d. H. Bruce and Inez Campbell; B.S. in Media Tech., Fed. City Coll., 1975; M.S. in Media Sci., U. D.C., 1979; grad. Foster Inst. Real Estate, 1985; m. John Lowe, Jan. 18, 1958 (div. Dec. 1975); children— Donna, Steven, Inez. Personnel clk. FCC, 1972-76; microfilm photographer Library of Congress, Washington, 1976-77, personnel clk., 1977, library technician, 1977— . Pres., Pentecostal Ch. Missionaries, 1974— . Recipient letter of commendation FCC, 1976. Mem. D.C. Library Assn., U. D.C. Alumni Assn. Democrat. Home: 1208 Gondar Ave Hyattsville MD 20785-4327 Office: Library of Congress 10 1st Ave SW Washington DC 20024-5105

LOWE, LISA, education educator, department chairman; BA in history, Stanford U., 1977; PhD in lit., U. of Calif., Santa Cruz, 1986. Prof. comparative lit. U. Calif. at San Diego, 1986—, chmn., lit. dept., 1998—2001. Exec. com. Divsn. on Sociol. Approaches to Lit. of the Modern Lang. Assn., 2001—; adv. bd. U. of Calif. Humanities Rsch. Inst., U. of Calif. President's Humanities Commn.; disting. faculty vis. Ctr. for Ideas and Soc. at U. of Calif., Riverside. Author: (book) Critical Terrains: French and British Orientalisms, 1991, Immigrant Acts: On Asian American Cultural Politics, 1996 (Book award in Cultural Studies from the Assn. for Asian Am. Studies, 1997); co-editor: The Politics of Culture in the Shadow of Capital, 1997. Fellowship, John Simon Guggenheim Meml. Found., 2003. Mem.: Nat. Coun. of the Am. Studies Assn. Office: U of Calif, San Diego Lit Dept 9500 Gilman Dr La Jolla CA 92093

LOWE, LYNN RAE, sculptor, educator, small business owner; b. Detroit, Dec. 24, 1946; d. Sidney Lewis and Beverly Monica (Shapero) Cohn; m. Sherwood Saul Swartz, Feb. 25, 1968 (div. Nov. 1978); children: Bradley, Damion; m. Buck Lowe (Dennis Michael Mellin), May 24, 1981 (dec. Sept. 2000)); children: Persephone, Dustin. Student, U. Colo., 1965-67; cert. master gardener, U. Ariz., 1990, BFA in Mixed Media summa cum laude, 1993. Gen. mgr. Sta. KOTO-FM, Telluride, Colo., 1981-83; publicity dir., actor SRO Theatre Troupe, Telluride, 1982-87; exec. dir. Gov.'s Cup and Pioneers of Skiing Internat., Telluride, 1984-88; tchr. art San Xavier Mission Sch., Tucson, 1990-93, founding pres. Lowe Co Motion, Telluride and Tucson, 1979—. Prodr. Telluride Jazz Festival, 1984-88, Ariz. Theatre Co. Temple of Music: Art Celebration, Tucson, 1988; dir. Telluride Film Festival, 1977—; cons. Colo. Coun. Arts and Humanities, Denver, 1980-81; mem. grants panel Tucson-Pima Arts Coun., 1991; bd. dirs. Nat. Film Preserve, Hanover, N.H., 1991-98; mem. adv. bd. Global Arts Project, Tucson, 1995-96; mem. adj. faculty Pima C.C., 1992—. One-woman shows Cathedral Heritage Found., Louisville, 1996, Sun Cities Mus., Ariz., 1997, Janice Epstein Mus. Gallery, West Bloomfield, Mich., 1998, Chase Freedman Gallery, West Hartford, Conn., 1999; author: Call Someplace Paradise, 1989; illustrator: Inner Journey, 1994; commns. include logo Am. Holistic Med. Nurses Assn., Boone, N.C., 1995, 99; work featured in jours., mags. and newspapers. Moderator Town of Telluride, 1984-88; bd. dirs. Project Graduation, Tucson, 1989; sponsor Tucson Med. Ctr. Aux.; coord. Meals on Wheels, Tucson, 1990-91; mem. adv. bd. Tucson Mayor's Task Force on Cultural Tourism, 1991; mem. fundraising steering com. Tucson Jewish Cmty. Ctr., 1994—. Recipient Niche award Niche mag., 1998. Mem. Internat. Sculpture Ctr., Nat. Mus. Women in the Arts, Rosicrucian Soc., Golden Key, Phi Kappa Phi. Avocations: teaching art, gardening, swimming, kayaking, entertaining. Home: 2425 E Caminito De Los Rancho Tucson AZ 85718-5907

LOWE, MARY FRANCES, federal government official; b. Ft. Meade, Md., Apr. 15, 1952; d. Benno Powers and Peggy Catherine (Moore) L. BA, Coll. William and Mary, 1972; MA, Fletcher Sch. Law and Diplomacy, 1974, MA Law and Diplomacy in, 1975; diplome, Grad. Inst. Internat. Studies U. Geneva, Switzerland, 1975; M.P.H. in epidemiology, Johns Hopkins Sch. Hygiene and Pub. Health, 1986. External collaborator ILO, Geneva, 1974; legis. asst. to U.S. Senator Richard S. Schweiker Washington, 1975-76; profl. staff mem. health and sci. rsch. subcom. U.S. Senate Com. Labor and Human Resources, Washington, 1976-81; exec. sec. U.S. Dept. HHS, Washington, 1981-85; sr. asst. to commr. program policy FDA, 1985-89; sr. asst. pesticide programs EPA, 1989-96; Pesticide Ch Comms., 1996-97; asst. Office Environ. Policy U.S. Dept. State, Washington, 1997-99; program advisor pesticide program govt. and internat. svcs. EPA, Washington, 1999—. Rep. U.S. delegations 34th and 35th World Health Assemblies, Geneva, NAFTA and WTO Coms., 1995—98; alt. trustee Woodrow Wilson Internat. Ctr. Scholars. Mem. Soc. for Epidemiologic Rsch., Am. Assn. World Health, Exec. Women in Govt., Soc. for Chem. Hazard Comm., Soc. Risk Analysis, Washington World Affairs Coun., Delta Omega. Home: 7920 Spotswood Dr Alexandria VA 22308-1125 Office: US EPA 1200 Pennsylvania Ave NW Washington DC 20460-0001 E-mail: lowe.maryfrances@epa.gov.

LOWE, MARY JOHNSON, federal judge; b. N.Y.C., June 10, 1924; m. Ivan A. Michael, Nov. 4, 1961; children: Edward H. Lowe, Leslie H. Lowe, Bess J. Michael. BA, Hunter Coll., 1952; LLB, Bklyn. Law Sch., 1954; LLM, Columbia U., 1955; LLD, CUNY, 1990. Bar: N.Y. 1955. Pvt. practice law, N.Y.C., 1955-71; judge N.Y.C. Criminal Ct., 1971-72; acting justice N.Y. State Supreme Ct., 1972-74; judge Bronx County Supreme Ct., 1974; justice N.Y. State Supreme Ct., 1977, 1st Jud. Dist., 1978; judge U.S. Dist. Ct. (so. dist.) N.Y., 1978-91, sr. judge, 1991—. Recipient award for outstanding service to criminal justice system Bronx County Criminal Cts. Bar Assn., 1974, award for work on narcotics cases Asst. Dist. Attys., 1974 Mem. Women in Criminal Justice, Harlem Lawyers Assn., Bronx Criminal Lawyers Assn., N.Y. County Lawyers Assn., Bronx County Bar Assn., N.Y. State Bar Assn. (award for outstanding jud. contbn. to criminal justice Sect. Criminal Justice 1978), NAACP, Nat. Urban League, Nat. Council Negro Women, NOW. Office: US Dist Ct 40 Foley Sq New York NY 10007-1502

LOWE, PAMELA MARY, art educator; d. Edsel L. and Mary Lou Harris; m. Thomas E. Lowe, Jr.. BA in visual arts, Ga. State U., Atlanta, 1981. Tchr. Turner Mid. Sch., Lithia Springs, Ga., 1982, Sweetwater Mid. Sch., Lawrenceville, 1982—83, Lassiter HS, Marietta, 1983—. Co-chmn. Renaissance faculty com. Lassiter HS; art club sponsor; ap: studio art tchr. Mem.: Nat. Art Educators Assn. Office: Cobb City Bd of Edn Lassiter HS 2601 Shallowford Rd Marietta GA 30066

LOWE, PATRICIA A. psychologist, educator; b. Landstuhl, Germany, July 31, 1957; (parents Am. citizens); d. Gerald H. and Hazel C. Lowe. BS magna cum laude, Boise State U., 1980; PhD, Tex. A&M U., 2000. Lic. psychologist Idaho, cert. sch. psychologist Idaho, Kans. Grad. rsch./tchg. asst. Tex. A&M U., College Station, 1995—99; psychology intern Warm Springs Counseling Ctr. and Tng. Inst., Boise, Idaho, 1999—2000, post-doctoral resident, 2000—01; prof. U. Kans., Lawrence, 2001—. Cons. for tech. initiative grant The Ind. Sch. Dist. of Boise City, 1999—2000; cons./tech. advisor to the U. Kans. Nat. Ctr. on Learning Disabilities U. of Kans., Lawrence, 2002—. Assoc. editor: book Encyclopedia of School Psychology; co-author: (test manual) Adult Manifest Anxiety Scale, (test) Adult Manifest Anxiety Scale-Elderly Version, Adult Manifest Anxiety Scale-Adult Version, Adult Manifest Anxiety Scale-College Version, (book) Clinical Applications of Continuous Performance Tests: Measuring Attention and Impulsive Responding in Children and Adults, Encyclopedia of School Psychology; contbr. chapters to books, articles to profl. jours. Faculty rep. U. Kans. Cir. K Svc. Orgn., Lawrence, 2001—03; univ. trainer Kans. Assn. Sch. Psychologists, 2001—02. Recipient Alumni award, Boise State U., 1980; Lechner Grad. Merit fellow, Tex. A&M U., 1995—96, Rsch. grantee, U. Kans., 2002, 2003. Mem.: APA, NASP, Psi Chi, Kappa Delta Phi, Phi Kappa Phi. Achievements include test development. Avocations: skiing, tennis, racquetball, swimming, running.

LOWELL, VIRGINIA LEE, librarian; b. San Jose, Calif., Nov. 21, 1940; d. Earnest S. and Dorothy (Givens) Greene; children: Michael Edward, Christopher Scott. Student, Reed Coll, 1958-61; BA, U. Calif., Berkeley, 1963; MSLS, Western Res. U., 1964. Cataloger Wittenberg U., Springfield, Ohio, 1965-66, John Carroll U., Cleve., 1966-68, Cuyahoga Community Coll., Cleve., 1968-70, cons., instr., 1970; head catalog dept. Cuyahoga County Pub. Library, Cleve., 1976-78; dir. tech. svcs. Cuyahoga County Pub. Libr., Cleve., 1979-89; dir. Jackson (Mich.) Dist. Libr., 1989—98; state libr. State of Hawaii, 1998—. Chmn. bd. trustees Ohionet, Columbus, 1987-89. Mem. ALA, Ohio Libr. Assn. (coord. automation and tech. div. 1988—), No. Ohio Tech. Svc. Librs. (chmn. 1988-89), Ohio Women Librs. (treas. 1987-89), Am. Mgmt. Assn., Mich. Libr. Assn. Democrat. Roman Catholic. Avocation: choral singing. Office: 465 S King St Rm B-1 Honolulu HI 96813

LOWENBERG, GEORGINA GRACE, retired elementary school educator; b. El Paso, Tex., Feb. 15, 1944; d. Eduardo Antonio and Grace Elizabeth (Fletcher) Orellana; m. Edward Daniel Lowenberg, June 14, 1968, (div. 1985); 1 child, Jennifer Anne. BSEd, U. Tex., El Paso, 1965, postgrad., 1965-66, U. St. Thomas, 1983. Permanent profl. teaching cert., Tex. Tchr. 5th grade El Paso Pub. Sch. Dist., 1965-70; tchr. 3d grade gifted, talented Ysleta Ind. Sch. Dist., El Paso, 1980—2002. Mem. com. Tex. State Textbook Selection Com., Austin, 1984-85, Tex. State TEAMS Math Adv. Com., Austin, 1986-87; sci. presentor Silver Burdett, Albuquerque, 1985-86; critic reader Scott-Foresman, Dallas, 1986; pres., v.p. Scotsdale Elem. Sch. PTA, El Paso, 1976-83, v.p. Eastwood Middle Sch. PTA, El Paso, 1984-85; mem. Eastwood Heights Elem. Sch. PTA, 1985-87; sec. Eastwood High Sch. Band Boosters, El Paso, 1985-89, Speech Boosters, 1986-88; life mem. Tex. State PTA, 1981—. Troop leader Brownie and Jr. Girl Scouts Am., El Paso, 1977-82; dir. Eaglette Dance Team, 1994—; vol. Eastwood Hts. Libr. Named Tchr. of Yr., Eastwood Heights Elem., 1983, Top Ten Dist. Tchr. of Yr., 1983. Mem. Assn. Tex. Profl. Educators (regional treas. 1987-88), Yseta and Tex. Ret. Tchrs. Assn. Roman Catholic.

LOWENSTEIN, ARLENE JANE, nursing educator, health facility administrator; b. Phila., Oct. 10, 1936; d. Nathan Morris and Rae (Greenburg) Needleman; m. Manfred Lowenstein, June 9, 1957; children: Jay David, Russell Scott. Diploma in nursing, Hosp. of U. Pa., Phila., 1957; BSN, Fairleigh Dickinson U., 1969; MA, NYU, 1974, PhD, U. Pitts., 1985. Staff and tchg. nurse Albert Einstein Med. Ctr., Hosp. U. Pa., 1957-59; instr. Middlesex County Coll., Edison, NJ, 1969-71; staff nurse Vis. Nurse Svc., N.Y.C., 1970-72; supr. obstet. and pediat. Middlesex Gen. Hosp., New Brunswick, NJ, 1972-74; dir. ambulatory & cmty. health Peter Bent Brigham Hosp., 1974-79, dir. nurse practitioner program, 1974-81; dir. surg. nursing Brigham and Women's Hosp., Boston, 1980—81; acting dir. nursing Peter Bent Brigham Hosp., Boston, 1978-80; assoc hosp. dir., dir nursing svc. U. Ky. Med. Ctr., Lexington, 1981-83; asst. prof. U. Pitts., 1983-85; prof. nursing, dept. chair. Med. Coll. Ga., Augusta, 1985-95; prof., dir. grad. program in nursing Mass. Gen. Hosp. Inst. of Health Professions, Boston, 1995—2003, prof. emeritus, 2003—. Contbr. articles to profl. jours. Bd. dirs. Sr. Citizens Coun. of Ctrl. Savannah River Area, Augusta, 1982-95. Mem. ANA, Coun. Grad. Edn. for Nursing Adminstrs. (chair 1990-92), Sigma Xi, Sigma Theta Tau. Avocations: opera, music, art. Home: 312 Lewis Wharf Boston MA 02110-3905 Office: Mass Gen Hosp Inst Health Professions Charleston Navy Yard 36 First Ave Boston MA 02129 E-mail: alowenstein@mghihp.edu.

LOWENTHAL, CONSTANCE, art historian, consultant; b. N.Y.C., Aug. 29, 1945; d. Jesse and Helen (Oberstein) L. BA cum laude, Brandeis U., 1967; AM, Inst. Fine Arts, NYU, 1969; PhD, Inst. Fine Arts, NYU, N.Y.C., 1976. Mem. faculty Sarah Lawrence Coll., Bronxville, N.Y., 1975-78; asst mus. educator Met. Mus. Art, N.Y.C., 1978-85; exec. dir. Internat. Found. Art Research, N.Y.C., 1985-98; dir. Commn. for Art Recovery World Jewish Congress, N.Y.C., 1998-2001; cons. art ownership disputes N.Y.C., 2001—. Bd. dirs. Ctr. for Edn. Studies, Inc. Regular contbr. Art Crime Update column Wall Street Jour., 1988-97; mem. editl. bd.: The Spoils of War, World War II and Its Aftermath: The Loss, Reappearance and Recovery of Cultural Property, 1997; contbr. articles to Mus. News and other profl. publs.

LOWENTHAL, SUSAN, realtor, artist; b. Munich, Nov. 30, 1946; came to U.S., 1949; d. Jerry and Gertrude (Wiestreich) L.; m. Alex J. Stolitzka, Oct. ll, 1987. BA, Bklyn. Coll., 1969. Exec. dir. Manhattan Girls Club, N.Y.C., 1969-73; conf. coord. Orton Soc., N.Y.C., 1973-77; v.p. Gemtique, N.Y.C., 1977-81; broker Prudential Bache, N.Y.C., 1981-83, Smith Barney, N.Y.C., 1983-85; pres., chief exec. officer Lowenthal Fin. Svcs., Inc., N.Y.C., 1985-89, fin. cons., money mgr., 1990-98; realtor, exclusive buyer agt. March Buyers Realty, 1995—. Designer/artist works sold in museum gift shops and pub. in nat. mags.; guest appearances on cable TV shows; pres. AcScents! Naturally. Artist, designer; designs published in maj. nat. mags. Jewish. Avocations: skiing, reading, bridge. Office Phone: 203-227-3343. E-mail: susan@acscentsnaturally.com., susan@bysusandesigns.com.

LOWERY, BARBARA J. psychiatric nurse, educator; RN, Reading Hosp. Sch., 1958; MSN, Villanova U., 1966; NSN, U. Pa., 1968; EdD, Temple U., 1973. Staff nurse, head nurse Danville State Hosp., Pa., 1958-62; unit and hosp. supr. Norristown (Pa.) State Hosp., 1960-63, instr. nursing edn., 1963-65; dir. nursing edn. Ea. Pa. Psychiat. Inst., 1968-69; instr. Sch. Nursing, U. Pa., Phila., 1970-72, assoc., 1972-73, from asst. prof. to assoc. prof., 1973-87, asst. provost, prof. nursing, 1987—, chmn. psychiat. mental health nursing, 1978-84, ombudsman, 1984-86, dir. Robert Wood Johnson clin. nurse scholars program, 1986—. Cons. in field. Author, co-author chpts. to books; assoc. editor Nursing Rsch., 1978-83. Fellow Am. Acad. Nursing; mem. NAS. Office: U Pa Sch Nursing Nursing Edn Bldg Rom 208 College Hall 420 Guardian Dr Philadelphia PA 19104-4210

LOWERY, DEBORAH GARRISON, freelance writer and editor; b. Johnson City, Tenn., Oct. 2, 1957; d. Clyde Mack and Joyce Dean (Stout) Garrison; m. David Ryan Lowery, Nov. 5, 1983; children: Caroline Nicole, Benjamin David. BS in Home Econs., U. Ga., 1979, MA in Journalism, 1981. Asst. editor So. Living Mag., Birmingham, 1981-87, assoc. editor, 1987-88; sr. editor Progressive Farmer Mag., Birmingham, 1988-92; mng. editor Cooking Light Mag., Birmingham, 1992-94, exec. editor, 1994; foods editor Oxmoor House Pub. Co., Birmingham, 1994-98. Charter mem. bd. advisors Coll. Family & Consumer Svcs. U. Ga., Athens, 1995-98; charter mem. work & family com. So. Progress Corp, Birmingham, 1991-97; media con. mem. Childhood Agrl. Injury Prevention Symposium Nat. Farm Medicine Ctr., 1992; owner, instr. Kids Can Cook! (children's cooking sch.), 1998—. Editor: (cookbook) Low Fat High Flavor Cookbook, 1995, Cooking Light Five-Star Recipes, 1996, Weight Watchers Light & Easy Cookbook, 1997, Weight Watchers Cook Quick Cook Healthy, 1997; coord. editor Countryplace Mag., 1991-97; freelance journalist, 1998—; contbr. articles to profl. jours. Sunday sch. tchr. Valleydale Bapt. Ch., Birmingham, 1997-98; parent coll. com. mem. Oak Mountain Elem. Sch., Birmingham, 1997-98. Recipient Nat. Bus. Home Economist Yr. Home Economists Bus., 1993, Ala. Home Economist Yr. Ala. Home Economists Bus., Birmingham, 1993; master writer award Am. Agrl. Editors Assn., 1992, Writer of Yr., 1991. Mem. Am. Assn. Family and Consumer Scis. (food and nutrition com. 1981-98, chmn. Birmingham group bus. sect. 1984-85), Ala. Assn. Family and Consumer Sci. (v.p. program devel. 1986-88). Avocations: herb gardening, inspirational writing. Home and Office: 3004 Stonehill Cir Birmingham AL 35244-3438 Fax: 205-980-5062. E-mail: writer1118@aol.com.

LOWERY, ELIZABETH, automotive executive; b. New Britain, Conn., Oct. 24, 1955; BBA cum laude, Ea. Mich. U., 1978; JD magna cum laude, Wayne State U., 1981. Ptnr. Honigman Miller Schwartz and Cohn; law clerk Mich. Supreme Ct. Chief Justice G. Mennen Williams, 1981—83; atty. GM, 1989—94, practice area mgr. environ. and energy, 1994—97, v.p. N.Am., gen. counsel, 1997—2000, v.p. environ. and energy, 2000—. Bd. dirs. World Environ. Ctr., Keystone Ctr., Haven, Women's Leadership Forum. Named One of 100 Most Influential Women, Crain's Detroit Bus., 2002. Office: GM Corp 300 Renaissance Ctr Detroit MI 48265-3000

LOWERY, SABRA ANNETTE, special education educator; d. Lonnie Drew and Shirley L. Lowery. BS, Mich. State U.; EdM, George Mason U.; Edn. Specialist, George Washington U. Elem. educator Fairfax (Va.) County Pub. Schs., 1991—2000, early childhood/elem. summer sch./stds. learning specialist, 2000—. Mem.: Coun. for Exceptional Children. Office: Fairfax County Pub Schs 10310 Layton Hall Dr Fairfax VA 22030 E-mail: sabra.lowery@fcps.edu.

LOWEY, NITA M. congresswoman; b. N.Y., July 5, 1937; m. Stephen Lowey, 1961; children: Dona, Jacqueline, Douglas. BS, Mt. Holyoke Coll., 1959. Community activist, prior to 1975; asst. sec. state State of N.Y., 1975-87; mem. U.S. Congress from 20th N.Y. dist., 1989-92, U.S. Congress from 18th N.Y. dist., 1993—. Mem. appropriations com., 1993—. Democrat. Office: US Ho of Reps 2329 Rayburn Ho Office Bldg Washington DC 20515-0001*

LOWRANCE, MURIEL EDWARDS, program specialist; b. Ada, Okla., Dec. 28, 1922; d. Warren E. and Mayme E. (Barrick) Edwards; B.S. in Edn., East Central State U., Ada, 1954; 1 dau., Kathy Lynn Lowrance Gutierrez. Accountant, adminstrv. asst. to bus. mgr. East Central State U., 1950-68; grants and contracts specialist U. N.Mex. Sch. Medicine, Albuquerque, 1968-72, program specialist IV, dept. orthopaedics, 1975-86; asst. adminstrv. officer N.Mex. Regional Med. Program, 1972-75. Bd. dirs. Vocat. Rehab. Center, 1980-84. Cert. profl. contract mgr. Nat. Contract Assn. Mem. Am. Bus. Women's Assn. (past pres. El Segundo chpt., Woman of Yr. 1974), AAUW, Amigos de las Americas (dir.). Democrat. Methodist. Club: Pilot (Albuquerque) (pres. 1979-80, dir. 1983-84, dist. treas. 1984-86, treas. S.W. dist., 1984-86, gov.-elect S.W. dist. 1986-87, gov. S.W. dist. 1987-88). Home: 3028 Mackland Ave NE Albuquerque NM 87106-2018

LOWREY, BARBARA R. federal official; BA, Mich. State U., 1963; MS, U. Wis., 1964; PhD, Mich. State U., 1970. Assoc. sec., ombudsman of bd. Bd. Govs. of Fed. Res. Sys., Washington. Chief staff support to Gov. Yellen on interagy. com. Women's Bus. Enterprises; bd. rep. NWBC, 1992-93. Office: Fed Res Sys Bd Mems Office 20th & C Sts NW Ofc Washington DC 20551-0001

LOWRIE, KATHRYN YANACEK, special education educator; b. Midland, Mich., Nov. 23, 1958; d. Frank Joseph and Jacqueline Ann (Sipko) Yanacek; m. David Bruce Lowrie, Mar. 14, 1987; 1 child, Alexandra Yanacek. BA in Psychology, Northea. U., 1980. Psychology technician Rsch. Inst. of Environ. Medicine, U.S. Army, Natick, Mass., 1980-81, computer programmer, 1981-83; assoc. recruiter Mgmt. Adv. Svcs., Burlington, Mass., 1983-85, v.p. mgmt. info. sys., 1985-86, exec. v.p., 1986-89; CEO Computer Careers, Raynham, Mass., 1989-90; v.p. G.R.S.I. Corp., Middleboro, Mass., 1990-94; owner S.B. Industries, Taunton, Mass., 1994-96; pres. Enviro-Screen, Inc., Taunton, 1996-97; sr. assoc. Franklin (Mass.) Key Assocs., 1997—99; contract recruiter, 1999—2001; spl. edn. tchr. J.E. Richards Mid. Sch., Lawrenceville, Ga., 2001—. Roman Catholic. Avocations: dance, reading, physical fitness, travel, motivational training. E-mail: kylowrie@hotmail.com.

LOWRY, KAREN M. biomedical research scientist, pharmacist; b. Stamford, Conn., July 8, 1945; d. Joseph John and Helen Elizabeth (Wykowski) Markovich; m. Atherton Clark Lowry Aug. 17, 1968; children: Atherton Clark Matthew, Suzanne Marie. BS summa cum laude, Fordham U., 1968; MS in Pharmacology, Cornell U., 1971; MA, St. Charles Sem., Wynnewood, Pa., 1983. Registered pharmacist, Pa. Rsch. asst. in biochemistry/molecular biology Thomas Jefferson Med. Sch., Phila., 1971-74; adj. prof. chemistry Holy Family Coll., Phila., 1975-76, Arcadia U., Glenside, Pa., 1984-87; sr. biochemist, lab. mgr. Beacon Rsch. Inc., Glenside, 1987-95; pharmacist Abington (Pa.) Meml. Hosp., 2000—; staff U. Pa. Health System/Presbyn. Med. Ctr., 2000. Asst. sec. Biocoat Inc., Ft. Washington, Pa., 1991-95; mem. sci. adv. bd. UHT, Dobbs Ferry, N.Y., 1987-95. Contbr. articles to profl. jours.; patentee in field. Libr. dir. Immaculate Conception Sch., Jenkintown, Pa., 1980-86; Am. sponsor Vietnamese refugees Cath. Social Svcs., Phila., 1975—. NSF rsch. participant, 1964-68; USPHS grantee, 1968-71 Mem. Am. Chem. Soc., GFWC Everywoman's Club of Glenside (publicity chair 1995-96, pres. 1996-99). Roman Catholic. Avocations: philosophy, growing roses, reading. Home: 631 Baeder Rd Jenkintown PA 19046-1555

LOWRY, LOIS (LOIS HAMMERSBERG), writer; b. 1937; Author: A Summer to Die, 1977, Find A Stranger, Say Goodbye, 1978, Anastasia Krupnik, 1979, Autumn Street, 1980, Anastasia Again, 1981, Anastasia at Your Service, 1982, The One Hundredth Thing About Caroline, 1983, Taking Care of Terrific, 1983, Anastasia, Ask Your Analyst, 1984, Us and Uncle Fraud, 1984, Anastasia on Her Own, 1985, Switcharound, 1985, Anastasia Has the Answers, 1986, Anastasia's Chosen Career, 1987, Rabbie Starkey, 1987, All About Sam, 1988, Number the Stars, 1989 (John Newbery medal 1990), Your Move, J.P.!, 1990, Anastasia at This Address, 1991, Attaboy, Sam!, 1992, The Giver, 1993 (John Newbery medal 1994), Anastasia Absolutely, 1995, See You Around, Sam!, 1996, Stay! Keeper's Story, 1997, Looking Back, 1998, Zooman Sam, 1999, Gathering Blue, 2000, Gooney Bird Greene, 2002, The Silent Boy, 2003, Messenger, 2004. Recipient Chgo. Tribune Young Adult Book prize, 2003. Address: 205 Brattle St Cambridge MA 02138-3345 Office: care Houghton Mifflin 222 Berkeley St Boston MA 02116-3748*

LOWRY, MARILYN JEAN, horticultural retail company executive; b. Greensburg, Pa., Oct. 19, 1932; d. Clifford Henry and Martha McCune (Whitehead) Bushyager; m. John Cathcart Lowry, June 14, 1958; children: Martha Kim Hultberg, John Ryan, Nancy Lynn. BS, Ind. U. of Pa., 1954; MEd, Pa. State U., 1958. Tchr. Jeannette (Pa.) pub. schs., 1954-57; grad. asst. Pa. State U., University Park, 1957-58; demonstration sch. tchr. Towson (Md.) U., 1958-59; sec.-treas. Lowry & Co., Inc., Phoenix, Md.,

1964—, 1987—. Master flower show judge Nat. Council State Garden Clubs, Inc., St. Louis, 1987—, landscape design critic, 1985—; master gardener U. Md. Extension Svc., 1984—. Mem. Lutherville Garden Club (pres. 1979—), Am. Assn. Nurserymen Aux. (pres. 1972), Federated Garden Clubs Md. (dir. dist. III 1981-83), Am. Nursery and Landscape Assn. (chmn. wholesale plant sales profits. 1999—). Republican. Presbyterian.

LOY, STEPHANIE LYNN, music educator; b. Oregon, Ohio, June 7, 1977; d. Larry Carl and Shirley Marie Loy. BA in Music Edn., Bowling Green State U., Ohio, 1999, postgrad. in Ednl. Adminstrn., 2002—. Music tchr. St. Peter Elem. Sch., Lorain, Ohio, 1999—2000, Lakota East Elem. Sch., Burgoon, Ohio, 2000—01; instrumental dir. Lakota Jr. High and H.S., Kansas, Ohio, 2001—. Track coach Lakota Jr. H.S., Kansas, Ohio, 2000—02; mus. dir. Lakota H.S., Kansas, Ohio, 2001—, cheerleading advisor, 2002—03, asst. athletic dir., 2002—. Softball coach Northwood Ch. of God, Ohio, 2001—, Christian edn. chairperson, 2001—. Named Christian Edn. Worker of the Yr., Northwood Ch. of God, 2000. Church Of God. Avocations: softball, collecting boyd's bears. Home: 1392 N Middlesex Dr W Genoa OH 43430

LOYD, MARTHA ROSE, forester; b. Sanford, Fla., Oct. 24, 1951; d. Charles W. and Geraldine (Greer) Rose; m. Randall Allen Loyd, Oct. 1, 1983 (div. Oct. 1998); children: Erin Leslie, Matthew Allen. BS in Forestry, U. Fla., 1978. Unit mgr. Scott Paper Co., Monroeville, Ala., 1978—86, regional mgr., 1986—93; mgr. silvicultural ops. Kimberly-Clark, Monroeville, 1993—99; divsn. forester Molpus Timberlands Mgmt., Huxford, Ala., 1999—2002; pres. Southeast Timberlands Mgmt., Monroeville, 2003—. Founder Monroeville Bus. Women, 1985; bd. dirs. YMCA, Monroeville, 1998—99. Mem.: Ala. Forestry Assn. (com. chairperson 1991—93). Avocations: gardening, travel, yoga, home improvement projects. Home: 456 Overlook Dr Monroeville AL 36460 Office: Southeast Timberlands Mgmt PO Box 477 Monroeville AL 36461

LOZANO, ARACELI E. foundation administrator, consultant; b. Laredo, Tex., Dec. 30, 1967; d. Juan Ovidio Jr. and Rosa F. Bautista; m. Romeo Lozano II, May 5, 1995. Student, Laredo C.C., 1986-87, 98-99. Human resource specialist, tng. coord. Sears Roebuck & Co., Laredo, 1986-91; office mgr. Santos & Assocs., Laredo, 1991-92; payroll mgr. Gonzalez, Farias, Guerra & Flores, Laredo, 1992-97; bus. devel. specialist Small Bus. Devel. Ctr., Laredo, 1997; dir. Laredo Devel. Found. Small Bus. Devel. Ctr., Laredo, 1997—. Mem. adv. bd. RCCI, Laredo, 1998—, Welfare to Work, Laredo, 1999—. Mem. Fin. Women's Assn., Laredo C. of C. (chair small bus. com. 1998-99), Laredo Bus. and Profl. Women's Assn. (sec. 1998-99, v.p. 1999-2000, pres. 2000—). Office: Laredo Devel Found 616 Leal St Laredo TX 78041

LOZANO-CENTANINO, MONICA CECILIA, publishing executive; b. L.A., July 21, 1956; d. Ignacio Eugenio and Marta Eloisa (Navarro) Lozano; m. Marcelo Centanino, Sept. 27, 1987; 1 child, Santiago Alberto. Student, U. Oreg., 1974—76; student San Francisco City Coll.; LHD (hon.), Occidental Coll., 1999. Mgr. Copy-Copia, Inc., San Francisco, 1980—85; mng. editor La Opinion, L.A., 1985—89, assoc. pub., 1989—91, assoc. pub., exec. editor, 1991—2000, pres., COO, 2000—04, pub., CEO, 2004—; pub. El Eco del Valle, San Fernando, Calif., 1990—91; v.p. Lozano Comm., 2000—04; sr. v.p. ImpreMedia LLC, 2004—. Bd. dirs. The Walt Disney Co., Union Bank Calif., Calif. Health Care Found., Tenet Healthcare Corp., Nat. Coun. La Raza; trustee SunAm. Asset Mgmt. Corp. Trustee U. So. Calif.; mem. bd. regents U. Calif., 2000—; bd. dirs. L.A. County Mus. Art, Venice Family Clinic, Ctrl. Am. Resource Ctr. Recipient Humanitarian award, Cen. Am. Refugee Ctr., L.A., 1989, Outstanding Achievement, Mex. Am. Opportunities Found., L.A., 1989. Mem. Nat. Assn. Hispanic Pubs., Nat. Assn. Hispanic Journalists, Calif. Hispanic Pubs., Am. Soc. Newspaper Editors, Calif. Chicano News Assn., Nat. Network Hispanic Women. Avocations: photography, reading, water sports. Office: La Opinion 411 W Fifth St Los Angeles CA 90013*

LOZEAU, DONNALEE M. state legislator; b. Nashua, N.H., Sept. 15, 1960; m. David Lozeau; 3 children. Attended, Rivier Coll. Mem. N.H. Ho. of Reps., former vice chair corrections and criminal justice com., vice chair rules com., legis. adminstrn. com., dep. spkr. Former chair ward five Rep. City Com.; commr. Nashua Airport Authority. Avocations: reading, outdoor sports, travel. Home: 125 Shore Dr Nashua NH 03062-1339 Office: NH Ho of Reps State Capitol Concord NH 03301

LOZOFF, BETSY, pediatrician; b. Milw., Dec. 19, 1943; d. Milton and Marjorie (Morse) L.; 1 child, Claudia Brittenham. BA, Radcliffe Coll., 1965; MD, Case Western Res. U., 1971, MS, 1981. Diplomate Am. Bd. Pediat. From asst. prof. to prof. pediatrics Case Western Res. U., Cleve., 1974-93; prof. pediatrics U. Mich., Ann Arbor, 1993—, dir. Ctr. for Human Growth and Devel., 1993—. Recipient Rsch. Career Devel. award Nat. Inst. Child Health and Human Devel., 1984-88. Fellow Am. Acad. Pediatrics; mem. Soc. for Pediatric Rsch., Soc. Rsch. in Child Devel. (program com. 1991-97), Soc. Behavioral Pediatrics (exec. com. 1985-88), Ambulatory Pediatric Soc. Office: Univ Mich Ctr Human Growth and Devel 300 N Ingalls St Ann Arbor MI 48109-2007

LU, MAY, psychologist, counselor, writer, watercolorist; b. China, Aug. 8, 1945; came to U.S., 1966; d. Conrad and Yvonne (Shaw) Cho; m. Tzu C. Lu, July 12, 1967; children: Tina, Tammy. MS, UCLA, 1969; PhD, U. Tex., Houston, 1979; MA, Norwich U., Burlington, Vt., 1990. Lic. marriage and family therapist. Counseling psychologist in pvt. practice, Houston, 1997—. Guest lectr. Family Inst., Houston, 1994, U. Houston, 1995, Chinese Cmty. Ctr., L.A., 1996, Chgo., 1998, Miami, Fla., 1999; spkr. and moderator in field. Author: Mental Health of the New Chinese American Elders, 1993, How Men and Women Communicate, 1994, How to Raise New Immigrant Chilren, 1999; watercolorist. English sec. Tex. Buddhist Assn., Houston, 1979—; trustee Inst. Chinese Culture, Houston, 1980-83; vol. counselor Chinese Sr. Assn., Houston, 1985-91, Chinese Health Ctr., Houston, 1980—. Recipient award as Best Informative Wirter Overseas, Taiwan Edn. Ministry, 1997. Mem. Watercolor Art Soc. Buddhist. Office: 1631 North Loop W Ste 630 Houston TX 77008-1536

LU, MI, computer engineer, educator; b. Chongqing, Sichuan, China, July 22, 1949; d. Chong Pu Lu and Shu Sheng Fan. MS, Rice U., 1984, PhD, 1987. Registered profl. engr. From asst. prof. to assoc. prof. Tex. A&M U., Coll. Sta., 1987-98, prof., 1998—. Stream chmn. 7th Internat. Conf. Computing and Info., Peterborough, Ont., Can., 1995; conf. chmn. 5th Internat. Conf. Computer Sci. and Informatics, 2000, 6th Internat. Conf., 2002. Assoc. editor Jour. Computing and Info., 1995—, Info. Sci., 1996-97, 2002--; contbr. articles to profl. jours. Mem. Computer Soc. of IEEE (sr.). Office: Tex A&M U Dept Elec Engring College Station TX 77843

LU, NANCY CHAO, nutrition and food science educator; b. Xian, China, May 29, 1941; came to U.S. 1963; d. Lun Yuan and Shu Mei (Tsang) Chao; m. Chyi Kang Lu, Mar. 19, 1966; 1 child, Richard H. BS, Nat. Taiwan U., 1963; MS, U. Wyo., 1965; PhD, U. Calif., Berkeley, 1973. Registered dietitian. Teaching asst. dept. nutritional sci. U. Wyo., Laramie, 1963, U. Calif., Berkeley, 1964, 70, teaching assoc. dept. nutritional sci., 1978, 79; lectr. dept. nutrition and food sci. San Jose State U., 1980-82, assoc. prof. dept. nutrition and food sci., 1982-87, prof. dept. nutrition and food sci., 1987—, acting assoc. dean, dir. divsn. health professions. Contbr. articles to profl. jours. Recipient Ellsworth Dougherty award, 1976, Calif. State U. Affirmative Action Faculty Devel. award, 1984, 85, 86, Meritorious Performance and Profl. Promise award San Jose State U., 1986, Most Outstanding Nutrition and Food Sci. Prof. award, 1989, 93; San Jose State U. Found. grantee, 1986-87, 89-90, 92-93, 93-94, 94-95, NIH grantee, 1975-76, 78-79, 73-75. Mem. Am. Dietetic Assn., Am. Inst. Nutrition, Inst. Food Technologists, Soc. Nematology, Soc. for Exptl. Biology and Medicine, Iota Sigma Pi, Sigma Xi. Office: San Jose State U Divsn Health Professions San Jose CA 95192 0001

LU, NINGPING, environmental chemist; b. Sichuan, China, June 18, 1941; d. Yiungdi and Jinghua (Liu) L.; m. Li Pin-Fun, July 23, 1964 (div. 1990); children: Ying, Nin. BS in Biophysics, Sichuan U., 1964; MS of Soil Chemistry, Auburn U., 1990, PhD in Environtl. Soil Chemistry, 1993. Dir. Atomic Agrl. Ins., Sichuan, 1983; rsch. assoc. Fertilizer Ins., Sichuan, 1985-86; postdoctoral rsch. assoc. Auburn U., 1993-94, Los Alamos Nat. Lab., 1994-97, tech. staff mem., 1997—. Vis. scientist Purdue U., West Lafayette, Ind., 1983-84, Auburn U., 1984-85; cons. UN Devel. Program in China, Beijing, 1997—. Contbr. over 70 articles to profl. publs. Mem. Agronomy Soc. of Am., Soil Sci. Soc. of Am., Am. Chem. Soc., N.Y. Acad. of Sci., Phi Kappa Phi. Achievements include development of remedial processes of radionuclide (e.g. uranium-238, cesium-137, plutonium-239, strontium-90, Americium-241, american-241, strantium-90) contaminated soils, surface water and ground water; utlization of municipal solid wastes on agricultural land; research in remediation of radionuclide contaminated soil, water and sites; actinide interactions with colloids of metal oxides, clays and silica; transport of radio-colloids in groundwater; stability, solubility and speciation of actinides at nuclear waste repository sites. Office: E-ET Los Alamos Nat Lab Ms J514 Los Alamos NM 87545-0001 E-mail: ningping@lanl.gov.

LUBBAT, NANCY PARMAR, secondary school educator; d. Mac and Annetta Parmar; m. Costandi Lubbat, Aug. 10, 1980; children: Charles, David. BS in Math., Troy State U., 1973; MA in Secondary Edn., U. Ala., 1974; counseling cert., U. Houston, 1985. Lic. day care dir. Tex., real estate broker Tex. Math. tchr. Baldwin County Bd. Edn., Daphne, Ala., 1974—79, Galena Park Ind. Sch. Dist., Houston, 1979—87, Sheldon Ind. Sch. Dist., Houston, 1990, Galena Park Ind. Sch. Dist., Houston, 1990—91, counselor, 1991—94, lead counselor, 1994—. Owner, broker Lubbat & Assocs., Houston, 1999—; owner, dir. Woodforest Christian Child Care, Houston, 1996—. Avocation: reading. Office: North Shore Jr HS 353 N Castlegony Houston TX 77049

LUBBERS, TERESA S. state legislator, public relations executive; b. Indpls., July 5, 1951; d. Richard and Evelyn (Ent) Smith; m. R. Mark Lubbers, Oct. 7, 1978; children: Elizabeth Stone, Margaret Smith. AB, Ind. U., 1973; MPA, Harvard U., 1981. Tchr. English Warren Ctrl. High Sch., 1973-74; pub. info. officer Office of Mayor Richard Lugar, 1974-75; dep. press sec., legis. asst. Office of U.S. Senator Richard Lugar, 1976-78; legis. rep. Nat. Fedn. Ind. Bus., 1978-80; dir. info. INC. Mag., 1981-82; press sec. Dielmann for Congress, 1982-83; pres. pub. rels. firm Capitol Communications, 1983—; mem. Ind. Senate from 30th dist., Indpls., 1992—. Co-founder, v.p. Richard G. Lugar Excellence in Pub. Svc. Series, 1990—; bd. dirs. Young Audiences Ind., Nat. Policy Forum. Bd. deacons Tabernacle Presbyn. Ch.; mem. cultural enrichment com. Immaculate Heart Sch., Meridian Kessler Neighborhood Assn., Rep. Profl. Women's Roundtable; mem. steering com. Forum Series, Girls Inc.; bus. mem. Broad Ripple Village Assn.; vol. Dick Lugar's 1974 Senate Campaign; pub. info. officer Mayor's Office, 1974-75; office mgr., Friends of Dick Lugar, 1976; senate staff Office of Senator Richard Lugar, 1976-78; adv. com. Ind. Sch. for Blind; bd. dirs. Brebeuf Prep. Sch., St. Vincent New Hope; cmty. adv. bd. Jr. League of Indpls.; exec. bd., crossroads coun. Boy Scouts of Am.; mem. devel. commn. White River State Park. Republican. Office: Ind Senate Dist 30 200 W Washington St Indianapolis IN 46204-2728

LUBBOCK, MILDRED MARCELLE (MIDGE LUBBOCK), former small business owner; b. Clebourne, Tex., Apr. 9, 1920; d. Richard Talmadge and Nell Bouregarde (Boykin) Hardin; m. Wilson Neibuhr Munz ; children: Pamela Ann Sanders, Timothy Ray Munz, Phyllis Glasscock; m. Charles William Lubbock, Aug. 12, 1990. Grad. high sch. and bus. sch., Houston. Asst. photographer Robinson Portraits, Houston; clk.-typist U.S. Naval Lighter-Than-Air Base, Houma, La., U.S. Naval Air Sta., Norfolk, Va.; sales distbr. Nina Ross Cosmetiques, Brenham, Tex., Midge's Health Food Store, Brenham, 1992-95. Contbr. poetry to various anthologies. Mem. libr. bd. Fortnightly Club, Brenham, 1970—, pres. arts dept.; pres. Brenham Fine Arts League, 1985. Recipient Golden Poet award, 1987-90, medal of honor World of Poetry, 1990. Mem. UDC (past pres.), Am. Legion Aux. (past pres.). Baptist. Avocations: oil painting, travel, poetry, reading, grandchildren. Home: 1501 E Stone St Brenham TX 77833-5050

LUBCHENCO, JANE, marine biologist, educator; b. Denver, Colo., Dec. 4, 1947; married; 2 children. BA, Colo. Coll., 1969; MS, U. Wash., 1971; PhD in Ecology, Harvard U., 1975; DSc (hon.), Princeton U. Asst. prof. ecology Harvard U., Cambridge, Mass., 1975—77; rsch. assoc. Smithsonian Inst., 1978—; from asst. prof. to assoc. prof. Oreg. State U., Corvallis, 1978—88, prof. zoology, 1988—, disting. prof., 1993—, Wayne and Gladys Valley prof. marine biology, 1995—; pres.-elect Internat. Coun. for Sci., Paris, 2001—02, pres., 2002—. Prin. investigator NSF, 1976—; mem. Nat. Sci. Bd., 1994, 2000. Named Oreg. Scientist of Yr., Oreg. Acad. Scis., 1994; fellow, John D. and Katherine T. MacArthur Found., 1993—98; Pew Scholar in conservation and environment, 1992, MacArthur fellow, 1993. Mem.: NAS, AAAS (pres. 1995—98), Am. Inst. Biol. Sci., Am. Soc. Zoologists, Am. Soc. Naturalists, Phycological Soc. Am. (nat. lectr. 1987—89), Ecol. Soc. Am. (mem. coun. 1982—84, chair awards com. 1983—86, nominating com. 1986, George Mercer award 1979). Achievements include research in population and community ecology, plant-herbivore and predator-prey interactions, competition, marine ecology, algal ecology, agal life histories, biogeography and chemical ecology. Office: Oreg State U Dept Zoology Cordley 3029 Corvallis OR 97331

LUBELL, ELLEN, writer; b. Bklyn., Apr. 7, 1950; d. Edward and Sonia Lubell. BA in Fine Arts, SUNY, Stony Brook, 1971. Contbg. editor Arts Mag., N.Y.C., 1972-79; founder, editor Womanart Mag., Bklyn., 1976-78; columnist Soho Weekly News, N.Y.C., 1977-79; contbr. Art in Am., N.Y.C., 1981-85; dir. pub. rels. Gerstman & Meyers Inc., N.Y.C., 1984-89; freelancer, columnist, publicist The Village Voice, N.Y.C., 1984-91; columnist, freelancer N.Y. Newsday, 1988—89; dir. comm. Inform, Inc., N.Y.C., 1991-95; comm. dir. Child Care Action Campaign, N.Y.C., 1995-99; freelance writer Star-Ledger, Newark, 1996-97; dir. pub. rels. The Childrens Aid Soc., N.Y.C., 1999—. Art Critics fellow Nat. Endowment for the Arts, 1978.

LUBENKOV, TERRY ANNE, broker, realtor; b. Cherry Point, N.C., 1948; d. John David and Eleanor Jane (Feild) Dunlop; m. Paul A. Lubenkov III, 1972; children: Byron, Ashley. BS in Edn., U. Ark., 1970. Tchr. North Kansas City (Mo.) Sch. Dist., 1970-72, Tucson Dist. #1, 1972-74, Dist. 86, Hinsdale, Ill., 1975, Dist. 74, Lincoln Wood, Ill., 1975—77, Dist. 106, Burr Ridge, Ill., 1977-80; realtor Century 21, LaGrange, Ill., 1979—98, Coldwell Banker Residential Brokerage, 1998—. Sub. tchr., LaGrange, 1988—. Recipient award N.Y. Marine Corp. U. Ark., 1966-70. Mem. AAUW (past pres. Western Springs area), Nat. Assn. Realtors, Ill. Assn. Realtors, La Grange Bd. Realtors, DuPage Bd. Realtors, Delta Gamma Alumnae (social chmn. 1978-80, sec. 1981-83, past pres. West Suburban Alumnae chpt.), Realtor Assn. West/South Suburban Chicagoland, N. Ill. Multiple Listing Svc., Burhham Park Yacht Club, LaGrange Field Club. Episcopalian. Office: Coldwell Banker Residential Brokerage 219 W Hillgrove LaGrange IL 60525-6129 Office Phone: 708-352-4840.

LUBETSKI, EDITH ESTHER, librarian; b. Bklyn., July 16, 1940; d. David and Leah (Aronson) Slomowitz; m. Meir Lubetski, Dec. 23, 1968; children: Shaul, Uriel, Leah. BA, Bklyn. Coll., 1962; MLS, Columbia U., 1965; MA in Jewish Studies, Yeshiva U., 1968. Judaica libr. Stern Coll. Yeshiva U., N.Y.C., 1965-66, acquisitions libr., 1966-69, head libr., 1969—. Author (with Meir Lubetski): (book) Building a Judaica Library Collection, 1983; author: The Jewish Woman: Recent Books, 1995; contbr. articles to profl. jours. Mem. exec. bd. Jewish Book Coun., 1998—. Mem.: ACRL, ALA, N.Y. Libr. Assn., Assn. Jewish Librs. (corr. sec. 1980—84, pres. N.Y. chpt. 1984—86, nat. v.p. 1984—86, nat. pres. 1986—88, Fanny Goldstein Merit award 1993, Life Membership award 2003). Home: 1219 E 27th St Brooklyn NY 11210-4622 Office: Yeshiva U Hedi Steinberg Libr 245 Lexington Ave New York NY 10016-4605 E-mail: Lubetski@ymail.yu.edu.

LUBIC, RUTH WATSON, health facility administrator, nurse midwife; b. Bucks County, Pa., Jan. 18, 1927; d. John Russell and Lillian (Kraft) Watson; m. William James Lubic, May 28, 1955; 1 child, Douglas Watson. Diploma, Sch. Nursing Hosp. U. Pa., 1955; BS, Columbia U., 1959, MA, 1961, EdD in Applied Anthropology, 1979; cert. in nurse midwifery, SUNY, Bklyn., 1962, DSc (hon.), 1993; LLD (hon.), U. Pa., 1985; DSc (hon.), U. Medicine and Dentistry, N.J., 1986; LHD (hon.), Coll. New Rochelle, 1992, Pace U., 1994. Staff nurse through head nurse Meml. Hosp. for Cancer and Allied Disease, N.Y.C., 1955-58; clin. assoc. Grad. Sch. Nursing N.Y. Med. Coll., N.Y.C., 1962-63; parent educator, cons. Maternity Ctr. Assn., N.Y.C., 1963-67, gen. dir., 1970-95, dir. clin. projects, 1995-97; project dir. Nat. Assn. of Childbearing Ctrs., Washington, 1997-99; pres., CEO D.C. Developing Families Ctr., 1998—2002, founder, pres. emeritus, 2003—, also bd. dirs.; pres., CEO, bd. dirs. D.C. Birth Ctr., 1998—. Cons. in midwifery, nursing and maternal and child health Office Pub. Health and Sci. HHS, 1995—97; adj. prof. divsn. nursing NYU, 1995—; bd. dirs., v.p. Am. Assn. World Health U.S. Com. WHO, 1975—94, pres. Am. Assn. World Health U.S. Com., 1980—81; mem. bd. maternal child and family health NRC, 1974—80; mem. Commn. Grads. Fgn. Nursing Schs., 1979—83, v.p., 1980—81, treas., 1982—83; bd. govs. Frontier Nursing Svc., 1982—92; bd. dirs. Pan Am. Health Edn. Found., pres., 1987—88; vis. prof. King Edward Meml. Hosp., Perth, Australia, 1991; Kate Hanna Harvey vis. prof. cmty. health nursing Frances Payne Bolton Sch. Nursing Case Western Res., 1991; Lansdowne lectr. U. Victoria, B.C., Canada, 1992; adj. prof. Sch. Nursing, Georgetown U., 1997—; Therese Dondero lectr. Am. Coll. Nurse-Midwives Found., 1995; Andrea Printy Meml. lectr. U. Minn., 1998; Kemble lectr. Sch. Nursing, U. N.C., Chapel Hill, 2000; Hugh P. Davis lectr. Emory U. Sch. Nursing, 2004. Author (with Gene Hawes): (book) childbearing: A Book of Choices, 1987; contbr. articles to profl. jours. Named Maternal-Child Health Nurse of the Yr., ANA, 1985, Disting. Alumna, U. Pa., 1992; named to Nursing Hall of Fame, 1999; recipient Letitia White award, Florence Nightingale medal, 1955, Nursing Practice award, U. Pa., 1980, Rockefeller Pub. Svc. award, 1981, Hattie Hemschemeyer award, 1983, Alumnae award, Sch. Nursing U. Pa., 1986, McManus medal, Tchrs. Coll. Columbia U., 1992, Disting. Svc. award, Francis Payne Bolton Sch. Nursing, 1993, Hon. Recognition, N.Y. State Nurses Assn., 1993, Nurse-Midwifery Faculty award, Columbia U., 1993, Spirit of Nursing award, Vis. Nurses Svc. N.Y., 1994, Maes-Macinnes award, Divsn. Nursing NYU, 1994, Hon. Recognition, ANA, 1994, Carola Warburg Rothschild award, Maternity Ctr. Assn., 1997, Healthy Babies Project award, 1998, Woman of Distinction award, Nat. Assn. Women in Edn., 1999; Irving Harris vis. scholar, Coll. Nursing U. Ill., 1999, MacArthur fellow, 1993. Fellow: AAAS, Soc. for Applied Anthropology, Am. Acad. Nursing (Living Legend award 2001); mem.: APHA (mem. com. on internat. health, sec. maternal and child health coun. 1982, mem. governing coun. 1986—89, mem. nominating com. 1987, mem. action bd. 1988—90), Vis. Nurse Svc. of N.Y. (Lillian Wald award 2003), Herman Biggs Soc. (sec.-treas. 1989—90), Am. Assn. Colls. Nursing (McGovern lectr. 1997), Nat. Assn. Childbearing Ctrs. (pres. 1983—91), Inst. of Medicine of NAS (Lienhard award 2001), Am. Coll. Nurse Midwives (v.p. 1964—66, pres.-elect 1969—70), N.Y. Acad. Medicine, Alpha Omega Alpha (hon.). E-mail: Rlubic@aol.com.

LUBIN, CAROL RIEGELMAN, political scientist; b. Montclair, N.J., Sept. 23, 1909; d. Charles A. and Lilian (Ehrich) Riegelman; m. Isador Lubin, Jan. 30, 1952 (dec. July 1978); 1 child, Ann L. Buttenwieser 1 stepchild, Alice Lubin Everit. BA, Smith Coll., 1930; MA, Columbia U., 1933, PhD, 1950. Rschr. Carnegie Endowment for Internat. Peace, N.Y.C., 1930-35; internat. staff Internat. Labour Office, Geneva, Switzerland, 1935-52; asst. to dir. Urban Studies Ctr. Rutgers U., 1960-64; cmty. planner City of Reston, Va., 1964-67; housing assoc., N.Y. Urban Coalition, 1968-70; social policy dir. United Neighborhood Houses, N.Y.C., 1970-80; editl. bd. Unemployment Compensation Commn., Washington, 1979-81; rep. Internat. Fedn. Settlements and Neighborhood Ctrs. at UN, 1982—, also bd. dirs. Co-author: Social Justice for Women: The Internat. Labour Orgn. and Women, 1991. Bd. dirs. Franklin and Eleanor Roosevelt Inst.; bd. dirs., sec. William Hodson Cmty. Ctr.; bd. dirs. Conf. Non-Govt. Orgns. Mem.: Smith Coll. Club N.Y., Women's City Club, Cosmopolitan Club, Nat. Women's Dem. Club, Phi Beta Kappa. Democrat. Home and Office: 1095 Park Ave New York NY 10128-1154

LUBKIN, GLORIA BECKER, physicist; b. Phila., May 16, 1933; d. Samuel Albert and Anne (Gorrin) B.; m. Yale Jay Lubkin, June 14, 1953 (div. Apr. 1968); children: David Craig, Sharon Rebecca. AB, Temple U., 1953; MA, Boston U., 1957; postgrad., Harvard U., 1974—75. Mathematician Fairchild Stratos Co., Hagerstown, Md., 1954, Letterkenny Ordnance Depot, Chambersburg, Pa., 1955-56; physicist TRG Inc., N.Y.C., 1956-58; acting chmn. dept. physics Sarah Lawrence Coll., Bronxville, N.Y., 1961-62; v.p. Lubkin Assocs., electronic cons., Port Washington, N.Y., 1962-68; assoc. editor Physics Today Am. Inst. Physics, N.Y.C., 1963-69, sr. editor, 1970-84, editor, 1985-94, editl. dir., 1994-00; editor-at-large, 2001—03; editor emerita, 2004—. Cons. in field; mem. Nieman adv. com. Harvard U., 1978-82; co-chmn. search/adv. com. Theoretical Physics Inst., U. Minn., 1987-89, co-chmn. oversight com. 1989—; mem. mng. com. Westinghouse Sci. Writing Prizes, 1988-91; mem. selection com. Knight Fellowships, 1990. Contbr. articles to profl. publs. Gloria Becker Lubkin Professorship of Theoretical Physics established in her honor U. Minn., 1990; Nieman fellow, 1974-75. Fellow: AAAS (chair nominating com. for sect. B physics 1989), Am. Phys. Soc. (founding mem. com. on status of women in physics 1971—72, exec. com. forum on physics and soc. 1977—78, exec. com. history of physics divsn. 1983—86, 1992—95, 1998—, coun. mem. 1998—, exec. bd. 2000—01, com. on coms. 2000—02, chair Lilienfeld prize com. 2002, com. on coms. 2004, audit com. 2004—); mem.: Com. Concerned Journalists, DC Sci. Writers Assn., Nat. Assn. Sci. Writers, NY Acad. Scis. (mem. The Scis. pub. com. 1992—93), Sigma Pi Sigma. Jewish. Office: Am Inst Physics One Physics Ellipse College Park MD 20740 E-mail: glubkin@aip.org.

LUBKIN, VIRGINIA LEILA, ophthalmologist; b. N.Y.C., Oct. 26, 1914; d. Joseph and Anna Fredericka (Stern) L.; m. Arnold Malkan, June 6, 1944 (div. 1949); m. Martin Bernstein, Aug. 28, 1949; children: Ellen Henrietta, James Ernst, Roger Joel, John Conrad. BS summa cum laude, NYU, 1933; MD, Columbia Coll. Physicans & Surgeons, 1937. Diplomate Am. Bd. Ophthalmology. Intern Harlem Hosp. Med. Ho., N.Y.C., 1938-40; asst. resident neurology Montefiore Hosp., N.Y.C., 1940, asst. resident gen. pathology, 1940-41, fellow in ophthalmology, 1941-42; asst. resident grad. basic sci. P & S Ophthalmology Harkness Eye Inst., 1941-42; resident ophthalmology Kings County Hosp., Bklyn., 1942-43, Mt. Sinai Hosp., N.Y.C., 1943-44; attending ophthalmologist, asst. and assoc. clin. prof. emeritus Mt. Sinai Sch. Medicine, 1944—; also sr. attending ophthalmic surgeon, assoc. plastic surg. N.Y. Eye and Ear Infirmary; pvt. practice N.Y.C., 1945-90; rsch. prof. N.Y. Med. Coll., Valhalla, 1983—. Co-creator, now chief of rsch. bioengineering lab. N.Y. Eye and Ear Infirmary (name now The Aborn Eye Rsch. Ctr.), N.Y.C., 1978—; rschr. piezoelectric aspects of ocular tissues; creator first grad. course in oculoplastics and bi-yearly symposia in devel. dyslexia Mt. Sinai Sch. Medicine; educator courses in psychosomatic ophthalmology Am. Acad. Ophthalmology, 1950—60, educator course in complications of blepharoplasty, 1980—90; bd. dirs. Jewish Guild for the Blind; tchr. surg. ophthalmology in French Cameroon Presbyn. Mission, 1951; lectr. in numerous countries including India, 76; lectr. in numerous countries including, India, 92, Pakistan, 76, Pakistan, 84, China, 78, Sri Lanka, 79, South Africa, 82, Singapore, 84, Thailand, 84, Argentina, 86, Peter Island, 87; ednl. dir. Aborn Eye Rsch. Lab. N.Y. Eye and Ear Infirmary, 2001—; hon. attending surgeon N.Y. Eye and Ear Infirmary; rsch. asst. in hematology Mt. Sinai Hosp. with Dr. Nathan Rosenthal, 1937; with Dr. H. Abramson, 37; consulting ophthalmologist Sharon Hosp., Conn.; postgrad. Inst. N.Y. Eye and Ear Infirmary, 1959—71, Am. Acad. Ophthalmology, 1968, 1969—71, N.Y. Eye and Ear Infirmary, 1970, Mt. Sinai Sch. Medicine, 1970; vis. prof. U. San Marco, Lima, Peru, 1967; lectr., co-chmn., chmn., and organizer in field at various meetings, symposiums and confs.; course dir. Mt. Sinai Sch. Medicine, 1971, 73, asst. course dir., 72; dir., founder resident (with Prof. Martin Gersten and Richard Koplin) rsch. fund N.Y. Eye and Ear Infirmary, 1978; edn. dir. dept. biomedical engring. N.Y. Eye and Ear Infirmary, 1978; impartial specialist in ophthamology worker's compensation bd., 1979—. Author (with others): Ophthalmic Plastic and Reconstructive Surgery, 1989, (2d edit.), 1997; co-author: Tear Osmolarity in Canines; patentee topical estrogen for postmenopausal dry eye; contbr. articles to profl. jours., chapters to books, publs. Bd. dirs. Ctr. fo Environ. Therapeutics, 1995; mem. Jewish Guild for the Blind, 1987—. Grantee Intraocular Lens Implant Mfrs., 1989; recipient Merit award Am. Acad. Ophthalmology and Otolaryngology, 1966, Sr. award, 1989. Fellow ACS, AMA, AAAS, Am. Soc. Ophthalmic Plastic and Reconstructive Surgery (founding), Am. Assn. Ophthalmology and Otolaryngology (instr. 1955-71), Am. Soc. Ophthalmic Plastic and Reconstructive Surgery (charter mem., founder 1969), Am. Acad. Facial Plastic and Reconstructive Surgery, N.Y. Acad. Medicine, N.Y. Acad. Scis., Am. Acad. Ophthalmology (Sr. Honor award 1989), Am. Soc. Cataract and Refractive Surgery, PanAm. Soc. Ophthalmology, N.Y. Soc. Clin. Ophthalmology (officer, v.p. 1969-70, pres. 1970-71), Soc. Light Treatment and Biol. Rhythms, Phi Beta Kappa (Mandel chemistry prize), Alpha Omega Alpha. Home: 1 Blackstone Pl Bronx NY 10471-3607 Office: NY Eye and Ear Infirmary 310 E 14th St New York NY 10003-4201 Fax: 718-549-6848; 212-979-4574. E-mail: drvlubkin@aol.com.

LUCAS, BARBARA B. electrical equipment manufacturing executive; b. 1945; BA magna cum laude, U. Md., 1967; MA, Johns Hopkins U., 1968. V.p., sec. Equitable Bancorp, 1977-85; sr. v.p. pub. affairs, corp. sec. Black & Decker Corp., Balt., 1985—96, sr. v.p., pub. affairs, 1996—, corp. sec., 1996—. Bd. dirs. Provident Bankshares; chair bd. dirs. Greater Balt. Med. Ctr., Balt. Named one of The 100 Women to Watch in Corp. Am., Bus. Month. Mem.: Am. Soc. Corp. Secretaries (pres. Mid-Atlantic Regional chpt., nat. dir.). Office: Black & Decker Corp 701 E Joppa Rd Baltimore MD 21286-5502

LUCAS, CAROL LEE, biomedical engineer; b. Aberdeen, S.D., Feb. 13, 1940; d. Howard Cleveland and Sarah Ivy (Easterby) Nogle; m. Richard Albert Lucas, Feb. 26, 1961; children: Wendy Lee, Sean Richard. BA, Dakota Wesleyan U., 1961; MS, U. Ariz., 1967; PhD, U. N.C., 1973. Tchr. Spanish, Mitchell (S.D.) H.S., 1960-61; tchr. math., English and sci. U.S. Army, Furth, Germany, 1961-62; sys. analyst Cargill Inc., Mpls., 1962-65; rsch. assoc. U. N.C., Chapel Hill, 1973-76, lectr., 1976-77, asst. prof. curriculum in biomed. engring. and math., 1977-84, assoc. prof. dept. surgery, 1984-89, prof., 1989—, acting chmn. curriculum biomed. engring. and math., 1990-92, chmn. biomed. engring., 1992—2001; program dir. NSF, 2001—. NIH trainee, 1968-73. Contbr. articles to profl. jours. Mem. IEEE, Am. Heart Assn., N.C. Heart Assn., Biomed. Engring. Soc., Cardiovasc. Sys. Dynamics Soc., Am. Inst. Biol. and Med. Engrs. Democrat. Methodist. Home: 2421 Sedgefield Dr Chapel Hill NC 27514-6810 Office: U NC Sch Medicine Dept Biomed Engring 152 Macnider Hall Chapel Hill NC 27599-0001 E-mail: clucas@bme.unc.edu.

LUCAS, CATHERINE, biotechnology company executive; b. Casablanca, Morrocco, Apr. 28, 1954; came to US 1978; d. Igor Vinner and Denise Marguerite Eugenie Pichenot; m. Jody Leopold Lucas, Aug. 10, 1977 (div. Sept. 1987); 1 child, Joelle. BS in Chemistry-Biology, U. Scis., Paris, 1972; MS in Biochemistry, U. Scis., 1974, PhD in Biochemistry, 1978. NIH postdoctoral fellow Stanford U., Palo Alto, Calif., 1978-80; sr. rsch. scientist Tago Inc., Burlingame, Calif., 1981-84; mgr. R&D Daryl Labs., Santa Clara, 1984-85; scientist Genentech Inc., South San Francisco, 1985-89, sr. scientist, 1989-93; dir. quality control and assay devel. Cell Genesys Inc., Foster City, Calif., 1993-95; dir. analytical sci. Alza Corp., Palo Alto, 1995-96, sr. dir. analytical, 1996-99, exec. dir. analytical, 1999-2000, v.p. implant R&D, 2000—. Fellow French Nat. League Cancer, Paris, 1976-78, Philippe Found. and UNESCO, 1978-79. Mem. Am. Soc. Neurochemistry, Am. Assn. Clin. Chemistry, Calif. Tissue Culture Assn., N.Y. Acad. Scis., Calif. Separations Soc. Avocations: Tae Kwon Do, bicycling, skiing, knitting, painting. Office: Alza Corp 1900 Charleston Rd Mountain View CA 94043-1218 E-mail: catherine.lucas@alza.com.

LUCAS, DONNA, communications executive; m. Greg Lucas; 1 child, Katherine. Grad. in Journalism, U. So. Calif., 1982. Press sec. Gov. George Deukmejian; dir. pub. affairs State Treas. Office; CEO, pres. Nelson Comm. Group, Sacramento, NCG Porter Novelli, Sacramento. Bd. dirs. Am. Assn. Polit. Cons.; past gubernatorial appointee Calif. Commn. on Status of Women; bd. dirs. Capitol Focus; Calif. media dir. Rep. Nat. Conv., 1992; Calif. press sec. Pres. George Bush's 1988 campaign; past campaign mgr. State Treas., Tom Hayes. Office: NCG Porter Novelli 1215 K St Ste 2100 Sacramento CA 95814-3951

LUCAS, ELOISA B. tax consultant, management consultant; b. Manila, Philippines, Apr. 11, 1938; came to U.S., 1973; d. Florentino Olazabal Bonicacio and Amalia Granados Alvarez; m. Pablo Matias Lucas, Dec. 26, 1960; children: Judy Marie, Mary-Anne, Michaelangelo (dec.), Robert, Christine, Heidi Marie. BBA in Acctg., U. of the East, Manila, 1959. CPA, Philippines; cert. govt. fin. mgr., Va.; lic. life ins. agt., Calif. Gen. acct. Cal-Island Devel. Co., Tamuning, 1973-76, San Diego State U., 1980-84; acctg. mgr. EBL Assocs., San Diego, 1985-87; fed. auditor Def. Contract Audit Agy., San Diego, 1987-90; field auditor FEMA, Office of Insp.Gen., San Francisco, 1990-92; tax/fin. mgmt. cons. EBL & Assocs., San Diego, 1992—; life ins. agt. San Diego, 1984—. Fin. cons. Ukraine Fedn. Profl. Accts. and Auditors; advisor Citizen Democracy Corps, Washington. Bd. dirs., CFO, treas. Lucas Arts and Voices, Inc., San Diego, 1999—; mem. ch. choral group Santa Sophia Cath. Ch., Spring Valley, Calif., 1999—; sec. Filipino-Am. Cmty. of St. John of the Cross, Lemon Grove, Calif., 1984-86; vol. advisor Citizens Democracy Corps, Inc., Washington, 1997—. Recipient Leadership award U. of the East, 1958. Mem. Assn. Govt. Accts., Inst. Mgmt. Accts., Assn. Cert. Fraud Examiners. Avocations: music, concerts, art work, stamp collections. Office: EBL & Assocs 636 Broadway Ste 319 San Diego CA 92101-5410 E-mail: eblandassociates@yahoo.com.

LUCAS, GEORGETTA MARIE SNELL, retired educator, artist; b. Harmony, Ind., July 25, 1920; d. Ernest Clermont and Sarah Ann (McIntyre) Snell; m. Joseph William Lucas, Jan. 29, 1943; children: Carleen Anita Lucas Underwood, Thomas Joseph, Joetta Jeanne Lucas Allgood. BS, Ind. State U., 1942; MS in Edn., Butler U., 1964; postgrad., Herron Sch. of Art, 1961-65, Ind. U., Indpls. and Bloomington, 1960-62, 65. Music, art tchr. Jasonville City Schs., Ind., 1942-43, Van Buren H.S., Brazil, Ind., 1943-46, Plainfield City Schs., Ind., 1946-52, Met. Sch. Dist. Wayne Twp., Indpls., 1952-56, 59-68; art tchr. Met. Sch. Dist. Perry Twp., Indpls., 1968-81. Lectr. Art Educators Assn. Ind., Ind. U.-Bloomington, 1976. Illustrator: (book) Why So Sad, Little Rag Doll, 1963; artist (painting) Ethereal Season, 1966, (lithograph) Bird of Time, 1965-66; exhibited in group shows Hoosier Salon Art Exhibit, 1954, 56, 60, 62-65, 67, 68, 70, 72, 87, 94, N.Y. Lincoln Ctr., N.Y.C., 1994; represented in permanent collections Ind. State U., Ind.-Purdue U.-Indpls. Jane Voorhees Zimmerli Art Mus., Rutgers U., N.J., Indpls. Pub. Sch. Collection; drummer with Hendricks County Ramblers, 1986—. Mem. NEA (life), Nat. Assn. Women Artist, Ind. Artist Craftsmen, Inc. (hon., pres. 1979-85, 87, 88, scholarship chmn. 1986—, bd. dirs. 1986—), Ind. Fedn. Art Clubs (hon., pres. 1986-87, counselor 1988-91, bd. dirs. 1991—, parliamentarian 1992-94, conv. mgr. 1999, Best of Show 1997), Hoosier Salon, Ind. State U. Mortar Bd., Art Edn. Assn. Ind. (life), Nat. League Am. Pen Women (Ind. state art chmn. 1984-96, Best of Show award 1983, 97, pres. Indpls. br. 1994-96, Ind. State Assn. pres. 1998-2000, front cover drawing Pen Women Nat. Mag. 1994), Fine Art for State Ind. (Internat. Women's Yr. fine art chmn. 1977), Ctrl. Ind. Artists (hon.), Alpha Delta Kappa (life, Ind. state chmn. of art 1973-77, pres. 1972-74, represented by painting in nat. hdqrs.-Kansas City, Mo., Fidelis Delta first v.p.), Retired Educators Sorority (1st v.p., pres. 1997-99), Order of Eastern Star. Republican. Methodist. Avocations: genealogy, travel, coin collecting/numismatics. Home and Office: 3192 E Main St Plainfield IN 46168-2721

LUCAS, JEANNE HOPKINS, state senator, retired educational administrator; b. Durham, N.C., Dec. 25, 1935; m. William Lucas. BA in French and Spanish, N.C. Ctrl. U., 1957, MA in Sch. Adminstrn., 1977. Tchr. French and Spanish, Durham, 1957-75; dir. staff devel., 1977-90; sch. adminstr., 1973-93; dir. pers. and cmty. rels., 1991; ret., 1993; mem. N.C. Senate, Raleigh, 1993—. Vice chmn. appropriations on gen. govt. com., health care com., ways and means com., mem. appropriations/base budget com., edn. and higher edn. com., judiciary I com., chmn. children and human resources com.; mem. black caucus N.C. Legislature; congl. dist. chmn., 1986. Mem. Durham Com. on Affairs Black People; active ARC, Habitat for Humanity; mem. N.C. Dem. Exec. Com.; chmn. Durham County Dem. Exec. Com., 1984; presinct sec., former chmn. Durham Dem. Com.; mem. plan of orgn. Dem. Com. Mem. NEA, N.C. Assn. Educators, Durham County Assn. Educators, NAACP, Links (past pres. Durham chpt.), Delta Sigma Theta. Democrat. Baptist. Office: 620 Legis Office Bldg 300 N Salisbury St Raleigh NC 27603-5925 also: PO Box 3366 Durham NC 27702-3366

LUCAS, KAREN, music educator; d. Clemon Willis and Celina Lucas. BS, Nazareth Coll., 1984; M in Music Edn., Mansfield U., 1986. Cert. music tchr. K-12 N.Y., 1990. Dir. bands Olinville Jr. H.S., Bronx, 1987—87, Kensington H.S., Buffalo, 1987—94; tchr. dist. wide music Geneva Mid. Sch., 1994—2001; dir. band Geneva H.S., 2001—03; tchr. dist. wide music Geneva Mid. Sch., 2003—. Playground supr. Geneva Recreation Dept., 1998—2001; unit supr. Nassau County AHRC, Hunter, 1989—90, athletic dir., 1987—89, camp counselor, Hunter, 1985—87. Guest conductor Rochester All City Elem. Band, Finger Lakes Concert Band. Bd. mem. Boys & Girls Club of Geneva, 2001—; commr. Geneva Human Rights Commn., 2003—. Mem.: N.Y. State Music Adminstrs., N.Y. State Music Educators Assn., Finger Lakes Music Educators Assn., Music Educators Nat. Conf., N.Y. State Band Dirs. Assn. Baptist. Avocations: music, softball, bicycling, camping, golf. Home: 188 High St Geneva NY 14456 Office: Geneva Mid Sch 63 Pulteney St Geneva NY 14456-2307 Personal E-mail: lucask@usadatanet.net.

LUCAS, KAREN WILLIAMS, controller; b. Ottawa, Can., Nov. 22, 1960; came to U.S., 1981; d. Lloyd George and Irene Katherine Williams; m. Ken W. Lucas, Apr. 18, 1981 (div. Apr. 1999); children: Kennith, James, Nicholas. AA with high honors, Broward C.C., 1990; BBA cum laude, Fla. Atlantic U., 1996, post grad. Cert. mgmt. acct., fin. mgmt., 2000. Asst. contr. EHP/Carico, Ft. Lauderdale, Fla., 1981-84; staff acct. MAP Builders, Coral Springs, Fla., 1984-86; contr. Conviber Co. Inc., Ft. Lauderdale, 1986-89, Commerce Group, Deerfield Beach, Fla., 1991-96, Purosys.. Inc., Ft. Lauderdale, 1996—2003, Urecoats Industries, Inc., Deerfield Beach, Fla., 2003, Purosys., Inc., Ft. Lauderdale, 2003—. Mem. Inst. Mgmt. Acct. (bd. 2000-2001), Beta Gamma Sigma.

LUCAS, TAMMI MICHELLE, music educator; b. Tifton, Ga., Nov. 27, 1971; d. Louis Elvin Lucas and Faye Wynema Allmond. B of Music Edn., Troy State U., 1995. Tchr. music W. Bainbridge Elem., Ga., 1995—96, Potter St. Elem., Bainbridge, 1996—97; dir. band Hutto Mid. Sch., Bainbridge, 1997—. Active ch. choir. Mem.: Profl. Assn. Ga. Educators, Ga. Music Educators Assn. (sec. 1999—). Republican. Baptist. Home: 1505 Lakewood Dr Bainbridge GA 39819

LUCAS-TAUCHAR, M. FRANCES, university administrator; b. Jackson, Miss., Oct. 24, 1956; d. Aubrey and Ella Lucas; m. Paul Tauchar, Dec. 29, 1990; children: Michael, Anna Catherine. BA in Comms., Miss. State U., 1978; MA in Higher Edn. Adminstrn., U. Ala., 1980, PhD in Higher Edn. Adminstrn., 1985; postgrad., Harvard U., 1989. Resident life coord. U. Ala., Tuscaloosa, 1979-83; asst. dean for student life Miss. State U., Starkville, 1983-86, v.p. for student affairs Baldwin-Wallace Coll., Berea, Ohio, 1986-92; v.p., dean for campus life Emory U., Atlanta, 1992—. Faculty mem. Nat. Housing Tng. Inst., Gainesville, 1993, Mid-Mgrs. Inst., 1991-93, 94-95. Author: NASPA Journal, 1990, 91, College Student Affairs Journal, 1994, About Campus Journal, 1996. Mem. Nat. Assn. of Student Pers. (Greek rels. chair 1985—), The Nat. V.P.'s Group, So. Assn. of Coll. Student Affairs, Nat. Interfraternity Conf., Am. Coll. Pers. Assn., Assn. of Fraternity Advisors, Nat. Assn. of Student Pers. Adminstrs. (assoc. dir. Mid-Mgrs. Inst. 1993-94), Omicron Delta Kappa. Office: Emory U Campus Life 605 Asbury Cir Atlanta GA 30322-1006

LUCCHETTI, LYNN L. career officer; b. San Francisco, Aug. 21, 1939; d. Dante and Lillian (Bergeron) L. AB, San Jose State U., 1961; MS, San Francisco State U., 1967; grad., U.S. Army Basic Officer Course, 1971, U.S. Army Advanced Officer Course, 1976, U.S. Air Force War Coll., 1983, Sr. Pub. Affairs Officer Course, 1984. Media buyer Batten, Barton, Durstine & Osborn, Inc., San Francisco, 1961-67; producer-dir. Sta. KTVA-TV, Anchorage, 1967-68; media supr. Bennett, Luke and Teawell Advt., Phoenix, 1968-71; commd. 1st lt. U.S. Army, 1971, advanced through grades to lt. col., 1985, col., 1989, brig. gen. nom., 1993, officer, 1971-74, D.C. N.G., 1974-78, U.S. Air Force Res., 1978-99; program advt. mgr. U.S. Navy Recruiting Command, 1974-76; exec. coordinator Joint Advt. Dirs. of Recruiting (JADOR), 1976-79; dir. U.S. Armed Forces Joint Recruiting Advt. Program (JRAP) Dept. Def., Washington, 1979-91, resources mgr. Exec. Leadership Devel. Program, 1991-94. Author: Broadcasting in Alaska, 1942-1966. Active Vols. of ARC. Decorated U.S. Army Meritorious Svc. medal, Nat. Def. medal, U.S. Air Force Longevity Ribbon, U.S. Navy Meritorious Unit Commentation, Dept. Def. Joint Achievement medal, 1984, N.Mex. Legion of Merit, 1999; Sigma Delta Chi journalism scholar, 1960. Mem. Women's Affairs Asn., AF Pub. Affairs Alumni Assn. Home: 16775 W Cathedral Rock Ct Surprise AZ 85387 E-mail: lynn_lucchetti@excite.com.

LUCCI, SUSAN, actress; b. Scarsdale, N.Y., Dec. 23, 1946; d. Victor and Jeanette L.; m. Helmut Huber, 1969; children: Liza Victoria, Andreas Martin. BA, Marymount Coll., 1968. Portrays Erica in TV series All My Children, 1970—; appearances in other series include: Fantasy Island, The Love Boat, The Fall Guy; TV films: Invitation to Hell, 1985, Mafia Princess, 1985, Ebbie, 1995, Seduced and Betrayed, 1995, (mini-series) Anastasia: The Mystery of Anna Anderson, 1986, Haunted by Her Past, 1988, Lady Mobster, 1988, The Bride in Black, 1990, The Women Who Sinned, 1991, Double Edge, 1992, Between Love and Hate, 1993, French Silk, 1994, Blood on Her Hands, 1998; host of spl. with Tony Danza 99 Ways to Attract the Right Man. Recipient 20 Emmy nominations and 1 Emmy award for best actress in daytime drama series, numerous other awards. Office: All My Children 320 W 66th St New York NY 10023-6397 also: care Sylvia Gold ICM 8942 Wilshire Blvd Beverly Hills CA 90211-1934*

LUCE, Mrs. HENRY See HADLEY, LEILA

LUCE, PRISCILLA MARK, public relations executive; b. NYC, Feb. 4, 1947; d. S. Carl and Patricia (Greenfield) Mark; m. Robert Warren Luce, July 19, 1969; children: James Warren, David Mark. BA, U. Pa., 1968. Adminstrv. asst. Phila. Mus. Art, 1968-69; asst. dir. pub. info. Mt. Holyoke Coll., South Hadley, Mass., 1969-71; v.p. Barnes & Roche, Inc., Phila., 1971-82; mgr. civic programs TRW Inc., Cleve., 1982-85, mgr. cmty. rels., 1985-88, mgr. external comm., 1988-90, dir., pub. affairs and advt., 1990-92, v.p. TRW info. sys. and svcs. comms., 1992-94, v.p. mktg. and orgn. comm., 1994—2001, v.p. corp. comm., 2001—03. Trustee New Orgn. for the Visual Arts, Cleve., 1983-97, pres., 1984-86; trustee Cmty. Info. Vol. Action Ctr., Cleve., 1984-86, Albert M. Greenfield Found., Phila., 1989—, pres., 1999—; trustee Cleve. State U. Found., 1996—, chmn. devel. com. 1998—, vice-chmn. 1999—; trustee Bus. Vols. Unltd., Cleve., 1998-2003; trustee WVIZ/PBS, WCPN Radio, 1997—, chmn. pub. rels. com., 1998-2001; chmn. media and mktg. com. Cleve. Today, 1999-2001; trustee Ohio Chamber Orch., Cleve., 1986-92, chmn. devel. com. 1987-88, chmn., trustee, 1991-92, exec. v.p., 1990-91; mem. steering com. Cleve. Art Festival, 1983-84, Mayor's Cultural Arts Planning Task Force, Cleve., 1985-87; trustee Ret. Sr. Vol. Prog., 1991, Western Res. Hist. Soc., 1999-2002; leadership devel. prog. participant United Way Svcs., Cleve., 1983, cons., 1983-85; steering com. Bus. Volunteerism Coun. of Cleve., 1984-92; comm. adv. com. Work in NE Ohio Coun., 1991-94. Recipient Woman of Profl. Excellence award, YWCA of Cleve., 1990. Mem.: Nat. Assn. Mfrs. Commns. Coun., Arthur W. Page Soc. Republican.

LUCENTE, ROSEMARY DOLORES, retired academic administrator; b. Renton, Wash., Jan. 11, 1935; d. Joseph Anthony and Erminia Antoinette (Argano) Lucente. BA, Mt. St. Mary's Coll., 1956, MS, 1963. Tchr. pub. schs., L.A., 1956-65; supr. tchr., 1958-65; asst. prin., 1965-69; prin. elem. sch., 1969-85, 86-99; dir. instrn., 1985-87; ret., 1999. Nat. cons., lectr. Dr. William Glasser's Educator Tng. Ctr., 1968—; nat. workshop leader Nat. Acad. for Sch. Execs.-Am. Assn. Sch. Adminstrs., 1980; L.A. Unified Sch. Dist. rep. for nat. pilot of Getty Inst. for Visual Arts, 1983-85, 92-98, site coord., 1983-86, team leader, mem. supt.'s adv. cabinet, 1987-98. Recipient Golden Apple award Stanford Ave. Sch. PTA, Faculty and Cmty. Adv. Coun., 1976, resolution for outstanding svc. South Gate City Coun., 1976, resolution for commitment to youth L.A. city Coun., 1996; named Woman of Yr., Calif. State Senate, 1997. Mem. NAESP, L.A. Elem. Prins. Orgn. (v.p. 1979-80), Assn. Calif. Sch. Adminstrs. (charter mem.), Assn. Elem. Sch. Adminstrs. (vice chair chpt. 1972-75, 79-80), Assn. Adminstrs. L.A. (charter mem.), Pi Theta Mu, Kappa Delta Pi (v.p. 1982-84, Hon. Educator award 1998), Delta Kappa Gamma, Phi Delta Kappa (Cert. of Recognition of Svc. on Membership Com. 2000). Democrat. Roman Catholic.

LUCERO, ANNE, critical care nurse; b. Lynwood, Calif., Aug. 21, 1954; d. Kenneth and Dorothy Irene (Berkland) Boulter; m. Emmett Ronald Lucero, Jan. 15, 1977 (div. June 1993); children: Christina Marie, Kathleen Anne. BSN, Calif. State U., Chico, 1976; MSN in Nursing Edn., Calif. State U., San Jose, 2001. RN, 1976, CCRN 1983, ACLS. Staff nurse Watsonville Cmty. Hosp., Calif., 1977-78, staff nurse/relief charge critical care, 1979-2000; part-time faculty Sch. Nursing, Cabrillo Coll., Aptos, Calif., 1992-2000, full-time faculty, 2000—. Leader Campfire Boys and Girls, Santa Cruz Co., 1984-90, Bethel Guardian Internat. Order Job Daughters, 1993-98. Mem. Calif. Nurses Assn. (nurse rep. 1979-83, bd. dirs. 1980-91, political action com. 1989-91, legis. laison congressman, 1982-92), Am. Nurses Assn. (delegate 1990-92), Calif. Tchrs. Assn., Sigma Theta Tau. Avocations: golf, walking, bike riding, reading. E-mail: lucerolady@aol.com.

LUCIA, MARILYN REED, physician; b. Boston; m. Salvatore P. Lucia, 1959, (dec. 1984); m. C. Robert Russell, (dec. 2000); children: Elizabeth, Walter, Salvatore, Darryl. AB with highest honors, U. Calif., Berkeley, 1951; MD, U. Calif., San Francisco, 1956. Cert. in psychiatry and child psychiatry Am. Bd. Psychiatry and Neurology. Intern Stanford U. Hosp., 1956-57; NIMH fellow, resident in psychiatry Langley Porter, U. Calif., San Francisco, 1957-60; NIMH fellow, resident in child psychiatry Mt. Zion Hosp., San Francisco, 1960-62; NIMH fellow, in cmty. psychiatry U. Calif., San Francisco, 1966—68, clin. prof. psychiatry, 1982—. Founder, cons. Marilyn Reed Lucia Child Care Study Ctr., U. Calif., San Francisco; cons. Cranio-facial Ctr., U. Calif., San Francisco; No. Calif. Diagnostic Sch. for Neurologically Handicapped Children; dir. children's psychiat. svc. Contra Costa County Hosp., Martinez. Fellow Am. Psychiat. Assn. (disting. life), Am. Acad. Child Psychiatry; mem. Am. Cleft Palate Assn., San Francisco Med. Soc., Phi Beta Kappa. Office: 350 Parnassus Ave Ste 602 San Francisco CA 94117-3608

LUCIANO, ROSELLE PATRICIA, advertising executive, editor; b. Bklyn., Feb. 10, 1921; d. Giacomo Roberto and Francesca Rosa (Ruvolo) Rubino; m. Anthony Vincenzo Luciano, Nov. 24, 1946; 1 child, Nino Vincenzo Luciano. Attended, NYU. College shop mgr. Abraham & Straus, Bklyn., 1939-41, advtg. copywriter, 1941-44; fashion editor Syndicated MB Reports, N.Y.C., 1945-48; advtg. mgr., fashions copywriter Macy's 34th St., N.Y.C., 1949-54; publicist, adminstr. Fun With Prodns., N.Y.C., 1959-69; chair, adminstr. U.U. Plandome Forum, Manhasset, N.Y., 1970-78, UU Veatch Found., Manhasset, N.Y., 1979-84; dir. devel. IALRW Literacy For Women Program, Great Britain and India, 1984—. Coord. numerous workshops in field for various orgns.; served as spkr., editor, writer, publicist, 1984—. Operator political booth Democratic Party, Garden City, 1984, 88, 92; founder R.P.L. Literacy Fund for Women, 1996—. Recipient Best Advtg. Ad of the Yr. award Women's Wear Daily, 1954, Citizen of the Yr. award Carle Place Schs., 1965, award for outstanding leadership and encouragement for working women Women-On-the-Job, Inc., N.Y., 1987, Susan B. Anthony award U. U. Women;s Fedn., 1997. Unitarian Universalist. Avocations: environmental activism, opera, ballet, theater, travelling.

LUCID, SHANNON W. biochemist, astronaut; b. Shanghai, Jan. 14, 1943; d. Joseph Oscar and Mary Wells; m. Michael F. Lucid, 1968; children: Kawai Dawn, Shandara Michelle, Michael Kermit. BS in Chemistry, U. Okla., 1963, MS in Biochemistry, 1970, PhD in Biochemistry, 1973. Sr. lab. technician Okla. Med. Rsch. Found., 1964-66, rsch. assoc., from 1974; chemist Kerr-McGee, Oklahoma City, 1966-68; astronaut NASA Lyndon B. Johnson Space Ctr., Houston, 1979—, mission specialist flights STS-51G and STS-34, mission specialist on Shuttle Atlantis Flight, 1991; mission specialist flight STS-58 NASA, 1993, mission specialist flight STS 76 & 79, 1996; mission specialist stationed on Space Station Mir, 1996. Recipient Space award Aviation Week and Space Tech., 1997; first woman to fly on the shuttle three times; remained aloft 188 days in shuttle Mir. Address: NASA Johnson Space Ctr CB-Astronaut Office Houston TX 77058

LUCIUS, MARY ALBUS, dietician; b. Harvey, N.D., Feb. 26, 1949; d. Walter Jake and Julia Bertha (Fehr) Albus; m. Robert Bruce Lucius, Dec. 29, 1972; children: David, Ruth. BS in Food and Nutrition, N.D. State U., 1971; MEd in Applied Nutrition, U. Cin., 1977. Lic. dietitian, Ohio; cert. diabetes educator. Intern in diatetics Miami Valley Hosp., Dayton, Ohio, 1971-72; staff dietitian Grandview Hosp., Dayton, Ohio, 1972-76, chief nutritionist, 1976-77; staff nutritionist Wright State U., Dayton, Ohio, 1977-81, chief nutritionist, 1981-83; clin. dietitian Sycamore Hosp., Kettering, Ohio, 1983-97; sr. clin. dietitian Sycamore Hosp./Kettering (Ohio) Med. Ctr., Kettering, Ohio, 1997—. Part-time instr. biol. chemistry Wright

State U., 1986-89; part-time instr. Andrews U. Cup Dietetic students, Barrien Springs, Mich., 1987-90; mem. adv. com. Greene County (Ohio) 4-H, 1997—. Jr. church leader, choir mem., leader 1st and 2d grade Pioneer Clubs, Voyager group Cmty. Bapt. Ch., Beavercreek, Ohio, 1982-94. Mem. Am. Dietetics Assn. (registered dietitian), Ohio Dietetic Assn. (chmn. cmty. nutrition 1985), Dayton Dietetics Assn. (program chmn. 1990, bd. dirs 1981-82). Avocations: antiques, needlework, bicycling, gardening. Home: 4289 Shakertown Rd Beavercreek OH 45430-1035 Office: Sycamore Hosp/Kettering Med Ctr 2150 Leiter Rd Miamisburg OH 45342-3660

LUCKE, BETTY JEAN, dressmaker; b. Pitts., July 6, 1926; d. George Michael and Emma Mae (Burris) Brilhart; m. Winston Slover Lucke, Sept. 13, 1947 (div. Sept. 1963); children: Nancy, Robert, Susan. ADN, St. Luke's Sch. Nursing, N.Y.C., 1947. RN, N.Y. Floor nurse orthopedics Mass. Gen. Hosp., Boston, 1947-49; nurse Palo Alto (Calif.) Med. Clinic, 1950-53; self-employed dressmaker Menlo Park, Calif., 1960—. Clothing Leader 4-H of San Mateo County, Calif., 1960-71; 4-H Club Leader, Alpine Valley 4-H, Calif., 1969-72. Democrat. Avocations: gardening, reading. Office: Bonasue 1172 Chestnut St Menlo Park CA 94025-4312

LUCKERT, MARLA JO, state supreme court justice; b. Goodland, Kans., July 20, 1955; d. William Gottleib and Gladys Iona (Rohr) L.; m. Steven. K. Morse, May 25, 1980; children: Sarah, Alisa. BA, Washburn U., 1977, JD, 1980. Bar: Kans. 1980, U.S. Dist. Ct. Kans. 1980, U.S. Ct. Appeals (10th cir.) 1980. Assoc. Goodell, Stratoon, Edmond & Palmer, Topeka, 1980—; chair Criminal Law Adv. Comm., Kans. Jud. Coun., Kans., 1992; chief judge Third Jud. Dist., Kans. Supreme Ct., Kans.; justice Kans. Supreme Ct., Kans., 2003—. Adj. prof. Washburn Univ. Sch. Law, Topeka, 1980-81, 1990—; pres. Women Attys. Assn. Kans., Topeka, 1988-89. Author: Kansas Consent Manual, 1988, Record Relations Guide, 1988, Kansas Law for Physicians, 1989. Pres. Mobile Meals of Topeka (Kans.), Inc., 1987-89, Mobile Meals of Topeka (Kans.) Found., 1989—; co-chair YWCA Nominating Com., Topeka, 1988-89. Recipient Woman of Excellence Award, YWCA/Topeka, Kans. Mem. ABA (co-chair young lawyers health law com. 1988-90), Am. Acad. Hosp. Attys., Kans. Assn. Hosp. Attys., Kans. Assn. Def. Counsel (bd. dirs. 1988—, disting. svc. award 1990), Kans. Bar Assn. (pres. young lawyers 1989-90, outstanding svc. award 1990), Topeka Bar Assn. (chair law day pubs. com.). Office: Kansas Judicial Ctr 301 SW 10th Ave Topeka KS 66612-1507

LUCKEY, DORIS WARING, civic volunteer; b. Union City, NJ, Sept. 17, 1929; d. Jay Deloss and Edna May (Ware) Waring; m. George William Luckey, Mar. 29, 1958; children: G. Robert, Jana Elizabeth, John Andrew. AB, U. Rochester, 1950; CLU, Am. Coll., Bryn Mawr, Pa., 1957. With pers. dept., supr. life dept. Travelers Ins. Co., Rochester, NY, 1952-58; agt. asst. life underwriting Mass. Mut. Ins. Co., Rochester, NY, 1958. Chair, various past offices Bd. Coop. Ednl. Svc. and State Edn. Dept. Vocat. Tech. Adv. Com., Rochester and Albany, NY, 1975—2003, pres. Rochester, 1975—85, Monroe County Sch. Bd. Assn., Rochester, 1980—81; v.p. Penfield (N.Y.) Sch., 1978—81; various fin. ednl. and speaking engagements LWV, 1983—, chair spkr. bur. (Rochester Metro chpt.); mem., past pres. William Warfield Scholarship Fund Bd.; coord. Young Artist Competition Penfield Symphony Orch; former adv. to bd. St. John's Home for Aging Bd., former mem. fin., pension and pers. com., former bd. dir., former exec. com.; pres. Leslie Norwood Carter Music Scholarship Fund; vol. numerous other civic, cultural, ch. and artistic orgn.; former pres. new investments United Ch. Christ, Genesee Valley, trustee former ch. coun., former pres. ch. coun., former chair ch. and min. com., co-chair; property trustee Brighton United Ch. Christ, chair pastoral search com., 2001—02, co-chair investment com., co-chair long-range planning com. Mem. AAUW (past pres. Greater Rochester br., past bd. dir., dist. 1 state rep.), LWV (co-chmn. nominating com. Rochester metro, chair of spkr. bur. Rochester Metro chpt.), Genesee Valley Assn. (response team sexual harrassment in clergy NY conf. United Ch. of Christ). Republican.

LUCKMAN, SHARON GERSTEN, arts administrator; b. Sioux City, Iowa, Oct. 10, 1945; d. Robert S. and Libbie (Izen) Gersten; m. Peter Luckman, Nov. 22, 1968 (div. 1979); children: Melissa, Gregory; m. Paul Shapiro, Dec. 13, 1981. BS, U. Wis., 1967; cert. Inst. Not-For-Profit Mgmt., Columbia U., 1982. Dir. 92d St YM/YHA Dance Ctr., N.Y.C., 1978-86; dir. devel. & new ventures Twyla Tharp Dance Found., N.Y.C., 1986-87, exec. dir., 1988; dir. Vol. Lawyers for Arts, N.Y.C., 1988-92; dir. devel. Alvin Ailey Dance Found., N.Y.C., 1992—95, exec. dir., 1995—. Dance tchr. 92nd St. Y, N.Y.C., 1963-78, Nassau C.C., Garden City, N.Y., 1963-78, Long Beach (N.Y.) Pub. Schs., 1963-78; dir. Brant Lake (N.Y.) Dance and Sports Ctr., 1980-86; bd. dirs. Dance USA. Chairperson Laban/Bartenieff Inst. Movement Studies, N.Y.C., 1984-87. Democrat. Jewish. Office: Alvin Ailey Dance Found Inc 211 W 61st St 3d Fl New York NY 10023-7832

LUCKTENBERG, JERRIE CADEK, music educator; b. July 19, 1930; d. Ottokar Theodore and Sara (Hitchcock) Č.; m. George Lucktenburg, 1953 (div. 1984); children: Judith, Kathryn, Ted. MusB, Curtis Inst., 1952; MusM, U. Ill., 1953; D of Mus. Arts, U. S.C., 1983. Concertizing as soloist and in chamber groups, Europe, Korea, Australia, U.S., 1954—96; assoc. prof. music Converse Coll., Spartanburg, SC, 1960—84; artist tchr., chmn. string dept. S.C. Gov.'s Sch. of Arts, Greenville, 1983—97; prof. music, chmn. string dept. U. So. Miss., Hattiesburg, 1984—96; concertmaster Pensacola (Fla.) Symphony, Meridian (Miss.) Symphony, 1986—96, Greater Spartanburg (S.C.) Philharm., 1996—2003. Author: The Joy of Shifting and Double Stops, a Violinist's Guide to Ease and Artistry, 1991; contbr. articles to profl. jours.; leader numerous workshops and clinics. Fulbright grantee State Acad. Music, Vienna, 1956-57; Ford Found. grantee, 1966-67; recipient Heart of Gold award The Arlington Assisted Living Facility, Hattiesburg, Miss., 1994, Tchr. Recognition award nat. winner Music Tchrs. Nat. Assn., 1974, Excellence in tchg. award, U. Southern Miss., 1990, Alumni Citation Outstanding Achievement as a performer and educator, U.S.C., 1991; citation for Exceptional Leadership and Merit award, 1992. Mem. Am. String Tchrs. Assn. (life; founding pres. Miss. chpt. 1985, jour. reviewer 1987—; Music Tchrs. Nat. Assn. (chmn. S.C. chpt. 1979-82, strings chmn. Miss. chpt. 1987-90), Music Educators Nat. Conf., Suzuki Assn. of Ams., Pi Kappa Lambda. Home: 311 Saranac Dr Spartanburg SC 29307-1141

LUCKY, ANNE WEISSMAN, dermatologist; b. N.Y.C., May 11, 1944; d. Jacob and Gertrude (Tetelman) Weissman; m. Paul A. Lucky, May 19, 1972; children: Jennifer, Andrea. BA, Brown U., 1966; MD, Yale U., 1970. Diplomate Nat. Bd. Med. Examiners, Am. Bd. Pediatrics/subspecialty of pediatric endocrinology, Am. Bd. Dermatology (pres. 1998—). Intern and resident in pediatrics The Children's Hosp. Med. Ctr., Boston, 1970-73; fellow in human genetics and pediatrics Yale U. Sch. Medicine, New Haven, Conn., 1973-74, resident in dermatology, 1979-81, instr. pediatrics, 1980-81, assoc. prof. dermatology and pediatrics, 1981-83; clin. assoc. Reprodn. Rsch. Br./Nat. Inst. Child Health/NIH, Bethesda, Md., 1974-76; asst. prof. pediatrics Wyler Children's Hosp./Pritzker Sch. Med./U. Chgo. Hosps., 1976-79; assoc. prof. dermatology, pediatrics U. Cin. Coll. Medicine, 1983-88; pvt. practice Dermatology Assocs. of Cin, Inc., 1988—; pres. Dermatology Rsch. Assocs., Inc., Cin., 1988—; dir. Dermatology Clinic Children's Hosp. Med. Ctr., Cin., 1989—. Vol. prof. dermatology and pediatrics U. Cin. Coll. Medicine, 1988-94. Editorial bd. Pediatric Dermatology, 1982—, Archives of Dermatology, 1983-94; contbr. numerous articles to profl. jours., publs. Recipient the Janet M. Glasgow Meml. Scholarship, Am. Women's Med. Assn., 1970, the Ramsey Meml. Scholarship award Yale U. Sch. Medicine, 1968, others; grantee USPHS, 1964-66, 67, 68-70, NIH, 1977-79, 79-82, 82-87, 84-87, 87-93, others. Mem. Lawson Wilkins Pediatric Endocrine Soc., Soc. for Pediatric Endocrinology (bd. dirs. 1984-87, pres. 1990-91), Am. Acad. Dermatology, Soc. Investigative Dermatology, Soc. for Dermatologic Genetics of the Am. Acad. Dermatology, Endocrine Soc., Acad. Medicine/Cin. Women's Faculty Assn./The Children's Hosp. Med. Ctr., Women's Derm. Soc. (bd. dirs. 1993—), Ohio State Med. Assn., Soc. Pediatric Rsch., Cin. Derm. Soc. (pres. elect 1995-96), Phi Beta Kappa, Sigma Xi, Alpha Omega Alpha. Office: Derm Assocs of Cin 7691 5 Mile Rd Cincinnati OH 45230-4348

LUCOFF, KATHY ANN, art advisor; b. L.A., Jan. 28, 1953; d. Marvin and JoAnn Ruth (Blaugrund) Miller Lucoff; m. Martin Gary Godin, Apr. 26, 1992. BFA, Calif. Coll. Arts & Crafts, Oakland, 1974. Asst. dir. L.A. Louver Gallery, Venice, Calif., 1976-78; instr. Santa Monica (Calif.) Coll., 1977; prin. Kathy Lucoff Arts Adv. Svcs., 1978—; instr. Dept. of Continuing Edn. Rice U., Houston, 1987-88. Bd. dirs. Univ. Art Mus., Long Beach, Calif.; art critic KABC Talk Radio, 1980-85. Art advisor: Poets Walk, Pub. Art Program, CBS Med. Art Ctr., L.A. C. of C. Pub. Art Programs, Burbank (Calif.) Empire Ctr. Avocations: travel, cooking, horseback riding. Office: 10520 Wilshire Blvd Ste 604 Los Angeles CA 90024-4595 Office Phone: 310-441-1040.

LUDDINGTON, BETTY WALLES, library media specialist; b. Tampa, Fla., May 11, 1936; d. Edward Alvin and Ruby Mae (Hiott) L.; m. Robert Morris Schmidt, Sept. 20, 1957 (div. Dec. 1981); children: Irene Schmidt-Losat, Daniel Carl Schmidt. AA, U. South Fla., 1979, BA in Am. Studies and History, 1980, MA in Libr., Media and Info. Studies, 1982, EdS in Gifted Edn., 1986. Cert. tchr. media and gifted edn., Fla. Media intern Witter Elem. Sch., spring 1982; media specialist Twin Lakes Elem. Sch., 1982-84, Just Elem. Sch., 1984-87, Blake Jr. H.S., 1987-88, Dowdell Jr. H.S. (now Dowdell Mid. Sch.), 1988—. Educator Saturday enrichment program for gifted children U. South Fla., springs 1980, 84, 85; participant pilot summer program in reading and visual arts Just Elem. Sch., 1987; educator gifted edn. program in visual and performing arts Kingswood Elem. Sch., summers 1985, 86, gifted edn. program in video camera Apollo Beach Elem. Sch., summer 1989, Gifted Enrichment Prog. Imagi-lympics 2012, Maniscalco Elem. Sch., 1998, others. Author: (book of poetry) Aaron Tippin: A Hillbilly Knight, 1993; contbr. articles and poems to various books and periodical publs., 1986—. Parent vol. media ctr. Witter Elem. Sch., 1976-78; tchr. sponsor Storytelling Club, Dowdell Jr. H.S., 1994-95; news media liaison, tchr. vol. Dowdell Jr. H.S., 1993-96. Recipient Student Affairs Golden Signet award U. South Fla., 1980, Parent award for continuing support of Fla. chpt. # 39 Am. Indsl. Arts Student Assn., 1987-88, Editor's Choice awards for outstanding achievement in poetry Nat. Libr. of Poetry, 1996; nominee Tchr. of Month, Sta. WTSP-TV, 1994; recognized for contbn. of motivational activity for Sunshine State Young Reader's Award program Fla. Assn. for Media in Edn., Inc., 1985; named to Internat. Poetry Hall of Fame, 1996. Mem. Internat. Soc. Poets (Disting. mem. 1995), Hillsborough Classrm. Tchrs. Assn. (grantee 1988, 90), Hillsborough Assn. Sch. Libr. Media Specialists, Clan Wallace Soc. (life), Phi Kappa Phi, Kappa Delta Pi, Phi Alpha Theta (pres., v.p., rep. to honors coun. 1980, 81, Outstanding Student award), Omicron Delta Kappa (treas., chairperson, del., mem. selection com. 1981, Leslie Lynn Walbolt book award), Pi Gamma Mu. Episcopalian. Avocations: poetry, books, cats, country music. Home: 1032 E Robson St Tampa FL 33604-4344

LUDDY, PAULA SCOTT, nursing educator; b. Plymouth, MA, May 29, 1945; d. James Bernard Scott and Margaret Elizabeth Legge Scott; m. Robert Thomas Luddy, May 20, 1944; children: Scott, Shawn. BSN, Bowie State U., 1993; MSN, 1996. RN Mass., 1966, Md., 1970. Educator Group Health Assn., Washington, 1983—87; ob/lactation cons. Dr. Rafiq Mian, Cheverly, Md., 1984—94; childbirth educator Childbirth Edn. Assn., Washington, 1971—95; staff nurse Prince George Hosp. Ctr., Cheverly, Md., 1981—87, patient educator, 1987—2002; coord./home interviewer Prince George Med. Soc., Prince George County, 1994—2002. Mem. adj. faculty dept. nursing Prince George's C.C., 1997—. Recipient Award of Excellence in Health Care, Assn. Women's Health, 2000, Hero for Babies, March of Dimes, 2002, Excellence in Edn. award, Prince George's C. of C. Bd. Edn., 2001.

LUDGUS, NANCY LUCKE, lawyer; b. Palo Alto, Calif., Oct. 28, 1953; d. Winston Slover and Betty Jean Lucke; m. Lawrence John Ludgus, Apr. 8, 1983. BA in Polit. Sci. with honors, U. Calif., Berkeley, 1975; JD, U. Calif., Davis, 1978. Bar: Calif. 1978, U.S. Dist. Ct. (no. dist.) Calif. 1978. Staff atty. Crown Zellerbach Corp., San Francisco, 1978-80, Clorox Co., Oakland, Calif., 1980-82, Nat. Semiconductor Corp., Santa Clara, Calif., 1982-85, corp. counsel, 1985-92, sr. corp. counsel, asst. sec., 1992-2000, assoc. gen. counsel, asst. sec., 2000—. Contbr. articles to profl. jours. Mem. ABA, Am. Corp. Counsel Assn., Calif. State Bar Assn., Santa Clara County Bar Assn., Phi Beta Kappa. Democrat. Avocations: travel, jogging, opera. Office: Nat Semiconductor Corp 2900 Semiconductor Dr # G3135 Santa Clara CA 95051 E-mail: nancy.lucke.ludgus@nsc.com.

LUDIN, PAMELA S. accountant; b. Camden, N.J., Sept. 13, 1960; d. Edward Nelson and Arlene June Rubenstein Ludin; m. Stewart Neal Abramson, Apr. 17, 1988; children: Matthew, Ethan. BS in Econs., U. Pa., 1981. Cert. mgmt. acct. Asst. staff acct. KPMG Peat Marwick, Phila., 1981-82; contr. Lombard Med. Assn., Phila., 1984-87; staff acct. Scripps Meml. Hosp., La Jolla, Calif., 1987-90; contr./Univ. Womens Healthcare Assocs. U. Pitts. Med. Ctr., 1990-94; dir. ops. Bookminders Inc., Pitts., 1994—2002; treas. Three Rivers Cmty. Found., 2002—. Fin. com. mem. Three Rivers Cmty. Found., Pitts., 1998—. Mem. Am. Soc. Women Accts. (nat. dir. 1997-99, Women of Achievement award 1999). Home: 522 Glen Arden Dr Pittsburgh PA 15208-2809 Office: Bookminders Inc Ste 100 700 River Ave Pittsburgh PA 15212-5907 E-mail: pludin@bookminders.com.

LUDOLF, MARILYN MARIE KEATON, lay worker; b. Morganton, N.C., July 19, 1932; d. Charles Jefferson and Dora Esther (Whitener) Keaton; m. Edwin Forrest Ludolf, Dec. 22, 1957; children: David Forrest, Jonathan Charles. BA, Lenoir Rhyne, 1954. Youth worker Cen. Bapt. Ch., Greenville, S.C., 1964-71, Park Bapt. Ch., Rock Hill, S.C., 1958-64; with coll. students Becks Bapt. Ch., Winston Salem, N.C., 1971-89; lay worker singles Calvary Bapt. Ch., Winston Salem, 1989—. Youth seminar leader youth activities Park Bapt., Rock Hill, S.C.; youth-Sunday sch. Tng. Union-All areas of Ch. Work, Greenville, S.C. and Winston Salem, N.C.; pub. spkr., sem. leader, Women's Conf. Keynoter. Author: Freed by Faith; contbr. to Guideposts and Bapt. publs. Chmn. Christian Women's Club Luncheon, Winston Salem, 2000-2002. Mem. Old Town Woman's Club (pres. 1975-77, Woman of Yr. 1977). Republican. Home: 3745 Whitehaven Rd Winston Salem NC 27106-2530

LUDWIG, KAREN, actor; b. San Francisco; d. David Ludwig and Patricia Figel. Attended, SF State Coll. Acting tchr. Conn. State Coll., Waterford, 1974, NYU with Andre Gregory's Manhattan Project, 1973—75, with Joseph Chaikin and Jean-Claude van Itallie, Tel Aviv, 1977, The Working Theater, New York, 1975—77, Pa. State Coll., 1980—81, Weist-Barron Sch., 1982—88, C.W. Post Coll., Long Island U., 1982, NYU Tisch Sch of Arts, 1985—87, The Lee Strasberg Inst., 1988—91; private acting coach General Hosptial Soap Opera, 1994—95; acting tchr. Am. Musical Theater of San Jose, 1995—97, Am. Conservatory Theater, 1996—97, UCLA, Dept. Entertainment Studies, 1996—98, The Howard Fine Acting Studio, 1995—2002, USC Sch. of Cinema/TV, 1996—2002, Director's/Actors Workshop, 2001—02, NYU Film Sch., 2003—. Dir.: (various theater productions), 1973—; actor: (Broadway plays) Prelude to a Kiss, Broadway Bound, Bosoms and Neglect, The Devils, The Deputy; (films) Thirteen Days, Stranger in This House, Citizen Cohn, Stanley & Iris, Manhattan, Ruby's World; (TV series, TV appearances) Law and Order SVU, The District, Judging Amy, Family Law, Party of Five, Promised Land, A Mother's Wish, N.Y.P.D. Blue, E.R., Chicago Hope, Picket Fences, Dream On, Murphy Brown, Knots Landing; (plays) The Seagull, Museum, Messiah, The Miracle Worker. Democrat. Jewish. Home: 55 Bethune St 823H New York NY 10014

LUDWIG, LAURA LONSHEIN, poet; b. Bklyn., July 26, 1955; d. Howard Lonshein, Gloria Lonshein; m. Ray Ludwig. Student, Franconia Coll., 1975—77. Writer Self-Employed, New York, NY, 1991—. Resident poet Joe Franklin Memory Lane Radio Show, WOR-AM, New York City, 1999—; screenwriter Joe Franklin Prodns., Inc., New York City, 1999—. Author (poetry, satires): Robo-Sapiens, 2001; author: (screenplays) Sounds Like a Plot, 2001, Reflections for the Renaissance, 2004; co-author (with Richard Ornstein): Of the Desk; prodr.(actress): classical concerts, ballet, opera, stage, short screenplays and T.V. programs, : (TV series) Earth is not on Tape;, co-author. Recipient Guardian Angel award, Hope for Children Found., 1999; grantee, N.Y. State Coun. for the Arts. Avocation: Robo-Sapiens available through City Lights Books (San Francisco CA), Barnes & Noble.com, Amazon.com, the Elmer Holmes Bobst Library/ New York University, New York Public Library. Home: 71 Joel M Austin Rd N Cairo NY 12413 Office Phone: 518-622-9747.

LUDWIG, MARTHA, biochemist, educator; BA, PhD, Cornell U.; MA, U. Calif., Berkeley. Postdoctoral fellow Harvard U., MIT; prof. dept. biol. chemistry U. Mich., Ann Arbor, 1967—. Mem.: NAS. Office: Dept Biological Chemistry Univ Mich Ann Arbor MI 48109

LUECHTEFELD, MONICA, retail executive; From gen. mgr. So. Calif. Region to exec. v.p. E-Commerce Office Depot, Inc., Delray Beach, Fla., 1993—2000, exec. v.p. E-Commerce, 2000—. Office: Office Depot Inc 2200 Old Germantown Rd Delray Beach FL 33445

LUECKE, PAMELA, professor, former editor; BA in Philosophy, Carleton Coll., 1974; MA in Journalism, Northwestern U., 1975; MBA, U. Hartford, 1979. Features reporter Hartford Courant, Hartford, Conn., 1975—79; bus. editor The Louisville Times, Louisville, 1981—84; various positions The Courier-Journal, Louisville, 1981—89; asst. mng. editor/metro Hartford Courant, Hartford, Conn., 1989—95, deputy mng. editor, 1995; editorial page editor Lexington (Ky.) Herald-Leader, 1995—96, editor, v.p., 1996—2000, editor, sr. v.p., 2000—01; prof., Reynolds Chair Dept. Journalism and Mass Comm., Washington and Lee Univ., Va., 2001—. Office: Washington & Lee Univ Lexington VA 24450

LUEDER, DIANNE CAROL, library director; b. Racine, Wis., Aug. 5, 1944; d. James Richard and Margaret Ann Helland; m. Roland Herman Lueder, Aug. 29, 1981 (dec. July 1993); children: Daniel Lee Bertelsen, Barbara Marie Lantz. BA, U. Wis.-Parkside, Kenosha, 1972; MLS, U. Wis., Milw., 1979. Ref./outreach libr. Elk Grove Village (Ill.) Libr., 1979-80; dir. Bartlett (Ill.) Pub. Libr., 1980-84; asst. exec. dir. DuPage Libr. Sys., Geneva, Ill., 1984-88; pres. Lueder Enterprises, Inc., Wauconda, Ill., 1988—2003; exec. dir. Roselle (Ill.) Pub. Libr., 1990—2001; libr. dir. Menomonie (Wis.) Pub. Libr., 2001—. Author: Administrator's Guide to Library Building Maintenance, 1992. V.p. Roselle Pub. Libr. Found., 1994-2001. Mem.: ALA, Wis. Libr. Assn., Menomonie Woman's Club, Rotary, Optimist Club. Lutheran. Avocations: flying, travel, learning Norwegian language. Home: 343 Red Cedar St Menomonie WI 54751 Office: Menomonie Pub Libr 600 Wolske Bay Rd Menomonie WI 54751 Office Phone: 715-232-2164. E-mail: dclueder@wwt.net.

LUETSCHWAGER, MARY SUSAN, transportation company professional; b. Bloomingdale, Ind., Nov. 19, 1937; d. William Blaine Shade and Goldina VandaVeer (Newlin) Brown; children: Roger, Tisa, Julia, Angela, Robert, William; m. Bruce E. Luetschwager, Sept. 9, 2000. Grad. high sch., Rockville, Ind. Sec., treas. Tri-State Transport, Inc., 1968-73; road driver Roadway Express, Chicago Heights, Ill., 1977—, safety team capt., 1991-92, 94. Completed Passport Tour (Abate), 1990, 94, 2000; mem. Roadway Express Dist. Road Team Dist. 12, 1995-97. Past mem. newsletter com. focus group Roadway Express; mem. focus group Kenworth Driver's Bd., 1992—; active Motorcycle Safety Found., Basic Rider Course; instr. 1999-, ABATE of Ind., Ind. Dept. of Edn. Recipient truck driving competition awards and motorcycle rally trophies, 3d place 8/48 rally Motorcycle Endurance Rider's Assn., 1996; 1st woman to finish on a Harley-Davidson motorcycle World Famous Iron Butt Rally, 1995, finished 6th place out of 78 starts and 61 finishers in 8th Iron Butt Rally, 1997, placed 3d in twin-trailer truck driving championships in Ill., 2000; placed 2nd in competition at Delta Nu Alpha truck driving fraternity in Rockford Ill, 2001, 1st pl. award (grand champion overall) in twin-trailer divsn. of truck driving championships, Ill., 2001; named Ill. TDC Sportsman of the Yr., 1995. Mem. Am. Motorcycle Assn., Am. Bikers Aim Toward Edn., Am. Radio Relay League, Harley Owners Group (newsletter editor Calumet region chpt. 1994-96, Hammond, Ind., asst. dir. Calumet region chpt. 1996-99, 2002, historian, 2000—, sec. 2004), Ladies of Harley. Avocations: motorcycle endurance riding, amateur radio. Home and Office: PO Box 316 Griffith IN 46319-0316

LUFT, CECILE E. music educator; b. Brooklyn, NY, May 14, 1925; d. Jacob and Sophie Burrows; m. Morris Luft; children: Tamara, Leslie Noymer. Diploma in piano, Juilliard School of Music, N.Y.C., 1946; MA, C.W. Post U., Brookville, N.Y., 1985—87. Choir dir. Temple Beth El, Bellmore, NY, 1953—56; music dir. Reform Jewish Congregation, Westbury, NY, 1960—68; music tchr. Pvt. Lessons, Merrick, NY, 1950—2001; music dir. Camp Rosemont & Roselake, Honesdale, Pa., 1967—68. Choir dir. Evangelical Covenant Ch., Floral Park, NY, 1986—2001. Mem.: Assn. Piano Tchrs. Long Island Inc. Avocations: travel, swimming.

LUGO, LORENA PEARL, elementary school educator, band director; b. Miami, Arizona, May 27, 1971; d. Alexander Michael and Donna Gail Candelaria; m. Robert Moses Lugo, Sept. 25, 1993; children: Ciara Avelina, Hailey Aurelia, Samuel Alexander. BA music edn., U. Ariz., 1993. Cert. tchg. K-12 Ariz., 1993. Elem. gen. music tchr. Gallego Elem. Sch., Tuscon, 1994; elem. band dir. Nogales Unified Sch. Dist., Nogales, Ariz., 1994—. Dir. and founder Nogales Elem. Honors Band (Cruz County), Nogales, Ariz., 1994—2000, Santa Cruz County Cmty. Band, Nogales, Ariz., 2000—; dir. and organizer Santa Cruz County Elem. Music Festival, 1999; bd. mem. Young Audiences of Santa, Nogales, Ariz., 2002—; dir. and organizer Santa Cruz County Elem. Music Festival, 2003; dir. Southern Ariz. Honor Band, Tucson, 2003—; music coord. Nogales Unified Schools, Nogales, Ariz. Arranger (elem. level music) various works and titles, 1994—; author: (music book) Essential Elements Supplemental, 1996. Recipient Outstanding Music Tchr., Lincoln Elem. Sch., Nogales, Ariz., 1995, commendation, Nogales Unified Sch. Dist., 1996. Mem.: Prof. Educators of Nogales, Ariz. Music Educators Assn., Music Educators Nat. Conf. Roman Catholic. Achievements include superior with distinction rating at music festivals 1996, 1998, and 2003. Excellent rating in music festival 2000. The performance at Ariz. Music Educators Convention Phoenix, 1997. Home: 143 Calle Tiburon Rio Rico AZ 85648-7305 Office: Nogales Unified Sch Dist 310 W Plum Nogales AZ 85621

LUGO, SONIA I. pharmacist, educator; d. Ruben Lugo and Ana Mercedes Lopez; m. Homero A. Monsanto, July 21, 1984. BS of Pharmacy, U. P.R., San Juan, 1982; MS, Purdue U., 1987; PhD, U. Md., 1994. Registered pharmacist. Asst. prof. Sch. of Pharmacy, U. PR., San Juan, 1993—97; assoc. prof. Sch. of Medicine, San Juan, 1996—98, Sch. of Pharmacy, U. PR., San Juan, 1997—. Vis. prof. U. Panama, 2001. Contbr. rsch. articles to profl. jours. Cancer awareness activist Coalicion para prevenir cancer de mama y cervix, San Juan, 1999—2002; coord. fund raising Susan G. Komen, San Juan, 1997—2002. Recipient Cancer Edn. and Prevention

Cert. of Recognition, Cancer Info. Ctr. and P.R. Cancer Ctr., 2000. Master: PRIDCO (scholar 1991—94); fellow: Am. Found. for Pharm. Edn.; mem.: Am. Assn. of Colls. of Pharmacy, Am. Assn. of Pharm. Scientists, Am. Pharm. Assn. (student's chpt. co-advisor 1996—2002). Office: U PR Sch Pharmacy PO Box 365067 San Juan PR 00936-5067 Personal E-mail: slugo@rcm.upr.edu. E-mail: slugo@rcm.upr.edu.

LUHRS, CARO ELISE, internal medicine physician, administrator, educator; b. Dover, N.J., Jan. 21, 1935; d. Albert Weigand and Ethel Adelaide (Voss) L. BA, Swarthmore Coll., 1956; MD, Harvard U., 1960. Diplomate Am. Bd. Internal Medicine; cert. personal fitness trainer, fitness instr., strength and conditioning specialist. Instr., asst. prof. medicine, dir. hematology labs. Georgetown Univ. Hosp., Washington, 1964-68; White House fellow USDA, Washington, 1968-69, spl. asst. to Sec. of Agr., 1969-73; dir. health and med. divsn. Booz, Allen & Hamilton, Washington, 1973-77; v.p., med. dir. EHE/Nat. Health Svcs., Washington, 1977-78; physician Washington, 1978—; med. dir. Hummer Cos., Washington, 1989-99; clin. prof. family medicine Georgetown U., Washington, 1991-99. Trustee Swarthmore (Pa.) Coll., 1975-79; bd. dirs. USDA Grad. Sch., Washington, 1970-74, The Pillsbury Co., 1973-89, White House Fellow Found., Washington, 1979; bd. regents Uniformed Svcs. U. of Health Scis., Bethesda, Md., 1980-85; cons. Office Sci. and Tech. Policy, The White House, 1977-80; with D.C. Mayor's Adv. Com. on Emergency Med. Svcs., 1980-84; mem. adv. com. hazardous materials EPA, 1970-76. Recipient Disting. Svc. award Uniformed Svcs. U. Health Scis., 1985. Fellow ACP, Royal Soc. Medicine; mem. AMA, Am. Coll. Sports Medicine, Med. Soc. D.C., Cosmos Club.

LUHRS, CAROL, physician; b. N.Y.C., Dec. 29, 1951; d. Eugene Frederick and Jane Elsie Luhrs; m. David Robert Blumenthal, Apr. 12, 1981; children: Alex Michael, Kelly Anne. BA, Hunter Coll., 1973; MD, SUNY, Bklyn., 1977. Diplomate Am. Bd. Internal Medicine, Am. Bd. Hematology and Med. Oncology, Am. Bd. Palliative Medicine. Intern, resident in internal medicine Kings County Hosp.-Downstate Med. Ctr., Bklyn., 1977-80; fellow in hematology/oncology Bklyn. VA Med. Ctr., 1980-83, staff physician, 1983-84, NIH postdoctoral trainee in hematology, 1984-86, staff physician, 1986-94, chief hematology/oncology sect., 1995—; asst. prof. SUNY Hlth. Scis. Ctr., Bklyn., 1986-94, assoc prof. clin. medicine, 1996—. Contbr. articles to profl. jours. NIH grantee, 1986-91, VA grantee, 1992-95. Mem. Am. Soc. Hematology, Am. Fedn. Clin. Rsch., Am. Soc. Clin. Oncology. Office: Bklyn VA Med Ctr 800 Poly Pl Brooklyn NY 11209-7104

LUHTA, CAROLINE NAUMANN, airport manager, flight educator; b. Cleve., Mar. 26, 1930; d. Karl Henry and Fannie Arletta (Harlan) Naumann; m. Fred Harlan Jones, July 2, 1955 (div. 1961); m. Adolph Jalmer Luhta, Dec. 12, 1968 (dec. 1993); 1 child, Katherine Louise. BA, Ohio Wesleyan U., 1952; BS magna cum laude, Lake Erie Coll., Painesville, Ohio, 1977. Rsch. chemist Standard Oil Co. Ohio, Cleve., 1952-68; office mgr. Adolph J. Luhta Constrn. Co., Painesville, 1968-83; acct. Thomas Y. Ellis, CPA, Painesville, 1978; bd. dirs. Painesville Flying Svc., Inc., 1968—, flight instr., 1970—, pres., 1993—. Bd. dirs. Concord Air Park, Inc., Painesville, 1968—, pres. 1993—; accident prevention counselor FAA, Cleve., 1975-85. Contbr. articles to profl. jours. Trustee Northeastern Ohio Gen. Hosp., Madison, 1973-83, chmn. bd. 1980-82; trustee Internat. Women's Air and Space Mus., Cleve., 1989—, treas. 1991-95, pres., 1997—; trustee Concord Twp., 1992—. Recipient Aerospace award Cleve. Squadron, Air Force Assn., 1966, Woman of Achievement award Lakeland C.C., 1999, Harvey High Sch. Alumni Assn. Hall Fame, 2001. Mem. Nat. Assn. Flight Instrs., Exptl. Aircraft Assn., Aircraft Owners and Pilots Assn., Ninety-Nines (life, chmn. All-Ohio chpt. 1969-70, Achievement award 1965, Amelia Earhart Meml. scholar 1970), Silver Wings (life), Order Ea. Star, Alpha Delta Pi (life). Avocations: air racing (Powder Puff Derby, All Women's Internat. Air Race). Office: Painesville Flying Svc Inc 12253 Concord Hambden Rd Painesville OH 44077-9566 E-mail: cluhta@iwasm.org.

LUIS, BELINDA, graphic designer; b. Luanda, Angola, June 15, 1967; came to U.S., 1979; Crispiniano and M. CArmo (Antunes) L. BA in Liberal Arts, Seton Hall U., 1990. Art dir. Luso Americano Newspaper, Newark, 1990-95; pres., owner On Design Graphics, Matawan, N.J., 1995—. Office: On Design Graphics 12 Arrowsmith Ct Matawan NJ 07747-3553 E-mail: ondesign@aol.com.

LUJAN, ROSA EMMA, bilingual specialist, trainer, consultant, assistant principal, assistant principal; b. El Paso, Tex., May 17, 1949; d. Rosendo G. and Petra (Rubalcava) López; m. Daniel Lujan, Feb. 21, 1976; children: Lorena Janel, Daniel Omar, Carina Viani, Crystal Rose. BA in Elem. Edn., U. Tex. El Paso, 1972, MS in Edn., 1978, postgrad., 1988, N.Mex. State U. Tchr. Ysleta Ind. Sch. Dist., El Paso, 1972-74, bilingual tchr., 1974-90, immigrant tchr., 1990—, now bilingual program supr. project mariposa. Cons. Internat. Acad. Coop. Learning, 1994; mem. Tex. Task Force on Profl. Preparation and Profl. Devel.; nat. bd. dirs. profl. tchg. stds. com. English as a New Lang., 1994; cooperating tchr. U. Tex. El Paso, 1978—; tchr. tnr. Ysleta Ind. Sch. Dist., 1980—; rschr. tnr. Johns Hopkins, U. Tex. El Paso, Haifa U., Israel, 1988—; mentor tchr. U. Tex. El Paso, El Salvador C.A., Boise, Idaho, 1990—; bd. dirs. Nat. Bd. for Profl. Tchg. Stds. Editor: (bilingual newsletter) El Chisme Bilingüe, 1986—. Pres. Ysleta Assn. Bilingual Edn., 1975-76, SW Assn. Bilingual Edn., El Paso, 1990-91; mem. Mt. Carmel Sch. Bd., El Paso, 1991-94, Tex. Com. Student Learning, Austin, 1992—. Named Tex. Tchr. of Yr., Tex. Edn. Agy., 1991-92, Tex. Elem. Tchr. of Yr., 1991-92. Mem. Nat. Assn. Bilingual Edn., Tex. Assn. Bilingual Edn., Phi Kappa Phi, Delta Kappa Gamma, Kappa Delta Pi. Democrat. Roman Catholic. Avocations: reading, sewing, traveling, dance. Office: Ysleta Ind Sch Dist 9600 Sims Dr El Paso TX 79925-7200

LUKENS, E.A. NANCY, language educator, writer; b. Washington, June 10, 1945; d. Horace Churchman and Lettie Robinson (Witherspoon) Lukens; 1 child, Hanna Sophie. BA, Coll. Wooster, 1967; MA, U. Chgo., 1969, PhD, 1973. Cert. translator Am. Translator's Assn. Libr. asst. Fairfax (Va.) County Schs., 1960—62; clk. Army Judge Advocate Gen., Arlington, Va., 1963; freelance translator, 1970—; lectr. in German U. Chgo., 1969—72; asst. prof. German Coll. Wooster, Ohio, 1972—78, assoc. prof. German, 1978—85, U. N.H., Durham, NH, 1985—95, chmn. Dept. German, 1985—95, prof. German and Women's Studies, 1995—. Cons. Trinity Films, Berlin, 1981—82, various jours., 1982—. Author: Büchner's Valerio and the Theatrical Fool Tradition, 1977; translator, editor: Daughters of Eve: Women Writers of the German Democratic Republic, 1993; ; translator: Sanctorum Communio, 1998, Fiction from Tegel Prison, 2000. Peace activist Seacoast Peace Response, Portsmouth, 2001—; press liaison Coalition for Pub. Sanctuary, Wooster, 1983—85; bd. dirs. Portsmouth (N.H.) Black Heritage Trail, 1995—. Fellow, Am. Coun. Learned Socs., 1980—81, Alexander von Humbolt Found., 1980—82; grantee, NEH, 1987—88. Mem.: Internat. Dietrich Banhoeffer Soc. (mem. editl. bd. 1986—2002), Children's Lit. Assn., Women in German, German Studies Assn., Modern Lang. Assn., Am. Assn. Tchrs. German, Phi Beta Kappa. Mem. Soc. Friends. Avocations: singing, writing, reading, time with family, swimming. Office: Dept Langs Lit and Cultures Univ NH Library Way Durham NH 03824

LUKER, KRISTIN, sociology educator; b. Sam Francisco, Aug. 15, 1946; d. James Wester and Bess (Littlefield) L. BA, U. Calif., Berkeley, 1968; PhD, Yale U., 1974. Postdoctoral fellow U. Calif., Berkeley, 1974-75, asst. prof. sociology San Diego, 1975-81, assoc. prof., 1981-85, prof., 1985-86, co-dir. women's studies program, 1984-85, prof. jurisprudence and social policy and sociology Berkeley, 1986—. Doris Stevens prof. women's studies, prof. sociology Princeton (N.J.) U., 1993-95. Author: Taking Chances: Abortion and the Decision Not To Contracept, 1976 (hon. mention Jessie Bernard award), Abortion and the Politics of Motherhood, 1984 (Charles Horton Dooley award, 1985). Bd. dirs. Ctr. for Women's Studies and Svcs., San Diego, Ctr. for Pupulation Otions, Washington. Grantee Guggenheim Found., 1985. Mem. Am. Sociol. Assn., Sociologists for Women in Society. Office: U Calif Jurisprudence and Social Policy 2240 Piedmont Ave Berkeley CA 94720-2150

LUKEY, JOAN A. lawyer; b. Malden, Mass., Dec. 28, 1949; d. Philip Edward and Ada Joan (Roberti) L.; m. Philip Davis Stevenson. BA magna cum laude, Smith Coll., 1971; JD cum laude, Boston Coll., 1974. Bar: Mass. 1974, U.S. Dist. Ct. Mass. 1975, U.S. Ct. Appeals (1st cir.) 1976, U.S. Supreme Ct. 1985. Assoc. Hale & Dorr, Boston, 1974-79, jr. ptnr., 1979-83, sr. ptnr., 1983—. Mem. Joint Bar Com. on Judicial Appointments, Mass., 1985-87, steering com. Lawyers' Com. for Civil Rights Under the Law, Boston, 1987-90. Fellow: Internat. Acad. Trial Lawyers, Am. Coll. Trial Lawyers (state com. 1993—2000, chair 1997—99, regent 2002—); mem.: ABA, Boston Bar Assn. (mem. coun. 1987—90, chair litigation sect. 1990—92, v.p. 1998—99, pres.-elect 1999—2000, pres. 2000—01), Mass. Bar Assn., Boston Club. Office: Hale & Dorr 60 State St Boston MA 02109-1816

LUKOMSKY, VERA, musicologist, pianist, music educator; b. St. Petersburg, Russia, May 30, 1947; came to U.S., 1990; d. Eugene and Sofia (Levin) L.; m. Alexander Lukomsky, Sept. 21, 1966; children: Eva Jane, Daniel. BA in Music, Rimsky-Korsakov Coll. Music, St. Petersburg, 1968; MA in Music, St. Petersburg Conservatory, 1973; postgrad., U. Calif. San Diego, 1992-98. Instr. music State Coll. Music, Novgorod, Russia, 1972-73; instr. Inst. Culture, St. Petersburg, 1972-75, Rachmaninov Sch. Music, St. Petersburg, 1975-89; instr., owner Allegro Piano Studio, Solana Beach, Calif., 1990—; lectr., asst. condr. U. Calif. San Diego, 1997-98; choral dir. San Diego H.S. and Meml. Jr. H.S., 1999-2000. Adj. prof. Nat. U., San Diego, 1999—. Author: The Analysis of Harmony in the Course of Solfeggio and Ear Training, 1985; contbr. articles to profl. jours. Recipient 1st pl. award Third Russian Republic Methodology Competition for Instrs. of Music and Art, 1983, Hendrikson fellowship U. Calif. San Diego, 1994-95. Mem. Am. Musicological Soc., Music Tchrs. Nat. Assn., Music Tchrs. Assn. Calif. (cert. of excellence 1999, 2000, 01, 02). Avocations: reading, travel, playing chamber music, theater, movies.

LUM, JEAN LOUI JIN, nursing educator; b. Honolulu, Sept. 5, 1938; d. Yee Nung and Pui Ki (Young) L. BS, U. Hawaii, Manoa, 1960; MS in Nursing, U. Calif., San Francisco, 1961; MA, U. Wash., 1969, PhD in Sociology, 1972. Registered nurse, Hawaii. From instr. to prof. Sch. Nursing U. Hawaii Manoa, Honolulu, 1961-95, acting dean, 1982, dean, 1982-89, prof. emeritus, 1995—. Project coordinator Analysis and Planning Personnel Svcs., Western Interstate Commn. Higher Edn., 1977; extramural assoc. div. Rsch. Grants NIH, 1978-79; mem. mgmt. adv. com. Honolulu County Hosp., 1982-96; mem. exec. bd. Pacific Health Rsch. Inst., 1980-88; mem. health planning com. East Honolulu, 1978-81; mem. rsch. grants adv. coun. Hawaii Med. Svcs. Assn. Found., Nat. Adv. Coun. for Nursing Rsch., 1990-93. Contbr. articles to profl. jours. Trustee Straub Pacific Health Found., Honolulu; bd. dirs. Friends of the Nat. Inst. of Nursing Rsch., 1994-97. Recipient Nurse of Yr. award Hawaii Nurses Assn., 1982; named Disting. Practitioner in Nursing, Nat. Acads. of Practice, 1986; USPHS grantee, 1967-72. Fellow Am. Acad. Nursing; mem. Am. Nurses Assn., Am. Pacific Nursing Leaders Conf. (pres. 1983-87), Council Nurse Researchers, Nat. League for Nursing (bd. rev. 1981-87), Western Council Higher Edn. for Nurses (chmn. 1984-85), Western Soc. for Research in Nursing, Am. Sociol. Assn., Pacific Sociol. Assn., Assn. for Women in Sci., Hawaii Pub. Health Assn., Hawaii Med. Services Assn. (bd. dirs. 1985-92), Western Inst. Nursing, Mortar Bd., Phi Kappa Phi, Sigma Theta Tau (Kupuna award 2003), Alpha Kappa Delta, Delta Kappa Gamma. Episcopalian. Office: U Hawaii Manoa Sch Nursing Webster Hall 2528 The Mall Honolulu HI 96822

LUM, VIOLA DORIS, music educator, personal financial analyst; b. San Benito, Tex., Apr. 3, 1928; d. Ernest Lee and Jewell Avis (Hughes) Marley; m. S.E. Lum, Dec. 25, 1949; children: Donald Gene, Karen Ann Lum Boer. Tchg. cert., St. Louis Inst. Music, 1947, advanced tchg. cert., 1959. Lic. ins. and securities dealer, Tex. and Okla.; cert. PFA. Instr. music Tarkington Sch., Cleveland, Tex., 1947-53; tchr. piano Cleveland, Pasadena and Conroe, Tex., 1953—, Lifestyle Christian Sch., Conroe, 1986-96; newspaper editor Southwestern Gospel Music Assn., Pasadena, 1975-85; fin. analyst Primerica Fin. Svc., Conroe, 1987—. Newspaper pub. Southwestern Gospel Music Assn., Pasadena, 1975-85; beauty cons. Mary Kay Cosmetics, 1982-90; traveled nationwide with Kingdom Seekers, Inc., gospel music ministry, 1970-87. Treas. East Side Assembly of God Ch., Conroe, 1987-94, pianist, Riverside, 1987—. Mem. NASD, Nat. Piano Guild (chmn., hon. tchr. 1993-2001), Music Tchrs. Nat. Assn., Tex. Music Tchrs. Assn. (chmn. Divsn. I, student affiliate coun. 1994—), Conroe Music Tchrs. (pres. 1991-94, Tchr. of Yr. 1994, 2003), Cypress Creek Music Tchrs. Assn. (v.p. 1998-2000, Selected Tchr. of the Yr. 1998). Avocations: photography, coin collecting, computers. Home: 13082 Cleveland Rd Conroe TX 77304-4174 Office: Primerica Fin Svcs 1712 N Frazier St Ste 212B Conroe TX 77301-1380 E-mail: vdlum@txucom.net.

LUMBYE, BETSY, editor; BA in English, U. Va., 1977. Reporter Colo. Springs Sunday, Knoxville Jour., Tenn., asst. city editor, city editor; metro editor The Record, Stockton; mng. editor The Herald, Rock Hill, SC, 1994—97; asst. mng. editor Fresno (Calif.) Bee, 1997, mng. editor, 1998—. Office: Fresno Bee 1626 E St Fresno CA 93706-2098

LUMGAIR, MARY ELIZABETH, energy executive; b. Houston, Mar. 18, 1977; Student, Baylor U., 1995—99. Sys. support group SourceNet Solutions, Houston, 1999—2000, assoc. cons., 1999—2000; bus. analyst Reliant Energy, Houston, 2000—03, supr., 2003—. Vol. Moonlight Bicycle Ramble, 2002, 5K Komen Race for the Cure/The Susan G. Komen Breast Cancer Found., 2002, MS150 Rider, Houston, 2003, Channel 11 Food Dr., 2003. Mem.: Am. Mktg. Assn. (v.p. comm. 1998—99). Achievements include Created Community Assistance Program Name for Reliant Energy (CARE Program: Community Assistance by Reliant Energy). Avocations: equestrian, running, fishing. Office: Reliant Energy 1201 Louisiana Houston TX 77002 E-mail: mlumgair@hotmail.com.

LUMMIS, CYNTHIA MARIE, state official, lawyer; b. Cheyenne, Wyo., Sept. 10, 1954; d. Doran Arp and Enid (Bennett) L.; m. Alvin L. Wiederspahn, May 28, 1983; children: Annaliese Alex. BS, U. Wyo., 1976, BS, 1978, JD, 1985. Bar: Wyo. 1985, U.S. Dist Ct. of Wyo. 1985, U.S. Ct. of Appeals (10th cir.) 1986. Rancher Lummis Livestock Co., Cheyenne, 1972—; law clk. Wyo. Supreme Ct., Cheyenne, 1985-86; assoc. Wiederspahn, Lummis & Liepas, Cheyenne, 1986—; treas. State of Wyo., 1999—. Mem. Wyo. Ho. Judiciary Com., 1979-86, Ho. Agriculture, Pub. Lands & Water Resources Com., 1985-86, Wyo. State Senate, 1993-94, Senate Judiciary Com., 1993-94, Senate Mines, Minerals, Econ. Devel. Com., 1993-94, U. Wyo. Inst. for Environment and Natural Resource Policy and Rsch.; chmn. County Ct. Planning Com., Wyo., 1986-88, Ho. Rev. Com., 1987-92, Joint Revenue Interim Com., 1988-89, 91-92; mem. adv. bd. U. Mont. Ctr. for the Rocky Mountain West, 1998—. Sec. Meals on Wheels, Cheyenne, 1985-87; mem. Agrl. Crisis Support Group, Laramie County, Wyo., 1985-87; mem. adv. com. U. Wyo. Sch. Nursing, 1988-90; mem. steering com. Wyo. Heritage Soc., 1986-89. Mem.: Rep. Women's (Cheyenne) (legis. chmn. 1982). Republican. Lutheran. Office: State Treasurer 200 W 24th St Cheyenne WY 82002-0001*

LUMMUS, CAROL TRAVERS, artist, printmaker; b. Hyannis, Mass., Nov. 2, 1937; d. Frank and Doris (Brown) Travers; m. Bertrand W. Lummus, Jan. 27, 1962; children: Sarah Travers, Jonathan Ames. Student, Walnut Hill Sch., Natick, Mass., 1952-55; AA, Colby-Sawyer Coll., New London, N.H., 1957; student, U. Geneva, 1960-62. Artist, printmaker. Mem. art adv. panel N.H. Commn. on Arts, 1980. One-woman shows include Hammerquist, N.Y.C., 1979, La Galeria, San Mateo, Calif., 1980, Alice Bingham, Memphis, 1980, P.S. Gallery, Ogunquit, Maine, 1980, 927 Gallery, New Orleans, Saint Gaudens Nat. Hist. Site, Cornish, N.H., exhibited in group shows at All New Eng. Show, 1975—76, Currier Mus., Manchester, N.H., 1976, 1980, Fitchburg (Mass.) Mus., 1975—76, Inst. Brasil-Estados Unidos, Brazil, 1978, Hobe Sound (Fla.) Gallery, 1976—, Payson-Waldron, Portland, Maine, 1982, Nat. Assn. Women Artists, 1994, 1999, Royal Miniature Art Soc., London, 1995, C.C.C.C. Gallery, Phila., 1999, Inspires Gallery, Oxford, Eng., 2000, Cove Gallery, Wellfleet, Mass., 2002, Gallery Z, Providence, 2003, Represented in permanent collections Springfield (Utah) Mus., Snow Coll., Ephraim, Utah, Georgetown U., Washington, Ogunquit Mus. Art, Family Tree Gallery, Portsmouth, N.H.; illustrator Cin. mag., Yankee mag. Recipient Rosmond de Kalb award Currier Mus., 1975, 1st prize Fitchburg Mus. Art, 1973, award Miniature Painters and Gravers Soc., Washington, 1996. Mem. Cape Cod Performing Arts Assn. (bd. dirs.), Mass. League N.H. Craftsmen, Nat. Assn. Women Artists N.Y., Barnstable (Mass.) Yacht Club. Episcopalian. Home (Winter): Box 525 Barnstable MA 02630 Home (Summer): 7 Railroad Ave Barnstable MA 02630

LUMPE, SHEILA, state commissioner, former state legislator; b. Apr. 17, 1935; m. Gustav H. Lumpe, 1958. AB, Ind. U.; postgrad., Johns Hopkins U.; MA, U. Mo. Formerly mem. Mo. Ho. of Reps.; now . Mo. Pub. Svc. Commn. Active Women's Polit. Caucus; bd. dirs. Mo. Humanities Coun., Partnership for Outstanding Schs. Democrat. Home: 320 Washington St Apt 201 Jefferson City MO 65101-1570 Office: Pub Svc Commn PO Box 360 Jefferson City MO 65102-0360

LUMPKIN, BEVERLEY CARSON, reporter, producer; b. Richmond, Va., Dec. 19, 1948; d. Robert Joseph Lumpkin and Dorothy Louise Phillips; m. Francis Joseph Stefanovich, Jr., Aug. 29, 1967 (div. 1972). BA, George Wash. U., 1984. Clk. Richmond Newspapers, 1967; mgr. bakery shop Harrington's Ltd., Hayes, England, 1968—69; clk. Alder Miles Druce Ltd., Hayes, England, 1969—70, Ctl. Nat. Bank, Richmond, 1970—72; legal sec. Browder, Russell, Little & Morris, Richmond, Va., 1972—75; adminstrv. asst. Fed. Election Commn., Wash., 1976—77; investigator U.S. Ho. of Reps., Wash., 1977—81, Goldstein Investigations, Washington, 1981—82; reporter, prodr. ABC News, Wash., 1982—. Participant various programs ABA-CEELI, Wash., 1998—99. Author: (weekly on-line column, abcnews-.com) Halls of Justice. Homeland Security fellow, NY Times Found., Coun. Fgn. Rels., 2002. Avocations: gardening, reading, music, volunteering at local theatres. Office: ABC News 1717 DeSales St NW Washington DC 20036 Office Phone: 202-222-7830. E-mail: beverley.c.lumpkin@abc.com.

LUMPKIN, MARGARET CATHERINE, retired education educator; b. Franklinton, N.C., Apr. 13, d. Willie Lee Lumpkin and Margaret (Ray) Pollock. BS, U. N.C., Greensboro, 1944; MS, Wellesley Coll., 1945; EdD, Oreg. State U., 1956. Instr. Mary Washington Coll., Fredricksburg, Va., 1945-48; from asst. prof. to prof. edn. Oreg. State U., Corvallis, 1948-87; co-owner, dir. The Reading Place, Corvallis, 1990-97; ret., 1997. Owner, co-dir. Camp Tamarack, Deschutes Nat. Forest, Sisters, Oreg., 1953-80; v.p. Britton & Assocs., Corvallis, 1972-2000; pres. Lake Creek Lodge, Inc., Sisters, 1974—2003; condr. workshops on lang. simplification, 1978-87; cons. on textbook selection criteria and lic. readability program Oreg. Legislature, Oreg. Edn. Dept.; resource person, cons. on lang. simplification pub. documents State of Oreg., 1979-89. Co-author: A Consumers Guide to Sex, Race and Career Roles in Public School Texts, 1977, Readability—A Consumers Guide, 1976-80, 17 Consumers Guides to Readability of Text Book Series; contbr. articles on reading improvement, devel. and psychology to profl. jours. Founding mem., bd. dirs. Youth Outreach., Inc., Corvallis, 1971-77; treas., sec., v.p., pres. Linn Benton Womens Polit. Caucus, Corvallis, 1977-87; founding voter, mem. Oreg. Womens Polit. Caucus, 1972—. Recipient meritorious award for rsch. in reading Project Innovation, Chula Vista, Calif., 1977, svc. award Oreg. Womens Polit. Caucus, 1980, nat. award for rsch. in reading Reading Improvement jour., 1978; grantee U.S. Office Edn., 1985-88, also other small grants. Mem. AAUW, ACLU (Liun-Benton bd. dirs. 1992-96), Phi Kappa Phi. Avocation: travel. Home and Office: 7565 NW Mountain View Dr Corvallis OR 97330-9751

LUNA, PATRICIA ADELE, marketing executive; b. Charleston, S.C., July 22, 1956; d. Benjamin Curtis and Clara Elizabeth (McCrory) L. BS in History, Auburn U., 1978, MEd in History, 1980; MA in Adminstrn., U. Ala., 1981, EdS in Adminstrn., 1984, postgrad. in Adminstrn. Cert. tchr., Ga., Ala. History tchr. Harris County Mid. Sch., Ga., 1978-79, head dept., 1979-81; residence hall dir. univ. housing U. Ala., 1981-83, asst. dir. residence life, 1983-85; intern Cornell U., Ithaca, N.Y., 1983; dir. mktg. Golden Flake Snack Foods, Inc., Birmingham, Ala., 1985-89; sr. v.p. Quest U.S.A., Inc., Atlanta, 1989-90; pres. Promotion Mgmt. Group, Inc., Montgomery, Ala., 1990—. Cons. Capital Campaigns; lectr. in field. Author: Specialization: A Learning Module, 1979, Grantsmanship, 1981, Alcohol Awareness Programs, 1984, University Programming, 1984, Marketing Residential Life, 1985, The History of Golden Flake Snack Foods, 1986, Golden Flake Snack Foods, Inc., A Case Study, 1987, Cases in Strategic Marketing, 1989, Cases in Strategic Management, 1990, Frequency Marketing, 1992. Fundraiser U. Ala. Alumni Scholarship Fund, Tuscaloosa, 1983, Am. Diabetes Assn., Tuscaloosa, 1984, Urban Ministries, Birmingham, 1985-88; fundraiser, com. chmn. Spl. Olympics, Tuscaloosa, 1985; chmn. Greene County Relief Project, 1982-89; bd. dirs. Cerebral Palsy Found., Tuscaloosa, 1985-86; lay rector and com. chmn. Kairos Prison Ministry, Tutwiler State Prison, Ala., 1986-92; lobbyist, com. chmn. task force Justice Fellowship, 1988-91; bd. dirs. Internat. Found. Ewha U., Seoul, Korea, 1988-91; chmn. bd. dirs. Epiphany Ministries, 1991-98; bd. dirs. Hunting Coll. Fine Arts, chairperson, Coll. Ministries, Whitfield Meml. United Meth. Ch., 1999-2000, chmn. capital fund campaign, 2000, chmn. stewardship bd. discipleship, 2000-02; chair Ala.-West. Fla. conf. United Meth. Ch., 2002, chair bd. discipleship, 2003—; bd. dirs. Acad. for Spiritual Formation, 1997-99; com. chmn. Emmaus Ministry, 1985—; chmn. Chrysalis steering com., 1995-97; mem. bd. devel. Upper Rm. Ministries. Recipient Nat. award Joint Coun. Econ. Edn., 1979, Rsch. award NSF, 1979, Harry Denman Evangelism award, 2001; named to Hon. Order Ky. Cols. Commonwealth of Ky., 1985. Mem. Sales and Mktg. Execs. (chmn. com. 1985-86), Leadership Ala. (pres. 1982-83), Am. Mktg. Assn. (Disting. Leadership award 1987, Commemorative Medal of Honor 1988), Assn. Coll. and Univ. Housing Officers (com. chmn. 1983-85), Nat. Assn. Student Personnel Officers, Snack Food Assn. (mem. mktg. com. and conf. presenter), Internat. Coun. Shopping Ctrs. (Merit award 1991, program com.), Commerce Exec. Soc., Omega Rho Sigma (pres. 1983-84), Omicron Delta Kappa, Phi Delta Kappa, Kappa Delta Pi, Phi Alpha Theta. Republican. Methodist. Avocations: skiing, tennis, community/church work, public speaking. E-mail: patluna@charter.net.

LUNA PADILLA, NITZA ENID, photography educator; b. San Juan, P.R., Mar. 13, 1959; d. Luis and Carmen Iris (Padilla) Luna. BFA, Pratt Inst., 1981; MS, Brooks Inst., 1985. Instr. U. P.R., Carolina, 1981-82, Cultural Inst., San Juan, 1988; prof. photography U. Sacred Heart, Santurce, P.R., 1987—; assoc. dir. communication ctr. U. Sagrado Corazon, Santurce, P.R., 1989-90. Contbr. articles to profl. publs.; one-woman shows P.R. Inst. Culture, 1988, Art and History Mus., San Juan, 1989, 94, 96, U. P.R., 1989, 90, Brooks Inst. Phototography, Santa Barbara, Calif., 1990, Miriam Walsh Gallery, Glenwood Springs, Colo., 1991, Mus. Ponce, 1991, Spokane

(Wash.) C.C., 1994, Centro Europa, San Juan, 1996, Galería de Arte, P.R., 1996; exhibited in group shows Santa Barbara Mus. Art, 1987, Coll. of Santa Fe, N.Mex., 1988, Durango (Colo.) Arts Ctr., 1988, 90, Laband Art Gallery, L.A., 1989, Cultural Ctr., Vercelli, Italy, 1989, Univ. Union Gallery Calif. Poly. State U., 1990, Coconino Ctr. Arts, Flagstaff, Ariz., 1990, Centro Cultural Washington Irving, Madrid, 1991, L.A. County Fair, 1991 Museo del Grabado Latinoamericano, San Juan, 1992, 93, 94, P.R. Inst. Culture, 1994, Hostos Art Gallery, N.Y.C., 1996, The Platinum Gallery, Sante Fe, 1996, Gallería Botello, San Juan, 1996, The Queens Mus., N.Y.C., 1997, The Platinum Gallery, N.Y.C., 1997, Arsenal, San Juan, 1997, Wis. Union Art Gallery, U. Wis., 1998; in permanent collections; juror Fotografia de prensa "Mandin,", 1991-92. MacDowell Colony grantee, Instituto de Cultural Puertorriqueña grantee, 1993, 94, 96. Mem. Soc. Photog. Edn., Friends of Photography. Roman Catholic. Avocations: painting, aerobics. Office: U Sagrado Corazón PO Box 12383 San Juan PR 00914-8505 E-mail: ritzaluna@prte.com.

LUNARDINI, CHRISTINE ANNE, writer, historian, school administrator; b. Holyoke, Mass., Jan. 27, 1941; d. Virgil Joseph and Christine Hildegarde (Cavanaugh) L. AA, Holyoke C.C., 1973; BA, Mt. Holyoke Coll., 1975; MA, Princeton U., 1979, PhD, 1981. Instr. history Princeton (N.J.) U., 1981-85; adminstrv. asst. Refco Inc., N.Y.C., 1985-87; assoc. prof. Pace U., N.Y.C., 1987-91; freelance writer, N.Y.C., 1991—; exec. asst. to pres. Lynn Chase Designs, Inc., N.Y.C., 1999-2000; dir. devel. St. Michael Acad., N.Y.C., 2000—. Vis. assoc. prof., Barnard Coll., Columbia U., N.Y.C., 1984-85; project mgr., sr. editor Carlson Pub., Bklyn., 1992-93. Author: From Equal Suffrage to Equal Rights: Alice Paul and the National Woman's Party 1910-1928, 1986, The American Peace Movement in the 20th Century, 1994, What Every American Should Know About Women's History, 1996, Women's Rights, 1996; editor, project mgr.: Black Women in America, An Historical Encyclopedia, 2 vols., 1993 (Dartmouth medal 1994), Columbia Guide to American Women: The Nineteenth Century, 1999; mem. editl. adv. bd. Am. Heritage Multi Media, Am. Heritage: Women in Am., 1994—. Princeton U. fellow, 1975-79, Woodrow Wilson nat. fellow, 1980, AAUW nat. fellow, 1980-81. Mem. NOW, Women's Bond Club N.Y., Phi Beta Kappa. Democrat. Episcopalian. Home: 26 Beaver St New York NY 10004-2311 Office: 425 W 33rd St New York NY 10001 E-mail: lunar127@aol.com.

LUND, DORIS HIBBS, retired dietitian; b. Des Moines, Nov. 10, 1923; d. Loyal Burchard and Catharine Mae (McClymond) Hibbs; m. Richard Bodholdt Lund, Nov. 9, 1946; children: Laurel Anne, Richard Douglas, Kristi Jane Lund Lozier. Scholar, Duchesne Coll., 1941-42; BS, Iowa State U., 1946; postgrad., Grand View Coll., 1965; MS in Mgmt., Iowa State U., 1968. Registered dietitian, lic. dietitian. Clk. Russell Stover Candies, Omaha, 1940-42; chemist Martin Bomber Plant, Omaha, 1942-43; Dietitian Grand Lake (Colo.) Lodge, 1946; tailoring instr. Ottumwa Pub. Schs., 1952-53; cookery instr. Des Moines Pub. Schs., 1958-62; dietitian Calvin Manor, Des Moines, 1965; home economist Am. Wool Coun./Am. Lamb Coun., Denver, 1963-65, The Merchandising Group of N.Y., 1965-68, Thomas Wolff, Pub. Rels., 1968-70; home economist weekly TV program Iowa Power Co., 1968-70; cons. in child nutrition programs Iowa Dept. Edn., Des Moines, 1970-95; ret. Nutritioneering, Ltd., 1995. Mem. Iowa Home Economists in Bus. (pres. 1962-63), PEO. Pres. Callanan Jr. H.S. PTA, 1964, Roosevelt H.S. PTA, 1966; amb. Friendship Force Internat., 1982—; alliance mem. Des Moines Symphony; guild mem. Civic Music Des Moines Met. Opera; mem. Civic Music Guild, Bot. Ctr. Des Moines, Des Moines Art Ctr., Des Moines Civic Ctr.; chmn. Met. Opera Previews; pres. Ctrl. Presbyn. Mariners, Des Moines; ruling elder, clk. of session Ctrl. Presbyn. Session, Des Moines, 1972—78; bd. dirs. Ctrl. Found., Ctrl. Pastor Seeking Nomination Com., 1996; chair cmty. concerns Calvin Cmty. Found., 1998, chair support and edn., 1999—. Duchesne Coll. 4 yr. scholar. Mem. Am. Dietetic Assn., Iowa Home Economists in Bus. (pres. 1962-63), PEO, Pi Beta Phi (pres. 1945-46). Republican. Avocations: international travel, writing, sailing, sewing, cooking. Home: 105 34th St Des Moines IA 50312-4526

LUNDBERG, SUSAN ONA, musical organization administrator; b. Mandan, N.D., Mar. 15, 1947; d. Robert Henry and Evelyn (Olson) L.; m. Paul R. Wick, July 2, 1972 (div. May 1976); 1 child, Melissa. BA, Stephens Coll., 1969; MLS, Western Mich. U., 1970; MPA, Calif. State U., Fullerton, 1980. Children's and reference libr. Bismarck (N.D.) Pub. Libr., 1970-71; reference libr. U. Tenn., Knoxville, 1971-72; coord. children's svcs. Orange County (Calif.) Pub. Libr., 1972-75; exec. dir. Bismarck-Manda Orch. Assn., 1992—. Exec. dir., founder Sleepy Hollow Summer Theatre, Bismarck, 1990—; trustee Gabriel J. Brown Trust, Bismarck, 1989—. Exhibitions include of paintings Scandinavian Threads of Inheritance, 2002. Chair Nat. Music Week N.D., 1990—, Friends of the Belle, 1994—; chair small budget orchs. Am. Symphony Orch. League, 2000-03. Named Outstanding Leaders of Yr. Bismarck Tribune, 1995. Mem. Calif. Libr. Assn. (pres. children's svcs. 1971-72), Bismarck Art Assn. (pres. 1982-84), Bismarck Art and Galleries Assn. (bd. dirs. 1985-2000, pres. 1986-88, Honor Citation award 1992), Jr. Svc. League. Lutheran. Avocations: painting, singing. Home: 112 Ave E W Bismarck ND 58501

LUNDEEN, MARGA LAIRD, art educator; b. Mpls., July 16, 1927; d. John Pierce and Gertrude Laird; m. Lyle August Lundeen; children: Richard, Cathrine, John, David. Student, U. Minn., Mpls. Sch. Art (now Mpls. Coll. Art and Design. Tchr. drawing and art history Stephens Sch. for Girls, Mpls. Portraits, Botanicals, Murals and Decorative Works. Avocations: walking, writing, naturalist.*

LUNDEN, JOAN, television personality; b. Fair Oaks, CA, Sept. 19, 1950; d. Erle Murray and Gladyce Lorraine (Somervill) Blunden; m. Michael Krauss, 1978 (div. 1992); children: Jamie Beryl, Lindsay Leigh, Sarah Emily; m. Jeff Konigsberg, 2000; children: Kate Elizabeth, Max Aaron. Student, Universidad de Las Americas, Mexico City, U. Calif., Calif. State U., Am. River Coll., Sacramento, Calif. Began broadcasting career as co-anchor and prodr. at Sta. KCRA-TV and Radio, Sacramento, 1973-75; with Sta. WABC-TV, N.Y.C., 1975—97, co-anchor, 1976-80; co-host Good Morning America, ABC-TV, 1980-97; host spl. report TV for Whittle Comm.; host Everyday with Joan Lunden, 1989, Behind Closed Doors With Joan Lunden, 1994-2000 (ABC), 2000- (A&E); pres., host Women's Supermarket Network; film appearances include: Macho Callahan, 1970, What About Bob?, 1991, Free Willy 2, 1995, Conspiracy Theory, 1997; spl. appearances: (TV series) Murphy Brown, 1992, 93, LateLine, 1998; Author: Good Morning, I'm Joan Lunden, 1986, Joan Lunden's Mother's Minutes, 1986, Your Newborn Baby: Everything You Need to Know, 1988, Joan Lunden's Healthy Cooking, 1996, Joan Lunden's Healthy Living, 1997, Joan Lunden's A Bend in the Road Is Not the End of the Road, 1998, Wake-Up Calls: Making the Most Out of Every Day, 2000; syndicated columnist: Parent's Notes. Recipient Outstanding Mother of Yr. award, Nat. Mother's Day Com., 1982; Albert Einstein Coll. of Yeshiva U. Spirit of Achievement award; Nat. Women's Polit. Caucus award; NJ Divsn. of Civil Rights award; Baylor U. Outstanding Woman of the Year award; Decoration for Disting. Civilian Svc., US Army. Office: LMNO Prodns PO Box 4361 Los Angeles CA 90028 also: Creative Artists Agy c/o Debra Goldfarb 9830 Wilshire Blvd Beverly Hills CA 90212-1825 also: Rm 4332 1271 Avenue Of The Americas New York NY 10020-1401*

LUNDERGAN, BARBARA KEOUGH, lawyer; b. Chgo., Nov. 6, 1938; d. Edward E. and Eleanor A. (Erickson) Keough; children: Matthew K., Mary Alice. BA, U. Ill., 1960; JD, Loyola U., Chgo., 1964. Bar: Ill. 1964, Ga. 1997, U.S. Dist. Ct. (no. dist.) Ill. 1964, U.S. Tax Ct. 1974. With Seyfarth Shaw LLP, Chgo., 1964—, ptnr., 1971-98, of counsel, 1998—. Fellow Am. Coll. Trust and Estate Counsel; mem. ABA (com. on fed. taxation), Ill. Bar Assn. (coun. sect. on fed. taxation 1983-91, chair 1989, coun. sect. on trusts and estates sect. coun. 1992-97, sec. 1996-97, editl. bd. Ill. Bar Jour. 1993-96), Chgo. Bar Assn. (chmn. trust law com. 1982-83, com. on fed. taxation). Office: Seyfarth Shaw LLP 55 E Monroe St Ste 4200 Chicago IL 60603-5863 Office Phone: 312-269-8826.

LUNDGREN, CISSI, artist, poet; b. Östersund, Sweden, Jan. 20, 1920; d. Bror Oskar and Julia Erika Lundgren; m. Sven Harry Monvik, Sept. 23, 1939 (dec. Aug. 1996); 1 child, Hans. Student, Konstfack Skola, Stockholm, 1937-39, Coll. Art, pvt. art schs., 1939-44, King Coll., Toronto, 1960-62. One-woman shows include Örebro, 1941; exhibited in group shows at London, 1950-52, Can., 1952-73, Vieneese Biennale, 1963-64, N.Y. State, 1962-70., L.A. and Thousand Oaks, Calif., 1988—; represented in permanent collection Seamens Ch., San Pedro, Calif.; contbr. poetry numerous anthologies, 1988—. Recipient publs. and editors awards, 1990-98. Mem. Am. Scandinavian Found. (life), Internat. Soc. Poets (life), Vasaorden, Sons of Norway, Color and Form, North Valley Art League.

LUNDGREN, RUTH WILLIAMSON WOOD (RUTH LUNDGREN WILLIAMSON WOOD), public relations executive, writer; b. Bklyn. d. John William and Hanna (Carlson) L.; m. W. F. Williamson, Dec. 17, 1949 (dec.); children: John Ross (dec.), Mark Ward; m. John Earle Wood, Aug. 27, 1988 (dec.). Student, Bklyn. Coll., 1936-41, Columbia U., 1942. Assoc. editor Everywoman's mag., 1940-42; pub. relations staff exec. J.M. Mathes Advt. Agy., 1942-45; dir. pub. relations Pan-Am. Coffee Bur., 1945-48; pres. Ruth Lundgren Ltd., N.Y.C., 1948-92. Pub. Ruth Lundgren Newsletter, 1950-58; writer daily column St. Petersburg (Fla.) Times, 1956-60; contbg. editor, writer monthly column Motor Boating and Sailing mag., 1962-80; contbr. to popular profl. publs. Home: PO Box 267 Sterling MA 01564-0267

LUNDIN, SHIRLEY MATCOUFF, pre-school administrator, adult education educator, consultant; b. Chgo., Feb. 6, 1935; d. William and Emma Martha (Graf) Matcouff; m. Roy Charles Lundin, Sept. 1, 1956; children: Michael Roy, Laura Marie Lundin Simpkiss, Bethel Anne Lundin-Martinez. BA in Liberal Arts, Northwestern U., 1957; M in Adult Continuing Edn., Nat. Louis U., 1981; Myers Briggs Type Indicator Interpreter, Assn. for Psychol. Type, 1995. Cert. Vol. Adminstrn., 1991. Dir. HeadStart Ctr. Cmty. Action Program, Evansville, Ind., 1974-76; edn. coord. HeadStart Comty. Action Program in Evansville, 1976-78; asst. program coord. parent edn. program Triton Coll., River Grove, Ill., 1979-80; trainer/field advisor Comty. Econ. Devel. Agt. HeadStart for Child Devel. Assoc. Credential, Chgo., 1981-83; adult devel./program cons. Chgo. Field Ctr. Girl Scouts USA, N.Y.C., 1983-88; coord. vol. svcs. Frank Lloyd Wright Home and Studio Fedn., Oak Park, Ill., 1988-91; adj. faculty, vol. mgmt. curriculum coord. Wm. Rainey Harper Coll., Palatine, Ill., 1995—2001; cons., trainer, prin. Lundin & Assocs., Indian Head Park, Ill., 1991—. Trainer workshops and seminars in field of vol. program adminstrn.; trainer Heartland Internat. in U.S. and Belarus, 1998-; cons. in field. Co-author (manual) How to Start a Parent Cooperative Preschool, 1980; contbr. articles to profl. jours. Interim dir., bd. pres. Vol. Ctr., Oak Park, 1990—95; Am. vol. for internat. devel. Nat. Forum Fedn., Washington, 1996—97; mem. com. study of infrastructure Village of Oak Park, 1996; internat. trainer Heartland Internat., 1997—; regional chair Unitarian Universalist Svc. Com., Boston, 1977—80; bd. dirs. Sr. Citizens Ctr., Oak Park and River Forest, 1996—2001, pres., 1998—2001. Mem.: Assn. for Psychol. Type, Chgo. Assn. Psychol. Type, Chgo. Area Tech. Assistance Providers (newsletter editor 1992—94), Assn. Vol. Adminstrn. (bd. dirs., program chair, regional conf. chair Metro Chgo. 1995, profl. devel. com. Metro Chgo. 1993—97), Assn. Vol. Adminstrn. Internat. (mem. regional coun. 1992—95, profl. devel. com., tng. coord. bylaws chair 1995). Avocations: archaeology, choral singing, dream work, travel, family.

LUNDSTROM, MARJIE, newspaper editor and columnist; Grad., U. Nebr. Columnist, editor, nat. corr. The Denver Post, 1981-89; with The Sacramento Bee, 1989-90, 91—; nat. corr. Gannett News Svc., Washington, 1990-91. Recipient Pulitzer Prize for nat. reporting, 1991. Office: The Sacramento Bee PO Box 15779 Sacramento CA 95852-0779*

LUNDSTROM, PATRICIA, state government administrator; b. Deadwood, S.D., Feb. 5, 1959; d. Leon and Mary (Munoz) L.; m. Rick Easley, June 8, 1985. BA, N.Mex. State U., 1981, MA, 1984. Exec. dir. N.W. N.Mex. Coun. Govts., Gallup. Bd. dirs. Gallup Mcpl. Credit Union. Mem. Kiwanis (bd. dirs.), Phi Sigma Alpha. Address: 208 W Coal Ave Gallup NM 87301-6306

LUNDY, BARBARA JEAN, training executive; b. Chicago, Feb. 2, 1950; Tchr., facilitator Red Rocks Cmty. Coll., Golden, Colo., 1986—90, AMI, St. Luke's Hosp., Denver, 1986—90; tchr. Arapaho Cmty. Coll., Denver, 1991—95; tng. mgr. Denver Options, 1995. Mediator U. Denver; dir. Am. Poets and Fiction Writing. Author, poet, editor Market Mountain Writer's, 1978-81; co-author: You Can Collect Child Support, 1989; contbg. author Directory of Am. Poets and Fiction Writer's. Profl. vol. VIDA Vol., Pueblo, Colo., 1971-73; vol. dir. Legal Aid Soc., Denver, 1980-85; bd. mem., editl. bd. Colo. Women's Polit. Caucus, Denver, 1980-81; state commn. mem. Colo. Child Support Commn., Denver, 1984-85; co-founder Kids in Need Support (KINS), Denver, 1986-87; com. mem. Denver Dist. Ct.: Bench, Bar, Cmty. Rels. Com., Denver, 1987-89. Mem. Assn. Persons Supported Employment (spkr. nat. conv. 1998); Hayna Writer's. Avocations: science, history and philosophy reading, piano, writing. Office: Denver Options 5250 Leetsdale Dr Ste 200 Denver CO 80246-1451 Office Phone: 303-636-5814. Personal E-mail: barbjlundy@earthlink.net. Business E-Mail: blundy@denveroptions.org.

LUNDY, JACKELYN RUTH, consulting firm owner, economist, researcher; b. Palo Alto, Calif., Nov. 8, 1951; d. Jack E. and Ruthe A. (Rose) L.; 1 child, Maia Rose. BA, U. Calif., Davis, 1973, MS, 1976, PhD, 1987. Staff rsch. assoc. U. Calif., Davis, 1976-80; tech. assistance officer Nat. Consumer Coop. Bank, Washington, 1980-82; assoc. analyst Calif. Office Econ. Opportunity, Sacramento, 1982-87; assoc. dir. agroecology program U. Calif., Santa Cruz, 1987-93, acting dir. Ctr. for Agroecology, 1993-97; owner Lundy and Assocs., Palo Alto, Calif., 1997—. Contbr. numerous articles to profl. jours. Bd. dirs. Internat. Tree Crops Inst., Davis, 1983—, Assoc. Coops., Richmond, Calif., 1994-96; mem. supervisory com. Santa Cruz Cmty. Credit Union, 1987-97. Fellow Resources for Future, 1988, leadership fellow Kellogg Found., 1991-94. Avocations: breeding and training golden retrievers, storytelling, tennis, piano. Office: Lundy and Assocs 598 Loma Verde Ave Palo Alto CA 94306-3032

LUNDY, SADIE ALLEN, small business owner; b. Milton, Fla., Mar. 29, 1918; d. Stephen Grover and Martha Ellen (Harter) Allen; m. Wilson Tate Lundy, May 17, 1939 (div. 1962); children: Wilson Tate Jr., Houston Allen, Micheal David, Robert Douglas, Martha Jo-Ellen. Degree in acctg., Graceland Coll., 1938. Acct. Powers Furniture Co., Milton, 1939-40; acct., v.p. Lundy Oil Co., Milton, 1941-52; controller First Fed. Savs. & Loan, Kansas City, Mo., 1953-55, Herald Pub. Co., Indepenence, Mo., 1956-58; mgr. Baird & Son Toy Co., Kansas City, 1959-62; regional mgr. Emmons Jewelers N.Y., Kansas City, 1963-65; owner, pres. Lundy Tax Svc., Independence, 1965-85; corp. sec.- treas., purchasing mgr. Optimation, Inc., Independence, 1974-85, mgr., 1985—2001; COO Wasber Industries LLC, Independence, 2001—. Contbr. articles to profl. jours. Mem. com. Neighborhood Coun., Independence, 1985. Mem.: Am. Bus. Women's Assn., Independence C. of C. (mem. com. 1965—85), Independence Women's Club. Republican. Reorganized Ch. Of Jesus Christ Of Latter-Day Saints. Avocations: counseling, swimming, bicycling. Home and Office: PO Box 520238 Independence MO 64052-0238 E-mail: slundy@comcast.net.

LUNDY, SHEILA EDWARDS, lawyer; b. Balt., Nov. 29, 1954; d. James Morris and Christine Anne E.; children: Tiffany D., Christopher R. BA, U. Balt., 1978, JD, 1991. Bar: U.S. Ct. Appeals Md. 1992, U.S. Dist. Ct. Md. 1994. Adminstrv. specialist BWI Airport, Md. Aviation Adminstrn., Balt., 1988-91, risk mgmt. specialist, 1991-92; staff atty. Md. Office Atty. Gen. Glen Burnie, 1992-94, asst. atty. gen., 1994—. Faculty The Md. Inst. for Continuing Profl. Edn. of Lawyers, 1999. Mem. Mt. St. Josephs H.S. Mother's Club, Balt., 1997—. Mem. Am. Inns of Ct., Md. Bar Assn. (mem. lawyer counseling com. 1998—), Paca-Brent Joint Inn of Ct., Anne Arundel County Bar Assn. (mem. com. 1994—, bd. trustees 1999), U. Balt. Alumni Assn., Paca-Brent Inn of Ct. (bd. dirs. 1999), Monumental Bar Assn. Democrat. Roman Catholic. Avocations: gardening, reading, old movies.

LUNDY-SLADE, BETTIE B. retired electronics professional; b. Marinette, Wis., Feb. 16, 1924; d. Adolph Gustav and Bertha Julian (Keller) Limberg; m. George Wesley Lundy II, Nov. 11, 1951 (div. 1956); children: George Wesley III, Genise Wynell, Charles Edward; m. Jim Donovan Slade, July 20, 1973. Lic. vocat. nurse, psychiat. technician, Calif. With Allis Chalmers, Milw., 1942-44, Gen. Dynamics, San Diego, 1959-65, Tetedyne Ryan, San Diego, 1966-76, Cubic, San Diego, 1976-86; ret., 1986. Author: (poetry) Do You Have a Minute, 1991, (biography) Growing Up on a Farm During the Depression, 1995, Book III Wistful Wanderings, 1992; artist over 100 paintings, 1986—. Den mother Boy Scouts Am., San Diego; Sunday sch. tchr. Luth. Ch., San Diego. With USN Waves, 1944-50. Recipient Sen. Cashman award Marinette, Wis., 1937, Letter of Appreciation Mother Teresa, 1992, Gen. Norman Schwarzkoph, 1993, Queen Elizabeth, 1993. Mem. Internat. Soc. Poets (life), Nat. Parks & Conservation, Smithsonian Assocs., Peal Ctr. Christian Living, Nat. Audubon Soc., Nat. Mus. Women in Arts. Republican. Avocations: soft sculpture, crocheting, short stories and poetry, oil, acrylic and water color painting. Home: 6315 Thorn St San Diego CA 92115-6908

LUNG, AURISTELA R. music educator; b. Barranquilla, Colombia, Jan. 14, 1955; arrived in U.S., 1958; d. Julio Rodríguez Buelvas and Estela Merlano Rodríguez. BA in Music Edn., U. Tex.-Pan Am. U., 1996; MA in Spanish Lit., U. Tex.-Pan. Am., 2000. Cert. bilingual educator, all-level music tchr. Missionary Jehovah's Witnesses, Colombia, 1982—85; piano tchr., owner Starr County Piano Studio, Rio Grande City, Tex., 1990—; 4th grade bilingual tchr. Rio Grande City Ctrl. Ind. Sch. Dist., 1997—99; instr. South Tex. C.C., Rio Grande City, 1999—. Vol. educator Jehovah's Witnesses, Roma, Tex., 1986—. Mem.: Magic Valley Music Tchrs. (sec. 1998—), Tex. Faculty Assocs., Tex. Music Tchrs. Assn., Phi Kappa Phi. Jehovah'S Witness. Avocations: reading, crocheting, travel, cat. Home: PO Box 804 Rio Grande City TX 78582 Office Phone: 956-488-5857.

LUNGARO CID, LISA, educational association administrator; b. Baton Rouge; children: Carina, Eddie. BA, San Francisco Coll. for Women; MA, U. Chgo.; cert. in non-profit mgmt., Case Western Res. U.; postgrad., Yale U., Columbia U. Educator pvt. schs., New Orleans, San Francisco; dir. comm. Girl Scouts, New Orleans, 1978—80, assoc. CEO, 1980—83; CEO Girl Scouts Ctrl. Md., 1993—. Mem. United Way Agy. Exec. Steering Com., 1995—2000, chair, 1998. Active Jr. League Adv. Bd., 1997—99, Coppin State, Am. Humanics Adv. Bd., 1999—, Md. Student Svc. Alliance Adv. Bd., 2000; mem. edn. com. Greater Balt. Com., 2000; active Gov.'s Coun. on the Status of Girls, 2000. Named to, Md. Top 100 Women, 1991; recipient Cert. of Honor for Svc. to San Diego County, 1991. Mem.: Network 2000 (sec. 1997—99). Office: Girl Scouts Ctrl Md 4806 Seton Dr Baltimore MD 21215

LUNZ, ELLEN DEITELBAUM, speech and language pathologist; b. Chgo., Dec. 18, 1950; d. Louis Walter and Marjorie Jaffe; m. Robert Edward Lunz, July 27, 1974; children: Rebecca Gwen, Jennifer Caitlin. BS with honors, U. Wis., 1972; MS with honors, U. Mich., 1973. Cert. speech-lang. pathologist, Ill.; cert. clin. competence speech-lang. pathology Am. Speech Hearing Assn.; cert. speech-lang. pathologist Chgo. Bd. Edn. Speech pathologist Chgo.-Read Mental Health Ctr., 1973-74, Ont. Ministry Health, Toronto, Can., 1974-76, Rimland Sch. for Austistic Children, Evanston, Ill., 1976-77, 3 C's Med. Ctr., Chgo., 1977-79, Chgo. Bd. Edn., 1979-1989, Julia Molloy Ctr., Morton Grove, Ill., 1989-91, Chgo. Home Health Care Groups, 1991—; pvt. practice Chgo., 1979—. Mem. Dem. Party of Ill., Wilmette, 1983—. Mem. Nat. Assn. Down Syndrome, Chgo. Down Syndrome Assn., League of Women Voters, North Suburban Speech-Lang. Assn., Ill. Speech Hearing Assn. Jewish. Avocations: photography, modern dance, reading, travel. Home: 808 Leyden Ln Wilmette IL 60091-2159 Office: Chgo Bd Edn Courtenay Sch 1726 W Berteau Ave Chicago IL 60613-1811

LUPTON, MARY HOSMER, retired small business owner; b. Olympia, Wash., Jan. 2, 1914; d. Kenneth Winthrop and Mary Louise (Wheeler) Hosmer; m. Keith Brahe-Wiley, Oct. 12, 1940 (dec. Apr. 1955); children: Sarah Hosmer, Wiley Guise, Victoria Brahe-Wiley; m. Thomas George Lupton, Nov. 27, 1965 (dec. Feb. 1989); 1 stepson, Andrew Henshaw Lupton. Student, Gunston Hall Jr. Coll., 1932-33; BS in Edn., U. Va., 1940. Ptnr. Wakefield Press, Earlysville, Va., 1940-55; owner, operator Wakefield Forest Bookshop, Earlysville, 1955-65, Forest Bookshop, Charlottesville, 1965-85, Wakefield Forest Tree Farm, 1955-85. Contbr. articles to profl. mags. Corr. sec. Charlottesville-Albemarle Civic League, 1963-64; sec. Instructive Vis. Nurses Assn., Charlottesville, 1961-62; chmn. pub. info. Charlottesville chpt. Va. Mus. Fine Arts, 1970-77; mem. Albemarle County Forestry Com., 1961-62; bd. dirs. Charlottesville-Albemarle Mental Health Assn., 1980-82, 89-91. Mem. AAUW, DAR (Am. Heritage com. chmn. 1983-85, 89-91), Assns. of U. Va. Libr., New Eng. Hist. Geneal. Soc., Conn. Soc. Genealogists, Geneal. Soc. Va. Hist. Soc., Albemarle County Hist. Soc., Va. Soc. Mayflower Descs. (asst. state historian 1979-82), LWV, Soc. Mayflower Descs., Am. Soc. Psychical Rsch., Brit. Soc. Psychical Rsch., Nature Conservancy, Charlottesville Soc. of Friends, Jefferson Soc., Cornerstone Soc. (charter), Lawn Soc. (charter), Chi Omega. Address: 2610 Barracks Rd Rm H252 Charlottesville VA 22901-2121

LURENSKY, MARCIA ADELE, lawyer; b. Newton, Mass., May 4, 1948; BA magna cum laude, Wheaton Coll., 1970; JD, Boston Coll. Law Sch., 1973. Bar: Mass. 1973, D.C. 1990, U.S. Dist. Ct. (we. dist.) Wis. 1978, U.S. Dist. Ct. Mass. 1974, U.S. Ct. Appeals (1st cir.) 1974, U.S. Ct. Appeals (3d cir.) 1982, U.S. Ct. Appeals (4th cir.) 1984, U.S. Ct. Appeals (5th cir.) 1995, U.S. Ct. Appeals (8th cir.) 1985, U.S. Ct. Appeals (9th cir.) 1976, U.S. Ct. Appeals (10th cir.) 1995, U.S. Ct. Appeals (11th cir.) 1982, U.S. Ct. Appeals (fed. cir.) 1989, U.S. Claims Ct. 1989, U.S. Supreme Ct. 1979. Atty. U.S. Dept. Labor, Washington, 1974-90, Fed. Energy Regulatory Commn., U.S. Dept. Energy, Washington, 1990—. Mem. Phi Beta Kappa. Office: Fed Energy Regulatory Commn 888 1st St NE Washington DC 20426-0002

LURIA, MARY MERCER, lawyer; b. Boston, Dec. 29, 1942; d. Albert and Mabel (Jacomb) Mercer; m. Nelson J. Luria, June 19, 1967. AB, Radcliffe Coll., 1964; LLB, Yale U., 1967. Bar: N.Y. 1968. Assoc. Simpson, Thacher & Bartlett, N.Y.C., 1967-68, Hale & Dorr, Boston, 1968-69, Satterlee & Stephens, N.Y.C., 1969-74, ptnr., 1974-86, Patterson, Belknap, Webb & Tyler, N.Y.C., 1986-97, Davis & Gilbert, N.Y.C., 1997—. Mem. ABA, N.Y. State Bar Assn., Assn. Bar City N.Y. Avocations: gardening, photography. Office: Davis & Gilbert 1740 Broadway Fl 20 New York NY 10019-4379 Office Phone: 212-468-4800. E-mail: mluria@dglaw.com.

LURIA, ZELLA HURWITZ, psychology educator; b. N.Y.C., Feb. 18, 1924; d. Hyman Hurwitz and Dora (Garbarsky) H.; m. Salvador Edward Luria, Apr. 18, 1945; 1 child, Daniel David. BA, Bklyn., 1944; MA, Ind. U., 1947, PhD, 1951. lic. clin. psychologist, Mass. Ford Found. post-doctoral fellow U. Ill., Urbana, 1951-53, Russell Sage found. fellow, 1953-56, clin.

researcher, 1954-58; asst. prof. psychology Tufts U., Medford, Mass., 1958-62, assoc. prof., 1962-70, prof., 1970—2003, prof. emerita, 2003. Psychiatry lectr. Mass. Gen. Hosp., Boston, 1970-79; vis. scholar Stanford U., 1977, 83; vis. prof. UCLA, 1992, U. Mich., 1993. Sr. author: Psychology of Human Sexuality, 1979, Human Sexuality, 1987. Pro-bono psychol. assessment Physicians for Human Rights, 1997—; state bd. dept. edn. Planned Parenthood of Mass., 2001—. Postdoctoral fellow USPHS, Paris, 1963-64, Bunting fellow Radcliffe Coll., 1989-90; Mellon Found. Faculty grantee Wellesley Coll., 1979-80. Mem.: AAUP (Tufts U. pres. 1986—), New Eng. Psychol. Assn. (pres. 1971—72). Office: Tufts Univ Dept Of Psychology Medford MA 02155

LURIE, ALISON, writer; b. Chgo., Sept. 3, 1926; children: John, Jeremy, Joshua. AB, Radcliffe Coll., 1947. Lectr. English Cornell U., 1968-73, adj. assoc. prof. English, 1973-76, assoc. prof., 1976-79, prof., 1979—98. Author: V.R. Lang: A Memoir, 1959, Love and Friendship, 1962, The Nowhere City, 1965, Imaginary Friends, 1967, Real People, 1969, The War Between the Tates, 1974, Only Children, 1979, The Language of Clothes, 1981, Foreign Affairs, 1984, The Truth About Lorin Jones, 1988, Don't Tell the Grownups, 1990, Women and Ghosts, 1994, The Last Resort, 1998, Familiar Spirits, 2001, Boys and Girls Forever, 2003. Recipient award in lit. Am. Acad. Arts and Letters, 1978, Pulitzer prize in fiction, 1985; fellow Yaddo Found., 1963-64, 66, Guggenheim Found., 1965, Rockefeller Found., 1967, Prix Femina Etranger, 1989. Home: 1409 Hanshaw Rd Ithaca NY 14850 E-mail: al28@cornell.edu.

LURIE, NICOLE, former health science association administrator; BA, U. Pa., 1975, MD, 1979; MSPH, UCLA, 1982. Resident UCLA, 1982; cons. RAND Corp., Santa Monica, Calif.; asst. prof. medicine UCLA; asst. to assoc. prof. U. Minn., prof. medicine and pub. health, 1985-98, dir. primary care rsch. and edn., dir. divsn. gen. and internal medicine; prin. dep. asst. sec. for health Office Pub. Health and Science, Washington, 1998—2001; senior researcher Rand Corp., 2002—. Former sr. assoc. editor Health Svcs. Rsch. Recipient Henry J. Kaiser Found. Faculty Scholar award, 1987, Nellie Westerman Prize for Rsch. in Ethics, 1987, Young Investigator award Assn. Health Svcs., 1990, Heroine in Health Care award Minn. Women's Consotium, 1994, award Am. Soc. Clin. Investigation, 1995, Article of Yr. Assn. Health Svcs., 1996, spl. recognition for Physical-Led Rsch. Minn. Physicians, 1997. Mem.: Soc. Gen. Internal Medicine (coun., treas., pres.), Inst. of Medicine. Office: Rand Corp 1200 South Hayes St Arlington VA 22202-5050

LUSCH, JENNIFER RENEE, music educator, consultant; b. Lansdale, Pa., June 9, 1976; d. Warren Dean Jr. and Cheryl Toni Wenger; m. Francis Xavier Jr. Lusch, June 22, 2002. MusB in Edn., Temple U., Phila., 1998. Cert. Microsoft Word 2000 specialist, Microsoft Excel 2000 specialist; music tchr. N.J., Pa. String instr. Lumberton (N.J.) Twp. Sch. Dist., 1998—; instrumental pvt. instr. Guitar Guild and Music Acad., Cinnaminson, NJ, 1998—; computer tchr. Ednl. Tech. Tng. Ctr. of Burlington (N.J.), 2003—. Trumpet, french horn musician Golden Eagle Cmty. Band, Mt. Holly, NJ, 1999—; violinist Philharm. of So. N.J., Voorhees, 2002—. Mem.: South Jersey Band and Orch. Dirs. Assn., Music Educators Nat. Conf. Roman Catholic. Avocations: music, computers, crafts. E-mail: teachumusic@aol.com.

LUSCHNIG, CECELIA EATON, humanities educator; b. N.Y.C. d. James Cottrell and Olive Semmes (Finlay) Eaton; m. Lance J. Luschnig, Mar. 4, 1970. BA, CCNY, 1962, MA, U. Cin., 1963, PhD, 1972. Instr. Ohio U., Athens, 1966—70; interim asst. prof. U. Wash., Seattle, 1973—74; asst. prof. U. Idaho, Moscow, 1975—77, assoc. prof., 1977—82, prof. classics, 1982—2003, prof. emeritus, 2003—. Mem. adv. coun. Tenn. Gov.'s Sch., Martin, 1985—86; mem. editl. bd. Scholia, Durban, South Africa, 1993—97; co-dir. NEH Secondary Edn. Inst., Moscow, 1987—88. Author: An Introduction to Ancient Greek: A Literary Approach, 1976, Latin and Literacy: An Essay on How and Why to Revive Latin in the Schools, 1978; author: (with L.J. Luschnig) ETYMA: An Introduction to Vocabulary Building from Latin and Greek, 1982, Etymidion: A Student's Workbook for Vocabulary Building, 1985; author: Vocabula: A Course in Latin Vocabulary Building, 1987, Time Holds the Mirror: A Study of Knowledge in Euripides' Hippolytus, 1988, Tragic Aporia: A Study of Europides' Iphigenia at Aulis, 1988, Etymidion II, 1994, The Gordon's Severed Head: A Study of Euripides' Alcestis, Electra and Phoenissae, 1995; author: (with H.M. Rocsman) A Commentary on Euripides' Alcestis, 2003. Recipient Excellence in Tchg. award, Am. Philogical Assn., 1979, Disting. Faculty award, Phi Kappa Phi, 1986. Mem.: Classical Assn. of Pacific NW (editor 1976—86). Democrat. Avocations: crossword puzzles, cooking, reading, sculpture. E-mail: luschnig@uidaho.edu.

LUSK, GLENNA RAE KNIGHT (MRS. EDWIN BRUCE LUSK), librarian; b. Franklinton, La., Aug. 16, 1935; d. Otis Harvey and Lou Zelle Knight; m. John Earle Uhler, Jr., May 26, 1956; children: Anne Knight, Camille Allana; m. 2d, Edwin Bruce Lusk, Nov. 28, 1970. BS, La. State U., 1956, MS, 1963. Asst. librarian Iberville Parish Library, Plaquemine, La., 1956-57, 1962-68; tchr. Iberville Parish Pub. Schs., Plaquemine, 1957-59, Plaquemines Parish Pub. Schs., Buras, La., 1959-61; dir. Iberville Parish Library, Plaquemine, 1969-89; chmn. La. State Bd. Library Examiners, 1979-89; pres. Camille Navarre Gallery, Ltd., Zachary, La., 1989-94. Mem. Iberville Parish Econ. Devel. Council, Plaquemine, 1970-71; sec. Iberville Parish Bicentennial Commn., 1973—; mem. La. Bicentennial Commn., 1974; bd dirs. McHugh House Mus., 1991-92. Named Outstanding Young Woman Plaquemine, La. Jr. C. of C., 1970. Mem. La. (sect. chmn. 1967-68), Riverland (sec. 1973-74) libraries assns., Capital Area Libraries (chmn. com. 1972-74). Republican. Episcopalian. Author: (with John E. Uhler, Jr.) Cajun Country Cookin', 1966, Rochester Clarke Bibliography of Louisiana Cookery, 1966, Royal Recipes from the Cajun Country, 1969, Iberville Parish, 1970. Home: 13291 Legacy Ct Baton Rouge LA 70816-7936

LUSK, MARY MARGARET, music educator; b. Athens County, Ohio, Mar. 17, 1936; d. Raymond Edward and Clara Grace (Johnston) Sanborn; m. Harold Waldo Mowery, Jan. 3, 1953 (div. Apr. 1961); children: Margaret Maria Barnhill, Harold Waldo 2nd; m. Ned Eugene Lusk, June 22, 1961; children: Bonita Jean Denig, Amy Beth Noykos, Melissa Kae Pfenning. Student, Ashland Jr. Coll., Russell, Ky., 1955-56, Ohio No. U., 1957. Apprentice music tchr., Nelsonville, Ohio, 1951-53; pvt. music tchr., 1951—. Traveling pianist Princeton Sem. Summer Mission Tour, summers 1949-52; ch. and youth camp music instr., 1953-60; adjudicator Teen Talent Contests, Ctrl. and Northwestern Ohio, 1968—; organist Patrick Heinl Funeral Home, 1976-88, Bayliff and Eley Funeral Home, 1988—. Columnist Wapakoneta Daily News, 1987-90; author of poetry. Dir., leader The Singing Lusk Family, 1975—; mem. Ohio Alliance for Arts Edn., 2002—; min. music Ch. of the Nazarene, Wapakoneta, Ohio, 1968—76, Cridersville, Ohio, 1976—83, First Presbyn. Ch., St. Marys, Ohio, 1984—85, United Meth. Ch., Botkins, Ohio, 1986—88, Salem United Meth. Ch., Wapakoneta, 1988—99; organist Byron Ch., Fairborn, Ohio, 2000—03. Mem. Music Tchrs. Nat. Assn., Ohio Music Tchrs. Assn., Northwestern Ohio Music Tchrs. Assn. Republican. Avocations: reading, writing, traveling, collecting precious miniature pianos, collecting precious moments figurines. Home: 920 Springwood Ln Wapakoneta OH 45895-9236

LUSKY, JOANN, psychotherapist, coach; b. Chgo., Ill., June 20, 1947; d. Frank Indurante, Ann Marie Indurante; 1 child, Amy. BA in Sociology and Edn., Coll. of St. Catherine's, St. Paul, 1969; MSW, Portland State U., 1971. Diplomate in Clin. Social Work Am. Bd. Examiners, 1987. Dir. residential facilities program Columbia River Mental Health Ctr., Vancouver, Wash., 1971—76; psychotherapist JoAnn Lusky, Vancouver, 1976—2000, pres., exec. coach, 2000—. Dir., cons. Residential Facilities Program, Vancouver, Wash., 1973—76; exec. coach, Portland, Oreg., 2001—. Author: Survival Skills for New and Used Mothers, 1979, Executive Coaching Tool Kit, 2002. Pres. Vancouver Trade Club, 1988; bd. dirs. Children's Home Soc., Vancouver, 1985. Named Bus. Assoc. of Yr., Am. Bus. Women's Assn., 1990. Fellow: Rotary; mem.: NAFE, NASW (Diplomate in Clin. Social Work 1987). Avocations: hiking, backpacking, travel, gardening, snorkeling. Office: 500 W 8th St Ste 215 Vancouver WA 98660

LUSTED, DONA SANDERS, music educator, consultant, organist; b. Washington, Oct. 2, 1951; d. Troy Harry and Rosemarie (Klemann) Sanders; m. Barry Emile Lusted, Nov. 7, 1982; children: Lori Marie, Luke Alan. Degree in ch. music, Evang. Landeskirchen Musik., Dusseldorf, Germany, 1969; BS in Music Edn. and German, Jacksonville State U., 1973; MM in Piano Performance, La. State U., 1975, PhD in Music, 1984. Instr. Northeastern Okla. State U., Tahlequah, 1975-76, Baker (La.) Mid. Sch., 1976-77; organist First United Meth Ch., Tahlequah, 1975-76; assoc. dir. music, organist Broadmoor United Meth. Ch., Baton Rouge, 1977—; pvt. music instr. Okla., Ala., La., 1969—; instr. La. State U., Baton Rouge, 1978-79. Dir. Summer Music and Arts/Theater Camp, Baton Rouge, 1987—; adjudicator Okla. Fedn. Music Clubs, Muskogee, 1976, Bayouland Choral Festival, Nichols State U., Thibadoux, 1994, 2000, Baton Rouge Choral Soc., 1978-79; co-founder/co-dir. South La. chpt. Choristers Guild, 1994-2000. Mem. Am. Guild Organists, Music Tchrs. Nat. Assn., La. Fedn. Music Clubs, Baton Rouge Piano Tchrs. Methodist. Avocations: swimming, reading, traveling. Home: 10709 Waverland Dr Baton Rouge LA 70815-5056 Office: Broadmoor United Meth Ch 10230 Mollylea Dr Baton Rouge LA 70815-4698

LUSTENADER, BARBARA DIANE, human resources specialist; b. Albany, N.Y., Nov. 26, 1953; d. Charles Elmer and Janet Barbara (Bergh) Setzer; m. Robert Alan Lustenader, May 20, 1972. BA in English, Coll. St. Rose, Albany, 1974; MA in English, SUNY, Oswego, 1979; postgrad., Northwestern U. Cert. sr. profl. human resources, compensation profl., cert. tng. generalist, instrnl. designer, tng.facilitator, master trainer, acad. cert. diplomate. Tchr. English Port Byron (N.Y.) Ctrl. Schs., 1974-79; sales exec. Miller/Hahn, Auburn, NY, 1979—80; exec. asst. to v.p. devel. Wells Coll., Aurora, 1980-83, adminstrv. asst. to pres., 1983-85, assoc. dir. admissions, 1985-87; asst. div. mgr. human resources Yaskawa Electric Am., Inc., Northbrook, Ill., 1987-89, divsn. mgr. corp. adminstrn. and human resources, 1989-90, dir. adminstrn. and human resources, br. mgr., 1990-94; pres. Lake Assocs., Inc., Albany, 1994—. Adj. instr. Coll. St. Rose, 2002—; spkr. in field. Mem. Lake County Youth Conservation Corps, Ill., 1993—96, chmn. 501(3)(c) com., 1993—94; bd. dirs., vol., co-chmn. Friends Schweinfurth Meml. Art Ctr., Auburn, 1983; bd. dirs., sec., chmn. human resource com., mem. nominating com. YWCA Lake and McHenry Counties, 1995—97; bd. dirs., co-chair student chpts. Capital Region Human Resources Assn., 2001—02, v.p., 2002—, chair website mgmt. com., 2002—03, pres., 2001—04. Mem.: LWV (fin. chmn. Cayuga County, N.Y. chpt. 1984—86, Mundelein chpt. 1988—90, 1996—97, bd. dirs.), ASTD, N.Y. State Soc. for Human Resource Mgmt., Inc. (certification dir.), Am. Acad. Cert. Cons. and Experts, Am. Soc. Healthcare Human Resource Assn., Am. Acad. Cert. Consultants and Experts, Capital Region Human Resource Assn. (bd. dirs. 2001—02, v.p. bd. dirs. 2002—03, pres. 2003—), Conn. Bus. and Industry Assn., Bus. Coun. N.Y. State, Lake County Women in Mgmt. (awards com. 1991, 1994, chair program com. 1994—96, awards com. 1995, chair 1996, Women of Achievement award 1996), Am. Soc. Healthcare Human Resource Adminstrs., WorldatWork, No. Ill. Bus. Assn. (co-chmn. pers. generalists roundtable 1987—97, compensation com. 1989—2000, human resources policies and practices com. 1989—2000, Outstanding Individual Contbr. award 1995), No. Ill. Soc. Human Resource Mgmt. (fin. com. 1990, cert. com. 1995—96, program com. 1996—97, Profl. Excellence award 1995), Nat. Women in Mgmt. Orgn. (Charlotte Danstrom award 1996), Basically Bach (devel. com. 1991). Office: Lake Assocs Inc 18 Thatcher St Albany NY 12207-3009

LUSTENBERG, MICHELLE WILLIAMSON, gifted and talented educator; b. Rabbit Hash, Ky., Mar. 22, 1968; d. Rita Ryle and Kenny Dean Williamson; m. Jeffrey Alan Lustenberg, Aug. 5, 1989; children: Michayla Jullaine, Madison Marta, Maya Victoria, Mikinley Grace. B, M, No. Ky. U. Cert. Teacher Nat. Bd. for Profl. Tchg. Standards Bd., 2002. Elem. art tchr. No. Elem., Butler, Ky., 1992—95; mid. sch. art tchr. Phillip A. Sharp Mid. Sch., Butler, Ky., 1995—2001; gifted and talented tchr. Pendleton County Schools, Falmouth, Ky., 2001—. Arts & humanities lead tchr. Phillip A. Sharp Mid. Sch., Butler, Ky., 2002—; Ky. cac com. for arts & humanities Ky. Dept. of Edn., Frankfort, 1999—2002; artfest coord. Ky. Art Edn. Assn., Richmond, 2000—, v.p., 1998—2001; southeastern region mid. level dir. Nat. Art Edn. Assn., Reston, Va., 2002—03; evening of the arts coord. Pendleton County Schools, Falmouth, Ky., 1997—, summer enrichment tchr., 1995—. Contbr. monotypes Licking Valley Review. Coord. of Pendleton county's walk for a cure Am. Diabetes Assn.; team capt. for sharp mid. sch. relay for life team Am. Cancer Soc.; bible sch. tchr. East Bend Bapt. Ch., Rabbit Hash, Ky. Grant, Very Spl. Arts Ky., 1996, Ky. Sch. to Work, 1997, Pendleton County 109 Environ. Bd., 1996, Ky. Art Edn. Assn., 1998, Pendleton County 109 Environ. Bd., 1997, 1998, 1998, grant, 1999, 2000. Mem.: Ky. Art Edn. Assn. (artfest coord. 1999—2003, Mid. Sch. Art Educator of the Yr. 2000, 2001), Ky. Assn. for Gifted Edn., East Bend Bapt. Ch. Independent-Republican. Bapt. Achievements include 2000 & 2001 Kentucky Middle School Art Educator of the Year; 2000-01 Pendleton County Chamber of Commerce Teacher of the Year; 1998-99 & 2000-01 Phillip A. Sharp Middle School Teacher of the Year; 1997 & 2001 Who's Who Among American Teachers; 1996-97 Pendleton County Conservation District Teacher of the Year; 2001 Esteemed Educator Citations from Kentucky House Representative Tom McKee and Senator Katie Stine. Avocations: parenting, digital photography, printmaking, sewing, learning. Home: 1245 Baker Williams Rd Corinth KY 41010 Office: Pendleton County Schools 35 Wright Rd Butler KY 41006 Personal E-mail: mlustenberg@aol.com. E-mail: mlustenber@pendleton.k12.ky.us.

LUSTICA, KATHERINE GRACE, marketing executive, artist, consultant; b. Bristol, Pa., Nov. 20, 1958; d. Thomas Lustica and Elizabeth Delores (Moyer) De Groat. Student, Hussian Sch. Art, Phila., 1976-78, Rider Coll., 1980-82, U. Utah, 1993—. Comml. artist, illustrator Bucks County Courier Times Newspapers, Levittown, Pa., 1978-82; account exec. Trenton (N.J.) Times Newspapers, 1982-84; promotions and account exec. Diversified Suburban Newspapers, Murray (Utah) Printing, 1984-88; pub. Barclays Ltd. Salt Lake City, 1988-97; mktg. dir. Bora Bora Trading Co., Murray, Utah, 1997; mktg. mgmt. Clear Channel Entertainment, 1998—. Cover artist, illustrator Accent mag., Bristol, 1978-82; freelance artist, 1978-98; advt. and creative cons. Everett & Winthrop Products Group, Salt Lake City, 1988-90, Multi Techs. Internat., Salt Lake City, 1990-91. Newcombe scholar, 1981-82. Mem. Golden Key. Presbyterian. Avocation: black belt tae kwon do. Office: 419 E 100 S Salt Lake City UT 84111-1801

LUSTIG, SUSAN GARDNER, occupational therapist; b. Beloit, Wis., Apr. 27, 1942; d. James and Sally Howell; m. Karl Lustig, Aug. 16, 1969 (div. 1997); children: Kurt, Daniel, Benjamin, David, Amy, Richard, Lauren. BS with distinction, U. Minn., 1965. Lic. occupl. therapist. Occupl. therapist Minn. State Hosp., Hastings, 1965-66; occupl. therapy cons. Hawaii Divsn. Vocat. Rehab., Honolulu, 1966-67; occupl. therapist Kaneohe (Hawaii) State Hosp., 1967, Minn. VA Hosp., Mpls., 1967-68, unit supervisor, 1968-70; chief occupl. therapist, occupl. therapy dept. mgr. Avery Health Care Sys., Newland, N.C., 1997-2000; established occupational therapy depts. Autumn Care Marion.Autumn Care, Drexel, NC, 2000—01, occupl. therapist, 2001—. Mem Nat. Bd. Cert. Occupl. Therapy, 1997—. Pres. LaSalle County (Ill.) Med. Aux., 1976—78; tutor, mentor Burke County Elem. Sch. Students; organist New Life Bapt. Ch., Newland, NC, 2003—, Crossmore (NC) 1st Bapt. Ch., 1999—2001; organist, pianist, dir. of music Linville River Bapt. Ch.; organist, Sunday sch. tchr. Long Ridge Bapt. Ch., 2001—03; bd. dirs. Harrison County Sheltered Workshop, 1971—72, Ottawa (Ill.) Pub. Health Nursing, 1976—78, Cooking for Christ, 1998—2002, Heartland Christian Acad. Sch., 1986—88, Diversified Industries, Port Angeles, Wash., 1980—82. Mem.: N.C. Occupl. Therapy Assn., Nat. Bd. for Cert. of Occupl. Therapists, Am. Occupl. Therapy Assn. Republican. Baptist. Avocations: organ, antiques, woodcarving, ice skating, reading. Home: 15 Little Cow Camp Rd Newland NC 28657-8704

LUSTREA, ANITA, radio personality; b. Blue Hill, Maine, May 28; m. Bob Lustrea; 1 child, John. Radio host Sta. WMBI, Chgo. Office: WMBI 820 LaSalle Blvd Chicago IL 60610

LUTERMAN, ALISON GINA, poet; b. State College, Pa., Oct. 19, 1958; d. David Maurice and Carolyn Darling Luterman; m. Alan George Sagan, July 11, 1987 (div. Aug. 1997). BFA in Poetry, U. Mass., 1981. Tchr. poetry Calif. Poets in Schs., Alameda, 1992—, Contra Costa, 1992—. Adj. faculty Holy Names Coll., Oakland, Calif., 1993—. Author: The Largest Possible Life, 2001, (plays) The Perfect Mother, 2003. Recipient Poetry Ctr. prize, Cleve. State U., 2000—01, Oberon Poetry prize, 2002. Mem.: PEN, Calif. Poets in Schs. Avocations: poetry, theater, singing. Home: 2187 38th Ave Oakland CA 94601

LUTEY, JOYCE LOUISE, real estate broker; b. Canton, Ohio, Jan. 11, 1946; d. William Clayton and Virginia Ruth (Wilgus) Sommers; m. Paul E. Lutey (dec. Feb. 2002); children: David Michael Calhoun, Traci Lyn Calhoun Tedrick. Student, U. Chattanooga, 1963-65, Mansfield Bus. Coll., Canton, Ohio, 1991-93, Assoc in Bus. Adminstrn., 1993. Cert. property mgr. Property mgr. Niebel Realty, North Canton, Ohio, 1981-85, Century 21 Americana Properties, St. Petersburg, Fla., 1987, Royal Estate Mgmt. Corp., Canton, 1989-90; pres., broker Greystone Group, Canton, 1989-99, Ostendorf-Morris Co., Canton, 1993-96; office leasing cons. Remax/Sedona, Ariz., 1999-2000; receptionist, asst. property mgr. Coldwell Banker First Affiliate, Sedona, Ariz., 2000—01; asst. property mgr. Coldwell Banker, Mabery-Cottonwood, Ariz., 2001—02; adminstr. Legg Mason Wood Walker Brokerage Firm, 2002—; receptionist Legg Mason Wood Walker Brokerage, 2003—. Mem. AARP, Women's Coun. Realtors (phone chmn. 1982, publicity chmn. 1983, treas. 1984, pres.-elect 1985, phone com. 1990), Canton/Massilon-St. Petersburg Bd. Realtors (program com. 1982-85, bldg. com. 1985, equal opportunity in housing com. 1990), Nazir Caldron Supreme Caldron (past Mighty Chosen One), Order Ea. Star (Delta chpt. # 539), VFW Auxiliary, Elks. Avocations: music, reading. Home: 3408 Cypress Trail # A103 West Palm Beach FL 33461 E-mail: honeybear@spamcop.net.

LUTHER-LEMMON, CAROL LEN, elementary school educator; b. Waverly, N.Y., May 8, 1955; d. Carl Rose and Mary Edith (Auge) Luther; m. Mark Kevin Lemmon, June 21, 1986; children: Mattew C. Lemmon, Cathryn M. Lemmon. BS, Ithaca Coll., 1976; MS in Edn., Elmira Coll., 1982. Cert. elem. and secondary tchr. Pa., N.Y. Reading aide Waverly Ctrl. Schs., 1978-80; tchr. reading N.Y. State Divsn. Youth, Lansing, 1981-82; tchr. title I reading, mem. student assistance program and instrnl. support team Rowe Mid. Sch., Athens (Pa.) Area Sch. Dist., 1982-94; tchr. Title I reading Lynch Elem. Sch., 1995—. Robotics team advisor Waverly HS, 2003. Basketball coach Youth Activities Dept., Athens, 1982—85, asst. softball coach, 1990—91; mem. ad hoc com. Waverly Sch. Dist., 1990—91; mem. Goal G parents & edn. mid sch. implementation team WINGS-Waverly in Global Soc., Waverly Ctr. Sch. Dist. Strategic Plan; active Girls' Softball League, Waverly, 1978—80, commr., 1980; mem. Valley Chorus, Pa. and N.Y., 1983—86, 1998—2002, Village of Waverly Recreation Commn., 1999—; robotics advisor Waverly H.S., 2003—; bd. dirs. Waverly Cmty. Ch., 1976—78; choir mem. Meth. Ch., Waverly, 1976—90, 1997—, adminstrv. bd., 1995, trustee, 1996, chmn. bd. trustees, 2001—03; bd. dirs. SACC, 1995—96. With USAR, 1977—83. Mem.: AAUW (v.p. Waverly br. 1982—83, pres. 1992—97), ASCD, N.Y. State Reading Assn., Chemung Area Reading Coun., Am. Legion Aux. (girl's state rep. 1972, girl's state chmn. 1976—80, Waverly post counsclor 1977). Republican. Home: 490 Waverly St Waverly NY 14892-1102 Office: Athens Area Sch Dist Pennsylvania Ave Athens PA 18810-1440 E-mail: ccmml@stny.rr.com.

LUTON, MARY KATHERINE, language educator; b. Iwakuni, Japan, Aug. 4, 1965; d. Jonathan Paul and Heloise Price Luton. BA French, Va. Wesleyan Coll., 1987; MA French, U. Va., 1989, PhD French, 1997. Grad. tchg. asst. U. Va., Charlottesville, 1988—95; vis. instr. Sweet Briar (Va.) Coll., 1996; asst. prof. Charleston (S.C.) Southern U., 1997—. Bd. dirs. Alliance Francaise, Charleston, SC. Author: (novels) La Comtesse de Segur, 1999. Vol. Elem. Sch., Summerville, SC, 2001—. Mem.: Children's Literature Assn. (mem. internat. com.), Modern Lang. Assn., Am. Assn. Tchrs. French. Avocations: photography, cooking, scrapbooks, travel. Office: Charleston Southern U Dept Lang Visual Arts PO Box 118087 Charleston SC 29423-8087

LUTTE, CAROLE ANNE, music educator; b. Allentown, Pa., Aug. 18, 1963; d. Robert George and Betty Mae Lutte; m. David Lee Hendricks; children: Taylor James Hendricks, Michaela Anne Hendricks. MusM, West Chester (Pa.) U., 1994. Cert. in the art of tchg. Pa. Instrumental tchr. Allentown Sch. Dist., 1985—86, Easton (Pa.) Area Mid. Sch., 1986—89, Easton Area H.S., 1989—. Freelance musician. Recipient Outstanding Tchr. award, Lehigh U., 1992. Mem.: Music Educators Nat. Conf. (assoc.), Pa. Music Educators Assn. (assoc.; pres. 1993—95). Home: 1051 N 23rd St Allentown PA 18104 Office: Easton Area HS 2601 William Penn Hwy Easton PA 18045

LUTTRELL, GEORGIA BENA, musician; b. Carbondale, Ill., Oct. 24, 1927; d. George Newton and Phyllis Bena (Gent) Gher; m. Claude Edward Luttrell, Mar. 25, 1964 (dec. Aug. 1987). BA, So. Ill. U., 1947; MusM, Northwestern U., Evanston, Ill., 1948; postgrad., various univs. Asst. prof. music Huntingdon Coll., Montgomery, Ala., 1948-50; music supr. Community Unit Dist. 2 Williamson County, Marion, Ill., 1950-53; music tchr. Dubois Grade Sch., Springfield, Ill., 1953-55; dir. choral music Feitshas High Sch., Springfield, 1955-67; chairperson music dept. Springfield S.E. High Sch., 1967-83; ind. music coord./pianist Springfield, 1983—. Accompanist various soloists and choirs, 1944—; accompanist Ill. Music Educators Assn., 1956-66; talent adjudicator Ill. High Sch. Assn., 1957-89, Ill. Elem. Sch. Assn., 1957-89. Pianist Springfield Symphony Orch., 1954-55; author (poet): American Poetry Anthology, 1988, Love's Greatest Treasures, 1989. Dir. choirs Douglas United Meth. Ch., Springfield, 1964-72; choir dir. Unity Ch., Springfield, 1981-85; vol. vocalist Ill. Symphony Chorus, formerly Springfield Symphony Chorus, 1986—. Grantee Carnegie Rsch. Found., 1949, State of Ill., Evanston Twp. High Sch., 1968. Mem. Internat. Platform Assn. (gov., music dir., pianist), Ill. Ret. Tchrs. Assn. Avocations: swimming, writing, sewing, dance, crafts, travelling.

LUTTRELL, MARY LOU, elementary school educator; b. Monroe County, Iowa, June 22, 1929; d. Forrest Charles and Catherine Cecilia (Stone) Sutcliffe; m. John Joseph, June 24, 1950; children: John S. (dec.), William A., Mary Elizabeth. AA, Ottumwa Heights Coll., 1949; BS in Elem. Edn., No. Ariz. U., 1969. Cert. tchr., N.Mex. 5th grade tchr. Albia (Iowa) Pub. Schs., 1949-51; 6th grade tchr. Chariton (Iowa) Pub. Schs., 1953-59, Cortez (Colo.) Pub. Schs., 1959-61, Cathedral Elem. Sch., Gallup, N.Mex., 1962-69; 5th grade tchr. Farmington (N.Mex.) Pub. Schs., 1969-90, sci.-math. advisor, 1994—; prin. Sacred Heart Sch., Farmington, 1990-92. Mem. N.Mex. history curriculum writing com. Farmington Pub. Schs., 1978-79. Pres. Lucas County Iowa Edn. Assn., 1957-58. Recipient Robert H. Taft Inst. Govt. award Robert H. Taft Found., 1976. Mem.

N.Mex. Assn. Edn. Retirees, San Juan County Assn. Edn. Retirees (v.p. 1997, pres. 1998). Roman Catholic. Avocations: travel, reading, bridge. Home: 600 W 20th St Farmington NM 87401-3994

LUTZ, CARLENE, educational association administrator; b. Chgo., Feb. 4, 1946; d. John Calvin Sr. and Helen (Kwast) L. BS in Edn., No. Ill. U., 1967; MA in Edn., U. Conn., 1971; adminstrv. endorsement, Chgo. State U., 1988. Cert. early childhood edn., tchr. kindergarten-grade 9. 2d grade tchr. Chgo. Pub. Schs., 1967-73, reading resource tchr., 1973-79, ESEA coord., 1979-80, upper grade lang. arts, 1980-89, reading resource tchr., 1989-92; asst. dir. Chgo. Tchrs. Union Quest Ctr., 1992—. Trainer ednl. rsch. and dissemination and critical thinking programs, Chgo., 1986—. Editor (pamphlet) EPDA Project, Pictorial Report, 1971. Ill. State scholar Ill. State Scholarship Commn., 1964; EPDA fellow U.S. Dept. Edn., 1971. Mem. ASCD, Internat. Reading Assn., Am. Fedn. Tchrs., Chgo. Tchr. Union, Ella Flagg Young Assn., Delta Kappa Gamma, Phi Delta Kappa. Home: 125 Acacia Cir Apt 613 Indianhead Park IL 60525-9037 Office: Chgo Tchrs Union Quest Ctr 222 Merchandise Mart Plz Ste 400 Chicago IL 60654-1103

LUTZ, CHARLENE JOYCE, special education educator, consultant; b. Santa Monica, Calif., Feb. 16, 1947; d. Frederick Pusant and Margaret Jane (Vartian) Samuelson; m. Arnold Anthony Lutz, Jan. 4, 1980 (div. Mar. 1987); children: Stara Lynn, Mista Lea; m. Gerald Anthony Howells, June 23, 1967 (div. June 1976); 1 child, Russell Allen Howells. BA in Psychology, UCLA, 1973; MEd, Calif. State U. LA, 1974; JD, U. West Los Angeles, 1994. Cert. tchr., tchr. learning handicapped, c.c. tchr., psychology resource specialist Calif. Tchr. spl. edn. Los Angeles County Office Edn., Downey, Calif., 1975—83; tchr. master tng. Calif State U., L.A., 1976—79; tchr. spl edn., resource specialist Centinela Valley Union H.S. Dist., Lawndale, 1983—85, program spl. coord., 1985—91; tchr. spl. edn. L.A. Unified Sch. Dist., 1991—95, resource specialist, 1995—2002. Cons. expert witness, LA, 1994—; tchr. master training Nat. U., Inglewood, Calif., 2001—02; career transition coord. LA Unified Sch. Dist., 2002. Author: Quick 'N' Easy Learning Tasks, 1986. Mem. Nat. Taxpayer's Union, Washington, 1995—, Howard Jarvice Taxpayer's Assn., L.A., 1995—. Mem.: NEA, Calif. Tchrs. Assn., United Tchrs. L.A., Pi Lambda Theta, Phi Delta Kappa. Libertarian. Avocations: gardening, walking, travel, cooking. Home: 7313 Earldon Ave Playa Del Rey CA 90293 E-mail: chlbestamerican@msn.com.

LUTZ, KAREN, finance company executive; Started in mgmt. tng. program European Am. Bank, Long Island City, NY, 1976, exec. v.p., 1992—2001; v.p. & regional mgr. Citibank N.A., Long Island City, NY, 2001—. Mem. exec. mgmt. group European Am. Bank; sec. bd. trustees Hofstra U. Co-pres. Long Island Fund for Women and Girls; bd. dirs. Nassau County Mus. of Art, Women on the Job, Long Island Women's Agenda; adv. bd. Nassau County Coalition Against Domestic Voilence, Girl Scouts Am., Nassau County; co-chair UCP Gt. Suffolk's Gala; co-chair golf outing Putt-ing Families First. Mem.: Consumer Bankers Assn. (bd. dirs.). Office: Citibank NA 3818 Queens Blvd Long Island City NY 11101*

LUTZE, RUTH LOUISE, retired textbook editor, public relations executive; b. Boston, Apr. 19, 1917; d. Frederick Clemons and Louise (Rausch) L. BA with honors, Radcliffe Coll., 1938; postgrad., Boston U., 1938-39. Tchr. Winthrop (Mass.) Pub. Schs., 1938-39; with pub. rels. dept. Boston City Club, 1939-42; sr. projects editor D.C. Heath & Co., Lexington, Mass., 1942-82. Book reviewer, lectr., cons. on pub. rels., lectr. textbook publ. Bd. dirs. Winthrop Improvement and Hist. Assn., 1980—; vol. tchr. Boston Pub. Schs., 1967-77; mem. Winthrop Rep. Town Com., 1970—; v.p. 1st Luth. Ch. Boston, 1986, deacon, 1980—. Recipient cert. appreciation for vol. in edn., Kiwanis Club of East Boston, 1972. Mem. Radcliffe Club Boston. Avocations: volunteer work, theatre, birdwatching, reading, art exhibits. Home: Winthrop, Mass. Died Aug. 17, 2002.

LUU, JANE, astronomer; Asst. prof. astronomy Harvard U., Cambridge, Mass. Recipient Annie Jump Cannon award Am. Astron. Soc., 1991. Office: Harvard U Dept Astronomy 60 Garden St # 15 Cambridge MA 02138-1516

LUZ, VIRGINIA OLIVAR, dietician; b. Antique, Philippines, May 21, 1934; came to U.S., 1960; d. Adriano and Expectacion Xavier (Salazar) Olivar; m. Zosimo Umali Luz, 1965; children: Cecilia Luz-Cariaga, Patricia Ann Luz-Holgado, Melinda M. Luz-Royall. BS in Nutrition, U. Philippines, 1957. Registered dietitian, Am. Dietetic Assn. Dietetic intern Brigham Women's Hosp., 1961-62; clin. dietitian Lemuell Shattuck Hosp., Jamaica Plain, Mass., 1962-63, Temple U. Hosp., Phila., 1963-65, Santa Cabrini Hosp., Montreal, Can., 1966-67, Roxborough Meml. Hosp., Phila., 1966; chief dietitian Nazareth Hosp., Phila., 1967-77; clin. dietitian Temple U. Hosp., Phila., 1977-87, Nazareth Hosp., Phila., 1994—; gen. renal nutritionist Biomed. Applications (name now Fresenius Med. Care), Phila., 1987—. Historian Mutya Philippine Dance Co., 1990—. Founder Mutya Philippine Dance Co., St. Augustine, Church Hall, Phila., 1990—; lectr., historian Pub. Grade Schs., Phila., 1963; pres. Filipino Am. Assn. Phila., Girard Avenue, 1980-82, Phila. Philippine Lions Club, 1982-84. Named Mother of Yr., Filipino Am. Assn. Phila., 1981; recipient Cultural Appreciation award Gov.'s Commn. on Heritage, Pa., 1995. Mem. Am. Dietetic Assn., Coun. on Renal Nurtition Network, Mutya Philippine Dance Co. Roman Catholic. Avocations: folklorist, modeling ethnic, drama, singing. Home: 706 Sunflower Ave Langhorne PA 19047-3748 Office: Nazareth Hosp & Fresnius Med Care 6201 Holme Ave Philadelphia PA 19152

LYALL, KATHARINE C(ULBERT), academic administrator, economist, educator; b. Lancaster, Pa., Apr. 26, 1941; d. John D. and Eleanor G. Lyall. BA in Econs., Cornell U., 1963, PhD in Econs., 1969; MBA, NYU, 1965. Economist Chase Manhattan Bank, N.Y.C., 1963-65; asst. prof. econs. Syracuse U., 1969-72; prof. econs. Johns Hopkins U., Balt., 1972-77, dir. grad. program in pub. policy, 1979-81; dep. asst. sec. for econs. Office Econ. Affairs, HUD, Washington, 1977-79; v.p. acad. affairs U. Wis. Sys., 1981-85; prof. of econ. U. Wis., Madison, 1982—; acting pres. U. Wis. Sys., Madison, 1985-86, 91-92, exec. v.p., 1986-91, pres., 1992—. Bd. dirs. Marshall & Ilsley Bank, Alliant, Carnegie Found. for Advancement of Tchg. Author: Reforming Public Welfare, 1976, Microeconomic Issues of the 70s, 1978. Mem. Mcpl. Securities Rulemaking Bd., Washington, 1990-93. Mem. Am. Econ. Assn., Assn. Am. Univs., Phi Beta Kappa. Home: 6021 S Highlands Ave Madison WI 53705-1110 Office: U Wis Sys Office of Pres 1720 Van Hise Hall 1220 Linden Dr Madison WI 53706-1559 E-mail: klyall@uwsa.edu.

LYBARGER, MARJORIE KATHRYN, nurse; b. Holland, Mich., Apr. 23, 1956; d. Richard Simon and Mary Kathryn (Homan) Den Uyl; m. John Steven Lybarger, Aug. 22, 1981; children: Ashley Ann, Ryan Christopher. BA in Psychology, Biola U., Calif., 1979, BS in Nursing, 1984. RN, Calif. Staff nurse Presbyn. Intercommunity Hosp., Whittier, Calif, 1985-86, Healthcare Med. Ctr., Tustin, Calif., 1986-88; staff nurse med.-telemetry unit Friendly Hills Regional Med. Ctr., La Habra, Calif., 1988-90; staff nurse telemetry unit Riverside (Calif.) Community Hosp., 1990-93; staff nurse med. telemetry unit St. Anthony's Ctrl. Hosp., Denver, 1993-94; clin. RN 1 cardiovascular intermediate care unit St. Anthony's Ctr., Denver, 1994-98, staff RN, 1998—, case mgr., 1999—2002; staff RN float pool, case mgr. Luth. Med. Ctr., Wheatridge, Colo., 2002—. Mem. Gamma Phi Beta. Republican. Avocations: snowskiing, swimming, tennis. Home: 8489 W 95th Dr Broomfield CO 80021-5330 E-mail: mklyb@aol.com.

LYCARDI, JOAN C. artist; b. Chgo., June 6, 1946; d. Tony P. Wojciechowski and Clara M Botwinski; m. Larry Rodriguez; children: Christopher Melnyk, Gregory Melnyk, Kerry Melnyk, Stephanie Rodriguez, Louis Rodriguez. Student, Am. Acad. Art, Chgo., 1979—81. Art dir. Rauch & Assocs., Orland Park, Ill., 1980—81; advt. asst. Vondrak Publs., Chgo., 1981—83; small bus. owner Cleaning Cruise, Chgo., 1984—2003. Pub. rels. Vondrak Publs., Chgo., 1982. Artist (ency.) Encyclopedia of Living Artists, 1988, (book) The Chicago Art Review, 1989, Midway Review, 1981—82; exhibitions include Ft. Wayne Mus. Art, 1987—88, Lincoln Cultural Arts Found., 1988, Mamaroneck artists Guild, 1988, Dell Arte' Players, Ink People, 1988, Amos Eno Gallery, Soho, N.Y., 1987, Greeley Nat. Art Mart, 1987, one-woman shows include Monroe Gallery, Chgo., 1986, Matrix Gallery, Sacramento, Calif., 1988, Arc Gallery, Chgo., 1989, New Dimensions, Inc., 1990, exhibited in group shows at Riverbend Studios, Blue Island, Ill., 2003. Artist for newsletter and logo design SW Women Working Together, Chgo., 1981—82; mem. selection com. for pub. art Chgo. Pub. Libr., 1994; bd. mem. SW Women Working Together, Chgo., 1981. Recipient 1st pl., Chgo. Ridge Art Ctr., 1982, 2d pl. watercolor, S.W. Cultural Arts League, 1981—82, 3d pl. graphics, Fine Arts League, La Junta, Colo., 1987, 2d pl. drawing, Emerald City Classic Internat. Competition, Wichita, Kans., 1988. Avocations: random acts of kindness, study of natural history, writing, fishing, gardening. Home: 5229 West 64th St Chicago IL 60638 Personal E-mail: inki@ameritech.net.

LYCETT, SARA F. See FINNEGAN, SARA ANNE

LYDICK, NANCY M. psychologist; b. Belville, Tex., June 18, 1942; d. John Samuel Jr. and Dale (Crawford) McCelvey; m. Larry Stuart Lydick (div.); children: L. Drew, Todd W.; m. M'Baye Fara Gaye, Sept. 23, 1999. BA in Psychology, Antioch U., West L.A., 1980; MA in Marriage, Family and Child Counseling, Azusa Pacific U., L.A., 1982; PhD in Gen. Psychology, U.S. Internat. U., San Diego, 1994. Lic. Marriage and Family Therapist Calif., Pa. Intern Calif. Family Study Ctr., 1982, L.A. Psychiat. Ctr., 1993—94; drug counselor, dual diagnosis Parkside Recovery/ Dept Human Svcs., Phila., 1999—, dir. family program, 2002—; pres., CEO For Love of the Family, Inc., 2004—. Presenter confs. and workshops Various Assns. and Groups, in U.S. and Can.; dir. workshops Dream, Sex Edn., Adolescents, Eating Disorders; interat. spkr. Women, Youth and Family (an Islamic perspective). Author (producer and dir.): (TV series) Women in Islam, 1996; author: (producer and host) Healing from the Heart, 1998; columnist (monthly mag. article) Ask Nasiha. Nat. Fellowship Ahmadu Bamba Internat. Sufi Sch.; presenter Development in Literacy; pres. Khidmatul Khadim Internat. Sufi Sch.; Vol. thrift shop, Big Sisters program, fund raiser Fort Worth Jr. League, Tex., 1965—73; vol. book mobile Nat. Coun. Jewish Women, Fort Worth, 1964. Mem.: Phila. Assn. Marriage and Family Therapy, Acad. Family Mediators, Assn. Family and Conciliation Cts., Assn. Play Therapy, Internat. Assn. Eating Disorders Specialists, Am. Psychol. Assn., Calif. Assn. Marriage and Family Therapy (clin. mem.), Am. Assn. Marriage and Family Therapy (clin. mem.), Kappa Kappa Gamma (Epsilon Alpha chpt.). Islam. Office: Parkside Recovery 5000 Parkside Ave Philadelphia PA 19131 E-mail: nm.lydick@verizon.net.

LYDON, AMANDA, chef; Chef Truc, Metro Brasserie, Boston, 2001—. Named Best New Chef, Boston Mag., 2000; named one of Best Young Chefs in Am., Food & Wine Mag. Office: Metro Brasserie 1815 Massachusetts Ave Cambridge MA 02140

LYDON, KERRY RAINES, elementary school educator; b. Urbana, Ill., Dec. 31, 1948; d. Irving Isaac and Charlotte Austine (Butler) Raines; m. Michael Mario Lydon, Aug. 17, 1970; children: Scott Michael, Heather Anne. BA, U. Md., 1970; early childhood Montessori credential, Ctr. for Montessori Tchr. Edn., 1984. Exec. dir. Cumberland County Mental Health Assn., Fayetteville, N.C., 1980-82; dir. Montessori Sch. Fayetteville, 1983—, adminstr., 1990—2001, bd. dirs. Workshop presenter in field. Author: A Birthday for Blue, 1989; editor, creator (newsletter) Connections, 1980-82; author, illustrator (activity newsletter) Montessori Mailbox, 1985, Montessori Mailbox-Parents Pages, 1998. Mem. Am. Montessori Soc., Authors Guild. Office: Montessori Sch Fayetteville 1201 Cape Ct Fayetteville NC 28304-4404

LYERLA, KAREN DALE, special education educator; b. Kansas City, Kans., Aug. 2, 1948; d. Dale Donelly Lyerla, Alberta Pauline Cromer-Lyerla. BS, U. Kans., 1970, MS Honors, 1972, postgrad., U. Tex. Cert. Tchg. Tex., Kans. Tchr. learning disabled, homebound tchr. Round Rock H.S., Tex., 1973—75; tchr. learning disabled Lawrence H.S., Lawrence Alternative H.S., Kans., 1975—77, 1995—96, Lawrence H.S., Kans., 1977—95, 1996—, chair, spl. edn. dept., 2002—. Cons., ctr. rsch. in learning U. Kans., Lawrence, 1980—, tchr. strategy girl's basketball team, 1989—90; mem., faculty adv. commn. Lawrence H.S., Kans.; mem. Lawrence Leadership Coun., Kans.; mem., moderator Scholar's Bowl; dist. USD 497; trainer inspiration software, read and write gold software; assessment coord. Author: The Paragraph Writing Strategy, 1990, Pre-Writing Organizers, 2001, Thesis Statement, 2001, Themewriting: Format, Steps, Structure and Introductions, 2002, Themewriting: Body and Conclusions, 2002. Grantee Kans. Child Svc. Demostration Ctr.-Project STILE, 1984-1988. Mem.: Assn. Children with Learning Disabilities, Coun. on Exceptional Children (presenter Kans. Fedn. 1986, presenter 65th ann. conf. 1987), One Hundred Good Women, River City Women's Club (historian 1975—), Phi Delta Kappa. Avocations: exercise, reading, sports, music, travel. Home: 746 Alabama Lawrence KS 66044 Office: Lawrence High Sch USD 497 1901 Louisiana Lawrence KS 66046

LYERLY, ELAINE MYRICK, advertising executive; b. Charlotte, N.C., Nov. 26, 1951; d. J.M. and Annie Mary (Myrick) L.; m. Marc Rauch, Jan. 17, 1987. AA in Advt. and Comml. Design, Cen. Piedmont Community Coll., 1972. Freelance designer Sta. WBTV, Charlotte, N.C., 1972; fashion illustrator Matthews Belk, Gastonia, N.C., 1972-73; designer Monte Curry Mktg. and Communication Svcs., Charlotte, 1973-74, exec. v.p., 1974-77; pres. Repro/Graphics, Charlotte, 1975-77, Lyerly Agy. Inc., Charlotte, 1977—. Organizing dir. First Trust Bank. Illustrator: Mister Cookie Breakfast Cookbook, 1985. Former chmn. regional blood com. Greater Carolinas chpt. ARC, 1990-93, mem. nat. implementation com., 1991, chair nat. conv., 2001, mem. nat. bd. govs., 2002—, Red Cross, nat. exec. com. and vice chair pub. support; bd. dirs. United Way, 1996, YMCA, Women's Impact Fund, 2003—, Levine Mus. of New South; bd. dirs., chair Child Care Resources, Inc., 2003—, Women's Impact Fund, 2002--; mem. bd. advisors Belmont Abbey Coll. Named Bus. Woman of Yr., Shearson Lehman Hutton/Queens Coll., 1989, N.C. Young Careerist Bus. and Profl. Women's Club, 1981; recipient ACE award Women in Comms., 1993, CPCC Hagemeyer award, 1996, Schley Lyons Leadership Charlotte award, 1999, Bus. Jour. Top 25 Women of Achievement award 2001. Mem. Women Execs., Women Bus. Owners (adv. coun., Leadership award 1990, Woman Bus. Owner of Yr. award 1994), Pub. Rels. Soc. Am. (Counselors Acad. 1985—), Charlotte C. of C. (bd. dirs., diversity coun., long-range planning com., Bus. Woman of Yr. award 1985), Hadassah. Republican. Jewish. Office: Lyerly Agy Inc 4819 Park Rd Charlotte NC 28209-3274 E-mail: elyerly@lyerly.com.

LYJAK CHORAZY, ANNA JULIA, pediatrician, medical administrator, educator; b. Braddock, Pa., Feb. 25, 1936; d. Walter and Cecilia (Swiatkowski) Lyjak; m. Chester John Chorazy, May 6, 1961; children: Paula Ann Chorazy Peters, Mary Ellen Chorazy-Cuccaro, Mark Edward Chorazy. BS, Waynesburg Coll., 1958; MD, Women's Med. Coll. Pa., 1960. Diplomate Am. Bd. Pediat. Intern St. Francis Gen. Hosp., Pitts., 1960-61; resident in pediat., tchg. fellow Children's Hosp. of Pitts., 1961-63, pediatrician, devel. clinic, 1966-75; pediat. house physician Western Pa. Hosp., Pitts., 1963-66; med. dir. Rehab. Instn. Pitts., 1975-98, Children's Inst., Pitts., 1998—2001, interim med. dir., 2002—03. Clin. asst. prof. pediat. Children's Hosp. Pitts. and U. Pitts. Sch. Medicine, 1971—94, clin. assoc. prof. pediat., 1994—2001; pediat. cons. Children's Home Pitts., 1985—2001. Author chpts. to books. Co-chmn. EACH Joint Planning and Assessment, Pitts., 1980-85; mem. adv. com. 10th Nat. Conf. on Child Abuse, Pitts., 1993. Recipient Miracle Maker award Children's Miracle Network, 1995. Fellow Am. Acad. Pediat.; mem. Pitts. Pediat. Soc. Avocations: reading, comedy, theatre, music, opera. Home: 131 Washington Rd Pittsburgh PA 15221-4437 Office Phone: 412-420-2268. Personal E-mail: cjcajc@comcast.net.

LYLE, VIRGINIA REAVIS, retired archivist, genealogist; b. Nashville, Apr. 19, 1926; d. Damon Ashley and Nellie Alice (Vaughan) R.; m. John Reid Lyle, Sept. 25, 1943; 1 child, Judith L. Haggard. BA, Vanderbilt U., 1974, MLS, 1975. Cert. genealogist, archivist. Administrv. officer Commerce Union Bank, Nashville, 1961-70, 75-78; rsch. asst. R.C.H. Mathews, Jr., Nashville, 1970-75, 78-79; genealogist Nashville, 1980; archivist Metro Nashville-Davidson County Archives, Nashville, 1981-93; ret., 1993; organizing sec. Friends of Metro Archives, 1994-95. Sec. Homecoming '86 Metro Steering Com. for Tenn., 1986; mem. Pub. Libr. Bd., 1978-81; historian, archivist Dalewood United Meth. Ch., 1995—. Mem. Tenn. Archivists, Nat. Geneal. Soc., DAR, Ladies Hermitage Assn., Soc. Am. Archivists, Acad. Cert. Archivists, Woman's Club of Nashville (adv. bd.), Historical Soc. Hopkins Co., Nat. Trust Historical Preservation, Middle Tenn. Genealogical Soc., Century Soc. Geo. Peabody Coll., Vanderbilt Univ. Methodist. Home: 1421 Eastland Ave Nashville TN 37206-2626

LYMAN, PEGGY, artistic director, dancer, choreographer, educator; b. Cin., June 28, 1950; d. James Louis and Anne Earlene (Weeks) Morner; m. David Stanley Lyman, Aug. 29, 1970 (div. 1979); m. Timothy Scott Lynch, June 21, 1982 (div. 1997); 1 child, Kevin Kynch. Grad. h.s., Cin. Solo dancer Cin. Ballet Co., 1964-68, Contemporary Dance Theater, 1970-71; chorus dancer N.Y.C. Opera, 1969-70; Radio City Music Hall Ballet Co., 1970; chorus singer, dancer Sugar, Broadway musical, N.Y.C., 1971-73; prin. dancer Martha Graham Dance Co., N.Y.C., 1973-88, rehersal dir., 1989-90; artistic dir. Martha Graham Ensemble, N.Y.C., 1990-91; faculty Martha Graham Sch., 1975—; co-artistic dir. Dance Conn., Hartford, 1998-2000. Head dance divns. No. Ky. U., 1977—78; artistic dir. Peggy Lyman Dance Co., N.Y.C., 1978—89; asst. prof. dance, guest choreographer Fla. State U., Tallahassee, 1982—89; guest choreographer So. Meth. U., Dallas, 1986; adjudicator Nat. Coll. Dance Festival Assn., 1983—; co-host To Make a Dance, QUBE cable TV, 1979; mem. guest faculty Am. Dance Festival, Durham, NC, 1984; site adjudicator NEA, 1982—84; tchr. Sch. Dance Conn., 1992—, East Conn. Concert Ballet, 1992—94; guest faculty Wesleyan U., Middletown, Conn., 1992; guest artist Conn. Coll., 1993; chair dance divsn. Hartt Sch., U. Hartford, Conn., 1994—2001; dir. dance divsn. Hartt Sch., U. Hartford, Conn., 2002—; freelance master tchr. internat. univs. Prin. dancer (TV spls.) Dance in America, 1976, 79, 84; guest with Rudolph Nureyev (CBS-TV) Invitation to the Dance, 1980; guest artist Theatre Choreographique Rennes, Paris, 1981, Rennes, France, 1983; Adelaide U., 1991; site dir. Martha Graham's Diversion of Angels for student concert U. Mich., 1992, Martha Graham's Panorama, U. Ill., Champaign-Urbana, 1993, Towson State U., 1997, Martha Graham's Diversion of Angels for Dutch Nat. Ballet, 1995, Diversion of Angels and Acts of Light for Dance Conn., 1998, Ballet Argentino, 1999; choreographer: Conundrum (solo), 1982, Mantid (group), 1984, Roll, Spin, Draw, or Fold (group), 1984, Chope Dance (solo), 1985, Mirror's Edge (group), 1986, No Gavotte Bach (group), 1995, Interior Landscapes (group), 1997, Family Portrait (group), 1999, Yes, Is A World (group), 2002; co-creator (with John Feierabend) Move It (CD/DVD), 2003. Founding mem. Cin. Arts Coun., 1976-78. Mem. Am. Guild Mus. Artists. Office: Hartt Sch Dance Divsn 224 Farmington Ave Hartford CT 06105-3501 Office Phone: 860-525-9396 x 27. E-mail: lyman@hartford.edu.

LYN, JEAN, interior designer; b. Charlotte, N.C., Nov. 22, 1946; d. Frederic C. and Justine Keith Mayer; m. Nicolae Umberto Pollcappelli, July 15, 1976 (div. Apr. 1982). AA, Stephen's Coll., 1966; BA with honors in Interior Arch., U. Ky., 1968. Designer Loeffler Johnson, Ludnberg, Pitts., 1970—73, Morganell-Heumann & Assocs., L.A., 1973—76; design ptnr. Inventor Policappelli, 1976—81; prin., owner Jean Lyn & Assocs., 1981—. Achievements include design of copyright for eco homes; founder environmental endowments. Avocations: Bikram yoga, philosophy, hiking, bicycling, climbing.

LYNAM, GLORIA, elementary school educator; d. Abraham and Diana Beatrice Gerber; m. Roger Lynam. B Arts and Scis. with honors, U. Conn., 1973; MEd, Coll. St. Joseph Vt., 1991. Vt. profl. educator. Tchr. middle sch. lang. arts Rutland (Vt.) Town Sch., 1998—. Editor: student poetry anthologies, comic books. Grantee, Chapbooks for Learning, 1999, Excellence in Edn. grantee, SHOPA Found., 1999—2000, No strings art, Chaffee Art Gallery, 1999, Nat. writing project, Vt., 1999. Mem.: New Eng. League of Middle Schs. Assn., Vt. Assn. Middle Level Edn., Nat. Coun. Tchrs. Eng., Northern Vt. Artists Assoc., Vt. Watercolor Soc. Avocations: writing, reading, mountain biking, walking, watercolors.

LYNCH, ANNETTE PETERS, literature educator; b. Marion, Ind., Oct. 23, 1922; d. Frank Robert and Delight Kindle (Simmons) Peters; m. Thomas Millard Lynch, Aug. 24, 1949 (div. Jan. 1975); children: Robert Millard, Susan D.L. Marks, David Barrett. BA, Ind. U., 1944, MA, 1945; PhD, Occidential Coll., 1961. Instr. Ind. U., Bloomington, 1945-49, Glendale (Calif.) Coll., 1949-50, Occidential Coll., L.A., 1950-55; prof. Mt. San Antonio Coll., Walnut, Calif., 1955-93. Adj. assoc. prof. Calif. State U., L.A., 1954-58; treas. Coll. English Assn., So. Sect., Calif., 1956-57, v.p., 1957-58, pres., 1958-59, staff mem. Writer's Day Mt. San Antonio Coll., Calif., 1972-93; leader poetry workshops. Author: Ways Around the Heart, 1988; author of poems; editor Mt. San Antonio Literary Mag., 1981-89. Vol. South Pasadena Pub. Libr., 1993—. Mem. Poetry Soc. Am., Acad. Am. Poets, Calif. State Poetry Soc., Beyond Baroque Literary Arts Ctr. Democrat. Avocations: dress designing, purse making, pottery collecting, movies. Home: 833 Garfield Ave South Pasadena CA 91030-2819

LYNCH, BARBARA, chef, restaurant owner; m. Charles Petri. Chef Figs, Boston, Rocco's, Boston, 1993—95; exec. chef Galleria Italiana, Boston, 1995—98; chef, owner No. 9 Park, Boston, 1998—; owner B&G Oysters, Ltd., Boston, 2003—. Subject : (documentaries) Amuse Bouche - A Chef's Tale; Boston 24/7. Named Ten Best New Chefs, Food & Wine mag., Best Chef, Northeast, James Beard Found., 2003. Office: 9 Park St Boston MA 02108

LYNCH, BEVERLY PFEIFER, education and information studies educator; b. Moorhead, Minn. d. Joseph B. and Nellie K. (Bailey) Pfeifer; m. John A. Lynch, Aug. 24, 1968. BS, N.D. State U., 1957, L.H.D. (hon.); MS, U. Ill., 1959; PhD, U. Wis., 1972. Librarian Marquette U., 1959-60, 62-63; exchange librarian Plymouth (Eng.) Pub. Library, 1960-61; asst. head serials div. Yale U. Library, 1963-65, head, 1965-68; vis. lectr. U. Wis., Madison, 1970-71, U. Chgo., 1975; exec. sec. Assn. Coll. and Research Libraries, 1972-76; univ. librarian U. Ill.-Chgo., 1977-89; dean Grad. Sch. Libr. and Info. Sci. UCLA, 1989-94, prof. Grad. Sch. Edn. and Info. Studies, 1989—; interim pres. Ctr. for Rsch. Librs., Chgo., 2000-01. Sr. fellow, vis. scholar UCLA, 1982. Author: (with Thomas J. Galvin) Priorities for Academic Libraries, 1982, Management Strategies for Libraries, 1985, Academic Library in Transition, 1989, Information Technology and the Remaking of the University Library, 1995. Recipient Cert. of Appreciation, Chinese Am. Librs. Assn., 2001; named Acad. Libr. of Yr., 1982, one of top sixteen libr. leaders in Am., 1990; fellow Indo-U.S. Subcommn. on Edn. and Culture, 1992-93. Mem. ALA (pres. 1985-86, coun. 1998-, com. on accreditation 1999-2002, chair 1999-2000), Nat. Info. Stds. Orgn. (bd. dirs. 1996-, vice chair 1999-2001, chair 2001-03), Rare Book Sch. U. Va.(bd. dir.), Acad. Mgmt., Am. Sociol. Assn., Assn. for the Study of Higher Edn.,

Bibliog. Soc. Am., Scottish Libr. Assn. (hon.), Caxton Club, Grolier Club, Book Club Calif., Phi Kappa Phi. Office: UCLA Grad Sch Edn Info Mailbox 951520 Los Angeles CA 90095-1520 Office Phone: 310-206-4294. E-mail: bplynch@ucla.edu.

LYNCH, CAROL, director special services, psychologist; d. Joseph Louis and Ellen (Birish) Dobkowski; 1 child, Eric Alexander. BA, William Paterson Coll., 1966; MA, NYU, 1970, PsyD, 1984. Lic. psychologist, N.J., N.Y. Tchr. Bloomfield (N.J.) Pub. Schs., 1966-68, psychologist, 1970-87; dir. spl. svcs. Waldwick (N.J.) Pub. Schs., 1987—, acting supt. schs., 1995-96, 98. Adj. clin. prof. NYU, N.Y.C., 1983-86 adj. prof. Montclair (N.J.) State Coll., 1984-85. Mem. prof. alumni coun. Sch. Edn., Health and Nursing, NYU, 1989—91; alumni coun. chair Sch. Edn., NYU, 1991—93, sec., 2002—03; sec., bd. trustees First Church of Religious Sci., New York, NY, 2001—. NYU fellow, 1981-82; recipient Best Practice award N.J. State Dept. Edn. for Fast Families Program, 1995, Disting. Grad. Brian E. Tomlinson Meml. award NYU, 1995, Exemplary Practice award N.J. Adminstrs. Assn./N.J. Sch. Bds. "Crisis Response Initiative," 2002. Mem. APA (sch. psychology task force 1989-90), N.J. Psychol. Assn. (treas. 1985-86, Sch. Psychologist of Yr. 2003), Nat. Assn. Sch. Psychologists (del. 1984-88), N.J. Assn. Sch. Psychologists (pres. 1982-83, Sch. Psychologist of Yr. 2003), Ea. Ednl. Rsch. Assn. (pres. 1993-95), Bergen County Assn. Lic. Psychologists (bd. dirs. 1991-93), NYU Sch. Psychology Alumni Assn. (founder 1988-92), Ramapo Valley Adminstrs. (v.p. 1996-98, pres. 1998—). Avocations: skiing, antiques collecting, tennis, gourmet cooking. Home: 124 Frank Ct Mahwah NJ 07430-2963 Office: Waldwick Pub Schs 155 Summit Ave Waldwick NJ 07463-2133 E-mail: drcarollynch@msn.com.

LYNCH, CARYN A. government agency administrator; b. Camden, N.J., Feb. 23, 1974; d. P.R. Larro, Carol A. Larro; m. Patrick Brian Lynch. BA, Trenton State Coll., 1996; M in Govt. Adminstrn., U. Pa., 2000. Dep. dir. briefings N.J. Gov.'s Office, Trenton, 1997—99, dir. briefings, 1999—2001; dir. govt. rels. Del. River and Bay Authority, New Castle, 2001—. Assoc. editor: Fels Jour. City and State Affairs, 2000. Vol. Get Out the Vote Rep. State Com., Trenton, NJ, 1997. Scholar Brian Stack Meml. Internship scholar, Trenton State Coll. Pres.'s Office, 1994. Mem.: Internat. City & County Mgmt. Assn.

LYNCH, CATHERINE GORES, social work administrator; b. Waynesboro, Pa., Nov. 23, 1943; d. Landis and Pamela (Whitmarsh) Gores; m. Joseph C. Keefe, Nov. 29, 1981; children: Shannon Maria, Lisa Alison, Gregory T. Keefe, Michael D. Keefe. BA magna cum laude with honors, Bryn Mawr Coll., 1965; postgrad., Cornell U., 1966-67. Cert. police instr. Mayor's intern Human Resources Adminstrn., N.Y.C., 1967; rsch. asst. Orgn. for Social and Tech. Innovation, Cambridge, Mass., 1967-69; cons. Ford Found., Bogota, Columbia, 1970; staff Nat. Housing Census, Nat. Bur. Statistics, Bogota, 1971; evaluator Foster Parent Plan, Bogota, 1972; rsch. staff FEDESARROLLO, Bogota, 1973 74; dir. Dade County Advocates for Victims, Miami, Fla., 1974 86; asst. to dep. dir. Dept. Human Resouces, Miami, 1986-87, computer liaison, 1987-88, asst. adminstr. placement svcs. program, 1988-89; exec. dir. Health Crisis Network, Miami, 1989-96; liaison HIV cmty. svc. State of Fla. Health and Rehab. Svcs., 1996-97; program ops. adminstr. adult protective svcs. Fla. Dept. Children and Families, 1997-2000; dir. grants mgmt. U. Miami Sch. Nursing, 2000—03; ann. giving and grants mgr. Audubon of Fla., 2003—. Guest lectr. local univs. Participant, co-chmn. various task forces rape, child abuse, incest, family violence, elderly victims of crime, nat. state, local levels, 1974-86, 99—2000; developer workshops in field; participant, chair, co-chair task forces on HIV/AIDS impact; long term care, children and AIDS, AIDS orgnl. issues, 1991-96; mem. gov.'s task force on victims and witnesses, gov.'s task force on sex offenders and their victims, gov.'s Red Ribbon panel on AIDS, 1992-93, gov.'s interdepartmental work group, 1993-96; mem. ednl. rev. com. Am. Found AIDS Rsch., 1991-96; vice chair Metro-Dade HIV Svcs. Planning Coun., 1991-93; active Fla. HIV Svcs. Adv. Coun., 1991-96; rev. panel Fed. Spl. Projects of Nat. Significance, 1994, 96; adv. coun. Metro Dade Social Svcs., 1995-96; v.p. Dade County Healthy Start Coalition, 2002—; cert. expert witness on battered women syndrome in civil and criminal cts. Contbr. writings to field to publs. Bd. dirs. Healthy Start Coalition of Miami-Dade County, 2002—. Recipient various pub. svcs. awards including WINZ Citizen of Day, 1979, Outstanding Achievement award Fla. Network Victim Witness Svcs., 1982, Pioneer award Metro-Dade Women's Assn., 1989; Fulbright scholar U. Central de Venezuela, Caracas, 1965-66; Lehman fellow Cornell U. Mem. Nat. Orgn. of Victim Assistance Programs (bd. dirs. 1977-83, Outstanding Program award 1984), Fla. Network of Victim/Witness Programs (bd. dirs., treas. 1980-81), Am. Soc. Pub. Adminstrs., Dade County Fedn. Health and Welfare Workers, Fla. Assn. Health and Social Svcs. (Dade county chpt., treas., 1979-80), LWV (bd. dirs. Dade County chpt. 1988-92), Fla. Consortium Sch.-Based Health Ctrs. (sec. 2001-03), Healthy Start Coalition of Miami-Dade County (v.p. 2002-). Office: Audubon of Fla 444 Brickell AveSte 850 Miami FL 33131 Office Phone: 305-371-6399. E-mail: clynch@audubon.org.

LYNCH, CHARLOTTE ANDREWS, retired communications executive, consultant; b. Fall River, Mass., Mar. 25, 1928; d. Alan Hall and Florence (Worthen) Andrews; m. Francis Bradley Lynch, June 7, 1952; children: Sarah Faldetta, Richard, Stephen, William. AB in Philosophy, Radcliffe Coll., 1950; postgrad., U. Bridgeport, 1969-71. Adminstrv. asst. Mass. Congl. Confs. and Missionary Soc., Boston, 1951-52; journalist Town Crier newspaper, Westport, Conn., 1968; asst. dir. devel. Cape Cod Hosp., Hyannis, Mass., 1975-76; parish adminstr. S. Congl. Ch., Centerville, Mass., 1976-83; cons. to ethnic advt. agy. Loiminchay, Inc., N.Y.C., 1992-98; ret. Mem. Radcliffe Club Cape Cod (v.p. 1990-97, pres. 1997-2000, exec. com. 1990-2000), Harvard Club of Boston. Republican. Roman Catholic. Avocation: travel.

LYNCH, DIANE, volunteer; d. Gerald Charles and Karen L. Lynch; 1 child, Thomas. Diploma, Diesel Inst. of Am., Md., 1998. Firefighter MIFRI, Md., cert. tree care Md., 1994. Forest and pks. employee Md. Conservation Corps., Anapolis, 1993—94; firefighter Bowmans Addition Vol. Fire Dept., Cumberland, Md., 1993—95; environ. coord. AmeriCorps Frostburg (Md.) St. U., 1995; cook Penn Alps Restaurant, Grantsville, Md., 2001. Coun. mem. Md. Conservation Corps, 1994. Vol. Boy Scouts of Am., 2002. Avocations: fishing, camping, cooking. Mailing: 96 Jackson St Lonaconing MD 21539

LYNCH, JANET NICHOLS, English language educator, writer; b. Sacramento, Calif., Oct. 3, 1952; d. William Rolland and Lena Donna (Graifemberg) Nichols; m. Timothy Edward Lynch, June 30, 1984; children: Caitlin Grace, Sean Nichols. BA in Music, Calif. State U., Sacramento, 1974; MusM in Piano, Ariz. State U., 1976; MFA in Creative Writing, Calif. State U., Fresno, 2002. Music instr. De Ariza Coll., Cupertino, Calif., 1980—90, Skyline Coll., San Bruno, Calif., 1981—90; critic Children's Book Rev. Mag., Altadena, Calif., 1995—97; music and English instr. Coll. of the Sequoias, Visalia, Calif., 1995—. Author: (book) American Music Makers, 1990, Women Music Makers, 1992, (juvenile novel) Casey Wooster's Pet Care Service, 1993; contbr. short stories to anthologies. Mem.: Calif. Assn. Tchrs. English, Nat. Guild Piano Tchrs. Avocations: competing in triathlons and marathons, swimming, running, bicycling. Office: Coll of the Sequoias Dept English 915 S Mooney Blvd Visalia CA 93277

LYNCH, JESSICA, military officer; b. Palestine, W. Va., Apr. 26, 1983; d. Gregory O. and Deadra Lynch. Army Pvt. First Class, Hon. Med. Disability Discharge, 2003. Decorated Purple Heart, Bronze Star, POW Medal; recipient Miss Congeniality, Wirt County Fair. Achievements include first POW/MIA recovered from Operation: Iraqi Freedom; subject of songs, poems, tributes, TV movies and reports; subject of Rick Bragg biography: I Am A Soldier Too: The Jessica Lynch Story, 2003; created the Jessica Lynch Found. to educate children of veterans.*

LYNCH, LORETTA, state agency administrator; JD, Yale U. Ptnr. Keker & Van Nest; dir. Gov. Davis' Office of Planning & Rsch.; pres. Calif. Pub. Utilities Commn., San Francisco, 2000—. Office: CPUC 505 Van Ness Ave San Francisco CA 94102

LYNCH, LORETTA E. lawyer, former prosecutor; b. Durham, N.C., May 21, 1959; d. Lorenzo Lynch. Grad., Harvard Coll., 1981; JD, Harvard U., 1984. Bar: N.Y., U.S. Dist. Ct. (ea. dist. NY), U.S. Dist. Ct. (so. dist. NY), U.S. Ct. Appeals (2nd cir.). Litigation assoc. Cahill, Gordon & Reindel, 1984-90; with Office of U.S. Atty. for Ea. Dist. of N.Y., 1990—2001; chief L.I. offices, 1994-98; chief asst. U.S. States Atty., 1998—99; U.S. atty. ea. dist. N.Y. U.S. Dept. Justice, Bklyn., 2000—01; ptnr. Hogan & Hartson LLP, 2002—. Instr. Dept. Justice Criminal Trial Advocacy Prog.; adj. prof. St. John's Univ. Sch. Law; bd. dir. Fed. Reserve Bank N.Y., Office of the Appellate Defender; trustee Nat. Inst. Trial Advocacy; mem. Magistrate Judge Selection Panel Ea. Dist. N.Y., Judicial Screening Panel of Sen. Charles Schumer, NYC Charter Revision Commn. Bd. dirs. Nat. Inst. Law and Equity. Mem.: Ea. Dist Com. on Civil Litigation, Fed. Bar. Coun., Assn. Bar N.Y.C. Criminal Law Com. (chair). Avocations: reading, tennis. Office: Hogan & Hartson 875 Third Ave New York NY 10022

LYNCH, MARGARET A. state legislator; b. Keene, N.H., Sept. 10, 1939; 4 children. BA, Keene State Coll., 1979. Ret. coll. adminstr.; mem. dist. 19 N.H. Ho. of Reps., mem. appropriations com., fin. com. Roman Catholic. Home: 94 Hurricane Rd Keene NH 03431-2107 Office: NH Ho of Reps State Capitol Concord NH 03301

LYNCH, NANCY ANN, computer scientist, educator; b. Bklyn., Jan. 19, 1948; d. Roland David and Marie Catherine (Adinolfi) Evraets; m. Dennis Christopher Lynch, June 14, 1969; children: Patrick, Kathleen (dec.), Mary. BS, Bklyn. Coll., 1968; PhD, MIT, 1972. Asst. prof. math. Tufts U., Medford, Mass., 1972-73, U. So. Calif., Los Angeles, 1973-76, Fla. Internat. U., Miami, 1976-77; assoc. prof. computer sci. Ga. Tech. U., Atlanta, 1977-82, MIT, Cambridge, 1982-86, prof. computer sci., 1986—, NEC prof. software sci. and engrng., 1996—. Ellen Swallow Richards chair MIT, 1982-87, Cecil H. Green chair, 1994-96. Contbr. numerous articles to profl. jours. Fellow Assn. Computing Machinery. Roman Catholic. Office: MIT NE43-365 Lab for Computer Sci Cambridge MA 02139

LYNCH, PATRICIA GATES, broadcasting organization executive consultant, former ambassador; b. Newark, Apr. 20, 1926; d. William Charles and Mary Frances Lawrence; m. Mahlon Eugene Gates, Dec. 19, 1942 (div. 1972); children: Pamela Townley Gates, Lawrence Alan Gates; m. William Dennis Lynch. Student, Dartmouth Inst., 1975. Broadcaster Sta. WFAX Radio, Falls Ch., Va., 1958—68; pub. TV host Sta. WETA, Washington, 1967—68; broadcaster NBC-Radio, Europe, Iran, USSR, 1960—61; internat. broadcaster, producer Voice of Am., Washington, 1962—69; staff asst. to First Lady The White House, Washington, 1969—70; host Voice of Am. Breakfast Show, Morning show, 1970—86; U.S. amb. to Madagascar and the Comoros, 1986—89; dir. corp. affairs Radio Free Europe/Radio Liberty, Washington, 1989—94; chmn. bd. Assn. Diplomatic Studies & Tng.-Fgn. Svc. Inst. Dept. State, Arlington, Va., 1998—. Worldwide lectr., 1968—86; adv. com. Ind. Fed. Savs. and Loan Assn., Washington, 1970—86. Author stories on Am. for English teaching dept. Radio Sweden, 1967—68, others on internat. broadcasting. Chair internat. svc. com. Washington chpt. ARC, 1979—86; bd. visitors Duke U. Primate Ctr., Durham, NC. Recipient Pub. Svc. award, U.S. Army, 1960; grantee USIA, 1983. Mem.: Washington Inst. Fgn. Affairs (bd. dirs.), Am. News Women's Club, Am. Women in Radio and TV (Washington chpt. pres. 1966—67), Coun. Am. Ambs. (v.p., bd. dirs.), Am. Acad. Diplomacy (bd. dirs. 2003—). Republican. Episcopalian. Avocations: reading, volunteer work, wildlife conservation. Fax: 410-586-9336.

LYNCH, PRISCILLA A. nursing educator, therapist; b. Joliet, Ill., Jan. 8, 1949; d. LaVerne L. and Ann M. (Zamkovitz) L. BS, U. Wyo., 1973; MS, St. Xavier Coll., Coll., 1981. RN, Ill. Staff nurse Rush-Presbyn.-St. Luke's Med. Ctr., Chgo., 1977-81, psychiat.-liaison cons., 1981-83, asst. prof. nursing, unit dir., 1985—. Mgr. and therapist Oakside Clinic, Kankakee, Ill., 1987—; mem. adv. bd. Depressive and Manic Depression Assn., Chgo., 1986—; mem. consultation and mental health unit Riverside Med. Ctr., Kankakee, 1987—; speaker numerous nat. orgns. Contbr. numerous abstracts to profl. jours., chpts. to books. Bd. dirs. Cornerstone Svcs., ARC of Ill. Recipient total quality mgmt. award Rush-Presbyn.-St. Luke's Med. Ctr., 1991, named mgr. of the quarter, 1997, Wayne Lerner Leadership award, 1998. Mem. APNA, ISPN, Ill. Nurses Assn. (coms.), Coun. Clin. Nurse Specialists, Profl. Nursing Staff (sec. 1985-87, mem. coms.). Presbyterian. Home: 606 Darcy Ave Joliet IL 60436-1673 Office Phone: 312-942-5100. E-mail: priscilla_lynch@rush.edu.

LYNCH, SANDRA LEA, federal judge; b. Oak Park, Ill., July 31, 1946; d. Bernard Francis and Eugenia Tyus Lynch; married; 1 child. AB in Philosophy, Wellesley Coll., 1968; JD cum laude, Boston U., 1971. Bar: Mass. 1971, U.S. Supreme Ct. 1974. Law clk. to Hon. Raymond J. Pettine U.S. Dist. Ct., Providence; asst. atty. gen. Commonwealth of Mass., Boston, 1974; gen. counsel Mass. Dept. Edn., Boston, 1974—78; ptnr. Foley, Hoag & Eliot, Boston, 1978—95; judge 1st cir. U.S. Ct. Appeals, Boston, 1995—. Contbr. articles to profl. jours. Past co-chair leading industries com. Greater Boston C. of C. Recipient Disting. Alumnae award, Boston U. Law Sch., 1993, Wellesley Coll., 1997, Disting. Svc. award, Planned Parenthood, 1991. Mem.: ABA, Boston Bar Assn. (pres. 1992—93, Jud. Excellence award 2001), Mass. Bar Assn., Nat. Assn. Women Judges, Women's Forum. Office: US Ct Appeals One Courthouse Way Ste 8710 Boston MA 02210-3010

LYNCH, SHARON GLYNN, neurologist, educator; b. Lake Charles, La., July 23, 1958; d. Lynden Wayne and Martha (Schunke) L. BS, U. South Ala., 1979; MD, U. Ala., 1984. Diplomate Am. Bd. Psychiatry and Neurology. Intern in internal medicine U. Utah, 1984-85, resident in neurology, 1985-88, postdoctoral fellow in immunogenetics, 1988-91; assoc. prof., dir. multiple sclerosis clinic U. Kans. Med. Sch., Kansas City, 1991—. NIH grantee, 1996. Mem. AAAS, Am. Acad. Neurology, Nat. Multiple Sclerosis Soc. (bd. dirs. Mid-Am. chpt. 1995—, postdoctoral fellow 1988-91, Profl. Svcs. award 1993, 97, grantee 1987, 91), Soc. for Creative Anachronism. Avocations: harp, tapestry weaving, cooking. Office: U Kans Med Sch Dept Neurology 3901 Rainbow Blvd Kansas City KS 66160-0001

LYNCH, SHERRY KAY, counselor; b. Nov. 20, 1957; d. Robert Emmett and Norma Lea Lynch. BA, Randolph-Macon Woman's Coll., 1979; MS, Emporia State U., 1980; PhD, Kans. State U., 1987. Vocat. rehab. counselor Rehab. Svcs., Topeka, 1980-81, cmty. program cons., 1981-86; counseling intern Winthrop Coll., Rock Hill, S.C., 1986-87; counselor Ripon (Wis.) Coll., 1987-90, Va. Poly. Inst. and State U., 1991—. Mem. exec. com. Sexual Assault Counseling Program, Topeka, 1983-86, recruitment coord., 1983-86, counselor, 1981-86, Nat. Singles Conf. Planning Com., Green Lake, Wis., 1987-90; area admissions rep. Randolph-Macon Woman's Coll., Lynchburg, Va., 1981-87; mem. Student Outreach Schs. coun. Northbrooke Hosp., 1988-90; mem. Student Affairs Devel. Com., 1991-94, chairperson, 1992-94, mem. Sexual Assault Victim Edn. and Support Com., 1991-95, Wellness Com., 1993-2000, Leadership Resource Team, 1994-96; bd. dirs., sec. Ripon Chem. Abuse and Awareness Program, 1987-90; bd. dirs. New River Family Shelter, sec., 1993-98, chair pers. com., 1999-2000; pro bono counselor Mental Health Assn. of New River Valley, 2002—; clin. mental health counselor certification exam com. Nat. Bd. Cert. Counselors, 1996—. Bd. dirs. Haymarket Sq. Homeowners Assn., 1992—, treas., 1993—; chairperson ch. and soc. com. Blacksburg United Meth. Ch., 1992-94, mem. coun. ministries, 1992-94; asst. class agt. Class of 1979, Randolph-Macon Woman's Coll., 2000—. Recipient Kans. 4-H Key award Ext. Svc. of Kans. State U., 1974; named Internat. 4-H Youth Exch. Amb. to France, 1977. Mem. Nat. Rehab. Counseling Assn. (bd. dirs. 1982-88, chairperson br. devel. subcoun. 1982-87, chairperson policy and program coun. 1987-88), Gt. Plains Rehab. Counseling Assn. (newsletter editor 1982-85, bd. dirs. 1983-87, pres. 1984-85, sec. 1986-87), Gt. Plains Rehab. Assn. (bd. dirs. 1983-85, awards chairperson 1984-85), Kans. Rehab. Counseling Assn. (bd. dirs. 1983-86, pres. 1984-85), Kans. Rehab. Assn. (bd. dirs. 1982-85, advt. chairperson 1983-85), Topeka Rehab. Assn. (bd. dirs. 1982-85, sec. 1982-83, pres. 1983-84), Am. Counseling Assn., Am. Coll. Pers. Assn. (chair-elect commn. VII counseling and psychol. svcs. 1995-96, chair 1996-98, past chair 1998-99, directorate body 1989-93, 95-99, membership commn. 1990-93, planning com. 1997-99, sec. 2000-02, exec. coun. 2000-02, Outreach and Advocacy Core Coun., sec. 1999-2000), Wis. Coll. Pers. Assn. (bd. dirs. 1988-90), Assn. for Specialists in Group Work, Va. Coll. Pers. Assn. Republican. Methodist. Avocation: tennis. Home: 2700 Newton Ct Blacksburg VA 24060-4112 Office: Va Tech Counseling Ctr 240 McComas Hall Blacksburg VA 24061 E-mail: sklynch@vt.edu.

LYNCH-POLANSKY, PATRICIA, health services executive; Diploma, Englewood (N.J.) Hosp., 1963; BSN, U. Pa., 1965; postgrad., Family Inst. of Westchester, 1979-81; MS in Cmty. Health, Rutgers U., 1981; postgrad., Columbia U., 1985-90. RN, N.J., Pa. Staff nurse Presbyn. Hosp., U. Pa., Phila., 1965-67; staff nurse, in-svc. instr. Mountainside Hosp., Montclair, N.J., 1973-77, asst. dir. nursing, 1977-78; v.p. nursing Union Hosp. an affiliate Saint Barnabas Health Care System, Union, N.J., 1980-82, v.p., 1982-84, v.p., COO, 1984-86, exec. v.p., adminstr., 1986-94, exec. v.p., COO, 1995-96; pres. The Millennium Group, Lewes, Del., 1995-97; exec. dir. divsn. law and pub. safety N.J. Bd. of Nursing, Newark, 1997—. Med. surg. clin. instr. Mountainside Hosp., 1977-79; adj. faculty Fairleigh Dickinson U., Rutherford, N.J., 1978-80; adj. faculty NYU, 1985—, U. Medicine and Dentistry of N.J., 1992-95, U. Pa., 1994—. Benefit com. Nutcracker, 1980-83; vol. Bloomfield chpt. Pop Warner Football Orgn.; vol. Montclair chpt. Boy Scouts Am.; vol. Am. Cancer Soc.; bd. dirs. Children of Chernobyl Relief Fund, 1992-97. Recipient Govs. Nursing Merit award Profl. Advanced Practice in Nursing, 1991; named Outstanding Alumna U. Pa. Coll. of Nursing, 1993. Mem. ANA, Am. Mgmt. Assn., Am. Orgn. of Nurse Execs., Am. Osteopathic Assn., Am. Coll. of Healthcare Execs., Am. Coll. of Osteopathic Healthcare Execs., Am. Pub. Health Assn., N.J. Assn. of Osteopathic Healthcare Exec., N.J. Hosp. Assn., N.J. State Nurses' Assn. (Adminstr. of Yr. award 1987, Roll of Honor 1992), N.J. League for Nursing, Nat. League for Nursing, Am. Heart Assn., Englewood Hosp. Sch. of Nursing Alumni Assn., U. Pa. Alumni Assn., William Custis Harrison Soc., Rutgers U. Alumnae Assn.

LYNCH SCHUSTER, JANICE MARIE, freelance/self-employed writer; b. Washington, Aug. 27, 1962; d. G. Dent and Mary Hourihan Lynch; m. Anthony Fowler, May 22, 1988 (div. Dec. 22, 1994); children: Conor Michael Fowler, Meredith Rose Fowler, Mary Alyson Lynch; m. Erik Stefan Schuster, Jan. 8, 1997; children: Devan P. Schuster, Chad J. Schuster, Ian Joseph. BS in Math., Guilford Coll., 1985; MFA in Creative Writing, Am. U., 1989. Freelance writer, Riva, Md., 1990—; comm. dir. Ams. for Better Care of the Dying, Washington, 1997—2003. Author: (non-fiction) Handbook for Mortals: Guidance for People Facing Serious Illness, 1999, Improving Care for the End of Life: A Sourcebook for Clinicians and Health Care Professionals, 2000. Mem.: Washington Ind. Writers. Avocations: swimming, reading. Home: 421 Granville Rd Riva MD 21140 Personal E-mail: abcdwriter421@aol.com.

LYNDRUP, PEGGY B. lawyer; b. Winnipeg, Can., Mar. 27, 1949; BS in Edn. magna cum laude, U. N.D., 1969; MEd, Kent State U., 1971; JD summa cum laude, U. Louisville, 1979. Bar: Ky. 1979, U.S. Dist. Ct. (we. dist.) Ky. 1979, U.S. Dist. Ct. (ea. dist.) Ky. 1981. Atty. Greenebaum Doll & McDonald, PLLC, Louisville, 1979—. Recipient Disting. Alumnus award U. Louisville Sch. Law, 1989; Brandeis scholar. Mem. ABA, Louisville Bar Assn. (pres. 1989). Office: Greenbaum Doll & McDonald PLLC 3300 National City Tower Louisville KY 40202 E-mail: pbl@gdm.com.

LYNE, DOROTHY-ARDEN, secondary school educator; b. Orangeburg, N.Y., Mar. 9, 1928; d. William Henry and Janet More (Freston) Dean; m. Thomas Delmar Lyne, Aug. 16, 1952 (div. June 1982); children: James Delmar, Peter Freston, Jennifer Dean. BA, Ursinus Coll., 1949; MA, Fletcher Sch. Law and Diplomacy, 1950. Assoc. editor World Peace Found., Boston, 1950-51; editorial assoc. Carnegie Endowment Internat. Peace, N.Y.C., 1951-52; dir. Assoc. of Internat. Rels. Clubs, N.Y.C., 1952-53; editor The Town Crier, Westport, Conn., 1966-68; editorial assoc. Machinery Allied Products Inst., Wash., 1959-63; tchr. Helen Keller Mid. Sch., Easton, Conn., 1967-89. Vice chmn. Cooperative Edn. Svcs., Fairfield, 1983-85. Editor: Documents in American Foreign Rels., 1950, Current Rsch. in Internat. Affairs, 1951. Chmn. Westport Zoning Bd. of Appeals, 1976-80, Westport Bd. of Edn., 1985-87; vice chmn. Westport Bd. of Edn., 1980-85; mem. Westport Charter Revision Commn., 1966-67. Republican. Episcopalian.

LYNE, SUSAN MARKHAM, former broadcast executive; b. Boston, Apr. 30, 1950; d. Eugene and Ruth (Lally) L.; m. George Crile III; children: Susan Markham, Jane Halle; stepchildren: Katherine Murphy, Elizabeth McCook. Assoc. editor City Mag., San Francisco, 1975-76; west coast editor New Times, San Francisco, 1976-77, mng. editor N.Y.C., 1978, The Village Voice, N.Y.C., 1978-82; v.p. creative devel. IPC Films, N.Y.C., 1982-85; ptnr. Lazar/Lyne Films, N.Y.C., 1985-86; founding editor Premiere mag., N.Y.C., 1987-96; exec. v.p. Walt Disney Motion Picture Group, 1996—98; exec. v.p. movies and miniseries ABC Entertainment, 1998—2002, pres., 2002—04. Bd. dirs. Lifetime Network, 1996—, Pub. Theater. Mem. Am. Soc. Mag. Editors (bd. dirs. 1993-96).

LYNN, BARBARA MICHELE, judge; b. Binghamton, N.Y., Sept. 19, 1952; d. Stanley Donald and Nelda Ruth (Brounstein) Golden; m. Michael Paige Lynn, Aug. 12, 1973; children: Tara Paige, Whitney Reed. BA with distinction, U. Va., 1973; JD summa cum laude, So. Meth. U., 1976. Bar: U.S. Dist. Ct. (no. dist.) Tex. 1976, U.S. Ct. Appeals (5th and 11th cirs.) 1981, U.S. Dist. Ct. (we. dist.) Tex. 1983, U.S. Dist. Ct. (ea. dist.) Tex. 1986, U.S. Dist. Ct. (so. dist.) Tex. 1991, U.S. Supreme Ct. 1987. Assoc. Carrington, Coleman, Sloman & Blumenthal, Dallas, 1976-83, ptnr., 1983-99; judge U.S. Dist. Ct., Dallas, 2000—. Instr. Nat. Inst. Trial Advocacy, 1979—. Master Higginbotham Inn of Ct.; fellow Am. Coll. Am. Coll. Trial Lawyers; mem. ABA (chmn. comml. litigation 1989-91, dir. of divs. 1992-93, coun. litigation sect. 1993-96, sect. chair 1998-99), Am. Bar Found., Dallas Assn. Young Lawyers, Dallas Bar Assn. (bd. dirs. 1985-88), Tex. Bar Found., Dallas Bar Found. Office: US Dist Ct 1100 Commerce St Rm 15e26 Dallas TX 75242-1495

LYNN, D. JOANNE, physician, ethicist, health services researcher; b. Oakland, Md., July 2, 1951; d. John B. and Mary Dorcas (Clark) Harley; m. Barry W. Lynn; children: Christina, Nicholas. BS summa cum laude, Dickinson Coll., 1970; MD cum laude, Boston U., 1974; MA in Philosophy and Social Policy, George Washington U., 1981; MS Clin. Evaluative Scis., Dartmouth Coll., 1995. Diplomate Am. Bd. Internal Medicine. Resident internal Medicine The George Washington U. Med. Ctr., 1974-77; emergency rm. physician, triage physician Washington VA Hosp., 1977-78;

faculty assoc. for medicine and humanities divsn. experimental programs George Washington U., Washington, 1978-81, dir. divsn. aging studies, 1988-92, prof. health care scis. and medicine, 1991-92, assoc. chairperson dept. health care scis., 1990-92, dir of the Ctr. to Improve the Care of the Dying, 1995-2000; prof. medicine, cmty. and family medicine, sr. assoc. Ctr. Evaluative Clin. Scis. Dartmouth-Hitchcock Med. Ctr., Hanover, N.H., 1992-95, assoc. dir. Ctr. for Aging, 1992-95; dir. RAND Ctr. for Improve Care of the Dying, Arlington, Va., 2000—02; pres. Ams. for Better Care of the Dying, 1995—; dir. The Washington Home Ctr. for Palliative Care Studies, 2002—. Robert Wood Johnson clin. scholar George Washington U., 1977-78, sr. fellow Ctr. Health Policy Rsch., 1991-92; asst. dir. med. studies The Pres. Commn. for Study of Ethical Problems in Medicine and Biomed. and Behavioral Rsch., 1981-83; med. dir. The Washington Home, 1983-89, Hospice of Washington, 1979-91, George Washington Cancer Home Care Program and Home Health Svcs. of The Washington Home, 1990-92, staff physician, 1979-92; fellow Hastings Ctr., 1984—; mem. working group on guidelines for care of terminally ill, 1985-87, rsch. project on ethical issues in care and treatment of chronically ill, 1985-87, working group on new physician-patient relationship, 1991-94, v.p., 1987, chair fellows nominating com., 1991; mem. coordinating coun. on life-sustaining med. treatment decision making by cts. Nat. Ctr. State Cts., 1989-93; fellow Kennedy Inst., 1991; mem. geriat. and gerontology adv. com. Dept. Vet. Affairs, 1991-97; mem. bioethics com. Vets. Health Adminstrn., 1991-93; active Washington Area Seminar on Sci., Tech., and Ethics, 1982-92, Nat. Clin. Panel on High-Cost Hospice Care, Washington, 1991; presenter in field. Author: (with J. Harrold) Handbook for Mortals: Guidance for People Facing Serious Illness, 1999, (with A. Kabamell and J. Lynch Schuster) Improving Care for the End of Life: A Sourcebook for Health Care Managers and Clinicians, 2000; author chpts. to books; mem. editl. bd. The Ency. of Bioethics, 1994-95; mem. adv. editl. bd. Biolaw, 1983, The Hospice Jour., 1984—, Med. Ethics for the Physician, 1985-92, Med. Humanities Rev., 1986—, Cambridge Quar., 1991-95; contbr. articles, revs. to profl. jours. Peter Jeffries and Jeanne Arnold scholar, 1973; recipient Wellington Parlin Sci. Scholarship award, 1979, Dr. Bertha Curtis prize Boston U. Med. Sch., 1974, Nat. Bd. award Med. Coll. Pa., 1992. Fellow ACP (mem. subcom. on aging 1986-91), Am. Geriatrics Soc. (mem. com. public policy 1983-98, mem. ethics com. 1988, chair subcom. on ethics and policy 1986, chair ethics com. 1991-98, bd. dirs. 1991-97); mem. AAAS, APHA, Am. Fedn. Clin. Rsch., Am. Health Care Assn. (mem. task force on AIDS 1987-89), Am. Hosp. Assn. (mem. spl. com. on biomedical ethics 1983-85, 89-94), Am. Med. Dirs. Assn., Am. Soc. Law and Medicine, Am. Coll. Health Care Adminstrs. (mem. nat. adv. com. wandering patients 1987-88), Nat. Inst. on Aging (mem. senile dementia of Alzheimer's type, mem. rsch. ethics task force 1981-82, Am. Geriatrics Soc. rep. 1984-86), Soc. Health and Human Values (mem. gov. coun. 1981-84), Inst. Medicine (mem. com. on future issues in med. tech. devel. 1992-94), N.H. Med. Soc., Soc. Health and Human Values (mem. gov. coun. 1981-84), Internat. Hospice Inst. (mem. physician's adv. com. 1984-86), Med. Soc. D.C. (mem. legis. affairs com. 1985-92, vice chairperson 1991-92), Soc. Gen. Internal Medicine (mem. editl. adv. bd. Jour. 1988-91), Inst. of Medicine, Americans for Better Care of the Dying (pres.). Home: The Washington Home Ctr for Palliative Care Studies 4200 Wisconsin Ave NW 4th Fl Washington DC 20016 E-mail: JLynn@medicaring.org.

LYNN, ENID, retired artistic director; b. Hartford, Conn., Oct. 30, 1947; d. Morton S. Rosenthal and Harriet (Schloss) Rosenthal; m. John L. Dollard, Aug. 28, 1983. AA, Hartford Coll. for Women, 1967; BFA, Hartt Sch., West Hartford, Conn., 1997. Dir. Sch. of Hartford Ballet, 1971—2001; dir. dance divsn. Hartt Sch., West Hartford, 1994—2001; co-artistic dir. Hartford Ballet, 1998—2001. Evaluator Nat. Assn. Schs. of Dance, Reston, Va., 1980, pres., mem. of bd., 1979—98; cons. in field. Choreographer Hartt Sch., 1970—73, Hartford Ballet, 1970—79; co-author: textbooks on dance, 1985, 87. Mem. task force Dance USA, Washington, 1991, 1993, 1994. Recipient Renaissance award, Greater Hartford Downtown Coun., 1976, Women in Leadership award, YWCA, 1983. Mem.: Conn. Assn. for Health, Phys. Edn., Recreation and Dance, Conn. Alliance for Arts Edn. (bd. dirs. 1992—, Profl. Merit award 1995).

LYNN, EVADNA SAYWELL, investment analyst; b. Oakland, Calif., June 16, 1935; d. Lawrence G. Saywell; m. Richard Keppie Lynn, Dec. 28, 1962; children: Douglas, Melisa. BA, MA in Econs., U. Calif., Berkeley. CFA. With Dean Witter, San Francisco, 1958-61, 70-71, Dodge & Cox, San Francisco, 1961-69; fin. analyst, v.p. Clark, Dodge & Co., San Francisco, 1971-73, Wainwright Securities, N.Y.C., 1977-78; 1st v.p. Merrill Lynch Capital markets, N.Y.C., 1978-90; sr. v.p. Dean Witter Reynolds, N.Y.C., 1990-97; forest products cons., San Francisco, 1997—. Mem. Assn. for Investment Mgmt. and Rsch., San Francisco Security Analysts (treas. 1973-74), Fin. Women's Club San Francisco (pres. 1967). Office: Apt F 1824 Jackson St San Francisco CA 94109-2873

LYNN, EVELYN JOAN, state senator, consultant; b. N.Y., Feb. 2, 1930; d. Leo A. and Helen (Shep) Hoes. BA in Psychology, Queens Coll., N.Y., 1950; MA English and Edn., Stetson U., 1969; EdD, U. Fla., 1979. Cons. for bus., edn. and govt., 1979—; rep. Fla. Ho. Dist. 27, Fla., 1994—2002. Bd. dirs. Boys and Girls Clubs; mem. adv. bd. Annie and Casey Found. Mem. Nat. Coun. State Legislators (com. vice chair). Home: PO Box 4236 Ormond Beach FL 32175-4236

LYNN, JUDITH, opera singer, artist, voice teacher; b. Chgo. d. Louis Leo and Mollie (Rudman) Cogan; m. Filippo Joseph DeStefano, Dec. 26, 1965. Student, LA Conservatory Music & Art, 1959-62, U. Vienna, 1964; Hon. Tchg. Degree, Conservatorio de Musica, Maracay, Venezuela, 1987; student, Fashion Inst. Tech., 1987-91; pvt. student music and voice, Filippo De Stefano; coaching, Giuseppe Pais, Lina Pagliughi, Felix Popper, Ruth and Mario Chamlee, Richard Hageman; student art, Albert & Yolanda Pels, Opera Linca De Stefano, Caracas, Venezuela. Sec.-treas. De Stefano Presents, N.Y.C., 1991—. V.p., mus. adminstr., 1983-87; sec., treas. De Stefano Presents, Inc., NYC, 1991—. Exhibited paintings at Casade la Cultura, Maracay, Venezuela, Bayside NY in the Bayside Hist. Soc., House of George in NYC, NY Hilton, and Towers, and The Pen and Brush Club, paintings such as Galeria EuroAmericano, Caracas, Ateneo de Los Teques Recipient 1st prize (voice) Ebell of LA, 1960, winner Am. Opera Auditions, 1963 (debut in Milan, Italy), 3d prize painting Salon Imagen and Grumbacher, Venezuela, 1984. Assoc. mem. Am. Watercolor Soc. Office: The Ansonia/Studio 14-40 2109 Broadway New York NY 10023-2106 E-mail: jlynnart@mindspring.com., destefanopresent@mindspring.com.

LYNN, KRISTINA, journalist, actress, writer, producer; b. Dayton, Ohio, Apr. 18, 1954; d. Donald Louis Craddock and Carol Rose (Righthouse) Guthrie; m. Gerald Lee Diez, Oct. 19, 1985 (div. Aug. 1988). BA with honors in Speech, English and Theatre, U. West Ga., 1976; postgrad. in Psychology, Ga. State U., 1978. Tchr., drama dir. Redan H.S., Stone Mountain, Ga., 1976-78; co-hostess Am. Radio Network, Balt., 1988-90; co-host, interviewer WNTR Radio, Washington, 1988-91; pres., owner Lynn Prodns., L.A., Atlanta, N.Y.C., 1985—. Spkr., tchr., coord. Learning Annex, Washington, 1987-91; corr. Joan Rivers Show, N.Y.C., 1992, Geraldo Show; corr., reporter Paramount TV, L.A., 1993-99; corr. celebrity reporter E Entertainment TV, L.A., 1995-96; corr., reporter, anchor Backstage Prodns., Nashville, 1994-97; host Dishin' Up Country T.V., Dishin' Up In the Country Kitchen, Vital Force Entertainment; mem., film festival asst. chair Women in Film, Washington, N.Y.C., 1988-92; talent coord. One Light Project, Dream Castle Prodns., 1999. Dir. (theatre) Plaza Suite, 1977 (1st place region competition award 1977), Sorry Wrong Number, 1978 (2d place region competition award 1978). Bd. dirs. Child Savers, Inc., Rockville, Md., 1991-96, fund raiser, 1991-96. Mem. AFTRA (mem. outreach program 1996, press dir. world music awards, Monaco), N.Am. Rec. Industry and Songwriters Assn., Talk Radio Assn. (bd. dirs. 1996), Nashville Songwriters Assn., Screen Actors Guild (vol. womens com. 1985), Women in Music Bus. Assn. (chmn. com. 1994-95), Phi Kappa Phi, Phi Alpha Gamma. Democrat. Roman Catholic. Avocations: singing, songwriting, dance, filmmaking, swimming. Home: 8750 Mount Rushmore Dr Alpharetta GA 30022-6888 E-mail: klyn30022@yahoo.com.

LYNN, LORETTA WEBB (MRS. OLIVER LYNN JR.), singer; b. Butcher Hollow, Ky., Apr. 14, 1935; d. Ted and Clara (Butcher) Webb; m. Oliver V. Lynn, Jr., Jan. 10, 1948; children— Betty Sue Lynn Markworth, Jack Benny (dec.), Clara Lynn Lyell, Ernest Ray, Peggy, Patsy. Student pub. schs. Sec.-treas. Loretta Lynn Enterprises; v.p. United Talent, Inc.; hon. chmn. bd. Loretta Lynn Western Stores. Country vocalist with MCA records, 1961— (numerous gold albums); most recent album Just a Woman, 1985, (with Conway Twitty) Making Believe, 1988, Greatest Hits Live, 1992, The Country Music Hall of Fame, 1991, Country's Favorite Daughter (reissue), 1993. Author: Coal Miner's Daughter, 1976; appearance (TV movie) Loretta Lynn: The Seasons of My Life, 1992, Big Dreams and Broken Hears: The Dottie West Story, 1995; discs include (boxed set) Honky Tonk Girl: The Loretta Lynn Collection, 1994, (MCA special products) Hymns, 1995, Christmas Without Daddy, 1995, On Tour #1, 1996, On Tour #2, 1996, 20th Century Masters: The Millenium Collection, 1999, Still Woman Enough, 2000. Hon. rep. United Giver's Fund, 1971. Named Country Music Assn. Female Vocalist of Year 1967, 72, 73, Entertainer of Year, 1972, named Top Duet of 1972, 73, 74, 75; recipient Grammy award 1971, Am. Music award 1978, named Entertainer of Decade, Acad. Country Music 1980; inducted into Country Music Hall of Fame, 1988; first country female vocalist to record certified Gold album. Office: care United Talent Inc PO Box 23470 Nashville TN 37202-3470

LYNN, NAOMI B. academic administrator; b. N.Y.C., Apr. 16, 1933; d. Carmelo Burgos and Maria (Lebron) Berly; m. Robert A. Lynn, Aug. 28, 1954; children: Mary Louise, Nancy Lynn Francis, Judy Lynn Chance, Jo-An Lynn Cooper. BA, Maryville (Tenn.) Coll., 1954; MA, U. Ill., 1958; PhD, U. Kans., 1970. Instr. polit. sci. Cen. Mo. State Coll., Warrensburg, Mo., 1966-68; asst. prof. Kans. State U., Manhattan, 1970-75, assoc. prof., 1975-80, acting dept. head, prof., 1980-81, head polit. sci. dept., prof., 1982-84; dean Coll. Pub. and Urban Affairs, prof. Ga. State U., Atlanta, 1984-91; chancellor U. Ill., Springfield, 1991-2001, chancellor emerita, 2001—. Cons. fed., state and local govts., Manhattan, Topeka, Altanta, 1981-91; bd. dirs. Bank One Springfield; bd. trustees Maryville Coll., 1997—. Author: The Fulbright Premise, 1973; editor: Public Administration, The State of Discipline, 1990, Women, Politics and the Constitution, 1990; contbr. articles and textbook chpts. to profl. pubs. Bd. dirs. United Way of Sangamon County, 1991-98, Ill. Symphony Orch., 1992-95, Urban League, 1993-99, Ill. State Mus. Soc., 2002—. Recipient Disting. Alumni award Maryville Coll., 1986; fellow Nat. Acad. Pub. Adminstrn. Mem. Nat. Assn. Schs. Pub. Affairs and Adminstrn. (nat. pres.), Am. Soc. Pub. Adminstrn. (nat. pres. 1985-86), Am. Polit. Sci. Assn. (mem. exec. coun. 1981-83, trustee 1993—96, Am. Assn. State Colls. and Univs. (bd. dirs.), Midwest Polit. Sci. Assn. (mem. exec. coun. 1976-79), Women's Caucus Polit. Sci. (pres. 1975-76), Greater Springfield C. of C. (bd. dirs. 1991-99, mem. U.S. Senate jud. nominations commn. State Ill. 1999-2001), Cosmos Club, Pi Sigma Alpha (nat. pres.). Presbyterian.

LYNN, SHARON, artist; b. Bethesda, Md., Apr. 1, 1952; d. Jean Doris (McDermott) Jacobs; m. Necdet Senhart, Oct. 24, 1976; 1 child, Ben. BA, SUNY, N.Y.C., 1994. Art dir. Pompeii Prodns., N.Y.C.; v.p. Bliss Street, Inc. Solo exhibitions at Pierce Coll., Athens, Greece, Beachcomber, Jacksonville Beach, Fla., Halstead's, N.Y.C., Bot. Gardens, N.Y.C.

LYNOTT, MARGARET, state legislator; b. Trinidad, W.I. Mem. Swanzey Zoning Bd., 1988-91, mem. planning bd., 1988-96, chair, 1991-93; mem. S.W. Regional Planning Commn., 1992—; mem. dist. 11 N.H. Ho. of Reps., Concord, 1996—, mem. state-fed. rels. and vets. affairs coms., 1996—. Pres. Shamrock Real Estate Inc. Mem. Kiwanis (past pres., sec. Winchester chpt. 1993—). Office: NH State Legis State House Concord NH 03301

LYON, JOANNE B. psychologist; b. Little Rock, June 2, 1943; d. F. Ike and Marie (Graham) Beyer; m. James S. Lyon, Dec. 1971 (div. Sept. 1975), m. John M. Lofton, May 22, 1983 (dec. Feb. 1990). BA, Webster U., 1966; MEd, U. Mo., St. Louis, 1976, PhD, 1986. Lic. psychologist, Kans. Reading specialist Rockwood Sch. Dist., St. Louis, 1976-79; psychology cons. handicapped component St. Louis Head Start, 1982-83; intern Topeka State Hosp., 1983-84; dir. partial hosp. programs Family Svc. & Guidance Ctr., Topeka, 1985-89; pvt. practitioner and joint owner Shadow Wood Clin. Assocs., Topeka, 1989—, adminstr., 1999-2000. Clin. supr. Family Svc. and Guidance Ctr., Topeka, 1989-93; psychology adv. bd. Behavioral Scis. Regulatory Bd., 1996-98. Mem. exec. bd. Interfaith of Topeka, 1995-99, I Have a Dream Coalition, 1994-98; bd. dirs. Temple Beth Sholom Sisterhood, 1997-2000, Temple Beth Sholom, 1997-2000, Torah Learning Ctr., 2000—. Sherman scholar U. Mo., St. Louis, 1982. Mem. APA, Kans. Psychol. Assn., Am. Orthopsychiat. Assn., Soc. for Personality Assessment. Jewish. Home: 10027 Mackey Cir Overland Park KS 66212 Office: 8340 Mission Rd Prairie Village KS 66206 also: Ste 100 3669 SW Burlingame Topeka KS 66611

LYON, JOYCE, artist, art educator; b. N.Y., June 11, 1943; d. Emil and Irene Altura Selborn. BA, Barnard Coll., 1964, Pratt Inst., Bklyn., 1966; MFA, U. Minn., ., 1970. Cmty. educator various, Mpls., 1972—78; artist adv. WARM and CETA; dir. Feminist Perspectives, Womens Art Registry of Minn., 1981—85; asst. prof. dept. art U. Minn., Mpls., 1985—90, assoc. prof. dept. art, 1990—; adj. prof. Mpls. Coll. of Art and Design, 1990—96. Cons. mentor program WARM, Mpls., 2002—03; juror, artist fellowships Minn. State Arts Bd., 1993, 94. Exhibitions include Groveland Gallery, Mpls., 1997—, Dialogue in Place: Joyce Lyon & Andrea Thoma, U. Leeds and U. Minn., 2000, Witness and Legacy: Contemporary Art about the Holocaust, Minn. Mus., 1995—2002; author: Conversations with Rzeszow, 1992. Mem.: Women's Art Registry of Minn. (steering com., founding mem.), Coll. Art Assn. Avocation: gardening. Home: 2201 Dudley Ave Saint Paul MN 55108 Office: Art Dept Univ Minn 405 21 Ave S Minneapolis MN 55455

LYON, MARTHA SUE, research engineer, retired military officer; b. Oct. 3, 1935; d. Harry Bowman and Erma Louise (Moreland) Lyon. BA in Chemistry, U. Louisville, 1959; MEd in Math., Northeastern Ill. U., 1974; postgrad., McGeorge Sch. Law, 1981-82, Northwestern Calif. U., 1999—, George Washington U., 1995—96. Cert. tchr. Ill., Ky. Rsch. assoc. U. Louisville Med. Sch., 1959-61, 62-63; commd. ensign USNR, 1965; advanced through grades to commr. USN, 1983; instr. instrumentation chemistry Northwestern U., Evanston, Ill., 1968-70; tchr. sci., chemistry, gifted math. Waukegan (Ill.) pub. schs., 1970-75; phys. scientist Libr. of Congress, Washington, 1975-76; rsch. engr. Lockheed Missiles & Space Co., Sunnyvale, Calif., 1976-77; instr., assoc. chmn. dept. physics U.S. Naval Acad., Annapolis, Md., 1977-80; analyst sys. analysis divsn. Office of Chief of Naval Ops. Staff, Washington, 1980-81; comdg. officer Naval Rsch. Ctr., Stockton, Calif., 1981-83; mem. faculty Def. Intelligence Coll., 1983-85; program mgr. Space and Naval Warfare Sys. Command, 1985-86; commdg. officer PERSUPPACT Memphis, 1986-88; program mgr. Space and Naval Warfare Sys. Command, 1988-91; sect. chief Def. Intelligence Agy., 1991-95. Chief marching divsn. Nat. Homecoming Parade and N.Y.C. Regional Parade Task Force Desert Storm, 1991; contractor mgr. supporting spl. asst. to Sec. of Def. for Gulf War Illnesses Investigations, 1997—98; pro bono work for Class Act Group; Fla. chpt. svc. officer, comdr. dist. 4 DAV. Mem. citizen rev. panel Fla. Foster Care Project Marion County, 1999; mem. exec. com. Marion County Dem. Grantee, Am. Heart Assn., 1960—62, 1997—98, NSF, 1971, 1982. Mem.: Pvt. Investigators Assn. Va., Evidence Photographers' Internat. Coun., Internat. Soc. Bassists, Internat. Conf. Women in Sci. Engring. (protocol chair), Am. Soc. Photogrammetry, Am. Statis. Assn., Am. Fedn. Musicians, Soc. Women Engrs., Am. Chem. Soc., Mensa, Order Eastern Star, Delta Phi Alpha, Zeta Tau Alpha. Achievements include development of processes used in archival photography. E-mail: mslyon@att.net

LYON, MARY LOU, retired secondary school educator; b. Wichita, Kans., Sept. 18, 1926; d. Theodore Joseph and Hazel Pearl (Johnson) Cochran; m. William Madison Lyon, Mar. 15, 1944 (div. July 1970); children: William Madison, Jr., Theodore Richard. AA, Coll. San Mateo, Calif., 1958; BA with distinction and honors, San Jose (Calif.) State U., 1960, lifetime secondary credential, 1961, MA, 1967. Cert. secondary edn. tchr., Calif. Tchr. Los Gatos (Calif.) HS, 1961, Blach Jr. HS Los Altos (Calif.) Elem. Dist., 1961-62, Homestead High, Fremont Union HS Dist., Cupertino, Calif., 1962—93, Metropoltitan Adult educator program, San Jose, 1986—. Tchr. San Jose State U. Extension, Cupertino, 1974-76, Fremont Union High Sch. Adult Edn., 1977; various offices Calif. Coun. for Social Studies, Sacramento, 1962-80; historian, photographer Anza Trek Observance Bicentennial, Santa Clara County (Calif.) Bicentennial Commn., 1975-76; cons. Calif. map Hearne Bros. Map Co., 1981; speaker Genealogical Soc., San Jose Hist. Mus., Calif. Hist. Soc., Menlo Park Hist. Soc., Tulare County Hist. Soc., others. Author, editor (pamphlet) Social Sci. Rev., 1975-76, San Francisco Westerners News from Telegraph Hill 1995-, Santa Clara County Trailblazers, 1997-2002; ; author, numerous books on Santa Clara County, photographer (one-woman show) Cupertino Hist. Soc., 1975; photographer: (textbook) Addison Wesley, 1980, Chair of site & times Conf. Calif. hist. soc., 1985—; commr. Santa Clara County Hist. Heritage, 1994—2003; delegate Calif. State Sesquicentennial commn. for CCHS, 1998—2000. Recipient history honor, Phi Alpha Theta, 1959—60, Award of excellence for tchng. Calif. history, Conf. of Calif. Hist. Soc., 1973, Honored as an Achiever, Santa Clara County Penwomen, 1976, Coke Wood award, Conf. of Calif. Hist. Soc., 1994, 1997, award of merit, Calif. Pioneers of Santa Clara County, 1999, Pres. award, Conf. of Calif. Hist. Soc., 1999, 2002. Mem. Conf. Calif. Hist. Soc. (various offices 1973—, pres. 1983-84), Oreg.-Calif. Trail Assn. (publicity com. Calif.-Nev. Hawaii br. 1985—), Nat. Oreg.-Calif. Trail Assn., Westerners Internat. (bd. dirs.); mem. Cupertino Hist. Soc., San Jose Hist. Soc. (cons.), Santa Clara County Hist.Heritage Commn., Santa Clara County Pioneers, Golden Gate Park Assoc., Heritage Coun. of Santa Clara County, Lewis & Clark Hist. Assoc., Nat. Parks & Conservation Assoc., Menlo Park Hist. Soc., San Jose Hist. Mus. Assoc., Santa Fe Trail Assoc., Tulare County Hist. Soc., San Franciso Corral of Westerners sheriff, 1995, others. Democrat. Presbyterian. Avocations: photography, traveling, lecturing, western history. Home: 879 Lily Ave Cupertino CA 95014-4261

LYONS, BERYL BARTON ANFINDSEN, advertising executive; b. Jersey City, Dec. 12, 1925; d. Edward I. and Beatrice (Means) Anfindsen; m. Robert Lyons, Dec. 18, 1954; children: Susan E.L. Paglia, Robert Jr., Christopher B. Student, Traphagen Sch. Fashion Illustration, summer 1943-44, St. Elizabeth Coll., N.J., 1945-46; BA, Coll. N.Y.U., 1949. With Lord & Taylor, N.Y.C., 1949-52; jr. exec. Hahne & Co., Newark, 1952; hostess Statler Hotel, L.A., 1952; model Powers Modeling Agency, N.Y.C., 1952; mdse. demonstration REH, Wayne, N.J., 1978-94, Prestige Promotion, Wayne, 1978-94, McKenzie Assoc., Cape Cod, Mass., 1994-97; with promotional advt. dept. Checkers Product Servicing, Hopkinton, Mass., 1997—, Promotional Advt., Saco, Maine, 1997—2004, Fraser & Wagner, Scituate, Mass., 1997—2004, Suray Promotions, 2000—04. With Avon, 1971-2004, team leader, asst. mgr., 1971-78. Author numerous poems. Election worker Livingston, N.J., 1991, 92, 93. Scholar Phoenix Art Sch., 1944. Mem.: AAUW (life), Lunenburg Women's Club. Republican. Presbyterian. Avocations: art illustration, poetry, aerobic and aqua exercies, reading, grandchildren. Home: 500 Pennsylvania Ave Apt 208 Leominster MA 01453-7413

LYONS, ELISABETH HELENE, peer counselor; b. Hanover, N.H., Dec. 19, 1950; d. John B. and Mary P. (Johnson) Lyons. BA in Sociology-Psychology, Annhurst Coll., 1973; MEd in Counseling and Psychotherapy, Notre Dame Coll., Manchester, N.H., 1990. Active supportive svcs. to elderly Hanover Terrace Healthcare, 1981-86; mem. Com. on Accessiblity for Persons with Disabilities, Town of Hanover, 1986; active supportive svcs. Hanover Hill Health Care Ctr., Manchester, 1989-91; vol. Manchester Mental Health Ctr., 1991-92; active supportive svcs. to elderly Mt. Carmel Nursing Home, Manchester, 1991-92; peer support facilitator Granite State Ind. Living Found., Concord, N.H., 1983-86, 89—, activities planning com., 1990—, devel. com., 1991-92, bd. dirs., 1991—, svc. com., 1991—, pers. com., 1992—, by-laws com., 1994—; vol. Hospice, 1984—; mem. parish liaison com. St. Marie's Parish, 1991—, chair, 1992; mem. Manchester Transit Authority Adv. Bd., 1992—; social svc. vol. McKerley Health Care Ctr., Ridgewood, Manchester, 1992-95; mem. evaluation and assessment com. Statewide Ind. Living Coun., Concord, 1994, adminstrn. com., 1994—, pub. info. and liaison com., 1994—, exec. com., 1995—; bd. trustees Crotched Mountain Found., 1995—, program and svc. com., 3d vice chair, 1996—. Named Vol. of Yr., Gov. Sununu, Concord; recipient Peer Support Facilitator award, 1986, 89, 90, 91. Mem. ACA, N.H. Assn. Mental Health Counselors, N.H. Assn. Counseling and Devel. Roman Catholic. Avocation: reading. Home: 245 Main St Manchester NH 03102-4017

LYONS, GLORIA ROGERS, medical, surgical nurse, clinical nurse specialist; b. Durham, N.C., Sept. 2, 1940; d. Roy Lee Rogers and Annie Bullock; m. James Lyons, Dec. 26, 1965; children: Jamesia, Anthony. BSN, Winston-Salem State U., 1962; MS, Tex. Woman's U., 1979. Cert. clin. nurse specialist. Charge nurse obstetrics Duke U. Med. Ctr., Durham, NC, 1962—65; charge nurse ob-gyn. John Hopkins Hosp., Balt., 1966; pub. health nurse Long Branch Pub. Health Agency, Long Branch, NJ, 1968; clin. rsch. nurse Clin. Rsch. Labs, Edgewood Arsenal, Md., 1966—68; charge nurse surgery Long Branch Med. Ctr., Long Branch, NJ, 1968—69; instr. LVN program Marlboro (N.J.) State Hosp., 1969—70; house supr. R.E. Thomason Gen. Hosp., El Paso, Tex., 1970—73; staff nurse emergency Darnall Army Cmty. Hosp., Fort Hood, Tex., 1974; coord. med.-surg. I Ctrl. Tex. Coll., Killeen, 1974—2003, prof. emeritus, 2003—. Mem.: Tex. Retired Tchrs. Assn., Delta Sigma Theta.

LYONS, LINDA, health science association administrator; BA, U. Calif.; MD, Harvard Med. Sch.; internal med. training, UCLA Med. Ctr. Sr. v.p. Scripps Clinic Med. Group, San Diego, Calif.; sr. v.p., health svcs., chief med. officer PacifiCare Health Systems, 1996—. Former chmn. Unified Med. Group Assn.; founding pres., chmn. Calif., Assn. Healthcare Provider Found.; bd. mem. Med. Quality Commn. Office: PacifiCare Health Sys 3120 W Lake Center Dr Santa Ana CA 92704-6917

LYONS, MARY E. academic administrator; b. Calif. BA, Sonoma St. Univ., 1971; MA, San Diego St. Univ., 1976; Ph.D, Sonoma St. Univ., 1983. Prof. Franciscan School of Theology, Berkeley, Calif., 1984—90; pres. Calif. Maritime Acad., Vallejo, 1990-96, Coll. of St. Benedict, St. Joseph, Minn., 1996—2003, Univ. San Diego, 2003—. Office: Office of the President Univ San Diego 5998 Alcala Pk San Diego CA 92110-2492

LYONS, MAXINE EVADNEY, small business owner, poet; b. Kingston, Jamaica, Nov. 7, 1962; arrived in U.S., 1995; d. Ezekiel West and Eunice May Hitnarinesingh; m. Norman W. Lyons, Dec. 31, 1989. AS, No. U. West Indies, Mandeville, Jamaica, 1985. Tchr. Continuation HS, Jamaica, 1980—81; sec. Precision Arts Ltd., Jamaica, 1986—88; sec., receptionist Speed-O-Graphic Printer, Jamaica, 1988—89; asst. mgr. Astra Hotel, Jamaica, 1990—91; sec. Jamaica Transformer Co., 1991—92. Owner Jamaica Pl., Bronx, 2000—; host poetry readings Magic Pot Restaurant, Bronx. Contbr. poetry to An Hour at Sunrise, 2000 (Editor's Choice award),

Poetry's Elite: The Best of Poetry 2000, 2000 (Editor's Choice award), TV appearance Good Day NY, Fox Channel 5, 2002, Bronxnet TV, 2002 (named Small Bus. of Week, 2002). Achievements include mounted commemorative poem entitled "Double Towers" used to raise funds for Jamaican victims of 9/11. Avocations: poetry, short stories, cooking, catering, music. Home: 3003 Grace Ave Bronx NY 10469 Office: Maroon Books PO Box 682 Bronx NY 10462 E-mail: info@maroonco.com., poettothemax@hotmail.com.

LYONS, MOIRA K. state legislator; b. Trenton, N.J. BA, Georgian Ct. Coll.; student, Miami U. Mem. Conn. Ho. of Reps., mem. appropriations com., chmn. transp. com., 1985—92, appt. dep. ho. spkr., 1993-95, majority leader, 1995—99, deputy spkr., 1993—94, spkr., 1999—. Bd. dirs. Conn. Women's Hall of Fame, Hartford, Workplace, Inc., Bridgeport, CTE (anti-poverty agency), the Women's Business Devel. Ctr., Jackie Robinson Hall of Fame, SoundWaters Community Ctr. for Environ. Edn.; Curriculum Adv., Leadership Fairfield Co. program, SACIA. Good Housekeeping magazine award for Women in Govt., 2000, Conn. Assoc. of Public Schools Superintendents Disting. Svc. award, 2000, Conn. Coalition for Land Preservation, 2000, Conn. Coalition of Police and Corrections Officers of Conn. Legis. Leadership award, 2000, Junior League of Stamford-Norwalk Cmty. Leadership award, Greenways Coun. Recognition award, Nat. Assoc. of Women Business Owners, Hartford Coll. for Women's Pioneer Woman of the Year award, 1999, Conn. Fedn. of Business and Professional Women's Clubs President's Courage award, 1999, Henry Toll Fellowship, Bice Clemow award, Conn. Coun. on Freedom of Information, March 2002, Conn. Nurturing award, April, 2002. Mem., Gov.'s Coun. on Econ. Competitiveness and Tech., Drugs Don't Work Sch., Campus, Cmty. and Youth Com. Democrat. Office: Legislative Office Bldg Rm 4105 Capital Ave Hartford CT 06106-1591 E-mail: Moira.Lyons@po.state.ct.us.*

LYONS, NATALIE BELLER, family counselor; b. Havana, Cuba, Apr. 3, 1926; d. Herman Lawrence and Jennie (Engler) B.; widowed, Apr. 18, 1986; children: Anne, Sara. Degrree in Surveying and Land Appraising, BS, Inst. Vedado, Havana, 1943; BA, U. Mich., 1946; MEd, U. Miami, Fla., 1967. Family counselor, mem. staff furniture design and mfg. co. George B. Bent Co., Gardner, Mass., 1953-58; tchr. H.S., Winchendon, Mass., Hollywood, Fla., 1962, parochial sch., Ft. Lauderdale, Fla., 1963-64; family counselor Miami, 1967—; project dir. Cen. Am. fisheries program Peace Corps, 1972-74. Counselor Svc. Corp. of Ret. Execs., Miami, 1993; bd. dirs. mem. Com. for Accuracy in Mid-East Reporting in Am. Pres. Miami region Hadassah, 1989—91; mem. cmty. rels. coun. Greater Miami Jewish Fedn., 1985—; bd. dirs. Miami Civic Music Assn., 1985—; nat. women's divsn. Am. Soc. for Technion, 1991—, pres., 2000—; co-chmn. Pro-Israel Rally, Tri County, 1991; co-chmn Joint Action Com., Miami, 1989—91; founder, dir. Cmty. Inst. Jewish Studies, Hollywood, Fla., 1962—64; tng. dir. Los Amigos de las Ams., 1975—2002. Recipient Leadership award Hadassah, 1987, honoree Am. Soc. for Technion Scholarship Fund, 1991; named Woman of Yr., Hadassah, 1991. Mem.: Am. Inst. Tech. (nat. pres. women's divsn.), Israel Inst. Tech. (pres. so. region 1996—2000), Am. Soc. for Technion (nat. pres. 2001—), Svc. Corps. of Ret. Execs. (bd. dirs. 1997—). Democrat. Avocations: travel, reading, antiques, family, performing arts. E-mail: Lyons.den@mindspring.com.

LYONS, VIRGINIA, state legislator; b. Auburn, N.Y., Sept. 24, 1944; m. Richard Lyons; children: Emily, Helen. AB in Zoology/Psychology, Drew U., 1966; MS in Nutritional Biochemistry, Rutgers U., 1968; EdD Adminstrn./Planning/Policy, U. Vt., 1988. Asst. prof. Middlesex County Coll., 1968-71; prof. biology Trinity Coll., Burlington, Vt., 1973-2000, coord., dir. allied health, 1978-2000; mem. Vt. Senate from Chittenden County, Montpelier, 2001—. Mem. Chittenden County Reg. Impact Task Force, 2000, Vt. League of Cities/Towns Quality of Life Commn., 2000, County Elected Ofcls., 1998-2000; alt. mem. Chittenden County Reg. Planning Commn., 1998-2000; chmn. Williston Select Bd., 1997-2000; clk. Sch Bd., 1984-86; mem. Williston Cmty. Schs. Edn. Fund, 1998-2000, Williston Federated Ch. Social Concerns Com., 1983-87; former bd. dirs. Channel 17. Mem. Sigma Xi (adv. bd. 1993-2000, nat. bd. dirs. 1995-98, reg. dir. 1995-98, pres. 1988-93), Cochran Ski Club (pres. 1986-89). Democrat. Office: 241 White Birch Ln Williston VT 05495

LYSTAD, MARY HANEMANN (MRS. ROBERT LYSTAD), sociologist, author; b. New Orleans, Apr. 11, 1928; d. James and Mary (Douglass) Hanemann; m. Robert Lystad, June 20, 1953; children: Lisa Douglass, Anne Hanemann, Mary Lunde, Robert Douglass, James Hanemann. AB cum laude, Newcomb Coll., 1949; MA, Columbia U., 1951; PhD, Tulane U., 1955. Postdoctoral fellow social psychology S.E. La. Hosp., Mandeville, 1955-57; field rsch. social psychology Ghana, 1957-58, 1968, 1986; chief sociologist Collaborative Child Devel. Project, Charity Hosp. La., New Orleans, 1958-61; feature writer African div. Voice Am., Washington, 1964-73; program analyst NIMH, Washington, 1968-78, asso. dir. for planning and coordination div. spl. mental health programs, 1978-80; chief Nat. Ctr. for Prevention and Control of Rape, 1980-83, Ctr. Mental Health Studies of Emergencies, 1983-89; pvt. cons. specializing on mental health implications social and econ. problems Bethesda, Md., 1990—. Cons. on youth Nat. Goals Research Staff, White House, Washington, 1969-70. Author: (nonfiction) Social Aspects of Alienation, 1969, As They See It: Changing Values of College Youth, 1972, Violence at Home, 1974, A Child's World As Seen in His Stories and Drawings, 1974, From Dr. Mather to Dr. Seuss: 200 Years of American Books for Chidlren, 1980, At Home in America, 1983; (fiction for children) Millicent the Monster, 1968, James the Jaguar, 1972, Jennifer Takes Over P.S. 94, 1972, Halloween Parade, 1973, That New Boy, 1973, Play Ball, 1997; editor: Innovations in Mental Health Services to Disaster Victims, 1985, Violence in the Home: Interdisciplinary Perspectives, 1986, Mental Health Response to Mass Emergencies: Theory and Practice, 1988. Recipient Spl. Recognition award USPHS, 1983, Alumna Centennial award Newcomb Coll., 1986. Home and Office: 4900 Scarsdale Rd Bethesda MD 20816-2440

LYTHCOTT, MARCIA A. newspaper editor; d. William and Florence; m. Stephen Lythcott (dec.). BA in journalism, U. Wisc., Madison. Assoc. food guide editor Chicago Tribune, Ill., editor, style section, editor, home section, 1993—94, op-ed editor, 1995—. Office: Chicago Tribune 435 N Michigan Ave Chicago IL 60611-4066

LYTLE, DEBORA SCHUBERT, art educator; b. Sweetwater, Tex., Nov. 4, 1962; d. Freddie Jerrald and Velma Louise Schubert; m. Clarence Jerry Lytle; 1 child, Christopher Jaret. AA, Western Tex. Coll., Snyder, 1983; BFA, Tex. A&M U., Commerce, 1983—87. Cert. K-12 tchr. Tex. A&M U. - Commerce, 1987. Dir. and instr. Tex. A&M U. - Commerce Children's Ctr., Commerce, Tex., 1987—89; HS art instr. Quinlan (Tex.) Ind. Sch. Dist., 1989—90, Sulphur Springs (Tex.) Ind. Sch. Dist., 1990—95; artist Debora Schubert Lytle Studio, Cumby, Tex., 1995—, art instr., 1995—, Paris Jr. Coll., 2004—. Judge, artistic discovery Congl. HS Art Competition, Commerce, Tex., 2001—03; judge, HS scholarship competition Tex. A&M U., Commerce, 2000—01. Exhibitions include North Tex. Area Art League, 1992, Surya Gallery Juried Exhbn., 1992, Tex. Visual Artists Membership Exhbn., 2000, Breckenridge (Tex.) Fine Arts Juried Exhbn., 2003, Represented in permanent collections Tex. A&M U., Commerce, Uniformed Fire Officers Assn. Mem.: Dallas Visual Artists, Pastel Soc. Southwest, Am. Soc. Classical Realism, Tex. Visual Artists Assn., Am. Soc. Portrait Artists (assoc.), The Portrait Soc. of Am. (assoc.). Home and Studio: Debora Schubert Lytle Studio 274 CR 4734 Cumby TX 75433 Office Phone: 903-886-4664.

LYTTON, LINDA ROUNTREE, marriage and family therapist, consultant; b. Suffolk, Va., Mar. 30, 1951; d. John Thomas and Anne Carolyn (Edwards) Rountree; m. Daniel Michael Lytton, June 23, 1973; 1 child, Seth Daniel. BS, Radford U., 1973; MS, Va. Poly. Inst. and State U., 1992. Collegiate profl. cert.; lic. profl. counselor, Va., 1995; lic. marriage and family therapist, 1997. Tchr., cons. Fauquier County Pub. Schs., Warrenton, Va., 1973-74, Chesterfield County Pub. Schs., Richmond, Va., 1974-78, Williamsburg (Va.)-James City Pub. Schs., 1979-83, Prince William County Pub. Schs., Manassas, Va., 1983-89; hist. area interpreter Colonial Williamsburg Found., 1978-79; outpatient therapist Prince William County Community Svcs. Bd., 1989-91, emergency svcs. therapist, therapist cons., 1991-93; marriage and family therapist Menninger Care Sys., Inc., Manassas, 1993-99; pvt. practice Ashton Profl. Ctr., 1996—. Cons. Horizons for Learning, Inc., Richmond, 1989—. Great Books Leader, 1993—. Mem. Am. Assn. Marriage and Family Therapy, Va. Assn. Marriage and Family Therapy, Internat. Assn., Marriage and Family Counselors, Sigma Kappa (life). Avocations: tennis, biking, boating, water skiing. Home: 12046 Market Square Ct Manassas VA 20112-3214 also: Fairfield Office Pk 12890 Harbor Dr Woodbridge VA 22192-2921 E-mail: llyttonlmft@comcast.net.

MA, CHUNG-PEI MICHELLE, astronomer, educator; BS, PhD, MIT, 1993. From asst. prof. to assoc. prof. physics and astronomy U. Pa., Phila., 1996—2001; assoc. prof. astronomy U. Calif., Berkeley, 2001—. Contbr. articles to profl. jours. Recipient Annie J. Cannon award, 1997, 1st prize Taiwan Nat. Violin Competition, 1983, Cottrell Scholars award Rsch. Corp., 1999, Lindback award for Disting. Tchg., U. Pa., 1999; Alfred P. Sloan fellow, 1999; Sherman Fairchild fellow, 1993. Mem. Phi Beta Kappa. Achievements include research in the formation and evolution of galaxies and large scale structure in the Universe; performed numerical simulations of the clustering of dark matter in various cosmological models of structure formation from the Early Universe until the present day; computation of the temperature variations imprinted on the cosmic microwave background radiation which provides a snapshot of the infant Universe. Office: U Calif Berkeley Dept Astronomy 601 Campbell Hall Berkeley CA 94720

MA, JING-HENG SHENG, language educator; b. Beijing, Mar. 15, 1932; arrived in U.S., 1963; d. Xue Shu and Guo Ying (Yin) Sheng; m. Wei-Yi Ma, Sept. 28, 1958; children: Lyou-fu, Syau-fu. BEd, Taiwan Normal U., 1958; MA, Philippine Women's U., 1963; MA in Applied Linguistics, U. Mich., 1971, PhD in Linguistics, 1983. Instr. Chinese Cornell U. Extension Program, Taipei, Taiwan, 1959-62; lectr. Chinese U. Mich., Ann Arbor, 1963-84; assoc. prof., chairperson dept. East Asian langs. Williams Coll., Williamstown, Mass., 1984-88. Vis. prof. Chinese dept. Wellesley Coll., 1988-89, prof., chair dept., 1989-92, 95-98, Mayling Soong prof. Chinese studies, 1997, chair dept., 2000—. Author: Chinese Language Patterns, 1985, A Study of the Mandaring Chinese Verb Suffix Zhe, 1986, At Middle Age: A Learning Guide for Students of Chinese, 1988, 2nd edit. 1991, Strange Friends: A Learning Guide for Students of Chinese, 1989, 2nd edit. 1991, Great Wall: A Learning Guide for Students of Chinese, 1990, 2d edit., 1993, The True Story of Ah Q: A Learning Guide for Students of Chinese, 1992, Difficult Points in Chinese Grammar, 1992, others; co-author: HyperChinese: The Grammar Modules (CD), 1993, Chinese Unmasked: Grammatical Principles and Applications, 1994, HyperChinese: The Pronunciation Modules, 1995, Drills and Quizzes in Mandarin Chinese Pronunciation, 1999, Keys to Chinese Character Writing, 2000, (book and CD) Learning Through Listening: An Introduction to Chinese Proverbs and Their Origins, 2002. Mem. Chinese Lang. Tchrs. Assn. (exec. bd. 1990-93), Assn. for Asian Studies, Internat. Soc. for Chinese Lang. Tchg. (bd. dirs. 1997—). Home: 10 Nonesuch Dr Natick MA 01760-1041

MA, XING, optical engineer; b. Jianjin, People's Republic of China, Dec. 15, 1954; d. Tai and Suwen (Yu) M.; m. Tianxiang Liu, Sept. 28, 1984; children: Patrick, Alex. BS in Physics, Normal U. Tianjin, China, 1980; PhD in Elec. Engring., U. New South Wales, Sydney, Australia, 1995. Optical engr. Electronic Material Co., Tianjin, China, 1981-86; rsch. asst. U. New South Wales, Sydney, Australia, 1987-94; rsch. engr. Dept. Comm. RMIT, Melbourne, Australia, 1994-97; sr. fiber optics engr. E-TEK Dynamics, San Jose, Calif., 1998—. Chief tech leader for design of new products: CADM and 5 part WDM device. Mem. IEEE. Avocations: coin collecting, shell collecting, swimming, volleyball. Office: E-TEK Dynamics 1865 Lundy Ave San Jose CA 95131-1834 E-mail: xing.ma@etek.com.

MAAR, ROSINA, medical organization executive; BS, Ga. Inst. Tech., 1984; MD, Morehouse Sch. Medicine, 1988. Cert. internal medicine Ga., N.C. Intern and resident in internal medicine Emory U. Sch. Medicine, Atlanta, 1991; physics lab. instr. Ga. Inst. Tech., Atlanta, 1981-84; rsch. asst. Emory U., Atlanta, 1985-86; med. evaluator maternal and infant project Grady Meml. Hosp., Atlanta, 1987-88; contract physician Wesley Woods Geriatric Hosp., Atlanta, 1989-90; contract physician, program dir. Piedmont Hosp./Spinal Shepard Ctr., Atlanta, 1989-91; med. dir. Cellcor, Inc., Atlanta, 1991-92, corp. med. dir. Newton, Mass., 1992-93; med. scientist med./regulatory svcs. Quintiles, Inc., Research Triangle Park, N.C., 1993-94, dir. med. svcs., 1994-95, v.p. clin. ops., 1995—, sr. v.p. strategic mgmt., until 1999; COO Clinicor, Inc., Austin, Tex., 1999—. Contbr. articles and abstracts to med. jours. Mem.: AMA, ACP, Am. Bd. Internal Medicine (diplomat). Office: Clinicor Inc 1717 W 6th St Austin TX 78703-4773

MAARBJERG, MARY PENZOLD, office equipment company executive; b. Oct. 2, 1943; d. Edmund Theodore and Lucy Adelaide (Singleton) Penzold; m. John Peder Maarbjerg, Oct. 20, 1966; 1 child, Martin Peder. AB, Hollins Coll., 1965; MBA, Wharton Sch., Pa., 1969. Cons. bus. and fin., Stamford, Conn., 1977-78; corp. staff analyst Pitney Bowes, Inc., Stamford, 1978-80, mgr. pension and benefit fin., 1980-81, dir. investor rels., 1981-85; v.p. planning and devel. Pitney Bowes Credit Corp., Norwalk, Conn., 1985-86, treas., v.p. planning, 1986-94; v.p. mktg. devel. and mng. dir. Asia Pacific Bowes Fin. Svcs., 1994-95, v.p. ops. and mng. dir., 1995-97; v.p. corp. svcs. Pitney Bowes, Inc., Stamford, 1997-99, v.p. real estate and adminstrn., 1999-2001, v.p. adminstrn. and process integration, 2001—. Bd. dirs. Stanford Dental Ctr., 2003—; mem. cmty. bd. U. Conn., Stanford, 2003—; bd. dirs. Person-to-Person, 2004—. Mem. adv. com. City of Stamford Mcpl. Employees Retirement Fund, 1980-85; mem. fin. adv. com. YWCA, Stamford, 1982-86; bd. dirs. Stamford Symphony, 1985-95, Vis. Nurses Assn., 1984-86, Am. Recorder Soc., 1986-98, Am. Classical Orch., 1999-2002; bd. dirs. Stamford Partnership, chmn., 1998-2003; bd. dirs., treas. Amherst Early Music, 2000—. Fellow Royal Statis. Soc.; mem. Fin. Execs. Inst., Phi Beta Kappa. Office: Pitney Bowes Inc 1 Elmcroft Rd Stamford CT 06926-0700

MAAS, JANE BROWN, advertising executive; b. Jersey City; d. Charles E and Margaret (Beck) Brown; m. Michael Maas, Aug. 30, 1957; children: Katherine, Jennifer. BA, Bucknell U., 1953; postgrad., U. Dijon, France, 1954; MA, Cornell U., 1955; LittD, Ramapo Coll., 1986, St. John's U., 1988. Assoc. producer Name That Tune TV Program, N.Y.C., 1957-64; v.p. Ogilvy and Mather Inc., N.Y.C., 1964-76; sr. v.p. Wells, Rich, Greene, Inc., N.Y.C., 1976-82; pres. Muller Jordan Weiss Inc., N.Y.C., 1982-89, Earle Palmer Brown Cos., N.Y.C., 1989-92, chmn., 1992-94, chmn. emeritus, 1994—. Co-author: (book) How to Advertise, 1975, Better Brochures, 1981, Adventures of a Advertising Woman, 1986, The New How to Advertise, 1992, Christmas in Wales: A Homecoming, 1994. Bd govs comt Scholastic Achievement, 1985—92; active Girl Scouts US, NY, 1970—76; mem adv bd William E Simon Grad Sch Bus, Univ Rochester, 1989—; pub dir AIA, 1993—95; trustee Bucknell Univ, Lewisburg, 1976—86, Fordham Univ, NY, 1983—91. Named Woman of the Yr, NY Advert, 1986; recipient Matrix Award, Women in Communications, 1980. Mem.: AIA (hon.), Am Assn. Advt. Agys. (bd govs), Am Archtl. Found (regent 1993—2000), Phi Beta Kappa. Avocations: creative writing, jogging. Home: 3 Meadow Way Westhampton Beach NY 11978 E-mail: janemaas@att.net.

MAATSCH, DEBORAH JOAN, manufacturing executive; b. Lincoln, Nebr., Mar. 26, 1950; d. Leon F. Forst and Jarolyn J. Hoffman Forst Conrad; m. Gordon F. Maatsch, Mar. 14, 1969; children: Jason, Diana. BS, U. Nebr., 1976; MBA, U. Phoenix, 1997. Accredited tax advisor; IRS enrolled agt. Acct., supr. US Civil Svc., Heidelberg, Germany, 1971—73; paralegal Mattson Rickets Davies et al, Lincoln, Nebr., 1976—87; tax cons., 1981—; paralegal Wade Ash Woods & Hill, P.C., 1986—94; sr. trust adminstr. Investment Trust Co., 1994—96; compliance officer Nelson, Benson and Zellmer, Inc., 1995—96; pres. DGJD Inc., 1993—; contr. Arena Devel., Inc., 1996—2000; pres. Boyd Industries, Inc., 2001—. Mem. Park County Sr. Wellness Team, 1999—; mem. bus. adv. bd. Ponderosa HS, 1994-98. Contbr. articles to profl. jour. Event chmn., vol. Jefferson Cmty. Ctr., 1999—; bd. dirs. JCCA, 2001-03, pres., 2002-03; bd. dirs. Kids Roundup, 2002—; coord. Jefferson Hist. Preservation Fund; mem. Women's C. of C. Mem. Doane Coll. Alumni Assn. (dir. 1989-93). Avocations: travel, outdoor activities, horses. Office: DGJD Inc PO Box 267 Jefferson CO 80456-0267 also: Boyd Industries Inc PO Box 315 Boyd TX 76023 E-mail: dgjdinc@bemail.com.

MABEE, SANDRA IVONNE, timpanist, percussionist, educator, clergyman; b. Hato Rey, P.R., Jan. 13, 1955; d. Nelson Custudio Noriega and Norma Ruth (Eiseman) Lee; m. Carl Mabee, 1980; 1 child, Rebecca Lee. BA in Bibl. Studies summa cum laude, Patten Coll., 1977; BM magna cum laude, San Francisco Conservatory, 1983; MA in Music cum laude, Calif. State U., Hayward, 1985; PhD in Religion, Christian Bible Coll., N.C., 2000. Ordained min. Evang. Ch. Alliance, 1991, Unveiled Christ Ministries, 1997; cert. Evangelical Tchr.'s Tng. Assn. Prin. timpanist Bay Area Women's Philharm., San Francisco, 1980—; prof. music Patten Coll., Oakland, Calif., 1983-89, chairperson profl. studies divsn., 1986-88; min. of music El Cerrito (Calif.) Christian Ctr., 1988-91; prof. music Hayward Christian Sch., 1988-91; intern pastor, dir. music ministry Trinity Ch., Oakland, Calif., 1991-92; pastor, dir. music ministries Unveiled Christ Ministries, Calif., 1992—2003; prof. music Las Positas Coll., 1996—; founder, pastor Up to Zion Ministries. Tympanist, percussionist various orchs., Bay Area, Calif., 1977—; pvt. tchr. music lessons, Bay Area, 1977—; percussion ensemble Patten Coll., Oakland, 1983-84; producer sing-it-yourself Messiah Patten Coll., Oakland, 1986; guest dir. choral Landmark Ministries, Oakland, 1990; seminar instr., Landmark Sch. Ministries, Oakland, 1990, Internat. Radio Broadcast, 1998. Prison ministry vol. Alameda County Jail, Oakland, 1990, Vacaville Fed. Prison, Follow-up Ministries; vol. rest home, Oakland, 1985—, Assn. of Christian Schs. Inc./Song Shop; founder Tracy Percussion Ensemble, 1999—. San Francisco Conservatory scholar, 1980-83; named Outstanding Young Woman of Am., 1986, 87, winner concerto soloist Redwood Symphony, 1988, for Outstanding Svc. to Teaching Profession A.B.I. Mem. Percussive Arts Soc., Hymn Soc. of Am., Sarasota Acad. Christian Counseling, Am. Assn. Christian Counselors. Office Phone: 209-640-1519. E-mail: drsm@uptozion.org.

MABREY, VICKI, news correspondent, anchor; b. St. Louis; BA in Polit. Sci. cum laude, Howard U., 1977. AFTRA tng. reporter Sta. WUSA-TV, Washington, 1982-84; gen. assignment reporter Sta. WBAL-TV, Balt., 1984-92; corr. CBS News, Dallas, 1992-95, London, 1995-98, 60 Minutes II, N.Y.C., 1998—. Recipient 2 Emmy awards, 1996, 2 Emmy awards, 1997. Office: c/o 60 Minutes II 524 W 57th St New York NY 10019-2902

MACAFEE, SUSAN DIANE, reporter; b. Feb. 1944; Attended, Foothill Coll. Disc jockey with news, pub. affairs; engr., editor, prodr. Sta. KZSU-Stanford U., Calif., 1975-80; freelance reporter, broadcast journalist, 1975—. Writer, prodr., engr. editor, narrator 25 original nationwide news stories and furnished story material for numerous radio stas. and networks, TV stas. including NPR, Pacifica, ABC, NBC and CBS networks, BBC radio and TV, Channel 9 Australia, numerous newspapers and magazines; rschr., documentor and author: Agent Orange Pilot Nutritional Detox Program, 1986, (5-part series) Food-Diet-Crime, Behavior and Learning Disability Connection, 1986; author, prodr., engr., editor and narrator: Treatment of Refractory Eosinophilia Myalgia Syndrome Associated with the Injestion of L-Tryptophan Containing Products, Parts I and II, 1990; interviewer, recorder, transcriber: A Historical Prospective of Vitamin C With Linus Pauling, 1991; researcher, documentor, writer Postscipt: Interactions of Glutathione, Ascorbic Acid HIV and AIDS, 1992, Neural Tube Defects and Folic Acid, 1995, Chromium - A New Treatment for Adult Type II (Maturity Onset) Diabetes, 1996. The Legality and Use of Bone Wax, 1997, 1999. V.p. Calif. Coll. Young Reps., 1967; sec., asst. to Nat. Field Dir. Coll. Young Reps., Rep. Nat. Com., Washington, 1968; dir. precinct orgn. Calif. State Assembly Campaign, San Francisco Rep. Ctrl. Com., 1968. Recipient 3 Nat. awards Young Rep. Nat. Com., 1967-68. Home and Office: 334 Paseo De Golf Green Valley AZ 85614-3319

MACALUSO, MARY MARGARET, nurse, educator; b. Poughkeepsie, N.Y., Oct. 25, 1954; d. Joseph William and Margaret Frances (Stickler) Schultz; m. Joseph Edwin Macaluso, Nov. 24, 1990; 1 child, Gary Daniel Graham. AAS in Nursing, Dutchess C.C., Poughkeepsie, 1974; BSN, Regents Coll., 1987. RN N.Y., Ga.; cert. nephrology nurse, peritoneal dialysis nurse. Home care coord. St. Francis Hosp., Poughkeepsie, 1977-92; renal nurse clinician Abbott Renal Care, Chgo., 1992-94; nephrology nurse specialist Nat. Med. Care, Rockleigh, N.J., 1994-97, Spectra Renal Mgmt., Fremont, Calif., 1997—. Cons. Abbott Renal Care, Chgo., 1989-92; bd. dirs. Bd. Nephrology Examiners, Bonent, 1991-93, v.p., 1993-96, pres., 1996-99; spkr. in field. Contbr. articles to profl. pub. Mem. Am. Assn. Nephrology Nurses, Nat. Kidney Found., Sigma Theta Tau. Roman Catholic. Avocations: singing, fine art, needlework, gardening. Home: 3040 Water Brook Dr SW Conyers GA 30094-5630 Office: Spectra Renal Mgmt 488818 Kato Rd Fremont CA 94538-7364

MACARTHUR, CAROL JEANNE, pediatric otolaryngology educator; b. Glendale, Calif., Aug. 23, 1957; d. Seth Gerald and Barbara Jeanne (Shaw) MacA.; m. Geoffrey Buncke, Dec. 14, 1990; children: Keith Davis, Michelle Jeanne. BS, Occidental Coll., 1979; MD, UCLA, 1984. Diplomate Am. Bd. Otolaryngology. Intern U. Calif., Davis, 1984-85, resident in otolaryngology, 1985-90; fellow in pediatric otolaryngology Boston Children's Hosp., 1990-91; instr. dept. otolaryngology U. Calif.-Davis, Sacramemto, 1989-90; clin. fellow in otology and laryngology Harvard U. Med. Sch., Boston, 1990-91; asst. prof. U. Calif., Irvine, 1991—2002, asst. prof. dept. pediatrics, 1993-98, program dir. dept. otolaryngology-head and neck surgery, 1992-95; staff dept. otolaryngology Oreg. Health Scis. U., Portland, 2002—. Recipient investigator devel. award Am. Acad. Facial Plastic and Reconstructive Surgery, 1993. Fellow ACS, Am. Acad. Pediatrics; mem. Am. Soc. Pediat. Otolaryngology, Soc. for Ear, Nose and Throat Advances in Children, Am. Acad. Otorhinolaryngology-Head and Neck Surgery, Alpha Omega Alpha. Home: 4018 Canal Woods Ct Lake Oswego OR 97034 Office: Oreg Health Scis U Dept Otolaryngology 3131 SW Sam Jackson Park Rd Portland OR 97201-3011

MACARTHUR, DIANA TAYLOR, advanced technology executive; b. Santa Fe, July 7, 1933; widowed; children: Elizabeth Tschursin, Alexander Tschursin. BA, Vassar Coll., 1955. Cons. economist Checchi & Co., 1957-61; v.p., dir. Thomas J. Deegan Co., 1961-62; dep. chief West Africa Peace Corps, 1963, reg. program officer for North Africa, Near East, South Asia, 1964, dir. divsn. pvt. and internat. orgns., 1965-66; pvt. cons., 1966-74; program mgr. Aerospace Divsn. Gen Elec. Co., 1974-76; pres. Consumer Dynamics, 1977-80; v.p., dir. Dynamac Internat. Inc., 1980-88, chmn., pres., CEO, 1988—; chmn., CEO Rsch. Analysis and Mgmt. Corp., 1988-92. Pres. Fgn. Traders, Inc., 1980—86. Trustee Menninger Found., Topeka, 1972—, Lady Bird Johnson Wildflower Ctr., 1985-; mem. Pres.'s Com. of Adv. on Sci. and Tech., 1994-01; citizens adv. bd. to the Pres. Coun. on Youth Opportunity, 1966-70; served on CSIS Strengthening of

Amer. Com., 1992, Nat. Benefits from Nat. Lab. Com., 1993, Sr. Policy on Nat. Challenges, 1996, Geopolitics of Energy Com., 2000; mem. The Chancellor's Adv. Coun. U. System of Md.; bd. visitors U. Md. Biotech. Inst.; adv. com. Ctr. Strategic & Internat. Studies; bd. dirs. Atlantic Coun. USA; bus. adv. coun. Ctr. for China-U.S. Coop., U. Denver. Mem. Coun. on Competitiveness, Business-Higher Edn. Forum (mem. exec. com.), Tech. Coun. Md. (mem. exec. com.), Los Alamos Nat. Lab. Found. (bd. mem.), Phi Beta Kappa. Office: Dynamac Internat Inc 2275 Research Blvd Rockville MD 20850-3268 E-mail: dmacarthur@dynamac.com.

MACARTHUR, SANDRA LEA, financial services executive; b. Springfield, Mass., July 21, 1946; d. John J. MacArthur and Catherine E. (Lantry) Mason; m. Edgar A. Dunn, June 23, 1973 (div. Mar. 1980); 1 child, Jonathan H.; m. Robert M. Cruickshank, Sept. 15, 1984. AA, Bradford Coll., 1966; BA, Simmons Coll., 1973; MBA, Babson Coll., 1983. Asst. dir. rental properties Wintergreen Resort, Charlottesville, Va., 1978-79; treas., ptnr. Elan, Inc., Boston, 1983-84; agt. State Mut. Am., Newton Center, Mass., 1985-86; sr. account officer Fidelity Investments Instl. Svcs., Boston, 1986-87, mgr. client svcs., 1987-88, assoc. market mgr., 1988-89; market mgr. Fidelity Instl. Retirement Svcs. Co., Boston, 1989-90, v.p. mktg., 1990-92, v.p. comm. prodn., 1992-96; v.p. Investment Svcs., Boston, 1996-2000; v.p. account mgmt. Fidelity Investments, Devonshire Custom Pub., Boston, 2000—02; v.p. client svcs. Fidelity Ad Agy., Boston, 2002—. Mem. Alumni Bd. of MacDuffie Sch., Beta Gamma Sigma. Democrat. Episcopalian. Avocations: bridge, tennis, golf. Home: 47 Westchester Rd Jamaica Plain MA 02130-3451 Office: Fidelity Investments 82 Devonshire St Boston MA 02109-3605

MACASKILL, BRIDGET, finance company executive; b. Aug. 5, 1948; M in bus., Edinburgh Coll. Commerce. Joined Oppenheimer Funds, Inc., N.Y.C., 1983, pres./CEO, 1995—2001, chmn., 2000—01; ind. consultant Merrill Lynch, 2003—. Non-exec. dir. J Sainsbury plc, Prudential plc, 1999—2001, 2003—.*

MACAVINTA-TENAZAS, GEMORSITA, family physician; b. Numancia, Aklan, Phillippines, Dec. 18, 1938; came to U.S., 1967; d. Dominador Zalazar and Georgina Estrada (Tabanera) Macavinta; m. Salvador Torrefiel Tenazas Jr., Apr. 18, 1963; children: Alan, Alex, Albert, Alfred. BA, Far Ea. U., Manila, 1959, MD, 1964. Diplomate Am. Bd. Family Practice. Intern North Gen. Hosp., Manila, 1963-64; pvt. practice Manila, 1965-67; extern Chinese Gen. Hosp., Manila, 1965-67; with St. Joseph Med. Ctr., Burbank, Calif., 1967-69; chief cytotechnologist Cancer Screening Svcs., North Hollywood, Calif., 1969-73; resident in family practice medicine Health Scis. Ctr., Tex. Tech. U., Lubbock, 1974-75; staff physician VA Outpatient Clinic, L.A., 1975—. Recipient physician recognition awards AMA, 1973-85, 92-94; named Mrs. Akron, 1986, Disting. Alumna, Aklan Acad., Philippines, 1991, Most Outstanding Parent award Builders Lions Club, 1995, Citizen of Yr. Builders Lions Club, 1996, Outstanding Physician Club Filipino, 1996, one of 10 Outstanding Women of Nation, Uliran, 1997, Mrs. Philippine Am., 2000. Fellow Am. Acad. Family Physicians; mem. Philippine-Am. Assn. Family Physicians (bd. govs. 1996, 2002—, sec. 1998, outstanding leader award 2000, sec. 1998-2002), Am. Assn. Family Physicians (named Mrs. Philippines), Calif. Acad. Family Physicians, Filipino Asian-Pacific VA Employees Soc. (pres. L.A. chpt. 1988—), Assn. Philippine Physicians in Am. (named Mrs. Mindanao, 2002), Aklanons of Am. (pres. 1988—, bd. govs. 1998-2000, 1st Mrs. Aklan 1986-89), Far Ea. U. Med. Alumni Assn. (asst. sec. 1988—). Roman Catholic. Avocations: dance, singing, sewing, piano playing, gardening. Office: VA Outpatient Clinic 425 S Hill St Los Angeles CA 90013-1110

MACBRIDE, ELIZABETH CUMMINGS, editor, writer, media consultant; b. Albuquerque, Feb. 12, 1971; d. John William and Carol King Cummings; m. Stephen James MacBride, Sept. 27, 1997; 1 child, Lillian Nancy. BA in Journalism, U. Md., 1993. Editor Diamondback, College Park, Md., 1992—93; staff writer Ctrl. Penn Bus. Jour., Harrisburg, Pa., 1993—96, Sunday News, Lancaster, 1999—2001; editor Ctrl. Penn Bus. Jour., Harrisburg, 1999—2001; mng. editor Crain's N.Y. Bus., N.Y.C., 2001—03. Cons. Mennonite Ctrl. Com., Akron, Pa., 2000, 02. Sec. Com. to Prevent Teen Pregnancy, Lancaster, Pa., 1999—2000. Mem.: Assn. of Area Bus. Pubs., Soc. Profl. Journalists. Avocations: antique jewelry, antique books. Office: 309 W Prospect Ave State College PA 16801

MACCALLUM, LORENE (EDYTHE MACCALLUM), pharmacist; b. Monte Vista, Colo., Nov. 29, 1928; d. Francis Whittier and Berniece Viola (Martin) Scott; m. David Robertson MacCallum, June 12, 1952; children: Suzanne Rae MacCallum Barslund and Roxanne Kay MacCallum Batezel (twins), Tracy Scott, Tamara Lee MacCallum Johnson, Shauna Marie MacCallum Bost. BS in Pharmacy U. Colo., 1950. Registered pharmacist, Colo. Pharmacist Presbyn. Hosp., Denver, 1950, Corner Pharmacy, Lamar, Colo., 1950-53; rsch. pharmacist Nat. Chlorophyll Co., Lamar, 1953; relief pharmacist, various stores, Delta, Colo., 1957-59, Farmington, N.Mex., 1960-62, 71-79, Aztec, N.Mex., 1971-79; mgr. Med. Arts Pharmacy, Farmington, 1966-67; cons. pharmacist Navajo Hosp., Brethren in Christ Mission, Farmington, 1967-77; sales agt. Norris Realty, Farmington, 1977-78; pharmacist, owner, mgr. Lorene's Pharmacy, Farmington, 1979-88; tax cons. H&R Block, Farmington, 1968; cons. Pub. Svc. Co., N.Mex. Intermediate Clinic, Planned Parenthood, Farmington; first woman registered pharmacist apptd. N.Mex. Bd. Pharm., 1982-92. Author numerous poems for mag. Advisor Order Rainbow for Girls, Farmington, 1975-78. Mem. Nat. Assn. Bds. Pharmacy (com. on internship tng., com. edn., sec., treas. dist. 8, mem. impaired pharmacists adv. com., chmn. impaired pharmacists program N.Mex., 1987—, mem. law enforcement legis. com., chmn. nominating com. 1992), Nat. Assn. Retail Druggists, N.Mex. Pharm. Assn. (mem. exec. coun. 1977-81), Order Eastern Star (Farmington). Methodist. Home and Office: 75 Trew Creek Rd Durango CO 81301-8307

MACCALLUM, MARTHA, correspondent; BA, St. Lawrence U. Anchor, reporter Sta. WBIS-TV, N.Y.C.; anchor, reporter, prodr. Wall St. Jour. T.V., N.Y.C., 1992-96; corr. Bus. News, CNBC, Ft. Lee, N.J. Office: CNBC 2200 Fletcher Ave Fort Lee NJ 07024-5005

MACCARTHY, TALBOT LELAND, civic volunteer; b. St. Louis, Jan. 28, 1936; d. Austin Porter Leland and Dorothy (Lund) Follansbee; m. John Peters MacCarthy, June 21, 1958; children: John Leland MacCarthy, Talbot MacCarthy Payne. BA, Vassar Coll., 1958. Sec., treas. Station List Pub. Co., St. Louis, 1975-85, pres., 1985-90. Hon. trustee Robert E. Lee Meml. Assn., Arts and Edn. Coun. Greater St. Louis, pres., 1978-80, emerita; past vestry mem. St. Michael and St. George Ch., 1997-00; past trustee St. Louis Art Mus., St. Louis Merc. Libr. Assn., Family & Children's Svc. Greater St. Louis, Health and Welfare Coun., Greater St. Louis, Jr. Kindergarten St. Louis Page Park YMCA, Scholarship Found. St. Louis, Friends St. Louis Art Mus. Bd., Ch. St. Michael and St. George Sch. Bd., Mid-Am. Arts Alliance; chmn. Mo. Arts Coun., 1980-85; past chmn. Vol. Action Ctr. Greater St. Louis; past vice chmn. bd. dirs. Mary Inst.; past pres. Jr. League St. Louis; mem. Nat. Coun. Arts, 1985-91; mem. nat. coun. for Sch. of Art Washington U.; bd. dirs. Sheldon Art Galleries; trustee Seabury-Western Theol. Sem. Recipient Woman of Achievement citation St. Louis Globe Democrat, 1979, Mo. Citizens for Arts/Arts Advocacy award, 1987, Mo. Arts Award, 1993. Mem. Vassar Club St. Louis (past pres.), Mary Inst. Alumnae Assn. (past pres.), Colonial Dames Am., Garden Club St. Louis, Belvedere Club (Charlevoix, Mich.; bd. dirs.). Republican. Episcopalian. Avocations: tennis, visual arts, performing arts.

MACCHIAROLO, ELIZABETH ANN, music educator; b. Woodbury, N.J., Apr. 29, 1963; d. Nick T. and Virginia (Vance) Macchiarolo. MusB in Edn. and Music Therapy, Henderson State U., 1985; MEd in Elem. Edn., U. North Tex., 1996. Cert. music tchr. preK-12 Tex., gen. elem. tchr. grades 1-8 Tex. Elem. music specialist North Little Rock (Ark.) Sch. Dist., 1986—87, Grapevine-Colleyville Ind. Sch. Dist., Euless, Tex., 1987—97, Birdville Ind. Sch. Dist., North Richland Hills, Tex., 1997—. Staff devel. trainer Birdville Ind. Sch. Dist., North Richland Hills, Tex., 2002—; cons./trainer Ctr. for Educator Devel. in Fine Arts, San Antonio, 2001—, workshop presenter Tex. Music Educators Assn., San Antonio, 1997—2003. Author: (musical play) The Wacky Wound-Up Watch; contbr. articles to ednl. jours. Vol. usher Bass Performance Hall, Fort Worth, Tex., 1998—99; team in tng. mentor Leukemia/Lymphoma Soc., Dallas, 2001—03; exec. bd. mem. Bear Creek and ACFT PTA's, Euless and North Richland Hills, Tex., 1991—2003. Mem.: Ctr. for Educator Devel. in Fine Arts, Music Educators Nat. Conf., Assn. of Tex. Profl. Educators, Tex. Music Educators Assn. (workshop presenter 1997—), Delta Omicron (life), USA Triathlon. Avocations: marathon running, triathlons and duathlons, travel, tap dancing, part time work for Texas Rangers and Dallas Stars. Office: Acad at Carrie F Thomas Elem 8200 O'Brian Way North Richland Hills TX 76180

MACCLOSKEY, RUTH BLAIR See PARRIS, REBECCA

MACCOBY, ELEANOR EMMONS, psychology educator; b. Tacoma, May 15, 1917; d. Harry Eugene and Viva May (Johnson) Emmons; m. Nathan Maccoby, Sept. 16, 1938 (dec. Apr. 1992); children: Janice Carmichael, Sarah Maccoby Blunt, Mark. BS, U. Wash., 1939; MA, U. Mich., 1949, PhD, 1950. Study dir. div. program surveys USDA, Washington, 1942-46; study dir. Survey Rsch. Ctr. U. Mich., Ann Arbor, 1946-48; lectr., rsch. assoc. dept. social rels. Harvard U., Cambridge, Mass., 1950-58; from assoc. to full prof. Stanford (Calif.) U., 1958-87, Barbara Kimball Browning prof., 1979, chmn. dept. psychology, 1973-76, prof. emeritus, 1987—. Author: (with R. Sears and H. Levin) Patterns of Child-Rearing, 1957, (with Carol Jacklin) Psychology of Sex Differences, 1974, Social Development, 1980, (with R.H. Mnookin) Dividing the Child: Social and Legal Dilemmas of Custody, 1992, (with Buchanan and Dombusch) Adolescents after Divorce, 1996, The Two Sexes: Growing Up Apart, Coming Together, 1998; editor: (with Newcomb and Hartley) Readings in Social Psychology, 1957, The Development of Sex Differences, 1966. Recipient Gores award for Excellence in Tchg., Stanford U., 1981, Disting. Contbn. to Ednl. Research award Am. Ednl. Rsch. Assn., 1984, Lectureship award Soc. for Devel. and Behavioral Pediats., 2002. Fellow APA (pres. Divsn. 7, 1971-72, G. Stanley Hall award 1982), Soc. for Rsch. in Child Devel. (pres. 1981-83, mem. governing coun. 1963-66, Disting. Sci. Contbn. award 1987), Am. Psychol. Soc. (Disting. Sci. Contbns. award 1988); mem. NAS, AAAS, Am. Acad. Arts and Scis., Inst. Medicine, Western Psychol. Assn. (pres. 1974-75, Lifetime Achievement award 2004), Inst. for Rsch. on Women and Gender, Social Sci. Rsch. Coun. (chmn. 1984-85), Consortium of Social Sci. Assns. (pres. 1997-98), Am. Psychol. Found. (Life Achievement award 1996). Democrat. Home: 729 Mayfield Ave Palo Alto CA 94305-1016 Office: Stanford U Dept Psychology Stanford CA 94305-2130 E-mail: Maccoby@psych.stanford.edu.

MACCORMACK, JEAN F. academic administrator; d. George and Helen MacCormack. BA, Emmanuel Coll., Boston, 1969; MEd, U. Mass., Amherst, 1978, EdD, 1979. Assoc. dean Coll. of Edn. U. Mass. Boston, 1984—87, acting dean Coll. of Edn., 1984—85, assoc. chancellor, 1987—88, vice chancellor arts and fin., 1988—95, interim chancellor, 1995—96, dep. chancellor and vice chancellor arts and fin., 1996—99, chancellor Dartmouth, 1999—. Mem. South Coast Econ. Devel. Partnership, 1999, Joint CEO Group, 2000, Racial and Ethnic Access and Fairness Adv. Bd., 2001; chair South Coast Edn. Compact, 2000; mem. vis. com. U. So. Maine New Eng. Assoc. of Sch. and Coll., 2000—01; ex-officio mem. U. Mass. Dartmouth Libr. Archive Campaign, 2001; bd. mem. South Coast Health Sys., Inc., 2002; mem. marine sci. com. Fall River CEO Group, 2003, mem. med. device com., 03, mem. south coast edn. com., 03; mem. Regional Competitiveness Coun., 2003. Vice chair bd. govs. New Bedford Oceanariun, 1999, chair edn and rsch. com., 1999, trustee, chair edn. com., 2000; trustee Artworks! at Dover St., 2000, mem. edn. com, 2000, mem. pers. com., 2000; trustee Global Learning Charter Sch., 2000; bd. mem. Greater New Bedford Workforce Investment Bd., 2000, mem. legis. affairs and pub. info. com., 2000, mem. youth coun., 2000; mem. New Bedford Econ. Devel. Coun., 2000; corporator Child and Family Svcs., Inc., 2002; incorporator Home Aged People in Fall river, 2003; corporator Narragansett Fin. Corp. Citizens - Union Savs. Bank, 2003; mem. pres.'s coun. New Bedford Symphony Orch., 2003; mem. leadership coun. New Bedford Whaling Mus. Mem.: YMCA of Southeastern Mass., WHALE, Am. Assn. of State Coll. and U., U. Mass. Dartmouth Libr. Assoc. E-mail: jmaccormack@umassd.edu.

MACCOY, MARILYN, physical education educator, volleyball coach; b. Ossining, N.Y., Oct. 30, 1940; d. Cecil and Henrietta (Authouse) MacC. BS, Boston U., 1962; MA, Adelphi U., 1969. Permanent cert. in edn. and coaching, N.Y. Coach varsity girls volleyball Mepham H.S., Bellmore, N.Y., 1962—, coach varsity boys volleyball, 1987—, coach varsity girls badminton, 1980-86, coach varsity girls tennis, 1962-80. Rep. Sect. 8 H.S. Sports Assn., 1990—; mem. Boys Volleyball Exec. Coun., Nassau County, 1990—; mem. Com. for Girls and Women in Sports Day, SUNY, 1995. Mem. PTA Bellmore Merrick Sch. Dist., 1962—. Named Girls Volleyball Coach of Yr., Nassau County, 1992, 96, 97; recipient Outstanding Achievement Coaches award N.Y. State Coaches Assn., 1992, Nat. Award for Outstanding Contbrns. to Girls' and Women's Sports, 1993; coached Nassau County volleyball championship teams, 1976, 88, 89, 92, 93. Mem. Nassau County H.S. Assn., Nassau County Boys and Girls Volleyball Coaches Assn. Republican. Congregationalist. Avocations: traveling, gardening, athletics, animal activist and volunteer. Office: W C Mepham H S 2401 Camp Ave Bellmore NY 11710-3029

MACDONALD, ERIN E. healthcare company executive; With Sierra Health Svcs. Inc. and predecessor firms, 1978—, ops. mgr. Southwest Med. Assocs.; dir. ops. HPN Sierra Health Svcs. Inc., Reno, Nev., v.p. HMO Ops., pres. HPN, 1984, v.p. HMO and ins. ops., 1989-92, pres. SHL, 1990, sr. v.p. ops. Office: Sierra Health Svcs 2724 N Tenaya Way Las Vegas NV 89128

MACDONALD, KAREN CRANE, occupational therapist, geriatric counselor; b. Denville, N.J., Feb. 24, 1955; d. Robert William and Jeanette Wilcox (Crane) M.; m. Geno Piacentini, Oct. 22, 1993. BS, Quinnipiac U., 1977; MS, U. Bridgeport, 1982; PhD, NYU, 1998. Cert. occupl. therapist. Occupational therapist, coord. of spl. care unit Jewish Home for the Elderly, Conn., 1987-92, N.Y. Inst., N.Y.C., 1984-86; pvt. practice Fairfield County, Conn., 1977-88; occupl. therapist Rehab. Assocs., Fairfield, Conn., 1993-96; instr. Houjatonic Cmty. Coll., Conn. Instr. NYU, 1985—89, Quinnipiac Coll., 1986—92, Housatonic CC, Bridgeport, Conn., 2002; lectr., cons. in field. Contbr. articles to profl. jours. Youth leader, deacon Union Meml. Ch., Stamford, Conn., 1980-88; deacon Southport Congl. Ch., 1992-94; chair consumer com. Alzheimer's Coalition of Conn., 1991-92. Teaching fellow NYU, 1983-86. Mem. AAAS, World Fedn. Occupl. Therapy, Am. Occupl. Therapy Assn. (scholar 1985, coun. edn.), Conn. Occupl. Therapy Assn. (gerontology liaison 1980-83), Am. Bd. Disability Analysts, NY Acad. Scis., Pi Lambda Theta. Avocations: poetry writing, quilting. Home: 198 Glenbrook Rd Bridgeport CT 06610-1149

MAC DONALD, MARGARET CLARK, retired real estate agent; b. Lewiston, Maine, Dec. 20, 1929; d. Arthur Bailey and Blanche (Plummer) Clark; m. John Edward Mac Donald, June 16, 1951 (dec. July 1988); children: Cornelia Ann Roberts (dec.), Edward Clark, Susan Mac Donald Moynahan. BS, Skidmore Coll., 1951. Bus. rep. N.Y. Bell Co., N.Y.C., 1951-52; show room mgr. Bonnie Doone, N.Y.C., 1952-53; interior decorator Susan Wang, N.Y.C., 1953-54; designer Maggie Mac Donald Interiors, Miami, Fla., 1960-64; owner, sec. Atlantic Millwork, Inc., Miami, 1964-88; assoc. realtor Keyes Co. Realtors, Miami, 1995-98. Pres. Homemaker Svc. Dade County, Cmty. Vol. Svc. Bur., 1967-68; pres. Jr. League Miami, Inc., 1969-70, chmn. sustaining mems., 1982; pres. Vis. Nurse Assn. Dade County, Fla., Inc., 1975-77; pres., past treas. Metropolitans, 1983-84; second v.p., spl. events chmn. The Vizcayans, 1984-85; pres. Dade County Nat. Soc. Colonial Dame Am., 1988-89; pres. Colonial Dame of Am. XVII, 1989-90, rec. sec., 1998-99. Mem. Nat. DAR (Biscayne chpt., del. conf. Washington, corr. 1998-99), Daus. Colonial Wars, Founders and Patriots (v.p. 2000). Avocations: reading, tennis. Home: 13480 Wansteadt Pl Bristow VA 20136-5728

MACDONALD, SHEILA DE MARILLAC, company executive; MBA, Harvard U. Prin. Tex. Transaction Mgmt. Co., Fair Winds Corp., Houston, 1990—. Chpt. 11 trustee, 1997-99; pres., CEO Bristol Resources Corp., 2000. Mem. Harvard Club N.Y., Met. Club, Petroleum Club. E-mail: sheilamacdonald@sbcglobal.net.

MACDOUGALL, FRANCES KAY, marketing consultant; b. Saginaw, Mich., Mar. 25, 1937; d. Frank King and Emily Runke Beck; m. Kenneth Jacobus, 1958 (div. 1969); m. Robert Louis Gilmore, 1972 (div. 1979); children: Peter Gilmore (dec.), Christoper Gilmore; m. Colin Kennedy MacDougall, 1981 (div. 1993). BA, Northwestern U., 1958; MBA, Loyola U., 1974; postgrad., Northwestern U. Sr. corp. analyst Am. Hosp. Supply, Inc., Evanston, Ill., 1969-71; rsch. assoc. Am. Hosp. Assn., Chgo., 1971-72; product mgr. Litton Med. Products, Elk Grove, Ill., 1972-74; cons. Technomic Cons., Chgo., 1974-79; mktg. dir. Just Jobs, Inc., Chgo., 1980-81; sr. cons. The Chgo. Group, Inc., Chgo., 1981-88; sr. assoc. SWF Cons. Group, Ft. Myers, Fla., 1988—. Dir. Ruth Cooper Ctr., Ft. Myers, 1988—; com. chmn. Lee County Infrastructure Task Force, 1988. Hon. scholar Nat. High Sch. Inst. Northwestern U., Evanston, 1954. Mem. Abbey Springs Country Club, Forest Country Club, Southwest Fla. Jazz Soc. Avocations: adventure travel, golf, bridge, writing poetry, music. Home: 16689 Waters Edge Ct Fort Myers FL 33908-4304

MAC DOWELL, ANDIE (ROSE ANDERSON MAC DOWELL), actress; b. Gaffney, S.C., Apr. 21, 1958; m. Paul Qualley (div.); 3 children ; m. Rhett Hartzog, 2001. Spokesmodel L'Oreal cosmetics and haircare. Films include: Greystoke, 1984, St. Elmo's Fire, 1985, sex, lies and videotape, 1989, Green Card, 1990, Hudson Hawk, 1991, The Object of Beauty, 1991, The Player, 1992, Ruby, 1992, Groundhog Day, 1993, Luck, Trust and Ketchup, 1994, Short Cuts, 1993, Four Weddings and a Funeral, 1994, Bad Girls, 1994, Unstrung Heroes, 1995, Michael, 1996, Multiplicity, 1996, The End of Violence, 1997, Town and Country, 1998, Shadrack, 1998, The Scalper, 1998, The Muse, 1999, Muppets From Space, 1999, Just the Ticket, 1999, Harrison's Flowers, 2000, Town & Country, 2001, Crush, 2001, Ginostra, 2002; TV movies include The Secret of the Sahara, 1988, Women and Men 2: In Love There Are No Rules, 1991, On the Edge, 2000, Dinner With Friends, 2001, Jo, 2002; prodr. Just the Ticket, 1999; TV guest appearances include Spenser: For Hire, 1985, Clive Anderson All Talk, 1996, Muppets Tonight!, 1997, The Practice, 2003. Office: ICM 8942 Wilshire Blvd Beverly Hills CA 90211-1934*

MACDUFF, ILONE MARGARET, music educator; b. Berwyn, Ill., Jan. 30, 1938; d. Albert Kenneth Hinckle and Dorothy Lydia Ardina Lange; m. James Donald Macduff, Jr., Apr. 2, 1959; children: Gordon Scott, James Alexander, Charles Colin. MusB, U. Idaho, 1976. Internat. rep. Boy Scouts Am., 1983—93; mem. Thurston County (Wash.) Hist. Commrs., 1984—98; active Boy Scouts Am., Tumwater, Wash., 1968—93, dist. Cub Scout program chmn., 1973—75, mem. coun. Pow Wow staff, 1973—76; founder Cub Scout Day Camp, Tumwater Area Coun., 1973; chmn. Coun. Scout-O-Rama, 1979, 1980, 1981; mem. coun. Eagle bd. Boy Scouts Am., 1985—90; dir. monthly musicales State Captial Mus., 1970—74. Recipient Single and Double awards, Nat. Fedn. Music Clubs, 1969, 1977, Silver Beaver award, Boy Scouts Am., 1981, Disting. Commr. award, 1981, Lamb award, 1987. Mem.: Olympia Music Tchrs. Assn. (pres. 2003—), Music Tchrs. Nat. Assn. (Olympia chpt. voice auditions chair 2001), Gordon Setter Club Am. (chmn. nat. dog show 2003), Puget Sound Gordon Setter Club (treas. 1998—2000, show chmn. 2003). Lutheran. Avocation: photography. Home: 8524 Delphi Rd SW Olympia WA 98512

MACE, JERILEE MARIE, opera company executive; BA in Speech Comm. and Mgmt. magna cum l, Simpson Coll., 1991. Mem. adminstrv. staff Des Moines Metro Opera, 1976, dir. mktg., exec. dir., 1988—. Developer OPERA Iowa, Des Moines Metro Opera; cons. various opera cos. On-site evaluator NEA; grad., bd. dirs. Greater Des Moines Leadership Inst.; founding mem. Warren County Leadership Com. Named Iowa Arts Org. of Yr., 2000; recipient Outstanding Achiever award, Ft. Dodge C. of C., 1994, Best Kept Secret award for bus. excellence, Greater Des Moines Partnership 2001, Women of Influence award, Des Moines Bus. Record, 2001; fellow exec., OPERA Am., 1993. Office: Des Moines Metro Opera 106 W Boston Ave Indianola IA 50125-1836 E-mail: jerimace@aol.com.

MACEK, PAMELA KAY, tax specialist, business executive; b. Mt. Plesant, Mich., Nov. 20, 1951; d. Harold D. and Betty Mae (Merrifield) Reynolds; m. Robert M. Macek, Jr., May 3, 1969; children: Kerry, Kristene, Robert. Student, Calif. Coast U., Calif. State U., San Bernardino, N.Am. Sch. Acctg., Newport Beach, Calif. Cert. tax preparer, Calif. Pvt. practice tax preparation; CFO Arrow Industries, Anaheim, Calif. Mem. Inland Soc. Tax Preparers, NAFE, Employer Adv. Coun. (award for Treas. and V.P., cert. appreciation). Address: 4637 Orly Pl Riverside CA 92507-5819

MACER-STORY, EUGENIA ANN, writer; b. Mpls., Jan. 20, 1945; d. Dan Johnstone and Eugenia Loretta (Andrews) Macer; divorced; 1 child, Ezra Arthur Story. BS in Speech, Northwestern U., 1965; MFA, Columbia U., 1968. Writing instr. Polyarts, Boston, 1970-72; theater instr. Joy of Movement, Boston, 1972-75; artistic dir. Magik Mirror, Salem, Mass., 1975-76, Magick Mirror Comm., 1977—. Author: Congratulations: The UFO Reality, 1978, Angels of Time, 1982, Project Midas, 1986, Dr. Fu Man Chu Meets the Lonesome Cowboy: Sorcery and the UFO Experience, 1991, 3d edit., 1994, Gypsy Fair, 1991, The Strawberry Man, 1991, Sea Condor/Dusty Sun, 1994, Awakening to the Light-After the Longest Night, 1995, Battles with Dragons: Certain Tales of Political Yoga, 1993, 2d edit., 1994, Legacy of Daedulus, 1995, The Dark Frontier, 1997, Troll and Other Interdimensional Invasions, 1999, Congratulations: The UFO Reality, 2000, Vanishing Questions, 2000, Carrying Thunder, 2002, Crossing Jungle River, 1998, Doing Business in the Adirondacks; True Tales of the Bizarre and Supernatural, 2003, (poetry book) The Merry Piper's Hollow Hills, 2003; (plays) Fetching the Tree, Archaeological Politics, 1986, Strange Inquiries, Divine Appliance, 1989, The Zig Zag Wall, 1990, The Only Qualified Huntress, 1990, Telephone Taps Written Up for Tabloids, 1991, Wars with Pigeons, 1992, Conquest of the Asteroids, 1993, Commander Galacticon, 1993, Meister Hemmelin, 1994, Six Way Time Play, 1994, Radish, 1996, Setting Up for the World Trade Centaur, 1996, Mister Shooting Star, 1998, Wild Dog Casino, 1999, Magic Mirror Space Installation at 515 Greenwich Street, 1999-2001, The Old Gaffer From Boise (at Gallery 113), 2000, The Redecoration According to Currier (at Gallery 113), 2001, (play) Ars Chronicon Sylvestre (at Theatre for the New City), 2002, Swords of the Equinox, 2003, New Life Expo, New Yorker Hotel, N.Y.C., 2003, Sayeed/Sayeeda, New Yorker Hotel, N.Y.C., 2003, others; philosophy writer; contbr. articles to profl. jours.; author (poetry): in Woodstock Times, Lamia Ink!, Manhattan Poetry Rev., Sensations, Kore, The Rift mag., Poet's House, Poetry Publ. Showcase, Poetry.com Anthology, 2000, Theatre for the New City Festivals, 1997—, others; feature writer: Newspeak Pubs., 1995, Paranoia Mag., 2002; editor Yankee Oracle Gazette, 1999; personal appearance as profl. clairvoyant (TV documentary) Haunted Houses, 1996, UFO Desk, Sta. WBAI radio shows, 1996-2001, Star People Confs., 1998—; interviewer: Interview and Occult Investigations, Magonia Mag.

Online, 1998, Paranoia Mag., 2000, Infinity Factory: exhbn. paintings Barcelona, Spain, 1999, 2000, 02, Magick Mirror Comm. Installation, 1999-2001, 515 Greenwich Gallery, So-Ho, N.Y., 1999, City Art Gallery, Stockholm, 2000, 04, Gam'Art Diffusion, Port Frejus, France, 2003, Kelikian Gallery, Beirut, 2002, 03, Holland Art Fair, The Hague, 2003, BCN Art-Directe Gallery, Barcelona, Spain, 2003. Shubert fellow, 1968. Mem. Am. Soc. Dowsers, Dramatists Guild (spkr., interviewer on radio shows and internet confs.), Theosophical Soc. Democrat. Avocations: swimming, outdoor activities, hiking. Office: Magick Mirror Comm PO Box 741 New York NY 10116-0741 E-mail: MagickMirr@aol.com.

MACEWAN, BONNIE, librarian; b. Memphis, Tenn., Sept. 10, 1950; m. Thomas Manig. BA, Whitter Coll., 1972; M, U. Denver, 1978. Humanities libr. Ctl. Mo. State Coll., Warrensburg, 1978—84; art, archaeology and music libr. U. Mo., Columbia, 1984—91; asst. dean collections Pa. State U., University Park, 1991—. Mem.: ALA (vice chair/chair-elect collection mgmt. and develop. sect. 2001—). Office: Pa State Univ 510 Paterno Libr University Park PA 16802

MACFARLAND, MIRIAM KATHERINE (MIMI MACFARLAND), writer; b. Trenton, NJ, June 21, 1949; d. James and Merrianne (Collins) MacF.; children: Bridget Lorraine MacFarland, Chloe Merrianne Griffin. Attended, Rutgers U., 1976-78, U. Pa., 1981-83, Oxford U., Eng., 1988; B in Liberal studies with distinction, U. Okla., 2000; MFA, L.I. Univ., 2002. Programmer analyst R&D Computer Sci. Corp., Naval Air Devel. Ctr., Warminster, Pa., 1977-81; programmer analyst NASA Ames Rsch. Ctr., Moffett Field, Calif., 1978; staff writer Aydin Controls, Inc., Ft. Washington, Pa., 1981-82; writer Banc Tec, Inc., Okla. City and Dallas, 1983-95; cons. engr. MCI Comm. Internat., Rye Brook, NY, 1984-86, Western Union Internat., N.Y.C., 1984, RCA Global Comm., Ft. Lee, NJ, 1985; cons. engr., writer Siemens Med. Sys., Iselin, NJ, 1988-98; adj. asst. prof. English and writing Southampton Coll. L.I. Univ., 2001—02. Guest spkr. U. Ctrl. Okla., Edmond, 1994, Americorp Patch project, Okla. City, 1995; mem. dean's student adv. com. U. Okla., 1999-2000. Author plays, journalism; numerous lit. rev.; CONTACT II, Hightimes Mag., The Bloomsbury Rev.; Another Chgo. Mag.; Renovated Lighthouse; author: 14 books, numerous poems; contbr. chpts. to books, articles to profl. jours. Mem. Dem. Nat. Com. L.I. U. fellow in writing, award, GAPA, 2000—02. Mem.: Associated Writing Programs, Southampton Coll. Alumni Assn., Phi Kappa Phi. Home and Office: PO Box 1669 Norman OK 73070-1669 E-mail: mimimac621@aol.com.

MACGILLIVRAY, LOIS ANN, organization executive; b. Phila., July 8, 1937; d. Alexander and Mary Ethel (Crosby) MacG. BA in History, Holy Names Coll., 1966; MA in Sociology, U. N.C., 1971, PhD in Sociology, 1973. Joined Sisters of Holy Names of Jesus and Mary, 1955. Research asst. U. N.C., Chapel Hill, 1969-70, 71-72, instr. sociology, 1970-71; sociologist Rsch. Triangle Inst., Durham, N.C., 1973-75, sr. sociologist, 1975-81; dir. Ctr. for Population and Urban-Rural Studies, Research Triangle Inst., Durham, 1976-81; pres. Holy Names Coll., Oakland, Calif., 1982-92, mem. steering com. Symposium for Bus. Leaders, 1982-92; prin. owner Svc. Orgns.: Planning and Evaluation, Chapel Hill, 1994—. Vis. scholar dept. sociology U. N.C., Chapel Hill, 1992-94; mem. policy bd. U. Oakland Met. Forum, co-convenor panel on edn. and youth. Bd. dirs. Oakland Coun. Econ. Devel., 1991-96; bd. dirs. Bay Area Biosci. Ctr., 1990-92, mem. adv com., 1992-94. Mem. Am. Sociol. Assn., Assn. Ind. Calif. Colls. and Univs. (exec. com. 1985-92, vice chmn. 1989-92), Regional Assn. East Bay Colls. and Univs. (past pres., bd. dirs. 1982-92). Avocation: birding. Home and Office: 101 N Hamilton Rd Chapel Hill NC 27517-5627

MACGOWAN, SANDRA FIRELLI, publishing executive, publishing educator; b. Phila., Nov. 9, 1951; d. William Firelli and Barbara (Gimbel) Kapalcik. BS in Biology, BA in English, Pa. State U., 1973, MA in English Lit., 1978. Cert. supervisory analyst N.Y. Stock Exchange. Editor McGraw-Hill Pub. Co., N.Y.C., 1979-81; sr. acquisitions editor Harcourt Brace Jovanovich, Inc., N.Y.C., 1981-82; sr. editor The Coll. Bd., N.Y.C., 1982-88; v.p., head editorial CS First Boston Corp., N.Y.C., 1988-94; v.p. supervisory analyst internat. rsch. SBC Warburg, N.Y.C., 1994-96; v.p., supervisory analyst internat. rsch. Arnhold and S. Bleichroeder, N.Y.C., 1996—2003; ops. dir. instnl. rsch. Natexis Bleichroeder Inc. (formerly Arnhold and S. Bleichroeder), N.Y.C., 2003—. Part time assoc. prof. pub. NYU Sch. Continuing Edn., N.Y.C., 1985—. Author: 50 College Admission Directors Speak to Parents, 1988. Democrat. Avocations: art, reading, travel. Office: Natexis Bleichroeder Fl 44 1345 Avenue Of The Americas New York NY 10105-4300

MACGRAW, ALI, actress; b. Pound Ridge, N.Y., Apr. 1, 1939; m. Robert Evans, 1970 (div.); 1 child, Joshua; m. Steve McQueen, 1973 (div.). Ed., Wellesley Coll. Former editorial asst. Harper's Bazaar Mag.; former asst. to photographer Melvin Sokolsky. Actress in films including Goodbye, Columbus, 1969, Love Story, 1971, The Getaway, 1973, Convoy, 1978, Players, 1979, Just Tell Me What You Want, 1979, Natural Causes, 1994, Glam, 2001; TV mini-series The Winds of War, 1983, China Rose, 1983, Dynasty, 1985, Falcon Crest; TV movies Survive the Savage Sea, 1992, Gunsmoke, The Hollywood Fashion Machine, 1995: the Long Ride, 1993; author: (autobiography) Moving Pictures, 1991. Address: PO Box 284 Tesuque NM 87574-0284

MACGREGOR, SHAWNA ANNE, lawyer, educator; b. San Jose, Calif., Aug. 31, 1943; d. Jules and Tatiana MacGregor. BA in History, UCLA, 1965; JD, U. Miami Law Sch., 1970. Bar: Ohio 1971, Mich. 1972. Ptnr. Meriks, MacGregor, & Scott, Dayton, Ohio, 1972—. Lectr. Ohio State U. Law Sch., 1990—. Mem.: ABA, Ohio Lawyers Assn. (v.p. 2003—). Democrat. Avocations: antique weapons, magic. Office: Meriks MacGregor & Scott 4125 Colemere Cir Dayton OH 45415-1908

MACH, MICHELE R. special education educator; b. E. Chgo., Ind., Aug. 25, 1949; d. Chester J. and Irene M. Franciski; m. Daniel W. Mach, Apr. 18, 1975; 1 child, William B. BA, Purdue U., 1972, MS in Edn., 1975; reading specialist, Ind. U., 1978. Endorsement in learning disabilities and mildly mentally handicapped Ind. Least Restrictive Environ. facilitator and spl. edn. tchr. N.W. Ind. Spl. Edn. Coop., Crown Point, 1975—, tchr. learning disabilities Griffith, 1975—78, tchr. mildly mentally handicapped Highland, 1978—, tchr. autistic spectrum, 1978—; tchr. gifted and talented Highland Pub. Schs., 1980—84; tchr. St. John Sch., Ind., 1972—75; Least Restrictive Environ. facilitator Southridge Sch., Highland, 1975—. Mentor first year tchrs. N.W. Ind. Spl. Edn. Cooperative, Crown Point, 1985—. Remedial reading tutor Tradewinds, Merrillville and Hammond, Ind., 1977—82; tchr./leader St. Thomas More Ch., Munster, Ind., 1996. Named one of Outstanding Elem. Tchrs. Am., Diocese of Gary, 1975. Mem.: Coun. Exceptional Children, Hammond Area Reading Coun. Avocations: knitting, writing, reading. Home: 25 Beverly Pl Munster IN 46321 Office: Southridge Sch 9221 Johnston St Highland IN 46322

MACH, RUTH, principal; m. Stan Mach; 2 children. Grad., Truman State U., 1958; M, U. Mo.; PhD, St. Louis U. Cert. elem. sch. adminstr., reading specialist, tchr. of learning disabled, tchr. behaviorally disturbed. Tchr. Affton Sch. Dist., Lindbergh Sch. Dist.; elem. sch. prin. Mehlville Sch. Dist.; prin. Meramec Elem. Sch., Clayton, Mo. Bd. dirs. Truman State U. Found.; apptd. bd. govs. Truman State U., 1995—. Mem.: ASCD, St. Louis Suburban Prins. Assn. (past pres., Disting. Prin. award), Conf. on Edn., Mo. Assn. Elem. Sch. Prins. (Disting. Elem. Prin. award), Nat. Assn. Elem. Sch. Prins. Office: Meramec Elem Sch 400 S Meramec Clayton MO 63105

MACHADO, KETY GONZALEZ, mathematician, educator; d. Antolin and Maria Gonzalez. BS, Ashland U., 1967. Cert. math. tchr. N.J., 1979, bilingual N.J., 1994. Math tchr. Piscataway (N.J.) H.S., 1982—92; bilingual math tchr. New Brunswick (N.J.) H.S., 1992—. Office: New Brunswick High School 1125 Livingston Ave New Brunswick NJ 00050

MACHAMER, CYNTHIA G. editor, writer; d. Joseph A. Kinard and Gail T. Mazourek; m. Thomas R. Machamer, June 29, 1984; children: Elliott, Makenna. BA in writing, Houghton (N.Y.) Coll., 1985. Editor, writer Houghton (N.Y.) Coll., 1985—. Mem.: Women in the Arts. Avocation: photography. Home: 9978 State Rte 19 Houghton NY 14744 Office: Houghton Coll 1 Willard Ave Houghton NY 14744

MACHIN, BARBARA E. lawyer; b. Kansas City, Mo., Mar. 26, 1947; d. Roger H. and Doris D. (Dunkel) Elliott; m. Peter A. Machin, June 1, 1969; 1 child, Andrew D. BS in Sec. Edn., U. Kans., 1969, MA in Curriculum Devel./Anthropology, 1973; JD, U. Toledo Coll., 1978. Bar: Ohio 1978, U.S. Dist. Ct. (no. dist.) Ohio 1978, U.S. Ct. Appeals (6th cir.) 1981, U.S. Supreme Ct. 1987. Instr. rsch. and writing U. Toledo Coll. of Law, 1978-79; law clerk Lucas County Ct. of Common Pleas, Toledo, 1979-80; assoc., ptnr. Doyle, Lewis & Warner, Toledo, 1980-87; assoc. Shumaker, Loop & Kendrick, Toledo, 1987-92; gen. counsel U. Toledo, 1993—. Pres., v.p., mem. bd. trustees Toledo Legal Aid Soc., 1983-93; pres. Toledo Civil Trial Attys., 1990-93; trustee Esworth Found., 1993-96. Contbr. articles to profl. jours. Mem. house corp. bd. Gamma Phi Beta Sorority, 1985—; mem. bd. trustees Epworth Found., 1993—, St. Luke's Hosp., 1994—. Mem. Ohio State Bar Assn., Toledo Bar Assn., Toledo Women's Bar Assn., Toledo Civil Trial Attys. (pres. 1983-92). Home: 414 Grenelefe Ct Holland OH 43528-9232 Office: U of Toledo Office of the Gen Counsel 3620 University Hall 2801 W Bancroft Toledo OH 43606

MACHT, AMY, real estate executive, foundation manager; b. Balt., Mar. 18, 1954; d. Philip Romm and Lois Lerner (Kleiman) M.; m. George Richmond Grose II, June 7, 1981; children: Eloise Macht Grose, Madeleine Macht Grose. BA, U. Pa., 1974; BArch, U. Md., 1978. Archtl. designer, draftsperson Hord, Coplan & Macht, Balt., 1978-81; pres., mgr. Morton & Sophie Macht. Found., Balt., 1978—; real estate mgr. Regional Mgmt., Inc., Balt., 1981-86, real estate broker, pres., CEO, 1986—. Mem. bd. Associated Jewish Cmty. of Balt. (1985-95), dir. Charles Crane Family Found., Balt., 1995—, adv. bd. Johns Hopkins Sch. of Pub. Health, Balt., 1995-2001. Home: 1412 Labelle Ave Baltimore MD 21204-6613 Office: Regional Management Inc 11 E Fayette St Baltimore MD 21202-1679

MACHTIGER, HARRIET GORDON, retired psychoanalyst; b. N.Y.C., July 27, 1927; d. Michael J. and Miriam D. (Rand) Gordon; m. Sidney Machtiger, Feb. 7, 1948; children: Avram Coleman, Marcia Gordon, Bennett Rand. BA, Bklyn. Coll., 1947; diploma with distinction, U. London, 1966, PhD, 1974. Cert. psychologist, Pa. Tchr. Phila. Pub. Schs., 1962-64; cdnl. therapist Child Guidance Tng. Ctr., London, 1966-68. Sch. Psychol. Svc./Inner London Edn. Authority, 1968-70; therapist Paddington Day Hosp., London, 1970-71, London Ctr. for Psychotherapy, 1971-74, Staunton Clinic U. Pitts., 1974-78; pvt. practice Pitts., 1976-2000; ret., 2000. Pres. C.G. Jung Ctr., Pitts., 1976-81; cons. in field. Active S.W. Pitts. Cmty. Mental Health, 1976-78, dir. Pitts. program Inter Regional Soc. Jungian Analysts, 1975-85. Recipient Pa. Dept. Edn. award for disting. contributions to advancement in edn., 1962, Social Sci. Rsch. Coun. award, 1973. Mem. Pa. Psychol. Assn., Brit. Psychol. Soc., Brit. Assn. Psycho therapists. Home: 6562 Jog Palm Dr Boynton Beach FL 33437-3925

MACIEL, PATRICIA ANN, development professional; b. Providence, Jan. 13, 1940; d. Raymond Wallace Sr. and Elizabeth Josephine (Kelly) Ross; m. John Maciel Jr., July 24, 1963; children: Kelly Patricia, Christopher John. EdB, R.I. Coll., 1961, MA in Tchg., 1976. Cert. tchr., R.I. Tchr. 3rd tchr. Pawtucket (R.I.) Pub. Schs., 1961-62; tchr. 5th and 6th grades Providence Pub. Schs., 1962-63; tchr. Pawtucket and Providence Pub. Schs., 1963-72; tchr., curriculum coord. Holy Name Sch., Providence, 1972-80; dir. edtl. programming Basic Skills, Inc., Providence, 1980-83; dir. devel./pub. rels. IN-SIGHT, Warwick, R.I., 1983-88; coord. ann. giving and spl. events St. Joseph Health Svcs. R.I., North Providence, R.I., 1988-2000; pvt. fundraising cons., 2000—. Editor, author newsletter IN-SIGHT News, 1980-83. Sec. exec. bd. Holy Name Sch., 1972-80; pres. employee activities com. St. Joseph Health Svcs. R.I., 1991-93; founding mem., pres. Friends of the Pawtucket Pub. Libr., 1966; pres. Pawtucket Jr. Woman's Club, 1965; publicity chair Middlebridge Assn., South Kingstown, R.I., 1989-90; mem. Narrow River Preservation Assn., South Kingstown, 1976—; mem. Save the Bay, State of R.I., 1987—; ex officio mem. R.I. Coll. Found., 1992-94, corporate bd. dirs., 1996-97, sec., 1997-99, v.p., 1999-2001, pres., 2001-03, immediate past pres., 2003—, chair ad hoc com. capital campaign, 2000-01, vice chair alumni capital campaign, 2001—; rev. com. United Way S.E. New England, 1999, 2002, 03; mem. adv. bd. Villa at St. Antoine, 2002-, mktg. coord., instr., RI Coll. Outreach Program, 2004-. Recipient Alumna of Yr award Rhode Island Coll., 1992. Mem. R.I. Coll. Alumni Assn (treas. exec. bd. 1990-92, chair ann. fund dr. 1990-92, chair class reunion 1981, 86, 91, class news sec. 1972-78, pres. 1992-94). Roman Catholic. Avocations: swimming, boating, walking, bicycling. Home: 3 Hunters Run North Providence RI 02904 E-mail: jmjpam@aol.com.

MACILWAINE, MARY JARRATT, public relations executive; b. Clifton Forge, Va., Oct. 29, 1942; d. Robert Bell and Mary Louise (Wood) J. BA, Mary Baldwin Coll., Staunton, Va., 1964; cert. bus., Katharine Gibbs Sch., Boston, 1965. Staff asst. com. on agr. U.S. Ho. of Reps., 1975-81; asst. sec. food and consumer services Dept. Agr., 1981-85; v.p. Wampler & Assocs. Inc., Washington, 1985-86; pres. Jarratt & Assocs., Inc., Washington, 1986-90; asst. to pres and CEO Va. Nat. Bank, Charlottesville, 2000—. Editor various legis. reports. Republican. Episcopalian. Home: 1149 Marion Dr Charlottesville VA 22903-4649 E-mail: mmacilwaine@virginianb.com.

MAC INNES, VIRGINIA LEWIS, real estate broker; b. Bklyn., Oct. 14, 1921; d. James Parker and Daisy Emerson (Larom) Lewis; m. David Mac Innes, Aug. 31, 1940; children: Suzanne Larom, David Bruce, Janet Elizabeth, Diane Emerson. BS in Econs. and Bus. Mgmt., Empire State Coll. SUNY, Albany, 1992. Lic. real estate broker, N.Y. Broker Terrace Realty, Forest Hills, N.Y., 1967—. Pres. Women's Guild St. Luke's Episcopal Ch., Forest Hills, 1963-65; v.p. Citizens Inquiry on World Trade Ctr., N.Y.C., 1965-68; pres. Oquaga Lake Improvement Assn., Deposit, N.Y., 1965-66; chmn. Bicentennial Commn., Cmty. Bd. # 6, Queens, N.Y., 1976-77; pres. Am. Legion Aux. Unit # 630, Forest Hills, 1976-77; v.p. Forest Hills C. of C., 1982-83, bd. dirs. 1978-79; organizing pres. Remsen Family Revolutionary Cemetery Coalition, Forest Hills, 1983. Mem. AAUW, Benjamine Romaine Soc. NSDAR (regent 1960-62), Nat. Soc. Children Am. Revolution (organizing pres. 1954, dir. N.Y. State 1957-60), Daus. of Brit. Empire, Colonial Dames XVII Century, Moorings Club, Women's Club of forest Hills, Inc. (past pres. 1968-70). Republican. Avocations: writing, photography. Home: 2205 N Southwinds Blvd Apt 207 Vero Beach FL 32963-4324 Office: Terrace Realty 16 Station Sq Forest Hills NY 11375-5234

MACIUSZKO, KATHLEEN LYNN, librarian, educator; b. Nogales, Ariz., Apr. 8, 1947; d. Thomas and Stephanie (Horowski) Mart; m. Jerzy Janusz Maciuszko, Dec. 11, 1976; 1 child, Christina Aleksandra. BA, Ea. Mich. U., 1969; MLS, Kent State U., 1974; PhD, Case Western Res. U., 1987. Reference libr. Baldwin-Wallace Coll. Libr., Berea, Ohio, 1974-77, dir. Conservatory of Music Libr., 1977-85; dir. bus. info. svcs. Harcourt Brace Jovanovich, Inc., Cleve., 1985-89; staff asst. to exec. dir. Cuyahoga County Pub. Libr., Cleve., 1989-90; dir. Cleve. Area Met. Library System, Beachwood, Ohio, 1990; media specialist Cleve. Pub. Schs., 1991-93, Berea (Ohio) City Sch. Dist., 1993—. Author: OCLC: A Decade of Development, 1967-77, 1984; contbr. articles to profl. jours. Named Plenum Pub. scholar, 1986. Mem. Spl. Librs. Assn. (pres. Cleve. chpt. 1989-90, v.p. 1988-89, editor newsletter 1988-89), Baldwin-Wallace Coll. Faculty Women's Club (pres. 1975), Avocation: music. Office: Midpark HS 7000 Paula Dr Middleburg Heights OH 44130

MACIVOR, CATHERINE J. lawyer; b. Royal Oak, Mich., Aug. 17, 1960; d. Angus Stewart and Hazel (Arnold) M. BA magna cum laude, Boston U., 1983; JD, U. Miami, 1989. Bar: Fla. 1992. Atty. Richard & Richard, P.A., Miami, 1990-94; pvt. practice Miami, 1994-96, Franklin & Marbin, P.A., North Miami Beach, 1996—. Tem. Fla. Bar (family law sect., appellate law sec.), DAR. Episcopal. Avocation: swimming. Office: Franklin and Marbin Citicentre Ph 2 290 NW 165th St North Miami Beach FL 33169-6457

MACK, CAROLE, financial consultant; b. N.Y.C., Feb. 28, 1943; d. August and Anne Cahier; m. Arthur R. Mack II, Aug. 21, 1965; children: Arthur R. Mack III, Alan R., John Wendell Howard. Student, Zion U. Customer svc. Blue Cross-Blue Shield, Rochester, NY; instr. baton twirling The Wine Country Club, Naples; owner Carriage House Christian Bookstore; real estate broker, owner Carole Mack Realty; consumer loan officer Citifinancial, Asheville, NC. Sec. Finger Lakes Bd. Realty, Penn Yan; real estate appraiser bd. assessors Town of Milo; bd. dirs. Keuka Housing Coun. Author: (songbook) Ascending the Holy Hill, 1993. Treas. Mt. Zion Christian Assembly, Penn Yan, 1990—98. Republican. Avocations: gardening, music, omnichord. Home: 219 Adams Hill Rd Asheville NC 28806

MACK, JUDITH COLE SCHRIM, political scientist, educator; b. Cin., Aug. 9, 1938; d. James Douglas and Cathleen (Cole) Schrim; m. Thomas H. Mack, Jan. 3, 1968; children: Robert Michael, Cathleen Cole. AB with high distinction, U. Ky., 1960; AM, Radcliffe Grad. Sch., 1962; MPhil, Columbia U., 1988, postgrad., 1986—. Tchr. Lexington (Ky.) Sch., 1962-63, instr. Russian Emory U., Atlanta, 1963-64, Kent (Ohio) State U., 1964-65; instr. Hunter Coll., N.Y.C., 1988-90; adj. lectr. Barnard Coll., N.Y.C., spring 1991, 92; instr. Douglass Coll. Rutgers U., New Brunswick, NJ, 1992—93. Rsch. asst. sociology dept. U. Ky., 1961; rsch. asst. Russian and E. European Studies Ctr. UCLA, 1965—67, rsch. asst. Security Studies Ctr., 1967—68; adj. lectr. Hunter Coll., N.Y.C., 1988; presenter in field. Chmn. state pub. affairs com. N.J. Jr. Leagues, 1979—80; bd. dirs. Children's Aide Adoption Soc., Hackensack, NJ, 1979—90, v.p., 1985—90; bd. dirs. Assn. Children N.J., Newark, 1982—, v.p., 1983—88, chair spl. events, 1999; trustee Divsn. Youth and Family Svcs., Trenton, NJ, 1982—91, v.p., 1983—88; others; trustee Dumbarton Ho., Washington; mem. Millburn-ShortHills County Rep. Com., 1994—, corr. sec., 1994—96, chmn., 1996—98. Woodrow Wilson fellow, Radcliffe Coll., 1960—61, Nat. Def. fellow, 1961—62. Mem.: Mortar Bd., Nat. Soc. Colonial Dames Am. (N.J. treas. 1995—2001), Phi Sigma Iota, Phi Beta Kappa. Episcopalian. Avocations: bridge, cooking, ballet, theater, movies. Home: 657C Del Parque Dr Santa Barbara CA 93103

MACK, JULIA COOPER, retired judge; b. Fayetteville, N.C., July 17, 1920; d. Dallas L. and Emily (McKay) Perry; m. Jerry S. Cooper, July 30, 1943; 1 dau., Cheryl; m. Clifford S. Mack, Nov. 21, 1957. BS, Hampton Inst., 1940; LL.B., Howard U., 1951; JD (hon.), U. D.C., 1999. Bar: D.C. 1952. Legal cons. OPS, Washington, 1952-53; atty.-advisor office gen. counsel Gen. Svcs. Adminstrn., Washington, 1953-54; trial appellate atty criminal div. Dept. Justice, Washington, 1954-68; civil rights atty. Office Gen. Counsel, Equal Employment Opportunity Commn., Washington, 1968-75; assoc. judge Ct. Appeals, Washington, 1975-89; sr. judge DC Ct. of Appeals, Washington, 1989—2001. Mem. Am., Fed., Washington, Nat. Bar Assns., Nat. Assn. Women Judges. Home: 1610 Varnum St NW Washington DC 20011-4206

MACK, KELLY, newscaster; BA magna cum laude, U. Announcer / prodr. "Public Radio in Mississippi", affiliate of Nat. Public Radio, Jackson, Miss., 1984; anchor, reporter WAPT-TV & WLBT-TV, 1985—87; anchor WXIA-TV, Atlanta, 1987—91; gen. assignment reporter, fill-in anchor WNBC TV, New York, 1993—94; gen. assignment reporter NBC 4, Los Angeles, 1994—97, co-anchor, Channel 4 News at 6pm, 1997—2001, co-anchor, Today in LA, 2001—. Office: NBC4 3000 W Alameda Ave Burbank CA 91523*

MACK, MARY ELKIN, counselor; b. Louisville, Aug. 17, 1955; d. Ralph Gentry and Gayle Susan (Rorrer) Elkin; m. Charles Edward Mack III, Oct. 3, 1994; children: Charles E. IV, Christopher, Heather Conn, Amy Ott, Nick Ott. BS in Recreation & Park Adminstrn., Ea. Ky. U., 1994; Masters degree, U. N.C. Charlotte, 1998. Contract editor Medusa Aggregates Corp., Lexington, Ky., 1978-80; sr. area supr./ops. dir. Domino's Pizza Inc., 1981-90; area supr. U.S. Census Bur., 1992; intern Ten Broeck Psychiat. Hosp., Louisville, 1994; counseling intern Mecklenburg County Schs., Hawthorne Middle Sch., Charlotte, 1996, Cabarrus Family Recovery Systems, Concord, N.C., 1996; counseling intern NOVA: Batterer's Edn./Counseling program Mecklenburg County, Charlotte, 1996—. Cons./trainer Jr. Achievement, Nashville, 1984-90; victim advocate Victims Assistance, Charlotte, 1995—; charter mem. bd. dirs. Ptnrs. Found., Domino's Pizza Inc., Ann Arbor, Mich., 1985—; vol. Charlotte Mental Health Assn., 1995—. Recipient Outstanding Citizen award Councilman Rod Williams, Nashville, 1985. Mem. Am. Coun. Assn.(ACA), Am. Therapeutic Recreation Assn.(ATRA), Am. Mental Health Counselors Assn.(AMHCA), Winston Cup Racing Wives Auxillary, Psi Chi, Chi Sigma Iota, Kappa Delta Pi. Avocations: auto restoration, boating. Office: 886 Carter Dr SW Calabash NC 28467-2537

MACK, VALERIE LIPPOLDT, music educator, performing arts educator, freelance/self-employed choreographer; b. Wichita, Kan., Aug. 30; d. Vaughn Lippoldt and Velma Miller; m. Tom M. Mack, Aug. 7, 1987; children: Stevie, Zane. BA, Bethany Coll., Lindsborg, Kan., 1983; BME, Wichita State Univ., Wichita, Kan., 1987, MME, 1993. Dance instr. Bethany Coll., Lindsborg, Kans., 1981—83; aerobics instr. Mary Mayt Fitness, Wichita, Kans., 1984—86; ballet, tap instr. Kans. Dance Acad., Wichita, Kans., 1986—87; choreographer Wichita State Univ., Wichita, Kans., 1987—95; vocal music H.S. instr. Maize H.S., Maize, Kans., 1986—87; lead vocal and dance instr. Butler C.C., El Dorado, Kans., 1987—. Clinician Emporia State Univ., Emporia, Kans., 1998—2003; producer, bd. mem. Miss Wichita, Miss Bulter, Wichita, Kans., 1983—2003; artistic dir. Butler Showchair Showcase, El Dorado, Kans., 1993—2003. Choreographer (plays) 100 Years Of Broadway, Carnegie Hall, 2000, (video) Mary Mayta Fitness for Life, 1986; performer: (video) Mary Mayta Fitness for Life, 1986; contbr.: chpt. Warm-Ups for Choral Directors, 2003. Praise choir, praise team dir. Risen Savior Luth. Ch., Wichita, Kans., 1994—, bells, chimes, Sunday sch., 1994—; prod., bd. mem. Miss Wichita, Wichita, Kans., 1988—2002; bd. mem. Alzeimeir Assn., Wichita, Kans., 1995. Mem.: Music Educators Nat. Conf. Republican. Luth. Avocations: dance, travel, Broadway shows. Home: 4104 Plum Tree St Wichita KS 67226 Office: Butler Cmty CC 901 S Haverhill Rd El Dorado KS 67042

MACKAY, CYNTHIA JEAN, music educator; b. Kane, Pa., Apr. 30, 1943; d. Theodore Elmer and Frances Agnes (Bertch) Johnson; m. Angus James Mackay, Dec. 30, 1972; children: Shannon Leslie, Brendan Douglas. BS, Mansfield (Pa.) State Coll., 1965; cert., U. Calif., San Diego, 1972. Cert. basic tchg., Oreg.; std. life tchg. credential, Calif; cert. music educator K-12, Tex. Instr. vocal music Camp Curtin Jr. H.S., Harrisburg, Pa., 1965-69, Lincoln Jr. H.S., Oceanside, Calif., 1969-73, Poynter Jr. H.S., Hillsboro, Oreg., 1973-75; tchr. piano Collingswood, N.J., 1976-94, Spring,

Tex., 1976-94; tchr. music Holmsley Elem. Sch., Houston, 1995—. Organist 1st Meth. Ch., Kane, 1958-61; part-time organist 1st Presbyn. Ch., Mansfield, 1961-65; piano accompanist, 1958—. Ednl. docent Houston Symphony League, 1985-92, creator Alice Flores Scholarship Competition, 1988; dist. vol. music coord., Klein, Tex., 1987-88; mem. Cypress Woodlands Jr. Forum, North Houston, Tex., 1988-94, pres. PTO Haude Elem., Spring, Tex., 1988-89, Strack Intermediate, Spring, 1991-92; 1st v.p. Klein Oak Strutters Booster Club, 1992-93. Mem. Tex. Music Educators Assn., Cypress Creek Music Tchrs. Assn. (corr. sec.). Republican. Presbyterian. Avocation: travel. Home: 3419 Blue Cypress Dr Spring TX 77388-5808

MACKAY, GAIL, librarian; b. New Castle, Ind., Nov. 13, 1948; d. Frederick Earl and Rosemary (Garvey) Brown; children: Heather E., Douglas F. BA in English, Purdue U., 1971; MLS, Ball State U., 1973. Cert. tchr., libr., Ind. English tchr. Taylor H.S., Kokomo, Ind., 1977-84; libr. Ind. U., Kokomo, 1992—. Author and presenter. Pres., Tribal Trails coun. Girl Scouts U.S.A., 1995—, nat. cert. instr. of trainers, 1992—. Thank Badge, Girl Scouts, 1989. Mem. ALA, Ind. U. Librs. Assn. (chair profl. devel. 1994), Ind. Libr. Fedn. (co-chair instrn. sect. 1994—). Roman Catholic. Office: Ind U Kokomo PO Box 9003 Kokomo IN 46904-9003

MACKAY, GLADYS GODFREY, adult education educator; b. Buffalo, N.Y., Sept. 17, 1915; d. Joseph Edwin and Hazel Winifred (Brown) Godfrey; m. James Albert MacKay, July 11, 1944 (wid. June 1997); children: Michael Paul, Cynthia Louise. BS, Cornell U., 1936; MA, Tchrs. Coll., Columbia U., 1940; postgrad., Case Western Res. U., Cleve., 1948-50. Cert. tchr. N.Y. Asst. home demonstration agt. Cornell U., N.Y., 1936-38; tchr. rural vocat. home econs. Consolidated Schs., Gilbertsville, N.Y., 1938-39; jr./sr. h.s. home econs. tchr. City Pub. Sch., Peekskill, N.Y., 1940-42; home econs. instr. Mather Coll./Cleve. Coll., Western Res. U., Cleve., 1946-48; marriage counselor/probation officer Lucas County Ct of Domestic Rels., Toledo, 1950-51; tchr./psychologist, spkr.'s bur. Family Health Assn. and Cen. Sch. of Practical Nursing, Cleve., 1951-54. Rep. to nat. consumer-retailer coun. for AAUW, Am. Stds. Assn., N.Y.C., 1940-42; mem. com. setting textile color-fastness stds. for FTC, Am. Stds. Assn., 1941; mem. task force to develop health edn. curriculum, Cleve. Heights Bd. of Edn., Ohio, 1967-69; mem. adv. bd. Children's Svcs., Cleve., 1963-65; mem. mental health com. Fedn. for Cmty. Planning, Cleve., 1977-78, others. Active Coun. on World Affairs, Cleve., 1960-76, in chg. fgn. doctors at Univ. Hosp., VA Hosp.; presenter Cleve. Growth Assn., 1964, Ohio Citizen's Coun., Columbus, 1974-77, others; presenter Met. Health Planning Corp., Cleve., 1978, chair Health Edn. Conf., 1978. Lt. USNR, 1942-46, WWII. Recipient Navy Commendation; named to Nat. Inst. of Pub. Affairs Conf. on Met. Problems, Washington, 1968. Mem. AAUW (life, honoree Ohio Wall of Fame 2000), Case Western Res. Univ. Women's Club (bd. mem. Sch. Medicine), Cleve. Acad. of Medicine Aux., Pi Lambda Theta, Alpha Xi Delta. Presbyterian. Avocations: travel, reading, creative thinking. Achievements include being one of first 2 women to fly Navy antisubmarine Patrol NAS, Norfolk, Va., 1943. Home: 162 Kendal Dr Oberlin OH 44074-1907

MACKAY, PATRICIA MCINTOSH, psychotherapist; b. San Francisco, Sept. 12, 1922; d. William Carroll and Louise Edgerton (Keen) McIntosh; m. Alden Thorndike Mackay, Dec. 15, 1945; children: Patricia Louise, James McIntosh, Donald Sage. AB in Psychology, U. Calif., Berkeley, 1944, elem. tchg. credential, 1951; MA in Psychology, John F. Kennedy U., Orinda, Calif., 1979; PhD in Nutrition, Donsbach U., Huntington Beach, Calif., 1981. Cert. marriage, family and child counselor. Elem. tchr. Mt. Diablo Unified Sch. Dist., Concord, Calif., 1950-60; exec. supr. No. Calif. Welcome Wagon Internat., 1960-67; wedding cons. Mackay Creative Svcs., Walnut Creek, Calif., 1969-70; co-owner Courtesy Calls, Greeters and Concord Welcoming Svcs., Walnut Creek, 1971-94; marriage, family and child counselor, nutrition cons., Walnut Creek, 1979—. Coord. Alameda and Contra Costa County chpts. Parents United Internat., 1985—, pres. region 2, bd. dirs., 1992; bd. dirs. New Directions Counseling Ctr., Inc., 1975-81, founder, pres. aux., 1977-79. Bd. dirs. Ministry in Marketplace, Inc.; founder, dir. Turning Point Counseling; active Walnut Creek Presbyn. Ch.; bd. dirs., counseling dir. Shepherd's Gate, shelter for homeless women and children, 1985-92, Contra Costa County Child Care Coun., 1993-95. Recipient award New Directions Counseling Ctr., 1978, yearly awards Neo-Life Co. Am. Prestige Club, 1977-856, Cmty. Svc. award Child Abuse Prevention Coun., 1990, 92, 94. Mem. AAUW, Am. Assn. Marriage and Family Therapists, U. Calif.-Berkeley Alunni Assn. (sec. 1979-94), Walnut Creek C. of C., Prytanean Alumnae, Soroptomists (bd. dirs. Walnut Creek 1976, 86), Delta Gamma. Republican. Home: 1101 Scots Ln Walnut Creek CA 94596-5432 Office: Ste 12 1399 Ygnacio Valley Rd Walnut Creek CA 94598-2815

MACKENZIE, NANCI, gas company executive; m. Len Mackenzie, 1988. Co-founder (with Sue Palmer) Lucky Lady Oil Co., 1976—82; founder, pres. USGT/Aquila (formerly U.S. Gas Transp. before sale to Aquila), Dallas, 1986—2001. Office: USGT/Aquila 2711 N Haskell Ave Ste 2050 Dallas TX 75204-2965

MACKERETH, BEVERLY D. state representative; b. Wash., DC, Jan. 27, 1958; m. Michael Mackereth; children: Casey, David, Nicholas, Shannon. BA, Frostburg State U., 1979. Dir. Office of Dist. Atty's. Child Abuse Unit/Victim/Witness Program, 1987—95; programs mgr. Office of the Dist. Atty., York County, Pa., 1987—97; dep. dir. Govs. Cmty. Partnership for Safe Children, 1997—99; exec. dir. Healthy York County Coalition, York Health Sys.; Pa. state rep., 2001—. Com. woman Spring Grove Borough, 1993—94, planning commn., 1994, borough coun., 1994—97, mayor, 1997—. Mem. Spring Grove Scholarship Found., 1997—. Mem.: Rep. Club of York, Rotary Club of York. Republican. Office: 52B E Wing Harrisburg PA 17120-2020 E-mail: bmackere@pahousegop.com.

MACKETY, CAROLYN JEAN, laser medicine and nursing consultant; b. Chgo., Feb. 27, 1932; d. Gerald J. and Minnette (Buis) Kruyf; m. Robert Martin, Oct. 3, 1952 (div.); m. Armand Mackety, Apr. 15, 1972 (div.); children: Daniel, David, Steven, Martin, Laura Fitzgerald. RN, Hackley Hosp., Muskegon, Mich., 1969; BA, Coll. St. Francis, Joliet, Ill., 1977; MA, Columbia Pacific U., San Rafael, Calif., 1987; A in Ministry, Western Theol. Sem., Holland, Mich., 1998. Dir. surg. svcs. Grant Med. Ctr., Columbus, Ohio, 1981-84; pres. Laser Cons., Inc., Chgo., 1984-86; v.p. Laser Ctrs. Am., Cin., 1986-88; nursing adminstr. Med. Ctr. Hosp., Burlington, Vt., 1988-91; cons. Colan, Inc., Holland, Mich., 1991—93; commd. program assoc. First Reformed Ch., Holland, Mich., 1998—2001; edn. dir. Cragmor Christian Reformed Ch., Colorado Springs, Colo., 0200, dir. congl. life, 2002—. Dir. perioperative svcs. Mercy Hosp., Muskegon, Mich., 1991-95, dir. critical care and emergency rm., 1996-98, continuous quality improvement instr.; mgmt. infor. systems workgroup Sister O Mery Corp., Farmington, Mich. Contbr. articles to profl. jours. Deacon 1st Reformed Ch., Holland, Mich., 1992-2001, parish nurse, 1995-98, leader children in worship, 1994—; vol. Good Samaritan Ministeries, Holland, 1998-2001. Recipient nursing excellence award Am. Soc. for Lasers Medicine and Surgery, 1991. Mem. Assn. Operating Rm. Nurses (mem. nursing practice com., data element com.), Am. Soc. Laser Medicine (nursing excellence award 1992), Mich. Orgn. Nurse Execs. Office: Cragmor Christian Reformed Ch Colorado Springs CO 80907

MACKEY, PATRICIA ELAINE, university librarian; b. Balt., July 29, 1941; d. Timothy and Hazel Mozelle (Davis) M. BA in Anthropology, CUNY, 1978; MLS, Columbia U., 1981. Asst. libr. I, European Exch. Sys., Mainz-Kastel, Germany, 1966-68; interlibr. loan asst. Poly. U., Bklyn., 1968-72, Rockefeller U., N.Y.C., 1972-73, sr. libr. asst., 1974-80, libr., 1981-91, univ. libr., 1991—. Mem. various libr. coms., N.Y.C., 1991—. Chair pub. svc. scholars program Hunter Coll. CUNY, 1992—; bd. trustees Met. N.Y. Libr. Coun., 2000—. Named to, Hunter Coll. Hall of Fame, 2002. Mem.: ALA, Assn. Coll. and Rsch. Librs., N.Y. State Libr. Assn., Hunter Coll. Alumni Assn. (bd. dirs. 1998—, 2d v.p. 1998—2002). Democrat. Roman Catholic. Avocations: reading, chess, gardening. Office: Rockefeller U Libr RU Box 263 1230 York Ave New York NY 10021-6307 Office Phone: 212-327-8909. Business E-Mail: mackey@rockefeller.edu.

MACKIEWICZ, LAURA, advertising agency executive; Formerly with D'Arcy Advt.; with BBDO, Chgo., 1973—, now sr. v.p., dir. broadcast and print svcs. Office: BBDO Chgo 410 N Michigan Ave Ste 8 Chicago IL 60611-4273

MACKINNIS, ANN PHELPS, municipal government and land use management executive; b. Hartford, Conn., Sept. 3, 1936; d. George Henry and Margaret Louise (Stewart) Phelps; m. Frank Reader MacKinnis, Mar. 15, 1957 (div. Dec. 1980); children: Robert Phelps, John Stewart. AS in Retailing summa cum laude, Lasell Jr. Coll., 1956; BSBA summa cum laude, Coll. of St. Elizabeth, 1988. Acctg. clk. Washington Aluminum Co., Balt., 1975—76; adminstrv. aide Town of Morristown, NJ, 1978—, adminstrv. officer planning and zoning bd., 1986—, mgr. divsn. land use adminstrn., zoning officer, 1986—. Trustee Christmas on the Green, Morristown, 1978-86; adj. prof. Rutgers U. Editor: Morristown Master Plan, 1978-79; also author of ordinances and pamplets. Mem. Morris County Bldg. Ofcls. Assn., Dover, N.J., 1995—, Rutgers Club, New Brunswick, 1998—, Calvert Marine Mus., Solomons Island, Md., 1997—; mem. Mayor's Design Rev. Com., Morristown, N.J., 2001—. Recipient Women of Accomplishment, Outstanding Acad. Achievement, Coll. of St. Elizabeth, 1985, Scholastic Achievement award, 1988. Mem. N.J. Planning Ofcls. (Achievement in Planning award 1997), N.J. Assn. Planning and Zoning Adminstrs. (pres. 1996-99, bd. dirs. 1992—, chmn. edn. and cert. commn. 1999—), Morristown Town Coun. (Achievement in Planning award 1997), Rutgers Club, Calvert Marine Mus. Republican. Protestant. Avocations: sailing, travel, reading, jigsaw and word puzzles. Home: 14 Cromwell Dr Morristown NJ 07960-4602 Office: Town of Morristown 200 South St Morristown NJ 07960-0914 E-mail: A-Mackinnis@TownofMorristown.org.

MACKINNON, CATHARINE ALICE, lawyer, law educator, legal scholar, writer; d. George E. and Elizabeth V. (Davis) MacKinnon. BA in Govt. magna cum laude with distinction, Smith Coll., 1969; JD, Yale U., 1977, PhD in Polit. Sci., 1987. Vis. prof. Harvard U., Stanford U., Yale U., others, Osgoode Hall, York U., Canada, U. Basel, Switzerland; prof. of law U. Mich., 1990—. Long term vis. prof. U. Chgo., 1997—; co-dir. project Equality Now, Legal Alliance Women, 2001—. Author: Sexual Harassment of Working Women, 1979, Feminism Unmodified, 1987, Toward a Feminist Theory of the State, 1989, Only Words, 1993, Sex Equality, 2001, Women's Lives, Men's Laws, 2004; co-author: In Harm's Way, 1997, Directions in Sexual Harassment Law, 2003. Office: U Michigan Law School Ann Arbor MI 48109-1215

MACKINNON, PEGGY LOUISE, public relations executive; b. Florence, Ariz., June 18, 1945; d. Lacy Donald Gay and Goldie Louise (Trotter) Martin; m. Ian Dixon Mackinnon, Oct. 20, 1973. BA, San Jose State U., 1967, postgrad., 1968. Cert. secondary tchr., Calif. Tchr. Las Lomas H.S., Walnut Creek, Calif., 1968-69; edn. officer Ormond Sch., Sydney, Australia, 1970-72; tchr. Belconnen H.S., Canberra, Australia, 1972-73; temp. exec. sec. various orgns., London, 1973-75; mktg. mgr. Roadtown Wholesale, Tortola, British Virgin Islands, 1975-80; sr. v.p., gen. mgr. Hill & Knowlton Inc., Denver, 1981-96; pres. Peggy Mackinnon Inc., Denver, 1996—. Bd. dirs. Rocky Mountain Poison and Drug Found., Denver, 1984-87, Denver C. of C., Boy Scouts Am., Denver coun. Avocations: tennis, skiing, fishing, travel. Home and Office: Apt 21 9200 Cherry Creek South Dr Denver CO 80231-4018

MACKINNON, SALLY ANNE, retired fast food company executive; b. Chgo., Apr. 20, 1938; d. Eugene and Anne Elizabeth (Jones) MacK. BA, Smith Coll., 1960; postgrad., U. Ark., 1961-62. Brand mgr. Speidel div. of Textron, Providence, 1967-70; mktg. mgr. Candy Corp. Am., Bklyn., 1970-72; v.p. account service William Esty Advt., N.Y.C., 1972-76; mktg. mgr. R.J. Reynolds Tobacco, Winston-Salem, N.C., 1976-84, v.p. new brands, 1984-86; v.p. new products mktg. Ky. Fried Chicken, Louisville, 1986-88; ret., 1988. Democrat. Episcopalian. Avocations: photography, travel. Home: 7500 E Boulders Pkwy # 20 Scottsdale AZ 85262

MACKLIN, ELIZABETH (JEAN), poet, editor; b. Poughkeepsie, N.Y., Oct. 28, 1952; d. Edward Carlyle and Margaret Jean (Herkenratt) Wood; m. Francis Gerald Macklin, Jr., Jan. 12, 1974 (div. Mar. 1979). BA, SUNY, Potsdam, 1973. Poetry editor Wigwag Mag., N.Y.C., 1989-91; query editor The New Yorker, N.Y.C., 1978-99. Author: (poetry collections) A Woman Kneeling in the Big City, 1992, You've Just Been Told, 2000; co-translatr: (book) In a Paper Boat, 1989; translator: Basque Lit. Series, U. Nev., 2003—, (CD-book) Too Old, Too Small; Maybe; contbr. poems and essays to popular mags., including The New Yorker, The Nation, The New Republic, Paris Review, others. Fellow in poetry Guggenheim Found., N.Y.C., 1994; recipient award in poetry Ingram Merrill Found., N.Y.C., 1990, Amy Lowell Poetry Traveling scholarship, 1998-99. Mem. Author's Guild, PEN Am. Ctr. (exec. bd. 1995-96). Home: 207 W 14th St Apt 5F New York NY 10011-7140 E-mail: elizabethmacklin@writersartists.net.

MACKLIN, ERICKA MONIQUE, career planning administrator; b. Fort Gordon, Ga., June 17, 1971; d. Charles Richard and Constance M. Macklin. MS, Nova SouthEastern U., 2001. Family resource coord. Augusta Housing Authority, Augusta, Ga., 1996—97; title II coord. Augusta Tech. Inst., 1997—99; career advisor Richmond/Burke Job Tng. Authority, 1999—2002, Clayton Coll. and State U., Morrow, 2002—. Personal E-mail: emacklin17@aol.com.

MACKLIN, RUTH, bioethics educator; b. Newark, Mar. 27, 1938; d. Hyman and Frieda (Yaruss) Chimacoff; m. Martin Macklin, Sept. 1, 1957 (div. June 1969); children: Meryl, Shelley Macklin Taylor. BA with distinction, Cornell U., 1958; MA in Philosophy, Case Western Res. U., 1966, PhD in Philosophy, 1968. Instr. in philosophy Case Western Res. U., Cleve., 1967—68, asst. prof., 1968—71, assoc. prof., 1971—76; assoc. for behavioral studies The Hastings Ctr., Hastings-on-Hudson, NY, 1976—80; vis. assoc. prof. Albert Einstein Coll. Medicine, Bronx, NY, 1977—78, assoc. prof., 1978—84, prof. dept. epidemiology and social medicine, 1984—. Cons. NIH, 1986—; advisor WHO, Geneva, 1989—; mem. White House Adv. Com. on Human Radiation Experiments, Washington1994; chair ethical rev. com. UNAIDS, Geneva, 1996—2001. Author: Man, Mind and Morality, 1982, Mortal Choices, 1987, Enemies of Patients, 1993, Surrogates and Other Mothers, 1994, Against Relativism, 1999, Double Standards in Medical Research, 2004; contbr. articles to ethics, law and med. jours. Fellow: APHA, Am. Soc. Law, Medicine and Ethics, Inst. Medicine NAS, The Hastings Ctr., Am. Philosophys. Assn. (life); mem.: Am. Soc. Bioethics and Humanities (bd. dirs. 1997—99), Internat. Assn. Bioethics (bd. dirs., pres. 1999—2001). Democrat. Office: A Einstein Coll Medicine Dept Epidemiology Population Health 1300 Morris Park Ave Bronx NY 10461-1926

MACKNIGHT, CAROL BERNIER, educational administrator; b. Quincy, Mass., Apr. 12, 1938; d. Harold Nelson and Marguerite (Norris) Bernier; m. William J. MacKnight, Aug. 19, 1967. BS, Ithaca Coll., N.Y., 1960; MM, Manhattan Sch. Mus., N.Y.C., 1961; Dipl., Fontainebleau Sch. Music/Art, France, 1963; EdD, U. Mass., 1973. Asst. to supt. Falmouth (Mass.) pub. schs., 1975-76; dir. bus., mgmt., engring. prog. Sch. Bus. Adminstrn. U. Mass., Amherst, 1976-79, assoc. dir. continuing edn., 1979-82, dir. Office Instructional Tech., 1982—. Trustee New Eng. Regional Computer Program, Inc., 1986—92; bd. dirs. Info. Sys. and Bus. Exch., 1992—93; keynote spkr. Australian Soc. for Computers in Learning In Tertiary Edn. Conf., Adelaide, 1996; conf. chair Transforming Practice with Tech., 2002. Editor: Jour. Computing in Higher Edn., 1988—, Jour. Info. Sys. for Mgrs., 1992—93; mem. editl. rev. bd.: Jour. of Computer-Based Instrn., 1988—2002, author/editor: computer progs.; contbr. articles to profl. jours. CDC grantee, 1986, Regents of Boston grantee, 1988, Lilly Fellow Mentor, 1991-92. Mem. ACM, Assn. for Computing Machinery, Educom, Soc. Applied Learning Techs. (bd. dirs. 2003—), New England Regional Computer Program. Avocations: music, photography, tennis, hiking, skiing. Office: Norris Consulting and Pub PO Box 2593 Amherst MA 01004

MACKUS, ELOISE L. food products company executive; Asst. gen. counsel J.M. Smucker Co., Orrville, Ohio, 1994-99, dir. internat., 1999, v.p., gen. mgr. internat. market, 2000—. Office: 1 Strawberry Ln Orrville OH 44667-1241

MACLACHLAN, PATRICIA, author; b. Cheyenne, Wyo., Mar. 3, 1938; d. Philo and Madonna (Moss) Pritzkau; m. Robert MacLachlan, Apr. 14, 1962; children: John, Jamie, Emily. BA, U. Conn., 1962. Tchr. English Bennett Jr. High Sch., Manchester, Conn., 1963-79. Vis. lectr. Smith Coll., Northampton, Mass., 1986—. Author: The Sick Day, 1979, Arthur, for the Very First Time, 1980 (Golden Kite award Soc. Children's Book Writers 1980), Moon, Stars, Frogs, and Friends, 1980, Through Grandpa's Eyes, 1980, Cassie Binegar, 1982, Mama One, Mama Two, 1982, Tomorrow's Wizard, 1982, Seven Kisses in a Row, 1983, Unclaimed Treasures, 1984 (Boston Globe/Horn Book award 1984), Sarah, Plain and Tall, 1985 (Golden Kite award 1985, Scott O'Dell Historical Fiction award 1985, John Newbery medal 1986, Jefferson Cup award Va. Libr. Assn. 1986, Christopher award 1986, Garden State Children's Book award N.J. Libr. Assn. 1988), The Facts and Fictions of Minna Pratt, 1988 (Parent's Choice award Parent's Choice Found. 1988), Three Names, 1991, Journey, 1991, All the Places to Love, 1993, Baby, 1993, Skylark, 1994, What You Know First, 1995, Caleb's Story, 2001; author (screenplays): Sarah Plain and Tall, 1988, Skylark, 1992, Journey, 1992. Bd. dirs. Children's Aid Family Svc. Agency, 1970-80. Recipient numerous awards for children's fiction. Office: Curts Brown Ltd c/o Marilyn Marlow 10 Astor Pl Fl 3D New York NY 10003-6935*

MACLAINE, SHIRLEY, actress; b. Richmond, Va., Apr. 24, 1934; d. Ira O. and Kathlyn (MacLean) Beatty; m. Steve Parker, Sept. 17, 1954 (div.); 1 child, Stephanie Sachiko. Ed. high sch. Broadway appearances include Me and Juliet, 1953, Pajama Game, 1954, films appearances The Trouble With Harry, 1954, Artists and Models, 1954, Around the World in 80 Days, 1955-56, Hot Spell, 1957, The Matchmaker, 1957, The Sheepman, 1957, Some Came Running, 1958 (Fgn. Press award 1959), Ask Any Girl, 1959 (Silver Bear award as best actress Internat. Berlin Film Festival), Career, 1959, Can-Can, 1959, The Apartment, 1959 (Best Actress prize Venice Film Festival), Children's Hour, 1960, The Apartment, 1960, Two for the Seesaw, 1962, Irma La Douce, 1963, What A Way to Go, The Yellow Rolls Royce, 1964, John Goldfarb Please Come Home, 1965, Gambit and Woman Times Seven, 1967, The Bliss of Mrs. Blossom, Sweet Charity, 1969, Two Mules for Sister Sara, 1969, Desperate Characters, 1971, The Possession of Joel Delaney, 1972, The Other Half of the Sky: A China Memoir, 1975, The Turning Point, 1977, Being There, 1979, A Change of Seasons, 1980, Loving Couples, 1980, Terms of Endearment, 1983 (Acad. award 1984, Golden Globe-Best Actress), Cannonball Run II, 1984, Madame Sousatzka, 1988 (Best Actress Venice Film Festival, Golden Globe-Best Actress), Steel Magnolias, 1989, Waiting For the Light, 1990, Postcards From the Edge, 1990, Defending Your Life, 1991, Used People, 1992, Wrestling Ernest Hemingway, 1993, Guarding Tess, 1994, Evening Star, 1995, Mrs. Winterbourne, 1996, Carolina, 2003; TV appearances Shirley's World, 1971-72, Shirley MacLaine: If They Could See Me Now, 1974-75, Gypsy in My Soul, 1975-76, Where Do We Go From Here?, 1976-77, Shirley MacLaine at the Lido, 1979, Shirley MacLaine...Every Little Movement, 1980 (Emmy award 1980), TV movie appearances Out On A Limb, 1987, (directorial debut) Bruno, 2000, TV mini-series Joan of Arc, Salem Witch Trials, 2002; prodr., TV movies These Old Broads, 2001; co-dir. documentary: China The Other Half of the Sky; star U.S. tour stage musical Out There Tonight, 1990; author: Don't Fall Off the Mountain, 1970, The New Celebrity Cookbook, 1973, You Can Get There From Here, 1975, Out on a Limb, 1983, Dancing in the Light, 1985, It's All in the Playing, 1987, Going Within: A Guide for Inner Transformation, 1989, Dance While You Can, 1991; editor: McGovern: The Man and His Beliefs, 1972, My Lucky Stars, 1995, The Camino, 2000, Out On A Leash: Exploring The Nature of Reality and Love, 2003. Address: C/O ICM 8942 Wilshire Blvd Beverly Hills CA 90211-1934*

MACLEAN, JUDITH E. writer, editor; b. L.A., May 13, 1946; d. Fred M. and Dorothy C. (Schmidt) MacL. BA, Rice U., 1969; postgrad., Duquesne U., 1970-71; postgrad. lang. study, Sorbonne U., 1966. Family therapist Families Together, Pitts., 1974-76; reporter In These Times, Chgo., 1976-77; co-chmn. New Am. Movement, Chgo., 1977-79; editor Am. Soc. on Aging, San Francisco, 1980-85; freelance writer, editor San Francisco, 1986—. Instr. U. Calif. Berkeley ext., San Francisco, 1994-95, Support Ctr., San Francisco, 1992-93. Co-author: (book) Women Take Care, 1986; author: Rosemary and Juliet, 2004; contbr. articles/stories to publs. Newsletter editor: Harvey Milk Lesbian and Gay Dem. Club, San Francisco, 1982-85, polit. action chmn., 1986-87; mem. nat. com. New Am. Movement, Pitts., 1972-76; mem. Nicaragua Solidarity Brigarde, Leon, Nicaragua, 1986. Named Vol. of Yr. Harvey Milk Lesbian and Gay Dem. Club, San Francisco, 1986. Avocations: cross-country skiing, backpacking, hiking, sea kayaking.

MACLEAN, RHONDA, information technology executive; m. Lynn Maclean. Various positions to sr. mgr. computer and comm. security The Boeing Co., 1982—96; dir. corp. info. security Nations Bank (now Bank of Am.), 1996; sr. v.p. Bank of Am., 1998—. Tech. adv. Pres. Nat. Security Telecom. Adv. Com. Fin. Services Risk Assessing, 1997; private sector coord. for fin. services industry public/private partnership on critical infostructure protection and homeland security Dept. of Treasury, 2002—. Mem. bd. adv. U. NC, Charlotte Coll. of Info. Tech. Named Women of Vision, Information Security mag., 2003, one of the 50 Most Powerful People in Networking, Networking World mag., 2003. Mem.: Fin. Services Info. Security Analysis Ctr. (FS/ISAC) (adv. to bd. dirs.), Internat. Inst. Info. Integrity (vice chmn. mem. Adv. Com.), Banking Industry Tech. Secretariat (elected mem. of Security Laboratory Governance Bd.). Office: Bank of Am Corp 100 N Tryon St Charlotte NC 28255*

MACLELLAND, JACKIE LYNN, English educator; b. Kaufman, Tex., Nov. 13, 1940; d. Grady and Juanita (Richman) Hill; m. C.G. MacLelland III, Dec. 18, 1965; children: Charles G. IV, Russell, Stephanie. BA, U. Tex. Dallas, Richardson, 1980; MFA in Painting and Drawing, Tex. Woman's U., 1986, MA, 1990, PhD, 1995. Pres., co-owner Ambience, Mesquite, Tex., 1965-84; pres. MacLelland & Son, Inc., Mesquite, 1990-95; editor Women's Caucus for Art, Phila., 1990-92, asst. to nat. pres., 1990-92; instr. art history Trinity Valley C.C., Terrell, Tex., 1990-95; dir. galleries Collin County C.C., Plano, Tex., 1994-95; prof. English Baiko Jo U., Shimonoseki, Japan, 1995—. Head Cambridge Acad., 1997—. Author: High Heels, 1994; contbr. articles to profl. jours. Planning mem. Planning and Zoning, Mesquite, 1970's; com. mem. Performing Arts Co., Mesquite, 1980's. Lavon B. Fulwiler scholar Tex. Woman's U., Denton, 1993. Mem. Phi Kappa Phi. Mailing: PO Box 852261 Mesquite TX 75185-2261 Home: PO Box 852261 Mesquite TX 75185-2261 Office: Baiko Jo Univ Shimonoseki 751 Japan

MACLENNAN, AMY MARIE, poet; b. San Mateo, Calif., Jan. 11, 1967; d. Hugh William MacLennan and Barbara Jean Tompkins. BS in Psychology, U. Calif., Davis, 1989; MA in English, Notre Dame de Namur U., Belmont, Calif., 2003. Bd. dir. The Sat. Poets, San Mateo, Calif. Co-author: So Luminous the Wildflowers, An Anthology of Calif. Poets; contbr. poetry to mags.; dir.: (non-profit org.) The Saturday Poets. Featured reader San Luis Obispo (Calif.) Poetry Festival, 2003, 2001, Petaluma (Calif.) Poetry Walk, 2002, Sacramento (Calif.) Poetry Ctr., 2003. Recipient 1st pl., Ina Coolbrith Cir. Poetry Contest, 2003, Honorable mention, Inland Empire Calif. Writers Club Writing Contest, 2003. Mem.: MLA, Tchrs. & Writers, Poetry Soc. Am., Acad. Am. Poets, PEN Ctr. USA, Calif. Writers Club. Home: 2379 Lyall Way Belmont CA 94002 Personal E-mail: amaclennan@earthlink.net.

MACLENNAN, BERYCE WINIFRED, psychologist; b. Aberdeen, Scotland, Mar. 14, 1920; came to U.S., 1949, naturalized, 1965; d. William and Beatrice (MacRae) Mellis; m. John Duncan MacLennan, Nov. 29, 1944. BSc with honors, London Sch. Econs., 1947; PhD, London U., 1960. Diplomate Am. Bd. Clin. Psychology; cert. group therapist, trauma specialist. Group psychotherapist, youth specialist cons., N.Y.C. and Washington, 1949-63; dir. Ctr. for Prevention Juvenile Delinquency and New Careers, Washington, 1963-66; sect. chief NIMH, Mental Health Study Ctr., Adelphi, Md., 1967-70, chief, 1971-74; regional adminstr. Mass. Dept. Mental Health, Springfield, 1974-75; sr. mental health adv. GAO, Washington, 1976-90; pvt. practice, specialist psychotherapy Bethesda, Md., 1990—. Clin. prof. George Washington U., 1970—; group therapy cons. D.C. Mental Health Svcs., 1993-2002, Washington Assessement and Therapy Svcs., 1992—; lectr. Montgomery C.C., 1988-91, Washington Sch. Psychiatry Geropsychiatric Program, 1997—; mem. tech. adv. com. Prince George's County Mental Health Assn., 1968-84; cons. Washington Bus. Group on Health, 1990-91, KOBA, 1991; leader Trauma Psychotherapy Groups, 2002-03, Hebrew Home Rsch. Inst. Elder Housing Socialization and Memory Improvement Groups, 2000-02. Mem. NIMH Prevention Intervention Rsch. Task Force, 1990-91, Montgomery County Victims Assistance Programs, 1990-95; v.p. Compliance, Federally Employed Women, 1979-81; pres. Glenecho chpt. Older Women's League, 1993-94. Fellow APA, Am. Orthopsychiat. Assn.; disting. fellow Am. Group Psychotherapy Assn.; mem. Washington Mushroom Club. Democrat.

MACLIAMMOIR, SANDRA JEAN, journalist, columnist, educator; b. Liverpool, England, Feb. 28, 1944; arrived in U.S.A., 1998; d. Charles McWilliams and Edna Kendall; children: Fon, Tara, Conn, Sarah. Diploma in Journalism, London (Eng.) Sch. Journalism, 1986; BA with hons. in English, Lasalle U., 2001; MA in English, Fla. State U., 2003; MFA in English, U. Miami, 2003—. Writer Sunday Ind., Dublin, 1989—93; columnist So. Star, Skibbereen, Ireland, 1986—99; tchg. asst. Fla. State U., Tallahassee, 2001—03, U. Miami, Fla., 2003—. Author: The Secret Life of Joan Moriarty, 1995, Phoebe, 2001. Mem.: Nat. Soc. Colllegiate Scholars, Alpha Sigma Lambda, Lambda Iota Tau. Democrat. Home: The Aston 409 3000 Coral Way Miami FL 33145 Office: U Miami Coral Gables FL 33146

MACMANUS, SUSAN ANN, political science educator, researcher; b. Tampa, Fla., Aug. 22, 1947; d. Harold Cameron and Elizabeth (Riegler) MacM. BA cum laude, Fla. State U., 1968, PhD, 1975, MA, U. Mich., 1969. Instr. Valencia C.C., Orlando, Fla., 1969-73; rsch. asst. Fla. State U., 1973-75; asst. prof. U. Houston, 1975-79, assoc. prof., 1979-85, dir. MPA program, 1983-85; rsch. assoc. Ctr. Pub. Policy, 1982-85; prof., dir. PhD progam Cleve. State U., 1985-87; prof. pub. adminstrn. and polit. sci. U. South Fla., Tampa, 1987—, chair dept. govt. and internat. affairs, 1987-93, disting. univ. prof., 1999. Vis. prof. U. Okla., Norman, 1981—; field rsch. assoc. Brookings Inst., Washington, 1977—82, Princeton (N.J.) U., 1979—, Cleve. State U., 1982—83, Westat, Inc., Washington, 1983—; summer field rsch. assoc. Columbia U., N.Y.C., 1979, Nat. Acad. Pub. Adminstrn., Washington, 1980. Author: Revenue Patterns in U.S. Cities and Suburbs: A Comparative Analysis, 1978, Federal Aid to Houston, 1993; author: (with others) Governing A Changing America, 1984; author: (with Francis T. Borkowski) Visions for the Future: Creating New Institutional Relationships Among Academia, Business, Government, and Community, 1989; author: Reapportionment and Representation in Florida: A Historical Collection, 1991, Doing Business with Government: Federal, State, Local and Foreign Government Purchasing Practices for Every Business and Public Institution, 1992, Young v. Old: Generational Combat in the 21st Century, 1996; author: (with Elizabeth R. MacManus) Citrus, Sawmills, Critters & Crackers: Life in Early Lutz and Central Pasco County, 1998; author: Targeting Senior Voters, 2000; author: (with Elizabeth R. MacManus) The Lutz Depot, 2000; editor: Mapping Florida's Political Landscape: The Changing Art and Politics of Reapportionment and Redistricting, 2002; editor: (with Thomas R. Dye) Politics in States and Communities, 11th edit., 2003; writer: manuals in field, mem. editl. bd.: various jours; contbr. articles to jours., chpts. to books. Bd. dirs. Houston Area Women's Ctr., 1977, past pres., v.p. fin., treas.; mem. LWV, Gov.'s Coun. Econ. Advisers, 1988-90, Harris County (Tex.) Women's Polit. Caucus, Houston; bd. dirs. USF Rsch. Found., Inc.; chair Fla. Elections Commn., 1999-2003; mem. Fla. Gov.'s Coun. Econ. Advisers, 2000—. Recipient U. Houston Coll. Social Scis. Tchg. Excellence award, 1977, Herbert J. Simon award for best article in 3d vol., Internat. Jour. Pub. Adminstrn., 1981, Theodore & Venette Askounes-Ashford Disting Scholar award U. South Fla., 1991, Disting. Rsch. Scholar award, 1991, Tchg. Excellence award, 1999; Ford Found. fellow, 1967-68; grantee Valencia C. C. Faculty, 1972, U. Houston, 1976-77, 79, 83; Fulbright Rsch. scholar, Korea, 1989; Choice mag. award, 1996; named Disting. Univ. Prof., 1999; rsch. fellow Fla. Inst. of Govt., 2000—. Mem. Am. Polit. Sci. Assn. (program com. 1983-84, chair sect. intergovtl. rels., award 1989, mem. exec. coun. 1994—, pres.-elect sec. urban politics 1994-95, pres. sect. urban politics 1995-96), So. Polit. Sci. Assn. (v.p. 1990-91, pres.-elect 1992-93, pres. 1993-94, V.O. key award com. 1983-84, best paper on women and politics 1988, Diane Blair award 2001), Midwest Polit. Sci. Assn., Western Polit. Sci. Assn., Southwestern Polit. Sci. Assn. (local arrangements com. 1982-83, profession com. 1977-80), ASPA (nominating com. Houston chpt. 1983, bd. mem. Suncoast chpt., pres.-elect 1991, Lilly award 1992), Policy Studies Orgn. (mem. editl. bd. jour. 1981—, exec. coun. 1983-85), Women's Caucus Polit. Sci. (portfolio pre-decision rev. com. 1982-83, projects and programs com. 1981, fin.-budget com. 1980-81), Fla. Polit. Sci. Assn. (pres. 1997-98, Manning Dauer Disting. Fla. Polit. Sci. award 2001), Acad. Polit. Sci., Mcpl. Fin. Officers Assn., Phi Kappa Phi (Artist/Scholar award U. South Fla. 1997), Phi Beta Kappa, Pi Sigma Alpha (mem. exec. coun. 1994-96, pres. 2000-02), Pi Alpha Alpha. Methodist. Home: 2506 Collier Pky Land O Lakes FL 34639-5228 Office: U South Fla Dept Polit Sci Tampa FL 33620 E-mail: samacmanus@aol.com.

MAC MASTER, HARRIETT SCHUYLER, retired elementary school educator; b. Maxbass, ND, Nov. 5, 1916; d. Hugh Riley and Christine (Park) Schuyler; m. Jay Myron Mac Master, May 27, 1944; children: Jay Walter, Robert Hugh, Anne Schuyler. BS, postgrad., Coll. N.J., 1971; grad., Inst. for Children's Lit., 1993. With staff spl. govt. WWII project Office Sci. R & D, 1943-44; tchr. Woodfern Elem. Sch., Neshanic, N.J., 1972-87; ret., 1987. Freelance writer elem. sci. program Silver Burdett Co., 1983. Elite mem. Nat. Rep. Congl. Com.; active Grace United Meth. Ch. Named Republican of Yr. from Fla., 2001. Fellow AAUW, LWV. Republican. Home: 230 NE 22nd Ave Cape Coral FL 33909-2820

MAC MILLAN, JANET SUSAN, elementary school educator, education educator; b. Elizabeth, New Jersey, Sept. 25, 1948; d. Edmund Anthony Palmieri and Marian Lucille Korn; m. Thomas Raymond Mac Millan, Apr. 7, 1973; children: Ryan, June, Lisa, RaeAnne, Michael. BA Elem. edn., Felician Coll., Lodi, N.J., 1966—70; MS Spl. edn. reading, Dowling Coll., Oakdale, N.Y., 1993—95. Cert. teaching N.Y., N.J., and N. Mex., 1970. Elem. sch. tchr. Hillside Sch. Dist., Hillside, NJ, 1970—73, Alamogordo Sch. Dist., Alamogordo, N.Mex., 1973—75; elem. art tchr. St. Patrick Sch., Smithtown, NY, 1990—93; elem. art tchr. St. Phillip and St. James Sch., St. James, NY, 1990—93; pre-sch. tchr. St. Patrick Sch., Smithtown, NY, 1993—95; elem. sch. tchr. Mid. County Sch. Dist., Centereach, NY, 1995—99; reading masters Supr. Dowling Coll., Oakdale, NY, 1996—98, adj. prof. of literacy edn., 1998—; reading, academic intervention tchr. Mid. County Sch. Dist., Centereach, NY, 1999—. Mem.: Alpha Upsilon Alpha, Alpha Beta Chpt. (treas. 2000—). Roman Catholic. Avocations: reading, writing a children's book, creative writing. Home: 33 Suburban Lane Nesconset NY 11767-1730

MACMILLAN, SHANNON ANN, professional soccer player; b. Syosset, N.Y., Oct. 7, 1974; Student in social work, U. Portland. Profl. soccer player San Diego Spirit, 2001—03. Mem. U.S. Nat. Women's Soccer Team, 1993—, including silver medal World Univ. Games team, 1993, gold medal U.S. Olympic Team, 96; mem. U.S. Women's Under-20 Nat. Team, 1993—94, including championship Internat. Women's Tournament, France, 1993; mem. LaJolla (Calif.) Nomads club soccer team, winning state club championship, 1991, 92, Japanese Women's Profl. League, 1996, 97. Named 1995 Soccer Am. Player of Yr., Female Athlete of Yr., 1993, 1995, U. Portland, World Cup Champion, 1999; named to San Diego Union Tribune All-Acad. team; recipient Mo. Athletic Club award, 1995, Hermann award, U. Portland, 1995, Bill Hayward award, 1995, Silver medal, Sydney Olympic Games, 2000. Office: US Soccer Fedn 1801-1811 S Prairie Ave Chicago IL 60616

MACMURREN, MARGARET PATRICIA, secondary education educator, consultant; b. Newark, Nov. 4, 1947; d. Kenneth F. and Doris E. (Lounsberry) Bartro; m. Harold MacMurren, Nov. 21, 1970. BA, Paterson State U., 1969; MA, William Paterson Coll., 1976; postgrad., Jersey City State Coll., 1976— Tchr. Byram (N.J.) Twp. Schs., 1969-77; learning cons., child study team coord. Andover Regional Schs., Newton, N.J., 1977—. Mem.: NEA, Andover Regional Edn. Assn. (pres. 1986—87), Sussex County Assn. Learning Cons. (pres. 1982—83, 1993—94, sec.-treas. 1991—92, v.p. 1992—93), N.J. Learning Assn., N.J. Edn. Assn. Avocations: skiing, dance, weightlifting, travel, reading. Home: 4 Systema Pl Sussex NJ 07461-2833 Office: Andover Regional Schs 707 Limecrest Rd Newton NJ 07860-8801 Office Phone: 973 940 1234 246. Business E-Mail: haroldm@nac.net.

MACNAMARA, ANN MARGARET, artist, art educator; b. Chgo., Sept. 21, 1947; d. John Bernard and Margaret Jane O'Connor; m. John R. MacNamara; children: Meghan, Coleen, John, Katie, Bill, Dan, Pat. BA, Manhattanville Coll., 1969; MA, U. Chgo., 1970. Mem., dir. West Hubbard Gallery, Chgo., 1980—82; art instr. Barat Coll., Lake Forest, Ill., 1980—82; reviewer The New Art Examiner, Chgo., 1982—85; artist-in-residence Field Mus. Natural History, Chgo., 1990—. Adj. asst. prof. Sch. Art Inst., Chgo., 1990—; art instr. in field. One-woman shows include Roger Ramery Gallery, 1984, Vedantz Gallery, 1996, Union League Club, 1998, Field Mus., 1999, Aron Packer Gallery, 2002, Represented in permanent collections Field Mus. Faculty Enrichment grantee, Sch. Art Inst., 2003. Avocations: hiking, kayaking. Office: Field Mus Natural History Roosevelt Rd and Lake Shore Dr Chicago IL 60605

MACO, TERI REGAN, accountant, engineer; b. Allentown, Pa., Nov. 4, 1953; d. Francis M. and Jacqueline K. (Becker) Regan; m. Bruce F. Maco, Oct. 1, 1983; children: Adam S., Alex M. BSChemE with honors, Lehigh U., 1975; MBA with distinction, U. New Haven, 1979; cert. in sci., West Chester U., 1994. Supr. Ivory, Procter & Gamble Mfg. Co., S.I., N.Y., 1975-77; asst. mgr. processing Chesebrough Ponds, Inc., Clinton, Conn., 1977-81, sec. and bd. dirs. credit union, 1980; group supr. McNeil Consumer Products, Ft. Washington, Pa., 1981-83; mgr. processing Johnson & Johnson, Ft. Washington, Pa., 1983-84, mgr. nat. planning, 1984-87, group mgr. acctg., 1987-93; pres. Child Placement Network, Inc., Norristown, Pa., 1989-93; tchr. Phoenixville (Pa.) H.S., 1993-94; treas. Borough of Collegeville, 1995-97; pres. T. Maco & Assocs. LLC, Collegeville, 1996—. Treas. United Fund Collegeville-Trappe, Inc., 1996—2000; developer computer-based tng. program. Author: Capital Asset Pricing Model: Capital Budgeting Applications (NAA Manuscript award, 1979). Recipient Achievement award, Johnson & Johnson, 1989, 1992. Democrat. Roman Catholic. Home and Office: T Maco & Assoc 4183 Ironbridge Dr Collegeville PA 19426-1189 Office Phone: 610-489-7215. E-mail: tmaco@juno.com.

MACON, JANE HAUN, lawyer; b. Corpus Christi, Tex., Sept. 26, 1946; d. E.H. and Johnnie Mae (De Mauri) Haun; m. R. Laurence Macon, Sept. 6, 1969. BA in Internat. Studies, U. Tex., 1967, JD, 1970. Bar: Tex. 1971, Ga. 1971, U.S. Dist. Ct. (we. dist.) Tex. 1973, U.S. Ct. Appeals (5th and 11th cirs.) 1973. Legal staff Office Econ. Opportunity, Atlanta, 1970-71; trial atty. City of San Antonio, 1972-77, city atty., 1977-83; ptnr. Fulbright & Jaworski, LLP, San Antonio, 1983—. Pres. Internat. Women's Forum, Washington, 1987-89; mem. Com. of 200, 1988—; bd. dirs. Siebert Fin. Corp., N.Y. Legal counsel Nat. Women's Polit. Caucus, 1981—. Named to San Antonio Hall of Fame, 1984; named one of Rising Stars, 1984. Fellow Tex. Bar Found., Tex. Bar Assn. (chmn. women and the law 1984-85, client security fund com.), Southwest Research Found.; mem. San Antonio Bar Assn., San Antonio Young Lawyers Assn., Women Lawyers Tex. (pres. 1984-85), Tex. Banking Bd., Bexar County Women's Bar Assn. Democrat. Baptist. Home: 230 W Elsmere Pl San Antonio TX 78212-2349 Office: Fulbright & Jaworski LLP 300 Convent St Ste 2200 San Antonio TX 78205-3720

MACON, MYRA FAYE, retired library director; b. Slate Springs, Miss., Sept. 29, 1937; d. Thomas Howard and Reba Elizabeth (Edwards) M. BS in Edn., Delta State U., 1959; MLS, La. State U., 1965; postgrad., U. Akron, Ohio; EdD, Miss. State U., 1977. Librarian Greenwood (Miss.) Jr. High Sch., 1959-62, Greenwood High Sch., 1962-63, Grenada (Miss.) High Sch., 1963-64; library supr. Cuyahoga Falls (Ohio) City Schs., 1964-71; assoc. prof. U. Miss., Oxford, 1971-83; dir. libraries Delta State U., Cleve., 1983-95. Editor: School Library Media Services for Handicapped; editor: ANRT Newsletter, Miss. Libraries; contbr. articles to profl. jours. Mem. ALA, Southeastern Library Assn., Miss. Library Assn., Exch. Club, Phi Delta Kappa, Beta Phi Mu, Delta Kappa Gamma, Omicron Delta Kappa. Home: RR 3 Box 215A Calhoun City MS 38916-9323

MACPHAIL, WENDY ROWENA, art educator, artist; b. East Orange, N.J., Apr. 25, 1949; d. Robert Stephen and Rowena Marian (Hermann) MacPhail; m. Arthur Jefferson Brigham, May 22, 1999. BA, Montclair (N.J.) State U., 1971, MA, 1984. Tchr. art Morris Mus., Morristown, NJ, 1968—70; tchr. art environ. edn. Millburn (N.J.) Township Pub. Schs., 1970—88, Aspen (Colo.) Sch. Dist., 1988—. Instr. art Adams State Coll., Alamosa, Colo., 1999—; bd. dirs. CLEARING Mag., Portland, Oreg.; bd. trustees Aspen (Colo.) Ctr. Environ. Studies, 1990—96; project mgr. 1000 ft. wall Aspen (Colo.) Sch. Dist. Author: Hawk's Message, 1997; contbr. articles to profl. jours. Bd. dirs. environ. edn. Roaring Fork Valley Alliance Environ. Edn., Old Snowmass, Colo., 1990—96. Named Tchr. of Yr., N.J. Conservation Dept., 1986. Mem.: Colo. Assn. Art Edn. Avocations: hiking, canoeing, painting, writing, camping. Home: PO Box 544 Snowmass CO 81654 Office: Aspen School Dist 235 High School Rd Aspen CO 81611

MACPHERSON, ELLE, model; b. Sydney, Australia, Mar. 29, 1964; m. Gilles Bensimon, May 24, 1986 (div.) Appeared on covers of Sports Illustrated swimsuit edit., 1986, 87, 88, 94, Elle, Cosmopolitan, Self; film appearences include Husbands and Wives, 1992, Sirens, 1994, If Lucy Fell, 1996, Jane Eyre, 1996, The Mirror Has Two Faces, 1996, The Edge, 1997, Batman and Robin, 1997, Beautopia, 1998, With Friends Like These, 1998, South Kensington, 2001; TV mini-series, A Girl Thing, 2001; TV appearance in Friends, 1999-2000. Office: Artist Mgmt Penn House B 414 E 52d St New York NY 10022

MACPHERSON, SHIRLEY, clinical therapist; b. Bayonne, N.J., June 16, 1934; d. Alexander Phillip and Milldred (Gurstelle) Gottlieb; m. Duncan MacPherson, Jan. 2, 1981; children from previous marriage: Suzanne Pugsley, Brett Barber. BS, Columbia U., NYU, 1951; MS, Juilliard Sch. Music, 1955; MEd, Calif. State U., Northridge, 1967; MA in Psychology, Pepperdine U., 1992; PhD in Psychology, Pacific Western U., 1998. Concert pianist Norman Seman Prodns., N.Y.C., 1952-61; indsl. health educator Am. Med. Internat., L.A., 1968-70; cons., lectr. Hosp. Mgmt. Corp., L.A., 1970-80; regional dir. Control Data Corp., L.A., 1980-86; outplacement specialist Ind. Cons., L.A., 1986-90; psychologist, intern Airport Marina Counseling Svcs., L.A., 1990-93; staff psychologist Forensic Psychology Assocs., Sherman Oaks, Calif., 1993-94; staff clin. psychologist Pacific Psychologist Assocs., L.A., 1992-94; clin. therapist employee profiling and crisis intervention MacPherson Relationship Counseling, L.A., 1993—. Author: Rx for Brides, 1990, Understanding Your Man, 1998. Vol. Cmty. Alliance to Support and Empower, L.A., 1994-96, South Bay Free Clinic, L.A., 1995-97; mem. Town and Gown Scholarship program, U. So. Calif., L.A. Mem. AAUW, APA, Calif. Psychol. Assn., L.A. Psychol. Assn., L.A. World Affairs Coun., Am. Bd. Hypnotherapy, Am. Assn. Humanistic Psychology, Am. Assn. Suidiology, Juilliard Alumni Assn., Pepperdine Allumni Assn., Internat. Wound Ballistics Assn. Avocations: french and italian, piano, studies. E-mail: Shirlmac@ix.netcom.com.

MACQUEEN, CHER, interior designer, retired newscaster, sportscaster; b. Kansas City, Mo., Mar. 20, 1952; d. Ira Raymond and Peggy Estelle (Turner) Milks. AA in Liberal Arts, L.A. Valley Coll., 1982; BS in Liberal Studies, Excelsior Coll., Albany, N.Y., 1993; grad., Barbizon Sch. Modeling, 1996; postgrad., Calif. State U., San Bernardino, 1998—; cert. in Interior Design, U. Calif., Riverside, 2002. Lic. radio-TV operator. Personnel specialist U.S. Army, Honolulu, 1973-75, adminstrv. specialist San Francisco, 1975-77, broadcast journalist Vicenza, Italy, 1977-80; radio traffic specialist Armed Forces Radio and TV, L.A., 1980-84, radio prodn. specialist, 1984-86, supr. broadcast support specialist Sun Valley, Calif., 1986-90, broadcast support mgr., 1990-91, internal info. mgr., 1991-94, news and sports specialist, 1994-99; owner The Keilani Co., Highland, Calif., 2003—. Mem.: DAV (life), Am. Soc. Interior Designers (allied mem., co-chair (Inland/Palm Springs chpt.), bd. dirs. Inland/Palm Springs chpt. 2003—04), Pacific Pioneer Broadcasters, Women in Mil. Svc. for Am. (charter), Armed Forces Broadcasters Assn. (v.p. L.A. chpt. 1991—93). Avocations: crafts, crocheting. Home: PO Box 276 Highland CA 92346-0276

MACTIER, ANN DICKINSON, state agency administrator; b. Ravenna, Nebr., June 29, 1922; d. Robert Smith and Carrie (Clark) Dickinson; m. James Allan Mactier, Feb. 26, 1944; children: James Allan II, Judith Ann, Robert Dickinson. BS, Northwestern U., 1944; BA, U. Nebr., Omaha, 1963, MA, 1969. Owner, mgr. Ponca Hills Riding Acad., Omaha, 1966-73; cmty. coord. Coll. Fine Arts, U. Nebr., Omaha, 1974-75; mem. Nebr. State Bd. Edn., 1996—, v.p., 2001—. Mem. Omaha Jr. League, 1944—57; mem. exec. com. Riverfront Devel. Corp., Omaha, 1973—79; founder, pres. Florence Arts Coun., Omaha, 1975—79; mem. Omaha Pub. Schs. Bd. Edn., 1983—98; mem. steering com. Coun. Urban Bds. Edn., 1996—98; bd. dirs. Coun. Great City Schs., 1984—89. Home: 3811 N Post Rd Omaha NE 68112-1209 E-mail: mactier@starband.net.

MAC WATTERS, VIRGINIA ELIZABETH, singer, music educator, actress; b. Phila. d. Frederick-Kennedy and Idoleein (Hallowell) Mac W.; m. Paul Abée, June 10, 1960. Grad., Phila. Normal Sch. for Tchrs., 1933; student, Curtis Inst. Music, Phila., 1936. With New Opera Co., N.Y.C., 1941-42; artist-in-residence Ind. U. Sch. Music, 1957-58; assoc. prof. U. Ind. Sch. Music, 1958-68, prof. voice, 1968-82, prof. emeritus, 1982—. Singer: leading roles Broadway mus. Rosalinda, 1942-44, Mr. Strauss Goes to Boston, 1945, leading opera roles New Opera Co., N.Y.C., 1941-42, San Francisco, 1944, N.Y.C. Ctr., 1946-51; leading soprano for reopening of Royal Opera House, Covent Garden, London, 1947-48, Guatemala, El Salvador, Cen. Am., 1948-49; debut at Met. Opera, N.Y.C., 1952; TV spls. on NBC include Menotti's Old Maid and the Thief, 1949, Would-be Gentleman (R. Strauss), 1955; leading singer with Met. Opera Co. on coast to coast tour of Die Fledermaus, 1951-52,, Met. Opera debut, N.Y.C., 1952, leading soprano Cen. City Opera Festival, Colo., 1952-56; performed with symphony orchs. in U.S., Can., S.Am.; concert recitalist U.S., Can., 1950-62; opened N.Y. Empire State Music Festival in Ariadne auf Naxos (Strauss), 1959; soloist Mozart Festival, Ann Arbor, Mich. Recipient Mile award Album Familiar Music, 1949, Ind. U. Disting. Tchg. award, 1979; named One of 10 Outstanding Women of the Yr.; Zeckwer Hahn Phila. Mus. Acad. scholar, 1941-42; MacWatters chair donated by New Auer Grand Concert Hall, U. Ind. Sch. Music. Mem. Nat. Fedn. of Music Clubs, Nat. Soc. Arts and Letters, Nat. Soc. Lit. and Arts, Soc. Am. Musicians, Nat. Assn. Tchrs. of Singing, Internat. Platform Assn., Sigma Alpha Iota. Clubs: Matinee Musical (hon. mem. Phila., Indpls. chpts.). Achievements include having only original recorded version of Zerbinetta aria from Ariadne auf Naxos (Strauss). Home: 3800 Arlington Rd Bloomington IN 47404-1347 Office: Ind U Sch Music Bloomington IN 47405

MACWILLIAMS, DIANE, communications executive; m. Bill MacWilliams. Degree in Fine and Applied Arts, U. Ill. Designer Arthur Andersen & Co.; pres., CEO, founder Quicksilver Assocs., Inc., Chgo., 1976—. Office: Quicksilver Assocs Inc 18 W Ontario St Chicago IL 60610-3809

MACZULSKI, MARGARET LOUISE, event marketing professional, meeting manager; b. Detroit, Apr. 01; d. Bohdan Alexander and Olga Louise (Martinuick) M. BS, Mich. State U.; cert. E-Commerce Mgmt., DePaul U., 2000. Cert. meeting mgr. Mgr. meetings Nat. Assn. Realtors, Mktg. Inst., Chgo., 1977-82, mgr. mktg., 1982-83; regional sales mgr. Fairmont Hotels, Chgo., 1982; dir., mgr. trade shows and confs. Capital Cities Am. Broadcasting Co./Pub. Div., Wheaton, Ill., 1983-85; mgr. meeting and conf. planning Soc. Human Resource Mgmt., Alexandria, Va., 1985-90; mgr. meeting and conv. planning Kraft Foods, Glenview, Ill., 1990-95; cons. meetings and spl. events Chgo., 1996-98; sr. mgr. meeting and travel svcs. Coll. Am. Pathologists, Northfield, Ill., 1998-2000; conv. mgr. Common, A User Group, 2001—02, cons. spl. events, 2002—. Mem. Meeting Planners Internat., Greater Washington Soc. Assn. Execs. (past chmn. site inspection com.), Soc. Corporate Meeting Planners, Am. Soc. Assn. Execs., Mich. State U. Alumni Assn. (treas. D.C. chpt. 1987-90), Soc. for Corp. Mtg. Planners, Assn. Forum, Profl. Conf. Mgmt. Assn. Republican. Roman Catholic. Avocations: piano, swimming, skiing. Home: 849 W Lakeside Pl 3 East Chicago IL 60640-6693 E-mail: gwenraz@hotmail.com.

MADARIAGA, LOURDES MERCEDES, accountant; b. Sagua La Grande, Cuba, July 10, 1959; came to U.s., 1967; d. Jose I. and Mercedes (Estrada) M. AA with honors, Miami Dade C.C., 1978; BBA, Fla. Internat. U., 1981. Staff/audit mgr. Pub. Svc. Commn., Miami, Fla., 1981-89; sr. acct. Price Waterhouse, Miami, 1990-92; staff analyst Regulated Industries, Miami, 1992; CFO, YWCA, Miami, 1992-93; chief fiscal dir. Little Havana Activities and Nutrition Ctrs. of Dade County, Miami, 1993-96; CFO, N.W. Dade Ctr., Miami, 1996-97; cons., sole practitioner acctg. and tax svcs., Miami, 1997-99; pres. Madariaga & Assocs., Inc., acctg. and tax svcs., Miami, 1999—. Vol. League Against Cancer, Miami, 1991—; co-chair GESU Centennial Alumni Reunion, Miami, 1996; treas., mem. host com. Willy Chirino Found., 1999-2000. Mem. Am. Soc. Woman Accts. Democrat. Roman Catholic. E-mail: lmmadariaga@aol.com.

MADAWICK, PAULA CHRISTIAN, artist, educator; b. Ft. Worth, Feb. 14, 1945; d. Tucker Paul Madawick and Lois (Percy) Long; m. Thomas J. Huggins III, Jan. 23, 1965 (div. Jan. 1981); children: Jonathan, James. Student, Sch. Visual Arts, N.Y.C., 1962-92, SUNY, Purchase, 1989-90; B in Visual Studies, Empire State Coll., 1992. Artist asst. Jasper Johns, A. Warhol, Robert Rauschenberg, N.Y.C., [illegible]; asst. art dir. Elois Display Co., Bronx, N.Y., 1980-83; real estate broker Jan Connor, Realtor, N.Y.C., 1983-92; instr. drawing Rockland Ctr. for Art, West Nyack, 1993, 1994, 1999—; gallery dir. Edward Hopper House Art Ctr., Nyack, N.Y., 1993-98, exec. dir., 1996-99; gallery dir. O.C.C. Art Ctr., Demarest, N.J., 2000—. Adj. prof. SUNY Empire Coll. and Rockland Coll., Hartsdale, N.Y., 1994-2001; mem. panel Snug Harbor Cultural Ctr., S.I., 1997; artist-in-residence Blue Hill Cultural Ctr., Pearl River, N.Y., 1994. Contbr. Creative Colored Pencil Landscape, 1996, Realist Painting After Edward Hooper, 1996, The Best of Colored Pencil #2 and #3, 1993, 94; represented in collections at Snake Island Rsch., Toronto, Chase Manhattan Bank, N.A., Bergen Mus. Art and Sci. Mem. Arts Coun. Rockland County, 1990—, Rockland Ctr. for the Arts, 1977—. Recipient Ted and Carol Shen drawing award Silvermine Guild Arts Ctr., 1999, Rockland County Exec. award for visual art, 2002; grant Vt. Studio Ctr., 1998. Mem. Colored Pencil Soc. Am. (signature mem., nat. workshop instr. 1999). Avocations: cycling, hiking. Studio: 159 Piermont Ave Piermont NY 10968-1259

MADAY, CHRISTINE VERGA, artist, illustrator; b. NY; d. John Richard and Joan Margaret Verga; m. Joseph Edward Maday III; 1 child, Sandra Lynn. AAS, Fashion Inst. Tech., SUNY, N.Y.C., 1974. Textile designer trainee Massaki Design Studio, N.Y.C., 1974; textile artist Farid Kahn Designs, Unlimited, N.Y.C., 1974-76; display asst. Sears, Roebuck & Co., 1983—; freelance artist for greeting cards, illustrations, textile and surface designs and fine art paintings Sears Mktg. Lead. Recipient Watercolor award State of N.Y., 1981, 92; Newsday Art contest award, 1996, Decorative Artist's Workbook Mag. award, 1996, award of Excellence Village Art Club, 2002, award of Excellence Tri-County Artists, 2002.

MADDALENA, LUCILLE ANN, management consultant; b. Plainfield, N.J., Nov. 8, 1948; d. Mario Anthony and Josephine Dorothy (Longo) M.; m. James Samonte Hohn, Sept. 7, 1975; children: Vincent, Nicholas, Mitchell. AA, Rider U., 1968; BS, Monmouth U., 1971; EdD, Rutgers U., 1978. Newscaster, dir. pub. rels. Sta. WBRW, Bridgewater, N.J., 1971-73; editor-in-chief Commerce mag., New Brunswick, N.J., 1973-74; dir. pub. rels. Raritan Valley Regional C. of C., New Brunswick, N.J., 1973-74; aide pub. relations to mayor City of New Brunswick, 1974; dir. comm. United Way Cen. Jersey, New Brunswick, 1974-77; mgmt. cons. United Way Am., Alexandria, Va., 1977-78; pres., owner Maddalena Assocs., Chester, N.J., 1978—; sr. cons. United Rsch. Co., Morristown, N.J., 1980-81; sr. ptnr., dir. OCD Group, Parsippany, N.J., 1984-87; chmn. bd. dirs. OCD Group (subs. Xicom Inc.), Morristown, N.J., 1988; pres. Morris Bus. Group, Chester, 1989—. Adj. faculty Somerset County Coll., Bridgewater, N.J., 1970, Fairleigh Dickinson U., 1980; guest lectr. Rutgers U., New Brunswick, N.J., 1975-80; designer publicly offered seminars for Bell Atlantic, 1992-98; cons. change Howmet, Alloy, Dover, N.J., 1993-98; consortium trainer Johnson & Johnson, 1988—; developer redesign program Howmet Alloy Divsn., 1994; instr. on-line worldwide grad. mgmt. program Seton Hall U., 1999-2001; profl. mentor to execs. in maj. firms, 1990—. Author: A Communications Manual for Non-Profit Organizations, 1980; editor New Directions for Instl. Advancement, 1980-81. Chmn. pers. com., police com. Chester Borough Coun., 1984-87; pres. Chester Consolidation Study Commn., 1990. Recipient Mayor's Commendation City of New Brunswick, 1973, Chester Borough, N.J., 1988. Mem. AAUW, LWV, Nat. Assn. Press Women, N.J. Elected Women Officials, Kappa Delta Pi. Clubs: N.J. Sled Dog Assn. Republican. Roman Catholic. Avocations: writing, working with non-profits. Home: 75 Melrose Dr Chester NJ 07930-2321 Office: Morris Bus Group PO Box 641 Chester NJ 07930-2920 E-mail: lucille@morrisbusinessgroup.com.

MADDEN, ALICE DONNELLY, lawyer; b. St. Louis, Dec. 9, 1958; d. William Joseph and Katherine (Kinsella) Donnelly; m. Peter Gerard Madden, Aug. 3, 1985; children: Thomas Joseph, Jackson Joseph. BA in Psychology, U. Colo., 1981, JD, 1989. Bar: Colo. 1989, U.S. Dist. Ct. Colo. 1989, U.S. Ct. Appeals (10th cir.) 1989. Assoc. Fairfield & Woods, P.C., Denver, 1989-94, Clayton & Stone, Boulder, Colo., 1994-96. Bd. dirs. Boulder County (Colo.) Land Trust, 1991-96, sec., 1992, pres., 1994; bd. dirs. Shannon Estates Homeowners Assn., Boulder, Colo., 1989-92; dir. alumni rels. U. Colo. Sch. of Law, 1997—. Mem. ABA, Colo. Bar Assn., Denver Bar Assn. (ct. reform com. 1991), Boulder County Bar Assn., Colo. Women's Bar Assn. Democrat. Avocations: skiing, hiking, reading. Office: U Colo Sch of Law PO Box 401 Boulder CO 80309-0401

MADDEN, CHERYL BETH, state legislator; b. Burke, S.D., Nov. 15, 1948; d. Herman and Ida Denker; m. Michael K. Madden, 1977; children: Pamela, Jessica, Rachel. Grad. high sch. Mem. S.D. Ho. of Reps., Pierre, 1992-98, mem. edn., health and human svc. coms.; mem. S.D. Senate from 35th dist., Pierre, 1999—. Chaplain, chmn. Fedn. Rep. Women. Address: 63 Langdon Rd Buffalo WY 82834-9341

MADDEN, GLENDA GAIL, sales professional; b. Norman, Okla., Aug. 30, 1949; d. John Samuel Jr. and Z. June (Pence) M. BA in Polit. Sci., Okla. Coll. Liberal Arts, 1970. Account clk. U. Okla. Press, Norman, 1977-78, advt. asst., 1978-80, asst. supr., 1980-81, sales mgr., 1981-98, asst. dir. mktg., 1998—. Avocations: home renovation, antiques, reading, genealogy. Office: Univ Okla Press 4100 28th Ave NW Norman OK 73069-8218

MADDEN, TERESA DARLEEN, insurance agency owner; b. Dallas, Aug. 4, 1960; d. Tommy Joe Frederick Dodd and Mary Helen (Sterner) Smith; m. Kim Ashley Madden, June 2, 1989. Student, Tex. Tech U., 1978-81. Cert. ins. counselor. With personal lines svc. Charles R. Ervin Ins., Midland, Tex., 1981, Bryant Scalf Ins., Richardson, Tex., 1981-82; with comml. ins. svc. Street & Assocs. Inc., Dallas, 1982-84; with comml. ins. sales/svc. Hotchkiss Ins., Dallas, 1984-85; mgr. sales Abbott-Rose Ins. Agy., Dallas, 1985-89; owner Glenn-Madden & Assocs. Ins., Dallas, 1990—. Methodist. Office: Glenn Madden & Assocs Inc 13601 Preston Rd Ste 106E Dallas TX 75240-4906 E-mail: dmadden@glenn-maddeninsurance.com.

MADDEN, THERESA MARIE, elementary school educator; b. Phila., Feb. 12, 1950; d. James Anthony and Marie Margaret (Clark) Madden. BA in Social Sci., Neumann Coll., 1977; postgrad., Beaver Coll., Immaculata Coll. Cert. tchr. Pa., prin. Pa. Tchr. elem. grades St. Anthony Sch., Balt., 1971-73, St. Mary-St. Patrick Sch., Wilmington, Del., 1973-74, Queen of Heaven Sch., Cherry Hill, N.J., 1974-77, St. Bonaventure Sch., Phila., 1977-78, 79-83, St. Stanislaus Sch., Lansdale, Pa., 1978-79; substitute tchr. various schs. Phila., 1983-84; tchr. 8th grade math. St. Cecilia Sch., Phila., 1984-94; tchr. math., vice prin. Corpus Christi Sch., Lansdale, Pa., 1994-99; tchr. grades 6-8 St. Maria Goretti Sch., Hatfield, Pa., 1999—. Mem. vis. team Mid. States Assn., Phila., 1992, Phila., 97, Phila., 99, Phila., 2000, Phila., 02, chair, 03; presenter workshops. Mem.: Assn. Tchrs. Math. Phila. and Vicinity, Pa. Coun. Tchrs. Math., Nat. Coun. Tchrs. Math. Roman Catholic. Avocations: crocheting, cross stitch, baking, horseback riding, walking. Office: St Maria Goretti Sch Cowpath Rd Hatfield PA 19440

MADDEN, VICKY J. brokerage house executive; b. Aug. 30; m. Robert Madden; 1 child, Jennifer. Bachelors, Lafayette Coll., Pa. V.p. Alliance Fin. Group, Ft. Myers, Fla., brokerage mgr. Adv. bd. mem. Soc. Fin. Svc. Profls., Ft. Myers; program chair SWF Assn. of Ins. and Fin. Advisors, Ft. Myers. Chair making it on purpose Jr. League of Ft. Myers. Office: Alliance Fin Group 14021 Metropolis Ave Fort Myers FL 33912

MADDEN, WANDA LOIS, nurse; b. Augusta, Kans., Apr. 26, 1929; d. George W. and Lillian B. (Dobyns) Provost; m. Laurence R. Madden, June 3, 1947 (div. 1961); children: Matthew, Mark, Luke, John, Michele. ADN, Pasadena City Coll., 1970; postgrad., Calif. State U. Consortium, 1986. RN, Calif.; ordained to ministry Am. Fellowship Ch., 1995. CCU nurse Huntington Meml. Hosp., Pasadena, Calif., 1970-71, ICU Community Hosp., Pico Rivera, Calif., 1971-72; CCU nurse Queen of the Valley Hosp., West Covina, Calif., 1973-74; ICU supr. Visalia (Calif.) Community Hosp., 1974-77, 89-90, ICU nurse, 1978, San Miguel Hosp. Assn., San Diego, 1978-79; supr. Casa Blanca Corp., San Diego, 1979-80; dir. nursing Visalia Convalescence Hosp., 1981-89, Westgate Gardens Convalescent Ctr., Visalia, 1990; psychiat. staff nurse Mill Creek Hosp., Visalia, 1990-91; AIDS case mgr. Tulare County Health Svcs., 1993-95; assoc. lay pastor Met. Cmty. Ch. of Sequoias, Visalia, 1994-95; pastor Tulare County Rainbow Cmty. Ch., 1995—. Mem. Tulare County HIV Care Consortium, Tulare County HIV-AIDS Edn. and Prevention Planning Com.; gay and AIDS activist, Tulare County; mem. AIDS Outreach Ministry in Home & Hosp. and Outreach to Gay/Lesbian and Transgender Cmty. Home and Office: 332 Pleasant St Roseville CA 95678-1555

MADDING, CLAUDIA, agricultural products executive; b. Detroit, Dec. 27, 1950; d. Clarence Irving and Theresa Flemming; m. John Eldon Madding, Apr. 4, 1979; children: Jonathan, Bryan, Collin. Student, Millikin U., 1969, Richland C.C., Decatur, Ill., 1979-80. Stenographer State of Ill., Springfield, 1968-74; adminstrv. asst. Archer Daniels Midland Co., Decatur, 1979-93, asst. sec., 1993—2001, exec. asst. to chmn. bd., 1994—2001, pres. ADM found., asst. sec., 1997—, exec. asst. to chmn. emeritus, exec. asst. to chmn. bd., 1999—, sec. to exec. com., 1999—2001. Bd. dirs. Hickory Point Bank, Decatur, Ill. Bd. dirs. United Way of Decatur, Decatur Club; past bd. dirs. Jr. Achievement Decatur, Holy Family Sch.; adv. bd. The Parent Project for Duchenne, Muscular Dystrophy Rsch., Inc., Middletown, Ohio; bd. St. Teresa H.S. Mem.: Country Decatur. Roman Catholic. Avocations: reading biographies, watching 1930-40's movies, foreign stamp collecting. Home: 16 Oakridge Dr Decatur IL 62521-4600 Office: Archer Daniels Midland Co 4666 E Faries Pkwy Decatur IL 62526-5666

MADDOX, MARJORIE LEE (MARJORIE LEE MADDOX-HAFER), English educator; b. Columbus, Ohio, Mar. 24, 1959; d. William Maddox and Roberta Lee (Clark) Scurlock; m. Gary R. Hafer, June 5, 1993. BA in Lit., Wheaton Coll., 1981; MA in English, U. Louisville, 1985; MFA in Poetry, Cornell U., 1989. Editor The Cobb Group, Louisville, 1983-87; instr. U. Louisville, 1982-85, Cornell U., Ithaca, N.Y., 1987-90; asst. prof. English Lock Haven (Pa.) U., 1990-95, assoc. prof. English, 1995—99, prof., 1999—. Author: Perpendicular As I, 1994 (Sandstone Pub. Nat. Poetry Book award), How to Fit God into a Poem, 1993, Ecclesia, 1997, When the Wood Clacks Out Your Name, 2000; contbr. more than 260 poems to profl. publs. Bread Loaf scholarship, Catskill Poetry scholarship; recipient Acad. of Am. Poets prize, Cornell's Chasen award, Paumoanok Poetry award 2000, nominated Puchcart prize 3 times; Va. Ctr. for the Creative Arts fellowship; Pa. State System of Higher Edn. grant. Mem. AWP, MLA. Episcopalian. Avocation: travel.

MADDOX, WILMA, health facility administrator; Grad., Truman State U., 1979. Bus. mgr. Vision Care Assocs., Macon, Maine. Bd. govs. Truman State U., 1994—; mem. Ko. K-16 Coalition; mem. bd. edn. Macon County R-I Sch. Dist.; vol. aftersch. program Macon United Meth. Ch. Mem.: Am. Found. for Vision Awareness (past pres. Mo. affiliate). Office: Vision Care Associates 1705 Prospect Drive Macon MO 63552

MADDOX-ADAMS, SHERRY, secondary school educator; Tchr. E.L. Connally Sch., Atlanta. Recipient Excellence Tchg. award, Nat. Coun. Negro Women, 2001, Chevy Malibu Tchg. Excellence award, Atlanta Jour.-Constitution Honor Roll Tchr. award; fellow, Earth Watch Inst.; Fulbright Meml. Fund Tchr. scholar, Japan. Mem.: Nat. Bd. for Profl. Tchg. Stds. (bd. mem.). Office: EL Connally Sch 1654 S Alvarado Terr SW Atlanta GA 30311

MADDOX-HAFER, MARJORIE LEE See MADDOX, MARJORIE LEE

MADGETT, NAOMI LONG, poet, editor, publisher, educator; b. Norfolk, Va., July 5, 1923; d. Clarence Marcellus and Maude Selena (Hilton) Long; m. Julian F. Witherspoon, Mar. 31, 1946 (div. Apr. 1949); 1 child, Jill Witherspoon Boyer; m. William H. Madgett, July 29, 1954 (div. Dec. 1960); m. Leonard P. Andrews, Mar. 31, 1972 (dec. May 1996). BA, Va. State Coll., 1945; MEd, Wayne State U., 1956; PhD, Internat. Inst. for Advanced Studies, 1980; LHD (hon.), Siena Heights Coll., 1991, Loyola U., 1993; DFA (hon.), Mich. State U., 1994. Reporter, copyreader Mich. Chronicle, Detroit, 1946; svc. rep. Mich. Bell Telephone Co., Detroit, 1948-54; tchr. English pub. high schs. Detroit, 1955-65, 66-68; rsch. assoc. Oakland U., Rochester, Mich., 1965-66; mem. staff Detroit Women Writers Conf. Ann. Writers Conf., 1968—; lectr. English U. Mich., 1970-71; assoc. prof. English Eastern Mich. U., Ypsilanti, 1968-73, prof., 1973-84, prof. emeritus, 1984—; editor-pub. Lotus Press, 1974—. Editor Lotus Poetry Series, Mich. State U. Press, 1993-98. Author: (poetry) Songs to a Phantom Nightingale (under name Naomi Cornelia Long), 1941, One and the Many, 1956, Star by Star, 1965, 70, Pink Ladies in the Afternoon, 1972, 90, Exits and Entrances, 1978, Phantom Nightingale: Juvenilia, 1981, Octavia and other Poems (Creative Achievement award Coll. Lang. Assn.), 1988, Remembrances of Spring: Collected Early Poems, 1993; Octavia: Guthrie and Beyond, 2002; (textbook) (with Ethel Tincher and Henry B. Maloney) Success in Language and Literature B, 1967, A Student's Guide to Creative Writing, 1980; editor: (anthology) A Milestone Sampler: 15th Anniversary Anthology, 1988, Adam of Ife: Black Women in Praise of Black Men, 1992; In Her Lifetime tribute Afrikan Poets Theatre, 1989. Participant Creative Writers in Schs. program. Recipient Esther R. Beer Poetry award Nat. Writers Club, 1957, Disting. English Tchr. of Yr. award, 1967; Josephine Nevins Keal award, 1979; Mott fellow in English, 1965, Robert Hayden Runagate award, 1985, Creative Artist award Mich. Coun. for the Arts, 1987, award Nat. Coalition 100 Black Women, 1984, award Nat. Coun. Tchrs. English Black Caucus, 1984, award Chesapeake/Virginia Beach chpt. Links, Inc., 1981, Arts Found. Mich. award, 1990, Creative Achievement award Coll. Lang. Assn., 1988; Arts Achievement award Wayne State U., 1985, The Black Scholar Award of Excellence, 1992; Am. Book award, 1993, Mich. Artist award, 1993; Creative Contbrs. award Gwendolyn Brooks Ctr. Black Lit. and Creative Writing Chgo. State U., 1993, Lifetime Achievement award Furious Flower, 1994, George Kent award, 1995, Lifetime Achievement award Gwendolyn Brooks Ctr., 2003; Naomi Long Madgett Poetry award named for her, 1993—, Alain Locke award Detroit Inst. Arts, Friends of African and African Am. Art, 2003; inducted Sumner H.S. Hall of Fame, St. Louis, 1997, Nat. Lit. Hall Fame for Writers of African Descent, Chgo. State U., 1999, Mich. Women's Hall of Fame, 2002; named Poet Laureate, City of Detroit, 2001—. Mem. NAACP, Coll. Lang. Assn., So. Poetry Law Ctr., Langston Hughes Soc., Detroit Women Writers, Charles H. Wright Mus. of African Am. History, Detroit Inst. of Arts, Fred Hart Williams Geneal. Soc., Alpha Kappa Alpha. Congregationalist. Home: 18080 Santa Barbara Dr Detroit MI 48221-2531 Office: PO Box 21607 Detroit MI 48221-0607 E-mail: nlmadgett@aol.com.

MADIGAN, LISA, state attorney general; BA, Georgetown U., 1988; attended, Loyola U. Asst. dean adult, continuing edn., dir. Sr. Acad. Lifelong Learning Wrights Family Coll. Wilbur Wright Coll., with positive alts. project; mem. Ill. Senate, Springfield, 1999—2003, mem. appropriations, local govt. coms., mem. senate appropriations com., joint com. adminstrv. rules; litigator Sachnoff & Weaver, Ltd., Chgo.; served as Dem. Senate Edn. Com., 1998; atty. gen. State of Ill., 2003—; co-chmn. Bd. dirs. AIDS Living Rememberance Com. Mem. Ill. Bar Assn., Women's Bar Assn. Ill., Chgo. Bar Assn. Democrat. Office: Atty Gen James R Thompson Ctr 100 W Randolph St Chicago IL 60601

MADIGAN, RITA DUFFY, career education coordinator; b. N.Y.C., Jan. 22, 1919; d. Anthony F. and Mary ([illegible]) Duffy; m. John Callahan Madigan, May 1, 1943; children: John C., James A., Paul F. BA in English History, Our Lady of Good Counsel Coll., 1940; M of Adminstrn., U. Bridgeport, 1963, postgrad., 1970. Tchr. English City of Bridgeport (Conn.), 1961-63, Birkshire Jr. High Sch., Birmingham, Mich., 1963-66; career counselor East Side Mid. Sch., Bridgeport, 1969-71; coord. career edn. Ctrl. HS, Bridgeport, 1972—99, ret., 1999. Recipient State SCOVE award, 1986, CCCA Meritorious award, 1993, Meritorious award Teikyo Post Univ, 1993, Meritorious award for svc. to cmty. Girl Scouts of Am., 1996. Mem. AAUW, NEA, Conn. Edn. Assn., Conn. Career Counselors Assn., Bridgeport Edn. Assn., St. Joseph's Ladies League (bd. dirs. 1992-94), Bridgeport U. Alumnae Assn. Republican. Roman Catholic. Avocations: skiing, golf, tennis, sailing, travel. Home: 44 Chatham Dr Trumbull CT 06611-3262

MADISON, PAULA, broadcast executive; b. N.Y.C. married; 1 child. Grad., Vassar Coll., 1974. Asst. city editor Dallas Times Herald; investigative bur. reporter Ft. Worth Star - Telegram, 1980; reporter Syracuse Herald Jour.; cmty. affairs dir. WFAA-TV, Dallas, 1982—84, news mgr., 1984—86; news dir. KOTV-TV, Tulsa, 1986—87; exec. news dir. KHOU-TV, Houston, 1987—89; asst. news dir. WNBC, N.Y.C., 1989—96, v.p., news dir., 1996—2000; v.p., sr. v.p. diversity NBC, N.Y.C., 2000—02; pres., gen. mgr. KNBC, L.A., 2000—. Bd. trustees Vassar Coll. Named Disting. African-Am. New Yorker, N.Y.C. Comptroller Alan Hevesi; recipient Ida B. Wells award, Nat. Assn. Black Journalists', 1998, Ellis Island medal of honor, Nat. Ethnic Coalition of Orgns., 1999, President's award, NAACP, 2001, Frederick C. Patterson award, United Negro College Fund, 2001, Diversity award, Nat. Assoc. Minority Media Execs., 2002, Woman of the Year, Los Angeles County Commn. for Women, 2002, Excellence in Media Award, Calif. NOW Chap., 2003, TRISCCORT award, Tri-State Catholic Com. on Radio and TV, Asian-Pacific Am. Corp. Impact award, Org. Chinese Americans Greater Los Angeles Chap. Image award Corp. Achievement. Mem.: N.Y. Assn. Black Journalists, Nat. Assn. Black Journalists. Office: NBC 4 3000 West Alameda Ave Burbank CA 91523*

MADISON, SUE WOOD, state legislator; b. Uchitomari, Okinawa, Feb. 10, 1948; d. Roy and Lyda (Camille) Wood; m. Bernard L. Madison; children: Eva, Blair. BS, La. State U., 1970, MS, 1976. Planning commr. City of Fayetteville, Ark., 1984-88; justice of peace Washington County, Ark., 1991-94; state rep., 1995—2000; state senator, 2003—. Property mgr., owner. Democrat. Presbyterian. Avocation: gardening. Home: 573 N Rockcliff Rd Fayetteville AR 72701-3809

MADISON, VICKI DIANNE, retired music educator; b. Paducah, Ky., July 17, 1947; d. Warren G. Dunkerson and Vernelle Frances Phillips Dunkerson; m. David Norris Madison, June 6, 1969; 1 child, Philip Warren. MusB, Murray State U., 1965—70. Yamaha Keyboard Lab Instr. Yamaha Corp., 2001, Orff/Schulwerk Level I Orff/Schulwerk, 2000. Music specialist k/12 Marshall County Schools, Benton, Ky., 1970—98, 1998—; adj. instr. Murray State U., Murray, Ky., 2001—; organist /pianist First Bapt. Ch. of Calvert City, Calvert City, Ky., 1976—. Mem./sect. leader Paducah Symphony Chorus, Paducah, Ky., 1999—2002. Sec. Calvert City Lions Club, Ky., 1996—97, pres., 1998—99, dir., 2003—, pres., 1998—2000, dir., 2003—; councilwoman Calvert City City Coun., Ky., 1999—, coun. rep., 1999—; state historian for Ky.. choral directors Am. Choral Directors Assn., Okla. City. Recipient Ky. Col., Commonwealth of Ky., 1996, Lion of the Yr., Calvert City Lions Club, 1998, Ky. Elem. Music Tchr. of the Yr., Ky. Music Educators Assn., 1996, Mid. Sch. Music Tchr. of the Yr., First Dist./Ky. Music Educators Assn., 1996—97. Mem.: Am. Choral Directors Assn./Ky. Chpt. (historian 1996—2003), Ky. Music Educators Assn. of Music Educators Nat. Conf. (elected/apptd. bd. rep. 1992—), Ky. Allianes for Arts Edn. (treas. 2003). Democrat-Npl. Bapt. Avocation: travel. Home: 1940 Camelot Drive Calvert City KY 42029

MADLOCK, YVONNE, city health department administrator; m. Lawrence Madlock; 3 children. BS, Wellesley Coll.; MAT, Wesleyan U., Middletown, Conn.; studied, U. Tex. Sch. Pub. Health. Adminstr., bur. personal health svcs. Shelby Co. Divsn. Health Svcs., Memphis, dir., 1995—. Bd. pres. Cmty. Inst. for Early Childhood; bd. dirs. W. Tenn. Area Health Edn. Ctr., Memphis Leadership Inst., Cmty. Found. of Greater Memphis, Shelby Co. Ground Water Quality Control Bd. Mem.: Nat. Assn. City and County Health Officials (bd. dirs.). Office: Shelby Co Divsn Health Svcs 814 Jefferson Ave Memphis TN 38103

MADONNA, (MADONNA LOUISE VERONICA CICCONE), singer, actress, producer; b. Bay City, Mich., Aug. 16, 1958; d. Sylvio and Madonna Ciccone; m. Sean Penn, Aug. 16, 1985 (div. 1989); m. Guy Ritchie, 2000; 2 children, Lourdes, Rocco. Student, U. Mich., 1976-78. Dancer Alvin Ailey Dance Co., N.Y.C., 1979; CEO Maverick Records, L.A. Albums include Madonna, 1983, Like a Virgin, 1985, True Blue, 1986,(soundtrack)Who's That Girl, 1987, (with others) Vision Quest Soundtrack, 1983, You Can Dance, 1987, Like a Prayer, 1989, I'm Breathless: Music From and Inspired by the Film Dick Tracy, 1990, The Immaculate Collection, 1990, Erotica, 1992, Bedtime Stories, 1994, Something to Remember, 1995, (soundtrack) Evita, 1996, Ray of Light, 1998 (Grammy award for Best Pop Album 1999), (with others) Austin Powers, The Spy Who Shagged Me soundtrack, 1999, Music, 2000, GHV2: Greatest Hits Volume II, 2002, American Life, 2003; film appearances include A Certain Sacrifice, 1980, Vision Quest, 1985, Desperately Seeking Susan, 1985, Shanghai Surprise, 1986, Who's That Girl, 1987, Bloodhounds of Broadway, 1989, Dick Tracy, 1990, Shadows and Fog, 1992, Truth or Dare, 1991, Body of Evidence, 1992, A League of Their Own, 1992, Dangerous Game, 1993, Blue in the Face, 1995, Four Rooms, 1996, Girl 6, 1996, Evita, 1996 (Golden Globe, 1997), The Next Best Thing, 2000, Swept Away, 2002; Broadway theater debut in Speed-the-Plow, 1987, stage appearance in Up for Grabs, 2002; TV appearances include Happy Birthday Elizabeth: A Celebration of a Life, 1997, Will & Grace, 2003; author: Sex, 1992, The English Roses, 2003. Office: 8491 W Sunset Blvd Ste 485 West Hollywood CA 90069-1911 Address: Maverick Recording Co 9348 Civic Center Dr Ste 100 Beverly Hills CA 90210-3606*

MADORI, JAN, art gallery director; Founder, CEO Personal Preference Inc., Bolingbrook, Ill., 1979—. Named Illinois/Northwest Indiana Entrepreneur of the Year, Ernst & Young; named to U. Illinois Entrepreneurship Hall of Fame. Office: Personal Preference Inc 800 Remington Blvd Bolingbrook IL 60440-4800

MADRID, OLGA HILDA GONZALEZ, retired elementary education educator, association executive; b. San Antonio, May 4, 1928; d. Victor A. and Elvira Ardilla Gonzalez; m. Sam Madrid, Jr., June 29, 1952; children: Ninette Marie, Samuel James. Student, U. Mex., San Antonio, St. Mary's U.; BA, Our Lady of Lake U., 1956, MEd, 1963. Cert. bilingual tchr., adminstr., Tex. Sec. Lanier HS San Antonio Ind. Sch. Dist., San Antonio, 1945-52; tchr. Collins Garden Elem. Sch., Storm Elem. Sch., San Antonio Ind. Sch. Dist., San Antonio, 1963-92; tutor Dayton, Ohio, 1952-54. Bd. dir., sch. rep. San Antonio Tchr. Coun., 1970-90; chair various coms. Collins Garden Elem., 1970-92. Elected dep. precinct, senatorial and state Dem. Conv., San Antonio, 1968—; apptd. commr. Keep San Antonio Beautiful, 1985; life mem., past pres. San Antonio YWCA; bd. dir. Luth. Gen. Hosp., Nat. Conf. Christians and Jews, Cath. Family and Children's Svc., St. Luke's Luth. Hosp.; nat. bd. dir. YWCA, 1985-96, also mem. exec. com.; mem. edn. commn. Holy Rosary Parish, 1994—; mem. bus. assoc.

com. Our Lady of the Lake U., 1995—. Recipient Outstanding Our Lady Lake Alumni award Our Lady Lake U., 1975, Guadalupana medal San Antonio Cath. Archdiocese, 1975, Yellow Rose Tex. citation Gov. Briscoe, 1977; Olga H. Madrid Ctr. named in her honor, YWCA San Antonio and San Antonio City Coun., 1983; Lo Mejor De Lo Nuestro honoree San Antonio Light, 1991, honoree San Antonio Women's History Month Coalition, 1996; named Our Lady of Lake Outstanding Alumna, 1999, one of five women honored for promoting literacy and cultural heritage with a sch. wall mural titled "Mis Palabras, Mi Poder", 2002. Mem. San Antonio Bus. and Profl. Women, Inc. (mem. exec. com.), Salute Quality Edn. (honoree 1993), Delta Kappa Gamma (Theta Beta chpt., mem. exec. com.). Avocations: reading, gardening. Home: 2726 Benrus Blvd San Antonio TX 78228-2319

MADRID, PATRICIA A. state attorney general; BA in English and Philosophy, U. N.Mex., 1969, JD, 1973; cert., Nat. Jud. Coll., U. Nev., 1978. Bar: N.Mex. N.Mex. State Dist. Judge, 1978—84; atty. gen. State of N.Mex., 1999—. Named Latina Atty. of Yr., Nat. Hispanic Bar Assn., 2001. Democrat. Office: Atty Gens Office PO Drawer 1508 Santa Fe NM 87504-1508

MADRY-TAYLOR, JACQUELYN YVONNE, educational administrator; d. Arthur Chester and Janie (Cowart) Madry; 1 child, Jana LeMadry. BA, Fisk U., 1966; MA, Ohio State U., 1969; EdD, U. Fla., 1975. Cert. Inst. for Ednl. Mgmt., Harvard U., 1981. Tchr. Spanish Terry Parker Sr. High Sch., Jacksonville, 1967-72; instr. U. Fla., Gainesville, 1972-75; asst. to v.p. for acad. affairs. Morris Brown Coll., Atlanta, 1975-76; dean for instructional svcs. No. Va. Community Coll., Annandale, Va., 1976-83; dean undergrad. studies Bridgewater (Mass.) State Coll., 1983-92, exec. asst. to acting pres., 1988, acting v.p. acad. affairs, 1988-90; dir. Acad. Leadership Acad. Am. Assn. State Coll. and Univs., Washington, 1992-94; dir. ednl. programs and svcs. United Negro Coll. Fund Hdqs., 1994-97; pres. JYM Assocs., 1999—. Cons. to colls., univs. and orgns., 1997-99; cons. W.K. Kellog Found., 1993-97; bd. dirs. Bridgewater State Coll. Early Learning Ctr., 1984-88; evaluator U.S. Dept. State/Fgn. Svc., Washington, 1982—, U.S. Dept. Edn., 1989—; pres. JYM Assocs., 1999—. Vice chmn. No. Va. Manpower Planning Coun., Fairfax County, Va., 1981. Recipient Cert. Achievement Bridgewater State Coll. Black Alumni, 1988, Women Helping Women award Soroptimist Internat., 1980, Outstanding Young Women Am. award, 1976, 78; named Personalities of South, 1977; recipient Outstanding Tchr./Student Rels. Humanitarian award B'nai B'rith, 1972. Mem. Pub. Mem. Assn. U.S. Fgn. Svc., Soroptimist Internat., Boston Club (v.p. 1986-88), Jack and Jill of Am., Inc., Pi Lambda Theta, Phi Delta Kappa, Alpha Kappa Alpha, Links Inc. (Reston, Va. chpt.). Methodist. Avocations: playing piano, bike riding. Home and Office: 12274 Angel Wing Ct Reston VA 20191-1119 Fax: 703-716-4364. E-mail: jkemt@aol.com.

MADSEN, BARBARA A, state supreme court justice; BA, U. Wash., 1974; JD, Gonzaga U., 1977. Pub. defender King and Snohomish Counties, 1977—82; staff atty. Seattle City Atty.'s Office, 1982—84, spl. prosecutor, 1984—88; judge Seattle Mcpl. Ct., 1988—92; justice Washington Supreme Ct., Olympia, 1993—. Office: Wash Supreme Ct PO Box 40929 Olympia WA 98504-0929*

MADSEN, SUSAN ARRINGTON, writer; b. Logan, Utah, Aug. 25, 1954; d. Leonard J. and Grace F. Arrington; m. Dean Madsen, Aug. 20, 1974; children: Emily, Rebecca, Sarah, Rachel. BS in Journalism, Utah State U., 1975. Mem. adj. faculty Logan Latter-day Saints Inst. Religion, 1991-95. Author: Christmas: A Joyful Heritage, 1984, The Lord Needs a Prophet, 1990, I Walked to Zion: True Stories of Young Pioneers on the Mormon Trail, 1994, Growing Up in Zion: True Stories of Young Pioneers Building the Kingdom, 1996, The Second Rescue: The Story of the Spiritual Rescue of the Willie and Martin Handcart Pioneers, 1998, (with Leonard J. Arrington) Sunbonnet Sisters: True Stories of Mormon Women and Frontier Life, 1984, Mothers of the Prophets, 1987; contbr. numerous articles to Collier's Ency. Yearbooks. Chair Hyde Pk. (Utah) Bd. Adjustments, 1985-94. Honoree Utah State U. Nat. Women's History Week, 1985; recipient Cmty. Svc. award Nat. Daus. Utah Pioneers, 1990. Mem. Lds Ch. Avocations: horseback riding, snow skiing, genealogy, family activities.

MADY, BEATRICE M. artist; d. Raymond J. and Beatrice A. Mady; m. David W. Cummings. Student, Bklyn. Mus. Art Sch.; BFA, U. Dayton; MFA, Pratt Inst. Asst. prof. graphic arts St. Peter's Coll., Jersey City. One-woman shows include Rockville Centre (N.Y.) Pub. Gallery, 1976, Jersey City Visual Art Gallery, 1988, Caldwell (N.J.) Coll., 1991, Johnson & Johnson Consumer Products divsn., Skillman, N.J., 1993, Rabbet Gallery, New Brunswick, N.J., 1996, Maurice M. Pine Gallery, Fair Lawn, N.J., 1997, exhibited in group shows at Newark Mus., 1982, Summit (N.J.) Art Ctr., 1985, Gallery Jupiter, Little Silver, N.J., 1986, Morris Mus., Morristown, N.J., 1987, Yuma (Ariz.) Art Ctr., 1989, Van Vorst Gallery, Jersey City, 1990, City Without Walls Gallery, Newark, 1993, 1998, Rabbet Gallery, New Brunswick, 1995, Watchung (N.J.) Arts Ctr., 1996, Seton Hall U. Law Sch., Newark, 1996, 2000, 2000, Merck Corp. Hdqs., White House, N.J., 1997, Ben Shahn Gallery, Wayne, N.J., 1998, Represented in permanent collections Dayton (Ohio) Art Inst., Pfizer, Morris Plains, N.J., Ortho Dermatol., Skillman, Janssen Pharmaceutia, Titusville, N.J., Bristol-Meyers Squibb, Plainsboro, Lawrenceville, N.J., Johnson & Johnson, New Brunswick, Sydney & Francis Lewis Found., Richmond, Va., Drew U. Mus., Madison, N.J., Arenol Chem. Corp., N.Y.C., Goetz and Mady-Grove, Jericho, N.Y. Grantee, Ford Found., 1978; Painting fellow, Pratt Inst., Bklyn., 1977—78, N.J. State Coun. Arts, 1985. Mem.: Coll. Art Assn.

MAEDA, J. A. data processing executive, consultant; b. Mansfield, Ohio, Aug. 24, 1940; d. James Shunso and Doris Lucille Maeda; m. Robert Lee Hayes; 1 child, Brian Sentaro Hayes. BS in Math., Purdue U., 1962, postgrad., 1962-63, Calif. State U., Northridge, 1968-75; cert. profl. designation in tech. of computer operating systems and tech. of info. processing, UCLA, 1971. Cons., rsch. asst. computer ctr. Purdue U., West Lafayette, Ind., 1962-63; computer operator, sr. tab operator, mem. faculty Calif. State U., Northridge, 1969, programmer cons., tech. asst. II, 1969-70, supr. acad. applicatons, EDP supr. II, 1970-72, project tech. support coord. programmer II, office of the chancellor, 1972-73, tech. support coord. statewide timesharing tech. support, programmer II, 1973-74, acad. coord., tech. support coord. instrn., computer cons. III, 1974-83; coord. user svcs. info. ctr., mem. tech. staff IV CADAM INC subs. Lockheed Corp., Burbank, Calif., 1983-86, coord. user svcs., tech. specialist computing dept., 1986-87; v.p., bd. dirs. Rainbow Computing, Inc., Northridge, 1976-85; dir. Aki Tech/Design, Northridge, 1976—. Mgr. mktg. thaumaturge Taro Quipu Cons., Northridge, 1987—; tech. cons. Digital Computer Cons., Chatsworth, Calif., 1988; computer tech., fin. and bus. mgmt., sys. integration, 1988—90; tech. customer software support Collection Data Sys., Westlake, Calif., 1991; sr. tech. writer info mgmt. divsn. Sterling Software, 1992—2000; sr. tech. writer, quality analyst Computer Assocs. Internat., Inc., 2000—. Contbr. articles and photos to profl. jours. Mem.: DECUS (ednl. spl. interest group 1977—83, ednl. steering com. RSTS/E 1979—82), SHARE, IEEE, Soc. for Tech. Comm. Avocations: photography, photojournalism, vintage automobiles. Office: Computer Assocs Internat Inc 8511 Fallbrook Ave Ste 100 West Hills CA 91304

MAES, PETRA JIMENEZ, state supreme court justice; widowed; 4 children. BA, U. N.Mex., 1970, JD, 1973. Bar: N.Mex. 1973. Pvt. pratice law, Albuquerque, 1973-75; rep., then office mgr. No. N.Mex. Legal Svcs., 1975-81; dist. judge 1st Jud. Dist. Ct., Santa Fe, Los Alamos, 1981-98; chief judge, 1984-87, 92-95; chief justice Supreme Ct. N.Mex., 1998—. Active S.W. coun. Boy Scouts Am., mem. dist. coms.; presenter pre cana St. John's Cath. Ch.; bd. dirs. Nat. Ctr. on Women and Family Law; chairperson Tri-County Gang Task Force; mem. Gov.'s Task Force on Children and Families, 1991-92; mem. adv. com. Santa Fe County Jail, 1996. Mem. N.Mex. Bar Assn. (elderly law com. 1980-81, alternative dispute resolution com. 1987-92, code of jud. conduct com. 1992—, juvenile cmty. corrections svcs. com. chairperson), Hispanic Women's Coun. (charter). Office: Supreme Court NMex PO Box 848 Santa Fe NM 87504-0848

MAFFRE, MURIEL, ballet dancer; b. Enghien, Val D'Oise, France, Mar. 19, 1966; came to U.S., 1990; d. Bernard and Monique (Berteaux) M. Diploma, Paris Opera Ballet Sch., 1981; Baccalauréat (hon.), France, 1984. Dancer Hamburg Ballet, Fed. Republic Germany, 1983-84; soloist Sarragoza Ballet, Spain; premiere danseuse Monte Carlo Ballet, Monaco, 1985-90; prin. dancer San Francisco Ballet, 1990—. Guest artist with Berlinor Staatsoper and Lines Contemporary Ballet. Recipient 1st prize Nat. Conservatory, Paris, 1983, Grand prize and Gold medal Paris Internat. Ballet Competition, 1984, Isadora Duncan award, 1990. Office: San Francisco Ballet 455 Franklin St San Francisco CA 94102-4471

MAGARIAN, KAREN S. chiropractor, consultant; b. Bronx, N.Y., May 19, 1957; d. Nazareth and Phyllis (Wolkoff) Magarian. BS in Rehab. Counseling, Boston U., 1979; BS in Human Biology, Nat. Coll. of Chiropractic, Lombard, Ill., 1984; DC, L.A. Coll. of Chiropractic, Whittier, Calif., 1987; MA in Family Therapy, Phillips Grad. Inst., North Hollywood, Calif., 1994. Lic. chiropractor, Calif., Mass.; cert. sex educator and counselor, Am. Assn. Sex Educators, Counselors & Therapists; diplomate Am. Acad. Pain Mgmt. Office mgr., counselor Women's Reproductive Health Ctr., Boston, 1978-82; pres., CEO Womanspirit Consulting, Boston, L.A., 1978—, med. tching. assoc. L.A., 1990—; pres., CEO Advantage Representatives, L.A., 1993—. Rschr. L.A. Coll. Chiropractic, 1986-87. Author: Turning Dreams Into Reality, 1995; editor: Chiropractic College Admissions and Curriculum Directory. Peer counselor Boston U. Speak Easy, 1976-79; pres., Woman's Health Coun., Nat. Coll. Chiropractic, 1982 83; v.p., Woman's Health Coun., L.A. Coll. of Chiropractic, 1986-87. Mem. AAUW, APHA, Nat. Coun. on Women's Health, Am. Assn. Sex Educators, Counselors and Therapists, Sexuality Info. and Edn. Coun. of the U.S., Acad. Family Mediators, Am. Acad. Pain Mgmt., Assn. Humanistic Psychology. Avocations: camping, yoga, gardening, swimming, horseback riding.

MAGEE, ELIZABETH SHERRARD, civic organization volunteer; b. Rock Island, Ill., Sept. 11, 1922; d. Benjamin Harrison and Helen Lucile (Williams) Sherrard; m. Harber Homer Hall, June 15, 1944 (div. 1949); 1 child, John Sherrard Hall; m. Curtis Lyness Johnson, Dec. 18, 1951 (dec. July 1957); children: Peter Hays Johnson, Julie Jaye Johnson Kimball; m. Robert Milton Magee, Sept. 21, 1963 (dec. 1988); 1 child, Robert Decker (dec. 1983). Student, Augustana Coll., Rock Island, 1940-42. Office mgr., sec. Chgo. Motor Club, Rock Island, 1942-44; personal shopper M.L. Parker Co., Davenport, Iowa, 1945-46. Mem. Jr. Bd. Rock Island, 1944—65, ARC nursing duties, Rock Island, 1971—75, Presbyn. Women Rock Island, 1960—99; clerk of session Broadway Presbyn. Ch., 1990—93, 1995—98, 2002. Mem. DAR (state rec. sec. 1995-97, divsn. I dir. 1997-99, editor Biennial Procs. Ill. State Orgn. 1995-97, state vice regent 2000-03), Internat. Order Kings Daus. and Sons, P.E.O. Sisterhood (past pres., sec., treas.). Republican. Presbyterian. Avocations: computers, stamps, coins. Home: 17575 Warner Castle Rd Orion IL 61273-9181

MAGERKO, MAGGIE HARDY, lumber company executive; d. Joseph Hardy; m. Peter Magerko. Pres. Nemacolin Woodlands Resort & Spa, 1987—, 84 Lumber Co., Eighty Four, Pa., 1994—. Office: 84 Lumber Co 1019 Route 519 Eighty Four PA 15330*

MAGGIOLO, PAULETTE BLANCHE, writer; b. Ballon, France, Mar. 2, 1922; d. Fernand Epinal and Blanche Audineau; m. Anthony Maggiolo, Dec. 29, 1946 (dec. Sept. 1982); children: Denise, Daniel, Annette. MA Columbia U., 1966; D Fgn. Lang.s, Middlebury U., 1972. Tchr. French lit. Lycee of Le Mans, France, 1942—45; head fgn. lang. dept. Leonia H.S., NJ, 1955—88; tchr. French Loud Fairfax C.C., Middletown, Va., 1990—97. Author: The Guilty Teacher, 1999. Home: 207 S Church St Woodstock VA 22664

MAGILL, DODIE BURNS, early childhood education educator; b. Greenwood, S.C., July 10, 1952; d. Byron Bernard and Dora Curry B.; children: Charles Towner II, Emily Curry. BA, Furman U., 1974; MEd, U. S.C., 1978. Cert. tchr., early childhood, elementary, elementary principal, supv., S.C. Kindergarten tchr. Sch. Dist. Greenville County, 1974-83; early childhood edn. instr. Valdosta (Ga.) State Univ., 1983-84; dir. lower sch. Valwood Sch., Valdosta, 1984-86; kindergarten tchr. Sch. Dist. Greenville County, 1986—. Tchr.-in-residence S.C. Ctr. for Tchr. Recruitment, Rock Hill, 1993, mem. policy bd.; workshop presenter and lectr. in various schs. and sch. dists. throughout U.S., 1974—; chmn. S.C. Pub. Kindergarten Celebration, 1994; giv. S.C. State Readiness Policy Group; mem. Southeastern Region Vision for Edn. Adv. Bd., S.C. Coun. Ednl. Collaboration. Demonstration tchr. S.C. ETV (TV show) Sch. Begins with Kindergarten. Mem. Gov. of S.C.'s State Readiness Policy Group, Southeastern Regional Vision for Edn. Adv. Bd., South Carolina Ctr. Tchr. Recruitment Policy Bd. Recipient Ralph Witherspoon award S.C. Assn. for Children Under Six; named Tchr. of Yr., Greenville County, 1992, 93, State of S.C., 1993, S.C. Tchr. of Yr. Coun. of Chief State Sch. Officers, 1993, 94. Mem. Assn. for Childhood Edn. Internat., S.C. Tchr. Forum (chmn. 1993-94), S.C. Early Childhood Assn., Alpha Delta Kappa. Presbyterian. Office: Partee Elem Sch 4350 Campbell Rd Snellville GA 30039-6922 Fax: 770-982-6923.

MAGILL, NANCY GENE, microbiologist, educator; b. Seneca Falls, N.Y., Sept. 3, 1957; d. Malcolm Eugene and Ruth Shirley (Holcomb) M.; m. Michael John Rosenfeld, July 4, 1997. BS, Allegheny Coll., 1979; MS, Cornell U., 1982, PhD, 1988. Postdoctoral fellow dept. biochemistry health ctr. U. Conn., Farmington, 1988-95; rschr., microbiologist, molecular biologist divsn. of infectious diseases R.I. Hosp., Providence, 1995—98; asst. prof. Dept. Biology Coe Coll., Cedar Rapids, Iowa, 1998—2003; instr. Dept. Sci. and Math. Kirkwood C.C., Cedar Rapids, 2003—. Instr. dept. biology R.I. Coll., Providence, 1996-98; instr. dept. biomed. scis. Salve Regina U., New Port, R.I., 1997-98. Vol. Macintosh tutor R.I. Libr., Providence, 1996. Mem. AAAS, Am. Soc. Microbiology, Union Concerned Scientists (mem. coun. undergraduate rsch.). Avocations: music, folk dancing, literature, aerobics. Home: 3510 Plum Grove Ct NE Cedar Rapids IA 52402-7609 E-mail: ngmagill@hotmail.com.

MAGILL, SHERRY, foundation administrator; m. Robert J. Willis. BA, U. Ala., 1974, MA, 1976; PhD, Syracuse U., 1984. V.p., dep. to pres. Washington Coll., Md.; program officer for edn. Jessie Ball duPont Fund, Jacksonville, Fla., 1991-93, exec. dir., 1993-2000, pres., 2000—. Sr. moderator Aspen Inst.; founding exec. dir. Wye Faculty Seminar. Former chair Fla. Funders Group, state bd. dirs. P.A.C.E. Ctr. for Girls; former bd. dirs. Leadership Jacksonville; former chair jud. nominating commn. Fla. State Supreme Ct. Mem. Southeastern Coun. Founds. (bd. dirs.), Jacksonville Women's Network (bd. dirs.). Office: Jessie Ball DuPont Fund One Independent Dr Ste 1400 Jacksonville FL 32202-5011 E-mail: smagill@dupontfund.org.

MAGINNIS, SHERRY ANN, musician, educator, composer; b. Oak Ridge, Tenn., May 6, 1957; d. James John and Barbara Jeanne (Engle) Maginnis. MusB, U. Tenn., 1999. Saxophone/oboe instr. Sch. Music Arts, Oak Ridge, 1984—87; woodwinds specialist Maryville (Tenn.) City Schs., 1988—92; founder Woodwinds Studio and Pub., Knoxville, 1992—. Bd. dirs. Sch. of Music Arts; guest artist World Saxophone Congress, Washington, 1986, Kawasaki, Japan, 88; prin. oboe Nat. Cmty. Band, 1986—90, prin. saxophone, 1992—. Author: (calendar) Saxophone-365 Days a Year, 1982, (pamplet) Perfect Pamplet Packet for Young Woodwinders, 1982, (video) How to Trick Your Kid into Teaching You Saxophone, 1989; composer: Sonata # 1 for Alto Saxophone, 1986, Periwinkles for Alto Saxophone with Wind Ensemble, 1988. Established saxophone/oboe scholarship for talented, low income musicians Sch. Music Arts, Oak Ridge, 1985. Mem.: Literacy Coun., Internat. Assn. Jazz Educators, N.Am. Saxophone Alliance. Home: 228 Cansler Ave Knoxville TN 37921

MAGLACAS, A. MANGAY, nursing researcher, educator; BSN, Vanderbilt U.; MPH, U. Minn.; DPH, Johns Hopkins U.; DSc (hon.), U. Ill. Former chief sci. for nursing devel. health manpower divsn. WHO, Geneva, Switzerland, 1976-89, regional nurse adviser Southeast Asia Office Delhi, India, 1972-75. Internat. health/nursing cons., 1989—; adj. prof. Coll. Nursing, U. Ill., Chgo., 1990-2000; various vis. prof. positions in several countries, 1990—. Former mem., bd. dirs. Internat. Coun. Nurses, 1989-93; fgn. assoc. NAS Inst. Medicine, 1988—. Rockefeller fellow, 1964-67; Fulbright-Smith-Mundt scholar, 1952-54; recipient Outstanding alumni award Vanderbilt U., 1986, Internat. Pub. Health Leadership award Johns Hopkins U., 1992, Outstanding Profl. award for Nursing, Profl. Regulation Commn. of Philippines, 2000, Profl. Recognition award U. Philippines, 1989, Disting. Achievement award Philippine Nurses Assn., 1989, Outstanding Alumni award U. Philippines Sch. Nursing, 1987, Disting. Leadership award USA Commn. on Grads. of Fgn. Nursing Schs., 2002; named Woman of Yr. Am. Rsch. Inst. Bd. Internat. Rsch., 1988, named Most Outstanding Paulinian St. Paul's U., Philippines, 2002. Fellow Royal Coll. Nursing U.K. (hon.). Office: 70 Rue De La Prulay CH-1217 Meyrin Geneva Switzerland

MAGLIO, GESOMINA V. clinical social worker; MSW, Fordham U., 1982, PhD in Social Welfare, 1995. Diplomate Am. Bd. Examiners in Clin. Social Work. Clin. social worker, psychotherapist, N.J., 1984—; pvt. practice, 1984—; pres. Soft Sci. Inc., Far Hill, NJ, 2000. Adj. prof. Coll. of St. Elizabeth, Convent Station, N.J., 1996. Fellow Am. Orthopsychiat. Assn.; mem. NASW, Acad. Cert. Social Works,, N.Y. State Soc. Clin. Social Workers, Nat. Registry Health Care Providers in Clin. Social Work.

MAGLIONE, LILI, artist, consultant; b. Manhasset, N.Y., Jan. 30, 1929; d. Angelo and Mary (Marciano) M.; m. Bernhart H. Rumphorst, June 1, 1957; children: Catherine, Douglas. AD, Traphagen Sch., N.Y.C., 1950; student, Art Students League, N.Y.C., 1950-52. Fashion artist Butterick Pattern Co., N.Y.C., 1952-53; fashion art cons. Miss. America Inc., N.Y.C., 1953-54; dept. head fashion art office Simplicity Pattern Co., N.Y.C., 1953-58, fashion art cons., 1958-62; art dept. cons. Nassau County Mus., Roslyn, N.Y., 1984-86; dir. decorative affairs Harbor Acres Assn., Port Washington, N.Y., 1987-89, Sands Point (N.Y.) Mus., 1989-91; art cons. Horst Design Assocs., Huntington, N.Y., 1992—. One-woman shows include Palm Gallery, Southampton, N.Y., 1980, Art Internat., Chgo., 1985, Isis Gallery, Port Washington, 1987, Gallery 84, N.Y.C., 1989, 1991, 1993; artist (one-woman retrospective shows include) Harkness Gallery, 1978, James Hunt Barker Gallery, 1984, Sands Point Mus., 1988, Fairfield U., 1995; exhibitions include Nat. Arts Club, N.Y.C., 1997; contbr. poetry Nat. Libr. Poets, 1997, Artists Mag., 1998, Am. Artist Mag., 1999, Internat. Artist Mag., 2002 (Master Painter of the World, 2002). Hon. trustee Parents TV Coun., 2000—. Named Master Painter, Internat. Artists Mag., 2002; recipient Winner Art Expo 98, B.J. Spoke Gallery, N.Y.C., 1998, Manhattan Arts Internat. Critics Choice award, 1998, Artists Mag. Ann. Competition finalist, 2001, Liquetex Purchase award, 1998, Amsterdam award of excellence, 1998, award for acrylic painting, Nat. Arts Club, N.Y.C., 1998, Art Calendar Centerfold award, 1998, award of merit, Allied Artists of Am., 1999, cert. of merit, Art Calendar mag., 1999, Award of Excellence, Manhattan Arts Internat., 2000, award, Nat. Assn. Women Artists, 2000. Mem.: Nat. Soc. Painters in Acrylic and Casein (Meml. award 2001, best in show award Pen and Brush 2001, finalist Artists Mag. ann. competition 2001), Portrait Soc. Am. Inc., Internat. Soc. Poets, Nat. Mus. Women in the Arts, Nat. Assn. Women Artists (Meml. award 2001, Salmagundi Meml. award 2001). Roman Catholic. Avocations: horticulture, flower arrangement, nutrition, music, child care. Home: 7 Harmony Rd Huntington NY 11743-2315 Office Phone: 631-673-3022. E-mail: maglione@optonline.net.

MAGNABOSCO-BOWER, JENNIFER LYNN, mental health professional; b. Champaign, Ill., Aug. 14, 1963; d. Peter Thomas and Gail Gwendolyn Magnabosco; m. Anthony G. Bower, July 12, 1997. BA, MA, U. Chgo., 1985; MPhil, Columbia U., 1995, PhD, 2001. Staff therapist Postgrad. Ctr. for Mental Health, N.Y.C., 1988-90; rsch. assoc. Grad. Sch. Bus. Decision Rsch. Lab., U. Chgo., 1985—86, 1993—94, Ctr. for Psychiat. Rehab., U. Chgo., 1994; adminstr., rsch. assoc. Ctr. for the Study of Social Work Practice, N.Y.C., 1991-92, project mgr., 1995-96, dir. adminstrn. and ops., 1994-97; mental health cons. Wayne, Pa., Redwood City and L.A., Calif., 1998—2000; assoc. policy rschr. RAND, Santa Monica, Calif., 2001—. Ad hoc tech. rev. com. Dept. of Health and Human Svcs., Substance Abuse and Mental Health Svcs. Adminstrn., Ctr. for Mental Health Svcs., Rockville, 1997-99. Author, co-editor: Outcomes Measurement in the Human Services: Cross Cutting Issues and Methods (NASW Press Best Seller 1997-98); co-author: Cultural Contingencies: Behavior Analytic Perspectives, 1997; manuscript reviewer Jour. Behavioral Health Svcs. and Rsch., 2001—; book reviewer Adminstn. in Social Work, 2001—. Mem. AAAS, Am. Psychol. Assn., Am. Pub. Health Assn., U. Chgo. Alumni Assn. (bd. govs., v.p., Young Alumni Citation 1997, Vol. Leadership All Univ. award). Democrat. Avocations: tennis, piano playing, doll and fan collecting, fundraising, history ancient civilizations. Office: 1700 Main St PO Box 2138 Santa Monica CA 90407-2138 Home: 807 18th St Apt 4 Santa Monica CA 90403-1950

MAGNAN, RUTHANN, nurse, social worker; b. Camden, N.J., July 6, 1953; d. Kenneth Clifford and Mary (Gilbert) Hall; m. Frank W. Magnan, Dec. 21, 1974; children: Robert, Michele, Johnathan. LPN, Cumberland County Vocat.-Tech.; AAS in Nursing, Regents U., 1997. Cert. social worker, N.J. Nurse Newcomb Hosp., Vineland, N.J., 1982-89, Bridgeton (N.J.) Nursing Ctr., 1989-95, 98—, asst. adminstr., 1993-95; nurse So. State Prison, Delmont, N.J., 1996-98. Avocations: bowling, gardening. Home: 319 Buck Rd Glassboro NJ 08028-3307

MAGNER, MARJORIE, bank executive; BS in Psychology, Bklyn. (N.Y.) Coll.; MS, Purdue U. Mng. dir. Chem. Tech. Divsn. Chemical Bank; from mem. staff Commercial Credit to chmn., CEO Citigroup, N.Y.C., 1997—2003, chmn., CEO Global Consumer Group, 2003—. Bd. trustees Bklyn. (N.Y.) Coll.; mem. dean's adv. coun. Krannert Sch. Mgmt. Purdue U. Bd. dirs. Welfare to Work Partnership, Dress for Success Worldwide, Port Discovery Children's Mus., Balt., Md. Bus. Roundtable Edn. Named One of 50 Most Powerful Women in Am. Bus., Fortune Mag., 2001, 2002, 2003. Office: Citigroup 399 Park Ave New York NY 10022*

MAGNESS, RHONDA ANN, microbiologist; b. Stockton, Calif., Jan. 30, 1946; d. John Pershing and Dorothy Waneta (Kelley) Wetter; m. Barney LeRoy Bender, Aug. 26, 1965 (div. Jan. 1977); m. Gary D. Magness, Mar. 5, 1977; children: Jay D.(dec.), Troy D. BS, Calif. State U., 1977. Med. asst. C. Fred Wilcox, MD, Stockton, 1965-66; clk. typist Dept. of U.S. Army, Ft. Eustis, Va., 1967, Def. Supply Agy., New Orleans, 1967-68; med. asst. James G. Cross, MD, Lodi, Calif., 1969, Arthur A. Kemalyan, MD, Lodi, 1969-71, 72-77; med. sec. Lodi Meml. Hosp., 1972; lab. aide Calif. State U., Sacramento, 1977; phlebotomist St. Joseph's Hosp., Stockton, 1978-79; microbiologist Dameron Hosp. Assn., Stockton, 1980—. Active Concerned Women Am., Washington, 1987—. Mem.: San Joaquin County Med. Assts. Assn., Calif. Assn. Clin. Lab. Technologists, San Francisco Offshore, Nat.

Geog. Soc., Nat. Audubon Soc., Jobs. Daus. (chaplain 1962—63). Baptist. Avocations: boating, birdwatching, sewing, reading. Home: 9627 Knight Ln Stockton CA 95209-1961 Office: Dameron Hosp Lab 525 W Acacia St Stockton CA 95203-2405

MAGNUS, [illegible], music educator; b. Langdon, N.D., June 10, 1946; d. Merle Francis and Mary B. (Belanus) Blair; m. R. Bruce Magnus, June 17, 1967; children: Ryan, Malia, Carmen. BS in Composite Music Edn., U. N.D., 1968. Cert. level 1 Tech. in Music Edn. Tchr. music Starkweather Pub. Sch., ND, 1968—69, Neche Pub. Sch., ND, 1969—74, Milton-Osnabrock Pub. Sch., Milton, ND, 1980—90, Border Ctrl. Pub. Sch., Calvin, ND, 1992—. Tchr. music Langdon Pub. Sch., ND, 1981—; dir. honor choir Devils Lake Pub. Sch., ND, 2001; dir. cmty. choirs Walhalla Cmty., 1971, 72, Neche Cmty., 1973, 89, 2002. Named N.D. Music Tchr. of Yr., 2003; named one of 50 Music Tchrs. Who Make A Difference, 2003. Fellow: 3-H Homemakers, Order Ea. Star (chaplain 1994). Episcopalian. Avocations: reading, exercise, technology. Office: Border Ctrl Pub Sch Hiway 20 N Calvin ND 58323*

MAGNUSON, KAREN M. editor; m. Tod Myers. City editor Sturgis (Mich.) Daily News; writer, bur. mgr. UP Internat., Ill., Iowa, Utah and Calif.; various mgmt. positions Daily News, L.A.; editor Oxnard (Calif.) Press-Courier, Calif.; mng. editor Valley Times, Pleasanton, Calif., 1994—97, Wichita (Kans.) Eagle, 1997—99, Rochester (NY) Dem. and Chronicle, 1999—2001, editor, v.p. news, 2001—. Mem.: AP Mng. Editors (vice chmn. journalism studies 2002—). Office: Rochester Dem and Chronicle 55 Exchange Blvd Rochester NY 14614-2001*

MAGNUSON, NANCY, librarian; b. Seattle, Aug. 15, 1944; d. James Leslie and Jeanette (Thomas) M.; 2 sons, Daniel Johnson, Erik Johnson. BA in History, 1977; MLS, U. Wash., 1978. With. King County Libr. System, Seattle, 1973-80; rsch. asst. Free Libr. Phila., 1980-81; asst. libr. Haverford (Pa.) Coll., 1981-87; libr. dir. Goucher Coll., Balt., Md., 1987—. Contbr. to profl. publs. Mem. ALA (com. on status of women in librarianship, various others), Online Computer Libr. Ctr. Users Coun., Md. Libr. Assn., Congress Acad. Libr. Dirs., NOW, Women's Internat. League for Peace and Freedom, Balt. Bibliophiles, Jane Austen Soc. N.Am. Democrat. Office: Goucher Coll Julia Rogers Libr 1021 Dulaney Valley Rd Baltimore MD 21204-2753

MAGOON, NANCY AMELIA, art association administrator; b. N.Y.C., Apr. 19, 1941; d. Jack and Norma Harriet (Hirschl) Parker; m. Robert Cornelius Magoon, Mar. 16, 1978; children: Adam Glick, Peri Curnin. Student, Cornell U., 1958-59. Gallerist Hokin Gallery, Miami, 1986-89; sec. Nat. Found. Advancement in Arts, 1989-94; nat. coun. mem. Aspen Art Mus., 1985—, Aspen Ballet, 1985—. V.p. Ctr. for Fine Arts, Miami, 1984-94, Miami City Ballet, 1990-94. Bd. dirs. Cmty. Alliance Against AIDS, 1990-92; coun. mem. Susan Komen Breast Cancer, Aspen, 1994—; hon. trustee Ctr. for Fine Arts, Miami Beach, 1996; trustee Site Santa Fe, 1996; mem. nat. coun. Jazz Aspen, 1999—; mem. collectors com. Nat. Gallery, Washington, 2000; bd. dirs. Aspen Cmty. Found., 2000. Named one of Outstanding Women in Miami, 1992; NEA grantee, 1995. Avocations: skiing, golf, fly fishing, skeet and clay target shooting.

MAGRILL, ROSE MARY, library director; b. Marshall, Tex., June 8, 1939; d. Joe Richard and Mary Belle (Chadwick) M. BS, E. Tex. State U., 1960, MA, 1961; MS, U. Ill., 1964, PhD, 1969. Asst. to dean women E. Tex. State U., Commerce, 1960-61, librarian II, 1961-63; teaching asst. U. Ill., Urbana, 1963-64; instr. to asst. prof. E. Tex. State U., Commerce, 1964-67; asst. prof. Ball State U., Muncie, 1969-70; asst. prof. to prof. U. Mich., Ann Arbor, 1970-81; prof. U. N. Tex., Denton, 1981-99; dir. libr. E. Tex. Bapt. U., Marshall, 1987-2001. Accreditation site visitor ALA, Chgo., 1975—; cons. in field. Co-author: Building Library Collections, 4th edit. 1974, Library Technical Services, 1977, Building Library Collections, 5th edit. 1979, Acquisition Management and Collection Development in Libraries, 2d edit. 1989; author: Family of Faith, 1998. Trustee Memphis Theol. Sem., 1988-98; treas. Mission Synod of Cumberland Presbyn. Ch., 1989—; mem. bd. fin. Trinity Presbytery, 1989—; sec.-treas. Harrison County Hist. Commn., 1995—; trustee Hist. Found., 1999—; sec. Nat. Conv. Cumberland Presbyn. Women, 2000—02, chmn. bd., 2003—; bd. dirs. Presbyn. HIst. Soc. of S.W., 2000—. Recipient award Cumberland Presbyn. History, 1995. Mem. ALA (RTSD Resources Sect. pub. award 1978), Tex. Libr. Assn. Home: 804 Caddo St Marshall TX 75672-2414

MAGSIG, JUDITH ANNE, retired early childhood education educator; b. Saginaw, Mich., Nov. 9, 1939; d. Harold Howard and Catherine Louise (Barstow) Gay; m. George Arthur Magsig, June 22, 1963; children: Amy Catherine, Karl Joseph. BA, Alma Coll., 1961. Cert. tchr., early childhood tchr., Mich. 1st grade tchr. Gaylord (Mich.) Schs., 1961-64, spl. edn. tchr., 1965-67, kindergarten tchr., 1968-99; violin tchr. Concord Acad. Antrim, Mancelona, Mich., 2003—. Instr. Suzuki violin method; second violinist Traverse (Mich.) Symphony Orch., 1985-92, Cadillac (Mich.) Symphony Orch., 1999-2000, Gaylord Chamber Orch., 2001—, Great Lakes Chamber Orch., 2001—. Mem. ASCD, NEA, Mich. Edn. Assn., Gaylord Edn. Assn. (historian 1997-99), Assn. for the Edn. of Young Children, Assn. for Childhood Edn. Internat., Suzuki Assn. Am., Am. String Tchrs. Assn., Music Tchrs. Nat. Assn., Order Eastern Star (chaplain 1997-98, warder 1999-2000, electa 2000—), Spirits of the North, Alpha Delta Kappa (pres. Beta Rho chpt. 1980-82, 84-86, treas. 1996-2000, music chmn. Mich., v.p. Beta Rho chpt. 2000-02, pres. 2002—). Methodist. Avocations: cross-stitch, camping, canoeing, sewing. Home: 2130 Evergreen Dr Gaylord MI 49735-9165 Office: Musik Haus 2300 S Otsego Ave Gaylord MI 49735-1869 Business E-Mail: gjmagsig@avci.net.

MAGSINO, MARISSA ESTIVA, internist, pediatrician; b. San Pablo, Laguna, The Philippines, Oct. 5, 1961; came to U.S., 1990; d. Rodelo Estiva and Mercy Balandan; m. Winston Q. Magsino, July 27, 1990; children: Ryan, Eryn. BS in Zoology, U. Philippines, Quezon City, 1982; MD, U. of East Ramon Magsaysay, Quezon City, 1986. Diplomate Am. Bd. Internal Medicine, bd. eligible Am. Bd. Pediat. Resident in medicine and pediat. U. Medicine and Dentistry N.J., Newark, 1992-97; pvt. practice, Orlando, Fla., 1997—. Internist, mem. active staff Orlando Regional Hosp., 1997—, Fla. Hosp., Orlando, 1997—; pediatrician, mem. active staff Health Ctrl. Hosp., Orlando, 1997—; med. dir. Bestchoice. Mem.: Am. Home Care Physicians, Philippine-Am. Med. Soc. Ctrl. Fla. Achievements include research in geriatric medicine and women's health. Office: Ste 7425 Conroy-Windermere Rd Orlando FL 32835 Home: 9073 Heritage Bay Cir Orlando FL 32836-5063

MAGUIRE, CHARLOTTE EDWARDS, retired pediatrician; b. Richmond, Ind., Sept. 1, 1918; d. Joel Blaine and Lydia (Betscher) Edwards; m. Raymer Francis Maguire, Sept. 1, 1948 (dec.); children: Barbara, Thomas Clair II (dec.). Student, Stetson U., 1936—38, U. Wichita, 1938—39; BS, Memphis Tchrs. Coll., 1940; MD, U. Ark., 1944; LHD (hon.), Fla. State U., 2002. Intern, resident Orange Meml. Hosp., Orlando, Fla., 1944-46, med. staff., 1944—69, instr. nurses, 1947-57; resident Bellevue Hosp. and Med. Ctr., NYU, NYC, 1954—55; staff mem. Fla. Santarium and Hosp., Orlando, 1946-56, Holiday House and Hosp., Orlando, 1950-62; mem. courtesy and cons. staff West Orange Meml. Hosp., Winter Garden, Fla., 1952-67; active staff, chief dept. pediat. Mercy Hosp., Orlando, 1965-68; med. dir. childrens med. svcs., asst. sec. Fla. Dept. Health and Rehab. Svcs., 1969—71, med. dir. med. svcs. and basic care, 1975-84; med. exec. dir., med. svcs. divsn. worker's compensation Fla. Dept. Labor, Tallahassee, 1984-87; chief of staff physicians and dentists Ctrl. Fla. divsn. Children's Home Soc. Fla., 1947-56; dir. Orlando Child Health Clinic, 1949-58; pvt. practice Orlando, 1946—68; asst. regional dir. HEW, 1970-72; ret., 1987. Asst. dir. health and sci. affairs Dept. Health Edn. & Welfare, Atlanta, 1971-72, Washington, 1972-75; pediat. cons. Fla. Crippled Children's Commn., 1952-70, dir., 1968-70; med. dir. Office Med. Svcs. and Basic Care, sr. physician Office of Asst. Sec. Ops., Fla. Dept. Health and Rehab. Svcs.; clin. prof. dept. pediat. U. Fla. Coll. Medicine, Gainesville, 1980-87; mem. Fla. Drug Utilization Rev., 1983-87; real estate salesperson Investors Realty, 1982-2003; bd. dirs. Stavros Econ. Ctr. Fla. State U., Tallahassee; pres.'s coun. Fla. State U., U. Fla., Gainesville; Charlotte Edwards Maguire eminent scholar chair and scholarships for qualified students, 1999. Mem. profl. adv. com. Fla. Ctr. for Clin. Svcs. at U. Fla., 1952-60; del. to Mid-century White House Conf. on Children and Youth, 1950; U.S. del from Nat. Soc. for Crippled Children to World Congress for Welfare of Cripples, Inc., London, 1957; pres. of corp. Eccleston-Callahan Hosp. for Colored Crippled Children, 1956-58; sec. Fla. chpt. Nat. Doctor's Com. for Improved Med. Svcs., 1951-52; med. adv. com. Gateway Sch. for Mentally Retarded, 1959-62; bd. dirs. Forest Park Sch. for Spl. Edn. Crippled Children, 1949-54, mem. med. adv. com., 1955-68, chmn., 1957-68; mem. Fla. Adv. Coun. for Mentally Retarded, 1965-70; dir. ctrl. Fla. poison control Orange Meml. Hosp.; mem. orgn. com., chmn. com. for admissions and selection policies Camp Challenge; participant 12th session Fed. Exec. Inst., 1971; del. White House Conf. on Aging, 1980; dir. Stavros Econ. Ctr. Fla. State U.; trustee Fla. State U. Found., 1998—, mem. campaign com. Charlotte Edwards Maguire Eminent Scholarship named in her honor Fla. State U.; named Outstanding Woman in Our Cmty. AAUW, Tallahassee, 2002. Mem. AMA (life), Nat. Rehab. Assn., Am. Congress Phys. Medicine and Rehab., Fla. Soc. Crippled Children and Adults, Ctrl. Fla. Soc. Crippled Children and Adults (dir. 1949-58, pres. 1956-57), Am. Assn. Cleft Palate, Fla. Soc. Crippled Children (trustee 1951-57, v.p. 1956-57, profl. adv. com. 1957-68), Mental Health Assn. Orange County (charter mem.; pres. 1949-50, dir. 1947-52, chmn. exec. com. 1950-52, dir. 1963-65), Fla. Orange County Heart Assn., Am. Med. Women's Assn., Am. Acad. Med. Dirs., Fla. Med. Assn. (life, chmn. com. on mental retardation), Orange County Med. Assn., Orange Med. Soc. (life), Fla. Pediat. Soc. (pres. 1952-53), Fla. Cleft Palate Assn. (counselor-at-large, sec.), Nat. Inst. Geneal. Rsch., Nat. Geneal. Soc., Assn. Profl. Genealogists, Tallahassee Geneal. Soc., Fla. State U. Found. Inc. (bd. dirs. Stavoris Ctr. for Econ. Edn.), Capital City Tiger Bay Club, Fla. Econs. Club, Francis Eppes Soc. Fla. State U., Econ. Club Fla., Governors Club. Home: 4158 Covenant Ln Tallahassee FL 32308-5765

MAGUIRE, MARTHA ELENOR ERWIN (MARTIE MAGUIRE), musician; b. York, Pa., Oct. 12, 1969; d. Paul and Barbara Erwin; m. Ted Seidel, 1995 (div.); m. Gareth MaGuire, Aug. 10, 2001. Student, So. Meth. U. Performer Blue Night Express, 1984—89; fiddle player, violinist, vocalist Dixie Chicks, 1989—. Performer: (albums) LIttle Ol' Cowgirl, 1992, Thank Heavens for Dale Evans, 1992, Shouldn't a Told You That, 1993, Wide Open Spaces, 1998 (Album of Yr., Acad. Country Music, 1998, Best Country Album, Grammy Awards, 1998, Best Country Artist Clip of Yr., Billboard Awards, 1998, Maximum Vision Clif of Yr., Billboard Awards, 1998, Best Selling Album, Can. Country Music Award, 1999, Song of Yr. (Country), WB Radio Music Awards, 1999, Album of Yr., Acad. Country Music, 1999), Fly, 1999 (Best Country Album, Grammy Awards, 1999, Best Selling Album, Can. Country Music Awards, 2000, Internat. Album, British Country Music Awards, 2000, Country Album of Yr., Billboard Awards, 2000, Album of Yr., Acad. Country Music, 2000, Album of Yr., CMA, 2000), Home, 2002 (Favorite Country Album, Am. Music Awards, 2002, Best Recording Package, Grammy Awards, 2002, Best Country Album, Grammy Awards, 2002), Top of the World Tour: Live, 2003. Named Top New Country Artist, Billboard, 1998, Most Significant New Country Act, Country Monitor, 1998, Group of Yr., CMA, 1998, Top Vocal Group, Acad. Country Music, 1998, Internat. Rising Star, British Country Music Awards, 1999, Country Artist of Yr., Rolling Stone, 1999, Artist of Yr. (Country), WB Radio Music Awards, 1999, Favorite New Artist (Country), AMA, 1999, Vocal Group of Yr., CMA, 1999, Country Artist of Yr., Billboard, 1999, 2000, Vocal Group of Yr., CMA, 2000, Entertainer of Yr., 2000, ACM, 2000, 2001, Vocal Group of Yr., 2001, Favorite Musical Group or Band, People's Choice Awards, 2001, Favorite Country Band, Am. Music Award, 2002, Vocal Group of Yr., Country Music Assn. Award, 2002, Country Duo/Group of Yr., Billboard, 2002; recipient Horizon award, CMA, 1998, others. Office: Monument Sony Nashville 34 Music Sq East Nashville TN 37203*

MAGUIRE, MILDRED MAY, chemistry educator, magnetic resonance researcher; b. Leetsdale, Pa., May 7, 1933; d. John and Mildred (Sklarsky) Magura. BS in Chemistry, Carnegie-Mellon U., 1955; MS in Phys. Chemistry, U. Wis., 1960; PhD in Phys. Chemistry, Pa. State U., 1967. Devel. chemist Koppers Co., Monaca, Pa., 1955-58; rsch. chemist Am. Cyanamid Co., Stamford, Conn., 1960-63; asst. prof. chemistry Waynesburg (Pa.) Coll., 1967-70, assoc. prof., 1970-74, prof., 1974—. Leverhulme vis. prof. U. Leicester, Eng., 1980-81, summer 1989; cons. Pitts. Energy Tech. Ctr., summers 1978-86; faculty rsch. participant Oak Ridge Assoc. Univs., 1978-80, 82-85; U.S. del. Internat. Conf. Phys. Chemists, China, 1996, Sci. and Tech. Conf., India, 1997. Contbr. articles to sci. jours., chpt. to book. Sec. Waynesburg Women's Club, 1981-82; citizen amb. People to People Program, 1996, 97. Recipient Woman of the Yr. award AAUW, Waynesburg, 1983; Cottrell grantee Rsch. Corp. N.Y., 1970-71; Leverhulme vis. fellow U.K., 1980-81; Curie Internat. fellow AAUW, U.K., 1980-81; Robert West Superconductor Rsch. Grantee, Univ. Wis., 2001-02. Mem. AAUP, AAAS, Am. Chem. Soc.; Spectroscopy Soc. of Pitts.; Pitts. Soc. of Analytical Chemists. Avocations: gardening, painting, swimming, classical music, reading. Home: 1550 Crescent Hills Waynesburg PA 15370-1654 Office: Waynesburg Coll College St Waynesburg PA 15370 E-mail: mmaguire@waynesburg.edu.

MAGUIRE-ZINNI, DEIRDRE, federal community development management analyst; b. Bklyn., Oct. 21, 1954; d. James Michael and Dorothy Ursula (Gronske) Maguire; m. Nicholas A. Zinni, Aug. 27, 1977, now div.; 1 child, Miles Angelo. BA with honors, SUNY, Stony Brook, 1976; MSP, Fla. State U., 1981. Housing specialist Suffolk Community Devel. Corp., Coram, N.Y., 1977-78; planner Palm Beach County Housing and Community Devel., West Palm Beach, Fla., 1980-83, sr. planner, 1983-84, mgr. adminstrn. and ops., 1984-87; fed. community planning and devel. rep. HUD, Jacksonville, Fla., 1987-88, community planning and devel. specialist, Entitlement Cmtys. Divsn. Washington, 1988-91, asst. dir. entitlement communities, 1991-94, dir. entitlement communities divsn., 1994-99, mgmt. analyst office of CFO, 1999—2001; sr. mgmt. analyst Office of Cmty. Planning and Devel. Dep. Asst. Sec. for Ops., 2001—. Staff liaison Affordable Housing Task Force, West Palm Beach, 1985-86, Fla. Community Devel. Assn., 1985-87. Democrat. Roman Catholic. Avocations: reading, baking. E-mail: Deirdre_Maguire-Zinni@hud.gov.

MAGYARY, CYNTHIA MARIE, elementary school educator, music educator; b. New Brighton, Pa., June 3, 1956; d. Nicholas (m) Magyary and Mary Helen Bedo-Magyary. BS in Music Edn., BS in Elem. Edn., Geneva Coll., 1978. Elem. music tchr. Wilmington Area Sch. Dist., New Wilmington, Pa., 1983—. Youth choir dir. Neshannock Presbyn. Ch., New Wilmington, Pa., 2001. Mem.: Wilmington Area Educators Assn. (sec.), Pa. State Educators Assn., Pa. Music Educators Assn. Avocations: piano, golf, swimming, sewing, reading. Office: New Wilmington Elem 450 Wood St New Wilmington PA 16142 Home: 168 Orchard Terrace Dr New Wilmington PA 16142

MAHAFFEY, MARYANN, councilwoman; b. Burlington, Iowa, Jan. 18, 1925; m. Herman Dooha; 1 child, Susan. BA, Cornell Coll., 1946, LHD (hon.), 1995; MSW, U. So. Calif., 1951. Legis. rep., chair Mich. Social Work Coun., 1965-68; founder, chair City of Detroit Task Force on Hunger & Malnutrition, 1969-74; council member, pres. pro tem City of Detroit, 1974—; emeritus prof. Wayne State U., Detroit, 1990—. Pres. Detroit City Coun., 1991-98. Del. founding conv. Nat. Women's Polit. Caucus, 1971-73; chair, founder Mich. Statewide Nutrition Commn., 1973-83; designer, initiator Detroit Police Dept. Rape Crisis Ctr. and Family Trouble Clinic of Detroit, Family Svc. and Police, 1974-75; del. IWY, Mexico City, 1975, Houston, 1978; dep. chair U.S. Conf. on Families, 1979-81; chair human devel. com. Nat. League of Cities, 1990; chair Mich. del. to UN Conf. Women, Beijing, 1995; summer recreation dir. Nat. Intercollegiate Christian Coun. in Concentration Camp for Japanese Ams., 1945; trainer, integrator Brownie Troop Indpls. Girl Scouts, 1951-52; organizer Welfare Rights, Detroit, 1961; founder Nat. Peace and Disarmament Com. NASW, 1962-69, pres., 1975-77; founder Women in Social Welfare, 1972-74; author policy of women's rights, Internat. Fedn. Social Workers, 1987; mem. exec. com. Internat. Fedn. Social Workers, 1984-86. Mem. NAACP (life), Am. Orthopsychiat. Assn. (pres. 1984-85), Japanese Am. Citizens League, Women in Mcpl. Govt. (pres. 1995, adv. bd. 1996—, mem. NLC policy adv. coun. 1997—), Nat. Coun. Negro Women (life). Office: 1340 City County Bldg Detroit MI 48226

MAHAFFIE, LYNN BOYNTON, lawyer, government official; b. Bronxville, N.Y., Feb. 21, 1965; d. Edmund Stratton and Jane (Bodorff) Boynton; m. Matthew Barton Mahaffie, Aug. 4, 1990; children: Shelby Alice, Grace Cooper. BBA, George Washington U., 1987; JD, U. Pa., 1990. Bar: Pa. 1990, D.C. 1991. Assoc. atty. Brownstein, Zeidman & Lore, Washington, 1990-93; mgmt. & program analyst U.S Dept. Edn., Washington, 1993—2002, dir. GEAR UP Program, 2002—. George Washington U. Bd. Trustees scholar, 1984-86. Mem. Nat. Fin. Mgmt. Hon. Soc., Beta Gamma Sigma. Democrat. Home: 6302 Wynkoop Blvd Bethesda MD 20817-5932 Office: US Dept Edn 1990 K Street NW Washington DC 20006

MAHAN, JACQUELINE FRANCIS, artist, educator; b. Cornwall, N.Y., Apr. 23, 1969; d. Patrick Anthony and Sandra Jon Mahan. AFA, Rockland C.C., Suffern, N.Y., 1990; B in Art Edn., St. Thomas Aquinas Coll., Sparkill, N.Y., 1994; M in Art Edn., Coll. New Rochelle, 1999. Cert. pub. sch. tchr. N.Y. Tchr. Valley Cottage (N.Y.) Elem. Sch., 1996—, Tarrytown (N.Y.) Hall Sr. Home, 2001—02, Continuing Edn. Art classes in, North Rockland. Exhibitions include Kiss Expo, N.Y., Balt., Md.; author: (poetry) various anthologies, (children's book) The Courtyard Duck, 2004. Mem.: N.Y. State Art Tchrs. Assn., Nat. Art Edn. Assn. Office: Valley Cottage Elem Sch 26 Lake Rd Valley Cottage NY 10989

MAHDAVIANI, MIRIAM, choreographer, educator; Student, Sch. Am. Ballet, 1968. Past mem., instr. Balanchine Co. Choreographer Jacob's Pillow Dance Festival, 1986, 87, Am. Music Festival N.Y.C. Ballet, 1988. Choreographer (ballets) N.Y.C. Ballet's Am. Music Festival, 1988, Dance Preludes Dancer's Emergency Fund Benefit, N.Y.C., 1991, Images, N.Y.C., 1992, Images Maggio Danza Festival, Florence, Italy, 1994, Correlazione N.Y.C. Ballet, 1994; dancer over 40 ballets including Ballo Della Regina, Coppelia, Donizetti Variations, Jewels, Raymonda Variations, La Valse. Office: Pacific Northwest Ballet 301 Mercer St Seattle WA 98109-4600

MAHER, FRAN, advertising agency executive; b. June 22, 1938; d. Edward Stephan and Virginia Rose (Harrington) Maher; m. Anthony Peter Petrella, Sept. 17, 1957; children: Roland, Louis, Marcus; m. Brian L. Coffey, June 19, 1993. Grad. scholar, U. Minn., 1957; student, Spectrum Inst., 1968—71; BA summa cum laude, Kean Coll., 1979; grad., Nanjing U., China, 2000. Diplomate acupuncture NCCAOM, 2001. Office mgr. Lead Supplies, Inc., Mpls., 1957—59; freelance artist and writer Warren, NJ, 1968—72; prin. Visuals, Warren, 1974—79; pres. Fran Maher, Inc., Bound Brook, NJ, 1980—99, wellness educator, 1996—; pvt. practice acupunture Warren. Bd. dirs. Parent Edn. Advocacy Tng. Ctr., Alexandria, Va., 1979—85; officer Friends of Weigand Farm, Milton, NJ, 1977—80, Somerset County Assn. Retarded Citizens, 1982—, pres., bd. dirs., 1987—89; officer, bd. dirs. Assn. Retarded Citizens N.J., 1987—89, chair residential quality life com., 1991—94; bd. trustees Peoplecare Ctr., Inc., 1990—93; bd. dirs. Somerset County Coalition on Affordable Housing, 1991—92; rep. Congress of States, The Arc of USA, 1993—95; founding mem. Flintlock Boys' Club. Recipient N.J. Art Dirs. Show award, 1978, 1st pl. award in graphics, Watchung Art Ctr., 1980. Mem.: Somerset County C. of C. (bd. dirs. 1989—94, chair affordable housing 1990—93).

MAHER, FRANCESCA MARCINIAK, lawyer, former air transportation executive; b. Chgo., Oct. 27, 1957; BA, Loyola U., 1978, JD, 1981. Ptnr. Mayer, Brown & Platt, Chgo., 1981—84, 1987—93; v.p. law, corp. sec. UAL Corp., Elk Grove Village, Ill., 1993-97, v.p., gen. counsel, sec., 1997-98, sr. v.p., gen. counsel, sec., 1998—2003; spl. counsel Mayer, Brown, Rowe & Maw, Chgo., 2003—. Bd. dirs. YMCA Met. Chgo., Lincoln Park Zool. Soc. Mem. Ill. Humane Soc. (pres. 1996-98). Office: Mayer Brown Rowe & Maw LLP 190 S LaSalle St Chicago IL 60603-3441 E-mail: fmmaher@mayerbrownrowe.com.*

MAHER, IRENE, newscaster; b. Hampton, Va. married. BA in Theatre and Speech, Coll. of William and Mary. Weekend weather anchor, med. reporter WAVY-TV, Portsmouth/Norfolk, Va.; health reporter WFLA-TV, Tampa, Fla., 1985, co-anchor, med. editor. Named Health Communicator of Yr., Fla. Hosp. Assn., 1994; recipient award, Am. Cancer Soc., Am. Heart Assn., Fla. Dietetic Assn., Tampa Bay Soc. Profl. Journalists, Fla. Dental Assn., Mental Health Assn. Hillsborough County, Comm. Media award, Fla. Nurses Assn. Office: WFLA-TV PO Box 1410 Tampa FL 33601

MAHER, LISA KRUG, editor; b. N.Y.C., Nov. 11, 1952; d. George William and Rita (Earle) Krug; m. Barney Rosset, Nov. 5, 1980 (div. Dec. 1990); 1 child, Chantal; m. Richard Maher, July 29, 2000. BA magna cum laude, Smith Coll., 1974; MA, Columbia U., 1976. Editor Latin Am. Series, N.Y.C., 1976-86; gen. editor Grove Press, N.Y.C., 1987-89; mng. editor Aperture, N.Y.C., 1987-90; pvt. practice N.Y.C., 1990—. Writer and editor UNICEF, N.Y.C., 1995—. Author: James Baldwin, 1989, Thurgood Marshall, 1993 (Outstanding Book For Teenagers award 1994). Mem. Phi Beta Kappa

MAHER, VIRGINIA JONES, art historian, educator; b. Milw., Oct. 11, 1941; d. Frederick Thomas Murphy and Virginia June Harmon; m. William H. Jones, Aug. 22, 1964 (dec. Nov. 23, 1982); children: William H. Jones Jr., Michael J. Jones, Megan Jones Townsend; m. J. Thomas Maher, III, May 14, 1994. BS, U. Wis., Milw., 1964, MA in Art History, cert. art mus. studies, U. Wis., Milw., 1994. Tchr. French and English Custer H.S., Milw., 1964; curatorial asst. Kohler Art Ctr., Sheboygan, Wis., 1993; curator fine arts commn. Cathedral of St. John, Milw., 1995—2003; instr. art history Cardinal Stritch U., Milw., 1997—99, Peninsula Art Sch., Fish Creek, Wis., 2001—04. Freelance writer, Milw., 1994—2004; guest art curator Miller Art Mus., Sturgeon Bay, Wis., 2000. Organizer Friends of Art History, Milw., 2000—03; hist. preservation Jr. League Evanston, Ill., 1980—81, lectr. art in the sch., 1978—80; bd. dirs. Peninsula Art Sch., Fish Creek, 2000—04, Wis. Heritages Inc., Milw., 1996—99, Am. Heritage Soc. Milw. Art Mus., 1994—98. Named Writer of Yr. award, Metalsmith Mag., 1998; recipient Grad. of Last Decade (G.O.L.D.) award, U. Wis., Milw., 2000. Mem.: Contemporary Art Soc. Milw. Art Mus., Womans Club Wis., Alpha Phi. Roman Catholic. Avocations: art collecting, painting, gardening. Home: 5611 Schauer Rd Sturgeon Bay WI 54235

MAHESH, SHRIPRIYA, Internet company executive; b. Madras, India, Aug. 28, 1973; came to U.S., 1995; d. K. and Shrimathi (Iyengar) Mahesh. Diploma, Nat. Inst. Info. Tech., Madras, 1993; BA in Econs., Madras U., 1993; MBA, Harvard U., 1997. Exec. asst. to CEO Lucas-TVS, Madras, 1993-94; mgr. new products Sundaram Brake Linings, Madras, 1994-95; summer assoc. Citibank N.Am., N.Y.C., 1996; assoc. Mitchell Madison Group, Cambridge, Mass., 1997-99; dir. E-Commerce NextCard Inc., San

Francisco, 1999—. Bd. dirs. TVS Global, Madras. Founder, trustee Values Art Found., Madras, 1995—. Hindu. Avocations: Karate, photography, tennis, bicycling, music. Office: NexCard Inc 595 Market St Ste 1800 San Francisco CA 94105-2827

MAHEU, SHIRLEY, Canadian legislator; b. Montreal, Que., Can., Oct. 7, 1931; d. George William Johnson and Bertha Hunt; m. René Albert Maheu, Sept. 5, 1953; children: Ronald, Richard, Daniel, Marc. Diploma, O'Sullivan Bus. Coll. Cert. ins. broker. Ins. broker; mcpl. councillor City of Saint-Laurent, Canada, 1982-88; mem. City of Saint-Laurent Mcpl. Coun., 1982—86; mem. from Saint-Laurent Cartierville Ho. of Commons, Canada, 1988-96; mem. Can. Senate, Ottawa, Canada, 1996—. Pres. Saint-Laurent br. Red Cross Soc. Mem.: Saint-Laurent C. of C. Roman Catholic. Office: Canadian Senate Wellington St EB Rm 263 Ottawa ON Canada K1A 0A4*

MAHFOUZ, ILHAM BADREDDINE, artist; b. Damascus, Syria, Jan. 2, 1956; came to U.S., 1972; d. Abdul Rahman Badreddine and Zabia Zebian Keilani; m. Abdul Razak Mahfouz, Aug. 27, 1972; children: Ruba, Rodwan. BFA in Painting, Ea. Mich. U., 1992; cert. interior design, La Salle U., 1979. Mem. Student Artist Gallery/Ea. Mich. U., Ypsilanti, 1991-92, Access, Dearborn, Mich., 1990-93; tchr. ceramic, painting, mixed media Pontiac (Mich.) Art Ctr., 1997-2001; tchr. ceramic, mixed media Birmingham Bloomfield (Mich.) Art Ctr., 1999—; Arabic lang. instr. U. Detroit Mercy, 2001—; tchr. Pontiac Art Ctr., 1997—. Ceramics and mixed media tchr. Pontiac Creative Art Ctr., Mich., 1997-2000; tchr. art Internat. Sch., Farmington Hill, Mich., 1997; co-founder Alternative Artists Group, 1994—; tchr. Lake Orion Sch. Author: poetry; one-woman shows include The Cultural Assn., Franklin, Mich., 1989, Islamic Cultural Inst., Auburn Hills, Mich., 1989, M.Y.N.A. Art Show, Franklin, 1991—92, Alternative Artist Space Gallery, Southfield, Mich., 1997, Trapper Alley Gallery, Detroit, 1998, Urban Park Gallery, 1998, Pontiac Creative Art Ctr., 2000, exhibited in group shows at Common Ground Gallery, Windsor, Ont., Can., 1994, Arab World Festival, Detroit, 1994, Agora Gallery, N.Y.C., 1994, 1998, Mich. Sci. and Rsch. Devel., Dearborn, 1995, Pontiac Artists Studio Tour, 1996, Arab/Latino Art Show, Detroit, 1996, Oak Park Libr., Mich., 1997, Pontiac Art Ctr., 1997, Friendship Fedn., El-Cajon, Calif., 1997, Contemporary Mus., 1999—2000, Pontiac Creative Art Ctr., 1999—2000, Farmington Hills (Mich.) Festival of Art, 2000, Dream of Humanity, Southfield, 2000, Swedish-Am. Mus. Ctr., Chgo., 2001, Bagly House, Detroit, 2001, numerous others; contbr. articles to profl. jours. including Arab Am. Jour., Al-Dar Al Arabi, 2000; subject of articles Al-Dar Al Arabi mag., Manhattan Arts Internat., 1993, New Art Internat., 2000. Recipient Merit award Manhattan Arts Internat., N.Y., 1993, 1st prize McKenny Union's Art Show, Ea. Mich. U., 1991, Earth and Art Gallery, Milford, Mich., 1990. Mem. Internat. Muslimah Women Artists Group (pres. 1997-98), Golden Key. Islamic. Avocation: arabic and conversational spanish languages. E-mail: ilhamart@hotmail.com.

MAHLENDORF, URSULA RENATE, literature educator; b. Strehlen, Silesia, Germany, Oct. 24, 1929; came to U.S., 1953; Student, Oberschule an der Hamburgerstraße, Bremen, Fed. Republic Germany, 1950, U. Tübingen, Fed. Republic Germany, 1950-52, Brown U., 1953-57, MA in English Lit., 1956, PhD in German Lit., 1958, student, Bonn (Fed. Republic Germany) U., 1953, London U. Teaching asst. Brown U., Providence, 1953-57; from acting instr. to prof. German U. Calif., Santa Barbara, 1957—93, assoc. dir., campus coord. edn. abroad program, 1967—69, chmn. dept. Germanic and Slavic langs. and lits., 1980-83, assoc. dean Coll. Letters and Sci., 1986-89, emeritus, 1993—. Chmn. symposium in honor of Harry Slochower, 1977; campus coord. edn. abroad program U. Calif., 1967-69, assoc. dir., 1969-72; co-chair Nietzsche symposium Dept. Germanic and Slavic Langs. and Lits., U. Calif., Santa Barbara, 1981. Author: The Wellsprings of Literary Creation, 1985; editor: (with John L. Carleton) Man for Man: A Multi-Disciplinary Workshop on Affecting Man's Social and Psychological Nature through Community Action (Charles C. Thomas), 1973, Dimensions of Social Psychiatry, 1979, (with Arthur Lerner) Life Guidance through Literature, 1992; assoc. editor Am. Imago, Am. Jour. Social Psychiatry, Jour. Evolutionary Psychology; contbr. more than 90 articles to profl. jours. Recipient Alumni award, 1981; rsch. grantee U. Calif., 1974—; Fulbright fellow, 1951-52. Mem. MLA, Am. Assn. for Aesthetics and Art Criticism (past pres. Calif. div.), Assn. for applied Psychoanalysis (profl. mem.), Am. Assn. Social Psychiatry (councillor 1977-81), Internat. Assn. Social Psychiatry (treas. 1978-83). Avocations: sculpting, woodcarving. Home: 1505 Portesuello Ave Santa Barbara CA 93105-4626 Office: U Calif Dept Dept Germanic Semitic Slavic Studie Santa Barbara CA 93106

MAHMUD, SHIREEN DIANNE, photographer; b. Chittagong, Pakistan, Oct. 4, 1949; came to U.S., 1974; d. Mohammed Mazhurul Qudus and Mumtaz Mahal Begum; m. Abdul Wazed Mahmud, Apr. 10, 1966 (div. 1996); children: Sharmin, Anita. BA in Mass Comm., U. Hartford, 1982. Part-time med. sec., Middletown, Conn., 1979-82; freelance photographer, 1985—; typist Aetna Ins. Co., Middletown, 1991; freelance photographer Conn. Post. Prodr. feature program Storer Cable Comm., Clinton, Conn., 1991-95; freelance photojournalist Middletown Press, Durham Gazette, Middletown, 1991-95; mem. Bridgeport Regional Bus. Coun., 1997. Literacy vol. Russell Libr., Middletown, Conn. Mem. AAUW, Nat. League Am. Pen Women, Internat. Soc. Poets (Hall of Fame award 1997), Conn. Soc. Poets, Conn. Songwriter's Assn., Internat. Platform Assn. Home: 2612 North Ave Unit G-4 Bridgeport CT 06604-2324

MAHON, BARBARA JOANNE, art educator; b. Helena, Mont., Apr. 29, 1944; d. Charles Everett Mark and Rachel Alberta Barber; m. Archie Calvin Mahon, Oct. 17, 1939; children: Mark Warren, Hobart Scott, Tara Lane Mahon Eckstrom. BS, Mont. State U., 1967, postgrad., 1968—79, Calif. State U. Hayward, 1968—79. Tchr. John M. Horner Jr. H.S., Fremont, Calif., 1968—79, Trinity Jr.-Sr. H.S., Coquille, Oreg., 1988—91; prin., tchr. Crusader Christian H.S., North Bend, Oreg., 1993—98; instr. painting Southwestern Oreg. C.C., Coos Bay, 2002—; founder, ptnr. Artist Loft Gallery, North Bend, 2003—. Mem.: Fremont Unified Tchr.'s Assn. (pres., v.p. 1976—79), Bay Area Artist's Assn. (pres. 2002—), Watercolor Soc. Oreg., Women's Aglow Internat. (publicity chmn. 2000—01, chmn., v.p.). Republican. Avocation: gardening. Home and Office: 97541 Kadora Ln North Bend OR 97459*

MAHON, MARINNA FAIRBANK, secondary education educator, writer, consultant; b. Phila., Dec. 27, 1940; d. Joseph Aloysius and Marie Josephine (McMahon) McNulty; m. Robert L. Fairbank (div. 1980); children: Wendy Anne, Elsa Marie. BA in History and Polit. Sci., Rosemont (Pa.) Coll., 1963; postgrad., Spanish-Am. Bilingual Inst., Mexico City, 1974-79, John Carroll U., 1991-93, Case Western Res. U., 1995-96. Cert. secondary tchr., Ohio. Substitute tchr. Cleveland Heights-University Heights (Ohio) Bd. Edn., 1982-92, 97—; cons. in writing, manuscript rschr., copywriter Mahon Enterprises, Chagrin Falls, Ohio, 1988—. Substitute tchr. Shaker Heights (Ohio) Sch. Bd., 1989-94, Mayfield Heights (Ohio) Bd. Edn., 1990-92, Orange Village Sch. Dist., Beachwood, Ohio, 1996-97; tutor, mem. substitute faculty Beaumont Sch., Cleveland Heights, 1996-97; writer, coord. nat. newsletter on stress reduction Am. Mensa Ltd., Dallas, 1990-96, writer, rschr., coord. nat. newsletter on entrepreneurship, 1994-96. Contbr. poetry to various pubs. Vol., capt. local fund raising Sta. WTTW, pub. TV, Chgo., 1969-70; fund raiser Humane Soc., Mexico City, 1976; vol. Natural History Mus., Cleve., 1987-89; vol. exhbn. tour guide Cleve. Art Mus., summer 1997. Recipient Sound of Poetry award Nat. Libr. Poetry, 1995; tchr. devel. scholr John Carroll U., 1990-93. Mem. NAFE, Am. Mensa (program chmn. Cleve. 1988-90), Smithsonian Assocs. Avocations: writing, abstract prints artist, hiking, swimming, reading. Office: Cleve Heights-Univ Heights Bd Edn 2155 Miramar Blvd University Heights OH 44118-3301

MAHON, MAXINE, performing company executive; BA in Sociology, San Diego (Calif.) State U. Dancer Starlight Opera, San Diego (Calif.) Ballet, Calif. Ballet Co., Nat. Ballet, Washington; dir., founder Calif. Ballet Co., San Diego, 1968—. Choreographer (films) Being John Malkovich, (plays) The Masked Ball, Seattle (Wash.) Opera Co., 2002, Toronto (Can.) Opera Co., 2003. Recipient Headliner of Yr. in Arts award, San Diego (Calif.) Press Club; grantee, NEA. Office: California Ballet Company 4819 Ronson Ct San Diego CA 92111*

MAHONE, BARBARA JEAN, automotive company executive; b. Notasulga, Ala., Apr. 19, 1946; BS, Ohio State U., 1968; MBA, U. Mich., 1972; program for mgmt. devel., Harvard U., 1981. Sys. analyst GM, Detroit, 1968-71, sr. staff asst., 1972-74, mgr. career planning, 1975-78, dir. pers. adminstrn. Rochester, N.Y., 1979-81, mgr. indsl. rels. Warren, Ohio, 1982-83, dir. human resources mgmt. Chevrolet-Pontiac-Can. group, 1984-86, dir. gen. pers. and pub. affairs Inland divsn., 1986-88, gen. dir. pers. Indland Fisher Guide divsn. Detroit, 1989-91, gen. dir. employee benefits, 1991-93, dir. human resources truck group Pontiac, Mich., 1994—2000, exec. dir. human resources, 2001—. Chmn. Fed. Labor Rels. Authority, Washington, 1983-84, Spl. Panel on Appeals; dir. Metro Youth; mem. bd. govs. U. Mich. Alumni. Bd. dirs. ARC, Rochester, 1979-82, Urban League Rochester, 1979-82, Rochester Aea Multiple Sclerosis; mem. human resources com. YMCA, Rochester, 1980-82; mem. exec. bd. Nat. Coun. Negro Women; mem. allocations com. United Way Greater Rochester. Recipient Pub. Rels. award Nat. Assn. Bus. and Profl. Women, 1976, Mary McLeod Bethune award Nat. Coun. Negro Women, 1977, Senate resolution Mich. State Legislature, 1980; named Outstanding Woman, Mich. Chronicle, 1975, Woman of Yr., Nat. Assn. Bus. and Profl. Women, 1978, Disting. Bus. Person, U. Mich., 1978, one of 11 Mich. Women, Redbook mag., 1978. Mem. Nat. Black MBA Assn. (bd. dirs., nat. pres. Disting. Svc. award, bd. dirs., nat. pres. Outstanding MBA), Women Econ. Club (bd. dirs.), Indsl. Rels. Rsch. Assn., Internat. Assn. for Pers. Women, Engring. Soc. Detroit. Republican. Home: 175 Kirkwood Ct Bloomfield Hills MI 48304-2927 Office: MC 483-585-227 585 South Blvd Pontiac MI 48341-3146

MAHONEY, CATHERINE ANN, artist, educator; b. Macon, Mo., Nov. 18, 1948; d. Joe H. and Berniece Joyce (Garnett) Dickson; m. Michael W. Mahoney, July 19, 1969; children: Karin Lynn Mahoney Broeker, Ryan Michael. BS in Edn. with honors, Truman U., Kirksville, 1969. Mo. state life cert. for tchg. art. Elem./secondary art instr. Bucklin (Mo.) R-I Schs., 1970-74; pvt. art instr. Groom (Tex.) Artist's Assn., 1974-75; substitute tchr. Gasconade R-I Schs., Hermann, Mo., 1977-89; pvt. art instr. Colorful Brushes Studio, Hermann, Mo., 1987—; elem./secondary art instr. Crosspoint Christian Schs., Union, Mo., 1994-98. Pres. City of Hermann Arts Coun., 1983-87, membership chmn., 1980-82; dir. Summertime Children's Watercolor Workshops, Colorful Brushes, Hermann, 1987—. One-woman shows at Truman U., Kirksville, 1969, Capitol City Art Guild, Jefferson City, Mo., 1983, Kolbe Gallery of Art, Hermann, 1984, Colorful Brushes Studio, Hermann, 1987-94; designer Sister Cities Emblem City of Hermann/Arolsen, Germany, 1989, 20 ft. histl. mural, Gasconade County; works published in: Best of Watercolor: Texture, 1998, The Artful Home 2, 2004. Pres. Hermann Parent-Tchr. Orgn., 1985—87; leader 4-H, Girl and Boy Scouts, Hermann, 1982—95; organist, pianist, tchr. Hermann Cath. and Bapt. Chs., 1977—97, E. Free Ch., 1997—. Named Outstanding Young Woman of Yr., Hermann Jaycees, 1984, 1st place award Mo. Artists Collection, Mo. Pub. Svc., Sedalia, Mo., 1992, 3d place award and purchase prize Watercolor USA, Springfield (Mo.) Art Mus., 1995, 1st place award Arts Rolla Art Show, 1999. Mem.: Mo. Watercolor Soc. (bd. mem. 1998—2004, signature, M. Graham Mdse. award 2003), Oil Painters Am., St. Louis Artist Guild (mem. art sect., Hon. Mention 1993, 1998, 2002), Watercolor USA Honor Soc. (hon. Art Show award 1995), Okla. Watercolor Assn. (assoc. included Art Show 1989), Nat. Watercolor Soc. (assoc. included Nat. Art Show 1995). Avocations: piano, reading, embroidery, sewing, knitting. Home: 1058 Old Stonehill Hermann MO 65041 Office: Colorful Brushes Studio 126 E 4th St Hermann MO 65041-1130 E-mail: camahoney@ktis.net.

MAHONEY, DONNA MARIE, psychotherapist; b. Oak Park, Ill., Mar. 13, 1961; d. Thomas Joseph and Eileen Mary Mahoney. MA, Loyola U., 1989; PhD, Inst. Clin. Social Work, 2000. Acad. advisor Triton Coll., River Grove, Ill., 1984-87; psychotherapist Centrum Clinic, Oak Park, 1989—97; psychotherapist, case mgr. Kenneth Young Ctrs., Elk Grove, Ill., 1989-96; psychotherapist Anxiety and Stress Ctr., Orland Park, Ill., 1996—. Adj. faculty Argosy U., Rolling Meadows, Ill., 2002, Loyola U., 2003. Contbr. articles to profl. jours. Mem. Anxiety Disorders Assn. Am., Obsessive Compulsive Fedn., Ill. Soc. Clin. Social Work, Chgo. Assn. Psychoanalytic Psychology. Democrat. Avocations: aerobics, music. Home: 712 Bell Ave La Grange IL 60525

MAHONEY, HEATHER M. social worker; b. Boston, June 2, 1970; d. Nicholas P. and Margaret DiMarino; life ptnr. July 17, 1999. BA, Quinnipiac Coll., 1992; MS, So. Conn. State U., 1996. Social worker DSS, Chelsea, Mass., 1997; clinician Boston Children's Svcs., 1997—98, Mass Halfway, Inc., Boston, 1998—99, Riverside Sch., Lowell, Mass., 1999; program mgr. The Bridge of Ctrl. Mass., Northboro, 2000—02; clinician Y.O.U., Inc., Baldwinville, Mass., 2002—. Program dir. BRAGLY, Brockton, Mass., 1996—99; mem. Youth Group Network Mass., Boston, 1996—99.

MAHONEY, JILL ELIZABETH, music educator; b. Phoenix, Oct. 2, 1961; d. John Richard and Janet Louise Mahoney. Student, Grand Canyon Coll., 1979—80; MusB, Ariz. State U., 1984, postgrad., 1984—89. Secondary tchg. cert. grades K-12 with music endorsement. Music tchr. Avondale (Ariz.) Elem. Sch. Dist., Ariz., 1984—85; band/instrumental music tchr. Peoria Unified Sch. Dist., Glendale, Ariz., 1985—. Honor band condr. Isaac Mid. Sch., Phoenix, 1997; honor orch. condr. Paradise Valley (Ariz.) Unified Dist., 1998. Editor: (newsletter) PEA Educator, 1989—91 (Sch. Bell award, 1991). Recipient Pride in Peoria award, 1994, Raymond Skills Leadership in Tchg. award, 2002. Mem.: Ariz. Music Educators Assn. (v.p. 1997—99, condr. Elem. All State Band 2000, George C. Wilson Leadership award 1999), Am. String Tchrs. Assn., Internat. Assn. Jazz Educators. Avocations: gardening, music, reading. Home: 2154 W Earll Dr Phoenix AZ 85015 Office: Marshall Ranch Elem Sch 12995 N Marshall Ranch Glendale AZ 85304

MAHONEY, JOAN, law educator; AB, AM, U. Chgo.; JD, Wayne State U.; PhD, Cambridge U. Assoc. Honigman Miller Schwartz and Cohn, Detroit; mem. law faculty U. Mo., Kansas City, 1980—94; mem. faculty, dean Western New Eng. Coll. Law, 1994—96; mem. faculty Wayne State U. Law Sch., Detroit, 1994—, dean, 1996—. Contbr. articles to profl. jours., chpts. to books. Office: Wayne U Law Sch 471 W Palmer Detroit MI 48202

MAHONEY, JOËLLE KATHERINE, astrological consultant, communications educator; b. Amiens, France, Jan. 6, 1948; came to U.S., 1953; d. Louis James and Regine (LeClercq) Dennis; m. John William Christopher Mahoney, Aug. 14, 1971. AA, Boro Manhattan C.C., 1971; BA, Adelphi U., 1982; postgrad., Hofstra U., 1989—. Profl. cert. in astrology; cert. master practitioner neurolinguistic programming; cert. neurolinguistics programming. Tri-lingual translator N.A. Bogdan Co., N.Y.C., 1967-71; practicing astrologer Long Island, N.Y., 1971-74; founding pres. Astrological Rsch. Centre and Tng. Inst. Ltd., Mineola, N.Y., 1974-84; internat. astrological cons. Brewster, N.Y., 1984—. Pres. French Regional Alliance for Nat. Costume Edn., 1999—. Author: Concept I, II and III, 1974, In Search of Time, 1989. Vol. fund raiser Americares, New Canaan, Conn., 1991-94, Silver Hill Hosp., New Canaan, 1992-94, City Harvest, N.Y.C., 1995-97; amb. All Nations Universal Pageant Orgn., 1998-99. Named Mrs. France, 1996, Mrs. All Nations Universal, 1997; named amb.-at-large All Nations Universal Orgn., 1998. Mem. Astrologers Guild Am. (pres. 1980-83), Congress of Astrological Orgns. (v.p. 1981-84). Avocations: equitation, oil painting, writing, fitness, animal welfare. Home: 5 Fair Meadow Dr Brewster NY 10509-4617

MAHONEY, MARGARET A. federal judge; b. 1949; BA, Coll. St. Catherine, 1971; JD, U. Minn., 1974. Bankruptcy judge U.S. Bankruptcy Ct. Dist. Minn., 1984-87, U.S. Bankruptcy Ct. (so. dist.) Tex., 1987-89; ptnr. Weil, Gotshal & Manges, 1989-93; chief bankruptcy judge U.S. Bankruptcy Ct. (so. dist.) Ala., Mobile, 1995—2002, bankruptcy judge, 1993—. Office: 201 Saint Louis St Mobile AL 36602-2919 Fax: 251-441-5612. E-mail: margaret_mahoney@alsb.uscourts.gov.

MAHONEY, MARGARET ELLERBE, foundation executive; d. Charles Hallam and Leslie Nelson (Savage) M. BS magna cum laude, Vanderbilt U., 1946; LHD (hon.), Meharry Med. Coll., 1977, U. Fla., 1980, Med. Coll. Pa., 1982, Williams Coll., 1983, Smith Coll., 1985, Beaver Coll., 1985, Brandeis U., 1989, Marymount Coll., 1990, Mt. Sinai Sch. Medicine, 1992, Rush U., 1993, SUNY, Bklyn., 1994, N.Y. Med. Coll., 1995. Fgn. affairs officer State Dept., Washington, 1946-53; exec. assoc., assoc. sec. Carnegie Corp., N.Y.C., 1953-72; v.p. Robert Wood Johnson Found., Princeton, NJ, 1972-80; pres. Commonwealth Fund, N.Y.C., 1980-94, MEM Assocs., Inc., N.Y.C., 1995—. Spkr. in field. Contbr. articles to profl. jours. Trustee John D. and Catherine T. MacArthur Found., 1985—2002, Smith Coll., 1988—93, Columbia U., 1991—96, Carnegie Found. Advancement of Tchg., 1963—2001, Arthur Ashe Found., 1997—; vis. fellow Sch. Arch. and Urban Planning, Princeton U., 1973—80; bd. dirs. Coun. on Found., 1982—88; mem. N.Y.C. Commn. on the Yr. 2000, 1985—87, MIT Corp., 1984—89; bd. govs. Am. Stock Exch., 1987—92, Skillbuilders Fund, 1993—, Am. Skin Assn., 1994—, Classroom Inc., 1996—; mem. adv. bd. Office of Med. Examiner, N.Y.C., 1987—; vice chmn. N.Y.C. Mayor's Com. for Pub./Pvt. Partnerships, 1990—93; bd. dirs. Alliance for Aging Rsch., 1987—, Overseas Devel. Coun., 1988—2001, Nat. Found. Ctrs. for Disease Control and Prevention, Inc., 1994—, chmn., 1996—98; mem. vestry Parish of Trinity Ch., 1982—89, 1991—95. Recipient Frank H. Lahey Meml. award, 1984, Women's Forum award, 1989, Walsh McDermott award, 1992, Disting. Grantmaker award Coun. Founds., 1993, Edward R. Loveland award ACP, 1994, Spl. Recognition award AAMC, 1994, Merit medal Lotos Club, 1994, Terrance Keenan Leadership award in health philanthropy Grantmakers in health, 1995, Distinction award Am. Skin Assn., 1998, Rsch. Am. award, 1999, Hon. Classmate Class of 1976 award Princeton U., 2001, Picker Inst. award, 2003. Mem. AAAS, Inst. Medicine of NAS, Am. Acad. Arts and Scis., Am. Philos. Soc., Coun. Fgn. Rels., Fin. Women's Assn. N.Y., N.Y. Acad. Medicine, N.Y. Acad. Scis., Alpha Omega Alpha. Office: MEM Assocs Inc 521 5th Ave Rm 1801 New York NY 10175-0088 Office Phone: 212-297-0500.

MAHONEY, MARGARET ELLIS, accountant; b. Detroit, Mar. 17, 1929; d. Seth Wiley and Mildred Elizabeth (Hill) Ellis; m. Stephen Bedell Smith, Mar. 15, 1956 (div. Oct. 1962); 1 child, Laura Elizabeth; m. Patrick John Mahoney, Sept. 1, 1972 (dec.). BA, Butler U., 1953. Copywriter Hook Drugs Inc., Indpls., 1953; continuity dir. Sta. WXLW, Indpls., 1954-57; ptnr. Steve Smith and Assocs. Advt., Indpls., 1956-62; account mgr. Sive Advt., Cin., 1963-64, Associated Advt., Cin., 1964-65; copywriter SupeRX Drugs Inc., Cin., 1965-72; promotion writer U.S. News and World Report, Washington, 1974; asst. mgr. advt. Drug Fair, Alexandria, Va., 1975-82; dir. advt. Cosmetic and Fragrance Concepts Inc./DBA Cosmetic Ctrs., Beltsville, Md., 1982 89; advt., prodn. cons. Nat. Red Cross, Galladet U., Washington, 1989-94; asst. to real estate agt. Carmel, Ind., 1994-96; editl. cons., mem. svc. rep., acctg. clk. Angie's List, Carmel, Ind., 1996—. Vestrywoman St. Matthews Episcopal Ch., Cin., 1969-71; vol. jr. achievement hosp. chmn. Sleepy Hollow Citizens Assn., Falls Church, Va., 1973; vol. resident assoc. program Smithsonian Instn., Washington, 1989-94; chmn. membership and pub. rels. Friends Chinn Park Regional Libr., Woodbridge, Va., 1991-94; vol. Indpls. Art Ctr. Gift Shop, 1997—, Prince William Symphony Orch., Prince William County Voter Registration Bd. Mem. Potomac Valley Aquarium Soc. (past treas., past sec., editor jour.), Am. Cichlid Assn. (nat. pub. rels. chair 1985 90), Delta Delta Delta. Avocations: swimming, reading, needlework, travel, computers. Home: 9850 Greentree Dr Carmel IN 46032-9099 Office Phone: 317-803-3961. E-mail: mmah317@aol.com.

MAHONEY, MARY, hotel executive; b. Orlando, Fla., Dec. 20, 1959; Various positions Days Inn of Am., Inc., 1980—90; founder Targa Internat., Inc, 1990—94; dir. preferred vendor mktg. Cendant Corp., dir. market devel., 1994—96, v.p. mktg., Howard Johnson, 1996-98, pres., CEO, Howard Johnson Internat. Inc., 1998—2003, sr. v.p., member relations and customer support, Fairfield Resorts, 2003—. Adv. bd. William F. Harrah Coll. Hotel Admin., UNLV. Mem. state bd. Junior Achievement, NJ; bd. dirs. Nat. Academy's Found. Travel & Tourism. Named Most Powerful Women in Travel Travel Agt. mag., 1997, 98, 99, Next Generation of Hot New Marketers list Brandweek. Mem.: Am Hotel & Lodging Assoc. Coun. Inns & Suites (audit com., fin. com.), Hospitality Industry Hall of Honor. Office: Fairfield Resorts 8669 Commodity Cir Orlando FL 32819

MAHONY, SHEILA ANNE, broadcast executive; b. Yonkers, N.Y., Jan. 30, 1942; d. Paul Ambrose and Grace (Sullivan) M.; m. Charles A. Riggs, July 7, 1983; stepchildren: Charles Riggs, Julia Riggs. BA, Newton Coll. Sacred Heart, Mass., 1963; JD, Fordham U., 1967. Asst. corp. counsel Law Dept. City of N.Y., N.Y.C., 1967-72; regional dir. Cable TV Info. Ctr., The Urban Inst., Washington, 1972-74, gen. counsel, 1974-75, exec. dir., 1976-77, Carnegie Commn. on Future of Pub. Broadcasting, N.Y.C., 1977-79; v.p. govt. rels. Cablevision Systems Corp., Woodbury, N.Y., 1980-95, sr. v.p. comm. and pub. affairs, 1995-99, exec. v.p. comm., govt. and pub. affairs, 1999—, dir., 1988—. Mem. exec. com. CSPAN, 2000—. Author: Keeping PACE With the New Television, 1979. Dir. C-SPAN, Washington, 1990—, Found. for Minority Interests in Media, N.Y.C., 1992—; bd. dirs. Lustgarten found., 2000—, Legal Aid Soc. of N.Y., 2000—. Mem.: Legal Aid Soc. (bd. dirs. 2000—), Cable TV and Telecom. Assn. N.Y. (dir. 1995—, 1st vice chair 1997—2001, chair 2001—03), Cable TV Pub. Affairs Assn. (dir. 1994—98), Lustgarten Found. for Pancreatic Cancer Rsch. (bd. dirs. 1999—). Office: Cablevision Systems Corp 1111 Stewart Ave Bethpage NY 11714-3581

MAHOSKY, NANCY LYNNE, secondary school educator; b. Pitts., Oct. 5, 1951; d. Alfred Charles and Eva Marie (Bruni) Melani; m. Henry John Mahosky, Jr., July 25, 1987. BS, Indiana U. Pa., 1973; MS, Duquesne U., 1977. Cert. tchr., Pa. Tchr. math. and computer sci. Blackhawk Sch. Dist., Beaver Falls, Pa., 1973—. NSF grantee, 1991. Mem. AAUW. Home: 1904 17th St Beaver Falls PA 15010-2627 Office: Blackhawk HS 500 Blackhawk Rd Beaver Falls PA 15010-1410

MAICKI, G. CAROL, former state senator, consultant; b. Holden, Mass., July 16, 1936; d. John Arne and Mary Emily (Bumpus) Mannisto; m. Henry J. Maicki, May 4, 1957; children: Henry III, Matthew, Scott, Julia, Mary. BA, U. Mich., 1978. Exec. dir. Sweetwater County Task Force/Sexual Assault, Rocksprings, Wyo., 1978-81; program mgr. Family Violence/Sexual Assault, Cheyenne, Wyo., 1981-85; coord. S.D. Coalition Against Domestic Violence and Sexual Assault, Black Hawk, 1985-90; state senator S.D. Legislature, Pierre, 1990-92. Cons. Black Hawk, 1990—, Nat. Coalition Against Domestic Violence, 1987; spkr. Nat. Coalition Against Sexual Assault, Portland, Oreg., 1987, 96, Rutger Ctr. for Women in Politics, San Diego, 1991, Gov.'s Conf., Las Vegas, Nev., 1997; mem. planning com. Office for Victims of Crime, U.S. Justice, Phoenix, 1989; expert witness state and fed. cts., 1990—. Author: (manuals) Operating Standards, 1984, Rules and Regulations, 1986, Shelter Procedures, 1987,

Administrative Procedures, 1995, Responders to Rope, 1996, Cultural Competency, 2001. Com. mem. Health and Human Svc. State Legislature, Pierre, 1990-92, local govt., 1990-92; commn. mem. local govt. study commn., Pierre, 1990-92; bd. dirs. Crisis Intervention Svcs., 1991-99, Dakotah territory, 1996—; apptd. def. adv. com. on women in svcs. Sec. of Def., 1995-97; apptd. exec. com. def. adv. com. on women in the svcs., 1996-97; founder Women's Connection, Inc., 1996; mem. Dacotah Terr. Youth Devel., Inc. Recipient award Gov. Wyo., 1985, Spirit of Peace award Women Against Violence, Rapid City, 1993, U.S. Dept. of Justice award, 1994, fellowship Share Our Strength, 1996-98, Equity award S.D. chpt. AAUW, 1996, Failure is Impossible award Rapid City, 1998. Mem. S.D. Alliance for Mentally Ill, Rapid City Womens Network, S.D. Advocacy Network for Women. Democrat. Avocations: reading, crosswords, gardening. Home: PO Box 375 Black Hawk SD 57718-0375 E-mail: gcarol@starband.net.

MAIDON, CAROLYN HOWSER, director; b. Chgo., May 13, 1946; d. Lloyd Earl and Esther Lillian (Beck) Howser; m. Charles Randall Maidon, Nov. 21, 1970; children: Randall Scott, April Janel. BS in Edn., Okla. State U., 1968; MS in Edn., N.C. State U., 1984, postgrad., 1987—. Tchr. biology and English Cary (N.C.) High Sch., 1968-71; grad. instr. N.C. State U., Raleigh, 1984-85, asst. affirmative action officer, 1985-89, asst. dir. univ. undesignated program, 1989-95; dir. tchr. edn., 1995-99; coord. MentorNet N.C. State U., Raleigh, 2000—; chief, tchr. edn. sect. N.C. Dept. Pub. Instrn., 1999-2000. Home: 4204 Belnap Dr Apex NC 27502-5378 Office: NC State U PO Box 7632 Raleigh NC 27695-7632

MAIER, DONNA JANE-ELLEN, history educator; b. St. Louis, Feb. 20, 1948; d. A. Russell and Mary Virginia Maier; m. Stephen J. Rapp, Jan. 3, 1981; children: Alexander John, Stephanie Jane-Ellen. BA, Coll. of Wooster, 1969; MA, Northwestern U., 1972, PhD, 1975. Asst. prof. U. Tex. at Dallas, Richardson, 1975-78; asst. prof. history U. No. Iowa, Cedar Falls, 1978-81, assoc. prof., 1981-86, prof., 1986—. Cons. Scott, Foresman Pub., Glenview, Ill., 1975-94; editl. cons. Children's Press, 1975-76, Macmillan Pubs., 1989-90, Harper-Collins Pubs., 1994. Co-author: History and Life, 1976, 4th edit., 1990; author: Priests and Power, 1983; co-editor African Economic History, 1992—; contbr. articles to profl. jours, Encyclopedia Britannica. Mem. Iowa Dem. Cen. Com., 1982-90, chmn. budget com., 1986-90; chmn. 3d Congl. Dist. Cen. Com., 1986-88. Fulbright-Hays fellow, Ghana, 1972, Arab Republic Egypt, 1987; fellow Am. Philos. Soc., London, 1978; recipient Iowa Bd. Regents Faculty Excellence award, 1996, U. No. Iowa Rsch. Assignment, Tanzania, 2002-04. Mem. African Studies Assn., AAUW (fellow Ghana 1973), pres. Quota Internat. of Waterloo, 1999-2000, Quota Club. Home: 219 Highland Blvd Waterloo IA 50703-4229 Office: U No Iowa Dept History Cedar Falls IA 50614-0001 E-mail: Donna.Maier@uni.edu.

MAIER, PAULINE, history educator; b. Apr. 27, 1938; d. Irvin Louis and Charlotte (Winterer) Rubbelke; m. Charles Steven Maier, June 17, 1961; children: Andrea Nicole, Nicholas Winterer, Jessica Elizabeth Heine. AB, Radcliffe Coll., 1960; postgrad., London Sch. Econs., 1960-61; PhD in History, Harvard U., 1968; LLD (hon.), Regis Coll., 1987; DHL (hon.), Williams Coll., 1993. Asst. prof. then assoc. prof. history U. Mass., Boston, 1968-77; Robinson-Edwards prof. history U. Wis., Madison, 1977-78; prof. history MIT, Cambridge, Mass., 1978—, William R. Kenan Jr. prof. history, 1990—. Dept. head, MIT, 1979-88, mem. coun. Inst. Early Am. History, 1982-84; trustee Regis Coll., 1988-93; trustee Commonwealth Sch., 1991-96; bd. mgrs. Old South Meeting House, 1987-97, bd. advisors Internat. Ctr. Jefferson Studies, 2000-. Author: From Resistance to Revolution: Colonial Radicals and the Development of American Opposition to Britain, 1765-1766, 1972, The Old Revolutionaries: Political Lives in the Age of Samuel Adams, 1980, The American People: A History, 1986, American Scripture: Making the Declaration of Independence, 1997; co-author: Inventing America, 2002. Recipient Douglass Adair award Claremont Grad. Sch.-Inst. Early Am. History, 1976, Kidger award New Eng. History Tchrs. Assn., 1981; fellow Nat. Endowment Humanities, 1974-75, 88-89, Charles Warren fellow, 1974-75, Guggenheim fellow, 1990. Mem. Orgn. Am. Historians (mem. exec. bd. 1978-82), Am. Hist. Assn. (mem. nominations com. 1983-85, chmn. 1985), Soc. Am. Historians, Am. Antiquarian Soc. (mem. exec. coun. 1984-89), Colonial Soc. Mass. (mem. exec. coun. 1990-93), Mass. Hist. Soc., Am. Acad. Arts and Scis., The Hist. Soc. (bd. govs. 1998—). Home: 60 Larchwood Dr Cambridge MA 02138-4639 Office: MIT E51-279 77 Massachusetts Ave Cambridge MA 02139-4307 E-mail: pmaier@mit.edu.

MAIERLE, BETTE JEAN, director nursery school; b. Greenville, Mich., Sept. 8, 1933; d. Clinton and Bonnie (Briggs) Peckham; m. Ronald Matthew Maierle, Aug. 27, 1960; children: Steven, Suzanne Maierle-Liesé, Peter, AnneMarie Maierle Krepela, Laura. AD in Secretarial Sci., Davenport Univ., 1952; BA in Speech Pathology, Mich. State U., 1956; MA in Human Devel. and Resources, Wayne State U., 1976. Speech pathologist Ferndale (Mich.) Schs., 1956-60; tchr. of deaf Walled Lake (Mich.) Schs., 1960-61; tchr. spl. edn. Troy (Mich.) Schs., 1961-69; part time theme reader Detroit Pub. Schs., 1964—65; speech pathologist Birmingham (Mich.) Schs., 1967—89; tchr. spl. edn. Avondale Schs., Auburn Hills, Mich., 1965—; owner, dir. Meadowbrook Nursery Sch., Troy, 1968—; speech pathologist Mich. Sch. for Deaf and Blind, Flint, Mich., 1991-97. Fruit and vegetable insp. USDA, Traverse City, Mich., summers 1990-95. Vol. St. Daniel's Cath. Ch., Clarkston; vol. Rep. Party, Clarkston. Republican. Roman Catholic. Avocations: travel, antiques. Home: 8220 Reese Rd Clarkston MI 48348-2742 Office: Meadowbrook Nursery 6995 Livernois Rd Troy MI 48098-1572 Office Phone: 248-879-0473. E-mail: betty_ron@hotmail.com.

MAILLET, LUCIENNE, humanities educator; b. Lewiston, Maine, Apr. 16, 1934; d. Leon J. and Alice (Lizotte) Thibault; m. Daniel J. Maillet, July 14, 1956; 1 child, Daniel Jr. BA in Chemistry, Bates Coll., 1956; MA in Edn., George Washington U., 1963; MLS, Cath. U., 1969; cert. of profl. devel. and library and info. scis., CUNY, 1975; DLS, Columbia U., 1982; MBA, L.I. U., 1999. Librarian Conn. Park Elem. Sch., 1965-69, Southwoods Jr. High Sch., 1969-70; head curriculum materials and audiovisual ctr. CUNY, York Coll., Jamaica, NY, 1970-75; asst. prof. Palmer Sch., Long Island U., Brookville, NY, 1975-84, dean, 1984-89, prof., 1975—. Mem. Am. Library Assn., Am. Soc. Info. Sci., Assn. Colls. and Rsch. Libraries, Spl. Libraries Assn., N.Y. Library Club, Assn. Library and Info. Sci. Edn., Beta Phi Mu. Home: 77 Andrew St Manhasset NY 11030-2309 Office: Long Island Univ Palmer Sch Libr & Info Sci CW Post Campus Greenvale NY 11548 Office Phone: 516-299-2175. E-mail: lmaillet@liu.edu.

MAIMON, ELAINE PLASKOW, English educator, university provost, campus chief executive officer; b. Phila., July 28, 1944; d. Louis J. and Gertrude (Canter) Plaskow; m. Morton A. Maimon, Sept. 30, 1967; children: Gillian Blanche, Alan Marcus. AB, U. Pa., 1966, MA, 1967, PhD, 1970. Asst. prof. Haverford (Pa.) Coll., 1971-73; lectr. Arcadia U., Glenside, Pa., 1973-75, asst. prof., dir. writing, 1975-77, assoc. prof., 1977-83, assoc. dean, 1980-84, assoc. v.p., prof. English, 1984-86; adj. assoc. prof. U. Pa., Phila., 1982-83; assoc. dean of coll. Brown U., Providence, 1986-88; dean, prof. English Queens Coll. CUNY, Flushing, N.Y., 1988-96; campus CEO, provost Ariz. State U. West, Phoenix, 1996—; v.p. Ariz. State U., 1996—; chancellor U. Alaska, Anchorage, 2004—. Nat. bd. cons. NEH, 1977-81; mem. adv. bd. Cox Comm., 1997-2001; bd. dirs. Arrowhed Cmty. Bank. Co-author: Writing in the Arts and Sciences, 1981, A Writer's Resource, 2003; co-editor: Readings in the Arts and Sciences, 1984, Thinking, Reasoning and Writing, 1989, A Writer's Resource, 2003. Trustee Heard Mus., Phoenix, 1999—. Recipient Golden Heart award, Today's Ariz. Woman, 2000, Women of Distinction award, YMCA, Maricopa County, 2001, YWCA award in Edn., 2002, World award, Girl Scouts Am., Ariz. Cactus-Pine Coun., 2002, Woman of Vision award, Phoenix Bus. Jour.; Elaine Maimon award for Excellence in Writing named in her honor, Arcadia U., 1994. Mem.: MLA (exec. com., tchg. of writing divsn.), Am. Assn. Colls. and Univs. (exec. bd. 2002—), Conf. on Coll. Composition Comm. (exec. com. 1985-87), ACE Nat. Commn. Women, Nat. Coun. Tchrs. English (nominating com. 1986—87, teaching of writing divsn. 1991), Phi Beta Kappa. Home: 20726 N 55th Ave Glendale AZ 85308-9342 Office: Ariz State U W PO Box 37100 4701 E Thunderbird Rd Phoenix AZ 85069-7100 Office Phone: 602-543-7001. E-mail: elaine.maimon@asu.edu.

MAIN, EDNA DEWEY (JUNE MAIN), education educator; b. Hyannis, Mass., Sept. 1, 1940; d. Seth Bradford and Edna Wilhelmina (Wright) Dewey; m. Donald John Main, Sept. 9, 1961 (div. Dec. 1989); children: Alison Teresa Main Ronzon, Susan Christine Main Leddy, Steven Donald. Degree in merchandising, Tobe-Coburn Sch., 1960; BA in Edn., U. North Fla., 1974, MA in Edn., 1979, M in Adminstrn. and Supervision, 1983; PhD in Curriculum and Instrn., U. Fla., 1990. Asst. buyer Abraham & Straus, Bklyn., 1960-61; asst. mdse. mgr. Interstate Dept. Stores, N.Y.C., 1962-63; tchr. Holiday Hill Elem. Sch., Jacksonville, Fla., 1974-86; instr. summer sci. inst., 1984-92; prof. edn. Jacksonville U., 1992—, dir.. masters program in integrated learning and ednl. tech. Instr. U. Fla., 1987—90, U. N. Fla., 1990—92; cons. Assn. Internat. Schs. Africa, 1994—97. Co-author: (book) Developing Critical Thinking Through Science, Book I, 2001, Developing Critical Thinking Through Science, Book II, 2002. Rep. United Way, 1981—86; tchr. rep., chpt. leader White Ho. Young Astronaut Program, 1984—85; team leader NSF Shells Elem. Sci. Project. Named Fla. Prof. of the Yr., Carnegie Found., 2002, Jacksonville U. Prof. of Yr., 2003; recipient Innovative Excellence in Tchg., Learning and Tech. award, Internat. Coll. Conf., 1999, Outstanding Alumni award, U. N. Fla., 1999, Eve award for Edn., 2001, Apple Disting. Educator award, 2003—04. Mem.: ISTE, ASCD, Nat. Sci. Tchrs. Assn. (Sci. Tchrs. Achievement Recognition award 1983), Kappa Delta Pi, Delta Kappa Gamma, Phi Delta Kappa, Phi Kappa Phi. Episcopalian. Office: Jacksonville U 2800 University Blvd N Jacksonville FL 32211-3394 E-mail: main750@bellsouth.net.

MAIN, PATRICIA ENGLANDER, investor; b. London, Apr. 8, 1931; d. Harry Norman and Eve (Roth) Englander; m. Arnold M. Singer, June 11, 1950 (div. May 1963); m. Frank Graham Main, Apr. 30, 1966 (div. Apr. 1981); m. Franklin Walter Mohney, Aug. 10, 1981 (dec. May 1991); children: Lisa Nicole Kelly, Susan Jennifer Kerschner, Jacqueline Eve Singer. Student, Mt. Holyoke Coll., 1948-50. Dir. pub. rels. Contemporary Arts Mus., Houston, 1962-64; relocation sales assoc. Paul Reinke Corp., Cherry Hill, N.J., 1964-69; account exec. Relocation Realty Svc. Corp., N.Y.C., 1972-76, v.p. ops., 1976-79; owner Patricia Mohney Gallery, Reading, Pa., 1981-84; v.p. Venture Components Corp., N.Y.C., 1984-92; pvt. investor N.Y.C., 1992—. Trustee, bd. mem. Reading Art Mus., 1980-83; mem. bus. and profl. com. N.Y.C. Ballet, 1985-95; mem. com. denominational affairs All Souls Ch., N.Y.C., 1998—. Mem. Mt. Holyoke Coll. Alumnae Club (bd. dirs. 1969-77, pres. 1977-79). Office: 65 E 76th St Ste 3B New York NY 10021-1844

MAINELLA, FRANCES P. federal agency administrator; b. Groton, Conn. BS cum laude, U. Conn.; MS cum laude in Counseling, Ctrl. Conn. State Coll.; PhD in Pub. Svc. (hon.), Ctrl. Conn. State U., 2002. H.S. phys. edn. tchr. Vernon Pub. Sch., Rockville, Conn., 1969—77; asst. ctr. dir. Tallahassee Parks and Recreation Dept., 1977—78; dir. recreation Town of Lake Park, Fla., 1978—83; exec. dir. Fla. Recreation and Park Assn., Tallahassee, 1983—89; dir. divsn. Recreation and Parks Fla. Dept. Environ. Protection, 1989—2001; dir. Nat. Park Svc., U.S. Dept. Interior, Washington, 2001—. Spkr. in field. Contbr. numerous articles to profl. publs. Co-chair Com. for Preservation of the White House, mem. adv. coun. on hist. preservation; bd. trustees John F. Kennedy Ctr. for Performing Arts; liaison White House Hist. Soc.; sec., treas. Nat. Park Found.; mem. Am. Folklife Bd.; past pres. Nat. Assn. State Park Dirs.; past bd. mem. Am. Acad. Park and Recreation Adminstr.; past mem. Fla. Commn. Ttourism; past officio bd. mem. Fla. Recreation and Park Assn.; past mem. Gov.'s Mansion adv. com.; past bd. mem. Fla. Gov.'s Coun. on Phys. Fitness and Sports; past sec., bd. dirs. Spl. Olympics; past pres. Tallahassee Soc. Assn. Execs.; past chair United Way Drive for Tallahassee Soc. Assn. Execs.; past bd. dirs. Tallahassee Leon County Convention and Visitors Bur.; bd. dirs. Ford's Theatre Soc., Wolf Trap Found. for Performing Arts. Recipient Disting. Svc. award, Nat. Assn. Recreation Resource Planners, 1996, Woman of Distinction award, Girl Scout Coun. of Apalachee Bend, 1998, Pugsley medal, Am. Acad. Park and Recreation Adminstrn., 1998, Disting. Svc. award, Nat. Assn. State Park Dirs., 1999, Senator Bob Williams award, State of Fla., 2001, Sheldon Coleman Outdoors award, 2002, Walter T. Cox Pub. Svc. Achievement award, Clemson U., 2002. Mem.: Nat. Recreation and Park Assn. (congress planning com. 1984, 1987, past chair coun. exec. dirs., pres. 1997—, Harold D. Meyer Profl. award 2000). Office: US Dept Interior Nat Park Svc 1849 C St NW Washington DC 20240*

MAINES, NATALIE LOUISE, musician; b. Lubbock, Tex., Oct. 14, 1974; d. Lloyd Maines and Tina; m. Michael Tarabay, May 1997 (div. Jan. 1999); m. Adrian Pasdar, June 24, 2000; 1 child, Jack Slade Pasdar. Student, Tex. Tech., Berklee Sch. Music. Performer Dixie Chicks, 1995—. Performer: (albums) Wide Open Spaces, 1998 (Maximum Vision Clip of Yr., Billboard, 1998, Best New Country Artist Clip of Yr., Billboard, 1998, Best Country Album, Grammy Awards, 1998, Album of Yr., Acad. Country Music, 1998, Best Selling Album, Can. Country Music Awards, 1999, Song of Yr. (Country), WB Radio Music Awards, 1999, Album of Yr., ACM, 1999), Fly, 1999 (Best Country Album, Grammy Awards, 1999, Best Selling Album, Can. Country Music Awards, 2000, Internat. Album, British Country Music Awards, 2000, Country Album of Yr., Billboard, 2000, Album of Yr., ACM, 2000, Album of Yr., CMA, 2000), Home, 2002 (Favorite Country Album, Am. Music Awards, 2002, Best Recording Package, Grammy Awards, 2002, Best Country Album, Grammy Awards, 2002). Named Most Significant New Country Act, Country Monitor, 1998, Top New Country Artist, Billboard, 1998, Group of Yr., CMA, 1998, Top Vocal Group, Acad. Country Music, 1998, Country Artist of Yr., Rolling Stone, 1999, Top Country Artist, Billboard, 1999, Internat. Rising Star, British Country Music Awards, 1999, Artist of Yr., WB Radio Music Awards, 1999, Favorite New Artist (Country), AMA, 1999, Vocal Group of Yr., CMA, 1999, Country Artist of Yr., Billboard, 1999, Entertainer of Yr., CMA, 2000, ACM, 2000, 2001, Vocal Group of Yr., 2001, Favorite Musical Group or Band, People's Choice Award, 2002, Vocal Group of Yr., Country Music Assn. Awards, 2002, others; recipient Horizon award, CMA, 1998. Office: Monument Sony Nashville 34 Music Sq East Nashville TN 37203

MAINWARING, SUSAN ADAMS, recreational facility executive; b. Detroit, Apr. 30, 1948; BA in Elem. Edn., Elmira Coll., 1970. Elem. tchr. The Am. Sch., Mexico City, 1971—73; travel cons. Columbus, Ohio, 1973—80; dist. sales mgr. Top Brands, Inc., Columbus, 1980—85, v.p., CEO Cleve., 1985—89; exec. dir. Classic Chamber Concerts, Naples, Fla., 1998—. Office: Classic Chamber Concerts PO box 10393 Naples FL 34101

MAINWARING-HEALEY, PEPPER, equestrian, writer; b. Wollaston, Mass., May 13, 1923; d. Herbert James and Marion Jessie (Imrie) Mainwaring; m. A.D. Healey, June 23, 1950; children: Eric, Robin. BS, Simmons Coll., 1948. Advanced lic. riding instr., Mass. Head of riding Camps and Riding Ctrs., N.E. U.S., N.Y., 1942-50, Foxhollow Sch., Lennox, Mass., 1948-50; owner, dir. High Hickory Dressage Farms, Framingham, Mass., 1953—, Langdon, NH, 1986—. Trainer horses and riders for dressage and eventing; dir. Farm Bur. Fedn., Ashland, Mass., 1989—. Author: You and Your Pony, 1972; contbr. articles in profl. jours. Thanks Be to Grandmother Winifred Found. grantee; named NHHC Horseperson of Yr., 2002. Mem. U.S. Dressage Fedn., N.Am. Sheep Dog Soc., N.E. Border Collie Club (sec.-treas. 1960-80), N.E. Welsh Pony Soc. (hon. life). Achievements include lifelong involvement with equestrian therapy for the handicapped with special emphasis on teaching older women with hidden disabilties. Avocations: swimming, tennis, cross-country skiing, sailing, craftsman working in enamels on copper and silver.

MAIO, ELSIE REGINA, communications consultant; b. Bklyn., Dec. 20, 1951; d. Ralph Joseph and Joan Anne (McNally) M. BA summa cum laude, CUNY, 1977. Editor Smith Barney Co., N.Y.C., 1977-78; sr. editor Dean Witter, N.Y.C., 1978-79, Instl. Investor mag., N.Y.C., 1979-80; comm. cons. McKinsey & Co., N.Y.C., 1980-83; founding prin. Maio Assocs., Guttenberg, N.J., 1986-89; sr. v.p. Lippincott & Margulies, N.Y.C., 1989-94; sr. ptnr. Diefenback Elkins, N.Y.C., 1994-96; pres. Maio and Co., Inc., 1996—. Spkr. in field. Bd. dirs. Sisters of Mercy of Ams. Mem. Soc. Profl. Journalists. Avocations: human potential movement, watercolor painting. Office: Maio & Co Inc 2 Fifth Ave New York NY 10011 E-mail: emaio@maioandco.com.

MAIOCCHI, CHRISTINE, lawyer; b. N.Y.C., Dec. 24, 1949; d. George and Andreina (Toneatto) M.; m. John Charles Kerecz, Aug. 16, 1980; children: Charles George, Joan Christine. BA in Polit. Sci., MA in Polit. Sci., Fordham U., 1971, JD, 1974; postgrad., NYU, 1977—. Bar: N.Y. 1975, U.S. Dist. Ct. (so. and ea. dists.), N.Y. 1975, U.S. Ct. Appeals (2nd cir) 1975. Law clk. to magistrate U.S. Dist. Ct. (so. dist.) N.Y., N.Y.C., 1973-74; atty. corp. legal dept. The Home Ins. Co., N.Y.C., 1974-76; asst. house counsel corp. legal dept. Allied Maintenance Corp., N.Y.C., 1976; atty. corp. legal dept. Getty Oil Co., N.Y.C., 1976-77; v.p., mgr. real estate Paine, Webber, Jackson & Curtis, Inc., N.Y.C., 1977-81; real estate mgr. GK Techs., Inc., Greenwich, Conn., 1981-85; real estate mgr., sr. atty. MCI Telecom. Corp., Rye Brook, N.Y., 1985-93; real estate and legal cons. Wallace Law Registry, 1994-96; sr. assoc. counsel Met. Transp. Authority, 1996-99, dep. gen. counsel, 1999—. Lectr. Practicing Law Inst., N.Y.C., NY, 1999—. Mem.: ABA, Indsl. Devel. Rsch. Coun. (program v.p. 1985, Profl. award 1987), Nat. Assn. Corp. Real Estate Execs. (pres. 1983—84, treas. 1984—86, bd. dirs. 1995—, exec. v.p. N.Y. chpt. 2000—01), The Corp. Bar (sec. real estate divsn. 1987—89, chmn. 1990—92), Women's Bar Assn. Manhattan, NY. Bar Assn., Dobbs Ferry Women's Club (program dir. 1981—92, 1994—96, publicity dir. 1992—94), Jr. League Club. Avocations: sports, theatre, gardening. Home: 84 Clinton Ave Dobbs Ferry NY 10522-3004 E-mail: cmaiocch@mtahq.org.

MAITOZA, COLLEEN, professional sports team executive; Gen. mgr., co-owner Sacramento (Calif.) Sirens, 2001—. Achievements include an undefeated 2003 season in the Independent Women's Football League; the Sacramento Sirens won the 2003 Independent Women's Football League Championship against the New York Sharks. Office: Sacramento Sirens PO Box 15920 Sacramento CA 95813-9998*

MAJERS, ELIZABETH LOUISE, lawyer; b. Chgo., Sept. 25, 1958; m. Roger Daniel Majers Bonds; children: Katelyn Christine Majers, Kellyanne Louise Majers. BS, U. Ill., 1979; JD, Ind. U., 1982. Bar: Tex. 1982, Ill. 1983; CPA, Ill. Tax atty. Exxon Co., U.S.A., Houston, 1982-83; assoc. Chapman and Cutler, Chgo., 1983-90, ptnr., 1990-92, capital ptnr., 1992-97, McDermott, Will & Emery, Chgo., 1998—. Spkr. in field, 1983—. Fellow Am. Coll. Investment Counsel (past pres. 1995-97, pres., v.p. 1993-95, trustee 1991—). Avocations: golf, cooking, photography, travel. Office: McDermott Will & Emery 227 W Monroe St Ste 4400 Chicago IL 60606-5096 E-mail: emajers@mwe.com.

MAJETTE, DENISE, congresswoman; b. Bklyn., May 18, 1955; d. Voyd and Olivia Majette; m. Rogers Mitchell Majette; 2 children. BA, Yale U., 1976; JD, Duke U., 1979. Atty. Legal Aid Soc. Winston-Salem, NC, 1981—83; law asst. Ga. Ct. Appeals, 1984—89; ptnr. Jenkins Nelson & Welch, 1989—92; spl. asst. atty. gen. State of Ga., 1991—92; adminstrv. law juste Ga. State Bd. Workers' Compensation, 1992; judge State Ct. of DeKalb County, 1993—2002; congresswoman 4th Dist. Ga. U.S. Ho. Reps., 2003—; mem. budget, edn. and workforce, and small bus. ho. coms. Grad. Leadership DeKalb, 1992; mem. Kidney Caucus; former com. mem. Miller Grove PTA; past mem. vestry Episcopal Ch. of Holy Cross; former pres. DeKalb Lawyers Assn.; mem. Childcare Com. YMCA, Decatur; mem. adv. bd. Jr. League DeKalb County; mem. Congl. Black Caucus, Congl. Caucus on India and Indian Ams.; mem. steward bd. Antioch AME Ch. Recipient Judge's Cmty. Recognition award, Black Law Students' Assn., Ga. State U. Coll. Law, 2001, You Go Girl award, Ga. Assn. Black Women Attys., 2003. Democrat. Office: 1517 Longworth House Office Bldg Washington DC 20515-1004*

MAJOR, ALICE JEAN, lawyer; b. Denver; m. Kent H. Major, Feb. 16, 1997; children: David, Thomas, Kassie, Samantha, Cameron, Eve, Zoë, Emma. BS in Bus., U. Colo., 1984, MBA, 1986; JD, U. Kans., 1987. Bar: Mo. 1987, Kans. 1988, U.S. Dist. Ct. Kans. 1988, Colo. 1990, U.S. Dist. Ct. Colo. 1991, U.S. Ct. Appeals (3d cir.) 1993, U.S. Supreme Ct. 1994. Atty. Legal Aid of Western Mo., Kansas City, 1987-88, Spencer, Fane, Britt & Browne, Kansas City, 1988-91; mcpl. and county atty. City and County of Denver, 1991—. Spkr. Colorado Springs mtg. Colo. County Attys. Assn., 1992. Vol. Denver Dumb Friends League, Denver, 1996—. Recipient ribbons and awards for paintings. Mem. Alfred A. Arraj Inn of Ct. (barrister mem.). Avocations: art, skiing, fishing. Office: City Attys Office City and County of Denver 1437 Bannock St Rm 353 Denver CO 80202-5375

MAJOR, CAROLYN LEDFORD, counselor; b. Hopkinsville, Ky., Nov. 6, 1962; d. Robert Howard and Martha Virginia (Aldridge) Ledford; m. James Kent Major, May 15, 1982; children: Ella Ashley, Madison Edward. BS, Murray (Ky.) State U., 1983, MS, 1985. Cert. tchr. K-12 phys. edn., history, elem. counselor. Elem. phys. edn. tchr. Christian County Bd. of Edn., Hopkinsville, Ky., 1984-91, elem. guidance counselor, 1991—. Mem. Am. Assn. Sch. Counselors, Ky. Assn. Sch. Adminstrs., Alpha Omicron Pi. Baptist. Home: 2421 Kings Chapel Rd Cadiz KY 42211-9737 Office: Ind Hills Elem Sch 313 Blane Dr Hopkinsville KY 42240-1338

MAJOR, FLORA HOELTING, music educator; b. Platteville, Wis., Feb. 4, 1933; d. Carl Albert Hoelting and Louise Christina Sieber; m. Gordon Major, July 30, 1955; children: Eleanor, Philip, Thomas. B.Mus.Edn., U. Dubuque, Iowa, 1955; MA in Tchg., Sacred Heart U., Fairfield, Conn., 1987. Music tchr. Guttenberg Schs., Iowa, 1955—56; 4th grade tchr. New Vernon Schs., NJ, 1956—59; 6th grade tchr. Luth. Schs., Cleve., 1971—74; music tchr. Toledo Pub. Schs., 1976—79, Norwalk Pub. Schs., Conn., 1979—2004. Organist, choir dir. Pilgrim United Ch., Cleve., 1970—74, Faith United Ch. Christ, Toledo, 1977—79, East Ave. Meth. Ch., Norwalk, 1989—. Active Knopp campaign, Dem. Party, Norwalk, 2001. Avocations: reading, bicycling, travel. Home: 112 Gillies Ln Norwalk CT 06854

MAJOR, MARY JO, dance school artistic director; b. Joliet, Ill., Dec. 5, 1955; d. George Francis and Lucille Mae (Ballun) Schmidberger; m. Perry Rex Major, June 9, 1979. AA, Joliet Jr. Coll., 1976; BA, Lewis U., 1978; MS, Ill. State U., 1983; postgrad., No. Ill. U., Nat. Louis U., Gov.'s State U., Olivet Nazarene U., Aurora U. Cert. tchr., Ill. Tchr., softball coach St. Rose Grade Sch., Wilmington, Ill., 1977-78; tchr., coach volleyball, basketball, softball Reed Custer High Sch., Braidwood, Ill., 1978-79; pvt. tutor, 1979; tchr. Coal City (Ill.) Middle Sch., 1980—, basketball coach, 1980-84; owner, dir., choreographer Major Sch. Dance, Inc., Coal City, 1984—; owner Technique Boutique, 1991—. Aerobics instr. Wilmington Park Dist., 1977-82, Coal City Shape Shoppe, 1980-82; cheerleading sponsor Joliet Jr. Coll., 1976-77, aerobics instr., 1980-81; pvt. dance instr., Coal City, 1981; dancer, choreographer Coal City Bi-Centennial Celebration, 1981, Coal City Community Celebration, 1982; founder Major Motion Dancers,

1984—; tchr., Russia, 1990; dancer, choreographer various performances for ch. and civic orgns.; televised half-time performance and tour Citrus Bowl. Commd. to choreograph and appear in video prodn.: Jacinta, Not an Ordinary Love, The Patty Waszak Show A Bit of Branson, 1995—; performer on televised Easter Seals Telethon from the Empress Casino, Joliet. Mem. Arts Coun. Co-op. Recipient Proclamation of Achievement award Dance Olympus, Chgo., 1986-2003, Best Choreographer award 1990, Merit award Tremaine Dance Conv., 1991-92; named Best Actress, Joliet Kiwanis, 1989, Best Musician, 1990. Mem. NEA, Ill. Edn. Assn., Coal City Cmty. Unit Edn. Assn. Office: Major Sch Dance Inc 545 E 1st St Coal City IL 60416-1643

MAJORS, BETTY-JOYCE MOORE, genealogist, writer; b. Tullahoma, Tenn., Nov. 22, 1930; d. Frank Russell and Willie Eveline (Cope) Moore; m. Charles Anderton Majors, June 19, 1953; children: Robert Cope Majors, Carolyn Lynn (Majors) Diehl. Student, Israel Conservatory of Music, Jerusalem, 1951; BS, Mid. Tenn. State U., 1952. Pub. sch. music tchr., Lynchburg, Tenn., 1953-54; computer programmer AEDC, Arnold Air Force Station, Tenn., 1954-86; genealogist, author, lectr., 1986—. Author: DeKalb County, Tennessee Genealogy from Settlement Books, 1992, Warren County, Tennessee Deed Book A, 1992, Warren County, Tennessee Will Books, 3 vols., 1992-95; co-author: Warren County, Tennessee Annotated Cemetery Books, 4 vols., 1994-99. Chmn. Coffee County Tenn. Records Commn., Manchester, Tenn., 1990—, also archivist, Coffee County Tenn., 1997—. Mem.: DAR (state chmn. 1980—82), Plantagenet Soc., Soc. Descs. Knights Most Noble Order of Garter, Colonial Order of Crown, Ams. of Royal Descent, Magna Charta Dames (state chmn. 1972—73), Sons and Daus. of Pilgrims (state officer 1981—82), USD1812 (chpt. officer 2000—01), Colonial Dames XVII Century (nat. officer 1979—83). Avocations: reading, cooking. Home: 111 Oak Park Dr Tullahoma TN 37388-4677

MAJURE, ALLISON SCOTT, product marketing professional; b. Sigonella, Sicily, Italy, June 17, 1960; d. Oscar Lamar and Barbara Exie (Scott) Majure; m. Walter Clifford Barkley; children: Miles Majure Barkley, Jack Majure Barkley BA in History of Sci., U. Calif., Berkeley, 1996. Pub. affairs exec. Inst. Humane Studies, Menlo Park, Calif., 1983-85; pub. affairs cons. Pacific Rsch. Inst., San Francisco, 1986-88; litigation sec. Brobeck, Phleger & Harrison, San Francisco, 1988-92; pvt. asst. Danielle Steel, San Francisco, 1992; sales/mktg. support specialist BARRA, Berkeley, 1992-95; advt. mgr. Daily Californian Newspaper, Berkeley, 1995-96; product mktg. mgr. PeopleSoft, Pleasanton, Calif., 1996-2000; pres. JustWrite, Castro Valley, Calif., 1999—; product mktg. mgr. Kana Comms., Redwood City, Calif., 2000—. Ann. fundraising campaign chair St. Vincent de Paul Soc. San Francisco, 1992; mem. Calif. Reps. for Choice, San Francisco, 1990-92. Mem. U. Calif. Berkeley Alumni Assn., Women in Tech. Republican. Presbyterian. Avocations: swimming, poetry, hiking. Office: Kana Comms 740 Bay Rd Redwood City CA 94063-2469

MAKAREC, KATHERINE, psychologist, educator; b. Sudbury, Ont., Can., Apr. 15, 1960; d. Antin Makarec and Gertrude Chyka; m. Stephen John Taylor, July 5, 1997. Diploma in counseling, Humber Coll., 1981; BA, Laurentian U., Sudbury, 1985; MA, York U., Toronto, Ont., 1990, PhD, 1995. Post doctoral fellow U. Toronto, 1995—97; asst. prof. William Paterson U., Wayne, NJ, 1997—. Faculty advisor Psi Chi William Paterson U., Wayne, 1997—, faculty advisor Psychology Club, 1998—, dept. chair, 2002—. Contbr. articles to profl. jours. Named Ont. Grad. Scholar, 1991—95; fellow, Nat. Sci. and Engring. Rsch. Coun., 1995—97; grantee, William Paterson U., 1998, 1999. Mem.: APA, Brain, Behavior and Cognitive Sci., Am. Psychol. Soc. Avocations: hiking, swimming, stained glass. Office: William Paterson U 300 Pompton Rd Wayne NJ 07470

MAKEPEACE, MARY LOU, former mayor; 2 children. BA in Journalism, U. N.D.; MPA, U. Colo., Colorado Springs. Tchr. Am. Sch., Tananarive, Madagascar; asst. to Def. Attaché Am. Embassy, Prague, Czechoslavakia; adult edn. officer Ramstein AFB, Germany; case worker, adminstr. El Paso County Dept. Social Svcs., 1974-82; exec. dir. Cmty. Coun. Pikes Peak Region, 1982-84; dist. 1 rep. City Colorado Springs, 1985-97, vice mayor, 1997, mayor, 1997—2003; exec. dir. Leadership Pike's Peak, Colo. Springs, 2003—. Exofficio mem. Econ. Devel. Coun. Bd. Dirs.; chair Econ. Devel. Com., Task Force City Svcs. to Srs., urban affairs com. Pikes Peak Area Coun. Govts.; apptd. Colo. Space Adv. Coun.; adj. prof. U. Colo.; ex-dir. leadership Pikes Peak Mem. steering com. Imagination Celebration; sr. advisor Palmer Found., Pikes Peak Partnership; mem. Nat. League Cities Leadership Tng. Coun.; past mem. Colo. Mcpl. League Exec. Bd., 1st United Meth. Ch. Gates Found. fellow, 1992; recipient Svc. Mankind award Centennial Sertoma Club, 1985, Mary Jean Larson Cmty. Svc. award Girl Scouts Wagon Wheel Coun., 2002, Spence Vanderlin Pub. Ofcl. award Am. Pub. Power Assn., 2002, Outstanding Cmty. award Econ. Devel. Corp., 2003; named Super Woman Women's Health Ctr., 1988, Best City Councilmem. Springs Mag., 1991; honored Women in Your Life dinner Women's Found. Colo., 2002. Mem. Am. Soc. Pub. Adminstrn., Pi Alpha Alpha. Office: Leadership Pikes Peak 219 W Colorado Ave Colorado Springs CO 80903*

MAKER, AZMAIRA HAMID, psychologist, educator; b. Karachi, Pakistan, Jan. 14, 1968; arrived in U.S., 1987; d. Hamid and Mumtaz M.; m. Zia Agha, Aug. 3, 2001. BA, Vassar Coll., Poughkeepsie, N.Y., 1991; PhD, U. Mich., Ann Arbor, 1996. Postdoctoral fellow U. Mich., Ann Arbor, 1997, 1999, lectr., 1997, 1999; asst. prof. Calif. State U., San Bernadino, 1999—2000, Ill. Sch. Profl. Psychology, Chgo., 2000—02, Marquette U., Milw., 2002—; pvt. practice Karachi, 1998. Cons. NGO's, Karachi, 1998—. Contbr. articles, chapters to books. Mem.: APA. Democrat. Muslim. Avocations: cooking, swimming, travel. Office: Marquette U Psychology Dept Schroeder Complex Milwaukee WI 53201

MAKI, HOPE MARIE, artist, sculptor, illustrator, poet, educator; b. St. Joseph, Mo., Jan. 14, 1938; 3 children. Host TV art show Channel 6, Fort Walton Beach, Fla.; owner art sch., gallery; art tchr., 1957—. Exhibited in shows at Arts-Inter-Salon Int des Sekneurs de L'Art, Chateauneuf du Pape, France, 1994, Salon Int des Seigneurs de L'Art, Palais des Congres Marseille, 1994, Mountserrat Gallery, N.Y.; represented in permanent pvt. and pub. collections; created art for the blind, 1963—; Author and illustrator: Trader Jon His Life, 2001. Named One of Best New Poets Am. Poetry Assn., 1987, 88, 89; recipient Award of Poetic Achievement, Amherst Soc., recognition of outstanding achievements in art edn. Cox Comm., 2000; poem placed in spl. collection Statue of Liberty Nat. Monument, 1992. Mem. Nat. Mus. of Women in the Arts. Avocation: poetry. Home: 3985 Langley Ave Pensacola FL 32504-8371

MAKKREEL, KAREN EMIKO, lawyer; b. San Diego, Feb. 1, 1969; d. Rudolf and Frances Tanikawa Makkreel. BA cum laude, U. Calif., San Diego, 1991; JD, U. Calif., San Francisco, 1994. Bar: Calif. 1995, U.S. Ct. Appeals (D.C. cir.) 1996, U.S. Ct. Appeals (fed. cir.) 1997, U.S. Ct. Fed. Claims 1997, U.S. Supreme Ct. 2002. Gen. atty. Office of Chief Counsel U.S. Customs Svc., Washington, 1996—99; atty.-advisor Office of Gen. Counsel U.S. Dept. of Treasury, Washington, 1999—2002; asst. chief counsel Office of Chief Counsel U.S. Customs and Border Protection, Tampa, Fla., 2002—. Active Capitol Hill United Meth. Ch., Washington, 1996—2002. Japanese Am. Citizenship League Mike Masaoka Congl. fellow, Hon. Robert T. Matsui, U.S. Ho. of Reps., 1994—95. Mem.: Asian Pacific ABA.

MAKRI, NANCY, chemistry educator; b. Athens, Greece, Sept. 5, 1962; came to the U.S., 1985; d. John and Vallie (Tsakona) M.; m. Martin Gruebele, July 9, 1992; children: Alexander Makris Gruebele, Valerie Gruebele Makri. BS, U. Athens, 1985; PhD, U. Calif., Berkeley, 1989. Jr. fellow Harvard U., Cambridge, Mass., 1989-91; from asst. prof. to assoc. prof. U. Ill., Urbana, 1992-99, prof., 1999—. Recipient Beckman Young Investigator award Arnold & Mabel Beckman Found., 1993, Ann. medal Internat. Acad. Quantum Molecular Sci., 1995, Camille Dreyfus Tchr.-Scholar award The Camille and Henry Dreyfus Found., 1997, Agnes Fay Morgan award Iota Sigma Pi, 1999, physics prize Bodossaki Found., 1999; named NSF Young Investigator, 1993; Packard fellow for sci. and engring. David and Lucile Packard Found., 1993, Sloan Rsch. fellow Alfred Sloan Found., 1994, Cottrell scholar Rsch. Corp., 1994; univ. scholar U. Ill., 1999. Fellow: AAAS, Am. Phys. Soc. Home: 2722 Valley Brook Dr Champaign IL 61822-7634 Office: U Ill Urbana Dept Chem 601 S Goodwin Ave Urbana IL 61801-3709 E-mail: nancy@makri.scs.uiuc.edu.

MAKUPSON, AMYRE PORTER, television station executive; b. River Rouge, Mich., Sept. 30, 1947; d. Rudolph Hannibal and Amyre Ann (Porche) Porter; m. Walter H. Makupson, Nov. 1, 1975; children: Rudolph Porter, Amyre Nisi. BA, Fisk U., 1970; MA, Am. U., Washington, 1972. Asst. dir. news Sta. WGPR-TV, Detroit, 1975-76; dir. pub. rels. Mich. Health Maintenance Orgn., Detroit, 1976-77; mgr. pub. affairs, news anchor Sta. WKBD-TV, Southfield, Mich., 1977—, Children's Miracle Network Telethon, 1989—. Mem. Co-Ette Club, Inc., Met. Detroit Teen Conf. Coalition; mem. adv. com., bd. dirs. Alzheimers Assn.; bd. dirs. com. March of Dimes; pres. bd. dirs. Detroit Wheelchair Athletic Assn.; bd. dirs. Providence Hosp. Found., Sickle Cell Assn., Kids In Need of Direction, Drop-out Prevention Collaborative, Merrill Palmer Inst., Skillman Found. Recipient 5 Emmy awards 3 Best Commentary/Best Anchor, Best Interview/Discussion Show, 24 Emmy nominations NATAS, Editl. Best Feature award AP, Media award UPI, Oakland County Bar Assn., TV Documentary award, Detroit Press Club, Bishop Gallagher award Mental Illness Rsch. Assn., Svc. award Arthritis Found. Mich., Mich. Mchts. Assn., DAV, Jr. Achievement, City of Detroit, Salvation Army, Spirit award City of Detroit, Spirit award City of Pontiac, Golden Heritage award Little Rock Bapt. Ch., 1993, Neal Shine award outstanding contbn. Nat. Soc. Fundraising Execs., Virginia Merrick award outstanding contbn. Christ Child Soc., Outstanding Achievement award Tuskegee Airmen, Best Feature Story award Mich. Assn. Broadcasters; named Media Person of the Yr., So. Christian Leadership Conf., 1994, Humanitarian of the Yr., March of Dimes, 1995. Mem. Pub. Rels. Soc. Am., Am. Women in Radio and TV (Outstanding Achievement award 1981, Outstanding Woman in TV Top Mgmt. 1993, Mentor award 1993), Women in Comm., Nat. Acad. TV Arts and Scis., Detroit Press Club, Ad-Craft, Howard U. Nat. Gold Key Honor Soc. (hon.). Roman Catholic. Office: 26955 W 11 Mile Rd Southfield MI 48034-2292

MALASANOS, LOIS JULANNE FOSSE, nursing educator; b. LaPorte City, Iowa, Sept. 1, 1928; d. Lewis Reginald and Henrietta Marie Fosse; widowed; 1 child, Toree. BSN, U. Tex., 1948; BA in Gen. Sci., U. Iowa, 1952; MA in Nursing Edn., U. Chgo., 1959; PhD in Physiology, U. Ill., 1973. Assoc. dir. nursing U. Iowa Hosps., Iowa City, 1950 51, staff charge nurse, 1951; instr. operating room Sch. Nursing, Michael Reese Hosp., Chgo., 1951-58; charge nurse, med.-surg. U. Chgo., Billings Hosp., 1952-59; pvt. duty nurse Ill., 1959-63; charge nurse, maternal-infant nursing Weiss Meml. Hosp., Chgo., 1963-66; asst. prof. Loyola U., Chgo., 1966-69; teaching asst. in physiology U. Ill., Chgo., 1969-73, assoc. prof., assoc. head gen. nursing dept. Coll. Nursing, 1973-76, prof., assoc. head gen. nursing dept., 1976-80; prof., dean Coll. Nursing U. Fla., Gainesville, 1980-95, Disting. Svc. prof., 1995—. Instr. anatomy and physiology Cook County Hosp., Chgo., 1973; lectr. endocrinology Chgo. Coll. Osteopathic Medicine, 1973-80; active Pres. Clinton's Task Force on Health Care, 1993; cons. Am. Assn. Med. Colls., 1977-78, Am. Heart Assn., 1977-94, Am. Jour. Nursing, 1978-79, Gainesville (Fla.) Vets. Ctr., 1980-95, Lake Butler Receiving Ctr., 1980—; chair Deans and Dirs. of Fla. Colls. Nursing, 1981-89; chair edn. com. State Bd. Nursing, 1983-87, chair probable course com., 1984—; vis. prof. Dokuz Eylul U., Izmir, Turkey, 1995-96; cons., presenter in field. Co-author, editor: Manual of Medical Surgical Nursing, 1983, Translating Comitment to Reality, 1986, Health Assessment, 1977 (Am. Jour. Nursing Book of Yr. award 1977), 4th edit., 1989; editor: Vital Signs, 1981-90, Fla. Cancer Nursing News, 1983-84; co-editor: Fla. Nursing Rev., 1986-90; mem. editl. rev. bd. Image, 1980-96; editl. cons. Nursing, 1982-94; manuscript referee Rsch. in Nursing and Health, 1980-94, Jour. Profl. Nursing, 1985-94, Turkish Jour. Nurse Rshc.; chairperson adv. com. Nursing Outlook, 1986-91, Peer Rev., 1986-94; contbr. more than 100 articles, revs. to profl. jours. Nursing com., scholarship com. and rsch. rev. com. Am. Cancer Soc., Tampa, Fla., 1980-94. Recipient Bronze medal Fla. Heart Assn., 1986, Silver medal Fla. Heart Assn., 1989, 93; named Disting. Alumnus U. Tex. Med. Br., 1985; named to Disting. Faculty, Albany State U., 1988, Hall of Fame, U. Tex. Med. Br., 1992; NEH fellow, 1981; Fulbright awardee to Turkey, 1995-96, 2001-02. Mem. ANA (mem. coun. nurse rschrs.), AACN, AAAS, AAUP, Am. Acad. Nursing (mem. pub. com. 1986-89) Am. Assn. Higher Edn., Am. Assn. Colls. Nursing, Fla. Nurses Assn. (mem. dist. 10), N.Y. Acad. Sci., Fla. League Nursing, Nat. League Nursing (chair, mem. coun. baccalaureate and higher degree program, Dirs. award 1995, site visitor for program rev. 1980—, bd. rev. for accreditation 1993-2002, Outstanding Leadership in Nursing Edn. award 2002), Fla. State Bd. Nursing (probable cause com.), So. Regional Edn. Bd., Sigma Xi, Sigma Theta Tau (Outstanding Leadership award 2003), Phi Kappa Phi (pres. 1987-88). Office: U Fla Coll Nursing PO Box 100187 Gainesville FL 32610-0187 E-mail: malaslj@nursing.ufl.edu.

MALBON, LOUISE, nursing educator, hypnotherapist; b. Fayetteville, N.C., Feb. 13, 1956; d. Margaret Bess and John Bullard, Fletcher Bess (Stepfather); children: Lessel Malbon, III, Lawrence A., Leslie. Assoc. Applied Scis., Excelsior Coll., 1987. Cert. CPR instr., ACLS instr.; RN; cert. clin. hypnotherapist. Clin. resource nurse educator DC Gen. Hosp., Washington, 2001—02; ambulatory svs. coord. Wash. Hosp. Ctr., Washington, 2002. ACLS instr. Wash. Adventist Hosp. Tng. Ctr., Takoma Park, 2002—. Author: Caring Enough to Change, 2002. Cmty. activist 8th Precinct Civic Assn., Chillum, 1987—2002. Named 100 Extra Ordinary Nurses, Sigma Theta Tau Internat. Honor Soc. Nursing, 2001. Mem.: Emergency Nurses Assn. Democrat. Baptist. Home and Office: Fresh Start Hypnotherapy and Pub 5405 13th Avenue Chillum MD 20783 Personal E-mail: LSMLB@AOL.COM. Business E-Mail: Freshstarthypnotherapy-.com.

MALCOLM, DAWN GRACE, family physician; b. L.A., Nov. 3, 1936; d. Thomas N. and Grace S. (Salisian) M. BA, UCLA, 1959; MD, Med. Coll. Pa., 1973. Diplomate Am. Bd. Family Practice. Tchr. elem. music Fullerton (Calif.) Sch. Dist., 1960-61; tchr. Ahlman Acad., Kabul, Afghanistan, 1961-65; intern and resident in family practice Kaiser Found. Hosp., L.A., 1973-76; family physician So. Calif. Permanente Med. Group, L.A., 1976—. Mem. faculty family practice residency program Kaiser Found. Hosp., L.A., 1976—. Fellow Am. Acad. Family Physicians. Office: So Calif Permanente Med Grp 4747 Sunset Blvd Los Angeles CA 90027-6021

MALCOLM, GLORIA J. small business owner; b. Atlanta, Apr. 16, 1956; d. George and Norella Camp; m. Ericka Monique Malcolm. B in Bus. Mgmt., DeKalb Coll., Atlanta. Team leader MS Soc., Atlanta; cons., advisor Home Testing Inst., NYCq; rep., organizer Nielsen TV, Dunedin, Fla.; mem. Alliance Orgn., Memphis; assoc., advisor Joyner Hutcheson Rsch., Atlanta; owner, pres. GJM Profl. Cleaning Svc., Inc., East Point, Ga. Bd. dirs. Atlanta FCU. Mem.: Nat. Female Execs. Assn., Bldg. Trader Assn. Avocations: travel, reading, volleyball, tennis, bicycling. Home: PO Box 490365 Atlanta GA 30349 Office: GJM Profl Cleaning Svc Inc 2111D Pointview Dr East Point GA 30344

MALCOLM, MOLLY BETH, political party official, counselor; BAS in Elem. Edn. with high honors, So. Meth. U., 1976; MS in Counseling and Guidance, Tex. A&M U.-Texarkana, 1988. Lic. profl. counselor, lic. chem. dependency counselor, Tex. Tchr. pub. schs., Ark., Tex., Okla., 1977-87; elem. counselor Texarkana (Ark.) Schs., 1987-89; drug. abuse prevention and counseling specialist Region VII Edn. Svc. Ctr., Kilgore, Tex., 1989-90; drug free schs. student assistance coord. Longview (Tex.) Ind. Sch. Dist., 1990-92; counseling and student svcs. coord. Texarkana (Tex.) Ind. Schs., 1992-93; owner, counselor Malcolm Cons., 1993—; field dir. Max Sandlin for Congress Campaign, 1996; dist. cmty. outreach coord. Congress Max Sandlin, Tex. 1st Dist., 1997-98; state chair Tex. Dem. Party, 1998—2003. Contbr. publs. and curricula. Active Dem. Nat. Com., 1998-2003, exec. com., 2000-2003; active Presbytery of the Pines, Synod of the Sun Presbyn. Ch. USA, Pine Street Middle Sch. PTA; pres. Texarkana Ind. Sch. Dist., 1993-94; deacon First Presbyn. Ch., Texarkana; advisor career devel. U. Tex. Chi Omega, 1999-2001; Texarkana bd. dirs. Susan G. Komen Race for the Cure. Named one of Rising Stars in Politics, Campaigns and Elections Mag., 2000, Pres.' award Ark. Counseling Assn., 1989, Hon. Bill Clinton Gov. Ark. Traveler award, 1989, Texarkana Alumni Achievement award Tex. A&M U., 1989, Winnsboro ISD Disting. Alumni award, 2003, Tex. Women's Polit. Caucus Blazing New Trails award Tex. Lyceum Assn., Inc., 2001-. Mem. NAACP (life), Tex. Counseling Assn. (Disting. Svc. award 1993, 96), Tex. Mental Health Counselors Assn., Tex. Sch. Counselors Assn., Tex. Assn. for Multicultural Counseling and Devel. (chair awards com. 1994), N.E. Tex. Counseling Assn., Assn. State Dem. Chairs (co-chair resolution com. 1999-2001, exec. com., treas. exec. com. 2001-2004), Tex. Rural Cmtys. Bd., Clinton Birthplace Found. Bd., Texarkana Mus. Sys. Bd., Texarkana Hist. Landmark Preservation Commn., Texarkana Regional Arts and Humanities Coun., Inc.(mem. AMAX adv. bd. 2004-), Better Orgn. New Downtown Bd., Tex. Dem. Women (pres. 1997-99, Mem. of Yr. 1998), Leadership Texarkana Alumi Assn. (adv. bd. 1996-99), Jr. League Texarkana, Leadership Tex. Alumnae Assn. (life, adv. bd. 1996-99), Ark. PTA (life), DAR, Tex. A&M U. at Texarkana Alumni Assn. (life, Achievement award 1989), So. Meth. U. Alumni Assn. (life), Rotary Internat., Psi Chi (v.p. 1987-89), Delta Kappa Gamma (pres. chpt. 1988-89), Chi Omega (pres. chpt. alumni assn. 1998-99), Dem. Nat. Com., Texarkana C. of C. (mil. affairs com.), Tex. Lyceum Assn. (bd. dirs.), Am. Legion. Office: Malcolm Consulting PO Box 6282 Texarkana TX 75505

MALDONADO, JUDITH ANN BATORSKI, art association administrator; b. Eden, N.Y., Oct. 8, 1949; d. John Michael and Ethel (Owens) B.; m. Michael J. Rocco (div. Oct. 1980); 1 child, Flora; m. Maximino Maldonado Jr., Oct. 13, 1997. Student, Colo. Springs Coll. Bus., 1981; AS in Fine Arts, Suffolk C.C., 1983; BA, SUNY, Stonybrook, 1985, MA, 1987; postgrad., Columbia Coll. Chgo. Film Sch., 1985. Caretaker, asst. mgr. Farmer's Shared Home, Danbury, N.H., 1979-80; cert. educator Assn. for Childbirth at Home, Internat., L.A., 1980; accts. payable clk. Pikes Peak C.C., Colorado Springs, Colo., 1981-82; office mgr. Three Village Meals-on-Wheels, Stonybrook, 1984; grad. sec. art dept. SUNY, 1986-87, art gallery intern Fine Arts Ctr., 1987; dir. ops., dir. master classes and free concerts Islip Arts Coun., East Islip, N.Y., 1987-89; cons. N.Y. State Coun. on the Arts, N.Y.C., 1989—; co-owner, cons. Fire and Earth Designers and Feng Shui Consultants, Patchogue, N.Y., 1999—. Participant Arts in Bus. Mgmt. seminar Citibank/ABC, N.Y.C., 1987, cmty. leaders luncheon Fox Channel 5, N.Y.C., 1987; asst. to dir. Newsday's L.I. Summer Arts Festival Cmty. Affairs Dept., 1989, Suffolk County Motion Picture and TV Commn., Hauppauge, N.Y., 1988—, Summer Film Festival, 1988-90; cons. N.Y. State Coun. Arts, 1989-90, cons., 1990-91; interior decorator Trans-Designs, 1992; ind. contractor KM-Matol Corp, Que., Can., 1993; intern Nat. Inst. Inner Healing, Rich in Mercy Inst.; Feng Shui cons., 1998; interior design cons. Black Hat Sect. Tibetan Buddhism Feng Shui, 1999. Photographs included in Photography Forum's Coll. Photography Ann., 1985. Campaign dir. Food for Poland, Colorado Springs, 1982; organizer Granite State Alliance, Portsmouth, N.H., 1979, Safe 'n' Sound anti-nuclear campaign, Shoreham, N.Y., 1979; grad. rep. Sch. Continuing Edn. SUNY Stonybrook, judicial com. on acad. standing, SUNY Stonybrook, 1986-87; vol. Vietnam Vets. Theatre Ensemble, 1988, New Community Cinema, Huntington, N.Y., 1988; active exec. com. Dowling Coll. Spring Tribute Concert, Oakdale, N.Y., 1989; asst. to dir. Newsday Community Rels. Dept. L.I. Arts 89, 1989; founding mem. com. L.I. Green Party, Brookhaven Twp., 1990—; participant Life in the Spirit seminar Cath. Charismatic Renewal, N.Y., 1992; tchr. Our Lady of Mt. Carmel Ch., N.Y., 1991—; active Pastoral Coun., 1992—. Mem. Internat. Platform Soc., Contemporary Hispanic Artists of L.I. (advisor to bd. dirs. Ctrl. Islip 1988-89). Roman Catholic. Avocations: screen-writing, poetry, photography, interior design and decoration, therapeutic touch healing. Home: 40 W 4th St Patchogue NY 11772-2171 also: 1075 Bay Shore Ave Bay Shore NY 11706-2738

MALDONADO-BEAR, RITA MARINITA, economist, educator; b. Vega Alta, P.R., June 14, 1938; d. Victor and Marina (Davila) Maldonado; m. Larry Alan Bear, Mar. 29, 1975. BA, Auburn U., 1960; PhD, NYU, 1969. With Min. Wage Bd. & Econ. Devel. Adminstr., Govt. of P.R., 1969-70; asst. prof. econs. Manhattan Coll., 1970-72; assoc. prof. econs. Bklyn. Coll., 1972-75; assoc. prof. fin. & econs., undergrad./grad. divsn. Stern Sch. Bus. NYU, 1975-81, prof., 1981—2004, prof. emerita, 2004—. Vis. assoc. prof. fin. Stanford (Calif.) Grad. Bus. Sch., 1973-74; acting dir. markets, ethics & law, NYU, 1993-94; cons. Morgan Guaranty Trust Co., N.Y.C., 1972-77, Bank of Am., N.Y.C., 1982-84, Res. City Bankers, N.Y.C., 1978-87, Swedish Inst. Mgmt., Stockholm, 1982-91, Empresas Master of P.R., 1985-90. Author: Role of the Financial Sector in the Economic Development of Puerto Rico, 1970; co-author: Free Markets, Finance, Ethics and Law, 1994; contbr. articles to profl. jours. Bd. dirs. Medallion Funding Corp., 1985-87; mem. NYU Senate and Faculty Coun., 1995—, chair fin. com., 1996—; apptd. adv. bd. dirs. equity & diversity in ednl. environs. Mid. States Commn. Higher Edn., 1991—; trustee Securities Industry Assn., N.Y. Dist. Econ. Edn. Found., 1994—; chair NSF, Nat. Vis. Com. Curriculum Devel. Project Networked Fin. Simulation, 1995—; econ. cons. Inst. Women of Color, Nat. Coun. Black Women Cmty. Svcs. Fund, 2000—; trustee Bd. Edn., Twp. Mahwah, N.J., 1991-92. P.R. Econ. Devel. Adminstrn. fellow, 1960-65, Marcus Nadler fellow, NYU, 1966-67, Phillips Lods Dissertation fellow, 1967-68. Mem. Am. Econs. Assn., Am. Fin. Assn., Metro. Econ. Assn. N.Y., Assn. Social Econs. (trustee exec. coun. 1994-96). Home: 95 Tam O Shanter Dr Mahwah NJ 07430-1526 Office: Mgmt Edn Ctr 44 W 4th St Ste 9-190 New York NY 10012-1106

MALE, CYNTHIA LEE, elementary school educator, artist; b. Charleston, W.Va., Jan. 21, 1949; d. Frederick West McClure and Dorthy Dee Francis; children: Mundi Morning, Jamison Grey. BA, W.Va. U., 1970; MA, Vt. Coll./Norwich U., 1984; MFA, Savannah Coll. of Art and Design, 2000. Educator Liberty County Schs., Hinesville, Ga., 1975—77, Ft. Stewart Dependents, Hinesville, 1978—80, Good Hope Sch., St. Croix, 1982—92, Country Day Sch., St. Croix, 1992—. Educator U. S.C., Beaufort and Hilton Head I., 2003. Author: (slide/lecture) Approaching Our Heritage Through Art, 1988. Organizer, curator Internat. Youth Art, Nat. Gallery of Art, Washington, 1999. Fellow Artists in the Schs. grantee, V.I. Coun. on Arts, St. Croix, 1986—96; grantee, Theatre Dance, St. Croix, 1983; Artists in the Schs. grantee, V.I. Coun. on Arts, St. Croix, 2003. Office: St Croix Country Day Sch RR 1 Box 6199 Kingshill VI 00850

MALEK, MARLENE ANNE, healthcare advocate, foundation administrator; b. Oakland, Calif., June 22, 1939; d. William and Yolanda (Stella) McArthur; m. Frederic Malek; children: Frederic William, Michelle A. duPont. Degree in nursing, Marymount U. Vice chmn. bd. dirs Marymount U., Arlington, Va.; presdl. appointee bd. dirs. Kennedy Ctr., 2002—; mem. adv. bd. Second Genesis, Bethesda, Md.; bd. dirs. Nat. Mus. Women in Arts, World Wildlife Found. Coun.; mem. collectors com. Nat. Gallery of Art;

pres. Friends of Cancer Rsch., Washington; presdl. appointment to Nat. Cancer Adv. Bd., 1991-96; mem. bd. overseers Duke U. Cancer Ctr.; mem. Nat. Dialogue on Cancer. Episcopalian. Avocations: cross country skiing, road biking.

MALEWITZ, JOAN, elementary school educator, library and information scientist; b. Dec. 15, 1947; d. Benjamin and Minnie Malewitz. B in Elem. Edn., Queens Coll., 1968, M in Elem. Edn., 1972, MLS, 1992. Cert. tchr. N-6 N.Y. Tchr., sch. libr. media specialist PS 160Q, Jamaica, NY, 1968—. Children's book reviewer Kirkus Revs., N.Y.C., 2000—. Recipient Success award, Citibank, N.Y.C., 1994. Mem.: ALA, Beta Phi Mu. Avocations: reading, travel, New York City history. Home: 62-95 Saunders St Rego Park NY 11374 Office: PS 160Q 109-59 Inwood St Jamaica NY 11435

MALEY, PATRICIA ANN, preservation planner; b. Wilmington, Del., Dec. 25, 1955; d. James Alfred and Frances Louise (Fenimore) M.; m. Scott A. Stone, Dec. 7, 1991 (div. June 1994). AA, Cecil C.C., 1973; BA, U. Del., 1975, MA, 1981. Cert. secondary tchr., Del. Analyst econ. devel. City of Wilmington, 1977-78, evaluation specialist, 1978-80, planner II mayor's office, 1980-86, cons. preservation, 1986-87; dir. Belle Meade Mansion, Nashville, 1987-88; dir. planning, devel. Children's Bur. of Del., Wilmington, 1988; prin. preservation planner Environ. Mgmt. Ctr., Brandywine Conservancy, Chadds Ford, Pa., 1988-92; planning cons., 1992-95; design review and preservation commn. coord. Wilmington Dept. Planning, 1995—, code enforcement constable, 1997—. Cons. cultural resources M.A.A.R. Inc., Newark, Del., 1987, ITC Cons., Wilmington, 1985-86; mem. Planned Approach to Comty. Health, Wilmington, task force for Wilmington Enterprise Comty. Health Benchmarking Project. Contbg. photographer America's City Halls, 1984; author numerous Nat. Register nominations, 1980-86; 88—. Pres., founder Haynes Park Civic Assn., Wilmington, 1977-80; photographer Biden U.S. Senate Campaign, New Castle County, Del., 1984; sec. parish coun. Our Lady Fatima Roman Cath. Ch., 1985-86, choir dir., 1983-87; mem. com. on design & renovation of worship spaces Diocese of Wilmington, also mem. Diocesan com. on music; bd. dirs. Del. Children's Theatre; music dir. St. Elizabeth Ann Seton parish, Bear, Del., 1988—, mem. long range planning com./demographics. U. Del. fellow, 1976-77. Mem.: Del. Inst. for Planning and Design (bd. dirs. 2002—), New Castle County (Del.) Bd. Realtors, Am. Planning Assn. (exec. com. Del. chpt. 1997, elected state chpt. treas. 1997, 1999, 2001), Am. Inst. Cert. Planners (cert. planner), Nat. Trust Hist. Preservation, Del. Hist. Soc., Nat. Pastoral Musicians Assn., Pi Sigma Alpha. Democrat. Avocations: photography, choral, piano, organ music. Office: City of Wilmington Dept Planning 800 N French St Fl 7 Wilmington DE 19801-3590 Office Phone: 302-576-3113. E-mail: trish1225@aol.com.

MALIA, ELIZABETH A. state representative, state legislator; Degree, Boston Coll. State rep. legis., Mass., 1998—. Com. mem. Ward 11 Dem. Com., Pub. Svc., ho. vice-chair; com. mem. Pub. Safety, transp. Mem.: Network for Women in Polit. and Govt. Democrat. Office: State Ho Rm 540 Boston MA 02133 also: Dist Office 72 Child St Jamaica Plain MA 02130

MALIHAN, AMIE A. physician; b. Kalibo, Aklan, Philippines, Nov. 19, 1950; came to U.S., 1974; d. Guadencio Rabe and Anastacia (Alvarez) M. BS in Pre-Med., U. Philippines, Manila, 1971; MD, U. of the East RMMC, Manila, 1976. Cert. Am. Bd. Plastic Surgery. Gen. surgery residency tng. Morristown (N.J.) Meml. Hosp., Columbia-Presbyn. Med. Ctr., N.Y., 1979-83; chief residency tng., gen. surgery Meml.-Sloane Kettering Cancer Ctr., 1983-84; plastic and reconstructive surgery N.Y. Hosp.-Cornell Med. Ctr., 1984-86; pvt. practice N.Y.C., 1986—. Fellow AMA, ACS, Med. Soc. State of N.Y., Richmond County Med. Soc.; mem. Am. Soc. Plastic Surgery. Roman Catholic. Avocation: golf. Home: 1025 Todt Hill Rd Staten Island NY 10304-1323 Office: 161 Madison Ave Ste 9sw New York NY 10016-5405 also: 5046 Amboy Rd Staten Island NY 10312-4834

MALIK, SHAZIA MUMTAZ, education educator, researcher; b. Mangla, Pakistan, Aug. 2, 1973; d. Mumtaz Ahmed Malik, Bader-un-nisa Mumtaz Malik; m. Mansoor Ahmed Malik, Sept. 1, 2001. BA in Applied Social Sci. with honors, Coventry (Eng.) U., 1994; PhD in Psychology, U. Birmingham, Eng., 1998. Tchg. asst. Sch. Psychology U. Birmingham, 1994—98; endnl. officer Brit. Ednl. Comm. and Tech. Agy., Coventry, 1998—99; postdoctoral rschr. Inst. Edn. U. Warwick, Coventry, 1999—2002; postdoctoral rsch. fellow dept. edn., dept. psychol. and brain scis. Dartmouth Coll., 2002—. Presenter U. Birmingham, U. Warwick, 1994—2002, U. Glasgow, Scotland, 1995, U. Bristol, England, 1998, Cheltenham and Gloucester Coll. Higher Edn., 2000. Author book; contbr. articles to profl. jours. Grantee, Rsch. Machines plc, U.K., 1999-2002. Avocations: travel, reading. Home: Meadow Brook Village Bldg 3 Apt 13 West Lebanon NH 03784 Personal E-mail: mumtaz_shazia@hotmail.com.

MALIK, T. SOPHIA, political scientist, educator; b. Franklin, La., Mar. 2, 1962; d. Leeds and Audrey Marie Moreau; 1 child, Imran Ul-Haque. BA in History, U. Houston, 1996; M in Liberal Arts, U. St. Thomas, 2002. Cert. in secondary edn. Tex., 1996. Tchr. Langham Creek H.S., Houston, 1996—99, Cypress Springs H.S., 1999—2003; asst. prof. polit. sci. Cy-Fair Coll., Houston, 2003—. Prin. Bear Creek Islamic Sunday Sch., 1994—96; sponsor Houston Area Model U.N., 1997—2003; mem. adv. bd. Global Classrooms, Houston, 2002—. Mem. Tex. Coalition to Abolish Death Penalty, Houston, 2000—03, Harris County Democrats, Houston, 1998—2003. Finalist Tchg. Tolerance, Anti-Deflamation League Houston, 1999; nominee Disney Tchr. of Yr., Walt Disney Co., 1999; Fulbright Meml. fellow, Fulbright Meml. Fund, 1998, James Madison fellow, James Madison Fellowship Found., 2000. Mem.: Nat. Polit. Sci. Honors Soc. (chpt. U. St. Thomas 2001), S.W. Social Sci. Assn., Nat. Social Studies Coun., Cy-Fair Social Studies Coun., Am. Polit. Sci. Assn. D-Liberal. Avocation: travel. Office: Cy-Fair Coll Houston TX 77084 Personal E-mail: t.s.malik@nhmccd.edu.

MALINOWSKI, MARYELLEN, photographer, artist; b. Oak Park, Ill., Oct. 10, 1961; d. Richard A. and Mary Jo (Curran) Lamz; m. Preston Malinowski; children: Nicole, Brielle, Demi. Student, Internat. Acad. Merch./Design, Chgo., 1985, Maine Photog. Workshops, Rockport, 1996, Elgin (Ill.) C.C., 1993-94. Owner Visual Elements, Dundee, Ill., 1992-94; owner, dir. The Infrared Light Gallery, St. Charles, Ill., 1994—; represented by Fraser Gallery, Washington; prin., owner Elighten Pub., St. Charles, 2004—. Spkr. in field. Author: The Sacred Light, 1999; exhibited infrared photography in shows. Founder, bd. dirs. The Sacred Light Found. Recipient awards for photography; People's Choice award Women's Work Exhbn., Woodstock, 1995, 1st place Georgetown Internat. Fine Art Exhbn., Washington, 1997; recipient Ill. Women's Works Scholarship, 1996. Mem. Kodak Profl. Network, Luminos Printmakers Guild, Nat. Mus. Women in Arts. Home: 6N 779 IL RT 31 Saint Charles IL 60175 Office: The Infrared Light Gallery PO Box 1281 Saint Charles IL 60174 Office Phone: 630-584-8068. E-mail: maryellen@infraredlight.com.

MALINOWSKI, PATRICIA A. community college educator; b. Buffalo, N.Y., Jan. 19, 1950; d. Raymond J. and Emily M. (Ferek) Cybulski; m. Leonard T. Malinowski, July 12, 1975; children: Adam, Christopher. BA, SUNY, Fredonia, 1971; MEd, Bowling Green State U., 1972. Asst. prof. devel. studies Finger Lakes C.C., Canandaigua, NY, 1987-92, assoc. prof., 1992-96, prof. devel. studies, 1996—, chair devel. studies dept., 1991—. Editor: Rsch. and Tchg. in Devel. Edn., 1990—; contbr. articles to profl. jours. Active Literacy Vols., Canandaigua, 1994—2000; counselor Boy Scouts Am., 1998—; active Canandaigua PTO, 1998—; youth adv. com. St. Mary's Ch., Canandaigua, 2000—; mem. sch. bd. St. Mary's Sch., Canandaigua, 1993—99; parish coun. youth adv. com. St. Mary's Ch., Canandaigua, 2002—, liturgy com., 2002—. Nominee ATHENA, 2002; recipient Excellence in Profl. Svc. award, N.Y. State Chancellor, 1993, Disting. Svc. award, Finger Lakes C.C., 1988, 2000, Pelican award, Boy Scouts Am., 2002. Mem.: NADE (edn. bd. 1994—, Outstanding Publ. award 1995), N.Y. Coll. Learning Skills Assn. (v.p., sec., conf. chair 1987—, Outstanding Profl. Svc. award 1995), N.Y. State English Coun., N.Y. State Reading Assn., Nat. Coun. Tchrs. English, Internat. Reading Assn. (editl. bd. 1994—), Nat. C.C. Chair Acad. (editl. bd. 1992—), Phi Delta Kappa. Avocation: Avocations: family, reading, travel, walking. Office: Finger Lakes CC 4355 Lakeshore Dr Canandaigua NY 14424-8347 Office Phone: 585-394-3500 x7389. Business E-Mail: malinopa@flcc.edu.

MALKIEL, NANCY WEISS, dean, historian, educator; b. Newark, Feb. 14, 1944; d. William and Ruth Sylvia (Puder) Weiss; m. Burton G. Malkiel, July 31, 1988. BA summa cum laude, Smith Coll., 1965; MA, Harvard U., 1966, PhD, 1970. From asst. to assoc. prof. history Princeton (N.J.) U., 1969-82, prof., 1982—, master Dean Mathey Coll., 1982-86, dean coll., 1987—. Author (as Nancy J. Weiss): (book) Charles Francis Murphy, 1858-1924: Respectability and Responsibility in Tammany Politics, 1968; author: (with others) Blacks in America: Bibliographical Essays, 1971, The National Urban League, 1910-1940, 1974, Farewell to the Party of Lincoln: Black Politics in the Age of FDR, 1983 (Berkshire Conf. of Women Historians prize, 1984), Whitney M. Young Jr., and the Struggle for Civil Rights, 1989. Trustee Woodrow Wilson Nat. Fellowship Found., 1975—, chmn. bd. trustees, 1999—; trustee Smith Coll., Northampton, Mass., 1984—94. Fellow, Woodrow Wilson Found., 1965, Charles Warren Ctr. Studies in Am. History, 1976—77, Radcliffe Inst., 1976—77, Ctr. Advanced Study Behavioral Scis., 1986—87. Mem.: So. Hist. Assn., Orgn. Am. Historians (chmn. status women hist. profession 1972—75), Am. Hist. Assn., Phi Beta Kappa. Democrat. Jewish. Office: Princeton U Office Dean Of College Princeton NJ 08544-0001

MALKIEWICZ, ELIZABETH MARY, art director; b. Buffalo, Mar. 26, 1943; d. Frank Joseph and Jennie (Ferner) Tomaselli; m. Thaddeus F. Malkiewicz, June 13, 1975 (dec. Oct. 1995) A in Comm. Art, Bryant & Stratton Bus. Inst., Buffalo, 1987. Art dir. Langston Hughes Ctr., Buffalo, 1988-89; art dir., designer Adventures Mktg., Buffalo, 1988-89; exec. dir. to executrix Sisti Art Gallery, Buffalo, 1990-94; pres., art instr. The Personal Planner Co. Books/Art/Writing Svcs., Buffalo, 1995—. Group shows include Bryant & Stratton Bus. Inst., Buffalo, 1985-87, Big Orbit Gallery, Buffalo, 1987-95, Lewiston Italian Art Ctr., 1988-89, Buffalo Soc. Artists, 1989-91, Perimeter Gallery, Buffalo, 1990-96, Carnegie Art Ctr, 1993-96, Fine Line Gallery, Buffalo, 1995-96, Buffalo Hist. Soc. Photo Show, 1996, Buffalo Past & Present, 1997, Kenmore Art Show, 1997; author The Personnal Planner, The Patriots Planner. Exec. asst. to dir. Ashford Hollow Arts Found., Buffalo, 1974-94, asst. after sch. art program, 1989, cons.; active Alzheimer's Assn., 1995—. Mem. Carnegie Art Inst. Democrat. Roman Catholic. Home and Office: 25 Eugene St Ste #4 Buffalo NY 14216

MALLEIN, DARLA J. social studies educator; BS in Secondary Edn., Emporia State U., 1980, MS, 1994; PhD in Curriculum and Instrn., Kans. State U., 2003. Tchr. Americus Elem. Sch., 1981-83; 8-12th grade lang. arts, yearbook LeRoy H.S., 1983-87; 9-11th grade lang. arts Emporia H.S., 1987-88; 8th grade social studies Emporia Mid. Sch., 1988—2001; social studies edn. specialist Emporia State U., 2001—, asst. prof. social scis. edn., 2003. Adj. faculty Emporia State U. Coll. Liberal Arts and Scis., 1998. Contbr. articles to profl. jours. Named Outstanding Young Educator Kans. Jaycees, 1996, Wal-Mart Tchr. of Yr. 1998, Kans. Tchr. of Yr. 1998; grantee Emporia Middle Sch. PTO, 1992, Southeastern Kans. Edn. Found., 1995, 7 grants Southwestern Bell Execellence in Edn., 1991-95, Emporia Schs. Found., 1998, 99, Michael Jordan Found. grant, 2000. Mem. NEA (chair comms. com. 1997-99, bd. edn. liaison 1995-99, others), Kans. Coun. for the Social Studies (state bd. dirs. 1994—, pres. 2003-04, others), Nat. Coun. for the Social Studies, Phi Kappa Phi, Phi Delta Kappa. Home: 1901 Meadowlark Ln Emporia KS 66801-6125 Office Phone: 620-341-5567. E-mail: malleind@emporia.edu.

MALLERS, LINDA RAE, music educator; b. Decatur, Ill., Sept. 16, 1955; d. Richard Camp and Martha Joan (Hiser) Myers; m. Charles Edwin Mallers, Sept. 1, 1979 (div. May 2002); children: Justin Charles, Paul Bryan, Scott Richard. B in Music Edn., Ea. Ill. U., 1997. Lic. musikgarten. Music educator Palatine (Ill.) Sch. Dist. 15, 1979—86; pvt. piano instr. Sleepy Hollow, Ill., 1987—2001; music educator Musikgarten, West Dundee, Ill., 1995—2001, Elgin (Ill.) Sch. Dist. U-46, 2001—03. Ch. organist First Congl. Ch., West Dundee, 1995—. Mem.: NEA, Ill. Music Educators Assn., Music Educators Nat. Conf. Mem.United Ch. Of Christ. Avocations: reading, sewing. Home: 910 Holly Ct Sleepy Hollow IL 60118

MALLIA-HUGHES, MARIANNE, medical writer; b. Davenport, Iowa, Feb. 14, 1948; d. Norman Bramblett and Mary Jane (Hilkemeyer) Hagar; m. Michael L. Hughes; 1 child from previous marriage, Lindsay Sharyn Mallia. BA in English, U. Iowa, 1970. Cert. tchr. Tchr. tech. writing Houston Ind. Sch. Dist., 1970—76; med. writer Tex. Heart Inst., Houston, 1976—; editl. cons. Tex. Heart Inst. Jour., Houston, 1977—87, head sci. publ., 1986—, sr. med. writer, 1994—. Instr. Sch. Allied Health Sci. and Sch. Pub. Health U. Tex., 1990—94. Editor: Techniques in Cardiac Surgery, 1984; editor: (with Denton A. Cooley) Surg. Treatment of Aortic Aneurysms, 1985; editor: (essays) Reflections and Observation, Denton A. Cooley, MD, 1985, (handbook) Heart Owner's Handbook, 1995; bd. editors: Life Sci., 2002. Fellow: Am. Med. Writers Assn. (core curriculum cert. 1984, instr. 1985—, advanced curriculum cert. 1989, honor roll workshop leader 1992—, bd. dir., exec. com. 1996—, pres. 2002—03, writer and advanced core curriculum); mem.: Women in Comm. (cert. editor in life sci., Matrix Aaward 1996—2000), Coun. Biology Editors, Pi Beta Phi. Office: Tex Heart Inst PO Box 20345 Houston TX 77225-0345 Home: 3779 Tangley St Houston TX 77005-2031 Business E-Mail: mmallia@heart.thi.tmc.edu.

MALLIN, JENNIFER, internet company executive, writer; b. N.Y.C., Nov. 28, 1961; d. Joel and Judith (Young) Mallin; m. Henry S. Edelson, May 25, 1991; 1 child, Alexandria Elizabeth. BA cum laude, Brandeis U., 1983. Fashion model print and TV, N.Y.C., 1979-86; art dealer, dir. Foxworth Gallery, N.Y.C., 1983-84; writer fiction and poetry, N.Y.C., 1983—; pres., chmn. JM Ageless.com., N.Y.C., 1999—. Author: (novel) The Bamboo Heart, 1999; author poetry and art revs. Recipient award for Poem of Yr., Am. Libr. of Poetry, 1985. Avocations: equestrian show jumping, collecting contemporary art, travel.

MALLING, MARTHA HALE SHACKFORD, social worker, educator; b. Atlanta, Aug. 20, 1944; d. James Atkins and Ada Vernon (Morrow) Shackford; m. Heinrich Valdemar Malling, July 18, 1969; children: Richard, Kevin, Kirsten. Student, U. Tenn., 1968-70; BA in Psychology, U. NC, 1978, MSW, 1983; postgrad., Tavistock Clinic, London, 1987-88. Cert. clin. social worker NC, 1991, LCSW NC, 2000. Lab. technician in genetics NC State U., Raleigh, 1964-66, Oak Ridge (Tenn.) Nat. Lab., 1966-67; spl. edn. tchr. Hill Learning Ctr. Durham (NC) Acad., 1978-81; social worker II IDTU Children's Inst. John Umstead Hosp., Butner, NC, 1983-84; clin. social worker Duke U. Med. Ctr., Durham, NC, 1985-87, U. NC Hosps., Chapel Hill, 1989-90; social work clin. specialist Child-Outpatient Clinic Dorothea Dix Hosp., Raleigh, NC, 1990—; pvt. practice Chapel Hill and Durham, 1990—. Peer counselor Office Continuing Edn. Duke U., Durham, 1976—77; crisis counselor and tng. team mem. Orange-Person-Chatham Mental Health Ctr., Chapel Hill, 1979—82; workshop leader N.C. State Tchrs. Duke U. Med. Ctr., Durham, 1986, diabetes day workshop leader, 87; adj. instr. U. NC Sch. Social Work, 1996—2001, mem. adv. com. on field edn., 1999—, adj. asst. prof., 2001—. Co-chair PTA Carolina Friends Sch., Durham, 1978—79, chmn. children's sect. art festival, 1978—81. Scholar VA, State of NC, 1964. Mem.: C. G. Jung Soc. (mem.-at-large 1989—90), Assn. Cert. Social Workers, NC Soc. Clin. Social Work (exec. bd. dirs., treas. 1990—94, co-chair com. psychoanalysis 1995—97). Democrat. Presbyterian. Avocations: hiking, design, music, reading. Home: 3200 Winged Elm Ln Chapel Hill NC 27514-9530 Office: Dix Hosp Child Outpatient Clinic 820 S Boylan Ave Raleigh NC 27603-2246 Office Phone: 919-733-5344.

MALLO-GARRIDO, JOSEPHINE ANN, advertising agency owner; b. Agana, Guam, Mar. 20, 1955; d. Benjamin Corneja and Salvacion (Lacuesta) Mallo; m. John Marco Haniu Garrido, Feb. 16, 1980; children: Josiah Michael (dec.), Jordan Thaddeus. Student, U. Guam, Agana, 1972-74; BA in Journalism, Seattle U., 1976; MBA, Pepperdine U., 1982. Reporter Pacific Daily News, Agana, 1976, features editor, 1977-78, asst. city editor, 1978-79; copy editor features Honolulu Star-Bull., 1979-81; advt. copywriter Advt. Factors, Honolulu, 1981-83; communications specialist Liberty House, Honolulu, 1983-84; editor, advt. copywriter Safeway Stores Inc., Oakland, Calif., 1984-88; features writer Tracy (Calif.) Press, 1988-91; mktg. mgr. ComputerLand of Guam, Maite, 1992-93; mktg. officer Citibank, Agana, 1993-94; owner JMG Advt., 1994—. Newspaper graphics cons. Pacific Daily News, 1984. Editor/writer Foods Unltd., 1984-88, Tracy Community Hosp. Health Beat and Update, 1988-91; editor Pacific Voice, 1977-78; contbr. articles to profl. jours. Vol. Engaged Encounter, Honolulu, 1989, Trans-Pacific Yacht Race, Honolulu, 1983, United Way, Oakland, 1986; advt. coord. Easter Seals, Oakland, 1987; organist St. Patrick's Ch., Honolulu, 1980—84, Immaculate Heart of Mary Ch., Toto, Guam, 1994—; mem. adv. bd. Cath. Social Svcs., Agana, Guam, 1993—97, bd. dirs., 1997—, bd. trustees, 2002—. Recipient Cert. Achievement award Advt. Age Mag., 1985, Cert Appreciation award Am. Heart Food Festival, 1985, Best in the West award Am. Advt. Fedn., 1986, Retail Nutrition award Nat. Potato Promotion Bd., 1986, Spl. Achievement award Newspaper Spl. Sect. Mother's Day/Father's Day Coun., 1989, 90, Best Feature Story 2d place Calif. Newspaper Pubs. Assn., 1989, 1st place Classified Advt. Assn., 1989, 1st place appetizer Spam Food Festival, 1991. Mem. Guam C. of C. (media coord. 1993-95), Citiclub (exec. sec. 1994-95). Roman Catholic. Avocations: piano, travel, Karate.

MALLON, MEG, professional golfer; b. Natick, Mass., Apr. 14, 1963; Student, Ohio State U., 1983-87. Prof. Golfer LPGA Tour, 1987—. Mem. Solheim Cup Team, 1992, 94, 96, 98, 2000, 2002, 2003 Named Female Player of Year, Golf Writers Assn. of Am., 1991, one of the LPGA's top 50 players and tchrs., LPGA's 50th Anniversary, 2000. Achievements include winner 15 career LPGA victories including: Mazda LPGA Championship, 1991, U.S. Women's Open, 1991. Avocations: music, sports, travel. Office: care LPGA 100 International Golf Dr Daytona Beach FL 32124-1082

MALLORY, PATRICIA JODY, museum curator; b. De Ridder, La., Sept. 22, 1951; d. William Buford and Gwendolyn (singletary) M. BBA, La. State U., 1979. Mgr. Harpers Records, De Ridder, 1979-83; dir. pub. rels. Goldband Records, Lake Charles, La., 1983-89; mgr. Bargain Time, Baton Rouge, 1989-91, Hills Music, De Ridder, 1991-96; sales and mktg. exec. Krok Radio, De Ridder, 1996-97; mus. curator Beauregard Parish, De Ridder, 1997—. Leader blues band Blues Horizon. Drummer Goldband Studios, 1971-83, Lake Charles; drummer recs. include Blessed Rain (Blue Rain), 1987, Drenched (Blue Rain), 1989, Saturday Nights and Sunday Mornings (OFB), 1987. Active Beauregard Econ. Devel., De Ridder; mem. main street promotions com.; mem. bd. dirs. Downtown Mchts. Assn., Beauregard Assn. Retarded Citizens. Named one of Best Unsigned Drummers, Promark, 1995. Mem. Percussive Arts Soc., Daus. of Confederacy, Humane Soc., People for Ethical Treatment Animals, Nat. Geog. Soc., World Wildlife Fund. Avocations: music, travel. Home: 501 S Stewart St Deridder LA 70634-4955

MALLORY-PARKER, SUZANNE, performing arts educator; b. Boston, Jan. 21, 1957; d. Edward Alexander and Sally Mae Mallory; children: Krystle Mallory Parker, Lauren Katherine Parker. B in Music Edn., Va. Commonwealth U., 1978, EdM, 1997. Collegiate profl. lic. Commonwealth Va., 2003. Vocal music tchr. Chesterfield County (Va.) Pub. Schs., 1979—97, instrnl. specialist for performing arts, 1997—. Curriculum devel. /cons. in performing arts; guest condr. Henrico County Pub. Schs., 1992, 98, Youth Jam Choir, 1998, Hanover County Pub. Schs., 1999. Mem., oboist Petersburg (Va.) Symphony Orch., 1979—2002; vol. Fan Free Clinic, Richmond, Va., 1995—96; youth ministry sponsor Christian Actors Standing for Truth New Deliverance Evangelistic Ch., Richmond, 1999—2002. Recipient MCD award, Chesterfield Edn. Assn. Mem.: Va. Music Educators Assn. (sec. treas. adminstrv. sect. 2000—03), Assn. Curriculum and Devel. (assoc.), Music Educators Nat. Conf. (assoc.), Alpha Delta Kappa (hon.). Office: Chesterfield County Pub Sch 2318 McRae Rd Richmond VA 23235 Personal E-mail: ssmp121@aol.com. E-mail: suzanne_m-parker@ccpsnet.net.

MALLOW, KATHLEEN KELLY, accountant; b. Chgo., Dec. 27, 1946; d. Robert Henry Kelly and Irene Alice Smith Kelly; m. Kenneth R. Mallow, July 9, 1983; children: Heather K. Peet, Christopher C. Mallow, Daniel S. Peet. BSc in Acctg., De Paul U., 1971; MBA, Keller Grad. Sch., 1986. Asst. supr. Dept. Fin. Instns. State of Ill., Chgo., 1994—, review examiner, 1994—. Mem. working group of edn. and tng. Commn. of Status of Women, Ill. Mem. AAUW (bd. dirs., past pres. 1971—), Home of the Sparrow. Home: 1219 E Plate Dr Palatine IL 60074-7260 Office: State of Ill Dept Fin Instns 100 W Randolph St Ste 15-700 Chicago IL 60601-3234

MALLOY, SANDRA MIRIAM, information specialist; b. Pitts., Sept. 22, 1953; d. David Leonard and Frances (Hershkowitz) M.; m. William Edward O'Brien, June 22, 1992. BA, UCLA, 1975; MLS, U. So. Calif., 1976. Asst. reference libr. Health Scis. Libr. Tex. Tech U., Lubbock, 1978-79, El Paso Pub. Libr., Tex., 1979-81; reference libr. Health Scis. Libr. U. Calif., Davis, 1981, reference libr. Shields Libr., 1982; rsch. dir. Am. Internat. Data Search, Sacramento, 1983, Info. on Demand, Berkeley, Calif., 1983-87; western region mktg. rep. ORBIT Search Svc., Mac Lean, Va., 1987-89; sr. info. specialist Business Wire, San Fransisco, 1989—. Contbr. articles to profl. jours., also East Bay Express newspaper, 1988—. Mem. Spl. Librs. Assn., Phi Beta Kappa. Avocations: reading, cooking, aerobics, ballet, sports. Office: Business Wire 44 Montgomery St Fl 39 San Francisco CA 94104-4602

MALM, MIA, actress; b. Ann Arbor, Mich., Oct. 18, 1962; d. William P. and Joyce A. (Rutherford) M. Student, San Francisco Sch. of the Arts, Herbert Berghof Studios, N.Y.C.; studied with Maria Vegh. Dance instr. Marin Ballet Sch., 1978-79. Appeared in (stage prodns.) Make Mine Disco, 1979, Dancin', 1981-83, 42nd Street, The Showgirl Musical, 1986, (films) Moscow on the Hudson, Curtain Call, 1984, Joan-Lui, A Chorus Line, 1985, Ishtar, (TV) Dance Through Time, 1978. Mem. Actors' Equity Assn., Screen Actors Guild, AFTRA, NOW, Planned Parenthood. Avocations: drawing, watercoloring, reading. Office: care Landslide Mgmt 928 Broadway New York NY 10010-6008

MALM, RITA H. securities executive; d. George Peter and Helen Marie (Woodward) Pellegrini; m. Robert J. Malm, Apr. 19, 1970. Student, Packard Jr. Coll., 1950-52, N.Y. Inst. Fin., 1958, Wagner Coll., 1955. Sales asst. Dean Witter & Co., N.Y.C., 1959-63, asst. v.p., compliance dir., 1964-74; v.p., dir. Securities Ind. Assocs., N.Y.C., 1969-72; CEO Muriel Siebert & Co., Inc., N.Y.C., 1981-83; pres., founder Madison-Chapin Assocs., N.Y.C., 1984-89; pres. Hayward Malm Securities, Ltd., 1989-93; pres., founder Concord Stuart, Inc., 1993—. Art mktg. cons. Author: Dying On Wall Street, 1996; author NASD Series 63 Blue Sky Uniform Securities Agent State Law Exam for Potential Stock Brokers, NASD Stockbroker Examination, NASD Series 6 primer. Bd. dirs. Head Start, 1996—. Mem. NAFE (bd. dirs.), Am. Caner Soc. (bd. dirs. Jupiter/Tequesta chpt. 1992-95), Profl. Women's Network (founder Palm Beach and Martin Counties 1991), Women's Bond Club N.Y. (dir., v.p. program chmn., pres. 1980-82), Cornell U. Club Ea. Fla. (bd. dirs. 1995). Address: PO Box 8603 Jupiter FL 33468-8603

MALME, JANE HAMLETT, lawyer, educator, advisor; b. N.Y.C., Dec. 2, 1934; d. Robert T. and Minnie (Means) Hamlett; m. Charles I. Malme, June 17, 1961; children: Robert H., Karen I. AB, Brown U., 1956; cert., U. Kobenhavn, Copenhagen, Denmark, 1959; JD, Northeastern U., 1977. Bar: Mass., 1977. Counsel Mass. Tax Commn., Boston, 1978-79; chief bur. local assessment Mass. Dept. Revenue, Boston, 1978-90; prin. Mcpl. Mgmt. and Taxation Cons. Svcs., Hingham, Mass., 1990—; fellow Lincoln Inst. Land Policy, Inc., Cambridge, Mass., 1993—. Faculty Lincoln Inst. Land Policy, Inc., Cambridge, 1989—; adv. property tax OECD, Paris, 1993-97; legal adv. property tax USAID, Russia, 1995-99, Korea Tax Inst., 1995-96, Poland, 1998-99, Slovenia, 2001-04, Lithuania, 2002-04. Author: (with Joan Youngman) Internat. Survey of Taxes on Land and Buildings, 1994, Development of Property Taxation in Countries in Transition, 2001; contbr. articles profl. jours. Trustee Old Ship Ch., Hingham, 1992-97; treas. Betty Taymor Scholarship Fund, Boston, 1992—; pres. Network for Women in Politics and Govt., McCormack Inst., Boston, 1992-94, mem. adv. com. Ctr. for Women in Politics and Pub. Policy, U. Mass., Boston, 1998—. chmn. Friends of Old Ship Meeting House Trust, 2002-04. Mem. Internat Assn. Assessing Officers (founder, state and prov. adminstrv. sec., legal com. 1997-, Presidential citation 1983), Mass. Assn. Assessing Officers (hon. lifetime), Mass. Bar Assn., Nat. Tax Assn. (program com. 1998-99), Nat. Assn. Tax Adminstrs. (chair property tax sect. 1988). Unitarian Universalist. Avocations: community service, women in politics, travel.

MALMSTADT, MARY JANE, music educator; b. Milwaukee, Wis., Apr. 12, 1923; d. Daniel Monte and Angela Marie LaFata; m. Robert Guy, June 25, 1949 (dec. Apr. 1998); children: Keith Robert, Deborah Jean. BS in Music Edn., U. Wis., 1945; postgrad., U. Wis., Marinette and Madison, 1950—83. Music tchr. K-12 NeKoosa (Wis.) Pub. Schs., 1945—46; music tchr. 9-12 Marinette (Wis.) H.S., 1946—51; music tchr. K-6 Elem. Schs., Marinette, 1965—85; ch. organist and pianist Pioneer Presbyn. Ch., Marinette, 1970—; pvt. piano tchr. Marinette, 1955—2001. Bd. dirs. Tri-City Cmty. Concerts, Wis. Mem.: Golden Soc. of Alumni/U. Wis. Milw., Gen. Fedn. of Women's Club (pres. 1988). Presbyterian. Avocation: oil painting, gardening, reading, travel, floral arrangements. Home: 1303 Elizabeth Ave Marinette WI 54143

MALO, MICHELE LEE, marketing professional; b. Chgo., Dec. 21, 1972; d. William Reining and Candyce Lee Collins; m. James John Malo, Oct. 4, 2003. B of Advt., U. Nebr., 1996; MBA with honors, Lake Forest U., 2003. Mktg. asst. Allied Domecq, Chgo., 1996—98, field mktg. specialist, 1998—2000; asst. promotions mgr. Kraft Foods, Glenview, 2000—02, assoc. promotions mgr., 2002—03, assoc. bus. mgr., 2003—04; customer mktg. mgr. Kellogg's, Elmhurst, Ill., 2004—. Mem.: Young Execs. Club, Women's Food Svc. Forum, Am. Mktg. Assn., Alpha Sigma Alpha Windy City Alumnae Chpt. Avocation: softball. Office: Kelloggs 545 Lamont Rd Elmhurst IL 60126 E-mail: esmalo@yahoo.com.

MALONE, CLAUDINE BERKELEY, financial and management consultant; b. Louisville, May 9, 1936; d. Claude McDowell and Mary Katharine (Smith) M.; B.A., Wellesley Coll., 1963; M.B.A., Harvard U., 1972. Systems engr. IBM Corp., Washington, 1964; sr. systems analyst Crane Co., Chgo., 1966; controller, mgr. data processing Raleigh Stores, Washington, 1967-70; asst. prof. Harvard U., 1972-76, assoc. prof., 1977-81; pres., CEO, Fin. and Mgmt. Consulting Inc., Bethesda, Md., 1981—; visiting prof., Georgetown U., 1982-84, U.Va, 1984-87; dir. Scott Paper Co., Houghton Mifflin Co., Campbell Soup Co., Boston Co., Dart Group Inc., Hasbro Inc., 1994-, Novell Inc., 2003-; trustee Penn Mut. Life Ins. Co. Chmn. Bus. for Reagan-Bush Com. Mass., 1980; trustee Wellesley Coll., 1982— . Recipient Candace award, 1982. C.P.A., Md. Mem. Assn. Women C.P.A.s, UN Assn., Wellesley Coll. Alumnae Assn. Episcopalian. Club: Washington Wellesley. *

MALONE, LISA A. federal agency administrator; b. Mobile, Ala. BJ, U. Ala., 1984; M in Mgmt., Fla. Inst. Tech., 1995. Accredited pub. rels. profl. Fla. Pub. Rels. Assn., 1992, cert. pub. rels. counselor Fla. Pub. Rels. Assn., 1996. With NASA Kennedy Space Ctr., Fla., 1984—, news chief media svc. br., 1993—95, chief media svcs. br., spokeswoman, 1995—, dir. external relations and bus. development, 2004—. Recipient Exceptional Service Medal, NASA, 2001. Office: NASA Kennedy Space Ctr Mail Code XA-E Kennedy Space Center FL 32899

MALONE, NANCY, actress; b. Queens Village, N.Y. d. James and Bridget (Sheilds) M. Freelance actress, dir., producer, writer. Performer (TV series) The First Hundred Years, Naked City, The Long, Hot Summer (Best Performance by an Actress award); Broadway debut in Time Out For Ginger, other stage performances include Major Barbara, The Makropoulis Secret, A Touch of the Poet, The Trial of the Catonsville Nine; touring performances include The Chalk Garden, The Seven Yr. Itch, A Place For Dolly; actress (films) The Violators, I Cast No Shadow, An Affair of the Skin, Intimacy, The Trial of the Cantonsville Nine, The Man Who Loved Cat Dancing, Capricorn One; producer (TV series) including Bionic Woman, 1978, Husbands, Wives and Lovers, 1978, The Great Pretender, 1984, (special) Bob Hope: The First 90 Years, 1993 (Emmy award, Outstanding Variety, Musical or Comedy Special, 1993), Womanspeak, 1983; dir. (TV series) Dynasty, 1984-87, Hotel, 1984-87, Colbys, 1985, Cagney and Lacey, 1987, Star Trek Voyager, 1997, Burning Zone, 1997, Fame l.A. 1997-98, Rosie O'Niel (Emmy nomination), Sisters (Emmy nomination), Melrose Place, 1992-99, Beverly Hills, 1990-2000, Picket Fences, Judging Amy, 1999-, Resurrection Blvd., 2000-02; producer, dir. (film) There Were Times Dear, 1986 (John Muir Trustees award, Cine Golden Eagle, Blue Ribbon); founder Nancy Malone Prodns., 1975, Lilac Prodns., 1979. Fellow Leaky Found.; mem. Am. Film Inst. (mem. founder), Women in Film (trustee, Chrystal award, Founders award 1996). Office: Guild Mgmt PHA 9911 W Pico Blvd Los Angeles CA 90035-2703

MALONEY, CAROLYN BOSHER, congresswoman; b. Feb. 19, 1948; d. R.G. and Christine (Clegg) Bosher; m. C.H.W. Maloney, 1976; children: Christina, Virginia. Student, Greensboro Coll. Various sr. staff positions N.Y. State Assembly and Senate, 1977-82; mem. N.Y.C Council dist. 8, 1983-93, U.S. Congress from 14th N.Y. dist., Washington, 1993—; mem. fin. svcs. com., ranking mem. subcom. domestic monetary policy, tech. and econ. growth; mem. fin. instns. and consumer credit subcom., internat. monetary policy and trade subcom.; mem. govt. reform and oversight com.; mem. joint economic com. Past chmn. Common Cause; active Assn. for a Better N.Y., Manahattan Women's Polit. Caucus. Mem. NAACP, Nat. Orgn. Women, Hadassah. Democrat. Home: 49 E 92nd St Apt 1A New York NY 10128-1326 Office: US Ho of Reps 2331 Rayburn HOB Washington DC 20515-0001*

MALONEY, CHERYL ANN, foundation, consultant, business executive; b. Mpls., Aug. 30, 1949; d. Arlie Chester and Mary Dawn (Holm) M. AA, U. Minn., 1969, BA in Speech and Theatre, 1972; MA in Theology/Spirituality, Coll. St. Catherine, St. Paul, 1989, MA cert. in Pastoral Ministry, 1990; postgrad., Calif. Inst. Integral Studies, 1994—95; DMin, U. Creation Spirituality, 2001. Cert. grantsmanship, Calif., financial mgmt. Assn. Gov. Accts. Bus. adminstr. Al's Auto Crushing, Inc., Mpls., 1980-81; rsch. assoc. St. Paul Ramsey Med. Ctr., 1981-83; cons. Autowoman Consulting, Mpls., 1982—; adjustor Dependable Auto Appraisal, Inc., Bloomington, 1983; dir. mktg. and devel. Health Recovery Center, Mpls., 1983-85; dir. sales and mktg. Dashe and Thomson, Mpls., 1987-89, Fredrickson Comm., Mpls., 1989-91; chaplain U. St. Thomas, St. Paul, 1989-90; ind. cons. Mpls., 1991-94; dir. devel. Sisters of Holy Family, Fremont, Calif., 1994-98; co-owner, co-founder Bras for Body and Soul, Fremont, 1995—; dir. Fremont Festival Arts, 1998; co-founder & exec. dir. HERS Breast Cancer Found., Fremont, 1999—. Dir. Women's Network, Mpls., 1974—77; dir. cultural arts City of Bloomington, Minn., 1977—78; spkr. U. Bethlehem, Israel, 1993; tchr. Holy Childhood High Sch., Jamaica, 1992; presenter M.R.A. Internat. 50th Anniversary Conf., Caux, Switzerland, 1996; prodr. Keep Abreast-Walking Together for HER 5K Run/Walk, 2000, 01, 02, 03; dir. devel. Sisters Holy Family, editor Family of Friends Newsletter, co-coord. Women's Spirituality Workshop series, 1996—97; participant World Media Forum, 1996—; cons. Sisters of St. Joseph of Carondelet, St. Paul, 1992—94; assoc. exec. dir. San Mateo Cmty. Colls. Found., 2000; ofcl. photographer Internat. Women's Ecumenical Decade Chs. Solidarity Women, 1993; quality cons. Goodwill Designer Showcase Mag., 1975, Mpls., 1971—94; contbr. Women's Network Directory, 1976, Streams from the Sacred River, 1998. Presenter Internat. Youth Leadership Conf., Brazil, 1993, 1993, 1993, coord., 1996; presenter Reaching Beyond Borders, San Diego, 1996; cmty. organizer Mpls. Crime Prevention Program, 1979—80; dir. Gov.'s Com. Women in Econ. Concern, St. Paul, 1972—77; co-founder HERS Found., Calif., 1999; state Dem. del. St. Paul, 1976; U.S. rep. Gov.Gen's Conf., Jamaica, 1992; coach, youth leader Unity South Ch., Bloomington, 1967—93; coach Ind. Ch., Mpls., 1984—92; chaplain U. St. Thomas, St. Paul, 1989—92, chair women and religion com.; outreach min. Unity of Valley, Minn., 1990—93; lay consociate Sisters St. Joseph, 1992, apptd. peace and justice commn. and comm. adv. bd., 1993—95; chair 125th Anniversary Celebration Sisters of the Holy Family, 1997. Recipient Celtic Studies award Coll. St. Catherine, St. Paul, 1988; honoree Hamnline U., St. Paul, 1993; Great Lakes Region scholar, 1986. Mem.: Nat. Women's Bus. Adv. Com., Am. Assn. Breast Care Specialists (pres. 2002), Nat. Assn. Self-Employed (women's nat. adv. coun. 2003), M.R.A. Internat. (nat. team planners for M.R.A. N.Am. and S.Am. activities, conf. presenter), Sales and Mktg. Execs. Am., Mission San Jose C. of C. (pres. 1999—2000, sec. 2000—01, co-founder olive festival 2001—), Minn. Coun. Quality (editor newsletter 1993—94), Le Group (co-founder), Self-Employed Women's Rotary (co-dir. 1982—94), Mpls. Women's Rotary (parliamentarian 1980—, bd. dirs. 1990—94), Commonwealth Club Calif. Independent. Avocations: integrating spirituality and work, cultural arts, sports, international relations. Home: PO Box 3273 Fremont CA 94539-0327 Office: HERS Breast Cancer Found Inc 38775 Stivers St Ste C Fremont CA 94536 E-mail: cheryl@hersfund.org.

MALONEY, KRISTEN, gymnast; b. Hacketstown, N.J., Mar. 10, 1981; d. Richard and Linda. Mem. U.S. Gymnastics Team, 1994—2001, UCLA Gymnastics Team, 2000—. Mem. U.S. World Championships Team, 1997, 99, U.S. Gymnastics Team Sydney Olympics, 2000. Recipient numerous awards, 1st pl. Am. Classic, 1997, 98, 1st pl. (3) Foxsport Challenge, Sydney, 1997, 1st team, 1st balance beam, 1st floor exercise 1st AA, Internat. Team Championships, 1998, 1st team, 1st AA, Pacific Alliance Champaionships, Winnipeg, Can., 1998, 1st balance beam Goodwill Games, 1998, others. Mem. Parketts Club. Avocations: reading, music, movies, shopping. Office: UCLA Women's Gymnastics PO Box 24044 Los Angeles CA 90024

MALONEY, MARY D. lawyer; BA, U. Akron, 1984; JD summa cum laude, Cleve. State U., 1987; LLM, Case Wester Res. U., 1995. Bar: Ohio 1987. With Jones Day, Cleve., 1987—, ptnr., 2001—. Mem.: Ohio State Bar Assn. Office: Jones Day North Point 901 Lakeside Ave Cleveland OH 44114-1190*

MALONEY, MARYNELL, lawyer; b. Hutchinson, Kans., Jan. 14, 1955; d. Robert Edgar and Marian Ellen (Benson) Baker; m. Michael D. Maloney, Nov. 30, 1977; children: Michelle M., Erica O., Dennis Jr. BA, Oberlin Coll., 1975; MA, Trinity U., San Antonio, 1978; JD, St. Mary's U., San Antonio, 1980. Cert. by Tex. bd. of legal specialization. Assoc. Law Offices Pat Maloney, P.C., San Antonio, 1981-82; ptnr., owner Maloney & Maloney, San Antonio, 1982—. Bd. dirs. San Antonio Internat. Keyboard Competition, 1988-90; bd. govs. St. Peters/St. Joseph's Children's Home, San Antonio, 1989-92. Mem. ACLU of Tex. (bd. dirs. 1990—, v.p. 1995-96, SACLU 1990—), Am. Trial Lawyers Assn., State Bar Tex., Tex. Trial Lawyers Assn. (assoc. bd. dirs. 1989-90, bd. dirs. 1991-2002, dir. emeritus 2002—, cert. personal injury trial law), San Antonio Bar Assn., San Antonio Trial Lawyers Assn. (pres. 1991-92). Democrat. Avocations: reading, writing, film. Office: Maloney & Maloney PC 2000 Milam 115 E Travis San Antonio TX 78205

MALONEY, RITA, radio personality; With Sta. WBVP, Pitts., news dir.; radio host Sta. WCCO radio, Mpls. Named one of Pitts. 50 Finest Young Profls.; recipient Best Regularly Scheduled Newscast award, 3 AIR awards for Best Traffic Reporter, Best Spot News Coverage award, Pa. AP. Office: WCCO 625 2nd Ave S Minneapolis MN 55402

MALONEY, THERESE ADELE, insurance company executive; b. Sept. 15, 1929; d. James Henry and F. Adele (Powers) M. BA in Econs., Coll. St. Elizabeth, Convent Station, N.J., 1951; AMP, Harvard U., 1981. CPCU. With Liberty Mut. Ins. Co., Boston, 1951-94, asst. v.p., asst. mgr. nat risks, 1974-77, v.p., asst. mgr. nat. risks, 1977-79, v.p., mgr. nat. risks, 1979-86, sr. v.p. underwriting mktg. and adminstrn., 1986-87, exec. v.p. underwriting, policy decision, 1987-94, also bd. dirs.; pres. and bd. dirs. subs. Liberty Mus. (Bermuda) Ltd., 1981-94, LEXCO Ltd.; cons. Exec. Svc. Corp., 1994—2002. Bd. dirs., dep. chmn. Liberty Mut. (U.K.) Ltd., London; bd. dirs. Liberty Mut. Ins. Co., Liberty Mut. Fire Ins. Co., Liberty Mut. Life Assurance Co., Liberty Fin. Cos.; mem. faculty Inst. Northeastern U., Boston, 1969—74; mem. adv. bd., risk mgmt. studies Ins. Inst. Am., 1977—83; mem. adv. coun. Suffolk U. Sch. Mgmt., 1984—96; mem. adv. coun. to program in internat. bus. rels. Fletcher Sch. Law and Diplomacy, 1985—94; cons. Exec. Svc. Corp., Boston, 1994—2002. Trustee Coll. St. Elizabeth, N.J., 1993-02. Mem. Soc. CPCUs (past pres. Boston chpt.), Univ. Club, Boston Club, Neighborhood Club of Quincy.

MALOTT, ADELE RENEE, editor; b. St. Paul, July 19, 1935; d. Clarence R. and Julia Anne (Christensen) Lindgren; m. Gene E. Malott, Oct. 24, 1957 BS, Northwestern U., 1957. Coordinator news KGB Radio, San Diego, 1958-60; asst. pub. relations dir. St. Paul C. of C., 1961-63; night editor Daily Local News, West Chester, Pa., 1963-65; editor, co-pub. Boutique and Villager, Burlingame, Calif., 1966-76; sr. editor mag. The Webb Co., St. Paul, 1978-84; editor GEM Pub. Group, Reno, 1985-2001. Faculty Reader's Digest Writers' Workshops. Co-author: Get Up and Go: A Guide for the Mature Traveler, 1989, The Mature Traveler's Book of Deals, 1997; columnist The Mature Traveler, 1989—. Recipient numerous awards Soc. Am. Travel Writers, Nat. Fedn. Press Women, Calif. Newspaper Pubs. Assn., San Francisco Press Club, Calif. Taxpayers Assn., White House Citations. Mem. Internat. Assn. Bus. Communicators (Merit award 1984), Press Women Minn. (numerous awards), Press Women Nev., Soc. Am. Travel Writers (v.p. 1999, chair Western chpt. 1996-98, pres. 2002-). Avocations: historical research, golf, travel, photography, reading. E-mail: maturetrav@aol.com.

MALOUF, PAMELA BONNIE, film editor, video editor; b. Reseda, Calif., July 9, 1956; d. Jubert George and Marguerite I. (Llido) Malouf. AA in Cinema with honors, Valley CC, 1976. Asst. film editor various film studios including Paramount, 20th Fox, CBS/MTM, and others, 1976-80; post prodn. coordinator, supr. David Gerber Co., Culver City, Calif., 1981-82; post prodn. coord. Paramount TV, L.A., 1982-84; sole proprietor Trailers, Etc., North Hollywood, Calif., 1984-85; film and video editor Paramount Pictures, L.A., 1985-86; film editor Universal Studios, Universal City, 1987-89; film, video editor New World TV, L.A., 1991-92; associate dir. Tri-Star TV, Studio City, Calif., 1992-93; film and video editor various studios, Studio City, 1993—. Owner, mgr. Choice Editing Sys., Northridge, Calif., 1993—. Film and video editor : (TV series) Rude Awakening; Strong Medicine; Anna Says; Magnificent 7; A Year in the Life; MacGyver; Call to Gloray; The Making of Shogun; Nightingales; Mission Impossible, Muder C.O.D., I'll Take Romance; Get a Life; A Fire in the Dark; The Fifth Corner; Stong Medicine; (TV films) Search for Grace; Eyes of Terror; Then There Was One; Sweet Bird of Youth; Without You I'm Nothing; All in the Family; Rockford Files; Is There Life Out There?; Thrill, Breaking Free; Something Borrowed...Something Blue; A Time to Stay Goodbye?; An Unexpected Life; A Father For Brittany; Love Song, Custody of the Heart, 2000; Snap Decision, The Familiar Stranger, Taking Back Our Town, 2001; asst. film editor : (films) King of Gypsies, Star Wars, others; film and video editor : (TV series) Casino. Mem.: Dirs. Guild Am., Acad. TV Arts and Scis., Am. Cinema Editors, Acad. Magical Arts, Inc., Tri-Network (pres. 1979—80), Internat. Alliance Theatrical Stage Employees and Moving Picture Machine Operators U.S. and Can. Democrat. Roman Catholic. Avocations: water-skiing, skiing, sand castle building, script writing.

MALOW-IROFF, MICHELINE SUSAN, psychologist, educator; b. Hamtramck, Mich., Nov. 2, 1959; d. Raymond Henry Malow and Cynthia Marie Bishop; m. Marc Steven Iroff, Sept. 30, 1961; children: Dana Malow Iroff, Erika Malow Iroff. BS, Mich. State U., 1981; MEd, CUNY, 1998, PhD, 2001. Lic. sch. psychologist N.Y. Sch. psychologist developmental presch. Hosp. Clinic Home Care, Bklyn., 1997—; asst. prof. dept. elem. and early childhood edn. Queens Coll.-CUNY, Flushing, 1996—, tchg. fellow coll. liaison, 2002—03. Contbr. articles to profl. jours. Grantee PSC CUNY33 grantee, Rsch. Found. CUNY, 2002—03, PSC CUNY34 grantee, 2003—. Mem.: APA, Soc. for Rsch. on Adolescence, Soc. for Rsch. on Child Devel. Avocations: travel, reading, skiing. Office: Queens Coll-CUNY Dept Elem Edn 65-30 Kissena Blvd Flushing NY 11367 Office Phone: 718-997-5314. E-mail: mmalowir@qc1.qc.edu.

MALOY, FRANCES, librarian; MLS, SUNY Albany. Leader of the access services divsn. Emory U. Gen. Libraries, 1992—; v.p. Assoc. Rsch. and Coll. Libraries, 2003—; dir., pub. services Hamilton Coll. Mem. bd. dirs. ACRL; chmn. ACRL Nominations Com. and ACRL Com. on Ethics. Office: 50 East Huron St Chicago IL 60611

MALSON, VERNA LEE, special education educator; b. Buffalo, Wyo., Mar. 29, 1937; d. Guy James and Vera Pearl (Curtis) Mayer; m. Jack Lee Malson, Apr. 20, 1955; children: Daniel Lee, Thomas James, Mark David, Scott Allen. BA in Elem. Edn. and Spl. Edn. magna cum laude, Met. State Coll., Denver, 1975; MA in Learning Disabilities, U. No. Colo., 1977. Cert. tchr., Colo. Tchr.-aide Wyo. State Tng. Sch., Lander, 1967-69; spl. edn. tchr. Bennett Sch. 29J, Colo., 1975-79, chmn. health, sci. social studies depts., 1977-79; spl. edn. tchr. Deer Trail Sch., Colo., 1979-98, chmn. careers, gifted and talented, 1979-87, spl. edn./presch. tchr., 1992-98, ret., 1998. Course cons. Regis Coll., Denver, 1990; mem. spl. edn. parent adv. com. East Central Bd. Coop. Ednl. Services, Limon, Colo. Colo. scholar Met. State Coll., 1974; grantee Colo. Dept. Edn., 1979, 81; recipient Cert. of Achievement, Met. State Coll., 1993. Mem. Coun. Exceptional Children, Bennett Tchrs. Club (treas. 1977-79), Kappa Delta Pi. Republican. Presbyterian. Avocations: coin collecting, reading, sports. Home: PO Box 208 Edgerton WY 82635-0208

MALTBY, FLORENCE HELEN, library science educator; b. Sumner, Iowa, Mar. 2, 1933; d. Harold George and Blanche Theresa (Gritzner) Garland; m. George Robert Maltby, June 3, 1964 (dec. Oct. 1985); 1 child, Patricia Garland Maltby Clark. BA, U. No. Iowa, Cedar Falls, 1954; MS in Libr. Sci., U. Ill., 1960, cert. advanced study librarianship, 1967. Elem. sch. libr. Barrington (Ill.) Pub. Sch., 1954-57, USAF Dependent Sch. Europe, Sculthorpe, Eng., 1957-58, Ramstein, Fed. Republic of Germany, 1958-59, Wiesbaden, Fed. Republic of Germany, 1960-61; grad. asst. U. Ill., Champaign, 1959-60; reference asst., instr. Libr. Cen. Mich. U., Mt. Pleasant, 1961-63; asst. prof. libr. sci. Southwest Mo. State U., Springfield, 1963-66, 67-80, assoc. prof. libr. sci., 1980-97; instr. libr. sci. U. Ill., Champaign, 1966-67; archivist Diocese of Springfield-Cape Girardeau, 2001—. Evaluator North Cen. Assn., Springfield, 1989, Dept. Elem. and Secondary Edn., Mo. Sch. Improvement, 1989; com. mem. Children's Lit. Festival, Springfield, 1990, treas., 1991. Contbr. to Masterplots II: Juvenile and Young Adult Fiction, 1991, 97. Mem. AAUP, ALA, Assn. Libr. and Info. Sci. Edn., Mo. Assn. Sch. Librs. (mem. standards rev. com. for state sch. libr. media standards 1994), Assn. Cath. Diocesan Archivists, Beta Phi Mu, Alpha Beta Alpha, Kappa Delta Pi. Roman Catholic. Avocations: reading, playing organ and piano, cert. literary braille transcriber.

MALVILLE, NANCY JEAN, anthropologist; b. Ft. Collins, Colo., July 24, 1937; d. Philip Grant and Florence Rebekah (Eyre) Koontz; m. John McKim Malville, Mar. 26, 1960; children: Katherine Malville Shipan, Leslie Malville Ellwood. BA, Coll. Wooster, 1959; MA, U. Colo., 1971, MA, 1982, PhD, 1987. Rsch. assoc. dept. anthropology U. Colo., Boulder, 1988—2004, asst. prof. adj. dept. anthropology, 2004—. Contbr. rsch. articles to profl. jours. Avocations: skiing, hiking, mountain climbing, music, viola. Office: U Colo Dept Anthropology PO Box 233 Boulder CO 80309-0233

MAMAYEK, TELLY, radio personality; married; children: Emily, Nathan. BA Journalism, U. Wis., 1985. With Stas. WBIZ/WJJK Radio, Eau Claire, Wis., Stas. KZIO/WDSM Radio, Duluth, Minn., Sta. WNIU Pub. Radio, DeKalb, Ill., Sta. WCKY Radio, Cin., Sta. WCCO Radio, Mpls., 1991—, morning news editor, anchor. Mem.: Minn. AP Broadcast Bd., Minn. Chpt. Profl. Journalists (pres.). Avocation: bicycling. Office: WCCO 625 2nd Ave S Minneapolis MN 55402

MAMER, LOUISAN ELIZABETH, home economist, journalist; b. Hardin, Ill., Aug. 28, 1910; d. Louis H. and Anna Mary Elizabeth (Mies) M.; m. Arthur Chris Hagen, Mar. 20, 1954. BA, U. Ill., 1931; Journalism Cert., USDA Grad. Sch., Washington, 1963. Cert. gemologist; cert. home economist; cert. in family and consumer scis. Tchr. sci., home econs., drama Erie Twp. H.S., Erie, Ill., 1931-34; 4-H county agt. Whiteside County Extension, Morrison, Ill., 1931-34; tchr. h.s. and adult groups DeKalb Twp. H.S., DeKalb, Ill., 1934-35; practice tchr., supr. No. Ill. U., DeKalb, 1934-35; specialist Regional Home Electrification/Ill., Iowa, Nebr., 1937-41, 1941-46; youth liaison specialist Hdqrs. Home Electrification, 1952-60; edn. clk., rev. head, writer Rural Electrification Adminstrn., Washington, 1935-37; media work, tng. specialist USDA Hdqrs., REA Program, Washington, 1946-81; freelance writer-editor, Washington, 1981—. Info. officer Rural Lines stories and newsletter author, 1960-70, mem. svcs. officer, 1960-70, tng. officer, acting chief, 1970-80. Writer 6 leaflets, various manuals and outlines, articles and informational pieces. With nutrition and safety programs ARC and REA, St. Louis, 1941-45; involved in demonstrations for the poor D.C. Citizens Svc. Coun., Washington, 1953-60; orgnl. fund raiser for U. Ill., 1975—; involved in numerous other civic activities. Mem. Illuminating Engring. Soc. (emeritus), World Future Soc., Elec. Women's Round Table (area chair 1968, 89-98), Consumer Fedn. Am., Am. Coun. on Consumer Interests, Nat. Consumers League, Women in Energy, Women's Coun. of Energy and the Environment, Am. Assn. Family and Consumer Scis., Women's Internat. Network of Utility Profls. (chair 1999), Phi Beta Kappa, Phi Upsilon Omicron, Alpha Lambda Delta. Avocations: lapidary and gem appraisal, riding and jumping, square dancing, reading and writing, play coaching. Home: The Ontario 2853 Ontario Rd NW Apt 422 Washington DC 20009-2241 Fax: (202) 328-3975.

MAMLOK, URSULA, composer, educator; b. Berlin, Feb. 1, 1928; d. John and Dorothy Lewis; m. Dwight G. Mamlok, Nov. 27, 1947. Student, Mannes Coll. Music, 1942-45; MusB, Manhattan Sch. Music, 1955, MusM, 1958. Faculty dept. music NYU, 1967-74, CUNY, 1971-74; prof. composition Manhattan Sch. Music, N.Y.C., 1968—2003. Composer numerous works including Variations and Interludes for 4 percussionists, 1973, Sextet, 1977, Festive Sounds, 1978, When Summer Sang, 1980, piano trio Panta rhei, 1981, 5 recital pieces for young pianists, 1983, From My Garden for solo viola or solo violin, 1983, Concertino for wind quintet, strings and percussion, 1984, Der Andreas Garten for voice, flute and harp, 1986, Alariana for recorder, clarinet, bassoon, violin and cello, 1986, 3 Bagatelles for harpsichord, 1987, 5 Bagatelles for clarinet, violin, cello, 1988, Rhapsody for clarinet, viola, piano Inward Journey for Piano, 1989, Sonata for violin and piano, 1989, Music for flute, violin, cello, 1990, Girasol, a sextet for flute, violin, viola, cello and piano, 1991, Constellations for orch., 1993, Polarities for flute, violin, cello, piano, 1995, Festive Sounds for Organ, String Quartet II, 1996-97, Two Thousan Notes for Piano, 2000-01, Confluencies for Clarinet, Violin, Cello, Piano, 2002, Rückblick for Saxophone and Piano, 2002. Recipient Opus One Rec. award Am. Composers Alliance, 1987, Serge Koussevitzky Found. commn., 1988, Walter Hinrichsen award Acad. Inst. Arts and Letters, 1989, commn. San Francisco Symphony, 1990; Nat. Endowment Arts grantee, 1974, Am. Inst. Acad. Arts and Letters grantee, 1981, 89, Martha Baird Rockefeller grantee, 1982; John Simon Gugenheim fellow, 1995. Mem. Am. Soc. Univ. Composers, Am. Women Composers, N.Y. Women Composers, Internat. League Women Composers, Am. Music Ctr., Internat. Soc Contemporary Music (bd. dirs.), Fromm Found. Commn., Am. Guild Organists Continuum Commn. Address: 315 E 86th St New York NY 10028-4714

MAMPRE, VIRGINIA ELIZABETH, communications executive; b. Chgo., Sept. 12, 1949; d. Albert Leon and Virginia S. (Joboul) M. BA with honors, U. Iowa, 1971; Masters degree, Ind. U., 1972; spl. cert., Harvard U., 1981. Cert. tchr. Harris Intern WTTW-TV Sta., Chgo., 1972, asst. dir., 1972-73; prod. and dir. WSIU/WUSI-TV Sta., Carbondale, Ill., 1973-74; instr. So. Ill. U., Carbondale, 1972-77; prog. and prod. mgr. WSIU/WUSI-TV, Carbondale, 1974-77; prog. dir. KUHT-TV Sta., Houston, 1977-83; pres. Victory Media, Inc., Houston, 1984-89, Mampre Media Internat., Houston, 1984—. Cons. Corp. Pub. Broadcasting, Washington, 1981—83; bd. dirs. TVPC; program bd. Ea. Ednl. Network; spkr., presenter in field Europe, Asia, Australia, S. Am. Contbg. author/editor to mags. including Focus, 1989, News & Views, 1987-88, In the Black, 1984-93, Festivals; creator: (report card campaign) Multi-media, U.S., 1985—; exec. prodr. TV spls., pub. affairs and info., 1977-83 (awards 1978-91). Pres. Child Abuse Prevention Coun., Houston, 1984—97; chmn. exhbns. Mayor's 1st Hearing, Children and Youth, Houston, 1985—88; rep. Houston 2nd World Conf. on Mayors, Japan, 1989; bd. govs. Houston Read Commn., pres., 1995—2001; mem. nat. faculty Ctr. Children's Issues, 1995—97; v.p. Episcopal Ch. Women; chair adv. bd. Houston Read Commn., 1993—2001; pres. bd. dirs. Houston Fin. Coun., 1983—; bd. dirs. Child Abuse Prevention Network, 1990—97; chmn. bd. dirs., gala chair Crime Stoppers Houston, 1984—99; founder, bd. dirs. Friends of WSIU-TV, 1974—77; chmn. St. Kevork/ACYO Nat. Sports Fair, St. John the Divine, 1990; mem. exec. bd. Nat. Com. To Prevent Child Abuse, 1990—97; pres., bd. dirs. Fedn. Houston Profl. Women Found., 1996; bd. dirs. Humanities Tex., 1998—, Tex. Coun. Humanities, Operation Rainbow, 1997—, pres. bd. gala chair. Fellow W.K. Kellogg Found., Battle Creek, Mich., 1987-90; recipient award for Excellence Pres. Pvt. Sector, White House, Washington, 1987, Ohio State U., Columbus, 1983, Feddersen award for excellence in Pub. TV Ind. U., Bloomington, 1981, Heritage award Child Abuse Prevention Coun., 1990, Dona J. Stone Founders award Nat. Assn. for Prevention of Child Abuse, 1990; named among Outstanding Women Vols. for community, civic and profl. contbns., Fedn. Houston Profl. Women, 1989; honoree Woman on Move, 1997. Mem.: Culinary Guild Houston, Internat. Festivals Events. Assn. (sec. 1994—, bd. dirs., creator Mampre Media Internat. Leadership Devel.), Profls. in Culinary Arts (pres. 2002—), TV Program Conf. (sec. bd. 1990—), Ctr. Bus. Women's Devel., Nat. Assn. Programming TV Execs., Nat. Assn. Ednl. Broadcasters (presenter nat. conv. 1975—76), Houston Fed. Profl. Women (del. 1986—93, chmn. 1994—, pres.), Am. Women in Radio and TV (bd. dirs. 1985—, nat. v.p. 1986—90, award 1987, pres. Houston chpt. 1990), Dau. of the King, Ch. of the Christ in the Arts (chair), Dephians, Tex. Lyceum (v.p., bd. dirs. 1990—96). Republican. Episcopalian. Avocations: photography, swimming, sailing, languages, travel. Office: Mampre Media Internat 5123 Del Monte Dr Houston TX 77056-4391

MAMUT, MARY CATHERINE, retired entrepreneur; b. Calabria, Italy, Oct. 17, 1923; came to U.S., 1928; d. Carmelo Charles and Caterina (Tripodi) Cogliandro; m. Michael Matthew Mamut, May 15, 1954; children: Anthony Carl, Charles Terrance. Student, Stenotype Comml. Coll., 1946-50. Sec. to pres. Thomas Goodfellow, Inc., Detroit, 1942-50; asst. to v.p. R.G. Moeller Co., Detroit, 1951-52; sec. to pres. United Steel Supply Co., Detroit, 1952-54; sec. to libr. Farmington (Mich.) Schs., 1962-68; real estate agt., 1969; owner, mgr. Crystal Fair, Birmingham, Mich., 1969-88, ret. Tchr. Stenotype Comml. Coll., Detroit, 1952-54. Vol. Henry Ford Mus., Dearborn, Mich., 1989-90, Greenfield Village, 1989-90, West Bloomfield Libr., 1993-95. Recipient World Lifetime Achievement award Am. Biog. Inst. U.S.A., 1993. Mem. Am. Bus. Women's Assn., Birmingham-Bloomfield C. of C., Profl. Secs. Internat, NAFE. Roman Catholic. Avocations: reading, music, art, theater. Home: 7423 Coach Ln West Bloomfield MI 48322-4022

MANAHAN, ANNA, actress; b. Ireland, Oct. 18, 1924; Student, Gaiety Sch. Acting. Actress Edwards/MacLiammoir Co., Nat. Theatre, London, Walter Kerr Theatre, N.Y.C. Appeared in numerous theatrical prodns., including The Rose Tattoo, Moon for the Misbegotten, Bloomsday, Entertaining Mr. Sloane, The Killing of Sister George, Cat on a Hot Tin Roof, the Gingerbread Lady, Lovers (Tony nomination), Live Like Pits, The Plough and the Stars (Oliver award nomination), The Leenana Trilogy, the Loves of Cass Maguire, I do Not Like Thee Dr. Fell, the Shaughraun, the Matchmaker, The Taylor, Ansty, Dr. Fell, The Beauty Queen of Leenane (Tony award 1998), The Matchmaker, 2002, Sive, 2002, numerous others; TV appearances include Me Mammy, The riordans, Leave it to Mrs. O'Brien, the Irish RM, (TV/films) the Bill, Lovejoy, 1986, Young Indiana Jones Chronicles, 1992, the Treaty, Blind Justice, Hear My Songs, 1991, Clash of the Titans, 1981, A Man of No Importance, 1994, Woman Found Dead in Elevator, 2000, On the Edge, 2000, Black Day at Black Rock, 2001, others. Recipient Tony award, Theatre World award, Freedom of City award, 2002. Office: Walter Kerr Theatre 219 W 48th St New York NY 10036-1423

MANASC, VIVIAN, architect, consultant; b. Bucharest, Romania, May 19, 1956; d. Bercu and Bianca (Smetterling) M.; m. William A. Dushenski, Feb. 25, 1984; children: Peter Gabriel, Lawrence Alexander. BS in Architecture, McGill U., Montreal, Que., Can., 1977, BArch, 1979; MBA, U. Alta., Edmonton, 1982. Architectural insp. Transport Can., Edmonton, 1977-79; project architect Bell Spotowski Architects, Edmonton, 1980-82; asst. dir. design constrn. Edmonton Pub. Schs., 1982-84; mgr., prin. Ferguson, Simek, Clark Architects Ltd., Edmonton, 1985-88; mng. dir. FSC Groves Hodgson Manasc Architects Ltd., Edmonton, 1988-97; pres. Manasc Isaac Archs., Edmonton, 1997—. Adj. asst. prof. of architecture, U. Calgary; bd. dirs. Can. Archtl. Accreditation Bd. Contbr. articles to profl. jours. Co-chair innovative practice group in arch. United Way Edmonton, sect. chair, cabinet mem., Edmonton, 1980-82; mentor RAIC Syllabus Program, Edmonton, 1982-88; bd. dirs. Econ. Devel. Edmonton. Scholar McGill U., 1974. Fellow Royal Archtl. Inst. Can. (bd. dirs.); mem. Alta. Assn. Archs., Manitoba Assn. Archs., B.C. Assn. Archs., Saskatchewan Assn. Archs., Coun. Edn. Facility Planners, Nat. Coun. Jewish Women (past pres. Edmonton sect.), Jewish Fedn. Edmonton (v.p. planning). Avocations: travel, photography, writing. Fax: (780) 426-3 70. E-mail: vivian@miarch.com.

MANCHIP, NANCY, special education educator; b. Fremont, N..H., Mar. 24, 1958; d. Dale Lloyd and Vivian Mae Manchip; m. Steve Burk, June 26, 1990. BS in Edn., Ctrl. Mich. U., 1979, MA in Edn., 1984. Cons. Zeeland Pub. Schs., Zeeland, Mich., 1984—86; tchr. spl. edn. Fremont Pub. Schs., 1980—84, Hopkins Pub. Schs., Mich., 1986—. Vol. local animal shelters. Avocations: antiques, gardening. Office: Hopkins HS 333 Clark St Hopkins MI 49328

MANCINELLI-CAHILL, MAGGIE, theater director; married; 1 child. Co. dir. Playwrights Preview Prodns., Manhattan, NY, 1991—95; artistic dir. Capital Repertory Theatre, Albany, NY, 1995—. Creator Urban Express, N.Y.C. Office: Capital Repertory Theatre 111 N Pearl St Albany NY 12207-2208*

MANCINI, GILDA MARIANN, musician, music educator; b. Detroit, Apr. 15, 1933; d. Peter and Rose Mancini. AA, L.A. City Coll., 1971. Tchr. Cath. Schs., L.A., Detroit, Unified Sch. Sys., L.A. Mem.: Third Order St. Dominic. Jewish. Avocations: painting, drawing. Home: Apt 212 3882 Dobie Rd Okemos MI 48864-3791

MANCINI, LOIS JEAN, elementary school educator; b. Pitts., May 1, 1944; d. Edward Walter and Margaret Jane Freidhof; m. George John Mancini, July 7, 1967; children: Robin Jennifer, Lori Jean. MEd, Rutgers U., 1988. Cert. elem. tchr. N.J., prin. N.J. Tchr. Moorestown (N.J.) Bd. Edn., Cinnaminson (N.J.) Bd. Edn., Andover (N.J.) Bd. Edn. Author: Mortimer Goose, 1998. Pres. Westampton N.J. Bd. Edn., 1993—. Named Tchr. of Yr., State of N.J., 1996. Mem. NEA, N.J. Edn. Assn., N.J. Sch. Bds. Assn. (pres. bd. dirs. 1993). Presbyterian. Avocations: reading, travel. Home: 57 Tarnsfield Rd Mount Holly NJ 08060-2363 E-mail: mancinil@mtps.middle.com.

MANCINI, MARILYN ELIZABETH, education educator; d. Fredric James and Margaret Ione Lee; m. Ernest Anthony Mancini, Dec. 27, 1969; children: Lisa, Lauren. AA, Gulf Park Coll., Long Beach, Miss., 1967; BS, So. Ill. U., 1969; MA, U. Ala., 1985. Copywriter Sta. WLDS-FM, Jacksonville, 1970, Sta. WINI-FM, Carbondale, Ill., 1970; instr., advising coord. U. Ala., 1986—. Bd. dirs. Caring Days, Tuscaloosa, 1997—; bd. trustees Cottey Coll., Nevada, Mo., 2000—. Program devel. Tombigbee Girl Scouts, Tuscaloosa, Ala., 2002—. Mem.: Assn. Educators in Journalism and Mass Comms., Am. Adv. Assn. Presbyterian. Avocations: boating, swimming, fishing, hiking, making bread. Office: Univ Ala PO Box 870172 Tuscaloosa AL 35487-0172 E-mail: mancini@apr.ua.edu.

MANCINI, MARY CATHERINE, cardiothoracic surgeon, researcher; b. Scranton, Pa., Dec. 15, 1953; d. Peter Louis and Ferminia Teresa (Massi) M. BS in Chemistry, U. Pitts., 1974, MD, 1978; PhD in Anatomy and Cellular Biology, La. State U. Med. Ctr., 2000; M in Med. Mgmt., U. Tex. Southwestern, 2002. Diplomate Am. Bd. Surgery (speciality cert. critical care medicine), Am. Bd. Thoracic Surgery. Intern in surgery U. Pitts., 1978-79, resident in surgery, 1979-87; fellow pediatric cardiac surgery Mayo Clinic, 1987-88; asst. prof. surgery, dir. cardiothoracic transplantation Med. Coll. Ohio, Toledo, 1988-91; assoc. prof. surgery, dir. cardiothoracic transplantation La. State U. Health Scis. Ctr., Shreveport, 1991-98, prof. surgery, chief cardiothoracic surgery, 1999—2002; dir. cardiovascular rsch. Willis Knighton Med. Ctr., 1991—. Med. advisor Total Artificial Heart Devel., ABIOMED Corp. Author: Operative Techniques for Medical Students, 1983; editor-in-chief: Cardiothoracic Surgery and Transplantation EMedicine Textbooks; contbr. articles to profl. jours. Mem. physicians adv. bd. Rep. Com. Recipient Pres. award, Internat. Soc. Heart Transplantation, 1983, Charles C. Moore Tchg. award, U. Pitts., 1985, Internat. Order of Merit award, 1995, Nina S. Braunwald Career Devel. award, Thoracic Surgery Found., 1996—98, Nat. Leadership award, Rep. Com., 2000, Disting. Alumni award, U. Pitts. Dept. Chemistry, 2002; grantee Am. Heart Assn., 1988, Whittaker, 1998, NIH, 2000. Fellow ACS, AHA, Am. Coll. Chest Physicians, Internat. Coll. Surgeons (councillor 1991—); mem. Assn. Women Surgeons, Am. Surg. Assn., Am. Assn. Thoracic Surgery, Am. Physiol. Soc., So. Surg. Assn., Rotary (gift of life program 1991). Roman Catholic. Achievements include first multiple organ transplant in La; first pediatric heart transplant in La., 1993. Office: La State U Med Ctr 1501 Kings Hwy Shreveport LA 71103-4228 Office Phone: 318-675-6154.

MANCINI BROWN, SHEREE L, education educator, writer; b. Cincinnati, Ohio, June 4, 1956; d. Albert B and Mildred Mancini; m. Gary M Brown, June 25, 1976; children: Ryan Asher Brown, Allison Rose Brown. BA, Coll. of Mt. St. Joseph; student, Xavier U., 1999—. Reporter No. Ky. Recorder/Cath. Telegraph, Cin., 1996—; dir. of writing ctr. Coll. of Mt. St. Joseph, Cin., 1999—2000. Adj. prof. english/comm. Coll. of Mt. St. Joseph, Cin., 1998—. Author: (essays) Italian America, The Kit Kat Review, (short stories) Drought.

MANCINO, ANNE ROCHELLE, surgeon; b. Little Rock, June 9, 1958; d. Ronald Greer and Patricia Joyce (Glass) Thompson; m. Michael John Mancino, Nov. 26, 1994; 1 child, Parker Kathleen. BA in Molecular Biology, Vanderbilt U., 1980; MD, U. Ark., 1984. Intern U. Louisville, 1984-87, resident in surgery, 1989-92; fellow in endocrine rsch. Mass. Gen. Hosp./Harvard Med. Sch., Boston, 1988-89; asst. prof. surgery U. Miss., Jackson, 1992-98; fellow diseases of the breast U. Ark., Little Rock, 1998—2000, asst. prof. surgery, 1998—2002, assoc. prof. surgery, 2002—, dir. student edn. dept. surgery, 2002—. Dir. student edn. dept. surgery U. Miss., 1992-98. Contbr. articles to profl. jours. Lt. col. U.S. Army, 1991. Fellow ACS; mem. Am. Assn. Endocrine Surgeons, Assn. for Surg. Edn., Assn. Acad. Surgeons, Alpha Omega Alpha. Democrat. Roman Catholic. Avocations: singing, boating. Office: U Ark Medical Sciences 4301 W Markham St # 725 Little Rock AR 72205-7101

MANDABACH, CARYN, television producer; m. Paul Mandabach; children: Marisa, Jon. Pres. Carsey-Werner Co., Studio City, Calif., 1987—; co-founder Oxygen Media, NYC, 1998—. Prodr.: (TV series) The Cosby Show, Roseanne, A Different World, Grace Under Fire, Cybill, Third Rock from the Sun, That 70's Show. Bd. dirs. The Center Theatre Group, The Curtis Sch., AFI Third Decade C. Recipient Emmy for The Cosby Show, Humanitas award, People's Choice award, Peabody award. Office: Oxygen Media 75 9th Ave New York NY 10011-7006

MANDARINO, CANDIDA ANN, education educator, consultant; b. Buffalo, N.Y., July 26, 1944; d. Amerigo and Adelaide (Alfieri) Mandarino. BS in Edn., SUNY, Buffalo, 1966; MA in Ednl. Psychology, Calif. State U., Long Beach, 1974; postgrad. in interior and environ. design, 1980—85; PhD in Psychology, Berne U., Wolfboro Falls, N.H., 2000. Tchr. on spl. assignment Norwalk (Calif.)-La Mirada Unified Sch. Dist. Office, 1990—99; mentor/master tchr.; literacy and resource specialist Los Alisos Middle Sch., Norwalk, 1999—2000; prin. Escalona Elem. Sch., La Mirada, 2000; ednl. trainer, cons. K-12 and univs. Heuer Corp., N.Y.C., 2001. Spkr., presenter in field. Mem.: Tchrs. Assn. Norwalk-LaMirada Area, Calif. Tchrs. Assn., Assn. Supervision and Curriculum Devel., Pi Lambda Theta. Home: 178 Roycroft Ave Long Beach CA 90803

MANDEL, ADRIENNE ABRAMSON, state legislator; b. Irvington, N.J., Sept. 30, 1936; d. Nathaniel and Florence (Lebovitz) Abramson; m. Emanuel Mandel, 1958; children: Lisa Mandel-Trupp, David. BA, Rutgers U., 1958; MA, George Washington U., 1984. Chairwoman, vice chairwoman Precinct 13-56, 1979-94; parole officer, social svc. case worker N.J. Dept. Inst. & Agencies, 1958-60; survey interviewer U.S. Census Bur., 1973-77; monitoring and evaluation specialist Divsn. Labor Svc., Montgomery County Govt., 1979-81; asst. dir. Sr. Ctr. Divsn. Elder Affairs, Dept. Family Resources, 1981-84; staff asst. Office Chief Adminstr., 1984-85; legis. rep. Office Intergovt. Rels., 1985-94; mem. Md. State Legislature, 1995—, mem. commerce govt. matters com., 1995—2002, mem. health and govt. ops. com., 2003—, dep. majority whip, 2003—. Pres. Women's Caucus, 2002-03; bi-county chair Montgomery County Del., 1999—; health issues chair Nat. Order Women Legislators, 1999—; mem. exec. bd. Nat. Found. Women Legislators, 2004—. Recipient Woman of Valor award B'nai B'rith Women, 1972; named amont Md. Top 100 Women, 2002, 04. Mem. Women's Polit. Caucus, Mothers Against Drunk Driving, Md. Govt. Rels. Assn., Montgomery County Ethnic Heritage Festival, LWV, Alpha Psi Omega, Delta Phi Delta.

MANDEL, CHARLOTTE, poet, literature educator, editor; m. Irwin D. Mandel; children: Carol, Nora, Richard. BA, Brklyn. Coll., 1944; MA, Montclair State U., 1977. Editor Saturday Press, U. Montclair, NJ, 1982—; poetry tchr. Barnard Coll. Ctr. Rsch. on Women, N.Y.C., 1995—. Poet in classroom various schs. & colls., 1975—. Author: (poetry) Sight Lines, 1998, The Marriages of Jacob, 1991, The Life of Mary, 1988, A Disc of Clear Water, 1981; editor: Saturday's Women, 1982. Office: Saturday Press PO Box 43534 Upper Montclair NJ 07043

MANDEL, KARYL LYNN, accountant; b. Chgo., Dec. 14, 1935; d. Isador J. and Eve (Gellar) Karzen; m. Fredric H. Mandel, Sept. 29, 1956; children: David Scott, Douglas Jay, Jennifer Ann. Student, U. Mich., 1954-56, Roosevelt U., 1956-57; AA summa cum laude, Oakton Community Coll., 1979. CPA, Ill; registered investment advisor; lic. life ins. provider. Pres. Excel Transp. Service Co., Elk Grove, Ill., 1958-78; tax mgr. Chunowitz, Teitelbaum & Baerson, CPA's, Northbrook, Ill., 1981-83, tax ptnr., 1984—. Sec-treas. Lednam, Inc., Coffee Break, Inc.; mem. acctg. curriculum adv. bd. Oakton C.C., Des Plaines, Ill., 1987—; pres. Lednam Enterprises, LLC, 2001—. Contbg. author: Ill. CPA's News Jour., Acctg. Today. Recipient State of Israel Solidarity award, 1976. Mem. AICPA, Am. Soc. Women CPA, Women's Am. ORT (pres. Chgo. region 1972-74, v.p. midwest dist. 1975-76, nat. endowment com., nat investment adv. com.), Ill. CPA Soc. (chmn. estate and gift tax com. 1987-89, legis. contact com. 1981-82, pres. North Shore chpt., award for Excellence in Acctg. Edn., Bd. dirs. 1989-91), Chgo. Soc. Women CPA, Chgo. Estate Planning Coun., Nat. Assn. Women Bus. Owners, Lake County Estate Planning, Coun., Greater North Shore Estate Planning Coun. Office: 401 Huehl Rd Northbrook IL 60062-2300 E-mail: KLM@CTBLTD.COM.

MANDEL, LESLIE ANN, investment advisor, business owner, author; b. Washington, July 29, 1945; d. Seymour and Marjorie (Syble) Mandel; m. Arthur Herzog III. BA in Art History, U. Minn., 1967; cert., N.Y. Sch. Interior Design, 1969. Cert. Brailled Libr. Congress. Pres. Leslie Mandel Enterprises, Inc., N.Y.C., 1968—; sr. v.p. Maximum Entertainment Network, L.A. and N.Y.C., 1988-90; pres. Rich List Co., 1968—; pres., CEO Mandel Airplane Funding and Leasing Corp., N.Y.C., Hong Kong, China and Mongolia, 1990—; CEO Mandel-Khan Inc., Ulaanbaatar, Mongolia, 1994—, keep hers, keep his, 2002—. Fin. advisor Osmed, Inc., Mpls., 1986—, Devine Comm./Allen & Co., NY, Del., Utah, N.Mex., NY, N.Y. WUWV, Utah KBER, WKTC-AM-FM, 1984—89, Am. Kefir Corp., N.Y.C., 1983—89, Shore Group (Internat., Guyana), Flight Internat., 1991—; owner The Rich List Co., 150 internat. catalogs, mags. and fundraising lists; joint venture Mongolian Ind. Broadcasting Channel, Ulaanbaatar, 1995; pres., owner Mandel Airplane Funding and Leasing Corp.; rep. Israeli Govt. IAI Satellite, China, Romania, Costa Rica, Mongolia, Amos Satellite Network, China, 1992—; advisor rep. Gt. Wall Corp., Long March Corp., China, 1992—, Chinese Silk, 1993—, Am. Oil Refinery, 1993—; bd. dirs. Coastal Equipment Co., Bristol Airlines; cons. Exclusive Miat Airlines, Mongolia; purchasing agt. People's Republic of China-Aircraft; advisor Aeropostalis, Mexico, 1994—95; photographer; lectr. UN Internat. Direct Mail; advisor Aruba Airlines, Mexicana Airlines; aircraft agt., bd. dirs. Lazorlines Landing Equipment, 1997—; lease Estafada Airlines 757-200-C, 2000—, Chile Airlines 757-200C, 2002; advisor Guyana 2000 Airlines. Photographer: Vogue, 1978, New Earth Times, 1995, Fortune mag.; Braille transcriber: The Prophet (Kalil Gibran), 1967, Getting Ready for Battle (R. Prawe Jhabuala), 1967; exec. prodr. film: Hospital Audiences, 1975 (Cannes award 1976); author: Hungry at the Watering Hole, Gardiners Island, 1636-1990, 1989, Expedition: In the Steps of Ghengis Kahn, 1994; advisor Port Libertè Ptnrs., 1988-94; contbr. articles to profl. jours. Fin. advisor Correctional Assn., Osborn Soc., 1977—; founder, treas. Prisoners Family Transportation and Assistance Fund, N.Y., 1972-77; judge Emmy awards of Acad. TV Arts and Scis., N.Y.C., 1970; bd. dirs. Prisoners Assn., 1990; chmn. U.S.A. com. Violeta B. de Chamarro for Pres. of Nicaragua Campaign. Recipient Inst. for the Creative and Performing Arts fellowship, N.Y.C., 1966, Appreciation cert. Presdl. Inaugural Com., Washington, 1981. Fellow N.Y. Women in Real Estate, Explorers Club (lectr. on Mongolia, fin. com.); mem. Com. on Am. and Internat. Fgn. Affairs, Lawyers Com. on Internat. Human Rels., Bus. Exec. Nat. Security, Venture Capital Breakfast Club, The Coffee Club House, Sigma Delta Tau, Sigma Epsilon Sigma. Democrat. Avocations: painting, writing, fishing, canoeing, horseback riding, breeding cockatiels. Home: 4 E 81st St New York NY 10028-0235 Office: Mandel-Khan Inc PO Box 97 care Boldbaatar Mandel Kahn Ulaanbaatar 210648 Mongolia also: Leslie Mandel Enterprises PO Box 294 Wainscott NY 11975-0294 also: PO Box 29A Wainscott NY 11975-0029

MANDEL, RUTH BLUMENSTOCK, politics educator, educational association administrator, researcher; b. Vienna; came to U.S., 1947; d. Michael and Lea (Schmelzer) Blumenstock; m. Barrett John Mandel, June 18, 1961 (div. 1976); 1 child, Maud S.; m. Jeffrey Lucker, Feb. 24, 1991. BA, Bklyn. Coll., 1960; MA, U. Conn., 1962, PhD, 1969. Part-time instr. dept. English U. Conn., 1960-66; lectr. dept. English U. Pitts., 1968-70; asst. prof. dept. English Rider Coll., 1970-71; asst. prof. Eagleton Inst. Politics Rutgers U., 1973-78, assoc. prof., 1978-85, prof., 1985-94, ednl. coord. Ctr. Am. Woman and Politics, Eagleton Inst. Politics, 1971, dir. ednl. programs and adminstrn., 1971-73, dir., 1973-94, bd. govs., prof. politics, 1994—, dir. Eagleton Inst. Politics, 1995—. Organizer Conf. Women in Legis. Leadership, 1985, Conf. Newly Elected Women Legis., 1989; founder Pub. Leadership Edn. Network; designer Nat. Edn. Women's Leadership; TV appearances include CBS Evening News, Nightline, Good Morning Am., Today, Charlie Rose, Nightly Bus. Report; lectr. in field. Author: In the Running: The New Woman Candidate, 1983, The Impact of Women in Public Office: An Overview, 1991; co-editor: The Douglas Series on Women's Lives and the Meaning of Gender; mem. editorial bd. Signs: Jour. Women in Culture and Soc., Women & Politics: Jour. Rsch. and Policy Studies; exec. prodr. (documentary) Not One of the Boys, 1984; contbr. articles to newspapers and mags. including USA Today, Working Woman, Ms. Cons. women in power com. Nat. Commn. on Observance Internat. Women's Yr., 1975; mem. state coordinating com. N.J. Internat. Women's Yr. Conf., 1976, co-chairperson nominating com., 1977; N.J. del. U.S. Nat. Women's Conf., Houston, 1977; mem. Mercer County Commn. Status of Women, 1977-84; appointed by gov. of N.J. Commn. to Study Need and Necessary Fiscal Commitments for Creating Chair Women's Studies at Douglass Coll., 1982, chair com. acad. needs; participant The Women's Dialogue—U.S./U.S.S.R., 1984; mem. program com. Women and Constitution, 1988; organizer Nat. Hispana Leadership Initiative, Ctr. Am. Women and Politics segment, 1988; bd. dirs. Nat. Coun. Rsch. Women, 1985-92, vice-chair, 1989-91, chairperson bd. com. on future, 1988-89; mem. Nat. Commn. Renewal Am. Democracy, 1992-93;appointed by Pres. of U.S. to Holocaust Meml. Coun., 1991; mem. search com. for dir. U.S. Holocaust Meml. Mus., 1992-93, com. collections and acquisitions; appointed by Pres.

Clinton vice chairperson U.S. Holocaust Meml. Coun., 1993, 96-01; Mary Louise Smith chair in women and politics Iowa State U., 1997-98. Named one of N.J.'s Most Powerful Women, N.J. Monthly, 1983; recipient Douglass medal Associate Alumnae Douglass Coll., 1989, Barbara Boggs Sigmund award Women's Political Caucus N.J., 1992, Jerseyan of Week award Sunday Star-Ledger, 1992, Woodrow Wilson Pub. Svc. award Gov. N.J. Award Program, 1992, Breaking the Glass Ceiling award Women Execs. in State Govt., 1998, 21st Century Leadership award Nat. Women's Hall of Fame, 1996, Gloria Steinem Woman of Vision award Ms. Fedn. for Women, 1996, Achievement award LWV of N.J., 1996. Office: Rutgers U Eagleton Inst Politics New Brunswick NJ 08901

MANDEL, TRUDY ANN, medical/surgical nurse, theology studies educator; b. Madison, Wis., Jan. 18, 1948; d. Robert Charles and Helen Oakley (Nemec) Johnson; m. Lawrence Neil Mandel, Sept. 6, 1969 (dec. Sept. 1994); adopted children: Edward Ryan, Shawn Michael 1 child, Todd Allen. RN, Mt. Sinai Hosp. Sch. Nursing, Milw., 1969; M in Religious Edn., Meadville/Lombard Theol. Sem., 1997. RN Wis.; cert. dir. religious edn. Nursing care coord. Green Tree Nursing Home, Glendale, Wis., 1980-82; nursing supr. Family Hosp. Nursing Home, Milw., 1982-85; owner, operator Youth Emporium, Grafton, Wis., 1984-88; staff nurse Outreach Healthcare, Brown Deer, Wis., 1987-90; dir. religious edn. Unitarian Church North, Mequon, Wis., 1990—; pvt. practice nurse, nursing care coord., case mgr. Mequon, 1992—. Foster care cons. Parent Children's Svc. Soc., Milw., 1994—. Leader Webelos cub scout pack Boy Scouts Am., Grafton, 1980—81, treas. troop 839, 1983—85; bd. dirs. Luth. Social Svc. Day Care for Elderly, Mequon, 1987—89; pres. Grafton SBA, 1985—88; mem. United for Diversity, Mequon, 1996—. Named one of Olympic torch bearer, Olympic Com., Atlanta, 1996. Mem.: Liberal Religious Educators Assn., Foster Parents Assn. (Foster Parent of the Yr. 1995). Democrat. Unitarian Universalist. Home: 1055 12th Ave Grafton WI 53024-1964 Office: Unitarian Church North 13800 N Port Washington Rd Mequon WI 53097-1738

MANDELBAUM, JEAN, director, educator; b. N.Y.C., May 19, 1934; d. Nathan Frank and Ann (Rubee) Isaacson; m. Bernard David Mandelbaum, March 25, 1956; children: Eric, Carl Steven. BA, U. Mich., Ann Arbor, 1955; MS, Bank Street Coll. of Edn., N.Y.C., 1959; PhD, N.Y.U., N.Y.C., 1978. Tchr. Marble Hill Nursery Sch., N.Y.C., 1957-60; music, movement specialist Horace Mann Sch. for N. Years, N.Y.C., 1968-73; ednl. cons. N.Y. State Dept. of Edn., Albany, N.Y., 1976-80; instr., asst. prof. The City Coll., N.Y.C., 1973-81; adj. faculty Bank Street Coll. of Edn., N.Y.C., 1986—; dir. All Souls Sch., N.Y.C., 1981—. Validator and mentor Nat. Acad. of Early Childhood Programs, Washington, 1986—; bd. dirs. Ind. Schs. Admissions Assn. of Greater N.Y., N.Y. State Assn. for the Edn. of Young Children; adv. bd. N.Y.C. UN Children's Fund, N.Y.C., 1992-95. Mem. adv. bd. N.Y.C. Parents in Action. Home: 55 E End Ave New York NY 10028-7928 Office: All Souls Sch 1157 Lexington Ave New York NY 10021-0495

MANDERS, SUSAN KAY, artist; b. Burbank, Calif., Dec. 29, 1948; d. Gus H. and Erika (Stadelbauer) M.; m. Allan D. Yasnyi, Dec. 18, 1992; children: Brian Mallut. Attended, U. Guadalajara, 1969; BA, Calif. State U., 1971; postgrad., Otis Parsons, L.A., 1985, Royal Coll. of the Arts, London, 1987; grad., Silicon Digital Arts. Owner, dir., tchr. The Art Experience Sch. and Gallery, Studio City, Calif., 1978—. Cons. in field. Exhibitions include UN World Conf. on Women, Beijing, 1996, L.A., N.Y., Chgo., Beverly Hills, Irvine, San Francisco, New Orleans, 1990—, prin. works include Steel Sculpture., Harry Ross Industries, 2003, Represented in permanent collections Nat. Mus. of Women in the Arts, Smithsonian, Wash. D.C., prin. works include Athens (Greece) Summer Olympic Games, 2004. Docent UCLA; active Tuesday's Child, Pillars of Hope Project San Fernando Valley County Fair, 1995. Mem. AAUW, L.A. Art Assn., Beverley Hills Art Assn., Nat. Mus. Women in the Arts, Nat. Assn. Univ. Women, L.A. County Mus. of Art, Dada, L.A., Mus. Contemporary Art Coun., Women in Animation, Nat. Assn. Univ. Women, Vidamation Assn. (bd. dirs.). Office: The Art Experience 11830 Ventura Blvd Studio City CA 91604-2617 Office Phone: 818-995-0009. Personal E-mail: susanmanders@aol.com.

MANDLER, JEAN MATTER, psychologist, educator; b. Oak Park, Ill., Nov. 6, 1929; d. Joseph Allen and May Roberts (Finch) Matter; m. George Mandler, Jan. 19, 1957; children: Peter Clark, Michael Allen. Student, Carleton Coll., 1947-49; BA with highest honors, Swarthmore Coll., 1951; PhD, Harvard U., 1956. Rsch. assoc. lab. social rels. Harvard U., 1957-60; rsch. assoc. dept. psychology U. Toronto, Ont., Can., 1961-65; assoc. rsch. psychologist, lectr. U. Calif. at San Diego, La Jolla, 1965-73, assoc. prof., 1973-77, prof. psychology, 1977-88, prof. cognitive sci., 1988-2000, rsch. prof., 2000—; mem. adv. com. memory and cognitive processes NSF, 1978-81. Hon. rsch. fellow U. Coll., London, 1978-89, vis. prof., 1990—; hon. mem. Med. Rsch. Coun. Cognitive Devel. Unit, 1982-98. Author: (G. Mandler) Thinking: From Association to Gestalt, 1964, Stories, Scripts and Scenes, 1984, The Foundations of Mind: Origins of Conceptual Thought, 2004; assoc. editor Psychol. rev., 1970-76; mem. editl. bd. Child Devel., 1976-89, Discourse Processes, 1977-94, Jour. Exptl. Psychology, 1977-85, Text, 1979-97, Jour. Verbal Learning and Verbal Behavior, 1980-88, Lang. and Cognitive Processes, 1985—, Cognitive Devel., 1990-99, Jour. Cognition and Devel., 1999—; contbr. articles to profl. jours. Pres. San Diego Assn. Gifted Children, 1968-71; v.p. Calif. Parents for Gifted, 1970-71; mem. alumni council Swarthmore Coll., 1975-78. NIMH research grantee, 1968-81; NSF research grantee, 1981-99. Fellow: APA (mem. exec. com. divsn. 3 1983—85), Am. Acad. Arts and Scis.; mem.: Soc. Exptl. Psychologists, Cognitive Devel. Soc., Cognitive Sci. Soc., Psychonomic Soc. (mem. governing bd. 1982—87, chmn. 1985—86), Phi Beta Kappa. Office: U Calif San Diego Dept Cognitive Sci La Jolla CA 92093-0515

MANDRACCHIA, VIOLET ANN PALERMO, psychotherapist, educator; b. N.Y.C. d. Anthony and Anna (Yetto) Palermo; m. John J. Mandracchia (dec. 1979); children: Dona Williams, Anne Marino, Marisa, John, Matthew, Lisa Williams. Student, Coll. Mt. St. Vincent; BA, St. John's U.; MA, Bklyn. Coll.; cert. in ednl. adminstrn. & supervision, Hofstra U.; MSW, SUNY, Stony Brook, 1990; advanced study in psychotherapy, L.I. Gestalt Ctr., 1988-92. LCSW, registered RCSW N.Y.; cert. secondary sch. adminstr., supr., English and social studies, practitioner Eye Movement Desensitization and Restructuring. Tchr. English Bay Ridge H.S., Bklyn., Ctrl. Islip (N.Y.) H.S., Smithtown (N.Y.) H.S.; asst. prin. Shoreham-Wading River (N.Y.) H.S., 1981-87; prin. West Islip (N.Y.) H.S., 1981-83; pvt. practice as psychotherapist Stony Brook and Manhattan, 1990—. Satellite psychotherapist Health House, Islandia, N.Y., 1988-97, supr., 1990-97. Active Suffolk County (N.Y.) Human Rights Commn., 1979-84, 88-92; chair adv. bd. Office for Women, Suffolk County, 1986-89; treas. bd. dirs. Women's Ctr., SUNY, Farmingdale, N.Y., 1985-87; chair Women's Equal Rights Coalition, Suffolk County, 1979-84, 88-92; chair North Fork Task Force in Arts, Suffolk County, 1977-79. Recipient Woman of Yr. award Suffolk County Exec. Office for Women, 1989; named Citizen of Yr., Smithtown LWV, 1984, Educator of Yr., Suffolk County Exec. & Women's Equal Rights Coalition, 1982; practitioner writing grantee Harvard U. Grad. Sch. Edn., 1981. Mem. NASW, NOW, Nat. Assn. Secondary Sch. Prins. Avocations: writing, film, theater, travel, painting. Home: 15 Shore Oaks Dr Stony Brook NY 11790-1417 Office: 211 Thompson St New York NY 10012-1365 Office Phone: 212-979-5650. E-mail: vmandr6889@aol.com.

MANDRAVELIS, PATRICIA JEAN, retired healthcare administrator; b. Hanover, N.H., May 7, 1938; d. William J. and Ruth E. (Darling) Bartis; m. Anthony M. Mandravelis, Nov. 8, 1959; children: Michael A., Tracy J. Diploma in nursing, Nashua (N.H.) Meml. Hosp. Sch. Nursing; BS in Psychology, Sociology, New Eng. Coll.; MBA, So. N.H. Coll., 1989. Cert. nursing adminstr., advanced nursing adminstr. Staff nurse Nashua Meml. Hosp. (name now So. N.H. Regional Med. Ctr.), 1959-60, obstet. nurse, 1962-65, charge nurse, 1969-71, supr., 1971-76, assoc. dir. nursing, 1976-81, dir. nursing, 1981-83, asst. exec. dir. nursing, 1983-87, v.p. nursing, 1987-91; v.p. ops., chief operating officer Nashua Meml. Hosp., 1991-95; v.p. cmty. health and wellness S. N.H. Regional Med. Ctr., Nashua, 1995—2000. Mem. healthcare transition fund State of NH, 1996—2002, Nashua Bd. for Continuum Care, 1997—2000. Contbr. articles to profl. jours. V.p. Nashua chpt. ARC, 1985—87; mem. citizens adv. bd. W.R. Grace, 1989—95; mem. Bd. Neighborhood Health Ctr. Greater Nashua, 1996—2000, pres., 2000; mem. allocations com. United Way Greater Nashua, 1997—; mem. Bridges, 1996—, bd. pres., 2000—02; loaned exec. United Way of Greater Nashua, 1996—; bd. dirs. deNicola Women's Ctr., Nashua, NH, 1987—95, Nashua Vis. Nurse Program, 1986—88, Home Health Hosp., 1988—94, chmn. bd., 1991—93, vice chmn. bd., 1993—94. Mem. Am. Coll. Healthcare Execs., Nat. League of Nursing, Am. Nurses Assn., Am. Orgn. Nurse Execs., N.H. Assn. Pub. Health, N.H. Nurses Assn., N.H. Orgn. Nurse Execs., Sigma Theta Tau. Avocation: antiques.

MANDRELL, BARBARA ANN, singer, entertainer, actress, producer, writer; b. Houston, Dec. 25, 1948; d. Irby Matthew and Mary Ellen (McGill) M.; m. Kenneth Lee Dudney, May 28, 1967; children: Kenneth Matthew, Jaime Nicole, Nathaniel. Grad. high sch. Country music singer and entertainer, 1959—, performed throughout U.S. and in various fgn. countries; mem., Grand Ole Opry, Nashville, 1972— ; star TV series Barbara Mandrell and the Mandrell Sisters, 1980-82, Barbara Mandrell: Get to the Heart, 1987; albums include Midnight Oil, Treat Him Right, He Set My Life To Music (Grammy award, Dove award 1983), This Time I Almost Made It, This is Barbara Mandrell, Midnight Angel, Barbara Mandrell's Greatest Hits, Christmas at Our House, 1987, Morning Sun, 1990, Greatest Country Hits, 1990, Standing Room Only, 1993; star TV series Barbara Mandrell and the Mandrell Sisters, 1980-82, TV movie Burning Rage, 1984, TV specials Barbara Mandrell, Something Special, 1985, The Lady is A Champ, (TV) The Wrong Girl, 1999, Stolen from the Heart, 2000; guest star TV series The Commish, Touched By an Angel, Dr. Quinn, Medicine Woman, Baywatch, Diagnosis Murder, (TV series) Sunset Beach, 1997-98, Touched By an Angel, 1994, Love Boat: The Next Wave, 1998, others; author (with George Vecsey): Get To the Heart: My Story, 1990; co-exec. (TV) Get to the Heart: The Barbara Mandrell Story, 1997; discs include No Nonsense, 1990, Key's in the Mailbox, 1991, The Best of Barbara Mandrell, 1992, The Ultimate Barbara Mandrell, 1994, The Barbara Mandrell Collection, 1995, Fooled By a Feeling, 1995. Named Miss Oceanside, Calif., 1965; Named Most Promising Female Singer, Acad. Country and Western Music, 1971; Female Vocalist of Yr., 1978; Female Vocalist of Yr., Music City News Cover Awards, 1979; Female Vocalist of Yr., Country Music Assn., 1979, 81, Entertainer of Yr., 1980, 81, 95; People's Choice awards (9), 1983-87. Mem. Musicians Union, Screen Actors Guild, AFTRA, Country Music Assn. (v.p.) Mem. Order Eastern Star. Home: PO Box 620 Hendersonville TN 37077-0620 Office: Creative Artists Agy 3310 W End Ave Fl 5 Nashville TN 37203-1028

MANDRELL, MARION D. psychology educator; b. Piedmont, S.C., July 6, 1929; d. Haynie Marion and Varnell Osteen Dowis; m. Nelson Eugene Mandrell, Aug. 16, 1952; children: Nelson Eugene Mandrell, Jr., Jeanne Caroline. BA, Carson Newman Coll., 1950; MA, So. Bapt. Theol. Sem., 1952; MEd, Clemson U., 1977. Social worker Louisville and Jefferson County Children's Agy., Louisville, 1952—53; pastor's wife First Bapt. Ch., Walhalla, SC, 1954—64; prof. Anderson (S.C.) Coll., 1965—91, prof. emeritus, 1991—. Recipient Annie Dove Denmark award, Anderson Coll. Alumni Assn., 2000. Mem.: AAUW (v.p.), Mental Health Assn. (bd. mem., sec., state del.). Democrat. Baptist. Avocations: travel, volunteering. Home: 905 Pine Cone Trail Anderson SC 29621

MANDRY, CHRISTINE M. public adminstator; b. Waukegan, Ill., June 16, 1964; d. James and Linda (Lambert) LaPonsie; m. Dennis Robert Mandry; children: Sherri Ann, Casey Lynn, Nicole, Rebekah. BS, Auburn U., 2000; MPA, Auburn U., Montgomery, 2003. Cert.: (legal asst.); victim svcs. officer. Records tech. Adminstrv. Office of Cts., Montgomery, Ala.; restitution coord. Dist. Attorney's Office, Montgomery, 2000—. Softball coach Millbrook Girls Softball League; vol. VOCAL (Victims of Crime and Leniency). Mem.: Nat. Orgn. Victim Assistance, Am. Soc. for Pub. Adminstrs. Home: 40 Green Ct Deatsville AL 36022 Office: Dist Atty's Office 100 South Lawrence St Montgomery AL 36102 Office Phone: 334-832-2545. Business E-Mail: christinemandry@mc-ala.org. E-mail: cmandry@justice.com.

MANEKER, DEANNA MARIE, advertising executive; b. Albany, N.Y., Dec. 13, 1938; d. Marion K. and Florence R. (Krell) Colle; m. Morton Maneker, Sept. 15, 1957 (div. Feb., 1981); children: Meryl C., Amy J., Marion Kenneth. AB, Barnard Coll., 1960. Dir. circulation Westchester Mag., Mamaroneck, N.Y., 1971-73; pub. Change Mag., New Rochelle, N.Y., 1973-78; gen. mgr. Ctr. for Direct Mktg., Westport, Conn., 1978-81, sr. v.p. The Stenrich Group, Glen Allen, Va., 1981-88, exec. v.p., 1988-94; COO Martin Direct (formerly The Stenrich Group), Glen Allen, Va., 1994-96, exec. v.p. database, fulfillment, call ctr. svcs., 1995-97; exec. v.p. Relationship Group The Martin Agy., Richmond, Va., 1997—. Home: 206 Tamarack Rd Richmond VA 23229-7039 Office: The Martin Agency One Shockoe Plz Richmond VA 23219-4132

MANEKER, ROBERTA S(UE), public relations executive; b. N.Y.C., July 9, 1937; d. Maxwell Roy and Esther (Gerson) Scheff; m. Hannan Wexler, June 4, 1961 (div. 1983); children: Daniel, Joanna; m. Morton M. Maneker, June 1, 1985. BA, Oberlin Coll., 1957. Mng. editor True Love mag., N.Y.C., 1960-62; publicity dir. Capt. Kangaroo, CBS, N.Y.C., 1962-66; syndicated columnist Oleg Cassini, N.Y.C., 1967-69; freelance writer, N.Y.C., 1967-70; dir. pub. rels. Direct Mktg. Assn., N.Y.C., 1983-85, v.p. pub. rels., 1985-87; v.p. pub. rels. Christie's, N.Y.C., 1987-91, sr. v.p. corp. comm./mktg., 1991—. dir. Lechters, Inc. Ford Found. scholar, 1953-57. Mem. Oberlin Coll. Alumni Assn. (pres. 1989-91), Phi Beta Kappa. Home: 30 E 65th St New York NY 10021-7013 Office: Christie's 20 Rockefeller Plz New York NY 10020-1902

MANELLA, NORA M. federal judge; BA in Italian with highest honors, Wellesley Coll., 1972; JD, U. So. Calif., 1975. Bar: Calif. 1976, U.S. Ct. Appeals (5th cir.) 1976, D.C. Ct. Appeals 1978, U.S. Dist. Ct. (ctrl., so., no. and ea. dists.) 1980-81, U.S. Ct. Appeals (9th cir.) 1982. Law clk. to Hon. John Minor Wisdom U.S. Ct. Appeals (5th cir.), New Orleans, 1975-76; legal counsel Subcom. on Constn., Senate Com. on Judiciary, Washington, 1976-78; assoc. O'Melveny & Myers, Washington and L.A., 1978-82; asst. to U.S. Atty. U.S. Dept. Justice, L.A., 1982-90, trial asst. major crimes, 1982-85, dep. chief, criminal complaints, 1986-87, chief criminal appeals, 1988-90; judge L.A. Mcpl. Ct., 1990-92; justice pro tem Calif. Ct. Appeals (2nd dist.), 1992; judge L.A. Superior Ct., 1992-93; U.S. atty. (ctrl. dist.) Calif. U.S. Dept. Justice, L.A., 1994-98; judge U.S. Dist. Ct. (ctrl. dist.) Calif., L.A., 1998—. Instr. U.S. Atty. Gen. Advocacy Inst., 1984-86, Calif. Jud. Coll., 1992-93; mem. Atty. Gen.'s Adv. Com., 1994-95. Mem. editl. bd. State Bar Criminal Law Newsletter, 1991-92. Mem. adv. bd. Monroe H.S. and Govt. Magnet, 1991-94; acad. specialist USAID Delegation, 1993; judge L.A. Times Cmty. Partnership Awards, 1993; bd. councilors Law Sch. U. So. Calif., 1996—. Mem. Am. Law Inst., Calif. Judges Assn., Nat. Assn. Women Judges, Calif. Women Lawyers, Women Lawyers of L.A., Order of the Coif. Office: US Dist Ct 312 N Spring St Los Angeles CA 90012-4701 E-mail: Arlene_Chavez@cacd.uscourts.gov.

MANER, DIANA, financial consultant; b. Brooklyn, N.Y., Aug. 3, 1961; BS, Va. Union U. Rsch. asst. Dean Witter Reynolds, N.Y.; fin. analyst Primerica Fin. Svcs., Atlanta; fin. counselor CitiStreet Retirement Svcs., Atlanta. Adv. bd. Acad. of Fin., Clayton Co., Ga. Mem.: World Changers Ch. Internat.

MANESS, ELEANOR PALMER, research analyst; b. Raleigh, N.C., June 24, 1935; d. Oren Alston and Lillian Way Palmer; m. Charles B. Maness, Feb. 1, 1955 (dec. July 1989); children: Reid, Brian, Teresa. BA, Meredith Coll., 1958. Tchr. St. Timoth Sch., Raleigh, 1958—64; rsch. analyst N.C. State U., Raleigh, 1966—99; cons., 1999—. Contbr. articles to sci. jours. Recipient L.M. Ware Rsch. award, Am. Soc. for Hort. Sci., 1974, Excellence in Environment Rsch. award, Fed. Hwy. Adminstrn., 1997. Presbyterian. Avocations: hiking, swimming, gardening, rock hunting, fishing. Home: 2104 Gray Walsh Dr Wilmington NC 28405

MANEY, CHERYL LITTLE, art educator, arts facilitator; b. Monroe, N.C., May 28, 1965; d. Thomas Ward and Frances Parker Little; m. Johnny M Maney, Apr. 1, 2000; children: Christopher, Megan. BA Creative, U. of NC, Charlotte, NC, 1983—89. Cert. NC K-12 Visual Arts Tchg. NC, 1989, Early and Mid. Childhood Art Nat. Bd. for Profl. Tchg. Standards, 2002. Visual arts tchr. NC, Charlotte-Mecklenburg Schools, Charlotte, NC, 1989—; arts tchr. Betty Stoval Spectrum of the Arts Program, Charlotte, NC, 1995—99, lead tchr., 2000—; arts facilitator Charlotte-Mecklenburg Schools, Charlotte, NC, 2002—; school-based dir. Blumenthal Performing Arts Center's Edn. Inst., Charlotte, NC, 2002—; tchr. mentor Charlotte-Mecklenburg Schools, Charlotte, NC, 2002—. Tchr. adv. coun. Mint Mus. of Craft and Design, Charlotte, NC, 1999; mentor to new charlotte-mecklenburg visual arts teachers Charlotte-Mecklenburg Schools, Charlotte, NC, 2000—; assessment devel. com. Opera Carolina: Music! Words! Opera!, Charlotte, NC, 2001—; tchr. adv. coun. Penland Exhbn., Mint Mus. of Craft and Design, Charlotte, NC, 2003—. Co-editor: (curriculum guide) Curriculum and Alignment Guide for Charlotte-Mecklenburg Schools; bookmaking artist/instructor (workshop) NC Art Educators State Conf. Named N.C. Art Educator of Yr., 2003; recipient Scholar, World Affairs Coun., 2001; grantee, Charlotte World Affairs Coun., 2002, NC Parent Tchr. Assn., 2002. Mem.: Nat. Art Educators Assn. Avocations: photography, bookmaking, outdoors person. Office: Charlotte-Mecklenburg Schools 2400 Hildebrand Street Charlotte NC 28216 Personal E-mail: jcmaney@msn.com.

MANEY, LOIS JEAN, postmaster; b. Marion, N.C., May 1, 1945; d. Frank Shannon and Virginia Mae (Helton) M.; m. Arthur Edison Walker, Sept. 21, 1963 (div. June 1982); 1 child, Linda Jean Walker; m. Anthony Joseph Paterno, July 7, 1984 (div. Apr. 1988). Grad. h.s., Nebo, N.C. Lace trimmer Shadowline Inc., Morganton, N.C., 1965-77; distbn. window clk. U.S. Postal Svc., Glen Alpine, N.C., 1977-79, Morganton, N.C., 1979-88, supr. mails and delivery, 1988-90, supt. postal ops., 1990-93, postmaster, 1993—2002, Jefferson, NC, 2002—. Postal co-chair Western Piedmont Postal Customer Coun., Western N.C., 1996—. Pres. Burke County Stamp Club, Morganton, 1996. Mem.: Burke County C. of C., Quaker Meadows Golf Club. Avocations: golf, scuba diving, exercise-walking. Office: US Postal Svc 410 E Main Street Jefferson NC 28640

MANGAHAS, CRYSTAL TECCA, market researcher; b. Houston, Aug. 19, 1971; d. Robert Lee Sr. and Georgia Nell (Aiken) Tecca; m. Jeff Lizan Mangahas, May 28, 1994. BA in Bus. Adminstrn., U. Wash., 1993; MBA, NYU, 2000. Asst. dir. new student programs U. Wash., Seattle, 1993-95; project coord. PERQ/HCI (formerly Healthcare Comms. Inc.), Princeton, NJ, 1995—2000; mgr. Kurt Salmon Assocs., San Bruno, Calif., 2000—. Active Literacy Vols. of Am. Office: KSA 950 Elm Ave Ste 300 San Bruno CA 94066 Home: 71 Raymond Heights Petaluma CA 94952

MANGAN, MONA, association executive, lawyer; b. Pittston, Pa., Dec. 29, 1945; d. Joseph H. and Mona C. Mangan; m. Roy N. Watanabe, Oct. 24, 1987 (div. 1999); 1 child, Julia. BA, Lock Haven U., 1966; AM, Duke U., 1969; JD, Columbia U., 1975. Bar: N.Y. 1976, U.S. Dist. Ct. (ea. and so. dists.) N.Y. 1979. Mem. congrl. staff Sen. Wayne Morse of Oreg., 1967-68; staff atty. U.S. Dept. Labor, N.Y.C., 1975-79; trial atty. EEOC, N.Y.C., 1979; asst. exec. dir. Writers Guild Am. East Inc., N.Y.C., 1979-84, assoc. exec. dir., 1984, exec. dir., 1984—. Recipient Gross award for contbn. to journalism Lock Haven U., 1984. Mem.: AFL-CIO (v.p., v.p. dept. for profl. employees), ABA, N.Y. NATAS (treas. 2000—), NATAS (bd. govs. 2001—), Internat. Affiliation Writers Guilds (treas.), Unions for Performing Arts (treas.), Pan Am. Fedn. Arts, Mass Media and Entertainment Unions (v.p. 1993—), Coalition on Motion Picture and TV Unions (v.p.), Assn. Bar City of N.Y., Nat. Policy Assn., Columbia U. Law Sch. Alumni Assn. Office: Writers Guild Am East Inc 555 W 57th St New York NY 10019-2925

MANGAN, PATRICIA ANN PRITCHETT, statistician; b. Hammond, Ind., Feb. 4, 1953; d. Edward Clayton and Helen Josephine (Mills) Pritchett; m. William Paul Mangan, Aug. 30, 1980; 1 child, Ryan Christopher. BS in Maths. and Stats., Purdue U., 1975, MS in Applied Stats., 1977. Tobacco devel. statistician R.J. Reynolds Tobacco Co., Winston-Salem, N.C., 1978-82, R&D statistician, 1982-86, sr. R&D statistician, 1986-90, sr. staff R&D statistician, 1990-93; dir. software devel. ARJAY Equipment Corp., Winston-Salem, N.C., 1993-96; sr. staff scientist R.J. Reynolds Tobacco Co., Winston-Salem, 1996-99; statis. analyst N.C. Bapt. Hosp., Winston-Salem, 1999-2000; staff specialist N.C. Baptist Hosp., 2000—. Cons. Lab. for Application of Remote Sensing, West Lafayette, Ind., 1976-77; statis. engr. Corning Glass Works, Harrodsburg, Ky., 1977. Editor Jour. of Sensory Studies, 1992-95; contbr. articles to sci. jours. Rep. United Way, Winston-Salem, 1985. Recipient G.R. DiMarco award, 1990, 96, Excaliber award for Outstanding Performance, 1991, 93. Mem. Am. Statis. Assn., Wash. Statis. Assn., Purdue Alumni Assn. E-mail: pmangan@wfubmc.edu.

MANGIPANO, ADELE C. librarian, educator; b. New Orleans, Aug. 3, 1947; d. Santo Anthony and Adele Simmons Mangipano; 1 child, Benjamin Santo Shane. BA, U. New Orleans, 1969, MEd, 1978; MLS, La. State U., 1991. Cert. sch. libr. cert. La. Tchr. St. Bernard Parish Schs., Chalmette, La., 1969—71, Jefferson Parish Schs., Metairie, La., 1971—77, libr., 1978—94, Tuscaloosa (Ala.) City Schs., 1994—95, Holy Cross Sch., New Orleans, 1995—. Pres. spl. com. Faxnet, New Orleans, 2001—02. Author: (newsletter) La. Sch. Librs., 1987. Mem.: Nat. Cath. Libr. Assn. (sect. head, bd. dirs. H.S. sect. 2002—05), Greater N.O. Cath. Libr. Assn. (v.p., pres. 1999—2003), Coun. for Internat. Visitors (bd. dirs. 1985—86), Toastmasters (officer, Toastmaster Entrepreneur 1998), Camellia Club of New Orleans. Democrat. Roman Catholic. Avocations: reading, gardening, dance, bicycling. Home: 3732 Lilac Ln Metairie LA 70001 Office: Holy Cross Sch 4950 Dauphine Sch New Orleans LA 70117-4318 E-mail: amangipano@yahoo.com.

MANGLONA, RAMONA V. state attorney general, judge; b. 1967; BA, U. Calif., 1990; JD, U. N.Mex., 1996. Bar: New Mex. Bar Assn. 1997, No. Mariana Islands Bar Assn. 1997. Asst. atty. gen.; atty. gen. No. Mariana Islands, Saipan, 2002—; assoc. judge Commonwealth Superior Ct., 2003—. Office Phone: 670-236-9751.

MANGO, CHRISTINA ROSE, psychiatric art therapist; b. Garden City, N.Y., May 13, 1962; d. Camillo Andrew and Dorothy Mae (Harrison) Mango; m. Keith Hurdman, Sept. 11, 1993 (div. 2001); children: Clarissa Rose Hurdman, Andrew James Hurdman. BFA summa cum laude, Coll. of New Rochelle, 1984; MA, NYU, 1987. Registered art therapist; bd. cert. structural family therapy tng.; cert. psycho-edn. multi family therapy tng.

Art therapist Bronx Mcpl. Hosp. Ctr., 1984-88; clin. supr. Fordham-Tremont Cmty. Mental Health Ctr., Bronx, 1988-98, unit dir., 1998—. Art therapy fieldworker Bronx State Hosp., 1984, art therapy intern Bronx Children's Hosp., 1985, Saint Lukes Hosp., N.Y.C., 1986. Contbr. articles to profl. jours. Mem. N.Y. Art Therapy Assn., No. N.J. Art Therapists Assn., Am. Art Therapy Assn. Home: 234 Garfield St Haworth NJ 07641-1420 E-mail: crm07641@aol.com.

MANGOLD, SYLVIA PLIMACK, artist; b. N.Y.C., Sept. 18, 1938; d. Maurice and Ethel (Rein) Plimack; m. Robert Mangold. Student, Cooper Union, 1956-59; BFA, Yale U., 1961. Exhibited one-person shows Daniel Weinberg Gallery, San Francisco, 1974, 75, Fischbach Gallery, N.Y.C., 1974, 76, Fischbach, 1974, 76, Annemarie Verna Gallery, Zurich, 1978, 91, 97, Droll-Kolbert Gallery, N.Y.C., 1978, 80, Young Hoffman Gallery, Chgo., 1980, Ohio State U., Columbus, 1980, Pa. Acad., 1981, Contemporary Arts Mus., Houston, 1981, Madison Art Ctr., (Wis.), 1982, Brooke Alexander, Inc., 1982, 83, 84, 85, 86, 89, 92, 95, Duke Art Mus., N.C., 1982, Rhona Hoffman Gallery, Chgo., 1982, 85, Tex. Gallery, 1986, Fuller Goldeen Gallery, San Francisco, 1987, U. Mich, Ann Arbor, 1992, Minn. Inst. Arts, 1992, Grunwald Ctr. for Graphic Arts, UCLA, 1992, Neuberger Mus. Art, SUNY, Purchase, 1993, Davison Art Ctr., Wesleyan U., Middletown, Conn., 1993, Albright-Knox Art Gallery, Buffalo, 1994, Wadsworth Atheneum, Hartford, Conn., 1994, Blaffer Gallery U. Houston, 1994, Mus. Fine Arts, Boston, 1994, Herbert F. Johnson Museum, 1998, Cornell U., Ithaca, N.Y., 1998, Alexander and Bonin, N.Y.C., 2000, 2003; group shows at Young Hoffman Gallery, Chgo., 1979, Walker Art Ctr., Mpls., 1979, Droll-Kolbert Gallery, 1979, Denver Art Mus., 1979, U. So. Calif., 1979, Honolulu Acad. Art, 1979, Oakland Mus., (Calif.), 1979, Univ. Art Mus. of U. Tex.-Austin, 1979, Cornell U., Ithaca, N.Y., 1979, The New Museum of Contemporary Art, N.Y.C., 1979, Nat. Museum, Belgrade, Yugoslavia, 1979, Internat. Biennial Ljibljana, Yugoslavia, Phoenix Art Mus., 1979, Art Latitute Gallery, N.Y.C., 1980, Thorpe Intermedia Gallery, Sparkhill, N.Y., 1980, U. Colo. Art Galleries, Boulder, 1980, Nina Freudenheim Gallery, Buffalo, 1980, U.S. Pavillion of Venice Biennial, 1980-81, Indianapolis Museum of Art, 1980, Civici Musei e Gallerie di Storia e Arte, Sala Ajace, Udine, Italy, 1980, Young Hoffman, Chicago, 1980-81, Delahurty, Dallas, 1980, Museum of Modern Art, 1981, Wesleyan U. Art Gallery, 1981, Davison Art Ctr., Middleton, Conn., 1981, Virginia Museum of Fine Arts, Richmond, 1981, Oakland Museum, Calif., 1981, Inst. Contemporary Art of U. Pa., Phila., 1980-81, Yale U. Art Gallery, 1981, San Antonio Mus. Art, 1981, Indpls. Mus. Art, 1981, Tucson Mus. Art, 1981, Pa. Acad., 1981, Mus. Art of Carnegie Inst., Pitts., 1981, Brooke Alexander, Inc., N.Y.C., 1982, Ben Shahn Ctr. Visual Arts, 1982, Castle Gallery, Coll. of New Rochelle, N.Y., 1983, Thomas Segal Gallery, Boston, 1982-83, Siegel Contemporary Art, N.Y., 1983, Freedman Gallery, Albright Coll., Reading, Pa., 1983, Fuller Goldeen, San Francisco, 1983, Yale U. Art Gallery, New Haven, 1983-84, 86, Wilcox Gallery, Swarthmore, Pa., 1984, The Hudson River Mus., Yonkers, N.Y., 1984, Sardonia Art Gallery, Wilkes Coll., Wilkes-Barre, Pa., 1985, Kent State U. Gallery, Ohio, 1985, Brooke Alexander, N.Y., 1985, John C. Stoller Co., Minn., 1985, Knight Gallery, Spirit Sq. Arts Ctr., Charlotte, N.C., 1986, Mus. Art, R.I. Sch. Design, Providence, 1986, Yale U. Gallery, 1986, CUNY, 1986-87, Lorence Monk Gallery, N.Y.C., Vanquard Gallery, Phila., 1986-87, Aldrich Mus., Ridgefield, 1986-87. Flander's Contemporary Art, Mpls., 1987, Annemarie Verna Galerie, Zurich, 1988, U. N.C., 1988, R.I. Sch. Design, 1988, Grace Borgenicht Gallery, N.Y.C., 1988, Fay Gold Gallery, Atlanta, 1988, U. N.C., Greensboro, Three Rivers Arts Festival, Pitts., 1989, Cin. Art Mus., New Orleans Mus. Art, Denver Art Mus., Pa. Acad. Fine Arts, 1989, U. Mich., 1992, Mpls. Inst. Arts, 1992, Grunwald Ctr. Graphic Arts, UCLA, L.A., Neuberger Mus. Art, SUNY Purchase, 1993, Davison Art Ctr., 1993, Montgomery Glasoe Fine Art, Mpls., 1993, Yale U. Art Gallery, New Haven, 1993, Daniel Weinberg Gallery, Santa Monica, Calif., 1993, Museum of Fine Arts, Boston, 1993, Barbara Mathes Gallery, N.Y.C., 1993, Nina Freudenheim Gallery, Buffalo, 1993, Kansas City Gallery of Art, U. Mo., 1994, Midtown Payson, N.Y.C., 1994, Katonah Museum of Art, N.Y., 1994, Rhona Hoffman Gallery, Chgo., 1994, Feigen Inc., Chgo., 1994, Brooke Alexander, N.Y.C., 1994, Elga Wimmer Gallery, N.Y.C., 1995, Aargauer Kunsthaus Aarau, Austria, 1995, The Am. Acad. of Arts and Letters, N.Y.C., 1995, Andre Zarre Gallery, N.Y.C., 1996, Aspen Art Museum, Colo., 1996, The Am. Acad. of Arts and Letters, N.Y.C., 1996, Anne Marie Verna Gallery, Zurich, Switzerland, 1997, Queens Museum of Art, 1997, Aspen Art Museum, 1997, U. Gallery, Fine Arts Ctr., U. Mass., Amherst James Graham & Sons, N.Y.C., 1997, The Museum of Modern Art, 1997, Seattle Art Museum, 1997, State U. N.Y., 1998, N.Y.C. Dowd Fine Arts Gallery, 1998, The Am. Acad. of Fine Arts and Letters, 1998, Karen McCready Fine Art, 1999, Alexander and Bonin, N.Y.C., 1999, Henry Art Gallery, Seattle, 2000; exhibited in permanent collections, Albright-Knox Art Gallery, Buffalo, Allen Meml. Art Mus., Oberlin, Ohio, Bklyn. Mus., Dallas Mus. Fine Arts, Detroit Inst. Art, Mus. Fine Arts, Houston, Indpls. Mus. Art, Madison (Wis.) Art Ctr., Milw. Art Mus., Yale U. Art Gallery, Mus. Modern Art, N.Y.C., Mus. Fine Arts, U. Utah, Tampa (Fla.) Mus., Walker Art Mus., Mpls., Whitney Mus. Am. Art, N.Y., Weatherspoon Art Gallery, Greensboro, N.C., Wadsworth Athenaeum, Hartford, U. Mich., Utah Mus. Fine Art, Museum of Fine Arts, Boston, N.Y.C. Public Library, Smith Coll. Museum, Northampton, Mass., Achenbach Found. for Graphic Arts, San Francisco, St. Louis Art Museum, The Tampa Museum. Achievements include work reviewed in newspapers and mags.

MANHART, MARCIA Y(OCKEY), art museum director; b. Wichita, Kans., Jan. 14, 1943; d. Everett W. and Ruth C. (Correll) Yockey; children: Caroline Manhart Sanderson, Emily Alexandrea Morrison. BA in Art, U. Tulsa, 1965, MA in Ceramics, 1971. Dir. edn. Philbrook Art Ctr., Tulsa, 1972-77, exec. v.p., asst. dir., 1977-83, acting dir., 1983-84; exec. dir. Philbrook Mus. Art (formerly Philbrook Art Ctr.), Tulsa, 1984—. Instr. Philbrook Art Ctr. Mus. Sch., Tulsa, 1963-72; gallery dir. Alexandre Hogue Gallery, Tulsa U., 1967-69; NEH Challenge Grant panelist, 1991, presenter to AAM Conv., 1991; MAAA Craft Fellowship panelist, 1988, 93, NEA Craft Fellowship panelist, 1990; NEA spl. exhbn. panelist, 1996; curator nat. touring exhibit Nature's Forms/Nature's Forces: The Art of Alexandre Hogue, 1984-85; co-curator internat. exhbn.: The Eloquent Object, 1987-90; curator Sanford and Diane Besser Collection exhbn., 1992. Author essays in field. Vis. com. Smithsonian Instn./Renwick Gallery, Washington, 1986; cultural negotiator Gov. George Nigh's World Trade Mission (Okla.), China., 1985; com. mem. State Art Coll. of Okla., 1985—; mem. Assocs. of Hillcrest Med. Ctr., 1983-88, exec. com., 1985-88; com. mem. Neighborhood Housing Services, 1985-87; mem. City of Tulsa Arts Commn., 1996—; steering com. Harwelden Isnt. for Aesthetic Edn., 1983; com. mem. River Parks Authority, 1976; mem. Jr. League of Tulsa Inc., 1974-78; adv. panel mem. Nat. Craft Planning Project, NEA, Washington, 1978-81; craft adv. panel mem. Okla. Arts and Humanities Council, 1974-76; juror numerous art festivals, competitions, programs; reviewer Inst. Mus. Services, Washington, 1985, 88, 92, 95, 98; auditor Symposium on Language & Scholarship of Modern Crafts, NEA and NEH, Washington, 1981; nominator MacArthur Fellows Program, 1988; panelist Lila Wallace Reader's Digest Internat. Artists Fellowship, 1992, panelist Pew Charitable Trust, 1996. Recipient Harwelden award for Individual Contbrn. in the Arts, 1989, Gov.'s award State of Okla., 1992. Mem. Assn. Am. Mus., Assn. Art Mus. Dirs., Art Mus. Assn. Am., Mountain Plains Assn. Mus., Am. Craft Coun., Okla. Mus. Assn., Tulsa Met. C. of C. (bd. dirs. 1997-99), Rotary, Phi Beta Kappa. Office: Philbrook Mus Art PO Box 52510 Tulsa OK 74152-0510 E-mail: mmanhart@philbrook.org.

MANHART, SHAWNA HOPE, music educator; b. L'anse, Mich., Oct. 7, 1972; d. Darlene Jill Swanson-Reno; m. Matt Paul Manhart, June 15, 1996. MusB, No. Mich. U., 1990—96; MusM, Wayne State U., 1999—2001. Professional Education Dept. of Edn./ State of Mich., 2002. Elem. music specialist Port Huron Area Sch. Dist., Mich., 1997—98; pvt. lesson instr. Self-employment, Port Huron, Mich., 1998—; dir. of bands Chippewa Mid. Sch., Port Huron, Mich., 1998—. Co-drum maj. NMU Marching Band, Marquette, Mich., 1992; musician for pit orchestras Various cmty. theaters, Port Huron, St. Clair, Mich., 1995—; horn player St. Clair County C.C. Band, Port Huron, Mich., 2000—01. Assn. rep. Port Huron Edn. Assn., Mich., 2003—. Mem.: Mich. Edn. Assn., Port Huron Edn. Assn., Women's Band Dir. Assn., Mich. State Band and Orch. Associaton, Chippewa Mid. Sch. P.T.S.A., The Nat. Assn. for Music Edn. Avocations: aerobics, reading, exercise, kickboxing, movies.

MANHEIM, CAMRYN, television and film actress; b. N.J., Mar. 8, 1961; BFA, UC Santa Cruz, 1984; MFA, NYU, 1987. Star (TV series) The Practice, 1997—, appeared in (TV films) Jackie's Back!, 1999, The Loretta Claiborne Story, 2000, (TV miniseries) The 10th Kingdom, 2000; actor: (films) Bonfire of the Vanities, 1990, The Road to Wellville, 1994, Jeffrey, 1995, Eraser, 1996, Romy and Michele's High School Reunion, 1997, David Searching, 1998, Wide Awake, 1998, Mercury Rising, 1998, Happiness, 1998 (Nat. Bd. Rev. award, 1998), Fool's Gold, 1998, Joe the King, 1999, What Planet are You From?, 2000; prodr., performer Kiss My Act, 2000; actor: (films) East of A, 2000, The Laramie Project, 2002, Just Like Mona, 2003; appeared on TV shows Law and Order, Touched By an Angel, New York Undercover, Ally McBeal, Oh Baby, Chicago Hope, Will and Grace, star (one-woman show) Wake Up, I'm Fat, 1995, theater appearances include N.Y. Shakespeare Festival, Lincoln Ctr., Yale Repertory, N.Y. Theatre Workshop, Classic Stage Co., Home for Contemporary Theater. Recipient Obie award, 1995, Emmy award as best supporting actress, 1998, Golden Globe award, 1999, Quality TV for Viewers award, 1999. Office: Creative Artists Agy 9830 Wilshire Blvd Beverly Hills CA 90212*

MANION, KAY DAUREEN, newspaper executive; b. St. Francis, Kans., Feb. 7, 1943; d. Edward William and Martha Dankenbring; children: Todd, Jon, Bandel. AS in Mktg. and Art, Western Nebr. C.C., 1990; postgrad., Colby (Kans.) C.C., 1992-95, Ft. Hays (Kans.) State Coll., 1997—. Various banking positions, Kans. and Nebr., 1960-73; mgr. Alliance (Nebr.) Area C. of C., 1974-79; bridal cons., dept. mgr. Hatch Drug, Alliance, 1980-85; bridal cons. Herbergers, Scotts Bluff, 1986-88; salesperson, script writer Sta. KIMB, Kimball, 1989-90; med. records analyst Dunn Med. Equipment and Svcs., Inc., Colby, 1990-93; graphic designer Quad County Star, Oakley, Kans., 1993-95; news asst., advt. sales rep. Sherman County Star, Goodland, Kans., 1995-97; fin. and office mgr. Steinke Farm Svcs., Holdredge, Nebr., 2000—. Freelance creative designer, 1988—; dir. tng. H.S. Distributive Edn. Clubs Am., Alliance, 1980-85, CETA, Alliance, 1976-79; advt. mgr. Russell Daily News, Russell Record, 1997—. Bd. dirs., sec. Alliance Cmty. Improvement Com., Alliance, 1974-79; mem. Oakley Tourism Com., 1994-96. Named Businesswoman of Yr. Alliance Area C. of C., 1978, One of the Oustanding Young Women in Am., 1976, 78; recipient Disting. Svc. award Jaycees, Alliance, 1979. Mem. Am. Legion Aux., Eagles Ladies' Aux., Phi Theta Kappa. Republican. Methodist. Avocations: art, drawing, photography, nature, music. Home: P O Box 193 Logan KS 67646-0193

MANION, KELLEY MICHELLE, surgical technician; b. Farmington, Mo., June 4, 1971; d. John Herbert and Karen Ruth Jones; m. Deron Carl Manion, June 22, 1991 (div. Oct. 1995); 1 child, Kylee Danielle. AA, Mineral Area Coll., Park Hills, Mo., 1993; Diploma/Operating Room Tech., Mineral Area Regional Med. Ctr., Farmington, Mo., 1996. Cert. surg. technician 1996. Surg. technician Parkland Health Ctr., Farmington, Mo., 1996—2003, The Surgery Ctr. of Farmington, 2003; treas. JK Svcs./EGifts 4All, Farmington, Mo., 2000—.

MANIS, LAURA GLANCE, retired psychology educator; b. Chgo., May 25, 1924; d. Nathan Glance and Minnie Walters; m. Jerome G. Manis, May 31, 1949; children: Robert, Lisa Neela. BEd, Chgo. State U., 1945; MA, Western Mich. U., 1965. Elem. sch. tchr. City Chgo., 1945-47; aptitude, personality assessor Johnson O'Conner Human Engring. Co., Chgo., 1947-49; pers. dir. Dr.'s Hosp., N.Y.C., 1949-52; counselor Climax (Mich.) H.S., 1965-66; psychol. counseling assoc. prof. Western Mich. U., Kalamazoo, 1966-83, assoc. prof. emerita, 1983—. Co-founder, dir. Women's Ctr., Western Mich. U., 1975-83, developer of women's studies, chair, 1979-73. Author: (manual) Woman Power, 1977, Assertion Training, 1983, revised edit., 1998, Training for Alzheimer's Group Leaders, 1984, Finding Your Voice, With Lisa N. Manis, 2001; contbr. articles to profl. jours. Pres. League Women Voters, Kalamazoo, 1964-66; v.p. ACLU, Kalamazoo, 1978-82; chair Hawaii State Legis. Co. AARP, Honolulu, 1994-95; pres. bd. dirs. Alzheimer's Assn. Hawaii, Honolulu, 1988-90; apptd. to State Health Planning Commn., Honolulu, 1995—2001; bd. mem. Planned Parenthood, 1978-82; chair Coalition for Affordable Long Term Care, Honolulu, 1998-2004. Recipient Women Pioneer award Mich. Women Lawyer's Assn., Detroit, 1978, Women of Yr. award Commn. on Status of Women, Kalamazoo, 1980, Outstanding Sr. Vol. award Gov. First Lady Awards, Honolulu, 1993, Outstanding Alumna of Yr. Western Mich. U., 1995, Honoree Hawaii State Legislature, 2003. Mem. Hawaiian Women in Sci. (bd. dirs. 1982-97), AARP (state legis. com. chair 1995), Honolulu Acad. Art. Avocations: swimming, snorkeling, watercolors, traveling, reading.

MANKILLER, WILMA PEARL, tribal leader, retired; b. Stilwell, Okla., Nov. 18, 1945; d. Charley and Clara Irene (Sitton) M.; m. Hector N. Olaya, Nov. 13, 1963 (div. 1975); children: Felicia Marie Olaya, Gina Irene Olaya; m. Charlie Soap, Oct. 13, 1986. Student, Skyline Coll., San Bruno Coll., 1973, San Francisco State Coll., 1973-75; BA in Social Sci., Union Coll., 1977; postgrad., U. Ark., 1979; DHL (hon.), U. New Eng., 1986; PhD in Pub. Svc. (hon.), R.I. Coll., 1989; DHL (hon.), Yale U., 1990; PhD (hon.), Dartmouth Coll., 1991; LLD (hon.), Mills Coll., 1992. Cmty. devel. dir. Cherokee Nation, Tahlequah, Okla., 1977-83, dep. chief, 1983-85, prin. chief, 1985-95; Montgomery fellow Darmouth Coll., 1996. Author: Mankiller: A Chief and Her People, 1993; co-editor: The Readers Companion to the History of Women in the U.S., 1998. Recipient Donna Nigh First Lady award Okla. Commn. for Status of Women, 1985, Am. Leadership award Harvard U., 1986, Elizabeth Blackwell award, 1996, Dorothy Height Lifetime Achievement award, 1997, Presdl. Medal of Freedom, 1998; inducted Okla. Women's Hall of Fame, 1986. Avocations: reading, writing. Home: PO Box 308 Park Hill OK 74451-0308

MANLEY, AUDREY FORBES, retired academic administrator, pediatrician, military officer; b. Jackson, Miss., Mar. 25, 1934; d. Jesse Lee and Ora Lee (Buckhalter) Forbes; m. Albert Edward Manley, Apr. 3, 1970. AB with honors (tuition scholar), Spelman Coll., Atlanta, 1955; MD (Jesse Smith Noyes Found. scholar), Meharry Med. Coll., 1959; MPH, Johns Hopkins U.-USPHS traineeship, 1987; LHD (hon.), Tougaloo (Miss.) Coll., 1990, Meharry Med. Coll., Nashville, 1991; LLD (hon.), Spelman Coll., 1991, Tskegee U., 1998; DSc (hon.), Coll. New Rochelle, 1998, Morehouse Coll., 2002, U. Del., 2002. Diplomate: Am. Bd. Pediatrics. Intern St. Mary Mercy Hosp., Gary, Ind., 1960; from jr. to chief resident in pediatrics Cook County Children's Hosp., Chgo., 1960—62; NIH fellow neonatology U. Ill. Rsch. and Ednl. Hosp., Chgo., 1963—65; staff pediatrician Chgo. Bd. Health, 1963—66; practice medicine specializing in pediatrics Chgo., 1963—66; assoc. Lawndale Neighborhood Health Ctr. North, 1966—67; asst. med. dir., 1967—69; asst. prof. Chgo. Med. Coll., 1966—67; instr. Pritzker Sch. Medicine, U. Chgo., 1967—69; asst. dir. ambulatory pediatrics, asst. dir. pediatrics Mt. Zion Hosp. and Med. Center, San Francisco, 1969—70; med. cons. Spelman Coll., 1970—71, med. dir. family planning program, chmn. health careers adv. com., 1972—76; med. dir. Grady Meml. Hosp. Family Planning Clinic, 1972—76; with Health Services Adminstrn., Dept. Health and Human Services, 1976—97; commd. officer, advanced though grades to rear adm. USPHS, 1976—97; chief genetic diseases services br. Office Maternal and Child Health, Bur. Community Health Services, Rockville, Md., 1976—81; acting assoc. adminstr. clin. affairs Office of Adminstr. Health Resources and Services Adminstrn., 1981—83, chief med. officer, dep. assoc. adminstr. planning, evaluation and legis., 1983—85; sabbatical leave USPHS Johns Hopkins Sch. Hygiene and Pub. Health, 1986—87; dir. Nat. Health Service Corps.; asst. surgeon gen., 1988; dep. asst. Sec. for Health USPHS/HHS, 1989—93, acting asst. Sec. Health, 1993, dep. asst. Sec. Health/intergovtl. affairs, 1993—94; dep. surgeon gen., acting dep. asst. sec. for minority health USPHS, 1994—95, acting surgeon gen., 1995—97; pres. Spelman Coll., 1997—2002, pres. emerita, 2003—. Mem. U.S. del. UNICEF, 1990-94, Am. Acad. Family Physicians (pub. adv. bd.), Am. Coun. Learned Socs., Am. Med. Assn. Minority Affairs Consortium (sr. advisor), Ctrs. for Disease Control Found. (bd. visitors), Morehouse Sch. Medicine (clin. Prof. Pediats., Pub. Health Lectr.), Rollins Sch. Pub. Health Emory U (Commrs., Adv. Coun., Ga. Leadership Commn. Organ, Tissue, Blood Marrow donation amont African Ams. Author numerous articles, reports in field. Trustee Spelman Coll., 1966-70; The Coll. Fund(UNCF (com. Archives, Hist. Govtl. Affairs Com.), Coun. Fgn. Rels., bd. dirs. coun. Ind. Colls.; bd. dirs. March of Dimes, 1998, Nat. Merit Scholarship Corp., Nat. Minority Mil. Mus. Found. Edl. Adv. Coun., Am. Cancer Soc. Found., CDC Found., Compas Compact, Downtown Atlanta Chpt. Rotary, Atlanta 2000 Adv. Com., adv. bd. Atlanta Regional Health Summit, Commerce Club, Ga. Found. Ind., Food and Drug Adv. Com. Rear adm. USPHS, ret. USPHS. Recipient Meritorious Svc. award USPHS, 1981, Mary McLeod Bethune award Nat Coun. Negro Women, 1979, Dr. John P. McGovern Ann. Lectureship award Am. Sch. Health Assn., Disting. Alumni award Meharry Med. Coll., 1989, Spelman Coll. 108 Founder's Day Convocation, 1989, Disting. Svc. medal USPHS, 1992, Hildrus A. Poindexter award OSG/PHS, 1993, numerous other svc. and achievement awards. Fellow Am. Acad. Pediatrics; mem. Nat. Inst. Medicine of Nat. Acad. Sci., Nat. Med. Assn., APHA, AAUW, AAAS, Spelman Coll. Alumnae Assn., Meharry Alumni Assn., Operation Crossroads Africa Alumni Assn., Atlanta C. of C., Rotary, Delta Sigma Theta (hon.), Phi Beta Kappa. Address: 2807 18th St NW Washington DC 20009

MANLEY, CATHEY NERACKER, interior design executive; b. Rochester, N.Y., Feb. 10, 1951; d. Albert John and Eleanor (Roberts) Neracker; m. Keith Howard Manley, Dec. 2, 1972 (div. Sept. 1977). AS, Endicott Jr. Coll., Beverly, Mass., 1971. Interior designer Bayles Furniture Co., Rochester, 1971-78, dir. mktg. and design, 1978-81; pres. Fabric PRO-TECTION Rochester, 1982—; bus. cons. Susanne Wiener & Assocs., Stamford, Conn., 1981—; owner Cathey Manley Assocs., Rochester and Clearwater, Fla., 1981—. Cons. Womens' Career Ctr., Rochester, 1976—. Contbr. to book: What Do You Say To A Naked Room, 1981; designer TV show Great American Home; writer, hostess video How to Sell Accessories. Mem. bldg. com. Rochester Health Assn., 1978-83; dir. Family Service of Rochester at Greece (N.Y.), 1973-76, Town of Greece Youth Bd., 1973-77; founder "The Point", Greece, 1971. Fellow Interior Design Soc. (pres. Rochester chpt. 1977-78, nat. bd. dirs. 1977—, nat. pres. at Chgo. 1983-85). Home: 1154 Edgemere Dr Rochester NY 14612-1506

MANLEY, JOAN A(DELE) DANIELS, retired publishing executive; b. San Luis Obispo, Calif., Sept. 23, 1932; d. Carl and Della (Weinmann) Daniels; m. Jeremy C. Lanning, Mar. 17, 1956 (div. Sept. 1963); m. Donald H. Manley, Sept. 12, 1964 (div. 1985); m. William G. Houlton, May 31, 1991. BA, U. Calif., Berkeley, 1954; DBA (hon.), U. New Haven, 1974; LLD (hon.), Babson Coll., 1978. Sec. Doubleday & Co., Inc., N.Y.C., 1954-60; sales exec. Time Inc., 1960-66, v.p., 1971-75, group v.p., 1975-84, also bd. dir.; circulation dir. Time-Life Books, 1966-68, dir. sales, 1968-70, pub., 1970-76; chmn. bd. Time-Life Books Inc., 1976-80. Vice chmn. bd. Book-of-the-Month Club, Inc., N.Y.C., until 1984; supervising dir. Time-Life Internat. (Nederland) B.V., Amsterdam, until 1984; bd. dirs. Dreyfus Founders Funds, Sara Lee Corp., R.R Donnelley & Sons. Past trustee Mayo Found., Rochester, Minn., Nat. Repertory Orch., William Benton Found.; former mem. adv. coun. Stanford U. Bus. Sch., Haas Sch. Bus. U. Calif. Named to Direct Mktg. Hall of Fame, 1993; U. Calif.-Berkeley fellow, 1989. Mem. Assn. Am. Pubs. (past chmn.).

MANLEY, JUDITH L. director; b. Columbus, Ohio; B in Bus., Ohio State U., 1970; MEd, Xavier U., 1986. Copy writer advt. agy., Columbus, 1970—74; program asst. Ohio State U., Columbus, 1974—. Advisor, counselor dept. Spanish and Portuguese Ohio State U., Columbus, 1991—. Author poems. Area commr. Greater Hilltop Area Commn., Columbus, 1989—; bd. mem. Greater Hilltop Cmty. Devel. Corp., Columbus, 1989—; alumnae Leadership Columbus, Columbus, 1993. Named Vol. of the Month, Children's Hosp., Columbus, 2002. Mem.: ACA. Avocations: writing, photography, music, theater.

MANLEY, MICHELLE S. social worker, educator; b. Norwich, N.Y., Dec. 15, 1965; d. Thomas Frederick Jr. and Joann (Castaldy) M. BS in Psychology, Syracuse U., 1987, MSW, 1990. Cert. social worker, N.Y. Preventive social worker sch. based program Salvation Army, Syracuse, N.Y., 1990-93, social worker teen violence intervention program, 1993-94, dir. sch. based adolescent pregnancy and parenting svcs., 1994-98, interim dir. daycare, 1999, dir. women's shelter, 1999—. Adj. prof. Cazenovia Coll., N.Y., 1997—. Bernard B. Given scholar Syracuse U., 1984-87, Univ. scholar, 1989-90. Mem. NASW (chmn. women's issues com. Ctrl. N.Y. chpt. 1995-98), Acad. Cert. Social Workers. Democrat. Avocations: reading, sewing, various crafts. Office: Salvation Army 677 S Salina St Ste 1 Syracuse NY 13202-3513 also: 703 Scarboro Dr Syracuse NY 13209-2246

MANLEY, NANCY JANE, environmental engineer; b. Ft. Smith, Ark., Sept. 13, 1951; d. Eugene Hailey and Mary Adele (Chave) M. BSE, Purdue U., 1974; MSE, U. Wash., 1976; postgrad., U. Minn., 1976-77; grad., Air Command and Staff Coll., 1984, Exec. Leadership Devel. Program Dept. Def., 1988. Lic. profl. engr., Ga.; registered environ. mgr. Sanitary engr. Minn. Dept. Health, Mpls., 1976-77; sanitary engr. water supply EPA, Chgo., 1977, leader primacy unit water supply Atlanta, 1977-79, leader tech. assistance team, 1979-82; chief environ. and contract planning, project mgr. Grand Bay Range design USAF, Moody AFB, Ga., 1982-84, dep. base civil engr. Carswell AFB, Tex., 1984-86, Scott AFB, Ill., 1986-89, mem. tech. adv. com. Scott AFB master plan study Belleville, Ill., 1986-89, dep. base civil engr. Robins AFB, Ga., 1989-91, acting chief engr., 1990-91, chief pollution prevention divsn., dir. environ. mgmt., 1991-93; chief engr. divsn. 78 Civil Engr. Group, Robins AFB, Ga., 1993—. Mem. Fla. Tech. Adv. Com. for Injection Wells, Tallahassee, 1980-82, Nat. Implementation Team for Underground Injection Control Program, Washington, 1979-82, tech. panel Nat. Groundwater Protection Strategy Hearings, 1981; judge Internat. Sci. and Engring. Fair, 1986. Active various ch. support activities, 1969-74; sec. Perry Area Hist. Soc., 1991-93; vol. Meals-on-Wheels, Girl Scouts U.S., Ga. Voluntary Tech. Assistance Group, others, various locations, 1982—; founder, crisis intervention counselor Midwest Alliance, West Lafayette, Ind., 1970-74; active St. Louis Math. and Sci. Network Day, 1989, Adopt-a-Sch. Program, Lebanon, Ill., 1987-89; scientist by mail Boston Mus. Sci., 1989-99, Mathcounts, 1991—; mentor Purdue U., U. Washington, others, 1986—. Named Engr. of Yr., Robins AFB, 1997, 2000, 2003, Air Force Material Command, 1998, 2000, Ga. Engr. of Yr., Ga. Soc. Profl. Engrs., 2001, USAF Civilian Engr. of Yr., 2003, Fed. Engr. of Yr., 2004; recipient Recipient Presdl. Point of Light award, USAF, 1991, Disting. Govt. Svc. award, Dallas/Ft. Worth Fed. Exec. Bd., 1986, Lady of the Black Knights award, 19th Air Refueling Wing, 1991, Celebration of Women in Engring. award, Nat. Acad. Engring., 2000. Fellow ASCE (vol. Ga. sect.); mem. NSPE (chpt. bd. dirs. 1991-94, 97—, v.p. local chpt. 1994-95, pres.-elect local chpt. 1995-96, pres. 1996-97, 2001, nat. govt. and legis. affairs com. 1999—, state dir. 2000—), Soc. Women Engrs. (regional mem.-at-large rep. 1990-93, sr. mem. local officers 1979-82, 84-86), Am. Women in Sci., Soc. Am. Mil. Engrs. (local membership and contingency coms., local bd. dirs., profl. soc. liaison 1998, sec. 1999-2001, exec. bd. 2003—). Achievements include assignment as 1st woman dep. base civil engr. USAF, Carswell AFB; first woman engineer hired by U.S. Environmental Protection Agency. Office: 778 CES/CEC 775 Macon St Robins AFB GA 31098 Office Phone: 478-926-3533 28100. E-mail: nancy.manley@robins.af.mil., nanjmanley@cs.com.

MANLY, SARAH LETITIA, retired state legislator, ophthalmic photographer, angiographer; b. Greenville, S.C., Feb. 1, 1927; d. Victor Harris and Elsie Clippard (Burnett) Gillespie; m. Basil Manly IV, Sept. 11, 1947; children: Sarah Manly Cornish, Basil V, Jean Manly McDowell, Mary Manly Mounce. BS cum laude, Furman U., 1947; postgrad., MIT, 1972; MEd, Clemson U., 1974; postgrad., Cambridge (Eng.) U., 1981. Cert. physics tchr., Pa., S.C.; cert. retinal angiographer. Ward sec. Roper Hosp., Charleston, S.C., 1947; analytical chemist Parker Labs., Charleston, 1948; tchr. sci. Upper Darby (Pa.) Sch. Dist., 1961-63; tchr. physics Sch. Dist. Greenville (S.C.) County, 1963-64, 70-76; ophthalmic photographer Basil Manly IV, MD, Greenville, 1976-96; lectr. physics Clemson (S.C.) U., 1979-81. Cons. MIT, Cambridge, 1972-75, Georgetown U., Washington, 1974-76, NASA, Houston, 1974-76. Editor, cons. physics study guides MIT, 1972-75; editor lab. materials NASA, 1974-76; contbr. articles to profl. jours. Trustee Sch. Dist. Greenville County, 1976-88. Named S.C. Legislator of Yr., S.C. Sch. Bds. Assn., 1991, Hon. Alumnus of Phi Beta Kappa, 1994. Mem. Greenville County Med. Aux. (sec. 1953-54), Delta Kappa Gamma. Democrat. Baptist. Avocations: travel, reading, volunteering. Home: 2 Chanticleer Dr Greenville SC 29605-3106

MANN, EMILY BETSY, writer, artistic director, theater director; b. Boston, Apr. 12, 1952; d. Arthur and Sylvia (Blut) M.; m. Gary Mailman; 1 child, Nicholas Isaac Bamman. BA, Harvard U., 1974; MFA, U. Minn., 1976; D of Fine Arts (hon.), Princeton U., 2002. Resident dir. Guthrie Theater, Mpls., 1976-79; dir. BAM Theater Co., Bklyn., 1980-81; freelance writer, dir. N.Y.C., 1981-90; artistic dir. McCarter Theater Ctr. for the Performing Arts, Princeton, N.J., 1990—. Author: (plays) Annulla, An Autobiography, Still Life (6 Obie awards 1981, Fringe First award 1985), Execution of Justice (Helen Hayes award, Bay Area Theatre Critics Circle award, HBO/USA award, Playwriting award Women's Com. Dramtists Guild for Dramatizing Issues of Conscience 1986), Greensboro: A Requiem, Having Our Say (L.A. NAACP award for Best Play), Meshugah; co-author: (with Ntozake Shange) (musical) Betsey Brown; (screenplays) Fanny Kelly, The Winnie Mandela Story, Having Our Say (Christopher award, Peabody award), Having Our Say (Peabody award); dir. Hedda Gabbler, A Doll House, Annulla, Still Life (Obie award), Execution of Justice (Guthrie and Broadway), Betsey Brown, The Glass Menagerie, Three Sisters, Cat on a Hot Tin Roof, Twilight: L.A., 1992 (L.A. NAACP award for best dir.), The Perfectionist, The Matchmaker, Safe as Houses, The Mai, Betrayal, Fool for Love, The Cherry Orchard, Because He Can, Romeo and Juliet, All Over, The Tempest, Uncle Vanya (McCarter and Lo Jolla Playjpise); adaptor, dir. Miss Julie, Having Our Say (Tony nomination-direction of a play 1995, Dramatist Guild's Hull Warriner award, L.A. NAACP award), Greensboro, A Requiem, The House of Bernarda Alba, Meshugah, The Cherry Orchard, Because He Can, Romeo and Juliet, Uncle Vanya; translator: Nights and Days (Pierre Laville), 1985; pub. in New Plays U.S.A. 1, New Plays 3, American Plays and the Vietnam War, The Ten Best Plays of 1986, Out Front, Testimony: 4 Plays by Emily Mann, 1997; co-editor: Political Stages, 2002. Recipient BUSH fellowship, 1975-76, Rosamond Gilder award New Drama Forum Assn., 1983, NEA Assocs. grant, 1984, Guggenheim fellowship, 1985, McKnight fellowship, 1985, CAPS award, 1985, NEA Playwrights fellowship, 1986. Mem. Soc. Stage Dirs. and Choreographers, Theatre Comms. Group (v.p.), New Dramatists, PEN, Writers' Guild, Dramatists' Guild (exec. bd. mem.), Phi Beta Kappa.

MANN, JENNIFER L. state representative; b. Allentown, Pa., May 17, 1969; BA, Lehigh U., 1991. Office mgr. Instant Access, 1994—95, owner, 1995—98; Dem. com. person Allentown 18th Ward, 2d Dist., 1999—. Bd. mem. Jr. Achievement of Lehigh Valley, 1997—, Allentown Bus. Coun. of Lehigh County C. of C., 1998—; mem. Hamilton Pk. Crime Watch, 1998—; bd. mem. Mayfair Festival of the Arts, 1999—; commr. Pa. Commn. on Crime and Deliquency, 1999—; dir. Small Bus. Coun. West Pk. Civic Assn. Democrat. Office: 121B E Wing Harrisburg PA 17120-2020 E-mail: jlmann@pahouse.net.

MANN, JOAN ELLONA, artist, editor; b. Seattle, Aug. 21, 1931; d. Henry Hughes and Jeanetta Maurine (Baker)) Jacobsen; m. Hugh Mann, Sept. 2, 1955 (div. Aug. 1981); children: Susan, Kristi, Steven, Nancy, Roy. BA in Journalism, U. Wash., 1953, BFA in Sculpture, 1970, MFA in Sculpture, 1985. Reporter East Side Jour., Kirkland, Wash., 1953-55; med. editor Virginia Mason Med. Ctr., Seattle, 1965-69; info. specialist Continuing Edn. News Svc. U. Wash., Seattle, 1969-73; editor Seattle Arts Commn., 1973-77; pub. info. officer King County Arts Commn., Seattle, 1973-90; owner, mgr. Joan Mann, Editor, Seattle. Sculptures include multi-media floor sculpture Trident, Ship of Fools, 1988 (award); shows include U. Wash. Henry Gallery, 1971; group shows include Roscoe Louie Gallery, Seattle, 1975, Univ. Unitarian Gallery, 1978, U. Wash. Henry Gallery, 1987, U. Wash. Meany Hall, 1987, SJW Studios, Seattle, 1988, Seattle Ctr. Opera House, 1988, PNAC, Bellevue, 1988, Ctr. for Contemporary Art, Seattle, 1989. Precinct del. Wash. Dem. Com., Seattle, 1992. Recipient 2d and 3d place ann. awards Wash. Press Women, 1971, 1st prize Ctr. for Contemporary Art, 1989; travel grantee Goethe Inst., Berlin, 1988. Mem. Women in Comm. (Nat. Clarion award 1974), Allied Arts Seattle (adv. bd. 1990—), Seattle Art Mus. Roman Catholic. Avocations: photography, skiing, hiking on beaches, travel.

MANN, JUDITH WALKER, curator; b. Washington, Sept. 29, 1950; d. James Harold and Margaret Blackwell Mann; m. David Thomas Konig, Nov. 9, 1975; children: Madeleine Blackwell Mann Konig, William James Mann Konig. BA, Mt. Holyoke Coll., 1972; MA, Washington U., St. Louis, 1978, PhD, 1986. Adj. prof. Old Dominion U., Norfolk, Va., 1986—87, Webster U., Webster Groves, Mo., 1987—88, Univ. Coll., Washington U., 1987—88; curatorial asst. St. Louis Art Mus., 1988—91, asst. curator, 1991—97, curator, 1997—; adj. prof. Washington U., 1989; asst. prof. U. Mo., St. Louis, 1991—97. Author: (catalog) Baroque into Rococo: Seventeenth and Eighteenth Century Italian Paintings, 1997, Orazio and Artemisia Gentileschi, 2001; contbr. articles to profl. jours. Bd. dirs., trustee Eliot Chapel, Kirkwood, Mo., 1989—92; vol. NARAL, St. Louis, 1990—2002; bd. dirs. Webster Groves Sch. Dist. Fedn., 1992—94. Grantee, Nat. Endowment for the Arts, 1994, 2001, Kress Found., 2002. Mem.: 16th Century Studies Soc., Renaissance Soc. Am., Coll. Art Assn. Democrat. Unitarian. Avocations: travel, sewing, reading, cooking. Home: 500 Lee Ave Webster Groves MO 63119 Office: St Louis Art Mus One Fine Arts Dr Saint Louis MO 63110 Office Phone: 314-655-5218. E-mail: jmann@slam.org.

MANN, KAREN, consultant, educator; b. Kansas City, Mo., Oct. 9, 1942; d. Charles and Letha (Anderson) M. BA, U. Calif., Santa Barbara, 1964; MPA, Golden Gate U., 1975, PhD, 1994. Cert. lay min. Order of Buddhist Contemplatives. Mem., tchr. Sisters of Immaculate Heart, L.A., 1964-68; group counselor San Francisco and Marin County Probation Depts., 1968—70; parole agt. Calif. Dept. Corrections, Sacramento, San Francisco, 1970-86; rschr. and cons. Non-profit Orgnl. Devel., 1986—, Computer Applications for Persons with Disabilities, 1986—. Adj. faculty Grad. Theol. Uion, Berkeley, 1984—; Compuserve Disabilities Forum, 1985-2000; forum adminstr., 1988-2000; mem. faculty Golden Gate U., 1990. Co-author: Prison Overcrowding, 1979, Community Corrections: A Plan for California, 1980. Sec., bd. dirs. Spirit Rock Mediation Ctr., 1989-93; co-founder Network Ctr. for Study of Ministry, San Francisco, 1982; pres. San Francisco Network Ministries, 1980-82; mem. Disabled Children's Computer Resource Group, 1988-90, Spingwater Ctr. for Mediative Inquiry and Retreats, 1986-88; emotional support counselor Marin AIDS Project, 1992-97; bd. dirs. Siskiyou Humane Soc., pres., 2003—. Fellowship of Reconciliation, N.Y., 1970—, Buddhist Peace fellowship, 2000—. Office: 400 Shasta Ave Mount Shasta CA 96067 Office Phone: 530-925-2997. E-mail: blueroof@snowcrest.net.

MANN, LAURA SUSAN, editor; b. Houston, Sept. 20, 1958; d. Manfred Walter and Sally Mae (Hennels) Schaefer; m. Richard Drew Mann, Aug. 1, 1987; children: W. Cole, Devon S. BS in Physics cum laude, U. Houston, 1986. Mktg. sec. Vector Cable/Schlumberger, Sugar Land, Tex., 1981-83; adminstrv. asst. Bekaert Internat. Trade, Inc., Houston, 1983-84; polit. pollster, rsch. and teaching asst. U. Houston, 1984-86; flight contr. Johnson Space Ctr., NASA, Houston, 1986-91, mgr. grapple fixture subsystem, 1991-92, mgr. space sta. engring. configuration, 1992-93; part time beauty cons. Mary Kay cosmetics, 1992; contract editor R.G. Landes Co., Georgetown, Tex. Mem. tech. adv. com. flight telerobotic servicer Goddard Space Flight Ctr., NASA, Greenbelt, Md., 1989; mission ops. directorate rep. hand contr. commonality study, leader space shuttle payload and deployment system tech. team/space sta. flight compatability rev. Johnson Space Ctr., NASA, 1990; rsch. asst. medium energy physics expt. U. Houston at Brookhaven Nat. Lab., Upton, N.Y., 1985, 86; mem. configuration mgmt. process improvement team for Space Sta. Freedom Program, 1992-93. Pres. Durham Pk. Homeowners Assn., Houston, 1990-92; vol. Tex. Water Commn. Testing Program, 1994-95. Mem. Am. Horse Shows Assn., U.S. Combined Tng. Assn. (adult team co-coord. 1998), Greater Houston Hunter Jumper Assn. (bd. dirs. 1991-92, contbg. newsletter columnist 1991-92, Jr./Adult Jumper Champion 1990, 4th in open jumper ann. awards 1992), Third Coast Eventers (newsletter columnist 1995—, sec.-treas. 1996—), U. Houston Alumni Orgn., MENSA, Phi Theta Kappa. Avocations: horse showing, camping, walking, gardening. Home: 691 Meadow Bend Rd Bellville TX 77418-9625

MANN, MARIA, photojournalist, director; Dir. of photography Agence France-Presse for North Am., 1984, internat. editor; dir. of photography Toronto Sun; employed United Press Internat. World Hdqrs. Recipient Joseph Costa Award for Leadership and continuing svc. to photojournalists, NPPA, 2002, Kenneth P. McLaughlin Award, 2002. Mem.: Workshop Bd. of Dir., Nat. Press Photgraphers Assoc. Best of Photojournalism Contest (chairwoman), Latin Am. Photojournalism Workshop (co-organizer), Knight Found., Latin Am. Task Force. Office: Agence France Presse Dir of Photography 747 Third Ave New York NY 10017

MANN, TORI, secondary school educator; b. Barnesboro, Pa., Oct. 14, 1944; d. William and Anne Victoria Todhunter; m. Weldon Mann, Sr., Jan. 28, 1968; chilren: Weldon, Todd Hunter. BA in Psychology, Sterling (Kans.) Coll., 1966; MS in Spl. Edn., Calif. State U., Hayward, 1993. Cert. tchr., Calif. Tchr. Oakland (Calif.) Pub. Schs., 1990-92; tchr. social studies Stockton (Calif.) Unified Schs., 1992—. Mem. Coun. for Exceptional Children, Calif. Assn. for Resource Specialists. Avocations: reading, theater, travel. Office: Hamilton Mid Sch 2245 E 11th St Stockton CA 95206-3697

MANN-BONDAT, LYDIA RACHEL, writer, researcher; d. Jonathan Max Mann and Marie-Paule Therese Bondat; m. Michael Stafford Masland, Mar. 25, 2000; 1 child, Dayton Jonathan Mann Bondat-Masland. MS in Fgn. Svc., Georgetown U., 2002; BA, Harvard U., 1995. Admissions and fin. aid officer Grad. Sch. of Arts and Scis. Harvard U., Boston, 1996—98; program assoc. Partners in Health, Boston, 1998—2000; writer, rschr. Inst. for the Study of Internat. Migration, Washington, 2001—. Adv. bd. mem. Robert F. Kennedy Meml. Health and Human Rights Fellowship, 2002—03. Recipient Citizen Appreciation award, Harvard U. Police Dept., 1995; fellow, Georgetown U., 2000—02. Mem.: Youth Against AIDS (advisor 2002). Home: 242 11th St SE Washington DC 20003-2124 Personal E-mail: lm42@georgetown.edu.

MANNE, DEBORAH SUE, dental hygienist, educator; b. Vincennes, Ind., Nov. 20, 1954; d. Charles Kenneth and Susan Jane (Fox) Thornberry; m. Marshall Stanley Manne, Dec. 21, 1985. AA, Maplewoods C.C., Kansas City, Mo., 1973; BS in Dental Hygiene, U. Mo., 1975; BSN, St. Louis U., 1991, MSN in Oncology Nursing, 1998. RN, reg. dental hygienist, Mo. Dental hygienist Dr. Marshall S. Manne, St. Louis, 1978—2001, office nurse, 1991—2001; oncology nurse CIRCLE Barnes-Jewish Hosp., St. Louis, 1993—98; staff nurse Radiation Oncology Ctr. Barnes-Jewish Hosp. North, 1997; nurse educator Cancer Family Care, St. Louis, 1998; clin. asst. prof. divsn. dental hygiene Sch. Dentistry U. Mo., Kans. City, 1999—; clin. nurse John Krey Cancer Info. Ctr., St. John's Mercy Pratt Cancer Ctr., St. Louis, 2001—. Instr. dental hygiene dept. St. Louis C.C., Forest Pk., 1999—2000; clin. instr. So. Ill. U., Carbondale, 2000; coord., cons. Oncology Dental Support Svcs., St. Louis, 1992—; mem. curriculum rev. com. dental hygiene program St. Louis C.C., 1993; mem. adv. bd. ACCESS Dental Hygiene Jour., 1994—2003; editl. bd. Jour. of Dental Hygiene, 2003—; reviewer Oncology Nursing Forum, 2003—; pilot reviewer Clin. Jour. of Oncology Nursing, 2003—. Contbr. articles to profl. jours. Chair Gt. Am. Smokeout, 1992; mem. Breast Cancer task force, 1994—98; bd. dirs, v.p. Am. Cancer Soc., St. Louis, 1992—93, mem. profl. adv. com. Wellness Cmty., St. Louis, 1994—; chmn. Tobacco-Free Mo. Super Coalition, St. Louis, 2000. Recipient Vol. Recognition award, Am. Cancer Soc., 1995, Irene Newman award, 1997, Susan Brockman-Bell Humanitarian award, U. Mo. Kans. City Dental Hygiene Alumni Assn., 2000. Mem. Am. Dental Hygienists Assn. (council on pub. rels., coun. on edn.), Oncology Nursing Soc. (chair oral care focus group, pres.-elect St. Louis chpt. 1998, pres. 1999, editor patient edn. sig newsletter 1999-2000), Mo. Dental Hygienists' Assn. (pres.), Greater St. Louis Hygienists' Assn. (pres.), Sigma Phi Alpha, Sigma Theta Tau. Avocations: walking, raising golden retrievers. Home: 11617 Larkmont Dr Creve Coeur MO 63141-6907

MANNER, JENNIFER FOUSE, social worker; b. Balt., June 15, 1964; d. Richard Erb and Patricia Ann (Matthews) Fouse; m. David Bruce Manner, Aug. 16, 1986; 1 child, Jessica Lynn. BA in Psychology, Hope Coll., 1986; MS in Social Adminstrn., Case Western Reserve U., 1988. Lic. ind. social worker, Ohio; cert. chem. dependency counselor. Adolescent continuing care coord. Lakeland Inst. Lorain (Ohio) Cmty. Hosp., 1988-90; dir. Laurelwood Counseling Ctr., Mayfield Heights, Ohio, 1990-93; field instr. Mandel Sch. Applied Social Scis. Case Western Res. U., Cleve., 1991-95; ind. social worker, chem. dependency counselor Elyria, Ohio, 1993—. Lectr. in field; adj. instr. Lorain County C.C., 1998—, Baldwin Wallace Coll., 2004-. Mem. NASW, Psi Chi. Democrat. Presbyterian. Avocations: canoing, writing children's books, skiing. Home: 6641 Myrtle Hill Rd Valley City OH 44280-9300 Office: Psychiat & Psychol Svcs 412 E River St Elyria OH 44035-5231 E-mail: JenniferManner@zoominternet.net.

MANNERS, PAMELA JEANNE, middle school educator; b. Holyoke, Mass., Mar. 20, 1951; d. Francis Edward and Helen Mary (Kurtyka) Herbert; div. 1985; children: Tracy, Kristen. BA, U. So. Miss., 1986, MEd, 1993. Cert. elem. edn. K-3, 4-8, secondary Eng., Social Studies; cert. elem. prin., secondary prin., elem. and secondary adminstrn. Registrar Michel Mid. Sch., Biloxi, Miss., 1987-88, tchr. Eng. and Social Studies, 1988-90, tchr. reading/law related edn., 1990-95; curriculum coord. Biloxi Pub. Schs., 1995-98; administrator Fernwood Jr. High Sch., Biloxi Pub. Schs., 1998-2000; dir. ABA Reading Curriculum Program, 1989-95; prin. Michel Jr. H.S., Biloxi Pub. Schs., 2000—. Law-related edn. trainer Miss. Law-Related Edn. Ctr., Jackson, 1990-2002; law-related trainer Ctr. Civic Edn., Calabasas, Calif., 1993; law-related trainer Constitutional Right Found., 1994-2002. Participant program Lawyer in Every Class Miss. Bar Assn., Jackson, 1990-93 On-site target grantee Miss. Bar/Dept. Justice, 1992; A+ Site recognition U.S. Dept. Edn. Mem. Leadership Gulf Coast C. of C. (edn. com. 1996—). Roman Catholic. Office: Biloxi Pub Schs 1400 Father Ryan Ave Biloxi MS 39530 E-mail: PamonCoast@aol.com.

MANNERS, RUTH ANN, writer; b. Keene, Ohio, Aug. 6, 1919; d. George Frank and Eva Barbara (Bissantz) Bauer; m. David X. Manners, Feb. 22, 1945; children: Paul, Jonathan, Michael, Timothy. BA, Randolph-Macon Woman's Coll., 1941; student, Art Students League, N.Y.C., 1941-43. V.p. David X. Manners Co. Inc., Norwalk, Conn., 1966-82. Author: Today's Woman Prize Kitchens, 1964, Today's Woman Sewing Simplified, 1965, (with William Manners) The Quick and Easy Vegetarian Cookbook, 1978 (Tastemaker award for cookbook excellence 1979), The New Quick and Easy Vegetarian Cookbook, 1993. Office: David X Manners Co Inc 107 Post Rd E Westport CT 06880-3410

MANNES, ELENA SABIN, film and television producer, director; b. N.Y.C., Dec. 3, 1943; d. Leopold Damrosch and Evelyn (Sabin) M. BA, Smith Coll., 1965; MA, Johns Hopkins U., 1967. Rschr. Pub. Broadcast Lab. Nat. Ednl. TV, N.Y.C., 1968-70; writer Sta. WPIX-TV, N.Y.C., 1970-73; assignment editor Sta. ABC-TV, N.Y.C., 1973-76; prodr., writer Sta. WCBS-TV, N.Y.C., 1976-80; prodr. CBS News, N.Y.C., 1980-87, Pub. Affairs TV/Bill Moyers PBS Documentaries, N.Y.C., 1987-90. Ind. documentary dir. and prodr., 1987—. Recipient Emmy award NATAS, 1984, 85, 87, 90, 94, 96, 2002, Peabody award, 1985, Cine Golden Eagle award, 1988, 90, 93, 94, 95, 99, Robert F. Kennedy Journalism award, 1989, DGA awards, 1987, 90. Mem. Writers Guild Am., Dirs. Guild Am., Am. Film Inst. (dir. Workshop for Women). Avocations: tennis, still photography.

MANNING, ALLEEN BLESI, art educator, artist; b. Cin., Nov. 26, 1950; d. Samuel and Edith Alleen Blesi; m. Shayne Manning, Dec. 12, 1986. BFA in Fine Arts, U. Cin., 1972, MA in Art Edn., 1974. Tchr. art Cin. Pub. Schs., 1974—94, Mariemont City Schs., Cin., 1994—. Mem.: Volcano Art Ctr., Nature Conservancy, Ohio Art Educators Assn., Contemporary Art Ctr., Cin. Art Mus., Cin. Zoo, Oxbow Inc. Republican. Avocations: hiking, snorkeling, swimming, birdwatching. Home: 5850 Given Rd Cincinnati OH 45243

MANNING, BLANCHE M. federal judge; b. 1934; BEd, Chgo. Tchrs. Coll., 1961; JD, John Marshall Law Sch., 1967; MA, Roosevelt Univ., 1972; LLM, Univ. of Va. Law Sch., 1992; DHL (hon.), Chgo. State U., 1998. Asst. states atty. State's Atty.'s Office (Cook County), Ill., 1968-73; supervisory trial atty. U.S. EEOC, Chgo., 1973-77; gen. atty. United Airlines, Chgo., 1977-78; asst. U.S. atty. U.S. Dist. Ct. (no. dist.) Ill., 1978-79, assoc. judge Cir. Ct. of Cook County, 1979-86, circuit judge, 1986-87; appellate court judge Ct. of Review Ill. Appellate Ct., 1987-94; district judge U.S. Dist. Ct. (no. dist.) Ill., Chgo., 1994—. Tchr. A. O. Sexton Elem. Sch. James Wadsworth Elem. Sch., Wendell Phillips H.S. Adult Program, Morgan Park H.S. Summer Sch. Program, South Shore H.S. Summer Sch. Program, Carver H.S. Adult Edn. Program; lectr. Malcolm X C.C., 1970-71; adj. prof. NCBL C.C. of Law, 1978-79, DePaul Univ. Law Sch., 1992—; tchg. team mem. Trial Advocacy Workshop, Harvard Law Sch., U. Chgo. Law Sch., 1991—; chmn. Com. on Recent Devels in Evidence, Ill. Judicial Conf., 1991; faculty mem. New Judges Seminar, Ill. Judicial Conf.; past faculty mem. Profl. Devel. Seminar for New Assoc. Judges, Cook County Cir. Ct.; past mem. bd. dirs., trained intervenor Lawyers' Assistance Program, Inc.; past mem. adv. coun. Lawyer's Asst. Program, Roosevelt U. Former trustee Sherwood Music Conservatory Bd.; clarinetist Cmty. Concert band Chgo. State U.; saxophonist Jazz ensemble, Chgo. State U. Jazz Band, jazz band Diversity. Mem. Cook County Bar Assn. (second v-p 1974), Nat. Bar Assn., Nat. Judicial Coun., Ill. Judicial Coun. (treas. 1982-85, chmn. 1988, chmn. judiciary com. 1992), Ill. State Bar Assn. (past mem. bd. dirs. Lawyers Assistance Program Inc.), Am. Bar Assn. (fellow 1991), Chgo. Bar Assn. (clarinetist Symphony Orch., saxophonist), John Marshall Law Sch. Alumni Assn. (bd. dirs.), Chgo. State Univ. Alumni Assn. (bd. dirs.). Office: US Dist Ct 2156 US Courthouse 219 S Dearborn St Ste 2050 Chicago IL 60604-1800

MANNING, BRENDA ARGOSY, painter; b. New Britain, Conn., Mar. 29, 1940; d. Henry Joseph and Ann Shebed Argosy; m. John Schultz Manning, Sept. 4, 1961; children: Gregory, Allyson Manning Jaye. Grad., Art Inst. Pitts., 1960; attended, Art Students League, N.Y.C., 1987—88. Freelance illustrator, 1960—; portrait painter, 1988—. Docent, lectr. chair New Britain Mus. Am. Art, New Britain, Conn., 1974—92, mem. acquisition & loan commn., 1996—; chmn., bd. mem.Art for the Cure Komen Conn. Race for the Cure, 1995—99. Exhibitions include Town & Country Club Hartford, Conn., 1989, one-woman shows include Sec. of State's Office, Hartford, Conn., 1991, exhibitions include Lily Pad Gallery, Charleston, R.I., 1995, one-woman shows include Seabury Cmty., Bloomfield, Conn., 1998, exhibitions include Hartford Fine Art & Framing, East Hartford, Conn., 1998, one-woman shows include Mooreland Hill Sch., Kensington, Conn., 1999, exhibitions include U. Conn. Med. Ctr., Farmington, Conn., 2000, New Britain Mus. Am. Art, 2001. Mem.: Univ./Cmty. Women's Forum (adv. com.), Nat. Women in Arts, New Britain Art League, Meriden Arts & Crafts Assn., West Hartford Art League, Conn. Pastel Soc., Conn. Acad. Fine Arts. Avocations: golf, travel, reading. Home: 118 Mooreland Rd Kensington CT 06037

MANNING, ELAINE S. retired art educator; b. Andalusia, Ala., July 17, 1946; d. Finis Murland and Nina Holmes Smith. BS in Edn., 1970; diploma in cosmetology, McArthur St. Tech. Coll., 2000. Cert. art tchr. Dept. of Edn., Ala. Art & elem. tchr. Montezuma Christian Acad., Andalusia, 1970—71; art tchr. Andalusia H.S., 1971—2001; ret., 2001. Mem.: NEA, Watercolor Soc. Ala., Nat. Watercolor Soc., Nat. Mus. Women in Arts, Ala. Art Edn. Assn., Andalusia Assn. Educators, Ala. Edn. Assn., Alpha Delta Kappa.

MANNING, JOAN ELIZABETH, health association administrator; b. Davenport, Iowa, July 7, 1953; d. George John and Eugenie Joan (Thomas) Stolze; m. Michael Anthony Manning, July 30, 1977. BA, U. No. Iowa, 1975; MPH, U. Minn., 1990. Traveling collegiate sec. Alpha Delta Pi Nat. Sorority, Atlanta, 1975—76; recreational therapist Americana Healthcare Ctr., Mason City, Iowa, 1976—81; communication coord. Area Agy. on Aging, Mason City, 1981—83; exec. dir. United Way Cerro Gordo County, Mason City, 1983—85, Health Fair of the Midlands, Omaha, 1985—87; dir. health services ARC, Omaha, 1987—90, COO, 1990—95, CEO, Pacific Northwest region, 1995—. Vis. rsch. prof. Niels Bohr Inst., Denmark, 1995-96. Bd. dirs. YMCA of U.S.A., Chgo., 1981-83, Mason City YMCA, 1980-84, Mason City Parks and Recreation Bd., 1983-85, Camp Fire Coun., 1989—, Potters Therapy House, 1989—; mem. spl. adv. bd. Cerro Gordo County Human Svcs. Bd., 1983-85; mem. spl. activities com. Omaha Wellness Coun. of Midlands, 1986-89; chmn. wider opportunity task force Great Plains (Nebr.) Girl Scouts U.S., 1986-89; bd. dirs. Omaha South YMCA, Cath. Charities; mem. Jr. League of Omaha. Mem. U. Minn. Alumnae Assn., Suburban Rotary, Alpha Delta Pi. Republican. Roman Catholic.

MANNING, JUDITH HUBERT, state legislator, real estate executive; b. Oct. 24, 1942; children: Hank, Elizabeth. Postgrad., U. Vienna (Austria), 1963-64; BS in Edn., U. Ga., 1964. Tchr. soc. studies Coll. Pk. H.S., Fulton County, Ga., 1966-67, McEachern Middle Sch., Cobb County, Ga., 1967-69; past real estate agent, broker Manning Properties, Marietta, Ga.; co-owner, real estate agent, broker, appraiser property mgmt., leasing, sales and appraisal firm; mem. Ga. House of Reps., Atlanta, 1997—. Mem. Retirement Com., Natural Resources Com., Banks and Banking Com.; active Women Leaders Summit, 1995, 96; mem. edn. task force Am. Legis. Exch. Coun. Del. 7th dist. Rep. Party Convention; past adv. pres. ARC; mem. Atlanta Regional Commn., Cobb Emergency Aid, Cobb Youth Leadership; mem. Girls, Inc., past chair, bd.dirs.; bd. dirs. Jubilee Fine Arts Fesival, OpenGate, Gateway Vis. and Info. Ctr., Dept. Family and Children Svcs.; past bd. dirs. Cobb Symposium, Vol. Atlanta; publicity chair, past bd. dirs. YMCA; vol. Kennestone Hosp.; vol. task force, exec. mem. United

Way; 1st pres. Vol. Cobb-Marietta; vice-chmn. Friends of the Park; historian, past bd. dirs. Ptnrs. Fund; participant Women Leaders Summit, 1995-96. W. Wyman Pilcher Jr. Meml. scholar; recipient Leadership Cobb Class of 1984-85, Leadership Ga. Class of 89-90, Disting. Leadership award Nat. Assn. Cmty. Leadership, 1989, Phoenix award Cobb County Bd. Realtors, 1996. Mem. Nat. Assn. Realtors, Cobb-Marietta Jr. League, Hon. Comdrs. Assn., The Walker Sch. Parents Assn., Assn. Metro Atlanta DFCS (co-vice chmn.). Home: 830 Whitlock Ave SW Marietta GA 30064-3034 Office: Legis Office Bldg Rm 607 Atlanta GA 30334

MANNING, MARTHA MARY, writer, psychologist; b. Chgo., Aug. 18, 1952; d. John Eugene and Mary Louise M.; m. Brian J. Depenbrock, Oct. 20, 1973; 1 child, Keara. BA with high honors, U. Md., College Park, 1974; MA, Cath. Univ. Am., 1978, PhD, 1981. Postdoctoral fellow McLean Hosp./Harvard Med. Sch., Boston, 1981-83; asst. prof. George Mason U., Fairfax, Va., 1983-88; pvt. practice Alexandria, Va., 1994-96. Psychology instr., 1989-93. Author: A Season of Mercy, 1985, Undercurrents: A Life Beneath the Surface, 1995, Chasing Grace, 1996; co-author: Restoring Intimacy: A Patients Guide to Maintaining Relationships During Depression, 1999, All Seasons Pass: Grieving & Miscarriage, 2000; columnist, Salt of the Earth, 1993-96; contbr. to popular mags. including Health, Mirabella, New Woman, Ladies' Home Jour., Glamour, U.S. Cath., N.Y. Times Book Review, Family Therapy Networker, Washington Post. Recipient Merit award Associated Ch. Press, 1994, 96, Best Mag. Column Cath. Press Assn., 1995, Presdl. award for Patient Advocacy, Am. Psychiat. Assn., 1996, Stephen Logan award Nat. Alliance for Mentally Ill. Office: Arielle Eckstut James Levine Comm Inc care FWI 307 7th Ave 1904 New York NY 10001

MANNING, NANCY CHRISTINE, elementary school educator; d. Alexander Anthony and Millie (Burczak) Pawlikowski; m. Richard Wayne Manning. BS in Elem. Edn. cum laude, East Stroudsburg U., 1971. Cert. Family Math. instr. Rutgers U., 1994. Tchr. Green Twp. Bd. Edn., Greendell, NJ, 1971—2003; ret. Treas. Green Twp. Edn. Assn., Greendell, 1978—2002. Recipient Tchr. Recognition award, NJ Dept. Edn., 1993. Avocations: reading, gardening, cooking, baking.

MANNING, SYLVIA, English studies educator; b. Montreal, Que., Can., Dec. 2, 1943; came to U.S., 1967; d. Bruno and Lea Bank; m. Peter J. Manning, Aug. 20, 1967; children— Bruce David, Jason Maurice BA, McGill U., 1963; MA, Yale U., 1964, PhD in English, 1967. Asst. prof. English Calif. State U.-Hayward, 1967-71, assoc. prof., 1971-75, assoc. dean, 1972-75; assoc. prof. U. So. Calif., 1975-94, prof., assoc. dir. Ctr. for Humanities, 1975-77, assoc. dir. Ctr. for Humanities, 1975-77, chmn. freshman writing, 1977-80, chmn. dept. English, 1980-83, vice provost, exec. v.p., 1984-94; prof. English U. Ill., Champaign, 1994—, v.p. for acad. affairs, prof. English, 1994—, interim chancellor Chgo., 1999-2000, chancellor, 2000—. Author: Dickens as Satirist, 1971; Hard Times: An Annotated Bibliography, 1984. Contbr. essays to mags. Woodrow Wilson fellow, 1963-64, 66-67 Mem. MLA, Dickens Soc. Office: U of Ill Office of Chancellor 2833 University Hall 601 S Morgan St Chicago IL 60607-7100

MANNIX, ALICIA GUTMAN, artist, marketing consultant; b. Jawor, Poland, Jan. 25, 1953; arrived in U.S., 1969; d. Abram Mendel and Anna Domnikoff Gutman; m. David Robert Mannix, May 13, 1977 (div. Dec. 15, 1989); children: Aletta, Ezra, Thomas Wray. BA in Art History, U. Md., 1975; MA in Liberal Arts, Johns Hopkins U., 1980. Pres. Bus. Dynamics, Inc., Portland, Oreg., 1979—82; dir. comms. United Way, Portland, 1982—84, Balt., 1985—88; dir. mktg. Graphic Press, Klamath Falls, Oreg., 1989—91; mktg. cons. Ashland, Oreg., 1995—99; artist, 1999—. Jewish. Avocations: reading, meditation, yoga, interior design, doing nothing. Home: 1520 Windsor St Ashland OR 97520 E-mail: alicia@aliciamannix.com.

MANNO, RITA, state agency administrator; b. Buffalo, Sept. 11, 1946; d. Anthony Joseph and Irene Pawlowski; m. Donald F. Manno, July 11, 1970; children: Kimberly, Rebecca. Student, Exetr (Eng.) U., 1965-66; BA, Canisius Coll., Buffalo, 1967; MA, U. Wis., 1968. State polit. editor Courier-Post, Cherry Hill, N.J., 1980-93; press sec. Gov. Christine Whitman, N.J., 1994-95; dir. comms. N.J. Dept. Health and Sr. Svcs., 1996—. Mem. exec. bd. Nat. Pub. Health Info. Coalition, 1996—. Recipient Best of Gannett award Gannett Corp., 1990-93; Knight scholar, 1993. Mem. N.J. C. of C. (N.J. 300 Women 1998-99). Avocations: hiking, weight training, movies, motorcycles. Office: NJ Dept Health and Sr Svcs PO Box 360 Trenton NJ 08625-0360

MANNWEILER, MARY-ELIZABETH, painter; b. Norwood, Ohio, June 23, 1916; d. Wilbur Lawrence Young and Augusta Minnis (Newman) Davis; m. Robert Mays Lang, Sr., May 25, 1940 (dec. July 1981); children: Robert Mays Lang, Jr., Gary Davis Lang, Julianna Elizabeth Lang Crawford; m. Gordon Bannatyne Mannweiler, Apr. 17, 1982(dec. Aug. 2001). Student, Miami U., Oxford, Ohio, 1935-37. Portrait painter; permanent collections; donated (with husband) stained glass window to Congl. Ch., Naugatuck, Conn. Past pres. Athena Club, Freeport, N.Y., Woodbury (Conn.) Women's Club, 1977-78, Watertown (Conn.) Art League; past dir. Waterbury (Conn.) Symphony Orch.; pres. Mannweiler Found., Naugatuck, Conn.; trustee YMCA, Naugatuck; mem. scholarship com. Naugatuck H.S., 2003. Recipient blue ribbons for artwork; Paul Harris fellow Rotary, 2001; music room named in honor of Mr. and Mrs. Mannweiler Conn. Jr. Republic, Litchfield, 1997. Mem. DAR (regent Ruth Floyd Woodhull chpt. 1966-67, pres.). Home: 435 Hillside Ave Naugatuck CT 06770-2727

MANROSS, MARY, mayor; m. Larry; 4 children. BS in Polit. Sci. Mayor City of Scottsdale, Ariz., 2000—. Mem. Scottsdale (Ariz.) City Coun., 1992—. Chmn. Scottsdale (Ariz.) Parks and Recreation Commn., Maricopa Assn. Govts. Youth Policy Adv. Com.; bd. dirs. Ariz. Women in Mcpl. Govt.; mem. Planning Commn.; vice chmn. Scottsdale Bond Com.; mem. Sub-com. TPC-Westworld, City Ct., C. of C./Econ. Devel.; mem. Govs. Task Force on Urban Planning, Ariz. Town Hall, Nat. League of Cities Energy, Environment and Nat. Resource Policy Com.; mem. steering com. NLC Transp., Infrastructure and Svcs. Address: 3939 N Drinkwater Blvd Scottsdale AZ 85251-4433 Office: City Hall 3939 N Drinkwater Blvd Scottsdale AZ 85251-4433

MANSFIELD, ELAINE SCHULTZ, molecular geneticist, automation specialist; b. Boulder, Colo., Apr. 20, 1954; d. William Varley and Juanita M. (Zingg) M.; m. Gary G. Schultz, Nov. 24, 1983; children: Matthew, Greggory Mark. BA in Molecular Biology, San Jose State U., 1975; MS in Genetics, U. Calif., Berkeley, 1978, PhD in Genetics, 1983. Diplomate Am. Bd. Med. Genetics (fellow), Am. Bd. Clin. Molecular Genetics. Customer cons. IntelliGenetics, Mountain View, Calif., 1983-86; staff scientist Applied Biosys., Foster City, Calif., 1986-93; sr. staff scientist Molecular Dynamics, Sunnyvale, Calif., 1993-98; dir. pharmacogenomics diaDexus, LLC, Santa Clara, Calif., 1998-99; prin. scientist Aclara Bio Sci., Mountain View, 1999—. Lectr. in the field. Author (with others) Mutations in the Human Genome, 1993; contb. to profl. jours.; patentee in field. U. Calif. grantee, Chancellors Patent Fund grantee U. Calif., NIH SBIR grantee, 1995-99. Mem. AAAS, Am. Soc. Human Genetics, Am. Soc. Histocompatibility and Immunogenetics, Women in Sci., Black Masque (pres. 1975). Avocations: skiing, quilting. Office: Aclara Bio Sci 1288 Pair Ave Mountain View CA 94043

MANSFIELD, KAREN LEE, lawyer; b. Chgo., Mar. 17, 1942; d. Ralph and Hilda (Blum) Mansfield; children: Nicole Rafaela, Lori Michele. BA in Polit. Sci., Roosevelt U., 1963; JD, DePaul U., 1971; student U. Chgo., 1959-60. Bar: Ill. 1972, U.S. Dist. Ct. (no. dist.) Ill. 1972. Legis. intern Ill. State Senate, Springfield, 1966-67; tchr. Chgo. Pub. Schs., 1967-70; atty. CNA Ins., Chgo., 1971-73; law clk. Ill. Apellate Ct., Chgo., 1973-75; sr. trial atty. U.S. Dept. Labor, Chgo., 1975—, mentor Adopt-a-Sch. Program, 1992-95. Contbr. articles to profl. jours. Vol. Big Sister, 1975-81; bd. dirs. Altgeld Nursery Sch., 1963-66, Ill. div. UN Assn., 1966-72, Hull House Jane Addams Ctr., 1977-82, Broadway Children's Ctr., 1986-90, Acorn Family Entertainment, 1993-95; active Oak Park Farmers' Market Commn., 1996-2002; rsch. asst. Citizens for Gov. Otto Kerner, Chgo., 1964; com. mem. Ill. Commn. on Status of Women, Chgo., 1964-70; del. Nat. Conf. on Status of Women, 1968; candidate for del. Ill. Constl. Conv., 1969. Mem. Chgo. Council Lawyers, Women's Bar Assn. Ill., Lawyer Pilots Bar Assn., Fed. Bar Assn. Unitarian. Clubs: Friends of Gamelan (performer), 99's Internat. Orgn. Women Pilots (legis. chmn. Chgo. area chpt. 1983-86, legis. chmn. North Cen. sect. 1986-88, legis. award 1983, 85). Home: 204 S Taylor Ave Oak Park IL 60302-3307 Office: US Dept Labor Office Solicitor 230 S Dearborn St Fl 8 Chicago IL 60604-1505

MANSON, ANNE, music director; Grad., Harvard U.; postgrad., King's Coll., London, Royal Coll. Music, Royal Northern Coll. Music; studied with Norman Del Mar, James Lockhart. Music dir. Kansas City (Mo.) Symphony, 1998—. Condr. Mecklenburgh Opera, 1991, Endymion Ensemble, 1992-93, London Mozart Players, 1993-94, BBC Scottish Symphony and Iceland Symphony Orch., 1994-95, Northern Sinfonia, Resedentie Orch. in The Hague, Ensemble Inter Contemporain, Paris, 1996-97, Bournemouth Symphony Orch., Royal Scottish Nat. Orch., 1997-98. Dir. operas The Emperor of Atlantis, Die Weisse Rose, Manekiny, Hansel and Gretel, Marriage of Figaro, Cosi fan Tutte, The Magic Flute, Il Combattimento, Echoes, Royal Opera House, Don Pasquale, Don Giovanni, English Touring Opera, House of the Dead, Salzburg Festival, Lohengrin, Blood Wedding, 1992-93, Petrified, The Place Theatre, London, 1992, Brundibar, Queen Elizabeth Hall, London, 1993, Craig's Progress, 1994, Boris Godunov, Vienna State Opera, 1994, Vanessa, 1994-95, Rise and Fall of the City of Mahagonny, Netherlands Touring Opera, 1996, Dangerous Liaisons, Washington Opera, 1997, Voices, Berlin Biennale, 1997-98. Marshall scholar Royal Coll. Music; Conducting fellow Royal Northern Coll. Music. Office: Kansas City Symphony 1020 Central St Ste 300 Kansas City MO 64105-1663

MANSON, JOANN ELISABETH, endocrinologist; b. Cleve., Apr. 14, 1953; d. S. Stanford and Therese (Palay) M.; m. Christopher N. Ames, June 12, 1979; children: Jennifer, Jeffrey, Joshua Simon. AB magna cum laude, Harvard U., 1975; MD, Case Western Res. U., 1979; MPH, Harvard Sch. Pub. Health, 1984, DPH, 1987. Bd. cert. internal medicine; bd. cert. in subspecialty of endocrinology and metabolism. Intern and resident internal medicine NEDH, Harvard Med. Sch., Boston, 1979-82; fellowship in endocrinology U. Hosp. Boston, Mass., 1982-84; rsch fellow in medicine Brigham and Women's Hosp., Boston, 1984-87, Andrew W. Mellon Found. fellow, 1987-89; dir. endocrinology, co-dir. women's health Brigham and Women's Hosp., Divsn. Preventive Medicine, Boston, 1993—; chief Divsn. Preventive Medicine Brigham and Women's Hosp., Boston, 1999—; staff physician, consulting endocrinologist Harvard Vanguard Med. Assocs., Peabody, Mass., 1986—; prof. medicine Harvard Med. Sch., Boston, 1999—, Elizabeth Brigham prof. women's health, 2003—. Mem. editl. bd. Am. Jour. Preventive Medicine, 1992—, Jour. Women's Health, 1996—; author textbooks and monographs; contbr. more than 400 articles to profl. jours. Vol. physician Lynn (Mass.) Shelter for the Homeless, 1989-93; med. adv. bd. Harvard Health Letter, Boston, 1992—, Greater Boston (Mass.) Diabetes Soc., 1993—, Harvard Women's Health Watch, Boston, 1993—; vol. Am. Heart Assn., 1992—. Named Hero in Women's Health, Am. Health for Women Mag., 1997, one of Top 10 Champions of Women's Health, Ladies Home Jour., 2000, one of Top Docs for Women. Boston mag., 2001; recipient Connors award for outstanding leadership in women's health, 1999-, Woman in Sci. award, Am. Med. Women's Assoc., 2003, Henry I. Bowditch award for excellence in pub. health Mass. Med. Soc., 2002. Fellow ACP, ACE; mem. AMA, Am. Med. Women's Assn., Am. Heart Assn., Women's Health Initiative (mem. steering com.), Alpha Omega Alpha. Avocations: playing with my children, reading, hiking, music, travel. Home: 14 Washington St Beverly MA 01915-5820 Office: Brigham and Women's Hosp 900 Commonwealth Ave E Fl 3 Boston MA 02215-1204 Office Phone: 617-278-0871. Business E-Mail: jmanson@rics.bwh.harvard.edu.

MANSSON, JOAN, librarian, consultant; b. Sacramento, June 9, 1950; d. Gunnar Emanuel Månsson and Signe Evy Jönsson. BA in Fine Arts, N.J. City U., 1982, MA in Studio Art, 1983, postgrad., 1983-84; MLS, Rutgers U., 1985. Grad. asst. art dept. N.J. City U., Jersey City, 1982-84; tchg. asst. Rutgers Art Libr., 1984-85; pub. svcs. libr. Maitland (Fla.) Pub. Libr., 1986—; rsch. cons. Tradingwise, Casselberry, Fla., 1989—; ind. rsch. cons., 1995—; freelance illustrator, 2002—. One-woman shows include Maitland Pub. Libr., 1999, W.T. Bland Pub. Libr., 2000, Maitland Pub. Libr., 2001, 2003, Patio Escapes, 2003. Mem. ALA, Fla. Libr. Assn. (chair young adult network 1988-92, steering com. 1994-96, chair YA caucus 1996-97, Transformers Honor Roll 1996), Fla. Pub. Libr. Assn. (spkr. conf. 1988), Ctrl. Fla. Libr. Consortium (continuing edn. com. 1994-96), Cen. Fla. Reads (steering com. 2003-2004). Lutheran. Avocations: pastel artist, weaver, painter, writing, digital. Office: Maitland Pub Libr 501 S Maitland Ave Maitland FL 32751-5672 E-mail: jmansson@maitlandpubliclibrary.org.

MANTELL, SUZANNE RUTH, editor; b. West Orange, N.J., Nov. 26, 1944; d. Milton A. and Florence B. M.; m. Peter Gray Friedman, 1985; 1 child, Erica Mantell Friedman Student, U. Chgo., 1962; B.F.A., Pratt Inst., 1967. Formerly assoc. editor Harper's mag., N.Y.C., exec. editor, 1977-80; editor Harper's Bookletter, 1974-77, Learning Mag., 1980-81, Family Learning Mag., 1983-84; reader Book of the Month Club, 1985-87, 91-99; editor Travel Bookstore Catalogue, Banana Republic, 1985-87; assoc. editor The N.Y. Observer, N.Y.C., 1987-91; acting Book News editor Pubs. Weekly, 1992-93, contbg. editor, 1993—. Also lectr. mag. writing Stanford U., U. Calif. at Santa Cruz. Consulting editor Spelman Coll. Messenger, 1994-98; columnist L.A. Times Book Review, 1998-99; arts editor New Times L.A., 1999-2001; author Art of the State: Vermont, 1998. Mem. PEN, PEN West USA, Nat. Book Critics Circle. Home: 101 Warwick Pl South Pasadena CA 91030-4062

MANTYLA, KAREN, distance learning consultant; b. Bronx, N.Y., Dec. 31, 1944; d. Milton and Sylvia (Diamond) Fischer; 1 child, Michael Alan. Student, Rockland Community Coll., Suffern, N.Y., 1962, NYU, 1967, Mercer U., 1981. Mktg. coordinator Credit Bur., Inc., Miami, Fla., 1973-79; dist. mgr. The Research Inst. Am., N.Y.C., 1979-80, regional dir., 1980-85, field sales mgr., 1985-86, nat. sales mgr., 1986-87; nat. accounts mgr. The Rsch. Inst. Am., N.Y.C., 1989; v.p. sales Bur. Bus. Practice/Paramount Comm., Inc., Waterford, Conn., 1989-93; pres. Quiet Power, Inc., Washington, 1993—. Author: Consultative Sales Power, 1995, Interactive Distance Learning Exercises That Really Work, 1999, The 2000/2001 ASTD Distance Learning Yearbook, 2000, Blending e-Learning: The Power is in the Mix, 2001; co-editor The 2001/2002 ASTD Distance Learning Yearbook; co-author: Distance Learning: A Step-By-Step Guide for Trainers, 1997, Blending E-Learning: The Power is in the Mix, 2001. Bd. dirs. Federal Govt. Distance Learning Assn. Named to Distance Learning Hall of Fame, Fed. Govt. Distance Learning Assn., 2003. Mem. ASTD, Sales and Mktg. Execs. (past bd. dirs. N.Y. chpt., v.p. Ft. Lauderdale chpt. 1979), U.S. Distance Learning Assn. (editor Distance Learning News, mem. tech. and comm. com. Fla. chpt.), Nat. Assn. Women Bus. Owners, U.S. C. of C., Women Entrepreneurs. Avocations: antiques, tennis, writing, swimming. Home: 6500 Majestic Prince Loop Gainesville VA 20155 Office: Quiet Power Inc 1201 Pennsylvania Ave NW Washington DC 20004-2401 E-mail: quietpower@aol.com.

MANTZELL, BETTY LOU, school health administrator; b. Brookville, Pa., Oct. 16, 1938; d. Elmer William and Wilda Mae (Enterline) M. Diploma, Ind. (Pa.) Hosp. Sch. Nursing, 1959; BSN, Case Western Res. U., 1969, MA, 1978; cert. supr. ednl. adminstrn. Cleve. State U., 1983; cert. supr., John Carroll U., 1989. RN, Ohio, Pa. Oper. room nurse Univ. Hosps. of Cleve., 1963-69; sch. nurse various locations Cleve. Pub. Schs., 1969-85, coord. sch. nurses, 1976-85, acting asst. supr. health svcs., 1985-86, supr. health svcs., 1986—. Mem. adv. com. to baccalaureate nursing program Cleve. State U.; prevention of blindness adv. com. Cleve. Sight Ctr.; active All Kids Count Consortium Cleve. Dept. Pub. Health; mem. sch. health com. Acad. Medicine Cleve.; Frances Payne Bolton Sch. Nursing, mem. alumni assn.; clin. instr. cmty. health nursing Case We. Res. U., Cleve., 1988-90, women's connection; mem. coun. econ. opportunities Greater Cleve.; mem. adv. com. Headstart Health Svcs. Mem. Am. Sch. Health Assn., Nat. Assn. Sch. Nurses, Ohio Assn. Sch. Nurses, Northeastern Ohio Assn. Sch. Nurses, Ohio Assn. Secondary Sch. Adminstrs., Cleve. Coun. Adminstrs. and Suprs., Cleve. Med. Libr. Assn. Office: Buhrer Elem Sch 1600 Buhrer Ave Cleveland OH 44109 Office Phone: 216-623-3759.

MANUEL, VIVIAN, public relations executive; b. Queens County, N.Y., May 6, 1941; d. George Thomas and Vivian (Anderson) M. BA, Wells Coll., 1963; MA, U. Wyo., Laramie, 1965. Mgmt. analyst Dept. Navy, 1966-68; account supr. GE Co., N.Y.C., 1968-72, corp. rep. bus. and fin., 1972-76; dir. corp. comm. Standard Brands Co., N.Y.C., 1976-78; pvt. cons. N.Y.C., 1978-80; pres. V M Comm. Inc., N.Y.C., 1980-97; pub. info. officer Mont. Dept. Commerce, Helena, 1997—2002; adminstr. Gough, Shanahan, Johnson & Waterman, Helena, 2003—. Mem. com. Girls Club N.Y., 1983—84; mem. adv. bd. Glenholme Sch., 1991—92; mem. allocation com. United Way Mont., 1998—; bd. dirs. Am. Lung Assn. of No. Rockies, 1999—2002; trustee Wells Coll., 1983—90. Mem. AAUW, N.Y. Women in Comms. (bd. v.p. 1983-85, chair Matrix awards 1985), Women Execs. in Pub. Rels. (bd. dirs. 1985-88), Women's Econ. Roundtable. Address: 1400 Flowerree St Helena MT 59601-6024 Business E-Mail: vam161@bresnan.com.

MANUELIAN, LUCY DER, art educator, architecture educator; b. Arlington, Mass. AB in English lit., Radcliffe Coll.; MA in Art History, Boston U., 1975, PhD in Art History, 1980. Head teaching fellow Boston U., 1975-76; vis. lectr. Framingham State Coll., 1979-80; archivist Armenian Archtl. Archives Project, 1979-84; lectureship in Armenian art and architecture Tufts U., Harvard U., McGill U., Boston U., Boston Coll., U. Mass., 1984—89; Arthur H. Dadian and Ara Oztemel prof. Armenian art and archtl. history Tufts U., Medford, 1989—. Mus. cons. Dartmouth Coll.; lectr. Poly Inst., U. Erevan, USSR, U. Aarhus, Denmark, Courtauld Inst., England, McGill U., U. Mich., U. Pa., Harvard U., Brown U., U. Chgo., Columbia U., Northeastern U., UCLA, Dartmouth Coll., Wellesley Coll., Mt. Holyoke Coll., Queens Coll., Rutgers U., London Sch. Econs.; Libr. Congress lectr. Met. Mus. N.Y., cultural and cmty. orgns. U.S. and abroad; author/narrator 4 TV documentaries on Armenian art. Author: Armenian Architecture, 4 vols., 1981—88, Dictionary of Middle Ages, 1982—89, Dictionary of Art, The Gregorian Collection-Armenian Rugs, 1983, Weavers, Merchants and Kings: The Inscribed Rugs of Armenia, 1984; contbr. chapters to books, articles to profl. jours. Fellow to USSR, 1977-78, fellow Bunting Inst., Radcliffe Coll., 1971-73; Samuel H. Kress grantee Boston U., 1975, 78, Rsch. grantee Nat. Assn. for Armenian Studies and Rsch. to USSR, 1972, 78; sr. scholar grantee Am. Coun. Learned Socs./Soviet Acad. Scis., 1983; recipient Jack H. Kolligian award Nat. Assn. Armenian Studies and Rsch., 1981, Boyan award Armenian Students Assn., Woman of Achievement award Armenian Internat. Women's Assn., 1994, Kohar award Armenian Rugs Soc.; named to Boston U. Acad. Disting. Alumni, 1986, Armenian of Yr., Masons, 1990. Mem. Armenian Acad. Sci. (cons. Art Inst. symposium 1990—), Nat. Assn. Armenian Studies and Rsch. (adv. bd. 1991—), Soc. Armenian Studies, Aga Khan Program Islamic Architecture (affiliate), Middle East Studies Assn., Coll. Art Assn., Medieval Acad. Accademia Tiberina Rome (assoc.), Assn. Internat. Etudes Armeniennes, Nat. Assn. Armenian Studies & Rsch. (hon. life), Phi Beta Kappa (hon. Radcliffe Coll.). Achievements include research in archaeological projects using ground penetrating radar technology. Avocations: music, piano, tennis, the restoration of Medieval Armenian churches. Business E-Mail: lucy.manuelian@tufts.edu. E-mail: ldm@world.std.com.

MANUS, NANCY MANNING, writer, former social services administrator; b. Jesup, Ga., Jan. 13, 1945; d. Charlie Dalton and Zellie Adell (Flowers) Manning; children: Andrew Ceaphus, Kevin Charles, Thomas Lindsey. BA in Journalism, U. Ga., 1967. Ga. state merit sys. cert. caseworker, 1968, level II, 1969, eligibility supr., 1970. Case worker I Wayne County Dept. Family and Children Svcs., Jesup, 1968-69; case worker II Coffee County Dept. Family and Children Svcs., Douglas, Ga., 1969-70, eligibility supr., 1970-73; freelance writer Odum, Ga., 1975-80; dir. med. social svcs. Wayne Meml. Hosp., Jesup, 1981-98. Com. mem. Edn./Cons. Social Work Found. of Ga. Hosp. Assn., 1989-98. Vol. hosp. blood drive coord. Red Cross Low Country Chpt., Hinesville, Ga., 1982-87; mem. Adv. Coun. Health and Edn., Wayne County, Ga., 1985-98; assisted living cons. in cmty., 1992—. Recipient Recognition for Svc. award Red Cross Low Country Chpt., Hinesville, 1985. Mem. Ga. Soc. Social Workers in Health Care of Ga. Hosp. Assn. (dist. chmn. S.E. dist. 1996-97, sec. 1996-97, Com. Achievement award 1996, cert. appreciation service, 1997-98). Avocations: do-it-yourself building projects, gardening, exploring nature, dance, reading.

MANZI, SHARON ULRICH, education educator, social worker; b. Newton, N.J., Sept. 3, 1944; d. Robert Gustus and Jean Elizabeth Ulrich; m. Raffaele Manzi; children: Adele Campagna, Miriam, Michael, Raffaele Jr., Michelle Kochman. PhD, The Union Inst., Cin., 1977. Cert. social worker N.J., lic. mental health practitioner Ga., diplomate Am. Psychotherapy Assn., Am. Coll. Forensic Examiners, Inc.; cert. educator Ga. Instr. Southea. Sem. Ext., Aberdeen, Md., 1980—81; counselor, instr. Harford C.C., Belair, Md., 1980—82; exec. dir. Christian Homes for Children, Hackensack, NJ, 1982—94; instr. The King's Coll., N.Y.C., 1983—85; employment counselor N.J. Dept. Labor, Paterson, 1994—95; exec. dir. Literacy Vols. Am. - Bergen County, Hackensack, 1995—97; instr. South U., Savannah, Ga., 1997—2000; county svc. mgr., social svc. provider II Gateway Cmty. Svc. Bd., Pembroke, Ga., 1998—2001; instr. St. Leo U., Savannah, 1999—; spl. edn. tchr. Savannah-Chatham Pub. Sch., 2001—. Cons. MEANS' Mission, I.N.C., Savannah, 1995—. Author: Teenagers: Our Spiritual and Social Concern, 1997, 2d edit., 2003, Is Joy Vertical or Horizontal?, 1997, Manual for Better Business of a Non-Profit Christian Human Service Agency, 2000, Manual for Better Management of a Non-Profit Christian Maternity Home, 2000, Heaven Help the Called Ones, 2002. Named Outstanding Young Woman of Am., 1969, Young Career Woman of Balt., Bus. and Profl. Women's Balt. Club, 1969, Cmty. Leader of Am., 1970; recipient cert. of recognition, Slippery Rock State Coll., 1979, God and Svc. emblem, Girl Scouts Am., 1980. Baptist. Avocations: reading, bicycling, gardening. Home and Office: MEANS' Mission INC 12905 Canterbury Rd Savannah GA 31419-2705 Personal E-mail: sharon@rmanzi.com. E-mail: meansinc@rmanzi.com.

MAPLE, MARILYN JEAN, educational media coordinator; b. Turtle Creek, Pa., Jan. 16, 1931; d. Harry Chester and Agnes (Dobbie) Kelley; 1 child, Sandra Maple. BA, U. Fla., 1972, MA, 1975, PhD, 1985. Journalist various newspaper including Mountain Eagle, Jasper, Ala., Boise (Idaho) Statesman, Daytona Beach (Fla.) Jour., Lorain (Ohio) Jour.; account exec. Frederides & Co., N.Y.C.; prodr. hist. films Fla. State Mus., Gainesville, 1967-69; writer, dir., prodr. med. and sci. films and TV prodns. for 6 medically related colls. U. Fla., Gainesville, 1969—. Pres. Media Modes, Inc., Gainesville. Author: On the Wings of a Butterfly; columnist Health Care Edn. mag.; contbr. Fla. Hist. Quar. Recipient Blakslee award, 1969, spl. award, 1979; Monsour lectr., 1979. Mem. Health Edn. Media Assn. (bd. dirs., awards 1977, 79), Phi Delta Kappa, Kappa Tau Alpha. Home: 1927 NW 7th Ln Gainesville FL 32603-1103 Office: U Fla PO Box 16J Gainesville FL 32602-0016 E-mail: mmaple@atlantic.net.

MAPLE, OPAL LUCILLE, school psychologist; b. Canton, Ill., Nov. 15, 1935; d. Dwight Willard and Eileen Beatrice (Cadwalader) Beaty; m. Gilbert Roy Maple, June 30, 1967 (dec. 1985). BA, Wheaton (Ill.) Coll., 1958; MS, We. Ill. U., 1962. Cert. sch. psychologist, Ill. Tchr. Community Dist. #5, Cuba, Ill., 1958-60, Community Dist. #66, Canton, Ill., 1960-61; asst. dean women Moody Bible Inst., Chgo., 1961-64; sch. psychologist intern Chgo. Pub. Schs., 1964-65; sch. psychologist Peoria (Ill.) pub. schs., 1965-69, Waukegan (Ill.) pub. schs., 1969-81, Knox-Warren Spl. Edn., Galesburg, Ill., 1986-96, ret., 1996. Co-author pre-sch. test, 1975. Deaconess, treas. Antioch Evang. Free Ch., 1971-81; deaconess, fin. sec. Bethel Bapt. Ch., Galesburg, 1982-94. Mem. Cen. Ill. Sch. Psychologists Assn. (pres. 1967-68), Ill. Psychol. Assn. (sec. 1977-79), DAR, Knox County Genealogical Soc., Ill. Sch. Psychologists Assn. Republican. Baptist. Avocations: genealogical research, travel.

MAPLESDEN, CAROL HARPER, marital and family therapist, music educator; b. Phila., Aug. 27, 1947; d. Emmitt Dewain and Helen Esther (Davison) Harper; m. James Paul Maplesden, May 27, 1967; children: Andrew James, Elizabeth Elvira. BA, Holy Family Coll., Phila., 1979; MA, La Salle U., Phila., 1984. Cert. counselor Nat. Bd. Cert. Counselors, lic. profl. counselor of mental health Del., Pa. Child, youth and family therapist People Acting To Help (PATH), Phila., 1983-86, Benjamin Rush Cmty. Mental Health, Phila., 1987-88; clin. dir. N.E. Treatment, Phila., 1988-89; outpatient supr. Interact Com. Mental Health, Phila., 1989; program supr. Cath. Charities Christopher House, Trenton, N.J., 1989-90; dir. Carden Family Inst., Phila., 1984—, instr. keyboard, organist, vocal performer, vocal choir and handbell choir dir. Carden music dlv., 1993—. Seminar lectr. in Phila. area. Author: (piano course and audio tape) Young Beginnings Piano Course, Part I, 1993. Mem.: ACA, Internat. Assn. Marriage and Family Counselors, Daughters Am. Colonists, Daughters Union Vets. Civil War (Pa. state pres. 2001—02). Republican. Methodist. Avocations: history studies, genealogy, crafts.

MAPP, RHONDA, professional basketball player; b. Oct. 13, 1969; Ctr.-forward Charlotte Sting, 1997—. Named Kodak and Street & Smith All-Am., 1992, Street & Smith All-Am., 1990; named to, ACC All-Tournament Team, 1989, 1991, First-Team All-ACC, 1991, 1992. Office: Charlotte Sting 3308 Oak Lake Blvd # B Charlotte NC 28208-7707

MAPSTONE, KIMBERLY I. psychotherapist; b. Pitts., Apr. 24, 1958; d. Ralph M. and Irma S. (Sutton) M. Student, Allegheny County C.C., Pitts.; M in Human Svcs. summa cum lauda, Lincoln U., 1995. Lic. profl. counselor, cert. addiction counselor. Clk. stenographer II, clk. stenographer I Referee's Office, Unemployment Compensation Bd. Rev., Commonwealth of Pa., Pitts., 1977—90; counselor Creative Living Ctr., Pitts., 1991-96; pvt practice, 1996—. Bd. dirs. Visions of Healing, Ctr. Creative Living, Pitts., 1993—; presenter workshops and seminars Overeaters Anonymous, 1983—, Women United in Recovery, Inc., 1986—, Wilkinsburg Family Cmty. Fun Festival, 1991, Allegheny County C.C., 1991, Life-Work Ctr., 1992; vol. hotline counselor Pitts. Action Against Rape, 1987-88. Mem. Women's Bus. Network, Pi Gamma Mu. Home: 2207 Buena Vista St Pittsburgh PA 15218-2232

MARAFIOTI, KAYALYN A. lawyer; b. Rochester, N.Y., 1954; AB cum laude, Harvard U., 1976; JD, NYU, 1979. Bar: N.Y. 1980. Ptnr. Skadden, Arps, Slate, Meagher & Flom, N.Y.C. Note and comment editor NYU Jour. Internat. Law and Politics, 1978-79. Office: Skadden Arps Slate Meagher & Flom 4 Times Sq Fl 24 New York NY 10036-6595

MARAMAN, KATHERINE ANN, judge; b. Los Alamos, N.Mex., Aug. 13, 1951; d. William Joseph and Katherine Ann (Thorpe) Maraman. BA, Colorado Coll., 1973; JD, U. N.Mex., 1976. Bar: N.Mex. 1976, Guam 1978, Trust Territory Pacific Islands, Commonwealth of No. Mariana Islands, U.S. Ct. Appeals (9th cir.), U.S. Supreme Ct. Draftsperson N.Mex. Legis. Coun. Svc., Santa Fe, 1976—77; atty. Brooks & Klitzkie, P.C., Agana, 1977—84; pvt. practice Agana, 1985—88; counsel Office of Gov., Agana, 1988—94; judge Superior Ct., Agana, 1994—. Mem. asst. legis. counsel Guam Legis., Agana, 1977—80, mem. minority counsel, 1981—87; bd. dirs. Pub. Defender Svc. Corp., Agana, 1988—94. Trustee Guam Ter. Law Libr., 1994—; counsel Rep. Party, Agana, 1981—94; deacon First Presbyn. Reformed Ch., Agana; bd. dirs. Guam Rehab. and Workshop, Inc., Tumon, 1983—95. Mem.: Mem. Guam Bar Assn. Office: Superior Ct Guam 120 W Obrien Dr Hagatna GU 96910-5174

MARATOS-FLIER, ELEFTHERIA, medical educator, physician; b. N.Y.C., Dec. 15, 1951; d. Costas and Anna (Domenikos) Maratos; m. Jeffrey Scott Flier, Dec. 7, 1975; children: Sarah, Lydia. BS, NYU, 1972; MD, Mt. Sinai Sch. Medicine, N.Y.C., 1976. Intern and resident George Washington U. Hosp., Washington, 1976-78; resident Beth Israel Hosp., Boston, 1978-79; rsch. fellow Harvard Sch. Pub. Health, Boston, 1980-81; fellow Joslin Diabetes Ctr., Boston, 1981-82; instr. Brigham & Women's Hosp., Harvard Med. Sch., Boston, 1982-87, asst. prof., 1987—. Contbr. articles to Sci., Jour. Cell Biology, Jour. Virology, Jour. Clin. Investigation. Mary K. Iacocca Rsch. fellow, 1981. Mem. Am. Soc. Virology, Am. Microbiol. Assn., Am. Diabetes Assn., Phi Beta Kappa. Office: Joslin Diabetes Ctr One Joslin Pl Boston MA 02215 also: Brigham & Womens Hosp 75 Francis St Boston MA 02115-6110

MARATTA SNYDER, GRACE ELVIRA, volunteer; b. Jackson, Ohio, July 22, 1922; d. John William and Mary Ann (Lewis) Matthews; m. James Edward Maratta, Oct. 14, 1957 (div. May 1971); m. Price Knapp Snyder, Sept. 19, 1998. Student, Rio Grande Coll., 1940-41, Columbus Bus. U., 1941-42. Clk.-typist Ohio State Dept. Trans., Columbus, 1942-44; adminstrv. office mgr. Div of Police City of Columbus, 1944-77, ret., 1977; legis. agt. Police and Fire Retirees of Ohio, Reynoldsburg, 1978—. Trustee Columbus Police Sub-Relief Fund, 1967—, Adult Life Care Ctr., Reynoldsburg, Ohio, 1990—; lobbyist Police and Fire Retirees of Ohio, Columbus, 1978—. Past pres. Reynoldsburg Womens Civic Club, 1979-81, Reynoldsburg Womens Rep. Club, 1982-84; pres. Reynoldsburg Sr. Citizens Ctr., 1988—; trustee Wesley Ridge Retirement and Health Complex, 1996—. Recipient Disting. Svc. award Ohio Gen. Assembly, 1970, Cmty. Builders award Masonic Lodge 340, 1996; named Outstanding Svc. Sr. Citizen Reynoldsburg Jaycees, 1987, Outstanding Eldercare Work, Ohio State Dept. Aging, 1989; inducted into Ohio Sr. Citizens Hall of Fame, 1994. Mem. Columbus Police Retirees Assn. (Outstanding Svc. 1981). Republican. Methodist. Avocations: musical theatre, reading, tv watching, shopping, eating out. Office: Police & Fire Retirees 7335 E Livingston Ave Reynoldsburg OH 43068 E-mail: pfro@iwaynet.net.

MARAZITA, ELEANOR MARIE HARMON, retired secondary school educator; b. Madison County, Ind., Oct. 25, 1933; d. William Houston Harmon and Martha Belle (Savage) Hinds; m. Philip Marazita; children: Mary Louise, Frank, Dominic, Vincent, Elizabeth Faye, Candice Marie, Daniel William. BS in Home Econs., Ctrl. Mich. U., 1955; MA in Human Ecology, Mich. State U., 1971. Cert. vocat. home econs. tchr., K-Jr. Coll., cert. speech correction tchr. Tchr. adult edn., Mt. Pleasant, Mich., 1956; substitute tchr. North Branch (Mich.) Schs., 1961-64; tchr. Pied Piper Coop. Nursery Sch., Lansing, Mich., 1964-69, Lansing C.C., 1971-81, Grand Ledge (Mich.) H.S., 1969-98; ret., 2002. Mich. tchr. del. World Conf. Tchg. Profls., 1985, 98; adv. mem. Mich. Tchr. Competency Testing Program, 1992. Bd. dirs. Greater Lansing chpt. U.N., 1995-98; vol. St. Lawrence Mental Health Hosp., 1972-73, Listening Ear Crisis Intervention Ctr., 1973-77, Capital City Convalescent Home, 1969-73; chmn. study com. Delta Twp. Libr., 1969-73, Jr. League, 1969—; interviewer Youth for Understanding, 1978-83; active exch. student orientation program Mich. State U., 1977, exch. trips, 1979-82; mem. adv. bd. Mich. League Human Svcs., 1988-91, Eaton County Extension Svcs., 1988-91, Mich. Women's Assembly, 1986-91; mem. Friends of Waverly Libr., 1963—; participant 3rd Congress Educators Caucus, 1986-92; 4-H leader, 1950-65. Recipient State Tchr. Multicultural award, 1989, UN Global Educator award, 1991, State Tchr. Maureen Wyatt feminist award, 1996. Mem. AAUW, LWV, NEA (del. 1998, observer 2d ann. Ednl. Internat. Congress 1998), DAR (co-chair State Good Citizen 1999-2003), DAR (v.p. Cameo Club 2002—), PEO, Mich. Edn. Assn. (polit. action exec. bd. 1986-98, v.p. women's caucus 1986-93, Liz Siddell State Internat. Cultures award 1992), Circumnavigators Club (travel around world in one trip 1993), Century Club (travel in 100 countries outside U.S. 1994, Seven Continent award 2003, Globetrotter award 2003), Delta Kappa Gamma (co-chair State World Fellowship 1993-95, chair state legislation com. 1997-99, chpt. Women of Distinction award 1993), Phi Delta Kappa (Tchr. of Yr. Mich. State U. 1992). Avocation: travel. Home: 214 Farmstead Ln Lansing MI 48917-3015

MARAZITA, MARY LOUISE, genetics researcher; b. Cheboygan, Mich., June 13, 1954; m. Richard T. McCoy, 1984; 5 children. BS, Mich. State U., 1976; PhD in Genetics, U. N.C., 1980. Fellow U. So. Calif., 1980-82; statistician, instr. UCLA, 1982-86; asst. prof. human genetics Med. Coll. Va., 1986-93; dir. Cleft Palate-craniofacial Ctr. U. Pitts., 1993-00, head divsn. oral biology, 1999—, asst. dean for rsch. Sch. Dental Medicine, 2000-2001, assoc. dean rsch., 2001—. Instr. biomath. U. Calif., 1984-86; asst. prof. dentistry Med. Coll. Va., 1992-93; assoc. prof. human genetics and oral maxillofacial surgery U. Pitts., 1993-97, prof. human genetics and oral and maxillofacial surgery, 1997—. Fellow Am. Coll. Med. Genetics, Am. Cleft Palate Assn., Am. Soc. Human Genetics, Internat. Genetic Epidemiol. Soc., Internat. Assn. Dental Rsch. Achievements include research in genetics of cleft lip, cleft palate and other craniofacial anomalies, including statistical genetic analysis and gene mapping studies. Office: U Pitts Divsn Oral Biology/Genetics Ste 500 Cellomics Bldg/100 Technology Dr Pittsburgh PA 15219

MARBACH, DONNA MAUREEN, writer; b. King City, Calif., Dec. 9, 1948; d. William Edward and Elfriede Hendrika (Maurer) M.; m. John Andrew Feldmann, Sept. 14, 1969 (div. Aug. 1977); m. Joseph Patrick Brennan, Sept. 6, 1980; children: Brian Timothy, Erin Coleen, Shannon Margaret, Kevin Michael, Colin Riley. BA in Lit., U. Calif., Santa Cruz, 1971; MSEd, U. Pa., 1975. V.p. asst. for cmty. program and others U. Pa., Phila., 1971-75; program dir. Am. Lung Assn. of Phila., 1975-78; rehab. counselor Horizon House, Phila., 1978-79; employment and tng. mgr. City of Phila., 1979-84; v.p. adminstrn. Vols. of America, Rochester, N.Y., 1984-93; pres. Easter Seal Soc. of Monroe County, Rochester, 1993-94, bus. mgr. Scholars Choice, Rochester, 1995-97, mktg. specialist, exhibitor, 1997—; art tchr. Am. Sch. of GDL, Guadalajara, Mexico, 1999; freelance writer, artist Guadalajara, 1997—. Mem. PTA (treas.), Rochester, 1996-97, Browncroft Neighborhood Assn., 1984-97, Monroe Co. Foster Parents Assn., 1985-89, Del. Regional Planning Commn., Rochester, 1985-93, U. Calif. Alumni Assn.; pres. Rochester Interfaith Jail Ministry, 1988-92. Mem. Am. Craft Coun., Art and Cultural Coun. Rochester, Internat. Soc. Poets (disting. mem.), Poetry Soc. Am., Acad. Am. Poets, Internat. Womens Writing Guild, Nat. Mus. Women In Arts. Democrat. Roman Catholic. Avocations: fundraising, painting, teaching. Home: 1935 Penfield Rd Penfield NY 14526-1434

MARBURGER, DARLA A. federal agency administrator; d. Maynard and Dawn Marburger. BS in agr. Journalism, Tex. A&M U.; MS in agr. econ., Tex. A&M. Dep. asst. sec. US Dept. Edn., Off. Elem. Sec. Edn. Policy, Wash., 2002—; sr. policy analyst Tex. Senate Edn. Com., Tex.; Congl. adv., agr. nat. resources issues Tex. Leg., Tex., 1994. Vol. tchr. ESL. Office: US Dept Edn Policy Dept FOB-6 Rm 3W305 400 Maryland Ave SW Washington DC 20202 E-mail: darla.marburger@ed.gov.

MARBURY, VIRGINIA LOMAX, insurance and investment executive; b. Ruston, La., June 25, 1918; d. Dallas Daniel and Della (Southern) Lomax; m. William A. Marbury Jr., Sept. 5, 1943; children: Rebekah, Caroline. BA, La. Tech. U., 1936, LLD (hon.), 1987; MusB, La. State U., 1938. Exec. v.p. Marbury Corp., Ruston, La., 1944—; sec.-treas. Bankers Life La., Ruston, 1959—. 1st v.p., membership chmn. Lincoln Parish Mus. and Hist. Soc., Ruston, La., 1992—. Recipient Tower Medallion award La. Tech. U., 1991. Mem. Shreveport Symphony Soc. Republican. Episcopalian. Office: Marbury Corp 601 N Trenton St Ruston LA 71270-3840

MARCALI, JEAN GREGORY, retired chemist; b. Jermyn, Pa., May 29, 1926; d. John Robert and Anna Marie Gregory; m. Kalman Marcali, Oct. 6, 1956; children: Coleman, Frederick. Student, U. Pa., 1948-52, U. Del., 1971-72. Microanalyst E.I. du Pont de Nemours & Co., Deepwater, N.J., 1943-60, tech. info. analyst, organic chems. dept., 1960-64, tech. info. analyst info. systems dept. Wilmington, Del., 1964-67, sr. adviser tech. info., 1967-70, supr. tech. info., 1970-82, 85-89, supr. adminstrv. svcs. Ctrl. Rsch. Dept., 1982-85, cons., 1989-92, retired, 1992. Sec. Alfred I. Dupont Elem. PTA, 1971, pres. 1972; pres. PTA Brandywine Sch. Dist., 1973; mem. Wilmington Dist. Rep. Com., 1976—. Mem. Am. Chem. Soc. (treas. div. chem. info. 1976-81, chmn.-elect 1981, chmn. 1982, 83, div. councilor 1983-90), Am. Chem. Soc. (com. on chem. abstracts svc. 1983-85, 87-93, mem. joint bd. coun. com. on chem. abstracts svc. 1994-96, 98, 99, 2000, Del. sec. chem. lit. topical group, chmn. 1979-80, chem. vets. chmn.-elect 1999), Order Ea. Star, Du Pont Country. Lutheran. Home: 312 Waycross Rd Wilmington DE 19803-2950

MARCDANTE, KAREN JEAN, medical educator; b. Milw., Sept. 15, 1955; d. Willard Karl and Beth Elaine (Maule) Kohn; m. Mark Wendelberger, Aug. 5, 1978 (div. Sept. 1985); m. Anthony Marcdante, Oct. 17, 1998. Student, Marquette U., 1973-76; MD, Med. Coll. Wis., 1980. Diplomate Am. Bd. Pediat. Resident in pediat. Med. Coll. Wis. affiliated hosps., Milw., 1980-83; instr. pediat. Med. Coll. Wis., Milw., 1983-85, asst. prof. pediat., 1987-94, assoc. prof. pediat., 1994-2000, prof. pediat., 2000—, assoc. dean curriculum, 1997—2003, vice-chair edn. dept. pediat., 1994—; fellow in pediatric critical care U. Calif., San Francisco, 1985-87; vice chief staff Children's Hosp. Wis., Milw., 1995-97. Dir. Respiratory Care Svcs., 1992-98, Transport Program, 1998—; chief dept. pediat. Children's Hosp. Wis., 1991-95, dept. critical care 1993-95, mem. numerous coms., including care mgmt. steering com., 1994-98, critical care com., 1991—, pres.-elect, 2003--. Contbr. numerous articles to profl. jours. Recipient New Investigator award Assn. Am. Med. Colls., 1992, Cert. Leadership award YWCA and Marquette Electronics Found., 1992; grantee Dept. HHS, 1996—. Mem. Am. Acad. Pediat. (pub. rels. chair Wis. chpt. 1988-91, sec.-treas. 1990-95, v.p. 1995-96, chair careers and opportunities 1996-2001), Soc. Critical Care Medicine (chair task force on quality improvement pediat. 1994-96, quality indicator devel. work group 1997-98, Presdl. citation 1996, 97), Coun. on Med. Student Edn. in Pediat. (co-chair task force on tchg. methods 1991—, nominating com. 1993-95, exec. com. 1996-99, sec.-treas. 1997—). E-mail: kwendel@mail.mcw.edu.

MARCEAU, JUDITH MARIE, retired elementary school educator, small business owner; b. Gardner, Mass., Aug. 10, 1946; d. George Joseph and Bernice Victoria (Johnson) Babineau; m. James Victor Krymowski, Aug. 20, 1976 (div. Mar. 1985); children: Kathryn Victoria, Kenneth James; m. Glenn Francis Marceau, Aug. 30, 1989. Grad., Sch. Worcester Art Mus., 1967; BFA, Clark U., 1971. Tchr. elem. art Quabbin Regional Pub. Schs., Barre, Mass., 1967-70, Gardner (Mass.) Pub. Schs., 1970—2003, ret., 2003; propr. Babineau's Corner Antiques Shop, Hubbardston, 2003—. Author, editor: Fascinating Facts of Gardner, 1977, 2d edit., 1999, Hubbardston as Seen Through the Eyes of its Children, 1987; author numerous poems. Active Hubbarston Hist. Commn.; vol. Hubbarston Recycling Initiative; bd. dirs. Gardner Edn. Assn., 1975-86; bd. dirs. Youth Advocacy and Counseling Ctr., Gardner, 1979-82. Recipient Citation of Outstanding Edn. City of Gardner, 1994, 2000, Cert. of Commendation, Mayor of City of Gardner. Mem. Mass. Tchrs. Assn., Nat. Tchrs. Assn. Avocations: writing history, poetry, antiques, watercolor painting, sketching. Home: 221 Gardner Rd Hubbardston MA 01452-1655 Office: Babineau's Corner Antiques 221 Gardner Rd Hubbardston MA 01452 Office Phone: 978-632-2840.

MARCEAU, YVONNE, ballroom dancer, educator; b. Chgo., July 13, 1950; BFA, U. Utah, 1972; AA, Imperial Soc. Ballroom Dance. Ballet dancer Ballet West; ptnr. with Pierre Dulaine, 1976; founder, artistic dir. Am. Ballroom Theatre, N.Y.C., 1984-93; educator dance divsn. Julliard Sch., N.Y.C., 1993—. Guest tchr. Sch. Am. Ballet, N.Y.C.; tchr. ballroom dancing Juilliard Sch. Appearances include The Smithsonian Inst., JFK Ctr. for Performing Arts, N.Y. State Theater, N.Y.C., Sadlers Wells, London, (Broadway and London show) Grand Hotel, 1989-92, toured with Pierre Dulaine and Am. Ballroom Theatre worldwide. Recipient Recipient Brit. Theatrical Arts Championships 4 times, Spl. Astaire award, Dance Educator awards, Outstanding Achievement in Dance award Nat. Coun. Dance Am., 1992, Dance Mag. award, 1993.*

MARCEAUX, LINDA D'AUGEREAU, elementary school educator; b. Abbeville, La., Sept. 27, 1947; d. Charles d'Augereau, Jr. and Hazel Marie Bellot d'Augereau; m. Alex John Marceaux, Aug. 31, 1968; 1 child, Jana Nichole. BA, U. Southwestern La., 1988. Cert. elem. edn. grades 1-8, spl. edn. mild/moderate grades 1-12 generic Dept. Edn. State La. Spl. edn. grades 4th-6th behavior disorder/resource Lafayette (La.) Parish Sch. Bd., 1988—91, educator 4th grade, 1991—2000, educator 6th grade math, 2000—01, educator 8th grade math, 2001—03, educator 7th -8th grade math. honors, 2003—. Mem. Student La. Assn. Educators U. Southwestern La., Lafayette, 1983—88; membership chair Coun. for Exceptional Chil dren, 2001—02; mem. Lafayette Parish Assn. Educators, 1988—; pres. Student Coun. for Exceptional Children, U. SW La., 1986—88. V.p. KC Aux., Abbeville, La., 1983—85; pres. Parents for Progress, Meaux, La., 1983—85; coach/advisor Vermilion Boys Football League Cheerleaders, Abbeville, 1983—86; coach/asst. Vermilion Girls Basketball, Abbeville, 1985—87, cheerleader coach Milton Mid. Sch., 1992—2000; co-organizer, co-chair Wives of Workers, Tex. City, Tex., 1972—74. Nominee Outstanding Inclusion Tchr., Coun. for Exceptional Children, 1998—99, Tchr. award, Lafayette Edn. Found., 1999; recipient Coach's award, Universal Cheerleading Assn., 1999. Mem.: La. Tchrs. Mathematics (math tournament com., Principal's award com.), La. Fedn. Coun. Exceptional Children (state membership chair 2002—), Lafayette Paris Assn. Classroom Tchrs., La. Assn. Educators. Roman Catholic. Avocations: woodworking, motorcycling, travel. Home: 410 Quail Dr Lafayette LA 70508 Office: Paul Breaux Mid Sch Lafayette LA 70508

MARCH, JACQUELINE FRONT, retired chemist; b. Wheeling, W.Va., 1914; m. A.W. March (dec.); children: Wayne Front, Gail March Cohen. BS, Case Western Res. U., 1937, MA, 1939; postgrad., U. Chgo.; PhD, U. Pitts., 1945. Clin. chemist U. Chgo.; rsch. analyst Koppers Co.; info. scientist Union Carbide Corp., Carnegie-Mellon U., Pitts.; propr. March Med. Rsch. Lab. etiology of diabetes, Dayton, Ohio; ret. Guest scientist Kettering Found., Yellow Springs, Ohio; Dayton Found. fellow Miami Valley Hosp. Rsch. Inst.; chemistry faculty U. Dayton, computer/chem. info. scientist Rsch. Inst. U. Dayton; on-base prin. investigator Air Force Info. Ctr. Wright-Patterson AFB, 1969-79; chem. info. specialist Nat. Inst. Occupl. Safety and Health, Cin., 1979-90; propr. JFM Cons., Ft. Myers, Fla., 1990-93; ret., 1993; designer info. sys., spkr. in field. Contbr. articles to profl. jours. Active Retired and Sr. Vol. Program Lee County Sch. Dist., 1992-93, Lee County Hosp. Med. Libr., Rutenberg County Libr. Recipient Letter of Commendation, Girl Scouts U.S., 1931, Cert. of Recognition, U. Dayton, 1950, Outstanding Profl. Achievement award Affiliated Engring. and Sci. Found. of Dayton, 1978, others; Wyeth Gastrointestinal fellow Med. rsch. U. Chgo., 1940-42. Mem. AAUP (exec. bd. 1978-79), Am. Soc. Info. Sci. (treas. South Ohio 1973-75), Am. Chem. Soc. (emeritus, Fla. chpt., pres. Dayton 1977), Dayton Engring. Soc. (hon.), Soc. Advancement Materials and Process Engring. (Fla. chpt., pres. Midwest chpt. 1977-78), 60 Dayton Affiliated Tech. Socs. (Outstanding Scientist and Engr. award 1978), Alumni Assn. of Carnegie-Mellon U. (hon.), Sigma Xi (emeritus Fla. chpt., pres. Cin. fed. environ. chpt. 1986-87).

MARCH, KATHLEEN PATRICIA, judge; b. May 18, 1949; married; 2 children. BA, Colo. Coll., 1971; JD, Yale U., 1974. Bar: N.Y. 1975, Calif. 1978. Law clk. to hon. judge Thomas J. Griesa U.S. Dist. Ct. (so. dist.) N.Y., 1974-75; assoc. Cahill, Gordon & Reindel, N.Y.C., 1975-77; asst. U.S. atty. criminal div. Office of U.S. Atty. Cen. Dist. Calif., L.A., 1978-82; assoc. Adams, Duque & Hazeltine, L.A., 1982-85; ptnr. Demetriou, Del Guercio & Lovejoy, L.A., 1985-88; judge U.S. Bankruptcy Ct. Cen. Dist. Calif., L.A., Calif., 1988—. Bd. editors Yale U. Law Jour. Mem.: ABA, Fin. Lawyers Assn., L.A. Bankruptcy Forum (bd. dirs.), Nat. Assn. Women Judges, Women Lawyers Assn., L.A. County Bar Assn., Fed. Bar Assn., Phi Beta Kappa. Avocations: horseback riding, scuba diving, photography. Office: Roybal Fed Ct Bldg 255 E Temple St Ste 1460 Los Angeles CA 90012-3332

MARCHAK, MAUREEN PATRICIA, anthropology and sociology educator; b. Lethbridge, Alta., Can., June 22, 1936; d. Adrian Ebenezer and Wilhelmina Rankin (Hamilton) Russell; m. William Marchak, Dec. 31, 1956; children: Geordon Eric, Lauren Craig. BA, U. B.C., Vancouver, Can., 1958, PhD, 1970. Asst. prof. U. B.C., Vancouver, 1972-75, assoc. prof., 1975-80, prof., 1980—, head dept. anthropology and sociology, 1987-90, dean faculty arts, 1990-96, disting. scholar in residence Peter Wall Inst., 2000—, prof., dean emerita of arts, 2001—; sr. rsch. fellow Ctr. Internat. Rels. Liu Inst. for Study of Global Issues, 2002—. Author: Ideological Perspectives on Canada, 1975, 2d edit., 1981, 3d edit., 1988, In Whose Interests, 1979, Green Gold, 1983 (John Porter award 1985), The Integrated Circus, The New Right and The Restructuring of Global Markets, 1991, Logging the Globe, 1995, Falldown, Forest Policy in British Columbia, 1999, Racism, Sexism and the University, the Political Science Affair at UBC, 1996, God's Assassins. State Terrorism in Argentina in the 1970's, 1999 (Wallace J. Ferguson prize, Hon. Mention), Reigns of Terror, 2003; author, co-editor: Uncommon Property, 1987; mem. editl. bd. Can. Rev. Sociology and Anthropology, Montreal, Que., 1971-74, Studies in Polit. Economy, Ottawa, Ont., Can., 1980-87, Current Sociology, 1980-86, Can. Jour. Sociology, 1986-90, B.C. Studies, 1988-90, 2000—. Bd. dirs., chair ethics com. Univ. Hosp., 1992-93, Cedar Lodge Trust Soc., 1989-92; mem. adv. coun. Ecotrust, 1991-93, bd. dirs., 1993-97, Eco-trust Can., 1995-99; chmn. bd. dirs. B.C. Bldgs. Corp., 1992-95; mem. B.C. Forest Appeals Commn., 1992-2002; bd. govs. U. B.C., 1999-2001; bd. dirs. Pub. Svc. Employees for Environ. Ethics, 2002--; mem. sector study steering com. Can. Coun. Profl. Fish Harvesters, 2002--. Named Woman of Distinction, YWCA, 1999. Fellow Royal Soc. Can. (v.p. Acad. II 1994-98, pres. Acad. II 1998-2000); mem. Can. Sociology and Anthropology Assn. (pres. 1979-80, other offices), Internat. Sociol. Assn., Can. Polit. Sci. Assn., Assn. for Can. Studies, Forest History Soc. (mem. exec. com. 1991-92). Avocations: hiking, swimming, traveling, listening to music. Home: 4455 W 1st Ave Vancouver BC Canada V6R 4H9 Office: Univ BC - Ctr of Internat Rels Inst for Restudy of Global Issues 6303 NW Marine Dr Vancouver BC Canada V6T 1Z1 E-mail: pmarchak@interchange.ubc.ca.

MARCHESSEAULT, ANITA, music educator; b. Moosup, Conn., June 15, 1917; d. Henry Marchesseault and Rose Brault; ptnr. Anita. MusB, Laval U., 1950; MusM, Boston U., 1957, D Mus. Arts, 1970. Cert. music tchr. Music tchr. Schs. of Mt. Royal, Montreal, Que., Can., 1935-52; prof. music, piano and organ tchr., band dir. Notre Dame Coll., Manchester, N.H., 1952—. Ch. organist, pvt. piano tchr., Manchester, 1952—. Recipient Key to City. Mem. Music Tchrs. Nat. Assn. (cert. chair 1968—), N.H. Music Tchrs. Assn. (Music Tchr. of Yr. 1970). Home: 357 Island Pond Rd #1 Manchester NH 03109

MARCHETTI-PONTE, KARIN, lawyer, conservation consultant; b. Devens, Mass., Nov. 3, 1951; d. Robert Joseph and Patricia (Morico) M.; m. John J. Ponte, Jr.; children: Haley Warden, Henry Warden, Chrisopher W. Kaiser, John G. Ponte, Hannah Ponte. BA summa cum laude, U. Maine, 1975, JD, 1978. Bar: Mass. 1979, Maine, 1979. Reporter Sta. WGBH-TV, Portland, Maine, 1978-79; news anchorperson Sta. WMTW-TV, Poland Spring, Maine, 1977-78; atty., founder Advocates, Inc., Portland, 1979-80; assoc. corp. counsel City of Portland, 1980-83; vol. Peace Corps, Tunisia, South Africa, 1983-84; gen. counsel, clk. Maine Coast Heritage Trust, Topsham, Maine, 1985—; prin. Land Conservation Legal Svcs., Bernard, Maine, 1992—. Intsr. Land Trust Alliance, Washington, 1988—; mem. Land Conservation Leadership Program, Washington, 1997—, Conservation Fund, Washington. Co-author: Conserving Land with Conservation Easements, 1999, Conservation Easement Handbook, Easement Drafting Guide. Office: Land Conservation Legal Svcs PO Box 100 Bernard ME 04612-0100 also: Maine Coast Heritage Trust Topsham ME 04086 also: PO Box 100 Hebron ME 04238

MARCINEK, MARGARET ANN, nursing educator; b. Uniontown, Pa., Sept. 29, 1948; d. Joseph Hugh and Evelyn (Bailey) Boyle; m. Bernard Francis Marcinek, Aug. 11, 1973; 1 child, Cara Ann. RN, Uniontown Hosp., 1969; BSN, Pa. State U., 1970; MSN, U. Md., 1973; EdD, W.Va. U., 1983. Staff nurse Presbyn. U., Pitts., 1970-71; instr. nursing W.Va. U., Morgantown, 1973-77, asst. prof., 1977-80, assoc. prof., 1980-83, Calif. U. Pa., 1983-87, prof., 1987—, dept. chmn., 1985—. Program evaluator Commn. on Collegiate Nursing Edn., Nat. League for Nursing Accrediting Commn.; mem. adv. coun. In Home Health, Inc.; mem. adv. coun. Albert Gallatin VNA. Contbg. author: Critical Care Nursing; contbr. articles to profl. jours. Mem.: ANA, Commn. on Collegiate Nursing Edn. (site evaluator), Oncology Nursing Soc., Sigma Theta Tau. Office Phone: 724-938-4130. E-mail: marcinek@cup.edu.

MARCINKO, JACQUELINE MICHELE, social worker; b. Cleve., Oct. 11, 1965; d. Frank and Dorrine Ann (Barber) Turk; m. John Michael Marcinko, Nov. 21, 1992; 2 children. BA, U. Dayton, 1987; MSW, U. Ga., 1994; postgrad., Spring Hill Coll. Lic. master's social worker, Ga. Cottage supr. Village of St. Joseph, Atlanta, 1987-90; trainer, server Peasant Restaurants, Atlanta, 1990-92; case mgr. Dekalb Co., Atlanta, 1992; intern Laurel Heights Hosp., Atlanta, 1993-94; therapist Village of St. Joseph, 1994-95; youth min. Sacred Heart Cath. Ch., 1998—2001; mid. sch. coord. Christ The King Sch., 2001—, tchr. religion, 2001—. Vol. RCIA, AIDS ministry, parish pastoral coun., liturgy coord., Cathedral of Christ the King, Atlanta, 1988—; pres., treas. North Ga. Childcare Assn., Atlanta, 1988-89; vol. Summer Olympics, Atlanta, 1996, ARC DMHS, 1997—. Mem. NASW, Phi Alpha Theta. Democrat. Roman Catholic.

MARCINKO, KRISTY EILEEN, special education educator; b. Cleve., May 15, 1977; d. Allen McDonald and April Eileen Sutton; m. Gregory Thomas Marcinko, July 27, 2002. MEd, Ohio State U., 1995—2000. Cert. developmentally handicapped K-12 Ohio. Spl. needs preschool tchr. Columbus Pub. Schools, Ohio, 2000—02; preschool toddler tchr. North Country Acad., Saratoga Springs, NY, 2002—03; spl. edn. tchr. South Kitsap Sch. Dist., Port Orchard, Wash., 2003—. Mem.: Coun. for Exceptional Children.

MARCO, PATRICIA LOUISE, music educator; b. New Kensington, PA, July 23, 1947; d. Adam Paul and Mary Louise Chovanes; m. Donald Anthony Marco; children: Maria, Christina, Adam. BS, Ind. U. of Pa., 1969. Tchr., band dir. Kiski Area Sch. Dist., Vandergrift, Pa., 1969—. Founder Kiski Valley Cmty. Band, dir. Founding dir. Kiski Valley Cmty. Band. Recipient Disting. Citizen award, Leechburg Elks, 2002. Mem.: Pa. State Edn. Assn., Music Educators Nat. Conf., Assn. Concert Bands, Women Band Dirs. Internat., Delta Kappa Gamma.

MARCOLINA, KATHRYN WATKINS, personal and professional success coach; b. West Chester, Pa., Jan. 17, 1959; d. Dwain Joseph and Kathryn Gertrude (Wood) W.; m. Peter Jerome Marcolina, Feb. 11, 1984. BS in Edn., U. Del., Newark, 1981; MSW, Bryn Mawr (Pa.) Coll., 1985. Cert clin. social worker, N.C. Family therapist Family Svc. Burlington County, Mt. Holly, N.J., 1985-89, Family Svc. Lower Cape Fear, Wilmington, N.C., 1989-90, The Parkside Clinic, Wilmington, 1990-96, Cape Fear Pschol. and Psychiat. Svcs., Wilmington, 1996-97; student counselor U. N.C., Wilmington, 1997-98; personal and profl. success coach Wrightsville Beach, NC, 2000—. Mem. NASW (chairperson local chpt. 1992), Acad. Cert. Social Workers, N.C. Cert. Bd. Social Work. Avocations: protection of sea turtles and wetlands, environmental awareness, study of nutrition, health and healing. Home: 2301-F Cordgrass Bay Wrightsville Beach NC 28480

MARCOULLIS, ERATO KOZAKOU, ambassador; b. Limassol, Cyprus, Aug. 3, 1949; m. George Marcoullis; 1 child, Panos. Degree in law, U. Athens, Greece, 1972; degree in pub. law and polit. scis., Dept. Pub. Law and Polit. Scis., 1975; PhD Social Scis., U. Helsinki, Finland, 1979. Practice law, 1973—74; advisor Permanent Mission of Cyprus UN, 1980—83, attaché Permanent Mission of Cyprus, 1983—88; consulate gen. Cyprus, 1982—83; amb. extraordinary and plenipotentiary with concurrent accreditation to Finland, Lithuania, Latvia, Sweden, Iceland, Norway, Denmark, and Estonia, 1996—98; mem. 1st polit. divsn. Cyprus question Ministry Fgn. Affairs, 1989—93, dir. office of permanent sec., 1993—96, amb. extraordinary and plenipotentiary to U.S. with concurrent accreditation to Can., Brazil, Guyana, Jamaica, 1998—. Office: Embassy of Cyprus 2211 R St NW Washington DC 20008

MARCOUX, JULIA A. midwife; b. St. Helens, England, Aug. 7, 1928; d. Robert Patrick and Margaret Mary Theresa (White) Ashall; m. Albert Marcoux, Apr. 23, 1955; children: Stephen, Ann Marie, Richard, Michael, Maureen, Patrick, Margaret, Julie. Diploma, Withington Hosp., Manchester, England, 1950; grad., Cowley Hill Hosp., St. Helens, England, 1952; BS in Pub. Adminstrn., St. Joseph's Coll. RN, Conn.; lic. midwife, Conn. Nurse, labor, delivery rm. and nursery Day Kimbal Hosp., Putnam, Conn.; sch. nurse Marianapolis Prep. Sch., Thompson, Conn.; occupational nurse U.S. Post Office, Hartford, Conn.; pvt. duty and gerontology nurse Conn. Nurse cons. to day care babies, toddlers and pre-schoolers. Contbr. articles to profl. jours. Named Internat. Cath. Family of Yr., 1982.

MARCUCCIO, PHYLLIS ROSE, retired association executive, editor; b. Hackensack, N.J., Aug. 25, 1933; d. Filippo and Rose (Henry) Marcuccio. AB, Bucknell U., 1955; MA, George Washington U., 1976. Trainee Time, Inc., 1956—57; art prodn. for mags. of Med. Econs., Inc., 1958—60; mem. staff Nat. Sci. Tchrs. Assn., Washington, 1961—99; assoc. editor Sci. and Children, 1963, editor, 1964—93, dir. divsn. elem. edn., 1974—78, dir. divsn. program devel. and continuing edn., 1978—83, pub., 1993—99; dir. publs. Nat. Sci. Tchrs. Assn., 1983—99, assoc. exec. dir., 1990—99; pub. Dragonfly, 1996—99. Lectr., cons. in field. Author (photographer, illustrator numerous articles) ; co-author: Investigation in Ecology, 1972; editor: Science Fun, 1977, Science Fun, 2d edit., 1994; Selected Readings for Students of English as a Second Language, 1966; compiler: Opportunities for Summer Studies in Elementary Science, 1968, Opportunities for Summer Studies in Elementary Science, 2d edit., 1969, pub.: Sci. and Children, 1993—99, Dragonfly Mag., 1997—99. Apptd. commr. Rockville (Md.) Housing Authority, 1981—91, chairperson, 1984—86; bd. dirs. Nat. Sci. Resource Ctr., NAS, 1986—96, Hands on Sci. Outreach, Inc., 1991—2001; pres. East Rockville Civic Assn., 2000—. Recipient Citizenship medal, DAR, 1951, Golden Lamp award, Edpress, 1990. Mem., AAAS, NSTA (life), Dreams Environ. Edn. Ctr. (bd. dirs. 1989—98), Sci. Tchg. Assn. N.Y. (Outstanding Svc. to Sci. Edn. award 1987), Ednl. Press Assn. Am. (regional dir. 1969—71, sec. 1979—, Disting. Achievement award 1969, 1971—74, 1976, 1977, Eleanor Fishburn award 1978, Disting. Achievement award 1980, 1988, 1993, 1995), The Washington Forum, Washington edn. Press Assn. (treas. 1966—67, pres. 1975—76), Ohio Coun. Elem. Sch. Sci. (life), Nat. Assn. Industry Edn. Coop. (bd. dirs. 1980—86), Nat. Press Club (Silver Owl), Am. Nature Study Soc., Coun. Elem. Sci. Internat. (Internat. award for outstanding contbns. sci. edn. 1971, 1972, 1986, 1994), Kiwanis Internat., Sigma Delta Chi, Phi Delta Kappa, Phi Delta gamma, Theta Alpha Phi. Home: 406 S Horners Ln Rockville MD 20850-1556 E-mail: marcu@erols.com.

MARCUM, DEANNA BOWLING, library administrator; b. Salem, Ind., Aug. 5, 1946; d. Anderson and Ruby (Mobley) Bowling; m. Thomas P. Marcum, June 13, 1974; 1 child, Ursula. BA, U. Ill., 1967; MA, So. Ill. U., 1969; MLS, U. Ky., 1971; PhD, U. Md., 1991. Tchr. Deland-Weldon (Ill.) High Sch., 1967-68; instr. English U. Ky., Lexington, 1969-70, cataloging librarian, 1970-73, asst. to dir., 1973-74; asst. dir. pub. svcs. Joint U. Librs., Nashville, 1974-77; mgmt. tng. specialist Assn. Rsch. Librs., Washington, 1977-80; sr. cons. Info. Systems Cons., Inc., Washington, 1980-81; v.p. Coun. on Libr. Resources, Washington, 1981-89; dean Sch. Libr. and Info. Sch. Cath. U., Washington, 1989-92; dir. pub. svcs. and collections mgmt. Libr. of Congress, Washington, 1993-95, assoc. libr., 2003—; pres. Coun. on Libr. Resources and Info., Washington, 1995—2003. Adv. bd. So. Edn. Found., Atlanta, 1986-91; chmn. grants com. Coun. on Libr. resources, Washington, 1990-94. Author: Good Books in a Country Home, 1993, Development of Digital Libaries, An American Perspective, 2001; co-author: (with Richard Boss) The Library Catalog, 1980, On-Line Acquisitions Systems, 1981; contbr. articles to profl. jours. Pres., Commn. on Preservation and Access, 1995—. Mem. ALA, Am. Studies Assn., Orgn. Am. Historians, Am. Antiquarian Soc. (adv. bd. 1989—), Beta Phi Mu, Phi Kappa Phi. Home: 3315 Wake Dr Kensington MD 20895-3218 Office: Coun on Libr and Info Resources Ste 500 1755 Massachusetts Ave NW Washington DC 20036-2124 Office Phone: 202-707-6240. E-mail: dmarcum@loc.gov.

MARCUS, ADRIANNE STUHL, writer; b. Everett, Mass., Mar. 7, 1935; d. George Zachariah and Edith Delores (Cohen) Stuhl; m. Warren M. Marcus (div. 1981); children: Stacey Ann, Shelby Alice, Sarah Naomi; m. Ian Holroyde Wilson. AB, San Francisco State U., 1955, MA, 1961. Poet, 1955—; tchr. Coll. of Marin, 1965-79; food columnist San Francisco Chronicle, 1985-87; writer, 1968—. Author: The Moon is a Marrying Eye, 1969, The Chocolate Bible, 1975; co-author: Carrion House World of Gifts, 1980. Fellow Ossabaw, 1982, Yaddo Corp., 1985, Va. Ctr. for Creative Arts, 1993-95-97. Mem. PEN, Internat. Food Journalists and Writers, Acad. Am. Poets, Overseas Press Club. Democrat. Jewish. Avocation: creating doll houses. Home and Office: 79 Twin Oaks Ave San Rafael CA 94901-1915

MARCUS, CAROL A. information technology manager; b. Chgo., Ill. AA, Coll of Du Page, 1978; BS, Elmhurst Coll., 1992; MBA, Dominican U., 1998. From merchandising application devel. to info. tech. project mgr. Ace Hardware Corp., Oak Brook, Ill., 1979—2001, info. tech. project mgr., 2001—. Cons. in hist. preservation. Chmn. Villa Pk. Hist. Preservation Commn., Villa Park, Ill., 1985—. Mem.: Nat. Trust, Chgo. Architecture Found., Ill. Assn. Historic Preservation Commn. (chmn. 1998—), Villa Park His. Soc. (v.p. 1986—). Republican. Roman Catholic. Avocations: history, gardening, travel, photography. Office: Ace Hardware Corp 2200 Kensington Ct Oak Brook IL 60523-2100

MARCUS, KAREN MELISSA, foreign language educator; b. Vancouver, B.C., Can., Feb. 28, 1956; came to the U.S., 1962; d. Marvin Marcus and Arlen Ingrid (Sahlman) Bishop; m. Jorge Esteban Mezei, Jan. 7, 1984 (div. Mar. 1987). BA in French, BA in Polit. Sci., U. Calif., Santa Barbara, 1978, MA in Polit. Sci., 1981; MA in French, Stanford U., 1984, PhD in French, 1990. Lectr. in French Stanford (Calif.) U., 1989-90; asst. prof. French No. Ariz. U., Flagstaff, 1990-96, assoc. prof. French, 1996—2004, prof. French, 2004—. Cons. Houghton Mifflin, 1993, Grand Canyon (Ariz.) Natural History Soc., 1994. Vol., letter writer Amnesty Internat. Urgent Action Network, 1991-95; vol. No. Ariz. Aids Outreach Orgn., Flagstaff, 1994-95. Recipient medal for outstanding achievement in French, Alliance Française, Santa Barbara, 1978; named Scholarship Exch. Student, U. Geneva, Switzerland, 1979-80; doctoral fellow Stanford (Calif.) U., 1981-85. Mem. MLA, Am. Assn. Tchrs. French, Am. Coun. on the Tchg. Fgn. Langs., Am. Literary Translators Assn., Women in French, Coordination Internat. des Chercheurs Sur Les Litteratures Maghrebines, Phi Beta Kappa, Pi Delta Phi, Alpha Lambda Delta. Democrat. Jewish. Avocations: walking, yoga, reading, writing short stories. Office: No Ariz Univ Modern Lang Dept PO Box 6004 Flagstaff AZ 86011-6004 Office Phone: 928-714-9538. Business E-Mail: melissa.marcus@nau.edu.

MARCUS, KELLY STEIN, psychologist, health science association administrator; b. Baltimore, Md., July 11, 1968; d. Anthony Alan and Barbara Marlene Stein; m. Matthew Alexander Marcus, May 23, 1999; 1 child, Samantha Haleigh. MA, MEd, Columbia U., 1991—93; PhD, Yeshiva U./Ferkauf Grad. Sch. Psychology, Bronx, NY, 1993—98. Cert. psychologist NY, 1999, Pa., 2000. Med. sci. mgr., neuroscience divsn. Bristol-Myers Squibb, Co., Philadelphia, Pa., 2001—; assoc. rsch. scientist Yale U. Sch. Medicine, New Haven, 1999—2003; attending psychologist Thomas Jefferson U. Hosp. Dept. Psychiatry, Philadelphia, Pa., 2000—01; attending psychologist, dept. anesthesiology Thomas Jefferson U. Sch. Medicine, Jefferson Pain Ctr., Philadelphia, Pa., 2000—01; post doctoral fellow Yale Sch. Medicine, Dept. Psychiatry, New Haven, 1998—99; psychologist Assn. for the Help of Retarded Children, New York, NY, 1994—2000. Prin. investigator Young Investigator Grant, Yale Sch. Medicine, New Haven, 1999—2003; ad hoc reviewer Annals of Internal Medicine, 2000—03. Contbr. articles to medical jours. Recipient Young Investigator Award, Nat. Alliance for Rsch. in Schizophrenia and Depression, 1999, Leadership Award, Bristol-Myers Squibb, Co. Neuroscience Med. Sci. Divsn., 2002; fellow Pre-Doctoral Fellowship, Meml. Sloan Kettering Cancer Ctr., Nat. Inst. Mental Health, 1994-1997. Mem.: APA. Democrat-Npl. Jewish. Avocations: running, creative arts. Office Phone: 215-575-9254.

MARCUS, LINDA SUSAN, dermatologist; b. Bklyn. d. Nathaniel and Eugenia (Portnay) Marcus; m. Ronald Carlin, July 5, 1976; children: Robert Adam, Neal Marc. BS, Adelphi U., Garden City, N.J., 1970; MD, Downstate Med. Sch., Bklyn., 1975. Diplomate Am. Bd. Dermatology. Intern Long Island (N.Y.) Jewish Med. Ctr., 1975-76; resident in dermatology Columbia-St. Luke's, N.Y.C., 1976-77, Boston U.-Tufts U., 1977-79; pvt. practice Wyckoff, N.J., 1980—. Dir. dermatology Valley Hosp. Ridgewood. Contbr. articles to profl. jours. Mem. Am. Acad. Dermatology (chair pamphlet com.), Am. Soc. Dermatol. Surgeons, Internat. Soc. Dermatol. Surgeons, N.J. Dermatol. Soc. (program dir.). Avocations: swimming, ice skating. Office: 271 Godwin Ave Wyckoff NJ 07481-2057 Personal E-mail: sexyderm@earthlink.net.

MARCUS, MICHELLE, computer scientist; b. St. Louis, Jan. 17, 1975; d. David George and Barbara (Sands) Marcus. BS, Bradley U., 1997. Computer software programmer Enterprise Rent-A-Car, St. Louis, 1997—2000, REJIS, St. Louis, 2000—03, Maritz Inc., St. Louis, 2002—. Avocations: music, movies, football. Home: Apt 9 10394 Oxford Hill Dr Saint Louis MO 63146-5722 Office: 1395 N Highway Dr Fenton MO 63099

MARCUS, SANDRA L., special education educator, consultant; d. Edward Ronald Marconi and Susan Sara Levinson. BS, Wayne State U., 1976, EdM, 1985; PhD in Holistic Counseling, U. Metaphysics, L.A., 2002. Elem. tchr. Detroit Pub. Schs., 1977—82; clinician foster care Children's Ctr., Detroit, 1987—87; coord., social worker Neighborhood Family Svcs., Detroit, 1987—88; instr. spl. edn. San Diego C.C., 1989—98; edn. cons., adv. San Diego Regional Ctr. for the Developmentally Disabled, 2000—. Edn. cons. San Diego Regional Ctr. Author: Education and Spirit, 2004. Mem.: Coun. for Exceptional Children. Avocations: writing, spiritual research, painting, antiques, meditation.

MARCUSS, ROSEMARY DALY, economist; b. Stamford, Conn., Aug. 27, 1945; d. Eugene Lawrence and Margaret Mary (Murphy) Daly; B.A. in Econs. cum laude, Newton (Mass.) Coll., 1967; M.S., U. Md., 1973, Ph.D., 1979; m. Stanley J. Marcuss, July 6, 1968; children— Elena Daly, Aidan Stanley. Jr. staff economist President's Council of Econ. Advisers, 1968-70; economist, asst. to pres. Am. Fedn. State, County and Mcpl. Employees, Washington, 1973; economist, mgmt. cons. Data Resources, Inc., Washington, 1974-78; dep. asst. dir. tax analysis Congressional Budget Office, Washington, 1980-83, asst. dir. tax analysis, 1983-98; dep. dir. Bur. Econ. Analysis, Washington, 1998—. NSF fellow, 1970-73. Mem. Am. Econ. Assn., Nat. Tax Assn., Tax Inst. Am., So. Econ. Assn., Soc. Govt. Economists, Nat. Economists Club, Nat. Assn. Business Economists (v.p. 2003-), Washington Women Economists. Home: 4616 29th Pl NW Washington DC 20008-2105 Office: Congressional Budget Office 2nd & D Sts SW Washington DC 20515-0001

MARCY, JEANNINE KOONCE, retired educational administrator; b. Lake City, S.C., Dec. 22, 1935; d. Alton Earle Sr. and Bernice Eva (Gerrald) K.; m. Shawn Marcy Fuentes, Vanessa Marcy Ruebel. BA, Winthrop Coll., 1957; MS, Barry Coll., 1976. Tchr. Florence (S.C.) County Schs., 1957-59, Kershaw County Schs., Camden, S.C., 1959-61; tchr., dept. chmn. Dade County Pub. Schs., Miami, Fla., 1961-82, asst. prin., 1982-86, coord. personnel staffing, 1986-89, dir. cert., 1989-92, pers. adminstr., 1993-97; ret., 1997. Mem. collective bargaining team Dade County Pub. Schs., 1983-84, trainer tchr. assessment devel. systems, 1983-85, trainer master tchr. program, 1984-85; panelist nat. conv. Assn. Supervision and Curriculum Devel., Altanta, 1980; presenter in field. Campaign worker Bob Graham for Gov., Miami, 1980's, Janet Reno for State Dist. Atty., Miami, 1980's. Mem. Kappa Delta Pi, Alpha Delta Kappa. Republican. Episcopalian. Avocations: piano, organ, guitar, reading. Home: 3250 Cypress Glen Way Apt 417 Naples FL 34109-3876

MARDER, CAROL, advertising specialist and premium firm executive; b. Bklyn., Sept. 20, 1941; d. Simon and Sylvia (Rothstein) Cohen; m. Edwin Marder, Apr. 15, 1961; children: Elisa, Steven Alan, Susan. Prin. owner Boys Ego Retail Clothing, Englishtown, N.J., 1974-76; pres. Motivators, Inc., Old Bridge, N.J., 1976-83, Inkwell Promotions Corp., Morganville, N.J., 1983—. Cons. Specialty Advt. of N.Y., 1988—. Recipient citation Monmouth County Bd. Recreation Commrs., Lincroft, N.J., 1987. Mem. East Flatbush League Retarded Children (bd. dirs. 1965-69), Marlboro Chpt. Retarded Children (founder, pres. 1969-71, 73-74, bd. dirs. 1971-76), Marlboro Jewish Ctr. Sisterhood (bd. dirs. 1971-73), N.J. Women in Bus., Middlesex County C. of C., Western Monmouth C. of C. Democrat. Jewish. Avocations: golf, cooking, travel. Office: Inkwell Promotions 1020 Campus Dr W Morganville NJ 07751-1260

MARDER, NANCY GRACE, foundation executive; b. Chgo., Nov. 7, 1951; m. Benjamin Ned Shain; children: Alec, Michael, Jarret, David. MA, U. Mich., 1976; MA in Ednl. Adminstrn. and Supervision, Roosevelt U., 1997. Co-pres. LWV of Highland Park, Ill.; exec. dir., founder Infinity Found., Highland Park, 1997—. Chair Highland Park Human Rels. Commn.; bd. dirs. Ill. LWV, 1987—. Vol. Peace Corps, U.S. State Dept., Sierra Leone, 1973—75. Mem.: U. Mich. Alumni Assn. (life). Office: Infinity Found 1282 Old Skokie Rd Highland Park IL 60035 Office Phone: 847-831-8828. Personal E-mail: infinfound@aol.com.

MARDIS, ELMA HUBBARD, county administrator, consultant; b. Memphis, July 16, 1932; d. Walter Lee Sr. and Edith (Scott) Hubbard; m. William Columbus Mardis, Dec. 22, 1957; 1 child, Marlah Mardis-Phillips. BS, LeMoyne-Owen U., 1952; MEd, U. Ill., 1960; EdD, U. Tenn., 1974. Tchr. Memphis City Schs., 1952-75; asst. prof., coord. Bur. Ednl. Rsch., U. Tenn., Knoxville, 1975-80; instr. Shelby State C.C., Memphis, 1977-78; nat. dir. edn. PUSH Excel Program, Chgo., 1980-82; tchr. Memphis City Schs., 1982-84; dir. computer ctr. Memphis Urban League, 1984-94; exec. dir. Pvt. Industry Coun., Memphis, Shelby, Fayette Counties, Tenn., 1994—. Dir. Am. Tutoring Ctr., Memphis, 1982—; cons. Josten's Learning Corp., San Diego, 1997—. Editor: PUSH for EXCELLENCE, 1981; author instrnl. curriculum; contbr. articles to profl. jours. Mem., alumnus Leadership Memphis, 1980—; organizer/charter pres. River City chpt. The Links, Inc., Memphis, 1987-95; commr./vice chair Memphis Housing Authority, 1992—; mem. Tenn. Commn. on Children and Youth, Nashville, 1995—; bd. trustees Memphis Urban League, sec.; mem. NAACP, Memphis, 1997; sec. Second Congl. United Ch. of Christ, 1989-97. Recipient Disting. Grad. award LeMoyne-Owen Coll., 1988. Mem. Nat. Assn. Pvt. Industry Couns., Tenn. Assn. Pvt. Industry Couns., Southeastern Employment and Tng. Assn., So. Assn. Colls. and Schs. (cons., facilitator review team 1977—), Phi Delta Kappa, Kappa Delta Pi, Pi Lambda Theta, Alpha Kappa Alpha. Avocations: reading, traveling, working with children, community projects, basketball. Home: 2324 Bridgeport Dr Memphis TN 38114-5714 Office: 100 N Main St Ste 2810 Memphis TN 38103-0528

MARDUEL, ALIX, venture capitalist; Ptnr. Sofinnova Ventures, 1990—97; med. residency Paris; postdoctoral fellowship U. Calif., San Francisco, Stanford U.; mng. dir. Alta Partners, San Francisco, 1997—. Office: Alta Partners One Embarcadero Ctr Ste 4050 San Francisco CA 94111

MARECEK, JEANNE, psychologist, educator; b. Berwyn, Ill., May 28, 1946; d. Frank J. and Josephine (Serio) M. BS, Loyola U., Chgo., 1968; MS, Yale U., 1971, PhD, 1973. From asst. prof. to prof. psychology Swarthmore (Pa.) Coll., 1972—, chmn. dept., 1986-91, 94-95, 98—, head women's studies program, 1996—. Fulbright sr. lectr., Sri Lanka, 1988. Co-author: Making a Difference: Psychology and the Construction of Gender; contbr. numerous articles to profl. jours. and chpts. to books. Bd. dirs. Women in Transition, Phila., 1980-86; vice patron Nest, Hendala, Sri Lanka, 1995—; bd. dirs. Women's Therapy Ctr., Phila., 1996—. Fellow Swedish Collegium for Advanced Study in Social Scis., 1997; various fed. research grants. Mem. APA, Ea. Psychol. Assn., Assn. for Asian Studies, Am. Inst. Sri Lanka Studies (sec. 1995—). Office: Swarthmore Coll Dept Psychology 500 College Ave Ste 2 Swarthmore PA 19081-1306

MARECHAUX, TONI GROBSTEIN, engineer, consultant; b. Joliet, Ill., June 26, 1959; d. Samuel Grobstein; m. Otis Marechaux, Nov. 8, 1993. BS in Metall. Engring., U. Ill., Champaign-Urbana, 1977—80; PhD in Materials Sci., Case Western Res. U., Cleve., 1982—89. Prodn. engr. Nat. Steel Corp., Portage, Ind., 1981—82; materials engr. NASA, Cleve., 1985—94; program mgr. U.S. Dept. Energy, Washington, 1994—2001; dir., nat. materials adv. bd. Nat. Acads., Washington, 2001—. Office: Nat Acads 500 Fifth St NW Washington DC 20001 E-mail: tmarecha@nas.edu.

MAREK, JOYCELYN, publishing executive; m. Andrew Marek; children: Allison, Matthew. BBA, U. Houston, 1978; postgrad., Northwestern U., 1996, Hearst Mgmt. Inst., 1997-98. Rsch. analyst Houston Chronicle, 1978, chief analyst, 1978-84, asst. rsch. mgr., 1984-85, rsch. mgr., 1985-88, display advt. dir., 1988-90, mktg. dir., 1990-95, v.p. mktg. and electronic products, 1995—. Bd. dirs., exec. com. Sheltering Arms; mem. mktg. com. Houston Symphony; former bd. dirs. Houston Advt. Fedn. Mem. Am. Mktg. Assn. (edn./intern chair, past pres. Houston chpt.), Newspaper Assn. Am. (former chair market devel. and promotion coun.). Avocations: tennis, reading, golf. Office: Houston Chronicle PO Box 4260 Houston TX 77210-4260

MAREK, KIERSTEN L. social worker; b. Windham, Conn., Oct. 7, 1968; d. Leland J. and Ann Marie Stoppleworth; m. Kevin Michael Krcmarik; 1 child, Katrina. BA, Hunter Coll., 1990; MSW, Smith Coll., Northampton, Mass., 1996. LCSW, lic. ind. clin. social worker. Assoc. editor Merlyn's Pen, East Greenwich, RI, 1995—2001; clin. social worker Child and Family Svcs. Newport County, Newport, RI, 1996—98, R.I. Hosp., Lifespan, Providence, 1998—; assoc. editor Pif Mag., Seattle, 2001—; asst. editor The Hudson Rev., N.Y.C. Workshop tchr. Kmareka.com, Cranston, RI, 2002—; editor-in-chief Kmareka.com and Saga City, Cranston, RI, 2002—. Contbr. short stories to mags. and anthologies. Campaign vol. Kate Coyne-McCoy for Congress, Providence, 2001. Home: 109 Waterman Ave Providence RI 02910 Office: Kmareka dot com and Saga City 109 Waterman Ave Providence RI 02910 Personal E-mail: kmarek@kmareka.com. Business E-Mail: kmarek@kmareka.com.

MARENDT, CANDACE L. state legislator; Student, Ind. U. Mem. Ind. State Ho. of Reps. Dist. 94, mem. commerce and econ. devel. com., mem. judiciary and pub. safety com., vice-chmn. families, children and human affairs com. Mem. MIBOR, Circle City Child Care Assn., N.W. Roundtable, Pike, Wayne, Washington and Eagle Creek GOP Clubs. also: Electronics Divsn 302 W Washington St Rm 204 Indianapolis IN 46204

MAREZ, TRINNIE MARIE, marketing professional; b. Marietta, Ga., July 29, 1958; d. Felix Martin Marez and Linda Joan Higgins; m. Thomas Ian MacDougall Christopher (dec.); 1 child, Leyla Brianna. BA in Comm. cum laude, Ga. State U., 1987. Corp. comm. The Coca-Cola Co., Atlanta, 1987—94; dir. guest relations Olympic Games Day Tripper Program, Atlanta, 1995—96; meteorology programming & prodn. The Weather Channel, 1997—98; dir. mktg. Wild Oats Mkts., Inc., Nashville, 2001—. Prodr.: (films) Charlie's War, 2003, Heike and the Mermaid, 2004, Dodge City, 2004; (TV series) Lorianne Crook's Celebrity Kitchen, 2003, Great American Country, 2003—04. 1st lt., dir. pub. affairs Ga. Wing Hdqs. USAF, 1987—94, Dobbins ARB, Marietta, Ga. Decorated Award of Excellent Svc. The Ga. Wing, CAP, Search & Rescue award, Lifesaving award, Comdr.'s commendations, Unit Citation awards, Brewer Aerospace Edn. award. R-Conservative. Catholic. Avocations: literature, painting, writing, skiing, films. Personal E-mail: sunshinemoonbeam@netzero.net. E-mail: frnmktmgr@wildoats.com.

MARGALITH, HELEN MARGARET, retired librarian; b. N.Y.C., Nov. 19, 1914; d. Louis and Caroline (Stern) Fleischer; m. Aaron Margalith, Jan. 26, 1947 (dec.); children: Carol Lenore, Joan Louise. BA, Hunter Coll., 1936, MA, 1944; MLS, Columbia U., 1958. Editl. corr. Book of the Month Club, 1936-47; rschr. libr. N.Y.C. Bd. Edn., 1955-80; prof. pibr. Touro Coll., N.Y.C., 1980-90; mentor in libr. Empire State Coll., SUNY, 1991—. Cons. in field. Fellow Royal Soc. Medicine (libr. com., gerontology com., history of medicine com.); mem. Ch. and Synagogue Libr. Assn. (book reviewer), Internat. Honor Soc. Women in Edn., Delta Kappa Gamma. Democrat. Avocations: reading, travel, research. Home: 205 W End Ave Apt 25S New York NY 10023-4804

MARGED, JUDITH MICHELE, information technology educator; b. Phila., Nov. 27, 1954; d. Bernard A. and Norma Marged. Student, Drexel U., 1972-73; AA in Biology, Broward C.C., Ft. Lauderdale, Fla., 1975; BA in Biology, Fla. Atlantic U., 1977, BA in Exceptional Edn., 1980, MEd in Counseling, 1984; EdD in Early and Middle Childhood, Nova U., 1991; postgrad., Capella U., 2002—03. Cert. tchr., Fla.; cert. tech. trainer; Microsoft cert. sys. engr.; Microsoft cert. profl., trainer. Tchr. Coral Springs (Fla.) Mid. Sch., 1979-80, Am. Acad., Wilton Manors, Fla., 1980-83, Ramblewood Mid. Sch., Coral Springs, 1984-96; info. tech. prof. Am. InterContinental U., Plantation, Fla., 1999—2002. Creator programs for mid. sch. students and coll. curriculum. Author: A Program to Increase the Knowledge of Middle School Students in Sexual Education and Substance Abuse Prevention, An Alternative Education Program to Create Successful Learning for the Middle School Child At-Risk. Mem.: IEEE, Assn. for Career and Tech. Edn., Phi Delta Kappa. Home: 9107 NW 83d St Tamarac FL 33321-1509

MARGIOTTA, MARY-LOU ANN, application developer; b. Waterbury, Conn., June 14, 1956; d. Rocco Donato and Louise Antoinette (Carosella) M. AS Gen. Edn., Mattatuck C.C., Waterbury, 1982; BSBA, Teikyo Post U., 1983; MS Computer Sci., Rensselaer Polytech. Inst., 1989. Programmer analyst Travelers Ins. Co., Hartford, Conn., 1985-87; sr. programmer analyst Conn. Bank and Trust Co., East Hartford, Conn., 1987-88; programmer analyst Ingersoll-Rand Corp., Torrington, Conn., 1990-91; sr. programmer analyst Orion Capital Cos. Inc., Farmington, Conn., 1991-92; pres., prin., software engr. A.M. Consultants, New Britain, Conn., 1992—. Pres. C++ Spl. Interest Group, 1995-96; bd. dirs. Conn. Object Oriented Users Group, 1995-96; tech. team leader Computer Scis. Corp., East Hartford, Conn., 1998-, Asnuntuck C. C., Enfield, Conn., 2003; adj. prof. Ctrl. Conn. State U., New Britain, 2000, New Eng. Tech. Inst., New Britain, Conn., 2002. Mem. social action com. St. Helena's Parish, West Hartford, Conn., 1988-95; advisor Jr. Achievement, Waterbury, 1981-83; tutor Traveler's Ins. Co. Tutorial Program, West Hartford, 1986-87; trainer CPR, ARC, Hartford, 1986-87; mem. Lang. and Cultural Adoptation Programs, Conn. and Mass., 1998— Clayborn Pell grantee Post Coll., 1982-83, State of Conn. grantee, 1982-83; recipient Citation, Jr. Achievement, 1982; Bd. Trustees scholar Post Coll., 1982-83. Mem. IEEE (chairwoman membership devel., Conn. chpt.), Am. Aculturation Assocs. (bd. dirs.), Toastmasters Internat., Tau Alpha, Beta Gamma. Roman Catholic. Avocations: european travel, gourmet cooking, reading, tennis, golf. Home: 210 Brittany Farms Rd Ste E New Britain CT 06053-1282 Office Phone: 860-229-3496. E-mail: raebedet@aol.com.

MARGO, KATHERINE LANE, family physician, educator; b. Buffalo, June 3, 1952; d. Warren Wilson and Virginia (Penney) Lane; m. Geoffrey Myles Margo, Apr. 20, 1980; 1 child, Benjamin stepchildren: Jenny, Judy. BA, Swarthmore Coll., 1974; MD, SUNY Health Sci. Ctr., Syracuse, 1978. Resident physician St. Joseph's Hosp., Syracuse, 1979-82; attending physician Health Svcs. Assn., Syracuse, 1982-90, asst. med. dir. for quality assurance, 1985-90; asst. prof. family medicine SUNY-HSC at Syracuse, 1990-94; mem. residency faculty Harrisburg (Pa.) Hosp., 1994-2000; med. dir. Harrisburg Kline Family Practice Ctr., 1996-2000; assoc. residency dir. Harrisburg Family Practice Residency, 1997-2000; predoctoral dir. Dept. Family Practice Cmty. Medicine U. Pa., 2000—, asst. prof., assoc. dir. family practice residency, 2000—. Clin. assoc. prof. Allegheny Med. Sch., 1997—2000. Contbr. articles to profl. jours. Bd. trustees Pt. Choice, Syracuse, 1993—94; chair med. com. Planned Parenthood, Syracuse, 1984—94; bd. dirs. Planned Parenthood Susquehanna Valley, 1996—2000; active Friends of Chamber Music, Syracuse, 1985—94; keyboard player Old World folk Band. Recipient Excuplary Tchg. award, Pa. Acad. of Family Practice, 2003. Mem.: Am. Acad. Family Practitioners (v.p. Syracuse chpt.), Soc. Tchrs. of Family Medicine (chair group on predoctoral edn. 2003—04). Home: 426 Carpenter Ln Philadelphia PA 19119-3040 Office Phone: 215-662-8941. E-mail: margok@uphs.upenn.edu.

MARGOLIN, DEBORAH SUSAN, performance artist, educator, writer; b. N.Y.C., Sept. 8, 1953; d. Harold and Elaine Marjorie (Rose) M.; m. Neal Ira Kirschner, Sept. 3, 1990; children: Bennett Alexander, Molly Cara. BA cum laude, NYU, 1975. Founding mem. Split Britches Theater Co., N.Y.C., 1980—, solo performance artist, 1985—; workshop creator, instr. creative writing Interart Theater, N.Y.C., 1988—; instr. performance composition NYU, N.Y.C., 1994-97; Zale writer-in-residence Tulane U., New Orleans, 1997. Artist-in-residence Hampshire Coll., Amherst, Mass., 1989, U. Hawaii, Oahu, 1992. Playwright, 1980—; author: More Monologues for Women, 1996, Out of Character, 1996, Split Britches: Feminist Performance, 1996, Of All the Nerve: Deb Margolin Solo, 1998. Fac. instr. Yale U. Theater Studies program, 1998—; bd. govs. N.Y. Found. for Arts, 1993—94. Univ. honors scholar NYU, 1975; performance art fellow N.Y. Found. for Arts, 1990-91. Home: 106 Woodland Rd Montvale NJ 07645-1332

MARGOLIN, JEAN SPIELBERG, artist; b. N.Y.C., Oct. 12, 1926; d. Jack and Ida (Grossman) Spielberg and Bess Liebowitz Spielberg (stepmother); m. Paul Margolin, May 19, 1946 (dec. Mar. 1989). Student, Ind. U., 1951-55, Skowhegan Sch. Painting/Sculp., 1954. Tchr. painting and drawing Ind. U., Bloomington, 1954-55; curator group show Pace U. Gallery, N.Y.C., 1984. Paintings exhibited John Herron Art Mus., Indpls., 1952-55, J.B. Speed Art Mus., Louisville, 1953, Cin. Mus. Art, 1955, L.A. County Mus. Art, 1956, A.C.A. Gallery, N.Y.C., 1959-60, Pa. Acad. Fine Arts, Phila., 1962, Heckscher Mus., Huntington, N.Y., 1964, Skowhegan Benefit Exbhn., Nat. Arts Club, N.Y.C., 1974, Arthouse, Storrs, Conn., 1979, Landmark Gallery, N.Y.C., 1980-82, Pace U. Gallery, N.Y.C., 1980, 84, The Artists Choice Mus., Alex Rosenberg Gallery, N.Y.C., 1983; paintings exhibited by appointment only, N.Y.C., 1985—. Recipient 1st prize purchase award for painting Skowhegan Sch. Painting and Sculpture, 1954, scholar, 1954. Home: 4 Washington Square Vlg Apt 12S New York NY 10012-1908

MARGOLIS, GWEN, county commissioner; 4 children. Grad., Temple U. Mem. Fla. Ho. of Reps., 1974-79, Fla. Senate, 1980, chair fin., tax and claims com., chmn. appropriations com., senate pres., 1990-92; mem. dist. 4 Metro-Dade County Commn., Fla., 1994—, chairperson, commr. dist. 4. Bd. dirs. Holocaust Documentation Ctr. Fla. Internat. U.; chmn. Coconut Grove Playhouse, chmn., 1997—. Recipient Econ. Devel. award Fla. C. of C., 1992, Legislator of Yr. award Fla. C. of C., 1992, Good Govt. award Dade League of Cities, 1992, Fla. Motion Picture and TV award, 1992, Glass Ceiling award Fla. Fedn. Bus. and Profl. Women, 1992. Office: Office County Commr 111 NW 1st St Fl 2 Miami FL 33128-1902

MARGOLIS, PATT, minister; b. N.Y.C., July 24, 1951; d. Joseph and Cynthia Beckles; m. Ira Margolis, Dec. 16, 1972; children: Cynthia, Emily, Jessica. Student, Wagner Coll., S.I., 1969—70, SUNY, New Paltz, 1983—85; BA, Empire State Coll., Saratoga Springs, N.Y., 1998; MDiv, Union Theol. Sem., N.Y.C., 2002. Pvt. music tchr., Monroe, NY, 1978—97; choir dir. St. Paul Luth. Ch., Monroe, 1978—82, music dir./adminstr., 1982—87; handbell dir. Sacred Heart Ch., Monroe, 1987—97; substitute tchr. Monroe Woodbury Ctrl. Sch. Dist., Monroe, 1997; vicar St. Mary's Episc. Ch., N.Y.C., 2000—01; sr. pastor St. Thomas Luth. Ch., Ctrl. Nyack, NY, 2001—. Vicar King of Kings Luth. Ch., 1993—94; instr. DiaKonia, 2003—; mem. pastoral care com. Nyack Hosp., 2002—; bd. dirs. Women of the Evang. Luth. Ch., N.Y.C., Met. N.Y. Synod Diaconal Coun., House of Hope, Airmont, NY, Nyack Hosp. Fellow Maxwell fellow, Union/Auburn Sem., 2002. Mem.: NAACP, African American Luth. Assn. (scholarship). Lutheran. Avocations: music, quilting, exercise. Office: St Thomas Luth Ch Central Nyack NY 10960 Office Phone: 845-358-2068. Personal E-mail: pattmargolis@hotmail.com.

MARGOLIS, PEPPY SYLVIA (PEARL MARGOLIS), elementary education educator, consultant; b. Zalsheim, Germany, July 19, 1946; came to U.S., 1950; d. David and Sara (Cederbaum) Schwarzberg; m. Ira Allan Margolis, July 7, 1968 (div. June 1996); children: Lisa, Loryn. BA in Elem. Edn., Trenton State Coll., 1968; postgrad., Seton Hall U., 1995-98. Cert. elem. tchr., N.J. Tchr. 4th grade Thomas Jefferson Sch., North Arlington, N.J., 1969-70; tchr. 7th and 8th grade lang. arts Prospect Ave Sch., Ridgefield, N.J., 1970-71; tchr. 7th and 8th grade various schs., N.J., 1980-89; prin. Temple Sinai, Summit, N.J., 1990-94; coord. Holocaust program United Jewish Fedn. of Metrowest, Whippany, N.J., 1990—; asst. dir. N.J. State Holocaust Commn., Trenton, 1993—. Cons. to N.J. State Holocaust Commn.; edn. cons. March of the Living, 1990; curriculum cons. Pa. Jewish Coalition, Harrisburg, 1991-93; chair N.J. State Second Generation Conf., Kean Coll., Union, N.J., 1989-90. Primary author elem. curriculum Caring Makes A Difference K-8, 19941 contbr. articles to profl. jours. Recipient Edn. Recognition award Honey and Maurice Axelrod Anti-Defamation League, 1984. Mem. Hadassh (life, pres. 1980-81, Woman of Valor 1983, Nat. Leadership award 1987). Democrat. Jewish. Avocations: travel, writing, reading, swimming, dance.

MARGOLIS, SHERRY, newscaster; m. Jeff Zaslow, 1987; children: Jordan, Alexandra, Eden. BA in English, SUNY, Buffalo. Anchor and reporter WKBW-TV, Buffalo; reporter WJBK-TV, Detroit, 1984—, anchor "In the News", co-anchor 5am and noon news. Named Best Newscast in Mich., AP, 1990; recipient Best News Anchor Emmys, NATAS, 1993, 1999, Emmy Reporting, 2002. Office: WJBK-TV FOX 2 PO Box 2000 Southfield MI 48037-2000

MARGOLIS, SUSAN ELLEN, psychiatric clinical nurse specialist, artist; b. Cleve., May 11, 1955; d. William Nathan and Sarah Aranow Zuckerman; m. Larry S. Margolis; children: William Zuckerman, Jacob Nathan. BSN, U. Tex., 1981, MSN, 1989; PhD, Tex. Woman's U., 2000. RN, Tex.; cert. clin. nurse specialist-psychiat./mental health. Charge/staff nurse NurseFinders, Arlington, Tex., 1984-88; clin. asst. Post Oak Psychiatry Assocs., Waxahachie, Tex., 1988-89; team leader Ft. Worth (Tex.) Vet.'s Ctr., 1989-90; nursing instr. Tarleton State U., Stephenville, Tex., 1990; pvt. practice cons., educator, lectr., therapist Benbrook, Tex., 1991-92; geripsychiat. nurse therapist Ft. Worth Family Inst., 1992-93; dir. geriatric svcs. Psychiat. Ctr. of North Tex., DeSoto, 1993—2002; corp. psychiat. cons. VeriCare Inc., 2002—. Spkr. many profl. and cmty. burs., 1989-. Vol. Arlington (Tex.) Night Shelter, 1988-96, Presbyn. Night Shelter, Ft. Worth, 1997—; del. to China, Am. Del. Psychol. Nurses, 1990; foster parent; active local Orthodox synagogue. With U.S. Army, 1973-75; lt. USAF, 1982-83. Full chemistry scholar Stephen F. Austin State U., 1972; selected for individual study Royal Acad. Nursing, Edinburgh, Scotland, 1973. Mem. ANA, Tex. Nurse's Assn., Disabled Vet.'s Assn., U. Tex. at Arlington Alumni Assn., Tex. Woman's U. Alumni Assn., Sigma Theta Tau. Jewish. Avocation: stained glass art. Home: 10166 Trail Ridge Dr Benbrook TX 76126-9516 Office: 10166 Trail Ridge Dr Benbrook TX 76126 E-mail: margolis7@hotmail.com.

MARGRAVE, KATHY CHRISTINE, nurse anesthetist; b. Pittsburg, Kans., Oct. 23, 1957; d. James Raymond and Nancy Jeanne (Evans) M.; 1 child, Erica. BSN, Marymount Coll., Salina, Kans., 1980; MS, U. Kans., 1996. Med. surgery staff nurse St. Mary's Hosp., Manhattan, Kans., 1980; med./surg. staff nurse S.W. Jefferson Community Hosp., Louisville, 1980-81; commd. U.S. Army, 1981-93, advanced through grades to maj., 1991; operating rm. staff nurse Frankfurt Army Reg. Med. Ctr., W. Ger., 1981-85, Brooke Army Med. Ctr., San Antonio, 1985-88; sr. clin. staff nurse Dwight D. Eisenhower Army Med. Ctr., Fort Gordon, Ga., 1989-90, 91-94; 86th Evacuation Hosp., Saudi Arabia, 1990-91; neuro ICU staff nurse U. Hosp., Augusta, Ga., 1993-94; CRNA Anethesia Assoc. of Savannah, 1997—2003, locmtenens CRNA, 2003—. Faculty Acad. Health Scis., U.S. Army, Ft. Sam Houston, Tex. Mem.: Am. Assn. Nurse Anesthetists.

MARGULIES, JULIANNA, actress; b. Spring Valley, NY, June 8, 1966; BA, Sarah Lawrence Coll., 1989. Actress (film) Out for Justice, 1991, Traveller, 1997, Paradise Road, 1997, A Price Above Rubies, 1997, The Newton Boys, 1998, What's Cooking, 2000, Ten Unknowns, 2001 (Lucille Lortel Award for outstanding featured actress, 2001), The Man From Elysian Fields, 2001, Ghost Ship, 2002, Evelyn, 2002, (voice) Dinosaur, 2000, (TV) Murder, She Wrote, Law and Order, Homicide, Philly Heat, ER, 1994-2000 (Emmy award for supporting actress Drama, 1995, Golden Globe award winner, 1998, SAG award winner 1997, 98, 99), The Mists of Avalon, 2001, Jennifer, 2001, Hitler: The Rise of Evil, 2003 (theater) The Substance of Fire, At Home, Fefu and Her Friends, Living Expenses, Dan Drift, and Book of Names, The Vagina Monologues, 2000. Office: c/o William Morris Agency 151 S El Camino Dr Beverly Hills CA 90212*

MARGULIS, HEIDI, managed health care company executive; Licensure analyst Humana, Inc., 1985—95, v.p. govt. affairs, 1995—2000, sr. v.p. govt. affairs, 2000—. Mem. fed. adv. com. to streamline regulations to ensure quality health care svcs., 2002; mem. com. on Medicare edn. HFCA. Mem.: Women's Polit. Forum (bd. dirs.), Bus. and Profl. Women (pres. 1978—79), Bus. Roundtable, Health Care Leadership Coun., Am. Assn. Health Plans (policy, legis., advocacy and strategic planning coms.). Office: Humana Inc 500 W Main St Louisville KY 40202

MARGULIS, LYNN (LYNN ALEXANDER), evolutionist, educator; b. Chgo., Mar. 5, 1938; d. Morris and Leone (Wise) Alexander; m. Carl Sagan, June 16, 1957; children: Dorion Sagan, Jeremy Sagan; m. Thomas N. Margulis, Jan. 18, 1967; children: Zachary Margulis-Ohnuma, Jennifer Margulis di Properzio. AB, U. Chgo., 1957; A.M., U. Wis., 1960; PhD, U. Calif., Berkeley, 1965. Mem. faculty Boston U., 1966—68, asst. prof. biology, 1967—71, assoc. prof., 1971—77, prof., 1977—88, Univ. prof., 1986—88; Disting. Univ. prof. U. Mass., Amherst, 1988—. Sherman Fairchild Disting. scholar Calif. Inst. Tech., 1976—77; vis. prof. dept. microbiology U. Autónoma de Barcelona, Spain, 1986, Spain, 88; Disting. univ. prof. U. Mass. Author: Origin of Eukaryotic Cells, 1970, Symbiosis in Cell Evolution, 1981, Early Life, 1982, 2d edit., 2002, Symbiosis in Cell Evolution, 2d edit., 1993, Microcosmos Videos, 1999, Luminous Fish: Tales of Science and Love, 2003; editor (with Mitchell Rambler and René Fester): Global Ecology, 1989; editor: (with others) Handbook of Protoctista, 1990; editor: Looking at Microbes, An Introduction to the Microbiology Laboratory for Students, Symbiotic Planet, A New Look at Evolution, 1997; co-editor (with René Fester): Symbiosis as a Source of Evolutionary Innovation: Speciation and Morphogenesis, 1991; co-editor: Concepts of Symbiogenesis: A Historical and Critical Study of the Research of Russian Botanists, 1992, Environmental Evolution: Effects of the Origin and Evolution of Life on Planet Earth, 1992, Environmental Evolution: Effects of the Origin and Evolution of Life on Planet Earth, 2d edit., 2000, Glossary of Protoctista, 1993, What Is Sex?, 1998, Slanted Truths: Essays on Gaia, Evolution and Symbiosis, 1997, What is Life?, 1995, Diversity of Life: The Illustrated Guide to the Five Kingdoms, 2d edit., 1999; co-author: Five Kingdoms, 1982, 3d edit., 1009, Microcosmos, 1986, Origins of Sex, 1986, Garden of Microbial Delights, 1988, 2d edit., 1998, Biospheres From Earth To Space, 1988, Mystery Dance: On the Evolution of Human Sexuality, 1991, What Happens to Trash and Garbage: An Introduction to the Carbon Cycle, 1993, Living Sands: Mapping Time and Space with Forams, 2000, Early Life, 2d edit., 2002, Acquiring Genomes: A Theory of the Origins of Species, 2002; contbr. chapters to books, articles to profl. jours. Recipient Nat. Medal Sci., 1999, Humboldt Prize, 2002, Commonwealth of Mass. award; Guggenheim fellow, 1979. Fellow: AAAS; mem.: NAS, Soc. Evolutionary Protistology (co-founder). Office: U Mass Geosci Dept 611 No Pleasant St Amherst MA 01003-2820 Office Phone: 413-545-3244. Business E-Mail: celeste@geo.umass.edu.

MARIAN, VIORICA, psychologist, educator; b. Chisinau, Moldova, June 29, 1974; d. Nicolai T. Marian and Natalia M. Marian-Iurasco; m. Aswin Aalt van den Berg, Sept. 27, 1998; children: Aimee-Nicole Marian van den Berg, Nadia Ilse Marian van den Berg. BA magna cum laude, U. Alaska, 1994; MA, PhD, Cornell U., 2000. Rsch. and tchg. asst. Cornell U., Ithaca, NY, 1996—2000; asst. prof. dept. comm. scis. and disorders and dept. psychology Northwestern U., Evanston, Ill., 2000—. Contbr. articles to profl. jours., papers to confs. Recipient Best Paper award, Behavioral Sciences Conf. of the North, 1994, Dissertation award, Pres.'s Coun. of Cornell Women, 1998, Nat. Rsch. Svc. award, NIH, 1999—2000. Mem.: APA, Cognitive Sci. Soc., Midwestern Psychol. Assn. Achievements include research in bilingual language processing using eye-tracking and functional neuroimaging; language and memory in bilinguals. Avocations: travel, reading, arts. Office: Northwestern U 2240 Campus Dr Evanston IL 60208

MARIE, HEATHER, director, consultant; b. Houston, May 19, 1968; d. Ron and Cynthia Coffman. BA in Humanities, Trinity U., San Antonio, 1990, MA in Tchg., 1991. Cert. tchr. spl. edn. pre-sch.-12, elem. self-contained 1-6, elem. English 1-6, elem. history 1-6, English as 2d lang. pre-K-12. Life skills tchr. for students with mild-moderate disabilities Alief Ind. Sch. Dist., Houston, 1991—94, tchr. spl. edn. and literacy, 1994—96, dist.-wide behavior/inclusion specialist, 1996—99; ednl. cons. Stetson & Assocs., Houston, 1999—2001; dir. behavior programs Sopris West Ednl. Svcs., Longmont, Tex., 2001—. Mentor gifted/talented students Saturday Morning Experience, San Antonio, 1989—90; mentor, tutor h.s. students Upward Bound, San Antonio, 1990—94; adult literacy instr. Neuhaus Ctr., Houston, 1994—96; presenter in field. Author, cons.: sci. textbook McGraw-Hill Science 2000, 1998. Recipient Tchr.-Rschr. grant, NICHD. Mem.: CEC, Coun. for Children with Behavior Disorders, Assn. for Curriculum and Devel. Avocations: reading, running, hiking, water-skiing, working and playing with young people. Home: # B309 2800 Kalmia Ave Boulder CO 80301

MARIETTA, ELIZABETH ANN, industrial engineer; b. Oshkosh, Wis., Feb. 28, 1954; d. Frederick Damler and Connie Steiger Dempsey; children: Hunter H. Student, U. Autonima, Guadalajara, Mex., 1974; BA in Architecture, U. N.Mex., 1979. Project mgr. drafting Hutchinson, Brown & Ptnrs., Architects, Albuquerque, 1978-80; engr. facilities constrn. mgmt. divsn. Albuquerque Ops. Office, 1982-90, engr. quality engring. divsn., 1982-90, engr. budget and resources mgmt., 1982-90, site mgr. uranium mill tailings remedial action project, 1982-90; sect. chief indsl. tech. Bonneville Power Adminstrn., Portland, Oreg., 1990—. Employee support sounding bd. Bonneville Power Adminstrn., Portland, 1990-91, women's resource group, 1990-93. Mem. City Club Portland, 1990-91. Avocations: reading, sailing, travel, scuba diving. Home: 318 2nd St Lake Oswego OR 97034-3115

MARIN, ROSARIO, former federal agency administrator; b. Mexico City, Mex., Aug. 4, 1958; m. Alex Marin; children: Eric, Carmen, Alvaro. BS bus. adminstrn., Calif. State U., L.A., 1983, LLD (hon.), 2002; grad., Harvard U., 1998. With City Nat. Bank, Beverly Hills, 1981—86; chief legis. affairs Calif. Dept. Devel. Svcs., 1992—93; chair Calif. State Coun. Developmental Disabilities, 1994—96; asst. dep. dir. Calif. State Dept. Social Svcs., 1996—97; dep. dir. Gov.'s Office Cmty. Rels., L.A., 1997—98; mayor City of Huntington Park, Calif., 1999—2000; 41st U.S. treas. U. S. Dept. Treasury, Washington, 2001—03. Recipient Rose Fitzgerald Kennedy award, U.N., 1995, Excellence in Pub. Svc. award, Latino Perspective Conf., 2000, Alumna of the Year, Calif. State U., 2002. Office: Rosario Moran for US Senate 3199 Airport Loop Dr Ste D Costa Mesa CA 92626

MARINCOLA, ELIZABETH MARK, scientific society executive; b. New Haven, Conn., Aug. 31, 1959; d. James B.D. and Jean M. (Rambar) Mark; m. Francesco M. Marincola, Jan. 1, 1982; children: James Paul,

Paula Rambar, Rachel Angela. AB, Stanford U., 1981, MBA, 1986. Dir. devel. Stanford (Calif.) U. Hosp., 1987-90; dep. dir. policy rsch. analysis NIMH, Rockville, Md., 1990-91; exec. dir. The Am. Soc. Cell Biology, Bethesda, Md., 1991—. Mem. cell biology com. of visitors NSF, 2001; com. for divsn. on earth and life studies Nat. Acad. Sci., 2001—; mem. PubMed Ctrl. Nat. adv. com. Nat. Libr. of Medicine Nat. Inst. Health, 2000-03; 20th Annual Fae Golden Kass lectr. Harvard Med. Sch., 1999; mem. adv. bd. Krasnow Inst. for Advanced Study, George Mason U., 2002—; elected first citizen mem. Am. Soc. Cell Biology, 2003. Home: 10110 Chapel Rd Potomac MD 20854-4143 Address: Amer Society for Cell Biology 8120 Woodmont Ave Suite 750 Bethesda MD 20814-2762 E-mail: emarincola@ascb.org.

MARINE, SUSAN SONCHIK, analytical chemist, educator; b. Maple Heights, Ohio, Mar. 10, 1954; d. Stephen Robert and Gloria Ann (Hach) Sonchik; m. Michael David Marine; 1 child, Matthew Robert Marine. BS in Chemistry magna cum laude, John Carroll U., 1975; MS in Analytical Chemistry, Case Western Res. U., 1978, PhD in Phys. Chemistry, 1980. Asst. chemist Horizons Research Inc., Beachwood, Ohio, 1974-75; chemist specialist Standard Oil of Ohio, Warrensville Heights, Ohio, 1975-79; organic chemistry br. mgr. Versar, Inc., Springfield, Va., 1980-83; mgr. gas chromatography program IBM Instruments Inc., Danbury, Conn., 1983-87, radiation safety officer, 1985-87; expert witness, cons. Martin, Craig, Chester & Sonnenschein, Chgo., 1981-83; adv. engr. in advanced lithography IBM Corp., Essex Junction, Vt., 1987-95; vis. assoc. prof. chemistry Centre Coll., Danville, Ky., 1995-98; asst. prof. chemistry and biochemistry, coord. tech. program Miami U., Middletown, Ohio, 1998—2004; spl. term appointment energy sys. divsn. Argonne Nat. Lab., Ill., 2003—; assoc. prof. chemistry and biochemistry, coord. tech program Miami U., Middletown, Ohio, 2004—. Vis. asst. prof. chemistry and math. Heritage Coll., 1991—92; spkr. in field. Author: African Walking Safari, 1985; editl. adv. bd. Jour. Chromatographic Sci., 1977-93, guest editor, 1987. Mem. Danbury Conservation Commn., 1986-87, tchr. and tutor chemistry, 1985-89, 91-92, 94; troop leader Lake Erie coun. Girl Scouts U.S.A., 1971-80, Southwestern Conn., 1983-87; leader explorer post Cleve. coun. Boy Scouts Am., 1977-78; managerial advisor Jr. Achievement, Warrensville Heights, Ohio, 1977-78; judge State or Regional Sci. Fair, 1977, 80, 89-91, 99, 2000, Odyssey of the Mind, 1994; asst. leader Internat. Folk Dancers, Newtown, Conn., 1985-87; tchr. religion, 1981-84, 87-90, 93-94. Recipient Overall Best Paper award Eastern Analytical Symposium, 1984, First Gas Chromatograph award IBM Instruments Inc., 1985, contbn. award (tech. paper) 10th Internat. Congress of Essential Oils, Flavors, Fragrances, Washington, 1986. Mem. ASTM (exec. com. E-19 1985-2000, chmn. subcom. 1986-2000, vice chmn. arrangements 1994-98), Am. Chem. Soc. (chmn. membership com. Green Mountain sect. 1988-89, chair elect 1989-90, chmn. 1990-91, local coord. Nat. Chemistry Week 1991, 93-98, 2002-03, Phoenix award 1994, 97), Iota Sigma Pi (pres. N.E. Ohio chpt. 1978-79, mem.-at-large fin. mgr. 1993-97, nat. v.p. 1996-99, nat. pres. 1999-2002, immediate past pres. 2002-), No. Vt. Canoe Cruisers (treas. 1990-92), Green Mountain Steppers (sec. 1993-95), Centre Coll. Outdoors Club (faculty liaison 1996-98), Miami U. Middletown Chemistry Club (faculty liaison 2003—). Roman Catholic. Avocations: camping, dance, travel. Home: 4667 Sebald Dr Franklin OH 45005-5328 Office: Miami U Middletown 4200 E University Blvd Middletown OH 45042-3458 E-mail: mariness@muohio.edu.

MARINELLI, JANICE, broadcast executive; b. N.Y., 1958; m. Thomas Mazza; 3 children. BS in comm., St. John's U., N.Y. Rsch. analyst TeleRep; sr. rschr. Lorimar TV, Katz TV Group; acct. exec. Buena Vista TV, 1985, dir. sales western divsn., exec. v.p., 1996—99, pres., 1999—. Office: Buena Vista TV 500 S Buena Vista St Burbank CA 91521*

MARINEZ, RITA MARIA, writer; b. Miami, Fla., May 22, 1975; d. Jose Manolo Martinez and Mery Caridad Barrera. BA in English Cum Laude, BA in Women's Studies Cum Laude, Fla. Internat. U., 1996, MFA Suma Cum Laude, 2003. Clerical asst. St. Brendan Ch., Miami, Fla., 1993—99; writer Fla. Internat. U. Office Mktg. Media Rels., 2000—. Guest lectr. Fla. Internat. U., Miami, Fla., 2003—, 2001—02. Contbr. articles to profl. jours.; creative dir.: website TuTTi USA, 1997. Recipient Poetry award, Gulf Coast Assn. Creative Writing Tchrs. Conf., 2003, 12th Annual Fla. Internat. U. Literary Competition. Mem.: Delta Nat. English Honor Soc. Home: 8201 SW 30 St Miami FL 33155

MARING, MARY MUEHLEN, state supreme court justice; b. Devils Lake, N.D., July 27, 1951; d. Joseph Edward and Charlotte Rose (Schorr) Muehlen: m. David Scott Maring, Aug. 30, 1975; children: Christopher David, Andrew Joseph. BA in Polit. Sci. summa cum laude, Moorhead State U., 1972; JD, U. N.D., 1975. Bar: Minn., N.D. Law clk. Hon. Bruce Stone, Mpls, 1975-76; assoc. Stefanson, Landberg & Alm, Ltd., Moorhead, Minn., 1976-82, Ohnstad, Twichell, Breitling, Rosenvold, Wanner, Nelson, Neugebauer & Maring, P.C., West Fargo, N.D., 1982-88, Lee Hagan Law Office, Fargo, 1988-91; pvt. practice Maring Law Office, Fargo, 1991-96; justice N.D. State Supreme Ct., Bismarck, ND, 1996—. Women's bd. mem. 1st Nat. Bank, Fargo, 1977-82; career day speaker Moorhead Rotarians, 1980-83. Contbr. note to legal rev.; note editor N.D. Law Rev., 1975. Mem. ABA (del. ann. conv. young lawyers sect. 1981-82, bd. govs. 1982-83), Minn. Women Lawyers, N.D. State Bar Assn. (bd. govs. 1991-93), Clay County Bar Assn. (v.p. 1983-84), N.D. Trial Lawyers Assn. (pres. 1992-93), Internat. Soc. of Barristers, Nat. Assn. of Women Judges (dist. 10 dir. 2001-03). Roman Catholic. Office: ND Supreme Ct 600 E Boulevard Ave Dept 180 Bismarck ND 58505-0530

MARINI, ANN MARIE, medical researcher, educator; b. Stamford, Conn., May 27, 1949; d. Alfred Francis and Theresa Maryann Marini; m. Robert Henry Lipsky, Sept. 6, 1990; 1 child, Sarah. BA, Erskine Coll., 1971; PhD, Georgetown U., 1978, MD, 1980. Diplomate Am. Bd. Internal Medicine, Am. Bd. Psychiatry and Neurology. Med. resident U. Mass., Worcester, 1980-83; neurology resident Albert Einstein Coll. Medicine, Bronx, N.Y., 1983-86; post-doctoral fellow NIH, Bethesda, Md., 1986-93; staff neurologist Dept. Vet. Affairs, Washington, 1993-94; asst. prof. Uniformed Svcs. U. Health Scis., Bethesda, 1994-2001, assoc. prof., 2001—. Mem. Am. Acad. Neurology (tech. and therapeutics subcom. 1994-99), Soc. for Neurosci., Sigma Xi. Office: Uniformed Svcs U Health Scis 4301 Jones Bridge Rd Bethesda MD 20814-4712 E-mail: amarini@usuhs.mil.

MARINI, JANE MARIE, music educator; b. Rochester, N.Y., Nov. 30, 1959; d. Joseph Charles Puceta and Jeanne Marie Scharvogel; m. Claude Anthony Marini, Nov. 24, 1984; children: Anthony, Dominic, Christopher, Cecilia. BS in Music Edn., Nazareth Coll., Rochester, N.Y., 1981. Music tchr. Hochstein Music Sch., Rochester, NY, 1999—; mentor tchg. artist Wolf Trap Found.-Aesthetic Edn. Inst., Rochester, NY, 2002—. Music dir. Vacation Bible Sch., Fairport, NY, 1993—. Mem.: Orff-Schulwerk Assn. Am., Music Educator's Nat. Conf. Avocations: reading, computers. Home: 26 Sanibel Dr Fairport NY 14450 Office: Hochstein Music Sch 50 N Plymouth Ave Rochester NY 14614

MARINO, MARY Q. research scientist; b. Pueblo, Colo. d. Edward Anthony and Marie (Carroll) Qualkenbush; m. Rocco Marino, Jr. BA, Loretto Heights Coll.; postgrad., Cath. U. Am. Washington; lab. med. technologist, Huntington Meml. Hosp. Lic. clin. lab. scientist, Calif. Dept. Health Svcs. Biochemist Pasadena (Calif.) Clin. Lab.; chief med. technologist Children's Clinic, Pasadena. Mem. Am. Soc. Clin. Pathologists, Calif. Assn. Med. Lab. Technology, Cath. U. Am. Alumni Club. Avocations: music, art, photography.

MARINO, SHEILA BURRIS, education educator; b. Knoxville, Nov. 24, 1947; d. David Paul and Lucille Cora (Maupin) Burris; m. Louis John Marino, Dec. 19, 1969; children: Sheila Noelle, Heather Michelle. BS, U. Tenn., 1969, MS, 1971, EdD, 1976; postgrad., W.Va. U., Europe. Elem./early childhood tchr. Knoxville City Schs., 1969-71; cooperating tchr. U. Tenn., Knoxville, 1969-71; dir. early childhood edn./tchr. Glenville (W.Va.) State Coll., 1971-72, Colo. Women's Coll., Denver, 1972-73; asst. prof. edn. Lander U., Greenwood, S.C., 1973-75; instr., spl. asst. to coord. elem./early childhood edn. U. Tenn., 1975-76; prof. edn., dir. clin. experiences, asst. dean Lander U. Sch. Edn., 1976—93, dean, 1993-94, dir. sci. discovery program, 1995—, prof. edn., dir. tchg. fellows program, 1995—. Cons. in field; dir. Creative Activities Prog. for Children, Lander U., 1979—; mem. W.Va. Gov.'s Early Childhood Adv. Bd., 1971-72, Gov.'s Team of Higher Edn. Profls. on Comprehensive Plan for S.C. Early Childhood Edn., 1982. Contbr. articles to profl. jours. and books; author: International Children's Literature, 1989. Bd. dirs. Greenwood Lit. Coun., v.p., 1990, pres., 1991; bd. dirs. St. Nicholas Speech and Hearing Ctr., Greenwood, pres., 1992; bd. dirs. Old Ninety-Six coun. Girl Scouts U.S.A., 1987-92; vol. March of Dimes Program, Greenwood, 1987. Mem. AAUW (pres. 1990-92), AAUP, SNEA (state advisor 1981-88, 98-99), S.C. Student Edn. Assn., Piedmont Assn. Children and Adults with Learning Disabilities (pres. 1986-93, exec. bd.), Learning Disabilities Assn. S.C. (pres. 1990-94), S.C. Edn. Assn., S. C. Assn. for Children Under Six, So. Assn. for Children under Six, S.C. Assn. Tchr. Educators, Piedmont Reading Coun. (v.p. 1985-86, 90-91, pres. 1986-88, 91-92, 96-97), S.C. Coun. Internat. Reading Assn. (exec. bd. 1986-88, 91-96), Delta Kappa Gamma (pres. Epsilon chpt. 1984-88, 92-94, mem. exec. bd.), Pi Lambda Theta, Kappa Delta Pi (pres. U. Tenn. chpt. 1974-75), Phi Delta Kappa (v.p. 1988-90, pres. Lander U. chpt. 1990-91, 94-96). Democrat. Presbyterian. Avocations: reading, gardening, swimming, music, arts and crafts. Home: 103 Essex Ct Greenwood SC 29649-9561 Office: Lander U Stanley Avenue Greenwood SC 29649

MARINOFF, ISABELLA BLUMENSTOCK, English educator; b. Brussels, Dec. 28, 1946; came to U.S., 1948; d. Abraham Samuel and Ela Blumenstock; m. Philip Sherman Marinoff, July 23, 1972 (dec. Apr. 1993); children: Sarah, Rebecca. BA summa cum laude, Barnard Coll., 1967; MA, Yale U., 1968, PhD, 1980. Cert. English tchr. grades 7-12, N.Y. Lectr. Marymount Manhattan Coll., N.Y.C., 1979-80, Hunter Coll., N.Y.C., 1984-85, Bklyn. Coll., N.Y.C., 1988-91; asst. to coord. acad. devel. and planning Touro Coll., N.Y.C., 1991-95; tchr. AP English Hebrew Acad. Nassau County, Uniondale, NY, 1995—. Adj. asst. prof. Kingsborough C.C., N.Y.C., 1990-94; presenter in field. Contbr. articles to profl. jours. Fellow Woodrow Wilson Found., 1967, NDEA Title IV fellow Yale U., 1968. Mem. MLA.

MARION, ANN, school psychologist, educator; b. Mobile, Ala., Apr. 30, 1936; d. Edmund Charles and Lela Marie (Franklin) Guidroz; m. Donald Orrin Marion, June 25, 1965; children: Janet Marie, Kathryn Elizabeth. BA, Millsaps Coll., Jackson, Miss., 1963; MEd, U. So. Miss., Hattiesburg, 1972. Cert. tchr., cert. sch. psychologist, Miss. Classrm. tchr. Natchez-Adams Sch. Dist., Natchez, Miss., 1963-72, tchr. Title III ESEA, 1967-69, psychometrist, 1969-72, sch. psychologist, 1977-94; ret. Past pres. Mental Health Assn., Adams County Assn. for Child Protection; mem. Gov.'s Criminal Justice Task Force, 1991; bd. dirs. Natchez Child Protection Assn.; mem. craft com. Natchez Career and Tech. Ctr. Mem. Pilgrimage Garden Club, Nat. Rep. Assn., Phi Delta Kappa. Avocations: reading, study groups, bridge, collecting antiques, dollhouses. Home: 105 Mansfield Dr Natchez MS 39120-4930 E-mail: agmarion@netscape.net.

MARION, MARJORIE ANNE, English language educator, education consultant; b. Winterset, Iowa, May 6, 1935; d. Virgil Arthur and Marilyn Ruth (Sandy) Hammon; m. Robert H. Marion, Dec. 20, 1964; 1 child, Kathryn Ruth. BA, Colo. Coll., 1958; MA, Purdue U., 1969; postgrad., Inst. Mgmt. Lifelong Edn. Harvard U., 1981. Chairperson English dept. Lincoln-Way H.S., New Lenox, Ill., 1964-68; dir. pub. rels. U. St. Francis, Joliet, Ill., 1968-70, chairperson English dept., 1971-75, chairperson divsn. humanities and fine arts, 1975-79, coord. instrnl. devel., 1979-80, dir. continuing edn., 1980-84, acting v.p. acad. affairs, 1984-85, dean of faculty, 1985-89, assoc. prof. English, 1989-97, dir. Freshman Core Program, 1993-95; dir. Writing Ctr. Joliet, Ill., 1996; prof. emeritus U. St. Francis, Joliet, Ill., 1997—. Cons. to presdl. search U. St. Francis, 2001—02; mem. vis. team North Ctrl. Assn., Joliet and Lockport, Ill., 1975—79; lectr. at ednl. workshops and instns.; condr. writing workshops for adults returning to coll., 1995—; TV and radio appearances regarding lifelong edn., Chgo., St. Louis, Albuquerque, Phoenix, 1982—85; lectr. writing workshops. Author: A Guide to Writing for the Faint at Heart, 1996; author monograph; drama critic Joliet Herald News, 1970-82. Recipient Pres.'s award Coll. St. Francis, 1975. Mem. Am. Assn. Higher Edn., Nat. Coun. Tchrs. of English, Nat. Acad. Advising Assn. Roman Catholic. E-mail: rhmarion@msn.com.

MARION, SARAH KATHLEEN, music educator; b. Wenatchee, Wash., Mar. 31, 1974; d. John Alfred Braden and Diana Lee Black; m. Jim Johan Marion; children: Christina, Daniel. AAS, Wenatchee Valley Coll., Wenatchee, Wash., 1995. Pvt. piano instr., Wenatchee, 1990—; part-time instr. Wenatchee Valley Coll., Wenatchee, 2001. Sec. Family Issues and Awareness Team, Wenatchee, 2000—; at-large bd. mem. Wenatchee Free Meth. Ch., 2001. Mem.: Wenatchee Chpt. Wash. State Music Tchrs. Assn. (publicity chmn. 1997—99), Music Tchrs. Nat. Assn., Wash. State Music Tchrs. Assn., Phi Theta Kappa. Avocations: travel, languages, running, outdoor recreation. Home: 50-19th St NE East Wenatchee WA 98802

MARION, SUZANNE MARGARET, music educator; b. Hutchinson, Kans., May 6, 1938; d. Charles Myers and Margaret Lansden (Foster) Davis; m. Stuart Eli Marion, June 2, 1962; children: John Stuart, David Evan, Matthew Charles. BA in Psychology, U. Ariz., 1960; BA in Music, U. Houston, 1982. Psychiat. social worker Ariz. State Hosp., Phoenix, 1960-62; tchr. voice, theory, piano Houston Music Inst., 1978-81; pvt. practice Houston, 1970—. Performer Class Act, Houston, 1994—. Soloist Emerson Unitarian Ch. choir, Houston, 1983—2000. Voice scholarship Madrigal Club, 1964. Mem. Houston Tuesday Musical Club (pres. 1996-98), Treble Clef Club, Sigma Alpha Iota. Republican. Unitarian Universalist. Avocations: creative writing, study of spanish, computer, reading, working with dogs. Home: 910 Briarbrook Dr Houston TX 77042-2006

MARIOTTI, MARGARET, executive secretary; b. Derby, Conn., Nov. 1, 1956; d. Peter J. and Matrona (Iannotti) M. Student, Stone Sch. Bus., New Haven, 1975-76. Sec. Sikorsky Aircraft, Stratford, Conn., 1977—. Mem. Alpha Iota. Home: 411 Coram Ave Shelton CT 06484-3134 E-mail: mmmariotti@aol.com.

MARIUCCI, ANNE L. real estate development company executive; BA in Accounting/Finance, U. Ariz. In corp. fin. KPMG Peat Marwick, Am. Continental Corp.; v.p. corp. planning & devel. Del Webb Corp., 1982-86, pres, CEO Del Webb Investment Properties, 1986-87, sr. v.p., 1988—. Office: Del Webb Corp 6001 N 24th St Phoenix AZ 85016-2018

MARK, JUDI, actress, choreographer; b. Chgo., Mar. 20; d. Leonard and Dorothy March. BS in Edn., So. Ill. U.; postgrad., San Diego State U., U.S. Internat. U. Performing Arts. Dancer U.S. Internat. Dance Theatre, Balboa Park Theatre, San Diego. Founder, choreographer Judi Mark & Co.; dance instr. P.S. 190, N.Y.C., 1986—; elem. tchr. Dade County Schs., 1970-74. Appeared in (stage prodns.) West Side Story, The Rose Tattoo, The Rainmaker, Time and Involvement, (films) Deathtrap, 1982, Turk 182!, 1985, Private Resorts, 1986, (TV) Miami Vice. Mem. AFTRA. Jewish. Avocation: traveling.

MARK, LILLIAN GEE, educational administrator; b. Berkeley, Calif., Mar. 18, 1932; d. Pon Gordon and Sun Kum (Wong) Gee; m. Richard Muin Mark, June 20, 1954; children: Dean, Kim, Faye, Glenn, Lynne. BA in Psychology, U. Calif., Berkeley, 1954; MS in Christian Sch. Adminstrn., Pensacola Coll., 1987; HHD (hon.), Shasta Bible Coll., 2002. Supt. Alpha Beacon Christian Sch., San Mateo, Calif., 1976—. CEO, Alpha Beacon Christian Ministries. Author: Handbook for Parents and Students, 1983, How To Encourage Your Staff. Mem.: Internat. Fellowship Christian Sch. Adminstrs., Assn. Christian Sch. Internat., Christian Ministries. Republican. Avocations: tennis, swimming, piano, Bible study. Home: 384 Montserrat Dr Redwood City CA 94065-2806 Office: Alpha Beacon Christian Sch 1950 Elkhorn Ct San Mateo CA 94403 Business E-Mail: abcinfo@alphabeacon.org.

MARK, MARSHA YVONNE ISMAILOFF, artistic director; b. Bridgeport, Conn., Mar. 15, 1938; d. Nicholas and Louba (Foullon) Ismailoff; m. Robert Louis Mark, June 25, 1960; children: Robert, William, Staci. Ballet tng. with, George Balanchine, 1946-50, George Volodine, 1945-60, 65-69; student, Skidmore Coll., 1978-80, Vaganova Method Sch., Minsk, USSR, 1983, U. of the Arts, 1990. Founder Marsha Imailoff Mark Sch. of Ballet, Newtown, Conn., 1969—; artistic dir. Com. for Ballet Miniatures, Newtown, Conn., 1974—, Malenkee Ballet Repertoire Co., Newtown, Conn., 1980—. V.p. Cmty. Arts Project Ext., Newtown, 1987-91; artistic dir. Danbury (Conn.) Music Ctr., 1989; instr. for neurologically impaired Ripton Sch., Shelton, Conn., 1992; choreographed section of Nutcracker Ballet for Special Children; toured Russia with Malenkee Ballet Repertoire Co. Choreographer including original works: Mademoiselle Angot, 1974, Circus, 1975, Haydn Concerto, 1976, Evening at the Zoo, 1977, Match Girl, 1978, The Four Seasons, 1979, Malenkee Waltz, 1980, Magic Key, 1981, Midsummer Night's Dream, 1982, Macbeth A Witches Haunt, 1983, Etudes, 1984, Toy Boutique, Etudes, 1985, Under the Sea, 1986, Nutcracker, 1987, 88, 89, 90, 91, 92, 93, 94, 95, 96, 97, Mere, Mere, Mere, 1988, Ellis Island Memoirs, 1991, Moonlight Etudes, 1992, Echoes of Soft Thunder, 1995, Coppelia, 1998; premiered in Baku USSR. Hostess for artists from Russia, translator UN Hostess Com., N.Y.C., 1988; Russian translator Friends of Music, Newtown, 1990, Sacred Heart U., Fairfield, Conn., 1994. Home: Apt 10 1457 NE Ocean Blvd Stuart FL 34996-1538

MARK, REBECCA P. environmental services administrator; BA in Psychology, MA in Internat. Mgmt., Baylor U.; MBA with distinction, Harvard U. From mem. staff to v. chmn. Enron, Houston, 1982-, v. chmn.; chmn., CEO, bd. dirs. Azurix Corp., Houston, 1999—. Office: Azurix Corp 333 Clay St Ste 1000 Houston TX 77002-4000 Fax: 713-345-5290.

MARKEE, KATHERINE MADIGAN, librarian, educator; b. Cleve., Feb. 24, 1931; d. Arthur Alexis and Margaret Elizabeth (Madigan) M. AB, Trinity Coll., Washington, 1953; MA, Columbia U., 1962; MLS, Case Western Res. U., 1968. Employment mgr., br. store tng. supr. The May Co., Cleve., 1965-67; assoc. prof. libr. sci., data bases libr. Purdue U. Libr., West Lafayette, Ind., 1968—, libr. spl. collections, 1996—. Contbr. articles to profl. jours. Mem. ALA, AAUP, Spl. Librs. Assn., Ind. Online Users Group, Sigma Xi (Rsch. Support award 1986). Avocations: photography, sailing, gardening. Office: Purdue U Libr 504 W State St West Lafayette IN 47907-2058 E-mail: kmarkee@purdue.edu.

MARKERT, MARY LOUISE, pediatrics educator; MD, Duke U., 1982. Resident Duke U., Durham, N.C., 1982-84, assoc. prof. pediatrics, 1984—; chmn. American Board of Allergy & Immunology, 1998—. Office: Duke U Med Ctr PO Box 3068 Durham NC 27715-3068

MARKEY, CHARLOTTE NICOLE, psychologist, educator; b. Burlingame, Calif., Nov. 18, 1975; d. Richard Stephen and Arlene Marie Castro; m. Patrick Michael Markey Jr., Aug. 25, 2001. BS in Psychology, Santa Clara (Calif.) U., 1997; MA in Psychology, U. Calif., 2000, PhD in Psychology, 2002. Tchg. asst. U. Calif., Riverside, Calif., 1997—2002, lectr. psychology, 2002; asst. prof. Rutgers U., Camden, NJ, 2002—. Adj. faculty Mount San Jacinto Valley Coll., Menifee, Calif., 2001—02; rschr. Ctr. State Health Policy Rutgers U., 2002—, acting dir. Women's Studies Program, 2003—, adv. Women's Studies Program, 2002—, co-adv. Psi Chi, 2002—. Reviewer: Jour. Family Psychology, 2000—02, Jour. Personality, 2002—; assoc. editor Individual Differences Rsch., 2002—; co-author: Health Psychology, 2nd edition, Instructor's Manual, 2001, Advances in Psychological Research, 2002, Personality: Classic Theories and Modern Research, 2nd edition, Instructor's Manual and Test Bank, 2003; author: (chpt.) Handbook of Parenting, 2002, Trends in Social Psychology, 2003, Brain and Longevity, 2003; contbr. articles to profl. jours. Recipient Wilhelm Wundt award, Santa Clara (Calif.) U., 1997; grantee, U. Calif., 2001, Ctr. Children and Childhood Studies, Rutgers U., 2003; scholar Presdl. scholarship, Santa Clara (Calif.) U., 1996—97. Mem.: Acad. Eating Disorders, soc. Personality and Social Psychology, Soc. Rsch. Adolescence, Soc. Rsch. Child Devel., Am. Psychol. Assn. (scholarship 2000, scholarship We. chpt. 2003). Office: Rutgers University 311 North 5th Street Camden NJ 08102

MARKEY, MARGARET M. state legislator; m. Charles J. Markey. BS, The Berkeley Sch. Acct. exec. Projects In Knowledge; asst. dir. econ. devel. Queens Borough; dir. Tourism Borough of Queens; assemlbywoman N.Y. State, 1998—. Mem. Cmty. Bd. 2, Cmty. Bd. 5, Maspeth Chpt. Kiwanis. Mem.: Daughters of Erin (founder), Am.-Irish Legislators Soc. of N.Y. (treas.). Democrat. Office: 84-32 Grand Ave Elmhurst NY 11373

MARKGRAF, ROSEMARIE, real estate broker; b. Grantsburg, Wis., Oct. 31, 1934; d. Helen Elizabeth Pribil. BS, U. Wis., 1957, MS, 1958. Cert. tchr. Tchr. H.S., Wis., Conn, 1958-61; office mgr. Robert S. Palmer, Middletown, Conn., 1962-64; edn. adv. Girl Scouts U.S.A., N.Y.C., 1964-66; cmty. rels. assoc. Motion Picture Assn. Am., N.Y., 1967-69; mgr. The Chateau Inn, Stamford, N.Y., 1970-78; real estate salesman Atkins Realty, Ltd., Bklyn., 1979-80; real estate broker, prin. The Markgraf Group, Ltd., Bklyn., 1980—. Cons. Real Estate Counseling Group Conn., Storrs, 1963-91; pres. Tuff Transport, Inc., 1977-2000; adj. prof. Real Estate Inst. and Real Estate Edn. Ctrs., 1995—. Pres. Brownstone Rep. Club; candidate 12th Congl. Dist., Bklyn., 1998, 2000; exec. com. Kings County Rep. Com.; conservative candidate 52d State Assembly Dist., 2002, dist. leader. Mem. Real Estate Bd. N.Y., Steuben Soc. (v.p.), Yeats Soc. N.Y. Roman Catholic. Avocations: water aerobics, crossword puzzles, oenology. Home and Office: The Markgraf Group Ltd 60 Remsen St Brooklyn NY 11201-3453 Office Phone: 718-625-0808. Personal E-mail: rmarkgraf@att.net.

MARKHAM, CLAIRE AGNES (M. CLARE MARKHAM), retired chemistry educator, consultant; b. New Haven, Conn., Aug. 12, 1919; d. James J. and Agnes V. (Manning) M. BA, St. Joseph Coll., West Hartford, Conn., 1940; PhD, Cath. U. Am., 1952; DHL (hon.), St. Joseph Coll., 1989. Joined Sisters of Mercy, Roman Cath. Ch., 1940. Tchr. chemistry and math. Sacred Heart H.S., Waterbury, Conn., 1945-49; mem. faculty chemistry St. Joseph Coll., West Hartford, 1952-97, cons. instl. advancement, 1996—, prof. emeritus in chemistry, 1997—. Dept. chair St. Joseph Coll., 1959-70, dean grad. sch., 1979-87, asst. to pres. acad. affairs, 1987-95; dir. numerous tchr. insts., 1959-89; mem. vis. faculty Calvin's Lab., NSF, U. Calif., Berkeley, 1967-68. dir. CT Talent Prog., 2002-03. Contbr. articles to profl. jours.; editor sci. series McGraw Hill, 1956-60. Undersec. for Energy, Office of Policy and Mgmt., State of Conn., Hartford, 1977—79; mem. adv. com. Permanent Commn. Status of Women, Hartford, 1995—; mem. adv. coun. Dept. Higher Edn., State of Conn., Hartford, 1970—80; energy advisor Nat. Gov.'s Assn., 1977—79; bd. dirs. Conn. Energy Co-op, 2000—03. Recipient Equity award AAUW, 1992, Sci. Advocacy award, CSTA, 2002, award for outstanding sci. adv. Conn. Sci. Tchrs. Awsn., 2002;

Faculty fellow NSF, Trondheim, Norway, 1967, travel grantee, cons., Madras, India, 1974-77. Fellow Conn. Acad. for Edn.; mem. AAAS, Am. Chem. Soc. (councilor 1968-88, chair Conn. Valley sect. 1955-67, 20 Yr. award 1988), Conn. Acad. Sci. and Engring. (founding mem., chair tech. bd. 1994-98), Sigma Xi (sect. chair 1993-95). Democrat. Avocations: photography, music, literature. Home: 1678 Asylum Ave West Hartford CT 06117-2791 Office: St Joseph Coll West Hartford CT 06117 Office Phone: 860-231-5501.

MARKIN, KAREN MARY, research scientist, journalist; b. Hartford, Conn., Jan. 20, 1957; d. Walter Anthony Markin, Katherine Irene Markin; m. Benjamin Adams Cray, June 6, 1987; 1 child, Colleen Cray. BA, Clark U., 1979; MA, Ohio State U., 1986; PhD, U. N.C., 1993. Reporter The Day, New London, Conn., 1975—85; dir. rsch. devel. U. R.I., Kingston, RI, 1999—. Vice chair law divsn. Assn. for Edn. in Journalism and Mass Comm., Columbia, SC, 2003—04; dir. Ctr. for Humanities U. R.I., Kingston, 2001; proposal reviewer NSF, Arlington, 1999—2004, U.S. Dept. Edn., Washington, 1998—2001. Author (govt. publ.): Ballot Access, volumes 2-4, 1995. V.p. program AAUW, Middletown, RI, 1997—99, pres. Westerly, RI; program panelist AAUW Ednl. Found., 2002—. Mem.: Soc. Rsch. Adminstrs., Nat. Coun. Univ. Rsch. Adminstrs., Internat. Comm. Assn. Office: Univ Rhode Island Rsch Office 70 Lower College Rd Kingston RI 02881

MARKLE, CHERI VIRGINIA CUMMINS, nurse; b. N.Y.C., Nov. 22, 1936; d. Brainard Lyle and Mildred (Schwab) Cummins; m. John Markle, Aug. 26, 1961 (dec. 1962); 1 child, Kellianne. RN, Ind. State U. and Union Hosp., 1959; BS in Rehab. Edn., Wright State U., 1975; BSN, Capital U., 1987; postgrad. in nursing adminstrn., Wright State U., 1987-89; MS, Calif. Coll. Health Sci. Administration, 1994; postgrad., Columbia Pacific U., 1996-2000. Cert. clin. hypnotherapist Nat. Guild Hypnotherapists. Coordinator Dayton (Ohio) Children's Psychiat. Hosp., 1962-75; dir. nursing Stillwater Health Ctr., Dayton, 1975-76; rehab. cons. Fairborn, Ohio, 1976-91, N.Y.C.; sr. supr. VA, Dayton, 1977-85, nurse coord. alcohol rehab., 1985-86; DON Odd Fellows, Springfield, Ohio, 1987-88, Miami Christel Manor, Miamisburg, Ohio, 1988-99; DON, rehab. cons. NMS Tng. Sys., Dayton, 1989-91. Psychiat. nurse VA Med. Ctr., N.Y. Rehab., 1991, mem. com. women vets., 1991-93; advisor Calif. Coll. Health Sci. Newspaper columnist Golden Times, Clark County. Bd. dirs. Temple Universal Judaism, 1992, 97; mem. Town and Village Synagogue, 1999—. 1st lt. USAF, 1959-61. Mem. ANA (cert. adminstrn. 1983, cert. gerontology 1984), AAUW, Nurse Mgrs. Assembly, Gerontol. Nurse Assembly, Rehab. Soc., Nat. Guild Hypnotherapists, Internat. Assn. Counselors and Therapists, Nat. Coun. Jewish Women, Jewish War Vets. (sr. vice comdr. Post 1), Wright State U. Alumni Assn., Am. Legion (life), Hadassah, Women's City Club N.Y., Gilbert and Sullivan Soc., Internat. Consortium Parse Scholars, Alpha Sigma Alpha, Sigma Theta Tau. Democrat. Jewish. Avocations: cats, reading, music, needlework, swimming, grandchildren. E-mail: cherimarklern@yahoo.com.

MARKLE, SANDRA, publishing company executive; 7th grade sci. tchr., Ohio; pres. CompuQuest, Inc., Bartlett, Ill. Office: CompuQuest Inc 366 S Main St Bartlett IL 60103-4423

MARKLE, SHELLEY EKERMEYER, construction executive; b. Alexandria, Va., Sept. 4, 1972; d. Edward Conradi and Rosalind Bigham Ekermeyer. BA Hist. Preservation, BS Psychology, Mary Washington Coll., Fredericksburg, Va., 1994; M Urban Planning and Policy, U. Ill., 1998. Project cons. mgr. Isaiah Cmty. Devel. Group, Chgo., 1994—97, Monterrey Contractors, Inc., Chgo., 1997—2003, v.p., 2001—03, Millstone Properties, Inc., Chgo., 1999—2003; pres., owner Shelley Cons. Svcs., Chgo., 2000—. Elder, treas. Lawndale Cmty. Presbyn. Ch., Chgo., 2000—. Mem.: Nat. Trust for Hist. Preservation. Presbyterian. Avocations: soccer, travel, cross stitch. Office: Shelley Construction Services Co 2023 W Carroll Ave Ste F264 Chicago IL 60612 Office Phone: 312-829-4250.

MARKLEY, KATE, social worker, consultant; b. Jacksonville, Fla., Dec. 1, 1948; d. Elizabeth Kalt Tongue M. AA, Polk C.C., Winter Haven, Fla., 1969; BA, U. So. Fla., 1975; MSW, Fla. State U., 1982. Lic. clin. social worker; Diplomate in clin. social work; ACSW. Caseworker Polk County Social Svcs., Bartow, Fla., 1975-83; clin. social worker Children's Home Soc., Lakeland, Fla., 1983-98; pvt. practice Lakeland, Fla., 1998—. Adj. instr. Fla. So. Coll., Lakeland, Fla., 1984-87, Polk C.C., Winterhaven, Fla., 1988-89, Hillsborough C.C., Plant City, Fla., 1990—; social work cons. Winter Haven Physical Therapy, Fla. 1985-92, Gessler Clinic, Winter Haven, Fla., 2000—; bd. mem., sec., treas. Mental Health Assn. Polk County, Fla.; bd. mem. Polk C.C. (social svcs. tech. adv. bd.). Named Outstanding Young Careerist Bus. and Profl. Women, Lakeland, Fla., 1977. Mem. NASW (unit chair 1999-2001, former program chair). Avocations: travel, reading. Office: 2031 E Edgewood Dr Ste 3 Lakeland FL 33803-3601

MARKO, MARLENE, psychiatrist; b. N.Y.C., July 3, 1945; m. Loren R. Skeist; children: Marc, David, Sarah. BA, Sarah Lawrence Coll., 1967; MD, Mt. Sinai Sch. Medicine, 1972. Diplomate Am. Bd. Psychiatry. Intern Lenox Hill Hosp., 1973; resident Mt. Sinai Hosp., 1976; clin. instr. Mt. Sinai Sch. Medicine.

MARKOVICH, PATRICIA HELEN, economist; b. Oakland, Calif. MS in Econs., U. Calif., Berkeley; postgrad., Stanford U. Cert. emergency mgmt. planner. Pub. rels. Pettler Advt., Inc.; pvt. practice polit. and econs. cons.; aide to majority whip Oreg. Ho. of Reps.; lectr., instr. various Calif. instns., Chemeketa (Oreg.) Coll., Portland (Oreg.) State U.; commr. City of Oakland (Calif.), 1970-74. Chairperson, bd. dirs. Cable Sta. KCOM; econ. and emergency mgmt. cons. Mem. Piedmont (Calif.) Gen. Plan Commn.; mem. Econ. Devel. City of Berkeley, Calif. NSF grant Oreg. Grad. Rsch. Ctr., Lilly Found. grant. Mem.: Nat. Coordinating Coun. Emergency Mgmt., Mensa.

MARKOWITZ, DEBORAH LYNN, state government official; b. Tarrytown, N.Y., Sept. 14, 1961; d. Gerald Harvey and Sandra Lee (Schulner) M.; m. Paul William Markowitz, June 19, 1988; children: Aviva Lee, Sandra Rose, Ari David. BA with honors, U. Vt., 1982; JD magna cum laude, Georgetown U., 1987. Bar: Vt. 1988, U.S. Dist. Ct. Vt. 1989. Assoc. Covington & Burling, Washington, summer 1986; jud. law clk. Justice Peck-Vt. Supreme Ct., Montpelier, 1987-88; assoc. Langrack, Sperry & Wool, Burlington, Vt., 1988-90; dir. Law Ctr. Vt. League of Cities and Towns, Montpelier, Vt., 1990—97; devel. cons. Vt. Law Sch., South Royalton, 1997—; sec. of state State of Vt., 2000—. Adj. faculty Vt. Law Sch., South Royalton, 1992; examiner Vt. Bd. Bar Examiners, Montpelier, 1994-98. Contbr. articles to profl. jours. Bd. dirs. Ctrl. Vt. Cmty. Action Agy., Vt. Hist. Soc.; trustee Woodbury Coll. Mem. ABA (state and local govt. sect.), Vt. Bar Assn. (mcpl. com.), Internat. Mcpl. Lawyers Assn. (chair pers. sect. 1993—), Nat. Assn. Secs. of State, Nat. Mus. of Women in the Arts (bd. dirs. Vt. chpt.), Order of Coif. Democrat. Avocations: cross-country skiing, singing, sketching, gardening. Office: Sec of State Redstone Bldg 26 Terrace Street, PO Box 9 Montpelier VT 05609-0001*

MARKOWITZ, PHYLLIS FRANCES, retired mental health services professional, retired psychologist; b. Malden, Mass., Sept. 2, 1931; d. Abraham and Rose (Kaplan) Kalishman; children: Gary Keith, Carol Diane Donnelly. AB, Harvard U., 1972, EdM, 1974; EdD, Boston U., 1987. Lic. psychologist Health Svc. Provider; LCSW Mass. Rsch. asst. Boston Coll., Newton, Mass., 1971-73; social worker Combined Jewish Philanthropies, Boston, 1973-74; instr. Harvard U., Cambridge, Mass., 1974-75, counselor, 1974-79; supr. Dept. Social Svcs., Newton and Marlborough, Mass., 1979-88; area dir. case mgmt. and tng. Dept. Mental Health, Boston, 1988-94, area coord. medically-mentally ill, 1988—, chair consumer/family empowerment project, 1992-96. Area dir. Svcs. Integration, 1994—95, Clin. Affairs and Rehab., 1995—2000; project dir. Supported Employment Svcs., 1994—95; area Am. with Disabilities coord. Dept. of Mental Health, Boston, 1995—2000; instr. human devel. U. Mass., Boston, 1990—97. Grantee, Radcliffe Inst., 1972; Rsch. scholar, Boston U., 1981—82. Mem.: APA, Mass. Psychol. Assn. Avocations: music, opera, writing. Personal E-mail: drpmarkowitz@aol.com.

MARKOWSKI, SALLY HAMILTON, medical/surgical nurse; b. Waterbury, Conn., Jan. 10, 1971; d. Henry Joseph and Gladys Dorothy (Cole-Hamilton) Grycz; m. David Markowski Jr., Apr. 20, 1996; children: Erica Rose, Olivia Anne. BSN, Northeastern U., 1994; MSN, U. Phoenix Online, 2003. RN, cert. med.-surg. nurse, ACLS. Staff nurse Hosp. of St. Raphael's, New Haven, 1994—. Tchr. CPR. Home: 35 Autumn Ct Cheshire CT 06410

MARKS, ESTHER L. metals company executive; b. Canton, Ohio, Oct. 3, 1927; d. Jacob and Ella (Wisman) Rosky; m. Irwin Alfred Marks, June 29, 1947; children: Jules, Howard, Marilyn. Student, Ohio State U., 1945-46, Youngstown State U., 1946-47. V.p. Steel City Iron & Metal, Inc., Youngstown, Ohio. Pres. Jr. Hadassah, Youngstown, 1943-45, Pioneer Women, Youngstown, 1951, Anshe Emeth Sisterhood, Youngstown, Broadway Theatre League, Youngstown, 1958, B'nai B'rith Women, Youngstown, 1962, Dist. 2 B'nai B'rith Women, Cleve., 1969-70, Jewish Cmty. Ctr., Youngstown, Youngstown Area Jewish Fedn., 1988-90; v.p. United Way, Youngstown, 1991, chmn., 1996; grad. Leadership Youngstown, 1991; bd. Akiva Acad. Commn. for Jewish Edn., Temple El Emeth, Stambaugh Auditorium. Named Guardian of the Menorah B'nai B'rith, Youngstown, 1978; recipient B'nai B'rith Girls Alumda award, Washington, 1989, Woman of Valor award Jewish Fedn., 1996. Mem. LMV, YWCA, Ohio Hist. Soc. Democrat. Jewish. Avocations: knitting, organizational work. Home: 1295 Virginia Trl Youngstown OH 44505-1637 Office: 703 Wilson Ave Youngstown OH 44506-1445

MARKS, JOAN FLORENCE, social worker; b. N.Y.C., Apr. 1, 1945; d. Alfred and Ellen Josephine (Strauss) Kallos; m. Stephen Roy Marks, June 13, 1965; children: Peter Jay, Andrew Eric. BA, Clark U., 1965; MSW, Simmons Coll., 1968. Diplomate in social work, lic. clin. social worker; ACSW. Rehab. social worker Ea. Maine Med. Ctr., Bangor, 1974-75; outpatient clinician Cmty. Health and Counseling Ctr., Bangor, 1975-78; staff counselor U. Maine, Orono, 1978-79; lic. ind. practice social worker Turning Point, Bangor, 1978—. Co-dir. Axis Cons. and Tng., Austin, Tex., 1995—; clin. cons. Families and Children Together, Bangor, 1995—, Good Samaritan Agy., Bangor, 2000—, Maine Child Welfare Tng. Inst., Augusta, 1995—; mediator Austin Dispute Resolution Ctr., Austin, 1997-2000. Co-founder steering com. Rape Crisis Ctr., Bangor, 1972-77; mem. steering com. Spruce Run Women's Shelter, Bangor, 1977-85; vol. Maine Won't Discriminate, Bangor, 1994 95. Mem. NASW, Acad. Cert. Social Workers, Group Explorations Inst., Acad. Family Mediators, Austin Group Psychotherapy Soc. Avocations: travel, reading, mushrooming, nature walks, music. Home: 21 Grove St Orono ME 04473-4402 Office: Turning Point 96 Harlow St Ste 1 Bangor ME 04401-4925 also: Axis Cons and Tng 2525 Wallingwood Dr Ste 701 Austin TX 78746-6929

MARKS, LAURA B. psychologist; b. L.A., Feb. 9, 1967; d. Stuart and Marsha Marks. RN, BSN, U. So. Calif., L.A., 1990; MA, Calif. Sch. Profl. Psychology, Alhambra, 1994, PhD, 1996. RN, Calif.; diplomate Am. Acad. Pain Mgmt. Pain mgmt. fellow Brotman Med. Ctr., Culver City, Calif., 1996-97; dir. pain mgmt. Psychol. Svcs., L.A., Calif., 1997-99; pvt. practice Santa Monica, Calif., 1997—. Guest spkr. UCLA; dir. psychol. svcs. and pain mgmt. Pain Mgmt. Ctr., Beverly Hills, Calif., 1999; clin. dir. pain mgmt. unit, pain mgmt. psychologist Centinela Med. Hosp., Inglewood, Calif. Contbr. articles to profl. jours. Mem. APA, Am. Pain Soc., Am. Acad. Pain Mgmt., Internat. Assn. for the Study of Pain, Calif. Psychol. Assn., U. So. Calif. Alumni Assn. Office: Centinela Med Hosp 935 S Flower St Inglewood CA 90301-4110

MARKS, LILLIAN SHAPIRO, secretarial studies educator, author; b. Bklyn., Mar. 16, 1907; d. Hayman and Celia (Merowitz) Shapiro; m. Joseph Marks, Feb. 21, 1932; children: Daniel, Sheila Blake, Jonathan. BS, NYU, 1928. High sch. tchr., N.Y.C., 1929-30; tchr. Evalina de Rothschild Sch., Jerusalem, 1930-31; social worker United Jewish Aid Bklyn., 1931-32; tchr. Richmond Hill High Sch., 1932-40, Andrew Jackson High Sch., Cambria Heights, N.Y., 1940-71; mem. faculty New Sch. Social Rsch., N.Y.C., 1977-87; staff Vassar Summer Inst., 1946. Vol. tchr. English Israel schs., 1987—2000. Am. editor: Teeline, A System of Fast Writing, 1970; author: College Teeline, 1977, College Teeline Self Taught, 1988, Touch Typing Made Simple, 1985; contbr. articles to profl. lit. jours. Mem. Am. Fedn. Tchrs. Democrat. Home and Office: 300 E46 St 17J New York NY 10017

MARKS, MARILYN, company executive; b. 1952; BS, U. Tenn., 1975. Acct. Ernst & Ernst, Chattanooga, 1975-76, with Deloitte, Haskins & Sells Chattanooga, 1976-79; v.p. corp. planning The Dorsey Corp., Chattanooga, 1979-87; pres., chmn. of bd., CEO Dorsey Trailers, Atlanta, 1987-97, chmn. bd., 1997—. Office: Dorsey Trailers Inc 3850 W Main St Ste 806 Dothan AL 36305-1006

MARKS, MARTHA ALFORD, writer; b. Oxford, Miss., July 27, 1946; d. Truman and Margaret Alford; m. Bernard L. Marks, Jan. 27, 1968. BA, Centenary Coll., 1968; MA, Northwestern U., 1972, PhD, 1978. Tchr. Notre Dame High Sch. for Boys, Niles, Ill., 1969-74; teaching asst. Northwestern U., Evanston, Ill., 1974-78, lectr., lang. coord., 1978-83; asst. prof. Kalamazoo (Mich.) Coll., 1983-85; writer Riverwoods, Ill., 1985—. Cons. WGBH Edn. Found., Boston, 1988-91, Am. Coun. on the Tchg. of Fgn. Langs., 1981-92, Ednl. Testing Svcs., 1988-90, Peace Corps., 1993. Co-author: Destinos: An Introduction to Spanish, 1991, 96, Al corriente, 1989, 93, 97, Que tal?, 1986, 90; author: (workbook) Al corriente, 1989, 93; contbr. articles to profl. jours. Mem. Lake County (Ill.) Bd., Forest Preserve Commn., 1992-2002, Lake County Conservation Alliance; vice chmn. Friends of Ryerson Conservation Area Bd.; co-founder, pres. REP Am., Reps. for Environ. Protection. Office: REP America 3200 Carlisle Blvd # 228 Albuquerque NM 87110

MARKS, NORA MARALEA, retired secondary school educator; b. Tarentum, Pa., Aug. 17, 1939; d. Chauncey Holmes and Mary Hettie (Bartmas) Elliott; m. Donald Richard Jacobs, July 8, 1961 (div. June 1979); children: Matthew John Jacobs, Donna Marie Gentz; m. Carr Bishop Marks, June 24, 1989; 1 stepchild, Michele Binkley. BS in Edn., Temple U., 1961, MS in Music Edn., 1981, postgrad., Hofstra U., Westminster Choir Coll., Trenton, N.J. Choral dir. Upper Perkiomen Schs., East Greenville, Pa., 1961—67; music tchr. Valley Stream Schs., NY, 1973—79; choral dir. Gettysburg H.S., Gettysburg, Pa., 1979—2000. State sec. Pa. Rural Letter Carriers Assn., 1993—; handbell choir dir. Uriah United Meth. Ch., Gardners, Pa., 1984—, dir. instrumental ensemble, adult choir dir., asst. organist; music dir. Uriah United Meth. Ch. Daycare, Gardners, 2003—. Scholar, Berkshire Music Ctr., Mass., 1963. Mem.: NEA, Adams County Music Educators Assn., Am. Choral Dirs. Assn. Home: 1971 Shippensburg Rd Biglerville PA 17307

MARKS, SHIRLEY ISAACSON, artist; b. N.Y.C., July 12, 1928; d. Hyman Max and Rose (Rosen) Isaacson; m. Herman Marks, June 8, 1947; children: Paulette Marks Lebowitz, Jeffrey I. Dir. Diana Kan Workshops, Panama City Beach, Fla., 1996—. One-person shows include Phyliss Powers Art Gallery, 1984-86, Radisson Hotel, 1987, Biscayne Bay Marriot Hotel, 1988, Contemporary Art Ctr., Kingston, Jamaica, 1989, Pen and Brush, N.Y.C., 1992, A.E. Bean Backus Gallery, 1993, Elliot Mus., Stuart, Fla., 1996; group shows include Suntrust Gallery, 1995, Heim/Am. Gallery, Fisher Island, 1995, Wetz Gallery, 1996, Am. Artists Profl. League Allied Artists Am., N.Y., 1996, Jupiter Town Hall Gallery Art, 1997, Ga. Watercolor Soc., 1998, numerous others; represented in permanent collections So. Exposure Gallery, W. Palm Beach, Fla., Coconut Grove Gallery, Miami. Fundraiser, newsletter chmn. Theater Art League, Miami, Fla., 1977-98; bd. dirs., arts and crafts dir. Nat. Children's Cardiac Hosp., Miami, 1960-63; youth coord. Coral Gables B'nai B'rith, Miami, 1960-64. Numerous awards, incl. many best in shows. Mem. Am. Artist Profl. League (pres. 1993-95), Nat. Arts Club, Sumi Soc. Am., Fla. Profl. Artist Guild, Miami Watercolor Soc., Fla. Watercolor Soc., Ga. Watercolor Soc., Salmagundi Club. Democrat. Jewish. Avocations: photography, travel. Home: 9603 SW 69th Pl Miami FL 33156-3071 Fax: 305-666-1946.

MARKS, SUSAN COLLIN, foundation administrator; MA in internat. relations, U. Kent, Canterbury, 1987; BA in social anthropology, U. Cape Town, 1969. Exec. v.p. Search Common Ground, Washington; journalist, filmaker freelance, 1970-85. Exec. bed. Western Cape Peace Com.; chair Regional Police Cmty. Relations Com., Regional Transportation Com. Editor: Track Two jour., 1992. Recipient Peace fellowship, U.S. Inst. Peace, Washington, D.C., 1994. Mem. Women in Internat. Security (exec. bd.) Office: Search Common Ground 1601 Connecticut Ave NW Ste 200 Washington DC 20009-1035 Fax: 202-232-6718. E-mail: search@sfcg.org.

MARKUS, MAURA, bank executive; BA summa cum laude, Boston (Mass.) Coll.; MBA, Harvard U. Joined Citibank, N.Y.C., 1987, pres. North Am. Retail Distbr. Group, 2000—. Office: CBNA One Court Sq 49th Fl Long Island City NY 11120*

MARKWARD, CHERI D. music educator; b. Beatrice, Nebr., July 15, 1947; d. Clyde F. and Doris L. McPhetrige; m. Edward Markward, Feb. 11, 1967 (div. 1983); children: Anthony, Nstalie. MusB, R.I. Coll., 1982; MusM, Boston U., 1990. First violinist R.I. Philharmonic, Providence, 1973—2003; instr. Great Woods Ednl. Forum, Mass., 1988—93; asst. prof. music Wharton Coll., 1993—94, C.C. R.I., Warwick, 1993—. Adj. faculty Providence Coll., 1984—89. Mem.: R.I. Music Educators Assn., R.I. String Tchrs. Assn., Am. Fedn. Musicians. Independent. Office: CC RI 400 East Ave Warwick RI 02886

MARLAR, JANET CUMMINGS, retired public relations officer; b. Burnsville, Miss., Dec. 22, 1942; d. James E. and Juanita (Hale) Cummings; m. David C. Linton, May 21, 1961 (div. 1984); 1 child, Jeffory Mark; m. Thomas Gilbert Cupples, Mar. 5, 1984 (div. 1990); m. Fredrick Marlar, Nov. 19, 1994. Student, NE Miss. Jr. Coll., 1960-61, Memphis State U., 1975-76, Sheffield Tech. Ctr., Memphis, 1984-85. Property owner, Burnsville, 1974—, Glen, Miss., 1994—2003. Mem. bus. adv. com. Sheffield Tech. Ctr., 1997—; docent Curlee House, Corinth, Miss., 1989—; exec. bd. Internat. Heritage Commn., Memphis, 1987-92; ret.; pub. rels. officer Internat. Heritage Ethnic Festival, Memphis. Co-editor: Internat. Heritage Bull./Newsletter; contbr. articles to Tishomingo County Newspaper. Vol. Memphis Brooks Mus. Art, 1980—, mem. exec. co., pub. info. officer Bldg. Bridges for A Better Memphis, 1985—; pres. Eagle Watch Assn.; founder Janet C. Cupples Citizenship awards, Memphis City Inter-City Sch., 1975, Founded Citizenship award, 1975, Memphis City Schs.; founder, chair women's com. on crime City of Memphis, 1985—, chair Heritage-City of Memphis, chair internat. heritage program, 1987, 88—, Ethnic Outreach Neighborfest, 1988—; hon. mem. city coun., 1987; donor, exec. com. Women of Achievement, Inc., Memphis, 1986; mem. spkrs. bus. United Way of Greater Memphis, Friends of Shelby County Libr., 1986—, YMCA; chair ethnic outreach com. Neighborfest, Memphis, 1987, chairperson exec. com., 1988; amb. Memphis Internat. Heritage Commn., 1988; youth mentor Memphis Youth Leadership Devel. Inst.; internat. coord. Neighborfest '88; chairperson Internat. Heritage City of Memphis, 1987; mem. cmty. coun. Memphis City Schs., Memphis Cablevision Edn. Task Force; apptd. col. aide de camp to Gov. Ned McWherter of Tenn., 1988; apptd. hon. mem. Tenn. State Senator Steve Cohen's staff, 1989; sec. safety com. St. Francis Hosp., 1992, sec. Burnsville H.S. com., 1960; participant Vol. Miss. Food Network Distbn. for Disabled Persons, 1996; active Dem. Nat. Com., 1994—; founder Inter City Sch. Citizenship award, 1986; founder Burnsville Sch. Accelerated Reader Awards, 2000, Libr. award, Citizenship Essay award, 2001—, founder book donation program, Mr. Jim Cummings Citizenship essay awards, 2000; sec., pub. rels. officer Burnsville H.S. 1960 Exec. Com., 1994-2004; chair Burnsville High 1960 Book Donation Com., 2000-2004. Recipient 11 certs. of recognition Memphis City Coun., 1986-89, Outstanding Svc. to Pub. Edn. award 1986, merit award City of Memphis, 1987, Royal award HRH Prince Kevin, 1996; named Outstanding Female Participant, Neighborhood, Inc., 1987; honored by Pres. George Bush as Outstanding Vol., 1989; featured as one of top 1000 Vols. in Mid-South, 1989; Svc. award Cummings Sch., 1993; apptd. Hon. Memphis City Councilwoman, 1995-96; recognized by Gen. Colin Powell, 1997; Burnsville Libr. Project commended by First Lady, Laura Bush, 2002; recipient Outstanding Svc. award Memphis City Schs., 2002, 03. Mem. NAFE, NOW (2d v.p. Memphis chpt. 1987, del. nat. conf. 1987, 2d v.p.), Network Profl. Women's Orgn., NCCJ, Rep. Career Women, Memphis Peace and Justice Ctr., Women's Polit. Caucus Tenn., Nat. Children's Cancer Soc. (friend 1995-96). Methodist. Avocations: community service, writing, teaching.

MARLEAU, DIANE, Canadian government official; b. Kirkland Lake, Ont., Can., June 21, 1943; d. Jean-Paul and Yvonne (Desjardins) LeBel; m. Paul C. Marleau, Aug. 3, 1963; children: Brigitte, Donald, Stéphane. Student, U. Ottawa, Ont., 1960-63; BA in Econs., Laurentian U., Sudbury, Ont., 1976. With Donald Jean Acctg. Svcs., Sudbury, 1971-75; receiver mgr. Thorne Riddell, Sudbury, 1975-76; treas. No. Regional Residential Treatment Program for Women, Sudbury, 1976-80, Com. for the Industry and Labour Adjustment Program, Sudbury, 1983; mem. transition team Ont. Premier's Office, Toronto, 1985; firm adminstr. Collins Barrow-Maheu Noiseux, Sudbury, 1985-88; M.P. from Sudbury House of Commons, Ottawa, 1988—; min. of health for Can., 1993-96; min. of public works Canada, 1996-97; min. for internat. cooperation, min. responsible for La Francophonie, 1997-99; vice chair Fgn. Affairs Com., 2002—. Councilor Regional Municipality of Sudbury, 1980-85, chair fin. com., 1981; alderman City of Sudbury, 1980-85; mem. No. Devel. Coun., Sudbury, 1986-88; vice chair Nat. Liberal Standing Com. on Policy, 1989; chair Ont. Liberal Caucus, 1990; apptd. nat. exec. Liberal Party Can., 1990, assoc. critic Govt. Ops., 1990, Dep. Opposition Whip, 1991, assoc. critic Fin., 1992; vice chair standing com. fin., 1992. Chmn. fund-raising Canadian Cancer Soc., Sudbury, 1987-88; co-chmn. Laurentian Hosp. Cancer Care Svcs. fund-raising campaign, Sudbury, 1988; chair bd. govs. Cambrian Coll., 1987-88, bd. govs., 1983-88; mem. Sudbury and Dist. Health Unit Bd., 1981-82; mem. fin. com., bd. dirs. Laurentian Hosp., 1981-85; chair Can. Games for the Physically Disabled, 1983; apptd. Ont. Adv. Coun. Women's Issues, 1984. Recipient Paul Harris award, 1996. Mem. Sudbury Bus. and Profl. Women Club. Liberal Party Can. Avocations: playing piano, gardening, cooking. Office: House of Commons Parliament Bldgs Ottawa ON Canada K1A 0A6 also: 36 Elgin St Sudbury ON Canada P3C 5B4

MARLETT, JUDITH ANN, nutritional sciences educator, researcher; b. Toledo; BS, Miami U., Oxford, Ohio, 1965; PhD, U. Minn., 1972; postgrad., Harvard U., 1973-74. Registered dietitian. Therapeutic and metabolic unit dietitian VA Hosp., Mpls., 1966-67; spl. instr. in nutrition Simmons Coll., Boston, 1973-74; asst. prof. U. Wis., Madison, 1975-80, assoc. prof. dept. nutritional scis., 1981-84, prof. dept. nutritional scis., 1984—. Cons. U.S. AID, Leyte, Philippines, 1983; acting dir. dietetic program dept. Nutritional Scis. U. Wis., 1977-78, dir., 1985-89; cons. grain, drug and food cos., 1985—, adv. bd. U. Ariz. Clin. Cancer Ctr., 1987-95;

sci. bd. advisors Am. Health Found., 1988—; reviewer NIH, 1982—. Mem. editl. bd. Jour. Sci. of Food and Agrl., 1989—, Jour. Food Composition and Analysis, 1994-2000, Jour. of Nutrition, 2002—; contbr. articles to profl. jours. Mem. AAAS, NIH (Diabetes amd Digestive and Kidney Disease spl. grant rev. com., 1992-96), Am. Soc. Nutritional Scis., Am. Dietetic Assn., Am. Soc. Clin. Nutrition. Achievements include research and international speaker on human nutrition and disease, dietary fiber and gastrointestinal function. Office: U Wis Dept Nutritional Sci 1415 Linden Dr Madison WI 53706-1527 Office Phone: 608-972-5221. E-mail: jmarlett@nutrisci.wisc.edu.

MARLING, KARAL ANN, art history and social sciences educator, curator; b. Rochester, N.Y., Nov. 5, 1943; d. Raymond J. and Marjorie (Karal) M. PhD, Bryn Mawr Coll., 1971. Prof. art history and Am. studies U. Minn., Mpls., 1977—. Author: Federal Art in Cleveland, 1933-1943: An Exhibition, 1974, Wall-to-Wall America: America: A Cultural History of Post-Office Murals in the Great Depression, 1982, 2d edit., 2001, The Colossus of the Roads: Myth and Symbol Along the American Highway, 1984, 2d edit., 2000, Tom Benton and His Drawings: A Biographical Essay and a Collection of His Sketches, Studies and Mural Cartoons, 1985, Frederick C. Knight (1898-1797), 1987, George Washington Slept Here: Colonial Revivals and American Culture, 1876-1986, 1988, Looking Back: A Perspective on the 1913 Inaugural Exhibition, 1988, Blue Ribbon: A Social and Pictorial History of the Minnesota State Fair, 1990; author: (with John Wetenhall) Iwo Jima: Monuments, Memories, and the American Hero, 1991; author: Edward Hopper, 1992, As Seen on T.V.: The Visual Culture of Everyday Life in the 1950's, 1994, Graceland: Going Home with Elvis, 1995; editor (with Jessica H. Foy): The Arts and the American Home, 1890-1930, 1994; editor: Norman Rockwell, 1997, Designing the Disney Theme Parks: The Architecture of Reassurance, 1997, Merry Christmas! Celebrating America's Greatest Holiday, 2000, Looking North, 2003, Debutante, 2004, Old Glory Unfurled, 2004; contbr. essays to catalogs. Recipient Minn. Humanities Commn. award 1986, Minn. Book award History, 1994, Robert C. Smith award Decorative Arts Soc., 1994, Internat. Assn. of Art Critics award, 1998. Office: 1920 S 1st St Ste 1301 Minneapolis MN 55454-1190

MARLOW, AUDREY SWANSON, artist, designer; b. N.Y.C.; d. Sven and Rita (Porter) Swanson; student (scholarships) Art Students League, 1950-55; spl. courses SUNY (Stony Brook), L'Alliance Française m. Roy Marlow, Nov. 30, 1968. With Cohn-Hall-Marx Textile Studio, 1961-65, R.S. Assocs. Textile Studio, 1965-73; freelance designer, illustrator Prince Matchabelli, Lester Harrison Agy., J. Walter Thompson Agy., 1957-78; portrait and fine artist, Wading River, N.Y., 1973—; instr. Phoenix Sch. Design (N.Y.C.); illustrator children's books: Breads of Many Lands and 4H Club Bakes Bread, 1966, Anna Smith Strong and the Setauket Spy Ring, 1991, Timothy and the Acrobat, 1992; exhibits include: Nat. Arts Club, NAD, Parish Art Mus., South Hampton, N.Y., Guild Hall, East Hampton, N.Y., Portraits Inc., Lincoln Ctr., Chung-Cheng Art Gallery, St. John's U., Mystic (Conn.) Art Assn., Harbour Gallery, St. Thomas, V.I., Palais Rameau, Lisle, France, 1988, Sumner Mus., Washington, 1992, East End Arts & Humanities Coun., L.I., N.Y., 1996; one-person shows: Salmagundi Club, 1982, Rockefeller Gallery, N.Y.C., 1992; portrait commns. include: Millicent Fenwick, Harrison J. Goldin, Thomas R. Bayles, Mons. John Fagan, others. Trustee, Middle Island Public Library, 1972-76. Recipient John W. Alexander medal, 1976, award Council on Arts, 1978, award of excellence Cork Gallery, Lincoln Center, 1982; Grumbacher Bronze medal, 1983; Grumbacher Silver medal 1986; Best in Show award N.Y. Arts Council, 1986, Suburban Art League, 1993, Excellence award Town of Oyster Bay, 1995, Brookhaven Arts & Humanities Coun., 1996. Mem. Pastel Soc. Am. (award 1977, 80, 90), Am. Artists Profl. League (2 1st prize awards), Hudson Valley Art Assn. (award), Knickerbocker Artists (2 awards), Catharine Lorillard Wolfe Art Club (award 1982), Salmagundi Club (5 awards), Nat. League Am. Pen Women (Gold award, Gold medal of Honor, Best in Show 1990). Works represented at NYU, Longwood Pub. Libr., Sr. Citizen's Complex, Newark, St. Theresa of the Child Jesus Convent, Wading River Congl. Ch., L.I., pvt. collections. Home: 147 N Side Rd Wading River NY 11792-1112

MARLOW, LYDIA LOU, elementary school educator; b. Aledo, Ill., Aug. 21, 1954; d. Dwayne Elwood Irwin and Phyllis Jean (McKeown) Graff; m. Sidney G. Marlow Jr.; children: Erika Lynn, John Andrew. BA in Edn. with honors, Stephens Coll., 1976; MA in Reading, U. Mo., Kansas City, 1983. Cert. elem. tchr., Mo. Tchr. 2d grade Atlanta (Mo.) C-3 Sch. Dist., 1976-81; from tchr. headstart to tchr. 2d grade Independence (Mo.) Sch. Dist., 1982-92; reading clinician Santa Fe Trail & Procter Elem. Sch., Independence, 1993-99; Title 1 reading tchr. George Caleb Bingham 7th Grade Ctr., Independence, 1999-2000; gifted and talented tchr., 2001—. Adj. prof. children's lit. Webster U., Kansas City, Mo., 1994; developer program Focus on Reading, Independence, Mo., 1996; dept. chair, contbr. Missouri Reader, 1998—; presenter in field. Author: (novels) The Master Teacher: Memorable Moments, 2001; contbr. articles. Facilitator attention deficit hyperactivity disorder support group Caring Cmty. Santa Fe Trail Sch., Independence, 1996—97; rschr., author Truman Whistlestop Project, Independence, 1996—97; reading clinician Literacy Learning Ctr., Independence, 1997—2001. Recipient True Friend award Friends United Ednl. Support, Independence, 1994, Excellence in Tchg. award Govt. Employees Hosp. Assn., 1997, 2002. Mem.: Cmty. Assn. for the Arts, Children and Adults with Attention Deficit Disorder, Internat. Reading Assn. (local pres., publicity com. 1989—90, publicity co-chmn., editor Indep. IRA local 1991—93, editor Mo. state IRA 1992—95, Pres. award 1989), AAUW (publicity chair 1982—83), NEA (MNEA/Reliant grantee 1997), ASCD, Writers Club (coord. 1993—99, Editor's Choice 2001). Avocations: writing, gardening, reading, collecting antiques and elephant figurines. Home: 14609 E 44th St S Independence MO 64055-4810 Office: Christian Ott Elem School 1525 N Noland Rd Independence MO 64050 E-mail: Lydz14609@yahoo.com.

MARLOW, MARCIA MARIE, secondary school educator, publishing executive; b. Maywood, Calif., Jan. 24; d. George Murf Chandler and Zelda Marie Chandler; m. L. K. Higginbotham (dec. Dec. 23, 1998); children: Kevin Darrell Smith, Trisha Nicole Ailey Abbott, Shannon Marie Ailey Alexander, Bryan Chandler Ailey. A in Bus., No. Okla. Coll., 1980; BS in Edn., Mo. So. State Coll., 1984, cert. reading specialist, 1985, degree in art edn., 1993. Tchr. McDonald County Sch., Jane, Mo., 1984—88; owner Southwestern Steel, Inc., Grove, Okla., 1988—99, New Horizons Steel, Grove, Okla.; pub. Chandler Day Pub., Inc., Fairland, Okla., 1999—. Educator Wyandotte Pub. Sch., Okla., 2001—. Editor: (book) Murphy, The Littlest Elf, 2000; author: Love Verses, 2001; acrylic and oil paintings. Recipient Tchr. of the Yr., McDonald County Sch., Jane, Mo., 1988. Mem.: Brush and Palette Club, Phi Theta Kappa (life). Baptist. Avocations: art, singing, reading, horseback riding, gardening.

MARLOW, PATRICIA BAIR BOND, realtor; b. Altoona, Pa., Dec. 3, 1932; d. John Lesley and Gladys Marie Bair; m. Neal Nelson Jensen Bond, Aug. 7, 1953 (dec. July 1963); children: John Scott Bond, Lisa Suzanne Moody, Lesley Ann Stephen; m. Laurin Purcell Marlow, Apr. 4, 1967. Student, Mary Washington Coll., 1950-52. Realtor Everitt/Luby, Dallas, 1971-80; with Merrill Lynch, Dallas, 1980-89; realtor Adleta & Poston, Dallas, 1989—. Contbr. poetry to anthologies. Recipient Diamond Summit. Mem. Dallas Mus. Art, Dallas Arboretum, Les Femmes du Monde, Dallas Mus. Art League, Tex. Kidney Found. Avocation: watercolor painting. Home: 4531 Nashwood Ln Dallas TX 75244-7520 E-mail: patti@pattimarlow.com.

MARLOWE, WILLIE, artist, fine arts educator; b. Whiteville, N.C., Jan. 17, 1943; d. John David and Tessie Ernestine (McLawhorn) M.; m. Thomas Blakeslee Speight, July 11, 1980. Student, Pa. Acad. Fine Arts, Phila., 1964; BS, East Carolina U., 1965; MFA, U. Idaho, 1969, postgrad., Peace Coll., 1993. Instr. dept. art Skidmore Coll., Saratoga Springs, NY, 1970-74, mentor univ. without walls, 1972-74, instr. dept. art Columbia-Greene C.C., Hudson, NY, 1973-74; instr. Empire State Coll. SUNY, Albany, 1974; prof. Dept. Visual Arts Sage Coll., Albany, 1977—; chmn. The Sage Colls., Albany, 1979-81. Co-founder, tchr. Saratoga Arts Workshop, Saratoga Springs, N.Y., 1970-74; watercolor tchr. abroad Sage Colls., Scotland, Ireland, 2001; tchr. Somerville Coll., Oxford U., Eng., 1992; vis. artist U. Ga. studies abroad program, Cortona, Italy, 1989; vis. artist, Wexford Arts Ctr., Ireland, 1998, artist-in-residence for Ptnrs. of the Americas, Barbados, W.I., 1986, The Millay Colony for the Arts, Austerlitz, N.Y., 1999; artist selection com. Albany Ctr. Gallery, 1998; lectr. in field. One-woman shows include The Mint Mus. Art, Charlotte, N.C., 1971, Schenectady Mus., N.Y., 1975, Marist Coll., Poughkeepsie, N.Y., 1976, Stockton State Coll., Pomono, N.J., 1977, The Greenville Mus. Art, N.C., 1982, 97, Ann Grey Gallery The Casino, Saratoga Springs, N.Y., 1985, The Barrett Art Gallery Utica Coll. Syracuse U., N.Y., 1986, The Atrium Gen. Electric Corp. R&D Ctr., Schenectady, 1988, The Forum Gallery, Gütersloh, Germany, 1992, Albany Ctr. Gallery, 1992, 97, McHenry County Coll., Crystal Lake, Ill., The Main St. Gallery, Dobbs Ferry, 1995, The Wexford Arts Ctr., Ireland, 1998, The Saratoga Arts Ctr., Saratoga Springs, N.Y., 2000, Rathbone Gallery, Albany, 2001, Fondo del Sol Gallery and Visual Arts Ctr., Washington, 2002, Barrett Arts Ctr., Poughkeepsie, N.Y., 2002, Gallery C, Raleigh, 2003, others; exhibited in group shows at Art Ctr. for the Capital Region, Troy, N.Y., 2002, Reprize Internat. Invitational Show, Wexford Arts Ctr., Wexford, Ireland, 2002, Martinez Gallery, Troy, NY, 2002, Artemisia Gallery, Chgo., 2000, 03, Nexus Gallery, N.Y.C., 1997-99, The Gang Gallery, N.Y.C., Eng. & Co., London, 1993, Steinbaum-Krauss Gallery, N.Y.C., 1990, Stux Gallery, Boston, 1987, Nat. Mus. Women Arts, Washington, 1987, Westbeth Gallery, N.Y.C., 1994, Clocktower, N.Y.C., 1986, The Rice Gallery The Albany Inst. History & Art, 1986, Deborah Davis Fine Arts, Hudson, 2003, Firlefanz Gallery, Albany, 2004, Gallery 100, Saratoga Springs, 2004, others; represented in pvt. collections; represented in permanent collections Legis. Offices Empire State Plz., Albany, First Albany Corp., The Md. Dept. Econ. & Cmty. Devel., Balt., Quad Graphics, Boston, SUNY Albany, N.C. Nat. Bank, Charlotte, The Greenville Mus. Art, East Carolina U., Greenville, N.C., Boston Pub. Libr., The Budapest Gallery, Russell Sage Coll., Troy, N.Y., The Mint Mus. Art, Charlotte, N.C., Four Winds Ctr., Saratoga Springs, The Univ. Mus. SUNY Albany, Bullard and McLeod & Assocs., Inc., N.Y.C.; co-curator and curator for mail art shows. Recipient Purchase award in painting Hudson Mohawk Regional Ann., SUNY Albany, 1977, 95, 97, honorable mention in watercolor The Oswego Art Guild, N.Y., 1986, medal Internat. Art Competition Metro Arts, Inc., Scarsdale, N.Y., 1986, honorable mention in painting Third Ann. Nat. C.C. Miniature Painting Show, Lexington, 1987, Sywer award, 1995, and numerous others; N.Y. State Coun. on the Arts grantee Barrett Art Gallery Syracuse U., 1986, grantee Artists' Space, 1988, N.Y. Found. for the Arts. Mem. Nat. Assn. Women Artists, Albany Inst. History and Art, Fulton St. Gallery, Albany Ctr. Gallery, Woman's Caucus For Art. Avocations: painting, visual poetry, mail art.

MARMER, ELLEN LUCILLE, pediatric cardiologist, mayor; b. Bronx, N.Y., June 29, 1939; d. Benjamin and Diane (Goldstein) M.; m. Harold O. Shapiro, June 5, 1960; children: Cheri, Brenda. BS in Chemistry, U. Ala., 1960; MD, U. Ala., Birmingham, 1964. Cert. Nat. Bd. Med. Examiners; diplomate Am. Bd. Sports Medicine, Bd. Pediat., Bd. Qualified and Eligible Pediatric Cardiology, Bd. cert. sports medicine. Intern Upstate Med. Ctr., Syracuse, NY, 1964-65, resident, 1965-66; fellow in pediatric cardiology Columbia Presbyn. Med. Ctr.-Babies Hosp., N.Y.C., 1967-69; pvt. practice Hartford, Vernon, Conn., 1969—. Examining pediatrician child devel. program Columbia Presbyn. Med. Ctr.-Babies Hosp., N.Y.C., 1967, instr. pediat., 1967-69; dir. pediatric cardiology clinic St. Francis Hosp., Hartford, 1970-80; asst. state med. examiner, Tolland County, Conn., 1974-79; sports physician Rockville (Conn.) High Sch., 1976—; advisor Cardiac Rehab. com., Rockville, 1984-90; mem. bd. examiners Am. Bd. Sports Medicine, 1991—, chmn. credentials com., 1991-93. Mem. Vernon Town Coun., 1985-89; bd. dirs. Child Guidance Clinic, Manchester, Conn., 1970—; life mem. Tolland County chpt. Hadassah, v.p., 1969-70, pres., 1970-72, bd. dirs., 1973-74; mem. B'nai Israel Congregation and Sisterhood, Vernon, 1969—, chmn. youth commn., 1970-72; mayor Town of Vernon, 2003--. Recipient Outstanding Svc. award Indian Valley YMCA, 1985. Fellow Am. Acad. Pediat., Am. Coll. Cardiology, Am. Coll. Sports Medicine; mem. Conn. Med. Soc., Am. Heart Assn. (mem. coun. cardiovasc. disease in young 1969—, chmn. elect New Eng. regional heart com. 1990-91, mem. Heritage affiliate 1998—), Conn. Heart Assn. (bd. dirs. 1974-75, 83-84, pres. 1986-88), Heart Assn. Greater Hartford (bd. dirs. 1970-89, mem. exec. com. 1972-73, 79-84, pres. 1982-84), Tolland County Med. Assn. (sec. 1971-72), Vis. Nurse and Cmty. Care Tolland County, LWV (state program chairperson Vernon chpt. 1971-73). Democrat. Jewish. Avocation: sports. Office: 520 Hartford Tpke Vernon Rockville CT 06066

MAROHN, ANN ELIZABETH, health information management professional; b. Grand Rapids, Mich., Feb. 26, 1946; d. Luther Alfonse and Mary Inez (Pinkstaff) M. BS, Ind. U., l968; MS, SUNY, Buffalo, l978. Asst. med. record dir. Highland Park (Mich.) Gen. Hosp., 1968-70; asst. dir. med. record svcs. Meml. Hosp., Elmhurst, Ill., 1970-73; dir. med. record tech. program Alfred (N.Y.) State Coll., 1974-76; mem. faculty med. record adminstrn. dept. Lincoln Coll., Melbourne, Australia, 1977-78, Kean Coll., Union, N.J., l984-85, Med. U. S.C., Charleston, 1985-87; mem. faculty health record dept. Ferris State Coll., Big Rapids, Mich., l979-80; dir. health info. mgmt. Armstrong State Coll., Savannah, Ga., l980-84; dir. med. record dept. Tucson Gen. Hosp., 1988-89, N.D. State Hosp., Jamestown, 1990-92; cons. Prospective Payment Specialists, Tucson, 1992-93; health info. mgr. Sierra Med. Ctr., El Paso, Tex., 1993-94; dir. health info. mgmt. program Southern U., Shreveport, La., 1994-97; dir. health info. mgmt. N. VA Mental Health Inst., Falls Church, Va., 1997; dir. health info. tech. program Molloy Coll., Rockville Centre, N.Y., 1997-99; coord. health info. mgmt. program Santa Fe C.C., Gainesville, Fla., 1999—2001. Cons. Oglethorpe Ctr., Savannah, 1983-84. Columnist Australian Med. Record Jour., 1981-87, Communique, 1981-84, Palmetto Breeze, 1985-87, Progress Notes, 1984-85, 2000. Recipient disting. mem. award Ga. Med. Record Assn., 1984; fellow Aspen Inst., 1988. Mem. Assembly on Edn., Am. Health Info. Mgmt. Assn., Ariz. Health Info. Mgmt. Assn. (program chmn. 1988-89, sec. 1989—), Tex. Health Info. Mgmt. Assn. (dist. III v.p.), L.I. Health Info. Mgmt. Assn., Fla. Health Info. Mgmt. Assn., N.E. Fla. Health Info. Mgmt. Assn. (del. 2000 state house dels.; incoming pres.-elect, 2000—), Alachua County Vocat. Edn. Assn., Internat. Fedn. Health Record Orgns. Episcopalian. Avocations: swimming, reading, travel, photography, cooking. Home: Apt 26 800 NW 18th Ave Gainesville FL 32609-3583 Personal E-mail: aemarohn@aol.com.

MARONEY, JANE P. former state legislator, consultant; b. Boston, July 29, 1923; d. John Henry and Mary (Boland) Perkins; m. John Walker Maroney, July 7, 1956; children: Jane Maroney El Dahr, John Walker Jr. Student, Radcliffe Coll., 1940—41, Katharine Gibbs Sch., 1941—42; LHD (hon.), Goldey Beacom Coll., 1995. Elected ofcl. Del. Gen. Assembly, Dover, 1978-98; former project mgr. Milbank Meml. Fund, N.Y.C. Del. Family Law Commn., 1990—99, Health and Human Devel. Com., 1984—99; moderator, panelist Pub. Policy Conf., annually; past mem. Jr. League Wilmington (Del.); vice chair Creative Grandparenting, Inc., 1999—; pres. Lincoln Club of Del., 2002—03; trustee Christiana Care Health Sys., 2000—; mem. bd. Health and Nursing Scis. U. Del., 1998—; bd. dirs. YWCA, New Castle County, Family and Workplace Connection, Coord. Coun. Children with Disabilities, chmn., 1990—91; mem. adv. bd. Rockwood Mus., Del. Hospice, Girl Scouts Del., Del. Internat. Yr. of Family, March of Dimes, Coalition for Literacy, Inst. Human Behavior; bd. dirs. Afghanistan-Del. Cmtys. Together, 2001 , St. Michaels Sch. and Nursery, 2000—. Named 1 of 10 Best Rep. Legislators of Yr., Pres. Reagan, 1985; named to Woman's Hall of Fame, Del., 1990, Outstanding Legislator of Yr., Easters Seals of Del., 1998; recipient Outstanding Svc. to Children award, Acad. Pediat., Disting. Svc. award, Del. Bar Assn., Alfred R. Shands Disting. Svc. award, 1992, Order of Merit award, U. Del., 1993, J. Donaldson Brown Disting. Svcs. award, Children and Family Svcs. Del. to Dr. & Rep. Maroney, 1992, Nathan Davis award, AMA, 1996, Order of the First State award, Gov. of Del., 1998, Advocacy and Leadership in Children's Issues award, Epilepsy Found. Del., 2000, Outstanding Lifetime Contbn. award, Health Edn. Network Del., 2001, Cmty. Builder award, Nat. Conf. for Cmty. and Justice, 2001, Woman Pioneer award, Boy Scouts Am., 2001, Liberty Bell award, Del. State Bar Assn. Law Day, 2003, Carrie Chapman Catt award, Wilmington LWV, 2004. Roman Catholic. Avocation: travel. Fax: 302-478-2677.

MARONI, DONNA FAROLINO, biologist, researcher; b. Buffalo, Feb. 27, 1938; d. Enrico Victor and Eleanor (Redlinska) Farolino; m. Gustavo Primo Maroni, Dec. 16, 1974. BS, U. Wis., 1960, PhD, 1969. Project assoc. U. Wis., Madison, 1960-63, 68-74; Alexander von Humboldt fellow Inst. Genetics U. Cologne, Fed. Republic Germany, 1974-75; Hargitt fellow Duke U., Durham, N.C., 1975-76, rsch. assoc., 1976-83, rsch. assoc. prof., 1983-87; sr. program specialist N.C. Biotech. Ctr., Research Triangle Park, 1987-88, dir. sci. programs div., 1988-92, v.p. for sci. programs, 1992-94, ret., 1995. Mem. adv. com. MICROMED at Bowman Gray Sch. Medicine, Winston-Salem, NC, 1988—94; mem. sci. adv. bd. NC Biosci. Fund, LLC, 1998—99, Minority Sci. Improvement Alliance for Instrn. and Rsch. in Biotech, Ala. A&M U., Normal, 1990—91. Contbr. over 20 articles and revs. to profl. jours. Grantee NSF, 1977-79, NIH, 1979-82, 79-83, 82-87. Mem. Genetics Soc. Am., N.C. Acad. Sci., Inc. (bd. dirs. 1983-86), Sigma Xi (mem. exec. com. Duke U. chpt. 1989-90). Achievements include research in electron microscopy, evolution of chromosomes, chromosome structure, evolution of mitosis, and mitosis and fungal phylogeny.

MAROT, LOLA, retired accountant; b. Providence, Oct. 6, 1939; d. Frank and Iola (Lombardi) Ansuini; m. Joseph Marot (div. 1973); 1 child, David Joseph BA with distinction, U. R.I., 1973; postgrad., Bryant Coll. Bookkeeper Diamond Paper Box Co., Providence, 1958-69; export sales adminstr. Brite Industries, Providence, 1973-77; property svcs. asst. Met. Property and Liability Ins. Co., Warwick, R.I., 1977-79, buyer, 1979-83, sr. buyer, 1983-86, supr. printing adminstrn., 1986-87, expense control adminstr., 1987-88; acct. Dept. Adminstrn. State of R.I., Divsn. Ctrl. Svcs., 1992-99; ret., 1999. Mem. Univ. Soc. Providence (pres. 1978)

MARPLE, DOROTHY JANE, retired church executive; b. Abington, Pa., Nov. 24, 1926; d. John Stanley and Jennie (Stetler) M. AB, Ursinus Coll., 1948; MA, Syracuse U., 1950; Ed.D., Columbia U. Tchrs. Coll., 1969; L.H.D., Thiel Coll., 1965, Gettysburg Coll., 1979, Ursinus Coll., 1981; D. Humanitarian Services, Newberry Coll., 1977; DD, Trinity Luth. Sem., 1987. Counselor, asst., office dean undergrad. women Women's Coll., Duke, 1950-53; dean women, fgn. student adv. Thiel Coll., 1953-61; asst. social dir. Whittier Hall, Columbia Tchrs. Coll., 1961-62; exec. dir. Luth. Ch. Women, Luth. Ch. Am., Phila., 1962-75; asst. to bishop Luth. Ch. Am., 1975-85; coord. Transition Office Evang. Luth. Ch. Am., 1986-87; asst. gen. sec. ops. Nat. Coun. Chs. of Christ in U.S., N.Y.C., 1987-89. Coordinator Luth. Ch. in Am. commn. on function and structure, 1970-72 Home: 8018 Anderson St Philadelphia PA 19118-2936

MARPLE, JILL M. music educator; d. Milton (Pete) B. and Colleen Breshears; m. Paul W. Marple, June 28, 1998. AA, Yakima Valley CC, 1983; BA, Ctrl. Wash. U., 1985; M, Heritage Coll., Toppenish, Wash., 1993. Music, band instr. Kelso Sch. Dist., 1985—88; instrumental music dir. Naches (Wash.) Valley Sch. Dist., 1988—98, elem. music tchr., 1999—. Ruth Brown Meml. scholar, Yakima Valley CC, 1983. Mem.: Sophisticated Swing Band, Music Educator's Nat. Conf., Yakima Valley Cmty. Band (assoc.). Roman Catholic. Avocations: music, tutoring, reading, crafts, sewing. Personal E-mail: jmarple@naches.wednet.edu.

MARQUARDT, SANDRA MARY, activist, lobbyist, researcher; b. Dhahran, Saudi Arabia, Mar. 5, 1959; parents Am. citizens; d. Donald Edward and Mary Eleanor (Lindsay-Rea) M.; m. Hans Kristensen. BA, U. Wis., 1982. Editor, organizer Nat. Coalition Against the Misuse of Pesticides, Washington, 1983-87; rschr., author Environ. Policy Inst., Washington, 1987-88; rschr., lobbyist Greenpeace, Washington, 1988-95; rschr. Consumer's Union, 1995-96; program dir. Mothers and Others for a Livable Planet, San Francisco, 1996-97; coord. organic fiber coun. Organic Trade Assn., Richmond, Calif., 1997—. Authored reports on domestic and internat. pesticide use, bottled water, organic cotton, golf courses, sanitary products. Avocations: hiking, swimming, photography.

MARQUART, PETRA A. training consultant; b. Fairmont, Minn., July 16, 1948; d. Walter H. and Mavis I. Marquart. BA in Comms., Metropolitan State U., Mpls., 1998. Cert. trainer 1993, achieve global 1991, resident mgr. 1984, lic. realtor Minn., 1982. Prin. Petra Marquart and Assocs., Minnetonka, Minn., 1998—; tng. coord. Customized Tng. Svcs./Hennepin Tech. Coll., Plymouth, Minn., 1990—. Adj. instr./CRM cert. Minn. Multi Housing Assn., Bloomington, Minn., 1987—98; bd. dirs. edn. Minn. Multi Ho. Asssn., Bloomington, Minn., 1992—97; bd. dirs. ACE, Honeywell, Minn., 1994—98; cons. Mayo Clinic, Rochester, 1999—2001. Singer: (singer with ensemble) The 10th Story Window, 1973; author: (novels) The Power of Service: Keeping Customers for Life, 1998, (customer svc. tng. program) Mall of America's Guest Service Training, 1995, Svc. at the Ctr. - Fairview Hosps., 1997, First Bank Sys. - Customers First, 1996, Capri Svc.-Casinos Am., 1998, (Property Mgmt. Course Series) Introduction to Property Management, 1987; actor: (films, supporting role) The Crucible, 1965 (Best Actress, 1965). Stephen Minister Gethsemane Luth. Ch., Hopkins, Minn.; pres. NOW, Jackson, Minn., 1975—76. Lutheran. Avocations: fishing, golf, music. Office: Petra Marquart and Assocs PO Box 55 Hackensack MN 56452 Business E-mail: info@petramarquart.com.

MARQUEZ, MICHELLE F. elementary school educator; b. Las Vegas, Oct. 2, 1972; d. Frank Robert Marquez and Esther Elaine Armijo; children: Jonathon James Cordova, Jeremy Lee Cordova. AA, Luna Cmty. Coll., 1997; BA, N. Mex. Highlands U., 1998. Asst. tchr. Imagination Sta., Las Vegas, 1992—94; employment specialist Vistas Sin Limites, N. Mex. Highlands U., 1998—2001; tchr. West Las Vegas Sch., 2001—. V.p. PTO, Las Vegas, 2002—03.

MARQUIS, HARRIET HILL, social worker; b. Rocky Mount, N.C., Sept. 4, 1938; d. Robert Foster and Anne Ruth (Daughtry) Hill; m. James Ralph Marquis, Apr. 23, 1967; children: Margaret Anne, Karen Lee. BA in English, Meredith Coll., 1960; MA in English, Seton Hall U., 1971; PhD in English, Drew U., 1984; MSW, NYU, 1987; cert., N.Y. Sch. Psychoanalytic Psychotherapy, 1991, Inst. Study Psychotherapy & Psychoanalysis N.J., 1998. Tchr. English S.C. Pub. Schs., 1960-62, Peace Corps, Sierra Leone, West Africa, 1963-65; adj. prof. English Farleigh Dickinson U., Madison, 1983-85; psychotherapist Child Guidance & Family Svc. Ctr., Orange, N.J., 1987; staff clinician Esther Dutton Counseling Ctr., Morristown, N.J., 1987-90; psychotherapist Ctr. Evaluation & Psychotherapy, Morristown, N.J., 1990-93; pvt. practice Madison, N.J., 1990-98, Brevard, N.C., 1998—. Mem. Internat. Conf. Advancement of Pvt. Practice Clin. Social Work; speaker in field. Fellow N.C. Soc. Clin. Social Workers; mem. NASW (bd.

cert. diplomate in social work), Nat. Fedn. of Socs. for Clin. Social Work (nat. membership com. psychoanalysis in clin. social work). Democrat. Methodist. Avocations: reading, walking, writing, travel. E-mail: harrieth@brinet.com.

MARR, CARMEL CARRINGTON, retired lawyer, retired state official; b. Bklyn., June 23, 1921; d. William Preston and Gertrude Clementine (Lewis) Carrington; m. Warren Marr II, Apr. 11, 1948; children: Charles Carrington, Warren Quincy III. BA, Hunter Coll., 1945; JD, Columbia U., 1948. Bar: N.Y. 1948, U.S. Dist. Ct. (ea. dist.) N.Y. 1950, U.S. Dist. Ct. (so. dist.) N.Y. 1951. Clk. Dyer & Stevens, N.Y.C., 1948-49; pvt. practice N.Y.C., 1949-53; adviser legal affairs U.S. mission to UN, N.Y.C., 1953-67; sr. legal officer Office Legal Affairs UN Secretariat, 1967-68; mem. N.Y. State Human Rights Appeal Bd., 1968-71, N.Y. State Pub. Svc. Commn., 1971-86; cons. Gas. Rsch. Inst., 1987-91. Lectr. N.Y. Police Acad., 1963-67. Contbr. articles to profl. jours. Mem. N.Y. Gov.'s Com. Edn. and Employment of Women, 1963-64; mem. Nat. Gen. Svcs. Pub. Adv. Council, 1969-71; mem., former chmn. adv. coun. Gas. Rsch. Inst.; mem. chmn. tech. pipeline safety standards com. Dept. Transp., 1979-85; former mem. task force Fed. Energy Regulatory Commn. and EPA to examine PCBs in gas supply system; past chmn. gas com. Nat. Assn. Regulatory Utility Commrs.; past pres. Great Lakes Conf. Pub. Utilities Commrs., mem. exec. com.; mem. UN Devel. Corp., 1969-72; bd. dirs. Amistad Rsch. Ctr., New Orleans, 1970—, chmn. bd. dirs., 1981-94; bd. dirs. Bklyn. Soc. Prevention Cruelty to Children, Nat. Arts Stblzn. Fund, 1984-93, hon. bd. mem., 1998, Prospect Park Alliance, 1987-98; bd. visitors N.Y. State Sch. Girls, Hudson, 1964-71; mem. exec. bd. Plays for Living, N.Y.C., 1968-75; pres. bd. dirs. Billie Holiday Theatre, 1972-80; mem. nat. adv. coun. Hampshire Coll.; pres.'s coun. Tulane U., 1988-95. Mem. Phi Beta Kappa, Alpha Chi Alpha, Alpha Kappa Alpha. Republican. Episcopalian.

MARR, PHEBE ANN, retired historian, educator; b. Mt. Vernon, N.Y., Sept. 21, 1931; d. John Joseph and Lillian Victoria (Henningsen) Marr. BA, Barnard Coll., 1953; PhD, Harvard U., 1967. Rsch. assoc. ARAMCO, Dhahran, Saudi Arabia, 1960-62; dir. mid. east program Fgn. Svc. Inst., 1963-66; asst. prof. Stanislaus State Coll., Turlock, Calif., 1970-71, assoc. prof., 1971-74; assoc. prof. history U. Tenn., Knoxville, 1974-85, chmn. Asian studies program, 1977-79. Cons. ARAMCO, 1979-83. Author: The Modern History of Iraq, 1985, 2d edit., 2003; co-editor: Riding the Tiger: Middle East Challenge After the Cold War, 1993; contbr. articles to profl. jours. Bd. dirs. Mid. East Policy Coun., 2004. Rsch. fellow Mid. East Ctr., Harvard U., Cambridge, Mass., 1968-70, sr. fellow Nat. Def. U., Washington, 1985-97, Woodrow Wilson Ctr. fellow, 1998-99, Coun. on Fgn. Rels., U.S. Inst. Peace fellow, 2004-. Mem. Mid. East Inst., Mid. East Studies Assn. Home: 2902 18th St NW Washington DC 20009-2954 E-mail: marrphebe@aol.com.

MARRA, KACEY G. research scientist, educator; b. Washington, Pa., Sept. 24, 1970; d. John W. and Kathleen A. Gribbin; m. William M. Marra, Nov. 26, 1994; children: Ethan, LeeAnna. BS, U. Pitts., 1992, PhD, 1996. Postdoctoral fellow Emory U. Sch. Medicine, Atlanta, 1996—97; rsch. scientist Carnegie Mellon U., Pitts., 1998—2002; asst. prof. U. Pitts., 2002—. Mem. study sect. NIH, 2000—01; mem. panel rev. NSF, 2002—03. Contbr. articles to profl. jours. Organizer charity event Genesis, Washington, 2000—01. Named Rschr. of the Month, Pitts. Tissue Engring. Initiative, Inc., 1998; named one of PUMP's "40 under 40" Most Influential Pittsburghers, Pitts. Urban Magnet Project, 2001. Mem. Soc. Biomaterials Materials Rsch. Soc., Am. Chem. Soc., Tissue Engring. Soc. Roman Catholic. Avocations: reading, golf. Office: U Pitts 1555W BST 200 Lothrop St Pittsburgh PA 15261 Business E-Mail: marrak@upmc.edu.

MARRAM, ELLEN R. investment company executive; BS, Wellesley Coll., 1968; MBA, Harvard U., 1970. V.p. mktg. Nabisco Biscuit Co., 1981-86, pres. grocery divsn., 1987-93; pres. Tropicana Beverage Group The Seagram Co. Ltd., Bradenton, Fla., 1993-97, pres. and CEO Tropicana Products and Tropicana Beverage Group, 1997-98; pres., CEO EfDex, Stamford, Conn., 1999; mng. dir. N. Castle Partners, 2000—. Bd. dirs. Ford Motor Co., N.Y. Times Co., Eli Lilly and Co., The Conf. Bd., Advt. Coun. Bd. dirs. N.Y. Presbyn. Hosp., Lincoln Ctr. Theater, Families and Work Inst, Assocs. of Harvard Bus. Sch. Office: N Castle Partners 138 E Putnam Ave Greenwich CT 06830*

MARRERO, TERESA, lawyer; b. N.Y.C. d. Miquel Angel and Jovita (Otero) Marrero. BA in Bus., Marymount Manhattan Coll., 1988; JD, N.Y. Law Sch., 1991. Bar: N.Y. 1992. Lawyer FCC, Washington, 1991-93; lawyer firm Akin, Gump, Washington, 1993-94; lawyer Teleport Comms. Group, N.Y.C., 1994-98, AT&T, Basking Ridge, N.J., 1998—. Mem. ABA. N.Y.C. Bar Assn., N.Y. State Bar Assn., P.R. Bar Assn., Adirondack Hiking Club, Audubon. Avocations: ornithology, birdwatching, bicycling, hiking. Office: AT&T 295 N Maple Ave Rm 1124m1 Basking Ridge NJ 07920-1025

MARRETT, CORA B. science educator; b. Richmond, Va., June 15, 1942; d. Horace Sterling and Clora Ann (Boswell) Bagley; m. Louis Everard Marrett, Dec. 24, 1968. BA, Va. Union U., 1963; MS, U. Wis., 1965, PhD, 1968. Asst. prof. U. N.C., Chapel Hill, 1968-69; from asst. to assoc. prof. Western Mich. U., Kalamazoo, 1969-73; from assoc. prof. to full prof. U. Wis., Madison, 1973-97; asst. dir. NSF, Arlington, Va., 1992-96; provost, vice chancellor for acad. affairs U. Mass., Amherst, 1997—2001; sr. v.p.. for acad. affairs U. Wis. System, 2001—. Mem. sci. adv. panel U.S. Army, Washington, 1976-77; mem. Naval Rsch. Adv. Com., Washington, 1978-81, Pres. Commn. on the Accident at Three Mile Island, 1979; bd. govs. Argonne (Ill.) Nat. Lab., 1983-90, 96-99. Editor: Research in Race and Ethnic Relations, 1988, Gender and Classroom Interaction, 1990. Resident fellow NAS, 1973-74; fellow Ctr. for Advanced Study in Behavioral Scis., 1976-77. Mem. AAAS, ASA, Phi Kappa Phi. Avocations: reading, travel, film appreciation. Home: 7517 Farmington Way Madison WI 53717 Office: Office of Acad Affairs U of Wisconsin Syatem 1620 Van Hive Hall Madison WI 53706 E-mail: cmarrett@uwsa.edu.

MARRIOTT, MARCIA ANN, business and economics educator, health facility administrator; b. Rochester, N.Y., Mar. 21, 1947; d. Coyne and Alice (Schleper) M.; children: Brian, Jonathan. AA, Monroe C.C., Rochester, 1967; BS, SUNY, Brockport, 1970, MA, 1975; PhD, S.W. U. La., 1985. Program adminstr. N.Y. Dept. of Labor, N.Y.C., 1970-75; employment mgr. Rochester Gen. Hosp., 1975-77, salary adminstr., 1982-98, compensation mgr., 1996—; corp. dir. wage and salary dept. Gannett Newspapers, Rochester, 1977-80; compensation and benefits adminstr. Sybron Corp., Rochester, 1980-82; compensation mgr. Rochester Gen. Hosp., 1996—; dir. compensation Via Health, Rochester, 1995-98; pres. Compensation Link, 1997—; prof. Grad. Sch. Bus. Rochester Inst. Tech., 1998—2003, SUNY, Brockport, 1998—2003. Instr. N.Y. State Sch. Indsl. Rels., Cornell U., N.Y.C., 1976-79; assoc. prof. Rochester Inst. Tech., 1978—, Monroe C.C., 1981—, dir. career adv. coun., 1989—; assoc. prof. SUNY, Brockport; assoc. prof. Nazareth Coll., 1998; dir. Rochester Presbyn. Home, 1987-91, 96—, v.p. bd. dirs., 1997-98, pres. bd. dirs., 1998—; dir. area hosp. coun. Kidney Svc. Ctrs., Rochester, 1988-91; cons. in field. Author: (pamphlets) Guideline for Writing Job Descriptions, 1983, (manual) Career Planning Manual, 1985, (booklet) Guideline for Writing Criteria-Based Job Descriptions, 1988, Skill-based Job Descriptions: A Quality Approach, 1994, Redesigning the Performance Appraisal Process, 1996. Campaign mgr. Carter Campaign Commn., Rochester, 1975; mem. coun. Messiah Luth. Ch., Rochester, 1991-94. Davenport-Hatch Found. grantee, 1973, Wegman Found. grantee, 1975. Mem. Am. Compensation Assn., Single Adopted Parents Group (pres. 1988-93). Avocations: tennis, hiking, reading, swimming, skiing. Office: Rochester Gen Hosp 1425 Portland Ave Rochester NY 14621-3095

MARRON, AMY M. band director; m. John T. Marron, Aug. 16, 1997; 1 child, Sarah M. B in Music Edn., Fla. State U., 1995; MA in Music Edn., Eastman Sch. Music, Rochester, N.Y., 2002. Cert. tchr. music K-12 N.Y. H.s. band dir. Odyssey Sch., Rochester, 1996—. Religious edn. tchr., NY. Mem.: Music Educators Nat. Conf. (assoc.), Greece Performing Arts Soc. (assoc.).

MARRON, DARLENE LORRAINE, real estate company executive; b. Auburn, N.Y., July 20, 1946; d. William Chester and Elizabeth Barbara (Gervaise) Kulakowski; m. Edward W. Marron Jr., Apr. 28, 1973. BS cum laude, Rider U., 1968; MBA, NYU, 1970. Lic. securities broker. Dir. mktg. Am. Airlines, N.Y.C., 1970-79; asst. v.p. Merrill Lynch, N.Y.C., 1979-83; v.p. Kidder, Peabody & Co., N.Y.C., 1983-86; prin. Marron Bros. Realty Corp., Upper Saddle River, N.J., 1990—; prin. real estate fin. svcs. firm Hendrickson Advisors, LLC, 2000—. Avocations: pianist, flutist, skiing, fly fishing. Home: 9 Normandy Ct Ho Ho Kus NJ 07423-1217 Office: Marron Cos 118 State Rt 17 Upper Saddle River NJ 07458

MARROW, DEBORAH, foundation administrator; b. N.Y.C., Oct. 18, 1948; d. Seymour Arthur and Adele (Wolin) M.; m. Michael J. McGuire, June 19, 1971; children: David Marrow McGuire, Anna Marrow McGuire. BA cum laude, U. Pa., 1970, PhD, 1978; MA, Johns Hopkins U., 1972. Resch. asst. Phila. Mus. of Art, 1974-75; mng. editor Chrysalis Mag., L.A., 1978-80; asst. prof. Occidental Coll., L.A., 1979, 81-82; publs. coord. The J. Paul Getty Trust, L.A., 1983-84; program officer The Getty Grant Program, L.A., 1984-86, asst. dir., 1987-89, dir., 1989—; interim dir. The Getty Res. Inst., 1999—. Mem. internat. com. Coun. on Founds., Washington, 1992-96; mem. internat. adv. Group Nat. Endowment for the Arts, 1992; mem. adv. com. Calif. Cmty. Found., L.A., 1991—; mem. Excellence and Equity task force Am. Assn. of Mus., Washington, 1989-91. Author: The Art Patronage of Maria de Medici, 1982; contbr. articles to profl. jours. Chair cultural diversity com. The J. Paul Getty Trust, L.A., 1995-98; mem. Save Am.'s Treas. com., Nat. Trust for Historic Preservation in partnership with White Ho. Millenium Coun., 1998—; mem. trustees coun. on Penn Women, U. Pa., 1997—; bd. govs. U. Calif. Humanities Rsch. Inst., 2000—. Samuel H. Kress Found. fellow, N.Y.C., 1975-77. Mem. Coll. Art Assn. of Am., So. Calif. Assn. for Philanthropy (program com., 1988-89, 97), Grantmakers in the Arts, Art Table, Internat. Coun. of Mus. Office: The Getty Rsch Inst 1200 Getty Center Dr Ste 800 Los Angeles CA 90049-1600

MARS, JACQUELINE BADGER, food products executive; m. David Badger, 1961 (div.); 3 children ; m. Harold Vogel, 1986 (div.). Degree in anthropology, Bryn Mawr Coll., 1961. Co-owner Mars, Inc., McLean, Va., 1973—, corp. v.p., 1990—. Trustee Bryn Mawr Coll. Office: Mars Inc 6885 Elm St Mc Lean VA 22101

MARSDEN, HERCI IVANA, classical ballet artistic director; b. Omis-Split, Croatia, Dec. 2, 1937; d. Ante and Magda (Smith) Munitic; m. Myles Marsden, Aug. 10, 1957 (div. 1976); children: Ana, Richard, Mark.; m. Dujko Radovnikovic, Aug. 27, 1977; 1 child, Dujko. Student, Internat. Ballet Sch., 1955. Mem. corps de ballet Nat. Theatre, Split, 1954-58; founder Braecrest Sch. Ballet, Lincoln, R.I., 1958—, State Ballet of R.I., Lincoln, 1960—, artistic dir., 1976—. Artistic dir. U. R.I. Classical Ballet, Kingston, 1966—, lectr., 1966—. Office: Brae Crest School of Ballet 52 Chapman Ave Lincoln RI 02865-3809 E-mail: hmarsden@stateballet.com.

MARSDEN-ATLASS, LYNN DEAN, curator, museum administrator; d. Phillips Brooks Marsden Jr. and Marjorie Dean Marsden; children: Jessica Atlass, Kate Atlass. BA, Lake Forest Coll., Ill., 1972; MA, U. Chgo., 1976; Certificat de Langue Francaise, U. Paris IV, 1983. Dir. Consortium of Colleges Abroad, Paris, 1980—89; prof., art history Brit. Inst. in Paris, 1980—88; assoc. dir. Colby Coll. Mus. of Art, Waterville, Maine, 1989—98; curator Am. and contemporary art Chrysler Mus. of Art, Norfolk, Va., 1999—2003. Author: Power & Whimsy: A Private Collection of American Modernism; contbr. catalogue Maine in America; author: (collection catalogue) 100 Works from the 20th Century at the Colby College Museum of Art, (exhibition catalogue) American Realism Abroad. Site reviewer for mus. assessment programs Inst. of Mus. and Libr. Scis., Washington, 1997—2003; peer reviewer, accreditation visiting com. Am. Assn. of Museums, Washington, 1998—2003. Mem.: Va. Mus. Assn., Am. Assn. of Museums, ArtTable. Avocations: travel, art. Home: 5946 Glenhaven Crescent Norfolk VA 23508

MARSEE, SUSANNE IRENE, mezzo-soprano; b. San Diego, Nov. 26, 1941; d. Warren Jefferson and Irene Rose (Wills) Dowell; m. Mark J. Weinstein, May, 1987; 1 child, Zachary. Student, Santa Monica City Coll., 1961; BA in History, UCLA, 1964. Mem. voice faculty Am. Mus. and Dramatic Acad., N.Y.C., 1994-97, Pitts. Civic Light Opera Acad., 1997—, Duquesne U., 1998-2000; artist's lectr. Carnegie Mellon U., 2000—. Assoc. prof. La State U. Appeared with numerous U.S. opera cos., 1970—, including N.Y.C. Opera, San Francisco Opera, Boston Opera, Houston Grand Opera; appeared with fgn. cos., festivals, Mexico City Bellas Artes, 1973, 78, Canary Islands Co., 1976, Opera Metropolitana, Caracas, Venezuela, 1977, Spoleto (Italy) Festival, 1977, Aix en Provence Festival, France, 1977, Calgary, Alta., Can., 1986; recorded Tales of Hoffmann, ABC/Dunhill Records; TV appearances include Live from Lincoln Center, Turk in Italy, Cenerentola, 1989, Live from Wolftrap Roberto Devereux, 1975, Rigoletto, 1988, A Little Night Music, 1990, Marriage of Figaro, 1991, (PBS TV) Rachel, La Cubana; recs. and CDs Anna Bolena with Ramey, Scotto, Roberto Devereux with Beverly Sills, Roberto Devereux with Monserat Caballé Carreras, Tales of Hoffmann with Beverly Sills, Rigoletto with Quilico and Carreras; videotape Roberto Devereux with Beverly Sills. Recipient 2d place award Met. Opera Regional Auditions, 1968, San Francisco Opera Regional Auditions 1968; named winner Liederkranz Club Contest, 1970; Gladys Turk Found. grantee, 1968-69; Corbett Found. grantee, 1969-73; Martha Baird Rockefeller grantee, 1969-70, 71-72 Mem. AFTRA, Am. Guild Mus. Artists (past bd. dirs.), Nat. Assn. Tchrs. of Singing (past bd. dirs. for N.Y.). Democrat.

MARSELLA, JULIA, music educator; b. Cedarville, N.J., July 29, 1929; d. Joseph and Marion Marie (Sanza) Nardelli; m. Anthony Joseph Marsella, Apr. 4, 1971. Student of Percy Ross, Phila. Conservatory of Music; student of Joseph Arcaro, Phila. Mus. Acad. Ptnr. Nardelli Hardware, Cedarville, 1946—90; pvt. piano tchr. Cedarville, 1962—. Organist, choir dir. St. Michael's Ch., Cedarville. Mem. Cumberland County Hist. Soc., Cedarville Hist. Soc.; trustee Cedarville Libr., 2000. Roman Catholic. Avocations: painting, reading, travel, cooking. Home: 329 Main St Cedarville NJ 08311

MARSH, ALMA FERN, retired music educator, director, organist; b. Kincaid, Kans., Dec. 30, 1921; d. George William Marsh and Adora Verle Hummiston Marsh. BSE, Emporia State Tchrs. Coll., Kans., 1952; MS, Pitts. State Coll., Kans., 1969. Cert. tchg. Music tchr. 3 rural schs., Hepler, Bronson, Kincaid, Kans., 1940—43; music tchr. 1-8 Elmdale, Kans., 1943—45; music tchr. 1-6 Horton, Kans., 1945—47, Ellsworth, Kans., 1948—51, Pitts., Kans., 1952—71, Iola, Kans., 1971—87; music dir. and organist First Presbyn. Ch., Iola, Kans., 1971—. Viola 1st chair Iola area Symphony Orch., Kans., 1971—; percussion Iola City Band, Kans., 2000—. Mem. Iola Cmty. Theatre, Kans., 1971—. Mem.: NEA, Kans. Music Educators Assn., Music Educators Nat. Conf., Allen County Ret. Personnel Assn., Delta Kappa Gamma. Republican. Presbyn. Achievements include writing songs and arranging music as needed for elem. children and the ch. choir; mentoring children learning to play piano and string instruments. Avocations: painting, sewing, crocheting, music, cultral attractions. Home: 220 W Jackson Ave Iola KS 66749

MARSH, CAROL K. adult community administrator; b. Elloree, S.C., Sept. 15, 1933; d. William Conrad and Allie (Ulmer) Kemmerlin; m. Edward A. Peeples, Sept. 20, 1963 (div. Dec. 1988); 1 child, William E. Kemmerlin Peeples; m. Charles Marsh, March 15, 1953 (div. Sept. 1961), remarried May. 27, 1989; children: Shera Marsh Chupa, Mickee Brown. Operator So. Bell Telephone, Allendale, SC, 1951-54; bookkeeper Colonial Stores, Chamblis, Ga., 1955-57, Florence, SC, 1957-58; retail acct. Piggly Wiggly Carolina, Charleston, SC, 1958-65; ptnr. Southern Inventory Svc., Charleston, SD, 1976-85; substitute tchr./trainer Charleston County Schs., 1979-88; gen. mgr. Beachwood at the Heritage, Myrtle Beach, SC, 1988—. Ptnr. Marsh Contractors Ltd., 1990—. Contbr. poetry to Internat. Libr. Poetry. Bd. dirs. Mfrd. Housing Inst. S.C., Columbia, 1996—; life mem. Luth. Sem. Aux./So. Sem., Columbia; pres. Women of Evang. Luth. Ch. Am. St. Matthews Luth. Ch., 1984-86. Named Vol. of the Yr., Charleston County Schs., 1984. Mem. NAFE, Myrtle Beach C. of C., Am. Bus. Women's Assn. (pres. 1996-98, Woman of Yr. 1998), PTA (life, hon.), S.C. PTA (hon. life), Am. Soc. Notaries. Lutheran. Home: PO Box 3111 Myrtle Beach SC 29578-3111 Office: Beachwood at the Heritage 1712 Club House Dr Myrtle Beach SC 29577-5090 E-mail: ccc2x1@cs.com.

MARSH, CAROLE, author, photographer, publisher; b. Marietta, Ga., Mar. 22, 1946; CEO, Gallopade Internat., Peachtree City, Ga. Author more than 10,000 books and software including: (children's ednl. series) CArole Marsh State Books, Our Black Heritage Series, Smart Sex Stuff for Kids 7-17, Quantum Leap Books, The Naked Gourmet, Lifewrite and Propub Books, History Mystery Books, Lost Colony Collection; author curriculum materials based on state standards for all 50 state and Can. Recipient Top Honors, Nat. C. of C.; named Communicator of Yr., Assn. Bus. Communicators. Office: Gallopade Publishing Group 665 Hwy 74 S Peachtree City GA 30269

MARSH, CARYL AMSTERDAM, museum exhibitions curator, psychologist, advisor; b. N.Y.C., Mar. 9, 1923; d. Louis and Kitty (Weitz) Amsterdam; m. Michael Marsh, Sept. 3, 1942 (dec. 1993); children: Susan E., Anna L. BA, Bklyn. Coll., 1942; MA, Columbia U., 1946; PhD, George Washington U., 1978. Lic. psychologist, D.C. Asst. cultural attache Am. Embassy, Paris, 1946-48; psychologist D.C. Recreation Dept., 1957-69; spl. asst. Smithsonian Instn., Washington, 1966-73; curator exhbns. Nat. Archives, Washington, 1978-85, sr. exhbns. specialist, 1985-86; dir. traveling psychology exhbn. Am. Psychol. Assn., 1986-93, sr. advisor, 1993-95; chair humanities seminars in sci. mus. Assn. Sci. Tech. Ctrs., 1994—. Rsch. fellow exptl. gallery Smithsonian Instn., 1992; rsch. cons. Nat. Zoo, 1981-92, Smithsonian Folk Life Festival, Nat. Mus. Am. History, 1977-78; organizer Discovery Room Nat. Mus. Natural History, 1969-73; cons. Meyer Found., 1964-66; advisor Lemelson Ctr. for Study of Invention and Innovation, Nat. Mus. Am. History, 1999-2000. Editor: Exhibition: The American Image, 1979. Organizer Anacostia Neighborhood Mus., Washington, 1967, bd. dirs., 1974—, v.p. 1993—; sec. D.C. Commn. on Arts and Humanities, 1969-72; pres. Pre-Sch. Parents Coun., Washington, 1956-57; adv. bd. Youth Alive, 1997-99. Fellow Nat. Mus. Am. Art, 1975-77; vis. scholar Nat. Mus. Am. Art, 1978—; grad. fellow CUNY, 1945-46; scholar George Washington U.; noted for Disting. Contbn. to Pub. Understanding of Psychology, APA, 1993. Mem. AAAS, APA (Outstanding Svc. award 1992, Disting. Contbn. to Pub. Understanding of Psychology award 1993), D.C. Psychol. Assn., Am. Assn. Mus., Mus. Edn. Roundtable (bd. dirs. 1983-87). Home and Office: 10450 Lottsford Rd # 3011 Mitchellville MD 20721-2734

MARSH, CLARE TEITGEN, retired school psychologist; b. Manitowoc, Wis., July 7, 1934; d. Clarence Emil and Dorothy (Napiezinski) Teitgen; m. Robert Irving Marsh, Jan. 30, 1955; children: David, Wendy Marsh Tootle, Julie Marsh Domino, Laura Marsh Beltrame. MS in Ednl. Psychology, U. Wis., Milw., 1968. Sch. psychologist Milw. Pub. Schs., 1975-76; lead psychologist West Allis (Wis.)-West Milw. Pub. Schs., 1968-95; sch. psychologist Wauwatosa (Wis.) Pub. Schs., 1987; instr. Milw. Sch. Engring., 1989-90, Alverno Coll., 1990-91. NDEA fellow, 1966-68. Mem. Internat. Sch. Psychologists Assn., Nat. Assn. Sch. Psychologists (del.), Suburban Assn. Sch. Psychologists (pres. 1976-77, 86-87), Wis. Assn. Sch. Psychologists (pres. 1990-91, chmn. membership com. 1980-84, sec. 1985-89, chmn. conv. 1987), Wis. Fedn. Pupil Svcs., Menomee Falls Symphony Orchestra, Our Lord's United Meth. Ch., United Meth. Women (pres., 2003—), Phi Kappa Phi, Pi Lambda Theta (pres.), Kappa Delta Pi, Phi Delta Kappa, Sigma Tau Delta, Alpha Chi Omega. Home: 14140 W Honey Ln New Berlin WI 53151-2442

MARSH, JOAN KNIGHT, educational film, video and computer software company executive, publisher children's books; b. Apr. 8, 1934; d. E. Lyle and Ruth (Hopkins) Knight; m. Alan Reid Marsh, Sept. 27, 1958; children: Alan Reid, Clayton Knight. BA, Tex. Tech U., 1956. Owner, pres. MarshMedia, Kansas City, Mo., 1969—. Mem. ctrl. governing bd. Children's Mercy Hosp., 1996—; mem. coun. Family Study Ctr., U. Mo., Kansas City, 1983-89, Children's Relief Assn. Mercy Hosp., Kansas City, 1984—, pres., 1989-91; pres. Friends of Children's Mercy Hosp., 1996-98; chmn. The Jewel Ball, 1997, Great Ball of China II, 1999. Mem. Jr. League (sustaining chmn. 1982-84, Cmty. Svc. award 1999), Gamma Phi Beta. Republican. Presbyterian. Avocations: egyptology, filmology.

MARSH, LISA A. musician; b. Detroit, Jan. 25, 1954; d. Allen Howard Filbey and Mary Lee Sharpe; m. Brian James Marsh, May 2, 1975; children: Jennifer, Terra, Elise. AD in Nursing, Lane C.C., Eugene, Oreg., 1977; BS in Music, Portland (Oreg.) State U., 1984, MusM, 2001. RN. Staff nurse neurosurgery Sacred Heart Hosp., Eugene, 1977—79; staff nurse emergency Eugene Hosp. and Clinic, 1979—80; nurse educator emergency dept. Good Samaritan Hosp., Portland, 1980—95; piano instr. Portland, 1995—2002; prin. keyboardist Columbia Symphony Orch., Portland, 1994—2002; pianist Onyx Trio, Portland, 1998—2002; dir. coord. Movement Program for Pianists Portland State U., Portland, 2002—; adj. piano faculty Marylhurst U., Portland, 2003. Founder, dir. Taubman Portland Coop. Program, 1996—2002; tchg. asst. Taubman Inst., Williamstown, Mass., 1997—2002. Vocal accompanist Oreg. Episcopal Sch., Portland, 1999—2002. Mem.: Oreg. Music Tchrs. Assn. (state chair MusicLink 1997—98). Democrat. Episcopalian. Avocations: music composition, hiking, gardening. Office Phone: 503-227-6699. E-mail: l88marsh@comcast.net.

MARSH, MARTHA, hospital administrator; BS, U. Rochester; MPH, MBA, Columbia U. Pres. and CEO Matthew Thornton Health Plan, Dartmouth-Hitchcock Med. Ctr., 1986—94; sr. v.p., profl. svcs. and managed care and v.p, managed care U. Pa. Health Sys., 1994—98; COO U. Calif.-Davis Health Care Sys., 1999—2002; dir., Hosp. and Clinics U. Calif.-Davis Medical Ctr., 1999—2002; pres. and CEO Stanford (Conn.) Hosp. and Clinics, 2002—. Apptd. by Pres. Bush Nat. Infrastructure Adv. Coun., 2003; bd. dirs. Calif. Healthcare Assoc., Integrated Healthcare Assoc., Blue Cross of Calif. Hosp. Relations Com. Office: Stanford Hosp 300 Pasteur Dr Ste H3200 Stanford CA 94305*

MARSH, MELISSA, newscaster; m. Jim Harmston. BA in Comm., Campbell U. Cert. aerobics instr. AFAA. Intern WECT, Fayetteville, NC; gen. assignment reporter WTVD, Fayetteville, NC, 1998—99; asst. prodr. NBC 17, Raleigh, NC, 1999—2000, Tech Watch reporter, 2000—01, gen. assignment reporter, 2001—. Instr. aerobics Gold's Gym, Cary and Raleigh. Avocations: travel, snorkeling, scuba diving, reading, exercising. Office: NBC 17 Studios 1205 Front St Raleigh NC 27609

MARSH, MERRILYN DELANO, sculptor, painter; b. Larchmont, N.Y., Dec. 26, 1923; d. Merrill Potter and Hazel (Holmes) Delano; m. George Estabrook Marsh, Sept. 18, 1954; children: Merrill Delano, George Estabrook Jr., Robert Houston. Diploma, Sch. of Mus. of Fine Arts, Boston, 1946, cert., 1947; postgrad., Acad. Grande Chaumière, Paris, 1947-48. Art tchr. Choate Sch., Brookline, Mass., 1948, 49, Brookline Cmty. Ctr., 1948, 49; pvt. art tchr. Newton, Mass., 1948-49; comml. sculptor for display and mfg. cos., 1948-55; sculpture tchr. De Cordova Mus., Lincoln, Mass., 1950-54. Juror for numerous art exhbns., New Eng. area, 1954-55, 72-74. One-woman show at Copley Soc. of Boston, 1996; commd. 7 reliefs for Sch. for Environ., Levine Sci. Ctr., Duke U., Durham, N.C., 1994, bronze statue for cloister garden St. Andrew's Episcopal Ch., Wellesley, Mass., 1995, bronze portrait reliefs for Houston and Sargent Athletic awards Tufts U., Medford, Mass., 1997, 2 bronze reliefs, Ellis Oval Athletic Field Tufts U., 2001, bronze portrait relief of Clarence P. "Pop" Houston, Houston Hall, Tufts U., 1965, bronze portrait relief for Rocco J. Carzo Cage, Cousens Gymnasium, Tufts U., 2002, others. Mrs. David Hunt Sculpture scholar Mus. Fine Arts, 1947; recipient Katherine Thayer Hobson award Pen and Brush Soc., 1991, Best in Show award Juliani Gallery, 1991, Pres.'s Cup award for golf Wellesley (Mass.) Country Club, 1998. 2d Pl. award Wellesley Soc. Artists, 2003. Mem. Copley Soc. Boston (Copley master, Maria Maravigna award 1988, 1st prize in sculpture and large works 1994, other awards, 1983, 89), New Eng. Sculptors Assn. (bd. dirs. 1986, award 1988), Wellesley Soc. Artists (awards 1985, 87, 89, 91-92, 95, 2001-02, 2d pl. award 2003, bd. dirs. 1970, 88—, Hon. Mention award 2003), Cambridge Art Assn. (Jack Schultz award, 2000, other awards 1993-94). Republican. Episcopalian.

MARSH, MICHELE, former newscaster; married; 1 child. Anchor/reporter WABI-TV, Bangor, Maine, KSAT-TV, San Antonio, WCBS, 1979-96; co-anchor WNBC/News Channel 4 at 6 p.m., N.Y.C., 1996—2003. Recipient Emmy awards for Best Broadcast (3). Office: WNBC-TV 30 Rockefeller Plz New York NY 10112-0002*

MARSHAK, CELIA L. biochemist, educator; b. N.Y.C., Aug. 20, 1923; m. Alfred G. Marshak, Feb. 10, 1952 (dec. June 1972); children: David W., Daniel R. BA in Biology, Hunter Coll., N.Y.C., 1943; MA in Biochemistry, Columbia U., N.Y.C., 1946; PhD in Biochemistry, Columbia U., 1951. Lectr. Hunter Coll. of CUNY, N.Y.C., 1946—52; assoc. prof. Beaver Coll., Glenside, Pa., 1960—65; rsch. asst. prof. Tulane U. Coll. of Medicine, New Orleans, 1965—69; asst. dean San Diego State U., 1972—93, prof. emerita, 1993—. Cons. Sci. Careers, 1993—. Fellow: AAAS; mem.: Am. Chem. Soc., Sigma Xi, Phi Beta Kappa. Democrat. Jewish. Home: 430 Retaheim Way La Jolla CA 92037

MARSHAK, HILARY WALLACH, psychotherapist, owner, small business owner; b. N.Y.C., May 27, 1950; d. Irving Isaac and Suni (Fox) Wallach; m. Harvey Marshak, Jan. 1, 1981; children: Emily Fox, Jacob Randall. BA, U. Conn., Storrs, 1973; MSW, N.Y.U., 1992; cert., Inst. for Study of Culture, and Ethnicity, N.Y.C., 1994. Cert. social worker, N.Y.; qualified clin. social worker; cert. secondary English tchr., N.Y. Tchr. English. Glastonbury (Conn.) H.S., 1973; instr. English, U. Autonoma de Guerrero, Acapulco, Mexico, 1974; administrv. asst. 4M Pub. Svcs. Corp., N.Y.C., 1975, bus. mgr.; exec. v.p. Vitalmedia Enterprises Inc., N.Y.C., 1977-87, pres., CEO, 1987-2001; psychotherapist Fifth Avenue Ctr. Counseling and Psychotherapy, N.Y.C., 1992-95; pvt. practice, N.Y.C., 1992—; co-dir. Inst. for Advanced Thinking, N.Y.C., 2000—; asst. dir. adult undergrad. admissions Pace U., N.Y.C., 2003—. Mktg. cons. Frana Ltd., London, 1988-89; infertility counselor; v.p. Think Impossible, 2000—; asst. dir. adult admissions Pace U., N.Y.C., 2003—. Editor: Before the Bar, 1978-80, Guide to Higher Edn., 1980; reviewer vol 32, The Jour. of Sex Rsch. Founder Women's Radical Caucus, U. Conn., 1970; broadcaster Sta. WHUS; bd. dirs. N.Y. Theater Ballet, 1990—, Am. AIDS Assn., 1992-97; mem. writers coun. Writers in Performance series Manhattan Theater Club. Recipient 2nd Place Flowers Ulster County Agrl. Fair, New Paltz, N.Y., 1987, 1st Place Herbs, 1988. Mem. NASW (qualified clin. social worker), Soc. for Sci. Study of Sex, Sex Edn. and Info. Coun. of U.S., Nat. Coun. Family Rels., Am. Infertility Assn., Am. Soc. for Reproductive Medicine, Resolve. Jewish. Avocations: gardening, birdwatching, cooking, reading. Home and Office: 100 Jane St Apt 45 New York NY 10014-1750

MARSHALL, CAK (CATHERINE ELAINE MARSHALL), music educator, composer; b. Nashville, Nov. 24, 1943; d. Dean Byron and Petula Iris (Bodie) M. BS in Music Edn., Ind. U. Pa., 1965; cert., Hamline U., 1981, 82, 83, Memphis State U., 1985; MME, Duquesne U., 1992. Nat. registered music educator, 1993; vocal music tchr., Pa. Tchr. music Mars (Pa.) Area Sch. Dist., 1965-66; music specialist Fox Chapel (Pa.) Area Sch. Dist., 1966—, Duquesne U. City Music Ctr., Pitts., 1994-98; ednl. dir. Peripole-Bergerault, Inc., Salem, Oreg., 2001—. Orff specialist Chatham Coll. Fine Arts Camp, Pitts., 1977-91; instrn. rep. elem. curriculum Dist. I, Pitts., 1986-92; arts curriculum project Pa. Dept. Edn., 1988; level one basic Orff tchr. U. Wis.-Milw., 2002, U. South Fla., 2002, U. Fla., Gainesville, 2003. Author: (plays) The Rainbow Recorder, 1988, The Gift Disk Dilemma, 1989; composer, author: (play) Pittsburgh-The City with a Smile on Her Face, 1986, (holiday musical) The Dove That Could Not Fly, 1986, (book) Seasons in Song, 1987, (play) The Search for Happiness, 1990; composer: What Color Was the Baby, 1990, Kaia, 1990, Sing Praises To His Name, 1990, Go In Peace, 1990, Sing Unto The Lord, 1990, Simple Gift, 1991, I Love America, 1992, The Cost Is Correct Caper, 1993, The Adventures of Arffie, 1997, The Greatest Snow on Earth, 1997, A Second Grade "Informance", 1998, Stopping by Woods, 1999, A Play-Party Play-in, 1999, Give Thanks, 1999. Actor North Star Players, Pitts., 1975-80; soloist Landmark Bapt. Ch., Penn Hills, Pa., 1981-86, Bible Bapt. Ch., 1987; performer Pitts. Camerata, 1977-89; group leader Pitts Recorder Soc., 1985-86; soloist Grace Bapt. Ch., Monroeville, 1991— Willamette Master Chorus, 2002—. Recipient Citation of Excellence award Pa. Dept. Edn., 1996. Mem. NEA, Am. ORFF-Schulwerk Assn., Pitts. Golden Triangle Chpt. (pres. 1985—), Music Educators Nat. Confl., Pa. Music Educators Assn. (elem. jour. 1986—), Am. Recorder Assn., Pi Kappa Lambda. Baptist. Avocations: cake decorating, bargello, needlework, swimming, folk dancing. Office: Peripole-Bergerault Inc PO Box 12909 Salem OR 97309 Home: 2494 Percheron Ct SE Salem OR 97301-6273

MARSHALL, CAROL JOYCE, clinical project director; b. Mt. Holly, N.J., July 29, 1967; d. Oliver Jr. and Ruby Jean (Bennefield-Smith) M. BA in Biol. Scis., Rutgers U., 1985-89. Transplant-procurement coord. Nat. Disease Rsch. Interchange, Phila., 1989-90, supr. procurement dept., 1990-91, rsch. mgr., 1991-92; clin. rsch. data coord. U.S. Biosci., West Conshohocken, Pa., 1992-93; clin. rsch. project mgr. Covance, Inc., Princeton, N.J., 1993—. Avocations: piano, flute, calligraphy, swimming. Home: 54 Chapel Hill Rd Mount Laurel NJ 08054 Office: Covance Inc 210 Carnegie Ctr Princeton NJ 08540-6233

MARSHALL, CAROLYN ANN M. church official; b. Springfield, Ill., July 18, 1935; d. Hayward Thomas and Isabelle Bernice (Hayer) McMurray; m. John Alan Marshall, July 14, 1956 (dec. Sept. 1990); children: Margaret Marshall Bushman, Cynthia Marshall Kyrouac, Clinton, Carol Bentler. Student, De Pauw U., 1952-54; BSBA, Drake U., 1956; D of Pub. Svc. (hon.), De Pauw U., 1983; LHD (hon.), U. Indpls., 1990. Corp. sec. Marshall Studios, Inc., Veedersburg, Ind., 1956-89, exec. cons., 1989-93; sec. Gen. Conf., lay leader South Ind. conf. United Meth. Ch., Veedersburg, Ind., 1988-96; exec. dir. Lucille Raines Residence, Inc., Indianapolis, 1996—. Carolyn M. Marshall chair in women studies Bennett Coll., Greensboro, N.C., 1988; fin. cons. Lucille Raines Residence, Inpls., 1977-95. Pres. Fountain Ctrl. Band Boosters, Veedersburg, 1975-77; del. Gen. Conf., United Meth. Ch., 1980, 84, 88, 92, 96, 2000, pres. women's divsn. gen. bd. global ministries, 1984-88; bd. dirs. Franklin (Ind.) United Meth. Ch. Mem. United Meth. Ch. Home: 204 N Newlin St Veedersburg IN 47987-1358 Office: Lucille Raines Residence Inc 947 N Pennsylvania St Indianapolis IN 46204-1070 E-mail: cmarshall@sprintmail.com.

MARSHALL, CONSUELO BLAND, federal judge; b. Knoxville, Tenn., Sept. 28, 1936; d. Clyde Theodore and Annie (Brown) Arnold; m. George Edward Marshall, Aug. 30, 1959; children: Michael Edward, Laurie Ann. AA, L.A. City Coll., 1956; BA, Howard U., 1958, LLB, 1961. Bar: Calif. 1962. Dep. atty., City of L.A., 1962-67; assoc. Cochran & Atkins, L.A., 1968-70; commr. L.A. Superior Ct., 1971-76; judge Inglewood Mcpl. Ct., 1976-77, L.A. Superior Ct., 1977-80, U.S. Dist. Ct. Central Dist. Calif., L.A., 1980—. Lectr. U.S. Information Agy. in Yugoslavia, Greece and Italy, 1984, in Nigera and Ghana, 1991, in Ghana, 1992. Contbr. articles to profl. jours.; notes editor Law Jour. Howard U. Mem. adv. bd. Richstone Child Abuse Center. Recipient Judicial Excellence award Criminal Cts. Bar Assn., 1992, Ernestine Stalhut award; named Criminal Ct. Judge of Yr., U.S. Dist. Ct., 1997; inducted into Langston Hall of Fame, 2000; rsch. fellow Howard U. Law Sch., 1959-60. Mem. State Bar Calif., Century City Bar Assn., Calif. Women Lawyers Assn., Calif. Assn. Black Lawyers, Calif. Judges Assn., Black Women Lawyers Assn., Los Angeles County Bar Assn., Nat. Assn. Women Judges, NAACP, Urban League, Beta Phi Sigma. Office: US Dist Ct 312 N Spring St Los Angeles CA 90012-4701

MARSHALL, CORA MARIA, art educator, artist, researcher; b. Washington, Nov. 7, 1947; BFA, Howard U., Washington, 1971; MA in Edn., Bank St. Coll. of Edn. - Parsons Sch. of Design, N.Y.C., 1993; ArtsD, N.Y. U., N.Y.C., 1997. Assoc. prof., art edn. Ctrl. Conn. State U., New Britain, Conn., 1996—; curriculum and staff devel. specialist Alexandria City Pub. Schools, Va., 1971—98, tchr., 1971—98. Rschr. Ctrl. Conn. State U., New Britain, Conn., 1998. Exhibitions, Myths, Magic, and Meaning (Faculty Rsch. Grant, 2003). Mem. Greater New Britain (Conn.) Arts Alliance, 2003—. Recipient The Ednl. Opportunity Citation for Outstanding Contbn., Hartford Pub. Access TV, 2002, Award of Excellence in Edn., Alexandria Va. City Bd. of Edn., 1993, Excellence in Tchg. Award, Alexandria Va. C. of C., 1993, Outstanding Educator, The Gov.'s Sch. for the Humanities and the Visual and Performing Arts, 1993, Innovation in Practice, Nat. Found. for the Improvement of Edn. - Nat. Art Edn. Assn., 1990. Fellow: N.Y. U. (Grad. and Profl. Opportunity Fellowship 1995); mem.: Entitled: Black Women Artists (sec. 2001—0.), Nat. Assn. of African and Native Am. Studies, Nat. Art Edn. Assn., Kappa Delta Pi. Achievements include research in African and Native American Women Artists. Office: Ctrl Conn State U 1615 Stanley Street New Britain CT 06050 E-mail: marshallc@ccsu.edu.

MARSHALL, DALE ROGERS, academic administrator, political scientist, educator; b. Mar. 22, 1937; m. Donald J. Marshall; children: Jessica, Cynthia, Clayton. BA in Govt., Cornell U., 1959; MA in Polit. Sci., U. Calif., Berkeley, 1960; PhD in Polit. Sci. with distinction, UCLA, 1969. Lectr. in polit. sci. UCLA, 1969-70, U. Calif., Berkeley, 1970-72, from asst. prof. to prof. Davis, 1972-86, faculty asst. to vice chancellor acad. affairs, 1980-82, assoc. dean Coll. Letters and Scis., 1983-86; acting pres. Wellesley (Mass.) Coll., 1987-88, dean of coll., prof. polit. sci., 1986-92; pres. Wheaton (Mass.) Coll., 1992—. Mem. exec. bd. Calif. Assembly Fellowship Program, 1980-86; bd. trustees, bd. overseers Newton-Wellesley Hosp., 1989-93; bd. trustees Cornell U., Ithaca, N.Y., 1983-93, chair Cornell Fund, co-chair Coll. Arts and Scis. Capital Campaign, 1990-93; bd. trustees New Eng. Zenith Fund, New Eng. Mut. Life Ins. Co., 1995—; bd. dirs. Am. Student Assistance Guarantor, Am. Student Assistance Corp, 1994-2001. Author: (with John C. Bollens) Guide to Participation: Field Work, Role Playing Cases and Other Forms, 1973, (with Roger Montgomery) Housing Policy for the 80's, 1980, (with Rufus P. Browning and David H. Tabb) Protest is Not Enough: The Struggle of Blacks and Hispanics for Equality in Urban Politics, 1984 (APSA Ralph J. Bunche award for best book on ethnic rels. 1985, Gladys Kammerer award for best book in Am. policy 1985); editor: Urban Policy Making, 1979, (with David K. Leonard) Institutions of Rural Development for the Poor: Decentralization and Organizatonal Linkages, 1982, (with Rufus P. Browning and David H. Tabb, co-editor), Racial Politics in American Cities, 1990, 3d edit., 2003; mem. editl. bd. Am. Polit. Sci. Rev., 1972-76, Pub. Adminstrn. Rev., 1985-86; contbr. articles to profl. jours. Woodrow Wilson fellow, 1959-60, Calif. Regents fellow, 1966-67, 67-68; NSF grantee, 1976-78, 79-80; recipient Disting. Teaching award Significant Contbn. to Status of Women citation Chancellor's Com. on Status of Women at U. Calif. at Davis, 1978. Mem. Am. Polit. Sci. Assn. (mem. exec. coun. 1974-76, v.p. 1985-86, mem. nominating com. 1988-90), Western Polit. Sci. Assn. (mem. exec. coun. 1973-75, pres. 1984-85), Nat. Acad. Pub. Adminstrn., Nat. Assn. Ind. Colls. and Univs. (bd. dirs.), Assn. Ind. Colls. and Univs. Mass. (exec. com.), Mortar Bd., Phi Beta Kappa, Phi Kappa Phi. Office: Wheaton Coll Office of Pres Norton MA 02766 E-mail: dmarshal@wheatonma.edu.

MARSHALL, ELAINE FOLK, state official; b. Lineboro, Md., Nov. 18, 1945; d. Donald and Pauline Folk; m. Sol Marshall; 3 stepchildren. BS in Textiles and Clothing, U. Md., 1968; JD, Campbell U., 1981. Bar: N.C., U.S. Dist. Ct. (ea. and mid. dists.), U.S. Ct. Appeals (4th cir.), U.S. Supreme Ct. Owner retail bus., 1968-79; assoc. Bain Law Firm, Lillington, N.C., 1981-84; ptnr. Bain & Marshall, Lillington, 1985-92, Marshall & Marshall, Lillington, 1993-96; sec.of state State of N.C., 1997-. Legal advisor Bus. and Profl. Women, N.C., 1982-90; mem. 15th dist. N.C. Senate, 1993-94, N.C. Planning Comm., 1993-94, N.C. Cts. Commn., 1993-94. Bd. dirs. Harnett County United Way, 1987-97, N.C. 4-H Devel. Fund, Inc., 1990—, N.C. Rural Econ. Devel. Fund, 1993-95, N.C. Bd. Econ. Devel., 1993-94, 97—, N.C. Ctr. Pub. Policy Rsch., 1994—, N.C. Justice Acad. Found., 1994—; mem. Divine St. United Meth. Ch.; founding chmn., hon. chmn. Harnett HelpNet Children, 1992—; trustee Meredith Coll., 1997—. Recipient N.C. Friends Ext. award, 1992. Fellow N.C. Inst. Polit. Leadership (bd. dirs. 1996—); mem. Women's Forum N.C. Democrat. Office: Office Sec State 300 N Salisbury St Raleigh NC 27603-5925 Mailing: PO Box 29622 Raleigh NC 27626-0622*

MARSHALL, ELIZABETH, performing company executive; b. Elkins, W.Va., Sept. 5, 1966; d. Hollis Carl and Adrienne (Semones) Vance; m. Scott Marshall, June 20, 0198 (div. Mar. 1996); 1 child, Sarah Elizabeth. BA in Music Edn., Fairmont State Coll., 1989; MA in Music Edn., Duquesne U., 2002. Band dir. East Preston H.S., Terra Alta, W.Va., 1989—90; def. contractor Advanced Engring. Planning Corp., Rockville, Md., 1990—91; music instr. Frederick (Md.) County Bd. Edn., 1991—93; choral dir. Randolph County Bd. Edn., Elkins, 1994—. Adj. instr. Fairmont State Coll., Elkins, 2002—; W.Va. exec. bd. Music Educators Nat. Conf., 2000—; writing team content stds. W.Va. State Dept. Edn., 2002; all state choir chair W.Va. Music Educators, 2002—. Choral dir. First Bapt. Ch., Elkins, 1996—. Mem.: Phi Mu, Kappa Kappa Psi. Democrat. Baptist. Avocations: walking, travel, gardening. Home: 1016 S Kerens Elkins WV 26241

MARSHALL, ELIZABETH ANNETTE, auditor; b. Ft. Worth, Dec. 22, 1962; d. Joe Donald and Gail Annette Marshall. B of Bus. Adminstrn., Stetson U., 1986. CPA, Fla. Sr. pub. accts. auditor Auditor Gen., Tallahassee, Fla., 1987—. Mem. G.F.W.C. Tallahassee Jr. Woman's Club, 1988—, custodian of files, 1992, treas., 1993; mem. Tallahassee Winds Cmty. Band. Mem.: St. Andrews Soc., Daus. Am. Colonists, U.S. Daus. of 1812, Nat. Huguenot Soc., Fla. Inst. CPAs, DAR (chpt. regent 1997—99, Fla. rec. sec. 1999—2001), AICPA, UDC, Scottish Gaines Coun., Alpha Kappa Psi. Democrat. Presbyterian. Avocations: genealogy, cooking, travel, music (flute). Office: Auditor Gen 111 W Madison St Tallahassee FL 32399-1450 Home: 2413 McWest St Tallahassee FL 32303-7119

MARSHALL, ELLEN RUTH, lawyer; b. N.Y.C., Apr. 23, 1949; d. Louis and Faith (Gladstone) M. AB, Yale U., 1971; JD, Harvard U., 1974. Bar: Calif. 1975, D.C. 1981, N.Y. 1989. Assoc. McKenna & Fitting, LA, 1975-80; ptnr. McKenna, Conner & Cuneo, LA and Orange County, Calif., 1980-88, Morrison & Foerster, LLP, Orange County, 1988—2003, Manatt, Phelps & Phillips LLP, Orange County, 2003—. Mem. ABA (bus. law sect., mem. savs. inst. com., mem. asset securitization com., tax sect., mem. employee benefits com.), Orange County Bar Assn., Center Club (Costa Mesa, Calif.), Yale Club (N.Y.C.). Office: Manatt Phelps & Phillips LLP 695 Town Ctr Dr Costa Mesa CA 92626

MARSHALL, JANE PRETZER, newspaper editor; b. Chase County, Kans. married; 2 children. BS in Home Econs. and Journalism, Kans. State U., 1967; student, Tex. A&M, U. Mo., Tex. Christian U., Brite Divinity Sch. Asst. editor dept. agr. info. Tex. Agrl. Ext. Sta. Tex. A&M U., College Station, 1967-70; staff writer Gazette-Telegraph, Colorado Springs, Colo., 1970-72; editor corporate publ. Colorado Interstate, Colorado Springs, 1972-75; co-editor The Pampa (Tex.) News, 1975-78; exec. features editor Ft. Worth Star-Telegram, 1978-84; features editor Denver Post, 1984-88, Houston Chronicle, 1988—. Author: (children's book) Going for the Gold: Hakeem Olajuwon, 1996. Recipient 1st place for feature writing Tex. AP Mng. Editors Assn., 1978. Mem. Am. Assn. Sunday and Features Editors (bd. dirs., founding chairperson Features First), Women's Fund Health Edn. and Rsch. (bd. dirs.), Journalism and Women Symposium (1st pres.). Office: Houston Chronicle 801 Texas St Houston TX 77002-2996

MARSHALL, JEAN MCELROY, physiologist; b. Chambersburg, Pa., Dec. 31, 1922; d. Frank Lester and Florence (McElroy) M. AB, Wilson Coll., 1944; MA, Mt. Holyoke Coll., 1946; PhD, U. Rochester, 1951. Instr. Johns Hopkins U. Med. Sch., Balt., 1951-56, asst. prof., 1956-60; research postdoctoral fellow Oxford (Eng.) U., 1954-55; asst. prof. Harvard U. Med. Sch., Boston, 1960-66; asso. prof. physiology Brown U., Providence, 1966-69, prof., 1969-88, prof. emerita, 1988, E. Brintzenhof Prof. Med. Sci., 1987—; rsch. prof. medicine R.I. Hosp., 1988—2000; rsch. cons. C.V. Rsch. Inst., Boston Med. Ctr., 2000—02. Mem. physiology study sect. NIH, 1967-71, mem. tng. com. engring. in biology and medicine, 1971-74, mem. tng. com. lab. medicine, 1976-77; physiol. test com. Nat. Bd. Med. Examiners, 1972-76, neurobiology adv. com., 1977-80 Editor: The Initiation of Labor, 1964; mem. editorial bd. Jour. Pharmacology and Exptl. Therapeutics, 1963-69, Am. Jour. Physiology, 1969-73, Circulation Research, 1973-81; contbr. articles to profl. jours. Mem. Am. Physiol. Soc., Am. Pharmacol. Soc., N.Y. Acad. Scis., Soc. Reproductive Biology, Soc. Gen. Physiologists, Phi Beta Kappa, Sigma Xi. Home: 14 Aberdeen Rd Weston MA 02493-1733

MARSHALL, JO TAYLOR, social worker; b. N.Y.C. BA, Sarah Lawrence Coll., 1957; MSW, Columbia U., 1959. Cert. social worker, N.Y.; clin. diplomate. Caseworker Youth Cons. Svcs., 1960-62; program cons. Social Work Recruiting Ctr., 1962-63; casework supr. Louise Wise Svcs., 1963-68; faculty field instr. sch. social work Columbia U., N.Y.C., 1968-70; coord. social work vol. and student tng. programs St. Lukes/Roosevelt Hosp. Ctr., 1970-75; asst. dir. fieldwork, faculty lectr. in health care Columbia U., N.Y.C., 1975-78; dir. social work and psychiat. emergency svcs. Morristown Meml. Hosp., 1978—95; social worker pvt. practice, 1995—2002; ret., 2002. Adj. prof. Columbia U.; adv. bd., faculty Nat. Discharge Planning Inst. SUNY, Buffalo; prin. speaker, cons. Hosp. Assn. Pa., 1983, Mid-Atlantic Health Congress, 1985, VA, East Orange, N.J., 1986, Hosp. Assn. Tenn., 1987; adv. com. Rutgers GGrad. Sch. Social Work; mem. multidisciplinary state rev. com. for discharge planning standards in N.J. Contbr. articles to profl. jours.; produced and cons. on numerous film and TV prodns. The New Welcome Ter. at Columbia grad. sch. of social work is being named in her honor. Mem. NASW, Soc. Hosp. Social Wk. Dirs. (exec. bd., pres. N.J. chpt. 1988-89, chmn. nat. media task force). Address: 1230 Hillsboro Mile Hillsboro Beach FL 33062-1344 also: PO Box 40 Far Hills NJ 07931-0040

MARSHALL, JOAN See HELPERN, JOAN

MARSHALL, JOSIE, secondary school educator; b. American, Idaho, Dec. 26, 1942; BS, MS in Edn., U. Idaho. Nat. bd. cert. tchr. 1999. Tchr. Sacajawea Jr. H.S., Lewiston, Idaho. Recipient Idaho Middle Sch. Tchr. of the Yr. award, 1997—98; Tom Wright fellow. Mem.: Idaho Edn. Assn. (bd. mem.), Nat. Bd. for Profl. Tchg. Stds. (bd. mem.). Office: Sacajawea Jr HS 3610 12th St Lewiston ID 83501

MARSHALL, KAROLYN MARGARET, private school educator; b. Silver Spring, Md., Apr. 26, 1965; d. Kenneth Anthony Marshall, Sr. and Frances Elaine Marshall. BA in Econs., U. Md., College Park, 1988. Fin. counselor Consumer Credit Counseling Svc., San Antonio, 1990—92; tchr. Village Pky. Christian Sch., San Antonio, 1993—95, New Life Christian Acad., San Antonio, 1995—2001; cashier Wal-Mart Supercenter, San Antonio, 2000—02; pres. Proverbial Consultants, San Antonio, 1997—. Com. mem. Bellamy for U.S. Congress 2004, San Antonio, 2002—. Recipient Mentoring/Protege Program award, City Pub. Svc., San Antonio, 2002. Republican. Avocations: reading, teaching, church, journal writing, real estate. Office: Proverbial Consultants PO Box 760752 San Antonio TX 78245

MARSHALL, KATHLEEN, choreographer, theater director, theater producer; Mem. exec. bd. Soc. Stage Dirs. and Choreographers. Asst. choreographer (Broadway plays) Kiss of the Spider Woman, 1993—95, She Loves Me, 1993—94, Damn Yankees, 1994—95, choreographer Swinging on a Star, 1996, Victor/Victoria, 1995—97, 1776, 1997—98, Ring Round the Moon, 1999, Kiss Me, Kate, 1999—2001 (Tony nominee best choreography, 2001, Laurence Olivier nominee best choreography, 2002), Seussical, 2000—01, Follies, 2001, Little Shop of Horrors, 2003; dir.: (Broadway plays) Wonderful Town, 2003 (Tony nominee best dir. musical, 2004); choreographer (Broadway plays) Wonderful Town, 2003 (Tony nominee best choreography, 2004), (TV films) The Music Man, 2003. Office: Al Hirschfeld Theatre 302 W 45th St New York NY 10036*

MARSHALL, KATHRYN SUE, lawyer; b. Decatur, Ill., Sept. 12, 1942; d. Edward Elda and Frances M. (Minor) Lahniers; m. Robert S. Marshall, Sept. 5, 1964 (div. Apr. 1984); m. Robert J. Arndt, June 25, 1988 (dec. 1999); children: Stephen Edward, Christine Elizabeth. BA, Lake Forest Coll., 1964; JD, John Marshall Law Sch., Chgo., 1976. Intern U.S. Atty.'s Office, Chgo., 1974-76; mng. ptnr. Marshall and Marshall Ltd., Waukegan, Ill., 1976-84; pvt. practice Waukegan, 1984-93, Preemptive Solutions, Wash. Contbr. articles to profl. jours. Cert. jud. candidate Dem. party, Lake County, Ill.; mem. Camerata Soc., Lake Forest; bd. mem., v.p. Lake Forest (Ill.) Fine Arts Ensemble; bd. dirs. Island Hosp. Health Found.; mem. steering com. Equal Justice Coalition. Fellow: ABA (gov. 1993—96), Coll. Law Practice Mgmt., Ill. Bar Assn.; mem.: Navy League (life). Avocations: boating, reading, travel.

MARSHALL, LINDA LANTOW, pediatrics nurse; b. Tulsa, Dec. 13, 1949; d. Lawrence Lee and Lena Mae (Ross) Lantow; m. David Panke Hartson, Aug. 25, 1970 (div. 1982); children: Michael David, Jonathan Lee; m. Roger Nathan Marshall, Dec. 11, 1985; 1 child, Sarabeth Megan. A. U. Okla., 1970; BSN, U. Tulsa, 1983. Cert. pediatric nurse, 1995. Pediats. nurse Youthcare, Claremore, Okla., 1983-85, 87-98; staff nurse ICU Doctors Hosp., Tulsa, 1985-87; sch. nurse Wilson Tulsa Pub. Schs., 1998—. Bd. dirs. PTA Barnard, Tulsa, 1993-95; leader Brownie troop Girl Scouts U.S., Tulsa, 1994-95, leader jr. scouts, 1995—. Mem. Sigma Theta Tau. Avocation: gardening. Home: 2628 E 22nd St Tulsa OK 74114-3123 Office: Wilson Middle Sch 1127 S Columbia Ave Tulsa OK 74104-3928

MARSHALL, MARGARET HILARY, state supreme court chief justice; b. Newcastle, Natal, South Africa, Sept. 1, 1944; came to U.S., 1968; d. Bernard Charles and Hilary A.D. (Anderton) M; m. Samuel Shapiro, Dec. 14, 1968 (div. Apr. 1982); m. Anthony Lewis, Sept. 23, 1984. BA,

Witwatersrand U., Johannesburg, 1966; MEd, Harvard U., 1969; JD, Yale U., 1976; LHD (hon.), Regis Coll., 1993. Bar: Mass. 1977, U.S. Dist. Ct. Mass., U.S. Dist. Ct. N.H., U.S. Dist. Ct. D.C., U.S. Dist. Ct. (ea. dist.) Mich., U.S. Tax Ct., U.S. Ct. Appeals (1st, 11th and D.C. cirs.), U.S. Supreme Ct. Assoc. Csaplar & Bok, Boston, 1976-83, ptnr., 1983-89, Choate, Hall & Stewart, Boston, 1989-92; v.p., gen. counsel Harvard U., Cambridge, Mass., 1992-96; justice Supreme Jud. Ct. Commonwealth Mass., 1996-99, chief justice, 1999—. Mem. jud. nominating coun., 1987-90, 92; chairperson ct. rules subcom. Alternative Dispute Resolution Working Group, 1985-87; mem. fed. appts. commn., 1993; mem. adv. com. Supreme Judicial Ct., 1989-92, mem. gender equality com., 1989-94; mem. civil justice adv. group U.S. Dist. Ct. Mass., 1991-93; spl. counsel Jud. Conduct Commn., 1988-92; trustee Mass. Continuing Legal Edn., Inc., 1990-92. Trustee Regis Coll., 1993-95; bd. dirs. Internat. Design Conf., Aspen, 1986-92, Boston Mcpl. Res. Bur., 1990-94, Supreme Judicial Ct. Hist. Soc., 1990-94, sec., 1990-94. Fellow Am. Bar Found. (Mass. state chair); mem. Boston Bar Assn. (treas. 1988-89, v.p. 1989-90, pres.-elect 1990-91, pres. 1991-92), Internat. Women's Forum, Mass. Women's Forum, Boston Club, Phi Beta Kappa (hon.). Office: 1 Beacon St 3rd Floor Boston MA 02108*

MARSHALL, MARY JONES, civic worker; b. Billings, Mont.; d. Leroy Nathaniel and Janet (Currie) Dailey; m. Harvey Bradley Jones, Nov. 15, 1952 (dec. 1989); children: Dailey, Janet Currie, Ellis Bradley; m. Boyd T. Marshall, June 27, 1990. Student, Carleton Coll., 1943-44, U. Mont., 1944-46, UCLA, 1959. Owner Mary Jones Interiors. Founder, treas. Jr. Art Council, L.A. County Mus., 1953-55, v.p., 1955-56; mem. costume council Pasadena (Calif.) Philharm.; co-founder Art Rental Gallery, 1953, chmn. art and architecture tour, 1955; founding mem., sec. Art Alliance, Pasadena Art Mus., 1955-56; benefit chmn. Pasadena Girls Club, 1959, bd. dirs., 1958-60; chmn. L.A. Tennis Patron's Assn. Benefit, 1965; sustaining Jr. League Pasadena; mem. docent council L.A. County Mus.; mem. costume council L.A. County Mus. Art., program chmn. 20th Century Greatest Designers; mem. blue ribbon com. L.A. Music Ctr.; benefit chmn. Venice com. Internat. Fund for Monuments, 1971; bd. dirs. Art Ctr. 100, Pasadena, 1988—; pres. The Pres.'s L.A. Children's Bur., 1989; co-chmn. benefit Harvard Coll. Scholarship Fund, 1974, steering com. benefit, 1987, Otis Art Inst., 1975, 90th Anniversary of Children's Bureau of L.A., 1994; mem. Harvard Radcliffe scholarship dinner com., 1985; mem. adv. bd. Estelle Doheny Eye Found., 1976, chmn. benefit, 1980; adv. bd. Loyola U. Sch. Fine Arts, L.A., Art Ctr. Sch. Design, Pasadena, Calif., 1987—; patron chmn. Benefit Achievement Rewards for Coll. Scientists, 1988; chmn. com. Sch. Am. Ballet Benefit, 1988, N.Y.C.; bd. dirs. Founders Music Ctr., L.A., 1977-81; mem. nat. adv. council Sch. Am. Ballet, N.Y.C., nat. co-chmn. gala, 1980; adv. council on fine arts Loyola-Marymount U.; mem. L.A. Olympic Com., 1984, The Colleagues; founding mem. Mus. Contemporary Art, 1986; chmn. The Pres.'s Benefit L.A. Children's Bur., 1990; exec. com. L.A. Alive for L.A. Music Ctr., 1992; mem. exec. com. Children's Bur. of L.A. Found., 1992; chmn. award dinner Phoenix House, 1994, 96; bd. dirs. Andrews Sch. Gerontology, U. So. Calif., 1996—, Leakey Found., 1996—; bd. regents Children's Hosp. L.A., 1996—. Mem. Am. Parkinson Disease Assn. (steering com. 1991), Valley Hunt Club (Pasadena), Calif. Club (L.A.), Kappa Alpha Theta. Home: 10375 Wilshire Blvd Ste 8B Los Angeles CA 90024-4712

MARSHALL, MARYANN CHORBA, office administrator; b. Scranton, Pa., Apr. 18, 1952; d. Edward M. and Mildred (Polc) Chorba; m. Daniel V. Marshall III. BA, Emmanuel Coll., 1974. Personal, social sec. Jordan Embassy Mil. Office, Washington, 1974-76; exec. asst, office mgr. Jordan Embassy Info. Bur., Washington, 1976-81; asst. to pres. Nat. Press Club, Washington, 1982-91; adminstr. Harvard Bus. Sch. Club, Washington, 1995-96; co-coord. frontiers in clin. genetics lecture series George Washington U. Med. Ctr., Washington, 1999-2000; exec. sec. The Gridiron Club, Washington, 2001—. Mem. League Rep. Women. Republican. Roman Catholic. Office: The Gridiron Club Capital Hilton Hotel 1001 16th St NW Washington DC 20036 Home: Watergate South # 805 700 New Hampshire Ave NW Washington DC 20037 E-mail: MAMarshall@verizon.net

MARSHALL, NATALIE JUNEMANN, economics educator; b. Milw., June 13, 1929; d. Harold E. and Myrtle (Findlay) Junemann; m. Howard D. Marshall, Aug. 7, 1954 (dec. 1972); children: Frederick S., Alison B.; m. Phillip Shatz, May 27, 1988. AB, Vassar Coll., 1951; MA, Columbia U., 1952, PhD, 1963, JD, 1994. Instr. Vassar Coll., Poughkeepsie, N.Y., 1952-54, 59, 59-60, 63, dean studies, prof. econs., 1973-75, v.p. for student affairs, 1975-80, v.p. for adminstrn. and student services and prof. econs., 1980-91, prof. econs., 1991-94; teaching fellow Wesleyan U., Middletown, Conn., 1955-56; from asst. prof. to prof. SUNY, New Paltz, 1964-73; prof. econs. Vassar Coll., Poughkeepsie, N.Y., 1973-94; of counsel Donoghue, Thomas, Auslander & Drohan, Hopewell Junction, N.Y., 1997—. Editor: (with Howard Marshall) The History of Economic Thought, 1968; Keynes, Updated or Outdated, 1970; author: (with Howard Marshall) Collective Bargaining, 1971. Trustee St. Francis Hosp., 1979-88, Area Fund Dutchess County, 1981-87, Coll. New Rochelle, 1994-2000, Hudson Valley Philharm., 1985-92, pres., 1989-91. Mem. AAUP, Am. Assn. Higher Edn., Am. Econ. Assn., AAUW (v.p. N.Y. State div. 1964-66), Poughkeepsie Vassar Club (pres. 1965-67). Home: 157 Skidmore Rd Pleasant Valley NY 12569-5001 E-mail: Natalie_Marshall@vh.net.

MARSHALL, NAVARRE, retired secondary school educator; b. Stockton, Calif., Oct. 31, 1916; d. Winfield Scott and Elizabeth (Brophy) Baggett; m. Robert Frank Marshall, Aug. 10, 1947; 1 child, Roberta Navarre Marshall. BA, San Francisco State U., 1937; postgrad., U. Calif., Berkeley, 1945-47, U. Calif., Santa Cruz, 1970-72. Cert. elem.-jr. high tchr. Tchr. Pittsburg (Calif.) Sch. Dist., 1937-40, Martinez (Calif.) Sch. Dist., 1941-49, Pajaro Valley Sch. Dist., Watsonville, Calif., 1958-76; ret., 1976. Sec., sponsor Watsonville Friends of the Libr.; mem. Pajaro Valley Arts Coun., 1994, Pajaro Valley Hist. Assn. Mem. AAUW (sec. 1963-64, pres. Watsonville br. 1992-93, sec. 1994-95, publicity chair 1995-97), Calif. Tchrs. Assn., Order Ea. Star, Delta Kappa Gamma (charter pres. 1961-62), Libr. of Congress (nat. mem. 1995), Nat. Trust for Historic Preservation, Internat. Zeta Epsilon (charter pres. 1961-62, chpt. pres. 1986-88, scholarship chair 1984-86, 88-90, Woman Making History award 1994), Nat. Steinbeck Ctr. Democrat. Avocations: reading, bridge, travel.

MARSHALL, PENNY (C. MARSHALL), director, actress; b. N.Y.C., Oct. 15, 1943; d. Anthony W. and Marjorie Irene (Ward) M.; m. Michael Henry (div.); 1 child, Tracy Lee; m. Robert Reiner, Apr. 10, 1971 (div. 1979). Student, U. N.Mex., 1961-64. Appeared on numerous television shows, including The Odd Couple, 1972-74, Friends and Lovers (co-star), 1974, Let's Switch, 1974, Wives (pilot), 1975, Chico and the Man, 1975, Mary Tyler Moore, 1975, Heaven Help Us, 1975, Saturday Night Live, 1975-77, Happy Days, 1975, Battle of Network Stars (ABC special), 1976, Barry Manilow special, 1976, The Tonight Show, 1976-77, Dinah, 1976-77, Mike Douglas Show, 1975-77, Merv Griffin Show, 1976-77, Blansky's Beauties, 1977, Network Battle of the Sexes, 1977, Laverne and Shirley (co-star), 1976-83; TV films More Than Friends, 1978, Love Thy Neighbor, 1984, Challenge of a Lifetime, 1985, The Odd Couple: Together Again, 1993; guest appearances include Mary Tyler Moore, 1975, Happy Days, 1975, Chico and the Man, 1975, Mork & Mindy, 1978, Bosom Buddies, 1982, Taxi, 1983, The Simpsons (voice), 1990, Frasier, 2004, I'm With Her, 2004; appeared in motion pictures How Sweet It Is, 1967, The Savage Seven, 1968, The Grasshopper, 1970, 1941, 1979, Movers and Shakers, 1985, She's Having a Baby, 1988, The Hard Way, 1991, Hocus Pocus, 1993, Get Shorty, 1995; dir. films: Jumpin' Jack Flash, 1986, Big, 1988, Awakenings, 1990, A League of Their Own, 1992, Renaissance Man, 1994, The Preacher's Wife, 1996, The Time Tunnel: The Movie, 1999, Special Delivery, 1999, Riding in Cars with Boys, 2001, appeared in TV movie Jackie's Back, 1999; prodr. TV series A League of Their Own, 1993 (also dir. pilot), Dynasties, 2003; prodr. films Getting Away With Murder, 1995, With Friends Like These, 1998, Risk, 2003 Office: c/o William Morris Agy 151 El Camino Dr Beverly Hills CA 90212*

MARSHALL, ROSEMARY, state representative; married; 3 children. Cert. in pub. policy disputes, MIT-Harvard U.; student, U. Colo., Colo. State U. State rep. State of Colo., 2002—, mem. fin. com., mem. judiciary com. Mem.: NAACP, Colo. Bus. Women Profl. Assn. Democrat. Address: 3451 E 26th Ave Denver CO 80203 Office: State Capitol #271 200 E Colfax Ave Denver CO 80203 E-mail: rosemary.marshall.house@state.co.us.

MARSHALL, SARA, b. Greenport, N.Y., June 2, 1950; d. Clarence Richard and Loretta Elizabeth (Stelzer) Bennett; m. Harry J. Marshall, Oct. 12, 1974; children: Loretta Louise, Amy Jean. BSN, SUNY, 1973; MSN, U. Wis., 1979; postgrad., Tulane U., 1984. RN, Fla., N.J., N.Y., Pa., Wis. Commd. 2d. lt. U.S. Army, 1975—, advanced through grades to lt. col., 1992. Bd. dirs., com. chair South Jersey Coun. on AIDS, Haddon Hts., N.J., 1993—; task force Camden County (N.J.) AIDS, 1993—. Vol. Am. Heart Assn., 1995-96; active Am. Legion Aux., 1993—, Ladies Aux. of Elks., 1990—. Mem. Am. Legion, Rep. Club (pres. 1996—). Office: Cooper Hosp 3 Cooper Plz Rm 513 Camden NJ 08103-1438 Home: 825 Bailey Dr Sebastian FL 32958-5301

MARSHALL, SHEILA HERMES, lawyer; b. N.Y.C., Jan. 17, 1934; d. Paul Milton and Julia Angela (Meagher) Hermes; m. James Josiah Marshall, Sept. 30, 1967; 1 child, James J.H. BA, St. John's U., N.Y.C., 1959; JD, NYU, 1963. Bar: N.Y. 1964, U.S. Ct. Appeals (2d, 3d, 5th and D.C. cirs.), U.S. Supreme Ct. 1970. Assoc. LeBoeuf, Lamb, Greene & MacRae, N.Y.C., 1963-72, ptnr., 1973—95, of counsel, 1996—. Specialist in field. Mem. ABA, N.Y. State Bar Assn., Assn. of Bar of City of N.Y. Republican. Home: 325 E 72nd St New York NY 10021 Office: LeBoeuf Lamb Greene & MacRae 125 W 55th St New York NY 10019-5369 Office Phone: 212-424-8000.

MARSHALL, SHERYL, venture capitalist; b. Boston, Dec. 5, 1949; d. Donald Resnick and Ethel (Fatles) Liner; m. Jan A. Marshall, Sept. 9, 1973 (div. Oct. 1982); 1 child, Dana. BA, Emerson Coll., 1972; MBA with distinction, Simmons Coll., 1976. Account exec. Merrill Lynch, Boston, 1977-82; 1st v.p. Drexel Burnham Lambert, Boston, 1982-89, Smith Barney Harris Upham, Boston, 1989-93; v.p. Donaldson, Lufkin, Jenrette, Boston, 1993-99; founding ptnr. Axxon Capital, Boston, 1999—. Investment com. Roxbury (Mass.) C.C., 1987—; guest fin. reporter Fin. News Network, Boston, 1983-86, Sta. WCVB-TV, Needham, Mass., 1979-86; bd. dirs. Fed. Retirement Thrift Savs. Plan, 1995—. Bd. dirs. Wang Ctr. for Arts, Boston, 1977-79, Anti-Defamation League, Boston, 1980-86. Mem. Internat. Women's Forum (bd. dirs. 1988—). Democrat. Jewish. Office: Axxon Capital 28 State St 37th Fl Boston MA 02109

MARSHALL, SIRI SWENSON, lawyer; BA, Harvard U., 1970; JD, Yale U., 1974. Bar: N.Y. 1975. Assoc. Debevoise & Plimpton, 1974-79; atty., sr. atty., asst. gen. counsel Avon Products, Inc., N.Y.C., 1979-85, v.p. legal affairs, 1985-89, sr. v.p., gen. counsel, 1990-94, Gen. Mills, Inc., Mpls., 1994-99, sr. v.p. corp. affairs, gen. counsel, sec., 1999—. Bd. dirs. Jafra Cosmetics, Am. Arbitration Assn. Trustee Mpls. Inst. Arts. Office: Gen Mills Inc Number One Gen Mills Blvd Minneapolis MN 55426

MARSHALL, SUSANNE T. government agency administrator; Student, U. Maryland Branch Campus, Munich, American U. Legislative asst., 1981—82; Republican staff asst. House Govt Operations Comm., 1983—85; Republican staff Comm. on Governmental Affairs, 1985—2002; chmn. Merit Systems Protection Bd., 2002—. Office: US Merit Systems Protection Bd 1615 M Street NW Washington DC 20419

MARSHALL-DANIELS, MERYL, communications executive, mediator; b. L.A., Oct. 16, 1949; d. Jack and Nita Corinblit; m. Raymond Daniels, Aug. 19, 2000. BA, UCLA, 1971; JD, Loyola Marymount U., L.A., 1974. Bar: Calif. 1974. Dep. pub. defender County of L.A., 1975—77; sole practice L.A., 1977—78; ptnr. Markman and Marshall, L.A., 1978—79; sr. atty. NBC, Burbank, Calif., 1979—80, dir. programs, talent contracts bus. affairs, 1980, asst. gen. atty. N.Y.C., 1980—82, v.p., compliance and practices Burbank, 1982; v.p. program affairs Group W Prodns., 1987—89, sr. v.p. future images, 1989—91, TV prodr., Meryl Marshall Prodns., 1991—93; pres. Two Oceans Entertainment Group, 1991—. Chmn., Nat. Women's Polit. Caucus, Westside, Calif., 1978-80; mem. Calif. Dem. Ctrl. Com., 1978-79; mem. Hollywood Women's Polit. Com., 1988; bd. mem. George Foster Peabody Awards. Mem.: Women in Film, Acad. TV Arts and Scis. (treas. 1985, treas. 1993—97, bd. govs. 1989—2001, pres. 1997—99, chmn. bd., CEO 1999—2001). Democrat. Jewish. Office: Two Oceans Entertainment Group 2017 Lemoyne St Los Angeles CA 90026 E-mail: twoceans@aol.com.

MARSHALL-HARDIN, FLOY JEANNE, art school educator; b. Clinton, Oklahoma, July 30, 1949; d. James Edward and Mary Josephine (Mangold) Marshall; m. John Thomas Hardin Jr., June 2, 1992; m. Daniel Paul Ahern; 1 child, Jeanne Danielle Ahern ; m. Randall Lee Martin; 1 child, Mackenzie Jin Martin. BFA, U. Ariz, 1978, MA, 1982. Dir. Fenster Ranch Camp, Tucson, 1988—92, Yuma Sch. Dist., Yuma, Ariz., 1986—88, elem. art edn., 1986—88; art educator Sunnyside HS, Tucson, 1994—95, Oracle (Ariz.) Mid. Sch., Oracle, Ariz., 1996—98; elem. art edn. grades K-12 Knox County Schools, Knoxville, Tenn., 2002—. Exhibtor (fibers) Art Educators Exhibit, 2002—03. Mem. Colonial Williamsburg Found., Williamsburg, Va., 2003—. Mem.: Tenn. Art Educators Assn., Nat. Art Educators Assn., Tenn. Educators Assn., Nat. Educators Assn., Knoxville Mus. of Art, U. Ariz. Alumni Assn. Democrat. Methodist. Avocations: travel, fibers. Home: 109 Sanwood Rd Knoxville TN 37923-5549 Office: Knox County Sch Knoxville TN Office Phone: 865-386-3156. Personal E-mail: MADDIEROSE74@hotmail.com.

MARSI, JANICE MICHAELS, religious organization administrator; b. Buffalo, Feb. 23, 1948; d. Kenneth Vincent and Doris Mary (Cowell) Michaels; m. Frederick Stephen Marsi, May 4, 1973; children: Stephen Michaels, Katherine Michaels. BA, Elmira Coll., 1970; postgrad., U. Pa., 1970—72; MSW, Marywood U., 1978; MDiv summa cum laude, Drew Theol. Sch., 1992. Ordained min. United Meth. Ch., 1995. Caseworker County Dept. Social Svcs., Binghamton, NY, 1974—76; social worker Conf. Children's Home, Binghamton, 1976—78, dir. social svcs., 1978—82; minister First United Meth. Ch., Endicott, NY, 1997—2003; supt. Oneonta dist. Wyo. Annual Conf. United Meth. Ch., Sidney, NY, 2003—. Sec. Coun. Chs. Broome County, Binghamton, 1999—2001. Wheel of Seasons, 1985, Once Around the Sun, 1995; performer: (albums) When I Want to Sing, 2003. Chair bd. dirs. Children's Home Wyo. Conf., Binghamton, NY, 1998—2000; sec. YWCA, Binghamton, 1987—89. Democrat. Methodist. Avocations: travel, gardening, hiking, kayaking, music. Home: 1036 Powderhouse Rd Vestal NY 13850 Office: Office Supt Oneonta Dist PO Box 2159 Sidney NY 13838-2159

MARSTON, BETSY PILAT, newspaper editor; b. N.Y.C., July 6, 1940; d. Oliver and Alice (Riddle) Pilat; m. Ed Marston; children: Wendy, David. BA, U. Del., 1962; MS in Journalism, Columbia U., 1963. Producer WNET-TV, N.Y.C., 1967-74; host KVNF Pub. Radio, Paonia, Colo., 1995-96; editor High Country News, 1983—2002, Writings on the Range syndicate at HCN, 2002—. Democrat. Avocations: hiking, biking, yoga, african dance, reading. Home: PO Box 279 Paonia CO 81428-0279 Office: High Country News PO Box 1090 Paonia CO 81428-1090 Address: HIGH COUNTRY NEWS PO Box 1090 Paonia CO 81428-1090

MARSZALEK, MARILYN, elementary school educator; b. Ridgway, Pa., June 26, 1953; d. Joseph John and Marigrace Sidoni; m. John Joseph Marszalek, July 10, 1976; children: Lisa, Pamela, Kristyn. BS in Music Edn, Edinboro U., 1975. Tchr. 4th gr. Gen. McLane Sch. Dist., Edinboro, Pa., 1988—. Home: 313 Waterford St Edinboro PA 16412

MARTEL, EVA LEONA, accountant; b. Bristol, Conn., Feb. 14, 1945; d. Samuel L. and Irene A. (Beaulieu) Martel. BS in Acctg., N.H. Coll., 1986; MBA, Plymouth State U., 1990. Cert. mgmt. acct.; cert. continuing edn. educator. Accts. payable Elliot Hosp., Manchester, N.H., 1971-79, bookkeeper, 1979-84, dir. acctg., 1984-94; portfolio mgr. Optima Health Inc., Manchester, N.H., 1994-97, mgr. managed care contracting, 1997-98, dir. managed care, 1998-2000; exec. dir. managed care Elliot Hosp., 2000—. Adj. faculty N.H. Coll., 1991—; speaker Daniel Webster coun. Boy Scouts Am., Manchester, 1988, Med. Assts. Workshop, 1997; panel mem. ednl. seminar, 1993. Treas. N.H. Indian Cun., 1980-84; vol. United Way, Manchester, 1988—, accountexec., 1990, 91; mem. adv. coun. health care adminstrn. N.H. Coll., 1990, faculty advisor weekend program, 1990-91; vol. N.H. Heart Assn., 1990-92; bd. dirs. N.H. chpt. Am. Cancer Soc., 1991—; road race com. Elliot Hosp.; mem. scholarship com. Jewett Sch. Recipient Excellence in Tchg. award N.H. Coll., 2000. Mem. NAFE, Hosp. Fin. Mgmt. Assn., Speaker's Bur. (smoke free com., recycling com. 1991), IMA, Healthcare Fin. Mgmt. Assn. Roman Catholic. Avocations: physical fitness, reading, music, writing, teaching. Home: 129 Riverledge Dr Goffstown NH 03045-6203 E-mail: emartel@elliot-hs.org.

MARTEL, LISA, food service executive; Student, Regis Coll.; grad., Johnson and Wales Coll. Culinary Arts, 1986. Line cook then banquet chef The Bay Tower Room; chef Rebecca's, Boston, 150 Wooster St. and Remi, N.Y.C., The Sherry Netherlands Hotel, N.Y.C., 224 Boston St., Boston, 1990; chef, owner On the Park, Boston. Office: On the Park One Union Park Boston MA 02118

MARTENS, BETTY JOAN, music educator, elementary school educator; b. Rochester, Ind., July 14, 1954; d. Russell Dale and Bonnie Jean Walters; m. Mark Edward Martens, June 4, 1977; children: Katie Bess Walters Martens, Sadie Jean Walters Martens. BS, Ind. U., 1977, MS, 1979, MLS, 1996. 2nd grade tchr. Akron (Ind.) Elem. Sch., 1977—87, 1990—91, 6th grade tchr., 1987—90; 1st grade tchr. Columbia Elem. Sch., Rochester, Ind., 1991—92; 6th grade tchr. Rochester Mid. Sch., 1992—98, choral music dir., 1998—. Pres. Tippecanoe Valley Classroom Tchrs. Assn., Mentone, Ind., 1984—85, Mentone, 1986—87, bldg. rep. Active Rochester City Coun., 1979—82; dir. Bells of Grace Handbell Choir. Mem.: NEA, Rochester Classroom Tchrs. Assn., Ind. State Tchrs. Assn. Methodist. Avocation: piano. Home: 2297 W 600 N Rochester IN 46975 Office: Rochester Mid Sch 650 Zebra Ln Rochester IN 46975

MARTENSEN, BARBARA, electronics executive; BS in Math., U. Ariz. With Motorola Semiconductor Products, 1978—99; global info. officer Avnet, Inc., Phoenix, 1999—2001, corp. v.p., sr. v.p. integrated bus. solutions, 2001—. Office: Avnet Inc 2211 S 47th St Phoenix AZ 85034*

MARTH, MARY ELLEN (KIM MARTIN), entertainer; b. Atkinson, Minn., July 15, 1936; d. Sigvard B. Kanikkeberg and Beatrice M. (Lundberg) Wangen; m. T.A. Martinez (div.); m. Luther H. Marth (div.); children: Mitzie, Leslie, Tina, Allen. Entertainer The Kim Martin Show, 1960—. Band leader Kim Martin Show, 1960—; real estate owner Marth Properties, Mpls., 1972—. Author of poems, songs, articles, short stories, childrens books, historian, humanitarian. Sec. Hennepin County Adult Foster Care, Mpls, 1983—; mem. Summit Ministries, Colo, 1995, Columbia Heights Owners Assn., 1990—, Multi-Housing Assn., Mpls, 1993—, Vesterheim Geneal. Mus., 1990, Norwegian Am. Mus., 1988—. Named Queen of Country Music, Country Entertainers Assn., Mpls., 1977, Entertainer of Yr. 1978, Female Vocalist of Yr., 1978, Best Band of Yr., 1979, Songwriter of Yr., 1980. Mem. Winnesheik Geneal. Soc., Filmore County Hist. Soc., Vesterheim Geneal. Soc., Minn. Historical Soc. Lutheran. E-mail: kimtonem@aol.com.

MARTIKAINEN, A(UNE) HELEN, retired health education specialist; b. Harrison, Maine, May 11, 1916; d. Sylvester and Emma (Heikkinen) M. AB, Bates Coll., 1939, DSc (hon.), 1957; MPH, Yale U., 1941; DSc, Harvard U., 1964, Smith Coll., 1969. Health edn. sec. Hartford Tb and Pub. Health Assn., 1941-42; cons. USPHS, 1942—49; chief health edn. WHO, Geneva, 1949—74; chair internat. affairs AAUW-NC, 1986—94, rep. to N.C. Coalition on Aging, 2001—, bd. dirs., 2001—; mem. N.C. Health Adv. Bd. for Aging, 2001—. Hon. trustee Bridgton Acad., North Bridgton, Maine; mem. N.C. Women's Forum, 1984—; bd. dirs. N.C. Ctr. of Laws Affecting Women, Inc.; bd. dirs. West Triangle chpt. UNA-USA; chair residents health and social svcs. com., mem. residents coun., mem. residents com. for cmty. rels. Carol Woods. Recipient Delta Omega award Yale U., Nat. Adminstrv. award Am. Acad. Phys. Edn., Key award Bates Coll., Internat. Svc. award, France, 1953, Prentiss medal, 1956, Spl. medal, cert. for internat. health edn. svc. Nat. Acad. Medicine for France, 1959, Profl. award Soc. Pub. Health Educators, 1963, Benjamin Elijah Mays award Bates Coll. Alumni Assn., 1989, Legacy of Leadership honoree Pines of Carolina coun. Girl Scouts U.S., 2002; named to Hall of Fame, Bridgeton Acad., Maine, 2003. Fellow APHA (chmn. health edn. sect., Excellence award 1969); mem. AAUW, LWV, Women's Internat. League for Peace and Freedom, U.S. Soc. Pub. Health Educators, Internat. Union Health Edn. (Parisot medal, tech. adviser), Acad. Phys. Edn. (assoc.), N.C. Coun. Women's Orgns. (mem. coun. assembly 1988-92, Women of Distinction award 1989), Phi Beta Kappa. Home: 3113 Carol Woods 750 Weaver Dairy Rd Chapel Hill NC 27514-1443

MARTIN, AGNES, artist; b. Maklin, Sask., Can., 1912; arrived in U.S., 1932, naturalized, 1950; Student, Western Wash. State Coll., 1935-38; BS, Columbia U., 1942, MFA, 1952. One-woman shows include Betty Parsons Gallery, N.Y.C., 1958, 1959, 1961, Robert Elkon Gallery, 1961, 1963, 1972, 1976, Nicolas Wilder Gallery, L.A., 1963—66, 1967, Visual Arts Ctr., N.Y.C., 1971, Kunstraum, Munich, 1973, Pace Gallery, N.Y.C., 1975, 1976, 1977, 1978, 1979, 1980—81, 1981, 1983, 1984, 1985, 1986, 1989, 1991, 1992, 1994, 1995, Mayor Gallery, London, 1978, 1984, Galerie Rudolf Zwirner, Cologne, Fed. Republic Germany, 1978, Harcus/Krakow Gallery, Boston, 1978, Margo Leavin Gallery, L.A., 1979, 1985, Mus. N.Mex., Santa Fe, 1979, 1998, Richard Gray Gallery, Chgo., 1981, Garry Anderson Gallery, Sydney, 1986, Waddington Galleries Ltd., London, 1986, Stedelijk Mus., Amsterdam, 1991, Whitney Mus. Am. Art, N.Y.C., 1992, 2000, Wildenstein Gallery, Tokyo, 1993, Serpentine Gallery, London, 1993, Galerie Michael Werner, Cologne, 1994, Pace Wildenstein, N.Y.C., 1995, 1996, 1997, 1998, 2000, 2001, Santa Fe Mus. Fine Arts, 1994, Galerie Daniel Blau, Munich, 1996, Harwood Mus., Taos, N.Mex., 1997, 2002, Galeria 56, Budapest, 1998, Royal Botanic Garden, Edinburgh, Scotland, 1999, Anthony d'Offay Gallery, London, 2001, Menil Collection, Houston, 2002, exhibited in group shows at Carnegie Inst., Pitts., 1961, Whitney Mus. Am. Art, 1962, 1966, 1967, 1974, 1977, 1992, Tooth Gallery, London, 1962, Gallery Modern Art, Washington, 1963, Wadsworth Atheneum, Hartford, Conn., 1963, Solomon R. Guggenheim Mus., N.Y.C., 1965, 1966, 1976, Mead Corp., 1965—67, Mus. Modern Art, N.Y.C., 1967, 1976, 1985, Inst. Contemporary Art, Phila., 1967, Detroit Inst. Art, 1967, Corcoran Gallery Art, Washington, 1967, 1981, Finch Mus., N.Y., 1968, Phila. Mus. Art, 1968, Zurich Art Mus., Switzerland, 1969, Ill. bell Telephone Co., Chgo., 1970, Mus. Contemporary Art, 1971, Inst. Contemporary Art, U. Pa., Phila., 1972, Randolph-Macon Coll., N.C., 1972, Kassel, Fed. Republic Germany, 1972, Stedelijk Mus., Amsterdam, 1975, U. Mass, Amherst, 1976, Venice Biennale, 1976, 1980, Cleve. Mus. Art, 1978, Albright-Knox Gallery, Buffalo, 1978, Inst. Contemporary Art, Boston, 1979, ROSC Internat. Art Exhbn., Dublin, Ireland, 1980, Marilyn Pearl Gallery, N.Y.C.,

1983, Kemper Gallery, Kansas City Art Inst., 1985, Am. Acad. and Inst. Arts and Letters, N.Y.C., 1985, Charles Cowles Gallery, 1986, Moody Gallery Art U. Ala., Birmingham, 1986, Butler Inst. Am. Art, 1986, Art Gallery Western Australia, Perth, 1986, Mus. Contemporary Art, L.A., 1986, Mus. Fine Arts, Boston, 1989, Represented in permanent collections Mus. Modern Art, N.Y.C., Albright Knox Gallery, Aldrich Mus., Ridgefield Conn., Art Gallery Ont., Can., Australian Nat. Gallery, Canberra, Grey Art Gallery and Study Ctr., N.Y.C., Solomn R. Guggenheim Mus., High Mus. Art, Atlanta, Hirshhorn Mus. and Sculpture Garden, Washington, Israel Mus., Jerusalem, La Jolla (Calif.) Mus. Contemporary Art, L.A. County Mus. Art, Mus. Art R.I. Sch. Design, Providence, Mus. Modern Art, Neuegalerie der Stadt, Aachen, Fed. Republic Germany, Norton Simon Mus. Art, Pasadena, Calif., Stedelijk Mus., Amsterdam, Mus. Modern Art, Paris, Tate Gallery, London, Wadsworth Atheneum, Walker Art Ctr., Mpls., Whitney Mus Am. Art, Worcester (mass.) Art Mus., Yale U. Art Gallery, New Haven, Conn.; subject of various articles. Office: 414 Placitas Rd # 37 Taos NM 87571-2513

MARTIN, ALICE HOWZE, prosecutor; b. Memphis, Apr. 25, 1956; BSN, Vanderbilt U., 1978; JD, U. Miss., 1981. Bar: Tenn. 1981, Miss. 1981, Ala. 1989. Asst. U.S. atty. U.S. Attys. Office, Memphis, 1983-89; ptnr. Harris Harris & Martin, Florence, Ala., 1992—94; dist. mcpl. judge City of Florence, Ala., 1993—97; judge Cir. Ct. State of Ala., 1997—99; U.S. Atty. No. Dist. Ala., 2001—. Avocations: travel, skeet shooting.

MARTIN, ALISON CADY, interior designer; b. N.Y.C., May 12, 1949; d. Everett Ware Jr. and Ruth Anne (Payan) Cady; m. Robin Bradley Martin, Jan. 29, 1972 (div. 1979); m. Frederic Bradley Underwood, Oct. 8, 1988 (div. 1999). BA, Middlebury (Vt.) Coll., 1971. Pres. Alison Martin Interiors, Ltd., Washington, 1976—. Sec. Great Falls (Va.) Concert Series, 1983-88, treas., 1988-96. Mem. Colony Club (N.Y.C.). Republican. Episcopalian. Avocation: classical singing. Office: PO Box 949 Berryville VA 22611 E-mail: amiltd@shentel.net.

MARTIN, ANDREA LOUISE, actress, comedienne, writer; b. Portland, Maine, Jan. 15, 1947; Grad., Emerson Coll. Appearances include (plays) Hard Shell, 1980 (off-Broadway debut), Sorrows of Stephen, 1980, What's a Nice Country Like You Doing in a State Like This?, 1974, She Loves Me, My Favorite Year, 1993 (Tony award, Featured Actress in a Musical), (films) Cannibal Girls, 1973, Black Christmas, 1974, Wholly Moses!, 1980, Soup for One, 1982, Club Paradise, 1986, Innerspace, 1987, Martha Ruth and Eddie, 1988, Worth Winning, 1989, Boris and Natasha, 1989, Rude Awakening, 1989, Too Much Sun, 1991, Stepping Out, 1991, All I Want for Christmas, 1991, (voice) The Itsy Bitsy Spider, 1992, Striking Distance, 1993, Bogus, 1996, (voice) Anastasia, 1997, Wag the Dog, 1997, The Rugrats Movie (voice), 1998, Bartok the Magnificent, 1999 (TV) Second City TV, 1977-81, That Thing on ABC, 1978, Torn Between Two Lovers, 1979, The Robert Klein Show, 1981, Kate and Allie, 1982, The Comedy Zone, 1984, Late Night Film Festival, 1985, Second City Twenty-Fifth Anniversary, 1985, Martin Short Concert for the North Americas, 1985, The Smothers Brothers Comedy Hour, 1988, Poison, 1988, The Martin Short Show, 1994, Earthworm Jim, 1995, Life...and Stuff, 1997, Damon, 1998, others; (TV movie) Charles Dickens' David Copperfield, 1993, Gypsy, 1993, In Search of Dr. Seuss, 1994, Harrison Bergeron, 1995; TV host Women of the Night II, 1988, Second City Fifteen Anniversary Special, 1988, Andrea Martin: Together Again, 1989; actress/writer: TV series SCTV Network 90, 1981-83 (2 Emmy awards 1982, 83), TV pilot From Cleveland, 1980; also The Completely Mental Misadventures of Ed Grimley, 1988-90 (voice of Mrs. Freebus).

MARTIN, ANN, newscaster; b. Portland, Oreg. married; 1 child. BA in comm., U. Wash. Anchor, reporter KABC-TV, Los Angeles, 1980—94; anchor KCBS 2, Los Angeles, 1994—, anchor, CBS 2 News at 4 and 6pm, 1997—. Guest host Good Morning America. Mem. Nat. Charity League. Recipient Golden Mike Award for Best 30 min. newscast, 1993. Office: CBS 2 News 6121 Sunset Blvd. Los Angeles CA 90028*

MARTIN, BECKY ROGERS, state representative, realtor; b. Mullins, S.C., July 7, 1950; d. Phillip V. and Inez M. Rogers; m. Johnny Wayne Martin, July 11, 1969; children: Jayne Marie, Mollie Katherine. A, Columbia Jr. Coll., 1969. Realtor; state rep. dist. 8 S.C. Legis., 1997—, mem. edn. and pub. works com., 2d vice-chmn. ops. and mgmt. com. Mem. Center Rock Fire Dept. Bd.; county chmn. United Way; mem. March of Dimes, Clemson Parents Coun., Anderson & Oconee Legis. Del., Women's Caucus, Appalachian Regional Coun. Govts.; pacesetter Stennis Ctr. So. Women Pub. Svc., 1998—2000; mem. Women's Rep. Caucus; 1st vice chair Freshman Caucus. Mem.: SCSEA (state mem. chmn., chpt. pres.), Nat. Found. Women Legislators (state dir. 1998), Women's Profl. Orgn. Women in Govt., Assn. Realtors, S.C. Pub. Health Assn., State Employee's Assn., Women's Golfing Assn., Rotary. Republican. Office: State Capitol 326B Blatt Bldg Columbia SC 29211 Home: 1103 Hunters Trail Anderson SC 29625 E-mail: BRM@scstatehouse.net.

MARTIN, BEVERLY, federal judge; b. Macon, Ga. BA, Stetson U., Deland, Fla., 1976; JD, U. Ga., 1981. Bar: Ga. 1981. Assoc. Martin, Snow, Grant & Napier, Macon, Ga., 1981-84; trial and appellate ct. litigator, sr. asst. atty. gen. and dir. bus. and profl. regulation divsn. Office of Atty. Gen. State of Ga., Macon, 1984-94; asst. U.S. atty. mid. dist. Ga. Macon, 1994-98; U.S. atty. mid. dist. Ga. U.S. Dept. Justice, Macon, 1998-2000; dist. judge U.S. Dist. Ct. for No. Dist. Ga., Atlanta, 2000—. Mem. Ga. Bar Assn., Macon Bar Assn., Am. Judicature Soc., Ga. Assn. Women Lawyers, Lawyers Club of Atlanta. Office: US Dist Ct for No Dist Ga 2388 US Courthouse 75 Spring St SW Atlanta GA 30303

MARTIN, CAROL JACQUELYN, artist, educator; b. Ft. Worth, Tex., Oct. 6, 1943; d. John Warren and Dorothy Lorene (Coffman) Edwards; m. Boe Willis Martin, Oct. 6, 1940; children: Stephanie Diane, Scott Andrew. BA summa cum laude, U. N. Tex., 1965; MA, U. Tex., El Paso, 1967. Tchr. Edgemere Elem. Sch., El Paso, Tex., 1965—66, Fulmore Jr. H.S., Austin, Tex., 1966-67, Monnig Jr. H.S., Ft. Worth, 1967-68, Paschal H.S., Ft. Worth, 1968-69; instr. Tarrant County Jr. Coll., Ft. Worth, 1968-69, 71-72; press sec. U.S. Sen. Gaylord Nelson, Washington, 1969-71; instr. Eastfield CC, Dallas, 1981, Richland CC Dist., 1982; instr. Meml. Student Ctr. UPlus Tex. A&M U., 2002—03. Artist Vt. Studio Cty, 1998. Editor The Avesta Mag., 1964-65; exhibited in group shows at City of Richardson's Cottonwood Park, 1970-86, Students of Ann Cushing Gantz, 1973-85, Art About Town, 1979, 80, shows by Tarrant County and Dallas County art assns. Active Dallas Symphony Orch. League, Easter Seal Soc., Women's Auxiliary of Nexus, Dallas Hist. Soc., Women's Bd. of the Dallas Opera, Dallas Arboretum and Garden Club, Dallas County Heritage Soc., Nat. Mus. Women in Arts. Mem. Internat. Platform Assn., Mortar Bd., Alpha Chi, Sigma Tau Delta, Kappa Delta Pi, Delta Gamma. Democrat. Methodist. Avocations: travel, photography, snow skiing, oil painting. Address: 4055 Sweetwater Dr College Station TX 77845-9650

MARTIN, CAROLINE JUNE, state senator; b. Brownsville, Tex., Feb. 28, 1952; d. W.J. Funkhouser and Lucille Cherry; married. Owner jewelry store; mem. Okla. State Senate, 1994—. Mem. Agr. and Rural Devel., Appropriations, Edn., Sunset Rev., Tourism and Recreation, Transp. coms. Okla. State Senate. Promoted Chisholm Trail Commn. for Econ. Devel. through Tourism; mem. Eagle Forum of Okla., Christian Coalition; active Ray of Hope Ch., Comanche, Okla.; lobied for locally controlled edn., right-to-life and econ. devel. issues. Republican. Office: State Capitol Bldg 2300 N Lincoln Blvd Rm 529B Oklahoma City OK 73105-4805

MARTIN, CAROLYN A. (BIDDY MARTIN), provost; BA in English, Coll. of William and Mary, 1973; PhD in German Lit., U. Wis., 1985. Mem. faculty Cornell U., Ithaca, NY, 1983—, sr. assoc. dean Coll. Arts and Scis., 1977—2000, univ. provost, 2000—. Grad. field rep. for German studies Cornell U., 1991—96, grad. field rep., co-founder lesbian and gay studies, 1992—96, assoc. dir. program women's studies, 1997—04, chair dept. German studies, 1994—97. Author: numerous books; contbr. articles to profl. jours.; mem. edtl. bd.: Studies in Gender and Sexuality, New German Critique, Gay and Lesbian Quar., Diacritics, Signs, Women in German. Mem.: Phi Beta Kappa. Office: Office of the Provost Cornell U Ithaca NY 14853

MARTIN, CATHIE JO, political scientist, educator; b. Panama Canal Zone, U.S., Nov. 22, 1951; d. Robert M. Martin and Mary Jo Mackenzie; m. James R. Milkey, July 7, 1990; 2 children. BA, Carleton Coll., 1974; MSW, U. Wash., 1979; PhD, MIT, 1987. Asst. prof. Northwestern U., Evanston, Ill., 1988—90; prof. Boston U., 1990—. Vis. prof. Copenhagen U., Denmark, 2000—01; vis. scholar Russell Sage Found., N.Y.C., 1994—95. Author: (nonfiction) Shifting the Burden, 1991, Stuck in Neutral, 2000. Grantee grant, NSF, 1986, Robert Wood Johnson Found., 1992—93, German Marshall Fund, 2001. Mem.: Am. Polit. Sci. Assn. Home: 24 Woodcliff Rd Newton MA 02461 Office: Boston Univ Dept Polit Sci 232 Bay State Rd Boston MA 02461

MARTIN, CONNY, artist, educator; b. Lubbock, Tex., June 29, 1925; d. William Alex McDonald and Lola Craig; m. C. B. Martin; children: Jay Davis, Jody Knox. Student, U. No. Colo., 1943—45. Art tchr. pvt. studio, Lubbock, 1945—60; art tchr. Lubbock Art Assn., 1960—80. Leader painting workshops. Numerous exhbns. and one-woman shows; author: (book) Art Lives in West Texas, 2003; collections, Tex. Tech. U., Represented in permanent collections Internat. Cultural Ctr., Tex. Tech. U. Mem.: Nat. Mus. Women in the Arts, Lubbock Art Assn. (art tchr. 1960—80, past pres. 1996—98). Home: 4511 13th El Paso TX 79916

MARTIN, CYNTHIA MAREK, art educator; b. Petersburg, Va., May 22, 1957; d. Warren Harding and Lillie Mae Marek; m. Kent Michael McMillan, Oct. 4, 1980 (div. Feb. 1985); 1 child, Sarah Nichole McMillan ; m. Walter Eugene Martin, Aug. 11, 1995. AA in Comm. Art, Chowan Coll., 1977; BS in Art Edn., Atlantic Christian Coll., 1979; M in Ednl. Media, Va. State U., 1997. Cert. art tchr. K-12 Va. Interior decorator J.C. Penneys, Petersburg, 1984—85; visual merchandiser Thalhimer's, Richmond, Va., 1985—87; sales Capital Floors and Decorating, Richmond, 1987—89; art tchr. Colonial Heights Mid. Sch., Va., 1989—. Baptist. Avocations: gardening, kickboxing, swimming, painting, travel. Home: 7507 Duncan Rd Petersburg VA 23803 Office: Colonial Heights Mid Sch 500 Conduit Rd Colonial Heights VA 23834

MARTIN, DALE, health facility administrator; b. NYC, May 10, 1935; d. Byron Pink Molter and Ruth Nobel; m. Robert A. Wishart, Dec. 13, 1985; children from previous marriage: Elizabeth, Devon. BS, U. Conn., 1957. RN, cert. case mgr., disability mgmt. specialist, lic. rehab. counsellor, Mass. Dental asst., Hempstead, NY, 1951; with Wesson Maternity Hosp., Springfield, Mass., 1957—58, Huntington Hartford Meml. Hosp., Pasadena, Calif., 1958—59; office mgr. Indsl. By Products Inc., Kalamazoo, 1969—72, contr. Chgo., 1970—74; cons. Mgmt. Resources Inc., Broomall, Pa., 1978—81; cons., owner Martin-Collard Assocs., Inc., Monmouth Beach, NJ, 1980—84; cons., owner, chmn. bd. dirs. MCA, Inc., St. Helena Island, SC, 1984—. Bd. dirs. Consortium Advantage, Inc., St. Helena Island, Silvers Assocs., Plymouth, Mass., Low Country Human Devel. Ctr., Beaufort, SC, mentor program dir., 2001—04, exec. com., steering com., chmn. vol. program, 2001—04; cons. Viewfinder, Old Chatham, NY, 1987—99, Phoenix Inc., Global Explorations, Inc., 1987—99, Fallon Inc., Dr. Martens Shoe Distbr., 1998—2000, Retail Swap.com, 2000—02, shoespot.com, 2001—02; chmn. Okatie Acad. Tennis Benefit. Contbr. articles to profl. jours., 2001. Bd. govs. Rumson-Fair Haven HS, NJ, 1976—78; mem. corp. fundraising com. Beaufort Orch., 2003—; mem. Beaufort Orch. League, 2004; benefit tennis co-chair Jordan Hosp.-White Cliffs County Club. Mem.: Case Mgmt. Soc. Am., Mass. Nurses Assn. (chmn. image com. 1984—85, pub. info. com. 1986—89), Individual Case Mgmt. Assn., Internat. Assn. Psychosocial Rehab. Specialists, Nat. Rehab. Assn. (pvt. sector group), Nat. Assn. Rehab. Profls. in Pvt. Sector (forensic sect., past rep. region 1 to bd. dirs.), Beaufort Orch. League, Jr. League, Dataw Island Club (bd. dirs., social chmn. Tennis Assn. 2001—, com. visual arts 2003—, club recreation com. 2004—), Miles Grant Country Club (bd. dirs. Tennis Assn. 1997—2001, pres. 1998—2000), Jr. Women's Club, Mountain Lakes Ski Club (founder), Town Club (v.p.), Alpha Delta Pi, Sigma Theta Tau. Avocations: painting, tennis, croquet, N.J. state girls gymnastic judge, kayaking.

MARTIN, DENISE BELISLE, magazine editor; b. West Springfield, Mass., Sept. 15, 1940; d. Paul E. and Grace A. (St Onge) Belisle; m. Roger H. Martin, Jr., Aug. 18, 1962 (div.); 1 dau., Sara B. BA magna cum laude, Smith Coll., 1961; MA, Radcliffe Coll., 1962; postgrad., U. Minn., 1968-70. Vol. Peace Corps., Colombia, 1966-68; prodn. mgr. Soho Weekly News, N.Y.C., 1976-77, assoc. editor, 1977-78, mng. editor, 1978, arts editor, 1979; assoc. editor Portfolio, N.Y.C., 1979-80, exec. editor, 1980-84; sr. editor The American Lawyer, 1984-85, editor, 1985-86, exec. editor, 1986—, Money. Mem. Phi Beta Kappa Home: 35 Bond St New York NY 10012-2426 Office: Money Time & Life Bldg Rockefeller Ctr New York NY 10020

MARTIN, DIANA WILLIAMS, music educator; b. Morgantown, W.Va., Aug. 9, 1947; d. Earl and Winona Williams; m. Lawrence Douglas Martin, July 4, 1946; 1 child, Ryan Douglas. BA, Alderson-Broaddus Coll., 1969; MME, Duquesne U., 1975; student, Pa. Gov.'s Inst. Arts Educators, 2003—. Cert. music educator. Vocal music tchr., grades 7-12 Ctr. Area Sch. Dist., Center Twp., Pa., 1969—70; vocal music tchr., grades K-5 Moon Area Sch. Dist., Moon Twp., Pa., 1970—. Music dir. Trinity Choir Ministries, Aliquippa, Pa., 1972—; choir dir. ch. Ohio United Presbyn. Ch., Aliquippa, 1972—85; music dir. New Brighton Christian Assembly, New Brighton, Pa., 1986—2000; asst. choir and band dir. New Brighton Christan Assembly, 2000—; music coord. K-12 Moon Area Sch. Dist., Moon Twp., 2003—. Mem. mini-mission team CCNA, Tzaneen, South Africa, 1999, leader mini-mission team, 2000; music dir., advisor Trinity Choir Ministries, Aliquippa, Pa., 1976. Mem.: MENC, NEA, Moon Edn. Assn., Pa. State Edn. Assn., Pa. Music Educators Assn., Profl. Orgn. for Music Educators. Democrat-Npl. Avocations: singing, travel, crafts. Home: 438 Independence Rd Aliquippa PA 15001 Office: Moon Area Sch Dist 8353 University Blvd Moon Township PA 15108 Personal E-mail: dismusic@aol.com. E-mail: dmartin@masd.k12.pa.us.

MARTIN, DIANNE LESLIE, artist, educator; b. Boston, Apr. 8, 1940; d. James Donald and Ina (Mac Lerie) M.; m. William Paul Kennedy, June 15, 1961 (div. June 1978). BFA in Painting, RISD, 1965; MA in Painting, U. Iowa, 1968. Head art dept. Spence Sch., N.Y.C., 1971—95; represented by Markel/Sears Works on Paper, N.Y.C., 1991—98. Reader advanced placement art portfolios Ednl. Testing Svc., Princeton, N.J., 1993-98; mem. nat. devel. com. Advanced Placement Studio Art, 2002—. One woman exhbns. include Noho Gallery, N.Y.C., 1981, 82, 85, Leonarda Di Mauro Gallery, N.Y.C., 1984, 87; group exhbns. include Brooklyn (N.Y.) Mus., 1975, Women in the Arts Found., N.Y.C., 1978, Salgamundi Club, N.Y.C., 1979, Bjorn Lindgren Gallery, N.Y.C., 1982, Ethel Putterman Gallery, Orleans, Mass., 1982, 83, Queens (N.Y.) Mus., 1985, Newmark Gallery, N.Y.C., 1989, Mus. of the Nat. Arts Found., N.Y.C., 1989, Ceres Gallery, N.Y.C., 1990, Citicorp Ctr., Long Island City, N.Y., 1992, Broome St. Gallery, N.Y.C., 1997, Whitney Art Works, Greenport, N.Y., 2001, 02, Interchurch Ctr., N.Y.C., 2002, Noho Gallery, N.Y.C., 2003; represented in permanent collections David Rockefeller Jr., Pfizer, Inc., Pepsico, J.C. Penney, Inc., Southeast Bank, Manhattan Musicians Union, Warburg Pincus, Inc. Resident fellow Va. Ctr. Creative Arts Sweetbrier Coll., 1995.

MARTIN, DONNA LEE, publishing company executive, retired; b. Detroit, Aug. 7, 1935; d. David M. Paul and Lillian (Paul); m. Rex Martin, June 5, 1956; children: Justin, Andrew. BA, Rice U., 1957. Mng. editor trade dept. Appleton-Century-Crofts Co., N.Y.C., 1961-62; dir. publs. Lycoming Coll., Williamsport, Pa., 1966-68; editor Univ. Press of Kans., Lawrence, 1971-74; mng. editor Andrews McMeel Publ., Kansas City, Mo., 1974-80, v.p., editorial dir., 1980-95, v.p., editor-at-large, 1995-98; v.p. Universal Press Syndicate, Kansas City, 1980-98. Lectr. U. Mo., Kansas City, Johnson County Cmty. Coll., Kans.; free-lance writer, editor; cons. Kansas City Star Books. Author: (adaptation) Charles Dickens' A Christmas Carol: Adapted for Theatre; contbr. articles to profl. jours. Named Disting. Alumna Rice U., 1990. Mem. Ctrl. Exchange (Kansas City), The Groucho Club (London), Phi Beta Kappa. Home: 6810 W 66th Ter Shawnee Mission KS 66202-4147 E-mail: DLPMartin@msn.com.

MARTIN, FELICIA DOTTORE, mental health services professional, marriage and family therapist; b. Cleve., July 7, 1956; d. Vincent James and Roseanne Dottore; m. William Arthur Martin, Mar. 26, 1983; children: Trevor Matthew, Trent Michael. BA in Psychology, Calif. State U., 1983; MA in Marriage Family Therapy, Pacific Oaks Coll., 1995. Lic. marriage family therapist Calif., 1999. Therapist Florence Crittenton Svcs., Fullerton, Calif., 1995—99, clin. dir., 1999—2001; dir. mental health South Coast Children's Soc., Costa Mesa, 2001—. 1st v.p. Oxford Acad. Instrumental Music Program, Cypress, Calif., 2000—03; mem. of com. Team for Bldg. com. Partnerships, 2003—. Mem.: Am. Assn. Marriaage and Family Therapists. Home: 10401 Hedlund Dr Anaheim CA 92804 Office: South Coast Children's Soc 1620 Sunflower Costa Mesa CA 92626 Personal E-mail: fdm777@aol.com. E-mail: fmartin@sccskids.org.

MARTIN, HELEN ELIZABETH, educational consultant; b. West Chester, Pa., Feb. 19, 1945; d. Thomas Edwin and Elizabeth Temple (Walker) M. BA, The King's Coll., N.Y.C., 1967; MEd, West Chester U., 1970; postgrad., Goethe Inst., Freiberg, Fed. Republic Germany, 1979, Oxford (Eng.) U., 1979. Nat. bd. cert. tchr. adolescent/young adult sci., 2000. Tchr. math. and sci. Unionville (Pa.) H.S., 1967-99; ret., 1999; ednl. cons. Adj. prof. West Chester U., 1989—; mem. Carnegie Forum on Edn. and the Economy. Mem. Pa. Rep. State Com., 1982-90, Rep. Com. of Chester County, 1984-94. Named Alumna of Yr., The King's Coll., 1987; recipient State Presdl. award, 1989, Frank G. Brewer Civil Air Patrol Meml. Aerospace award, 1989, Outstanding Achievement award U.S. Dept. Commerce, 1993; Bus. Week/Challenger Seven fellow, 1991. Fellow Am. Sci. Affiliation; mem. AAAS, Nat. Bd. Profl. Tchg. Stds. (founding dir., 1987-94), Satellite Educators Assn. (pres. 1990-2000), Nat. Sci. Tchrs. Assn., Nat. Coun. Tchrs. Math., Nat. Sci. Tchrs. Assn. (internat. lectr. 1987), Assn. for Sci. Edn. in U.K. (internat. lectr. 1987). Home: PO Box 605 Unionville PA 19375-0605 E-mail: SatTeacher@aol.com.

MARTIN, IONA B. guidance counselor; d. Thearthur and Ora Dee Martin. Elem. Edn., Ala. State U., Montgomery, AL, 1976—78; M.Ed. Elem. Edn., Ala. State U., Montgomery, 1979—81; Sch. Counseling, Ala. State U., Montgomery, AL, 1987—89, Ednl. Adminstrn., 2002—03. Elem. tchr. Selma City Schools, Selma, Ala., 1978—95, sch. guidance counselor, 1995—. Pres. Ala. Counseling Assn. - Dist. VI, Selma, Ala., 2003—; workshop facilitator Ala. Counseling Assn. Conf., Mobile, Ala., 2002. Supporter NAACP, Baltimore, Md., 1985—2003, So. Poverty Law Ctr., Montgomery, Ala., 2002—03, United Way, Selma, Ala., 1980—2003, United Negro Coll. Fund, 1990—2003. Recipient Who's Who Among Students in Am. Jr. Colleges, 1975-1976, Elem. Tchr. Svc. Award (17 Years), Edgewood Elem. Sch., 1995, Honor Student Award, Ala. State U. Coll. of Edn., 1978; scholar Scholarship, Herff Jones Yearbook Co., 1978. Mem.: ASCD, Ala. Counseling Assn. (pres. 2003—), NEA, Ala. Edn. Assn., Toastmasters Internat. Democrat. Baptist. Avocations: piano, biking, model car collection, reading. Office: Cedar Park Elem Schl 1101 Woodrow Ave Selma AL 36701

MARTIN, IONE EDWARDS, social worker; b. Davenport, Okla., Sept. 11, 1912; d. Rila Dewitt and Mae Eliza (Brown) Edwards; m. Lawrence Joseph Martin, Aug. 9, 1946 (dec.); 1 child, David L. BA, Southwestern Coll., 1934; MSSW, St. Louis U., 1945. Caseworker Wichita (Kans.) Welfare, 1934-35; state child welfare worker Kans. Child Welfare, Topeka, 1937-38; social worker VA, Denver, 1949-51; psychiat. social worker Patton, Calif., 1953-55; med. social worker Colo. Gen. Hosp., Denver; sch. social worker Denver Pub. Schs., 1958-70. Lectr. local Questers and retirement homes; lectr. on bead heritage local Questers orgn., retirement facilities. Mem. AAUW (mem. book rev. group), NEA, Colo. Edn. Assn., Questers Internat. (pres. Aurora chpt. 1986-88, 92-93, lectr. 1996-97). Avocations: collecting and studying antiques, bridge.

MARTIN, JACQUELINE BRIGGS, author juvenile prose; b. Maine; m. Rich Martin; children: Sarah, Justin. Author: Bizzy Bones and Moosemouse, 1986, Bizzy Bones and the Lost Quilt, 1988, Bizzy Bones and Uncle Ezra, 1984, Button, Bucket, Sky, 1998, The Finest Horse in Town, 1992, Grandmother Bryant's Pocket, 1996 (Lupine award 1996), The Green Truck Garden Giveaway: A Neighborhood Story and Almanac, 1997, Good Times on Grandfather Mountain, 1992, Higgins Bend Song and Dance, 1997, Snowflake Bentley, 1998 (Caldecott Award 1999, Lupine Award 1998), Washing the Willow Tree Loon, 1995, The Lamp, The Ice and The Boat Called Fish, 2001, The Water Gift and the Pig of the Pig (Lupine award 2003), 2003, On Sand Island, 2003. Office: Houghton Mifflin Co Juvenile Dept Boston MA 02116

MARTIN, JEAN ANN, retired school system administrator, educator; b. Omaha, June 27, 1942; d. Clarid Fee and Frances Catherine (Dugan) McNeil; m. Robert William Martin, Dec. 28, 1968. BS, Pa. State U., 1963; MEd, U. Del., 1968; EdD, Wilmington Coll., 1997. Cert. English tchr., Pa., N.Y., Del., reading specialist, Va., N.Y., Del., secondary prin., reading supr., dir. of instrn., Del. Tchr. English Neshaminy Sch. Dist., Langhorn, Pa., 1963-65; tchr. English and reading Unionville (Pa.) Sch. Dist., 1965-68; tchr. reading Jamesville-DeWitt (N.Y.) Sch. Dist., 1968-69, South Colonie Sch. Dist., Albany, N.Y., 1969-70; tchr. English Bethlehem Ctrl. Sch. Dist., Delmar, N.Y., 1970-71, Smyrna (Del.) Sch. Dist., 1971-73; reading specialist, tchr. English Delmar (Del.) Sch. Dist., 1973-88; reading specialist Accomack (Va.) County Schs., 1988-93; sch. adminstr., ednl. diagnostician Del. Dept. Svc. for Children, Youth and Their Families, Middletown, 1994—2003. Adj. prof. Del. State U., 1997—99, Wilmington Coll., 2000—; chairperson H.S. Reading Task Force, Del. Commn. on Reading Success, 1999. Mem.: ASCD, Cedar Shores Condominium Assn. (sec.), Internat. Reading Assn. (ea. regional conf. gen. conf. chair 1997—99, regional conf. com. 1999—2001), Del. Assn. Sch. Adminstrs., Diamond State Reading Assn. (pres. 1985—86, editor DSRA Reader), Lions Club (New Castle, Del., pres. 2001), Alpha Delta Kappa (past pres. Theta chpt. and Del.). Home: 33 E 6th St New Castle DE 19720-5087 E-mail: jmart000@aol.com.

MARTIN, JEANNE DAVIS, forensic specialist, consultant, writer, editor; m. Timothy Jerome Martin, Mar. 30, 1990. BA Summa cum Laude, St. Leo Coll., St. Leo, Fla., 1981; MEd, Miss. State U., Miss. State, Miss., 1983, PhD, 1985. Sentencing mitigation specialist: Am. Acad. Experts Traumatic Stress, Profl. Acad. Custody Evaluators 2004; diplomate Am. Coll. of Forensic Examiners, 2001, Am. Psychotherapy Assn., 2000, cert. Clinical Forensic Counselor Am. Acad. of Forensic Counselors, 2000; lic. Profl. Counselor N.J., 1999. Pres., CEO Vanguard Consulting, Montgomery, Ala.,

2000—; webmaster, developer Various, Montgomery, Ala., 2001—; vis. counselor, lectr. Miss. State U., Miss. State, Miss., 1994—96, adj. prof. Miss. State, Miss., 1994—96; sr. trainer Anteon Corp., Montgomery, Ala., 1996—98; pres., CEO B & R ID Services, Inc., Montgomery, Ala., 1991—95; translator World Bank, Washington, 1988—89; dir. of devel. Kans. Newman Coll., Wichita, Kans., 1989—90; dir. Career Ctr., Pensacola Jr. Coll., Pensacola, Fla., 1985—88; adj. prof. Troy State U., Montgomery, Ala., 1990—; editor Psychol. Assessment Resources, Inc., Lutz, Fla., 1995—; writer Exam Master, Inc., Middletown, Del., 1996—; exec. dir. Al-Hajj, Inc., Montgomery, Ala., 2000—03; clin. dir. Seraaj Familly Homes, Inc., Montgomery, Ala., 1999—2003; pres. Ala. Therapeutic Foster Care Providers Assn., Inc., Montgomery, Ala., 2001—03; pres., CEO ShrinkingPrices.com, Montgomery, Ala., 2002—. Editor: (profl. jour.) Old South Publications, Inc.; pub. (profl. jour.) Old South Publications, Inc., Psychol. Assessment Resources, Inc., Exam Masters, Inc.; contbr. articles to profl. jour. Mentor Lighthouse Mentoring Program, Montgomery, Ala., 1998—2001; vol., mentor Boys Ranch, Pensacola, Fla., 1987—88; vol. Family Ctr. for Abused Children, Shreveport, La., 1985—86; state coord. Adoptee's Liberty Movement Assn., Columbus, Miss., 1982—84; vol. Santa Rosa Mental Health Clinic, Milton, Fla., 1980—83, Boys Club of Escambia County, Pensacola, Fla., 1986—89, Escambia County Boys Clubs, Montgomery, Ala., 1986—89, Montgomery County Dept. of Human Resources Quality Assurance, Montgomery, Ala., 1998—2000; chair Therapeutic Cmty. Task Force, Montgomery, Ala., 1999—2001. With US Army, 1977—80, Fort Eustis, VA. Recipient Outstanding Young Am., 1985, Outstanding Cmty. Svc., Escambia County Boys Clubs, 1988, Children's Advocate, Seraaj Family Homes, Inc., 2002. Mem.: APA, Am. Acad. Custody Evaluators, Am. Acad. Experts Traumatic Stress, Am. Psychotherapy Assn., Am. Coll. Forensic Examiners. Office: Vanguard Cons 529 S Perry St St 12 Montgomery AL 36104 E-mail: dr_jdm@vanguardconsulting.net.

MARTIN, JERRI WHAN, public relations executive; b. Aurora, Ill., Oct. 21, 1931; d. Forest Livings and Geraldeane Jeanette (Cutler) Whan; m. Charles L. Martin (div.); children: Vicki, Bill, Erica, Kevin. BMus, Wichita State U., 1952. Co-owner Sta. KCNY, San Marcos, Tex., 1957-70; correspondent Austin Am.-Statesman, 1959-85; co-owner Sta. KWFT, Wichita Falls, Kans., 1965-96. Cons. U.S. Office Econ. Opportunity, Austin, 1966 68, Tex. Ednl. Found., Inc., San Marcos, 1975—. Pres. Hays County Women's Polit. Caucus, Tex., 1985-89; officer Tex. Women's Polit. Caucus, 1990; del. State Dem. Convs., Dallas, Houston, 1982, 84, 96; bd. dirs. Ctrl. Tex. Higher Edn. Authority, San Marcos, 1982-87, Scheib Opportunity Ctr., San Marcos, 1983-90; bd. dirs., chm. Edwards Underground Water Dist., San Antonio, 1985-96; trustee Tex. Ednl. Found., Inc., 1991—; chair Citizen Rev. Commn., 2000—. Named Outstanding Reporter in Tex., Tex. Legis., 1960; inducted into San Marcos Hall of Fame, 1993; recipient Extraordinary Svc. award Trust for Pub. Land, 1994. Mem. San Marcos C. of C., LWV, Hays Women's Ctr. Office: Tex Ednl Found Inc PO Box 1108 San Marcos TX 78667-1108

MARTIN, JOANNE, social sciences educator; b. Salem, Mass., Sept. 25, 1946; d. Richard Drake and Nathalie (Ashton) M.; m. Beaumont A. Sheil, July 9, 1977; 1 child, Beaumont Martin Sheil. BA, Smith Coll., 1968; PhD in Social Psychology, Harvard U., 1977; PhD in Econs. and Bus. Adminstrn. (hon.), Copenhagen Bus. Sch., 2001. Assoc. cons. McBer & Co. (formerly Behavior Sci. Ctr. of Sterling Inst.), 1968-70, dir. govt. mktg., 1970-72; asst. prof. orgnl. behavior and sociology Grad. Sch. Bus., Stanford (Calif.) U., 1977-80; assoc. prof. grad. sch. bus. Stanford U., 1980-91, prof. grad. sch. bus., 1991—, dir. doctoral programs, grad. sch. bus., 1991-95, Fred H. Merrill prof. orgn. behavior and sociology, 1996—. Sec. adv. bd. Stanford U., 1995—96, vice chair adv. bd., 1996—97; vis. scholar Australian Grad. Sch. Mgmt. U. N.S.W., 1989—90, Copenhagen Bus. Sch., 1998, 2004; vis. scholar dept. psychology Sydney (Australia) U., 1989—90; Ruffin fellow bus. ethics Darden Grad. Sch. Bus. Adminstrn. U. Va., 1990; mem. bd. advisors iMahal; mem. internat. adv. bd. Internat. Ctr. for Rsch. in Orgnl. Discourse, Strategy and Change. Mem. editl. bd. Adminstrv. Sci. Qtrly., 1984—88, Jour. Social Issues, 1981—83, Acad. Mgmt. Jour., 1984—85, Social Justice Rsch., 1985—90, Jour. Mgmt. Inquiry, 1991—, Orgn., 1994—, Jour. Mgmt. Studies, 1996—, Gender, Work and Organization, 1998—; co-author: five books; contbr. articles to profl. jours. Recipient Centennial medal for contbns. to soc. Harvard U. Grad. Sch. Arts and Scis., 2002; Lena Lake Forrest Rsch. fellowship Bus. and Profl. Women's Found., 1978, James and Doris McNamara Faculty fellowship Grad. Sch. of Bus., Stanford U., 1990-91. Fellow: APA, Am. Psychol. Soc., Acad. Mgmt. (rep.-at-large 1983—85, divsn. program chair 1985—87, divsn. chair 1987—89, nat. bd. govs. 1992—95, we. divsn. Promising Young Scholar award 1982, Nat. Disting. Educator award 2000, We. Divsn. Sr. Scholar award 2003); mem.: Nat. Assn. Corp. Dirs. (adv. bd. 2000—). Office: Stanford U Grad Sch Bus Littlefield Ctr 353 Stanford CA 94305

MARTIN, JUDITH SYLVIA, journalist, author; b. Washington, Sept. 13, 1938; d. Jacob and Helen (Aronson) Perlman; m. Robert Martin, Jan. 30, 1960; children: Nicholas Ivor, Jacobina Helen. BA, Wellesley Coll., 1959; DHL (hon.), York Coll., 1985, Adelphi U., 1991. Reporter-critic, columnist Washington Post, 1960—83; syndicated columnist United Feature Syndicate, N.Y.C., 1978—; columnist Microsoft, 1996—. Critic-at-large Vanity Fair, 1983-84. Author: The Name on the White House Floor, 1972, Miss Manners' Guide to Excruciatingly Correct Behavior, 1982, Gilbert, 1982, Miss Manners' Guide to Rearing Perfect Children, 1984, Common Courtesy, 1985, Style and Substance, 1986, Miss Manners' Guide for the Turn-of-the-Millennium, 1989, Miss Manners on (Painfully Proper) Weddings, 1996, Miss Manners Rescues Civilization, 1996, Miss Manners' Basic Training: Communications, 1997, Miss Manners' Basic Training: Eating, 1997, Miss Manners' Basic Training: The Right Thing to Say, 1998, Miss Manners' Guide to Domestic Tranquility, 1999, Star-Spangled Manners, 2002. Bd. dirs. Washington Concert Opera, Friends of Scuola San Rocco. Mem. Cosmos Club, Literary Soc. Office: United Feature Syndicate 200 Madison Ave Fl 4 New York NY 10016-3911

MARTIN, JULIE, women's healthcare company executive; BA in Liberal Arts and Scis., MS in Exercise Physiology, San Diego State U. Propr. 2 cos., 1983-90; gen. mgr. Dale Fitzmorris, 1990-92; dir. health promotion Ctr. for Women's Medicine, 1993-96; co-CEO, As We Change, LLC, 1995-98; v.p. catalog ops. Women First HealthCare, Inc., San Diego, 1998—. Office: Women First HealthCare Inc 12220 El Camino Real Ste 400 San Diego CA 92130-2091 Fax: 619-509-1353.

MARTIN, JULIE A. retired insurance company executive; BS, Tex. Tech. U.; MS in Fgn. Svc., MBA in Fin., George Washington U. Dir. investment missions program Overseas Pvt. Investment Corp., investment ins. officer, regional mgr. ins. dept., mng. dir. L.Am. and Caribbean ins. dept., mng. dir. policy and underwriting, chief underwriter polit. risk ins. dept., dep. v.p. ins., v.p. ins., 1997—. Office: Overseas Pvt Investment Corp 1100 New York Ave NW Washington DC 20527-0001

MARTIN, JUNE JOHNSON CALDWELL, journalist; b. Toledo, Oct. 06; d. John Franklin and Eunice Imogene (Fish) Johnson; m. Erskine Caldwell, Dec. 21, 1942 (div. Dec. 1955); 1 child, Jay Erskine; m. Keith Martin, May 5, 1966. AA, Phoenix Jr. Coll., 1941; BA, U. Ariz., 1943, 59; postgrad., Ariz. State U., 1939, 40. Freelance writer, 1944—; columnist Ariz. Daily Star, Tucson, 1956-59, 70-94, book reviewer, 1970-94, co-founder Ann. Book and Author Event; editor Ariz. Alumnus mag., Tucson, 1959-70; ind. book reviewer, audio tape columnist Tucson, 1994—; coord. S.W. Books of Yr. sponsored by Tucson Pima Pub. Libr., Ariz., 2000—. Panelist, co-producer TV news show Tucson Press Club, 1954-55, pres., 1958. Contbg. author: Rocky Mountain Cities, 1949; contbr. articles to World Book Ency., and various mags. Mem. Tucson CD Com., 1961; vol. campaigns of Samuel Goddard, U.S. Rep. Morris Udall, U.S. amb. and Ariz. gov. Raul. Castro. Recipient award Nat. Headliners Club, 1959, Ariz. Press Club award, 1957-59, 96, Am. Alumni Coun., 1966, 70. Mem. Nat. Book Critics Circle, Ariz. Press Women, Jr. League of Tucson, Tucson Urban League, PEN U.S.A. West, Planned Parenthood So. Ariz., Tucson Press, Pi Beta Phi. Democrat. Methodist. Home: Desert Foothills Sta PO Box 65388 Tucson AZ 85728-5388

MARTIN, KATE ABBOTT, lawyer; b. Pasadena, Calif., Mar. 11, 1952; BA, Pomona Coll., 1973; JD, U. Va., 1977. Bar: D.C. 1978, U.S. Ct. Appeals (D.C. cir.) 1979, U.S. Supreme Ct. 1989. Assoc. Nussbaum, Owen & Webster, Washington, 1977-83, ptnr., 1983-88; dir. Nat. Security Litigation Project ACLU, Washington, 1988-92, dir. Ctr. for Nat. Security Studies, 1992—. Office: Gelman Libr 2130 H St NW Ste 701 Washington DC 20037-2521

MARTIN, KATHLEEN, medical center administrator; BS, RN, U. Bridgeport, 1964; MS, N.Y. Med. Coll., 1966; JD, Tulane U., 1991. RN, La, Conn., N.Y.; cert. nurse-midwife; bar: La. 1991. Instr. U. Mass. Sch. of Health Scis., Amherst, Mass., 1975-77, La. State U. Sch. of Nursing, New Orleans, 1978-79; nurse practitioner Planned Parenthood of La., 1986-88; pvt. practice in nurse-midwife New Orleans, 1978-80, 83-91; assoc. atty. Thompson & Lavender, New Orleans, 1991-95; nurse-midwife, coord. maternity svcs. Saint Thomas Health Svc., Inc., 1995-96; dir. WomanCare Midwife Ctr., Columbia Lakeland Med. Ctr., 1996—. Mem. Am. Coll. of Nurse-Midwives (treas., pres. 1996-98), La. Nurse Practitioners Assn., Nurse-Midwives Svc. Dirs. Network, La. Hosp. Assn. Office: Am Coll of Nurse-Midwives 818 Connecticut Ave NW Ste 900 Washington DC 20006-2702

MARTIN, KATHLEEN L. military officer, hospital administrator; BSN, Boston U., 1973; MS in Nursing Adminstrn., U. San Diego, 1992. Commd. ensign USN, 1973; advanced through grades to rear admiral Nat. Naval Med. Ctr.; staff nurse, then charge nurse in pediats. Naval Hosp., Camp Lejeune, NC, 1973—76, charge nurse pediat. ward Jacksonville, Fla., 1979—82; med. programs officer Navy Recruiting Dist., Phila., 1976—79; divsn. officer mil. medicine, credentials coord., risk mgr., quality assurance coord. Naval Med. Clinic, Pearl Harbor, Hawaii, 1982—86; head amb. med. nursing dept. Naval Hosp., San Diego, 1986—90; dir. nursing svcs. Naval Med. Clinic, Port Hueneme, Calif., 1992—93, commdg. officer, 1993—95, Naval Hosp., Charleston, SC, 1995—98, med. inspector gen., 1998—99; 19th dir. Navy Nurse Corps, 1998—99; comdr. Nat. Naval Med. Ctr., Bethesda, Md., 1999—. Decorated Legion of Merit (3), Def. Meritorious Svc. medal, Meritorious Svc. medal, Navy Commendation medal. Mem.: Assn. Mil. Surgeons of the U.S., Am. Acad. Amb. Care Nursing, Am. Coll. Healthcare Execs., Sigma Theta Tau. Office: National Naval Med Ctr 8901 Wisconsin Ave Bethesda MD 20889-5600

MARTIN, KATHRYN A. academic administrator; Dean Sch. Fine and Performing Arts Wayne State U., Detroit; chancellor U Minn, Duluth, 1995—. Office: University of Minnesota-Duluth Office of the Chancellor Admin Bldng 10 University Dr Duluth MN 55812-2496

MARTIN, KELLIE (NOELLE), actress; b. Riverside, Calif., Oct. 16, 1975; Movie and motion picture actress. Actress T.V. series Life Goes On, 1989, (voice) Taz-Mania, 1992, Christy, 1994-1995, Crisis Ctr., 1997, ER, 1998-2000, Fiona, 2002, others; movies and TV movies include Jumpin' Jack Flash, 1986, Secret Witness, 1988, Troop Beverly Hills, 1989, Matinee, 1993, If Someone Had Known, 1995, Her Last Chance, 1996, On The Edge of Innocence, 1997, About Sarah, 1999, All You Need, 2001, Malibus Most Wanted, 2003, Open House, 2003; voice characterization A Goofy Movie, 1995, also T.V. guest appearances. Office: c/o The Gersh Agy 232 N Canon Dr Beverly Hills CA 90210-5302

MARTIN, KIM See MARTH, MARY

MARTIN, LAURABELLE, real estate and farm land owner and manager; b. Jackson County, Minn., Nov. 3, 1915; d. Eugene Wellington and Mary Christina (Hansen) M.. BS, Mankato State U., 1968. Tchr. rural schs., Renville County, Minn., 1936-41, 45-50, Wabasso (Minn.) Pub. Sch., 1963-81; pres. Renville Farms and Feed Lots, 1982-86. Author: Hist. Biography of Joseph Renville, 1996; poet: Nat. Libr. Poetry (Silver Cup award, 2003). Pres. Wabasso (Minn.) Edn. Assn., 1974-75, publicity chmn., 1968-74; sec. and publicity agt. Hist. Renville Preservation Com., 1978-86; publicity chmn., sec. Town and Country Boosters, Renville, 1982-83. Recipient Outstanding Achievement in Poetry Award, Internat. Soc. Poets. Mem. Genealogy Soc. Renville County, Am. Legion Aux. Democrat. Lutheran. Avocations: antique furniture, travel, sewing, writing poetry. Home and Office: 334 NW 1201st Rd Holden MO 64040-9378

MARTIN, LEANNA WRIGHT, minister; d. Richard Martin and Theresa Wright; m. William Martin Jr.; children: Shenita, Jerrod, Shonda Sharon. Diploma, Bible Coll., L.A., 1974; student, United Theol. Sem., Monroe, 1977—79; cert., Bob Brooks Real Estate Sch., 1992. Cert. life and health ins. Pastor Ch. of Jesus Christ, Monroe, La., 1988—. Active Free Gift Bapt. Ch.; radio evangelist. Recipient Cmty. Svc. award, NAACP, 2000, Joe James Sr. Presdl. award, 2001. Democrat. E-mail: electlady8@aol.com.

MARTIN, LINDA GAYE, demographer, economist; b. Paris, Ark., Dec. 17, 1947; d. Leslie Paul and Margie La Verne (Thomas) Martin. BA in Math., Harvard U., 1970; MPA, Princeton U., 1972, PhD in Econs., 1978; DHL (hon.), Marlboro Coll., 2002. Dir. mgmt. info. sr. ctrs. bur. purchased social svcs. for adults City of N.Y., 1972—74; rsch. assoc., rsch. dir. U.S. Ho. of Reps. Select Com. on Population, Washington, 1977—79; rsch. assoc. East-West Population Inst., Honolulu, 1979—89, asst. dir., 1982—84; asst. prof. econs. U. Hawaii, Honolulu, 1979—81, assoc. prof., 1981—89, prof., 1989; dir. com. on population Nat. Acad. Scis., Washington, 1989—93; dir. domestic rsch. divsn., v.p. RAND, Santa Monica, Calif., 1993—95, v.p. for rsch. devel., 1995—99; pres. Population Coun., N.Y.C., 1999—. Mem. neurosci. behavior and sociology of aging rev. com. Nat. Inst. on Aging, Bethesda, 1991—95; chair panel on aging in developing countries NAS, Washington, 1987, mem. com. on population, 1993—99, mem. panel on internat. aging data, 1999—2001; mem. peer rev. oversight group NIH, 1998—. Editor: The ASEAN Success Story, 1987; co-editor: Demographic Change in Sub-Saharan Africa, 1993, The Demography of Aging, 1994, Racial and Ethnic Differences in the Health of Older Americans, 1997; author: (monograph) The Graying of Japan, 1989; contbr. articles to profl. jours. Mem. adv. coun. Woodrow Wilson Sch. Pub. and Internat. Affairs, Princeton U., NJ, 2000—. Recipient Fulbright Faculty Rsch. award, Coun. for Internat. Exch. of Scholars, 1988. Mem.: AAAS (adv. coun. 2003—), Population Assn. Am. (bd. dirs. 1991—93), Internat. Union for Sci. Study Population, Gerontol. Soc. Am. Democrat. Office: Population Council 1 Dag Hammarskjold Plz New York NY 10017-2220

MARTIN, LORNA CAMPBELL, English language educator; b. Ridgewood, N.J., June 28, 1967; d. Robert F. and Pearl Campbell; m. Michael Glenn Martin, July 8, 1995. BA in English, Wake Forest U., 1989. Cert. tchr., 1991. Tchr. English, soccer coach, yearbook advisor Pinecrest High Sch., Southern Pines, N.C., 1991—. Mem. N.C. English Tchrs. Assn., Nat. Soccer Coaches Assn., N.C. Soccer Coaches Assn. Presbyterian. Home: 114 Heather Ln Southern Pines NC 28387-7331 Office: Pinecrest HS PO Box 1259 Southern Pines NC 28388-1259

MARTIN, LORRAINE B. humanities educator; b. Utica, N.Y., Aug. 18, 1940; d. Walter G. and Laura (Bochenek) Bolanowski; m. Charles A. Martin; children: Denise M. Stringer, Tracy M. Weinrich. Student, SUNY, Albany, 1958-60, postgrad., 1992—; BA in English and Edn. magna cum laude, Utica Coll. of Syracuse U., 1977; MS in Edn. and Reading, SUNY, Cortland, 1979, CAS in Edn. Adminstrn., 1984; postgrad., Syracuse U., 1990—. Cert. nursery, elem. tchr., secondary tchr., sch. adminstr. and supr., sch. dist. adminstr., reading specialist, N.Y. From tchr. to reading specialist, adminstrv. intern Poland (N.Y.) Cen. Sch., 1972-84; instr. reading Utica Coll. of Syracuse U., summer 1982-84; adminstr. spl. edn. and chpt. 1 remedial program Little Falls (N.Y.) City Sch. Dist., 1984-85; adminstr. adult and continuing edn. Madison-Oneida Bd. Coop. Ednl. Svcs., Verona, N.Y., 1985-86; dir. gen. programs Herkimer (N.Y.) Bd. Coop. Ednl. Svcs., 1986-88. Prof. emeritus English, SUNY SLN Internet English 1, children's lit., intro. edn., and honors program Herkimer County C.C. of SUNY, 1988—, participant brainstorming session on underprepared students SUNY, 1993, trainer tchr. performance evaluation program N.Y. State Dept. Edn., Herkimer, 1984, facilitator effective schs. program, 1986-88; co-developer edn. degree program; cons. Two-Yr. Coll. Devel. Ctr. SUNY, 1985-89, tchr. trainer for the Writing Process; developed summer reading, writing and study skills course for Bridge program; tchr. asst. cert. program; cons. in field. Author: The Bridge Program-Easing the Transition from High School to College, 1990; editorial bd. Research and Teaching in Developmental Education; contbr. to Teaching Writing to Adults Tips for Teachers: An Idea Swap, 1989; textbook reviewer for pubs., 1993—. Vol. arts and crafts fair HCCC Found.; advisor Network for Coll. Re-Entry Adults; mem. Coun. of Profs., Parents Weekend Com. Recipient Leader Silver award for volunteerism 4-H Coop. Extension, Utica, 1980; HCCC Found. grantee, Writing grantee Readers's Digest. Mem. Internat. Reading Assn., Assn. Supervision and Curriculum Devel., Nat. Coun. Tchrs. English, Conf. on Coll. Composition and Communication, Phi Kappa Phi, Alpha Lambda Sigma. Avocations: English, current events, travel, public and satellite television, computers. Home: 7099 Crooked Brook Rd Utica NY 13502-7203 Office: Herkimer County Comm Coll SUNY Reservoir Rd Herkimer NY 13350-1545

MARTIN, LUCY Z. public relations executive; b. Alton, Ill., July 8, 1941; d. Fred and Lucille J. M. BA, Northwestern U., 1963. Adminstrv. asst., copywriter Batz-Hodgson-Neuwoehner, Inc., St. Louis, 1963-64; news reporter, Midwest fashion editor Fairchild Publs., St. Louis, 1964-66; account exec. Milici Advt. Agy., Honolulu, 1967; publs. dir. Barnes Med. Ctr., St. Louis, 1968-69; comms. cons. Fleishman-Hillard, St. Louis, 1970 74; comms. cons., CEO, pres. Lucy Z. Martin & Assocs., Portland, Oreg., 1974—. Spkr. Marylhurst Coll., 1991, 92, 93, Concordia Coll., 1992, Women Entrepreneurs of Oreg., 1992, Oreg. Assn. Hosps. and Health Sys. Trustees, 1992, Healthcare Assn. Hawaii, Honolulu, 1993, USBancorp for Not-for-Profits, 1993, Multnomah County Ret. Srs. Vol. Program, 1993, Healthcare Fin. Mgmt. Assn., N.W., 1993, Healthcare Comms. Oreg., 1994, Area Health Edn. Ctrs., OHSU/statewide, 1994, Columbia River chpt. Pub. Rels. Soc. Am., 1994, 96; spkr., workshop conducter Healthcare Assn. Hawaii, 1993, USBancorp Not-for-Profit, 1993, Healthcare Communicators Oreg., 1994, Pathways to Career Transition, 1995, among others; bd. dirs. Ctrs. Airway Sci., Oregon Coll. Arts & Crafts, 1989-95, Good Samaritan Hosp. Assn., 1991-94, Am. Mktg. Assn., Oreg. chap., 1992-93, Inst. Managerial and Profl. Women, 1992-94, YMCA Public Policy com., 1993-95, Jr. League Cmty. adv. bd., 1994—, Bus. Social Responsibility Steering com., 1996—, Ctrs. for Airway Sci. Bd., 1996—; spkr. in field. Featured in Entrepreneurial Woman mag.; contbr. articles to profl. jours. Chmn. women's adv. com. Reed Coll., Portland, 1977-79; mem. Oreg. Commn. for Women, 1984-87; bd. dirs. Ronald McDonald House Oreg., 1986, Oreg. Sch. Arts and Crafts, 1989—, Northwestern U. Alumni Coun., 1992 ; bd. dirs. Good Samaritan Hosp. Assocs., 1991-94, chair 1993-94; mem. pub. policy com. YMCA, 1993-95; mem. adv. bd. Jr. League, 1994—; mem. steering com. Bus. for Social Responsiblity, 1996—; bd. dirs. Ctrs. for Airway Sci., 1996—. Recipient MacEachern Citation Acad. Hosp. Pub. Relations, 1978, Rosey awards Portland Advt. Fedn., 1979, Achievement award Soc. Tech. Comms., 1982, Disting. Tech. Comm. award, 1982, Exceptional Achievement award Coun. for Advancement and Support Edn., 1983, Monsoon award Internat. Graphics, Inc., 1984, William Marsh Achievement award PRSA, 1998; named Woman of Achievement Daily Jour. Commerce, 1980. Mem. Pub. Rels. Soc. Am. (pres. Columbia River chpt. 1984, chmn. bd. 1980 84, Oreg. del. 1984-86, jud. panel N. Pacific dist 1985-86, exec. bd. health care sect. 1986-87, mem. Counselors Acad., Spotlight awards 1985, 86, 87, 88, nat. exec. com. 1987-91; William Marsh Achievement award 1998), Portland Pub. Rels. Roundtable (chmn. 1985, bd. dirs. 1983-85), Assn. Western Hosps. (editl. adv. bd. 1984-85), Best of West awards 1978, 80, 83, 87), Oreg. Hosp. Pub. Rels. Orgn. (pres. 1981, chmn. bd. 1982, bd. dirs. 1992-93), Acad. Health Service Mktg., Am. Hosp. Assn., Am. Mktg. Assn. (Oreg. chpt. bd. dirs. 1992-93), Am. Soc. Hosp. Mktg. & Pub. Rels., Healthcare Communicators Oreg. (conf. keynote speaker 1994), Internat. Assn. Bus. Communicators (18 awards 1981-87), Oreg. Assn. Hosps. (keynote speaker for trustee, 1991, speaker, 1993, bd. dirs. 1992-93), Oreg. Press Women, Nat. and Oreg. Soc. Healthcare Planning and Mktg., Women in Comms. (Matrix award 1977), Bus. for Social Responsibility (steering com. 1996—), Inst. for Managerial and Profl. Women (bd. dirs. 1992-94). Office: 1881 SW Edgewood Rd Portland OR 97201-2235 Fax: 503-227-1569. E-mail: lucyz@lzma.com.

MARTIN, LYNN MORLEY, former secretary of labor; b. Evanston, Ill., Dec. 26, 1939; d. Lawrence William and Helen Catherine (Hall) Morley; children from a previous marriage: Julia Catherine, Caroline; m. Harry D. Leinenweber, Jan. 1987; stepchildren: Jane, John, Stephen, Justin, Thomas Leinenweber. BA, U. Ill., 1960. Former tchr. pub. schs.; mem. Ill. Ho. of Reps., 1977-79, Ill. Senate, 1979-81, 97th-101st Congresses from 16th Ill. Dist., 1981-91; sec. Dept. of Labor, Washington, 1991-93; prof. Harvard Univ., 1993—. Co-chmn. Bush-Quayle Presdl. campaign, 1988. Named one of Outstanding Young Women in Am., U.S. Jaycees; named Rep. Woman of the Yr., 1989; named a Mother of the Yr., Nat. Mother's Day Com., 1992; 1st woman elected to leadership post in House of Reps., 1982. Mem. AAUW, Jr. League, Phi Beta Kappa (hon. doctorate). Republican. Office: Harvard Univ Cambridge MA 02138

MARTIN, MARCELLA EDRIC, retired community health nurse; b. Rosedale, Miss., Jan. 25, 1930; d. Amos and Alma Allen; m. Reuben Clifton Martin, Jan. 25, 1969; children: Brunetta, Jacqueline, Cornell, Constance. Student, Marygrove Coll., Detroit, 1971; ADN, Highland Park Sch. Nursing, Mich., 1979; ThB, Cmty. Bible Coll., Detroit, 1968. Lic. LPN. LPN VA Hosp., Ann Arbor, Mich., Crittendon Hosp., Detroit, Vis. Nurses Assn., Detroit. Instr. Charles H. Mason Bible Sch., Detroit, 1991—95; mem. C.O.G.I.C. Bus. owners Assn., 1982—. Author: (book) Women Who Struggle, 2001; prodr.: (plays) And Didn't Those Knees Bow, 2004. Founder Prime of Life Adult Foster Care Home, 1979, Somebody's Got To Care Min., 2003; mem. Nat. Campaign Tolerance-The Wall of Tolerance, 2003; missionary over women Chs. of God in Christ, 1986—2002; vol. Redford Geriatric Home, Mich., 1999—. Named to Wall of Tolerance, New Civil Rights Meml. Ctr., Montgomery, Ala., 2003; recipient Spirit of Detroit award, City of Detroit, 1978, 2000, 2002, Disting. Citizen of Detroit award, 1980, Testimonial Resolution award, 1985. Mem.: Detroit Writers Guild. Democrat. Pentecostal Ch. Avocations: reading, writing. Home: 25332 Shiawassee Cir Apt 106 Southfield MI 48034

MARTIN, MARCI, writer, former advertising specialist; b. Corsicana, Tex., Oct. 20, 1927; d. Roy Rhoston McNutt and Maggie Mae Price; m. Harold Durward Martin, May 31, 1947 (dec. Dec. 15, 1998); children: Jennifer Ann Martin Svihus, Gary(dec.). Student, North Tex. State U., 1945—46, So. Meth. U., 1946, Miracosta Coll., 1990—91. Bus. rep. Southwestern Bell, Dallas, 1946—55; advt. rep. Christian Sci. Monitor, San Diego, 1982—89. Author: Go To Hell and Make a U-Turn, 1996, rev. edit., 2000, Secrets and Lies, 2000, License To Steal, 2001, (short stories, essays, articles) The Muse on My Shoulder, 2001. Vol. prison chaplain, San Diego,

1989—95. Recipient 1st pl. for poetry, Nat. U., 1991, 3d pl. for essay, Writer's Jour., 2d pl. and hon. mention, Ann. Showcase Writers Club, 1994, Tangled Webs 2d pl., Jim Woods prize, 2002. Mem.: Sisters in Crime, Ariz. Mystery Writers (coord./pres. 1998—), Soc. Southwestern Authors (mentor 1998—), Mystery Writers Am. Avocation: golf. Home: 3011 W Sawmill Spring Trail Tucson AZ 85742

MARTIN, MARGARET GATELY, elementary school educator; b. Teaneck, N.J., July 24, 1928; d. Martin F. and Grace (Hammell) Gately; m. Phillips H. Martin, June 27, 1953 (div. 1977); children: Paul H., Patrick W., Thomas P. BA, Hunter Coll., 1950, MA, 1953. Cert. elem. tchr. N.Y. Tchr. Pub. Sch. # 5, Queens, N.Y., 1950-53, Wappingers Cen. Sch., Wappingers Falls, N.Y., 1953-55, Jamestown Pub. Schs., 1968—95; ret., 1996. Tchr. Wenzler Day Care and Learning Ctr., 2000—04; tchr. religious edn. St. Francis of Assissi, Centerville, Ohio, 2001. Citizen amb. to Pargue and Russia People to People, 1995; tchr. Sunday sch. Sts. Peter and Paul Ch., Jamestown, 1977—95. Mem.: AAUW (pres. 1980—82, 1992—94, Edn. Found. Program award 1985), NEA, Jamestown Tchrs. Assn. (membership chair 1976—78, sec. 1982—84), Green Thumb Garden Club (pres. 1986—88, 1996—, v.p. 1991—93, 1995—96), Jamestown Inter Club Coun. (pres. 1984—86, v.p. 1995—96, Woman of the Yr. 1991), Delta Kappa Gamma (corr. sec. 1988—90, membership chair 1991—94, v.p. 1994—96, pres. 1998—2000). Republican. Roman Catholic. Avocations: gardening, needlepoint, travel, theater, genealogy. Home: 3708 Wenzler Dr Kettering OH 45429-3366

MARTIN, MARILYN JOAN, library director; b. Golden Meadow, La., Jan. 17, 1940; d. Marion Francis Mobley and Audrey Virna (Goza) Sapaugh; m. James Reginald Martin, Dec. 16, 1958; children: James Michael, Linda Jill Michaels. BA in History, U. Wash., 1975, MLS, 1976; MA in Pub. History, U. Ark., 1992; PhD in Libr. Sci., Tex. Woman's U., 1993. Cataloger, reference libr. St. Martin's Coll., Lacey, Wash., 1976-78; asst. reference libr. Pacific Luth. U., Tacoma, 1978-85; serials libr. Henderson State U., Arkadelphia, Ark., 1985-86, collection devel. libr., 1987-88, dir. learning resources, 1989-95; dean libr. svcs. Rowan U., Glassboro, 1995—. Contbr. articles to profl. jours. Bd. dirs. N.J. Acad. Libr. Network; mem. exec. com. Tri-state Coll. Libr. Mem. ALA (rsch. com. 1993—, stds. com. 1994—), Assn. Coll. and Rsch. Librs. Republican. Avocations: walking, reading, collecting names. Office: Library Rowan U Glassboro NJ 08028-1701

MARTIN, MARILYN MANN, retired library media specialist; b. Greencastle, Ind., July 14, 1939; d. Emil Albert and Edith Costa Mann; m. Max Lee Martin; children: Michael Lee, Melanie Sue Martin Boesen. BS, Ind. State U., 1960, MS, 1970, 88. Tchr. Latin, sch. libr. Danville H.S., Ind., 1960; libr., media specialist Greencastle H.S., Ind., 1971—2002, ret., 2002. Mem. tech. connections com. Greencastle H.S., 1997-98; mem. exec. bd. Stone Hills Libr. Svcs., Bloomington, Ind., 1990-96. Mem.: NEA, ASCD, Greencastle Classroom Tchrs. (scholarship chmn. 1985—2002), Assn. Ind. Media Educators (dist. advocacy chmn. 1998), Ind. Coop. Libr. Svcs., Ind. Libr. Found., Ind. Ret. Tchrs. Assn., Phi Kappa Phi. Avocations: gardening, reading, volunteering.

MARTIN, MARY, secondary school educator; b. Detroit, May 17, 1954; d. Enos and Sara (Evans) M. AS, Highland Park C.C., 1975; BA, Wayne State U., 1975, MA in Teaching, 1981; postgrad., So. Calif. Sch. Ministry, Detroit, 1992—. Dietary aide Allan Dee Nursing Home, Detroit, 1972, Harper Hosp., Detroit, 1973, 74, nurse aide, 1974-75, respiratory technician, 1975-80, Dr.'s Hosp., Detroit, 1980; head cook, supr. Focus Hope, Detroit, 1981; substitute tchr. Detroit Bd. Edn., 1984-90, tchr. adult edn., 1990-93, tchr., 1993—. Interim advisor student coun. Wayne State U., Detroit, 1985. Sunday sch. teaching trainer People's Missionary Bapt. Ch., Detroit, 1986, del., 1984-87, mem. All Aid, 1984-87, mem. choir, 1984, usher, 1984; precinct del. 13th Congl. Dist., 1986-88, 90-92, model, 1985. Recipient Spirit of Detroit award Detroit City Coun., 1993, Spl. Congl. cert. Hon. Barbara Rose Collins, 1994, Proclamation, Wayne County Commr. George Cushingberry, 1994. Mem. Nat. Sociol. Honor Soc. Democrat. Avocations: reading, shopping, movies, golf, driving.

MARTIN, MARY ANNE, art gallery owner; b. Hoboken, N.J., Apr. 26, 1943; d. Thomas Philipp and Ruth (Kelley) Martin; m. Henry S. Berman, June 9, 1963 (div. 1976); 1 child, Julia Coyote. Student, Smith Coll., 1961-63; BA, Barnard Coll., 1965. Head dept. painting Sotheby Parke Bernet, N.Y.C., 1971-78; founder Latin Am. dept. Sotheby's, N.Y.C., 1977, sr. v.p., 1978-82; pres. Mary Anne Martin, Fine Art, N.Y.C., 1982—. Mem.: Art Dealers Assn. Am. (sr. v.p.). Avocations: art collecting, scuba diving. Office: Mary Anne Martin Fine Art 23 E 73rd St New York NY 10021-3522 E-mail: mamartin@mamfa.com.

MARTIN, MARY ELAINE, psychologist; b. Oct. 22, 1955; BA Theatre Arts, Humboldt State Univ., Arcata, Calif., 1980; MA Psychology, Pepperdine Univ., Malibu, Calif., 1984; PhD Clinical Psychology, Calif. Sch. Profl. Psychology, 1996. Lic. pschologist N.Y. Stagehand IATSE Local 504, Anaheim, Calif., 1983—2000; cmty. mental health specialist St. Mary's Hosp., Amsterdam, NY, 2000; psychologist N.Y. State office of Children & Family Svcs., Johnstown, NY, 2001—. Adv. bd. Trauma Intervention Program, Orange County, Calif., 1996—2000. Fellow: APA. Avocation: horseback riding. Office: Brookwood Secure Ctr PO Box 265 Claverack NY

MARTIN, MARY ELLEN, state legislator, human development specialist; b. Southfield, Mich. m. George Martin; 3 children. Student, Mercy Coll. Nursing; BS, Daniel Webster Coll., 1988. Human devel. specialist; mem. from dist. 34 N.H. State Ho. of Reps., mem. resources com., mem. recreation and devel. com. Home: 5 Lone Star Dr Nashua NH 03062-3411 Office: NH Ho of Reps State Capitol Concord NH 03301

MARTIN, MARY WOLF, newspaper editor; b. Corwith, Iowa, Nov. 6, 1930; d. Henry Herbert and Mabel M. (Keeney) Wolf; m. Charles William Martin, Oct. 16, 1950; children: Stephen C., Neal J., Sally Martin Kindell. Grad. high sch., Weyauwega, Wis. Corr. Britt (Iowa) News Tribune, 1946-47; staff writer Wheaton (Ill.) Daily Jour., 1963-65; reporter, photographer Rhinelander (Wis.) Daily News, 1967-69, news editor, 1969-74, mng. editor, 1974-76, Neenah-Menasha Northwestern, Neenah, 1976-80; editor Oshkosh Northwestern, 1980-94. Pres. Fox Valley Press Club, Oshkosh, 1982; bd. dirs. Goodwill Industries N.E. Wis., Menasha, 1978-86, Rape Crisis Ctr., Oshkosh, 1981-85, Fox Valley Arts Alliance, Appleton, Wis., 1980-85, Fox Valley Cmty. Tech. Coll., Oshkosh, 1986-92; trustee Paine Art Ctr. Arboretum, Oshkosh, 1990-93. Named Woman of Yr., Bus. and Profl. Women, Rhinelander, 1975, Vol. of Yr., Sexual Abuse Svcs., Oshkosh, 1989. Mem. Wis. Assoc. Press Mng. Editors (pres. Milw. 1985-86), Nat. Assoc. Press Mng. Editors, Am. Soc. Newspaper Editors, Media-Law Com. Wis. Bar Assn. Roman Catholic. Avocations: reading, travel, photography, golf. Home: 898 County Road Q Pelican Lake WI 54463-9409

MARTIN, MAUREEN FRANCES, medical educator; b. Montreal, Can., Feb. 12, 1950; d. Geoge Alguire and Frances Dorothy May (Brenner) M. BS, Concordia U., 1978; MD, McGill U., 1982. Fellowship in hepatobiliary surgery Lahey Clinic, Boston, 1988; fellowship in transplantation New England Deaconess Hosp., Boston, 1989; lectr. in anatomy McGill U., Montreal, 1984-88; instr. in surgery Harvard U., Boston, 1988-89; asst. prof. surgery U. Pitts., 1989-92; assoc. prof. surgery U. Iowa, Iowa City, 1992-99, dir. organ transplant, 1992-99; assoc. prof. surgery Harvard U., Boston, 1999—; chief divsn. liver surgery/transplantation, dir. Liver Ctr., Beth Israel Deaconess Med. Ctr., Boston, 1999—2002; chmn. surgery Kern Med. Ctr., Bakersfield, Calif., 2002—. Reviewer NIH, 1995, scientific advisor, 1994; principle investigator Cooperative Clin. Trials, Iowa City, 1994. Author: (with others) Current Trends in New Development, 1995; contbr. articles to profl. jours. Spkr. Rotary Club, Cedar Rapids, 1996, U. Iowa Alumni, Des Moines, 1996, Johns Hopkins, 1995; del. Citizen Amb. Program, Russia, 1995. Scholar Sandoz, 1990, McGill U., 1978-82, Concordia U., 1971-77. Mem. ACS, Midwest Surg. Assn., Am. Soc. of Transplant Surgeons, Am. Assn. for the Study of Liver Disease, Internat. Transplant Soc., United Network for Organ Sharing. Roman Catholic. Avocations: skiing, golf. Home: 2502 Twickenham Ct Bakersfield CA 93311- Office: 1830 Flower St Ste 3000 Bakersfield CA 93305-

MARTIN, MELISSA CAROL, radiological physicist; b. Muskogee, Okla., Feb. 7, 1951; d. Carl Leroy and Helen Shirley (Hicks) Paden; m. Donald Ray Martin, Feb. 14, 1970; 1 child, Christina Gail. BS, Okla. State U., 1971; MS, UCLA, 1975. Cert. radiol. physicist Am. Bd. Radiology, radiation oncology Am. Bd. Med. Physics. Asst. radiation physicist Hosp. of the Good Samaritan, L.A., 1975-80; radiol. physicist Meml. Med. Ctr., Long Beach, Calif., 1980-83, St. Joseph Hosp., Orange, Calif., 1983-92, Therapy Physics, Inc., Bellflower, Calif., 1993—. Cons. in field. Editor: (book) Current Regulatory Issues in Medical Physics, 1992. Fund raising campaign divsn. mgr. YMCA, Torrance, Calif., 1988-92; dir. AWANA Youth Club-Guards Group, Manhattan Beach, Calif., 1984—. Named Dir. of Symposium, Am. Coll. Med. Physics, 1992. Fellow Am. Coll. Med. Physics (chancellor western region 1992-95, treas. 2004-), Am. Assn. Physicists in Medicine (profl. coun. 1990-95, treas. 1998-2003, bd. dirs. 1994-2003), Am. Coll. Radiology (econs. com. 1992-95, govt. rels. com. 1998—, coucilor at large 2001-, commn. on med. physics 2002-); mem. Calif. Med. Physics Soc. (treas. 1991-98), Am. Soc. for Therapeutic Radiology and Oncology, Health Physics Soc. (pres. So. Calif. chpt. 1992-93), Am. Brachytherapy Soc. Baptist. Avocation: christian youth group dir. Home: 507 Susana Ave Redondo Beach CA 90277-3953 Office: Therapy Physics Inc 9156 Rose St Bellflower CA 90706-6420 Office Phone: 562-804-0611. E-mail: melissamartin@compuserve.com.

MARTIN, MILINDA, public relations executive; d. Charles Rodman and Milena (Kurilich) Martin; m. Simon David Goode, Apr. 6, 1985 (div. Aug. 3, 2000); children: Joseph Robert Goode, Sofia Marie Goode. BA in Econs., Tufts U., 1983; cert. in Econs., London Sch. Econs., 1982. Mgr., spl. events and pub. rels. I. Magnin, Beverly Hills, Calif., 1987—94; mgr., spl. events & pub. rels. Robinsons-May, North Hollywood, Calif., 1994—98, dir., spl. events and pub. rels., 1998—2003; v.p., spl. events and pub. rels. Robinsons-May/Meier & Frank, North Hollywood, Calif., 2003—. Retail chair Music Ctr. of Los Angeles County, L.A., Calif., 2001—. V.p. PTA., South Pasadena, Calif., 2001—; dir. Ford Theatre Found., L.A., Calif., 2000—; mentor Leukemia and Lymphoma Soc., L.A., Calif., 2001—03. Mem.: Fashion Group Internat. (publicity chair 1991—93), Am. Friends of the London Sch. Econs. Democrat. Avocations: bicycling, skiing, hiking, travel. Office: Robinsons-May/Meier & Frank 6160 Laurel Canyon Blvd North Hollywood CA 91606 Office Phone: 818-509-4975. E-mail: milinda_martin@robinsonsmay.com.

MARTIN, MOLLY ERDMAN, music educator; b. Cedar Rapids, Iowa, June 2, 1949; d. Bernard William and Madlyn O'Connor Erdman; 1 child, Elizabeth Anne. BA, Coll. St. Catherine, 1971; MusM, No. Ill. U., 1992. Cert. music educator Am. Orff-Schulwerk Assn., 1988. Vocal music tchr. Coll. Cmty. Sch. Dist., Cedar Rapids, Iowa, 1971, Naperville (Ill.) Sch. Dist. 203, 1972—79; elem. vocal music tchr. Bolingbrook (Ill.) Sch. Dist., 1980—81; vocal music specialist, dept. coord. Avery Coonley Sch., Downers Grove, Ill., 1981—92; dir. corp. and found. rels. No. Ill. U., DeKalb, Ill.; vocal music tchr. Indian Prairie Sch. Dist. 204, Naperville, 1993—. Choral dir. Young Naperville Singers, Naperville, Ill., 1986—87, profl. accompanist, 1971—, 1994—99, choral dir., 1997—2002, artist dir., 1999—2002; profl. accompanist St. Thomas the Apostle Ch., Naperville, Ill., 1994—2001. Mem. Jaycettes/Jaycees, Naperville, 1982—84; com. mem. Cmty. Concert Ctr. Planning Com., Naperville, 2000—02; liturgical life com. mem., profl. accompanist St. Raphael's Cath. Ch., Naperville, Ill., 1977. Mem.: Ill. Music Edn. Assn., Am. Choral Dirs. Assn., Music Educators Nat. Conf. (registered music educator 1995), Phi Beta Kappa, Kappa Gamma Pi. Avocations: travel, volunteer work, fund raising for cancer research. Home: 946 Heathrow Ln Naperville IL 60540 Office: Patterson Elem Sch 3731 Lawrence Dr Naperville IL 60564 E-mail: molly_martin@ipsd.org.

MARTIN, NANCY JANE, music educator; b. Dodge City, Kans., July 12, 1968; d. Emil and Emma Goldsberry; m. Peter Kip Martin; children: Sarah Ruth, Leah Joy. Bachelor of Music Education, Evangel U., 1990; Master's in Secondary Edn., S.W. Mo. State U., 1996. Elem. vocal music tchr. Mountain View Birch Tree RIII, Mo., 1990—91, Springfield R-12 Schs., Mo., 1991—. Adj. faculty S.W. Mo. State U., Springfield, 2000. Composer: (CD) Carry the Torch, 1996. Vol. pianist Oak Grove Assembly of God Ch., Springfield, 1986—. Mem.: Music Educators Nat. Conf. Avocations: swimming, tennis. Home: 1707 W Winchester Rd Springfield MO 65807

MARTIN, NANICE S. software company executive; Editor, writer numerous publs., including Tiger Beat, Seventeen; dir. software devel. Mattel, dir. online content; pres. PlanetGirl.com., Los Angeles. Author 4 books; prodr. CD-ROM Barbie Fashion Designer, also entertainment CD-ROMs. Office: PlanetGirlcom 1964 Westwood Blvd Ste 425 Los Angeles CA 90025-4651 Fax: 310-446-1405. E-mail: christiana@planetgirl.com.

MARTIN, PATRICIA, dean, nursing educator; BSN, U. Cin.; MS, Wright State U.; PhD, Case Western Res. U. Dir. nursing rsch., interim dean, assoc. prof. Wright State U. Contbr. articles to profl. jours. Office: Wright State U 168 University Hall Dayton OH 45435-0001

MARTIN, RANDI CHRISTINE, psychology educator; b. Salem, Oreg., May 24, 1949; d. Harold Raymond and Maxine Constance (Torgeson) M.; m. Lawrence P. Chan, Aug. 30, 1974. BA, U. Oreg., 1971; MA, Johns Hopkins U., 1977, PhD, 1979. Lectr. U. Calif., Santa Cruz, 1979-80; assoc. rsch. scientist Johns Hopkins U., Balt., 1980-82; asst. prof. Rice U., Houston, 1982-87, assoc. prof., 1987-93, prof., 1993—, chair psychology dept., 2002—. Assoc. editor Psychonomic Bulletin & Rev., Austin, Tex., 1995—; editl. bd. mem. Cognitive Neuropsychology, London, 1994—, Jour. Neurolinguistics, Cambridge, Eng., 1994—; contbr. articles to profl. jours. Recipient Claude Pepper award NIH Deafness and Comm. Disorders Inst., 1995—. Fellow APA; mem. Psychonomic Soc. (sec./treas. 1993-95, bd. dirs. 1997—), Acad. Aphasia (program com. 1990-93). Achievements include research in short term memory deficits in brain damaged patients. Office: Rice U Dept Psychology 6100 Main St Houston TX 77005-1892

MARTIN, SANDRA ANN, special education educator, writer; b. Sewickley, Pa., Feb. 9, 1954; d. Antoni S. and Marian M. Jankiewicz; m. Stephen Patrick Martin, June 26, 1976; children: Caitlin Lauren, Alyssa Ann. BS in Edn., Bloomsburg (Pa.) U., 1976; M in Edn., Shippensburg (Pa.) U., 1979. Learning disabilities and emotional support resource rm. tchr. southwestern sch. dist. Lincoln Intermediate Unit # 12 Emory Markle Intermediate Sch., Hanover, Pa., 1976—77; learning disabilities and emotional support tchr. grades 6-12 math, reading, and lang. arts resource rm. settings Lincoln Intermediate Unit # 12 New Oxford (Pa.) Jr. H.S., 1977—79, learning disabilities tchr. grades 7-9 math, reading, and lang. arts resource rm. settings, 1979—83; learning disabilities tchr. grades 6-8 math, reading, and lang. arts resource rm. settings New Oxford Mid. Sch., 1983—88, learning support tchr. grades 7-8 math, reading, and lang. arts resource rm. and inclusion settings Lincoln Intermediate Unit, 1988—96, learning support tchr. grades 7-8 math, reading, and lang. arts resource rm. and inclusion settings Conewago Valley Sch. Dist., 1996—. Spkr. in field, 2000—; supr. spl. edn. tchrs. Western Md. Coll. and Shippensburg U., 1997—98. Author: Breaking the Sound Barrier to Fluent Reading, Level 1, 2002, Mathopedia, Level 1, Level 2, 2003. Chaperone, dance instr. New Oxford Mid. Sch., 1990—2003, drama coach, 1977—85; chaperone, dance instr. Girl Scouts, New Oxford, 1991—99; fundraiser Immaculate Conception Ch., New Oxford. Finalist Pa. Tchr. of Yr., 2004; named one of Outstanding Educators of Adams County. Mem.: NEA, Pa. State Edn. Assn., Coun. Exceptional Children (divsn. learning disabilities), New Oxford Area C. of C. Avocations: travel, concerts, Broadway plays and musicals, antiques, spectator sports. Home: 316 Lincoln Way W New Oxford PA 17350 Office: Conewago Valley Sch Dist 130 Berlin Rd New Oxford PA 17350 Office Phone: 717-624-4513. E-mail: martins@conewago.k12.pa.us.

MARTIN, SARAH CARRIER, science educator; b. Carbondale, Ill., Sept. 16, 1957; d. Neil Alan and Faith Ruth Carrier; m. Corey Carrier Martin, Apr. 6, 1986 (div. July 1, 1994). BS, U. Ctrl. Fla., 1987; MS, U. Fla., 1992, PhD, 1999. Tchr. Sch. Bd. Alachua County, Gainesville, Fla., 1988—. Adj. asst. prof. U. Fla., Gainesville, 1997—2003; cons. in field. Contbr. articles to profl. jours. Active Move On, 2003. Recipient Popularization of Entomology award, Entomol. Soc. Am., 1992. Mem.: Nat. Sci. Tchrs. Assn., Ass. Edn. Tchrs. Sci. Democrat. Unitarian Universalist. Avocation: running marathons. Office: Norton Elementary School 2200 NW 45th Ave Gainesville FL 32605

MARTIN, SHEILA ANN, wife of Canadian Prime Minister; d. William and Sheila Cowan; m. Paul Martin, Sept. 11, 1965; children: Paul, Jamie, David. Degree, U. Toronto, 1964. Wife of Canadian Prime Minister, 2003—. Home: 24 Sussex Dr Ottawa ON Canada

MARTIN, SUSAN KATHERINE, librarian; b. Cambridge, Eng., Nov. 14, 1942; came to U.S., 1950, naturalized, 1961; d. Egon and Jolan (Schonfeld) Orowan; m. David S. Martin, June 30, 1962. BA with honors, Tufts U., 1963; MS, Simmons Coll., 1965; PhD, U. Calif., Berkeley, 1983. Intern libr. Harvard U., Cambridge, Mass., 1963-65, systems libr., 1965-73; head systems office gen. libr. U. Calif., Berkeley, 1973-79; dir. Milton S. Eisenhower Libr. Johns Hopkins U., Balt., 1979-88, exec. dir. Nat. Commn. on Libraries and Info. Sci., 1988-90; univ. libr. Georgetown U., Washington, 1990-2001, tchr., cons., 2001—; pres. SKM Assocs. Inc., 2001—; cons. dir. Marstons Mills Pub. Libr., 2003—. Mem. libr. com. Princeton (N.J.) U., 1987—95; mem. vis. com. Harvard U. Libr., 1987—93, 1994—2000; bd. overseers for univ. libr. Tufts U., 1986—2001, Tufts U. Sch. Arts and Scis., 2001—; cons. various librs. and info. cos., 1975—; mem. libr. adv. com. Hong Kong U. Sci. Tech., 1988—95; mem. acad. libr. adv. group U. Md. Sch. Librs. and Info. Scis., 1994—96; mem. adv. bd. ERIC, 1990—92; mem. Chadwyck-Healey N.Am. Adv. Com. on Lit. Online, 1997—99; vice chair, chair Chesapeake Info. and Rsch. Libr. Alliance, 1996—98; cons. libr. devel. & fundraising, 1998—; spkr. in field; mem. bd. trustees Marstons Mills Pub. Libr., 2002—03; bd. mem. adv. coun. Georgetown U. Libr., 2001—03. Author: Library Networks: Libraries in Partnership, 1986—87; editor: Jour. Libr. Automation, 1972—77; co-editor: Portal: Libraries and the Academy, 2000—; mem. editl. bd.: Advanced Tech./Librs., 1973—93, Jour. Libr. Adminstrn., 1986—2000, Libr. Hi-Tech., 1989—93, Jour. Acad. Librarianship, 1994—99; contbr. articles to profl. jours. Trustee Phila. Area Libr. Network, 1980—81; bd. dirs. Universal Serials and Book Exch., 1981—82, v.p., 1983, pres., 1984; trustee Capital Consortium, 1992—95; mem. bd. Potomac Internet, 1995—96; pres., trustee Marstons Mills Pub. Libr., 2002—03. Named Samuel Lazerow disting. lectr., Drexel U., 1984, L.I. U., 2002; recipient Simmons Coll. Disting. Alumni award, 1977; Coun. on Libr. Resources fellow, 1973. Mem.: ALA (coun. 1988—92, structure revision TF 1995—97, chair task force on external accrediting body 1999—2002), Assn. Coll. and Rsch. Librs. (pres. 1994—95, vis. program officer for scholarly com. 2002—03), Coalition for Networked Info. (leader working group 1990—92), Assn. Jesuit Colls. and Univ. Librs. (chair 1997—98), Libr. of Congress (optical disk pilot project adv. com. 1985—89), Assn. Rsch. Librs. (info. policy com. 1995—97, stats. com. 1998—2000), Libr. and Info. Tech. Assn. (pres. 1978—79), Rsch. Librs. Group (exec. com. 1985—87, gov.), Internat. Fedn. Libr. Assns. Commn. on Access to Info. and Freedom of Expression, Cranberry Shores Chorus (publicity coord. 2002—, v.p., Cranberry Shores Chorus 2003—), Sweet Adelines Internat., Cosmos Club (libr. com. 1986—96), Phi Beta Kappa (chair Georgetown U. chpt. 2000—01). Home and Office: 10 Colonial Farm Cir Marstons Mills MA 02648 Business E-Mail: martin@skmassociates.net.

MARTIN, SUSAN TAYLOR, newspaper editor; b. N.Y.C., Aug. 3, 1949; d. Lewis Randolph and Carolyn Emmons (Douthat) Taylor; m. James Addison Martin Jr., Nov. 15, 1975; 1 child, Steven Randolph. BA in Polit. Sci., Duke U., 1971. Reporter Ft. Myers (Fla.) News Press, 1972-75, Tampa (Fla.) Tribune, 1975-77, Associated Press, Detroit, 1977-78; bur. chief Detroit News, 1978-81; asst. city editor Orlando (Fla.) Sentinel, 1981-82; exec. bus. editor St. Petersburg (Fla.) Times, 1982-86, city editor, 1986-87, nat. corr., 1987-91, asst. mng. editor, 1991-93, dep. mng. editor, 1993-97, chief fgn. corr., 1997—. Trustee Poynter Fund, St. Petersburg, 1992—. Recipient Non-Deadline Reporting award Soc. Profl. Journalists, 1990, Investigative Reporting award, 1991, Feature, Depth Reporting award Fla. Soc. Newspaper Editors, 1990, Depth Reporting award, 1991. Mem. Suncoast Figure Skating Club. Democrat. Episcopalian. Avocations: figure skating, travel, antiques, reading. Home: 1312 51st Ave NE Saint Petersburg FL 33703-3209 Office: St Petersburg Times 490 1st Ave S Saint Petersburg FL 33701-4204

MARTIN, THERESA KAY, minister; b. Cookeville, Tenn., Apr. 3, 1949; d. Armon Nell and Mary Jo Hitchcock; m. Thomas Russell Martin, July 23, 1951; children: Stephen Thomas, Brian Hop Lee, Matthew Michael. BS in Bus. Mgmt., Tenn. Technol. U., 1971. Program of Alternate Studies Cumberland Presbyn. Ch./Tenn., 2001, ordained minister Tenn. Ga. Presbytery of the Cumberland Presbyn. Ch., 2001. Customer svc. rep. Xerox Corp., Chattanooga and Knoxville, Tenn., 1971—75; ptnr. Crescent Printing Co., Inc., Chattanooga, 1983—94; co-owner ProForma Crescent, Chattanooga, 1994—99; co-pastor Mt. Carmel Cumberland Presbyn. Ch., Laconia, Tenn., 1999—2002; sem. rels. assoc. Memphis Theol. Sem., 1999—2002; co-pastor Cumberland Presbyn. Ch., Hopkinsville, Ky., 2001—. Mem.: Kiwanis, Newcomers Club. Presbyterian. Avocations: reading, hiking. Office: Cumberland Presbyterian Church 2701 Faircourt Hopkinsville KY 42240

MARTIN, VIVIAN, soprano; b. Detroit, May 09; d. George W. and Lillie (Champion) M.; m. Clement A. McDowell. Student, Detroit Conservatory Music; BS in Edn., Wayne State U.; studied with, Nadia Boulanger, Germaine Martinelli, France, Samuel Margolis, N.Y.C., Paul Daubner, Munich, Elsa Verena, Berlin, Celeste Cole, Detroit. Educator Bd. of Edn., Detroit, N.Y.C. Soloist with Robert DeCormier Singers, Munich Philharm., Neurnberg Symphongy and Philharm. Chorus, 1970, Gävleborgs Symfoniorkester, Gavle, Sweden, 1978, Symphony Radio Concert, Paris, 1978, Warsaw Symphony Orch.; operatic debut as Leonora in La Forza del Destino, 1971; appeared in Antigone and Carmina Burana with Munich Philharm. Orch. and Chorus, Das ewige Evangelium with Nürnberg Symphony Orch. and Philharm. Chorus, L'Africaine in Ghent, Belgium, Oberon in Wexford (Ireland) Opera Festival, 1972, Bess from Porgy and Bess, Bratislava, 1979, Il Travatore, Constantza, 1980; performed with Royal Opera Ghent, Stadt Opera Essen, Badische Opera Karlsruhe, Stadt Opera Bonn, Mainz Opera, Royal Opera Lisbon, Portugal, Stadtheatre Bremen; TV broadcasts include BBC, BRT Belgium, Bratislava (Czechoslovakia) Philharm. Orch. and Opera, Bavarian Radio; rec. artist RCA, Concord Records, Concord Records, Halo Records; tour India, Iran, Afghanistan, U.S. State Dept., 1976; toured with Gävleborgo Symphony Orch., Sweden, 1981-84; appeared in opera concert on radio and TV,

Bucharest, 1979; sang Leonora in Il Travatore in opera festival, Constantza, Rumania, 1979; concerts in Belgrade, Tivoli Gardens, Copenhagen, Zagreb, Yugoslavia, 1979; opera concert tour of Sweden with Gävle Symphony Orch., 1979; soloist Belgium TV Flanders Expo, Gent, Belgium, 1990, concert tour Czechoslovakia, 1991, performed New Opera House, Maastricht, Holland with Limburgs Symphony Orchestra, 1992, Concert Koor, 1992, Olavshallen, Trondheim, Norway with Trondheim Symfoniorkester and Trondheim Kammerkor, 1993, concert tours U.S.A., 1994-96, soprano soloist Gershwin Gala Porgy and Bess, 1989-96, (with Philharm. Orch.) World of Gershwin, 1998; concert tours Belgium, Germany, (with St. Petersburg (Russia) Phil. Orch.) Shostakovich, 1998, (with Russian Nat. Symphony Orch.), Moscow, 1998; solo recitals festival St. Petersburg, 1998, Moscow, 1998. Recipient Jean Paul Alaux award Conservatoire de Fontianbleau, 18 singing scholarships and awards. Mem. AFTRA, Am. Guild Mus. Artists, Actors Equity Assn., New Initiatives for the Arts, Wayne State U. Alumni Assn., Alpha Kappa Alpha. Office: Dr Gosta Schwarck Intl Ltd 18 Groennegade 1st Fl DK-1007 Copenhagen K Denmark

MARTIN-BOWEN, LINDSEY, freelance writer; b. Kansas City, Kans., Aug. 4, 1959; d. Lawrence Richard and V. Marie Pickett; m. Frederick E. Nicholson (div.); 1 child, Aaron Frederick; m. Edwin L. Martin (div.); 1 child, Ki Elise; m. Michael L. Bowen (div. 1997). BA in English Lit., U. Mo., Kansas City, 1972, MA in English and Creative Writing, 1988, postgrad., 1991-94; JD, U. Mo. Kansas City Sch. Law, Kansas City, 2000. Bar: Mo. 2001. Tech. editor Office Hearings and Appeals, U.S. Dept. Interior, Washington, 1976-77; reporter, photographer Louisville Times, 1982-83; reporter, features editor Sun Newspapers, Overland Park, Kans., 1983-84; assoc. editor Modern Jeweler, Overland Park and N.Y.C., 1984-85; writer Coll. Blvd. News, Overland Park, 1985-89, KC View, Kansas City, Mo., 1988-89; editor Number One, Kansas City, Mo., 1986-88, cons., 1988-89; copywriter Sta KXEO/KWWR Radio, Mexico, Mo., 1989; editorial asst. New Letters, 1985—; features writer, columnist The Squire, Prairie Village, Kans., 1990-95. Instr. lit., fiction writing, intro. to journalism, reporting, English, cultural studies, tech. writing, acad. writing and lit. U. Mo., Kansas City, 1986-88, 97—, Johnson County C.C., 1988-95; fiction writer, 2002--; instr. world lit., writing Rockhurst U., 2002--; tchr. English and fiction Longview C.C., 1988-95, 97-98; instr. writing and mass comm. Webster U., 1990; instr. world lit., Am. lit., women in lit., creative writing Penn Valley C.C., 1993-97, faculty sponsor The Penn; owner, writer Paladin Freelance Writing Svc., Kansas City, 1988—; prodn. editor Nat. Paralegal Reporter, 1992-95, editor 1994-97, also columnist; staff writer, columnist NPR, 1992-; writing contest judge New Letters, 1987—2002; judge poetry contest BkMk Press, U. Mo., Kansas City, 1998—. Author: (novel) The Dark Horse Waits in Boulder, 1985, (poetry) Waiting for the Wake-Up Call, 1990, Second Touch, 1990, (fiction) Cicada Grove and Other Stories, 1992, (novel) Harvest, 2002, (novel) Denvie USA, 2003; contbr. poems, book revs., features, cartoon artwork, and photographs to numerous publs. including New Letters, Lip Service, Contemporary Lit. Criticism, UMKC Law Rev., River King Poetry Supplement, Thorny Locust, The Same, Coal City Rev., Black Bear Rev., The Kans. City Star; lead actress prodns. Coach House Players, 1969-70; extra HBO film Truman, 1995; staff mem., contbr. UMKC Law Rev., 1997-99. Campaigner McGovern for Pres. Campaign, Kansas City, 1971-72. Regents scholar, 1967; GAF fellow, 1986. Mem. U. Mo. Kansas City Alumni Assn. (media com. 1983-84), Phi Kappa Phi. Roman Catholic. Avocations: acrylic and oil painting, downhill skiing, music, Greek cooking, paralegal work. Office: U Mo Kansas City English Dept Cockefair Hall Rm 111 5100 Rockhill Rd Kansas City MO 64110-2481

MARTIN BURGHARD, STEPHANIE MARIE, pilot, educator; d. James Albert Martin and Barbara Jean Froebel, Marty Froebel (Stepfather); m. David Michael Burghard, Aug. 24, 1996. AAS in Aviation Tech. cum laude, Palo Alto Coll., San Antonio, 1994; B in Applied Arts and Scis. magna cum laude, S.W. Tex. State U., San Marcos, 2002. Lic. airline transport pilot Dept. Transp., FAA, airline transport pilot with Beechjet 400A type rating Dept. Transp., FAA, cert. flight instr. Dept. Transp., FAA. Flight instr. Alpha Tango Flying Svc., San Antonio, 1994—96, Ohio State U., Columbus, 1996—97; pilot MedFlight of Ohio, Columbus, 1997—2000, Flight Options (Raytheon Travel Air), Cleve., 2000—. Amelia Earhart Meml. scholar, The Ninty-Nines, 1995. Mem.: Aircraft Owners Pilot Assn., Women in Aviation Internat. Avocations: landscaping, photography, hiking. Office: Flight Options 26180 Curtiss-Wright Pky Cleveland OH 44143

MARTINDALE, CARLA JOY, retired librarian; b. Ladysmith, Wis., Sept. 9, 1947; d. Howard Walter and Audrey Elizabeth (Stanton) Martindale. BA, Mt. Senario Coll., 1970; MLIS, U. South Fla., 1990. Libr. Blackhawk Schs., South Wayne, Ind., 1975-79, Osceola County Libr., Kissimee, Fla., 1989-90, Fla. Tech. Coll., Orlando, 1991-92, Orlando Coll. South, 1993-98; ret., 1998; libr. U. of Ctrl. Fla., 2003—. Vis. prof. distance learning libr. St. Leo (Fla.) U., 1999—2002; chair libr. 21st curriculum Phillips Coll., Orlando, 1995, acad. com., 1993—98, accreditation steering com., 1996. Named libr. in her honor, Orlando Coll. South, 1995. Mem.: ALA, Fla. Libr. Assn. Avocations: reading, pets, stock investing. Home: 10 Chapel Lake Cir Quitman AR 72131 E-mail: carlajoy52@yahoo.com.

MARTIN-DEWITT, M. LORI, minister; b. Ida Grove, Iowa, June 15, 1955; d. Arthur Henry and Virginia Alice Martin; m. John Alan DeWitt. BS, No. Ariz. U., 1976; MDiv, Fuller Theol. Seminary, 1983; D in Ministry, U. Creation Spirituality, Oakland, Calif., 2000. Cert. Gestalt counselor S. Western Gestalt Ctr., Phoenix, 1999. Assoc. pastor, counselor Ch. on the Hill, Vallejo, Calif.; assoc. pastor Day Spring United Meth. Ch., Tempe, Ariz., 1985—88; pastor Safford (Ariz.) 1st United Meth. Ch., 1988—93, Faith United Meth. Ch., Phoenix, 1997—2001; sr. pastor Scottsdale (Ariz.) United Meth. Ch., 2001—. Bd. ordained min. Desert S.W. Conf. United Meth. Ch., Phoenix, episcopy bd., chair nominating com. Activist Valley Interfaith Project, Phoenix, 1998—99. Avocations: interior decorating, movies, pets, nature. Home: 10337 E Becker Ln Scottsdale AZ 85260 Office: Scottsdale United Meth Ch 4140 N Miller Rd Scottsdale AZ 85251

MARTINE, ANDREA SCHULTZ, secondary school educator; b. Washington, Aug. 24, 1945; d. George Norman and Grace Lois (DiBetetto) S.; m. Leonard Francis Martine, June 10, 1967 (div. Apr. 1978). BS, Duquesne U., 1967, MA, 1970; postgrad., U. Pitts., 1970—. Cert. English tchr., prin., Pa. English tchr. Allderdice H.S., Pitts., 1967—98, chair English dept., 1970-90, facilitator Ctrs. for Advanced Studies, 1990—95, advanced placement coord., 1995—98; academic coach English Beaver Area Sch. Dist., 1998—2000; ednl. assessment specialist Pa. Dept. Edn., Harrisburg, Pa., 2000—. Day care dir. Tot Town Day Care Ctr., Pitts., 1978-82; instr. English dept. Allegheny C.C., Pitts., 1982—; advanced placement English cons. Coll. Bd., Phila., 1986—. Contbr. chpts. to books; author curriculum in field. Vol. Mercy Hosp., Pitts., 1985-87; vol. various elections Rep. Party, Pitts., 1980—. Howard Heinz fellow, 1990-94, Harper Collins fellow, 1991; finalist Pa. Tchr. of the Yr., 1992. Mem. AAUW, Conf. Coll. Composition and Comm., Nat. Coun. Tchrs. English, Pa. Coun. Tchrs. English, Duquesne U. Alumni Assn. (bd. dirs. 1970-78, v.p. 1972-76), Tchr. of Yr. Orgn., Internat. Poetry Forum (mem. adv. bd. 1978—), Nat. Assn. Gifted Children, Alpha Delta Kappa (pres. Pa. Iota chpt. 1994-96). Roman Catholic. Avocations: photography, embroidery, writing. Home: 212 School Ln Mount Joy PA 17552-3127 Office: Pa Dept Education 333 Market Street 8th Floor Harrisburg PA 17126-0333 Office Phone: 717-787-4234.

MARTINEAU, LYNN, retail executive; Pres. western divsn. Home Depot, Atlanta. Office: Home Depot Inc 2455 Paces Ferry Rd SE Atlanta GA 30339-4024

MARTINELLI, JANET SUE, artist, educator; b. Glendale, Calif., June 6, 1944; d. Francis (Gus) C.F. and Mildred Nylene Minich; m. Harley Martinelli, 1965; 1 child, Bridey Elizabeth Chadwick. A, LaSalle Coll.; BS in Edn., Henderson State U., 1988. Cert. tchr. Ark. Tchr. high sch. art, music Amity Pub. Sch., 1994—96; tchr. k-12 Ouachita Pub. Schools, Donaldson, Ark., 1988—. E-mail: martins@ouachita.dsc.k12.ar.us.

MARTINES, EUGENIA BELLE, elementary school educator; b. Marion, Va., Feb. 28, 1939; d. Howard Kelly Gullion and Mary Enias Edwards-Gullion; m. Frank Fuentes Martines, May 23, 1959 (dec. Oct. 25, 1991). Student, Marion Jr. Coll., 1958; AA, Coll. of Sequoias, 1960; BEd, Calif. State U., Fresno, 1966; cert. in bilingual edn., Calif., 1996. Kindergarten tchr. Five Points (Calif.) Sch., 1962—63; 3d grade spl. edn. tchr., 6th grade and 1st grade tchr. Corcoran (Calif.) Joint Unified Schs., 1963—97. Mem. Kings County Citizens Adv. Bd. on Alcohol and Other Drugs, Hanford, Calif., 1986—2001, chmn., 1992; mem. Red Ribbon Com. on Kings County and Corcoran, 1989—2001, Kings County Health Adv. Bd., Hanford, 1997—2001, Kings County Master Plan on Alcohol and Other Drugs, Hanford, 1991—2001; tutoring students with dyslexia; credentials person region 6 Reform Party of Calif., 1997—. Recipient Poet Merit Silver Bowl award, Internat. Poet Soc., 2002. Mem.: NEA, Corcoran Faculty Assn., Calif. Tchrs. Assn., Internat. Soc. Poets, Soc. Children's Writers, Romance Writers of Am., Valley Writer's Network (pres. 1991—92), Fiction Writers' Connection, Photographers Assn., Kings County Critiquing (cofounder), PTA (life), Nat. Writers' Club. Reform. Roman Catholic. Avocations: reading, writing, breeding chihuahuas, political activism. Address: PO Box 458 Corcoran CA 93212-0458 E-mail: eugenia@savy2k.net., jingles@savypro.com.

MARTINEZ, ADRIANA, political organization worker, photographer; Student, U. Nev., Las Vegas; BA, Brooks Inst. Photography. Photography instr. C.C. So. Nev.; wedding photographer So. Nev. News Bur.; chair Nev. State Dem. Party, Las Vegas, 2003—. Mem.: PTA. Office: So Nev Dem Hdqrs Ste 496 1785 E Sahara Ave Las Vegas NV 89104

MARTINEZ, ALMA R. actress, theater director, educator; b. Monclova, Coahuila, Mex. Student, U. Guadalajara-Artes Plasticas, Mex., 1972-73, Ibero-Am. U., 1976, UNAM, Mexico City, 1976-77; BA in Theatre, Whittier Coll., 1984; MFA in Acting, U. So. Calif., 1995; postgrad., Stanford U., 1994- ; student, Jerzy Grotowski Para Theatre, Berkeley, Calif., 1977, Lee Strasberg Theatre Inst., Hollywood, Calif., 1982, Royal Acad. Dramatic Arts, London, Eng., 1987, Mnouchkine/Theatre du Soleil, Paris, 1993. Asst. prof. theatre arts U. Calif., Santa Cruz, 2001—. Appeared in plays including In the Summer House, Lincoln Ctr., N.Y.C., Greencard, Joyce Theatre, N.Y.C., Zoot Suit, Mark Taper Forum, L.A., Bocon, Mark Taper Forum, L.A., Macbeth, Oreg. Shakespeare Festival, The Skin of Our Teeth, Oreg. Shakespeare Festival, Hello Dolly, Long Beach Civic Light Opera, A Christmas Carol, South Coast Repertory, House of Blue Leaves, Pasadena Playhouse, Sundance Inst., Sundance, Utah, Fuente Ovejuna, Berkeley Repertory Theatre, Burning Patience, San Diego Repertory Theatre, Marriage of Figaro, Ariz. Theatre Co., Sons of Don Juan, Asolo Theatre, Fla., Wait Until Dark, Pa. Stage Co., La Carpa de los Rasquachis, Teatro Campesino; TV appearances include Gen. Hosp., Twilight Zone, Sequin, Corridos (Peabody award), Tough Love, Dress Gray, The Boys, In a Child's Name, The Gambler Returns, Quiet Killer, The New Adam 12 (series regular), 500 Nations, Nash Bridges (guest star); film appearances include Ballad of a Soldier, Jacaranda, The Novice, Trial by Terror, Dollie Dearest, Maria's Story, For A Loves One, Soldado Razo, Shattered Image, Zoot Suit, Barbarosa, Born in East L.A., Under Fire, among others; dir. (plays) Bed of Stone, 1996, La Gran Carpa de los Rasquachis, 1997, Heroes & Saints, 2001. Active Assistance with Alcohol and Sobriety Uniting Latinas, United L.Am. Youth, Med. Aid for El Salvador, Save the Children, the Christian Children's Fund; vol. and charity work in refugee camps in Ethiopia, India, Thailand, Sri Lanka, and The Philippines; bd. dirs. Mexican Mus., El Teatro Compresing. Recipient Cert. of Appreciation El Teatro Campesino, 1978, Recognition award Barrio Sta., 1980, Alumni Hall of Fame, El Rancho H.S., 1982, Outstanding Hispanic Alumni award Whittier Coll., 1984; co-recipient with Anthony Quinn and Edward James Olmos Hispanic Entertainer of Yr., The Equitable Co., 1987; Escobedo fellow Stanford U., 1996, Dorothy Danforth Compton Rsch. fellow, 1996. Mem. NATAS, AFTRA, SAG (John Dales scholar 1995-96, 98), TCG, Modern Lang. Assn., Assn. for Theatre in Higher Edn., Nat. Theatre Conf., Nat. Assn. Chicas and Chicano Studies, Actors Equity Assn. Address: JE Talent 323 Geary St #302 San Francisco CA 94102 Office: Univ Calif J-14 Theatre Arts Ctr Santa Cruz CA 95064 E-mail: almamar@catx.ucsc.edu.

MARTINEZ, CARMEN M. ambassador; b. Pensacola, Fla., July 1950; married; 1 child. MA in Medieval History, MS in Nat. Security and Strategic Resources. Various positions U.S. Fgn. Svc., Sao Paulo, Brazil, 1981, prin. officer, 1999—2002; chief of the consular sect. Quito, Ecuador, 1989—93; prin. officer U.S. consulate, Barranquilla, Colombia, 1993—94; numerous govt. positions, including dep. chief of mission Maputo, Mozambique, 1997—99; U.S. amb. to Burma, 2002—. Office: DOS Amb 4250 Rangoon Pl Washington DC 20521

MARTINEZ, DONNA F. federal judge; BA, U. Conn., 1973, MSW, 1975, JD, 1978. Bar: Conn. 1979. Corp. counsel City of Hartford, Conn., 1979-80; asst. U.S. atty. Office U.S. Atty., Hartford and New Haven, 1980-94; chief organized crime drug enforcement task force Dist. of Conn.., New Haven, 1989-94; magistrate judge U.S. Magistrate Ct., Hartford, 1994—. Instr. trial practice Yale U. Law Sch., New Haven, 1996-2001. Mem. Conn. Bar Assn., Fed. Bar Assn., Hispanic Bar Assn., Fed. Magistrate Judges Assn., Am. Inns of Ct. (past. v.p., past pres.), Am. Leadership Forum (bd. dirs.). Office: US Magistrate Ct 450 Main St Rm 262 Hartford CT 06103-3002

MARTINEZ, HERMINIA S. economist, banker; b. Havana, Cuba; came to U.S., 1960, naturalized, 1972; d. Carlos and Amelia (Santana) Martinez Sanchez; m. Mario Aguilar, 1982; children: Mario Aguilar, Carlos Aguilar. BA in Econs. cum laude, Am. U., 1965; MS in Fgn. Svc. (Univ. fellow); MS in Econs., Georgetown U., 1967, PhD in Econs., 1969; postgrad., Nat. U. Mex. Instr. econs. George Mason Coll., U. Va., Fairfax, 1967-68; researcher World Bank, 1967-69, indsl. economist, devel. econs. dept., 1969-71; economist World Bank Latin Am. (Ctrl. Am., Mex., Venezuala, Equador, Panama and Dominican Republic, Washington, 1971-79; sr. loan officer for Middle East and North Africa World Bank, 1977-81, sr. loan officer for Western Africa region, 1981-84, sr. economist Africa Region, 1988-91, prin. ops. officer pvt. sector fin. group Africa region, 1992-96, lead specialist, sub-regional mgr., 1996-2000; pvt. practice fin., econ. devel., 2000—. Contbg. author: The Economic Growth of Colombia: Problems and Prospects, 1973, Central American Financial Integration, 1975. Mid-Career fellow Princeton U., 1988-89. Mem. Am. Econ. Assn., Soc. Internat. Devel., Brookings Inst. Latin Am. Study Group. Roman Catholic. Home: 5145 Yuma St NW Washington DC 20016-4336 Office: World Bank 1818 H St NW Washington DC 20433-0001

MARTINEZ, IRIS, state senator; b. Chgo. 1 child. Grad., Northeastern U., U. Ill., Chgo. Mem. Ill. State Senate, Springfield, 2003—, mem. appropriations II com., health and human svcs. com. and sbucom. on health care, vice chhair com. on ins. and pensions, mem. subcom. on mandates. Liaison to Hispanic Ministry. Committeewoman Ill. Dem. State Com.; mem. Dem. Nat. Com. Democrat. Catholic. Office: Capitol M-106 Capitol Bldg Springfield IL 62706 also: District 3024 N Pulaski Rd Chicago IL 60641 also: Home office 3912 W Byron St #2W Chicago IL 60618

MARTINEZ, JEAN, newscaster; BA in journalism, U. Mo., 1985. Morning anchor, reporter WXII, Winston-Salem, NC, 1985—86; anchor, reporter KGBT, CBS affiliate, Harlingen, Tex., 1986—88; morning anchor KSAT, ABC affiliate, San Antonio, 1988, KCNC, CBS affiliate, Denver, 1988—95; anchor, reporter KTTV Fox 11, Los Angeles, 1995—. Host News for Kids, 1993—95. Office: KTTV Fox 11 1999 S Bundy Dr Los Angeles CA 90025-5235*

MARTINEZ, JOANNE, consultant; b. Phila., Jan. 19, 1950; d. Joseph F. and Nina Duvgoluk Olekszyk; m. Ernest J. Martinez; children: Kristin C., Erik J. BA, U. Pa., 1970; MBA, Adelphi U., 1973. Various position Internat. Paper and Singer Co., N.Y.C., 1977-82; v.p. Ambase Corp., N.Y.C., 1982-92, ADP, Roseland, N.J., 1992-94, Am. Banknote, N.Y.C., 1995-96; pres. Martinez Cons., Bklyn., 1996—. Bd. mem. ARC-Bklyn. chpt., 1989—. Achievements include placing 19th in 2004 indoor rowing world championships. Office: Martinez Consulting 594 E 5th St Brooklyn NY 11218-4916 Personal E-mail: jmartinez@pipeline.com.

MARTINEZ, JUDY PERRY, lawyer; b. New Orleans, La., Aug. 15, 1957; BS, La. State U., 1979; JD cum laude, Tulane U., 1982. Bar: La. 1982. Atty., chair Simon, Peragine, Smith & Redfearn, LLP, New Orleans, 1982—. Mem. Elmo B. Hunter Ctr. for Jud. Excellence, 1994—97; chairperson New Orleans Pro Bono Project, 1989. Fellow: Am. Bar Found., La. Bar Found. (life); mem.: ABA (commn. on women in the profession 1991—94, spl. advisor standing com. on fed. jud. 1994—95, bd. govs. 1996—99, exec. com. 1998—99, del.-at-large 1999—, gen. mem. sect. on litigation ABA Ho. of Dels. 2000—, nominating com. 1993—96, chair young lawyers divsn. 1990—91, chair commn. on domestic violence 1999—2001, young lawyers divsn. liaison to sect. litigation 1991—93, mem. exec. coun. young lawyers divsn. 1986—96, divsn. del. 1991—96), Am. Judicature Soc., Assn. for Women Attys., La. State Bar Assn. (chairperson minority involvement com. 1984—87, long range planning com. 1987—92, chairperson professionalism and quality of life com. 1992—93, chairperson post-conviction representation com. 1997—99), New Orleans Bar Assn. (chairperson young lawyers sect. 1986—87). Office: Simon Peragine Smith & Redfearn LLP 30th Fl Energy Ctr 1100 Poydras St New Orleans LA 70163-3000

MARTINEZ, MARGARET ANNE, education organization executive, psychologist; d. Henry John and Betty (Cuaron) Martinez; m. Victor Everett Arndt, Oct. 28, 1988. BA, Humboldt State U., Eureka, Calif., 1975; MS in Libr. Sci., Calif. State U., Fullerton, Calif., 1978; PhD in Instrnl. Psychology and Tech., Brigham Young U., Provo, Utah, 1999. Cert. in Information Systems USC, 1990. Rsch. and advanced info. specialist Dep. Under Sec. of Def. Rsch., Washington, 1987—88; info. specialist Def. Tech. Info. Ctr., Alexandria, Va., 1988—89; worldwide tng. & certification mgr. WordPerfect Corp., Provo, Utah, 1993—95; chief learning officer Tng. Pl., Inc., Oro Valley, Ariz., 1999—2000, CEO, 2000—; internat. tng. & certification mgr. WordPerfect, Eschborn, Germany, 1990—92. Bd. dirs. Alpine Media Corp., Inc., Provo, Utah; expert adv. bd. ElementK Corp., Rochestor, NY, 2001—. Researcher (instructional psychology research) Learning Orientation Research Program (Assn. for Computer Machinery Grad. Rsch. Award, 1999), (dissertation) An Investigation into Successful Learning-Measuring the Impact of Learning Orientation (a Primary Learner-Difference Variable) on Learning (Soc. for Tech. Communication (STC) Rsch. Award, 1999), (learning assessment instrument) Learning Orientation Questionnaire. Mem.: Assn. for the Advancement of Computing in Edn. Office: The Training Place Inc 743 W Bougainvillea Dr Oro Valley AZ 85737 Office Phone: 520-877-3991.

MARTINEZ, MARIA, computer software company executive; BA in elec. engring., U. PR; MA in computer engring, Ohio State U. Various mgmt. and engring. positions AT&T Bell Labs.; v.p., gen. mgr. Internet Connectivity Solutions Divsn. Motorola Inc.; CEO Embrace Network, Inc.; corp. v.p. comm. and mobile solutions unit Microsoft Corp. Named an Elite Woman, Hispanic mag., 2004; recipient several process and quality awards. Achievements include led Motorola's launching of first CDMA comml. sys. in world; played a leadership role in Bell Lab's devel. of UNIX sys. for symmetrics multiprocessing and high availability; patents for devel. and disk storage sys; launched first software platform and developed customer base for Embrace Networks, Inc; first female Hispanic named v.p. at Microsoft. Office: Microsoft Corp One Microsoft Way Redmond WA 98052-6399 Office Phone: 425-882-8080. Office Fax: 425-706-7329.*

MARTINEZ, MARIA DOLORES, pediatrician; b. Cifuentes, Cuba, Mar. 16, 1959; d. Demetrio and Alba Silvia (Perez) M.; m. James David Marple, Apr. 25, 1992. MD, U. Navarra, Pamplona, Spain, 1984. Med. diplomate. Resident in pediatrics Moses Cone Hosp., Greensboro, N.C., 1986-89; pvt. practice Charlotte, N.C., 1989-93, Mooresville, N.C., 1993-96; pediat. pulmonary fellow Univ. Med. Hosp., Tucson, 1996-99; pediatric pulmonologist, also in sleep medicine/transplants Duke U., Durham, N.C., 1999—, dir. pediat. lung transplant svcs., assoc. dir. sleep medicine lab., 2000—. Mem. AMA, Am. Acad. Pediatrics, N.C. Med. Soc., Mecklenburg County Med. Soc. Republican. Roman Catholic. Avocations: horseback riding, travel. Office: Duke U Med Ctr Dept Pediats PO Box 2994 Durham NC 27710-0001

MARTINEZ, NATALIE, newscaster; b. Buffalo; Degree, SUNY, Buffalo. Anchor, reporter, prodr. at upstate N.Y. radio and TV stations; reporter and weekend anchor WXAA-TV, Albany, NY, primary anchor; co-anchor weekend morning news and reporter WMAQ-TV, Chgo., 2001—. Mem.: UNAVOZ, Nat. League Female Execs., Nat. Assn. of Hispanic Journalists. Office: WMAQ-TV NBC Tower 454 N Columbus Dr Chicago IL 60611-5555

MARTINEZ, NICOLA MARIE, choreographer, educator; d. Elizabeth (Lovika) Allain and Pierre De Koninck(Stepfather), Michael Owen Mulholland; m. Raúl Paniagua Martínez, Dec. 31, 1999; 1 child, Mikaël Jonathan Mulholland. Student, Petit Séminaire de Québec, Que., Can., 1983; BA magna cum laude, U. Ottawa, 1988—91; MA, U. Calif., 1992—95, Doctoral Studies, 1994—96. Lectr., fine arts and communication Sul Ross State U., Alpine, Tex., 1997—2002, dir., sul ross ballet folklorico de las americas, 1997—2002; dir., desert islanders tahitian dance ensemble Desert Islanders Tahitian Dance Ensemble, Alpine, Tex., 1998—2002; dir., instrnl. tech. ctr. Sul Ross State U., Alpine, Tex., 1999—2002; coord., instrnl. design and curriculum devel. SUNY empire State Coll., Saratoga Springs, NY, 2002—. Dancer, choreographer, dir., performer various local, regional, nat. and internat. competitions, festivals, Sul Ross Ballet Folklorico and Desert Islanders Tahitian Dance Ensemble, Various, US and Mex., 1997—2002; project designer and project dir. wireless rural access collaborative, a region-wide wireless, Sul Ross State U., Alpine, Tex., 2000—02; sul ross state u. rep., tex. state u. sys. tech. com. Tex. State U. Sys., Austin, Tex., 2000—02; dir. Ballet Folklorico performance at the Jornadas Villistas in Parral, (Chihuahua, Mex.) Sul Ross State U., Alpine, Tex., 2000—02, Cinco de Mayo ballet folklorico presentation in the Rotunda State Capitol bldg., (Austin, Tex.)Sul Ross State U., Alpine, Tex., 2001; v.p. and bd. mem. Big Bend Players Cmty. Theatre, Alpine, Tex., 2002. Narrator, writer (contemporary tahitian dance enactment) Two Tahitian Creation Myths, writer, choreographer (play) Moe's Song; choreographer Deep Blue, Ote'a Atea, Ocean Moon, Otamu, A Solo for Sarah, Paea (Versions 1 and 2), Amazing Grace, Bora Bora, Vahine Tahiti. Grantee Competitive Discovery Grant, Tex. Telecom. Infrastructure Bd., 2000-2002. Achievements include first to Envision, research, and design a groundbreaking wireless distance-learning project, an ambitious, holistic, visionary e-learning delivery system. Home: P O Box 871 Saratoga Springs NY 12866 Office: SUNY Empire State Coll 3 Union Avenue Saratoga Springs NY 12866 Personal E-mail: nicolamartinez@msn.com. E-mail: nicola.martinez@esc.edu.

MARTINEZ, ROSE MARIE, health facility administrator; PhD, Johns Hopkins Sch. Hygiene and Pub. Health. Former asst. dir. health fin. and policy U.S. Gen. Acctg. Office; sr. health rschr. Mathematica Policy Rsch.; dir. IOM Bd. Health Promotion and Disease Prevention, 2002—. Office: 2101 Contitution Ave NW Washington DC 20418

MARTINEZ, VERA, academic administrator; b. San Bernardino, Calif., Nov. 12, 1939; d. Daniel Galvan and Adela (Machado) M.; 1 child, Stephanie Ann Murguia-Hammond. BA in Spanish, Calif. State U., 1962; MA in Sociology, U. Calif., Riverside, 1971, PhD in Ednl. Adminstrn., 1979. Spl. asst. to chancellor UCLA, 1979-81, dir., 1981-84; asst. dean Santa Monica (Calif.) College, 1984-85, dean, 1985-86, spl. assignment to pres., 1987-88, adminstrv. dean, 1990-92, 94-95, acting provost, 1992-94; pres. Fullerton (Calif.) Coll., 1995-98; vice chair instrnl. svcs. for dist. Fullerton, 1998-99; cons., 1999—. Presdl. appointee Nat. Institution Edn., Washington, 1971-75. Harvard fellow 1994. Mem. Cmty. Coll. League Calif., Calif. Assn. Cmty. Colls., Calif. Comm. Colls. (cons. chancellor's office 1992, bd. Latina Leadership 1988—), Nat. Network Hispanic Women (bd. dirs. 1980—). Home: 1041 Madison Pl Laguna Beach CA 92651-2805

MARTINEZ FALLON, ALMA URANIA, mechanical engineer; b. Constanza, Dominican Republic, Dec. 1, 1958; m. Stephen J. Brady. BSME, Old Dominion U., 1987. Engr. submarine design Newport News Shipbuilding, 1988-92, sr. engr. comml. design, 1992-95, engring. supr. aircraft carrier design, 1995-96, process mgr. process innovation, 1996—. Mem. ASME (mem. bd. on minorities and women 1996—), Soc. Women Engrs. (chmn. multi-cultural com. 1994-96, Disting. New Engr. 1997). Home: 2687 Heywood Ln Hayes VA 23072-4427

MARTINEZ-NEMNICH, MARICELA, realtor; b. Acapulco, Mex., June 24, 1949; arrived in U.S., 1995; d. Gilberto Martinez and Elena Errasquin; m. Guillerno Duran, Nov. 19, 1969 (div. Oct. 1983); children: Marisela, Veronica, Ana; m. Larry L. Nemnich, July 13, 1996. Lic. realtor. Mem.: Nat. Notary Assn. (pub. notary), Aurora Assn. Realtors, Nat. Assn. Realtors. Avocations: gardening, tennis, cooking. Home: 5617 S Winnipeg St Aurora CO 80015

MARTINO, CHERYL DERBY, insurance company secretary; b. Paterson, N.J., Jan. 19, 1946; d. Elles Mayo and Sarah Emma (Steele) D.; m. Leonard D. Martino, Nov. 4, 1995. BA, Elmira Coll., 1967; MBA, NYU, 1982. Tchr. Ramsey (N.J.) High Sch., 1967-70; contbns. analyst Met. Life Ins. Co., N.Y.C., 1970-83, fin. writer investments dept., 1983-93, asst. sec., 1994—. Bd. trustees United Meth. Ch. of Waldwick, N.J., v.p., 1989-91, pres., 1992-93, fin. sec., 2000—. Fellow Life Mgmt. Inst. (bd. dirs. Greater N.Y. chpt. 1984-91, pres. 1986, edn. coun. 1990-93), Life Mgmt. Inst. Edn. Coun. (nat. adminstrv. com. chmn. 1990-92, mktg. subcom. 1985-93), Nat. Orchestral Assn. (bd. dirs. 1990-92); mem. Elmira Coll. Alumni Club N.J. (exec. bd. 1982-87); mem. alumni bd. dirs. Elmira Coll.,1992—. Methodist. Office: Met Life 1 Madison Ave New York NY 10010-3603

MARTINO, DONNA FRANCES, newspaper sales administrator; BA, Coll. Mt. St. Vincent, 1969; MA, Columbia U., 1972. Cert. early childhood tchr., N.Y., N.J. Acct. mgr. Contra Costa Times, Walnut Creek, Calif., 1980-83; nat. acct. mgr. San Francisco Chronicle/Examiner, 1983-85; retail acct. exec. The N.Y. Times, N.Y.C., 1986—96, nat. acct. mgr., 1994-96; nat. sales mgr. pharms. advt. Newspaper Nat. Network, N.Y.C., 1996—2000; dir. pharm. Valassis Commn., 2000—02; cons., bd. mem. bus. mgr. Media Women, Inc., 2003—. Mem. Columbia U. Alumni Club Bergen/Passaic Counties (bd. dir., pres. 1998-2000). Avocations: sailing, rock climbing, antiques, art.

MARTINO MAZE, CLAIRE DENISE, nursing educator; d. Samuel Joseph and Clara Fusco Martino; 1 child, Elizabeth Raye Maze. AS in Nursing, Broward C.C., Coconut Creek, Fla., 1975; BSN, Fla. Atlantic U., 1994; MSN, Barry U., 2000, PhD in Nursing, 2004. RN Fla. Staff nurse Vanderbilt U. Hosp., Nashville, 1975—77; charge nurse Wilford Hall Med. Ctr., San Antonio, 1977—79; charge and staff nurse Dial-Rent-A-Nurse, Hialeah, Fla., 1980—82, Holy Cross Hosp., Ft. Lauderdale, Fla., 1982—85; office nurse Gyn. Office, Ft. Lauderdale, 1985—88; sch. and camp nurse Pine Crest Prep. Sch., Inc, Boca Raton, Fla., 1988—95; dir. nursing Venture Ambulatory Surgery Ctr., North Miami Beach, Fla., 1995—97; nurse educator Atlantic Tech. Ctr., Coconut Creek, Fla., 1997—2000; assoc. prof. nursing Palm Beach C.C., Lake Worth, Fla., 2000—02; asst. prof., nursing, dir. nursing resource ctr. Barry U., Miami Shores, Fla., 2002—. Nominating com. Sigma Theta Tau Internat., Iota XI Chpt., 1997—98; newsletter editor Sigma Theta Tau Internat., Lambda Chi Chpt., 2002—; presenter in field. Author: Nursing Care of Patients with Gastrointestinal Cancer: A Staff Development Approach, 2002. Mem. Nat. Org. for Women, Ft. Lauderdale, Fla., 1983—; bd. dirs. FNA Del., Fla. Nurses Assn., Ft. Lauderdale, Fla., 2001—. Decorated Army Svc. Ribbon 324 Combat Support Hosp., Nat. Def. Svc. medal 324th Combat Support Hosp., Army Res. Components Achievement medal 10/108 (PN/HS) Bn.; recipient faculty recognition, 10th Bn. PN Detachment, 1999; Fla. Nurses Found. grantee, 2000, Barry U. Mini Rsch. grantee, 2003. Mem.: NOW, ANA, Fla. Nurses Assn. (del. 2001), Nat. League Nurses, Sigma Theta Tau Internat. (nominating com. Iota Xi chpt. 1997—98, newsletter editor Lambda Chi chpt. 2002—, pres. elect). Office: Barry U 11300 NE 2nd Ave Miami Shores FL 66161-6695 E-mail: cmaze@mail.barry.edu.

MARTIN-O'NEILL, MARY EVELYN, advertising, marketing, business writing, sales training consultant; b. Lexington, Ky. d. George Clarke and Georgann Elizabeth (Bovis) M.; m. John Michael O'Neill, May 24, 1998. BA magna cum laude, Lindenwood Coll.; MA with honors, U. Ky. Asst. to pres. The Hamlets, Ltd/Park Place Country Homes, Louisville, 1984-85; advt. designer, copywriter Park Place Country Homes, Anchorage, Ky., 1985-86; creative dir. of advt., mktg., v.p., treas. Park Place Country Homes/Park Place Properties, Anchorage, Ky., 1986—; mktg. comm. specialist Mayfield Publ., Mountain View, Calif., 1998; curriculum developer Oracle Corp., Redwood Shores, Calif., 1998-2000; sr. info. designer/tech. writer BenefitPoint, Inc., San Francisco, 2000—02; sales tng. and mktg. comms. mgr. Applied Underwriters, San Francisco, 2002—. Founder, pres. Good Help Cons. Svcs., Louisville and Lexington, Maison Marche Advt. & Promotions, Louisville, 1989; instr. dept. English U. Ky., 1989—91; adj. prof. composition U. Louisville, 1991—97; vis. lectr. lit. Bellarmine Coll., Louisville, 1992; adj. prof. humanities Ind. U. S.E., 1991—95; instr. DeVry U., 2002—, Am. Intercontinental U., 2003—, City Coll. San Francisco, 2003—; prof. arts and humanities McKendree Coll., Louisville, 1993—97; lectr. San Francisco State U. Coll. Bus., 2000—; writer, historian Home Builders Assn. Louisville, 1996. Editor: (poetry mag.) The Griffin, 1979-80, Bus. Wire, 1997; contbr. series to mag., 1996. Mem. People for the Am. Way, Greenpeace. Recipient Spahmer creative writing award, 1979; Haggin fellow U. Ky., 1987; grantee U. Louisville, 1992-95. Mem. Am. Film Inst., Nat. Assn. Home Builders (affiliate), Ky. Film Artists Coalition, Women in Tech. Internat. Democrat. Avocations: weaving, screenwriting. Office: 915 Cole St # 300 San Francisco CA 94117

MARTINSON, IDA MARIE, nursing educator, physiologist, medical/surgical nurse; b. Mentor, Minn., Nov. 8, 1936; d. Oscar and Marvel (Nelson) Sather; m. Paul Varo Martinson, Mar. 31, 1962; children: Anna Marie, Peter. Diploma, St. Luke's Hosp. Sch. Nursing, 1957; BS, U. Minn., 1960, M.N.A., 1962; PhD, U. Ill., Chgo., 1972. Instr. Coll. St. Scholastica and St. Luke's Sch. Nursing, 1957—58, Thornton Jr. Coll., 1967—69; lab. asst. U. Ill. at Med. Ctr., 1970—72; lectr. dept. physiology U. Minn., St. Paul, 1972—82, asst. prof. Sch. Nursing, 1972—74, assoc. prof. rsch., 1974—77, prof., dir. rsch., 1977—82; prof. dept. family health care U. Calif., San Francisco, 1982—2003, chmn. dept., 1982—90. Vis. rsch. prof. Nat. Taiwan U., Def. Med. Ctr., 1981; vis. prof. nursing Sun Yat-Sen U. Med. Scis., Guang Zhou, China, Ewha Women's U., Seoul, Republic of Korea, Frances Payne Bolton Sch. Nursing, Case Western Res. U., Cleve., 1994—96; chair, prof. dept. health scis. Hong Kong Poly. U., 1996—2000. Author: Mathematics for the Health Science Student, 1977; Editor: Home Care for the Dying Child, 1976, Women in Stress, 1979, Women in Health and Illness, 1986, The Child and Family Facing Life Threatening Illness, 1987, Family Nursing, 1989, Home Health Care Nursing, 1989, Home Health Care Nursing, 2d edit., 2002; contbr. chapters to books, articles to profl. jours. Active Am. Cancer Soc. Recipient Book of Yr. award, Am. Jour. Nursing, 1977, 1980, 1987, 1990, Humanitarian award for pediat. nursing, 1993; fellow, Fulbright Found., 1991. Mem.: ANA, Inst. Medicine, Am. Acad. Nursing, Coun. Nurse Rschrs., Sigma Theta Tau, Sigma Xi. Lutheran. Address: 12149 E Movil Lake Rd NE Bemidji MN 56601

MARTINSON, RITA R. state legislator; b. Gloster, Miss., Sept. 11, 1937; d. D.M. and Beulah (LeDoux) Randall; m. William K. Martinson Sr., Aug. 2, 1958; children: Ginny Martinson Vampran, Karen Martinson McKie, W.K. Jr., Allen. BA in Polit. Sci., Millsaps Coll., 1991. Mem. Miss. Ho. of Reps., 1992—. Mem. Madison County Rep. Exec. Com., 1988-91; active Madison Arboretum, 1992—. Mem. Madison County C. of C. (Outstanding Citizen 1992), City of Madison C. of C., Madison County Rep. Women's Club, Ridgeland/Northpark Lions Club (past v.p. 1990-91), Ofcl. Miss. Women's Club (pres.), Rep. Elected Ofcls. Club (sec.). Roman Catholic. Avocations: flying, reading, gardening, photography. Home: 1472 Highway 51 Madison MS 39110-9095 Office: Miss State Ho of Reps PO Box 1018 Jackson MS 39215-1018

MARTIN-WEIKLE, MARY JANE, medical/surgical nurse; b. Hinton, W.Va., May 30, 1959; d. William Marshall and Nellie Marie Martin; m. Joseph Wayne Weikle, Feb. 14, 1991; 1 child, Joede Anne-Marie. AN, W.Va. Tech. Inst., Montgomery, 1991. RN Summers County Hosp., Hinton, 1982—94, Appalachian Regional Hosp., Hinton, 1994—. V.p. Econ. and Gen. Welfare for RNs Orgn., Charleston, W.Va., 1998—2000. Mem.: W.Va. Nurses Assn. (pres. Summers County chpt. 1998—2000, v.p. 2000—02). Democrat. Methodist. Avocations: genealogy, gardening, canning, quilting. Home: PO Box 104 Forest Hill WV 24935-0104

MARTONE, JEANETTE RACHELE, artist; b. Mineola, N.Y., June 5, 1956; d. John and Mildred Cecilia (Loehr) M. BFA, SUNY, Purchase, 1978. One woman shows include Ariel Gallery, N.Y.C., 1990, La Mantia Gallery, Northport, N.Y., 1994-96, Inter-Media Arts Ctr., Huntington, N.Y., 1996, St. Xavier U. SXU Gallery, Chgo., 2003; exhibited in group shows from 1980 to 2002 including Harbor Gallery, Cold Spring Harbor, 1980, Huntington Coun. Arts, 1986, Pindar Gallery, N.Y.C., 1987, Mills Pond House, Smithtown, N.Y., 1987, Suffolk County Exec. Offices, Hauppage, N.Y., 1988, La Mantia Gallery, Northport, N.Y., 1990, Nassau County Office Cultural Affairs, 1991, Ward-Nasse. Gallery, N.Y.C., 1991, Monsterrat Gallery, N.Y.C., 1991, Priscilla Redfield Roe Gallery, Bellport, N.Y., 1991, L.I. U., Brookville, 1992, Northport B.J. Spoke Gallery, Huntington, N.Y., 1992, Fischetti Gallery, N.Y., 1992, Artists Space, N.Y.C., 1992, N.Y. Botanical Gardens, Bronx, N.Y., 1993, Visions Gallery, Albany, L.I. U., Brookville, N.Y., 1994, Goodman Gallery, Southampton, N.Y., 1994, B.J. Spoke Gallery, Huntington, N.Y., 1994-95, 2003, Islip Art Mus., East Islip, N.Y., 1994, 2003, L.I. MacArthur Airport, Ronkonkoma, N.Y., 1995, The Stage Gallery, N.Y., 1997, Lightworks Gallery, Glen Cove, N.Y., 1997, Showcase 98, Smithtown Twp. Arts Coun., St. James, N.Y., 1998, Nat. League Am. Pen Women, Inc., 1999, N.Y. Open Ctr., N.Y.C., 1999, Cork Gallery, Lincoln Ctr., N.Y.C., 1999, Omni Gallery, Uniondale, N.Y., 1999, Nat. League of Am. Pen Woman Inc., Bienniel, Belmont, Calif., 2002, Nat. League of Am. Pen Woman, Inc., Smithtown, N.Y., 2001, St. John's U. 7th Annual Juried exhb., Jamaica, N.Y., 2001, Huntington Arts Coun., Huntington, N.Y., 2001, 2003, Smithtown Township Arts Coun., 2001, Marymount Manhattan Coll., N.Y.C., 2002, St. Xavier U. Gallery, Chgo., Ill., 2003, Marymount Manhattan Coll., N.Y., 2003; publs. include The Other Side Mag., 1997, 1999, 2000-03, The Artist's Mag., 1999, Art Calendar, 1995, 2000, 2004, Portrait Inspirations, 1997, The Best of Oil Painting, 1996; artwork published in profl. publs. Recipient Award of Excellence Gold medal Art League of Nassau County, 1993, Best in Show award Nat. League Am. PEN Women Artists, 1990, 92, Windsor and Newton award for oil Arts Coun. East Islip, N.Y., 1989, award of excellence Art League of Nassau County, 1987, 88, many best in shows including 1st Ann. Juried Art Exhibit, Brookhaven Arts and Humanities Coun., Farmingville, N.Y., 1996, Supervisor's award Babylon Citizens Coun. Arts Juried Exhbn., 1994, Bob Jones Glad Hand Press award Stamford Art Assn., 1995, Faber Biren Nat. Color award Stamford Art Assn., 1995, Ann. Mem. Art Forum award of Excellence, Smithtown, N.Y., 1999, Award of Excellence Smithtown Twp. Arts Coun. Mem. Show, St. James, N.Y., 1997, 1999, Nat. League of Am. Pen Woman, Inc. Belmont, Calif. award of Excellence, 2002, Catharine Lorillard Wolfe Art Club Inc. Portrait award, 2002, Anna Hyatt Huntington Horse's Head award for best painting, 2003, Art League of L.I., Huntington, N.Y., Pall Corp. award of excellence, 2003. Mem. Nat. League of Am. Pen Women, Catherine Lorillard Wolfe Art Club (Frank B. and Mary Anderson Cassidy Meml. award 1992, Award for Oil 1987Margaret Dole Portrait award 2002, Anna Hyatt Huntington Horse's Head award 2003), Allied Artists of Am. (John Young Hunter Meml. award 1993, Antonio Cerino Meml. award 1990, award of Excellence 1997), Hudson valley Art Assn., Knickerbock Artists of Am., Nat. Art League. Avocations: travel, reading, volunteer work. Home: 47 Summerfield Ct Deer Park NY 11729-5642

MARTONE, PATRICIA ANN, lawyer; b. Bklyn., Apr. 28, 1947; d. David Andrew and Rita Mary (Dullmeyer) Martone. BA in Chemistry, NYU, 1968, JD, 1973; MA in Phys. Chemistry, Johns Hopkins U., 1969. Bar: N.Y. 1974, U.S. Dist. Ct. (so. and ea. dists.) N.Y. 1975, U.S. Ct. Appeals (2d cir.) 1975, U.S. Ct. Appeals (1st cir.) 1981, U.S. Patent and Trademark Office 1983, U.S. Ct. Appeals (fed. cir.) 1984, U.S. Supreme Ct. 1984, U.S. Dist. Ct. (ea. dist.) Mich. 1985, U.S. Dist. Ct. (no. dist.) Calif. 1995. Tech. rep. computer timesharing On-Line Sys., Inc., N.Y.C., 1969-70; assoc. Kelley Drye & Warren, N.Y.C., 1973-77, Fish & Neave, N.Y.C., 1977-82, ptnr., 1983—. Adj. prof. NYU Sch. Law, 1990—; mem. adv. coun. Engelberg Ctr. Innovation Law & Policy, 1996—; participating atty. Cmty. Law Offices, N.Y.C., 1974—78; atty. Pro Bono Panel U.S. Dist. Ct. (so. dist.) N.Y., 1982—84; lectr. Practising Law Inst., N.Y.C., 1995—, Aspen Law & Bus., 1990—95, Franklin Pierce Law Sch., 1992—97, Lic. Exec. Soc.; chair, bd. dirs. N.Y. Lawyers for the Pub. Interest, 1996—98, vice chair, 1998—2000, 2002—, Legal Svcs., N.Y.C., 1991—95. Mng. editor NYU Law Sch. Rev. Law and Social Change, 1972-73; contbr. articles to profl. jours. Recipient Founder's Day award NYU Sch. Law, 1973; NSF grad. trainee Johns Hopkins U., 1968-69; NYU scholar, 1964-68. Mem. ABA, Assn. Bar City N.Y. (mem. environ. law com. 1978-83, trademarks, unfair competition com. 1983-86), Fed. Bar Coun., Fed. Cir. Bar Assn., Copyright Soc., Am. Chem. Soc., Licensing Execs. Soc., N.Y. Intellectual Property Law Assn., Univ. Club. Office: Fish & Neave Fl 49 1251 Ave of the Americas New York NY 10020-1105 Office Phone: 212-596-9000. E-mail: pmartone@fishneave.com.

MARTORANA, BARBARA JOAN, secondary school educator; b. NYC, Oct. 18, 1942; d. Samuel and Joan Renee (Costello) M. BA, St. John's U., Jamaica, N.Y., 1970, MS in English Edn., 1972; advanced cert. computers in edn., L.I. U., 1988, profl. diploma in edn. adminstrn., 1990. Cert. sch. dist. adminstr., sch. adminstr. and supr., tchr. English grades 7-12, NY, Ed.D, Lit. Studies, Hofstra U., Hempstead, NY, 2003. Exec. sec. Am. Petroleum Inst., NYC, 1960-65; exec. asst. to v.p. Goldring, Inc., NYC, 1965-67; exec. asst. Rsch. Inst. for Cath. Edn., NYC, 1967-69; English tchr. St. Martin of Tours Sch., Amityville, NY, 1970-77; Oceanside Jr. HS, NY, 1977-78, Freeport HS, NY, 1979—. Rec. sec. Freeport (N.Y.) Tchr. Ctr. Policy Bd., 1986-89; co-chair Middle States Steering Com., Freeport, 1988-90; chair Freeport (N.Y.) H.S. Shared Decision Team, 1992-93; adv. bd. L.I. Writing Project, Garden City, N.Y., 1993—, co-leader Summer Insts.; adj. prof. literacy studies dept. Hofstra U., N.Y., 1999—. Co-author: (textbooks) Writing Competency Practice, 1980, Writing Competency Practice-Revised and Expanded, 1989. With Seaford (NY) Rep. Club, 1975—. Mem. ASCD, Nat. Coun. Tchrs. English (conf. on English edn.), N.Y. State English Coun., L.I. Writing Project. Avocations: reading, writing, traveling. Office: Freeport HS 50 S Brookside Ave Freeport NY 11520-3144 Office Phone: 516-867-5300. E-mail: engteech@aol.com.

MARTYL, (MRS. ALEXANDER LANGSDORF JR.), artist; b. St. Louis, Mar. 16, 1917; d. Martin and Aimee (Goldstone) Schweig; m. Alexander Langsdorf, Jr., Dec. 31, 1941; children: Suzanne, Alexandra. AB, Washington U., St. Louis, 1938. Instr. art dept. U. Chgo.; artist in residence Tamarind Inst., U. N.Mex., Albuquerque, 1974 Solo shows include, Calif. Palace of Legion of Honor, 1956, Chgo. Art Inst., 1949, 76, Feingarten Galleries, N.Y.C., Beverly Hills and Chgo., 1961, 62, 63, St. Louis, 1962, Feingarten Gallery, N.Y.C., 1963, L.A., 1964, Kovler Gallery, Chgo., 1967, Washington U., St. Louis, 1967, U. Chgo. Oriental Inst. Mus., 1970, Deson&Zaks Gallery, 1973, Fairweather-Hardin Gallery, 1977, 81, 83, Ill. State Mus., 1978, Fermilab, 1985, 91, Bklyn. Mus., 1986, Oriental Inst. Mus., 1987, Gibbes Art Mus., Charleston, S.C., 1988, Fairweather-Hardin Gallery, 1988, Tokyo Internat. Art Expo, 1990, State of Ill. Art Gallery, Chgo., 1990, Expo Navy Pier, Chgo., 1993, Printworks Gallery Ltd., Chgo., 1995, 97, 99, 2002, 04, Navy Pier, Chgo., 2003, Oriental Inst. Mus., Chgo., Martyl: Nature/Artifice Ft. Wayne Mus. Art, 2000; represented in permanent collections, Met. Mus. Art, Chgo. Art Inst., Pa. Acad. Fine Arts, Ill. State Mus., Bklyn. Mus., DuSable Mus., Chgo., Los Angeles County Mus., Whitney Mus. Am. Art, Davenport (Iowa) Municipal Mus., St. Louis Art Mus., Washington U., U. Ariz., Arnot Gallery, Elmira, N.Y., Greenville (S.C.) Mus., Nat. Coll. Fine Arts, Hirshhorn Mus. and Sculpture Gallery, Rockford (Ill.) Mus. Recipient 1st prize City Art Mus., St. Louis, 1943, 44; Armstrong prize Chgo. Art Inst., 1947; William H. Bartels award, 1953; Frank Logan medal and prize, 1950; Walt Disney purchase award Los Angeles Museum; purchase prize Portrait of America competition, Colo. Springs Fine Arts Center, 1961; honor award for mural AIA, 1962, Outstanding Achievement award in the Arts YWCA, 1986; named Artist of Year Am. Fedn. Arts, 1958 Mem. Chgo. Network, Arts Club (Chgo.). Unitarian Universalist.

MARTYSKA, BARBARA, composer, performer, teacher; b. Phila., Nov. 16, 1936; d. Alexander Thomas and Sophia Victoria (Romanek) M.; m. Gerald Bernard Buckley, Dec. 29, 1956 (div. 1972); children: Regina Buckley-Fried, Sandra Buckley-Rusnov, Gerald Thomas Buckley, Paul David Buckley, Mary Elizabeth Buckley; m. James William Lieberman, Sept. 17, 1978. Freelance composer home studio, Allentown, Pa., 1980—; pvt. studio tchr. Allentown, 1971—, Cmty. Music Sch., Allentown, 1986-96; music for handicapped Good Shepherd Home, Allentown, 1986-91. Founder Second Sunday Salon performance series, 2001—; adjudicator various piano/composition competitions. Composer Cloud Watching, 1994, Two Minuets, 1995, In the Silence, 1996, Russian Legend, 1997, In the Still Hours, 1998; author (piano books) From Canyons to Highlands, 1995, Ancient Echoes, 1995, Adventures and Amusements, 1998, Ordinary and Extraordinary Animals, 1998. Recipient ASCAP spl. award, 1996-2003. Mem. ASCAP, Internat. Alliance Women in Music, Music Tchrs. Nat. Assn. (composition chair 1998-2000, pres. local chpt. 1995-97, v.p. local chpt. 1993-95), Nat. Fedn. Music Clubs (composers award merit 1993, 98). Avocations: reading, gardening. Home: 1716 Saratoga Ct Allentown PA 18104-1716 E-mail: BMmusic@fast.net.

MARTZ, JUDY HELEN, governor; b. Big Timber, Mont., July 28, 1943; m. Harry Martz, June 23, 1965; children: Justin, Stacey. Owner, operator Martz Disposal Svc., 1971—; skater U.S. World Speed Skating Team, Japan, 1963, U.S. Olympic Team, Innsbruck, Austria, 1964; exec. dir. U.S. High Altitude Speed Skating Ctr., Butte, Mont., 1985-89; field rep. Senator Conrad Burns, 1989—95; lt. gov. State of Mont., 1997-2001, gov., 2001—. Coach Mont. Amateur Speed Skating Assn.; bd. dirs. Youth Hockey Assn.; pres. adv. bd. U.S. Internat. Speed Skating Assn. Bd dirs. St. James Cmty. Hosp., Legion Oasis HUD Housing Project. Named Miss Rodeo Mont., 1963; inducted Butte Sports Hall of Fame, 1987. Republican.*

MARUCA, RITA, real estate company executive, real estate broker; b. Italy, Sept. 15, 1957; came to the U.S., 1974; d. Italo Talarico and Rosa Rotundo; m. Luigi Maruca, Oct. 27, 1973; children: Concetta, Italo, Anthony. Ed. in Italy. Mgr. FNY, Jackson Heights, N.Y., 1988-90, Era Vision, Corona, N.Y., 1990-91; salesperson Century 21 Sam & Raj, Corona, 1991-95, Era Today, Floral Park, N.Y., 1995-97; broker, owner Parkview Realty LLC, Corona, 1997—. Mem. Lions Internat. Office: Parkview Realty LLC 50-07 108th St Corona NY 11368

MARUOKA, JO ANN ELIZABETH, retired information systems manager; b. Monrovia, Calif., Jan. 1, 1945; d. John Constantine and Pearl (Macovei) Gotsinas; m. Lester Hideo Maruoka, Nov. 8, 1973 (div. Aug. 1992); stepchildren: Les Scott Kaleohano, Lee Stuart Keola. BA with honors, UCLA, 1966; MBA, U. Hawaii, 1971. Office mgr. and asst. R. Wenkam, Photographer, Honolulu, 1966-69; computer mgmt. intern and sys. analyst Army Computer Sys. Command, Honolulu, 1969-78; reservations mgr. Hale Koa Hotel, Honolulu, 1978-79; equal employment opportunity specialist U.S. Army Pacific Hdqs., Honolulu, 1979-80, computer specialist, 1980-87, supervisory info. sys. mgr., chief info. tech. plans and programs, 1987-2001; ret., 2001. Bd. dirs. High Performance Computing and Comm. Coun., Tiverton, R.I.; pacific v.p. Fedn. Govt. Info. Processing Couns., Washington, 1992-95. Mem. Nat. and Hawaii Women's Polit. Caucus, Honolulu, 1987—; pres. Fed. Women's Coun. Hawaii, Honolulu, 1976-77, advisor, 1977—; sec. Hawaii LWV, 2003—. Recipient Svc. award Fed. Women's Coun. Hawaii, 1986, EEO Excellence award Sec. of Army, 1989, Pacific Fed. Mgr. award Honolulu-Pacific Fed. Exec. Bd., 1990, Info. Resources Mgmt. award Interagy. Com. on Info. Resources Mgmt., 1991, Lead Dog Leadership award Fedn. Govt. Info. Processing Couns., 1993; named One of Fed. 100 (Execs.) of Yr., Fed. Computer Week, 1996. Mem. NAFE, Nat. Women's Polit. Caucus, AAUW, LWV, Armed Forces Comm.-Electronics Assn. (Hawaii chpt., Internat. award for Info. Resources Mgmt. Excellence 1992), Assn. U.S. Army (Pacific Fed. Mgr. award 1990), Federally Employed Women (advisor Aloha and Rainbow chpts. 1977—), Army Signal Corps Regtl. Assn. (Bronze Order of Mercury 1997, Silver Order of Mercury, 2001), Hawaii Intergovt. Info. Processing Coun. (pres. 1988-89, svc. award 1989), Hawaii LWV (sec.). Avocations: travel, reading, tai chi, support of performing arts.

MARUZO-BOLDUC, LISA MARIE, protective services official; b. Norwich, Conn., Oct. 19, 1956; Human Rels., Ea. Conn. State U., 1983—87. Police chief Willimantic Police Dept., Willimantic, Conn., 2003—, police capt., 1993—2003. Mem.: FBI Nat. Acad. Office: Willimantic Police Department 22 Meadow St Willimantic CT 06226 E-mail: wmtc.pol@snet.net.

MARVEL, L. PAIGE, judge; b. Easton, Md., Dec. 6, 1949; d. E. Warner Marvel and Louise Harrington Harrison; m. Robert H. Dyer, Jr., Aug. 9, 1975; children: Alex W. Dyer, Kelly E. Dyer. BA magna cum laude, Notre Dame Coll., 1971; JD with honors, U. Md., 1974. Bar: Md. 1974, U.S. Dist. Ct. Md. 1974, U.S. Tax Ct. 1975, U.S. Ct. Appeals (4th cir.) 1977, U.S. Supreme Ct. 1980, U.S. Ct. Claims 1981, D.C. 1985. Assoc. Garbis & Schwait, P.A., Balt., 1974-76, shareholder, 1976-85, Garbis, Marvel & Junghans, P.A., Balt., 1985-86; mem. Melnicove, Kaufman, Weiner, Smouse & Garbis, P.A., Balt., 1986-88; ptnr. Venable, Baetjer and Howard LLP, Balt., 1988-98; judge U.S. Tax Ct., Washington, 1998—. Mem. U. Md.

Law Sch. Bd. Vis., 1995—2001; mem. adv. com. U.S. Dist. Ct. Md., 1991—93; mem. Commr.'s Rev. Panel on IRS Integrity, 1989—91. Co-editor procedure dept. Jour. Taxation, 1989-98; contbr. chpts. to books, articles to profl. jours. Active Women's Law Ctr., 1974-85, Md. Dept. Econ. and Cmty. Devel. Adv. Com., 1978-80; trustee Loyola-Notre Dame Libr., Inc., 1996-2003. Recipient recognition award Balt. Is Best Program, 1981; named One of Md.'s Top 100 Women, The Daily Record, 1998; recipient MSBA Taxation section's Tax Excellence award, 2002. Fellow Am. Bar Found., Md. Bar Found., Am. Coll. Tax Counsel (regent 1995-98); mem. ABA (sect. taxation coun. dir. 1989-92, vice-chair com. ops. 1993-95, Disting. Svc. award, Jules Ritholz award 2004), Am. Law Inst. (advisor restatement of law third, law governing lawyers), Md. Bar Assn. (chmn. taxation sect. 1982-83, bd. dirs. 1988-90, 96-98, Disting. Svc. award), Balt. Bar Assn. (at-large exec. coun.), Am. Tax Policy Inst. (trustee 1997-98), Serjeant's Inn, Rule Day Club. Avocations: golf, music, travel. Home: 7109 Sheffield Rd Baltimore MD 21212-1628 Office: US Tax Ct 400 2d St NW Washington DC 20217-0001 Office Phone: 202-606-8871. E-mail: lawsoi@bellatlantic.net.

MARVIN, BARBARA JOYCE, writer; b. Garden City, N.Y., July 31, 1954; d. Roland Reed Jr. and Ruth Doris (Henze) Hummel; m. Lewis Beach Marvin III, July 5, 1977; children: Lewis Beach Marvin IV, Henze Louise, Maximilian Gardner. BA in English Lit., Finch Coll., 1975; postgrad., Marymouht Manhattan, 1975, Adelphi U., 1975. Ballerina Malibu Ballet by the Sea, 1980-98; owner animal sanctuary Moonfire Ranch, Malibu, 1957—. Author: Tales from Moonfire, 4 vols., 1995-98; author short stories, hist. love tales. Mem. Pacific Asian Mus., Malibu Libr. Mem. Met. Club (N.Y.), Malibu Ballet Soc. Republican. Avocations: ballet, exotic animals, vegetarianism, poetry and prose, fashion modeling, private investor. Home and Office: 23852 Pacific Coast Hwy # 349 Malibu CA 90265-4879

MARVIN, D. JANE, consumer products company executive; B in Econs., U. Sussex, Eng.; MBA, U. Mich. V.p. human resources Ameritech, Gen. Bus. Svcs., 1997—99; exec. v.p. human resources Covad Com. Group, Inc., 1999—2001, AT&T Wireless Svcs., Inc., Redmond, Wash., 2001—. Office: AT&T Wireless Svcs Inc NE Bldg 1 7277 164th Ave Redmond WA 98052

MARVIN, FREDA MARY, art educator, nurse; b. Everett, Wash., July 3, 1930; d. Robert Laffayette and Georgeina (Mahlstedt) Pressey; m. Donald Conrad Lawrence, 1950 (div. 1966); children: Linda, Karen, Donna, Betty; m. William Hammond Marvin, July 30, 1971. AA, San Jose City Coll., 1964; BS, Calif. State U., Fresno, 1974; cert., Beartooth Sch. Wildlife, 1995, 96. RN, Calif.; cert. sch. audiometrist Calif. Head nurse II Agnew State Hosp., San Jose, Calif., 1964-71; head nurse I Med. Ctr. Fresno (Calif.), 1971-72; intern nurse St. Agnes Hosp., Fresno, 1974-75; sch. nurse Teague Sch. Dist., Fresno, 1976-78; intensive care pvt. duty nurse Fresno, 1980-94; relief dir. nursing Sierra View Convescent Hosp., Fresno, 1995; art tchr. Marvin Art Studio, Prather, Calif., 1995—. Numerous two-women and group shows including Timberline Gallery, Oakhurst, Calif., Marvin Art Gallery, Prather, Calif. Fresno State Coll. scholar, 1973, 74; recipient Art award Clovis Art Guild, Soc. Western Artists Signature Show award, 1999. Mem. Soc. Western Artists (pres. 1994, 95, degree of honor 1993), Yosemite Western Artists (exec. bd. dirs. 1980-90, exec. bd. 1995, awards). Republican. Avocations: gardening, painting, reading, computer. Home: 14916 Garlock Ln Prather CA 93651-9731 Fax: 209-322-0904. E-mail: Bilfrema@msn.com.

MARVIN, URSULA BAILEY, retired geologist; b. Bradford, Vt., Aug. 20, 1921; d. Harold Leslie and Alice Miranda (Bartlett) Bailey; m. Lloyd Burton Chaisson, June 28, 1944 (div. 1951); m. Thomas Crockett Marvin, Apr. 1, 1952. BA, Tufts Coll., 1943; MA, Harvard/Radcliffe Coll., 1946; PhD, Harvard U., 1969. Rsch. asst. dept. geology U. Chgo., 1947-50; mineralogist Union Carbide Corp., N.Y.C., 1952-58; instr. dept. geology Tufts U., Medford, Mass., 1958-61; geologist Smithsonian Astrophysics Obs., Cambridge, Mass., 1961-98; lectr. geology Harvard U., Cambridge, 1974-92; sr. geologist emeritus Harvard-Smithsonian Ctr. for Astrophysics, Cambridge, 1998. Vis. prof. dept. geology Ariz. State U., Tempe, 1978; trustee Tufts U., 1975-85, trustee emeritus, 1988—; trustee U. Space Rsch. Assn., Columbia Md., 1979-84, chmn., 1982-83; sec.-gen. Internat. Commn. on History Geol. Scis., 1989-96, v.p. for N.Am., 1996—. Author: Continental Drift, 1973; contbr. chpt.: Astronomy from Space, 1983, The Planets, 1985, Les Météorites, 1996, James Hutton-Present and Future, 1999, The Earth Inside and Out: Some Major Contributions to Geology in the Twentieth Century, 2002; assoc. editor Earth in Space, Am. Geophys. Union, 1988-90; contbr. articles to profl. jours. Chair profl. accomplishments evaluation com. Smithsonian Astro-Phys. Obs., 1986-92, 2001—; mem. Lunar and Planetary Sci. Coun., Houston, 1987-91; chair Antarctic Meteorite Working Group NSF-NASA-Smithsonian Instn., 1993-99. Recipient Antarctic Svc. medal NSF, 1983, Sustained Superior Achievement award SAO, 1988, 93, 96, Lifetime Achievement award Women in Sci. and Engring., 1997, Lifetime Achievement award Harvard-Smithsonian Ctr. for Astrophysics, 1997; Asteroid Marvin named in her honor Minor Planet Bur. of Internat. Astron. Union, 1991, Marvin Nunatak (mountain peak rising through the Antarctic ice sheet) named in her honor U.S. Bd. on Geog. Names, 1992. Fellow AAAS, Meteoritical Soc. (pres. 1975-76), Geol. Soc. Am. (chmn. history of geology divsn. 1982-83, History of Geology award 1986); mem. Assn. Women in Sci., Am. Geophys. Union, History of Earth Scis. Soc. (pres. 1991), Sigma Xi (pres. Harvard-Radcliffe chpt. 1971-72). Avocation: worldwide birding. Office: Harvard-Smithsonian Ctr for Astrophysics 60 Garden St Cambridge MA 02138-1516 Office Phone: 617-495-7270. E-mail: umarvin@cfa.harvard.edu.

MARX, ANNE (MRS. FREDERICK E. MARX), poet; b. Germany; came to U.S., 1936, naturalized, 1938; d. Jacob and Susan (Weinberg) Loewenstein; m. Frederick E. Marx, Feb. 12, 1937; children: Thomas J., Stephen L. Student, U. Heidelberg, U. Berlin. Mem. staffs N.Y.C. Writers Conf., 1965, Iona Coll., 1964, 65, 70, Wagner Coll., 1965, Poetry Workshop, Fairleigh Dickinson U., 1962, 63, 64, Poetry Soc. Am. Workshop, 1970-71, 78-79; Bronxville Adult Sch. Lecture Series, 1972; bd. dir. poetry series Donnell Library Ctr. (N.Y. Pub. Library), 1970-74; poetry day chmn. Westchester County, 1959—; Poetry Day Workshop, Ark., 1966, 70, Ark. Writers Conf., 1971, South and West Conf., Ark., 1972; vis. poet So. U., 1979; tchr., poetry readings, Jakarta, Indonesia, summer 1979; poetry workshop leader Scarsdale Cultural Ctr., 1981-82; conv. speaker Nat. Fedn. State Poetry Socs., 1974, 81, 82; condr. symposium Immigrant Voices, Pa. State U., 1986; judge Chapbook Award Nat. Federation of Poetry Socs., 1994, 1996-97; judge various nat. poetry contests; ongoing project: Selected Poems from Half a Century, 1997—. Poet; more than 1500 poems published in nat. mags., anthologies, lit. jours. and newspapers; Author: Ein Buechlein, 1935, Into the Wind of Waking, 1960, The Second Voice, 1963, By Grace of Pain, 1966, By Way of People, 1970, A Time to Mend; selected poems, 1973; A Conversation with Anne Marx; 2 hour talking book for blind, 1974; Hear of Israel and Other Poems, 1975, 40 Love Poems for 40 Years, 1977, Face Lifts for All Seasons, 1980, 45 Love Poems for 45 Years, 1982, Holocaust: Hurts to Healings, 1984, German edit. Wunden und Narben, 1986; A Further Semester, 1985, Love in Late Season (New Poems by Anne Marx), 1993, Selected and New Poems, 2003; co-editor: Pegasus in the Seventies, 1973; contbr. to American Women Poets Discuss Their Craft, 1983, The Courage to Grow Old, 1989, A Collection of Essays by Ballantine Books, 1989; nat. editor poetry recs., Lamont Library at Harvard, stas. WFAS, WRNW, WEVD, WRVR, Voice of Am., The Pen Woman, 1986-88, Christian Sci. Monitor Anthology of Poems, 1989, Canadian Anthology, 1991, Irish Anthology, 1991, M. Rukeyser Anthology, 1999. Recipient Am. Weave Chapbook award 1960, Nat. Sonnet 1959, 67, 81, award World Order Narrative Poets, 1981-85 1959, 67, prizes Nat. Fedn. Women's Clubs 1959, 60, Nat. Fedn. State Poetry Socs. 1962, 65, 66, 73, 80-83, South and West Publn. award 1965, Greenwood prize Eng. 1966, 2d Ann. Viola Hayes Parsons award 1977, award Delbrook Center Advanced Studies 1978, 1st prize Nat. Essay Competition, 1990, N.Y. State Outstanding Writer award, 1991; named Poet of the Year N.Y. Poetry Forum, 1981; winner Chapbook competition Crossroads Press, 1984, Ann. Writer's Digest award, 1983-90; recipient N.Y. State 1st prize for Poetry, 1995. Mem. Poetry Soc. Am. (life, exec. bd. 1965-70, v.p. 1971-72, 2 fellowships, Cecil Hemley Meml. award 1974), Poetry Soc. Gt. Britain, Nat. League Am. Pen Women (pres. Westchester county br. 1962-64, North Atlantic regional chmn. 1964-66, nat. letters bd. 1972-74, biennial poetry workshop leader, nat. poetry editor 1974-78, N.Y. State lit. chmn. 1979-80, N.Y. State pres. 1982-84, 2d nat. v.p. 1984-86, nat. editor Pen Woman mag. 1986-88, contbg. editor 1990—, Biennial Book award 1976, Biennial awards (4), 1982, (2), 1984, Writer of Yr. 1991, N.Y. State Poetry award 1996, 1st prize Biennial Conv. 1998, established Anne Marx Sestina award 1998, Helen Sutton Booth Spl. Biennial award 2002), Acad. Am. Poets, Poet Soc. Pa., Composers, Authors and Artists Am., Inc. (poetry editor mag. 1973-78), Poets and Writers, Inc., N.Y. Poetry Forum (life). Achievements include being subject of story "An American by Choice, A Poet's Credo" pub. in The PEN Woman mag., Nov. 1988, The Courage to Grow Old, 1989, N.Y. Times interview "Finding Poetry in All of Life's Events," 1993; collected works N.Y. Pub. Libr.: Anne Marx Archives, 1992, early German material added to collection, 1994, Juvenile Diaries, 2000.

MARX, NICKI DIANE, sculptor, painter; b. L.A., Oct. 3, 1943; d. Donald F. and Ruth H. (Ungar) M. Student, U. Calif., Riverside, 1965, U. Calif., Santa Cruz, 1973. Represented by Nicki Marx Studio, Taos, N.Mex., Fred Kline Gallery, Santa Fe, N.Mex. One-woman shows include Palm Springs Desert Mus., 1977, Julie Artisans Gallery, N.Y.C., 1975, Phoenix Art Mus., 1975, Weston Gallery, Carmel, Calif, 1981, Kirk de Gooyer Gallery, L.A., 1982, Rocklands Gallery, Monterey, Calif., 1983, Fetish Gallery, Taos, 1988, Fenix Gallery, Taos, 1991, Earthworks, 1993, Lamberts, 1994, Stables Gallery, Taos, 1995, Fred Kline, 1995, Sun Cities Mus. Art, Ariz., 1996, Harwood Mus. Art, Taos, 1999, others; group exhbns. include E.P. Smith Gallery, Santa Cruz, 1994, Lumina Gallery, Taos, 1994, Cafe Gallery, Albuquerque, 1991, Bareiss Gallery, Taos, 1990, Ctr. for Contemporary Art, Santa Fe, 1989, Jordan Gallery, Taos, N.Mex., 1988, 89, Stables Art Gallery, Taos, 1988, 94, Albuquerque State Fair Grounds, 1986, San Francisco Mus. Modern Art, 1977, 78, The Elements Gallery, Greenwich, Conn., 1977, Pacific Design Ctr., L.A., 1976, Lantor Gallery, Inverness, Calif., 1976, numerous others; work included in sixteen invitational shows; represented in pub. collections IBM, Milford, Conn., N.Y.C., San Jose, Calif., Bank of Am., San Francisco, The Continental Group, Inc., Stamford, Conn., Cedars-Sinai Hosp., L.A., Farm Bur. Fedn., Sacramento, Calif., Sherman Fairchild Sci. Ctr., Stanford, Calif., Palm Springs (Calif.) Desert Mus., Univ. Mus., Ariz. State U. at Tempe, Mills Coll. Art Gallery, Berkeley, Calif.; exhibited in pvt. collections of Estate of Eugene Klein, Estate of Louise Nevelson, Estate of Georgia O'Keeffe, Fritz Scholder, Ray Graham, Bunny Horowitz, Sue and Otto Meyer, Burt Sugarman, Craig Moody, Paul Pletka, others; subject of numerous articles in jours. and mags. MacDowell Colony fellow, 1975; recipient Adolph and Esther Gottleib Found. grant, 1985. Studio: PO Box 1135 Ranchos De Taos NM 87557-1135 Office Phone: 505-758-4892.

MARYSCHUK, OLGA YAROSLAVA, artist, executive assistant; b. Greenwich, Conn., July 21, 1928; d. George and Rose Greshchyshyn M. BFA, Cooper Union Sch. Art/Arch., 1979. Exec. asst. I.M. Pei & Ptnrs., N.Y.C., 1966—92. One-woman shows include I.M. Pei & Ptnrs., Architects & Planners, N.Y.C., 1984, Fifth Street Gallery, N.Y., 1980, Ukrainian Can. Art Found., Toronto, 1980, Ukrainian Artists Assn. in USA, N.Y.C., 1979, Ukrainian Friendship Soc., 1971, Peter Cooper Gallery, N.Y., 1968; exhibited in group shows at Old New York Gallery, N.Y., 1998, 2000, Tenement Mus., N.Y., 1999, Ukrainian Inst., N.Y., 1999, Richmond (Calif.) Art Ctr., 1997, Chgo. Ctr. for Book and Arts, 1996, The Cooper Union, Houghton Gallery, N.Y.C., 1996, Michael Ingbar Gallery, N.Y.C., 1993-94, others; represented in permanent collection AT&T, Atlanta, C&S/Sovran Bank, Atlanta, Carter Wallace, N.Y., Kohn Pedersen Fox, Architects, N.Y.C., Mortgage Bankers Assn., Washington, Ternopil Regional Mus., Ukraine, Ukrainian Mus. of Fine Art, Kiev, United Way, Atlanta, West Allis Meml. Hosp., Milw., Consul Gen. Ukraine in N.Y. Founding mem. Fulton Art Fair, Bklyn., 1957; vol. Sta. WNYC, N.Y.C., 1992—, UNICEF, N.Y.C., 1999—. Scholarship Kiev State Art Inst., 1970-71; fellowship Ragdale Found., 1984, 86, Va. Ctr. for Creative Arts, 1982, 83. Unitarian Universalist. Avocations: tai chi, travel, writing, curatorial work. Home: 170 Avenue C Apt 2C New York NY 10009

MAS, BEVERLEY BERLIN, career planning advisor, counseling advisor; d. Hobart Irl Willits and Irene Ethel LaRue; m. Oscar Más, Apr. 30, 1977. BA in Psychology summa cum laude, Fla. Atlantic U., 2002. Secretarial supr. Irell & Manella Law Firm, Century City, Calif., 1981—91; freelance manuscript editor Palm Beach Gardens, Fla., 1991—99; academic advisor and counselor Palm Beach C.C., Palm Beach Gardens, 2002—, tutor English, biology, anatomy/physiology, 2002—; freelance life coach Palm Beach Gardens, 2002—. Trainer-recruiter Literacy Coalition Palm Beach County, Jupiter, Fla., 2000—02; presenter in field. Author short stories and poems. Group facilitator Murder and Suicide Survivors, L.A., 1994—95, Suicide Survivors, L.A., 1994—95; organizer, ofcl. Psychology Club Palm Beach C.C., Palm Beach Gardens, 1998—99, contbg mem. of president's strategic planning team, 1998—99, coll. amb. and student liaison; organizer of svc. of food and fin. svc. to needy families in cmty., v.p. of svc. Phi Theta Kappa Internat. Honors Soc., Palm Beach Gardens, 1998—99; ann. neighborhood vol. Am. Heart Assn., Palm Beach Gardens, 1999—2003, Am. Cancer Soc., Palm Beach Gardens, 1999—2003; leader Spl. Olympics, North Palm Beach, Fla., 1999—2000; organizer Halloween and Christmas parties for abused and underprivileged children Palm Beach County, Palm Beach Gardens, 1999—99; leader, vol. program for after-school tutorage Am. Reads Program, Jupiter, Fla., 2000—02; honoree, spkr., program presenter Nat. Collegiate Honors Coun. Nat. Convention, Chgo.; presenter Cognitive Aging Conf., Atlanta, 2000; v.p. Glenwood Homeowners' Assn., Palm Beach Gardens, 1998—99. Finalist Fla. Student of the Yr., Fla. Today, 1999, Top Ten Coll. Women, Glamour Mag., 2000; named to All USA Academic First Team, USA Today, 1999, All Fla. Academic First Team, Fla. State Legislature, 1999; recipient Spl. commendation as outstanding scholar in Ho. Resolution No. 9053, State Fla. Ho. Reps., 1999, State Poetry award, Fla. Collegiate Honors Coun., 2002, winning short story, Twentieth Century Lit. Conf., U. Louisville, Ky., 2002; scholar, Harriet L. Wilkes Honors Coll., Fla. Atlantic U., 2001; Guistewhite Scholar of the Yr., Phi Theta Kappa Internat. Honor Soc., 1999, Frederick DeHon scholar. Mem.: APA (life), SAG (life), Women in Edn. (assoc.), Fed. Assn. Cmty. Colls. (assoc.), Greater Found. Women's Coun. (life), People for the Ethical Treatment of Animals (life), Physicians' Com. for Responsible Medicine (life), Soc. for the Study of Peace, Conflict, and Violence (life), Nat. Alliance for the Mentally Ill (life), Am. Fed. Variety Artists (life), Amnesty Internat. (life; women's action coun.), Psi Beta (v.p. and chair edn. activities), Golden Key, Phi Kappa Phi, Phi Theta Kappa (Guistewhite scholar of the Yr. 1999), Nat. Soc. Collegiate Scholars (life). Achievements include research in age difference in effects of gaze avers; effects of age and encoding context on recognition of nouns and verbs; influences of task difficulty and time pressure on age differences in memory for activities. Home: 1502 15th Terr Palm Beach Gardens FL 33418-3613 Office: Palm Beach Community College 3160 PGA Blvd Palm Beach Gardens FL 33410-2893 E-mail: masb@pbcc.edu.

MASCHERONI, ELEANOR EARLE, marketing communications executive; b. Boston, June 6, 1955; d. Ralph II and Eleanor Forbes (Owens) Earle; m. Mark Mascheroni, May 30, 1981; children: Olivia Forbes, Isabella Starbuck, Rex Owens. AB, Brown U., 1977. Dept. adminstr. Sotheby Parke Bernet, N.Y.C., 1978-79; asst. dir. devel. Inst. Architecture and Urban Studies, N.Y.C., 1979-81; assoc. in pub. rels. Prudential Securities Inc., N.Y.C., 1981-84, asst. v.p., 1984-86, assoc. v.p., 1986-87, v.p., mgr., 1987—89, 1st v.p., dir. corp. commns., 1989—91; v.p. corp. comms. Zurich Scudder Investments, Inc., N.Y.C., 1991-95, prin., sr. v.p., dir. corp. comms., 1996-99, mng. dir., 1999—2001; CMO Ogilvy & Mather, 2001—. N.Y. Alumnae bd. govs. St. Timothy's Sch., Stevenson, Md., 1994—; trustee Hartley House, 2000—. Avocations: running, photography.

MASCILAK, J. comedienne, recording industry executive, theater producer, video specialist; b. Detroit, May 23, 1955; d. Joseph John and Gladys E. (Cook) M.; children: Joyce Rosebudd, Star-Angel. Grad., Osborn High Sch., Detroit, 1973. With Sunshire Floral Co., 1977-81; owner Joey's Flowers, 1981-84, 93—; with Joey's Corner, 1978-85, 93—, Pop-Rock Prodns., Ft. Worth, 1980-90; owner Tickle My Funny Bone Records, Ft. Worth, 1986—, Roc Records, Ft. Worth, 1988-89, Jammo Prodns., Ft. Worth, 1988—, J.M.I. Prodns., Ft. Worth, 1980-89, J.M.I. Pulser Graphics, Ft. Worth, 1980—, J.M.I. Used Records & Tapes, Ft. Worth, 1988-89, Rockavision, Ft. Worth, 1986—, Pop Rock Videos, Ft. Worth, 1990—; v.p. entertainment ROCKDOG Entertainment-ROCKDOG Records, Ft. Worth, 1989—; owner Flower King Co., 1993—, Rosebud's, 1993-94, 98—, Dirty White Boy Prodns., 1993. Comedian (comedy/audio) Jammo/High on Air, 1988, Jammo/On Warp Speed, 1988, Jammo/Lesbians, Rockers and the 90s, 1990, Jammo/Jam It Up and Rock 'N' Roll, 1991, Jammo/Jammo Jams!, 1992, Jammo/Emerald Dogs, 1994, Jammo/Pain, Shock and Roll! Shock-treatment, 1994, National Joey Jet/I've Been Touched, 1995, National Joey Jet/Eddie Crankn A Rock 'N' Roll Rebel, 1996, National Joey Jet/Live But Cheap, 1996, National Joey Jet/Live Butt Naked, 1997, Jammo/What Stinks?!, 1998, T-Girl Conressions, 1998, Freedom to Be You Freedom to Be Me; author: In Search of Shema, 1994, The Texas Whipping Boys, 1995, Daytrippers My Hippie Days, 1998, Kilroy was Here or Highway to Hell, 1996, The Rooster, 1994, Dirt Hell in Fort Worth Texas, 1998, Bad Dreams, 1998, Peace, Love, Happiness Time Out, 1995, Real Life Adventures, 1997; comedy tour Nat. Joey Jet, 1997-98. Active Amnesty Internat., Just Say No, Don't Do Drugs, Artist's for a Hate Free America, Rockers Agains Drunk Driving. Mem. Greenpeace, NOW, NAFE, D.A.R.E. Roman Catholic. Office: Nat Joey Jet Entertainment Co PO Box 9602 Fort Worth TX 76147-2602

MASCIOTRA, JANET MARIE, elementary school educator; d. Antonio and Eleanor Masciotra. AA summa cum laude, St. Petersburg (Fla.) Jr. Coll., 1986; BS magna cum laude, U. South Fla., 1989. Cert. tchr. Fla., Mass. Tchr. Tyrone Mid. Sch., St. Petersburg, Fla., 1989—96, Criminal Justice Acad., Pinellas Park, Fla., 1996—2000, Fairview Veterans Meml. Mid., Chicopee, Mass., 2000—. Mem. Kiwanis Internat., Boca Ciega, Fla., 1997—2000; vol. Dist. 7 VFW, Mass., 2000—03. Recipient Citizenship Edn. Tchr. of the Yr. award, Mass. VFW, 2002—03; Justice Tchg. Inst. fellow, Fla. State Supreme Ct., 1997, Conf. fellow, Vietnam Veterans Meml. Fund, 2003. Mem.: Ladies Aux. VFW (life), Delta Kappa Gamma. Avocations: Tampa Bay Buccaneers, volunteer work, travel, country music. Office: Fairview Veterans Meml Middle Sch 26 Memorial Ave Chicopee MA 01020

MASEK, BEVERLY, state representative; b. Anvik, Alaska, Sept. 30, 1963; m. Jan Masek; 1 child, Michael. Asst. mgr. Stuckagain Heights Lodge; bookkeeper Chena Hot Springs; operator Masek Racing Kennels; owner, operator Rustic Wilderness Lodge; spokesperson Alyeska Pipeline, Charter North, Payless Drug Stores; mem. Alaska Ho. of Reps., 1994—. Commr. Alaska Native Commn., Alaska Hist. Commn.; mem. state adv. com. U.S. Civil Rights Commn.; spkr. child abuse prevention program, goal setting and achievement program. Mem. Alaska Outdoor Coun., Hugh O'Brien Youth Found. Mem.: NRA, Alaska Boating Assn. Republican. Avocations: dog mushing, hiking, fishing. Office: Rm 403 State Capitol Juneau AK 99801-1182 Address: 600 E Railroad Ave Ste 1 Wasilla AK 99654

MASHIN, JACQUELINE ANN COOK, medical sciences administrator, nursing administrator; b. Chgo., May 11, 1941; d. William Hermann and Ann (Smidt) Cook; m. Fredric John Mashin, June 7, 1970; children: Joseph Glenn, Alison Robin. BS, U. Md., 1984; BSN, Cath. U. Am., Washington, 1993. Cert. realtor. Adminstrv. asst. CIA, Washington, 1963-66; asst. to mng. dir. Aerospace Edn. Found., Washington, 1966-74; exec. asst. to asst exec. dir. Air Force Assn., Washington, 1974-79; v.p., ptnrship. owner Discount Linen Store, Silver Spring, Md., 1979-81; asst. regional polit. dir. Office of Pres.-elect, Washington, 1980-81; confidential asst. to dir. Office of Personnel Mgmt. (US), Washington, 1981-83; spl. asst. to dep. dir. Office of Mgmt. and Budget, Washington, 1983-86; dir. internat. communications and spl. asst. to commr. Dept. of the Interior, Washington, 1986-89, cons., 1989-93; with Washington Hosp. Ctr., 1993—. Chmn., vol. coord. Mo. County Rep. Party, 1999; chmn. Bayclub, Mo. County Fedn. Rep. Women, 1999, 2000; mem. bd. rev. Dept. Health and Mental Hygiene Md. State Senate, Annapolis, Md., 2003—. Pres. Layhill Civic Assn., Silver Spring, Md., 1980; state chmn. Md.'s Reagan Youth Delegation, Annapolis, Md., 1980; state treas., office mgr. Reagan-Bush State Hdqrs. of Md., Silver Spring, 1980; mem. Women's Com. Nat. Symphony Orch.; pres. Rock Creek Women's Rep. Club, 1998, Montgomery County Rep. Party, 1999, Montgomery County Fedn. Rep. Women, 1999—; steering com. Wheaton Redevel. Program, 2001—; gov.'s adv. bd. Md. Bd. Health and Mental Hygiene. Mem.: Air Force Assn. (life), U.S. Capital Hist. Soc., Am. League Lobbyists, Aux. Salvation Army (life), Indian Springs Country Club. Republican. Avocations: golf, horseback riding, collecting wine glasses, hibel plates, lithos and lalique crystal. Home and Office: 2429 White Horse Ln Silver Spring MD 20906-2243 E-mail: Jaguar041@aol.com.

MASI, DALE A. research company executive, social work educator; b. N.Y.C. d. Alphonse E. and Vera Avella; children: Eric, Renee, Robin. BS, Coll. Mt. St. Vincent; MSW, U. Ill.; D Social Work, Cath. U. Lectr. Sch. Social Svcs., Ipswitch, Eng., 1970-72; project dir. occupational substance abuse program, asso. prof. Boston Coll. Grad. Sch. Social Work, 1972-79; dir. Office Employee Counseling Svc., Dept. Health/Human Svcs., Washington, 1979-84; pres. Masi Research Cons., Inc., 1984—; prof. U. Md. Grad. Sch. Social Work, 1980—; adj. prof. U. Md. Coll. Bus. and Mgmt., 1980—. Mem. IBM Mental Health Adv. Bd., 1990-95; cons. IBM, Toyota, Mobil Chm., The Washington Post, U.S. Ho. Reps., U.S. Postal Svc., White House, WHO, Bechtel Corp., other orgns. in pub. and pvt. sector; bd. advisors Nat. Security Inst., Wayside Youth and Family Support Network; USIA Ampart lectr. on alcohol, drugs and AIDS in the workplace; chair CMHS Jooint Industry Alliance, 2002—. Author: Human Services in Industry, Organizing for Women, Designing Employee Assistance Programs, Drug Free Workplace, AIDS Issues in the Workplace: A Response Model for Human Resource Management, The AMA Handbook for Developing Employee Assistance and Counseling Programs, Evaluating Your Employee Assistance and Managed Behavioral Care Program, Internat. Employee Assistance Anthology, Productivity Lost: Alcohol and Drugs in the Workplace; co-author: Shrink to Fit: Answers to Your Questions About Therapy; also over 40 articles. Named Disting. Scholar, Nat. Acad. Practice, 2001—; named to Employee Assistance Program Hall of Fame; recipient award, Employee Assistance Program Digest; fellow Fulbright fellow, 1969—70, 1994, AAUW postdoctoral fellow, NIMH, 1962—64; Fulbright Sr. Specialist Canidate, 2002. Mem. AAUW, NASW (Internat. Rhoda G. Sarnat award 1993), Acad. Cert. Social Workers, Employee Assistance Profls. Assn. (nat. individual achievement award 1983), Fulbright Assn. (nat. bd.). Democrat. Roman Catholic. Office: 2549 Virginia Ave NW Washington DC 20037-1903 E-mail: masirsrch@aol.com.

MASI, MARY ELIZABETH, editor, writer; b. Cambridge, Minn., Sept. 23, 1968; d. Edwin and Ruth Andrews; m. Thomas Allen Masi, Oct. 10, 1993. BA, Ambassador U., 1991; MA, St. Cloud State U., 1993. Coll.

writing instr. St. Cloud (Minn.) State U., 1991-93; asst. editor John Wiley and Sons, Inc., N.Y.C., 1994-97, editl. cons., 1997—. Author profl. publs. Mem. Priests for Equality, Dearborn, Mich., 1994, Christians Bib. Equality, Mpls., 2004, Nat. Parks and Conservation. Grantee St. Cloud State U., 1992, recipient Coard Meml. scholarship 1992. Mem. NOW. Avocations: writing reviews of books, gardening, learning langs., drawing.

MASINI, ELEONORA BARBIERI, futurist; b. Quirigua, Los Amates, Guatemala, Nov. 19, 1928; d. Vincenzo and Edith Frances (Fullerton) Barbieri; m. Francesco Maria Masini, Jan. 31, 1953; children: Alessandro, Andrea, Federico. LLD, U. Rome, 1952, D in Sociology, 1964. Dir. Ctr. of Forecasting Instituto Richerche Applicate Documentazione E Studi, Rome, 1972—75; rsch. dir. UNESCO, 1972—78, Centro Italiano Femminile, 1972—78; coord. projects UN Univ., 1978, 1984—90; chmn. social forecasting Pontifical Gregorian U., Rome, 1977—. Sec. gen. World Future Studies Fedn., Rome, 1975—80, pres., 1980—89, Women's Internat. Network Emergency and Solidarity. Author: Space for Man, 1972, Social and Human Forecasting, 1973, Social Indicators and Forecasting, 1977, Visions of Desirable Societies, 1983, Why Futures Studies?, 1993; editor: Women, Households and Change, 1991, The Future of Asian Cultures, 1993, Penser Le Futur, 2000. Named Fulbright fellow, 1951, Fulbright prof., U.S.A., 1986; recipient Fulbright fellow, 1985. Mem.: Club of Rome. Home and Office: Via Bertoloni 23 00197 Rome Italy

MASON, ANN DARLENE, real estate broker; b. Louisville, Mar. 2, 1934; d. James Robert and Lilly Mae (Hedgepeth) Noe; m. Dallas House, Dec. 23, 1953 (div. 1978); children: Dallas House, James House, Henry House, Jon House; m. Sidney E. Mason, Aug. 10, 1984; stepchildren: Bruce, Linda. Student, Fla. So. Coll., 1952-53, U. Ga., 1953-55, Ringling Sch. Art, Sarasota, Fla., summer 1952, Herr Krupp Art Sch., Ramstein, Germany, 1958-60, Manatee Jr. C.C., Sarasota, 1969. Lic. real estate broker. Real estate broker Harry Robbins Real Estate Office, Sarasota, 1994—; chmn. Health Effects of Lawncare Pesticides, Sarasota, 1986—. Real estate broker Arvida Corp., Merril L. Boomhower. Contbr. articles to profl. jours. V.p. Facts About Alternatives to Chem. Trespassing, 2000—; vice chair Sarasota Rally Against Malathion, 1997; mem. Coalition to Stop Children's Exposure to Pesticides, 1996; mem. Sarasota County Environ. Pest Mgmt. Adv. Bd.; mem. Sarasota County Mosquito Control Adv. Bd.; chair Health Effects Pesticides Task Force, 1986—97; pub. affairs com. Jr. League Sarasota, Inc., 1969. Named Sustainer of the Yr., Jr. League Sarasota, Inc., 1988—89. Mem.: PEO. Republican. Baptist. Avocations: swimming, sailing, sewing, public speaking, radio and TV talk shows. Home: 2290 Clematis St Sarasota FL 34239-3907 Office: Harry Robbins Real Estate Sarasota FL 34239 Fax: 941-954-0004.

MASON, ANNE R. HARDIN, municipal official; b. Hamlet, N.C., Dec. 19, 1931; d. William Herbert and Catherine Holder Robertson; m. C. Dwight Hardin, Jr., June 18, 1955 (dec. June 1972); 1 child, Charles David Hardin ; m. Robert L. Mason, Mar. 29, 1975 (dec. Mar. 1989); children: Shelly Mason Ivey, Jennifer Mason Fanjoy. BA, U.N.C., Greensboro, 1954. Tchr. North Sch., Gastonia, NC, 1954—55, Oakwood Sch., Hickory, NC, 1955—59, College Park Jr. H.S., Hickory, NC, 1972—77, Southwest Elem. Sch., Hickory, NC, 1977—81, College Park Mid. Sch., Hickory, NC, 1981—92. Chief judge Bd. Elections, Newton, NC, 1992—2003. Mem.: NEA, N.C. Assn. Educators. Democrat. Presbyterian. Avocations: bridge, garden club. Home: 771 9th St NW Hickory NC 28601

MASON, BARBARA FOUNTAIN, minister; d. Johnnie Lee and Eddie Fountain; m. William Lawrence Mason, June 12, 1956; children: Johnnie Ann Crawford, Lawrencina Mason Oramalu. AA, Calvary Bible Coll., Kansas City, Mo., 1977; BS Local Ch. Edn., Calvary Bapt. Bible Coll., Grandview, Mo., 1980; MA Ednl. Adminstrn., U.Mo., Kansas City, 1984. Pastor Little Flock Cmty. of Faith, Mpls., 1994—; tchr. Mpls. Pub. Schools, 1999—2003. Dir. Christian edn. Met. Missionary Bapt. Ch., Kans. City, Mo., 1977—90; asst. pastor Zion Bapt. Ch., Mpls., 1990—92; dir., ecumenical ptnrs. Greater Mpls. Coun. of Churches, 1993—94, dir., social policy, 1993—94. Bd. dirs. Salvation Army, Mpls., 1993—94, Battered Women's Orgn., Mpls., 1995—97; mem. Mayor's Coun. on Interfaith & Racial Partnerships, Mpls., 1996—98; bd. dirs. Exodus Cmty. Devel., Mpls., 2000—01; mem. Ministerial Alliance, Mpls., 1991—94; bd. dirs. Greater Mpls. Coun. of Churches, Mpls., 1992—93. Named Role Model for Youth, Bd. of Christian Edn., Met. Bapt. Ch., 1990; recipient Regional Workshop Facilitator, Nat. Bapt. Pub. Bd., 1988; grantee Multicultural Educators' Program, Mpls. Pub. Schools, 2001-2003. Mem.: LWV (bd. dirs. 1999—2001), Spl. Needs' Assn. Dfl. Baptist. Achievements include design of Designed summer camp; development of Developed a Christian pre-school; design of Designed a teacher training class; Designed a Bible Institute for lay leaders; development of Developed a prayer ministry; Developed outreach ministry; design of Designed curriculum for character development; Designed self-esteem program for juveniles; Founding Pastor of Little Flock Community of Faith. Home: 8712 Bass Creek Ave Minneapolis MN 55428 Office: Little Flock Comty Faith Ch 128 W 33rd Street Minneapolis MN 55408

MASON, BOBBIE ANN, novelist, short story writer; b. Mayfield, Ky., May 1, 1940; d. Wilburn A. and Christianna (Lee) M.; m. Roger B. Rawlings, Apr. 12, 1969. BA, U. Ky., 1962; MA, SUNY, Binghamton, 1966; PhD, U. Conn., 1972. Asst. prof. English Mansfield (Pa.) State Coll., 1972-79. Writer-in-residence, U. Ky., Lexington, 2001—. Author: Nabokov's Garden, 1974, The Girl Sleuth: A Feminist Guide to the Bobbsey Twins, Nancy Drew and Their Sisters, 1975, 2d edit., 1995, Shiloh and Other Stories, 1982 (Ernest Hemingway award, Nat. Book Critics Circle award nominee, Am. Book award nominee, PEN Faulkner award nominee), 2d edit., 2001, In Country, 1985, Spence + Lila, 1988, 2d edit., 1998, Love Life, 1989, Feather Crowns, 1993 (Nat. Book Critic's Circle award nominee, So. Book award), Midnight Magic, 1998, Clear Springs, 1999 (Pulitzer prize finalist), Zigzagging Down a Wild Trail, 2001 (So. Book award), Elvis Presley, 2003 (Ky. Literary award); contbr. regularly to the New Yorker, 1980—; contbr. fiction to The Atlantic, Redbook, Paris Rev., Mother Jones, Harpers, N.Am. Rev., Va. Quar. Rev., Story, Ploughshares, So. Rev., Crazyhorse, DoubleTake; contbr. works Best American Short Stories, 1981, 83, The Pushcart Prize, Best of the Small Presses, 1983, 86, 97. Recipient O. Henry Anthology awards, 1986, 88, Hillsdale prize, 1999; grantee Pa. Arts Coun., 1983, 89, Nat. Endowment Arts, 1983, Am. Acad. and Inst. Arts and Letters, 1984; Guggenheim fellow, 1984. Mem.: PEN, Author's Guild, Fellowship of So. Writers. Office: Internat Creative Mgmt care Amanda Urban Agt 40 W 57th St New York NY 10019-4001

MASON, CHERYL WHITE, lawyer; b. Champaign, Ill., Jan. 16, 1952; d. John Russell and Lucille (Birden) White; m. Robert L. Mason, Oct. 9, 1972; children: Robert L. II and Daniel G. BA, Purdue U., 1972; JD, U. Chgo., 1976. Bar: Calif. 1977. Assoc. O'Melveny & Myers LLP, L.A., 1976-81, 84-86, ptnr., 1987—; exec. dir. Public Counsel, L.A., 1981-84. Bd. dirs. Pub. Policy Inst. Calif. Chmn. State Bar, Legal Svcs. Trust Fund, 1987; trustee L.A. County Bar, 1985-88; bd. dirs. Challengers Boys and Girls Club, L.A., 1990—, Western Ctr. Law and Poverty, L.A., 1991-94; bd. dirs. James Irvine Found. Mem. ABA (co-chair environ. litigation commn. 1992-94, lawyer rep. 9th cir. jud. conf. 1993-94), Calif. Women Lawyers, L.A. County Bar Assn., Women Lawyers L.A., Black Women Lawyers L.A., Langston Bar Assn. Democrat. Office: O Melveny & Myers LLP 400 S Hope St Los Angeles CA 90071

MASON, CHRISTINE CHAPMAN, psychotherapist; b. El Paso, Tex., Sept. 17, 1948; d. Wilson A. and Mary (McGovern) Chapman; m. Gary R. Mason, Nov. 3, 1973; children: Ryan, Alison, Amanda, Sean. BA in Journalism, Tex. Tech. U., 1970; certificate, Am. U., 1973; MA, Marymount U., 1995, George Washington U., 1997, MA, 1998; PsyD, So. Calif. U., 2003. Cert. Paralegal 1985, Counselor, lic. Profl. Counselor. Flight attendant supr. Eastern Airlines, Washington, 1971—84; pres. Stratford Properties, Charles County, Md., 1980—; psychotherapist Charles County Mental Health Ctr., Loplata, Md., 1995—98, Eva Turner Elem. Sch., Waldorf, Md., 1999—. Dir. rehab. svc. Edgemeade, Waldorf, Md., 1999—2000; emergency psychiat. clinician St. Mary's Hosp., Leonardtown, Md., 1998—; psychotherapist Calvert Psychiat. Assn., Leonardtown, 1998—. Bd. dir. On Our Own of Charles County, Waldorf, Md., 1998—2000, Charles County Mental Health Authority, Waldorf, 1993—96. Mem.: Md. Assn. Counseling-Devel., Am. Counselors Assn. Republican. Roman Catholic. Home: 13535 Waverly Point Road Newburg MD 20664-2821

MASON, EILEEN B. federal administrator; b. Bklyn., 1943; m. Arthur Mason; children: Elizabeth, Laura. BA, Cornell U.; MPA, Am. U. Tchr. math. and reading Hephzibah High Sch., Ga.; editor Little Brown, Boston; music adv. panelist Md. State Arts Coun.; v.p. grants Arts and Humanities Coun., Montgomery County, Md.; mgr. and adminstr. U.S. NRC, FERC; sr. dep. chmn. NEA, Washington, 2001—, acting chmn., 2002—03. Performer: (violinist) Cornell U. Symphony, MIT Symphony, Augusta Symphony, Am. U. Symphony Orchestra. Mem.: Phi Alpha Alpha. Office: NEA 1100 Pennsylvania Ave NW Washington DC 20506

MASON, LOIS E. (J. DAY MASON), painter, poet, actress, educator; b. Boston, May 4, 1919; d. Harold Monroe and Orpah Cecil (Smith) Scheibe; m. Lucien Bunce Day, June 21, 1941 (div. 1954); children: Felicity, Christopher, Sarah; m. Frederick Dike Mason, Apr. 27, 1964 (dec.); children: Frederick Dike III, Victoria, Johanna. Student, U. Leiden, Netherlands, 1939; BA, Oberlin (Ohio) U., 1940; postgrad., Cranbrook Acad. Art, Bloomfield Hills, Mich., 1941. Set-up and tchr. art dept. Pingree Sch., Hamilton Mass.; TV, lectr. creative arts and writing, Mass. and Conn., 1949-58. Actress appearing in Alien Corn, Twelfth Night, Crucible, George Washington Slept Here, Philadelphia Story, Auntie Mame, Skin of our Teeth, Spoon River, Anything Goes, Call Me Madame, Seven Keys to Baldpate, Other People's Money, Quilters, Golden Pond, Cat on a Hot Tin Roof, Little Foxes, Lettice and Lovage, Close Ties, Grace and Glorie, others; set designer, decorator Auntie Mame, See How They Run, Tea House of the August Moon, Spoon River, Archie and Mehitable; author: Speaking to Strangers, 1987-88; one-woman shows include New Britain (Conn.) Mus., Am. Ballet, N.Y., Green Mountain Gallery, N.Y.C., Essex (Mass.) Inst., Marblehead Arts, Quadrom, Mast Cove, 6 Deering, Miles Hosp., Atty. Gen.'s Office, Kennebec Valley Art Assn., Chocolate Ch. Art Ctr., Maine Gallery, Kristina's, Oliver's, Islesboro Historic Soc., West Island Gallery, Bath, Maine. Ch. ladies com. Hamilton Hall, Salem, Mass., 1975—78; set designer Cmty. Theater, Swampscott, Mass., 1973—78. Recipient C. Law/Watkins fellowship Phillips Gallery, Mus., Washington, 1944-46. Mem. Nat. Assn. Women Painters, Conn. Acad., Silvermine, Maine Gallery, Kennebec Valley Arts, Chocolate Ch. Art Ctr., Marblehead Arts, Conn. Acad., Maine Writers and Publs. Avocations: cooking, sailing, gardening.

MASON, LUCILE GERTRUDE, fundraiser, consultant; b. Montclair, N.J., Aug. 1, 1925; d. Mayne Seguine and Rachel (Entorf) M. AB, Smith Coll., 1947; MA, NYU, 1968, 76. Editor ABC, N.Y.C., 1947-51; asst. casting dir. Compton Advt., Inc., N.Y.C., 1951-55, dir. and head casting, 1955-65; conf. mgr. Camp Fire Girls, Inc., N.Y.C., 1965-66; exec. dir. Assn. of Jr. Leagues of Am. Inc., N.Y.C., 1966-68; dir. div. pub. affairs Girl Scouts U.S.A., N.Y.C., 1969-71; dir. pub. rels. YWCA of City of N.Y., 1971-73; dir. community rels. and devel. Girl Scout Coun. of Greater N.Y., N.Y.C., 1973-76; dir. devel. Montclair Kimberley Acad., Montclair, N.J., 1976-78, Ethical Culture Schs., N.Y.C. and Riverdale, N.Y., 1978-80; pres. Lucile Mason & Assocs., Montclair, 1980-83; devel. officer founds. Fairleigh Dickinson U., Rutherford, N.J., 1983-85; dir. devel. Whole Theatre, Inc., Montclair, 1985-86, YMWCA of Newark & Vicinity, 1986-88; v.p. adminstrn. and fin. devel. Inst. Religion and Health, N.Y.C., 1988-90; dir. corp. and found. rels. Upsala Coll., East Orange, N.J., 1990-91; pres. Lucile Mason & Assocs., Montclair, 1991—. Vol. bd. counselors Smith Coll., 1964—74, chmn. theatre com., mem. exec. com., 1969—74; trustee Citizens Com. Presby. Meml. Iris Gardens of Montclair, 1992—98; trustee Friends of Barnet, 1994—95; v.p. Neighborhood Coun., Inc., Montclair, 1987—95, 1997—98, bd. dirs., 2000—01; mem. fund devel. com. Greater Essex County coun. Girl Scouts U.S., 1986—92. Mem.: Pub. Rels. Soc. Am., Assn. Fundraising Profls. (bd. dirs. N.J. chpt. 1983—86, mem. awards com. 1994, co-chair awards com. N.J. Conf. on Philanthropy 1995), Cmty. Agys. Pub. Rels. Assn. (membership chmn. 1973—76), Am. Women in Radio and TV (pres. N.Y.C. chpt. 1955—56), Smith Coll. Club Montclair (bd.dirs. 1986—90). Avocations: collecting pewter, gardening, concerts, plays. Home and Office: 142 N Mountain Ave Montclair NJ 07042-2350

MASON, MARGARET CRATHER, elementary school educator; b. Wilmington, Del, Aug. 15, 1945; d. William F. and Regina (Mays) Crather; children: Donna Lynn, R. Brian. BA, U. Del., 1968; postgrad., Loyola Coll. Balt., Del. State Coll.; M in Ednl. Leadership, Wilmington Coll. Cert. English, secondary and elem. tchr., elem. prin., Del. Secondary tchr. English, Podua Acad., Wilmington; elem. tchr. St. John the Beloved Sch., Wilmington; elem. tchr. sci. Christina Sch. Dist., Wilmington, asst. prin. elem. sch. Active numerous community orgns. and local ch. Recipient Fire Safety Edn. award New Castle County Vol. Firefighters. Mem. Del. Assn. Sch. Adminstrs.

MASON, MARILYN GELL, library administrator, writer, consultant; b. Chickasha, Okla., Aug. 23, 1944; d. Emmett D. and Dorothy (O'Bar) Killebrew; m. Carl L. Gell, Dec. 29 1965 (div. Oct. 1978); 1 son, Charles E.; m. Robert M. Mason, July 17, 1981. BA, U. Dallas, 1966; M.L.S., N. Tex. State U., Denton, 1968; M.P.A., Harvard U., 1978. Libr. N.J. State Libr., Trenton, 1968-69; head dept. Arlington County Pub. Libr., Va., 1969-73; chief libr. program Metro Washington Coun. Govts., 1973-77; dir. White House Conf. on Librs. and Info. Svcs., Washington, 1979-80; exec. v.p. Metrics Rsch. Corp., Atlanta, 1981-82; dir. Atlanta-Fulton Pub. Libr., Atlanta, 1982-86, Cleve. Pub. Libr., 1986-99; writer, cons., 1999—. Trustee Online Computer Library Ctr., 1984-97; Evalene Parsons Jackson lectr. div. librarianship Emory U., 1981; commr. Nat. Commn. Libr. Info. Svcs., 2001-02. Author: The Federal Role in Library and Information Services, 1983, Strategic Management for Today's Libraries, 1999; editor: Survey of Library Automation in the Washington Area, 1977; project dir.: book Information for the 1980's, 1980. Bd. visitors Sch. Info. Studies, Syracuse U., 1981-85, Sch. of Libr. and Info. Sci., U. Tenn.-Knoxville, 1983-85; trustee Coun. on Libr. Resources, Washington, 1992-2000. Recipient Disting. Alumna award N. Tex. State U., 1979, Herbert and Virginia White award, ALA, 1999; inducted into Ohio Libr. Coun. Hall of Fame, 1999. Mem. ALA (mem. council 1986—90), Am. Assn. Info. Sci., Ohio Library Assn., D.C. Library Assn. (pres. 1976-77) Home and Office: 811 Live Oak Plantation Rd Tallahassee FL 32312-2412 Personal E-mail: marilyngmason@earthlink.net. Business E-Mail: mgmason@oclc.org.

MASON, MARSHA, actress, theater director, writer; b. St. Louis; d. James and Jacqueline M.; m. Gary Campbell, 1965 (div.); m. Neil Simon, Oct. 25, 1973 (div.). Grad., Webster (Mo.) Coll. Performances include cast broadway and nat. tour Cactus Flower, 1968; other stage appearances include The Deer Park, 1967, The Indian Wants the Bronx, 1968, Happy Birthday, Wanda June, 1970, Private Lives, 1971, You Can't Take It With You, 1972, Cyrano de Bergerac, 1972, A Doll's House, 1972, The Crucible, 1972, The Good Doctor, 1973, King Richard III, 1974, The Heiress, 1975, Mary Stuart, 1982, Amazing Grace, 1995, Night of the Iguana, 1996; one-woman show off-Broadway, The Big Love, Perry St. Theatre, 1988, Lake No Bottom, Second Stage, 1990, Escape From Happiness, With Naked Angels, 1994, Amazing Grace, 1998, House, 1998, (London) Prisoner of Second Avenue, 1999; film appearances include Blume in Love, 1973, Cinderella Liberty, 1973 (recipient Golden Globe award 1974, Acad. award nominee), Audrey Rose, 1977, The Goodbye Girl, 1977 (recipient Golden Globe award 1978, Acad. award nominee), The Cheap Detective, 1978, Promises in the Dark, 1979, Chapter Two, 1979 (Acad. award nominee), Only When I Laugh, 1981 (Acad. award nominee), Max Dugan Returns, 1982, Heartbreak Ridge, 1986, Stella, 1988, Drop Dead Fred, 1990, I Love Trouble, 1994, Nick of Time, 1995, Two Days in the Valley, 1996; TV appearances include PBS series Cyrano de Bergerac, 1974, The Good Doctor, 1978, Lois Gibbs and the Love Canal, 1981, Surviving, 1985, Trapped in Silence, 1986, The Clinic, 1987, Dinner at Eight, 1989, The Image, 1990, Broken Trust, 1994, series Sibs, 1991, Dead Aviators, 1999; dir. (plays) Juno's Swans, 1987, Heaven Can Wait; dir. ABC Afternoon Spl. Little Miss Perfect, 1988; Frasier, 1997(Emmy Nom.), Me & My Shadows: The Judy Garland Story, 2001, author: Journey: A Personal Odyssey (Simon & Schuster), 2000. E-mail: douhlem@newmexico.com.

MASON, NANCY TOLMAN, retired state agency director; b. Buxton, Maine, Mar. 14, 1933; d. Ansel Robert and Kate Douglas (Libby) M. Grad., Bryant Coll., Providence, R.I., 1952; BA, U. Mass., Boston, 1977; postgrad., Inst. Governmental Services, Boston, 1985, The Auditor's Inst., 1988. Asst. to chief justice Mass. Superior Ct., Boston, 1964-68; cmty. liaison Action for Boston Cmty. Devel., Boston, 1968-73; mgmt. cons. East Boston Cmty. Devel. Assn., Boston, 1973-78; asst. dir. Mass. Office of Deafness, Boston, 1978-86; dir. of contracts Mass. Rehab. Commn., Boston, 1986-98; ret., 1998. Cons. Jos. A Ryan Assocs., Boston and Orleans, Mass., 1981-86, Radio Sta. WFCC, Chatham, Mass., 1987-91. Author: Bromley-Heath Security Patrols, 1974, Reorganization of East Boston Community Development Corporation, 1976, How to Start Your Own Small Business, 1981. Bd. dirs. Deaf-Blind Contact Ctr., Boston, 1988-91; vol. Am. Cancer Soc., Winchester, Mass., 1986-93, Tax Equity Alliance Mass., 1994; treas. Sunset Bay Condo Assn., 1998-99, bd. dirs. 1998-2001. Recipient Good Citizen award DAR, 1950, Community Svc. award Northeastern U., 1986, Gov.'s citation for outstanding performance, 1993; named to Outstanding Young Women of Am., 1965. Mem. NOW, NAFE, Mass. State Assn. Deaf, Mass. Rehab. Commn. Statewide Cen. Office Dirs. (chair 1995-98, MRC procurement mgmt. team 1997-98, co-chair Take Your Daughters to Work Day 1998-99). Democrat. Episcopalian. Avocations: reading, music, bridge, swimming, sign language. Address: 5 Elmwood Dr Saco ME 04072-2103

MASQUE, MARIA L. urban planner; b. Habana, Cuba, Oct. 1, 1956; d. Ada R. Garcia-Masque and Jose L. Masque. AA, Santa Fe C.C., 1983; BA Anthropology, U. Fla., 1987, MA Urban & Regional Planning, 1994. Dir. Inst. of Hispanic and Latino Cultures - U. of Fla., Gainesville, 1995—97; prin. planner North Ctrl. Fla. Regional Planning Coun., Gainesville, 1997—2000; sr. planner/project mgr. The Planning Ctr., Tucson, 2000—. Tech. adv. com. So. Ariz. Home Builders Assn., Tucson, 2000—, Santa Cruz River Corridor Study, City of Marana, 2000—01; mem. CANAMEX Trade Corridor Project, Tucson, 2000—02, Arizona/Sonora Mex. Project, Tucson, 2000—02, City of Douglas Focused Future II, 2001—02; cons., facilitator, steering com. Davis-Monthan AFB Airfield Compatibility Study, Tucson, 2001—03. Adv., vol. cons. Hist. Barrio Anita Neighborhood Orgn., Tucson, 2000—02; cons. City of Douglas Housing Authority, 2001—02, Pascua Yaqui Tribe, Ariz., 2001—; active El Presidio Neighborhood Orgn., Tucson, 2001—. Mem.: City of Bisbee Gen. Plan Update Steering Com. (facilitator 2003—), Davis-Monthan AFB JLUS (working group 2003—), Tres Rios del Norte River Study Task Force, Ariz. Planning Assn. Avocation: writing, traveling, networking, team building, horseback riding. Office: The Planning Center, Tucson 110 South Church St 6320 Tucson AZ 85701 Business E-Mail: mmasque@azplanningcenter.com.

MASSARO, LINDA P. science foundation executive; BS in Physics and Math., U. Richmond; MSA in Mgmt. Engring, George Washington U.; postgrad., Nat. Def. U., Fed. Exec. Inst. Structural engr. Naval Ship Rsch. and Devel. Ctr.; tech. info. specialist, phys. sci. adminstr., mgmt. analyst Naval Material Command; dep. br. chief USMC Hdqrs.; dep. adminstr. for mgmt. USDA, 1987-94, acting agy. adminstr., 1992-93; dep. asst. sec. for personnel U.S. State Dept., 1994-96; dir. Office Info. and Resource Mgmt. NSF, 1996—, also chief info. officer. Recipient Presidential Meritorious Rank award. Mem. Exec. Women in Govt., Orgn. Prof. Employees at Agr. (past pres.), Mgmt. Coun. at Agr. (past chmn.), Sr. Execs. Assn. (bd. dirs., co-founder fgn. affairs agy. chpt.).

MASSARO, TONI MARIE, dean, law educator; BS, Northwestern U., 1977; JD, Coll. William and Mary, 1980. With Vedder, Price, Kaufman and Kammholz; tchr. law Washington and Lee U., U. Fla.; former prof. law U. Ariz., Tucson, dean, Milton O. Riepe chair constl. law, 1999—. Vis. prof. law Stanford U., U. N.C., Johann Goethe U., Frankfurt, West Germany. Author: Constitutional Literacy: A Core Curriculum for a Multi-Cultural Nation; contbr. numerous articles to law revs. Office: U Ariz Coll Law Bldg 204a PO Box 210176 Tucson AZ 85721-0176 Fax: 520-621-9140. E-mail: massaro@nt.law.arizona.edu.

MASSARO, TRACI LYNN, special education educator; b. Gadsden, Ala., Jan. 16, 1969; d. James Michael Cushing and Sheltie Anna Griffin; m. Thomas Christopher Massaro, Aug. 18, 1992; children: Lorren Elizabeth, Ryan Thomas, Andrew Michael. BS in Spl. Edn., Jacksonville State U., 1992; M, Kennesaw State U., 2000. Tchr. Bartow County Schs., Cartersville, Ga., 1992-93, Douglas County Schs., Douglasville, Ga., 1993-99, Etowah County Schs., Gadsden, Ala., 1999—. Recipient Mamie Jo Jones scholarship, 1995, Hope Tchr. scholarship, 1996-98, Outstanding Grad. Student Special Edn. award, 1999, Pledge of Yr. award Gadsden City Coun., 2002. Mem. Coun. Exceptional Children (v.p. 1996-97, pres. 1997—), Kiwanis (Circle K, v.p. 1989-90. pres. 1990-91), Anchor Club (v.p. 1985-86, pres. 1986-87), Beta Sigma Phi (Gadsden City Coun. Pledge of Yr. 2002, Woman of Yr. 2003). Republican. Baptist. Avocations: crafting, sewing. Home: 505 Cosby St Gadsden AL 35903-6911

MASSEE, JUDITH TYLE, editor, educator; b. Portland, June 26, 1937; d. Axel Buch Tyle and Annette Dorothy Brown; m. Richard S. Tron, Aug. 15, 1970; m. Michael David Massee, Aug. 22, 1959 (div. Mar. 1968). BS, Portland State U., 1959; postgrad., U. Oreg., 1970. Recreational dir., dance specialist Bur. Pks. and Recreation, Portland, 1958—60; profl. dancer Broadway, Off-Broadway, N.Y.C., 1960—68; dir. dance dept. Reed Coll., Portland, 1968—98; ptnr., poetry editor Media Weavers LLC, Portland, 1998—. Adv. com. Portland Ctr. for Performing Arts, 1982—86. Choreographer (profl. production) New Savoy Opera Co., 1959—62; author: (poetry, anthology) Blooming in the Shade, 1997, (poetry book revs.) Writers NW Newspaper, 1997—. Design com. Performing Arts Ctr., Portland, 1980—86; mem. Multnomah County Arts Commn., Portland, 1982—86. Recipient Tchr. of Yr., Oreg. Dance Assn., 1992, Pacific NW Am. Assn. for Phys., Edn., Health, Recreation and Dance, 1993. Mem.: Oreg. Writers Colony (bd. mem. 1997—). Avocations: mentoring beginning writers/poets, reading. Home: 3415 SE Steele St Portland OR 97202

MASSENBURG, JOHNNYE SMITH, speech pathology/audiology services professional, minister; b. Durham, N.C., July 4, 1954; d. John Franklin and Florence Rowland Smith; m. C. Warren Massenburg, Aug. 4, 1990. BS in Speech Pathology and Audiology, Hampton (Va.) U., 1975; MS in Speech Pathology and Audiology, Towson (Md.) State U., 1978; PhD in Theology, Piedmont Theol. Sem., 2000. Lic. ordained minister Va. Speech pathologist and audiologist Balt. (Md.) City Schs., 1975—78, Durham (N.C.) City Schs., 1978—89; speech pathologist Richmond (Va.) City Schs., 1989—; prin., owner Massenburg & Massenburg Inc., Midlothian, 1990—; minister First Bapt. Ch., Midlothian, Va., 1998—. Named Woman of Yr., First Bapt. Ch., 1992; recipient Svc. award, Vets. Assn., 1993, 1994, 1998, Achievement award, Bus. Women Assn., 1994. Mem.: Am. Speech and Hearing Assn., Ministers Wives and Widows (treas. 1991—93). Democrat. Bapt. Avocations: singing, reading. Home: 13302 Farm Crest Ct Midlothian VA 23112 Office: Blackwell Elem Model School 1600 Everett St Richmond VA 23224 also: First Baptist Ch 13800 Westfield Drive Midlothian VA 23112 Office Phone: 804-780-5078.

MASSENGILL, BARBARA DAVES, artist; d. Raleigh Whitson Daves and Laura Hermena Cox; m. Thomas Allan Rudisill, Dec. 19, 1954 (div. Sept. 1986); children: Carol Marie Rudisill, Allan Daves Rudisill, Sandra Lynn Rudisill Porter; m. James Robert Massengill, Mar. 19, 1989. Student, U. N.C., 1952—55. Substitute tchr. Raleigh (N.C.) Pub. Schs., 1968—69; co-owner Tinker's Dam, Ltd., Raleigh, 1970's; asst. DP coord. N.C. Dept. NRCD, Raleigh, 1982—87; DP coord. N.C. Dept. Human Resources, Raleigh, 1987—90; ret., 1990; v.p. Del-Mar Enterprises, Inc., Raleigh, 1996—; owner, artist Studio # 12 Hwy. 152, Hillsboro, N.Mex., 2003. Author: (tng. manual) A Function Oriented Guide for the Client, 1990; one-woman shows include First Savings Bank, Truth or Consequences, N.Mex., 2003, Elephant Butte (N.Mex.) C. of C., 2003, Bank of the Southwest, Elephant Butte, 2003, Truth or Consequences, 2003, exhibited in group shows at Apple Festival, Hillsboro, 2003, Sierra County Fair, Truth or Consequences, 2003, Quality Inn, Elephant Butte, 2003 (1st Pl. award Balloon Regatta Logo Design Contest), Geronimo Springs Mus., Truth or Consequences, 2003, Truth or Consequences C. of C., 2003 (1st Pl. award Fiesta Poster Contest), Represented in permanent collections Alaska, Calif., NC, N.Mex., Tex. Mem.: Black Range Artists (v.p. 2004), Nat. Mus. Women in the Arts, Sierra Art Soc. (treas. 2003), Sierra County Hist. Soc., DAV Aux., Nat. League Am. Pen Women, Inc (Rio Grande br., N.Mex., treas. 2004). Democrat. Avocations: gardening, cake decorating, photography, geological study and collection, wildlife study and preservation. Home: HCR 31 Box 97A Caballo NM 87931 Office Phone: 505-895-3377. E-mail: bmassen@zianet.com.

MASSENGILL, BELINDA B. voice educator; b. Luxora, Ariz., Jan. 25, 1950; d. James Thurman and Sylvia Daniel Barber; m. Ollice A. Massengill; children: Steve, Kevin, Karen Massengill Pannell. BS, Blue Mountain Coll., 1981; MEd, U. Miss., 1991, Specialist in Edn., 1992. Cert. tchr., adminstr. Secondary sci. instr. West Union Attendance Ctr., Myrtle, Miss., 1983—88, Hickory Flat Attendance Ctr., Hickory Flat, Miss., 1988—98; vocat. dir. Benton County Sch. Dist., Ashland, Miss., 1998—. Mem.: NEA, Miss. Assn. Educators, Miss. Assn. Career and Tech. Edn. Home: 625 Massengill Rd Hickory Flat MS 38633 Office: Benton County Vocat Ctr 25 Industrial Dr Ashland MS 38603 Office Fax: 662-224-3629. Personal E-mail: bmass_1@yahoo.com.

MASSEY-BURZIO, VIRGINIA, librarian, writer; b. Greenfield, Mass., Apr. 5, 1943; d. Louis G. and Marie (Lamarche) Massey; m. Luigi Burzio, Dec. 1, 1978. BA, Trinity Coll., 1965; MLS, Drexel U., 1966. Cataloger Boston Pub. Libr., 1966—68; asst. docs. libr. Dartmouth Coll., Hanover, NH, 1968—71; docs. libr. Brandeis U., Waltham, Mass., 1971—73, head, docs. sect., 1973—83, head, reference dept., 1983—88, head, reader services, 1988—91; head, core libr. services U. Md., College Park, 1991; head, resource services dept. Johns Hopkins U., Balt., 1992—. Contbr. articles to jours. Recipient Isadore Gilbert Mudge award, Reference and User Services Assn., a divsn. of the ALA, 1999. Mem.: Assn. of Coll. and Rsch. Libraries, ALA. Achievements include development of Brandeis model of reference service. Avocations: creative writing, calligraphy, yoga. Office: Johns Hopkins University 3400 N Charles St Baltimore MD 21218 E-mail: vmb@jhu.edu.

MASSIE, ANNE ADAMS ROBERTSON, artist; b. Lynchburg, Va., May 30, 1931; d. Douglas Alexander and Annie Scott (Harris) Robertson; m. William McKinnon Massie, Apr. 30, 1960; children: Anne Harris Massie-Apperson, William McKinnon, Jr. Grad., St. Mary's Coll., Raleigh, N.C., 1950; BA in English, Randolph Macon Woman's Coll., 1952. Tchr. English E.C. Glass High Sch., Lynchburg, 1955-60. Juror Am. Watercolor Soc. Ann. Exhbn., 1998, Ctrl. Va. Watercolor Guild, 1996. Represented in permanent collections at Hotel de Ville, Rueil-Malmaison, France, L'Association des Amis de la Grande Vigne, Dinan, France, Randolph Macon Woman's Coll., Lynchburg Coll., Va. Episcopal Sch., Va. Sch. of Arts, Va. State Bar Assn., Richmond, St. John's Episcopal Ch. Bd. dirs. Lynchburg Hist. Found., 1968-81, 91-95, pres., 1978-81; bd. dirs. Lynchburg Fine Arts Ctr., 1992-98, Point of Honor Mus., 1988-99, collections com., 1970-, chmn. 1989-99; bd. dirs. Amazement Sq. Children's Mus., 1996-2004; trustee Va. Episcopal Sch., Lynchburg, 1983-89, Va. Ctr. for Creative Arts, 1999—; mem. Friends of Rivermont, 2000-, pres. 2000-02. Mem. Am. Watercolor Soc. (signature, Dolphin fellow 1993, Gold medal of Honor 1993), Nat. Watercolor Soc. (signature, Artist's Mag. award), Nat. League Am. Pen Women (pres. 1987, Best in Show 1994), Knickerbocker Artists (signature, Silver medal Watercolor 1993), Watercolor USA Honor Soc., Watercolor West (signature), Catharine Lorillard Wolfe Art Club (signature, medal of honor for water media, 2003), Allied Artists Am., Inc. (signature), Southern Watercolor Soc. (signature), Pa. Watercolor Soc. (artist mem., Best in Show 1992, 97, chmn. exhbns. 1986, pres. 1995-96), Nat. Arts Club (exhibiting artist mem.), Artists' Fellowship, Colonial Dames Am. (chmn. 1987-90), Hillside Garden Club (pres. 1974-76), Jr. League (editor 1953-72), Lynchburg Art Club (bd. dirs. 1995-96, chmn. 1981-4), Antiquarian Club. Episcopalian. Avocations: book club, gardening, tennis. Home: 3204 Rivermont Ave Lynchburg VA 24503-2028

MASSIE-BURRELL, TERRI L. educational association administrator; b. Balt., Mar. 29, 1964; d. Edward Forest and Eleanor Dease Massie; m. Robinson Burrell, Jr., Feb. 14, 1990; 1 child, Robinson Burrell III. BA, Howard U., 1986; MA, Johns Hopkins U., 1990; attending, U. MD, 1990—. Substitue tchr. Balt., Md., 1990—92; special educator Balt. City Pub. Schs., 1996—98; spl. educator Montgomery County Pub. Schs., Rockville, Md., 1998—2000; counselor Howard Cmty., Columbia, Md., 1999—2003; learning specialist Towson (Md.) U., 2000—02, faculty, 2001—, sr. dir., 2002—. Bd. mem. Md. State Rehab., Balt., 2001—; lectr. Towson (Md.) U., 1995—; co-chair Jack & Jill of Am., Balt., 2002—; pres. Howard U. Alumni, 1996—2001; adv. Delta Sigma Theta, Inc., Morgan State U., 1993—95. Recipient Presenters award, Balt. Tchrs. Union, 2001. Mem.: Learning Ctr. Coll. Reade and Learn. Assoc., Am. Coll. Personnel Assoc. Democrat. Roman Catholic. Avocation: singing. Office: Towson U Academic Achievement Ctr 8000 York Rd Baltimore MD 21252 E-mail: tmassieburrell@towson.edu.

MAST, BERNADETTE MIHALIC, lawyer; BS, Ohio State U., 1982; JD magna cum laude, Case Western Res. U., 1988. CPA; bar: Ohio 1988; cert. prodn. and inventory mgr., systems profl. 1985. With Jones Day, Cleve., 1988—, ptnr., 2000—. Mem.: Cleve. Bar Assn. (real estate sect.), Ohio State Bar Assn. Office: Jones Day North Point 901 Lakeside Ave Cleveland OH 44114-1190*

MAST, KANDE WHITE, artist; b. St. Louis, Mar. 10, 1950; d. Elliott Maxwell and Mary (Barritt) W. Student, U. Mo., 1968-70, Longview C.C., Kansas City, Mo., 1970-71. Portrait painter, free-lance artist, Albany, N.Y., 1973-74, Kansas City, 1974—; dir., tchr. Studio Kande, Sch. Fine Arts, Kansas City, 1983-86; founder, exec. dir. Art Ctr. Kansas City, 1986-90; behavioral foster parent, 1989—; master foster parent, 1992—. Mem. psychiat. diversion team, mental health rev. team Jackson County Divsn. Family Svcs., 1992-95. Portrait painter and free-lance artist. Pres., bd. dirs. Advocates for Children, Inc., 1996—; vol. Ozanam Home for Boys, Kansas City, 1987—, mem. adv. bd., 1991—; mem. Cmty. Response Team, Jackson County, Divsn. Family Svcs. Named Therapeutic Foster Parent of Yr., 1992. Mem.: Code Pink: Women for Peace, Nat. Mus. of Women in Arts (charter). Home and Office: 10243 Cedarbrooke Ln Kansas City MO 64131-4209

MASTEN, JACQUELINE GWENDOLYN, small business owner; b. Brunswick, Maine, Oct. 24, 1941; d. Ralph Henry Bennet and Phyllis Estelle Crooker; children from previous marriage: Geraldine Frances Bullwinkel, Jennifer Lynn. Diploma in Bus., Pluss Sch. of Business, Portland, Maine, 1966. Shop owner Hudson Chair Caning Svcs., Hudson, NH, 1982; data entry operator Digital Corp., Nashua, NH, 1980; real estate landlady Hudson, NH, 1996—. Author: A Shaker Poetry Poetic History Book: A Tribute to My Aunt Eldress Gertrude Soule Shaker, 2003; contbr. poems to books. Named 1999 Poet of the Year, Famous Poets Soc., Nev., 1999, World Champion Amature, Internat. Soc. of Poets, 2001; recipient Shakespear medallion of Excellence, 2002. Mem.: New Eng. Saddlebred and Pony Assn., Quartzsite Roadrunner Gem and Mineral Club. Avocation: Shaker poetry writing, shaker tape chair seating, silversmith, gem faceting, lapidary..

MASTERS, ANN BROWNING, education educator, poet; d. Shirley A. and William T. Browning; m. Jeremy A. Masters; 1 child, Forrest J. BA, U. Fla., 1973, MEd, 1976, PhD, 1992. Exec. dir. Jane Ho. Drug Abuse Prevention and Edn. Ctr., St. Augustine, Fla., 1975—77; consultation edn. coord. Tri-County Mental Health Svcs., St. Augustine, 1979—80; sr. case mgr., staff coord. St. Johns County Coun. Aging, 1981—85; academic advisor St. Johns River C.C., St. Augustine, 1985—96, prof. edn. program coord., 1996—. Author of poems; contbr. articles to profl. jours. Mem. St. Augustine Hist. Soc., Fla., 1996—2003, Menorcan Cultural Soc., 1990—2003; founding bd. mem Los Floridanos Soc., St. Augustine, Fla., 2000—03. Recipient Tchg. Excellence award, Nat. Inst. for Staff and Orgnl. Devel., 1998. Mem.: AAUW, Edn. Law Assn., Fla. Assn. of C.Cs. (chpt. pres. 1993), Los Floridanos Soc., Menorcan Cultural Soc., St. Augustine Hist. Soc.

MASTERS, ARLENE ELIZABETH, singer; b. Freeport, Ill., Oct. 6, 1960; d. Elmer and Mary (Green) Masters; m. Douglas Dewayne Burck (div.); 1 child, Douglas. Singer classic rock and blues; with The Blues Transit Band, A. Masters Publishing. Home: 2680 S Tissaw Road Cornville AZ 86325

MASTERS, BETTIE SUE SILER, biochemist, educator; b. Lexington, Va., June 13, 1937; d. Wendell Hamilton and Mildred Virginia (Cromer) Siler; m. Robert Sherman Masters, Aug. 6, 1960; children: Diane Elizabeth, Deborah Ann. BS in Chemistry, Roanoke Coll., 1959, D.Sc. (hon.), 1983; PhD in Biochemistry, Duke U., 1963. Postdoctoral fellow Duke U., 1963-66, advanced research fellow, 1966-68, assoc. on faculty, 1967-68; mem. faculty U. Tex. Health Sci. Ctr. (Southwestern Med. Sch.), Dallas, 1968-82, assoc. prof. biochemistry, 1972-76, prof., 1976-82, research prof. surgery, dir. biochem. burn research, 1979-82; prof. biochemistry, chmn. dept. Med. Coll. Wis., Milw., 1982-90; Robert A. Welch prof. chemistry, dept. biochemistry U. Tex. Health Sci. Ctr., San Antonio, 1990—. Mem. pharmacology toxicology rsch. rev. com. Nat. Inst. Gen. Med. Scis., NIH, 1975-79; mem. bd. sci. counselors Nat. Inst. Environ. Health Scis., 1982-86, chmn., 1984-86; mem. adv. com. on biochemistry and endocrinology Am. Cancer Soc., 1989-92, chmn., 1991-92, mem. coun. for extramural grants, 1998—; mem. phys. biochemistry study sect. NIH, 1989-90; vis. scientist Japan Soc. for Promotion Sci., 1978. Mem. editl. bd. Jour. Biol. Chemistry, 1976-81, 96-2001, Archives Biochemistry and Biophysics, 1991-94, Drug Metabolism and Disposition, 1993-, Nitric Oxide, Biology and Chemistry, 1996-, Internat. Union Biochemistry and Molecular Biology Life, 1999-; contbr. chpts. to books and articles, revs. and abstracts to profl. publs. Mem. coun. extramural grants Am. Cancer Soc., 1998-2000. Recipient Merit award Nat. Heart, Lung and Blood Inst., 1988-97, grantee, 1970—; recipient Excellence in Sci. award Fedn. Am. Socs. for Exptl. Biology, 1992; postdoctoral fellow Am. Cancer Soc., 1963-65, advanced rsch. fellow Am. Heart Assn., 1966-68, established investigator, 1968-73; rsch. grantee NIH, 1970—, Nat. Heart Lung Blood Inst., 1970—, Nat. Inst. Gen. Med. Scis., 1980—, Robert A. Welch Found., 1971-82, 90—; elected to Inst. Medicine of NAS, 1996. Fellow AAAS; mem. NIH (adv. com. to the dir. 2000—), Am. Soc. Biochemistry and Molecular Biology (nominating com. 1983, coun. 1985-86, awards com. 1992-96, fin. com. 1993-98, publs. com. 1994-97, pres.-elect 2001, pres. 2002-), Am. Soc. Pharmacology and Exptl. Therapeutics (exec. com. drug metabolism divsn. 1979-81, chmn. exec. com. 1993-94, bd. publs. trustees 1982-87, Bernard B. Brodie award 2000), Am. Chem. Soc., Assn. Am. Med. Colls. (adv. bd. biomed. rsch. 1995-98), Fedn. Am. Socs. for Exptl. Biology (bd. dirs. 1998—, v.p. 2001-2002), Internat. Union Biochemistry and Molecular Biology (nominating com. 1994-97, chair U.S. nat.com. 1997—), Sigma Xi, Alpha Omega Alpha. Office: U Tex Health Sci Ctr Dept Biochemistry 7703 Floyd Curl Dr MSC 7760 San Antonio TX 78229-3900 E-mail: masters@uthscsa.edu.

MASTERSON, CARLIN See GLYNN, CARLIN

MASTERSON, ELLEN HORNBERGER, accountant; b. Ft. Smith, Ark., Feb. 19, 1951; d. Evans Zacharias and Nancy Cravens (Eads) H.; m. Conrad J. Masterson, Jr., Sept. 26, 1987. BA, Emory U., 1973; MBA, So. Meth. U., 1978. CPA, Mass. Staff acct. Coopers & Lybrand, Boston, 1973, gen. practice ptnr. Dallas, 1985—97; CFO Am. Gen. Corp., Houston, 1997—99; ptnr. PricewaterhouseCoopers, N.Y.C., 1999—. Instr. Sch. Mgmt. and Adminstrv. Scis., U. Tex., Dallas, 1980-81. Bd. dirs. Shakespeare Festival Dallas, 1983-86, Leadership Dallas, 1985-86, USA Film Festival, 1986-88, Dental Health Program, Inc., 1986-88; mem. Jr. League, The 500, Inc.; workshop leader, vol. Cmty. Bd. Inst.; cons. Ctr. for Non Profit Mgmt. Mem. AICPA, Mass. Soc. CPAs, Tex. CPAs, So. Meth. U. MBA Alumni Assn., Kappa Kappa Gamma, Alpha Iota Delta, Beta Gamma Sigma. Presbyterian. Office: PricewaterhouseCoopers 1301 Ave of Americas New York NY 10019

MASTERSON, JULIE COSGROVE, photographer; b. LA, June 23, 1940; d. John Charles and Emilie Dohrmann Cosgrove; m. Justice William Anthony Masterson, Dec. 15, 1973; children: Mark, Mary, Barbara. BA, Stanford U., 1962. Tchr. South Pasadena (Calif.) Schs., 1964—72; with Flournoy for Gov., LA, 1972—73; fine art photographer, 1981—. Pres. Jr. League LA, 1980—81. Home: PO Box 190 Mendocino CA 95460

MASTERSON, MARY STUART, actress; b. N.Y.C., June 28, 1966; d. Peter and Carlin Glynn Masterson. Theatre appearances include Alice in Wonderland, 1982, Been Taken, 1985, The Lucky Spot, 1987, Lily Dale, 1987, Three Sisters, 1991; TV movies include Love Lives On, 1985, City in Fear, 1980, Lily Dale, 1996, On the 2nd Day of Christmas, 1997; films: The Stepford Wives, 1975, Heaven Help Us, 1984, At Close Range, 1985, My Little Girl, 1986, Gardens of Stone, 1987, Some Kind of Wonderful, 1987, Mr. North, 1988, Chances Are, 1989, Immediate Family, 1989, Funny About Love, 1990, Married To It, 1990, Fried Green Tomatoes, 1991, Benny and Joon, 1993, Bad Girls, 1994, Radioland Murders, 1994, Heaven's Prisoners, 1996, Bed of Roses, 1996, Digging to China, 1997, Dogtown, 1997, The Postman, 1997, The Florentine, 1998, The Book of Stars, 1999, Black and Blue, 1999, The Book of Stars, 2000, Leo, 2002, West of Here, 2002; dir., writer for Showtime 2000; TV guest appearances include Amazing Stories, 1985, Inside the Actors Studio, 1994. Office: Creative Artists Agency 9830 Wilshire Blvd Beverly Hills CA 90212-1825

MASTRACCHIO-HARDT, DINA RAPHAELLA, elementary school educator; b. New Haven, Conn., Feb. 16, 1974; d. David Anthony and Patricia Raphaella Mastracchio; m. Richard Louis Hardt, Jr., Aug. 11, 2001. BS in Sociology, So. Conn. State U., 1998; MEd, U. New Haven, 2001. Adminstrv. asst. Yale U., New Haven, 1998—99; tchr. St. Lawrence Sch., West Haven, Conn., 2000—01; tchr. elem. Orchard Hills Sch., Milford, Conn., 2001—. Dir., tchr. Enrichment Sch., Milford, 2000—. Avocations: acting, theater, travel, reading.*

MASTROIANNI, ANNA CATHERINE, law educator; b. New Haven, Conn., Dec. 21, 1960; d. Luigi Mastroianni; m. Gregory M. Shaw, Oct. 16, 1993; children: Ryan Michael Shaw, Ella Catherine Shaw. BA, BS, U. Pa., 1982, JD, 1986; MPH, U. Wash., 1997. Atty. Epstein, Becker and Green, PC, Washington, 1987—88; asst to D.C. fin. dir. Dukakis Bentsen Campaign, Washington, 1988—88; legal cons. NRC, Washington, 1988—89; atty. Green, Stewart & Farber PC, Washington, 1989—92; study dir. Inst. Medicine, NAS, Washington, 1992—94; assoc. dir. White Ho. Adv. Com. on Human Radiation Experiments, Washington, 1994—95; part time lectr. U. Wash. Sch. Law, Seattle, 1996—98, asst. prof., 1998—. Editor: (book) Women and Health Research: Ethical and Legal Issues of Including Women in Clinical Studies, 1994, Beyond Consent: Seeking Justice in Research, 1998, Ethics of Research with Human Subjects: Selected Policies and Resources, 1998; contbr. articles to profl. jours. Recipient faculty scholarship, Greenwall Found., 2002—. Office: Univ Wash Sch Law Wm H Gates Hall Box 353020 Seattle WA 98195-3020

MASTROPAOLO, JOAN ARENA, healthcare management executive; b. Bklyn., Oct. 20, 1958; d. Bartello and Margaret Arena; m. Frank A. Mastropaolo, Sept. 24, 1983. BA in Psychology, Queens Coll., 1981. Mgr. nat. accounts CIGNA Healthcare, Bloomfield, Conn., 1990—93, mgr. client svcs. N.Y.C., 1993—96, dir. client svcs. Jersey City, 1996—2002, asst. v.p., 2002—. Home: 355 South End Ave 14B New York NY 10280 Office: CIGNA Healthcare 499 Washington Blvd Jersey City NJ 07310

MATA, JOSEFINA, health education coordinator, educator; b. Juarez, Mex., Mar. 28, 1968; came to U.S., 1979; d. Angel and Irma Ulloa; m. Jesus Antonio Mata, Aug. 29, 1989; 1 child, Lizbeth Mata. BS, N.Mex. State U., 1991, MS, 1994, MPH, 1999; MBA, U. Phoenix, 2002. News translator Sta. RZOL Radio, El Paso, 1984-86; receptionist aid San Jacinto Sch., El Paso, Tex., 1985-86; nutritionist La Fe Clinic, El Paso, summer 1990; gang prevention and intervention counselor Families and Youth Inc., Las Cruces, N.Mex., 1992-93; health educator Adolescent Family Life, Las Cruces, 1993-95; health edn. and quality inspection coord. Ben Archer Health Ctr., Truth or Consequences, N.Mex., 1995-98; health edn. coord. La Clinica Familia, Las Cruces, 1998—. Mem. adv. bds. Corp. Extend in Svc., Las Cruces, 1993, Health Sci. Dept. N.Mex. State U., Las Cruces, 1995-98, Sierra County Adv. Sch., 1995-98, Am. Cancer Soc., Sierra County, N.Mex., 1995-98. Mem. cmty. involvement Kellog Found. N.Mex. state U., 1997; mem. Nat. Faculty Comenzando Bien March of Dimes Initiative. Grantee N.Mex. Dept. Health, 1994, 98, N.Mex. Teen Pregnancy Coalition peer edn. program, 1996-98; recipient Marathon Participation award Leukemia Soc. Am., 1996. Mem. MPH Assn., Am. Pub. Health Assn., USA Track & Field Assn., Mesilla Valley Track Club, Tobacco Free Coalition. Roman Catholic. Avocation: road racing. Office: La Clinica Familia 1100 S Main St Ste A Las Cruces NM 88005-2952

MATA, LINDA SUE PROCTOR, writer, consultant; b. Topeka, Oct. 22, 1950; d. Frank Robert and Anabelle Simpson Proctor; m. Robert William Mata, Aug. 29, 1980; children: Adrian Robert-Proctor, Christiana Nicole. BA in sociology, U. Cent. Okla., 1973; BA in edn., Pacific Luth. U., 1983; MBA, City U., Renton, Wash., 1999. Tchr. North Thurston Sch. Dist., Olympia, Wash., 1986—88; cons. Dept. Social and Health Svcs., Olympia, 1988—. Tchr. Kid's Outreach, Olympia, 2001—. Author: (book) Roads and Reminiscences (Poetry Award, 2003). Mem. Blacks in Govt., Olympia, 2001—03. With U.S. Army, 1977—81. Mem.: U. Okla. Alumni Assn. (assoc.). Avocations: travel, doll collecting, reading, camping, writing poetry. E-mail: matals@dshs.wa.gov.

MATALIN, MARY, political consultant; b. Chgo., Aug. 19, 1953; d. Steven and Eileen Matalin; m. Artie Arnold (div.); m. James Carville, Nov. 25, 1993; 2 children. Grad., Western Ill. Univ.; student, Hofstra Univ. With the Rep. Nat. Com., since the early 80's; polit. dir. George Bush's 1992 re-election campaign; co-host CNBC talk show, Equal Time, 1993—96; host The Mary Matalin Show; asst. to the Pres. and Counselor to the V.P., 2001—. Author (with James Carville): All's Fair, 1994; author: Letters to My Daughters, 2004; co-author (with Shelley L. Davis): Unbridled Power: Inside the Secret Culture of the IRS, 1997. Office: care The Mary Matalin Show PO Box 15129 Washington DC 20003-0129*

MATAN, LILLIAN KATHLEEN, secondary school educator, consultant, interior designer; b. Boston, Aug. 18, 1937; d. George Francis and Lillian May (Herbert) Archambault; m. Joseph A. Matan, Aug. 6, 1960; children: Maria, Meg, Tony, Elizabeth, Joan, Molly. BS, Seton Hall Coll., 1960; MA, San Francisco State U., 1984; EdD, U. San Francisco, 1999. Tchr. St. Jane de Chantal, Bethesda, Md., 1956-60; tchr. home econs. Surrottsville (Md.) H.S., 1960-61; tchr., head home econs. dept. Bruswick (Md.) H.S., 1972-73; designer Dudley Kelley and Assocs., San Francisco, Calif., 1976-84; designer (prin.) K. Matan Antiques and Interiors, Ross, Calif., 1985-87, designer Charles Lester Assocs., San Francisco, 1987-88; dean of students St. Rose Acad., San Francisco, 1988-90; dir., asst. devel. The Branson Sch., Ross, Calif., 1990-92; prin. St. Anselm Sch., San Anselmo, Calif., 1993-94; adminstrv. head Ring Mt. Day Sch., Tiburon, Calif., 1995-96; sabbatical, 1997-98. Ednl. cons. Head Start, Frederick County, Md., 1972-73. Pres. Cath. Charities, Marin County, Calif.; mem. Ecumenical Assn. for Housing, Marin County. Mem. KM (dame), Am. Soc. of Interior Designers, Am. Assn. Family and Consumer Scis., Serra Club, Phi Delta Kappa. Democrat. Home: PO Box 1140 Ross CA 94957-1140 E-mail: lmatan6561@aol.com.

MATASAR, ANN B. former dean, business and political science educator; b. N.Y.C., June 27, 1940; d. Harry and Tillie (Simon) Bergman; m. Robert Matasar, June 9, 1962; children— Seth Gideon, Toby Rachel AB, Vassar Coll., 1962; MA, Columbia U., 1964, PhD, 1968; M of Mgmt. in Fin., Northwestern U., 1977. Assoc. prof. Mundelein Coll., Chgo., 1965-78; prof., dir. Ctr. for Bus. and Econ. Elmhurst Coll., Elmhurst, Ill., 1978-84; dean Roosevelt U., Chgo., 1984-92; prof. Internat. Bus. and Fin. Walter E. Heller Coll. Bus. Adminstrn. Roosevelt U., 1992—. Dir. Corp. Responsibility Group, Chgo., 1978-84; chmn. long range planning Ill. Bar Assn., 1982-83; mem. edn. com. Ill. Commn. on the Status of Women, 1978-81 Author: Corporate PACS and Federal Campaign Financing Laws: Use or Abuse of Power?, 1986; (with others) Research Guide to Women's Studies, 1974, (with others) The Impact of Geographic Deregulation on the American Banking Industry, 2002; contbr. articles to profl. jours. Dem. candidate 1st legis. dist. Ill. State Senate, no. suburbs Chgo., 1972; mem. Dem. exec. com. New Trier Twp., Ill., 1972-76; rsch. dir., acad. advisor Congressman Abner Mikva, Ill., 1974-76; bd. dirs. Ctr. Ethics and Corp. Policy, 1985-90. Named Chgo. Woman of Achievement, Mayor of Chgo., 1978. Fellow AAUW (trustee ednl. found. 1992-97, v.p. fin. 1993-97); mem. Am. Polit. Sci. Assn., Midwest Bus. Adminstrn. Assn., Acad. Mgmt., Women's Caucus for Polit. Sci. (pres. 1980-81), John Howard Assn. (bd. dirs. 1986-90), Am. Assembly of Coll. Schs. of Bus. (bd. dirs. 1989-92, chair com. on diversity in mgmt. edn. 1991-92), North Ctrl. Assn. (commr. 1994-97), Beta Gamma Sigma. Democrat. Jewish. Avocations: jogging, biking, tennis, opera, crosswords. Office: Roosevelt U Coll Bus Adminstrn Dept Fin 430 S Michigan Ave Chicago IL 60605-1394 Office Phone: 312-281-3283. E-mail: amatasar@roosevelt.edu.

MATASEJE, VERONICA JULIA, sales executive; b. St. Ann's, Ontario, Can., Apr. 5, 1949; came to U.S., 1985; d. John and Anna Veronica M. Grad. H.S., Smithville, Can. Clk. typist, typesetter Crown Life Ins. Co., Toronto, 1966-70; typesetter Toronto Life/Calendar Mag., 1970-71; typesetter, exec.

sec. Cerebrus Prodns. Ltd., Toronto, 1971-74; pres. Veron Prodns. Ltd., Toronto, 1975-81, Acclaim Records Inc., Toronto, 1981-88; pvt. health care provider Las Vegas, 1989-94; retail sales mgr. Top Cats, Las Vegas, 1994-00; pres. Abracadabra Music Corp., 2000—. Campaign vol. Dist. Atty., Las Vegas, 1994; vol. pilot Angel Planes, Las Vegas, 1989. Avocations: gardening, interior design, showing cats, travel, music. Home: 4326 Caliente St Las Vegas NV 89119-3801 Office: Top Cats PO Box 61173 Las Vegas NV 89160-1173 E-mail: vm@abracadabramusic.com.

MATASOVIC, MARILYN ESTELLE, manufacturing executive; b. Chgo., Jan. 7, 1946; d. John Lewis and Stella (Butkauskas) M. Student, U. Colo. Sch. Bus., 1963-69. Owner, pres. UTE Trail Ranch, Ridgway, Colo., 1967—; pres. MEM Equipment Co., Mokena, Ill., 1979—; sec./treas. Marlin Corp., Ridgway, 1991—, v.p., sec.-treas., 1991—, pres., 2003—; sec.-treas. Linmar Corp., Mokena, 1991-93, pres., 2003—; ptnr. Universal Welding Supply Co., New Lenox, Ill., 1964-90; v.p. OXO Welding Equipment Co, Inc., New Lenox, 1964-90; ptnr. Universal Internat., Mokena, Ill., 1990—2003, owner, 2003—; ind. travel agt. Ideal Travel Concepts, Mokena, 1994—2003; mgr. Hereford Works Warehouse, Mokena, 1997—, owner, 2001—, Barnyardblvd.com, 2001—; ptnr. OXO Hereford Ranches, Ridgeway, Colo., 2003—. Co-editor newsletters. U.S. rep. World Hereford Conf., 1964, 68, 76, 80, 84, 96. Recipient Outstanding Hereford Woman award, 1999. Mem. Am. Hereford Aux. (charter, bd. dirs. 1989-94, historian 1990-92, v.p. 1992, pres.-elect 1993, pres. 1994), Am. Hereford Women (charter, pres. 1994, bd. dirs. 1994-96, award 1999), Am. Agri-Women, Colo. Hereford Aux., Ill. Hereford Aux. (sec. 1969-70, publicity 1970-72), U. Colo. Alumni Assn., Ill. Agri-Women, Las Vegas Social Register. Avocations: showing cattle, computers, travel. E-mail: herefordworks@usa.net.

MATEER, ANNE FRANCES, multi-media specialist, elementary school educator; b. Yonkers, N.Y. d. Alexander Gillespie and Anne Frances Votta; m. W. Bruce Mateer; children: Sandra Ann Rivera, Robert Bruce, Marjorie Elizabeth. BS, SUNY, Buffalo, 1962; M, C. W. Post Coll., L.I., 1987. Art educator Bd. Coop. Edn. Services, Suffolk County, NY, 1982—87; libr. media specialist, study skills instr. Elmwood Mid. Sch., East Northport, NY, 1987—. Mem. libr. adv. bd. Bd. Coop. Edn. Services, Suffolk County, 2002, mem. adv. bd., 2003—, 2004. Named Turnkey Tchr., Suffolk County Middle Sch./Jr. High Sch. Tchrs. in position of libr., 1989. Presbyterian. Avocations: reading, sailing, gardening, writing. Office: Elwood Mid Sch 478 Elwood Rd East Northport NY 11731-4831

MATEJKA, BARBARA A. draftsman; b. Sharon, Pa., Aug. 23, 1957; d. William L. and Mary B. Parker; m. Frank R. Matejka, Feb. 15, 1991; children: Shane A., Victoria L., Elizabeth L., Frank M. A in Archtl. Engring., Pa. State U., 1979. Cert. constrn. specifier Constrn. Specifications Inst. Draftsman Hunter Heiges Archs., Sharon, 1979—80; design draftsman Chgo. Bridge and Iron, Greenville, Pa., 1980—85; project mgr. HHSDR Archs./Engrs., Sharon, 1985—98, specifications writer, 1998—. Parent advisor Girl Scouts, Trumbull County, Ohio, 1994—; exec. bldg. com. Joseph Badger Sch. Dist., Trumbull County, Ohio, 2000—. Mem.: Constrn. Specifications Inst. Avocation: sewing. Office: HHSDR Archs and Engrs 40 Shenango Ave Sharon PA 16146

MATELIC, CANDACE TANGORRA, museum studies educator, consultant, museum director; b. Detroit, Aug. 21, 1952; d. Paul Eugene and Madeline Marie (Tangora) M.; m. Steven Joseph Mrozek, Sept. 17, 1983 (div. Sept. 1987); 1 child, Madeline Rose. BA, U. Mich., 1974; MA, SUNY, Oneonta, 1977; postgrad. doctoral studies, SUNY, Albany. Interpretive specialist Living History Farms, Des Moines, 1978-80; mgr. adult edn. Henry Ford Mus./Greenfield Village, Dearborn, Mich., 1981-82, mgr. interpretive tng., 1982-84; dir., prof. mus. studies Cooperstown grad. program SUNY, Oneonta, 1985-94; exec. dir. Mission Houses Mus., Honolulu, 1994-96, Historic St. Mary's City, Md., 1997-98; pres./CEO CTM Profl. Svcs., Inc., 1999—; founder, prin. The Cherry Valley Group, 2002—. Cons. history mus., 1979—; lectr., tchr. nat. and regional confs., workshops, seminars, 1979—; grant reviewer NEH and Inst. for Mus. Svc., Washington, 1982—, PEW Charitable Trusts, 2003; mem. guest faculty U. Victoria, B.C., 1993, 2000, 02, 03, author distance learning course, 2002—. Author: (with others) Exhibition Reader, 1992; co-author: A Pictorical History of Food in Iowa, 1980, Survey of 1200-Plus Museum Studies Graduates, 1988; contbr. articles and videos on mus. interpretation, tng. and mentoring in mus., 1979—; author conf. proceedings. Trustee Motown Hist. Mus., 1985—; bd. dirs. Hawaii Youth Opera Chorus, 1996. Mem. Am. Assn. State and Local History (sec., bd. dirs. 1988-93, program chmn. ann meeting 1988, mem. edn. com. 1996-99, co-chair task force on edn. and tng. 1994-96, faculty nat. workshop series 2001-03), designed profl. tng. workshop series, 1999-00, Assn. Living Hist. Farms and Agrl. Mus. (bd. dirs. 1980-88, pres. 1985, John T. Schlebecker award Lifetime Disting. Svc. 1996), Midwest Open Air Mus. Coordinating Coun. (founder, bd. dirs., pres. 1978-80, Candace Tangorra Matelic essay award competition established by MOMCC 2002), Am. Assn. Museums (mus. studies com. 1986-94), Internat. Coun. Museums, Nat. Trust for Hist. Preservation, Hawaii Museums Assn. (bd. dirs. 1994-96), So. Md. Mus. Assn. (bd. dirs. 1997-98), Historic House Initiative. Democrat. Roman Catholic. E-mail: ctmatelic@aol.com.

MATER, MAUD, lawyer; b. Portland, Oreg., May 12, 1947; BA in English, Case Western Reserve U., 1969, JD, 1972. Asst. gen. counsel Freddie Mac, McLean, Va., 1976-78, assoc. gen. counsel, 1978-79, v.p., dep. gen. counsel, 1979-82, v.p., gen. counsel, 1982-84, sr. v.p., gen. counsel, sec., 1984-98, exec. v.p., gen. counsel, sec., 1998—2003. Mem.: FBA, ABA (com. corp. gen. counsel), Washington Met. Corp. Counsel Assn., Conf. Bd. Coun. of Chief Legal Officers, DC Bar, Ohio Bar, Am. Arbitration Assn. (dir.), Am. Corp. Counsel Assn.

MATERA, FRANCES LORINE, elementary school educator; b. Eustis, Nebr., June 28, 1926; d. Frank Daniel and Marie Mathilda (Hess) Daiss; m. Daniel Matera, Dec. 27, 1973. Luth. tchrs. diploma, Concordia U., Seward, Nebr., 1947, BS in Edn., 1956; MEd, U. Oreg., 1963. Elementary tchr. Our Savior's Luth. Ch., Colorado Springs, Colo., 1954-57; tchr. 5th grade Monterey (Calif.) Pub. Schs., 1957-59; tchr. 1st grade Roseburg (Oreg.) Schs., 1959-60; tchr. several schs. Palm Springs (Calif.) Unified Sch. Dist., 1960—93; tchr. 3rd grade Vista del Monte Sch., Palm Springs, Calif., 1973-93; ret., 1993. Named Tchr. of the Yr., Palm Springs Unified Schs. Mem. Kappa Kappa Iota (chpt. and state pres.). E-mail: Franmatera7@aol.com.

MATERIA, KATHLEEN PATRICIA AYLING, nurse; b. Jersey City, Nov. 7, 1954; d. Donald Anthony and Muriel Cecilia (Joyce) Ayling; m. Francis Peter Materia, June 5, 1983; children: Christopher Michael, Donna Nicole. BSN, Fairleigh Dickinson U., 1976. RN, N.J.. Critical care nurse Palisades Gen. Hosp., North Bergen, N.J., 1976-87; grad. nurse, 1976-77; nurse critical care unit North Hudson Hosp., Weehawken, NJ, 1977-78. Mem. Alpha Sigma Tau. Democrat. Avocations: bowling, dance.

MATERO, JANET LOUISE, counselor, educator; b. Cadillac, Mich., Sept. 1, 1950; d. Leonard Egbert and Helen Marie (Peterson) Mattison; m. Michael Edgar Blanehard, Sept. 12, 1970 (div. Mar. 20, 1976); 1 child, Jennifer; Paul Abie Matero, June 20, 1987; stepchildren: Michael, Timothy. AA, Northwestern Mich. Coll., Traverse City, 1970; BA, Ctrl. Mich. U., Mt. Pleasant, 1977, MA, 1980; PhD with high distinction, Trinity Coll. and Sem., Newburgh, Ind., 1996. Lic. profl. counselor, Mich. Sch. social worker Adams Ctrl. Schs., Monroe, Ind., 1973-75; career devel. counselor Region 7B Employment/Tng. Consortium, Harrison, Mich., 1977-78, dir. counseling programs, 1978-81; dir. counseling Gogebie C.C., Ironwood, Mich., 1981-84, dean student svcs., interim pres., 1984-89; pvt. counselor Christian Counseling Svcs., Negaunee, Mich., 1990—. Mem. Pvt. Industry Coun., Mich. Manpower, Ironwood, 1983-89; chair bd. trustees planning com. Gogebic C.C., Ironwood, 1985-89, ednl. cons., 1990-91; mem. faculty curriculum rev. com. Trinity Coll., Newburgh, Ind., 1996—; condr. workshops and seminars, vol. ARC, Decatur, Ind., 1979-[illegible]; adult probation officer Isabella County Dist. Ct., Mt. Pleasant, Mich., 1975-80, Crisis Ctr., Ironwood, 1982-89; vol. counselor Women's Shelter, Marquette, Mich., 1993—. Mem. ACA, Am. Assn.. Christian Counselors, Mich. Counseling Assn., Mich. Assn. Marriage and Family Counselors, Internat. Assn. for Marriage and Family Counselors. Lutheran. Avocations: travel, cooking, sewing, gardening. Office: Christian Counseling & Cons Svcs Negaunee MI 49866 E-mail: jlmatero@portup.com.

MATESKY, NANCY LEE, music educator; b. West Point, Mo., Nov. 30, 1941; d. Enoch Ivy and Layla Nixon Miller; m. Michael Paul Matesky, Aug. 10, 1973; children: Angela Lynn, Michael Paul II. BS in Edn., U Ark., 1963, MS in Edn., 1971. Piano tchr. self employed, Tex.,Ark.,Wash., 1960—90; music tchr. Rogers Ark. Sch., 1963—64, Fayetteville (Ark.) Sch., 1964—65, Springdale (Ark.) Sch., 1965—70; instr. U Ark., Fayetteville, 1971—72; asst. prof. West Tex. State U, Canyon, 1972—75; prof. Shoreline Cmty. Coll., Seattle, 1976—. Founder, first pres. Ark. Elem. Music Educators Assn., 1965—67. Performer: Shoreline C.C., 1981—98, Seattle Art Mus., 2000, 2002, Matesky-Swisher Two Piano Duo. Named one of Outstanding Young Women in Am., 1968; recipient Outstanding Young Educator award, Jaycees, 1967. Mem.: Music Educators Nat. Conf., Music Tchr. Nat. Assn. (assoc.), Seattle Ladies Musical Club, Sigma Alpha Iota (Nat. Coll. Leadership award 1963, Nat. Alumnae Leadership award 2001). United Meth. Home: 23004 35th Ave S E Bothell WA 98021-8913 Office: Shoreline Cmty Coll 16101 Greenwood Ave N Seattle WA 98133 Office Phone: 206-546-4618.

MATHEIS, CHERYL, nonprofit association administrator; b. Buffalo, N.Y., May 15, 1951; d. Charles Wililam and Mary Aileen Matheis; m. Thomas Gillett Goodwin, Sept. 22, 1984; children: John Thomas Mary Claire. BA, Manhattanville Coll., 1973; JD, Cath. U. Am., 1978. Bar: D.C. 1978. Rsch. analyst Civil Rights Divsn. Dept. Justice, Washington, 1973-77; pvt. practice Washington, 1978-86; legis. rep. AARP, Washington, 1986-99, dir. state legis., 1999—. Mem. Am. Health Lawyers Assn., Women in Govt. Rels. Office: AARP 601 E St NW Washington DC 20049-0003

MATHENY, RUTH ANN, editor; b. Fargo, N.D., Jan. 17, 1918; d. Jasper Gordon and Mary Elizabeth (Carey) Wheelock; m. Charles Edward Matheny, Oct. 24, 1960. BE, Mankato State Coll., 1938; MA, U. Minn., 1955; postgrad., Universidad Autonoma de Guadalajara, Mex., summer 1956, Georgetown U., summer, 1960. Tchr., U.S. and S.Am., 1938-61; assoc. editor Charles E. Merrill Pub. Co., Columbus, Ohio, 1963-66; tchr. Confraternity Christian Doctrine, Washington Court House, Ohio, 1969-70; assoc. editor Jr. Cath. Messenger, Dayton, Ohio, 1966-68; editor Witness Intermediate, Dayton, 1968-70; editor in chief, assoc. pub. Today's Cath. Tchr., Dayton, 1970—2002, editor-in-chief emeritus, 2002—; editor in chief Catechist, Dayton, 1976-89, Ednl. Dealer, Dayton, 1976-80; v.p. Peter Li, Inc., Dayton, 1980—. Editl. collaborator: Dimensions of Personality series, 1969—; co-author: At Ease in the Classroom; author: Why a Catholic School?, Scripture Stories for Today: Why Religious Education?; freelance writer, 1943—. Bd. dirs. Friends Ormond Beach Library. Mem.: 3d Order St. Francis (eucharistic min. 1990—), Nat. Coun. Cath. Women. Home: 26 Reynolds Ave Ormond Beach FL 32174-7043 Office: Peter Li Inc Group 2621 Dryden Rd Ste 300 Dayton OH 45439 E-mail: chilermat@aol.com.

MATHER, ANN, film company executive; b. Stockport, Cheshire, Eng., Apr. 10, 1960; came to U.S., 1993; d. Robert Joseph and Theresa (Westhead) M. Grad., Cambridge U., Eng., 1981. CPA. Sr. Peat Marwick, London, 1981-84; sr. fin. analyst Paramount Pictures, London, 1984-85, European contr. Amsterdam, 1985-87, mgr. strategic planning N.Y.C., 1987-88; pres. art import/export Santa Fe Galleries, London/Santa Fe/San Diego, 1988-89; dir. fin. Polo Ralph Lauren Europe, Paris, 1989-91; European contr. life ins. div. AIG, Paris, 1991-92; dir. fin. and adminstrn. Europe internat. film distbn. div. The Walt Disney Co., Paris, 1992-93, v.p. fin. and adminstrn. Buena Vista Internat. Theatrical Divsn. Burbank, Calif., 1993-97, sr. v.p. fin. and adminstrn. Buena Vista Internat. Theatrical Divsn., 1998-99; exec. v.p., CFO Village Roadshow Pictures, 1999, Pixar Animation Studios, 1999—2004. Contbr. Descanso Gardens, La Canada, Calif., 1996. Recipient award for land values paper Royal Soc. Chartered Surveyors, 1981. Mem. Women in Film, Fin. Execs. Inst. (chmn. profl. devel. com.), Brit. Acad. Film and TV Arts. Avocations: skiing, horseback riding, travel, literature, film. Office: Pixar Animation Studios 1200 Park Ave Emeryville CA 94608*

MATHER, ELIZABETH VIVIAN, healthcare executive; b. Richmond, Ind., Sept. 19, 1941; d. Willie Samuel and Lillie Mae (Harper) Fuqua; m. Roland Donald Mather, Dec. 26, 1966. BS, Maryville (Tenn.) Coll., 1963; postgrad., Columbia U., 1965-66. Tchr. Richmond Cmty. Schs., 1963-67, Indpls. Pub. Schs., 1967-68; systems analyst Ind. Blue Cross Blue Shield, Indpls., 1968-71, Ind. Nat. Bank, Indpls., 1971; med. cons. Ind. State Dept. Pub. Welfare, Indpls., 1971-78, cons. supr., 1978-86; systems analyst Ky. Blue Cross Blue Shield, Louisville, 1988-89; contracts specialist Humana Corp., Louisville, 1989—. Active Rep. Cen. Com. Montgomery County, Crawfordsville, 1976-86, Centenary Meth. Ch., adminstrv. bd., 1990. Mem. DAR (treas. 1963-66, sec. 1978-86). Avocation: designing and sewing clothes. Home: 6106 Partridge Pl Floyds Knobs IN 47119-9427 Office: 500 W Main St Fl 6 Louisville KY 40202-2946 E-mail: emather@humana.com.

MATHER, MILDRED EUNICE, retired archivist; b. Washington, Iowa, July 25, 1922; d. Hollis John and Delpha Irene (Cummings) Whiting; m. Stewart Elbert Mather, Aug. 7, 1955; children: Julie Marie, Thomas Stewart(dec.). Cert., Burlington and Des Moines, 1941, 1947, Stenotype Inst., 1948. Typist Burlington Willow-Weave, 1941-42, Burlington Basket Co., 1942; clk. typist U.S. Dept. War, Washington, 1942-43; supr. internat. corf. U.S. Dept. State, Washington, 1949-52; bookkeeper Iowa Wesleyan Coll., Mt. Pleasant, 1952-55; clk. typist Herbert Hoover Presdl. Libr., West Branch, Iowa, 1964-69, archives technician, 1964-72, archivist, libr., 1972-92, ret., 1992. With WAC U.S. Army, 1943—46. Mem.: Order Ea. Star (worthy matron). Republican. Home: 1794 Garfield Ave West Branch IA 52358-9403

MATHER, RUTH ELSIE, writer; b. Waverly, Wash., Feb. 14, 1934; d. James Orrin and Leona Ezthelda (Mather) Tallman; m. Mike Nicholas Dakis, Apr. 20, 1958 (div. Nov. 1971); children: Cynthia Michelle, Martin Nicholas; m. Fred Junior Morgan, Nov. 20, 1971. BA with highest honors, Brigham Young U., 1961, MA, 1965; postgrad., U. Miss., 1977-78. Cert. secondary tchr., Idaho, cert. elem. tchr. and secondary tchr. grades 7-14, Calif. English tchr. Iglesia Jesucristo Rama Roma, Mexico City, 1955-56, Lemhi County Schs., Leadore, Idaho, 1962-66; English instr. Yonsei U., Seoul, Republic of Korea, 1973-74, U. Md. Far East Divsn., Seoul, 1975-77, Boise (Idaho) State U., 1978-79, Coll. of the Redwoods, Eureka, Calif., 1980-81; writer hist. video scripts History West Pub. Co., Oklahoma City, 1990—; screenwriter Frontier Images, Canyon Country, Calif., 1994—. Cons. on hist. video for PBS, A La Carte, San Francisco, 1994-95; guest expert on Secrets of the Gold Rush-PBS, 1995; cons. Western Mont. Coll. Schmittroth collection of electronically printed Western history books, Dillon, 1997—. Author: Hanging the Sheriff: A Biography of Henry Plummer, 1987, John David Borthwick: Artist of the Gold Rush, 1989, Gold Camp Desperadoes: Study of Crime & Punishment on Frontier, 1990, Vigilante Victims, 1991, Scandal of the West: Domestic Violence on the Frontier, 1998, The Bannack Gallows, 1998, The Cottonwood Murders: Unsolved, 1999; contbr. short stories, book revs., articles to encys. and profl. jours. Local campaign dir. Dem. Party, Arcata, Calif., 1969-70. Mem. Nat. Outlaw and Lawman Assn., Western Outlaw and Lawman Assn., Virginia City Preservation Alliance, People for the Ethical Treatment of Animals, Nat. Anti-Vivisection Soc., Physicians Com. for Responsible Medicine. Avocations: reading, hiking. Office: History West Pub Co PO Box 23133 Oklahoma City OK 73123-2133

MATHER, STEPHANIE JUNE, lawyer; b. Kansas City, Mo., Dec. 5, 1952; d. Edward Wayne and H. June (Kunkel) M.; m. Miles Christopher Zimmerman, Sept. 23, 1988. BA magna cum laude, Okla. City U., 1975, JD with honors, 1980. Lawyer Pierce, Couch, Hendrickson, Johnston & Baysinger, Okla. City, Okla., 1980-88, Manchester, Hiltgen & Healy, P.C., Okla. City, 1989-90; sr. staff counsel Nat. Am. Ins. Co., Chandler, Okla., 1990-98; atty. Ctr. for Edn. Law, Oklahoma City, 1998—. Asst. v.p. Lagere & Walkingstick Ins. Agy., Inc., Chandler, Okla., 1993-98. Co-chair Lincoln County Dem. Party, 1991-92, 95-97; v.p. Lincoln County Dem. Women, 1992-95, pres., 1995-97; bd. dirs. Lincoln County Partnership for Children, 1994—, Gateway to Prevention and Recovery, 1996-97. Mem. Okla. Bar Assn. (editor, bd. editors, 1992-99), Lincoln County Bar Assn. (mem. libr. bd. 1990—), Nat. Sch. Bds. Assn. (coun. of sch. attys. 1998—), Okla. State Sch. Bds. Assn. (coun. of sch. attys. 1998—, bd. dirs. 2002--), Lincoln County Profl. Women, Alpha Phi (treas. Ctrl. Okla. Alumnae 1997-99). Democrat. Avocations: reading, genealogy, ranching, cooking. Home: PO Box 246 Chandler OK 74834-0246 Office: 900 N Broadway Ave #300 Oklahoma City OK 73102-5828 E-mail: smather@cfel.com.

MATHERN, DEB, state legislator; 2 children., N.D. State Coll. of Sc.; grad. Credit Union mgmt., U. Wis. Mem. N.D. Senate from 45th dist., Bismark, 1999—. Bd. dirs. N. D. Credit Union League, 1999—. Recipient Profl. of the Year, 1997. Mem. Fargo C. of C., NDCUL and affiliates. Office: Dist 45 3228 2nd St N Fargo ND 58102-1109 E-mail: dmathern@state.nd.us.

MATHERS, MARGARET, reference librarian, archivist; b. Ada, Okla., Feb. 16, 1929; d. Robert Lee and Josiephine Margaret (Reed) Erwin; m. Coleman F. Moss, Sept. 1956 (div. 1966); children: Carol Lee Gibson-Taylor, Marilyn Frances; m. Boyd Leroy Mathers, Apr. 10, 1967 (div. 1987). BS in Music, Tex. U., 1950. Svc. rep. Gen. Tel. Co., Santa Monica, Calif., 1955-58; tchr. pvt. sch. Santa Monica, 1958-60; computer program and data analyst System Devel. Corp., Santa Monica, 1961-66; computer programmer Inst. Def. Analyses, Arlington, Va., 1966-70; typist, transcriber Edgewater, Md., 1971-80; sec. People Assisting the Homeless, 1992-94; proofreader, copy editor Farmington Daily Times, 1993-99, mem. editl. bd., libr., office mgr., 1999—. Pres. San Juan Coun. Cmty. Agys., 1986-87, treas., 1987-89, sec., 1989-90; cons. in field. Dir. San Juan Cath. Charities, Farmington, N.Mex., 1984-93, asst. dir., 1993-96, sec. bd. dirs., 1997-2000; chmn. county Libertarian Party N.Mex., San Juan County, 1985-99, sec. ctrl. com., 1988-92, mem. ctrl. com., 1988—; mem. selection com. Habitat for Humanity, 1990; mem. San Juan County Task Force on Housing, 1991, Task Force on Transp., 1991; mem. social justice com. Sacred Heart, Farmington, 1992; mem. adv. bd. San Juan County DNA Legal Aid, 1992, sec., 1993; sec. Cmty. Network Coun., 1992-94, treas., 1994—; treas. Neighborhood Watch, 1998—; minister Secular Franciscan Order, 1997-2001. Roman Catholic. Avocations: puzzles, politics, philosophy. Office: The Daily Times PO Box 450 Farmington NM 87499-0450

MATHES, DOROTHY JEAN HOLDEN, occupational therapist; b. Paterson, N.J., Mar. 13, 1953; d. Cornelius Fred and Dorothy Johanna (Ferguson) Holden; m. Clayton Derald Mathes, May 26, 1973 (div. Dec. 1984); children: Christy, Carl, Chuck, Chad; m. Elie Youssef Hajjar, Oct. 4, 1989 (dec. Dec. 1996). BS in Occupational Therapy, Tex. Woman's U., Denton, Tex., 1988; MA in Occupational Therapy, Tex. Woman's U., 1995. Lic. occupational therapist, Tex. Occupational therapy cons. Lakes Regional-SOCS Early Childhood Intervention, 1988-97, Denton (Tex.) State Sch., 1997—, Rehab. Svcs. Unltd., 2003—. Mem. Am. Occupational Therapy Assn., Tex. Occupational Therapy Assn. Avocations: gardening, reading, swimming. Home: 2608 Woodhaven St Denton TX 76209-1340 Office: Denton State Sch PO Box 368 Denton TX 76202-0368 E-mail: djmathes@verizon.net.

MATHESON, LINDA, retired social worker; b. Martna, Estonia, Mar. 29, 1918; came to U.S., 1962, naturalized, 1969; d. Endrek and Leena Endrekson; m. Charles McLaren Matheson, Feb. 5, 1955. Diploma, Inst. Social Scis., Tallinn, Estonia, 1944; MS, Columbia U., 1966, D in Social Work, 1974. Diplomate clin. social work. Social work officer UN Rehab. and Resettlement Assn., Germany, 1946-48; social worker Victorian Mental Hygiene, Australia, 1955-62; rsch. assoc., social work project dir. Arthritis Midway House, N.Y.C., 1966-68; rsch. Columbia Presbyn. Med. Ctr., N.Y.C., 1971-75; field instr. Columbia U. Sch. Social Work, 1977-79, Columbia Presbyn. Med. Ctr., NYU Sch. Social Work, 1989-90; ret., 1992. Family Found. fellow, 1966, 89-90; grantee NIMH, 1969-72. Mem. Nat. Assn. Social Workers, Nat. Wildlife Fedn., Ctr. for Study of Presidency, Internat. Platform Assn., United Leaders, BATUN, Baltic-Am. Freedom League, Smithsonian Assn., English Spkg. Union, Alliance Francaise, Columbia U. Alumni Assn., Met. Mus. N.Y. Lutheran. Home: 30-95 29th St Astoria NY 11102-2735

MATHESON, NINA W. medical researcher; Prof., dir. William H. Welch Med. Libr., Balt., 1985—94; prof. emeritus, Welch Med. Libr., Health Divsn. Adminstrn. Johns Hopkins U., Balt., 1994—. Named Disting. prof. nursing, Vanderbilt Sch. Nursing, 1976—82. Office: Johns Hopkins Univ c/o Barbara Todd 720 Rutland Ave Baltimore MD 21205-2109

MATHEWS, BARBARA EDITH, gynecologist; b. Oct. 5, 1946; d. Joseph Chesley and Pearl (Cieri) Mathews. AB, U. Calif., 1969; MD, Tufts U., 1972. Diplomate Am. Bd. Ob-Gyn. Intern Cottage Hosp., Santa Barbara, Calif., 1972-73, Santa Barbara Gen. Hosp., 1972-73; resident in ob-gyn Beth Israel Hosp., Boston, 1973-77; clin. fellow in ob-gyn Harvard U., Boston, 1973-76, instr., 1976-77; gynecologist Sansum Med. Clin., Santa Barbara, 1977-98; sr. scientist Sansum Med. Rsch. Inst., 1998—; med. dir., gynecologist Women's Health Svcs., Santa Barbara, 1998—. Faculty mem. ann. postgrad. course Harvard Med. Sch.; bd. dirs. Sansum Med. Clinic, 1989-96, vice chmn. bd. dirs., 1994-96; dir. ann. postgrad course UCLA Med. Sch. Bd. dirs. Meml. Rehab. Found., Santa Barbara, Channel City Club, Santa Barbara, Music Acad. of the West, Santa Barbara, St. Francis Med. Ctr., Santa Barbara; mem. citizen's contg. edn. adv. coun. Santa Barbara C.C.; moderator Santa Ba rbara Cottage Hosp. Cmty. Health Forum. Author: (with L. Burke) Colposcopy in Clinical Practice, 1977; contbg. author Manual of Ambulatory Surgery, 1982. Fellow ACOG, ACS; mem. AMA, Am. Soc. Colposcopy and Cervical Pathology (dir. 1982-84), Harvard U. Alumni Assn., Tri-counties Obstet. and Gynecol. Soc. (pres. 1981-82), Birnam Wood Golf Club (Santa Barbara), Phi Beta Kappa. Home: 2105 Anacapa St Santa Barbara CA 93105-3503 Office: 2235 De La Vina St Santa Barbara CA 93105-3815 Fax: 805-687-0012.

MATHEWS, BERNICE MARTIN, state legislator, small business owner; b. Jackson, Miss., Nov. 12, 1933; children: Arnold II, Anthony, Aileen, Barbara, Ruben, Clive, Allen (dec.). BSN, MEd, U. Nev. Small bus. owner; mem. Nev. Senate, Dist. 1 Washoe, Carson City, 1994—; mem. fin. com., human resources and facilities com. Nev. Senate, mem. legis. affairs and ops. com. City councilwoman, Reno; mem. Regional EMS Coun., 1974-85; past chair Reno Civil Svc. Commn., 1979-89; active Ch. Youth Dept., 1981-87, United Way Distbn. Com., 1992—, Nev. Women's Fund Adv. Bd., 1992—; bd. dirs. Trukee Meadows Boys and Girls Club, 1987—. Mem.

Nev. Nurses Assn., Commn. for Women. Democrat. also: Nev State Legis Bldg 401 S Carson St Rm 208 Carson City NV 89701-4747 Office: PO Box 7176 Reno NV 89510-7176 Fax: 706-687-8206; 702-673-2086. E-mail: bmathews@sen.state.nv.us.

MATHEWS, CAROLYN CAMMACK, secondary school educator; b. Jasper, Tex., Nov. 21, 1944; d. Bernard Ardean and Ettie Lee (Minton) Cammack; m. Jack Blanton Mathews, May 25, 1997. BBA, Lamar U., 1966; MBA, Sam Houston State U., 1975. Profl. tchg. cert. Tex. Sec. Exxon, Houston, 1966—67; bus. tchr. West Sabine Ind. Sch. Dist., Pineland, Tex., 1967—69, Bastrop (Tex.) Ind. Sch. Dist., 1969—70, Spring (Tex.) Ind. Sch. Dist., 1970—87, U. Wis., Eau Claire, 1987—89, Klein (Tex.) Ind. Sch. Dist., 1990—97, Nacogdoches (Tex.) Ind. Sch. Dist., 2002—. Mem. CATE adv. bd. Career and Tech.-Consumer Scis., Nacogdoches, 2001—02. Pres. Zeta Tau Alpha Frat., Nacogdoches, 2000—02. Mem.: Tex. Bus. Edn. Assn. (pres. 1992—93, Tchr. of Yr. 1986, 1994), Tex. Bus. Tech. Edn. Assn. (pres.-elect, Tchr. of Yr. 2003), Nat. Bus. Assn., West Sabine H.S. Alumni Assn. (treas. 2002—), Cum Concillo Study Club (treas. 2001—). Baptist. Avocations: volunteering, knitting, gardening. Home: 4318 Oak Creek Dr Nacogdoches TX 75965

MATHEWS, E. ANNE JONES, library educator and administrator, consultant; b. Phila; d. Edmond Fulton and Anne Ruth (Reichner) Jones; m. Frank Samuel Mathews, June 16, 1951; children: Lisa Anne Mathews-Bingham, David Morgan, Lynne Elizabeth Bietenhader-Mathews, Alison Fulton Sawyer. AB, Wheaton Coll., 1949; MA, U. Denver, 1965, PhD, 1977. Field staff Intervarsity Christian Fellowship, Chgo., 1949-51; interviewer supr. Colo. Market Rsch. Svcs., Denver, 1952-64; reference libr. Oreg. State U., Corvallis, 1965-67; program dir. Ctrl. Colo. Libr. Sys., Denver, 1969-70; inst. dir. U.S. Office of Edn., Inst. Grant, 1979; dir. pub. rels., prof. Grad. Sch. Librarianship and Info. Mgmt. U. Denver, 1970-76, prof., dir. continuing edn., 1977-80; dir. office libr. programs, office ednl. rsch., improvement US Dept. Edn., Washington, 1986-91; dir. Nat. Libr. Edn., Washington, 1992-94; cons. Acad. Ednl. Devel., Washington, 1994—; cons. mil. installation vol. edn. rev. Am. Coun. on Edn., 1990—; from asst. prof. to prof., 1977—85. Mem. adv. com. Golden H.S., 1973—77; faculty assoc. Danforth Found., 1974—84; mem. secondary sch. curriculum com. Jefferson County Pub. Schs., Colo., 1976—78; vis. lectr. Simmons Coll. Sch. L.S., Boston, 1977; mem. book and libr. adv. com. USIA, 1981—91; spkr. in field; cons. USIA, 1984—85; del. Internat. Fedn. Libr. Assns., 1984—93; mem. adv. coun. White House Conf. on Librs. and Info. Svcs., 1991; cons. Walden U., Mpls., 2001. Author, editor 6 books; contbr. articles to profl. jours., numerous chpts. to books. Mem. rural librs. and humanities program Colo. planning and resource bd. NEH, 1982—83; bd. mgrs. Friends Found. of Denver Pub. Libr., 1976—82; pres. Faculty Women's Club, Colo. Sch. Mines, 1963—64; bd. dirs. Jefferson County Libr. Found., 1996—, v.p., 1997—2000. Mem.: ALA (visionary leaders com. 1987—89, mem. coun. 1979—83, com. on accreditation 1984—85, orientation com. 1974—77, 1983—84, pub. rels. com.), English Speaking Union, Assn. Libr. and Info. Sci. Edn. (comm. com. 1978—80, program com. 1977—78), Colo. Libr. Assn. (pres. 1974, bd. dirs. 1973—75, continuing edn. com. 1976—80), Mountain Plains Libr. Assn. (profl. devel. com. 1979—80, pub. rels. and publs. com. 1973—75, continuing edn. com. 1973—76), Am. Soc. Info. Sci. (chmn. pub. rels. 1971), Naples Philharm. League, Pelican Bay Women's League Fla., Mountain Rep. Women's Club (v.p. 1997—2000), Mt. Vernon (Colo.) Country Club, Cosmos Club (Washington). Avocations: travel, reading, museum and gallery activities, volunteer work. Home (Summer): 492 Mount Evans Rd Golden CO 80401-9626 E-mail: afmathews2@earthlink.net.

MATHEWS, JENNIFER PAULINE, anthropologist, educator, archaeologist; b. Glendale, Calif., Feb. 11, 1969; d. Cynthia Ethel Lowry, Louis Paul Mathews, Alison McIlvane Turner (Stepmother), Gary L. Withrow (Stepfather). PhD in Anthropology, U. Calif., Riverside, 1998. Lectr. U. Calif., Riverside, Calif., 1998—99; asst. prof. Trinity U., San Antonio, 1999—. Co-dir. Yalahau Regional Human Ecology Project, Cancun, Quintana Roo, Mexico, 1998—. Grantee, NSF, 1997, Found. Advancement of Mesoamerican Studies, Inc., 1999—2000, Trinity U., 2000, 2002, 2004. Mem.: Alamo Pre-Columbian Soc. (bd. dirs. 2000—04, editor 2000—04), Soc. Am. Archaeology, Am. Anthropol. Assn. Avocations: travel, reading, exercising. Office: Dept Sociology and Anthropology One Trinity Pl San Antonio TX 00209 Office Phone: 210-999-8507. Office Fax: 210-999-8509. Business E-Mail: jmathews@trinity.edu.

MATHEWS, JESSICA TUCHMAN, executive, foreign policy expert; b. N.Y.C., July 4, 1946; d. Lester Reginald and Barbara (Wertheim) Tuchman; m. Colin D. Mathews, Feb. 25, 1978 (divorced); children: Oliver Max Tuchman, Jordan Henry Morgenthau. AB magna cum laude, Radcliffe Coll., 1967; PhD, Calif. Inst. Tech., 1973. Congrl. sci. fellow AAAS, 1973-74; profl. staff mem. Energy and Environment subcom. House Com. on Interior and Insular Affairs, Washington, 1974-75; dir. issues and rsch. Udall Presdl. campaign, 1975-76; dir. Office of Global Issues NSC staff, Washington, 1977-79, mem. editorial bd. The Washington Post, 1980-82; v.p., dir. rsch. The World Resources Inst., Washington, 1982-92; dep. to undersec. for global affairs U.S. Dept. State, Washington, 1993; sr. fellow Coun. on Fgn. Rels., Washington, 1993-97; columnist Washington Post, 1991-97; pres. Carnegie Endowment Internat. Peace, Washington, 1997—. Mem. numerous adv. panels Office Tech. Assessment, NAS, AAAS, EPA; adv. com. Air Products Corp., 1995—99; bd. dirs. Somalogic Inc. Trustee Rockefeller Found., Century Found., Nuc. Threat Initiative; mem. Coun. Fgn. Rels.; bd. dirs. Joyce Found., Chgo., 1984—91, Inter-Am. Dialogue, 1991—2000, Surface Transp. Policy Project, 1991—2003, Radcliffe Coll., 1992—96, Carnegie Endowment for Internat. Peace, Washington, 1992—, Rockefeller Bros. Fund, N.Y.C., NY, 1992—96, Brookings Instn., Washington, 1995—2001. Mem.: Inst. Internat. Econs. (adv. com.), Fedn. Am. Scientists (bd. dirs. 1985—87, 1988—92), Trilateral Commn. Democrat. Jewish. Office: Carnegie Endowment Internat Peace 1779 Massachusetts Ave NW Washington DC 20036-2109

MATHEWS, JOAN HELENE, pediatrician; b. Manchester, N.H., Feb. 3, 1940; d. John Barnaby and Helen A. Wlodkoski; m. Ernest Stephen Mathews, June 1, 1965; 3 children. BS, U. N.H., 1961; MD, Columbia U., 1965. Diplomate Am. Bd. Pediatrics. Med. intern Roosevelt Hosp., N.Y.C., 1965-66; pediatric resident Babies Hops. Columbia Presbyn. Med. Ctr., N.Y.C., 1966-68, pediatric endocrine fellow Babies Hosp., 1968-70; instr. clin. pediat. Columbia U. Coll. Physicians and Surgeons, N.Y.C., 1973-77; asst. prof. pediat. Cornell U. Med. Coll., N.Y.C., 1977-81; clin. instr. pediat. Harvard Med. Sch., Boston, 1985—2003, clin. asst. prof. pediat., 2003—; clin. assoc. children's svc. Mass. Gen. Hosp., Boston, 1985—. Fellow: Am. Acad. Pediat.; mem.: Phi Beta Kappa. Office: 777 Concord Ave Cambridge MA 02138-1053 Fax: (617) 876-5713. Office Phone: 617-876-6800.

MATHEWS, KATHLEEN ANN, social worker, psychotherapist; b. Minneapolis, Minn., Feb. 1, 1958; d. Lois Elaine Mathews, Wallace Edward Mathews; m. Bradley Scott Turner; children: Carsen Turner, Frances Turner. MSW, Columbia U., 1990; BS in Family Relationships, U. Minn., 1981. Lic. ind. clin. social work 1993. Supr. Home Front program Washburn Child Guidance Ctr., Mpls., 1993—, psychotherapist, 1998—, supr. Vision Program, 1997—2000; contract psychotherapist Chrysalis, A Center for Women, Mpls., 1994—98; program coord. Allendale Assn., Lake Villa, Ill., 1992—93; social worker Jewish Home and Hosp. for Aged, New York City, 1990—92. Mem.: NASW. Avocations: sewing, reading. Office: Washburn Child Guidance Ctr 2430 Nicollet Ave S Minneapolis MN 55404

MATHEWS, LAURIE A. state agency administrator; m. Andrew Holecek. BS in Environ. Biology, U. Colo., Boulder, 1974; M in Environ. Engring., Stanford U., 1976. Staff mem. U.S. Senate; water cons. DeLew Cather & Co.; asst. dir. Dept. Natural Resources; acting dir. Gov. Roy Romer's Policy Office; dir. State Colo., divsn. State Parks and Outdoor Recreation, Denver, 1991—. Bd. dirs. Nat. Assn. State Park Dirs. Bd. vols. Outdoor Colo. Office: State Colo Divsn State Parks & Outdoor Rec 1313 Sherman St Ste 618 Denver CO 80203-2240 Fax: 303-866-3206.

MATHEWS, LINDA MCVEIGH, newspaper editor; b. Redlands, Calif., Mar. 14, 1946; d. Glenard Ralph and Edith Lorene (Humphrey) McVeigh; m. Thomas Jay Mathews, June 15, 1967; children: Joseph, Peter, Katherine. BA, Radcliffe Coll., 1967; JD, Harvard U., 1972. Gen. assignment reporter L.A. Times, 1967-69, Supreme Ct. corr., 1972-76, corr., 1977-79, China corr., 1979-80, editor op-ed page, 1980-81, dep. nat. editor, 1981-84, dep. fgn. editor, 1985-88, editl. writer, 1988-89, editor L.A. Times Mag., 1989-92; corr. Wall Street Jour., Hong Kong, 1976-77; sr. prodr. ABC News, N.Y.C., 1992-93; nat. editor N.Y. Times, N.Y.C., 1993-96; editor USA Today, McLean, Va., 1997—. Lectr.; freelance writer. Author (with others): Journey into China, 1982, One Billion: A China Chronicle, 1983. Mem. Women's Legal Def. Fund, 1972-76; co-founder, pres. Hong Kong Montessori Sch., 1977-79; bd. dirs. Ctr. for Childhood. Mem. Fgn. Corrs. Club Hong Kong. Office: USA Today 7950 Jones Branch Dr Mc Lean VA 22108 Personal E-mail: LiMathews@aol.com. Business E-Mail: lmathews@usatoday.com.

MATHEWS, MICH, computer company executive; Grad., U. Brighton, England. With Gen. Motors; pub. relations cons., U.K div. Microsoft Corp., head corp. pub. rels. group, 1993, v.p. corp. comms., 1993—, mem., bus. leadership team, 1999—. Office: Microsoft Corp Comms one Microsoft Way Redmond WA 98052-6399

MATHEWS, SHARON WALKER, artistic director, secondary school educator; b. Shreveport, La., Feb. 1, 1947; d. Arthur Delmar and Nona (Frye) Walker; m. John William (Bill) Mathews, Aug. 14, 1971; children: Rebecca, Elizabeth, Anna. BS, La. State U., 1969, MS, 1971. Dance grad. asst. La. State U., Baton Rouge, 1969-71, choreographer, 1975-76; 6th grade tchr. East Baton Rouge Parish, 1971-72, health phys. edn. tchr., 1972-74; dance instr. Magnet High Sch., Baton Rouge, 1975—; artistic dir. Baton Rouge Ballet Theatre, 1975—; dance dir. Dancers' Workshop, Baton Rouge, 1971—; choreographer Baton Rouge Opera, 1989-94, Univ. H.S. Musical Theatre, 1998—; choreographer Baton Rouge Gilbert and Sullivan Soc. summer musical La. State U., 2000, 2001; choreographer Baton Rouge Little Theater, 2000, 2002. Author: East Baton Rouge Parish Dance Curriculum. Mem. La. Supts. Task Force for the Arts in Edn., 1999-2001; mem. La. Content Standards Com. for Dance, 2001; mem. East Baton Rouge Parish Curriculum Com. for Dance, 1997; mem. La. Arts Content Standards Com., 2002—; mem. La. Arts Consortium, 2000—; mem. La. Arts Content Revision Com., 2002-03. Named Dance Educator of Yr., La. Alliance for Health, Physical Edn., Recreation and Dance, 1986-87; recipient Mayor-Pres.'s award for Excellence in the Arts, 1999, Stream award S.W. Regional Ballet Assn. for artistic excellence, 1991, Mayor Pres.'s award for excellence in the arts, 1999; inducted into the Univ. H.S. Hall of Distinction, 2003, Baton Rouge Magnet H.S. Hall of Fame, 2003. Mem. Southwestern Regional Ballet Assn. (bd. dirs. 1981—, treas., exec. bd. dirs. 1989-92), La. Assn. for Health, Phys. Edn., Recreation and Dance (dance chairperson 1995). Republican. Baptist. Office: Baton Rouge Ballet Theater 11017 Perkins Rd Baton Rouge LA 70884

MATHIAS, ALICE IRENE, business management consultant; b. N.Y.C., Mar. 2, 1949, d. Murray and Charlotte (Kottle) M. BS in Math., Western New Eng. Coll., 1972. Programmer Carnation Co., L.A., 1973-78; programmer/analyst Cedars-Sinai Med. Ctr., L.A., 1978-79, Union Bank, L.A., 1979-81; group leader Kaiser Found. Health Plan, Pasadena, Calif., 1981-98; sr. cons. KPMG LLP, L.A., 1998—99; prin. Info. Tech. Mgmt., L.A., 1999—. Mem. NAFE, Am. Mgmt. Assn., L.A. County Mus. Art (sponsor), Smithsonian Inst., KCET Pub. TV, Choice In Dying, U.S. Holocaust Meml. Mus. (charter mem.), Caithness Collectors Club, Statue of Liberty Ellis Island Found. Home: 2031 Dracena Drive Apt 320 Los Angeles CA 90027 Office: Info Tech Mgmt 2031 Dracena Dr Ste 320 Los Angeles CA 90027

MATHIAS, BETTY JANE, communications and community affairs consultant, writer, editor, lecturer; b. Oct. 22, 1923; d. Royal F. and Dollie B. (Bowman) M.; 1 child, Dena. Student, Merritt Bus. Sch., 1941, 42, San Francisco State U., 1941-42. Asst. publicity dir. Oakland (Calif.) Area War Chest and Comty. Chest, 1943-46; pub. rels. Am. Legion, Oakland, 1946-47; asst. to pub. rels. dir. Cen. Bank of Oakland, 1947-49; pub. rels. dir. East Bay chpt. Nat. Safety Coun., 1949-51; propr., mgr. Mathias Pub. Rels. Agy., Oakland, 1951-60; publicity dir. U.S. Nat. Figure Skating Championships, Berkeley, Calif., 1957; gen. assignment reporter, teen news editor Daily Rev., Hayward, Calif., 1960-62; freelance pub. rels. and writing Oakland, 1962-66, 67-69; dir. corp. comms. Systech Fin. Corp., Walnut Creek, Calif., 1969-71; v.p. corp. comms. Consol. Capital cos., Oakland, 1972-79, v.p. comty. affairs Emeryville, Calif., 1981-84, v.p. spl. projects, 1984-85; v.p., dir. Consol. Capital Realty Svcs., Inc., Oakland, 1973-77, Centennial Adv. Corp., Oakland, 1976-77; comms. cons., 1979—. Cons. Mountainair Realty, Cameron Park, Calif., 1986-87; pub. rels. coord. Tuolumne County Visitors Bur., 1989-90; lectr. in field. Editor: East Bay Mag., 1966-67, TIA Traveler, 1969, Concepts, 1979-83; editor, writer souvenir program: Little House on the Prairie Reunion, 1998. Bd. dirs. Oakland YWCA, 1944-45, ARC, Oakland, So. Alameda County chpt., 1967-69, Family Ctr., Children's Hosp. Med. Ctr. No. Calif., 1982-85, March of Dimes, 1983-85, Equestrian Ctr. of Walnut Creek, Calif., 1983-84, also sec.; mem. Women's Ambulance and Transport Corps of Calif., Oakland, 1942-46; active USO and Shrine Hospitality Ctrs., Oakland, USO-Travelers Aid Soc., Oakland, 1942-46; publicist Oakland Area War Bond Com., 1943-46; adult and publs. adv. Internat. Order of the Rainbow for Girls, 1953-78; comms. arts adv. com. Ohlone (Calif.) Coll., 1979-85, chmn., 1982-84; mem. adv. bd. dept. mass comms. Calif. State U.-Hayward, 1985; pres. San Francisco Bay Area chpt. Nat. Reyes Syndrome Found., 1981-86; vol. staff Columbia Actors' Repertory, Columbia, Calif., 1986-87, 89; mem. exec. bd., editor newsletter Tuolumne County Dem. Club, 1987; publicity chmn. 4th of July celebration Tuolumne County C. of C., 1988; vol. children's dept. Tuolumne County Pub. Libr., 1993-97; vol. Ann. Comty. Christmas Eve Dinner, Sonora, Calif., 1988-96; mem. adv. com. Ride Away Ctr. for Therapeutic Riding for the Handicapped, 1995-96, vol. Hold Your Horses Therapeutic Riding Acad., 1997; vol. Tuolumne County Visitors Bur. and Film Commn., 1996-99. Recipient Grand Cross of Color award Internat. Order of Rainbow for Girls, 1955. Mem. Order Ea. Star (life, worthy matron 1952, publicity chmn. Calif. state 1955), East Bay Women's Press Club (pres. 1960, 84). Home: 20575 Gopher Dr Sonora CA 95370-9034

MATHIAS, MARGARET GROSSMAN, manufacturing company executive, leasing company executive; b. Detroit; d. D. Ray and Lila May (Skinner) Grossman; children: Deborah, Robert, Lesley, Jennifer, Mary. BA, Mt. Holyoke Coll.; cert., Am. Acad. Art. Artist and co-mgr. Mary Chase Marionettes, N.Y.C.; exec. v.p. Star Five Corp., Elkhart, 1975-88, pres., treas., chmn. bd., 1985-90; sec., chmn. bd. L & J Press Corp., Elkhart, Ind., 1985-91, also chmn. bd. dirs.; chmn., pres., CEO Magland Co., Elkhart, 1986—, Magco Inc., Elkhart, 186—; pres., chmn., CEO Tech Products, Inc., Elkhart, 1992—. Mem. fin. com. United Fund, Elkhart; mem. parents adv. bd. Furman U., Greenville, S.C., 1978-83, mem. art adv. bd. Mt. Holyoke Coll., South Hadley, Mass., 1982—; pres. Tri Kappa Service Orgn., Elkhart, 1965-66; trustee Stanley Clark Sch., South Bend, Ind., 1977-87; bd. dirs. Bridgework Theatre, Goshen, Ind., also Balt., 1996—; mem. adv. bd. Ruthmere 1910 House Mus. designated one of Am.'s castles, 1999—; instr., spkr. etiquette Montessori Schs., Elkhart, Ind., 1998—; vol. Dept. Edn., 2003, Art Inst. Chgo., 2003; weekly vol. dept. edn. Art Inst. Chgo. Recipient Lawson Top Sculpture Purchase award Midwest Mus. Am. Art, 1990. Mem. Elkhart C. of C. Clubs: Elcona Country (Elkhart), Woman's Athletic (Chgo.), Thursday (Elkhart) (pres. 1976). Republican. Avocations: sculpting, traveling, skiing. Home: 1077 Greenleaf Blvd Apt 101 Elkhart IN 46514-3562 Office: 429 S Main St Elkhart IN 46516-3210

MATHIEU, GAIL DENNISE, ambassador; b. N.J. m. Erick Mathieu; 1 child, Yuri. B in Spanish and Latin Am. Studies, Antioch Coll.; JD, Rutgers U. Bar: N.J., D.C. Dep. chief of mission in Accra; U.S. observer UNESCO, 1991—95; dep. dir. Pacific Island affairs Dept. State, 1995—97; dep. officer dir. of West African affairs Dept. of State, 1997—99; U.S. amb. to Niger, 2002—. Office: US Embassy in Turkmenistan rue Des Ambassades 11201 Niamey Turkmenistan*

MATHIEU, MICHELE SUZANNE, computer scientist, consultant; b. Chgo., Mar. 24, 1950; d. Joseph Edward Mathieu and Mary Ellen Fisher; m. Robert Steven Harris, May 1, 1988 (dec. Sept. 2000). BS in Mktg., Regents Coll., Albany, N.Y., 1998; cert. web site design, Columbia Coll., Chgo., 2000; cert. in Perl and CGI Scripting, San Diego C.C., 2003. Microsoft cert. profl. Broadcast coord. Grey-North Advt., Chgo., 1967-71; head drama dept. Patricia Stevens Coll., Chgo., 1972; instr. beginning acting Ted Liss Sch. Performing Arts, Chgo., 1973-75; project coord. grants and contracts Am. Dietetic Assn., Chgo., 1974-81, adminstr. govt. affairs, 1981-86, mgr. licensure comm., 1986-90, adminstr. nutrition svcs. payment systems, 1990-94, team leader, health care fin. team, 1994-97, dir. health care fin. team, 1998-00, dir. mem. web, 2000-01, dir. applications devel., 2001—02; technician Networks Plus Tech. Group, San Diego, 2003—04; pc imaging technician Knowledge Info. Solutions, San Diego, 2004—. Grant proposal cons. various performance arts, Chgo., 1978-2000; med. reporter, writer various internat. clients, 1994--; PC cons., Chgo., 1994-2002, San Diego, 2002—. Editor Legis. Newsletter, 1981-86; contbg. editor Nutrition Forum, 1986, Courier, 1987—2002; contbr. articles to profl. jours., mags., newspapers. Website project mgr. DigitalEve, Chgo., 2001. Ill. Arts Coun. grantee, 1981. Mem. Am. Soc. Assn. Execs. (Excellence in Govt. award 1989), WebSanDiego. Roman Catholic. Avocations: reading, fitness walking.

MATHIS, ALICIA, biologist; b. Meridian, Miss., May 7, 1960; d. Shirley Broadhead. BS, U. So. Miss., 1982, MS, 1985; PhD, U. Southwestern La., 1989. Tchg. asst. U. So. Miss., Hattiesburg, 1983—85; biologist U.S. Army Corps of Engrs., Vicksburg, Miss., 1985; tchg. asst. U. Southwestern La., Lafayette, 1985—89; post-doctoral fellow U. Sask., Saskatoon, Canada, 1990—93; prof. S.W. Mo. State U., Springfield, 1993—. Rev. panel NSF, 2001—01; mem. adv. bd. Ozark Ctr. for Wildlife Rsch., Reeds Spring, Mo., 1994—97. Editor: Herpetologica, 2004—; assoc. editor: Jour. Herpetology, 1997—2000, Behavioral Ecology and Sociobiology, 2000—03; contbr. articles to profl. jours., chapters to books. Fellow, Mountain Lake Biol. Sta., 1988; grantee, U.S. Fish and Wildlife Svc., 2001—03, Mo. Dept. Conservation, 1997—99, NSF, 1996, Sigma Xi, 1987, 1988. Mem.: Herpetologists League (councilor 2001—03), Am. Soc. of Ichthyologists and Herpetologists (symposium organizer 1997), Soc. for the Study of Evolution, Internat. Soc. for Behavioral Ecology, Animal Behavior Soc. (travel grantee 1993). Avocation: singing. Office: SW Mo State U 901 S National Ave Springfield MO 65807

MATHIS, DIANE, cell biologist, educator; BSc in Biology, Wake Forest U., 1971; MSc in Cell Biology, U. Rochester, 1976, PhD in Cell Biology, 1978. Postdoctoral fellow Lab. Génétique Moléculaire des Eucaryotes, Strasbourg, France, 1977—81; postdoctoral fellow Dept. Med. Microbiology Stanford (Calif.) U. Med. Ctr., 1981—83; sr. investigator Dept. Immunology Inst. Génétique et de Biologie Moléculaire et Cellulaire, Strasbourg, 1983—99; sr. investigator immunology and immunogenetics Joslin Diabetes Ctr. Harvard Med. Sch., Boston, 1999—, prof. medicine, 1999—. Vis. prof. Walter and Elisa Hall Inst., Melbourne, 1997—98; mem. adv. bd. Deutsches Rheuma-Forschungszentrum, Berlin, 1997—, Max Planck Inst. Immunology, Freiburg, Germany, 1997—, Walter and Eliza Hall Inst., Melbourne, 1998—, Peptimmune, 2000—, Inst. Pasteur, Paris, 2001—, Jackson Lab., Bar Harbor, Maine, 2001—, Riken Inst., Yokohama, Japan, 2001—, NIH Study Sect., 2001—. Mem. editl. bd.: European Jour. Immunology, 1988—2001, EMBO Jour., 1992—95, 1999—, Internat. Immunology, 1992—96, Immunology Today, 1992—2000, Sci., 1993—, Cell, 1994—; translator: Current Biology, 1994—2001; Jour. Exptl. Medicine, 1996—, Immunity, 1997—, Diabetes, 1999—, Modern Rheumatism, 2000—, EMBO Reports, 2000—, Current Sci. Faculty of 1000, 2001—; contbr. over 120 articles to profl. jours. Fellow, Damon Runyon-Walter Winchell Cancer Fund, 1977—81, Leukemia Soc. Am., 1981—83. Office: Joslin Diabetes Center One Joslin Place Boston MA 02215

MATHIS, KAREN MCHUGH, artist; b. Alma, Mich., June 13, 1945; d. James Edward and Nelda Ellen (Grubaugh) McHugh; m. John Prentiss Mathis, May 31, 1966; children: Lisa Lynne Mathis Kirkpatrick, Andy Prentiss. BS, So. Meth. U., 1965; BA, George Washington U., 1979. Cert. secondary tchr., Washington. Mem. gen. staff for spl. events Nat. Gallery Art, Washington, 1985-88. Paintings featured in The Best of Watercolor, 1995, 97, 99, Best of the Best, 2002; one-woman shows Landon Gallery, Landen Sch., Bethesda, Md., 1989, 93, Town Ctr. Gallery, Rockville, Md., 1990, Met. Meml. United Meth. Ch., Washington, 1990, Grenleaf Gallery, Nags Head, N.C., 1994, Yellow Barn Gallery, Glen Echo, Md., 1996, Albany (Ga.) Mus. Art, 1991, Gwinnett Fine Arts Ctr., Duluth, Ga., 1996, Howard Mandville Gallery, Kirkland, Wash., 1996, Gallery B.A.I., N.Y.C., 1998, 2002, Spectrum Gallery, Georgetown, Washington. Docent chmn. at Nat. Gallery of Art, Jr. League Washington, 1985, designer spl. exhibit project, 1986. Mem. Art League Washington, Ga. Watercolor Assn., N.W. Watercolor Assn. Democrat. Methodist.

MATHIS, MARSHA DEBRA, customer relations manager; b. Detroit, Dec. 22, 1953; d. Marshall Junior and Anita Willene (Biggers) M. BS, Fla. State U., 1978; MBA, Miss. Coll., 1982. With telecommunications dept. Fla. State Dept. Safety, Tallahassee, 1973-76; asst. to chmn. Tallahassee Savs. and Loan Assn., 1976-78; sales engr. Prehler, Inc., Jackson, Miss., 1978-82; mktg. mgr. Norand Corp., Arlington, Tex., 1982-87; v.p. mktg. and sales Profl. Datasolutions, Inc., Irving, Tex., 1987-88; v.p. mktg. and sales, ptnr. Target Systems, Inc., Irving, 1988-89, also bd. dirs.; v.p. mktg. Profl. Datasolutions, Inc., Irving, 1990—2002, Onvance, Atlanta, 2002, Fintech, Tampa, Fla., 2002—. Contbr. articles to industry trade jours. Advisor Am. Diabetes Assn., Jackson, 1983—, Diabetes Found. (Jackson) Miss., 1983-. Mem. Internat. Platform Assn., Nat. Adv. Group, Nat. Assn. Convenience Stores (Industry Task Force 1987-88). Republican. Roman Catholic. Avocations: scuba diving, sailing, reading, coin collecting. Home: 325 Old York Rd Irving TX 75063-4247 Office: Fintech Ste 100 4720 W Cypress St Tampa FL 33607

MATHIS, PRUDENCE MARCHMAN, real estate company executive; b. Throckmorton, Tex., Aug. 21, 1956; d. Jack Robert and Grace Alma Hurst Brockman; m. Leonard Renfro Marchman, June 8, 1974 (div. May 4, 1990); m. Jimmy Dale Mathis, June 9, 1990 (div. May 24, 1999); children: Jeremy Robert Marchman, Caitlin Breanne Marchman. Student, Mountain View Coll., 1985—90. Utility Constrn. Cert. Competent Person Utility Constrn., Tex., 1998. Comml. ins. & workers compensation clk. Lovett-Meredith Clinic, Olney, Tex., 1977—79; credit corr., accounts receivable clk., fin. inventory control analyst, accounts payable clk., bid clk. Am. Hosp. Supply Co., Grand Prairie, Tex., 1979—85; credit analyst/adjuster Gifford-Hill & Co., Inc., Dallas, 1985—88; acctg. clk. - part-time Roy Rabenaldt, CPA, Farmers Branch, Tex., 1988—89; office mgr. Evelyn Cannon Showroom of Women's Apparel, Dallas, 1989—90; asst. office mgr./payroll coord. Site Concrete, Inc., Grand Prairie, Tex., 1990—94; customer svc. rep./accounts receivable collector Occupl. Health Centers, Dallas, 1994—95; human resources mgr., benefits specialist Site Concrete, Inc., Grand Prairie, Tex., 1995—98; exec. adminstrv. asst. Kelly Services for Johnson & Johnson Med., Arlington, Tex., 1998—2000; travel coord. Galactic Mktg., Arlington, Tex., 2000—01; human resources mgr. Site Concrete, Inc., Grand Prairie, Tex., 2001—02, v.p., and co-owner Quest Residential & Comml. Properties, Ltd, Grand Prairie, Tex., 2002—. Trainer Site Concrete, Inc., Grand Prairie, Tex., 2001—02. Vol. Habitat for Humanity, Grand Prairie, Tex., 2001—03; vol. adult leader and facilitator Boy Scouts of Am., Grand Prairie, Tex., 1999—2003; chancel choir mem. First United Meth. Ch., Grand Prairie, Tex., 2001—02. Recipient Phi Theta Kappa Honors Frat., 1987—90. Mem.: NAFE (assoc.), Nat. Home Builders Assn., Home Builder's Assn. Greater Dallas, Soc. of Human Resource Managers (assoc.), Am. Bus. Women's Assn. (assoc.; former sec. 1999—2000), Dallas Ft. Worth Real Estate Investor Network (assoc.), Assn. of Ind. Real Estate Owners (assoc.). R-Liberal. Meth. Avocations: reading, singing, photography, crocheting, travel. Office: Quest Properties 4116 S Carrier Pkwy Ste 280-827 Grand Prairie TX 75052

MATHIS, SAMANTHA, actress; b. N.Y.C., May 12, 1970; d. Bibi Besch. Actress: (films) Forbidden Sun, 1989, Pump Up the Volume, 1990, This is My Life, 1992, FernGully: The Last Rainforest (voice), 1992, Super Mario Bros., 1993, The Music of Chance, 1993, The Thing Called Love, 1993, Little Women, 1994, Jack and Sarah, 1995, How to Make an American Quilt, 1995, The American President, 1995, Broken Arrow, 1996, Museum of Love, 1996, Sweet Jane, 1998, Waiting for Woody, 1998, Freak City, 1999, The Simian Line, 2000, American Psycho, 2000, Attraction, 2000, The Punisher, 2004; (TV movies) Aaron's Way: The Harvest, 1988, Cold Sassy Tree, 1989, American Nuclear, 1989, Extreme Close-Up, 1990, 83 Hours 'Til Dawn, 1990, To My Daughter, 1990, Harsh Realm, 1999, Mermaid, 2000, Collected Stories, 2002; (TV series) Knightwatch, 1988-89, Aaron's Way, 1988, Harsh Realm, 1999, First Years, 2001; (TV miniseries) The Mists of Avalon, 2001. Office: Creative Artists Agy care Rick Kurtzman 9830 Wilshire Blvd Beverly Hills CA 90212-1804

MATHIS, SHARON BELL, author, retired elementary educator and librarian; b. Atlantic City, Feb. 26, 1937; d. John Willie and Alice Mary (Frazier) Bell; m. Leroy F. Mathis, July 11, 1957 (div. Jan. 1979); children: Sherie, Stacy, Stephanie. BA, Morgan State Coll., 1958; M.L.S., Catholic U. Am., 1975. Interviewer Children's Hosp. D.C., Washington, 1958-59; tchr. Holy Redeemer Elem. Sch., Washington, 1959-65, Charles Hart Jr. H.S., Washington, 1965-72; spl. edn. tchr. Stuart Jr. H.S., Washington, 1972-74; libr. Benning Elem.Sch., Washington, 1975-76, Friendship Ednl. Ctr. (now Patricia R. Harris Ednl. Ctr.), 1976-95, ret., 1995. Writer-in-charge children's lit. div. D.C. Black Writers Workshop; writer-in-residence Howard U., 1972-73 Author: Brooklyn Story, 1970, Sidewalk Story, 1971 (Council on Interracial Books for Children award 1970), Teacup Full of Roses, 1972 (Outstanding Book of Yr. award New York Times 1972), Ray Charles, 1973 (Coretta Scott King award 1974), Listen for the Fig Tree, 1974, The Hundred Penny Box, 1975 (Boston Globe-Horn Book Honor book 1975, Newbery Honor Book 1976), Cartwheels, 1977, Red Dog Blue Fly: Football Poems, 1991 (Children's Book of Yr. award Bank St. Coll. 1992), Red Dog Blue Fly: An American Bookseller (Pick of the List 1995), Running Girl: The Diary of Ebonee Rose, 1997, Ray Charles, 2001. Mem. bd. advisers lawyers com. D.C. Commn. on Arts, 1972. Nominated Books for Brotherhood list NCCJ, 1970; recipient D.C. Assn. Sch. Librs. award 1976, Arts and Humanities award Archdiocese of Washington Black Secretariat, 1978; Weekly Reader Book Club fellow Bread Loaf Writers Conf., 1970, MacDowell Colony fellow, 1978. Roman Catholic.

MATHIS, VIRGINIA, federal judge; Apptd. magistrate judge U.S. Dist. Ct. Ariz., 1996. Office: 5025 US Courthouse 230 N 1st Ave Phoenix AZ 85025-0230

MATHISEN-REID, RHODA SHARON, international communications consultant; b. Portland, Oreg., June 25, 1942; d. Daniel and Mildred Elizabeth Annette (Peterson) Hager; m. James Albert Mathisen, July 17, 1964 (div. 1977); m. James Albert Mathisen, July 17, 164 (div. 1977); m. James A. Reid Sr., Jan. 1, 1991. BA in Edn., Music, Bible Coll., Mich., 1964. Cmty. rels. officer Gary-Wheaton Bank, Wheaton, Ill., 1971-75; br. mgr. Stiver Temporary Personnel, Chgo., 1975-79; v.p. sales Exec. Technique, Chgo., 1980-83; prin. Mathisen Assocs., Clarendon Hill., Ill., 1983—. Presenter seminars; featured speaker Women in Mgmt. Oak Brook Chpt., 1988.; cons. Haggai Inst., Atlanta; adv. mem. Nat. Bd. Success Group, 1986. Newsletter editor/publisher: 90th Divsn. Assn. (WWII Vets) 2001—. Mem. Downers Grove Twp. Precinct # 87 Rep. Com., 1998—; pres. chancel choir Christ Ch. Oak Brook, 1985—87; bd. dirs. Career Devel. Inst., Oak Brook, 1992—99, chair operational fin. com., 1997—98; bd. dirs. Crossroads Ministry Internat., 2000—; chmn. 1st Profl. Women's Seminar, 1995; judge Mrs. Ill., USI Pageant, 1994; exec. sec., treas. 90th Divsn. Assn., 2001—. Recipient Denby Steel award, 90th Divsn. Assn., 2001. Mem. Bus. and Profl. Women (charter mem., Woodfield chpt.), Execs. Club Oak Brook, Assn. Commerce and Industry (named Ambassdor of Month N.W. suuburban chpt. 1979), Oak Brook Assn. Commerce and Industry (membership com.), Women Entrepreneurs of DuPage County (membership chmn., featured speaker Ja 1988), Art. Inst., Willowbrook/Burr Ridge C. of C., 90th Divsn. Assn. (asst. sec., treas., 2001 Denby Steel award, editor newsletter), US Army WWII Vets. Orgn. (newsletter editor 2001-). Office: Mathisen Assocs 17 Lake Shore Dr Willowbrook IL 60527-2221

MATHON, LAUREN R. judge; b. L.A., Oct. 23, 1949; d. Benjamin D. and Sylvia M.; m. Marvin S. Maslin, Sept. 2, 1990. BA, U. Calif., Berkeley, 1971; JD, Lewis & Clark Law Sch., 1974; MA, U. Southern Calif., 1980. Bar: Calif. 1975, D.C. 1997. Dep. dist. atty. Dist. Atty's. Office, L.A. County, 1976-85; trial atty. Dept. Justice, Immigration & Naturalization Svc., El Centro, Calif., 1986; immigration judge Dept. Justice, Exec. Office Immigration Review, L.A., 1987-94; mem. Dept. Justice, Bd. Immigration Appeals, Falls Church, Va., 1995—. Avocation: yoga. Office: Bd Immigration Appeals 5107 Leesburg Pike Ste 2400 Falls Church VA 22041-3234

MATJASKO, M. JANE, anesthesiologist, educator; b. Harrison Twp., Pa., 1942; MD, Med. Coll. Pa., 1968. Diplomate Am. Bd. Anesthesiology. Resident in anesthesiology Md. Hosp., Balt., 1968-72; prof., chmn. anesthesiology U. Md., Balt., 1990—. Bd. dirs. Am. Bd. Anesthesiology. Mem. Am. Soc. Anesthesiologists, Assn. Univ. Anesthesiologists. Office: U Md Hosp Dept Anesthesiology 22 S Greene St Baltimore MD 21201-1544

MATKIN, JUDITH CONWAY, jewelry designer and manufacturer; b. Ontario, Oreg., Jan. 26, 1943; d. Edward Owen and Lois Lorraine Conway; m. Eltjo Emile Witkop, Feb. 23, 1963 (div. Jan. 1970); children: Gregory Lyn, Joella Monique, Bradley Michael; m. Reuel P. Matkin, Mar. 20, 1995; stepchildren: Chris, Marcie, Ryan. Grad. H.S., Ontario. Designer, sales rep. Jerome I. Silverman, Inc., N.Y.C., 1970-86, Gem East Corp., Seattle, 1986-87; designer Nova Stylings, Van Nuys, Calif., 1987-91, Bagley & Hotchkiss, Santa Rosa, Calif., 1991-94; designer, owner Judith Conway, Windsor, Calif., 1994—. Design cons. Jade and Gem Corp., Hong Kong, 1986; career fair advisor Gemol. Inst. Am., L.A., N.Y.C., 1990-99. Designer Diamond Internat. Awards, 1990, Jewelers of Am. Awards, 1991, Platinum Guild Internat., 1998. Lobbiest Parents of Blind Children, Oreg., 1978-79; pres. Lambda Chi Alpha Parents Orgn., Oreg. State U., Corvallis, 1983, 84, Lakeridge Parents Music Orgn., Lake Oswego, Oreg., 1984-85. Mem. Womans Jewelers Assn. (chairperson annual dinner 1990, Designer of the Yr. 1998), Jewelry Info. Ctr., Contemporary Design Group, Chaine Des Rotisseurs (dame de la chaine). Avocations: art collecting, wine and food, musical instruments and listening, boating, family activities. Office: Judith Conway Inc PO Box 956 Windsor CA 95492-0956 E-mail: judith@judithconway.com.

MATLIN, MARLEE, actress; b. Morton Grove, Ill., Aug. 24, 1965; m. Kevin Grandalski, Aug. 29, 1993; 3 children Attended William Rainey Harper Coll. Appeared in films Children of a Lesser God, 1986 (Acad. award for best actress, Golden Globe award), Walker, 1987, Linguini Incident, 1990, The Player, 1992, Hear No Evil, 1993, It's My Party, 1996, When Justice Fails, 1998, Freak City, 1999; TV films: Bridge to Silence, 1989, Against Her Will: The Carrie Buck Story, 1994, When Justice Fails, 1997, Dead Silence, 1997, Where the Truth Lies, 1999; TV series: Reasonable Doubts, 1991-93; guest star: Picket Fences, 1993, 94-96 (Emmy nomination, Guest Actress-Drama Series, 1994), Seinfeld, 1993 (Emmy nomination Guest Actress-Comedy Series, 1994), The Larry Sanders Show, 1992, Spin City, 1996, ER, 1999, Judging Amy, 1999, The West Wing, 2000—; author: Deaf Child Crossing, 2002 Office: care ICM 8942 Wilshire Blvd Beverly Hills CA 90211-1934

MATNEY, JUDY MCCALEB, secondary school educator; b. Dumas, Tex., Jan. 31, 1944; d. Alex Truman McCaleb and Minnie May Curley; m. Roy Matney II, Dec. 21, 1963 (div. Jan. 1999); 1 child, Roy Matney III. BS in Chemistry, U. Tex., 1965; MEd in Math., Southwestern U., San Marcos, Tex., 1967. Cert. tchr. math., tchr. biology, tchr. chemistry, tchr. physics. Tchr. Taylor Ind. Sch. Dist., Tex., 1965—66, Austin Ind. Sch. Dist., Tex., 1967—69, Fort Bend Ind. Sch. Dist., Sugar Land, Tex., 1975—, head dept. sci. Active state textbook rev. panel Tex. Edn. Agy., Austin, 2001; active gov.'s block grants State Tex., Austin, 1983. Named Tex. State Tchr., Tex. Edn. Agy., 1981; recipient Termann Engring. award, Stanford U., 1997, Southwestern Region U.S. AP Physics Tchr. award, Coll. Bd., 1997, Excellence in Sci. award, Exxon. Mem.: Nat. Sci. Tchrs. (Excellence in Sci. Tchg. award). Avocation: computer technology. Home: 2911 Blue Lakes Missouri City TX 77459 Office: FBISD PO Box 1004 Sugar Land TX 77487-1004

MATNEY, LOUISE HOFF, psychotherapist; b. L.A., Nov. 25, 1944; d. Kenneth Eugene and Dolores Emma White Hoff; m. Frits Boer, Aug. 31, 1966; children: Martin Boer, Dan Boer, Vanessa Boer; m. Greg Matney, June 29, 1997. Candidaats, U. Amsterdam, The Netherlands, Doctorandus, 1974; Master's, Antioch U. Pvt. practice. Author: Dictionary of Psychology, 1979. Cubmaster Boy Scouts Am., Topanga, Calif., 1983—84; pres. Waialua Hongwanji, 1999—2001. Mem.: Am. Assn. Marriage and Family Therapists, Assn. Advancement Gestalt Therapy. Buddhism. Avocation: art. Office: PO Box 25 Northfield MA 01360

MATORIN, SUSAN, social work administrator, educator; b. Boston, Jan. 9, 1943; d. Mervyn Donald and Eleanor (Marinoff) M.; m. Richard Charles Friedman, Nov. 24, 1978; 1 child, Jeremiah Simon. AB, Vassar Coll., 1964; postgrad., Columbia Sch. Social Work, 1966. Cert. social worker, N.Y. Chief social work Washington Heights Cmty. Svc., N.Y. State Psychiat. Inst., 1966-78; chief ambulatory social work in psychiatry Presbyn. Hosp., Columbia Med. Ctr., N.Y., 1978-81; dir. social work Payne Whitney Clinic of N.Y. Hosp., Cornell, 1981-97; program dir. Cornell Psychiatry IOP, 1997—. Mem. adv. coun., 2d vice chair Columbia U. Sch. of Social Work, 1994—; adj. assoc. prof. Columbia Sch. Social Work, 1977—; bd. trustees Selig Ednl. Inst. Jewish Bd. Family Svcs., N.Y.; spkr. in field. Contbr. articles to profl. jours. and books. Recipient Disting. Svc. award Columbia U., 1989, Centennial award, 1998. Fellow Am. Orthopsychiatry Assn.; mem. NASW (Met. chpt. licensing task force, bd. dirs.), Acad. Cert. Social Workers, Soc. for Social Work Adminstrs. in Health Care (N.Y. chpt. program co-chair 1994—, nominated Social Work Dir. of Yr. 1995). Democrat. Jewish. Avocations: family, playing piano, reading, walking, ballet and art. Home: 27 W 86th St Apt 9C New York NY 10024-3615 Office: Payne Whitney Clinic 525 E 68th St # 147 New York NY 10021-4870

MATSA, LOULA ZACHAROULA, social services administrator, educator; b. Piraeus, Greece, Apr. 16, 1935; came to U.S., 1952, naturalized 1962; d. Eleftherios Georgiou and Ourania E. (Fraguiskopoulou) Papoulias; m. Ilco S. Matsa, Nov. 27, 1953; 1 child, Aristotle Ricky. Student, Pierce Coll., Athens, 1948-52; BA, Rockford Coll., 1953; MA, U. Chgo., 1955. Diplomate clin. social worker; bd. cert. clin. social workers, N.Y. cert. social orkers, pub. employees fedn. Marital counselor Family Soc., Cambridge, Mass., 1955-56; chief unit II social svc. Queen's (N.Y.) Children's Psychiat. Ctr., 1961-74; dir. social svcs., supr.-coord. family care program Hudson River Psychiat. Ctr., Poughkeepsie, N.Y., 1974-91; supr. social work Harlem Valley Psychiat. Ctr., Wingdale, N.Y., 1991-93, Hudson River Psychiat. Ctr., 1993—. Field instr. Adelphi, Albany and Fordham univs., 1969—. Contbr. articles to profl. jours.; instrumental in state policy changes in treatment and court representation of emotionally disturbed and mentally ill. Fulbright Exch. student, 1952-53; Talcott scholar, 1953-55. Mem. NASW, Internat. Platform Assn., Internat. Coun. on Social Welfare, Acad. Cert. Social Workers, Assn. Cert. Social Workers, Pierce Coll. Alumni Assn. Democrat. Greek Orthodox. Home: 81-11 45th Ave Elmhurst NY 11373-3553

MATSON, FRANCES SHOBER, retired social worker; b. Cin., Mar. 21, 1921; d. Frank Lyford and Florence Leone (Bridgeford) Shober; student U. Cin., 1939-41, B.A., 1951, postgrad., 1951-52; M.S.W., U. Calif., 1956; Nat. Registry of Clin. Social Work; m. John Alan Matson, Dec. 2, 1942 (dec.). Diplomate Am. Bd. Examiners in Clin. Social Work. Councillor, County of San Mateo, 1956-57; therapist, supr. Center for Treatment and Edn. on Alcoholism, Oakland, Calif., 1957-63; pvt. practice social worker, Berkeley, Calif., 1960-64; supr. dept. social service County of Marin, Calif., 1966; psychotherapist Marin Inst., 1966-70, Oaknoll Naval Hosp., 1969; public health social worker Dept. Health County of Contra Costa (Calif.), 1972; psychotherapist Day Care Center for Schizophrenics, Contra Costa County Med. Services, 1972-74; dir. Martinez Mental Health Clinic, Contra Costa County Med. Services, 1974-81; coordinator adult outpatient services, edn., group therapy Contra Costa County Mental Health Center, 1981-88, ret., 1988. Amem. Nat. Assn. Social Workers, Acad. Cert. Social Workers, Internat. Transactional Analysis Assn., Marin Assn. Mental Health, Contra Costa County Mental Health Assn., Soc. Clin. Social Work. Home: 184 Cedarview Dr Shepherdsville KY 40165-6105

MATSON, PAMELA ANNE, environmental scientist, science educator; b. Eau Claire, Wis., Aug. 3, 1953; BS, U. Wis., 1975; MS, Ind. U., 1980; PhD, Oreg. State U., 1983. Prof. U. Calif., Berkeley, 1993—97, Stanford U., Calif., 1997—. Fellow MacArthur fellow, 1995. Fellow: Am. Acad. Arts & Scis.; mem.: Nat. Acad. Sci. Achievements include research in in interactions between the biosphere and the atmosphere; pioneer into the role of land-use changes on atmospheric change, analyzing the effects of greenhouse gas emissions resulting from tropical deforestization; in the effects of intensive agriculture on the atmosphere, especially the effects of tropical agriculture and cattle ranching; development of ways in which agricultural productivity can be expanded without causing off-site environmental consequences. Office: Stanford U Sch Earth Scis Stanford CA 94305-2210

MATSUI, CONNIE L. pharmaceutical executive; b. Piedmont, Calif. m. William Beckman; 2 children. BA, Stanford U., MBA, 1977. Various positions Wells Fargo Bank, 1977—91; sr. dir., planning and resource devel. IDEC Pharm., 1992—94, v.p., planning and resource devel., 1994—2000, sr. v.p., planning and resource devel., 2000—03; exec. v.p. corp. strategy and communication Biogen Idec Inc., 2003—. Nat. pres. Girl Scouts Am., 1999—2002. Office: Biogen Inc 14 Cambridge Ctr Cambridge MA 02142*

MATSUI, DOROTHY NOBUKO, elementary school educator; b. Honolulu, Jan. 9, 1954; d. Katsura and Tamiko (Sakai) M. Student, U. Hawaii, Honolulu, 1972-76, postgrad., 1982; BEd, U. Alaska, Anchorage, 1979, MEd in Spl. Edn., 1986. Clerical asst. U. Hawaii Manoa Disbursing Office, Anchorage, 1974-76; passenger service agt. Japan Air Lines, Anchorage, 1980; bilingual tutor Anchorage Sch. Dist., 1980, elem. sch. tchr., 1980—. Facilitator for juvenile justice courses Anchorage Sch. Dist., Anchorage Police Dept., Alaska Pacific U., 1992-93; mem. adv. bd. Anchorage Law-Related Edn. Advancement Project. Vol. Providence Hosp., Anchorage, 1986, Humana Hosp., Anchorage, 1984, Spl. Olympics, Anchorage, 1981, Municipality Anchorage, 1978, Easter Seal Soc. Hawaii, 1975. Mem. NAFE, NEA, Alaska Edn. Assn., Smithsonian Nat. Assoc. Program, Nat. Space Soc., Smithsonian Air and Space Assn., World Aerospace Edn. Orgn., Internat. Platform Assn., Nat. Trust for Hist. Preservation, Nat. Audubon Soc., Planetary Soc., Cousteau Soc., Alaska Coun. for the Social Studies, Alaska Coun. Tchrs. Math., World Inst. Achievment, U.S. Olympic Soc., Women's Inner Circle Achievement, U. Alaska Alumni Assn., World Wildlife Fund, Japanese-Am. Nat. Mus., Alpha Delta Kappa (treas. Alpha chpt. 1988-92, corr. sec. 1993-96, sgt. at arms 1996-98). Avocations: reading, sports, learning. Office: Anchorage Sch Dist 7001 Cranberry St Anchorage AK 99502-7145

MATSUMURA, VERA YOSHI, pianist; b. Oakland, Calif. d. Naojiro and Aguri Tanaka; m. Jiro Matsumura, Aug. 8, 1942; 1 son, Kenneth N. BA in Piano Pedagogy, Coll. Holy Names, Oakland, 1938; pvt. studies with F. Moss, M. Shapiro, L. Kreutzer, P. Jarrett. Mem. staff, pianist Radio Sta. KROW, Oakland, 1938-39. Numerous concert performances in Far East (Japan, Thailand), 1940—; numerous teaching appointments, 1940—; dir. Internat. Music Council, Berkeley, Calif., 1969—. Named to Hall of Fame, Piano Guild, 1968. Mem. Nat. Music Tchrs. Nat. Assn., Music Tchrs. Assn. Calif., Internat. Platform Assn., Alpha Phi Mu. Methodist. Home: 2 Claremont Cres Berkeley CA 94705-2324

MATTEO, CHRISTINE E. librarian; b. Jersey City, May 26, 1952; d. Peter J.G. and Doris Ella (Stoffel) Dirschauer; m. Joseph A. Matteo, Sept. 9, 1978. BA in Psychology, Washington Coll., Chestertown, Md., 1974; MLS, Rutgers U., 1977. Cert. libr., N.J. Sr. libr., br. mgr. Beachwood (N.J.) br. Ocean County Libr., 1976-78; prin. libr., br. mgr. Jackson br. Ocean County Libr., 1978-86; automation implementation mgr. Ocean County Libr., Toms River, N.J., 1986-89, supervising libr. ctrl. svcs., 1989-91, chief libr. pub. svcs., 1991-95, chief libr. tech., 1995—. Mem. exec. bd., treas. Ctrl. Jersey Regional Libr., Freehold, 1994-96, Customers of Dynix, Inc., Provo, Utah, 1989-91; editor, mem. steering com. Ocean Co. Libr. Master Plan, Toms River, 1984-85, 91-92, 97-98; mem. exec. bd. One Ease-E-Link, Toms River, 1998—2002. Mem. ALA, ASPCA, Humane Soc. U.S., N.J. Libr. Assn., Toms River Yacht Club, Earthwatch, Greenpeace, Tuckerton Seaport Soc. (charter), Toms River Seaport Soc., Environ. Def. Fund, Monmouth County SPCA, World Wildlife Fund, Animal Birth Control Inc., Associated Humane Socs., Humane Soc. U.S. Avocations: sailing, gardening, dog obedience, kayaking, science fiction. Office: Ocean County Libr 101 Washington St Toms River NJ 08753-7688 E-mail: matteo_c@oceancounty.lib.nj.us.

MATTERN, JOANNE, writer, educator; b. Nyack, NY, Mar. 5, 1963; d. Robert Frederick and Genevieve Porri Gise; m. James Jude Mattern, June 16, 1990; children: Christina Xinwei, Leanne Pengjing. BA in English, Hartwick Coll., 1985. Asst. editor Morrow Jr. Books, NYC, 1985—88; sr. editor, writer Troll Comms., Mahwah, NJ, 1988—95; freelance writer, 1995—. Author: (series) Wildlife of North America, 1998, Compete Like a Champion: Gymnastics, 1999, Barbie First-Grade Workbooks, 1999, Fisher-Price Little People Toddler Sticker Workbooks, 2000, Explorers, 2000—01, Working Together, 2001, Animal Geography, 2001, Safety First, 2000, Learning About Cats, 2000—01, Native Peoples, 2001, (children's books) Brer Rabbit in the Briar Patch, 1997, I Can't Believe My Eyes! Extraordinary Photos or Ordinary Things, 1997, Smart Thinking! Clever Ways Animals Make Their Lives Easier, 1997, Telling Time with Goofy, 1997, The Story of Molly Pitcher, 1999, The Trojan Horse, 1999, Big and Small, Homes for All: The Story of Bird Nests, 1999, From Flowers to Honey: The Story of Beekeeping, 1999, Mountain Climb, 1999, A Visit to the Past, 1999, Tower of Stone: The Story of a Castle, 1999, Claws and Wings and Other Neat Things, 2000, Power Rangers Power-Up Skills Learning Pads, 2000, Wishbone Adventures: Curse of Gold, 2000, Teletubbies Fun with Favorite Things Giant Coloring Activity Book, 2000, Animals Animals, 2001, People in the News: Tom Cruise, 2001, Nature's Greatest Hits, 2001, Reading Progress Indicators, 1998, Texas Assessment of Academic Skills, 2000, Reading Workbook, 2001, many others. Mem.: Soc. Children's Book Writers and Illustrators. Roman Catholic. Avocations: choral music, needlecrafts, church activities, reading, travel.

MATTERSON, JOAN MCDEVITT, physical therapist; b. Bryn Mawr, Pa., Feb. 24, 1949; d. William J. and Wanda Jean (Edwards) McD.; children: Brian, Jennie, Kira. BS in Biology, St. Joseph's U., Phila., 1973; cert. in Phys. Therapy, U. Pa., 1974. Assoc. pharmacologist, rschr. immunology and arthritis Prog. Phys. Therapy, P.A., Wilmington, Del., 1976-93, pediatric phys. therapist, 1974-81, pres., 1976-95; rehab. dir. Achievement Rehab.; phys. therapist Liberty Home Health, 1995—; rehab. dir. Office of Joan Matterson, 1995—, Integrated Health Svcs.- Kent, Smyrna, Del., 1996—; dir. rehab. Keystone Care Therapies, Media, Pa., 1997—, with Pain Mgmt. Ctr. Chester, Pa., 1999; with Hands on Health, Wilmington, 1999—2000; phys. therapist Hickory House Nursing and Rehab. Ctr., Honeybrook, Pa., 2000—. Lectr. in field of low level laser therapy. Dep. gov. Am. Biog. Rsch. Inst.; mem. adv. bd. Internat. Biog. Rsch. Inst., Cambridge, Eng. Mem. Am. Soc. Laser Medicine and Surgery, Internat. Platform Assn., Am. Acad. Pain (assoc.), Inst. Noetic Sci., Am. Bd. Forensic Examiners, North Am. Assn. Laser Therapy, Internat. Exec. Service Corp. Avocations: dance, skiing, cooking.

MATTESON, CAROL J. academic administrator; BS in Health Edn., Slippery Rock U. of Pa.; MS in Psychomotor Learning, U. Oreg.; PhD in Bus. Adminstrn., U. Pitts. Faculty Sturt Coll. of Edn., Slippery Rock U., U. Maine, Augusta, Rowan U., NJ; asst. to pres. Slippery Rock U. of Pa.; dean coll. of bus. Bloomsburg U., Pa., provost and v.p. academic affairs, 1992—95; exec. v.p. and provost Rowan U., NJ, 1995—2000; pres. Mt. Ida Coll., Newton, Mass., 2000—. Office: Mt Ida Coll 777 Dedham St Newton MA 02459*

MATTESON, CLARICE CHRIS, artist, educator; b. Winnipeg, Man., Can., Sept. 2, 1918; came to U.S., 1922; d. Sergis and Nina (Balter) Alberts; m. D.C. Matteson, 1956 (dec. 1976); children: Kemmer, Gretchen. BA, Met. State U., 1976; MA in Liberal Studies, Hamline U., 1986; PhD in Humanities, LaSalle U., 1995. Mem. Orson Welles' staff, Hollywood, Calif., 1945-46; owner Hilde-Gardes Co., L.A., 1952—56; instr. art North Hennepin C.C., Brooklyn Park, Minn., 1975-81; instr. continuing edn. for women U. Minn., 1980. Prodr., host TV program Accent on Art, St. Paul, 1979—; instr. art Lakewood C.C., 1979, U. Minn., Bloomington (Minn.) Sch. Dist., 1980-2004, Mpls. Sch. Dist., St. Paul Sch. Dist., 1981-2002, 03-04; guest artist Montserrat Gallery, Soho, N.Y.C., 1999; appeared as guest artist WCCO-TV, 1998; spkr. on TV, Nat. Am. Pen Women Spirituality and Creativity in Art, 2003. (one-woman shows) Decathlon Club, 1998, State Capital Rotunda, 1986, Lindbergh Home, 1988, Hamline U., 2002, exhibited (group shows) Mpls. Inst. Art, 1994—98, Art in Bloom, 1999—2002, St. Paul, 2000, Landmark Ctr., Hamline U., St. Paul, 2002, U. Minn. Womens Club, 2002, U. Minn. Womens Club Art Show, 2003, Fairmount Hotel, 2002; Exhibited in group shows at Art in Bloom, 1999—2003; (represented by) Gov. Ventura's Ofcl. Residence and now by Gov. Jim Pawlenty, 2003—04, Montserrat Art Gallery, N.Y.C., Gallery 416, Mpls., Jean Stephen Art Gallery, 1999—2002, Premier Gallery, 2001—02, (corr.) Schaumburg (Ill) Newspapers, 1962—68; prodr.: (TV series, host) Kids Art, 1995—, (series program) Internat. Cafe Internet Arts, 1996—; patentee plastic products; prodr.: Men Aware TV, 2001—02, Punt, Pass, or Pie TV, 2001—02; composer: I Want You Near; Exhibited in group shows at Women's Club, 2002—03, exhibited in group shows, Gov. Ventura's and Gov. Tim Pawlenty's, 2001—05; composer: You Make a Difference, God is in my Heart, Art Works Art is Everywhere. Active Minn. Orch. (WAMSO), Mpls., 1972—, vol. Recipient award for creative leadership Minn. Assn. for Continuing Adult Edn., 1977, Gold Cup award Bloomington Cable, 1989, Gov.'s Letter of Commendation, 1994; named Outstanding Grad. for past 25 yrs. Met. State U., 1997, Disting. Alumna John Marshall H.S., L.A., 2002, Outstanding Nominee of Grad. Students Met. State U., 2002; Park Cable TV grantee, 1982, Minn. Humanities Commn. grantee, 1985. Qem. ASCAP (award 1997-2003, award for popular music, 2003-04), AAUW (dir. arts com. 1989-90, bd. dirs. 1990-92), Am. Pen Women (Minn. chpt. 1994—, v.p. 1998), Internat. Biog. Assn. (dep. dir. Cambridge, Eng. 2001, participate art and comm. congress, 2001), Am. Composers Forum, Minn. Artists Assn., Minn. Territorial Pioneers (bd. dirs. 1995—, v.p. 1997-99, 1st v.p. 1999-2003, elected Minnesotan of Yr., 1999-2002, elected 1st v.p. 2003-04), Internat. Alliance for Women in Music, St. Paul Neighborhood Network (elected bd. dirs. TV station SPNN, 2002-04), N.Y. Neighborhood Network, Internat. Platform Speakers (award 1998), Mpls. Telecom. Network, Metro Cable Network, Adelphi Cable, Duluth-Superior Cable, NDT, Eagan. Avocations: tennis, dance, writing children's books, composing liturgical music. Home and Office: 2119 Sargent Ave Saint Paul MN 55105-1126

MATTESON, KARLA J. health science association administrator; BS in Chemistry, Beloit (Wis.) Coll., 1969; MS in Chemistry, Marquette U., 1976; PhD, Med. Coll. Wis., 1981. Postdoctoral fellow Baylor Coll. Medicine, Houston, 1981—83; former asst. dir. U. Tenn Devel. and Genetic Ctr., Knoxville; assoc. prof. med. genetics and pathology U. Tenn., Knoxville, 1986—, dir. biochem. and molecular genetics lab., 1986—; bd. dirs. Am. Bd. Med. Genetics, 1998—2001, exec. dir., 2001—. Fellow: Am. Coll. Med. Genetics; mem.: AAAS, Soc. for Inborn Metabolic Disorders. Office: U Tenn Grad Sch Medicine 1924 Alcoa Hwy Knoxville TN 37920-6999 also: Am Bd Med Genetics 9650 Rockville Pike Bethesda MD 20814-3998*

MATTEUCCI, SHERRY SCHEEL, former prosecutor; b. Columbus, Mont., Aug. 17, 1947; d. Gerald F. and Shirley Scheel; m. William L. Matteucci, Dec. 26, 1969 (div. June 1976); children: Cory, Cody. Student, Kinman Bus. U., 1965-66, Mont. State U., 1967-69, Gonzaga U., 1971-72; BS, Eastern Wash. State U., 1973; JD, U. Mont., 1979. Bar: Mont., U.S. Dist. Ct. Mont., U.S. Ct. Appeals (9th cir.), U.S. Supreme Ct. Mont. Spl. asst. Commr. Higher Edn., 1974-76; assoc. Crowley, Haughey, Hanson, Toole & Dietrich, Billings, Mont., 1979-83, ptnr., 1984-93; U.S. atty. Dist. of Mont., Billings, 1993—2001. Bd. visitors U. Mont. Law Sch., 1988—. Mem. editorial bd. U. Mont. Law Rev., 1977-78, contbg. editor, 1978-79. Bd. dirs. Big Bros. & Sisters, Billings, 1982-85, City/County Library Bd., Billings, 1983-93, Billings Community Cable Corp., 1986, chmn., 1987; vice chmn., bd. dirs. Parmley Billings Library Found. Named one of Outstanding Young Women in Am., 1983. Mem. ABA, State Bar Mont. (chmn. jud. polling com. 1985-87, chmn. women's law sect. 1985-86, trustee, sec., treas. 1988—), Yellowstone County Bar Assn. (dir. 1984-87, pres.-elect 1986-87, pres. 1987-88), Billings C. of C. (leadership com. 1986, legis. affairs com. 1984). Democrat. Mem. Unitarian Ch.

MATTHEW, LYN, sales executive, consultant, marketing professional, consultant; b. Long Beach, Calif., Dec. 15, 1936; d. Harold G. and Beatrice (Hunt) Matthew; m. Wayne Thomas Castleberry, Aug. 12, 1961 (div. Jan. 1976); children: Melanie Castleberry, Cheryl Castleberry, Nicole Castleberry, Matthew Castleberry. BS, U. Calif., Davis, 1958; MA, Ariz. State U., 1979. Cert. hotel sales exec., meeting profl., hospitality mktg. exec., hospitality mgmt. exec. Pres. Davlyn Cons. Found., Scottsdale, Ariz., 1979-82; cons., vis. prof. Art Bus., Scottsdale, 1982—; pres., dir. sales and mktg. Embassy Stes., Scottsdale, 1987-98; pres. Matthew Enterprises, Inc., Scottsdale, 1998—. Vis. prof. Maricopa CC, Phoenix, 1979—, Ariz. State U., Tempe, 1980—83; cons. Women's Caucus Art, Phoenix, 1983—88; coun. adminstr. Lynn Andrews Prodns., 2001—. Author: (book) The Business Aspects of Art, Book I, 1979, Book II, 1989, Marketing Strategies for the Creative Artist, 1985, Moxibustion Manual, 1999. Bd. dirs. Rossom Ho. and Heritage Sq. Found., Phoenix, 1987—88; trustee Hotel Sales and Mktg. Assn. Internat. Found., 1988—90, chmn., 1991—93, mem. exec. com., 1993—95. Recipient Cmty. Bldg. award, 2000. Mem.: Am. Orgn. Bodywork Therapies Asia (pres., state dir. 1999—2003), Ariz. Acad. Performing Arts (v.p. bd. dirs. 1987—88, pres. 1988—89), Soc. Govt. Meeting Planners (charter bd. dirs. 1987, nat. conf. co-chair 1993—94, Sam Gilmer award 1992), Meeting Planners Internat. (v.p. Ariz. Sunbelt chpt. 1989—91, pres. 1991—92, CMP cert. trainer 1995—, Supplier of the Yr. award 1988), Cert. Hospitality Mktg. Execs. (profl. designation tng. chair 1995), Hotels Sales and Mktg. Assn. Internat. (bd. dirs. 1985—90, pres. Great Phoenix chpt. 1988—89, regional dir. 1989—90, mktg. exec. 1998—), Ariz. Vocat. Edn. Assn. (sec. 1978—80), Ariz. Women's Caucus Art (pres. 1980—82, hon. advisor 1986—87), Nat. Women's Caucus Art (v.p. 1981—83), Women in Higher Edn., Ariz. Visionary Artists (treas. 1987—88), Women Image Now (Achievement and Contbn. in Visual Arts award 1983), Coun. Whistling Elk (worldwide coun. adminstr. 2001—).

MATTHEWS, BARBARA, state legislator; b. Nov. 26, 1939; m. Barry Matthews; 2 children. AA, Chabot Coll. Mgr. Calif. govt. affairs Albertson's; mem. Tracy (Calif.) Planning Commn., Tracy City Coun., 1991—2000; mem., dist. 17 Calif. State Assembly, 2000—. Mem. Tracy Econ. Devel. Com., Tracy "Main Street City" Com.; chair Agriculture Com.; mem. Arts, Entertainment, Sports, Tourism, and Internet Media Com., Higher Edn. Com., Water, Parks and Wildlife Com., Vets. Affairs Com., San Joaquin Waste Mgmt. Task Force. Mem. Delta Protection Commn.; bd. dirs. Tracy's Arts Leadership Alliance. Mem.: Soroptimist Internat. (Tracy-Daybreak). Democrat. Mailing: PO Box 942849 Rm 5155 Sacramento CA 95814 Office: 31 E Channel St St 306 Stockton CA 95202 also: 806 W 18th St Merced CA 95340

MATTHEWS, BARBARA CARIDAD, lawyer; d. Frederick Lawrence and Caridad Ofelia Matthews; m. Andrew Michael Danas, Nov. 6, 1999; 1 child, Lydia Marguerite Danas. B.Sc.F.S., Georgetown U., 1986; JD, LLM, Duke U., 1991. Bar: N.Y. 1992. Assoc. banking advisor Inst. Internat. Fin., Washington, 1992—94, banking advisor, regulatory counsel, 1996—2003; assoc. Morrison & Foerster, Washington, 1994—96; sr. coun., Fin. Svc. Com. House of Rep., 2003. Mem. editl. bd. Jour. Derivatives Use, Trading and Regulation, 1997—; contbr. articles to profl. jours., chapters to books. Pres. Friends Assisting the Nat. Symphony, Washington, 1998—99; bd. dirs. Young Audiences, Washington, 2000—; mem. exec. com. women's leadership group Boys & Girls Clubs Greater Washington, 2000. Fellow internat. law, Ford Found., 1991—92. Mem.: ABA, N.Y. State Bar Assn., Internat. Assn. Fin. Engrs., Pi Sigma Alpha, Alpha Sigma Nu. Avocations: photography, tennis, travel. Office: US Ho of Reps Rayburn House Office Bldg Rm 2129 Washington DC 20515 Business E-Mail: barbara.matthews@mail.house.gov.

MATTHEWS, ELIZABETH WOODFIN, law librarian, law educator; b. Ashland, Va., July 30, 1927; d. Edwin Clifton and Elizabeth Frances (Luck) Woodfin; m. Sidney E. Matthews, Dec. 20, 1947; 1 child, Sarah Elizabeth Matthews Wiley. BA, Randolph-Macon Coll., 1948, LLD (hon.), 1989; MS in Libr. Sci., U. Ill., 1952; PhD, So. Ill. U., 1972; LLD, Randolph-Macon Coll., 1989. Cert. law libr., med. libr., med. libr. III. Libr. Ohio State U., Columbus, 1952-59; libr., instr. U. Ill., Urbana, 1962-63; lectr. U. Ill. Grad. Sch. Libr. Sci., Urbana, 1964; libr., instr. Morris Libr. So. Ill. U., Carbondale, 1964-67; classroom instr. So. Ill. U. Coll Edn., Carbondale, 1967-70; med. libr., asst. prof. Morris Libr. So. Ill. U., Carbondale, 1972-74, law libr., asst. prof., 1974-79, law libr., assoc. prof., 1979-85, law libr., prof., 1985-92, prof. emerita, 1993—. Author: Access Points to Law Libraries, 1984, 17th Century English Law Reports, 1986, Law Library Reference Shelf, 1988, 5th edit., 2003, Pages and Missing Pages, 1983, 2d edit., 1989, Lincoln as a Lawyer: An Annotated Bibliography, 1991. Mem. AAUW (pres. 1976-78, corp. rep. 1978-88), Am. Assn. Law Librs., Postdoctoral Acad. Higher Edn., Beta Phi Mu, Phi Kappa Phi. Methodist. Home: 811 S Skyline Dr Carbondale IL 62901-2405 Office: So Ill U Law Libr Carbondale IL 62901

MATTHEWS, GLENNA CHRISTINE, historian; b. LA, Nov. 7, 1938; d. Glen Leslie and Alberta Marie (Nicolais) Ingles; m. James Duncan Matthews (div. Jan. 1978); children: Karen, David. BA, San Jose State U., 1969; MA, Stanford U., 1971, PhD, 1977. Assoc. prof. history Okla. State U., 1978-85. Author: Just a Housewife, 1987, The Rise of Public Woman, 1992; co-author: Running as a Woman, 1993, American Women's History: A Student Companion, 2000, Silicon Valley, Women, and the California Dream, 2002. Recipient The Sierra prize Western Assn. Women Historians; NEH fellow, 1998-99. Mem. Am. Hist. Assn., Orgn. Am. Historians.

MATTHEWS, JANICE C. financial consultant; b. Livingston, Mont., Apr. 7, 1955; d. Frank L. and A. Kathryn Hocevar; children: Amanda, Andrew. BS in Econs., Mont. State U., 1977. Sales rep. IBM, Boise; fin. cons. Merrill Lynch, Idaho Falls. Avocations: fishing, theater, biking. Home: 152 W Stone Run Ln Idaho Falls ID 83404 Office: 560 S Woodruff Ave Idaho Falls ID 83401-5298 E-mail: Janice_Matthews@ml.com.

MATTHEWS, KATHLEEN SHIVE, biochemistry educator; b. Austin, Tex., Aug. 30, 1945; d. William and Gwyn Shive; m. Randall Matthews. BS in Chemistry, U. Tex., 1966; PhD in Biochemistry, U. Calif., Berkeley, 1970. Post doctoral fellow Stanford (Calif.) U., 1970-72; mem. faculty Rice U., Houston, 1972—, chair dept., 1987-95, Wiess prof., 1989-96, Stewart Meml. chair, 1996—, dean natural scis., 1998—. Mem. BBCB study sect. NIH, Bethesda, Md., 1980-84, 86-88, BRSG adv. com., 1992-94; mem. adv. com. on rsch. programs Tex. Higher Edn. Coord. Bd., Austin, 1987-92; mem. undergrad. edn. initiative rev. panel Howard Hughes Rsch. Inst., Bethesda, 1991, mem. rsch. resources rev. panel, 1995, mem. predoctoral fellowships rev. panel, 2001, trustee S.W. Rsch. Inst., 2003—, Steering Com. Vinson & Elkins Women's Initiative Adv. Bd., 2001—. Mem. editl. bd. Jour. Biol. Chemistry, 1988-93, assoc. editor, 1994-99; contbr. 140 reviewed papers. Fellow AAAS; mem. Am. Soc. Biochemistry and Molecular Biology (nominating com. 1993-94, 96-97, fin. com. 2001-2002), Protein Soc., Biophys. Soc. (pub. affairs com. 2002—), Am. Chem. Soc., Phi Beta Kappa. Office: Rice Univ PO Box 1892 6100 Main St MS102 Houston TX 77005-1892 E-mail: ksm@rice.edu.

MATTHEWS, LOIS MARR, musician, music educator; b. Washington, July 10, 1928; d. Ralph Dorian and Ruth Hayes Marr; m. Richard Matthews, June 23, 1956; children: Julia Louise Pagio, Christine Dorian Trout, Melanie Marr Doss. BA, Wilson Tchrs. Coll., 1950; MA in Music, Columbia U., 1953. Organist Calvary Meth. Ch., Arlington, Va., Cmty. Meth. Ch., Meml. Bapt. Ch. Mem.: DAR, Am. Guild Organists. Methodist. Avocations: piano, organ, painting. Home: 6329 Arbor Way Elkridge MD 21075

MATTHEWS, MARY KOSTIELNEY, political organization worker, consultant; b. Detroit, July 6, 1947; d. Walter Anthony and Helen Clare Kostielney; m. Stephen Mark Matthews, Sept. 1, 1972; children: Jacob Kostielney, Stephanie Marie. Coord. Jackson County Dem. Comm., Mich., 1970—73; sales rep. Mich. Bell Tel. Co., 1973—75; campaign dir. Alex Perlos for Circuit Judge, 1986—86; coord. Jackson County field Lana Pollack for U.S. Congress, 1988—88; campaign dir. Jim Berryman for State Senate, Monroe, 1990—90; vol. coord. Lana Pollack for U.S. Senate, Ann Arbor, 1992—92; campaign dir. Rochefort for State Rep, Jackson, 1993—93, Sierra Club, Lansing, 1996—96, Stephen for Dist. Judge, Jackson, 2000—00, Eric C. White for Circuit Judge, 2002. Mem. Delta Dental Plan Mich., Okemos, 1987—92. Chair City of Jackson Charter Commn., 1995—97; coach Lumen Christi H.S. Quiz Bowl Team, 1996—2003; word giver and judge Scripps-Howard Spelling Bee, 1995—2003; co-founder, women's caucus Mich. Dem. Party, Detroit, 1969; mem., city commn. City of Jackson, 1981—85; mem. Diocese of Lansing Bd. Edn. and Formation, Lansing, 1991—97, chair, 1996—97; labor & delivery lamazeinstructor Childbirth Preparation Services, Jackson, 1976—80; dir. Monday-Friday Duplicate Bridge Club, 1995—2003; mem. bd. dirs. Mich. Shakespeare Festival, 1995—2003. Named Disting. Citizen, Jackson Citizen Patriot, 1997; recipient Susan B. Anthony award, Y Ctr. Women's Com., 1996. Avocations: reading, embroidery, travel, bridge.

MATTHEWS, MILDRED SHAPLEY, scientific editor, freelance writer; b. Pasadena, Calif., Feb. 15, 1915; d. Harlow and Martha (Betz) Shapley; m. Ralph Vernon Matthews, Sept. 25, 1937; children:: June Lorrain, Bruce Shapley, Melvin Lloyd, Martha Alys. AB, U. Mich., 1936. Rsch. asst. Calif. Inst. Tech., Pasadena, 1950-61; bilingual editor, rsch. asst. Astron. Obs. Merate-Milan and Trieste, Italy, 1960-70; rsch. asst. Lunar-Planetary Lab., editor space sci. series U. Ariz., Tucson, 1970-96; retired, 1996. Contbr. articles to Sky and Telescope, Astronomia. Recipient Masursky Meritorious Svc. award div. planetary sci. Am. Astron. Soc., 1993. Avocations: classical music concerts, especially opera, travel. Home: 1600 Milvia St Berkeley CA 94709-2012

MATTHEWS, RONDRA J. publishing executive; d. Nedra Plummer; m. Keith Matthews. BS in Behavioral Sci., High Point U.; MBA, Rollins Coll. Various mgmt. positions Orlando (Fla.) Sentinel Comms., 1980—99, v.p., gen. mgr., 1999—2000; pres., pub., CEO Daily Press, Newport News, Va., 2000—. Office: Daily Press 7505 Warwick Blvd PO Box 746 Newport News VA 23607*

MATTHEWS, WYHOMME S. retired music educator, academic administrator; b. Battle Creek, Mich., July 22, 1948; d. Woodrow R. and LouLease (Graham) Sellers; m. Edward L. Matthews, Apr. 29, 1972; children: Channing DuVall, Triston Curran, Landon Edward, Brandon Graham. AA, Kellogg C.C., 1968; MusB, Mich. State U., 1970, MA, MusM, Mich. State U., 1972. Cert. elem. and secondary tchr., Mich. Tchr., vocal music dir. Benton Harbor (Mich.) Pub. Schs., 1971-72, dir. vocal music, 1972; dir. edn. head start program Burlington (N.J.) County, 1972-73; pvt. music tchr., 1973-89; tchr. Southeastern Jr. H.S., 1986-87, W.K. Kellogg Jr. H.S., 1987-89; chair visual and performing arts dept. Kellogg C.C., Battle Creek, Mich., 1989-99, dir. Eastern acad. Ctr., 1999—2003, ret., 2003. Part-time instr. Kellogg C.C., 1973—, dir. Eclectic Chorale, 1973—, dir., organizer Kellogg C.C. Eclectic Chorale Sacred Cultural Festival, 1979—, judge various contests; artistic dir. Battle Creek Sojourner Truth Monument Presentation Day, 1999; presenter in field. Pres. Dudley Elem. Sch., 1981-85; active Battle Creek Pub. Schs. PTA, Pennfield Pub. Schs. PTA, Mt. Zion African Meth. Episc. Ch.; v.p. Life Care Amb. Bd., 1990-2003; bd. dirs. Leila Aboretum Soc.; mem. Battle Creek Cmty. Found., Glen Cross Arts and Infrasture Fund. Mich. State U. fellow, 1971; recipient Outstanding Cmty. Svc. award, 1975, Sojourner Truth award, 2000, George award City of Battle Creek, 2000. Mem. Mich. Music Tchr. Assn., Nat. Music Tchrs. Assn., Battle Creek Music Tchrs. Assn., Battle Creek Morning Music Club (bd. dirs.), Nat. Leadership Acad., Battle Creek Cmty. Concert Assn. Home: 466 Alton Ave Battle Creek MI 49017-3212 E-mail: wmatth5278@aol.com.

MATTHEWS ELLIS, BONNIE, management consultant; b. Fostoria, Ohio, Nov. 14, 1942; d. Blaine Garfield and Mildred Mae (Reed) Hummel; m. Gary Matthews, May 20, 1961 (div. Mar. 1978); children: Christopher, Jennifer, Jonathan; m. William C. Ellis, Sept. 20, 1998. BS, Bowling Green State U., 1965; MA, Ohio State U., 1973, PhD, 1978; postgrad., Franklin U., 1978. Accredited pub. rels. Coord. supplementary tng. Bowling Green (Ohio) State U., 1965-68; supervising tchr. Head Start, Rising Sun, Ohio, 1965-68; assoc. dir. Ohio Community Mental Health & Mental Retardation Assn., Columbus, 1974-77; dir. community programs Ohio Mental Health & Mental Retardation Adv. and Rev. Commn., Columbus, 1977-78; dir. pub. rels. Columbus Mus. Art, 1978-81; chmn., pres. Mgmt. Dimensions, Inc. dba MD Staffing, 1981—; pres. Matthews/Colburn Inc., 1984-86; mng. ptnr., chmn. Fund Raising Dimensions, 1990-92. Adj. prof. Franklin U., Columbus, 1974-85, Otterbein Coll., Westerville, Ohio, 1988-94; therapist, Columbus, 1989-94. Therapist, Columbus, 1989—. Mem. Pub. Rels. Soc. Am. (pres. 1986-87), Nat. Soc. Performance and Instrn., Ohio Bd. Realtors, Ohio State U. Pres. Club, Ohio State U. Alumni (life),Pres of Bd. All The World's A Stage; Bd. mem. The Macomb Symphony. Lutheran. Avocation: tennis. Home: 70901 Carnegie Ln Romeo MI 48065 Office: Mgmt Dimensions 2122 15 Mile Ste A Sterling Heights MI 48310

MATTIE, JEANNE MARIE, public relations and communications consultant; b. Sendai, Japan, Aug. 4, 1950; came to U.S., 1952; d. John D. and Edna H. M.; m. Donald J. Patrican, June 14, 1986; 1 child, Julian M. Patrican. BA, U. Del., 1970. Co-founder Cyrk, Inc., Gloucester, Mass., 1975-80; pres. Mattie Assocs., Inc., Boston and Franklin Lakes, N.J., 1980—. Office: Mattie Assocs Inc 707 Horseshoe Trl Franklin Lakes NJ 07417-1532 Fax: 201-848-7892. E-mail: jmmattie@aol.com.

MATTILA, MARY JO KALSEM, elementary and art educator; b. Canton, Ill., Oct. 26, 1944; d. Joseph Nelson and Bernice Nora (Milbauer) Kalsem; m. John Peter Mattila, Jan. 27, 1968. BS in Art, U. Wis., 1966; student, Ohio State U., 1972, Drake U., 1981; MS in Ednl. Adminstrn., Iowa State U., 1988. Cert. tchr., prin., supt., adminstr., art tchr., secondary tchr., Iowa. Tchr. 2d grade McHenry (Ill.) Pub. Schs., 1966-67, Wisconsin Hts. Schs., Black Earth, Wis., 1967-69; substitute tchr. Columbus (Ohio) City Schs., 1969-70; elem. art tchr. Southwestern City Schs., Columbus, 1972-73; adminstrv. intern Ames, Iowa, 1984-86; lead tchr. at Roosevelt Sch. Ames Cmty. Schs., 1986-87, art vertical curriculum chair, 1983-89, art educator, elem. and spl. edn., 1973—2003. Author articles. Active LWV, Ames, 1982—; fundraiser Altrusa, Ames, 1992—. Recipient Very Spl. Svc. award for Disting. Svc. in Very Spl. Arts, Gov. of Iowa, 1984. Mem.: Questers, Cen. Iowa Orchid Soc., Am. Orchid Soc. Avocations: collecting old stoneware jugs, growing orchids, reading. Home: 2822 Duff Ave Ames IA 50010-4710 Office: Ames Cmty Schs 120 S Kellogg Ave Ames IA 50010-6719

MATTIS, CONSTANCE MARIE, controller; b. Buffalo, Aug. 28, 1960; d. William James Pierce and Welma Rebecca Armstrong; m. Mark Eugene Mattis, Aug. 27, 1983; 1 child, Colleen. BS in Acctg., Plattsburgh State U., 1982; MBA, Gannon U., 2000. Acct. Appletree & Kern PC, CPAs, Erie, Pa., 1984-88, Zurn Industries, Inc., Erie, 1988-96; contr. Uniflow Mfg. Co., Erie, 1996—. Fin. advisor, rev. com. United Way of Erie County, 1998—. Bd. dirs. Our Lady of Mt. Carmel Sch., 1999-01. Mem. Inst. Mgmt. Accts. (dir. meetings/mem. attendance 1997—). Democrat. Roman Catholic. Avocations: golf, reading, boating, swimming. Home: 6003 Southland Dr Erie PA 16509-7833 Office: Uniflow Mfg Co 1525 E Lake Rd Erie PA 16511-1000 Fax: (814) 455-6336. E-mail: cmmattis@hotmail.com.

MATTLEMAN, MARCIENE SCHREIBER, organization executive; b. Phila., Jan. 26, 1930; d. Abner and Miriam (Lamm) Schreiber; m. Herman Mattleman, June 25, 1950; children: Ellen Mattleman Kaplan, Jon, Barbara. BS in Edn., Temple U., 1951, MEd in Elem. Edn., 1962, EdD, 1967. Tchr. elem. sch. Cheltenham (Pa.) Twp., 1951-53; reading tutor Lower Merion (Pa.) Twp. Schs., 1957-59; lectr., instr. English edn. Temple U., Phila., 1962-67, asst. prof., 1967-69, assoc. prof., 1969-72, prof., 1973-84; exec. dir. Phila. Mayor's Commn. on Literacy, 1984-88; founder, exec. dir. Phila. Futures, 1989-97; exec. dir. Phila. Reads, Mayor's Office, 1997—2000; literacy dir. Pub./Pvt. Ventures, 2000—02; exec. dir. After Sch. Activities Partnerships, 2002—. Bd. dirs. Phila. (Pa.) Futres, Jewish Cmty. Rels. Coun., Rural Edn. and Devel., City Year Phila., ARC of S.E. Pa. Author: 101 Activities for Teaching Reading, 1973, (with Herman Mattleman) Expanding Language Skills, 1981. Trustee C.C. Phila., 1985—2002; trustee Free Libr. Phila., 1987—99, chmn. bd. trustees, 1993—97; bd. dirs. Pub. Interest Law Ctr. Phila., 1986—; mem. Phila. Mayor's Commn. on Literacy, 1992—2002; mem. adv. bd. Nat. Inst. for Literacy, 1995—2002. Recipient Humanitarian award Am. Jewish Com., 1985, B'nai B'rith Educators, 1987, literacy award Keystone State Reading Assn., 1986, leadership honoree Luth. Settlement House, 1988, cert. of recognition Phila. Coun. Adminstrv. Women in Edn., 1988, humanities award Jewish Chaplaincy Svc., 1989, ann. award Phila. Com. on City Policy, 1991, Clarence Farmer award Phila. Commn. on Human Rels., 1991, alumni award Temple U. Coll. Edn., 1991, Gimbel award Med. Coll. Pa., 1993, ednl. leadership award Phila. United Negro Coll. Fund, 1991, Points of Light award The White Ho., 1994, gold medal Phila. Pub. Rels. Assn., 1995, Spectrum award ARC, 1996, annual award LWV, 1996, hon. mem. award Schoolmen's Club of Phila., 1997, Lifetime Achievement award Please Touch Mus., 1999; named One of 1000 Women for '90s, Mirabella mag., 1994, Woman of Distinction, Phila. (Pa.) Bus. Jour., 1998; named to Alumni Hall of Fame, Overbrook H.S., 1994. Democrat. Jewish. Avocations: reading, painting, sailing, canoeing, mentoring high school students. Office: ASAP 123 S Broad St Philadelphia PA 19109

MATTSON, CAROL LINNETTE, social services administrator; b. Frederic, Wis., Oct. 3, 1946; d. Clarence Waldemar and Lucille Anna Mathilda (Bengtson) Hedlund; m. Wesley Harlan Mattson, June 24, 1967; 1 child, Aaron Ray. BS, U. Wis., Menomonie, 1968. Home econs. tchr. Luck (Wis.) High Sch., 1968-72; clk. Daniels Twp., Siren, Wis., 1973-75; family living instr. Wis. Indianhead Tech. Inst., New Richmond, 1974-77; aging program dir. Polk County, Balsam Lake, Wis., 1977—. Treas., bd. dirs. Polk County Transp. for the Disabled and Elderly, Inc., Balsam Lake, 1978—; mem. com. Long Term Support Com., Balsam Lake, 1985—. Mem. Wis. Assn. Nutrition Dirs., Wis. Assn. Aging Unit Dirs. Lutheran. Avocations: reading, needlecraft. Office: Polk County Aging Programs 300 Polk County Plz Ste 20 Balsam Lake WI 54810-9096

MATUS, NANCY LOUISE, artist; b. Wichita, Kans., Jan. 22, 1955; d. Joseph John and Josephine Emily (Kulina) M.; m. Kenneth Lee Walker, Feb. 14, 1990. AA, Phoenix Coll., 1980; student, U. Ariz., 1978, 79, Ariz. State U., 1984, 85. Exhibited in group shows Ariz. Sate Capitol, Phoenix, 1985, Movimento Artistico del Rio Salado Gallery, Phoenix, 1986, 87, 89, 91, 92, Tempe (Ariz.) Arts Ctr., 1987, U. Ariz., Phoenix, 1987, Nat. Acrylic Painters Assn., Long Beach, Calif., 1996, Coos Bay (Oreg.) Art Museum, 1999, Coos Art Mus., 1999, Nat. Acrylic Painters Assn.-Westminster Gallery, London, 1999; represented in numerous pvt. collections, including loan to City of Phoenix, City Hall, 1998; work represented in Best of Acyrlic Painting, 1996, Creative Inspirations, 1997. Mem. Nat. Acrylic Painters Assn. (signature), Nat. Oil and Acrylic Painters Soc. (assoc.), Cottonwood Country Club, Catharine Lorillard Wolfe Art Club (assoc.). Address: 25802 S Cloverland Dr Chandler AZ 85248-6875

MATUS-MENDOZA, MARIADELALUZ, language educator, sociologist; b. Mexico City, Apr. 10, 1961; arrived in U.S., 1991; d. MariadelaPaz Matus-Mendoza; m. Geoffrey Fitch, Sept. 3, 1993. BA in English Lit. and Applied Lang., Mex. Autonoman U., Mexico City, 1984; MA, Temple U., 1993, PhD, 1999. Tchr. Mex. Autonomon U., 1984—91; tchg. asst. Temple U., Phila., 1991—94, adj. instr., 1994—95, LuSulle U., Phila., 1995—98,

U. Pa., Phila., 1996—99; asst. prof. Spanish U. Ctrl. Fla., Orlando, 1999—2001, Drexel U., Phila., 2001—. Cons. ETS, Princeton, NJ, 2001—. Mem.: MLA, Am. Assn. Tchrs. of Spanish and Portugese, Nat. Assn. Hispanic and Latino Studies. Roman Catholic. Office: Drexel Univ 229 N 33rd St Philadelphia PA 19104

MATUSOW, NAOMI C. state legislator; b. Nashville, Oct. 31, 1938; m. Gene R. Matusow; children: Gary, Jason. BA cum laude, Vanderbilt U., 1960; MA in Counseling and Guidance, NYU, 1966; JD, Pace U., 1979. Bar: N.Y. 1981. Editl. asst. Golden Press, 1960-62; tchr. math. N.Y.C. Pub. Schs., 1962-65, guidance counselor, 1965-67; pvt. practice as lawyer Armonk, 1981-92, White Plains, 1981-92; mem. N.Y. State Assembly, 1992—, chair librs. and edn. tech. com., mem. assembly coms., econ. devel.. environ. conservation, local govt., transp., consumer affairs, tourism, arts, sports devel., spkrs. steering com. Chmn. Women's Bus. Devel. subcom.; bd. dirs. Juvenile Diabetes Found. Westchester County. Mem. NOW, Nat. Women's Polit. Caucus. Office: 103 Old Hckory Way Bedford NY 10506-2000 E-mail: matusow@assembly.state.ny.us.

MATUSZAK, ALICE JEAN BOYER, pharmacy educator; b. Newark, Ohio, June 22, 1935; d. James Emery and Elizabeth Hawthorne (Irvine) Boyer; m. Charles Alan Matuszak, Aug. 27, 1955; children: Matthew, James. BS summa cum laude, Ohio State U., 1958, MS, 1959; postgrad., U. Wis., 1959-60; PhD, U. Kans., 1963. Registered pharmacist, Ohio, Calif. Apprentice pharmacist Arensberg Pharmacy, Newark, 1953-58; rsch. asst. Ohio State U., Columbus, 1958, lab. asst., 1958-59; rsch. asst. U. Wis., Madison, 1959-60, U. Kans., Lawrence, 1960-63; asst. prof. U. of the Pacific, Stockton, Calif., 1963-67, assoc. prof., 1971-78, prof., 1978—2000, prof. emerita, 2000—; order of Pacific, 2000. Vis. fgn. prof. Kobe-Gakuin U., Japan, 1992. Contbr. articles to profl. jours. Recipient Disting. Alumna award Ohio State U. Coll. Pharmacy, 1994, Profl. Frat. Assn. Career Achievement award, 2000; NIH grantee, 1965-66. Fellow Am. Pharm. Assn. (chmn. basic scis. 1990); mem. Am. Assn. Colls. of Pharmacy (chmn. chemistry sect. 1979-80, bd. dirs. 1993-95), Am. Inst. History of Pharmacy (exec. coun. 1984-88, 90-92, 92-95, chmn. contributed papers 1990-92, pres.-elect 1995-97, pres. 1997—, cert. of commendation 1990), Am. Chem. Soc., Internat. Fedn. Pharmacy, Acad. Pharm. Rsch. Sci. (pres. 1993-94), Coun. Sci. Soc. Pres., U.S. Adopted Names Coun. Review Bd., U.S. Pharmacopeial Conv., Clan Irwin Assn., Donald Salvatori Calif. Pharmacy Mus., Sigma Xi, Rho Chi, Phi Lambda Sigma, Phi Kappa Phi, Kappa Epsilon (Unicorn award, award of merit 1995, Merck Vanguard leadership award 2000), Lambda Kappa Sigma, Delta Zeta. Democrat. Episcopalian. Avocation: collecting historical pharmacy artifacts. Home: 1130 W Mariposa Ave Stockton CA 95204-3021 Office: U Pacific Sch Pharmacy Stockton CA 95211-0001

MATZ, DEBORAH, federal agency administrator; m. Marshall Matz; children: Hayley, Peter. BS, Cornell U.; MA, George Washington U. Cmty. devel. rep. U.S. Dept. Housing and Urban Devel.; legis. asst. Congressman Peter Peyser; dir. Office Tech. Assessment, U.S. Congress; economist Joint Econ. Com.; exec. officer Liaison Office N.Am. Food and Agrl. Orgn., UN; numerous positions including deputy asst. sec. adminstrn., chair loan resolution task force, chief of staff adminstrs. Farm Svc. Agy and Farmers Home USDA, 1993—2001; mem. Nat. Credit Union Adminstrn., Alexandria, 2002—. Office: Nat Credit Union Adminstrn 1775 Duke St Alexandria VA 22314-3428

MAU, C. S. **See SALERNO, CHERIE ANN**

MAUCH, DIANE FARRELL, music educator; b. Flushing, NY, Jan. 15, 1934; d. Edward Joseph Farrell and Adelaide Mary Hopkins; m. Robert Kurt Mauch, Aug. 24, 1963; children: Anneliese Farrell, Bronwen Adele. MusB, Manhattanville Coll., 1955; MusM, U. Mich., 1971; postgrad., Juilliard Sch. Music, Manhattan Sch. Music, Aspen Music Sch. Cert. tchr. Fla. Bd. Edn., ministry formation cert. Nat. Assn. Pastoral Musicians. Asst. prof. music Trevecca Coll., Nashville, 1973—77; music tchr. St. Bernard Acad., Nashville, 1976—82; music specialist Carrollton Sch., Coconut Grove, Fla., 1983—99; adj. prof. music U. Miami, Coral Gables, Fla., 1994—. Music rep. Sch. Arts Planning, Ann Arbor, Mich., 1969—72; dir. Liturgy Com., Nashville, 1975—83; adj. prof. music Scarritt Coll., Nashville, 1976—80, Miami (Fla.)-Dade C.C., 1983—90; dir. edn. Fla. Grand Opera, Miami, 1990—93; del. Children Cultural Coalition, Miami, 1990—93; music rep. Visual and Performing Arts Steering Com., Miami, 1991—94; opera cons. Opera Am., Washington, 1992—94; choir dir. St. Mary's, Manchester, Mich., 1966—69, St. Lawrence Ch., North Miami Beach, Fla., 1984—86; soloist St. Henry, Nashville, 1975—82, Ch. by the Sea, Bal Harbour, Mich., 1991—2001. Contbr. textbook Music! Words! Opera! Vols. II and III, 1991;, performer (radio, concert opera, oratorios). Chairperson Cmty. Concerts, Nashville, 1976—78; active Dade County Cultural Coalition, Miami, 1998—. Recipient Leadership award, Nat. Assn. Pastoral Musicians, Washington, 1980; grantee, NEA, 1977, NEH, 1991. Mem.: Miami Music Tchrs. Assn., Music Tchrs. Nat. Assn. (permanent nat. profl. cert., honors chair, v.p.), Nat. Assn. Tchrs. Singing (past officer, v.p., pres., auditions chair). Roman Catholic. Avocations: traveling, linguistics and languages, choral singing. Home: 10645-C SW 113 Pl Miami FL 33176 Office: U Miami Foster Bldg San Amaro Dr Miami FL 33124

MAUE, LETA JO, special education administrator; b. York, Pa., Dec. 7, 1951; d. Wilford Thomas and Helen Louise Myers; m. Frederick Robert Maue, Sept. 24, 1994; children: Frederick C., Patrick P. BS in Elem. Edn., Mansfield U., 1973; MA in Spl. Edn., Shippensburg U., 1979; Cert. in Supervision of Spl. Edn., Bloomsburg U., 1998. Cert. in reality therapy. Elem. tchr. Shikellamy Sch. Dist., Sunbury, Pa., 1973-76, spl. edn. tchr., 1986-90, instrnl. support diagnostician, 1990-97, spl. edn. supr., 1997—; tchr. of gifted York (Pa.) Suburban Sch. Dist., 1976-83. Dir. Camp Pennwood, York County Arc, 1982-83; staff devel. trainer Shikellamy Sch. Dist., 1991—, supt. leadership adv. coun., 1997—. Mem. Local Right to Edn. task force, Danville, Pa., 1997—; vol. Sunbury Revitalization, 1989-95; mem. Northumberland County Hist. Soc.; bd. dir. Susquehanna Valley Chorale, 1984-92; mem. coun.. Zion Luth. Ch., 1990-94, pres. coun., 1993-94, mem. choir, 1984—. Mem. Coun. for Exceptional Children awarded profl. spl. educator adminstrn. (CEC, 2001), William Glasser Inst., SAI Hon. Music Frat. Avocations: playing piano, singing, opera, travel, camping. Home: 168 N 11th St Sunbury PA 17801-2444 Office: Shikellamy Sch Dist 200 Island Blvd Sunbury PA 17801-1028

MAUGHAN, SUSAN IRENE, director; b. Youngstown, Ohio, Dec. 19, 1951; d. James Frances and Lorna Maxine (Leichter) Rogers; m. James William Maughan, Aug. 24, 1973; children: James Jr., Erin E.; 2 adopted children: Melissa E., Robert A. BS in Education, Kent State U., 1974, MS in Sch. Psychology, 1979, EdS, 1981; cert. drug/alcohol abuse couselor, Cadwalder Behavior Inst., Houston, 1987; EdD in Ednl. Leadership, Baylor U., 2001. Cert. tchg. educable mentally retarded; learning disabilities; behavior disorders; phys. edn.; child study certification; lic. psychol. assoc.; marriage and family therapist, Tex.; lic. chem. dependency counselor. Tchr. spl. edn. Warren Sch. Dist., Ohio, 1978-79; grad. asst., recreation for handicapped Kent State U., Ohio, 1979-80; intern, sch. psychologist Windham Sch. Dist., Ohio, 1980-81; assoc. sch. psychologist Friendswood Sch. Dist., Tex., 1981-85; psychol. assoc. Ruscelli Clinic, Webster, Tex., 1985-92; lic. specialist sch. psychology Santa Fe Sch. Dist., Tex., 1992—99; dir. spl. svcs. Marble Falls Sch. Dist., 1999—. Coord. Spl. Transitional Edn. Program Santa Fe Sch. Dist., 1992-94, Student Support Svcs., 1994—, instr. crisis prevention, 1994—; del. varios delegations; spkr. in field. Contbr. articles to profl. jours. Exec. bd. Leaders in Action Safer Soc., 2001—03. Democrat. Roman Catholic. Avocations: walking with dau., camping, volunteering, drawing. Home: PO Box 9085 Horseshoe Bay TX 78657-9085 Office: Marble Falls Sch Dist 2001 Broadway Marble Falls TX 78654

MAUKE, LEAH RACHEL, retired counselor; b. Newport, R.I., Aug. 29, 1924; d. Louis and Annie (Price) Louison; m. Otto Russell Mauke, June 18, 1950. BSBA, Boston U., 1946, MBA, 1948. Teaching fellow Boston U., 1946-48; head advt. dept. Endicott Coll., Beverly, Mass., 1948-66; guidance counselor Vineland (N.J.) Sr. High Sch., 1966-69, Black Horse Pike Regional Sch. Dist., Blackwood, N.J., 1969-86, ret., 1986. Vol. ARC, Vero Beach, Fla., 1988—. Boston U. fellow 1946. Mem. AAUW (life, pres. North Shore br. 1955-59, state fellowship chmn. 1957-58), NEA, N.J. Edn. Assn., Camden County Pers. and Guidance Assn. (sec. 1972). Avocations: reading, travel, crossword puzzles. Home: 2119 E Lakeview Dr Sebastian FL 32958-8519

MAUKSCH, INGEBORG GROSSER, nursing educator; b. Austria; d. Frederick and Claire (Tauber) G.; children from previous marriage: Lawrence Bernard, Valerie. PhD, U. Chgo., 1969; D.Sc. (hon.), Syracuse U., 1979. Valere Potter disting. svc. prof. nursing Vanderbilt U. Sch. Nursing, Nashville, sr. program cons. Robert Wood Johnson nurse faculty fellowships in primary care program, 1976—. Mem. Presdl. Com. on Nat. Health Inst. Author: (with M. Miller) Implementing Change in Nursing, 1981, Systematic Patient Medication Record Review, 1980; mem. editorial bd.: Nursing Outlook, Nurse Educator. Mem. U.S. Holocaust Meml. Council. Recipient Alumni Achievement award Columbia U., 1979 Mem. Am. Nurses Assn. (hon.), Am. Acad. Nursing, Nat. Acad. Scis., Tenn. Nurses Assn. Office: Sch Nursing Vanderbilt Hospital Nashville TN 37232-0001

MAUL, CAROL ELAINE, small business owner; b. Joliet, Ill., Feb. 28, 1953; d. Donald James and Virginia Olive (Wilson) Johnson; m. Richard Kester Maul, June 16, 1979. Student, Met. State Coll., 1971-76. Mgr. So-Fro Fabrics, Elgin, 1976-79; owner, operator Port Arthur Pie Co., Denver, 1985-87; freelance musician Denver, 1987—; owner CAMA Creative Mktg. Bus. Promotion, Profl. Voice Work. Prin. flutist Elgin Symphony Orch., 1976-79; mem. Denver Botanic Gardens. Mem. Colo. Rail Passenger Assn., Nat. Trust Hist. Preservation, Citizens for Classical FM Radio (bd. dirs.), Colo. Water Garden Soc., Denver Garden Railway Soc., Rocky Mtn. Koi Club. Independent. Episcopalian. Lodge: Job's Daughters (Honored Queen 1970-71). Avocations: needlepoint, calligraphy. Home and Office: 387 S Pontiac Way Denver CO 80224-1335

MAULE, THERESA MOORE, lawyer; b. Winner, S.D., Jan. 20, 1966; d. Robert James and Serrilyn Rae (Belmer) M.; m. Brian Lee Kramer, Nov. 25, 1996. BA summa cum laude, Dakota Wesleyan U., 1988; MA, U. S.D., 1990, JD, 1994. Bar: S.D., U.S. Dist. Ct. S.D., Lower Brule Sioux Tribal Ct., Rosebud Sioux Tribal Ct. Prosecutor Rosebud (S.D.) Sioux Tribal Ct., 1994-96; ptnr. Maule & Maule Law Offices, Winner, S.D., 1995—; prosecutor Lower Brule (S.D.) Sioux Tribal Ct., 1996—; states atty Tripp County, Winner, 1997—. Mem. Tripp County Child Protection Team, Winner, S.D., 1997—. Mem. ABA, S.D. Bar Assn., Nat. Dist. Attys. Assn., S.D. Trial Lawyers Assn., Bus. and Profl. Women (Young Careerist 1996), Phi Kappa Phi, Phi Alpha Theta. Republican. Episcopalian. Avocations: camping, ceramics. Office: Maule & Maule Law Offices PO Box 1831 Winner SD 57580-1031

MAULTSBY, MARILYN D. health science association administrator; b. Balt., 1953; BA, Case Western Res. U., 1975; MS, U. Cin., 1976. Dir. planning Md. Health Planning Commn., 1977—86; dir. regional policy Greater Balt. Com., 1986—88; dir. pub. policy BlueCross BlueShield Md., 1988—93, v.p. strategic planning and adminstrn., 1993—95; dir. devel. and mgmt. svcs. Fidelity Health Sys. Inc., 1996—98; exec. dir. Md. Health Care Found., 1998—. Chair Role Network 2000, Inc., 1995—; mem. Balt. City Bd. Fin., 1997—; mem., pres. Md. State Bd. Edn., 2002—; bd. mem. Md. Assn. Health Underwriters, N.W. Hosp. Ctr. Vice chair Bd. Associated Black Charities, 1996—98; chair nominating com. Md. Com. for Children, 1997—99; mem. Govs. Task Force on Charitable Giving, 1997—; chair, bd. mem. Associated Black Charities, 1998—; mem. audit and compliance com. LifeBridge Health, 1999—. Recipient Md. Top 100 Women award, Daily Record, 1998, 2000, 2002. Mem.: Omega Psi, Delta Sigma Theta. Office: Md State Bd Edn 200 W Baltimore St Baltimore MD 21201 also: Md Health Care Found 6470-C Dobbin Rd Columbia MD 21045

MAUMENEE, IRENE H. ophthalmology educator; b. Bad Pyrmont, Germany, Apr. 30, 1940; MD, U. Gottingen, 1964. Cert. Am. Bd. Ophthalmology, Am. Bd. Med. Genetics. Rsch. asst. U. Hawaii, 1968; vis. geneticist Population Genetics Lab., 1968-69; fellow dept. medicine Johns Hopkins U., 1969-71; ophthalmology preceptorship Wilmer Inst. Johns Hopkins Hosp., 1969-71, from asst. prof. to assoc. prof. Wilmer Ophthalmology Inst., 1972-87; prof. ophthalmology and pediatrics Wilmer Ophthalmology Inst., 1972—; dir. Johns Hopkins Ctr. Hereditary Eye Disease, Wilmer Inst., 1979—. Cons. John F. Kennedy Inst. Visually & Mentally Handicapped Children, 1974—; dir. Low Vision Clinic, Wilmer Inst., 1977-88; vis. prof. French Ophthalmology Soc., Paris & French Acad. Medicine, 1988; advisor Nat. Eye Inst. Task Forces, 1976, 81. Mem. AMA, Am. Soc. Human Genetics, Am. Acad. Ophthalmology, Assn. Rsch. Vision & Ophthalmology, Internat. Soc. Genetic Eye Disease, Am. Ophthal. Soc., Pan Am. Assn. Ophthalmology. Achievements include research in nosology and management of ophthalmic and general medical genetics; population genetics; computer application to genetic analysis; molecular genetics; over 200 publications on human genetics and eye diseases. Office: Johns Hopkins Ctr Hereditary Eye Diseases 600 N Wolfe St # 517 Baltimore MD 21287-0005 E-mail: jhched@jhmi.edu.

MAUN, MARY ELLEN, computer consultant; b. N.Y.C., Dec. 18, 1951; d. Emmet Joseph and Mary Alice (McMahon) M. BA, CUNY, 1977, MBA, 1988. Sales rep. N.Y. Telephone Co., N.Y.C., 1970-76, comml. rep., 1977-83, programmer, 1984-86; systems analyst Telesector Resources Group, N.Y.C., 1987-89, sr. systems analyst, 1990-95; pres. Sleepy Hollow (N.Y.) Techs., Inc., N.Y., 1995—. Corp. chmn. United Way of Tri-State Area, N.Y.C., 1985; recreation activities vol. Pioneers Am., N.Y.C., 1982—; active Sleepy Hollow Hist. Soc.; founder Mary Ellen Maun Philanthropic Found., 1998; Dem. dist. leader for Philipse Manor. Recipient Outstanding Community Service award, Calvary Hosp., Bronx, N.Y., 1984. Mem. N.Y. Health and Racquet Club, Road Runners. Avocations: antique restoration, classical music, skiing, running. Office: Sleepy Hollow Techs Inc 3 Farrington Ave Sleepy Hollow NY 10591-1302 Home: 539 Martling Ave Tarrytown NY 10591-4719

MAUNUS, EILEEN SUSAN, lawyer; b. Phila., June 18, 1958; d. Alan Jacob and Loretta Paula (Trachtenberg) M. BA, Temple U., 1979, JD, 1982. Bar: Pa. 1982, U.S. Supreme Ct. 1986, U.S. Dist. Ct. (ea. and mid. dists.) Pa. Law clk. Phila. Common Pleas Ct., 1982-83; asst. counsel Pa. Liquor Control Bd., Harrisburg, 1983-89, dep. chief counsel, 1989-96; chief adminstrv. law judge, 1996—. Pa. Bar Inst. lectr. on Pa. Alcohol Beverage Practice, 1987, 96, 2000, 2003. Contbr. articles to profl. jours. Mem. ABA (vice-chair alcohol beverage practice com. 1993—, editor The Bar 1993-97), Dauphin County Bar Assn. Avocations: furniture construction, sailing, tennis, travel, photography. Office: Office of Adminstrv Law Judge Brandywine Plaza 2221 Paxton Church Rd Harrisburg PA 17110-9600

MAUPIN, ELIZABETH THATCHER, theater critic; b. Cleve., Oct. 21, 1951; d. Addison and Margaret (Thatcher) M.; m. Jay Yellen, Dec. 29, 1995. BA in English, Wellesley (Mass.) Coll., 1973; M in Journalism, U. Calif., Berkeley, 1976. Editorial asst. Houghton Mifflin Co., Boston, 1973-74; reporter, movie critic Times-Standard, Eureka, Calif., 1976-78; theater and movie critic Chronicle-Telegram, Elyria, Ohio, 1978-79; movie critic Ledger-Star, Norfolk, Va., 1979-82; feature writer Va.-Pilot and Ledger Star, Norfolk, 1982-83; sr. theater critic Orlando (Fla.) Sentinel, 1983—. Fellow Nat. Arts Journalism program Columbia U., 1995-96. Fellow Nat. Critics Inst.; mem. Am. Theatre Critics Assn. (exec. com. 1993-99, chair 1996-99). Office: Orlando Sentinel 633 N Orange Ave Orlando FL 32801-1349

MAURER, ILLENE K. retired speech pathology/audiology services professional, volunteer; b. Ft. Wayne, Ind., June 14, 1935; d. Jack M. and Rose Hoffman Komisarow; m. Michael Ben Maurer, Dec. 23; children: Stacy, Larry, Betsy. BS in Speech, Northwestern U. Mem. People of Vision, Indpls. Mus. Art, Family Support Ctr. Aux., Theatre Arts Guild; immediate past chair devel. com. Meth. Hosp. Health Fedn., 2003—, com. mem. devel. com. and long-range planning com., 2003—; co-chair underwriting com. for arts/antiques show Meth. Hosp., Indpls., 2003—; bd. dirs., chmn. vol. com. Indpls. Symphony Orch., 2003—; vol. reader to preschoolers at nursery sch., 2003—; mem. Nat. Bd. Hadassah, 1982—86; pres., co-founder Ha'ima Hadassah, 1960; pres. Indpls. chpt. Hadassah, 1976; pres. Ill.-Ind. region Hadassah, 1982—85; pres. Congregation Beth-El Zedeck, Indpls., 1992—94; bd. dirs. Indpls. Opera, 1983—86; bd. dirs. women's com. Indpls. Symphony Orch., 2003—; bd. dirs. Ind. U. Hillel Bd. Advisers, 2003—. Named Vol. of Yr. in Arts and Edn. category, Cen. Ind., 1994; recipient Young Leadership award, Jewish Welfare Fedn., 1974, Sagamore of the Wabash, Gov. Evan Bayh, 1991, Living in 2 Civilizations award (Illene K. Maurer Day named in her honor), Jewish Reconstructionist Coll., 1996. Mem.: Jr. League Indpls. (hon.). Home: 7777 N Pennsylvania Indianapolis IN 46240

MAURER, KAREN ANN, special education educator; b. New Kensington, Pa., Apr. 5, 1954; d. James Clair and Carrie Carmella (Siciliano) Blissell; m. Kevin Michael Maurer, June 25, 1983; children: Kevin Shawn, Kari Ann, Katelyn Elisabeth. BS in Elem. Edn./Spl. Edn., Edinboro U. of Pa., 1976, MEd in Mental Retardation, behavior mgmt. specialist cert., Edinboro U. of Pa., 1979. Cert. Pa. Instructional II; cert. emotional support tchr. Tchr. of mental/phys. handicapped preschs. Dr. Gertrude A Barber Ctr., Erie, Pa., 1976-80; tchr. of primary socially/emotionally disturbed students N.W. Tri County Intermediate Unit, Edinboro, Pa., 1980-83; tchr. h.s. emotionally disturbed students Allegheny Intermediate Unit, Pitts., 1983-91, South Fayette Twp. Sch. Dist., McDonald, Pa., 1991—. Lead tchr. elem. spl. edn. dept. South Fayette Elem. Sch., McDonald, 1992-93; master tchr. elem spl. edn. dept. N.W. Tri-County Intermediate Unit, Edinboro, 1981-83; presenter staff devel. South Fayette Twp. Schs., McDonald, 1993. Life mem. Girl Scouts of Am., N.Y.C., 1998—; sponsor Multicultural Club of South Fayette H.S., McDonald, 1995—. Mem. Coun. for Exceptional Children, Pa. State Edn. Assn. (rep.), Pa. Assn. of Supervision and Curriculum Devel. (western region), Pa. Middle Sch. Assn. Democrat. Roman Catholic. Avocations: singing, sewing, church work. Home: 42 W Manilla Ave Pittsburgh PA 15220-2838 Office: South Fayette Twp Sch Dist 2250 Old Oakdale Rd Mc Donald PA 15057-2580 E-mail: maurer@southfayette.org.

MAURLAND, ANNE ELISABETH, potter; b. Oslo, Apr. 6, 1964; came to U.S., 1984; d. Harald and Unni Elisabeth (Bjanes) M. BA, Luther Coll., 1987; MA, Ill. State U., 1989. Potter Genszler Stoneware Designs, Briggsville, Wis., 1989-94, Decorah, Iowa, 1994—. Recipient Award of Excellence, Plaza Art Fair, 1995, 97, Old Orchard Crafts Fair, 1994, Best of Show award Art Fair on the Square, 1995, Excellence in Clay award Minn. Craft Fair, 1995, 98, Award of Merit Winter Park Sidewalk Art Festival, 1999, 3d place award Cherry Creek Arts Festival, 1999. Mem. Norwegian Assn. Arts and Crafts. Avocations: mountain biking, skiing, reading, piano playing, cooking. Studio: Elisabeth Maurland Studio 411 W Water St Decorah IA 52101-1731

MAURO, JEAN CRANSTOUN, music educator; b. Trenton, N.J., Oct. 22, 1954; d. Leroy Bruce and Evelyn (Weber) Cranstoun; m. Peter Randolph Mauro, Aug. 7, 1976; children: Gabriella Andrea, Eric Peter, Alexander Tristan. B in Music, U. Iowa, 1975; MA in Conducting, Trenton State Coll., 1990. Dir. orch. Grinnell (Iowa)-Newburg Schs., 1975—77; dir. orch., string quartet advisor West Windsor-Plainsboro Schs., Princeton Junction, NJ, 1978—. Dir. orch. Carnegie Hall John Baker Prodns., N.Y.C., 2002. Home: 6 Lucerne Dr Lawrenceville NJ 08648 Office: West Windsor Plainsboro HS 346 Clarksville Rd Princeton Junction NJ 08550

MAU-SHIMIZU, PATRICIA ANN, lawyer; b. Jan. 17, 1953; d. Herbert G. K. and Leilani (Yuen) Mau; 1 child, Melissa Rose. BS, U. San Francisco, 1975; JD, Golden Gate U., 1979. Bar: Hawaii 1979. Law clk. State Supreme Ct., Honolulu, 1979-80; atty. Bendet, Fidell & Sakai, Honolulu, 1980-81; legis. atty. Honolulu City Coun., 1981-83, House Majority Staff Office, Honolulu, 1983-84, dir., 1984-93; chief clk. Hawaii Ho. of Reps., 1993—. Mem. Hawaii Bar Assn., Hawaii Women Lawyers, Jr. League Hawaii. Democrat. Roman Catholic. Home: 7187 Hawaii Kai Dr Honolulu HI 96825-3115 Office: State House Reps 415 S Beretania St Rm 027 Honolulu HI 96813-2407 Office Phone: 808-586-6127.

MAUSKOPF, ROSLYNN R. prosecutor; b. Washington, 1957; BA, Brandeis U., 1979; JD, Georgetown U., 1982. Asst. dist. atty. N.Y. County Dist. Atty.'s Office, 1982—95, dep. chief spl. prosecution bur., 1992, chief frauds bur., 1993; insp. gen. State of N.Y., 1995—2002; U.S. atty. U.S. Dept. Justice, Ea. Dist. N.Y., Bklyn., 2002—. Chair Moreland Commn. N.Y.C. Schs., 1999. Office: Ea Dist NY 147 Pierrepont St Brooklyn NY 11201

MAUTNER, GABRIELLA, writer, educator; b. Chemnitz, Germany, Jan. 8, 1922; arrived in U.S., 1946; d. Norbert and Charlotte Regina (Cohn) Kramer; m. Fred Solinger, Mar. 1942 (div. Nov. 1951); 1 child, Tom David Solinger ; m. Ervin Mautner, July 24, 1954 (dec.); children: Daria Cohen, Eva. BA, San Francisco State U., 1972, MA, 1975. Tchr. creative writing San Francisco State U., 1975—77; tchr. comparative lit. Coll. of Marin, Kentfield, Calif., 1977—78; lectr. creative writing The Fromm Inst., U. San Francisco, 1981—2003. Author: (novels) Out of a Season, 1968, Lovers and Fugitives, 1986. Democrat. Avocations: swimming, yoga, literature, theater, music. Home: 7 Keats Dr Mill Valley CA 94941 E-mail: gabriellam@worldnet.att.net.

MAUZY, (MARTHA) ANNE, retired deaf educator, audiologist; b. Birmingham, Ala., June 1, 1929; d. Huell Olon and Verna Eleanor (Evans) Rogers; m. Billy Burton Rister, Mar. 30, 1951 (div. 1973); children: Melanie Kofnovec, Jennifer Tyson, Randy Rister; m. Oscar Holcombe Mauzy, Feb. 14, 1976 (dec. Oct. 2000); stepchildren: Catherine, Charles, James. BA, U. Tex., 1948; MEd, U. Houston, 1954. Cert. elem. tchr., tchr. of deaf, Tex.; lic. audiologist, Tex. Tchr. Aldine Schs., Houston, 1948-49, Spring Br. Schs., Houston, 1949-50, Victoria (Tex.) Schs., 1950-51, Pasadena (Tex.) Schs., 1951-55, Corpus Christie (Tex.) Schs., 1955-58; supr., dir. children's programs Speech and Hearing Inst., Houston, 1958-73; asst. prof. Speech and Hearing Inst. U. Tex., Houston, 1973-76, ret. Co-author (2 chpts. in book) Language and Learning of the Preacademic Child, 1985. Mem. Gov.'s Commn. for Women, Austin, 1983-86; mem. adv. coun. Coll. Edn., U. Tex., 1988—, chmn. centennial celebration, 1991; treas. Tex. Dem. Women (Outstanding Mem. 1992, chair fedn. conv. nat. Fedn. Dem. Women 1993); mem. U. Tex. Nursing Sch. Coun., 1999—, U. Tex. Adv. Coun. Athletics Found., 2002—. Recipient Disting. Alumni award Coll. of Edn. Univ. Tex., 1991. Mem. AAUW, Am. Speech and Hearing Assn., Tex. Speech and Hearing Assn. (sec. 1955-56, hon. award

1985), Tex. Speech-Lang.-Hearing Found. (pres. 1992-94), Senate Ladies Club (pres. 1983). Unitarian Universalist. Avocations: politics, educational opportunities through travel. Home: Apt 125 4100 Jackson Ave Austin TX 78731-6033

MAX, CLAIRE ELLEN, physicist; b. Boston, Sept. 29, 1946; d. Louis William and Pearl (Bernstein) M.; m. Jonathan Arons, Dec. 22, 1974; 1 child, Samuel. AB, Harvard U., 1968; PhD, Princeton U., 1972. Postdoctoral rschr. U. Calif., Berkeley, 1972-74; physicist Lawrence Livermore (Calif.) Nat. Lab., 1974—; dir. Livermore br. Inst. Geophysics and Planetary Physics, 1984-93, dir. univ. rels., 1993-2000; assoc. dir. Ctr. for Adaptive Optics, U. Calif., Santa Cruz, 2000—. Mem. Math.-Sci. Network Mills Coll., Oakland, Calif.; mem. com. on fusion hybrid reactors NRC, 1986, mem. com. on internat. security and arms control NAS, 1986-89, mem. com. on phys. sci., math. and applications NRC, 1991-94, mem. policy and computational astrophys. panels, astron. and astgrophys. survey NRC, 1989-91; mem. sci. steering com. W.M. Keck Obs., 1992-96, mem. adaptive optics sci. team, 1994—; mem. vis. com. Space Telescope Sci. Inst., 1996-2000, Hubble Space Telescope Second Decade Com., 1998-2000. Editor: Particle Acceleration Mechanisms in Astrophysics, 1979; contbr. numerous articles to sci. jours. Fellow AAAS (coun. rep. physics sect. 2001—), Am. Phys. Soc. (exec. com. divsn. plasma physics 1977, 81-82); mem. Am. Astron. Soc. (exec. com. divsn. high energy astrophysics 1975-76), Am. Geophys. Union, Internat. Astron. Union, Phi Beta Kappa, Sigma Xi. Achievements include rsch. on adaptive optics and laser guide stars for astronomy; astrophys. plasmas. Office: Lawrence Livermore Nat Lab PO Box 808 7000 East Ave # L413 Livermore CA 94550-9516 E-mail: max1@llnl.gov.

MAXFIELD, LOUISA FONDA GRIBBLE, executive secretary; b. Waco, TX, Sept. 27, 1924; d. Theodore Miles and Louise Irwin Gribble; m. Jack G.S. Maxfield, July 21, 1951 (dec.); children: Martha Woodson Maxfield Cottingham, Elizabeth Fonda. BA, Randolph-Macon Woman's Coll., 1945; M Liberal Arts, So. Meth. U., 1982. Editor, indsl. house organ Gen. Tire & Rubber Co., Waco, Tex., 1945—51; bus. mgr. Maxfield Clin./Hosp., Dallas, 1976—84, Covenant Presbyn. ch., Carrollton, Tex., 1984—99.

MAXFIELD, MARY CONSTANCE, management consultant; b. Washington, Mar. 16, 1949; d. Orville Eldred and Rose Mary (Stiarwalt) Maxfield; m. Robert Charles Kneip III, Aug. 21, 1971 (div. Apr. 1981); 1 child, Stephanie Alexandra; m. Richard Howard Cowles, May 16, 1981 (dec.); m. Phillip Walker, July 25, 1985 (div. June 1991); m. Michael Lee Beeman, Sept. 28, 2002. BA in History and Spanish, Va. Tech., 1970; MS in Occupl. Tech., U. Houston, 1996. Clk.-typist HEW, Social Security Adminstrn., New Orleans, 1971—72, svc. rep., 1972-73; mgmt. analyst Office Comptroller of Currency Treasury Dept., Washington, 1974-77, dir. mgmt. analysis divsn. U.S. Customs New Orleans, 1978-80, mgmt. analyst Houston, 1980-81, program analyst, 1981-82, chief data processing br., 1982-83, chief mgmt. analysis br., 1983-85, pres. Constance Walker Assocs., Inc., 1985-91, Maxfield Productivity Cons., Inc., 1991—; co-founder Inspired Learning Adventures, L.C., 2002; founder, pres. Anam Cara (handmade jewelry), 2002. Co-founder Supplier Registry; co-designer Kitchen 101 CD-ROm learning program. Author (with others): Team Approach to Problem Solving, 1991; author: Quality School Facilitator Training, 1992, Interpersonal Communications Skills, 1992, Introduction to Total Quality Schools, 1992, Tex. Leadership Ctr. DuPont LDP Tng., TQM Module, 1999, Total Quality Management, 1999, Strengthening Team Development, 1995, Internal Auditing to ISO 9000 Standards, 1995, Essential Facilitation Skills, 2000, Personnel Management in Food Service, 1995, Successfully Leading Change, 1996, Leading Change Through Site-Based Teams, 1996, Quality Tools 101, 1996, Introduction to ISO 9000, 1999, Benchmarking, 1999, Advanced Facilitation Skills, 2000, Developing and Evaluating Training, 2000, Presentation Skills for Change Agents, 2000, Successfully Managing Projects, 2001, Coaching for Performance, 2001, Everyday Creativity, 2001, Appreciative Inquiry, 2001, Kitchen 101, 2002, Conducting Value Added Assessments, 2002, Child Nutrition Course New Managers Playbook, 2004; contbr. numerous articles to profl. jours. Named Customs Woman of Yr., U.S. Customs, 1979, Fed. Exec. Bd. Woman of Yr., 1979, Cora Bell Wesley scholar, UDC, 1969; recipient Outstanding Performance award, 1979—85, Outstanding Svc. award, Office of Sec. of Treasury, 1976, Key to City, New Orleans, 1990. Mem. DAR, ASTD, Assn. Psychol. Type, Am. Soc. Quality, Assn. Quality and Participation (past pres. Houston chpt.), Treasury Hist. Assn., Daus. Rep. of Tex., Daus 1812, UDC, Va. Tech. Alumni Assn., Austin's Old 300 (founding), Delta Zeta. Episcopalian. Home and Office: Maxfield Productivity Cons Inc 8007 Liberty Elm Ct Spring TX 77379-6125

MAXMAN, SUSAN ABEL, architect; b. Columbus, Ohio, Dec. 30, 1938; d. Richard Jack Abel and Gussie (Brenner) Seiden; children: Andrew Frankel, Thomas Frankel, Elizabeth Frankel, Melissa, Abby, William Jr. Student, Smith Coll., 1960; MArch., U. Pa., 1977; HHD, Ball State U., 1993, U. Detroit Mercy, 1997. Registered profl. architect, Pa., Ohio, N.J., N.Y., Md., W.Va., Va., Maine, Mo., N.C., D.C. Project designer Kopple Sheward & Day, Phila., 1978-80; ptnr. Maxman & Sutphin, Phila., 1980-83; prin. Susan Maxman & Ptnrs., Phila., 1984—. Mem. bd. overseers Grad. Sch. Fine Arts U. Pa.; mem. corp. vis. com. MIT; bd. dirs. Found. Arch.; mem. Planning and Design Commn., Ga. Inst. Tech. Works include design of Women's Humane Soc. Animal Shelter, Bensalem, Pa. (Northeastern Sustainable Energy Assn.'s Comml. Bldg. award, 1994, Metal Constrn. Assn. award 1995, Gov.'s Award for Environ. Excellence 1997, AIA Pa. Hon. award 1997), Camp Tweedale-Freedom Valley Girl Scouts USA (AIA honor award, 1991), Cusano Environ. Edn. Ctr. at John Heinz Nat. Wildlife Refuge at Tinicum, Phila. (award) including U.S. Dept. Energy Fed. Energy Saver Showcase award, U.S. Dept. Interior Environ. Achievement award-,restoration Vernon House (honorable mention Remodeling Mag.), Germantown, Robert Lewis House (McArthur award 1985), Phila., Restoration Pennock Farmstead (Grand Prize Nat. Trust Historic Preservation 1995), Feasibility Study and Renovation of Old Main Pa. Hist. and Mus. Commn. Historic Preservation award, 1998, Kutztown U., Pa., sisters Servants of the Immaculate Heart of Mary Renovation of the Motherhouse (Mich. HIst. Preservation Network bldg. award 2003), Renovation of U. Pa. Nursing Edn. Bldg., Phila., Barbara C. Harris Camp and Conf. Ctr., Greenfield, N.H., Chestnut Hill Nat. Bank, Phila., Somerset (Pa.) Hist. Ctr., Seneca Rocks Visitor Ctr., Seneca Rocks, W.Va., Fort Necessity/Nat. Rd. Interpretive Edn. Ctr., Farmington, Pa., The Woods Residence Hall at Pa. State-Berks, Reading, others. Mem. Eco-Efficiency Task Force Pres. Coun. Sustainable Devel.; past chair Environ. Coun., Urban Land Inst.; mem. trustee's coun. for Pa. Women, U. Pa. Recipient Disting. Dau. Pa. award Gov. Tom Ridge, 1995, Excellence citation Engring. News Record, Shattering the Glass Ceiling award Women's Nat. Dem. Club, Mayor's commendation City Phila., citation Pa. Ho. Reps., Gov.'s award Environ. Excellence, 1997; named to Pa. Honor Roll of Women, Pa. Commn. for Women, 1996, named 1 of Pa.'s Best 50 Women in Bus. 1996. Mem. AIA (nat. pres. 1993, Pa. chpt. Honor award 1997), Pa. Women's Forum, Forum Exec. Women, Carpenter's Co. Phila. Avocations: swimming, gardening, sailing. Office: 1600 Walnut St Fl 2D Philadelphia PA 19103-5405

MAXSON, LINDA ELLEN, biologist, educator; b. N.Y.C., Apr. 24, 1943; d. Albert and Ruth (Rosenfeld) Resnick; m. Richard Dey Maxson, June 13, 1964; 1 child, Kevin. BS in Zoology, San Diego State U., 1964, MA in Biology, 1966; PhD in Genetics, San Diego State U./U. Calif., Berkeley, 1973. Instr. biology San Diego State U., 1966-68; tchr. gen. sci. San Diego Unified Sch. Dist., 1968-69; instr. biochemistry U. Calif., Berkeley, 1974; asst. prof. zoology, dept. genetics and devel. U. Ill., Urbana-Champaign, 1974-76, asst. prof. dept. genetics, devel. and ecology, ethology & evolution, 1976-79, assoc. prof., 1979-84, prof., 1984-87, prof. ecology, ethology and evolution, 1987-88; prof., head dept. biology Pa. State U., State College, 1988-94; assoc. vice-chancellor acad. affairs/dean undergrad. acad. affairs, prof. ecology and evolutionary biology U. Tenn., Knoxville, 1995-97; dean Coll. Liberal Arts & Scis., prof. biol. scis. U. Iowa, Iowa City, 1997—. Exec. officer biology programs Sch. Life Scis., U. Ill., 1981-86, assoc. dir. acad. affairs, 1984-86, dir. campus honors program, 1985-88; vis. prof. ecology and evolutionary biology U. Calif., Irvine, 1988; mem. adv. panel rsch. tng. groups behavioral biol. scis. NSF, 1990-94. Author: Genetics: A Human Perspective, 3d edit., 1992; mem. editl. bd. Molecular Biology Evolution; exec. editor Biochem. Sys. & Ecology, 1993-2001; contbr. numerous articles to scientific jours. Recipient Disting. Alumni award San Diego State U., 1989, Disting. Herpetologist award Herpetologists' League, 1993. Fellow: AAAS; mem.: Herpetologists League, Soc. Molecular Biology and Evolution (treas. 1992—94, sec. 1992—95), Soc. Study Evolution, Soc. for Study of Amphibians and Reptiles (pres. 1991), Am. Men and Women in Sci., Phi Beta Kappa. Office: U Iowa 240 Schaeffer Hall Iowa City IA 52242-1409 E-mail: linda-maxson@uiowa.edu.

MAXWELL, CARLA LENA, dancer, choreographer, educator; b. Glendale, Calif., Oct. 25, 1945; d. Robert and Victoria (Carbone) Maxwell. Student, Bennington Coll., 1963-64; BS, Juilliard Sch. Music, 1967. Mem. Jose Limón Dance Co., N.Y.C., 1965, prin. dancer, 1969—, acting artistic dir., 1977-78, artistic dir., 1978—. Lectr., tchr. in field. Dancer soloist Louis Falco Dance Co., 1967—71, Harkness Festival at Delacorte Theater, N.Y.C., 1964—, artist-in-residence Gettysburg Coll., 1970—, Luther Coll., Decorah, Iowa, 1971—, U. Idaho, 1973—, choreographer Function, 1970—, Improvisations on a Dream, 1970—, A Suite of Psalms, 1973—, Homage to José Linón, Place Spirit, 1975, Aadvark Brothers: Schwartz and Columbo Present Please Don't Stone the Clowns, 1975, Blue Warrior, 1975, Sonata, 1980, Keeping Still Mountain, 1987, dancer toured East and West Africa, 1969. Recipient Dance Mag. award, 1995; N.Y. State Cultural Coun. grantee, 1971. Home: 7 Great Jones St New York NY 10012-1135 Office: Jose Limon Dance Fedn 611 Broadway Fl 9 New York NY 10012-2608

MAXWELL, DOROTHEA BOST ANDREWS, volunteer; b. Greenville, Ill., Apr. 20, 1911; d. Samuel Washington and Viola Maud (Bost) Andrews; m. Richard Wesley Maxwell, June 1, 1935; children: Andrea Judith Maxwell Platz, Anne Dorothea Maxwell Walsh. BA with honors, diploma in piano, Greenville Coll., 1933; MusM, Northwestern U., 1937. Cert. primary and secondary tchr., music tchr., Mo. Dir. sch. music Spring Arbor (Mich.) Jr. Coll., 1933-34; tutor orthopedic handicapped children St. Louis Pub. Schs., 1950-56. Tour guide Mo. Bot. Garden, St. Louis, 1975—87; pres. The Wednesday Club St. Louis, 1983—85, archivist, 1985—92; guide tours of distinction St. Louis Symphony Soc., 1980—85; pres. Women's Assn., 2d Presbyn. Ch., St. Louis, 1956—58. Mem. Clan Maxwell Soc. U.S.A., Mo. Hist. Soc., St. Louis Genealogy Soc., Piano Club St. Louis, Washington U. Faculty women's Club, Mu Phi Epsilon. Republican. Congregationalist.

MAXWELL, JUDITH, think-tank executive, economist; b. Kingston, Ont., Can., July 21, 1943; d. James Ruffee and Marguerite Jane (Spanner) McMahon; m. Anthony Stirling Maxwell, May 8, 1970; children: David, Elizabeth Jane. B in Commerce, Dalhousie U., 1963, LLD, 1991; postgrad., London Sch. Econs., 1965-66; LLD, Queen's U., 1992. Researcher Combines Investigation Br. Consumer and Corp. Affairs, Ottawa, Can., 1963-65; econs. writer, mem. editorial bd. Fin. Times, Montreal, Que., Can., 1966-72; dir. policy studies C.D. Howe Inst., Montreal, 1972-80; cons. Esso Europe Inc., London, Eng., 1980-82, Coopers & Lybrand, Montreal, Que., 1982-85; chmn. Econ. Council Can., Ottawa, Ont., 1985-92; exec. dir. Queen's-U. Ottawa Econ. Projects, 1992—. Dir. Can. Found. for Econ. Edn., 1985-88, Inst. for Rsch. on Pub. Policy, 1987-88. Author: Energy From the Arctic, 1973; (with C. Pestieau) Economic Realities of Contemporary Confederation, 1980; (with S. Currie) Partnership for Growth: Corporate University Education in Canada, 1984. Active Ont. Premier's Coun., 1988-90, Nfld. and Labrador Sci. and Tech. Adv. Coun., 1988-90. Mem. Can. Assn. Bus. Econs. (pres. 1976-77), Montreal Econs. Assn. (pres. 1975-76). Office: Canadian Policy Rsch Networks 600-250 Albert St K1P 6M1 Ottawa ON Canada Office Phone: 567 7500.

MAXWELL, MARY ELLEN, school system administrator; Grad., St. Mary's Acad., 1961, N.C. Sch. Bds. Assn. Acad. Ret. child devel. adminstr. U.S. Naval Security Group Activity N.W., Chesapeake, Va.; chmn., mem. at large Currick County Bd. Edn., 1982—. Chairperson Currituck County Alcohol and Drug Task Force; bd. dirs. Colonial Coast Girl Scouts Coun.; mem. Edn. and Tng. Voluntary Partnership; active Albemarle Hopeline, Currituck County Relay for Life. Mem.: Nat. Coun. for the Accreditation of Tchr. Edn. (mem. exec. com.), Nat. Sch. Bds. Assn. (former pres. bd. dirs.), N.C. Sch. Bds. Assn. (bd. dirs.), Nat. Bd. for Profl. Tchg. Stds. (bd. mem.), Moyock Woman's Club, Currituck Christian Women's Club.

MAXWELL, MAUREEN KAY, media specialist, educator; d. William J. and Sylvia A. Maxwell. BA in History, MS Agr. and Resources Econs., Colo. State U. Legislative aide and press sec. U.S. Rep. Patricia Schroeder, Washington, 1982—90; asst. dir., population program The Wilderness Soc., 1993—96; sr. pub. rels. specialist Am. Acad. Family Physicians, 1998 Instr. self def. D.C. Self Def. Karate Assn., 1998—2003; chair D.C. Impact, 2003, bd. mem., 2000—03. Recipient Pillar of the School award, D.C. Self Def. Karate Assn., 2002. Mem.: Nat. Press Club. Avocations: writing, photography, reading, martial arts, travel. Office: Am Acad Family Physicians 2021 Massachusetts Ave NW Washington DC 20036 E-mail: mmaxwell@aafp.org.

MAXWELL-BROGDON, FLORENCE MORENCY, school administrator, educational consultant; b. Spring Park, Minn., Nov. 11, 1929; d. William Frederick and Florence Ruth (LaBrie) Maxwell; m. John Carl Brogdon, Mar. 13, 1957; children: Carole Alexandra, Cecily Ann, Daphne Diana. BA, Calif. State U., L.A., 1955; MS, U. So. Calif., 1957; postgrad., Columbia Pacific U., San Rafael, Calif., 1982-86. Cert. tchr., Calif. Dir. Rodeo Sch., L.A., 1961-64; lectr. Media Features, Culver City, Calif., 1964—; dir. La Playa Sch., Culver City, Calif., 1968-75; founding dir. Venture Sch., Culver City, Calif., 1974—, also chmn. bd. dirs. Bd. dirs., v.p. Parent Coop. Preschools, Baie d'Urfe Que., Can., 1964—; del. to Ednl. Symposium, Moscow-St. Petersburg, 1992, U.S./China Joint Conf. on Edn., Beijing, 1992, Internat. Confedn. of Prins., Geneva, 1993, Internat. Conf., Berlin, 1994, Internat. Confedn. of Sch. Prins., Helsinki, Finland, 2000, Edinburgh, Scotland, 2003. Author: Let Me Tell You, 1973, Wet'n Squishy, 1973, Balancing Act, 1977, (as Morency Maxwell) Framed in Silver, 1985; (column) What Parents Want to Know, 1961—; editor: Calif. Preschooler, 1961-74; contbr. articles to profl. jours. Treas. Dem. Congl. Primary, Culver City, 1972. Mem. NASSP, Calif. Coun. Parent Schs. (bd. dirs. 1961-74), Parent Coop. Preschs. Internat. (advisor 1975—), Pen Ctr. USA West, Mystery Writers of Am. (affiliate), Internat. Platform Assn. Liberatarian. Home: 10814 Molony Rd Culver City CA 90230-5451 Office: Venture Sch 11477 Jefferson Blvd Culver City CA 90230-6115 E-mail: morencee@aol.com.

MAY, AVIVA RABINOWITZ, music educator, linguist, musician; b. Tel Aviv; naturalized, 1958; d. Samuel and Paula Pessia (Gordon) Rabinowitz (div.); children: Chelley Mosoff, Alan May, Risa McPherson, Ellanna May/Gassman. AA, Oakton C.C., 1977; BA in Piano Pedagogy, Northeastern Ill. U., 1978. Folksinger, educator, musican Aviva May Studio/Piano and Guitar, 1948—; Sunday sch. dir. Canton (Ohio) Synagogue, 1952-54; nursery sch. tchr. Allentown (Pa.) Jewish Cmty. Ctr., 1954-56; Hebrew music tchr. Brith Shalom Cmty. Ctr., Bethlehem, Pa., 1954-62; Hebrew tchr. Beth Hillel Congregation, Wilmette, Ill., 1964-83; tchr. B'nai Mitzva, 1978; music dir. McCormick Health Ctrs., Chgo., 1978-79, Cove Sch. Perceptually Handicapped Children, Evanston, 1978-79; prof. Hebrew and Yiddish, Spertus Coll. Judaica, Chgo., 1980-89; Hebrew tchr. Anshe Emet Day Sch., 1989—, West Suburban Temple Har Zion, Oak Park, Ill., 1993—; music studio tchr. Cosmopolitan Sch., Chgo., 1992—. Tchr. continuing edn. Northeastern Ill. U., 1978-80, Niles Twp. Jewish Congregation, 1993—, also Jewish Cmty. Ctrs.; with Office Spl. Investigations, Dept. Justice, Washington; music dir. Temple Emanuel Rosenwald Sch. Composer classical music for piano, choral work, folk songs; developer 8-hour system for learning piano or guitar; contbr. articles to profl. jours. Recipient Magen David Adom Pub. Svc. award 1973; grantee Ill. State, 1975-79, Ill. Congressman Woody Bowman, 1978-79. Mem. Music Tchrs. Nat. Assn., Ill. Music Tchrs. Assn., Organ and Piano Tchrs. Assn., Am. Coll. Musicians, Ill. Assn. Learning Disabilities, North Shore Music Tchrs. Assn. (charter mem., co-founder), Sherwood Sch. Music, Friends of Holocaust Survivers, Nat. Yiddish Book Exch., Nat. Ctr. for Jewish Films, Chgo. Jewish Hist. Soc., Oakton C.C. Alumni Assn., Northeastern Ill. U. Alumni Assn. Democrat. Office: Aviva May Studio 410 S Michigan Ave Ste 920 Chicago IL 60605-1471 Office Phone: 773-348-8700. E-mail: arm801@aol.com.

MAY, DAWN ARLENE, counseling administrator; b. Owosso, Mich., Mar. 23, 1973; d. Ronald Robert Forcde and Donna Marie Schuyler; m. Christopher Allan May, Apr. 17, 1999; children: Christopher Allan, Jalen Isaiah. BS, Grand Valley State U., 1995; M in Counseling, We. Mich. U., 2000. Youth counselor St. John's Home, Grand Rapids, Mich., 1995—99, house mgr., 1999—2001, clin. case mgr., 2001—02, program dir., 2002—. Mem.: Am. Assn. Marriage and Family Therapy. Avocations: scrapbooks, softball, exercise. Home: 1945 Hollow Creek Dr SE Caledonia MI 49316 Office: St Johns Home 2355 Knapp St Grand Rapids MI 49505

MAY, ELAINE, actress, theatre and film director; b. Phila., Apr. 21, 1932; d. Jack Berlin; m. Marvin May (div.); 1 child, Jeannie Berlin; m. Sheldon Harnick, Mar. 25, 1962 (div. May 1963). ed. high sch., studied Stanislavsky method of acting withMarie Ouspenskaya. Stage and radio appearances as child actor; performed with Playwright's Theatre, in student performance Miss Julie, U. Chgo.; appeared with improvisational theatre group in night club The Compass, Chgo., 1954-1957, (with Mike Nichols) appeared N.Y. supper clubs, Village Vanguard, Blue Angel, also night clubs other cities; TV debut on Jack Paar Show, 1957; also appeared in Omnibus, 1958, Dinah Shore Show, Perry Como Show, Laugh Line, Laugh-In, TV spls.; comedy albums include Improvisations to Music, An Evening with Mike Nichols and Elaine May, Mike Nichols and Elaine May Examine Doctors; weekly appearance NBC radio show Nightline; appeared (with Mike Nichols) NBC radio show, N.Y. Town Hall, 1959, An Evening with Mike Nichols and Elaine May, Golden Theatre, N.Y.C., 1960-61; theater appearances include The Office, N.Y.C., 1966, Who's Afraid of Virginia Woolf?, Long Wharf Theatre, New Haven, Conn., 1980; dir. plays The Third Ear, N.Y.C., 1964, The Goodbye People, Berkshire Theater Festival, Stockbridge, Mass., 1971, various plays at Goodman Theatre, Chgo., 1983; dir., author screenplay, actress film A New Leaf, 1972; dir. films The Heartbreak Kid, 1973, Mikey and Nicky, 1976 (writer, dir. remake 1985), Ishtar, 1987 (also writer); appeared in films Luv, 1967, California Suite, 1978 (Acad. award Best Supporting Actress 1978), In The Spirit, 1990; co-author screenplay Heaven Can Wait, 1978, Birdcage, 1996, Primary Colors, 1998; author plays A Matter of Position, 1962, Not Enough Rope, 1962, Adaptation, 1969, Hot Line, 1983, Better Part of Valor, 1983, Mr. Gogol and Mr. Preen, 1991, (one act) Death Defying Acts, 1995; stage revue: (with Mike Nichols) Telephone, 1984; co-recipient (with Mike Nichols) Grammy award for comedy performance, Nat. Acad. Recording Arts & Scis., 1961; actress (film) Small Time Crooks, 2000. Office: care Julian Schlossberg Castle Hill Prodns Ste 1502 1414 Ave of the Americas New York NY 10019-2514

MAY, GEORGIANA, biologist, educator; PhD, U. Calif., Berkeley, 1987. Assoc. prof. dept. plant biology U. Minn., St. Paul. Contbr. articles to profl. jours. Recipient Alexopoulos prize Mycological Soc. Am., 1997. Achievements include research on the interactions of fungi with plants, evolution of fungal populations and their interactions with other organisms, evolution of gene structure and function in mating compatibility loci, determining the genetic basis of smut resistance in maize, the impact of agricultural practice on host/pathogen interactions. Office: U Minn Dept Plant Biology 220 Biological Sci Ctr 1445 Gortner Ave Saint Paul MN 55108 Fax: 612-625-1738. E-mail: gmay@maroon.tc.umn.edu.

MAY, GITA, language educator, literature educator; b. Brussels, Sept. 16, 1929; came to U.S., 1947, naturalized, 1950; d. Albert and Blima (Sieradska) Jochimek; m. Irving May, Dec. 21, 1947. BA magna cum laude, CUNY-Hunter Coll., 1953; MA, Columbia U., 1954, PhD, 1957. Lectr. French CUNY-Hunter Coll., 1953-56; from instr. to assoc. prof. Columbia U., N.Y.C., 1956—68, prof., 1968—, chmn., 1983-93, mem. senate, 1979-83, 86-88, chmn. Seminar on 18th Century Culture, 1986-89. Lecture tour English univs., 1965 Author: Diderot et Baudelaire, critiques d'art, 1957, De Jean-Jacques Rousseau à Madame Roland: essai sur la sensibilité préromantique et révolutionnaire, 1964, Madame Roland and the Age of Revolution, 1970 (Van Amringe Disting. Book award), Stendhal and the Age of Napoleon, 1977, Encyclopedia of Aesthetics, 1998, Dictionnaire de Diderot, 1999, French Women Writers, 1991, The Feminist Encyclopedia of French Literature, 1999; co-editor: Diderot Studies III, 1961; mem. editl. bd. 18th Century Studies, 1975-78, French Rev., 1975-86, 98—, Romanic Rev., 1959—, Women in French Studies, 2000—; contbg. editor: Oeuvres complètes de Diderot, 1984, 95; gen. editor: The Age of Revolution and Romanticism: Interdisciplinary Studies, 1990—, extensive essays on Diderot and George Sand in European Writers, 1984, 85, and on Rebecca West, Anita Brookner and Graham Swift in British Writers, 1996, 97, 99, Bayle, Fontenelle and Fénelon in Dictionary of Literary Biography, 2003, Voltaire's Candide (in Barnes and Noble Classics), 2003; contbr. articles and revs. to profl. jours. Decorated chevalier and officier Ordre des Palmes Acad.; recipient award Am. Coun. Learned Socs., 1961, award for outstanding achievement CUNY-Hunter Coll., 1963; named Outstanding Mentor, Women in French, 2003; Fulbright rsch. grantee, 1964-65; Guggenheim fellow, 1964-65, NEH fellow, 1971-72. Mem. AAUP, MLA (del. assembly 1973-75, mem. com. rsch. activities 1975-78, mem. exec. coun. 1980-83), Am. Assn. Tchrs. of French, Am. Soc. 18th Century Studies (pres. 1985-86, 2nd v.p. 1983-84, 1st v.p. 1984-85, One of Gt. Tchrs. award 1999, Outstanding Mentor), Soc. Française d'Etude du Dix-Huitième Siècle, Soc. Diderot, Am. Soc. French Acad. Palms, Soc. des Etudes Staëliennes, N.Am. Soc. for the Study of Jean-Jacques Rousseau, Soc. des Professeurs Français et Francophones d'Amérique, Phi Beta Kappa. Office: Columbia U Dept French/Romance Philol 516 Philosophy Hall MC4918 New York NY 10027 Business E-Mail: gm9@columbia.edu.

MAY, MARGRETHE, health educator; b. Tucson, Ariz., Oct. 6, 1943; d. Robert A. and Margrethe (Holm) M. BS in Human Biology, U. Mich., 1970, MS in Anatomy, 1986. Cert. surg. technologist. Surg. technologist Hartford (Conn.) Hosp., 1965-68, U. Mich. Hosps., Ann Arbor, 1968-70; asst. operating room supr. U. Ariz. Med. Ctr., Tucson, 1971-72; coord. operating room tech. program Pima Coll., Tucson, 1971-76; prof., coord. surg. tech. and surg. first asst. programs Delta Coll., University Center, Mich., 1978—99, coord., surg. first asst. distance edn. program, 1999—2003, coord. surg. tech. program, 2003—. Commr. Commn. on Accreditation of Allied Health Ednl. Programs, Chgo., 1994-97, Coun. Accreditation and Unit Recognition, 1994-96. Editor: Core Curriculum for Surgical Technology, 3d edit., 1990, Core Curriculum for Surgical First Assisting, 1993; contbr. articles to profl. jours. Mem. Assn. Surg. Technologists (bd. dirs. 1987-89, pres.-elect 1989-90, pres. 1990-91, on-site visitor program accreditation 1974—, chmn. exam writing com. 1981, liaison coun. on cert. co-chmn. 1977, chmn. 1978, sec.-treas. 1979, chmn. accreditation review com for edn. in surg. tech. 1994-97, Mich. state assembly AST bd. dirs. 2000—), Am. Soc. Law, Medicine and Ethics, Mich. Assn. Allied Health Professions (sec. 1994-97), Nat. Network Health Career Programs in

Two-Year Colls. Avocation: international health care issues and allied health education. Home: 2506 Abbott Rd Apt P-2 Midland MI 48642-4876 Office: Delta Coll Health And Wellness Divsn University Center MI 48710-0001 E-mail: mmay@alpha.delta.edu.

MAY, PHYLLIS JEAN, financial executive; b. Flint, Mich., May 31, 1932; d. Bert A. (dec.) and Alice C. (Rushton) Irvine; m. John May, Apr. 24, 1971 (dec. 1997). Grad., Dorsey Sch. Bus., 1957; cert., Internat. Corr. Schs., 1959, Nat. Tax Inst., 1978; MBA, Mich. U., 1970. Registered real estate agt; lic. life, auto and home ins. agent. Office mgr. Comml. Constrn. Co., Flint, 1962-68; bus. mgr. new and used car dealership Flint, 1968-70; contr. various corps., 1970-75; fiscal dir. Rubicon Odyssey Inc., Detroit, 1976-87, Wayne County Treas.'s Office, 1987-93; exec. fin. office Grosse Pointe Meml. Ch., 1993—. Acad. cons. acctg. Detroit Inst. Commerce, 1980-81; pres. small bus. specializing in adminstrv. cons. and acctg., 1982—; supr. mobile svc. stat., upholstery and home improvement businesses; owner retail bus. Pieces and Things. Pres. PTA Westwood Heights Schs., 1972; vol. Fedn. of Blind, 1974-76, Probate Ct., 1974-76; mem. citizens adv. bd. Northville Regional Psychiat. Hosp., 1988, sec., 1989-90; pres. La'Renaissance Condominium Assn., Atlantic City, N.J., 1996-2000, sec., 2000-02, 2004. Recipient Meritorious Svc. award Genesee County for Youth, 1976, Excellent Performance and High Achievement award Odyssey Inc., 1981. Mem. NAFE (bd. dirs.), Am. Bus. Women's Assn. (treas. 1981, rec. sec. 1982, v.p. 1982-83, Woman of Yr. 1982), Womens Assn. Dearborn Orch. Soc., Dearborn Community Art Ctr., Mich. Mental Health Assn., Internat. Platform Assn., Guild of Carillonneurs in N.Am., Pi Omicron (officer 1984-85, treas. 2002—). Presbyterian.

MAYBERRY, MARILYN MARIE, community outreach advocate-mediator; b. Whittier, Calif., Sept. 8, 1940; d. Michael Marius Mayberry and Alice Gayle Olson; m. Jock Andrews, May, 1959 (div. 1970); children: Mari Amelia, Dawn Evangeline, Katrina Inez, Gwendolen Gayle, Ethan Michael. Degree in sociology, Ft. Lewis Coll., Durango, Colo., 1996. Patient support advocate, burn ward Fitzsimmons Army Hosp., Denver, 1976-72; primary counselor Trained Colo. Gen. Sch. Medicine, Durango, 1969—; advocate-mediator (rape, sexual abuse, domestic violence) various cities, 1980—. Active ADA compliance-phys., Barrier Busters, Durango, 1990—, South Durango Neighborhood Assn., 1993—; active in pub. transp., welfare reform, women's occupl. health issues, Durango, 1980—. Mem. AAUW, NOW, Am. Legion Aux. Democrat. Unitarian Universalist. Avocations: gardening, youth tutoring and enrichment. Home and Office: 6173 W 10150 N Highland UT 84003-3418

MAYDEN, BARBARA MENDEL, lawyer; b. Chattanooga, Sept. 18, 1951; d. Eugene Lester Mendel and Blanche (Krugman) Rosenberg; m. Martin Ted Mayden, Sept. 14, 1986. AB, Ind. U., 1973; JD, U. Ga., 1976. Bar: Ga. 1976, N.Y. 1980. Assoc. King & Spalding, Atlanta, 1976-79, Willkie Farr & Gallagher, N.Y.C., 1980, Morgan Lewis & Bockius, N.Y.C., 1980-82, White & Case, N.Y.C., 1982-89; spl. counsel Skadden, Arps, Slate, Meagher & Flom, N.Y.C., 1989-95; mem. Bass, Berry & Sims PLC, Nashville, 1996—; lectr. Vanderbilt U. Sch. Law, Nashville, 1995-97. Mem. bd. visitors U. Ga. Sch. Law, Athens, 1986—89; mem. Leadership Nashville, 1999—2000; mem. adv. bd. Women's Fund of the Cmty. Found. of Mid. Tenn., 2001—; bd. dirs. YWCA, 2001—, Jewish Cmty. Ctr., 2001—02. Fellow Am. Bar Found. (life); mem. ABA (chair young lawyers divsn. 1985-86, ho. of dels. 1986—, commr. commn. on women 1987-91, commr. commn. opportunities for minorities in profession 1986-87, select com. of the house 1989-91, chmn. assembly resolutions com. 1990-91, membership com. of the house 1991-92, bd. govs. 1991-94, chair com. on rules and calendar 1996-98, chair bd. govs. ops. com., exec. com. 1993-94, task force long range fin. planning 1993-94, com. scope correlation of work 1998-2003, chair 2001-02, sec. bus. law sect. 2001-02, vice-chair 2002-03, chair-elect 2003-04), Nat. Assn. Bond Lawyers (bd. dirs. 1985-86), Bond Attys.' Workshop (chmn. 1986), N.Y. State Bar Assn. (ho. of dels. 1993-95), Assn. of Bar of City of N.Y. (internat. human rights com. 1986-89, 2d century com. 1986-90, com. women in the profession, 1989-92), N.Y. County Lawyers Assn. (com. spl. projects, chair com. rels with other bars), Am. Law Inst. Democrat. Jewish. Home: 4414 Herbert Pl Nashville TN 37215-4544 Office: Bass Berry & Sims PLC 315 Deaderick St Ste 2700 Nashville TN 37238-0002 E-mail: bmayden@bassberry.com.

MAYE, S. ELIZABETH BETH, artist, small business owner; d. James McKee Robinson and Patricia Dougherty MacGuigan; m. Chris Maye, Feb. 19, 1993; children: Jessica, Jack, Abigail, Charlie. BA, U. Okla., 1992. Reporter Ottawa (Can.) Sun Newspaper, 1993; contract editor Can. Parliament, Ottawa, 1994; field rep. Scholastic Book Fairs, Okla. City, 1996—98; journalist Okla. Bus. Jour., Okla. City, 1998—99; roster artist in residence Okla. Arts Coun., Okla. City, 1998—; prin., owner SEMantics, Inc., Okla., 1998—; instr. English No. Okla. Coll., Enid, 2003—. Alumni dir. Westminster Sch., Okla. City, 2000—03, mem. devel. bd. Author: So Many Questions, 2000, The Marble, 2001; editor: Everyone Hurts, Everyone Heals, 2002. Vol. Am. Jr. Leagues, Inc., Okla. City, 1997—2000; nursery organizer Our Lady's Cathedral, Okla. City, 1995—98. Recipient Artist's Recognition award, Dollie Smith Cancer Ctr., 1998. Mem.: Okla. Writers Fedn. Inc. Avocations: motherhood, reading, walking, running, water-skiing. Office: 2721 NW 153d St Edmond OK 73013

MAYER, BEATRICE CUMMINGS, civic worker; b. Montreal, P.Q., Can., Aug. 15, 1921; came to U.S., 1939, naturalized, 1944; d. Nathan and Ruth (Kellert) Cummings; BA in Chemistry, U. N.C., 1943; postgrad. U. Chgo., 1946; LHD (hon.)1991, Spertus Coll. Judaica, 1983, Kenyon Coll., 1987; m. Robert Bloom Mayer, Dec. 11, 1947 (dec.); children: Robert N., Mrs. Ruth M. Durchslag. Mem. vis. com. Sch. Social Svc. Adminstrn. U. Chgo., 1964—, dept. art, 1972—; dir. women's bd., 1973—, Art Inst. Chgo. (life trustee) 1984—; bd. dirs. Michael Reese Hosp. Corp., Chgo., 1974-1982—, bd. dirs. Spoleto Festival, 1980—1989; trustee Kenyon Coll., Gambier, Ohio, 1976-89, trustee emritus, 1989—; bd. fellows Brandeis U., Waltham, Mass., 1977—;trustee Anshe Emet Synagogue, Chgo., 1974—1990, (life trustee 1990-); trustee Mus. Contemporary Art, Chgo., 1974—1990, (life trustee 1990-); mem. adv. com. U.N.C. Ackland Mus. visiting com.1985-, Recipient Brandeis U. Disting. Community Service award, 1972, medallion Am. Jewish Com. Human Rights, 1976, Outstanding Achievement award in the Arts, YWCA Met. Chgo., 1979, Centennial Gold Medal for Disting. Community Service Jewish Theol. Sem., 1986, Alumni Laureate award Loyola Coll. Balt., 1984; named to Hall of Fame, Jewish Community Ctrs. Adult Services, 1987, Rosary Coll. Bravo award in Art, 1994, U. Chic. Alumni Nation award, 2001, Jewish Council on Urban Affairs Cmty. Svc. award, 2002.; Clubs: Tavern, Standard (Chgo.); Lake Shore Country (Glencoe, Ill.). Home: 160 E Pearson St # 3103 Chicago IL 60611-2148

MAYER, EVE ORLANS, retired public relations and marketing consultant, writer; b. Bklyn., Apr. 26, 1930; d. Abraham Salem Orlans and Rose V. Wissotsky; m. Sidney A. Mayer, Jun. 8, 1952; children: Marc Orlans Mayer and Jonathan Orlans Mayer. BA cum laude, Hunter Coll., 1951; MS, Columbia Univ., 1952. Asst. editor Human Interest Mag., N.Y.C., 1952-53; asst. prodr. Channel 5, N.Y.C., 1953-54; publicity writer NYU, N.Y.C., 1954-57; freelance writer N.Y.C., 1957—; publ. rels. dir. Parsons Sch. of Design, N.Y.C., 1970-74, 1979-84; owner, prin. Eve Orlans Mayer, Inc., N.Y.C., 1984-92. Contbr. articles to newspapers and mags.; ghost writer, speech writer:, interviewer : Steven Spielberg's Survivors of the Shoah Visual History Found., 1993—2000. Bd. dirs. CARING at Columbia, Columbia U. Coll. Phys. and Surg., 1991—2000; mem. alumni exec. com. Columbia U. Grad. Sch. Journalism, 1995—; mem. Dem. Congl. Campaign Com., 1995—. Recipient Columbia U. Alumni medal, 2002. Mem. Hadassah Women's Zionist Orgn. Am., World Jewish Congress, Anti-Defamation League, Am. Jewish Congress, NARAL, NOW, Planned Parenthood, Choice in Dying, Hemlock Soc., Mother's Voices, Emily's List, Phi Beta Kappa, Sigma Tau Delta. Democrat. Jewish. Avocations: theater, travel, friends, books, music. Home: 15 W 81st St Apt 8A New York NY 10024-6022 E-mail: eveomayer@aol.com.

MAYER, JOYCE HARRIS, artist; b. New York City, May 7, 1935; d. Harold and Dorothy Harris; m. Bernard Charles Mayer, Mar. 15, 1969; 1 child, Robert Charles. AAS, Inst. of Applied Art and Sci., N.Y.C., 1957. Sketcher Merrylen Cartooning Studio, 1952. Client contact, layout artist, Haire Publ., N.Y.C., 1957-59; art dir., Real Estate Forum, N.Y.C., 1959-60; Denhard and Stewart, N.Y.C., 1960-67; Herb Lubalin Graphic Art Award, 1964; self employed N.Y.C., 1967-71; co curator, New Orleans Mus. of Art, 1985. Among first women to have work pub. in Art Direction, 1964, exhibitions include N.Y. Inst. of Applied Arts and Sci., New Orleans Mus. of Art, 2003, Horizon Gallery, Royal Typographers, N.Y., Nat. Arts Club, Tulane Univ., Dominican Coll., Robinson Gallery, Mario Villa and Arthur Roger, New Orleans, TWEED Gallery, Plainfield, N.J., Barbara Gillman Gallery, Miami, Contemporary Art Ctr., New Orleans, Bruce Mus., Conn., Represented in permanent collections paintings, mono prints, and digital photographs in numerous collections in Europe and. U.S., Digital La., Contemporary Art Ctr., New Orleans, 2002, Biennale Internazionale dell Arte Contemporanea, Florence, Italy, 2003, N.C. Mus. Art, numerous others. Mem. Bd. Edn., Greenwich, Conn., 1978; art advisor Freeport McMoRan Art Collection, New Orleans, 1985; curator Mario Villa Gallery, New Orleans, 1989; juror Arts Coun., New Orleans, 1990. Recipient N.Y. Graphic Soc. award, 1976, medal in photography, Florence Biennale, 2003. Coll. Art Assn. Avocations: reading, theater, ballet, birdwatching. Home: 8 Golfview Dr Medford NJ 08055 Address: 34 Castle Rock Branford CT 06405 Office Fax: 609-953-2390. E-mail: joycehmayer@aol.com.

MAYER, KAY MAGNOR, writer; b. 1943; d. Frank J. and Harriet (Schnell) Magnor; m. Kenneth W. Mayer, May 2, 1943; children: Michael J., Patricia A., Mark T. Student, Northwestern U., 1938-43. News reporter Tampa Times, 1943; advt. copywriter Marshall Field & Co., Chgo., Earle Ludgin & Co., Chgo.; Henri, Hurst & McDonald Chgo., 1944-58; spl. editor, writer Scott, Foresman & Co., Glenview, Ill., 1966-71; freelance writer Columbia, 1971—. Recipient Press Women's awards, 1983, 84, 85, 89, 92, 93, 98. Mem. Nat. Fedn. Press Women, Ill. Press Women, Western History Assn., Soc. Southwestern Authors (dir. 1981-83), The Writers (hon. mem.), Glencoe, Ill. Home: 1000 Applewood Dr # 185 Roswell GA 30076-1375

MAYER, KRISTINE I. small business owner, writer; b. Tulsa, Okla., Dec. 11, 1959; d. Harry W. and Eleanor M. (Westphal) Meeker; m. Heinz C. Mayer, Jan. 18, 1986 (div. 1995); children: Justin, Forrest. BA in journalism, Okla. State Univ., 1987; MS in counseling psych., Northeastern State Univ., 1991. Mental health counselor Mayer Counseling Svcs., Inc., Tulsa, 1991-96; child welfare specialist State of Okla. Dept. Human Svc., 1996—2000; profl. gun seller Broken Arrow, Okla., 2000—. Mem. Am. Counseling Assn., Okla. Scholar Leadership, Psi Chi. Avocations: travel, equestrian sports, history, music, theatre.

MAYER, MARILYN GOODER, steel company executive; b. Chgo. d. Seth MacDonald and Jean (McMullen) Gooder; m. William Anthony Mayer, Nov. 14, 1959; children: William Anthony Jr., Robert MacDonald. Grad., Career Inst., Chgo., 1941; student, Lake Forest Coll., Ill., 1942. Adminstrv. asst. Needham, Louis & Brorby, Chgo., 1949-53; v.p. RMB Corp., Chgo., 1963-71, Mayer Motors, Ft. Lauderdale, Fla., 1965-74, Gooder-Henrichsen, Chicago Heights, Ill., 1975—. Dir. Barnett Bank, West Palm Beach, Fla. Trustee Gulf Stream (Fla.) Sch.; trustee emeritus St. Andrew's Sch., Boca Raton, Fla.; bd. dirs. Bethesda Hosp. Assn., Boynton Beach, Fla., pres. 1981-82; bd. dirs. Gulf Stream Civic Assn. Mem. Soc. Four Arts, Little Bath and Tennis Club (gov. of Gulf Stream). Avocation: travel. Home: 2925 Polo Dr Delray Beach FL 33483-7331

MAYER, MONA R. music educator; b. Hobbs, N.Mex., Mar. 13, 1945; d. A. D. and Mary Louise Summerville; m. Gary Martin Mayer, July 2, 1965; 1 child, Heather L. MusB of Edn., Ea. N.Mex. U., 1968, M of Elem. Edn., 1971. Cert. tchr. N.Mex., Pa. Elem. music tchr. Clovis (N.Mex.) Mcpl. Schs., 1974—75; mid. sch. music tchr. Upper Perkiomen Mid. Sch., 1974—75; music tchr. K-8 St. Philip Neri Parochial Sch., East Greenville, Pa., 1986—89; h.s. choir dir., elem. music tchr. Bethlehem (Pa.) Area Sch. Dist., 1994—96; elem. music tchr. Clovis Mcpl. Schs., 1996—.

MAYER, ROSEMARY, artist; b. Ridgewood, N.Y., Feb. 27, 1943; d. Theodore Albert and Marie Anne (Stumpf) M. AB magna cum laude, U. Iowa, 1964; postgrad., Bklyn. Mus. Art Sch., 1964-65, Sch. of Visual Arts, N.Y.C., 1967-69. Model Raphael Soyer, N.Y.C., 1968-74; writer Arts Mag., N.Y.C., 1972-75, Art in Am., N.Y.C., 1974-75. Vis. artist many schs. including Hartwick Coll., Oneonta, N.Y., 1976, Art Inst., Chgo., 1974; guest artist Nat. Endowment Workshop, Tyler Sch. Art, Phila., Mpls. Acad. Art and Design, 1981; adj. lectr. La Guardia C.C., CUNY, 1992—; adj. prof. L.I. U., 1988—; writer, speaker A.I.R. Gallery, N.Y.C., 1972-74. Translator: Pontormo's Diary 1983; author: Swatches, 1969, Surroundings, 1977. Grantee numerous orgns. including NEA, CAPS, 1976—. Democrat. Home: 55 Leonard St New York NY 10013-2928

MAYER, SUSAN, telecommunications company executive; b. Providence, Feb. 15, 1950; d. Frederick Augustus and Margaret Patience (Elvin) Cluck; m. James Douglas Mayer, Sept. 4, 1976; children: Catherine Paige, Julia Christina. BA, Boston U., 1971; MBA, Harvard U., 1979. Social worker Mass. Dept. Pub. Welfare, Boston, 1973-75, project mgr., 1975-77; cons. Boston Cons. Group, Boston, Munich, 1979-83, mgr., 1983-86; v.p. Communications Satellite Corp., Washington, 1986-91; gen. mgr. Comsat Video Svcs., 1988-90; cons., 1991-93; sr. v.p. MCI Comms. Corp., 1993—; pres. Sky MCI, 1996-97, MCI WorldCom Venture Fund, 1998—. Bd. dirs. Caliber Learning Network, Inc., Rhythms NetConnections, Inc., STG, Inc., WAM!NET, Inc., Sta. WETA, Channel 26. Active Connelly Sch. of the Holy Child. Mem.: Harvard (Boston). Home: 12429 Rivers Edge Dr Potomac MD 20854-1069 Office: MCI WorldCom Venture Fund 1133 19th St NW Washington DC 20036-3604

MAYER, SUSAN LEE, nurse, educator; b. N.Y.C., Feb. 10, 1946; d. Hans and Frieda (Schein) Abramson; m. Steven Mayer, June 24, 1973; children: Jason, Stuart, Richard, Deborah. BSN, Hunter Coll., 1968; MA, NYU, 1974; EdD, Columbia U., 1996; postgrad., Yeshiva U., 1986, Adelphi U., 1987. RN, N.Y.; cert. in gerontology; cert. tchr., N.Y. Staff nurse ICU-CCU Montefiore Hosp., Bronx, N.Y., 1968; organizer CCU Jewish Meml. Hosp., N.Y.C., 1968; supr., adminstr. Morrisania City Hosp., N.Y.C., 1969-76; instr. Adelphi U., Garden City, N.Y., 1977-78; substitute nurse Great Neck (N.Y.) Pub. Schs., 1980-90; rsch. asst. to dean Adelphi U. Sch. Nursing, 1987-88; dir. ambulatory edn. North Bronx Healthcare Network, 2001—. Staff nurse Winthrop U. Hosp., Mineola, NY, 1987—90, per diem nurse, 1987—90; instr. dept. nursing edn. Bronx Mcpl. Hosp. Ctr. (now Jacobi Med. Ctr.), 1990—96; asst. prof. Helene Fuld Coll. Nursing, 1996—2001; adj. instr. Bronx C.C., 1992, Queensborough C.C., 1987—89; adj. asst. prof. Iona Coll. Sch. Nursing; adj. assoc. prof. Tchrs. Coll./Columbia U., 1997—; field nurse coord. RN Home Care Winthrop U. Hosp., Mineola, 1996—2001; lectr. and presenter in field. Contbr. articles to profl. jours. including Nursing and Health Care. Bd. dirs. Great Neck Synagogue, 1981-91, v.p. Sisterhood, 1978-79, pres., 1979-81; former bd. dirs. Russell Gardens Assn.; founder Work for Share Zedek Hosp., 1977—; past pres., fin. sec. L'Chaim chpt. Hadassah Nurse Coun. N.Y. State Regents scholar, 1963. Mem. ANA, Assn. Orthodox Jewish Scientists, Am. Assn. Ambulatory Care Nurses, N.Y. Counties Registered Nurses Assn., N.Y. State Nurses Assn. (dist. 13 bd. dirs., past chmn. nurse practice com., past treas., past chair coun. ethical practice), Am. Assn. for History of Nursing, Nurses Edn. Alumni Assn. (past historian), Sigma Theta Tau, Kappa Delta Pi. Democrat. Home: 28 Laurel Dr Great Neck NY 11021-2827 Office Phone: 718-515-1438. E-mail: sm192@columbia.edu., susan.mayer@nbhn.net

MAYER, SUSAN MARTIN, art educator; b. Atlanta, Oct. 25, 1931; d. Paul McKeen and Ione (Garrett) Martin; m. Arthur James Mayer, Aug. 9, 1953; 1 child, Melinda Marilyn. Student, Am. U., 1949-50; BA, U. N.C., Greensboro, 1953; postgrad., U. Del., 1956-58; MA, Ariz. State U., 1966. Artist-in-residence Armed Forces Staff Coll., Norfolk, Va., 1968-69; mem. art faculty U. Tex., Austin, 1971—2003. Co-editor: Museum Education: History, Theory and Practice, 1989; author various mus. publs.; contbr. articles to profl. jours. Recipient award Austin Ind. Sch. Bd., 1985. Mem. Nat. Art Edn. Assn. (bd. dirs. 1983-87, award 1987, 91), Tex. Art Edn. Assn. (mus. edn. chair 1982-83, Mus. Educator of Yr. 1986), Tex. Assn. Mus. (mus. edn. chair), Austin Visual Arts Assn., Am. Assn. Mus.

MAYERI, BEVERLY, artist, ceramic sculptor, educator; b. N.Y.C., Nov. 2, 1944; d. Bernard and Cora (Wisoff) Howard; m. Earl Melchior Mayeri, Sept. 1, 1968; 1 child, Rachel Theresa. BA, U. Calif., Berkeley, 1967; MA in Art and Sculpture, San Francisco State U., 1976. Tchr. Foothill Coll., Los Altos Hills, 1990, Natsoulas Gallery, 1992, U. Minn., Mpls., 1993, Sonoma Stae U., Rohnert Park, Calif., 1994, Mendocino (Calif.) Art Ctr., 1995, Fresno State U., 1996, CCAC, Oakland, Calif., 1996, Edinboro (Pa.) U., 1997, Scropps Coll., Claremont, Clif., 1999, Cuesta Coll., San Luis Obispo, Calif., 2001, San Diego State U., 2002. Artist: solo exhibitions include Palo Alto (Calif.) Cultural Ctr., 1979, Ivory/Kimpton Gallery, San Francisco, 1981, 83, Garth Clark Gallery, N.Y., 1985, 87, Esther Saks Gallery, Chgo., 1988, 90, Dorothy Weiss Gallery, San Francisco, 1990, 92, 94, 96, 98, 2000, San Jose Inst. Contemporary Art, 1990, Robert Kidd Gallery, Birmingham, Mich., 1993, Perimeter Gallery, Chgo., 1998, Susan Cummins Callery, Mill Valley, Calif., 2002; group exhibitions include San Francisco Mus. of Art, Northern Calif. Clay Routes: Sculpture Now, 1979, Smithsonian Instn., Renwick Gallery, 1981, Prieto Meml. Gallery, Mills Coll., Oakland, Calif. 1982, Crocker Art Mus., San Francisco, 1983, Euphrate Gallery, De Anza Coll., Cupertino, Calif., 1984, 88, Fisher Gallery, U. So. Calif., L.A., traveled to Pratt Inst., N.Y.C., 1984, Arts Commn. Gallery, San Francisco, 1984, Signet Arts Gallery, St. Louis (two person show), 1984, Garth Clark Gallery, N.Y., 1985, Robert L. Kidd Gallery, Birmingham, Mich., Animals Contemporary Vision, Major Concepts: Clay, 1986, Fresno (Calif.) Arts Ctr. and Mus., 1987, Canton (Ohio) Art Inst., 1991, Soc. for Contemporary Crafts, Pitts., 1992, Triton Mus. of Art, Santa Clara, Calif., 1992, Nat. Mus. of History Taipei, Taiwan, 1993, Lew Allen Gallery, Santa Fe, New Mex., 1993, Perimeter Gallery, 1995, Duane Reed Gallery, St. Louis, 1997, Scripps Coll., 1999, LACMA, L.A., 2000, Calif. State U., Chico, 2001, Clay Studio, Phila., 2001; works in pub. and private collections include: Nat. Mus. History, Taipei, Canton Art Inst., Long Beach (Calif.) Parks and Recreation, L.A. Arts Commn., Mr. and Mrs. Eric Lidow, L.A., Alfred Shands, Louisville, Mrs. Audrey Landy, Atlanta, Karen Johnson Boyd, Racine, Wis., Alan and Esther Saks, Chgo., Gloria and Sonny Kamm, L.A. County Mus. Art. Founder Marin Women Artists, Marin County, Calif., 1974-84. Recipient fellowship visual artist NEA, Washington, 1982, 88; grantee: Marin Arts Coun., 1987, Virgina A. Groot Found., 1991. Avocations: painting, hiking, skiing, gardening, environmentalist. Office: Dorothy Weiss Gallery 3 Indian Gulch Rd Piedmont CA 94611-3527

MAYER LOSSING, EMILY ANN, city official; b. Havre, Mont., Jan. 24, 1972; d. Mark Joseph and Darleen May (O'Donnell) Mayer; m. Lyle Victor Lossing, June 8, 1996. AS in Bus. Adminstrn., Mont. State U.-No., 1999. Hostess Iron Horse Restaurant, Havre, 1990; asst. mgr. House of Fabrics, Havre, 1990-93; teller Bear Paw Credit Union, Havre, 1993-96; phone banker Mont. Dem. Party, 1994; city alderwoman City of Havre, 1995—; loan processor Heritage Bank, 1999; sec. Mont. State U. No. Coll. Nursing. Sec. Hauge Law Office, 1997; mem. Child Devel., Inc., 1999 Field organizer Friends of Max Baucus, Havre, 1996; hist. interpreter Ft. Assinniboine, Havre, 1997, Wahkpa Chu'gn Bison Kill, Havre, 1997; hist. interpreter, display presenter Havre Beneath the Streets, 1995—; state convention del. Hill County Dem. Ctrl. Com., 1996, chair adv. com., 1998—; sec. Hill County Dem. Women's Club, Havre, 1995-96, pres., 1997; precinctwoman precinct 2 Hill County Dem. Party, Havre, 1995—, 2d alt. state committeewoman, 1994-95, 1st alt., 1999; bd. dirs. Ft. Assinniboine Preservation Soc., 1997, sec.-treas.; bd. dirs. Russell County Tourism, 1997; co-chairwoman Havre Chamber Tourism Com., 1998; mem. Hist. Preservation Soc., 1996, officer, 2000; mem. Hi-Line Chpt. Credit Unions, 1993-96; mem. fire and police com. Havre City, 1995-97, fin. com., 1995-97, chairwoman park and recreation com., 1995-97, ordinance com., 1998—, water and sewer com., 1998—, labor negotiations com., 1998—; mem. adv. com. Havre City CI-75; re-established Havre Historic Preservation Commn., 1999, officer, 2000; record keeper Havre Cmty. Tourism Assessment Program, 1997-98; bus. devel. com. Havre Chamber, 1998—, legis. com., 1999; sec. H. Earl Clack Mus. Found., 1998—, co-chair bldg. grounds, 1998—; no. student justice Mont. State U., 1997-98, no. student chief justice, 1998; winter insert com. Russell county, 1998—; founder Havre Hist. Preservation Commn., 1999, officer, 2000. Named Precinctwoman of Yr. Mont. Dem. Party, 1996, Outstanding Young Montanian Montana Jaycees, 1999; recipient STAR Program award (4) Mont. Credit Union Network, Helena, Mont., 1994. Mem. Old Forts Trail Assn. (minute recorder 1997—, HOME program loan rev. com. 1998—, sec. 1997—), Bull Hook Blossoms Garden Club (rec. sec. 1998—), Nat. Trust Historic Preservation, Victorian Soc. Am. Roman Catholic. Avocations: collecting antiques, historic preservation, democratic party activities, community involvement, handworks. Home: 124 3rd St Havre MT 59501-3532

MAYERSOHN, NETTIE, state legislator; m. Ronald Mayersohn; children: Jeffrey, Lee. BA, Queens Coll., 1978. Exec. dir. N.Y. State Crime Victims Bd.; mem. N.Y. State Assembly, 1982—, chairperson assembly ho. ops. com., mem. legis. women's caucus, mem. various coms. Dist. leader 27th N.Y. State Assembly Dist.-Part A, 1972—. Past mem. Cmty. Bd. # 8, former chairperson youth com.; past chairperson Pomonok Cmty. Ctr.; founder, organizer Pomonok Neighborhood Ctr., Inc.; active Electchester Jewish Ctr., Israel Ctr. of Hillcrest Manor; N.Y. state del. Internat. Women's Conf., 1977; bd. dirs. Harry Van Arsdale, Jr. Meml. Assn. Recipient Builders of Brotherhood award Nat. Conf. Christians and Jews, 1977, Legislator of Yr. award N.Y. State chpt. NOW, 1989. Mem. Stevenson Regular Dem. Club, Inc. (exec. mem.), Alpha Sigma Lambda. Home: 67-11 Parsons Blvd Flushing NY 11365-2961 Office: NY State Assembly State Capitol Albany NY 12224

MAYERSON, SANDRA ELAINE, lawyer; b. Dayton, Ohio, Feb. 8, 1952; d. Manuel David and Florence Louise (Tepper) M.; m. Scott Burns, May 29, 1977 (div. Oct. 1978); 1 child, Katy Joy. BA cum laude, Yale U., 1973; JD, Northwestern U., 1976. Bar: Ill. 1976, N.Y. 1997, U.S. Ct. Appeals (7th cir.) 1976, U.S. Dist. Ct. (no. dist.) Ill. 1977, U.S. Dist. Ct. Md. 1989, U.S. Ct. Appeals (5th cir.) 1994, U.S. Dist. Ct. (so. and ea. dists.) N.Y. 1997, U.S. Ct. Appeals (2nd Cir.) 1997, U.S. Dist. Ct. (ea. dist.) Mich. 2000. Assoc. gen. counsel JMB Realty Corp., Chgo., 1979-80; assoc. Chatz, Sugarman, Abrams et al, Chgo., 1980-81; ptnr. Pollack, Mayerson & Berman, Chgo., 1981-83; dep. gen. counsel AM Internat., Inc., Chgo., 1983-85; ptnr. Kirkland & Ellis, Chgo., 1985-87; ptnr., chmn. bankruptcy group Kelley Drye & Warren, N.Y.C., 1987-93; ptnr., chmn. N.Y. bankruptcy group McDermott, Will & Emery, N.Y.C., 1993-99; ptnr., bankruptcy nat. practice group leader Holland and Knight, N.Y.C., 1999—. Examiner Interco chpt. 11, 1991. Contbr. articles to profl. jours. Bd. dirs. Jr. Med. Rsch. Inst. coun. Michael Reese Hosp., Chgo., 1981-86, Self Help Inc., 2000-; met. divsn. Jewish Guild for Blind, 1990-92; nat. legal afffairs com. Anti-Defamation League, 1990-; lawyers' exec. com. United Jewish Appeal; chair Holland & Knight Nat. Bankruptcy & Creditors Rights Group, 2001-. Named one of

Top 50 Women Litigators, Nat. Law Jour., 2001; assoc. fellow, Branford Coll., Yale U., 1993—. Mem. ABA (bus. bankruptcy com. 1976—, sec. 1990-93, chair avoiding powers subcom. 1993-96, chair claims trading subcom. 1997-2000, chair strategic planning subcom., 2000-), Ill. State Bar Assn. (governing council corp. and securities sect. 1983-86), Chgo. Bar Assn. (current events chmn. corp. sect. 1980-81), 7th Cir. Bar Assn., Yale Club (N.Y.C.). Democrat. Jewish. Office: Holland and Knight 195 Broadway Fl 24 New York NY 10007-3100

MAYES, MAUREEN DAVIDICA, physician, educator; b. Phila., Oct. 16, 1945; d. David and Marguerite Cecilia M.; m. Charles William Houser, Dec. 18, 1976; children: David Steven, Edward Charles. BA, Coll. Notre Dame, 1967; MD, Ea. Va. Med. Sch., 1976; MA in Pub. Health, U. Mich., Ann Arbor, 1994. Diplomate Am. Bd. Internal Medicine, Am. Bd. Rheumatology. Resident in internal medicine Cleve. Clinic Found., 1977-79, fellow in rheumatology, 1979-81; asst. prof. medicine W.Va. U., Morgantown, 1981-85, Wayne State U., Detroit, 1985-90, assoc. prof. medicine, 1990-97, prof. medicine, 1997—2001, U. Tex., Houston, 2002—. Dir. scleroderma unit Wayne State U., Detroit, 1991—; prin. investigator Scleroderma Registry NIH, 1994—; pres. Scleroderma Clin. Trials Consortium, 1998—2000. Author: The Scleroderma Book, 1999; contbr. articles to profl. jours. Pres. bd. United Scleroderma Found., 1988-89, pres. med. adv. bd., 1997—; bd. trustees Arthritis Found., Mich. Robert Wood Johnson scholarship EVMS, 1972, NIH fellow, 1993-94, NIAMS Sr. Rsch. fellowship, 1994; recipient Lower award Cleve. Clinic Found., 1981. Fellow: ACP, Am. Coll. Rheumatology (ctrl. region coun. 1995—97). Office: U Tex Health Sci Ctr 6431 Fannin Houston TX 77030

MAYES, MICHELE COLEMAN, lawyer; b. Los Angeles, Calif., July 9, 1949; BA, U. Mich., 1971, JD, 1974. Bar: Mich. 1974, U.S. Dist. Ct. 1974, Ea. Dist. of Mich. 1976, Ill. 1980, U.S. Supreme Ct. 1988, Pa. 1988. Adj. prof. Wayne State U., 1981—87; in-house counsel Colgate-Palmolive, 1992—2003; sr. v.p., gen. counsel Pitney Bowes Inc., 2003—. Mem.: ABA (mem. commn. on women in the profession 1992, co-chair, arbitration com. 1990—92). Office: Pitney Bowes Inc World Hdqs 1 Elmcroft Rd, Mail Stop MSC 6411 Stamford CT 06926-0700

MAYFIELD, JACQUELINE ROWLEY, business educator, department chairman; b. Detroit, Feb. 17, 1952; d. Ralph James and Worth Carpenter Rowley; m. Milton Ray Mayfield, Jr., June 2, 1991. BA in French, George Washington U., 1974, MBA in Mktg., 1979; MA in Tchg. (French), U. Chgo., 1975; PhD in Bus. Adminstrn., U. Ala., 1993. Tchr. French D.C. Pub. Schs., Washington, 1975—76; market rsch. analyst, product devel. coord. Blue Cross Blue Shield, Washington, 1979—82, product devel. specialist, health industry analyst Jacksonville, Fla., 1982—87; asst. prof. mgmt. Radford U., Va., 1992—95, Tex. A&M Internat. U., Laredo, 1995—99, assoc. prof., 1999—, co chair dept. mgmt. and mktg., 2001—02, dir. prof. devel. Coll. Bus., 2002—03. Pvt. practice orgnl. cons., Cotulla, Tex., 1992—. Named Outstanding Young Woman of Am., Outstanding Young Ams. Assn., 1983; recipient Best Paper in Orgnl. Behavior, Inst. Behavioral and Applied Mgmt., 1994, Citation of Excellence, Anbar Pub., 1999. Mem.: Acad. Mgmt., Phi Kappa Phi, Beta Gamma Sigma. Avocation: music, films, meteorology. Office: Tex A&M Internat U 5201 Univ Blvd Laredo TX 78041-1900 Business E-Mail: jmayfield@tamiu.edu.

MAYHAR, ARDATH FRANCES (FRANK CANNON), author; b. 1930; Ind. book cons., 1979—; dairyman, 1947-57; prin. East Tex. Bookstore, Nacogdoches, 1958-62; proofreader Capital Jour., Salem, Oreg., 1968-75; chicken farmer, 1976-78; proofreader Daily Sentinel, Nacogdoches, 1979-82; writer, 1982—; co-mgr. View From Orbit Bookstore, Nacogdoches, 1984—99; writing instr. Writer's Digest, 1982—. Author: How the Gods Wove in Kyrannon, 1979, The Seekers of Shar Nuhn, 1980, Soul Singer of Tyrnos, 1981, Warlock's Gift, 1982, Khi to Freedom, 1982, Runes of the Lyre, 1982, Golden Dream, 1983, Lords of the Triple Moons, 1983, Exile on Vlahil, 1984, The Saga of Grittel Sundotha, 1985, The World Ends in Hickory Hollow, 1985, Medicine Walk, 1985, Carrots and Miggle, 1986, The Wall, 1987, Makra Choria, 1987, Feud at Sweetwater Creek (as Frank Cannon), 1988, A Place of Silver Silence, 1988; (collaboration with Marylois Dunn) The Absolutely Perfect Horse, 1983; (collaboration with Ron Fortier) Trail of the Seahawks, 1987, Monkey Station, TSR, 1989; (as John Killdeer) Wild Country, The Untamed, Wilderness Rendezvous, Blood Kin, People of the Mesa, 1992, Island in the Lake, 1993, Towers of the Earth, 1994, Passage West, 1994, Far Horizons, 1994, Hunters of the Plains, 1995, (as Frances Hurst) High Mountain Winter, 1996, Riddles and Dreams, 2003. Home: 533 CR 486 Chireno TX 75937

MAYHO, LOIS MARY, social worker; b. New Orleans, Jan. 5, 1945; d. Joseph Herbert and Marguerite McConnell; m. David Louis Bartholomew Jr., June 25, 1965 (div. June 1986); children: Darlene Washington, David Louis Bartholomew III, m. David Edward Mayho, June 20, 1992. BSW, So. U. New Orleans, 1985, MSW, 1986; postgrad., U. New Orleans, 1986—87. LCSW, Diplomate in Clin. Social Work, cert. pub. mgr. Social worker, adoption specialist Child Protection, New Orleans, 1971—90, supr. Harvey, La., 1990—95, mgr. program Baton Rouge, 1995—2000, adminstr., 2000—. Bd. dirs. Nat. Assn. Family based Svcs., 1997—99; co-chair Interagency Coun. for Homelessness, Baton Rouge, 1999—. Mem.: New Orleans Assn. Black Social Workers (exec. com., membership chairperson 1985—95, Founders award 1987). Avocations: reading, swimming, walking. Home: 4624 Norwich Dr Baton Rouge LA 70814*

MAYLE, AMANDA LYNN, psychologist; b. Zanesville, Ohio, Feb. 18, 1975; d. Larry Wayne and Diana Jean (Chandler) Mayle; 1 child, Dwight Conway-Wayne Richards. AS, Ohio U., 1994, BS, 1996; D in Psychology, Wright State U., 2002. Psychol. asst. Wright State U., Dayton, Ohio, 1998—2001; intern Park Ctr., Inc., Ft. Wayne, Ind., 2001—02, staff psychologist, 2002—. Vis. fellow Columbia U., Manhattan, NY, 2001. Mem.: APA, Ohio Psychol. Assn. Baptist. Home: 6930 Selkirk Dr Fort Wayne IN 46816 Office: Park Center Inc Blufton IN

MAYNARD, CATHERINE, medical researcher; BS, U. Manchester. Mgr. core transgenic svcs. Imperial Cancer Rsch. Fund, 1988-92; various positions most recently assoc. dir. Animal Rsch. Svcs. and Microembryology, 1992-96; assoc. dir. animal rsch. svcs. & microembryology Abgenix, Inc., Fremont, Calif., 1996-98, dir. ops., 1998—. Office: Abgenix Inc 7601 Dumbarton Cir Fremont CA 94555-3616

MAYNARD, JOAN, education educator; b. Louisa, Ky., Oct. 18, 1932; d. Macon Scott and Jeanette (Thompson) Chambers; m. Frank Maynard Jr., June 15, 1951 (dec. Oct. 1988); children: Mark Steven, Julia Beth Maynard McFann, Robert Blake. BA, Wittenberg U., 1977; MEd, Wright State U., 1980, MEd, 1984. Tchr., reading specialist Mechanicsburg (Ohio) Exempted Village Schs., 1976—; pres. TOTT Publs. Inc., Bellbrook, Ohio, 1988—99; ret., 1999. Rep. Career Edn., Mechanicsburg, 1981-88, mem. Thompson Grant Com., Mechanicsburg, 1987-88. Author: Mud Puddles, 1988, Mud Pies, 1989. Vol. Mechanicsburg Schs. Levy, 1980, 82, 88, Congl. Race, Campaign County, Ohio, 1982, 84, 86; cons. Urbana U., Ohio, 1988-90, 91, 92, 93; tutor Laubach Lit. Action, Urbana, 1989-90, 91-93, 94. Recipient Thompson grant, 1982, 88, 92. Mem. AAUW (edn. chmn. Champaign County chpt. 1988-89, treas. 1989-90), Internat. Reading Assn., Champaign County Reading Coun. (treas. 1990-91), Midwestern Assembly Lit. Young People (treas. 1989-93), Kappa Delta Pi. Avocations: collecting children's lit. books, travel, reading. Home: 1546 Parkview Rd Mechanicsburg OH 43044-9779 Office: Exempted Village Schs 60 High St Mechanicsburg OH 43044-1071

MAYNARD, NATALIE RYSHNA, pianist, educator; b. Phila., Aug. 21, 1930; d. George Thomas Hook and Helen Agatha Reese; m. Harry Edgar Maynard, Jan. 30, 1960; children: Melanie Dawn, Amie Anne. Degree in piano performance, Juilliard Graduate Sch. Music, N.Y.C., 1952. Concert pianist Columbia Artists Mgmt., tours in U.S. and Europe, 1963-94; rec. artist Contemporary Records and Ambiphon Records, 1957-75; pvt. piano instr., 1985—; project dir. Title III and State Urban Edn. program N.Y.C. schs. Founder, chmn. edn. com. Sta. WNET/13-TV, N.Y.C., 1973—77; pres. Performers Conn., Westport, 1985—91, bd. dirs., 1982—; exec. dir. R. B. Fisher Found. Composer Awards, 1986—96; v.p. ednl. outreach Friends of Music Fairfield County, 1995—99. Bd. dirs. Friends of Channel 13, Nat. Friends of Pub. Broadcasting, 1971—82; apptd. to arts adv. com. Town of Westport, 1998—2000, 2000—, co-chair town millenium edn. com., 1998; mem. adv. bd. Stamford Symphony Orch. Recipient Outstanding Women Conn. award, Lt. Gov. Conn., 2003. Mem.: Conn. State Music Tchrs. Assn., Nat. Music Tchrs. Assn., Schubert Club.

MAYNARD, OLIVIA P. foundation administrator; m. S. Olof Karlstrom. BA, Geroge Washington U., 1959; MSW, U. Mich., 1971. Dir. Mich. Office Svcs. to Aging, 1983—90; tchr. Sch. Social Work U. Mich., Mich. State U.; tchr. Ctr. for Aging Edn. Lansing (Mich.) C.C.; pres. Mich. Prospect for Renewed Citizenship, Flint, Mich. Del. White House Conf. on Aging, 1995. Regent U. Mich., Ann Arbor; chmn. Mich. Dem. Party, 1973—82; candidate Lt. Gov. of Mich., 1990. Democrat. Office: Northbank Ctr Ste 406 432 N Saginaw St Flint MI 48502

MAYNARD, PAMELA RAE, architectural design firm executive; b. Granada Hills, Calif., Nov. 20, 1957; d. Raymond Herman Meyer and Rosemary R. Robertson; m. Richard Edward Maynard, May 21, 1988; 1 child, Matthew Austin. BS in Arch., Calif. Poly. U., Pomona, 1981. Cert. interior designer, Calif. Archtl. project mgr. HMC Group, Ontario, Calif., 1981—85, interior design, 1986—98, dir. interior design, 1998—, assoc., 1999, sr. assoc., 2002, prin., 2003—. Mem.: Internat. Interior Design Assn. (assoc.). Republican. Avocations: travel, art, literature. Office: HMC Group 3270 Inland Empire Blvd Ontario CA 91764

MAYNARD, VIRGINIA MADDEN, foundation administrator; b. New London, Conn., Jan. 29, 1924; d. Raymond and Edna Sarah (Madden) Maynard. BS, U. Conn., 1945; postgrad., Am. Inst. Banking, 1964-66, Cornell U., 1975. With Nat. City Bank (now Citibank), N.Y.C., 1954-79, asst. cashier, 1965-69, asst. v.p., 1969-74, v.p. internat. banking group, 1974-76, comptroller's div., 1976-79; v.p. First Women's Bank, N.Y.C., 1979-80; rep. Internat. Fedn. Univ. Women UN, 1982—2003. Rep. UN, 1997—; trustee fellowships endowment fund AAUW Ednl. Found., Washington, 1977—80, Va. Gildersleeve Internat. Fund Univ. Women, Inc., pres., 1987—93, bd. dirs., 1994—2000, Conf. Nongovtl. Orgns. Found., Inc., 1997—2004, treas., 1999—2004. Mem.: AAUW (fin. chmn. N.Y.C. br. 1976—79, bylaws chmn. 1979—83, adminstr. Meml. Fund 1983—92, 2000—, bd. dirs. 1992—94, 1996—99, Woman of Achievement 1976). Republican. Congregationalist. Home: 601 E 20th St New York NY 10010-7622

MAYNE, LUCILLE STRINGER, finance educator; b. Washington, June 6, 1924; d. Henry Edmond and Hattie Benham (Benson) Stringer; children: Patricia Anne, Christine Gail, Barbara Marie. BS, U. Md., 1946; MBA, Ohio State U., 1949; PhD, Northwestern U., 1966. Instr. fin. Utica Coll., 1949-50; lectr. fin. Roosevelt U., 1961-64, Pa. State U., 1965-66, asst. prof., 1966-69, assoc. prof., 1969-70; assoc. prof. banking and fin. Case-Western Res. U., 1971-76, prof., 1976-94, prof. emerita, 1994—, grad. dean Sch. Grad. Studies, 1980-84. Sr. economist, cons. FDIC, 1977-78; cons. Nat. Commn. Electronic Fund Transfer Sys., 1976; rsch. cons. Am. Bankers Assn., 1975, Fed. Res. Bank of Cleve., 1968-70, 73; cons. Pres.'s Commn. Fin. Structure and Regulation, 1971, staff economist, 1970-71; analytical statistician Air Materiel Command, Dayton, Ohio, 1950-52; asst. to promotion mgr. NBC, Washington, 1946-48; expert witness cases involving fin. instns. Assoc. editor: Jour. Money, Credit and Banking, 1980-83, Bus. Econs., 1980-85; contbr. articles to profl. jours. Vol. Cleve. Soc. for Blind, 1979—2004, Benjamin Rose Inst., 1995—; mem. policyholders nominating com. Tchrs. Ins. and Annuity Assn./Coll. Retirement Equities Fund, 1982-84, chair com., 1984; bd. dirs. Women's Cmty. Found., 1994-96. Grad. scholar Ohio State U., 1949; doctoral fellow Northwestern U., 1963-65. Mem. LWV (bd. dirs. Shaker Heights chpt. 1999--), Midwest Fin. Assn. (pres. 1991-92, bd. dirs. 1975-79, officer 1988-93), Phi Kappa Phi, Beta Gamma Sigma. Episcopalian. Home: 3723 Normandy Rd Cleveland OH 44120-5246 Office: Case Western Res U Weatherhead Sch Mgmt U Circle Cleveland OH 44106-7235

MAYNE, MARIANNE, special education educator; b. Salt Lake City, Sept. 4, 1968; d. Jack and Gwen Steele Mayne. AS, Utah Valley State Coll., 1994; BS, Utah State U., 1997; MEd, U. Utah, 1999. Summer tchg. asst. Alpine Sch. Dist., American Fork, Utah, 1987—98, presch. spl. edn. tchr. America Fork, Utah, 1998—99; asst. to prof. Utah State U., Logan, Utah, 1995—97; presch. spl. edn. tchr. Nebo Sch. Dist., Springville, Utah, 1999—. Mem.: NEA, CEC (divsn. early childhood), Nebo Edn. Assn., Utah Edn. Assn. Church Of Jesus Christ Of Latter-Day Saints. Avocations: reading, shopping, crafts, concerts, family. Home: 789 W 2600 N Pleasant Grove UT 84062 Office: Sage Creek Elem 1050 S 700 E Springville UT 84663

MAYO, CAROLYN, marketing professional, public relations executive; BA in Journalism, La. State U. Pub. rels. mgr. Houston dist. J.C. Penny; pvt. practice; shareholer, pres. Vollmer, 2002—. Supporter arts orgns., Gulf Coast area. Named 1 of city's top 50 woman bus. owners. Mem.: Pub. Rels. Soc. Am. Counselor's Acad., Pub. Rels. Soc. Am. (accredited mem.). Office: 808 Travis Ste 501 Houston TX 77002-5706

MAYO, KATHLEEN OWENS, librarian; b. Miami Beach, Fla., May 23, 1948; d. Edwin Shepherd and Theodora Winifred (Jones) Morris; m. Harold Anthony Mayo, June 30, 1972; children: Giuliana Nora, Adam Anthony. BS in Art Edn., Fla. State U., 1970, MS in Libr. Sci., 1971. Sch. libr. Funston & Hamilton Schs., Moultrie, Ga., 1971-72; libr. asst. Fla. State U., Tallahassee, 1972-73; libr. dir. Fla. State Hosp., Chattahoochee, 1973-78; libr. cons. State Libr. Fla., Tallahassee, 1978-89; mgr. cmty. access svcs. Lee County Libr. Sys., Fort Myers, Fla., 1989—. Editor Health Info at Your Library, 1987; (newsletter) Keystone Tech. Bull. Librs., 1979-89; co-editor: ADA Library Kit, 1994. Mem. rape task force/trauma ctr. Fort Myers, 1990-98; bd. dirs. Meals on Wheels Lee County, Fort Myers, 1993-97, Assn. Provider Orgns., Fort Myers, 1991-94, Friendship Vol. Ctr. Recipient Citizen of Yr. award SW Fla. Unit NASW, 1996. Mem. NOW, ALA, Assn. Specialized and Coop. Libr. Agys. (bd. dirs. 1979-81, Exceptional Svc. award 1991), ADA Assembly, Health Care Librs. (chair 1983-84), Pub. Libr. Assn. Bookmobile Svcs. (chair 1994-95, 99-2000), Fla. Libr. Assn. Democrat. Unitarian Universalist. Office: Lee County Libr Sys 21100 Three Oaks Pkwy Estero FL 33928 Office Phone: 239-390-3234. E-mail: Kmayo@leegov.com.

MAYS, CAROL JEAN, state legislator; b. Independence, Mo., July 16, 1933; m. Ronald H. Mays; children: Terri, Melanie, Hugh. Student, Baker U. State rep., chmn. consumer protection edn. appropriations com., mem. transp., ways & means & comm. coms. Mo. Ho. of Reps., Jefferson City. Restaurant owner. Mem. Mo. Restaurant Assn., Independence C. of C., Fairmount Comml. Club, Alpha Chi Omega. Democrat. Methodist. Home: 3603 S Hedges Ave Independence MO 64052-1167 Office: Mo Ho of Reps State Capitol Bldg 201 W Capitol Ave Rm 206A Jefferson City MO 65101-1556

MAYS, CAROLENE, state representative; 1 child, Jada. BA in Bus. Mgmt. and Mktg., Ind. State U. Various pos. in sales, corp. acct. mgmt., customer svc., and product distbn. Occidental Chem. Co., San Francisco, Dallas, and Mpls.; mgr. customer svc. and nat. accts. Mays Chem. Co.; pres., gen. mgr. The Indianapolis Recorder, 1998—; state rep. dist. 94 Ind. Ho. of Reps., Indpls., 2002—, mem. human affairs, judiciary, pub. health, and ways and means coms. Host, weekly TV news segment Community Link WISH-TV Ch. 8, Ctrl. Ind. Bd. dirs. Ind. Sports Corp. Bd., U. Indpls.; mem. Ind. Supreme Ct. Commn. for Racial and Gender Fairness; bd. dirs. Indpls. Downtown Mktg., Inc.; apptd. by mayor Indpls. Neighborhood Housing Partnership Bd.; adv. bd. Julian Ctr., NCAA Citizenship Through Sports Alliance/Common Ground; bd. dirs. Shrewsberry & Assocs., Peyton Manning's PeyBack Found.; apptd. by mayor Greater Indpls. Progress Com.; past bds. and coms. 2001 World Police and Fire Games Exec. Com., Indy Jazz Fest, Ind. Repertory Theatre, Ind. Sch. Champions, Ind. Pvt. Industry Coun., Girls, Inc., United Way's Ardeth Burkhart Series exec. com., Freetown Village Bd., chair Circle City Classic Coaches Luncheon 2000 NCAA Final Four Com., chair comm. World's Largest Christmas Tree, coord. Ind. Sch. Champions Camp, numerous other planning coms., workshops and speaking engagements. Named one of Women to Watch, Indpls. Bus. Jour.; recipient Disting. Alumni award, Ind. State U., Martin Luther King Ctr. Living the Legacy award, 2002, Media award, Ind. Black Expo, 2002, Trailblazer award, Women's Expo, 2001, Presdl. citation, Nat. Newspaper Pubs. Assn., 2000. Mem.: Nat. Coun. Negro Women (named Woman in the Bethune Tradition 2001), United Way Minority Key Club, Alpha Kappa Alpha (Regional Comm. award 2002). Democrat. Avocations: skiing, cooking. Office: Ind Ho of Reps 200 W Washington St Indianapolis IN 46204-2786

MAYS, JANICE ANN, lawyer; b. Waycross, Ga., Nov. 21, 1951; d. William H. and Jean (Bagley) M. AB (hon.), Wesleyan Coll., Macon, Ga., 1973; JD, U. Ga., 1975; LLM in Taxation, U. Georgetown, 1980. Bar: Ga. 1976. Tax counsel com. on ways and means U.S. Ho. Reps., Washington, 1975-88, chief tax counsel com. on ways and means, staff dir. subcom. select revenue measures, 1988-93, chief counsel, staff dir. com. on ways and means, 1993-95, minority chief counsel, staff dir. com. on ways and means, 1995—. Recipient Disting. Achievement in Profession Alumnae award Wesleyan Coll., 1998. Mem. Tax Coalition (past chair). Office: Ways & Means Com 1106 Longworth Office Bldg Washington DC 20515-0001

MAYS, JILL DUNCAN, social services administrator, counselor; b. Louisville, Apr. 17, 1966; d. Charles Henry Sr. and Ruth Ella (Bohannon) Duncan; m. Samuel Aaron Mays Sr., Dec. 28, 1991; children: Shelby Amaris, Samuel Aaron Jr., Jayce Allan. BA in Psychology, Emory U., 1988; MS in Cmty. Counseling, Ga. State U., 1992. Lic. profl. counselor, Ga.; master addiction counselor, nat. cert. counselor Nat. Bd. Cert. Counselors, Inc. Rsch. interviewer Emory U. Sch. Pub. Health, Atlanta, 1990-92; evening outpatient coord. Decatur (Ga.) Hosp., 1992-94; counselor The Atlanta Union Mission, 1992-94, dir. women and children's svcs., 1994—, Atlanta City Mission, 2000—. Cons. Intracultural Comm., Decatur, 1993-95, DeKalb County Dept. Youth Svcs., Decatur, 1993; com. mem. Atlanta Summit Against Poverty, 1997; bd. dirs. Zion Hill Cmty. Devel. Corp.; mem. com. DeKalb County Bd. Health/Divsn. Health Assessment and Promotion, 2002-03. Olympic Force coord. Atlanta Com. for the Olympic Games, 1995—96; mem. Atlanta Women Making a Mark, 2002. Mem.: Coun. Vol. Adminstrs., Assn. Gospel Rescue Missions, Am. Assn. Christian Counselors, Nat. Assn. for the Edn. Young Children, Alpha Kappa Alpha Sorority, Inc. Democrat. Baptist. Avocations: singing, reading, acting/playwriting. Office: The Atlanta Union Mission 921 Howell Mill Rd Atlanta GA 30318 E-mail: samnjam1@prodigy.net.

MAYS, LESLIE A. human resources specialist; b. Houston; BA, Tex. So. U. Pers. dir., city mgr. Peoples Express Airline; cons. Jane C. Edmonds and Assocs.; human resources dir. Reebok Internat. Ltd., 1989—94; mem. diversity dept. Gen. Mills, 1994—96; exec. dir. diversity Royal Dutch/Shell Oil Co., 1996—99, v.p., Global Group Diversity, 1999—. Mem.: Nat. Coalition 100 Black Women (bd. mem. 1997—2001, pres. 2001—). Office: Ste 1610 38 W 32nd St New York NY 10001-3816*

MAYSILLES, ELIZABETH, speech communication professional, educator; b. Sleepy Creek, W.Va. d. Evers and Rose (Scott) M. AB, W.Va. U.; MA, Hunter Coll., 1963; PhD, NYU, 1980. Announcer Radio Sta. WAJR, Morgantown, W.Va.; broadcaster Radio Sta. WGHF-FM, Rural Radio Network, N.Y.C.; group leader GMAC, N.Y.C.; instr. NYU, N.Y.C.; adj. prof. speech comm. Pace U., N.Y.C., 1978—2002; exec. adminstr. Am.-Scottish Found., N.Y.C., 1980-90; adminstrv. asst. Brit. Schs. and Univs. Found., Inc.; numerous radio and television appearances. Cons., lectr. in field. Vol. counselor Help Line, N.Y.C., 1971-75. Recipient Disting. Svc. award NYU Grad. Orgn., 1970-71. Mem. Internat. Platform Assn. (bd. govs. 1980—), N.Y. Acad. Scis., English-Speaking Union, Caledonian Club N.Y. (bd. dirs. 1994-96, chieftain 2001-02). Avocations: reading, swimming, gardening, travel in England and Scotland. Home: 155 E 77th St Apt 6F New York NY 10021-1955

MAZUR, RHODA HIMMEL, community volunteer; b. Bklyn., July 4, 1929; d. Morris and Gussie (Nadler) Himmel; m. Marvin Irwin Mazur, June 7, 1952; children: Jody, Amy, Leslie, Eric. Student, CCNY, CUNY. Bd. dirs. Newport News Social Svcs. Adv. Bd., 1979-84, Gov.'s Commn. Status Women, Richmond, 1981-84, Coun. Jewish Fedns., N.Y.C., 1985-87, Nat. Coun. Christians and Jews, 1985-89, Rodef Sholom Endowment Com., 1996—; v.p. Anti-Defamation League Regional Bd., Richmond, 1983-85, bd. dirs., 1985—; pres. Newport News Hadassah, 1984-85, United Jewish Cmty. Va. Peninsula Inc., Newport News, 1985-88, Rodef Sholom Sisterhood, 1997-98; active Newport News Task Force on Emergency Housing, 1984-85; chair fin. com. Peninsula Peace Edn. Ctr., Newport News, 1984-85; adv. bd. Friends of the Homeless, Inc., 1987-2000, pres., 1993-98, v.p., 1998-99; adv. bd. Associated Marine Inst., 1988-92; mem. social svcs. com. United Jewish Cmty. Va. Peninsula, 1995—, mem. campaign coun., 1999—; chair social action com. Rodef Sholom Temple, 1993-96, endowment com., 1998—; cmty. activist; bd. dirs., Peninsula Camp Fund, 2001—, Fed. Emergency Mgmt. Agy., 2001. Recipient Young Leadership award Jewish Fedn. Newport News, 1968, Brotherhood citation Nat. Conf. Christians and Jews, 1984, Anti-Defamation Leadership award, 1997. Democrat. Avocations: hand crafts, reading, music, photography. Home: 114 James River Dr Newport News VA 23601-3604

MAZZAFERRI, KATHERINE AQUINO, lawyer, bar association executive; b. Phila., May 14, 1947; d. Joseph William and Rose (Aquino) M.; m. William Fox Bryan, May 5, 1984 (div.); 1 child, Josefa Mazzaferri Bryan. BA, NYU, 1969; JD, George Washington U., 1972. Bar: D.C., 1972. Trial atty. EEOC, Washington, 1972-75; dir. litigation LWV Edn. Fund, Washington, 1975-78; dep. asst. dir. for advt. practices FTC, Washington, 1978-80, asst. dir. for product liability, 1980-82, asst. dir. for advt. practices, 1982; exec. dir., v.p. pub. svcs. activities corp. D.C. Bar, Washington, 1982—. Bd. dir. regulatory analysis project U.S. Regulatory Coun.; mediator D.C. Mediation Svc., 1982; vis. instr. Antioch Law Sch., Washington, 1985; mem. Bd. of Women's Bar Assn. Found., 1990-93; mem. FBA Meml. Found., 1991-96. Bd. dirs. River Rd. Unitarian Ch., 2001—, bd. dir., 2001—. Recipient Superior Service award FTC, 1979 Mem. ABA (rep. of the homeless project steering com. 1988-90), D.C. Bar, Womens Legal Def. (pres. 1972-73, bd. dirs. 1971-75, 76-79), FBA Meml. Found. Home: 5832 Lenox Rd Bethesda MD 20817-6070 Office: DC Bar 1250 H St NW Lbby 6 Washington DC 20005-5906

MAZZARIELLO, MARY C. state representative; b. Rutland, Vt., Oct. 18, 1944; LPN, Fanny Allen Sch. Nursing, Vt., 1964; postgrad., Castleton State Coll. Justice of the peace, Rutland; state rep. Vt. Ho. of Reps., 1996—.

Cons. in field; long-term care ombudsman, Bennington/Rutland County Office on Aging. Bd. dirs. Civil Authority, Rutland; mem. Rutland City Dem. Com., Rutland County Dem. Com. Office: 6 Tuttle Meadow Dr Rutland VT 05701-2543

MAZZILLI, ROSLYN, sculptor; b. Bklyn., July 30, 1941; d. Sol and Minna (Heller) Krawatsky; m. Ron Mazzilli (div. 1978); children: Darrin, Andrew; m. Gregg Melvin, Dec. 3, 1988. BA in Sculpture, San Jose State U., 1977, MA in Sculpture, 1981. Lectr. AAUW, Sacramento, 1984, Civic Arts Ctr., Walnut Creek, Calif., 1985, San Mateo (Calif.) Art Ctr., 1987, Mercer Island (Wash.) ARt Ctr., 1994, San Jose (Calif.) State U., 1996. Executed sculptures at Hyatt Regency, West Houston, Tex., 1983, Spectrum Ctr., Dallas, 1983, Pleasant Hill (Calif.) Cmty. Ctr., 1984, Chapman Coll., Orange, Calif., 1985, Calif. Plz., Walnut Creek, 1986, Koll Devel. Corp., San Jose, 1987, Belmont (Calif.) CalTrain Sta., 1987, Oakland (Calif.) City Ctr., 1988, Cucamonga Calif. Town Ctr., 1990, Emerson Elec. Corp., St. Louis, 1990, City of Mercer Island, 1993. others. Grantee Calif. Coun. for Arts, 1986. Mem. Pacific Rim Sculptors Group, Internat. Sculptors, Women's Caucus for Arts. Home: 1764 Hurley Mountain Rd Hurley NY 12443-5015

MAZZIO-MOORE, JOAN L. retired radiology educator, physician; b. Belmont, Mass., Oct. 26, 1935; d. Frank Joseph and Maria L. Mazzio; children: James Thomas, Edwin Stuart. BA in Chemistry and Theology, Emmanuel Coll., 1957; MA in Genetics and Physiology, Mass. Wellesley Coll., 1961; PhD in Genetics, Bryn Mawr (Pa.) Coll., 1964; MD, Phila. Coll. of Medicine, 1977, MSc in Radiology, 1981. Instr. in biochemistry Gwynedd Mercy Coll., Springhouse, Pa., 1963—65; instr. in genetics Holy Family Coll., Phila., 1965—66; instr. in anatomy Phila. Coll. of Medicine, 1971—77, instr., 1973—77, asst. prof., 1977—84; prof. W.Va. Sch. of Medicine, 1984—2003, ret.; rotating intern Phila. Coll. of Medicine Hosp., 1977—78, resident in radiology and radiation therapy, 1978—81; advanced through grades to lt. col. USAR, 1984—2002; med. dir. 91W transition program U.S. Army Med. Corps Reserves, divsn. surgeon, 80th divsn. (IT). Author: (with Dr. DiVirgilito) Essentials of Neuropathology, 1974. Treas. Hist. Soc. of Frankford, Phila., 1968—75, Sch. Mother's Assn., Devon, Pa., 1980—81; organist Ch. of Incarnation, W.Va., St. Charles Borromeo Ch., White Sulphur Springs, W.Va., 2001—04; lector St. Ann's Cath. Ch., Phoenixville, Pa., 1981—84. Col. med. corps U.S. Army, 1992—2003, ret. med. corps. U.S. Army, 2003. Mem. AAUP, Am. Acad. Family Physicians, Am. Assn. Women Radiologists, Am. Med. Women's Assn., Am. Osteo. Coll. of Radiology (life), Am. Soc. Clin. Oncology, Am. Soc. Therapeutic Readiologists, Hist. Soc. of Lewisburg (life), Pa. Osteo. Med. Assn., Pa. Osteo. Gen. Practitioner's Soc., Radiol. Soc. N.Am., Radiation Rsch. Soc., Res. Officers Assn. (life), W.Va. Soc. Osteo. Medicine, Greenbrier River Hike and Bike Trail. Home: RR 1 Box 179 Frankford WV 24938 Fax: 304-497-2752. E-mail: drjmoore@mail.wvnet.edu.

MAZZO, KAY, ballet dancer, educator; b. Evanston, Ill., Jan. 17, 1946; d. Frank Alfred and Catherine M. (Hengel) M.; m. Albert C. Bellas, 1978; children: Andrew, Kathryn. Student, Sch. Am. Ballet, 1959-61. Profl. debut in ballets U.S.A. 1961, touring Europe with co., performing for Pres. Kennedy at White House, 1961, joined N.Y.C. Ballet, 1962-80, soloist, 1965-69, prin. ballerina, 1969-80, prin. roles in world premiere of ballets including Tschaikowsky Suite No. #3, 1970, PAMTGG, 1971, Stravinsky Violin Concerto, 1972, Scherzo A La Russe, 1972, Duo Concertant, 1972, Sheherazade, 1975, Union Jack, 1976, Vienna Waltzes, 1977, Davidsbundlertanze, 1980; ballet tchr. Sch. Am. Ballet, 1980—; appeared as guest artist in leading roles with numerous cos. including Boston Ballet, Washington Ballet, Berlin Ballet, Geneva Ballet; appeared on TV in U.S., Can., Fed. Republic Germany. Recipient Mademoiselle Merit award 1970 Office: Sch Am Ballet 70 Lincoln Center Plz New York NY 10023-6548

MAZZONI, KERRY, former state agency administrator; b. 1951; children: Casey, Peter. BS in Child Devel., U. Calif., Davis. Mem. Calif. State Assembly, Sacramento, 1994—2000, mem. various coms. including edn., sch. facilities fin., banking and fin., utilities and commerce, and housing and cmty. devel.; sec. of edn. State of Calif., Sacramento, 2000—03. Trustee Novato Unified Sch. Dist. Bd., 1987—, pres., 1990, 1993. Named Marin County Sch. Trustee of Yr., 1992.

MBADUGHA, LORETTA NKEIRUKA AKOSA, social services administrator, consultant; b. Onitsha, Anambara, Nigeria, Dec. 10, 1957; d. James and Sylvia O. (Asika) Akosa; m. Christian Mbadugha; children: Kristen Ogechi, Kyle Kelechi, Kelsey Odinaka. Assoc., Langham Secretarial Coll., London, 1978; BS, Tex. So. U., Houston, 1981, MS, 1982; PhD, U. New Orleans, 2000, PhD in Higher Edn. Adminstrn., 2001. Program analyst Tex. So. U., Houston, 1982-84; sanitarian City of Houston Health Dept., 1984-85; adj. faculty So. U., New Orleans, 1981-90; asst. to exec. dir. YWCA, New Orleans, 1984-93; family rep. Jefferson Parish Human Svcs. Authority, New Orleans, 1993—2001; CEO Profl. Family Support Svcs., New Orleans, 1994—. Cons., founder, bd. mem. Camelot Providers, New Orleans, 1987—; bd. mem. United Svcs. AIDS Found., 1990-92; trainer Coun. for Early Childhood Profl. Recognition, 1987—; cons., trainer on child devel. State of La., 1987-89; exec. dir. Gilbert Acad.; asst. prof. edn. Dillard U. Sec. Chapel of Praise, 1997. Recipient Mayoral Cert. of Merit, New Orleans, 1991; Grace Hodge fellow YWCA, 1992. Mem. ACA, Nigeria Ebony Club for Women (pres. 1995). Home: 7141 Westhaven Rd New Orleans LA 70126-2132 Office: 7041 Real Ln New Orleans LA 70127

MCADOO, CLARISSA EILEEN, city agency administrator; b. Portsmouth, Va., Aug. 29, 1955; d. Clarence William Johnson and Catherine (Johnson) Barksdale; m. Anthony McAdoo, Oct. 1, 1995; children: Paris Simone. BA in Sociology, Va. State U., 1997. Social worker Soc. Aid Sickle Cell Anemia, Norfolk, Va., 1977-79; zoning inspector City of Portsmouth, 1979-84; zoning adminstr. City of Laurel, Md., 1984-86; asst. to dir. econ. and comml. devel. City of Hyattsville, Md., 1986-87; city planner City of Suffolk, Va., 1984-93; devel. ops. mgr. Norfolk Redevelopment and Housing Authority, Va., 1993-96; exec. dir. Suffolk Redevelopment and Housing Authority, Va., 1996—. Cons. Greater Downtown Devel. Com., Suffolk, 1997—; moderator, advisor Orlando Project Area Com., Suffolk, 1997—. Editor: A Guide to Giving Your Interview 100%, 1982. Mem. Women on Missions, East End Bapt. Ch., pres. 1987-96. Recipient Cmty. Svc. award Norfolk State U., 1995, Appreciation award Parker Riddick/Cypress Manor Resident Coun., 1997. Fellow Old Dominion U. Civic Leadership Inst.; mem. ASPA, Conf. Minority Pub. Adminstrs., Suffolk Civic Forum (spkr.), Energizers Unlimited (v.p. 1989-93), Pilot Club, Kiwanis (spkr.), Alpha Kappa Alpha. Democrat. Avocations: tennis, harpist, crystal collecting, reading. Office: Suffolk Redevelopment & Housing Authority 530 E Pinner St Suffolk VA 23434-3023

MCAFEE, CHERYL, architect; Grad, Ks. State Univ., 1979; grad., Harvard Univ. Grad. Sch. of Des., 1981. Prin./pres. Charles F. McAfee, Atlanta, 1998. Mem.: Atlanta Urban Design Commn. (bd. mem. 2002), AIA (chair of the Nat. 5th Annual Diversity Conference 1998), Nat. Org. of Minority Arch. (NOMA) (president 1998), Olympic Games in Atlanta (sr. mgr. arch. 1996). Office: Charles F McAfee 127 Peachtree St NE Atlanta GA 30303

MCAFEE, MARGARET ANNE, retired art educator; b. Denver, May 14, 1929; d. Abe I. and Anne M. Blomquist; m. George Lafayette Finn McAfee, July 22, 1972. AA, UCLA, 1947, BA, 1951; MA in Edn., Calif. State Coll., 1967. Cert. tchr. Calif. State Bd. Of Edn., 1955. Tng. tchr. UCLA, USC & Mt. St. Mary's Coll., 1955—66; art tchr. and dept. chmn. Hamilton Sr. HS, LA, 1952—69; tchr. and prof. of art emeritus LA (Calif.) C.C. Dist., 1969—89; assoc. tchr. art Saddleback C.C., Mission Viejo, Calif., 1990—2003. Cons. in field. Dir.: (TV series) How to Design, Make and Use Mosaic Projects In and Around the Home, 1961—66; contbr. articles to newspapers. Troop leader Girl Scouts Am., LA, 1949—50. Mem.: AAUW, Assn. Ret. Tchrs., The Enamelist Soc., Am. Fedn. Tchrs. Emeritus, Nat. Art Edn. Assn., Calif. Art Edn. Assn., Calif. Tchrs.' Assn., Phi Kappa Phi (hon.), Pi Lambda Theta (hon.). Avocations: gardening, drawing, cooking, reading, travel. Home: 27826 Torroba Mission Viejo CA 92692-2131 Personal E-mail: mgmcafee@cox.net.

MCALLISTER, LYNETTE J. financial consultant; b. Salt Lake City, July 17, 1961; d. Robert E. Cheney Sr. and Marie Jane Thurman; m. Robert Dale McAllister, May 16, 1986; children: Cherise Lynne, Ethan Trevor. Grad., Salt Lake City Coll. Med. and Dental Careers, 1986. Credit proof operator First Security Bank, Salt Lake City, 1979-81; dental asst. FHP of Utah (HMO), Midvale, 1981-84, Dr. Mark Blaisdell DDS, Bountiful, Utah, 1984-86; ops. mgr. First Security Investor Svcs., Salt Lake City, 1986-90, brokerage trader, 1990-96; fin. cons. Zions Investment Securities, Salt Lake City, 1996—. Mem. Fin. Women Internat. (edn. chair, sec. 1997—, Woman of Yr. 1997, com. festival of trees 1998). Avocations: camping, sports, crocheting, painting. Office: Zions Investment Securities One South Main St 3d Fl Salt Lake City UT 84111

MCALLISTER, NANCY ELIZABETH, music educator; b. New Haven, Conn., Oct. 23, 1962; d. Harold George Card and Lorraine Anna Murphy; m. Michael Patrick McAllister, July 30, 1994; children: Patrick Michael, Megan Ann. BA in Music Edn., U. Hartford, Conn., 1985; postgrad., So. Conn. State U., New Haven, 1990. Cert. pre-K to grade 12 music tchr. Conn., 1985, early childhood, elem., and mid. sch. tchr. Conn., 1990. Music educator, kindergarten through grade 6 Norwich Pub. Schs., Conn., 1985—86; music educator, kindergarten through grade 3 Clinton Pub. Schs., Conn., 1986—. Mem. Tchr. Evaluation Com., Clinton, Conn., 1988—89, Curriculum Planning and Adv. Coun., Clinton, Conn., 1989—; presenter Conn. Early Childhood Edn. Conf., 1992—93; mem. Arts Edn. Curriculum Devel., Clinton, Conn., 1996—98, Tchr. Evaluation Com., Clinton, Conn., 2001—. Catechism tchr. St. Mary's Ch., Clinton, Conn., 2002—. Recipient Clinton Tchr. of the Yr., Clinton Bd. of Edn., 2003-2004. Mem.: NEA, Am. Orff-Schulwerk, Orgn. of Am. Kodaly Educators, Nat. Assn. for Music Edn., Alpha Delta Kappa-TAU Chpt. (v.p. 1996—98). Roman Catholic. Avocations: gardening, sewing, hiking, walking, travel. Home: 1 Indian Dr Clinton CT 06413 Office: Lewin G Joel Jr Sch 37A Glenwood Rd Clinton CT 06413 E-mail: nmcallister@clintonpublic.org.

MCALPINE, MARY HELEN, nutritional science educator; b. Forkland, Ala., Aug. 21, 1959; d. Horace and Ceola McAlpine. BSc, Ala. A&M U., 1981; MSc, Calif. State U., 1989. Tchr. LA Unified Sch. Dist., 1991—. Mem.: Ala. Civic and Social Club, Zeta Phi Beta. Avocations: reading, cooking, travel. Home: 27030 Bolo Ct Corona CA 92883-6663 Office: Banning High School 1527 Lakme Ave Wilmington CA 90744

MCANALLY, ANN, puzzle constructor; b. Sioux City, Iowa, Jan. 13, 1920; d. Walter Peter and Clerce Ellen (Gregoire) Knudsen; m. Paul Edward McAnally, July 12, 1942; children: Kathleen, Thomas P., Gary Edward. AA in Bus., NBT, Sioux City, Iowa, 1937-39. Puzzle constructor Acrostics Network, 1993—. Poems pub. Internat. Soc. Poets.; author: All I Remember: A Memoir. Vol. Red Cross, Family Svcs. Recipient poetry awards, Internat. Soc. Editors Choice, honorable mention, Iliad Lit. Awards, President's award for Literary Excellence, Nat. Authors Registry, 2001. Mem. Internat. Poets Soc., S.W. League of Fine Arts (treas.), So. Az. Watercolor Guild, Mensa, Alpha Iota. Avocations: art, travel, mah jongg. Home: 451 N Meadow Drive Dammeron Valley UT 84783

MCANARNEY, ELIZABETH R. pediatrician, educator; b. N.Y.C., May 7, 1940; d. Henry Kellers and Kathryn (Blaney) McA. AB, Vassar Coll., 1962; MD, SUNY, Syracuse, 1966. Diplomate Am. Bd. Pediatrics in pediatrics and adolescent medicine. Intern, resident SUNY Upstate Med. Ctr., Syracuse, N.Y., 1966-68; fellow in behavioral pediatrics U. Rochester (N.Y.) Med. Ctr., 1968-70, sr. instr. pediatrics, 1969-71, asst. prof. pediatrics, 1971-77, assoc. prof. pediatrics, 1977-85, prof. pediatrics, 1985—, chair pediatrics dept., 1993—. Adv. com. Fertility and Maternal Health FDA, Bethesda, Md, 1987-92; mem. program adv. bd. Robert Wood Johnson Clin. Scholars Program, Princeton, N.J., 1995—. Editor: (books) Premature Adolescent Pregnancy, 1983, Identifying Social/ Psychological Antecedents of Adolescent Pregnancy, 1984, Textbook of Adolescent Medicine, 1992; co-author of nearly 200 papers, chpts., and comm. Recipient McNeil Outstanding Achievement award Soc. for Adolescent Medicine, 1989, Job Lewis Smith award Cmty. Pediat., Am. Acad. Pediat., 1990; named to Alumni Honor Roll, SUNY, 1998. Fellow AAAS; mem. Soc. for Pediatric Rsch., Am. Pediatric Soc. (mem. exec. coun. 1998—), Assn. for Med. Sch. Pediatric Chairs (pres. 1999—), Inst. Medicine, Nat. Acad. Sci. Achievements include determination of relationship between young maternal age and maternal/neonatal outcomes. Office: U Rochester Med Ctr Dept Pediatrics 601 Elmwood Ave Box 777 Rochester NY 14642-0001 E-mail: carole_berger@urmc.rochester.edu.*

MCANDREWS, SHANNON MARIE, elementary school educator; b. Kailua, Hawaii, Mar. 23, 1969; d. James Edward and Marie Louise Sniffen; m. Kenneth Lloyd McAndrews, Aug. 21, 1993; children: Logan Marie, Jordan Elizabeth. BS, San Diego State U., 1991; MS in Spl. Edn., U. San Diego, 1993. Tchr. San Diego Unified, 1992—93, Poway Unified, 1993—94, Ramona Unified, Ramona, Calif., 1995—. Mem.: Calif. Coun. Social Studies. Achievements include recognition as the first of 2 PATH program educators in Calif. Avocation: dance. Office: James Dukes Elem Sch 24908 Abalar Way Ramona CA 92065 E-mail: mcandrewsjd@aol.com.*

MCANENY, DEBORAH H. insurance company executive; b. 1980; Staff John Hancock Life Ins. Co., Boston, 1985—98, v.p., 1998—2000; sr. v.p. John Hancock Fin. Svcs., Inc. & John Hancock Life Ins. Co., Boston, 2000—02; dir. and CEO John Hancock Natural Resource Group, Boston, 2001—; exec. v.p. John Hancock Fin. Svcs., Inc. & John Hancock Life Ins. Co., Boston, 2002—; also bd. dirs. John Hancock Subsidiaries, Boston, 2002—. Office: John Hancock Fin Svcs Inc John Hancock Pl PO Box 111 Boston MA 02117

MCANIFF, NORA P. publishing executive; BA, CUNY. From mktg. info. mgr. to pres. People Mag. Time Inc., N.Y.C., 1982—98, pres. People Mag., 1998—2002, pub. Life Mag., 1992—93, pub. Teen People, 1997—98, exec. v.p., 2002—. Office: Time Inc 1271 Avenue of the Americas New York NY 10020-1300

MCARDLE, BARBARA VIRGINIA, elementary school educator; b. Worcester, Mass., Sept. 4, 1925; d. Patrick Michael Brosnan and Nora Catherine Ferriter; m. William Henry McARdle, June 20, 1956. BS in Edn., Worcester State Tchrs. Coll., 1947, MEd, 1953. Elem. grade tchr. Grove St. Sch., Spencer, Mass., 1947—48, Allen L. Joslin Sch., Oxford, Mass., 1948—56, Euclid Sch., St. Petersburg, Fla., 1957—63, Wood Lawn Sch., St. Petersburg, 1963—91. Sch. rep. Pinellas County Tchrs. Assn., St. Petersburg, 1957—91; active Boys and Girls Club of Am.; vol. Dem. Orgn., St. Petersburg. Named to Kindergarten Playground at Wood Lawn Sch. Mem.: St. Jude's Guild, St. Anthony's Guild. Roman Catholic. Home: 5266 26th Ave N Saint Petersburg FL 33710

MCARDLE, KATHLEEN ANN, elementary school educator; b. Newark, Oct. 13, 1954; d. James Michael and Sophie Veronica McArdle. BA, Coll. N.J., 1976; MFA in Painting, Pratt Inst., 1978. Cert. tchr. Caldwell Coll. Prodn. mgr. Deluxe Corp., Mountain Lakes, NJ, 1986—99; visual arts specialist Clifton Elem. Schs., NJ, 2000, L.V. Moore Mid. Sch., Roselle, NJ, 2000—03, Glen Rock Mid. Sch., NJ, 2003—. Mem.: NEA, Art Educators N.J., Nat. Art Edn. Assn. Democrat. Roman Catholic.

MCARDLE, PATRICIA ANNE, security company executive; b. Freeport, N.Y., Oct. 8, 1963; d. John Fergerson and Dorothy Patricia (Williamson) McA.; m. Robert Tyszkowski, Dec. 30, 1995. BBA, Pace U., 1985; MBA, N.Y. Inst. Tech., 1990; postgrad., John Jay Coll., 1993-94. Lic. pvt. detective, Mass., N.Y. Mfg. planner Grumman Aerospace, Milledgeville, Ga., 1981-82, Hazeltine Corp., Commack, N.Y., 1987-89; contracts analyst N.Y.C. Transit Authority, Bklyn., 1989-90, contracts mgr., 1991-92, acting dir. procurement, 1992-93; spl. investigator City of N.Y., 1993-96; prin., CEO, chmn. bd. dirs. P.M.T. Assocs. Inc., Boston, 1996—; CEO, pres., chmn. bd. dirs. Evidaunt Investigations, Inc., Boston, 1997—. Author: Handbook of Investigations, 1995. Event vol. U.S. Special Olympics, Hempstead, N.Y., 1992; mem. Redwood Libr. and Athenaeum, Newport, R.I. Recipient Silver Leader award DAV, 1997, 98, 99. Mem. Athenaeum (Boston, Newport, R.I.), Nat. Assn. Investigative Specialists, Tennis and Racquet Club (Boston), Redwood Libr. Republican. Avocations: reading, international travel. Office: Evidaunt Investigations Inc Prudential Ctr PO Box 990067 Boston MA 02199-0067 E-mail: evidaunt@aol.com.

MCARTHUR, LISA R. music educator, musician; d. Tremaine James and Judith Hammon McArthur. Ph.D. in Music Theory, U. of Ky., Lexington, Kentucky, 1995—99; MA in Music Theory, Kent State U., Kent, Ohio, 1990—94, MusM in Performance, 1990—93; MusB in Music Edn., SUNY Potsdam Coll., Crane Sch. of Music, Potsdam, New York, 1986—90. Grad. asst. Kent State U., Kent, Ohio, 1990—92; orch. dir., grades 4-12 Akron Pub. Schools, Akron, Ohio, 1993—95; grad. tchg. asst. U. of Ky., Lexington, Ky., 1995—98; assoc. prof. Campbellsville U., Campbellsville, Ky., 1998—. Clinician Emerson Flutes, Elkhart, Ind., 2000—; performer, Ky., and New York, 1990—; dir. Campbellsville U. Flute Ensemble, Campbellsville, Ky., 1998—. Author: (article) Flute Keys (periodical name), musician guest recital, (debut CD) Something Old, Something New, Something Borrowed, Something Blue, 2004; presenter at the National Flute Convention, at the In-Service Conference of the Kentucky Music Educators Association/Southern Division of the Music Educators National Conference. Named Coll./U. Educator of the Yr., Ky. Music Educators Assn., 2001; recipient Performer's cert., Crane Sch. of Music, 1990. Mem.: Nat. Assn. of Coll. Wind and Percussion Instructors, Nat. Flute Assn., Soc. for Music Theory, Coll. Music Soc., Music Educators Nat. Conf. (coll. chpt. advisor 1998—, state chpt. advisor 2003—), Ky. Music Educators Assn., Flute Soc. of Ky. (pres. 2000—), Sigma Alpha Iota (life). Achievements include Musical Composition for Flute and Percussion: Finding Peace (1998); Musical Composition: ...but deliver us from evil for Flute Ensemble (2001). Office: Campbellsville University UPO 1346 Campbellsville KY 42718 E-mail: lrmcarthur@campbellsville.edu.

MCATEE, PATRICIA ANNE ROONEY, medical educator; b. Denver, Apr. 20, 1931; d. Jerry F. and Edna E. (Hansen) Rooney; m. Darrell McAtee, Sept. 4, 1954; 1 son, Kevin Paul. BS, Loretto Heights Coll., 1953; MS, U. Colo., 1961; PhD, Union of Univs., 1976. Supr. St. Anthony Hosp., Denver, 1952-55; pub. health nurse, edn. dir. Tri-County Health Dept., Colo., 1956-58; adminstr. sch. health program Littleton (Colo.) Pub. Schs., 1958-60; asst. prof. community health, acad. adminstr. continuing edn. U. Colo., 1968-70; project dir. Western Interstate Commn. for Higher Edn., 1972-74; asst. prof. pediatrics, project co-dir. Sch. Medicine U. Colo., 1975—; mem. profl. svcs. staff Mead Johnson & Co., 1981—. Cons. Colo. Safety Coun.; treas. Vista Nueva Assocs. Editor: Pediatric Nursing, 1975-77. Chmn. bd. dirs. Found. for Urban and Neighborhood Devel.; mem. Arapahoe Health Planning Coun. Mem. NAS, APHA, Inst. Medicine, Nat. Bd. Pediatric Nurse Practitioners and Assocs. (pres.), Nat. Assn. Pediatric Nurse Practitioners (v.p.), Am. Acad. Polit. and Social Scientist, Nat. League Nursing, Western Soc. Rsch., Am. Sch. Health Assn., Sigma Theta Tau. Home: 877 E Panama Dr Littleton CO 80121-2531 Office: 4200 E 9th Ave Denver CO 80220-3706

MCATEER, DEBORAH GRACE, travel executive; b. NYC, Nov. 3, 1950; d. Edward John and Ann Marie (Cassidy) McA.; m. William A. Helms, Feb. 5, 1948 (div. 1993); children: Elizabeth Grace, Kathleen Marie, Margaret Ann; m. M. Lees Sherwood, Mar. 8, 1949 (div. 2002). Student, Montgomery Coll., 1969, Am. U., 1972. Sec. Polinger Co., Chevy Chase, Md., 1969-72, Loews Hotels, Washington, 1972-73; adminstr. asst. Am. Gas Assn., Arlington, Va., 1973-75; mgr. Birch Jermain Horton Bittner, Washington, 1975-77; asst. mgr. Travel Services, McLean, Va., 1977-79; founder, pres. Travel Temps, Washington, Atlanta, Phila., Miami and Ft. Lauderdale, Fla., 1979—; pres. Diversified Communications, Atlanta, 1990—; tchr. Ga. State U., Atlanta, 1996; pres. The Internet Employment Source, Atlanta, 1987—. Tchr. Montgomery Coll., Rockville, Md., 1980-84, Ga. State U., 1996. Mem. Christ Child Soc., Washington, 1975—; bd. dirs. Atlanta Ballet, 1995—. Mem. Internat. Travel Soc. (pres. 1983-84), Am. Soc. Travel Agts., Pacific Area Travel Assn., Inst. Cert. Travel Cons. (cert., life mem.), Nat. Assn. Women Bus. Owners (chair membership com. 1983-84), Women Bus. Owners Atlanta (bd. dirs. 1991—, pres. 1994), Women's Commerce Club, PROST (v.p. 1991), Atlanta Women in Travel. Republican. Roman Catholic.

MCAULIFFE, CATHERINE A. counselor, psychology educator, psychotherapist; b. Northampton, Mass., July 31, 1952; d. Francis G. and Emliy R. (Hanley) Ciarfella; m. Francis J. McAuliffe, Aug. 14, 1999; children: Richard Jr. DiPersio, Edward DiPersio, Mary Catherine DiPersio. BS in Elem. Edn., U. Conn., 1974; MS in Counseling, So. Conn. State U., 1988; postmaster's sch. counseling cert., Cen. Conn. State U., 1992. Cert. K-12 counselor, K-8 tchr. Conn., adult edn. tchr. 1st grade tchr. Granby (Conn.) Pub. Schs., 1974-75; pvt. psychotherapist Meriden, Conn., 1988—97; dir. counseling Paier Coll. Art, Hamden, Conn., 1988—91; h.s. counselor Sacred Heart H.S., Waterbury, Conn., 1990-91; sch. counselor Meriden Pub. Schs., Cheshire (Conn.) Pub. Schs., 1997—2000, Bridgeport (Conn.) Pub. Schs., 2001—. Pers. devel. counselor U. Conn., Waterbury, 1991—97; psychology instr. Paier Coll. Art, 1991—97. Scout leader Cub Scouts Am., Meriden, 1984-86, Girl Scouts Am., 1986-87; hospitality chairperson PTA, Meriden, 1984-85; vol. Rep. Party, Meriden, 1988. Mem.: Am. Assn. Christian Counselors, Conn. Sch. Counseling Assn., Conn. Sch. Counseling Assn., ACA, Phi Kappa Phi. Roman Catholic. Avocations: singing, directing choirs, playing keyboard, guitar, composing lyrics and music. Home: 15 Spring Glen Dr Meriden CT 06451-2720 Office: 265 George St Bridgeport CT 06604-3320

MCAULIFFE, JANE DAMMEN, religious studies and Islamic studies educator; BA in Classics and Philosophy, Trinity Coll., 1968; MA in Religious Studies, U. Toronto, 1979, PhD in Islamic Studies, 1984. Asst. prof. dept. religious studies U. Toronto, 1981-86, assoc. to full prof. dept. Middle East and Islamic studies, dept. study religion, 1992-99, chair dept. study of religion, dir. Ctr. Study of Religion, 1992-97; from asst. prof. to assoc. prof. history of religions and Islamic studies Candler Sch. Theology Emory U., Atlanta, 1986-92, assoc. dean Candler Sch. Theology, 1990-92; prof. Dept. for the Study of Religion, 1997-99; dean, prof. history and Arabic Georgetown Coll. Georgetown U., Washington, 1999—. Appointed Vatican Commn. for Religious Rels. with Muslims, 1994. Author: Qur'anic Christians: An Analysis of Classical and Modern Exegesis, 1991, 'Abbasid Authority Affirmed: The Early Years of al-Mansur, vol. 28, 1995; editor: Encyclopaedia of the Qur'an, 2001—; contbr. articles to profl. jours. Danforth Found. fellow, 1976-80, NEH Summer fellow, 1979-80, Charles Gordon Heyd fellow, 1980-81, Social Scis. and Humanities Rsch. Coun. doctoral fellow, 1981-84, Postdoctoral fellow, 1984-86, CASA II fellow, 1986, NEH Summer Faculty Travel fellow, 1989, NEH Rsch. fellow, 1992, Mellon fellow, 1994, Guggenheim fellow, 1996. Mem. Am. Soc. Study of

Religion, Am. Acad. Religion, Am. Oriental Soc., Can. Soc. Study of Religion, Mid. East Studies Assn. (Thesis award 1985), Soc. Values in Higher Edn. Office: Georgetown Coll Georgetown U PO Box 571003 Washington DC 20057-1003 Home: 1321 36th St NW Washington DC 20007

MCAULIFFE, ROSEMARY, state legislator; b. Seattle, Aug. 1, 1940; m. James McAuliffe; 6 children. BSN, Seattle U. Owner, mgr. Hollywood Sch. House; mem. Wash. Senate, Dist. 1, Olympia, 1993—; chair edn. com. Wash. Senate, mem. environ. quality and water resources com., mem. higher edn. com., co-chairperson joint select com. on edn. restructuring, mem. student conduct task force, mem. spl. edn. adv. coun., mem. food safety adv. coun. Bd. dirs. Northshore Sch., 1977-91, bd. pres., 1981-82; mem. Northshore Econ. Devel. Com., Together for a Drug-Free Youth Com., 1989; chairwoman Bothell Downtown Mgmt. Assn., 1987-90; del. Main St. Revitalization, Pacific N.W.; mem. conf. com. and diversion com. Northshore Juvenile Ct., 1978-80; mem. Lake Health Com., 1997-98. Mem. Wash. Sch. Dir.'s Assn. (legis. network rep. 1990-91), Assn. Children with Learning Disabilities, Northshore and Woodinville C. of C. Democrat. Office: 402A John Cherberg Bldg Olympia WA 98504-0001

MCBEE, MARY LOUISE, state legislator, former academic administrator; b. Strawberry Plains, Tenn., June 15, 1924; d. John Wallace and Nina Aileen (Umbarger) McB. BS, East Tenn. State U., 1946; MA, Columbia U., 1951; PhD, Ohio State U., 1961. Tchr. East Tenn. State U., Johnson City, 1947-51; asst. dean of women, 1952-56, 57-60; dean of women, 1961-63, U. Ga., Athens, 1963-67; world campus afloat adminstr., 1966-67; assoc. dean of students, 1967-72; dean of students, 1972-74; asst. v.p. acad. affairs, 1974-76; assoc. v.p. acad. affairs, 1976-86; v.p. acad. affairs, 1986-88. Author: College Responsibility for Values, 1980; co-author: The American Woman: Who Will She Be?, 1974, Essays, 1979,, 2d edit. 1981. Bd. dirs. Salvation Army, Athens, 1978—, United Way, Athens. Fulbright scholar, The Netherlands, 1956-57. Mem. Athens C. of C. (bd. dirs.). Democrat. Methodist. Avocations: gardening, tennis, hiking. Home: 145 Pine Valley Pl Athens GA 30606-4031 Office: Ga House of Reps State Capitol Atlanta GA 30334 E-mail: lmcbee@legis.state.ga.us.

MCBEE, SUSANNA BARNES, retired journalist; b. Santa Fe, N.Mex., Mar. 28, 1935; d. Jess Stephen and Sybil Elizabeth (Barnes) McBee; m. Paul H. Recer, July 2, 1983. AB, U. So. Calif., 1956; MA, U. Chgo., 1962. Staff writer Washington Post, 1957-65, 73-74, 77-79, asst. nat. editor, 1974-77; asst. sec. pub. affairs HEW, 1979; articles editor Washingtonian mag., 1980-81; assoc. editor U.S. News & World Report, 1981-86; news editor Washington Bur., Hearst Newspapers, 1987-89, asst. bur. chief, 1990—2003, ret., 2003; Washington corr. Life mag., 1965—69; Washington editor McCall's mag., 1970—72. Bd. dirs. Washington Press Club Found., 1992-95. Recipient Penney-Missouri mag. award, 1969, Hall of Fame award, Soc. Profl. Journalists, 1996, Sigma Delta Chi Pub. Svc. award, 1969, Hearst Eagle award, 1994. Mem. Nat. Press Club, Cosmos Club. Home: 5190 Watson St NW Washington DC 20016-5329

MCBRAYER, SANDRA L. educational director, homeless outreach educator; AA, San Diego Mesa Coll., 1981; BA in Applied Arts and Scis., San Diego State U., 1986, MA in Edn., 1990. Cert. presch.-kindergarten, grs. 1-12, adult edn., Calif. Tchr. asst. group homes Oz, The Bridge, Gatehouse, 1984-87; tchr. Hillcrest Receiving Home, 1987-88, Juvenile Hall, 1987-88, Comprehensive Adolescent Treatment Ctr., 1987-88; head tchr. the Monarch HS, 1988-96; CEO The Children's Initiative, San Diego. Lectr., cons. Ctrs. Careers Edn., Sch. Tchr. Edn. San Diego State U., 1990—; collaborator sch. dists. State Dept. Edn., Equity/Homeless Office, 1992—; staff devel. tng.; adj. prof. Coll. Edn., San Diego (Calif.) State U. Recipient award Exceptional Vols. Svc. Family Care Ctr., 1988, San Diego's 10 Leadership award Sta. KGTV, 1991, Celebrate Literacy award Internat. Reading Assn., 1992, Women of Vision in Edn. award LWV San Diego, 1992, Disting. Alumna of Yr.-Edn. award San Diego State U., 1992, Golden Bell award Calif. Sch. Bds. Found., 1992, Coun. of State Sch. Officers Nat. Tchr. of Yr. award 1994; named San Diego County Tchr. of Yr. by San Diego County Office of Edn., 1993, Calif. Tchr. of Yr. by State Dept. Edn., 1993, Nat. Tchr. of Yr., Pres. Clinton, 1994, Tech. Tchr. of Yr., Coun. on Tech. Tchr. Edn., 1994, Exceptional Svc. award Calif. State PTA, Humanitarian award Youth Advocacy Assn., Living Legacy award Internat. Women's Ctr.; recognized by local and nat. news media. Mem. NEA, Calif. Tchrs. Assn., Assn. Educators, Nat. Dropout Prevention Network, Calif. Homeless Coalition, Phi Kappa Phi. Office: The Childrens Initiative 4438 Ingraham St San Diego CA 92109

MCBREEN, MAURA ANN, lawyer; b. N.Y.C., Aug. 18, 1953; d. Peter J. and Frances S. (McVeigh) McB. AB, Smith Coll., 1975; JD, Harvard U., 1978. Bar: Ill. 1978. Ptnr. Kirkland & Ellis, Chgo., 1978-86, Isham, Lincoln & Beale (merged with Reuben & Proctor), Chgo., 1986-88, Baker & McKenzie, Chgo., 1988—. Mem. ABA, Chgo. Bar Assn., Midwest Pension Conf. Office: Baker & McKenzie 1 Prudential Pla 130 E Randolph Dr Ste 3700 Chicago IL 60601-6342

MCBRIDE, ANGELA BARRON, nursing educator; b. Balt., Jan. 16, 1941; d. John Stanley and Mary C. (Szczepanska) Barron; m. William Leon McBride, June 12, 1965; children: Catherine, Kara. BS in Nursing, Georgetown U., 1962, LHD (hon.), 1993; MS in Nursing, Yale U., 1964; PhD, Purdue U., 1978; D of Pub. Svc. (hon.), U. Cin., 1983; LittD (hon.), Purdue U., 1998; LLD (hon.), Ea. Ky. U., 1991; DSc(hon.), Med. Coll. of Ohio, 1995; LHD (hon.), U. Akron, 1997. Asst. prof., rsch. asst. inst. Yale U., New Haven, 1964-73; assoc. prof., chairperson Ind. U. Sch. Nursing, Indpls., 1978-81, 80-84, prof., 1981-92, assoc. dean rsch., 1985—91, interim dean, 1991—92, univ. dean, 1992—2003, disting. prof., 1992—; sr. v.p. acad. affairs, nursing Clarian Health Ptnrs., 1997—2003; Am. Acad. Nursing scholar-in-residence Inst. Medicine, 2003—04. Mem. Nat. Adv. Mental Health Coun., 1987—91; mem. adv. com. NIH Office of Women's Health Rsch., 1997—2001, NIH Office of Women's Health Rsch. Specialized Ctrs. Rsch. on Sex and Gender Factors, 2003—; mem. Yale U. Coun., 2000—; ext. acad. advisor Sch. Nursing, Hong Kong Polytechnic U., 2000—. Author: The Growth and Development of Mothers, 1973 (Best Book award 1973), Living with Contradictions, A Married Feminist, 1976, How to Enjoy A Good Life With Your Teenager, 1987; editor: Psychiatric-Mental Health Nursing: Integrating the Behavioral and Biological Sciences, 1996 (Best Book award 1996); compiler: Nursing and Philanthropy, 2000. Recipient Disting. Alumna award Yale U., Disting. Alumna award Purdue U., Univ. Medallion, U. San Francisco, 1993, Hoosier Heritage award, 2000, Disting. Nurse Educator award Coll. Mt. St. Joseph, Cin., 2000, Ross Pioneering Spirit award Am. Assn. Critical-Care Nurses, 2004; named Influential Woman in Indpls., Indpls. Bus. Jour./Ind. Lawyer, 1999, named HealthCare Hero Indpls. Bus. Jour., 2003; Kellogg nat. fellow; Am. Nurses Found. scholar, Salute to Women award Indpls. YMCA, 1999, Sagamore of Wabash, 1999. Fellow: Nat. Acads. Practice, Am. Acad. Nursing (dir. leadership devel. Bldg. Acad. Geriatric Nursing Capacity program 2001—, past pres.), APA (nursing and health psychology award divsn. 38 1995); mem.: Nat. Acad. Scis., Inst. of Medicine, Soc. for Rsch. in Child Devel., Midwest Nursing Rsch. Soc. (Disting. Rsch. award 1985), Sigma Theta Tau (past pres., mentor award 1993, disting. lectr 1995—99, Melanie Dreher award for contbns. as a dean 2001), Chi Eta Phi (hon.). Home: 744 Cherokee Ave Lafayette IN 47905-1872 E-mail: amcbride@iupui.edu.

MCBRIDE, BEVERLY JEAN, lawyer; b. Greenville, Ohio, Apr. 5, 1941; d. Kenneth Birt and Glenna Louise (Ashman) Whited; m. Benjamin Gary McBride, Nov. 28, 1964; children: John David, Elizabeth Ann. BA magna cum laude, Wittenberg U., 1963; JD cum laude, U. Toledo, 1966. Bar: Ohio 1966. Intern Ohio Gov.'s Office, Columbus, 1962; asst. dean women U. Toledo, 1963-65; assoc. Title Guarantee and Trust Co., Toledo, 1966-69; spl. counsel Ohio Atty. Gen.'s Office, Toledo, 1975; assoc. Cobourn, Smith, Rohrbacher and Gibson, Toledo, 1969-76; v.p., gen. counsel, sec. The Andersons, Maumee, Ohio, 1976—. Exec. trustee, bd. dirs. Wittenberg U., Springfield, Ohio, 1980-83; trustee Anderson Found., Maumee, 1981-93; mem. Ohio Supreme Ct. Task Force on Gender Fairness, 1991-94, Regional Growth Partnership, 1994—; chmn. Sylvania Twp. Zoning Commn., Ohio, 1970-80; candidate for judge Sylvania Mcpl. Ct., 1975; trustee Goodwill Industries, Toledo, 1976-82, Sylvania Cmty. Svcs. Ctr., 1976-78, Toledo-Lucas County Port Authority, 1992-99; chair St. Vincent Med. Ctr., 1992-99; founder Sylvania YWCA Program, 1973; active membership drives Toledo Mus. Art, 1977-87. Recipient Toledo Women in Industry award YWCA, 1979, Outstanding Alumnus award Wittenberg U., 1981. Fellow Am. Bar Found.; mem. ABA, AAUW, Ohio Bar Assn., Toledo Bar Assn. (pres., treas., chmn., sec. various coms.), Toledo Women Attys. Forum (exec. com. 1978-82), Pres. Club (U. Toledo exec. com.). Home: 5274 Cambrian Rd Toledo OH 43623-2626 Office: The Andersons 480 W Dussel Dr Maumee OH 43537-1690

MCBRIDE, ELIZABETH ANNE WILMORE, writer; b. Charlotte, N.C., Nov. 10, 1942; d. John Henry and Frances (Cox) Wilmore; divorced; children: John and Laura. BA in English, Rice U., 1964; MA in English & Creative Writing, U. Houston, 1982; student, Edward Albee Workshops, 1989-92. Instr. U. Houston, 1979—81, 1985—88; editor Lit. Mag., Houston, 1982-83, Domestic Crude, Houston, 1983-84; contbr. editor, columnist Artscene, 1989; editor rsch. papers for Naomi Kraus, U. Tex., Houston, 1990. Reader Houston Festival; judge Southwest Writers' Conf., 1984; bd. dirs. Lawndale Art and Performance Ctr.; panel mem. Seminar on Hispanic Art, U. Ariz., 1987-88. Guest curator Rice U., Houston, 1988, Glassel Sch., Houston, 1993, Houston Art League, 1997; contbr. author: (short stories) Her Work, Common Bonds, The Whole Story, Texas Short Stories II; reviewer The Houston Chronicle, 1980, ARTspace Mag., 1987-92, ARTnews, 1990-95, 2000, Pub. News, 1988-94, Sculpture Mag., 1989-90, Artscene Mag., 1984, Chelsea Mag., N.Y., and numerous others; poems: Vapor Trails, 1981, Diversions, 1982, Biloxi 1945, 1982, South Pacific Stars and Stripes, 1982, Kwajalein, 1983, Deep Sea Fishing With My Father, 1984, Everyday Places, 1985, Linguistics, 1987, Moctezuma's Headdress, 1992, I Bury My Father, 1993, Corazal, 1993, Inca Doves, 1993, O Corporeal, 1997; editor Ctr. for Big Bend Studies, Bosque Bonito, 2002; contbr. articles and short stories to profl. jours. and mags.; exhibited in group shows at Treebeards, 1995, The New Gallery, 1995, Lawndale Art Ctr., 1995, Diverse Works Alternative Space, 1996, Sally Sprout Gallery, 1996, Houston Pottery Guild and Gallery, 1997, 2000; one woman shows at Westenberg Gallery, Marfa, 2000, Big Bend Sentinel, Marfa, 2000, Devin Borden Hiram Butler Gallery, Houston, 2002, Terlingua Ho. Projects, Alpine, Tex., 2002, Highland Gallery, Marfa, 2003; represented in numerous pvt. collections, S.I. Assocs., Houston, Playwright, Long Island; writer-in-residence Chinati Found, 1995-96, art critic ArtLies Mag., Houston Tex. Vol. tchg. Hartman Jr. High, Roberts Elem. Sch., Valley of Peace, Belize, Marfa Tex. Libr.; mem. literacy events bd. Houston Festival, chmn. lit. arts panel, 1986; bd. dirs. lit. and humanities panel Cultural Arts Coun. Houston, 1987-88; mem. lit. panel Tex. Commn. Arts, 1988-89. Recipient Brazos for fiction prize, 1984; fellow MacDowell Colony, 1986, Edward Albee Found., 1990. Mem. Poets and Writers, League Women Voters (chmn. voters svc.); founding bd. mem. Zocalo Theater. Office: PO Box 5 Marfa TX 79843

MCBRIDE, JOYCE BROWNING, accountant; b. Ga., May 28, 1927; d. Eph and Zula (Harden) Browning; children: Jan Coffman, Gary, Kandie Van Affelen. Grad., So. Bus. U., 1947. Asst. contr. Hampton Ct. Knits, L.A., 1967—78; owner, mgr. McBride & Assocs. Bookkeeping Svc., 1978—. Address: 2925 Tyler Ct Simi Valley CA 93063-1742 E-mail: mcassoc7@aol.com.

MCBRIDE, JUDITH, elementary school educator; BFA in Interior Design, Utah State U., 1963; MFA, U. Wyo., 1980. Art tchr. Beitel Elem. Sch., Laramie, Wyo., Spring Creek Elem. Sch., Laramie, Centennial Valley Elem. Sch., Laramie. Named Wyo. State Tchr. of Yr., 1993. Office: Spring Creek Elem Sch 1203 Russell St Laramie WY 82070-4682

MCBRIDE, MARTINA, vocalist; b. Medicine Lodge, Kans., July 29, 1966; d. Daryl and Jeanne Schiff; m. John McBride, May 15, 1988; children: Delaney Katherine, Emma Justine. Vocalist Schiffters, 1975-86, assorted bands, Wichita, Kans.; represented by RCA Records, 1991—; backup singer Garth Brooks, 1992—93, European tour, 1994. Singer (popular): (albums) The Time Has Come, 1992, The Way That I Am, 1993 (Platinum), Evolution, 1997 (Triple Platinum), Wild Angels, 1995 (Platinum), WhiteChristmas, 1998 (Platinum), Emotion, 1999 (Platinum), Greatest Hits, 2001 (Dounble Platinum), Martina, 2003 (Gold), (songs) Sweet Dreams of You, 2003, Cheap Whiskey, 2003, (albums) (Group recording) Safe In The Arms Of Love, 2000, (various artists) Wrong Again, 2000, (soundtrack various artists) There You Are, 2000, (songs) You'll Get Through This, 2000, I Love You, 1999, (albums) (various artists) Girls Night Out, 1999, numerous recordings; performer (pop star): (tv appearances) In My Daughters Eyes, 2003, (tv appearances co-star Pat Benatar) CMT Crossraods, 2003, (tv appearances) Stand By You Man, 2003, (presenter of award) CMT Flameworthy Awards, 2003, (tv appearance) Nat. Anthem, 2003, (tv appearances) Today Show, 2002, (tv biograhy) Lifetime Intimate portrait, 2002, (tv appearance) The Tonight Show, 2001, Larry King Live, 2001, Live! Regis and Kathy Lee, 2001, numerous tv appearances. Nominee Top Female Vocalist, Acad. of Country Music, 1993, Video of the Yr. for "Independence Day", 1994, Horizon award, Country Muci Assn., 1994, Best Country Song for "Independence Day", Grammy, 1994, Best Country Collaboration with Vocals for "Own My Own" with Reba McEntire, Linda Davis, and Trisha Yearwood, 1995, Best Country Female Vocal Performance for "Safe In The Arms Of Love", 1995, Album of the Yr. for "Wild Angels", Country Music Assn., 1996, Vocal Event of the Yr. for "On My Own" with Reba McEntire, Linda Davis, and Trisha Yearwood., 1996, Album of the Yr. for "Wild Angels", 1996, Female Vocalist of the Yr., 1996, Best Country Collaboration with Vocals for "Still Holding You" with Clint Black, Grammy, 1997, Vocal Event of the Yr. for "Still Holding On" with Clint Black, Country Music assn., 1997, Single of the Yr. for "A Broken Wing", Country Music Assn., 1998, Video of the Yr. for "A Broken Wing", 1998, Single of the Yr. for "A Broken Wing", 1998, Female Vocalist of the Yr., 1998, Top Female Voclaist, Acad. of Country Music, 1998, Best Country Female Vocal Performance for "I Love You", Grammy, 1999, Female Vocalist of the Yr., Country Music Assn., 1999, Video of the Yr. for "A Broken Wing", Acad. of Country Music, 1999, Song of the Yr. for "A Broken Wing", 1999, Single of the Yr. for "A Broken Wing", 1999, Top Female Vocalist, 2000, Female Vocalist of the Yr., Country Music Assn., 2001, Top Female Vocalist, Acad. of Country Music, 2001, Best Female Country Vocal Performance for "Blessed", Grammy, 2002, Single of the Yr. for "Blessed", Country Music Assn., 2002, Video of the Yr. for "Concrete Angel", 2003, Female Vocalist of the Yr., Am. Music Awards, 2003; recipient Best Video of the Yr. for "Independence Day", The Gt. Brit. Music Awards, 1994, Breakthrough Artist Video for "My Baby Loves Me", Music Row Ind. Summit Award, 1994, Music Vidoe of the Yr. for "Independence Day", Country Music Assn. Awards, 1994, Best Southern Gospel, Country Gospel or Bluegrass Gospel for "Amazing Grace - A Country Salute To Gospel", Grammy Awards, 1995, Video of the Yr. for "Independence Day", TNN Music City News Award, 1995, Nashville Music Awards, 1995, Country Album of the Yr. for "Wild Angels", 1996, Video of the Yr. for "Safe In The Arms of Love", Nashville Music Award, 1996, Best Female Artist, Country Radio Music Awards, 1996, Video of the Yr. for "Safe In The Arms of Love", Nashville Music Awards, 1996, Gold Clio for Country Music Video of the Yr. for "Independence Day", Clio Awards, 1995, Female Vocalist of the Yr., Country Music Assn. Award, 1999, 2002, Country Female Artist of the Yr., Billboard Music Award, 2002, Top Female Vocalist, Acad. of Country music Awards, 2002, Female Video of the Yr. for "Blessed", CMT Flameworthy Awards, 2002, Female Vocalist of the Yr. award, Country Music Assn., 2003, Top Female Vocalist, Acad. of Country Music award, 2003, Favorite Female Artist, country, Am. Music Awards, 2003, Female Video of the Yr. for "Concrete Angel", CMT Flameworthy Award, 2003, Favorite Female Artist, Country Weekly, 2003. Address: RCA Records 1400 18th Ave S Nashville TN 37212-2809

MCBRIDE, MILDRED MAYLEA, retired elementary school educator; b. Bowerston, Ohio, Oct. 7, 1922; d. Harry Scott and Mary McGary (Mowl) McB.; 1 adopted child, Marjorie Mi Sang McBride. BS in Music, Baldwin-Wallace Coll., 1944; MA, Columbia U., N.Y.C., 1949. Cert. tchr., Ohio, Hawaii. Traveling music tchr. Tuscarawas County Del., 1944-45; tchr. elem. music Parma (Ohio) Schs., 1945-48, tchr. jr. h.s. music, 1946-48; tchr. h.s. gen. music, chorus Kamehameha Sch. for Girls, Honolulu, 1949-59; tchr. elem. music Tempe (Ariz.) Schs., 1959-60, Hawaii Pub. Sch. Sys., 1960-86, ret., 1986. Co-founder Elem., Intermediate, Gen. Music Interest Group, Honolulu, 1969-79. Author, editor: (biography) Meg!, 1996, Three Women of Kintail, 2001, 4 hist. novels; writer mus. plays. Helper Bowerston Pub. Libr., 1939, 48, 97—; bd. dirs. Hawaii Habitat for Humanity, Honolulu, 1986-93; mem. Honolulu Symphony Chorus; head soup kitchen, vol. Harris United Meth. Ch., Honolulu, 1990-96, mem. choir, 1975-96; libr. asst. Dormont Presbyn. Ch. Libr. Avocations: golf, travel, singing, cooking, enjoying daughter. Home: 2934 Espy Ave Pittsburgh PA 15216-2017

MCBRIDE, SANDRA TEAGUE, psychiatric nurse; b. Corinth, Miss., Sept. 13, 1958; d. Clarence R. and Alice (Ingram) T. AAS, Shelby State Community Coll., 1983; BSN, U. North Ala., 1987; MSN, Union U., 2001. RN, Miss., Tenn. Nurse supr. Alcorn County Care, Inc., Corinth, Miss., 1985-87; staff nurse Bolivar (Tenn.) Cmty. Hosp., 1988-90; shift supr. Tenn. Dept. of Corrections, West Tenn. High Security Facility, Ripley, 1990-91; staff nurse U.S. Med. Ctr. for Fed. Prisoners, Springfield, Mo., 1991 92, Western Mental Health Inst., Bolivar, 1992—.

MCBRIDE, SHARON LOUISE, counselor, technical communication educator; b. Peoria, Ill., Dec. 5, 1939; d. Ralph Cannon and Joyce Eliz (Shoff) McB.; m. Armond B. Ciota, Jr., Apr. 23, 1960 (div.); children: Matthew Ciota, Eliz Faron, Thomas Ciota, Nathan Ciota. BA, Bradley U., 1960, MA, 1987. Various positions to undergrad. student adviser Bradley U., Peoria, 1972—; instr. Ill. Ctrl. Coll., East Peoria, 1987—. Chmn. bd. trustees Greater Peoria Mass Transit. Trustee West Peoria Twp., 1984-96; sec.-treas. Ill. Twp. Trustees, 1993-96; chairperson West Peoria Zoning Bd. Appeals; mem. policy com. Peoria Pekin Urbanized Area Transp. Study. Mem.: Am. Assn. Women in C.C., Am. Pub. Transit Assn. (transit bd., Region IV rep.), Am. Soc. Engring. Edn., Rotary Club (Peoria North), Lions (bd. dirs. West Peoria chpt. 1984—97, precinct com.). Republican. Avocations: travel, community volunteer. Home: 2413 W Kellogg Ave West Peoria IL 61604-5011

MCBRIDE, TERESA, information systems specialist; b. Grants, N. Mex., Sept. 8, 1962; 1 child. Mem. staff Family Restaurant, Grants, N. Mex.; founder, pres., CEO McBride & Assocs., Albuquerque, 1986—. Office: McBride & Assocs 5555 Mcleod Rd NE Albuquerque NM 87109-2408

MCBURNEY, ELIZABETH INNES, dermatologist, physician, educator; b. Lake Charles, La., Dec. 24, 1944; d. Theodore John and Martha (Caldwell) Innes; divorced, 1980; children: Leanne Marie, Susan Eleanor. BS, U. Southwestern La., 1965; MD, La. State U., 1969. Diplomate Am. Bd. Internal Medicine, Am. Bd. Dermatology. Intern Pensacola (Fla.) Edn. Program, 1969-70; resident in internal medicine Boston U. and Carney Hosps., 1970-72; resident in dermatology Charity Hosp., New Orleans, 1972-74; staff physician Ochsner Hosp., New Orleans, 1974-80; assoc. head of dermatology Ochsner Clinic, New Orleans, 1974-80; clin. asst. prof. La. Health Scis., New Orleans, 1976-79, clin. assoc. prof., 1979-90, clin. prof., 1990—; clin. asst. prof. Tulane Health Scis., New Orleans, 1976-88, clin. assoc. prof., 1988-91, clin. prof., 1991—. Mem. courtesy staff Northshore Regional Med. Ctr., Slidell, La., 1985—; mem. staff Slidell Meml. Hosp., 1988—, chmn. CME courses, 1988—, pres.-elect med. staff, 2000-01, pres., 2001—02; regional dir. Mycosis Fungoides Study Group, Balt., 1974-94. Contbr. articles to profl. jours. Bd. dirs. Slidell Art Coun., 1988—, Camp Fire, New Orleans, 1979-83, Cancer Assn. New Orleans, 1978-83; juror Art in Pub. Places, Slidell, 1989. Recipient Disting. Woman Physician award AMA, 1999, Ian G. Pearson edn. meml. award, 2004. Fellow ACP; mem. Am. Soc. Dermatologic Surgery (treas. 1991-94, bd. dirs. 1988-91, pres. elect 1995-96, pres. 1996-97, Samuel Stegman award 2000), Am. Acad. Dermatology (bd. dirs. 1994-98), Am. Bd. Laser Medicine and Surgery (bd. dirs. 1991-96), La. Dermatologic Soc. (pres. 1989-90), St. Tammany Med. Soc. (pres. 1988), Phi Kappa Phi, Alpha Omega Alpha. Avocations: reading, gardening, fine art, music, film. Office: 1051 Gause Blvd Ste 460 Slidell LA 70458-2985

MCCABE, MARY WILLIAMSON, computer systems analyst; b. Memphis, Aug. 8, 1934; d. Edwin Lacey and Mary Maxine (Maners) Williamson; m. Henry Arthur McCabe, Sept. 22, 1973; stepchildren: Patrick, Anne, Kevin, Cathleen, John. BA, Rhodes Coll., 1956. Math. tchr. Bolton (Tenn.) High Sch., 1956-57; programmer/analyst Mallory AF Sta., Memphis, 1957-61; sr. systems specialist computer dept. GE, Huntsville, Ala., 1961-66; sr. systems specialist Honeywell Info. Systems, Phoenix, 1966-78, Honeywell Bull, Mpls., 1979-88. Pres. McCabe & Assocs., Inc., Minnetonka, Minn., 1990-91, v.p. 1992. Vol. Am. Cancer Soc., Minnetonka, 1980—91; co-dir. altar guild Christ Ch. Ascension, 2002—. Mem. Paradise Rep. Women's Club (cmty affairs chair 2002, 2d v.p. 2004—), Alpha Omicron Pi (v.p. Kappa Omicron chpt. 1955-56). Republican. Episcopalian. Avocations: reading, photography. Home: 15193 N 102d Way Scottsdale AZ 85255

MCCABE, MELISSA CHRISTINE, music educator, researcher; b. Kansas City, Mo., Feb. 19, 1975; d. Deborah Louise and Thomas Michael McCabe. MusB, Simpson Coll., 1996; postgrad., U. Mo., Kansas City, 2001—. Cert. K-12 music educator Iowa State Bd. Edn., Kans. State Bd. Edn. Band and choir tchr. Ind. Sch. Dist. of West Burlington, Iowa, 1997—2000; band and orch. tchr. Coronado Mid. Sch., Kansas City, Kans., 2000—. Pvt. music instr. Studio Saxophone Lessons, Olathe, Kans., 2001—; rschr. in field. Mem. Ch. of the Resurrection Adult Orch., Leawood, Kans., 2001—; dir. Ch. of the Resurrection Mid. Sch. Orch., Leawood, 2001—; mem. Midwest Winds, Stanley, Kans., 2002—, Midwest Sax Quartet, Kansas City, Mo., 2002—. Recipient Outstanding Voluntary Svc. award, Ch. of the Resurrection, 2002. Mem.: Kans. Music Educators Assn., Music Educators Nat. Conf., Women Band Dirs. Internat. Avocations: travel, scrapbooking, playing in music ensembles, reading. Home: 14212 S Brougham Dr Olathe KS 66062 Personal E-mail: melissamccabe@comcast.net.

MCCAFFERTY, BARBARA JEAN (BJ MCCAFFERTY), sales executive; b. Lincoln, Nebr., Dec. 6, 1940; d. Russell Rowley and Ruth Alice (Williams) Wightman; m. Eriks Zeltins, Dec. 29, 1962 (div. Oct. 1976); 1 child, Brian K. Zeltins; m. Charles F. McCafferty Jr., Oct. 3, 1981 (div. July 1986). Student, Drexel U., 1958-61; BS magna cum laude, Del. Valley Coll. Sci. and Agri., Doylestown, Pa., 1984; MBA in Mktg., LaSalle U., 1998. Dept. mgr. Strawbridge & Clothier, Neshaminy, Pa., 1968-73, asst. buyer Phila., 1973-76; office adminstr. Am. Protein Products, Croydon, Pa., 1976-78; tech. librarian Honeywell Power Sources Ctr., Horsham, Pa., 1978-85; sales dir. Colonial Life and Accident Ins., Wayne, Pa., 1985-86; adminstrn. mgr. Mobi Systems, Inc., Ft. Washington, Pa., 1986-88; spl. rep. Universal Mktg. Corp., Southampton, Pa., 1988-89; ind. contractor McCafferty Ins. Svcs., Doylestown, Pa., 1989—; bus. rsch. asst. Merck & Co., Inc., West Point, Pa., 1993—. Mem. alumni recruitment connection Delaware Valley Coll. Sci. and Agr. Mem. NAFE, Nat. Assn. Profl. Saleswomen, Options, Inc., Franklin Mint Collectors Soc., Optomists, Lenox Collections, High Point Athletic Club. Republican. Presbyterian. Avocations: aerobics, power walking, tennis, skiing, reading. Home: 224 Hastings Ct Doylestown PA 18901-2506

MCCAFFERTY, LORNA MARIE (LORNA SUPERNOR), computer electronics engineer; b. Boston, Oct. 25, 1957; d. David John and Kathryn June (Hamilton) Branagan; m. Harold Henry Supernor, Jr., July 19, 1975 (div. Oct. 1978); 1 child, Robert Douglas; m. Kenneth E. McCafferty, May 17, 1993. AS, Quinsigamond C.C., Worcester, Mass., 1979; cert. computer electronics, Marlboro Skills Ctr., 1980; student, Boston U., 1980-81, West Coast u., 1982-83, UCLA, 1983-85. Field svc. engr. Omnidata, Westlake Village, Calif., 1983-84; computer products specialist Hamilton/Avnet Electronics, Chatsworth, Calif., 1984-86; regional sales mgr. Schweber Electronics, Irvine, Calif., 1986-88; corp. mktg. mgr. Wyle Labs., Garden Grove, Calif., 1988-90; regional sales mgr. Avnet Computer Corp., Irvine, 1990-91, Banctec Svc. Corp., Irvine, 1991-92; sr. sales rep. Bell Atlantic, Brea, Calif., 1992-94; internet sales mgr. HLC-Internet, Irvine, 1995-96; pres. Star Seekers Internet Svcs., Denver, 1997—. Web designer in field. Named Boss of the Yr., Bus. Women's Assn., Orange County, Calif., 1990. Mem. Nat. Space Soc., Insts. Noetic Scis., Nat. Wildlife Fedn., Humane Soc. Avocations: sailing, biking, mountain back-roading, reading, internet surfing.

MCCAFFREY, CARLYN SUNDBERG, lawyer; b. N.Y.C., Jan. 7, 1942; d. Carl Andrew Lawrence and Evelyn (Back) Sundberg; m. John P. McCaffrey, May 24, 1967; children: John C., Patrick, Jennifer, Kathleen. Student, Barnard Coll., 1963; AB in Econs., George Washington U., 1963; LLB cum laude, NYU, 1967, LLM in Taxation, 1970. Bar: N.Y. 1974. Law clk. to presiding justice Calif. Supreme Ct., 1967-68; teaching fellow law NYU, N.Y.C., 1968-70, asst. prof. law, 1970-74; assoc. Weil, Gotshal & Manges, N.Y.C., 1974-80, ptnr., 1980—. Prof. in residence Rubin Hall NYU, 1971-75; adj. prof. law NYU, 1975—, U. Miami, 1979-81; lectr. in field. Contbr. articles to profl. jours. Mem. ABA (chmn. generation-skipping transfer tax 1979-81, 93—, real property pro ate and trust law sect.), N.Y. State Bar Assn. (exec. com. tax sect. 1979-80, chmn. estate and gift tax com. 1976-78, 95—, life ins. com. 1983-85, trusts and estates sect.), Assn. of Bar of City of N.Y. (matrimonial law com., chmn. tax subcom. 1984-86, Am. College Trusts & Estates Counsel (bd. regents 1992—, mem. exec. com. 1995—, pres. 2002--). Home: PO Box 232 Waccabuc NY 10597-0232 Office: Weil Gotshal & Manges 767 5th Ave Fl Concl New York NY 10153-0119 E-mail: Carlyn.mccaffrey@weil.com.

MCCAFFREY, JUDITH ELIZABETH, lawyer; b. Providence, Apr. 26, 1944; d. Charles V. and Isadore Frances (Langford) McC.; m. Martin D. Minsker, Dec. 31, 1969 (div. May 1981); children: Ethan Hart Minsker, Natasha Langford Minsker. BA, Tufts U., 1966; JD, Boston U., 1970. Bar: Mass. 1970, D.C. 1972, Fla. 1991. Assoc. Sullivan & Worcester, Washington, 1970-76; atty. FDIC, Washington, 1976-78; assoc. Dechert, Price & Rhoads, Washington, 1978-82, McKenna, Conner & Cuneo, Washington, 1982-83; gen. counsel, corp. sec. Perpetual Savs. Bank, FSB, Alexandria, Va., 1983-91; ptnr. Powell, Goldstein, Frazer & Murphy, Washington, 1991-92, McCaffrey P.A., 1992—. Contbr. articles to profl. jours. Mem. Leadership Collier, 1998. Mem. ABA (chair subcom. thrift instns. 1985-90), D.C. Bar Assn. (bd. govs. 1981-85), Fla. Bar Assn. (chmn. fin. svcs. com. 1999-2000, exec. coun. bus. law sect. 1998-), Women's Bar Assn. D.C. (pres. 1980-81), Collier County Women's Bar Assn. (pres. 1997-98), Gulf Coast Venture Forum (pres. 2001-03). Episcopalian. Avocations: travel, reading, martial arts, Spanish. Home: PO Box 2081 Naples FL 34106-2081 Office: McCaffrey PA 568 9th St S Ste 255 Naples FL 34102-6620

MCCAIN, BETTY LANDON RAY (MRS. JOHN LEWIS MCCAIN), political party official, state official; b. Feb. 23, 1931; d. Horace Truman and Mary Howell (Perrett) Ray; m. John Lewis McCain, Nov. 19, 1955; children: Paul Pressly III, Mary Eloise. Student, St. Marys Jr. Coll., 1948—50; AB in Music, U. N.C., Chapel Hill, 1952, LLD (hon.), 1998; MA, Columbia U., 1953; LittD (hon.), U. N.C., Wilmington, 1997; HHD (hon.), Wake Forest U., 1999; LLD (hon.), Barton Coll., 1999. Courier, European tour guide Ednl. Travel Assocs., Plainfield, NJ, 1952-54; asst. dir. YWCA, U. N.C., Chapel Hill, 1953-55; chmn. N.C. Dem. Exec. Com. (1st woman), 1976-79; mem. Dem. Nat. Com., 1971-72, 76-79, 80-85, chmn. sustaining fund, 1981, 88-91, mem. com. on presdl. nominations (Hunt Commn.), 1981-82, mem. rules com., 1982-85, mem. cabinet Gov. James B. Hunt, Jr., 1993-2001, sec. dept. cultural resources, 1993-2001; mem. State Dem. Exec. Com., 1971—99, 2001—. Mem. Winograd Commn., 1977-78; pres. Dem. Women of N.C., 1971-72, dist. dir., 1969-72; pres. Wilson County Dem. Women, 1966-67; precinct chmn., 1972-76; del. Dem. Nat. Conv., 1972, 88; mem. Dem. Mid-Term Confs., 1974, 78, mem. jud. coun. Dem. Nat. Com., 1985-89; dir. Carolina Tel. & Tel. Co. (now Sprint), 1981-97 (1st woman). Contbg. editor: History of N.C. Med. Soc. Sunday sch. tchr. 1st Presbyn. Ch., Wilson, 1970—71, 1986—88, 1990—92, mem. chancel choir, 1985—, deacon, 1986—92, chmn. fin. com., 1990—91, chair, 1992—; treas. Wilson on the Move, 1990—92; mem. Coun. on State Goals and Policy, 1970—72, Gov.'s Task Force on Child Advocacy, 1975—78; chmn. Wilson-Greene Morehead scholarship com., 1986—89; mem. career and personal counseling svc. adv. bd. St. Andrews Coll.; charter mem. Wilson Edn. Devel. Coun.; active Arts Coun. of Wilson, Inc.; N.C. Art Soc.; N.C. Lit. and Hist. Assn.; pres. Wilson County Mental Health Assn., bd. dirs., legis. chmn.; bd. govs. U. N.C., 1975—81, 1985—93, pers. and tenure com., 1985—91, chmn. budget and fin. com., 1991—93; bd. regents Barium Springs Home for Children, 2003—, chair Founds. com. Capital Campaign; bd. dirs. N.C. Mus. History Assocs., 1982—83, pres., 1982—83, membership chair, 1987—88; co-chmn. Com. to Elect Jim Hunt Gov., 1976, 1980, co-chmn. senatorial campaign, 1984; mem. N.C. Adv. Budget Com. (1st woman), 1981—85; chmn. State Employees Combined Campaign N.C., 1993; bd. visitors Peace Coll., Wake Forest U. Sch. Law, 1980—83, U. N.C., Chapel Hill; co-chmn. fund dr. Wilson Cmty. Theater; elder 1st Presbyn. Ch., 1992—; state bd. dirs. N.C., Am. Lung Assn., 1985—88; bd. dirs. Roanoke Island Commn.; USS/NC Battleship Commn., 1993—2001. Recipient state awards N.C. Heart Assn., 1967, Easter Seal Soc., 1967, Cmty. Svc. award Wilson Downtown Bus. Assocs., 1977, award N.C. Jaycees, 1979, 85, Women in Govt. award N.C. and U.S. Jaycettes, 1985, Alumni Disting. Svc. award U. N.C., Chapel Hill, 1993, Flora Mac Donald Scottish Heritage award, 1995, Carpathian award N.C. Equity, 1995, Pinnacle award, 1997, 1st winner Holderness-Weaver award U. N.C., Greensboro, 1999, Citizen of Yr. award Wilson C. of C., 2000, Ruth Coltrane Cannon award for hist. preservation Preservation N.C., 2000, N.C. State U. Sch. of Design award, 2000; named to Order of Old Well and Valkyries, U. N.C., 1952; named Dem. Woman of Yr., N.C., 1976. Mem.: DAR, UDC (historian John W. Dunham chpt.), Rotary Internat. (Paul Harris fellow 2003), N.C. Inst. Medicine (bd. dirs. 1993—), N.C. Sch. Arts (trustee 1993—2001), N.C. Equity (bd. dirs.), N.C. Soc. Internal Medicine Aux. (pres.), N.C. Symphony (trustee 2002—), Info. Resources Mgmt. Commn. N.C. (bd. dirs. 1993—2001), N.C. Agy. Pub. Telecom. (bd. dirs. 1993—2001), N.C. Found. for Nursing (bd. dirs. 1989—92), St. Mary's Alumni Assn. (regional v.p.), U. N.C. Chapel Hill Alumni Assn. (chmn. 2001—02, dir.), Nat. Soc. Colonial Dames Am. NC (pres., dir., parliamentarian med. auxs., local com. program co-chmn.), AMA Alliance (dir., nat. vol. health svcs. chmn., aux. liaison rep. AMA Coun. on Mental Health, aux. rep. Coun. on Vol. Health Orgns.), Wilson Country Club, Little Book Club, The Book Club (pres.), Pi Beta Phi. Home: 1134 Woodland Dr NW Wilson NC 27893-2122

MCCAIRNS, REGINA CARFAGNO, pharmaceutical executive; b. Phila., Dec. 23, 1951; d. Carmen Augustus and Regina Mary (Yost) Carfagno; m. Robert Gray McCairns Jr., Nov. 6, 1982. BS, Marymount Manhattan Coll., 1973; MS, Villanova U., 1976; cert. bus., U. Pa., 1982; MS, Temple U., 2001. Rsch. asst. Temple U. Med. Coll., Phila., 1973-77; mfg. supr. William H. Rorer, Ft. Washington, Pa., 1977-79; from mgmt. trainee, tech. asst. to validation coord. SmithKline & French Labs., Phila., 1979-87; mgr. validation svcs. SmithKline Beecham, Phila., 1987-96; quality assurance investigator pharm. tech. Glaxo Smith Kline, Upper Providence, Pa., 1996—99. Trustee Country Day Sch. of the Sacred Heart, 1993—99, PDA Sci. Found., 1997—. Mem. Parenteral Drug Assn. (bd. dirs. 1985-92, chmn. spring program 1988, 90, chmn. tng. com. 1986-88, chmn. nat. program com. 1990-93), Jefferson Med. Coll. Faculty Wives Club (v.p. 1988-90, program chmn., 1988-90, pres.-elect 1990-92, pres. 1992-94). Democrat. Roman Catholic. Avocations: golf, books. Office: Glaxo Smith Kline UW 2909 709 Swedeland Rd PO Box 5089 King Of Prussia PA 19406 E-mail: regina_c_mccairns@gsk.com.

MCCALEB, ANNETTE WATTS, executive secretary; b. Darbfork, Ky., Dec. 11, 1931; d. Benjamin Taylor and Suzanna Elizabeth (White) Watts; m. John Henry McCaleb, Oct. 23, 1962; children: Jonathan Jeffrey, Suzanna Elizabeth McCaleb Woodhead, Sarah Leslie McCaleb James. BS, U. Ky., 1954. Med. technologist Good Samaritan, Lexington, Ky., 1953-54; lab. supr. Charleston (W.Va.) Meml., 1954-58; chief med. technologist Meml. Hosp., Indpls., 1958-63; assoc. prof. UAMC, Little Rock, 1963-66; sec., treas., co-owner John H. McCaleb Constrn., Inc., Little Rock, 1966—. Justice of the peace Pulaski County Quorum Ct., Ark., 1989—; state bd. dirs. F.L.A.G., 1989-98. Mem. S.W. Kiwanis (pres. 1997-), Pulaski County Property Owners Assn. (pres. 1990-2000). Democrat. Baptist. Avocations: reading, crossword puzzles, gardening, sewing, swimming. Home and Office: 3900 Annette Ct Little Rock AR 72206-5357 Office Phone: 501-888-4253. E-mail: annmccaleb@sbcglobal.net.

MCCALEB, MARGARET ANNE SHEEHAN, application developer; b. Washington, Jan. 15, 1956; d. Rourke Joseph and Anne Marie (Fahy) Sheehan; m. Michael Ray McCaleb, May 2, 1987. Bachelors cum laude, Rosemont Coll., 1978; Masters, Cath. U., 1980. Co-dir. Media Analysis Project, Washington, 1980—81; dir., litigation support staff Morgan Associates, Washington, 1981—90; software devel. mgr. Adminstrv. Office of U.S. Cts., Washington, 1990—. Co-author: Over the Wire and On TV, 1983; contbr. articles to mags. and newspapers. Recipient scholarship, Cath. U., 1978—79, grant, Russell Sage Found., 1980—81. Roman Catholic. Office: Adminstrv Office US Cts 1 Columbus Cir NE Washington DC 20544

MCCALL, COLLEEN WHITING, social worker; b. Phoenix, Ariz., Nov. 18, 1951; d. Warren Grant and Eloise Udall Whiting; m. Chand Bhasker, Aug. 24, 2000; m. Daniel Wayne McCall, Nov. 29, 1974 (div. Nov. 5, 1994); children: Valerie LeeAnn, Lee Han. BA, Coll. of William and Mary, 1973; MS, Va. Commonwealth U., 1974; MSSW, U. Tex., Arlington, 1980. LCSW master social worker Tex., Acad. Cert. Social Workers NASW; lic. profl. counselor Tex., child care adminstr. Tex. Rehab. counselor Ea. Rehab. Ctr., Williamsburg, Va., 1974—75; pub. welfare worker Tex. Dept. of Human Svcs., Amarillo, 1976—77; caseworker Amarillo State Ctr., 1977—79; social worker Amarillo Ind. Sch. Dist., 1980—87; program dir. Tex. Dept. of Protective and Regulatory Svcs., Amarillo, 1989—93, regional dir., 1993—. Mem. and past chair Tex. State Child Fatality Rev. Team, Austin, 1994—. Mem., pres. Camp Fire, Amarillo, 1986—93, Rape Crisis and Domestic Violence Ctr., Amarillo, 1976—84. Recipient On Behalf of Youth award, Camp Fire Coun. of Amarillo, 1996, Women Helping Women, Soroptimist Internat. Amarillo, 1994, Career Achievement award, Amarillo Women's Network, 1994. Mem.: NASW (assoc. Social Worker of Yr. award Amarillo chpt. 1982, 1997). Episcopalian. Office: Tex Dept of Protective and Regulatory Svc 6200 I-40 W Amarillo TX 79106 E-mail: colleen.mccall@tdprs.state.tx.us.

MCCALL, DEBRA KNIGHT, art educator; d. Harry Dillard and Dorothy Jones Knight; m. Archie Bernard McCall, Jr., June 25, 2003; children: Payton Leigh, Gavin Blake. BA in Art Edn., East Carolina U., 1984. Art tchr. Charlotte (NC)-Mecklenburg Schs., 1984—. Officer PTA, Charlotte, 1984—; co-chair Sch. Leadership Planning Com., Charlotte, NC, Character Edn. Com., Charlotte; moderator Ramah Presbyn. Ch., Huntersville, NC. Mem.: Nat. Art Edn. Assn., NC Art Edn. Assn. Avocations: crafts, reading, cooking. Home: 14215 Hudson Park Ln Huntersville NC 28078 Office: Long Creek Elem 9213 Beatties Ford Rd Huntersville NC 28078

MCCALL, DOROTHY KAY, social worker, psychotherapist; b. Houston, July 18, 1948; d. Sherwood Pelton Jr. and Kathryn Rose (Gassen) McC. BA, Calif. State U., Fullerton, 1973; MS in Edn., U. Kans., 1978; PhD, U. Pitts., 1989. LCSW Pa., 1991; cert. aromatherapist Australasian Coll. Health Studies, 2002. Counselor/intern Ctr. for Behavioral Devel., Overland Park, Kans., 1976-77; rehab. counselor Niagra Frontier Voc. Rehab. Ctr., Buffalo, 1978-79; counselor/instr. dept. motor vehicles Driving While Impaired Program N.Y. State, 1979-80; alcoholism counselor Bry Lin Hosp., Buffalo, 1979-81; instr. sch. social work U. Pitts., 1984, 91; alcohol drug counselor The Whale's Tale, Pitts., 1984-86; sole practice drug and alcohol therapy Pitts., 1986—; faculty Chem. People Inst., Pitts., 1987-89; CEO Kingsbury Fragrances, Inc., 2004—. Guest lectr. sch. social work U. Pitts., 1982-87, 89; educator, trainer Community Mental Health Ctr., W.Va., 1986-87, Tenn., 1986; trainer Tri-Cmty. Sch. Sys., Western Pa., 1984-87; cons. Battered Women's Shelter, Buffalo, 1980, Buffalo Youth and Alcoholism Abuse program, 1980; lectr. in field. Mem. Spl. Adv. Com. on Addiction, 1981-83; bd. dirs. Chem. People, Task Force Adv. Com., 1984-86, Drug Connection Hot Line, 1984-86; co-founder Greater Pitts. Adult Children of Alcoholics Network, 1984; mem. adv. bd. Chem. Awareness Referral and Evaluation System Duquesne U., 1988-93; hon. bd. dirs. Pa. Assn. for Children of Alcoholics, 2000. Recipient Outstanding Achievement award Greater Pitts. Adult Children of Alcoholics Network, 1987, Disting. Svc. award Pa. Assn. for Children of Alcoholics, 1993; Nat. Inst. Alcohol Abuse tng. grantee, 1981; U. Pitts. fellow, 1983. Mem. Am. Acad. Experts in Traumatic Stress, NASW, Pa. Assn. for Children of Alcoholics (bd. dirs. 1987-99, v.p. 1990-94, hon. bd. dirs. 2000, Disting. Svc. award 1993), Employee Assistance Profls. Assn., Am. Soc. for Clin. Hypnosis, Nat. Assn. for Children of Alcoholics, Internat. Soc. for Study of Subtle Energies and Energy Medicine, Am. Recorder Soc. (Pitts. chpt.), Soc. Creative Anachronism. Democrat. Avocations: perfumery, film, reading, drawing, playing the recorder. Office: 673 Washington Rd Pittsburgh PA 15228-1917 Office Phone: 412-343-4066. E-mail: dmccallpa@earthlink.net.

MCCALL, JENNIFER JORDAN, lawyer; b. N.Y.C., Feb. 15, 1956; m. James W. McCall; children: Caroline, Hillary. BA cum laude in English Lit., Princeton U., 1978; JD, U. Va. Sch. Law, 1982; LLM in Taxation, NYU, 1988. Bar: N.Y. 1983, Calif. 2002. Assoc. Lord Day & Lord, N.Y.C., 1982-92; ptnr. Lord Day & Lord, Barrett Smith, N.Y.C., 1992-94; ptnr. Pvt. Client Group Cadwalader, Wickersham & Taft, N.Y.C., 1994—2003; ptnr. Pillsbury Winthrop, LLP, N.Y.C., 2003—, Palo Alto, Calif., 2003—. Trustee Charitable Founds. and Trusts and advisor to numerous high net worth individuals; spkr. in field on estate and tax planning and adminstrn. Co-author: Estate Planning for Authors and Artists, 1998; contbr. chpt. to Estate Tax Techniques. Steering com., Planned Giving Adv. Com., The Mus. of Modern Art; mem. Profl. Advisor's Coun., Lincoln Ctr., Inc.; trustee League for the Hard of Hearing, N.Y.C., 1992-2003, East Side House Settlement, Bronx, N.Y., 1995-2002, Chapin Sch., N.Y.C., 1998-2001; chairperson Ethel Gray Stringfellow Art Case Com., N.Y.C.; bd. trustees San Francisco Ballet. Fellow Am. Coll. Trust and Estate Counsel; mem. ABA (real property, probate and trust law sects.), N.Y. State Bar Assn. (com. on trusts and estates adminstrn.; chairperson subcom. on proposed legislation on executor's commns.), Calif. State Bar Assn. Office: Pillsbury Winthrop LLC 2470 Hanover St Palo Alto CA 94304 also: Pillsbury Winthrop LLC 1540 Broadway New York NY 10038

MCCALL, JUNIETTA BAKER, psychotherapist, minister; d. Cecil Stanford and Katherine Violet Baker; m. John Cornwall Pearson; children: Jonathan Seth, Jeremiah Brierly. BA, Beloit Coll., 1968; MDiv, Andover Newton Theol. Sch., Newton Centre, Mass., 1985, D of Ministry, 1991. Ordained min. United Ch. of Christ, 1983; cert. pastoral psychotherapist N.H., diplomate Am. Assn. Pastoral Counselors. Assoc. pastor South Congl. Ch., Concord, NH, 1980—85; dir. pastoral svcs. N.H. Hosp., Concord, 1985—. Dir. tng. Journeys Pastoral Counseling Ctr., Durham, NH, 1993—96; adj. faculty Andover Newton Theol. Sch., 1993—96. Author: Grief Education for Caregivers of the Elderly, 1999, A Practical Guide to Hospital Ministry, 2002, Bereavement Counseling, 2004. Avocations: qulting, gardening, antiques and collectibles. Office: NH Hosp 36 Clinton St Concord NH 03301 E-mail: jmccall@dhhs.state.nh.us.

MCCALL, LOUISE HARRUP, artist; b. Oklahoma City, July 8, 1925; d. Paul Louis and Lucile (Martin) Harrup; m. Robert Theodore McCall, July 20, 1945; children: Linda Louise, Catherine Anne. Student, Okla. State U., 1943-44, U. N.Mex., 1944-45, Art Inst., 1946; pvt. study, N.Y., 1955-65. Freelance artist, Chgo., 1946—48, Tarrytown, NY, 1949—53, Chappaqua, NY, 1953-67, 68-71, London, 1967, Paradise Valley, Ariz., 1971—; owner McCall Studios, Inc., Paradise Valley, 1986—. Exhibitions include Ariz. State U., 1999, Grace Mus., Abilene, Tex., 1999, Sky Harbor Millenium Traveling Show, 1999—2000, Ariz. State U. Club, 1999, Women Artists of Ariz., Wickenburg, 2001; artist with husband (murals) Air and Space Mus., Washington, 1975—76, Johnson Space Ctr., Houston, 1978, Disney Epcot Ctr., L.A., 1983, Phoenix Indsl. Commn., 1987, designed with husband windows of Valley Presbyn. Chapel, Scottsdale, Ariz., 1984, 2002, stained glass window Valley Presbyn. Ch. Libr., 2002, window of Sky Harbor Airport, Phoenix, 1998, Phippen Art Mus., Prescott, Ariz., 2003, artist (paintings in pvt. collections) H.R.H. Prince Fahd Bin Salman and H.R. Prince Sultan Bin Salman of Saudi Arabia, Mayo Clinic Collection, Scottsdale, 1997, designer meditation chapel for new cancer ctr., 2001; exhibitions include West Valley Art Mus., Phoenix, 2002; designed (stained glass window) Valley Presbyn. Ch. Libr., 2003, Libr. Valley Presbyn. Ch., 2002, designer Chapel for Va. G-Piper Cancer Ctr., Scottsdale. Fundraiser Crisis Nursery, Phoenix, 1984, Ariz. Hist. Soc., Phoenix, 1986, Scottsdale Cultural Ctr. 1990-92, Phoenix Art Mus., 1993-94, Scottsdale Art. Sch., 1996, 1994 Art Show O'Brien's Gallery, 1995 Art Show Peoria Sch. Dist.; ann. fund raiser Hospice Phoenix, 1983-92, Bot. Gardens Phoenix. Winner 1st Prize, State of Tex., 1943, 1st Prize, Jr. League Artists No. Westchester and N.Y., 1961. Mem. NASA Permanent Art Collection, Nat. Mus. Women in the Arts, Jr. League of Phoenix, Paradise Valley Country Club. Republican. Presbyterian. Avocation: speaking. Home and Office: 4816 E Moonlight Way Paradise Valley AZ 85253 Fax: 480-991-2099. E-mail: robtmccall@cox.net.

MCCALL-RODRIGUEZ, LEONOR, entrepreneur, consultant; b. Chgo., Feb. 21, 1958; d. Sixto Rodriguez Hernandez and Dolores Leonor Jimenez de Rodriguez; m. Dean W. McCall, July 14, 2002; stepchildren: Samantha Lynn McCall, Christopher Dean McCall. Licenciatura in Econs., Universidad Nacional Autónoma de México, Mexico City, 1982; MBA, Universidad de Las Americas, Mexico City, 1998. Lic. economist Secretaria de Educación Publica, Mexico. Mktg. mgr. Casa Pedro Domecq, Mexico City, 1984—90, Braun divsn. Gillette, Mexico City, 1990—91, PepsiCo-Frito Lay, Mexico City, 1991—97, La Opinion, L.A., 1999—2000; pres. Bus. and Mktg. Solutions, Mexico City, 1997—99; v.p. Face to Face Mktg., Inc., Pasadena, Calif., 2000—03; gen. mgr. Walker Advt., Inc., San Pedro, Calif., 2000; pres., founder Mira Promo, Inc., Redondo Beach, Calif., 2003—, Latino Speakers Bur., Redondo Beach, 2003—. Adj. prof. econs. Universidad Nacional Autónoma de México, Mexico City, 1982—84. Author: (short stories) Cuentos de Juanita La Ranita, 2004; editor, translator: novel La Quileña, 2004. Vol. art tchr. 1736 Family Crisis Ctr., L.A., 2000—03. Mem.: Mexican Am. Nat. Assn. (assoc.), Women's Bus. Entrepreneurs Nat. Coun. (assoc.), Nat. Assn. Women Bus. Owners (assoc.), Latin Bus. Assn. (assoc.). Democrat. Roman Catholic. Avocations: writing, reef aquaria, travel. Office: Mira Promo Inc 2018 Farrell Ave Unit B Redondo Beach CA 90278 Office Phone: 310-937-2789. E-mail: leonor@miraprom o.com.

MCCALL-THOMPSON, KATHLEEN SAMONE, actor, educator; d. Donald Leon and Jo Ann McCall; m. Luther Kent Thompson, Dec. 4, 1999; 1 child, Alexander Tucker. BA in Theater and Music, Moorhead State U., 1981; cert., London (Eng.) Acad. Music and Dramatic Art, 1982. Casting dir. asst. Michael Fendor Casting, 1982—86; events coord. asst. Lorelie Enterprise, 1994—97; actress. Actress Ala. Shakespeare Festival Acad., 1984—2003, instr., 1998—2003. Actor: (Broadway plays) M. Butterfly, (off-Broadway plays) Theme and Variations, Steel Magnolias, The Girl Next Door, A Capella Hardcore, Thanksgiving, numerous regional theatre prodns.; (TV series) Wings, St. Elsewhere, Houston Knights, Monsters, Loving, As The World Turns, Guiding Light; (plays, touring prodn.) Doubles, Macbeth, Arcadia, Disguises. Dir. First Ladies Art's Festival, Montgomery, Ala., 2000; organizer Montgomery (Ala.) AIDS Outreach Benefit, 1998, 1999, 2001, 2003; prodr. Lysistrata Project, Montgomery, 2003. Recipient Bessie award, 1998, Cleve. Morris award, 1990. Office: Alabama Shakespeare Festival 1 Festival Drive Montgomery AL 36117

MCCALLUM, LAURIE RIACH, lawyer, state government; b. Virginia, Minn., Aug. 19, 1950; d. Keith Kelvin and Maybelle Louella (Hanson) Riach; m. J. Scott McCallum, June 19, 1979; children: Zachary, Rory, Cara. BA, U. Ariz., 1972; JD, So. Meth. U., 1977. Bar: Wis. 1977. Consumer atty. Office of Commr. of Ins., Madison, Wis., 1977-79; asst. legal counsel Gov. of Wis., Madison, Wis., 1979-82; mng. ptnr. Petri and McCallum Law Firm, Fond du Lac, Wis., 1979-80; exec. dir. Wis. Coun. on Criminal Justice, Madison, 1981-82; commr. Wis. Pers. Commn., Madison, 1982—2002, chairperson, 1988—2002; commr. Wis. Labor and Industry Rev. Commn., 2002—03, sr. rev. atty., 2003—. Mem. gov.'s jud. selection com. Supreme Ct., 1993; dir. State Bar Labor Law Sect., Madison, 1988-91; faculty U. Wis. Law Sch., Madison, 1992, 93. Dir. Prevent Blindness Wis., Madison Symphony Orch., Wis. Women in Govt. Republican. Office: LIRC PO Box 8126 Madison WI 53708-8126

MC CANDLESS, BARBARA J. tax consultant; b. Cottonwood Falls, Kans., Oct. 25, 1931; d. Arch G. and Grace (Kittle) McCandless; m. Allyn O. Lockner, 1969. BS, Kans. State U., 1953; MS, Cornell U., 1959; postgrad. U. Minn., 1962-66, U. Calif., Berkeley, 1971-72. Enrolled agt. IRS. Home demonstration agt. Kans. State U., 1953-57; teaching asst. Cornell U., 1957-58, asst. extension home economist in marketing, 1958-59; consumer mktg. specialist, asst. prof. Oreg. State U., 1959-62; instr. home econs. U. Minn., 1962-63, research asst. agrl. econs., 1963-66; asst. prof. U. R.I., 1966-67; assoc. prof. family econs., mgmt., housing, equipment dept. head S.D. State U., 1967-73; asst. to sec. Dept. Commerce and Consumer Affairs, S.D., 1973-79, tax cons., 1980-91; revenue auditor Kans. Dept. Revenue, Topeka, 1991-2000; tax cons., 2001—. Mem. Am. Agrl. Econs. Assn., Am. Assn. Family and Consumer Scis., Am. Coun. Consumer Interests, Nat. Coun. on Family Rels., LWV, Kans. State U. Alumni Assn., Pi Gamma Mu. Address: 2135 SW Potomac Dr Topeka KS 66611-1450 E-mail: bmccandless@cox.net.

MCCANDLESS, CAROLYN KELLER, retired human resources executive; b. Patuxent River, Md., June 6, 1945; d. Stevens Henry and Betty Jane (Bethune) Keller; m. Stephen Porter McCandless, Apr. 22, 1972; children: Peter Keller, Deborah Marion. BA, Stanford U., 1967; MBA, Harvard U., 1969. Fin. analyst Time Inc., NYC, 1969-72, mgr. budgets and fin. analysis, 1972-78, asst. sec., dir. internat. adminstrn., 1978-85, v.p., dir. employee benefits, 1985-90; v.p human resources and adminstrn. Time Warner, Inc., NYC, 1990—2001. Bd. dir. Friends and Relatives of Institutionalized Aged, NY Svc. Program for Older People, Inc.; adv. bd. Booker T. Washington Learning Ctr. and Pres. Coun. Nat. Pub. Radio. Democrat. Mem. Unitarian Ch.

MCCANN, COLLEEN MARY, public affairs specialist, lobbyist; b. Phila., June 28, 1964; d. John Francis and Agnetta Marie (McLaughlin) McC. BA, Rutgers U., 1986. Staff asst. subcom. on commerce, transp. and tourism U.S. Congress, Washington, 1986; staff asst., legis. corr. U.S. Rep. Jim Florio, Washington, 1986-88, legis. asst., 1988-89; policy analyst Gov.-elect Jim Florio's Transition Team, 1989-91; legis. liaison Dept. of State, Trenton, N.J., 1990-93; v.p. The MWW Group, Trenton, 1993-99. Active N.J. Women's Polit. Caucus, 1990—; mem. govt. affairs alumni com. Rutgers U., trustee, 1994—. Democrat. Roman Catholic. Home: 815 Delancey Pl Ocean City NJ 08226-4137 Office: 150 W State St Ste 220 Trenton NJ 08608-1105

MCCANN, DIANA RAE, secondary school educator; b. Huron, S.D., Nov. 16, 1948; d. Ralph Henry and Rosina Agnes (Rowen) Yager; m. Gregory Charles McCann, 1974; children: Grant Christopher, Holly Ann. BS, S.D. State U., 1972. Tchr. Bon Homme 4-2, Tyndall, SD, 1972-74, 1976—, Avon (S.D.) Sch., 1975-76. Math. curriculum adv. bd., SD, 1992—; coord. Presdl. awards in math., SD, 1998—. Leader 4-H Club, 1986—; sec.-treas. 4-H Leaders Assn., 1992—2000; tournament coord. Bon Homme Youth Wrestling Club, 1986—93. Recipient Elem. Math. Presdl. award for Excellence in Math. Tchgs., NSF, 1993, Disting. Svc. award for Math. in S.D., 2003. Mem.: S.D. Coun. Tchrs. Math. (pres.-elect 1990—92, pres. 1992—94, treas. 1999—), Nat. Coun. Tchrs. Math. Avocation: gardening.

MCCANN, ELIZABETH IRELAND, theater, television and motion picture producer, lawyer; b. N.Y.C., Mar. 29, 1931; d. Patrick and Rebecca (Henry) McC. BA, Manhattanville Coll., 1952, PhD hon., 1983; MA, Columbia U., 1954; LLD, Fordham U., 1966; ArtsD (hon.), Manhattanville Coll., 1987; LitD (hon.), Marymount Coll., 1993. Bar: N.Y. 1966. Assoc. firm Paul, Weiss, Rifkind, Wharton & Garrison, N.Y.C., 1965-66; assoc. numerous theater mgmts. Robert Joffrey, Hal Prince, Saint Suber, Maurice Evans, 1956-68; mng. dir. Nederlander Orgn., N.Y.C., 1968-76; pres. McCann & Nugent Prodns., Inc., N.Y.C., 1976-86; mng. prodr. Tony Awards, N.Y.C., 2001—. Bd. dirs. City Ctr. Music and Dance, Marymount Coll. Prodr.: (play) My Fat Friend, 1975, Dracula (Tony award for most innovative prodn. revival, 1978), The Elephant Man, 1978 (Tony award for best play, 1979, Drama Critics award, 1978, Drama Desk award, 1978, Outer Critics Circle award 1978, Obie award 1978), Night and Day, 1979, Home, 1980 (Adelco award, 1980), Morning's at Seven, 1980 (Tony award for reproduction play/musical, 1980), Amadeus, 1980 (Tony award for best play, 1981, Drama Desk award, 1980), The Philadelphia Sotry, 1980, Piaf, 1981, Rose, 1981, The Dresser, 1981, Mass Appeal, 1981, Macbeth, 1981, The Floating Light Bulb, 1981, The Life and Adventures of Nicholas Nickleby, 1981 (Tony award for best play, 1982, Drama Critics Circle award, 1981), Good, 1982, All's Well That Ends Well, 1983, The Glass Menagerie, 1983, Total Abandon, 1983, Painting Churches, 1983, The Lady and the Clarinet, 1983, Cyrano de Bergerac/Much Ado About Nothing, 1984, Pacific Overtures, 1984, Leader of the Pack, 1985, Les Liaisons Dangereuses, 1987 (Drama Critics Circle award, 1987), Stepping Out, 1987, Orpheus Descending, 1989, Nick & Nora, 1991, Three Tall Women, 1995, A Midsummer Night's Dream, 1995, In the West End with Robert Fox, Ltd., 1996, Who's Afraid of Virginia Woolf?, 1996, A Delicate Balance, 1997, A View from the Bridge, 1998 (Tony award for best revival play, 1998), The Unexpected Man, 1998, A View from the Bridge (Tony award), 1999, Copenhagen, 2000 (Tony award for best play, 2000), Cobb, 2000, The Play About the Baby, 2001, Tuesdays with Morrie, 2002, The Goat, or Who is Sylvia?, 2002 (Tony award for best play, 2002), The Smell of the Kill, 2002, Beckee/Albee, 2003; TV show Piaf, 1981, Morning's at Seven, 1982, Pilobolus Dance Theatre, 1982; assoc. prodr. Orpheus Descending, 1990. Recipient Entrepreneurial Woman award Women Bus. Owners of N.Y., 1981, 82, James J. and Jame Hoey award for Interracial Justice, 1981, Spl Drama League award for co-producing the Life and Adventures of Nicholas Nickleby on Broadway, 1982, Dr Louis M. Spadero award Fordham Grad. Sch. Bus., 1982 E-mail: liz@weproduce.biz.*

MCCANN, GAIL ELIZABETH, lawyer; b. Boston, Aug. 25, 1953; d. Joseph and Ruth E. (Lagerquist) McC.; m. Stanley J. Lukasiewicz. AB, Brown U., 1975; JD, U. Pa., Phila., 1978. Bar: R.I. 1978, Mass. 1984, U.S. Dist. Ct. R.I. 1978, U.S. Dist. Ct. Mass. 1990. Ptnr. Edwards & Angell, LLP, Providence, 1978—. Bd. dirs. Caritas House, Inc.; mem. R.I. adv. coun. New Eng. Legal Found. Mem.: Am. Coll. Mortgage Attys., RI Bar Assn., Brown U. Alumni Assn. (past pres.). Avocations: hiking, travel, yoga. Office: Edwards & Angell LLP 2800 Financial Plz Providence RI 02903

MCCANN, JANET, language educator, poet; PhD, U. Pitts., 1974. Prof. Eng. Tex. A&M U., College Station, 1997—, coord. creative writing, 1999—2002. Author: (book) Looking for Buddha in the Barbed Wire Garden, Wallace Stevens Revisited, The Celestial Possible, (poetry) 1980 (Pudding Nat. Looking Glass Poetry Chapter Book Competition), Dialogue with the Dogcatcher, (poetry chapter book) Afterword (Franciscan U. Poetry Chapter Book Competition), Ghosts of Christmas (Chimera Connections Poetry Chapter Book Competition). Poetry Writing fellow, NEA, 1989. Roman Catholic. Office: Tex A&M Univ Dept English College Station TX 77843 E-mail: j-mccann1@tamu.edu.

MCCANN, JEAN FRIEDRICHS, artist, educator; b. N.Y.C., Dec. 6, 1937; d. Herbert Joseph and Catherine Brady (Ward) Friedrichs; m. William Joseph McCann, May 14, 1960; children: Kevin, Brian, Maureen McCann Breslin, William, James, Denis Gerard, Kathleen. Student, Caton-Rose Inst. Fine Arts, 1955-57; AAS, SUNY, Farmingdale, 1959; BS, SUNY-Empire State Coll., Binghamton, 1986; MA summa cum laude, Marywood Coll., 1987, MFA in Art summa cum laude, 1989; completed Kellogg Leadership Progam, Sch. Mgmt., SUNY, Binghamton, 1992; PhD, Nova Coll., 1995. Designer Patton Corp., N.Y.C., 1959-66; sub. art tchr. Owego-Apalachin Sch. Dist., 1968-88; tutor, evaluator Empire State Coll. SUNY, 1987—; dir. ArtSpace Gallery, Owego, N.Y., 1992-94. V.p. bd. dirs. Tioga County Coun. on Arts, 1990—91, pres., 1992—95; tchr. design and drawing Diàn Dà Shui Coll., Guiyang, Guizhou, China, 2001; demonstrator for various schs., ednl. TV and county museums. One-woman shows include IBM, Owego, 1972, Tioga County Hist. Soc. Mus., 1975, Nat. Hist. Ct. House, 1982, Visual Arts Ctr., Scranton, Pa., 1989—90, ArtSpace Gallery, 1991, MacDonald Art Gallery of Coll. Misericordia, Dallas, Pa., 1992, Plaza Gallery, Binghamton, 1992, Krembs Gallery, 1993, 2000, Wilson Gallery, Johnson City, N.Y., 1994, 2001, 2003, Countryside Gallery, Owego, N.Y., 1996, 2002, Meml. Gallery, SUNY, Farmingdale, 1998, exhibited in group shows at IBM, Owego, 1970, Roberson Ctr., Binghamton, 1972, Arnot Art Mus., Elmira, 1974, 1989, 1992, Nat. Exhibits at Arena, Binghamton, 1974—76, Riise Gallery, St. Thomas, 1975—78, Pennino's Gallery, Burlington, Vt., 1975—77, 1999, 2000, Visual Arts Ctr., Scranton, Pa., 1987, Tioga County Hist. Soc. Mus., 1990, ArtSpace Gallery, 1990, Contemporary Gallery, Scranton, 1992, 1996, Meml. Gallery, SUNY, Farmingdale, 1997, Artists Guild Gallery, 1993, 1999, 2000, Krembs Gallery, Binghamton, 1999, 2001, 2003, Schweinfurth Meml. Art Ctr., Auburn, N.Y., 2002, Represented in permanent collections Pres. George Bush, Congressman Matt McHugh, Sen. Tom Libous, Gov. George Pataki, pub. collections. Bd. dirs. Birthright of Owego, 1993—2003. Recipient N.Y. State Artisans award, 1982, Nat. Strathmore Silver award, 1989, 1st pl. in Graphic Arts award Jericho Arts Coun., 1994. Mem. Nat. Mus. Women in Arts (charter), Kappa Pi (pres. Zeta Omicron chpt. 1987-89, life), Artists Guild. Avocations: travel, read, visit museums. Home: 6403 Roberts Drive Victor NY 14564 Home (Winter): 1776 Atwater Ct Kissimmee FL 34746

MCCANN, JOYCE JEANNINE, retired elementary education educator; b. Council Bluffs, Iowa, Dec. 15, 1926; d. Clyde Oliver and Reva Arleta (Myers) Tisher; m. Daniel Steven McCann, Aug. 14, 1960 (div. 1968); children: Marianne Rose, Daniel Patrick. BA, UCLA, 1955. Elem. tchr. L.A. Unified Sch. Dist., 1968-92. Recipient grant L.A. Bd. Edn., 1986-87. Mem.: Profl. Educators L.A., PEO Sisterhood, Delta Kappa Gamma (pres. Zeta Xi chpt. 2000—01). Republican. Avocation: violinist.

MCCANN, MARY CHERI, medical technologist, horse breeder and trainer; b. Pensacola, Fla., July 29, 1956; d. Joseph Maxwell and Cora Maria (Underwood) McCann; m. John Coleman Riggs, July 3, 1999 (div. 2002). AA, Pensacola Jr. Coll., 1975; student, U. Md., 1977-78; BS in Biology, Troy State U., 1979; postgrad., U. Fla., 1979. Med. technologist Cape Fear Valley Med. Ctr., Fayetteville, N.C., 1981-85, Doctors Diagnostic Ctr., Fayetteville, 1985-86; sales rep. Waddell & Reed, Fayetteville, 1985-86; med. technologist Roche Biomed. Lab., Burlington, N.C., 1986-87; lab. mgr. Cumberland Hosp., Fayetteville, 1987-89; lab. dir. Naval Hosp., Pensacola, 1989-90, chemistry supr., 1990-96, night shift supr., 1996—2001; med. technologist Andalusia Regional Hosp., Andalusia, Ala., 2001—03, Ft. Walton Beach Med. Ctr., 2003—. With U.S. Army, 1976-77. Mem. Am. Soc. Clin. Pathologists (registrant), Am. Quarter Horse Assn., Japan Karate Assn., Arabian Horse Assn. Am. Republican. Avocations: Karate, guns, oil painting. Home: 300 Dogwood Dr Pensacola FL 32505-5323 Office: Cheri's Equines 300 Dogwood Dr Pensacola FL 32512 E-mail: C5horses@yahoo.com.

MCCANN, RENETTA, advertising executive; married; 2 children. BS in Speech, Northwestern U., 1978. Client svc. trainee Starcom, 1978, v.p., 1988, media dir., 1989, sr. v.p., 1995; CEO Starcom N.Am., Chgo., 1999—. Bd. mem. Audit Bur. Circulations Northwestern U., mem. adv. bd. Media Mgmt. Ctr.; bd. mem. Chgo. United. Named Media Maven, Advt. Age, 2001, Corp. Exec. of Yr., Black Enterprise, 2002, Advt. Woman of Yr., Women's Advt. Club Chgo., 2002; named one of 50 Women Who Are Changing the World, Essence, 2003; recipient Outstanding Women in Comm. award, Ebony, Vanguard award, Chgo. Mags. Assn., Media Strategies award, Bus. Week. Mem.: Am. Advt. Fedn. (mem. multicultural bus. practices leadership coun.), Am. Assn. Advt. Agys. (chair media policy com.). Office: Starcom NAm 35 W Wacker Dr Chicago IL 60601*

MCCANTS, ZAUDITU ESTHER, social worker; b. Chgo., Feb. 29, 1944; d. Lester and Dorothy D. Solobilings (McCants); 1 child, Zia P. Hill. BA, Calif. State U., 1966; MSW, Atlanta U., 1970; postgrad., Ill. Inst. Tech., Chgo., 1979, U. So. Miss., 1989. Lic. ind. clin. social worker, Washington; cert. social worker, Md., Miss. Counselor, dist. supr. Miss. Office of Youth Svcs., Jackson; psychiatric and med. social work therapist VA Med. Ctr., Washington, L.A., Chgo.; psychiatric social work therapist St. Elizabeth's Hosp., Washington; social work therapist Family and Children's Svcs., Nashville; social worker, child and family svcs. divsn. D.C. Dept. Human Svcs. Mem. NASW (foster care review bd. 1986, headstart policy coun. 1983-86), Acad. Cert. Social Workers, So. States Correctional Assn. Home: 4324 Castletower Ct White Plains MD 20695-3470

MCCARGAR, ELEANOR BARKER, artist; b. Presque Isle, Maine, Aug. 30, 1913; d. Roy and Lucy Ellen (Hayward) Barker; m. John Albert McCargar, Feb. 10, 1947; children: Margaret, Lucy, Mary. Cert. elem. sch. tchg., Aroostook State Normal Sch., Presque Isle, 1933; student, Acadia U., 1935-36; B of Sociology, Colby Coll., 1937; summer student, Harvard U., 1939; and, Cambridge Sch. Art, 1939; studied portrait painting with Kenneth Washburn, Thomas Leighton, Maria von Ridelstein, Jean Henry, 1957-67. Ltd. svc. credential in fine and applied arts and related techs. Calif. C.C. Tchr. sci. and geography Limestone (Maine) Jr. H.S., 1937-41; ins. claim adjuster Liberty Mut. Ins. Co., Boston, 1941-42, Portland, Maine, 1943; ARC hosp. worker 20th Gen. Hosp., Ledo, Assam, India, 1944-45; portrait painter Burlingame and Apple Valley, Calif., 1958—. Commns. include more than 800 portraits in 10 states and 4 fgn. countries. Recipient M. Grumbacher Inc. Merit award for outstanding contbn. to arts, 1977; named Univ. of Maine Disting. Alumnus in Arts, 1981. Avocations: canoeing, camping, travel, studying.

MCCARLEY, CAROLINE, state legislator; b. Birmingham, Ala., May 11, 1952; m. Dan Harkinson; three children. BA, Davidson Coll., 1974. Mem. Dist. 6 N.H. Senate, Concord, 1996—. Mem. econ. devel., edn., wildlife and recreation, pub. inst., HHS coms., vice-chair pub. affairs com. N.H. State Senate. Chmn. Rochester Sh. Bd., 1988—; incorporator N.H. Charitable Found., 1991—; founder, v.p. Rochester Lilac Family Fun Festival, 1993—. Mem. Rochester Vis. Nurse Assn. (pres. bd. dirs. 1995—). Office: PO Box 131 Rochester NH 03866-0131 also: NH State Legis State House Concord NH 03301

MCCARROLL, KATHLEEN ANN, radiologist, educator; b. Lincoln, Nebr., July 7, 1948; d. James Richard and Ruth B. (Wagenknecht) McC.; m. Steven Mark Beerbohm, July 10, 1977 (div. 1991); 1 child, Palmer Brooke. BS, Wayne State U., 1974; MD, Mich. State U., 1978. Diplomate Am. Bd. Radiology. Intern/resident in diagnostic radiology William Beaumont Hosp., Royal Oak, Mich., 1978-82, fellow in computed tomography and ultrasound, 1983, dir. divsn. emergency radiology, 2001—; radiologist, dir. radiologic edn. Detroit Receiving Hosp., 1984-2001, vice-chief dept. radiology, 1988-96, chief dept. radiology, 1996-2001. Pres.-elect med. staff Detroit Receiving Hosp., 1992-94, pres., 1994-96; mem. admissions com. Wayne State U. Coll. Medicine, Detroit, 1991-2001; trustee Detroit Med. Ctr., 1996-2001, dir. med. staff consolidation, 1996-97, mem. consol. med. exec. com., 1998-2001, chmn. credentials com., 1998-99, joint conf. com., 1998-99; officer bd. dirs. Dr. L. Reynolds Assoc., P.C., Detroit, 1991-94, 96-2001; presenter profl. confs.; assoc. prof. radiology Wayne State U. Sch. Medicine, Detroit, 1995—; health care cons./med. staff affairs, 1998—. Editor: Critical Care Clinics, 1992; mem. editorial bd. Emergency Radiology; contbr. articles to profl. publs. Named to Crain's Bus. Detroit, Detroit's 100 Most Influential Women, 1997. Mem.: AMA, Wayne/Oakland County Med. Soc., Mich. State Med. . Soc., Am. Soc. Emergency Radiologists (bd. dirs. 1996—2001, mem. exec. com. 1998—2001, bylaws com. 2001—), Am. Roentgen Ray Soc., Radio. Soc. N.Am., Am. Coll. Radiology (Mich. chpt. sec. 1995—98, alt. councilor 1999—2002, councilor 2002—, plain film and fluoroscopy accreditation com. 2003—), Phi Beta Kappa. Avocations: travelling, skiing, reading. Office: Wm Beaumont Hosp Dept Diag Radiology 3601 W 13 Mile Rd Royal Oak MI 48073

MCCARROLL, MARTHA HADLEY, music educator, conductor; b. Washington, Aug. 15, 1972; life ptnr. Ingalls Matt. MusB in Piano Performance, U. Tex. Austin, 1994, MusM in Piano Performance, 1996. Piano instr. San Francisco Cmty. Music Ctr., 1997—; dir. Hadley McCarroll piano studio Oakland, Calif., 1996—; pianist, condr. Bay Area Summer Opera Theater Inst., San Francisco, 2000—; rehearsal pianist Opera San Jose, Calif., 2002—, Berkeley Opera, Calif., 1999—; resident artist San Francisco Opera Ctr., 2003; repetiteur, pianist Berkeley Symphony Orch., 1999—2001. Pres. East Bay chpt. Calif. Assn. of Profl. Music Tchrs., Oakland, 1999—. Sec. Accendi Performances, Inc., Oakland, 2001. Recipient Shenson Faculty Artist Concert, San Francisco Cmty. Music Ctr., 1999, 2002; grantee, City of Oakland Craft and Cultural Art Dept., 2003; Faculty Enrichment Grant, San Francisco Cmty. Music Ctr., 2003. Master: Am. Liszt Soc.; mem.: Music Tchrs. Nat. Assn. (pres., East Bay chpt. 1999, Local Assn. Matching Grant 2002, 2003). Democrat-Npl. Home: 545 Valle Vista Ave Apt #4 Oakland CA 94610-1950 Personal E-mail: hadley@mirageensemble.com.

MCCARRON, MERNE CHRISTINE, writer, public relations consultant; b. Milw., July 30, 1959; d. James Warren and Jean Miren (Jones) Schwerdt; divorced; children: Wesley, Madeleine. BA in Journalism and French, U. Wis., 1981. Comm. specialist Wis. chpt. Am. Heart Assn., Milw., 1982-83; with employee comm. dept. Pillsbury Co., Milw., 1985-86; coord. pub. rels. Ellerbe Becket Inc., Mpls., 1986-89; prin., owner, mgr. Savoir Faire Comm., Mpls., 1989—. Mem. comm. adv. bd. Minnetonka (Minn.) Pub. Sch. Sys., 1996-99. Editor Minn. Splty. Physicians NetNews and Update newsletters, 1996-99; contbr. articles to profl. jours. Publicist Madison (Wis.) Art Ctr., 1983; mem. Encore adv. bd. YWCA, Mpls., 1989-91. Coll. scholar Homestead H.S., Mequon, Wis., 1977. Mem. Women in Comm., Profl. Women's Network, Internat. Assn. Bus. Communicators (internship coord. 1985-86). Avocations: international travel, art, photography, gardening, speaking french. Office: Savoir Faire Comm 5754 Holiday Ct Minnetonka MN 55345-5312

MCCARTER, KATHERINE SAUTER, association executive; b. Nov. 12, 1942; d. William Charles and Josephine RFosina (Schoenie) Sauter; m. Robert James McCarter, Dec. 6, 1969; 1 child, Emily Katherine. BA in Biology, Cedar Crest Coll., Allentown, Pa., 1964; MHA (EPA trainee), Johns Hopkins U., 1973. Chmn. sci. dept. Arundel (Md.) Jr. H.S., 1964—68; assoc. career devel. program Am. Lung Assn., N.Y.C., 1968; air conservation cons. Mass. Lung Assn., 1968—69; exec. dir. Met. Boston Citizen's Coalition Clean Air, 1968—69; cmty. health educator Environ. Health Adminstrn., Md. Dept. Health, 1971—76; dir. govt. rels. APHA, Washington, 1976—80, asst. exec. dir., 1980—83, assoc. exec. dir., 1984—97; exec. dir. Ecol. Soc. Am., Washington, 1997—. Mem. nat. air pollution manpower devel. adv. com. EPA, 1973—76. Mem. editl. adv. bd.: The AIDS Reference Guide, 1987. Bd. dirs. Nat. Coalition Health and Environment, 1980—82, Coalition for Health Funding, 1983—, treas., 1983—86, v.p., 1987—88, pres., 1989—94, past pres., 1994—97. Mem.: APHA, Coun. Engring. and Sci. Soc. Execs. (bd. dirs. 2003—). Home: 9027 Billow Row Columbia MD 21045-2343 Office: 1015 15th St NW Washington DC 20005-2605

MCCARTHY, BEA, state legislator; b. Great Falls, Mont., Apr. 17, 1935; d. Robert Joseph and Rose Mary (Krier) McKenna; m. Edward Joseph McCarthy, June 27, 1959; children: Colleen, Mary, Edward Jr., Patrick, John. BS in Elem Edn., Mont. State U., 1957. Tchr. 1st grade, Anaconda, Mont., 1968 ; mem. Mont. Ho. of Reps., Dist. 66, 1991-94, Mont. Senate, Dist. 29, Helena, 1997—. Mem. Mont. Bd. Regents, 1983-90, Mont. Bd. Edn., 1983-90. Mem. AAUW, Am. Legion Aux., Ladies Ancient Order Hibernians (past pres.), Phi Beta Phi, Delta Kappa Gamma. Democrat. Roman Catholic. Avocations: needlework, painting, reading. Home: 1906 Ogden St Anaconda MT 59711-1706 Address: Capitol Station Helena MT 59620

MCCARTHY, CAROLYN, congresswoman; b. Brooklyn, Jan. 5, 1944; LPN. With St. Francis and Winthrop Hosp., 1964—93; gun safety activist, 1994—97; mem. U.S. Congress from 4th N.Y. dist., 1997—. Mem. edn. and workforce com., fin. svcs., subcom. on fin. inst. and consumer credit, 21st century competitiveness. Recipient numerous awards, including being named one of Newsday's 100 L.I. Influentials, Congl. Quarterly's 50 Most Effective Legislators in Congress, one of nine Redbook Mag.'s "Mothers and Shakers", Ladies' Home Jour. list of America's 100 Most Important Women, and Advertising Age's list of Most Impact by Women in 1999; also honored by U.S. Women's Soccer Team and Oprah Winfrey. Democrat. Office: US Ho of Reps 106 Cannon Ho Office Bldg Washington DC 20515-3204

MCCARTHY, JANE MCGINNIS, retired consultant; b. Cleve., June 17, 1946; d. William Ashley and Dorothy Haverick McGinnis; m. Albert Gregory McCarthy III, May 23, 1981. AAS, Marymount U. (formerly Marymount Coll. of Va.), 1966. Adminstrv. asst. to the pres. and mgr. Marymount Coll. Va., Arlington, Va., 1966—72; confidential asst. to the exec. dir. Am. Inst. of Planners, Washington, 1972—76; exec. asst. Hunter Corp., 1976—77; office mgr., account exec. Koch Associates, Inc., 1977—81; intergovtl. rels. officer, office of the dep. undersecretary for intergovtl. rels. US HUD, 1981—82; cons. pvt. practice, Arlington, 1981—. Bd. dirs., mem. exec. com. Marymount Coll. Va. (now Marymount U.), Arlington, 1976—86; founding mem., rec. sec., chmn. Friends of Capital Children's Mus., Washington, 1981—88; bd. dirs., chair Support Our Aging Religious, Silver Spring, Md., 1993—99; campaign adminstr. St. Charles Borromeo Cath. Ch., Arlington, 2000—; tournament coord. Archbishop Borders Ann. Clergy Golf Tournament, Balt., 2000—02; vol. advisor, capital campaign Holy Cross Abbey, Berryville, Va., 2002—. Named Outstanding Young Women in Am., 1976, 1982; recipient Alumni Achievement award, Marymount U., 1994, award of Merit, Marymount U. Alumni Assn., 1985—91. Independent. Roman Catholic. Avocations: golf, travel. Home and Office: 4531 4th Rd N Arlington VA 22203 E-mail: auntiegreat@att.net.

MCCARTHY, JENNY, actress; b. Chgo. m. John Asher. Student Sch. Nursing, So. Ill. U. Appeared in films Things to Do in Denver When You're Dead, 1995, The Stupids, 1996, Baseketball, 1998, Diamonds, 1999, Scream 3, 2000, TV shows The Jenny McCarthy Show, 1997, Jenny, 1997-98; host game show Singled Out, MTV, 1995-96; featured photographs in Playboy mag., including as Miss Oct. 1993, then as Playmate of Yr. Address: c/o United Talent Agy 9560 Wilshire Blvd Ste 500 Beverly Hills CA 90212-2427

MCCARTHY, KAREN P. congresswoman, former state legislator; b. Mass., Mar. 18, 1947; BS in English, Biology, U. Kans., 1969, MBA, 1985; MEd in English, U. Mo., Kansas City, 1976. Tchr. Shawnee Mission (Kans.) South High Sch., 1969-75, The Sunset Hill (Kans.) Sch., 1975-76; mem. Mo. House of Reps., Jefferson City, 1977-94; cons. govt. affairs Marion Labs., Kansas City, Mo., 1986-93; mem. U.S. Congress from 5th Mo. dist., Washington, 1995—; mem. commerce com.; mem. Ho. Select Com. on Homeland Security. Rsch. analyst pub. fin. dept. Stearn Bros. & Co., 1984-85, Kansas City, Mo.; rsch. analyst Midwest Rsch. Inst., econs. and mgmt. scis. dept., Kansas City, 1985-86. Del. Dem. Nat. Conv., 1992, Dem. Nat. Party Conf., 1982, Dem. Nat. Policy Com. Policy Commn., 1985-86; mem. Ho. Commerce Com. Energy and Power, Telecom., Trade and Consumer Protection; co-chair Dem. Caucus Task Health Care Reform. Recipient Outstanding Young Women Am. award, 1977, Outstanding Woman Mo. award Phi Chi Theta, Woman of Achievement award Mid-Continent Coun. Girl Scouts U.S., 1983, 87, Annie Baxter Leadership award, 1993; named Conservation Legislator of Yr., Conservation Fed. Mo., 1987. Fellow Inst. of Politics; mem. Nat. Inst. of Politics; mem. Nat. Conf. on State Legis. (del. on trade and econ. devel. to Fed. Republic of Germany, Bulgaria, Japan, France and Italy, mem. energy com. 1978-84, fed. taxation, trade and econ. devel. com. 1986, chmn. fed. budget and taxation com. 1987, vice chmn. state fed. assembly 1988, pres.-elect 1993, pres. 1994), Nat. Dem. Inst. for Internat. Affairs (instr. No. Ireland 1988, Baltic Republics 1992, Hungary 1993). Democrat. Office: US House Reps 1436 Longworth HOB Washington DC 20515-2505*

MC CARTHY, KATHRYN A. physicist; b. Lawrence, Mass., Aug. 7, 1924; d. Joseph Augustine and Catherine (Barrett) McCarthy. AB, Tufts U., 1945, MS, 1946; PhD, Radcliffe Coll., 1957; DSc (hon.), Coll. Holy Cross, 1978; DHL (hon.), Merrimack Coll., 1981. Instr. physics Tufts U., 1946-53, asst. prof., 1953-59, assoc. prof., 1959-62, prof., 1962-95, emerita, 1995—, dean Grad. Sch., 1969-74, provost, sr. v.p., 1973-79. Rsch. fellow in metallurgy Harvard, 1957-59, vis. scholar, 1979-80; rsch. assoc. Baird Assocs., 1947-49, 51, Boston U. Optical Rsch. Lab., summer 1952; assoc. rsch. engr. U. Mich., summer 1957-58; dir. Mass. Electric Co., State Mut. Assurance Co.; chmn. Hallmark Health Systems, 1997—. Trustee Southeastern Mass. U., 1972-74, Merrimack Coll., 1974-83, Coll. Holy Cross, 1980-97; corporator Lawrence Meml. Hosp., 1975-97, dir., 1978-97. Fellow Optical Soc. Am., Am. Phys. Soc.; mem. Soc. Women Engrs. (sr.), Phi Beta Kappa, Sigma Xi. Roman Catholic. Office: Tufts U Dept Physics 4 Colby St Medford MA 02155-6013 Home: 1010 Waltham St Apt C362 Lexington MA 02421-8092 E-mail: kmccarbb[illegible]@aol.com

MCCARTHY, LYNN COWAN, genealogist, researcher; b. Panama City, Panama, Mar. 18, 1940; d. John Linus and Rose (Cowan) McC. BA, Mary Washington Coll., 1961; MSW, Va. Commonwealth U., 1969. Pub. asst. social worker Social Svc. Bur., Norfolk, Va., 1961-62; grad. resident advisor U. Ky., Lexington, 1962-63, head resident, 1963-64; child welfare worker Commonwealth of Ky., Lexington, 1964-67; asst. tng. specialist Commonwealth of Ky. Cabinet for Human Resources, Frankfort, 1969-71, tng. adminstr., 1971-74, child protective svcs. cons., 1974-81, employer svcs. supr., 1981-83; grants and contracts adminstr. Commonwealth of Ky. Dept. Librs. and Archives, Frankfort, 1983-94; profl. genealogist Frankfort, 1994—2002. Sec., exec. bd. Friends of Ky. Pub. Archives, Frankfort, 1994. Rschr. (TV prodn.) The Hatfields and McCoys: An American Feud, 1996; prodr. (video) The Family of Rose and Jack McCarthy, 1998. Vol. Habitat for Humanity, Inc., Ky., 1997-2000. Named Col. Hon. Order of Ky. Cols., 1994, Outstanding Profls. in Human Svcs., Am. Acad. Human Svcs., 1973. Mem. NASW, Nat. Geneal. Soc., Ky. Hist. Soc., Ky. Geneal. Soc., Va. Geneal. Soc., N.C. Geneal. Soc., Friends of Ky. Pub. Archives, Ky. Pub. Retirees, Acad. Cert. Social Workers, Assn. Profl. Geneaologists, Ky. Network Profl. Genealogists (co-founder 1999). Democrat. Methodist. Avocations: travel, bird-watching, photography, landscaping, spectator sports. Home: 929 Brookhaven Dr Frankfort KY 40601-4439

MCCARTHY, MARIANNE, government agency administrator; BA, UCLA; MA in Edn., U. No. Colo.; PhD in Psychology, UCLA. Prin. Woodview Calabasas Sch., Erikson H.S.; dir. edn. program NASA, 1996—. Vol. tchrs. asst. UCLA Neuropsychiat. Inst. Office: NASA Dryden Rsch Ctr PO Box 273 MS 4839 Edwards CA 93523-0273

MCCARTHY, MARY ANN, counselor, educator; b. Barstow, Calif., Jan. 16, 1954; d. Thomas Edward and Helen C. (Krutell) McC. BA in Psychology, San Francisco State U., 1975; MS in Counseling, Calif. State U., Fullerton, 1995. Cert. pupil pers. svcs., 1995. Br. mgr., asst. v.p. Great American First Savings, Orange County, Calif., 1981-88, dist. mgr., v.p., 1988-90; dir. re-entry ctr. Saddleback Coll., Mission Viejo, Calif., 1995; intern coord. Orange Coast Coll., Costa Mesa, Calif., 1995—, adj. counselor, 1997—; assoc. prof. counseling, counselor Saddleback Coll., Mission Viejo, Calif., 1996—. Adj. prof. counseling Orange Coast Coll., Costa Mesa, Calif., 1997; assoc. prof. counseling Irvine Valley Coll., Calif., 2004. Vol. Beverly Manor Convalescent Hosp., Laguna Hills, Calif., 1989-94, Mission Viejo Animal Shelter, 1996-97, Big sister Big Bros./Big Sisters Am., Mission Viejo, 1980-83; vol. and cmty. rep. Trauma Intervention Program, 2002—; mem scholarship and ednl. coms. Saddleback Valley C. of C., Laguna Hills, 1982-86; spkr. local schs. Saddleback Valley Vol. Network, Mission Viejo, 1982-86. Recipient Outstanding Young Woman Am. award, 1983; named Saddleback Valley Young Careerist, Bus. & Profl. Women, 1983. Mem. AAUW (past pres., editor, scholarship chair, pub. info. officer, sec. 1996-97), Am. Counseling Assn., Am. Coll. Counseling Assn., Calif. C.C. Counselor Assn., Calif. Assn. Counseling and Devel. Avocations: reading, travel. Home: 5 Martinique St Laguna Niguel CA 92677-5804 Office: Orange Coast Coll 2701 Fairview Rd Costa Mesa CA 92626-5563 also: Saddleback Coll 28000 Marguerite Pkwy Mission Viejo CA 92692-3635

MCCARTHY, MARY ARMAO, professional society administrator; b. N.Y.C., Mar. 4, 1947; d. John A. and Concettina D. (Conforti) Armao; m. J. Kevin McCarthy; children: Christine, Michelle, Michael. BA in English and Bus., SUNY, 1968. Instr. English, bus. Wolhoit Sch., Kenitra, Morocco, 1968, 69; ednl. cons. N.Y. State Edn. Dept., Albany, 1970-73; instr. Mildred Elley Sch., Albany, 1973-82; spl. project coord. N.Y. State Dept. Environ. Concervation, Albany, 1983-86; founding exec. dir. Dist. II Am. Coll. Ob-Gyn., Albany, NY, 1986—99. Bd. dirs. Ctr. Women in Govt., Albany, 1986-97, Hudson Valley Writers Guild, pres., 1999-, Panel of Am. Women. 1983-87, mem., 1973-89; mem. N.Y. State Women's Polit. Caucus, 1991—, N.Y. State Family Planning Advocates, 1988—, N.Y. State Civil Liberties Union, 1997—. Mem. NOW, N.Y. State Soc. Assn. Execs., N.Y. State Perinatal Assn., LWV (bd. dirs. 1982-86). Avocations: writing, swimming.

MCCARTHY, MARY ELIZABETH (BETH) CONSTANCE, conductor, educator, music educator; b. Chgo., Apr. 8, 1961; d. Thomas Joseph and Loretta Ann McCarthy. BA, North Ctrl. Coll., 1983; postgrad., Goethe Inst., 1991, Ea. Ill. U., 1993; MusM in Choral and Instrumental Edn. and Cognition and Vocal Performance, Northwestern U., 1999. Profl. cantor Joliet/Rockford Dioceses, Ill., 1979—; assoc. condr. Chorus Orch. Band Ill. Math. and Sci. Acad., Aurora, 1989—2000; site coord. gifted program Ill. Math. and Sci. Acad. at Ea. Ill. U., Charleston, 1990—95; soloist Lincoln Opera Co., Chgo., 1991—94; chmn. Dept. Fine Arts Rosary H.S., Aurora, 1993—; dept. chair music Aurora U., 1995—; condr., artistic dir. Fox Valley Festival Chorus, Aurora, 1999—. Profl. role coach pvt. students, Ill., 1989—; condr., music dir. dinner theatres, summer stock, Ill., 1990—; artistic cons. oratory and recitals, Ill., 1993—; adjudicator orchs., chorus, bands, Ill., 1993—; cons. to critique Nat. Stds. for the Arts, Ill., 1994; master class clinician various choral orgns., Ill., 1995—; guest condr. fine arts festivals, Ill., 2001—; host Cath. Conf. Fine Arts Festival Rosary H.S., Aurora, 2002. Sec. The Beta Fin. Group, Sycamore, Ill., 1995—2002; conservation mem. Salmon Unlimited-Ill. chpt., 1997; religious edn. tchr. St. Peter and Paul Ch., Naperville, Ill., 1980—, cantor, 1976—, Rite of Christian Initiation for Adults sponsor, 1995. Recipient Internat. Bel-Canto Vocal Competition Opera award, Bel-Canto Found., 1995; fellow Richter fellow for internat. rsch./study, North Ctrl. Coll., 1982. Mem.: AAUW, Lyric Opera Chgo., Ill. Music Educators' Assn., Music Educators' Nat. Conf., Fox Valley Music Educators' Assn., North Ctrl. Coll. Alumni Assn., Northwestern U. Music Sch. Alumni Assn. (bd. dirs. 1998—2001), Northwestern Club Chgo., Alpha Psi Omega, Beta Beta Beta, Phi Alpha Theta. Avocations: art, travel, running, boating, reading. Office: Aurora Univ Music Dept 347 S Gladstone Aurora IL 60506

MCCARTHY, MARY FRANCES, medical foundation administrator, not-for-profit fundraiser, consultant; b. Washington, Apr. 16, 1937; d. Joseph Francis and Frances (Oddi) McGowan; m. Charles M. Sappenfield, Dec. 14, 1963 (div. June 1990); children: Charles Ross, Sarah Kathleen; m. Daniel Fendrich McCarthy, Jr., Aug. 25, 1990 (dec. Apr. 1999); m. Cary Walter Allen, Nov. 30, 2002. BA, Trinity Coll., Washington, 1958; cert. in bus. adminstrn., Harvard U.-Radcliffe Coll., 1959; MA, Ball State U., Muncie, Ind., 1984. Systems engr. IBM, Cambridge, Mass., 1959-61; editl. asst. Kiplinger Washington Editors, 1961-63; feature writer pub. info. dept. Ball State U., 1984-85, coll. editor Coll. Bus., 1985-86, coord. alumni and devel., 1986-88, dir. major gift clubs and donor rels., 1988-90; dir. devel. Sweet Briar (Va.) Coll., 1990-91; adminstr. St. Mary's Hosp. and Med. Ctr. Found., Grand Junction, Colo., 1991—. Editor: A History of Maxon Corporation, 1986, Managing Change, 1986, Indiana's Investment Banker, 1987; assoc. editor Mid-Am. Jour. Bus., 1985-86. Participant Leadership Lynchburg, 1990, Jr. League; regional dir. IX Assn. for Healthcare Philanthropy, 1996—98, found. bd., 1997—; bd. dirs. Sr. Companions, Grand Junction, 1992—; mem. steering com. Mesa County Health Cmtys., 1992—; bd. dirs. Grand Junction Musical Arts, 1997—; trustee Women's Found. of Colo., 2000—; bd. dirs. Grand Valley Hospice, 2002—; mem. Mesa County Health Assessment, 1994—. Recipient Golden Broom award Muncie Clean City, 1989; svc. of distinction award Ball State U. Coll. Bus., 1990. Mem. Coun. for Advancement and Support of Edn., Assn. of Healthcare Philanthropy (regional 9 cabinet 1992—, bd. dirs. 1997—), Nat. Soc. Fundraising Execs. (cert., Colo. chpt. bd. dirs. 1994—), Rotary. Republican. Avocations: biking, walking, cross-country skiing, gardening.

MCCARTHY, NOBU, actress, performing company executive, educator; Adj. prof. Calif. State U. Artistic dir.: East West Players in Los Angeles, As The Crow Flies (Drama-Logue award), Sarcophagus, Come Back Little Sheba; dir. The Chairman's Wife, Webster Street Blues, And the Soul Shall Dance, (TV) China Beach, Island Son, Magnum P.I., Quincy, Farell to Manzanar, Playhouse 90, (feature films) Geisha Boy, Wake Me When It's Over, Karate Kid II, Pacific Heights. Office: Mark Taper Forum 5905 Wilshire Blvd Los Angeles CA 90036-4504

MCCARTHY, PAMELA MAFFEI, magazine editor; b. N.Y.C., May 28, 1952; d. Rudolph Paul Maffei and Mary Frances Maresca; m. Joseph Matthews McCarthy, Sept. 16, 1978; 2 children. Student, Trinity Coll., Dublin, Ireland, 1972-73; BA, Mt. Holyoke Coll., 1974. Mem. editorial staff Esquire mag., N.Y.C., 1974-76, copy editor, 1976-79, exec. editor, 1978-84; mng. editor Vanity Fair mag., N.Y.C., 1984-92, The New Yorker, N.Y.C., 1992-95, dep. editor, 1995-99, mng. editor, 1999—. Mem. Am. Soc. Mag. Editors Office: The New Yorker Advance Publications Inc 4 Times Sq New York NY 10036-6561

MCCARTHY, PATRICE ANN, lawyer; b. New Haven, Jan. 23, 1957; d. Robert Edmund and Faith Arline (Augur) McC.; m. Donald Allen Kirshbaum, Oct. 25, 1986; children: Lynn Anne, Sara. BA, Mt. Holyoke Coll., 1978; JD, U. Conn., 1981. Bar: Conn. 1981, U.S. Dist. Ct. Conn. 1981. Staff assoc. Conn. Conf. Municipalities, New Haven, 1981-83; legal counsel Conn. Assn. Bds. Edn., Hartford, 1983-88, gen. counsel, assoc. exec. dir. for govt. rels., 1988-91; dep. dir., gen. counsel, 1991—. Editor: Conn. Manual Bd. Policy Regulations and By-laws, 1987; contbr. articles to profl. jours. Mem. ABA, Nat. Sch. Bds. Assn. Coun. Sch. Attys. (bd. dirs. 1990-94), Am. Soc. Pub. Adminstrn. (coun. 1988—), Nat. Orgn. for Legal Problems in Edn., Conn. Bar Assn., Conn. Sch. Attys. Coun. (pres. 1988-89), Conn. Pub. Employers Labor Rels. Assn. (bd. dirs. 1985-88), Mt. Holyoke Club (v.p. 1986-88, pres. 1990-94). Office: Conn Assn Bds Edn 81 Wolcott Hill Rd Hartford CT 06109-1242

MCCARTHY, ROSE MARIE, medical/surgical nurse; b. Brooklyn, N.Y., May 18, 1951; children: Daniel, Devin. ADN, CUNY, 1973. RN NJ, Pa. Rn Downstate U., 1973—76, Atlantic City Med. Ctr., 1976—. Playboy Hotel & Casino, 1981—98; head nurse. Bd. mem. Am. Cancer Soc., Absecon, NJ, 1988—2003; past pres. Crimestoppers, Northfield, NJ, 1983—88. Mem.: Red Cross. Personal E-mail: bluerose46@aol.com.

MCCARTNEY, RHODA HUXSOL, farm manager; b. Floyd County, Iowa, June 30, 1928; d. Julius Franklin and Ruth Ada (Carney) Huxsol; m. Ralph Farnham McCartney, June 25, 1950; children: Ralph, Julia, David. AA, Frances Shimer, 1948; BA, U. Iowa, 1950. Mng. dir. McCartney-Huxsol Farms, Charles City, Iowa, 1969—; prin. trustee J.F. Huxsol Trusts, Charles City, Iowa, 1984—. Pres. Nat. 19th Amendment Soc., Charles City, 1991-2002, past pres., 2002—; mem. Terace Hill Commn., Des Moines, 1988-94; bd. dirs. Iowa Children and Family Svcs., Des Moines, 1963-68; mem. Iowa. Arts Coun., Des Moines, 1974-78. Named Woman of Yr., local C. of C., 2000. Mem. AAUW, Iowa LWV, PEO. Congregationalist. Avocations: church work, gardening, travel. Home: 1828 Cedar View Dr Charles City IA 50616-9129 Office: McCartney-Huxsol Farms 1828 Cedarview Rd Charles City IA 50616

MCCARTNEY, ROSE MARIE, minister; b. Ten Mile, W. Va., Aug. 20, 1953; d. Hayward Zane and Lillian Oliver Zirkle; m. Charles Michael Ray McCartney, Aug. 28, 1971 (div. Apr. 29, 1991); children: Steven Ray, Jamie Lee. BA, W.Va. Wesleyan Coll., 1992; MDiv, Meth. Theol. Sch., Ohio, 1996. Ordained Elder W.Va. Annual Conf. of United Meth. Ch. Co-owner, operator Mike's Fix It Shop, French Creek, W.Va., 1987—90; pastor Ellamore Charge United Meth. Ch., Buckhannon, W.Va., 1990—95, Sabro-Highland Charge United Meth. Ch., Morgantown, W.Va., 1995—97, Hodgesville Charge United Meth. Ch., Buckhannon, W.Va., 1997—99, Belington Charge United Meth. Ch., 1999—. Bd. mem. Sugar Creek Children's Home, Philippi, W.Va., 1999—, Heart and Hand, Philippi, W.Va., 1999—. Author: (poem) Today's Famous Poems, 2003. Mem.: Barbour County Ministerial Assn. (sec. 2000—). Methodist. Avocations: reading, writing, walking. Home: RR Box 226-5 Buckhannon WV 26201 Office: Belington Charge United Meth Ch 512 Beverly Pike Belington WV 26250 E-mail: pastorj@sunlitsurf.com.

MCCARTY, JUDY, councilman; b. June 4, 1940; m. Curt McCarty; 2 children. BS, Ind. U. Aide to Assemblyman Larry Stirling; del. UN Program for Local Environ. Initiatives, White House Conf. on Libr. and Info. Svcs.; city councilwoman 7th Dist., San Diego, 1985—. Chair select com. on govt. effeciency, fiscal reform, Mission Traisl Regional Pk. Task Force, natural resources, culture com., city rep. Pk. and Recreation Bd., San Diego Processing Corp., alt. rep. Met. Transit Devel. Bd., San Diego City Coun. Pres. Navajo Cmty. Recipient Local Legislator of Yr. award, Kate Sessions award Industry Environ. Assn. Methodist. Office: City San Diego 202 C St Fl 10 San Diego CA 92101-3860

MCCARTY, SHIRLEY CAROLYN, aerospace executive; b. Minot, N.D., May 2, 1934; d. Harry and Cecelia Marie (Engene) Wolhowe; m. John Myron McCarty, Apr. 3, 1958. BS in Bus. Adminstrn., U. N.D., 1958. Mem. tech. staff Douglas Aircraft, El Segundo, Calif., 1960-62, The Aerospace Corp., El Segundo, 1962-72, mgr., 1972-73, dir., 1973-79, prin. dir., 1979-89; gen. mgr., 1989—. Mem. adv. council Calif. State U., Northridge, 1979—, chmn., 1984-86; mem. indsl. adv. bd. Purdue U. Soc. Women Engrs., West Lafayette, Ind., 1979-82, 1985—. Named Woman of Yr. The Aerospace Corp., 1976, Pres.'s award, 1987; recipient Spl. Judges Award for Leadership, Los Angeles YWCA, 1977, Sioux Alumni Award, U. N.D, 1982, Achievement award Los Angeles County Commn. for Women, 1987. Mem. IEEE, Assn. for Computing Machinery, Soc. Women Engrs., Bus. and Profl. Women (Woman of Achievement 1984, Golden Nike award 1985), Women in Bus.(corp. achievement award, 1987), Women in Computing (founding mem., bd. dirs.). Avocations: raising and training siberian huskies, traveling, writing. Home: 357 Valley St El Segundo CA 90245-2932 Office: The Aerospace Corp 2350 E El Segundo Blvd El Segundo CA 90245-4691

MCCARTY, V.K. publisher, chaplain, librarian; b. Boston, June 26, 1948; d. Charles Osner and Dorothy June (McAlister) Long. BM, Mich. State U., 1969; MM, U. Louisville, 1972; cert. in theatre arts, U. London, 1972; student in Congl. Devel. Inst. Tng., St. Luke's Roosevelt Hosp., N.Y.C., 2002—. Advt. asst. Lansing (Mich.) State Jour., 1968-69; market rsch. cons. Sta. WKLO, Louisville, 1969-70; libr. Louisville Free Pub. Libr., 1970-72; v.p. assoc. pub. Gen. Media Inc., N.Y.C., 1979-2000; acquisitions libr. Gen. Theol. Sem. St. Mark's Libr., N.Y.C., 2000—; part-time acquisitions libr. United Theol. Sem. Burke Libr., N.Y.C., 2001—02; dir. Christian Formation, St. Paul's Ch., Chatham, NJ, 2002—03. Bd. dirs. B.F.T., Inc., N.Y.C. Dance editor Saturday Review Mag. Online, 1993-95. Master of ceremonies St. Ignatius of Antioch, N.Y.C., 1984-98; chaplaincy coord. St. Luke's Roosevelt Hosp., N.Y.C. Mem. N.Y. Liturgical Music Found. (steering com. 1982-84), N.Y. Ch. Club. Avocations: riding, ballet, preservation of Benedictine monasticism, Byzantine art. Office: Gen Theol Sem St Mark's Libr 175 9th Ave New York NY 10011-4977

MCCASKILL, CLAIRE, auditor; b. Houston, July 25, 1953; Auditor State of Mo., Jefferson City, 1999—. Democrat. Office: Mo State Auditors Off PO Box 869 Jefferson City MO 65102-0869 Fax: 573-751-6539.

MCCASLIN, KATHLEEN DENISE, child abuse educator; b. Poughkeepsie, N.Y., Aug. 4, 1962; d. Nancy Ann Gosselin; m. David Wayne McCaslin, Sept. 27, 1986 (dec. Oct. 1990); 1 child, LeAnn ; m. Larry Thomas Ward, July 14, 1998. BA, Adelphi Coll., 1984. Pub. speaker Impact Seminars, Littlestown, Pa., 1987-[illegible] McCaslin Internat., Guffey, Colo., 1994—; pub. speaker The Family Advocate, Guffey, Colo., 1997—. Founder We the People, Colorado Springs, Colo., 1982; vol. counselor/facilitator Beginning Experience, Harrisburg, Pa., 1991-94. Author: (books) Trusting in God, 1993, Respecting Yourself, 1993, Loss and Recovery, 1992, (cd audio) One Child's Journey to Freedom, 1998. Troop leader Girl Scouts U.S., Guffey, Colo., 1998-2000. Recipient Outstanding Grad. award Adelphi Coll., Colorado Springs, 1984. Mem. ASCPA, World Wildlife Fedn., Arbor Day Found., S.W. Indian Found. Avocations: reading, hiking, needlework, gourmet cooking, gardening. Office: McCaslin Internat PO Box 100 Guffey CO 80820

MCCASLIN, LATANYA, art educator; d. Frank and Eloise McCaslin. Student, U. Ala., Birmingham, 1987—92. Art lectr., Birmingham, 1992—; cultural arts dir. Sparkle Arts and Computers, Fairfield, Ala., 1992—. Active Dem. Nat. Com., Washington, Dem. Congl. Campaign Com., Washington. Home: 113 60th St Fairfield AL 35064

MCCASLIN, TERESA EVE, human resources executive; b. Jersey City, Nov. 22, 1949; d. Felix F. and Ann E. (Golaszewski) Hrynkiewicz; m. Gary A. McCue. BA, Marymount Coll., 1971; MBA, L.I. U., 1981. Adminstrv. officer Civil Service Commn., Fed. Republic Germany, 1972-76; personnel dir. Oceanroutes, Inc., Palo Alto, Calif., 1976-78; mgr., coll. relations Continental Grain Co., N.Y.C., 1978-79, corp. personnel mgr., 1979-81, dir. bus. redesign, internal cons., 1981-84; dir., human resources Grow Group, Inc., N.Y.C., 1984-85, v.p. human resources, 1985-86, v.p. adminstrn., 1986-89; corp. v.p. human resources Avery Dennison Corp., Pasadena, Calif., 1989-94; v.p. human resources Monsanto Co., St. Louis, 1994-97; sr. v.p. human resources and pub. rels. Conti Group Cos. (formerly Continental Grain Co.), N.Y.C., 1997—, exec. v.p. human resources & info. tech., 1999—. Mem. Am. Mgmt. Assn. (vice chair, fin. and exec. com., chair compensation com., mem. bd. trustees), Human Resources Coun. Roman Catholic. Avocations: skiing, traveling, golf. Office: Conti Group Cos 277 Park Ave New York NY 10172-0003

MCCAUGHAN, DELLA MARIE, retired science educator; b. Pass Christian, Miss., Apr. 10, 1928; d. John Jeff and Nora Bell Sims; m. Finley Brandt McCaughan, Aug. 2, 1952; children: Leona Grace McCaughan Clawson, Diana Kay McCaughan Rodwig. Assocs. Degree, Miss. Gulf Coast C.C., Perkinston, Miss., 1949; BS, U. So. Miss., 1951, MS, 1959, specialist degree in sci. edn., 1979. Cert. elem. and secondary edn. in sci. Miss. Sci. educator Biloxi (Miss.) Pub. Schs., 1951—58, chairperson dept. sci., educator, 1959—95; ret., 1995. Adj. instr. biology for gifted secondary students Johns Hopkins U., Balt., 1988—91; ind. contractor Miss.-Ala. Sea Grant Consortium, Biloxi, 1980—84; edn. advisor U.S. Senate (Office Senator Thad Cochran), Washington, 1991—92; ind. contractor, author Miss. Dept. Marine Resources, Biloxi, 1996—99. Author: Guide to Federal Programs for Mississippi Educators, 1992; editor: Marine Resources and History of the Mississippi Gulf Coast (vols. 1-4), 1998. Finalist Nat. Tchrs. Hall of Fame, 2002; named Congl. Einstein fellow, U.S. Senate, Washington, 1991—92; named to Miss. Hall of Master Tchrs., 1991; recipient Presdl. award for excellence in sci. and math. tchg., Washington, 1984, Tandy Tech. Scholars award, Tandy Corp., L.A., 1991. Mem.: Nat. Sci. Tchrs. Assn. (Nat. Disting. Svc. citation 1976), Assn. Presdl. Awardees in Sci. Tchg., Benevolent Protective Order of Elks. Avocations: reading, traveling. Home: 134 St Jude St Biloxi MS 39530

MCCAUGHEY ROSS, ELIZABETH P. (BETSY MCCAUGHEY), former lieutenat governor; b. Oct. 20, 1948; d. Albert Peterkin; m. Thomas McCaughey, 1972 (div. 1994); children: Amanda, Caroline, Diana. BA, Vassar Coll., 1970; MA, Columbia Univ., 1972, PhD, 1976. Public policy expert Manhattan Inst., N.Y.C.; lt. gov. State of N.Y., 1995—99. Asst. prof. Vassar Coll., 1979, Columbia U., 1980-84; chmn. Governor's Medicaid Task Force, 1994. Author: From Loyalist to Founding Father, 1980, Government By Choice, 1987; also articles including an article in The New Republic (Nat. Mag. award for Pub. Policy 1995). Recipient Bancroft Dissertation award, Richard B. Morris prize; Woodrow Wilson fellow, Herbert H. Lehman fellow, Honorary Vassar fellow, John Jay fellow, Post Doctoral Rsch. fellow NEH, 1984, John M. Olin fellow Manhattan Inst., 1993, sr. fellow Ctr. Study of the Presidency. Republican.

MCCAUL, ELIZABETH, investment advisor, former state agency administrator; BA in econ., Boston U., 1985; postgrad., Georgetown U. Congl. intern, 1981; investment banker, v.p. Goldman, Sachs & Co., 1985—95; chief of staff N.Y. State Banking Dept., 1995—96, first dep. supt. banks, 1996—97, acting supt. banks, 1997-2000, supt. banks, 2000—03; ptnr. Promontory Fin. Group, 2003—. Dir. Empire State Devel. Corp., State N.Y. Mortgage Agy., N.Y. State Job Devel. Authority, Harlem Cmty. Devel. Corp.; statutory mem. Cmty. Facilities Project Guarantee Fund. Scholar European Econ. Cmty., Inst. European Studies, Freiburg, Germany. Mem. Conf. State Bank Suprs. (bd. dirs., supervisory chmn., 2001-02, internat. bankers adv. bd.), Fed. Fin. Inst. Examination Coun., 2002-03. Office: Promontory Fin Group 1201 Pennsylvania Ave NW Ste 617 Washington DC 20004

MCCAULEY, DIANE LYNN, secondary school educator, music educator; b. Richland Center, Wis., Nov. 12, 1968; d. Milford Roy and Caroline Ann McCauley. BA, Luther Coll., 1991; MS, Cardinal Stritch U., 2003. Cert. PK-12 prin., dir. instrn., PK-12 instrumental music Wis. Grades 9-12 instrumental music tchr. Marathon (Wis.) Pub. Schs., 1991—97, Merrill (Wis.) Area Pub. Schs., 1997—. Music dir. Mt. Olive Luth. Ch., Schofield, Wis., 1992—2001; adjudicator Wis. Sch. Music Assn., Waunakee, 1992—. Fundraising vol. Performing Arts Found., Wausau, Wis., 1995; mem. scholarship com. Mt. Olive Luth. Ch., Schofield, 1997—2001; bd. dirs. Merrill Concert Assn., 1999—2001. Nominee Disney's Am. Tchr. award, Walt Disney Corp., 2002; named Outstanding Young Woman Am., Outstanding Young Ams., 1997. Mem.: Wis. Music Educators' Assn., Music Educators Nat. Conf., Nat. Band Assn. Avocations: walking, crafts, solo handbell ringing. Home: 602 Hollywood Dr #1 Merrill WI 54452 Office: Merrill HS 1201 N Sales St Merrill WI 54452 Business E-Mail: Diane.McCauley@maps.k12wi.us. E-mail: mccauley@dwave.net.

MCCAULEY, FLOYCE REID, psychiatrist; b. Braddock, Pa., Dec. 30, 1933; d. John Mitchel and Irene (Garner) Reid; m. James Calvin McCauley, July 15, 1955; children: James Stanley, Lori Ellen. BSN, U. Pitts., 1956; DO, Coll. Osteopathic Medicine, Phila., 1972. Diplomate Am. Bd. Forensic Medicine, Am. Bd. Forensic Examiners, bd. eligible in child and adult psychiatry. Intern Suburban Gen. Hosp., Norristown, Pa., 1972-73; resident in adult psychiatry Phila. State Hosp. and Phila. Mental Health Clinic, 1973-75; fellow Med. Coll. of Pa. and Ea. Pa. Psychiat. Inst., Phila., 1975-78; Chief child psychiatry inpatient unit Med. Coll. Pa., Phila., 1978-80; med. dir. Carson ValleySch., Flourtown, Pa., 1980-82; dir. outpatient psychiat. clinic Osteopathic Med. Ctr. Phila., 1980-86; staff psychiatrist Kent Gen. Hosp., Dover, Del., 1986-89; psychiat. cons. Del. Guidance Svcs. for Children, Dover, 1986-91; clin. dir. children's unit HCA Rockford Ctr., Newark, 1991-93; with Kid's Peace Nat. Hosp. for Kids in Crisis, 1993-95; staff psychiatrist St. Lukes Quakertown Hosp., 1996-98; cons. Interact Phila., 1996-98; staff psychiatrist Del. Guidance Svcs. for Children and Youth, Dover, 1998—2001. Psychiat. cons. Cath. Charities Day Treatment Program 3-6 Yr. Olds, Dover, Del., 1990—2003, Seaford (Del.) Br. New Eng. Fellowship Rehab., 1991—93; cons. Del. Guidance Day Treatment Program, 1990—2002; mem. Mental Health Code Rev. Com., Del., 1991; staff psychiatrist Kids Peace Nat. Hosp. for Kids in

Crisis, 1993—95, Penn Found., 1995—98; cons. psychiatrist Valley Day Sch., Morrisville, Pa., 2000—, Children's Svcs., Inc., Phila., 2002—. Mem. Mayor's Com. for Mental Health, Phila., 1983. Named to Chapel of Four Chaplains, Phila., 1983. Mem.: Am. Osteopathic Assn. Democrat. Methodist. Avocations: sewing, decorating, playing classical guitar, drawing, singing with copper penny players.

MCCAULEY, JANE REYNOLDS, journalist; b. Wilmington, Del., Oct. 22, 1947; d. John Thomas and Helen (Campbell) McC. BA, Guilford Coll., 1969. Editor, sr. writer Nat. Geographic Soc., Washington, 1970-90; freelance writer, editor, artist, 1990-96; exec. editor AM Quilter's Soc., 1996-97; freelance editor, writer, 1997—. Former owner Unique Native Crafts; tropical bird specialist. Author of 15 children's books; co-author award-winning travel books, art revs. Mem.: Children's Book Soc. E-mail: ritstuff4u@aol.com.

MCCLAIN, CINDY DUNSTAN, music educator; d. Kenneth Warren and Janet Lou Dunstan; m. Michael Austin McClain, June 1, 1987; children: Melinda Wrye Washington, John Michael Kritos. MusB in Vocal and Instrumental Edn. K-12, Lincoln U. of Mo., Jefferson City, 1977; MA in Piano Performance, Ctrl. Mo. State U., 1995. Dir., coord. music, adjudicator State Fair Coll., Sedalia, Mo., 1988—. Recipient Governor's award for excellence in tchg., State of Mo., 2000. Mem.: Mo. Assn. Dept. Schs. of Music, Mo. C.C. Assn., Music Educators Nat. Conf., Am. Choral Dirs. Assn. Office: State Fair Coll 3201 W 16th St Sedalia MO 65301 Office Phone: 660-530-5800. Personal E-mail: cmcclain@iland.net. E-mail: mcclain@sfcc.cc.mo.us.

MCCLAIN, LENA ALEXANDRIA, protective services official; b. Toledo, Ohio, Aug. 15, 1966; d. Lee Earl McClain, Mattie May Roberts-McClain; m. David Angelo Neyland, Aug. 4, 1990 (div. July 1995). AAS in Criminal Justice Adminstrn., Pikes Peak C.C., Colorado Springs, Colo., 1994; postgrad., U. Colo., 1994—95; BS in Criminology, U. So. Colo., 1996; postgrad., Spring Arbor U., Mich., 2001—02. Corrections officer Colo. Dept. Corrections, Colorado Springs, 1994—96, sgt., 1996—97, case mgr./lt., 1997—99; sr. resident specialist coord. N.W. Cmty. Corrections Ctr., Bowling Green, Ohio, 1999—2000; shift supr. Lucas County Dept. Wk. Release, Toledo, 2000—. Employee counsel, bd. dirs. Delta Correctional Ctr., 1998—99. Mem. Colo. Grievance Team, 1990; bd. dirs. Pub. Arts Commn., Delta, Colo., 1999; bd. dirs., liaison Nat. Assn. Blacks in Criminal Justice, Delta, 1998. With U.S. Army, 1987—90. Mem.: Am. Correctional Assn., Correctional Peace Officers Found., Phi Theta Kappa. Democrat. Avocations: golf, basketball, softball, chess, writing.

MCCLAIN, PAULA DENICE, political scientist, educator; b. Louisville, Jan. 3, 1950; d. Robert Landis and Mabel (Molock) McC.; stepdau. of Annette Williams McClain; m. Paul C. Jacobson, Jan. 30, 1988; children: Kristina L., Jessica A. BA, Howard U., Washington, 1972; MA, Howard U., 1974, PhD, 1977; postgrad., U. Pa., 1981-82. Asst. prof. dept. polit. sci. U. Wis., Milw., 1977-82; assoc. prof. and prof. pub. affairs Ariz. State U., Tempe, 1982-91; prof. govt. and fgn. affairs U. Va., Charlottesville, 1991-2000, chair govt. and fgn. affairs, 1994-97; prof. dept. polit. sci. Duke U., Durham, N.C., 2000—. Co-author: Can We All Get Along? Racial and Ethnic Minorities in American Politics, 1995, 3d edit. 2001, Race, Place and Risk: Black Homicide in Urban America, 1990; editor: Minority Group Influence, 1993; co-editor: Urban Minority Administrators, 1988. Mem. Nat. Conf. Black Polit. Scientists (pres. 1989-90), Am. Polit. Sci. Assn. (exec. coun. 1985-87, v.p. 1993-94), So. Polit. Sci. Assn. (exec. coun. 1992-95, v.p. 2002-03, pres.-elect 2004), Internat. Polit. Sci. Assn. (exec. com. 1997-2003, v.p. 1997-2003), Midwest Polit. Sci. Assn. (v.p. 2002-04). Office: Duke U Dept Polit Sci Perkins Libr PO Box 90204 Durham NC 27708-0204 E-mail: pmcclain@duke.edu.

MCCLAIN, VEDA, education educator, department chairman; BA in English, Wesleyan U., 1979; MS in Edn., U. Ctrl. Ark., 1992; PhD in Reading Edn., U. Ga., 1997. Elem. sch. tchr., Little Rock; reading instr. Upward Bound Project U. Ga., Philander Smith Coll., Little Rock; tchg. asst., rsch. asst. Nat. Reading Rsch. Ctr. U. Ga., Athens; instr. dept. reading edn. Ark. State U., State University, asst. prof. reading, assoc. prof. reading edn., dir. Minority Tchr. Scholars Program, chair dept. edn., 2001—. Reviewer Reading Excellence Grants Ark. Dept. Edn. Mem.: Ark. Literacy Tchr. Educators, Ark. Reading Assn. (chair student membership com.), S.E. Literacy Consortium, Nat. Coun. Tchrs. English, Nat. Reading Conf., Internat. Reading Assn., S.W. Ednl. Lab. (bd. mem. 2003—). Office: Ark State Univ PO Box 2350 State University AR 72467

MCCLANAHAN, KAY MARIE, government official, lawyer; b. Arkadelphia, Ark., Feb. 17, 1944; d. Allen William and Dorothy H. (Boon) McC.; m. George Townes Weaver, Jr., Aug. 20, 1966 (div. July 1987); 1 child, Shannon Marie Weaver Flanagan. B in Edn., U. Ark., 1966, JD, 1990; MA in Spanish, U. N.H., 1976. Bar: Ark. 1990. Staff atty. Adminstrv. Office Cts., Little Rock, 1990-92; acting dep. dir. Nat. Women's Bus. Coun., Washington, 1993-94; sr. program officer Devel. Assocs., Arlington, Va., 1995-96; confidential asst. to adminstr. Fgn. Agrl. Svc. USDA, Washington, 1996-97; U.S. rep. Inter-Am. Inst. Coop. Agr., Washington, 1997-99, coord. interregional instnl. rels. San Jose, Costa Rica, 1999—. Spkr. U.S. Info. Agy., Chile and Paraguay, 1994; election observer UN, El Salvador, 1994, OAS, Dominican Republic, 1996, 2000. Bd. dirs. Spanish Ednl. Devel. Ctr., Washington, 1996-99; commr. Sister Cities Commn., Little Rock, 1993; mem. Clinton-Gore Campaign, Ark. and Tex., 1992; dir. Alliance for Am., Nat. Order Women Legislators, Washington, 1994-95. Recipient scholarship Ark. Bar Found,. 1988; fellow U. N.H., 1977. Mem. Ark. Womens Lawyers Assn. (exec. bd. dirs. 1992-93), Ark. Bar Assn., Pulaski County Bar Assn. Avocations: singing, dance, nature activities, hiking. Office: Inter-Am Inst for Coop Agr San Isidro de Coronado #55-2200 San Jose Costa Rica E-mail: kaymcclan@hotmail.com.

MCCLEAN, LENORA JAMES, nursing educator, dean; b. Jesup, Ga., Apr. 22, 1937; d. Ealey and Mary (Howard) Hayes; m. Robert William McClean, July 13, 1963; children: Anne-Marie St. John, Sharman Danielle, Tara Lauren, Marshall Hayes. Asst. prof. nursing Fla. State U., Tallahassee, 1963-64; asst. prof. nursing Tchrs. Coll. Columbia U., N.Y.C., 1964-73; clinician Bronx Psychiat. Center, 1966-73; asst. prof., dean graduate studies Sch. Nursing Health Scis. Ctr., Stony Brook, 1973-79, prof., 1979—, assoc. dean academic affairs, 1979-80, acting dean, 1981—; chief nursing officer U. Med. Ctr. Cons. in field; chair subcom. alternative healthcare delivery patterns Cmty. Health Plan Suffolk, 1977; mem. search com. for chmn. OB/GYN Nassau County Med. Ctr., 1977-78, for chief of nursing V.A. Hosp., Northport, N.Y., 1983, planning com. rsch. and edn., 1983-86; planning group L.I. State Vets. Home, 1986-91, adv. group multidisciplinary opers., 1992; nursing adv. com. N.Y. State pub. svc. tng. program, 1988; faculty Comparative Health Care clin. study tour, U.S.-Morocco, 1990, Comparative Health Sys. Sino-Am. clin. study tour, China, 1982-91, Pediatric Nursing Soviet-Am. clin. study tour, 1981; researcher, presenter in field. Author: (with Dorothy Anderson) Identifying Suicide Potential, 1976; contbg. author: Comprehensive Psychiatric Nursing, 1979, 2d edit., 1982; contbr. numerous articles to profl. jours. Bd. dirs. Response Suffolk County, 1973-76; mem. cmty. adv. bd. transitional svcs., 1977, prof. adv. bd. chpt. Nat. Found.-March of Dimes Birth Defects, L.I. chpt., 1978-84, Blue Ribbon panel Suffolk County Infirmary, chair patient care subcom., 1989-90. Vis. fellow Sturt Coll. Advanced Edn., Bedford Park, South Australia, 1981-82; grantee. Mem. Am. Assn. Colls. Nursing (chair spl. interest group academic health sci. ctrs. 1990-93), Nat. League Nursing (coun. baccalaureate and higher degree programs), N.Y. State Nurses Assn. (v.p. 1980-82, reelected 1982, chair edn. com. 1978-80), Am. Nurses Assn., Coun. Deans of Nursing, Sr. Colls. and Univs. N.Y. State (-res. 1992), Sigma Theta Tau (Kappa Gamma chpt. 1988—). Democrat. Episcopalian. Office: SUNY Sch Nursing at Stony Brook U Hosp & Med Ctr Nicolls Rd T14 138 Ctr Stony Brook NY 11794-0001

MCCLELLAN, BETTY, county official; b. Norborne, Mo., Oct. 10, 1940; d. William Edwin and Kathryn Louise England; m. Gerald Louis McClellan, Dec. 6, 1958; childre; Tamela Stanek, Marsha Junge. Grad. high sch., Troy, Mo. Receptionist Nat. Pet Supply, St. Louis, 1958, Lincoln County Meml. Hosp., Troy, Mo., 1958-59; factory worker The Artemis Co., Troy, Mo., 1963-64; hatchery worker Trojan Hatchery, Troy, Mo., 1965-69; bookkeeper Silex (Mo.) Elevator, 1969-74, Agri-Foods, Troy, 1974-79; deputy recorder deeds Lincoln County Recorder, Troy, 1979-83; treas. Lincoln County, Troy, 1983—. Treas. Lincoln County Dem. Com., 1989-97, treas. women's club, 1974-80; bd. dirs., treas. Lincoln County Fair, 1996-98; coord. steering com. Congressman Harold Volkmer, Hannibal, Mo., 1977-95. Mem. Mo. County Treas. Assn., Order Ea. Star (sec. Silex chpt. 1986-93). Presbyterian. Avocations: crocheting, crafts, doll collecting, travel. Home: 721 Hwy E Silex MO 63377-2425 Office: Lincoln County Treas 201 Main St Troy MO 63379-1127

MC CLELLAN, CATHARINE, anthropologist, educator; b. York, Pa., Mar. 1, 1921; d. William Smith and Josephine (Niles) McClellan; m. John Thayer Hitchcock, June 6, 1974. AB magna cum laude in Classical Archaeology, Bryn Mawr Coll., 1942; PhD (Anthropology fellow), U. Calif. at Berkeley, 1950. Vis. asst. prof. U. Mo. at Columbia, 1952; asst. prof. anthropology U. Wash., Seattle, 1952-56; anthrop. cons. USPHS, Arctic Health Research Center, Alaska, 1956; asst. prof. anthropology, chmn. dept. anthropology Barnard Coll., Columbia U., 1956-61; asso. prof. anthropology U. Wis. at Madison, 1961-65, prof., 1965-83, prof. emeritus, 1983—, John Bascom prof., 1973. Vis. lectr. Bryn Mawr (Pa.) Coll., 1954; vis. prof. U. Alaska, 1973, 87. Assoc. editor: Arctic Anthropology, 1961; editor, 1975-82; assoc. editor: The Western Canadian Jour. of Anthropology, 1970-73. Served to lt. WAVES, 1942-46. Margaret Snell fellow AAUW, 1950-51; Am. Acad. Arts and Scis. grantee, 1963-64, Nat. Mus. Can. grantee, 1948-74 Fellow Am. Anthrop. Assn., Royal Anthrop. Inst. Gt. Britain and Ireland, AAAS, Arctic Inst. N.Am.; mem. Am. Ethnol. Soc. (sec.-treas. 1958-59, v.p. 1964, pres. 1965), Kroeber Anthrop. Soc., Am. Folklore Soc., Am. Soc. Ethnohistory (exec. com. 1968-71), Sigma Xi. Achievements include rsch. in archaeol. and ethnographic field investigations in Alaska and Yukon Territory in Can. E-mail: cmclellan@rivermead.org.

MCCLELLAN, DIXIE, secondary school educator; b. Freeburn, Ky., Dec. 4, 1940; d. Albert Eugene and Pauline (Lusk) McC.; m. Edward Lee Jessee, June 13, 1969 (div. Apr. 1975); m. Richard Joel McDuffee, July 2, 1996. BS in Edn., Concord Coll., Athens, W.Va.; MA in Polit. Sci., W.Va. U., 1972. Cert. secondary edn. tchr. Tchr. Roanoke County Schs., Salem, Va., 1959-62, Wyoming County Schs., Pineville, W.Va., 1962-64, Garrett County Schs., Oakland, Md., 1964-69, Preston County Schs., Kingwood, W.Va., 1969-72; Appalachian edn. specialist Appalachian Reigonal Com., Washington, 1972-77; rural devel. dir. Tenco Devel., Shelbyville, Tenn., 1977-81; exec. dir. Tenn. Export Devl. Assn., Nashville, 1982-85; pvt. cons. Nashville, 1985-89; tchr. Williamson County Schs., Nashville, 1989—. Chmn. Bedford County Adult Activity Ctr., Shelbyville, 1977-81; mem. Balance of State CETA Bd., Nashville, 1980-81; bd. dirs. Clan McClellan in Am., 1980-83. Writer monograph, grants, articles. Named to Outstanding Young Women of Am., 1979. Mem. Am. Polit. Sci. Assn., Profl. Educators Tenn. Republican. Episcopalian. Avocations: reading, gourmet cooking. Home: 2936 Spanntown Rd Arrington TN 37014-9123 Office: Centennial HS 5050 Mallory Ln Franklin TN 37067-1398 E-mail: McDuffee@mindspring.com.

MCCLELLAN, JOAN C. OSMUNDSON, retired art educator, artist; b. Milw., Jan. 5, 1934; d. Henry and Alma (Oyaas) Osmundson; m. Robert J. McClellan, Apr. 2, 1955 (dec.); children: Michael J., Linda A., Katherine M., Mary M. BS, SUNY, Buffalo, 1956; MA, Adelphi U., 1968; postgrad., SUNY, Buffalo, 1961, Hofstra U., 1966. Tchr. Harris Hill (N.Y.) Elem. Sch., 1957; art specialist Huth Rd. Sch., Grand Island, N.Y., 1958-59; art educator Prospect Ave Sch., East Meadow, N.Y., 1959-89, W.T. Clarke High Sch., East Meadow, 1959-89. Exhibited in group shows including Sarasota Art Assn., 1989, Art League of Manatee County, 1989, Federated Woman's Club, 1990, Englewood Artisan Guild, 1990 (Best of the Best award). Vol. English tchr. to Spanish immigrants, L.I., N.Y., 1987-88; vol. soup kitchen, Wyndauch, L.I., 1987-88. Mem.: AAUW, Sarasota Art Assn., Nat. Mus. Women in Arts, Englewood Artisan Guild (rec. sec. 1989—90, chair publicity com. 1997—98, bd. dirs.), Nat. League Pen Women (chair S.C. art com.), Venice Art League, Sea Grape Gallery, Charlotte County Art Guild, Rotonda West Federated Woman's Club (past pres., arts chmn. 1989—). Republican. Roman Catholic. Avocations: travel, cooking, gardening, computers, painting. Home and Studio: 8229 Palmview Ct Englewood FL 34224-7698 E-mail: artisjoan@earthlink.net.

MCCLELLAN, MARY ANN, pediatric nurse practitioner; b. Mar. 29, 1942; BS, Tex. Woman's U., 1964; MN, U. Wash., 1968-69; cert., U. Tex., Arlington, 1997. Cert. family life educator, CPNP, pediatric nurse practitioner; advanced RN practitioner, Okla. Charge nurse Baylor U. Med. Ctr., Dallas, 1964—65; pub. health staff nurse Dallas County Health Dept., Dallas, 1965—68; supervising nurse Okla. State Dept. Health, Oklahoma City, 1969—70, maternal-child health nurse cons., 1971; asst. prof. U. Okla. Coll. Nursing, Oklahoma City, 1971—72; from instr. to asst. prof. Harris Coll. Nursing Tex. Christian U., Ft. Worth, 1972—75; asst. prof. continuing edn. U. Okla. Coll. Nursing, Oklahoma City, 1976—79, asst. prof. baccalaureate program, 1979—96, mem. grad. faculty, 1991—. Cons. and lectr. in field. Contbr. chpts. to books, articles to profl. jours. Mem. Nat. Coun. on Family Rels., Okla. Family Resources Coalition, Nat. Assn. Pediatric Nurse Assocs. and Practitioners (Okla. chpt.), Assn. Faculty of Pediat. Nurse Practitioner Programs, So. Early Childhood Assn., Okla. Coun. on Family Rels., Okla. Early Childhood Assn., Sigma Theta Tau., Phi Kappa Phi. Office: U Okla Coll Nursing PO Box 26901 Oklahoma City OK 73126-0901

MCCLELLAN, STEPHANIE ANN, speech pathology/audiology services professional; b. Colorado Springs, Colo., Sept. 13, 1962; d. Jay and Ruthann Rash; m. Michael Allen McClellan, Sept. 14, 2001; 1 child, Evan James. AS in Interpreting for the Deaf, Northwestern Conn. C.C., Winsted, 1982; BS in Secondary Edn., Northwest Mo. State U., 1985; MS in Speech Lang. Pathology, Gallaudet U., 1990. Cert. clin. competence Am. Speech Lang. and Hearing Assn., 1991, lic. Del. State Bd. of Profl. Regulation, 2000. Speech lang. pathologist S.C. Sch. for the Deaf and Blind, Spartanburg, SC, 1990—93; chief of speech pathology svcs. in Europe USAF, England, 1993—99; speech lang. pathologist Smyrna, Del., 1999—. Pvt. practice interpreter, Lawrence, Kans., 1982—2003. Translator interpreter for the deaf. Cons. Smyrna Ch. of Christ Sch., Smyrna, Del., 2000—03. Capt. USAF, 1993—99, RAF Lakenheath, England. Recipient Vol. of Yr. award, S.C. Assn. for the Deaf, 1992. Mem.: Am. Speech Lang. Hearing Assn. (assoc.). Republican. Avocations: quilting, piano, travel, cooking. Home and Office: Speech and Lang Svcs 102 Hunting Way Smyrna DE 19977

MCCLELLAND, EMMA L. state legislator; b. Springfield, Mo., Feb. 26, 1940; m. Alan McClelland; children: Mike, Karen. BA, U. Mo., 1962. mem. appropriations, natural and econ. resources com., budget com., elem. and secondary edn. com., mcpl. corps. com., rules, joint rules and bills perfected and printed com., social services com., medicaid and elderly com. Dir. field office, corp. divsn. Mo. Sec. of State, St. Louis; committeewoman Gravois Twp.; mem. St. Louis County Rep. Cent. Com., Mo. Rep. State Com., Mo. Ho. of Reps., Jefferson City, 1991—; mem. appropriations, budget, edn., mcpl. corps., rules, joint rules and bills perfected and printed, social svcs., medicaid and the elderly coms. Bd. dirs. Ct. Apptd. Spl. Advocates, Family Support Network; elder Webster Groves Presbyn. Ch.; mem. Leadership St. Louis. Recipient Leadership award for govt. YWCA of St. Louis, Spirit of Enterprise award Mo. C. of C., Mental Health Assn. award for legis. svc., 1998, Mo. Child Adv. of Yr. award Mo. Child Care Assn., 1998. Mem. Webster Groves C. of C., Pi Lambda Theta. Republican. Presbyterian. Home: 455 Pasadena Ave Webster Groves MO 63119-3126 Office: Mo Ho of Reps State Capitol Building Jefferson City MO 65101-1556

MCCLELLAND, HELEN, music educator; b. Chgo., Dec. 5, 1951; d. Leon Leroy and Willie Jo (Darnell) McC.; (div. Sept. 1981); 1 child, Tasha Renee. Diploma in arts, Kennedy-King Coll., 1971; cert. in voice, Sherwood Music Coll., 1971-73; BS, Chgo. State U., 1975, MA in Adminstrn., 1983; D in Adminstrn. and Supervision, U. Calif., 1993. Tchr. Faulkner Sch., Chgo., 1975-78; tchr. music Harvey (Ill.) Pub. Sch. Dist. 152, 1978—. Dir. music Pleasant Green Missionary Bapt. Ch., Chgo., 1971—; mem. sch. bd. New World Christian Acad., Chgo., 1988—; bd. dirs. South Shore Drill Team, Chgo. Author: operetta So You Want to Be a Star, 1987. Cmty. worker People United to Save Humanity, Chgo., 1973, Harold Washington Orgn., Chgo., 1987; cmty. educator Chgo. Planned Parenthood, 1988; cmty. counselor Lincoln Cmty. Ctr., Chgo., 1975; mem. sch. bd. Dist. 160, 1994, now v.p.; mem. Ill. State Sch. Bd., 1997-98; bd. dirs. Operation P.U.S.H.; vice chmn. Ill. Assn. Sch. Bds., Ill. State Assn. Bd.; v.p. Sch. Dist. #160; ; mem. Grace M.B. Ch. Named Tchr. of the Yr., Faulkner Sch., 1976. Mem. Ill. Edn. Assn., NEA, Harvey Edn. Assn., Tennis Club, Traveling Club, Phi Delta Kappa, Pi Lambda Theta. Democrat. Baptist. Avocations: singing, bowling, piano. Home: 18029 Ravisloe Ter Country Club Hills IL 60478-5169

MCCLELLAND, PATRICIA G. minister; b. Warsaw, Mo., July 12, 1944; d. Gail Raymond and Martha Carolyn (Lewis) Easton; m. Lester E. McClelland, Aug. 18, 1974; 1 child, Melody. BS, U. Mo., 1968; MA, Drury Coll., 1972. Cert. tchr., Mo., Kans., Ill.; lic. counselor; ordained to ministry Unity Ch., 1986. Instr. U. Mo., Kansas City, 1968, 71-74, Park Coll., Parkville, Mo., 1968-70; spl. cons. Kansas City Pub. Schs., 1970-71; author edn. materials, 1975-78; instr. U. Wis., 1978-79; min. Milw., 1979-81; instr. Sem. Unity Sch. Christianity, 1983-85; co-min. Unity Ch. Pitts., 1985-86; sr. min. Unity Ch., Anderson, Ind., 1986-87, sr. minister Warren, Ohio, 1987-88, Massillon, Ohio, 1988-90; dir. housing Southwestern Coll., Winfield, Kans., 1990-91; min. specializing in ministry to women, cons., Lincoln, Nebr., 1991-93; co-min. Lindenwood Union Ch., Rockford, Ill., 1993—. Founding min. Council Bluffs Unity Ch.; tchr. pub. schs., Rochelle, Ill., 1994—2000; instr. Rockford (Ill.) Coll.; tchr., facilitator Skylight grad. program Rock Valley Coll., Janesville, Wis., 2002—; tchr. Belvidere Pub. Schs., 2002—, St. Xavier U., 2002—. Mem. NAFE, ASCD, TESOL, Nat. Assn. Self-Employed, Internat. New Thought Alliance, Internat. Platform Assn. Methodist/Unity. Home and Office: 7399 Bermuda Dr Rockford IL 61108-4486 E-mail: revpatmcc@yahoo.com.

MCCLENAHAN, MARY TYLER FREEMAN, civic and community volunteer; b. Richmond, Va., Apr. 6, 1917; d. Douglas Southall and Inez Virginia (Goddin) Freeman; m. Leslie Cheek Jr., June 3, 1939 (dec. Dec. 1992); children: Leslie III, Richard Warfield, Elizabeth Cheek Morgan; m. John Lorimer, Aug. 14, 1993. AB, Vassar Coll., 1937; LHD (hon.), St. Paul's Coll., 1977, Washington and Lee U., 1983, Va. Commonwealth U., 1993, Hollins Coll., 1993; HHD (hon.), U. Richmond, 1985; LHD (hon.) (hon.), Va. Union U., 2002. Author: (booklet) Death, The Key to Life, 1982, (with Alonzo T. Dill) A Visit to Stratford and the Story of the Lees, 1986, Douglas Southall Freeman: Reflections By His Daughter, His Research Associates and a Historian, 1986; contbr. articles to popular mags. Active Robert E. Lee Meml. Assn., Stratford, Va., 1964-95, hon. dir., 1995—; dame, bd. govs. Order of Hosp. St. John, N.Y.C., 1984—; bd. dirs. Maymont Found., 1982—, Va. Cmty. Devel. Corp., 1989—, Trees for Richmond, 1991—, Caucus for Future Ctrl. Va., 1992—, (hon.) Va. League Planned Parenthood (Outstanding Svc. award), 1952—; bd. dirs., exec. com. Richmond Renaissance, 1982-96; former bd. dirs., chair, adv. bd. Coun. Am.'s First Freedom; trustee Va. Union U., Richmond, 1985—, Va. Hist. Soc, (hon.), Black History Mus. and Cultural Ctr. of Va., Hist. Richmond Found.; chair, founder Richmond Better Housing Coalition, 1989—; vice-chair Conserve Va.; pres.'s coun. So. Environ. Law Ctr.; adv. bd. ARC, 1992—, Christian Children's Fund, 1993-95; adv. com. Girl Scouts U.S., Va; nat. com. Jefferson Poplar Forest Fund. Recipient Mary Mason Anderson Williams Preservation award Assn. Preservation Va. Antiquities, 1977, Barbara Ransome Andrews disting. vol. award Jr. League Richmond, 1982, Fair Housing award Housing Opportunities Made Equal, 1983, Brotherhood award Nat. Conf. Christians and Jews, 1983, Human Rels. award, 1984, Ten Outstanding Women award YWCA-Richmond, 1986, Sallie Wilson Peake Meml. award Housing Opportunities Made Equal, 1987, Charlotte J. Washington cmty. svc, award Richmond Urban League, 1988, Archtl. medal Am. Inst. Architects, 1991, Liberty Bell award Richmond Bar Assn., 1991, Faith in Action award Va. Coun. Churches, 1992, Outstanding Citizen award Civitan Club, 1992, Hope award Nat. Multiple Sclerosis, 1994; named Richmonder of Yr. STYLE mag., 1990, Va. Women Hall Fame Va. Coun. on Status Women, 1991, Flame Bearer of Edn. award United Negro Coll. Fund, 1995, Local Initiatives Support Corp. award, 1997, Lifetime Achievement award Urban League of Greater Richmond, 1999, Ne Plus Ultra award Va. Assn. Fund Raising Execs., 1999, Good Citizenship award SAR, 2000, Lettie Pate Whitehead Evans award Va. Theol. Sem., 2000, Mary Tyler McClenahan cmty. award, Richmond Cmty. Develop. Alliance, 2000, Lifetime Achievement in Philanthropy award, Assn. of Fund Raising Execs., 2001, Lee Integrity award Robert E. Lee Meml. Assn., 2002, Bridge Bldr. award Ptnrs. for Livable Cmtys., 2002. Mem. Richmond Urban Forum (founder, chair, hon.), AIA (hon.) Women's Club of Richmond, Cosmopolitan Club, The Acorn Club of Phila., Hroswitha Club, James River Garden Club, Va. Writer's Club, Richmond First Club (Good Govt. award, 1987), Omicron Delta Kappa, Phi Beta Kappa. Democrat. Episcopalian. Avocations: writing, literature, hist. preservation, gardening, urban devel. Home: 4703 Pocahontas Ave Richmond VA 23226-1720

MCCLINTOCK, JESSICA, fashion designer; b. Frenchville, Maine, June 19, 1930; d. Rene Gagnon and Verna Hedrich; m. Frank Staples (dec. 1964); 1 child Scott. BA, San Jose State U., 1963. Elem. sch. tchr., Marblehead, Mass., 1966-68, Long Island, N.Y., 1968, Sunnyvale, Calif., 1964-65, 68-69; fashion designer Jessica McClintock, Inc., San Francisco, 1969—. Active donor, AIDS and Homeless programs; scholarship sponsor Fashion Inst. Design and Merchandising. Recipient Merit award Design, 1989, Dallas Fashion award, 1988, Tommy award, 1986, Pres. Appreciation award, 1986, Best Interior Store Design, 1986, Calif. Designer award, 1985, Earnie award, 1981, numerous others. Mem. Coun. Fashion Designers of Am., Fashion Inst. Design & Merchandising (adv. bd. 1979—), San Francisco Fashion Industry (pres. 1976-78, bd. dirs. 1989). Office: Jessica McClintock Inc 1400 16th St San Francisco CA 94103-5181

MCCLINTOCK, MARTHA K. biologist, educator; AB, Wellesley College, 1969; MA in Psychology, U. Penn., 1972, Ph.D. in Psychology, 1974. With U. Chgo., 1976—, asst. prof., psychology and human devel., 1976, David Lee Shillinglaw Distinguished Svc. Prof. Psychology, dir., Inst. Mind & Biology. Chmn. biopsychology com., 1986—99; mem. neurobiology com., evolutionary biology com., human develop. com. Contbr. articles to profl. jours. Recipient Disting. Sci. Award for Early Career Contbn. to Psychology, APA, 1982, MERIT Award, NIMH, 1992, Edith Krieger Wolf Disting. Vis. Prof., Northwestern Univ., 1993, 2000, Henry G. Walter Sense of Smell Award, Sense of Smell Inst., 2001. elected mem., Inst. of Medicine, 1999, Acad. of Arts and Sciences, 1999. Office: U Chgo 5730 S Woodlawn Ave Chicago IL 60637*

MCCLINTOCK, SANDRA JANISE, writer, editor; b. Connersville, Ind., July 28, 1938; d. Owen Dale and Mary Janis (Tierney) M.; m. Harvey Miles Garrison, Jr., Aug. 1, 1959 (div. 1967); children: Heidi, Katherine, H. Miles III; m. Joseph Lloyd Fagen, May 15, 1969; 1 child, Adam Joseph. BA, Drake U., 1960; postgrad., Calif. State U., Fullerton, 1966-67; cert., Am. Grad. U., 1987. Lic. gen. contractor. Coord. copy desk Time Mag., N.Y.C., 1960-62; mem. graphics prodn. staff Times-Mirror Co., L.A., 1962-64; mgr. prodn. Miller Freeman Publs., Long Beach, Calif., 1964-68; supr. Design Svc., Anaheim, Calif., 1968-73; prin. Fagen Graphics, Long Beach, 1973-77, Palomar Publs., Ranchita, Calif., 1977-84; cons. Cons. & Designers, Anaheim, 1984-87; mgr. publs. Tracor Flight Systems, Inc., Santa Ana, Calif., 1987-88; coord. publs. Rockwell Internat. Corp., Anaheim, 1988-92; dir. comms. Terra Christa Comms., Tucson, 1992-93; tech. writer CH2M Hill, Santa Ana, Calif., 1993—97; editor South Coast Mags., San Clemente, Calif., 1993—; assoc. dir. SBC Comm., 1998—. Cons. Aerotest, Inc., Mojave, Calif., 1986, Voice Telecom Corp., Laguna Beach, Calif., 1986. Editor: Psychopharmacology, 1984, Joseph of Aramathea, 1982, Who is Who at the Earth Summit, 1992; guest editor Interface Age mag., 1976; contbg. editor Rockwell News in U.S. and Can., 1988. Bd. dirs. Vol. Fire Dept., Ranchita, 1979; fund raiser Dem. candidate Calif. Assembly, Orange county, 1964. Mem. NAFE, Nat. Mgmt. Assn., So. Calif. Astrological Network. Mem. Religious Sci. Ch. Avocations: architecture, astronomy, alternate medicine, travel, tennis. Home: 29491 Dry Dock Cv Laguna Niguel CA 92677-1643 Office: SBC 16755 Van Karman Rm 120 Irvine CA 92606

MCCLINTON, DOROTHY HARDAWAY, former business educator; b. Seguin, Tex., Jan. 4, 1925; d. George Washington and Rosetta (Hodge) Hardaway; m. Marion N. Hopkins Sr., Oct. 27, 1951 (div. Dec. 1982); 1 child, Marion N. Jr.; m. Elmer McClinton, Aug. 12, 1986; children: Thomas, Evelyn M., Nathaniel. BS, Huston-Tillotson Coll., 1947; MBEd, Tex. So. U., 1960. Tchr. Ball Elem. Sch., Seguin, 1947-49, Ball Mid. Sch., Seguin, 1949-54; clk., typist Kelly AFB, San Antonio, 1956-57; tchr. Ball High Sch., Seguin, 1957-64; tchr., dept. chair St. Philips Community Coll., San Antonio, 1964-86, prof. emeritus, 1986—. Audio visual tutorial cons. Media Systems Corp. subs. Harcourt Brace Jovanovich, Inc., 1978-86; mem. nat. rsch. rev. panel Ohio State U., 1983-84. Chair telethon United Negro Coll. Fund, San Antonio, 1990-92, 98; trustee Huston-Tillotson Coll., 1990—. Recipient Bus. Tchr. of Yr. award Tex. Bus. Edn. Assn., Austin, 1981-82, Acad. Achievement award Huston-Tillotson Coll., 1990-91; Inst. for Ednl. Ledership fellow St. Philip's Coll., San Antonio, 1984-85, Lifetime Achievement award San Antonio Black Achievement Awards, 1996; named Woman of Yr. St. Paul UMC, 1991; inductee Educators' Hall of Fame, Gamma Tau chpt. Phi Delta Kappa, 1993-94. Mem. Alamo Community Coll. Retirees, Top Ladies of Distinction (sgt.-at-arms 1987-92), Huston-Tillotson Coll. Alumni (pres. 1982-91, nat. pres. 1985-87) Delta Sigma Theta, Inc. (pres. 1972-74). Home: 1639 Lone Oak St San Antonio TX 78220-4223

MCCLINTON, JOANN, state legislator; m. Emory McClinton; 2 children. Grad., Washington High Sch. State rep. Ga. Ho. of Reps., Atlanta, 1992—, mem. children and youth, health and ecology state planning com., chmn. com. for arts and humanities. Democrat. Office: Ga House of Reps State Capitol SE Atlanta GA 30334

MCCLOSKEY, ANN FRANCES, elementary and secondary music educator; b. Jacksonville, Ill. d. Peter and frances Adorno Bonansinga; widowed; 1 child, William Peter. MusB, MacMurray Coll., 1930; MusM, Chgo. Mus. Coll., 1942. Music tchr. Pittsfield (Ill.) Pub. Schs., 1930-34, San Marino (Calif.) Schs., 1938; mem. voice tchg. faculty MacMurray Coll., Jacksonville, 1942-48, Thornton Jr. Coll., Harvey, Ill., 1965-73, Everett Dirksen Jr. H.S., Calumet City, Ill., 1965-73; pvt. voice and piano tchr. Lyon & Healy, Chgo., 1974-82. Concert mezzo soprano. Named Disting. Alumna, MacMurray Coll., 1995. Mem. Irving Music Tchrs., Nat. Music Tchrs. Home: 4137 Portland St Irving TX 75062-2953

MCCLOUD, ANECE FAISON, academic administrator; b. Dudley, N.C., May 29, 1937; d. J.D. Faison and Nancy Jane (Simmons) Faison-Cole; m. Verable Lancaster McCloud, June 1, 1959; children: Aja Siobhan, Carla Danette. BS, Bennette Coll., Greensboro, N.C., 1959; MA, U. Nebr., Omaha, 1989; Basic Mediations Skills, Ea. Mennonite Coll., 1994. Tchr. Lincoln Jr. High Sch., Greensboro, N.C., 1959-60, Woodbridge Airforce Base (Eng.), 1961-62; resident advisor and ednl. coord. Child Saving Inst., Omaha, 1967-71; asst. registrar for acad. records U. Nebr. Med. Ctr., Omaha, 1972-76, first dir. minority student affairs, 1976-85; assoc. dean of students Washington and Lee U., Lexington, Va., 1985—. Cons. Deans Forum on Revitalizing Health Profl. Edn., Dept. of Health and Human Svcs., 1985, Campus Alcohol Initiative, N.C. Gov.'s Inst. Alcohol and Substance Abuse, 1999—, Peer Rev., Health Careet Opportunity Program, 1982, 1984; cons. on simulated minority admissions Assn. Am. Med. Colls., Washington, 1979. Bd. mem., v.p. Rockbridge Area Housing Corp., Lexington, 1988-95; mem. Va. adv. com. U.S. Commn. on Civil Rights, 1995—; mem. Va. Identification Program for Advancement of Women in Higher Edn., 1995-96; treas. Mayor's Commn. on Status of Women, Omaha, 1977-78. Recipient Plaque for Outstanding Svc. to Washington and Lee Comty., 1994, Cert. Acknowledgement of Contbn. to Edn., Omaha Pub. Schs., 1984, Cert. Black History Month Spkr., VA Hosp., Omaha, 1983, Vol. Program award Girls Club of Omaha, 1977; grantee Health Career Opportunity, Disadvantaged Assistance Office, Dept. Health and Human Svcs., 1976, 80, 83. Mem. Am. Assn. for Higher Edn., Nat. Assn. For Women in Edn., Am. Coll. Personnel Assn., Assn. of Am. Med. Colls., Am. Assn. of Counseling and Devel., Nebr. Assn. for Non-White Concerns (past sec.), Nebr. Assn. of Collegiate Registrars and Admissions Officers (chair-person sub.-com. on minority affairs 1978-89), Nat. Assn. of Med. Minority Educators (vice coord. 1982-83). Democrat. Avocations: social research, writing, interior decorating. Office: Washington & Lee U Payne Hall 3 Lexington VA 24450

MCCLOUD, PATRICIA CAROLYN KAISER, nurse educator, consultant; d. Leonard George and Dorothy Caroline Louise (Klawuhn) K.; divorced; children: Scott William, Aaron Leonard, Brook Elizabeth Dorothy. Student, Washtenaw C.C., 1967; diploma magna cum laude, Mercy Sch. Nursing Detroit, Ann Arbor, Mich., 1969; BSN with honors, U. Mich., 1975, MS, 1977. Staff nurse dept. obstet. St. Joseph Mercy Hosp., Ann Arbor, 1970—; staff and evening charge nurse dept. obstet. Women's Hosp., Ann Arbor, 1975; from tchg. asst. to asst. prof. parent child nursing U. Mich., Ann Arbor, 1975-81; instr. dept. nursing Washtenaw C.C., Ann Arbor, 1988-90; lectr. divsn. acute, critical-long term care programs U. Mich. Sch. Nursing, Ann Arbor, 1991-92, lectr., course coord. divsn. acute, critical-long term care, 1992—. Camp nurse Interlochen Ctr. for the Arts, summer, 1993-94; mem. adj. faculty Concordia Coll., Ann Arbor, 1991-94; instr., cons. Nursing Edn. Consortium, Ann Arbor, 1994-95; instr. nursing Ea. Mich. U., Ypsilanti, summer, 1977; presenter in field; expert witness in field. Co-author: Test Item File, Being a Nursing Assistant, 1997, Instructor Guide, Being a Nursing Assistant, 1997; contbr. articles to profl. jours.; textbook reviewer. Co-chair benefit auction acquisitions com. Greenhills Sch., 1991—; choir coord. Ann Arbor Youth Chorale, 1992; choral mgr., bd. dirs. Boychoir of Ann Arbor, 1989-91, events coord., 1990-91; vol. March of Dimes, 1991, 97, Arthritis Found., 1994, Martin Luther King Jr. Sch., 1984-93; mgr. Summer Youth League Baseball, 1983-93; founder, block capt. Neighborhood Watch, 1982-94; co-leader Girl Scouts Am., 1992-93; pres. Ann Arbor Suzuki Inst., 1984-85, bd. dirs., 1982-84, dir. ann. workshop, 1984-85, chair fundraising com., 1982-83; choral asst., substitute tchr., Law Montessori Sch., 1988-89; dir. religious edn. St. Lukes Episcopal Ch., coord. vol. svcs., health fair com., 1989; past pres. Ann Arbor Cantata Singers, 2001-03. Shirley C. Titus scholar U. Mich. Mem. Sigma Theta Tau (Rho chpt. chmn. exec. bd. 1978-81, Rho chpt. membership com. 1977-81). Episcopalian. Avocations: choral performances, music, sports. Office: Univ Mich Sch Nursing 2177 Sch Nursing Bldg 400 N Ingalls St Ann Arbor MI 48109-2003

MCCLOY, ELIZABETH K. lawyer; b. 1959; BA, Dartmouth Coll., 1981; JD, Northwestern U., 1984. Bar: Ill. 1984. With Sidley Austin Brown & Wood, Chgo., 1984—, ptnr., 1993—. Office: Sidley Austin Brown and Wood Bank One Plz 10 S Dearborn St Chicago IL 60603*

MCCLURE, ANN CRAWFORD, judge, lawyer; b. Cin., Sept. 5, 1953; d. William Edward and Patricia Ann (Jewett) Crawford; m. David R. McClure, Nov. 12, 1983; children: Kinsey Tristen, Scott Crawford. BFA magna cum laude, Tex. Christian U., 1974; JD, U. Houston, 1979. Bd. cert. in family law and civil appellate law Tex. Bd. Legal Specialization. Assoc. Piro and Lilly, Houston, 1979-83; pvt. practice El Paso, Tex., 1983-92; ptnr. McClure and McClure, El Paso, 1992-94; justice 8th Ct. of Appeals, El Paso, 1995—. Past mem. Tex. Bd. Law Examiners, Bd. Disciplinary Appeals; mem. Family Law Specialization Exam Com., 1989—93; mem. civil appellate law adv. com. Tex. Bd. Legal Specialization; mem. Tex. Jud. Coun. Contbr. articles to profl. jours.; past editor The Family Law Forum; past contbg. editor: Texas Family Law Service; mem. editl. bd. Tex. Family Law Practice Manual, 1982-93; editl. cons. Matthew Bender Tex. Family Law Practice and Procedure. Mem.: Tex. Jud. Coun., El Paso Bar Assn. (sec. 2002—03, 2003—, treas. 2003—), Tex. Acad. Family Law Specialists (past dir.,), State Bar Tex. (family law sect. chair 1997—98, appellate law sect. chair 2000—01, appellate divsn. jud. sect. chair 2001—02). Democrat. Presbyterian.

MCCLURE, EVELYN SUSAN, historian, photographer; b. Milw., Mar. 11, 1940; d. Henry F. and Blanche E. Schuster; m. John C. McClure, Oct. 26, 1967; 1 child, Heather. BS, U. Wis., 1964. Cert. fine art photography, U. Calif. Adminstrv. asst. Northwestern U., Chgo., 1964-66, KGO-TV, San Francisco, 1966-70, Crocker Bank, San Francisco, 1980-86, Wells Fargo Bank, San Francisco, 1986-93; pub. Belle View Press, Sebastopol, Calif., 1993—. Author, photographer: Sebastopol, California - History, Homes & People 1855-1920, 1995 (Historic Scholarship award Sonoma County Hist. Soc. 1997), Sebastopol's Historic Cemetery, 2000; columnist Sonoma West Times and News, Sebastopol, 1998—. Exhbn. com. Sebastopol Ctr. Arts, 1995-97; bd. mem., publicity chair, newsletter editor, vol. Western Sonoma County Hist. Soc., Sebastopol, 1996; dir. W. Co. Mus., 1999—. Roman Catholic. Avocation: gardening. E-mail: belleview@monitor.net.

MCCLURE, JULIE ANNE, literature educator; b. Naperville, Ill., Mar. 9, 1967; d. Paul Robert and Linda Kay (Schlytter) McClure. BS in English, No. Ariz. U., 1989; AA in Paralegal Studies, Am. Inst., Phoenix, Ariz., 1991. Cert. tchr. Ill., Ariz. Paralegal/payroll profl. Corp. Personnel Svcs., Phoenix, 1992—92; paralegal Robert A. Kelley Jr. & Assocs., Scottsdale, Ariz., 1993—94; English educator Long Wood Acad., Chgo., 1998—99; corp. sec. MacWilliams Corp., Benton Harbor, Mich., 1993—; English educator Maria H.S., Chgo., 1999—. Office: Regina Dominican High Sch 701 Locust Rd Wilmette IL 60091-2298

MCCLURE, LAURA, state legislator; b. Hays, Kan., May 11, 1950; m. John D. McClure. Kans. state rep. Dist. 119, 1993—. Democrat. Friends Church. Office: Kans Ho of Reps State Capitol Topeka KS 66612

MCCLURE-BIBBY, MARY ANNE, former state legislator; b. Milbank, S.D., Apr. 21, 1939; d. Charles Cornelius and Mary Lucille (Whittom) Burges; m. D.J. McClure, Nov. 17, 1963 (dec. Apr. 1990); 1 child, Kelly Joanne Kyro; m. John E. Bibby, May 1, 1993 (dec. July 2003). BA magna cum laude, U. S.D., 1961; postgrad., U. Manchester, Eng., 1961-62; M of Pub. Adminstrn., Syracuse (N.Y.) U., 1980. Staff asst. U.S. Senator Francis Case, Washington, 1959-61; sec. to lt. gov. State of S.D., Pierre, 1963, with budget office, 1964; exec. sec. to pres. Frontier Airlines, Denver, 1963-64; tchr. Pub. High Schs., Pierre and Redfield, S.D., 1965-66, 68-70; mem. S.D. State Senate, Pierre, 1975-89, pres. pro tem, 1979-89, vice chmn. coun. of state govts., 1987, chmn. coun. of state govts., 1988; spl. asst. to Pres. Bush for intergovernmental affairs, 1989-92; exec. dir. S.D. Bush-Quayle Campaign, 1992. Vice chmn. sch. bd. Redfield Ind. Sch. Dist., 1970-74. Fulbright scholar, 1961-62, Bush Leadership fellow, 1977-80. Mem. Phi Beta Kappa. Republican. Congregationalist. Home: 822 8th Ave Brookings SD 57006-1314

MCCLUSKEY, SUSAN D. lawyer; b. Osmond, Nebr. d. Earle R. and Deloris C. (Olson) M.; m. Charles D. Gray, Feb. 17, 1980; children: Charles W., Johanna M. BA, U. Denver, 1973; JD, Cornell U., 1977; cert. sr. mgrs. in govt., Harvard U., 1992. Bar: D.C., 1977, U.S. Supreme Ct., 1993. Asst. counsel Nat. Treasury Employees Union and Panel Assoc., 1984-86, Fed. Svc. Impasses Panel, 1984-86; spl. asst. to exec. dir. Fed. Labor Rels. Authority, 1984-86, exec. asst. to chmn., 1986-89, chief counsel to chmn., 1989—. Methodist. Office: Fed Labor Relations Authority 607 14th St NW Ste 410 Washington DC 20005-2000

MCCLYMONDS, JEAN ELLEN, marketing professional; b. Richmond, Calif. d. Rollin John Lepley and Doris Ellen Baughman; m. Gareth Lynn McClymonds, Sept. 18, 1981. BS in Edn., U. Calif., Berkeley, 1970; M Bus. Communications, San Jose State U., 1987. Adminstr. sales Dohrmann Div. Envirotech, Santa Clara, Calif., 1970-74; supr. order processing Molectron Corp., Sunnyvale, Calif., 1974-79; mgr. mktg. svcs. Gould-Biomation, Santa Clara, 1979-84; dir. corp. communications Madic Corp., Santa Clara, 1984-86; dir. mktg. nat. accounts Skyway Freight Systems, Inc., Watsonville, Calif., 1986-89; pres. Just Mktg., Scotts Valley, Calif., 1989—. Pub. speaker various local orgns., 1984—. Contbr. articles industry jours., 1986—. Mem. Am. Trucking Assn. (outstanding svc. award 1997), Bus. Profl. Advt. Assn., Nat. Assn. Quality Control, Peninsula Mktg. Assn., Coun. Logistics Mgmt., San Jose Women in Bus. Republican. Avocations: speaking, dance, skiing. Office: 683 Uncle Billy Court Copperopolis CA 95228 E-mail: justmktng@aol.com.

MCCOLLAM, SHARON L. retail executive; BS in Acctg. CPA. Former acctg. Ernst and Young; divisional v.p., CFO Dole Food Co., Inc., 1993—2000; v.p. fin. Williams-Sonoma, Inc., San Francisco, 2000—01, sr. v.p., CFO, 2001—03, exec. v.p., CFO, 2003—. Office: Williams-Sonoma Inc 3250 Van Ness Ave San Francisco CA 94109

MCCOLLUM, BETTY, congresswoman; b. July 12, 1954; m. Douglas McCollum; 2 children. BS in Edn., Coll. St. Catherine. Retail store mgr., Minn.; mem. Minn. Ho. Reps., 1992-2000, mem. edn. com., environ. and natural resources com., mem. gen. legis. com., vet. affairs and elections com., mem. transportation and transit com., asst. majority leader, chair legis. commn. on econ. status of women, mem. rules and adminstrv. legis. com.; mem. U.S. Congress from Minn. 4th Dist., Washington, 2001—; mem. edn. and workforce com., resources com.; mem. Com. on Internat. Relations. Mem. St. Croix Valley Coun. Girl Scouts. Mem. VFW Aux., Am. Legion Aux. Democrat. Office: US Ho of Reps 1029 Longworth HOB Washington DC 20515*

MCCOLLUM, JEAN HUBBLE, medical assistant; b. Peoria, Ill., Oct. 21, 1934; d. Claude Ambrose and Josephine Mildred (Beiter) Hubble; m. Everett Monroe Patton, Sept. 4, 1960 (div. Jan. 1969); 1 child, Linda Joanne; m. James Ward McCollum, Jan. 2, 1971; 1 child, Steven Ward. Student, Bradley U., Ill. Cen. Coll. Stenographer Caterpillar Tractor Co., Peoria, 1952-53, supr. stenographer pool, 1953-55, adminstrv. sec., treas., 1955-60, sec., asst. dept. mgr., 1969-71; med. staff sec. Proctor Cmty. Hosp., Peoria, 1978-82; med. asst. Drs. Taylor, Fox and Morgan, Peoria, 1982-84; freelance med. asst. Meth. Hosp. and numerous physicians, Peoria, 1984-89; office mgr. bus. office Dr. Danehower, McLelland and Stone, Peoria, 1989—. Vol. tutor Northmoor Sch., Peoria, 1974-78; bd. dirs., mem. exec. com., chmn. patient rels. com., com. chmn. Planned Parenthood, Peoria, 1990-92; judge scholarship com. Bradley U., 2004, Region 2 Ill. State History Fair; hon. mem. scholarship com. Am. Indian Edn. Found. Recipient Outstanding Performance award Proctor Hosp., 1981, also various awards for svc. to schs., ch. and hosps. for mentally ill. Mem. Nat. Wildlife Fedn., Mensa Internat. (publs. officer, scholarship com., editor 1987-89, csholar com. 1993), Mothers League (treas. 1977), Willow Knolls Country Club (social com. 1989-90), Nature Conservancy (Seasons of the River event com. 2000—), World Wildlife Fund, Forest Park Found., Jacques Cousteau Soc., Wilderness Soc., Nat. Trust for Historic Preservation, Natural Resources Def. Coun., Religious Coalition for Reproductive Rights, USO, Am. Indian Educators Found. (hon., scholar com. 2004). Methodist. Avocations: socializing, reading, travel, theatre, yoga. Home: 6501 N Brookwood Ln Peoria IL 61614-2401

MCCOLLUM, SUSAN, elementary school educator; Grad., Butler County C.C.; BA in Edn., Emporia State U., 1974, MA in Edn., 1979. Nat. bd. cert. tchr. 1998. Tchr. Santa Fe Trail Sch. Dist., Carbondale (Kans.) Sch. Named Disting. Alumni, Emporia State U., 2002. Mem.: NEA, Nat. Bd. for Cert. Tchrs. in Kans. (state chair 2003—), Nat. Bd. for Profl. Tchg. Stds. (bd. mem. 2002—). Office: Carbondale Attendance Ctr 315 N 4th Carbondale KS 66414

MCCOMB, KARLA JOANN, educational curriculum and instruction administrator, consultant; b. Tacoma, July 23, 1937; d. John Frank and Lorraine Beatrice (Winters) Bohac; m. Russell Marshall McComb, Nov. 27, 1959 (div.); children: Marsha McComb Hayes, Kathleen McComb Bridge. Cert. instr. French, U. Paris, 1958; BA, Calif. State U., Sacramento, 1960; MS, Nova U., 1984. Cert. secondary tchr., Nev. Tchr. French and music Sacramento Waldorf Sch., 1960-62; tchr. French Red Bluff H.S., 1967-68; tchr. French and music Pocatello (Idaho) Schs., 1969-71; tchr., chairperson dept. Clark County Sch. Dist., 1971-76; curriculum cons. social sci., fgn. lang., profl. growth Las Vegas, 1976-84; cons. staff devel. and profl. growth, 1984-91; dir. staff devel., multicultural edn., substance abuse edn., 1993—. Cons. Taft Inst. Govt., Salt Lake City, 1977—, Tchr. Inservice, Follett Pub. Co., 1980-81. Author: A Cultural Celebration, 1980, Project MCE: Multicultural Education in the Clark County School District, 1992; editor The Nevada Holocaust Curriculum, 1987; author, prodr. Nevada Curriculum on the Holocaust, 1997. Coord. N ev. Close-Up Program, 1980-88; mem. Sacramento Symphony Orch., 1954-66, Nev. Humanities Com.; co-chair, pres. Nev. commn. Holocaust, 1996—; pres., bd. dirs. Ctr. Ind. Living, 1995—; v.p. Nev. Assn. Handicapped, 1994—, pres., 1996; bd. dirs. Love All People Youth Group, supt. Love All People Sch., 1983-93, prodr. staff devel. films, 1986—; mem. Nev. Work Force Devel. bd., 1997—, Gov. Workforce adv. bd., 1996—. Mem. Clark County Fgn. Lang. Tchrs. Assn. (pres.), Nat. Coun. Social Studies, Social Studies Suprs. Assn., Nev. Fgn. Lang. Tchrs. Assn. (pres. Outstanding Humanities Nevadan 1994), AAUW, Vegas Valley Dog Obedience Club (pres.), Jackpot Obedience Assn. (pres.). Democrat. Home: 1608 Hills Of Red Dr Unit 104 Las Vegas NV 89128-8418 Office: 601 N 9th St Las Vegas NV 89101-2536

MCCOMBS, CHARLINE, professional sports team executive; m. Red McCombs, 1950; children: Lynda, Marsha, Connie. DH(hon.), Southwestern U. Owner Minn. Vikings, Inc. Co-host Tex. Tuxedo fundraiser U. Minn., 1999; vol. Salvation Army, Cris Carter Viking Super Challenge; mentor San Antonio elem. schs.; mem. adv. bd. Friends of Ronald McDonald; bd. dirs. Las Casas Found., San Antonio, Susan G. Komen Breast Cancer Found., nat. adv. bd.; bd. dirs. Cancer Ctr. Coun.; former bd. dirs. Friends of Ronald McDonald, San Antonio; bd. dirs. McNay Art Mus., mem. art and edn. coms. Named Mother of Yr., Advance orgn.; recipient Trfoil award, Girl Scouts U.S., 1999, Spirit of Youth award, Boys Town, Sch. Arch. and Design award, U. Tex., Outstanding Philanthropist award, NAFE, Civic Virtue award, Freedom of Info. Found., Spirit of Philanthropy award, Non-Profit Resource Ctr. Office: 9520 Vikings Dr Eden Prairie MN 55344

MCCOMBS, KELLY FRITZ, dietician; b. Flemington, N.J., Sept. 23, 1968; d. John Frederick Fritz III and Joy Elaine Gallagher; m. Timothy Ronald McCombs, Aug. 31, 1996. BS, Ohio State U., 1997, MS, 1999. Cert. pharmacy technician. Pharmacy technician Riverside Meth. Hosp., Columbus, Ohio, 1989-99, med. rsch. asst., 1996-99; oncology pharmacy technician St. Anthony Regional Oncology Ctr., Columbus, 1990-91; intern Ohio State U., 1998—99; family and consumer sci. agt. N.C. Coop. Ext., Elizabeth City, 1999—2002; diabetes and health promotion dietitian Albemarle Regional Diabetes Care, Elizabeth City, 2003—. Co-author: Jour. Food Quality. Recipient Florence Hall award, 2000, Early Career award, 2002. Mem.: Am. Diabetes Assn., Coastal Diabetes Educators Assn., N.C. Extension Assn. Family and Consumer Scis., Soc. Nutrition Educators, N.C. Dietetic Assn., Am. Dietetic Assn., Elizabeth City Jr. Women's Club. Avocations: gardening, cooking.

MCCONNELL, LORELEI CATHERINE, retired library director; b. Port Jefferson, NY, Dec. 5, 1938; d. Alvin and Mary (McConnell) Philibert; m. Thomas McConnell, Jan. 20, 1962; children: Catherine, Michael. BA, Drew U., 1960; MLS, Rutgers U., 1963. Reference libr. Irvington (N.J.) Pub. Libr., 1963-90, dir., 1990-99; founder Irvington Literacy Program, 1986, dir., 1986-90; ret., 1999; cons., 2000—. Mem. exec. bd. Infolink, 1998-99. Mem. ALA, N.J. Libr. Assn. (mem. exec. bd. 1990-93, N.J. Libr. of Yr. 1993-94), Irvington (N.J.) C. of C. (exec. bd. 1992—, Civic award 1996), Beta Phi Mu. Home: 563 Park St Montclair NJ 07043-2027

MCCONNELL SERIO, SUZIE THERESA, former professional basketball player, professional basketball coach; b. Pitts., July 29, 1966; married; 4 children. BA, Pa. State U., 1988. Coach Oakland Cath. High Sch., Pitts.; guard Cleve. Rockers, WNBA, 1998—2000; head coach Oakland Cath. H.S., 1990—2003, Minn. Lynx, WNBA, 2003—. Recipient Gold medal Olympic Games, Barcelona, 1988, Bronze medal Olympic Games, Seoul, 1992, Sportsmanship award WNBA, 1998, 1999, Newcomer award, 1998; named to All-WNBA 1st team, 1988. Office: Minn Lynx 600 First Ave North Minneapolis MN 55403

MCCONNEY, MARY E. information technology executive; BA in physics & Environ. Studies, Whitman Coll., 1976; M in Econ., U. Pa., 1979, M in Urban Planning, 1980, PhD in Spatial Econ., 1983. Applied statistician U. Wash., 1977—85, U. Pa., 1977—85; applied statistician & database design NAS, 1985—88; pres. HiroSoft Internat. Corp., 1988—; CFO Sunhawk.com, Seattle, 1992—99, treas., 1999—. Contbr. articles to profl. jours. Office: Sunhawk.com Corp 223 Taylor Ave N Ste 200 Seattle WA 98109

MCCONNON, VIRGINIA FIX, dietician; b. Aberdeen, SD, July 20, 1932; d. Lavern Clyde and Janette Clare (Schmidt) Fix; m. Thomas James McConnon, Oct. 28, 1955; children: James Renaud, John Thomas, Paul Wilson. BS in Home Econ. (hon.), S.D. State U., Brookings, 1954. Registered dietitian Am. Dietetic Assn., 1955; cert. dietitian/nutritionist, N.Y., 1995. Dietetic intern U. Minn. Hosps., Mpls., 1955; therapeutic dietitian Northwestern Hosp., Mpls., 1955; dietitian Riley County Hosp., Manhattan, Kans., 1956; cons. dietitian Chautauqua County Office for the Aging, Mayville, N.Y., 1975-89. Treas. Aging Svcs. Dietitians of N.Y. State, 1976-90; mem. Chautauqua County Nutrition Coun., 1990-98. Bd. dirs. Hall Meml. Housing Corp., Jamestown, N.Y., 1995-2001, 2003—, Harbor House, Jamestown, N.Y., 1975-80, Chautauqua Region Multiple Sclerosis Soc., Jamestown, N.Y., 1983-86, Chautauqua Area Adult Day Care Ctrs., Jamestown, Dunkirk and Westfield, N.Y., 1990—; ch. clk., 1990-93,

2004—, diaconate, 1993-96, ch. coun., 1997-2003, ch. choir, 1946—. Named Chautauqua County Sr. Citizen of Yr., 1995. Mem. Am. Dietetic Assn., N.Y. State Dietetic Assn., Western N.Y. Dietetic Assn. Republican. Congregationalist. Avocations: singing, bridge, reading, travel. Home: 4465 Baker Street Ext Lakewood NY 14750-9762

MCCONVILLE, RITA JEAN, finance executive; b. Chgo., July 7, 1958; d. Daniel Joseph and Rosemary (Smolinski) McC. BA, Northwestern U., 1979; MBA, U. Chgo., 1982. CPA, Ill. Fin. analyst Miami Valley Hosp., Dayton, Ohio, 1982-85; sr. cons. Health Facilities Corp., Northfield, Ill., 1985-87; sr. fin. analyst Lyphomed, Inc., Rosemont, Ill., 1987-88, mgr. fin. planning, 1988-90; controller Videocart, Inc., Chgo., 1990-93, OptionCare, Inc., Bannockburn, Ill., 1993-97; v.p., CFO, sec. Akorn, Inc., Buffalo Grove, Ill., 1997—. Mem. Ill. CPA Soc. Office: Akorn Inc 2500 Millbrook Dr Buffalo Grove IL 60089-4694 Home: 177n Willow Blvd Willow Springs IL 60480-1644

MCCOOK, KATHLEEN DE LA PEÑA, university educator; b. Chgo. d. Frank Eugene and Margaret L. (de la Peña) McEntee; m. Philip G. Heim, Mar. 20, 1972 (div.); 1 child, Margaret Marie; m. William Woodrow Lee McCook, Oct. 12, 1991; stepchildren: Cecilia, Billie Jean, Nicole. BA, U. Ill., Chgo.; MA, Marquette U., U. Chgo.; PhD, U. Wis.-Madison. Reference librarian Elmhurst Coll. Libr., Ill.; dir. pub. svcs. Dominican U., River Forest, Ill.; lectr. U. Wis., Madison; asst. prof. library sci. U. Ill., Urbana; dean, prof. La. State U. Sch. Libr. and Info. Sci., Baton Rouge; dean grad. sch. La. State U.; dir. Sch. Libr. and Info. Sci., U. South Fla., 1993-99, prof., 1993—, coord. cmty. outreach, 2000—02, disting. univ. prof., 2002—; McCusker lectr. Dominican U., 2003—. Author: (wth K. Weibel) Role of Women in Librarianship, 1978, (with L. Estabrook) Career Profiles, 1983, (with William E. Moen) Occupational Entry, 1989, Adult Services, 1990, (with Gary O. Rolstad) Developing Readers' Advisory Services, 1993, Toward a Just and Productive Soc., 1994, Opportunities in Library and Information Science, 1997, (with B. Ford) Global Reach: Local Touch, 1998, Women of Color in Librarianship, 1998, (with B. Immroth) Library Services to Youth of Hispanic Heritage, 2000, A Place at the Table, 2000; contbr. essays to books, articles to profl. jours. Chmn. Equal Rights Amendment Task Force, Ill., 1977-79. South Count Coalition for Comty. Concerns, 1996-; mem. Eugene McCarthy campaign, U. Ill., Chgo., 1968; mem. La. Gov.'s Commn. for Women, 1985-88; bd. dirs. La. Endowment for Humanities, 1991-92; mem. exec. bd. Rural Social Svcs. Partnership, Hillsborough County, 1998-2001; mem. dem. exec. com., Hillsborough County, 2001-; dem. del. Fla. State Convention, 2002-03. Recipient Disting. Alumnus award U. Wis., 1991, award of merit Trejo Foster Found., 1999; named Bradshaw scholar Tex. Woman's Univ., 1994; named scholar in residence Chgo. Pub. Libr., 2003. Mem. ALA (com. chmn. 1980-, editor RQ jour. 1982-88, Pub. Librs. Jour. 1989-90, Am. Librs. adv. com. 1994-96, contbg. editor Am. Librs. 1999-2001, column editor RUSQ 2000-, RE-FORMA (bd. dirs. 1997-98, Latino Libr. of Yr. 2002, Equality award 1987, Adult Svc. award 1991, Futas Catalyst for Change award 1998), Assn. for Libr. and Info. Sci. Edn. (com. chmn. 1981-, pres. 1987-88, Pres. award 1997), Fla. Libr. Assn. (bd. dirs. 1995-98, Transformer award 1996), Tampa Bay Libr. Consortium (bd. dirs. 1994-97), Women Libr. Workers, Ruskin Civic Assn. (sec. 1997-99), Ill. Libr. Assn. (treas. 1981-83), Beta Phi Mu (50th Anniversary Disting. Mem. 1999, Dist. Lectr. award 2002, Disting. Svc. to Edn. of Librarianship, 2003), Cath. Libr. Assn. (Brubaker award for Outstanding Artid, 2003). Democrat. Roman Catholic. Avocation: reading. Office: U South Fla Sch Libr and Info Sci 4202 E Fowler Ave Stop Cis1040 Tampa FL 33620-7800 Home: PO Box 1027 Ruskin FL 33575 E-mail: kmccook@tampabay.rr.com.

MCCORD, JEAN ELLEN, secondary art educator, coach; b. Ilion, NY, Oct. 20, 1952; d. Harold Shepard and Marian Alice (Bernier) Shepard; m. Colin McCord, May 10, 1977 (div. Sept. 1993). AA, Mohawk Valley C.C., Utica, N.Y., 1972; BA, SUNY, New Paltz, 1975, postgrad., 1976-77; student, Coll. Santa Reparata Sch. Art, Florence, Italy, 2001. Cert. art educator, N.Y. Jr. kindergarten tchr. Norfolk (Va.) Naval Base, 1978-79; jr. kindergarten and art tchr. Sunnybrook Day Sch., Virginia Beach, Va., 1979-81; tchr. art Fisher Elem. Sch., Mohawk, N.y., 1982-84, Mechanicstown Sch., Middletown, N.Y., 1984-88, Middletown (N.Y.) Start Ctr., 1986-87, tchr. synergetic edn., Middletown Tchr. Ctr., 1986-87; pvt. portfolio tutor Middletown, 1989-91; tchr. art Middletown Elem. Summer Sch., 1989—, Middletown H.S., 1987-97; tchr. Maple Hill Elem., 1997—. Sec. of policy and exec. bds. Middletown Tchr. Ctr., 1988-91, chmn. policy and exec. bds., 1991-92; com. mem. Bicentennial of Edn.; advisor Nat. Art Honor Soc., 1989-97; coord. After Sch. Program for Youth at Risk, 1995—, tchr., 1992-94; internat. com. for comm. Cambridge U., 2001, Cultural Ednl. Exch., Japan, U.S., 2004. Actress, vocalist, designer in regional theatre, 1970—; artistic designer sch. plays and Creative Theatre Group; writer, dir. for local cabarets and charities; local muralist and portraitist, 1990—; set designer (off broadway) in NYC incl. Mother Posture, Seedless Grapes, The Pelican, New Village Prodns. benefit for AIDS, marquee 1st Theatre Mus. Village, Monroe, NY; performer Cancer Soc. Fundraiser, 1997, for John Brigham Meml. Scholarship Fundraiser, Ruthie Dino Marshall Fundraiser, others; producer, dir. Follies/Toys for Tots Campaign, 1997; exhibited in shows Lisbon, Portugal, 2001, Paramount Theatre, Middletown, NY, Cambridge, Eng., 2001, Vancouver, B.C., Can., 2002, Middletown Art Ctr., 2004, Middletown Art Ctr., N.Y.; executed mural M.H.S., Middletown, 2001; set designer, Dracula, 2003. County svc. coord. Orange County Youth-In-Govt. (adv. 1988-91), Goshen, NY, 1991-93; Odyssey of the Mind Coach, 1984-92; chair edn. and cultural sem., Lisbon, Portugal, 1999; chair edn. and culture comm., Vancouver, Can.; art and music comm., Vancouver, Can.; chmn., internat. comms. com. Internat. Edn. Culture Com.; mem. Internat. Art and Music Com., Vancouver, 2002, mem. multi-cultural com., 2002-2003; curriculum writer Middletown City Schs., 2003; founding mem. Nat. Campaign for Tolerance, Birmingham, Ala., 2003. Named for outstanding set design Times Herald Record, 1994; honored by Bd. Edn. Outstanding Educator, 1992, Apple award, 1999; named in S.W. Arts Mag., 2001, named Educator Yr. Am. Biog.Inst., 2003. Mem. Marine Corps League (hon.), NJROTC (hon. cadet 1997, Outstanding Contbn. to Arts award, Millenium Medal of Honor, 2000), Am. Biographical Inst. (chmn. ednl. culture com., 1999, mem. comms. com., chmn. edn. and culture com., 2002, art and music com., 2002, multicultural com., 2002), World Peace Diplomacy Forum. Episcopalian. Avocations: theatrical design, singing, calligraphy. Home: PO Box 4429 Middletown NY 10941-8429 Office: Middletown City Schs Wisner Ave Middletown NY 10940 Office Phone: 845-346-4900.

MCCORDUCK, PAMELA ANN, writer, educator; b. Liverpool, Eng., Oct. 27, 1940; came to U.S., 1946; d. William John and Hilda May (Bond) McC.; m. Joseph F. Traub, Dec. 6, 1969. Lectr. Columbia U., 1980-90. Author: Familiar Relations, 1971, Working to the End, 1972, Machines Who Think, 1979, The Fifth Generation, 1983. The Universal Machine, 1985, The Rise of the Expert Company, 1988, Aaron's Code, 1990, The Futures of Women, 1996. Mem. Am. PEN (bd. dirs. N.Y.C. chpt., 1986-94, v.p. 1994-96). Home: 445 Riverside Dr # 71 New York NY 10027-6801

MCCORKLE, RUTH, oncological nurse, educator; BS, U. Md., 1968; MA, U. Iowa, 1972, PhD, 1975. Staff nurse CCU Vancouver (Wash.) Med. Hosp., 1968-69; oncological clin. nurse specialist U. Iowa Hosps. and Clinics, Iowa City, 1971-73; instr. psychiat. nursing and oncological nursing Sch. Nursing, U. Iowa, Iowa City, 1974-75; from asst. prof. to prof. dept. cmty. health care sys. U. Wash., Seattle, 1975-85; prof. adult health and illness divsn. Sch. Nursing, U. Pa., Phila., 1986—, chairperson, 1988-89, dir. Ctr. Advancing Care in Serious Illness, 1989—, dir. cancer control Cancer Comprehensive Ctr., 1990-98; prof. nursing, chmn. doc program, dir. Ctr. Chronic Illness Sch. Yale U., New Haven, 1998—. Mem. nursing sci. rev. com. Nat. Ctr. Nursing Rsch., 1988-92. Contbr. articles to profl. jours. Fellow Am. Acad. Nursing; mem. ANA, NAS, Internat. Soc. Nurses Cancer Care (dir.-at-large 1983-89), Am. Assn. Cancer Edn., Oncology Nursing Soc. (charter mem., mem. rsch. com. 1981-82, dir.-at-large 1983-85). Office: Yale U 100 Church St S PO Box 9740 New Haven CT 06536-0740

MCCORMACK, GRACE LYNETTE, civil engineering technician; b. Dallas, Nov. 2; d. Audley and Janice Meredith (Metcalf) McC. Tech. degree, Durham's Coll., 1958; grad. in civil engring., El Centro Coll., 1972; grad. in advanced surveying, Eastfield, 1975. Cert. sr. engr. technician. Contract design technician various engring firms, Dallas, 1958-70; sr. design engr. technician City of Dallas Survey Div., 1970-80, street light div., 1980-95, ret. 1995. Mem. Unity Ch. Avocations: numerology, astrology, metaphysics, Egyptian-Arabian horses, lighting and designing black and white portrait photography. Home: 1428 Meadowbrook Ln Irving TX 75061-4435

MCCORMACK, MARJORIE GUTH, psychology educator, career counselor, communications educator, public relations consultant; b. Jersey City; d. Joseph and Vera Guth; m. Kevin T. McCormack, 1961. BA, St. Peter's Coll., 1974; MA, Jersey City State Coll., 1990. Editor AT&T, N.Y.C., 1952-60, libr., 1960-67, St. Peter's Coll., Jersey City, 1967-71; pub. rels. mgr. Blue Cross of N.J., Newark, 1971-81; instr. history, econs. St. Aloysius H.S., Jersey City, 1981-82; pub. rels. cons. Creative Pub. Rels. Assocs., Queensbury, N.Y., 1981—; prof. psychology Hudson County C.C., 1995-97. Adj. instr. comm. St. Peter's Coll., 1982-88; copy editor Glens Falls, (N.Y.) Post-Star, 1986; dir. career placement Hudson County C.C., 1988-91. Bd. mgrs. Am. Cancer Soc., Jersey City, 1978-79; mem., sec. parish coun. St. Aloysius Ch., 1981-85; mem. Jersey City Tenants Orgn., 1981-98, Rent Leveling Bd. Jersey City, 1983-86, St. Peter's Coll. Cmty. Chorus, 1988-94; 2d v.p., pub. rels. chair Sodality of the Children of Mary of St. Teresa, 1993-95. Mem. AAUP, AAUW, NAFE (pub. rels. chmn. 1980-82), Mid Atlantic Career Counselors Assn., N.J. Assn. Counseling and Devel., N.J. Edn. Assn., Jersey City Bus. and Profl. Women's Assn. (legis. chmn. 1975-77, Nat. program award 1976, State Press award 1982), Hudson County Women's Network. Avocations: music, theatre, gourmet cooking.

MCCORMACK, SHEILA ANN, network technician; b. Honeyeye Falls, N.Y., May 5, 1945; d. Paul Edgar and Lois Mildred (Landon) Hilbert; m. Howard L McCormack, July 6, 1977 (div. Sept. 27, 1988); children: Lori Lynn Shannon, Shawn Eric McCormack Sr. MCSE Burlington County Coll., 1981, cert. Contracting Officer's Representative U S Army Systems Command, Va, 1987; Organizational Leadership for Exec. U.S. Army Command and Gen. Staff Coll., 2000. Keypunch operator Dept. of Motor Vehicles, Trenton, NJ, 1964—65, McGraw-Hill Pub. Co., Hightstown, NJ, 1965—67. Keypunch operator Raytheons, Andover, Mass., 1967—69; keypunch supr. Salem Data Services, Salem, NH, 1969—71; data entry clk. Automation Mgmt. Office, Fort Dix, NJ, 1978—88; network mgr. Directorate of Info. Mgmt., Fort Dix, NJ, 1988—95, chief, network ops. ctr., 1995—. Author computer programs. Fund raising chairwoman Boy Scouts of Am., Browns Mills, NJ, 1977—79. Recipient High Performance of Excellence, Dept. of the Army, 1992. Achievements include development of program for the dept. of the Army which resulted in tangible benefits to Fort Dix; design of program for non-commissiones officers; development of computer program for Computer analysts at Fort Dix. Avocations: woodworking, reading, travel, needlecrafts, furniture restoration. Office: Directorate of Info Mgmt Bldg 5321 Delaware St Fort Dix NJ 08640

MCCORMICK, ALMA HEFLIN, writer, retired educator, psychologist; b. Winona, Mo., Sept. 2, 1910; d. Irvin Elgin and Nora Edith (Kelley) Heflin; m. Archie Thomas Edward McCormick, July 14, 1942 (dec.); children: Thomas, James, Kelly Jean. BA, Ea. Wash. Coll., 1936, EdM, 1949; PhD, Clayton U., 1977. Originator dept. severly mentally retarded Tri-City Pub. Schs., Richland, Wash., 1953, Parkland, Wash., 1955; co-founder, dir. Adastra Sch. for Gifted Children, Seattle, 1957-64; author profl. publs., novels. Editor: Cub Flyer, Western Story mag., Wild West Weekly; assoc. editor: Mexico City Daily News (English sect. of Novedades); contbr. articles to various publs., 1937—. One of the first Am. woman test pilot's, 1942. Mem. Am. Psychol. Assn., OX 5 Aviation Pioneers, Kappa Delta Pi. Republican. Roman Catholic. Home and Office: 10 E Pennington St Tucson AZ 85701-1506

MCCORMICK, DALE, state treasurer; b. N.Y., Jan. 17, 1947; BA, U. Iowa, 1970. Mem. Maine State Senate from 18th dist, 1991-96; treas. State of Maine, Augusta, 1999—. Author: Against the Grain, a Carpentry Manual for Women, 1977. Address: Maine State Treasury 39 St House Station Augusta ME 04333-0001*

MCCORMICK, DONNA LYNN, social worker; b. Austin, Minn., Aug. 13, 1944; d. Raymond Alois and Grace Eleanor (Hayes) Schrom; m. James Michael McCormick, Jan. 15, 1972. BA in Psychology, Coll. St. Catherine, 1966. Cert. substitute tchr. Camden County Coll., 2001. Caseworker Phila. County Bd. Pub. Assistance, 1968-70; sr. social worker San Francisco Dept. Human Svcs., 1986-97; interviewer dept. epidemiology and biostats. U. Pa., Phila., 1998-2000. Mem. Nature Conservancy, Consumer's Union, Emily's List. Mem.: AAUW, Coll. Nat Trust Hist. Preservation, Met. Opera Guild, Nat. Mus. Women Arts. Democrat. Avocations: reading, walking, wine tasting, letter writing, opera.

MCCORMICK, KAREN LOUISE, savings and loan association executive; b. San Jose, Calif., Nov. 22, 1954; d. Clifford Kaye Jr. and Margaret Elizabeth (Bigler) McC.; children: Crystal DeAnne, Sheralyn Rose McCormick. Grad. high sch., Mountain View, Calif., 1973; cert. Inst. Fin. Edn., Ariz. State U., 1987. Cashier, loan officer Santa Clara County Employees' Credit Union, San Jose, 1973-77; teller, loan officer First Fed. Savs. & Loan Assn. Port Angeles, Wash., 1977-83, v.p., br. mgr., 1983-87, v.p., adminstr. loan prodn., 1987-89, v.p., ass. dir. lending, 1989-90, sr. v.p., dir. lending, 1990—97, pres., CEO, 1997—. Bd. dirs., chair opns. com. Wash. Community Reinvestment Assn., Seattle, 1992-95.; mem. Wash. Savs. League Affordable Housing com., 1991; vice chair Wash. Fin. League, 2003-; chair bd. dirs. WFL Services (subsid. corp. of Wash. Fin. League), 2003-; past bd. mem. & pres. Thrift Inst. Adv. Coun. Contbr. articles to newspapers, 1989-91. Bd. dirs. Clallam County YMCA, 1992-95, Diversified Industries, Inc., Port Angeles, 1985-87, Port Angeles C of C; mem. Queen of Angels sch. bd., 1988-90; co-founder Olympic Peninsula Housing Coalition, 1992—; treas. Peninsula Coll. Found., past pres. Nor'Wester Rotary Club of Port Angeles. Named one of The Top 25 Most Powerful Women in Banking, US Banker mag., 2003. Mem.: America's Cmty. Bankers (pres. 2003). Avocations: creative writing, reading, music, travel. Office: First Fed Savs Port Angeles PO Box 351 Port Angeles WA 98362-0055*

MCCORMICK, KATHRYN ELLEN, prosecutor; b. Milw., Dec. 27, 1952; d. James Patrick and Kathryn Goss McCormick; 1 child, Joshua Patrick-Edwin Davis. BS cum laude, Ariz. State U., 1989; JD, U. Ariz., 1994. Bar: Ariz. 1994, U.S. Dist. Ct. Ariz. 1994; cert. peace officer Ariz. Police officer Scottsdale Police Dept., Ariz., 1972—77; investigator Maricopa County Atty.'s Office, Phoenix, 1977—80; spl. agt. Ariz. Atty. Gen.'s Office, Phoenix, 1980—91; def. atty. Maricopa County Pub. Defenders Office, Phoenix, 1994—98; prosecutor Securities divsn. Ariz. Corp. Commn., Phoenix, 1998—2002; dep. county atty. Office of County Counsel Govt. Rels., Phoenix, 2002—. Mem. consumer protection com. Ariz. State Bar, Phoenix, 1999—, mem. UPL adv. com., 2003—. Mem., pres. Tumbleweed Ctr. for Youth Devel., Phoenix, 1998—; commr. Phoenix Women's Commn., 1999—. Named Police Office of the Yr., Phoenix Exchange Club, 1975. Mem.: Ariz. Alliance for the Mentally Ill, Nat. Alliance for the Mentally Ill, Ariz. Women Lawyers Assn., Altered Tails Svc. Group. Avocations: gardening, swimming, hiking, reading. Home: 2034 W Edgemont Phoenix AZ 85009-1944 Office: Office of County Counsel 222 North Central Ste 1100 Phoenix AZ 85004 Office Phone: 602-506-8541.

MCCORMICK, MARIE CLARE, pediatrician, educator; b. Haverhill, Mass., Jan. 7, 1946; d. Richard John and Clare Bernadine (Keleher) McC.; m. Robert Jay Blendon, Dec. 30, 1977. BA magna cum laude, Emmanuel Coll., 1967; MD, Johns Hopkins U., 1971, ScD, 1978; MA, Harvard U., 1991. Diplomate Am. Bd. Pediat. Pediatric resident, fellow Johns Hopkins Hosp., Balt., 1971-75, rsch. fellow, 1972-75; asst. prof. U. Ill. Schs. Medicine & Pub. Health, Chgo., 1975-76; pediat. instr. Johns Hopkins Med. Sch., Balt., 1976-78; asst. prof. healthcare orgn. Johns Hopkins Sch. Hygiene & Pub. Health, 1978-81; asst. prof. pediat. U. Pa., Phila., 1981-86, assoc. prof. pediat., 1986-87, Harvard Med. Sch., Boston, 1987-91, prof. pediat., 1992—, 1st Sumner and Esther Feldberg prof. maternal/child health, 1996—; prof. Harvard Sch. Pub. Health, Boston, 1992—2003, chair maternal and child health, 1992—2003, prof. Soc., Human Devel. and Health, 2003—. Adj. assoc. prof. pediat. U. Pa., 1987-92; active attending physician, Johns Hopkins Hosp., 1976-81, asst. physician Children's Hosp. Phila., 1981-84, assoc. physician, 1984-86, sr. physician, 1986-87, assoc. pediatrician Brigham & Women's Hosp., 1987—; sr. assoc. in medicine Children's Hosp., 1987—; sr. assoc. in pediat. Beth Israel Deaconess Med. Ctr., 1987—; vis. prof. Wash. U., St. Louis, 1993; editl. bds. Health Svcs. Rsch., 1985-94, Pediat. in Rev., 1986-91, Pediat., 1993-99; assoc. editor Jour. Ambulatory Pediatric Assn., 1999—; adv. coun. Ctr. Perinatal & Family Health Brigham & Women's Hosp., 1991—; cons. to numerous coms., orgns. and bds. Contbr. articles to profl. jours. Adv. The David and Lucile Packard Found., 1993-95; bd. dirs. Family Planning Coun. S.E. Pa., 1984-87; chair com. child health Mayor's Commn. Phila., 1982-83. Named Henry Strong Denison scholar Johns Hopkins Sch. Medicine, 1971, Leonard Davis Inst.; Health Econs. fellow U. Pa. 1984, recipient Johns Hopkins U. Soc. Scholars award, 1995. Fellow Am. Acad. Pediat.; mem. AAAS, Inst. Medicine of NAS, Ambulatory Pediat. Assn. (Rsch. award 1996), Soc. Pediatric Rsch. (sr.), Am. Pediatric Soc., Am. Pub. Health Assn., Internat. Epidemiol. Assn., Assn. Health Svcs. Rsch., Ea. Soc. Pediatric Rsch., Soc. Pediatric Epidemiologic Rsch., Assn. Tchrs. Maternal and Child Health, Mass. Med. Soc., Norfolk Dist. Med. Soc., Mass. Pub. Health Assn., Johns Hopkins U. Soc. Scholars, NAS (nat. assoc.). Office: Harvard Sch Pub Health 677 Huntington Ave Boston MA 02115-6096 E-mail: mmccormi@hsph.harvard.edu.

MCCORMICK, MAUREEN OLIVEA, computer systems programmer; b. Toledo, Mar. 24, 1956; d. Richard Ernest and Rita Maureen (Pratt) McC. BS in Elem. Edn., Kent State U., 1978, MA Reading Specialization, 1980. Reading instr. Elyria City Schs., Elyria, Ohio, 1978-79; tchr. Wellington Village Schs., Wellington, Ohio, 1979-80; devel. edn. instr. Lorain County C.C., Elyria, 1980-83; computer programmer analyst Navy Fin. Ctr., Cleve., 1981-86, Naval Mil. Pers. Command, Arlington, Va., 1986; computer systems analyst Marine Corps Cen. Design & Programming Activity/MCDEC, Quantico, Va., 1986-87; computer systems programmer Navy Fin. Ctr., Cleve., 1987-91, Def. Fin. and Acctg. Svc.-Cleve./Info. and Tech., 1991-92, 1992-93, supervisory computer specialist, 1993—. Mem. Am. Soc. Mil. Compts., TransAtlantic Brides & Parents Assn. Avocations: swimming, travelling, crafts, golf. Home: 153 Burns Rd Elyria OH 44035-1510 Office: DFAS-CL/I&T 1240 E 9th St Cleveland OH 44199-2001

MCCORMICK, QUEEN ESTHER WILLIAMS, clergyman; b. Apr. 5, 1941; BA in Theology, Internat. Sem., 1986; MA in Theology, Logos Bible Coll., 1993, PhD in Ministry, 1996. Adj. prof. Internat. Sem., Plymouth, Fla., 1987,91,98; founder, pastor New Birth House of Prayer for All People, Ft. Lauderdale, Fla., 1980—; pres. CEO Compassionate Hearts-Serving Hands, 2000. Radio/TV min., 1974-97; gospel singer, 1946—. Author: The Elect Lady in Ministry, 3d edit., 1998. Office: PO Box 5712 Fort Lauderdale FL 33310-5712

MCCORMICK, TERRI, state legislator; b. Waupun, Wis., Oct. 24, 1956; married; 3 children. BS, U. Wis., 1980; postgrad., U. Windsor, Ont., Can., 1982, Lawrence U., 1993; MA, Marian Coll., 2000. Former edn. cons.; mem. Wis. State Assembly, Dist. 56, Madison, 2000—, mem. edn. reform, ins., judiciary, labor and workforce devel., pub. health and state/local fin. coms. Coach Xavier Mock Trial Team; mem. Winnebago County r. Mem.: Am. Legion Aux. Republican. Office: State Capitol Rm 127W PO Box 8953 Madison WI 53708-8953 Address: 3328 W Parkridge Ave Appleton WI 54914

MCCOURT, LISA, writer; b. Jacksonville, Fla., Sept. 2, 1964; d. Michael Lee and Bettye Jean McCourt; m. Gregory Vincent Combs; children: Lily-Kate Combs children: Tucker Combs. BS, Drew U., Madison, N.J., 1986. Author: (children's book) I Love You, Stinky Face, 1997 (National Parenting Publication Award (Nappa) Honors Award, 1998), The Rain Forest Counts!, 1997, The Long and Short of It, 1998 (chosen for The Original Art by the Society of Illustrators, 1998), Raptors!, 1997, Deadly Snakes, 1998, I Miss You, Stinky Face, 1999 (a PBS "Between the Lions" selection, 2001), Candy Counting, 1999, Rocket to the Moon, 1999, Construction Buddies; Dozer to the Rescue!, 1999, It's Time for School, Stinky Face, 2000, Construction Buddies; Dozer's Wild Adventure, 2000, Chicken Soup for Little Souls; The Best Night Out with Dad, 1997, Chicken Soup for Little Souls; The Never-Forgotten Doll, 1997 (Storytelling World Award; Honor Title, 1998), Chicken Soup for Little Souls; The Goodness Gorillas, 1997, Chicken Soup for Little Souls; The Braids Girl, 1998, Chicken Soup for Little Souls, A Dog of My Own, 1998 (IRA/CBC Children's Choice Award, 1998), Chicken Soup for Little Souls; The New Kid and the Cookie Thief, 1998, Chicken Soup for Little Souls; Della Splatnuk, Birthday Girl, 1999 (Storytelling World Award, Honor Title, 2000), Chicken Soup for Little Souls Family Collection, 1999, Chicken Soup for the Little Souls; 3 Colorful Stories to Warm the Hearts of Children, 2000, Love You Until. . ., 1999, (parenting book) 101 Ways to Raise a Happy Baby, 1999, (preteen book) Attitude--How to Be the Coolest Girl You Know, 2000, (children's book) Weird in the Wild; Wet 'n' Weird, 2000, Weird in the Wild; Hairy 'n' Weird, 2000, (parenting book) 101 Ways to Raise a Happy Toddler, 2000, (children's book) Good Night, Princess Pruney Toes, 2001, I Love You, Stinky Face board book, 2002, Merry Christmas, Stinky Face, 2002, (children's book) What's Inside My Body?, 2000, (children's book) Mysterious Space, 2000. Personal E-mail: lisa@lisamccourt.com.

MCCOY, CAROL P. psychologist, training executive; b. Bronxville, N.Y., June 14, 1948; d. Rawley Deering and Jane (Wiske) McC.; m. Lanny Gordon Foster, Nov. 29, 1975 (div. 1985). BA, Conn. Coll., 1970; MS in Psychology, Rutgers U., 1974, PhD in Psychology, 1980. Adj. instr. psychology Rutgers U., New Brunswick, N.J., 1974-75; faculty chair dept. social sci. Misericordia Hosp. Sch. Nursing, Bronx, N.Y., 1976-79; tng. and devel. cons. Chase Manhattan Bank N.A., N.Y.C., 1980-85, tng. mgr. internat. consumer banking div., 1985-88, tng. mgr. individual banking, 1988-91; dir. corp. tng. UNUM Life Ins. Co. Am., Portland, Maine, 1991-97, mgr. tng. quality assurance, 1997-99; pres. McCoy Trng./Devel. Resources, Falmouth, Maine, 1999—. Pres. Find-Your-Roots.com, 2002—. Author: Managing a Small HRD Department, 1993; editor: Managing the Small Training Staff, 1998. Mem. Am. Soc. Tng. and Devel., Am. Psychol. Assn. Avocations: genealogy, music, baseball cards. Home and Office: McCoy Tng/Devel Resources 11 Johnson Rd Falmouth ME 04105-1408 Office Phone: 207-781-7515. E-mail: cmccoy3333@aol.com.

MCCOY, DONNA LEE, elementary school educator; b. Columbus, Ohio, Dec. 12, 1960; d. Arthur Lee and Anna Margaret (Keefer) King; m. Russell Dean McCoy, Sept. 15, 1990; 1 child. BS in Elem. Edn., W.Va. State Coll.,

1990. Cert. tchr., W.Va. 1st grade tchr. Parsons (W.Va.) Elem. Sch., 1990-95, extended yr. tchr. kindergarten-3d grade, summer 1991-95; substitute tchr. Mason County Bd. Edn., 2003—. Core mem. Outcome Driven Devel. Model, Parsons Elem., Tucker County Bd. of Edn., 1990-95. Vol. Roosevelt Elem. Sch.; participant Regional Edn. Svc. Agy. VII Exemplary Tchg. Techniques Program, 1991. Recipient Exemplary Tchg. Techniques award Tucker County, 1994. Avocations: horses, tutoring for primary students.

MCCOY, EDNA ROSE, music educator; b. Man, W.Va., July 23, 1959; d. Van Buren and Ceceilia Curry; m. Lewis S. Mccoy, July 25, 1981; children: Steve, Laura. MEd in reading, East Tenn. State U., 1996—98; BS in music edn., W.Va. Inst. of Tech., 1977—81. Cert. Elementary Teacher Ky. and Va., 1992. Adult edn. tchr. and substitute Hopkins County Schools, Madisonville, Ky., 1987—92; primary grade tchr./gen. music tchr. Jenkins Ind. Schools, Jenkins, Ky., 1995—98; choir dir./ gen. music tchr. Perry County Schools, Viper, 1998—2000; choir dir./gen. music tchr. Pike County Schools, Pikeville, Ky., 2000—01; band and choir dir. Pound H.S. and J.W. Adams Combined Sch., Pound, Va., 2001—. Mem.: Music Educators Nat. Assn. (assoc.). Home: POBox 1078 Pound VA 24279 Personal E-mail: ednamccoy@naxs.net.

MCCOY, LOIS CLARK, emergency services professional, retired county official, magazine editor; b. New Haven, Oct. 1, 1920; m. Herbert Irving McCoy, Oct. 17, 1943; children: Whitney, Kevin, Marianne, Tori, Debra, Sally, Daniel. BS, Skidmore Coll., 1942; student, Nat. Search and Rescue Sch., 1974. Asst. buyer R.H. Macy & Co., N.Y.C., 1942-44, assoc. buyer, 1944-48; instr. Mountain Medicine & Survival, U. Calif., San Diego, 1973-74; cons. editor Search & Rescue Mag., 1975, Rescue Mag., 1988-97, editor, 1992-94, Press On Newsletter, 1992—2000. Coord. San Diego Mountain Rescue Team, La Jolla, Calif., 1973-75; exec. sec. Nat. Assn. for Search and Rescue, Inc., Nashville, La Jolla, 1975-80, comptr., 1980-82; disaster officer San Diego County, 1980-86, Santa Barbara County, 1985-91, ret.; pres. Nat. Inst. Urban Search & Rescue, Inc., 1987—; assoc. dir. Armed Forces Commns. and Electronics Assn., 2003—. Author: Search and Rescue Glossary, 1974; contbr. editor Rescue Mag., 1989-97; editor-in-chief Response! mag., 1982-86; editor Press On! Electronic mag., 1994—; mem. adv. bd. Hazard Monthly, 1991-99; contbr. articles to profl. jours. Cons. law enforcement divsn. Calif. Office Emergency Svcs., 1976-77; pres. San Diego Com. for L.A. Philharm. Orch., 1957-58; bd. dirs. Search and Rescue of the Californias, 1976-77, Nat. Assn. for Search and Rescue, Inc., 1980-87, pres., 1985-87, trustee, 1987-90, mem. Calif. OES strategic com., 1992-96; CEO Nat. Inst. for Urban Search, 1989—; mem. Gov.'s Task Force on Earthquakes, 1981-82, Earthquake Preparedness Task Force, Seismic Safety Commn., 1982-85, Army Sci. and Tech. Commn., 2003; mem. adv. coun. Nat. Meml. Inst. for the Protection from Terrorism. Recipient Hall Foss award for outstanding svc. to search and rescue, 1982, Diamond Safety award for outstanding work in emergency svcs., 1996; named to "The Fed. 100", 2002. Mem.: IEEE, Armed Forces Comm. and Electronics Assn. (named to Army Sci. and Tech. com. for Homeland Def. 2003—04), San Diego Mountain Rescue (hon.; life), Nat. Assn. Search and Rescue (life Svc. award 1985, 2002), Santa Barbara Amateur Radio Club. Episcopalian. Office: PO Box 91648 Santa Barbara CA 93190-1648 Office Phone: 800-767-0093. E-mail: niusr@cox.net.

MCCOY, MARILYN, university official; b. Providence, Mar. 18, 1948; d. James Francis and Eleanor (Regan) McC.; m. Charles R. Thomas, Jan. 28, 1983. BA in Econs. cum laude, Smith Coll., l970; M in Pub. Policy, U. Mich., l972. Dir. Nat. Ctr. for Higher Edn. Mgmt. Systems, Boulder, Colo., l972-80; dir. planning and policy devel. U. Colo., Boulder, l98l-85; v.p. adminstrn. and planning Northwestern U., Evanston, Ill., 1985—. Trustee One Group Funds. Co-author: Financing Higher Education in the Fifty States, 1976, 3d edit., 1982. Bd. dir. Evanston Northwestern HealthCare, 1988—, Mather Found., 1995—; trustee Carleton Coll., 2003—. Mem. Am. Assn. for Higher Edn., Soc. for Coll. and Univ. Planning (pres., v.p., sec., bd. dir. 1980—), Assn. for Instnl. Rsch. (pres., v.p., exec. com., publ. bd. 1978-87), Chgo. Network (chmn. 1992-93), Chgo. Econ. Club. Home: 1100 N Lake Shore Dr Chicago IL 60611-1070 Office: Northwestern U 633 Clark St Evanston IL 60208-0001

MCCOY, MARY NELL, music educator; d. James Albert Swope Jr. and Marjorie Gayle Swope; m. Gary Wayne McCoy, Nov. 28, 1968; children: Amy Annelle, Jason Todd, Joyce Elaine. MusB in Edn., Ctrl. Mo. State U., 1968; M in Ch. Music, S.W. Bapt. Theol. Sem., 1972. Cert. crosscultural, lang. and academic devel. State of Calif., 2000. Elem. music tchr. Knob Noster (Mo.) Elem. Sch., 1968—70; music cons. Internat. Mission Bd., Richmond, 1974—91; elem. music tchr. Bay Elem. Sch.-San Lorenzo Unified Sch. Dist., Calif., 1995—. Support provider for new tchrs. Beginning Tchr. Support and Assessment, San Lorenzo, 2001—; mentor tchr. Peer Assessment and Rev., San Lorenzo, 2001—; rep. Gifted and Talented Program, San Lorenzo, 2000—; adj. prof. Golden Gate Bapt. Theol. Sem., Mill Valley, Calif. Min. music First Bapt. Ch., Novato, Calif., 1992—96; interim min. music Petaluma (Calif.) Valley Bapt. Ch., 1997—99; children's choir leader Concord Korean Bapt. Ch., Martinez, Calif., 2000—03. Mem.: Calif. Tchrs. Assn. (assoc.), Calif. Music Educator's Conv. (assoc.), Music Educator's Nat. Conv. (assoc.), Calif. Parents, Tchrs. Assn., Phi Kappa Lambda. Democrat-Npl. Baptist.

MCCOY, MILDRED BROOKMAN, retired elementary education educator; b. Princeton, W.Va., Nov. 23, 1924; d. Ralph William and Nannie Mae (Tabor) Brookman; m. Julius Rossey McCoy, Apr. 12, 1945 (dec. 1980); children: Michael David, Alan Dale. BA, Shepherd Coll., 1976. Elem. tchr. Baltimore County Bd. Edn., Balt., 1957-67, Washington County Bd. Edn., Md., 1967-86, ret., 1986. Docent Washington County Hist. Soc., Hagerstown, Md., 1990—, Washington County Art Mus., 1997—. AAUW grantee, 1993. Mem. Md. Ret. Tchrs. Assn., Hagerstown Women's Club, PEO. Episcopalian. Avocations: antiquing, hiking, traveling, reading. Home: 18824 Preston Rd Hagerstown MD 21742-2716

MCCOY, SUE, retired surgeon, biochemist; b. Charlottesville, Va., Nov. 14, 1935; d. Hulburt Christopher and Evelyn (Savage) McC. AB, Radcliffe Coll., 1957; PhD, Johns Hopkins U., 1964; MD, U. Va., 1980, postgrad., 2001—. Diplomate Am. Bd. Surgery. Fellow in physiol. chemistry Johns Hopkins U., Balt., 1964-67; asst. prof. chemistry U. South Fla., Tampa, 1967-69; asst. prof. orthopedics U. Va., Charlottesville, 1969-73, asst. prof. surgery, 1973-78; resident in surgery Hosp. U. Pa., Phila., 1980-83; resident in surgery Cooper Hosp. Rutgers U. Med. Sch., Camden, N.J., 1983-85, asst. prof. surgery, 1985-86, East Tenn. State U., Johnson City, 1986-91, assoc. prof., 1991-2000, prof., 2000—01; ret. Mem. ACS, Am. Chem. Soc., N.Y. Acad. Sci., Royal Soc. Chemistry, Assn. for Acad. Surgery, Shock Soc., Internat. Soc. Oxygen Transport to Tissue, Am. Fedn. Clin. Rsch., Tenn. Med. Assn., Southeastern Surg. Congress, Assn. for Surg. Edn., Assn. for Women Surgeons, Tenn. Geriatric Assn., Am. Soc. for Parenteral and Enteral Nutrition, Sigma Xi. Achievements include research in hemorrhagic shock, aging, oxygen transport. Home: 8658 Batesville Rd Afton VA 22920

MCCRACKEN, CARON FRANCIS, computer company executive, consultant; b. Detroit, Jan. 12, 1951; d. WIlliam Joseph and Constance Irene (Kramer) McC. AS, Mott C.C., 1971; BS, Ctrl. Mich. U., 1973; MA, U. Mich., 1978; MBA in Fin. with hons., Wayne State U., 2003. Tchr. Elkton, Pigeon, Bayport (Mich.) High Sch., 1973—74, Davison (Mich.) Jr. High Sch., 1974-75; instr. Mott C.C., Flint, Mich., 1974-78; planning and rsch. specialist Flint Police Dept., 1977-79; campus coord., programmer Systems & Computer Tech. Corp. (now SunGard Data Sys., Inc.), Detroit, 1981-82; acad. specialist computing systems Systems & Computer Tech. Corp., Detroit, 1982-83, mgr. acad. computing systems, 1983-84, mgr. adminstrv. computing systems, 1984-85; communications analyst Fruehauf Corp., Detroit, 1985-86, sr. comms. analyst, 1986-87; account cons. US Sprint Communications Co., Detroit, 1987-89; account mgr. US Sprint Communications Corp., Detroit, 1989-90; sr. mgr. Technology Specialists, Inc., Phila., 1990-91, Digital Mgmt. Group, Detroit, 1991—92; sr. cons. info. tech. practice, tech. delivery svcs. PriceWaterhouseCoopers LLP, Detroit, 1992—. Adv. bd. CONTEL Bus. Networks, Atlanta, 1987. Contbr. articles to profl. jours. Vol. charitable and homeless orgns. including Coalition on Temporary Shelter, Core Cities, Paint the Town; undergrad. computer lab. cons., student mgr. computer sci. dept. Wayne State U., 1993-95, vol. computer cons. Bus. Sch., 1997-98; vol. tech. advisor on 1992 elections project City of Detroit; vol. St. Joseph's Mercy Hosp., Pontiac, Mich., 1995; chair of bd., pres., treas. Bloomfield Courts Condominium Assn., 1996-98; vol. Pub. TV WTVS, Detroit, 1996-99, vol., Pub. Radio Sta. WDET, Detroit, 1996-98; elected precinct del. for 4th precinct Bloomfield Twp., 2002-; vol. State Senatorial and U.S. Congressional re-elect. campaigns, 2002. Named to Beta Gamma Sigma MBA Hon. Soc., 2001. Mem.: Detroit Zool. Soc., Detroit Inst. Arts, Assn. Computing Machinery, Data Processing Mgmt. Assn., Alumni Assn. Wayne State U., Smithsonian Instn. (assoc.), Alumni Assn. U. Mich., Adventure Cycling Assn. (Missoula, Mont.), Women's Econ. Club of Met. Detroit (fin. com. 1999), Beta Gamma Sigma. Avocations: reading, athletics, personal research, international travel. Home: 100 W Hickory Grove H4 Bloomfield Hills MI 48304-2169 Office: PricewaterhouseCoopers LLP 400 Renaissance Ctr Ste 780 Detroit MI 48243-1501

MCCRACKEN, KATHRYN ANGELA, clinical social worker; b. Steubenville, Ohio, Apr. 24, 1943; d. Ned Edward and Anna Lucy (Cortez) White; m. William Floyd Grandinetti, Dec. 14, 1961 (div. 1971); children: Natalie, Jane Elizabeth; m. Dudley Ral McCracken, Aug. 13, 1972; children: Anne Louise, Dori Kate. AS in Fine Arts, Washtenaw Community Coll., Ypsilanti, Mich., 1986; MSW, U. Mich., 1988. Supr. nursing svc. Ypsilanti State Hosp., 1972-88; client svc. mgr. Monroe (Mich.) County Cmty. Mental Health, 1989-98, outpatient therapist, 1998-2000; pvt. practice, 2000—. Mem. NASW, APA. Democrat. Roman Catholic. Avocation: book collector. Office: EJ Wasilewski & Assocs 708 S Monroe St Monroe MI 48161-1430

MCCRACKEN, LINDA, librarian, commercial artist; b. Rochester, N.Y., Apr. 13, 1948; d. Frederick Hugh Craig and Shirley Betty (Shacter) Bickford; m. Alan Cheah, June 13, 1972 (div. 1978); m. Bruce E. McCracken, Sept. 23, 1978 (div. 1985); 1 child, Karen Elizabeth. BA in History, MLS, SUNY, Geneseo, 1970. Reference libr. Northeastern U., Boston, 1971-72; asst. libr. Burlington (Mass.) Pub. Libr., 1972-74; artist, writer, rschr. McCracken's, Marlow, NH, 1972—; rsch. asst. Data Resources, Inc., Lexington, Mass., 1974-76; asst. libr. N.H.. Vocat.-Tech. Coll., Manchester, 1985-87; libr. N.H. Hosp., Concord, 1987-99; med. libr. New London (N.H.) Hosp., 1999. Participant paintings Horseheads Mall Art Show (3d pl. award 1968); graphic artist Rare Coin Rev. mag., 1983; layout artist Market Media Guide, 1979; market rschr. Delahaye Group, Newington, N.H., 1993-94; author Burlington Times-Union, 1973, Pleasant News, 1987-88, Breene Briefings, 1998-99. Treas. Village Players, Wolfeboro, 1982-83; mem. pub. rels. com. Gov.'s Arts Coun., Wolfeboro, 1982. Mem. State Employees Assn. N.H., Mensa. Avocations: reading, hiking, kayaking, theater. Home and Office: PO Box 235 Marlow NH 03456

MCCRACKEN, PEGGY JANE, webmaster, publishing executive; b. Flomot, Tex., Jan. 31, 1935; d. Robert Houston and Sallie Ann (Matthews) Gunn; m. Leon V. McCracken, Apr. 18, 1951; children: David Leon McCracken, Peggy Lynn Goddard. Cashier CIT, Pecos, Tex., 1953-56; sec. Hwy. Dept. State of Tex., Pecos, 1958-59; sec. West Park Bapt. Ch., Pecos, 1961-71; reporter/mng. editor Pecos Enterprise, 1972-78, reporter/edit. page editor, Internet web page dir., 1988—99; news dir. Sta. KIUN-AM, Pecos, 1978-87; freelance writer Pecos, 1978-88; bus. mgr. and webmaster Pecos Enterprise, Tex., 1999—. Media rels. Emergency Mgmt., Pecos, 1993-99. Baptist. Home: 1804 S Park St Pecos TX 79772-5727 Office: Pecos Enterprise 324 S Cedar St Pecos TX 79772-3211

MCCRADY, BARBARA SACHS, psychologist, educator; b. Evanston, Ill., May 7, 1949; d. James Frederick and Margaret Maxine (Miller) Sachs; m. Dennis D. McCrady, June 13, 1969; 1 child, Eric Paul. BS, Purdue U., 1969; PhD, U. R.I., 1975. Lic. clin. psychologist. Clin. project evaluator Butler Hosp., Providence, 1974-75, chief psychol. assessment program, 1975-76, chief problem drinkers' project, 1976-83; assoc. prof. psychology Rutgers U., Piscataway, N.J., 1983-89, prof. psychology, 1989-2000, prof. II, 2000—. From instr. to assoc. prof. psychiatry Brown U., Providence, 1975-83; acting dir. Rutgers Ctr. Alcohol Studies, Piscataway, 1990-92; reviewer Nat. Inst. on Alcohol Abuse and Alcholism, Washington, 1979-82, extramural scientific adv. bd., 1989-93; cons. Inst. Medicine, Washington, 1988-89. Author: The Alcoholic Marriage, 1977; editor: Marriage and Marital Therapy, 1978, Directions in Alcohol Abuse Treatment Research, 1985, Research on Alcoholics Anonymous: Opportunities and Alternatives, 1993, Addictions: A Comprehensive Guidebook, 1999. Grantee Nat. Inst. on Alcohol Abuse and Alcoholism, 1979-83, 1988—. Fellow Am. Psychol. Assn. (past pres. divsn. addictions); mem. Assn. for Advancement Behavior Therapy, Rsch. Soc. on Alcoholism (bd. dirs., 1999-2003). Avocations: horseback riding, skiing, piano. Office: Rutgers U Ctr Alcohol Studies 607 Allison Rd Piscataway NJ 08854-8001 Office Phone: 732-445-0667. E-mail: bmccrady@rci.rutgers.edu.

MCCRADY, PRISCILLA I. advocate; b. Pitts., May 11, 1944; d. Thomas and Virginia Humphrey Jamison; m. William Duff McCrady; children: Thomas J., William Duff Jr., Caroline M. Rudolf. AA, Centenary Jr. Coll., Hackettstown, N.J., 1964; BA, Chatham Coll., 1981; M Pub. Mgmt., Carnegie Mellon U., 1989. Placement coord. Bradford Sch., Pitts., 1983—87; campaign mgr. M.C. Hunt Campaign, Pitts., 1985; trustee rep. The Shore Fund, Pitts., 1990—. Mem. women's com. Carnegie Mus., Pitts., 1978—; vice chmn. Carnegie Hero Fund, Pitts., 1990—; bd. mem. Leading Edn. & Advocay for Depression, 2001—, Frick Art and Hispanic Ctr., 2002—. Republican. Presbyterian. Avocations: golf, reading. Home: 5051 Castleman St Pittsburgh PA 15232

MC CRANN, DEBORAH THERESA, securities trader; b. N.Y.C., Sept. 12, 1953; d. John J. and Agnes C. (Booth) Di Tusa; m. Robert Thoman, Sept. 21, 1975 (div. Mar. 1979); m. Paul Francis Mc Crann, May 24, 1992; 1 child, Liam John. BS in Mgmt. and Comm. magna cum laude, Adelphi U., 1992. Lic. trader, registered rep. series 7, 23 and 24, N.Y. Stock Exch. From sec. to v.p. corp. fin. Lehman Bros., N.Y.C., 1977-83; instl. sales/trader, v.p. Hambrecht & Quist, N.Y.C., 1983-85; instl. sales/trader, dir., mng. dir. Smith Barney Inc., N.Y.C., 1985-99; v.p. NASDAQ trading Donaldson, Lufkin & Jenrette, N.Y.C., 1999—. Guest spkr., prodr. TV program Modern Marvels—The Stock Exchange, History Channel, 1997; featured in discussion of women in investment banking Traders Mag., 1996. Vol. homeless shelter St. Augustine, Park Slope, Bklyn., 1988-92. Mem. Mem. Security Traders Assn. N.Y. (chairperson instl. com. 1995—, bd. dirs. 1999-2002). Episcopalian. Avocations: skiing, reading, golf, gardening, herbology. Office: Donaldson Lufkin Jenrette 277 Park Ave Fl 7 New York NY 10172-3400

MCCRARY, EUGENIA LESTER (MRS. DENNIS DAUGHTRY MCCRARY), civic worker, writer; b. Annapolis, Md., Mar. 23, 1929; d. John Campbell and Eugenia (Potts) Lester; m. John Campbell Howard, July 15, 1955 (dec. Sept. 1965); m. Dennis Daughtry McCrary, June 28, 1969; 1 child, Dennis Campbell. AB cum laude, Radcliffe Coll.-Harvard U., 1950; MA, Johns Hopkins U., 1952; postgrad., Harvard U., 1953, Pa. State U., 1953-54, Drew U., 1957-58, Inst. Study of USSR, Munich, 1964. Grad. asst. dept. Romance langs. Pa. State U., 1953-54; tchr. dept. math. The Brearley Sch., N.Y.C., 1954-57; dir. Sch. Langs., Inc., Summit, N.J., 1958-69, trustee, 1960-69. Co-author: Nom de Plume: Eugenia Campbell Lester, (with Allegra Branson) Frontiers Aflame, 1987; film script adaptation (with John Gallagher) Frontier, 1998. Dist. dir. Ea. Pa. and N.J. auditions Met. Opera Nat. Coun., N.Y.C., 1960-66, dist. dir. publicity, 1966-67, nat. vice chmn. publicity, 1967-71, nat. chmn. public rels., 1972-75, hon. nat. chmn. pub. rels., 1976-99; bd. govs., chmn. Van Cortlandt House Mus., 1985-90. Mem. Nat. Soc. Colonial Dames Am. (bd. mgrs. N.Y. 1985-90), Met. Opera Nat. Coun., Soc. Mayflower Desc. (former bd. dirs. N.Y. soc., chmn. house com. 1986-89), Soc. Daus. Holland Dames (bd. dirs. 1982-87, 96—, 3d directress gen. 1987-92, directress gen. 1992-96), L'Eglise du St.-Esprit (vestry 1985-88, sr. warden 1988-90), Huguenot Soc. Am. (governing coun. 1984-90, 2000—, asst. treas. 1990-91, sec. 1991-95, 2d v.p. 1995-2000), Colonial Dames Am., Daus. of Cin., Colony Club (bd. govs. 1988-96), Causeries du Lundi. Republican. Episcopalian. Home: 24 Central Park S New York NY 10019-1629 Personal E-mail: elmccrary@aol.com.

MCCRAVEN, EVA STEWART MAPES, health service administrator; b. L.A., Sept. 26, 1936; d. Paul Melvin and Wilma Zech (Ziegler) Stewart; m. Carl Clarke McCraven, Mar. 18, 1978; children: David Anthony, Lawrence James, Maria Lynn Mapes. ABS magna cum laude, Calif. State U., Northridge, 1974; MS, Cambridge Grad. Sch. Psycholoy, 1987, PhD, 1991. Dir. spl. projects Pacoima Meml. Hosp., 1969-71, dir. health edn., 1971-74; ast. exec. dir., v.p. Hillview Cmty. Mental Health Ctr., Lakeview Terrace, Calif., 1974-99, exec. dir., 1999—, former dir. clin. svcs. Past dir. dept. consultation and edn. Hillview Ctr., developer, mgr. long-term residential program, 1986-90; former program mgr. crisis residential program, transitional residential program and day treatment program for mentally ill offenders, past dir. mentally ill offenders svcs.; former program dir. Valley Homeless Shelter Mental Health Counseling Program; dir. Integrated Svcs. Agy., Hillview Mental Health Ctr., Inc., 1993-98, dir. clin. programs, 1996-99, exec. dir. 1999—. Former pres. San Fernando Valley Coordinating Coun. Area Assn., Sunland-Tujunga Coordinating Coun.; bd. advisors Pacoima Sr. Citizens Multi-Purpose Ctr.; bd. dirs. N.E. Valley Health Corp., 1970-73, Golden Gate Cmty. Mental Health Ctr., 1970-73. Recipient resolution of commendation State of Calif., 1988, commendation award, 1988, spl. mayor's plaque, 1988, commendation awards for cmty. svcs. City of L.A., 1989, County of Los Angeles, 1989, Calif. Assembly, 1989, Calif. Senate, 1989, award Sunland-Tujunga Police Support Coun., 1989, Women of Achievement award Sunland-Tujunga Bus and Profl. Women, 1990. Mem. Health Svcs. Adminstrn. Alumni Assn. (past v.p.), Sunland-Tujunga Bus. and Profl. Women, LWV, Valley Philharm. Soc. Office: Hillview Cmty Mental Health Ctr 11500 Eldridge Ave Lake View Terrace CA 91342-6523

MCCRAW, KATHY, elementary school educator, special education educator; b. Spartanburg, S.C., Dec. 30, 1954; d. Perry Robert and Lillie Belle Stevens; children: Brooke Kathryn, Courtney Nicole. BA with highest honor, Clemson U., 1977; MA, Converse Coll., 1984. Tchr. spl. edn. Lugoff-Elgin Mid. Sch., Camden, S.C., 1977-80; resource tchr. Spartanburg H.S., 1980-97; resource tchr. and tchr. earth and phys. sci. Houston Elem. Sch. and McCracken Jr. H.S., Spartanburg, 1998; tchr. modified lang. arts Whitlock Jr. H.S., Spartanburg, 1999—, tchr. lang. arts, 2002—. Mem. com. writing state stds. for alternative diploma program and developing curriculum and materials. Mem. Coun. for Exceptional Children. Republican. Baptist. Avocation: painting. Home: 14 Somersett Dr Spartanburg SC 29301-6532

MCCRAY, ALEXA T. health science association administrator, director; PhD, Georgetown U., Washington, 1981. Faculty Georgetown U., Washington, 1981—84; rsch. staff mem. IBM T.J. Watson Rsch. Ctr., 1986; with Lister Hill Nat. Ctr. for Biomed. Comms., a divsn. Nat. Libr. of Medicine, NIH, Bethesda, Md., 1986—, dir. Contbr. articles to profl. jours.; co-editor-in-chief Methods of Information in Medicine, mem. editl. bd. Jour. Am. Med. Informatics Assn. Fellow: AAAS, Am. Coll. Med. Informatics; mem.: Internat. Med. Informatics Assn., Am. Med. Informatics Assn. (bd. dirs.), Inst. Medicine of NAS (past bd. dirs.). Achievements include research in in medical informatics. Office: Nat Library Medicine 8600 Rockville Pike Bethesda MD 20894

MCCRAY, DORIS RAINES, minister; b. Petersburg, Va., July 1, 1940; d. Linwood and Florence Raines; m. John McCray, Aug. 29, 1958; children: Ronald, Deborah Ramsey, Wayne, Donald. Student, Va. State U., 1980; BA, Richmond Va. Sem., 1986, MDiv, 1988. Notary pub. Assoc. min. Met. Ch., Petersburg, Va., 1982—84; assoc. pastor Good Shepherd Ch., 1985—86, asst. pastor, 1986—87, interim pastor, 1987—90; assoc. min. Met. Ch., 1990—2000; assoc. pastor Olive Br. Ch., Dinwiddie, 2000—. Counselor Southside Mental Health, Petersburg, 1984—90; chaplain Southside Regional Hosp., 1983—95. Sr. citizen mem. Sr. Adv. Com., Richmond, Va., 2002. Mem.: AARP. Democrat. Baptist. Avocations: reading, travel. Home: 1712 W Clara Dr Petersburg VA 23803 Office: Olive Br Ch 11119 Bovdton Plank Rd Dinwiddie VA 23841 E-mail: preacherdot@hotmail.com.

MCCRAY, NIKKI KESANGAME, professional basketball player; b. Collierville, Tenn., Dec. 17, 1971; BA, U. Tenn., 1995. Basketball player USA Women's Nat. Team, 1996, Washington Mystics, 1998—. Office: Washington Mystics MCI Ctr 601 F St NW Washington DC 20004-1605

MCCUE, JUDITH W. lawyer; b. Phila., Apr. 7, 1948; d. Emanuel Leo and Rebecca (Raffel) Weiss; m. Howard M. McCue III, Apr. 3, 1971; children: Howard, Leigh. BA cum laude, U. Pa., 1969; JD, Harvard U., 1972. Bar: Ill. 1972, U.S. Tax Ct. 1984. Ptnr. McDermott, Will & Emery, Chgo., 1995—. Dir. Schawk, Inc., Des Plaines, Ill.; past pres. Chgo. Estate Planning Coun. Trustee Chgo. Symphony Orch., 1995—, vice chair, 1998—2001. Fellow: Am. Coll. Trust and Estate Counsel (com. chair 1991—94, regent 1993—2000, com. chair 1998—2001, pres.-elect 2004—); mem.: Chgo. Bar Assn. (chmn. probate practice com. 1984—85, chair estate and gift tax divsn. of fed. tax com. 1988—89). Office: McDermott Will & Emery 227 W Monroe St Ste 3100 Chicago IL 60606-5096 E-mail: jmccue@mwe.com.

MCCUISTION, PEG OREM, retired hospice administrator; b. Houston, July 28, 1930; d. William Darby and Dorothy Mildred (Beckett) Orem; m. Palmer Day McCuistion, Sept. 4, 1949 (div. 1960); 1 child, Leeanne E. BBA, Southwest Tex. State, 1963; MBA, George Washington U., 1968; EdD, Wayne State U., 1989. Patient care adminstr. Holy Cross Hosp., Silver Spring, Md., 1968-79; exec. dir. Hospice of S.E. Mich., Southfield, 1979-86, Hospice Austin, Tex., 1987-94; CEO EMBI, Inc., Arlington, Tex., 1994—98; gen. mgr. Hospice Home Care, San Antonio, 2001—04, ret., 2004. Bd. dirs. Cmty. Home for the Elderly, Austin, 1989-92. Fellow Am. Coll. Health Care Execs. (membership com.); mem. Internat. Hospice Inst. (assoc.), Nat. Hospice Orgn. (chair standards and accreditation com.), Tex. Hospice Orgn. (pres. 1993-94), exec. com., standards and ethics com., edn. com., chair legis. com.), Mich. Hospice Orgn. (chair edn. com., bd. dirs.). E-mail: pegomc@wimberley-tx.com.

MCCULLAGH, JANICE MARY, adult education educator; b. Minneapolis, Minnesota, July 22, 1949; d. Byron Wilford and Miriam Helene McCullagh; m. Roy Denton Sparkman; children: Shane, Benjamin, Tess. BFA, Drake U., Des Moines, Iowa, 1967—70; MA, U. Iowa, 1970—72; PhD, U. Tex., 1972—80. Instr. No. State U., Aberdeen, SD, 1972—73, U. North Tex., Denton, Tex., 1973—75; tchr. aid, grad student U. Tex., Austin, Tex., 1977; asst. prof. U. Nebr., Lincoln, Nebr., 1978—84, Southwestern U., Georgetown, Tex., 1984—85; instr. Temple Coll., Temple, Tex., 1987—89; assoc. prof. art history Baylor U., Waco, Tex., 1989—. Author: (periodical articles) Arts Mag.; Art Bull.; Ceramics Monthly; Internat. Directory of Arts and Artists; New Art Examiner; and others, (book contributions) August Macke, Albert Block, Artistic and Lit. Perspectives; Karl Umlenf, The

Journey. Mem.: Coll. Art Assn., Historians of German and Central European Art and Architecture, German Academic Exch. Svc. Avocations: travel, photography. Office: Baylor U Dept Art PO Box 7263 Waco TX 76798

MCCULLEY, LANA JANEEN, museum administrator, consultant; b. Berwyn, Ill., Sept. 15, 1976; d. Russell Alan and Lila June (Jones) McCulley; 1 child, Matthew. BS in Family & Consumer Sci., Ill. State U., 1998. Norary pub. Ill., 2000. Asst. curator Lois Jett Costume Collection, Ill. State U., Normal, 1998, McLean County Mus., Bloomington, 1998; constrn. coord. Spectra Site Comm., Chgo., 1999—2002; estimator EFCOO Corp., Bolingbrook, 2002—. Cons. Tastefully Simple, 2002—. Pres. PEacock Pl. COndo Assn., Berwyn, Ill., 2003—. Grantee, United Meth. ORgn., Mekendree Coll., Lebanon, Ill., 1995. Mem.: Kappa Omicron Nu. Avocations: travel, art, cooking.

MCCULLOCH, ANNE MERLINE JACOBS, college dean; b. L.A., Mar. 20, 1948; d. Merlin Lee and Edna (Rammell) J.; m. Arlyn Cecil McCulloch, Sept. 17, 1977 (div. Mar. 1993); children: Justin Jacobs, Caroline Ranawn. BA, Coll. of Charleston, 1971; D of Arts, Idaho State U., 1975. Cert. secondary tchr., Idaho; cmty. coll. cert., Calif. Caseworker Dept. Social Svcs., Newport News, Va., 1970-71; asst. prof., then assoc. prof. polit. sci. Idaho State U., Pocatello, 1975-86, prof., 1986-89, grad. dir. polit. sci. dept., 1977-87; prof. Columbia (S.C.) Coll., 1989—, chmn. dept. history and polit. sci., 1991-98, interim dir. Leadership Inst., 1990-91, dean evening coll. and external programs, 1998—. Cons. Shoshone/Bannock Tribes, Ft. Hall, Idaho, 1986-87, 97; cons. S.C. ednl. TV film Snowbird Cherokee, 1993-95. Contbg. author: Native Americans and Public Policy, 1992; editor Native Am. Policy Network Newsletter, 1995—; assoc. editor Ency. Minorities in American Politics, 1999; contbr. articles to profl. jours. Mem. Idaho Gov.'s Blue Ribbon Econ. Commn., 1982-83; co-program chmn. Elizabeth Cady Stanton Conf., Columbia, 1995. Mem. Am. Polit. Sci. Assn. (coord. Native Am. studies 1995-96), So. Polit. Sci. Assn., So. Polit. Sci. Assn., Phi Kappa Phi, Pi Sigma Alpha, Phi Alpha Theta. Democrat. Mem. Lds Ch. Avocations: gardening, running, home remodeling. Home: 437 Southlake Rd Columbia SC 29223-6601 Office: Columbia Coll Evening Coll Columbia SC 29203 E-mail: amcculloch@colacoll.edu.

MCCULLOCH, LINDA, state official; b. Mont., Dec. 21, 1954; m. Bill McCulloch, 1978. BA in Elem. Edn., MA in Elem. Edn., U. Mont. Tchr. Pub. Schs, Mont., Ashland, Missoula, Bonner, 1978—95; rep. Mont. Ho. of Reps., Boise, 1995—2001; supt. pub. instrn. Mont., 2002—. Mem. juvenile justice, mental health, judiciary, Indian Affairs coms. Mont. Ho. Reps., 1997; minority caucus leader Ho. Reps., Helena, Mont., 1999; vice chair edn. com. Mont. Ho. Reps., 1999. Mem., officer PTA Assn., Helena, 1985—; bd. dirs. Missoula Developmental Svcs. Corp.; mem. adv. com. Missoula Youth Homes Foster Care. Recipient Mike and Maureen Mansfield Libr. scholaship, 1995, J.C. Penny Vol. Program award, 1998. Mem.: AAUW, LWV, Five Valleys Reading Assn., Mont. State Reading Coun., Mont. Fedn. Tchrs., Mont. Ednl. Assn., Mont. Libr. Assn. (Legislator of Yr. award 1997), Mont. Family Union, Montana Dem. Womens Club. Office: Mont Office Pub Instruction 1227 11th Ave Helena MT 59620-2501

MCCULLOCH, RACHEL, economics researcher, educator; b. Bklyn., June 26, 1942; d. Henry and Rose (Offen) Preiss; m. Gary Edward Chamberlain; children: Laura Chamberlain Gehl, Neil Dudley Chamberlain. BA, U. Pa., 1962; MA in Teaching, U. Chgo., 1965, MA, 1971, PhD, 1973; student, MIT, 1966-67. Economist Cabinet Task Force on Oil Import Control, Washington, 1969; instr., then asst. prof. Grad. Sch. Bus. U. Chgo., 1971-73; asst. prof., then assoc. prof. econs. Harvard U., Cambridge, Mass., 1973-79, assoc. prof., then prof. econs. U. Wis., Madison, 1979-87; prof. Brandeis U., Waltham, Mass., 1987—, Rosen Family prof., 1989—, dir. Lemberg Program in Internat. Econs. and Fin., 1990-91, dir. PhD program Grad. Sch. Internat. Econs. and Fin., 1994—2001. Mem. Pres.'s Commn. on Indsl. Competitiveness, 1983-84; mem. adv. coun. Office Tech. Assessment, U.S. Congress, 1979-88; cons. World Bank, Washington, 1984-86; mem. com. on internat. rels. studies with People's Republic of China, 1984-91; rsch. assoc. Nat. Bur. Econ. Rsch., Cambridge, 1985-93; mem. adv. com. Inst. for Internat. Econs., Washington, 1987—; faculty Advanced Mgmt. Network, La Jolla, Calif., 1985-92; mem. com. examiners econs. test Grad. Record Exam. Ednl. Testing Svc., 1990-96, chair, 1992-96; mem. discipline adv. com. for Fulbright scholar awards in econs. Coun. Internat. Exch. Scholars, 1991-93, chair, 1992-93; mem. adv. com. for Fulbright Chairs Program, 1997; cons. Global Economy Project, Edn. Film Ctr., 1993-94; mem. study group on pvt. capital flows to developing and transitional economies Coun. Fgn. Rels., 1995-96, acad. adv. panel, Fed. Reserve Bank of Boston, 1999—; faculty assoc. Harvard Inst. for Internat. Devel., 1997-2000; fellow Internat. Leadership Forum, 2001-. Author: Research and Development as a Determinant of U.S. International Competitiveness, 1978; contbr. articles to profl. jours. and books. Grantee NSF, 1975-79, Hoover Inst., 1984-85, German Marshall Fund of U.S., 1985, Ford Found., 1985-88, U.S. Dept. Edn., 1990-91, Schulhof Found., 2001-02. Mem. Am. Econ. Assn. (dir. summer program for minority students 1983-84, mem. executive com., 1997-2000), Internat. Trade and Fin. Assn. (bd. dirs. 1993-95). Home: 10 Frost Rd Lexington MA 02420-1904 Office: Brandeis U Dept Econs MS 021 Waltham MA 02454 E-mail: mcculloch@brandeis.edu.

MCCULLOH, JUDITH MARIE, editor; b. Spring Valley, Ill., Aug. 16, 1935; d. Henry A. and Edna Mae (Traub) Binkele; m. Leon Royce McCulloh, Aug. 26, 1961. BA, Ohio Wesleyan U., 1956; MA, Ohio State U., 1957; PhD, Ind. U., 1970. Asst. to dir. Archives of Traditional Music, Bloomington, Ind., 1964-65; asst. editor U. Ill. Press, Champaign, 1972-77, assoc. editor, 1977-82, sr. editor, 1982-85, exec. editor, 1985—, dir. devel., 1992—2003; asst. dir., 1997—. Advisor John Edwards Meml. Forum, Los Angeles, 1973—. Mem. Editorial Bd. Jour. Am. Folklore, Washington, 1986-90; co-editor Stars of Country Music, 1975; editor (LP) Green Fields of Ill., 1963, (LP) Hell-Bound Train, 1964, Ethnic Recordings in America, 1982; gen. editor Music in American Life series. Trustee Am. Folklife Ctr., Libr. of Congress, Washington, 1986-2004, chair, 1990-92, 96-98. Fulbright grantee, 1958-59; NDEA grantee, 1961, 62-63; grantee Nat. Endowment for the Humanities, 1978; recipient Disting. Achievement citation Ohio Wesleyan U. Alumni Assn., Disting. Svc. award Soc. for Am. Music, Lifetime Achievement award Belmont U. Curb Music Industry, Disting. Achievement award Internat. Bluegrass Music Assn. Fellow: Am. Folklore Soc. (exec. bd. 1974—79, pres. 1986—87, exec. bd. 2001—03); mem.: Am. Musicological Soc., Am. Anthropol. Assn., Soc. Am. Music (1st v.p. 1989—93), Soc. for Ethnomusicology (treas. 1982—86). Democrat. Office: U Ill Press 1325 S Oak St Champaign IL 61820-6903 E-mail: jmmccull@uillinois.edu.

MCCULLOUGH, EILEEN (EILEEN MCCULLOUGH LEPAGE, ELLI MCCULLOUGH), financial consultant, writer, editor, educator; b. Phila., Oct. 16, 1946; d. Charles Norman and Marie Teresa (Inglesby) McCullough; m. Clifford Bennett LePage Jr., Mar. 6, 1970; children: Clifford Bennett III, Alexander Pierce. BA in English and Secondary Edn., George Washington U., 1969; MEd in Gifted Edn., Temple U., 1972. Cert. secondary sch. tchr.; registered securities rep. Record-keeper child growth and devel. program Children's Hosp. of Phila., 1965; with advt. dept. Phila. Inquirer, 1966-67; with ops. control U.S. Civil Svc. Commn., Washington, 1967-69; mgr. N.J. Bell Telephone, Trenton, 1969; researcher Temple U., Phila., 1969-71; tchr. Wyomissing (Pa.), 1972-77; fin. cons. various orgns., 1984-93; cons. EMLCommunications Cons. Co., Reading, 1994—. Adj. instr. Reading (Pa.) Area C.C., 1978-81; lectr. English Albright Coll., Reading, 1981-84; founding mem. Common Cents Investment Club, 1983-93; founding and mng. ptnr. Klein LePage McCullough Partnership, Ocean City, N.J., 1982-96; presenter in field. Author: The Clue in the Snow, 1959; editor: 1st Complete Pocket Guide to Atlantic City Casinos, 1984, The Autobiography of Capt. Michael Kevolic, 1986; photographer Cherry Hill Mtg. Bd. dirs. Nat. Found. March of Dimes, Reading, 1969-75, chmn., 1974-75; bd. sch. dirs. Wyomissing Area Sch. Dist., 1984-92; bd. dirs. Wyomissing Pub. Libr., Reading, 1980-85; asst. chmn Region 8 Pa. Sch. Bds. Assn., 1989-91; dir. Saturday Morning Sch., Assn. for Children with Learning Disabilities, Reading, 1970; acting sec. Berks County Commn. for Women, Reading, 1993; active Reading Community Players, 1980; past bd. mem. Berks Ballet Theatre; past vol. Berks C. of C.; vol. mus. guide Reading Pub. Mus. and Art Gallery, 1999-2002, Berks County Chpt Am. Red Cross, 1997; presenter Green Circle, Reading Berks Human Rels. coun., Reading Pub. Schs., 1998-99. Fellow Pa. writing project; mem. AAUW (life; topic chmn.), Am. Assn. Individual Investors (life), Internat. Platform Soc., Women's Internat. Fedn. for World Peace. Avocations: dance, singing. Home and Office: EMLCommunications Cons Co 10 Phoebe Dr Reading PA 19610-2857 Office: NJ Br PO Box 65 Somers Point NJ 08244 E-mail: akaellimay@aol.com.

MCCULLOUGH, KATHRYN T. BAKER, social worker; b. Trenton, Tenn., Jan. 5, 1925; d. John Andrew and Alma Lou (Wharey) Taylor; m. John R. Baker, Sept. 30, 1972 (dec. Oct. 1981); m. T.C. McCullough, May 14, 1988. BS, U. Tenn., 1945, MSW, 1954; postgrad., U. Chgo., 1950, Vanderbilt U., 1950-51. Lic. social worker, Tenn.; emeritus diplomate in clin. social work Am. Bd. Examiners. Home demonstration agt., agrl. extension svc. U. Tenn., Hardeman County, 1946-49; Dyer County, 1949-50; dir. med. social work dept. Le Bonheur Children's Hosp., Memphis, 1954-57; chief clin. social worker clinic mentally retarded children U. Tenn. Dept. Pediatrics, Memphis, 1957-59; clin. social worker Children's Med. Ctr., Tulsa, 1959-60; dir. med. social work dept. Coll. of Medicine U. Tenn., Memphis, 1960-69; dir. community svcs. regional med. program Coll. of Medicine, 1969-76; dir. regional clinic program Child Devel. Ctr. Coll. of Medicine, 1976-85; mem. faculty Coll. of Medicine, Coll. of Social Work U. Tenn., Memphis, 1960-85; social worker admissions rev. bd. Arlington Devel. Ctr., Memphis, 1976-98. Cons. Tenn. Dept. Children's Svcs., 1999—2003. Author 14 books. Commr. Dist. I, Gibson Utility Dist., Shelby County, Tenn., 1990—98; former bd. dirs. Am. Heart Assn., Am. Cancer Soc., Am. Lung Assn., United Cerebral Palsy, Goodwill Industries, AGAPE Child and Family Svcs., Health and Welfare Planning Coun., Shelby County Head Start, Greater Memphis Day Care Assn.; advisor AGAPE Child and Family Svcs., 1998—2001, field. rep., 2003—; mem. bd. visitors U. Tenn. Coll. Social Work, Knoxville, 2000—; active Gibson County Fedn. Dem., 1985—98, Dem. Party orgns., 1946—. Fellow: Am. Assn. Mental Retardation (life); mem.: AAUP, Tenn. Conf. on Social Welfare, Acad. Cert. Social Workers, Sigma Kappa Sorority (life). Mem. Ch. of Christ. Avocations: piano, organ, symphony. Home: 627 Riverside Yorkville Rd Trenton TN 38382-5917

MCCULLOUGH, MARY W. social work educator, therapist; b. Phila., Aug. 14, 1945; d. Harry and Mildred (Steel) Werner; children: Phoebe, Abbé. BA, Millersville (Pa.) U., 1968; MSW, U. N.C., 1971; PhD, Temple U., 1991. LCSW Pa. Caseworker Dept. Pub. Welfare, Reading, Pa., 1968-69, social worker Chester, Pa., 1971-73, Mental Health Ctr., Chester, 1973-76, Phila. Family Ctr., 1976-77; asst. prof. West Chester (Pa.) U., 1977-94, assoc. prof., 1994-97, prof., 1997—. Author: Black and White Women as Friends: Building Cross-race Friendships, 1999, With Nat. Guard. Recipient various acad. and svc. awards. Mem.: Nat. Comm. Assn. (chair women's caucus 1995—97). Democrat. Avocations: travel, gardening, snorkeling. Office: West Chester U 509 Main St West Chester PA 19383-0001 Home: 700 N Franklin St #222 West Chester PA 19380-2334

MCCULLY, EMILY ARNOLD, illustrator, writer; b. Galesburg, Ill., 1939; d. Wade E. and Kathryn (Maher) Arnold; m. George E. McCully, 1961 (div. 1975); children: Nathaniel, Tad. BA, Brown U., 1961; MA, Columbia U., 1964; LittD (hon.), Brown U., 2002. Author: How's Your Vacuum Cleaner Working? O'Henry Collection, 1977, A Craving, 1982, (novel) Picnic, 1984 (Christopher award), First Snow, 1985, (novel) Life Drawing, 1986, The Show Must Go On, 1987, School, 1987, You Lucky Duck!, 1988, New Baby, 1988, The Grandma Mix-up, 1988, The Christmas Gift, 1988, Zaza's Big Break, 1989, Grandma's at the Lake, 1990, The Evil Spell, 1990, Speak Up, Blanche!, 1991, Mirette on the Highwire, 1992 (Caldecott medal 1992), Grandma's at Bat, 1993, The Amazing Felix, 1993, My Real Family, 1994, Crossing The New Bridge, 1994, Little Kit, or: The Industrious Flea Circus Girl, 1995, The Pirate Queen, 1995, The Ballot Box Battle, 1996, The Bobbin Girl, 1996, Popcorn at the Palace, 1997, Starring Mirette and Bellini, 1997, an Outlaw Thanksgiving, 1998, Beautiful Warrior, 1998, Mouse Practice, 1999, Monk Camps Out, 2000, The Orphan Singer, 2001, Four Hungry Kittens, 2001; illustrator: Sea Beach Express, 1966, The Seventeenth Street Gang, 1966, Rex, 1967, Luigi of the Streets, 1967, That Mean Man, 1968, Gooney, 1968, Journey From Peppermint Street, 1968 (Nat. Book award 1969), The Mouse and the Elephant, 1969, The Fisherman, 1969, Tales from the Rue Brocca, 1969, Here I Am, 1969, Twin Spell, 1969, Hobo Toad and the Motorcycle Gang, 1970, Slip! Slop! Gobble!, 1970, Friday Night is Papa Night, 1970, Maxie, 1970, Steffie and Me, 1970, The Cat and the Parrot, 1970, Gertrude's Pocket, 1970, Go and Hush the Baby, 1971, Finders Keepers, 1971, Ma n Da La, 1971 (Bklyn. Mus. award 1976, N.Y. Pub. Libr. award 1976), Hurray for Captain Jane!, 1971, Michael Is Brave, 1971, Finding Out With Your Senses, 1971, Henry's Pennies, 1972, Jane's Blanket, 1972, Grandpa's Long Red Underwear, 1972, Girls Can Too!, 1972, The Boyhood of Grace Jones, 1972, Black Is Brown Is Tan, 1973, Isabelle the Itch, 1973, When Violet Died, 1973, That New Boy, 1973, How To Eat Fried Worms, 1973, Jenny's Revenge, 1974, Her Majesty, Grace Jones, 1974, Tree House Town, 1974, I Want Mama, 1974, Amanda, the Panda and the Redhead, 1975, The Bed Book, 1976, My Street's A Morning Cool Street, 1976, Professor Coconut and the Thief, 1977, Martha's Mad Dog, 1977, That's Mine, 1977, Where Wild Willie, 1978, No Help At All, 1978, Partners, 1978, The Twenty-Elephant Restaurant, 1978, What I Did Last Summer, 1978, The Highest Hit, 1978, I and Spraggy, 1978, Edward Troy and the Witch Cat, 1978, My Island Grandma, 1979, Whatever Happened to Beverly Bigler's Birthday?, 1979, Last Look, 1979, Ookie-Spooky, 1979, The Black Dog Who Went Into the Woods, 1980, How I Found Myself at the Fair, 1980, How We Got Our First Cat, 1980, Oliver and Allison's Week, 1980, Pajama Walking, 1981, The April Fool, 1981, I Dance in My Red Pajamas, 1982, The Halloween Candy Mystery, 1982, Go and Mush the Baby, 1982, Mitzi and the Terrible Tyrannosaurus Rex, 1983, Best Friend Insurance, 1983, Mail-Order Wings, 1984, Gertrude's Pocket, 1984, Fifth Grade Magic, 1984, The Ghastly Glasses, 1985, Fourth of July, 1985, The Explorer of Barkham Street, 1985, Wheels, 1986, Lulu and the Witch Baby, 1986, Richard and the Vratch, 1987, Molly, 1987, Molly Goes Hiking, 1987, Jam Day, 1987, The Boston Coffee Party, 1988, The Take-Along Dog, 1989, Selene Goes Home, 1989, The Magic Mean Machine, 1989, It Always Happens to Leona, 1989, The Grandpa Days, 1989, Dinah's Mad, Bad Wishes, 1989, Stepbrother Sabotage, 1990, Lulu Goes to Witch School, 1990, The Day Chubby Became Charles, 1990, The Christmas Present Mystery, 1990, Sky Guys to White Cat, 1991, Meatball, 1991, Leona and Ike, 1991, The Butterfly Birthday, 1991, Yankee Doodle Drumsticks, 1992, One Very Best Valentine's Day, 1992, Meet the Lincoln Lions Band, 1992, Jingle Bells Jam, 1992, In My Tent, 1992, Anne Flies the Birthday Bike, 1993, Amzat and His Brothers, 1993, Leo the Magnificent, 1996, Old Home Day, 1996, The Divide, 1997, Rabbit Pirates, 1999, Sing a Song of Piglets: A Calender in Verse, 2002.

MCCUNE, LINDA WILLIAMS, artist, educator; b. Dyersburg, Tenn., Sept. 29, 1950; d. Willard Charles and Margie Harrison Williams; m. William Derryman McCune II, Dec. 30, 1972; children: Nova Lauran, Tayce Caitlin. BFA, U. Tenn., 1974, postgrad., 1974-77; MFA, U. S.C., 1982. Cert. tchr. Tenn., S.C. Artist-illustrator U. Tenn., Knoxville, 1970-72; art history commentator Sta. WSJK-TV, Knoxville, 1971-72; artistic designer Morristown (Tenn.) Theatre Guild, 1971-78; artist in residence Morristown City Sch. Sys., 1972-77; asst. prof. art Walters State C.C., Morristown, 1973-77; display designer Laminite-Laminall Corp., Morristown, Tenn., 1975-76; co-owner Upstairs Gallery, Morristown, 1976-78; art cons. Allendale (S.C.) County Sch. Sys., 1979-80; co-owner Studio III Frame Shop, Allendale, 1979-86; grad. asst. U. S.C., Columbia, 1980-82, teaching assoc. Allendale, Walterboro, 1980-86; dir. Summer Art Series for Youth, Tryon, N.C., 1987-89; artist in residence S.C. Arts Commn. Residency Program, Columbia, 1987-89; mem. art faculty, leader fine arts Greenville (S.C.) Technical Coll., 1989—; grad. student advisor Vt. Coll., Montpelier, 1996—. Mem. fine arts com. Morristown C. of C., 1974—79, bicentennial com., 1975—76; sec. visual and environ. design panel Tenn. Arts Commn., Nashville, 1975—79; mem. fine arts com. Cmty. Devel. Bd., Allendale, 1980, downtown renovations com., 80; chmn. exhbns. com. Allendale County Arts Gallery and Mus., Allendale County Arts Coun., 1984—; mem. bd. Southeastern Art Assn., New Art Examiner Mag., Chgo., 1989—90; lectr. in field. One person shows include Archtl. Bldg. Gallery, U. Tenn., Knoxville, 1970, Morristown-Hamblen Libr., 1971, Walters State C.C., Morristown, 1974, 78, Jonesboro (Tenn.) Gallery, 1975, Appalachia State U., Boone, N.C., 1976, Emory and Henry Coll., Bristol, Va., 1976, Carrol Reese Mus. ETSU, Johnson City, Tenn., 1976, Kingsport (Tenn.) Fed., 1977, Rose Cultural Ctr. Mus., Morristown, 1978, U. S.C., Allendale, 1979, Weekend Gallery, Columbia Mus., 1980, Barnwell (S.C.) County Mus., 1982, Copland Wahl House, Columbia, 1982, Columbia Mus. Arts and Scis., 1983, Spirit Sq. Art Ctr., Charlotte, 1985, Nexus Contemporary Arts Ctr., Atlanta, 1986, Asheville (N.C.) Art Mus. Civic Ctr., 1990, Converse (S.C.) Coll., 1995, 291 Gallery, Greenville, 1996, Taylors (S.C.) First Bapt. Ch., 1997, Coastal Carolina U., Myrtle Beach, S.C., 1997, U. S.C., Spartanburg, 1997, S.C. Archives and History Ctr., Columbia, 1998, Pickens Mus., 2000, North Greenville Coll., 2002, Fine Arts Ctr. Kershaw, Conn., 2001; exhibited in group shows at Dublin Art Mus., Knoxville, 1974, Austin Peay State U., Nashville, 1976, Spoletto Festival at Dock St. Theatre, Charleston, S.C., 1979, Beaufort (S.C.) Art Assn., 1979, 80, 81, Miss. Mus. Art, Jackson, 1981, Tampa (Fla.) Mus., 1983, Alexandria Mus. Art, La., 1983, Roanoke (Va.) Mus. Fine Arts, 1983, McKissick Mus., Columbia, 1982, 83, 93, 95, 96, 98, 2000, Tucson Mus., 1983, Hunter Mus. Art, Chattanooga, 1985, Arrowmont Sch. Arts and Crafts, Gatlinburg, Tenn., 1985, Spartanburg (S.C.) Arts Ctr., 1985, Allendale County Mus., 1986, Columbia Mus. Arts and Scis., 1986, 90, The Upstairs Gallery, Tryon, N.C., 1987, 88, Women's Art Registry Minn., Mpls., 1986, Furman U., Greenville, 1988, 93, 97, 99, S.C. State Mus., Columbia, 1989, 92, 94, 99, 2000, 01, U. Ky., Lexington, 1990, Vista Arts Gallery, Columbia, 1991, Ownesboro (Ky.) Mus. Fine Arts, 1991, Havens Gallery, Columbia, 1992, Asheville Art Mus., 1993, Greenville County Mus., 1990, 93, 2001, 2002, Lee Hall Gallery, Clemson (S.C.) U., 1985, 95, Greenville Tehnical Coll., 1996, 97, 99, 2000, 01, U. S.C., Spartanburg, 1996, Columbia, 1996, Mobile (Ala.) Mus. Art, 1996, NationsBank Plz., Columbia, 1997, 2000, Rocky Mount (N.C.) Art Ctr., 1997, Fayetteville (N.C.) Mus. Art, 1997, Koller Gallery, Washington, 1997, The White House, Washington, 1998, 2001, Greensboro (S.C.) Cultural Art Ctr., 1998, Zone One Contemporary Gallery, Asheville, 1998, Lander U., Greenwood, S.C., 1998, North Charleston (S.C.) Rhodes Cultural Ctr. City Gallery, 1999, Wachovia Bank Bldg. Gallery, Greenville, 1999, Ashville, N.C., Arboretum, 2000, Burroughs-Chapin Mus., Myrtle Beach, S.C., 1999, Longwood Ctr. in the Visual Arts Farmville, Virginia, 2001, Brevard Coll., Brevard, N.C., 2000, Hartz Witzer Gallery, Charlotte, N.C., 2001, Wingate U., Wingate, N.C., 2001, Accessibility, Sumpter, S.C., 2001, 02, Moore Coll. Art and Design, Phila., Pa., 2002, W.H. Moring Gallery, Ashboro, N.C., 2002, Fine Arts Ctr., Greenville, S.C., 2003, Anderson Co. Art Ctr., 1999, 2000, 02, 03, Florence Mus. Art, S.C., 2003, Elon Coll., Burlington, N.C., 2003, U. N.C., Asheville, 2003, Meredith Coll., Raleigh, 2003, City Gallery and Redux Gallery, Charleston, 2003, Eastern Carolina U. Sch. Art, 2004, many others; contbr. articles to various publs. Tchr. Taylors (S.C.) First Bapt. Ch., 1988—; active PTA Bd., Buena Vista Elem., Greer, S.C., 1991-92. Recipient award, Tenn. Water Color All-State Show, 1974, Beaufort Art Assn. Exhbn., 1979, 1980, 1981, McKissisk Mus. Exhbn., 1982, Sandoz SCRA Regional Exhbn., 1986, Seneca County Art Coun. Exhibit, 1998, 1999, Upstate Visual Arts Millenium Exhbn., 2000, Andenson Arts Coun., 1999, 100 yrs. 100 artist award, S.C. State Mus., 2000; grantee, S.C. Visual Arts, 2001—02, S.C. Visual Arts Commn., 2001. Mem. Southeastern Coll. Art Assn., Upstate Visual Artists, Tri State Sculptors (S.C. state rep.), Wash. Sculptors Group, Met. Arts Coun. Avocations: traveling, visiting antique shows, collecting vintage broaches. Office: Greenville Tech Coll Visual Arts Dept PO Box 5616 Greenville SC 29606-5616 E-mail: sculp999@bellsouth.net., linda.mccune@gvltec.edu.

MCCUNE, SARA MILLER, foundation executive, publisher; b. N.Y.C., Feb. 4, 1941; d. Nathan M. and Rose (Glass) M.; m. George D. McCune, Oct. 16, 1966 (dec. May 1990). BA, Queens Coll., 1961. Asst. to v.p. sales Macmillan Pub. Co., N.Y.C., 1961-63; sales mgr. Pergamon Press Ltd., Oxford, England, 1963-64; pres., pub., founder Sage Publs. Inc., N.Y.C., 1965-66, pres., pub. Beverly Hills, Calif., 1966-83, pub., chmn. Newbury Park, Calif., 1984—; bd. dirs. Sage Publs. Ltd., London, chmn. 1990-95; bd. dirs. Sage Publs. India, New Delhi; pres. McCune Found., Newbury Park, Calif., 1990—. Mem. bd. dirs. UCSB Comm. Dept. Adv. Bd., Santa Barbara, Calif., 1994—, USCB Bd. Trustees, 1994—, The Fielding Inst., 1994—, Am. Acad. Pol. Scis., Phila., 1994—. Bd. dirs. USCB Found. Bd. Trustees, 1994—, sec., 1996-97, treas., 1997-98, vice chair, 1998—. Mem. Am. Evaluation Assn. (spl. award for disting. contbns. 1988). Office: Sage Publications Inc 2455 Teller Rd Newbury Park CA 91320-2234

MCCURDY, DONNA T. food products company executive; Degree in math., Case Western Res. U.; MBA, James Madison U. CPA, Va. Dir. acctg. Delmonte Corp., Charlottesville, Va.; CFO pvt. found. Charlottesville; corp. contr. Rocco Inc., Harrisonburg, Va., 1990-95, sr. v.p., CFO, 1996—. Mem. Phi Beta Kappa. Office: 1 Kratzer Ave Harrisonburg VA 22801-3939

MCCURDY, GISELA ANN, physician; b. Breslau, Germany, Aug. 10, 1917; came to U.S., 1951; d. Ernst and Elizabeth (Schimpff) Wohl; m. Frank C. McCurdy, Aug. 22, 1959 (dec. July 1986); 1 child, Carole Ann. BS, U. Perugia, Italy, 1939; MD, U. Graz, Austria, 1951. Lic. Ill. Med. State Bd., 1953. Rotating intern Chgo. Meml. Hosp., 1952-53; pathology resident Michael Reese Hosp., Chgo., 1953-54; internal medicine resident Belmont Hosp., Chgo., 1954-55; staff physician Mcpl. Tuberculosis Sanitarium, Chgo., 1955-58, sr. staff physician, 1958-65; dir. employees health Mt. Sinai Hosp., Chgo., 1965-70; staff physician Neighborhood Health Clinic, Chgo., 1970-72; pvt. practice Chgo., 1972-75; student health physician Cir. Campus U. Ill., Chgo., 1975-82. Mem. AMA, NOW, Planned Parenthood. Avocations: painting, sculpting, creative writing, walking.

MCCURLEY, MARY JOHANNA, lawyer; b. Baton Rouge, La., Oct. 3, 1953; d. William Edward and Leora Elizabeth (Block) Trice; m. Carl Michael McCurley, June 6, 1983; 1 stepchild, Melissa Reneé McCurley. BA, Centenary Coll., 1975; JD, St. Mary's U., 1979. Bar: Tex. 1979; cert. family law. Assoc. Martin, Withers & Box, Dallas, 1979-82; Raggio & Raggio, Inc., Dallas, 1982-83; ptnr. Bruner, McColl, McColloch & McCurley, Dallas, 1983-87; assoc., ptnr. Selligson & Douglass, Dallas, 1987-90; jr. ptnr. Koons, Fuller, McCurley & VanderEykel, Dallas, 1990-92; ptnr. McCurley, Orsinger, McCurley, & Nelson, Dallas, 1992—. Contbr. articles to profl. jours. Adv. Women's Service League, Dallas, 1993—. Mem.: Dallas Bar Assn., Tex. Acad. Family Law Specialist, Tex. State Bar Assn. (sec. 2001, vice-chair 2001, treas. 2001, chair 2003—, family law coun.), Dallas Bar Assn. (chair family law sect. 1985), Am. Acad. Matrimonial Lawyers (treas. Tex. chpt. 1993—95, sec. 1995—96, pres. 1997, pres. Tex. chpt. 1997—98, bd. govs. 2000, nat. sec. 2000—01, nat. v.p. 2003, nat. bd.

dirs.). Methodist. Avocations: golf, travel, jogging, horseback riding. Home: 4076 Hanover Ave Dallas TX 75225-7009 Office: McCurley Orsinger McCurley & Nelson LLP 5950 Sherry Ln Ste 800 Dallas TX 75225-6533 E-mail: maryjo@momn.com.

MCCURRY, MARGARET IRENE, architect, interior and furniture designer, educator; b. Chgo., Sept. 26, 1942; d. Paul D. and Irene B. McC.; m. Stanley Tigerman, Mar. 17, 1979. BA, Vassar Coll., 1964. Registered architect, Ill., Mass., Mich., Tex., Wis., Pa., Ind., Fla.; registered interior designer, Ill. Design coord. Quaker Oats Co., Chgo., 1964-66; sr. interior designer Skidmore, Owings & Merrill, Chgo., 1966-77; pvt. practice architect Margaret I, Chgo., 1977-82; ptnr. Tigerman, McCurry, Chgo., 1982—. Vis. studio critic Art Inst. Chgo., 1985-86, 88, 98, lectr., 1988, 98; vis. studio critic U. Ill., Chgo., Miami U., Oxford, Ohio, 1990; juror Internat. furniture awards Progressive Architecture mag., N.Y.C., 1986, advt. awards, 1988; juror design grants Nat. Endowment for Arts, Washington, 1983; NEA Challenge Design Rev., 1992; peer reviewer design excellence program Gen. Svcs. Administrn., 1992—; juror, Wis., Minn., Calif., Va., Washington, Pitts., Ky., Ga. Conn. Soc. Architects, Detroit, N.Y.C., Memphis, Austin, L.A. chpts. AIA, Am. Wood Coun., AIA Students Design Competition, 1993. Author: Margaret McCurry: Constructing 25 Short Stories, 2000; contbr. Chgo. Archtl. Club Jour.; designer, contbr. archtl. exhibit Art Inst. Chgo., 1983-85, 93, 99, Chgo. Hist. Soc., 1984, Gulbenkian Found., Lisbon Portugal, 1989, Chgo. Athenaeum, 1990, Gwenda Jay Gallery, 1992, Women of Design Traveling Exhbn., 1992-96; archtl. drawings and models in permanent collection Art Inst. Chgo. and Deutsches Architektur Mus., Frankfurt. Chmn. furniture sect. fundraising auction Sta. WTTW-TV, PBS, Chgo., 1975-76; mem. Chgo. Beautiful Com., 1968-70; pres. alumni coun. Grad. Sch. Design, Harvard U., 1997-2000; bd. dirs. Architecture and Design Soc. Art Inst. Chgo., 1988-97, mem. textile adv. bd. textile dept. Loeb fellow Harvard U., 1986-87; recipient Builders Choice Grand award Builders Mag., 1985, Interior Design award Interiors Mag., 1983, Dean of Architecture award Chgo. Design Source and the Merchandise Mart, 1989, Designer of Distinction award ASID, 2002; inducted into Interior Design Hall of Fame, Interior Design Mag., 1990. Fellow AIA (v.p. bd. dirs. Chgo. chpt. 1984-89, chair 1993, nat. design com., lectr. Colo. chpt. 1985, nat. conv. 1988, 97-98, Monterey Design Conf. 1989, Washington Design Ctr. 1989, Nat. Honor award 1984, Nat. Interior Architecture award 1992, 98, Disting. Bldg. award Chgo. chpt. 1984, 86, 91, 94, 99-2000, Disting. Interior Architecture award 1981, 83, 88, 91, 97, product display Neocon award 1985, 88, Gold award best of Neocon 1998, ALA Silver Medal Design award 2003), Coll. of Fellows AIA, Internat. Interior Design Assn., Chgo. Network, Am. Soc. Interior Designers (v.p. bd. dirs. Chgo. chpt., Nat. Design award 1992, 94, Ill. chpt. Design award 1994, Ill. chpt. Merit award 1994, Designer Distinction award, 2002), Chgo. Archtl. Club, Arts Club Chgo., Womens Athletic Club, Harvard Alumni Assn. (dir. 2000—). Episcopalian. Avocations: drawing, writing, travel, golf, gardening. Office: Tigerman McCurry Archs 444 N Wells St Chicago IL 60610-4501 Office Phone: 312-644-5880. Business E-Mail: mimccurry@tigerman-mccurry.com.

MCCURRY, STEPHANIE, historian, educator; BA, U. Western Ont., 1981; MA, U. Rochester, 1983; PhD, SUNY, Binghamton, 1988. Asst. prof. U. Calif., San Diego, 1988—94, assoc. prof., 1994—98, Northwestern U., Evanston, Ill., 1998—. Mem. grad. student award com. CCHWP-CGWH/Berkshire Conf. Women Historians, 1993, 94; mem. award selection com. NEH, 1995; dir. Calif. History Project U. Calif., San Diego, 1996—98; dir. Alice Berline Kaplan Ctr. for the Humanities Northwestern U., Evanston, 2002—03; reviewer Oxford U. Press, U. N.C. Press, Harvard U. Press, U. Ill. Press, Johns Hopkins U. Press, U. Ga. Press; referee Am. Hist. Rev., Jour. Am. History, Gender and History, Jour. So. History, Ark. Hist. Quarterly; lectr. in field. Author: Masters of Small Worlds: Yeoman Households, Gender Relations and the Political Culture of the Antebellum South Carolina Low Country, 1995 (nominated for Pulitzer prize in history, 1995); contbr. articles to profl. jours. Recipient Frances Weir prize for history and lit., U. Western Ont., 1981, John Hope Franklin prize, Am. Studies Assn., 1996; fellow, John Simon Guggenheim Meml. Found., 2003; grantee, Am. Coun. Learned Socs., 1990; Rush Rhees and History Dept. fellow, U. Rochester, 1981—83, Doctoral fellow, Social Scis. and Rsch. Coun. Can., 1983—85, Smithsonian Instn., 1985—86, AAUW, 1986—87, Vis. scholar, Inst. for Rsch. on Women and Gender, Stanford U., 1994—95. Mem.: Am. Hist. Assn. (mem. Joan Kelly prize com. 1997—99), So. Assn. Women Historians (chair Willie Lee Rose prize 1999, mem. A. Elizabeth Taylor prize com. 1996, Willie Lee Rose prize 1997), So. Hist. Assn. (chair Francis B. Simkins award com. 1999—2001, mem. program com. ann. meeting 1997, Charles Sydnor prize 1996, Francis Butler Simkins prize 1997), Orgn. Am. Historians (co-chair program com. 2003). Office: Northwestern Univ Dept History Harris Hall #202 1881 Sheridan Rd Evanston IL 60208

MCCUTCHEN, TAMMY DEE, federal agency administrator; b. Kewanee, Ill., Oct. 20, 1965; BA, Western Ill. U.; JD, Northwestern U. Clk. U.S. Ct. Appeals (7th cir.), 1991—92; assoc. Skadden, Arps, Slate, Meagher and Flom, Chgo., 1992—95, Matkov, Salzman, Madoff anf Gunn, 1995—99; sr. counsel Hershey Foods Corp., 1999—2001; adminstr. wage and hour divsn. U.S. Dept. Labor, Washington, 2001—. Office: US Dept Labor 200 Constitution Ave NW Washington DC 20210

MCDANIEL, ANNA S. language educator; b. Van Buren, Ark., Dec. 10, 1940; d. John Dean and Virginia (Linn) Maurer; m. Johnny F. McDaniel, June 30, 1987; children: Johnny Lee, Elisabeth Rice, Kyle Page. BA, Sonoma State U., 1978; MEd, Texas A&M, 1989. Cert. Tex. tchr. Educator-English Spkrs. Other Langs. Dallas Ind. Sch. Dist., Dallas, 1987—2004; coord. Critical World Langs. Bryan Adams H.S., Dallas, 1989—; ret., 2004. Contbr. mags. including Education West Mag., 2001. Named Outstanding Russian Facilitator, Russian Am. Ctr., Dallas, Tex., 2000; recipient Process Innovation award, Kenesis Corp., 2001. Mem.: DAR. Conservative. Episcopalian. Avocation: travel.

MCDANIEL, JAN, television station executive; b. St. Louis, June 27, 1951; BA in Journalism, U. Mo., 1973. Pres., gen. mgr. Sta. KAKE-TV, 1991-96; gen. mgr. Sta. WCCO-TV, Mpls., 1996—. Mem. Women in Comm. Office: Sta WCCO-TV 90 S 11th St Minneapolis MN 55403-2414

MCDANIEL, JANET B. principal; b. Fort Carson, Colo., Mar. 03; d. Atsuko Barber; m. Robert M. III McDaniel, July 31, 1982; children: Robert IV, Kristin. BS in Secondary Edn., Gardner-Webb Coll., Boiling Springs, N.C., 1983; MS in Prin.-Sch. Adminstrn., Appalachian State U., Boone, N.C., 2000. Interpreter for the deaf Western Piedmont C.C., Morganton, NC, 1982—83; tchr. Burke County Pub. Schs., Morganton, 1983—96, N.C. Sch. for the Deaf, Morganton, 1996—98, prin., 1998—. Coach Nat. Sci. Olympiad, 1990—92. Named Tchr. of the Yr., Burke County Pub. Schs./Hildebran Jr. H.S., 1984, 1985, Burke County Pub. Schs./Liberty Jr. H.S., 1990, Lioness of the Yr., 1984, Region 7 Sci. Tchr. of the Yr., 1991. Office: North Carolina Sch for the Deaf 517 W Fleming Dr Morganton NC 28655

MCDANIEL, MYRA ATWELL, lawyer, former state official; b. Phila., Pa, Dec. 13, 1932; d. Eva Lucinda (Yores) Atwell; m. Reuben Roosevelt McDaniel Jr., Feb. 20, 1955; children: Diane Lorraine, Reuben Roosevelt III. BA, U. Pa., 1954; JD, U. Tex., 1975; LLD, Huston-Tillotson Coll., 1984, Jarvis Christian Coll., 1986. Bar: Tex. 1975, U.S. Dist. Ct. (we. dist.) Tex. 1977, U.S. Dist. Ct. (so. and no. dists.) Tex. 1978, U.S. Ct. Appeals (5th cir.) 1978, U.S. Supreme Ct. 1978, U.S. Dist. Ct. (ea. dist.) Tex. 1979. Asst atty. gen. State of Tex., Austin, 1975-81, chief taxation div., 1979-81, gen. counsel to gov., 1983-84, sec. of state, 1984-87; asst. gen. counsel Tex. R.R. Commn., Austin, 1981-82; gen. counsel Wilson Cos., San Antonio and Midland, Tex., 1982; assoc. Bickerstaff, Heath & Smiley, Austin, 1984, ptnr., 1987-96; mng. ptnr. Bickerstaff, Heath, Smiley, Pollan, Kever & McDaniel, Austin, Tex., 1996—2000, of counsel, 2003. Mem. asset. mgmt. adv. com. State Treasury, Austin, 1984-86; mem. legal affairs com. Criminal Justice Policy Coun., Austin, 1981-8, Inter-State Oil Compact, Oklahoma City, 1981-86, bd. dirs. Austin Cons. Group, 1983-86; mem. Jud. Efficiency Coun., Austin, 1995-96; lectr. in field. Contbr. articles to profl. jours., chpts. to books Del. Tex. Conf. on Librs. and Info. Sci., Austin, 1978, White House Conf. on Librs. and Info. Scis., Washington, 1979; mem. Libr. Svcs. and Constrn. Act Adv. Coun., 1980-84, chmn., 1983-84; mem. long range plan task force Brackenridge Hosp., Austin, 1981; clk. vestry bd. St. James Episcopal Ch., Austin, 1981-83, 89-90; bd. visitors U. Tex. Law Sch., 1983-87, vice chmn., 1983-85; bd. dirs. Friends of Ronald McDonald House Ctrl. Tex., Women's Advocacy, Inc., Capital Area Rehab. Ctr.; trustee Episcopal Found. Tex., 1986-89, St. Edward's U., Austin, 1986—, chmn. acad. com., 1988-2002, vice chair, 2002-; chmn. divsn. capital area campaign United Way, 1986; active nat. adv. bd. Leadership Am.; trustee Episcopal Sem. S.W., 1990-96, Assn. Governing Bds. Univs. and Colls., Leadership Edn. Arts Program, 1995—; adv. bd. mem. Women Basketball Coaches Assn., 1996-99; bd. dirs. U.Tex. Law Sch. Found., 1997-98, Wells Fargo Cmty. Bd., Ctrl. Tex., 2000—; trustee Episcopal Health Charities, 1997—. Recipient Tribute to 28 Black Women award Concepts Unltd., 1983; Focus on women honoree Serwa Yetu chpt. Mt. Olive grand chpt. Order of Eastern Star, 1979, Woman of Yr. Longview Metro C. of C., 1985, Woman of Yr. Austin chpt. Internat. Tng. in Communication, 1985, Citizen of Yr. Epsilon Iona chpt. Omega Psi Phi, Lone Star Girl Scout Coun. Women of Distinction, 1997, Profiles in Power Austin Bus. Jour., 1999, Silent Samaritan award Samaritan Counseling Ctr., 2000. Master Inns of Ct.; mem. ABA, Am. Bar Found., Tex. Bar Found. (trustee 1986-89), Travis County Bar Assn., Travis County Women Lawyers' Assn., Austin Black Lawyers Assn., State Bar Tex. (chmn. Profl. Efficiency & Econ. Rsch. subcom. 1976-84), Golden Key Nat. Honor Soc., Longhorn Assocs. for Excellence in Women's Athletes (adv. coun. 1988—), Order of Coif (hon. mem.), Omicron Delta Kappa, Delta Phi Alpha. Democrat. Office: Bickerstaff Heath Smiley Pollan Keever & McDaniels 1700 First Bank Plz 816 Congress Ave Austin TX 78701-2443 Office Phone: 512-472-8021. E-mail: mmcdaniel@bickerstaff.com.

MCDANIEL, OLA JO PETERSON, retired social worker, educator; b. Hot Springs, Ark., Sept. 17, 1951; d. Milton Paul and Ella Floyd (Dickerson) Peterson; m. Daniel Tillman McDaniel, June 11, 1994; 1 child, Cadra Peterson. B Music Edn., Henderson State Coll., Arkadelphia, Ark., 1973; MA in Edn., Lindenwood Colls., St. Charles, Mo., 1983, cert. in social studies, 1977. Cert. tchr., Mo., Ark. Faculty Sch. Dist. St. Charles, 1974-84; adj. faculty Garland County C.C., Hot Springs, 1988-90; social worker Ark. Dept. Human Svcs., Hot Springs, 1990-94; substitute tchr. Hot Springs Sch. Dist., 1994-95; tutor St. Michael's Sch., Hot Springs, 1995—96; substitute tchr. Mt. Pine (Ark.) Sch. Dist., 1997-98. Substitute tchr. Mt. Pine Sch. Dist., 1997-98; soloist Congr. House of Israel, Hot Springs, 1965-73; cons. scholarships Hot Springs Music Club, 1988; const. student performance Garland County C.C., Hot Springs, 1988. Author, contbr. (learning activities) 3 R's for the Gifted: Reading, Writing, Research, 1982. Active Hot Springs Mid. Sch. PTO, 1996—98; vol. Hot Springs H.S.; founding mem. Friends of the Clinton Presdl. Libr., Nt. Campaign for Tolerance, 2003; hon. mem. Nat. Steering Com. to Reelect the Pres., Washington, 1995; mem. Dem. Nat. Com., Washington, 1994—, Pres.'s 2d Term Com., Washington, 1997; vol. Hot Springs Mayoral Campaign, 1993, Dem. Gubernatorial campaign, Hot Springs, 1990, Dem. campaign U.S. Congress Dist. 4, 2000; historian Virginia Clinton Kelley Dem. Women's Club of Garland County; mem. Dem. Ctrl. Com. of Garland County; vol. Garland County Dem. Hdqs., 2002. Recipient certs. of appreciation, St. Chrysostom's Am. Episcopal Ch., Hot Springs, 1990, Nat. Mus. Am. Indian, Washington, 1995, Alpha Chi, 1997, Hot Springs Mid. Sch., 1998, Parent Vol. award, 1998, Gov.'s Vol. Excellence award, 1997, 1998, cert. of recognition, Dem. Nat. Com., 2002. Mem.: AAUW, Nat. Campaign for Tolerance. A project of the Southern Poverty Law Center, Clinton Birthplace Foundation, Lindenwood Alumni, Henderson Alumni, Nat. Mus. Women in Arts (cert. appreciation 1997). Democrat. Roman Catholic. Avocations: advocate of welfare reform, reading, music. Home: 102 Woodberry St Hot Springs National Park AR 71913-2806

MCDANIEL, SARA SHERWOOD (SALLY MCDANIEL), trainer, consultant; b. St. Louis, Apr. 24, 1943; d. Edward Leighton and Dolores Edic (Pitts) Sherwood; m. Allen Polk McDaniel, Dec. 29, 1967; children: James Polk, Fontaine Maury. AA, Mt. Vernon Coll., 1963; BS, Vanderbilt U., 1965. Tchr. Kanawha Valley Schools, Charleston, W.Va., 1965-66, Fulton County Schools, Atlanta, 1966-68, Trinity Sch., 1969-71; tournament dir. Atlanta Classic, 1972-77; dir. alumni affairs Leadership Atlanta, 1988-89; pvt. practice cons., trainer Atlanta, 1988—. Bd. dirs. AID Atlanta, The High Mus. Art, Leadership Coun. Kennedy Ctr. of Vanderbilt U., UNICEF-Atlanta, The Atlanta Women's Found., Leadership Atlanta. Bd. dirs. Girl Scouts U.S., Ga., High Mus. Art, Atlanta Opera, UNICEF Atlanta, Aid Atlanta, Fine Art Collectors; active Com. on Women and Minorities for 1996 Olympics; mem. exec. com. Leadership Atlanta, Jr. League; mem. Friends of Spelman; trustee Mt. Vernon Coll.; bd. chair Atlanta Women's Fund. Mem. Am. Soc. Trainers and Dirs., Atlanta Women's Network (bd. dirs., pres.), Vanderbilt U. Alumni Assn., Alumni Assn. Peabody Coll., The Atlanta Girls Sch. Presbyterian.

MCDANIEL, SUE POWELL, writer, speaker; b. Jefferson City, Mo., Mar. 13, 1946; d. Ernest Gayle and Ruth Angeline (Raithel) Powell; m. Walter Lee Zimmerman, Aug. 14, 1966 (div. 1980); m. Olin Cleve McDaniel, June 23, 1985 (div. 2002). BS in Edn., U. Mo., 1968, MEd in Edn., 1977, EdS, 1980, PhD, 1985. Cert. tchr., Mo. Tchr. Jefferson City Pub. Schs., 1968-80; fiscal assoc. Mo. Coordinating Bd. for Higher Edn., Jefferson City, 1980-90; exec. dir. Mo. Women's Coun., Jefferson City, 1990-99; exec. dir. Skillpath Seminars, 2000—03; pres. Alternatives, Jefferson City, Mo., 1999—; dir. Heisinger Hope Found., 2004. Author: (with C. Dixon) Learning, Changing, Leading: Keep to Success in the 21st Century, 1998, I.M. Heart, 2004; co-author: Missouri Women Today, 1993, Status of the Women, 1994,. Mem. Zonta Internat. Avocations: reading, music, drawing, flower garden, photography. Home: 1600 Stadium Blvd Jefferson City MO 65109-2418

MCDANIELS, AUDREY EVELYN, microbiologist; b. Grants Pass, Oreg., Feb. 11, 1928; d. Charles Pixley and Ruby Clark Best; divorced; 1 child, David Douglas. BS in Microbiology, Oreg. State U., 1950; BS in Edn., U. Wash., 1964; MS in Gen. Scis., Oreg. State U., 1965; PhD in Environ. Sci., U. Mich., 1980. Jr. scientist GE, Hanford, Wash., 1950-53; microbiologist City of Seattle, 1954-57, Wash. State Pub. Health, Seattle, 1957-60; 4th grade tchr. Amity (Oreg.) Elem., 1965-68; biology tchr. Rainier (Oreg.) H.S., 1968-72; microbiologist EPA, Cin., 1980—. Home: 1029 Fashion Ave Cincinnati OH 45238 Office: US EPA 26 W Martin Luther King Dr Cincinnati OH 45268

MCDARRAH, GLORIA SCHOFFEL, editor, author; b. Bronx, N.Y., June 22, 1932; d. Louis and Rose Schoffel; m. Fred W. McDarrah, Nov. 5, 1960; children: Timothy, Patrick. BA in French, Pa. State U., 1953; MA in French, NYU, 1966. Editorial asst. Crowell-Collier, N.Y.C., 1957-59; exec. asst. to pub. Time Inc., N.Y.C., 1959-61; libr., tchr. N.Y.C. Pub. Schs. and St. Luke's Sch., 1972-76; exec. asst. to pres. Capital Cities Communications Inc., N.Y.C., 1972-76; analyst N.Y.C. Landmarks Preservation Commn., 1976-79; project editor Grosset & Dunlap Inc., N.Y.C., 1979-80; sr. editor Prentice Hall trade div. Simon & Schuster Inc., N.Y.C., 1980-88; pres. McDarrah Media Assocs., N.Y.C., 1988—. Editor book rev. The Picture Profl., 1989—; book reviewer Pub.'s Weekly, 1994—. Author: Frommer's Guide to Va., 1992, Frommer's Guide to Va. 2d edit., 1994—95, Frommer's Atlantic City and Cape May, 1984, Frommer's Atlantic City and Cape May 4th edit., 1991, Frommer's Atlantic City and Cape May 5th edit., 1993—95, The Artist's World 2d edit., 1988, Photography Encyclopedia, 1999; co-author: Museums in N.Y. 5th edit., 1990, Photography Marketplace, 1975, The Beat Generation: Glory Days in Greenwich Village, 1996, Anarchy, Protest and Rebellion and the Counter-Culture That Changed Am., 2003; co-editor: Exec. Desk Diary Saturday Rev., 1962—64; contbg. editor (quar.): Dollarwise Traveler, Fodor's Cancun, Cozumel, Yucatan Peninsula, Fodor's Ariz.

MCDAVID, JANET LOUISE, lawyer; b. Mpls., Jan. 24, 1950; d. Robert Matthew and Lois May (Bratt) Kurzeka; m. John Gary McDavid, June 9, 1973; 1 child, Matthew Collins McDavid. BA, Northwestern U., 1971; JD, Georgetown U., 1974. Bar D.C. 1975, U.S. Ct. Appeals (fed. cir.) 1975 (D.C. cir. 1976), U.S. Supreme Ct. 1980, U.S. Ct. Appeals (5th cir.) 1983, (9th cir.) 1986. Assoc. Hogan & Harston, Washington, 1974-83, ptnr., 1984—. Gen. counsel ERAmerica, 1977-83; mem. antitrust task force Dept. Defense, 1993-94, 96-97; mem. antitrust coun. U.S. C. of C., 1994—; advisor Bush adminstrn. transition team, 2001. Contbr. articles to profl. jours. Participant Clinton and Bush adminstrn. transition team FTC. Mem. ABA (antitrust sect., vice chmn. civil practice com. 1986-89, sect. 2 com. 1989-90, chmn. franchising com. 1990-91, coun. mem. 1991-94, program officer 1994-97, vice chair 1997-98, chair-elect 1998-99, chair 1999-2000, immediate past chair, governing com. of forum on franchising 1991-97), ACLU, U.S. C. of C. (antitrust coun. 1995—), Washington Coun. Lawyers, D.C. Bar Assn., Fed. Bar Assn., Womens Legal Def. fund. Democrat. Office: Hogan & Hartson 555 13th St NW Washington DC 20004-1109 E-mail: jlmcdavid@hhlaw.com.

MCDAVID, SARA JUNE, librarian; b. Atlanta, Dec. 21, 1945; d. William Harvey and June (Threadgill) McRae; m. Michael Wright McDavid, Mar. 20, 1971. BA, Mercer U., 1967; MLS, Emory U., 1969. Head librarian Fernbank Sci. Ctr., Atlanta, 1969-77; dir. rsch. libr. Fed. Res. Bank of Atlanta, 1977-81; mgr. mem. services SOLINET, Atlanta, 1981-82; media specialist Parkview High Sch., Atlanta, 1982-84; ptnr. Interncontinental Travel, Atlanta, 1984-85; librarian Wesleyan Day Sch., Atlanta, 1985-86; mgr. info. svcs. Internat. Assn. Fin. Planning, Atlanta, 1986-90; dir. rsch. Korn Ferry Internat., Atlanta, 1990-95; Atlanta rsch. coord. Lamalie Amrop Internat., Atlanta, 1995-98; dir. practice splty. teams LAI Ward Howell, 1998; prin. McDavid Rsch. Assocs., Atlanta, 1998-99; lead rschr. The Boston Consulting Group, Atlanta, 1999—. Bd. dirs. Southeastern Library Network, Atlanta, 1977-80, vice chmn. bd., 1979-80. Contbr. articles to profl. jours. Pres., mem. exec. com. Atlanta Humane Soc., 1985-86, bd. dirs. aux., 1978-90. Mem. Ga. Libr. Assn. (v.p. 1981-83), Spl. Librs. Assn. (treas. libr. mgmt. divsn. 1998-2000, editor Libr. Mgmt. Quar. 1996-98, 2002). Home: 1535 Knob Hill Dr NE Atlanta GA 30329-3206 Office: Boston Consulting Group Inc 600 Peachtree St NE Ste 3800 Atlanta GA 30308-2218 E-mail: mcdavid.sara@bcg.com.

MCDEMMOND, MARIE VALENTINE, academic administrator, consultant; b. New Orleans, Feb. 4, 1946; d. George Graham and Marie Valentine (Prudeaux) McD.; m. Louis Saulny, June 15, 1966 (div. 1972); children: Alan Peter, Eric W. Reid; m. Roy Russell Mouton, Sept. 18, 1987. BA, Xavier U., 1968; MEd, U. New Orleans, 1971; postgrad, SUNY, Albany; EdD, U. Mass., 1985. Tchr. Kohn Jr. High Sch., New Orleans, 1968-70; dir. Community Leadership Program, New Rochelle, N.Y., 1970-72, Community Leadership Consortium, Westchester County, N.Y., 1972-73; assoc. Higher Edn. Opportunity Program Office, Albany, N.Y., 1973-74; instr. dept. edn. Ithaca (N.Y.) Coll., 1974; with bus. office, dept. acctg. Bronx (N.Y.) Phychiatric Ctr., 1974-77; assoc. higher edn. N.Y. State Bd. Regents, Albany, 1977-78; dir. fin. Mass. Bd. Regional Community Colls., Boston, 1979-80; assoc. vice chancellor U. Mass., Amherst, 1980-84; v.p. budget & fin. Atlanta U., 1984-85; asst. v.p. for fin. Emory U., Atlanta, 1985-86; pres. McDemmond & Assoc., Boca Raton, Fla., 1986-89; asst. prof. edn. U. New Orleans, 1987-88; asst. v.p. adminstrn. & fin. Fla. Atlantic U., Boca Raton, 1988-89, v.p. adminstrn. & fin., 1990-96; pres. Norfolk (Va.) State U., 1996—. Adj. asst. prof. Coll. New Rochelle, N.Y., 1971-73; adj. prof. edn. U. Mass., Amherst, 1984; hostess Sta. WTCC, Springfield, Mass., 1983-84; lectr. in economic redevel., 1989. Author tng. course. Civil svc. examiner State N.Y., Albany, 1976-78; precinct coord. Democrats for Jackson, Amherst, 1984; advisor Palm Beach Judicial Bldg., West Palm Beach, Fla., 1991. Named Fla. Woman Who Makes a Difference Nat. Assn. Women Bus. Owners, 1990. Mem. Bus. and Profl. Women's Club Am. (Woman of Achievement award 1991), New England Minority Women (pres. 1982-84), So. Assn. Coll. and Bus. Officers (exec. com. 1991—), Nat. Assn. Coll. and Univ. Bus. Officers, Coun. Minority Edn. (pres. 1982-84). Roman Catholic. Avocations: gardening, reading. Office: Norfolk State U 700 Park Ave Norfolk VA 23504-8090

MCDERMID, MARGARET E. information technology executive, engineer; B in bus., Mary Baldwin Coll.; MBA, U. Richmond. With Stone and Webster Engring. Corp.; joined Va. Power, 1982, various positions engring. & construction dept., 1982—86, dir. adminstrv. svcs., 1986—98; v.p. info. tech., CIO Dominion Resources Inc., 1998—2000, sr. v.p. info. tech., CIO, 2000—. Mem. apptd. by Gov. Gilmore CIO Adv. Bd., 2000. Active with United Way, Big Brothers, Big Sisters; bd. trustees Mary Baldwin Coll.; found. bd. J. Sargeant Reynolds Cmty. Coll.; bd. dirs. Greater Richmond Tech. Coun., Children's Mus. Richmond Bus. Com., CIO Forum; mem. Va. Rsch. and Tech. Adv. Coun. Achievements include first woman to enter the Apprentice Program at Newport News Shipyard where she completed the Patternmaker's program. Office: Dominion Resources Inc 120 Tredegar St Richmond VA 23219 Office Phone: 804-819-2000.*

MCDERMOTT, AGNES CHARLENE SENAPE, philosophy educator; b. Hazelton, Pa., Mar. 11, 1937; d. Charles G. and Conjetta (Ranieri) Senape; children: Robert C., Lisa G., Jamie C. BA, U. Pa., 1956, PhD, 1964; postgrad., U. Calif.-Berkeley, 1960—61, U. Amsterdam, Netherlands, 1965, U. Wis., 1967—69. Instr. math. Drexel Inst. Tech., Phila., 1962-63; asst. prof. philosophy SUNY-Buffalo, 1964-65, Hampton Inst., Va., 1966-67; asst. prof. U. Wis.-Milw., 1967-70; assoc. prof. philosophy U. N.Mex., Albuquerque, 1970-80, prof., dean grad. studies, 1981-86; dean in residence Coun. of Grad. Schs., Washington, 1985-86; provost, v.p. acad. affairs CUNY, 1986-89, prof. philosophy, 1986-91; dean for acad. and student affairs, cons. Albuquerque Acad., 1991-93; ind. cons. Corrales, N.Mex., 1993—. Vis. assoc. prof. U. Wash., Seattle, 1974, U. Calif.-Berkeley, 1973-74, U. Hawaii, Honolulu, 1975; vis. prof. U. Calif.-Berkeley, 1980; vis. prof. Semester at Sea, U. Pitts., fall 1994; bd. dir. Juvenile Diabetes Rsch. Found.; lectr., panelist in field. Author: An Eleventh Century Buddhist Logic of 'Exists', 1969, Boethius' Treatise on the Modes of Signifying, 1980; compiler, editor anthology: Comparative Philosophy: Selected Essays, 1983; rev. editor Phil. East West, 1986—; contbr. articles and stories to profl. and literary jours. Active Albuquerque Care Alliance, 1988-2000. AAUW postdoctoral fellow, 1965-66; NEH Younger Humanist fellow, 1971-72; faculty rsch. fellow U. N.Mex., 1978, 79, 80; U. Pa. grad. fellow, 1961-62; S. Fels Found. fellow, 1963-64; U. Pa. tuition scholar; Pa. Hist. Soc. scholar Mem. N.Y. Acad. Scis., Am. Philos. Soc., Am. Philos. Assn. (exec. com. 1977-80), Assn. Asian Studies (exec. com. 1977-80), Am. Oriental Soc., Western Assn. Grad. Schs. (pres. 1986-87), N.Mex. Juvenile Diabetes Rsch. Found., Phi Beta Kappa, Pi Mu Epsilon. Democrat. Avocations: skiing, fly-fishing. E-mail: mcdcott@aol.com.

MCDERMOTT, ALICE, writer; b. Bklyn., June 27, 1953; married; 3 children. BA, SUNY, Oswego, 1975; MA, U. N.H., 1978. Instr. U. Calif., San Diego, Am. U., Washington; lectr. in English U. N.H.; writer-in-residence Lynchburg Coll., Va., Hollins Coll., Va., Johns Hopkins U., Balt. Author: A Bigamist's Daughter, 1982, That Night, 1987 (Pulitzer Prize finalist, Nat. Book Award finalist, L.A. Times Book Prize finalist), At Weddings and Wakes, 1992, Charming Billy, 1998 (Nat. Book Award); contbr. short stories to numerous profl. publs. Recipient Whiting Writers award. Office: Farrar Straus and Giroux 19 Union Sq W New York NY 10003*

MCDERMOTT, LUCINDA MARY, ecumenical minister, teacher, philosopher, poet, author, psychologist; b. Lynwood, Calif., June 3, 1947; d. R. Harry and Cathrine Jaynne (Redmond) Boand. BA, U. So. Calif., L.A., 1969; MS, Calif. State U., Long Beach, 1975; PhD, Saybrook Inst., San Francisco, 1978. Pres. Environ. Health Systems, Newport Beach, Calif., 1976-90; founder, pres. Forerunner Publs., Newport Beach, 1985—, Life-Skills Learning Ctr., Newport Beach, 1985—; founder, dir. Newport Beach Ecumenical Ctr., 1993—. Founder, dir., Tri Delta Mgmt.; pres. bd. dirs., The Boand Family Found. Author: Bridges to Another Place, 1972, Honor Thy Self, Vol. I and II, 1973, Hello-My-Love-Good Bye, 1973, Life-Skills for Adults, 1982, Au Courants, 1983, Life-Skills for Children, 1984, Myrika-An Autobiographical Novel, 1989, White Knights and Shining Halos: Beyond Pair Bonding, 1996, (musical screen play) The Good Life, 1997. Mem. APA, Calif. Psychol. Assn., Truthsayer Minstrels (founder, dir. 1996—), Alpha Kappa Delta, Kappa Kappa Gamma. E-mail: Dr.McD@sbcglobal.net.

MCDERMOTT, PATRICIA ANN, nursing administrator; b. Bklyn., July 10, 1943; d. John J. and Lillian J. (Sweeney) Skelly; m. Joseph Kevin McDermott, Oct. 5, 1963; children: Colleen Mary, John Joseph. Diploma, Kings County Hosp Sch. Nursing, Bklyn., 1963; BS in Health Care Adminstrn., St. Francis Coll., Bklyn., 1979. Staff nurse Kings County Hosp., Bklyn., 1963-66, head nurse outpatient dept., 1966-74; evening supr. Park Nursing Home, Rockaway Park, N.Y., 1974-83; day supr. Hyde Park Nursing Home, Staatsburg, NY, 1984-85, DON, 1985—96, Victory Lake Nursing Ctr., Hyde Park, N.Y., 1996-97. NY State evaluator for nurses aides, 1988—; PRI assessor; MDS coord. Active local Girl Scouts U.S.A., 1971-78, Boy Scouts Am., 1978-82, Stella Maris Parents Club, 1978-82, St. Francis de Sales Altar and Rosary Soc., 1970-83; active St. Francis de Sales Little League, 1978-80, also softball coach, 1974-77; elected tax collector Town of Clinton, N.Y., 1999—; dance com. chair St. Peter's, Hyde Park, N.Y., 1998-2002. Dutchess County Salute to Women honoree, 1997. Home: 184 Shadblow Ln Clinton Corners NY 12514-2834

MCDERMOTT, RENÉE R(ASSLER), lawyer; b. Danville, Pa., Sept. 26, 1950; d. Carl A. and Rose (Gaupp) Rassler; m. James A. McDermott, Jan. 1, 1986. BA, U. So. Fla., 1970, MA, 1972; JD, Ind. U., 1978. Bar: Ind. 1978, N.C. 1999, U.S. Dist. Ct. (so. and no. dists.) Ind. 1978, U.S. Ct. Appeals (7th cir.) 1979, U.S. Ct. Appeals (9th cir.) 1985. Law clk. to presiding judge U.S. Dist. Ct. (no. dist.) Ind., Ft. Wayne, 1978-80; assoc. Barnes & Thornburg, Indpls., 1980-84, ptnr., 1985-93; pvt. practice Nashville, Ind., 1994-99, Tryon, NC, 1999—. County atty. County of Brown, Ind., 1994-98. Editor-in-chief Ind. U. Law Jour., 1977-78. Bd. visitors Ind. U. Law Sch., Bloomington, 1979—; bd. dirs. Pacolet Area Conservancy, 1999—, v.p., 2000-02, pres., 2003; bd. dirs. Foothills Equestrian Trail Assn., 1999-2002. Fellow Ind. Bar Found. (chair 1998-99), Am. Bar Found. (life); mem. ABA (bus. sect. coun. 1995-98, chmn. environ. controls com. 1991-95, liaison to standing com. on environ. law bus. law sect. 1991-98), Ind. State Bar Assn. (chmn. young lawyers sect. 1985-86, chmn. environ. law sect. 1989-91), Fellows of Ind. Bar. Found. (chair 1998-99), Polk County Cmty. Found. (bd. dirs. 2000-, chair exceptional dstbns. com. 2000-02), Order of Coif. Avocations: scuba diving, horseback riding, music, reading, hiking. Home and Office: 845 Fox Run Ln Tryon NC 28782-9758 E-mail: rmcdermott@alltel.net.

MCDEVITT, SHEILA MARIE, lawyer, energy company executive; b. St. Petersburg, Fla., Jan. 15, 1947; d. Frank Davis and Marie (Barfield) McD. AA, St. Petersburg Jr. Coll., 1966; BA in Govt., Fla. State U., 1968, JD, 1978. Bar: Fla. 1978. Research asst. Fla. Legis. Reference Bur., Tallahassee, 1968-69; adminstr., research assoc. Constitution Revision Commn. Ga. Gen. Assembly, Atlanta, 1969-70; adminstrv. asst., analyst Fla. State Sen., Tallahassee, Tampa, 1970-79; assoc. McClain, Walkley & Stuart, P.A., Tampa, Seminole, Fla., 1979-81; govtl. affairs counsel Tampa Electric Co., 1981-82, corp. counsel, 1982-86; sr. corp. counsel TECO Energy, Inc., Tampa, 1986-89, asst. v.p., 1989-92, v.p., asst. gen. counsel, 1992-99, corp. compliance officer, 1993-99, v.p., gen. counsel, 1999—2001, sr. v.p., gen. counsel, chief legal officer, 2001—. Mem. Worker's Compensation adv. coun. Fla. Dept. Labor, Tallahassee, 1984-86; trustee St. Leo U., 1999—, vice chair, 2001; mem. bd. visitors Fla. State U. Coll. Law, 1996—, chmn., 2003; mem. bd. advisors The Centre for Women, 1998—, Met. Ministries, 1996—; mem. ethics adv. bd. U. Tampa Ctr. for Ethics, 1997-99; mem. jud. nominating commn. 13th Jud. Cir., 2001—; mem. Fla. bd. govs. State Univ. sys., 2004. Bd. dirs. Vol. Ctr. Hillsborough County, Tampa, 1984-85, Fla. Aquarium, 1999-2000; bd. dirs. Lowry Park Zoo Soc., 1999—2004, chmn., trustee, 1986-94, also legal advisor; bd. dirs. Hillsborough County Easter Seal Soc., 1994-95; mem. Fla. Rep. Exec. Com., Tallahassee, 1974-75, Hillsborough County Rep. Exec. Com., 1974-75; mem. transition team for Fla. Gov. Bob Martinez, 1986-87; mem. Fed. Jud. Adv. Commn., 1989-93; mem. Fla. Humanities Coun., 2000—04; mem. WW Women's Leadership, 2004—. Mem ABA, Fla. Bar (vice chmn., then chmn. energy law com. 1984-87, jud. nominating procedures com. 1986-91, jud. adminstrn. selection and tenure com. 1991-93), Hillsborough Bar Found. (trustee 2002-), Hillsborough County Bar Assn. (chmn. law week com. 1990, corp. counsel com. 1986-87, internat. law com. 1994-95) corporate counsel of the yr. award, 2001-02, Am. Corp. Counsel Assn. (bd. dirs. Ctrl. Fla. chpt. 1986-87), Hillsborough County Bar Found., Tampa Club, Tiger Bay Club, Tampa Yacht and Country Club. Roman Catholic. Avocations: photography, bicycling, reading, boating. Office: TECO Energy Inc PO Box 111 702 N Franklin St Fl 5 Tampa FL 33602-4440

MCDIARMID, LUCY, English educator, author; b. Louisville, Mar. 29, 1947; m. Harris B. Savin, Oct. 13, 1984; children: Emily Clare, Katharine Eliza. BA, Swarthmore (Pa.) Coll., 1968; MA, Harvard U., 1969, PhD, 1972. Asst. prof. Boston U., 1972-74; from asst. prof. to assoc. prof. Swarthmore Coll., 1974-81; asst. prof. U. Md. Baltimore County, Balt., 1982-84; prof. Villanova (Pa.) U., 1984—. Vis. prof. English Princeton U., 1995; mem. exec. com. Am. Conf. for Irish Studies, 1987-91, v.p., 1995-97, pres., 1997-99, past pres., internat. rep., 1999—2001. Author: Saving Civilization: Yeats, Eliot and Auden Between the Wars, 1984, Auden's Apologies for Poetry, 1990; co-editor: Selected Writings of Lady Gregory, 1995, High and Low Moderns: Literature and Culture, 1889-1939, 1996, The Irish Art of Controversy, 2005; contbr. articles to profl. jours. NEH fellow, 1981-82; ACLS grantee, 1976, Bunting Inst. fellow, 1981-82, Guggenheim fellow, 1993-94; vis. fellow N.Y. Inst. Humanities, 1993-95. Mem. MLA (exec. com. Twentieth Century Lit. divsn.), Internat. Assn. for Study Anglo-Irish Lit. (Am. sec.-treas. 1994-96), Phi Beta Kappa. Home: 1931 Panama St Philadelphia PA 19103-6609 Office: Villanova U Dept Of English Villanova PA 19085

MCDIVITT, KAREN LOUISE, psychologist, writer; b. Las Animas, Colo., Jan. 10, 1953; d. Frank Junior and Ida Ruth (Lopkoff) Woods; m. Michael Wayne McDivitt, June 20, 1977; children: David Eric, Elisabeth Kay. BA, U. Colo., 1974, MA, 1975; PhD, U. Denver, 2000. Spl. edn. tchr. Denver Pub. Schs., 1976-77; diagnostician Colo. Boys' Ranch, LaJunta, Colo., 1977-78; real estate developer LaJunta, 1980-87; bus. mgr. McDivitt Law Firm, Colorado Springs, Colo., 1989-94; freelance writer, 1994—. Sec. Nat. Charity League, Colorado Springs, 1996-97; den leader Boy Scouts Am., LaJunta, 1986-89; pres. PTA, Colorado Springs, 1993-94. Mem. AAUW, APA, Nat. Assn. for Edn. Young Children, U. Colo. Alumni Assn. (bd. dirs. 1986-89), Nat. Writers Club. Republican. Methodist. Avocations: piano, skiing, cooking, reading. Home: 545 Bear Paw Ln N Colorado Springs CO 80906

MCDONALD, ANNE B. state legislator; b. Syracuse, N.Y. BS, LeMoyne Coll.; MS, Syracuse U. Mem. Commn. on Aging, Stamford, Conn., 1969-76, chair, 1972-76; mem. State Adv. Coun. on Aging, 1977-80, Bd. of Edn., Stamford, 1980-87, pres., 1984-85; chmn. Housing Authority, Stamford, 1988-90; mem.. Conn. Ho. of Reps., Hartford, 1991—. Democrat. Home: 53 Courtland Hill St Stamford CT 06906-2306 Office: Conn Ho of Reps Legislative Bldg Capitol Ave Hartford CT 06106

MCDONALD, AUDRA ANN, actress; b. Berlin, July 3, 1970; d. Stanley and Kathryn McDonald; m. Peter Donovan, Sept. 10, 2000; 1 child, Zoe Madeline Donovan. BFA in Voice, Juilliard Sch., 1993; attended, Sch. Arts., Calif. Stage appearances include (regional) Man of La Mancha, Evita, The Wiz, A Chorus Line, Grease, Anything Goes, The Real Inspector Hound, (Broadway) The Secret Garden, Man of La Mancha, 1989, Carousel, 1994 (Tony award best featured actress in a musical, 1994, Outer Critics Circle award outstanding actress in a musical, 1994), Master Class, 1995-97 (Tony award best featured actress in a musical, 1996, L.A. Ovation award best featured actress in a musical, 1996), Ragtime, 1998-99 (Tony award best featured actress in a musical, 1998), Sweeney Todd, 2000, A Raisin in the Sun, 2004 (Tony nom. best featured actress in a play, 2004); (TV series) Bill Cosby pilot, 1996, Mister Sterling, 2003 (TV Movies) Having Our Say: The Delaney Sisters' First 100 Years, 1999, Annie, 1999, The Last Debate, 2000, Wit, 2001 (Emmy award nom. best supporting actress, 2001) (Films) Seven Servants, 1996, The Object of My Affection, 1998, Cradle Will Rock, 1999, It Runs in the Family, 2003, The Best Thief in the World, 2004; concert performances include S'Wonderful, Some Enchanted Evening, Christa Ludwig and James Levine Recital, Revelation in Courthouse Park, Requiem Canticles. Recipient Theatre World award, 1994, Drama League award distinguished achievement in musical theatre, 2000. Office: c/o The Gersh Agy 130 W 42nd St Ste 1804 New York NY 10036-7901*

MCDONALD, BRENDA DENISE, librarian; b. Waco, Tex., Feb. 15, 1954; d. William Dale and Ella Mae (Parrott) Maness; m. Jeffrey L. McDonald, May 26, 1979; 1 child, Sean Thomas. BA in History, William Jewell Coll., 1975; MLS, U. Okla., 1976; MA in History, U. Tex., El Paso, 1988. Libr. govt. documents and periodicals Hardin Simmons U., Abilene, Tex., 1977-79; head documents and maps library U. Tex., El Paso, 1979-84; law libr. Scott Hulse Marshall Feuille Finger and Thurmond, El Paso, 1984-88; govt. documents libr. St. Louis Pub. Library, 1988-90, coord. info. svcs., 1990-95, dir. ctrl. pub. svcs., 1995-98, dir. ctrl. and regional svcs., 1999—. Jamestown Soc. fellow, 1988. Mem. ALA, Am. Law Library Assn., Spl. Libraries Assn., Beta Phi Mu. Office: St Louis Pub Library 1301 Olive St Saint Louis MO 63103-2389 E-mail: bmcdonald@slpl.lib.mo.us.

MCDONALD, CASSANDRA BURNS, lawyer; b. Aberdeen, Md., Aug. 28, 1963; d. Charles Franklin and Elizabeth (Connor) Burns; 1 child, Christopher. AB, Dartmouth Coll., Hanover, N.H., 1985; JD, Cornell U., 1990. Bar: Conn. 1991, U.S. Dist. Ct. Conn. 1992, U.S. Dist. Ct. (ea. and so. dists) N.Y. 1992. Atty. Cummings & Lockwood, Stamford, Conn., 1990—94, 1996—2002; v.p. legal affairs & compliance Luxury Mortgage Corp., 2002—. Mem. Women's Leadership Conf., Conn., 1998—; 1st v.p. The Links, Inc., Fairfield County, 2000—04; bd. dirs. Waveny Care Ctr., New Canaan, Conn., 2000—, Fairfield County Cmty. Found., 2001 . Mem.: ABA, Dartmouth Lawyers Assn., Lawyers for Children Am., Inc., Stamford/Norwalk Bar Assn., Conn. Bar Assn., Nat. Bar Assn., Black Alumni Dartmouth, Dartmouth Club of Fairfield County, Delta Sigma Theta. Baptist. Avocations: travel, reading, tennis. Office: Luxury Mortgage Corp 1 Landmark Sq Ste 100 Stamford CT 06901 E-mail: cbmcdonald@luxurymortgage.com.

MCDONALD, CHRISTIE ANNE, Romance languages and literature educator, writer; b. N.Y.C., May 4, 1942; d. John Denis and Dorothy (Eisner) McD.; m. Eugene Augustus Vance, June 11, 1965 (div. June 1986); children: Adam Vance, Jacob Vance; m. Michael David Rosengarten, Dec. 4, 1987. AB, Mt. Holyoke Coll., 1964; PhD, Yale U., 1969; MA (hon.), Harvard Coll., 1994. Acting instr. Yale U., New Haven, 1968-69; asst. prof. French U. Montreal, Que., Can., 1969-77, assoc. prof. French, 1977-83, prof., 1983, 86-93; prof. modern langs. Emory U., Atlanta, 1984-86; prof. romance langs. and. lits. Harvard U., Cambridge, Mass., 1994—, chmn. romance langs. and lits., 2000—. Author: The Dialogue of Writing, 1985, Dispositions, 1986, The Proustian Fabric, 1991; editor: The Ear of the Other, 1988, Transpositions, 1994. Recipient Clifford prize Am. Assn. 18th-Century Studies, 1994-95. Mem. Royal Soc. Can., Chevalier Palmes Académiques. Office: Harvard U 431 Boylston Hall Cambridge MA 02138 Office Phone: 617-495-2547.

MCDONALD, ELIZABETH LYNNE, speech pathology/audiology services professional; b. Watertown, N.Y., Aug. 24, 1955; d. Kenneth George McDonald and Helen Elizabeth Bunce; 1 child, Sarah Liu Wen. BS in Speech Pathology, SUNY, Geneseo, 1976; MA in Speech Pathology, Ohio State U., 1978. Lic. speech pathology N.Y., cert. tchr. speech/hearing handicapped N.Y. Speech therapist Jeff-Lewis BOCES, Glenfield, NY, 1976—77; speech pathologist Onondaga ARC, Syracuse, NY, 1978—81, North Syracuse Early Edn. Program, North Syracuse, NY, 1981—. Presenter insvc. classes, various feeding and comm. topics, 1980—; presenter grad. classes Syracuse U., 1979—. Bd. mem. CNY Geneal. Soc., Syracuse, 1986—92, Adoptive Family Network, Syracuse, 1999—2001, UCC Nursery Sch., Liverpool, NY, 1998—. Mem.: Am. Speech/Lang. Hearing Assn. (cert.). Mem. United Ch. Of Christ. Avocations: scrapbooks, genealogy, Chinese culture classes, crafts. Home: 110 Single Dr North Syracuse NY 13212 Office: North Syracuse Early Edn Program 205 S Main St North Syracuse NY 13212 E-mail: baslm@yahoo.com.

MCDONALD, FRANCES D. government official, editor, lawyer; b. Washington, July 6, 1949; BA, U. Va., 1971; JD, Cath. U. Am., 1981. Bar: Va. 1982. Legal publs. specialist Office Fed. Register. Nat. Archives and Records Adminstrn., Washington, 1980-82, atty., 1982-86, dir. legal svcs., 1986-91, dir. presdl. and legis. divsn., 1991-96, mng. editor, 1996—. Mem. Pi Gamma Mu. Office: Office Fed Registr Nat Archives-Recs Adminstrn 800 N Capitol St Rm 700 Washington DC 20408-0001 Office Phone: 202-741-6002. Business E-Mail: frances.mcdonald@nara.gov.

MC DONALD, GAIL FABER, musician, educator; b. Jersey City, Oct. 24, 1917; d. Samuel and Jennie (Weiss) Faber; m. George Walther, Nov. 17, 2000; children from previous marriage: Lora McDonald Ferguson, Charles McDonald, Henry McDonald. Diploma, Mannes Music Sch., N.Y.C., 1938; BA, U. Md., 1962; MusM, Cath. U., 1968; DMus Arts, U. Md., 1977. Legis. asst. Capitol Hill, 1943-46; pvt. tchr. piano and music theory Washington and Md., 1950—. Piano soloist Nat. Gallery Art, 1977; rec. artist Educo Records; lectr., performer Bach Sinfonias and Mendelssohn's Complete Songs Without Words; recorded complete solo piano works of Daniel Gregory Mason. Author: Muzio Clementi and the Gradus Ad Parnassum, 1968. Mem. D.C. Music Tchrs. Assn., Md. Music Tchrs. Assn. (pres. 1977—), D.C. Fedn. Music Clubs, Nat. Guild Piano Tchrs. (adjudicator 1972-2003), Friday Morning Music Club (performing mem.). Address: 801 N Monroe St Apt 602 Arlington VA 22201-2372

MCDONALD, JINX, interior designer; b. Kingston, Jamaica, Aug. 5, 1946; d. Leonard Fraser and Norma Dawn (Phillips) McConnell; m. C. John McDonald, Dec. 20, 1965 (div. Nov. 1993); children: Sarah, Minka. Interior design/journalism, St. Godric's Coll., Hampstead, Eng., 1967; interior design, Tuxedo Ctr., Atlanta, 1986. Owner/pres. Internat. Accents, Inc., Atlanta, 1986—91; interior designer Style, Inc., Naples, 1991—95, Forum Design group, Inc., Naples, Fla., 1995—2000; prin., owner Jinx McDonald Designs, Inc., Naples, Fla., 2000—. Cons. interior design. Recipient Sand Dollar award, Collier Bldg. Industry Assn., 1999, 2002, 2003, Design of Distinction, Naples Illustrated, 2002, Pinacle award, 2003. Mem. Am. Soc. Interior Design (allied mem.), Interior Design Soc., Nat. Abortion and Reproductive Rights Action League, Natural Resources Def. Coun. Democrat. Anglican. Home and Studio: 7536 San Miguel Way Naples FL 34109-7162 Office: Jinx McDonald Designs Inc 5603 Naples Blvd Naples FL 34109-2023 E-mail: jinxmcdonald@yahoo.com.

MCDONALD, JOANNE, business executive; b. San Diego, June 10, 1947; d. Paul and Dolores (Paganucci) McD. BA, U. Md., 1970. High tech. exec. ENSCO, Inc., Springfield, Va., 1981—, v.p. adminstrn. and human resources, 1992—, bd. dirs., 1994—. Office: ENSCO Inc 5400 Port Royal Rd Springfield VA 22151-2312

MCDONALD, JULIE JENSEN, writer, educator; b. Fiscus, Iowa, June 22, 1929; d. Alfred Julius Jensen and Myrtle Petra (Faurschou) Jensen Petersen; m. Elliott Raymond McDonald Jr., May 6, 1952; children: Beth, Elliott Raymond III. BA, U. Iowa, 1951; LLD, St. Ambrose Coll., 1972. Women's editor Rockford (Ill.) Newspapers, 1951—52; feature writer, reviewer Quad-City Times, Davenport, Iowa, 1963—83; lectr. journalism St. Ambrose Coll., Davenport, 1974—2000; feature writer, reviewer, columnist Dispatch, Argus, Leader, Quad Cities, Iowa, 1983—; bd. dirs. Midwest Writing Ctr., Quad Cities. Author 12 novels including Amalie's Story, 1970, biography Ruth Buxton Sayre, 1986, history Pathways to the Present, 1977, biography My Brother, Grant Wood, 1993. Trustee Davenport Mus. Art, 1986-2003; precinct committeewoman Rep. Party, Davenport, 1955-60. Recipient Isabel Bloom award for the arts Women's Encouragement Bd., 1989, Johnson Brigham award Iowa Libr. Assn., 1983, Friends of Am. Writers award, 1979. Mem. Iowa Press Women, Nat. Fedn. Press Women (1st pl. award Nat. Comms. Contest 1988), Scottish Am. Soc. (sec.), Danish Sisterhood. Presbyterian. Avocations: playing clarinet, swimming. Home: 2802 E Locust St Davenport IA 52803 Business E-Mail: McDonaldJulie@ambrose.sau.edu.

MCDONALD, LOIS ALICE, elementary school educator; b. Grand Rapids, Mich., Feb. 19, 1930; d. Embert and Ruth Alfareta (Priest) Grooters; m. Ronald Gerard McDonald, July 17, 1954; children: Rodney Mark, Wendy Louise. BS, Western Mich. U., 1952, MA, 1974. Cert. elem. permanent tchr., Mich. Kindergarten and elem. tchr. Chalmers Sch., Algoma Twp., Sparta, Mich., 1952-54; elem. tchr. Loucks Sch., Peoria, Ill., 1955-56, Lakeside Sch., East Grand Rapids, Mich., 1957-58, Clyde Park Sch., Wyoming, Mich., 1958-63, 64-76; tchr. kindergarten Gladiola Sch., Wyoming, 1963-64; elem. tchr. Pinery Park Elem. Sch., Wyoming, 1976-85, Rogers Lane Sch., Wyoming, 1985-91; ret., 1991. Dir. John Knox Food Pantry, 1991—96; vol. Red Cross & West Mich. Trails of Girl Scouts, 1998—2002; ch. sch. supt. John Knox Presbyn. Ch., 1968—73; mem. Chancel Choir, 1977—98; bd. of dir. Second Harvest Gleaners of West Mich., 1993—2001. Mem.: MEA-NEA (lifc). Home: 33 13 Mile Rd NE Sparta MI 49345-9342

MCDONALD, MARIANNE, classicist; b. Chgo., Jan. 2, 1937; d. Eugene Francis and Inez (Riddle) McD.; children: Eugene, Conrad, Bryan, Bridget, Kirstie (dec.), Hiroshi. BA magna cum laude, Bryn Mawr Coll., 1958; MA, U. Chgo., 1960; PhD, U. Calif., Irvine, 1975; doctorate (hon.), Am. Coll. Greece, 1988; diploma (hon.), Am. Archaeol. Assn.; DLitt (hon.), U. Athens, 1994, U. Dublin, 1994, Aristotle U., 1997, U. Thessalonika, 1997, Nat. U. Ireland, 2001. Instr. Greek, Latin, English, mythology, cinema U. Calif., Irvine, 1975-79; founder, rsch. fellow Thesaurus Linguae Graecae Project, 1975-97. Tchg. asst. U. Calif., Irvine, 1974; vis. prof. U. Ulster, Ireland, 1997, U. Dublin, 1990—, Univ. Coll. Dublin, 1999, 2002; adj. prof. theatre U. Calif., San Diego, prof. theatre and classics, 1994—; bd. dirs. Centrum. Author: (novels) Terms for Happiness in Euripides, 1978, Semilemmatized Concordances to Euripides' Alcestis, 1977, Cyclops, Andromache, Medea, 1978, Heraclidae, Hippolytus, 1979, Hecuba, 1984, (critical books) Hercules Furens, 1984, Electra, 1984, Ion, 1985, Trojan Women, 1988, Iphigenia in Taurus, 1988, Euripides in Cinema: The Heart Made Visible, 1983; translator: The Cost of Kindness and Other Fabulous Tales (Shinichi Hoshi), 1986, Views of Clytemnestra, Ancient and Modern, 1990, Classics and Cinema, 1990, Modern Critical Theory and Classical Literature, 1994, A Challenge to Democracy, 1994, Ancient Sun/Modern Light: Greek Drama on the Modern Stage, 1990, Star Myths: Tales of the Constellations, 1996, Sole Antico Luce Moderna, 1999, Mythology of the Zodiac: Tales of the Constellations, 2000, Antigone by Sophocles, 2000, Mythology of the Zodiac, 2000, Sing Sorrow: Classics, History, Heroines in Opera, 2001; translator: (with Michael Walton) Euripides Andromache, 2001; editor (with M. McDonald and Michael Walton): Six Greek Tragedies, 2002; editor: (with Michael Walton) Amid Our Troubles: Irish Versions of Greek Tragedy, 2002, Canta la tua Pena, 2002; editor: The Living Art of Greek Tragedy, 2003. Bd. dirs. Am. Coll. of Greece, 1981-90, Scripps Hosp., 1981, Am. Sch. Classical Studies, 1986-; mem. bd. overseers U. Calif., San Diego, 1985-; nat. bd. advisors Am. Biog. Inst., 1982—; pres. Soc. for the Preservation of the Greek Heritage, 1990-, Asian Am. Repertory Theatre, 2003; founder Hajime Mori Chair for Japanese Studies, U. Calif., San Diego, 1985, McDonald Ctr. for Alcohol and Substance Abuse, 1984, Thesaurus Linguarum Hiberniae, 1991-, Hiroshi McDonald Mori Performing Arts Ctr. Recipient Ellen Browning Scripps Humanitarian award, 1975, Disting. Svc. award U. Calif.-Irvine, 1982, 2001, Irvine medal, 1987; named one of the Cmty. Leaders Am., 1979-80, Philanthropist of Yr., 1985, Headliner San Diego Press Club, 1985, Philanthropist of Yr. Honorary Nat. Conf. Christians and Jews, 1986, Woman of Yr. AHEPA, 1988, San Diego Woman of Distinction, 1990, Woman of Yr. AXIOS, 1991; recipient Bravissimo gold medal San Diego Opera, 1990, Gold Medal Soc. Internationalization of Greek Lang., 1990, Athens medal, 1991, Piraeus medal, 1991, award Desmoi, 1992, award Hellenic Assn. of Univ. Women, 1992, Acad. of Achievement award AHEPA, 1992, Woman of Delphi award European Cultural Crr. Delphi, 1992, Civis Universitatis award U. Calif., San Diego, 1993, Hypatia award Hellenic U. Women, 1993, Am.-Ireland Fund Heritage award, 1994, Contribution to Greek Letters award Aristotle U. Thessaloniki, 1994, Mirabella Mag. Readers Choice One of 1000 Women for the Nineties, 1994, citations from U.S. Congress and Calif. Senate, Alexander the Gt. award Hellenic Cultural Soc., 1995, made hon. citizen of Delphi and gold medal of the Amphiktuonon, Del. Bus. award for Fine Arts San Diego Bus. Jour., 1995, Vol. of Decade Women's Internat. Ctr., 1994, 96, Gold Star award San Diego Arts League, 1997, Golden Aeschylus award Inst. Nat. Drama Antkg. Siracusa, 1998, Women Who Mean Bus., Fine Arts award San Diego Bus. Jour., 1998, Fulbright award, 1999, Ellis Island award, 1999, Spirit of Scripps award 1999; Theatre Excellence award KPBS Patte, 2001, Laud and Laurels, U. Calif. Disting. Alumni award Hellenic Cultural Soc. San Diego, 2003, Sledgehammer Theatre award, 2003, New Path award, 2003. Mem. MLA, AAUP, Am. Philol. Assn. (disting. svc. award 1999), Soc. for the Preservation of the Greek Heritage (pres.), Libr. of Am., Am. Classical League, Philol. Assn. Pacific Coast, Am. Comparative Lit. Assn., Modern and Classical Lang. Assn. So. Calif., Hellenic Soc. (coun. award 2000), Calif. Fgn. Lagn. Tchrs. Assn., Internat. Platform Assn., Royal Irish Acad., Greece's Order of the Phoenix (commdr. 1994), KPBS Prodrs. Club, Hellenic Univ. Club (bd. dir.). Avocations: Karate, harp (medieval), skiing, diving. Home: PO Box 929 Rancho Santa Fe CA 92067-0929 Office: U Calif at San Diego Dept Theatre La Jolla CA 92093 E-mail: mmcdonald@ucsd.edu.

MCDONALD, MARILYN A. academic assistant; b. Des Moines, Nov. 7, 1932; d. Edmund and Alice Groomes; m. Thomas Edwin McDonald, Feb. 12, 1955 (dec. June 1991); children: Deborah Sue, Thomas Groomes, Sarah

Alice, Janet Louise. BS, Iowa State U., 1954. Instr. Sch. Home Econs. Iowa State U., Ames, 1955; tchr. civics and English Evanston Twp. H.S., Evanston, 1956; home economist Pub. Svc. Co., Northbrook, Ill., 1957; substitute tchr. Ft. Worth Ind. Sch. Dist., 1973—76, mid. sch. tchr., 1976—92; exec. asst. dept. neurosurgery U. Tex. Med. Sch., Houston, 1994—. Founding mem., mem. issues com. Save Our ER, Houston, 2001; mem., discussion leader Bible Study Fellowship, Ft. Worth and Houston, 1983—2000; elder First Presbyn. Ch., Houston. Mem.: Mortar Bd., Omicron Nu, Phi Kappa Phi. Avocations: tennis, reading, travel. Office: U Tex Med Sch Dept Neurosurgery 6431 Fannin Ste 7 148 Houston TX 77030

MC DONALD, MEG, public relations executive; b. Santa Monica, Calif., Oct. 11, 1948; Dir. radio & TV svcs. Fran Hynds Pub. Rels., 1969-75; owner, CEO Mc Donald Media Svcs., 1975—. Recipient Buccaneer award PIRATES, 1980, 82, Prisms award Pub. Rels. Soc. Am., 1981, Pro awards Publicity Clubs. of L.A. Mem. Pub. Rels. Soc. Am. (sec. 1985), Radio ane TV News Assn. of So. Calif. (mem. bd. dirs. 1973-88), Publicity Club of L.A. (pres. 1979-80), L.A. Advt. Women (v.p. 1984-85), Print Interactive Radio and TV Ednl. Soc. (pres. 1998-00), Radio and TV News Assn. Office: Mc Donald Media Svcs 11076 Fruitland Dr Studio City CA 91604-3541

MCDONALD, PAMELA JANE, educational media specialist; d. Edd Reed and Dortha Mae McDonald. BA, Fla. State U., 1974, MS, 1981. Cert. profl. educator's cert. pre-K-12 Dept. Edn., Fla. Ednl. media specialist Max Bruner, Jr. Mid. Sch., Ft. Walton Beach, Fla., 1974—. Recipient extended access grant, Dept. Edn., 2001. Mem.: ALA, Fla. Assn. for Media in Edn. Avocations: travel, genealogy, reading. Office: Max Bruner Jr Mid Sch 322 Holmes Blvd NW Fort Walton Beach FL 32548

MCDONALD, PATRICIA ANN, legislative administrator; d. Alfred Keith and Mercelene (Eberlee) McD. BA with distinction, U. Mich., 1973. Writer, photographer Jackson (Wyo.) Hole Guide, 1974; asst. mktg. mgr. Grand Targhee Ski Area, Alta, Wyo., 1975; back country ranger Grand Teton Nat. Pk., Moose, Wyo., 1973-76; legis. dir. U.S. Sen. Malcolm Wallop, Washington, 1977-84; spl. asst., western field rep. to sec. Dept. of Interior, Denver, 1984-85; dir. comm. Steve Schuck for Gov., Denver, 1985-86; exec. dir. pub. lands coun., dir. pub. lands Nat. Cattlemen's Assn, Washington, 1986-90; pres. McDonald and Assocs., Washington, 1990, 95-96; chief of staff for U.S. Sen. Malcolm Wallop, Washington, 1991-94; Rep. staff dir. U.S. Senate Com. on Energy and Natural Resources, Washington, 1994; chief of staff U.S. Rep. Barbara Cubin, Washington, 1996-2000, Sen. Conrad Burns, Washington, 2000—. Republican. Avocations: dance, skiing, snowboarding, hiking, boating. Home: 4525 Macomb St NW Washington DC 20016-2752 Office: US Senate Senate Office 187 Dirksen Rd Ofc Washington DC 20510-0001

MCDONALD, REBECCA ANN, natural gas company executive; b. Phoenix, June 14, 1952; d. William Robert and Regenia Lucille (Hall) Kennedy; m. John Edward McDonald Sr., May 26, 1977; 1 child, John Edward Jr. BS, Stephen F. Austin State U., 1973. Project procurement mgr., buyer Fluor Engrs. and Constructors, Houston, 1974-79; pvt. practice cons. Houston, 1979-81; devel. mgr. Panhandle Ea. Pipeline, Houston, 1981-82, mgr. customer rels., 1982-84, mgr. sales, 1984-85; mgr. gas sales Panhandle Trading Co., Houston, 1985-88, v.p., gen. mgr., 1988-90; v.p. Strategic Planning Tenneco Gas Co., 1990—. Cert. power trainer Situation Mgmt. Systems, Plymouth, Mass., 1981—. Pres. bd. trustees The Chinquapin Sch., Highlands, Tex., 1986—; mem. Houston Jr. Forum, 1986—. Mem. Natural Gas Men of Houston (bd. dirs. Houston chpt.), Am. Soc. Tng. & Devel. (membership chair 1975-76, Most Valuable Mem. award 1976), Am. Bus. Women (hon. nom. bd.). Episcopalian. Office: Tenneco Gas Co 1010 Milam St Houston TX 77002-5312

MCDONALD, ROXANNE MARIE, English language educator, writer; b. Newport, N.H., July 31, 1958; d. Robert Malcolm McDonald and June Carmen Hall; m. Shahram Bahreyni, Aug. 1983 (div. Apr. 1989). BA in English, San Francisco State U., 1989, MA in English, cert. coll. composition tchr., San Francisco State U., 1994. Assoc. prof. English Skyline Coll., San Bruno, Calif., 1994—2003; instr. English Acad. Art, San Francisco, 1995—96; PM coord. Skyline Coll. Learning Ctr., San Bruno, 1999; instrnl. coord. A Plus, San Mateo, Calif., 1996—97; instrnl. aide Skyline Coll. Acting Learning Ctr., San Bruno, 1999—2003; coord. Skyline Coll. Learning Ctr. English Assistance Lab., San Bruno, 2003, instr. record, 2003. Creator, advisor critical jour. Spiritive, San Bruno, 1996—98. Author: (liner notes for albums and CDs) Calif. Art and Jazz Ensemble; contbr. poetry to anthologies (Nat. Libr. Poetry 3d prize). Mem. moveon.org, 2003. Mem.: Amnesty Internat., Tchrs. and Writers. Democrat. Avocations: needlepoint, restoring Monte Carlo SS, computer and board games, art salons, theater. Personal E-mail: roxanne.mcdonald@sbcglobal.net. Business E-Mail: mcdonald@smccd.net.

MCDONALD, SALLY J. lawyer; b. West Lafayette, Ind., Feb. 15, 1964; d. Homer C. and Esteleen M. (Bowman) McD.; m. Richard M. Levin, Oct. 16, 1993. BS, Ind. U., 1986; JD, Duke U., 1990. Bar: Ill. 1990. Assoc. Bell, Boyd & Lloyd, Chgo., 1990-92, Piper Rudnick, Chgo., 1992-98, hiring ptnr., 1998—99, co-nat. hiring ptnr., 1999—. Gen. counsel Gtr. Chgo. Food Depository, 1995-99. Contbr. chpt. to book. Mem. Chgo. Bar Assn. (bd. mgrs. 1998-2000, chair Young Lawyers sect. 1996-97, Maurice Weigle award 1994), Chgo. (Ill.) Bar Found.

MCDONALD, SARANNE, human services professional; b. Dallas, Jan. 9, 1952; d. Egbert Paul and Lucile Sara (Templeton) McD. BS, So. Meth. U., 1974; M of Urban Affairs, U. Tex., Arlington, 1982. Asst. Commn. on Children, Dallas, 1974-75; caseworker Adult and Family Svcs., Waukegan, Ill., 1975-76; rschr. CPI, Inc., Dallas, 1977-80; adminstrv. analyst City of Arlington, Tex., 1980-85; coord. Takilma (Oreg.) People's Clinic, 1985-91; dir. Commn. for Children, Grants Pass, Oreg., 1991—. Grantwriter Evergreen Data Svcs., 1978—; trainer Developing Capable People, Josephie, Oreg., 1997—. Bd. dirs. Ill. Valley Citizens Bd., Cave Junction, Oreg., 1990—, Our Valley Clinic, Grants Pass, 1992-95; mem. Project Awareness, Grants Pass, 1993. Avocation: cross country skiing. Office: Josephine County 500 NW 6th St Grants Pass OR 97526-2063

MCDONALD, SHARON HOLLIDAY, special education educator; b. Farmington, Mo., Jan. 15, 1948; d. Charles Douglas and Edythe Murriel Holliday; m. Gayle Dean McDonald, Feb. 14, 1969; children: Leslie Douglas, Mry Elizabeth. BS in Edn., U. Mo., 1969; MS in Edn., Kans. State U., 1973. Cert. K-9 tchr., learning disabilities, behavioral disabilities, mental retardation, social studies, composition, Kans. Tchr. spl. edn. Ottumwa (Iowa) Pub. Schs., 1969, Washington (Iowa) Cmty. Schs., 1969-71, Unified Sch. Dist. 336, Holton, Kans., 1971-75, 80-81, 82—. Mem. student improvement team Jackson Heights Elem. Sch., Holton, 1999—. Sunday sch. tchr. 1st United Meth. Ch., Holton, 1991-95, mem. Lady Belles, 1993—, chmn. adminstrv. coun., 1995, del. ann. conf., 1996. Named Outstanding Nutrition Educator, Midland Dairy Coun., 1994. Mem. NEA, Coun. for Exceptional Children (cert. profl. recognized spl. educator), Kans. Edn. Assn., Holton Edn. Assn., Pilot Club (pres. Holton 1980, 2000), Delta Kappa Gamma (membership com. Holton 1998-00). Republican. Avocations: music, needlework, reading. Home: 15587 222nd Rd Holton KS 66436-1406 Office: Jackson Heights Elem Sch 12763 266th Rd Holton KS 66436-8717

MCDONALD, SUSAN, publishing executive; V.p., CFO San Jose (Calif.) Mercury News. Office: San Jose Mercury News 750 Ridder Park Dr San Jose CA 95190-0001

MCDONALD, TERRE REESE, elementary school educator; b. Blackwell, Okla., Dec. 3, 1954; d. Darrell Dean and Ruth Jeanette Reese; m. Mark Lee McDonald, July 30; children: Aaron Lee, Sara Jen, Jairus Reese, Leah Kristen. AA, No. Okla. Jr. Coll., Tonkawa, 1975; BME, Okla. State U., 1977; postgrad., Okla. U., U. Ctrl. Okla. Music tchr. grades 1-5 Mustang Valley Elem. Sch., Mustang, Okla., 1977—80; spl. edn. asst. Blackwell (Okla.) Mid.-High Sch., 1981; music tchr. grades 4-5 Blackwell Elem. Sch., 1984—85; music tchr. grades 1-5 Lakehoma Elem. Sch., Mustang, 1987—88, Mustang Trails Elem. Sch., 1990—91, Lakehoma Elem. Sch., Mustang, 1991—. Co-founder Children's Mus. Theatre, Mustang, 1991—; precinct chmn. Rep. Party, Blackwell, 1988, campaign advisor Mustang, 1995; campaign mgr. State Legis. Race, Blackwell, 1988; bd. dirs. Mustang Arts Coun., 1980—. Named Tchr. of the Yr., Lakehoma Sch., 1994; recipient Jim Thorpe award, Jim Thorpe Com., 1973. Mem.: Mustang Area Reading Assn., Music Educators Nat. Conf., Phi Theta Kappa. Republican. Methodist. Avocations: sewing, sporting events, concerts. Home: 616 N Bluebird Way Mustang OK 73064 Office: 906 S Heights Dr Mustang OK 73064-3542

MCDONALD, THERESA BEATRICE PIERCE (MRS. OLLIE MCDONALD), church official, minister; b. Vicksburg, Miss., Apr. 11, 1929; d. Leonard C. Pierce and Ernestine Morris Templeton; m. Ollie McDonald, Apr. 23, 1966. Student, Tougaloo Coll., 1946-47, U. Chgo. Indsl. Rels. Ctr., 1963-64; BA in Sociology with deptl. honors, Roosevelt U., 1997; student, Chgo. Theol. Sem., 1997—. Ordained to Gospel Ministry, 1997. Vol. rep. Liberty Bapt. Ch., Am. Legion Aux., VA West Side Hosp., Chgo., 1971-73; nat. instr. ushers dept. Prog. Nat. Bapt. Conv. Inc., Washington, 1973-75, nat. sec. ushers dept., 1975-76, v.p. at large, 1980-82, chmn. pers. com., 1982-84; mem. faculty Congress of Christian Edn., 1978-85; mem. pub. rels. staff Liberty Bapt. Ch., Chgo., 1973-79, trustee, 1987-91; asst. Christian edn. dir. Maryland Ave. Bapt. Ch., Chgo., 1995-99; assoc. min. Md. Ave. Bapt. Ch., Chgo., 1997—, dir. Christian edn., 2000—02. Cons., lectr. in field; Sunday ch. sch. tchr.; bible class instr.; guest speaker TV and radio programs. Participant White House Regional Confs., 1961. Recipient Christian Svc. award Prog. Nat. Bapt. Conv. Inc., 1986, 92, 94, Disting. Svc. award, 1990-94, Dedicated Svc. award, 1998. Mem. VFW (life mem. Hunt aux. 2024), Bethlehem Bapt. Dist. Assn. Chgo. (asst. sec. 1982-84), Ch. Women United in Greater Chgo. (Ecumenical Actions com. 1981-83), Am. Legion (Outstanding Svc. award 1972, 73), Bapt. State Conv. Ill. (life), Order Ea. Star. Address: 9810 S Calumet Ave Chicago IL 60628-1432

MCDONALD, WYLENE BOOTH, former nurse, pharmaceutical sales professional; b. Kinston, N.C., Sept. 29, 1956; d. Wiley Truett and Hilda Grey (Brinson) Booth; m. Robert H. McDonald; stepchildren: Stephanie Lynn, Robin Leigh. BSN, Barton Coll., 1979; MSN, East Carolina U., 1984. Pub. health nurse Sampson Co. Health Dept., Clinton, N.C., 1979-81; pub. health coord. New Hanover Co. Health Dept., Wilmington, N.C., 1981-83; med. ctr. liaison Cape Fear Valley Med. Ctr., Fayetteville, N.C., 1984-85; profl. sales rep. Merck, Human Health Div., West Point, Pa., 1985-88; hosp. specialist sales rep. Human Health divsn. Merck, West Point, Pa., 1988-90, sr. prostate health specialist rep., 1990-94, exec. cardiovascular specialist, 1995—, exec. specialty rep., 1997-98, exec. hosp. specialist, 1998-2001, bus. mgr., 2001—. Speaker Coastal Area Perinatal Assn., 1983, Career Week, U. N.C. Sch. Bus., Wilmington, 1987, 88, 89, 93. Fundraiser March of DImes, Fayetteville, 1987, Wilmington, 1991, Am. Heart Assn., Wilmington, 1991-93. Named one of Outstanding Young Women of Am., 1981. Mem. ANA, AAUW, N.C. Nurses Assn., N.C. Pub. Health Assn., Masters Club, Sigma Theta Tau. Avocations: exercising, biking, reading, traveling. Home and Office: 108 Seapath Est Wrightsville Beach NC 28480-1964

MCDONALD RACKLEY, COLLETTE LYNN, management consultant; b. N.Y.C., Nov. 21, 1966; d. Robert Louis and Catherine L. (Morris) McD.; m. Richard Rackley, Jr., Sept. 2, 1989; 1 child, Richard III. Student, U. Tenn., 1984, Ga. State U., 1985, 87. Account mgmt. coord. Hutchenshutze Advt., Atlanta, 1987-89; office mgr., exec. asst. to pres., CEO ACT III Broadcasting, Inc., Atlanta, 1989-92; mktg. asst. Price Waterhouse, LLP, Atlanta, 1992, mktg. programs specialist, 1992-93; market rsch. analyst Coopers & Lybrand LLP, Atlanta, 1993, sr. assoc., mktg. rsch. and programs, 1994-96; sr. assoc. new bus. devel. and mktg. comms. Hartsfield Group, Atlanta, 1996; project mgr., sr. cons. Innovative Search Group, LLP, Atlanta, 1996; dir. of rsch. Egon Zehnder Internat., Atlanta, 1996—. Cons., advisor B&C Travel, Inc., College Park, Ga., 1995—, RCR Cons., Atlanta, 1996—. Mem. Nat. Black MBA Assn., Am. Mktg. Assn., Soc. Human Resource Mgmt., Soc. Competitive Intelligence Profls., Exec. Search Roundtable, NAFE. Democrat. Mem. World Changers Ch. Internat. Avocations: internet, travel, non-fiction. Office: Egon Zehnder Internat 3475 Piedmont Rd NE # 1900 Atlanta GA 30305-2987 E-mail: cmrackley@mailexcite.com.

MCDONALD-UMBAYEMAKE, LINDA, librarian, rehabilitation counselor; b. Cleve., Feb. 19, 1953; d. Charles Morgan and Helen Loretta (Ballard) McDonald; children: Manu, Kumar, Bari, Mayi, Thurayya, GlennChinua. AA, Cuyahoga C.C., Cleve., 1980; BA, Kent State U., 1984; MLS, Tex. Woman's U., 1989; MRC, U. Ky., 1998. Dir. African Am. Ctr. Toledo-Lucas County Pub. Libr., Toledo, 1989; libr. young adult, correctional and homebound Cuyahoga County Pub. Libr., Warrensville, Ohio, 1989-90; libr. supr. Western N.Mex. Correctional Facility, Grants, 1990; instr., libr. supr. Santa Fe C.C., 1990; libr. supr. Ga. Dept. Corrections, Buford, 1991; instr. head circulation Ky. State U., Frankfort, 1992-93, instr./ILL/reference libr., 1993-96; pub. svcs. asst. libr. Owensboro C.C., 1996; substitute tchr. Franklin County Pub. Schs., Frankfort, 1997—98; offender rehab counselor, substance abuse program Luther Luckett Correctional Ctr., 1998—99; collection devel. specialist Book Wholesalers Inc., 1999-2000; STAR program coord. U. Akron, Ohio, 2001—02; br. mgr. East Cleve. Pub. Libr. Caledonia Br., Cleve., 2001—. Founder Lumbay, 1997—; mem. Kent Ohio Cable Commn., 2003—. Apptd. to Ky. Foster Care Rev. Bd., 1999—2000; child support, visitation com. Franklin County Family Ct., Ohio, 1999—2000; mem. Bd. Elections Franklin County. Mem.: NAMI, Nat. Rehab. Assn., Black Caucus of ALA (chair new mem. orientation com. 1994—96, membership com. 1989—96, ALA Shirley Olofson com. 1993—96, mem. minority recruitment com. 1993—96), Chi Sigma Iota. E-mail: lumbay2000@yahoo.com.

MCDONEL, JENNIFER SUTTON, music educator; b. Parkersburg, W.Va., July 30, 1970; d. Cullen Burdette and Sharon Jones Sutton; m. James Andrew McDonel, Aug. 3, 1991; children: Katherine Elaine, Grant Brooks. B in Music Edn. summa cum laude, Ohio State U., 1992; MA in Music Edn., U. Rochester, 1997. Cert. music tchr. grades K-12 Ohio. Instrumental music educator West Carrollton (Ohio) City Schs., 1992—98; lic. kindermusik educator Kimberly's Kindermusik, Lebanon, Ohio, 1999—; cert. musikgarten educator Lebanon, 2002—; music educator Lebanon City Schs., 2003—. Sch. music adv. bd. Dayton (Ohio) Philharm. Orch., 1996—97; adjudicator Ohio Music Educators Assn., Ohio. Author: A Joyful Noise, 2004. Mem.: Gordon Inst. for Music Learning (exec. sec. 2002—), Music Educators Nat. Conf. Republican. Methodist. Avocations: running, quilting, reading. Office: Gordon Inst for Music Learning PO Box 528 Lebanon OH 45036-0528

MCDONNELL, BARBARA, lawyer; B, Univ. Ill.; M, Univ. Iowa; JD magna cum laude, Univ. Pa. Law Sch. With Sherman & Howard, 1982-87; staff atty. Colo. Ct. Appeals, 1988-89; law clerk Phila.; legal adv. Gov. Romer, dep. dir. policy and rsch., 1989-90; exec. dir. Colo. Dept. Human Svcs., 1991-99; chief dep. atty. gen. Office of Atty. Gen., Denver, 1999—. Rep. Nursing Adv. bd., team leader Policy Acad. Team on Families & Children At Risk. Office: Office Atty Gen 1525 Sherman St Denver CO 80203-1702

MCDONNELL, G. DARLENE, retired business educator; b. South Bend, Ind., Mar. 3, 1939; d. Roy Edward and Gizella Elizabeth Stroup; m. Dennis Eugene McDonnell, June 22, 1968; children: Lori, Jamie. BS, MA, Ball State U., 1962. Lic. real estate broker. Tchr. bus. edn. South Bend Cmty. Sch. Corp., 1962—2002, ret., 2002. Chmn. dept. bus. edn. LaSalle H.S., South Bend Cmty. Sch. Corp., 1972—95, BOA adv. bd., 1973—93. Co-editor (bus. edn. practice set simulation): Aaron's Insurance Agency, 1981. Mem.: Ind. Bus. Edn. Assn. (membership chmn.), Ind. State Tchrs. Assn., Bus. Office Assn. (intracurricular student sponsorship 1972—95), Delta Kappa Gamma, Kappa Delt Pi, Delta Pi Epsilon. Avocations: reading, golf. Home: 20440 Miller Rd South Bend IN 46614

MC DONNELL, LORETTA WADE, lawyer; b. San Francisco, May 31, 1940; d. John H. and Helen M. (Tinney) Wade; m. John L. McDonnell, Jr., Apr. 27, 1963 (div.); children: Elizabeth, John L. III, Thomas. BA, San Francisco Coll. for Women, 1962; MA, Stanford U., 1963; grad., Coro Pub. Affairs Tng. Program for Women, 1976; JD, Golden Gate U., 1989. Bar: Calif. 1990. H.S. tchr. East Side Union H.S. Dist., San Jose, Calif., 1962-63; project coord. Inter Agy. Collaboration Effort, Oakland, Calif., 1977; legal asst. Pacific Gas and Elec. Co., San Francisco, 1980-89, coord., 1989-90, atty., 1990—. Assoc. editor The Antiphon, 1971-74. Chmn. spkrs. panel Focus on Am. Women, 1973-74; bd. dirs. Alameda County Vol. Bur., 1973-74, St. Paul's Sch., 1974-75, Carden Redwood Sch., 1975-77; budget panelist United Way of Bay Area, 1975-77; cmty. v.p. Jr. League, 1976-77, nat. conv. del., 1976. Mem. Jr. League Oakland-East Bay, Inc., Stanford Alumni Assn. Democrat.

MCDONNELL, MARY THERESA, travel service executive; b. N.Y.C., Nov. 9, 1949; d. John J. and Mary B. (Lunney) McD.; m. Robert T. Barber, Oct. 7, 1989 (dec. Nov. 7, 1999). Mgr. Kramer Travel Agy., White Plains, N.Y., 1967-79; owner, mgr. New Trends Travel, Rye, N.Y., 1979-90, Honey Travel Inc., Rye, N.Y., 1990—. Office: Honey Travel Inc 11 Elm Pl Rye NY 10580-2918 Office Phone: 914-921-0455. Personal E-mail: mtbarber1@yahoo.com., honeytravel@yahoo.com.

MCDONOUGH, ANN PATRICE, ice skater; b. Korea, May 29, 1985; Grad. high sch. Figure skater competing numerous events including State Farm U.S. Championships, 1999—, Jr. Grand Prix, Norway, Mex., 2000, World Jr. Championships, 2001—02, Four Continents Championships, 2002—03, Campbell's Classic, 2002—03, Smart Ones Skate Am., 2002, ABC Sports Internat. Figure Skating Challenge, 2003, Cup of China, 2003, numerous other competitions. Recipient numerous 1st place awards including, Gardena Spring Trophy, Southwestern Sectional, Midwestern Sectional, Jr. Grand Prix Final, Southwestern Regional, World Jr. Championships, numerous 2d place awards including, Jr. GLlrand Prix Norway, World Jr. Championships, Nebelhorn Trophy, Campbell's Class, Smart Ones Skate Am. Office: US Figure Skating Hdqrs 20 First St Colorado Springs CO 80906*

MCDONOUGH, BRIDGET ANN, music theatre company director; b. Milw., June 19, 1956; d. James and Lois (Hunzinger) McD.; m. Gregory Paul Opelka, Sept. 20, 1986 (div. Aug. 1993); m. Robert Markey, Feb. 29, 2000. BS, Northwestern U., 1978. Bus. mgr. Organic Theater Co., Chgo., 1979-80; mng. dir., founder Light Opera Works, Evanston, Ill., 1980—. U.S. rep. European Congress Musical Theatre, 1995. Founder, mem. Chgo. Music Alliance, 1984—, pres., 1995-98; mem. Ill. Arts Alliance; bd. dirs., Nat. Alliance for Musical Theatre, 2001—, sec., 2001—; bd. dirs. Evanston Convention Visitors Bur., 1999-2002; mem. alumni adv. bd. Northwestern U. Sch. Speech, 1999-2002. Recipient Women on the Move award Evanston YWCA, 1991. Mem. Evanston C. of C. (bd. dirs., 1993-99), Rotary (pres. Evanston chpt. 1999-2000). Avocation: birding. Office: Light Opera Works 927 Noyes St Evanston IL 60201-6206

MCDONOUGH, KAYE (KATHRYN SUSAN MCDONOUGH), poet, playwright; b. Pitts., Aug. 8, 1943; d. Edward Arthur and Lucille Marie (Bechman) M.; 1 child, Nile Joseph Corso. Student, Vassar Coll., 1961-63, Boston U., 1964-65; BA, U. Calif., Berkeley, 1967; MFA in writing and poetry, Sarah Lawrence Coll., 2002. Adj. lectr. U. Conn., Ea. Conn. State U., Quinnipiac U. Author: (book/play) Zelda: Frontier Life in America, 1978; contbr. poems to City Lights Rev., 1994, City Lights Jour., 1978, City Lights Anthology, 1974, The Stiffest of the Corpse, 1989, Exquisite Corpse, 1985, Cafe Society, 1978, Umbra, Gale Research Contemporary Authors Autobiography Series, 1998, Outlaw Bible of Am. Poetry,1999, The Baby Beats and the Second San Francisco Renassance, 2002, the Beat Generation in San Francisco (by Bill Morgan), 2003, others; poetry readings at San Francisco Poetry Festival, 1976, Polyphonix Franco-Am. Poetry Festival, Paris, 1979, Shakespeare & Co., Paris, 1979, Santa Cruz Poetry Festival, 1982, Poetry Ctr. San Francisco State Coll., 1984, Cody's Bookstore, Berkeley, 1992, others; play performed at St. Clement's Theatre, N.Y.C., 1978-79, U. Cambridge, New Zealand, 1979, The Glass Factory, Salt Lake City, 1980. Poet Big Mountain Navajo/Hopi Support Com. Benefit, San Francisco, 1981, Anti-Nuclear Proposition 15 Benefit, San Francisco, Internat. Women's Day Benefit, San Francisco, El Salvador Benefit, San Francisco. Home: 236 Santa Fe Ave Hamden CT 06517-1532

MCDONOUGH-TREICHLER, JUDITH DIANNE, medical educator, consultant; b. L.A., Aug. 15, 1938; d. William Charles and Eleanor (Lewis) Anderson; m. Raymond Milan McDonough, Mar. 2, 1957 (div. Oct. 2, 1974); children: Joyce Churchill, Steven McDonough, Jill Cannon; m. John Rex Treichler, June 2, 1985. BS in Health Edn., Calif. State U., Long Beach, 1978; MS in Health Care Adminstrn., U. LaVerne, Calif., 1981; PhD in Pub. Health, Loma Linda U., Calif., 1991. Cert. registered nurse, Calif., health edn. specialist nat. Commn. for Health Edn. Credentialing. Dir. health edn. Nat. Med. Enterprises, Lakewood, Calif., 1972-80, Taif, Saudi Arabia, 1980-82, health educator Manila, Philippines, 1983; dir. health promotion and edn. Med. Ptnrs. US Family Care, Montclair, Calif., 1992-97; adj. faculty prof. U. LaVerne, Calif., 1986—, U. Phoenix, Ontario, Calif., 1996—, Crafton Hills Coll., Yucaipa, Calif., 1997—; owner, exec. v.p. JJS Health Edn. Cons., Rancho Cucamonga, Calif., 1996—. Rsch. asst. Loma Linda (Calif.) U., 1995-97; adv. bd. mem. Cerritos (Calif.) Coll., 1975-80, U. LaVerne, Calif., 1996—. Contbr. articles to profl. jours. Contbg. mem. La Liga Flying Samaritans, Rosario Mex., 1978-80, Friendship For Animals, Rancho Cucamong, Calif., 1995—. Recipient Dean's fellowship Loma Linda (Calif.) U., 1988. Mem. APHA, Calif. Scholarship Fedn., Nat. Coun. Against Health Fraud, World Clowns Assn., Clowns of Am. Internat., Calif. State U. Alumni Assn., Alpha Gamma Sigma. Avocation: clowning. Office: U LaVerne Dept Health Svcs Mgmt 1950 3d St La Verne CA 91750 Home: 5152 Breckinridge Ave Banning CA 92220-7153

MCDORMAND, FRANCES, actress; b. Ill., June 23, 1957; m. Joel Coen, 1984; 2 children. Student, Yale U. Sch. Drama. Stage appearances include Awake and Sing!, N.Y.C., 1984, Painting Churches, N.Y.C., 1984, The Three Sisters, Mpls., 1985, N.J., 1991, All My Sons, New Haven, 1986, A Streetcar Named Desire, N.Y.C., 1988, Moon for the Misbegotten, 1992, Sisters Rosensweig, N.Y.C., 1993, The Swan, N.Y.C., 1993, To You, the Birdie!, 2002, Far Away, 2002; TV appearances include The Twilight Zone, The Equalizer, Spencer: For Hire, Hill Street Blues, (series) Hunter, 1984, Legwork, 1986-87, Twilight Zone, 1986, State of Grace, 2001; film appearances include Blood Simple, 1984, Crime Wave, 1986, Raising Arizona, 1987, Mississippi Burning, 1988 (Academy award nominee), Chattahoochee, 1990, Darkman, 1990, Miller's Crossing, 1990, Hidden Agenda, 1990, The Butcher's Wife, 1991, Passed Away, 1992, Short Cuts, 1993, Beyond Rangoon, 1995, Plain Pleasures, 1996, Fargo, 1996 (Academy award for Best Actress in a Leading Role, 1997), Lone Star, 1996, Primal Fear, 1996, Palookaville, 1996, Paradise Road, 1997, Johnny Skidmarks, 1998, Madeline, 1998, Talk of Angels, 1998, Wonder Boys, 1999, Almost Famous (Academy award nominee, Brit. Acad. award nominee, Golden Globe nominee, SAG nominee), Man Who Wasn't There, 2001, City by the Sea, 2002, Something's Gotta Give, 2003, (TV movies) Scandal Sheet, 1985, Vengeance: The Story of Tony Cimo, 1986, Crazy In Love, 1992, Good Old Boys, 1995, Hidden in America, 1996. Office: Endeavor Talent Agy LLC 9701 Wilshire Blvd Fl 10 Beverly Hills CA 90212

MCDOUGAL, AMY NICOLE, poet; b. Canton, Ohio, USA, Apr. 20, 1979; d. Ronald Eugene McDougal and Marica Jo Casey. Assoc. mem. Acad. of Am. Poets, New York City, NY, 1999—. Author: (Poem) Poets of the New Millineum, 2000, Hidden Roots (England), 2000, Candlelight Poetry Jour., 1997. Min. (door to door) Jehovah's Witnesses, 1995—. Mem.: KSPS, Acad. of Am. Poets. Jehovah'S Witnesses.

MCDOWELL, ANNIE R. retired counselor; b. Lawtey, Fla., Sept. 12, 1934; d. Elbe and Rebecca (Strong) Hamilton; m. John D. Buckhanon, July 12, 1953 (div. June 1962); 1 child, Levon Buckhanon. BA, Fla. A&M U., Tallahassee, 1967; MEd, U. Ctrl. Fla., 1972; M in Guidance Counseling, Rollins Coll., 1975. Tchr. Orange County Pub. Schs., Orlando, Fla., 1967-73; equal opportunity counselor, coord. Valencia C.C., Orlando, 1973-97; ret., 1997. Mem. Valencia Black Adv. Bd., Orlando, Fla., 1973—, President's Status of Women, 1989—, Sisters Alive, Orlando, 1993—, Orlando Partnership, 1994—. Recipient Appreciation award African-Am. Cultural Soc./Valencia Coll., 1995. Mem. Mem. Nat. Hook-Up of Black Women (Honors ward 1988, pres. 1989), Friendship Club, Negro Coun. Women, Gamma Delta Pi. Democrat. Baptist. Home: 1549 Lawndale Cir Winter Park FL 32792-6160

MCDOWELL, DONNA SCHULTZ, lawyer, educator; b. Cin., Apr. 23, 1946; d. Robert Joseph and Harriet (Parronchi) Schultz; m. Dennis Lon McDowell, June 20, 1970; children: Dawn Megan, Donnelly Lon. BA in English with honors, Brandeis U., 1968; MEd, Am. U., 1972; C.A.S. with honors in Reading, Johns Hopkins U., 1979; JD with honors, U. Md., 1982; MS, Hood Coll., 1995; postgrad., U. Md. Bar: Md. 1982; cert. tchr. reading K-12, D.C.; advanced profl. cert. in English, Biology and Reading, Md. Instr. Anne Arundel & Prince George's C.C., Severna Park and Largo, Md., 1977-78; coll. adminstr. Bowie State Coll. (Md.), 1978-79; assoc. Miller & Bortner, Lanham, Md., 1982-83; sole practice Lanham, 1983-87, Gaithersburg, Md., 1987—; sci. tchr. D.C. Pub. Schs., 1999-2000; chair dept English Montgomery County Pub. Schs., 2000—, English lit. tchr., 2002—03. Ednl. cons.; presenter in field. Chmn. Housing Hearing Com., Bowie, 1981-83; trustee Unitarian-Universalist Ch., Silver Spring, Md., 1979-83; bd. dirs. New Ventures, Bowie, 1983, Second Mile (Runaway House), Hyattsville, Md., 1983; officer Greater Laytonsville Civic Assn., 1989; founding mem. People to Preserve, Laytonsville; mem. Solid Waste Adv. Com., Montgomery County, Md.; election judge; presenter NCTE, SOMIRA, NCPS. Recipient Am. Jurisprudence award U. Md., 1981; Michael Jordan grantee, 2000, D.C. Pub. Schs grantee, 2000. Mem. Phi Kappa Phi. Democrat. Avocations: gardening, reading, bluebirds, movies. Home: 24308 Hipsley Mill Rd Gaithersburg MD 20882-3132 E-mail: DonnaSMcD@aol.com.

MCDOWELL, ELAINE, retired federal government executive, educator; b. Balt., June 28, 1942; d. McKinley and Lena (Blue) McDowell; children: Nathan H. Jr. Murphy, Michael W. Murphy. BA, Morgan State U., Balt., 1965; MSW, U. Md., 1971, PhD, 1988. Drug abuse adminstr., acting regional dir. State Md. Drug Abuse Adminstrn., Balt., 1971-72; social sci. analyst, pub. health advisor Nat. Inst. Drug Abuse, Rockville, MD, 1972-76, dep. dir., dir. div. community assistance, 1976-82, dep. assoc. dir. for policy devel., 1981-82, dir. div. prevention and communications, 1982-85; exec. asst. to adminstr. Alcohol, Drug Abuse & Mental Health Adminstrn., Rockville, Md., 1985; dep. dir. Nat. Inst. on Drug Abuse, Rockville, MD, 1985-88; dir. Ctr. for Substance Abuse Prevention, 1988-96; acting adminstr. Alcohol, Drug Abuse and Mental Health Adminstrn., Rockville, Md., 1992, Substance Abuse and Mental Health Svcs. Adminstrn., Rockville, Md., 1992-94. Expert cons. in substance abuse, treatment, and mental health fields; prof. Morgan State U., Balt. Chmn. non-alcoholic internat. gen. svc. bd. Alcoholics Anonymous, 2001—; active Presbyn.. Ch. U.S.A., Balt., 1998—; bd. dirs. Rosalynn Carter Inst. for Human Devel. Recipient Outstanding Leadership in Improving Health Care in Black Cmty. award Nat. Med. Assn., 1989, Secretary's commendation HHS, 1989, Disting. Svc. award, 1990, Nat. Coun. on Alcoholism and Drug Dependence Ind., Pres. award for outstanding fed. leadership, 1991, Presdl. Meritorious Exec. Rank award, 1991, Presdl. Meritorious Disting. Rank award, 1993. Mem.: NASW, Sr. Execs. Assn. E-mail: JLuvenia@aol.com.

MCDOWELL, ELIZABETH MARY, retired pathology educator; b. Kew Gardens, Surrey, Eng., Mar. 30, 1940; came to U.S., 1971; d. Arthur and Peggy (Bryant) McD. B Vet. Medicine, Royal Vet. Coll., London, 1963; BA, Cambridge U., 1968, PhD, 1971. Gen. practice vet. medicine, 1964-66; Nuffield Found. tng. scholar Cambridge (Eng.) U., 1966-71; instr. dept. pathology U. Md., Balt., 1971-73, asst. prof., 1973-76, assoc. prof., 1976-00, prof., 1980-96, ret., 1996. Co-author: Biopsy Pathology of the Bronchi, 1987; editor: Lung Carcinomas, 1987; contbr. over 120 articles to sci. jours., chpts. to books. Rsch. grantee NIH, 1979-92. Avocations: conservation education, gardening, swimming. Home: 9715 Branchleigh Rd Apt 3 Randallstown MD 21133-2158

MCDOWELL, JENNIFER, sociologist, composer, playwright, publisher; b. Albuquerque; d. Willard A. and Margaret Frances (Garrison) McD.; m. Milton Loventhal, July 2, 1973. BA, U. Calif., 1957; MA, San Diego State U., 1958; postgrad., Sorbonne, Paris, 1959; MLS, U. Calif., 1963; PhD, U. Oreg., 1973. Tchr. English Abraham Lincoln H.S., San Jose, Calif., 1960-61; free-lance editor Soviet field, Berkeley, Calif., 1961-63; editor, pub. Merlin Papers, San Jose, 1969-80, Merlin Press, San Jose, 1973—; rsch. cons. sociology San Jose, 1973—; music pub. Lipstick and Toy Balloons Pub. Co., San Jose, 1978—; composer Paramount Pictures, 1982-88; music pub. Abbie & Dolley Records, 2003—. Tchr. writing workshops; poetry readings, 1969-73; co-producer radio show lit. and culture Sta. KALX, Berkeley, 1971-72. Author: (with Milton Loventhal) Black Politics: A Study and Annotated Bibliography of the Mississippi Freedom Democratic Party, 1971 (featured at Smithsonian Inst. Spl. Event 1992), Contemporary Women Poets, 1977; co-author: (plays off-off Broadway) Betsy and Phyllis, 1986, Mack the Knife Your Friendly Dentist, 1986, The Estrogen Party To End War, 1986, The Oatmeal Party Comes to Order, 1986, (plays) Betsy Meets the Wacky Iraqi, 1991, Bella and Phyllis, 1994; contbr. poems, plays, essays, articles, short stories, and book revs. to lit. mags., news mags. and anthologies; rschr. women's autobiog. writings, contemporary writing in poetry, Soviet studies, civil rights movement, and George Orwell, 1962—; writer: (songs) Money Makes a Woman Free, 1976, 2004, 3 songs featured in Parade of Am. Music, 1976-77; co-creator mus. comedy Russia's Secret Plot To Take Back Alaska, 1988, (CDs) Our Women Are Strong, 2002, The Wearing of the Green Burkas, 2003, She, A Tapestry of Women's Lives, 2004. Recipient 8 awards Am. Song Festival, 1976-79, Bill Casey Award in Letters, 1980; doctoral fellow AAUW, 1971-73; grantee Calif. Arts Coun., 1976-77. Mem. AAUW, Am. Assn. for Advancement of Slavic Studies, Soc. Sci. Study of Religion, Am. Sociol. Assn., Dramatists Guild, Phi Beta Kappa, Sigma Alpha Iota, Beta Phi Mu, Kappa Kappa Gamma. Democrat. Office: c/o Merlin Press PO Box 5602 San Jose CA 95150-5602 E-mail: jeditorphd@earthlink.net.

MCDOWELL, KAREN ANN, lawyer; b. Ruston, La., Oct. 4, 1945; d. Paul and Opal Elizabeth (Davis) Bauer; m. Gary Lee McDowell, Dec. 22, 1979. BA, U. La., Monroe, 1967; JD, U. Mich., 1971; diploma, John Robert Powers Sch., Chgo., 1976, Nat. Inst. Trial Advocacy, 1990. Bar: Ill. 1973, Colo. 1977, U.S. Dist. Ct. (so. dist.) Ill. 1973, U.S. Dist. Ct. Colo. 1977. Reference libr. assoc. Ill. State Library, Springfield, 1972-73; asst. atty. gen. State of Ill., Springfield, 1973-75; pvt. practice Boulder, Colo., 1978-79, Denver, 1979—. Mem. So. Poverty Law Ctr.; mem. hate violence task force, Colo. Lawyers Com.; bd. dirs., foster mom for young kittens Recycled Critter Rescue. Mem.: DAR, ABA, Colo. Women's Bar Assn. (editor newsletter 1982—84), Denver Bar Assn., Colo. Bar Assn. (legal fee arbitration com.), Am. Assn. Retired Persons, Survivors United Network (legal coord. 1992—93), Ams. of Royal Descent, Toastmasters Internat. (Able Toastmaster Bronze 1992), Colonial Dames, Survivors United Network Profls. (exec. com. 1992), Mensa (local sect. Ann Arbor, Mich. 1968), Nat. Soc. Magna Carta Dames, Colonial Order of Crown, Sovereign Colonial Soc., Alpha Lambda Delta, Sigma Tau Delta, Phi Alpha Theta. Avocations: stamp collecting/philately, chess, needlework, dinosaurs, horatio alger stories. Office: 1525 Josephine St Denver CO 80206-1406 E-mail: kamcdowell@qwest.net.

MCDOWELL, SHERRIE LORRAINE, secondary school educator; b. Manchester, Ky., Apr. 20, 1948; d. Alonzo and Madge Loudean (Christensen) Garrison; m. Gary Lynn McDowell, July 11, 1970; 1 child, Marc Ryan. BA, U. No. Colo., 1970; MA, Lesley Coll., 1989; postgrad., U. Wyo. Cert. tchr., Wyo.; nat. bd. cert. tchr. adolescence and young adulthood English lang. arts, 2000. Tchr. English St. Mary's Cath. Sch., Cheyenne, Wyo., 1971-72; instr. homebound program Laramie County Sch. Dist., Cheyenne, 1978-84; English instr. Cen. High Sch., Cheyenne, 1984—. Wyo. coach Nat. Tournament of Acad. Excellence, 1988-90. Mem. NEA (Assembly rep. 1993-2003, cadre trainer state level women's leadership tng. program 1995—), AAUW (sec. 1975-77), Wyo. Edn. Assn. (chair profl. standards and practices commn. 1995-1999, chair summer Inst. 1996-99, co-chmn. local activities Read Across Am. 1999, rep. for del. assembly 1993-2003), Nat. Coun. Tchrs. English (recorder Boston Conv. 1996), Cheyenne Tchrs. Edn. Assn. (edn. assn. del. 1992-2000, chair instrnl. issues 1995, co-chair pub. rels. 1988-90, editor ACCENTS 1988-90, 2002-2003, sec. 1995-96, at-large rep. 2000-01), Wyo. Assn. Tchrs. English (presenter), Wyo. Chautauqua Soc. (pres. 1985-86, bd. dirs. 1984-85), Delta Kappa Gamma (state scholarship chair 1989-90, pres. chpt. 1988-90). Home: 100 Grandview Ct Cheyenne WY 82009-4912 Office: Ctrl H S 5500 Education Dr Cheyenne WY 82009-4008

MCDUFFIE, MARCIA JENSEN, pediatrics educator, researcher; b. Phila., Apr. 10, 1949; d. John Calvin and Agnes Margaret (Jakob) J.; children: Kathryn Steere, Joanna Steere, Michael. Student, Duke U., 1967-69; BA cum laude with honors in Biochemistry, U. Pa., 1971; MD with honors, U. N.C., 1981. Diplomate Am. Bd. Pediat. Pediat. intern U. Colo. Health Scis. Ctr., Denver, 1981-82, resident in pediat., 1982-84, asst. prof., 1987-93, rsch. mem. Barbara Davis Ctr. for Childhood Diabetes, 1989-93; postdoctoral fellow div. basic immunology dept. medicine Nat. Jewish Ctr. for Immunology and Respiratory Medicine, Denver, 1984-87; assoc. prof. U. Va. Health Scis. Ctr., Charlottesville, 1993—. Assoc. editor Jour. Immunology, 1992-94; mem. editl. bd. Diabetes, 1995—; contbr. articles to profl. jours. Recipient career devel. award Juvenile Diabetes Found., 1992-95, rsch. grantee Juvenile Diabetes Found., 1991-95, 96—, Am. Diabetes Assn., 1994—, NIH, 1996—. Mem. Soc. for Pediatric Rsch., Am. Assn. Immunologists. Office: U Va Health System Dept Pharmacology Mr-4 Rm 5116 Charlottesville VA 22908-0001

MCDUNN, ADRIENNE, human behavior consultant; b. Moorhead, Minn., June 16, 1953; d. Adrian James and Virginia Ann McDunn. Student, U. Lancaster, Eng., 1976; BA, U. Minn., 1981; M of Adult Edn., N.C. State U., 1992. Cert. in divorce, family, civil mediation; facilitation; diversity application. Tng. mgr. Cambar Bus. Sys., Charleston, S.C., 1983-85; sr. application cons. Mgmt. Sci. Am., Hamden, Conn., 1985-89; sr. engagement mgr. McKinsey & Co., Atlanta, 1989-91; cons., mediator Dispute Settlement Ct., Durham, N.C., 1991-93; exec. v.p. Personalysis Corp., Houston, 1993—2003; v.p. strategic learning Providence Health Sys., Seattle, 2003—. Mediator in dist. ct. Civil Ct. Sys., Raleigh and Durham, 1991-93; guest lectr. Student Leadership Ctr., N.C. State U., Raleigh, 1992-93. Mem. ASTD (membership dir. 1992), Orgn. Devel. Network, Phi Kappa Phi. Office: Providence Health System 506 2nd Ave Ste 1200 Seattle WA 98104

MCDYER, SUSAN SPEAR, academic administrator; b. Bridgeton, N.J., July 18, 1948; d. Wallace H. and Oleta (Craddock) Spear; 1 child, Kristine Beth. AS, Widener U., 1968. Dir. fin. & personnel U. Pitts., 1986-87, dir. major gifts, assoc. dir. campaign for 3d century, 1987-89, exec. dir. univ. resources devel., dir. campaign 3d century, 1989-91; v.p. univ. rels., dir. campaign Gannon U., Erie, Pa., 1991—. Presenter in field. Bd. dirs. Discovery Sq., First Night Erie. Mem. AAUW, NAFE, Nat. Soc. Fundraising Exec., Am. Med. Colls. (pub. affairs com. 1989-91), Assn. Am. Med. Colls. (pub. affairs com. 1989-91), Coun. Advancement & Support Edn., St. Vincent Health System (bd. corps.), Erie Club, The Newcomen Soc. U.S., Presque Isle Partnership (dir.), C. of C. (dir.).

MCEACHERN, JOAN, medical association administrator; b. East Los Angeles, Calif., Feb. 28, 1937; d. Chester Manwell Biffi and Doris May Horrocks; m. Wayne Ellery McEachern, Sept. 8, 1961 (dec. Mar. 1992); children: Marc Alan, David Wayne, Eric John. AA, East Los Angeles Coll., 1957. Sec. Flour Corp., City of Commerce, Calif., 1957-61; volunteer art tchr. Yorkville Schs., Yorkville, IL, 1975-1983; office supr. McKeoun-Dunn Ambulance, Oswego, Ill., 1992-97. Author: Illinois Association for Home and Community Education—An Aim for the Homemaker: 75 Years of Education and Outreach, 1999. Mem. Kendall County 4-H, various coms., 1975-2000, mem. Ill. 4-H Found., 1988-97, sec. exec. com. 1990-97; del. Ill. 4-H Salute to Excellence, Washington, 1985; mem. various state coms. in 4-H, 1979-94, developed 4-H project books; ext. adv. coun. U. Ill., 1994-97; pres. Kendall County Homemakers Ext. Assn., 1982-84; adv. coun. Yorkville Schs. Curriculum Com., 1974-76, pres. 1975-76; started Picture Person Art Appreciation program, Yorkville Schs., 1976, chmn., 1975-81; vol. art tchr., 1975-83, others. Recipient Yorkville Area Humanitarian award City of Yorkville Human Svcs. Com., 1983, Disting. Svc. award award Kendall County Homemakers Ext. Assn., 1985, Kendall County Friend of 4-H award, 1989, numerous others. Mem.: Am. Women for Internat. Understanding (bd. dirs. 2002—, membership chair 2003—), Associated Country Women of the World (pubs. and promotions com. 2001—04), Ill. Assn. Home and Cmty. Edn. (pres. 1994—97), Nat. Vol. Outreach Network (pres. 1998—2001), Kendall County Hist. Soc. (newsletter editor 1992—2001), Yorkville Women's club. Avocations: water color painting, skiing, photography, travel, reading. Home and Office: 137 Riverside Dr Yorkville IL 60560-9471 E-mail: mcskikat@usa.com.

MCEACHERN, SUSAN MARY, information technology specialist; b. Royal Oak, Mich., May 3, 1960; d. Donald Keith and Lois Jean (Robison) McE.; m. James Paul Corbett, Jan. 8, 1983 (div. 1999). BS, Mich. State U., 1982; MBA, New Mex. State U., 1985. LPN, Cmty. Coll. Denver, 2004. From acct. adminstr. trainee to acct. adminstr. IBM, El Paso, Tex., 1985-89, customer support rep. Southfield, Mich., 1989-90, sr. adminstrv. specialist, 1991-92, adv. customer support rep., 1992-93, fin. analyst Boulder, Colo., 1993-95, database adminstr., analyst, 1995, team leader, 1995-2000, project mgr., internet, 2000—02. Cons. Integrated Sys. Solutions Co., Dallas, 1990-93. Author: Treasury of Poetry, 1992; editor-in-chief Online Newsletter for Polycystic Ovarian Syndrome Assn., 1998-2000; asst. editor Bull. for Nat. Polycystic Ovarian Syndrome Assn., 1998-2000; profl. flutist PSC Players, 1997-2001; prin. flutist Celebration Christian Ctr., 1996-2000. Vol. supr. Easter Seals, Southfield Mich., El Paso, Tex., 1978-88, Crisis Pregnancy, Las Cruces, New Mex., 1982-86, Multiple Sclerosis, Mich., 1983, Longmont (Colo.) Vol. Assn., 1994. Recipient Photography award Mich. State Fair, 1991, 92. Mem. IBM Club (v.p.), Creative Designs (pres. 1994—, Nat. Sci. and Engring. vol. rep. 1994), Polycystic Ovarian Syndrome Assn. (pres. Colo. chpt. 1997-2000, Outstanding Vol. award 1999, Internat. Dir. Med. Rsch.), Women of the Moose (chair health awareness 1998-99, apptd. officer Argus 1999-2000, Acad. Friendship award 2000). Avocations: computers, swimming, white-water rafting, photography, flute. Home: 1736 Collyer Longmont CO 80501-2077 E-mail: sbrightandsunny@aol.com.

MCELHINNEY, SUSAN KAY (KATE ECHEVERRIA) (KATE MCELHINNEY), executive assistant; b. Greeley, Colo., May 20, 1947; d. Glenn Eugene and Maxine (Filkins) McE.; m. Ben Echeverria, 1997. Student, U. N.C., 1965-67, U. Kans., 1969, U. Colo., 1971-72, 80. Adminstrv. sec. Colo. Pub. Defender, Denver, 1970-74; clk. Colo. Dist. Ct., Boulder, 1974-80; legal asst., office mgr. Law Office Ben Echeverria, San Marcos, Calif., 1986-97; exec. asst. Palomar (Calif.) C.C., 1997—. Mem. black tie fund raising com. Palomar C.C., 1991-92. Republican. Avocations: reading, golf, travel, animal advocate, gardening. Home: 57 Santa Ana Loop Placitas NM 87043-9437

MCELLIGOTT, ANN THERESA, accountant; b. Portland, Oreg., Nov. 18, 1942; d. Frank J. and Florence L. (Swanson) McE.; m. Forrest G. Hawkins, Sept. 9, 1961 (div. Sept. 1982); children: Michelle, Brenda, Sandra; m. Bruce N. Braunsten, Dec. 10, 1999. Student, Portland Community Coll., 1971-72; BS, Portland State U., 1974; MS, U. Oreg., 1994. CPA, Oreg. Staff acct. Coopers & Lybrand, Portland, 1974-76, in-charge acct., 1976-78, audit mgr., 1978-83; reporting and gen. ledger mgr. Tektronix, Beaverton, Oreg., 1983-86, group acctg. mgr., 1986-97, dir. facilities gen. svcs., 1997—. Bd. dirs. Campfire Girls, Portland, 1979-81, treas., 1988-91, v.p.; bd. dirs. Neighborhood House, 1998—, treas., 1999—. Recipient Guleck award Campfire Girls, 1986. Mem. AICPA, Oreg. Soc. CPA's. Avocations: bridge, walking, theater. Office: Tektronix PO Box 500 PO Box 55-075 Beaverton OR 97077-0001

MCELROY, ABBY LUCILLE WOLMAN, financial advisor; b. Washington, Oct. 16, 1957; d. M. Gordon and Elaine (Mielke) Wolman; m. Peter J. McElroy, Mar. 15, 1986; children: Abel Hurst, Leo Frederick. BA, St. Lawrence U., 1979; MS, Ind. U., 1981. 1st v.p. investment Salomon Smith Barney, Westport, Conn., 1986-99, Pridential Securities Inc., Westport, 1999—. London Group Study Exch. grantee Rotary Internat., 1989. Avocations: golf, squash, tennis, lacrosse, swimming, skiing, painting, art history, langs. Office: Wachovia Securities One Morningside Dr N Westport CT 06880

MCELROY, LINDA SUE, retired elementary school educator; b. Stephenville, Tex., Sept. 14, 1945; d. E. J. McElroy Sr. and Margaret Walsworth McElroy. BME, Tarleton State U., 1974, MEd, 1980. Cert. English as Second Lang. 1992, Elem. Edn. 1980. With Evant (Tex.) Ind. Sch. Dist., 1968—80, tchr. k-2, 1979—80; tchr. 1st and 2nd grade Lingleville (Tex.) Ind. Sch. Dist., 1981—85; elem. music tchr. Granbury Ind. Sch. Dist., Granbury, Tex., 1985—87; spl. edn. tchr. Mineral Wells Ind. Sch. Dist., Mineral Wells, Tex., 1987—88; tchr. ESL and music Huckabay Ind. Sch. Dist., Stephenville, 1988—2003; mgr. Stephenville Mus., 2003—. Sec./treas. Tex. State Gospel Singing Conv. Mem.: AAUW (pres. 1988), Assn. Tex. Profl. Educators. Methodist. Avocations: singing, reading. Home: 2643 W Washington Stephenville TX 76401 Office: Stephenville Mus 525 E Washington Stephenville TX 76401

MCELROY, MARY M. (MICKIE MCELROY), educational writer; b. Ft. Worth, June 29, 1944; d. Kennedy King and Maurine (Davenport) McElroy; m. James William Salterio Jr., Aug. 24, 1966 (div. Aug. 1968); m. Michael John Waters, Dec. 13, 1975 (div. Aug. 1983). BA, U. Tex., 1966, MA, 1970; M in Ednl. Adminstrn., Western Wash. U., 1989. Cert. secondary sch. adminstr., classrm. tchr. math., Latin, history. Classrm. tchr. various schs., Wash. and Tex., 1970-78, 80-89, instrnl. cons. in math. Region XIII Ednl. Svc. Ctr., West Tex., 1979-80; asst. prin. Stevens Mid. Sch., Port Angeles, Wash., 1989-90; bus. owner Office on Call, Seattle, 1991-96; dir. edn. Tex. Soc. Profl. Engrs., Austin, 1996-98; curriculum developer Tchg. Tech., Inc., Austin, 1998-99, corp. trainer, 1998-99; devel. editor Thinkwell, Austin, 1999—2001; editor, writer Kamico Instrnl. Media, Austin, 2001—. Dir. Regional Math. Competition, Everett, Wash., 1981-84; chair Com. to Improve Comm., Everett, 1986-87. Author: Powerpoint for Educators, 1998, The Internet and Social Studies in the Classroom, 1999, Designing Web Pages for Libraries, 1998. Dir. Magnolia Summerfest, Magnolia C. of C., Seattle, 1992-94; bd. dirs. Big Bros., Big Sisters, Port Angeles, Wash., 1989-90. Named Networker of Yr., Western Wash. Entrepreneurs Assn., 1992. Mem. Nat. Coun. Tchrs. Math., Wild Bunch, Beta Sigma Phi. Democrat. Avocations: painting, reading, travel, photography. Home: 2712 Deeringhill Dr Austin TX 78745-5112 E-mail: mickiemc@alumni.utexas.net.

MCELROY, MAURINE DAVENPORT, financier, educator; b. Eastland, Tex., Sept. 28, 1913; d. William Fred and Mary Ewell (Johnson) Davenport; m. Kennedy King McElroy, Aug. 9, 1937 (dec. Mar. 1996); children: Mary M., Kennedy King Jr. BA, Tex. Tech U., 1937; MA, Hardin-Simmons U., 1941; PhD, U. Tex., 1964. Tchr. Eastland West Ward Elem. Sch., 1933-39, Eastland H.S., 1939-41, Miller H.S., Corpus Christi, Tex., 1951-54, Ray H.S., Corpus Christi, 1954-57; instr. Del Mar Coll., Corpus Christi, 1957-59; prin. Birdville H.S., Ft. Worth, 1942-43; feature writer Ark. Dem.-Gazette, Little Rock, 1948-51; assoc. prof. emeritus dept. English U. Tex., Austin, 1964—. Cons. in field. Contbr. articles to profl. publs. Patron art museums, theatrical orgns., hist. preservation; sponsor Shelter for Abused Women and Children; fin. mgr. trusts. Mem. AAUW, Am. Assn. Colls. Tchg. English, Coll. English Assn. (life), Renaissance Soc. Am. Avocations: travel, reading, theatre, horticulture. Home: 3215 Gilbert St Austin TX 78703-2221 Office: U Tex Austin Dept English Parlin Hall 108 Austin TX 78712

MCELVEEN-HUNTER, BONNIE, ambassador; b. S.C., Jan. 1945; m. Bynum M. Hunter, Sr.; 1 child, Bynum M. Hunter Jr. Pres., CEO, owner Pace Comm., Inc.; U.S. amb. to Finland Dept. of State, Helsinki, 2001—. Chmn. Alexis de Tocqueville Soc., United Way Greater Greensboro, NC; bd. mem. United Way Am., chair nat. women's leadership giving campaign; chair Women in Philanthropy Summit, Washington; internat. bd. mem. Habitat for Humanity; bd. mem. Internat. Women Build Habitat for Humanity, Habitat for Humanity First Ladies Build. Office: DOS Amb 5310 Helsinki Pl Washington DC 20521

MCELWEE, DORIS RYAN, psychotherapist; b. Calif., Feb. 15, 1931; d. Dennis M. and Emma A. (Klockau) Ryan; m. Charles B. McElwee, Feb. 6, 1959; children: Brent, Gregg, Cynthia; m. Craig A. Thomson, May 6, 1988. BA, Millikin U., Decatur, Ill.; MA, U. Ariz.; PhD, U. So. Calif., UCLA, Temple U. Sr. therapist Am. Inst. Family Rels., Burbank, Calif., 1969—, grad. faculty, 1972-85; psychotherapist in pvt. practice Burbank and Arcadia, Calif., 1970—; grad. faculty Chapman Coll., 1973-75, Pepperdine U., L.A., 1975-78; psychotherapist Calif. Family Study Ctr., Burbank, 1985-90. Guest expert Phil Donahue Show. Co-author: Techniques of Marriage and Family Counseling, Suicide Prevention for College Students, A Place to Rest Your Heart; contbr. articles to Ladies Home Jour. Bd. dirs. NOW, Pasadena, Calif.; mem. Arcadia Assistance League, Las Alas Orgn. Recipient Merit award, Millikin U., 1983. Mem.: Self Esteem Task Force, So. Calif. Assn. Marriage and Family Therapy, Calif. Assn. Marriage and Family Therapists, Am. Assn. Marriage and Family Therapy, Group Psychotherapy Assn. So. Calif. (v.p., exec. bd. dirs.), Panhellenic Assn., Psi Chi, Pi Beta Phi. Republican. Lutheran. Avocations: travel, gardening.

MCELWREATH, SALLY CHIN, corporate communications executive; b. N.Y.C., Oct. 15, 1940; d. Toon Guey and Jean B. (Wong) Chin; m. Joseph F. Callo, Mar. 17, 1979; 1 child, R.J. McElwreath III. BA, Pace Coll., 1963;

MBA, Pace U., 1969. Copywriter O.E. McIntyre, N.Y.C., 1963-65; editl. asst. Sinclair Oil Corp., N.Y.C., 1966-70; account exec. Muller, Jordan & Herrick, N.Y.C., 1970-71; regional mgr. pub. rels. United Airlines, N.Y.C., 1971-79; dir. corp. comm. Trans World Airlines, N.Y.C., 1979-86; v.p. pub. rels. TWA Mktg. Svcs., Inc., N.Y.C., 1986-88; ptnr. The Comm. Group, N.Y.C., 1988-90; gen. mgr. corp. comm. Ofcl. Airline Guides, 1990-91; v.p. corp. comm. Macmillan, Inc., 1991-93, cons. N.Y.C., 1993-94; sr. v.p. corp. comm. Utilicorp United, Inc., Kansas City, 1994—2001, Utilicorp United, Inc. (now Aquila Inc.), Kansas City, 2003—. Pub. affairs officer USNR, 1973-2000. Ret. Capt. Named Woman of Yr., YWCA, 1980, Alumnus of Yr., Pace U., 1976. Mem. N.Am. Pub. Rels. Assn. (vice chair 2003-04), N.Y. Airline Pub. Rels. Assn. (chmn. 1978-79), Wings Club (N.Y.C.). Avocations: sailing, skiing, harpsichord. Office: Aquila Inc 20 W 9th St Kansas City MO 64105-1704 E-mail: sallymc79@aol.com.

MCELYEA, JACQUELYN SUZANNE, accountant, real estate consultant; b. Dallas, July 19, 1958; d. Owen Clyde and Mary Lou (Cockerill) Harvey; m. James E. McElyea, June 11, 1983. BBS, Tex. A&M U., 1980. CPA, Tex. Acctg. mgr. Oxford Tex. Devel., Dallas, 1980-81; staff to dir. PriceWaterhouseCoopers, Dallas, 1981—. Pres. Nat. Assn. Corp. Real Estate, Dallas. Co-author: Real Estate Accounting Reporting, 1995. Bd. dirs. Am. Diabetes Assn., Dallas, 1996-97. Mem. AICPA, Nat. Assn. Real Estate Cos., Tex. Soc. CPAs. Presbyterian. Avocations: animals, cooking. Office: PriceWaterhouse Coopers 2001 Ross Ave Ste 1800 Dallas TX 75201-2933 E-mail: smcelyea@home.com.

MCENTIRE, REBA N. country singer; b. McAlester, Okla., Mar. 28, 1955; d. Clark Vincent and Jacqueline (Smith) McE.; m. Narvel Blackstock, 1989; 1 child, Shelby Steven McEntire Blackstock. Student elem. edn., music, Southeastern State U., Durant, Okla., 1976. Rec. artist Mercury Records, 1978-83, MCA Records, 1984—. Albums include Whoever's in New England (Gold award), 1986, What Am I Gonna Do About You (Gold award), 1987, Greatest Hits (Gold award, Platinum award, U.S., Can.), 1987, Merry Christmas To You, 1987, The Last One To Know (Gold award), 1988, Reba (Gold award 1988), Sweet 16 (Gold award 1989, U.S.), Rumor Has It (Gold award 1991, Platinum award 1992, Double Platinum 1992), Reba Live (Gold award 1990, Gold award 1991, Platinum award 1991), For My Broken Heart, 1991, Forever in Your Eyes, 1992, It's Your Call, 1992, Read My Mind, 1994, Starting Over, 1995, Reba compilation video (Gold award, Platinum award 1992), Reba Live (video), 1995, What If It's You, 1996, Celebrating 20 Years (video), 1996, If You See Him, 1998, Forever Reba, 1998, Star Profile, 1999, So Good Together, 1999, Secret of Giving: A Christmas Collection, 1999; author: (with Tom Carter) Reba: My Story, 1994; actress: (films) Tremors, 1990, The Little Rascals, 1994, North, 1994, One Night at McCool's, 2000, (TV films) The Gambler Returns: The Luck of the Draw, 1991, The Man From Left Field, 1993; actress, exec. prodr. TV films Is There Life Out There?, 1994, Forever Love, 1998, Secret of Giving, 1999; other TV appearances include Country Gold, 1982, Bob Hope Winterfest Christmas Show, 1987, (video) Wrestlemania VIII, 1992, (TV series) Disney's Hercules, 1998, A Salute to Dustin Hoffman, 1999; appeared on TV series Evening Shade, One Life to Live, Frasier, The Roseanne Show. Spokesperson Middle Tenn. United Way, 1988, Nat. and State 4-H Alumni, Bob Hope's Hope for a Drug Free Am.; Nat. spokesperson Am. Lung Assn., 1990-91. Recipient numerous awards in Country music including Disting. Alumni award Southeastern State U., Female vocalist award Country Music Assn., 1984, 85, 86, 87, Grammy award for Best Country Vocal Performance, 1987, 2 Grammy nominations, 1994, Grammy award, Best Country Vocal Collaboration for "Does He Love You" with Linda Davis, 1994, Entertainer of Yr. award Country Radio Awards, 1994, Female Vocalist award, 1994; named Entertainer of Yr., Country Music Assn., 1986, Female Vocalist of Yr. Acad. Country Music, 1984, 85, 86, 87, 92, Top Female Vocalist, 1991, Am. Music award favorite female country singer, 1988, 90, 91, 92, 93, Am. Music award, 1989, 90, 91, 92, Best Album, 1991, Favorite Female Vocalist, 1994, Favorite Female Vocalist, Peoples Choice Award, 1992, Favorite Female Country Vocalist, 1992, 93, Favorite Female Vocalist, TNN Viewer's Choice Awards, 1993, Favorite Female Country Artist, Billboard, 1994, Favorite Country Album award Am. Music Awards, 1995, Favorite Female Country Vocalist award Am. Music Awards, 1995, Favorite Female Vocalist award People's Choice Awards, 1995, Top Female Vocalist of Yr. award Acad. Country Music, 1995, Entertainer of Yr. award Acad. Country Music, 1995, Favorite Female Vocalist award TNN Viewer's Choice Awards, 1995, Star on the Walk of Fame, 1999. Mem. Country Music Assn., Acad. Country Music, Nat. Acad. Rec. Arts and Scis., Grand Ol' Opry, AFTRA, Nashville Songwriters Assn. Inc. Avocations: golf, shopping, being with narvel and shelby, horse racing, raising horses.

MCEUIN, DOROTHEA L. (DOTTIE MCEUIN), counseling administrator; b. Decatur, Tex., Mar. 28, 1944; d. James Allen and Josephine Arlice (Malone) Lewis; m. Grady Raymond Jr. McEuin, Mar. 25, 1967; children: Ray, Malinda, Allie, Ryan. BBA in Edn., North Tex. State U., 1967. Cert. spl. edn., autistic and emotional disturbance, counseling. Sec. AAlie I. Miller Ins., Denton, Tex., 1962; sec., receptionist North Tex. State U./Bapt. Student Union, Denton, 1962—63, North Tex. State U. Student Union, Denton, 1963—66; co-owner Denison (Tex.) Glass and Mirror, 1967—71, Denton Glass and Mirror, 1981—88; tchr., counselor Denton H.S., 1987—. Mem. Citizen's Police Acad., Denton, 2000. Mem.: Tex. Edn. Assn., Coun. for Exceptional Children, Epsilon Sigma Alpha (sec., v.p., pres. 1967—71, treas., sec. 1971—74). Baptist. Avocations: movies, gardening. Office: Denton HS 1007 Fulton St Denton TX 76201

MCEVOY, FRANCES JANE COMAN, writer, editor; b. Phoenix, May 11, 1929; d. James Lindley Coman and Pearl Catherine Bruns; m. Joseph Francis McEvoy, Nov. 10, 1956 (dec. Oct. 1997); children: David L., Stephen C., Anne G. BA, Ariz. State U., 1951; postgrad., Boston U., 1959—60. Editor Helios Lit. Mag. Ariz. State U., Tempe, 1948—50; editor Am. Acad. Arts and Scis., Boston, 1951—52; reporter Waltham (Mass.) News Tribune Dailey, 1952—54, State House News Svc., Boston, 1952—55; press sec. Senator Leslie B. Cutler, Boston, 1954—55; asst. publicity dir. Boston (Mass.) U., 1955—56; writer features Boston (Mass.) Herald, 1975—80; writer, contbr. Dell Horoscope Astrologers Newsletter, 1980—98; editor Geocosmic Mag. Nat. Coun. Geocosmic Rsch., 1984—. Author: Power of Yod & Quincuux, 1998, Out of Bounds Moon and Planets, 2002; contbr. articles to jours.; portrait artist, 1970—2002. Mem. pub. rels. com. Greater Boston Com., 1954, Rep. State Com., Boston, 1955. Mem.: Women's Edn. and Ind. Union, De Cordova Mus. (Lincoln, Mass.), Boston Mus. Fine Arts, Bostonian Soc., DAR, Tenn. Hist. Soc., New Eng. Hist. and Geneal. Soc., Daus. Colonial Wars. Avocations: painting, writing, historic research. Home and Office: 209 Common St Belmont MA 02478

MCEVOY, GRACE ELIZABETH, photographer; b. Patterson, N.J., Nov. 18, 1961; d. Charles Joseph and Mary Hayes (Lyons) McEvoy-French. BS in Media Arts, U. S.C., 1986. Photographer McKissick Mus., Columbia, S.C., 1983-86; freelance photographer, Austin, Tex., 1986-89; photographer Austin History Ctr., 1989—. Mem. peer panel Austin Arts Commn., 1993, chmn. adv. panel, 1994—; judge Tex. Media Awards, Austin, 1994—; bd. dirs. Diverse Arts; cons. Austin, 1996—. Photographer, rschr. Art in Pub. Places, Austin, 1993; photographer Progressive rts Collective, Austin, 1992-94. Recipient svc. award Austin Parks and Recreation Dept., 1994, Mayor of Austin, 1994, 95, Progressive Arts Collective, 1994. Mem. Tex. Photog. Soc., Tex. Fine Arts Assn. Democrat. Avocations: gourmet cooking, ceramics. Office: Austin History Ctr 810 Guadalupe St Austin TX 78701-2314

MCEVOY, NAN TUCKER, publishing company executive, olive rancher; b. San Mateo, Calif., July 15, 1919; d. Nion R. and Phyllis (de Young) Tucker; m. Dennis McEvoy, 1948 (div.); 1 child, Nion Tucker McEvoy. Student, Georgetown U., 1975. Newspaper reporter San Francisco Chronicle, 1944-46, N.Y. Herald Tribune, N.Y.C., 1946-47, Washington Post, 1947-48; rep. in pub. rels. John Homes, Inc., Washington, 1959-60; spl. asst. to dir. U.S. Peace Corps, Washington, 1961-64; mem. U.S. delegation UNESCO, Washington, 1964-65; dir. Population Coun., Washington, 1965-70; co-founder, dep. dir. [illegible] Inc., Washington, 1970-74; former chmn. bd. Chronicle Pub. Co., San Francisco, 1975-95, dir. emeritus, 1995—. Mem. nat. bd. dirs. Smithsonian Instn., Washington, 1994—; bd. dirs. Am. Farmland Trust; mem. coun. Brookings Instn., Washington, 1994—; mem. U. Calif. San Francisco Found., 1993—; dir. emeritus Nat. Mus. Am. Art; mem. Nat. Coun. Fine Arts Museums; formerly arbitrator Am. Arbitration Assn., Washington. Named Woman of Yr., Washingtonian Mag., 1973. Mem. Am. Art Forum, Burlingame Country Club, The River Club, Commonwealth Club of Calif., World Affairs Coun., Villa Taverna. Avocations: overseeing marin county, california olive grove ranch producing fine extra virgin olive oil. Office: 655 Montgomery St Ste 1430 San Francisco CA 94111-2635

MCEVOY, SHARLENE ANN, law educator; b. Derby, Conn., July 6, 1950; d. Peter Henry Jr. and Madaline Elizabeth (McCabe) McE. BA magna cum laude, Albertus Magnus Coll., 1972; JD, U. Conn., West Hartford, 1975; MA, Trinity Coll., Hartford, 1980, UCLA, 1982, PhD, 1985. Bar: Conn., 1975. Pvt. practice, Derby, 1984—; asst. prof. bus. law Fairfield (Conn.) U. Sch. Bus., 1986—92; adj. prof. bus. law, polit. sci. Albertus Magnus Coll., New Haven, 1978-80, U. Conn., Stamford, 1984-86; acting chmn. polit. sci. dept. Albertus Magnus Coll., 1980; assoc. prof. law Fairfield U., 1992-98, prof. bus. law, 1998—. Chmn. Women's Resource Ctr., Fairfield U., 1989-91. Staff editor Jour. Legal Studies Edn., 1989-94; reviewer Am. Bus. Law Assn. jour., 1988—, staff editor, 1995—; sr. articles editor N.E. Jour. Legal Studies in Bus., 1995-96. Mem. Derby Tercentennial Commn., 1973—74; justice of the peace City of Derby, 1975—83; alt. mem. Parks and Recreation Commn., Woodbury, 1995—99; v.p. N.E. Acad. Legal Studies in Bus., 2001—02, 2001—02, pres-elect., program chair, 2003, pres., 2003—; editor-in-chief N.E. Jour. of Legal Studies, 2003—04; mem., treas. Woodbury Dem. Town Com., 1995—96, corr. sec., 1996—98; bd. dirs. Valley Transit Dist., Derby, 1975—77. Recipient Best Paper award N.E. Regional Bus. Law Assn., 1990, Best Paper award Tri-State Regional Bus. Law Assn., 1991; Fairfield U. Sch. Bus. rsch. grantee 1989, 91, 92, Fairfield U. rsch. grantee, 1994. Mem. ABA, Conn. Bar Assn., Acad. Legal Studies in Bus., Mensa (coord. SINISTRAL spl. interest group 1977—). Democrat. Roman Catholic. Avocations: running, sailing, tennis, swimming. Office: 198 Emmett Ave Derby CT 06418-1258 E-mail: samcevoy@mail.fairfield.edu.

MCEVOY-JAMIL, PATRICIA ANN, English language educator; b. Butler, Pa, June 26, 1955; d. Joseph Lawrence McEvoy and Janet Ann (McConnell) Beier; m. M. Jamal Jamil, Nov. 23, 1977; 1 child, Amirah M. MA in TESOL, Monterey Inst. Internat. Studies, 1984; MA in English, U. Notre Dame de Namur, 1995; EdD, U. San Francisco, 1996. Calif. C.C. credential for life. Instr. ESL City Coll. San Francisco, 1989-98, Can. Coll., Redwood City, Calif., 1989-98; lectr. ESL Stanford U., 1989—97, U. Notre Dame de Namur, 1991—98; co-owner, v.p. bd. MPA Co. Investments, Inc., Houston, 1998—. Presenter in field; vis. prof. EFL, Georgetown U., Washington, summer 1999; adj. ESL instr. U. Houston-Downtown, 2000-02, Mus. Fine Arts, Houston. Mem. leadership coun. So. Poverty Law Ctr.-contributed to Jimmy Carter Ctr.; ptnr. mem. Habitat for Humanity Internat.; team leader Rep. Party. Recipient ELITE Patron of Honor award, ELITE Stanford (Calif.) Hosp., 1989, 1990, Wall of Tolerance Award; faculty rsch. grant, U. Notre Dame de Namur, 1984, doctoral rsch. grant, U. San Francisco, 1992—93. Mem. AAUW, NAFE, Nat. Coun. Tchr. English, Tchr. English to Speakers Other Lang., Nat. Mus. Women Arts, Nat. Trust Historic Preservation, Phi Delta Kappa. Avocations: tennis, swimming, bicycling. Office: 5850 San Felipe Ste 500 No 117 Houston TX 77057 E-mail: docpamjam@hotmail.com.

MCEWEN, IRENE RUBLE, physical therapy educator; b. Columbus, Ohio, May 19, 1943; d. John Mitchell and Isabel (Ruble) McE. BS in Phys. Therapy, U. Wash., 1965, MEd in Ednl. Psychology, 1973; PhD in Spl. Edn., Purdue U., 1989. Cert. pediatric clin. specialist Am. Bd. Phys. Therapy Spltys. (pediatric splty. coun.); lic. phys. therapist, Okla., Wash. Phys. therapist St. Vincent Hosp., Portland, Oreg., 1965-69; head phys. therapist Lowell Sch., Seattle, 1970-76; physiotherapist Spastic Centre of New South Wales, Mosman, Australia, 1976-77; head phys. therapist Seattle Sch. Dist., 1977-84; phys. therapist Mesa Pub. Sch., Ariz., 1984, Roosevelt Sch. Dist., Phoenix, 1984-86; rsch. fellow Purdue U., West Lafayette, Ind., 1986-89; tech. specialist Ind. Augmentative and Alternative Communication Tech. Team, West Lafayette, 1988-89; assoc. prof. phys. therapy U. Okla. Health Sci. Ctr., Oklahoma City, 1989-97, prof. phys. therapy, 1997—, Presbyn. Health Found. Presdl. prof., 1998, George Lynn Cross rsch. prof., 2003. Rschr., presenter in field. Mem. editl. bd., dep. editor, editor: Case Reports Phys. Therapy; co-editor: Physical and Occupational Therapy in Pediatrics; contbr. Mem.: Rehab. Engring. and Assistive Tech. Soc. N.Am., Internat. Soc. Augmentative and Alternative Comm., Coun. Exceptional Children, Assn. for Persons with Severe Handicaps, Am. Phys. Therapy Assn. (Margaret L. Moore Outstanding New Acad. Faculty mem. award 1992, Dorothy Briggs Sci. Inquiry award 1993, sect. on pediat. rsch. award 1998, sect. on pediat. Bud DeHaven Svc. award 2001), Am. Assn. Mental Retardation, Am. Acad. Cerebral Palsy and Devel. Medicine, Alpha Eta, Sigma Xi, Phi Kappa Phi. Office: U Okla Dept Rehab Sci PO Box 26901 Oklahoma City OK 73190-1090 Office Phone: 405-271-2131. E-mail: irene-mcewen@ouhsc.edu.

MCEWEN, JOAN GRACE (JOANIE LAWRENCE), actress, recording industry executive; b. Hopkinsville, Ky., Oct. 15, 1932; d. Joseph Thomas McEwen and Thelma Irene (Grace) Fox; m. John E. Bills Jr. (dec.); children: Jennifer Jones, John E. III, James L., Robert J. Student, U. Tenn., Knoxville, 1950-53, U. Tenn., Nashville, 1961-62, Aquinas Jr. Coll., 1962-63, Alvin Ailey Dance Theatre, N.Y.C., 1977, Lee Strasberg Theatre Inst., N.Y.C., Neighborhood Playhouse, 1995-97. Ballet instr., Nashville, 1960-68; adminstr. Shelby Singleton Records, Nashville, 1968-70; from adminstrv. asst. to gen. mgr. Sta. WLAC, Nashville, 1970-73; nat. dir. promotion Mercury Records, Chgo., 1973-76, Pvt. Stock Records, Inc., N.Y.C., 1976-78, Arista Records, Inc., L.A., 1978-87; pres. Joan Lawrence Entertainment, Nashville, 1987—. Active Nashville Symphony Guild. Mem. SAG, AFTRA, Nashville Symphony Assn., Cheekwood Arts. Republican. Avocations: skiing, tennis, horseback riding, golf.

MCEWEN, LAURA, publishing executive; m. James McEwen; 1 child, Sean. BA, Fordham U. Pub. New Woman, Snow Country Mag.; sr. pub. Harpers Bazaar, Family Circle; pub. YM Mag., 2000—03; v.p., pub. dir. Readers Digest Mag., 2003—. Mem., planning com. Mag. Pub. of Am., 2003. Mem.: Fragrance Found., N.Y. Advt. Club, Advt. Women of N.Y., Fashion Group Internat. (bd. dirs.), Cosmetic Exec. Women (bd. dirs.). Office: Readers Digest Mag Box 200 Pleasantville NY 10572-0200

MCEWEN, RUTH, foundation administrator; b. Kieghley, Kans., Dec. 29, 1912; d. Henry Kennedy and Mary Estelle (Erdley) Shaffer; m. Theodore Reginald McEwen, Aug. 1, 1942 (dec. Apr. 1976). BMus, Colo. Women's Coll., Denver, 1933; BA, Colo. State Coll. Edn., 1936; MA, U. So. Calif., L.A., 1940. Tchr. music Arvada (Colo.) H.S., 1937-42. Author: Poems From a Couch, 1995. Pres. Rocky Ridge Music Ctr. Found., Estes Park, Colo., 1955-67, Denver Symphony Guild, 1972-79; trustee Golden (Colo.) Symphony, 1950-56, Denver Symphony, 1970-72, Young Musicians of Colo. Found., 1987—; tchr. sr. citizens art YMCA, 1990—; adv. bd. Coll. Music, U. Colo., Boulder, 1980-95; advisor Met. Opera Auditions, 1980—, Young Musicians Found., Denver, 1989—; founder, advisor Young Musicians Competition, Denver Symphony, 1972-76; clinician, adjudicator master classes, 1950—; pres. Lakewood Woman's Club, 1960-62; bd. govs. Jefferson Family YMCA, Lakewood, 1990-93; founder Jefferson Youth Symphony, 1950. Recipient Svc. award Golden Symphony, 1955, Disting. Svc. award Coll. Music, U. Colo., 1988, Eiber St., 1988. Mem. Colo. State Music Tchrs. Assn., Music Tchrs. Nat. Assn., Silver and Gold Book, Century Club, Mu Phi. Republican. Methodist. Avocations: travel, fishing, swimming. Home: 9650 W 11th Ave Lakewood CO 80215-4602

MCFADDEN, MARY JOSEPHINE, fashion industry executive; b. N.Y.C., Oct. 1, 1938; d. Alexander Bloomfield and Mary Josephine (Cutting) McF.; m. Philip Harari; 1 child, Justine. Ed., Sorbonne, Paris, Traphagen Sch. Design, 1957, Columbia, 1959-62; DFA, Internat. Fine Arts Coll., 1984. Pub. rels. dir. Christian Dior, N.Y.C., 1962—64; merchandising editor Vogue South Africa, 1964—65, editor, 1965—69; polit. and travel columnist Rand (South Africa) Daily Mail, 1965—68; founder sculptural workshop Vukutu, Zimbabwe, 1968—70; spl. projects editor Vogue U.S.A., 1973; pres. Mary McFadden, Inc., N.Y.C., 1976—; ptnr. MMcF Collection by Mary McFadden, 1991—. Bd. dirs., advisor Sch. Design and Merchandising Kent State U., Eugene O'Neill Meml. Theatre Ctr.; mem. profl. com. Cooper-Hewitt Mus., Smithsonian Inst., Nat. Mus. of Design; designer Collection by Mary McFadden, 2000, Mary McFadden Collection, 2003, Earth-BOUND, N.Y.C., 2003; lectr. U. Phila., 2004, Dept. Ancient Near Eastern Art, Met. Mus. Art, 2004. Fashion and jewelry designer, 1973—; maj. retrospective of fashion, textiles and jewels at Allentown (Pa.) Art Mus., 2004; author introduction Mary McFadden High Priestess of High Fashion, 2004. Advisor Nat. Endowment for Arts; active local Police Athletic League, We Care About N.Y., CFDA-Vogue Breast Cancer Initiative, Beth Israel Hosp., The Chemotherapy Found.; curator emeritus Cannan Found., 1973-85; founding trustee Robert Redford's Sundance Inst., 1978-83; trustee Devi Ahilya Bai Holkal Meml. Charitable Trust, Maheshwar, Indore, India. Recipient Am. Fashion Critics award-Coty award, 1976, 78, 79, Audemars Piguet Fashion award, 1976, Rex award, 1977, award More Coll. Art, 1977, Pa. Gov.'s award, 1977, Roscoe award, 1978, Pres.'s Fellows award RISD, 1979, Neiman-Marcus award of excellence, 1979, Design Excellence award Pratt Inst., 1993, award N.Y. Landmarks Conservancy, 1994, NU Breed Fashion award, 1996, Marymount Coll. Fashion award, 1996, Legends award N.Y., 2001, Lifetime Achievement award South Am. Press Assn., Miami, Fla., 2002, Pratt Legions award, 2002, Spirit of Design award Phila. U., 2004; named to Fashion Hall of Fame, 1979; fellow RISD. Mem. Fashion Group (bd. dirs. 1981-82), Council of Fashion Designers Am. (past pres.). Office: Mary McFadden Inc 525 E 72nd St New York NY 10021 Office Phone: 212-772-1125. E-mail: MMcF@aol.com.

MCFADDEN, NANCY ELIZABETH, lawyer; b. Wilmington, Del., Oct. 20, 1958; d. William P. and Mary Elizabeth (Adams) McF. BA, San Jose State U., 1984; JD, U. Va., 1987. Judicial clk. Hon. John P. Wiese U.S. Claims Ct., Washington, 1987-88; atty. O'Melveny & Myers, Washington, 1988-91; deputy communications dir. Office of Pres.-Elect, Washington, 1992-93; asst. atty. gen. U.S. Dept. Justice, Washington, 1993, prin. deputy assoc. atty. gen., 1993-95; gen. counsel Dept. Transp., Washington, 1996—. Nat. deputy polit. dir. Clinton for Pres. Campaign, 1992, nat. surrogate dir. Clinton-Gore for Fres. Campaign, 1992.

MCFADDEN, ROBBYN KILBANE, interior designer, public policy specialist, artist, advocate; b. Chgo., Oct. 5, 1951; d. Robert Harrison and Adrienne Fay (Seyring) Kilbane; m. James E. McFadden Jr., Dec. 20, 1975; 1 child, Ryan James. BFA, U. Ill., 1969-74; Diploma in Interior Design, Harper Coll., Chgo., 1976. Designer Euromarket Designs, 1978-83; project cons. Volo Interiors, 1983-90; educator, art and design dept. Coll. of Lake County, 1981-83; owner, prin. Design Perspectives, 1983—. Design cons. Law Offices of Patricia Hogan, Monadnock Bldg., Chgo., 1989; project designer retail space Historic Harbor House, Waukegan, Ill., 1988, others. Pub. design commns. include Hunterdon Art Ctr. Archival Print System, 1994, Cleve. Edn. Fund. Historic Dallas Bldg., 1998, Kids First Festival, Lake County, Ill., 1998, numerous others; pvt. commns. include residences in Ill., N.J., Ohio, Calif. Mem. adv. com. to internat. programs LWV USA, Washington, 1994—; nat. bd. dirs. UNIFEM/UN Devel. Fund for Women, N.Y.C., 1999—; fundraiser, pub. policy advocate Ctr. for the Humanities and Environment, Jackson Hole, Wyo., 1992-95; adv. mem., cons. Com. for Pub. Art, Cleve., 1995-97; vis. svcs. cons. Art Inst. Chgo., 2003—; specialist advisor Lake County Women's Coalition Arts, 2003—; mem. women's bd. Hist. Genesee Theater, Lake County, Ill. Recipient Carrie Chapman Catt award LWV, Cleve., 1998. Mem. LWV (bd. dirs. Ill. chpt., Lake County pres. 2003—), Am. Soc. Interior Designers (allied), Interior Design Soc./Nat. Home Furnishings Assn., PEO, Lake County Dem. Women (bd. dirs.). Avocations: painting, golf. Personal E-mail: indezyn@aol.com.

MCFADIN, HELEN LOZETTA, retired elementary education educator; b. Tucumcari, N.Mex., Sept. 7, 1923; d. Henry J. and LaRue Altha (Ford) Stockton; m. John Reece McFadin, July 3, 1946; 1 child, Janice Lynn McFadin Koenig. AB in Edn./Psychology, Highlands U., Las Vegas, N.Mex., 1956; MA in Teaching, N.Mex. State U., 1968; postgrad., U. N.D., 1965, St. Leo's Coll., St. Leo, Fla., 1970. Cert. tchr., K-12 reading/psychology specialist, N.Mex. Tchr. 1st and 2d grades Grant County Schs., Bayard, N.Mex., 1943-44; tchr. 4th grade Durango (Colo.) Pub. Schs., 1946-48; tchr. 2d grade Artesia Pub. Schs., Loco Hills, N.Mex., 1955; tchr. 3d grade Alamogordo (N.Mex.) Pub. Schs., 1957-66, h.s. reading specialist, 1966-72, elem. reading specialist, 1972-77, tchr. 4th grade, 1977-82, reading tchr. 7th grade, dept. chair, 1982-87; ret. N.Mex. State U., Alamogordo, 1987, instr. edn., 1987-90. Organizer reading labs. h.s., elem. schs., Alamogordo, 1966-77, designer programs and curriculum, 1957-89; presenter/cons. in field; cons. Mary Kay Cosmetics; rep. Excel Telecomms., Inc. Contbr. articles to profl. jours. Local and dist. judge spelling bees and sci. fairs Alamogordo Pub. Schs., 1987-98. Recipient Literacy award Otero County Reading Coun., 1986; inducted in Women's Hall of Fame, Alamogordo Women's Clubs, 1989. Mem. Am. Bus. Women's Assn. (pres. 1986-87, v.p. local chpt. 1999-00, named Woman of the Yr. 1988, 2003), NEA (del. 1957-87, Dedicated Svc. award 1987), N.Mex. Edn. Assn., Internat. Reading Assn. (mem. Spl. League of the Honored 1985, pres. 1975-76), N.Mex. Reading Assn. (bd. dirs. 1988-94, del. to 1st Russian reading conf. 1992, Dedicated Svc. award 1994), Tularosa Basin Hist. Soc., Beta Sigma Phi (pres. local chpt. 1998-99, formed new master chpt. 1999, Golden Cir. Anniversary award 2002), Kappa Kappa Iota (local pres. Kappa Conclave 1998-00, state officer, nat. com., co-chair nat. conv. 2000-02, Disting. Educator Emeritus Cert. of Merit 1988, VIP award 2000, 2002). Republican. Baptist. Avocations: reading, fashion modeling. Home: 2364 Union Ave Alamogordo NM 88310-3848

MCFADYEN, LIANE, state representative; m. Paul Ray; 1 child. BA, Adams State Coll., 1991, MS, 1993. State rep., dist. 45 Colo. House Rep., Denver, 2000—; owner Rocky Mountain Specialized Cleaning, Pueblo, Colo., Alliance Bus. Strategies, Pueblo. Mem. Info. and Tech. Com., Transp. and Energy Com. Democrat. Office: State Capitol #307 200 E Colfax Ave Denver CO 80203

MCFALL, CATHERINE GARDNER, poet, critic, educator; b. Jacksonville, Fla., July 10, 1952; d. Albert Dodge and Joan (Livingston) McF.; m. Peter Forbes Olberg, Oct. 21, 1978; 1 child, Amanda Olberg. Baccalaureat, U. Paris, 1973; AB magna cum laude, Wheaton Coll., Norton, Mass., 1974; MA, Johns Hopkins U., 1975; PhD, NYU, 1990. Editl. asst., short story editor Ladies' Home Jour., N.Y.C., 1975-77; adminstrv. dir. Poetry Soc. Am., N.Y.C., 1981-83; instr. writing NYU, N.Y.C., 1983-87, asst. dir. Poetics Inst., 1984-86; asst. prof. humanities Cooper Union, N.Y.C., 1990-98. Adj. asst. prof. English Hunter Coll., N.Y.C. Author: Jonathan's

Cloud, 1986, Discovery, 1989 (Nation award), Naming the Animals, 1994, The Pilot's Daughter, 1996; editor: Made with Words, 1998; contbr. poetry and revs. to mags. including Paris Rev., Atlantic Monthly, N.Y. Times, others. Bd. dirs. Yaddo, 2003—. MacDowell Colony fellow, 1980, 86, Yaddo fellow, 1981, 84, 91, 93, 97, 99, Nat. Arts Club Poetry scholar Bread Loaf Writers Conf., 1983. Mem. MLA, Poets and Writers, Poetry Soc. Am., Nat. Book Critics Cir. E-mail: cathgm@aol.com.

MCFARLAND, JANE ELIZABETH, librarian; b. Athens, Tenn., June 22, 1937; d. John Homer and Martha Virginia (Large) McFarland. AB, Smith Coll., 1959; M in Divinity, Yale U., 1963; MS in LS, U. N.C., 1971. Tchr. hist. and religion Northfield Schs., Mass., 1961-62; head librarian reference and circulation Yale Divinity Library, New Haven, Conn., 1963-71; head librarian Bradford (Mass.) Coll., 1972-77; reference librarian U. Tenn., Chattanooga, Tenn., 1977-80; head librarian reference dept Chattanooga-Hamilton County Bicentennial Library, Tenn., 1980-86, acting dir., 1986, dir., 1986—. Mem. Chattanooga Library Assn., Tenn. Library Assn., Southeastern Library Assn., Am. Library Assn., Phi Beta Kappa. Democrat. Roman Catholic. Avocations: reading, travel, needlework. Home: 1701 Estrellita Cir Chattanooga TN 37421-5754 Office: Chattanooga-Hamilton County Libr 1001 Broad St Chattanooga TN 37402-2620

MCFARLAND, KAY ELEANOR, state supreme court chief justice; b. Coffeyville, Kans., July 20, 1935; d. Kenneth W. and Margaret E. (Thrall) McF. BA magna cum laude, Washburn U., Topeka, 1957, JD, 1964. Bar: Kans. 1964. Sole practice, Topeka, 1964-71; probate and juvenile judge Shawnee County, Topeka, 1971-73; dist. judge Topeka, 1973-77; assoc. justice Kans. Supreme Ct., 1977-95, chief justice, 1995—. Mem. Kans. Bar Assn., Women Attys. Assn. Topeka., Topeka Bar Assn. Office: Kans Supreme Ct Kans Jud Ctr 301 SW 10th Ave Topeka KS 66612-1507 Fax: (785) 291-3274.

MCFARLAND, LYNNE VERNICE, pharmaceutical executive; b. San Antonio, Tex., June 3, 1953; d. Earle Clifford and Avis Marie (Jones) Olson; m. Marcus Joseph McFarland, July 27, 1975. BS in Microbiology, Portland State U., 1975, MS, 1980; PhD in Epidemiology, U. Wash., 1988. Cert. Pub. Health. From rsch. asst. to lab. supr. U. Oreg. Health Sci. Ctr., Portland, 1977-82; intern Wash. State Pub. Health Labs, Seattle, 1983; from tchg. asst. dept. epidemiology to rsch. asst. U. Wash., Seattle, 1984-88, from rschr. to lectr. dept. med. chemistry, 1988, rsch. assoc. prof., 1991—; dir. scientific affairs Biocodex, Inc., Seattle, 1988—2001; project dir. diabetes rsch. U. Wash., 2001—. Reviewer McGraw-Hill Book Co., N.Y.C., 1982; editorial reviewer Ob-Gyn, L.A., 1989-2000, Jour. of Infect Diseases, 1991, 95—, Vet. Adminstrn., 1991; also review for gastroenterology, 1990-03, clin. infectious diseases, 1995-03. Reviewer Gastroenterology; contbr. articles to profl. jours. Lobbyist environ. issues Wash. State Biotech. Assn., Seattle, 1990; vol. Literacy Plus, Seattle, 1990. Recipient Poncin scholarship, Seafirst Bank, Seattle, 1985-88. Mem. Am. Soc. Microbiology, Soc. for Epidemiol. Rsch., Soc. Microbiol. Ecology and Diseases (bd. dirs. 1997-2001), Wash. Assn. Epidemiology. Avocations: photography, piano, flute, poetry, sports. Office: 6727 Rainier Ave S Seattle WA 98118

MCFARLANE, BETH LUCETTA TROESTER, former mayor; b. Osterdock, Iowa, Mar. 9, 1918; d. Francis Charles and Ella Carrie (Moser) Troester; m. George Evert McFarlane, June 20, 1943 (dec. May 1972); children: Douglas, Steven (dec.), Susan, George. BA in Edn., U. No. Iowa, 1962, MA in Edn., 1971. Cert. tchr. Tchr. rural and elem. schs., Iowa, 1936-50, 55 56; elem. tchr. Oelwein Cmty. Schs., Iowa, 1956-64, jr. high reading tchr., 1964—71, 1983; city council Oelwein, 1981-82; mayor of Oelwein, 1982-89. Evaluator North Cen. Accreditation Assn. for Ednl. Programs; mem. planning team for confs. for Iowa Cities, N.E. Iowa, 1985; v.p. N.E. Iowa Regional Coun. Econ. Devel., 1986-89; mem. Area Econ. Devel. Com. N.E. Iowa, 1985, Legis. Interim Study Com. on Rural Econ. Devel., 1987-88; mem. policy com. Iowa League Municipalities, 1987-88. V.p. Fayette County Tourism Coun., 1987-88; mem. Iowa State steering com. on road use tax financing, 1988-89; chmn. bd. govs. Oelwein Cmty. Ctr., 1990-94, bd. govs., 2001—; chmn. bldg. and fin. com. Reorganized LDS/Cmty. of Christ Ch. Bldg., 1980—, dist. ch. fin. com., 1992-2001, dist. ch. revolving loan com., 1982-00. Named Iowa Reading Tchr. of Yr., Internat. Reading Assn. Iowa, 1978; recipient Outstanding Contbn. to Reading Coun. Activities award Internat. Reading Assn. N.E. Iowa, 1978, State of Iowa's Gov.'s Leadership award, 1988. Mem.: Oelwien Area C. of C. (bd. dirs. 1986—89, Humanitarian award 1987), Oelwein Area Ret. Sch. Pers. (pres. 1994—96), Oelwein Bus. and Profl. Women (Woman of Yr. 1983), MacDowell Music and Arts Orgn. (pres. 1978—80), N.E. Iowa Reading Coun. (pres. 1975—77), Area Univ. Women (pres. 1999—2000), Delta Kappa Gamma (pres. 1980—82). Republican. Mem. Cmty. Of Christ Ch. Avocations: hiking, refinishing antiques, gardening, walking, creative sewing. Home: 512 7th Ave NE Oelwein IA 50662-1326

MC FARLANE, KAREN ELIZABETH, concert artists manager; b. St. Louis, Jan. 2, 1942; d. Nicholas and Bonita Margaret (Fults) Walz; m. Ralph Leo McFarlane, Nov. 30, 1968 (div.); children: Sarah Louise.; m. Walter Holtkamp, June 19, 1982. B.Mus.Ed. (Presser Music Found. scholar), Lindenwood Coll., 1964. Public sch. music tchr., St. Louis County, 1964-66; music asst. Riverside Ch., N.Y.C., 1966-70; dir. music Park Ave. Christian Ch., N.Y.C., 1974-81; also pres. Murtagh/McFarlane Artists, Inc., Cleve., 1976-88; pres. Karen McFarlane Artists, Cleve., 1989-2000. Mem. Am. Guild Organists, Nat. Assn. Performing Arts Mgrs. and Agts., Inc., Internat. Soc. Performing Arts Adminstrn. Democrat. Presbyterian. Office: 2385 Fenwood Rd Cleveland OH 44118 E-mail: karen@concertorganists.com.

MCFARLIN, BARBARA L. secondary school educator, small business owner; d. Edward H. and Alyce A. Debenjak; m. William B. McFarlin, Aug. 7, 1976; children: Christalynne A., William Cristofer. BS in Edn., Miami U., Oxford, Ohio, 1976; postgrad., U. Ariz. and Pima C.C., U. Akron, Malone Coll., Kent State U., Moody Bible Inst., Chapman U. Cert. tchr. Ohio, Ariz., Ill. Owner, cons. McFarlin Enterprises, Aurora, Ohio, 1985—97; instr. Kent (Ohio) State U., 1996—97; tchr. Valley Christian Acad., Aurora, 1989—97; supr. Aurora Shores Comty., Aurora, 1986—97; co-owner Splatter Matters, Tucson, 1997—; tchr., coach Pusch Ridge Christian Acad., Tucson, 1997—; pool supr., staff devel. Pima County, Tucson, 2003—. Mem. devel. and scheduling team Valley Christian Acad., Aurora, 1991—96; counselor, tchr. Crisis Pregnancy Ctr., Tucson, 2003. Mem. safety coun. adv. bd. ARC, Tucson, 1972—, instr.-trainer Cleve. and Portage Cty, Ohio, 1972—, vol. instr. Sarasota, Fla. and Chgo., 1972—. Avocations: swimming, reading, hiking. Office: Pusch Ridge Christian Acad 9500 N Oracle Rd Tucson AZ 85737

MCFARLIN, DIANE HOOTEN, publisher; b. Lake Wales, Fla., July 10, 1954; d. Ruffie Denton Hooten and Anna Loraine (Peeples) Huff; m. Henry Briggs McFarlin, Aug. 28, 1976 (div. 1993). BS, U. Fla., 1976. Reporter Sarasota (Fla.) Jour., 1976-77, asst. news editor, 1977-78, city editor, 1978-82; asst. mng. editor Sarasota (Fla.) Herald Tribune, 1983-84, mng. editor, 1985-87; exec. editor Gainesville (Fla.) Sun, 1987-90; from exec. editor to assoc. publ. Sarasota Herald-Tribune, 1990-99, publ., 1999—. Adv. bd. U. Fla. Coll. Journalism and Comm., 1987—; Pulitzer juror Columbia U., 1995-96, 2001-02. Mem. accrediting coun. Edn. in Journalism and Mass Comms., 1994-96. Recipient Alumna of Distinction award U. Fla., 1999. Mem. Am. Soc. Newspaper Editors (com. chair 1992, 94, 96, 2000, bd. dirs. 1994—, treas., sec., v.p. 2001, pres. 2002), Fla. Soc. Newspaper Editors (sec.-treas. 1993, v.p. 1994, pres. 1995). Office: Sarasota Herald-Tribune PO Box 1719 Sarasota FL 34230-1719 also: 801 S Tamiami Trail Sarasota FL 34236-7824

MCFARLIN, SHANNON DIANNE, writer, researcher; b. St. Louis, Mo., May 26, 1954; d. Marion Amos and Dolores Jeannette McFarlin; m. David Lamar Maywhoor, Mar. 17, 1973 (div.). BA cum laude, Murray State U., Murray, Ky., 2002. Newspaper reporter Daily Std., Celina, Ohio, 1973—96, Wapakoneta Daily News, Wapakoneta, Ohio, 1996—96. Writer Bowling Green State U. Pub. Rels. Office, Bowling Green, Ohio, 1997—99, Paris Post-Intelligencer, Paris, 2003—; featured speaker, on vanished black communities for Black History Month Ohio State Univ., Lima, Ohio, 1999. Sec. Henry County Dem. Women, Paris, Tenn., 2000—03. Nominee Pulitzer Prize, 1991; recipient Winner, Hellman/Hammett Award, Human Rights Watch, 2000, First Pl., Investigate Reporting, Ohio AP, 1991; grantee Vanished Black Communities Project, The Ohio Hist. Preservation Soc., 1980. Mem.: Alpha Sigma Lambda, Alpha Chi, Pi Sigma Alpha, Phi Alpha Theta. D-Liberal. Achievements include Panelist, The Journal, WBGU-TV, Bowling Green, Ohio, about vanished black communities, February and October, 1999; research in vanished black communities in pre and post Civil War era, funded by Ohio Historical Preservation Soc., grant finalized in 1980, but rsch.continues today. Avocations: running, racquetball, gardening, walking, birdwatching. Home: 713 Park St Paris TN 38242 Personal E-mail: shannonmcfarlin@hotmail.com.

MCFATE, PATRICIA ANN, foundation executive, science educator; b. Detroit, Mar. 19, 1936; d. John Earle and Mary Louise (Bliss) McF.; m. Sidney Norman Graybeal, Sept. 10, 1988. BA (Alumni scholar), Mich. State U., 1954; MA, Northwestern U., 1956, PhD, 1965; MA (hon.), U. Pa., 1977. Assoc. prof. English, asst. dean liberal arts and scis. U. Ill., Chgo., 1967-74, assoc. prof. English, assoc. vice chancellor acad. affairs, 1974-75; assoc. prof. folklore Faculty Arts and Scis., U. Pa., Phila., 1975-81; prof. tech. and soc. Coll. Engring. and Applied Sci., 1975-81, vice provost, 1975-78; dep. chmn. Nat. Endowment for Humanities, Washington, 1978-81; exec. v.p. Am.-Scandinavian Found., N.Y.C., 1981-82, pres., 1982-88; sr. scientist Sci. Applications Internat. Corp., Mc Lean, Va., 1988—, program dir. Ctr for Nat. Security Negotiations, 1988—; cons. UN, 1994-95. Vis. assoc. prof. dept. medicine Rush U., Chgo., 1970-85; bd. dirs. First Union Corp.; mem. sr. adv. panel Dept. Def., 1998—. Author: The Writings of James Stephens, 1979, Uncollected Prose of James Stephens, 1983; exec. producer Northern Stars, 1985, Diego Rivera: I Paint What I See, 1989, The Bear in the Skies, 1998, contbr. articles in fields of sci. policy and lit. to various jours. Mem. Arms Control and Non-Proliferation Adv. Bd., Dept. of State, 1995-2001; mem. disting. adv. panel Sandia Nat. Labs.; bd. dirs. Raoul Wallenberg Com. of U.S., Swedish Coun. Am., Santa Fe Cmty. Found., Santa Fe Opera, Lensic Performing Arts Ctr. Decorated officer Order of Leopold II Belgium, comdr. Order Icelandic Falcon, comdr. Royal Order of Polar Star (Sweden), comdr. Order of Lion (Finland), comdr. Royal Norwegian Order Merit, Knight 1st class Royal Order Dannebrog (Denmark); U. Ill. Grad. Coll. faculty fellow, 1968; Swedish Bicentennial Fund grantee, 1981 Fellow N.Y. Acad. Scis.; mem. AAAS (chmn. com. on sci., engring. and pub. policy 1984 87, com. on sci. and internat. security 1976-79, 88-93), Coun. on Fgn. Rels., Acad. Scis. Phila. (founding mem., corr. sec. 1977-79), Theta Alpha Phi, Omega Beta Pi, Delta Delta Delta. E-mail: patricia.a.mcfate@saic.com.

MCFEATTERS, ANN CAREY, journalist; b. Colorado Springs, Colo., June 27, 1944; d. Norman Cromer and Mildred Harriet Carey; m. Dale B. McFeatters, Sept. 27, 1969; children: Dale C., Matthew C., Kirsten C. BA, Marquette U., 1966. Reporter Evansville (Ind.) Press, 1966-68, Pitts. Press, 1969, Washington Daily News, 1969-70, Scripps Howard News Svc., Washington, 1970-99; Washington bur. chief The Pitts. Post-Gazette and The Toledo Blade, Washington, 1999—. Named to Hall of Fame Soc. Profl. Journalists, 1998; recipient Disting. Svc. award Scripps Howard News Svc., 1999. Mem. Nat. Press Found. (chmn. 1996-98), Washington Press Club (pres. 1980-81), The Gridiron Club. Office: Block News Alliance 529 14th St NW Ste 955 Washington DC 20045 E-mail: amcfeatters@nationalpress.com.

MCGANN, LISA B. NAPOLI, language educator; b. West Hartford, Conn., Sept. 07; d. James Napoli; m. Edward Harrison McGann, Jr. BA, Vassar Coll., 1980; MA, Columbia U., 1983, postgrad., 1991-95; MA, Middlebury Coll., 1987. Cert. tchr. French, ESL and Italian, Conn. Cmty. English program coord. Tchrs. Coll. Columbia U., N.Y.C., 1982-83; mgr. English tchg. com. Jr. League N.Y., N.Y.C., 1983-84; asst. dir. ESL Fordham U., N.Y.C., 1988-89; ESL instr. Laguardia C.C., CUNY, Long Island City, N.Y., 1983—, Columbia U., 1983-96. ESL instr. Yale U., 1988, 89; ESL specialist, tchr. UN, N.Y.C., 1990. Big sister Highland Hts., New Haven, 1976-77; ESL tchr. Boys and Girls Club, Astoria, N.Y., 1992. Recipient awards and scholarships. Mem. Nat. TESOL Soc., Am. Assn. Tchrs. Italian, Italian-Am. Hist. Soc., Nat. Italian Am. Found. (coun.), The Statue of Liberty-Ellis Island Found., Inc. Roman Catholic. Avocations: ballet, reading, travel, real estate, tennis.

MCGARITY, MARGARET DEE, federal judge; b. 1948; BA, Emory U., 1969; JD, U. Wis., 1974. Bar: Wis. 1974. Pvt. practice, 1974-87, bankruptcy judge U.S. Dist. Ct. (ea. dist.) Wis., 1987—. Lectr. on marital property, bankruptcy and family law Fed. Judicial Ctr., Nat. Conf. Bankruptcy Judges, State Bar Wis., Nat. Child Support Enforcement Assn., others. Co-author: Marital Property Law in Wisconsin, 2d edit. 1986, Collier Family Law and the Bankruptcy Code, 1991. Mem. Nat. Conf. Bankruptcy Judges, State Bar Wis., Nat. Assn. Women Judges, Milw. Bar Assn., Assn. Women Lawyers, Thomas E. Fairild Inn, Am. Coll. Bankruptcy, Am. Bankruptcy Inst. Office: 162 US Courthouse 517 E Wisconsin Ave Milwaukee WI 53202-4500

MCGARRY, CARMEN RACINE, historian, artist; b. Plattsburgh, N.Y., Dec. 15, 1941; d. Allyre Joseph and Annette Cecile (Roy) Racine; sep.; children: Suzanne, John Jr., Annette, Patrick. BA, Coll. St. Rose, 1962. Tchg. cert. Ill.; lic. real estate broker, Ill.; cert. interior designer, Ill. Tchr. Chgo. Bd. Edn., 1962-69; comptr., mgr., broker K&G Bldg. Mgmt., Chgo., 1969-90; rsch. asst. U. Chgo., 1985-89. Author: Magnificent Mile: A History of Hillsboro Beach, 1998; designer and creator stained glass windows St. Anne's Shrine, Isle La Motte, Vt., 1995. V.p. Women's History Coalition, Broward County, Ft. Lauderdale, Fla., 1993—2002; com. mem. County Health Fair, Broward County, 1994—; bd. dirs. Hillsboro Lighthouse Com., 1994—, Broward 2000, Broward County League of Cities, 1998-2003; chmn., bd. mem. adv. coun. Area Agy. on Aging, Ft. Lauderdale, 1996—, chmn., 1998-; mem. adv. bd. Fla. Dept. Edler Affairs, 2003-04; chmn. for women's hall of fame Broward County, 1996-98; rep. for srs. on transp. Disadvantaged Coord. Bd. Broward County, 1999-; town commr. Hillsboro Beach, 1999-2003. Recipient Cmty. Svc. award Cystic Fibrosis Found., 1999, First Lady of Broward County award 2000; named to Women's Hall of Fame Broward County, 2001. Golden Choice award from Gov. Bush, 2003. Mem. ASID, Stained Glass Assn. Am., Women's League Hillsboro (bd. mem. 1993—), Broward County Hist. Commn., Hillsboro Beach Hist. Commn. (founder, pres.), Deerfield Beach Rotary (dir. 1996—, pres. 1999-2000, Cooper-Kirk award for hist. rsch. and preservation 1999), First Ladies of Broward County, 1991. Avocations: traveling, writing. Home: 1073 Hillsboro Mile Hillsboro Beach FL 33062-2139 E-mail: ctlm@aol.com.

MCGARRY, DIANE E. marketing professional; b. Oakland, Calif., July 13, 1949; Doctorate (hon.), The Ryerson Sch. Bus. Mgmt.; D of Commerce (hon.), St. Mary's U., Halifax, Nova Scotia; LLD (hon.), U. Waterloo, Can. Sales rep. to sr. v.p./gen. mgr. ea. customer ops. group Xerox Corp., Ft. Wayne, Ind., 1973-99, corp. v.p. gen. mktg. Stamford, Conn., 2000—. Bd. dirs. Can. Life Fin. Inc., Toronto, Omnova Solutions, Fairlawn, Ohio; spkr. in field. Office: 800 Long Ridge Rd Stamford CT 06902-1227

MCGARRY, MARCIA, retired community service coordinator; b. Washington, Dec. 9, 1941; d. Emil Sylvester and Bernice B. (Bland) Busey. BS, Morgan State U., 1964. Cert. tchr., law enforcement officer, Fla. Payroll clk., jr. acct. U.S. Dept. Labor, Washington, 1964-65; English tchr. Taiwan, 1968-70; tchr. Monroe County Sch. Bd., Key West, Fla., 1971-81; exec. dir. Monroe Assn. Retarded Citizens, Key West, 1977-79; dep. sheriff Monroe County Sheriff's Dept., Key West, 1979-83, 86-90; probation/parole officer Fla. State Dept. Corrections, Key West, 1983-91; law enforcement instr. Fla. Keys C.C., 1983-91; cmty. svc. coord. City of Bradenton, 1991-2000; domestic violence specialist II Broward County Sheriff Dept., 2001—. Mem. rev. bd. City of Bradenton Police Dept., 1996—2000, mem. cmty. rels. com., 1996—2000. Active local polit. campaigns; co-founder day schs. for under-privileged children; former mem. Big Bros./Big Sisters Am., mem. com., 1985-86, former bd. dirs., Spouse Abuse, former bd. dirs.; bd. dirs. Adv. Coun. Orange-Ridge Elem., 1991-93; bd. dirs. mayor's com., chmn. task force Drug Free Cmtys., 1991-94, bd. dirs., 1996-2001; bd. dirs. Human Rels. Commn., 1991-93, Drug Free Schs. and Cmty. Adv. Coun., 1991-98, T.O.T.S. (These Our Tots), Inc., 1998-2000; former mem. adv. coun. Byrd Edn. Found., Sweet Adelines Internat., 1992-94, commr. 12th Jud. Nominating Commn., 1992-99, cons., facilitator Cultural Diversity Conflict Resolution Workshops, Manatee County High Schs. and Bradenton Police Dept.; attendance adv. com. Bayshore High, 1993, multicultural com., 1994, former rep. Women's Forum; former dir. choir Luth. Ch.; founding mem. Comprehensive Neighborhood Support Network; mem. adv. bd. Manatee County Sheriff's Dept., 1994-2000, mem. hiring rev. bd., 1997-2000. Recipient Appreciation cert., Lions Club, 1978, 1979, Career Week award, Harris Elem. Sch., 1981, Glynn Archer Elem. Sch., 1989, Trainers award, Probation/Parole Acad., 1987, Cert. of Acknowledgement for Cmty. Svc., AAUW, 1995, awadrd, Vol. Army for the War on Drugs, 1989. Mem. NAFE, Fla. Police Benevolent Assn., Fla. Women in Govt. (mem. Manatee County chpt.), Ecumanical Luth. Ch. of Am. (elected consultation conm. Fla. Synod 1989), Key West Profls., Luth. Ch. Women, Delta Sigma Theta (v.p. 1990-91, corr. sec. 1993-95). Office Phone: 954-831-7045. Personal E-mail: marciadnc@aol.com.

MCGEADY, SISTER MARY ROSE, retired religious organization administrator; b. Hazelton, Pa., June 28, 1928; d. Joseph James and Catherine Cecilia (Mundie) McG. BA in Sociology, Emmanuel Coll., 1955; MA in Clin. Psychology, Fordham U., 1961; DHL (hon.), St. John's U., Queens, N.Y., 1982, Coll. New Rochelle, N.Y., 1991, Fordham U., 1991, Niagara U., 1991, Coll. St. Rose, Albany, N.Y., 1991, DePaul U., 1991. Joined Daus. of Charity St. Vincent De Paul, Roman Cath. Ch., 1946. Dir. Astor Home Clinics, Rhinebeck, N.Y., 1961-66; exec. dir. Nazareth Child Care Ctr., Boston, 1966-71; dir. mental health Cath. Charities Bklyn., 1971-79, assoc. exec. dir., 1987-90; dir. Kennedy Child Study Ctr., N.Y.C., 1979-81; provincial supr. Daus. of Charity St. Vincent DePaul, Albany, 1981-87; pres., chief exec. officer Covenant House, N.Y.C., 1990—2003. Bd. dirs. Cardinal Cooke Health Care Ctr., N.Y.C., Meninger Found., Kans., Ctr. for Human Devel., Washington. Author: Catholic Special Education, 1979. Mem. N.Y. State Mental Health Svcs. Coun., Albany, 1983-90, N.Y. State Mental Health Planning Coun., Albany, 1986-91, Cath. Charities USA, 1966—. Recipient svc. award N.Y.C. Dept. Mental Health, 1988, Encouragement award Cath. U. Am., 1991. Roman Catholic. Home: 75 Lewis Ave Brooklyn NY 11206-7015 Office: Covenant House 346 W 17th St New York NY 10011-5089

MCGEE, CARRIE L. artist; BA, Immaculate Heart Coll., L.A., 1976. One-woman shows include Penine Hart Gallery, N.Y.C., 1989, The Greater Nashville Arts Found., 1995, Cheekwood Mus. Art, Nashville, 1996, Internat. Austausch Ateliers Region Basel, Basel, Switzerland, The Lowe Gallery, Atlanta, 1998; group shows at Penine Hart Gallery, N.Y.C., 1989, 90, 93, Cheekwood Mus. Art, Nashville, 1993, The Gallery on Broadway, Nashville, 1993, Bell Gallery, Memphis, 1994, AKA Gallery, Nashville, 1994, Zeitgeist, Nashville, 1995, 96, Southeastern Ctr. for Contemporary Art, Winston-Salem, N.C., 1997, Cumberland Gallery, Nashville, 1998, others. Fellow MacDowell Colony, N.H., 1989-90; fellow NEA/So. Arts Fedn. Visual Arts, 1996; named Internat. Austausch Ateliers Basel Exchange Artist, Christoph Merian Found., 1997.

MCGEE, JANE MARIE, retired elementary school educator; b. Paducah, Ky., Nov. 3, 1926; d. William Penn and Mary Virginia (Martin) Roberts; m. Hugh Donald McGee, Oct. 11, 1946; children: Catherine Jane McGee Bacon, Nancy Ann McGee McManus. BS in Elem. Edn., Murray State U., 1948; cert. in gifted edn., Nat. Coll. Edn., 1976. Tchr. Hazel (Ky.) Pub. Schs., 1948-49, Pittsford (Mich.) Pub. Schs., 1949-50, Leal Elem. Sch., Urbana, Ill., 1950-53, Cleveland Elem. Sch., Skokie, Ill., 1953-57; pvt. tutor, pre-sch. tchr., 1953-61; tchr. Woodland Park Elem. Sch., Deerfield, Ill., 1968-83; ret., 1983; beauty and skin care cons. Mary Kay Cosmetics, Gunnison, Colo., 1984—; co-owner Eagles Nest B&B, 1996—2002. Soprano Western State Coll. and Cmty. Chorus, Gunnison, 1986-97, European concert tour, 1990. Mem. AAUW, Top o' the World Garden Club (sec. 1984—2002, winner first place at numerous garden club shows). Republican. Baptist. Avocations: flower arranging, crafts, knitting, bird watching, rock collecting. Home: 109 San Juan Dr Sequim WA 98382-9326

MCGEE, LINDA MACE, judge, lawyer; b. Marion, N.C., Mar. 20, 1949; d. Cecil Adam and Norma Jean (Hogan) Mace; m. B. Gary McGee, Dec. 19, 1970; children: Scott Adam, Jeffrey Sean. BA, U. N.C., 1971, JD, 1973. Bar: N.C. 1973. Exec. dir. N.C. Acad. Trial Lawyers, Raleigh, 1973-78; assoc. Finger, Watson & di Santi, Boone, N.C., 1978-80; ptnr. Finger, Watson, di Santi & McGee, Boone, 1980-89, di Santi, Watson & McGee, Boone, 1989-95; judge N.C. Ct. of Appeals, 1995—. Mem. trustee panel U.S. Bankruptcy Ct., Greensboro, N.C., 1980-82; bd. dirs. Legal Services of N.C., Raleigh, 1980-84; mem. N.C. Bd. Law Examiners, 1986-93. Vice-chairperson Watauga County Coun. on Status of Women, Boone, 1979-82; trustee Caldwell C.C. and Tech. Inst., Hudson, N.C., 1980-89; mem. exec. bd. N.C. Assn. C.C. Trustees, 1983-85; trustee Caldwell C.C., 1981-89; mem. Pub. Edn. Commn., 2000—. Mem. ABA, ATLA, AAUW, LWV, ABA Found., Am. Law Inst., N.C. Assn. Women Attys. (charter, treas. 1980-84, chair jud. divsn. 1997, Gwyneth B. Davis award 1997, Outstanding Judge of Yr. award 1999), N.C. Bar Assn. (bd. govs. 1983-86, co-chair lawyers in schs. com., Pro Bono Svc. award, 1992, jud. divsn. Outstanding Judge of Yr. award 1999), N.C. Acad. Trial Lawyers (bd. govs. 1993-95), N.C. State Bar, Boone C. of C. (bd. dirs. 1982-85), N.C. Bus. and Profl. Womens Clubs (chair polit. action com. 1982-83, Young Career Woman 1980), Boone Bus. and Profl. Women's Club (Woman of Yr. 1980), N.C. Women's Forum. Democrat. Presbyterian. Home: PO Box 9068 Hickory NC 28603-9068 Office: PO Box 888 Raleigh NC 27602-0888

MCGEE, LYNDA PLANT, guidance counselor; b. L.A., Nov. 22, 1960; d. Larry Earle and Dolores (Balin) Plant; m. William Granville McGee, Dec. 21, 1996; 1 child, Roman Earle. BA in English Edn. cum laude, Xavier U., 1984; MEd in Counseling Psychology, U. Ill., 1986; cert. in coll. counseling, UCLA, 1997. Pupil pers. svcs. credential in counseling. English tchr., decathalon coach Dorsey H.S., L.A., 1986-94; English tchr. St. Monica Cath. H.S., Santa Monica, Calif., 1994-98, Downtown Magnets H.S., LA, 1998—2000, guidance counselor, 2000—; faculty advisor Teach for Am., 2003. Instr. Crenshaw-Dorsey Adult Sch., 1988-89; ind. coll. counselor, L.A., 1999—. Author: Active Learning Through Teacher Research, 1997. Mem. sch. decision making coun. Downtown Magnets H.S., L.A., 1998-99; bd. dirs. urban schs. com. UCLA, mem. h.s. initiative com., 2000. Fellow Nat. Endowment, 1994, 2000, UCLA, 1996, 97. Mem. Nat. Assn. Coll. Admission Counselors, Calif. Assn. Sch. Counselors, West of Westwood Homeowners Assn. (bd. mem.), Multiracial Americans of So. Calif. (bd. mem.), Western Assn. Coll. & Admission Counselors, Order Ea. Star, Zeta

Phi Beta. Democrat. Avocations: reading, traveling, acting. Office: Downtown Magnets HS 1081 W Temple St Los Angeles CA 90012-1513 Office Phone: 213-481-0371 ext. 5133. E-mail: sisofe@aol.com.

MCGEE, PATRICIA K. state legislator; m. Mike McGee, 1960; foster children: Ann, Carol, Norma. AA, Alfred State Coll. Asst. to the dean Jamestown C.C., Cattaraugus, N.Y.; mem. N.Y. State Assembly, Albany, 1987-98, vice chmn. minority joint conf. com., ranking minority mem. assembly higher edn. com., assembly intern com., ranking minority mem. assembly transportation com., mem. assembly standing com. on environ. conservation and higher edn. com., appointed asst. minority wip.; mem. dist. 56 N.Y. Senate, Albany, 1998—. Mem. legis. commn. on Hazardous and Toxic Waste and Rural Resources Commn.; rep. task force mem. on Econ. Devel. and the Future of SUNY; guest speaker Chautauqua Inst. Mem. 219 Liaison Com., Farm Bur., Portville Parent Tchr Assn., Cattaraugus County Tourist Bur. Mem. Am. Legis. Exchange Coun., Nat. Conf. State of State Legis., Nat. Order of Women Legis., N.Y. State Fire Safety Consortium, VFW, Am. Legion, Disabled Am. Vets. Office: Westgate Plz 700 W State St Olean NY 14760-2346 also: 814 Legislative Office Bldg Albany NY 12247

MCGEE, SHERRY, retail executive; b. Honolulu, Hawaii, Nov. 16, 1957; d. Winnie R. Johnson; 1 child, Michael L. BS, Wayne State U., 1987, MBA, 1991. Divsn. sales mgr. CDI Corp., 1978-89; sales tng. cons. McGee & Co., 1990-92; dir. mktg. Bartech, Inc., 1992-97; founder, pres. Apple Book Ctr., 1996—. Vol. Jr. Achievement. : Apple Book Center 18843 Gainsborough Rd Detroit MI 48223-1341 E-mail: apple001@aol.com.

MCGEER, EDITH GRAEF, neurological science educator; b. NYC, Nov. 18, 1923; d. Charles and Charlotte Annie (Ruhl) Graef; m. Patrick L. McGeer, Apr. 15, 1954; children: Patrick Charles, Brian Theodore, Victoria Lynn. BA, Swarthmore Coll., 1944; PhD, U. Va., 1946; DSc (hon.), U. Victoria, 1987, U. B.C., 2000. Research chemist E.I. DuPont de Nemours & Co., Wilmington, Va., 1946-54; research assoc. div. neurological sci. U. B.C., Vancouver, Can., 1954-74, assoc. prof., 1974-76, prof., acting head, 1976-83, prof., head., 1983-89, prof. emerita, 1989—. Author: (with others) Molecular Neurobiology of the Mammalian Brain, 1978, 2d. edit., 1987; editor: (with others) Kainic Acid as a Tool in Neurobiology, 1978, Glutamine, Glutamate, and GABA, 1983; contbr. articles to profl. jours. Decorated officer Order of Can.; recipient citation, Am. Chem. Soc., 1958, Rsch. award, Clarke Inst., 1992, Lifetime Achievement award, Sci. Coun. B.C., 1995, Hon. Alumnus award, 1996, cert., Internat. Sci. Inst., 2001, medal of svc., Dr. Cam Coady Found., 2003. Fellow Can. Coll. Neuropsychopharmacology, Royal Soc. of Can.; mem. Can. Biochemical Soc., Internat. Brain Rsch. Orgn., Internat. Soc. Neurochemistry, Soc. Neuroscience, Am. Neurochemical Soc. (councilor 1979-83), North Pacific Soc. Neurology and Psychiatry (hon. fellow), Lychnos Soc., Sigma Xi, Phi Beta Kappa Office: U BC Divsn Neurol Scis 2255 Wesbrook Mall Vancouver BC Canada V6T 1Z3 E-mail: mcgeer@interchange.ubc.ca.

MCGEHEE, SHARON, school system administrator; Tchr. Ramona Elem. Sch.; prin. Berlyn Elem. Sch., Lehigh Elem. Sch.; with personnel svcs. Ontario-Montclair Sch. Dist., Calif., dir. certificated personnel and staff devel., asst. supt., dep. supt., 1998—2000, supt., 2000—. Office: Ont-Montclair Sch Dist 950 W D St Ontario CA 91762*

MCGERVEY, TERESA ANN, technical information specialist; b. Pitts., Sept. 27, 1964; d. Walter James and Janet Sarah (Donehue) McG. BS in Geology, Calif. U. Pa., 1986, MS in Earth Sci., 1988; MLS, Cath. U. Am., 1998. Phys. sci. technician U.S. Geol. Survey, Reston, Va., 1989-90; editor, indexer Am. Geol. Inst., Alexandria, Va., 1990-91; cartographer Def. Mapping Agy., Reston, 1991-93; tech. info. specialist Nat. Tech. Info. Svc., Springfield, Va., 1993-2000, Dept. of Def., Arlington, Va., 2000—. Intern dept. mineral scis. Smithsonian Instn., 1985—86. Mem.: AAUW, ALA, Geosci. Info. Soc. Personal E-mail: tamgervey@starpower.net.

MCGHEE, CARLA RENEE, professional basketball player; b. Peoria, Ill., Mar. 6, 1968; Degree in Sports Mgmt. with honors, U. Tenn., 1990. Basketball player USA Women's Nat. Team Olympics, 1996; profl. basketball player Orlando (Fla.) Miracle, 1999—.

MCGHEE-HENSEL, KAREN SUE, music educator; b. McPherson, Kans., Oct. 15, 1954; d. Herbert and Marcelyn McClain; m. John Hensel, July 10, 1999; children: Sharon McGhee, Sean McGhee. MusM in Edn., U. Mo. Dir. orch. Pratt H.S., Kans., 1977—79, Shawnee Mission North H.S., 1979—. Recipient Crystal Apple, Fox 4 News, 2001. Mem.: Sigma Alpha Iota. Achievements include Develop Outstanding Orchestra Program. Home: 8014 W 54th Terr Overland Park KS 66202 Office: Shawnee Mission North High Sch 7401 Johnson Dr Shawnee Mission KS 66202 Personal E-mail: kmcghee99@yahoo.com. E-mail: nomcghee@smsd.org.

MCGIBBON, PHYLLIS ISABEL, art educator, artist; b. Madison, Wis., Jan. 9, 1961; d. W. Henry and G. Louise McGibbon. BFA, U. Wis., 1983, MFA, 1988. Luther Gregg Sullivan vis. artist Wesleyan U., Middletown, Conn., 1989-91; asst. prof. art Pomona Coll., Claremont, Calif., 1991-94, Wellesley (Mass.) Coll., 1994-97, assoc. prof., 1997—. Artist residency Bemis Ctr. for Contemporary Art, Omaha, 1995, Millay Colony, Austerlitz, N.Y., 1996, Va. Ctr. Creative Arts, Sweet Briar, 1997. Solo art installations include Davison Art Ctr., Middletown, Conn., 1990, Orange County Ctr. for Contemporary Art, Santa Ana, Calif., 1992, Sushi Performance and Visual Art, Inc., San Diego, 1994, Davis Mus. and Cultural Ctr., Wellesley, 1996, John Michael Kohler Arts Ctr., Sheboygan, Wis., 1998. Recipient award Elizabeth Greenshields Found., Montreal, Can., 1991, award Western States Arts Found. NEA, 1992, award Art Matters, Inc., N.Y.C., 1994; fellow Kala Inst., Berkeley, Calif., 1992-93, individual artist fellow Nat. Endowment for Arts 1995. Mem. Coll. Art Assn., Am. Print Alliance. Office: Wellesley Coll Dept of Art Jewett Arts Ctr Wellesley MA 02481

MCGILL, GRACE ANITA, retired occupational health nurse; b. Lawrence, Mass., Mar. 8, 1943; d. Joseph John and Tina Mary (Sicurella) Tabacco; m. Howard L. McGill, Jr., Feb. 28, 1965 (dec. Mar. 2003); children: Cynthia, Deborah, David. RN, Mass. Gen. Hosp., 1963; BS, Lesley Coll., 1987; MS in Mgmt., Lesley Grad. Sch., 1990. Cert. occupl. health nurse Am. Bd. Occupl. Health Nurses, Inc. Nurse Phillips Acad., Andover, Mass., 1963-65, 97th Gen. Hosp., Frankfurt, Germany, 1966, Highsmith-Rainey Hosp., Fayetteville, N.C., 1968, Lawrence (Mass.) Gen. Hosp., 1969-78, Baldpate Psychiat. Hosp., Georgetown, Mass., 1978-79; nursing staff St. Joseph's Hosp., Lowell, Mass., 1980-81, head nurse, 1981-83; occupl. health nurse Wang Labs., Inc., Lowell, 1983-87, corp. safety specialist, 1987-90; health svcs. adminstr. Loral Infrared and Imaging Sys., Inc., Lexington, Mass., 1990-93; supr. health svcs. Osram Sylvania, Inc., Danvers, Mass., 1993-95; occupl. health nurse Occupl. Health Strategies, Inc., Chelmsford, Mass., 1995—98; ret., 1998. Contract instr. Sch. Pub. Health Harvard U.; occupl. health nurse Sts. Meml. Med. Hosp. ; past chair Am. Bd. Occupational Health Nurses, 1997—99. Pres. Cape Cod Hosp. Aux., 2001—03; dir. Cape Cod Healthcare Found. Bd., 2001—03. Recipient MA Medique Leadership grant, 1999. Mem. Am. Assn. Occupl. Health Nurses, Mass. Gen. Hosp. Nurses Alumnae Assn., Lesley Coll. Alumnae. Episcopalian. Avocations: music, piano, organ. Home: 30 Marsh Side Dr Yarmouth Port MA 02675

MCGILL, JENNIFER HOUSER, non-profit association administrator; b. Abingdon, Va., Mar. 3, 1957; d. Mason L. and Margaret Jane Houser; m. James B. McGill, July 15, 1978; children: Melissa Diane, Mark James. AA, Va. Highlands C.C., Abingdon, 1978; BA, U. S.C., 1980. Reporter, editor Sumter (S.C.) Daily ITEM, 1980-81; assoc. editor Sandlapper Mag., Columbia, S.C., 1981-82; membership editor Assn. for Edn. in Journalism/Mass Comm., Columbia, 1982-83, adminstrv. asst., 1984-85, exec. dir., 1985—. Mem. nat. steering com. Journalist-in-Space Project, Columbia, 1985-86; mem. exec. com. Coun. Nat. Journalism Orgns., 2003—; co-exec. dir. Coun. Comm. Assocs., 2003—. Mem. [illegible] Club (3d v.p. 1990-91, 2d v.p. 1991-92). Avocations: reading, cooking, biking. Office: Assn Schs Journalism & Mass Comm 234 Outlet Pointe Blvd Columbia SC 29210-5667

MCGILL, SYLVIETTE DELPHINE, editor; b. Southern Pines, N.C., Feb. 17, 1964; d. Sylvester Nicholson and Josephine Graham Flowers; m. Michael Anthony McGill, Aug. 7, 1982; children: Vindell, Miranda. BS in Bus., Liberty U., 1992. Tchr. Aldine Sch. Dist., Houston, 1993-94; mng. editor Upscale mag., Atlanta, 1995—. Mem. Mag. Assn. Ga., Atlanta Assn. Black Journalists (Soft Feature award 1998), Nat. Coun. Negro Women. Avocations: singing, traveling. Office: Upscale Mag 600 Bronner Bros Way SW Atlanta GA 30310-2040

MCGILLICUDDY, JOAN MARIE, psychotherapist, consultant; b. Chgo., June 23, 1952; d. James Neal and Muriel (Joy) McG. BA, U. Ariz., 1974, MS, 1976; PhD, Walden U., 1996. Cert. nat. counselor. Counselor ACTION, Tucson, 1976; counselor, clin. supr. Behavioral Health Agy. Cen. Ariz., Casa Grande, 1976-81; instr. psychology Cen. Ariz. Coll., Casa Grande, 1978-83; therapist, co-dir. Helping Assocs., Inc., Casa Grande, 1982—, v.p., sec., 1982—; cert. instr. Silva Method Mind Devel., Tucson, 1986—. Mem. Mayor's Com. for Handicapped, Casa Grande, 1989-90, Human Svcs. Planning, Casa Grande, 1985-95. Named Outstanding Am. Lectr. Silva Mind Internat., 1988-99. Mem. ACA. Avocations: jogging, singing. Office: Helping Assocs Inc 1901 N Trekell Rd Casa Grande AZ 85222-1706

MCGINN, LORETTA, food service administrator; b. S.I., N.Y., May 23, 1934; d. Francis Aloysious and Maryan (Russell) Byrne; m. Thomas A. McGinn, Jan. 21, 1956 (dec. Nov. 1991); children: Thomas A.J., Consuelo, Marianne Byrne, Julia Gaetano, Laura. BA, Coll. S.I., 1979; MSW, Rutgers U., 1989. Sec. S.I. (N.Y.) Hosp., 1975-82; office mgr. Cmty. Svc. Soc. N.Y., N.Y.C., 1982-85; exec. dir. N.Y. RSVP/SERVE, N.Y.C., 1985-90, Meals in Wheels, S.I., 1990-93, pres., CEO, 1993—. Bd. dirs. S.I. Cares, 1993-96; officer S.I. Interagy. Coun., 1984-90; sec., treas., v.p., pres. S.I. United Way, 1985—. Mem. AAUW, NAFE, Nat. Assn. Fundraising Execs., Nat. Assn. Meal Programs, Rotary. Roman Catholic. Avocations: handcrafts, walking, decorating, painting. Office: Meals on Wheels 304 Port Richmond Ave Staten Island NY 10302-1700

MCGINN, MARY J. lawyer, insurance company executive; b. St. Louis, Apr. 9, 1947; d. Martin J. and Janet McGinn; m. Bernard H. Shapiro, Sept. 6, 1971; children: Sara, Colleen, Molly, Daniel. BA, Dominican U., River Forest, Ill., 1967; JD, St. Louis U., 1970. Bar: Mo. 1970, Ill. 1971. Atty. tax div. U.S. Dept. Justice, Washington, 1970-73; atty. Allstate Ins. Co., Northbrook, Ill., 1973—, v.p., dep. gen. counsel, 1980—. Mem. ABA, Am. Coll. Investment Counsel, Assn. Life Ins. Counsel. Roman Catholic. Home: 155 N Buckley Rd Barrington IL 60010-2607 Office: Allstate Ins Co 3075 Sanders Rd Ste G5A Northbrook IL 60062-7127 E-mail: mmcginn@allstate.com.

MCGINN, MARY LYN, real estate company executive; b. New Orleans, Aug. 12, 1949; d. Dan Creedon and Millicent Virginia (White) Midgett; m. Walter Lee McGinn, Mar. 14, 1985. BA, La. State U., 1970, MA, 1972; PhD, U. So. Miss., 1976; MBA, Loyola Coll., 1990. Cert. comml.-investment mem., cert. property mgr., master appraiser. Dir., prof. Dillard U., New Orleans, 1972-76, Loyola U., New Orleans, 1976-80; sr. v.p. Equity Investment Svcs., Inc., New Orleans, 1980-84; pres. Mgmt. Svcs. Group, Inc., New Orleans, 1984-85, Assoc. Investment Svcs. Inc., New Orleans, 1985-87, Northshore Property Mgmt., Inc., New Orleans, 1985-87; asst. v.p. USF&G Realty, Balt., 1987-89, v.p., 1989-90; exec. mng. dir. Galbreath Co., 1990—98; exec. v.p. CB Richard Ellis, 1998—2001; pres. Lin-Chris Assocs., L.P., 2001—. Cons. colls. and univs., 1976—. Bd. dirs. Pitts. Zoo, Salvation Army, Jr. Achievement. Mem. Nat. Assn. Corporate Real Estate Execs., Bldg. Owners and Mgrs. Assn., Comml.-Investment Council, Nat. Assn. Master Appraisers. Avocations: tennis, golf, skiing.

MCGINNIS, MARY LOUISE, mental health services professional; b. Tampa, Fla., July 1, 1957; d. Harold Glen and Peggy Joyce (Hawley) McG.. AA in Education, Hillsborough Cmty. Coll., 1979; BA in Psychology, U. So. Fla., 1991, MA in Counselor Edn., 1995. Cert. legal asst.; diplomate Am. Psychotherapy Assn.; lic. mental health counselor, nat. cert. counselor. Pvt. practice, 1995—. Adj. instr. Hillsborough Cmty. Coll., Tampa, 1992—; mem. Fla. Bar Grievance Com. (13th cir.). Bd. chmn. Bd. of Social Ministry, Holy Trinity Luth. Ch., 1991-92. Mem.: Tampa Bay Assn. Marriage and Family Therapy, Am. Assn. of Christian Counselors, Nat. Assn. Legal Assets, Am. Mental Health Counseling Assn., Golden Key, Psi Chi, Pi Gamma Mu, Phi Kappa Phi. Lutheran. Office: 1308 W Sligh Ave Tampa FL 33604-5902 Office Phone: 813-963-7373.

MCGINNIS, PATRICIA GWALTNEY, nonprofit organization executive; b. Goldsboro, N.C., July 19, 1947; d. Thomas McKim Gwaltney and Patricia Anne (Watkins) Schools; m. James Michael McGinnis, Aug. 4, 1978; children: J. Brian, Katherine B. BA, Mary Washington Coll., 1969; MPA, Harvard U., 1975. Dir. spl. studies U.S. Dept. Commerce, Washington, 1975-76; prof. staff mem. U.S. Senate Budge Com., Washington, 1976-77; dep. assoc. dir. U.S. Office Mgmt. and Budget, Washington, 1977-81; sr. cons. Cresap, McCormick and Paget, Inc., Washington, 1981-82; prin. The FMR Group, Inc., Washington, 1982-94; pres., CEO Coun. for Excellence in Govt., Washington, 1994—. Mem. exec. alumni coun. Kennedy Sch. Govt., Harvard U., Cambridge, Mass., 1992-96; dir. Primark Corp., Waltham, Mass., 1995-2000; mem. assoc. coun. George Washington Sch. Bus. and Pub. Adminstrn., 1996-99; bd. dirs. Brown Shoe Co., St. Louis, Imagitas, Inc., Newton, Mass.; bd. visitors U. Md. Sch. Pub. Affairs. Contbr. articles to profl. jours. Office: Coun for Excellence in Govt 1301 K St NW Ste 450W Washington DC 20005-3397

MCGINN MILLER, JANET SCRIVNER, elementary school educator, writer; b. Roy Bert Scrivner and Wanda Lou Jeffcoat; m. Glenn Richard Miller, Dec. 29, 2000; m. David George McGinn, Aug. 8, 1987 (dec. Nov. 21, 1993); children: Bryan George Loveless, Kyle Andrew McGinn, Kelly Anita Molly McGinn. BS magna cum laude, Slippery Rock State Univ., 1979—80; MA, U. of Ariz., 1987—95. Ariz. Tchg. Cert. K-8 Ariz. State Edn. Dept., 1983. Eighth grade tch. tchr. Tucson Unified Sch. Dist., 2001—, math improvement tchr., 2001; eighth grade math tchr Sunnyside Sch. Dist., Tucson, 1986—94; sixth grade math/sci. tchr. Window Rock Unified Sch. Dist., Ft. Defiance, Ariz., 1984—86. Sponsor Falcon Crest presents (student movie projects) Booth-Fickett Magent Sci. Mid. Sch., Tucson, 2001—. Author: (book) Widowed Without Warning, (screenplay) A Part of We. Mem. PTA, Tucson, Sagaro Del La Vista Neighborhood Assn., Tucson, 2002—03. Recipient Lambda Epsiolon Delta, Nat. Elem. Edn. Hon., 1981. Mem.: NYC Writers Assn., Soc. of Southwestern Authors, Tucson Edn. Assn. Liberal. Avocations: web page designer, sewing. Personal E-mail: author1@cox.net.

MCGLYNN, MARGARET G. pharmaceutical executive; BS in Pharmacy, SUNY, Buffalo, 1982, MBA in Mktg., 1983. Profl. rep. Merck & Co., Inc., Whitehouse Sta., NJ, 1983—84, mktg. analyst, 1985—86, promotion mgr., 1986, product mgr., 1987—89, dir. bus. devel., 1987—89, 1989—90, sr. dir. mkt. planning, 1990—91, exec,. dir. nat, consumer mktg. U.S. human health, 1991—93, v.p. bus. mgmt. and devel. U.S. human health, 1993, sr. v.p. managed care U.S. human health, 1994—95, sr. v.p. bus. planning proposals and analysis Merck-Medco Managed Care, 1994, sr. v.p. health and utilization mgmt., Merck-Medco Managed Care L.L.C., 1995—98, sr. v.p. world wide human health mktg., 1998—2001, exec. v.p. customer mktg. and sales U.S. human health, 2001—03, pres. U.S. human health, 2003—. Mem. dean's adv. coun. U. Buffalo Sch. Mgmt. Office: Merck & Co Inc One Merck Dr PO Box 100 Whitehouse Station NJ 08889-0100

MCGLYNN, MARILYN HUTCHISON, medical/surgical nurse, educator; d. John Read Glass and Carolyn Jean Cabana; m. Timothy Patrick Wayne K. Hutchison, Dec. 9, 1978; 1 child, Brittany Lynn Hutchison. B.Gen. Studies in Health and Fitness, Valdosta State U., Ga., 1995; ADN, Abraham Baldwin Coll., Tifton, Ga., 1998. RN Ga., 1999. X-ray technician/nursing asst. Dr. John P. Kendrick, Valdosta, Ga., 1986—88; fitness dir./specialist Lowndes-Valdosta YMCA, Valdosta, 1988—93; health and safety dir. ARC, Valdosta, 1994; adj. instr. Valdosta Tech. Coll., 2001—; chart auditor/matrix coder South Ga. Med. Ctr., Valdosta, 1999—. Patient care assistance adviser Valdosta Tech. Coll., 2001—03; fitness specialist Lowndes-Valdosta YMCA, Ga., 1991—94. Mem. Rotary Club, Valdosta, Ga., 1996—97. Mem.: NAFE (none), Ga. Nurses Assn. (licentiate; none). Methodist. Avocations: walking, reading, movies, photography.

MCGOLDRICK, KATHRYN ELIZABETH, anesthesiologist, educator, writer; b. Worcester, Mass., 1946; MD, Cornell U., 1970. Diplomate Am. Bd. Anesthesiology. Intern N.Y. Hosp.-Cornell Med. Ctr., 1970—71; resident anesthesiology Peter Bent Brigham Hosp., Boston, 1971—73; fellow pediat. anesthesiology Children's Hosp. Med. Ctr., Boston, 1973—74; prof. anesthesiology Yale U., New Haven, 1992—2001; prof., chmn. dept. anesthesiology N.Y. Med. Coll., Valhalla, 2001—. Med. dir. ambulatory surgery Yale-New Haven Hosp., 1991—2001. Editor-in-chief Survey of Anesthesiology, 1995—; mem. editl. bd. Anesthesia Web, 1999—. V.p., trustee Wood Libr.-Mus. Anesthesiology, 1998—2001, pres., 2001—. Fellow Am. Coll. Anesthesiology; mem. AMA, Am. Soc. Anesthesiologists, Conn. State Soc. Anesthesiologists (pres. 1998-2000), Assn. Univ. Anesthesiologists, Acad. Anesthesiology, Soc. Ambulatory Anesthesia (pres-elect 2003, pres. 2004). Office: Dept Anesthesiology NY Med Coll Valhalla NY 10595

MCGOVERN, MAUREEN ANN, curator; b. Chgo., Nov. 1, 1952; BA, No. Ill. U., 1976; MA, NYU, 1994. Media specialist Young and Rubicam, Chgo., 1976-79; corp. media specialist Darcy Benton and Bowles, N.Y.C., 1979-81; media and video prodns. specialist N.Y. Daily News, N.Y.C., 1981-85; dir. visual and creative svcs. Telecomms. Cons. and Planning, Inc., N.Y.C., N.J., 1986-92; curator Corp. Art Planning, Inc., N.Y.C., 1986—, Akari Light Sculptures, 1989-90, Willis-Corroon, N.Y.C., 1991—; corp. art cons. Timken Co., Canton, Ohio, 1998-99. Exhbn., corp. identity specialist for various fine art and new media prodns., N.Y.C., 1986—; artwork verification authenticator of Nadelman sculpture, 1990; corp. curator Hamilton Corp. Fin. Ltd., London; art lectr. N.Y. Pub. Schs., 1990-95, NYU, 1997—; U.S. curatorial participation "John Byrne at 60," Paisley Mus., Scotland, 2000; cons. for placement of an important contemporary collection with a major Am. U., 2001, others. Author: A Guide to Commerce of Art, 2000; co-curator multi-media exhbn. U.S. Atty. So. Dist. N.Y., 1987. Com. vol. Am. Diabetes Assn. Recipient award Weiboldt Found., 1978; Ill. State scholar, 1970; Barat scholar, 1997— Mem. Nat. Assn. for Corp. Art Mgmt., Am. Assn. Museums (assoc.), Appraisal Assn. Am. (affil.), N.Y. Chamber of Commerce, Assn. Ind. Video and Filmmakers, N.Y. New Media Group, Phi Sigma Tau. Avocations: art collecting, golf, fundraising art, media and charitable organizations. Office: Corp Art Planning Inc 27 Union Sq W Ste 407 New York NY 10003-3305 E-mail: corporateartplanning@e-architect.com.

MCGOWAN, DIANE JOYCE, psychologist; b. Johnstown, Pa., Oct. 8, 1949; d. Harry William and Alice LaVerne Schmidt; m. Vincent George McGowan, June 10, 1967; children: Kimberly, Christopher, Chad, Vincent Jr. BA in Psychology, Indiana U. of Pa., 1993; MS in Counseling Psychology, Frostburg State U., 1997. Caseworker County Mental Health, Johnstown, Pa., 1994; rsch. asst. Frostburg (Pa.) State U., 1994—96; outpatient therapist Bedford (Pa.) County Mental Health, Bedford, 1996—97, Cambria County Mental Health, Johnstown, Pa., 1997—98; drug and alcohol counselor Cove Forge Charter Renewal Ctr., Johnstown, 1997; psychol. svcs. specialist, sex offender program coord. Pa. Dept. Corrections, Houtzdale, 1998—. Avocations: travel, reading, gardening, crafts. Office: SCT-Houtzdale Po Box 1000 Houtzdale PA 16698 Home: 6930 Aspen St Allendale MI 49401-9600

MCGOWAN, JOAN YUHAS, development researcher; b. Trenton, N.J., Feb. 13, 1955; d. Bernard Joseph and Estelle (Gray) Yuhas; children: Matthew Sheehan, Allison Joo Ok. BA summa cum laude, The Coll. N.J. (formerly Trenton State Coll.), 1977. Cert. tchr. N.J., 1977. Tchr. Blessed Sacrament Sch., Trenton, 1977; intake officer Mercer County Juvenile Ct, Trenton, 1978-82; rsch. dir. Audits and Surveys, Princeton, N.J., 1982-85; project dir. The Gallup Orgn., Princeton, 1985-86, Hase/Schannen Rsch. Assocs., Princeton, 1986; devel. rschr. Coll. NJ, 1986—2003; ind. rsch. cons. J.A.M.S. Cons., 2002—. Guest lectr., Thomas Jefferson U., Rutgers U., Helene Fuld Sch. Nursing; guest speaker local television programs. Author: Waiting: The Hopes and Frustrations of a Childless Couple, 1983; contbr. articles to various publs. Pres. Resolve, Inc., Phila, 1982; mem. Holt Internat. Children's Svcs., Trenton, 1984-85, Incarnation Altar Rosary Soc., Trenton, 1988—, Holy Name Soc., Trenton, 1989—; treas, area contact, Homeward Bound, Inc., 1996-2000. Recipient Think and Suggest award State of N.J., 1977, Meritorious award Trenton State Coll., 1989. Mem.: New Eng. Devel. Rschrs. Assn. (mentor, Retirees award for extraordinary efforts and dedication, TCNJ 2003), Assn. Profl. Rschrs. for Advancement, Am. Fedn. Tchrs., Villa Park Civic Assn., Operation Scarlet (assoc.). Democrat. Roman Catholic. Avocations: reading, family activities, rescue dogs, piano, music. Home: 941 Lyndale Ave Trenton NJ 08629-2409 E-mail: sadiemae@snip.net.

MCGOWAN, MONICA S. performing company executive, sales executive; b. Rapid City, SD, June 2, 1954; d. Elmer E. and Ora Virginia Flatt; m. Joseph E. McGowan, Sept. 25, 1981. BS in music edn., Chadron State Coll., 1972—76. Artistic dir. Twin Cities Bronze, Lakeville, Minn., 1999—; handbell sales rep. - minn. Schulmerich Bells, Lakeville, 2003—; dir. of handbells Shepherd of the Valley Luth. Ch., Apple Valley, 1995—2002, Gethsemane Luth. Ch., Minnetonka, 1993—96, St. Paul's United Meth. Ch., Mendota Heights, 1993—95, First United Meth. Ch., Natchitoches, La., 1992—93, St. Stephen Episcopal Ch., Edina, Minn., 1988—91, Good Samaritan United Meth. Ch., Edina, 1987—91; purchasing sec. Al Johnson Constrn. Co., Bloomington, 1979—82. Bd. dirs. Am. Guild of English Handbell Ringers, Inc., Centerville, Ohio, 1995—2003, spl. interest dept. chair, 1999—2003; chime rep. Area VII, Am. Guild of English Handbell Ringers, Inc., Lakeville, Minn., 1994—95; chair Area VII, Am. Guild of English Handbell Ringers, Lakeville, Minn., 1995—2002. Mem.: Twin Cities Bronze, Music Educators Nat. Conf., Am. Guild of English Handbell Ringers, Inc. (area chair 1995—2002, dept. chair 1999—2003), Order of the Ea. Star. Office: Twin Cities Bronze 9399 Birch Lane Lakeville MN 55044

MCGOWAN, ROSE, actress; Actor: (films) Encino Man, 1992, The Doom Generation, 1995, Bio-Dome, 1996, Kiss & Tell, 1996, Scream, 1996, Going All The Way, 1997, Nowhere, 1997, Lewis & Clark & George, 1997, Seed, 1997, Phantoms, 1998, Southie, 1998, Devil in the Flesh, 1998, Jawbreaker, 1999, Sleeping Beauties, 1999, Ready to Rumble, 2000, The Last Stop, 2000, Monkeybone, 2001, Strange Hearts, 2001, Vacuums, 2002;

(TV films) God Is In the T.V., 1999, The Killing Yard, 2001; (TV series) Charmed, 2001—, (TV appearances) True Colors, 1990—, What About Joan, 2001—. Office: Internat Creative Mgmt 8942 Wilshire Blvd Beverly Hills CA 90211-1934*

MCGOWEN, SANDRA GRANT, interior designer; b. Shreveport, La., Dec. 4, 1942; d. Ellis Elva and Mary Lou (McMahen) Grant; m. Norman Douglas McGowen, Mar. 14, 1964 (dec. 1972); children: Amanda Laine, Norman Douglas Jr. BS in Home Econs., La. Tech. U., 1965; BA in Visual Arts and Interior Design, Ga. State U., 1978. Interior designer Rich's, Atlanta, 1978-85; dir. design Comml. Interior Designs, Atlanta, 1985; pres. McGowen Interiors Inc., Atlanta, 1985—. Adj. prof. Brenau Univ., 1995; coord. interior design Brenau Univ., Atlanta campus, 1996—. Elder Presbyn. Ch., 1986; bd. dirs. Niskey Lake, Atlanta, 1986; design judge March of Dimes, Birmingham, Ala., 1987. Fellow: Am. Soc. Interior Designers (newsletter editor 1986, 87, treas. 1987, 88, pres. Ga. chpt. 1990-91, nat. bd. 1991-93, Presdl. citation 1981, 87, 96); mem.: Nat. Trust for Hist. Preservation, Mercedes Benz Club Am. (sec. Peachtree sect.), High Mus. Art., Ga. Trust for Hist. Preservation, Atlanta City Sales Club (pres. 2000—, chmn. bd. 2001—), Gamma Phi Beta (pres. Mother's Club. U. Ga. 1987-88). Republican. Presbyterian. Home and Office: 720 Old Saddle Lane Alpharetta GA 30004 Office Phone: 678-867-0066. Personal E-mail: mcgowenint@mindspring.com.

MCGRADY, CORINNE YOUNG, design company executive; b. N.Y.C., May 6, 1938; d. Albert I. and Reda (Bromberg) Young; m. Michael Robinson McGrady; children: Sean, Siobhan, Liam. Student, Bard Coll., Annandale-on-Hudson, N.Y., 1960, Harvard U., 1968—69. Founder, pres. Corinne McGrady Designs; designer Corinneware (joint venture Corinne McGrady Designs and Boston Warehouse Trading Corp.), East Northport, NY, 1970—. Exhibited in group shows at Mus. Contemporary Crafts, N.Y.C., 1969—70, Smithsonian Instn., 1970—71, Pompidou Ctr., Paris, 1971, Mus. Sci. and Industry, 1970, exhibitions include Guild Hall Show, Southampton, N.Y., 1968, Hecksher Mus., 1968; patentee cookbook stand. V.p. Women's Internat. League for Peace and Freedom, Huntington, NY, 1971; mem. bldg. com. Timberland Lib Hoodsport, 1996—97. Recipient Design Rev. award, Indsl. Design, 1969, 1970, Instant Supergraphic Indsl. Design Rev. award, 1971. Home and Office: PO Box 27 Lilliwaup WA 98555-0027

MCGRADY, PHYLLIS, television producer; Exec. prodr. PrimeTime Live, N.Y.C., Turning Point; with ABC, 1977—; v.p. and exec. prodr. spl. programming ABC News, 1998—2000; exec.-in-charge Good Morning Am., 1999—; sr. v.p. primetime, early morning and news program devel. ABC News, 2000—. Office: PrimeTime Live 147 Columbus Ave Fl 3D New York NY 10023-5900

MCGRAIL, JEANE KATHRYN, artist, educator, poet, curator; b. Mpls., May 1, 1947; d. Robert Vern and Mary Virginia (Kees) McGrail. BS, U. Wis.-River Falls, 1970; MFA, Cranbrook Acad. Art, 1972; postgrad., Sch. of Art Inst. of Chgo., 1985, Ill. Inst. Tech., 1993. Group exhbn. include Saginaw Art Mus., Mich., 1972, Met. Mus. Art, Miami, Fla., 1974, Lowe Mus. Art, Coral Gables, Fla., 1974, 76, Miller Galleries, Coconut Grove, Fla., 1978, 80, Cicchinelli Gallery, NYC, 1980-82, Harper Coll., 1984, Contemporary Art Ctr. Arlington, Arlington Heights, Ill., 1984, 85, 86, 94, Evanston Art Ctr., 1985, South Shore Cultural Ctr., Chgo., 1990, N.A.M.E. Gallery, 1990, Artemisia Gallery, Chgo., 1991, 92, 93, 94, North Lakeside Art Ctr., Chgo., 1991, 94, 95, Ceres Gallery, NYC, 1992, Harper Coll., Ill., 1993, Environ. Concerns, Chgo., 1993, North Pk. Coll., Chgo., 1993, Franklin Square Gallery, Chgo., 1994, 95, 96, Space 900 Gallery, Chgo., 1994, 95, 96, 97, 98, 99, Chuck Levitan Gallery, NYC, 1995, Riverwest Art Ctr., Milw., 1995, Nat. Mus. Women in the Arts, Wash., 1996, Gallery 1040, 1997-, "Red", Chgo., 1998, Oakton Coll. Gallery, Ill., 1999-, Women's Works, Woodstock, Ill., 1999, "Paint It Siver", ARC Gallery, Chgo., 1999, Past/Present, Chgo., 1999, "Blue", Northeastern Ill. U.,Chgo., 2000, Then and Now, Chgo., 1999, Norris Cultural Ctr., St. Charles, Ill., 1999, others; represented in permanent collections at Chgo. Mus. Sci. and Industry, U. Chgo., Mus. Photography, Chgo., Miami-Dade Pub. Libr., U. Wis.-River Falls, MacGregor Found., Printmakers Workshop, NYC, Norman R. Eppnik Art Gallery Emporia State U., Kans., 2000, Mini Print Internat. Exhbn., Binghamton, NY, 2000, Yale U. Med. Libr., 2000, Columbia U. Med. Ctr., 2000, Mini Print Internat. of Cadaques, Spain, Macy Gallery, Providence, RI, 2000, Brickton Gallery, Pk. Ridge, Fla., 2001, Mini Print Internat. of Cadaques, Spain, 2001-04, Last of Primaries, Coll. of Lake Co., 2003-, Ukrainian Mus. Contemporary Art, Chgo., 2003, others; solo exhbn. include Gallery at the Commons, Chgo., 1982, Truman Coll. Gallery, Chgo., 1991, C.G. Jung Inst., Evanston, Ill., 1992, Carlson Tower Gallery, Chgo., 1994, Olcott Ctr. Gallery, Theosophical Soc. Am., Wheaton, Ill., 2001; pub. "Mosaic", 1992, The Best of Printmaking, 1997; contbr. publ. to profl. jour. Cranbrook Acad. Art scholar, 1971; CAAP grantee Dept. Cultural Affairs City Chgo, 1992; recipient Poster Competition award Vizcaya Mus., 1974; Print award Auction WPBT, 1979. Mem. Coll. Art Assn., Chgo. Women's Caucus for Art (bd. dirs. 1992-93, sec.), Chgo. Artists Coalition. Democrat. Studio: 1040 W Huron St LL5 Chicago IL 60622-6591 Office Phone: 312-882-8512. E-mail: jkmc@jeanemcgrail.com.

MCGRANERY, REGINA C. judge; b. Phila., Nov. 7, 1945; BA magna cum laude, Trinity Coll., 1967; JD, U. Va., 1970. Law clk. to Chief Judge Edward M. Curran U.S. Dist. Ct. DC Dist., 1971-73; asst. U.S. atty. Washington, 1973-84; asst. gen. counsel for litigation U.S. Cath. Conf., 1984; adminstrv. appeals judge benefits rev. bd. Dept. Labor, Washington, 1995—. Contbr. articles to profl. jours. Mem. Am. Inns of Ct., Fed. Bar Assn. (disting. svc. award 1990). Roman Catholic. Office: Dept Labor Benefits Rev Bd 800 K St NW Ste 500 Washington DC 20001-8004

MCGRATH, ANNA FIELDS, retired librarian; b. Westfield, Maine, July 4, 1932; d. Fred Elber and Nancy Phyllis (Tarbell) Fields; m. Bernard McGrath (div.); children: Timothy, Maureen, Patricia, Colleen, Rebecca. BA, U. Maine, Presque Isle, 1976; MEd, U. So. Maine, 1979; MLS, U. R.I., 1982. Libr. U. Maine, Presque Isle, 1976-86, assoc. libr. dir., 1986-89, interim libr. dir., 1989-92, dir., 1992-94, spl. collection libr., 1994-97, ret., 1997. Editor: County: Land of Promise, 1989. Mem. Friends of Aroostook County Hist. Ctr. at Libr., U. Maine-Presque Isle; mem. Plymouth (Mass.) Spiritualist Ch. Mem. Inst. Noetic Scis., Am. Mensa. E-mail: amcgrath@maine.edu.

MCGRATH, CHRYSTYNE MARY, retail clothing store owner; b. New Haven, Dec. 16, 1968; d. Walter Gerard and Geraldine Mary (Ward) Pieper; m. David Vincent McGrath, Aug. 10, 1991. Student, Stone Acad., 1988-89, U. New Haven, 1990-91. Sales rep. Exclusively Children's, Guilford, Conn., 1984—; front desk clk. Marriott, Trumbull, Conn., 1988-89, Waters Edge, Westbrook, Conn., 1989-90; asst. mgr. Brooks-Hirsh, Hamden, Conn., 1990-91; owner Chrystyne's (formerly Exclusively Jrs.), Guilford, 1991-96, Exclusively Children's and Chrystyne's, Guilford, 1995—, Chrystyne's. Chairperson The Bus. Devel. Team. Mem. Guilford Bus. Devel. Team; pres. Heat & Eat program Guilford Welfare Dept.; chair Taste All of Guilford. Mem. Nat. Assn. Women Bus. Owners, Guilford C. of C. (bd. dirs.). Roman Catholic. Avocations: crafts, gardening. Home: 1451 West St Guilford CT 06437-1022 Office: Exclusively Children's 1250 Boston Post Rd Guilford CT 06437-2452

MCGRATH, EILEEN MARIE, pediatric nurse; b. N.Y.C., June 13, 1961; d. Patrick J. and Bridget K. (Dolphin) McG. BS in Nursing, Coll. New Rochelle (N.Y.), 1983, M in Nursing Adminstrn., 1990. Cert. pediatric nurse. Staff pediatric nurse Montefiore Med. Ctr., Bronx, N.Y., 1983-86; lic. practical nurse med./surg. New Rochelle Hosp., 1982-83; pvt. duty nurses aide Kingsbridge Jewish Nursing Home, Bronx, N.Y., 1978-80; patient care coord. Montefiore Med. Ctr., Bronx, 1986—; exec. dir. Am. Med. Women's Assoc, Alexandria, Va., 2001—02, exec. v.p., CEO, 2002—. Mem. Am. Assn. Nurses Network, Inc., N.Y. State Nurses Assn.

MCGRATH, ELEANOR BURNS, editor, writer; b. Gloucester, Mass., July 28, 1952; d. Edward James and Julia Ann (Holloran) McG.; m. Paul Allen Witteman, May 5, 1984; 1 child, Katharine McGrath Witteman. AB magna cum laude, Mt. Holyoke Coll., 1974. Rschr. Time-Life Books, N.Y.C., 1974-76; reporter, staff writer, edn. editor Time Mag., N.Y.C., 1976-86; sr. editor Women's Sports and Fitness Mag., San Francisco, 1986-87; spl. corr. Time Mag., San Francisco, 1988; sr. editor, articles editor Self Mag., N.Y.C., 1991-98; editor Time Mag./Princeton Rev. Coll. Guide, 2000—. Journalist-in-residence U. Mich., Ann Arbor, 1984-85. Author: My One and Only: The Special Experience of the Only Child, 1989; editor: One Earth, 1990. Trustee Mt. Holyoke Coll., South Hadley, Mass., 1976-79; pres. Greater N.Y. Athletic Assn., N.Y.C. 1980-84. Time fellow Duke U., 1981. Mem. N.Y. Rd. Runners Club. Avocation: distance running. Home: 110 Riverside Dr New York NY 10024-3715 E-mail: elliemcgrath@timemagazine.com.

MCGRATH, JUDITH, broadcast executive; b. Scranton, PA, 1952; BA English, Cedar Crest Coll., Allentown, PA. Copy chief Glamour mag.; sr. writer Mademoiselle; copywriter Nat. Advt., Phila.; copywriter, on-air promotion Warner Amex Satellite Entertainment Corp. (predecessor to MTV), 1981; editl. dir. MTV, sr. v.p., creative dir., 1988—92, exec. v.p., creative dir., 1992—93, co-pres., creative dir., 1993—94, pres., 1994—96, MTV, MTV2, 1996—2000, pres. MTV Group, chmn. Interactive Music, 2000—02; pres. MTV Networks Music Group, 2002—. Trustee emeritus Nat. Campaign to Prevent Teen Pregnancy; bd. dirs. Rock the Vote. Named Humanitarian of Yr., T.J. Martell Found. Leukemia, Cancer and AIDS Rsch., 2003; recipient Cable Ace Award, 1993, Founders award, Rock the Vote, 2001, Friend of the Children award, Harlem Children's Zone, 2001. Office: MTV 1515 Broadway Fl 25 New York NY 10036-8901*

MCGRATH, KATHRYN BRADLEY, lawyer; b. Norfolk, Va., Sept. 2, 1944; d. James Pierce and Kathryn (Hoyle) Bradley; children: Ian M., James D. AB, Mt. Holyoke Coll., 1966; JD, Georgetown U., 1969. Ptnr. Gardner, Carton & Douglas, Washington, 1979-83, dir. div. investment mgmt. SEC, Washington, 1983-90; ptnr. Morgan Lewis, Washington, 1990—2002, Crowell & Moring, LLP, Washington, 2002—. Named Disting. Exec. Pres. Reagan, 1987. Mem. Fed. Bar Assn. (exec. council securities law com.). Office: Crowell & Moring LLP 1001 Pennsylvania Ave NW Washington DC 20004 E-mail: kmcgrath@crowell.com.

MCGRATH, MARY HELENA, plastic surgeon, educator; b. N.Y.C., Apr. 12, 1945; d. Vincent J. and Mary M. (Manning) McG.; children: Margaret E. Simon, Richard M. Simon. BA, Coll. New Rochelle, 1966; MD, St. Louis U., 1970; MPH, George Washington U., 1994. Diplomate Am. Bd. Surgery, Am. Bd. Plastic Surgery, lic. physician Calif. Resident in surg. pathology U. Colo. Med. Ctr., Denver, 1970-71, intern in gen. surgery, 1971-72, resident in gen. surgery, 1971-75, chief resident in gen. surgery, 1975-76; resident in plastic and reconstructive surgery Yale U. Sch. Medicine, New Haven, 1976-77, chief resident plastic and reconstructive surgery, 1977-78; fellow in hand surgery U. Conn.-Yale U., New Haven, 1978; instr. in surgery divsn. plastic and reconstructive surgery Yale U. Sch. Medicine, New Haven, 1977-78, asst. prof. plastic surgery, 1978-80; attending in plastic and reconstructive surgery Yale-New Haven Hosp., 1978-80, Columbia-Presbyn. Hosp., N.Y.C., 1980-84, George Washington U. Med. Ctr., Washington, 1984-2000, Children's Nat. Med. Ctr., Washington, 1985-2000, Loyola U. Med. Ctr., 2000—02, U. Calif., San Francisco, 2003—, Hines VA Hosp., 2001—02, San Francisco (Calif.) VA Ctr., 2003—, San Francisco (Calif.) Gen. Hosp., 2003—; asst. prof. plastic surgery Columbia U., N.Y.C., 1980-84; assoc. prof. plastic surgery Sch. Medicine, George Washington U., Washington, 1984-87, prof. plastic surgery, 1987-2000, Loyola U. Med. Ctr., 2000—02, U. Calif., San Francisco, 2003—. Attending physician VA Hosp., West Haven, Conn., 1978-80; attending in surgery Hosp. Albert Schweitzer, Deschapelles, Haiti, 1980; historian., bd. dirs. Am. Bd. Plastic Surgery, 1991-95; guest examiner certifying exam., 1986-88, 95-2003; specialist site visitor Residency Rev. Com. for Plastic Surgery, 1985, 87, 91, 94; presenter, cons. in field; senator med. faculty senate George Washington U., bd. govs. Med. Faculty Assocs. Co-editor: (with M.L. Turner) Dermatology for Plastic Surgeons, 1993; assoc. editor: The Jour. of Hand Surgery, 1984-89, Annals of Plastic Surgery, 1984-87, Plastic and Reconstructive Surgery, 1989-95, Contemporary Surgery, 1999—, Annals of Surgery, 2004—; advt. editor Plastic and Reconstructive Surgery, 2003—; contbr. book chpts.: Problems in General Surgery, 1985, Human and Ethical Issues in the Surgical Care of Patients with Life-Threatening Disease, 1986, Problems in Aesthetic Surgery, Biological Causes and Clinical Solutions, 1986; guest reviewer numerous jours.; contbr. articles to profl. jours. Recipient numerous rsch. grants, 1978—. Fellow ACS (D.C. chpt. program ann. meeting chmn., 1992, pres. 1994-95, bd. govs. 1995-98, exec. com. 1996-97, chmn. adv. coun. for plastic surgery 1995-98, regent 1997—); mem. AAAS, Am. Surg. Assn., Am. Assn. Hand Surgery (exec. sec. 1988-90, 1st prize ann. resident contest 1978, other coms.), Am. Assn. Plastic Surgeons (trustee 1997-2000), Am. Burn Assn., Am. Soc. for Aesthetic Plastic Surgery, Am. Soc. Maxillofacial Surgeons, Am. Soc. Plastic and Reconstructive Surgery (chmn. ethics com. 1985-87, chmn. device/tech. evaluation com. 1993-94, chmn. workforce task force 1997-2000, bd. dirs. 1994-96, chmn. endowment bd. dirs. 2000—, ednl. found. bd. dirs. 1985-96, treas. 1989-92, v.p. 1992-93, pres.-elect 1993-94, pres. 1994-95), Am. Soc. Reconstructive Microsurgery (edn. com. 1992-94), Am. Soc. Surgery of Hand (chmn. 1987 ann. residents' and fellows conf. 1986-87, rsch. com. 1988-90), Assn. Acad. Chmn. Plastic Surgery (bd. dirs. 1999—), Assn. Acad. Surgery, Chgo. Soc. Plastic Surgeons (treas. 2001-02), Calif. Soc. Plastic Surgeons, San Francisco Surg. Soc., Chgo. Surg. Soc., Internat. Soc. Reconstructive Surgery, Met. D.C. Soc. Surgery Hand (pres. 1995-97), N.Y. Surg. Soc., Northeastern Soc. Plastic Surgeons (chmn. sci. program com. 1991, treas. 1993-96, pres. 1997-98), Plastic Surgery Rsch. Coun. (chmn. 1990), Surg. Biology Club III, The Wound Healing Soc. Office: U Calif San Francisco Divsn Plastic Surgery 1635 Divisadero Ste 520 San Francisco CA 94115 Office Phone: 415-476-3727. E-mail: mcgrathm@surgery.ucsf.edu.

MCGRATH, SYLVIA WALLACE, historian, educator; b. Montpelier, Vt., Feb. 27, 1937; d. George John and Martha Eloise (Cooper) Wallace; m. W. Thomas McGrath, June 11, 1966; children: Sandra Jean, Charles George. BA, Mich. State U., East Lansing, 1959; MA, Radcliffe Coll., Cambridge, 1960; PhD, U. Wis., Madison, 1966. Tchr. Falmouth (Mass.) Pub. Schs., 1960-61, M. County Day Sch., C. Madera, Calif., 1961-62; asst. prof. history Stephen F. Austin State U., Nacogdoches, Tex., 1968-73, assoc. prof. history, 1973-87, prof. history, 1987—, Regents' prof., 1994-95, chair history dept., 2000—. Author: (book) Charles Kenneth Leith, Scientific Advisor, 1971; book reviewer: various jours. including Jour. of Am. History, Jour. So. History, Forest and Conservation History, Southwestern Hist. Quarterly, East Tex. Hist. Jour., Environ. History Review, ISIS, Science Books and Films, Legacies, various jours; contbr. chpts. to books, articles to encyclopedias. Mem. Orgn. Am. Historians, Tex. Assn. Coll. Tchrs. (regional v.p. 1992-93), So. Hist. Assn., History Sci. Soc., Soc. History of Tech., Forest History Soc., Am. Soc. Environ. History. Presbyterian. Home: 216 N Mound St Nacogdoches TX 75961-5030 Office: PO Box 13013 Nacogdoches TX 75962-0001

MCGRATTAN, MARY K. state legislator; b. N.Y.C. RN, St. Catherine's Hosp. Sch. of Nursing. Mem. town coun. Town of Ledyard, Conn., 1977-83, mayor, 1983-91; pres. Conn. Conf. of Municipalities, 1990-91; mem. Conn. Ho. of Reps., Hartford, 1993—. Mem. Ledyard Dem. Town Com. Address: 13 Lynn Dr Ledyard CT 06339-1312 Office: Conn Ho of Reps State Capitol Hartford CT 06106 Fax: 860-464-7079. E-mail: Mary.McGrattan@po.state.ct.us.

MCGRAW, A. MICHELLE, music educator; b. Gallipolis, Ohio, Oct. 30, 1975; d. Herbert Garland Biggs Sr. and Carrie Musick Biggs; m. Hurston Shane McGraw, July 29, 1999. BS in Music Edn., U. Rio Grande, 1999. Tchr. music K-6 Clay Local Sch. Dist., Portsmouth, Ohio, 1999—2000; tchr. music K-12 We. Local Sch. Dist., Latham, Ohio, 2000—02, Ea. Local Sch. Dist., Beaver, Ohio, 2003—. Pianist teen Sun. sch. Bethesda Chapel Freewill, Jackson, Ohio, 2001—. Republican. Baptist.

MCGRAW, JANET GOLLER, executive secretary, office coordinator; b. Tulsa, Sept. 23, 1936; d. Walter Henry and Caroline Wilhelmina (Pedersen) Goller; m. Russell McGraw, Oct. 11, 1958; children: Theresa McGraw-French Janssen, Jeanne McGraw Garalis, Mary McGraw Mink, Alice McGraw Lively. Cert. in acctg., DeKalb C.C., 1983, cert. profl. sec., 1986; cert. of mgmt., U. Ga., 1988; AAS in office sys., DeKalb C.C., 1993. Cert. profl. sec., 1985. Sec. to mgr. Merrill, Lynch, Pierce, Fenner & Smith, Miami Beach, Fla., 1954-59; sec. to v.p. Am. Bonded Mortgage Co., Miami, Fla., 1960-62; sec. John Nicholas, Miami, 1962-72; exec. sec. to fire chief, coord. office DeKalb County Fire Services, Decatur, Ga., 1973-98; adminstrv. asst. Ga. Inst. Tech., 2000—. Mem. Bus. Adv. Coun. GoodwillIndustries, 1975-98, DeKalb Tech. Inst. Bus. Adv. Com. (chmn. Secretarial Sci. com. 1998—), Peachstate Fed. Credit Union Supervisory Com. Recipient Disting. Leadership award, 1988. Mem. NAFE, Profl. Sec. Internat. (membership com. 1985-86, ways and means com. 1985-86, publicity com. 1986-87, Statewide Sec. of Yr. award 1989, 1991, DeKalb chpt. sec. 1989-90, pres. 1991-92, 92-93, sec. bd. Ga. divsn. 1994-95, v.p. 1995-96, pres. elect 1996-97, pres. 1997-98, Mem. of Yr. award 1994), Internat. Assn. Adminstrv. Profls. (co-coord. 17th ann. Ga. divsn. student conf. 1999).

MCGRAW, LAVINIA MORGAN, retired retail company executive; b. Detroit, Feb. 26, 1924; d. Will Curtis and Margaret Coulter (Oliphant) McG. AB, Radcliffe Coll., 1945. Mem. Phi Beta Kappa. Home: 2501 Calvert St NW Washington DC 20008-2620

MCGRAY, DEANNA GAIL, retired elementary school educator; b. LI, Feb. 2, 1940; d. Lewis Rapport and Muriel Helen Rosing-Mack; m. William Franklin McGray, Aug. 17, 1989; children: David Aaron, Mark Edward; m. Meyer Grossman, Dec. 20, 1959 (div.). BA, Calif. State U., Northridge, 1964. Tchr. Canton (Ohio) City Schs., 1959—61, Sulphur Springs Sch. Dist., Canyon Country, Calif., 1962—64, 1969—88, LA Unified Sch. Dist., San Fernando Valley, Calif., 1988—96, Nestle Ave Sch., Tarzana, Calif., 1996—2002; ret., 2002. Vol. Food Pantry, Woodland Hills, Calif., 2003, Nestle Ave Sch., Tarzana, Calif., 2002—03; vol. Grandparent Reading Program Topanga (Calif.) Pub. Libr.; mem. Brandeis U. Nat. Women's Com. Mem.: AAUW. Democrat. Jewish. Avocations: hiking, canoeing, bicycling, reading, travel. Home: 1621 gunnison Tr Topanga CA 90290

MCGREEVY, MARY SHARRON, former psychology educator; b. Kansas City, Kans., Nov. 10, 1935; d. Donald and Emmy Lou (Neubert) McG.; m. Phillip Rosenbaum (dec.); children: David, Steve, Mariya, Chay, Allyn, Jacob, Dora. BA in English with honors, Vassar Coll., 1957; postgrad., New Sch. for Social Rsch., NYU, 1958-59, Columbia U., 1959-60, U. P.R., 1963-65, U. Mo., 1965-68, U. Kans.; PhD with distinction, U. Calif., Berkeley, 1969. Exec. Doubleday & Co., N.Y.C., 1957—60; chief libr. San Juan Sch., PR, 1962—63; NIMH drug rschr. Russell Sage Found., Clinico de los Addictos, Rio Piedras, PR, 1963—65; psychiat. rschr. U. PR Med. Sch., PR, 1963—65; psychiat. researcher U. Kans. Med. Ctr., Kansas City, 1966—68; rsch. assoc. Ednl. Rsch., 1965—69; from assoc. prof. to disting. prof. U. Calif., Berkeley, 1968—69, ret., 1969. Yacht owner Encore; lectr. in philosophy; founder Simone de Beauvoir Cir., Inc. Author: (poetry) To a Sailor, 1989, Dreams and Illusions, 1993, Wedding: A Celebration, 1998, The Red Hibiscus, 2000, Irish Poems, 2000, The Swan, 2001, Sea Poems, 2002, Memoir of Annette Van Howe, 2002; contbr. articles to profl. jours. Mem. U.S. Holocaust Meml. Mus., Women in the Arts. Nat. Gallery, Jewish World Congress, 2000—, Friends Everglades, Nat. Wildlife Assn., Nat. Coun. Jewish Women (photographer 2000-), 1999—; publicity chair Nat. Coun. Jewish Women, 2000—02; vol. Broward County Hist. Commn., Friends of the Libr., Ft. Lauderdale Libr., 1969—, Broward County Libr. Found., FAU Wimberly Libr. Found.; mem. Naval Air Sta. Ft. Lauderdale Hist. Assn., 1994—, Am. Friends of Bodleian Libr., Oxford, England, Irish Cultural Inst., Ft. Lauderdale, Ft. Lauderdale Hist. Soc., Nat. Trust Hist. Preservation, Frances Loeb Lehman Art Gallery, Vassar Col., Ctr. de las Artes, Miami, Friends of Modern Mus. Art, Friends of the Guggenheim, Friends of Met. Mus. Art, Nelson-Atkins Mus. Art, Nat. Gallery of Art of Ireland, Norton Mus. Art, Palm Beach, Friends of Mus. of Art, Ft. Lauderdale, Friends of U. Mo. Libr., Johnson County Mental Health Assn., Pine Crest Columns Soc., Ft. Lauderdale Philharm. Soc., Menninger Found., 1997—, Navy League Broward County; founder Dora Achenbach McGreevy Poetry and Philosophy Found., Inc., 1989—, exec. dir., 1989—, Pius X Cath. Women's Club, active Fla. Atlantic U. Found., 1993. Recipient Cert. for Svc. Broward County Hist. Commn., 1994, Nat. Women's History Project award, 1995; honored by Broward County Women's Hist. Coalition, 1996; Sproul fellow, Bancroft Libr. fellow, Russell Sage Found. fellow; postdoctoral grant U. Calif. Mem.: NOW, AAUW (corr. sec. 1991—95, bd. dirs. 1991—2001, Jeanne Faiks meml. scholarship fund com. 1992—98, Nat. Ednl. Found. book brunch com. 1994—98, chair cultural events 1995—, chair 1998, rec. sec. 1998—2002, book brunch com. 2000—01, photographer, honoree Ednl. Found. Fund 1993, cert. appreciation 2000), Fla. Women's Consortium, Southwestern Philosophy Assn., Soc. Phenomenology and Existentialism, Nietzsche Soc., Fla. Philosophy Assn. (spkr. 1991, 1993, chair self in philosophy 1994), Mo. Sociol. Assn., Poets of the Palm Beaches (yearly poetry anthology 1992—, 1st prize free verse ann. contest 1996), South Fla. Poetry Inst. (yearly poetry anthology 1991—98), Union of Concerned Scientists, Women in Psychology, Nat. Acad. Poets, Nat. Women's History Project Orgn., Internat. Soc. Universal Dialogue, Am. Philos. Assn., Nat. Women's Political Caucus, Pem-Hill Alumni Assn., Vassar Alumni Assn., Secular Humanists (bd. dirs. 1992—98, program chair 1995—98, publicity chair 1998—99), Oxfam Am., Smithsonian Instn., Fla. State Poets Assn., Inc., Broward Women's Hist Coalition (bd. dirs. 1991—98, archivist 1991—98, ad hoc com., Hall of Fame Women's History awards 1989—98), Fla. Atlantic U. Chamber Music Soc., Libr. Congress, Sierra (conservation com. 1979—, co-chair beach clean-up 1993, archivist 1993—95, Redwoods chpt. 1997, newspaper reporter, environ. com.), Vassar Club (N.Y., Kansas City, South Fla. and Palm Beach chpts.). Democrat. Roman Catholic. Achievements include first to use methodone treatment and rehabilitation at drug clinic in Puerto Rico. Avocations: poetry, painting, sailing, tennis, the beach.

MCGREGOR, MARY, professional athletics manager; Degree, Carleton U.; postgrad., McGill U. Exec. dir. Can. Rhythmic Gymnastics Fedn.; acquatics dir. Dalhousie; exec. dir. Water Ski Can., 1984—92; former exec. dir. Can. Assn. for Advancement of Women and Sport, 1992—2000; CEO Can. Interuniv. Athletic Union, Ottawa, Canada, 2000—. Mission staff Commonwealth Games, 1998; mem. adv. com. Minister's Task Force on Sport Policy; spkrs. bur. Female Athlete's Motivating Excellence; bd. dirs. Can. Sport and Firness Adminstrn. Centre. Mem.: Commonwealth Games Assn. Can. Office: Can Interuniv Athletic Union 801 King Edward Ste N205 Ottawa ON K1N 6N5 Canada E-mail: mcgregor@universitysprot.ca.

MCGREGOR, RUTH VAN ROEKEL, state supreme court justice; b. Le Mars, Iowa, Apr. 4, 1943; d. Bernard and Marie Frances (Janssen) Van

Roekel; m. Robert James McGregor, Aug. 15, 1965. BA summa cum laude, U. Iowa, 1964, MA, 1965; JD summa cum laude, Ariz. State U., 1974. Bar: Ariz. 1974, U.S. Dist. Ct. Ariz. 1974, U.S. Ct. Appeals (9th cir.), U.S. Supreme Ct. 1982. Assoc. Fennemore, Craig, von Ammon, Udall & Powers, Phoenix, 1974-79, ptnr., 1980-81, 82-89; law clk. to justice Sandra Day O'Connor U.S. Supreme Ct., Washington, 1981-82; judge Ariz. Ct. Appeals, 1983-98, vice chief judge, 1993-95, chief judge, 1995-98; justice Ariz. Supreme Ct., 1998—, vice chief judge, 2002—. Mem. disciplinary commn. Ariz. Supreme Ct., 1984-89, City of Mesa jud. adv. bd., 1997—. Mem., newsletter editor Charter 100, Phoenix, 1981—; bd. dirs., mem. Ctr. for Law in Pub. Interest, Phoenix, 1977-80. Mem. ABA (chmn. state memberships 1985—), Ariz. Bar Assn. (disciplinary com. 1984—), Ariz. Judges Assn. (exec. com. 1990—, sec. 1991-92, v.p. 1992-93, pres. 1993-94), Nat. Assn. Women Judges (chair first time attendees com. 1990-91, 1994 conv. com.; exec. com. 1995—). Lodges: Soroptomists. Democrat. Lutheran. Office: Arizona Supreme Court 1501 W Washington St Phoenix AZ 85007-3231

MCGREW, PAMELA KAY, health facility administrator; b. Amarillo, Tex., Sept. 22, 1966; d. Leo Copeland, June Copeland; m. Mike McGrew; 1 child, Bradley. MSW, Our Lady of Lake U., 1994; BSW, Abilene Christian U., 1988. Lic. master social worker 1995. Specialist eligibility Tex. Dept. Human Svcs., Abilene, 1988—94; rep. Child Care Licensing Tex. Dept. Protective and Regulatory Svcs., Abilene, 1994—96, investigator Child Care, 1996—97; dir. social work Windcrest Alzheimer's Care Ctr., Abilene, Tex., 1999—2002, dir .of resident svc., 2002, asst. adminstr., 2002—. Chair Abilene Aging Cluster, 2001—. Mem.: NASW (vice chairperson 2001—). Office: Windcrest Alzheimer's Care Center 6050 Hospital Dr Abilene TX 79606 Business E-Mail: pkmcgrew@sears-methodist.com.

MCGRORY, MARY KATHLEEN, retired academic administrator, humanities educator; b. N.Y.C., Mar. 22, 1933; d. Patrick Joseph and Mary Kate (Gilvary) McG. BA, Pace U., 1957; MA, U. Notre Dame, 1962; PhD, Columbia U., 1969; DHL, Albertus Magnus Coll., 1984; LLD, Briarwood Coll., 1990; DHL, Trinity Coll., 1991. Prof. English Western Conn. State U., Danbury, 1969-78; dean arts and scis. Ea. Conn. State U., Willimantic, 1978-80, v.p. for acad. affairs, 1981-85; pres. Hartford (Conn.) Coll. for Women, 1985-91; sr. fellow U. Va. Commonwealth Ctr., Charlottesville, 1991-92; exec. dir. Soc. Values in Higher Edn./Georgetown U., Washington, 1992-96; chair dept. rhetoric, lang. and culture U. Hartford, dir. profl. and tech. writing. Pres. MKM Assocs., Holland, Mass., 1983—. Author: Yeats, Joyce & Beckett, 1975. Bd. dirs. Hartford Hosp., 1985-93; chmn. bd. govs. Greater Hartford Consortium Higher Edn., 1989-90. Fels Found. fellow, 1966-67, NEH summer fellow, 1975; Ludwig Vogelstein Found. travel grantee, 1973. Mem. New Eng. Jr. Community and Tech. Coll. Coun. (v.p. 1988-91), Am. Assn. Higher Edn., Med. Acad. of Am., Greater Hartford C. of C. (bd. dirs. 1989-91), Hartford Club (bd. dirs. 1988-91). Avocations: writing, swimming, piano. Address: 44 Forest Dr Holland MA 01521-9702

MCGUIRE, CAROLE BAKER, legislative staff member; b. Seattle, Dec. 26, 1951; BA, Western Wash. U., 1974. Staff aide Sen. Warren Magnuson, 1974-76; legis. analyst Budget Com., 1976-81, legis. and budget analyst, 1981-85, dir. appropriations activities, 1985—, asst. staff dir., 1995—. Office: Budget Com 621 Senate Dirksen Office Bldg Washington DC 20510-0001

MCGUIRE, LESIL L. state representative; b. Portland, Oreg., Jan. 22, 1971; m. Scott McCracken. Degree in Speech Comm. and Polit. Sci., Willamette U., 1993, JD, 1998. Legis. and press aide U.S. Senator Ted Stevens, 1993—95; legal intern U.S. Atty., 1996; law clerk Oreg. Dept. Justice, 1996—98; mem. Alaska Ho. of Reps., 2000—; judiciary com. Vol. Habitat for Humanity; mentor Bush Elem. Sch. Mentor Program; vol. Salem's Women's Crisis Ctr. Mem.: Young Rep., Anchorage Rep. Women's Club, Am. Diabetes Assn. Republican. Avocations: fishing, skiing, flying, scuba diving, reading. Office: Rm 118 State Capitol Juneau AK 99801-1182 Address: 716 W 4th Ave Ste 430 Anchorage AK 99501-2133

MCGUIRE, LILLIAN (ELIZABETH) HILL, historian, researcher, retired education educator, writer; b. Middlesex County, Va., Jan. 17, 1928; d. Howard Garfield Hill, Sr. and Malissie O'Neal (Carter) Hill; m. Charles Edward McGuire, Aug. 11, 1957 (dec. July 30, 1997); children: Brenda Colette, Gina Renae, Laura Jane Fortune Battle. Student, Hampton Inst., 1946—48; BS, Morgan State U., 1951. Primary and Secondary Tchg. Cert. Va. Dept. of Edn. Classroom tchr. Richmond County Sch. Sys., Warsaw, Va., 1951—65, Essex County Sch. Sys., Tappahannock, Va., 1965—88; adult edn. tchr. Rappahannock C.C., Warsaw, Va., 1989—94; adult edn. tchr. Essex County Sch. Sys., Tappahannock, 1989—94. Pres. Essex Edn. Assn., Tappahannock, 1982—86, editor-news letter, 1982—88; historian Va. Ret. Tchrs. Assn., Blacksburg, 1995—97. Author: (book) The Vista of a Century: History of the Southside Rappahannock Baptist Association and Allied Bodies, 1977, Our Spiritual Heritage: History of First Baptist Church Tappahannock, VA, 1993, Uprooted & Transplanted: From Africa to America; Focus on African Americans in Essex County, VA, 2000. Charter mem. Essex County Mus., Tappahannock, 1996; mem. NAACP Essex County Br., Tappahannock, 1950, Essex County Hist. Soc., Tappahannock, 1996. Named Outstanding Elem. Sch. Tchr. of Am., Bd. of Advisors, Washington, 1974; recipient Honor award, Essex Edn. Assn., Tappahannock, 1977, Disting. Svc. award, 1982. Mem.: Rappahannock Indsl. Acad. Alumni Assn. (historian 1975), Morgan State U. Nat. Alumni Assn., Dist. A of Va. Ret. Tchrs. (life; historian 1988). Democrat-Npl. Bapt. Achievements include at the request of The Library of Virginia, Lillian has successfully researched the life of a former Essex County slave-turned politician-born in 1820. (Completed March 1, 2003). Avocations: writing, puzzles, travel, fitness. Home: 445 Marsh St PO Box 143 Tappahannock VA 22560

MCGUIRE, MARY JO, state legislator; b. Mpls., 1956; BA in Bus. Adminstrn., Coll. of St. Catherine, 1978; JD, Hamline U., 1988; postgrad., Harvard U., 1995-97. Mem. Minn. Ho. of Reps., 1988—, mem. judiciary com., judiciary fin. divsn., vice chair family and early childhood edn. fin. divsn., mem. govt. ops., chair data practices subcom., lead minor mem. Democrat. Home: 1529 Iowa Ave W Saint Paul MN 55108-2128 Office: Minn Ho of Reps State Ho Office Bldg Saint Paul MN 55155-0001

MCGUIRE, PATRICIA A. lawyer, academic administrator; b. Phila., Nov. 13, 1952; d. Edward J. and Mary R. McGuire. BA cum laude, Trinity Coll., 1974; JD, Georgetown U., 1977. Bar: Pa. 1977, D.C. Ct. Appeals 1979. Program dir. Georgetown U. St. Law Clinic, Washington, 1977-82; asst. dean for devel. and external affairs Georgetown U. Law Ctr., Washington, 1982-89; pres. Trinity Coll., Washington, 1989—. Adj. prof. law Georgetown U., 1977-82, Georgetown Law Ctr., 1987—; commr. Mid. States Commn. on Higher Edn., 1991—; bd. dirs. Acacia Group, Elderhostel, Inc. Editor: Street Law Mock Trial Manual, 1984; contbr. articles to profl. jours. Trustee Trinity Coll., 1986—; bd. dirs. Assn. Cath. Colls. and Univs., 1991—, Eugene and Agnes Meyer Found.; mem. adv. bd. Merion Mercy Acad. and Sisters of Mercy, 1990—; bd. dirs. Nat. Assn. Ind. Colls. and Univs.; mem. commn. govt. rels. Am. Coun. Edn.; bd. dirs. Women's Coll. Coalition; adv. bd. Coll. Access Network; mem. dollar coin design adv. com. U.S. Mint; bd. vis. Joint Mil. intelligence Coll. Recipient Daytime Emmy, TV Acad., N.Y.C., 1979-80. Mem. ABA, Assn. Am. Law Schs. (instl. advancement 1985—), Coun. for the Advancement and Support of Edn., Trinity Coll. Alumnae Assn. (pres. 1986-89) Democrat. Roman Catholic. Office: Trinity Coll Office of the President 125 Michigan Ave NE Washington DC 20017-1091 E-mail: president@trinitydc.edu.

MCGUIRE, ROBIN CHRISTINE, special education educator; b. Sacramento, Jan. 6, 1966; d. Michael Anthony Endicott and Virginia Ellen Nagel; m. Scott Gregory McGuire, July 21, 1991; children: Cash Heyden, Reese Jackson, Shane Christopher. AA, Green River C.C., Auburn, Wash., 1986; BEd, Ctrl. Wash. U., 1991; M Tech., City U., Renton, Wash., 1998. Cert. tchr. Wash. Spl. edn. tchr. [illegible] Hill, Kent, Wash., 1991—2002, chmn. integrated program dept., 1994—2002; tchr. George T. Daniel Elem., 2002—. Avocations: sports, camping, reading. Home: 15249 SE 280th St Kent WA 98042

MCGUIRE, SANDRA LYNN, nursing educator; b. Jan. 28, 1947; d. Donald Armstrong and Mary Lue (Harvey) Johnson; m. Joseph L. McGuire, Mar. 6, 1976; children: Matthew, Kelly, Kerry. BSN, U. Mich., 1969, MPH, 1973, EdD, 1988, MSN, 1997. Staff nurse Univ. Hosp., Ann Arbor, Mich., 1969; pub. health nurse Wayne County Health Dept., Eloise, Mich., 1969-72; instr. Madonna Coll., Livonia, Mich., 1973; pub. health coord. Plymouth Ctr. for Human devel., Northville, Mich., 1974-75; asst. prof. cmty. health nursing U. Mich., Ann Arbor, 1975-83; asst. prof. U. Tenn., Knoxville, 1983-88, assoc. prof., 1990—, gerontol. nurse practitioners program coord., 1998—, chair MSN program Coll. Nursing. Dir. Kids Are Tomorrow's Srs. Program, 1988—; resource person Gov.'s Com. Unification of Mental Health Svcs. in Mich.; spkr. profl. assns. and workshops. Author (with S. Clemen-Stone and D. Eigsti)): Comprehensive Community Health Nursing, 1981, Comprehensive Community Health Nursing, 5th edit., 1998, Comprehensive Community Health Nursing, 6th edit., 2002. Bd. dirs. Ctr. Understanding Aging, 1987-93, v.p., 1995; bd. dirs. Mich. chpt. ARC, 1980-83, Knoxville chpt., 1984-85; founder Knoxville Intergenerational Network, 1989. Recipient John W. Runyan, Jr. Cmty. Health Nursing award U. Tenn. Memphis, 2002; USPHS fellow, 1972-73, Robert Woodruff fellow Emory U., 1996-97, Hewlett Innovative Tech. fellow U. Tenn., Knoxville, 1999-00, Profl. Devel. awardee U. Tenn. Knoxville, 1996-97, 99-2000. Mem. ANA, Tenn. Nurses Assn., Nat. Conf. Gerontol. Nurse Practitioners, Nat. Gerontol. Nursing Assn., Mich. Pub. Health Assn. (chmn. mental health sect. 1976, dir., co-chmn. residential svcs. com. 1976-79, chmn. health svcs. 1979-82), Nat. Assn. Retarded Citizens, Mich. Assn. Retarded Citizens, Nat. Coun. on Aging, Ctr. for Understanding Aging (v.p. 1994-95), Plymouth (chmn. residential svcs. com. 1975-77), Tenn. Assn. Retarded Citizens, So. Nursing Rsch. Soc., Sigma Theta Tau, Pi Lambda Theta, Phi Kappa Phi. Home: 11008 Crosswind Dr Knoxville TN 37922-4011 Office: 1200 Volunteer Blvd Knoxville TN 37996 E-mail: smcguire@utk.edu.

MCGUIRE, SUSAN GRAYSON, legislative staff member; BA in Polit. Sci., U. Mich., 1962. Legis. asst. select com. on equal ednl. opportunity U.S. Senate, Washington, 1970-73; staff dir. subcom. on employment opportunities U.S. Ho. of Reps., Washington, 1973-84, staff dir. com. on edn. and labor, 1984-91; pub. policy cons. McGuire & Assocs., Cedar Crest, N.Mex., 1991-93; exec. dir. Indian Arts and Crafts Assn., Albuquerque, 1995-98; state dir. U.S. Senator Jeff Bingaman, Albuquerque, 1998—. Pres. N.Mex. Arts and Crafts Fair, Albuquerque; sec. bd. dirs. Albuquerque Literacy Program; active N.Mex. Clinton for Pres. Com., 1992. Office: 625 Silver Ave SW Ste 130 Albuquerque NM 87102-3185 Fax: 505-346-6780. E-mail: Susan_McGuire@Bingaman.senate.gov.

MCGUIRL, MARLENE DANA CALLIS, law librarian, educator; b. Hammond, Ind., Mar. 22, 1938; d. Daniel David and Helen Elizabeth (Baludis) Callis; m. James Franklin McGuirl, Apr. 24, 1965. AB, Ind. U., 1959; JD, DePaul U., 1963; MALS, Rosary Coll., 1965; LLM, George Washington U., 1978; postgrad., Harvard U., 1985. Bar: Ill. 1963, Ind. 1964, D.C. 1972. Asst. DePaul Coll. of Law Libr., 1961-62, asst. law libr., 1962-65; ref. law librarian Boston Coll. Sch. Law, 1965-66; libr. dir. D.C. Bar Libr., 1966-70; asst. chief Am.-Brit. Law Divsn. Libr. of Congress, Washington, 1970, chief, 1970-90, environ. cons., 1990—; counsel Cooter & Gell, 1992-93; adminstr. Washington Met. Transit Authority, 1994—. Libr. cons. Nat. Clearinghouse on Proverty Law, OEO, Washington, 1967-69, Northwestern U. Nat. Inst. Edn. in Law and Poverty, 1969, D.C. Office of Corp. Counsel, 1969-70; instr. law librarianship Grad. Sch. of U.S. Dept. of Agr., 1968-72; lectr. legal lit. Cath. U., 1972; adj. asst. prof., 1973-91; lectr. environ. law George Washington U., 1979—; judge Nat. and Internat. Law Moot Ct. Competition, 1976-78, 90—; pres. Hamburger Heaven, Inc., Palm Beach, Fla., 1981-91, L'Image de Marlene Ltd., 1986-92, Clinique de Beautè Inc., 1987-92, Heads & Hands Inc., 1987-92, Horizon Design & Mfg. Co., Inc., 1987—; dir. Stoneridge Farm Inc., Gt. Falls, Va., 1984—. Contbr. articles to profl. jours. Mem. Georgetown Citizens Assn.; trustee D.C. Law Students in Ct.; del. Ind. Democratic Conv., 1964. Recipient Meritorious Svc. award Libr. on Congress, 1974, letter of commendation Dirs. of Pers., 1976, cert. of appreciation, 1981-84. Mem. ABA (facilities law libr. Congress com. 1976-89), Fed. Bar Assn. (chpt. council 1972-76), Ill. Bar Assn., Women's Bar Assn. (pres. 1972-73, exec. bd. 1973-77, Outstanding Contbn. to Human Rights award 1975), D.C. Bar Assn., Am. Bar Found., Nat. Assn. Women Lawyers, Am. Assn. Law Libraries (exec. bd. 1973-77), Law Librarians Soc. of Washington (pres. 1971-73), Exec. Women in Govt. Home: 3416 P St NW Washington DC 20007-2705 E-mail: mmcguirl@wmata.com.

MCGUNIGLE, DOROTHY GREENE, interior designer, artist; b. Providence, Jan. 24, 1914; d. Dutee Thomas and Carrie May (Stewart) Greene; m. Douglas Campbell McGunigle, June 14, 1941 (dec. 1958); children: Jane Douglas (dec.), Bruce Campbell. Grad., R.I. Sch. Design, 1935, BFA (hon.), 1990. Interior designer Healy & Helgeson, Providence, 1935-36, Merriam Co., Providence, 1936-43; mgr. interior decorating dept. Shepard Co., Providence, 1960-70; owner Dorothy McGunigle Interiors, East Greenwich, R.I., 1970-95. Tchr. adult edn. Providence YMCA, 1958-59, Cranston High Sch., 1962, Warwick High Sch., 1964, East Greenwich High Sch., 1970-71; art shows include: Providence Art Club, 1972, 74, 76, 78, 80, 82; Indsl. Nat. Bank, Providence, 1974, 76; Warwick Pub. Library, 1980; cons. hist. restoration Varnum House Mus., 1963— . Paintings represented in permanent collection R.I. Hist. Soc. Bd. dirs. East Greenwich Preservation Soc., 1972—77, chmn. consultation com. hist. restoration. Recipient Hon. Mem. award Continental Ladies, Varnum House Mus., 1970; top 3% interior designers in Am., 1989, top 1% internat. designers, 1990. Mem. AID and ASID (visited fgn. designers in Greece, Spain, Portugal, Turkey, Austria, Italy, Switzerland, France, England, Sweden, Denmark, Finland, Norway, Russia to exchange ideas on projects), Providence Art (picture custodian 1974-85, chmn. ladies bd. 1978-79), Providence Pottery and Porcelain (pres. 1981-83), Colonial Dames, Mayflower Descendants, DAR, R.I. Sch. Design Alumni Assn.

MCHALE, CATHERINE A. lawyer; b. Chgo., Aug. 20, 1964; d. Edward Michael and Nancy Ruth (Martin) McH. BA, Fordham U., 1992; MDiv, Harvard U., 1996; JD, Columbia U., 1999. Press attaché Karl Lagerfeld N.A., N.Y.C., 1988-90; tutor The Learning Ctr., N.Y.C., 1990-92; curatorial asst. Peabody Mus., Cambridge, Mass., 1993-95; asst. to dir. Harvard Native Am. Program, Cambridge, 1995-96; cons. The Drawing Ctr., N.Y.C., 1996-97; with Sonnenschein Nath & Rosenthal, N.Y.C., 1998—2000, Kay & Boose LLP, N.Y.C., 2000—. Author book chpt., poems, articles. Vol. The Repatriation Found., N.Y.C., 1997-99, Vol. Lawyers for the Arts, N.Y.C., 1997-99; mentor Mock Trial Program, N.Y.C., 1999; vol. N.Y. Cares, 2000—, N.Y. Hospice, 2001—. Charlotte Newcombe scholar, 1989, Vera Bellus scholar, 1994, Harland Fiske Stone scholar, 1999. Mem. Am. Acad. Religion, Soc. for Study of Native Am. Religious Traditions. Democrat. Avocations: reading, skiing, cooking. Office: Kay & Boose LLP 1 Dag Hammarskjold Plaza New York NY 10017

MCHALE, JUDITH A. (JUDITH OTTALLORAN), broadcast executive, lawyer; b. N.Y.C., 1947; m. Michael McHale; 2 children. B in politics, U. Nottingham, Eng.; JD, Fordham U.Law Sch., 1979. Atty. Battle, Fowler, N.Y.C.; gen. counsel MTV networks, Discovery Comm., Inc., 1987, sr.. v.p. and gen. counsel, exec. v.p. and gen. counsel, pres. and COO, 1995—. Mem. Md. State Bd. of Edn., 1997—2001; bd. dirs. Polo Ralph Lauren, John Hancock Co., Potomac Electric Power Co., Host Marriott Corp., Cable in the Classroom, Vital Voices Global Partnership, Africa Soc., [illegible], Sister-to-Sister Everyone Has a Heart Found. Office: Discovery Comm 7700 Wisconsin Ave Bethesda MD 20814*

MCHAN, MARTHA ELAINE, purchasing agent; b. Crescent City, Calif., June 8, 1956; d. Ralph Calvin and Martha Mae Smith; m. Ronnie Crawford McHan, Aug. 5, 1983 (div. Aug. 1991); children: Lesley Dawn, Brandon Shawn, Jeffrey Todd. Student, Pines Vocat. Sch., Pine Bluff, Ark., 1977, 80. Cert. profl. legal sec. Legal sec., adminstrv. asst., office mgr. Rando O. Lewis, Atty. at Law, Luling, La., 1980-83, Baim Law Firm, Pine Bluff, 1984-85; sec. to dep. dir. U.S. Army Pine Bluff Arsenal Directorate of Materiel, Pine Bluff, 1985-90, sec. to dir., purchasing agt., 1990—. Treas., mem. exec. bd. White Hall (Ark.) Elem. Football League. Mem. Pine Bluff Arsenal Women's Club (pres.). Avocations: reading, children's activities, gravestone rubbing. Office: US Army Pine Bluff Arsenal B23-370 Sibert Rd Pine Bluff AR 91602-9500

MCHENRY, ANITA PETEI, historian, archaeologist; b. Coffeyville, Kans., Mar. 2, 1949; d. Woodrow Wilson Gordon and Erva Odile (Crevier) Hardy; m. Gray Richard McHenry, Dec. 12, 1981; children: Carrie Ann, Thomas Owen. BS in Anthropology, U. Calif., Riverside, 1992; MA in History, U. San Diego, 1997. Archaeologist, historian Gallegos & Assocs., Carlsbad, Calif., 1990-96; pub., owner GP Mktg., Escondido, Calif., 1996—. Exec. dir. Valley Ctr. (Calif.) History Mus., 2001—; vol. archivist Valley Ctr. Libr., 1996—; v.p. hist. com. Friends of Valley Ctr. Libr., 1996—. Author: History of Valley Center, 1997, San Diego and Honolulu, A PhotoJournal Through a Sailor's Eye 1920-1943, 2002. Active Nat. Trust Historic Preservation. Fellowship grant, U. San Diego, 1995—96. Mem. Soc. Calif. Archaeology, San Diego Hist. Soc., Smithsonian Assn., San Diego County Archaeol. Soc., Phi Alpha Theta. Avocations: historical research, genealogy, archaeology, reading. Home and Office: GP Mktg 28338 Mountain Meadow Rd Escondido CA 92026-6907 E-mail: gpmch@att.net.

MCHOES, ANN MCIVER, academic administrator, computer systems consultant; b. San Diego, June 17, 1950; d. Donald Anthony and Ann Mae McIver; children: A. Genevieve, Katherine Marie. BS in Math., U. Pitts., 1973, MS in Info. Sci., 1986. Tech. writer Westinghouse Electric Corp., Pitts., 1973—79; pres. McHoes & Assocs., Pitts., 1981—; dir. enrollment svcs. Chatham Coll., Pitts., 2002—. Mem. adj. faculty computer sci., Carlow Coll., Pitts., 1992—, Duquesne U., 1997-99; cons. Westinghouse Electric Corp., 1988-99, PNC Bank, Pitts., 1988—, CBS Corp., 1996-99, Intel, 1998—, McDonalds Corp., 1998-2001, commonwealth of Pa. Healthy Women Project, 1998—; vis. lectr. Pa. State U., State College, 1990-91; judge Pa. Jr. Acad. Sci., Pitts., 1993—; vol. tutor Greater Pitts. Literacy Coun., 1996-98; webmaster NVR Mortgage, 1998-2000; bd. dirs. Pitts. Playback Theatre, 2000-2001. Co-author: Understanding Operating Systems, 1991, 2d edit., 1997, 3d edit., 2000 (used in colleges and univs., North Am., Europe, Africa, Asia and Australia); assoc. editor: (4-vol. ency.) Computer Science for Students, 2002. Recipient 2001 Texty Excellence award Text and Academic Authors Assn., 2001. Mem. IEEE Computer Soc., Assn. Computing Machinery, Info. Sys. Security Assn. (chpt. sec. 1991-94, v.p. 1995-96, membership chair 1994—), Pa. Mid. Sch. Assn. (conf. exhibit chair 1996-97). Avocations: travel, tennis, golf. Office: Chatham Coll Braun Hall Woodland Rd Pittsburgh PA 15232

MCHOSE, ALISON LITTELL, assemblywoman; b. May 24, 1965; BS in govt. and politics, U. of Md. Assemblywoman N.J. Gen. Assembly, 2003—. Mem. Franklin Econ. Devel. Com., 1995—; adv. bd. Sussex County Office of Aging, 1997—; mem. Sussex County 250th Com., 2002—. Republican. Office: 61 Spring St 3d Fl Newton NJ 07860 E-mail: AswMcHose@njleg.org.

MCHUGH, ANNETTE S. artist, educator, playwright; b. Greensburg, Pa., May 31, 1926; d. Daniel Karl Shirey and Marian Grabill Kurtz; m. John Edward McHugh Jr., Nov. 24, 1948. Student, Ind. State Tchrs. Coll., Pa., 1945—47, Pa. State U., 1947—49, State Coll. Pa., 1980, student, 1981, Art Alliance Ctrl. Pa., 1981—85, ARt Alliance Ctrl. Pa., 1985—90. File & locate clk. FBI, Washington, 1944—45; sec. to asst. dean edn. Pa. State U., University Park, 1947—49, sec. to exec. dir., 1962, pers. sec. phys. plant; test adminstr. Pa. State Employment Office, Bellefonte, 1962—65; editl. asst., prodn. sec. Sta. WPSX-TV, 1977—79; tchr. traditional chinese brush painting Art Alliance Ctrl. Pa., Lemont, Pa., 2001—03. Playwright, dir.: Those Were the Days, 1979, We've Come A Long Way Ladies, 1984, Every Night is Opening Night on Broadway, 1989, Madame Pres....Ladies of the Club, 1994, Celebrate State College, 1996. V.p., bd. dirs. Univ. Park Airport, University Park, 1957—62; bd. dirs., flower show chmn. Penn. State Garden Days, University Park, 1957—59; bd. dirs. Art Alliance Ctrl. Pa., 1981—82, pres., 1983, Nittany Coun. Rep. Women, 1961; pres. women's assn. State Coll. Presbyn. Ch., State Coll., Pa., 1971—73, deacon State College, Pa., 1965—71, elder, 1971—74, bd. sec. Recipient State of Pa. award, Pa. Coun. Rep. Women, 1961—62, Pub. Rels. award, Am. Cancer Soc., 1980, 2d pl. art award, Pa. Fedn. Women's Club, 1987. Mem.: Pa. State U. Woman's Club (chair book and play rev., co-editor), State Coll. Woman's Club (pres. 1959—61, past v.p., past pres., art, garden and drama dept. chair). Republican. Presbyterian. Avocations: gardening, photography, reading, golf.

MCHUGH, CARIL EISENSTEIN DREYFUSS, art dealer, art gallery director, consultant; b. New Haven, Conn. d. Irving and Gertrude (Lax) Eisenstein; m. Barney Dreyfuss II (div.); children: Caryn, Barney III (Terry), Andrew, Evan; m. James Marshall McHugh Jr., Dec. 31, 1976. BA, Smith Coll. Libr. archivist, mem. staff art rental Washington Gallery of Modern Art, 1963-67; asst. to curator of prints and drawings Nat. Mus. Am. Art, Washington, 1967-69; dir. Studio Gallery, Washington, 1970-75; dir., ptnr. Parsons-Dreyfuss Gallery, N.Y.C., 1976-80; dir. Frank Marino Gallery, N.Y.C., 1981, Humphrey Fine Art, N.Y.C., 1988-90, Gregory Gallery, N.Y.C., 1995-96; freelance curator, adv. bd. Hugo de Pagano Gallery, 1997—2000; rschr. Barnett Newman Found., N.Y.C., 2001—. Art cons., writer, N.Y.C., 1982—; arranger exhbns. Nat. Mus. Am. Art, Washington, 1968-69, USIA, Washington, 1976, Automation House, N.Y.C., 1983. An Homage to Betty Parsons exhbn., 2000, Portraits by Tom Block/Amnesty Internat. Exhbn., 2002, essays to catalogs, articles to profl. mags. Bd. dirs. Women's Nat. Dem. Club, Washington, 1972-76, Friends of the Corcoran, Washington, 1972-76, Smith Club of Washington, 1974-76; Sophia Smith Assoc. Smith Coll., Northampton, Mass., 1985, 90, 95, 2000, Women in the Arts, 1995—. Avocations: reading, hiking, swimming, designing accessories, writing poetry. Home: 241 Central Park W Apt 9C New York NY 10024-4545

MCHUGH, HEATHER, poet; b. Calif., Aug. 20, 1948; BA, Radcliffe Coll., 1970; MA, U. Denver, 1972. Assoc. prof. English SUNY, Binghamton, 1976-82; prof. English, Milliman writer-in-residence U. Wash., Seattle, 1983—. Vis. prof. Columbia U., 1987; Holloway lectr. U. Calif., Berkeley, 1987; judge Nat. Poetry Series book award, 1986, 95. Author: (poetry) Dangers, 1977, A World of Difference, 1981, To the Quick, 1987, Shades, 1988, Hinge & Sign: Poems, 1968-93, 1994 (Nat. Book award nomination 1994), The FAther of the Predicaments, 1999, (essays) Broken English: Poetry and Partiality, 1993; translator: D'Apres Tout: Poems by Jean Follain, 1981; (with Nikolai Popov) Because the Sea Is Black: Poems by Blaga Dimitrova, 1989, (with Nikolai Popov) Glottal Stop: 101 Poems by Paul Celan, 2000, (with David Konstan) Cyclops of Euripides, 2000. Recipient Harvard U./Pollock prize, 1995, Lila Wallace/Reader's Digest

Writer's award, 1996, PEN Voelcker prize, 2000. Mem. Acad. Am. Poets (chancellor 1999), Am. Acad. Arts and Scis. Office: U Washington Dept English Box 354330 Seattle WA 98195-4330

MCHUGH, MAURA, professional basketball coach; b. Worcester, Mass. m. Greg Olson. Grad. magna cum laude, Old Dominion U., 1975; MS in Phys. Edn., Pa. State U., 1977. Grad. asst. Pa. State U., Univ. Pk., 1977, asst. basketball coach, 1978-80; basketball coach U. Okla., Norman, Ariz. State, Tempe, 1988-93; exec. dir. Bus. Coun. for Alcohol Edn., Phoenix, 1993-97; head basketball coach Long Beach (Calif.) StingRays, 1997—. Named Big Eight Coach of Year, 1977, Converse Nat. Coach of Year, 1977. Achievements include being awarded one of first ever women's basketball scholarships at Old Dominion U.; No. 1 ranking academically at Old Dominion U.; advancing to NCAA Sweet 16 postseason play in 1986. Address: Long Beach Stingrays 1900 Embarcadero Rd Ste 110 Palo Alto CA 94303-3310 also: Long Beach Stingrays 230 California St Ste 510 San Francisco CA 94111-4331

MCILWAIN, CLARA EVANS, agricultural economist, consultant; b. Jacksonville, Fla., Apr. 5, 1919; d. Waymon and Jerusha Lee (Dickson) Evans; m. Ivy McIlwain, May 15, 1942 (dec. 1987); children: Ronald E., Carol A. McIlwain Edwards, Marilyn E. McIlwain Moody, Ivy J. McIlwain Lindsay. BS, U. D.C., 1939; MS Agrl. Econs., U. Fla., 1972. Notary pub., Va.; lic. life and health ins. agt., Md., Va., D.C. Statis. asst. Hist. and Statis. Analysis Div., Washington, 1962-67; statistician Econ Devel. Div. USDA, Washington, 1967-70, 72, agrl. economist, 1972-74; program analyst Office Equal Opportunity, USDA, Washington, 1974-79; staff writer Sci. Weekly, Chevy Chase, Md., 1988-89; ins. agt. A.L. Williams, Primerica, Camp Springs, Md., 1990-95; min. New Light Mission Ministries, Clinton, Md., 1995—; prof. English Potomac Coll., Herndon, Va., 2003. Workshop coord. Author: Steps to Eloquence, 1989; co-author (Min. Carol M. Edwards): Blazing the Trail to the Kingdom of God, Old Testament and New Testament, 2001; contbr. to profl. publs. Dist. coord., instr. Youth Leadership and Speechcraft, Toastmasters Internat., Washington area, 1972-78; tchr., bd. dirs. Sat. Tutorial Enrichment Program, Arlington, Va., 1988-89; mem. network Christian women; min. to sr. citizens New Light Mission Mins., Clinton, Md., 1999-2002; asst. in strategic bus. planning advanced environ. rsch., 1995-2002. Rockefeller Found. scholar, 1970-72. Mem.: Internat. Assn. Home Bus. Entrepreneurs, Nat. Assn. Agrl. Econs., So. Assn. Agrl. Economists, Am. Assn. Notaries, Internat. Platform Assn., Toastmasters Internat. (past pres. Potomac club, Gavel award 1976, Able Toastmaster award 1978). Avocations: teaching public speaking, tutoring, attending conventions. Office: Evans Unlimited 6612 Denny Pl Mc Lean VA 22101-5505 Office Phone: 703-883-0664. E-mail: phyllis52003@yahoo.com.

MCINERNEY, ELLEN EUSTIS, management consultant; b. Bayshore, N.Y., Feb. 22, 1946; d. John Joseph Sr. and Ellen Eustis McI. AAS, Marjorie Webster Coll., 1966; postgrad., NYU, 1967 78. Pers. mgr. The Slick Corp., N.Y.C., 1968-70; supr. employment Am. Express Travelers Cheque, N.Y.C., 1970-72; mgr. human resources Gulf & Western Industries, Inc., N.Y.C., 1972-74; dir. staffing The N.Y. Times Co., N.Y.C., 1974-78; sr. v.p. Daniel A. Silverstein Assoc., Inc., N.Y.C., 1979-84; ptnr. Claveloux, McCaffrey, McInerney & Co., Green Farms, Conn., 1984—; COO Wentworth USA, Inc., Auckland, New Zealand, 1995—98; ptnr., bd. dirs. OSIRIS Group, LP, N.Y.C., 1995—98; CEO WARP Group, LLC, N.Y.C., 1996. Pres., COO, bd. dirs. Global Securitization, Inc., Parlin, N.J., 1994-96, bd. dirs. Blumberg Investments, N.Y.C.; mem. coun., bd. dirs. alcoholism and drug abuse Sullivan County Inc., 1995—; bd. cons. The Recovery Ctr. Bd. dirs. Stepping Stones Found., Bedford Hills, N.Y., 1998-99, Liberation Passion Project, 1994-2004. Mem. Nurse healers profl. assoc., Inc., Shanti Nilaya, Internat. Health Rsch. Network. Democrat. Tibetan Buddhist. Avocations: cross country skiing, asian and tibetan mythology, healing and martial arts. Home and Office: PO Box 38 55 John George Rd Grahamsville NY 12740 Office Phone: 845-985-7606. E-mail: eustis@warwick.net.

MCINERNEY, NOREEN LINDA, lawyer; b. Evergreen Park, Ill., Sept. 27, 1971; d. Patrick Joseph and Florence Murphy; m. Michael Joseph McInerney, June 4, 1995; children: Cortney Marie, Neive Renee. BAS in Econs., U. Ill., 1993; JD, Ill. Inst. Tech., 1996. Bar: Ill. 1996. With First Chgo., Chgo., 1997; atty. Griffin & Gallagher, Palos Hills, Ill., 1997—. Mem.: ABA, Clare Assn., Ill. State Bar Assn. Roman Catholic. Avocations: running, bicycling, reading. Office: Griffin & Gallagher 10001 S Roberts Rd Palos Hills IL 60465 Business E-Mail: linda@griffingallagher.com.

MCINTOSH, AMY BENNETT, publishing/internet company executive; b. Cin., Apr. 14, 1958; d. Robert Charles McIntosh and Nancy Allensworth Drysdale; m. Jeffrey Ross Toobin, May 31, 1986; children: Ellen Frances Toobin, Adam Jerome Toobin. AB, Harvard U., 1980, MBA, 1984. Various positions Am. Express, N.Y.C., 1984-99, v.p. mktg., 1991-93, sr. v.p. mktg., 1993-95; v.p. consumer mktg. Bell Atlantic (previously Nynex), N.Y.C., 1995-98, pres., CEO, Network Data, Inc., 1998-2000; CEO Zagat Survey, N.Y.C., 2000—02; sr. v.p. Mktg. Product Solutions D&B, 2002—. Rsch. analyst Bain & Co., Boston, 1980-82. Chmn. bd., Teach for Am.-N.Y., N.Y.C., 1997—. Mem. Internet Industry Assn. Am. (bd. mem. 1998-2000).

MCINTOSH, CAROLYN MEADE, retired educational administrator; b. Waynesburg, Ky., Oct. 21, 1928; d. Clarence Hobert and Sarah Letitia (Bentley) Meade; m. Edgar G. McIntosh, Aug. 21, 1948; children: Wayne, Jeanne, Penny, Jimmi, Carol. BS, Miami U., Oxford, Ohio, 1962; MEd, Xavier U., Cin., 1966. Elem. tchr., Ohio, 1961-79; prin. New Richmond (Ohio) Sch. Dist., 1980-91, ret., 1991. Tchr. Clermont County Adult Edn. Program, 1970-95, Clermont County dir.of Headstart 1971-72, Clermont County Rep. to Ohio elem. adminstr., 1985-87, Pres. Clermont and Brown County adminstr., 1988-89; apptd. student achievement liaison team, New Richmond Bd. Edn. Editor Ret. Tchrs. Newsletter. Pres. New Richmond Bd. Edn.; v.p. U.S. Grant Vocat. Sch. Bd. Edn.; mem. Clermont County Excellence in Edn. Com.; mem. edn. adv. com. Clermont Coll., mem. long range planning com., 1999; ; mem. adv. bd. Bethany Children's Home; mem. Clermont 2001 Com.; mem. Rep. Ctrl. Com. of Clermont County; mem. New Richmond Continuous Improvement Com., 1999; mem. Clermont County Kids Voting Com.; mem. com. Renaissance New Richmond; judge Clermont/Brown County Lit. Coun. Ann. Spelling Bee. Recipient New Richmond Adminstr. of the Yr. award City of New Richmond, 1989; named citizen of yr. Monroe Twp., 1996; selected for sr. leadership charter class, Clermont 2000—. Mem. AAUW, ASCD, NAESP, Nat. Sch. Bd. Assn., Ohio Sch. Bd. Assn., Ohio Assn. Elem. Sch. Adminstrs. (all county legis. liaison), Ohio County Ret. Tchrs. Assn., Clermont County Ret. Tchrs. Assn. (pres.), Order Eastern Star, Clermont County Comm. Svcs. Bd. (apptd. 1998), Phi Delta Kappa, Delta Kappa Gamma (pres. chpt.). Baptist.

MCINTOSH, CECILIA ANN, biochemist, educator; b. Dayton, Ohio, Apr. 30, 1956; d. Russell Edward McIntosh and Geraldine Rita (Cochran) Slemp; m. Kevin Smith Schweiker, May 28, 1978 (div. Mar. 1989); children: Katrina Lynn McIntosh Schweiker, Rebecca Sue McIntosh Schweiker. BA in Biology cum laude, U. South Fla., 1977, MA in Botany, 1981, PhD in Biology, 1990. Rsch. assoc. U. South Fla., Tampa, 1981-86; sci. mentor Ctr. for Excellence, U. So. Fla., Tampa, 1984-90; tchg. and rsch. asst. dept. biology U. South Fla., Tampa, 1986-90; postdoctoral fellow dept. biochemistry U. Idaho, Moscow, 1990-93; asst. prof. dept. biol. scis. East Tenn. State U., Johnson City, 1993-98, assoc. prof., 1998—2004, prof., 2004—, grad. student coord., 1997—2003; adj. assoc. prof. dept. biochemistry Quillen Coll. Medicine East Tenn. State U., Johnson City, 1995—; metabolic biochemistry program dir. NSF DMCB, 2003—04; asst. dean Sch. Grad. Studies, 2004—. Sci. mentor U. So. Fla. Ctr. for Excellence, Tampa, 1984-90; rsch. forum judge Coll. Medicine Rsch. Forum, East Tenn. State U., Johnson City, 1994—; program dir. biomolecular sys. NSF, 2003—. Contbr. articles to sci. jours. including Plant Sci., Plant Physiology, Archives Biochemistry and Biophysics. Sci. fair judge East Tenn. Regional Sci. Fair, Johnson City, 1994—. Grantee USDA, 1994—, East Tenn. State U. Rsch. Devel. Coun., 1994-2002, USDA NRI, 1998-2001, 2003-05; co-grantee Howard Hughes Med. Inst., 2000—. Mem. Am. Assn. Women in Sci., Am. Soc. Plant Biologists, Phytochem. Soc. N.Am. (treas. 1998-2002), Sigma Xi (sci. fair workshop coord. Appalachian chpt. 1995, Dissertation award 1991). Achievements include characterization of new enzyme in plant flavonoid biosynthesis; biochemical characterization of plant mitochondrial membrane tricarboxylate and phosphate transporters and TCA cycle enzymes. Office: East Tenn State U Dept Biol Scis Box 70 703 Johnson City TN 37614-0703 E-mail: mcintosc@mail.etsu.edu.

MCINTOSH, DEBORAH V. elementary school educator; b. Detroit, Feb. 3, 1950; d. Hubert Harvey and Lillian Ethel Mobley; divorced; Courtney James, Carlyn D'Nita, Corey Harvey. BS, U. Mich., 1974; MEd, U. Detroit, 1994. Cert. elem. edn. tchr. K-8. Employment counselor Businessman's Clearinghouse, Chgo., 1977-79; corp. mgr. trainee Sears, Roebuck & Co., Chgo., 1977-78, retail dept. mgr. Hamilton, Ohio, 1978-81; asst. store mgr. Kayo Oil, Ft. Worth, 1983-84; substitute tchr. St. Brigid & St. Cecilia Schs., Detroit, 1986-92; classroom tchr. Highland Park (Mich.) Pub. Schs., 1994—. Tchr. facilitator Project Link, Highland Park, 1997—; mem. edn. & tech. team Jason Project, Lamphere/Highland Park Sch. Dist., 1998-2000; mem. elem. sci. curriculum devel. team Highland Park Pub. Schs., 1998—; co-chairperson Cortland Acad. Social Comm., Highland Park, 1999-2000; mem. Web-based Sci. Rsch. Grant (Eisenhower Found.), Lawrence Technical Inst., Southfield, Mich., 1999-2000. Vol. Mothers Against Drunk Driving, Livonia, Mich., 1993-96; Earth Day chairperson Cortland Acad. chpt. Earth Day Orgn., Highland Park, Mich., 1999-2000. Named for Excellence in Edn., Wayne County Rsch. Edn. Svc. Agy., 1998, 99. Mem. ASCD, Benjamin Banneker Assn., Detroit Area Coun. Tchrs. Math., Met. Detroit Sci. Tchrs. Assn., Highland Park Fedn. of Tchrs. (strategy team 1994), Alpha Kappa Alpha. Democrat. Avocations: reading, poetry and short story writing, gardening, collecting crystal miniatures. Office: Cortland Acad 138 Cortland St Detroit MI 48203-3511

MCINTOSH, ELAINE VIRGINIA, nutrition educator; b. Webster, S.D., Jan. 30, 1924; d. Louis James and Cora Boletta (Bakke) Nelson; m. Thomas Henry McIntosh, Aug. 28, 1955; children: James George, Ronald Thomas, Charles Nelson. BA magna cum laude, Augustana Coll., Sioux Falls, S.D., 1945; MA, U. S.D., 1949; PhD, Iowa State U., 1954. Registered dietitian. Instr., asst. prof. Sioux Falls Coll., 1945-48; instr. Iowa State U., Ames, 1949-53, rsch. assoc., 1955-62; postdoctoral rsch. assoc. U. Ill., Urbana, 1954-55; asst. prof. human biology U. Wis., Green Bay, 1968-72, assoc. prof., 1972-85, prof., 1985-90, emeritus prof., 1990—, writer, cons., 1990—, chmn. human biology dept., 1975-80, asst. to vice chancellor, asst. to chancellor, 1974-76. Author 3 books including American Food Habits in Historical Perspective, 1995, Lewis and Clark: Food, Nutrition, and Health, 2003; contbr. numerous articles on bacterial metabolism, meat biochemistry and nutrition edn. to profl. jours. Fellow USPHS, 1948-49. Mem. Am. Dietetic Assn. Avocation: traveling. Office: U Wis Green Bay ES 307A Human Biology 2420 Nicolet Dr Green Bay WI 54311-7001

MCINTOSH, MAGGIE, state legislator; b. Quinton, Kans., Dec. 22, 1947; AA, Independent Jr. Coll., 1967; BAE, Wichita State U., 1970; MS, ADS, Johns Hopkins U., 1987. Adminstr., tchr. Balt. City Pub. Schs., 1972-78; adj. instr. continuing edn. Cantonville (Md.) C.C., 1978-79; cmty. svc. planner, grants analyst Commn. on Aging and Retirement Edn., Balt., 1979-85; del. Dist. 44 Md. State Delegation, 1992-94, del. Dist. 42, 1995—, mem. appropriations com., 1993—, mem. econ. matters com., 1992—. Del. Dem. Nat. Conv., 1980; mem. Dem. State Ctrl. Com., 1986—; state dir. U.S. Senator Barbara A. Mikulski, 1988-92. Office: Md Ho of Reps State Capitol Annapolis MD 21401 also: Lowe House Office Bldg 84 College Ave Rm 141B Annapolis MD 21401-1693 Address: 6615 Reisterstown Rd Ste 301 Baltimore MD 21215-2689

MCINTOSH, TERRIE TUCKETT, lawyer; b. Ft. Lewis, Wash., July 20, 1944; d. Robert LeRoy and Elda (Perry) Tuckett; m. Clifton Dennis McIntosh, Oct. 13, 1969; children: Alison, John. BA, U. Utah, 1967; MA, U. Ill., 1970; JD, Harvard U., 1978. Bar: N.Y. 1979, Utah 1980. Assoc. Hughes, Hubbard & Reed, N.Y.C., 1978-79, Fabian & Clendenin, Salt Lake City, 1979-84, shareholder, 1984-86; staff atty. Questar Corp., Salt Lake City, 1986-88, sr. atty., 1988-92, sr. corp. counsel, 1992—. Instr. philosophy Douglass Coll. Rutgers U., New Brunswick, N.J., 1971-72; mem. adv. com. civil procedure Utah Supreme Ct., Salt Lake City, 1987—; mem. jud. nominating com. 5th Cir. Ct., Salt Lake City, 1986-88. Mem. Utah State Bar (ethics and discipline screening panel 1989-96, vice chair ethics and discipline com. 1996-99, co-chair law related edn. com. 1985-86), Women Lawyers of Utah (chair exec. com. 1986-87), Salt Lake Legal Aid Soc. (trustee 1999—), Harvard Alumni Assn. Utah (bd. dirs. 1987—), Phi Beta Kappa, Phi Kappa Phi. Office: Questar Corp PO Box 45433 180 E 1st S Salt Lake City UT 84111-1502

MCINTYRE, ANITA GRACE JORDAN, lawyer; b. Louisville, Ky., Jan. 29, 1947; d. Blakely Gordan and Shirley Evans (Grubbs) Jordan; m. Kenneth James McIntyre, Oct. 11, 1969; children: Abigail, Jordan Kenneth. BA, Smith Coll., 1969; JD, U. Detroit, 1975. Bar: Mich. 1975, U.S. Dist. Ct. (ea. dist.) Mich. 1975, U.S. Dist. Ct. (we. dist.) Mich. 1979, U.S. Ct. Appeals (6th cir.) 1979. Ptnr. Rollins White & Rollins, Detroit, 1975-79; vis. assoc. prof. Detroit Coll. Law, 1979-81; assoc. Tyler & Canham, Detroit, 1981-82; prin. Anita G. McIntyre, P.C., Grosse Pointe, Mich., 1982-87, 91—; of counsel Nederlander Dodge & Rollins, Detroit, 1987-90; assoc. Damm & Smith, P.C., Detroit, 1990-91. Hearing panel chmn. Atty. Discipline Bd., 1985—. Editor, author (case notes) U. Detroit Jour. Urban Law, 1975; contrbr. articles to profl. jours. Sec. Berry Subdivsn. Assn., Detroit, 1975-77; pres. Smith Coll. Club Detroit, 1982-86; mem. parents bd. U. Liggett Sch., Grosse Pointe, Mich., 1991,95; vice chair state pub. affairs com. Mich. State Coun. Jr. Leagues, 1998-2000, chair, 2001-. Mem.: Wayne County Juvenile Trial Lawyers Assn., Wayne County (Mich.) Probate Bar Assn., State Bar Mich., Edgemont Park Assn. (sec.), Jr. League Detroit (chair pub.affairs com. 1998—2001, vice chair Mich. state pub. affairs com. 1999—2001, chair 2001—02). Episcopalian. Avocations: skiing, swimming, needle point. Office: 15324 Mack Ave Ste 201 Grosse Pointe Park MI 48230 E-mail: agmcintyr@cs.com.

MCINTYRE, ELIZABETH JONES, multi-media specialist, educator; b. Teaneck, N.J., July 17, 1939; d. Paul J. Jones and Ann Cecilia O'Leary; m. John Peter McIntyre, Jan. 30, 1960; children: John P. III, Paul M., Patricia M., Maura M. Student, Rosemont Coll., 1957—59; BS in Edn., Seton Hall U., 1961; degree, Caldwell Coll., 1976. Cert. Tchr. N.J., 1976, Libr. N.J., 1976. Tchr. 4th grade Corpus Christi Sch., Hasbrouck Heights, NJ, 1960—61; media specialist Gould & Grandview Sch., North Caldwell, NJ, 1961—63, Parsippany Twp. Sch., Parsippany, NJ, 1974—2000. Grantee, Parsippany Bd. Edn., 1981, 1989. Mem.: AAUW, Women of Irish Heritage. Republican. Roman Catholic. Avocations: gardening, reading. Home: 12 South Tamarack Drive Brielle NJ 08730

MCINTYRE, JERILYN SUE, university administrator; b. June 24, 1942; d. Frank Otto and Maxine (Ward) McIntyre; m. W. David Smith. Student, Stanford U., Italy, 1962; AB in History with distinction, Stanford U., 1964, MA in Journalism, cert. Summer Radio-TV Inst., Stanford U., 1965, tchrs. cert., 1968; PhD in Comms., U. Washington, 1973; postgrad. Inst. Ednl. Mgmt., Harvard U., 1993. Corr. World News Bureau McGraw-Hill Pub. Co., L.A., 1965-67; asst. prof. dept. mass comm. Chico (Calif.) State Coll., 1968-70; asst. prof. Sch. Journalism U. Iowa, Iowa City, 1973-77; assoc. prof., prof. dept. comm. U. Utah, Salt Lake City, 1977-2000, assoc. dean Coll. Humanities, 1984-88, assoc. v.p. acad. affairs, 1988-90, interim pres., 1997, v.p. acad. affairs, 1990-98; pres. Ctrl. Wash. U., Ellensburg, 2000—. Dir. Wall St. Jour. Publs. Workshop, Chico State Coll., 1968; mem. edn. adv. bd. NFL, 1996; mem. exec. com. coun. acad. affairs Nat. Assn. State Univs. and Land Grant Coll., 1995—98, chair, 1997; mem. steering com. Utah Edn. Network, 1995—98. Editl. asst. Chemical Week Mag., 1965-66, World News Bureau, 1966-67; mem. editl. bd. Journalism History; co-author: Symbols & Society; contbr. articles to profl. jours., chpts. to books. Mem. Utah Women's Forum. Named a David P. Gardner fellow, 1984; recipient Yesterday's Girl Scout Today's Successful Woman, Utah Girl Scout Coun., 1996. Mem.: AAUW (Salt Lake City chpt. Disting. Woman 1994), Assn. Edn. in Journalism and Mass Comm. Office: 400 E University Way Ellensburg WA 98926-7501

MCINTYRE, JUDY, social worker, state representative; b. Tulsa, Okla., May 31, 1945; d. Garland O. Eason, Del (Stepfather) and Jeanne (Hughes) Phillips; BS in Social Work, U. Okla., 1967, MS in Social Work, 1979. Social worker Dept. Human Svcs. in Child Welfare, Okla.; rep. Ho. Reps., State of Okla., Okla. City, 2002—. Mem. speaker's leadership team Okla. Ho. Reps., Okla. City, 2002—, mem. common edn., higher edn., human svcs., pub, health coms., 2002—. 1921 Race Riot Design Com.; Greenwood Redevel. Authority; mem., pres. Tulsa Sch. Bd. Named Fellow, Ctr. for Am. Women and Politics/Eagleton Inst. Politics, Rutgers U. Leadership Inst., 2002. Mem.: Com. Workers of Am., NAACP. Democrat. Office: 2300 N Lincoln Blvd Rm 301 Oklahoma City OK 73105 Home and Office: PO Box 48548 Tulsa OK 74148 E-mail: mcintyreju@lsb.state.ok.us.

MCINTYRE, LINNEA ANDREN, landscaping company executive; b. Point Pleasant, N.J., July 21, 1950; d. Carl Walter and Eva Helen (ReMillong) Andren; m. Kevin McIntyre, 1987; 1 child, Kasara Megan. BS in Elem. Edn., Trenton State Coll., 1972; cert. master gardener, Pa. State U. Owner Plants by Design, Upper Black Eddy, Pa., 1975—. Mem. Am. Hort. Soc., Pa. Hort. Soc. Avocations: sailing, snow skiing, gardening. Home and Office: Plants by Design 1306 River Rd Upper Black Eddy PA 18972 Office: Plants by Design 1306 River Rd Upper Black Eddy PA 18972 E-mail: linnea@plantsbydesign.com.

MCINTYRE, LOLA MAZZA, music educator; b. Hammond, Ind., Sept. 23, 1955; d. Tony and Isabell Emma Mazza, Wanda Marie Mazza (Stepmother); m. William Russell McIntyre; children: William, Alexander. BMus, Hope Coll., Holland, Michigan, 1978; MMus, U. Tenn., 1989. Cert. nat. cert. piano 1991, Mich. Music Tchg. K-12 1978, Ind. applied music tchg. 2002. Music tchr. Saugatuck (Mich.) Pub. Schs., 1978—79; owner, tchr. The Studio of Holland, Holland, Mich., 1979—81; parish dir. music ministries Lafayette Diocese of Ind., Carmel, Ind., 1991—97; pvt. piano tchr. Carmel, Ind., 1976—; assoc. adj. prof. piano U. Indpls., 2001—. Prodr.: (Audio Recording) Alleluia!, 1996; author: (Multi-media Instructional CD-ROM) Bach's Musette, 2000. Friend Mus. Miniature Enthusiasts, Carmel, 2001—; docent Indpls. Symphony Orch., 1999. Recipient Concerto Competition award, Hope Coll., 1977. Mem.: Ind. Piano Tchrs. Guild (web designer, webmaster 2001—), Gtr. Indpls. Piano Tchrs. Assn. (v.p., theory chmn. 2000—02), Ind. Music Tchrs. Assn. (state advisor, music tech. 2001—02), Music Tchrs. Nat. Assn., Delta Omicron (life; chpt. pres. 1977—78, Star of Delta Omicron 1978). Roman Catholic. Avocations: miniatures, golf, quilting, travel, concerts. Office: U Indpls Music Dept 1400 E Hanna Ave Indianapolis IN Personal E-mail: lmcintyre@indy.rr.com. Business E-Mail: lmcintyre@uindy.edu.

MCINTYRE, LOUISE S., income tax consultant; b. Cin., Jan. 29, 1924; d. George Washington and Bertha (McDaniels) Sullivan; m. Harry McIntyre Jr., Jan. 18, 1947; children: Carol L., Patricia A., Harriet L., Harry J., Brenda R. AA, Mira Costa Coll., Oceanside, Calif., 1972; grad. in auditing, Nat. Tax Practice Inst., 1989. Enrolled agt. Hydraulic testor Paterson Field, Fairfield, Ohio, 1942-45; control clk. Hickam Field, Honolulu, 1945-47; clk.-typist Patterson Field, Fairfield, 1947-49, Camp LeJeune, Jacksonville, N.C., 1951-56; sec., bookkeeper Mission Bowl, Oceanside, 1973-79; income tax cons. Oceanside, 1974—. Mem. Oceanside Human Rels. Commn., 1970; bd. dirs. Armed Forces YMCA, Oceanside, 1969-71, Oceanside Christian Women's Club, 1988-91, North County Concert Assn. Aux., 1993-96; active PTA, Girl Scout U.S. Mem. Inland Soc. Tax Cons. (bd. dirs. 1988—), Am. Soc. Women Accts. (v.p. 1989-90), Enrolled Agts. Palomar, Nat. Assn. Enrolled Agts., Nat. Soc. Pub. Accts., Calif. Assn. Ind. Accts., Palmquist PTA (hon. life). Avocations: bowling, dance, crafts, interior decorating, cake decorating. Home: 328 Camelot Dr Oceanside CA 92054-4515

MCINTYRE, VICKY JOYCE, business owner; b. Glasgow, Mont., Dec. 12, 1952; d. Frank Smith Jr. and Mary Helen (Smith) McIntyre; m. John Peter Oleksey, Jr., Aug. 7, 1976 (div. May l984); l child, Kathryn Elizabeth. Student, U. Colo., 1973-76, U. Md., Fed. Republic Germany, 1977-81; BSBA, U. Phoenix, 1984; MBA, Boise State U., 1988. Cert. quality analyst, quality award examiner, Minn.; cert. Myers Briggs Personality Typing, Star Performance and ISO 9000 auditor. Keytape operator 1st Security Bank, Glasgow, l968-7l; programmer analyst Baldwin Data Svcs., Denver, 1973-76; acctg. technician dept. non-appropriated funds U.S. Govt., Ramstein, Fed. Republic Germany, 1977-79, systems operator dept. non-appropriated funds, 1979-80; programmer analyst II, United Banks Colo., Denver, l982-85; programmer analyst Moore Fin. Group, Boise, Idaho, l985-87, career developer, 1987-88; mgr. quality assurance West One Bancorp, Boise, 1988-90; mgr. quality assurance software products Bankers Systems, Inc., St. Cloud, Minn., 1991-93, sr. bus. analyst, 1993-95; owner Applied Bus. Strategies, St. Cloud, Minn., 1995—; exec. dir., founder Ctrl. Minn. Quality Coun., 1996-99; prof. St. Cloud State U., 1997—2002; asst. prof. mgmt. Coll. St. Benedict, 2002—. Dir. bus. program St. Cloud State U., 2000—01. Mem. pers. com., leader single parents group 1st Presbyn. Ch., Boise, 1988-89; bd. dirs. St. Cloud All-City H.S. Marching Band, 1995-96, Forum of Exec. Women, 1996. Recipient Outstanding Project Chmn. award, Jaycee of Month award U.S. Jaycees-Idaho, 1989, Staff Officer of Yr., 1991, Project Chmn. of Yr. 1991, Ambassador, 1993; named Statesman Minn. Jaycees, 1993, Single Parent of the Yr., 1994. Mem. Am. Bus. Women's Assn. (v.p. Boise chpt. 1987-88, Woman of Yr. award 1987), Capitol Jaycees (v.p. for mgmt. devel. 1989), Sartell Jaycees (pres. 1992-93, state del. 1993-94). Republican. Episcopalian. Avocations: skiing, camping. Home: 2808 21st Ave S Saint Cloud MN 56301-9063 Office: 2808 21st Ave S Saint Cloud MN 56301-9063

MC INTYRE, VONDA NEEL, writer; b. Aug. 28, 1948; d. H. Neel and Vonda Barth (Keith) McI. BS, U. Wash., Seattle, 1970. Author: The Exile Waiting, 1976, 85, Dreamsnake, 1978 (Hugo award, Nebula award), Fireflood and Other Stories, 1979, The Entropy Effect, 1981, The Wrath of Khan, 1982, Superluminal, 1983, The Search for Spock, 1984, Barbary, 1986, Enterprise: The First Adventure, 1986, The Voyage Home, 1986, Starfarers, 1989, Transition, 1991, Metaphase, 1992, Nautilus, 1993, Star Wars: The Crystal Star, 1994, The Moon and the Sun, 1997 (Nebula award); editor: (with Susan Janice Anderson) Aurora: Beyond Equality, 1976. Mem. ACLU. Recipient Nebula award, 1973, 78 Mem. Sci. Fiction Writers Am., Planetary Soc., Cousteau Soc., NOW, Space Studies Inst., Authors Guild, Greenpeace, Nature Conservancy.

MCINTYRE-IVY, JOAN CAROL, data processing executive; b. Port Chester, N.Y., Mar. 1, 1939; d. John Henry and Molly Elizabeth (Gates) Daugherty; m. Stanley Donald McIntyre, Aug. 24, 1857 (div. Jan. 1986); children: Michael Stanley McIntyre, David John McIntyre, Sharon Lynne McIntyre; m. James Morrow Ivy IV, June 1, 1988. Student, Northwestern U., 1956-57, U. Ill., 1957-58. Assoc. editor Writer's Digest, Cin., 1966-68; instr. creative writing U. Ala., Huntsville, 1974-75; editor Strode Pubs., Huntsville, 1974-75; paralegal Smith, Huckaby & Graves (now Bradley, Arant, Rose & White), Huntsville, 1976-82; exec. v.p. Micro Craft, Inc.,

Huntsville, 1982-85, pres., 1985-89, ceo, chmn. bd., 1989—; also bd. dirs., co-owner. Author: numerous computer operating manuals for law office software, 1978—; co-author: Alabama and Federal Complaint Forms, 1979; editor: Alabama Law for the Layman, 1975; contbr. numerous articles to profl. jours. Hon. scholar Medil Sch. Journalism Northwestern U., 1956. Mem. Huntsville Literary Soc. (bd. dirs. 1976-77). Republican. Methodist. Office: 123 Fairington Rd NW Huntsville AL 35806-2249 E-mail: verdictsos@aol.com.

MCJUNKIN, EVON MARIE LLOYD, minister; b. Erie, Pa., Mar. 2, 1959; d. Thomas and Jane Lloyd; m. Paul Harvey McJunkin, July 20, 1937; 1 child, Anna Maria. MDiv, Union Theol. Sem. Va., 1987; MEd, Edinboro U. Pa., 1983; BA, Westminster Coll., 1981. Ordained Min. of Word and Sacrament Presbyn. Ch., 1987. Pastor First Presbyn. Ch., U.S.A., Port Allegany, Pa., 2001—; interim pastor Girard Presbyn. Ch., Pa., 2000—01; designated pastor Perkins Presbyn. Ch., Erie, 1997—2000; pastor Faith United Ch. Presbyn., Clifton, Kans., 1991—97; interim pastor Sebring Presbyn. Ch., Ohio, 1991; pastor Concord Presbyn. Ch., Salem, Ohio, 1987—91, Ellsworth Presbyn. Ch., Ohio, 1987—91; devel. reading tchr. Gen. McLane Sch. Dist., Edinboro, Pa., 1982—84. Mem. ministry com. Presbytery of Lake Erie, Pa., 2003—, moderator Worship Life com., Pa., 1999—2001; pres. Port Allegany Area Ministerium, 2002—. Mem., pres. C. of C., Clifton, Kans., 1992—97. Mem.: Artisans Club, Port Allegheny, Pa. (pres. 2002—03). Achievements include Represented Eastminster Presbytery of Ohio in negotiation of a partnership with the Evangelical Presbyterian Church, Ghana in 1988. Avocations: watercolor painting, reading, singing. Office: First Presbyterian Ch 12 Church St Port Allegany PA 16743

MCKAGUE, SHIRLEY, state representative; b. Nampa, Idaho, Dec. 4, 1935; m. Paul McKague; children: Rhonda, Van, Dan, Randy, Rick, Robert. Grad., Nampa H.S., 1953. Legal sec. Carey Nixon, 1964—78; columnist Valley Times, 1980—82; co-owner Paul's Meridian Stinker, 1970—; state rep. dist. 20B Idaho Ho. of Reps., Boise, 1996—, mem. commerce and human resources, and transp. and def. coms., vice chmn., revenue and taxation com. Mem. Miss Meridian Pageant com.; mem. Rep. Precinct Com., 1986—. Mem.: Meridian C. of C., Idaho Farm Bur. Republican. Office: State Capitol PO Box 83720 Boise ID 83720-0038

MCKAMEY, FRANCES HELENE, music educator; b. Tacoma, Wash., Nov. 14, 1958; d. G. Robert and Frances K. McKamey. AAS, Ft. Steilacoom C.C., Tacoma, Wash., 1979; BA in Edn., Pacific Luth. U., Tacoma, Wash., 1981. Cert. tchr. Wash. Summer music camp staff Pacific Luth. U., Tacoma, 1980—83; sub. tchr. Bethel Sch. Dist., Spanaway, Wash., 1982; instrumental and voice tchr. Pateros Sch. Dist., Wash., 1982—84; dir. elem. band program John F. Kennedy Meml. H.S., Burien, Wash., 1984—. Min. music to local chs., Tacoma, Seattle, Wash., 1979—; trumpet tchr., Tacoma, 1979—. Mem.: Nat. Catholic Band Assn., Music Educators Nat. Assn., First Catholic Slovak Ladies Assn. Roman Catholic. Avocations: reading, sports. Office: John F Kennedy Meml HS 140 S 140th St Burien WA 98168

MCKAY, DONNA, legal association administrator; V.p. devel. U.S. Fund for UNICEF; dir. program funding Planned Parenthood, N.Y.C., devel. dir., v.p. for external affairs Chgo.; dir. devel. ACLU, N.Y.C. Office: ACLU 18th Fl 125 Broad St New York NY 10004

MC KAY, EMILY GANTZ, civil rights professional; b. Columbus, Ohio, Mar. 13, 1945; d. Harry S. and Edwina (Bookwalter) Gantz; m. Jack Alexander McKay, July 3, 1965. BA, Stanford U., 1966, MA, 1967. From pub. info. specialist to rsch. assoc. Cmty. Action Pitts., 1967-70; freelance cons., 1969-70; pub. rels. and materials specialist Met. Cleve. JOBS Coun., 1971-72; rsch. and mgmt. cons. BLK Group, Inc., Washington, 1970-73; dir. tech. products Am. Tech. Assistance Corp., McLean, Va., 1973-74; rsch. and mgmt. cons. CONSAD Rsch. Corp., Pitts., 1974-76, v.p., 1976-78; spl. asst. to pres. for planning and eval. Nat. Coun. La Raza, Washington, 1978-82, v.p. rsch., advocacy & legislation, 1981-88, exec. v.p., 1983-88, cons. to pres., 1988-90, v.p. instl. devel., 1991-93, sr. v.p. instl. devel., 1993-94. Pres. Mosaica: Ctr. for Nonprofit Devel. and Pluralism, 1994—; cons. resource devel. New Israel Fund, 1989-91; cons. City of Cleve., Nat. Assn. Cmty. Devel., Nat. Coun. La Raza, 1975-78, Ford Found., 1989, Nat. AIDS Network, 1988-89, Am. Cultural Ctr., Israel, 1990, 2000, Nat. Hispana Leadership Inst., 1993; vol. orgnl. cons. SHATIL, Jerusalem and cmty. based groups in Israel, 1987—; guest faculty Union Inst. Grad. Sch.; adj. faculty Sch. Internat. Svc. Am. U., Washington, 1995—; mem. faculty Salzburg (Austria) Seminar on Leadership, 2003. Author devel. tng. materials and HIV/AIDS tech. assistance materials. Co-chmn. Citizens Adv. Com. to D.C. Bar, 1986-87; mem. Mayor's Commn. Coop. Econ. Devel., 1981-83; non-lawyer bd. govs. D.C. Bar, 1982-85; exec. com., bd. dirs. Indochina Resource Action Ctr., 1982-92; bd. dirs. exec. com. Southeast Asia Resource Action Ctr., 1993-97; co-chmn. Citizens Commn. Adminstrn. Justice, 1982-84; exec. com. Coalition on Human Needs, 1981-88; Washington area steering com. New Israel Fund, 1989-91; co-chmn. adv. com. to Washington dist. office dir. Immigration and Naturalization Svc., 1984-88; chair Refugee Women in Devel., 1987-90, vice-chair, 1990-94; nat. adv. bd. Project Blueprint United Way of Am., 1992-94, diversity com., 1994-96; vice-chair, treas. Fund for the Future of Our Children, 1994—; sec. bd. dirs. New Bosnia Fund, 1995-99, U.S. vice-chair, 1997-99; bd. advisors Internat. Ctr. for Residential Edn., 1994-96; bd. dirs. Mary's Ctr. Maternal and Child Care, 1995-2000, treas., 1996-2000; treas., bd. dirs. AVODAH: The Jewish Svc. Corps., 1996-99; bd. dirs. Acad. of Hope, 2001—; bd. dirs. Nat. Hispana Leadership Inst., 1997-2003, treas., 1998-2003; working group Memorandum of Understanding between HHS and Israeli Ministry of Labour and Social Welfare, 1990-94, chair subcom Youth at Risk, 1992-94; adv. merit sel. panel Superior Ct. D.C., 1987-90; planning task force US-Israel Women to Women, 2000-01. Recipient I. Pat Rios award Guadalupe Ctr., 1988; Ford Found. nat. honors fellow, 1966-67. Mem. NAACP, Nat. Coun. La Raza, Phi Beta Kappa. Democrat. Home: 3200 19th St NW Washington DC 20010-1006 Office: 1522 K St NW Ste 1130 Washington DC 20005-1225 E-mail: Emily@mosaica.org.

MCKAY, JOANE WILLIAMS, dean; b. New Underwood, S.D., June 5, 1939; d. Gene Edward and Saxon Molly (Guptill) Williams; m. Donald Jerome McKay, June 5, 1964; children: Marc Donald, Troy Daniel. BA, Augustana Coll., Sioux Falls, S.D., 1961; MS, Iowa State U., 1986, PhD, 1990. Pub. sch. tchr., Wyo., Iowa and S.D., 1980-89; dir. field experience Iowa State U., Ames, 1989-91; grad. coord. U. Nev., Las Vegas, 1991-94; assoc. dean U. No. Iowa, Cedar Falls, 1994-97; dean St. Cloud (Minn.) State U., 1997—. Columnist, Riverton (Wyo.) Ranger, 1966-72, Ames Daily Tribune, 1974-84. Named Tchr. of Yr., Nat. Tchr. of Yr. Awards, 1988. Mem. Assn. Tchr. Educators (chair global task force 1996), Am. Assn. Colls. for Tchr. Edn. (chair spl. interest group 1997). Office: St Cloud State U 720 4th Ave S Saint Cloud MN 56301-4498

MCKAY, KAY, academic administrator; Student, No. Ariz. U., 1961—65. Pres. Ariz. Bd. Regents, Phoenix, 1998—. Cons. in staff/mgmt. rehab. Exec. dir. Big Bros./Bis Sisters, Flagstaff, Ariz.; superior ct. mediator Conconino County, Ariz.; mem. jud. rev. and selection bd., Ariz.; bd. dirs. Flagstaff Med. Ctr., Ariz. Health Care, Inc. Office: Ariz Bd Regents Ste 230 2020 N Central Ave Phoenix AZ 85004

MCKAY, LAURA L. banker, consultant; b. Watonga, Okla., Mar. 3, 1947; d. Frank Bradford and Elizabeth Jane (Smith) Drew; m. Cecil O. McKay, Sept. 20, 1969; 1 child, Leslie. BSBA, Oreg. State U., 1969. Cert. cash mgr., Treasury Mgmt. Assn. New br. rsch. U.S. Bank, Portland, Oreg., 1969-80, cash mgmt. officer, 1980-82, asst. v.p., 1982-87, v.p., 1987-94; founder, cons. LLM Cons., Milw., 1994-97; co-founder, mng. ptnr. DMC & Assocs. LLC, Portland, 1997—2001; v.p. treasury mgmt., sales mgr. West Coast Bank, 2000—. Cert. trainer Achieve Global and Edge Learning. Chmn. Budget Com., North Clackamas Sch. Dist., 1982-84. Mem. ASTD, Assn. for Fin. Profls., Nat. Assn. Bank Women (chmn. Oreg. group 1979-80), Portland Cash Mgrs. Assn., Portland C. of C. Republican. Office: PO Box 8000 Wilsonville OR 97070 Office Phone: 503-454-0416. E-mail: mckayl@wcb.com.

MCKAY, RENEE, artist; b. Montreal, Que., Can. came to U.S., 1946, naturalized, 1954; d. Frederick Garvin and Mildred Gladys (Higgins) Smith; m. Kenneth Gardiner McKay, July 25, 1942; children: Margaret Craig, Kenneth Gardner. BA, McGill U., 1941. Tchr. art Peck Sch., Morristown, N.J., 1955-56. One woman shows include Pen and Brush Club, N.Y.C., 1957, Cosmopolitan Club, N.Y.C., 1958; group shows include Weyhe Gallery, N.Y.C., 1978, Newark Mus., 1955, 59, Montclair (N.J.) Mus., 1955-58, Nat. Assn. Women Artists, Nat. Acad. Galleries, 1954-78, N.Y. World's Fair, 1964-65, Audubon Artists, N.Y.C., 1955-62, 74-79, N.Y. Soc. Women Artists, 1979-80, Provincetown (Mass.) Art Assn. and Mus., 1975-79; traveling shows in France, Belgium, Italy, Scotland, Can., Japan; represented in permanent collections: Slater Meml. Mus., Norwich, Conn., Norfolk (Va.) Mus., Butler Inst. Am. Art, Youngstown, Ohio, Lydia Drake Libr., Pembroke, Mass., Nat. Arts Club, N.Y.C., Provinceton Mus.- Mass., Provincetown, many pvt. collections. Recipient Jane Peterson prize in oils Nat. Assn. Women Artists, 1954, Famous Artists Sch. prize in watercolor, 1959, Grumbacher Artists Watercolor award 1970, Solo award Pen and Brush, 1957, Sadie-Max Tesser award in watercolor Audubon Artists, 1975, Peterson prize in oils, 1980, Michael Engel prize Nat. Soc. Painters in Casein and Acrylic, 1983. Mem. Nat. Assn. Women Artists (2d v.p. 1969-70, adv. bd. 1974-76), Audubon Artists (pres. 1979, dir. oils 1986-88), Artist Equity (dir. 1977-79, v.p. 1979-81), N.Y. Soc. Women Artists, Pen and Brush, Nat. Soc. Painters in Casein and Acrylic M.J. Kaplan prize 1984, Nat. Arts Club, Provincetown Art Assn. and Mus., Key West Art Assn., Cosmopolitan Club.

MCKAY-WILKINSON, JULIE ANN, minister, marriage and family therapist; b. Washington, D.C., Feb. 26, 1953; d. Charles William and Evelyn Loretta (Starr) McKay; m. Grover Gene Wilkinson, Jan. 13, 1990; 1 child, Angela Starr Gotti. AS, Camden County Coll., 1975; BA, Rowan U., 1978; grad., Unity Sch. Christianity, Lee's Summit, Mo., 1997. Cert. pastoral addictions counselor, and lic. addictions counselor, co-dependency counselor. Probation officer York County Probation, Pa., 1983—86; therapist pvt. practice, York, 1985—90, New Insights, York, 1985—87, Clare Ctr., York, 1987—90; founder, min., therapist Unity Christ Ch., Lubbock, Tex., 1997—. Editor: (monthly newsletter) Spiritual Lifelines, 1997—. Chairperson Christmas toy dr. Unity Christ Ch., 1997—. Mem.: Lubbock Ecimenical Orgn. Democrat. Avocations: gardening, music, animals, movies. Office: Christ Unity Church 7300 Mallard Creek Rd Charlotte NC 28262 Home: 2540 Pickway Dr Charlotte NC 28269 E-mail: revjulie3@aol.com.

MCKEAGE, ALICE JANE, computer programmer; b. Saginaw, Mich., Mar. 27, 1948; d. Donald William and Genevieve Francis McK.. BS in Edn., Ctrl. Mich. U., Mt. Pleasant, Mich., 1970. Tchr. Madison Dist. Pub. Schs., Madison Heights, Mich., 1970—79; computer programmer Retail Mgmt. Svcs., Birmingham, Mich., 1980—82, 3 PM, Livonia, Mich., 1982—85, Am. Fin. Cons. Co., Troy, Mich., 1985—87, Cats Co., Troy, 1988—90, Ford Motor Co., Dearborn, Mich., 1990—. Interviewee (TV show) Straight Talk About Gays in the Workplace, 2001. Co-founder gay, lesbian, bisexual transgender employee network Ford Motor Co., 1994; co-founder Race Matters, Detroit gay, lesbian, bisexual, transgender discussion group on racism and sexism, 2000; mem. steering com. Main St. Pride, Royal Oak, Mich., 1996, outreach co-chair, 1997; bd. dirs. Affirmations Gay Lesbian Bisexual Transgender Cmty. Ctr., Ferndale, 2000—03. Recipient Cmty. Svc. award, Gay Lesbian Bisexual Transgender Pride, 1999, Spirit of Detroit award, Detroit City Coun., 2001, Unity award, Race Matters Gay, Lesbian, Bisexual Transgender Pride awards, 2002, Jan Stevenson award, Affirmations Gay and Lesbian Cmty. Center, 2004. Mem.: Out and Equal Workplace Advs. (charter). Democrat. Avocations: softball, gardening, hiking. Office: Ford Motor Co The American Rd Dearborn MI 48121

MCKEAN, MAUREEN CATHERINE, city official, systems analyst; b. Babylon, N.Y., Aug. 25, 1956; d. Donald Joseph and Alba Erminia (Frasco) McK.; m. Kenneth Raymond Crockett, Apr. 7, 1982; 1 child, Nicholas. BA, SUNY, Buffalo, 1977; postgrad., U. Tex., 1979-81, 86. Staff devel. specialist City of Austin, Tex., 1985-89, sys. support specialist I, 1989-90, sys. support specialist II, 1990-96, sys. analyst, 1996—, project mgr. automated customer assistance process, 1996—. Mem. bd. Employee Learning Program, Austin, 1992—. Bd. dirs. Pilot Parent, ARC, Austin, 1989-90; pres. Capital Area Autism Soc., Austin, 1992-94, bd. dirs., 1994—. Avocations: photography, antique refinishing, tropical aquarium. Home: 811 W Gibson St Austin TX 78704-2345 Office: City of Austin 206 E 9th St Austin TX 78701-2516

MCKEE, CATHERINE LYNCH, law educator, lawyer; b. Boston, June 7, 1962; d. Robert Emmett and Anne Gayle (Tanner) Lynch; m. Bert K. McKee Jr., Dec. 25, 1990; children: Timothy Kingston, Shannon Lancaster. BA in Biol. Sci., U. Calif. Berkeley, 1984; JD, U. San Diego, 1988. Bar: Calif. 1988, U.S. Dist. Ct. (cen., so. and ea. dists.) Calif. 1989, U.S. Ct. Appeals (9th cir.) 1989. Assoc. Parkinson, Wolf, Lazar & Leo, L.A., 1988-89, McCormick & Mitchell, San Diego, 1989-91; prof. Mt. San Antonio Coll., Walnut, Calif., 1994—, mock trial coach, 1994—2000, dir. paralegal program, 1999—2003. Cert. rev. hearing officer, Orange County, 1994—; legal counsel Imperial Valley Lumber Co., Valley Lumber and Truss Co., 1998—; coach nat. champion C.C. mock trial team, 2000; mem. acad. senate exec. coun. Mt. San Antonio Coll., 1996-2000, chmn. campus equivalency com., 1999, chair paralegal program adv. com., 1999-2003; mem. East San Gabriel Valley regional occupl. program adv. com., 2003—. Contbr. weekly newspaper column, 1993-99; prodr., star videos An Attorney's Guide to Legal Research on the Internet, 1998, 99; co-author: Jeff and Catherine's World's Best List of Legal (and Law-related) Internet Sites. Chair scholarship com. U. Calif. Alumni Assn., Berkeley, 1995—; capt. auction team SCATS Gymnastics, 2000—02. Named Cmty. Person of Yr. Diamond Bar C. of C., 1995. Mem. NEA, State Bar Calif. (probation monitor 1993—), Ea. Bar Assn. L.A. (trustee 2000—), Calif. Tchrs. Assn., Am. Inns of Ct., Calif. Assn. Lanterman-Petris-Short Hearing Officers. Avocations: weight lifting, photography, reading. Office: Mount San Antonio Coll 1100 N Grand Ave Walnut CA 91789-1341 E-mail: cmckee@mtsac.edu.

MCKEE, CHARLOTTE HICKERSON, music educator; b. Richmond, Va., Oct. 15, 1953; m. David McKee; 3 children. BME, Shenandoah Coll. & Conservatory of Music, Winchester, Va., 1976; MEd, Va. Tech., Blacksburg, Va., 1986. Cert. post graduate tchg. cert. Va., creating original opera level 3 cert., Orff-Schulwerk, level 1 cert. Elem. sec. music tchr. Sumner County Sch., Gallatin, Tenn., 1976—79; elem. music tchr. Loundon County Sch., Leesburg, Va., 1979—84, Montgomery County Sch., Christiensburg, Va., 1987—, music specialist elem., mid. sch., dir. choir Blacksburg, Va., 1987—. Cultural dir. PTA-Margaret Beeks Elem. Sch., Blacksburg, Va., 1989—2000; mem. Roanoke Symphony Orch. Edn. Com., 1996—98, Montgomery County Music Task Force, Christiansburg, Va., 1996—98, Va. Music Educators Assn. Standard of Learning Rewrite Com., 1995—96. Mem.: Nat. Edn. Assn., Am. Choral Dir. Assn., Music Educators Nat. Conf. Avocations: reading, walking, sewing. Office: Blackburg Mid Sch 3109 Prices Fork Rd Blacksburg VA 24060

MCKEE, ELEANOR SWETNAM, retired principal; b. Del Norte, Colo., Oct. 21, 1934; d. William Wayne and Harriet Norris Swetnam; children: Tim, David, Christopher. BA in Secondary Edn., Adams State Coll., 1960; MA in Elem. Edn., U. So. Colo., 1976; postgrad., U. Hawaii, 1976—78. Tchr. Nenana Schs., Alaska, 1964—76; prin. Railroad Sch. Dist., Healy, Alaska, 1976—89; journalist Prism Enterprises, LaJunta, Colo., 1991—93; curriculum writer Internat. Found. for Edn. and Self Help, Malawi, 1998—99; prin. Am. Grade Schs., Phoenix, 1998—99; tchr. Phoenix Christian Acad., 1999—2001; prin. Beaver Sch./Yukon Flats Sch. Dist., Ft. Yukon, Alaska, 2001—02; ret., 2002. Contbr. articles to profl. jours. Tchr. vol. Migrant Edn., Rocky Rd., Colo., 1991—95. Mem.: N.C. Writers Network, Alaska Edn. Assn. (sec. 1979—80), Orton Soc. Republican. Episcopalian. Avocations: hiking, theater, cooking, piano, mountain biking. Home: 279 W Puainako St Hilo HI 96720-3176

MCKEE, MARGARET JEAN, federal agency administrator; b. New Haven, June 20, 1929; d. Waldo McCutcheon and Elizabeth McKee. AB, Vassar Coll., 1951. Staff asst. United Rep. Fin. Com., N.Y.C., 1952, N.Y. Rep. State Com., N.Y.C., 1953—55, Crusade for Freedom (name later changed to Radio Free Europe Fund), N.Y.C., 1955—57; researcher Stricker & Henning Rsch. Assocs., Inc., N.Y.C., 1957—59; exec. sec. New Yorkers for Nixon (name later changed to N.Y. State Ind. Citizens for Nixon Lodge), N.Y.C., 1959—60; asst. to Raymond Moley, polit. columnist N.Y.C., 1961; asst. campaign com. Louis J. Lefkowitz for Mayor, N.Y.C., 1961; rsch. programmer, treas. Consensus, Inc., N.Y.C., 1962—67; spl. asst. to U. S. Senator Jacob K. Javits NY, 1967—73; adminstr. asst., 1973—75; dep. adminstr. Am. Revolution Bicentennial Adminstrn., 1976, acting adminstr., 1976—77; chief of staff Perry B. Duryea (minority leader) N.Y. State Assembly, 1978; pub. affairs cons., 1979—80; dir. govt. rels. Gen. Mills Restaurant Group, Inc., 1980—83; exec. dir. Fed. Mediation and Conciliation Svc., 1983—86; mem. Fed. Labor Rels. Authority, 1986—89, chmn., 1989—94; mem. Nat. Partnership Coun., 1993—94; chmn. adv. bd. Workplace Solutions, 1996—. Mem. U.S. Adv.Commn. on Pub. Diplomacy, 1972—82; dir. scheduling and spkrs.' bur. N.Y. Com. to Re-elect the Pres., 1972; mem. bd. govs. Women's Nat. Rep. Club, N.Y.C., 1963—66; mem. N.Y. State Bingo Control Commn., 1965—72; pres. Bklyn. Heights Slope Young Rep. Club, 1955—56; co-chmn. Bklyn. Citizens for Eisenhower-Nixon, 1956; chmn. 2nd Jud. Dist. Assn. N.Y. State Young Rep. Clubs, Inc., 1957—58, vice chmn., mem. bd. govs., 1958—60, v.p., 1960—62, pres., 1962—64; mem. exec. com. Fedn. Women's Rep. Clubs N.Y. State, Inc., 1960—64; asst. campaign mgr. Kenneth B. Keating for Judge Ct. Appeals, NY, 1965; dir. scheduling Gov. Rockefeller campaign, 1966, Sen. Charles E. Goodell campaign, 1970; dir. planning and strategy Conn. Reagan-Bush campaign, Hartford, 1980; mem annual fund adv. com. Vassar Coll., 1992—96, chmn. 50th Reunion, 2001. Mem.: Nat. Assn. Olmsted Parks (bd. trustees 2003—, bd. dirs.), New Eng. Hist. Geneal. Soc. (mem. adv. coun. 2001—03, bd. trustees 2003—), Nat. Women's Edn. Fund. (mem. bd.), Exec. Women on Govt. (chmn. 1986), Nat. Soc. Colonial Dames, Vassar Club (past dir., Bklyn.), Am. Newspaper Women's Club, Jr. League of Bklyn. (past dir.). Republican. Episcopalian. Home: 532 S Brooksvale Rd Cheshire CT 06410-3515 also: 3001 Veazey Ter NW Apt 1225 Washington DC 20008-5407

MCKEEL, LILLIAN PHILLIPS, retired education educator; b. Rocky Mount, N.C., Aug. 23, 1932; d. Ellis Elma and Lillian Bonner (Archbell) Phillips; m. James Thomas McKeel Jr., July 23, 1955; children: Sarah Lillian McKeel Youngblood, Mary Kathleen McKeel Welch. BA, U. N.C., 1954; MEd, Pa. State U., 1977, DEd, 1993. Tchr. State Coll. (Pa.) Area Schs., 1964-90; instr. Pa. State U., University Park, 1990-93; asst. prof. Shippensburg (Pa.) U., 1993—2001; ret., 2001. Mem. of panel NSTA Book Rev. Panel/Outstanding Sci. Tradebooks for Children, Washington, 1992; faculty sponsor Shippensburg U. Sch. Study Coun., 1993-95. Contbr. articles to profl. jours. Recipient Presdl. award for Excellence in Sci. and Math. Tchng., NSF, Washington, 1990; finalist Tchr. of Yr. program Pa. Dept. Edn., Harrisburg, 1992, cert. Recognition, Hon. Robert Casey/Gov., Harrisburg, Pa., 1991; named Achieving Women of Penn State, Pa. State U., 1993. Mem. Nat. Sci. Tchrs. Assn., Soc. Presdl. Awardees, Assn. Edn. Tchrs. in Sci., Coun. Elem. Sci. Internat., Phi Delta Kappa (Disting. Svc. award 1992), Pi Lambda Theta, Phi Kappa Phi. Avocations: photography, collecting antique toys. Home: 637 Wiltshire Rd State College PA 16803 E-mail: lmcke637@aol.com.

MCKEEL, SHERYL WILSON, pharmacist; b. Nashville, Apr. 6, 1957; d. Robert Lewis and Norma Anne (Cox) Wilson; m. Vaughn Allen McKeel, Apr. 22, 2000. BS in Biology, David Lipscomb U., 1979; BS in Pharmacy, Auburn U., 1985. Lic. pharmacist, Tenn. Student extern/intern East Alabama Med. Ctr., Opelika, Ala., 1982-86; staff pharmacist Metro Nashville Gen. Hosp., 1987-95, PharmaThera, Inc., Nashville, 1995-99, Mid. Tenn. Mental Health Inst., Nashville, 1999-2000. Flutist Nashville Cmty. Concert Band, 1973-97; presch. tchr. Donelson Ch. of Christ, 1988—; active Lipscomb U. Cmty. Chorus, 1998—. Mem. Am. Pharm. Assn., Am. Soc. Health Sys. Pharmacists, Am. Soc. Parenteral and Enteral Nutrition, Tenn. Soc. Health Sys. Pharmacists, Nashville Area Pharmacists Assn. Democrat. Avocations: art, music, reading, cooking, sewing. Home: 1439 McGavock Pike Nashville TN 37216-3231 Personal E-mail: mckeelsw@prodigy.net.

MCKEEN, ELISABETH ANNE, oncologist; b. New Castle, Pa., Oct. 13, 1950; d. Richard Douglas and Harriette Elisabeth McK; m. Barry Nixon Walker; children: Anne, Matthew. BS in Biology, Rensselaer Polytech. Inst., 1974; MD, Albany Med. Coll., 1974. Diplomate Nat. Bd. Med. Examiners, Am. Bd. Internal Medicine, Am. Bd. Med. Oncology, Am. Bd. Hospice and Palliative Medicine; cert. in familial cancer assessment and mgmt. Intern Emory U. Affiliated Hosps., Atlanta, 1974-75, resident, 1975-76; fellow cancer epidemiology Nat. Cancer Inst., Bethesda, Md., 1976-78; fellow med. oncology Georgetown U. Hosp., Washington, 1978-79; clin. instr. in medicine Georgetown U. Hosp., Washington, 1979-82; clin. asst. prof. U. Fla., Gainesville, 1987—; from assoc. to ptnr. Harris & McKeen MDs, P.A., W. Palm Beach, Fla., 1982-90; Palm Beach Oncology/Hematology Good Samaritan Med. Ctr., W. Palm Beach, 1993—, Helen and Harry Gray Cancer Inst., 1997—. Clin. investigator Nat. Cancer Inst., Bethesda, Md. 1979-82; med. dir. Hospice Palm Beach County, 1985-93, faculty, 1990; chmn. med. edn. com. Palm Beach County chpt., 1983—; cons. assoc. dept. medicine Duke U., Durham, N.C., 1994—; med. dir. cancer genetics and counseling, Dr. Mary Tarzian Cancer Genetic Program, 1997—; med. dir. Norma E. and Miles M. Zisson Comprehensive Breast Ctr. Good Samaritan Med. Ctr., W. Palm Beach, 1997—; staff mem. St. Mary's Hosp., West Palm Beach, chair pharmacy and therapeutic com., 1992-93, transfusion com. 1989-90; mem. quality assurance, 1987-88, pharmacy and therapeutic 1991-92, continuing edn. com., 1992-93; cons. Palm Beach Gardens Med. Ctr., Palm Beach Gardens, Fla., 1982—; co-chmn. breast com. Duke Comprehensive Cancer Ctr., 1993—. Contbr. articles to profl. jours. including Am. Jour. Human Genetics, Am. Soc. Human Gentics, Proceedings Am. Soc. Clin. Oncology, Am. Assn. Cancer Rsch., Jour. Nat. Cancer Inst., Lancet, Annals Internal Medicine, Internat. Jour. Cancer; speaker to sci. groups and in ednl. insts. Fla. Chmn. med. edn. com. Am. Cancer Soc., Palm Beach County, 1983—, bd. dirs. 1984-88; mem. speaker's bur. VNA, 1984-88; bd. dir. S. Fla. chpt. Susan G. Komen Breast Cancer Found., Dallas, 1991—; peer reviewer cancer related pain guideline for health care providers Agy. for Health Care Policy and Rsch. and Pain Mgmt. Panel, 1992. Fellow ACP; mem. AMA, Am. Acad. Hospice Physicians (bd. dirs. 1988—, chmn. edn. and tng. com. 1988—), So. Assn. for Oncology, Fla. Soc. Clin. Oncology (bd. dirs. 1991-93, legis., legal and ethics com. 1992-93), Israel Cancer Assn. (regional sci. bd.), Am. Soc. Breast Disease, Am. Soc. Clin. Oncology, Palm Beach County Med. Soc., Am. Soc. Internal Medicine, Fla. Cancer Control and Rsch. Adv. Bd., Gilda's Club of S. Fla. (profl. adv. bd.). Office: Helen & Harry Cancer Inst Palm BEach Cancer Institute 1309 N Flagler Dr West Palm Beach FL 33401-3406 E-mail: elisabeth.mckeen@pbcancer.com.

MCKEEN, SALLY WERST, volunteer; b. Phila., July 28, 1934; d. Harry Kenneth and Doris Callaway Werst; m. Chester M. McKeen, Jr., Nov. 6, 1999 (div.); 1 child, Stephen Harry Werst. BFA, U. Tex., 1956; postgrad., U. Wis., 1975. Intern UN, N.Y.C., 1956; adminstrv. asst. Free Europe Com., Munich, 1958—59; writer, editor U.S. Army Forces Southern Command, Fort Amador, Canal Zone, 1963—75; editor 5th Army Inf. Divsn. Mech., Fort Polk, La., 1975—76; dep. chief of pub. affairs U.S. Army Corps. of Engrs., Dallas, 1976—79, chief pub. affairs Memphis, 1979—83, Fort Worth, Tex., 1983—94. Vol. Harris Meth. Hosp.; bd. dirs. Union Gospel Mission; active U. Christian Ch., deacon, Stephen Minister; bd. dirs. Boy Scouts Am., Women's Policy Forum, YMCA Camp Carter, Ct. Apptd. Spl. Advocates for Children, ARC, Exec. Svc. Corps., Tarrant Area Food Bank; regional dir. Leadership Tex.; chair Leadership Fort Worth, Huguley Meml. Med. Ctr. Hospice, Salvation Army Fort Worth/Tarrant Area; bd. dirs., chair Cancer Care Svcs.; bd. dirs. Cmty. Found. North Tex.; sec. bd. dirs.. Meals on Wheels Endowment; sec. bd. dirs. Women's Ctr. Tarrant County; bd. dirs. Girl Scouts Am.; mem. capital campaign steering com. Goodwill Industries; active in pub. rels. and devel. coms. Crime Prevention Resource Ctr.; coms. Alzheimer's Assn.; bd. visitors McDonald Observatory U. Tex.; bd. dirs. Learning Ctr. North Tex., Cmty. Hospice of Tex.; commr. Tex. Commn. on Law Enforcement. Decorated Meritorious Civilian Svc. medal U.S. Army; named Outstanding Women of Fort Worth, 1998; recipient Nat. Leadership award, Nat. Assn. for Cmty. Leadership, 1999, Citizen of the Week award, KRLD Dallas, 1998, Sr. Vol. of Yr. award, United Way, 1997, Vol. of Yr. award, Salvation Army, 1977. Mem.: Panamanian/Am. Soc., Pub. Rels. Soc. Am. (Fort Worth co founder, pres., Silver Anvil and Silver Quill awards 1983), Nat. Soc. Fundraising Execs. (bd. dirs., Vol. Fundraiser of Yr. award 1998), Fort Worth Rotary Club (dir., sec. 1993—95, Paul Harris fellow), Kappa Alpha Theta. Republican. Home: 2310 Woodsong Trail Arlington TX 76016

MCKEE-RYAN, FRANCES M, education educator; d. Sonja M and Stephen F McKee; m. David P Ryan, Sept. 27, 1997; children: Alexander D Ryan children: William S Ryan. PhD, Ariz. State U., 2002. Asst. prof. of mgmt. W.Va. U., 2000—02; asst. prof. of orgnl. behavior Oreg. State U., 2002—. Contbr. articles to profl. jours. Mem.: APA, Soc. for Indsl. and Orgnl. Psychology, Acad. of Mgmt., Sigma Iota Epsilon, Phi Kappa Phi, Golden Key Honor Soc., Beta Gamma Sigma, Alpha Gamma Delta (pres., leadership cons. 1991—93), Delta Sigma Pi. Christian. Avocations: reading, walking, hiking. Office: Oregon State University 200 Bexell Hall Corvallis OR 97331

MCKELLY, BEVERLY, artist, educator; m. Patrick McKelly, Dec. 25, 1984; 1 child, Joshua Benjamin. Ch. sec. Sonlight Foursquare Ch., Glenwood Springs, Colo., 1990—91. Mem.: NAFE (assoc.).

MCKELRATH, HEIDI LEE, real estate closing agent; d. Howard Clark and Betty Lee McKelrath. BA, U. Colo., Boulder, 1987; MBA, U. Phoenix, Denver, Colo., 2000. Real estate closing agt. Security Title, Lakewood, Colo., 1993—. Key user Security Title, Greenwood Village, Colo., 2002—. Mem.: German - Am. C. of C. Avocations: travel, skiing, ice skating. Home: 401 S Oak St Denver CO 80226

MCKELVEY, JUDITH GRANT, lawyer, educator, university dean; b. Milw., July 19, 1935; d. Lionel Alexander and Bernadine R. (Verdun) Grant. BS in Philosophy, U. Wis., 1957, JD, 1959. Bar: Wis. 1959, Calif. 1968. Atty. FCC, Washington, 1959-62; adj. prof. U. Md., Europe, 1965; prof. law Golden Gate U. Sch. Law, San Francisco, 1968-99, dean, 1974-81. Mem. State Jud. Nominees Evaluation Commn., 1981-82. Contbr. to: Damages Book, 1975, 76. Bd. dirs. San Francisco Neighborhood Legal Assistance Found. Fellow Am. Bar Found.; mem. ABA, Wis. Bar Assn., Calif. Bar Assn., San Francisco Bar Assn. (dir. 1975-77, chmn. legis. com., sec.-treas., pres.-elect 1980-83, pres. 1984), Calif. Women Lawyers (1st pres.), Law in a Free Soc. (exec. com.), Continuing Edn. of Bar (chmn. real estate subcom., mem. joint adv. com.), Legal Svcs. to Children Inc. (pres. 1987-89), San Francisco Neighborhood Legal Assistance Found. (dir. and exec. com. 1985-87), Lawyers Com. for Urban Affairs (dir. and exec. com. 1985-87, co-chairperson 1988-90). Office: Golden Gate U Sch Law 536 Mission St San Francisco CA 94105-2921

MCKELVY, NIKKI KAY, nurse; b. Honolulu, May 16, 1956; d. Donald and Virginia Katherine (Davis) McK.; m. David Stuart Murry, Dec. 9, 1978 (dec. 1992); children: Ryan Cobb, Caleb Murry. AA, Saddleback Coll., 1989; BSN, Dominican Coll., 1994. RN. Customer svc. clk. United Parcel Svc., Little Rock, 1974-78; resident/extern Vets. Hosp., Montrose, N.Y., 1993-94; staff nurse Harrison (Ark.) Nursing Ctr., 1995-96, 99; sub. tchr. Branson (Mo.) Sch. Dist., 2000—. Salesperson Nana's Fashions for Kids, 1999—2000. Fellow Sigma Theta Tau; mem. Nursing Assn. Dominican Coll. (v.p.). Democrat. Roman Catholic. Avocations: reading, swimming, travel. Home: 255 Bunker Rd Harrison AR 72601-7529

MCKENNA, JEANETTE ANN, archaeologist; b. N.Y.C., Aug. 6, 1953; d. Edward Patrick and Ann Jeanette (O'Brien) McKenna; children: Stephanie Jane, Daniel Glen Edward. AA in Phys. Edn., Mount San Antonio Jr. Coll., 1974; BA in Anthropology, Calif. State U., Fullerton, 1977, MA in Anthropology, 1982; postgrad., Ariz. State U., 1981-84, U. Calif., Riverside, 1991-92. Field archaeologist Archaeol. Rsch., Inc., Costa Mesa, Calif., 1976-79; rsch. asst. Calif. State U., 1979; lab. dir. Environ. Rsch. Archaeologists, L.A., 1978-79; staff archaeologist Ariz. State U., Tempe, 1979-82; rsch. archaeologist Soil Systems, Inc., Phoenix, 1982-84, Sci. Resource Surveys, Huntington Beach, Calif., 1984-87; co-owner, prin. Hatheway & McKenna, Mission Viejo, Calif., 1987-89; owner, prin. McKenna et al., Whittier, Calif., 1989—; dir. Divsn. Cultural Resource Mgmt. Svcs. EIP Assocs., Chino, Calif., 1996-97. Contbr. numerous articles to profl. jours. and reports. Bd. dirs. Whittier Conservancy, 1987-98, interim treas., 1994, pres., 1994-95, bd. dirs. Residents' Voice, 1998—. Recipient Gov.'s award for Hist. Preservation/Calif., The Whittier Conservancy, 1995. Mem. Soc. Profl. Archaeologists (bd. dirs. 1993-97), Archaeol. Inst. Am., Am. Soc. Conservation Archaeology, Am. Mus. Natural History, Soc. Am. Anthropology, Ariz. Archaeol. Coun., Ariz. Hist. Found., Calif. Hist. Soc., Nat. Arbor Day Found., Nat. Parks and Conservation Assn., Nat. Trust for Historic Preservation, Soc. Calif. Archaeology, Soc. Hist. Archaeology, S.W. Mus. Assn., Wilderness Soc., Whittier Conservancy, Southwestern Anthrop. Assn., Gene Autry Western Heritage Mus. Assn., Nature Conservancy, Smithsonian Assocs., Sierra Club, otehrs. Democrat. Roman Catholic. Avocations: traveling, reading, hiking, camping, gardening. Office: McKenna et al 6008 Friends Ave Whittier CA 90601-3724

MCKENNA, MARGARET ANNE, university president; b. R.I., June 3, 1945; d. Joseph John and Mary (Burns) McK.; children: Michael Aaron McKenna Miller, David Christopher McKenna Miller. BA in Sociology, Emmanuel Coll., 1967; postgrad., Boston Coll. Law Sch., 1968; JD, So. Meth. U., 1971; LLD (hon.), U. Upsala, N.J., 1978, Fitchburg (Mass.) State Coll., 1979, Regis Coll., 1982; D Community Affairs, U. R.I., 1979; LLD (hon.), Emmanuel Coll., 2000. Bar: Tex. 1971, D.C. 1973. Atty. Dept. Justice, Washington, 1971-73; exec. dir. Internat. Assn. Ofcl. Human Rights Agys., Washington, 1973-74; mgmt. cons. Dept. Treasury, Washington, 1975-76; dep. council to Pres. White House, Washington, 1976-79; dep. undersec. Dept. Edn., Washington, 1979-81; dir. Mary Ingraham Bunting Inst., Radcliffe Coll., Cambridge, Mass., 1981-85; v.p. program planning Radcliffe Coll., Cambridge, 1982-85; pres. Lesley U., Cambridge, 1985—. Bd. dirs. Dominion Resources, Inc., Cisco Learning Inst., The Jason Found. for Edn. Bd. dirs. Am. Assn. Coll. for Tchr. Edn., Coun. for Higher Edn. Accreditation, Datatel Scholars Found.; chmn. higher edn. task force Clinton Transition, 1992-93; chmn. edn. task force Mayor Thomas Menino Transition Com., 1994; bd. overseers Peabody Essex Mus. Recipient Outstanding Contribution award Civil Rights Leadership Conf., 1978; named Woman of Yr. Women's Equity Action League, 1979, Outstanding Woman of Yr. Big Sister Assn., 1986, Pinnacle award for Lifetime Achievement, Lelia J. Robinson award Women's Bar Assn. Mass., 1996, Valeria Addams Knapp award, The Coll. CLub, 1995; named Margaret A. McKenna Day, Gov. DePrete, R.I. Mem. Boys Scouts Am., Big Sisters Ass. Boston, Y.W.C.A. Cambridge, Women's Equity Action League, Nat. Women's Polit. Conf., Nat. Assn. Official Human Rights Agencies. Democrat. Office: Lesley Univ Office of the President 29 Everett St Cambridge MA 02138-2702

MCKENNEY, GLADYS HOLDEMAN, educational consultant, artist, storyteller; b. Jackson, Mich., Jan. 5, 1928; d. Walter Ray and Florence Hester (Barthel) Holdeman; m. Robert Dorion McKenney, June 10, 1950; children: Wayne Brian, Cathleen Renee (dec.), Michael Brent, Marcia Lynn, Linda Denise. BA in Psychology, Mich. State U., 1949; MEd in Guidance, Wayne State U., 1963, EdD, 1979. Permanent tchg. cert. Mich. State Bd. Edn. H.S. English tchr. Beaverton (Mich.) Pub. Schs., 1950-51; H.S. social studies tchr. Rochester (Mich.) Schs., 1965-83; pres. McKenney Ednl. Cons., Rochester, 1982—, ind. and family counseling, 1983-87, creator, spkr. Women's History Project, 1984—. Author, actress (one-woman play) Our Fabulous Foremothers--A Celebration, 1984, (audio tape) Votes for Women, 1990; sculpture, artist, mus. exhibitor. Pres. North Oakland NOW, Rochester, 1979-80. Chataqua Presenter grantee Mich. Humanitites Coun., 1992-96. Mem. AAUW (Rochester ednl. found. chair 1995-96), LWV, Mich. Assn. Ret. Sch. Pers., Mich. Women's Studies Assn., Storyteller's Guild. Avocations: reading, walking, drawing, painting, music. Office Phone: 248-651-8328.

MCKENNEY, IRENE JUNE, business manager, former educator; b. Hutchinson, Minn., June 8, 1930; d. William Paul and Ethel Ida (Laabs) Radtke; widowed, Feb. 1985; children: Judy Floy, Kent Floy, Timothy Floy, Jane Floy, Paul Floy, m. 2d, June 30, 1990. Std. elem. tchg. cert., Wartburg Coll., 1950; BS, Westmar Coll., 1963; MS, N.D. State U., 1970, Drake U., 1979. Cert. elem. tchr., Iowa, Minn.; cert. secondary tchr., Iowa. Tchr. 1st grade pub. sch., Emmetsburg, Iowa, 1950-52, LeSuer, Minn., 1952-53, Olivia, Minn., 1953-54; substitute tchr. pub. sch. LeMars and Osage, Iowa, 1960-75; secondary tchr. Carroll (Iowa) H.S., 1975-90; psychologist Des Moines Area C.C., Carroll, 1980-83; bus. mgr. N.W. Iowa Radiology, P.C., Storm Lake, Iowa, 1990—. Instr. Parent Effectiveness, Iowa, 1972-75, Tchr. Effectiveness, Carroll, 1976-78. Pres. Iowa Luth. Pastor's Wives, Des Moines, 1974-76; bd. dirs. Ingham Okoboji Luth. Bible Camp, 1992—. Mem. AAUW, Profl. Assn. Health Care Mgrs. (cert., bus. mgr. 1990—). Republican. Lutheran. Avocations: singing in church choir, teaching sunday school, church work, playing piano, reading. Home: PO Box 901 1700 W 5th St Storm Lake IA 50588-3032

MCKENNEY, MURIEL ANITA, art educator, engineer; b. Chgo., Ill., Aug. 26, 1923; d. Myron Bedrose and Salome Mary (Attarian) Donchian; m. William James McKenney, Feb. 21, 1949; children: Mary Dierker, William James III, Christine, James, Audrey, Bruce. BFA U. Colo., 1983. Editor, writer Aurora (Colo.) Advocate Newspaper, 1965—70; engr. drafting, writer, editor AT&T, Englewood, Colo., 1970—90; art tchr. City of Aurora, Colo., 1991—. Recipient 1st pl., U. Colo., 1982, City of Aurora, 1995. Mem.: Denver Art Mus., Aurora Artist Guild (adv. bd. 1995, 1st pl. award 1996), Denver Botanic Gardens (advisory, program chair 1996, spl. events 1992—, SCFD award 1996). Avocations: marionettes, dance, painting, gardening, ballet. Home: 408 S Xanadu St Aurora CO 80012

MCKENZIE, KAY BRANCH, public relations executive; b. Atlanta, Feb. 12, 1936; d. William Harllee and Katherine (Hunter) Branch; m. Harold Cantrell McKenzie, Jr., Apr. 11, 1958; children: Ansley, Katherine, Harold Cantrell III. Student, Sweet Briar Coll., 1955, Emory U., 1956-57. Account exec. Hill and Knowlton Inc., Atlanta, 1979-80, account supr./dir. S.E. govt. rels., 1981-83; ptnr. McKenzie, Gordon & Potter, Atlanta, 1983-85; pres. McKenzie & Assocs. Inc., Atlanta, 1986-89; sr. v.p. Manning Selvage & Lee, Atlanta, 1989-93; v.p. comm. and creative svcs. 1996 Atlanta Paralympic Games, 1993-96; v.p. comm. and devel. U.S. Disabled Athletes Fund, 1997—. Mem. Commn. on Future of South, 1974; co-chmn. John Lewis for Congress, Atlanta, 1986; regional bd. dirs. Inst. Internat. Edn., 1987-93. Fellow Soc. Internat. Bus. Fellows (bd. dirs. 1983-85, 92-93, v.p. 1986-88); mem. Pub. Rels. Soc. Am., Ga. C. of C. (bd. dirs. 1983-97), Leadership Atlanta, Ga. Internat. Horse Park Found. (bd. dirs. 1993-98). Democrat. Episcopalian. Office: 280 Interstate N Cir Ste 450 Atlanta GA 30339 Home: 209 N Forest Ave Marietta GA 30060 E-mail: kmckenzie@blazesports.com.

MCKENZIE, MARY BETH, artist; b. Cleve. d. William Jennings and Mary Elizabeth (McCray) McK.; m. Tony Mysak, May 8, 1974; children: Zsuzsa McKenzie Mysak, Maria McKenzie Mysak. Student, Mus. Fine Arts, Boston, 1964-65, Cooper Sch. Art, Cleve., 1965-67; diploma, NAD, N.Y.C., 1974. Painting instr. NAD, 1981—, Art Students League, 1995—. Author: A Painterly Approach, 1987; contbr. articles to profl. jours.; one-woman shows include Nat. Arts Club, N.Y.C., 1976, FAR Gallery, 1980, Perin and Sharpe Gallery, New Canaan, Conn., 1981, Frank Caro Gallery, N.Y.C., 1988—89, Joseph Keiffer Gallery, 1991, Union County Coll., 1998, exhibited in group shows at Sindin Gallery, N.Y.C., 1985—86, Ice Collection, 1995—96, Susan Conway Gallery, Washington, Galerie Yoramgil, Beverly Hills, Met. Mus. Art, 2001, Represented in permanent collections The Butler Mus. Am. Art, Met. Mus. Art, N.Y.C., Mus. City of N.Y., NAD, Art Students League of N.Y., Nat. Mus. Women in the Arts, N.Y. Hist. Soc., Mus. Am. Art, Smithsonian Instn., Bklyn. Mus. Art, New Britain Mus. Am. Art, N.Y. Hist. Soc., Galerie Yoramgil, Beverly Hills, Calif. Recipient Nat. Scholastic award Mus. Fine Arts, Boston, numerous awards including Thomas B. Clark prize and the Isaac N. Maynard prize Nat. Acad. Design, Greenshields Found. grantee, Stacey Found. grantee. Mem. Nat. Acad. Design, Pastel Soc. Am. (Best In Show, Award of Exceptional Merit, Exhbn. Com. award), Allied Artists Am. (Gold medal, The Jane Peterson award, Grumbacher Cash award, Silver medal), Audubon Artists (Pastel Soc. Am. award). Home: 525 W 45th St New York NY 10036-3414

MCKENZIE-ANDERSON, RITA LYNN, psychologist; b. Boston, Nov. 25, 1952; d. Wallace Andrew and Angelina Rita (Bagnoli) McK; m. Brien Anderson, Oct. 22, 1994; 1 child, Liam Wallace. BA, Framingham State Coll., 1974; MEd, Northeastern U., 1975; PhD, Temple U., 1983. Lic. psychologist, Mass. Pvt. practice, Fairfield, Conn., 1984-86; psychologist Johnson Life Ctr., Springfield, Mass., 1986-87, dir. outpatient therapy, 1987-88; pvt. practice Springfield, 1988—; investigator Springfield (Mass.) Juvenile Ct., 1989—. Adj. faculty Holyoke (Mass.) Community Coll., 1989-90, Springfield Tech. Community Coll., 1989-90; dir. day treatment DuBois Day Treatment Ctr., Stamford, Conn., 1982-86; cons. psychologist Community Care Mental Health Ctr., Springfield, 1989-97, Spofford Hall Treatment Ctr., Ludlow, Mass., 1991-92. Trustee Northampton (Mass.) State Hosp., 1989-93; mem. organizing com. Week of Young Child, Springfield, 1988-93; bd. dirs. Stop Abuse Against Kids. Mem. Women Bus. Owners Alliance, Zonta Internat. Office: 380 Union St Ste 14 West Springfield MA 01089-4123

MCKEON, JUDITH C. horticulturist, writer; b. Phila., Pa., Mar. 2, 1950; d. Catherine Rush and Henry McKeon; life ptnr. Anne Swoyer. AS in Horticulture, Temple U., 1984, BA in English, 1987; MLA, U. Pa., Phila., 2003. Chief horticulturist Morris Arboretum, U. Pa., Phila., 1991—99, rosarian, 1984—99. Adj. prof. English Arcadia U., Glenside, Pa., 2001—. Author: The Encyclopedia of Roses: An Organic Guide, 1995, Gardening With Roses, 1997; contbr. Home: 497 Ripka St Philadelphia PA 19128 Personal E-mail: jmckeon@dca.net.

MCKEOWN, H. MARY, lawyer, law educator; b. West Palm Beach, Fla., Sept. 17, 1952; d. Honore Stephen McKeown and Margaret Berg McKeown Growney; m. Jon Henry Barber, Sept. 18, 1981; children: Sean Patrick, Mary Kathleen. AA, St. Petersburg Jr. Coll., Fla., 1970; BA in Polit. Sci. and Sociology, U. South Fla., 1972; JD cum laude, Samford U., 1976. Bar: Fla. 1976, U.S. Dist. Ct. (mid. dist.) Fla. 1977, U.S. Ct. Appeals (5th and 11th cirs.) 1981, U.S. Supreme Ct. 1992. Asst. state atty. 6th Jud. Ct., Clearwater, Fla., 1976-90; ptnr. Growney, McKeown & Barber, St. Petersburg, 1976—. Adj. prof. Stetson Coll. of Law, St. Petersburg, 1990—. Chairperson Child Welfare Std. and Tng. Coun., 1995—98; mem. nominee qualifications rev. com. Health and Human Svcs. Bd. Dist. 5, 1992—2000; mem. Study Commn. Child Welfare, 1990—91; leader Girl Scouts U.S., 1991—2001. Recipient Victim Advocacy award Pinellas County Victims Rights Coalition, 1984, Law and Order award Elks, Pinellas County, 1991. Mem.: St. Petersburg Bar Assn., Fla. Bar Assn., Acad. Fla. Trial Lawyers, Phi Alpha Delta. Office: 7455 38th Ave N Saint Petersburg FL 33710-1228

MCKEOWN, LORRAINE LAREDO, travel company executive, writer; b. N.Y.C., Mar. 20, 1928; d. Frank A. and May (Collins) Laredo; m. William Taylor McKeown, July 9, 1964; children: Beth Ellison, Kate Taylor, Suzanne Harris. Talent agt. Carl Eastman, N.Y.C., 1960-65; cooking/travel columnist Camping Jour./Boating Jour., N.Y.C., 1968-70; travel agt. Beecher Travel, N.Y.C., 1968-70; founding ptnr. Computer Travel Info., N.Y.C., 1984, v.p., pres., 1985-90, CEO, 1990—. Contbr. articles to various publs. Bd. dirs. Chapin-Brearley Exch., N.Y.C., 1980, Howland Cultural Ctr., 2002—, Howland Cultural Ctr., 2002—. Mem. Freelance Assocs., Beacon Conservation Coun. E-mail: mckeown@bestweb.net.

MCKEOWN, MARY MARGARET, federal judge; b. Casper, Wyo., May 11, 1951; d. Robert Mark and Evelyn Margaret (Lipsack) McKeown; m. Peter Francis Cowhey, June 29, 1985; 1 child, Megan Margaret. BA in Internat. Affairs and Spanish, U. Wyo., 1972; JD, Georgetown U., 1975. Bar: Wash. 1975, D.C. 1982. Assoc. Perkins Coie, Seattle, 1975—79, Washington, 1979—80; White House fellow U.S. Dept. Interior and White House, Washington, 1980—81; ptnr., mem. exec. com. Perkins Coie, Seattle, 1981—98, mng. dir. strategic planning and client rels., 1990—95; judge U.S. Ct. Appeals for 9th Cir., Seattle, 1998—2001, San Diego, 2001—. Trustee The Pub. Defender, Seattle, 1982—85; rep. 9th Cir. Judicial Conf., San Francisco, 1985—89; mem. gender bias task force, 1992—93; jud. conf. Com. on Codes of Conduct, 2001—; exec. com. 9th Cir., 2001—. Author: Girl Scout's Guide to New York, 1990; contbr. chpt. to book and articles to profl. jours. Nat. bd. dirs. Girl Scouts U.S., N.Y.C., 1976—87; mem. exec. com. Corp. Coun. for the Arts, Seattle, 1988—98; bd. gen. counsel Downtown Seattle Assn., 1986—89; mem. exec. com. Wash. Coun. Internat. Trade, 1994—; bd. mem. YMCA Greater Seattle, 1998—; bd. dirs. Family Svcs., Seattle, 1982—84. Named one of 100 Young Women of Promise, Good Housekeeping, 1985, Washington's Winningest Trial Lawyers, Washington Jour., 1992, Top 50 Women Lawyers, Nat. Law Jour., 1998; recipient Rising Stars of the 80's award, Legal Times Washington, 1983; fellow Japan leadership, 1992—93. Fellow: ABA (ho. of dels. 1990—); mem.: Nat. Assn. Iolta Programs (bd. dirs 1989—91), Wash. Women Lawyers (bd. dirs., pres. 1978—79), Legal Found. Wash. (trustee, pres. 1989—90), Seattle-King County Bar Assn. (trustee, sec. 1984—85, Outstanding Lawyer award 1992), Wash. Bar Assn. (chmn. jud. recommendations 1989—90), Fed. Bar Assn. (trustee western dist. Wash. 1980—90), White House Fellows Found. (bd. dirs. 1998—, pres. 2000—01). Avocations: travel, classical piano, hiking, gourmet cooking, tennis. Office: US Ct Appeals 401 West A St Ste 2000 San Diego CA 92101-7908 E-mail: Judge_McKeown@ca9.uscourts.gov.*

MCKEOWN, REBECCA J. principal; b. Wayne, Okla., Apr. 4, 1937; d. William S. and Ila Rebekah (Mitchell) Lackey; m. Loren Ferris, Apr. 5, 1958; children: Michael, Thomas, Nancy, David. BS, Okla. State U., 1966; MEd, U. Okla., 1976. Cert. elem. tchr., elem. prin. 6th grade tchr. Ponca City (Okla.) Pub. Schs., 1966-67; 1st and 6th grade tchr. Peru Elem. Sch., Auburn, Nebr., 1967-69; 4th grade tchr. Woodland Hills Sch., Lawton, Okla., 1971-76; asst. prin. Douglass Learning Ctr., Lawton, Okla., 1976-78; prin. Lincoln Elem. Sch., Lawton, Okla., 1978-84, Hugh Bish Elem., Lawton, Okla., 1984—. Recipient Disting. Achievement award Lawton Bd. Edn., 1992, Adminstr. of Yr. award Lawton Area Reading Coun., 1993, Arts Adminstr. of Yr. award Okla. Alliance for Arts, 1993, Nat. Blue Ribbon Sch. Recognition award 1993-94, D.A.R.E. Adminstrn. award Lawton Police Dept., 1993. Mem. ASCD, Okla. Reading Coun., Okla. ASCD, Lawton Area Reading Coun., Elem. Prins. Assn. (pres. 1986-87), PEO Sisterhood. Democrat. Methodist. Avocations: reading, walking, music, cooking. Home: 3122 NW Denver Ave Lawton OK 73505-3864 Office: Lawton Pub Schs 751 NW Fort Sill Blvd Lawton OK 73507-5421

MCKEOWN-MOAK, MARY PARK, educational consultant; d. John Paton and Sophie Cichon Park; m. Lynn Martin Moak, Oct. 4, 1997; children: David Lynn Moak, Susan Marie Moak; m. James Charles McKeown, Jan. 2, 1965 (div.); children: Jeffrey Charles McKeown, Pamela Lynn McKeown; m. Kenneth Forbis Jordan, Jan. 2, 1982 (div. Sept. 1993). BA, Mich. State U., E. Lansing, 1962—66; MA, Mich. State U., E. Lansing, Mich., 1965—66; Phd, U. of Ill., Urbana-Champaign, 1968—74. Cert. Tchr. Mich., 1966, real estate agent Ill., 1977. Bus. mgr. U. of Ill. Found., Champaign, Ill., 1974—77; sch. fin. specialist, asst. prof. of pub. adminstrn. Ill. Bd. of Edn., Sangamon State U., Springfield, Ill., 1977—80; assoc. dir. of fin. and facilities Md. State Bd. for Higher Edn., Annapolis, Md., 1980—87; dir. of strategic planning Ariz. State U., Tempe, Ariz., 1987—94; assoc. exec. dir. and sr. fin. officer Ariz. Bd. of Regents, Phoenix, 1994—98; ptnr. MGT Am., Inc., Austin, Tex., 1998—. Sec. Ariz. Chpt. of Phi Delta Kappa, Tempe, Ariz., 1987—91; pres. Fiscal Issues Spl. Interest Group, Am. Edn. Rsch. Assn., Washington, 1990—91; pres. and chair Futures Planning Spl. Interest Group Am. Edn. Rsch. Assn., Washington, 1992—93; pres. Am. Edn. Fin. Assn., Denver, 1996—97. Contbr. articles to profl. jours. Pres. Coll. of Bus. Faculty Wives, Champaign, Ill., 1971—73; troop leader Girl Scouts, Boy Scouts, Champaign, Ill., 1974—78; treas. Champaign-Urbana PTA Coun., Champaign, Ill., 1978—80; pres., v.p., sec. Alameda Estates Homeowners Assn., Tempe, Ariz., 1988—95. Mem.: Travis Audubon Soc. Avocations: gardening, travel, birdwatching. Home: 8800 Gallant Fox Road Austin TX 78737 Office: MGT Am Inc 502 E 11th Street Ste 300 Austin TX 78701 Office Phone: 512-476-4697. E-mail: mmoak@mgtamer.com.

MCKERROW, AMANDA, ballet dancer; b. Albuquerque; d. Alan and Constance McKerrow; m. John Gardner. Student, Met. Acad. Ballet, Bethesda, Md., Washington Sch. Ballet. With Washington Ballet Co., 1980-82, Am. Ballet Theatre, N.Y.C., 1982—, soloist, from 1983, prin. dancer, 1987—. Toured Europe with Washington Ballet; danced in Margot Fonteyn Gala at Metropolitan Opera House; featured in Pavlova Tribute film, also many guest appearances; leading roles in Ballet Imperial, La Bayadere, Manon, Birthday Offering, Dim Lustre, Donizetti Variations, Giselle, Graduation Ball, The Leaves Are Fading, Nine Sinatra Songs, The Nutcracker, Pillar of Fire, Requiem, Romeo and Juliet, The Sleeping Beauty, Les Sylphides, Push Comes to Shove, Symphony Concertante, Symphonic Variations, Theme and Variations, Stravinsky Violin Concerto, Swan Lake, Triad, Duets, Etudes, Coppelia, Voluntaries and Rodeo; created leading role in Bruch Violin Concerto No. 1, Some Assembly Required and Agnus De Mille's The Other. Recipient N.Y. Woman award for dance, 1991; co-winner gold prize for women Moscow Internat. Ballet Competition, 1981. Office: Am Ballet Theatre 890 Broadway New York NY 10003

MCKILLIP, PATRICIA CLAIRE, operatic soloist; b. Milw., Apr. 28; d. Lester J. and Ruth J. (Lohneis) McK.; m. Mark Richard McKillip, June 16, 1990. BA in English-Drama, Creative Writing, Lit., Alverno Coll., 1980, MusB in Applied Music, 1981; postgrad., Wis. Conservatory of Mus.,

1981-82; MS in Fine Arts Edn., U. Wis., Milw., 1996; postgrad., The Juilliard Sch., 1982-84, Am. Acad. Dramatic Arts, 1983-84, Adelphi U., 1984; MA in English-Creative Writing and Lit., U. Wis., Milw., 1997; postgrad., Milw. Inst. Art and Design, 2003—. Soloist Amadeus Opera Co.; instr. vocal music seminars various high schs., N.Y. Co-founder, co-dir. The Masque Consort, N.Y.C., 1990-91, exec. v.p., 1991; v.p., co-founder Creative Learning [illegible] Inst. Cardinal Stritch Coll., Milw., 1994—. Performed with numerous opera cos. including The Florentine Opera Co., Music Under the Stars Prodns., Milw. Opera Co., Westchester Lyric Opera Co., Profl. Opera Workshop at Lincoln Ctr., Met. Opera Co., N.Y. Grand Opera Co., Monteverdi Opera Guild Prodns., Republic Opera Co., La Puma Opera Co., and other chamber, theater and folk groups; puppeteer, costumer, designer Puppet Art Troupe; performed in over 50 mus. shows and prodns., 6 solo recitals, also medieval concerts, choruses, orchestras, oratorio; 42 other recitals; author: (poetry and artwork) Springdrift, 2003; contbr. poetry to lit. publs. Exec. v.p. Masque Consort, a multi-media theatrical orgn. Music dept. scholar Alverno U.; named Woman of Yr., Am. Biographical Inst. Bd. Internat. Rsch., 2003. Mem. AFTRA, SAG, Nat. Assn. Music Tchrs., Music Educators Nat. Conf. (treas.), Internat. Platform Assn., Wis. Fedn. Music Clubs, Music Clubs Am., Am. Guild Mus. Artists, Q'ahal-Liturgical Music Soc., Acad. Am. Poets, Milw. Artists Resource Network, Walker's Point Ctr. for Arts, Delta Omicron (v.p., chaplain, warden Gamma Gamma chpt., WMA State and Regional Vocal award 1978, Star of Delta Omicron award 1980, 40 music medals from state and dist. WSMA), Alpha Sigma Tau. Democrat. Roman Catholic. Avocations: dance, creative writing, art. Home: 4860 S 69th St Greenfield WI 53220-4452 E-mail: pcmckil@aol.com.

MCKIM, RUTH ANN, antique dealer; b. Keokuk, Iowa, Nov. 26, 1932; d. Carl Edward and Ruby Irene (Martin) McKim; m. William James Ashbrook, Aug. 15, 1959 (div. 1974); children: Leslie McKim, Diane Hodges. BS, U. Louisville, 1955, MS in Community Devel., 1977. Co-dir. art therapy Norton-Children's Hosps. Inc., Louisville, 1956-67; dir. art therapy Ky. Bapt. Hosp., Louisville, 1955-56, NKC Hosps. Inc., 1957-59; researcher Bd. Aldermen, Louisville, 1976; pub. relations staff Dept. Consumer Affairs, Louisville, 1976-78; realtor assoc. Century 21, Louisville, 1979-86; fin. planner Nat. Life Vt., Louisville, 1986—; tutor Ky. Assn. Specific Perceptual-Motor Disability, Louisville, 1970-74. Author: Banking Survey, 1977. Sec., treas. ch. sch. 2nd Presbyn. Ch., Louisville, 1975-76, arts festival com., 1975-77; chmn., coordinator Louisville Food Day, 1978; canvasser Voter Registration, Louisville, 1976, 78, 82; vol., art donor Pub. Broadcasting System, Louisville, 1985-88; active Rep. Nat. Com., Rep. Presdl. Task Force, Nat. Rep. Senatorial Com., Nat. Rep. Congl. Com.. Scholar Allen R. Hite Art Inst., 1952-54, Bd. Realtors scholar, 1979—; recipient Rep. Presdl. Legion of Merit medal and The Order of Merit. Mem. Louisville Craftsmans Guild (life), Ky. Artists and Craftsmen, Inst. Community Devel. Assn., U. Louisville Alumni Assn. Republican. Avocations: oil and acrylic painting. Home: No 43 410 Mockingbird Valley Rd Louisville KY 40207-1318

MCKINLEY, DEBRA LYNN MCKINLEY, small business owner, dog show judge, real estate agent; b. Albuquerque, July 8, 1954; d. Francis Marion and Bonnie Marie (Byard) McKinney; m. René John Krier II, Sept. 7, 1974 (div. June 1989); children: René John Krier III, Lynn Marie Krier; m. Eugene Randon McKinley, Sept. 7, 1991 (dec. Aug. 26, 2000). Lynn Marie Krier Lyne m. Jebb Scott Lyne, June 30, 2001. Grad., Taunton (Mass.) H.S., 1972, John Powers, Phila., 1973. Lic. judge Am. Kennel Club, real estate agent S.C. Judge Am. Kennel Club, N.Y.C., 1983—; owner, pres. Charleston Gas Light. Contbr. articles to jours. in field. Founder Taunton Young Reps., 1971-72; com. woman Taunton Rep. Party, 1972; treas. Rowan Rep. Women, Salisbury, N.C., 1993-94; treas. Salisbury Symphony Guild, 1991-94, pres., 1994-95; pres. bd. dirs. Salisbury Symphony Soc., 1996-97; pres. concert choir, 1994-95. Named Miss Rehobeth, Miss. Am. Pageants, Taunton, 1972, Miss Lansdale (Pa.), Miss USA Pageants, 1973. Mem. DAR (sec. Elizabeth Maxwell chpt. 1997-98), Cabarrus Kennel Club (pres. 1984). Presbyterian. Avocations: master gardener, showing championship dogs, entertaining, volunteer work, genealogy. Home: One Ocean Point Isle Of Palms SC 29451 Office Phone: 888-958-0023. E-mail: dmckinley@mindspring.com.

MCKINLEY-HAAS, MARY, artist; b. St. Louis; d. Lee Carrington and Florence (Dowden) McK.; m. Saul Haas; children: Christopher, Matthew. BA, Smith Coll.; student, Art Students League, 1973-74, Nat. Acad. Design, 1965-66, Studio and Forum Stage Design. Head costume design dept. ABC-TV, NYC, 1968-73. Solo exhbns. include Tarlowe Gallery, Westhampton Beach, N.Y., 1974, Fontbonne Gallery, St. Louis, 1977, Gallery Yssa, N.Y.C., 1979, Vered Gallery, East Hampton, N.Y., 1981, Netherlands Bank & Ludlow-Hyland Gallery, N.Y.C., 1981, U. Tex., Austin, 1988, RVS Fine Art, Southampton, N.Y., 1990, TSS Gallery, N.Y.C., 1992, U. Tex., Austin, 1992, TAI Gallery, N.Y.C., 1999; group exhbns. include Guild Hall, East Hampton, N.Y., 1974, 75, 76, 78, 81, 85, 96, Parrish Art Mus., Southampton, 1975, 76, 78, 81, Water Mill Mus., 1983, 92, Vared Gallery, East Hampton, N.Y., 1985, Lincoln Ctr., N.Y.C., N.Y., 1989, 90, Queens Coll. Art Ctr., Flushing, N.Y., 1991, Dorothy Chandler Pavillion, L.A., Calif., 1993, Stony Brook U. Art Gallery, N.Y., 1994, Women in Art and Culture, Beijing, 1995, Elite Gallery, Moscow, 1995, Nat. Mus. Women in Arts, Washington, 1996, Soho 20 Gallery, N.Y.C., 1998—. Canajoharie (N.Y.) Libr. and Art Ctr., 2000, Weill Cornell Med. Libr., N.Y.C., 2002, others; represented in permanent collections at Nat. Mus. of Women in the Arts, Washington, Tari Women's Cultural Ctr., Papua, New Guinea, Fontbonne Coll., St. Louis, No. Trust Naples (Fla.); also numerous pvt. collections; costume designer for Broadway and network TV shows, Harkness Ballet, Holiday on Ice, others. Mem. United Scenic Artists, Women in the Arts, N.Y. Artists Equity. Address: 280 Lafayette St Loft5B New York NY 10012-3303

MCKINNEY, BETSY, state legislator; b. Bangor, Maine, Mar. 24, 1939; BS, Bentley Coll., 1972. Accountant, N.H.; mem. dist. 24 N.H. Ho. Rep., mem. budget com., 1977-81, 87-88, mem. regulated revenues com. Del. N.H. Constl. Conv., 1984. Treas. Friends of the Libr., 1988—; chmn. Old Home Day, 1990, treas., 1978—; chmn. Rockingham County Exec. Com., 1991-92; mem. Londonderry Charter Commn., 1995; mem. Libr. Bldg. Com., 1995-96; treas. N.H. OWLs, 1994—. Recipient Citizen of the Yr. award City of Londonderry, 1987. Mem. Londonderry C. of C. (treas. 1980-88). Republican. Roman Catholic. Home and Office: 3 Leelynn Cir Londonderry NH 03053-2326

MCKINNEY, BETTY LOUISE, musician; b. Dunkirk, N.Y., Aug. 24, 1948; d. Bert Edward and Elizabeth Louise Bullock; m. Timothy Patrick McKinney, Feb. 12, 1972; children: Aaron Patrick, Galen Adam. MusM in Performance, SUNY, Fredonia, 1975. Music educator Ripley (N.Y.) Ctrl. Sch. Dist., 1972—81, Mercyhurst Coll., Erie, Pa., 1983—91. 2d clarinet Erie Chamber Orch., 1990—2003. Avocation: walking. Home: 4725 Conrad Rd Erie PA 16510-3815 Personal E-mail: blmck48@lycos.com.

MCKINNEY, CARA LYNN, music educator; b. Lake Forest, Ill., Mar. 19, 1967; d. Gordon LeRoy and Jeanne Crista Nereim; m. Franklin Connor McKinney, July 31, 1988. BA in Music Edn., U. Ctrl. Fla., 1990, Master's in Ednl. Leadership, 1997. Cert. music educator K-12 Fla. Band dir. Deltona H.S., Fla., 1990—94, Deltona Mid. Sch., 1994—. Chair Volusia All County Band Volusia County Schs., Fla., 1995—97, Fla., 2002. Mem.: Music Educators Nat. Conf., Fla. Music Educators Assn., Fla. Bandmasters Assn. (dist. chair 1998—2000, exec. bd. dirs. 1998—2000). Presbyterian. Avocations: gardening, camping, hiking.

MCKINNEY, CAROLYN, educational association administrator, educator; BS in Early Childhood Edn., U. N.C., Greensboro; M in Elem. Edn., Gardner-Webb U. Elem. sch. tchr. Winston-Salem/Forsyth County Schs.; elem. tchr. Sedge Garden Sch. Math. and Sci.; 2n and 3d gr. tchr. Kernersville Elem. Sch.; tchr. Gen. Greene Sch., Guilford County; pres. N.C. Assn. Educators, Raleigh, 2001—. Mem.: NEA (alt. dir. bd. dirs.), N.C. Assn. Educators (bd. dirs., Terry Sanford award for excellence in edn. [illegible]), Forsyth [illegible] Classroom Tchrs. (pres.). Office: NC Assn Educators PO Box 27347 Raleigh NC 27611

MCKINNEY, CYNTHIA ANN, former congresswoman; b. Atlanta, Georgia, Mar. 17, 1955; d. Billy and Leola McKinney. BA, U. So. Calif., 1978; postgrad., Ga. State U., U. Wis.; Tufts U. Former instr. Clark Atlanta U., Atlanta Met. Coll.; mem. Ga. Ho. of Reps., 1988-92, U.S. Congress from 4th and 11th Ga. dist., 1993—2003; mem. banking and fin. svcs. com., com. housing and cmty. devel. 103rd Congress from 11th Ga. dist.; mem. internat. rels. com. internat. ops. and human rights 103rd-106th Congress from 11th Ga. dist., mem. nat. security com.; mem. NAACP, congress. black caucus and prog. caucus; Frank H.T. Rhodes Class of '56 prof. Cornell U., Ithaca, NY, 2003—. Vis. prof. Cornell U., Ithaca, NY, 2003—. Recipient Diplomatic fellow, Spellman Coll., 1984. Democrat. Office: Cornell U Rhodes Class of '56 Profs Ithaca NY 14853*

MCKINNEY, ERICA KIMBERLY, city official; b. Apr. 5, 1971; BA, Vassar Coll., 1993; JD, U. Miami, 1996. Sr. adminstrv. asst. Mayor's Office, City of Miami, Fla., 1994-96, project rep. dept. planning, 1996; policy advisor Mayor's Office Miami Dade County, Fla., 1996—. Mem. tech. com. Overtown Adv. Bd., Miami, 1994-96. Participant Leadership Miami, 1995; alt. mem. bd. alt. boundary com. Dade County Pub. Schs., Miami, 1995—; bd. dirs. Miami-Kagoshima (Japan) Sister Cities Com., 1996-97; bd. dirs. Suited for Success, Miami, 1997—; acting pres., reunion chmn. class of 1993, Vassar Coll., 1993—. Minority scholar Nat. Trust for Hist. Preservation, 1992; fellow U.S. Coun. on Legal Edn., 1993-96. Mem. Alpha Kappa Alpha (policy action chmn. 1995—). Office: Met-Dade County Mayor's Office 111 NW 1st St Ste 2910 Miami FL 33128-1930 Home: 14615 NE 5th Ave Miami FL 33161-2151

MCKINNEY, PATRICIA J. automobile company executive; Student, Memphis State U. Various positions in automotive bus., 1968-96; pres., owner Nissan of Brandon, 1996—. Mem. Nat. Auto Dealers Assn., Auto Import Assn., Tampa New Car Dealers Assn., Brandon C. of C. Office: 9920 Adamo Dr Tampa FL 33619-2618

MCKINNEY, SALLY VITKUS, state official; b. Muncie, Ind., Aug. 6, 1944; d. Robert Brookins and Mary (Mann) Gooden; m. Alan George Vitkus (div. Jan. 1979); m. James Larry McKinney, Feb. 1, 1986. AA, William Woods U., 1964; BS, U. Ariz., 1966; postgrad., U. Nev., Las Vegas, 1966-68. Tchr. Las Vegas Day Sch., 1972—76; salesperson Globe Realty, Las Vegas, 1976—79; owner, pres. Realty West, Las Vegas, 1979—96; chief investigator State of Nev. Real Estate Divsn., 1996—2000; prin., owner McKinney Realty, Las Vegas, 2000—; corp. broker, dir. bus. and devel. Real Estate Temps, Las Vegas. Rec. sec. Clark County Rep. Cen. Com., Las Vegas, 1982, 1st vice chmn., 1985; vice chmn. Nev. Rep. com., 1986, chmn., 1987-88; mem. Assistance League Las Vegas; state chmn. Nev. Rep. Party. Recipient award Nat. Assn. Home Builders, 1981, 82, 83. Mem. Nat. Assn. Realtors, Las Vegas Bd. Realtors, Greater Las Vegas C. of C., Gen. Fedn. Womens Clubs (nominee Outstanding Young Woman Am. 1979, exec. bd. 1980-82), Jr. League Las Vegas, Mesquite Club (chmn. pub. affairs com. 1986-87, past pres., secret witness exec. bd. 1994-96, vice chmn.). Presbyterian. Avocations: bridge, fly fishing. Home: 511 Mountain Dell Ave Henderson NV 89012-2509

MCKINNEY, SHANNON J. retired secondary school educator; b. Huntingburg, Ind., Sept. 12, 1942; d. Lester Maxey and Clarice V. Corn; m. David E. McKinney, May 18, 1963; children: David E. Jr., Karla K. BS, Oakland City U., 1965; MA, U. Evansville, 1971. Tchr. Plainville (Ind.) H.S., 1965—66, Barr-Reeve H.S., Montgomery, Ind., 1966—67, Dale (Ind.) H.S., 1967—69, East Gibson Sch. Corp., Oakland City, Ind., 1969—2001; ret., 2001. Author: (poetry) Apple Skins, 2001, (novels) Fences, 2002; contbr. articles, short story to profl. publs. Sec., bldg. rep., v.p. East Gibson Classroom Tchr.'s Assn., Oakland City. Recipient Hon. Mention, Rising Sun Fund Poetry Competition, 2002. Mem.: NEA, Ind. State Tchr.'s Assn. Avocations: gardening, writing, camping, travel, photography. Home: 1542 E Arthur Church Rd Winslow IN 47598

MCKINNIE, NANCY ELLIOTT, bank executive; b. Jackson, Miss., Feb. 28, 1952; d. Morelle A. and Elaine (Heard) Elliott; m. William D. McKinnie, May 18, 1974. BA in English Lit., Memphis State U., 1974, MBA in Fin., 1980. Office mgr. Group Ins. Analysts, Memphis, 1972-75; pension adminstr. Conn. Gen. Life, Memphis, 1975-77; trust officer 1st Tenn. Bank, Memphis, 1977-79, v.p. trust sales, 1979-82, v.p., mgr. corp. trust sales, 1982-86, v.p. cash mgmt., 1986-87, pres. Bartlett, 1987-92, sr. v.p. Memphis, 1992—. Trustee, past pres. U. Memphis Found., 1978-96; sec./treas., charter mem. U. Memphis Women's Leadership Coun., 1996-97; past pres. Civitan Club, Bartlett, Exch. Club, Bartlett, Hardin County Meals on Wheels. Mem. Leadership Memphis (grad.). Unitarian Universalist. Avocations: hiking, biking, yachting, reading.

MCKINSEY, ELIZABETH, humanities educator, consultant; b. Columbia, Mo., Aug. 10, 1947; d. J. Wendell and A. Ruhamah (Peret) McK.; m. Thomas N. Clough, June 18, 1977; children: Emily, Peter. BA, Radcliffe Coll., 1970; PhD, Harvard U., 1976. From instr. to asst. prof. English Bryn Mawr (Pa.) Coll., 1975-77; from asst. to assoc. prof. English Harvard U., Cambridge, Mass., 1977-85; dir. Bunting Inst. Radcliffe Coll., Cambridge, 1985-89; dean Carleton Coll., Northfield, Minn., 1989—2002, prof., 2002—. Author: Niagara Falls: Icon of the American Sublime, 1985; contbr. articles and revs. to profl. jours. and lit. mags. NEH fellow, 1980; Carnegie Found. for the Advancement of Tchg. vis. scholar, 2003. Mem. MLA, Am. Conf. Acad. Deans, Nat. Coun. for Rsch. on Women (assoc.), Am. Studies Assn., Nat. Assn. Women in Edn., Phi Beta Kappa (pres. Iota of Mass. chpt. 1986-89). Home: 815 2nd St E Northfield MN 55057-2308 Office: Carleton Coll 1 N College St Northfield MN 55057-4001 E-mail: emckinse@carleton.edu.

MCKNIGHT, MAMIE, commissioner; Ret. H.S. and coll. educator; part-time dir.Tex. PreFreshman Engring. Program U. Tex., Dallas; commr. Tex. Hist. Commn., Austin, 1999—. Assoc. dir. Louis Stokes Alliance for Participation Program in Engring., Math. and Sci.; dir. re-opening and operation Juanita Craft Civil Rights House, Dallas, 2000—; chmn. Dallas Landmark Commn.; founding dir. Black Dallas Remembered, Inc. Office: PO Box 12276 Austin TX 78711-2276

MCKNIGHT, PAMELA ANN, art educator; b. Morristown, N.J., Sept. 29, 1959; d. Edward Harold Spreen and Juliet Ann Dorigo; m. William A. McKnight, Mar. 11, 1995; m. Benjamin A. Mall, May 25, 1985 (div. Aug. 15, 1994); children: Victoria A. Mall, Katherine Rose Mall. BA, Oral Roberts U., Tulsa, 1981; MA in Art Edn., U. North Tex., 2004. Cert. tchr. all level art Tex., 1981, elem. tchr. 1-8 Tex. Art tchr. Our Lady of Sorrows, McAllen, Tex., 1983—87, Mary Hoge Jr. High, Weslaco, Tex., 1987—89, Lamar Jr. High, McAllen, Tex., 1989—90, Martha Turner Reilly Elem., Dallas, 1991—2001, Bradfield Elem., Highland Park, Tex., 2002—. Art tchr. Dallas Mus. of Art, Dallas, 2002—. Recipient Profl. Achievement Award, Highland Pk. Ind. Sch. Dist., 2003; Marcus fellow, Edward and Betty Marcus Found. and North Tex. Inst. for Educators on the Visual Arts, 2001. Mem.: Nat. Art Edn. Assn. (assoc.), Tex. Art Edn. Assn. (assoc.; regional rep. 2001—03), Tex. Parent Tchr. Assn. (life; cultural arts chair 1996—2001, Life Membership Award 2000), Phi Kappa Phi (assoc.). Avocations: travel, reading, art. Office: Highland Park ISD 4300 Southern Ave Dallas TX 75205 E-mail: mcknigp@hpisd.org.

MCKOWEN, DOROTHY KEETON, librarian, educator, consultant; b. Bonne Terre, Mo., Oct. 5, 1948; d. John Richard and Dorothy (Spoonhour) Keeton; m. Paul Edwin McKowen, Dec. 19, 1970; children: Richard James, Mark David. BS, Pacific Christian Coll., 1970; MLS, U. So. Calif., 1973; MA in English, Purdue U., 1985, PhD, 2003. Libr.-specialist Doheny Libr., U. So. Calif., L.A., 1973-74; asst. libr. Pacific Christian Coll., 1974-78; serials cataloger Purdue U. Librs., 1978-88; head children's and young adult svcs. Kokomo-Howard County Pub. Libr., Ind., 1988-89, coord. children's and tech. svcs., 1989-91; cataloger, network libr. Ind. Coop. Libr. Svcs. Authority, 1991-2001; libr. cons. and contractor, 2001—. Mem. adj. faculty.C.C. of Ind., 2001—. Mem. ALA, MLA, Soc. Early Americanists, Assn. for Libr. Collections and Tech. Svcs. (bd. dirs. 1986-90, 95-96, vice chair, chair-elect coun. of regional groups 1986-88, chair 1988-90, conf. program com. 1986-88, internat. rels. com. 1986-88, micropub. com. 1986-87, subject analysis com., membership com. 1988-90, planning and rsch. com. 1988-90, chair program initiatives com. 1991-93, orgn. and bylaws com. 1991-92, 99-2001), Network OCLC Svc. Mgrs. (MARC Task Force 2000-01), Ind. Coun. Libr. Automation (bibliog. stds. task force), Ind. Libr. Fedn. (chair tech. svcs. divsn. 1984-85), Ohio Valley Group Tech. Svcs. Libr. (chmn. 1985-86). Republican. Home: 7625 Summit Ln Lafayette IN 47905-9729 E-mail: mckowen@remconline.net.

MCKOWN, MARTHA, minister, writer; b. Dixie, Ky., May 29, 1933; d. John William and Dora Ellen (Melton) Powell; m. Leslie Henry McKown, June 22, 1957; children: Karen Marie McKown Lee, Liana Jane McKown Edenfield. AB in English, Evansville Coll., 1955; M of Religious Edn., Boston U., 1957; MDiv, Christian Theol. Sem., 1978. Ordained elder Meth. Ch., 1979. Dir. ch. edn. Maple St. Congl. Ch., Danvers, Mass., 1957-58, Temple United Meth. Ch., Terre Haute, Ind., 1973-75; pastor East Park United Meth. Ch., Indpls., 1979-80; assoc. pastor Trinity United Meth. Ch., Evansville, Ind., 1980-82; pastor Faith United Meth. Ch., Princeton, Ind., 1982-85, St. Paul United Meth. Ch., Poseyville, Ind., 1985-89. Author: Palm Sunday Parade, 1995; contbr. articles to various pubs. Pastoral counselor Pike County (Ind.) Hospice, 1993-96; mem. So. Ind. Conf. United Meth. Ch.; rep. Red Bird Missionary Conf., 1995—2002; pres. joint archives North and South Ind. confs., 1998-99, South Ind. Conf. United Meth. Hist. Soc., 2000-03; mem. Southern Ind. Conf. Archives pres. South Ind. Conf. United Meth. Hist. Soc., 2000-03, Southern Ins. Conf. Archives History Commn., 1996—2004; bd. dirs. Evansville United Meth. Youth Home, 1994—2002. Mem. Ohio Valley Writers Guild, Tri-State Geneal. Soc., Woman's Club, Browning Club (pres. 1996-97). Democrat. Avocations: gardening, family, swimming, walking, reading. Home and Office: 7944 Meadow Ln Newburgh IN 47630-2842

MCKUNE, ELIZABETH WALTER, education educator, psychologist; b. Albany, Mo., Mar. 27, 1968; d. Giles and Judith Walter; m. Joseph McKune; children: Margaret, Katherine. B in ednl. studies, U. Mo., 1990, M in edn., 1991; EdD, U. Louisville, 1999. Lic. Psychologist, cert. Psychology Ky. Bd. Examiners, 2000. Admissions counselor III U. Louisville, 1995—96; pre-doctoral intern Western Ky. Internship Consortium, Hopkinsville, 1996—97; cert. psychol. assoc. CARITAS Pain Mgmt. Ctr., Louisville, 1997—98; temp. lic. psychol. Innovance Pain Care Ctr., Louisville, 1998—99; lic. psychol. Ky. Justice Cabinet, LaGrange, Ky., 1999—; clin. faculty Spalding U., Louisville, 2000—; ptnr., v.p. Health Enhancement Resources, Louisville, 2002—. Mem.: APA - Divsn. 38, Am. Psychol. Assoc., Ky. Psychol. Assoc. (pres. elect 2003—), Beta Sigma Phi-Gamma (sec. 2001—03).

MCLACHLAN, SARAH, composer, musician; b. Halifax, Nova Scotia, Jan. 28, 1968; Founder, performer Lilith Fair. Albums include Touch, 1989, Solace, 1991, Live EP, 1992, Fumbling Towards Ecstasy, 1994, Freedom Sessions, 1995, Rarities, B-Sides, and Other Stuff, 1996, Surfacing, 1997, Mirrorball, 1999, Sarah McLachlan Remixed, 2001, Afterglow, 2003; appearances include Gravity, 1991, Island of Circles: A Nettwork C, 1991, No Alternative, 1993, Christmas at Mountain Stage, 1994, Testimonial Dinner: the Songs of Xt, 1995, Memories of the Soul Shack Survivor, 1996, Heroine, 1996; worked with Delerium, Donovan. Recipient Best Female Pop Vocal Performance award Grammy, 1997, 1999, Best Pop Instrumental Performance award, 1997. Office: c/o Arista Records 6 W 57th St New York NY 10019-3901 also: Nettwork Mgmt 1650 W 2nd Ave Vancouver BC V6J 4R3 Canada*

MCLACHLIN, BEVERLEY, Canadian supreme court chief justice; b. Pincher Creek, Alta., Can., Sept. 7, 1943; m. Roderick McLachlin (dec. 1988); 1 child, Angus ; m. Frank E. McArdle, 1992. BA, MA in Philosophy, LLB, U. Alta., LLD (hon.), 1991, U. B.C., 1990, U. Toronto, 1995, York U., 1999, Law Soc. Upper Can., 2000, U. Ottawa, 2000, U. Calgary, 2000, Brock U., 2000, Simon Fraser U., 2000, U. Victoria, 2000, U. Alberta, 2000, U. Lethbridge, 2001, Bridgewater State Coll., 2001, Mt. St. Vincent U., 2002, U. PEI, 2002, U. Montreal, 2003. Bar: Alta. 1969, B.C. 1971. Assoc. Wood, Moir, Hyde and Ross, Edmonton, Canada, 1969—71, Thomas, Herdy, Mitchell & Co., Fort St. John, Canada, 1971—72, Bull, Housser and Tupper, Vancouver, 1972—75; lectr., assoc. prof., prof. with tenure U. B.C., 1974—81; appointed to County Ct., Vancouver, 1981; justice Supreme Ct. of B.C., 1981—85, B.C. Ct. of Appeal, Canada, 1985—88; chief justice Supreme Ct. of B.C., Canada, 1988; justice Supreme Ct. Can., Ottawa, Canada, 1989—2000, chief justice Can., 2000—. Co-author: B.C. Supreme Court Practice, B.C. Court Forms, Canadian Law of Arch. and Engring.; contbr. articles to profl. jours. Office: Supreme Ct Bldg 301 Wellington St Ottawa ON Canada K1A 0J1

MCLAIN, THELMA LOUISE, retired librarian; b. Sparks, Okla., Nov. 18, 1918; d. Grant Leroy and Emma Evelyn (Ellington) Spoonemore; m. Bruce McLain, Nov. 27, 1943 (div. June 1948). BA, Tex. Woman's U., Denton, 1940; MLS, U. Tex., 1959. Cert. tchr., Tex. Sch. libr. supr. Works Progress Adminstrn., Waco, Tex., 1940-41; tchr. 5th grade Donna (Tex.) Pub. Schs., 1941-42; h.s. libr. Rosenburg (Tex.) Pub. Schs., 1942-43; bookmobile libr. Houston Pub. Libr., 1943-44; county libr. Morgan County Libr., Versailles, Mo., 1946-49; h.s. libr. Harlingen (Tex.) Pub. Schs., 1950-52; asst. order libr. U. Tex. Libr., Austin, 1953-56; head rsch. and reference Pan Am. U. Libr., Edinburg, Tex., 1957-74; asst. prof. Pan Am. U., Edinburg, 1970-74; co-owner Custom Ladies Dress Designs, McAllen, Tex., 1972-75. Selling arts and crafts, 1975—. Exhibited paintings oil and acrylics spons. by McAllen Art Mus., Hidalgo County Art League, McAllen, McAllen Jr. League, Rio Grande Valley Art League, Harlingen, Willacy County Art League, Raymondville, Tex., others; author: Long Trail Awinding--My Family's History, 1993. Recipient awards for art. Mem. Order of the Daus. of the King (sec. chpt. 1992—). Episcopalian. Avocations: needlecrafts, especially cloth dolls of original design.

MCLANE-ILES, BETTY LOUISE, academic administrator, educator, writer; b. Chgo., Mar. 15, 1951; d. Clifford I. (Mac) and Genevieve (Cohn) McLane; m. Lawrence (Larry) Irvine Iles, Dec. 28, 1983. BA, French U., Ariz., 1973, MA, 1975; PhD, French U., Ill., 1982. French instr. U. Ariz., Tucson, 1973—76, U. Ill., Champaign-Urbana, 1976—77; adminstr. asst., rschr. small bus. com. Ho. of Reps., Washington, 1977—78; French instr. U. Ill., Champaign-Urbana, 1978—79; lectr. Lycée Henri IV, Paris, 1979—80; French instr. U. Ill., Champaign-Urbana, 1980—81; prof. French, Truman State U., Kirksville, Mo., 1982—. Rsch. asst. econ. and bus. rsch. divsn. U. Ariz., Tucson, 1970—73; co-chmn. fgn. lang. dept. Truman State U., 1996—98, co-chmn. French dept., 1982—88, 1990—92, 1999—2000. Author: Uprooting and Integration in the Writings of Simone Weil, 1987, (plays) The Lost Duchess, 1996; contbr. articles to profl. jours. Faculty advisor Amnesty Internat., Kirkville, Mo., 1997—; faculty advisor Coll. Greens, Truman State U., 1998—. Mem.: MLA, Chgo. Playwrights Network, Assn. internationale des Études Québécoises, Nat. Fraternity of Student Musicians, Internat. Women Playwrights Assn., Mo. Writers Guild, Pi Delta Phi (founder, faculty co-advisor Iota Tau chpt. 1984), Phi Kappa Phi, Phi Beta Kappa. Jewish. Avocations: writing, swimming, travel, drawing. Office: Truman State Univ Dept French Kirksville MO 63501

MCLAREN, KAREN LYNN, advertising executive; b. Flint, Mich., Feb. 14, 1955; m. Michael L. McLaren, June 18, 1974. AA, Mott Community Coll., Flint, 1976; BA, Mich. State U., 1978. Writer Sta. WGMZ-FM, Flint, 1979-84; writer, producer Tracy-Stephens Advt., Flint, 1984-87; pres. McLaren Advt., Troy, Mich., 1987—. Contbr. articles to profl. jours. Mem. centennial com. Wolverine region ARC, 1981, pub. rels. com., 1981-84; vol. coord., pub. rels. tour guide Whaley Hist. Ho., Flint, 1980-91; home designer, tour guide Romeo (Mich.) Hist. Home Tour, 1992; mem. Nat. Trust for Hist. Preservation, 1991-95; com. chair Crim Festival of Races, Flint, 1992, 93, 94, 95; active Sta. WFUM-Pub. TV, Flint, 1980-91; panelist career fair Modona U., Livonia, Mich., 1994, 95, 96, 97; ad book chair Juvenile Diabetes Found./Detroit Evening of Brilliance, 1997; mem. Oakland Regional Bd. Barbara Ann Karmanos Cancer Instn., 1999. Recipient 3 awards, 2 Nat. Health Care Mktg. Competition awards, Women's Adv. Club Detroit Pres.'s award, 1994. Mem. NAFE, Women's Advt. Club Detroit (scholar chmn. 1988-88, bd. dirs. 1989, 92-93, chmn. scholarship fundraiser 1991, co-chmn. career fair 1989, 90, 92, career fair panelist 1993, v.p. 1990, pres. 1991, amb. 1992, chmn. woman of yr. award 1994-96, by-laws chmn. 1994), Women's Econ. Club Detroit (progam com. 1996, workplace of tomorrow com. 1996, vice chair 1997, chair 1999). Office: 3001 W Big Beaver Rd Ste 306 Troy MI 48084-3104

MCLAUCHLEN, JENNIFER, art dealer; b. Montclair, N.J., May 19, 1966; d. James Robert III and Kathleen Ann Carew McLauchlen; m. Joseph Robert de Sane, June 21, 1998. BA, Marymount Coll., 1986, Stony Brook U., 1993. Studio asst. Elaine de Kooning, Easthampton, N.Y., 1987-88, Willem de Kooning, Easthampton, 1988-93; archives dept. rschr. Leo Castelle Gallery, N.Y.C., 1993; lic. appraiser Hamptons Appraisal Corp., Southampton, N.Y., 1994-98; sales assoc. McLauchlen Real Estate, Southampton, 1994-98; owner McLauchlen Gallery, Ltd., Southampton, 1998—. Staff reporter The Easthampton Star, 1994-96. Benefit chairperson Water Mill (N.Y.) Cmty. Club, 1993-94; benefits com. mem. Parrish Art Mus., Southampton, 1995-97, Southampton Cultural Ctr., 1998-99, bd. dirs., 1999—, Guild Hall Easthampton. Mem. Water Mill Cmty. Club Address: 444 N Sea Road Southampton NY 11968

MCLAUGHLIN, CAROLYN LUCILE, elementary school educator; b. Pensacola, Fla., June 16, 1947; d. John Franklin and Mamie Lou (Rayburn) Wells; m. Richard Allen McLaughlin, Sept. 5, 1969; children: Allen Wayne, Kristen Lynn. BA, U. West Fla., 1970. Cert. early childhood, elem. edn. tchr., ESOL. Elem. tchr. Santa Rosa Sch. Bd., Milton, Fla., 1970—2003, reading specialist tchr., 2002—03. Lobbyist for edn. State Fla. Legis. Com., 2001—03. Mem. County Tchr. Edn. Coun., Santa Rosa, v.p., 1995—97, pres., 1998—2000, 2001—03; youth ch. tng. tchr., music and youth dir., Sunday sch. youth tchr. Billory Bapt. Ch., East Bay Bapt. Ch., Midway Bapt. Ch., 1970—95, Navarre Bapt. Ch.; dir. Bible Sch. Holley Assembly God, 2001. Grantee Jr. League 1986, 91-99, Chpt. II Fed. grantee Elem. and Secondary Edn. Act, 1992. Mem.: Santa Rosa Reading Assn. (treas. 2001—03), Santa Rosa Profl. Educators (dist VII rep., negotiations team com., county calendar com., sec. county restructuring steering com., county curriculum com., tchr. of yr. com.), Fla. Reading Assn., Internat. Reading Assn. (v.p. Santa Rosa chpt. 1998—99, pres.-elect 1999—2000, pres. 2001—03), Navarre C. of C. (edn. com. 1998—2001, 2001—03), Kiwanis (children priority one com. 1998—2001). Home: 3586 Ginger Ln Navarre FL 32566-9616 E-mail: richcarol@cs.com, mclaughlincl@mail.santarosa.klz-fl.us.

MCLAUGHLIN, CATHERINE G. healthcare educator; AB, Randolph-Macon Woman's Coll., 1971; MS in Econs., U. Wis., 1978, PhD in Econs., 1980. Prof. health mgmt. and policy U. Mich., 1983—, dir. Econ. Rsch. Initiative on the Uninsured, prof. dept. health mgmt. and policy, dir. Robert Wood Johnson Found. Scholars in Health Policy Rsch. Program. Dir. U. Mich. component Agy. for Healthcare Rsch. and Quality's Ctr. of Excellence on Managed Care Markets and Quality. Contbr. articles to profl. jours.; sr. assoc. editor Health Svcs. Rsch. Office: U Mich Dept Health Mgmt and Policy 109 S Observatory M3166 SPH II Ann Arbor MI 48109-2029 Business E-Mail: cmcl@umich.edu.

MCLAUGHLIN, DARA DAWN, freelance/self-employed writer, freelance/self-employed artist; b. Buffalo, N.Y., Jan. 9, 1951; d. Elaine Iris Cacciato nee Ebert; m. Matthew Militello, Mar. 27, 1971 (div.); children: Santo R Militello, Marla Elaine Militello, Daina Lynn Militello Richards. Diploma, Grover Cleve. HS, 1969. Freelance writer, Rio Rancho, N.Mex., 1990—; freelance artist, 1999—; artist-in-residence V.S.A. Arts of N.Mex., Albuquerque, 2000. Cons. Ind. Living Resource Ctr., Albuquerque, 1996—, V.S.A. Arts of N.Mex, Albuquerque, 1999—; tchr. various cmty. ctrs. and librs., Albuquerque; spkr. in field. Author: A Map Of This World. Tchr. creative writing Cmty. Ctrs. and Librs., Albuquerque, 1996—2003. Named Women On The Move, State of N.Mex, 2001; recipient Human Rights award, 2002; grantee, Friends, 2003. Mem.: Clarence (N.Y.) C. of C., So. Poverty Law Ctr., S.W. Writers. Avocations: cooking, interior decorating, swimming, event planning. Personal E-mail: darasarts@yahoo.com.

MCLAUGHLIN, GOLDIE CARTER, music educator; b. Martinsville, Mo., Aug. 15, 1906; d. Silas Franklin and Fannie Elizabeth (Creekmore) Carter; m. William Coleman McLaughlin, Jan. 5, 1935 (dec. 1970). AA, Palmer Coll., Albany, Mo., 1925; student, U. N.Mex., 1929-31, State Coll., Maryville, Mo., 1930, U. Calif., San Diego. Cert. tchr. Mo., N.Mex., Calif. Grade sch. tchr. Pawnee (Mo.) Sch. Dist., 1927-28; tchr. Hollister (Mo.) City Schs., 1925-29, Russelville (Mo.) Pub. Schs., 1929-30, Dona Ana County Pub. Schs., Las Cruces, N.Mex., 1930-35; engineering draftman Tool Design Dept. North Island Naval Air Station, 1942-46; pvt. music tchr. Napa, Calif. and El Paso, Tex., 1972—.

MCLAUGHLIN, JEAN WALLACE, art director, artist; b. Charlotte, N.C., Dec. 19, 1950; d. John Mason and Caroline (Garner) McL.; m. Thomas Hudson Spleth, Jan. 1991. BA, U. N.C., 1972; postgrad., Calif. Coll. Arts & Crafts, 1983-85; MA, N.C. State U., 1994. Spl. projects coord. Divsn. of the Arts, Dept. Cultural Resources, Raleigh, N.C., 1975-77; arts program coord. Gov.'s Adv. Coun. for Persons with Disabilities, Raleigh, 1978-79; visual and literary arts coord. N.C. Arts Coun., Raleigh, 1979-82; pvt. practice arts cons. San Francisco, 1982-85; visual arts sect. dir. N.C. Arts Coun., Raleigh, 1985-98; dir. Penland (N.C.) Sch. Crafts, 1998—. Art educator Charlotte (N.C.) Latin Sch., 1973-75; panelist and spkr. in field. Author: The Arts in the Churches and Synagogues of North Carolina, 1976; prodr. (book) Public Art Dialogue: SE, 1988. Bd. mem. New Langton Arts, San Francisco, 1983-85, N.C. World Ctr., Raleigh, 1988-91; program com. mem. Fiberworks, Berkeley, 1984-85. Mem. Nat. Assn. Artists Orgns., N.C. Ats Advs., Am. Assn. Mus., Am. Crafts Coun., New Langton Arts, Internat Sculpture Ctr., Art Table, Inc., N.C. Mus. Art, Southeastern Ctr. for Contemporary Art, Mint Mus. Craft and Design, Smithsonian. Avocations: gardening, traveling, reading, writing, making art.

MCLAUGHLIN, JOAN B. literature and writing educator, writer; BA, Nicholls State U., 1968; MA, La. State U., 1970; PhD, U. Tex., 1975. Tchg. asst. La. State U., New Orleans, 1968-70; tchg. asst., asst. instr. U. Tex., Austin, 1970-75; asst. prof. Clemson (S.C.) U., 1975-82, assoc. prof., 1982-87; ind. edn. cons., workshop leader, writer, 1987—. Contbr. articles to profl. jours. Mem. MLA.

MCLAUGHLIN, JUDITH ANN, secondary school educator; b. Newark, Mar. 11, 1950; BA, Moravian Coll., 1972; MS Edn. Adminstrn., Gweynedd Mercy Coll., 2000. Cert. spl. educator 1976, sec. prin. 2000. Continuing edn. adminstr. Pa. State U., Abington, Pa., 1973—75; spl. educator Wordsworth Acad., Fort Washington, Pa., 1975—85; spl. educator, chairperson Coun. Rock Sch. Dist., Newtown, Pa., 1985—. Dir. St. Paul's Presch. Ctr., Warrington, Pa., 1975—85, Friends of the Libr. Ctr., Doylestown, 1998—. Mem.: ASCD, Coun. for Exceptional Children, Nat. Assn. Tchrs. of English, James Michener Art Mus., Phi Delta Kappa (sec. 1999—). Avocations: old home restoration, gardening, reading, vocal music. Office: Coun Rock HS 62 Swamp Rd Newtown PA 18940 E-mail: judymcl@hotmail.com.

MCLAUGHLIN, MARGARET BROWN, adult education educator, writer; b. Miami Beach, Fla., Aug. 24, 1926; d. J. Clifford and Grace Lindsey (DuPre) Brown; m. Francis Edward McLaughlin, Oct. 30, 1982 (dec.). BA cum laude, U. Miami, 1946; MA, Duke U., 1949; PhD, Tulane U., 1976. Instr., lectr. in English U. Miami, Coral Gables, Fla., 1946-47, 56-61, 73-91, 2000; English tchr. Narimasu Am. Sch., Tokyo, 1963-65; asst. prof. Manchester Coll., North Manchester, Ind., 1965-67; instr. Miami-Dade C.C., 1977, 81; dir. writing workshop for fgn. students U. Miami Sch. Medicine, 1991-92; adj. prof. English, Asian and Liberal studies Fla. Internat. U., Miami, 1997—. Prodr. Dade County Cable TV series Caribbean Writers and Their Art, 1991; prodr., host cable tv series Haiti Cherie, 1993-94. Contbr. articles to popular mags. and newspapers; contbr. play reviews to Internet pub. Trustee Mus. Sci., Miami, 1977-78. Mem. Am. Lit. Assn. (Henry Adams Soc.), Egyptology and Asian Civilizations Soc. Miami (bd. dirs., pres. 1976-78, 83-85), South Fla. Internat. Press Club (scholarship chmn. 2002—), South Fla. Writers' Assn. Avocations: writing, travel, editing, civic speaking. Home and Office: 1621 S Bayshore Dr Miami FL 33133-4201 Office Phone: 305-858-7224. E-mail: mjmbjb711@aol.com.

MCLAUGHLIN, MARGUERITE P. state legislator, logging company executive; b. Matchwood, Mich., Oct. 15, 1928; d. Harvey Martin and Luella Margaret (Livingston) Miller; m. George Bruce McLaughlin, 1947; children: Pamela, Bruce Jr., Cynthia. Owner, operator contract logging firm, Orofino, Idaho; mem. Idaho Ho. of Reps., 1978-80, Idaho Senate, 1980—, asst. Dem. Leader, 1990-93, Dem. leader, 1997-98. Chair Democrat Caucus, 1995-96; mem. Senate Fin. Com., 1987—, Gov.'s Adv. Coun. Workers Compensation, 1990-96, State of Idaho Endowment Fund Investment Bd., 1991-95, legis. coun., 1989-94, 95—. Mem. State of Idaho Job Tng. Coun., 1989-98, State Ins. Fund Commn., 1998—; trustee Joint Sch. Dist. 171, 1976-80; pres. Oro Celebration, Inc. Office: Idaho State Senate State Capital Boise ID 83720-0001

MCLAUGHLIN, ROSEMARY, horse trainer, state representative; b. Royalton, Vt., July 15, 1952; m. Tom Wells; 1 child, Katie. Student, Vt. Tech. Coll., 1969—70, Reed Coll., 1971—73. Prin., owner Hitching Post Farm, Royalton, Vt., 1973—; rep. Vt. State Ho. Reps., 2003—. Mem. Royalton (Vt.) Selectboard, Royalton (Vt.) Sch. Bd., 1990—96. Democrat. Home: 273 Rousseau Rd South Royalton VT 05068

MCLAUGHLIN, SHERRY, association administrator; m. Art McLaughlin; 3 children. With Emil H. Dutler unit 177 Am. Legion Aux., 1956, unit pres., 3d dist. pres., Dept. of Iowa pres., 1985—86, nat. v.p., nat. pres., 2001—; counselor Iowa Girls State. Chmn. Aux. Emergency Fund; mem. numerous coms. Am. Legion Aux. Vol. Iowa Vets. Home, Iowa Braille, Vinton-Shellsburg Schs., Union Sch.; Ct. apptd. spl. advocate; confirmation tchr. Trinity Luth. Ch. Recipient Gov.'s Vol. of the Yr. award, 1999, 2000. Office: American Legion Auxiliary 777 N Meridian St 3rd Flr Indianapolis IN 46204

MCLAUGHLIN, SYLVIA CRANMER, volunteer, environmentalist; b. Denver, Dec. 24, 1916; d. George Ernest and Jean Louise (Chappell) Cranmer; m. Donald Hamilton McLaughlin, Dec. 29, 1948; children: Jean Katherine McLaughlin Shaterian, George Cranmer McLaughlin. AB, Vassar Coll., 1939. Co-founder Save San Francisco Bay Assn., Berkeley-Oakland, Calif., 1961-99, pres., 1993-95. Bd. dirs. Ptnrs. for Liveable Cmtys., Washington, 1975-78; mem. waterfront adv. com. City of Berkeley, Calif., 1964-68; sec., bd. dirs. Resource Renewal Inst., 1980—, Citizens for Eastshore State Park, 1980—; founder, bd. dirs. Pub. Trust Group, Oakland, Calif., 1997—; mem. awards com. Berkeley Cmty. Fund, 1998—; mem. adv. bd. Greenbelt Alliance, San Francisco, 1982—; mem. nat. adv. coun. Trust for Pub. Land, San Francisco, 1986—, Ecocity Builders, Berkeley, 1990—. Mem. Nat. Aubudon Soc. (bd. dirs. 1970-76), Nat. Recreation and Parks Assn. (bd. dirs. 1974-78), East Bay Conservation Corps (bd. dirs. 1985-97), Student Conservation Assn. (bd. dirs. 1979-84). Avocations: outdoor activities, adventure and travel, reading, children and grandchildren, working out. Home: 1450 Hawthorne Ter Berkeley CA 94708-1804

MCLEAN, DIANNE KAY, music educator; b. Galveston, Tex., Nov. 21, 1948; d. George Edmund and Juanita Arlette (Nuss) Duytschaever; m. John Robert Clendenen, Mar. 17, 1979 (div. Apr. 1996); children: Kimberly Clendenen, Robert Clendenen, Amy Clendenen, Laurie Clendenen, John Clendenen. BA in Psychology, Lamar U., 1970; AA in Music magna cum laude, Coll. of the Mainland, 1992; tchr. cert. in music, U. Houston, 1995. Cert. all level music preK-12 tchr. Tex., elem. tchr. grades 1-8 Tex. Ballet, tap, jazz, acrobatics, ballroom dance instr. various studios, Houston, 1970—72; music, dance, piano tchr. The Studio of Performing Arts, Santa Fe, Tex., 1988, 1989; owner, dir. keyboard, voice and dance studio Talent Unlimited, Galveston County, Tex., 1989—. Choreographer, choral dir. The Studio of Performing Arts, Santa Fe, 1988—90; choral dir. Santa Fe H.S. and Jr. High, 2000, 01, 02; music dir., instr. K.E. Little Elem. Sch., Bacliff, Tex., 2002—. Author: The Poetry of Dianne McLean, vol. 1, 1986, The Poetry of Dianne McLean, vol. 2, 1987; composer: (book of songs) The Greatest of These is Love, 1988. Vol. crisis worker Crisis Hotline-Mental Health, Galveston, Tex., 1975—76; vol. tchr., crisis worker The Bridge-Women's Shelter, Pasadena, Tex., 1994; ch. choral dir. and accompanist Galveston County, Tex., 1991—2002. Mem.: Bay Area Dance, Tex. Music Educators Assn., Phi Theta Kappa, Alpha Lambda Delta. Avocations: music, movies, reading, dance. Home: 5621 Avenue G 1/2 Santa Fe TX 77510

MCLEAN, DONNA, federal agency administrator; BS in Polit. Sci., M of Pub. Affairs, Ind. U. Mem. staff U.S. Ho. of Reps.; asst. adminstr. fin. svcs. FAA; asst. sec. Office Budget and Programs, CFO U.S. Dept. Transp., Washington, 2001—. Office: US Dept Transp Budget and Programs 400 7th St SW Washington DC 20590

MCLEAN, JULIANNE DREW, concert pianist, educator; b. Stoneham, Mass., Sept. 12, 1928; d. Benjamin Drew and Elizabeth Anna McLean; m. Carmelo Addario, Oct. 18, 1958 (dec.); 1 child, Angela Elizabeth Addario. BMusic, Conservatory of Music, Kansas City, Mo., 1949, MMusic, 1950. Concert pianist NAC, U.S., Europe, Near and Far East, 1956—; tchr. pvt. classes, Kans., Hawaii, Va., 1956—; rec. artist Wichita State U., 1987—; lectr. in field. Musician: appearances on TV; musician: (invited pianist) Survivors of Andrea Doria Reunion; musician: live on Vatican Radio. Bd. dirs. Maud Powell Found., Falls Church, Va., 1995—. Recipient scholarships. Mem. Mu Phi Epsilon. Roman Catholic. Avocation: cooking.

MCLEAN, KATHERINE, photographer, artist; b. Washington, Feb. 6, 1950; d. Melvin Anselm and Louise Victoria-Ruth (Kiefer) J.; m. Gordon Kennedy McLean, Dec. 30, 1970; children: Jason Richard, Jesse J. Student, Phila. Coll. Art, 1970; BA summa cum laude, U. Pa., 1986. Freelance designer, med. illustrator, Phila., 1975-86; freelance photographer, artist Phila., Pitts., 1985—. Asst. film editor, prodn. asst. Visionaries Film & Video, Phila., 1984-87; coord. membership and edn. Silver Eye Ctr. for Photography, Pitts., 1993-94. Painter: Art of the State, 1997 (1st pl. award 1997), Wonder Boy, 1999; photographer: Photo Opportunity, 1991 (Juror's award 1991). Vol. Associated Artists Pitts., 1990-99. Mem. Group A, Pitts. Soc. Artists (Juror's award 1992). Avocations: reading, gardening, travel, movies, dogs. Home: 125 Quail Hill Rd Pittsburgh PA 15238-1835

MCLEAN, SUSAN O'BRIEN, artist; b. Bronxville, N.Y., Dec. 13, 1944; d. Francis Joseph O'Brien and Mildred Maud Brooks; m. John Allan McLean, Oct. 2, 1965; children: John Allan Cameron, Jennifer Brooks, Christopher O'Brien. Student, Chestnut Hill Coll., Pa., 1962-63, Church Stile Studio Schs., Cobham, Surrey, Eng., 1981-86, St. Martins Sch. Art, London, 1982-83. One-woman shows include Boathouse Gallery, Walton-on-Thames, 1989; exhibited in group shows at Royal Inst. Painters in Watercolor, London, Royal Soc. Portrait Painters, London, 1987, Pastel Soc., London, 1985, 86, Cape Cod Art Assn., Falmouth Artist's Guild, Creative Arts Ctr., Chatham, Copley Soc., Duxbury Art Complex; represented in permanent collection Cape Mus. of Fine Arts, Dennis. Mem. Copley Soc. (Copley Artist), Cape Cod Art Assn. (artist mem., Grumbacher Gold Medal award for painting All New Eng. Show 1997). Home: 36 Donna Ave Osterville MA 02655-1714 E-mail: jacsusie@mindspring.com.

MCLEER, LAUREEN DOROTHY, drug development and pharmaceutical professional; b. N.Y.C., Feb. 5, 1955; d. William Myers and Una Lee (Massey) McLeer. BS, Columbia U., 1977; MBA, U. London, 1981. RN N.Y., D.C., state reg. nurse, Eng., registered state nurse, Wales. Staff nurse NYU Med. Ctr., N.Y.C., 1977-78; charge nurse Scripps Clinic and Rsch. Found., La Jolla, Calif., 1979-80; clin. rschr. Ayerst Labs., N.Y.C., 1982; sales rep. Pfizer, Inc., N.Y.C., 1983-87, Cahners Pub. Co., N.Y.C., 1988-89; dir. bus. devel. Pro Clinica, N.Y.C., 1990-91; account supr. Salthouse Torre Norton, Inc., Rutherford, N.J., 1992-93; dir. bus. devel. Med. & Tech. Rsch. Assocs., Inc., Wellesley, Mass., 1993-94; sr. project dir. Quiltiles Inc., Arlington, Va., 1994-99; project mgr. product devel. and commercialization Aventis Pharms., Inc., Berwyn, Pa., 1999—2002; clin. trial mgmt. leader AstraZeneca, LP, Wilmington, Del., 2002—. Mem. com. for healthcare issues and legis. United Hosp. Fund, N.Y.C., 1992—94. Chmn. Help Our Neighbors Eat Yr. 'Round, N.Y.C., 1987—89; trustee Murray Hill Com., N.Y.C., 1988—90; bd. dirs. East Midtown Svcs. for Older People, 1987—94; vol. nurse Whitman Walker Clinic, 1995—99; bd. dirs. Cecil Land Trust, 2002—, Eastern Shore Land Conservancy, 2003—. Mem.: Drug Info. Assn., Regulatory Affairs Profl. Soc. Home: PO Box 681 Chesapeake City MD 21915 Office: AstraZeneca LP 1800 Concorde Pike Wilmington DE 19802-4034 E-mail: laureen.mcleer@astrazeneca.com.

MCLELLAN, A. ANNE, Canadian government official; b. Hants County, N.S., Can., Aug. 31, 1950; d. Howard Gilmore and Joan Mary (Pullan) McL. BA, Dalhousie U., LLB, 1974; LLM, King's Coll., U. London, 1975. Bar: N.S., 1976. Asst. prof. law U. N.B., Can., 1976-80; assoc. prof. law U. Alta., Edmonton, Can., 1980-89, assoc. dean faculty of law, 1985-87, prof. law, 1989-93, acting dean, 1991-92; M.P. for Edmonton West Ho. of Commons, Can., 1993—; min. of nat. resources Govt. of Canada, Ottawa, 1993—97, min. of energy, mines and resources, 1993—95, min. of forestry, 1993—95, fed. interlocutor for metis and non-status Indians, 1993—97, min. justice and atty. gen. of Canada, 1997—2002, min. of health, 2002—03, dep. prime min., 2003—, min. of public safety and emergency preparedness, 2003—. Commentator on Can. Charter of Rights and Freedoms and on human rights issues. Contbr. articles to profl. publs. Past bd. dirs. Can. Civil Liberties Assn., Alta. Legal Aid; past v.p. U. Alta. Faculty Assn. Office: Office of the Prime Min Langevin Block 80 Wellington St K1A 0A2 Ottawa ON Canada E-mail: McLellan.A@parloge.ca.*

MCLEMORE, CAROL LEE, accountant; b. Newnan, Ga., Sept. 29, 1962; d. Fredrick William and Lucy Ann (Yarbrough) Lange; m. Charles H. McLemore, Oct. 11, 1996. BBA in Acctg., West Ga. Coll., 1988, M of Profl. Accountancy, 1995. CPA Ga. State Bd. Accountancy. Advanced staff auditor Ga. Dept. of Audits, Atlanta, 1988-93; fiscal officer Cmty. Action for Improvement, LaGrange, 1993-94; grant acct. Columbus (Ga.) Consol. Govt., 1994-98; staff acct. Robinson, Grimes & Co., P.C., 1998—2000; adj. acctg. instr. So. Union State Cmty. Coll., Valley, Ala., 2002—; acct., CFO Pine Mt. (Ga.) Ace Hardware, 2003—. Mem. AICPA, Inst. Mgmt. Accts., Ga. Soc. CPA's. Republican. Baptist. Avocations: tennis, reading. Office Phone: 706-663-2205. E-mail: carolmclemore@bellsouth.net.

MCLEMORE-WHEELER, LINDA M. literature educator; b. Akron, Ohio, Oct. 26, 1970; d. Lee and Catherine White; m. William A. Wheeler, June 10; children: Elizabeth Wheeler, Jordan Wheeler, Austin Wheeler. BA in English, Jackson State U., Miss., 1988—92, MA in English, 1995—97. Computer instr. Johnson Elem., Jackson, Miss., 1992—96; English instr. Coahoma C.C., Clarksdale, Miss., 1998—2000, Jackson State U., Jackson, Miss., 2000—. Editor: (cookbook) Heart and Soul: Student Recipes for Everyday Living. Vol. Couples Ministry Outreach, Jackson, Miss., 2000—01. Mem.: Miss. Assn. for Devel. Edn., Nat. Coun. for the Teachers of English, Writer's Guild, Alpha Epsilon Lambda (sec. 1995), Phi Kappa Phi. Baptist. Avocations: piano, reading, singing, poetry. Office: Jackson State Univ 1400 John R Lynch St Jackson MS 39217 E-mail: linda.m.wheeler@jsums.edu.

MCLENDON, DOROTHY, school psychologist; b. Crawfordsville, Ind., Feb. 20, 1918; d. Joseph Newton and Dora (Ryall) Fullenwider; m. Hiram James McLendon, May 23, 1942; 1 child, Hiram James McLendon, Jr. AB, Olivet Coll., Kankakee, Ill., 1942; MA, Boston U., 1945, EdD, 1970. Diplomate Am. Bd. of Profl. Psychology. Spl. edn. tchr. Kingsley Schs., Belmont Jr. High, Boston, 1943-46, 56-57; lectr. Homerton Coll., Cambridge, England, 1946-47; sch. psychologist Alameda County Schs., Oakland, Calif., 1949—51, Berkeley Pub. Schs., 1951—52, Paris Am. Army Dependent Sch., France, 1957-58, Brookline (Mass.) Pub. Schs., 1958-81; pvt. cons. Cambridge, Mass., 1981—; cons. Cocoa, Fla., 1981—. Address: 1660 Rosetine St Cocoa FL 32926-5502

MCLENNAN, BARBARA NANCY, international tax specialist; b. N.Y.C., Mar. 25, 1940; d. Sol and Gertrude (Rochkind) Miller; m. Kenneth McLennan, Aug. 14, 1962; children: Gordon, Laura. BA magna cum laude, CCNY, 1961; MS, U. Wis., 1962, PhD, 1965; JD, Georgetown U., 1983. Bar: DC 1983, U.S. Ct. Internat. Trade 1988, U.S. Ct. Appeals (DC cir.) 1988, U.S. Supreme Ct. 1988, Va. 1991; cert. accredited valuation analyst Nat. Assn. Career Valuation Analysts, 2004. From asst. prof. to assoc. prof. Temple U., Phila., 1965—78; budget analyst Com. Budget, U.S. Ho. of Reps., Washington, 1978—81; legis. asst. fin. and budget Senator Dan Quayle, Washington, 1981—84; internat. tax specialist IRS U.S. Dept. Treasury, Washington, 1984—89; dep. asst. sec. trade, info. and analysis U.S. Dept. Commerce, Washington, 1989—91; prin., atty.-at-law Bitonti and Wilhelm, PC., McLean, Va., 1991—93; staff v.p. govt.-legal affairs consumer electronics group Electronic Industries Assn., Washington, 1993—94, staff v.p. tech. policy, consumer electronics group, 1994—95; v.p. Van Scoyoc Assocs., Washington, 1995—96; cons. on tax related issues in U.S., former Soviet Union, and West Bank and Gaza McLean, Va., 1996—. Sr. polit. scientist SRI-Internat., Arlington, Va., 1971—74; vis. prof. Am. Coll., Paris, 1975—76; cons. UNESCO, Paris, 1977—78. Author: (book) Comparative Political Systems, 1975; contbr. articles to profl. jours. Mem. parents adv. coun. Randolph-Macon Coll., Ashland, Va., 1989—92. Fellow NDEA, 1962—65. Mem.: ABA, Va. Bar Assn., Fed. Bar Assn., DC

Bar Assn., Am. Soc. Assn. Execs., Phi Beta Kappa. Home: 1620 Harbor Rd Williamsburg VA 23185 E-mail: barb.mcl@cox.net.

MCLENNAN, BERNICE CLAIRE, human resources professional; b. Malden, Mass., Dec. 26, 1936; d. Ralph Cyril Worth and Alice Seaman (Hunter) Worth Barrett; m. Hubert Earle McLennan, Oct. 28, 1961; 1 child, Cynthia Alice. Student, Moody Bible Inst., 1958, Salem State Coll., 1988, Bentley Coll., 1989. Youth dir. Faith Evangelical Ch., Melrose, Mass., 1971-77; adminstrv. asst. Boston Redevel. Authority, 1977-85, adminstr. coord., 1985-87, asst. sec. to the authority, 1981—2002, dir. human resources, 1988-95, asst. dir., 1995-99, dep. dir. for human resources, 1999—2002; human resources cons., 2003; ret., 2003. Moderator Faith Evangelical Ch., Melrose, 1985-88, Christian edn. chair, 1973-76. Sec. Melrose (Mass.) Sch. Com., 1983-85; vol. Boston (Mass.) Youth Campaign, 1989, 90; bd. dirs. Chime Time Children's Ctr., Melrose, 1998-99; mem. 1st Bapt. Ch. of Melrose, 1999--. Mem. Internat. Pers. Mgmt. Assn., Assn. Affirmative Action Profls., Christian Edn. Com. Avocations: Christian edn., women's issues, drug/alcohol edn. Home: 31 Botolph St Melrose MA 02176-1126

MCLEOD, JACQUELYN H. special education educator; b. Magee, Miss., Aug. 12, 1951; d. M.C. McLeod and Othella Granthom-Jones; children: Martina D. Gillis, Aishah S. Bashir, Quwana S. Bashir, Jafar H. Bashir, Husniyah B.T. AA, Contra Costa C.C., San Pablo, Calif., 1984; BS, U. Calif., Davis, 1988; studied in edn. leadership program, admin. credentials, Mills Coll., 2004. Multi-subject tchg. credential Calif., 1989, mid./moderate spl. edn. tchg. credential Calif., 2000. Gen. edn. tchr. W. Contra Costa Unified Sch. Dist., Richmond, Calif., 1989—97, spl. edn. tchr., 1998—. Story teller Unity Ch. of Richmond, 1990—97; tutor S. Berkeley Cmty. Ch., Berkeley, Calif., 2002—03; instr. English lang. Internat. Found. Edn. and Self-Help, Awassa, Ethiopia, 1997—98. Founding mem. Lest We Forget Planning Com., Berkeley, 1995; coun. rep. United Tchrs. of Richmond, Richmond, Va., 1993—97, 2003—; mem. E. Bay Local Asian Devel. Corp., Oakland, Calif., 2003—; co-founder Conscious New African Women Healing Collective, Richmond, 2000—. Mem.: Calif. Tchrs. Assn., United Tchrs. Richmond (coun. rep. 1993—97). Democrat. Avocations: travel, hiking, reading. Home: 1049 18th St Richmond CA 94801 Office: West Contra Costa Unified School Dist 1108 Bissell Ave Richmond CA 94801

MCLIN, RHINE LANA, mayor, former state legislator; b. Dayton, Ohio, Oct. 3, 1948; d. C. Josef, Jr. and Bernice (Cottman) McL. BA in Sociology, Parsons Coll., 1969; MEd, Xavier U., 1972; postgrad. in law, U. Dayton, 1974-76; AA in Mortuary Sci., Cin. Coll., 1988. Lic. funeral dir. Tchr. Dayton Bd. Edn., 1970-72; divorce counselor Domestic Rels. Ct., Dayton, 1972-73; law clk. Montgomery Common Pleas Ct., Dayton, 1973-74; v.p., dir., embalmer McLin Funeral Homes, Dayton, 1972—; mem. Ohio Ho. of Reps. from 36th & 38th dists., Columbus, 1988-94, Ohio Senate from 5th dist., Columbus, 1994—2002; mem. Ways & Means Com.; controlling bd., ins. commerce comn. ranking mem.; state and local govt. com. Columbus; minority whip Ohio Senate, Columbus, 1998—2002; mayor City of Dayton, 2003—. Instr. Central State U., Wilberforce, Ohio, 1982-97; mem. Ohio Tuition Trust Authority. Mem. Dem. Nat. Com., Children's Def. Fund. Toll fellow; Paul Harris fellow; Flemming fellow; BLLD fellow; named Ohio Legislator of Yr., Ohio Social Workers Assn., 1999. Mem. Nat. Funeral Dirs. Assn., Ohio Funeral Dirs. Assn., Montgomery County Hist. Soc., NAACP (life), Nat. Coun. Negro Women (life), Delta Sigma Theta. Office: City Hall 2nd Fl 101 W Third St Dayton OH 45402*

MCLOUGHLIN, CAROL A. health facility administrator; b. Bklyn., July 2, 1955; d. Edward Francis and Bernadette (Lynch) McLoughlin. BA Sociology, SUNY, Binghamton, 1977; MSW, SUNY, Stony Brook, 1980. Cert. social worker N.Y., 1981. Adoption supr. St. Christopher's Home, Glen Cove, NY, 1980—85; social worker Creedmoor Psychiatric Ctr., Queens Village, NY, 1985—91, treatment team leader, 1991—96, Bronx Psychiatric Ctr., NY, 1996—98; chief mental health treatment svcs. Manhattan Psychiatric Ctr., N.Y.C., 1998—. Mem.: ACSW, NASW. Avocations: rescuing feral cats, gardening, travel, attending dance concerts, taking care of dogs and cats. Home: 9-15 166th St Apt 5C Whitestone NY 11357 Office: Manhattan Psychiatric Ctr Ward's Island New York NY 10035 Business E-Mail: mafm@omh.state.ny.us.

MCMAHON, CHRISTINE CAROLINE, sales professional, trainer, consultant; b. Cambridge, Mass., Oct. 12, 1961; d. Pauline Regina and Guy Lawson Keans; m. Duke Paul McMahon, Oct. 15, 1995; 1 child, Cherise Elizabeth. BS, Boston Coll., 1983. Spkr., trainer, cons. Christine McMahon & Assoc., Milwaukee, Wis., 1995—; dist. mgr. Nabisco Biscuit Co., Milwaukee, Wis., 1991—94; regional dir. Slim-Fast Foods, New York, NY, 1989—91; unit mgr. Procter & Gamble, Boston, 1983—89. Columnist (articles) Secrets of Successful Negotiating. Exec. bd. mem. United Cerebral Palsy, Milwaukee, Wis., 1995—2003. Mem.: Womens Bus. Owners Network (bd. mem. 1996—2003, found.), Sales & Mktg. Executives Internat., Nat. Speakers Assn. Office: Christine McMahon & Associates 1563 S 101st Street Milwaukee WI 53214 E-mail: christinemcmahon-.com.

MCMAHON, JANET MANKIEWICH, critical care nurse; b. Rockville Centre, N.Y., Apr. 23, 1957; d. Matthew J. and Lois May (Johns) Mankiewich; m. Michael T. McMahon, July 12, 1985; children: Shannon and Sandy (twins), Patrick. BSN, Adelphi U., 1980. RN, N.Y., Va.; cert. BLS instr., ACLS. Nurse St. Francis Hosp., Roslyn, N.Y.; charge nurse L.I. Jewish Hillside Med. Ctr., New Hyde Park, N.Y., Alexandria (Va.) Hosp., Mary Washington Hosp., Fredricksberg, Va., Mt. Vernon (Va.) Hosp., George Washington U. Hosp., Washington; nurse Potomac Hosp., Woodbridge, Va. Mem. AACCN. Home: 4803 Kempair Ct Woodbridge VA 22193-4631

MCMAHON, LINDA E. sports association executive; b. New Bern, N.C., Oct. 4, 1948; m. Vincent K. McMahon, Aug. 6, 1966; children: Shane, Stephanie. Degree, East Carolina U. Co-founder, bd. dirs. World Wrestling Fedn. Entertainment, Inc., Stamford, Conn., 1980—, pres., 1993—, CEO, 1997—. Office: WWFE Corp Hdqs 1241 E Main St Stamford CT 06902

MCMAHON, MARGOT ANN, sculptor, art educator; b. Lake Forest, Ill., Apr. 15, 1957; d. William Franklin and Irene Mary (Leahy) McM.; m. Daniel Joseph Burke, June 25, 1988; children: Brendan McMahon Burke, Mary Irene McMahon Burke, Aubrey McMahon Burke. BA, Hamline U., 1979; MFA, Yale U., 1984. Sculpture asst. Hamline U., St. Paul, 1978; editl. artist World Book Ency., Chgo., 1979-82; tchg. asst. Yale U., New Haven, 1982-84; tchr. Yale Summer Sch., Norfolk, Conn., 1983; mem. sculpture faculty Sch. of Art Inst., Chgo., 1986-89; lectr. Art Inst. Assocs., Chgo., 1989—, DePaul U., Chgo., 1998. Vis. artist Sch. of Art Inst., 1992, 96, St. Xavier Coll., Chgo, 1995; presenter in field. Prin. works include sculptures and mural at St. Patrick Ch., Lake Forest, Ill., John D. MacArthur State Park, North Palm Beach., Fla., DePaul U., One Northfield Plz., Northfield, Ill., Lake Bluff, Ill., St. Mary's Sch., Lake Forest, Robert Irwin Park, Homewood, Ill., Highwood (Ill.) Pub. Libr., St. Francis Retreat Ctr., Oak Brook, Ill., Chgo. Botanic Garden, Northfield Pub. Libr., Beye Sch., Oak Park, Ill.; represented in permanent collections Chgo. Hist. Soc., Chgo. Horticultural Mus., DePaul U., John D. and Catherine T. MacArthur Found., Lake Forest H.S., Mobil Oil Internat., Fairfax, Va., Mus. Contemporary Art, Chgo., Nat. Portrait Gallery, Smithsonian Instn., Washington, Sch. of St. Mary, Lake Forest, Silberline Co., Inc., Tamaqua, Pa., Tuthill Corp., Hinsdale, Ill., Yale U., and numerous pvt. collections; represented in DeBilzan Gallery, Santa Fe, N.Mex. Bd. dirs. Palette and Chisel, Chgo., 1989, Oak Park Area Arts Coun., 1999, Nat. Mus. of Women in the Arts, 1999—; mem., exhibitor Deerpath Art League, Lake Forest, 1990-00, Hyde Park Art Ctr., Chgo., 1992—, Oak Park Area Arts Coun., 1992—, Chgo. Arts Club. Recipient Fellowship award Barat Coll., 2000, Rose Phillipine Duchasne award, 2000; grantee Retirement Rsch. Found., Chgo., 1989, Ragdale Found., 1993, Steans Family Found., 1991. Mem. Internat. Sculpture Soc., Nat. Sculpture Soc. (Alex B. Hexter award 1991), Renaissance Soc., Ragdale Found., Mus. Contemporary Art, Arts Club of Chgo. Roman Catholic. Avocations: book clubs, sailing, music, softball. Home: 310 S Humphrey Ave Oak Park IL 60302-3528 E-mail: mmcmahom@mediaone.net.

MCMAHON, MARIBETH LOVETTE, physicist; b. Bradford, Pa., June 8, 1949; d. James Harry and Jospehine Rose (Sylvester) Lovette; m. Frank Joseph MaMahon, Nov. 19, 1976 (div.). BS in Math., BS in Physics, Pa. State U., 1971, MS in Physics, 1974, PhD in Physics, 1976. Research asst. Pa. State U., 1971-76; advanced research and devel. engr. GTE Sylvania, Danvers, Mass., 1976-78; sr. physicist 3M Co., St. Paul, 1978-79, market devel. supr., 1979-83; market devel. mgr. Galileo Electro-Optics Corp., Sturbridge, Mass., 1983-84; product mgr. Varian Assocs., Lexington, Mass., 1984-85; mktg. dir. Bowmar, Acton, Mass., 1985-86; pres. Kilduff Inc., Peoria, Ariz., 1986—. Recipient Cert. in Appreciation of Service Pa. State U., 1971 Mem. Optical Soc. Am., Assn. Women in Sci., Assn. Physicists in Medicine, Sigma Pi Sigma, Sigma Chi Home and Office: 11327 N 82nd Dr Peoria AZ 85345-5895

MCMAHON MASTRODDI, MARCIA A. secondary school educator, artist, writer; b. Akron, Ohio, Dec. 26, 1953; d. James R. and Marla June McMahon; m. Dennis W. Mastroddi, Aug. 22, 1987. BA in Art, Ursuline Coll., 1978; MA in Art, Case Western Res. U., 1980; student, Cleve. Inst. Art. Cert. K-12 art tchr., Ill. Instr. art Cuyahoga C.C., Warrensville Heights, Ohio, 1978-87; lectr. art Spoon River Coll., Canton, Ill., 1989, Ill. Ctrl. Coll., Peoria, 1990; tchr. art CBS Alternative H.S., Beardstown, Ill., 1993-95, Ursuline Acad., Springfield, Ill., 1996-97, Dist. 186, Springfield, 1997-98; tchr. art, chmn. dept. Tower Hill (Ill) Consol. Unified Sch. Dist. 66, 1999—. Lectr. art for gifted Lincoln Land C.C., Springfield, part-time 1995-98, Art Inst. Online, divsn. Pitts. Art Inst.; featured guest spkr. Case Western Res. U., Cleve., 1980, Shard Hill Art Gallery, Farmington, Ill., 1989, Bot. Garden, 1998, Ursuline Coll., Cleve., 1979, Peoria Art Guild, 1990—, Ill. State Mus., Springfield, 1995—, Unity Gallery, 1999—, Rushville (Ill.) Arts Coun., 1999, Taste of Champaign (Ill.) Art Ctr. Sq. Show, 1999, Lincoln Prairie Trail Art Show, 2001; author: Diana Speaks to the World, 2002, Princess Diana's Message of Peace: An Extraordinary Message of Peace for Our Current World, 2004; prin. works include, U.S., Europe, and Can.; pub. in (with Princess Diana's messages) Channeling Anthoogy for September 11th (www.spiritwritings.com). Houseparent Am. Youth Hostels, 1988-89. Recipient svc. award for tchr. Cuyahoga C.C., 1989, Rosie Richmond award Springfield Area Arts Coun., 1998. Mem. Prairie State Orchid Soc., Ill. tate Mus. Soc., Washington Park Bot. Gardens, Tower Hill Art Club. Mem. Unity Ch. Avocations: designing jewelry, hiking, sketching, portraiture, collecting antiques. E-mail: marcia@ctitech.com., dianaspeaks@hotmail.com.

MCMANIGAL, PENNY, artist; b. Orange, Calif., 1936; d. Howard R. and Helen L. Hineman; m. Paul G. McManigal, Aug. 22, 1959; children: Lisa Anne, Scott Paul. BA, Pomona Coll., 1958. Tchr. Fern Leaf Elem., Fullerton, Calif., 1958—59, Springhill Elem., Lafayette, Calif., 1959—63; master tchr. San Jose State U., Lafayette, 1962—63; tchr.-writer art curriculum Eastbluff Elem., Newport Beach, Calif., 1974—79. One-woman shows include Pennswood Gallery, Newtown, Pa., 1990, Internat. Mus. 20th Century Art & Culture, Laguna Beach, Calif., 1991, U. Calif., Irvine, 1992, The Beckman Ctr., 1993, UN 4th NGO World Conf. on Women, China, 1995, Claremont Forum Gallery, Claremont, Calif., 1999, UN Ch. Ctr., NYC, 2002, St. Paul's Chapel, 2002, world co-creative interactive project Weaving the Dream!, 1997—2003, numerous internat. locations, exhibited in group shows at Irvine Fine Arts Ctr., Irvine, Calif., 1999, Anaheim Mus., Anaheim, Calif., 1999, L.A. County Fair, Edn. Bldg., 2000, dA Gallery, Pomona, Calif., 2001, 2002, numerous others, Peace for Our Children painting presented to Mikhail Gorbachev, Pres. George H.W. Bush, Desmond Tutu, others. Artistic amb. People to People Internat., 2000; del. and group co-creative leader UN 4th NGO World Conf. on Women, China, 1995, UN Commn. on the Status of Women, NY, 2002; founder and pres. Parents Who Care, Newport Beach, 1982—86; city arts commr. City of Newport Beach, 1966—71. Named to Hall of Fame, Fullerton Union H.S., 1985; recipient Outstanding Vol. Svc. to the Arts award, City Coun., 1982, Silver Anchor award for outstanding cmty. svc., C. of C. Newport Beach, 1985, Outstanding Contbn. to Edn. award, Orange County Dept. Edn., 1988, Clara Barton Spectrum awards, Orange County chpt. ARC, 1995, Artistic Contbn. award, ARC, 1995. Avocations: genealogy, writing. Home: 16 Inverness Ln Newport Beach CA 92660 Office: PO Box 9426 Newport Beach CA 92658-9426

MCMANIGAL, SHIRLEY ANN, university educator, dean emerita; b. Deering, Mo., May 4, 1938; d. Jadie C. and Willie B. (Groves) Naile. BS, Ark. State U., 1971; MS, U. Okla., 1976, PhD, 1979. Med. technologist, 1958-75; chair dept. med. tech. U. So. Miss., Hattiesburg, 1979-83, Tex. Tech U. Health Scis. Ctr., Lubbock, 1983-87, dean Sch. Allied Health, 1987-97. Gov.'s appointee to statewide health coord. coun., 1994-97. Leadership Tex., 1992; Lt. Alumnae Regl. dir., 1994-97. Recipient Citation, State of Tex., 1988; named Woman of Yr., AAUW, Tex. div., 1990, Woman of Excellence in Edn. YWCA, Lubbock, 1990. Mem.: AAUW (Tex. bd. dirs. 1990—94, mem. ednl. found. internat. fellows panel 1994—98, chair 1998—2001), Tex. Soc. Med. Tech. (Educator of Yr. 1990), Tex. Soc. Allied Health Professions (pres. 1990—91), So. Assn. Allied Health Deans at Acad. Health Ctrs., Nat. Assn. Women in Edn., Am. Soc. Med. Tech., Clin. Lab. Mgmt. Assn. (chair edn. com. 1989, 1991), Phi Beta Delta, Alpha Eta. Home: 24633 Ivory Cane Dr 103 Bonita Springs FL 34134 E-mail: smcmnigal@comcast.net.

MCMANN, EDITH BROZAK, performance artist, visual artist; b. Totowa, N.J., Mar. 26, 1929; d. Henry and Lena (Ulmer) Brozek; m. Frank Richard McMann, May 26, 1957; children: Robert, Stephen. Dance student, Sch. Am. Ballet, N.Y.C., 1945-57; art student, Westchester Art Workshop, Art Students League, N.Y.C., 1976-84; B in Profl. Studies in Dance and Visual Arts, SUNY, 1984; MS in Studio Art, Coll. of New Rochelle, 1989. Performing artist Alicia Alonso's Nat. Ballet Cuba tours, 1948-50, George Balanchine's N.Y.C. Ballet, 1950-57; visual artist N.Y.C., 1970—; intern Silvermine Coll. Art, 1989. (exhibitions) Depicting Dance in Art, Gutman Gallery, White Plains, 1990, Xavier Gallery, New Rochelle, N.Y., 1989—94, Mamaroneck Artist Guild Gallery, Larchmont, N.Y., 1990—, Beaux Arts Exhibits, 1991—94, Manhattanville Coll., Purchase, N.Y., 1991, Town Ctr. Gallery, Mamaroneck, 1993—, N.Y.C. Ballet, Lincoln Ctr., N.Y., 1993—, Westbeth Gallery, N.Y.C., 1994, Hammond Mus., Salem, N.Y., 1994, Town House Gallery, Stamford, Conn., 2000—, Tower Perrins, Stamford, 2000—02, (represented in archives) Libr. of Performing Arts, Lincoln Ctr., N.Y.C., N.Y.C. Ballet Archives, Nat. Mus. for Women in Arts, Washington, (also in pub. and pvt. collections), U.S., abroad, performing artist (ballets) Alicia Alonso's Nat. Ballet Cuba, Mex., Ctrl. Am., South Am., 1948—50, Apollo, Sleeping Beauty, Pas de Quatre, Ensayo Symphonica, George Balachine's N.Y.C. Ballet, 1950—57, U.S., Can., Europe, Swan Lake, Symphony C, Con Amore, Nutcracker. Recipient numerous awards for sculpture, painting and graphics including Cert. of Merit U.S. Senator-N. Spano, 1989, U.S. State Assemblyman-R. Brodsky, 1989, Letter of Appreciation U.S. Senator Pat Moynihan, 1989, Letter of Congratulations U.S. Congressman -B. Gilman, 1989. Mem. Allied Artist of Am., Hudson River Contemporary Artists, Nat. Mus. for Women in Art, Silvermine Guild of Artists, Scarsdale Art Soc., Stamford Art Assn., Mamaroneck Artists Guild (bd. dirs. assoc. rep. 1990-91, receiving com. 1992). Home: 10 Burkewood Rd Hartsdale NY 10530-2933

MCMASTER, BELLE MILLER, religious organization administrator; b. Atlanta, May 24, 1932; d. Patrick Dwight and Lila (Bonner) Miller; m. George R. McMaster, June 19, 1953; children: Lisa McMaster Stork, George Neel, Patrick Miller. BA, Agnes Scott Coll., 1953; MA, U. Louisville, 1970, PhD, 1974. Assoc. corp. witness Presbyn. Ch. USA, Atlanta, 1974-77, dir. corp. witness, 1977-81, dir. div. corp. and social mission, 1981-87, dir. social justice and peacemaking unit Louisville, 1987-93; acting dir. program women in theology and ministry Candler Sch. Theology Emory U., 1993-96, dir. advanced studies Candler Sch. Theology, 1995—2003. Vice-moderator chs. commn. internat. affairs World Coun. Chs., 1984-91, mem. Justice, Peace and Creation Commn., 1991-99; chair commn. internat. affairs Nat. Coun. Chs., NYC, 1986-89, v.p., 1990-95, chair ch. world svc. and witness unit com., 1990-95, exec. bd., 1990-2003; chair fin. com. Ch. World Svc. and Witness Unit Com., NC, 1997-99, bd. dirs., 1999-2003. Author: Witnessing to the Kingdom, 1982, book columnist "What I Have Been Reading" in Church and Society Magazine, 1993-2001; contbr. articles to profl. jours. Pres. League of Women Voters, Greenville, S.C., 1963-64; bd. dirs. Interfaith Housing, Atlanta, 1975-81. Danforth fellow, 1969-74. Mem.: MLA, Soc. for Values in Higher Edn., Acad. Am. Religion, Phi Beta Kappa. Presbyterian. E-mail: bmcmast@emory.edu.

MCMASTER, JULIET SYLVIA, English language educator; b. Kisumu, Kenya, Aug. 2, 1937; emigrated to Can., 1961, naturalized, 1976; d. Sydney Herbert and Sylvia (Hook) Fazan; m. Rowland McMaster, May 10, 1968; children: Rawdon, Lindsey. BA with honors, Oxford U., 1959; MA, U. Alta., 1963, PhD, 1965. Asst. prof. English U. Alta., Edmonton, Can., 1965-70, assoc. prof., 1970-76, prof. English, 1976-86, Univ. prof., 1986—2000, prof. emeritus, 2000—. Author: Thackeray: The Major Novels, 1971, Jane Austen on Love, 1978, Trollope's Palliser Novels, 1978, (with R.D. McMaster) The Novel from Sterne to James, 1981, Dickens the Designer, 1987, Jane Austen the Novelist, 1995, Reading the Body in the Eighteenth-Century Novel, 2004; co-editor: Jane Austen's Business, 1996, Cambridge Companion to Jane Austen, 1997; gen. editor Juvenilia Press, 1993-2002; illustrator/editor children's picture book: (by Jane Austen) The Beautifull Cassandra, 1993; contbr. articles to profl. jours. Fellow Can. Coun., 1969-70, Guggenheim Found., 1976-77, Killam Found., 1987-89; recipient Molson prize in Humanities for Outstanding Contbn. to Canadian Culture, 1994. Fellow Royal Soc. Can.; mem. Victorian Studies Assn. Western Can. (founding pres. 1972), Assn. Can. Univ. Tchrs. English (pres. 1976-78), MLA, Jane Austen Soc. N.Am. (dir. 1980-91). E-mail: juliet.mcmaster@ualberta.ca.

MCMATH, ELIZABETH MOORE, graphic artist; b. Iredell, Tex., Feb. 20, 1930; d. Fred William and Elizabeth Carol (Smith) Moore; m. Charles Wallis McMath, Jan. 16, 1978 (dec. Dec. 1990); children: Charles Wallis, John Seals. BA, BS in Advt. Design, Tex. Woman's U., Denton, 1951; grad. gemologist, Gemol. Inst. Am., L.A., 1977. Layout artist Leonard's Dept. Store, Ft. Worth, Tex., 1951-52; artist/bookkeeper Bud Biggs Studio, Dallas, 1953; sec./artist Squire Haskins Studio, Dallas, 1953-54; artist/art dir. Dowdell-Merrill, Inc., Dallas, 1954-58; owner/artist Moore Co., Dallas, 1958-90. Mem. Stemmons Corridor Bus. Assn., Dallas, 1988-89. Mem. Dallas/Ft. Worth Soc. Visual Comm. (founder), Tex. Woman's U. Nat. Alumnae Assn., Greater North Tex. Orchid Soc. (treas. 1987), Daylily Growers of Dallas (sec. 1989-90, 1st v.p. and program chmn. 1992), Internat. Bulb Soc., Native Plant Soc. Tex. (publicity chmn. Trinity Forks chpt. 1991-02, pres. 1998, sec. 1999-2001, 2002-03, Elm Fork chpt., master naturalist Tex. 2001-2003), Fort Worth Orchid Soc. Presbyterian. Avocations: ranching, horticulture, plant propagation, lost wax casting, gemstone cutting. Home: PO Box 1068 Denton TX 76202-1068

MCMEEKIN, DOROTHY, botany, plant pathology educator; b. Boston, Feb. 24, 1932; d. Thomas LeRoy and Vera (Crockatt) McM. BA, Wilson Coll., 1953; MA, Wellesley Coll., 1955; PhD, Cornell U., 1959. Asst. prof. Upsala Coll., East Orange, N.J., 1959-64, Bowling Green State U., Ohio, 1964-66; prof. natural sci. Mich. State U., East Lansing, 1966-89, prof. botany, plant pathology, 1989—. Author: Diego Rivera: Science and Creativity, 1985; contbr. articles to profl. jours. Mem. Am. Phytopath. Soc., Mycol. Soc. Am., Soc. Econ. Bot., Mich. Bot. Soc. (former bd. dirs.), Mich. Women's Studies Assn., Sigma Xi, Phi Kappa Phi. Avocations: gardening, sewing, travel, drawing. Home: 1055 Marigold Ave East Lansing MI 48823-5128 Office: Mich State U Dept Botany-Plant Pathology 100 N Kedzie Hall East Lansing MI 48824-1031 E-mail: mcmeekin@msu.edu.

MCMICHAEL, JEANE CASEY, real estate company executive, educator; b. Clarksville, Ind., May 7, 1938; d. Emmett Ward and Carrie Evelyn (Leonard) Casey; m. Norman Kenneth Wenzler, Sept. 12, 1956 (div. 1968); m. Wilburn Arnold McMichael, June 20, 1978. Student Ind. U. Extension Ctr., Bellermine Coll., 1972-73; student, Ind. U. S.E., 1973—, Kentuckiana Metroversity, 1981—; grad. Realtors Inst., Ind. U., 1982. Grad. Leadership Tng., Clark County, Ind.; lic. real estate broker, Ind., Ky.; master Grad. Realtors Inst., Cert. Residential Splst., Cert. Real Estate Broker. Owner, pres., mgr. McMichael Real Estate, Inc., Jeffersonville, 1979-88, 91-98; mgr., owner Buzz Bauer, 1979-88, 88-91; mng. broker Parks & Weisberg Realtors, Jeffersonville, Ind., 1989-96; instr. pre-license real estate Ivy Tech. State Coll., 1995-96, ISTR Real Estate Tng. Concepts, Inc. Pres. congregation St. Mark's United Ch. of Christ, 1996, mem. long range plan and property acquisition, 1996-98; pres. Mr. and Mrs. Class, chmn., fin. trustee, bus. adv., chmn. devel. com., 1993, 94, chmn. com. long range planning, 1997; chmn. bd. trustees Brooklawn Youth Svcs., 1988-95, chmn., 1994-96; bd. dirs. Noah's Ark, Inc., 1998-99, sec./treas., 1999—; chmn. social com. Rep. party Clark County (Ind.); v.p. Floyd County Habitat for Humanity, 1991, 94-95. Recipient cert. of appreciation Nat. Ctr. Citizen Involvement, 1983; award Contact Kentuckiana Teleministries, 1978. Mem. Nat. Assn. Realtors (nat. dir. 1989—), Ind. Assn. Realtors (state dir. 1987—, quick start spkr. 1989-91), Nat. Women's Coun. Realtors (state pres., chmn. coms., state rec. sec. 1984, state prs. 1985-86, Nat. Achievement award 1982, 83, 84, 85, 86, 87, 88, 89, 90, nat. gov. Ind. 1987, v.p. region III 1988, Ind. Honor Realtor award 1982—), Women's Coun. of Realtors (spkr. 1990-94, Mem. of Yr. 1988), Ky. Real Estate Exch., So. Ind. Bd. Realtors (program chmn. 1986-87, bd. dirs., pres. 1988—, Realtor of Yr. 1985, instr. success series 1989-92, Snyder Svc. award 1987, Omega Tau Rho award 1988, excellence in Edn. award 1989), Ind. Assn. Realtors (state dir. 1985—, bd. govs. instr./trainer, spkr. 1989-94, chair bd. govs. 1991), Toastmasters (pres. Steamboat chpt.), Psi Iota Xi. Office: McMichael Properties Inc 23 Arctic Springs Jeffersonville IN 47130-4701

MCMILLAN, ADELL, retired educational administrator; b. Portland, Oreg., June 22, 1933; d. John and Eunice A. (Hoyt) McM. AB in Social Sci., Whitman Coll., 1955; MS in Recreation Mgmt., U. Oreg., 1963. Program dir. Erb Meml. Union, U. Oreg., Eugen, 1955-68; program cons. Willard Straight Hall, Cornell U., Ithaca, N.Y., 1966-67; assoc. dir. Erb Meml. Union, U. Oreg., Eugene, 1968-75, dir., 1975-91, dir. emeritus, 1992—. Editor, co-author: College Unions: Seventy-Five Years, 1989; interviewer, editor oral history interviews, 1978, 92-94, 96; author: A Common Ground--Erb Memorial Union 1950-2000, 2004. Bd. dirs. United Way, Lane County, Oreg., 1976-83, 87-97, 98—,pres., 1982-83, 88-90; commr. Eugene City Planning Commn., 1992—; mem. Hist. Rev. Bd., 1992—; mem. Tree Commn., 1992-93; bd. dirs., treas., 1994-95, Eugene Opera Co., 1992-2000; bd. dirs. Eugene Pub. Libr. Found., 2002—; pres.-elect City Club of Eugene, 2003—. Named Woman of Yr. Lane County Coun. Orgns., Eugene, Oreg., 1985; re-named Erb Meml. Union Art Gallery, U. Oreg. as Adell McMillan Art Gallery, 1998. Mem. Assn. Coll. Unions-Internat. (v.p. 1977-80, pres. 1981-82, Butts-Whiting award 1987, hon. 1992, editor Vets. newsletter, 1993-2000, bd. dirs. 2004—), Zonta Club of Eugene, Zonta Internat. (pres. 1984-86, dist. treas. 1990-92, 92-94), Emerald Valley

Women's Golf Club (pres. 1995). Democrat. Episcopalian. Avocations: golf, reading. Office: 55 W 39th Ave Eugene OR 97405-3344 Office Phone: 541-344-6305. E-mail: adellmcm@darkwing.uoregon.edu.

MCMILLAN, BETTIE BARNEY, English language educator; b. Fayetteville, N.C., Mar. 14, 1941; d. Booker T. and Sarah Estelle (Barney) McM.; children: Gregory L., Kenneth A., Ronald D., Pamela M., Deirdre Y., Michael A. BA in Psychology/Sociology, Meth. Coll., 1978. Program supr. Adminstrv. Office of the Cts.-Guardian Ad Litem Program, Raleigh, N.C.; English instr. Cmty. Coll., Fayetteville, N.C.; info. specialist, case mgr. Big Bros./Big Sisters, Fayetteville. Author: A Plea For Love, 1995, The Language of Love (award of merit 2002), Fires of Passion (Pres. award for literary excellence, Nat. Authors Registry, 2003), (song) Love Is Waiting, 2003, (poems) I Am Love, Language of Love, 2002; contbr. Celebrations of Honor: a collection of poems and essays from around the world, 2003. Leader, nat. officer United Order of Tents, Norfolk, Va., 1982-92; vol. N.C. Guardian Ad Litem, Raleigh, 1992—; mem. Atlanta Com. for Olympic Games, 1996. Recipient Copyright award plaque Copywright award, 1996, Poet Merit award Nat. Libr. Congress, 1995, Shakespeare Trophy of Excellence, 2002, Poet of Yr. Medallion, 2002, Pres. award for Lit. Excellence, 2003. Mem. Internat. Soc. of Poets (Disting. mem., 1995-96, Poets Choice award 1995), Sigma Omega Chi. Baptist. Avocations: reading, writing, literary works, community volunteer, gardening, travel. Home: 5509 Ramshorn Dr Fayetteville NC 28303-2736

MCMILLAN, HELEN BERNEICE, sales executive; b. Huntington, Ark., Jan. 27, 1932; d. James Louis and Edna Lorene (Repass) Harrison; m. James Edward McMillan, May 10, 1950; children: Dianna Kaye Carter, Connie Sue Sadler. BBA, Dallas Bapt. U., 1993. Sewing machine operator Bobbinoak Corp., Fort Smith, Ark., 1949-50; greeting card decorator Hallmark Corp., Leavenworth, Kans., 1950-54; office clk. Sears Roebuck & Co., Lawton, Okla., 1955-57; grocery checker Safeway Grocery, Moberly, Mo., 1957-58; asst. retail mgr. Army & Air Force Exch., Leesville, la., 1962-74, buyer ladieswear Dallas, 1974-90, merchandise mgr. Munich, 1990-93; sales assoc. Hallmark Cards, Grand Prairie, Tex., 1994—. Recipient Achievement award Nat. Assn. Purchasing Mgmt., Dallas, 1988. Mem. NAFE, Fashion Group Internat. Republican. Avocations: doll collecting, ceramics, aerobics, gardening, fashion. Home: 609 Redwood Dr Grand Prairie TX 75052-6734

MCMILLAN, JULIA A. pediatrician; b. Pinehurst, N.C., July 10, 1946; MD, SUNY, Syracuse, 1976. Intern SUNY Upstate Med. Ctr., Syracuse, 1976-77, resident in pediatrics, 1977-78, 79-80, fellow in infectious diseases, 1979-81; mem. staff Johns Hopkins U. Hosp., Balt.; assoc. prof. Johns Hopkins U., Balt., dep. dir., residency program dir., prof., vice-chair med. edn., 1996—; chair. Am. Bd. of Pediatrics, Chapel Hill. Author: Oski's Pediatrics: Principles and Practice, 3d edit., 1999, The Best of the Whole Pediatrician Catalogs, I-III, 1984, The Whole Pediatrician Catalog: A Compendium of Clues to Diagnosis and Management, 1977. Mem. ASM, IDSA, Am. Acad. Pediatrics. Office: Johns Hopkins Hosp Dept Pediatrics 600 N Wolfe St Dept Baltimore MD 21287-0005*

MCMILLAN, MARY BIGELOW, retired minister, volunteer; b. St. Paul, July 30, 1919; d. Charles Henry and Allison (McKibbin) Bigelow; m. Richard McMillan, June 26, 1943; children: Richard Jr., Charles B., Douglas D., M. Allison, Anne E. BA, Vassar Coll., 1941; MDiv, United Theol. Sem. Twin Cities, 1978, DDiv (hon.), 1989. Ordained to ministry Presbyn. Ch., 1978. Asst. min. House of Hope Presbyn. Ch., St. Paul, 1978-82; interim pres. United Theol. Sem. Twin Cities, New Brighton, Minn., 1982-83, ret., 1987. Contb. author: The Good Steward, 1983. Regional dir. Assn. Jr. Leagues, N.Y.C., 1959—61, pres. St. Paul chpt., 1957—59; vice chair Ramsey County Welfare Bd., St. Paul, 1962—66, St. Paul Health and Welfare Planning Coun., 1964—70, F.R. Bigelow Found., St. Paul, 1988—95, also 1st vice chair; 1st vice chair, trustee Wilder Found., 1973—89; active Presbyn. Homes Found., 1996—; trustee Minn. Ch. Found., Mpls., 1984—99, United Theol. Sem. Twin Cities, 1977—89, also chmn. bd. trustees; bd. dirs. Inst. for Ecumenical and Cultural Rsch., Collegeville, Minn., 1982—2003. Recipient award for community planning United Way, 1965, also for yr. round leadership, 1973, Leadership in Community Svc. award YWCA, 1980, Sisterhood award NCCJ, Mpls., 1989; named Disting Alumna award St. Paul Acad. and Summit Sch., 1988 Mem.: Univ. Club, New Century Club. Avocations: golf, knitting, reading. Home: 2925 Lincoln Dr #713 Roseville MN 55113

MCMILLAN, TERRY L. writer, educator; b. Port Huron, Mich., Oct. 18, 1951; d. Edward McMillan and Madeline Washington Tillman; 1 child, Solomon Welch. BA in Journalism, U. Calif., Berkeley, 1979; postgrad., Columbia Univ., N.Y.C., 1979. Instr. U. Wyoming, Laramie, 1987-88; prof. U. Ariz., Tucson, 1988-91. Author: Mama, 1987, Disappearing Acts, 1989, Waiting to Exhale, 1992, How Stella Got Her Groove Back, 1996, A Day Late & A Dollar Short, 2001; editor: Breaking Ice: An Anthropology of Contemporary African-American Fiction, 1990; screenwriter (with Ron Bass) (movies) Waiting to Exhale, 1995, How Stella Got Her Groove Back, 1998. Recipient National Endowment for the Arts fellowship, 1988.

MCMILLEN, SARAH ANNE, marriage and family therapist, adult education educator; b. Salina, Kans., June 17, 1979; d. Dale Alvin and Cherie Louella Knopf; m. Gregory Michael McMillen, July 14, 2001; 1 child, Alexander Xavier. BA in psycho., Kans. Wesleyan U., 1998; MS in counseling psycho., Calif. Bapt. U., 2001. Lic. marriage and family therapist. Clin. program dir. Focus on the Future, Salina, 2002—03; instr. Little House Adult Learning Ctr., Salina, 2002, Cloud County Cmty. Coll., Concordia, Kans., 2003—; clin. psycho. intern Mercy Regional Health Ctr., Manhattan, Kans., 2003—. Exec. dir. interim Focus on the Future, 2002. Mem.: Kans. Assn. of Marriage and Family Therapists (assoc.), Am. Assn. of Marriage and Family Therapists (assoc.). Avocations: painting, motorcycling.

MCMILLER, ANITA WILLIAMS, leasing company executive; b. Chgo., Dec. 23, 1946; d. Chester Leon and Marion Claudette (Martin) Williams; m. Robert Melvin McMiller, July 29, 1967 (div. 1980). BS in Edn., No. Ill. U., 1968; MBA, Fla. Inst. Tech., 1979; M of Mil. Arts and Sci., U.S. Army Command & Gen. Staff Coll., 1990; postgrad., U.S. Army War Coll., Carlisle, Pa., 1993-94. Social worker Cook County, Chgo., 1968-69; recruiter analyst, dir. pers. State of Ill., Chgo., 1969-75; commd. 1st lt. U.S. Army, 1975, advanced through grades to col., 1996; dep. comdr., ops. officer Bremerhaven (Germany) Terminal, Ft. Eustis, Va. and Okinawa; comdr. 1320th Port Batt, 1991-93; comdr. 1320th Port Battalion U.K. Terminal, Felixstowe, Great Britain, 1991-93; dep. legis. asst. to Chmn. Joint Chiefs of Staff The Pentagon, Washington, 1994-98; pres., CEO Trove Internat., 1999—2002; v.p. ATC Leasing, Kenosha, Wis., 1999—; cons. Trove Internat., Washington, 2002—. Instr. Ctrl. Tex. Coll., Hanau, Germany, 1981-83, Phillips Bus. Coll., Alexandria, Va., 1983-84, City Colls. Chgo., 1987-89. Editor: Rocks, Inc. Pictoral Album, 1996, Alpha Kappa Alpha 75th Commemorative Album, 1997; contbr. articles to profl. jours. Child adv., foster mother Army Cmty. Svc., Hanau, 1980-83; tutor Parent-Tchr. Club Hanau Schs., 1981-83; vol. Vis. Nurses Assn. No. Va., 1983-85; coord., English tutor Adopt-a-Sch. Project, Washington, 1983-85; treas. Bremerhaven Girl Scouts Coun., 1987-89; bd. dirs. Project 2000, Boys and Girls Club of Kenosha. Mem.: NAACP, Internat. Coach Fedn., Links, Inc., Nat. Assn. Women Bus. Owners, Nat. Coun. Negro Women, Army Women's Profl. Assn., Internat. Platform Assn., Am. Hist. Assn., Rocks, Inc., Fedn. Bus. Profl. Women, Am. Mgmt. Assn., Assn. for Study Life and History, Am. Soc. for Quality, Assn. U.S. Army, World Affairs Coun., Nat. Def. Transp. Assn. (bd. dirs., v.p.), Army-Navy Club (Washington), Jr. League Washington, Am. Legion, Brit. Legion, Alpha Kappa Alpha. Avocations: skiing, golf, running, historical research. Home: 5127 Heritage Ln Alexandria VA 22311

MCMILLION, MARGARET KIM, foreign service officer; b. New Brighton, Pa., Nov. 4, 1951; d. Theodore M. and Margaret Jane (Houlette) McM. BA, Eisenhower Coll., 1973; MPIA, U. Pitts., 1975; cert., Nat. War Coll., 1990. Analyst, intern Gulf Oil Corp., Pitts., 1974; polit. and consular officer U.S. Embassy, Kigali, Rwanda, 1975-77, consular officer Taipei, Taiwan, 1977-79; travel svcs. officer Am. Inst. in Taiwan, Taipei, 1979; desk officer Office of West African Affairs U.S. Dept. of State, Washington, 1979-81; with tng. dept. Fgn. Svc. Inst., Washington, Rep. of South Africa, 1981-82; polit. officer. tng. dept. U.S. Embassy, Pretoria, Rep. of South Africa, 1982-85; with Thai lang. tng. dept., Washington, 1985-86; prin. officer U.S. Consulate, Udorn, Thailand, 1986—89; asst. dir. Office of Korean Affairs, Udorn, 1990-91; spl. asst. under sec. for polit. affairs U.S. Consulate, Udorn, 1991-92; polit. counselor U.S. Embassy, Bangkok, 1992—95; dep. chief Mission in Vientiane, Laos; dir. Office for Analysis of Africa, Bur. Intelligence and Rsch., 1999—2001; U.S. amb. to Rwanda, 2001—. Presbyterian. Achievements include speaks French, Afrikaans, Thai and Lao. Avocations: swimming, hiking, music, reading. Office: US Mission to Rwanda 377 Blvd de la Revolution Kigali BP 28 Rwanda*

MCMINN, VIRGINIA ANN, human resources consulting company executive; b. Champaign, Ill., Apr. 7, 1948; d. Richard Henry and Esther Lucille (Ellis) Taylor; m. Michael Lee McMinn, Dec. 29, 1973. BA in Teaching of English, U. Ill., 1969; MS in Indsl. Rels., Loyola U., Chgo., 1985. Pers. sec. Solo Cup Co., Urbana, Ill., 1972-74; pers. asst. Rust-Oleum Corp., Evanston, Ill., 1974-75, asst. pers. mgr., 1974-80, mgr. employee rels. Vernon Hills, Ill., 1980-81, mgr. human resources, 1981-84; dir. human resources Field Container Corp., Elk Grove Village, Ill., 1984-87; regional mgr. human resources Hartford Ins. Corp., Chgo., 1987-90; owner, pres. McMinn & Assocs., Ltd., Palatine, Ill., 1988—; founder S.W. Human Resources Group, Chandler, Ariz., 1995. Instr. bus. and mgmt. divsn. Trinity Coll., Deerfield, Ill., 1984-85; instr. bus. and social scis. Harper Coll., Palatine, Ill., 1990-93; bd. dirs. Nierman's Hard-To-Find Sizes Shoes, Chgo., Ariz. SmallBus. Assn.; ptnr. ManagersAdvantage.com, 2002; spkr. in field. Bd. dirs. Ill. Crossroads coun. Girls Scouts USA, Elk Grove, 1988-92, Ariz. Small Bus. Assn., 2004—; mem. Ill. Com. to Implement Clean Indoor Air Act, Chgo., 1990-91; past mem. adv. bd. Coll. of Lake County, 1982-84. Mem. Soc. for Human Resource Mgmt., Nat. Network Sales Profls. (program chmn. 1990-93), Women in Mgmt. (chpt. Leadership award corp. category, past pres.), Ariz. Employers' Coun., Ariz. Small Bus. Assn. Avocations: reading, golf, crafts. Office Phone: 480-726-0343. Business E-Mail: ginny@mcminnhr.com.

MCMORROW, MARGARET MARY (PEG MCMORROW), retired secondary school educator; b. N.Y.C., Dec. 18, 1924; d. Patrick Joseph and Ellen Veronica (Quinn) McIntyre; m. Joseph Patrick McMorrow, Oct. 12, 1948; children: Linda Karen, Robert Michael (dec.), Patrice Ann, Jane Ellen. BS, Queens Coll., 1946; MS in Edn., Hofstra U., 1959. Space controller Am. Airlines Co., N.Y.C., 1946-48; bus. rep. N.Y. Telephone Co., N.Y.C., 1948-52; tchr. Elwood Sch. Dist, Huntington, N.Y., 1965-89, ret., 1989. Fellow Elwood Tchrs. Assn., L.I. Scribes, N.Y. State United Tchrs., Mensa; mem. Elwood Ret. Tchrs. Assn., Alpha Lambda Omicron. Roman Catholic. Avocation: calligraphy.

MCMORROW, MARY ANN G. state supreme court chief justice; b. Chgo., Jan. 16, 1930; m. Emmett J. McMorrow, May 5, 1962; 1 dau., Mary Ann. Student, Rosary Coll., 1948-50; JD, Loyola U., 1953. Bar: Ill. 1953, U.S. Dist. Ct. (7th dist.) Ill. 1960, U.S. Supreme Ct. 1976. Atty. Riordan & Linklater Law Offices, Chgo., 1954—56; asst. state's atty. Cook County, Chgo., 1956-63; sole practice Chgo., 1963-76; judge Cir. Ct. Cook County, 1976-85, Ill. Appellate Ct., 1985-92, Supreme Ct. Ill., 1992—. Faculty adv. Nat. Jud. Coll., U. Nev., 1984. Contbr. articles to profl. jours. Mem. Chgo. Bar Assn., Ill. State Bar Assn., Women's Bar Assn. of Ill. (pres. 1975-76, bd. dirs. 1970-78), Am. Judicature Soc., Northwestern U. Assocs., Ill. Judges Assn., Nat. Assn. Women Judges, Advocates Soc., Northwest Suburban Bar Assn., West Suburban Bar Assn., Loyola Law Alumni Assn. (bd. govs. 1985—), Ill. Judges Assn. (bd. dirs.), Cath. Lawyers Guild (v.p.), The Law Club of the City of Chgo., Inns of Ct. Office: Supreme Ct of Ill 160 N La Salle St Chicago IL 60601-3103

MCMULLEN, JENNIFER ANNE, secondary school educator; b. Abilene, Tex., May 16, 1970; d. Robert Milton McMullen, Sr. and Ouida Anne (Mitchell) McMullen. BA cum laude, Harding U., 1992, MEd, 1994. Tchr. Ctrl. Ark. Christian Sch., North Little Rock, 1994—95; instr. First Class Driving Sch., Bossier City, La., 1995—; tchr. for homebound, hospitalized teenagers Caddo Parish Sch. Bd., Shreveport, La., 2001—; tchr. BASE Ctr., Bossier Parish Sch. Bd., La., 2002—. Mem.: ASCAP, Southern Songwriters Guild (sec.). Avocations: singer, songwriter, musician, youth group support team mem.. Personal E-mail: dixiegarden@aol.com.

MCMULLEN, SHARON JOY ABEL, life coach, marriage and family therapist; b. Peoria, Ill., June 21, 1933; d. Richard Glen Abel and Harriet Bernice Copland; m. David Winston McMullen, Dec. 27, 1956; children: David Paul, Jeniffer Joy. BA, UCLA, 1955; MA in Marriage and Family Therapy, St. Joseph Coll., 1996. Lic. marriage and family therapist, Conn.; life cert. tchr. Calif. Counselor First Ch. of Christ, Wethersfield, Conn., 1996—2003, Stafford Family Svcs., Stafford Springs, Conn., 1996—2003. Vol. staff asst. Master Therapists Workshop Series, U. Conn. Health Ctr., 1996-2003; life coach. Chair counseling task force 1st Ch. of Christ, Wethersfield, 1997-98, co-founder, team tchr. couples ministry, co-facilitator pre-marital workshops, 1997-2002. Mem. Am. Assn. of Marriage and Family Therapists (advocacy com. 1997-98), Calif. Assn. of Marriage and Family Therapists, Am. Assn. of Pastoral Counselors, Am. Assn. of Christian Counselors. Democrat. Avocations: reading, genealogy, gardening, walking. Home: 1755 Vallecito Dr San Pedro CA 90732 E-mail: sm@dmcma.com.

MCMULLIN, JOYCE ANNE, general contractor; b. Tulsa, Jan. 6, 1952; d. Junior Lawrence Patrick and Carol Anne (Morris) McM.; m. David Lawrence Tupper, Jan. 1, 1980 (div. May 1982). BFA, Calif. Coll. Arts and Crafts, 1973. Interior designer Design Assocs., Oakland, Calif., 1974; interior designer, sales rep. Sullivan's Interiors, Berkeley, Calif., 1975; supr. bldg. maintenance Clausen House, Inc., Oakland, 1975-82; owner New Life Renovation, Lafayette, Calif., 1981—; bldg. inspector Contra Costa County, 2002—. Contbr. articles to mags., newspapers. Mem. Contra Costa Coun., Nat. Trust Historic Preservation. Mem. AAUW, Am. Plywood Assn., We. Regional Builders Assn., NAFE, Bus. and Profl. Women, Contra Costa County Women's Network, Self-Employed Tradeswomen (sec. 1984), Contra Costa Coun., Leads Club. Avocations: oil painting, needlework, antique restoration, gardening, travel. E-mail: newliferenovate@prodigy.net.

MCMULLIN, RUTH RONEY, publishing executive, trustee, management fellow; b. N.Y.C., Feb. 9, 1942; d. Richard Thomas and Virginia (Goodwin) Roney; m. Thomas Ryan McMullin, Apr. 27, 1968; 1 child, David Patrick. BA, Conn. Coll., 1963; M Pub. and Pvt. Mgmt., Yale U., 1979. Market rschr. Aviation Week Mag., McGraw-Hill Co., N.Y.C., 1962-64; assoc. editor, bus. mgr. Doubleday & Co., N.Y.C., 1964-66; mgr. Natural History Press, 1967-70; v.p., treas. Weston (Conn.) Woods, Inc., 1970-71; staff assoc. GE, Fairfield, Conn., 1979-82; mng. fin. analyst GECC Transp., Stamford, Conn., 1982—84; credit analyst corp. fin. dept. GECC, Stamford, Conn., 1984-85; sr. v.p. GECC Capital Markets Group, Inc., N.Y.C., 1985-87; exec. v.p., COO, CEO, John Wiley & Sons, N.Y.C., 1987—90, pres., CEO; CEO Harvard Bus. Sch. Pub. Corp., Boston, 1991-94; mem. chmn.'s com., acting CEO UNR Industries Inc., Chgo., 1991-92, also bd. dirs.; mgmt. fellow, vis. prof. Sch. Mgmt. Yale U., New Haven, 1994-95; chairperson trustees Eagle-Picher Personal Injury Settlement Trust, 1996—; chairperson Claims Procesing Facility, Inc., 1998—. Bd. dirs. Bausch & Lomb, Rochester, N.Y.; vis. prof. Sch. Mgmt., Yale U., New Haven, 1994-95. Mem. dean's adv. bd. Sch. Mgmt. Yale U., 1985—92; bd. dirs. Yale U. Alumni fund, 1986—92, Yale U. Press, 1988—99, Math. Scis. Edn. Bd., 1990—93; bd. dirs., treas. Mighty Eighth Air Force Heritage Mus., 2000—03; chmn. Mighty Eighth Found., 2003—; bd. dirs. Savannah Symphony, 1999—2003, The Landings Club, 2002—. Mem. N.Y. Yacht Club, Stamford Yacht Club, Yale Club. Avocations: sailing, skiing, golf, tennis. Home: 8 Breckenridge Ln Savannah GA 31411-1701 Office: Eagle Picher Trust P O box 206 652 Main St Cincinnati OH 45202-2542 E-mail: rrmcmullin@aya.yale.edu.

MCMURRY, IDANELLE SAM, educational consultant; b. Morganfield, Ky., Dec. 6, 1924; d. Sam Anderson and Aurelia Marie (Robertson) McM. BA, Vanderbilt U., 1945, MA, 1946. Tchr. English Abbot Acad., Andover, Mass., 1946-50, Hockaday Sch., Dallas, 1951-54, San Jacinto High Sch., Houston, 1954-55; dean of girls Kinkaid Sch., Houston, 1955-63; headmistress Harpeth Hall Sch., Nashville, 1963-79, Hockaday Sch., Dallas, 1979-89; ret.; now pvt. sch. cons. The Edn. Group, Dallas. Bd. dirs. Ednl. Records Bur., 1979-85, trustee, 1980-85. Bd. dirs. Tex. council Girl Scouts U.S., 1980-82, Town North YMCA; trustee Winston Sch., 1979-85, Spl. Care Sch., 1979-81, Asheville Sch., Manzano Day Sch. Mem. Nat. Study Sch. Evaluation (bd. dirs. 1979-83), Headmasters Assn., Nat. Assn. Ind. Schs. (bd. dirs. 1974-84, acad. com. 1974-79, sec. 1978-80, chmn. 1980-84), So. Assn. Ind. Schs. (pres. 1974-75), Tenn. Assn. Ind. Schs. (pres. 1967-68), Mid-South Assn. Ind. Schs. (pres. 1972-73), Ind. Schs. Assn. S.W. (v.p. 1967—), Nat. Assn. Prins. Schs. for Girls (sec. 1970-72, pres. 1975-77, coun. 1970-79), Nat. Assn. Secondary Sch. Prins., Country Day Sch. Headmasters Assn. (exe. com. 1984-87, v.p. 1988-89), So. Assn. Colls. and Schs. (adminstrv. coun. 1974-77, ctrl. reviewing com. 1972-77, vice chmn. secondary commn. 1975-76, chmn. 1976-77, bd. dirs. 1976-81), Ladies Hermitage Assn., Vanderilt Aid Soc. (sec. 1971-73, pres. 1994-96), Ind. Edn. Svcs. (trustee 1980-88, chmn. 1986-88), Susan Komen Found. (adv. bd.), Belle Meade Club, Centennial Club, Phi Beta Kappa, Pi Beta Phi. Democrat. Presbyterian. Office: 5 Strawberry Hill Nashville TN 37215-4118

MCNABB, CORRINE RADTKE, librarian; b. Detroit, Dec. 18, 1956; d. Eugene R. and Dorothy A. (Dorosz) Radtke; m. Daniel M. McNabb, Oct. 6, 1978; children: Brynne Catherine, Kalen Daniel. BA, Aquinas Coll., 1978; MS, Drexel U., 1982, cert. advanced study, 1997. Cert. tchr., Pa., 1997. Assoc. Nat. Libr. Medicine, Bethesda, Md., 1982-83; dir. libr. svcs. Carbondale (Pa.) Gen. Hosp., 1983-85; libr. dir. Interboro Libr., Peckville, Pa., 1985-86; reference libr. U. Scranton, Pa., 1986-87; libr. Cmty. Med. Ctr., Scranton, 1987-95; elem. libr. Carbondale Area Sch. Dist., 1995-96, Mountain View Sch. Dist., Kingsley, Pa., 1996—; adj. faculty Univ. Scranton, 2002—. Bd. dirs. Carbondale Pub. Libr., 1993—. Mem. ASCD, ALA, Pa. Sch. Librs. Assn. Roman Catholic. Avocations: reading, travel, walking. Home: RR 1 Box 1104 Carbondale PA 18407-9015 Office: Mountain View Elem Libr RR 1 Box 339A Kingsley PA 18826-9778 Office Phone: 570-434-2181. E-mail: santafe13@hotmail.com.

MCNALLY, CONNIE BENSON, magazine editor, publisher, antiques dealer; b. Chgo. d. Peter D. and Joanna Agriosthates; m. Dick Benson, Nov. 19, 1955 (div. mar. 1961); 1 child, Douglas; m. William C. McNally, July 27, 1975. Student, Univ. Wis., 1954-55; BA, Baylor, 1962. Midwest supr. Slenderella Internat., Chgo., 1955-59; dir. John Roberts Powers Sch., Dallas, 1960-62; backgammon tchr., profl. Racquet Club, Palm Springs, Calif., 1969-75, La Costa (Calif.) Resort, 1973-75; antique dealer Palm Springs, 1975—; ptnr. Carriage Trade Antiques, 1975-78; owner, mgr. McNally Co. Antiques, 1978—; editor, pub. Silver Mag., Inc., Rancho Santa Fe, Calif, 1993—. Mem. Am. Assn. Antique Dealers, Antique Dealers Assn. Calif., Country Firends (vol. chair 1985-87, area dir. 1988-89, publicity chair 1990-91, program chair 1992-93, corr. sec. 1994-95, bd. dirs.), Social Svc. League La Jolla, Soc. Am. Silversmiths, Rancho Santa Fe Rep. Women's Club. Avocations: equestrian, gourmet cook. Office: Silver Mag Inc PO Box 9690 Rancho Santa Fe CA 92067-4690

MCNAMARA, ANN DOWD, medical technologist; b. Detroit, Oct. 17, 1924; d. Frank Raymond and Frances Mae (Ayling) Sullivan; m. Thomas Stephen Dowd, Apr. 23, 1949 (dec. 1980); children: Cynthia Dowd Restuccia, Kevin Thomas Dowd; m. Robert A. McNamara, June 15, 1985. BS, Wayne State U., 1947. Med. technologist Woman's Hosp. (now Hutzel Hosp.), Detroit, 1946-52, St. James Clin. Lab., Detroit, 1960-62; supr. histo-pathology lab. Hutzel Hosp., Detroit, 1962-72, Mt. Carmel Mercy Hosp., 1972-87, ret., 1987. Docent Domino's Ctr. Architecture & Design, Ann Arbor, Mich. 1988. Mem. Am. Soc. Clin. Pathologists, Am. Soc. Med. Technology, Mich. Soc. Med. Technology, Nat. Soc. Histotechnology, Mich. Soc. Histotechnologists, Wayne State U. Alumni Assn., Smithsonian Assos., Detroit Inst. Arts Founders Soc. Home: 2488 Signature Dr Pinckney MI 48169

MCNAMARA, ANNE H. lawyer, corporate executive; b. Shanghai, Republic of China, Oct. 18, 1947; came to U.S. 1949; d. John M. and Marion P. (Murphy) H. AB, Vassar Coll., 1969; JD, Cornell U., 1973. Bar: N.Y. 1973, Tex. 1981. Assoc. Shea, Gould, Climenko & Casey, N.Y.C., 1972-76; from asst. corp. sec. to corp. sec. Am. Airlines, Inc., Dallas, 1976-88, v.p. pers. resources, 1988; sr. v.p., gen. counsel Am. Airlines (AMR Corp.), Dallas, 1988—. Bd. dirs. Louisville Gas & Electric Co., LG&E Energy Corp., Sabre Group Holdings, Inc. Office: Am Airlines Inc Dallas/Fort Worth Airport PO Box 619616 Dallas TX 75261-9616

MCNAMARA, BRENDA NORMA, secondary school educator; b. Blackpool, Lancashire, Eng., Aug. 8, 1945; arrived in U.S., 1946; d. Milford Hampson and Nola (Welsby) Jones; m. Michael James McNamara, July 19, 1969. BA in History, Calif. State U., Long Beach, 1967; postgrad., Calif. State U., various campuses, 1967—. Cert. secondary tchr. and lang. devel. specialist Calif. Tchr. history West HS, Torrance, Calif., 1968—, dept. chair, 1989-99, 2000—. Cons. Golden State Exam. in History Calif. State Dept. Edn., 1998; state del. NEA Annual Meeting, 2000, 02, local del., 03; cons. in field. Co-author: (book) World History, 1988. Western Internat. Studies Consortium grantee, 1988. Mem.: NEA, Am. Hist. Assn., Nat. Coun. Social Studies, So. Calif. Coun. Social Studies, Torrance Tchrs. Assn. (bd. dirs. 1992—), Calif. Coun. Social Studies, Calif. Tchrs. Assn. Avocations: travel, theater, mystery reading, gourmet cooking. Office: West H S 20401 Victor St Torrance CA 90503-2255

MCNAMARA, JULIA MARY, academic administrator, foreign language educator; b. N.Y.C., Dec. 13, 1941; d. John P. and Julia (Dowd) McNamara. BA in History and French, Ohio Dominican Coll., 1965; MA in French, Middlebury Coll., 1972; MPhil, Yale U., PhD in French Lang. and Lit., 1980; DHL (hon.), Sacred Heart U., Hamden, Conn., 1984. Mem. faculty St. William Sch., Pitts., 1963-64, Holy Spirit Sch., Columbus, Ohio, 1964-65, Newark (Ohio) Cath. High Sch., 1965-66, Northwest Cath. High Sch., West Hartford, Conn., 1966-69, St. Vincent Ferrer High Sch., N.Y.C., 1969-70, St. Mary's High Sch., New Haven, 1971-74; lectr. french Albertus Magnus Coll., New Haven, 1976-80, dean of students, 1980-82, acting pres., 1982-83, pres., 1983—. Prof. French Albertus Magnus Coll., 1981—; mem. Conn. Health and Edn. Facilities Authority, Hartford, 1983—; chair Conn. Conf. Ind. Colls., Hartford, 1990-92, sec.-treas. 1986—, chmn., 1990-92; lectr. in field; assoc. fellow Yale U., Morse Coll.; bd. dirs. New

Haven Savs. Bank. Chairperson United Way Greater New Haven, 1987; bd. dirs. St. Mary's High Sch., New Haven, 1982-91, ARC, New Haven Savs. Bank, 1990—; trustee Yale-New Haven Hosp., 1984— (chair med. com., 1989-91 vice chair bd., 1991-), chair, Yale-New Haven Health Sys.; adv. bd. Bank of Boston-Conn., 1983-87; adv. com. Jr. League Greater New Haven, 1985; trustee Hartford Sem., 1985-91. Fulbright fellow, Paris, 1977-78; Yale U. fellow, 1971-70, Am. Council on Edn. fellow, 1981; recipient Disting. Woman in Leadership award New Haven YWCA, 1984, Veritas award Providence Coll., 1987, Greater New Haven Jr. Achievement Ann. award, 1990. Mem. Fulbright Alumni Assn., New Haven C. of C. (bd. dirs. 1984-90), New England Assn. Schs. and Colls. (appeals bd. 1986-88). Roman Catholic. Office: Albertus Magnus Coll Office of the President 700 Prospect St New Haven CT 06511-1224*

MCNAMARA, MARGARET M. pediatrician; MD, U. Conn., 1990. Diplomate Am. Bd. Pediatrics. Resident in pediatrics U. Calif., San Francisco; chief of pediatrics U. Calif. San Francisco/Mount Zion Pediatric Practice, San Francisco. Office: UCSF Mount Zion Pediat Practice 2330 Post St Ste 320 San Francisco CA 94115-3466

MCNAMARA, MARY E. nonprofit executive, asset manager, minister; b. Mpls., Dec. 18, 1943; d. Edward Emmanuel and Gladys Theresa (Mattson) Bjorklund; m. Peter Alexander McNamara II (div.); children: Peter Alexander III, Nathaniel Paul. BA, Carleton Coll., 1965; MDiv, Harvard U., 1968. Cert. fin. planner. Program dir. St. Peter's Ch., N.Y.C., 1968-72, program dir., dep. exec., 1977-80; program dir. Ctr. Ch. on-the-Green, N.Y.C., 1972-74; program developer Westminster Presbyn. Ch., Springfield, Ill., 1974-77; assoc. Gen. Assembly Coun. Presbyn. Ch. (USA), N.Y.C., 1980—86; dir. not-for-profit sector City of N.Y., 1986—90; pres., exec. dir. Interchurch Ctr., N.Y.C., 1990-99; exec. v.p. Union Theol. Sem., N.Y.C., 1999—. V.p. Pathways for Youth, Bronx, NY, 1987—96; pres. Morningside Area Alliance, N.Y.C., 1991—98; parish assoc. Fifth Ave. Presbyn. Ch., 1998—2002. Moderator Presbyn. N.Y.C., 1995—96, chair com. on ministry, 1992—95, chair implementation task force, 1996—98; chmn. bd. dirs. exec. com. Presbyn. Conf. Ctr., Stony Point, 1996—2002; bd. dirs. Union Theol. Sem., 1996—99, Blanton/Peale Inst. on Religion and Health, 1994—2001, Wartburg Adult Care Cmty., 1999—, chair elect, 2001—03, chair, 2003—, chmn. pers. com., exec. com., 2001—03. Home: 99 Claremont Ave Apt 621 New York NY 10027-5711 Office: Union Theol Sem 3041 Broadway New York NY 10027-5710

MCNAMARA-RINGEWALD, MARY ANN THÉRÈSE, artist, educator; b. Hempstead, N.Y., Apr. 11, 1935; d. William George Schlichtig and Alice Agnes Rakeman; m. Raymond Anthony McNamara, Apr. 22, 1957 (div. Sept. 1975); children: Thomas William, Raymond Gerard, William Daniel, Peter Joseph, James Francis Jude; m. John Drew Ringewald, Feb. 17, 1984. BS, Fordham U., 1957, Barbizon Sch., NYC, 1953; M in Studio Arts, Adelphi U., 1972; postgrad., Parsons Sch. Design, 1973-75; student, Art Students League, N.Y.C., 1973-74; postgrad., Goddard Coll., Calif., 1986-87; student, Progoff Intensive Jour. Program, N.Y.C., 1999—, Cape Cod Sch., 1993. Cert. elem. edn. and art N.Y. Elem. sch. art tchr. Dept. Edn., Freeport, N.Y., 1957-58, Farmingdale, NY, 1967; jr. and h.s. art tchr. Massapequa (N.Y.) Sch. Dist., 1970-90; owner, pres. South Shore Creative Arts Ctr., Massapequa, 1975; pvt. art tchr. various locations, 1970-90. Illustrator Doubleday, Inc., N.Y.C.; art advisory bd. Chesapeake Coll, Wye Mills, Md., 1995— (lectr., 1998, 99, 2000), Snow Princess, Fordham U., 1954; symposium coord. Hofstra U., N.Y.; lectr. Naples Philharm., 1992; judge, lectr. in field; architectural designer, M.E, 1977, M.D., 1988-, F.L., 1990. One-woman shows include Fordham U., 1954, Andonia Gallery, Massepequa, N.Y., 1974, Isis Gallery, Islip, N.Y., 1974, For the Birds, Salisbury, Conn., 1978, Harguen Gallery, Pt. Jefferson, N.Y., 1979, Adelphi U., Garden City, N.Y., 1992, Wohlfarth Gallery, Washington, 1994-95, SpanBauer Gallery Naples, Fla., 1996, Naples Philharmonic, Naples, Fla., 1992, Gallery 44, Millbrook, N.Y., 1997-98; groups shows: Acad. of Arts, Easton, Md., 1993. works exhibited at Kennedy Gallery, Key West, Fla., 1997-99, Chesapeake Coll., Md., 1998-99; represented in pvt. collections General Motors, The Benedictines, Prudential Life, St. Michael's Maritime Mus., Yupo Corp., Japan; illustrator: From a Lighthouse Window, Chesapeake Bay Maritime Mus., 1992 (Best of Balt. Book award 1993, Book award Tabasco N.Y.C. 1994); original poetry published. Pres. AAUW, L.I., 1969-71; bd. dirs. L.I. (N.Y.) Art Tchrs. Assn., 1973-76; docent U.S. Fish and Wildlife Svc., Washington, 1994-95; mem. Am. Farmland Trust; vol. Delmarva Chpt., ARC, 2001-. Recipient Nat. Middle Sch. Art Tchrs. award, Nassau County Middle Sch. Art Tchrs. Assn., 1988, Very Spl. Arts Festival for Handicapped, 1977, Festival of Creation, Diocese of RVC, 1975, Catalyst, 1975; named to Outstanding Young Women of Am., 1969; works featured in Nat. Anthology of Poetry, 1953. Mem. Internat. Welcome Fla. Assn. Series (lectr. 1994—), Nat. League Am. Pen Women (founder, pres. Naples, Fla. br. 1995—), Nat. Gallery Art (copyist 1993—), Order of the Benedictines (oblate 1990—), Working Artists Forum (Easton, Md.), NY State Art Tchrs. Assn. (bd. mem. 1972-80). Roman Catholic. Avocations: horticulture, travel, illuminations, music, poetry. Address: Marafour 5493 Anderby Dr Royal Oak MD 21662 Office: Marafour Studio 27098 Del Ln Bonita Springs FL 34135-4409

MCNAMEE, SISTER CATHERINE, theology studies educator; b. Troy, N.Y., Nov. 13, 1931; d. Thomas Ignatius McNamee and Kathryn McNamee Marois. BA, Coll. of St. Rose, 1953, DHL (hon.), 1975; MEd, Boston Coll., 1955, MA, 1958; PhD, U. Madrid, 1967. Grad. asst. Boston Coll., 1954-55; asst. registrar Boston Coll. (Grad. Sch.), 1955-57; mem. faculty Coll. St. Rose, Albany, N.Y., 1960-65, acad. v.p., 1968-75; dir. liberal arts Thomas Edison Coll., Trenton, 1975-76; pres. Trinity Coll., Burlington, Vt., 1976-79, Coll. St. Catherine, St. Paul, 1979-84; dean Dexter Hanley Coll., U. Scranton, Pa., 1984-86; pres. Nat. Cath. Ednl. Assn., Washington, 1986-96; sr. scholar Ctr. for Cath. Studies, U. St. Thomas, St. Paul, Minn., 1996-2000; prof. U. Catolica, Talca, Chile, 2000—. Bd. dirs. Am. Forum for Global Edn. Trustee assoc. Boston Coll. Spanish Govt. grantee, 1965-67; OAS grantee, 1967-68; Fulbright grantee, 1972-73 Mem. Inter-Am. Confedn. Cath. Edn., Internat. Orgn. Cath. Edn., Nat. Cath. Ednl. Assn., Internat. Fedn. Cath. Univs., Delta Epsilon Sigma. Roman Catholic. Home: Casilla 712 Talca Chile E-mail: cmncsj@chilesat.net.

MCNAMEE, LINDA ROSE, broadcast executive; b. Holyoke, Mass., Oct. 1, 1969; d. Robert Dean and Jacqueline Marguerite Mashia. BA, Smith Coll., 1991; CSS, Harvard U., 2002. Cert. elem. tchr. level 1-6 Mass., FCC restricted radiotelephone operator permit. Instr. Learning Skills, Inc., Northampton, Mass., 1991-92; traffic asst. Sta. WGBY-TV, Springfield, Mass., 1992-93, air/traffic contr., 1993-94, asst. dir. broadcast ops., 1994-95; learning resources coord. Sta. WXEL-TV, West Palm Beach, Fla., 1995-96, ops. mgr., 1996-97, dir. ops., 1997; broadcasting coord. Sta. WGBH-TV, Boston, 1997-2000, traffic supr., 2000—03, devel. coord., 2003—. Mem. PBS Traffic Adv. Com., Alexandria, 1998—2001, vice chmn., 2000—01, mem., 2003. Dist. com. mem. Squanto dist. Boy Scouts Am., Brockton, Mass., 1997—99, Knox Trail Coun., 2000—; assoc. advisor Stoughton (Mass.) Police Explorer Post # 57, 1998—2000, Newton (Mass.) Police Explorer Post # 300, 1999—2001, Emergency Svcs. Post # 525, Waltham, Mass., 2001—; dir. Children's Handbell Choir, 1998—2003. Home: 5 Manning St Burlington MA 01803- Office: Sta WGBH 125 Western Ave Boston MA 02134-1008 Fax: 617-300-1022. E-mail: linda_mcnamee@wgbh.org.

MCNANAMY, EVE WEEKS, clinical psychologist, marriage therapist; b. N.Y.C., Feb. 14, 1933; BEd, U. Miami, 1957, MEd, 1958, PhD in Clin. Psychology, 1966. Lic. clin. psychologist and marriage and family therapist, Fla. Practicum in counseling and psychotherapy dept. medicine U. Miami, Fla., 1959-60; psycho. counselor Lighthouse for the Blind, Miami, 1960-61; clin. intern Jackson Meml. Hosp., Miami, 1961-62; psychol. counselor Bascom-Palmer Eye Inst., Miami, 1962-64; staff psychologist Long Term Illness Project, Miami, 1964-65; clin. psychologist Jackson Meml. Hosp., Miami, 1965-66; comty. programs dir. Mental Health Assn., Miami, 1965-67; psychologist Children's Psychiat. Ctr., Miami, 1967-68, Maxine Baker Mental Health Clinic, Miami, 1966-69, pvt. practice as psychologist Miami, 1968—. Mem. med. staff Health South Larkin Hosp., Health South Dr.'s Hosp., Harborview Hosp., Grant Ctr. Deering Hosp., Former Homestead Air Force Base Hosp., Charter Hosp. Miami, South Miami Hosp., Miami Children's Hosp. Miami, Bapt. Hosp. Mem. advocate program AAUW, Miami; active Big Sisters of Miami, Ednl. Guidance Svc., Inc., Jr. League Miami, Miami Palmetto Sr. H.S. Feeder Sys., Protestant Social Svcs. Seagull Orientation, Rec. for Blind and Dyslexic, Miami, South Dade Mental Health Found., Women's Alcoholic Edn. Ctr.; counselor, cystic fibrosis and multiple sclerocis clinics, Baptist Health. Recipient Presdl. award for svc. to Com. of Total Employment, 1967, Haddassah Myrtle Wreath award for outstanding comty. svc. in mental health field, 1965, Comty. Headliner's award Women in Comms., 1983, Women of Yr. award Am. Cancer Soc., 1989, Trailblazer's award Women's Com. of One Hundred, 1992, Women of Yr. award Comty. Coalition for Women's History, 1992; grantee Fla. Coun. Tng. and Rsch. in Mental Health, 1957-63; scholar U. Miami, 1957-66; Marsdon Found. fellow for outstanding student in psychology, 1958-62. Fellow Internat. Coun. Sex Edn. and Parenthood, Am. Orthopsychiat. Assn.; mem. APA, Am. Assn. for Marriage and Family Therapy, Am. Soc. Adolescent Psychiatry, Nat. Vocat. Rehab. Assn., Coun. for Exceptional Children, Southeastern Psychol. Assn., Fla. Soc. Clin. Hypnosis, South Fla. Vocat. Rehab. Assn., Dade County Psychol. Assn., South Dade C. of C., Greater South Miami C. of C., Zonta Club Coral Gables. Avocations: attending opera and plays, walking, swimming, reading. Office: PO Box 560458 Miami FL 33256-0458

MCNEELY, BONNIE L. (K.W. ROWE JR.), retired internist and educator; b. Cin., Nov. 26, 1930; d. William Vernuel and Lydia LaBelle McNeely; m. Kenneth Wyer Rowe, Jr., Sept. 18, 1969; children: Christopher, Amy, Gregory, Laurel. BS, U. Cin., 1952, MD, 1956. Intern Cin. Gen. Hosp., 1956-57, resident in surgery, 1957-58, resident in internal medicine, 1958-60, fellow in cardiology, 1960-61; mem. faculty, dir. med. ctr. health svc. U. Cin. Coll. Medicine, 1961-88; dir. pers. health and employee health svcs. Conemaugh Meml. Med. Ctr., Johnstown, Pa., 1989-97; ret., 1997. Elder, Seventh Presbyn. Ch., Cin. Mem.: Ohio Med. Assn. Republican. Avocations: carpentry, outdoor activities, reading, stamp collecting, gardening.

MCNEELY, DELORES, banker; b. Ft. Bragg, N.C., Dec. 28, 1949; d. Rayfield O. and Ann Gloria Ozier; m. James Leon Bell, Sept. 21, 1968 (div. June 1986); 1 child, Jeffrey Demarco; m. Robert Arthur McNeely, June 25, 1988. Human resources cert., San Diego State U., 1984; cert. in banking, Pacific Coast Banking Sch., 1997. From mgmt. trainee to sr. v.p. Union Bank of Calif., San Diego, 1972—. Chief of staff San Diego Urban Bankers, 1989-99, pres. 1993-94; mem. Econ. Devel. task force, 1993. Home: 922 Cordova St San Diego CA 92107-4224 Office: Union Bank of Calif 530 B St Ste 1610 San Diego CA 92101-4410

MCNEELY, JUANITA, artist; b. St. Louis; d. Robert Hunt and Alta B. (Green) McN.; m. Jeremy Lebensohn, Mar., 1982. BFA, Washington U. St. Louis, 1959; MFA, So. Ill. U., 1964. Prof. figure drawing So. Ill. U., Carbondale, 1962-64; prof. drawing Chgo. Art Inst., 1964-65; prof. drawing and painting Western Ill. U., Macomb, 1965-67; prof. painting Suffolk (N.Y.) Coll., 1969-82; artist, 1959—; art tchr., 1962—. Adj. prof. painting Parsons Sch. Art, N.Y.C., NYU; artist-judge art exhbn. White House, Washington, 1994; art judge, spkr. Very Spl. Arts, Washington, 1990-96. One-person shows include Elaine Benson Gallery, Bridgehampton, L.I., N.Y., 1994; represented in print and painting collections Nat. Mus. Art, Taipei, Taiwan, Palacio de Las Bellas Artes, Mexico City, Oakleigh Collection, Boston, Bryn Mawr Coll., and others; represented in galleries Evelyn Amis Gallery, Can., 1980-84, Soho 20 Gallery, N.Y.C., 1980-82, Prince St. Gallery, N.Y.C., 1970-80; included in books, including Self Portrait by Women Painters. Named to honor roll, Veteran Feminists Am., 2003. Studio: 463 West St New York NY 10014-2010

MCNEELY, PATRICIA GANTT, journalism educator; b. Winnsboro, S.C., Dec. 2, 1939; d. William Adolphus and Alice (Woodson) Gantt; m. Alfred Raymond McNeely, Apr. 8, 1960; children: Allison Patricia, Alan David. BA, Furman U., 1960; MA, U. S.C., 1975. Reporter Greenville (S.C.) News, 1958-60, Columbia (S.C.) Record, 1960-66, 66-72, news editor, 1979-80; reporter The State, Columbia, 1965-66; prof. journalism U. S.C., Columbia, 1972—, Eleanor M. and R. Frank Mundy prof. of journalism, 2000—, dir. print and electronic sequence, 2000—. State mgr. Voter News Svc., N.Y., 1972—; workshop dir. Reader's Digest, Pleasantville, N.Y., 1985—. Mem. Assn. for Edn. in Journalism and Mass Comm. (sec. mag. divsn. 1995-96, head newspaper divsn. 1988-89, standing profl. freedom and responsibility com. 1995-98). Office: Univ SC Coll Journalism Mass Comm Blossom At Assembly Sts Columbia SC 29208-0001

MCNEES, PAT (PATRICIA ANN MCNEES), writer, editor; b. Riverside, Calif., Jan. 30, 1940; d. Glenn Harold and Eleanor Maxine (McCoskrie) McN.; m. Anthony V. Mancini, Apr. 22, 1967 (div. 1978), 1 child, Romana Mancini. BA, UCLA, 1961; postgrad., Stanford U., 1961-63. Instr. English Stanford U., Palo Alto, Calif., 1962-63; assoc. editor Harper & Row, N.Y.C., 1963-66; editor Fawcett Publishers, N.Y.C., 1966-70; ind. writer and editor N.Y.C., Washington, 1970—. Cons. clients include World Bank 1987—, UN, Rockefeller Found., Nat. Sci. Found., NIH. Author: Dancing: A Guide to the Capital Area, 1987, An American Biography: An Industrialist Remembers the 20th Century, 1995, By Design, 1997, YPO: The First 50 Years, 2000, New Formulas for America's Workforce: Girls in Science, and Engineering, 2003, Building Ten at Fifty: 50 Years of Clinical Research at the NIH Clinical Center, 2003; editor: (anthologies) Contemporary Latin American Short Stories, 1974, Dying: A Book of Comfort, 1996; contbr. articles to mags. including New York Mag., Washington Post. Mem. Am. Soc. Journalists and Authors, Authors Guild, PEN, Nat. Assn. Sci. Writers. Avocations: dance, cooking. E-mail: pmcnees@nasw.org.

MCNEIL, BARBARA JOYCE, radiologist, educator; b. Cambridge, Mass., Feb. 11, 1941; d. Archibald Pius and Katherine (Joyce) McNeil. AB, Emmanuel Coll., 1962; MD, Harvard U., 1966, PhD, 1972. Diplomate Am. Bd. Nuc. Medicine. Intern Mass. Gen. Hosp., Boston, 1966—67, resident in nuclear medicine, 1971—73; prof. radiology and clin. epidemiology Harvard Med. Sch. and Brigham & Women's Hosp., Boston, 1983—, dir. ctr. for cost effective care, 1980—93; chmn. dept., Ridley Watts prof. health care policy Harvard Med. Sch., 1988—. Chmn. Blue Cross-Mass. Hosp. Assn. Fund for Coop. Innovation, 1981—87; mem. Prospective Payment Assessment Commn., 1983—91; mem. nat. adv. coun. Agy. for Health Care Policy, Rsch. and Evaluation, 1991—96. Editor: Critical Issues in Medical Technology, 1982; contbr. articles to profl. jours. Fellow: AAAS, Am. Coll. Nuc. Physicians (Presdl. award 1995); mem.: Soc. Nuc. Medicine, Am. Coll. Radiology, Inst. Medicine (coun. 1991—), Am. Acad. Arts and Scis. Office: Harvard Med Sch Dept Health Care Policy 180 Longwood AveRm 202-A Boston MA 02115-5821

MCNEIL, LORI MICHELLE, professional tennis player; b. San Diego, Dec. 18, 1963; d. Charlie Mc. Student, Okla. State U., 1981-83. 8th ranked woman USTA; winner mixed doubles (with Jorge Lozano) French Open, 1988; now ranked 101st USTA, 1999. Achievements include Pro Tour Singles titles such as Colorado Classic, 1992, Japan Open, 1992. Office: US Tennis Assn 70 W Red Oak Ln White Plains NY 10604-3602

MCNEIL, SUE, transportation system educator; b. Newcastle, Australia, June 17, 1955; d. George Peers and Norma (Avard) McGeachie; m. John Franklin McNeil, Dec. 4, 1976; children: Sarah, Emily. BS, U. Newcastle, Newcastle, Australia, 1976; B.E., U. Newcastle, 1978; MS, Carnegie Mellon U., 1981, PhD, 1983. Registered profl. engr., N.J. Asst. works engr. N.S.W. Dept. Main Rds., Singleton, Australia, 1977-79; transp. engr. Garmen Assocs., Montville, N.J., 1983-84; vis. lectr. Princeton U., Princeton, N.J., 1984-85; asst. prof. MIT, Cambridge, Mass., 1985-87, Carnegie Mellon U., Pitts., 1988-90, assoc. prof. to prof., 1990—2000; dir. The Brownfields Ctr., Mellon U. Carnegie, 1998—2000; dir. Urban Transp. Ctr. U. Ill., Chgo.; prof. Coll. Urban Planning and Pub. Affairs, 2000—. Assoc. editor Jour. Infrastructure Sys.; contbr. articles to profl. jours. Doctoral dissertation fellow AAUW, 1982-83; named Presdl. Young Investigator, NSF, 1987-92. Mem.: ASCE (chmn. facilities mgmt. com. 1988—94), Transp. Rsch. Bd. (exec. com. 2004—), INFORMS (assoc.), Inst. Transp. Engrs. (assoc.). Office: U Ill Urban Transp Ctr MC357 412 S Peoria St Ste 340 Chicago IL 60607-7063 Office Phone: 312-996-9818.

MCNEILL, MAXINE CURRIE, county official; b. Rockingham, N.C., Oct. 17, 1934; d. Daniel Franklin and Lollie Mae (Davis) Currie; m. James Albert McNeill, May 5, 1956; children: James C., David A., Jon S., Ellen F. BSN, Wingate Coll., 1986; MPH, U. N.C., 1991. Cert. nurse practitioner; cert. in women's ambulatory health care. Dir. nursing svc., Hamlet, N.C., 1967-69; sch. nurse Rockingham, N.C., 1970-72; dir. Richmond County Home Health Agy., Rockingham, 1972-74; pub. health nurse Scotland County Health Dept., Laurinburg, N.C., 1974-75, nurse practitioner, 1975-79, Laurinburg Surg. Clinic, 1979-80; nursing supr. Scotland Count Health Dept., Laurinburg, 1980-82, Richmond County Health Dept., Rockingham, N.C., 1982-88; local health dir. Montgomery County Health Dept., Troy, N.C., 1988-92; nurse practitioner Richmond OBGYN, Rockingham, N.C., 1992-93, Bladen County Health Dept., 1993-95; dir. daily ops. St. Joseph Home Health Agy., Troy, N.C., 1995-96; nurse practitioner Health Care Connections, Raeford, NC, 2001—02. Staff nurse, relief supr. Richmond Meml. Hosp., Rockingham, N.C., 1955-67; mem. Maternal-Health Liason Com., 1990-91, N.C. State Pers. Liason Com., 1990-91. Mem. ANA, N.C. Nurses Assn. (disting. achievement award dist. V 1986), N.C. Pub. Health Assn. (dist. 12), N.C. Assn. Local Health Dirs., N.C. Dist. V Perinatal Assn., Kiwanis, Sigma Theta Tau. Democrat. Presbyterian. Avocations: reading, boating, dance, needlework, friends. Home: 5080 Woodrun On Tillery Mount Gilead NC 27306-9550 E-mail: maxinecm@carolina.net.

MCNEILL, SUSAN, real estate marketing and sales professional; b. Prescott, Ariz., Feb. 26, 1936; d. Glenn S. and Alma Johnson Hunter; m. Richard G. Bryant, Dec. 19,1 956 (div. Apr. 1971); children: Robert (dec.), Kathleen; m. Kenneth I. McNeill, Nov. 23, 1972; 1 child, John. BA, U. Ariz., 1957. Real estate owner Seaview Properties, Palos Verdes, Calif., 1978-82; real estate mktg. staff Coldwell Banker, Palos Verdes, 1982-99, Summit Group, Palos Verdes, 1999-2000, ReMax, Palos Verdes, 2001—. Art tchr., dir. Arts Unlimited Chadwick Sch., Palos Verdes, 1982-90; owner Bright Ideas, Palos Verdes, 1982—; founder Art At Your Fingertips, Palos Verdes. Bd. dirs. Norris Theater, Palos Verdes C. of C. Recipient Cmty. Svc. award City of L.A., 1993; named Palos Verdes Citizen of Yr., 2000. Mem. Palos Verdes Arts Ctr. (bd. dirs., exhbn. curator). Home: 32735 Seagate Dr Palos Verdes Peninsula CA 90275-5886 also: PO Box 2370 Palos Verdes Peninsula CA 90274-8370 Office: 63 Malaga Cove Plz Palos Verdes Estates CA 90274

MCNEILL-MURRAY, JOAN REAGIN, volunteer consultant; b. Atlanta, July 8, 1936; d. Arthur Edward and Annie May (Busby) Reagin; children: Thomas Pinckney, Clyde Reagin. Student, U. Louisville, 1955-57; BA, U. Tenn., Chattanooga, 1976; D of Music Mgmt. (hon.), Kharkov Philharm. Inst. Music, 2002. Founding pres. Family and Children's Svcs. Assocs., Chattanooga, 1987-88, bd. dirs., 1996—; bd. dirs. Chattanooga Symphony and Opera Assn., 1984-88, 99—, pres., 1984-87; pres. Chattanooga Ballet Assn., 1986-88; bd. dirs. U. Chattanooga Found., 1986-89, A.I.M. Ctr. of Chattanooga, 1997—, Eos Orch., N.Y.C., 1998—; v.p. devel. Chattanooga Cares, 1997—; chair Spl. needs and Svcs. for the Elderly of Chattanooga, 1997—; mem. bd. dirs. Hosanna House, 2001—; mem. vol. coun. bd. dirs. Am. Symphony Orch. League, Washington, 1986-96; pres.-elect, 1992-93, pres., 1993-95; bd. dirs. Hosanna House of Chattanooga, pres., 2002-2003; chmn. new millenium internat. conducting competition Kharkov (Ukraine) Philharm., 2002-, Vakhtang Jordania Music Found., 2002-. Recipient Outstanding Svc. award U. Tenn., Chattanooga, 1988; named Chattanooga's Disting. Woman, 1999. Mem. U. Tenn. Chattanooga Alumni Assn. (pres. 1985-86), Golden Key, Order of Omega, Sigma Kappa Found. (trustee 1992-98, sec. 1993-94, pres. 1994-98, Colby award for volunteerism 1990). Republican. Episcopalian. Office: 7457 Preston Cir Chattanooga TN 37421-1839 E-mail: clownjoni@aol.com.

MCNEIL STAUDENMAIER, HEIDI LORETTA, lawyer; b. Preston, Iowa, Apr. 7, 1959; d. Archie Hugo and Heidi (Waltert) McN.; m. L. William Staudenmaier III; children: Kathleen Louise McNeil Staudenmaier, Jacob William Staudenmaier. BA in Journalism and Broadcasting with distinction, U. Iowa, 1981, JD with distinction, 1985. Bar: Ariz. 1985, U.S. Dist. Ct. Ariz. 1985, U.S. Ct. Appeals (9th cir.) 1985, U.S. Ct. Appeals (10th cir.) 1990. Sports journalist The Daily Iowan, Iowa City, 1977-81, Quad City Times, Davenport, Iowa, 1981-82; ptnr. Snell & Wilmer, Phoenix, 1985—. Judge pro tem, Maricopa County, Phoenix, 1992—, Ariz. Ct. Appeals, 1998—. Mem. ABA (mem. domestic violence commn. 1995-98, Ho. of Dels. 1995-98, 2001—, chair young lawyers career issues com. 1992-93, mem. affiliate assistance program com. 1992-93, dir. 1993-94, spl. projects coord. 1994-95, bus. law sect., editor-in-chief Bus. Law Today, co-chair fellows program), Internat. Assn. Gaming Attys., Internat. Masters of Gaming Law (prs. 2003), Ariz. Bar Assn. (Indian law sect. exec. coun. and chair, 1995-99, young lawyers exec. coun. 1991-94), Maricopa County Bar Assn. (bd. dirs. 1991—, young lawyers divsn. 1987-93, pres. 1991-92, 99-2000), Ariz. Women Lawyers, Phoenix Assn. Def. Counsel, Native Am. Bar Assocs., Phi Beta Kappa, Phi Eta Sigma. Lutheran. Avocations: running, golf, skiing, hiking, bicycling.

MCNELIS, KATHLEEN ANN, medical/surgical nurse; b. Grosse Pointe Farms, Mich., Nov. 3, 1955; d. Thomas Clement and Priscilla Warras McNelis; m. Rodrigue Estimé, Oct. 2, 1980; children: Stephen R., Michael T., David P. Diploma in Nursing, Harper Hosp., 1973; BSc in Nursing, Wayne State U., 1983; MSc in Nursing, Oakland U., 1996. RN Mich., 1975, cert. registered nurse anesthetist, Mich., 1996. Staff nurse Harper Hosp., Detroit, 1975—77, Hosp. Albert Schweitzer, Deschapelles, Haiti, 1978—80, Detroit (Mich.) Med. Ctr., 1980—93, cert. RN anesthetist, 1996—99, Providence Hosp., Southfield, Mich., 2000—. Vol. anesthetist Hosp. Albert Schweizer, 2001—; clin. instr. Wayne State U., Detroit, 1996—99, Providence Hosp., 2000—. Contbr. articles to profl. jours. Team capt. for cert. RN anesthetists Komen Detroit (Mich.) Race for Cure, 2001—. Mem.: ANA, Mich. Assn. Nurse Anesthetists (co-chmn. pub. rels. 2001—), Am. Assn. Nurse Anesthetists. Roman Cath. Avocations: reading, music, films, travel. Home: 28048 Pierce Southfield MI 48076 Office: Providence Hospital W 9 Mile Southfield MI 48075

MCNULTY, KATHLEEN ANNE, clinical social worker, psychotherapist, business consultant; b. Hackensack, N.J., Oct. 6, 1958; d. Alfred Edward and Gertrude Natalie (Currie) McN.; m. Henry Stanislaw Kowal, Sept. 16, 1988. BA, Rutgers U., 1980; MSW, Smith Coll., 1984; postgrad., Fielding Grad. Inst., 2001—. Lic. marriage and family therapist. Mental health aide Belleville (N.J.) Mental Health Clinic, 1980-82; clin. social worker Albert Einstein Coll. Medicine, Bronx, N.Y., 1984-86, Family Guidance Bergen, Hackensack, 1986-87, Cliffwood Mental Health Ctr., Englewood, N.J., 1986-87; pvt. practice Rutherford, N.J., 1987-99, Ridgewood, N.J., 1999—. Cons. Meadowlands Weight Control, Rutherford, 1988—, St. Lukes-

Roosevelt Hosp. Ctr., N.Y.C., 1988. Contbr. articles to profl. jours. Mem. Am. Orthopsychiat. Assn., Acad. Cert. Social Workers (cert.), Nat. Assn. Social Workers. Avocations: painting, singing, sports, poetry.

MCPARTLAND, PATRICIA ANN, health educator and administrator; b. Passaic, NJ; d. Daniel and Josephine McP. BA, U. Mo., 1971; MCRP, MS in Preventive Medicine, Ohio State U., 1975; EdD in Higher and Adult Edn., Columbia U., 1988; cert. distance edn., Tex. A&M U., 2000, cert. distance edn. web pub. cert., 2001. Cert. health edn. specialist, distance edn. web pub., grants specialist; workforce devel. profl. Sr. health planner Merrimack Valley HSA, Lawrence, Mass., 1977—79; planning cons., adminstr. Children's Hosp., Boston, 1979—80; exec. dir. Assn. for Workforce Alternatives, Rsch. & Devel., Inc., Marion, Mass., 1980—. V.p., cons. New Bedford (Mass.) Cmty. Health Ctr, 1993—94; chmn. edn. and tng. com. Health and Human Svc. Coalition, 1988—89; mem. project expert panel Office of Minority Health, 1997—2003; mem. New Eng. Regional Minority Health Conf. Com., 1997—99; vis. lectr. Bridgewater State Coll.; lectr. in field; project expert panel Office Minority Health's Culturally and Linguistically Appropriate Svcs.; mem. New Eng. Regional Minority Health Conf. Com., 2001—03. Mem. editl. bd. Jour. Healthcare Edn. and Tng., 1989-93; author: Promoting Health in the Workplace, 1991; reviewer Qualitative Health Rsch. Jour.; contbr. articles to profl. jours. Vol. spkr. March of Dimes Found., Wareham, Mass., 1992-93; coll.-wide vocat. Cape Cod C.C., Hyannis, Mass., 1989—; planning adv. 2nd Internat. Symposium, Pasco, Wash., 1992; v.p. New Bedford chpt. Am. Cancer Soc., 1985-90. Recipient award Excellence in Continuing Edn. Nat. AHEC Ctr. Dirs. Assn., 1994, 95, 96, 97, Sec.'s awards for Outstanding Progam in Community Health, Nat. Cancer Inst., Washington, 1990. Mem.: APHA, Nat. Assn. Workforce Devel. Profls. (bd. dirs.), Nat. Planning Conf. (mem. com. 1984—87), Southeastern Mass. Health Planning (bd. dirs., sec. 1982—87), Inst. for Disease Prevention (steering com. 1982—). Avocations: writing, acting, dance, theater, travel. Home: PO Box 1116 Marion MA 02738-0020 Office: Assn for Workforce Alternatives Rsch & Devel Inc PO Box 69 2 Spring St Marion MA 02738-1519 Office Phone: 508-748-0837. E-mail: pmcpartland@comcast.net., smahec@tiac.net.

MCPETERS, SHARON JENISE, artist, writer; b. San Bernardino, Calif., Oct. 17, 1951; d. Cecil L. and Mary I. (Tanner) McP.; 1 child, Angela M. Bunduru. BA in Journalism and English, U. So. Calif., 1981. Proofreader Ventura (Calif.) Coll., 1979. Prin. works include My Professors, 1993, Interpretations, 1994, The Thoughts of Socrates, 1995, Self Portrait, 1995, Happiness, 1996, My True Self, 1998, Czechoslovakia 1923, 1999, Liszt, 1999, Portrait of Ten Artists, 2000; author: (autobiography) A Human Mind, 1997, (novels) Domestic Symphonies, 1986, The Broken Heart of the World, 1999, An Illuminated Manuscript, 1994, (short stories) The Library of Heaven, 2000, A Girl Without A Name, 2001, A Sanctified Heart, Selected Poems, 1974-2002, 2003, An Intellect's Goodness, 2004. Avocation: philosophical reading.

MCPHAIL, JOANN WINSTEAD, writer, publisher, art dealer; b. Trenton, Fla., Feb. 17, 1941; d. William Emerson and Donna Mae (Crawford) Winstead; m. James Michael McPhail, June 15, 1963; children: Angela C. McPhail Morris, Dana Denise McPhail Gaizutis, Whitney Gold McPhail Casso. Student, Fla. So. Coll., 1959-60, St. John's River Jr. Coll., Palatka, Fla., 1960-61, Houston (Tex.) C.C. With Jim Walter Corp., Houston, 1961-62; receptionist, land lease sec. Oil and Gas Property Mgmt. Inc., Houston, 1962-63; sec. to mng. atty. State Farm Ins. Co., Houston, 1963-64; saleswoman, decorator Oneil-Anderson, Houston, 1973; sec. Law Offices of Ed Christensen, Houston, 1980-82; advt. mgr. Egalitarian Houston (Tex.) C.C. Systems, 1981; fashion display artist, 1985-86; entrepreneur, writer, art agt. Golden Galleries and Antiques, Houston, 1990-95; owner, property mgr. APT Investments, 1994-98; lyricist, publisher Anna Gold Classics, 1995—, writer song lyrics, 1996—. Freelance writer, photographer: Elegance of Needlepoint, 1970, S.W. Art Mag., A Touch of Greatness, 1973, Sweet 70's Anthology, The Budding of Tomorrow, 1974 (award); columnist, photographer: Egalitarian: Names Can be Symbols, Design Your Wall Covering, Student Profile, 1981, National Library of Poetry, Fireworks (award), 1995; contbr. poetry various publs.; playwright, 1993—; screenwriter, 1996—; writer, pub. The Missing Crown, religious drama World Wide Christian Radio, Sta. KCBI-FM, KYND-AM, and other radio stas., 1996—, baby publ. Hello...World...Hello, 1997; author: (poetry) The Budding of Tomorrow, 1997; music pub., 1999—. Vol. PTO bd. Sharptown Middle Sch. Mem. ASCAP, Manuscriptors Guild. Methodist. Home: 361 N Post Oak Ln Apt 333 Houston TX 77024-5950

MCPHAIL-GEIST, KARIN RUTH, secondary school educator, real estate agent, musician; b. Urbana, Ill., Nov. 23, 1938; d. Wilber Harold and Bertha Amanda Sofia (Helander) Tammeus; m. David Pendleton McPhail, Sept. 7, 1958 (div. 1972); children: Julia Elizabeth, Mark Andrew; m. John Charles Geist, June 4, 1989 (div. 1995). BS, Juilliard Sch. Music, 1962; postgrad., Stanford U., 1983-84, L'Academia, Florence and Pistoia, Italy, 1984-85, Calif. State U., 1986-87, U. Calif., Berkeley, 1991, 92. Cert. tchr., Calif.; lic. real estate agt., Calif. Tchr. Woodstock Sch., Musoorie, India, 1957, Canadian, Tex., 1962-66, Head Royce Sch., Oakland, Calif., 1975-79, 87—, Sleepy Hollow Sch., Orinda, Calif., 1985-2001; realtor Freeholders, Berkeley, Calif., 1971-85, Northbrae, Berkeley, Calif., 1985-92, Templeton Co., Berkeley, 1992—99. Organist Kellogg Meml., Musoorie, 1956-57, Mills Coll. Chapel, Oakland, 1972—; cashier Trinity U., San Antonio, 1957-58; cen. records sec. Riverside Ch., N.Y.C., 1958-60; sec. Dr. Rollo May, N.Y.C., 1959-62, United Presbyn. Nat. Missions, N.Y.C., 1960, United Presbyn. Ecumenical Mission, N.Y.C., 1961, Nat. Coun. Chs., N.Y.C., 1962; choral dir. First Presbyn. Ch., Canadian, Tex., 1962-66; assoc. in music Montclair Presbyn. Ch., Oakland, 1972-88; site coord., artist, collaborator Calif. Arts Coun. Artist; cons. music edn. videos and CD Roms Clearvue EAV, Chgo., 1993—. Artist: produced and performed major choral and orchestral works, 1972-88; prodr. Paradiso, Kronos Quartet, 1985, Magdalena, 1991, 92, Children's Quest, 1993—. Grantee Orinda Union Sch. Dist., 1988. Mem. Berkeley Bd. Realtors, East Bay Regional Multiple Listing Svc., Calif. Tchrs. Assn., Commonwealth Club (San Francisco). Democrat. Home: 7360 Claremont Ave Berkeley CA 94705-1429

MCPHEARSON, GERALDINE JUNE, medical/surgical nurse; b. Red Bud, Ill., June 3, 1938; d. Arthur and Viola (Liefer) Althoff; children: Deborah, Michael, Belinda, Sabrina. Diploma, Evang. Deaconess Hosp. Sch. Nursing, St. Louis, 1959. RN. Sch. nurse San Antonio Ind. Sch. Dist.; head nurse Bethesda Gen. Hosp., St. Louis; supr. Am. Blood Components, Inc., St. Louis; nurse mgr. Meml. Hosp., Belleville, Ill. Coord. arthritis svc. staff Meml. Hosp. Mem. Nat. Assn. Orthopaedic Nurses (1st pres., sec., v.p., organizer Ill. chpt.).

MCPHEE, MARTHA, literature educator; BA magna cum laude, Bowdoin Coll., 1987; MFA, Columbia U., 1994. Fiction tchr. Gotham Writer's Workshop, N.Y.C., 1993—97; adj. prof. creative writing Columbia U., 1997—99; writer, asst. prof. creative writing Hofstra U., 2002—. Author: (novels) Bright Angel Time, 1998, Gorgeous Lies, 2002, (nonfiction) Girls: Ordinary Girls and Their Extraordinary Pursuits, 2000; translator: Crossing the Threshold of Hope, 1994, author short stories; contbr. articles to publs. Fellow, John Simon Guggenheim Meml. Found., 2003. Office: Hofstra Univ Hempstead NY 11549-1000

MCPHEE, NORMA HOWATT, publishing executive, author; b. Dunkirk, N.Y., June 24, 1928; d. Walter Bruce and Hattie Calista (Holcomb) Howatt; m. Richard Samuel McPhee, Jan. 5, 1951; children: Julia Ellen, Jonathan Bruce, James Robert, Keith Richard. BS in Music Edn., SUNY, Fredonia, N.Y., 1950, student, 1966, Immaculata Coll., Media, Pa., 1988, U. Pa., Phila., 1988. Music edn. Lake Shore Ctrl. Sch., Angola, N.Y., 1951-52; pvt. music tchr. Oxford, N.Y., 1956-59, New Britain, Conn., 1959-63; chapel musician USAF, 1963-85; chapel, ch. drama, program dir., 1957—; free lance writer, 1963—; founder, CEO Jason & Nordic Pub., Hollidaysburg, Pa., 1988—. Vol. music edn., therapy staff The Children's Ctr., Montgomery, Ala., 1984-85, Old Forge Sch., Middletown, Pa., 1986-91. Author: Danny and The Merry Go Round, 1988, How About a Hug, 1988, Patrick and Emma Lou, 1989, Andy Opens Wide, 1990, Sarah's Surprise, 1990, A Smile From Andy, 1990, Fair and Square, 1991, Andy Finds a Turtle, revised 1998, Sensitivity and Awareness, 1998, Leah's Night of Wonder, 1999, Of Easter Eggs and Things, 2000. Mem. AAUW, The Author;s Guild, Inc., Authors LEague Am. Republican. Protestant. Avocations: swimming, theater arts, camping, reading, sewing. Home: 424 N Montgomery St Hollidaysburg PA 16648-1432 Office: Jason & Nordic Publishers PO Box 441 Hollidaysburg PA 16648-0441

MCPHEE, PENELOPE L. ORTNER, foundation executive, television producer, writer; b. Louisville, Nov. 24, 1947; d. Alvin B. and Loyce L. Ortner; m. Raymond Hunter McPhee, Aug. 25, 1973; 1 child, Cameron McPhee Baker. BA with honors, Wellesley Coll., 1969; MS in Journalism, Columbia U., 1970. Dir. pub. rels. Am. Sch. in Switzerland, Lugano, 1970-71; writer, rschr. Sta. WTVJ-TV, Miami, Fla., 1972-73; prof. journalism and film Fleming Coll., Florence, Italy, 1972-73; freelance writer, prodr. Miami, 1973-80; exec. prodr. for cultural programming Sta. WPBT-TV, Miami, 1980-88; instr. documentary filmmaking Fla. Internat. U., 1987-88; ind. TV prodr., cons., 1988-90; program officer arts and culture Knight Found., Miami, 1990-96, v.p., chief program officer, 1996—. Author: Martin Luther King, Jr.: A Documentary, Montgomery to Memphis, 1976 (Best of Books award ALA 1983), Beauty Ency., 1978, King Remembered, 1986, Your Future in Space, 1986; contbg. author: Underwater Photography for Everyone, 1978. Trustee Dade County Art in Pub. Places Trust, 1985, vice chmn., 1988-89, chmn., 1989-90; trustee Grantmakers in the Arts, 1992-98, chmn. 1995-96, Southeastern Coun. on Foundations, 1999—, Coun. on Founds., 1998-2002; adviser Indep. Sector Comm. com., 1999—. Recipient Iris award Nat. Assn. TV Program Execs., 1983, Children's Programming award Corp. for Pub. Broadcasting, 1982, local program award Corp. Pub. Broadcasting, 1984, 90, Emmy award, 1984, 88, N.Y. State Martin Luther King, Jr. Medal of Freedom, 1986; Sackett scholar Columbia U., 1970. Mem. Miami Wellesley (v.p. 1976-80, admissions rep. 1980-85, 1989-90). Office: 2 S Biscayne Blvd Ste 3800 Miami FL 33131-1808 E-mail: Mcphee@knightfdn.org.

MCPHERON, JOANN MARIE, music educator, poet; b. Racine, Wis., Feb. 19, 1938; d. Joseph Eugene-Reath and Ann Bernadette (Mostek) Stetka; m. Lamont Preston McPheron II, Oct. 14, 1961; children Dawn Marie and Lamont P. III (twins). Student, U. Wis., Parkside, 1958-60. Adminstrv. asst. Racine County Social Svc. Dept., Wis., 1958-63; pvt. piano, music theory tchr. Racine, 1970—. Contbr. poems to anthologies and mags.; performer Racine Summer Theater, 1957. Asst. programs Children's Theatre, Racine, 1975; chmn. Minority Scholarship Program, 1970; active Roosevelt Sch. PTA, 1968—74; vol. All Saints Hosp., 2002—, Performing Arts Ctr., Milw., 1994—97; mem. Milw. Zoo, Art Inst. Chgo., United Performing Arts, Milw., Milw. Art Mus.; vol. fundraiser Miller Ride for the Arts, 1994—2000, AIDS March, Milw.; contbr. Racine Arts Coun.; bd. dirs. St. Luke's Hosp. Aux., Racine, Wis., 1992—98. Recipient award for poetry Racine Art Coun., 1990; nominated Graduates of Distinction William Horlick H.S., Racine, 1992. Fellow Wis. Fellowship of Poets; mem. Racine Music Tchrs. Assn., Wis. Music Tchrs. Assn., Music Tchrs. Nat. Assn., Root River Poets. Mem. Unitarian Universalist Ch. Avocations: grandchildren, poetry, walking, gardening, painting. Home: 516 Augusta St Racine WI 53402-4408

MCPHERSON, ALICE RUTH, ophthalmologist, educator; b. Regina, Sask., Can., June 30, 1926; came to U.S., 1938, naturalized, 1958; d. Gordon and Viola (Hoover) McP. BS, U. Wis., 1948, MD, 1951, DSc (hon.), 1997. Diplomate Am. Bd. Ophthalmology. Intern Santa Barbara (Calif.) Cottage Hosp., 1951-52; resident anesthesiology Hartford (Conn.) Hosp., 1952; resident ophthalmology Chgo. Eye, Ear, Nose and Throat Hosp., 1953, U. Wis. Hosps., 1953-55; ophthalmologist Davis and Duehr Eye Clinic, Madison, Wis., 1956-57; clin. instr. U. Wis., 1956-57; fellow retina svc. Mass. Eye and Ear Infirmary, 1957-58; ophthalmologist Scott and White Clinic, Temple, Tex., 1958-60; practice medicine specializing in ophthalmology and retinal diseases Houston, 1960—. Staff Meth., St. Luke's, Tex. Children's Hosps., Harris County Hosp. Dist., Houston; clin. asst. prof. Baylor Coll. Medicine, Houston, 1959-61, asst. prof. ophthalmology, 1961-69, clin. assoc. prof., 1969-75, clin. prof., 1975-98, prof., 1998—; cons. retinal diseases VA Hosp., Houston, 1960—, Ben Taub Hosp., Houston, 1960—; mem. adv. com. for active staff appt. sect. ophthalmology Meth. Hosp., 1986-91, mem equipment com., 1993-95, mem. grievance panel, 1997; vol. clin. faculty appts. and promotions com., 1993—; bd. dirs. Highlights of Ophthalmology; v.p. N.Am. Highlights of Ophthalmology Internat. Editor: New and Controversial Aspects of Retinal Detachment, 1968, New and Controversial Aspects of Vitreoretinal Surgery, 1977, Retinopathy of Prematurity: Current Concepts and Controversies, 1986. Amb. Houston Ballet, mem. Houston Ballet Found.; mem. pres.'s coun. Houston Grand Opera, condrs. cir. Houston Symphony, mem Houston Symphony Soc.; mem. campaign for 80s Baylor Coll. Medicine; mem. Assn. for Cmty. TV, BBB, Physicians' Benevolent Fund, South Tex. Diabetes Assn. Inc., Jr. League Houston; bd. dirs. U. Wis. Found., Madison. Recipient Award of appreciation KT Eye Found., 1978, Woodlands Medal for Outstanding Contbn. to the Econ. Devel. of Cmty., 1988, spl. recognition award Assn. for Rsch. in Vision in Ophthalmology, Crystal award Recognizing Generous Support-Ptnrs. with an Eye for Vision Found. Am. Acad. Ophthalmology, 2000, Benjamin Boyd Humanitarian award Pan Am. Assn. Ophthalmology, 2001, Philip Corboy Meml. award Disting. Svc. Ophthalmology, 2002, Women of Vision Houston Delta Gamma Found., 2002; Alice R. Mc Pherson Lab. for Retina Rsch. dedicated Baylor Ctr. for Biotech., 1988; Alice R. Mc Pherson Day proclaimed in her honor Mayor of City of Houston, Mar. 12, 1988. Fellow: ACS (credentials and Tex. credentials com., com. on applications), Am. Acad. Ophthalmology (2nd v.p. 1979, vice chmn. program devel. found. bd. trustees 1993—, com. for pub. and profl. rels., bd. dirs. opthalmology ednl. trust fund found., honor award 1956, sr. honor award 1986, guest of honor 1998 meeting); mem.: AMA, Highlights Ophthal. Internat., Schepens Internat. Soc. (sec. 1986—93, v.p. 1993—95, pres. 1995—97), Internat. Med. Assembly S.W. Tex., French Ophthal. Soc., U. Wis. Ophthal. Alumni Assn. (founding pres. 1990—93, founded Alice R. McPherson lectureship 1994), Assn. Rsch. Surgeons, Pan Am. Assn. Ophthalmology Found., Tex. Ophthal. Assn., So. Med. Soc., Rsch. to Prevent Blindness, Pan Am. Assn. Opthalmology (v.p. 1991—92, pres. elect 1992—95, AJO lectr. 1993, pres. 1995—97, pres. found. 1997—, bd. dirs., membership com., Benjamin Boyd Humanitarian award 2001), Macula Soc. (credentialing com. 1992—), Internat. Soc. Eye Rsch. (credentials com. 1992—), Houston Ophthal. Soc. (pres. 1990—91, credentials com.), Harris County Med. Soc., Am. Bd. Laser Surgery, Am. Soc. Contemporary Ophthalmology (Charles Schepens Hon. award), Internat. Coll. Ocular Surgeons (vice regent 1991), Retina Soc. (v.p. 1976—77, pres. 1978—79, credentials com.), Am. Med. Women's Assn., Internat. Coll. Surgeons (vice regent 1991—), Tex. Med. Assn., Vitreous Soc., Jules Gonin Club (assoc.). Achievements include research in vision and ophthalmology. Office: Tex Med Ctr 6560 Fannin St Ste 2200 Houston TX 77030-2715

MCPHERSON, GAIL, advertising and real estate executive; b. Fort worth; d. Garland and Daphne McP. Student, U. Tex.-Austin; BA, MS, CUNY. Advt. sales exec. Harper's Bazaar mag., NYC, 1974—76; sr. v.p., fashion mktg. dir. L'Officiel/ USA mag., NYC, 1976—80; fashion mgr. Town & Country Mag., NYC, 1980—82; v.p. advt. and mktg. Ultra mag., NYC, 1982—84; fragrance, jewelry and automotive mgr. M. Mag., NYC, 1984—85; sr. real estate sales exec. Fredric M. Reed & Co., Inc., NYC, 1985—88; AT&T security system rep. Home-Watch Inc., Amarillo, Tex., 1989—92; sales rep. Universal Comm., Dallas, 1992—94; acct. exec. Corp. Mktg., Inc., Dallas, 1994—98; sales rep. Pub. Concepts, LP, Dallas, 1998—. N.Y. sponsor Southampton Hosp. Benefit Com.; mem. jr. com. Mannes Sch. Music, NYC, Henry St. Settlement, NYC, Dallas Mus. Art (PM) League. Mem. Fashion Group NY, Advt. Women N.Y., Real Estate Bd. NY, U. Tex. Alumni Assn. of NY (v.p.), Amarillo C. of C. (commn. com.), Corviglia Club, Doubles, El Morocco Club (mem. jr. com.), Le Club. Republican. Presbyterian. Home: 17850 Sunmeadow Dr Apt 2009 Dallas TX 75252-5382

MCPHERSON, MARY PATTERSON, charitable foundation executive; b. Abington, Pa., May 14, 1935; d. John B. and Marjorie Hoffman (Higgins) McP. AB, Smith Coll., 1957, LL.D., 1981; MA, U. Del., 1960; PhD, Bryn Mawr Coll., 1969; LLD (hon.), Juniata Coll., 1975, Smith Coll., 1981, Princeton U., 1984, U. Rochester, 1984, U. Pa., 1985; LittD (hon.), Haverford Coll., 1980; L.H.D. (hon.), Lafayette Coll., 1982; LHD (hon.), U. Pa., 1985, Med. Coll. Pa., 1985. Instr. philosophy U. Del., 1959-61; asst., fellow and lectr. dept. philosophy Bryn Mawr Coll., 1961-63, asst. dean, 1964-69, assoc. dean, 1969-70; dean Bryn Mawr Coll. (Undergrad. Coll.), 1970-78, assoc. prof., from 1970; acting pres. Bryn Mawr Coll., 1976-77, pres., 1978-97, pres. emeritus, 1997—; v.p. The Andrew W. Mellon Found., 1997—. Bd. dirs. Agnes Irwin Sch., 1972-90, Shipley Sch., 1972-90, Phillips Exeter Acad., 1973-76, Wilson Coll., 1976-79, Greater Phila. Movement, 1973-77, Internat. House of Phila., 1974-76, Josiah Macy, Jr. Found., 1977—, Carnegie Found. for Advancement Teaching, 1978-86, Univ. Mus., Phila., 1977-79, University City Sci. Center, 1979-85, Brookings Inst., 1984-90, Phila. Contributionship, 1985—, Carnegie Corp. N.Y., 1985-94, Nat. Humanities Ctr., 1986-91, Amherst Coll., 1986-98, Humanity in Action, Inc., 1997—, Goldman Sachs Asset Mgmt., 1997—, The Spencer Found., 1993—, Am. Sch. Classical Studies, 1996—, Bank St. Coll., 1998—, Smith Coll., 1998—. Mem. Am. Philos. Soc., Am. Acad. of Arts and Scis., Cosmopolitan Club. Office: The Andrew W Mellon Found 140 E 62nd St New York NY 10021-8124 Office Phone: 212-838-8400.

MCPHERSON, SHERRY LYNN, social worker; b. Bklyn., Mar. 8, 1969; d. George Cephano and Mary Sue McPherson. BA, Hofstra U., 1992; MSW, Adelphi U., 1996. Cert. sch. social worker. Program coord. Colonial Youth and Family Svcs., Mastic, NY, 1993; sch. social worker Cmty. Counseling Ctr., Franklin Square, NY, 1996—97; cons. Elmont Pre-Kindergarten, NY, 1997, Glen Cove Child Day Care, NY, 1997—98; sch. social worker Patchogue-Medford Schs., NY, 1997—. Mem.: NASW, NAACP, Sch. Social Work Assn. Am., Nat. Assn. Black Social Workers (treas. 2002—), Black/Hispanic Alumni Assn. Hofstra U., Lupus Found. Roman Catholic. Avocations: travel, baseball. Office: Patchogue Medford Sch Sys 241 S Ocean Ave Patchogue NY 11772*

MCPHERSON, VANZETTA PENN, magistrate judge; b. Montgomery, Ala., May 26, 1947; d. Luther Lincoln and Sadie Lee (Gardner) P.; m. Winston D. Durant, Aug. 17, 1968 (div. Apr. 1979); 1 child, Raegan Winston; m. Thomas McPherson Jr., Nov. 16, 1985. BS in Speech Pathology, Howard U., Washington, 1969; MA in Speech Pathology, Columbia U., 1971, JD, 1974. Bar: N.Y. 1975, Ala. 1976, U.S. Dist. Ct. (so. dist.) N.Y. 1975, U.S. Dist. Ct. (mid. dist.) Ala. 1980, U.S. Ct. Appeals (2d cir.) 1975, U.S. Ct. Appeals (11th cir.) 1981, U.S. Supreme Ct. Assoc. Hughes, Hubbard & Reed, N.Y.C., 1974-75; asst. atty. gen. Ala. Atty. Gen. Office, Montgomery, 1975-78; pvt. practice Montgomery, 1978-92; magistrate judge U.S. Dist. Ct. (mid. dist.) Ala., Montgomery, 1992—. Former co-owner Roots & Wings, A Cultural Bookplace, Montgomery, 1989—2000. Dir. Ala. Shakespeare Festival, Montgomery, 1987—, Montgomery Symphony Orch., 1995-98; chmn. trustees Dexter Ave. King Meml. Bapt. Ch., Montgomery, 1988; chmn. Leadership Montgomery; bd. mem. Lighthouse Counseling Ctr., Montgomery, 1981-84, Montgomery County Pub. Libr., 1989-90; v.p. Lanier H.S. Parent Tchr. Student Assn., Montgomery, 1990-91, Metro-Montgomery YMCA, 2000—, Ala. Arts Coun., 2001-. Recipient cert. Ala. Jud. Coll.; named Woman of Achievement Montgomery Advertiser, 1989, Boss of Yr. Montgomery Assn. Legal Secs., 1992. Mem. ABA (law office design award 1985), FBA (pres. Montgomery chpt.), Nat. Bar Assn., Ala. State Bar Assn. (chmn. family law sect. 1989-90), N.Y. State Bar Assn., Montgomery Inn of Cts. (master bencher 1992—), Ala. Black Lawyers Assn. (pres. 1979-80). Office: US Dist Ct Mid Dist Ala PO Box 1629 One Church St Montgomery AL 36104

MCPHILLEN, LAURI, financial analyst, product manager, educator; BA in Psychology summa cum laude, U. Calif., Irvine, 1995; MBA, Brigham Young U., Provo, Utah, 1997. Fullcharge bookkeeper McGee Electric, Pomona, Calif., 1987—89; mktg. mgr., adminstrv. mgr. U. Calif., Irvine, 1989—95; sr. product mgr., bus. analyst Novell, Inc., Provo, Utah, 1996—2001; educator Coastline Regional Occupl. Programs, Garden Grove, Calif., 2002—. Pres., adult leader for youth group The LDS Ch., Tulsa, Okla., 1980—87; elected rep., verano residents' coun. U. Calif., Irvine, 1993—95. Recipient Outstanding Coach award, Novell Edn., 2001. Mem.: Women in Tech., Acad. and Profl. Women, Golden Key Nat. Honor Soc., Psi Chi. Avocations: hiking, time with family and friends, reading, outdoor activities, exercising. Home: PO Box 5325 Irvine CA 92616

MCQUAID, PATRICIA A. information systems educator; b. Cleve., May 19, 1954; d. Thomas F. and Sophia (Mihailoff) McQ. BS in Acctg., Case-Western Res. U., 1978; MBA, Eastern Mich. U., 1982; MS in Computer Sci. and Engring., Auburn U., 1988, PhD in Computer Sci. and Engring., 1996. Cert. info. sys. auditor. Sr. EDP audit analyst COMERICA Bank, Detroit, 1978-81; sr. EDP auditor The Bendix Corp., Southfield, Mich., 1981-83; lectr. in acctg. Ea. Mich. U., Ypsilanti, 1983-84; instr. info. sys. U. Cin., 1984-85; instr. computer sci. and engring. Auburn (Ala.) U., 1985-92; instr. info. sys. Auburn U., Montgomery, 1992-96; assoc. prof. Calif. Poly. State U., San Luis Obispo, 1996—. Chair program com. North, Ctrl., South Am. 2nd World Congress for Software Quality; spkr. in field. Contbr. articles to profl. jours. Recipient Best Rsch. Paper in Field of Software Metrics Fifth European Conf. Software Quality European Orgn. Quality, 1996. Mem. Am. Soc. Quality (software divsn., program com. N.Am., C.Am., S.Am. 1998—).. Avocations: raising lizards, pool, golf. Office: Calif Poly State U Coll Bus - MIS San Luis Obispo CA 93407

MCQUARRIE, BEATRICE SUE, financial analyst, director; b. Lancaster, N.H., June 17, 1956; d. Elliott A. and Elaine G. (Enman) Kenison; m. Kevin F. McQuarrie; children: Bernard J., Michael F. AS, Fisher Jr. Coll., 1980; BGen Studies cum laude, U. N.H., Durham, 1984; postgrad., U. Md., 1992-94. CPA, CMA, Md. Acct. Sch. Adminstrn. Unit 36, Whitefield, N.H., 1980-82; sch. bus. adminstr. Sch. Adminstrn. Unit 58, Groveton, N.H., 1982-86; pvt. practice fin. cons. Whitefield, 1986-91; acct. Village at Maplewood, Bethlehem, N.H., 1988-90; adj. faculty mem. Berlin (N.H.) Vocat. Tech. Coll., 1990-91; asst. treas. Bank of Glen Burnie, Md., 1991—2000; sr. acct. Crestar Leasing Corp., 2000—01; mgr. fin. analysis Md. Environ. Svc., 2001—. Vol. IRS, Whitefield, 1991; active Arundel Gambrills H.S., Gambrills, Md., 2002—, Four Season Cmty. Assn., Gambrills, 1991—; active Gambrills Odenton Recreation Coun., 1992—; FIFA and fedn. soccer referee, 2000-. With U.S. Army, 1974-77. Mem. Inst. Mgmt. Accts. (cert.), Md. Assn. CPAs, Am. Legion. Avocations: tennis, skiing, reading. Office: Md Environ Svc 2011 Commerce Park Dr Annapolis MD 21401

MCQUEEN, DEVA REVELL, minister; b. West Point, Miss., June 29, 1949; d. Jeptha Rye Revell and Lela Glenda Ward; m. Paul Scott McQueen, Nov. 9, 1999; m. John Douglas Williams, Oct. 7, 1969 (div. June 1988); children: John Forrest, Eva Christine. BS, Univ. Memphis, 1971; MA in Religion, Fla. State Univ., 1988; MDiv, Austin Presbytn. Theol. Sem., 1994. Cert. tchg. cert. Tenn., Miss., Ala., Fla., Wash. Tchr. lang. arts Pub. Schs.,

Rossville, Tenn., 1971—72, Aberdeen, Miss., 1972—75, Barbour County, Ala., 1978—81, Medart, Fla., 1982—85; dir. Christian edn. Presbyn. Ch., Tallahasee, Fla., 1986—88, Marianna, Fla., 1988—89, Kalispell, Mont., 1989—90, designated pastor Deer Lodge, Mont., 1994—97, interim pastor Gt. Falls, Mont., 1999—2000, Medford, Oreg., 2001—02, Longview, Wash., 2003—. Bd. mem. Mont. Assoc. of Chs., Kalispell, Mont., 1990, Gt. Falls, Mont., 2000. Author: (poetry) Hungry Heart News, 1996. Sponsor Children's Friendship Project, No. Ireland, Mont., 1996; key club Kiwanis Internat., Deer Lodge, Mont., 1995—96. Recipient Scholarship, Austin Presbyn Theological Sem., 1994. Mem.: Assoc. Presbyn. Christian Educators. Democrat. Presbyn. Avocations: walking, writing, poetry. Home: 139 Stone Way Chehalis WA 98532

MCQUEEN, REBECCA HODGES, health care executive, consultant; b. Dothan, Ala., July 20, 1954; d. Edward Grey and Shirley Louise (Varner) Hodges; m. David Raymond McQueen, Mar. 5, 1982; children: Matthew David, Owen Grey. BS, Emory U., 1976, MPH, 1979. Research assoc. North Cen. Ga. Health Systems Agy., Inc., Atlanta, 1979-80; assoc. dir. Health Services Analysis, Inc., Atlanta, 1980-82; med. group adminstr. Southeastern Health Services, Inc./Prucare, Atlanta, 1982-84; sr. v.p., COO SouthCare Med. Alliance, Atlanta, 1985-93; pres., CEO, PROMINA N.W. Health Network, Atlanta, 1993-96; sr. v.p. managed care PROMINA Health Sys., Atlanta, 1996-97; exec. dir. Principal Health Care, Inc., Pensacola, Fla., 1997-99; v.p. managed care and quality improvement West Fla. Regional Med. Ctr., Pensacola, 1999—. Cons. North Cen. Ga. Health Systems Agy., 1980-81, Region 4 HHS, Atlanta, 1980-82, instr. Applied Stats., Washington, 1980-82; mem. Health Data com. and Health Cost subcom. Atlanta Healthcare Alliance, 1985—; cons. Atlanta Com. for the Olympic Games, 1992. Contbr. articles to profl. jours. Adviser to med. support panel Atlanta Com. for Olympic Games; mem. Planned Parenthood-Atlanta, Ga. Coun. on Child Abuse; campaign coord. United Way. Recipient rsch. award Nat. Conf. on High Blood Pressure Control, 1981; nominee Woman of Achievement award YWCA. Mem. APHA (women's caucus com.), ACLU, NOW, Am. Coll. Healthcare Execs. (diplomate), Women Healthcare Execs., Covenant Hospice (bd. dir.), ARC/Gateway (bd. dir), Five Flags Rotary (bd. dir.), Am. Managed Care and Rev. Orgn. (presenter nat. conf. 1989), Assn. Emory Alumni (bd. govs., pres. 1999-2000), Rotary (Five Flags club), Delta Omega, Delta Delta Delta. Democrat. Methodist. Office: West Florida Regional Med Ctr 8383 N Davis Hwy Pensacola FL 32514-6039

MCQUEEN, REGENIA, writer; b. Summerville, SC, Oct. 29, 1945; d. William McQueen and Mary Stoutamire-McQueen; m. John Ray Sanders Teasley, Oct. 11, 1961; children: John Ray Sanders Teasley, Tonya Teasley, Ieishia Teasley, Nairobi Teasley, Rhodesia Teasley, Donnish Lindsey Teasley, DeJong Lindsey Teasley. A, Cin. Tech. Coll., 1985; cert., Blackstone Sch. of Law, Dallas, 2000. Clk. Western-So. Life Ins., Cin., 1967-72, IRS, Covington, Ky., 1985-87. Author: Regenia McQueen: Born to Search, 2000, Nairobi Teasley: 1-1/2 Hour Defenseless Lamb, 2001, Witnesses to the Impossible Dreams, 2002, Regenia McQueen Life Stolen, Name, Land, Oil, Government and History, Theft in South Carolina, 2003, Regina McQueen Documents in Theft in South Carolina, 2004, Nairobi Teasley: Unlawfully Made Guilty until Lawfully Proven Innocent, 2004. V.p. 13th St Tenant Assn., 1979-85; trustee Owning the Realty, 1983-85; Rosa Parks co-chmn. Wall of Tolerance award Nat. Campaign for Tolerance, 2002. Recipient Achievement award, Ho. of Reps., Ohio, 2000. Avocations: researching, writing. Mailing: PO Box 15311 Covington KY 41015

MCQUIGG, MICHELE BERGER, state legislator; b. Bay Shore, N.Y., Sept. 2, 1947; m. F. Clancy McQuigg; children: Heather Lukes, Katie Schneider. BS, Mary Washington Coll., 1968; MS, Va. Polytech. Inst. & State U., 1978. Mem. Va. State Legis., 1998—, mem. cts. of justice com., mem. counties cities & towns com., mem. labor & commerce com., cts. justice labor, commerce gen.laws counties, cities, town, 1998—. Republican. Episcopalian. Office: Gen Assembly Bldg PO Box 406 Richmond VA 23218-0406 E-mail: del-mcquigg@house.state.va.us., michele@mcquigg.com.

MCQUOWN, ELOISE, librarian; b. Santa Monica, Calif. d. Franklyn King and Paula (Rogers) McQ. BA, U. Utah, Salt Lake City, 1965; MLS, Rutgers U., New Brunswick, N.J., 1968; MS, U. Utah, Salt Lake City, 1976. Libr. U. Utah Librs., Salt Lake City, 1969-80, head access svcs., 1980-84; asst. dir.adminstrv. svcs. San Francisco State U., 1984-89, libr. instrnl. and rsch. svcs., 1989—. Conf. workshop leader Calif. Libr. Assn., Oakland, 1993; conf. spkr. Utah Libr. Assn., St. George, 1989, Am. Libr. Assn., Chgo., 1984, libr. cons. Children's Ctr., Salt lake City, 1970-73. Author: Business Information, 1974; contbg. editor: Network, 1978-84; contbr. articles to profl. jours. Del. Dem. Nat. Conv., N.Y.C., 1976, 80; candidate Utah State Legis., Salt Lake City, 1980. Recipient Susa Young Gates award Utah Women's Polit. Caucus, 1975; named Disting. Woman of Yr. in Utah., Salt Lake City, 1979. Mem. ALA, Assn. Coll. and Rsch. Librs., Calif. Faculty Assn. (chair polit. action, legis. com. 1995—, dir. voter registration project. 1996, chair statewide legis. polit. action com. 1999—, statewide bd. dirs. 1999—). Democrat. Avocations: travel, tennis, human rights. Office: San Francisco State U Library 1630 Holloway Ave San Francisco CA 94132-1722

MCRAE, KAREN K. state legislator; b. Detroit, Feb. 19, 1944; m. Gossett W. McRae; 2 children. BSL, Georgetown U., 1965. Mem. N.H. Ho. of Reps.; vice chmn. sci., tech. and energy com. Active Goffstown Conservation Com., 1972—, chmn., 1975-79. Mem. Georgetown U. Alumni Assn. (class rep. 1975—). Avocations: skiing, gardening, gourmet cooking, baking, reading. Home: 469 Black Brook Rd Goffstown NH 03045-2931 Office: NH Ho of Reps 107 N Main St Rm 105 Concord NH 03301-4993

MCRAE, MARION ELEANOR, critical care nurse; b. Kingston, Ont., Can., Sept. 19, 1960; d. James Malcolm and Madeline Eleanor (MacNamara) McR. BSN, Queen's U., Kingston, 1982; MSN, U. Toronto, 1989, ACNP diploma, 2001. RN, Calif., CCRN; cert. BCLS, ACLS. Staff nurse thoracic surgery Toronto (Can.) Gen. Hosp., 1982-83, staff nurse cardiovascular ICU, 1983-85; nurse clinician critical care Michael's Hosp., Toronto, 1985-87; external critical care clin. tchr. Ryerson Poly. Inst., Toronto, 1986-87; staff nurse cardiovascular ICU The Toronto Hosp.-Toronto Gen. Divsn., 1987-89; clin. nurse specialist cardiac surgery The Toronto Hosp., 1989-90; clin. nurse II cardiothoracic ICU UCLA Med. Ctr., 1990-92, clin. nurse III cardiothoracic ICU, 1992-2000; nurse practitioner cardiovasc. surgery Toronto Gen. Hosp., 2000—. Mem. critical care nursing adv. bd. George Brown Coll., Toronto, 1987-88. Contbr. articles to profl. nursing jours. Recipient Open Master's fellowship U. Toronto, 1987-88, M. Keyes bursary Toronto Gen. Hosp., 1988-89, Nursing fellowship Heart and Stroke Found. Ont., 1988-89, Outstanding Svc. award UCLA Med. Ctr., 1994, Cardiothoracic ICU Nurse of Yr. award UCLA, 1995. Mem. AACN, Am. Heart Assn. Coun. on Cardiovascular Nursing. Office: Toronto Gen Hosp 4C 452 585 University Ave Toronto ON Canada M5G 2N2 E-mail: marion.mcrae@uhn.on.ca.

MCRANEY, JOAN KATHERINE, artist; b. Magee, Miss., Mar. 21, 1936; d. Harold Bryce and Ruth Katherine (Graves) McRaney; m. William Cummings Hollis, Mar. 14, 1966 (div. June 1970); m. Richard Felder, 1997. BFA, Inst. Allende, San Miguel de Allende, Mex., 1975; postgrad., U. So. Miss., 1990—; pvt. study, Miss. sculptor Dan Askew, 1999-2000. Profl. portrait artist and contemporary sculptor, McComb, Hattiesburg, Miss., 1979—. Lectr. Lauren Rogers Mus. Art, Laurel, Miss., 1996; artist-in-residence Gethsemane Project, Hattiesburg, Miss., 2002. Exhibitions include Inst. Allende Gallery, 1973, Bellas Artes Gallery, San Miguel de Allende, 1974, Gulf South Gallery, McComb, 1982—84, Images '84, Miss Pavilion, New Orleans World Fair, 1984, Cottonlandia Mus., Greenwood, Miss., 1985—86, Woods Gallery So. Artists Invitational, U. So. Miss., 1990, Saenger Gallery, Hattiesburg, 1990, Woods and Locke Gallery, U. So. Miss., 1992—96, Lucille Parker Gallery, William Carey Coll., 1993, Miss. Collegiate Art Competition, Lauren Rogers Mus. Art, Laurel, Miss., 1996, Meridian (Miss.) Mus. Arts, 1997, USM Mus. Art, 1998, Lauren Rogers Mus., 1999, [illegible] Gallery, Hattiesburg Downtown Gallery Walk, 1999, 2000, Impressions Gallery, 2000, 2001, McComb Pub. Libr., 2000, Southwest C.C., 2002. Recipient Louie B. Holmes Meml. award, McComb, 1980, 81, hon. mention Nat. Portrait Seminar, Houston, 1981, 1st pl. Pastel award South Miss. Art Assn. Cloverleaf Show, 1992, 1st pl. Drawing award, 1992, Dean's Outstanding Creativity award, 1993, 94, 1st pl. Painting award Umpteenth Ann. Student Show, Woods Gallery, 1995, Fred A. Waits Endowment, 1995, 1st pl. Drawing award, 1995, Best of Show award (mixed media sculpture), Miss. Collegiate Art Competition, 1997, Best of Sculpture award Best of Show (mixed media sculpture) Dept. Art Annual Student Exhbn., 1998, honored by Hattiesburg Arts Coun., 1998; winner juried competition Laurel Arts League, 1999, Meridian Mus. Art, 1999. Mem.: Golden Key Soc., Kappa Delta. Avocations: canoeing, photography, yoga, meditation, cooking. Home: PO Box 94 Hattiesburg MS 39403 E-mail: refelder@netdoor.com.

MCREE, CELIA, composer, singer, actress, writer, producer; b. Memphis; d. John Louis and Leta Gwendolyn (Phillips) McR. Student, Phila. Coll. Art (U. of Arts), 1976-77, Herbert Berghof Studio, 1989, Playwrights Horizon Theater, 1989; cert. with distinction, Nat. Acad. Paralegal Studies, Christian Bros. U., 1992. Pres. Mother Records, Memphis, 1984—, You Should Meet My Mother (Publishing), Memphis, 1984—, Wild Thing Music, Memphis, 1987-99, Mother Prodns., Memphis, 1986—; producer, host Indian Talk, WEVL-FM90, Memphis, 1992-95; ptnr. The Cinema Group, N.Y.C., 1997—. Artist, group and solo exhbns. including Eads Gallery, Grover Cleveland Arts Inst., Phila. Mus. Natural History; screenwriter, film scoring; singer, writer (nat. album) including Celia McRee/Back From Under, 1985 (ASCAP Spl. Pop award 1985-86, 86-87), Archives of Modern Music NY., Celia McRee/Passion, 1994; composer, arranger, producer, pub. background and feature music ABC Network, Cable TV and Radio; signature model for KeTukla, 1st Native Am. fashion designer; co-writer Circle of Love, 1999. Entertainer Vets. Bedside Network, N.Y.C., 1981. Recipient cert. of scholarly distinction Nat. Acad. for Paralegal Studies, 1992, cert. of appreciation United Music Heritage, 1990, spl. pop award ASCAP, 1982-84, 87-93, 95-96, 96-97, 97-98, 98-99, 99-2000, 2000-01, Henrietta Hickman Morgan writing award DAR; named Female Pop Songwriter and Female Pop Vocalist of Yr., Entertainer Indi-Assn., 1994, Female Vocalist and Female Entertainer of Yr., 1995; named Most Popular Female Entertainer, Entertainer Indi-Assn., 1996, Female/Artist/Entertainer, 1996, 97, Eia's Female Entertainer/Writer, 1997. Mem. AFTRA, ASCAP, NARAS, Nat. Mus. of the Am. Indian (charter), Animal Legal Def. Fund, N.Y. Acad. Sci., Humane Soc. U.S., Mensa, Memphis Kennel Club. Office: Mother Prodns 5159 Wheelis Dr # 110 Memphis TN 38117-4519

MCREYNOLDS, MARY MAUREEN, small business owner; b. Tacoma, July 15, 1940; d. Andrew Harley and Mary Leone (McGuire) Sims; m. Gerald Aaron McReynolds, Dec. 10, 1964. BA, U. Oreg., 1961; PhD, U. Chgo., 1966; postgrad., San Diego State U., 1973-75. NIH postdoct. fellow U. Tex., Austin, 1966-68, mem. adj. faculty, 1980-82, mem. biosafety com., 1981—2003; rsch. assoc. Stanford U., Calif., 1968-71; chemist assoc. Syva Co., Palo Alto, Calif., 1972; environ. splst. County of San Diego, Calif., 1973-75; dept. head City of Austin, 1976-84; chief environ. officer, 1984-85; utility environ. mgr., 1985-92; mgr. environ. and regulatory svcs., 1992—2003; prin., owner McReynolds Winery, 1998—. Dir. Ctr. Environ. Rsch., 1992-2003; part-time mem. faculty Austin C.C., 1993-98; cons. enologist Mirassou Vineyards, San Jose, Calif., 1969-72; lectr. Wright Inst., Berkeley, Calif., 1971-72; instr. San Diego State U., 1974-75. Editor: Dist. 56 newsletter, 1989-90; contbr. articles to profl. jours. Mem. Austin-Saltillo Sister City Assn., 1980-99; U.S.-Mex. Sister Cities del., 1983-85; sponsor, chaperone Tex.-SouthAustralia Youth Exch., 1986; active Leadership Austin, 1987-88; mem. Austin-Adelaide Sister City Com., 1986—, chmn., 1989-91, sec., 1992-96; bd. dirs. Internat. Hospitality Coun. Austin, 1989-96; mem. steering com. Colo. River Clean Rivers; mem. adv. panel Lake Austin. USPHS tng. grantee U. Chgo., 1961-66. Mem.: Tex. Assn. Met. Sewage Agys. (sec. 1994, v.p. 1995, pres. 1996), Am. Inst. Cert. Planners (cert.), Am. Planning Assn., Water Environment Fedn. (v.p. local chpt. 1988—89, pres. 1990—91, sect. rep. 1991—94), Tex. Hill Country Winery Assn. (bd. dirs. 2003—), Sweet Adelines (bd. dirs. Tex. Star chpt. 1998—2001), Toastmasters Internat. (club pres. 1981, area gov. 1981—82, div. lt. gov. 1982—83, Able Toastmaster 1983, Dist. 56 Table Topics award 1986, Disting. Toastmaster award 1987, club pres. 1988, Able Toastmaster Bronze award 1990, Able Toastmaster Silver award 1993, club pres. 2000—01, Competent Leader award 2001, Outstanding Toastmaster Dist. 56), Soroptimists (dir. Soroptimist Manor 1978—80, 1983—85, pres. chpt. 1985—87, rep. youth citizenship award com. 1986—88, chpt. dir. 1987—88, chmn. south central region UN com. 1988—90, rep. youth forum com. 1990—92, chpt. corr. sec. 1999—2001), Zeta Tau Alpha. Avocations: gourmet food and wine, barbershop singing. Office: McReynolds Winery 706 Shovel Mountain Rd Round Mountain TX 78663

MCSHANE, ROSEMARY, lawyer; b. Tucson, May 4, 1950; d. John B. and Jean Ann Jacobson McShane; m. James Allen Dator, Sept. 4, 1981; 1 child, McShane Allen Dator. BA, U. Hawaii, 1973; JD, William S. Richardson Sch. Law, 1981. Pvt. practice, Honolulu, 1981-82; lawyer corp. counsel, family support divsn. City and County of Honolulu, 1983-89; lawyer dept. atty. gen., social svcs. divsn. State of Hawaii, Honolulu, 1989-93; adminstr., head hearings officer dept. atty. gen. Office Child Support Hearings, State of Hawaii, Honolulu, 1993-95; atty., divsn. head dept. corp. counsel, family support div. City and County of Honolulu, 1995—. Contbg. author: (book) Our Rights, Our Lives, 3d edit., 1996, (manual) Hawaii Divorce Manual, 3d edit., 1996. Mem. Hawaii Women Lawyers (bd. dirs. 1995-97, 99—, v.p. 1997-98, pres. 1998-99), Hawaii State Bar Assn., William S. Richardson Sch. Law Alumni Assn. Office: Dept Corp Counsel Family Support Divsn # 703 204 Makee Rd Honolulu HI 96815-3978

MCSHANE-HALIK, CHRISTINE DENISE, secondary school educator; b. Chgo., Aug. 3, 1952; d. Thomas Carl McShane and Carmen Rosita Williamson, Joseph Richard Thune (Stepfather); m. John Halik, Sept. 17, 1977; children: Sarah Elizabeth Halik, Jenna Victoria Halik, Travis Justin Halik. Diploma, Valparaiso H.S., Ind., 1970. Clk./switchboard operator/dietary help/office manager:emergency dept./bus. clk. Porter Meml. Hosp., Valparaiso, Ind., 1967—71; med. sec./receptionist/office fin. coord. Midwest Pain Clinic, Michigan City, Ind., 1994—95; ednl. instrnl. asst./ alternative edn. supr. LaPorte H.S., Ind., 1996—; co-sponsor/coord. Girl Reserves/LaPorte H.S., Ind., 2001—; liasion Americorps, LaPorte, Ind., 2002—; instrnl. supr./co-coordinator/data entry Project Extended Day/LaPorte H.S., Ind., 2001—; receptionist/sec./front office mgr. Thomas P. Konicke, M.D., Chesterton, Ind., 1971—73; clk. United Parcel Svc., Westville, Ind., 1974—77; med. records clk./transcriptionist trainee LaPorte Hosp., Ind., 1979—81; clk./receptionist/data entry Star Staffing Svcs., LaPorte, Ind., 1993—96. Computer vol. help St John's Luth. Sch., LaPorte, Ind., 1990—93; mem. Hoosier Alternative Learning Options, Ind., 1997—; girls softball coach LaPorte Parks & Recreation, Ind., 1998—2001. Calligraphy, The Hound (Merit for Participation (Chgo. artist display), 1979). Treas. St John's Athletic Com., LaPorte, Ind., 1993—96. Recipient Award of Appreciation for Coaching & Participation, LaPorte Pk. & Recreation Dept., 2001. D-Liberal. Catholic. Avocations: equestrian, art, travel, writing, conservation/ecology. Home: 1519 Indiana Ave LaPorte IN 46350 Office: LaPorte HS 602 'F' St LaPorte IN 46350 Office Fax: 1-219-324-2142. Personal E-mail: laughingravydaze@yahoo.com. E-mail: chalik@lpcsc.k12.in.us.

MCSHAY, YVONNE MANGRAM AL'MEDIA, English educator, consultant; b. Jacksonville, Fla., Dec. 2, 1944; d. Demous Wesley and Georgia Mae (Brown) Mangram; children: Juli Von, Lisa Ann Henderson. BS, Edward Waters Coll., 1963; MS, Ind. U., 1973. Asst. dir. Planned Parenthood, South Bend, Ind., 1971-72; dist. mgr. Avon Cosmetics, Cinn., 1972-74; tchr. English Polk County Schs., Lakeland, Fla., 1974-92; prof. English Polk C.C., Winter Haven, Fla., 1992—. Owner, dir. POLM Yvonne's Ednl. Techniques, Lakeland. Author (booklet) Rainbow, 1982. Participant Leadership Lakeland VIII, 1990, Focus on Leadership/Ledger, 2003; mem., 1st v.p. NAACP, Lakeland, 1990; organizer, pres. North Lakeland Friends of Libr., 1990-92. Mem. AAUW (v.p. 1989-90, Woman of Yr. 1991), Am. Assn. Women in C.C. (1st v.p.-elect 1996—), Fla. Devel. Edn. Assn. (pres. 2003), Phi Delta Kappa, Delta Kappa Gamma (2nd v.p. 2004), Alpha Kappa Alpha. Home: 202 Pinehurst St Lakeland FL 33805-2862 Office: Polk CC 999 Avenue H NE Winter Haven FL 33881-4256

MCSORLEY, RITA ELIZABETH, adult education educator; b. Baraboo, Wis., Feb. 13, 1947; d. Charles Gervase and Bertie Ellen (Baker) Collins; m. William David McSorley III, June 6, 1967; children: William David IV, Kathryn Rita, Stephen Charles, Matthew Thomas. B Liberal Studies, Mary Washington Coll., Fredericksburg, Va., 1988; MEd, U. Va., Charlottesville, 1994. Adult edn. instr. Waipahu (Hawaii) Cmty. Sch. for Adults, 1989-91, literacy coord., 1990-91; dir. religious edn. Marine Meml. Chapel, Quantico, Va., 1992-94; adult edn. instr. Prince William County Schs., Quantico, 1992-93; coord. computer assisted lang. learning project Literacy Coun. No. Va., Falls Church, 1995-96; ednl. cons. Fairfield Lang. Techs., Harrisonburg, Va., 1996-97; adult edn. coord. N.E. Ind. Sch. Sys., San Antonio, 2000—. Mem. sch. bd. Quantico Dependent Schs., 1980-82; vol. Boy Scouts Am., Quantico and Pearl City, Hawaii, 1985-97. Mem. TESOL, U. Va. Alumni Assn. Roman Catholic. Avocations: quilting, genealogical research, travel. Office: NEISD 10333 Broadway San Antonio TX 78217 E-mail: rmcsor@neisd.net.

MCSPADDEN, LETTIE, political science educator; b. Battle Creek, Mich., Apr. 9, 1937; d. John Dean and Isma Doolie (Sullivan) McSpadden; m. Manfred Wilhelm Wenner, Apr. 3, 1962; children: Eric Alexis, Adrian Edward. AB, U. Chgo., 1959; MA, U. Calif., Berkeley, 1962; PhD, U. Wis., 1972. Fgn. svc. officer Dept. State, Washington, 1961-63; rsch. assoc. Dept. HEW, Washington, 1965-67; asst. prof. polit. sci. U. Ill., Chgo., 1972-79, assoc. prof. polit. sci., 1979-88; prof. and chair dept. polit. sci. No. Ill. U., De Kalb, 1988-94, prof. dept. polit. sci., 1994—. Author: One Environment Under Law, 1976, The Environmental Decade in Court, 1982, United States Energy and Environmental Interest Groups, 1990. Mem. Am. Polit. Sci. Assn., Midwest Polit. Sci. Assn., Law and Society Assn., Pub. Policy Assn., Audubon Soc., Sierra Club. Democrat. Office: No Ill U Dept Polit Sci Dekalb IL 60115 Home: Apt 328 500 S Clinton Chicago IL 60607-4089

MCSWEENEY, FRANCES KAYE, psychology educator; b. Rochester, N.Y., Feb. 6, 1948; d. Edward William and Elsie Winifred (Kingston) McSweeney. BA, Smith Coll., 1969; MA, Harvard U., 1972, PhD, 1974. Lectr. McMaster U., Hamilton, Canada, 1973-74; asst. prof. Wash. State U., Pullman, 1974-79, assoc. prof., 1979-83, prof. psychology, 1983—, chmn. dept. psychology, 1986-94, vice provost for faculty affairs, 2003—. Cons. in field. Contbr. articles to profl. jours. Woodrow Wilson fellow, Sloan fellow, 1968—69, NIMH fellow, 1973. Fellow: APA, Am. Psychol. Soc.; mem.: Assn. Behavior Analysis, Psychonomic Soc., Phi Kappa Phi, Sigma Xi, Phi Beta Kappa. Home: 860 SW Alcora Dr Pullman WA 99163-2053 Office: Wash State U Dept Psychology Pullman WA 99164-4820 Office Phone: 509-335-3508.

MCTAGUE-DOUGHERTY, AMY ELIZABETH, speech pathology/audiology services professional; d. Edward Patrick and Eileen Frances McTague; m. Patrick C. Dougherty, July 12, 1997; 1 child, Emma Louise Dougherty. BS, Loyola Coll., Balt., 1993, MS, 1995. Cert. clin. competence Am. Speech Lang. Hearing Assn., speech lang. pathologist N.J. Augmentative comm. specialist Cerebral Palsy of Monmouth and Ocean Counties, Inc., Wanamassa, NJ, 1995—; augmentative comm. cons. Prentke Romich Co., Wooster, Ohio, 1997—99; comm. instr. Temple U., Phila., 1999. Adj. prof. Richard Stockton Coll. N.J., Pomona, 1999—2001. Named Employee of the Quarter, Cerebral Palsy of Monmouth and Ocean Counties, 1996. Mem.: Am. Speech Lang. Hearing Assn., Internat. Soc. of Augmentative and Alternative Comm., U.S. Soc. of Augmentative and Alternative Comm., N.J. Speech Lang. Hearing Assn. (co-chair augmentative and alternative comm. com. 1998—99). Roman Catholic. Achievements include development of Vocabulary program for communication devices. Avocations: bicycling, gardening, walking. Office: Cerebral Palsy of Monmouth and Ocean Counties 1701 Kneeley Blvd Asbury Park NJ 07712 Office Phone: 732-493-5900. Personal E-mail: pat.doug@verizon.net.

MCTAGUE-STOCK, NANCY A. painter, printmaker; b. Brooklyn, Dec. 26, 1957; d. Walter James McTague and Mary Louise Tazewell; m. Robert Stock, Oct. 2, 1982; children: Benjamin Stock, Rebecca Stock. BFA, Va. Commonwealth U., 1979. V.p. of design R.S. Designs, Inc., New York, NY, 1985—92; art hist. lectr. Weston Public Schs., Conn.; originator and facilitator Landscapes into Tuscany Painting Tours, Italy, 1997—99; self-employed painter and printmaker Wilton, Conn., 1996—; faculty mem. Silvermine Sch. of Art, New Canaan, Conn., 2000—. Vis. artist lectr. Wilton Arts Festival, Wilton, Conn., 2000—01; lectr. Silvermine Sch. Art, New Canaan, Conn., 2001; monotype instructor Creative Arts Festival, Westport, Conn., 2001; lectr. Art Lecture Series, Conn., 2000; mem. faculty Green Farms Acad., Conn., 2002—. Exhibitions include Hamsphire Coll. Main Gallery, Mass., 2001, The Swedish Am. Mus., Chgo., 2001, Silvermine Galleries, Conn., 2001, Milford Ctr. Arts, Milford, Conn., 2001, Catherine J. Smith Gallery, Appalachian State Univ., N.C., 2001, Solon H. Borghlum Galley, Conn., 2001, Laura Barton Gallery, Westport, Conn., 2001, Left of the Bank Gallery, Old Greenwich, Conn., 2001, John Slade Ely Gallery, New Haven, Conn., 2001, Conn. Graphic Arts Ctr., Norwalk, Conn., 2001, Attleboro (Mass.) Mus., 2002, Am. Print Alliance Traveling Exhbn., 2002, U. Conn., Stamford, 2002, Jeffrey Weiss Gallery, Conn., 2002 (Drawing award Nat. Arts Program), Ctr. Contemporary Printmaking, Norwalk, Conn., 2002, Westport (Conn.) Arts Ctr., 2002, Higgins Art Gallery, Cape Cod, Mass., 2002, Capital C.C., Hartford, Conn., 2003, Silvermine Hays Gallery, Conn., 2003, Carriage Barn Gallery, New Cannan, Conn., 2003, Hays Gallery, New Canaan, 2003, Attleboro Mus., 2003, numerous others; contbr. articles The Weston Forum, 1998, to jours., 2001; exhibitions include Ctr. for Contemporary Printmaking, Norwalk, Conn., 2002, Westport Arts Ctr., Conn., 2002, Hays Gallery, New Canaan, Conn., 2003, Carriage Barn Gallery, Conn., 2003, Capital Cmty. Coll., Hartford, Conn., 2003. Named landscape painter, Darien Land Trust, Conn.; recipient Juror's award, 21 Ann. Conn. Artists Exhbn., 2001, Honorable Mention award, Stamford Mus., 2000, Rembrandt Award for Excellence in Graphic Art, Silvermine Galleries, 1999, Printmaking award, Landscape, Stamford Art Assn., 1997, Drawing award, Nat. Arts Educators' Exhbn., 2003. Mem.: Conn. Women Artists, Women's Caucus of Art, Monotype Guild of New England, Am. Print Alliance. Avocations: art history, cooking, gardening. Office: The Painting Studio PO Box 5054 Westport CT 06881-5054 Business E-Mail: nmsstudio1@aol.com.

MCTYER-CLARKE, WANDA KATHLEEN, interior designer; b. St. Louis, Apr. 06; d. Wiley and Lorain Howard. BSBA, St. Louis U., 1982; MS in Econs., So. Ill. U., Edwardsville, 1989; postgrad., Sheffield Sch. Interior Design, N.Y.C.; MBA in Organizational Behavior, Heriot-Watt U. Sch. Bus. Edinburgh Sch., Scotland, 1997; cert., N.Y. Sch. of Interior Design, 1995. Cert. nutritionist, aerobic dance instr., folk art paint technique instr.; decorative painters cert. Plaid Co. OSCI. Sec. St. Louis U.; substitute tchr., aerobic dance instr. St. Louis Bd. Edn.; caseworker Mo. Div. Family Social Svcs., St. Louis; interior designer St. Louis; with McTyer-Clarke

Designs, 1992-96. Block capt. Operation Brightside (cert. of appreciation); Ms. Mahogany Social Clubs 2d Runner Up, 1981-82, Miss Galaxy 1st Runner-Up, 1984. Alpha Kappa Alpha scholar, Sigma Ghamma Rho scholar, Washington Tabernacle Ch. scholar, Cotillion de Leon's Alternate scholar. Address: PO Box 142673 Saint Louis MO 63114-0673

MCVEIGH-PETTIGREW, SHARON CHRISTINE, communications consultant; b. San Francisco, Feb. 6, 1949; d. Martin Allen and Frances (Roddy) McVeigh; m. John Wallace Pettigrew, Mar. 27, 1971; children: Benjamin Thomas Pettigrew, Margaret Mary Pettigrew. BA with honors, U. Calif.-Berkeley, 1971; diploma of edn., Monash U., Australia, 1975; MBA, Golden Gate U., 1985. Tchr., adminstr. Victorian Edn. Dept., Victoria, Australia, 1972—79; supr. Network Control Ctr. GTE Sprint Comms., Burlingame, Calif., 1979—81, mgr. customer assistance, 1981—84, mgr. state legis. ops., 1984—85, dir. revenue programs, 1986—87; comm. cons. Flores, Pettigrew & Co., San Mateo, Calif., 1987—89; telemktg. Apple Computer Inc., Cupertino, Calif., 1989—94; prin. The Call Ctr. Group, San Mateo, Calif., 1995—. Telecomm. cons. PPG Svcs., 1994—; telecomm. spkr. Dept. Consumer Affairs, Sacramento, 1984. Panelist Wash. Gov.'s Citizens Coun., 1984; founding mem. Maroondah Women's Shelter, Victoria, 1978; organizer nat. conf. Bus. Women and the Polit. Process, New Orleans, 1986; mem. sch. bd. Boronia Tech. Sch., Victoria, 1979. Recipient Tchr. Spl. Responsibilities award, Victoria Edn. Dept., 1979. Mem.: Women's Econ. Action League, Am. Telemktg. Assn. (bd. dirs. 1992), Peninsula Profl. Women's Network, Am. Mgmt. Assn., Women in Telecom. (panel moderator Sann Francisco 1984). Democrat. Roman Catholic.

MCVEY, ALICE LLOYD, social worker; b. N.Y.C., Mar. 21, 1935; d. George John and Alice Wood (Lloyd) Mc Vey. MS, Syracuse U., 1970; M of Profl. Svc., N.Y. Theol. Sem., 1977; cert. pastoral counseling, Postgrad. Ctr. Mental Health, 1977; cert. in gerontology, Adelphi U., 1983; MSW, Fordham U., 1991. Tchr. elem. Schs. in Diocese of Bklyn., 1955-66; tchr. biology Holy Family High Sch., Huntington, N.Y., 1966-75; regional superior Sisters of St. Joseph, Brentwood, N.Y., 1975-82; pastoral minister to older adults Our Lady of Grace Ch., West Babylon, N.Y., 1982-96, dir. parish social min. office, 1996—. Mem. Acad. Cert. Social Workers. Avocations: gardening, birding, hiking.

MCVEY, DIANE ELAINE, accountant; b. Wilmington, Del., Apr. 20, 1953; d. C. Granville and Margaret M. (Lindell) McV. AA in Acctg., Goldey Beacom Coll. (Del.), 1973, BS in Acctg., 1980; MBA in Mgmt., Fairleigh Dickinson U., 1985. Acct. Audio Visual Arts, Wilmington, 1973; cost acct. FMC Corp., Kennett Sq., Pa., 1973-75; asst. acct. NVF Corp., Kennett Sq., 1978-80; staff analyst GPU Nuclear, Parsippany, N.J., 1980-93; staff acct., 1993-95, GPU Svc., Morristown, 1995-2000, Reading, Pa., 2000—, FirstEnergy, 2001—. Owner, Demac Cons., Dover, N.J., 1988-2000, Reading, 2000—. Elder First Presbyn. Ch., Rockaway, N.J., 1986—, session mem., 1988-91; commr. to bd. adjustment, Dover, N.J., 1994-2000. With U.S. Army, 1975-78. Mem. Assn. MBA Execs. Republican. Presbyterian. Avocations: reading mystery books, writing and performing music, needlework. Office: 2800 Pottsville Pike Reading PA 19601 E-mail: d.mcvey@gpu.com., d.e.mcvey@worldnet.att.net.

MCVEY, TERESA LYNN, special education educator; b. Emporia, Kans., May 26, 1962; d. Robert Dale and Marleen Kay Lane; m. Ron Lee McVey, June 12, 1998; 1 adopted child, Kay Lynn children: Amber, Jason Denton, Derek. BS in Elem. Edn., Emporia State U., 1984, MS in Spl. Edn., 1991. Early childhood spl. edn. tchr., autism cons. Tri-County Spl. Edn. Coop. # 607, Independence, Kans., 1986—; adj. tchr. Independence C.C., Kans., 1986—, instr. Upward Bound, 1997—. Bd. dirs. Big Bro./Big Sister, Indepenedence, Kans.; chairperson Tot Olympics, 1995. Mem.: Kans. Nat. Edn. Assn. (pres. 1996—). Avocations: travel, dance. Home: 2088 CR 2700 Caney KS 67333

MC VIE, CHRISTINE PERFECT, musician; b. Eng., July 12, 1943; m. John McVie (div.); m. Eddy Quintela. Student art sch., pvt. student sculpture. Singer, keyboardist, Fleetwood Mac, from 1970; albums with Fleetwood Mac include: Fleetwood Mac, 1968, Fleetwood Mac in Chicago, 1969, Then Play On, 1969, English Rose, 1969, Kiln House, 1970, Future Games, 1971, Bare Trees, 1972, Penguin, Mystery To Me, 1973, Heroes Are Hard to Find, 1974, Fleetwood Mac, 1975, Rumours, 1977, Tusk, 1979, Fleetwood Mac Live, 1980, Mirage, 1982, Jumping at Shadows, 1985, Tango in the Night, 1987, Greatest Hits, 1988, Behind the Mask, 1990, The Dance, 1997; solo albums include Christine Perfect, 1969, Christine McVie, 1984; composer: songs including Spare Me a Little of Your Love, Don't Stop, You Make Loving Fun, Over and Over, Hold Me, Songbird, Got a Hold on Me, Heroes Are Hard to Find, Little Lies, As Long as You Follow, Save Me, Skies the Limit. Office: care Warner Bros Records 3300 Warner Blvd Burbank CA 91505-4632

MCWADE, JESSICA CHRISTY, marketing professional; b. Malden, Mass., May 10, 1956; d. Stanley Bernard and Doris Marie McWade; children from previous marriage: Zachary, Jackson. BS, Boston U., 1978; MBA, NYU, 1980; MPA, Harvard U., 1987; cert. econs., Stockholm Sch. Econs., 1980. Photographer Gov.'s Office, Boston, 1976—78; dep. press sec. Mayor's Office, City of Boston, 1982—84; dir. corp. rels. BankBoston, 1987—94, internat. loan officer, 1984—87; dir. corp. comms. Textron, Providence, 1994—95; v.p. corp. affairs Raytheon Co., Lexington, Mass., 1996—98; pres. McWade Group, Burlington, Mass., 1998—. Pres. World Affairs Coun. Boston, 1992—96. Active The Coun. Fgn. Rels., N.Y.C., 1993—; allocations committeewoman United Way of Mass Bay, Boston, 1989—94; treas. Whittier St. Neighborhood Health Ctr., Boston, 1990—93. Comdr. USNR, 1980—. Decorated Navy Commendation medal, Navy Achievement medals; named Ten Outstanding Young Leaders, Boston Jaycees, 1987; recipient Twice a Citizen award, USNR Assn., 1985; fellow, The Salzburg Seminar, 1998, The British-Am. Fellowship, 1994. Roman Catholic. Office: McWade Group 10 Maple Ridge Dr Burlington MA 01803 Business E-Mail: jmcwade@mcwadegroup.com.

MCWETHY, PATRICIA JOAN, educational association administrator; b. Chgo., Feb. 27, 1946; d. Frank E. and Emma (Kuehne) McW.; m. H. Frank Eden; children: Kristin Beth, Justin Nicholas. BA, Northwestern U., 1968; MA, U. Minn., 1970; MBA, George Washington U., 1981. Geog. analyst CIA, McLean, Va., 1970-71; rsch. asst. NSF, Washington, 1972-74, spl. asst. to dir., 1975, assoc. program dir. human geography and regional sci. program, 1976-79; exec. dir. Assn. Am. Geographers, Washington., 1979-84, Nat. Assn. Biology Tchrs., Reston, Va., 1984-95, Nat. Sci. Edn. Leadership Assn., Arlington, Va., 1995-97; edn. dir. Nat. Alliance for Mentally Ill, Arlington, 1998-99. Prin. investigator grant on biotech. equipment ednl. resource partnership NSF, 1989-93, NSF funder internat. symposium on Basic Biol. Concepts: What Should the World's Children Know?, 1992-94; co-prin. investigator NSF grant, 1995-97; mem. chmn.'s adv. com. Nat. Com. Sci. Stds. and Assessment, 1992-95; mem. Commn. for Biology Edn., Internat. Union Biol.. Sci., 1988-97; mem. exec. com. Alliance for Environ. Edn., 1987-90, chmn. program com., 1990; condr. seminars in field; lectr. in field. Author monograph and papers in field; editor handbook. NSF grantee, 1989-93, 95-97; NSF fellow, 1968-69; recipient Outstanding Performance award, NSF, 1973. Mem. Phi Beta Kappa.

MCWHINNEY, MADELINE H. (MRS. JOHN DENNY DALE), economist, director; b. Denver, Mar. 11, 1922; d. Leroy and Alice (Houston) McW.; m. John D. Dale, June 23, 1961; 1 child, Thomas Denny. BA, Smith Coll., 1943; MBA, NYU, 1947. Economist Fed. Res. Bank, N.Y.C., 1943-73, chief fin. and trade statis. divsn., 1955-59, mgr. market stats. dept., 1960-65, asst. v.p., 1965-73; pres. First Women's Bank, N.Y.C., 1974-76, Dale, Elliott & Co., Inc., Red Bank, N.J., 1977-97. Trustee Retirement System Fed. Res. Bank, 1955-58; vis. lectr. N.Y.U. Grad. Sch. Bus., 1976-77; mem. N.J. Casino Control Commn., 1980-82, Women's Econ. Round Table, 1978-89, chmn. 1987-88; bd. govs. Am. Stock Exch., 1977-81; trustee Monmouth Mus., 1995—, Vis. Nurse Assn. Ctrl. Jersey, 1995—, Planned Parenthood Ctrl. Jersey, 1995-2003, Carnegie Corp. N.Y., 1974-82, Central Savs. Bank of N.Y., 1980-82, Monmouth Conservatory of Music, 2002—; trustee Charles F. Kettering Found., 1975-93, chmn. 1987-91; trustee Inst. Internat. Edn., 1975—, Investor Responsibility Rsch. Ctr., Inc., 1974-81; asst. dir. Whitney Mus. Am. Art, 1983-86; dir. Atlantic Energy Co., 1983-93; trustee The Mgrs. Funds, 1983-2004; mem. adv. com. profl. ethics N.J. Supreme Ct., 1983-98. Trustee Monmouth Conservatory of Music, 2002—. Recipient Smith Coll. medal, 1971, Alumni Achievement award NYU Grad. Sch. Bus. Adminstrn. Alumni Assn., 1971, NYU Crystal award, 1982. Mem. Am. Fin. Assn. (past dir.), Money Marketeers (v.p. 1960, pres. 1961-62), Alumni Assn. Grad. Sch. Bus. Adminstrn. NYU (dir. 1951-63, pres. 1957-59), Soc. Meml. Ctr., N.J. Com. for Humanities, Phi Beta Kappa Fellows (v.p. 1979-87). Office: PO Box 458 Red Bank NJ 07701-0458 Home: 192 Heritage Court Little Silver NJ 07739

MCWHIRTER, GLENNA SUZANNE (NICKIE MCWHIRTER), retired newspaper columnist; b. Peoria, Ill., June 28, 1929; d. Alfred Leon and Garnet Lorene (Short) Sotier; m. Edward Ford McWhirter (div.); children: Suzanne McWhirter Orlicki, Charles Edward, James Richard. BS in English Lang. and Lit., U. Mich., postgrad., 1960-63. Editl. asst. McGraw-Hill Pub. Co., Detroit, 1951-54; staff writer Detroit Free Press, Inc., Detroit, 1963-70, asst. city editor, 1971-77, columnist, 1977-88, Detroit News Inc., Detroit, 1988-97; advt. copy writer Campbell-Ewald Co., Detroit, 1967-68; ret., 1997. Author: Pea Soup, 1984 Winner 1st Place Commentary award UPI, Mich., 1979; 1st Place Columns AP, Mich., 1978, 81; 1st Place Columns Detroit Press Club Found., Mich., 1978; Disting. Service award State of Mich., 1985 Mem. Women in Comm. (Headliner award 1978), Alpha Gamma Delta. Avocations: flower gardening, interior design. Home: 495 Lake Shore Ln Grosse Pointe Woods MI 48236

MCWHIRTER, JAMILA LEANN, choral conductor; d. John Robert and Lenora Evelyn Lucy; m. R. Mark McWhirter, Oct. 27, 1995. MusB, S.W. Bapt. U., 1989; MA, Ctrl. Mo. State U., 1995; postgrad., U. Mo., 2002—. Cert. tchr. elem. and secondary edn. Mo. Choral music tchr. Plato R-V Sch. Dist., Plato, Mo., 1989—92, fine arts dept. chairperson Morgan County R-2 Sch. Dist., Versailles, Mo., 1992—2002; choral dir. Stephens Coll., Columbia, Mo., 2002—; choral dir./music educator U. of Mo., Columbia, Mo., 2002—; adj. faculty Ctrl. Mo. State U., Warrensburg, Mo., 1995—2000; excel adj. faculty Mo. Bapt. Coll., St. Louis, 1997—2002. Adjudicator/clinician Mo. Music Educator's Assn., Mo., 1989—, Mo. Choral Dirs. Assn., Mo., 1989—; choral dir. Ctrl. Mo. State U. Summer Music Camp, Warrensburg, Mo., 1997—2000; applied voice instr., Mo., 1989—. Dir.: (numerous choral performances), (musical) Camelot; singer: (musicals) Oklahoma;Wizard of Oz; Anything Goes; dir.: (yuletide feasts); contbr. articles to profl. jours. Dir. Versailles Cmty. Chorus, Versailles, Mo., 1992—94; musical dir./bd. advisor Royal Theater Arts Coun., Versailles, 1992—2001; min. of music Second Bapt. Ch., Lebanon, Mo., 1989—92; asst. min. of music Trinity So. Bapt. Ch., Versailles, 1992, chair pers. com., 1999—2003. Recipient Tom Mills Choral award, U. of Mo. Columbia; scholar Post Grad. Tchg. assistantship, U. of Mo., Regents scholar, Ctrl. Mo. State U., S.W. Bapt. U., Vocal Performance scholar. Mem.: West Ctrl. Mo. Music Educator's Assn. (jr. high choral v.p. 1996—98), Classroom Tchrs. Assn. (vice-president 1994—95), Mo. State Tchrs. Assn., West Ctrl. Mo. Choral Dirs. Assn. (dist. rep. 1998—2000), West Ctrl. Mo. Music Educator's Assn. (pres. 2002—), Mo. Music Educator's Assn. (Selected for Choral Performance at State Conv. 1999), Mo. Choral Dirs. Assn. (state treas. 2000—04), Pi Kappa Lambda. Avocations: horseback riding, reading, swimming, fishing, hiking.

MCWHORTER, DIANE, writer; b. Birmingham, Ala. Postgrad., Wellesley Coll. Writer, N.Y.C. Contbr. The N.Y. Times, USA Today, Harpers, The Nation, The New Republic, Newsday, People, Talk, The Wall Street Journal, The Washington Post, others (Pulitzer prize for gen. nonfiction, 2002); author: Carry Me Home. Recipient Pulitzer prize for gen. Non-Fiction, 2002. Office: Simon and Schuster 1230 Ave of the Americas New York NY 10020

MCWHORTER, KATHLEEN, orthodontist; b. Houston, May 29, 1953; d. Archer and Lucile (Taft) McW. BA summa cum laude, U. Houston, 1986; DDS with honors, Baylor Coll., 1990. Mgr. Am. Internat. Rent-A-Car, Houston, 1974-79; mktg. researcher Concoco Oil Co., Houston, 1979-83; orthodontist Baylor Coll. Dentistry, Dallas, 1990—. Presenter Am. Assn. Dental Rsch., Montreal, Que., Can., 1988, Cin., 1990; rsch. fellow Baylor Coll. Dentistry, Dallas, 1987, 88, 89. Contbr. articles to profl. jours. Mem. ADA, Am. Assn. Orthodontists, Am. Assn. Women Dentists, Am. Assn. Dentistry for Children, Internat. Assn. Dental Rsch., Am. Assn. Dental Rsch., Tex. Dental Assn., Dallas County Dental Soc., The Crescent Club. Avocations: tennis, walking, music, water skiing. Office: Baylor U Coll Dentistry Dept Orthodontics 3302 Gaston Ave Dallas TX 75246-2027

MCWILLIAM, JOANNE ELIZABETH, retired religion educator; b. Toronto, Ont., Can., Dec. 10, 1928; d. Cecil Edward and Edna Viola (Archer) McW.; children, Leslie Mary Giroday, Elizabeth Dewart, Sean Dewart, Colin Dewart; m. C. Peter Slater, June 6, 1987. BA, U. Toronto, 1951, MA, 1953, U. St. Michael's, Toronto, 1966, PhD, 1968; DD honoris causa, Queen's U., Kingston, Ont., 2003. Asst. prof. religious studies U. Toronto, 1968-74, assoc. prof., 1974-87, prof., 1987, chairperson dept. religious studies, 1990-92, 93-94; Mary Crooke Hoffman prof. of Dogmatic Theology The Gen. Theol. Sem., N.Y.C, 1994-99; ret., 1999. Author: The Theology of Grace of Theodore of Mopsuestia, 1971, Death and Resurrection in the Fathers, 1986; editor: Augustine: Rhetor to Theologian, 1991, Toronto Jour. Theology. Mem. Can. Soc. for Patristic Studies (pres. 1987-90), Conf. Anglican Theologians (pres. 1990-91), Can. Soc. for the Study of Religion, Can. Theol. Soc., Am. Theol. Soc., Am. Acad. Religion. Anglican. Home: 59 Duggan Ave Toronto ON Canada M4V 1Y1 E-mail: joanne.mcwilliam@utoronto.ca.

MCWILLIAMS, DAWN SUZANNE, marketing professional, consultant; b. Rochester, N.Y., July 4, 1963; d. Richard Joseph Jr. and Donna Charlotte Bleier; m. Michael L. McWilliams, Oct. 11, 1986; children: Megan L., Adam M. BFA, Rochester Inst. Tech., 1985, MBA, 2000. Mgr. creative svcs. Visual Horizons, Rochester, 1986—89; assoc. dir. pub. affairs U. Rochester, 1989—2000, dir. mktg., 2000—; owner, co-founder Strategic Mktg. Assn., Rochester, 2001—. Presenter in field. V.p. adv. bd. Rochester Inst. Tech. Coll. Bus., 2001—. Named one of 40 Under 40, Rochester Bus. Jour., 2002; recipient Cir. of Excellence award, CASE, 2003. Mem.: Am. Mktg. Assn. (bd. dirs. Rochester chpt. 2003—), Univ. and Coll. Designers Assn., Rochester Inst. Tech. Alumni Network (founder, co-chair), Rochester Women's Network. Avocations: gardening, reading, swimming, walking. Home: 456 Dewey St Churchville NY 14428 Office: U Rochester 2-211B Carol Simon Hall Rochester NY 14627 Business E-Mail: mcwilliams@simon.rochester.edu.

MCWILLIAMS, MARGARET ANN, home economics educator, author; b. Osage, Iowa, May 26, 1929; d. Alvin Randall and Mildred Irene (Lane) Edgar; children: Roger, Kathleen. BS, Iowa State U., 1951, MS, 1953; PhD, Oreg. State U., 1968. Registered dietitian. Asst. prof. home econs. Calif. State U., L.A., 1961-66, assoc. prof., 1966-68, prof., 1968-92, prof. emeritus, 1992—, chmn. dept., 1968-76; pres. Plycon Press, 1978—. Author: Food Fundamentals, 1966, 7th edit., 1998, Nutrition for the Growing Years, 1967, 6th edit., 1999, Experimental Foods Laboratory Manual, 1977, 5th edit., 2000, Lifelong Nutrition, 2001, (with L. Kotschevar) Understanding Food, 1969, Illustrated Guide to Food Preparation, 1970, 8th edit., 1998, (with L. Davis) Food for You, 1971, 2d edit., 1976, The Meatless Cookbook, 1973, (with F. Stare) Living Nutrition, 1973, 4th edit., 1984, Nutrition for Good Health, 1974, 2d edit., 1982, (with H. Paine) Modern Food Preservation, Fundamentals of Meal Management, 1978, 4th edit., 2005, (with H. Heller) The World of Nutrition, 1984, Foods: Experimental Perspectives, 1989, 4th edit., 2000, Food Around the World: A Cultural Perspective, 2003. Chmn. bd. Beach Cities Symphony, 1991-94. Recipient Alumni Centennial award Iowa State U., 1971, Profl. Achievement award, 1977; Phi Upsilon Omicron Nat. Founders fellow, 1964; Home Economist in Bus. Nat. Found. fellow, 1967; Outstanding Prof. award Calif. State U., 1976. Mem. Am. Dietetic Assn., Inst. Food Technologists, Phi Kappa Phi, Phi Upsilon Omicron, Omicron Nu, Iota Sigma Pi, Sigma Delta Epsilon, Sigma Alpha Iota. Home: PO Box 220 Redondo Beach CA 90277-0220

MEAD, CHRISTINA DYKSTRA, church administrator; BA, U. Wis., Madison; MS in Pub. Adminstrn., NYU. Exec. asst. to chief exec. for fin. N.Y.C. Health and Hosps. Corp.; exec. McKinsey & Co. Internat. Cons.; v.p., CFO Reading is Fundamental; CFO Washington Nat. Cathedral, 2000—. Trustee Shipley Sch., Bryn Mawr, Pa., Campaign for Wis.; House of Ruth Washington, DC. Office: Washington Nat Cathedral Massachusetts & Wisconsin Aves NW Washington DC 20016-5098

MEAD, PRISCILLA, state legislator; b. Columbus, OH, Feb. 7, 1944; m. John L. Mead; children: John, Willian, Neel, Sarah. Student, Ohio State U. Councilwoman, Upper Arlington, Ohio, 1982-90; mayor, 1986-90; mem. Ohio Ho. of Reps. from 28th dist., Columbus, 1992-2000, Ohio Senate from 16th dist., Columbus, 2001—. Mem. Franklin County Child Abuse and Neglect Found., Coun. for Ethics and Econs. Recipient Svc. award Northwest Kiwanis, Woman of Yr. award Upper Arlington Rotary, Citizen of Yr. award U.S. C. of C. Mem. LWV, Upper Arlington Edn. Found., Jr. League Columbus, Upper Arlington C. of C., Delta Gamma. Republican. Home: 2281 Brixton Rd Columbus OH 43221-3117 Office: Ohio Ho of Reps State House Columbus OH 43215

MEADE, BIRGITTA ROSEMARY, elementary school educator; b. Denmark, July 18, 1961; d. Carol Rugland and Roger Meade. MS, Mont. State U., 2003. Cert. tchr. Nat. Bd. for Profl. Tchg. Stds., 2000. Tchr. North Winneshiek Cmty. Sch., Decorah, Iowa, 1995—. Home: 1978 Colonel Taylor Rd Decorah IA 52101-7471 Office: North Winneshiek Cmty Sch Decorah IA Personal E-mail: bmeade@n-winn.k12.ia.us.

MEADE, DOROTHY WINIFRED, retired educational administrator; b. N.Y.C., Jan. 26, 1935; d. Percival and Fraulien Franklin; m. Gerald H. Meade (div. 1987); 1 child, Myrla E. BA in Am. History, Queens Coll., Flushing, N.Y., 1970; MA in Corrective Reading, Bklyn. Coll., 1975; BA in Religious Edn., United Christian Coll., Bklyn., 1980; postgrad., Bklyn. Coll., 1984. Tchr. social studies cluster Pub. Sch. 137, Bklyn., 1979-83, curriculum coord. Follow Through Program, 1984-88, adminstrv. intern, 1983-84; staff developer social studies Cen. Sch. Dist. 23, Bklyn., 1988-89, dist. coord. Project Child, 1989-91. Mem. faculty Coll. of New Rochelle, Bklyn., 1994-97. Participant Crossroads Africa, 1958; active Agape Tabernack Internat. Fellowship, 2000; former mem. Ch. of the Master; theol. intern Mt. Lebanon Bapt. Ch., 2001. Mem. African Christian Tchrs., N.Y. Pub. Sch. Early Childhood Edn., N.Y. Geography Inst., Women Organizing, Mobilizing Bldg. Pentecostal. Avocations: bicycling, swimming, roller skating, singing, traveling. Home: 538 E 86th St Brooklyn NY 11236

MEADORS, MARYNELL, former professional basketball coach, sports team executive; B.Health, Phys. Edn. and Recreation, Mid. Tenn. State U., 1965, M. Physiology of Exercise, 1966. Basketball coach Tenn. Tech., 1970-86, Fla. State U., 1986-96; head coach, gen. mgr. Charlotte Sting, 1997-99; dir. scouting Miami Sol, 1999—. Named Ohio Valley Conf. Coach of the Yr., 1978, 83, Metro Conf. Coach of Yr., 1990, Conf. Co-Coach of the Yr., 1991; inductee Tenn. Tech. Hall of Fame, 1992, Ohio Valley Conf. Hall of Fame, 1992. Achievements include appearing in NCAA record book in all-time coaching longevity records section (ranks third in most games coached, 786, fifth in most seasons, 26 and seventh in victories, 495). Office: Miami Sol SunTrust Internat Ctr One SE 3rd Ave Ste 2300 Miami FL 33131 Fax: 786-777-1629. E-mail: mmeadors@heat.com.

MEADOW, LYNNE (CAROLYN MEADOW), theater producer; b. New Haven, Nov. 12, 1946; d. Frank and Virginia R. Meadow BA cum laude, Bryn Mawr Coll., 1968; postgrad., Yale U., 1968-70. Dir. Theatre Communications Group, 1978-80. Adj. prof. SUNY, Stony Brook, 1975-76, Yale U., Circle in the Sq., 1977-78, 89-91, NYU, 1977-80; theatre and music/theatre panelist Nat. Endowment for Arts, 1977-88; artistic advisor Fund for New Am. Plays, 1988-90. Artistic dir. Manhattan Theatre Club, N.Y.C., 1972—; guest dir. Nat. Playwrights Conf., Eugene O'Neill Theatre Ctr., 1975-77, Phoenix Theatre, 1976; dir. Ashes for Manhattan Theatre Club and N.Y. Shakespeare Festival, 1977; prodr. off-Broadway shows Ain't Misbehavin', 1978, Crimes of the Heart, 1981, Miss Firecracker Contest, 1984, Frankie and Johnny, 1987, Eastern Standard, 1988, Lisbon Traviata, 1989, Lips Together, Teeth Apart, 1991, Four Dogs and a Bone, 1993, Love! Valour! Compassion!, 1994; dir. Principia Scritoriae, 1986, Woman in Mind, 1988 (Drama Desk award), Eleemosynary, 1989, Absent Friends, 1991; dir. Broadway prodn. A Small Family Business, 1992, The Loman Family Picnic, 1993, Nine Armenians, 1996(Drama Desk nominee), Captains Courageous: The Musical, 1999, The Tale of the Allergist's Wife, 2000; (dir. Broadway prodn. and nat. tour) The Tale of the Allergist's Wife, 2000, Last Dance, 2003, Rose's Dilemma, 2003; co-prodr. off-Broadway and Broadway show Mass Appeal, 1981. Recipient Citation of Merit Nat. Coun. Women, 1976, Outer Circle Critics award 1977, Drama Desk award, 1977, Obie award for Ashes, 1977, Margo Jones award for Continued Encouragement New Playwrights, 1981, Critics Circle award Outstanding Revival on or off Broadway for Loot, 1986, Lucille Lortel award for Outstanding Achievement, 1987, Spl. Drama Desk award, 1989, N.Y. Drama Critics Circle award Best Fgn. Play for Aristocrats, 1989, Torch of Hope award, 1989, Manhattan Mag. award, 1994, Lee Reynolds award League Profl. Theatre Women, 1994; named Northwood Inst. Disting. Woman of Yr., 1990, Person of Yr., Nat. Theatre Conf., 1992, SDCF "Mr. Abbott" award, 2003. Office: Manhattan Theatre Club 311 W 43rd St Fl 8 New York NY 10036-6413

MEADOWS, JOYCE KATHERINE, nurse; b. Detroit, Mich., Aug. 12, 1944; d. Jesse O. and Katherine Rita Meadows; 1 child from previous marriage, Katherine Cherine. Diploma LAC USC Sch. Nursing, 1977, Enterostomal Therapy Cert., 1979. RN. RN, cons., educator, Calif., 1968—97; nurse Jerry Pettis Meml. Vets. Hosp., Loma Linda, Calif., 1978—81; educator, specialist, Vis. Nurse Assn., Inland County, Riverside, Calif., 1981—84; educator, specialist Vis. Nurse Assn., Sacramento, 1984—86, Vis. Nurse Assn., Orange County, Tustin, Calif., 1986—90; wound, ostomy specialist, educator Vis. Nurse Assn., Inland County, Riverside, Calif., 1997—. Chair nursing subcom. Dept. of Aging, Sacramento, Calif., 1991; cons. to FHP model for govt. HMO system, Fountain Valley, Calif., 1990—96; spkr. in field. Contbr. articles to profl. publs. Educator, cons. Ostomy Assn., Riverside, Calif., 1981—84. Recipient Hands and Heart award with commendation, Max Cleland VA Adminstrn., Washington, D.C., 1980. Avocation: candlemaking, writing poetry and stories. Home: 28323 Birdie St Moreno Valley CA 92555 Office: Vis Nurse of Inland County PO Box 1649 Riverside CA 92502

MEADOWS, JUDITH ADAMS, law librarian, educator; b. Spartanburg, SC, June 5, 1945; d. Thomas Taylor and Virginia (Dayton) Adams; m. Bruce R. Meadows; children: Beth Ann Blackwood, Ted Adams Meadows.

BA, Am. U., 1967; MLS, U. Md., 1979. Law libr. Aspen Sys. Corp., Gaithersburg, Md., 1979-81; dir. Fairfax (Va.) Law Libr., 1981-84, State Law Libr., Helena, Mont., 1984—. Vis. prof. U. Wash., Seattle, 1994; adj. prof. U. Great Falls, Mont., 1989-96; presiding ofcl. Gov.'s Conf. on Libr. Info. Svc., Helena, Mont., 1991. Author: (book chpts.) From Yellow Pads to Computers, 1991, Law Librarianship, 1994; contbr. articles to profl. jours. [illegible] Helena Presents, 1980-92, Holter Mus. Art, 1995-2002, Mont. Supreme Ct. Commn. on Tech., Mont. Supreme Ct. Commn. on Self-Represented Litigants, Mont. Equal Justice Task Force, 2001—, Helena Edn. Found., v.p., 2003. Recipient Disting. Svc. award State Bar of Mont., 1991. Mem. Am. Assn. Law Librs. (treas. 1992-95, v.p. 1996—, pres. 1997-98, past pres. 1998—), N.W. Consortium of Law Librs. (pres.), Mont. Libr. Assn. (sec. 1986-88). Avocations: gourmet cooking, cross-country skiing, reading. Office: State Law Libr Mont PO Box 203004 Helena MT 59620-3004

MEADOWS, PATRICIA BLACHLY, art curator, civic worker; b. Amarillo, Tex., Nov. 12, 1938; d. William Douglas and Irene Bond Blachly; m. Curtis Washington Meadows, Jr., June 10, 1961; children: Michael Lee, John Morgan. BA in English and History, U. Tex., 1960. Program dir. Ex-Students Assn., Austin, Tex., 1960-61; co-founder, dir. Dallas Visual Art Ctr., 1981-86, curator, 1987-98, bd. dirs., 1981-99, pres. bd. dirs., 1982-85, founder The Collectors, 1988; founder, prin. cons. Art Connections, Dallas, 1996—; sr. v.p. Hall Fin. Group Ltd., 1999—. Exhbn. dir. Tex. bd. Nat. Mus. Women in Arts, Washington, 1986-91; mem. acquisition com. Dallas Mus. Art, 1988-92; chmn. adv. bd. Oaks Bank and Trust, 1993-96; juror numerous exhibits, Dallas and Tex.; spkr. on arts subjects; cons. city, state and nat. project concerning arts; chmn. bd. dirs. State-Thomas TIF Zone #1, 1994-99, bd. dirs. 1989-99. Author: (art catalogues) Critic's Choice, 1983-97, Texas Women, 1989-90, Texas: reflections, rituals, 1991; organizer many exhbns. including Presenting Nine, D-Art Visual Art Ctr., 1984, Mosaics, 1991-97, Senses Beyond Sight, 1992-93. Bd. dirs. Mid-Am. Arts Alliance, Kansas City, Mo., 1989-93, Tex. Bd. Commerce, Austin, 1991-93, Women's Issues Network, Dallas, 1994-96; bd. dirs. Dallas Summit, 1989-95, pres., 1993-94, mem. 1988—; mem. Charter 100, 1993—, Dallas Assembly, 1993—, Leadership Tex., 1987; co-founder, mem. steering com. Emergency Artists Support League, Dallas, 1992-99; mem. originating task force Dallas Coalition for Arts, 1984; also others. Recipient Dedication to Arts award Tex. Fine Arts Assn., 1984, Assn. Artists and Craftsmen, 1984, Southwestern Watercolor Soc., 1985, Flora award Dallas Civic Garden Ctr., 1987, James K. Wilson award TACA, 1988, Maura award Women's Ctr. Dallas, 1991, Disting. Woman award Northwood U., 1993, Excellence in the Arts award Dallas Hist. Soc., 1993, Legend award Dallas Visual Art Ctr., 1996. Mem. Tex. Assn. Mus., Arts Dist. Mgmt. Assn. (bd. dirs., exec. com. 1984-92, Artists and Craftsmen Assn. (pres. bd. dirs. 1982-83), Dallas Art Dealer's Assn. (pres. 1997-99). Presbyterian. Office: Hall Financial Group 6801 Gaylord Pkwy Ste 100 Frisco TX 75034-8545 E-mail: pmeadows@hallfinancial.com.

MEADOWS, VICKERS B. federal agency administrator; Grad., Green Mountain Coll. Procuremen, dir. presdl. gifts White House, Washington, 1989—89, spl. asst. to the v.p. for adminstrn., 1985—89; dep. dir., dir. exec. svc. Dept. Transp., Washington, 1989—93; dir. adminstrn. Gov. Bush, 1995—2000; spl. asst., dir. White House Mgmt. White House, Washington, dir. adminstrn. Bush-Cheney Transition; asst. sec. for adminstrn. office, CIO, Dept. HUD, Washington, 2002—. Republican. Office: Dept HUD Adminstrn Office 451 7th St SW Washington DC 20410-1047

MEADS, MINDY, merchandising and design executive; BS, U. Ill. With Denver Dry Goods, 1974—78; sr. v.p., v.p., merchandising administr., v.p., store mgr., jeans collection buyer R.H. Macy and Company Inc., 1978—89; operating exec. The Limited, 1989—90; v.p., gen. merchandising mgr. Lands End, 1991—94, sr. v.p. merchandising and design, 1994—96; sr. v.p., gen. merchandising mgr., merchandising design planning and allocation Gymboree Corp., 1996—98; exec. v.p. merchandising and design Lands End, 1998—2003; gen. mgr. apparel Sears Roebuck and Co., 2003—04, exec. v.p., 2003—; pres. Lands End, 2003—, CEO, 2004—. Office: Sears Roebuck and Co 3333 Beverly Rd Hoffman Estates IL 60179*

MEAGHER, DEIRDRA M. lawyer; b. N.Y.C., Aug. 15, 1949; d. Pearse P. and Katherine M. Meagher. BA, Mercy Coll., Dobbs Ferry, N.Y., 1970; MS, Mich. State U., East Lansing, 1972; JD, Seton Hall U. Sch. of Law, Newark, 1992. Bar: N.J. 1994, D.C. 1994, U.S. Patent and Trademark Office 2000. Systems engr. EDS Corp., Plano, Tex., 1973—77; tech. assoc. Merck & Co., Inc., Rahway, NJ, 1977—81; info. tech. cons. Fords, NJ, 1981—85; project leader Hartz Mountain Corp., Secaucus, NJ, 1985—88; summer law assoc. Friedman Siegelbaum, Roseland, NJ, 1991—91; assoc., law clk. Selitto, Behr & Kim, Metuchen, NJ, 1991—95; assoc. Glynn & Assocs., P.C., Flemington, NJ, 1995—. Author: Vendor's Guide to Computer Contracting. Chair cmty. affairs commn. Metuchen Diocesan Coun. for Cath. Women, Metuchen, NJ, 1983—89; recorder Rec. for the Blind and Dyslectic, Princeton, NJ, 1999—2000; com. mem. Condominium Assn. Bldg. and Grounds Com., Flemington, NJ, 2001; mem. Ladies Ancient Order of Hibernians, Somerville, NJ, 2001; Confraternity of Christian Doctrine tchr. St. Janes Ch., Woodbridge, NJ, 1986—87; parish pastoral coun. rep., sec. St. Joseph Ch., East Millstone, NJ, 1995—98; lector, visitor to homebound, and rosary altar soc. mem. St. Magdalen de Pazzi Ch., Flemington, NJ, 2000. Roman Catholic. Achievements include development of system specifications and workflows on numerous computer systems including manufacturing, telephony, pharmaceutical and medical claims; patents for software and electro-mechanical inventions. Avocations: swimming, folk dancing, tennis. Home: 4 Colts Ln Flemington NJ 08822 Office: Glynn & Assocs PC 24 Mine St Flemington NJ 08822 Personal E-mail: drdmeag@netzero.com.

MEAGHER, SANDRA KREBS, artist; b. N.Y.C., Dec. 18, 1936; d. Oswald Armand and Ella Katherine (Coleman) Krebs; m. John Forsyth Meagher, Oct. 15, 1966. BA, Smith Coll., Northampton, Mass., 1958. Author, artist: (book of drawings and poetry) NORA, 1991. Vice chmn. bd. dirs. Stoneleigh-Burnham Sch., Northampton, 1984-87. Recipient fellowship Va. Ctr. for the Creative Arts, Mt. San Angelo, Va., 1993, Vt. Studio Ctr., Johnson, Vt., 1997. Mem. Art/Place Gallery (pres. 1993), Silvermine Guild of Artists, Rowayton Arts Ctr., Art Students League (life).

MEAKER, MARIJANE AGNES, author; b. Auburn, N.Y., May 27, 1927; d. Ellis R. and Ida T. M. BA, U. Mo., 1949; PhD (hon.), Southampton Coll., 1996. Author: novels (under own name) Sudden Endings, 1965, Hometown, 1967, Game of Survival, 1969, Don't Rely on Gemini, 1971, Shockproof Sydney Skate, 1972, 2d edit., 1990; (under pseudonym M.E. Kerr), Dinky Hocker Shoots Smack, 1972, Gentlehands, 1978, If I Love You, Am I Trapped Forever, 1973, I'll Love You When You're More Like Me, 1977, Is That You, Miss Blue?, 1975, Love is a Missing Person, 1975, The Son of Someone Famous, 1975, Little Little, 1981 (Soc. Children's Books Writers award 1982), What I Really Think of You, 1982, Me Me Me Me Me: Not a Novel (Best Books for Young Adults ALA), 1983, Him She Loves?, 1984, I Stay Near You (Best Books for Young Adults ALA), 1985, Night Kites, 1986, Fell, 1987, Fell Back, 1989, Fell Down, 1990; (under pseudonym Mary James) Shoebag, 1990, The Shuteyes, 1993, Frankenlouse, 1994, Shoebag Returns, 1996, (M.E. Kerr) Linger, 1993, Deliver Us from Evie, 1994, Hello, I Lied, 1997, Blood on the Forehead, 1998, What Became of Her, 2000, Slap Your Sides, 2001, Highsmith, 2003, (M.E. Kerr) Snakes Don't Miss Their Mothers, 2003. Recipient Notable Children's Book award ALA, 1972, Book of Yr. award Sch. Library Jour., 1972, 77, 78, Christopher award, 1978, Night Kites award ALA, 1986, Margaret A. Edwards award ALA, 1993, Lifetime Achievement award, The Publishing Triangle, 1998, Lifetime Achievement award The Knickerbocker, 1999, Lifetime Achievement award ALAN, 2000. E-mail: mekerr13@aol.com.

MEAL, LARIE, chemistry educator, researcher, consultant; b. Cin., June 15, 1939; d. George Lawrence Meal and Dorothy Louise (Heileman) Fitzpatrick. BS in Chemistry, U. Cin., 1961, PhD in Chemistry, 1966. Rsch. chemist U.S. Indsl. Chems., Cin., 1966-67; instr. chemistry U. Cin., 1968-69, asst. prof., 1969-75, assoc. prof., 1975-90, prof., 1990—, rschr., 1980—. Cons. in field. Contbr. articles to profl. jours. Mem. [illegible], N.Y. Acad. Scis., Am. Chem. Soc., NOW, Planned Parenthood, Iota Sigma Pi. Democrat. Avocations: gardening, yard work. Home: 2231 Slane Ave Norwood OH 45212-3615 Office: U Cin 2220 Victory Pky Cincinnati OH 45206-2822

MEALS, PAMELA F. publishing executive; b. Ill. 1 child, Laura. Student, We. Oreg. State Coll. With advtsg. The Oreg. Statesman and Capital Jour., Salem; advtsg. mgr. The Idaho Statesman, Boise, 1979, pres., publ., 1994-99; publ. Coffeyville (Kans.) Jour., 1979-82, The Palladium-Item, Richmond, Ind., 1982-85, The Olympian, Olympia, Wash., 1985-94, Bellingham Herald, Bellingham, Wash., 1999—. Bd. dirs. Boise Pub. Schs. Edn. Found., Idaho Shakespeare Festival, Albertson Coll. Annual Fund, FUNDSY, William Allen White Found. Mem. Boise Area C. of C. (bd. dirs.), Rotary Club, Idaho Bus. Coun., Pacific N.W. Newspaper Assn. (bd. dirs.), Newspaper Assn. Am. Office: The Bellingham Herald 1155 N State St Ste 1 Bellingham WA 98225-5086

MEANS, ROSALINE, business executive, business educator; b. Manila; came to U.S., 1952; d. Cheng Peng and Lu Chong (Siy) Limtiuco; m. Cyril Chestnut Means, Jr., Nov. 8, 1958 (dec. Oct., 1992); children: Elizabeth Rose Thayer Means, Annette Thayer Means, Cyril III. AA in Pre-law, U. Santo Tomas, Manila, The Philippines, 1949; BS in Comm. Edn., U. East, Manila, 1951; MA in Edn., U. Iowa, 1953; postgrad., CUNY, 1956-58. Tchr. Chinese Rep. Sch., Manila, 1947-52; corp. dir. and officer various cos. and corps., 1950-70; edn. specialist U. Hosp. Sch., Iowa City, 1952-53; lectr. SUNY Urban Ctr., Bklyn., 1967-73; adj. lectr. cmty. coll. CUNY, 1969-72, various positions, 1973-84; adj. prof. L.I. U., Bklyn., 1978; lectr. Ednl. Opportunity Ctr., Bklyn., 1973-95. Author: First Steps in Conversation, 1954; stage performances include Two for the Seesaw, The Defender, Stage Door. Mem. Legis Adv. Com. N.Y. State Senate, 11th Dist., 1990; treas. PSC/CUNY. Recipient Cmty. Leaders and Noteworthy Ams. award, 1975-76, formal recognition Bus. and Profl. Women of Cape Ann, 1996; named Goddess of Arts-Beauty Queen, 1954, Miss Fashion Model of Yr., 1954; finalist Mrs. N.Y. Am. Beauty Pageant, 1990. Mem. Liedenkranz of City of N.Y. (music libr. and treas.). Avocations: classical music, fishing, boating. Home: 13 Salt Island Rd Gloucester MA 01930-1972

MEARA, ANNE, actress, playwright, writer; b. Bklyn., Sept. 20; d. Edward Joseph and Mary (Dempsey) M.; m. Gerald Stiller, Sept. 14, 1954; children: Amy, Benjamin. Student, Herbert Berghoff Studio, 1953-54. Apprentice in summer stock, Southold, L.I. and Woodstock, N.Y., 1950-53; off-Broadway appearances include A Month in the Country, 1954, Maedchen in Uniform, 1955 (Show Bus. off-Broadway award), Ulysses in Nightown, 1958, The House of Blue Leaves, 1970, Bosoms and Neglect, 1986, After-Play, 1996; Shakespeare Co., Two Gentlemen of Verona, Ctrl. Park, N.Y.C., 1957, Romeo and Juliet, 1988; Broadway plays: Spookhouse, 1982, Eastern Standard, 1989, Anna Christie, 1993 (Tony nomination Best Supporting Actress); film appearances include The Out-of-Towners, 1968, Lovers and Other Strangers, 1969, The Boys From Brazil, 1978, Fame, 1979, Nasty Habits (with husband Jerry Stiller), 1976, An Open Window, 1990, Mia, 1990, Awakenings, 1991, Reality Bites, 1994, Daytrippers, 1997, The Fish in the Bathtub, 1998, Southie, 1999, The Independent, 2001, Like Mike, 2002, comedy act, 1963—; appearances Happy Medium and Medium Rare, Chgo., 1960-61, Village Gate, Phase Two and Blue Angel, N.Y.C., 1963, The Establishment, London, 1963, QE II, 1990; syndicated TV series Take Five with Stiller and Meara, 1977-78; numerous appearances on TV game and talk shows, also spls. and variety shows; rec. numerous commls. for TV and radio (co-recipient Voice of Imagery award Advt. Bur. N.Y.); star TV series Kate McShane, 1975, Archie Bunker's Place, 1979, Alf, 1986-88; other TV appearances The Sunset Gang, 1990, Avenue Z Afternoon, 1991, Murphy Brown, 1994, Homicide, 1996 (Emmy nomination), Will and Grace, 2002, Sex in the City, 2002-04, The King of Queens, 2003-04, Good Morning Miami, 2003; (TV movie) Jitters, 1997, All My Children, 1994-99, (TV movie) What Makes a Family, 2001; writer, actress TV movie The Other Woman, 1983 (co-recipient Writer's Guild Outstanding Achievement award 1983), Alf, To Make Up to Break Up, The Stiller and Meara pilot; author, actor (play) After-Play, 1996; author (play) Down the Garden Paths, 2000; video host (with Jerry Stiller) So You Want to Be an Actor? Recipient Outer Critic's Cir. Playwriting award for After-Play, 1995, 4th ann. Alan King award in Jewish Humor, 2003.

MEARS, CATHERINE LOUISE, principal; b. Bremerton, Wash., Nov. 28, 1942; d. Edgar Verne and Marie (Lande) Combelic; m. Willard Albert Mears, Oct. 2, 1976; children: Christopher Neil, Kelly John. AA, Yakima (Wash.) Valley Coll., 1965; EdB, Ctrl. Wash. U., Ellenburg, 1968, MEd, 1975. Cert. dir. spl. edn. programs. Tchr. spl. edn. Sunnyside (Wash.) Sch. Dist., 1968—2001, spl. edn. dir., 1978—2001, prin., 1978—. Leader 4-H Clubs Am., Wash., 1963—2003. Named Educator of the Yr., State of Wash., 1999, Sunnyside C. of C., 1999. Mem.: Assn. Wash. Sch. Prins., Delta Kappa Gamma (pres.). Lutheran. Avocations: gardening, reading, sports. Home: 2941 Hornby Rd Grandview WA 98930 Office: Sunnyside Sch Dist 3800 Van Belle Rd Outlook WA 98938 Office Phone: 509-837-3352. Business E-Mail: mearswa@bantonrea.com.

MEBANE, BARBARA MARGOT, artistic director, choreographer; b. Sylacauga, Ala., July 21, 1947; d. Audrey Dixon and Mary Ellen (Yaikow) Baxley; m. James Lewis Mebane, Dec. 31, 1971; 1 child, Cieson Brooke. Grad., Brookhaven Coll., Dallas. Line performer J. Taylor Dance Co., Miami, Fla., 1964-65; sales mgr. Dixie Readers Svc., Jackson, Miss., 1965-67; regional sales mgr. Robertson Products Co., Texarkana, Tex., 1967-75; owner, pres. Telco Sales, Svc. and Supply, Dallas, 1976-90; dir. The Dance Factory performing co., Lewisville, Tex.; owner, artistic dir. Dancers Workshop Studios, Inc., Lewisville. Mem. Dance Masters, Miami, 1975—; mgr., choreographer music videos for pay/cable TV, 1985—; prodr. theatrical/musical shows to profl. theatre, coll. dists. and high schs; pub. speaker in field of positive thinking for women. Author: Paper on Positive Thinking, 1983. Sponsor Cancer Rsch. Ctr., Dallas, Flower Mound Bus. Womens Group; hon. chmn. Rep. State Com., Tex.; founder arts devel. and outreach DWSI for underpriveledged children. Named Bus. Woman of the Yr., Gov. Anne Richards, Tex., 1994. Mem. Nat. Fedn. Ind. Businesses, Internat. Register of Profiles Cambridge, Eng., Female and Minority Owned Bus. League, PDTA (Dallas Dance Coun.). Avocations: working with children, teaching dance, writing. Office: Dancers Workshop 705 S Mill Lewisville TX 75057

MEBANE, FELICIA EUGENIA, health policy, news media educator, researcher; b. Greensboro, N.C., Mar. 23, 1967; d. William E. Mebane, Joyce G. Mebane. BSPH, U. N.C., 1989, MSPH, 1994; PhD, Harvard U., 1998. Fin. mgmt. trainee GE, Hickory, NC, 1989—92; post-doctoral fellow Harvard U., Cambridge, Mass., 1998—2001; asst. prof. health policy, politics and comms. U. N.C., Chapel Hill, 2001—. . Avocations: travel, reading, running, dance. Business E-Mail: fmebane@unc.edu.

MEDAGLIA, ELIZABETH ELLEN, small business owner; b. Boston, Jan. 22, 1970; d. Anthony Joseph Medaglia, Jr. and Catherine Louise (Nardelli) Medaglia. BA in Sociology, Coll. of the Holy Cross, 1991; postgrad., Cornell U., 1995—97; cert. in therapeutic massage and hydrotherapy, Finger Lakes Sch. Massage, 1999; M in Acupuncture, Acad. for Five Element Acupuncture, 2003. Lic. massage therapist N.Y., nat. cert. therapeutic massage and bodywork, lic. acupuncturist Mass., diplomate acupuncture (NCCAOM), cert. MT educator Finger Lakes Sch. Massage, 2nd degree Reiki, clean needle technique Council Coll. Acupuncture and Oriental, Pan Gu Shengong instr. Litigation legal asst. Ropes & Gray, Boston, 1991—95; founder, pres. DancingPhoenix LLC, Newton, Mass., 2003—. Fundraiser, cmty. vol. City Year, Mass., 1992—95; intake test vol. Literacy Vol. Am., Mass., 1994—95; [illegible] Boston Area Rape Crisis Ctr., 1995. Mem.: Am. Acupuncture Coun., Ctr. for Balance, Newton-Needham C. of C., Theosophical Soc. Boston, Acupuncture and Oriental Medicine Alliance, Am. Massage Therapy Assn., Newton Hist. Soc. Office Phone: 617-869-6371.

MEDAGLIA, MARY-ELIZABETH, lawyer; b. Suffern, N.Y., Oct. 13, 1947; d. Joseph Mario and Edith Elizabeth (Price) M. BA, Sweet Briar Coll., 1969; JD, U. Va., 1972. Bar: Va. 1972, D.C. 1974, U.S. Ct. Appeals (D.C. cir.) 1974, U.S. Supreme Ct. 1980, U.S. Ct. Appeals (4th, 5th, 9th and 11th cirs.) 1981, U.S. Ct. Appeals (10th cir.) 1982, Md. 1990, U.S. Ct. Appeals (2d cir.) 1998. Law clk. to judge D.C. Ct. Appeals, Washington, 1972-74; asst. atty. U.S. Atty.'s Office, Washington, 1974-79; deputy solicitor Fed. Labor Relations Authority, Washington, 1979-82, acting solicitor, 1982; assoc. Jackson & Campbell P.C., Washington, 1982-84, ptnr., 1984—. Sec. D.C. Bar, 1983-84, bd. govs. 1984-87. Fellow Am. Bar Found.; mem. ABA (chmn. TIPS com. on ins. coverage litigation 1989-91, ho. of dels. 1981-83), D.C. Bar Assn. (bd. dirs. 1980-83, chmn. young lawyers sect. 1980-81), Women's Bar Assn. D.C. (pres. 1982-83), Charles Fahy Am. Inn of Ct. (pres. 1990-92), Fedn. Def. and Corp. Counsel, Am. Soc. Writers on Legal Subjects, Phi Beta Kappa. Office: Jackson & Campbell PC South Tower 1120 20th St NW Ste 300S Washington DC 20036-3437 Office Phone: 202-457-1612. E-mail: LMedaglia@jackscamp.com.

MEDEL, REBECCA ROSALIE, artist; b. Denver, Mar. 26, 1947; d. Natividad and Josefa (Apodaca) M. BFA, Ariz. State U., 1970; MFA, UCLA, 1982. Asst. prof. fibers dept. head Tenn. Technol. U., Smithville, 1983-88; lectr. Dept. of Design, UCLA, 1989-91; studio artist, 1991—; assoc. prof. Tyler Sch. Art Temple U., 1995—. Lectr. N.C. State U., Raleigh, San Diego State U., SUNY, Purchase, 1992, Penland Sch. Asheville, N.C., Textile Study Group, N.Y.C., Calif. Coll. of Arts & Crafts, Oakland, Calif., San Jose State U., Am. Ctr., Kyoto, Japan, City Ctr., Sapporo, Japan, 1986; vis. artist U. N.D., 1985. One-woman shows include Thirteen Moons Gallery, Santa Fe, 2003, Brown Grotta Gallery, Wilton, Conn., 1996, Neuberger Mus. of Art, Purchase, N.Y., 1992-93, Bellas Artes Gallery, N.Y.C., 1991, N.D. Mus. Art, Grand Forks, 1985, Maya Behn Galerie, Zurich, 1984, UCLA, 1982, Thirteen Moons Gallery, Santa Fe, 2003; two-person exhbns. include Heath Gallery, Atlanta, 1987, Maya Behn Gallerie, 1986; group shows include Bellas Artes Gallery, Santa Fe, N.Mex., 1992, N.C. State U. Gallery, 1992, Portland Art Mus., 1995, Madison (Wis.) Art Ctr., 1995, Santa Monica (Calif.) Art Gallery, 1995, Maya Behn Gallerie, 1991, Mus. Van Bommel-Van Dam, Venlo, Netherlands, 1990, Palo Alto Cultural Ctr., 1990, Barbican Ctr. Concourse Gallery, London, 1998, Montclair (N.J.) State U. Gallery, 1998, Art Inst. Chgo., 1999, Yokohama (Japan) Mus. Art, 1999, Biennial 2000, Del. Art Mus., Wilmington, L.A. Mus. Art, 2000, Soc. Contemporary Crafts, Pitts., 2001, Westport Arts Ctr., Conn.,, 2003, many others. Recipient bronze medal Triennial of Tapestry, 1985; visual artist fellow Nat. Endowment for Arts, 1986, 88, fellow for emerging visual artists So. Arts Fedn. NEA, 1985; Pew fellow in the arts, 1999, 2003, fellow Pa. Coun. on Arts, 2001, 03; scholar to Arcosanti, Nat. Endowment for Arts, 1986, 88. Home: 2920 Meyer Ave Glenside PA 19038-1920 Office Phone: 215-782-2728.

MEDEROS, CAROLINA LUISA, public policy consultant; b. Rochester, Minn., July 1, 1947; d. Luis O. and Carolina (del Valle) Mederos. BA, Vanderbilt U., 1969; MA, U. Chgo., 1971. Adminstrv. asst. Lt. Gov. of Ill., Chgo., 1972; sr. research assoc. U. Chgo., 1972; project mgr., cons. Urban Dynamics, Inner City Fund and Community Programs Inc., Chgo., 1972-73; legis. asst. to Senate pres. Ill. State Senate, Chgo. and Springfield, 1973-76; program analyst Dept. Transp., Washington, 1976-79, chief, trans. assistance programs div., 1979-81, dir. programs and evaluation, 1981-88, chairwoman, sec.'s safety rev. task force, 1985-88, deputy asst. sec. for safety, 1988-89; cons. Patton Boggs LLP, Washington, 1990—. Recipient award for Meritorious Achievement, Sec. Transp. 1980, Superior Achievement award U.S. Dept. Transp., 1981, Sec.'s Gold Medal award for Outstanding Achievement, 1986, Presdl. Rank award, 1987. Home: 2723 O St NW Washington DC 20007-3128 Office: Patton Boggs LLP 2550 M St NW Washington DC 20037-1350 Office Phone: 202-457-5653. E-mail: cmederos@pattonboggs.com.

MEDICI, ROCHELLE, psychologist, brain researcher; b. Morris, Minn., Dec. 31, 1933; d. Albert and Johanna (Ulvestad) Johnson; m. Michael A. Medici, July 4, 1970 (div. 1995); 1 child, Bianca Cristina. BA magna cum laude, U. Minn., 1954, PhD, 1962. Lic. psychologist, Calif. USPHS postdoctoral fellow U. Minn., Mpls., 1965-67; asst. biologist Calif. Inst. Tech., Pasadena, 1967-68; assoc. prof. anatomy Brain Rsch. Inst., UCLA, 1968-79; pvt. practice neuropsychology, San Marino, Calif., 1980—. Cons. AEC, Washington, 1976, WHO, Washington, 1976, Neuroscis. Rsch. Program, Boston, 1977. Rschr. numerous publs.; contbr. articles to profl. jours (Nature, Brain Research, et al) Mem. APA, AAAS, Explorers Club, Phi Beta Kappa. Democrat. Avocations: music, art, travel, politics, literature. Home: 2220 El Molino Pl San Marino CA 91108-2317

MEDICUS, HILDEGARD JULIE, retired dentist, orthodontist, educator; b. Frankfurt, Germany, July 25, 1928; came to U.S., 1961, naturalized, 1995; d. Gustav and Elizabeth Berta (Neunhoeffer) Schmelz; m. Heinrich Adolf Medicus, June 15, 1961. DMD, U. Marburg, W. Germany, 1953; orthodontics diploma, U. Düsseldorf, W. Germany, 1957. lic. dentist, N.Y. Postdoctoral fellow dental sch. U. Zürich, Switzerland, 1957; postdoctoral fellow U. Liège, Belgium, 1958, Forsyth Dental Ctr., Boston, 1959, orthodontic rsch. affiliate, 1963—74; sch. dentist Pub. Sch. Sys., Zürich, 1975—76; dental hygiene instr. Hudson Valley C.C., Troy, NY, 1976—77; pvt. practice Troy, NY, 1977—89. Active Hudson Mohawk Swiss Soc. Mem. AAUW, ADA, European Orthodontic Soc., German Orthodontic Soc. Presbyterian. Achievements include study of functional orthodontic appliances and growth and development. Home: 1 The Knoll Troy NY 12180-7284

MEDIN, JULIA ADELE, mathematics educator, researcher; b. Dayton, Ohio, Jan. 16, 1929; d. Caroline (Feinberg) Levitt; m. A. Louis Medin, Dec. 24, 1950; children: Douglas, David, Thomas, Linda. BS in Maths. Edn., Ohio State U., 1951; MA in Higher Edn., George Washington U., 1977; PhD in Counseling and Edn., Am. U., 1985. Cert. tchr., Fla., Md. Rsch. engr. Sun Oil Co., Marcus Hook, Pa., 1951-53; tchr. maths. Montgomery County Pub. Schs., Rockville, Md., 1973-88; asst. prof. maths. U. Ctrl. Fla., Orlando, 1988-90, sr. ednl. technologist Inst. for Simulation and Tng., 1990-99; sr. assoc. Mgmt. and Ednl. Tech. Assocs., 1999—. Adv. steering com. U.S. Dept. Edn. Title II, Washington, 1985-89; sr. math. educator, rschr. Inst. for Simulation and Tng., Orlando, 1988-90; judge, co-chair GII Nar. Awards; co-acad. advisor I/ITSEC Conf.; condr. nationwide rsch. project on effective use of technology in the classroom; spkr. in field. Author: Loc. of Cont. and Test Anxiety of Mar. Math. Studies, 1985; contbg. author: Math for 14 & 17 Yr. Olds, 1987; editor: Simulation and Computer-Based Technology for Education; contbr. articles to profl. jours. Dem. committeewoman Town of Monroeville, Pa., 1962; religious sch. dir. Beth Tikva Religious Sch., Rockville, 1971; cons. Monroeville Mental Health, 1960. Mem. Nat. Coun. Tchrs. Math., Math. Assn. Am. (task force on minorities in math.), Women in Math. in Edn., Nat. Coalition for Tech. in Edn. and Tng., Phi Delta Kappa, Kappa Delta Pi. Home and Office: 11401 Ridge Mist Ter Potomac MD 20854-7002 E-mail: jmedin@comcast.net.

MEDINA, JANIE, not-for-profit fundraiser; b. Bronx, June 24, 1956; d. Luis A. and Aida Diaz Medina. Paralegal Cert., CUNY, 1997, BA, 1988. Adminstrv. asst. Planned Parenthood of N.Y.C., 1979—83; events coord. Mt. Sinai Children's Ctr. Found., N.Y.C., 1984—98; spl. events assoc. Mt. Sinai NYU Health, N.Y.C., 1998—. Cons. Latino Heritage Mo. Mt. Sinai Med. Ctr., 2000—01. Lobbyist, 1981—83; recording sec. Mt. Sinai Children's Ctr. Found., N.Y.C., 1991—98; vol. Mike Bloomberg for Mayor, N.Y.C., 2001, Latino Expo, 2001, Kids of NYU, 2000—01; pres. 615 Pelham Pkwy. North Tenants Assn., 1981—82; vol. Fundraising Day N.Y., 2002, N.Y. Internat. Latino Film Festival, 2002. Mem.: N.Y. Women's Agenda, Coun. of Protocol Execs., Women in Devel., Alpha Sigma Lambda.

MEDINA, KATHRYN BACH, book editor; b. Plainfield, N.J. d. F. Earl and Elizabeth E. Bach; 1 child from previous marriage. BA, Smith Coll.; MA, NYU. With Doubleday Pub. Co., Inc., N.Y.C., 1965-85; exec. editor, sr. v.p. Random House, N.Y.C., 1985—. Assoc. fellow Jonathan Edwards Coll., Yale U., New Haven, 1982—; fellow Bunting Inst., 1994—95; cons., 1995—96, Coun. Fgn. Rels. Editor books by James Atlas, Peter Benchley, Amy Bloom, Tom Brokaw, Anita Brookner, Ethan Canin, Michael Chabon, Robert Coles, Agnes deMille, E.L. Doctorow, Jane Fonda, Max Frankel, Henry Louis Gates, Jr., Carol Gilligan, Mary Gordon, David Halberstam, Kathryn Harrison, John Irving, Tracy Kidder, Wynton Marsalis, Bobbie Ann Mason, James A. Michener, Sandra Day O'Connor, Jane Pauley, Anna Quindlen, Nancy Reagan, James Reston, William Safire, Maggie Scarf, Gloria Steinem, Christopher Tilghman, Alice Walker, Daniel Yergin, Wynton Marsalis, others.

MEDINA, SANDRA, social worker, educator; b. Tulsa, Oct. 4, 1947; d. James and Erleen (Austin) Meeks; m. Michael Sellman, 1966 (div. 1979); children: Rhainnie, Morgan; m. Ernest Medina, Aug. 21, 1985; 1 child, Brendyn. Cert., Community Coll. of Denver, 1975; BS summa cum laude, Met. State Coll., Denver, 1981; MSW, U. Denver, 1983, postgrad. Lic. clin. social worker, Colo. Dir. Lafayette (Colo.) Presch./Playtime, 1973-75, Bennett (Colo.) Non-Denominational Presch., 1975-76; intern. in clin. social work Brighton (Colo.) Schs., 1981-82; adminstrv. social work intern Jefferson County (Colo.) Schs., 1982-83; med. social worker Las Animas County Health Dept., Trinidad, Colo., 1983-85, psychiat. social worker Colo. State Hosp., Pueblo, 1985-89; clin. social worker PsychCare, Greeley, 1990-92; counselor high sch. U. Northern Colo. Lab. Sch. Instr. Trinidad State Jr. Coll., 1984-85; field instr. N.Mex. Highlands U., Las Vegas, 1986-87, U. So. Colo., Pueblo, 1988-89; adj. prof. social work U. Denver, 1996-97; asst. prof. social work, practicum coord. Chadron State Coll., 1997-99. Mem. exec. com. Gov.'s Task Force on Child Abuse, Denver, 1985; bd. dirs. Adams County Rep. Advs. for Children Today, Denver, 1978-79; chairperson membership com. Met. Child Protection Coun., Denver, 1982-83. Mem. NASW. Democrat. Presbyterian. E-mail: bestmedfam@netscape.net.

MEDLAR, DEBORAH STARKEY, secondary school educator; b. Devils Lake, N.D., Sept. 13, 1952; d. Harold Lee and Ruth Adele (Swan) Starkey; m. Richard Lee Medlar, July 21, 1978; children: Noah, Ira. BA cum laude, Jamestown Coll., N.D., 1976. Tchr. Egeland H.S., ND, 1976—77, Dickinson H.S., ND, 1977—79, Trinity H.S., Dickinson, ND, 1988—; adj. lectr. Dickinson State U., ND, 2001—. Tchr. cons. Nat. Geog. Soc. Mem.: APA, N.D. Geog. Alliance, Nat. Coun. for Social Studies. Office: Dickinson State Univ 291 Campus Dr Dickinson ND 58601 Business E-Mail: deborah.s.medlar@dsu.nodak.edu.

MEDLER, MARY ANN L. federal judge; JD, St. Louis U., 1983. Atty. Thompson Coburn, St. Louis, 1983-85; asst. cir. atty. Office of Cir. Atty. of City of St. Louis, 1985-92; atty. Union Pacific R.R., St. Louis, 1992-93; magistrate judge U.S. Dist. Ct. (ea. dist.) Mo., St. Louis. Office: 111 S 10th St Rm 13S Saint Louis MO 63102 E-mail: Mary_Ann_Medler@MOED.USCOURTS.gov.

MEDLIN, VERONICA B. benefits compensation analyst; b. New Orleans, May 28, 1965; d. Noel Back and Lola Verdin; m. John E. Medlin, Apr. 28, 1989; children: Brandt Thomas, Julia Noel. Cert. QKA Am. Soc. Pension Actuaries. Retirement plan adminstr. Deloitte & Touche, LLP, New Orleans, 1989—94; mgr. retirement & investment svcs. Pan-Am. Life, New Orleans, 1994—. Co-author: (textbook) LOMA's Foundation of Customer Service Textbook. Bd. dirs. Bellemeade Civic Assn., Gretna, La., 2002—03.

MEDVEDOW, JILL, museum director; BA, Colgate U., 1976; M of Art History, Inst. Fine Arts N.Y., 1978. With Met. Mus. Art, N.Y.C., Franklin Furnace; founder Contemporary Art Ctr., Seattle; program mgr. New Eng. Found. Arts, Boston; dep. dir. contemproary art Isabella Stewart Gardner Mus., Boston, 1991-97; dir. Inst. Contemporary Art, Boston, 1998—. Cons., founder VitaBrevis. Office: Inst Contemporary Art 955 Boylston St Boston MA 02115-3194 E-mail: info@icaboston.org.*

MEEHAN, LIL EUPHRASIA THERESE, poet; b. Boston, Nov. 14, 1942; d. George Leo Meehan and Elizabeth Catherine Dalton Meehan; m. Daniel Charles McGrath, Dec. 19, 1964 (div. Aug. 1968); 1 child, Christopher. Prodn. staff U.S. Mint, San Francisco, 1980—85; freelance author, 1985—. Author (song poems): The True American, 1986, The Robe, 2000, Eyes, 2000, Emblem of Your Character, 2000, Peace Be With You, 2000, That's Our Baby Tim, 2000, Ten Years Ago That Day, 2000, So Beautiful and Rare, 2000, Even Though, 2001, Don't Let Go, 2001, Bubbles, 2001, The Best Present, 2001, You Have Arisen, 2001, Heartfelt Love in USA, 2001, Winds of Winter, 2001, Mother of Mercy, 2002. With Nat. Guard U.S. Army, 1976. Democrat. Roman Catholic. Avocations: reading, writing, swimming, basketball. Home: #503 120 N Broadway Santa Maria CA 93454

MEEHAN, SANDRA GOTHAM, corporate financial executive, consultant; b. Tokyo, June 9, 1948; d. Fred C. and Evelyn (Dirr) Gotham; m. James P. Jenkins June 15, 1970 (div.); m. Dayton T. Carr, Dec. 27, 1986 (div. 1989), m. Michael J. Meehan, Jan. 16, 1992. Student, Stanford-in-France, Tours, 1968-69; BA, Stanford U., 1970, MA, 1971. Acct. exec. Young & Rubicam Inc., N.Y.C., 1972-78, acct. supr., 1978-80; pres. Gotham Prodns., N.Y.C., 1980-82; v.p., mgmt. supr. Ogilvy & Mather, N.Y.C., 1982-85; v.p. Steuben Glass, N.Y.C., 1985-88; sr. v.p. Siegel & Gale, N.Y.C., 1988-92; prin. Gotham Meeham Ptnrs., N.Y.C., 1992-97, mng. ptnr., 1998—. Sr. v.p., dir. corp. comm. Bionutrics, Inc., 1997-98; cons. Congl. coms., FDA, FTC for exec. program Am. Assn. Advt. Agys., Washington, 1978-80; cons. Ctr. Arctic Studies Sorbonne, Paris, in U.S. and Can., 1980-82; seminar dir. N.Y. chpt. Women in Bus., N.Y.C., 1983-84. Author, editor: TV documentary Inuit! The Universal Cry of the Eskimo People, 1981. Trustee, bd. dirs. Rensselaerville (N.Y.) Inst., Checkerboard Film Found.; dirs. coun. Paris Rev. of Books; N.Y.C. Mayor's rep. to Bd. of Botanical Gardens, 2001-04 Mem.: Young Profls. Group Fgn. Policy Assn. (organizing chair 1980—81), Writers Guild Am. Home: 220 E 73rd St New York NY 10021-4319 Office: Gotham Meehan Ptnrs 220 E 73rd St Ste 5G New York NY 10021-4319 Fax: 212-628-6747. Office Phone: 212-628-6810.

MEEK, CARRIE P. former congresswoman; b. Tallahassee, Fla., Apr. 29, 1926; 3 children. BS, Fla. A&M U., 1946; MS, U. Mich., 1948. Mem. Fla. Ho. of Reps., Tallahassee, 1979-82, Fla. Senate, Tallahassee, 1982—93, U.S. Congress from 17th Fla. dist., 1993—2002; mem. appropriations com.; mem. subcommittee on Treasury, Postal Svc. and Gen. Gov., subcommittee on VA, HUD, and Ind. Agencies. Recipient Benjamin Franklin award for outstanding pub. svc., Suncoast Tiger Bay Club, 2004. Democrat.*

MEEK, VIOLET IMHOF, retired dean; b. Geneva, Ill., June 12, 1939; d. John and Violet (Krepel) Imhof; m. Devon W. Meek, Aug. 21, 1965 (dec. 1988); children: Brian, Karen; m. Don M. Dell, Jan. 4, 1992. BA summa cum laude, St. Olaf Coll., 1960; MS, U. Ill., 1962, PhD in Chemistry, 1964. Instr. chemistry Mount Holyoke Coll., South Hadley, Mass., 1964-65; asst. prof. to prof. Ohio Wesleyan U., Delaware, Ohio, 1965-84, dean for ednl. svcs., 1980-84; dir. annual programs Coun. Ind. Colls., Washington, 1984-86; assoc. dir. sponsored programs devel. Rsch. Found. Ohio State U., Columbus, 1986-91, dean, dir. Lima, 1992—2003; ret., 2003. Vis. dean U. Calif., Berkeley, 1982, Stanford U., Palo Alto, Calif., 1982, reviewer GTE Sci. and Tech. Program, Princeton, N.J., 1986-92, Goldwater Nat. Fellowships, Princeton, 1990-98. Co-author: Experimental General Chemistry, 1984; contbr. articles to profl. jours. Bd. dirs. Luth. Campus Ministries, Columbus, 1988-91, Luth. Social Svcs., 1988-91, Americom Bank, Lima, 1992-98, Art Space, Lima, 1993—, Allen Lima Leadership, 1993—, Am. House, 1992—, Lima Vets. Meml. Civic Ctr. Found., 1992—; chmn. synodical coms. Evang. Luth. Ch. Am., Columbus, 1982; bd. trustees Trinity Luth. Sem., Columbus, 1996—; chmn. Allen County C. of C., 1995—, chair bd. dirs., 1999; bd. dirs. Lima Syphomy Orch., 1993—, pres. bd. dirs., 1997— Recipient Woodrow Wilson Fellowship, 1960. Mem. Nat. Coun. Rsch. Adminstrs. (named Outstanding New Profl. midwest region 1990), Am. Assn. Higher Edn., Phi Beta Kappa. Avocations: music, skiing, woodworking, civil war history, travel. Home: 209 W Beechwold Blvd Columbus OH 43214-2012 Office: Ohio State U 4240 Campus Dr Lima OH 45804-3576

MEEKER, MARY, stock brokerage executive; BA, DePauw U.; MBA, Cornell U. Tech. rsch. analyst Salomon Bros., Cowen & Co.; mng. dir. Internet, new media and PC software equity rsch. Morgan Stanley, Dean Witter, Discover & Co. (now Morgan Stanley), N.Y.C., 1991—. Office: Morgan Stanley 1585 Broadway New York NY 10036-8200 Fax: 212-761-0472. E-mail: mmeeker@ms.com.*

MEEKISON, MARYFRAN, writer; b. Napoleon, Ohio, Apr. 9, 1919; d. Frank J. and Elizabeth (Keyes) Shaff; m. David Meekison, June 17, 1939; children: Maureen Meekison Houppert, David Francis, Beth Ann. Student, St. Mary's Coll., Notre Dame, Ind., 1936-39. Hist. writer, photographer, Napoleon, 1963—, St. Augustine Ch., 1983—. Author: (photographer) Canal Days to Modern Ways Revisited, 1984, History of St. Augustine's 1882-1982, History of St. Augustine Ch., 1983, centennial edit.; (brochure) Canal Days to Modern Ways, 1963; mem. editorial adv. bd. Courier mag., 1989-91; contbr. articles to numerous mags. Steering com. Napoleon Susquicentennial, 1984; trustee Napoleon Pub. Lib., 1976-01. Recipient Spl. citation Courier Alumnae mag., also numerous photography and writing awards, Pres.'s medal, St. Mary's Coll., Notre Dame, Ind., 1991; named Citizen of Yr., Napoleain Area C. of C., 1990; named to St. Mary's Coll. Athletic Hall of Fame Notre Dame, 2001. Mem. Alumnae Assn. St. Mary's Coll. (bd. dirs. 1985-91), Literary Club. Democrat. Roman Catholic. Avocations: tennis, sailing. Home: PO Box 253 Napoleon OH 43545-0253

MEEKS, CINDY LOU, special education educator; b. Arkansas City, Kans., June 24, 1952; d. William Neal and Lucille Lorraine Fildes; m. David Charles Meeks, May 31, 1980; children: Bardo Marshall, Katie Desiree'. MS, Emporia State U., 2003. Cert. tchr. Kans. State Bd. Edn., 2001. Para educator Usd #465, Winfield, Kans., 1993—99, spl. edn. tchr., 1999—. Mem. Am. Cancer Soc., Arkansas City. Scholar, Cowley County Spl. Services Coop., 4. Mem.: NEA (assoc.), Kans. Edn. Assn. (assoc.), Coun. for Exceptional Children (assoc.). Avocations: sewing, crafts, travel. Office: Arkansas City High School 1200 Radio Ln Arkansas City KS 67005

MEESE, CELIA EDWARDS, pharmaceutical company executive; b. San Diego, May 10; d. Roy Clifford Edwards and Bessie Lucille (Lang) Hill; m. Jed D. Meese; 1 child, Scott Edwards Meese. BA, U. Wis.; BA (hon.), U. Taiwan. Pres. Vitaline Corp., Ashland, Oreg., 1972—; v.p. RenalChem, Inc., San Jose, Calif., 1982-90, Formulations Tech., Inc., Oakdale, Calif., 1982—; dir., trustee Oreg. Shakespeare Festival Endowment, Pacific Retirement Svcs., Medford, Oreg. Mem. Pharm. Mfrs. Assn., Mensa. Home: 88 Granite St Ashland OR 97520-2711

MEESE, FRANCES MILDRED, library administrator; b. Ottawa, Ohio, Feb. 5, 1915; d. Berl Butler Blauvelt and Clara Bell Atkinson-Blauvelt; m. Ward Richard Meese; children: John Butler, Paul Richard, Jane Claire Meese-Jones. BS Edn., U. Colo., Colorado Springs, CO, 1974. Certified Teacher Colo. State, 1974, Tutor Certificate Laubach Literacy Action, Colo. Springs, 1986, Choral & Music Direction U. Denver, Library Science So. Colo. State, Organ Music Technique Colo. Coll., 1974. Dental asst. Dr. John R. White, DDS, Ft. Wayne, Ind., 1934—42; bigade chapel organist Ft. Carson Army Post, Fort Carson, Colo., 1961—73; med. libr. (original organizer) Meml. Hosp., Colorado Springs, Colo., 1958—85; tchr., english as a second lang. Sch. Dist. #3, Security, Colo., 1985—98. Leader Cub Scouts, Girl Scouts; charter mem. Soli Deo Gloria Choir, Colorado Springs, Colo., 1973; mem. Colo. Springs Chorus, Colorado Springs, Colo., 1957—58, Colo. Springs Chorale, Colorado Springs, Colo., 1958—74. Avocation: church organist. Home: 808 Dahlia Dr Colorado Springs CO 80911

MEGAHY, DIANE ALAIRE, physician; b. Des Moines, Iowa, Oct. 12, 1943; d. Edwin and Georgiana Lee Raygor; m. Mohamed H. Saleh Megahy, Sept. 20, 1969; children: Hassan, Hamed, Hala, Heba. MD, U. Alexandria, Egypt, 1981. Diplomate Am. Bd. Family Practice. Intern Univ. Hosp., Alexandria, Egypt, 1982-83; resident Siu Family Practice, Belleville, Ill., 1987—90; physician St. Joseph's Hosp., Highland, Ill., 1988—2001; med. coord. Tri-County Radiation Oncology, 2001—. Mem. steering com. on domestic violence 3d Jud. Cir. Ct., co-chmn. health care subcom. Mem. emergency med. svcs. coun. Madison and St. Clair Counties, Ill. Mem.: AAUW, AMA, Ill. State Med. Soc. (del. internat. med. grad. com.), So. Ill. Med. Assn. (past pres.), Ill. Coalition for Injury Prevention, Safe Kid Ill. Avocations: student education in local schools, domestic violence education. Home: 2 Bay Meadow Pl Belleville IL 62223 Office: 7300 Twin Pyramid Pkwy Belleville IL 62223 Fax: 618-234-1793. Office Phone: 618-277-5882. E-mail: dialmeg@msn.com.

MEGGERS, BETTY J(ANE), anthropologist, researcher; b. Washington, Dec. 5, 1921; d. William Frederick and Edith (Raddant) M.; m. Clifford Evans, Sept. 13, 1946. AB, U. Pa., 1943; MA, U. Mich., 1944; PhD, Columbia U., 1952; D (hon.), U. de Guayaquil, Ecuador, 1987, U. Fed. Rio de Janeiro, Brazil, 1994, U. Nat. La Plata, Argentina, 1997, U. Católica de Goiás, Brazil, 1999. Instr. anthropology Am. U., Washington, 1950-51; rsch. assoc. Smithsonian Instn., 1954—, expert, 1981—; founder, pres. Taraxacum Inc., 1977—. Hon. prof. U. de Azuay, Ecuador, 1991. Author: Environmental Limitation on the Development of Culture, 1954, Ecuador, 1966, Amazonia, 1971, 2d edit., 1996, Prehistoric America, 1972, Evolucion y Difusion Cultural, 1998, Ecologia y Biogeografia de la Amazonia, 1999, (with Clifford Evans) Archeological Investigations at the Mouth of the Amazon, 1957, Archeological Investigations in British Guiana, 1960, (with Clifford Evans and Emilio Estrada) Early Formative Period of Coastal Ecuador, 1965, (with Clifford Evans) Archeological Investigations on the Rio Napo, Eastern Ecuador, 1968; editor: Prehistoria Sudamericana, 1992. Recipient award for sci. achievement Washington Acad. Sci., 1956; gold medal 37th Internat. Congress of Americanists, 1966; Order Al Merito Govt. Ecuador, 1966; Order Bernardo O'Higgins Govt. Chile, 1985; Sec.'s Gold medal for exceptional service Smithsonian Instn., 1986; Order Andres Bello Govt. Venezuela, 1988; Order Al Mérito por Servicios Distinguidos Govt. Peru, 1989. Fellow: AAAS, Assn. Tropical Biology (hon.; councilor 1976—78, pres.-elect 1982, pres. 1983); mem.: Ecol. Soc. Am., New Eng. Antiquities Rsch. Assn., Academia Nacional Historia Ecuador (corr.), Am. Anthrop. Assn. (exec. sec. 1959—61), Museo Antropológico de la Cultura Andina (hon.), Soc. Am. Archeology (exec. bd. 1962—64), Am. Ethnol. Soc., Anthrop. Soc. Wash. (treas. 1955—60, v.p. 1965—66, pres. 1966—68), Phi Beta Kappa, Sigma Xi. Home: 1227 30th St NW Washington DC 20007-3410 Office: Smithsonian Instn Washington DC 20560-0001

MEGHAN, MURRAY PATRICE, director; d. Edward Joseph and Carol Ann Murray. B in Gen. Studies, Kent State U., 1999, M in Edn., 2001. Adminstrv. & programming asst. Gilda's Club N. Coast Ohio, Ashtabula, Ohio, 1998—99; area coord. residence life St. Joseph's U., Phila., 2001—. Vol. Gilda's Club Bucks & Montgomery Counties, Pa., 2002—03. Named Outstanding Young Women of Am., 1997; scholar, Regional Entry Level Inst., 2002. Avocations: painting, reading. Office: Saint Josephs U Residence Life Office 5600 City Ave Philadelphia PA 19131 Personal E-mail: megsju2000@yahoo.com. Business E-Mail: mmurray@sju.edu.

MEGHERIAN, YEFKIN, sculptor; b. Troy, N.Y., Mar. 23, 1924; d. Haroutiun DerBedrosian and Nevart DerVartanian; m. Vartan Megherian, Nov. 30, 1947 (dec. Jan. 1984); children: Gay Zarman, Lori Christine, Narrek Khachig, Talin Yefkin. BA, SUNY, Albany, 1945, MA, 1946; AS in Fine Arts, Queensborough C.C., N.Y.C., 1994. Cert. tchr. secondary schs. N.Y., tchr. primary grades N.Y., ancillary cert. tchr. art Bd. Edn., N.Y.C. H.S. sci. tchr. Warwick (N.Y.) Valley Ctrl. Sch., 1946—47; tchr. N.Y.C. Bd. Edn., 1967—85; sculptor, 1986—. Ch. sch. supr. St. James Armenian Ch., Evanston, Ill., 1947—55, Armenian Ch. of the Holy Martyrs, Bayside, NY, 1955—72; sec. coun. for religious edn. Diocese Armenian Ch., N.Y.C., 1956—61, mem. adv. bd. for bronze doors of cathedral, 2002—. Prin. works include Statue of Pope John Paul II, Vatican Mus., Rome, Bust of Vazken I, Catholicos of All Armenians, St. Gregory Illuminator Ch., Westchester, N.Y., Bust of Archbishop Tiran Nersoyan, Libr. Armenian Seminary, Westchester, Bas-relief, St. Vartan Armenian Cathedral, N.Y.C., St. Peter Armenian Ch., Watervliet, N.Y., medallion, Med. Mus., Wroclaw, Poland, Alex Manoogian Mus., St. John Armenian Ch., Southfield, Mich., exhibitions include Queensborough C.C., N.Y.C., Canon House Office Bldg. Rotunda, Washington, pvt. collections. Mem.: Nat. Assn. Women Artists, Pen and Brush, Inc. (Tallix Foundry award 1996, Merit award 2000, Compleat Sculptor 2003), Fedn. Internat. de la Medaille, Nat. Mus. Women in the Arts, Am. Medallic Sculpture Assn. (bd. dirs. 1997—2000, co-chair medallic sculpture exhbn. 2000), Nat. Sculpture Soc. Avocations: painting, travel, opera, ceramics, reading. Home: 218-37 Grand Central Pkwy Queens Village NY 11427 Office Phone: 718-217-6285

MEGIVERN, DEBORAH MARY, social worker, educator; d. John Paul and Peggy Laraine Megivern, Charlene Megivern (Stepmother); life ptnr. Douglas Andrew Foster, Oct. 4, 2003; children: Eric Alden Foster, Elliot Nielsen Foster. PhD, U. Mich., 2001. Asst. prof. Washington U., St. Louis, 2003—; postdoctoral rsch. assoc. Ctr. for Memtal Health Svcs. Rsch. Wash. U., St. Louis, 2001—03; program evaluator GLASER Project U. Mich., Ann Arbor, 2000—, instr. Social Work Sch., 1999—2001. Author: (book chpt.) Reclaiming Class: Women, Poverty, and the Promise of Higher Education. Rsch. com. mem. Internat. Assn. of Psychosocial Rehab. Svcs., Washington, 2003—. Mem.: NASW, Am. Psychol. Assn. (Todd Husted award 2001). D-Liberal. Avocation: travel. Office: Washington University One Brookings Dr Campus Box 1093 Saint Louis MO 63130-4899 E-mail: dmegivern@wustl.edu.

MEHRING, NANCY, medical and surgical nurse, administrator; b. Lorain, Ohio, June 13, 1943; d. d. Stacy C. and Mary B. (Sascik) Jezewski; m. Frank Mehring, July 16, 1966; children: Gregory M., Stacey M. Diploma, M.B. Johnson Sch. Nursing, Elyria, Ohio, 1964; BSN, U. Akron, 1984. Staff nurse, asst. head nurse, head nurse Elyria Meml. Hosp., 1964-84, admission coord., mgr., 1984-2000; nurse mgr. P.A.T. and Ambulatory Care Ctr.; onsite mgr. Amherst (Ohio) Hosp., 2000—. Mem. adv. com. U. Akron Outreach Program. Mem. ANA, Ohio Nurses Assn., M.B. Johnson Sch. Nursing Alumni Assn., Lorain County Dist. Nurses Assn., Sigma Theta Tau.

MEHRLANDER, CARMIE, retail executive; Office: Bombay Co Inc PO Box 161009 Fort Worth TX 76161-1009

MEHTA, EILEEN ROSE, lawyer; b. Colver, Pa., Apr. 1, 1953; d. Richard Glenn and Helen (Wahna) Ball; m. Abdul Rashid Mehta, Aug. 31, 1973. Student, Miami U., 1971-73; BA with distinction, Fla. Internat. U., 1974; JD cum laude, U. Miami, 1977. Bar: Fla. 1977, U.S. Dist. Ct. (so. dist.) Fla. 1977, U.S. Ct. Appeals (11th cir.) 1981. Law clk. to presiding judge U.S. Dist. Ct. (so. dist.) Fla., Miami, 1977-79; asst. atty. County of Dade, Miami, 1979-89; shareholder Fine Jacobson Schwartz Nash Block & England, Miami, Fla., 1989-94; ptnr. Eckert Seamans Cherin & Mellott, Miami, 1994-98, Bilzin Sumberg Baena Price & Axelrod, Miami, 1998—. Lectr. in field; v.p., bd. dirs. Mehtatron Enterprises, Inc., Miami, Shalimar Homes Inc., Anderson, S.C. Miami U. scholar, 1971-73. Mem. Fla. Bar Assn., Dade County Bar Assn. Office: Bilzin Sumberg Baena Price & Axelrod 2500 Wachovia Fin Ctr Miami FL 33131

MEI, DOLORES MARIE, research administrator; b. Ludlow, Mass., Sept. 3, 1955; d. Paul John and Pauline Lavoie M.; m. Jack Irwin, June 28, 1981 (div. Feb. 1988); 1 child, Robert Aaron. AB in Psychology cum laude with honors, Smith Coll., 1977; MA, Columbia U., 1979, M of Philosophy, 1980, PhD, 1981. Rsch. assoc. Columbia U., Henry Krumb Sch. Mines, N.Y.C., 1981-82; mem. staff Office Ednl. Rsch., Bklyn., 1982-83, evaluation mgr., 1983-96; dep. exec. dir. Divsn. of Assessment and Accountability, N.Y.C. Dept. Edn., N.Y.C., 1997—2001, exec. dir., 2001—03, sr. instrnl. mgr. assessment and accountability, 2003—. Ind. cons. N.Y. Zool. Soc., Bronx, 1980-82, 86-97. Recipient Nat. Rsch. Svc. award Nat. Inst. Mental Health, 1979-80. Democrat. Roman Catholic. Avocations: walking, bicycling. Home: 138 71st St Apt 1F Brooklyn NY 11209-1141 Office: Divsn of Assessment and Accountability New York City Dept Edn 52 Chambers St Rm 309 New York NY 10007

MEIDES, HOLLY SUE, music educator; b. Buffalo, Dec. 15, 1968; d. Richard Henry and Margaret Ann Meides. MusB, Potsdam Coll., N.Y., 1991; MusM, Potsdam Coll., 1992. Cert. tchr. music K-12 NY, 1991. Gen. music tchr. Amherst Ctrl. Schs., NY, 1993; orch./band dir./tchr. Lancaster Ctrl. Schs., Lancaster, NY, 1993—. Sec./clarinetist Akron Cmty. Band, Akron, NY, 1984—; solo adjudicator Erie County Music Educator's Assn., East Aurora, NY, 1995—. Recipient Departmental scholar, Crane Sch. of Music, 1991, Presdl. scholar, Potsdam Coll., 1987—91, Presdl. fellow, 1991—92, Gold award, Girl Scouts of Am., 1986. Mem.: NY State Sch. Music Assn., Am. String Tchrs. Assn., Erie County Music Educators Assn., Music Educators Nat. Conf., Maroon Key Soc. (hon.), Pi Kappa Lambda (hon.), Kappa Delta Pi (hon.), Gamma Sigma Sigma (life), Sigma Alpha Iota (life). Roman Catholic. Home: 7061 Maple Rd Akron NY 14001 Office: William Street Sch 5201 William St Lancaster NY 14086 Office Phone: 716-686-3800. Personal E-mail: strings15@aol.com.

MEIDHOF, SISTER PATRICIA E. school system administrator; b. Metuchen, N.J., Dec. 12, 1932; d. Herbert Michael and Anette (Gaffney) Meidhof. BE, Coll. St. Elizabeth, Convent Sta., N.J., 1962; MA, Fairfield Univ., Conn., 1973. Cert. tchg. Dept. Edn., N.J., 1968, Dept. Edn., N.J., 1977, Dept. Edn., N.J., 1988. Tchr. St. Anastasia Sch., Teaneck, NJ, 1951—60, St. Philip Sch., Saddle Brook, NJ, 1960—86; prin. St. Francis Sch., Ridgefield, NJ, 1986—. Mem.: Nat. Pastoral Musician Assn., Nat. Cath. Edn. Assn. Mailing: St Francis Sch 110 Mt Vernon St Ridgefield Park NJ 07660

MEIER, ARLENE, retail executive; CFO, exec. v.p.,& sec Kohl's Corp., Menomonee Falls, Wis., 1994-. Office: Kohls Corp N56 W 17000 Ridgewood Dr Menomonee Falls WI 53051

MEIER, DEBI DAWN, secondary school educator; b. Salem, Oreg., Nov. 17, 1962; d. James Leo and Dawn Cathy Meier. B, Western Oreg. State Coll., Monmouth, 1986; M, Oreg. State U., Corvallis, 2001. Lic. TSPC counselor Oreg., 2001. Phys. edn. and health tchr. Curtis Sch., L.A., Calif., 1986—97; phys. edn. tchr. Sisters (Oreg.) Elem. Sch., 1997—98; phys. edn. and health tchr., counselor Riddle (Oreg.) Jr./Sr. High Sch., 1998—2001; [illegible] Hill City, Oreg., 2001—. Named to Sports Hall of Fame, McNary HS, 2002. Democrat. Avocations: hiking, travel, sports, reading, photography. Personal E-mail: ebiday31@netzero.net.

MEIER, DEBORAH, principal; M in History, U. Chgo.; degree (hon.), Harvard U., Yale U., Brown U., Columbia Tchrs. Coll. Co-founder, prin. N.Y. Ctrl. Park East Elem. and Secondary Sch.; co-prin. Mission Hill Elem. Sch., Roxbury, 1997—. Bd. mem. Nat. Acad. Edn., Ctr. for Collaborative Edn., Boston, Panasonic Found., Fairtest. Author: The Power of Their Ideas: Lessons to America from a Small School in Harlem, 1995, Will Standards Save Public Education, 2000, In Schools We Trust, 2002, Creating Communities of Learning in an Era of Testing and Standardization; mem. editl. bd.: The Nation, Dissent and the Harvard Education Letter; contbr. articles to profl. jours. Trustee Ednl. Alliance and Educators for Social Responsiblity. Recipient MacArthur award; Sr. Annenberg fellow, 1994—97. Mem.: Coalition of Essential Scis., Nat. Bd. for Profl. Tchg. Stds. (founding mem.), Carnegie Found. for Advancement in Edn. (bd. mem., vice chair). Office: Mission Hill Elem Sch 67 Alleghany St Boston MA 02120

MEIER, HEATHER M. music educator; m. Christopher J. Meier. MusB, Mich. State U., 1998. Band/orch. dir. Jefferson County Schs., Golden/Lakewood, Colo., 1999—2000; band dir. Westview Mid. Sch., Longmont, Colo., 2000—. Elective chair dist. mid. sch. design/spec com. St. Vrain Valley Schs., Longmont, 2001—02. Mem.: Nat. Band Assn., Music Educators Nat. Conf., Mich. State U. Alumni Assn. (life), Sigma Alpha Iota (life; chpt. pres. 1997—98, Alpha B Province Leadership award 1998, Sword of Honor 1997).

MEIER, NANCY JO, nursing consultant; b. Sidney, Nebr., Dec. 15, 1951; d. Donald William and Clara Jo (Miller) M. BA, Midland Luth. Coll., 1974; diploma in Nursing, Immanual Hosp. Sch. Nursing, Omaha, 1974; MS in Nursing Edn., Tex. Women's U., 1978. RN, Tex. Staff nurse St. Lukes Episcopal Hosp./Tex. Heart Inst., Houston, 1974-75, Park Plaza Hosp., Houston, 1976; clin. nursing specialist Houston Thoracic and Cardiovascular Assn., 1977-78; instr. clin. nursing Cedar Sinai Med. Ctr., Los Angeles, 1978-79; dir. dept. nursing edn. Los Angeles New Hosp., 1979-80; ind. cons. nursing edn. Los Angeles, 1980-81; systems support specialist IVAC Corp., San Diego, 1981-83; med. specialist, advt. account exec. Kenneth C. Smith & Assocs., La Jolla, Calif., 1983-87; ind. nursing cons. San Diego, 1987—. Cons. nursing edn. Nat. Med. Enterprises, Saudi Arabia, 1980-81, Nursing Services Internat., Los Angeles, 1980, Grossmont Hosp., San Diego, 1985; instr. cardiac life support Los Angeles chpt. Am. Heart Assn., 1978-84; lectr. in field. Organist United Meth. Ch., Sidney, 1967-69, Immanual Sch. Nursing, 1971-74, Meml. Luth. Ch., Houston, 1977-78; bd. dirs. Bluffs of Fox Run Homeowners Assn., San Diego, 1984-85, pres., 1985-86. Mem. Am. Nurses Assn., Am. Assn. Operating Room Nurses, Med. Mktg. Assn., Sigma Theta Tau. Republican. Lutheran. Avocations: sewing, skiing, diving. Home and Office: 1405 6th St Gering NE 69341-2922

MEIERHENRY, JUDITH KNITTEL, judge, lawyer; b. Burke, SD, Jan. 20, 1944; d. Adolph John and Anna Elizabeth (Voos) Knittel; m. Mark Vernon Meierhenry, May 14, 1961; children: Todd, Mary. BA in English, U. S.D., 1966, MA, 1968, JD, 1977. Bar: S.D. 1977. H.S. tchr. English Plattsmouth (Nebr.) Pub. Schs., 1966-67; instr. U. S.D., 1968-70, Hiram Scott Coll., Scottbluff, Nebr., 1970; tchr. Todd County Pub. Schs., Mission, S.D., 1971-74; ptnr. Meierhenry, DeVaney, Krueger & Meierhenry, Vermillion, S.D., 1977-79; cabinet sec. S.D. Dept. Labor, Pierre, 1980-84; cabinet sec. edn. and cultural affairs State S.D., 1983-84; sr. mgr., asst. gen. counsel Citibank S.D., 1985-88; cir. ct. judge State S.D., 1988—2002; justice S.Dak. Supreme Ct., 2002—. Mem.: Nat. Assn. Women Judges, SD Bar Assn. Office: South Dakota Supreme Ct 425 N Dakota Ave Sioux Falls SD 57104-2400 E-mail: jmeierh@aol.com.

MEIKLEJOHN, MINDY JUNE (LORRAINE MEIKLEJOHN), political organizer, realtor; b. Staunton, Colo., June 9, 1929; d. Edward H. and Erna E. (Schwabe) Mindrup; m. Alvin J. Meiklejohn, Apr. 25, 1953; children: Pamela, Shelley, Bruce, Scott. Student, Ill. Bus. Coll., 1948, Red Rocks C.C., 1980-81. Pvt. sec. Ill. Liquor Commn., 1948-51, David M. Wilson, Ill. Sec. of State's Office, 1951-52; flight attendant Continental Airlines, 1952-53, pvt. sec. to mgr. flight svcs. office, 1953-54; orgnl. dir. Colo. Rep. Party, Denver, 1981-85, mem. Ctrl. Com., 1987—. Campaign coord. Hank Brown's Exploratory Campaign for Gov., 1985, mgr. Hank Brown for Congress, 1985-86; dep. campaign dir. Steve Schuck for Gov., 1985-86; vice chmn. 2d Congl. Ctrl. Com. Colo.; active campaigns; del., alt. to various county, state, dist. and nat. assemblies and convs.; Colo. chmn. Citizens for Am., 1987-96; realtor, sales assoc. Metro Brokers, Inc.; mem. polit. action com. Jefferson County Bd. Realtors; bd. dirs. Humphrey Meml. Park and Mus., 1996—, Sci. and Cultural Facilities Dist., 1989-94, Jefferson County chpt. Am. Cancer Soc., 1987-91, Jefferson Found., 1991-97; apptd. trustee Harry S. Truman scholarship Found., 1991; mem. Jefferson County Hist. Commn., Colo., 1974-82, pres., 1979; vol. Jefferson County Legal Aid Soc., 1970-74; vice chmn. Jefferson County Rep. Party, 1977-81, exec. com., 1987; vice chmn. Colo. State Rep. Party, 1981-85; chmn. Rep. Nat. Pilot Project on Volunteerism, 1981; mem. adv. coun. Peace Corps, 1982-84; sect. chmn. Jefferson County United Way Fund Drive; mem. exec. bd. Colo. Fedn. Rep. Women; pres. Operation Shelter, Inc., 1983-99; chair bd. dirs. Rocky Mountain Butterfly Consortium, 1996—; state chair Citizens for Am., 1987-96. Mem. Jefferson County Women's Rep. (edn. chmn. 1987-91). Home: 7540 Kline Dr Arvada CO 80005-3732

MEIL, KATE, sculptor; b. N.Y.C., June 15, 1925; d. Jacob and Becky (Lichtman) Meil; 1 child, Maria Rebecca Black. BBA in Acctg., CCNY, 1949. Acct. chem., printing, garment, machine and tool, film/car ind., 1943-91. Sculptor: Mein Kind, 1976, Determined to Be, 1977, Inner Mirror, 1979, Zeyda, 1980, Meydele, 1985, Remembering, 1987, Single Parent, 1988, Survivors, 1989, Einstein, 1991, We Too Have Dreams, 1992, Sage, 1992, Alone Together, 1995, Woody Guthrie, Pete Seeger; carvings: Love, Grief, Determined and Alice in Wonderland; exhibits include Can. Nat. Exhibit, 1989, Cork Gallery, N.Y.C., 1994, Ethical Culture Soc., N.J., 1997, Puffin Gallery, N.Y., 1997, Puffin Cultural Forum, Teaneck, N.J., 1998, No. N.J. Woodcarvers Ann. Nat. Juried Exhbn., 1998 (many ribbons advanced woodcarving). Leader Hudson Ave. Area Residents Assn., Edgewater, 1973. Recipient Red and Blue ribbons, N.J. Woodcarving and Wildlife Art Shows (intermediate category), 1987—95, 3d Place ribbon, Bergen County Dept. Parks, 1991—92, 2nd Place, 1994—95, 3rd Place, Ringwood State Manor exhibit of Salute to Women in the Arts, 1992. Mem. Salute to Women in Arts, Whittle Ones, Ethical Culture Soc., Palisades Nature Assn. Avocations: chess, theater, folk dancing.

MEILAN, CELIA, food products executive; b. Bklyn., Jan. 21, 1920; d. Ventura Lorenzo and Susana (Prego) Meilan. Student, CCNY, 1943—46. Codes and ciphers translator security divsn. U.S. Censorship Office, N.Y.C., 1942-46; sec., treas. Albumina Supply Co., N.Y.C., 1946-55; co-founder, co-owner, sec., treas., fin. officer Internat. Proteins Corp. (now AnimalFeeds Internat. Corp.), Clark, NJ, 1955-86, exec. v.p., 1986-92, pres., 1992-94, chair emeritus, bd. dirs., 1994—, v.p., co-owner, 1998—. Bd. dirs. Pesquera Taboquilla, Panama City, Panama, Inversiones Pesqueras S.A., British Virgin Islands; v.p., bd. dirs. Atlantic Shipers of Tex. Inc., Port Arthur, 1989; bd. dirs. Atlantic Shippers Inc., Morehead City, NC, Empacadora Nacional S.A., Panama City; v.p., dir. AnimalFeeds, Internat., Santiago, Chile. Named One of Top 50 Women Bus. Owners, Working Woman Mag./Nat. Found. Women Bus. Owners, 1994, 1995. Mem.: Nat. Found. Women Bus. Owners, Spanish Benevolent Soc. (bd. dirs. 1955—62). Avocation: Avocations: travel, [illegible]

MEINER, SUE ELLEN THOMPSON, gerontologist, nurse practitioner, nursing educator and researcher, legal nurse consultant; b. Ironton, Mo., Oct. 24, 1943; d. Louis Raymond and Verna Mae Thompson; m. Robert Edward Meiner, Mar. 5, 1971; children: Diane Romeril, Suzanne. AAS, Meramec C.C., 1970; BSN, St. Louis U., 1978, MSN, 1983; EdD, So. Ill. U., Edwardsville, 1991. RN, Mo., Nev.; cert. gerontol. nurse practitioner; cert. clin. specialist in gerontol. nursing. Staff RN St. Joseph's Hosp., St. Charles, Mo., 1976-78; nursing supr. Bethesda Gen. Hosp., St. Louis, 1975-76, 71-74; adult med. dir. Family Care Ctr.-Carondelet, St. Louis, 1978-79; program dir., lectr. Webster Coll./Bethesda Hosp., Webster Groves, Mo., 1979-82; diabetes clin. specialist Washington U. Sch. Medicine, St. Louis, 1982; chmn. dept. nursing, asst. prof. St. Louis C.C., 1983-88; vis. nurse assoc. St. Louis, 1970—71; chmn. dept. nursing, asst. prof. Barnes Hosp. Sch. Nursing, 1988-89; instr. U. Mo., St. Louis, 1989; assoc. prof. St. Charles County C.C., St. Peters, Mo., 1990-92, Deaconess Coll. of Nursing, 1991-93; patient care mgr. Deaconess Hosp., St. Louis, 1993-94; assoc. prof. Jewish Hosp. Coll. of Nursing and Allied Health, 1994-99; gerontol. nurse, rschr. Wash. U. Sch. Med., St. Louis, 1996-2000; asst. prof. nursing U. Nev. Coll. Health Scis., Las Vegas, 2000—. Nat. dir. edn. Nat. Assn. Practical Nurse Edn. and Svc., Inc., St. Louis, 1984-86; mem. task force St. Louis Met. Hosp. Assn., 1987-88; mem. adv. com. Bd. Edn. Sch. Nursing, St. Louis, 1986-90; grant cood. Kellogg Found. Gerontology and Nursing, 1991-92; project dir. NIH Grant Washington U. Sch. Medicine, St. Louis, 1996—2000; mem. editorial bd. Geriatric Nursing Journ., 1999-2002; legal nurse cons. Author and editor profl. books; contbr. articles to profl. jours. Chmn. bd. dirs. Creve Coeur Fire Protection Dist. Mo., 1984-89; vice chmn. Bd. Cen. St. Louis County Emergency Dispatch Svc., 1985-87; asst. leader Girl Scouts U.S., St. Louis, 1975; treas. Older Women's League, St. Louis, 1992-93. Recipient Woman of Worth award Gateway chpt. Older Women's League, 1993. Mem.: ANA, Am. Soc. of Aging, Nat. League for Nursing, Am. Nurses Found., Am. Coll. Nurse Practitioners, Am. Acad. Nurse Practitioners, Job's Daus. (guardian 1979—80), Order Ea. Star (chaplain 1970), Creve Coeur C. of C., Sigma Theta Tau (fin. chmn. 1984, archivist 1985—87, Zeta Kappa chpt. v.p. 2001—03), Kappa Delta Pi, Sigma Phi Omega (Iota chpt. pres. 1990—91). Avocations: travel, reading. Home and Office: 3722 Violet Rose Ct Las Vegas NV 89147-7400 E-mail: sue.meiner@ccmail.nevada.edu., agingwell2002@msn.com.

MEIS, REBECCA G. orchestra director; b. Hays, Kansas, Jan. 24, 1950; d. John Wesley and Esther Frederika Kraus; m. Raymon Charles Meis, Jr., Aug. 4, 1979. MusB, Fort Hays State Univ., Hays, Kans., 1972; MusM, Wichita State Univ., Kans., 1977. Strings tchr. Salina Pub. Sch., Kans., 1973—79, Kans. City, Kans. Pub. Sch., 1979—80; orch. dir. Olathe Pub. Sch., Kans., 1980—. Prin. violist Hutchinson Symphony, Hutchinson, Kans., Overland Pk. Symphony, Overland Pk., Kans.; sect. violist Kans. City Civic Orch., Kans. Recipient Orch. Tchr. of the Yr., N.E. Dist. Kans. Music Educators Assn., 2002—03. Mem.: Am. String Tchr. Assn. (sec. 2002—, bd. mem. 1988—90). Avocations: reading, needlepoint. Home: 9311 W 150th St Overland Park KS 66221 Office: Olathe North High Sch 600 E Prairie St Olathe KS 66061

MEISELAS, SUSAN CLAY, photographer; b. Balt., June 21, 1948; d. Leonard and Murrayl (Groh) M. BA, Sarah Lawrence Coll., 1970; EdM, Harvard U., 1971; DFA (hon.), Parsons Sch./New Sch., N.Y.C., 1988, Art Inst. of Boston, 1996, Trinity Coll., Hartford, 1999. Photographic cons. Cmty. Resources Inst., N.Y.C., 1972-74; artist-in-residence S.C. Arts Commn., 1974-75; photography tchr. New Sch., N.Y.C., 1975; free-lance photographer Magnum Photos, N.Y.C., 1976—, v.p., 1986-91. Author: Carnival Strippers, 1976, revised 2d edit., 2003, Nicaragua, 1981, Kurdistan: In the Shadow of History, 1997, Pandora's Box, 2001, Encounters with The Dani, 2003; co-editor: El Salvador, 1983; editor: Chile from Within, 1991; editor Learn to See, 1974; co-dir.: (film) Living at Risk, 1985, Pictures from a Revolution, 1991. Recipient Robert Capa gold medal Overseas Press Club, 1979, Leica award of excellence New Sch., 1981, Photojournalist of Yr. award Am. Soc. Mag. Photographers, 1981, award Nat Endowment for Arts, 1987, Hasselblad Found., 1994, Maria Moors Cabot prize Columbia U., 1994; MacArthur fellow, 1992. Office: Magnum Photos Inc 151 W 25th St New York NY 10001-7204 E-mail: susan@magnumphotos.com.

MEISENBECH, ANNETTE MARIE, elementary school educator; b. Milw., Apr. 15, 1958; d. August Albert and Margaret Mary Tarnowski; m. Michael Ralph Meisenbech, Sept. 25, 1981; children: Robert, Julie, Sara. AA, U. Wis. Ctr., Sheboygan, 1979; BS, Lakeland Coll., 1997. Co-owner M&M Landscaping, Sheboygan, 1982—92; tchr. 8th grade Sts. Peter & Paul Sch., Kiel, Wis., 1997—99; tchr. alternative mid. sch. Sheboygan Area Sch. Dist. Farnsworth Mid. Sch., 1999—. Forensics coach Farnsworth Mid. Sch., 2000—. Religious edn. tchr. Immaculate Conception Parish, Sheboygan, 2001—. Roman Catholic. Avocations: sewing, counted cross stitch, gardening, walking, water-skiing. Home: 824 N 17th St Sheboygan WI 53081 Office: Farnsworth Mid Sch 1017 Union Ave Sheboygan WI 53081 E-mail: meisen@charter.net.

MEISNER, MARY JO, editor; b. Chgo., Dec. 24, 1951; d. Robert Joseph and Mary Elizabeth (Casey) M.; 1 child, Thomas Joseph Gradel. BS in Journalism, U. Ill., 1974, MS in Journalism, 1976. Copy editor Wilmington (Del.) News Jour., 1975-76, labor and bus. reporter, 1976-79; labor and gen. assignment reporter Phila. Daily News, 1979, city editor, 1979-83, met. editor, 1983-85; PM city editor San Jose (Calif.) Mercury News, 1985-86, met. editor, 1986-87; city editor The Washington Post, 1987-90; mng. editor The Ft. Worth Star-Telegram, 1991-93; editor and v.p. The Milw. Jour., 1993-95; editor, sr. v.p The Milw. Jour. Sentinel, 1995-97; editor, vice chmn. Cmty. Newspaper Co., 1997—. Mem. AP Mng. Editors (bd. dirs. 1992-95), Am. Soc. Newspaper Editors, Internat. Press Inst. (bd. dirs. 1994-2000, Pulitzer prize juror 1994, 96). Mass. Newspaper Pubs. Assn. (bd. dirs. 1997—). Office: Cmty Newspaper Co 254 2nd Ave Needham MA 02494-2811

MEISSNER, KATHERINE GONG, city official; b. Stockton, Calif., 1955; BA, U. Phoenix, Stockton, Calif., 1999. Mem. comty. planning dept. staff City of Stockton, Calif., 1982-85, exec. asst. city clk., 1985-96, city clk., 1996—. Office: City Stockton Office City Clk 425 N El Dorado St Stockton CA 95202-1997

MEISTER, KAREN OLIVIA, secondary school educator; b. Newark, May 19, 1944; d. Bernice Hendricks Huebner; children: Christin, Brian, Erin. BA, Kean Coll., 1966, MA, 1987. Tchr. Union (N.J.) Bd. Edn., 1970-74; instr. Roselle (N.J.) Bd. Edn., 1982—; adj. prof. Union County Coll., 1987—92, Raritan Valley Cmty. Coll., Somerset, 1992—; Ind. Cons. Mary Kay Inc. Trainer Lit. Vol. Am., 1989-91. Mem. NEA, N.J. Edn. Assn., Internat. Reading Assn., N.J. Reading Assn., Suburban Reading Coun. Avocation: antiques. Office: Harrison Sch 310 Harrison Ave Roselle NJ 07203-1495

MEITIN, DEBORAH DORSKY, cantor; b. Cleve., July 25, 1951; d. Irving and Rosalind (Lewis) D.; m. Samuel R. Meitin, Dec. 6, 1987. BS, Mich. State U., 1973; M Health Adminstrn., Ohio State U., 1981. Cert. med. technologist. Med. technologist U. Hosps., Cleve., 1974-79; adminstrv. dir. surgery and anesthesiology Cleve. Met. Gen. Hosp., 1981-86; sr. cons. Ernst & Whinney, Chgo., 1986-87; sr. v.p. Diversified Health Search, Maitland, Fla., 1988-89; pres. Health Search Cons., Altamonte Springs, Fla., 1989-91. Sr. cons. Ernst & Young, Orlando, 1991-92, mgr., 1992-94; sys. analyst Fla. Hosp., Orlando, [illegible] bd. profl. women's group Jewish Fedn., Chgo., 1986-87; mem. coms. Jewish Cmty. Ctr., Chgo., 1986-87, Orlando, Fla., 1990-97, v.p., 1991-94; bd. dirs. Michael Reese Hosp.-Jr. Med. Rsch. Coun., Chgo., 1986-87, Temple Israel, Orlando, 1989-2000, sec., 1996-98; co-chmn. Shalom Orlando, 1998-2000. Fellow Am. Coll. Healthcare Execs.; mem. Ctrl. Fla. Healthcare Exec. Group (pres. 1995-97), Ohio State U. Grad. Program in Health Adminstrn. Alumni Assn. (bd. dirs. 1982-84), Phi Kappa Phi, Beta Beta Beta. Democrat. Avocations: folk dancing, travel, vocalist. Home: 877 Victoria Terr Altamonte Springs FL 32701 Office: 555 Markham Woods Rd Longwood FL 32779 E-mail: dmeitin@cfl.rr.com.

MEITNER, ERIKA, poet, education educator; d. John Gad and Betty Meitner. BA, Dartmouth Coll., 1992—96; MFA, U. of Va., 1999—2001. Analyst Andersen Consulting, New York, NY, 1997—98; tchr. NYC Bd. of Edn., Brooklyn, NY, 1998—99; instr. U. of Va., Charlottesville, Va., 2000—01, U. of Wisconsin-Madison, Madison, Wis., 2001—02; asst. prof. U. of California-Santa Cruz, Santa Cruz, Calif., 2003—. Assoc. editor Meridian, Charlottesville, Va., 2001—; instr. U. of Wisconsin-Madison, Madison, Wis., 2001—02; asst. prof. U. of California-Santa Cruz, Santa Cruz, Calif., 2003—; assoc. editor Meridian, Charlottesville, Va., 2001—. Author: (books of poetry) Inventory at the All-Night Drugstore. Recipient Judith Siegel Pearson award, Wayne State U., 2002; Diane Middlebrook Poetry fellowship, Wis. Inst. for Creative Writing, 2001—02, John N. Wall fellowship, Sewanee Writer's Conf., 2003, Henry Hoyns fellowship, U. of Va., 1999—2001, Reynolds fellowship, Dartmouth Coll., 1996—97, Summer Residency, Va. Ctr. for Creative Arts, 2002.

MEITNER, PAMELA, lawyer, educator; b. Phila., Aug. 23, 1950; d. Alfred Victor Meitner and Claire Jane (Carroll) Harmer; m. William Bruce Larson, Sept. 13, 1980; 1 child, William Bruce, Jr. BS in chem. enging., Drexel U., 1973; JD, Del. Law Sch., 1977. Bar: Del. 1977, U.S. Dist. Ct. Del. 1977, U.S. Patent and Trademark Office 1977. Engr. DuPont Co., Deepwater, N.J., 1973-77, lawyer Wilmington, Del., 1977. Prof. Del. Law Sch., Wilmington, 1985-89. Commr. State Emergency Response Com., Dover, Del., 1986-90, 97—. Mem. Del. Bar Assn. Clubs: DuPont Country (Wilmington) (bd. govs. 1984-85). Home: 211 Welwyn Rd Wilmington DE 19803-2951 Office: DuPont Co Legal Dept 1007 S Market St Wilmington DE 19801-5227

MELAMED, CAROL DRESCHER, lawyer; b. N.Y.C., July 12, 1946; d. Raymond A. and Ruth W. (Schwartz) Drescher; m. Arthur Douglas Melamed, May 26, 1983; children: Kathryn, Elizabeth; children from previous marriage: Stephanie Weisman, D. Wynne Brown. AB, Brown U., 1967; MAT, Harvard U., 1969; JD, Cath. U. Am., 1974. Bar: Md. 1974, D.C. 1975, U.S. Ct. Appeals (D.C. cir.) 1975, U.S. Dist. Ct. D.C. 1981, U.S. Supreme Ct. 1982. Tchr. English Wellesley (Mass.) H.S., 1968-69; law clk. U.S. Ct. Appeals (D.C. cir.), Washington, 1974-75; assoc. Wilmer, Cutler & Pickering, Washington, 1975-79; assoc. counsel The Washington Post, 1979-95, v.p. govt. affairs, 1995—. Mem. Phi Beta Kappa. Office: The Washington Post 1150 15th St NW Washington DC 20071-0002

MELANSON, DOROTHY, political organization administrator; b. Boston, Mass, Sept. 21, 1953; AS, Westbrook Coll., Maine, 1980. Com. woman Maine Dem. Nat., Maine, 1996; chairwoman Dem. Com., Cumberland County, Maine, 1996—2002; com. woman Maine Dem. Nat., Maine, 2000; Presdl. Elector Maine, 2000; com. woman Maine Dem. Nat., 2001—03; chairwoman Maine Dem. Party, 2003—; registered nurse Maine Med. Ctr., Maine. A longtime dem. party activist. Office: Maine Dem Party Chair PO Box 5258 12 Spruce St Augusta ME 04332

MELANSON, SUSAN C. small business owner; b. Boston, May 6, 1946; d. Arthur Wood and Marion (Saunders) Chapman; m. Arthur S. Melanson. AA, Colby-Sawyer Coll., 1966; BA, Hiram Coll., 1970. Founder, pres. Gem Island Software, Reading, Mass., 1985-90, dir. Carlisle, Mass., 1990-93; property mgr. Finard & Co., Burlington, Mass., 1993-98; founder, herbalist Oak Hill Farm, South Hiram, Maine, 1995—; co-owner High Acres Maple Syrup. Co-owner Washington Kennel; breeder, trainer, racer Siberian and Alaskan huskies. Author: Wentworth-By-The-Sea, 1969: A Novel. Class historian Wellesley High Class, 1964. Mem. Omicron Beta. Avocations: genealogy, growing medicinal herbs, collecting Inuit art, Native American Studies.

MELBY, JANET NIEUWSMA, research scientist; b. Strasburg, ND, June 17, 1950; d. Peter E. and Johanna A. Nieuwsma; m. Russell J.A. Melby, May 17, 1975; children: Kristin Joye, David Alan Russell. BS in Child Devel. and Family Rels., BA in Sociology, N.D. State U., 1972, MS in Child Devel. and Family Rels., 1974; PhD in Child Devel., Iowa State U., 1988. Grad. tchg. asst. N.D. State U., Fargo, 1973—74; instr. S.D. State U., Brookings, 1974—78, asst. prof., 1978—84; grad. rsch. asst. Inst. for Social & Behavioral Rsch., Iowa State U., Ames, 1984—88; rsch. assoc. Iowa State U., Ames, 1988—93, asst. scientist, 1993—94, assoc. scientist, 1994—2001, rsch. scientist, 2001—. Adj. assoc. prof. human devel. and family studies Iowa State U., Ames, 2002—; cons. on observational rsch., 1992—; manuscript reviewer, 1992—. Contbr. chapters to books, articles to profl. jours. Pres. Lord of Life Luth. Ch., Ames, 1996, 1997; bd. mem., youth chairperson Bethesda Luth Ch., Ames, 2000—. Mem.: Soc. Rsch. in Child Devel., Am. Psychol. Assn., Groves Conf. on Marriage and Family, Am. Assn. Family and Consumer Scis. (cert. in family and consumer scis.), Nat. Coun. on Family Rels. (cert. family life educator), Phi Upsilon Omicron, Phi Kappa Phi, Phi Upsilon Omicron (Founders fellow 1987). Lutheran. Home: 2106 Hunziker Dr Ames IA 50010 Office: Inst for Social and Behavioral Rsch 2625 N Loop Dr Ames IA 50010 Office Phone: 515-294-8144.

MELCHER, ELIZABETH (ELIZABETH MELCHER WINGER), musician; b. Phoenixville, Pa., Oct. 1, 1965; d. William Diehl Lober and Caroline Merroth Melcher; 1 child, Amy Elizabeth Winger. MusB, The Curtis Inst. Music, 1987; MusM, The Juilliard Sch., 1990; DMA, Eastman Sch. Music, 1994. Fellow in ch. music Christ and Stephen's Episc. Ch., N.Y., 1988—89; asst. organist Brick Presbyn. Ch., N.Y., 1989—90; organist/choirmaster Ch. of Ascension, Rochester, NY, 1991—94; min. music Ascension Luth. Ch., Balt., 1994—97; dir. music The Luth. Ch. St. Andrew, Silver Spring, 1997—2001; min. music The Ch. Good Shepherd, Burke, Va., 2001—03; organist/choirmaster Grace and Holy Trinity Episc. Ch., Richmond, Va., 2003—. Asst. organist John Wanamaker Grand Ct. Organ, Phila., 1985—87; pvt. tchr. organ and piano, 1999—. Organist: CD recording Pageant, 2001. Recipient 2d prize, Naples (Fla.) Internat. Organ Festival Competition, 1993, Arthur Poister Nat. Organ Competition, 1995, 1988. Mem.: Am. Guild Organists (recitalist, adjudicator various competitions, Finalist Nat. Young Artists competition 1996, First prize Nat. Young Artists competition 1991). Avocations: tennis, swimming, reading, concerts, travel. Office: Grace and Holy Trinity Episc Church 8 North Laurel St Richmond VA 23220-4797 Office Phone: 804-359-5628 ext. 20. Office Fax: 804-353-2348. E-mail: melcherwinger@networkrichmond.com.

MELCHER WINGER, ELIZABETH See MELCHER, ELIZABETH

MELCONIAN, LINDA JEAN, state legislator, lawyer; b. Springfield, Mass. d. George and Virginia Elaine (Noble) Melconian. BA, Mt. Holyoke Coll.; MA, George Washington U.; JD, George Mason U. Asst. counsel to Spkr. Thomas P. O'Neill, Jr. U.S. Ho. of Reps., Washington, 1111; pros.atty.

Hampden County Dist. Atty., Springfield, Mass.; state senator Mass. Gen. Ct., Boston, 1983—, former majority leader Mass. State Senate. Instr. Mt. Holyoke Coll.; Our Lady of the Elms Coll., Baypath Coll.; incorporator Springfield Coll. Ex Officio trustee Ella T. Grasso Found., Conn.; active Dem. State Com., Mass. Home: 257 Fort Pleasant Ave Springfield MA 01108-1521 Office: Mass State Senate Rm 511B Boston MA 02133 E-mail: lmelconi@senate.state.ma.us.

MELEIS, AFAF IBRAHIM, nurse sociologist, educator, clinician, researcher; b. Alexandria, Egypt, Mar. 19, 1942; d. Abdel Baki Ibrahim and Soad Hussein Hassan; m. Mahmoud Meleis, Aug. 21, 1964; children: Waleed, Sherief. BS magna cum laude, U. Alexandria, 1961; MS, UCLA, 1964, MA, 1966, PhD, 1968; D of Pub. Svc. (hon.), U. Portland, 1989. Instr. U. Alexandria, 1961-62; acting instr. UCLA, 1966-68, asst. prof. nursing, then assoc. prof., 1968-75; assoc. prof., dean Health Inst., Kuwait, 1975-77; prof. nursing U. Calif., San Francisco, 1977—2001, also dir. Study Immigrant Health and Adjustment; dean Univ. of Penn. Sch. of Nursing, 2002—. Vis. prof. colls. in Sweden, Brazil, Japan, Saudi Arabia, Kuwait, Egypt; 1st Centennial prof. Columbia U., N.Y.C., 1992-94; cons., speaker in field. Author: theoretical Nursing: Development & Progress, 1985 (Book of Yr., am. Jour. Nursing, 1985), 2d edit., 1991, 3d edit., 1997; contbr. articles to rsch. and profl. jours. Recipient Helen Hahm award U. Calif. Sch. Nursing, San Francisco, 1981, Teaching awards U. Calif., San Francisco, 1981, 85, Pres. Hosni Mubarak medal of Excellence, 1990; Kellogg Internat. fellow, 1986-89. Fellow Am. Acad. Nursing; mem. Coun. Nurse Researchers, Western Soc. Research in Nursing, Am. Nurses Assn. Avocations: jogging, symphony, reading, international affairs, women's issues. Office: Univ Penn Sch Nursing 420 Guardian Dr Rm 465 NEB Philadelphia PA 19104-6096

MELENDEZ, ROSA MARIA, protective services official; b. Salt Lake City, Oct. 24, 1952; Diploma, Wash. State Criminal Justice, 1978. U.S. marshall We. dist. U.S. Marshall Svc., Wash., 1994—. Office: 300 US Courthouse 1010 5th Ave Seattle WA 98104-1195

MELESIO, KATHRYN MARY, oncological nurse, educator; b. Binghamton, N.Y., June 20, 1961; d. Frank Conrad and Mary Anne (Stazinski) Dombroski; m. James. W. Vandyke, Nov. 5, 1982 (div. Nov. 1986); 1 child, Jason; m. Faustino Soto Melesio, Apr. 25, 1987; children: Benjamin, Faustino, Andrew. RN, Ill.; cert. trauma nurse specialist, RN intravenous therapy, pediatric advanced life support, oncology cert. nurse, ACLS, RN cert., CPR Instr. Nurse Kimberly Nurses, Long Beach, Calif., 1982-85; nurse oncology St. Therese Med. Ctr., Waukegan, Ill., 1985-86, Am. Internat., Zion, Ill., 1986-89, N.W. Community Hosp., Arlington Heights, Ill., 1989-90, cons. clin. nursing, 1990-97; staff nurse Manpower Agy., Waukegan, Ill., 1992-95; clin. instr. McHenry C.C., Crystal Lake, Ill., 1993-96; instr. Harper Coll., Palatine, Ill., 1995—2000; home care nurse Home Vitality Inc., 1997; nurse educator Bard Access Systems, Chgo., 1997—99; dir. infusion svcs. PSA Healthcare, 1997—99; orthop. nurse Centegra Healthcare Sys., McHenry, Ill., 1999—2001, nurse ambulatory treatment svcs., 2001—02, boriatric nurse coord., 2002—. IV task force Northwestern Healthcare Network. Contbr. articles to profl. jours. Mem. Nat. Intravenous Nurses Soc., Ill. Intravenous Nurses Soc. (spkr. in field, pres.-elect 1995-96, pres. 1996-97, presdl. advisor 1997-98), Ill. Coalition Nursing Orgns. Roman Catholic. Avocations: reading, cross stitch, coaching soccer, swimming, arts and crafts.

MELICH, GAYLE PETERS, writer; b. Gainsville, Fla., June 10, 1938; d. Carlton Powell and Martha (Watson) Peters; m. Michael Edward Melich, Apr. 25, 1970. BS, Ariz. State U., Tempe, 1961; postgrad., San Diego Coll. Bus., 1971. Employee benefits cons. Gen. AniLine & Film Corp., N.Y.C., 1963-65; transp. mgr. Compton Advt. Inc., N.Y.C., 1966-70; adminstr. Beauvoir, The Nat. Cathedral Elem. Sch., Washington, 1972-74, 79-80; exec. dir. Nat. Women's Polit. Caucus, Washington, 1981-83, 84-85; writer, event mgr. Niceville, Fla., 1986—. Cons Nat. Women's Polit. Caucus Archives Project, Schlesinger Libr., Radcliffe, 1991; charter mem., chair Okaloosa County (Fla.) Commn. on Status of Women, 1995—, vice chair, 1999. Editor Procs. Global Summit of Women, 1997, 98. Bd. dirs., pres. Nat. Women's Edn. Fund, Washington, 1979-88; bd. dirs. Child Care Svcs., Inc., Okaloosa County, 1995-96; campaign chair No. to Billboards, Niceville, 1995; co-mgr. Global Summit of Women, London, 1998, event organizer, Miami, Fla., 1997; bd. trustees, pres. Okaloosa County Heritage Mus., Valparaiso, Fla., 1997—. Mem. LWV, AAUW, Am. Bus. Women's Assn. (Fla. Women's Hall of Fame chair 1994), Nat. Women's Polit. Caucus Va. (No. Va. chair 1980-81). Avocations: gardening, theater, travel. Office: Okaloosa County Commn on Status of Women PO Box 1651 Niceville FL 32588-1651

MELICIA, KITTY, human resources administrator, foundation administrator; b. San Jose, Calif., June 25, 1955; d. Philip Louis and Jeanne Cattano; m. Salvatore James Melicia, Dec. 31, 1983 (div. Oct. 1999); children: Jessica, Krystyne. AAS in Computer Bus., Heald Bus. Coll., 1997-98. Office mgr. Southland Corp., San Jose, 1978-83; human resources admin. Sierracin EOI, San Jose, 1983-85; founder, exec. dir., pres. Candlelighters Childhood Cancer Found., Seaside, Calif., 1994—; human resources adminstr. SPCA Monterey County, Monterey, Calif., 1999—. Bd. dirs. Monterey County (Calif.) Bd. Health. Contbr. essay to profl. pub. Pres. PTA Ord Terrace Sch., Monterey, 1993-96. Mem. Ctrl. Coast Human Resource Assn., Soc. Human Resources Mgmt. Address: 1426 San Pablo Ave Apt C Seaside CA 93955-3983 E-mail: buzymom@hotmail.com., kmelicia@spcamc.org.

MELINSKI, MARGARET, realtor; b. Port Washington, Wis., May 13, 1952; d. Henry and Margret Emma Schinker. A.in Liberal Arts, Concordia Coll., Mequon, Wis., 1995; grad. in massage therapy, Lakeside Sch., Milw., 1996. Lic. real estate broker Wis. Dance instr. Fred Astaire Studio, Wis., 1972—74; real estate salesperson M and M Properties, West Bend, Wis., 1978—. Massage therapist, 1996. Home and Office: 3757 Hwy NN West Bend WI 53095

MELKA, JANET PATRICIA, medical/surgical nurse; m. Thomas Melka; children: Michael, Nicolette. RN. With Surgery Ctr. Marin Marin Gen. Hosp., Greenbrae, Colo., 2002—; RN first asst. Homeroom parent Neil Cummins Sch., Core Madera, Calif., 1996—. Mem.: AORN. Avocations: art, stained glass, weaving, gardening, hiking.

MELLERT, LUCIE ANNE, writer, photographer; b. Charleston, W.Va., June 6, 1932; d. Wilbur Conant and Grace Martin (Taylor) Frame; m. William Jennings Mellert, March 15, 1957; 1 child, James Floyd Kelly III. Student, Mason Coll. of Music Fine Arts, Charleston, 1937-49, W.Va. U., Morgantown, 1950-51. Pub. rels. exec., asst. treas., office mgr. J. H. Milam, Inc., Dunbar, W.Va., 1959-71; pub. rels. exec., office mgr. Hallcraft, Inc., Dunbar, 1972-74; office mgr. Kanawha Stone Co. Inc., Nitro, W.Va., 1975-78; freelance writer Dunbar, 1978—; freelance writer, photographer Charleston, W.Va., 1978—. Beautification commr. City of Dunbar, 1969-72; activity coordinator, program dir. Dunbar Bicentennial Com., 1971; founder, coordinator Dunbar City wide Beautification and Improvement Com., 1969-72; coord. Kanawha County Elem. Students Anti-Litter Program, Planting the Seed, 1996-2003; donated paintings W.Va. Cultural Ctr., 1990-2004; pres. United Meth. Women of St. Marks; active U. Charleston Builders, Friends of Avampato Discovery Mus., W.Va. Humanities Coun., Friends of W. Va. Culture and History. Recipient West Virginian award, Gov. Cecil Underwood, 2000, Gov. Bob Wise, 2001, West Va. Vol. Spirit award, W. Va. Women's Commn., 2003. Mem. Nat. Mus. Women in the Arts, Nat. Fedn. Press Women, Pioneer Women's (past pres.), Libr. of Congress Assn., Kanawha Valley and Nat. Trust Hist. and Preservation Soc., East End Assn., Women of Moose, Woman's Club Charleston, Charleston Women's Forum, Am. Bus. Women's Assn., W.Va. Soc.Assn. Execs., Mental Health Assn., Mid Atlantic Arts Found., South Charleston Lions Club, other mus. Methodist. Avocations: church activities, piano, music, travel, art. Home: 1604 Virginia St E Charleston WV 25311-2114

MELLI, MARYGOLD SHIRE, law educator; b. Rhinelander, Wis., Feb. 8, 1926; d. Osborne and May (Bonnie) Shire; m. Joseph Alexander Melli, Apr. 8, 1950; children: Joseph, Sarah Bonnie, Sylvia Anne, James Alexander. BA, U. Wis., 1947, LLB, 1950. Bar: Wis. 1950. Dir. children's code revision Wis. Legis. Coun., Madison, 1950-53; exec. dir. Wis. Jud. Coun., Madison, 1955-59; asst. prof. law U. Wis., Madison, 1959-66, assoc. prof., 1966-67, prof., 1967-84, Voss-Bascom prof., 1985-93, emerita, 1993—. Assoc. dean U. Wis., 1970-72, rsch. affiliate Inst. for Rsch. on Poverty, 1980—; mem. spl. rev. bd. Dept. Health and Social Svcs., State of Wis., Madison, 1973—2002. Author: (pamphlet) The Legal Status of Women in Wisconsin, 1977, (book) Wisconsin Juvenile Court Practice, 1978, rev. edit., 1983, (with others) Child Support & Alimony, 1988, The Case for Transracial Adoption, 1994; co-editor: Child Support: The Next Frontier, 1999; contbr. articles to profl. jours. Bd. dirs. Am. Humane Assn., 1985-95, Frank Lloyd Wright - Wis., 2004; chair A Fund for Women, Madison, Wis., 2002, 2003. Named one of five Outstanding Young Women in Wis., Jaycees, 1961; rsch. grantee NSF, 1983; recipient Belle Case LaFollette award for outstanding svc. to the profession, 1994, award for Outstanding Contbn. to Advancement of Women in Higher Edn., 1991, award for Lifelong Contbn. to Advancement of Women in the Legal Prof., 1994, Rotary Sr. Svc. award, Madison, Wis., 2002. Fellow Am. Acad. Matrimonial Lawyers (exec. editor jour. 1985-90); mem. Am. Law Inst. (cons. project on law of family dissolution), Internat. Soc. Family Law (v.p. 1994-2000, 02—), Wis. State Bar Assn. (reporter family law sect.), Nat. Conf. Bar Examiners (chmn. bd. mgrs. 1989, editl. adv. com.). Democrat. Roman Catholic. Avocations: walking, swimming, collecting art. Home: 2904 Waunona Way Madison WI 53713-2238 Office: U Wis Law Sch Madison WI 53706 E-mail: msmelli@wisc.edu.

MELLINK, MACHTELD JOHANNA, archaeologist, educator; b. Amsterdam, Holland, Oct. 26, 1917; came to U.S., 1949; d. Johan and Machteld (Kruyff) M. BA, U. Amsterdam, 1938, MA, 1941; PhD, Utrecht (Netherlands) U., 1943; LLD (hon.), U. Pa., 1987, Anatolian U., Turkey, 1990. Faculty Bryn Mawr Coll., 1949-88, prof. classical and Near Eastern archaeology, 1962-88, chmn. dept., 1955-83; staff mem. excavations Tarsus, Turkey, 1947-49, Gordion, Turkey, 1950-74; field dir. excavations Karatas-Semayuk, Lycia, Turkey, 1963—; staff mem. Troy, 1988—. Rsch. assoc. U. Mus., U. Pa., 1955-82, cons. scholar, 1982—. Author: Hyakinthos, 1943, A Hittite Cemetery at Gordion, 1956; author: (with Jan Filip) Frühe Stufen der Kunst-Propyläen Kunstgeschichte XIII, 1974; editor: Dark Ages and Nomads c. 1000 B.C., 1964, Troy and the Trojan War, 1986, Elmali-Karatas I, 1992, II, 1994; author: Kizilbel, An Archaic Painted Tomb Chamber in Northern Lycia, 1998; contbr. articles to profl. jours. Recipient Lucy Wharton Drexel medal U. Pa. Mus., 1994—. Fellow Am. Acad. Arts and Scis.; mem. Archaeol. Inst. Am. (pres. 1981-84, gold medal 1991), German Archaeol. Inst., Am. Oriental Soc., Am. Philos. Soc.; corr. mem. Royal Netherlands Acad. Scis., Austrian Archaeol. Inst. (corr.), Türk Tarih Kurumu (hon.), Am. Rsch. Inst. Turkey (v.p. 1977-87, pres. 1988-92). Home: 264 West Montgomery Ave Haverford PA 19041-1531

MELLO, DAWN, retail executive; b. Lynn, Mass. Student, Modern Sch. Fashion and Design, Boston. Model; asst. to fashion dir. B. Altman & Co., N.Y.C., fashion dir., 1971—75; from corp. buying officer to v.p. and gen. merchandise mgr. May Dept. Stores Co.; v.p., fashion dir. to exec. v.p., dir. fashion merchandising Bergdorf Goodman, N.Y.C., 1975—84, pres., 1984—89, 1994—99; creative dir. Gucci, 1989—94; cons. Dawn Mello and Assocs., N.Y.C., 1999—. Office: Dawn Mello and Assocs Inc 12 W 57th St # 802 New York NY 10019*

MELLON, NANCY SCOTT, arts therapist; b. Syracuse, N.Y., Apr. 25, 1941; d. Sydney Walter and Helen Claire (Dann) Stringer. BA, Wellesley Coll., 1962; MA in Lit., CCNY, 1972; MA in Expressive Therapy, Lesley Coll., Cambridge, Mass., 1993. Cert. secondary sch. tchr. Tchr. high sch. English, 1962-75; Waldorf educator children/adults, 1977—; dir. Story Arts, Cambridge, Mass., 1982-90; intern expressive therapy Harvard Cmty. Health Plan/New Eng. Meml. Hosp., Boston, 1991-93; dir. Sch. Therapeutic Storytelling, 1996—; faculty Sch. Storytelling Emerson Coll., Sussex, U.K., 1992—. Ednl. advisor tchrs., schs. 1982—; co-leader symposia, 1992—; conf. presenter. Author: Storytelling and the Art of Imagination, 1992, Art of Storytelling, 3d edit., 2003; poetry in various publs. Mem. League of New Eng. Storytellers. Avocations: language, music, poetry writing, biodynamic gardening. Office: 82 Gage Rd Wilton NH 03086-5807

MELLOR, ANNE KOSTELANETZ, English literature educator; b. Albany, N.Y., July 15, 1941; d. Austin John Tidaback and Dorothy Jane (Gannett) Gannett; m. Ronald John Mellor, June 6, 1969; 1 child, Blake. BA summa cum laude, Brown U., 1963; PhD, Columbia U., 1968. Asst. prof. Stanford (Calif.) U., 1966-73, assoc. prof., 1873-80, prof., 1980-86, Watkins U. prof., 1983-85; prof. UCLA, 1986—. Cons. BBC, London, 1993, Melvin Bragg's South Bank Show, London, 1994, Discovery Channel, Washington, 1995. Author: 14 books including Blake's Human Form Divine, 1974, English Romantic Irony, 1980, Mary Shelley, 1986, Romanticism and Gender, 1993, Mothers of the Nation, 2000; mem. editl. bd. Nineteenth-Century Contexts, European Romantic Rev., Ninteenth-Century Lit., Women's Studies. Recipient fellowship J.S. Guggenheim Found., 1972-73, 83-84, NEH, 1977-78, Am. Coun. for Learned Socs., 1983-84. Mem. MLA (adv. bd. publs. 1994-97, adv. bd. conf. on romanticism 1995-98 recipient Keats-Shelley Assn. Disting. Scholar award, 1999). Avocations: theater, hiking, snorkeling, ballet, opera. Home: 2620 Mandeville Canyon Rd Los Angeles CA 90049-1004 Office: UCLA Dept English 405 Hilgard Ave Dept English Los Angeles CA 90095-9000

MELMAN, CYNTHIA SUE, special education educator; b. Pottsville, Pa., Nov. 13, 1946; d. Earl J. and Lillian (Zubroff) M. BA in English, Lebanon Valley Coll., 1969; MEd, Western Md. Coll., 1978. Advanced prof. cert. Md. State Dept. Edn. English tchr. Susquehanna Twp. Sch. Dist., Harrisburg, Pa., 1969-70; tchr. of the deaf Am. Sch. for the Deaf, West Hartford, Conn., 1978-80; sign lang. interpreter for the deaf Montgomery County Pub. Schs., Rockville, Md., 1980-81, tchr. of the deaf/hard of hearing, 1981—. In-svc. program masters plus 30, Montgomery County Pub. Schs., Rockville, 1982-96, base sch. rep. for energy saving and recycling program, 1994-95. Co-author: (one workbook in a series) Writing Sentences, 1981. Mem.: NEA, Montgomery County Assn. for Hearing Impaired Children. Avocations: theater, movies, music, reading, walking.

MELMON, ELYCE EDELMAN, literature educator, writer; b. Milw., May 15, 1937; d. Albert Lloyd and Anita Ruth Edelman; m. Kenneth Lloyd Melmon, June 9, 1957 (dec. Apr. 2002); children: Bradley Scott, Debra Wynne. BA, Dominican Coll., San Rafael, Calif., 1971, M in English, 1975. Freelance writer, 1955—; English tchr. Dominican Coll., San Anselmo, Calif., 1975—77, San Domenico, San Anselmo, Calif., 1976—79; head English dept., tchr. Woodside Priory, Portola Valley, Calif., 1979—81, Castilleja Sch., Palo Alto, Calif., 1981—97. Vol. tchr. OICW, Menlo Park, Calif., 1996—98, Eastside Coll. Prep., East Palo Alto, Calif., 1998—. Author: (poetry, plays, and articles) Vehicle, 2003. Mem.: Drama League, Acad. Am. Poets, Am. Jewish Congress, Amnesty Internat. Democrat. Jewish. Avocations: music, piano, harp, gardening, flower arranging. Home: 51 Cragmont Way Woodside CA 94062

MELNICK, ALICE JEAN (AJ MELNICK), counselor; b. St. Louis, Dec. 25, 1931; d. Nathan and Henrietta (Hausfater) Fisher; m. Harold Melnick, May 24, 1953; children: Susan, Vikki, Patrice. BJ, U. Tex., Austin, 1952; MEd, U. North Tex., 1974. Lic. profl. counselor. Reporter San Antonio Light, 1952-53; instr. journalism project Upward Bound So. Meth. U., Dallas, 1967-71. Instr. writing El Centro Dallas County C.C., Dallas, part time 1972-74; instr. human devel. Richland C.C., Dallas, part-time 1974-79; tchr. English, journalism and psychology Dallas Ind. Sch. Dist., 1969-81; counselor Ursuline Acad., 1981-94; part-time instr. human devel. Sante Fe C.C.; freelance documentary photographer. Mem. Dallas Sports Car Club, N.Mex. Jewish Hist. Soc., Temple Beth Shalom. Jewish. Home: 101 Monte Alto Rd Santa Fe NM 87508-8865 E-mail: aj@melnick.net.

MELNICK, JODI, dancer; Mem. Twyla Tharp Dance Co., 1991—; tchr. dance, choreographer, collaborator. Performer with Sara Rudner, with Dennis O'Connor, with Vicky Shick, with Yoshiko Chuma, with Susan Rethorst.

MELOY, JUDITH MARIE, humanities educator; b. Pitts., Oct. 22, 1951; d. John C. and Miriam Meloy. BA, Denison U., 1973; MST, U. Dayton, 1982; PhD, Ind. U., 1986. Admissions counselor Denison U., Granville, Ohio, 1973—74; tchr. Centerville (Ohio) City Schs., 1978—83; program evaluation Conn. State Dept. Edn., Hartford, 1987—89; prof. Vt. State Colls., Castleton, 1989—. Dept. chair, 1994—95; chair tchg. and scholarship com., 2001—03; faculty fellow, 1996—97. Author: (book) Writing the Qualitative Dissertation: Understanding by Doing, 1994, Writing the Qualitative Dissertation: Understanding by Doing, 2d edit., 2002. Cmty. Svc., Castleton, 1998—; mem. Hayes Found. Bd., 1992—. Office: Castleton State Coll Castleton VT 05735

MELROY, PAMELA ANN, astronaut; b. Palo Alto, Calif., Sept. 17, 1961; d. David and Helen M.; m. Christopher Wallace. BS in Physics and Astronomy, Wellesley Coll., 1983; MSc in Earth and Planetary Scis., MIT, 1984. Commd. 2nd lt. USAF, 1983, advanced through grades to lt. col.; co-pilot KC-10, aircraft comdr., instr. pilot Barksdale AFB, Bossier City, La.; test pilot C-17 Combined Test Force; shuttle pilot NASA, Houston, pilot STS-92. Decorated Air Force Meritorious Svc. medal with oak leaf cluster, Air medal with oak leaf cluster, Aerial Achievement medal with oak leaf cluster, Expeditionary medal with oak leaf cluster. Mem. Soc. Exptl. Test Pilots, Order of Daedalians, 99s. Avocations: theatre, tap and jazz dancing, reading, cooking, flying. Office: Astronaut Office/CB NASA Lyndon B Johnson Space Ctr Houston TX 77058

MELTEBEKE, RENETTE, career counselor; b. Portland, Oreg., Apr. 20, 1948; d. Rene and Gretchen (Hartwig) M. BS in Sociology, Portland State U., 1970; MA in Counseling Psychology, Lewis and Clark Coll., 1985. Lic. profl. counselor, Oreg.; nat. cert. counselor; Veriditas trained labyrinth facilitator. Secondary tchr. Portland Pub. Schs., 1970-80; project coord. Multi-Wash CETA, Hillsboro, Oreg., 1980-81; coop. edn. specialist Portland C.C., 1981-91; pvt. practice career counseling, owner Career Guidance Specialists, Lake Oswego, Oreg., 1988—. Mem. adj. faculty Marylhurst (Oreg.) U., 2003—, Portland State U., 1994—, Lewis and Clark Coll., 2001—; assoc. Drake Beam Morin Inc., Portland, 1993-96; career cons. Managed Health Network, 1994—, Career Devel. Svcs., 1990—, Life Dimensions, Inc., 1994; presenter Internat. Conf., St. Petersburg, Russia, 1995. Rotating columnist Lake Oswego Rev., 1995-99; creator video presentation on work in Am. in 5 langs., 1981. Pres. Citizens for Quality Living, Sherwood, Oreg., 1989, mem. Leadership Roundtable on Sustainability for Sherwood, 1994-95, bd. dirs. Bus. for Social Responsibility for Oreg. and Southwestern Wash., 1999, 2000. Recipient Esther Matthews award for outstanding contbn. to field of career devel., 1998. Mem.: Assn. for Humanistic Psychology (presenter nat. conf. Tacoma 1996), Oreg. Career Devel. Assn. (pres. 1990), Nat. Career Devel. Assn., Willamette Writers. Avocations: walking, swimming, bicycling, cross-country skiing, photography. Home: 890 SE Merryman St Sherwood OR 97140-9746 Office: Career Guidance Specialists 15800 Boones Ferry Rd Ste C104 Lake Oswego OR 97035-3492

MELTON, JUNE MARIE, nursing educator; b. St. Louis, Oct. 16, 1927; d. Thomas Jasper and Alice Marie (Sloas) Hayes; m. Malcolm Adrian Essen, July 12, 1947 (dec. July 1978); children: Alison, William, Terrence, Mark, Cathleen, Melodie; m. Denver A. Melton, Sept. 6, 1989 (dec.). Grad., Jewish Hosp. Sch. Nursing, 1948; student, U. Mo., Lincoln U., U. Colo., Stephens Coll., U. S.W. RN, Mo.; nurse ARC. Instr. home nursing U. Mo., Columbia, 1948-49; acting dir. nurses, 1957-68; supr. instr., obstet. supr. Charles E. Still Hosp., Jefferson City, Mo.; supr. nurse ICU, primary nurse St. Mary's Health Ctr., Jefferson City; health dir. Algoa Correctional Instn., Jefferson City, 1979-83; home health vis. nurse A&M Home Health, Jefferson City, 1983-96, parish nurse, 1998—. Mem. adv. bd. A&M Home Nursing, Jefferson City; instr. GED Lincoln U., Jefferson City; participant study of premature baby nursing U. Colo., 1964. Vol. ARC, Belle-Rolla, Mo., instr. home nursing; missionary to Togo, West Africa Mo. Synod. Luth. Ch., 1996—97, parish nurse, 1998—, harvester for Christ, 1999—; parish nurse Yeleta Luth. Mission, 2002. Mem. U.S. Nurse Corps. Democrat. Lutheran. Avocations: fishing, sewing, reading, traveling. Home: 704 Golden Village Apt 1-D New Bloomfield MO 65063

MELTON, ROBERTA LYNN-KONG, financial consultant; b. Des Moines, Iowa, July 18, 1957; d. William T. and Isabelle Marie Kong. BA in Econs., Drake U., Iowa, 1978; MA in Sci, Tech. and Pub. Policy, George Washington U., 1986. Office mgr. Internat. Mgmt. and Devel., Alexandria, Va., 1989—92; ops. mgr. Children's Nat. Med. Ctr., Washington, 1992—96; program mgr. Md. Indsl. Partnerships, College Park, 1996—2000; sr. bus. devel. Prince George's County Econ. Devel., Lanham, Md., 2000—01; asst. dir. investment fin. group Md. Dept. Bus. and Econ. Devel., Balt., 2001—03; v.p. Women in Bio, Washington, 2002—. Pres. Asian Pacific Am. C. of C., Honolulu, 1988—89; adv. MIT Enterprise Forum Bd., Arlington, Va., 2002—. Dir.: (Christian theater) Parables and Miracles, 1996—. Recipient Vol. of Yr., Des Moines YMCA, 1973.

MELTZER, E. ALYNE, elementary school educator, social worker, volunteer; b. Jersey City, May 16, 1934; d. Abraham Samuel and Fannie Ruth (Nydick) Meltzer. BA, Mich. State U., 1956. Acctg. clk. Louis Marx Co. Inc., N.Y.C., 1957-60; tchr. social studies Haverstraw HS, NY, 1960-61; tchr. Sachem Ctrl. Sch. Dist., Farmingville, NY, 1961-63, East Paterson Sch. Dist., NJ, 1964-65; case worker dept. social svc. Human Resource Adminstrn., N.Y.C., 1966-89. Mem. Yorkville Civic Coun., 1988—93; policy advisor Senator Roy Goodman Adv. Com., Albany, 1987—90; mem. Temple Shaaray Tefila. Recipient Sabra Soc. Plaque award, State of Israel New Leadership Divsn., N.Y.C., 1979, Prime Min. Club Plaque award, State of Israel Bonds, 1986—87, 1996, Pin award, 1986—87, 1990, 1994—96, others. Mem.: AAUW, Jewish Genealogy Soc., Assn. Ref. Zionists Am., Am. Jewish Com., Internat. Coun. Jewish Women (participant Jerusalem seminar 1991), Nat. Coun. Jewish Women (life; participant nat. conv. 1987, Albany Inst. 1987, Washington Inst. 1987, N.E. dist. conv. 1988, Albany Inst. 1988, Israel Summit V 1988, Washington Inst. 1989, sec. sect. pub. affairs com. 1990—93, mem. state and sec. pub. affairs com. 1990—, Albany Inst. 1991, Washington Mission 1991, co-chair Hunger Program Sunday Family Soup Kitchen 1991—93, nat. Israel affairs com. 1991—96, bd. dirs. N.Y. sect. 1991—, Jewish/Israel affairs com. sect. 1991—, Washington Inst. 1992, participant nat. conv. 1993, Albany Inst. 1993, chair Roosevelt Island Svcs. 1993—2003, participant nat. conv. 1996, Israel Roundtable 1996—99, co-chair fundraising jour. 1998—2000, co-chair sec. Yad B'Yad (Hand in Hand with Israel) cmty. svc. project 1999—, film festival com. Eleanor Leff Jewish Women's Resource Ctr. 2001—02, co-chair sec. Jewish/Israel Affairs com. 2001—, life mem. N.Y. and Rockland County sects., Outstanding Vol. award 1973—74, 1990—91,

Donor award 1987—93, 1996), Jewish Hist. Soc. N.Y., Mich. State U. Alumni Orgn. (life; sec. N.Y. chpt. 1959—60), Mothers and Others, Rockland County Jewish Home for the Aged (life), Women's League for Israel (life), Hadassah (life), Sierra Club.

MELVILLE, CATHY LOUISE, administrative assistant; b. Johnstown, Pa., May 08; d. Charles Richard and Doris Louise (Fritz) Galbraith; m. Roger Daniel Melville, Nov. 27, 1976; 1 child, Melissa Lynn. Mail clk. Johnstown (Pa.) Bank and Trust Co., 1972-73, steno-clk., sec., 1973-81; human resources clk. BT Fin. Corp., Johnstown, 1982-94, human resources officer, 1994—99, payroll specialist, 1999—2002; adminstrv. asst. The Closing Specialists, Ligonier, Pa., 2002—. Treas. West Fairfield Cemetery Assn., 1980—; reader Johnstown Radio Reader, 1993—; asst. troop leader Girl Scouts U.S., Fairfield, 1994-2000; asst. treas. Laurel Valley Band Parents, 1996-2000; elder, ch. auditor local Presbyn. ch., Sunday sch. tchr., various coms. Mem. Order Eastern Star. Presbyterian. Home: 244 Beaufort Rd New Florence PA 15944

MEMBIELA, ROYMI VICTORIA, marketing professional, consultant; b. Havana, Cuba, June 25, 1957; arrived in U.S., 1970; d. Rolando Angel Membiela and Migdalia Amand; m. Terry D McCandlish, July 22, 2003. BS in Mktg., Barry U., 1986. Lic. real estate assoc. Fla. Dir. new bus. and Hispanic market devel. specialist Miami (Fla.) Herald Pub. Co., 1977—94; pres. Mktg. Americas Group, Coral Gables, Fla., 1994—98; cons. Internat. Consulting Partners, Inc, Miami, 1998—99; sr. v.p. Kelley Swofford Roy, Coral Gables, 1999—2002; pres. Roymi Membiela & Associates, Inc, Miami Beach, Fla., 2002—. Community activist (mentorship of women) Miami Dade County Parks & Recreation (In the Co. of Women, 2003). Bd. mem. UNIDAD Hispana, Miami Beach, Fla., 2001—03, Spanish-Am. League Against Discrimination, Miami, 1999—2003; bd. dirs. Vizcaya Trust Fund, Miami, 2000—02; cmty. activist, women's mentor Miami Dade County Parks & Recreation; chmn. Cmty. Rels. Bd. City of Miami Beach, 2002—03; mem. State of Fla. Bd. of Architecture and Interior Design, Tallahassee, 2002—03; bd. dirs. Miami Dade County Housing Fin. Authority, Miami, 2002—03; chmn. Miami Dade County Hispanic Affairs Adv. Bd., Miami, 1998—2002; mem. Miami Dade County Cmty. Rels. Bd., Miami, 2001—02; bd. dirs. Miami-Dade Expy. Auth., 2004—, Miami Beach Cultural Arts Coun., 2004—. Recipient Achievement award for Hispanic Women, VISTA Mag., 1997, Corp. Hispanic Bus. Adv. award, U.S. Hispanic Chamber of Commerce, 1993. Mem.: Greater Miami C. of C. (assoc.), Pub. Rels. Soc. of Am. (assoc.), Camara Comercio Latina (assoc.), Assn. Women in Comm. (assoc.). Avocations: travel, reading, public speaking, mentoring. Office: Roymi Membiela & Associates 6538 Collins Avenue #125 Miami Beach FL 33141 Office Phone: 305-868-1655. Personal E-mail: roymi@membiela.com. E-mail: roymi@membiela.com.

MENAKER, SHIRLEY ANN LASCH, psychology educator, academic administrator; b. Jersey City, July 22, 1935; d. Frederick Carl and Mary Elizabeth (Thrall) Lasch; m. Michael Menaker, June 4, 1955; children: Ellen Margaret, Nicholas. BA in English Lit., Swarthmore Coll., 1956; MA, Boston U., 1961; PhD in Clin. Psychology, 1965. Adminstrv. asst. N.J. State Fedn. Dist. Bds. Edn., Trenton, 1956-59; trainee clin. psychology Mass. Mental Health Ctr., Boston, 1960-61; intern clin. psychology Thom Guidance Clinic for Children, Boston, 1961-62; research assoc. ednl. psychology U. Tex.-Austin, 1964-67, asst. prof. ednl. psychology, 1967-70, assoc. prof., 1970-79, assoc. dean grad. sch., 1975-77; psychology cons. Research and Devel. Ctr. for Tchr. Edn., 1965-67, faculty investigator, 1967-74; assoc. prof. counseling psychology U. Oreg., Eugene, 1979-85, prof., 1985-87, assoc. dean grad. sch., 1979-84, acting dean grad. sch., 1980-81, 82-83, dean grad. sch., 1984-87; assoc. provost for acad. support and classroom mgmt., prof. U. Va., Charlottesville, 1987—2004, prof. emeritus, 2004—. Contbr. articles to profl. jours. Bd. dirs. Nat. Grad. Record Exam Bd. and Policy Council-Test of English as Fgn. Lang., Ednl. Testing Services, 1984-88. NIMH fellow, 1963-64.

MENARD, JOAN M. state legislator; BS, Bridgewater State Coll., 1967; MEd, Boston U., 1971; postgrad., Boston Coll., 1997—. Mem. Mass. Senate, Boston, 1979—; majority whip Mass. Ho. of Reps., Boston, 1984, 92-96, asst. majority whip, 1991, mem. house rules and joint rules coms., house vice chairperson election laws; elem. tchr. Somerset (Mass.) Pub. Schs., 1966-70, spl. edn. tchr., 1970-74, adminstr. spl. needs, 1974-78. Bd. dirs. Fall River Five Cents Savs. Bank, Steppinstone. Mem. adv. bd. Southeastern Mass. Labor Ctr.; chair Dem. State Com., 1993-95, del., 1980; chairwoman Mass. Dem. Party, 1997—2001, State Senator, Mass. Rep. Party, Somerset, Mass., 2000-. Mem. LWV, NOW, Women's Polit. Caucus, Somerset Cath. Womens Club, Bus. and Profl. Women's Club. Democrat. Office: 27 Water St Ste 309 Wakefield MA 01880

MENARD, LYSSA, psychologist, educator; PhD, Pacific Grad. Sch. Psychology, 2001. Lic. clin. psychologist Ill. Bd. Psychology, 2002. Rsch. asst. U. Calif., San Francisco, 1993—2001; rsch. asst./tchg. asst. Pacific Grad. Sch. Psychology, Palo Alto, Calif., 1996—2000; instr. Foothill C.C., Chgo., 1999—2000; psychology intern Hines VA Hosp./Loyola U. Med Sch., Chgo., 2000—01; psychology fellow U. Chgo., 2001—02. Dissertation fellow, Soroptimist Internat., 2000—01. Mem.: APA, Am. Pain Soc., Soc. Behavioral Medicine. Office: Rush-Presbyterian-St Luke's Med Ctr Prof Bldg III 550 1725 W Harrison St Chicago IL 60612

MENCER, C. SUZANNE, federal agency administrator; m. John Mencer; children: Jessie, Alex. BA in Spanish, Ohio State U. Tchr. Spanish, 1968—78; spl. agt. FBI, 1978—85, supervisory spl. agt., 1985—90, supr., 1990—98; pvt. cons. Anti-Terrorism Tng., Denver; exec. dir. dept. pub. safety State of Colo., Denver, 2000—03. Office: Naval Security Sta Nebraska and Massachusetts Avenues NW Washington DC 20393*

MENCER, JETTA, lawyer; b. Coshocton, Ohio, Apr. 7, 1959; d. William J. and Virginia M. (Fry) M. BS, Ohio State U., 1980, JD, 1983. Bar: Ohio, U.S. Dist. Ct. (so. dist.) Ohio. Assoc. Berry, Owens & Manning, Coshocton, 1983-86; asst. pros. atty. Coshocton County, 1983-86, Licking County, Newark, Ohio, 1986-88, asst. atty. gen., 1988-95; pvt. practice Coshocton, 1995-96; prosecuting atty. Coshocton County (Ohio) Prosecutor's Office, 1997-2001; atty. Lee Smith & Assocs., Columbus, Ohio, 2001—03; pvt. practice Columbus, 2003—. Treas. Coshocton County Dem. Cen. & Exec. Coms., 1984-86; chmn., 1986-88; sec., bd. dirs. Heart Ohio Girl Scout Council, Inc., Zanesville, Ohio, 1985-87; fin. chmn., bd. dirs. YMCA, Coshocton, 1985-87. Mem. Ohio State Bar Assn., Coshocton County Bar Assn., Lions Club. Democrat. Methodist. Office: 967 Delaware Ave Columbus OH 43201 E-mail: jmencer@columbus.rr.com.

MENDELSOHN, CAROL S. television producer; Student, Smith Coll., Cornell U. Writer CSI and CSI: Miami CBS, LA; with Securities and Exchange Commn.; atty. Washington; writer Fame NBC, LA; with Stephen J. Cannell; exec. prodr. Melrose Pl. NBC, 1990—99; exec. prodr. CSI CBS, LA, 2000—. Author: (TV series) Clifford the Big Red Dog, CSI (nominated Emmy Outstanding Drama Series award, 2002, 2003, nominated TV Prodr. of Yr. award, 2003, 2004), CSI: Miami, Gabriel's Fire, Hardcastle & McCormick, J.J. Starbuck, Melrose Place, Providence, Stingray, Teenage Mutant Ninja Turtles, Wiseguy, (films) To Brave Alaska.*

MENDELSON, ELLEN B. radiologist, educator; MD, Northwestern U. Feinberg Sch. Medicine, 1980. Cert. diagnostic radiology 1984. Intern to resident, diagnostic radiology NW U. Meml. Hosp., Chgo., 1981—84, fellowship, 1984—85; radiologist Western Penn Hosp., Pitts.; bd. mem. Monongahela Valley Hosp., Pa.; assoc. prof., radiology U. Pitts. Sch. Medicine; prof. radiology NW U., Feinberg Sch. Medicine, Chgo.; dir. breast imaging NW Meml. Hosp. Office: NW U Feinberg Sch Medicine 675 N St Clair Galter 13th Fl Chicago IL 60611 Address: NW Meml Hosp 251 E Huron St Chicago IL 60611

MENDELSON, JOAN RINTEL, lawyer; b. N.Y.C., July 19, 1941; d. Leon and Myra Rintel; m. Neil H. Mendelson, July 30, 1959; children: Debora C., Marie Mendelson Piccarreta. BA with high distinction, with honors in Zoology, Ind. U., 1962, MA, 1963; JD, U. Ariz., 1974. Bar: Ariz. 1975. Co-founder and co-dir. Catonsville Coop. Nursery Sch., Md., 1967—69; assoc. Law Offices of Ann Bowen, Tucson, 1975—76; pvt. practice Tucson, 1977—80; asst. atty. gen. Office of Atty. Gen., Tucson, 1980—2000. Instr. biology U. Md. Balt. County, Catonsville, 1968; spl. magistrate Tucson City Ct., 1984—91; mem. Pima County Child Fatality Rev. Bd., Tucson, 1982—; mem. legal counsel Gov.'s Task Force on Sch. Age Child Care, Phoenix, 1984—86; mem. Pima County Citizen Rev. Bd., Tucson, 2000—; mem. child abuse team Ariz. Health Scis. Ctr., Tucson, 1983—2000; mem. ad hoc com. on child protective svcs. and related child welfare issues Ariz. Legislature, Phoenix, 1994—2000, mem. legal and statutory reform subcom. ad hoc com. on child protective svcs. and related child welfare issues, 1994—2000, chair sys. and policy changes subcom. ad hoc com. on child protective svcs. and related child welfare issues, 1996—2000; mem. model ct. steering com. Pima County Juvenile Ct., Tucson, 1996—2000, mem. model ct. workgroup, 1998—2000; mem. emergency juvenile rules com. Ariz. Supreme Ct., Phoenix, 1998—99, mem. juvenile rules com., 1999—2000, mem. ct. improvement project adv. workgroup, 1998—2003; mem. Pima County Interagency Task Forces on Custodial Interference, Tucson, 1997—2000, Pima County Child Adv. Ctr. Adv. Bd., Tucson, 1997—99; mem. child adv. clinic adv. bd. Coll. Law U. Ariz., Tucson, 1998. Three Yr. Master's Program fellow, Ford Found., 1961, Pre-doctoral fellow, NSF, 1962. Mem.: Sigma Xi, Phi Beta Kappa. Office: PO Box 30192 Tucson AZ 85751-0192

MENDELSON, LOTTIE M. retired pediatric nurse practitioner, writer; b. Portland, Oreg., June 4, 1937; d. Esther Layton-Murphy, James A. Murphy; m. Robert Mendelson, June 22, 1958; children: David, Tamara Mendelson-Hefetz, Mark, Michelle Rosenbloom. BS, U. Portland, 1958; MS, Oreg. Health Scis. U., 1972, Pediat. Nurse Practitioner, 1978. RN 1958, cert. pediat. nurse practitioner, 1978. Pediat. nurse practitioner Pediat. Assocs., Portland, Oreg., 1980—98; ret., 1998. Co-author: Raising Your Baby and Young Child, The New Parent's Question and Answer Book, 1992, editor (founder) Pediat. newsletter, 1984-97. Bd. dirs. Jewish Family and Child Svc., Portland, 1993—98. Mem.: Woman's Divsn. Oreg. Israel Bonds (chairperson 1981—85). Avocations: tennis, travel. Home: 5455 SW 87th Ave Portland OR 97225-1713 Personal E-mail: bbxmnr@aol.com.

MENDENHALL, HOLLIE CHRISTINE, music educator; b. Lancaster, Pa., Dec. 9, 1977; d. Edd Charles and Deborah Ann Monskie; m. Darin Michael Mendenhall, June 24, 2000. BS in Music Edn., Millersville (Pa.) U., 1999. Elem. music tchr. Hempfield Sch. Dist., Landisville, Pa., 2000; mid. sch. music tchr. Sch. Dist. of Lancaster, Lancaster, Pa., 2000—02; elem. music tchr. Donegal Sch. Dist., Marietta, Pa., 2002—; piano and voice tchr. Hollie's Mendenhall's Music Studio, Lancaster, Pa., 1999—. Mem.: NEA, Music Educators Nat. Conf. Republican. Lutheran. Avocations: African drumming, softball, travel, cross stitch, reading. Office: Donegal Sch Dist Marietta PA Personal E-mail: holliem306@comcast.net.

MENDEZ, ANGELA M. small business owner; b. Elmhurst, N.Y., Apr. 27, 1972; d. Paulina Magdalena Mendez, Rodolfo Alfonso Mendez; life ptnr. Marlene T. Monday. BA, So. Conn. State U., 1999. Co-author: Essential Love: poems about mothers and fathers, daughters and sons, 1999; contbr. poems to poetry jours. Mem.: Conn. Poetry Soc. (v.p. 1998—99, Joseph Brodine Nat. Poetry award 1997). Roman Catholic. Avocations: reading, painting, travel, poetry. Home: PO Box 26401 West Haven CT 06516 Personal E-mail: poemlovr@yahoo.com. Business E-Mail: poemlover@2cgdesigns.com.

MENDEZ, C. BEATRIZ, obstetrician, gynecologist, educator, gynecologist, consultant; b. Guatemala, Apr. 21, 1952; d. Jose and Olga (Sobalvarro) M.; m. Mark Parshall, Dec. 12, 1986. BS in Biology and Psychology, Pa. State U., 1974; MD, Milton Hershey Coll. Medicine, 1979. Diplomate Am. Bd. Ob-gyn.; cert. in advanced operative laparoscopy and hysteroscopy Accreditation Coun. for Gynecologic Endoscopy, Inc. Resident in ob-gyn. George Washington U., Washington, 1979-83; pvt. practice Santa Fe, 1985-95, Locum Tenens, 1996; contract physician Lovelace Health Sys., Albuquerque, 1996-98; clin. instr. dept. ob-gyn. U. N.Mex. Sch. Medicine, Albuquerque, 1983—85, 1996—98; pvt. practice anti-aging medicine, 2001—02; cons. to med. facilities; med. dir. The Sterling Inst., 2001—02, Med. Spa Profl. Alliance, 2002—; med. cons. Med. Spa Conf., 2001—. Bd. dirs. Hershey (Pa.) Coll. Medicine, 1977—82; chair perinatal com. St Vincent's Hosp., Santa Fe, 1986—89, mem. quality assurance com., 1986—95, chief ob-gyn., 1992—94; Vol. physician Women's Health Svcs., Santa Fe, 1995—96; clin. instr. dept. ob-gyn. U. N. Mex. Sch. Medicine, Albuquerque, 1997—; med. dir. The Sterling Inst., Santa Fe; med. advisor Med. Spas Conf., 2001—. Med. advisor: MedicalSpa Mag., 2001—. Vol. Women's Health Svcs., Santa Fe, 1985-95. With USPHS, 1983-85. Mosby scholar Mosby-Hersey Med. Sch., Hershey, 1979. Fellow: ACOG (Continuing Edn. award 1986—); mem.: AMA (Physician Recognition award 1986—), Residents Assn. George Washington U. (co-founder 1981—83), Am. Soc. Coloscopy and Cervical Pathology, Am. Fertility Soc., Internat. Soc. Endoscopy, Am. Assn. Gynecol. Laparascopists, Am. Acad. Anti-aging Medicine. Democrat.

MENDEZ, DEBORAH, parochial school educator; b. Delran, N.J., Mar. 7, 1973; d. Robert Barry and Mary Lou Sause; m. John Mendez, Mar. 7, 1997. BS, St. John's U., 1995; postgrad., Nova Southeastern U., Ft. Lauderdale, Fla. Cert. tchr., Fla. Tchr. Our Lady of Refuge Sch., Bklyn., 1996-97, Annunciation Sch., Hollywood, Fla., 1997—. Active Annunciation Parish, 1997—. Mem. St. John's U. Alumni Assn. Roman Catholic. Home: 7161 SW 10th St Pembroke Pines FL 33023-1644 Office: Annunciation Sch 3751 SW 39th St Hollywood FL 33023-6252 E-mail: jmendez6@bellsouth.net.

MENDEZ, OLGA A. state legislator; b. Mayaguez, P.R. BA, U. P.R.; MEd, Columbia U., 1960; PhD in Ednl. Psychology, Yeshiva U., N.Y.C., 1975. Previously assoc. prof. SUNY-Stony Brook, research psychologist Albert Einstein Coll. Med., N.Y.C., dep. commr. N.Y.C. Agy. for Child Devel.; mem. from dist. 28 N.Y. Senate, Albany, 1978—. Del. Dem. Nat. Conv., 1980, leadership position, 1984—, sec. minority conf., 1992—, chairperson conf. Home: 87 E 116th St New York NY 10029-1103 Office: N Y State Senate State Capitol 420 State Capitol Bldg Albany NY 12247

MENDIETA, RAQUELIN MARIA DE LA CONCEPCION, artist; b. Havana, Cuba, Aug. 4, 1946; came to the U.S., 1961; d. Ignacio Alberto and Raquel de San José (Oti) M.; m. Donald Raymond Holmes, Aug. 26, 1967 (div. Dec. 1973); m. James William Auman, Aug. 9, 1975 (div. July 1977); m. Thomas Joseph Harrington, May 17, 1978 (div. 2002); children: Raquel Cecilia, Paulette Ana, Shambhavi Elvira, Neel Miguel, Vitthal Pablo. Student, Mt. Mercy Coll., 1963-65; BA in Studio Art, U. Iowa, 1970, postgrad., 1970-72, MA in Edn., 1977. Pvt. practice exhbns. cons., 1987—. Cons. The Mus. Contemporary Art, N.Y.C., 1987, Galerie Lelong, N.Y.C., 1991—, Arts Alliance of Haverstraw, N.Y., 1992, Carla Stellweg Fine Arts, N.Y.C., 1993; humanities adv. bd. Fondo del Sol Visual Arts Ctr., Washington, 1990-93, co-chair exhbns., 1993-97; ednl. coord. Fondo del Sol, Washington, 1991; adj. prof. L.Am. studies Jersey City State Coll., 1991; trustee Arts Alliance Haverstraw, 1992-94; ednl. program specialist The Bronx (N.Y.) Mus. Arts, 1995-96; art dir., music cons. Corazon Prodns., Inc., Miami, Fla., 1996-98; lectr. in field. One woman shows include Rockland C.C., 1990, 96, Café Teatro Julia de Burgos, N.Y.C., 1993, Visceglia Arts Ctr., Caldwell, N.J., 1993, Ludwig Found. Galleries, Ltd., Havana, 2000; permanent collections Bronx Mus. Arts, Mus. of the Art Inst. Chgo. Trustee, liaison [illegible]; rep. to daycare coalition U. Parents Care Collective, Iowa City, 1971-75; vocat. advisor, arts supr. Bedford Hills (N.Y.) Correctional Facility for Women, 1985; mem. Hispanic Heritage Com., Rockland C.C., 1990-93, Hispanic Coalition Rockland County, N.Y., 1991-94. Recipient Cert. of Merit, Town of Ramapo, County of Rockland, 1992, Cert. of Recognition for developing arts programs Hispanic Coun. Rockland County, Haverstraw, 1992, Cert. of Merit, The Assembly of N.Y. State, 1993, award for contbns. to Am. art in sculpture Fondo del Sol Visual Arts Ctr., Washington, 1993. Mem. Arts Alliance of Haverstraw (hon., bd. dirs. 1993-94, trustee 1995—), Coast to Coast Nat. Women Artists of Color. Democrat. Siddha Yoga. Avocations: writing, music, personal computing, meditation, chanting. Home: 11615 SW 135th Pl Miami FL 33186-4429

MENDIOLA, ANNA MARIA G. mathematics educator; b. Laredo, Tex., Dec. 21, 1948; d. Alberto and Aurora (Benavides) Gonzalez; m. Alfonso Mendiola Jr., Aug. 11, 1973; children: Alfonso, Alberto. AA, Laredo C.C., Tex., 1967; BA, Tex. Woman's U., 1969, MS, 1974. Tchr. math. Laredo Ind. Sch. Dist., 1969-81; instr. math. Laredo C.C., 1981—, organizer Jaime Escalante program, 1991-92; tech. prep. com. mem., 1991-92; ednl. coun., sec. Christen Mid. Campus, 1992-94; mem. site based campus com. Martin H.S., 1994-2000. Vis. instr. St. Augustine Sch., Laredo. 1987-88; evaluator So. Assn., Corpus Christi, 1981, So. Assn. Colls. and Schs., United H.S., 1991; mem. quality improvement coun. Laredo C.C., 1993-94; mem. instrn. coun. Laredo C.C., 1995-96; participant SC3 Calculus Reform Inst., NSF, 1996; mem. adv. com. on core curriculum Tex. Higher Edn. Coord. Bd., 1997-99, mem. adv. com. on transfer issues and field of study, 2000—; mem. Laredo C.C. self-study steering com. So. Assn. Colls. and Schs. Reaffirmation, 1997-99, coord. honors program, 1999—; math. dept. chair 2002[00bf]; faculty assoc. NSF-LCC Rio Grande River Project, 1998-2000. V.p., bd. dirs. Our Lady of Guadalupe Sch., Laredo, 1988-91; sec. Laredo C.C. Faculty Senate, 1986-87, v.p., 1995-96, pres., 1996-97, mem. curriculum com., 2003[00bf]; rep. Laredo Ind. Sch. Dist. Parent Adv. Coun., 1997-98. Recipient Teaching Excellence award NISOD, 1993; named LCC Innovator of the Month, 1998. Mem. AAUW (pres. 1979-81, v.p. 1987-89, scholarship chair 1993-94, membership chair 1994-95, bylaws chair 1996-97, pub. policy chair 1997-99), Am. Math. Assn. Two-Yr. Colls., Tex. State Tchrs. Assn., Tex. C.C. Tchrs. Assn. (campus rep., sec. math. sect. 1997-98, vice chair math. sect. 1998-99, chair math. sect. 1999-2000, chair audit com. 1999-2000, co-chair membership com. 2001-02, mem. profl. devel. com., 2003—), Tex. Woman's U. Alumnae Assn., Blessed Sacrament Altar Soc., Delta Kappa Gamma (membership chair 1993-96, v.p. 2000-02). Democrat. Roman Catholic. Office: Laredo CC West End Washington St Laredo TX 78040 E-mail: amendiola@laredo.edu.

MENDIUS, PATRICIA DODD WINTER, editor, educator, writer; b. Davenport, Iowa, July 9, 1924; d. Otho Edward and Helen Rose (Dodd) Winter; m. John Richard Mendius, June 19, 1947; children: Richard, Catherine M. Graber, Louise, Karen M. Chooljian. BA cum laude, UCLA, 1946; MA cum laude, U. N.Mex., 1966. Cert. secondary edn. tchr., Calif., N.Mex. English teaching asst. UCLA, 1946-47; English tchr. Marlborough Sch. for Girls, L.A., 1947-50, Aztec (N.Mex.) High Sch., 1953-55, Farmington (N.Mex.) High Sch., 1955-63; chair English dept. Los Alamos (N.Mex.) High Sch., 1963-86; sr. technical writer, editor Los Alamos Nat. Lab., 1987—. Adj. prof. English, U. N.Mex., Los Alamos, 1970-72, Albuquerque, 1982-85; English cons. S.W. Regional Coll. Bd., Austin, Tex., 1975—; writer, editor, cons. advanced placement English test devel. com. Nat. Coll. Bd., 1982-86, reader, 1982-86, project equality cons., 1985-88; book selection cons. Scholastic mag., 1980-82. Author: Preparing for the Advanced Placement English Exams, 1975; editor Los Alamos Arts Coun. bull., 1986-91. Chair Los Alamos Art in Pub. Places Bd., 1987-92; chair adv. bd. trustees U. N.Mex., Los Alamos, 1987-93; pres. Los Alamos Concert Assn., 1972-73, 95-98, 2000-04, pres., 2003-04; chair Los Alamos Mesa Pub. Libr. Bd., 1990-94, chair endowment com., 1995-99. Mem. Soc. Tech. Communicators, AAUW (pres. 1961-63, state bd. dirs. 1959-63, Los Alamos coordinating coun. 1992-93, pres. 1993-94, 2002-04, sec. 2001-04), DAR, Order Ea. Star, Mortar Bd., Phi Beta Kappa (pres. Los Alamos chpt. 1969-72, 99, v.p. 1996-99, pres. 2000-01, dir. 2002-04), Phi Kappa Phi, Delta Kappa Gamma, Gamma Phi Beta. Avocations: swimming, reading, hiking, astronomy, singing. Home: 124 Rover Blvd Los Alamos NM 87544-3634 Office: Los Alamos Nat Lab Diamond Dr Los Alamos NM 87544 E-mail: mendius@qwest.net., pmendius@lanl.gov.

MENDOZA, LYDIA, vocalist; Mem. El Cuarteto Carta Blanca. Recordings include: Mal Hombre, 1934; performances include Smithsonian Bicentennial Festival of Am. Folklife, Carter Presdl. Inauguration; author (compiled by Chris Strachwitz and James Nicolopulos): Lydia Mendoza: A Family Autobiography, 1993; author: (with Y. Broyles-Gonzales) Lydia Mendoza: My Life and Music, 2001. Named a Nat. Treasure, Smithsonian Instn.; named Nat. Heritage fellow, Nat. Endowment for the Arts, 1982; named to Tex. Hall of Fame; recipient Nat. Medal of Arts, Nat. Assn. for Chicana and Chicano Studies Lifetime Achievement Cmty. award, 1999, Nat. Medal of Arts, Am. Heritage award. Office: c/o Arhoolie Records 10341 San Pablo Ave El Cerrito CA 94530-3123 E-mail: chris@arhoolie.com.

MENDOZA, MARTHA, reporter; b. L.A., Calif., 1969; BA, U. Calif. Santa Cruz, 1988. Reporter Madera Tribune, Bay City News Svc., Santa Cruz County Sentinel; nat. investigative reporter Associated Press, San Jose, Calif., 1995—. Co-author: The Bridge at No Gun Rl: A Hidden Nightmare from the Korean War, 2001. Recipient Pulitzer prize, 2000, Alumni Achievment award, U. Calif. Santa Cruz, 2002; John S. Knight fellow, Stanford U., 2001. Office: Associated Press 675 N 1st St San Jose CA 95112

MENDOZA, MELISSA ANN, lab administrator, technologist; b. San Antonio, Dec. 15, 1973; d. Clifford Allen Waseham and Guadalupe Stout; m. Gabriel Mendoza, Aug. 30, 1998; children: Sevin, Devin. Cert. in phlebotomy, U. Tex., Brownsville, 1994, AAS, AIA, U. Tex., Brownsville, 1995. Phlebotomist, med. lab. technician, breath alcohol technician Valley Regional Med. Ctr., Brownsville, 1996—2000, nightshift lab. supr., 1998—2000; med. technologist, clin. lab. scientist, lab. mgr., order entry computer coord. Brownsville Surg. Hosp., 2000—. Blood donor ARC, Harlingen, Tex., 1995—. Mem.: NAFE, Tex. Soc. Am. Med. Technologists (assoc.), Am. Soc. Clin. Pathologists (assoc.), Am. Med. Technologists (assoc.). Avocations: photography, painting, crafts, kickboxing, kickball. Home: 3005 Old Alice Rd 1100-C Brownsville TX 78521 Office: Brownsville Surg Hosp 4750 N Expressway Brownsville TX 78526 Personal E-mail: mmendoza@ies.net.

MENDOZA, RUTH, art educator; b. San Antonio, Nov. 17, 1941; d. Rudy Aleman and Lucy (Lopez) Hernandez. BS, Howard Payne U., 1965; M of Liberal Arts, So. Meth. U., Dallas, 1981. Cert. tchr., Tex. Tchr. Woodsboro (Tex.) Ind. Sch. Dist., 1966-69, Corpus Christi (Tex.) Ind. Sch. Dist., 1970-73, Grand Prairie (Tex.) Ind. Sch. Dist., 1974—. Cons. State Textbook Com., Grand Prairie, 1988. Mem. com. First Bapt. Ladies Ministry, Grand Prairie, 1992-95; translator The Master's Builders, Grand Prairie, 1990—. Recipient Hon. Life membership Tex. Congress of Parents and Tchrs., 1979. Mem. AAUW, Nat. Mus. Women in Arts, Tex. PTA, Dallas Mus. Art. Avocation: art related activities.

MENEBROKER, ANN, special education educator, writer; b. Washington, D.C., Mar. 30, 1936; d. Harold Godfrey Reynolds Jr. and Edith Louise (Ellis) Reynolds; children: Audrey St Violet, Lauri Solari, Sue McElligot. Dir.'s asst. Artists' Contemporary Gallery, Sacramento, 1990—2000; instrnl. asst. in spl. edn. Natomas Sch. Dist., Sacramento, 2000—. Co-editor: (anthology) Landing Signals, 1985, Watching from the Sky, 1990; author: (poetry collection) Trying for the Ten Ring, 2000, Walking the Dog, Selected Poems 1959-1989, 2003. Avocations: art, rare book collecting, music, walking. Home: 10 Azorean Ct Sacramento CA 95833-1142

MENENDEZ, BELINDA, broadcast executive; Student, St. Andrews U., Scotland. With internat. TV sales Televisa, 1986—95; mgr. TV sales Cisneros; internat. tv distbn. ops. mgr. Michael Solomon's S.I.E.; exec. v.p. sales Studio Canal (formerly Canal Plus DA); co-pres. Universal TV Distbn., Universal City, Calif., 2001—. Office: Universal TV Distbn USA Bldg 1440/3030 100 Universal City Plaza Universal City CA 91608-1002*

MENENDEZ, TERESA, communications executive; d. Jose Ramon and Martha Moraima Menendez; m. Richard Smith, June 16, 1978; children: Scott Ryan Smith, Brett Tyler Smith, Analise Nicole Smith. B, Fla. State U., 1975. Hispanic market rsch. analyst Kenneth Hollander Assocs., Atlanta, 1977—80; owner / pres. Menendez Internat., Miami and Key West, Fla., 1988—; owner Rsch. Resources, Atlanta, 1980—88; interviewer / supr. Comm. Rsch. Ctr., Tallahassee, 1971—77. Ethnic edn. subcommittee mem. Advt. Rsch. Found., New York, NY. Author: (hispanic research) Market Research: A Magazine of Management and Applications; speaker (various university & high school campus); author: (hispanic research) The U.S. Hispanic Report, Potentials in Marketing, Marketing News; contbr. speaker Se Habla Español Conference; speaker (association of national advertisers), (mexican american grocery association), (point of purchase advertising institute), (various national corporate headquarters). Recipient Judge, Se Habla Espanol Conf. Hispanic Advt. Mem.: NAFE, Assn. of Hispanic Advt. Agencies, Qualitative Rsch. Consultants Assn., Mktg. Rsch. Assn., Am. Mktg. Assn. Democrat-Npl. Mem. Assembly Of God Ch. Achievements include design of Established National Field Service Network; Hispanic Definition for Marketing; development of Defined Systems for Qualifying and Research Hispanics Domestically & Abroad. Avocations: fishing / boating, cooking / baking, travel. Office: Menendez International 1331 White Street Key West FL 33040 E-mail: menendezlh@aol.com.

MENES, PAULINE H. state legislator; b. N.Y.C., July 16, 1924; d. Arthur B. and Hannah H. Herskowitz; m. Melvin Menes, Sept. 1, 1946; children: Sandra Jill Menes Ashe, Robin Joy Menes Elvord, Bambi Lynn Menes Gavin. BA in Bus. Econs. and Geography, Hunter Coll., N.Y.C., 1945. Economist Quartermaster Gen. Office, Washington, 1945-47; geographer Army Map Svc., Washington, 1949-50; chief clk. Prince George's County Election Bd., Upper Marlboro, Md., 1963; substitute tchr. Prince George's County H.S., Md., 1965-66; mem. Md. Ho. of Dels., Annapolis, 1966—, mem. judiciary com., 1979—, parliamentarian, 1995—. Com. on rules and exec. nominations, Md. Ho. of Dels., Annapolis, 1979-94, 95—, chmn. spl. com. on drug and alcohol abuse, 1986—, chmn. Prince George's County del., 1993-95. Mem. Md. Arts Coun., Balt., 1968-95, Md. Commn. on Aging, Balt., 1975-95; bd. dirs. Prisoner's Aid Assn., Balt., 1971-94. Recipient Internat. Task Force award Women's Yr., 1977, Ann London Scott Meml. Excellence award NOW, 1976; named to Hall of Fame Hunter Coll. Alumni Assn., 1986, Women's Hall of Fame Prince George County, 1989. Mem. NOW, Nat. Conf. State Legislators (com. on drugs and alcohol 1987), Nat. Order Women Legislators (pres. 1979-80), Women's Polit. Caucus, Bus. and Profl. Women. Avocations: theater, music, dance show attending, stamp collector. Home: 3517 Marlbrough Way College Park MD 20740-3925 Office: Md Ho of Reps Rm 210 Lowe State Office Bldg Annapolis MD 21401

MENG, M. KATHRYN, lawyer; JD, Fordham U. Former dist. ct. bur. chief criminal divsn. Legal Aid Soc. Nassau County; ptnr. Cianciulli & Meng, P.C., Uniondale, NY. Dean Nassau Acad. Law; adj. prof. Nassau C.C. Columnist Nassau Lawyer. Bd. dirs. Sara's Ctr.; mem. outreach adv. com. St. Brigid's Ch., Westbury, eucharistic ministr. Mem.: ABA (del.), Nassau Legal Aid Soc. (former pres., former bd. dirs.), Attys. to the Bar (com. character and fitnss for admission 1983—), Criminal Cts. Bar Assn. (former pres., former bd. dirs.), N.Y. State Bar Assn. (del.), Nassau County Bar Assn. (pres., former chair civil rights com., former chair lawyer's assistance com., former mem. judiciary com.). Office: Cianciulli & Meng PC PO Box 246 773 Hampstead Tpke Uniondale NY 11553-0246

MENINGALL, EVELYN L. educational media specialist; b. Dothan, Ala., July 22, 1935; d. Earl and Luella Koonce; m. A. Richard Meningall, Jan. 17, 1958; children: Dawn, Tracy, Richard. BS in Edn., Wayne State U., 1975; MLS, Rutgers U., 1979. Cert. ednl. media specialist Dept. Edn. State N.J., elem. sch. dept. Dept. Edn. State N.J., profl. librs. cert. Dept. Edn. State N.J. Tchr. Detroit Bd. Edn., 1975—76; libr. East Brunswick (N.J.) Pub. Libr., 1978—80; ednl. media specialist Piscataway (N.J.) Bd. Edn., 1980—98; ret., 1998. Author poetry. Active New Detroit, Inc., Delta Sigma Theta Sorority Ctrl. Jersey; vol. tutor/reader pub. schs.; vol. to holisitic score English tests Plainfield (N.J.) H.S.; recording sec. Scholarship Fund of St. Paul AME Ch. Mem.: ALA, Ednl. Media Assn., Nat. Sorority Phi Delta Kappa, Inc. (life; basileus 1987—89, exec. advisor 1989—91). Ame Church. Avocations: writing poetry, reading, fishing. Home: 23 Vauxhall Rd East Brunswick NJ 08816-1719

MENKEL-MEADOW, CARRIE JOAN, law educator; b. N.Y.C., Dec. 24, 1949; d. Gary G. and Margot (Sinn) Menkel; m. Robert Gary Meadow, Aug. 22, 1971. AB magna cum laude, Columbia U., 1971; JD cum laude, U. Pa., 1974; LLD (hon.), Quinnipiac Coll. Law, 1995. Bar: Pa. 1974, U.S. Ct. Appeals (3d cir.) 1975, Calif. 1979, D.C., 1997. Dir. legal writing U. Pa. Law Sch., Phila., 1974-75, clin. supt., lectr., 1976-79; staff atty. Cmty. Legal Svcs., Phila., 1975-77; prof. UCLA, 1979—, prof. law, 1979-99, Georgetown Law Ctr., Washington, 1996—; holder Phyllis Beck chair Temple U. Law Sch., Phila., 1999. Vis. prof. law Harvard Law Sch., 2001; panel mem. NAS, Washington, 1986—87, NSF, Washington, 1987—90; cons. ABA, Chgo., 1979—84; dir. UCLA Ctr. for Conflict Resolution, 1994—99, Georgetown-Hewlett Program on Conflict Resolution and Problem Solving, 2001—. Author: Mediation: Theory, Practice and Policy, 2000, Dispute Processing: Theory, Practice and Policy, 2003, What's Fair: Ethics for Negotiators, 2004; contbr. articles to profl. jours. Chairperson Ctr. for Study of Women, UCLA; bd. dirs. Western Ctr. on Law and Poverty, L.A., 1980-86; chair CPR Commn. on Ethics and ADR. Recipient William Rutter Found. for Tchg. award, 1992, 1st prize for Acad. Scholarship on Alternative Dispute Resolution Ctr. for Pub. Resources, 1983, 91, 98. Mem. Soc. Am. Law Tchrs. (trustee), Assn. Am. Law Schs. (alt. dispute resolution sect., law and social sci. sect., women in law sect., accreditation com. 1987-90), Ctr. for Law and Human Values (bd. dirs.), Law and Soc. Assn. (trustee), Am. Bar Found. (bd. dirs., sec., exec. com. 1994—), Am. Law Inst., Acad. Civil Trial Mediators, Phi Beta Kappa. Democrat. Office: Georgetown Law Ctr 600 New Jersey Ave NW Washington DC 20001-2075 E-mail: meadow@law.georgetown.edu.

MENKEN, JANE AVA, demographer, educator; b. Phila., Nov. 29, 1939; d. Isaac Nathan and Rose Ida (Sarvetnick) Golubitsky; m. Matthew Menken, 1960 (div. 1985); children: Kenneth Lloyd, Kathryn Lee; m. Richard Jessor, Nov. 13, 1992. AB, U. Pa., 1960; MS, Harvard U., 1962; PhD, Princeton U., 1975. Asst. in biostats. Harvard U. Sch. Pub. Health, Boston, 1962-64; math. statistician NIMH, Bethesda, Md., 1964-66; research assoc. dept. biostats., Columbia U., N.Y.C., 1966-69; mem. research staff Office of Population Research Princeton U., N.J., 1969-71, 75-87, asst. dir., 1978-86, assoc. dir., 1986-87, prof. sociology, 1980-82, prof. sociology and pub. affairs, 1982-87; prof. sociology and demography U. Pa., Phila., 1987-97, UPS Found. prof. social scis., 1987-97, dir. Population Studies Ctr., 1989-95; prof. sociology U. Colo., Boulder, 1997—, faculty assoc. Population Program, Inst. Behavioral Sci., 1997—; dir. Population Aging Ctr., 2000—, Inst. Behavioral Sci., 2001—, disting. prof., 2002—. Mem. social scis. and population study sect., NIH, Bethesda, Md., 1978-82, chmn., 1980-82, population adv. com. Rockefeller Found., N.Y.C., 1981-93, com. on population and demography, NAS, Washington, 1978-83, com. on population, 1983-85, 1996-2002, chair 1998-2002, com. nat. stats., 1983-89, com. on AIDS research, 1987-93, chair 1990-93; co-chair panel data and rsch. priorities for arresting AIDS in sub-Saharan Africa, 1994-96, Com. on Behavioral and Social Scis. and Edn., 1991-97, sci. adv. com., Demographic and Health Surveys, Columbia, Md., 1985-90, Nat. Adv. Child Health and Human Devel. Council, 1988-91;dirs. adv. com. NIH, 1995-2000, adv. coun. Fogarty Internat. Ctr., 2000-02, cons. Internat. Centre for Diarrhoeal Disease Research, Bangladesh, Dhaka, 1984—. Author: (with Mindel C. Sheps) Mathematical Models of Conception and Birth, 1973; editor: (with Henri Leridon) Natural Fertility, 1979, (with Frank Furstenberg, Jr. and Richard Lincoln) Teenage Sexuality, Pregnancy and Childbearing, 1981, World Population and U.S. Policy: The Choices Ahead, 1986; contbr. articles to profl. jours. Bd. dirs. Alan Guttmacher Inst., N.Y.C., 1981-90, 93-2000, African Population and Health Rsch. Ctr., Nairobi, Kenya, 2000—. Nat. Merit scholar, 1957; John Simon Guggenheim Found. fellow, 1992-93, Ctr. for Advanced Study in Behavioral Scis. fellow, 1995-96. Fellow AAAS, Am. Statis. Assn.; mem. NAS, Inst. of Med., Am. Acad. Arts and Scis., Population Assn. Am. (Mindel Sheps award 1982, pres. 1985), Am. Pub. Health Assn. (Mortimer Spiegelman award 1975), Am. Sociol. Assn., Soc. for Study of Social Biology, Internat. Union for Sci. Study of Population (coun. 1989-97), Sociol. Research Assn. (exec. com. 1991-96, pres. 1996). Office: U Colo IBS#1 483 UCB Boulder CO 80309-0483 E-mail: menken@colorado.edu.

MENKIN, EVA L. marriage and family therapist; b. Berlin, June 26, 1923; came to the U.S., 1934; d. Henry O. and Tamara G. Fuchs; m. Fred Landecker, Sept. 10, 1942 (div. 1972); children: Judy Hoffman, David, Anita, Peter; m. David B. Menkin, Feb. 17, 1974. BA in Psychology, Goddard Coll., 1971, MA in Marriage and Family Counseling, 1973. Lic. marriage and family therapist. Intern Beverly Manor Convalescent House, L.A., 1972, Winsor Manor Retirement Home, Glendale, Calif., 1972; intern, counselor So. Calif. Counseling Ctr., L.A., 1973-76; pvt. practice Westchester Ctr. for Counseling and Psychotherapy, L.A., 1975-76; pvt. practice psychotherapy Santa Barbara, Calif., 1976—. Coord. daytime programs for older adults Rutgers U., 1968-70; instr. UCLA Ext., 1974, Felicia Mahood Ctr., L.A., 1975, U. Calif., Santa Barbara, 1977-78; field faculty Goddard and Antioch Colls., 1976-81; cons., therapist Arthritis Found., Santa Barbara, 1976-80; cons. Sanctuary House, 1976-80, Santa Barbara City Coll., 1981, Casa Dorinda Residential Retirement Home, Santa Barbara, 1983-84. Co-authro: (with B. Weininger) Aging is a Lifelong Affair, 1978; contbr. articles to profl. jours. Mem. Am. Assn. Marriage and Family Therapy, Calif. Assn. Marriage and Family Therapists, Gerontol. Soc. Am. Home: 1011 Mission Ridge Rd Santa Barbara CA 93103-1618 E-mail: dmenkin@aol.com

MENNA, SARI, artist, educator; b. San Fracisco, Sept. 29, 1932; m. Ferdinand Carl Menna, Mar. 10, 1949; children: Mark, Diane Menna Clarke. BFA cum laude, Hunter Coll. of CUNY, N.Y.C., 1968, MFA, 1974, post grad., N.Y. U., N.Y.C., 1987—93. Lic. tchr. N.Y. Bd. Edn., 1971. Substitute tchr. Massapequa Pub. Schs., L.I., NY, 1968—69; tchr. art N.Y.C. Bd. Edn., 1971—95; ret., 1995. Vol. art tchr. Pres.' Econ. Opportunity Cu., L.I., 1967—68; organizer juried art shows Amity Art League, 1964—67; tchr. cultural workshop Amityville Workshop, L.I., 1968. Mini-park, N.Y.C., 1974, calendar and cover art, Women Artists, 1983, exhibitions include Salute to Women, Washington and Nairobi, 1991, Women's Art, N.Y.C., 1992, Paintings and Paperworks, CUNY, 1992, Small Works, Kirkland, Wash., 1993, Garden of Delights, Bklyn., 1994, Family Values, N.Y.C., 1994, Hallelujah 94, 1994, Visions of Reality, Madison, N.J., 1995, A Woman's Pl., N.Y.C., 1995, Points of View, 1995, ADA: Women and Info. Tech., Chgo., 1995—96, The World's Women On Line, Beijing, Tempe, Ariz. and online, 1995—96, Fine Arts Mus., L.I., 1996, Openings 96, N.Y.C., 1996, Diversity, 1997, Small Statement Show, Bklyn., 1997, Painterly Forms, N.Y.C., 1997, BWAC 4th Ann. Pier Show, NJ, 1998, Flat Iron Gallery, Peekskill, N.Y., 1999, Broome St. Gallery, Soho, N.Y.C., 2000, WIA PART II, Canojohri, N.Y., 2000, Represented in permanent collections Nat. Mus. of Women in the Arts, Washington, Women's Interart Collections, N.Y.C., in pvt. collections, exhibited in group shows at Pier Show, N.Y.C., N.Y. Pres. Creative Women's Collection, N.Y.C., 1982—85; mem. Women's Caucus Art (N.Y.C. chpt.), 1982—91; mem. Queens Coun. on Art, 2001—04. Mem.: Creative Women's Collective, Women in the Arts Found, Inc.

MENSH, SUZANNE COOPER, state official; b. Atlantic City, Aug. 29, 1929; d. Paul Joel and Jennie Jean Cooper; m. H. David Mensh, Dec. 18, 1949; children: Paul Jay, Spencer Lee; m. Saul Brown, Feb. 17, 1985. Grad. high sch., Balt. Assoc. judge Orphans' Ct., Balt., 1962-66, chief judge, 1966-85; clk. of ct. Circuit Ct. for Baltimore County, Balt., 1986—. Mem. jud. ethics com. Judiciary of Md., Balt., 1992-99. Active Balt. Dem. Com., 1962—; mem. Nat. Coun. Jewish Women; pres. Balt. Zionist Fedn., 1989-93; former mem. found. bd. Towson State U.; former mem. bd. dirs. Jewish Nat. Fund; former condr. estate planning seminars N.W. Hosp. Ctr., also formr mem. found. bd. Named Woman of Yr. Aux. Baltimore County Gen. Hosp. (now N.W. Hosp. Ctr.), 1989. Mem. Md. Circuit Ct. Clks. Assn. (past pres.), Hadassah (life), Na'Amat (life). Jewish. Avocations: walking, decorating, entertaining, violin. Home: 303 Glatisant Pl Baltimore MD 21208-1400 Office: Circuit Ct Clk's Office County Cts Bldg 401 Bosley Ave Baltimore MD 21204-4420

MENZA, CLAUDIA MARCELLA, literary agent; b. N.Y.C., June 11, 1947; d. John Gaetano and Antonina (di Lorenzo) M.; m. James R. Forker, May 29, 1971 (div. 1980); m. Charles Anthony Frye, Dec. 16, 1989 (dec. Oct. 1994). BA, Oberlin Coll., 1969. Asst. editor Evergreen Rev., N.Y.C., 1969-73; gen. editor, prodn. mgr. Grove Press, Inc., N.Y.C., 1973-83; sr. editor Art Dir. News, N.Y.C., 1983-85; pres. Claudia Menza Lit. Agy., N.Y.C., 1983—. Cons. Riverrun Press, N.Y.C., 1983-96; guest lectr. Tex. A&M U., Prairie View, Tex., 1986, NYU, N.Y.C., 1986-87; cons., panelist Nat. Civil Rights Mus. Conf. The Power of the Word, Memphis, 1995; panelist NYU, 1998, The New Sch., N.Y.C., 2000, The Lost State Writers Conf., Greeneville, Tenn., 2000, Harlem Book Fair, 2001; panelist African Am. Lit. Conf., Raleigh, NC, 2003. Author: Cage of Wild Cries, 1990, The Lunatics Ball, 1994, (plays), 2002; co-author: The Dream Book: An Anthology of Writing by Italian-American Women, 1985 (Am. Book award, 1985); actor: Damned Pub. Riverside Studios, 1999. Working mem. Congress of Racial Equality, Hempstead, N.Y., 1961, Student Nonviolent Coord. Com., Oberlin, Ohio, 1965, Students for Dem. Soc., Oberlin, 1965, The West Village Com., N.Y.C., 1980. Mem. PEN, Internat. Platform Assn., Acad. Am. Poets, Italian-Am. Writers Assn., Assn. Authors Reps. Avocations: reading, music, theater. Office: Claudia Menza Lit Agy 1170 Broadway Ste 807 New York NY 10001-7507

MENZEL, IDINA, actress, lyricist; b. May 30, 1971; d. Stuart and Helene Mentzel; m. Taye Diggs, 2003. BFA in drama, Tisch Sch. Arts, NYU. Actor: (Broadway plays) RENT, 1995—97 (Tony award nominee), Aida, 2001, Funny Girl, 2002, Wicked, 2003— (Tony award nominee, Best Actress in a Musical, 2004); (plays) The Wild Party, 1999, Summer of '42, 2000, Hair, 2001, The Vagina Monologues, 2002; singer: (albums) Still I Can't Be Still, 1998, Here, 2004; actor: (films) Kissing Jessica Stein, 2001, Just a Kiss, 2002, The Tollbooth, 2004; composer: (songs) Follow If You Lead for film "The Other Sister", 1999. Office: Gershwin Theater 222 W 51st St New York NY 10019*

MENZEL, MARYBELLE PROCTOR, volunteer; b. Milledgeville, Ga., Feb. 5, 1940; d. Ennis Hall Proctor and Sara (Evans) McCarthy; m. Robert John Menzel, Sept. 1, 1961; children: Blake, John, Craig. BA cum laude, Wesleyan Coll., Macon, Ga., 1962; MA with highest distinction, U. Ctrl. Fla., 1986. Cert. highest level tchr. Fla. Tchr. Spaulding Jr. H.S., Griffin, Ga., 1962, East Syracuse (N.Y.) Minoa H.S., 1964—65, Coral Gables (Fla.) H.S., 1965—66; dir. Gerber Child Care Ctr., Indialantic, Fla., 1981, Brevard C.C. Coop Presch., Melbourne, Fla., 1982—85; adj. instr. English and Humanities Brevard C.C., Cocoa, Fla., 1985. Mem.: AAUW (Nat. award Fundraising AAUW Ednl. Found. 2001, Garden of Victories award 1993), Colo. AAUW (dir. ednl. found. 2000—01, pres. elect 2001—02, pres. 2002—, state exec. bd., mem. women's lobby), Wesleyan Coll. Million Dollar Women, Nat. Mus. Women in the Arts (friend), Nat. Mus. Women's History (charter), Nat. Trust for Historic Preservation, Phi Kappa Phi. Democrat. Methodist.

MEOLA, JANICE GRACE, lawyer; b. Newark, Jan. 10, 1966; d. William Frank and Rose Marie Meola. BS in Fin., Pa. State U., 1988; JD, U. N.C., Chapel Hill, 1991. Bar: N.J., D.C., U.S. Dist. Ct. N.J. Jud. clk. Superior Ct. of N.J., Jersey City, 1991-92; litigation assoc. Bumgardner, Hardin & Ellis, Springfield, N.J., 1992-94; environ. counsel CNA Ins. Cos., Cranbury, N.J., 1994-96; assoc. counsel Suburban Propane, L.P., Whippany, N.J., 1996-98, counsel, 1998-99, gen. counsel, sec., 1999—. Mem. ABA, Am. Corp. Counsel Assn., N.J. Corp. Counsel Assn. (bd. dirs.), Am. Soc. Corp. Secs., Propane Gas Def. Assn. Office: Suburban Propane LP PO Box 206 240 Route 10 Whippany NJ 07981-0206 Home: 625 Binghampton Ln Livingston NJ 07039-8260

MERCER, EVELYN LOIS, retired guidance counselor; b. Ellensboro, N.C., Apr. 25, 1934; d. Milton Bernadine Robinson Sr. and Lois Lenora Robinson; m. Theodore Roosevelt Mercer Sr. (div. June 1978); children: Theodore Roosevelt Jr., Brian Vincent, David Lemuel. BS in Math., Livingstone Coll., 1957; MEd in Guidance and Counseling, U. Cin., 1972; student, U. Akron, 1973, Miami U., Ohio, 1973—75, U. Akron, 1974. Cert. math tchr. Ohio, 1963, guidance counselor Ohio, 1972, lic. profl. counselor Ohio Counselor & Social Worker Bd., 1984. Math tchr. Jackson County Pub. Schs., Gumberry, NC, 1957—60, Cin. Pub. Schs., Cin., 1963—72, guidance counselor, 1972—73, Winton Woods City Sch. Dist., Cin., 1973—94, ret., 1994. Mem. adv. com. conselor edn. U. Cin., Cin., 1975—76; admissions adv. bd. Cin. Tech. Coll., Cin., 1975—81, The Ohio State U., Columbus, Ohio, 1982—85; nursing sch. adv. bd. Deaconess Hosp. Sch. Nursing, Cin., 1983—88; dir. Sch. Counseling Cons. Svc., Cin., 1994—, Charlotte, NC, 1994—. Docent Mint Mus., Charlotte; mem. housing commn. City of Forest Park, Cin., 1974—76; Dem. precinct exec. Hamilton County Bd. Elections, Cin., 1974—96. Named Outstanding Counselor of Yr., Inroads of Cin., 1984. Mem.: NEA, AAUW (pres. Charlotte br. 2001—03), Am. Assn Coll. Admissions Counselors, Ohio Assn. Coll. Admissions Counselors, Ohio Sch. Counselors Assn., Ohio Edn. Assn., Livingstone Coll. Alumni Assn., U. Cin. Alumni Assn., Nat. Assn. Advancement for Colored People, Les Birdies Golf Club Charlotte (founder 1999, pres. 1999—2001), Order of Eastern Star, Zeta Phi Beta. Democrat. Methodist. Avocations: golf, travel, bridge, volunteering, gardening. Home and Office: 4101 Rye Mill Ct Charlotte NC 28277

MERCER, FRANCES DECOURCY, artist, educator; b. Centreville, Miss., June 14, 1944; d. John Homer Jr. and Patricia Powers (Given) Mercer. BA in English Lit., U. Miami, 1969, MA in History of Art, 1971; MFA in Painting, San Francisco Art Inst., 1974. Cert. tchr. Fla. Instr. South Fla. Art Inst., Hollywood, Fla., 1979—81; tchg. asst. San Francisco Art Inst., 1974; instr. Broward C.C., Ft. Lauderdale, Fla., 1979—83; owner 17th St. Galleries, Ft. Lauderdale, 1984—91; tchr. Broward County Sch. Bd., 1980—82; adj. prof. Fla. Atlantic U., 1979—80. Exhibited in group shows at Grove Art Gallery, Coconut Grove, Fla., 1973, Emanuel Walter Gallery, San Francisco, 1975, The Lucian LaBaudt Gallery, 1976, The Both Up Gallery, Berkeley, Calif., 1976, Discover Ctr., Ft. Lauderdale, 1980, Nova U. Artoberfest, Art and Culture Ctr. Hollywood, 1981, Indian Hammock Hunt and Riding Club, Okeechobee, Fla., 1998, A.E. Backus Gallery and Mus., Ft. Pierce, Fla., 2000, pvt. collections. Scholar Tuition scholar, San Francisco Art Inst., 1972, 1973, 1974. Avocations: photography, trail hiking, kayaking, golf, sailing. Home: #200 Blue Heron Ln 32801 Hwy 441 Okeechobee FL 34972 E-mail: fmercer@floridawatercolors.com

MERCER, NANCY OWENS DUNN, art industry purchasing agent, artist, educator; d. Martin Erwin and Eunice Lorraine Owens; m. Kyle L Mercer, Feb. 11, 1956. Customer svc. mgr. Tex. Art Supply, Houston, 1987—90, retail ops. mgr., 1990, store mgr., 1992—93, spl. events coord., 1993—; staff devel. instr. All sch. districts, Tex., 1993—; buyer/trend forcaster Tex. Art Supply, Houston, 1994—. Publication in anthologies, Shattered Glass, exhibition of paintings, Orange Streamers series. Recipient Friend of Art Edn., Tex. Art Educators Assn., 2002. Mem.: Women in Visual & Lit. Arts (founder, Houston 1993), Glass Art Soc. Home: 7121 Brendam Ln Houston TX 77072 Office: Texas Art Supply 2001 Montrose Blvd Houston TX 77006 Personal E-mail: nancynkyle@aol.com. E-mail: ndunn@texasart.com.

MERCHANT, NATALIE ANNE, musician, singer; b. Jamestown, N.Y., Oct. 26, 1963; d. Tony and Ann Merchant; 1 child. Lead singer band 10,000 Maniacs, 1981-1993; solo artist, 1993—; founder Myth Amer. Records LLC, 2003—. Albums with 10,000 Maniacs include Human Conflict Number Five, 1982, Secrets of the I Ching, 1983, The Wishing Chair, 1986, In My Tribe, 1987, Blind Man's Zoo, 1989, Hope Chest, 1990, Our Time in Eden, 1992, 10,000 Maniacs MTV Unplugged, 1993; solo album Tigerlily, 1995, Ophelia, 1998, Live In Concert, 1999, Motherland, 2001, Natalie Merchant, 2001, Motherland, 2001, The House Carpenter's Daughter, 2003; composer soundtracks: Felicity, 1998, Earthlings, 2003. Office: Myth Amer Records 660 Madison Ave 10th Fl New York NY 10021*

MERCHANT, SHARON J. state legislator; b. West Palm Beach, Fla., Aug. 30, 1963; BS in Internat. Affairs, Fla. State U., 1986. Exec. v.p. Equipment Rental Svc.; mem. Fla. Ho. of Reps., Tallahassee, 1992—; vice chair Palm Beach Legis. Del., 1993-94, chair, 1994-95. Chair Com. on Transp. and Econ. Devel. Appropriation Fiscal Responsibility Coun., 1996-97; mem. Com. on Utilities and Comms. Econ. Impact Coun., 1996-97, Com. on Water and Resource Mgmt. Govtl. Responsibility Coun., 1996-97. Mem. small bus. adv. bd. Fla. Atlantic U.; mem. Fla. Def. Conversion and Transition Commn., Transp. Task Force, Seminole Boosters, Big Bros./Big Sisters, Young Reps. Palm Beaches, Palm Beach County Republican Exec. Com. Recipient Roll Call Fla. C. of C., 1993, 94, 95, 96, 97, Champion for Econ. Devel. award Rep. Caucus, 1994; named Legis. of Yr. Assn. Retarded Citizens, 1995. Mem. Am. Legis. Exch. Coun., Nat. Assn. Women Bus. Owners, Nat. Assn. Women in Constrn., Northside Rep. Club, Rep. Club Palm Beaches. Episcopalian. Avocations: softball, golf, gym, walking. Home: 824 US Highway 1 North Palm Beach FL 33408-3873 Office: Fla Capitol 401 S Monroe St Rm 221 Tallahassee FL 32301-2034

MERCHLEWITZ, ANN ELIZABETH, lawyer; b. Decatur, Ill., Oct. 31, 1958; d. Thomas Lee and Joyce Ann (Hofman) Burford; m. Mark Anthony Merchlewitz, Aug. 20, 1983; children: Daniel Thomas, Emily Ann, Frank John. BA summa cum laude, Ill. Coll., Jacksonville, 1980; JD, U. Notre Dame Law Sch., Notre Dame, 1983; MA, Saint Mary's U. Minn., Winona, 1996. Staff atty. Southern Minn. Reg. Legal Svcs., Winona, Minn., 1983-84; asst. county atty. Winona County Attys. Ofc., 1984-92; spec. counsel to pres. Saint Mary's Coll. of Minn., 1992-96, v.p., gen. counsel, 1996—. Mem. Physician Recruitment Task Force, Winona, 1994-96; exec. dir. The Minn. Prep. Schs., 1999-2000; bd. dirs. Merchants Bank, Saint Anne of Winona. Chairperson Winona Area Cath. Schs. Bd., Winona, 1992-94; v.p.

Winona County Hist. Soc., 1994-96; chair, bd. dirs. Cath. Charities, Diocese of Winona, 1993—; bd. dirs. Winona City Charter Commn., 1993-2000. Recipient Outstanding Woman of Law and Govt. Winona YWCA, 1989. Mem. Winona County Bar Assn., (v.p. 1994), Minn. Planned Giving Coun., Nat. Assn. of Coll. and Univ. Attorneys, Phi Beta Kappa. Roman Catholic. Avocations: reading, piano, volunteer work. Office: St Marys U of Minn 700 Terrace Hts # 30 Winona MN 55987-1321

MERCIER, EILEEN ANN, corporate financial executive; b. Toronto, Ont., Can., July 7, 1947; d. Thomas Sidley and Frances Katherine (Boone) Falconer; m. Ernest Cochrane Mercier, Feb. 8, 1980; children: Jenny, Sheelagh, Peter, Michael, Stuart. BA with honors, Waterloo Luth. U., 1968; MA, U. Alta., Can., 1969; fellow, Instn. Can. Bankers, 1975; MBA, York U., 1977. Mgr. corp. fin. Toronto-Dominion Bank, 1972-78, portfolio mgr. TD capital; dir., U.S. comm. ops. Canwest Capital Corp., Toronto, 1978-81; mgr. fin. strategy & planning Gulf Can. Ltd., Toronto, 1981-86, mgr. corp. fin.; v.p. The Pagurian Corp., Toronto, 1986-87; v.p., treas. Abitibi-Price, Inc., Toronto, 1987-88, v.p. corp. devel., 1989-90, sr. v.p., CFO, 1990-95. Bd. dirs. Hydro One, Inc., TeeKay Shipping Corp., The CGI Group Inc., Winpak Ltd., ING Bank Can., Quebecor World, Inc., Shermag Ltd. Past chmn., mem. bd. govs. Wilfrid Laurier U., Waterloo, Ont., York U., U. Health Network. Recipient Outstanding Bus. Leader award Sch. Bus. and Econs., Wilfrid Laurier U., 1991, Award for Outstanding Contbn. Schulich Sch. of Bus. York U., 1997. Office: 199 Cranbrooke Ave Toronto ON Canada M5N 1M6

MERCIER, LINDA ANN, secondary school educator; b. Salem, Mass., Nov. 6, 1947; d. Joseph Emile and Maroin Ann (Freeman) Mercier. BS in Secondary Edn., Salem State Coll., 1972; MS in Edn., Lesley Coll., 1997. Advanced cert. tchg. social studies 1998. Tchr. St. John's, Peabody, Mass., 1972—76, St. Pius, Lynn, Mass., 1986—91, Palo Verde H.S., Las Vegas, 1991—. V.p. Social Studies Coun. Nev., 1998—. Scholar Fulbright Meml. Fund, Japan, 2001. Avocations: photography, writing. Home: 3208 Beaconshores Cir Las Vegas NV 89117 Office: 333 S Pavilion Center Dr Las Vegas NV 89144-4001

MERCIER, RITA, mayor; Mem. Lowell (Mass.) City Coun., 1996—2002; mayor State of Mass., Mass., 2002—. Com. organizer Com. to Elect Senator Henry Jackson for Pres., Bklyn., Senator Edward Kennedy Re-election Com., Com. to Protect Jobs, The Use of Convenient Containers (The Bottle Bill); bd. dir. Friends Coun. Aging. Mem.: East End Club (mem. ladies auxilliary), Greek Am. Legion, Post 662 VFW (mem. honor guard). Office: 375 Merrimack St Lowell MA 01852

MERCURI, JOAN B. museum administrator; b. N.Y.C. BA, Va. Commonwealth U., 1984. Mgmt. positions various corps., Ill., 1986-96; exec. dir. Frank Lloyd Wright Home and Studio Found., Oak Park, Ill., 1996—; pres., CEO Frank Lloyd Wright Preservation Trust, Oak Park, 2000—. Mem. Am. Assn. Museums, Nat. Trust for Hist. Preservation, Frank Lloyd Wright Bldg. Conservancy, Am. Soc. Assn. Execs., Assn. Fundraising Profls., Board Source.

MEREDITH, MARY J. secondary school educator; b. Wichita, Kans., Nov. 26, 1945; d. Harold William and Anna Augusta Meredith. BS Kans. State Tchrs. Coll., 1967, MS Emporia State Univ., 1971. Tchr. jr. high Santa Anna (Calif.) Unified Schs., 1968—72, tchr. sr. h.s., 1972—. Volleyball/track coach Saddleback H.S., Santa Ana, Calif., 1973—83; union rep. NEA, CTA, SAEA, Santa Ana, 1969—76; tchr. advisory com. SAUSA/State of Calif., County of Orange, Santa Ana, 1968—2001. Program organizer Operation History Now - Desert Storm Sch. Alumni Support Group, Santa Ana, 1990—91; cultural exch. coord. Anti-Defamation League, Orange County, Calif., 1990. Mem.: NEA, Hist. Preservation Soc., San Clemente Hist. Soc. Democrat. Home: 210 S Calle Seville San Clemente CA 92672

MEREDITH, MERI HILL, reference librarian, educator; b. Riverside, Calif., May 30, 1943; d. William Beans and Marie Louise (Zantzinger) Hill; m. William Rinehardt Meredith, Mar. 17, 1970 (div.); children William Rinehardt III, Sarah Daingerfield Meredith. AB in French, George Washington U., Washington, 1967; MLS, Ind. U., 1980. Cataloger Ind. U., Bloomington, 1980-81; bus. libr. Cummins Engine Co., Columbus, Ind., 1981-88; pres. Info. and Comm. Rsch., Inc., Columbus, 1989-92; reference libr. Ohio State U. Bus. Libr., 1992—. Bd. dirs. Sch. of Libr. and Info. Sci., Ind. U., Bloomington; pres., co-founder Ind. On-Line Users Group, Indpls. Mem. AAUP, Spl. Librs. Assn., Acad. Libr. Assn. of Ohio. Republican. Roman Catholic. Home: 1800 Lafayette Pl Apt A1 Columbus OH 43212-1609 Office: Ohio State U Bus Libr Raymond E Mason Hall 250 W Woodruff Ave Columbus OH 43210-1133 E-mail: meredith.18@osu.edu.

MERIDETH, SUSAN CAROL, business administration educator; b. St. Louis, May 25, 1956; d. George Getzel Brody and Jacquie Jean Lammers; m. John Wolf Merideth, July 28, 1979; children: Laura, Michelle. AAS, St. Louis C.C., 1977; BS, Fontbonne U., 1979; Master of Bus. Adminstrn., Maryville U., 1994. Presch. tchr. various instns., San Diego, 1979—82, Greater San Diego Health Plan, San Diego, 1985—87; supr. Cmty. Care Network, San Diego, 1987—90; mgr. St. John's Mercy Med. Ctr., St. Louis, 1990—95; contracts mgr. Nashua Eye Assocs., Nashua, 1996—98; practice mgr. Found. Med. Ptnrs., Nashua, 1998—99; assoc. prof. bus. adminstrn. Hesser Coll., Manchester, NH, 2000—. Mem.: AAUP, Nat. Bus. Edn. Assn., Phi Theta Kappa (faculty advisor Alpha Nu Upsilon chpt. 2002—, mem. Pi Kappa chpt.). Office: Hesser Coll 3 Sundial Ave Manchester NH 03103

MERINI, RAFIKA, foreign language, cultures and literatures educator; b. Morocco; d. Mohamed M. and Fatima Merini. BA in English cum laude, U. Utah, 1978, MA in Romance Langs. and Lits., 1981; postgrad., U. Wash., 1980-82; cert. in translation, SUNY, Binghamton, 1988, PhD in Comparative Lit., 1992. Tchg. asst. U. Utah, Salt Lake City, 1978-80, U. Wash., Seattle, 1980-82; adminstrv. asst., tchr. French, interpreter The Lang. Sch., Seattle, 1982-83; lectr. Pacific Luth. U., Tacoma, spring 1983; instr. French and Spanish Ft. Steilacoom C.C. (now Pierce C.C.), 1983—85; tchg. asst. dept. romance langs. SUNY, Binghamton, 1985-87, tchg. asst. women's studies dept., summer 1988, tchg. asst. comparative lit. dept., 1986-88; vis. instr. humanities and French Union Coll., Schenectady, NY, 1988—89; vis. instr. dept. fgn. langs. and lits. Skidmore Coll., Saratoga Springs, N.Y., 1989-90; asst. prof. dept. modern and classical langs. State U. Coll., Buffalo, 1990—96, assoc. prof. dept. modern and classical langs., 1996—. Coord. Buffalo State Coll. women's studies interdisciplinary unit State U. Coll., Buffalo, 1993-99, adviser French Club, 1990-93; founder, dir. Trois-Pistoles French Immersion Program, U. Western Ont.-Buffalo State Coll., 1994, 95; presenter, spkr., conf. organizer in field. Author: Two Major Francophone Women Writers, Assia Djebar and Leïla Sebbar: A Thematic Study of Their Works, 1999, 2d printing, paperback edit., 2001; mem. editl. bd. Jour. Middle Eastern and North African Intellectual and Cultural Studies; contbr. articles to profl. jours. Grantee Nat. Defense Student award U. Utah, 1974; also numerous other grants and awards. Mem. MLA (grantee), Am. Assn. Tchrs. French, Women in French, Conseil Internat. d'Etudes Francophones, Pi Delta Phi, Soc. Hon. Française, Kappa Theta (hon.). Home: PO Box 1063 Buffalo NY 14213-1063 Office: State Univ Coll-Buffalo Modern & Classical Langs 1300 Elmwood Ave Buffalo NY 14222-1095 E-mail: merinir@buffalostate.edu.

MERK, ELIZABETH THOLE, investment company executive; b. Salt Lake City, July 29, 1950; d. John Bernard and Emily Josephine (Knotek) Thole; m. J. Eliot Merk, July 26, 1996 (div.); 1 child from previous marriage, William Lance Ulich. BA, U. Hawaii, Hilo, 1984, paralegal cert. cum laude, 1989; postgrad.in bus. adminstrn., U. Hawaii, Manoa, 1985-86. Lic. gen. agt. Hawaii, Tex.; registered investment advisor, stock broker Hawaii, Tex., Calif., Utah. Regional archtl. rep. Lightolier, Inc., Salt Lake City, 1978-80; group sales rep. FHP/Utah, Salt Lake City, 1980-81; health net rep. Blue Cross Corp., L.A., 1981-82; v.p. fin. Bus. Support Systems, Hilo, 1983-89; rep. Prudential Ins. and Fin. Svcs., Honolulu, 1989-97; registered rep. Pruco Securities Corp. subs. Prudential Ins. & Fin. Svcs., 1989-97; acct. exec. Dean Witter Reynolds, 1997-98; adv. assoc., registered prin. Mutual Svc. Corp., 1998—2001; adv. assoc., registered rep. Centaurus Fin. Inc., 2001—. Docent Lyman House, 1984-85, L.A. County Mus. of Art, 1980-81, S.L.C. Art Mus., 1970-80; bd. dirs. YWCA, Hawaii Island, 1980-91, 1st v.p., 1988. Named YWCA Vol. of Yr., 1991, Top 25 Women owned Firms in Hawaii, Pacific Bus. News, 2001, 2002, 2003, Women Who Mean Bus. in Hawaii, Pacific Bus. News, 2001, 2002, 2003; named to Ct. of the Table Million Dollar Round Table, 2000; recipient Nat. Quality award 1991, 92, 93, 94, Nat. Sales Achievement award NAIFA, 1992, 93; Paul Harris fellow Rotary Internat., 1997. Fellow: Life Underwriters Tng. Coun.; mem.: AAUW (bd. dirs. Hilo chpt. 1987—89, fundraiser chmn. Kona chpt. 1992, Steven Bufton grantee 1985), Securities Industry Assn., Million Dollar Round Table (mem. ct. of the table 2000, mem. Top of the Table 2001—04), Nat. Assn. Ins. and Fin. Advisors (charter mem.), Nat. Assn. Life Underwriters (legis. rep. West Hawaii chpt. 1995—97), Am. Bus. Women's Assn. (pres. Nani O Hilo chpt. 1995—96, membership chmn. 1996—97, inner circle 1997—), Outdoor Circle, Soroptimists. Roman Catholic. Office: 118 Kamehameha Ave Hilo HI 96720 Office Fax: 808-883-8399.

MERKERSON, S. EPATHA, actress; b. Saginaw, Mich., Nov. 28, 1952; BFA, Wayne State U. Broadway and Off-Broadway productions include The Piano Lesson, I'm Not Stupid (Obie award 1992); appeared in films including Terminator II, Jacob's Ladder, Navy Seals, Loose Cannons, Random Hearts, 1999, The Rising Place, 2001, Radio, 2003, Jersey Girl, 2004; television guest appearances include The Cosby Show, Equal Justice, Elysian Fields, Moe's World; television series roles include Pee Wee's Playhouse, Mann & Machine, Here & Now, Law & Order; A Place for Annie, 1994, A Mother's Prayer, 1995, Breaking Through, 1996, An Unexpected Life, 1998, Exiled, 1998. Nominated for Tony award, 1990, Drama Desk award, 1990, Helen Hayes award, 1990, L.A. Theater Critics award, 1990. Office: Law & Order c/o Universal Television 100 Universal City Plz Universal City CA 91608-1002*

MERLIS, ANNETTE FORBES, artist; b. Omaha, Sept. 20, 1925; d. Isadore and Gertrude (Gold) Forbes; m. Sidney Merlis, Aug. 11, 1946; children: Gale B. Tauberer, Michael H., Laurence M. BS in Journalism, Creighton U., 1947; postgrad., New Sch. Group exhbns. include: Roads Gallery, N.Y.C., 1975, Parrish Art Mus., Southampton, N.Y., 1976, Northport Galleries, N.Y., 1980, Gallery Three, Sayville, N.Y., 1986, Anthony Giordano Gallery, Oakdale, N.Y., 1988, Elaine Benson Gallery, Bridgehampton, N.Y., 1990, Islip (N.Y.) Art Mus., 1993, 94, 95, 96, 99, 2001, Nese Alpan Gallery, Roslyn, N.Y., 1997, 98, 2000, Heckscher Mus., 2000, Nassau County C.C., 2003, St. John's U., Jamaica, N.Y., 2000, various others; solo exhbits include: Mallette Gallery, Garden City, N.Y., 1974, Northport Galleries, 1984, Port Washington (N.Y.) Libr., 1996, Nese Alpan Gallery, Roslyn, N.Y., 1998, Alpan Gallery, Huntington, N.Y., 2002, 03, 04; represented in permanent collection Islip (N.Y.) Art Mus. Recipient Elizabeth Morse Genius Found. award, 1997. Mem. Nat. Assn. Women Artists (medal of honor 1997, Miriam Halpern award 2001, Elizabeth Erlanger award 1998).

MERLY, MIRIAM NAVEIRA, state supreme court justice; b. Santurce, P.R., July 28, 1934; married; 2 children. BA, Mount St. Vincent Coll., N.Y., 1956; JD, U. P.R. Law Sch., 1960; LLM, Columbia U., 1969; postgrad., Leiden U., Holland, 1971-72; LLD, U. Georgetown Sch. Law, 1990. Law clerk P.R. Supreme Ct., 1963-71, asst. atty. gen. Dept. Justice, 1966-73, asst. solicitor gen. Dept. Justice, 1973-76, assoc. justice, 1985—, pres. judicial commn. on gender bias, 1992—; tchr. Law Sch. U. P.R., 1971-72; atty. pvt. practice, 1976-85; prof. Sch. Law Inter-Am. U. Office: Supreme Ct PO Box 2392 San Juan PR 00902-2392

MERMELSTEIN, BETTY JANE, elementary school educator; d. William O. Nelson, Jr. and Barbara Lou Nelson; m. Alan Z. Mermelstein, Jan. 20, 1974; children: Joshua Michael, Daniel James. BS, Plattsburgh State U., 1973; M in Reading Edn., Calif. State U., Fullerton, 1989. Cert. tchr. Ariz., 1992. Tchr. Bolton (Conn.) Coop. Nursery Sch., 1984—85, Lynwood (Calif.) Unified Sch. Dist., 1985—86; substitute tchr. Irvine and Santa Ana (Calif.) Unified Sch. Dists., 1986—88; tchr. Saddleback Valley Unified Sch. Dist., Mission Viejo, Calif., 1988—92; substitute tchr. Kyrene and Tempe Sch. Dists., Phoenix and Tempe, Ariz., 1992—93; tchr. Mesa (Ariz.) Pub. Schs., 1993—. Contbr. articles to mags., jours. and newspapers. Grantee French resources, Oriental Lodge #20, Mesa, 2003.

MERMELSTEIN, ISABEL MAE ROSENBERG, financial consultant; b. Houston, Aug. 20, 1934; d. Joe Hyman and Sylvia (Lincove) Rosenberg; m. Robert Jay Mermelstein, Sept. 6, 1953 (div. July 1975); children: William, Linda, Jody. Student, U. Ariz., 1952, Mich. State U., 1974, Lansing (Mich.) C.C., 1975. Exec. dir. Shiawassee County YWCA, Owosso, Mich., 1975-78; real estate developer F&S Devel. Corp., Lansing, Mich., 1978-79, Corum Devel. Corp., Houston, 1979-81; adminstrv. fin. planner, sr. citizen cons. Investec Asset Mgmt. Group, Inc.; owner Ins. Filling Svcs. Sr. Citizens, 1985-98; guardian VA, 1990—. Author: For You! I Killed the Chicken, 1972. Mem. Older Women's League, Houston, 1st Ecumenical Coun. Lansing, Nat. Mus. Women in Arts, Judaica Mus., Houston, Mus. Fine Arts, Houston, Mus. Natural Sci., Houston; bd. mem. Holocaust Mus., Houston; mem. African-Jewish Dialogue Group, Houston. Recipient State of Mich. Flag, 1972, Key to City, City of Lansing, 1972-73. Mem. Nat. Assn. Claims Assistance Profls., Afro-Am. Jewish Dialogue Group, Internat. Women's Pilot Orgn. (the 99's), Jewish Geneal. Soc., Internat. Directorate Disting. Leadership, Zonta, Licoma, B'nai B'rith, Hadassah, Nat. Fedn. Temple Sisterhoods, Wellington Soc., Flew All Women's Transcontinental Air Race (Powder Puff Derby 1972, 73). Republican. Jewish. Avocations: flying, gourmet cooking, needlepoint, knitting, skiing. Home: 1400 Hermann Dr Unit 16B Houston TX 77004-7138

MERRICK, BEVERLY GEORGIANNE, journalism, communications educator; b. Troy, Kans., Nov. 20, 1944; d. Horace Buchanan Merrick and Vola Yolantha (Clausen) Maul; m. John Douglas Childers, July 10, 1963 (div. 1998); children: John Kevin, Pamela Christine, Jessica Faye. BA in Journalism with honors, BA in English with honors, Marshall U., 1980, M Journalism, 1982; M Creative Writing, Ohio U., 1986, cert. in Women's Studies, 1984, PhD in Mass Comm. with honors, 1989. Reporter, photographer Ashland (Ky.) Daily Ind., 1981; tchr., instr. Albuquerque Pub. Schs., 1986—89; gen. assignment reporter, photographer Rio Rancho (N.Mex.) Observer, 1986; editor, rsch. cons. Ins. Pub. Law, Sch. of Law U. N.Mex., Albuquerque, 1990; asst. prof. Ga. So. U., Statesboro, 1991—94; assoc. prof. dept. mass comm. U. S.D., Vermillion, 1994; from asst. to assoc. prof. dept. journalism and mass comm. N. Mex. State U., Las Cruces, 1995—; faculty, photographer the Washington Ctr., 1999; sabbatical N.Mex. State U., 2002—03; mng. editor, features and photo editor, newspaper exec., Custer County chief Cmty. Newspapers Holdings Inc., 2002—03. Part-time tchr., tchg. assoc. Ohio U. Athens, 1981—84; part-time copy editor Albuquerque Tribune, 1991; vis. prof. East Carolina U., Greenville, NC, 1989—90; adj. prof. Embry-Riddle U., Kirtland AFB, N.Mex., 1989, Kirtland AFB, 91; organizer diversity conf., 1st amendment conf. Ga. So. U.; mem. session MIT, 1989; chair campus com. N. Mex. State U.; faculty Wash. Ctr. Nat. Women in Leadership Interns Program, 1999; leadership trainer N.M. No. U., Abiquiu, 1999; photographer/journalist Comstock Windmill Festival, Comstock Rock Festival, Comstock Godstode, 2003; presenter in field. Author: (poetry) Navigating the Platte, 1996, Pearls for the Casting, 1987, Closing the Gate, 1993, (monograph) Jane Grant, The New Yorker and Ross, 1999, (poetry) Zephyr Ear, 2003, The Worm in the Eye, 2003, Liver of the White Buffalo, 2003, I Am a Great-Grandchild of Grand Island, 2003; photographer, documentary reporter. (TV films) Windmill Festival, Comstock Rocks, Godstock, 2003; contbr. poems to profl. pubs., jours., chapters to books. Pub. rels. liaison Nat. Convention Bus. and Profl. Women, Albuquerque, 1988; pres. Albuquerque Bus. and Profl. Women, 1986-87, Rio Rancho Civic Assn., 1987-89, So. Ohio Improvement League, 1973-76; pres. bd. dirs. Pine Creek Conservancy Dist., 1976-83; chair Ted Turner and Jane Fonda Com., 1996, Sam Donaldson Native Sun Benefit Com., 1999; gov., girls State counselor, N.M., 2000; chair poster contest on media literacy Las Cruces Pub. Schs., So. N.Mex. Literacy Coun.; organizer Hepatitis C spkrs. tour, New Mex., 2003. Named Truly Fine Citizen of Ohio, Ohio Gen. Assembly, 1973, Outstanding Homemaker of Ohio, Gov. of Ohio, 1974, Outstanding Citizen, N.Mex. Legislature, 1988; grantee Reader's Digest, 1980, 83; John Houk Meml. grantee W.Va. Women's Conf., 1982; fellow Nat. Women's Studies Inst., Lilly Found., 1983, Freedom Forum Ethics, 1995, Am. Newspaper Inst., 1995; Newsday fellow Am. Soc. Newspaper Editors, 1998; E.W. Scripps scholar, 1984; recipient Silver Clover award 4-H, Writing award Aviation/Space Writers Assn., 1981, 1st place open rsch competition Nat. Assn. Women's Deans, Adminstrs. and Counselors, 1990 award 16th Ann. Gov.'s Awards for Outstanding N.Mex. Women, 2001; rsch. grantee N.Mex. State U., 1996. Mem. Soc. Profl. Journalists, Assn. for Edn. in Journalism and Mass Comm. (mem. nat. conv. com. 1993-94, vice head mag. divsn. 1995-96, head mag. divsn., 1996-97, chair southwest colloquium 1998), S.W. Edn. Coun. for Journalism and Mass Comm. (conf. chair 1998, bd. dirs. 1999-2002), Western Journalism Historians Assn. (conf. chair Berkeley Sch. Journalism 1999), N.Mex. State Poetry Soc. (pres. 1987-89), Sigma Tau Delta. Home: 985 Ivydale Dr Las Cruces NM 88005-0927

MERRIER, HELEN, actress, writer; b. Chgo., Mar. 10, 1932; d. Miner Thompson and Helen (Hembree) Coburn; m. Tim Meier, Dec. 23, 1954; 1 child, William Frank. BA, Mills Coll., 1954; BS, Northwestern U., 1955. Radio roles include Ma Perkins, One Man's Family, Standard School House of the Air, 1934-52; stage roles include Finian's Rainbow, 1952, The Happy Time, 1952, The Night of January 16th, 1952, No Exit, 1953, Tiger at the Gates, 1953, Caeser and Cleopatra, 1953, The Cocktail Party, 1953, Streetcar Named Desire, 1953, Misalliance, 1956, Cry the Beloved Country, 1956, Cat in a Tin Roof, 1963, Take Me Along, 1966, Caucasian Chalk Circle, 1967, The Devils, 1968, Electra, 1969, Jean Harlow and Billy the Kid, 1969, Three-Penny Opera, 1969, A Shot in the Dark, 1970, Private Lives, 1970, The Importance of Being Earnest, 1971, Forty Carats, 1972, Paris is Out!, 1972, A Christmas Carol, 1973, The Sea Gull, 1975, Something more than Ordinary, 1976, Three Dollar Bill, 1976, Maid to Marry, 1977, Scrooge, the musical, 1984, Prisoner of Second Avenue, 1985, Tom Sawyer, 1986, Comedy of Errors, 1987, Juno and the Paycock, 1987, Woman of the Year, 1989, Time and the Conways, 1991, Cinderella, 1991, Sweeney Todd, 1991, The Birds, 1993, Dreams of Defiance (rev.), 1994, Lady Lucinda's Scrapbook (solo play), 1996-98, As You Like It hike, 1998-99, A Midsummer Night's Dream hike, 1999, 2001, Vieux Carre, 1999, Woman Talk (cabaret), 1999—, Healthy- Minded Little Old Lady Songs (solo cabaret), 2000—, William Inge Festival, 2000, Robin Hood hike, 2000-01, Rip van Winkle hike, 2001, Stephen Foster in Song and Story (solo cabaret), 2001—, Eleemosynary, 2002. Recipient The Spirit of Theater award, 2000, Disting. Svc. award The Salvation Army, 2000. Mem. Victory Svcs. Club (London), Arts Club Chgo. Home: 915 Linden Ave Wilmette IL 60091-2712 Personal E-mail: hmerrier@@worldnet.att.net .

MERRIFIELD, SUSAN RUTH, education educator; b. Stoneham, Mass., Jan. 8, 1949; d. Stephen and Jean D. (McCormack) Merrifield; m. Bruce Wilfred Roberts; 1 child, Margaret Susan. BA, U. Mass., 1971; MA, Goddard Coll., 1973; MEd, U. Maine, 1981; EdD, Harvard U., 1989. Instr. English U. Mass., Boston, 1973—77, rschr., 1973—74; tchr. corps., instr. edn. U. Maine, Orono, 1979—82; program dir. edn. Lesley Coll., Lesley U., Cambridge, Mass., 2000—02; prof. English edn. Lesley U., Cambridge, Mass., 1990—. Adult learning disabilities specialist, 1985—93; joint task force tchr. edn. Bd. Regents, Mass., 1987—88. Author: (chpt.) When Children Don't Learn, 1998; contbr. articles to profl. jours. Woodrow Wilson fellow, 1987—88. Mem.: Am. Ednl. Rsch. Assn. Democrat. Avocations: poetry, writing. Office: Lesley U Lesley Coll 27 Mellen St # 12 Cambridge MA 02138 Office Phone: 617-349-8937.

MERRIFIELD, THERESA L. assistant principal, consultant; b. N.Y.C., Aug. 26, 1970; d. Theresa B. Brown. MEd in Adminstrn. and Supervision in Adminstrn. and Supervision, Bowie (Md.) State U., 1999. Cert. adminstrn. and supervision I Md. State Dept. of Edn., 2000. Vice prin. Prince George's County Pub. Schs., Upper Marlboro, Md., 2000—; nat. tchrs. exam (praxis i) instr. Prince George's County Pub. Schools, Upper Marlboro, Md., 2002—. Ednl. cons. DTM Global Enterprise, Temple Hills, Md., 2003—. Cons. Sisters from the Heart, Camp Springs, Md., 2001—03. Mem.: Assn. Sch. Adminstrs. (assoc.; n/a). Personal E-mail: ther.merrifield@pgcps.org.

MERRIHEW, MARY ALBEE, counselor; b. St. Johnsbury, Vt., May 5, 1928; d. Gertrude Frances Butterfield and Reginald Terrill Albee; m. Ray Lincoln Merrihew, Aug. 10, 1985; m. John Wallace Chugg, June 17, 1947 (div.); children: John Lewis Chugg, Rosalie Marguerite Chugg, James Wallace Chugg, Steven Arthur Chugg, Judy Frances Chugg. BA, Burlington Coll., 1979—82; MA in counseling psychology, Vt. Coll. of Norwich U., 1982—84. Lic. Alcohol & Drug Counselor State of Vt., 1982, cert. Clinical Supervisor Vt. Addiction Professionals Assn., 1993, Senior Alcohol & Drug Counselor Vt. Addiction Professionals Assn., 1988, National Certified Alcohol & Drug Counselor Nat. Counselor Reciprocity Commn., 1990. Instr. in substance abuse Burlington Coll., Burlington, Vt., 1979—81; charge clin. counselor Howard Mental Health, Burlington, Vt., 1979—82; counselor & ho. mgr. Grace Ho., Rutland, Vt., 1982—85; co-founder & pres. Counseling Ctr. for Human Potential, Rutland, Vt., 1985—; substance abuse counselor State of Vt. and others, Morrisville & Burlington, Vt. Dir. Associated Psychotherapists of Vt., Rutland, Vt., 1996—; certification bd. Vt. Addiction Professionals Assn., Newport, Vt., 1985—94, sec., 1984—88; trustee Burlington Coll., Vt., 1979—82; dir. Maple Leaf Farm Assn., Underhill, Vt., 1967—68. Author: (books of poetry) Some of Those Good Old Days; soloist includes 6 ch. choirs. Spkr. on small colleges Joint session of Vt. Legislature, Montpelier, Vt., 1983; testimony U.S. Senate Edn. Com., Brattleboro, Vt., 1982; testimony honoring senator pell U.S. Edn. Com., Providence, 1984. Recipient Vt. Women Making A Difference award, Castleton State Coll., 1994; Pell Edn. grant, U.S. Govt., 1980. Avocation: reading. Home: 41 Burnham Ave Ste 1 Rutland VT 05701-3407 Office: Counseling Ctr for Human Potential 41 Burnham Ave Ste 1 Rutland VT 05701-3407 Personal E-mail: maray2@adelphia.net.

MERRILL, CONNIE LANGE, chemical company executive; b. Baytown, Tex., Oct. 18, 1950; d. Monroe Edison and Doris Marie Lange; m. James Tyler Merrill, Jan. 1, 1977; m. William Edward Terry, Sept. 19, 1969 (div. 1975); 1 child, Adam Maxwell. BS in Chemistry, N.C. State U., 1977; PhD in Chemistry, Rice U., 1981. Rsch. chemist detergents Shell Chem. Co., Houston, 1981-88, venture devel. mgr. olefins and detergents, 1988-90, quality performance mgr., 1990-93, coatings mktg. mgr. resins, 1993-96, global bus. coord. thermoset performance products, 1996-98; practice leader global diversity consultancy Shell Group of Cos., London, 1998-99; mgr. mergers and acquisitions Shell Chems. Ltd., Houston, 1999—. Spkr. in field. Inventor R&D detergent; contbr. articles to profl. jours. Mem. Am. Chem. Soc. (bd. dirs. local chpt. 1983-88), Chem. Specialty Mfrs. Assn. (chmn. 1986-90), Houston Bus. Forum (bd. dirs. 1991-93), Nat. Paint and Coatings Assn. Avocations: scuba diving, underwater photography, travel. Office: Shell Chems 910 Louisiana St Houston TX 77002-4916

MERRILL, DENISE, state legislator; b. Calif. BA, U. Conn., 1988; JD, San Francisco Law Sch. Bar: Calif. 1978. Tchr. Vershire Sch., 1979-81; exec. dir. Consortium Law-Related Edn., 1983-92; cons. State Dept. Edn., Conn., 1984-91; mem. Dist. 54 Conn. State Ho. of Reps., 1993-99, dep. majority leader, 1999—. Mem. Mansfield Bd. Edn., 1991-93. Office: 148 Coventry Rd Mansfield Center CT 06250-1400

MERRILL, JEAN FAIRBANKS, writer; b. Rochester, N.Y., Jan. 27, 1923; d. Earl Dwight and Elsie (Fairbanks) M. BA, Allegheny Coll., 1944; MA, Wellesley Coll., 1945. Feature editor Scholastic Mags., 1947-50; editor Lit. Cavalcade, 1956-57; publs. div. Bank St. Coll. Edn., 1964-65. Children's books include Henry, the Hand-Painted Mouse, 1951, The Woover, 1952, Boxes, 1953, The Tree House of Jimmy Domino, 1955, The Travels of Marco, 1956, A Song for Gar, 1957, The Very Nice Things, 1959, Blue's Broken Heart, 1960, Shan's Lucky Knife (Jr. Lit. Guild selection), Emily Emerson's Moon, 1960 (Jr. Lit. Guild selection), The Superlative Horse (Jr. Lit. Guild selection), 1961 (Lewis Carroll Shelf award 1963), Tell About the Cowbarn, Daddy, 1963, The Pushcart War (Lewis Carroll Shelf award), 1964 (Boys Club Am. Jr. Book award), High, Wide & Handsome, 1964 (Jr. Lit. Guild selection), The Elephant Who Liked to Smash Small Cars, 1967, Red Riding, 1968, The Black Sheep, 1969, Here I Come—Ready or Not!, 1970, Mary, Come Running, 1970, How Many Kids are Hiding on My Block?, 1970, Please, Don't Eat My Cabin, 1971, The Toothpaste Millionaire (Dorothy Canfield Fisher Meml. award 1975-76), 1972 (Sequoyah award 1977), The Second Greatest Clown in the World, 1972, The Jackpot, 1972, The Bumper Sticker Book, 1973, Maria's House, 1974, The Girl Who Loved Caterpillars, 1992; poetry books edited include A Few Flies and I, 1969; libretto for chamber opera Mary Come Running, 1983. Fulbright fellow India, 1952-53 Mem. Authors League, Vt. Arts. Coun., Vt. Inst. Natural Sci., Vt. Nat. Resources Coun., Fulbright Assn., Women's Internat. League Peace and Justice, Sierra Club, Audobon Soc., Phi Beta Kappa.

MERRILL, JUDITH ROBIN, artist; b. Ann Arbor, Mich., Mar. 9, 1924; d. Charles Jerome and Cornelia Charlotte (Boutell) M.; m. Paul W. Pencke, Jan. 30, 1943 (div. 1965); children: Michael D., Laura C., Liza, William B.; m. Arthur D. Hall III, 1997. Student, Conservatory Art, Ft. Lauderdale, Fla., 1938-41, Am. Acad. Art, Chgo., 1941-42, Moore Coll. Art, Phila., 1976, 77,78. Office mgr. R.H. Bolster, MD, Paoli, Pa., 1963-68, head order dept., staff artist Betsy Ross Co., Paoli, 1968-76; office mgr. M.P. Erdman, AIA, Haverford, Pa., 1980-91. Judge Nat. Vets. Art Festival, Coatesville, Pa., 1995. One woman shows include Lippincott Gallery, Phoenixville, Pa., 1990, Artworks, Kennett Square, Pa., 1990, Montgomery Sch., Chester Springs, Pa., 1991, Cecil County Arts Coun., Elkton, Md., 1992, North St. Studio, Elkton, 1993, Picture Show, Havre de Grace, Md., 1994, Willow Valley, Lancaster, Pa., 1998, Ctr. for Creative Arts, Yorklyn, Del., 1999; 2-person show at Art First 2003, Fredericksburg, Va.; exhibited in group shows at Sketch Club, Phila., Woodmere Art Mus., Chestnut Hill, Pa., Am. Coll., Bryn Mawr, Pa., Brandywine Nursing Sch. Invitational, Coatesville, Pa., Sunset Hill Gallery, Westchester, Pa., Catherine Lorillard Wolfe Club, N.Y.C., Poldi Hirsch Meml. Nat. Show, Havre De Grace, Md., Pa. State, Delaware Campus, Media, Pa., Chester County Invitational Show, West Chester, Pa., Phila. Country Club, Gladwyne, Pa., Yellow Springs Ann. Art Show, Chester Springs, Pa., Birchrun Gallery, Birchrunville, Pa., The Studio, Swarthmore, Pa., Cabrini Coll. Invitational Show, Radnor, Pa., Moore Coll. Art, Phila., Fleisher Gallery, Miami Beach, Fla., Celebration of Arts--Govt. House, Annapolis, Md. Mem. Cecil County Arts Coun., 1992-95, Del. Art Mus., 1995, Woodmere Art Mus., 1991-95. Recipient 2nd prize oils Impressions XII Am. Coll., Bryn Mawr, Pa., 1993, Best in Show award St. Citizens Show, Elkton, Md., 1993, 1st and 2nd prizes Chestertown (Md.) Art League, 1995, 2nd prize oils 5th Nat. Juried Exhbn., Havre de Grace, Md., 1995, 2nd prize Chester County Art Assn., 1994-95, Best in Show award Md., You are Beautiful, 1993, Mansion Inn award Bianco Gallery, 1997, Excellence award Cecil County Arts Coun., 1997, Best of Portrait Painting award North Light Books, 1996. Mem. Nat. League Am. Pen Women, Chester County Art Assn., Woodmere Art Mus., Cecil County Arts Coun., Coun. Del. Artists. Home: 11301 N Club Dr Fredericksburg VA 22408-2056

MERRILL, LYNDA MAE, real estate broker; b. Bklyn., Jan. 30, 1948; d. Bernard and Edith Zucker; m. Dennis Alan Merrill, Feb. 14, 2000; m. Joe John Romero, Apr. 28, 1979 (dec. Apr. 18, 1996); children: Jason Matthew Romero, Derek Austin Romero. AA, L.A. City Coll., 1967. Cert. accreditation Relocation Resources, Inc., 1994. Legal sec. Heaton & Wright, Las Vegas, Nev., 1978—82, Lionel, Sawyer & Collins, Las Vegas, 1982—85; broker, saleswoman Western Properties, ERA, Las Vegas, 1985—90; broker, co-owner Properties Plus, Inc., Las Vegas, 1990—93; broker, saleswoman Coldwell Banker Premier, Las Vegas, 1993—2000, Merit Realty, Las Vegas, 2000—; broker, owner Merrill Realty Group, Inc., Las Vegas, 2002—. Author: (poetry) Reflections of The Inward Silence, The Fisherman, Night Stalker. Chairwoman residential com. North Las Vegas (Nev.) C. of C., 1990—91; mem. sponsorship com. Silverado Little League, Las Vegas, 1995—97; programs Comml. Real Estate Women, Las Vegas, 2003—03. Recipient Most Sales award, Greater Las Vegas Assn. Realtors, 1988, 1990. Mem.: Nat. Assn. Realtors, Nev. Assn. Realtors, Comml. Real Estate Women. Avocations: golf, writing, drawing. Office: Merrill Realty Group Inc 5613 S Eastern Ave Las Vegas NV 89119 Office Phone: 702-895-7427. E-mail: lynda@merrillrealty.lvcoxmail.com.

MERRILL, MARTHA, library media educator; b. Anniston, Ala., Apr. 21, 1946; d. Walter James and Polly (McCarty) M. BA, Birmingham-So. Coll., 1968; MS, Jacksonville (Ala.) State U., 1974; PhD, U. Pitts., 1979. Social worker Tuscaloosa (Ala.) County Dept. Human Resources, 1968-71, Calhoun County Dept. Human Resources, Anniston, 1971-73; social scis./bus. libr. Jacksonville State U., 1974-86, prof. instrnl. media, 1987—. Editor: Reference Services and Media, 1999; co-author: Dictionary for School Library Media Specialists, 2001. Mem. Friends of Libr. bd. Anniston-Calhoun County Pub. Libr., 1984—. Recipient Ala./SIRS Intellectual Freedom award, Intellectual Freedom Com., Ala. Libr. Assn., 1992, Ala. Beta Phi Mu chpt. Libr. of Yr. award, 1997. Mem. ALA (exec. bd., Intellectual Freedom Round Table 1987-93), Ala. Libr. Assn. (pres. 1990-91, Disting. Svc. award 1995), Ala. Assn. Coll. and Rsch. Librs. (pres. 1989-90), Southeastern Libr. Assn. (chair intellectual freedom com. 1986-88, chair resolutions com. 1990-92). Office: Jacksonville State U Coll Edn Dept Ednl Resources Jacksonville AL 36265 Office Phone: 256-782-5011. E-mail: mmerrill@jsucc.jsu.edu.

MERRILL, MARY MARGARET, secondary school educator; b. Chicago, Ill., July 29, 1949; d. Alex John and Helen Vivian Hrymak; children: Elizabeth Mary Wiley, John Courtney Merrill, III. BS, Memphis State U., 1971; M in Edn., Mid. Tenn. State U., 1976, Ednl. Specialist, 2003. Cert. tchr. Tenn., 1971. Tchr. Rutherford County, Readyville, Tenn., 1972—; tutor YMCA, Murfreesboro, Tenn., 1999—2003. Leader Girl Scouts, Mufreesboro, Tenn., 1986—91; asst. leader Cub Scouts, Murfreesboro, Tenn., 1988—90; mem. START Standing Together as Advocates for Responsible Testing, Mufreesboro, Tenn., 2002—03. Mem.: NEA, Rutherford Edn. Assn. (officer), Tenn. Edn. Assn., Assn. for Supervision and Curriculum Devel., Alpha Gamma Delta (officer). Avocations: reading, gardening, cross stitch. Home: 1406 Beasley Court Murfreesboro TN 37130 Office: Kittrell Sch 7801 Woodbury Hwy Readyville TN 37149

MERRILL, NORMA, video producer, copy writer; b. Whittier, Calif., Apr. 7, 1925; d. Parmer Leroy and Roosevelt Miller; m. Zadoc Ensign Merrill, Nov. 13, 1944; children: Cindy, Sally, Libby, Dadoc Ensign, Tawny. Grad., Albany (Oreg.) H.S., 1942. Asst. society editor Dem.-Herald, Albany, 1944-45; video prodn. coord. Upstairs Prodns., Portland, Oreg., 1980-91; video assoc. prodr. ZM Assocs., Portland, 1991—. Bd. dirs. Upstairs Prodns. Lyricist; copy writer for TV and vidio prodns. The Winter Winds of Hell, 1998. Republican. Mem. Four-Square Christian Ch. Avocations: travel, grandchildren, great grandchildren. Home: 4062 SW Pendleton St Portland OR 97221-3449

MERRILL, WENDY JANE, insurance company executive; b. Waterbury, Conn., Dec. 4, 1961; d. David Kenneth and Jane Joy (Nevius) Merrill; m. Aidan T. Harrison (div. Nov. 1998); children: Christopher Harrison, Charlotte Harrison, Ryan Harrison; m. Michael G. Kelly, Oct. 2, 1999. BA in Journalism, George Washington U., Washington, 1981; MBA in mgmt., Cornell U., 1992. Intern in edn. HEW, Washington, summer 1978, writer, summer 1979; rsch. asst. dep. health svcs. adminstrn. George Washington U., Washington, 1979-81; sec. Nat. Assn. Beverage Importers, Washington, 1981; account exec. Staff Design, Washington, 1982; adminstrv. aide Internat. Food Policy Rsch. Inst., Washington, 1983-86; program assoc. Acad. for Ednl. Devel., Washington, 1986-87; pvt. practice cons. Washington, 1987-88; adminstrv. mgr. food and nutrition policy program Cornell U., Ithaca, 1988-92; cons. in mgmt. of med. practices Med. Bus. Mgmt., Ithaca, 1994-95; realtor Century 21 Alpha, 1995-97; compensation mgr. Santa Clara (Calif.) U., 1996-98; sr. compensation analyst Stanford (Calif.) U., 1998-99; human resources cons. Siemens Info. and Comm. Networks, 2000; compensation and benefits mgr. Kana Comms., 2000-2001; U.S. compensation mgr. KLA-Tencor, 2001—02; pres. The Benefits Source Ins. Svcs. Inc., Calif., 2003—. Cons., editor George Washington U., 1986; cons., rapporteur Internat. Food Policy Restaurant Inst., Washington and Copenhagen, Denmark, 1987; cons., adminstr. Hansell & Post, Washington, 1987-88, Cornell U., Washington and Ithaca, 1988; pvt. practice cons., 2001—. Sponsor Worldvision, Tanzania, 1988-91. George Washington U. scholar, 1979-81. Mem. AMA, Soc. for Human Resources Mgmt., Sigma Delta Xi (scholar 1980). Democrat. Episcopalian. Avocations: piano, hiking, swimming. Home: 745 S Mary Ave Sunnyvale CA 94087 E-mail: wendy@benefits-source.org.

MERRILL WARNER, VERONIQUE, psychologist; b. Dansville, NY, Mar. 14, 1965; d. Raymond Greiner Merrill and Monique Marcelle Francette Monnot; m. Michael V. Warner, May 17, 1991; children: Jeremy Raymond Warner, Miranda Caline Warner, Valerie Cosette Warner. B cum laude, Occidental Coll., 1987; MA, Calif. Sch. Profl. Psychology, L.A., 1997, D in Psychology, 1999. Lic. psychologist Calif. Bd. of Psychology, 2001. Bookkeeper Carol L. Strop, CPA, Glendale, Calif., 1987—91, Very-unique Bus. Svcs., Sierra Madre, Calif., 1991—99; lic. psychologist-contractor Bienvenidos Children's Ctr., Altadena, Calif., 2001; outpatient unit coord. Enki Health and Rsch. Systems, Inc., Covina, Calif., 1999—2001, supervising psychologist, 2001, clinic mgr. Pico Rivera, Calif., 2001—. Testing supr. Enki Health & Rsch. Systems, Inc., Pico Rivera, 2001—; field tng. supr. U. of La Verne, Calif., 2001—; ambs. of change task force mem. Enki Health & Rsch. Systems, Inc., Covina, 2000—01; tchr. asst. Assessment Lab. Calif. Sch. of Profl. Psychology, L.A., 1997—99, field tng. supr., 2003—; mem. dissertationcom. U. La Verne. Author (singer/songwriter): (compact disc/songbook) I'm a Kid, Too. Vol. Pasadena (Calif.) Mental Health Ctr., 1994—95; team mom AYSO; vol. Grace Miller Elem. Sch., La Verne, Calif., 2002—03, Sierra Madre Sch., Sierra Madre, Calif., 2000—02. Mem.: APA (licentiate), Psi Chi (pres. 1987). Democrat. Avocations: singing, theater, writing, reading, gardening. Office: Enki ELA Youth & Family Svcs 4400 Rosemead Blvd Suite 12 Pico Rivera CA 90660 Personal E-mail: doc.vmw@verizon.net.

MERRIM, LOUISE MEYEROWITZ, artist, actress; b. N.Y.C. d. Leo and Jeanette (Harris) Meyerowitz; m. Lewis Jay Merrim, June 27, 1948; children: Stephanie, Andrea Merrim Goff (dec.). BFA, Pratt Inst., 1947; MFA, Columbia U., 1951; postgrad., Post Coll., 1971-72, New Sch., 1977-78. Art tchr. pub. schs., N.Y.C., 1947-51, Port Washington, N.Y., 1970-83. One-woman shows include Plandome Gallery, L.I., Isis Gallery, N.Y., San Diego art Inst., Pan Pacific Hotel, San Diego; exhibited in group shows at Nassau County Fine Arts Mus. (Bronze award), Heckscher Mus. (Nora Mirmont award), Nat. Acad., Nat. Assn. Women Artists (Medal of Honor, Charlotte Whinston award), Audubon Artists (Stephen Hirsch Meml. award), Cork Gallery, Warner Comm. Gallery, L.I. Art Tchrs. (two awards of excellence), L.I. Art Tchrs. Award Winners Show, Pt. Washington Libr. Invitational, Glen Cove (2nd prize), Manhasset Art Assn. (best in show, five 1st prizes), San Diego Art Inst., San Diego Mus. Art (Gold award), Oceanside Mus. Art, Hank Baum Gallery, San Francisco, Tarbox Gallery, Clark Gallery, Knowles Gallery, San Diego, Golden Pacific Arts Gallery, San Diego, Henry Chastain Gallery, Scottsdale, Boehm Gallery/Palomar Coll., Hyde Gallery/Grossmont Coll., Timmons Gallery, Rancho Santa Fe, Calif.; included in permanent collection of San Diego Mus. Art; appeared in numerous theatrical prodns. including Fiddler on the Roof, Barefoot in the Park, N.Y., Anything Goes, The Musical Comedy Murders of 1940, Anastasia (Drama award), Fiddler on the Roof, The Music Man, What's Wrong With this Picture?, Marvin's Room, San Diego, The Foreigner; dir. Under Milkwood; dir., appeared in Spoon River Anthology. Mem. Nat. Assn. Women Artists, N.Y. Soc. of Women Artists, Contemporary Artists Guild of N.Y., Audubon Artist (N.Y.), San Diego Art Inst., Artists Guild of San Diego Art Mus. (pres. 1993), Artists Equity, Actors Alliance. Avocations: tennis, poetry, travel. Home: 3330 Caminito Vasto La Jolla CA 92037-2929 E-mail: louisemer@hotmail.com.

MERRIMAN, DEBORAH JOY, marriage and family therapist; b. Springfield, Mass., Feb. 15, 1954; d. James I. and Flora W. (Stewart) M.; m. Frank T. Apple, Oct. 1, 1972 (div. Feb. 1986); children: Adam, April; m. James E. Hughes, Sept. 7, 1990 (div. 1998). AS, Bay Path Coll., 1979; BA, U. Mass., 1990; MEd, Cambridge Coll., 1992; cert. Advanced Grad. Study, U. Mass., 1996; postrad., Saybrook Grad. Sch. Lic. marriage and family therapist, Mass.; cert. alcohol and drug addiction counselor, Mass., Conn. Family counselor The Blue Ridge Ctr., Bloomfield, Conn., 1992-93; counselor, case mgr. U. Mass. Ctr. for Counseling and Acad. Devel., Amherst, Mass., 1994-95; psychiat. social worker Ctr. for Behavioral Health, Hartford, Conn., 1995-96; sr. faculty Cambridge Coll., Springfield, Mass., 1994—; psychotherapist Enfield (Conn.) Clinicians, 1994—. Counseling psychology program coord. Cambridge Coll., Springfield, 1997—; founder, chairperson Women for Continuing Edn., Bay Path Coll., Longmeadow, Mass., 1976-78; cmty. AIDS educator Latino Health Inst., Dept. Pub. Health, Boston, 1992-93. Mentor Women's Partnership, Springfield C. of C., 1992; forum coord. Family Therapy Network, Washington, 1996—; presenter ProVisions V, Conn. AIDS Action Coun., Hartford, 1996; clin. supr. The Salvation Army, Springfield, 1997—. William Ross scholar in human svcs. U. Mass., 1990. Mem. Women's Faculty Assn. (founder, chairperson 1996—), Am. Assn. Marriage and Family Therapy (assoc. mem., clin. mem.), Nat. Assn. Alcohol and Drug Counselors, Phi Delta Kappa. Pentecostal. Avocations: artwork, dream analysis, star trek fan. Home: 1114 Parker St Springfield MA 01129-1004 Office: Cambridge Coll 570 Cottage St Springfield MA 01104-3219

MERRIS, DONNA ROSE, lawyer; b. Bluffs, Ill., Nov. 25, 1939; d. Donald Doyle and Helen Louise (Frohwitter) M.; children: Laura Katherine Merris Huffman, Kristen Rose Merris Huffman. BS in Edn., Ill. State U., 1961; MMus, Northwestern U., 1965; JD, Bklyn. Law Sch., 1987. Bar: N.Y. 1989, N.J. 1989. Dir. instrumental music Lanark (Ill.) Pub. Schs., 1961-64, Winchester (Ill.) H.S., 1965-66; dir. music edn. Malden (Mass.) Pub. Schs., 1966-74; instr. music Mannes Coll. Music, N.Y.C., 1974-80; exec. dir. Bklyn. Music Sch., 1977-85; spl. asst. U.S. Atty. U.S. Dist. Ct. (so. dist.) N.Y., N.Y.C., 1988-90; asst. gen. counsel Office of the Comptroller, N.Y.C., 1990-94; gen. counsel Mayor's Office of Contracts, N.Y.C., 1994-99; adminstrv. law judge Office of Adminstrv. Trials and Hearings, N.Y.C., 1999—. Adv. bd. Bklyn. Music Sch., 1986—; trustee Nat. Guild Cmty. Schs. of the Arts, N.Y.C., 1993-99. Mem. Assn. Bar City of N.Y. Office: 40 Rector St Fl 6 New York NY 10006-1705 E-mail: dmerris@nyc.rr.com.

MERRITT, CAROLYN, government agency administrator; Diploma, Radford U. Mngr. of solid and hazardous waste and environmental health and safety Champion Intl. Corp., 1988—94; sr. project mngr. RMT/Jones and Neuse, Inc., Houston, 1994; sr. v.p. for Environment, Health and Safety IMC Global Inc., Northbrook, Ill.; chmn, CEO U.S. Chemical Safety and Hazard Investigation Board, 2002—. Office: 2175 K Street NW Ste 400 Washington DC 20037

MERRITT, DEBORAH FOOTE, state legislator, vocational coordinator; b. Peterborough, N.H., June 19, 1961; d. William Lewis and Mary Elizabeth (Moore) Foote. BA in Sociology, Bowdoin Coll., 1983; MPA, U. N.H., 1994. Tchr. math. Buckley Sch., Sherman Oaks, Calif., 1983-84, Chaminade Coll. Prep. Sch., Canoga Park, Calif., 1984-85; saleswoman Smith Barney, L.A., 1985-87, B.R. Stickle & Co., Chgo., 1987; trader Harris Trust, Chgo., 1988-90; bus. mgr. Merritt Chiropractic, Durham, N.H., 1990-94; state rep. N.H. Gen. Ct., Concord, 1993—; marketer Devel. Svcs. of Strafford County, Dover, 1994; residential counselor Our House, Dover, 1994; vocat. coord. Riverbend Cmty. Mental Health, Concord, N.H., 1995-98; dir. programs and ops. Divsn. Elderly and Adult Svcs., Concord, 1998—. Bd. dirs. Our House, 1993-94, counselor, 1994-95; adv. bd. health & human svcs. dist. coun. Inst. Disability. Mem. NOW, N.H. Women's Lobby, Gt. Concord C. of C., Planned Parenthood No. New Eng., Women's Legis. Lobby (vice chair Strafford County del. 1994-95, chmn. 1996—), N.H. Assn. for the Blind (bd. dirs.). Democrat. Home: 40 Rumford St Concord NH 03301-3910 Office: Divsn Elderly & Adult Svcs 129 Pleasant St Concord NH 03301-3852

MERRITT, JEAN, consulting firm executive, psychotherapist; b. N.Y.C., Oct. 29, 1952; d. Harry and Ruth (Happel) Packman; m. Richard L. Kashinsky, Aug. 2, 1976 (div.); m. Richard L. Merritt, May 5, 1985 (div. June 2002); children: Courtney Morgan, Melissa Morgan Grad. high sch., Bayside, N.Y. From contr. to v.p., sec., treas. Kaswol Corp., Richmond Hill, NY, 1973—85; corp. exec. Federated Cons. Svc., Inc., Bayside, NY, CFO Jupiter, Fla., 1985—2002, psychotherapist, 2004—. Coach Queens Spl. Olympics, 1985. Mem. Nat. Trust for Hist. Preservation, Nat. Fedn. Wildlife, Ctr. for Environ. Edn., Defenders of Wildlife, Nat. Resource Def. Coun., Humane Soc. of U.S., Sierra Club, Amnesty Internat. Presbyterian. Avocations: flying, art collecting, painting, interior design, gourmet cooking. Home: 520 W 43 StApt 2K New York NY 10036 Office Phone: 917-319-0184. E-mail: jeanie22m@aol.com.

MERRITT, JERALYN E. lawyer; b. N.Y.C., N.Y., Sept. 28, 1949; BA, Case Western Res. U., 1971; JD, U. Denver, 1973. Bar: Colo. 1974, (U.S. Dist. Ct. Colo.), U.S. Ct. Appeals (10th cir.) 1981, (N.Y.) 1990, U.S. Supreme Ct. 1990, (Ariz.) 1999, U.S. Ct. Appeals (9th cir.). Mem. legal adv. bd. Martindale-Hubbell LexisNexis, 1996—; mem. editl. bd. Matthew Bender Criminal Publs., 1999—; lectr. law U. Denver Coll. Law, 2001—. Fellow: Am. Bd. Criminal Lawyers (mem. bd. govs. 1994—); mem.: ABA (criminal justice sect. coun. 2000—), Colo. Criminal Def. Bar, Denver Bar Assn., Colo. Bar Assn., Nat. Assn. Criminal Def. Lawyers (bd. dirs. 1995—2001, sec. 2002—, co-chair/vice-chair legis., Internet, and innocence project coms. 1995—, 1st Ann. Marshall Stern award for outstanding legis. achievement 1995). Office: Ste 1700 950 17th St Denver CO 80202

MERRITT, MARY JANE, community volunteer; b. Milford, Mass., Feb. 6, 1942; d. Theodore and Rosemary Edith (Box) Bothfeld; m. Thomas Butler Merritt, July 23, 1966; children: Thomas Butler Jr., Haidee Soule, Theodore Bothfeld. AB, Boston U., 1964. Tchr. Perceptual Edn. Rsch. Ctr., Inc., Sherborn, Mass., 1964-66, Tenacre Country Day Sch., Wellesley, Mass., 1966-67, Head Start, Nashua, N.H., 1995-96; with ARC Bloodmobile, 1997-2001. Pres. Colonial Garden Club, Hollis, N. H., 1987-90; chmn. Governing Com. of Charles J. Nichols Fund, Hollis, N.H., 1989-95; mem. Master Plan Study com., Hollis, N.H., 1989-91; pres. Amherst Villagers Chpt. of The Questers, Inc., Amherst, N.H., 1995-97; pres. Hollis Woman's Club, 1999-2001. Recipient Community Svc. award Town of Hollis, N.H., 1993. Mem. Alpha Phi. Home: PO Box 516 Littleton NH 03561-0516

MERRITT, NANCY-JO, lawyer; b. Phoenix, Sept. 24, 1942; d. Robert Nelson Meeker and Violet Adele Gibson; children: Sidney Kathryn, Kurt, Douglas. BA, Ariz. State U., 1964, MA, 1974, JD, 1978. Bar: Ariz. 1978, U.S. Dist. Ct. Ariz. 1978, U.S. Ct. Appeals (9th cir.) 1984. Shareholder Fennemore Craig, P.C., Phoenix. Author: Understanding Immigration Law, 1993; sr. editor: Immigration and National Law Handbook, 1993—; contbr. articles to profl. jours. Chair bd. dirs. TERROS, 1995-97. Fellow Ariz. Bar Found.; mem. ABA, Am. Immigration Lawyers Assn. (chairperson Ariz. chpt. 1985-87, several coms., Pro Bono award), Ariz. Bar Assn. (immigration sect.), Nucleus Club. Democrat. Avocations: modern literature, south american literature, hiking, gardening. Office: Fennemore Craig PC 3003 N Central Ave Ste 2600 Phoenix AZ 85012 E-mail: njmerritt@fclaw.com.

MERRITT, SANDRA LEE, educational consultant; b. Manchester, Iowa, Sept. 16, 1949; d. Roy Thomas Atkinson and Lavon Blanche Williams; m. William Joseph Merritt, June 18, 1988; children: Michelle Ann McClure, Staci Lynn Shaffer. MA in Edn., U. No. Iowa, 1999. First grade tchr. Center Point (Iowa)-Urbana Schools, 1971—2002, reading recovery tchr., 2000—02; inclusion resource specialist Grant Wood Area Edn. Agy., Cedar Rapids, Iowa, 2002—. Contbr. articles to profl. jours. Recipient Spl. Tchr. award, Greater Cedar Rapids Cmty. Found., 2002. Mem.: NEA, ASCD, Coun. for Exceptional Children, Iowa State Edn. Assn., Iowa Assn. for the Edn. of Young Children (sec. 1999—2002). Home: 900 Maplewood Dr Center Point IA 52213 Office: Grant Wood Area Education Agency 4401 6th St SW Cedar Rapids IA 52404 Office Phone: 319-399-6783. Personal E-mail: slmerritt@msn.com. E-mail: smerritt@aea10.k12.ia.us.

MERSCHAM, CARRIE, psychologist; b. Rochester, N.Y., May 22, 1971; d. Robert Francis and Barbara Lee McCrudden; m. Lonnie W. Merscham, Dec. 12, 1998. BA in History, U. Va., 1993; MA in Counseling, U. Denver, 1995; D in Psychology, U. No. Colo., 2001. Lic. clin. psychologist Colo. Acad. counselor DU Learning Effectiveness Program, Denver, 1994—95; therapist Third Way Ctr., Denver, 1995—98; career counselor U. No. Colo. Career Svcs. Ctr., Greeley, 1998—99; predoctoral intern Denver Health Med. Ctr., 2000—01; mental health therapist Mental Health Corp. Denver, 2001—; pvt. psychologist Denver, 2001—. Sec. of the bd. LTrain Electric, Inc., Golden, Colo., 2000—; spkrs. bur. vol. Mental Health Assn. Colo., Denver, 2001—. Co-chair Sunset Com., 2002—04. Mem.: APA, Colo. Psychol. Assn. (vol. legis.com. 2001—02, co-chair legis.com. 2002—04, chair legis.com 2004—, Pres. award legis. com. 2003, Pres. award Sunset com. 2003). Avocations: hiking, horseback riding, cooking, reading. Office: Ste 220 919 Jasmine St Denver CO 80220

MERSEL, MARJORIE KATHRYN PEDERSEN, lawyer; b. Manila, Utah, June 17, 1923; d. Leo Henry and Kathryn Anna (Reed) Pedersen; m. Jules Mersel, Apr. 12, 1950; 1 child, Jonathan. AB, U. Calif., 1948; LLB, U. San Francisco, 1948. Bar: D.C. 1952, Calif. 1955. Pvt. practice, Beverly Hills, Calif., 1961—71, L.A., 1997—; staff counsel Dept. Real Estate State of Calif., L.A., 1971—97. Pub. counsel, 2000—02. Active L.A.-Guangzhou Sister City. Mem.: ABA, Current Affairs Forum, World Affairs Coun., So. Calif. Women Lawyers Assn. (treas. 1962—63), Trial Lawyers Assn., L.A. County Bar Assn., Beverly Hills Bar Assn., Beverly Hills C. of C., L.A.-Guanghou Sister City Assn., Sierra Club, L.A. Athletic Club. Home: 13007 Hartsook St Sherman Oaks CA 91423-1616 Office: Dept Real Estate 107 S Broadway Ste 8107 Los Angeles CA 90012-4402

MERSKEY-ZEGER, MARIE GERTRUDE FINE, retired librarian; b. Kimberley, South Africa, Oct. 10, 1914; came to U.S., 1960, naturalized, 1965; d. Herman and Annie Myra (Wigoder) Fine; m. Clarence Merskey,

Oct. 8, 1939 (dec. 1982); children: Hilary Pamela Merskey Nathe, Susan Heather Merskey Sinistore, Joan Margaret Merskey Schneiderman; m. Jack I. Zeger, July 15, 1984 (dec. Jan. 1997). Grad., Underwood Bus. Sch., Cape Town, South Africa, 1934; BA, U. Cape Town, 1958, Diploma in Librarianship, 1960. Sec. to Chief Rabbi Israel Abrahams, South Africa, 1945-49; sec. Jewish Sheltered Employment Coun., 1954-[illegible]; reference libr. New Rochelle (N.Y.) Pub. Libr., 1960-63; rsch. libr. Consumers Union, Mt. Vernon, NY, 1963-66; asst. readers svcs., head union catalog Westchester Libr. Sys., 1966-69, trustee, 1989-93, v.p., 1991; dir. Harrison (N.Y.) Pub. Libr. and West Harrison Br., 1969-84; acting dir. Mamaroneck (N.Y.) Free Libr., 1987-88, also trustee, 1988-93. Author: History of the Harrison Libraries, 1980; contbg. author: Celebration, Village of Mamaroneck Centennial, 1895-1995, History of Town/Village of Harrison Tricennial, 1696-1996; editor: Harrison Highlights and Anecdotes, 1989, (cookbook) On Harrison's Table, 1976; author articles. Pub. edn. officer USCG Aux Flotilla 63; bd. dirs Shore Acres Point Corp., Mamaroneck, 1985-89; program dir. Friends of the Mamaroneck Libr., 1993—. Recipient Brotherhood award B'nai B'rith, 1974; named Woman of Yr., Harrison, 1984. Mem. ALA, N.Y. Libr. Assn. (adult edn. com. for continuing edn. 1971-75, adult svcs. com. 1973-75, vice chmn. 1975, exec. bd. 1981-82), Westchester Libr. Assn., Pub. Libr. Dirs. Assn. (tech. svcs. com. chmn. Westchester County 1971, exec. bd. 1974-75, vice chmn. 1975), Charles Dawson History Ctr. (co-founder 1980, bd. dirs. 1980—), Mamaroneck Hist. Soc. Home: 316 S Barry Ave Mamaroneck NY 10543-4201

MERTENS, JOAN R. museum curator, art historian; b. N.Y.C., Oct. 10, 1946; d. Otto R. and Helen H. M. BA, Radcliffe Coll., 1967; PhD, Harvard U., 1972. Curatorial asst. Met. Mus. Art, N.Y.C., 1972-73, asst. curator, 1973-76, assoc. curator, 1976-81, curator Greek and Roman dept., 1981—, curator, adminstr., 1983-90, mem. editorial bd. Mus. Jour., 1976—; adj. prof. NYU, Inst. Fine Arts, 1992—. Author: Attic White-Ground*Its Development, 1977, Greek Bronzes in the Metropolitan Museum of Art, 1985, (with others) Ancient Art from Cyprus: The Cesnola Collection in the Metropolitan Museum of Art, 2000. Mem. Archaeol. Inst. Am., German Archael. Inst. (corr. mem.) Home: 124 E 84th St New York NY 10028-0915 Office: Met Mus Art Fifth Ave at 82nd St New York NY 10028

MERTENS, LYNNE G. retail executive; CEO, pres. Waller, The Graphics Resource, San Francisco, Calif. Office: Waller 339 Harbor Way South San Francisco CA 94080-6919 Fax: 650-589-0578.

MERTZ, ANNE MORRIS, writer, researcher, journalist, educator; b. Indpls., Sept. 29, 1913; d. Theodore Hatfield and Lisette Susanna (Krauss) Morris; m. Walter Day Mertz, June 29, 1937; children: Suzanne Day Mertz Smalloy, Elizabeth Morris Mertz O'Brien, Walter Day Jr., Theodore Morris. BA cum laude, Randolph-Macon Woman's Coll., Va., 1935. cert. tchr. Pa. 1935. Tchr. ch. sch. Germantown Unitarian Ch., Phila., 1935—50; tchr. Yeadon (Pa.) Sch. Dist., 1935—40; religious edn. dir. Unitarian Ch., Wilmington, Del., 1950—60; mus. guide Hagley Mus., Wilmington, 1964-76; travel writer, lectr., 1965—. Author: (booklets) History of Delaware Colonial Dames Headquarters, 1990, 2001, History of Delaware Mayflower Society, 1993, (books) Morris Migration: A Saga of Forbears and Descendants, 1996, 2000, 2001, Windows into Pilgrim Life and Seven Mayflower Ancestors, 1998, Memoirs of Washington in the Eighteen Sixties Including the Witnessing of Lincoln's Assassination, 2001; author: (with others) Reaching the Summit, 1999, America at the Millennium, 2000; contbr., rschr. (articles) many jours., newspapers, mags., Libr. of Congress Archives, Phila. Inquirer, Wayne Suburban, Ardmore Suburban, Greenville Cmty. News, Wilmington News Jour., Sarasota Herald Tribune, Brandenton Herald, Venice Gondolier, Mayflower Quar., Baby Talk Mag., Del. Geneal. Jour., Hockessin Cmty. News, Bank Notes, Dartmouth Coll. and Randolph-Macon Woman's Coll. Mag. Vol. mus. guide Winterthur Mus., Wilmington, 1956—60; active pres.'s adv. bd. Wilmington Trust of Fla., Stuart, 1990—93; bd. dirs. Wilmington Music Sch., 1952—73, Family Svcs. Del.; spkr., dir., hon. bd. dirs. United Fund Planning Com., Wilmington, 1957—65; hon. bd. dirs. Children and Families First, 1995—; hon. bd. mem. Family and Children's Svcs.; pres. Travelers Aid Soc., Wilmington, 1954—56, Randolph-Macon Woman's Coll. Alumnae of No. Del., 1949—51, 1965—68; nat. v.p. Randolph-Macon Woman's Coll. Alumnae Assn., Lynchburg, Va., 1961—64. Mem.: AAUW (nat. and local life mem., Wilmington Br. chair trustees, 1st v.p. 1970—75, Scholarship-Grant named for her 1940—), Nat. League Am. PEN Women (active Sarasota and Fla.), Del. Colonial Dames (spkr., rschr., oral history interviewer), Del. Hist. Soc., Mayflower Soc. (life; Del. state pres. 1990—93, bd. dirs., gold medal), Del. Geneal. Soc. Avocations: world travel, flowers, gardening, genealogy, embroidery. Home (Summer): 726 Loveville Rd # 904 Hockessin DE 19707-1513 Home (Winter): 1526 Pelican Point Dr # 145 Sarasota FL 34231-6792 E-mail: mertz.wd@.com.

MERTZ, DOLORES MARY, farmer, state legislator; b. Bancroft, Iowa, May 30, 1928; d. John Francis and Gertrude (Erickson) Shay; m. H. Peter Mertz (dec. 1983), Dec. 27, 1951; children: Peter, Mary Simpson, David, Ann Cornicelli, Helen Powell, Janice, Carol. AA, Briar Cliff Coll., 1948. Pres. Coun. Cath. Women, Sioux City, Iowa, 1986-88; state regent Cath. Daus. Am., Iowa, 1988-94; county supr. Kossuth County, Iowa, 1983-89; mem. Iowa Ho. of Reps., Des Moines, 1989—. Dem. precinct com. person, Kossouth County, Iowa, sec. 1975—. Recipient Womens Leadership award Iowa Lakes Community Coll., 1988; named Woman of Yr. Beta Sigma Phi Internat., West Bend, Iowa, 1989; recipient Iowa Lakes Community Coll. Disting. Svc. award, 1992, Guardian of Small Businesss award. Mem. Soroptomist Internat. (Woman of Distinction award 1987), Drama Club (pres. 1970's). Liberal. Roman Catholic. Office: Iowa Ho of Reps State Capitol Des Moines IA 50319-0001 Home: 607 110th St Ottosen IA 50570-8504

MERY, NAOMI MERY, music educator; b. El Paso, Tex., Jan. 13, 1959; d. Arturo and Maria Refugio de la Torre; m. Robert Charles Mery, July 16, 1983; 1 child, Robert Joseph. MusB in piano, U. Tex., El Paso, 1983. Tchg. k-12 Tex., 1983, tchg. music Ed K-12 Colo., 2001. Instr. cert. yamaha piano Phoenix Yamaha Sch., 1985—85, Rocky Mt. Yamaha Sch., Denver, 1985—88; tchr. pvt. piano Schroeder Baldwin Studios, El Paso, Tex., 1980—83, Home Studio, Co. Springs, Colo., 1989—93, 2001—02; tchr. music Divine Redeemer Cath. Sch., Co. Springs, 1990—2002; choir, music, theatre Gorman Pub. Mid. Sch., Co. Springs, 2002—. Studio supr. Schroeder Baldwin Studios, El Paso, Tex., 1980—83; arts assembly coord. Divine Redeemer Cath. Sch., Colorado Springs, Colo., 1996—2002. Dir.: (plays) Elem Mid. Sch. Theatre. Music tchr. Divine Redeemer Cath. Sch., Co. Springs, Colo., 1990—2002. Recipient Mortar Bd. Honor Roll Assn. award, Mortar Bd. honor Roll Assoc., 1981, 1982; scholar Piano Competition, 1st Place, Sigma Alpha Iota Music Frat., 1982; Piano Dept. scholarship, U. Tex. El Paso, 1978—80. Mem.: Colo. Music Educators Assn. (licentiate), Music Educators Nat. Conf. (licentiate), Music Teachers Nat. Assoc. (corr.). Avocations: sewing, shopping, movies, concerts. Home: 1935 Chapel Hills Dr Colorado Springs CO 80920 Personal E-mail: naomimery@pcisys.net.

MESA, YOLANDA DEL CARMEN, artist; b. Medellin, Colombia, Dec. 14, 1953; came to U.S., 1983; d. John and Lucia (Hoyos) M.; m. Nicholas George Sperakis, Feb. 1, 1984; 1 child, Constanza. Student, Art Inst., Medellin, Colombia, 1972-75, San Fernando Sch. Fine Arts, Madrid, Spain, 1976-77, Pratt Graphic Ctr., 1983-84, Art Students League N.Y., 1982-83. Tchr. graphic design Svc. of Nat. Apprenticeship, 1976-77, Art Inst., Medellin, 1979-81, U. de Los Andes, Santafe de Bogota, Colombia, 1990, 93. One-woman shows include Museo de Antioquia, Medellin, 1976, Ctrl. Libr. Gallery, Medellin, 1979, La Mancha Blanca Gallery, Cali, Colombia, 1980, Galerie Taub, Phila., 1983, Gal A.R.T. Gallery, Bogota, Colombia, 1985, Aura Gallery, Mexico City, 1985, Mus. Contemporary Hispanic Art, N.Y.C., 1986, Die Alte Reithalie, Stuttgart, Germany, 1986, Galeria Gasa Negret, Bogota, 1987, Galerie Leopold, Hamburg, Germany, 1988, Volksbank, Weinheim, Germany, 1989, Museo Rayo, Valle, Colombia, 1991, Galeria Gartner/Torres, 1992, Santa Fe de Bogota, Colombia, 1992, 93, Galeria Gartner/Uribe, Bogata, 1996, Mused de Arte Moderno de Cartagena, Columbia, 1996, Centro Colombo-Americano, Bogota, others; group shows include Museo de la Universidad de Antioquia, Medellin, 1977, Partes Gallery, Medellin, 1980, Nat. Exhbn. Art, Medellin, 1981-87, Mus. Contemporary At, Bogota, 1982, 84, Chronocide Gallery, N.Y.C., 1986, La Jeune Peinture, Paris, 1987, Galeria El Museo, Bogota, 1989, Art Forms Gallery, Redbank, N.J., 1990, Maximillian Gallery, N.Y.C., 1990, Sindin Gallery, N.Y.C., 1993, Museo de Arte Moderno De Cartagena, Colombia, 1993, XXXV Salon Nacional de Artistas, Bogata, Columbia, 1993, Sindin Gallery, N.Y., Bienal Internat. de Arte Valpaiso, Chile, 1994, IV Salon de Dibujo-Museo de Arte Moderno, Santo Domingo, Republican Dominicana, 1994, Mirate-Feria de Arte Internat., Bogota, 1996, Pop Art Fundacion Gilberto Alzate Auendano, Bogota, 1997, Galeria El Museo, Bogota, Stands Alon Stephen Gang Gallery, Inc., Chelsea, N.Y., 1998, Nexus Project Gallery, N.Y.C., 2004, Museo Rayo, Roldanillo Valle, Columbia, 2004, others; represented various permanent collections.

MÉSAVAGE, RUTH MATILDE, language educator; BS Dance, Juilliard Sch.; MA, Hunter Coll., 1972; MPhil French, Yale U., 1975, PhD French, 1979; cert., Inst. Michelangelo, Florence, Italy, 1980; postgrad., U. Laval, Quebec, Canada, 1985; cert., Russian State Hydrometeorol. U., St. Petersburg, 2002. Tchg. asst. Yale U., 1973—74, 1975—76, instr., 1974, 1975—76; asst. prof. SUNY, Plattsburgh, 1977—79; asst. prof. French Wake Forest U., 1979—81; asst. prof. French and dance Rollins Coll., Winter Park, Fla., 1981—84, assoc. prof. French and dance, 1984—90, prof. French, 1990—, prof. French and dance, 1990—94, dir. Quebec studies, 1986, 1989, 1991, 1993, 1996; assoc. prof. U. Stendhal-Grenoble III, 1993—95. Instr., dir. intermediate French Yale Summer Lang. Inst., 1974, 75; vis. instr. Middlebury Coll., 1976—77, Ecole Française d'Été Middlebury Coll., 1977. Contbr. over 40 articles to scholarly publs. and textbook. Recipient Cert. of Excellence, Summer Russian Sch./Middlebury Coll., 2001; scholar scholarship, Svcs. Culturels Français de l'Ambassade de France and Ctrs. Internat. Bus. Edn. and Rsch. San Diego State U. and U. Ill.; Yale U. fellow, ., 1971—76, Jack B. Critchfield grantee, 1983, Summer grantee, Rollins Coll., 1984, Govt. Canada, 1985, Jack B. Critchfield grantee, 1986, 1991, 1992, Individual Devel. grantee for rsch. on French Que., 1992, Svcs. Culturels Françaises de l'Ambassade de France and Ctrs. Internat. Bus. Edn. and Rsch. San Diego State U. and U. Ill. scholar. Mem.: Soc. des Profs. Français en Amérique, Am. Soc. 18th Century Studies, Soc. Internat. d'Etude du Dix-Huitième Siècle, Assn. for Canadian Studies in the U.S., L'Assn. des littératures Canadiennes et Québécoise, Am. Coun. for Québec Studies, Am. Assn. Tchrs. French, Conseil Internat. d'Etudes Francophones, Soc. Profs. Français et Francophones d'Amérique. Office: Dept Modern Lang and Lit Rollins Coll Winter Park FL 32789

MESCH, HELENE W. retired social worker; b. Jersey City, N.J., Mar. 5, 1928; d. Emanuel and Belle Weiser; m. Morris Mesch, June 5, 1949 (dec. Sept. 26, 1997); children: Michael, Robert, Cheryl, Richard. BA, U. Buffalo, 1949; MSW, SUNY, Buffalo, 1992. Cert. social worker N.Y. Caseworker, sr. caseworker Erie County Dept. Social Svcs., Buffalo, 1949—53, 1958—60, 1978—88; tchg. asst. W. Seneca (N.Y.) Devel. Ctr., 1976—77; evaluator Erie County (N.Y.) Reevaluation Program, 1975—76; social worker Erie County Health Dept., Buffalo, 1986; social work supr. Erie County Dept. Social Svcs., Buffalo, 1988—95; social worker Amherst (N.Y.) Sr. Svcs. Ctr., 1999—2000. Group facilitator Amherst Sr. Svcs., 2000. Classroom vol. Buffalo Pub. Sch., 2001. Mem.: NASW, Women's Club, SUNY. Avocations: bridge, genealogy, reading.

MESCHKE, DEBRA JOANN, polymer chemist; b. Elyria, Ohio, Oct. 22, 1952; d. Loren Willis and JoAnne Elizabeth (Meyer) M. BS, U. Cin., 1974; MS, Case Western Res. U., 1976, PhD, 1979. Sr. chemist Union Carbide Corp., South Charleston, W.Va., 1979-82, project scientist, 1982-85, chair research and devel. Exempt Women's Group, 1980-81, chair research and devel. Ctr. Safety Team, 1981-82, coordinator Polymer Methods Course, 1982-83, project scientist Tarrytown, N.Y., 1985-86; sr. prin. research chemist Air Products and Chems. Inc., Allentown, Pa., 1986-88, chmn. waste disposal com., 1986-88; rsch. scientist Union Carbide Corp., South Charleston, W.Va., 1988-95, sr. rsch. scientist, 1995—2001; process leader The Dow Chem. Co., 2001—. Author chpts. in textbooks; patentee in field. Bd. dirs. Overbrook Home Owners Assn., Macungie, Pa., 1987. Case Western Res. U. grad. fellow, 1974-79. Mem. AAAS, Am. Chem. Soc. (Polymer div.), Iota Sigma Pi. Avocations: gardening, reading, automobiles, water sports, skiing. Home: 2022 Parkwood Rd Charleston WV 25314-2244

MESHOLAM, RAQUELLE ILYSE, neuropsychologist, researcher; b. Bklyn., Nov. 16, 1971; d. Solomon and Isabelle Helene Mesholam. PhD(hon.), Drexel U., Philadelphia, PA, 1999. Lic. clin. neuropsychologist Mass., 2000, registered health svc. providers in psychology Mass., 2000, lic. health svc. provider Mass., 2000. Instr. in psychiatry Harvard Med. Sch., Boston, 2000—, supervising neuropsychologist Commonwealth Rsch. Ctr., 2000—. Chair, website com. Mass. Mental Health Ctr., Boston, 2000—. Author (presenter): (poster session) Elucidating elderly minor depression through verbal learning and memory profiles, Clinical response to treatment in first episode schizophrenia: Clozapine versus haloperidol, Risk factors for suicidality in patients with schizophrenia or schizoaffective disorder, Cognitive function in first episode schizophrenia: Clozapine versus haloperidol, Clozapine reduces alcohol drinking in Syrian golden hamsters.; author: (principal investigator) (research grant) Schizophrenia and comorbid substance use disorder: Clozapine, olfaction and reward. (NARSAD Young Investigator Award, 2003); author: (abstract) Archives of Clinical Neuropsychology, Joumal of the International Neuropsychology Society; author: (presenter) (poster session) Olfactory identification deficit in elderly schizophrenia and Alzheimer's Disease, Olfaction in neurodegenerative disease: A meta-analysis of olfactory function in Alzheimer's and Parkinson's diseases.; contbr. articles to profl. jours. Recipient Young Investigator award, Nat. Alliance for Rsch. in Schizophrenia and Depression, 2003. Master: Mass. Mental Health Ctr Website Com. (chair); mem.: APA, Mass. Psychol. Assn., Mass. Neuropsychology Soc., Internat. Neuropsychological Soc., Nat. Acad. of Neuropsychology. Office: Commonwealth Rsch Ctr Harvard Med Sch Mass Mental Health Ctr 74 Fenwood Rd Boston MA 02115 E-mail: rmesholam@hms.harvard.edu.

MESROBIAN, ARPENA SACHAKLIAN, publisher, editor, consultant; b. Boston; d. Aaron H. and Eliza Sachaklian; m. William J. Mesrobian, June 22, 1940 (dec.); children: William S.(dec.), Marian Elizabeth (Mrs. Bruce MacCurdy). Student, Armenian Coll. of Beirut, Lebanon, 1937-38; AA, Univ. Coll., Syracuse (N.Y.) U., 1959, BA magna cum laude, 1971; MSsc, Syracuse U., 1993. Editor Syracuse U. Press, 1955-58, exec. editor, 1958-61, asst. dir., 1961-65, acting dir., 1965-66, editor, 1968-85, assoc. dir., 1968-75, dir., 1975-85, 87-88, dir. emeritus, 1985. Dir. workshop on univ. press. pub. U. Malaysia, Kuala Lumpur, 1985; cons. Empire State Coll. Book rev. editor: Armenian Rev., 1967-75; author: (book) Like One Family: The Armenians of Syracuse, 2000; mem. publs. bd. Courier, 1970-94; mem. adv. bd. Armenian Rev., 1981-83; contbr. numerous articles, revs. to profl. jours. Pres. Syracuse chpt. Armenian Relief Soc., 1972-74; sponsor Armenian Assembly, Washington, 1975; mem. mktg. task force Office of Spl. Edn., Dept. Edn., 1979-84, Adminstrn. of Developmental Disabilities, HHS; mem. publs. panel Nat. Endowment for Humanities, Washington; bd. dirs. Syracuse Girls Club, 1982-87; pres. trustees St. John the Bapt. Armenian Apostolic Ch. and Cmty. Ctr., 1991-95. Named Post-Standard Woman of Achievement, 1980; recipient Chancellor's award for disting. service Syracuse U., 1985; Nat. award U.S. sect. World Edn. Fellowship, 1986; N.Y. State Humanities scholar. Mem. Women in Communications, Soc. Armenian Studies (adminstrv. council 1976-78, 85-87, sec. 1978, 85-87), Syracuse U. Library Assocs. (v.p. 1983-88), Am. Univ. Press Services (dir. 1976-77), [illegible] Armenian Community Center, Assn. Am. Univ. Presses (v.p. 1976-77), UN Assn. (bd. dirs. 1983-88, v.p. 1985), Phi Kappa Phi, Alpha Sigma Lambda. Mem. Armenian Apostolic Ch. (past trustee). Club: Zonta of Syracuse (pres. 1979-80, 1st v.p. 1985-86, dist. historian Dist. 2 Zonta Internat. 1993-96).

MESSERLE, JUDITH ROSE, medical librarian, public relations director; b. Litchfield, Ill., Jan. 16, 1943; d. Richard Douglas and Nelrose B. Wilcox; m. Darrell Wayne Messerle, Apr. 26, 1968; children: Kurt Norman, Katherine Lynn. BA in Zoology, So. Ill. U., 1966; MLS, U. Ill., 1967. Cert. med. libr. Libr. St. Joseph's Sch. Nursing, Alton, Ill., 1967-71, dir. med. info. ctr., 1971-76, dir. info. svcs., 1976-79; dir. ednl. resources and cmty. rels. St. Joseph's Hosp., 1979-84; dir. Med. Ctr. Libr. St. Louis U., 1985-88; libr. Francis A. Countway Libr. Harvard Med. Sch. and Boston Med. Libr., 1989—. Cons., 1973—; instr. Lewis and Clark Coll., 1975, Med. Libr. Assn. Bd. dirs. Family Svcs. and Vis. Nurses Assn., Alton, 1976-79. Fellow AAAS, Med. Libr. Assn. (search com. for exec. dir. 1979, dir. 1981-84, pres. 1986-87, legis. task force 1986-90, task force for knowledge and skills 1988-92, nominating com. 1996); mem. OCLC (spl. libr. adv. com. 1994-98), AMA (com. on allied health edn. and accreditation 1991-94), Assn. Acad. Health Sci. Libr. Dirs. (editl. bd. for ann. stats. 1989-94, Region 8 adv. bd. 1992-93, joint legis. task force 1992—, pres. 1993, charting the future task force 2001-03, scholarly communication task force 2003-), Am. Med. Informatics Assn. (planning com. 1990, publs. com. 1994-96, ann. mtg. com. 1996-98), Ill. State Libr. Adv. Com., Midwest Health Sci. Libr. Network (divsn. health sci. coun.), St. Louis Med. Librs., Hosp. Pub. Rels. Soc. St. Louis, Nat. Libr. Medicine (biomed. libr. rev. com. 1988-92). Office: Countway Libr Medicine 10 Shattuck St Boston MA 02115-6011

MESSERSMITH, STEPHANIE HUNT, nursing administrator; b. Key West, Fla. BSN, U. Hawaii, 1978; MSN, George Mason U., 1996. RN, Md., Va., DC; cert. case mgr.; diplomate Am. Bd. Quality Assurance & Utilization Rev. Physicians. Staff nurse Paul H. Weisshaar, MD, Burke, Va., 1986-89; nurse case mgr. Resource Opportunities, Inc., Vienna, Va., 1989-92; analyst State and Fed. Assocs., Vienna, Va., 1992-95; cons. Springfield, Va., 1995-97; ambulatory case mgr. Kaiser Permanente, Springfield, Va., 1997-98, quality improvement coord. Rockville, Md., 1998-99, project mgr., 1999-2000, sr. mgr. Springfield, Va., 2000—. Mem. People to People, Managed Helath Care Del., South Africa, 2000. Co-author: (coloring book for children with cancer) Do You Know What This Is All About?, 1978 (Best Regional Project Am. Cancer Soc. 1978). Mem. Am. Bd. Quality Assurance and Utilization Review Physicians, 1998—, Case Mgmt. Soc. Am., Case Mgmt. Soc. Nat. Capital Area (bd. dirs. 1994). Office: Kaiser Permanente Mid-Atlantic States 2101 E Jefferson St Rockville MD 20852-4908

MESSIER, IRENE M. state legislator; b. Manchester, N.H., May 9, 1923; m. Armand Messier; 3 children. Student, N.H. Sch. Acctg. and Fin. Mem. from dist. 50 N.H. State Ho. of Reps., mem. environ. and agr. com. Del. Constnl. Conv., 1984; mem. Manchester Rep. City Com., ward 10 Rep. chmn. and ballot inspector; mem. Hillsborough County Exec. Com.; mem. Mayor's Liaison Commn.; active ARC. Mem. LWV, Manchester Cmty. Concerts Assn. (bd. dirs., officer), Greater Manchester Rep. Women's Club. Home: 40 New Gate Cir Manchester NH 03102-5147 Office: NH State Senate State Capital Concord NH 03301

MESSIN, MARLENE ANN, plastics company executive; b. St. Paul, Oct. 6, 1935; d. Edgar Leander and Luella Johanna (Rahn) Johnson; m. Eugene Carlson (div. 1972); children: Rick, Debora, Ronald, Lori; m.. Willard Smith (dec. 1975); m. Frank Messin, Sept. 24, 1982; 5 stepchildren. Bookkeeper Jeans Implement Co., Forest Lake, Minn., 1952-53, 1953—57, Great Plains Supply, St. Paul, 1960-62, Plastic Products Co., Inc., Lindstrom, Minn., 1962-75, pres., 1975—; co-owner, treas. Gustaf's Fine Gifts, Lindstrom, 1985—. Bookkeeper Trinity Luth. Ch., Lindstrom, 1976-81. Recipient award, Diversity 2000/Woman-Owned Bus. in Minn. Mem. Soc. Plastic Engrs., Swedish Inst., Soc. Plastic Industry, Minn. State Hist. Soc., Chgo. County Hist. Soc. Home: 28968 Olinda Trl Lindstrom MN 55045-9429 Office: 30355 Akerson St Lindstrom MN 55045-9456

MESSING, CAROL SUE, communications educator; b. Bronx, N.Y. d. Isidore and Esther Florence (Burtoff) Weinberg; m. Sheldon H. Messing; children: Lauren, Robyn. BA, Bklyn. Coll., 1967, MS, 1970. Tchr. N.Y.C. Bd. Edn., 1967-72; prof. lang. arts Northwood U., Midland, Mich., 1973—2004, prof., 1993—. Owner Job Match, Midland, 1983-85; cons. Mich. Credit Union League, Saginaw, 1984-87, Nat. Hotel & Restaurant, Midland, 1985-89, Univ. Coll. program, Continuing Edn. program, Northwood U., 1986—, Dow Chem. Employee's Credit Union, 1988—. Author: (anthology) Symbiosis, 1985, rev. edit., 1987, Controlling Communication, 1987, rev. edit., 1993, Creating Effective Team Presentations, 1995; co-author: PRIMIS, 1993. Mem. LWV, Nat Coun. Tchrs. English, Kappa Delta Pi, Delta Mu Delta (advisor). Avocations: reading, sewing. Office: Northwood U 4000 Whiting Dr Midland MI 48640-2311

MESSING, DEBRA, actress; b. Bklyn., Aug. 15, 1968; m. Daniel Zelman; 1 child. Actor: (films) Walk in the Clouds, 1995, McHale's Navy, 1997, Prey, 1997, Celebrity, 1998, Mothman Prophecies, 2002, Hollywood Ending, 2002, Along Came Polly, 2004; (TV series) Ned and Stacey, 1995, Prey, 1998, Will & Grace, 1998— (Emmy award best actress in a comedy, 2003), numerous TV guest appearances, including Seinfeld, Partners, NYPD Blue. Office: c/o Gersh Agy 232 N Canon Dr Beverly Hills CA 90210*

MESSING, KAREN, occupational health researcher; b. Springfield, Mass., Feb. 2, 1943; BA, Harvard U., 1963; MSc, McGill U., 1970, PhD in Biology, 1975. Rsch. asst. biochemistry Jewish Gen. Hosp., Montreal, Can., 1970-71; NIH fellow genetics Boyce Thompson Inst. Plant Rsch., 1975-76; prof. ergonomics U. Quebec, Montreal, 1976—, dir. Ctr. Study Biol. Interactions & Environ. Health, 1990—95, 2000—03, dir. grad. ergonomics program, 1999-2000. Disting. fellow Que. Coun. for Social Rsch., 1995-97, Can. Inst. Health Rsch., 2001—; invited rschr. Inst. Cancer Montreal, 1983-95, Sweden Nat. Inst. Working Life, 1997-98; mem. bd. dirs. Quebec Sci. & Tech. Mus., 1984-86, Quebec Coun. Social Affairs, 1984-90. Author: One-Eyed Science: Occupational Health and Working Women, 1998, Integrating Gender in Ergonomic Analysis, 1999; editor: Women and Health, Policy and Practice in Health and Safety, Internat. Jour. Health Svcs., Recherches Feministes Salud y Trabajo, Policy and Practice in Health and Safety; co-editor: Women's Health at Work, 1998. Mem. Am. Pub. Health Assn., Assn. Can. Ergonomists. Office: Univ Que at Montreal CP 8888 succursale Centre-ville Montreal QC Canada H3C 3P8 E-mail: messing.karen@uqam.ca.

MESSINGER, MARINA TRABANINO, real estate investor; b. Guatemala, Central America, July 3, 1923; came to U.S., 1953; d. Jose Mariano and Romelita (Barrios) Trabanino; m. Max Oral Messinger, May 31, 1958 (Mar. 1978); children: Katherina, Alex. Student, U. San Carlos, 1948-51, Fac. Economia, 1956. Clk. sec. Ministerio de Economia, Guatemala, 1946-47; acctg. sec. Afiansadora Guatemalteca, Guatemala, 1948-49; with acctg. dept. De Sola Co. Coffee Exp., Guatemala, 1950-53; CPA Watson CPA, San Francisco, 1953-55; with acctg. dept. Arthur J. Fritz Co., San Francisco, 1956, Wilbur Ellis Co., San Francisco, 1957-58; Spanish tchr. Mercy H.S., Bulingame, Calif., 1961-64; real estate investor Calif., 1978—.

Pres. Cath. Charities Aux., San Mateo, 1969; active Exch. Students, Guatemala, 1961, San Mateo County, Calif., 1969; sec. Las Cadetes de Cristo, Guatemala, 1944-46. Home: 101 Barroilhet Ave San Mateo CA 94401-3704

MESSINGER, PENNY, historian, educator; b. Branchland, W.Va., Feb. 23, 1965; d. Wendell and Martha Hazelett Messinger; m. Phillip G. Payne, Sept. 9, 1989; children: Laurel Ann Payne, Russell Paul Payne. BA in History, Marshall U., 1986; MA in History, Ohio State U., 1991, PhD in History, 1998. Adj. prof. St. Bonaventure (N.Y.) U., 1999—2003, acad. skills specialist Higher Edn. Opportunity Program, 2000—03; asst. prof. Daemen Coll., Amherst, NY, 2003—. Mem.: Nat. Assn. Devel. Edn. Office: Daemen Coll History and Govt Dept 4380 Main St Amherst NY 14226 Home: 365 Center St East Aurora NY 14052-2236

MESSMAN-MOORE, TERRI LYN, psychologist, educator; b. Lincoln, Nebr., Mar. 25, 1970; d. Larry D. and Lavonne Andrea Messman; m. Derrick Dean Moore, Aug. 12, 1995. BA, U. Nebr., 1992; MS, Okla. State U., 1994, PhD, 1999. Lic. clin. psychologist Ohio, 2002. Postdoctoral fellow Ctr. for Trauma Recovery U. Mo., St. Louis, 1999—2000; asst. prof. Miami U., Oxford, Ohio, 2000—. Cons. Ctr. for Trauma Recovery U. Mo., St. Louis, 2000—. Contbr. articles to profl. jours. Fellow, Okla. State U. Found., 1993; scholar, Alpha Phi Nat. Sorority, 1997; Superior scholar, U. Nebr. Coll. Arts and Scis., 1992. Mem.: APA, Midwestern Psychol. Assn., Assn. for the Advancement Behavior Therapy, Psi Chi, Phi Beta Kappa, Alpha Phi (treas. 1991—92). Office: Miami University Dept Psychology Benton Hall Oxford OH 45056

MESZAROS, PEGGY S. academic administrator; BS, Austin Peay State U.; MS, U. Ky.; PhD, U. Md. Dept. head Hood Coll.; dean human environ. scis. U. Ky.; assoc. dean, dir. acad. affairs Okla. State U.; dean Coll. Human Resources, prof. family and child devel. Va. Tech.; sr. v.p., provost Va. Poly. Inst. and State U., Blacksburg, 1995-2000, William E. Lavery prof. human devel., 2000—. Mem. Nat. Higher Edn. Com., Nat. Ext. Com. Mem. Am. Assn. Family and Consumer Scis., Kappa Omicron Pi. Office: Va Poly Inst and State U Blacksburg VA 24061-0202

METALLO, FRANCES ROSEBELL, mathematics educator; b. Jersey City, N.J. d. Vincenzo James and Lucille (Frank) M. BA in Math., Jersey City State Coll., 1985, MA in Math. Edn., 1987. Math. tchr. Emerson High Sch., Union City, N.J., 1990-92; math tchr. gifted/talented program Jefferson Annex Woodrow Wilson Sch. Dist. Union City, 1992-95; math tchr. Woodrow Wilson Sch., Dist. Union City, 1995—. Adj. tchr. math. Hudson County C.C., 1987—, Jersey City State Coll., 1986—, tutor, 1983-86; reviewer for Nat. Coun. Tchrs. Math mag., A Plus for Kids Tchr. Network, 1994, grantee 1993, 96 Contbr. articles to profl. publs.; author, History of the Abacus and Study of Sorubah, The Abaacus: It's History and Application Module 17, A concise Dictionary of Math and Symbols, Smile, Basic Algebra is Fun. Nominee Pres. award for sci. and math tchg. Mem. Nat. Coun. Tchrs. Math., Assn. Math. Tchrs. of N.J., Alumni Assn. Jersey City State Coll., Math. Assn. Am., Am. Soc. Prevention of Cruelty to Animals, Assn. of Women in Math., Am. Math. Soc., Dozenal Soc., Kappa Delta Pi, Phi Delta Kappa. Avocations: developing classroom math. materials, crochet, embroidery, piano. Office: 80 Hauxhurst Ave Weehawken NJ 07086-6837

METCALF, CINDY W. political organization administrator; Former chair Vt. Dem. Party, Montpelier; chief of staff Office of the Lt. Gov., Montpelier, Vt., 2001—. Office: 115 State St Drawer 33 Montpelier VT 05633

METCALF, ELYSE N. small business owner; b. Hamilton, Ohio, Nov. 8, 1959; d. Turner W. Metcalf and Irene V. Madden-Metcalf. Cert. profl. freelance ct. reporter, 1983—99; owner, propr. Elyse's Passion, Cin., 1999—. Sexual advocate, educator, 1999—; cons. obscenity prosecutions, 2000—. Recipient Reuben Sturman spl. achievement award, Adult Video News, 2002, First Amendment award, Cavr.com, 2001. Office: Elyse's Passion 1569 Chase Ave Ste 4 Cincinnati OH 45223 E-mail: elysespassion@aol.com.

METCALF, GINGER (VIRGINIA) ARVAN, psychotherapist, consultant; b. Decorah, Iowa, Aug. 19, 1953; d. Theodore Gerald Arvan and Norma Jean Ellickson; m. Michael James Metcalf, Feb. 22, 1985; children: Jason Alan, Rachel Teresa Metcalf-Lange; children: Matthew Lee Canterbury, Aimee Elizabeth Canterbury. BS cum laude in Nursing, Wash. State U., 1975; MS magna cum laude in Clin. Psychology, Ea. Wash. U., 1990. Lic. mental health counselor Nat. Bd. Counselor Certification, Wash., 1993. Therapist, case mgr. Spokane (Wash.) Mental Health, 1990—94; pvt. practice psychotherapist Spokane, 1994—. Cons. Mentor Program, Spokane, 1996; clin. cons. Luth. Cmty. Svc., Spokane, 2001—. Ct. apptd. spl. adv. Spokane (Wash.) Juvenile Ct., 1984—90. Mem.: Am. Profl. Soc. Abuse of Children. Democrat. Lutheran. Avocations: sprint triathalons, quilting. Office: Ginger Arvan Metcalf Ms Rn 1005 N Pines Road Suite 340 Spokane WA 99206 Personal E-mail: gingamet@comcast.net.

METCALF, KAREN, retired foundation executive; b. Reading, Mass., Dec. 12, 1936; d. Albion Edmund and Natalie Viola (Ives) M. AB, Vassar Coll., 1958; MBA, Harvard U., 1968. CFA. Sec. Radio Liberty Com., N.Y.C., 1958-60; rsch. asst. Air Inc., Cambridge, Mass., 1960-64; sys. analyst Keydata Corp., Watertown, Mass., 1964-66; customer edn. cons. Interactive Data Corp., N.Y.C., 1968; portfolio mgr. Scudder, Stevens & Clark, N.Y.C., 1969-81; v.p. fin. and adminstrn. N.Y. Cmty. Trust, N.Y.C., 1981—2002. Episcopalian. Avocations: travel, opera.

METCALF, PAULINE CABOT, architectural historian; b. Providence, Mar. 31, 1939; d. George Pierce Metcalf and Pauline Pumpelly (Cabot) Metcalf Wykeham-Fiennes. BA, Sarah Lawrence Coll., 1960; MS in Hist. Preservation, Columbia U., 1978. Interior decorator Thedlow, Inc., N.Y.C., 1962-65; assoc. ptnr. Richard A. Nelson, Inc., N.Y.C., 1966-75; pvt. practice PCM Interiors, N.Y.C., 1975—. Cons. for interior restorations and renovations for hist. bldgs.; lectr. in field. Author, editor: Ogden Codman and the Decoration of Houses, 1988. Trustee RISD, Providence, 1989—, Preservation Soc. Newport Co., 1998—; bd. dirs. Victorian Soc. Am., 1984-94, adv. bd., 1995—; bd. dirs. Edith Wharton Restoration, Lenox, Mass., 1984—. Winterthur fellow, 1995-96. Mem. Canterbury Choral Soc., Nat. Soc. Colonial Dames, Decorator's Club, Art Club Providence, Cosmopolitan Club. Avocations: choral singing, gardening, skiing, tennis.

METROS, MARY TERESA, librarian; b. Denver, Nov. 10, 1951; d. James and Wilma Frances (Hanson) Metros. BA in English, Colo. Women's Coll., 1973; MA in Librarianship, U. Denver, 1974. Adult svcs. libr. Englewood Pub. Libr., Colo., 1975—81, mgr. adult svcs., 1983—84; sys. cons. Dataphase Sys., Kansas City, Mo., 1981—82; circulation libr. Westminster Pub. Libr., Colo., 1983; supr. pub. svcs. Tempe Pub. Libr., Ariz., 1984—90, libr. dir., 1990—. Mem.: ALA, Mt. Plains Libr. Assn., Libr. Adminstrn. and Mgmt. Assn., Ariz. Libr. Assn., Pub. Libr. Assn. Democrat. Office: Tempe Pub Libr 3500 S Rural Rd Tempe AZ 85282-5405 Office Phone: 480-350-5551.

METTEE-MCCUTCHON, ILA, municipal official, retired career army officer; b. Mobile, Ala., May 1, 1945; d. John Martin and Anna Ruth (Cleveland) Mettee; m. John Robert McCutchon, Oct. 13, 1974; 1 child, Erin Tempest. BS, Auburn (Ala.) U., 1967, MS, 1969; grad., various army schs. Rsch. psychologist VA Hosp., Tuskegee, Ala., 1967-69; clin. psychologist U. Ala. Med. Ctr., Birmingham, 1969-71; commd. 1st lt. U.S. Army, 1971, advanced through grades to col., 1992. Officer in charge Alcohol and Drug Abuse Rehab. Ctr., Presidio, San Francisco, 1971-73; strategic intelligence officer 8th Psychol. Bn., 1973-75; tactical intelligence officer, ops. officer, co. comdr. 525th MI Brigade (Airborne), Ft. Bragg, N.C., 1976-79; project officer Command, Control, Comms. and Intelligence Directorate, Combined Arms Combat Devel. Activity, Ft. Leavenworth, Kans., 1979-82; student Command and Gen. Staff Coll., 1982-83; ops. officer Army Spl. Security Group, Washington, 1983-86; Def. Lang. Inst. Presidio of Monterey, 1986-87; chief U.S. So. command Joint Intelligence Ctr., Republic of Panama, 1987-89; comdr. 741st M.I. Bn., Ft. Meade, Md., 1989-91; U.S. Army War Coll., 1991-92; strategic intelligence officer Internat. Military Staff NATO, Brussels, Belgium, 1992-94; comdr. Presidio of Monterey and Ft. Ord, Calif., 1994-96, chief base realignment and closure/environ. mgmt., 1996-97, ret. with honors, 1997. Elected to Marina City Coun., 1998, Rep. ctrl. com. Monterey County, 2000, Mayor City of Marina, 2002--; apptd. housing cmty. and econ. devel. policy com. League Calif. Cities', 1999—. Decorated Army Commendation medal (3), Meritorious Svc. medal (4), Def. Meritorious Svc. medal (1), Army Achievement award (2), Legion of Merit (2), Def. Superior Svc. medal (1); named Woman of Yr. Marina, 2001, Philanthropist of Yr., 2001. Mem. NAFE, Nat. Assn. Univ. Women, Nat. Women's Polit. Caucus, VFW, Assn. U.S. Army, Alumni Assn. U.S. Army War Coll., WAC Found., Women in NATO, Am. Legion (post 694), Ft. Ord Alumni Assn. (adv. bd.), Girl Scouts of Monterey Bay (bd. dirs.), Cmty. Human Svcs. (bd. dirs.), Rotary Internat. (local chpt.), Monterey Rep. Women, Marina C. of C., Marina Bus. Assn., Marina Larger Libr. Com. Home: 3181 DeForest Rd Marina CA 93933 Office: City Hall City of Marina 211 Hillcrest Ave Marina CA 93933-3534

METTY, THERESA M. communications executive; Degree in Bus., Harvard U. Leader Associated Spring Divsn. Barnes Group, Inc., 1975—95; with IBM, 1995—98; v.p. global procurement IBM, 1998—2000; from sr. v.p. and gen. mgr. supply chain Personal Comms. Sector Motorola Inc., Schaumberg, Ill., 2000—03, sr. v.p. and chief procurement officer, 2003—. Active purchasing coun. Mfrs. Alliance Productivity and Innovation; bd. dirs. The Inst. Supply Mgmt., Nat. Minority Supplier Devel. Coun., Women's Bus. Enterprise Nat. Coun.; spkr. in field. Office: Motorola Inc 1303 E Algonquin Rd Schaumburg IL 60196*

METZ, MARY SEAWELL, foundation administrator, retired academic administrator; b. Rockhill, S.C., May 7, 1937; d. Columbus Jackson and Mary (Dunlap) Seawell; m. F. Eugene Metz, Dec. 21, 1957; 1 dau., Mary Eugena. BA summa cum laude in French and English, Furman U., 1958; postgrad., Institut Phonetique, Paris, 1962-63, Sorbonne, 1962-63; PhD magna cum laude in French, La. State U., 1966; HHD (hon.), Furman U., 1984; LLD (hon.), Chapman Coll., 1985; DLT (hon.), Converse Coll., 1988. Instr. French La. State U., 1965-66, asst. prof., 1966-67, 1968-72, assoc. prof., 1972-76, dir. elem. and intermediate French programs, 1966-74, spl. asst. to chancellor, 1974-75, asst. to chancellor, 1975-76; prof. French Hood Coll., Frederick, Md., 1976-81, provost, dean acad. affairs, 1976-81; pres. Mills Coll., Oakland, Calif., 1981-90; dean of extension U. Calif., Berkeley, 1991-98; pres. S.H. Cowell Found., San Fransisco, 1999—. Vis. asst. prof. U. Calif. Berkeley, 1967-68; mem. commn. on leadership devel. Am. Coun. on Edn., 1981-90, adv. coun. Stanford Rsch. Inst., 1985-90, adv. coun. Grad. Sch. Bus., Stanford U.; bd. dirs. PG&E, SBC Comms., Inc., Union Bank, Longs Drug Stores, S.H. Cowell Found. Author: Reflets du monde francais, 1971, 78, Cahier d'exercices: Reflets du monde francais, 1972, 78, (with Helstrom) Le Francais a decouvrir, 1972, 78, Le Francais a vivre, 1972, 78, Cahier d'exercices: Le Francais a vivre, 1972, 78; standardized tests; mem. editorial bd. Liberal Edn., 1982— . Trustee Am. Conservatory Theater. NDEA fellow, 1960-62,, 1963-64; Fulbright fellow, 1962-63, Am. Council Edn. fellow, 1974-75 Mem. Western Coll. Assn. (v.p. 1982-84, pres. 1984-86), Assn. Ind. Calif. Colls. and Univs. (exec. com. 1982-90), Nat. Assn. Ind. Colls. and Univs. (govt. rels. adv. coun. 1982-85), So. Conf. Lang. Teaching (chmn. 1976-77), World Affairs Coun. No. Calif. (bd. dirs. 1984-93), Bus.-Higher Edn. Forum, Women's Forum West, Women's Coll. Coalition (exec. com. 1984-88), Phi Kappa Phi, Phi Beta Kappa. Address: PO Box 686 Stinson Beach CA 94970-0686 also: 9 Regulus Ct Alameda CA 94501-1015 Office: SH Cowell Found 120 Montgomery St San Francisco CA 94104-4303

METZER, PATRICIA ANN, lawyer; b. Phila., Mar. 10, 1941; d. Freeman Weeks and Evelyn (Heap) M.; m. Karl Hormann, June 30, 1980. BA with distinction, U. Pa., 1963, LLB cum laude, 1966. Bar: Mass. 1966, D.C. 1972, U.S. Tax Ct. 1988. Assoc., then ptnr. Mintz, Levin, Cohn, Glovsky and Popeo, Boston, 1966—75; assoc. tax legis. counsel U.S. Treasury Dept., Washington, 1975-78; shareholder, dir. Goulston & Storrs, P.C., Boston, 1978-98; stockholder Hutchins, Wheeler & Dittmar, P.C., Boston, 1998—2002; of counsel Vacovec, Mayotte & Singer LLP, Newton, Mass., 2003—. Lectr. program continuing legal edn. Boston Coll. Law Sch., Chestnut Hill, Mass., spring, 1974; lectr. grad. tax program Boston U. Law Sch., 2001—03; mem. adv. com. NYU Inst. Fed. Taxation, N.Y.C., 1981—87; mem. practitioner liaison com. Mass. Dept. Revenue, 1985—90; spkr. in field. Author: Federal Income Taxation of Individuals, 1984; mem. adv. bd. Corp. Tax and Bus. Planning Rev., 1996—; mem. authors' panel Jour. Passthrough Entities, 2003—, mem. editl. bd. Am. Jour. Tax Policy, 1995-98; contbr. articles to profl. jours., chpts. to books. Bd. mgrs. Barrington Ct. Condominium, Cambridge, Mass., 1985-86; bd. dirs. University Road Parking Assn., Cambridge, 1988—; trustee Social Law Libr., Boston, 1989-93. Mem. ABA (tax sect., vice-chair publs. 2000-02, mem. coun. 1996-99, chmn. subcom. allocations and distbns. partnership com. 1978-82, vice chmn. legis. 1991-93, chmn. 1993-95, com. govt. submissions, vice liaison 1993-94, liaison 1994-95, North Atlantic region, coliaison 1995-96, N.E. region, regional liaison meetings com.), FBA (coun. on taxation, chmn. corp. taxation com. 1977-81, chmn. com. partnership taxation 1981-87), Mass. Bar Assn. (coun. tax sect. 2001-), Boston Bar Assn. (coun. 1987-89, chmn. tax sect. 1989-91), Am. Coll. Tax Counsel (bd. regents 1999-2004), Boston Estate Planning Coun. (exec. com. 1975, 79-82). Avocation: vocal performances (as soloist and with choral groups). Office: Vacovec Mayotte & Singer LLP Two Newton Pl Ste 340 255 Washington St Newton MA 02458-1634 Office Phone: 617-964-0500.

METZGER, DELORES VIRGINIA, social services professional; b. Balt., Feb. 25, 1952; d. Arthur Willard and Delores Fredricka Maxwell; m. Albert Timothy Metzger, Apr. 15, 1972; children: Brian Timothy, Damien Phillip. AA degrees, Dundalk C.C., 1975, 89; BA, U. Balt., 1992; MSW, U. Md., 1994. Lic. social worker. Child support enforcement agt. Dept. Human Resources, Balt., 1983-85, adminstrv. reviewer Family Investment Adminstrn., 1985-87, asst. field supr., 1987-90, field supr., 1990-95, program mgr., 1995-96, mgmt. analyst, 1997-99, program analyst Social Svcs. Adminstrn., 1999—. Chair hospitality com. PTA High Point Elem. Sch., 1980-90; ch. vol. Our Daily Bread, Balt. Mem. Loyal Order of the Moose. Avocations: reading, bowling, contestant on wheel of fortune. Office: Dept Human Resources 311 W Saratoga St Baltimore MD 21201-3500

METZGER, KATHLEEN ANN, computer systems specialist; b. Orchard Park, N.Y., Aug. 4, 1949; d. Charles Milton and Anna Irene (Matwijow) Wetherby; m. Robert George Metzger, Aug. 29, 1970 (div. June 1988). BS in Edn. cum laude, SUNY Coll., Buffalo, 1970; postgrad., SUNY, Fredonia, 1975. Cert. secondary tchr. Math. tchr. Crestwood High Sch., Mantua, Ohio, 1970-71; sec., bookkeeper Maple Bay Marina, Lakewood, N.Y., 1972; math., bus. tchr. Falconer (N.Y.) High Sch., 1972-76; bookkeeper Darling Jewelers, Lakewood, 1977-78; computer operator Ethan Allen Inc., Jamestown, N.Y., 1978-79, So. Tier Bldg. Trades, Jamestown, 1979; program analyst TRW Bearings Divsn., Inc., Jamestown, 1980-82; cons. Fla. Power Corp., St. Petersburg, 1982-2000; lead IT analyst Progress Energy, St. Petersburg, 2000—. Vol. Christmas Toy Shop. Mem. Assn. Info. Tech. Profls., St. Petersburg Second Time Arounders Marching Band Color Guard, Kappa Delta Pi. Republican. Roman Catholic. Avocations: travel, photography, boating, watching football and hockey, driving corvette. Home: 8701 Blind Pass Rd Apt 110 Saint Petersburg FL 33706-1463 Office: Progress Energy Fla 100 Central Ave Saint Petersburg FL 33701-3324

METZLER, RUTH HORTON, genealogical educator; b. Eden, New York, Aug. 4, 1927; d. John Morris and Bernice Louise (Horton); m. Henry George Metzler, Sept. 4, 1948; children: Kathleen, Ronald, Janice, Margaret. Attended, Wheaton Coll., 1945-48; BA (hon.), Wilmington Coll., 1956; MLS, State Univ. of N.Y., Geneseo, 1962. Cert. tchr., libr. media splty., N.Y. Cataloging typist Peoria Pub. Libr., Ill., 1949-52; cataloging asst. Wilmington Coll. Libr., Ohio, 1953-56; sch. libr. K-12 Nunda Ctrl. Sch., NY, 1956-65; head libr. media ctr. Irondequoit H.S., Rochester, NY, 1965-84; pres. Rochester Geneal. Soc., NY, 1989-93; instr., lectr. Rochester Mus. and Sci. Ctr., NY, 1990—. Author of several family histories. Organizing instr. Genealogy workshops, Rochester Mus. and Sci. Ctr; contbg. lectr. Nat. Geneal. Conf., Rochester, 1990; others. Mem. N.Y. Libr. Assn.,;N.Y. State Tchr. Retirement Sys.; New Eng. Hist. and Geneal. Soc.; Kodak Geneal. Soc., N.Y.; State Coun. of Geneal.; Genealogy Round Table of Monroe County (del. 1996—); Rochester Geneal. Soc.; Geneal. Educators (organizing mem. 1996). Republican. Baptist. Avocations: family history photography, genealogy, writing.

METZNER, BARBARA STONE, university counselor; b. St. Louis, June 9, 1940; d. Wendell Phillips and Lois Custer (Rake) Metzner. AB, Ind. U., 1962, MS, 1964, EdD, 1983; BA, Purdue U., 1979. Asst. dean students U. Ill., Urbana, 1964-68; undergrad. advisor UCLA, 1968-69; asst. dean students Ohio State U., 1969-72; student affairs officer San Diego State U., 1972-76; sr. counselor Ind. U. - Purdue U., Indpls., 1976—. Supr. Ednl. Testing Svc., Indpls., 1980-90; cons. editl. bd. Nat. Acad. Advising Assn., Manhattan, Kans., 1987-93; adj. prof. Ind. U., 1987—; mgr. Info. Svcs. Univ. divsn. Ind. U.-Purdue U., Indpls., Ind., 1989-91. Contbr. articles to profl. jours., chpts. to books. Mem. Marion County Precinct Election Bd., 1980-92; mem. exec. com. Ind. Allied Health Assn., 1983-84; VIP escort Pan Am. Games, 1987. Spencer Found. grantee, 1985. Mem. AAAS, APA, Am. Edn. Rsch. Assn., Assn. Instl. Rsch., Kappa Alpha Theta (vol. charity benefits 1980-90), Phi Beta Kappa. Avocations: tennis, chinese cooking, fine arts. Office: IUPUI 815 W Michigan St Indianapolis IN 46202-5199

MEUNIER, MONIQUE, dancer; b. L.A. Studied with Irena Komoskova, studied with Yvonne Mounsey; student, Sch. Am. Ballet, 1988. Mem. corps de ballet N.Y.C. Ballet, 1990—97, soloist, 1997—98, prin., 1998—2002, soloist Am Ballet Theatre, NYC, 2002—. Dancer (ballets) Agon, Apollo, Harlequinade, The Nutcracker, Swan Lake, Tschaikovsky Piano Concerto No. 2, Vienna Waltzes, The Sleeping Beauty, Ash, Delight of the Muses, A Schubert Sonata, Slavonic Dances. Office: Am Ballet Theatre 890 Broadway New York NY 10003

MEURY, VERONICA KMEC, foundation administrator; b. Pitts., Mar. 18, 1946; d. Andrew William and Veronica Constance (Rudzik) Kmec; m. John Nicholas Meury, Jr., Oct. 29, 1966; children: John III, Matthew, Mark. BA, U. Pitts., 1963-68. Bus. office supr. Pacific Telephone, L.A., 1969-71; asst. dir. svcs. Honolulu Club, 1981-84; nat. coord. Second Chance Hot-Line, Pitts., 1985-86; project chmn. Internat. Organ Transplant Forum, Pitts., 1985-87; exec. dir. Transplant Recipients Internat., Pitts., 1987-93; dir. membership & devel. Helen Clay Frick Found., Pitts., 1993—2004; mgr. Soc. Automotive Engrs. Found., Warrendale, Pa., 2004—. Bd. dirs. AIDS Task Force, Pitts., Family Resources, Pitts., Industry, Univ. roundtable for enhancing Engring. Edn., Garrett Morgan Tech. and Transportation Futures Prog., DOT, Wash. Campaign coord. June Delano for Commr., Pitts., 1989; bd. dirs. Jr. League Pitts., 1986—; pres. Symphony Guild of Honolulu, 1983-84; grad. Leadership Pitts., Class 6, 1989; assoc. vol. The Nat. Ctr., Washington, 1989; adv. mem. Mt. Lebanon Sch. Dist., Pitts., 1987; ordained elder Presbyn. Ch. Recipient Outstanding Svc. award Sta. KDKA-TV and Presbyn. U. Hosp., 1985, Anne D. Johnston award Jr. League Pitts., 1992. Mem. Am. Coun. Transplantation (bd. dirs.), Assn. of Jr. Leagues Internat. (area pub. rels. liaison), ACT Patient & Family Forum, Mt. Lebanon Garden Arts (program chair 1987-88). Avocations: gardening, travel, reading, gourmet cooking. Office: Soc Automotive Engrs Found 400 Commonwealth Dr Warrendale PA 15086-7511 also: SAE Automotive Hdqs 755 W Big Beaver Ste 1600 Troy MI 48084

MEYER, ALICE VIRGINIA, state official; b. N.Y.C., Mar. 15, 1921; d. Martin G. and Marguerite Helene (Houzé) Kliemand; m. Theodore Harry Meyer, June 28, 1947; children: Robert Charles, John Edward. BA, Barnard Coll., 1941; MA, Columbia U., 1942. Tchr. pub. schs., Elmont, N.Y., 1942-43; tchr. Fairlawn (N.J.) High Sch., 1943-47; office mgr., sales rep. N.Y.C., 1948-55; substitute tchr. Pub. Schs., Easton, Conn., 1965-72; state rep., asst. minority leader Conn. State Legislature, Hartford, 1976-93. Mem. Ct. Bd. of Govs. for Higher Edn., 1993—, vice-chair, chair. bd. govs. for higher edn. Mem. Edn. Commn. of the States, 1985—87; life trustee Discovery Mus., 1980—; trustee United Way Regional Youth Substance Abuse Project, Bridgeport, 1983—93; vice chmn. Easton Rep. Town Com., 1970—78; mem. strategic planning com. Town of Easton, 1993—; vice chmn. ct. adv. coun. on intergovtl. rels., 1988—; mem. Conn. Commn. on Quality Edn., 1992—93; supporter Conn. Small Towns, 1988; mem. Conn. Humanities Coun., 1974—76, Conn. Film Commn., 1985—88; co-chair Com. on State Plan of Conservation and Devel., 1985—87; mem. Lt. Gov.'s Commn. on Mandate Reduction, 1995; sec. Easton Free Sch. Scholarship Fund, 1980—; pres. Barnard Class of 1941, 1996—; justice of the peace, 2001—; ct. adv. coun. career and vocat. edn., 1980—88; bd. dirs. 3030 Park, 1993—; Fairfield County Lit. Coalition Bridgeport, 1988—94. Named Legislator of Yr. Conn. Libr. Assn., 1985; Guardian Small Bus. grantee Nat. Fedn. Ind. Bus., 1987; honoree Fairfield YWCA Salute to Women, 1988, Conn. Assn. Small Towns, 1990; named grant to AAUW Fellowship Fund, Bridgeport Br., 1970, Conn. State AAUW, 1974; recipient Conn. Friends of Libr. Hon. award, 1984, Disting. Svc. award Conn. State Coun. on Voc/Tech. Edn., 1986, Sacred Heart U. Ctr. for Policy Issues award, 1988, citation Conn. Bd. for Acad. Affairs, 1992, citation Charter Oak Coll., 1993, Spl. Day Recognition, Town of Weston, 1993, Cert. of Recognition, Town of Westport, 1993, Citation for Fostering Open Access to Higher Edn., AAUW, 1994, Disting. Rep. award Easton Rep. Town Com., 2000, Pub. Svc. award Com. Sec. of State, 2003, others. Mem.: LWV, AAUW (local pres. 1976, bd. dirs. 1982), Nat. Order Women Legislators (regional dir. 1987—, past pres. Conn. chpt.), Conn. Assn. Sch. Adminstrs. (hon.), Bus. and Profl. Women. Congregationalist. Avocations: swimming, sailing, bridge. Home: 18 Lantern Hill Rd Easton CT 06612-2218

MEYER, AMY ALLEN, counselor; b. McKinney, Tex., Aug. 29, 1956; d. Tom Wallace Jr. and Patsy Ruth (Paysinger) Allen; children: Emily, Allison; m. Kurt Meyer. BS, North Tex. State U., 1978; MEd, U. North Tex., 1993. Lic. profl. counselor, Tex.; registered play therapist. Tchr. McKinney Ind. Sch. Dist., 1978-81, St. Peters Sch., McKinney, 1986-93; freelance counselor McKinney, 1991—2002. Chmn. organ com. 1st Bapt. Ch., 1994-95, organist, 1986—, children's choir dir., 1976-96; numerous other civic and school coms. Named to Outstanding Young Women of Am., 1988. Mem. ACA, Tex. Assn. for Play Therapy, Assn. Play Therapy. Avocations: music, handwork, tennis. Office: 9741 Preston Rd Ste 106 Frisco TX 75034

MEYER, ANDREA PEROUTKA, small business owner; b. Prague, Czechoslovakia, Nov. 29, 1963; came to U.S. 1970; d. George and Alena Peroutka; m. Dana Charles Meyer, Oct. 16, 1983. BA in Liberal Arts, U. Tex., 1985, M in Libr. of Info. Sci., 1986. Libr. IBM, Austin, Tex., 1985-86; rsch. specialist Career Track Seminars, Boulder, Colo., 1986-88; founder, pres. Working Knowledge, Boulder, 1988—. Project mgr. Interesting Orgns. Database for MIT, 1995—; cons. The Tom Peters Group, Palo Alto, Calif., 1989-95. Author: (workbooks) Stress Management Strategies, 1987, How to Give Presentations, 1988; co-author: (audio tape) How to Set Up a Corporate Library, 1989; co-editor Briefing Book for Inventing the Organizations of the 21st Century, 1995-96; assoc. editor Inside Decisions, 1995-96; contbr. chpts. to 3 books. Recipient Ray C. Janeway scholarship, Tex. Libr. Assn., 1985, Philip Morris scholarship, 1981 85. Mem. Planning Forum (v.p. comm., bd. dirs, Denver chpt.), Product Devel. and Mgmt. Assn. (newsletter editor), Toastmasters, Mensa (chmn. scholarship com.), Pres.'s Assn., European Consortium of Info. Cons., Phi Beta Kappa. Avocations: reading, hiking, writing, travel. Home and Office: 515 Forest Ave Boulder CO 80304-2550 E-mail: dcmeyer@knewbiquity.com.

MEYER, ANN JANE, human development educator; b. N.Y.C., Mar. 11, 1942; d. Louis John and Theresa Meyer. BA, U. Mich., 1964; MA, U. Calif., Berkeley, 1967, PhD, 1971. Asst. prof. dept. human devel. Calif. State U., Hayward, 1972-77, assoc. prof., 1977-84, prof., 1984—. Mem. APA. Office: Calif State U Dept Human Devel Hayward CA 94542 Business E-Mail: ameyer@csuhayward.edu.

MEYER, BETTY JANE, former librarian; b. Indpls., July 20, 1918; d. Herbert and Gertrude (Sanders) M.; B.A., Ball State Tchrs. Coll., 1940; B.S. in L.S., Western Res. U., 1945. Student asst. Muncie Public Library (Ind.), 1936-40; library asst. Ohio State U. Library, Columbus, 1940-42, cataloger, 1945-46, asst. circulation librarian, 1946-51, acting circulation librarian, 1951-52, adminstrv. asst. to dir. libraries, 1952-57, acting asso. reference librarian, 1957-58, cataloger in charge serials, 1958-65, head serial div. catalog dept., 1965-68, head acquisition dept., 1968-71, asst. dir. libraries, tech. services, 1971-76, acting dir. libraries, 1976-77, asst. dir. libraries, tech. services, 1977-83, instr. library adminstrn., 1958-63, asst. prof., 1963-67, asso. prof., 1967-75, prof., 1975-83, prof. emeritus, 1983—; library asst. Grandview Heights Public Library, Columbus, 1942-44; student asst. Case Inst. Tech., Cleve., 1944-45; mem. Ohio Coll. Library Center Adv. Com. on Cataloging, 1971-76, mem. adv. com. on serials, 1971-76, mem. adv. com. on tech. processes, 1971-76; mem. Inter-Univ. Library Council, Tech. Services Group, 1971-83; mem. bd. trustees Columbus Area Library and Info. Council Ohio, 1980-83. Ohio State U. grantee, 1975-76. Mem. ALA, Assn. Coll. and Research Libraries, AAUP, Ohio Library Assn. (nominating com. 1978-81), Ohioana Library Assn., Ohio Valley Group Tech. Services Librarians, No. Ohio Tech. Services Librarians, Franklin County Library Assn., Acad. Library Assn. Ohio, PEO, Beta Phi Mu, Delta Kappa Gamma. Club: Assn. Faculty and Profl. Women Ohio State U. Home: Apt B138 6000 Riverside Dr Dublin OH 43017

MEYER, CHERYL LORRAINE, music educator; b. Camp Breckenridge, Ky., Feb. 10, 1953; d. Stanley O. and Arliss L. Boyum; m. Jon C. Meyer, Aug. 1973; children: Sarah, Erik. MusB, U. Wis., Madison, 1975. Elem. music specialist Sch. Dist. 102 of La Grange, La Grange Park, Ill., 1975—76, Sch. Dist. 92 1/2, Westchester, Ill., 1976—77, Appleton (Wis.) Area Sch. Dist., 1985—. Conductor Lawrence Arts Acad. Girl Choir, Appleton, 1992—. Named Appleton Elem. Educator of Yr., Mielke Found., 2001. Mem.: Wis Choral Dirs. Assn., Am. Choral Dirs. Assn., Music Educators Nat. Conf. Office: Jefferson Elem Sch 1000 S Mason St Appleton WI 54914

MEYER, DIANE CHRISTINE, social worker; b. Meadowbrook, Pa., May 9, 1963; d. Robert Francis and Carole Ann Meyer; children: Stephen Francis, Alexander Gerard, Robert Nathaniel. BA in Psychology, LaSalle U., Phila., 1989. Childcare supr. St. Mary's Villa, Ambler, Pa., 1989—91; caseworker Bucks County Children & Youth, Doylestown, Pa., 1991—2001, casework supr., 2001—. Democrat. Roman Catholic. Avocation: reading. Home: 4218 Miladies Ln Doylestown PA 18901 Office: Bucks County Children and Youth 4259 W Swamp Rd Doylestown PA 18901

MEYER, ELEANOR CATHERINE, artist, educator; b. Milw., Aug. 17, 1917; d. Aloysius and Elinore (Matt) Grosspietsch; divorced; children: Marc Jan, Gregory George. Student, Layton Art Sch., 1935—40; degree in Bible, Moody Bible Inst., Chgo., 1953. Artist Milw. Iron Works, 1940—43; supr., tchr. State of Mo., Kansas City, 1965—72; freelance tchr. Kansas City, 1976—2003, Mountain View, Ark., 1976—2003. Works exhibited in 4 one-person shows, collections, Stargap Gallery, Little Rock and Fayetteville, Ark., one-woman show Stargap Ballery, 1996; contbr. pen and ink drawing for newspaper, 1994—; author: (cartoon book) Cartooning with Cathe, 1995, (poetry) Tomorrow Never Knows, 1995. Sec., treas. Stone County Rep. Party, 1982, 94, 96. Mem. Mid-South Watercolors (signature mem.). Republican. Pentecostal. Avocations: writing, teaching, painting. Home: Mountain Lodge Apts 221 King Ave Apt 19 Mountain View AR 72560

MEYER, ELLEN ADAMS, arts and small business development specialist; b. Sacramento, Calif., Nov. 1, 1947; d. Joseph Robert Hobson and Mary Ellen (Adams) Fort; m. Jeffrey Norman Meyer, June 18, 1966 (div. 1975); children: Zoe Ingrid, Lara Alixandra; m. Glenn Charles Madrid, June 12, 1991; 1 child, Zachary Adams Cabezuela Madrid. BFA in Studio Painting, U. Oreg., 1979; MBA in Mgmt., Sul Ross State U., 1999. Artist Studio in a Sch. Assn., N.Y.C., 1982-84; mng. dir. for artist Donald Judd, 1984-91; exec. dir. Byrd Hoffman Found., N.Y.C., 1991-92; dir. Akira Ikeda Gallery, N.Y.C., 1992-94; arts cons. N.Y.C. and Marfa, Tex., 1994—; with Sml. Bus. Devel. Ctr. Sul Ross State U., Alpine, Tex., 2000—. Adj. prof. depts. bus. adminstrn. and art Sul Ross State U., 2000. Exhbns. include U. Oreg.-Gallery 141, 1978, Photography Gallery, N.Y.C., 1979, Pub. Image, N.Y.C., 1980, A's, N.Y.C., 1981, Interart Gallery, N.Y.C., 1982, City Gallery, N.Y.C., 1983, Artist's Space, N.Y.C., 1984, Sul Ross State U., Alpine, Tex., 1996, Nueva Vida Gallery, Alpine, 1997. Sec. City Zoning Adjustment, Marfa, 1997, alt. bd. mem., 2000; bd. dirs. Watermill Found., N.Y.C., 1991—93, Pub. Image Gallery, N.Y.C., 1981—84, Marfa Studio of Arts, 2001; sec. bd. dirs. Chinati Found., 1988—91. Democrat. Episcopalian. Office: PO Box 278 Marfa TX 79843-0278 E-mail: elenadam@yahoo.com.

MEYER, ELLEN L. academic administrator; BA and MS Geo Wash U. Vp for mktg and exten, dean of cont studies and dir of exten prog and summer sch Minneapolis College of Art and Design; dir of cont ed and spec prog RI Sch of Design; pres. Atlanta Coll. Art, 1992—. Mem.: National Black Arts Festival Bd of Dir, Metro Atlanta Arts Fund Adv Bd, vice chair, bd of dir, Atl Reg Consortium for Higher Ed. Achievements include 1992-93 graduate, Midtown Leadership Program, Atlanta; 1994 graduate, Leadership-Atlanta. Office: Atlanta Coll Art President 1280 Peachtree St NE Atlanta GA 30309-3502

MEYER, FRANCES MARGARET ANTHONY, elementary and secondary school educator, health education specialist; b. Stella, Va., Nov. 15, 1947; d. Arthur Abner Jr. and Emmie Adeline (Murray) Anthony; m. Stephen Leroy Meyer, Aug. 2, 1975. BS, Longwood Coll., 1970; MS, Va. Commonwealth U., 1982, PhD, 1996. Cert. tchr., Va. Health, phys. edn., and dance tchr. Fredericksburg (Va.) City Pub. Schs., 1970-89; AIDS edn. coord. Va. Dept. Edn., Richmond, 1989-90, health edn. specialist, 1990-94, comprehensive sch. health program specialist, 1994—2003; edni. cons. Fredericksburg, Va., 2003—. Mem. rev. bd. Nat. Commn. for Health Edn. and Credentialing, Inc., conf. and profl. devel. rev., 1996-2000. Author (with others): Elementary Physical Education: Growing through Movement-A Curriculum Guide, 1982; contbr. articles to profl. jours. Dir. Va. Children's Dance Festival, 1981—96, 1997—; vol. ARC, Fredericksburg, 1976—84, 1997—2001, Va. affiliate AHA, 1982—93, 1999—2001; mem. ctrl. steering com. Health, Mental Health and Safety in Schs. Nat. Guidelines Project, Am. Acad. Pediat., 2000—02; Va. Affiliate Am. Cancer Soc. Richmond, Va.; mem. Public Health Edn.Coun., Comprehensive Sch. Health Edn. Team, Va. Alliance Adolescents and Sch. Health, 1990—; bd. dirs. Va. HIV/AIDS Network ARC, 1997—2001. Recipient gov.'s medal for substance abuse and prevention edn. State of Va., 1997, Alumni Cmty. Svc. award Va. Commonwealth U., 1998, Youth Edn. award for Leadership in the healthy devel. of children Am. Cancer Soc., 2002, Disting. Leadership in Phys. Edn. award Nat. Assn. Sport and Phys. Edn., 2004. Fellow: North Am. (honor) Soc. Health, Phys. Edn., Recreation, Sport and Dance; mem.: AAPHERD (chmn. divsn. 1970—, So. dist. applied strategic planning com. chair 2002—04, past v.p., nominating com., social justice com., strategic planning com., So. Dist. honor award 1995, pres.'s recognition award 1997, svc. award 1997, So. Dist. honor award 1999, nat. honor award 1999), ASCD, AAUW (com. 1989—90, 1995—), NEA, Dance Edn. Orgn. (charter mem.), Va. Assn. for Health, Phys. Edn., Recreation and Dance (various coms. 1970—, health edn. editor Va. Jour. 1994—, past pres., Tchr. of Yr. 1983, Va. Honor award 1988, Va. Pioneer award 2003), Va. Alliance for Arts Edn. (adv. bd. 1980—83, 1989—90, 1994—96), Am. Coll. Health Assn. (curriculum and tng. rev. panel 1992—94), Soc. State Dirs. Health, Phys. Edn. and Recreation (legis. affairs com. 1994—98, mem. applied strategic planning com. 1994—2001, pres.-elect 1997, pres. 1998, past pres. 1999, think tank chair 2000—02, applied policy & legis. com. 2002—, Healthis acad. rev. com. 2001—03, Presdl. award 1996, Presdl. Recognition award 1997, 2000, Simon A. McNeely Honor award 2000, Julian B. Smith award 2004), Va. Health Promotion and Edn. Coun. (bd. dirs. 1990—96), Internat. Coun. for Health, Phys. Edn., Recreation, Sport and Dance (internat. commns. for health edn. and commn. for dance and dance edn., mem. jour. articles rev. com.), Va. Mid. Sch. Assn., Va. Edn. Assn., Nat. Mid. Sch. Assn., Nat. Dance Assn. (bd. dirs. 1996—, pres. 2001—03, Presdl. citation 1998, svc. award 1998, 2000, Pres.'s Merit award 2001), Nat. Network for Youth Svcs. (adv. bd. 1994—98, rev. panel), Longwood Coll. Alumni Coun. (bd. dirs. 1987—90), Delta Kappa Gamma (pres. Beta Eta chpt. 1988—90). Baptist. Avocations: travel, dance, swimming, reading, theatrical performances.

MEYER, GAIL BARRY, retired real estate broker; b. Athens, Ga., Oct. 13, 1940; d. John Carlton and Addie Lorene (Harris) Barry; m. Leo Marcus Meyer Jr., July 2, 1960; Rand Marcus, Brian Kevin, Kelli Paige. Cert., Grad. Realtors Inst., 1979. Cert. residential specialist, rape counselor. Assoc. broker, owner So. Realty, Statesboro, Ga., 1977-80; assoc. broker Zetterower-Olliff Realty, Statesboro, 1980-84, Century 21, Johnny Cobb Realty, Statesboro, 1984-99. Pres., v.p., treas. Citizens Against Crime, Statesboro, 1990—; pres. Victim Witness Assistance Program, Statesboro, 1990—; mem. Georgians for Victims Justice, Parents and Childrens Counsel, 1998-2004. Recipient Deen Day Smith award C. of C. and Statesboro Herald News, 1989. Mem.: NARAL, AAUW, MADD, NOW (pres. 1980—, v.p., treas.). Roman Catholic. Avocation: reading. Home: 274 Parkway Dr Athens GA 30606-4950 Office Phone: 706-546-6696. E-mail: gail586@charter.net.

MEYER, HELEN BERNADINE, financial services company executive; b. Ireton, Iowa, Mar. 2, 1929; d. Adolph J. and Haldora J. (Barnes) Opdahl; m. W. Thomas Logan, Nov. 19, 1955 (div. Mar. 1961); 1 stepchild, Thomas C. Logan ; m. William James Meyer, Oct. 19, 1968 (dec. Aug. 1993); 1 adopted child, H.B. Kris. Student, Sch. Mpls. Inst. Art, 1946-49. NASD registered rep., Iowa, Minn. Advt. artist, writer, mgr. Lawton Co., Cinn., 1949-51; illustrator, acct. exec. Simons Advt., N.Y.C., 1951—53; asst. advt. mgr. Max Wiesen & Sons, Inc., N.Y.C., 1953-54, Mays Dept. Store, Bklyn., 1954-55; advt. and pub. rels. dir. Dayton's-Fantle's, Sioux Falls, S.D., 1955-66; comml. illustrator Meyer Advt., Worthington, Minn., 1967-69, comml. and continuity writer electronic media, 1970-76; regional promotions dir. shopping mall devel. Developers Diversified, Cleve., 1977-79; fin. svcs. exec. Meyer Ins. and Investment, Worthington, 1980—. Charter mem. Advt. Artist Guild, 1960-66, dir., 1963-64. Charter treas., pres. Zonta Internat., Sioux Falls, 1957-66; pub. rels., promotions staff Am. Cancer Soc., Worthington, 1972-77. Lutheran. Achievements include patent for surgical support. Home: 29744 290 St Worthington MN 56187 Office Phone: 888-526-2482.

MEYER, HELEN M. judge; BSW, U. Minn.; JD, William Mitchell Coll. Law. Cert.: Nat. Bd. Trial Advocacy (civil trial specialist). Ptnr. Pritzker & Meyer, 1987—96, Meyer and Assocs., 1996—2002; assoc. justice Minn. Supreme Ct., St. Paul, 2002—. Mem. Jud. Merit Selection Commn., Minn. Mem.: Acad. Cert. Trial Lawyers, Minn. Trial Lawyers Assn. (bd. dirs.), Minn. State Bd. Legal Cert. (bd. dirs.), Minn. State Bar Assn. (cert. civil trial specialist). Office: Minn Jud Ctr 25 Reverend Dr Martin Luther King Jr Blv Saint Paul MN 55155

MEYER, JENNE L. marketing professional; b. Cudahy, Wis., Apr. 5, 1975; d. James M. Palasz and Linda J. Rozek; m. Ross Q. Meyer. BA in Internat. Rels., U. Wos., Milw., 1996; MBA, Cardinal Stritch U., 1999; postgrad., Capella U., 2003—. Market analyst Generac Portable Products, Jefferson, Wis., 1996—99; mgr. market devel. Harley-Davidson, Milw., 1999—. Mem.: Nat. Assn. State Motorcycle Safety Adminstrs., Soc. Consumer Psychology, Am. Mktg. Assn., Phi Eta Sigma. Office: Harley-Davidson 3700 W Juneau Ave Milwaukee WI 53208 E-mail: jenne.meyer@harley-davidson.com.

MEYER, JUDITH CHANDLER PUGH, history educator; b. Detroit, Oct. 22, 1948; d. Howard Chandler and Margaret Elizabeth (Bentley) Pugh; m. Paul Rudolph Meyer Jr., Aug. 17, 1974; children: Matthew Paul, Timothy Chandler. BA, Lawrence U., 1970; MA, U. Iowa, 1972, PhD, 1977. Tchg. asst. U. Iowa, Iowa City, 1974-76; instr. Ind. Cen. U., Indpls., 1977-78; asst. prof. history Smith Coll., Northampton, Mass., 1978-79; lectr. Fairfield (Conn.) U., 1985, 87, 89; lectr. in history U. Conn., Stamford, 1981-89, asst. prof. history Waterbury, 1989-95, assoc. prof. history, 1995—. Author: (monograph) Reformation in La Rochelle: Tradition and Change in Early Modern Europe, 1500-1568, 1996; contbr. articles to profl. jours. NDEA fellow U. Iowa, 1970-73, Fulbright fellow, Paris and La Rochelle, France, 1973-74, jr. faculty summer fellow and rsch. grantee The Rsch. Found., U. Conn., 1991-92. Mem. Am. Hist. Assn., Soc. for Reformation Rsch., 16th Century Studies Conf. Methodist. Avocations: reading, music, travel, hiking. Home: 184 College Park Dr Fairfield CT 06824 Office: U Conn-Waterbury 32 Hillside Ave Waterbury CT 06710-2217

MEYER, JUDY L. science educator, director; BS in Zoology, U. Mich.; MS in Zoology, U. Hawaii; PhD in Ecology, Cornell U. Co-dir. River Basin Sci. and Policy Ctr., Athens, Ga.; Disting. Rsch. prof. Inst. Ecology U. Ga. Mem. com. Nat. Acad. Scis./NRC; mem. Improving Nat. Water Quality Assessment Program USGS; elected U.S. nat. rep. Internat. Assn. Theoretical and Applied Limnology; chair sci. and tech. adv. com., bd. dirs. Am. Rivers; chair edn. and sci. adv. com., bd. dirs. Upper Chattahoochee Riverkeeper; bd. dirs. Ga. Land Trust Svc. Ctr. Recipient Creative Rsch. medal, U. Ga. Rsch. Foun.; grantee, NSF, EPA, U.S. Dept. Agr., U.S. Dept. Energy, U.S. Forest Svc., U.S. Geol. Survey, U.S. Fish and Wildlife Svc., Ga. Dept. Natural Resources, Turner Found. Fellow: AAAS; mem.: Nat. Coun. Sci. Soc. Pres. (exec. com.), Ecol. Soc. Am. (v.p., pres.). Office: River Basin Sci and Policy Ctr 201 N Milledge Ave Athens GA 30602-5482

MEYER, LISA MARIE, elementary school educator; b. Livonia, Mich., Nov. 15, 1961; d. James Theo and Dolores Lola Bishop; m. John Melville Meyer, May 22, 1982; children: Jessica Ellen, Brittany Allyssa. AA, Henry Ford C.C., Dearborn, Mich., 1981; B in Music Edn., Ea. Mich. U., 1987; M in Elem. Edn., Wayne State U., 1991. Cert. tchr. music edn., elem. edn. Mich. Elem. music tchr. Detroit Pub. Schs., 1987—89; music tchr. Dearborn Pub. Schs., 1989—95, music resource tchr., 1995—. Adj. instr. William Tyndale Coll., Farmington Hills, Mich., 1986—; cons. Ideas, LLC, West Norwalk, Conn., 2000—; mem. adv. bd. Ward Pre-Sch., Northville, Mich., 1987—90. Named one of Best 100 for Music Edn. in Am., Music Tchr. Nat. Assn., 2001; recipient Named one of Best of 100 for Music Edn. in Am., 2002. Mem.: Mich. Music Educator Assn. (Outstanding Adminstr. award 2001, 2002), Am. Orff Schulwerk Assn., Nat. Assn. Music Edn. Avocations: singing, camping, hiking. Home: 43069 Devon Ln Canton MI 48187 Office: Dearborn Pub Schs 18700 Audette Dearborn MI 48124 E-mail: meyerl@dearborn.k12.mi.us.

MEYER, LOIS KATHRYN, graphic artist; b. Bellingham, Wash., Mar. 19, 1926; d. William Sam and Coralie Anne (Johnson) M. BA, Western Wash. State U., 1963. Graphic artist Whatcom County Pub. Libr., Bellingham, 1963—78; studio painter, print-maker Bellingham, 1963—79, San Diego, Pismo Beach, Calif., 1982—. One-woman shows include Gallery West and Gallery 217, Bellingham, Panaca Gallery, Bellevue, Wash., Choice, Inc., San Francisco, Whatcom Mus. of Art, Bellingham; group shows include Seattle Art Mus., Nat. Watercolor Exhibn., Pacific N.W. Arts and Crafts, Bellevue, N.W. Wash. Regional Artists Traveling Exhibit, Whatcom Mus. History and Art Invitational Exhibn., Anacortes (Wash.) Arts and Crafts Exhibit; works in pvt. collections Western Wash. State U., Bellingham, Skagit Valley Coll., Mt. Vernon, Wash., First Fed. Bank, Burlington, Wash. Home: 10025 El Camino Real #103 Atascadero CA 93422

MEYER, LYNN NIX, lawyer; b. Vinita, Okla., Aug. 10, 1948; d. William Armour and Joan Ross Nix; children: Veronica, Victoria, David. BA, Baldwin Wallace Coll., 1978; JD, Case Western Res. U., 1981. Bar: Ky. 1982, Colo. 1984. Paralegal Texaco Devel., Austin, Tex., 1976-77; legal asst. Alcan Aluminum, Cleve., 1977-79; assoc. Wyatt, Tarrant & Combs, Lexington, Ky., 1982-83; ptnr. Meyer, Meyer & Assocs., P.C., Denver, 1984-85; gen. counsel Carbon Fuels Corp., 1985-95; in pvt. practice Denver, 1996-97; asst. gen. counsel products Gambro, Inc., Lakewood, Colo., 1997—. Mem. ABA, Colo. Bar Assn., Ky. Bar Assn., Arapahoe County Bar Assn. Home: 10487 E Ida Ave Englewood CO 80111-3746 Office: 10810 W Collins Ave Lakewood CO 80215-4439 E-mail: lynn.meyer@gambrobct.com.

MEYER, MARGARET ELEANOR, microbiologist, educator; b. Westwood, Calif., Feb. 8, 1923; d. Herman Henry and Eleanor (Dobson) M. BS, U. Calif., Berkeley, 1945; PhD, U. Calif., Davis, 1961. Pub. health analyst USPHS, Bethesda, Md., 1945-46; swine Brucellosis control agt. Dept. Agr., Davis, 1946-47; bacteriologist U. Calif., Davis, 1947-61; research microbiologist U. Calif. (Sch. Vet. Medicine), 1961-77, prof. vet. pub. health and microbiologist exptl. sta., 1977—; research microbiologist U. Calif. Med. Sch., Los Angeles, 1961-77; supr. Brucella identifications lab. WHO, U. Calif.-Davis, 1964—, prof. vet. pub. health, 1973—; also dir. M.A. program in preventive vet. medicine. Cons. subcom. on Brucella Internat. Com. Bacterial Taxonomy, 1962—, mem., 1966—; mem. 5th Pan Am. Congress Veterinary Medicine, Venezuela, 1966; mem. Internat. Congress Microbiology, Moscow, 1966, Mexico City, 1970, Munich, Ger., 1978, mem., officer, Eng., 1986; mem. Internat. Conf. Culture Collections, Tokyo, 1968; mem. adv. com. to Bergey's Manual Determative Bacteriology, 1967; cons. in resident Pan Am. Health Orgn., Zoonoses Lab., Buenos Aires, 1968; mem. brucellosis tech. adv. com. U.S. Animal Health Assn., 1977; FAO cons. on brucellosis control in dairy animals, Tripoli, Libya, 1981, mem. 3d internat. brucellosis symposium, Algiers, 1983; cons. Alaska Dept. Fish and Game, 1976, FAO, Libya, 1981, Bering Straits Reindeer Herders Assn., Nome, Alaska, 1981; invited speaker Internat. Symposium on Advances in Brucellosis Rsch., Tex. A&M U., 1989, Internat. Bison Conf.; resident cons. on brucellosis control in sheep and goats Am. Near East Refugee Aid, East Jerusalem, 1989; cons. on brucellosis in Yellowstone Nat. Pk., Nat. Pk. Svc., 1991—; invited mem. nat. symposium on brucellosis in the Greater Yellowstone Area, Jackson Hole, Wyo., 1994; cons. on brucellosis control in livestock for Armenia, 1994—. Contbr. articles to profl. jours. Bd. dirs. Carmichael Park and Recreation Dist., Calif., 1975; mem. Sacramento County Grand Jury, 1999-2000. Recipient Research Career Devel. award USPHS-NIH, 1963 Fellow Am. Pub. Health Assn., Am. Acad. Microbiology; mem. Soc. Am. Microbiologists, N.Am. Conf. Animal Disease Research Workers, Am. Coll. Vet. Microbiologists (hon. affiliate), U.S. Animal Health Assn. (chmn. brucellosis tech. advisory com. 1978-79), Internat. Assn. Microbiol. Socs. (mem. 1st intersect. congress 1974), AAUW, No. Calif. Women's Golf Assn., U. Calif. Alumni Assn., Sigma Xi. Clubs: U. Calif. Faculty (Davis); El Dorado Royal Country (Shingle Springs, Calif.); Reno Women's Golf. Home: 5611 Fair Oaks Blvd Carmichael CA 95608-5503 Office: U Calif Sch Vet Medicine Dept Epidemiology & Preventive Medicine Davis CA 95616

MEYER, MARGARET VAUGHAN, librarian, educator; b. Phila., Mar. 13, 1919; d. Clifford and Fannie (Lehman) Vaughan; m. Donald Rupert Meyer, Sept. 3, 1949 (dec. Mar. 2002); children: Karen, Frederick E., Julie Meyer Ramos. BEd, UCLA, 1942; MLS, U. So. Calif., 1967. Elem. tchr. Indio Sch. Dist., Indio, Calif., 1942-43, Lawndale Sch. Dist., Lawndale, Calif., 1943-44, L.A. Unified Schs., 1946-53; program libr. City of Pasadena Libr., Pasadena, Calif., 1965-85. Co-author (Spanish-English): Centeno Collection-Annotated, 1977; author (biog. and notes, 2 CDs): Clifford Vaughan classical music. Organizer, chmn. libr. com. PTA, L.A., 1961—64, hon. life mem., 1964; vol. Com. Solidarity People of El Salvadore, L.A., 1985—97; mem. Citizens Com. Save Elysian Park, L.A., 1987—, L.A. County Mus. Art, 1986—, Friends of Pasadena Pub. Libr., 1986—. Mem.: ALA (del. 1967—80), L.A. Pub. Libr., Libr. Found. (charter mem.), Calif. Libr. Assn., Am. Fedn. Tchrs. (exec. bd. L.A. chpt.), Denishawn Repertory Dancers (hon. bd. dirs.), Sierra Club. Avocations: music, reading, swimming, gardening, games. Home: 1525 Upshur-NW Washington DC 20011

MEYER, NORMA WEINTRAUB, conductor; b. Phila., Dec. 9, 1949; d. Israel and Barbara Gertrude Weintraub; m. Joshua Lee Meyer, June 16, 1968; children: Adam Samuel, Ranaan Louis. MusB in Piano Performance, Phila. Musical Acad., 1968; MusM in Piano Performance, Temple U., 1970. Cert. music tchr. grades K-12 N.J., supr. N.J. Pvt. piano instr., 1965—; music instr. grades K-8 Vare Elem. Sch., Phila., 1974—78; orch. dir. Washington Twp. H.S., Sewell, NJ, 1985—91, 1999—, Chestnut Ridge Middle Sch., Sewell, 1991—99. Mem. solo and ensemble com. N.J. Am. String Tchrs.' Assn., 1985—87. Mem.: NJ Edn. Assn., Music Educators' Nat. Conf., South Jersey Band and Orch. Dirs. (orch. libr., mgr. 1985—2002), Piano 4. Democrat. Jewish. Avocations: fitness. Office: Washington Twp HS 509 Hurffville Cross Keys Rd Sewell NJ 08080

MEYER, PAULETTE ANN, history educator; b. Newport, Oreg., Feb. 20, 1945; d. Paul Merrill and Shirley (Cooper) Billbe; m. Richard John Meyer, Jan. 9, 1965; children: Erika Meyer, Rodrick Meyer. AB in History, Stanford (Calif.) U., 1966, AM in Edn., 1967; PhD, U. Minn., 1997. Cert. secondary tchr., Calif. Instr. world history U. Minn., Mpls., 1992; instr. European intellectual history S.W. State U., Marshall, Minn., 1994; lectr. history of biology, world history Humboldt State U., Arcata, Calif., 1995—2001. Presenter in field. Author: They Met in Zürich-German and Russian Women Physicians, 1997, From 'Uncertifiable' Medical Practice to the Berlin Clinic of Women Doctors: The Medical Career of Franziska Tiburtius, 1999, Maternal Feminism and Physiatrie: Dr. Anna Fischer-Dückelmann (M.D. Zürich, 1896) Critiques German Academic Medicine, 2002, Dr. Marie Zakrzewska (1829-1902) and the Reform of Medical Institutions, 2004. Action chair LWV, Humboldt; bd. suprs. Recreational Trails Com., Humboldt. Fellowship U. Minn., 1989; Nat. Merit scholar. Mem. Western Assn. of Women Historians (sem. presenter 1995), Columbia History of Science Group (seminar presenter 1996). United Methodist. Avocation: training arabian horses. Home: 1615 SE 58th Ave Portland OR 97215-3414 E-mail: meyer@quik.com.

MEYER, PEARL, executive compensation consultant; b. N.Y.C. d. Allen Charles and Rose (Goldberg) Weissman; m. Ira A. Meyer. BA cum laude, postgrad., NYU. Statis. specialist, exec. comp. div. Gen. Foods Corp., White Plains, NY; exec. v.p. and cons. Handy Assocs., Inc., N.Y.C., NY; founder, pres., chair Pearl Meyer & Ptnrs., N.Y.C., NY, 1989—. Lectr. exec. compensation confs. and seminars. Contbr. articles to profl. jours. Recipient Entrepreneurial Woman award, Women Bus. Owners N.Y. Mem.: Pers. Accreditation Inst., Women's Econ. Roundtable, Soc. Human Resources Mgmt. (cert. accredited pers. diplomate), WorldatWork, Am. Mgmt. Assn., Women's Forum, Sky Club, Sedgewood Club, Phi Beta Kappa, Beta Gamma Sigma, Pi Mu Epsilon. Office: Pearl Meyer & Ptnrs 445 Park Ave New York NY 10022-2606

MEYER, PRISCILLA ANN, Russian language and literature educator; b. Aug. 26, 1942; d. Herbert Edward and Marjorie Rose (Wolff) M.; m. William L. Trousdale, Sept. 15, 1974; 1 dau., Rachel V. BA, U. Calif., Berkeley, 1964; MA, Princeton U., 1966; PhD, 1971. Lectr. in Russian lang. and lit. Wesleyan U., Middletown, Conn., 1968-71, asst. prof., 1971-75, assoc. prof., 1975-88, prof., 1988—. Vis. asst. prof. Yale U., 1973, adv. coun. dept. Slavic lang. and lit. Princeton U., 1998-2002. Co-editor: Dostoevsky and Gogol, 1979; editor: Life in Windy Weather (by Andrei Bitov), 1986, author: Find What the Sailor Has Hidden: Vladimir Nabokov's Pale Fire, 1988; co-editor: Essays on Gogol: Logos and the Russian Word, 1992; co-editor: Nabokov's World, 2001; translator stories; mem. editl. bd. Slavic and East European Jour., 1999—; contbr. articles to profl. jours. Scholar Internat. Rsch. and Exch. Bd., 1973; grantee Ford Found., 1964-68, 70; hon. vis. fellow Sch. Slavonic and East European Studies London U., 1997, 2001. Mem. Am. Coun. Tchrs. Russian (dir. 1983-86), Am. Assn. Tchrs. Slavic and East European Studies, Internat. Vladimir Nabokov Soc. (v.p. 1983-85, 2002-04, pres. 1985-87, 2004-), Tolstoi Soc., Dostoevsky Soc., Conn. Acad. Arts and Scis. Office: Russian Dept Wesleyan U Middletown CT 06459-0001 Office Phone: 860-685-3127. E-mail: pmeyer@wesleyan.edu.

MEYER, PUCCI, newspaper editor; b. N.Y.C., Sept. 1, 1944; d. Charles Albert and Lollo (Offer) M.; m. Michael V. McGill, Oct. 28, 2001. BA, U. Wis., 1966. Asst. editor Look mag., N.Y.C., 1970-71, editorial asst. Paris, 1967-69; reporter Newsday, Garden City, L.I., N.Y., 1971-73; style editor N.Y. Daily News Sunday Mag., N.Y.C., 1974-76, assoc. editor, 1977-82, editor, 1983-86; sr. editor Prodigy, White Plains, N.Y., 1987; spl. projects editor N.Y. Post, N.Y.C., 1988-89, style editor, 1990-92, food editor, 1992-93, assoc. features editor, 1993—94, travel editor, 1994—2004. Contbr. articles to various nat. mags. Recipient Pulitzer prize as mem. Newsday investigative team that wrote articles and book The Heroin Trail, 1973.

MEYER, RUTH KRUEGER, museum administrator, educator, art historian; b. Chicago Heights, Ill., Aug. 20, 1940, d. Harold Rohe and Ruth Halbert (Bateman) Krueger; m. Kenneth R. Meyer, June 15, 1963 (div. 1978); 1 child, Karl Augustus BFA, U. Cin., 1963; MA, Brown U., 1968; PhD, U. Minn., 1980. Lectr. Walker Art Ctr., Mpls., 1970—72; instr. U. Cin., 1973—75; curator Contemporary Arts Ctr., Cin., 1976—80; dir. Ohio Found. Arts, Columbus, 1980—83, Taft Mus., Cin., 1983—93; prof. Miyazaki (Japan) Internat. Coll., 1994—2001, Art Acad. Cin., 2002—; sr. curator Solway Gallery, Cin., 2003—. Adj. prof. The Union Inst., Cin., 1994. Pub. Dialogue Mag., Columbus, 1980-83; author: (exhbn. catalogues) Sandy Rosen Vestal Vases, 1986, Oblique Illusion: An Installation by Rick Paul, 1986, David Black an American Sculptor, 1985, Brad Davis: The Pines, 1984, The American Weigh, 1983, New Epiphanies, 1982, (with others) The Tafts Collection: The First Ten Years of Its Development, 1988, The Tafts of Pike St., 1988, (exhbn. catalogue) The History of Travel: Paintings by William Wegman, 1985-90, 1990, The Artist Face to Face: Two Centuries of Self-Portraits from the Paris Collection of Gerald Shurr, 1989, Tributes to the Tafts, 1991, The Taft Museum: Its Collection and Its History, 1995; (with Madeleine Fidell-Beaufort) Collecting in the Gilded Age: Art Patronage in Pittsburgh, 1997, Water de Gruyter BErlin, 2000, others; contbr. articles to profl. jours. Recipient rsch. award Kress Found., 1967, 76; named Chevalier in the Order of Arts and Letters, Govt. of France, 1989. Mem. Internat. Assn. Art Critics, Coll. Art Assn. Democrat. E-mail: ruthkmeyer@yahoo.com.

MEYER, SUSAN MOON, speech language pathologist, educator; b. Hazleton, Pa., Mar. 8, 1949; d. Robert A. and Jane W. (Walters) Moon; m. John C. Meyer Jr., Feb. 16, 1989; children: Chris, Scott. BS, Pa. State U., 1971, MS, 1972; PhD, Temple U., 1983. Cert. tchr., Pa. Speech-lang. pathologist, instr. Elmira (N.Y.) Coll., 1973-74; speech-lang. pathologist Arnot-Ogden Hosp., Elmira, 1973-74; supr. Sacred Heart Hosp. Speech and Hearing Ctr., Allentown, Pa., 1974-75; speech-lang. pathology instr. Kutztown (Pa.) U., 1975-78, asst. prof., 1978-82, assoc. prof., 1982-85, prof., 1985—. Owner Speech and Lang. Svcs., Allentown, 1975-87; cons. Vis. Nurses Assn., Allentown, 1975-85, Home Care, Allentown, 1975-85. Author: Survival Guide for the Beginning Speech-Language Clinician, 1998. Mem. Am. Speech-Lang.-Hearing Assn. (cert., councilor 1986-89, numerous Continuing Edn. awards), Pa. Speech-Lang.-Hearing Assn. (cert., v.p. profl. preparation 1985-89, Appreciation award 1987-89, 2001), Northea. Speech and Hearing Assn. Pa. (pres. 1984-86, Outstanding Dedication award 1985, Honors of the Assn. award 1999), Coun. Suprs. Speech-Lang. Pathology and Audiology. Avocations: family activities, cross-country skiing, British sports cars, reading. Bus. Office: Kutztown U Dept Speech-Lang Kutztown PA 19530 E-mail: smeyer@kutztown.edu.

MEYER, SUSAN M. lawyer; b. 1943; BA in Philosophy and Psychology, Marquette U.; JD, Fordham U. Officer, investigator Washington Met. Police Dept.; gen. counsel Beatrice Consumer Durables, Northbrook, Ill., G.D. Searle & Co., Skokie, Ill.; sr. counsel Beatrice Cos., Inc., Chgo., 1986-91; v.p., sec., dep. counsel Gen. Instrument Corp., Chgo., 1991-98; v.p., sec., gen. counsel United Stationers Inc., Des Plaines, Ill., 1998—. Office: 2200 E Golf Rd Des Plaines IL 60016-1246

MEYERS, ABBEY S. foundation administrator; b. Bklyn., Apr. 11, 1944; m. Jerrold B. Meyers, Oct. 23, 1966; children: David, Adam, Laura. AAS, N.Y.C. Community Coll., 1962; LHD (hon.), Alfred U., 1994. Comml. artist various advt. agys., N.Y.C., 1962-65; dir. patient svcs. Tourette Syndrome Assn., Bayside, N.Y., 1980-85; exec. dir., founder Nat. Org. for Rare Disorders, Danbury, Conn., 1985—, pres. U.S. commr. Nat. Commn. on Orphan Diseases, Washington, 1986-89; mem. subcom. Human Gene Therapy NIH, Bethesda, Md., 1989-92; mem. recombinant DNA adv. com. NIH, 1992-96; mem. Health Care Payor Adv. Commn. on Conn. Commn. on Hosps. and Health Care, 1992-94; mem. FDA Biol. Response Modifiers Com., 1995-99; mem. DHHS Nat. Human Rsch. Protection Adv. Com., 2000-2002. Author: (with others) Orphan Drugs and Orphan Diseases: Clinical Reality and Public Policy, 1983, (with others) Cooperative Approaches to Research and Development of Orphan Drugs, 1985, (with others) Tourette Syndrome: Clinical Understanding and Treatment, 1988, (with others) Physicians Guide to Rare Diseases, 1992. Bd. dirs. Nat. Orphan Drug and Device Found., N.Y.C., 1982-85; leader Coalition to Pass Orphan Drug Act of 1983, 1979-82. Recipient Pub. Health Svc. award HHS, 1985, Commr.'s Spl. citation FDA, 1988. Mem. Nat. Health Coun. (bd. dirs. 1989-94), Alliance of Genetic Support Groups (bd. dirs. 1987-89), European Orgn. for Rare Disorders (hon. pres. 1997—). Avocations: reading, horseback riding. Office: Nat Orgn for Rare Disorders PO Box 1968 Danbury CT 06813-1968 E-mail: orphan@rarediseases.org.

MEYERS, AMY, museum director; m. Jack Meyers; 1 child, Rachel. BA, U. Chgo.; PhD in Am. Studies, Yale U. Rschr. Dumbarton Oaks; rschr. Ctr. for Advanced Study in Visual Arts, Nat. Gallery; curator Am. Art, Henry E. Huntington Libr., Art Collections and Bot. Gardens, San Marino, Calif.; dir. Yale Ctr. for Brit. Art; prof. art Yale U. Adj. faculty Calif. Inst. Tech.; vice chair, Huntington rep. Assn. Rsch. Insts. in History of Art, 1995—2000. Co-editor (with Margaret Pritchard): Empire's Nature: Mark Catesby's New World Vision; co-editor: (with Alan Trachtenberg and Neil Gray Jr.) Classic Essays on Photography. Office: Yale Ctr for Brit Art PO Box 208280 1080 Chapel St New Haven CT 06520-8280

MEYERS, ANN ELIZABETH, sports broadcaster; b. San Diego, Mar. 26, 1955; d. Robert Eugene and Patricia Ann (Burke); m. Donald Scott Drysdale, Nov. 1, 1986; children: Donald Scott Jr., Darren John, Drew Ann. Grad., UCLA, 1978. Profl. basketball player N.J. Gems, 1979-80; profl. basketball player Ind. Pacers NBA, 1979; sports broadcaster Ind. Pacers, 1979-80; sportscaster men's basketball U. Hawaii, Honolulu, 1981-82; sportscaster men's and women's basketball UCLA, 1982-84, 89—; sportscaster volleyball, basketball, softball, tennis ESPN, 1981—; sportscaster Olympic Games ABC, L.A., 1984; sportscaster volleyball, softball, tennis, basketball, soccer Sportsvision, 1985-87; sportscaster volleyball, basketball, softball Prime Ticket, 1985-97; sportscaster CBS-TV, 1991—, ESPN Women's Basketball, Fox Women's Basketball, WNBA-NBC World Championships; sportscaster Olympic Games NBC, Sydney, Australia, 2000. Sportscaster Goodwill Games, WTBS, 1986, 90; sportscaster basketball NBC and ESPN, 1996-97, WNBA, NBA, ESPN, 1996—. Winner Silver medal Montreal Olympics, 1976, Gold medal Pan Am. Games, 1975, Silver medal, 1979, All-Am. UCLA, 1975, 76, 77, 78; 1st woman named to Hall of Fame UCLA, 1987; named to Women's Sports Hall of Fame, 1987, Orange County Sports Hall of Fame, 1985, Calif. H.S. Hall of Fame, 1990, Basketball Hall of Fame, 1993, Nat. H.S. Hall of Fame, 1995, NBC Hoop It Up, 1995, 96, 97, Cath. Youth Orgn. Hall of Fame, 1996, Women's Basketball Hall of Fame, 1999. Office: c/o Lampros and Roberts 16615 Lark Ave Ste 101 Los Gatos CA 95032-7645

MEYERS, CHRISTINE LAINE, marketing and media executive, consultant; b. Detroit, Mar. 7, 1946; d. Ernest Robert and Eva Elizabeth (Laine) M.; 1 child, Kathryn Laine; m. Oliver S. Moore III, May 12, 1990. BA, U. Mich., 1968. Editor indsl. rels. diesel divsn. Gen. Motors Corp., Detroit, 1968; nat. advt. mgr. J.L. Hudson Co., Detroit, 1969-76, mgr. internal sales promotion, 1972-73, dir. pub., 1973-76; nat. advt. mgr. Pontiac Motor divsn., Mich., 1976-78; pres., owner Laine Meyers Mktg. Cos., Inc., Troy, Mich., 1978—; founder, owner CORP! Mag., 1998—. Dir. Internat. Inst. Met. Detroit, Inc. Contbr. articles to profl. publs. Bus. adv. coun. Ctrl. Mich. U., 1977-79; pub. adv. com. on jud. candidates Oakland County Bar Assn.; adv. bd. Birmingham Cmty. Hosp., Bank of Am., 1999-2001; bd. dirs. YMCA, Mich., 1992-98, Haven, 1997—, Automation Alley, Oakland County, 1999—. Named Mich. Ad Woman of Yr., 1976, one of Top 10 Working Women, Glamour mag., 1978, one of 100 Best and Brightest Advt. Age, 1987, one of Mich.'s top 25 female bus. owners Nat. Assn. Women Bus. Owners, One of Top 10 Women Owned Bus., Mich., 1994; recipient Vanguard award Women in Comm., 1986, Lifetime Achievement award Northwood U., 2002. Mem. Internat. Assn. Bus. Communicators, Adcraft Club, Women's Advt. Club (1st v.p. 1975), Women's Econ. Club (pres. 1976-77), Internat. Women's Forum Mich. (founding pres. 1986-97), Internat. Inst. Detroit (bd. dirs. 1986-89), Detroit C. of C., Troy C. of C., Mortar Bd., Quill and Scroll, Pub. Rels. Com. Women for United Found., Founders Soc. Detroit Inst. Arts, Fashion Group, Pub. Rels. Soc. Am., First Soc. Detroit (exec. com. 1970-71), Kappa Tau Alpha. Home: 5165 Longmeadow Rd Bloomfield Hills MI 48304-3657 Office: Laine Meyers Mktg Cos Inc 3645 Crooks Rd Troy MI 48084-1642 Office Phone: 248-458-2677. E-mail: cmyers@corpmagazine.com.

MEYERS, JAN, retired congresswoman; b. Lincoln, Nebr., July 20, 1928; m. Louis Meyers; children: Valerie, Philip AA in Fine Arts cum laude, William Woods Coll., 1948; BA in Communications (hon.), U. Nebr.-Lincoln, 1951; LittD, William Woods Coll., 1986; LLD (hon.), Baker U., 1993. Mem. Overland Park (Kans.) City Coun., 1967-72; pres. Overland (Kans.) Park City Council; mem. Kans. Senate, 1972-84, chmn. pub. health and welfare com., local govt. com.; mem. 99th-103rd Congresses from 3rd Kans. Dist., 1985-97, mem. com. internat. rels., chmn. sml. bus. com., mem. com. on econ. and ednl. opportunities. Chmn. pub. health and welfare com., chmn. local govt. com., vice chmn. transp. com., vice chmn. utilities com. Kans. Senate. 3rd Dist. co-chmn. Bob Dole for U.S. Senate, 1968; chmn. Johnson County Bob Bennett For Gov., 1974; mem. Johnson County Cmty. Coll. Found.; bd. dirs. Johnson County Mental Health Assn.; mem. fundraising com. Johnson County Am. Cancer Soc.; mem. com. for Ctr. for Aging, Kans. U. Med. Ctr.; bd. dirs. Johnson County Libr. Assn. Recipient Outstanding Elected Ofcl. of Yr. award Assn. Cmty. Mental Health Ctrs. Kans., Woman of Achievement Matrix award Women in Communications, Disting. Service award Bus. and Profl. Women Kansas City, William Woods Alumna award of distinction, Cmty. Svc. award Jr. League Kansas City, 1st Disting. Legislator award Kans. Assn. C.C.s, Outstanding Svc. award Kans. Library Assn., United Community Services, Kans. Pub. Health Assn., award Gov.'s Conf. Child Abuse and Neglect, Outstanding Legislator award Kans. Action for Children, Friend award Nat. Assn. County Park and Recreation Ofcls., 1987, Disting. Alumna award, 1991, Spirit of Enterprise award U.S. C. of C., Guardian of Small Bus. award Nat. Fedn. Ind. Bus. Mem. LWV (past pres. Shawnee Mission) Methodist.

MEYERS, LINDA DEE, federal agency administrator; b. Chgo., Dec. 31, 1945; m. L. Richard Meyers; 2 children. BA in Phys. Edn. & Health with honors, Goshen Coll., 1968; MS in Nutrition, Colo. State U., 1974; PhD in Human Nutrition, Cornell U., 1978. Tchr. Swaneng Hill Secondary Sch., 1968-71; staff Bioteko Rural Coop., Serowe, Botswana, 1972; rsch. asst. dept. food sci. and nutrition Colo. State U., 1973-74; scientist Nat. Ctr. Health Statistics HHS, Washington, 1976-78, sr. nutrition advisor, 1986—, dep. dir. & team leader nutrn., environ. hlth. & sci. coord., 1996—; exec. dir., food & nutrition bd. Inst. of Med. of the Nat. Academies, Washington, 2003—. Contbr. articles to profl. jours. Mem. APHA, Am. Soc. Nutritional Scientists, Am. Soc. Clin. Nutrition, Am. Soc. Nutritional Scis., Omicron Nu, Phi Kappa Phi. Office: Inst of Med 500 Fifth St NW Washington DC 20001*

MEYERS, MARLENE O. retired health facility administrator; m. Eugene Meyers; children: Lori, Lisa, Dean. BSN, U. Sask., 1962; postgrad., U. Oslo, Norway, 1973; MSc, U. Calgary, Alta., Can., 1976; continuing edn., Harvard U., 1980, Banff Sch. Mgmt., 1985, U. Western Ont., Can., 1993; EMT-B, Scottsdale C.C., 2000. RN, Ariz. Various nursing positions, Alta. and B.C., Can., 1962-69; instr., chair Mount Royal Coll. Allied Health, Calgary, 1969-82; asst. exec. dir. Rockyview Hosp., Calgary, 1982-85; v.p. patient svcs. Calgary Gen. Hosp., 1985-91, pres., CEO, 1991-95, Meyers and Assocs. Health Care Mgmt. Cons., Calgary, 1995—98; clin. nurse Scottsdale Behavioral Health Ctr., 1999—. Surveyor Can. Coun. on Health Facilities Accreditation, 1986-97; mem. adv. com. for South Caucasus Health info. project, Can. Adv. Com. Named Calgary Woman of Yr. in field of Health, 1982; recipient Heritage of Svc. award, 1992. Mem. Alta. Assn. RNs (hon.), Can. Coll. Health Svcs. Orgn., Can. Exec. Svcs. Orgn., Can. Soc. for Internat. Health (bd. dirs. 1997-2001, South Caucasus adv. com. 2001—), Rotary Internat. Home and Office: 244 Osprey Cir Hope ID 83836-9664 also: 10464 E Cannon Dr Scottsdale AZ 85258-4929

MEYERS, MARSHA LYNN, retired social worker; b. Springfield, Ohio, Dec. 3, 1948; d. Dennis Wathan and Juanita E. (Ratliff) Easterling; m. Wade Trent Meyers, Oct. 5, 1974; children: Lindsay Dionne, Whitney Jane. BA in Sociology, Olivet Nazarene U., 1972. Lic. social worker, Ohio. Formerly social work coord. Mercy Meml. Hosp. and Home Health Care, Urbana, Ohio. Former bd. dirs. Champaign County chpt. Am. Cancer Soc.; mem. adv. bd. Mercy Meml. Hosp. Home Health Care Hospice. Named Social Worker of the Yr. for excellence in small depts. Ohio Soc. Hops. Social Workers, 1995, Social Worker of Yr., Cedarville U. chpt. Phi Alpha Theta, 2000. Mem. Soc. of Hosp. Social Work Dirs., Nat. Assn. Christian Social Workers (past v.p.). Home: 223 College St Urbana OH 43078-2405

MEYERS, MARY ANN, foundation administrator, writer, consultant; b. Sodus, N.Y., Sept. 30, 1937; d. Harold Galpin and Clarice Mildred (Daniel) Dye; m. John Matthew Meyers, Aug. 22, 1959; children: Andrew Christopher, Anne Kathryn. BA magna cum laude, Syracuse U., 1959; MA, U. Pa., 1965, PhD, 1976. Editorial asst. Ladies' Home Jour., Phila., 1959-62; editor, asst. dir. news bur. U. Pa., Phila., 1962-65, asst. to pres., 1973-75, univ. sec., lectr. Am. civilization, 1980-90; contbg. writer The Pennsylvania Gazette, Phila., 1965—97; dir. coll. rels., editor Haverford Horizons, lectr. in religion Haverford (Pa.) Coll., 1977-80; pres. The Annenberg Found., St. Davids, Pa., 1990-92; v.p. for external affairs Moore Coll. Art and Design, Phila., 1995-97; sr. fellow The John Templeton Found., Radnor, Pa., 1997—. Vis. com. dept. biology U. Pa., 1996—2002; mem. bd. advisors The Peter Gruber Found., St. Thomas, U.S. V.I., 2001—. Author: A New World Jerusalem, 1983, Art, Education and African American Culture: Albert Barnes and the Science of Philanthropy, 2004; contbg. author: Death in America, 1975, Gladly Learn, Gladly Teach, 1978, Coping with Serious Illness, 1980, Religion in American Life, 1987; contbr. articles to profl. jours. Judge recognition program Coun. for Advancement and Support Edn., Washington, 1977—78, chair creative editing and writing workshop, 1978; mem. Picker Found. Program on Human Qualities in Medicine, N.Y.C., Phila., 1980—83; del. Phila.-Leningrad Sister Cities Project, 1986; trustee U. Pa. Press., 1985—; vice chmn. U. Pa. 250th Anniversary Commn., 1987—90; mem. steering com. of bd. trustees U. Pa., Annenberg Sch. for Comm., 1990—92; mem. adv. bd. U. Pa., Annenberg Ctr. for the Performing Arts, 1990—98; mem. bd. overseers U. Pa., Sch. Arts and Scis., 1990—97; mem. steering com. of bd. trustees Annenberg Ctr. for Comm., U. So. Calif., L.A., 1990—92, The Annenberg Washington Program in Comm. Policy Studies of Northwestern U., Washington, 1990—92; dir., sec. Am. Acad. Polit. and Social Sci., 1992—, World Affairs Coun. Phila., 1990—93; dir. Diagnostic and Rehab. Ctr., Phila., 1993—2002. Recipient Excellence award Women in Communications, Inc., 1973-74, award for pub. affairs reporting Newsweek/Coun. for Advancement and Support Edn., 1977, Silver medal Coun. for Advancement and Support Edn., 1986. Mem. Am. Acad. Polit. and Social Sci. (sec. and dir. 1992-), Cosmopolitan Club, Sunday Breakfast Club, Phi Beta Kappa (mem. steering com. Delaware Valley chpt. 1995-97). Roman Catholic. Home: 217 Gypsy Ln Wynnewood PA 19096-1112

MEYERS, NANCY JANE, screenwriter, producer, director; b. Phila., Dec. 8, 1949; d. Irving H. and Patricia (Lemisch) M. BA, Am. U., Washington, 1971. Dir.: (films) The Parent Trap, 1998, What Women Want, 2000, Somethings Gotta Give, 2003; prodr.: (films) Private Benjamin (Acad. award nominee, Writers Guild award 1980), Baby Boom, 1987, Father of the Bride, 1991, A Place to be Loved (assoc. prodr.), 1991, I Love Trouble, 1994, Father of the Bride Part II, 1995, Ted Hawkins: Amazing Grace (co-prodr.), 1996, What Women Want, 2000, The Affair of the Necklace, 2001, Something's Gotta Give, 2003; wrote.: (films) Private Benjamin, 1980, Irreconcilable Differences, 1984, Protocol, 1985, Baby Boom, 1987, Father of the Bride, 1991, Once Upon A Crime..., 1992, I Love Trouble, 1994, Father of the Bride Part II, 1995, The Parent Trap, 1998, Something's Gotta Give, 2003. Mem. ASCAP, Acad. Motion Picture Arts and Scis., Writers Guild Am. West. Office: Creative Artists Agy 9830 Wilshire Blvd Beverly Hills CA 90212-1825*

MEYERS, PAMELA SUE, lawyer; b. Lakewood, N.J., June 13, 1951; d. Morris Leon and Isabel (Leibowitz) M.; m. Gerald Stephen Greenberg, Aug. 24, 1975; children: David Stuart Greenberg, Allison Brooke Greenberg. AB with distinction, Cornell U., 1973; JD cum laude, Harvard U., 1976. Bar: N.Y. 1977, Ohio 1990. Assoc. Stroock & Stroock & Lavan, N.Y.C., 1976-80; staff v.p., asst. gen. counsel Am. Premier Underwriters, Inc., Cin., 1980-96; legal counsel Citizens Fed. Bank, Dayton, Ohio, 1997-98; gen. counsel, sec. Mosler Inc., Hamilton, Ohio, 1998—2001. Bd. dirs. Hamilton County Alcohol and Drug Addiction Svc. Bd., 1996-2000, Adath Israel Synagogue, 1999—. Mem. Cin. Bar Assn., Harvard Club of Cin. (pres. 1998-99, bd. dirs. 1993-2000), Phi Beta Kappa. Jewish. Avocations: piano, reading, tennis. Home: 3633 Carpenters Creek Dr Cincinnati OH 45241-3824 E-mail: psmeyers@fuse.net.

MEYERSON, BARBARA TOBIAS, elementary school educator; b. Rockville Centre, N.Y., May 17, 1928; d. Sol and Hermine (Sternberg) Tobias; m. Daniel Meyerson, Sept. 4, 1962 (dec. Apr. 1989); children: George D., Barbara Meyerson Ayers. BEd, SUNY, New Paltz, 1948; postgrad., NYU, Hofstra U. Tchr. kindergarten Dix Hills (N.Y.) pub. schs., Hicksville (N.Y.) pub. schs., Valley Stream (N.Y.) pub. schs.; tchr. 6th grade Flushing (N.Y.) Bd. Edn. Dist. commr. Boy Scouts Am., mem. tng. staff, organizer new units; founder, sec. Repertory Theatre, Rio Rancho, N.Mex.; bd. dirs. Italian Am. Assn., Rio Rancho; vol. Rio Rancho City Hall Pub. Offices; vol. reading and spl. edn. classes Rio Rancho Pub. Schs; chmn. Rio Rancho Park and Recreation Bd. Commrs.; dep. publicity chmn. State of N.Mex., Mayor's Task Force City Honorees, 2003-04. Mem. ACE, VFW Aux. (pres. dist. 11), United Fedn. Tchrs. Home: 6127 Cottontail Rd NE Rio Rancho NM 87124-1545 E-mail: barbtobias@aol.com.

MEZACAPA, EDNA S. music educator, elementary school educator; b. Flint, MI, Jan. 23, 1948; d. Jack E. and Vlasta A. Tremayne; m. Nicklas A. Mezacapa, July 25, 1970; children: Amy Anne, Sara Marie. MusB, Heidelberg Coll., Tiffin, Ohio, 1970. Gen. music tchr. Bellevue (Ohio) City Schs., 1969—73; youth choir dir. Findlay Episc. Ch., Findlay, Ohio, 1975—78; subs. tchr. Rochester (N.Y.) Schs., 1979—81; youth choir dir. Ch. of the Epiphany, Rochester, 1979—81; music tchr., K-8 St. Mary's Cath. Sch., Kalamazoo, 1981—82, St. Ludmila Cath. Sch., Cedar Rapids, Iowa, 1984—86; tchr. Christian edn. Calvary Episc. Ch., Rochester, Minn., 1986—87; subs. music tchr., 1-6 Rochester City Schs., Rochester, Minn., 1988—90, music tchr., 1-6, 1990—. Dir. Calvary Episc. Youth Choir, 1995—96, Suzuki Orch., 2001—03. Dir. youth choir Calvary Episcopal Ch., 1996—97; dir. Suzuki Orch., 2001—03.

MICEK, ISABELLE, music educator; b. Shelby, Nebr., July 28, 1922; d. Thomas Adolph and Julia Lucy (Triba) M. MusB in Piano Performance, St. Louis Inst. Music, 1943; postgrad., Peabody Conservatory, 1971; MusM in Piano Pedagogy, St. Louis Inst. Music, 1972. Instrumental/vocal tchr. various elem. and secondary schs., Hull, Ill., 1943-45, Oakland, Iowa, 1945-46; pvt. piano/vocal/theory instr. Columbus, Nebr., 1946—. Participated internat. workshops, Honolulu, 1980, Calgary, 1990, Graz, Austria, 2000. Pres. N.E. Dist. Nebr. Music Tchrs. Assn., 1949-56, Cmty. Concert Assn., Columbus, 1965-67; advisor Birthright Columbus, 1992—. Recipient Medallion of Merit award Art Publ. Soc., St. Louis, 1957; scholar U. Mexico, Mexico City, 1950, Royal Conservatory, London, 1952, Staatlichen Hochschule, Munich, 1963, St. Cecilia Conservatory, Rome, 1966, Manuel de Falla Conservatore, Buenos Aires, 1974. Mem. Music Tchrs. Nat. Assn., Nebr. Music Tchrs. Assn., Nat. Guild (adjudicator 1993-98). Democrat. Roman Catholic. Avocations: gardening, reading, concerts, speaker for modern problems high school classes. Home: 2115 18th St Columbus NE 68601-4531

MICHAEL, CAROL M. utilities executive, consultant; b. Hermiston, Oreg., Mar. 16, 1938; d. Delbert and Lois Eilene Mackan; m. Robert J. Michael, June 8, 1956; 1 child, Lee Eric. BA in Bus. and Coms., Eastern Washington U., 1988; MA in Applied Behavioral Sci., Leadership Inst. of Seattle, 1992. Cert. mgr., Inst. Cert. Profl. Mgrs. Sec. GE Co., Richland, Wash., 1955-66, Battelle-N.W., Richland, Wash., 1966-70; adminstrv. asst. Westinghouse Hanford, Richland, Wash., 1970-73, adminstrv. mgr., 1973-77, Wash. Pub. Power Supply Sys., Richland, Wash., 1977-83, quality cons.,

1985-96; total quality mgr. Brownsville (Tex.) Pub. Utilities Bd., 1996—2002. Contract cons. U. Tex., Brownsville, 1998—2001. Facilitator City of Brownsville, 1997—, Cameron County, Harlingen, Tex., 1997-99. Named Woman of Yr. Bus. and Profl. Women's Orgn., State of Wash., 1972. Mem. Assn. for Quality and Participation, ASTD, Assn. for Records Mgrs. and Adminstrs. Avocations: fishing, shopping. Home: 950 S Garcia St Unit 321 Port Isabel TX 78578-4018 Office: 950 S Garcia # 321 Port Isabel TX 78578

MICHAEL, DOROTHY ANN, nursing administrator, naval officer; b. Lancaster, Pa., Sept. 20, 1950; d. Richard Linus and Mary Ruth (Hahn) M.; m. Juan Roberto Morales, July 15, 1995. Diploma, RN, Montgomery Hosp. Sch. Nursing, Norristown, Pa., 1971; BSN, George Mason U., 1980; MSN, U. Tex. Health Sci. Ctr., 1985. Commd. ensign USN, 1970, advanced through grades to capt. Nurse Corps, 1994, staff nurse Nat. Naval Med. Ctr., 1971-73, charge nurse Naval Hosp. Guantanamo Bay, Cuba, 1973-74, charge nurse Naval Regional Med. Ctr. Phila., 1974-76, charge nurse Naval Hosp. Keflavik, Iceland, 1977, Bethesda, Md., 1980-84; sr. nurse, asst. officer-in-charge Br. Med. Clinic Naval Weapons Ctr., China Lake, Calif., 1986-89; coord. quality assurance Naval Hosp., Oakland, Calif., 1989-92, assoc. dir. inpatient nursing, 1992-93; divsn. officer USNS Mercy, Persian Gulf, 1990-91; assoc. dir. surg. nursing Naval Hosp., Oakland, 1993-95, dir. nursing svc. Great Lakes, Ill., 1995-98; dep. comdr. Naval Ambulatory Care Ctr., Newport, R.I., 1998-2001; ret. Splty. advisor to dir. Navy Nurse Corp., Navy Med. Command, Washington, 1983-84. V.p. Deepwood Homeowners Assn., Reston, Va., 1978-82; advisor, com. mem. Reston Found., 1979. Decorated Navy Commendation medal, Meritorious Svc. medal, Legion of Merit; recipient R.W. Bjorklund Mgmt. Innovator award, Kern County, Calif., 1988, Comdr.'s award for outstanding professionalism in pub. health support, 1988. Mem. VFW, Vietnam Vets. Am., Am. Legion, Sigma Theta Tau. Roman Catholic. Home: 3324 Susquehanna Rd Dresher PA 19025 E-mail: dotjuan@aol.com.

MICHAEL, MARILYN CORLISS, music educator, mezzo soprano; d. Charles Bernard and Peggy Clarice Michael. MusB in Voice, U. Kans., 1976, MusM in Vocal Performance, 1977; EdD in Curriculum and Instrn., U. Sarasota, Argosy U., 2002. Instr. voice U. Kans., Lawrence, 1976—77, dir. vocal program Midwest Music and Art Camp, 1976—77; prof. voice Eckerd Coll., St. Petersburg, Fla., 1980—88; prof. voice, opera and humanities St. Petersburg Coll., 1994—, dir. Summer Vocal Inst., 2003—. Dir. music, organist Chapel By-the-Sea, Clearwater Beach, Fla., 1980—. Singer: (vocal performer) Carnegie Hall debut as mezzo-soprano soloist in, (cd vocal recording on Erasmus label) Von ewiger Liebe, and other songs by Johannes Brahms, (opera vocal competition) Suncoast Opera Guild (1st Pl. winner, 1980), (soloist with Fla. Orch.) Mahler Symphony no. 2, Julius Rudel conducting, (soloist with London Bach Choir) Mozart Requiem American tour with Sir David Willcocks conducting, (soloist with Stuttgart Sommerfest) mezzo soloist with Bach Cantatas with Helmuth Rilling conducting, (recital soloist) Lieder recitals at Toynbee Hall, London, England. Mem.: Am. Guild Organists, Opera Am., Nat. Assn. Teachers of Singing, Pinellas Opera League, Pi Kappa Lambda, Phi Kappa Phi. Conservative. Roman Catholic. Achievements include research in Songs by Women Composers; development of Summer Vocal Institute in collaboration with leading Metropolitan Opera tenor, Enrico di Giuseppe; design of honors humanities curriculum utilizing Multiple Intelligences. Avocations: swimming, dogs, antiques. Home: 2935 Robinwood Ln Palm Harbor FL 34684 Office: St Petersburg Coll 6605 5th Ave N Saint Petersburg FL 33710 E-mail: michaelm@spcollege.edu.

MICHAEL, NOREEN, commissioner, educator; Commr. of edn. Virgin Islands Dept. Edn., Charlotte, 2002—. Office: Commr of Education 44-46 Kongena Gade St Thomas VI 00802

MICHAEL, SANDRA DALE, biomedical educator, biomedical researcher; b. Sacramento, Jan. 23, 1945; d. Gordon G. and Ruby F. (Johnson) M.; m. Dennis P. Murr, Aug. 12, 1967 (div. 1974). BA, Calif. State Coll., Sonoma, 1967; PhD, U. Calif., Davis, 1970. NIH predoctoral fellow U. Calif., Davis, 1967-70, NIH postdoctoral fellow, 1970-73, asst. rsch. geneticist, 1973-74; asst. prof. SUNY, Binghamton, 1974-81, assoc. prof., 1981-88, prof. reproductive endocrinology, 1988—, dept. chair, 1992-2000. Adj. prof. dept. ob-gyn. SUNY Upstate Med. U., Syracuse; mem. NIH Reproductive Endocrinology Study Sect., 1991-95; cons., presenter in field; grant reviewer NIH, NSF, USDA and others. Mem. editl. bd. Reproductive Biology and Endocrinology, Am. Jour. Reproductive Immunology; contbr. articles to profl. jours. Vice chair Tri Cities Opera Guild, Binghamton, 1987-90, chair, 1990-92; mem. Harpur Forum, Binghamton, 1987—, SUNY Found., Binghamton, 1990-96. Fulbright Sr. scholar Czech Republic, 1994; grantee NIMH, 1976-79, Nat. Cancer Inst., 1977-80, 83-87, Nat. Inst. Environ. Health Scis., 1979-80, NSF, 1981-83, NIH, 1987—. Fellow: AAAS; mem.: N.Y. Acad. Sci., Soc. for Exptl. Biology and Medicine, Women in Endocrinology, Am. Soc. for Immunology of Reprodn. (editl. bd.), Soc. for Study of Fertility, Soc. for Study of Reprodn., Endocrine Soc., Sigma Xi. Avocations: golf, skiing, bridge, opera, literature. Office: Binghamton U Dept Biol Scis Binghamton NY 13902 E-mail: smichael@binghamton.edu.

MICHAELS, CINDY WHITFILL (CYNTHIA G. MICHAELS), educational consultant; b. Plainview, Tex., Aug. 31, 1951; d. Glenn Tierce and Ruby Jewell (Nichols) Whitfill; m. Terre Joe Michaels, July 16, 1977. BS, W. Tex. State U., 1972; MS, U. Tex., Dallas, 1976; postgrad. cert., E. Tex. State U., 1982; grad., Garland Citizens Police Acad., 2000. Registered profl. ednl. diagnostician Tex., cert. supr. gen. and spl. edn., elem. edn. tchr., K-8 English tchr., spl. edn. tchr. generic and mental retardation Tex. Gen. and spl. edn. tchr. Plano (Tex.) Ind. Sch. Dist., 1972-76; dependents' sch. tchr. U.S. Dept. Def., Office of Overseas Edn., Schweinfurt, Germany, 1976-77; asst. dir. edn. dept. spl. edn. Univ. Affiliated Ctr., U. Tex., Dallas, 1977-80; asst. to acting dir. edn., dept. pediat., Southwestern Med. Sch. Univ. Affiliated Ctr., U. Tex. Health Sci. Ctr., Dallas, 1980-82; dir. Collin County Spl. Edn. Coop., Wylie, Tex., 1982-89; dir. spl. svcs. Terrell (Tex.) Ind. Sch. Dist., 1989-92; cons. for at-risk svcs. instrnl. svcs. dept. Region 10 Edn. Svc. Ctr., Richardson, Tex., 1992-93, cons. for staff devel., 1993-95; cons. Title I Svcs., 1995-96; ind. rep. Am. Comm. Network, 1995—; owner Strategic Out-Source Svcs., Garland, Tex., 1996—. Regional cons., presenter, spkr. Region 10 Adminstrs. Spl. Edn., Dallas, 1982—92; grant reviewer Tex. Edn. Agy., Austin, 1984, state conf. presenter, spkr., 92, Tex. Assn. Bus. Sch. Bds., Houston, 1991; cons. S.W. regional tng. program educators U. So. Miss., 1992—93; regional coord. HS mock trial competition State Bar Tex., 1993; regional liaison Tex. Elem. Mentor Network, 1993—96; state presenter Tex. Vocat. Educators Conf., 1994; ednl. cons. Strategic Outsource Svcs., 1996—. Active Dance-A-Thon United Cerebral Palsy, Dallas, 1986; area marcher March of Dimes, Dallas, 1990, Park Cities Walkathon Multiple Sclerosis, 1994, 1995; bd. dirs. New Beginnings Ctr. Domestic Violence Agy., 2001—. Named Outstanding Young Women in Am., 1981; grantee, Tex. Edn. Agy., 1990—92, Job Tng. & Partnership Act, 1991, Carl Perkins Vocat. Program, 1991. Mem.: Tex. Coun. Adminstrs. Spl. Edn. (region 10 chairperson 1985—87, state conf. presenter 1989, 1992), Garland Citizens Police Acad. Alumnae, Alpha Delta Pi (Richardson alumnae, philanthropy chair 1988, v.p. 1989—91, 1994—2000, v.p., sec. 1993—94). Avocations: aerobics, skiing, travel, dance. Home: 2613 Oak Point Dr Garland TX 75044-7809 also: 232 Broadmoor Alto NM 88312

MICHAELS, HELENE, broadcast executive; m. Geoffrey De Stefano, 2000. Pres. Columbia Tristar TV, Culver City, Calif. Office: Columbia Tristar TV 9336 Washington Blvd Culver City CA 90232-2628

MICHAELS, JENNIFER TONKS, foreign language educator; b. Sedgley, England, May 19, 1945; d. Frank Gordon and Dorothy (Compston) Tonks; m. Eric Michaels, 1973; children: Joseph, David, Ellen. MA, U. Edinburgh, 1967, McGill U., 1971, PhD, 1974. Teaching asst. German dept. Wesleyan U., 1967-68; instr. German dept. Bucknell (Pa.) U., 1968-69; teaching asst. German dept. McGill U., Can., 1969-72; prodn. asst. Pub. TV News and Polit. program, Schenectady, N.Y., 1974-75; from asst. prof. to assoc. prof. Grinnell (Iowa) Coll., 1973-87, prof., 1987—. Vis. cons. German dept. Hamilton Coll., 1981; cons. Modern Lang. dept. Colby Coll.; panelist NEH, 1985; spkr. in field. Author: D.H. Lawrence, The Polarity of North and South, 1976, Anarchy and Eros: Otto Gross' Impact on German Expressionist Writers, 1983, Franz Jung: Expressionist, Dadaist, Revolutionary and Outsider, 1989, Franz Werfel and the Critics, 1994; contbr. numerous articles, revs. to profl. jours. Mem. MLA, Am. Assn. Tchrs. of German, Soc. Exile Studies, German Studies Assn. (sec. treas. 1991-92, v.p. 1992-94, pres. 1995-96, numerous coms.). Democrat. Avocations: music, travel, reading. Office: Grinnell Coll German Dept PO Box 805 Grinnell IA 50112-0805 E-mail: michaels@grinnell.edu.

MICHAELS, MARION CECELIA, newswriter, editor, news syndicate executive; b. Black River Falls, Wis. d. Leonard N. and Estelle O. (Payne) Doud; m. Charles Webb (div.); children: Charles, David, Robert; m. Mark J. Michaels (div.); 1 child, Merry A. Student, MIT, 1962-64, U. Wis., 1971-76, BS in Bus. Edn., 1978, MS in Spl. Edn., 1981. Mgr., instr. bus. program Blackwell Job Corps Ctr., 1987-89; mgr. Michaels Secretarial Svc., Black River Falls, Wis., 1979-83; columnist, editor Michaels News, Black River Falls, 1983—, pres., 1989—. Hon. appt. rsch. bd. advisors Am. Biog. Inst., 1996-2001. Author: The Little Cowboy: Pursuing Dana's Dream, 1998, September's Song, 2003—, Dana's Dream, 2004; columnist Single Parenting, 1983—94, Parenting Plus, 1990—, editor, contbr. (column) Surviving Single, 1990—95, To Read or Not, 1985—2004, Report From Planet Earth, 1985—2004, Travel Tidbits, 1991—95, Surviving Sane, 1995—98. Chmn. Brockway Cmty. Orgn., 1969-71; chair, counselor Brockway Youth Group, 1970-72; chmn. labor com. Dem. Platform Com., Wis., 1975-76; candidate State Assembly, 1978, 82; co-founder Franklin Delano Roosevelt Meml., 1997; mem. LWV. Named to Internat. Poetry Hall of Fame, 1997. Mem.: Assn. Rsch. and Enlightenment, Physicians for Social Responsibility, Union Concerned Scientists, Internat. Soc. Poets (Poet of Yr. nominee 1997, 1999, Internat. Poet of Merit award 1999, Poet of Yr. nominee 2000, 2001, 2002, 2003), Women's History Mus. (charter mem.), Wilson Ctr., League of Conservation Voters, Inst. for Noetic Sci., Amnesty Internat., Pub. Citizen, Am. United, Nat. Parks, Clean Wis., So. Poverty Law Ctr., Natural Resources Def. Coun., Co-op Am., Nat. Trust for Pub. Edn., Friends of the Earth, Peale Ctr. for Positive Living, Nat. Com. to Protect Soc. Security and Medicare, Common Cause, Internat. Fund for Animals, Phi Delta Kappa, Pi Omega Pi. Avocations: singing, dance, walking, swimming.

MICHALAK, MELANIE S. music educator; d. Richard F. and Sue T. Michalak. Diploma in Ethnomusicology and Polish Studies, Jagiellonian U., Krakow, Poland, 1975; MusB, Coll. of Mt. St. Joseph, Cin., 1976; MusM, DePaul U., Chgo., 1982. Cert. music, English and drama tchr. Ill., 1976, dressage L judge U.S. Dressage Fedn., 1994. Jr. high music tchr. St. Jude The Apostle Sch., South Holland, Ill., 1978—80; choral dir., music master tchr. & lab program supr. DePaul U. Lab Sch. Project at Oscar Mayer Sch., Chg., 1980—82; dir. of choral music Evergreen Park Cmty. H.S., Ill., 1982—. Author of ednl. publs. Chgo. Symphony Orch., 1990—93; mus. freestyle composer, designer, and choreographer, Tinley Park, Ill. Author (and photographer): (educational film) The Polish-American Experience: A Legacy of Honor; author: (and designer) Chgo. Symphony Orch. Youth Concerts Guide For Teachers, musical freestyle performance articles; co-author: THE BEAT Chgo. Symphony Orchestra Youth Concert Guides for Students; conductor & composer (CD) A Concert Of Gratitude - Hawaii, conductor & arranger (CD) EPCHS Madrigals: A Musical Journey. Past pres. S.W. Polish Soc., Chgo., 1982—87; sec. Homeowners' Assn., Tinley Park, Ill., 1999—2003. Named Outstanding Music Educator, World of Music Festivals, 1994; named one of Women In Am. Music: Role Models of Creativity, U. Wis., Madison, 1993; recipient Lifetime Achievement award, S.W. Polish Soc., 1984; honored for Preservation of The Italian Madrigal, Mayor of Florence, Italy, 1999. Mem.: Evergreen Park Tchrs. Union, Ill. Choral Dirs. Assn., Ill. Music Educators Assn., Ill. Dressage and Combined Tng. Assn. (numerous awards), U.S. Dressage Assn. (awards 1989, 1994, 1995). Avocations: dressage competitor, dressage competition judge, author, composer and arranger. Office: Evergreen Park Cmty HS 9901 S Kedzie Ave Evergreen Park IL 60805 Personal E-mail: MSMmusic@sbcglobal.net. E-mail: mmichalak@evergreenpark.org.

MICHALEK, SUZANNE M. biology educator; b. Chgo., July 19, 1944; BS, Ill. State U., 1967, MS, 1968; PhD in Microbiology, U. Ala., 1976. Rsch. asst. microbiology and immunology Nat. Inst. Dental Rsch. NIH, Bethesda, Md., 1972-76, fellow microbiology and immunology, 1977-79; investigator Inst. Dental Rsch. U. Ala., Birmingham, 1980-85, scientist, 1985—, sr. investigator Rsch. Ctr. Oral Biology, 1988—. Mem. Am. Soc. Microbiology, Am. Assn. Immunologists, Internat. Assn. Dental Rsch., Am. Assn. Dental Rsch., Soc. Exptl. Biology and Medicine. Office: U Ala Rsch Ctr in Oral Biology Bbrb 258 845 S 19th St Birmingham AL 35294-0001

MICHALS, LEE MARIE, travel agency administrator; b. Chgo., June 6, 1939; d. Harry Joseph and Anna Marie (Monaco) Perzan; children: Debora Ann, Dana Lee, Jami. BA, Wright Coll., 1959. Cert. travel specialist and cons., destination specialist. Internat. travel sec. E.F. MacDonald Travel, Palo Alto, Calif., 1963-69; pres. Travel Experience, Santa Clara, Calif., 1973-88; ptnr. Cruise Connection, Mountain View, Calif., 1983-85; travel specialist Allways Travel, Sunnyvale, Calif., 1992-98; adminstrv. asst. Ventures Extraordinaire, Inc., San Mateo, Calif., 1998—. Former stars rep. Hertz, Ritz Carlton, Marriott Hotels, various airlines and tour cos. Mem. Am. Soc. Travel Agts., Inst. Cert. Travel Agts., Bay Area Travel Assn., Pacific Area Travel Agts., San Jose Women in Travel (organizing pres. 1971, 1st v.p. 1989, del. to internat. fedn. women's travel orgn. 1997-99). Office: Sutter Travel 693 E Remington Dr #A Sunnyvale CA 94087

MICHALSKI, JEANNE ANN, human resources professional; b. Tampa, Fla., Nov. 7, 1958; d. Enrique and Mary Ellen (Bandi) Escarraz; m. Michael John Michalski, Nov. 24, 1984. BA in Psychology, U. South Fla., 1979, MA in Indsl. Psychology, 1983, PhD in Indsl. Psychology, 1990. Human resource coord. GTE Data Svcs., Tampa, 1984-86, mgmt. cons., 1986-87, mgr. human resource planning, employment office, 1987-88, mgr. human resource, 1988-89; mgr. testing and performance mgmt. GTE Telephone Ops., Irving, Tex., 1989-90, mgr. continuity planning and performance mgmt., 1990-94; asst. v.p. human resources planning Burlington No., Fort Worth, 1994-95; asst. v.p. staffing and devel. Burlington No. Santa Fe, Fort Worth, 1995—. Cons. Herb Meyer Assocs./TECO, Tampa, 1983-84, Mail Prescriptions, Tampa, 1989-90. Campaign worker Dem. state legislator election, St. Petersburg, Fla., 1980; mem. Polit. Action Com., Irving, 1989-90. Grad. fellowship scholar U. South Fla., 1979. Mem. APA, Soc. for Indsl./Orgnl. Psychologists, Dallas/Ft. Worth Indsl. Orgn. Psychologist Group, Human Resource Planning Soc. Roman Catholic. Home: 505 Woodland Trl Keller TX 76248-2634 Office: Burlington No 3000 Continental Plz Fort Worth TX 76161

MICHAUD, NORMA ALICE PALMER, paralegal, real estate investor; b. Concord, N.H., May 6, 1946; d. Leon Charles and Goldie May (Maxfield) Palmer (both dec.); m. Bob Michaud, July 21, 1973; 1 child, Derrick Charles. AAS in Bus. Mgmt., Mississippi County C.C., 1994; student, State Tech., Memphis, 1994-99. With United Life & Accident Ins. Co., Concord, N.H., 1965-68, 71-74; data processor Blue Cross/Blue Shield, Concord, 1968-71; with Daniel Law Firm, 1994—95, Walter Lee Bailey & Assocs., 1996—98, Shuttleworth, Williams, Harper, Waring & Derrick, 1999; adminstr. U.S. Govt., 1972—2003, Bogin, Munns & Munns, 2004; house renovator, real estate owner Blytheville, Ark., 1986—. Mem. Bus. Profls. Am. (chpt. v.p. 1994), Phi Theta Kappa. Methodist. Avocations: reading, painting, travel. Home: 14626 Gateway Pointe Cir Apt 14201 Orlando FL 32821 5166

MICHEL, AIMEE KATHERINE, theater director, educator; b. Baton Rouge, La., Mar. 12, 1962; d. Melvin Maurice Michel and Elizabeth Nell Dubus; m. John Kevin Lawson, Oct. 28, 2001; 1 child, Sebastian Louis. BA with honors in French & Theatre, La. State U., 1985; MFA in Theatre Directing, Tulane U., 1990. Assoc. artistic dir. Playmakers Profl. Theatre, Baton Rouge, 1990—93; dir. apprentice program Actors Theatre of Louisville, Louisville, 1993—94; artistic dir. The Drama League, N.Y.C., NY, 1994—96, The Shakespeare Festival at Tulane, New Orleans, 1996—. Freelance theatre dir., various, 1990—. Dir.: (plays) various Shakespearean. Fellow Foreign Study fellow, Coun. for Devel. of French, 1980, The Dirs. Project fellow, The Drama League, 1990, Boris Segal fellow, Williamstown Theatre Festival, 1990. Avocations: gardening, reading, walking.

MICHEL, ELIZABETH CHENEY, social reform consultant; b. Pitts., Feb. 11, 1951; d. George Philip and Charlotte Elizabeth (Cowser) Cheney; m. Raymond Joseph Michel, Oct. 21, 1973 (div. June 1997); children: Keith Raymond, Grant Petersen. BA, Rollins Coll., 1973; M in Comm., U. Ctrl. Fla., 1988, PhD, 1992. Vis. prof. Univ. Ctrl. Fla., Orlando, Fla., 1989-92; assoc. prof., chair comm. program Mars Hill (N.C.) Coll., 1993-99; comms. cons., v.p. Comms. Strategies-Healthcare.com, Corp., 1999-2000; dir. change mgmt. Ga. Tech. Authority, 2001—. Pres. Kairos Commn. Strategies, Atlanta, 1998—; bd. dirs. Biltmore Inst., 1997—, cons., 1996—; bd. dirs. Commn. on Industries of the Mind, Atlanta; vice-chair 21st Century Comm., 1996—; project coord. for joint comm. with Chinese Acad. Social Scis., China; del. to Consortium for Global Edn., China, 1998; vis. prof. comm. Kennesaw State U.; mem. internat. del. to Conf. on Environ. Sustainability, Shanghai, 2000, Implementation Strategies for SMEs, Networking 2000, Paris, 2000; v.p. Systems and Strategies; mem. bd. advisor Atlantic U. Chinese Medicine, 2000—, chair bd. dirs., 2001—. Author: 4 Simple Steps to Communications that Connect! and Kairos Community Strategies Interactive CD-ROM, 2000; chief editor: An Orchestra of Voices: Making the Argument for Press and Speech Freedom in the People's Republic of China, 2000; contbr. articles to mag. Bd. dirs. Atlanta Women's Network, 2000—01. Internat. Rsch. grant Appalachian Coll. Assn., 1994, 96, 97, Mellon Found., 1994, 95, 96, 97; Vis. Rsch. fellow Chinese Acad. Social Scis., 1996, 97. Mem.: Women's Network, Brit. Am. Bus. Group, Am. Educators Journalism and Mass Comm., Nat. Comm. Assn., Atlanta Coun. on Internat. Rels., Dem. Women's forum, Metro Atlanta C. of C., Women's Commerce Club, Ga. Exec. Women's Network, Atlanta Women's Network-Strategic Planning, Kappa Delta Phi, Phi Kappa Phi. Presbyterian. Avocations: acting. music, postmodernism, drawing.

MICHEL, MARY ANN KEDZUF, nursing educator; b. Evergreen Park, Ill., June 1, 1939; d. John Roman and Mary Kedzuf; m. Jean Paul Michel, 1974. Diploma in nursing, Little Company of Mary Hosp., Evergreen Park, 1960; BSN, Loyola U., Chgo., 1964; MS, No. Ill. U., 1968, EdD, 1971. Staff nurse Little Co. of Mary Hosp., 1960-64; instr. Little Co. of Mary Hosp. Sch. Nursing, 1964-67, No. Ill. U., DeKalb, 1968-69, asst. prof., 1969-71; chmn. dept. nursing U. Nev., Las Vegas, 1971-73, prof. nursing, 1975—, dean Coll. Health Scis., 1973-90; pres. PERC, Inc.; mgmt. cons., 1993—95. Mgmt. cons. Nev. Donor Network, 1993; mem. So. Nev. Health Manpower Task Force, 1975; mem. manpower com. Plan Devel. Commn., Clark County Health Sys. Agy., 1977-79, mem. governing body, 1981-86; mem. Nev. Health Coordinating Coun., Western Inst. Nursing, 1971-85; mem. coordinating com. assembly instnl. adminstrs. dept. allied health edn. and accreditation AMA, 1985-88; mem. bd. advisors So. Nev. Vocat. Tech. Ctr., 1976-80; sec.-treas. Nev. Donor Network, 1988-89, chmn. bd., 1988-90. Contbr. articles to profl. jours. Trustee Desert Spring Hosp., Las Vegas, 1976-85; bd. dirs. Nathan Adelson Hospice, 1982-88, Bridge Counseling Assocs., 1982, Everywoman's Ctr., 1984-86; chair Nev. Commn. on Nursing Edn., 1972-73, Nursing Articulation Com., 1972-73, Yr. of Nurse Com., 1978; moderator Invitational Conf. Continuing Edn., Am. Soc. Allied Health Professions, 1978; mgmt. cons. Nev. Donor Network, 1994-95, Donor Organ Recovery Svc., Transplant Recipient Internat. Orgn., S.W. Eye Bank, S.W. Tissue Bank. Named Outstanding Alumnus, Loyola U., 1983; NIMH fellow, 1967-68. Fellow Am. Soc. Allied Health Professions, 1991, (chair nat. resolutions com. 1981-84, treas. 1988-90, sec's. award com. 1982-83, 92-93, nat. by-laws com. 1985, conv. chair 1987); mem. AAUP, Am. Nurses Assn., Nev. Nurses Assn. (dir. 1975-77, treas. 1977-79, conv. chair 1978), So. Nev. Area Health Edn. Coun., Western Health Deans (co-organizer 1985, chair, 1988-90), Nat. League Nursing, Nev. Heart Assn., So. Nev. Mem. Hosps. (nursing recruitment com. 1981-83, mem. nursing practice com. 1983-85), Las Vegas C. of C. (named Woman of Yr. Edn.) 1988, Slovak Catholic Sokols, Phi Kappa Phi (chpt. sec. 1981-83, pres.-elect 1983, pres. 1984, v.p. Western region 1989-95, editl. bd. jour. Nat. Forum 1989-93), Alpha Beta Gamma (hon.), Sigma Theta Tau, Zeta Kappa. Office: U Nev Las Vegas 4505 S Maryland Pky Las Vegas NV 89154-9900

MICHELINI, SYLVIA HAMILTON, auditor; b. Decatur, Ala., May 16, 1946; d. George Borum and Dorothy Rose (Swatzell) Hamilton; m. H. Stewart Michelini, June 4, 1964; children: Stewart Anthony, Cynthia Leigh. BSBA summa cum laude, U. Ala., Huntsville, 1987. CPA, Ala.; cert. govt. fin. mgr., fraud examiner. Acct. Ray McCay, CPA, Huntsville, 1987-88; auditor Def. Contract Audit Agy., Huntsville, 1989-92; auditor-office of inspector general George C. Marshall Space Flight, Center, Ala., 1992-97; contr. Hamilton Hotels, Inc., 1997-2001. Exec. bd. Decatur City PTA, 1976-78; pres., v.p. Elem. Sch. PTA, Decatur, 1977-79; leader Girl Scouts U.S. and Cub Scouts, Decatur, 1972-77; active local ARC, 1973-77. Mem. AICPA, AAUW (chpt. treas. 1988-90), Nat. Assn. Accts. (dir. community svc. 1987-88, v.p. adminstrn. and fin. 1988-89, pres. 1989-90, nat. com. on ethics 1990-91), Nat. Notary Asns., Am. Soc. Women Accts. (chpt. treas. 1989-90, dir. chpt. devel. 1989-90), Assn. Govt. Accts. (sec. 1992-93, chmn. pub. rels. 1993-94), Ala. Soc. CPAs (profl. ethics com. 1993-94), Inst. Internal Auditors (dir. awards and recognition 1996-97, sec. 1999-2001, 2003—), Inst. Mgmt. Accts. (v.p. comms., dir. program book 1991-94, Dixie coun. dir. newsletters 1992-93, dir. ednl. programs 1992-93, 93-94, nat. com. ethics, 1990-97, nat. fin. com. 1997-98), Ala. Soc. CPAs (govtl. acctg. and auditing com. 1994-95), Inst. Mgmt. Accts. (nat. bd. dirs. 1994-97, nat. fin. com. 1997-98), Phi Kappa Phi. Baptist. Avocations: reading, walking, sewing, research, music. Home and Office: 2801 Sylvia Dr SE Decatur AL 35603-5643 E-mail: michelin@hiwaay.net.

MICHELLE, STEFL, music educator, choral director, soprano; b. Mt. Pleasant, Pa., Feb. 4, 1970; BS in music edn., Ind. U. of Pa., 1987—91, student, 1991—2001, Duquesne U., 1991—2001. Pa. State Tchg. Cert. - Level II Pa., 1991. Music educator Connellsville Area Sch. Dist., Pa., 1991—; asst. to the min. music First Presbyn. Ch., Greensburg, Pa., 1996—, soprano soloist, 1996—. Mem.: NEA, Connellsville Area Edn. Assn., Pa. State Edn. Assn., Pa. Music Edn. Assn., Music Educator's Nat. Conf., Am. Choral Directors Assn., Delta Omicron (life; delta sigma - chaplain - historian 1989—90). Christian. Avocations: biking, walking, hiking, swimming, travel. E-mail: mstefl@casdfalcons.org.

MICHELMAN, KATE, advocate; married; 3 daughters. Dir. Planned Parenthood, Harrisburg, Pa., 1980-85; pres. Nat. Abortion and Reproductive Rights Action League, Washington, 1985—. Spkr. in field. Named one of 100 Most Powerful Elites in the Nation's Capitol Washingtonian Mag., named a fellow of John F. Kennedy Sch. Govt.'s Inst. of Politics Harvard U., 1994. Office: Nat Abortion Rights Action League 1156 15th St NW Ste 700 Washington DC 20005-1744

MICHELS, DIA LOREN, publishing executive, writer; b. L.A., Oct. 22, 1958; d. Lawrence Michels and Elaine Phyllis Cooper; m. John Anthony Gualtieri, Oct. 13, 1985; children: Akaela Michels-Gualtieri, Zaydek Michels-Gualtieri, Miralah Michels-Gualtieri. BA in Econ., Brandeis U., 1980. Mktg. staff Convergent Solutions, Wash., DC, 1982—89; freelance writer Wash., DC, 1989—98; pres. Platypus Media, LLC, Washington, 1998—. Guest spkr. Turning the Pages, Washington, 2001—; guest expert RIFNet, Washington, 2002—; guest instr. Smithsonian Resident Associates Program, Washington, 1999—; guest commentator Pub. Radio Internat., Washington, 1997—. Author: (book) A Woman's Guide to Yeast Infections, 1992, Milk, Money & Madness: The Culture and Politics of Breastfeeding, 1995 (Winner Book award Am. Med. Writer's Assn., 1997), If My Mom Were A Platypus: Animal Babies and Their Mothers, 2001, Zack in the Middle, 2001, Breastfeeding at a Glance: Facts, Figures and Trivia about Lactation, 2001, Breastfeeding Annual International 2001, 2001, Look What I See! Where Can I Be? In the Neighborhood, 2001, Look What I See! Where Can I Be? At Home, 2002, Look What I See! Where Can I Be? With My Animal Friends, 2002, Look What I See! Where Can I Be? Visiting China, 2003, Look What I See! Where Can I Be? At the Synagogue, 2003; editor: Breastfeeding Facts for Fathers, 2003. Creative dir. Watkins After-Sch. Enrichment Program, Washington, 1996—2001. Mem.: Small Press Assn. of N.Am., Publishers' Mktg. Assn., Wash. Ind. Writers, Woman's Nat. Book Assn., Am. Soc. of Journalists and Authors. E-mail: dia@platypusmedia.com.

MICHELS, FRANCES G. management company executive; Sr. v.p., supr. svcs. Morrison Mgmt. Splsts., Smyrna, Ga., 1996—. Office: Morrison Mgmt Specialists 1955 Lake Park Dr Ste 400 Smyrna GA 30080

MICHELS, PATRICIA A. insurance agent; b. Colorado Springs, Colo., Jan. 14, 1954; d. George A. and G. Elizabeth (Bradshaw) M. BA in Edn., U. No. Colo., 1976. CLU. Tchr. Douglas (Ariz.) Sch. Dist., 1976-80; ins. agt. Bankers Life & Casualty, Colorado Springs, 1983—. Mem. long-term care adv. panel Colo. Divsn. of Ins., Denver, 1995—. Sec., bd. dirs. Sr. Resource Coun., Colorado Springs, 1996-97, health care issues chmn., 1995—. Mem. Colorado Springs Assn. Life Underwriters (govtl. affairs chmn. 1994-97, profl. devel. chmn. 1997—, bd. dirs., sec.-treas. 1997-98, v.p. 1999-00), Am. Soc. CLUs and ChFCs, U.S. Figure Skating Assn. Republican. Episcopalian. Avocations: figure skating, ice dancing, oil and watercolor painting, travel, genealogy. Office: Bankers Life and Casualty PO Box 8135 Colorado Springs CO 80933-8135

MICHELS, RUTH YVONNE, retired cytotechnologist, consultant; b. Denver, Aug. 23, 1942; d. James John Crumb and Ruth Marie Hoglund; m. Robert Allen Michels, June 5, 1960; children: Danna Lynn Michels Hardy, Anita Kay Michels Bornschein. AS, Mesa State Coll., Grand Junction, Colo., 1973. Registered cytotechnologist Am. Soc. of Clin. Pathologist, 1974. Rsch. cytotechnologist St. Mary's Hosp. & Med. Ctr., Grand Junction, Colo., 1973—83, clin. cytotechnologist, 1983—85, cytology/histology supr., 1985—93; edn. coord. -cytology program Grand Junction campus U. Utah, Salt Lake City, 1987—88, clin. instr., 1988—93; cons. Shandon, Inc., Pitts., 1988—99; dir. of ops. Saccomanno Rsch. Inst., Grand Junction, Colo., 1993—99; cons. Bayer Diagnostic, Emeryville, Calif., 1999—2001; cytotechnologist - call in position Cmty. Hosp., Grand Junction, Colo., 2000—; cons. Inspire Pharms., Inc., Durham, NC, 2000—01; rsch. cons. Opacity, Inc. (Bio-Imaging Tech.), Grand Junction, Colo., 2001—. Mem. nat. adv. com. Am. Soc. of Cytology, Phila., 1990—92; chmn. quality assurance com. on pap smears Colo. State Dept. of Health Women's Health Initiative, Denver, 1991—94; mem. adv. com. on papanicolaou technique: approved guidelines Nat. Com. for Clin. Lab. Stds., Wayne, Pa., 1993—94; human subjects adv. com. mem. U.S. Dept. of Energy, Washington, 1993—99; exec. com. ASSIST - Colo. Dept. of Pub. Health, Denver, 1994—99. Author: (sci. paper) Cancer in Children, Pulmonary Cytologic Specimens using the Shandon Megafunnel (Nat. Soc. of Histology Sci. Paper of the yr., 1998), Geno Saccomanno, MD, Ph.D. Pioneer Pathologist 1915 -1999, Examination of p53 Alterations and Cytokeratin Expression in Sputa Collected from Patients Prior to Histologic Diagnosis of Squamous Cell Carcinoma., Concurrent Flourescence In Situ Hybridization and Immunocytochemistry for the Detection of Chromosome Abberations in Exfoliated Bronchial Epithelial Cells., Cytologic Evaluations of Pulmonary Infiltrates: Tumor vs. Inflammation, (tech. video) The Saccomanno Brush Wash Collection Tube; contbr. documentary film - universal studios Early Warning Lung Cancer; author (presenter): (presentation) Early Detection of Lung Cancer, (human subjects meeting) Educating the Nations IRBS, (lung cancer seminar) Where Do We Go From Here?; author: (sci. paper) The Cytologic Diagnosis of Small Cell Carcinoma of the Lung., A comparison of Saccomanno Smear Slides and the New Large Format Cytospin, Megafunnel Slides of sputum Specimens. Co-chmn. Drug Free Mesa County, Grand Junction, Colo., 1999—2003; mem. Rocky Mountain Divsn. Am. Cancer Soc., Denver, 1995—2003, Colo. Divsn. Am. Cancer Soc., Denver, 1974—95; chmn. bd. dirs. Colo. Divsn. Am. Cancer Soc., Denver, 1991—92; stakeholder on peer rev. grant application com. - cell cycle and growth Nat. Home Office - Am. Cancer Soc., Atlanta, 2000—03. Named Vol. of Yr., Colo. divsn. Am. Cancer Soc., 1982; recipient St. Geroge medal, Nat. Home Office, Am. Cancer Soc., 1995, Bonnie Forquer award for substance abuse prevention, Drug Free Mesa County and the Mesa County Dept. of Pub. Health, 2002, Disting. Alumni award, Mesa State Coll., 2003. Mem.: Internat. Acad. of Cytology (assoc.), Am. Soc. of Cytology (assoc.), Sigma Xi Sci. Rsch. Soc. (assoc.). Independent-Republican. Lutheran. Achievements include patents for Cell Block Collection Method and Apparatus for Cytology Specimens; Cytological Sampling Method and Device using a liquid Based Fixative for Pap smears; Cytological Sampling Method and Device for non gynecological cytology specimens. Avocations: creative writing, reading, family & friends, bike riding, outdoors activities. Home: 2151 Hawthorne Ave Grand Junction CO 81506-4164 Personal E-mail: rmichels@acsol.net.

MICHELSON, GERTRUDE GERALDINE, retired retail company executive; b. Jamestown, N.Y., June 3, 1925; d. Thomas and Celia Rosen; m. Horace Michelson, Mar. 28, 1947 (dec. Apr. 2002); children: Martha Ann (dec.), Barbara Jane. BA, Pa. State U., 1945; LLB, Columbia U., 1947; LLD with honors, Adelphi U., 1981; DHL with honors, New Rochelle Coll., 1983; LLD with honors, Marymount Manhattan Coll., 1988; PhD in Policy Analysis, Rand Grad. Sch., 2002. Mgmt. trainee Macy's N.Y., 1947-48, various mgmt. positions, v.p. employee personnel, 1963-70, sr. v.p. labor and consumer rels., 1970—72; sr. v.p. pers. labor and consumer rels. Macy & Co., Inc., 1972-79, sr. v.p. external affairs, 1979-80, R.H. Macy & Co., Inc., 1980-92, sr. advisor, 1992-94; ret., 1995. Chmn. Helena Rubinstein Found.; bd. dirs. Markle Found.; chmn. emeritus bd. trustees Columbia U.; life trustee Spelman Coll.; past pres. bd. overseers Tchrs. Ins. and Annuity Assn. of Am. Coll. Retirement Equities Fund. Recipient Disting. Svc. medal Pa. State U., 1969. Mem. N.Y.C. Ptnrship. (vice chmn.), Women's Forum, Econ. Club N.Y. Home: 70 E 10th St New York NY 10003-5102 Office: Federated Dept Stores Inc 151 W 34th St New York NY 10001-2101

MICHELSON, LILLIAN, librarian, researcher; b. N.Y.C., June 21, 1928; d. Louis and Dora (Keller) Farber; m. Harold Michelson, Dec. 14, 1947; children: Alan Bruce, Eric Neil, Dennis Paul. Vol. Goldwyn Libr., Hollywood, Calif., 1961-69; owner Former Goldwyn Rsch. Libr., Hollywood, 1969—; ind. location scout, 1973—. Mem. Motion Picture Libr. Found., 2002—, Friends L.A. Pub. Libr. Mem.: Acad. Motion Picture Arts and Scis. Office: c/o Dreamworks SKG Rsch Libr 1000 Flower St Glendale CA 91201-3007 Office Phone: 818-695-6445. E-mail: hmichelson@dreamworks.com.

MICHIE, SARA H. pathologist, educator; b. Tulsa, Okla., Jan. 3, 1955; BS in Biology, Stephen F. Austin U., 1977; MD, U. Tex., Houston, 1981. Diplomate Am. Bd. Pathology. Resident anatomic pathology Stanford (Calif.) U. Med. Ctr., 1981—83, postdoctoral fellow immunology dept. pathology, 1983—84, 1986—87, postdoctoral fellow diagnostic immunopathology, 1984—85; resident dept. pathology U. Iowa, Iowa City, 1985—86, postdoctoral fellow, 1986; assoc. investigator lab. svc. VA Hosp., Palo Alto, Calif., 1988—89, staff physician, 1989—, assoc. investigator, 1990—91; clin. instr. pathology dept. Stanford U., 1989—92, asst. prof. pathology, 1992—. Contbr. articles to profl. jours. Recipient Rsch. award, Am. Diabetes Assn., 1996. Mem.: Bay Area Flow Cytometry Group, Soc. Investigative Pathology, Am. Soc. Investigative Pathology, Alpha Omega Alpha, Sigma Xi. Office: VA Hosp Palo Alto 3801 Miranda Ave Stop 154F Palo Alto CA 94304-1207

MICHNEY-HEIPP, KAREN MARIE, secondary education educator; b. Cleve., Aug. 9, 1965; d. Robert Joseph and Kathleen Karen (Lewicki) M.; m. R.T. Heipp. BA in Elem. Edn. summa cum laude, Wilmington Coll., 1987; MA in Religious Studies, John Carroll U., 1989. Joined as lay co-mem. Congregation of St. Joseph, Roman Cath. Ch., 1995. Co-instr. acad. resources, then substitute instr. Wilmington (Ohio) Coll., 1983-87; grad. asst. dept. religious studies John Carroll U., University Heights, Ohio, 1987-89, rsch. asst., 1989; tchr. theology Trinity H.S., Garfield Heights, Ohio, 1989-91, St. Joseph Acad., Cleve., 1991—99, dir. at risk spl. edn. program, 1996—98, retreat dir., 1989-95, facilitator adult edn., 1993, dept. chmn., 1994—99. Contbr. articles to religious publs. Mem. AAUW, Nat. Cath. Educators Assn., Nat. Assembly Religious Women, Ohio Assn. Women in Edn., Ctr. for Women and Religion, Women's Ordination Conf., Futurechurch (outreach com. Cleve.), Phi Beta Kappa. Democrat. Office: 14523 Orchard Park Ave Cleveland OH 44111-2116

MICHNICH, MARIE E. health policy analyst, consultant, educator; M Health Svs. Adminstrn., DrPH Health Svs Rsch., UCLA. Asst. prof. health svs. U. Washington; sr. exec. v.p. Health Policy, Am. Coll. Cardiology Clin. Practice and Sci. Svs. Divsn.; dir. Health Policy Programs and Fellowships Nat. Acad. Scis. Inst. Medicine, 2002—. Cons, spkr. in field; legis. asst. health policy Medicare, Medicaid, maternal and child health; legis. asst. U.S. Senate Majority Leader Robert Dole; mem. several nat. health policy groups. Robert Wood Johnson Health Policy fellow. Mem.: Am. Pharm. Assn. Found. (1st pub. mem. bd. dirs. 2002—), Robert Wood Johnson Health Policy Fellows Program (mem. adv. bd., dir.), Health Care Quality Alliance (former chmn.). Office: Office Health Policy Programs & Fellowsh 500 5th St NW Washington DC 20001

MICK, MARGARET ANNE, communications executive; b. Phila., Apr. 24, 1947; d. Charles Philip and Helen Margaret (Amig) Maurer; m. Donald Kenneth Mick, Sept. 8, 1979. BS with honors, Pa. State U., 1969; MA, NYU, 1972. Assoc. producer Visual Edn. Corp., Princeton, N.J., 1972-73; program devel. specialist AEtna Life & Casualty, Hartford, Conn., 1973-78, sr. program devel. specialist, 1978 81, mgr. audiovisual communications, 1981-82, dir. audiovisual and mktg. communications, 1982-84, dir. mktg. communications, 1984-86, dir. bus. devel., 1986-88, asst. v.p. customized communications, 1988-96; pres. Sachem Comm., Guilford, Conn., 1996-97; cons. Watson Wyatt Worldwide, 1997—. Juror EFLA Am. Film Festival, Hartford, 1977-79. Writer, dir., producer TV films including (edn1.) PAC Man in the Money Works. Recipient Apex award, 2000, 01, 03, Dalton Pen award Yale-New Haven Hosp., 2003. Mem. Info. Film Producers Am. (chmn. 1981, treas. 1982, Conn. Valley Chpt.), Internat. TV Assn. (chmn. 1983), Hartford Women's Network, Mature Market Inst., Bus. and Profl. Advt. Assn. Republican. Avocations: gardening, reading, dance. Home and Office: 483 Colonial Rd Guilford CT 06437-3127

MICKELSON, RHODA ANN, speech pathology/audiology services professional; b. Rugby, N.D., Oct. 22, 1952; d. Oliver Roger and Doris Marie Stutrud; m. Edward Carl Mickelson, June 27, 1981; children: Alison Marie, Brittany Ann, Elizabeth Ann Marie. BS, Minot State Univ., N.D., 1974; MEd, Univ. N.D., Grand Forks, N.D., 1996. Speech lang. pathologist Lake Region Spl. Edn. Unit, Cavalier County, ND, 1974—76; elem. edn. tchr. Mt. Pleasant Schs., Rolla, ND, 1976—80; elem. tchr. Larimore Pub. Sch., ND, 1980—81; speech lang. pathologist Turtle Mountain Cmty. Sch., Belcourt, ND, 1981—82; disabilities coord., speech pathologist Turtle Mountain Head Start, Belcourt, ND, 1982—91; speech lang. pathologist Turtle Mountain Cmty. Sch., Belcourt, ND, 1991—. Bd. dirs. Internat. Ragtop Festival, Rolla, ND, 1997; com. mem. Boys & Girls Club of Am., Rolla, ND, 2001. Mem.: CEC, WELCA, Elks. Luth. Avocations: travel, reading.

MICKELSON, STACEY, state legislator; BA, Minot State U., 1994. Govt. rels. dir. Artspace Projects, Inc.; rep. Dist. 38 N.D. Ho. of Reps., 1994-2000, mem. fin. and taxation com., vice-chmn. transp. com. Mem. interim taxation, adminstrv. rules coms. Bowhay Inst. for Legis. Leadership and Devel. fellow. Mem. Am. Coun. Young Polit. Leaders, Darden Program Emerging Polit. Leaders, Flemming Fellows. Home: 410 Groveland Ave #702 Minneapolis MN 55403

MICKIEWICZ, ELLEN PROPPER, political and social science educator; b. Hartford, Conn. d. George K. and Rebecca (Adler) Propper; m. Denis Mickiewicz; 1 son, Cyril. BA, Wellesley Coll.; MA, Yale U., PhD, 1965. Lectr. dept. polit. sci. Yale U., 1965-67; asst. prof. dept. polit. sci. Mich. State U., East Lansing, 1967-69, assoc. prof., 1969-73, prof., 1973-80; prof. dept. polit. sci. Emory U., Atlanta, 1980-88, dean Grad. Sch. Arts and Scis., 1980-85, Alben W. Barkley prof. polit. sci., 1988-93; James R. Shepley prof. pub. policy, prof. polit. sci. Duke U., Durham, N.C., 1994—, dir. DeWitt Wallace Ctr. for Comm. and Journalism Terry Sanford Inst. Pub. Policy, 1994—. Vis. prof. Kathryn W. Davis Chair Wellesley Coll., 1978; vis. com. dept. Slavic lang. and lit. Harvard U., 1978-85, vice chmn. vis. com. Russian Rsch. Ctr., Harvard U., 1986-92; mem. subcom. on comms. and society Am. Coun. Learned Socs./Soviet Acad. Scis., 1986-90; mem. com. on internat. security studies, Am. Acad. Arts and Scis., 1988-90; fellow The Carter Ctr., 1985—, dir. Commn. on Radio and TV Policy; mem. area adv. com. for Ea. Europe and USSR, Coun. for Internat. Exch. Of Scholars, 1987-90; mem. acad. adv. coun. The Kennan Inst. for Advanced Russian Studies, 1989-93; mem. bd. overseers Internat. Press Ctr., Moscow, 1995; dir., commr. Commn. Radio and TV Policy, 1990. Author: Soviet Political Schools, 1967, Media and the Russian Public, 1981, Split Signals: Television and Politics in the Soviet Union, 1988 (Electronic Book of Yr. award Nat. Assn. Broadcasters and Broadcast Edn. Assn. 1988); co-author: Television and Elections, 1992, Television/Radio News and Minorities, 1994, Changing Channels: Television and the Struggle for Power in Russia, 1997, revised and expanded edit., 1999; editor: Soviet Union Jour., 1980-90; co-editor: International Security and Arms Control, 1986, The Soviet Calculus of Nuclear War, 1986; editor, contbr.: Handbook of Soviet Social Science Data, 1973; mem. editl. bd. Jour. Politics, 1985-88, Harvard Internat. Jour. Press/Politics, 1995—, Polit. Comms., 1996—, Polit. Comm., 1995—. Founder, 1st chmn. bd. dirs. Opera Guild of Greater Lansing, Inc., 1972-74. Recipient Outstanding Svc. to Promote Dem. Media in Russia award Journalists Union of Russia, 1994; Ford Found. Fgn. Area Tng. fellow, 1962-65, Guggenheim fellow, 1973-74; Sigma Xi grantee, 1972-74, John and Mary R. Markle Found. grantee, 1984-88, 94-96, 95—, Ford Found. grantee, 1985, 88-91, 92—, Rockefeller Found. grantee, 1985-87, W. Alton Jones Found. grantee, 1987-88, Eurasia Found. grantee, 1993-94, Carnegie Corp. of N.Y. grantee, 1996—. Mem. Am. Assn. for Advancement Slavic Studies (bd. dirs. 1978-81, mem. awards com., mem. endowment com. 1984-86, pres. 1987-88), Am. Polit. Sci. Assn.,Internat. Studies Assn. (v.p. N.Am. 1983-84), Dante Soc. Am., So. Conf. Slavic Studies (exec. com. 1983-84), Counc. Fgn. Rels. Office: Duke U Sanford Inst Pub Policy PO Box 90241 Durham NC 27708-0241

MICKLE, DELORIS B. credit manager, artist; b. Erwin, N.C., Mar. 3, 1951; d. Lewis Hart and Essie Lee Blue; m. Joseph Mickle, Feb. 22, 1970 (div. Jan. 7, 1976); children: Joseph Mickle Jr., Miranda Lanette. Grad. in Graphic Comml. Art, Nova U., 1990; cert. in Electronic Comm., Innovative Tng. Inc., 1998; cert. in Intranet Ware 4.11 Adminstrn., Ctrl. Piedmont C.C., 1998. Sec., key punch op. IBM, White Plains, NY, 1969—73; pheripheral and computer op. S.C. Dept. Mental Health, Columbia, 1973—77; record clk. AT&T, White Plains, 1980—84, reports clk. White Plains and Herndon, Va., 1984—94, billing clk. Charlotte, NC, 1994—. Artist, designer (book cover) 10 Minutes Past Too Late, 2001, photographer (pub.) The Awakening At Hains Point, 2000, patentee in field. Mem. Pioneers, Charlotte, 1990—. Recipient award, Internat. Libr. Photography, 2001. Mem.: Nat. Mus. Women in Arts. Home: 6401 Woodbridge Rd Charlotte NC 28227 Office: Dee's Art and Design 6401 Woodbridge Rd Charlotte NC 28227

MIDDEL, MARJORIE, social worker, consultant; MSW, U. Mich., 1980. Cert. social worker Mich., 1982, sch. social worker Mich., 1981, employee assistance profl. Employee Assistance Profls., 1986, addictions counselor Mich., 1990. EAP mgr. Multi Resource Ctr., Southfield, Mich., 1982—84; br. mgr. Ford Motor Co. Contract, Dearborn, Mich., 1985—88; cons. Middel & Assocs., Traverse City, Mich., 1986—; dir. Munson Alcohol and Drug Treatment Ctr., Traverse City, 1988—94; sch. social worker Traverse City Area Pub. Schs., 2000—. Field instr. U. of Mich., Ann Arbor, Mich., 1984—86; huron valley chpt. pres. Employee Assistance PA, Traverse City, Mich., 1985—87; chemcial dependency study group Governor's Task Force, Lansing, Mich., 1987—87; pres. Employee Assistance Soc. of N.Am., Chicago, Ill., 1987—96; adv. bd. mem. Grand Traverse Families in Action, Traverse City, Mich., 1989—94; task force on alcohol and other drugs Grand Traverse Chamber of Commerce, Traverse City, Mich., 1989—94; active Leadership Grand Traverse Grand Traverse Area C. of C., Traverse City, 1990—90; adv. bd. mem. Traverse City Area Drug Free Schools Com., 1992—94; field instr. Grand Valley State U., Grand Rapids, Mich., 2000—; spkr. in field. Assoc. editor: Jour. Employee Assistance Quar. Vol. No. Mich. Gymnastics, Traverse City, 1998—2002, Inside Out Volleyball, Traverse City, 2003—03; pres. and other bd. positions Employee Assistance Soc. N.Am., Chgo., 1987—96. Grantee Drug Free Schools Grant, State of Mich., 1996, 1997, 1998, 1999. Mem.: NASW (ACSW).

MIDDLEBROOK, DIANE WOOD, English language educator, writer; b. Pocatello, Idaho, Apr. 16, 1939; d. Thomas Isaac and Helen Loretta (Downey) Wood; m. Jonathan Middlebrook, June 15, 1963 (annulled 1976); 1 child, Leah Wood ; m. Carl Djerassi, June 21, 1985. BA, U. Wash., 1961; MA, Yale U., 1962, PhD, 1968; LittD (hon.), Kenyon Coll., 1999. Asst. prof. Stanford (Calif.) U., 1966-73, assoc. prof., 1973-83, prof., 1983-2001, prof. emerita, 2002—, dir. Ctr. for Rsch. on Women, 1977-79. Author: Walt Whitman and Wallace Stevens, 1974, Worlds into Words: Understanding Modern Poems, 1980, Anne Sexton, A Biography, 1991, Suits Me: The Double Life of Billy Tipton, 1998, Her Husband: Hughes and Plath, a Marriage, 2003; editor: Coming to Light: American Women Poets in the Twentieth Century, 1985; author: (poetry) Gin Considered as a Demon, 1983. Founding trustee Djerassi Resident Artists Program, Woodside, Calif., 1980—83, chair, 1994; trustee San Francisco Art Inst, 1993. Finalist Nat. Book award, 1991; recipient Yale Prize for Poetry; fellow Ind. Study, NEH, 1982—83, Bunting Inst., Radcliffe Coll., 1982—83, Guggenheim Found., 1988—89, Rockefeller Study Ctr., 1990. Mem.: MLA, Authors Guild, Royal Soc. for the Arts (London), Biographers Club. Avocations: collecting art, theater. Home: 1101 Green St Apt 1501 San Francisco CA 94109-2012 Office: Agent Georges Borchardt 136 E 57th St New York NY 10022 E-mail: dwm@stanford.edu.

MIDDLETON, LINDA CHARLENE, humanities educator; b. Honolulu, Feb. 19, 1955; d. Charles Richardson and Rita Virginia Middleton. BA, U. Hawaii, 1976; Ph.D., U. of Hawaii, Manoa, Honolulu, Hawaii, 1986—93; MA, UC, Berkeley, California, 1976—78. Lectr. dept. English U. Hawaii, Honolulu, 1993—96, instr. dept. English, 1996—2002, asst. prof. dept. English, 2002—. Contbr. articles to profl. jours. Pres. Children's Lit. Hawaii, Honolulu, 2002—03. Recipient Francis Davis award, 2003—04. Mem.: AAUW, MLA, Women's Caucus for Modern Lang., Nat. Conv. Tchrs. of English. Avocations: writing, aerobics. Office: Dept English U Hawaii Manoa 1733 Donaghho Rd Honolulu HI 96822 E-mail: lmiddlet@hawaii.edu.

MIDDLETON, LINDA JEAN GREATHOUSE, lawyer; b. Poplar Bluff, Mo., Sept. 22, 1950; d. Casper Scott and Anna Garnelle (Qualls) Greathouse; m. Roy L. Middleton, Sept. 27, 1969. BS cum laude, Ark. State U., 1972; JD, Baylor U., 1974. Bar: Tex., 1974; CPCU, CLU. Asst. v.p., asst. sec., atty. Equitable Gen. Ins. Co., Ft. Worth, 1977-81; gen. counsel, corp. sec. Chilton Corp., Dallas, 1981-83; mgr. pub. affairs Fina Oil and Chem., Dallas, 1983-85, corp. sec., sr. atty., 1983—. Sec. Parliamentarian, Dallas, 1985—. Sec. Homeowners Assn., Dallas, 1981—. Mem. Tex. Bar Assn., Dallas Bar Assn. Baptist. Avocations: oil painting, sewing, piano. Office: 615 Lakeshore Dr Little Elm TX 75068-5036

MIDDLETON, MARY, secondary school educator; b. Lackawana, N.Y., Nov. 13, 1942; d. Arthur Jordan and Kathryn (Sternburg) M. BS in Edn., Ohio State U., 1965; postgrad., Akron U., 1970, Cleve. State U., 1981-84. Profl. cert. in edn. Tchr. Columbus (Ohio) Schs., 1966-68, Brooklyn (Ohio) Schs., 1968-98. Co-dir. C.A.R.E. (Chem. Abuse Reduced through Edn.), Brooklyn (Ohio) City, 1986-95, Englist dept. chair, acad. team advisor Brooklyn (Ohio) Schs., 1987-98; mem. dimensions of learning task force Bklyn. Schs., 1997; core team mem. Comprehensive Mgmt., 1996-98. Contbr. articles to profl. jours. Campaign worker North Olmsted (Ohio) Dem. club, 1988, 92, 96; recreation dir. Country Club Condominiums, 1992-2000. Recipient N.E. Ohio Writing Project fellowship Martha Holden Jennings, Cleve. State U., 1985. Mem. Cinnamon Woods Condominiums Assn. (bd. dirs., pres.), Re-elect the Pres. Com., Ohio State U. Alumni Assn. Pres.'s Club, Neighbors Who Care (pub. rels. com., editor), Phi Mu. Methodist. Avocations: swimming, reading, travel, tennis. Home: 24026 S Sunny Side Dr Sun Lakes AZ 85248

MIDDLETON, TERESA MUIR, Internet company executive, researcher; b. London; d. Francis Robert and Marjorie Banwell Muir; children: Christopher, Andrew, Claire. BSc, Syracuse U., 1978; MBA, Pepperdine U., 1982. Rschr. SRI Internat., Menlo Park, Calif., 1970—90, program mgr., 1990—94, assoc. dir., 1994—98, assoc. dir. emeritus, 1998—; CEO PatchWorx, Inc., Menlo Park, 1998—. Founding dir. Nat. Cristina Found., Greenwich, 1989—; mem. com. Nat. Conf. Tech. and Disabilities, Northridge, 1989; chmn. Virtual Reality Conf., Menlo Park, 1991; rschr. in field. Editor: Virtual Worlds: Real Challenges, 1991. Dir. telecom. for the deaf Deafnet Dissemination Project, 1984. Recipient Mimi award, SRI Internat., 1997. Avocations: swimming, music, travel. Office: Patchworx Inc 333 Ravenswood Ave BS372 Menlo Park CA 94025 Personal E-mail: tmiddleton@aol.com. Business E-Mail: tmiddleton@patchworx.org.

MIDDLETON, WANDA KAREN LEE, songwriter, poet, minister; b. Balt., Mar. 13, 1958; d. Willie James and Dorothy Lee Middleton; m. Ronald L. Greene, May 6, 2000; children: Ryan Middleton, Willie Lee, Russell Lee, DaWoyne, Bryan, Tiffanee, Rashell. Student, Bay Coll. Md., 1976—78, Balt. C.C., 1979—80; AA in Div. (hon.), Universal Ministries; cert. in early childhood edn., Stratford Career Inst., 2001; cert. in nutrition and fitness, Profl. Career Inst., 2001; BA in Gospel Music (hon.), Universal Ministries, 2003. Cert. Nutrition and fitness. Home health aide Kelly Health Care, Towson, Md., 1976—78; recreation worker Fed. Hill Nursing Home, Balt., 1979—80; vol. St. Joseph Hosp., Towson, 1981—83; clk. Def. Investigative Svc., Washington, 1984—86; dietary asst. Amu Retirement Home, Montgomery County, Md., 1987—. Recipient Editors Choice award,

Nat. Libr. Poetry, 1996, Pub. award, Cader Publs., 1996. Mem.: English Conversation Club. Church For All. Avocations: writing, travel, Bible study, exercise, family games. Address: PO Box 4054 Rockville MD 20849 E-mail: middletonlee22@yahoo.com.

MIDGETT, CAROL WICKHAM, mathematics educator, consultant; d. Walter [illegible] and Edna [illegible]; m. [illegible] Midgett, III, June 30, 1968; children: John Dameron, Todd Cameron. BA, Barton Coll., 1966; MEd, U. N.C., 2003. Cert. Nat. Bd. Cert. Tchr., Nat. Bd. for Profl. Tchg. Stds. Dir. Christian edn. United Meth. Ch., Goldsboro, NC, 1966—68; tchr. Elsa Williams Needle Art Sch., West Townsend, Mass., 1972—86, Johnson County Schs., Smithfield, NC, 1968—70, Carteret County Schs., Beaufort, NC, 1970—74, Brunswick County Schs., Southport, NC, 1986—2000; tchr. in residence U. N.C., Wilmington, 2000—. Ednl. cons., 1988—. Contbr. chpt. to book Classroom Assessment, 1997, articles to profl. jours. Contbr., worker Habitat for Humanity, Wilmington; mem. gov. tchr. adv. com. Gov. Office N.C., 1995—2000. Recipient Presdl. award in math., NSF, 1991, award for video No Greater Calling, PBS, 2000. Mem.: ASCD, N.C. Coun. Tchrs. Math. (elem. v.p. 1999—2001), Nat. Coun. Tchrs. Math. (writing team stds. 2000 1996—2000, lesson plan coord. Illuminations, project coord. 2001—03). Methodist. Avocation: needlecrafts. Home: 1002 Bussells Turn Southport NC 28461 Office: U NC Wilmington NC 28403-5991 E-mail: midgettc@uncw.edu.

MIDLER, BETTE, singer, entertainer, actress; b. Honolulu, Dec. 1, 1945; m. Martin von Haselberg, 1984; 1 child, Sophie. Student, U. Hawaii. Debut as actress (films), Hawaii, 1965, mem. cast Fiddler on the Roof, N.Y.C, 1966—69, Salvation, 1970, Tommy, Seattle Opera Co., 1971, nightclub concert performer on tour U.S., from 1972; appearance Palace Theatre, N.Y.C., 1973, Radio City Music Hall, 1993, TV appearances include The Tonight Show, Bette Midler: Old Red Hair is Back, 1978, Gypsy, 1993 (Golden Globe award best actress in a mini-series or movie made for television, 1994, Emmy nomination, Lead Actress - Special, 1994), Seinfeld, 1996, Diva Las Vegas, 1997, Murphy Brown, 1998, appeared Clams on The Half-Shell Revue, N.Y.C., 1975, recs. include The Divine Miss M, 1972, Bette Midler, 1973, Broken Blossom, 1977, Live at Last, 1977, The Rose, Thighs and Whispers, 1979, Songs for the New Depression, 1979, Divine Madness, 1980, No Frills, 1984, Mud Will Be Flung Tonight, 1985, Beaches (soundtrack), 1989, Some People's Lives, 1990, Bette of Roses, 1995, Bathhouse Betty, 1998, Bette, 2000; actor: (films) Hawaii, 1966, The Rose, 1979 (Academy award nomination best actress, 1979), Divine Madness, 1980, Jinxed, 1982, Down and Out in Beverly Hills, 1986, Ruthless People, 1986, Outrageous Fortune, 1987, Oliver and Company (voice), 1988, Big Business, 1988, Beaches, 1988, Stella, 1990, Scenes From a Mall, 1991, For the Boys, 1991 (Academy award nomination best actress, 1991), Hocus Pocus, 1993, Get Shorty, 1995, The First Wives Club, 1996, That Old Feeling, 1997, Get Bruce, 1999, Isn't She Great, 1999, Drowning Mona, 2000; appeared in cable TV (HBO) prodn. Bette Midler's Mondo Beyondo, 1988; author: A View From A Broad, 1980, The Saga of Baby Divine, 1983; exec. prodr., composer (TV show) Bette, 2000, exec. prodr. Some of My Best Friends, 2001, (films) Divine Secret of the Ya-Ya Sisterhood, 2002. Recipient After Dark Ruby award, 1973, Grammy awards, 1973, 1990, spl. Tony award, 1973, Emmy award for NBC Spl., Ol' Red Hair is Back, 1978, 2 Golden Globe awards for The Rose, 1979, Golden Globe award for The Boys, 1991, Emmy award The Tonight Show appearance, 1992. Office: Endeavor Entertainment care Adam Venit 9701 Wilshire Blvd Fl 10 Beverly Hills CA 90212*

MIEDEMA, BARBARA JANE, music educator; b. Quincy, Ill., July 30, 1953; d. Bliss Marion and Virginia Ellen Crosby Branson; m. Lawrence Ray Miedema, Aug. 2, 1980; children: Jeffrey Branson, Jonathan Crosby, Emily Elizabeth. BS in Music Edn., U. Ill., 1975. Cert. tchr. Ill., 1975, Ind. Music tchr. Sheridan Elem. Sch., Ill., 1975—77, Quincy Pub. Schs., Ill., 1977, Bradley Bourbonnais Cmty. H.S., Ill., 1978—81, Northview Mid. Sch., Indpls., 2000—. Pvt. voice and piano tchr. Cub Scout leader Crossroads of Am. coun. Boy Scouts Am., Indpls., 1989—94; Girl Scout leader Girl Scouts of Hoosier Capital Coun., Indpls. Grantee Profl. Devel. Show Choir Camps of Am., Wash. Twp. Edn. Found., 2002, Profl. Devel. Tech. Inst. for Music Educators, 2003. Mem.: NEA, Wash. Twp. Edn. Assn., Ind. Edn. Assn., Tech. Inst. of Music Educators, Am. Choral Dirs. Assn., Ind. Music Educators Assn., Music Educators Nat. Conf.

MIEL, VICKY ANN, city official; b. South Bend, Ind., June 20, 1951; d. Lawrence Paul Miel and Virginia Ann (Yeagley) Hernandez. BS, Ariz. State U., 1985. Word processing coordinator City of Phoenix, 1977-78, word processing adminstr., 1978-83, chief dep. city clk., 1983-88, city clk. dir., 1988—. Assoc. prof. Phoenix Community Coll., 1982-83, Mesa (Ariz.) Community Coll., 1983; speaker in field, Boston, Santa Fe, Los Angeles, N.Y.C. and St. Paul, 1980—. Author: Phoenix Document Request Form, 1985, Developing Successful Systems Users, 1986. Judge Future Bus. Leaders Am. at Ariz. State U., Tempe, 1984; bd. dirs. Fire and Life Safety League, Phoenix, 1984. Recipient Gold Plaque, Word Processing Systems Mag., Mpls., 1980, Green Light Productivity award City of Phoenix, 1981, Honor Soc. Achievement award Internat. Word Processing Assn., 1981, 1st Ann. Grand Prize Records Mgmt. Internat. Inst. Mcpl. Clks., 1990, Olsten Award for Excellence in Records Mgmt., 1991, Tech. Award of Excellence, 1995. Mem. ASPA, Assn. Info. Systems Profls. (internat. dir. 1982-84), Internat. Inst. Mcpl. Clks. (cert., 2d v.p. 1996-97, 1st v.p. 1997-98, pres. 1998-99, tech. award of excellence 1995, immediate past pres. 1999-2000), Am. Records Mgrs. Assn., Assn. Image Mgmt., Am. Mgmt. Assn. Office: City Phoenix 200 W Washington St Ste 1500 Phoenix AZ 85003-1611

MIELE, DENISE MARIE, special education educator; b. South Hampton, New York, Nov. 19, 1970; d. Anthony DelPercio and Barbara Ann Ruzas; m. Joseph Miele. BA, Coll. New Rochelle, N.Y., 1999; MS, Lehman Coll., Bronx, N.Y., 2003. Spl. educator Yonkers Bd. of Edn., Yonkers, NY, 1999—. Recipient Magna Cum Laude, Coll. of New Rochelle, N.Y., 1999, Kappa Gamma, 1999, Psi Chi, 1999. Mem.: Coun. for Exceptional Children, Parent Tchr. Assn., Yonkers Fedn. of Teachers. Avocations: running, water sports, travel, reading, music.

MIELKE, NANCY E. music educator; b. Savanna, Ill., Apr. 13, 1944; d. Edward H. and Isabelle M. Mielke. BS in Elem. Edn. and Music with honors, Western Mont. Coll., 1965; M in Music Edn., U. Mont., 1974; postgrad., U. Nev. Cert. tchr. Nev. 2d grade tchr. Missoula (Mont.) Sch. Dist., 1965—69, Washoe County Sch. Dist., Reno, 1969—70; elem. gen. music tchr. grades K-6 and spl. edn., mid. sch. choral and handbell dir. grades 6-8 Carson City (Nev.) Sch. Dist., 1970—. Presenter in field. Music dir., childrens, adult and handbell choirs, organist, pianist First United Meth. Ch., Carson City, 1973—. Mem.: Am. Guild English Handbell Ringers, Am. Recorder Soc., Am. Guild Organists, Am. Choral Dirs. Assn., Internat. Soc. for Music Edn., Music Educators Nat. Conf., Delta Kappa Gamma (chpt. pres. 1995—99, state music chair 1995—97, Rose of Recognition 1998). Republican. United Methodist. Avocations: gardening, hiking, skiing, reading, needlework. Home: 4098 Northgate Ln Carson City NV 89706

MIERA, LUCILLE CATHERINE MIERA, artist, retired art educator; b. Socorro, N.Mex., Nov. 25, 1931; d. Stephen Maurice and Carmen Rosela (Baca) Miera; m. Vito Modesto Miera Jr., Aug. 22, 1953; children: Stephanie Lucille Miera Mansfield, Jennifer Ann Miera Eberhart. BA, U. N.Mex., 1973, MA, 1976, Ednl. Specialist Sch. Adminstrn., 1984. Cert. tchr., adminstr., N.Mex. Apprentice land surveying and draftsmen Stephen M. Miera, Regional Land Surveyor, Albuquerque, 1946-49; typist Albuquerque Abstract & Title, 1950; typist, engring. draftsman U.S. Army Corps Engrs., Albuquerque, 1950-57; engring. draftsman U.S. Dept. Interior, Albuquerque, 1957-59; art tchr., art dept. chair Albuquerque Pub. Sch. Sys., 1973-93, reviewer curriculum devel. plan jr. high schs.; reviewer mid. schs.; ret. Prof. asst. U. N.Mex., Albuquerque, 1974; mid. sch. articulation rep. Taylor Middle Sch., Albuquerque, 1974-83; art rep. North Ctrl. Evaluation Middle Sch., Albuquerque, 1978; pres., art tchr. N.Mex Art League, Albuquerque, 1996, 97, 99; founder art program Emeritus Acad. Tech. Vocat. Inst., 1997; art tchr. bd. dirs. 1997— [illegible] include Mus. Art, Toledo, Ohio, 1964, Kirtland AFB Officers Club, Albuquerque, 1967—68, U. N.Mex., 1969—76, 1999—2000, Albuquerque Pub. Schs. Adminstrn. Bldg., 1973—93, United Bank N.Mex., 1982, Albuquerque C. of C., 1999, exhibited in group shows at N.Mex. State Fair Fine Arts Gallery, N.Mex. State Fair Hispanic Art Gallery, Scottsdale Village Cir. Art Gallery, Old Town Albuquerque De Colores Soaring Eagle and La Hacienda Galleries, Coronado Airport Gallery. Mem., flyer distbr. Rep. Party, Albuquerque, 1954; poll clk. Bernalillo County, Albuquerque, 1960; leader Campfire USA, Albuquerque, 1966, 80; treas. Manzano Band, Albuquerque, 1977; pres. Glenwood Neighborhood Assn., Albuquerque, 1984-87; pres., nat. area dir. Res. Officers Assn. Ladies, Washington, 1989-91. Mem. Nat. Mus. Women's Art (charter), Nat. Hist. Soc., N.Mex. Assn. Educators Ret., N.Mex. Watercolor Soc., N.Mex. Res. Officer Ladies (pres.), N.Mex. Archdiocesan Coun. Cath. Women (pres. 1974), Epsilon Sigma Alpha. Avocations: travel, instructing and displaying art to promote art in the community. Home: 4405 Glenwood Hills Dr NE Albuquerque NM 87111-4260 E-mail: lmierart@aol.com.

MIEROW, SHARON ANN, special education educator; b. Milw., Aug. 9, 1950; d. Leonard Norbert and Esther Marie (Kramer) Banaszynski; children: Natalie Ann, Noelle Marie. MusB, St. Norbert Coll., 1972. Educator music Alverno Coll. Young Peoples Arts, Milw., 1980-85, Cullins Lake-Pointe Elem. Sch., Rowlett, Tex., 1988-90, Naamen Forest High Sch., Garland, Tex., 1990-92; educator spl. edn. Dobbs Elem. Sch., Rockwall, Tex., 1992-96, Nebbie Williams Elem. Sch., Rockwall, Tex., 1996—; educator music pvt. practice, Rockwall, Tex., 1992—. In-home instr. for families with children who have autism. Cantor O.L.O.L. Cath. Ch., Rockwall, 1996, 97. Named Tchr. of Yr., 1989-90, 97-98. Mem. Nat. Music Tchrs. Assn., Tex. Music Tchrs. Assn., Garland Music Tchrs. Assn., Mu Phi Epsilon. Democrat. Avocations: family, reading, travel, musicals, theater. Home: 1009 Signal Ridge Pl Rockwall TX 75032-5414 Office: Nebbie William Elem Sch 350 Dalton Rd Rockwall TX 75087-7061

MIERS, HARRIET E. lawyer; b. Dallas, Aug. 10, 1945; BS, So. Meth. U., 1967, JD, 1970. Bar: Tex. 1970. Pres. Locke Purnell Rain Harrell, PC, Dallas. Chair Tex. Lottery Commn.; bd. dirs. Capstead Mortgage Corp., Coamerica Bank, Tex. Comments editor Southwestern Law Jour., 1969-70. Former mem.-at-large Dallas City Coun.; trustee Southwestern Legal Found. Named 1 of 50 Top Women Lawyers Nat. Law Jour., 1998. Fellow Am. Bar Found., Tex. Bar Found. (life); mem. ABA (jour. bd. editors, ho. dels., chair credentials and admissions com., election law com., bus. and cmty. activities), Dallas Bar Found., Dallas Bar Assn. (pres. 1985, chmn. bd. dirs. 1981), State Bar Tex. (pres. 1992-93, dir. 1986-89), Attys. Liability Assurance Soc. (bd. dirs.). Office: Locke Purnell Rain Harrell 2200 Ross Ave Ste 2200 Dallas TX 75201-6776 E-mail: hemiers@lprh.com.

MIGALA, LUCYNA J. journalist, arts administrator, radio station executive; b. Krakow, Poland, May 22, 1944; came to U.S., 1947, naturalized, 1955; d. Joseph and Estelle (Suwala) M.; m. Frank A. Cizon, Oct. 9, 1998. Student, Loyola U., Chgo., 1962-63, Chgo. Conservatory of Music, 1963-70; BS in Journalism, Northwestern U., 1966. Radio announcer, prodr. Sta. WOPA, Oak Park, Ill., 1963-66; writer, reporter, prodr. NBC News, Chgo., 1966-69, 69-71; prodr. NBC local news, Washington, 1969; prodr., coord. NBC network news, Cleve., 1971-78, field prodr. Chgo., 1978-79; v.p. Migala Comms. Corp., 1979—. Program and news dir., on-air personality Sta. WCEV, Cicero, Ill, 1979—; lectr. City Colls., Chgo., 1981, Morton Coll., 1988. Columnist Free Press, Chgo., 1984-87. Founder, artistic dir., gen. mgr. Lira Ensemble (formerly The Lira Singers), Chgo., 1965—, Artist-in-residence, Loyola U., Chgo.; mem., chmn. various cultural coms. Polish Am. Congress, 1970-80; bd. dirs. Nationalities Svcs. Ctr., Cleve., 1973-78; bd. dirs., v.p. Cicero-Berwyn Fine Arts Coun., Cicero, Ill., 1980-87; mem. City Arts I and II panels Chgo. Office of Fine Arts, 1986-89, 94; v.p. Chgo. chpt. Kosciuszko Found., 1983-86; bd. dirs. Polish Women's Alliance Am., 1983-87, Ill. Humanities Coun., 1983-89, mem. exec. com., 1986-87; bd. dirs. Ill. Arts Alliance, 1989-92; founder, gen. chmn. Midwest Chopin Piano Competition (later Chgo. Chopin Competition), 1984-86; founding mem. ethnic and folk arts panel Ill. Arts Coun., 1984-87, 92-94; mem. Polonia Census 2000 Com.; bd. dirs.Polish-Am. Leadership Initiative, Chgo., 2001—. Decorated Cavalier's Cross of Merit govt. of Poland; recipient AP Broadcasters award, 1973, Emmy award NATAS, 1974, Cultural Achievement award Am. Coun. for Polish Culture, 1990, award of merit Advocates Soc. Polish Am. Attys., 1991, Human Rels. Media award City of Chgo., 1992, Outstanding Achievement award Minister of Fgn. Affairs Rep. of Poland, 1994, Civic Achievement award Polish Am. Hist. Assn., 2000, Nat. Creative Arts award Polish Am. Hist. Soc., 2003; Washington Journalism Ctr. fellow, 1969. Mem. Soc. Profl. Journalists. Office: Sta WCEV 5356 W Belmont Ave Chicago IL 60641-4103 also: The Lira Ensemble 6525 N Sheridan Rd # Sky905 Chicago IL 60626-5344 Office Phone: 773-508-7040. E-mail: limgala@liraensemble.com.

MIGDAL, RUTH AIZUSS, sculptor, educator; b. Chgo., Aug. 17, 1932; d. Joseph and Anna (Smith) Aizuss; m. Norman Bernard Migdal, June 20, 1954 (div. Oct. 1967); children: Allison, James; m. James Allison Brown, Jan. 29, 1997; adopted son, Sam Migdal-Brown. BFA, Sch. of Art. Inst. of Chgo., 1954; MFA, U. Ill., 1958. Art tchr. grades 2-8 Sunset Ridge Sch., Northfield, Ill., 1958-60; art instr. Columbia Coll., Chgo., 1967-68; lectr. U. Ill., Chgo., 1968-69; asst. prof. Malcolm X Coll., Chgo., 1969-81, Loop Coll. (now Harold Washington Coll.), Chgo., 1981-84; from assoc. prof. to prof. Harold Washington Coll., Chgo., 1984-96, prof. emeritus, 1996—. Emeritus bd. dirs. Victory Garden Theater, Chgo.; artist sculptor Virginia Lust Gallery, N.Y.C., U. Ill., Springfield, 1995; vis. artist lectr. U. Mont., Missoula, 1988, Soc. of Arts, Religion and Contemporary Culture, N.Y.C., 1996. One-person shows include U. P.R., San Juan, 1956, Tacoma (Wash.) Mus., 1964, Veridian Gallery, N.Y.C., 1978, Elaine Starkman Gallery, N.Y.C., 1986, Virginia Lust Gallery, N.Y.C., 1992, U. Ill., Springfield, 1995, Foundry metal Art Gallery, 2002-03; exhibited in group shows Am. Gallery, N.Y.C., 1962, Tacoma Mus., 1964, Springfield Art Assn., 1979, Viridian Gallery, N.Y.C., 1985, Albright Knox Gallery, Bronx, 1985, Elaine Starkman Gallery, N.Y.C., 1985, Rockford Art Mus., 1986, Wolf Gallery, Townsend, Wash., 1991, U. Ill., Springfield, 1995, Women Made Galery, Arts Pl. Studio Gallery, Chgo., Jan Wilson Gallery, Sun Valley, Idaho, Art Inst. of Chgo., 1998, Arts Club of Chgo., 1964-2001, Chgo. Art Open, 1998, 99, 2001, 03, Gallery on the Lake, 2003, Beverly Art Ctr., Morgan Pk., Ill., 2003, Foundry Metal Art Gallery;Contbr. art revs. and articles to radio and publs. Recipient William Bartel prize Art Inst. Chgo., 1961, Pauline Palmer prize Art Inst. Chgo., 1973; Arts Coun. grantee Ill. Arts Coun., 1981, Spl. Assistance grantee, Ill. Arts Coun., 1995. Mem. Chgo. Artist's Coalition (founding mem., 1st chairperson 1974-75), Coll. Art Assn., Internat. Sculpture Ctr., Women's Caucus for Art, Arts Club Chgo. Avocations: art, reading, walking, traveling, visiting museums. Home: 2238 N Geneva Ter Chicago IL 60614-3716

MIGEON, BARBARA RUBEN, pediatrician, geneticist; b. Rochester, N.Y., July 31, 1931; d. William Saul and Sara (Gitin) Ruben; m. Claude Jean Migeon, Apr. 2, 1960; children: Jacques Claude, Jean-Paul, Nicole. BA, Smith Coll., 1952; MD, SUNY, Buffalo, 1956. Diplomate Am. Bd. Pediatrics; cert. in med. genetics. Pediatric residency The Johns Hopkins U., Balt., 1956-59; fellow in endocrinology Harvard U. Med. Sch., Boston, 1959-60; fellow in genetics The Johns Hopkins Sch. Medicine, Balt., 1960-62, assoc. prof. pediatrics, 1970-79, joint appointment in biology, 1978—, prof., 1979—, founding dir. PhD program in human genetics, 1979-89. Mem. Genetics Study Sect., NIH, Bethesda, Md., 1975-77, Mammalian Genetics Study Sect., NIH, Bethesda, 1977-79, Human Genome Study Sect., NIH, Bethesda, 1991-93. Contbr. more than 100 rsch. papers to profl. publs. [illegible], recipient Outstanding Woman Physician award Med. Coll. Pa.; Vis. investigator Carnegie Instn. of Washington, 1975, Exch. prof. Guys Hosp., 1986. Mem. Am. Pediatric Soc., Am. Soc. Human Genetics. Office: Inst Genetic Medicine CMSC 10-04 The Johns Hopkins U Baltimore MD 21287-0001

MIGIELICZ, GERALYN, photojournalist; b. St. Louis, Feb. 15, 1958; d. Edward J. and Mary Ann (McCarthy) M. BJ, U. Mo., 1979. Photographer Emporia (Kans.) Gazette, 1979-80; chief photographer St. Joseph (Mo.) News-Press & Gazette, 1980-83; photo editor, photographer Seattle Times, 1984; picture editor Rocky Mountain News, Denver, 1985-86; graphics editor San Jose (Calif.) Mercury News, 1986-92, dir. photography, 1992—. Mem. faculty Poynter Inst., U. Mo. Workshop, Latin Am. Photojournalism Conf. Recipient Individual Editing awards Soc. Newspaper Designers, 1988-98, Editing awards, 91-98; named for Overall Excellence in Editing, Picture of Yr. Contest, U. Mo., 1993. Office: San Jose Mercury News 750 Ridder Park Dr San Jose CA 95131-2432

MIGIMOTO, FUMIYO KODANI, retired secondary school educator; b. Oxnard, Calif, Jan. 2, 1918; d. Katsutaro and Yoshio Kodani; m. Tadao Migimoto, June 1956. BA, UCLA, 1939, cert. teaching, 1940; MA, Oberlin Coll., 1953; cert. in teaching, U. Hawaii, 1956. Cert. secondary tchr., Calif., Hawaii. Asst. to dean of coll. Oberlin Coll., Ohio; English tchr. Jackson Coll., Honolulu, Hawaii State Dept. Edn., Honolulu; retired. Mem. textbook evaluation com. Hawaii. Author many poems, editor, military newsletters 1993-1999. Hawaii State Dept. Edn. grantee. Mem ASCD, Internat. Soc. Poets, Pan-Pacific S.E. Asia Women's Assn. Hawaii (past exec. v.p.), Hawaii Edn. Assn., Hawaii State Retired Tchr. Assn., Oahu Retired Tchr. Assn., Alliance for Drama Edn., UCLA Alumni Assn., Oberlin Alumni Assn., Poetry Acad., Alpha Delta Kappa (past chpt. exec. pres., chmn. frat. edn.). Home: 999 Wilder Ave Apt 303 Honolulu HI 96822-2628

MIGLIN, MARILYN, cosmetics executive; Student, Northwestern U. Profl. ballerina; model Marshall Fields; founder, owner Marilyn Miglin Cosmetic Co., 1963—. Active Mayor Richard M. Daley's spl. com. tourism; officer Chgo. Conv. and Tourism Bur.; apptd. Gov. James Edgar Econ. Devel. Bd.; past pres. Oak St. Coun.; founder Women of Destiny (mentoring program). Named in her honor Marilyn Miglin Day, Chgo., 1998. Office: 120 E Oak St Chicago IL 60611-1204

MIGUEL, JENNIFER MARIE, adult education educator; b. Loma Linda, Calif., July 31, 1974; d. Gerhard Arnold and Joyce Louise Steudel; m. Russell Charles Miguel, Sept. 6, 2003. BA in Theatre Arts, Gettysburg (Pa.) Coll., 1996; MA in English, Coll. of Staten I., 2003. Cert. tchr. N.Y. Sec. music dept. Gettysburg Coll., 1992, shop supr. theater dept., 1993—96; advt. mgr. The Gettysburgian, 1995—96; carpenter, driver Noble Theatrical, Inc., Bklyn., 1996—97; admin. asst. Northwestern Mut. Life, N.Y.C., 1997—98, The New 42d St., Inc., N.Y.C., 1998—99; rsch. asst. Cooper Stevens, N.Y.C., 1999; counselor A Very Spl. Pl., Staten I., 1999—2000; vet. technician Animal Hosp. of Staten I., 1999—2000; music tchr. Sunnyside Music Sch., Staten I., 1999—2002; tchr. Moore Cath. H.S., Staten I., 2001, Bklyn. Studio Sch., 2001—, South Shore Adult Edn., Bklyn., 2002. Treas., co. mgr. Theatre SanGreal, Inc., Staten I., 2001—03. Dir.: (plays) Cowboy Mouth, About You, About Me, About Us, Day of Absence, Women and Wallace; stage mgr. Dante's Paradiso, Macbeth, The Tempest, City of Hope; contbr. poetry to anthologies. Mem.: Alpha Phi Omega (life). Avocations: travel, music, cooking, reading. Personal E-mail: msteudel@si.rr.com.

MIHAL, SANDRA POWELL, systems analyst; b. Balt., Dec. 15, 1941; d. Sanford William and Mary Louise (Barry) Powell; m. James George Anderson, June 15, 1963; children: Robin Marie, James Brian, Melissa Lee, Derek Clair; m. Charles Turner Barber, Apr. 18, 1978; stepchildren: Gretchen Jayco, Katrina Hope; m. Ladislaw Paul Mihal, May 25, 1991; stepchildren: Alexander Paul, Suzie May, Natasha Elizabeth, Rudy Darius. BA, Mt. St. Agnes Coll., 1963; MA, N.Mex. State U., 1970, Purdue U., 1975; EdD, Vanderbilt U., 1990. Cert. tchr., Md. Tchr. Ridgely-Dulaney Jr. H.S., Towson, Md., 1964; grad. asst. N.Mex. State U., Las Cruces, 1967—69; acad. advisor, instr. polit. sci. Purdue U., West Lafayette, Ind., 1974—78; prof., acad. sys. analyst U. So. Ind., Evansville, 1978—82; assoc. prof., chair dept. computer info. sys. Henderson (Ky.) C.C., 1982—88; prof. computer tech., divsn. chair Anne Arundel C.C., Arnold, Md., 1988—91; computer sys. analyst immigration and naturalization svc. Dept. of Justice, Washington, 1991—92, Glynco, Ga., 1995—; dep. program mgr. distributed learning Fed. Law Enforcement Training Ctr., Homeland Security, Glynco, Ga., 2002—. Bd. dirs. Ind. Polit. Sci. Assn., Muncie, 1984-88, Internat. Studies Assn.-Midwest, Chgo., 86-88; pres. Ky. Acad. Computer Users' Group, Lexington, 1985-86; mem. telecom. adv. bd. C.C. Sys., Annapolis, Md., 1990-91; computer sys. network analyst CLARC Svcs., Pt. Charlotte, Fla., 92-95; adj. prof. history and polit. sci. Edison C.C., Punta Gorda, Fla., 1993-95. Author: Learning By Doing BASIC, 1983, Computers Learning By Doing, 1984; contbr. to several profl jours. 1980-90; author, spkr. series Faculty/Staff Edison CC 94, Ednl. Tech. Nova U., 1995. Block coord. several neighborhood assns.; computer adv. bd. Henderson County Sch., 1982-88; chmn. Newburgh (Ind.) Youth Orgn., 78-86; judge Sci. Fair, Annapolis, 1988-90; nomination bd. Ky. Higher Edn. Assn., 1989-91; mem. Charlotte Chorale, Port Charlotte, 1992-94, Peace River Power Squadron, Port Charlotte, 1994-96. Coast Guard Aux., 1995-97. Md. State Tchr. Bd. Edn. scholar, 1960-63; fellow Sloan Found., 1973-75, U. Ky., 1984. Mem. Soc. Applied Learning Tech., Assn. Computing Machinery (v.p. 85—), Am. Legion, Pi Gamma Mu. Democrat. Mem. Ch. Of Christ. Avocations: sailing, swimming, cooking, playing the dulcimer. Home: 112 Oak Ridge Rd Brunswick GA 31523-9741 Office Phone: 912-267-2591.

MIHELIC, TRACEY L. lawyer; b. Lake Forest, Ill., Sept. 12, 1965; BA, Ill., 1990. With Gardner, Carton & Douglas, Chgo., 1990—2000, ptnr., 1998—2000, Baker & McKenzie, Chgo., 2000—. Mem.: ABA, Internat. Emissions Trading Assn., Emissions Mktg. Assn., Ill. State Bar Assn. Office: Baker and McKenzie One Prudential Plz 130 E Randolph Dr Chicago IL 60601*

MILLER, SUSAN DIANE, artist; b. NYC; d. Charles and Alyce Mary (Gebhardt) Knapp. BFA, SUNY, 1988; MFA, U. North Tex., 1992. Scenic designer Forestburgh (N.Y.) Playhouse, 1989; adj. prof. Tex. Christian U., Ft. Worth, 1992-94; lectr. U. Tex., Dallas, 1995-99, SUNY, New Paltz, 1999—. Treas. mem. 500X Gallery, Dallas, 1991-92. One-woman shows include Western Tex. Coll., 1993, Brazos Gallery, Richland Coll., 1993, Women & Their Work Gallery, 1995 (Gallery Artists Series award, 1995), A.I.R. Gallery, 1996, Milagros Contemporary Art, 1996, Pentimenti Gallery, Pa., 1997, Plano Art Ctr., 1999, Orange County C.C., 2000, Continental Gallery, 2001, Marie Park Studios, 2001, Weir Farm Trust, Plano Art Ctr., 2003; resident artist Weir Farm Nat. Hist. Trust. Recipient 4th Nat. Biennial Exhbns. Grand Purchase award, 1991, Mus. Abilene award, 1992, Lubbock Art Festival Merit award, 1992, 2d pl. award, Matrix Gallery, 1995, Hon. Mention award 3d Biennial Gulf of Mex. Exhbn., 1995, 1st place award, Soho Gallery, 1996, Juror's Choice award, Bucking the Texan Myth Exhbn., 1998, hon. mention, Susquehanna Art Mus., 1998, 1999, Faculty Devel. award, 2001, NYSCA award, 2003. Mem. Coll. Art Assn. Office: PO Box 775 Sparrow Bush NY 12780-0775

MIKAN, KATHLEEN JOYCE KEHRER, medical/surgical nurse, educator; b. Galion, Ohio; BSN cum laude, Ohio State U., Columbus, 1961; MSN, U. Colo., Denver, 1963; PhD, Mich. State U., East Lansing, 1972; postdoctoral, U. Utah, Salt Lake City, 1991. Staff nurse Ohio State U. U. Hosp., Columbus, 1961; asst. instr. Ohio State U., Columbus, 1961-62, instr. med.-surg. nursing, team nursing and fundamentals of nursing, 1963-65; asst. prof. Mich. State U., East Lansing, 1965-67, co-dir. multi-media project, 1967-69; asst. prof. Case Western Res. U., Cleve., 1970-72, assoc. in nursing, 1970-74, program dir. Health Sci. Communications Ctr., 1971-74, ednl. specialist primary health practitioner program, 1972-74, assoc. prof., 1972-74, adminstrv. officer, 1973-74; dir. learning resources U. Ala., Birmingham, 1974-91, prof., 1974—, mem. faculty post master fellowship program in oncology nursing edn., 1980-83, media dir., 1984-87, 1985-89, project faculty, cost mgmt. edn. for nurses contract, 1986-88, media expert, 1988-91, prof., 1974—. Nurse Camp Taconic, Pittsfield, Mass., summers, 1961, 62; mem. planning com. 5th Nat. Learning Resources Conf. U. Tex., San Antonio, 1994; SCAMC referee for paper selection Ann. Symposium on Computer Applications in Med. Care, 1985—; out of state expert rsch. proposal reviewer La. Edn. Quality Support Fund State of La. Bd. Regents, 1990; cons. expansion of learning resource capacity and computer utilization to various schs. nursing; mem. spl. project review panel divsn. of Nursing HEW, 1989—; mem. adv. bd. dirs. The Soc. Nursing Profls., 1991—; speaker, presenter in field; cons. WHO, Indonesia, 1995; sec. Univ. Ala. Birmingham Faculty Senate, 1995-97. Manuscript reviewer FOCUS, 1984—; author (with Eula Aiken) In Computer Applications in Nursing Education and Practice, 1992; contbr. articles to profl. jours. Mem. Lung Resource Ctr. Com. Ala. Lung Assn., 1980-90, community health and program support com., 1990—. Recipient Red Ribbon award Am. Film Festival Case Western Res. U., 1972, Bronze award Internat. Film and TV Festival Case Western Res. U., 1972. Fellow Am. Acad. Nursing (Svc. cert. 1990); mem. ANA (coun. on computer applications in nursing), Assn. for Ednl. Communications and Tech., Nat. League for Nursing (nat. forum on computers in health care and nursing, coun. on nursing informatics), Ala. Instrl. Media Assn., Ala. Lung Assn., Ala. State Nurses Assn., Am. Acad. of Nursing (pub. rels. com. 1987-90), Ohio State U. Nursing Alumnae Assn., U. Colo. Alumni Assn., U. Colo. Sch. of Nursing Alumni, Lambda Alpha Delta, Sigma Theta Tau (Internat. Officer award 1985-91, heritage com. 1985-91, sec. 1985-91, publ. com. 1987-91, Internat. Heritage award, chair 1991, co-chair resolutions com. biennial conv. 1991, co-chair voting com. biennial conv. 1991, libr. sci. com. 1991—, evaluation visitor 1991, installing officer 1992), Phi Kappa Phi, Am. Nurses Found. Century Club.

MIKELL, NANCY THERESA, pharmacist; b. Memphis, Sept. 14, 1952; d. George Edwards Goodman and Mary Elizabeth Parrish; m. Robert Doyle Mikell, Jr., Jan. 10, 1976. BS in Pharmacy, U. Miss., 1975. Staff pharmacist HMO Hunter Found., Lexington, Ky., 1976—77, VA Med. Ctr., Lexington, 1977—80, St. Francis Hosp., Charleston, SC, 1980—82, VA Med. Ctr., Charleston, 1982—83, IV specialist pharmacist, 1983—88, supr. pharmacy svcs., 1988—98, dir. pharmacy svc., 1998—. Bd. advisors Trident Tech. Sch., Charleston, 1995—, MUSC Sch. Pharmacy, Charleston, 1997—. Active Friends of the Libr. Charleston County Libr., 1985—; mem. Carolopolis award com. Preservation Soc., Charelston, 1991—; active Harris Teater Consumer Bd., Charelston, 1997—. Mem.: DAR (vice regent 2001—03), Southeastern Soc. Health Sys. Pharmacists (pres. 2001—02, Lillian Price award 2001—02, Svc. award 2002—03), U.S. Daus. 1812 (state registrar 2000—03), United Daus. of the Confederacy (chaplain 1999—2001), Phi Lambda Sigma. Republican. Presbyterian. Avocations: museum volunteer, war and wardrobe, reading, watercolor. Home: 79 Pitt St Charleston SC 29403

MIKES, JUDITH PAULINE, music educator; b. Winnipeg, Manitoba, Canada, Dec. 4, 1949; d. Austen Geoffrey Trevallyn-Jones and Alfea Louisa Jones; m. Loniel Jerry Mikes, Aug. 2, 1975; children: Heather Autumn, Steven Loniel. MusB, Miami U., Oxford, Ohio, 1972; MEd, Kent State U., 1974. Cert. tchg. Music K-12 Ohio Dept. Edn., 1984, Permanent Tchg. Cert. - Spl. Edn. Ohio Dept. Edn., 1985, cert. Nat. Bd. Early Middle Childhood Music Nat. Bd. Profl. Tchg. Stds., 2002. Tchr. spl. edn. Stow-Munroe Falls City Schs., 1974—77, tchr. music, 1972—. Dir. Sto-Notes, Stow, Ohio, 1982—, Stow Youth Symphony, 1987—; inaugural mem. clarinetist Stow Chamber Orch., 1998—. Selected exhibitor (capital conf.) Tchg. Music Literacy With Recorders (Student Achievement Fair, 2002), (capital conference) Music, Math, and Graphing with Tech. (Student Achievement Fair, 2003), presenter (conf.) Nat. Bd. for Profl. Tchg. Standards, Wash. D.C., 2003, Greater Akron Math. Educators Soc. Conf., 2004. Mem. PTA, Stow Munroe Falls, Ohio, 1972—2003, reflection's contest adjudicator, 1997—2003. Recipient Disting. Alumni award, Exceptionally Talented Children All Am. Youth Show Choir, 1992, Golden Rule award, JC Penny, 1996, 25 Yrs. Svc. award, Ohio Music Educators Assn., 2001, Master Cadre Tchrs. Tech., Summit Edn. Initiative, 2003, Outstanding Educator Yr., Fishcreek Elem. PTA, 2003, Recognition of Excellence award, Ohio Coalition Bd. Cert. Tchrs., 2003, Govs. Ednl. Leadership award, Ohio, 2003, grantee Impact II Disseminator Grant award, Summit Edn. Initiative, 2003—04. Mem.: Ohio Music Educators Assn., Music Educators Nat. Conf., Parent Tchr. Assn. (second v.p. 1976—77), Stow Teachers Assn. (bldg. rep. 1975—77), North East Ohio Educators Assn., Ohio Edn. Assn., NEA, Orgn. of Am. Kodaly Educators, North Coast Kodaly Assn. (coll. liaison 2002—), Midwest Kodaly Music Educators Assn. Achievements include design of published Exemplar on the World Wide Web, Music Literacy with Recorders; published Exemplar on the World Wide Web, Graphing Orchestras. Home: PO Box 1646 Stow OH 44224 Office: Fishcreek Elementary School 5080 Fishcreek Rd Stow OH 44224 Personal E-mail: judithpm@aol.com. E-mail: st_mikes@mail.neonet.k12.oh.us.

MIKESELL, PAMELA PRESTWOOD, guidance counselor; b. Waukegan, Ill., May 16, 1945; d. Robert Milton and Ann Sandra (Subotka) Prestwood; m. Jan Erwin Mikesell, Dec. 25, 1965; children: Danielle Marie, Lisa Michelle. Grad., Western Ill. U., 1967, Western Md. Coll., 1975. Dir. Fairfield (Pa.) Sch. Bd., 1988-92; councilwoman Carroll Valley (Pa.) Boro, 1996—. Mem. NEA, Pa. Edn. Assn., Littlestown Edn. Assn. (pres. 1985-87, 91-93, 2002-), Pa. Sch. Counselors Assn., Delta Kappa Gamma (pres. 1996-98). Democrat. Episcopalian. Home: 6 Meadow Trl Fairfield PA 17320-8220

MIKIEWICZ, ANNA DANIELLA, marketing and international business exporter; b. Chgo., Dec. 22, 1960; d. Zdislaw and Lucy (Magnusewska) M. BS in Mktg., Elmhurst Coll., 1982; postgrad., Triton Coll. Asst. to midwestern regional mgr. Melster Pub. Co., Chgo., 1983; sales rep. First Impressions, Elk Grive, Ill., 1984; asst. to Midwestern dist. mgr. Airco Ind. Gases, Broadview, Carol Stream, Ill., 1985; customer svc. & ops. mgr. Yamazen USA, Inc., Schaumburg, Ill., 1985-88; nat. sales & mktg. coord. Kitamura Machinery U.S.A. Inc., 1988-95; mktg. mgr. Beth Lee Boutique, 1995-97; internat. bus. export control sales coord. MHI Machine Tool USA, Inc. subs. Mistubishi Heavy Industries, 1997-99; internat. bus. asst. to exec. v.p. sales America Excel, Inc., Palatine, Ill., 1999—; internat. bus. Brazil Market JST Sales Am., Inc., Palatine, 2000—. Named Chgo. Polish Queen Polish Am. Culture Club, 1983-84. Mem. NAFE. Republican. Roman Catholic.

MIKKELSEN, BARBARA BERRY, retired retail executive, rancher; b. Wichita Falls, Tex., June 16, 1942; d. Marshall Keith Berry and Louie Arlene Williams; m. John Hardie Mikkelsen, Nov. 24, 1967. BA, Tulane U., New Orleans, La., 1965. Pres. White Rabbit, Inc, Vernon, Tex., 1980—96, Plum Creek Farms, Inc, Vernon, Tex., 1985—. Adv. bd. Vernon Humane Soc., Tex., 1983—2003; mem. Adv. Bd. for Vernon State Hosp., Vernon, Tex., 1974; mem. of bd. Vernon Boys and Girls Club, Vernon, Tex., 1969—2003; chmn. spl. events Santa Fe Opera, 2003—04, mem. of bd., 2003—, Anson County Hist. Soc., Wadesboro, NC, 1988—89, Red River Valley Mus., Vernon, Tex., 1983—2000, Wilbarger Country Hist. Soc., Vernon, Tex., 1988—99; pres. Vernon Jr. League, Vernon, Tex., 1969—71, mem. of bd., 1971—76, Broadway Theatre League, Wichita Falls, Tex., 1970—72. Recipient 25 Yr. Award, Vernon Boys and Girls Club, 1994, Donor, Vernon Humane Soc., 1984. Avocations: raising and training horses, art, travel, opera, theater. Home: 1288 Este Ln Santa Fe NM 87501 Office: 2429 Texas St Vernon TX 76384 Personal E-mail: eagle505@earthlink.net.

MIKLES, ALICIA GENEVIEVE, artist, publishing executive; b. Syracuse, N.Y., Feb. 22, 1970; d. Stephen Philip Mikles and Janice Mary Wagner; m. Daniel Ethan Green, Aug. 1, 1998. BFA summa cum laude, Syracuse U., 1992. Design asst. HarperCollins Pub., N.Y.C., 1993—94, staff designer, 1994—98, design supr., 1998—99, assoc. art dir., 2000—02, art dir., 2003—. Portfolio reviewer Soc. Children's Book Writers and Illustrators, Roanoak, Va., 1998; collabor Inst. Aesthetic Modulation, 2000—. Designer Violet and Claire, 2000, The Boy of a Thousand Faces, 2001 (Children's Trade 3d pl. award Bookbinder's Guild N.Y., 2001, Young Adult 1st pl. jacket award Bookbinder's Guild N.Y., 2001), Loser, 2003.

MIKULSKI, BARBARA ANN, senator; b. Balt., July 20, 1936; d. William and Christine (Kutz) M. BA, Mt. St. Agnes Coll., 1958; MSW, U. Md., 1965; LLD (hon.), Goucher Coll., 1973, Hood Coll., 1978, Bowie State U., 1989, Morgan State U., 1990, U. Mass., 1991; DHL (hon.), Pratt Inst., 1974. Tchr. Vista Tng. Ctr. Mount St. Mary's Sem., Balt.; social worker Balt. Dept. Social Services, 1961-63, 66-70; mem. Balt. City Council, 1971-76, 95th-99th Congresses from 3d Md. Dist., 1977-87; U.S. senator from Md., 1987—; sec. Dem. Conf. 104th-106th Congress. Adj. prof. Loyola Coll., 1972-76; mem. U.S. Senate labor and human resources com., 1987—, ranking mem. subcom. on aging, 1993—; mem. appropriations com., 1987, ranking mem. subcom. on vets., housing, and ind. agys., 1987—. Bd. visitors U.S. Naval Acad. Recipient Nat. Citizen of Yr. award Buffalo Am.-Polit. Eagle, 1973, Woman of Yr. Bus. & Profl. Women's Club Assn., 1973, Outstanding Alumnus U. Md. Sch. Social Work, 1973, Govt. Social Responsibility award, 1991. Mem. LWV. Democrat.*

MIKUMO, AKIKO, lawyer; b. Kyoto, June 18, 1953; BA, U. Calif., Berkeley, 1978; JD, NYU, 1982. Assoc. Weil, Gotshal & Manges LLP, N.Y.C., 1982—90, ptnr., 1990—, head U.S. practice London, 1998—2000. Mem.: ABA (mem. com. on corp. law 1993—), Assn. of the Bar of the City of N.Y. Office: Weil Gotshal & Manges LLP 767 Fifth Ave New York NY 10153*

MILANO, ALYSSA, actress; b. N.Y.C., Dec. 19, 1972; d. Thomas M. and Lin Milano. Student, Bel Air Prep. Sch., L.A. Appeared on TV series Who's the Boss?, 1984-92, Melrose Place, 1997-98, Charmed, 1998- (also prodr.); appeared in TV movies The Canterville Ghost, 1986, Dance'Til Dawn, 1988, Conflict of Interest, 1992, Candles in the Dark, 1993, Casualties of Love: The Long Island Lolita Story, 1993, Confessions of a Sorority Girl, 1994; appeared in various TV spls.; on TV shows Body by Jake, 1988, The Arsenio Hall Show, 1989, various shows for American Treasury, 1989, To Brave Alaska, 1996; film actress Old Enough, 1982, Commando, 1985, Speed Zone, 1989, Where the Day Takes You, 1992, Little Sister, 1992, Double Dragon, 1993, Embrace of the Vampire, 1995, At Home with the Webbers, 1993, The Surrogate, 1995, Public Enemy # 1, 1995, No Fear, 1996, Glory Daze, 1996, Jimmy Zip, 1996, Below Utopia, 1997, Hugo Pool, 1997, Buying the Cow, 2002, Kiss the Bride, 2002, Dickie Roberts: Former Child Star, 2003; stage debut in Annie, various cities, 1980-81; stage appearances include All Night Long, Second Stage Theatre Co., N.Y.C., 1984, Jane Eyre, Theatre Opera Music Inst., N.Y.C., others; TV guest appearances include The Outer Limits, 1995, Spin City, 1996, Fantasy Island, 1998; prodr. Below Utopia, 1997. Recipient Best Supporting Actress award Youth Films Awards; Silver prize Tokyo Music Festival, 1989. Mem. SAG, AFTRA, Actors' Equity Assn.*

MILANOVICH, NORMA JOANNE, training and development company executive; b. Littlefork, Minn., June 4, 1945; d. Lyle Albert and Loretta (Leona) Drake; m. Rudolph William Milanovich, Mar. 18, 1943 (dec.); 1 child, Rudolph William Jr. BS in Home Econs., U. Wis., Stout, 1968; MA in Curriculum and Instrn., U. Houston, 1973, EdD in Curriculum and Program Devel., 1982. Instr. human svcs. dept. U. Houston, 1971-75; dir. videos project U. N.Mex., Albuquerque, 1976-78, dir. vocat. edn. equity ctr., 1978-88, asst. prof. occupational edn., 1982-88, coord. occupational vocat. edn. programs, 1983-88, dir. consortium rsch. and devel. in occupational edn., 1984-88; pres. Alpha Connection Tng. Corp., Albuquerque, 1988—; exec. dir. Trinity Found., 1991—; pres. Athena Leadership Ctr., 1999—. Adj. instr. Cen. Tng. Acad., Dept. Energy, Wackenhut; mem. faculty U. Phoenix; adj. faculty So. Ill. U., Lesley Coll., Boston; lectr. in field. Author: Model Equitable Behavior in the Classroom, 1983, Handbook for Vocational-Technical Certification in New Mexico, 1985, A Vision for Kansas: Systems of Measures and Standards of Performance, 1992, Workplace Skills: The Employability Factor, 1993; editor: Choosing What's Best for You, 1982, A Handbook for Handling Conflict in the Classroom, 1983, Starting Out...A Job Finding Handbook for Teen Parents, Going to Work...Job Rights for Teens; author: JTPA Strategic Marketing Plan, 1990, We, The Arcturians, 1990, Sacred Journey to Atlantis, 1991, The Light Shall Set You Free, 1996; editor: Majestic Raise newsletter, 1996—, Celestial Voices newsletter, 1991—; conf. presenter in field. Del. Youth for Understanding Internat. Program, 1985—90; mem. adv. bd. Southwestern Indian Poly. Inst., 1984—88; com. mem. Region VI Consumer Exch. Com., 1982—84; coord. various countries Worldwide Conf. for Peace on Earth, 1999—2004; coord. Customized Leadership Programs, 2004; bd. dirs. Albuquerque Single Parent Occupational Scholarship Program, 1984—86. Grantee N.Mex. Dept. Edn., 1976-78, 78-86, 83-86, HEW, 1979, 80, 81, 83, 84, 85, 86, 87. Mem. ASTD, Am. Vocat. Assn., Vocat. Edn. Equity Coun., Nat. Coalition for Sex Equity Edn., Am. Home Econs. Assn., Inst. Noetic Scis., N.Mex. Home Econs. Assn., N.Mex. Vocat. Edn. Assn., N.Mex. Adv. Coun. on Vocat. Edn., Greater Albuquerque C. of C., NAFE, Phi Delta Kappa, Phi Upsilon Omicron, Phi Theta Kappa. Democrat. Roman Catholic. Office: Athena Leadership Ctr Scottsdale AZ 85259 E-mail: info@athenalctr.com.

MILBRATH, MARY MERRILL LEMKE, quality assurance professional; b. Evanston, Ill., Aug. 13, 1940; d. William Frederick and Martha Merrill (Slagel) Lemke; m. Gene McCoy Milbrath, Aug. 22, 1964; children: Elizabeth Ann, Sarah Toril Jeanne. BA in Biology, Albion Coll., 1962; MS in Plant Pathology, U. Ariz., 1966. Microbiologist Abbott Labs., North Chicago, Ill., 1962; toxicologist U. Ariz., Tucson, 1965-67, U. Ill., Urbana, 1976-77, entomologist, 1978; plant pathologist State of Oreg., Salem, 1979, chemist, 1980-82; quality auditor Siltec Corp., Salem, 1983-84, quality control supr., 1985-91, quality auditing mgr., 1992-97, implementor ISO 9002, 1995, implementor ISO 9001 Quality Std., 1996, quality assurance dir., 1997—2002; implementor ISO 14001 Silitec Corp., Salem, 1998; pres. MLM Enterprises, 2002—. Active Ill. Emergency Svcs.toxic sub task force U. Ill., Urbana, 1978; mem. Responsible Corp. Citizens Com., Salem, 1989-96. Mem. citizens adv. com. Sch. Bd., Urbana, 1976-78; campaigner Oreg. 5th Dist. Race, Salem, 1984, Oreg. Nat. Abortion Rights Assn. League, Salem, 1986; bd. dirs. Tribute to Outstanding Women, YWCA, 1992, 93, 94, 95; vol. Tree Giving, 1991, 92. NDEA fellow U.S. Dept. Def., 1962; elected Woman of Achievement, YWCA, 1997. Mem. AAUW (chmn. interest group), Am. Soc. for Quality (cert. quality auditor exam writing com. 1993, 95, exam rev. 1996, 98, 2002, spkr. nat. conf. 1999), Willamette U. House Corp. (treas. 1982-85, v.p. 1991-96, mem.-at-large 2000—, treas. 2001--), Delta Gamma (treas. Salem Alumnae chpt. 1981-85, pres. Salem Alumnae chpt. 1987-89, scholarship advisor Willamette U. chpt. 1986-90). Avocations: family activities, travel, painting. Office: Mitsubishi Silicon Am 1351 Tandem Ave NE Salem OR 97303-4105

MILBRETT, TIFFENY CARLEEN, professional soccer player; b. Portland, Oreg., Oct. 23, 1972; Degree in comms. mgmt., U. Portland. Mem. U.S. Women's Nat. Soccer Team; profl. soccer player N.Y. Power, 2001—03. Mem. championship team, Montricoux, France, 1993. Named World Cup Champion, 1999; recipient Gold medal, Centennial Olympic Games, 1996, 3d place medal, 1995, Silver medal, World Univ. Games, 1993, Sydney Olympic Games, 2000. Office: c/o US Soccer Fedn 1801 S Prairie Ave # 1811 Chicago IL 60616-1319

MILBURN, DIANE SUZANE, healthcare industry executive, writer; b. Houston, Tex., Aug. 13, 1961; d. Samuel Milburn and Margaret Russow-Milburn. BA in Journalism, U. Houston, 1986. Rsch. libr. Houston (Tex.) Post Newspaper, 1981—86; gen. assignment reporter Houston (Tex.) Sun Newspaper, 1987—91; acct. clk. Allstak Med., Houston, 1992—95; acct. supr. I.G. Gold, Inc., Houston, 1996—2001; founder, dir. Margaret Russaw Caregivers Found., Houston, 2001—. Vol. Tex. Legis. Black Caucus, Houston and Austin, Tex., 1995—97; chmn. W.Va. Ch. and Soc., Houston, 1996—2000. Mem.: NAACP, Nat. Family Caregivers Assn., African Am. Leadership Network, Cancare Houston. Avocations: gold trading, reading, drawing, community service. Office: MRCF Inc PBM 332 PO Box 710350 Houston TX 77271

MILDVAN, DONNA, infectious diseases physician; b. Phila., June 20, 1942; d. Carl David and Gertrude M.; m. Rolf Dirk Hamann; 1 child, Gabriella Kay. AB magna cum laude, Bryn Mawr Coll., 1963; MD, Johns Hopkins U., 1967. Diplomate Am. Bd. Internal Medicine and Infectious Diseases. Intern, resident Mt. Sinai Hosp., N.Y.C., 1967-70, fellow, infectious diseases, 1970-72; asst., assoc. prof. clin. medicine Mt. Sinai Sch. Medicine, N.Y.C., 1972-87; prof. clinical medicine Dept. Medicine, Mt. Sinai Sch. Medicine, N.Y.C., 1987-88, prof. medicine, 1988-94; physician-in-charge infectious diseases Beth Israel Med. Ctr., N.Y.C., 1972-79, chief, div. infectious diseases, 1980—; prof. medicine Albert Einstein Coll. of Medicine, N.Y.C., 1994—. Mem. AIDS charter rev. com., NIH/Nat. Inst. Allergy and Infectious Diseases, Bethesda, 1987—; cons. FDA, Rockville, 1987—, Ctrs. for Disease Control, Atlanta, 1985-86; among first to describe AIDS, "Pre-AIDS", AIDS Dementia, 1982, among first to study AZT, 1986; Keynote speaker, II Internat. Conf. on AIDS, Paris, 1986 and other achievements in field; Sophie Jones Meml. lectr. in infectious diseases U. Mich. Hosps., 1984. Contbr. numerous articles to profl. jours; co-editor two books, several book chpts. and abstracts on infectious diseases and AIDS. Grantee N.Y. State AIDS Inst., 1986-87; Henry Strong Denison scholar Johns Hopkins U. Sch. Medicine, 1967; recipient Woman of Achievement award AAUW, 1987; contract for antiviral therapy in AIDS, Nat. Cancer Inst./Nat. Inst. Allergy and Infectious Diseases, 1985-86, subcontract Nat. Inst. Allergy and Infectious Diseases, ACTU, 1987-99, prin. investigator, 2000—. Fellow Infectious Diseases Soc. Am.; mem. Am. Soc. Microbiology, AAAS, Harvey Soc., Internat. AIDS Soc. Democrat. Jewish. Avocation: old movies. Office: Beth Israel Med Ctr 1st Ave New York NY 10003-7903

MILES, AMY E. recreational facility executive; With Pricewaterhouse-Coopers, LLC, 1989—98; sr. mgr. Deloitte & Touche, 1998—99; from sr. v.p. fin. to exec. v.p., CFO, treas. Regal Entertainment Group, Englewood, Colo., 1999—2000, exec. v.p., 2000—, CFO, 2000—, treas., 2000—. Office: Regal Entertainment Group 9110 East Nichols Ave Ste 200 Englewood CO 80112

MILES, CHRISTINE MARIE, museum director; b. Madison, Ind., Mar. 2, 1951; d. Leland Weber and Mary Virginia (Geyer) M. BA, Boston U., 1973; MA, George Washington U., 1982; postgrad., Mus. Mgmt. Inst., 1985. Curatorial asst. Mus. City of N.Y., 1973-75; art gallery dir. South Street Seaport Mus., N.Y.C., 1975-77; rschr. The Octagon, AIA Found., Washington, 1978-80; dir. Fraunces Tavern Mus., Washington, 1980-86, Albany (N.Y.) Inst. History and Art, 1986—. Bd. dirs. SUNY-Albany Found. Author, writer/coordinator, compiler of catalogs in field. Mem. Arts Commn. City of Albany; pres. Gallery Assn. N.Y. State, 1991-93, Mus. Assn. N.Y. State. Mem. Am. Assn. Mus. Office: Albany Inst History and Art 125 Washington Ave Albany NY 12210-2296

MILES, DEBORAH H. language educator; b. New Haven, Conn., July 25, 1953; d. Frederick T. and Jean Robert Hinners; m. Douglas Stuart Miles, Dec. 23, 1978; 1 child, Brendan Douglas. BA magna cum laude, Albertus Manus Coll., 1971—75; MA, So. Conn. State Univ., 1975—80. English tchr. Regional Dist. 17, Haddam, Conn., 1975—99, cirriculum coord., 1999—2001, instrnl. specialist, 2001—; adj. instr. Quinnipiac Univ., Hamden, Conn., 1989—2000. Contbr. articles book reviews in periodicals, 1980—99. Mem. Middlesex C. of C., Middletown, Conn., 2000—. Recipient Celebration of Excellence, State of Conn., 1989. Mem.: Conn. Tchr. Assn., Nat. Tchr. Assn., Nat. Council of Tchrs. of English. Avocations: reading, films, creative writing, gardening. Office: Regional District 17 95 Little City Rd Higganum CT 06441-4323

MILES, ELIZABETH JANE, social worker; b. Upper Fairmount, Md., Mar. 13, 1927; d. Harry Budd Miles and Elizabeth Thomas. AA, St. Mary's Coll., St. Mary's City, Md., 1947; BA, Scarritt Coll., 1949; MSW, Vanderbilt U., 1951. Dir. Christian edn. Meth. Ch., Gaithersberg, Md., 1952—53; mgr., owner Edn. Assn., Pitts., 1954—60, Frontier Press, Balt., 1960—70; social worker, bd. dirs. Home-Coming Mental Health, Bel Air, Md., 1970—90; resident supr. VA Home Programs, Perry Point, Md., 1990; pvt. cons. in field. Mem. bd. Commn. on Aging, Somerset County, Md., 1990—; deaconess Meth. Ch..., Balt., 1951—52; bd. dirs. Country Retreat-Christian Retreat, Bradenton, Fla., 1991—. Scholar, Md. State Senator, 1945, Meth. Missionary Bd. Mem.: Nat. Hist. Trust Assn., Bus. and Profl. Club. Republican. Methodist. Avocations: horses, antiques, restoring family home. Home (Summer): PO Box 144 Manokin MD 21836

MILES, JOAN FOWLE, journalist, writer; b. Woburn, Mass., Aug. 5, 1921; d. Donald Adams and Ethel Adelaide (Wallace) Fowle; m. Stephen Lewis Miles, Sept. 8, 1945; children: Joanna Miles Griffith, Dierdre Miles Burger. BA, Mt. Holyoke Coll., 1943; cert. in pub., Radcliffe Coll., 1948. Copy clk. NBC, N.Y.C., 1943-44; editl. asst. Robert St. John, N.Y.C., 1944-45; cmty. rels. cons. Lahey Clinic, Burlington, Mass., 1978—95; dir. student art project Lahey Clinic Med. Ctr., Burlington, 1983—2002. Profl. svcs. chair Eliot Cmty. Human Svcs., Lexington, Mass., 1988-98; mem. legis. action com. Coop. Met. Ministries, Newton, Mass., 1994-98. Author: Burlington--The Growth Years, 1990, Aftermath-The Last Twenty-Five Years of Burlington History, 1998; editl. writer Burlington Times Union, 1964-68. Sch. bldg. need and sites com. Town of Burlington, 1964-68; mem. Burlington Sch. Com., 1968-86, Lahey Clinic Med. Ctr. Cmty. Benefit Initiative Com., 1996-2002; founder, pres. Burlington Cmty. Scholarship Found./Dollars for Scholars, 1988-2003; mem. parish coun. United Ch. of Christ Congrgational, Burlington. Named Outstanding Citizen, Town of Burlington, 1976; Joan F. MIles Libr. named in her honor Burlington Sch. Com., 1986. Democrat. Avocations: writing, reading, gardening, working out, theater/dance.

MILES, JOANNA, actress, playwright, director; b. Nice, France, Mar. 6, 1940; came to U.S., 1941, naturalized, 1941; d. Johannes Schiefer and Jeanne Miles; m. William Burns, May 23, 1970 (div. 1977); m. Michael Brandman, Apr. 29, 1978; 1 child, Miles. Grad., Putney (Vt.) Sch., 1958. Mem. Actors Studio, Playwrites and Dirs. Workshop, N.Y.C., 1966; co-founder, mem. L.A. Classic Theatre, 1986. Founder, mem. Playwrights Group/LAWW, 1991-98, L.A. Writer's Workshop, 1996-98. Appeared in: (motion pictures) The Way We Live Now, 1969, Bug, 1975, The Ultimate Warrior, 1975, Golden Girl, 1978, Cross Creek, 1983, As Is, 1986, Blackout, 1988, Rosencrants and Guildenstern are Dead, 1991, The

Rhinghart Theory, 1994, Judge Dredd, 1994, Alone, 1996; numerous television films including In What America, 1965, My Mothers House, 1963, Glass Managerie, 1974, Born Innocent, 1974, Aloha Means Goodbye, 1974, The Trial of Chaplain Jensen, 1975, Harvest Home, 1977, Fire in the Sky, 1978, Sophisticated Gents, 1979, Promise of Love, 1982, Sound of Murder, 1983, All My Sons, 1987, The Right to Die, 1987, The Habitation of Dragons, 1991, Heart of Justice, 1991, Water Engine, 1991, Cooperstown, 1992, Legionnaires, 1992, Life Lessons, 1992, Willing to Kill, 1992, The American Clock, 1993, Dark Reflections, 1993, Outcry, 1994, Everything to Gain, 1995, Small Vices, 1998, Crossfire Trail, 1999, Thin Aire, 1999; episodes in numerous TV series including: Barney Miller, Dallas, St. Elsewhere, The Hulk, Trapper John, Kaz, Cagney and Lacey, Studio 5B, 1989, Star Trek: The Next Generation, 1990, 91, Life Stories, 1991, HBO Life Stories, 1993, Total Security, 1997, Nothing Sacred, 1998, Chicago Hope, 1998-99, ER, 2000, Family Law, 2000; stage plays include Once in a Life Time, 1963, Cave Dwellers, 1964, Drums in the Night, 1968, Dracula, 1968, Home Free, 1964, One Night Stands of a Noisy Passenger, 1972, Dylan, 1973, Dancing for the Kaiser, 1976, Debutante Ball, 1985, Kramer, 1977, One Flew Over the Cuckoo's Nest, 1989, Growing Gracefully, 1990, Cut Flowers, 1994; performed in radio shows Sta. KCRW Once in a Lifetime, 1987, Babbit, 1987, Sta. KPFK, Grapes of Wrath, 1989, The White Plague, Sta. KCRW, 1991, Chekhov Short Stories, Sta. KCRW, 1992; playwright, v.p. Brandman Productions; author; (plays) Ethanasia, A Woman in Reconstruction, Hostages, Feathers, On the Shelf. Pres. Children Giving to Children. Recipient 2 Emmy awards, 1974, Women in Radio and TV award, 1974, Actors Studio Achievement award, 1980, Dramalogue award, 1996; nominated Golden Globe, 1994. Mem. Acad. Motion Picture Arts and Scis., Acad. TV Arts and Scis., Dramatists Guild Office: Brandman Prodns 2062 Vine St Apt 5 Hollywood CA 90068-3928 also: The Artists Agy 10000 Santa Monica Blvd Los Angeles CA 90067-7007 E-mail: jmilesb@aol.com.

MILES, LAVEDA ANN, advertising executive; b. Greenville, S.C., Nov. 21, 1945; d. Grady Lewis and Edna Sylvia (Mahaffey) Bruce; m. Charles Thomas Miles, Nov. 10, 1974; 1 child, Joshua Bruce. A in Bus. Adminstrn., North Greenville Jr. Coll. Traffic mgr. WFBV-TV, Greenville, 1968-74; pub. svc. dir., traffic mgr. WTCG-TV, Atlanta, 1974-75; traffic mgr. Henderson Advt. Co., Greenville, 1975-77, broadcast coord., 1977-79, dir. broadcast bus., 1979-82, v.p., dir. broadcast bus., 1982-89, bus. mgr. creative dept., 1989-91, dir. creative svcs., 1991-93, sr. v.p., 1994-96, v.p., dir. creative svcs., 2000—; owner Altamont Mktg., 1996-99. Mem. Leadership S.C., 1994-95; bd. dirs. Boys Home of the South, 2003—. Named one of 100 Best and Brightest Women, Ad Age and Advt. Women of N.Y., 1988. Mem. Advt. Fedn. Greenville (sec. 1979-81), Greenville Ad Club (sec. 1999-2000, pres. 2000—, Silver medal awrd 2003). Republican. Baptist.

MILES, SUZANNE LAURA, dean; b. Omaha, Nebr., Feb. 17, 1953; d. Ronald Ray Miles and Marian Genene (Ganaros) Pflasterer; m. Robert Hill Mason, July 7, 1975; children: Miles, Maraka. BS, Northwestern U., 1975; MA, Ariz. State U., 1978; PhD, U. Ariz., 1992. Cert. coll. tchr., Ariz. Admissions advisor Oakland U., Rochester, Mich., 1979-83; faculty U. Phoenix, Tucson, 1984—; ednl. program planner Pima Cmty. Coll., Tucson, 1991-92, assoc. dean of instrn., 1992-97, dean math. and comms. arts, 1997—. Co-chair instnl. climate task force Pima C.C., 1995—, EC project adminstr., 1995-97; adj. lectr. U. Ariz., 1997—; presenter in field. Vice chair U. High Parent Bd., Tucson, 1996—; moderator Rincon Congrl. Ch., Tucson, 1997-98; hospice vol. Tucson Med. Ctr., 1994—. Kellogg fellowship League for Innovation, U. Tex., 1997—; recipient Omaha North High Outstanding Alumni award, 1995. Mem. AAUW (Tucson chpt. corp. rep. 1996—), Am. Assn. of Women in C.C. (PCC chpt. pres. 1996-97), Way Up Women's Orgn. (Ariz. chpt. conf. com. 1995-97). Republican. United Ch. of Christ. Avocations: theatre, dance, travel, camping. Home: 6492 E Sun Cir Tucson AZ 85750-1932 Office: Pima Cmty Coll Downtown 1255 N Stone Ave Tucson AZ 85709-3002

MILES-CLARK, JEARL, olympic athlete, track and field; b. Gainesville, Fla., Sept. 4, 1966; m. J.J. Clark, Nov. 30, 1996. BA in Business, Ala. A&M, 1988. Winner N.C.A.A. Divsn. II Nats. 400m, 1985; mem. U.S.A. Olympic Team, 1992, 1996. Achievements include world Champion 400m, 1993, USA Outdoor 800m champion, 1st pl. 400 meter, Verizon Millrose Games, 400 meter USA Outsdoor champ, 2002, 1st pl., Oracle Open, 2002, ranked #1 in the US at 400meter, #2 in US at 800 meter by Track and Field News, 2002. Office: c/o USA Track & Field 1 Rca Dome Ste 140 Indianapolis IN 46225-1023

MILES-LA GRANGE, VICKI, judge; b. Oklahoma City, Okla., Sept. 30, 1953; d. Charles and Mary (Greenard) Miles. BA, Vassar Coll., 1974; LLB, Howard U., 1977; cert., U. Ghana, West Africa; DHL (hon.), Oklahoma City U., 1995. Legis. aide Spkr. House Rep. Carl Albert, 1974-76; law clerk Judge Woodrow Seals U.S. Dist. Ct. (so. dist.), Tex., 1977-79; fellow, atty. criminal divsn. U.S. Dept. Justice, Washington, 1979-83; asst. dist. atty. Dist. Atty.'s Office, Oklahoma County, 1983-86; pvt. practice Oklahoma City, 1986-93; mem. Okla. Senate (Dist. 48), 1987-93; U.S. atty. U.S. Dept. Justice, Oklahoma City, Okla., 1993-94; judge U.S. Dist. Ct. (we. dist.), Oklahoma City, 1994—. Bd. trustees Vassar Coll. Mem. ABA, Nat. Bar Assn., Okla. Bar Assn., Am. Inns Ct. Democrat. Baptist. Office: US Dist Judge US Courthouse 200 NW 4th St Ste 5011 Oklahoma City OK 73102-3031

MILEWSKI, BARBARA ANNE, pediatrics nurse, neonatal/perinatal nurse practitioner, critical care nurse; b. Chgo., Sept. 11, 1934; d. Anthony and LaVerne (Sepp) Witt; m. Leonard A. Milewski, Feb. 23, 1952; children: Pamela, Robert, Diane, Timothy. ADN, Harper Coll., Palatine, Ill., 1982; BS, Northern Ill. U., 1992; postgrad., North Park Coll. RN Ill., cert. CPR instr. Staff nurse N.W. Cmty. Hosp., Arlington Heights, Ill., Resurrection Hosp., Chgo.; nurse neonatal ICU Children's Meml. Hosp., Chgo.; day care cons. Cook County Dept. Pub. Health; owner, CEO Child Care Health Cons. CPR instr. Stewart Oxygen Svcs., Chgo., Harper Coll., Children's Meml. Hosp.; instr., organizer parenting and well baby classes and clinics; health coord. CEDA Head Start; mem. adv. bd. Cook County Child Care Resource and Referral; dir. Albany Park Head Start. Vol. Children's Meml. Hosp., Boy Scouts Am. Mem.: Am. Mortar Bd., Sigma Theta Tau.

MILHOLLAND, SANDRA JANE, marriage and family therapist; b. Nashville, July 16, 1944; d. Dan Harding and Frances Jane (Harris) Woodroof; m. Thomas Alva Milholland, June 5, 1966; children: Kay Elizabeth Milholland Orr, Matthew Thomas. BS in Psychology, Abilene Christian U., Abilene, Tex., 1984; MS in Psychology, Abilene Christian U., 1988, MS in Marriage and Family Therapy, 1991. Lic. marriage and family therapist Tex., profl. counselor Tex. Ct. reporter Curtis D. Ruff Ct. Reporters, Lubbock, Tex., 1973—79; with U.S. Probation Svc., Abilene, 1979—90; marriage therapist Abilene, 1990—; prison psychologist Tex. Tech. Correctional Health Care, Abilene, 1995—. Author: Prelude to Joy, 2001 (Disting. Family Ministry award Pepperdine U., 2003); contbr. numerous articles to profl. jours.; contbg. editor: Upreach mag., 1980—85, Christian Woman mag., 2000—. Vol. cmty. police Abilene Police Dept., 2001—; bd. dirs. Clear Fork Rehab. Ctr., Abilene, 1999—2000. Named Outstanding Alumnus, Okla. Christian U., 1986. Mem.: Abilene Writers Guild, Tex. Assn. Marriage and Family Therapy, Am. Assn. Marriage and Family Therapy. Ch. Of Christ. Avocations: race walking, gourmet cooking, tea parties, reading, motortriking.

MILIORA, MARIA TERESA, chemist, psychotherapist, psychoanalyst, educator; b. Somerville, Mass., June 29, 1938; d. Andrew and Maria Civita (Gallinaro) Migliorini. BA cum laude, Regis Coll., 1960; PhD, Tufts U., 1965; MSW, Boston U., 1985. Rsch. asst. Tufts U., Medford, Mass., 1960-64, rsch. assoc., 1965-66; assoc. prof. Suffolk U., Boston, 1965-68, 1968-71, prof., 1971—, chmn. dept. chemistry, 1972-84, presdl. search com., 1980, faculty rep. strategic planning com., 1992—; faculty Boston Inst. for Psychotherapy, 1992-96, Tng. and Rsch. Inst. for Self Psychology, N.Y.C., 1994—. Rsch. assoc. Bio-Research Inst., Cambridge, Mass., 1968. Author: Narcissism, the Family, and Madness, 2000, The Scorsese Psyche on Screen, 2004; contbr. articles to profl. jours. Faculty rep. to trustees Joint Coun. on Univ. Affairs, Suffolk U., 1973-77, 79-81; convenor Pres.'s Commn. on Status of Women, 1974-78, speaker ednl. policy com., 1972-73; chair cultural diversity CLAS Curriculum, 1991—. Mem. AAUP (chpt. pres. 1970), NASW, Am. Chem. Soc. (alt. councillor 1976-82, councillor 1979-82, bd. dirs. Northeastern sect. 1976-80, chmn. pub. rels. sect. 1977-79), Mass. Acad. Clin. Social Work, Nat. Assn. for Advancement Psychoanalysis, Nat. Membership Com. on Psychoanalysis, Sigma Xi (chpt. pres. 1972-73), Sigma Zeta (chpt. sect. 1970-80), Alpha Lambda Delta, Delta Epsilon Sigma. Home: 41 Irving St Newton MA 02459-1611 Office: Suffolk University Beacon Hill Boston MA 02114 E-mail: Theresa0369@comcast.net.

MILITELLO, MICHELLE LEIGH, securitization specialist; b. Phila., Mar. 29, 1975; d. Ralph James and Kathleen Joan Lovuolo; married, May 24, 2003. BBA, James Madison U., 1997. Adminstrv. asst.-securitization ING, N.Y.C., 1997—98, analyst-securitization, 1998—2000, assoc.-securitization, 2000—. Vol. Make-A-Wish, N.Y.C., 1997—; coord., team leader N.Y. Cares, 2000—. Avocation: teaching dance aerobics. Office: ING 1325 Ave of the Americas New York NY 10019

MILITELLO, ROBERTA JAN, artist, illustrator, designer; b. L.I., N.Y., July 28, 1959; d. William S. and Hilde (Lauterbach) M.; m. Thomas Schiel, Sept. 12, 1987 (div.); 1 child, Tara Schiel. BFA magna cum laude, SUNY, Albany, 1981; postgrad., Acad. Fine Art, Munich, 1983-84. Freelance artist, N.Y., 1981-91; instr. painting and drawing Cmty. Sch., Munich, 1991-93, BMW, Munich, 1991-93; freelance illustrator N.Y., 1993—; web adminstr. Cornell U. Coll. Vet. Medicine, Ithaca, NY, 1997—99; web developer Cornell U., Ithaca, NY, 1999—2003, multi-media developer, 2003—. One-woman shows include Univ. Art Gallery, Albany, 1980; exhibited in group shows at Schenectady Mus., 1980, Limner Gallery, East Village, N.Y., 1988, Pasing (Germany) Culture Ctr., 1990, Gasteig Culture Ctr., Munich, 1990, Blutenburg Castle, Munich, 1991, Leppert & Schiel, Rastatt, Germany, 1992, Women's Rights Nat. Hist. Pk., Seneca Falls, N.Y., 1993-94. Grantee City of Munich, 1990, Philip Morris Performance Series, 1990, Art in Architecture, Germany, 1990. Mem. Woodstock Art Assn. (bd. dirs. 1981-87), German Artist Union. Avocation: music.

MILKEY, VIRGINIA A. state legislator; b. Brattleboro, Vt., Jan. 27, 1950; BA, Middlebury Coll., 1972. Mem. Vt. Ho. of Reps., Montpelier, 1991—. Dir. Ret. and Sr. Vol. Program of Windham County.; co-founder, bd. dirs. Bonnyvale Environ. Edn. Ctr.; bd. dirs. Alliance for Bldg. Cmty.; mem. Brattleboro Agrl. Adv. Com.; mem., exec., health, life and state/fed. rels. coms. of Nat. Conf. Ins. Legislators. Rep. Brattleboro Town Meeting; corporator Brattleboro Meml. Hosp. Mem. Nat. Assn. Ret. and Sr. Vol. Program Dirs., New Eng. Assn. Ret. and Sr. Vol. Program Dirs., Vt. Nat. Sr. Svc. Corps. Dirs. Assn. Home: 266 Meadowbrook Rd Brattleboro VT 05301-2581

MILKMAN, BEVERLY L. federal agency administrator; b. Ft. Pierce, Fla., Jan. 9, 1945; d. Robert George and Annette (Leatherwood) Lyford; m. Raymond H. Milkman, Feb. 27, 1972; 1 child, Katherine. BA magna cum laude, U. Ariz., 1967; MLA with honors, Johns Hopkins U., 1972; MA, George Washington U., 1978. Rsch. analyst Peat, Marwick, Mitchell & Co., 1967-69, program analyst, 1970-72, spl. asst. to dep. sec., 1972-74, spl. asst. to asst. sec., 1974-80, dir. office tech. assistance, 1980-81, dir. office of planning, tech. assistance, rsch. and evaluation, 1981-86, dep. dir. grant programs, 1986-88; exec. dir. Com. for Purchase from People Who are Blind or Severely Disabled, 1988—. Assoc. editor Economic Development Quarterly; contbr. articles to profl. publs. Recipient Disting. and Meritorious Exec. Rank awards, 1993, 96. Office: Com Purchase from People Who Are Blind or Severely Disabled 1215 Jefferson Davis Hwy Arlington VA 22202-4302

MILKMAN, MARIANNE FRIEDENTHAL, retired city planner; b. Berlin, May 13, 1931; arrived in US, 1957; d. Ernst Leopold and Margarethe (Goldschmidt) Friedenthal; m. Roger Dawson Milkman, Oct. 18, 1958; children: Ruth, Louise, Janet, Paul. BA, Cambridge (Eng.) U., 1952, MA, 1956; teaching diploma, London U., 1953. Tchr. biology Milham Ford High Sch., Oxford, Eng., 1953-57; teaching fellow, rsch. asst. U. Mich., Ann Arbor, 1957-59; sci. dir. Children's Sch. Sci., Woods Hole, Mass., 1971-72; planning technician dept. planning and program devel. City of Iowa City, 1975-76, planner I, 1976-79, assoc. planner, 1979-85, coord. comty. devel., 1986-96; ret., 1996. Bikeways chmn Project Green, Iowa City, 1968—75; chmn. comprehensive plan com. Town of Falmouth, 2002—. Fellow, English Speaking Union, 1957—58; scholar State, Cambridge Univ and London Univ, 1949—53, Fulbright Traveling, Univ Mich, 1957. Mem.: Nat Community Develop Asn, Nat Asn Housing and Redevelopment Offs, Am Planning Asn (secy-treas Iowa chpt 1982—84, vpres 1984—86, pres 1986—88, chmn univ relations comt 1987—91, Pres's Award 1988). Jewish. Avocations: mountain hiking, wild flowers, music. Home: 12 Fells Rd Falmouth MA 02540-1626

MILLANE, LYNN, retired town official; b. Buffalo, Oct. 14, 1928; d. Robert P. and Justine A. (Ross) Schermerhorn; m. J. Vaughan Millane, Jr., Aug. 16, 1952; children: Maureen, Michele, John, Mark, Kathleen. EdB, U. Buffalo, 1949, EdM in Health Edn., 1951. Coun. mem. Amherst (N.Y.) Town Bd., 1982—96, dep. town supr., 1990-96, supr., 1996—. Founder, liaison 1st adult day svcs. adv. bd. Town of Amherst, 1988, liaison to ad hoc cable TV com., 1992—96, liaison to Amherst C. of C., 1993—96, 1st records mgmt. adv. bd., liaison ethics bd., 1994—; legis. liaison SUNY Family Violence Clin. Sch. Law, Buffalo, 1997—98; pres. E.J. Meyer Hosp. Jr. Bd., 1962—64; commr. N.Y. State Ethics Commn., 1999—; mem. adv. bd. N.Y. State Office Aging, 1996—, chair adv. bd., 1997—; bd. dirs. Kaledia Health, 1998—2000. Pres. Aux. to Erie County Bar Assn., 1966-68, Womens Com. Buffalo Philharm. Orch., 1976-78, v.p. adminstrn., 1975-76, v.p. pub. affairs, 1974-75, chair. adv. bd., 1979-82; v.p. Buffalo Philharm. Orch. Soc., Inc., 1976-78, coun. mem., trustee, 1979-87, bd. overseers, 1987-92; dir. 8th jud. dist. N.Y. State Assn. Large Towns, 1989-91; bd. dirs. oper. bd. Millard Fillmore Suburban Hosp., 1992-98; 1st v.p. Fams for 17, 1980-82, Friends of Baird Hall SUNY, Buffalo, 1980-82; exec. bd. Womens Exec. Coun. Erie County Rep. Com., 1969-71, Longview Protestant Home for Children, 1979-85, 2d v.p., 1982-85; bd. dirs. Amherst br. ARC, 1982-91, by-laws com., 1981, 84, chair sr. concerns com., 1982-91, liaison code of ethics com., 1987-89; nat. music com. Womens Assn. for Symphony Orchs. in Am. and Can., 1977-79; coun. mem. Am. Symphony Orch. League; sec. Amherst Sr. Citizens Adv. Bd., 1980-81, liaison from Amherst Town Bd., 1982-96; liaison to the Alternate Fuel and Clean Cities Com., 1994-96; dir.-at-large cmty. adv. coun. SUNY, Buffalo, 1981-91; co-assoc. chair maj. gift divsn. capital campaign Daeman Coll., 1983-84, trustee, 1998—; chair mem. com. Daeman Coll Trustees, 2003—; co-chair Women United Against Drugs Campaign, 1970-72; founding mem. Lunch and Issues, Amherst, 1981—; edn. com., bd. dirs. Network in Aging of Western N.Y., Inc., 1982-89, housing com., 1987-89; bd. dirs. Amherst Elderly Transp. Corp., 1982-99; committeeman dist. Town of Amherst Rep. Com.; treas. Town and Country Rep. Club, 1980-81; nominating com. Fedn. Rep. Womens Clubs Erie County, 1980; del. N.Y. State Govs. Conf. on Aging, 1995, White House Conf. on Aging, 1995, named mem. aging svcs.; mem. Erie County indsl. Devel. Agy. Erie County Regional Devel. Corp., 1996—; mem. adv. bd. Amherst Symphony Orch., 2003; vol. life project Greater Buffalo chpt. ARC, 2002-04, mem. svc. to older adults com., 2002-04. Named Homemaker of Yr., Family Circle mag., 1969, Woman of Substance, 20th Century Rep. Women, 1983, Woman of Yr., Buffalo Philharm. Orch. Soc., Inc., 1982, Outstanding Woman in Cmty. Svc., SUNY, Buffalo, 1985; recipient Good Neighbor award, Courier Express, 1978, Merit award, Buffalo Philharm. Orch., 1978, edn. Rep. Womens Clubs Erie County award, 1982, Disting. Svc. award, Town of Amherst Sr. Ctr., 1985, Amherst Adult Day Care and Vis. Nurses Assn., 1994, Susan B. Anthony award, nterclub Coun. Western N.Y., 1991, Cmty. Svc. award, Amherst Rep. Com., 1991, D.A.R.E. award, Town of Amherst Police Dept., 1994, Amherst South Rotary Club, 1997, Outstanding Cmty. Svc. award, Amherst Sr. Citizen Found., 1997, Lynn Millane Cmty. Svc. award named in her honor, Rep. honoree, award for svc., Town of Amherst Youth Bd., 1996, award for care and assistance to sr. citizens of N.Y. State, Batavia Nursing Home, 2000, Woman of Distinction award, NY State Senate, 2003; fellow hon. Paul Harris fellow. Mem. Amherst C. of C. (VIP dinner com. 1984), LWV, SUNY Buffalo Alumni Assn. (life, presdl. advisor 1977-79), Amherst Symphony Orch. Assn. (bd. dirs. 1981-87, roster chair. 1982-84, nominating chair 1985-86, vice-chair 50th ann. com. 1994—), Amherst Rep. Womens Club (bd. dirs. 1963-65, 99), Zonta (pres. Amherst chpt. 1986-88, Zontian of Yr. 1992), Pi Lambda Theta (hon.).

MILLAR, SALLY GRAY, nurse; b. Madison, Wis., Dec. 8, 1946; d. William Llewellyn and Janet Josephine (Dean) M. Student, U. Iowa, 1964-65; R.N., St. Joseph Hosp. Sch. Nursing, 1968; MBA, Simmons Coll. Grad. Sch. Mgmt., 1985. Staff nurse Bryn Mawr (Pa.) Hosp., 1968-69; team leader, cardiac surg. intensive care unit Mass. Gen. Hosp., Boston, 1969-78, head nurse, respiratory/surg. intensive care unit, 1978-81, clin. nurse leader, intensive care nursing service, 1981-85, project dir. patient classification system, 1985-86, dir. nursing info. systems, 1986-97, dir. svcs., 1997—99; patient care svcs. Info. Sys., 1999—; dir. Office of Patient Advocacy, 1997—. Editor: Focus on Critical Care, 1978-80; editor-in-chief: Methods in Critical Care, 1980, Procedure Manual for Critical Care, 1985. Mem. Am. Assn. Critical Care Nurses (pres. 1980-81, dir. 1976-82), Soc. Critical Care Medicine. Republican. Roman Catholic. Home: 849 Boston Post Rd E Apt 3E Marlborough MA 01752-3700 Office: Mass Gen Hosp 32 Fruit St Boston MA 02114-2620

MILLENDER-MCDONALD, JUANITA, congresswoman, school system administration; b. Birmingham, Ala., Sept. 7, 1938; d. Shelly and Everlina (Dortch) M.; m. James McDonald III, July 26, 1955; children: Valeria, Angela, Sherryll, Michael, Roderick. BS, U. Redlands, Calif., 1980; MS in Edn., Calif. State U., L.A., 1986; postgrad., U. So. Calif. Manuscript editor Calif. State Dept. Edn., Sacramento; dir. gender equity programs L.A. Unified Sch. Dist.; mem. U.S. Congress from 37th Calif dist., Washington, 1996—; mem. small bus. com., transp. and infrastructure com.; mem. Ho. Com. on Ho. Adminstrn.; tchr., sch. adminstr., 1981—90; Carson mayor pro-tempore; mem. Calif. Assembly, 1992—96, Jt. Com. Libr., Dem. Homeland Security Task Force, New Democrat Coalition, Regional Whip. City councilwoman, Carson; bd. dirs. S.C.L.C. Pvt. Industry Coun. Policy Bd., West Basin Mcpl. Water Dist., Cities Legis. League (vice chmn.; mem. Nat. Women's Polit. Caucus; mem. adv. bd. Comparative Ethnic Tng. U. So. Calif.; founder, exec. dir. Young Advocates So. Calif. Mem. NAACP, NEA, Nat. Assn. Minority Polit. Women, NAFE, Nat. Fedn. Bus. and Profl. Women, Assn. Calif. Sch. Adminstrs., Am. Mgmt. Assn., League African Women, L.A. World Affairs Coun., Nat. Female Execs., Nat. Coun. Jewish Women, Carson C. of C., Phi Delta Kappa. Democrat. Office: US House Reps 1514 Ho Office Bldg Washington DC 20515-0537*

MILLER, ALICE, state representative; b. L.I., Mar. 3, 1939; d. Edward and Alice Miller. BA, Bennington Coll., 1960; MS, Bank St. Coll., 1964; postgrad., NYU, 1966. Adminstrv. planning mgr. Roche Diagnostics, N.J., 1989-93; state rep. Vt. Ho. Reps., 1996—. Vice-chmn. Bd. Selectman, Shaftbury, Vt., 1994—; dir. Nat. Follow Through Program, Brattleboro, Vt., 1968-77; dir. Student Affairs, Bennington Coll., 1977-88. Mem. Bennington Profl. Women, Workforce Investment Bd., Bennington Learning Inst., Vt. Film Commn., New England Bd. Higher Ed.

MILLER, ALICE ANN, state utilities regulation executive; b. Des Moines, June 8, 1955; d. Edwin and Ethel (Kjaer) Barker; m. Mark Miller, Nov. 25, 1977; children: Eric, Katherine (Katie). BA in Edn., U. Iowa, Iowa City, 1974, MA in English, 1976; MBA, SUNY, Albany, 1991. Rsch. asst. N.Y. Dept. Pub. Svc., Albany, 1981-82, utility rates analyst, 1982-85, utility ops. examiner, 1985-90, chief utility rates analyst, 1990—. Mem. Phi Beta Kappa, Beta Gamma Sigma. Avocations: travel, skiing, hiking, camping. Office Phone: 518-474-2350.

MILLER, ALISA DOROTHY NORTON, artist; b. Wellsville, N.Y., Nov. 18, 1920; d. Oak Duke and Gladys Virginia (Dexter) Norton; Rochester Inst. Tech., 1968-69, San Jose State U., 1981; A.A. in Fine Arts, West Valley Coll., Saratoga, Calif., 1983; m. Robert E. Miller, Oct. 12, 1974; children by previous marriage— Richard, Linda, Michael. Airline stewardess Colonial Airlines, N.Y.C., 1944-45; art supr. Eastman Kodak Co., Rochester, 1962-70; exec. sec. 3M Corp., Rochester, 1970-72; med. sec., asst., Los Gatos, Calif., 1972-76; portrait artist Art Studio, Los Gatos, 1976—1990 ; one-man show: Norton Gallery, Rochester, 1972; group shows include: Glossinger Cultural Mus., Xenia, Ohio, 1964, Rosicrucian Mus., San Jose, Calif., 1981, Triton Mus., Santa Clara, Calif., 1982; represented in permanent collections: Glossinger Cultural Mus., also numerous pvt. collections. Home and Office: 2561 Sadies Drive Hollister CA 95023-8320

MILLER, ALYSON REBECCA, school psychologist; b. Smithtown, N.Y., Mar. 9, 1974; d. Zachary and Diane Eileen Miller. Ph.D., Hofstra U., Hempstead, NY, 1996—2001. Cert. sch. psychologist N.Y., 2003. Counselor S.E. Nassau Guidance Ctr., Seaford, NY, 1999—; sch. psychologist East Islip Sch. Dist., Islip Terrace, 2002—. Recipient James McClintock award Excellence Psychology, Drew U., 1996. Mem.: APA (assoc.), Nat. Assn. Sch. Psychology (assoc.), Am. Assn. Suicidology (assoc.). Office: East Islip Sch Dist Craig B Gariepy Ave Islip Terrace NY 11752 Personal E-mail: alymiller2002@yahoo.com. E-mail: amiller@eischools.org.

MILLER, ANDREA LYNN, library science educator; b. Warren, Pa., Sept. 25, 1957; d. Harlan Kermit and Hazel Adeline Samuelson; m. Michael Edward Miller, oct. 16, 1953; 1 child, Lena. BS in Edn., Clarion U., 1978, MA in English, 1982, MSLS, 1991; PhD in Info. Scis., U. Pitts., 1997. English tchr. Redbank Valley Sch. Dist., New Bethlehem, Pa., 1979-86, sch. libr. media specialist, 1986-92; assoc. prof. libr. sci. Clarion (Pa.) U., 1992—, dir. Inst. for Study and Devel. of Sci. Libr. Info. Ctrs., 2000—, dept. chair and program dir. dept. libr. sci., 2002—. Distance edn. trainer Cmty. Agile Ptnrs. in Edn., Bethlehem, 1999—, Ctr. for Distance Edn., Pa. State Sys. Higher Edn., Harrisburg, 1999—. Contbg. author: Powerful Public Relations with Full-time Results, 2d edit., 2001; author profl. devel. workshop in field. Trustee Clarion Free Pub. Libr., 1993-99. Recipient Laura Braun scholarship, 1993; grantee Pa. State Sys. Higher Edn., 1999. Mem. ALA, ASCD, Assn. Libr. and Info. Sci. Edn., Pa. Assn. Ednl. Comms. and Tech., Assn. Pa. State Coll. and Univ. Facilities (chmn. nominating com. 1995-97), Assn. Libr. Svc. to Childen, Young Sch. Librarians (chmn. Highsmith rsch. grant award 1999-2001), Pa. Sch. Librarians Assn. (co-chmn. state curriculum com. 1998-2002), Internat. Assn. Sch. Librarians, Assn. Ednl. Comms. and Tech., Delta Kappa Gamma. Democrat. Baptist. Avocations: travel, golf, biking. Home: 35 Ross St Clarion PA 16214 Office: Clarion U Pa 840 Wood St Clarion PA 16214 Fax: (814) 393-2150. E-mail: amiller@clarion.edu.

MILLER, ANNIE CHRISTMAS, secondary school educator; b. Greenville, N.C., Dec. 22, 1947; d. Oliver Miller and Maggie Gaylord; children: Kwan, Kia. BS, Elizabeth City State U., 1970; MA, U. D.C., 1977. Expungent aide FBI, Washington, 1982—86; tchr. D.C. Pub. Schs., Washington, 1987—. Adv. mem. World Wildlife Fund, Washington, 1985—, Teen Life Choices, Washington, 1997—; gleaners Washington Area Gleaning Network, Arlington, Va., 1990—; mem. Nat. Campaign for Tolerance, Washington, 2000—. Named Internat. Tchr. of Yr., World Affairs Coun., 2001; recipient Kelly Miller Pen Pal Club award, Samuel Pardoe Found., 1996, Program Excellence award, Ptnrs. Am., 1997; fellow Ptnrs. Am. Internat. fellow, W.K. Kellogg Found., 1998; scholar Fulbright scholar, World Affairs Coun., 2001. Democrat. Avocations: reading, travel. Home: 531 42nd St NE Washington DC 20019

MILLER, BARBARA KENTON, retired librarian; b. N.Y.C., Sept. 21, 1934; d. Robert Alfred and Kathleen Hope (Levy) Kenton; m. John Arnold Miller, June 15, 1955; children: Valerie Ann Miller, Jennifer Karen Kraft. BA with distinction, Finch Coll., 1960; MLS, C.W. Post, 1976. Cert. libr., N.Y. Libr., cons. archivist Coun. Fgn. Rels., N.Y.C., 1977-2000; ret., 2000. Cons. archivist Coun. on Fgn. Rels. Mem. Spl. Librs. Assn., Beta Phi Mu. Avocations: dogs, golf, tennis. Office: Coun Fgn Rels 58 E 68 St New York NY 10021-5953 E-mail: bkmiller55@aol.com.

MILLER, BARBARA STALLCUP, development consultant; b. Montague, Calif., Sept. 4, 1919; d. Joseph Nathaniel and Maybelle (Needham) Stallcup; m. Leland F. Miller, May 16, 1946; children: Paula Kay, Susan Lee, Daniel Joseph, Alison Jean. BA, U. Oreg., 1942. Women's editor Eugene Daily News, Oreg., 1941-43; law clk. J. Everett Barr, Yreka, Calif., 1943-45; mgr. Yreka C. of C., 1945-46; N.W. supr. Louis Harris Assocs., Portland, Oreg., 1959-62; dir. pub. rels., fund raising Columbia River coun. Girl Scouts U.S.A., 1962-67; pvt. practice pub. rels. cons. Portland, Ohio, 1967-72; adviser, student publs., asst. prof. comms. U. Portland, 1967-72, dir. pub. rels. info., asst. prof. comms., 1972-78, dir. devel., 1978-79, exec. dir. devel., 1979-83; assoc. dir. St. Vincent Med. Found., 1983-88; dir. planned giving Good Samaritan Found., 1988-95; planned giving cons., 1995—. Contbr. articles to profl. jours. Pres. bd. dirs. Vols. of Am. of Oreg., Inc., 1980-84, pres. regional adv. bd., 1982-84; chmn. bd. dirs. S.E. mental Health Network, 1984-88; nat. bd. dirs. Vols. of Am., Inc., 1984-96; pres., bd. dirs. Vol. Bur. Greater Portland, 1991-93; mem. U. Oreg. Journalism Advancement Coun., 1991-2003. Named Oasis Sr. Role Model, 1992, Ont. Presdl. Citation, Oreg. Communicators Assn., 1973, Matrix award, 1976, 80, Miltner award U. Portland, 1977, Communicator of Achievement award Oreg. Press Women, 1992, Willamette Valley Devel. Officers award, 1992 (Barbara Stallcup Miller Profl. Achievement award 1992). Mem. Nat. Coast Trail Assn. (pres. bd. dirs. 1997-2003), Nat. Soc. Fundraising Execs., Nat. Planned Giving Coun., Women in Comm. (NW regional v.p. 1973-75, Offbeat award 1988), Nat. Fedn. Press Women, Oreg. Press Women (dist. dir.), PRSA (dir. local chpt., Marsh award 1989), Oreg. Fedn. Womens Clubs (comms. chmn. 1978-80), Alpha Xi Delta (found. trustee, editor 1988-95), Portland Zenith (pres. 1975-76, 81-82, 2002—). Unitarian Universalist. Home and Office: 1706 Boca Ratan Dr Lake Oswego OR 97034-1624 Personal E-mail: bmiller@teleport.com.

MILLER, BEBE, choreographer; b. N.Y.C., Sept. 20, 1950; BA in Fine Arts, Earlham Coll., 1971; MA in Dance, Ohio State U., 1975. Owner Bebe Miller Co., N.Y.C., 1985—; prof. dance Ohio State U., 2002—. Bd. dirs. Dance USA, Dance Theater Workshop, Danspace Project; tchr. U. Ill., Champaign/Urbana, UCLA, NYU, Mt. Holyoke Coll., Movement Rsch., N.Y.C., Sarah Lawrence Coll., U. Minn., Mills Coll., Middlebury Coll., Va. Commonwealth U., Tex. Women's U., Cal Arts and Stanford U. Choreographer (theatre) Tiny Sisters in the Enormous Land, 1995, Going to the Wall, 1998, (original works) Oreg. Ballet Theatre, Boston Ballet, Dayton Contemporary Dance Co. and others. Recipient 2 Bessie awards, award, Am. Choreographer, 1988, Young Artists Recognition award, Dewars, 1990; fellow, Creative Artists Pub. Svc., 1984, Nat. Found. for Arts, 1984, Nat. Endowment for Arts, 1985—88, John Simon Guggenheim Found., 1988. Office: Bebe Miller Co 54 W 21st St Ste 502 New York NY 10010

MILLER, BETH MCCARTHY, television director; Dir.: (TV series) Saturday Night Live, 1975, 1995—, The Jon Stewart Show, 1993—, The Colin Quinn Show, 2002, (TV spl.) Eagles: Hell Freezes Over, 1994—, Nirvana Unplugged, 1994—, James Taylor Live, 1998—, Saturday Night Live: The Best of Adam Sandler, 1999—, Saturday Night Live Christmas, 1999—, Saturday Night Live: 25th Anniversary, 1999, America: A Tribute to Heroes, 2001, NBC 75th Anniversary Spl., 2002, Saturday Night Live: The Best of Will Ferrell, 2002, GQ Men of the Yr. Awards, 2003; dir., prodr.: MTV Video Music Awards, 2003. Nominee Outstanding Directorial Achievement in Musical/Variety award, DGA, 2000, 2004, Emmy award, 1999, 2000, 2003; recipient Outstanding Directorial Achievement in Musical/Variety award, DGA, 2001, 2002. Office: Saturday Night Live 30 Rockefeller Plaza 50th St and 6th Ave New York NY 10112*

MILLER, BETTY BROWN, freelance writer; b. Altus, Ark., Dec. 21, 1926; d. Carlos William and Arlie Gertrude (Sublett) Brown; m. Robert Wiley Miller, Nov. 15, 1953; children: Janet Ruth, Stephen Wiley. BS, Okla. State U., 1949; MS, U. Tulsa, 1953; postgrad., Am. U., 1966-68. Tchr. LeFlore (Okla.) H.S., 1947-48, Osage Indian Reservation H.S., Hominy, Okla., 1948-50, Jenks (Okla.) H.S., 1950-51; instr. Sch. Bus. U. Tulsa, 1950-51; tchr. Tulsa pub. schs., 1951-54; instr. Burdette Coll., Boston, 1954-55; reporter Bethesda-Chevy Chase Tribune, Montgomery County, Md., 1970-73; freelance writer, contbr. newspapers and mags., 1973—. V.p. Kenwood Park (Md.) Citizens Assn., 1960; mem. Ft. Sumner Citizens Assn., editor newsletter, 1969; mem. Md. State PTA, editl. coord. leadership conf., 1973-74; founder, chair Montgomery County Forum Edn., 1970-75; trustee Friends Valley Forge Nat. Hist. Park; bd. dirs. Friends Curtis Inst. Music; mem. Nat. Mus. Women in the Arts, Musical Fund Soc. Phila.; trustee adv. Help the Aged. Mem.: DAR, PEO, Union League Phila. (past mem. ladies com., mem. ladies adv. com.), The Nat. Gravel Soc., Internat. Platform Assn., Montgomery County Press Assn., Nat. Soc. Arts & Letters (past editor mag., bd. dirs. pub rels., past nat. corr. sec.), Huguenot Soc. Pa. (v.p. 1989—92, pres. 1993—95, past bd. dirs., hon. v.p. 1997—), Nat. League Am. Pen Women (former budget chmn., past nat. treas.), Soc. Descendants of Washington's Army at Valley Forge (past. nat. comdr. in chief, past inspector gen. Nat. Huguenot Soc., past. mem. gen. coun.), Acorn Club Phila., Sedgeley Club (pres. Phila. 1985—88), Washington Club, U.D.C., Adventures Unltd. (chmn. Washington chpt.), Capital Spkrs. Club Washington (past pres.), Melba T. Croft Music Club, Order Ea. Star (life). Republican. Address: PO Box 573 Valley Forge PA 19481-0573

MILLER, BETTY SUE, counselor; b. Hopkinsville, Ky., June 11, 1960; d. Gerald and Mable (Lee) M. AA, Hopkinsville C.C., 1980; BS, Murray (Ky.) State U., 1982; MEd, U. North Tex., 1987; M of Ednl. Counseling, U. Phoenix, 1995. Cert. tchr., Colo.; cert. spl. svcs., Colo.; cert. K-12 counselor. Tchr. Dallas Ind. Sch. System, 1982-89, Jefferson County Sch. Dist., Wheat Ridge, Colo., 1989-96, sch. counselor Littleton, Colo., 1996—; counselor Karlis Family Ctr., Lakewood, Colo., 1995—. Instr. Colo. State U., Denver, 1992; lic. profl. counselor. Editor The Round Table Literary mag., 1980. Mem. ACA, Am. Assn. of Christian Counselors, Jefferson County Edn. Assn., Jefferson County Internat. Reading Assn. (bldg. rep. 1991-96), Am. Sch. Counselor Assn. Avocations: drama, reading, arts and crafts, decorating. Office: Summit Ridge Middle Sch 11809 W Coal Mine Ave Littleton CO 80127-4849

MILLER, BEVERLY WHITE, former college president, educational consultant, consultant; b. Willoughby, Ohio, 1923; d. Joseph Martin and Marguerite Sarah (Storer) White; m. Lynn Martin Miller, Oct. 11, 1945 (dec. 1986); children: Michaela Ann, Craig Martin, Todd Daniel, Cass Timothy, Simone Agnes. AB, Western Res. U., 1945; MA, Mich. State U., 1957; PhD, U. Toledo, 1967; LHD (hon.), Coll. St. Benedict, St. Joseph, Minn., 1979; LLD (hon.), U. Toledo, 1988. Chem. and biol. researcher, 1945-57; tchr. schs. in Mich., also Mercy Sch. Nursing, St. Lawrence Hosp., Lansing, Mich., 1957-58; mem. chemistry and biology faculty Mary Manse Coll., Toledo, 1958-71, dean grad. div., 1968-71, exec. v.p., 1968-71; acad. dean Salve Regina Coll., Newport, R.I., 1971-74; pres. Coll. St. Benedict, St. Joseph, Minn., 1974-79, Western New Eng. Coll., Springfield, Mass., 1980-96, pres. emerita, 1996—. Higher edn. cons., 1996—; cons. U.S. Office Edn., 1980; mem. Springfield Pvt. Industry Coun./Regional Employment Bd., exec. com., 1982-94; mem. Minn. Pvt. Coll. Coun., 1974-79, sec., 1974-75, vice chmn., 1975-76, chmn., 1976-77; cons. in field. Author papers and books in field. Corporator Mercy Hosp., Springfield, Mass. Recipient President's citation St. John's U., Minn., 1979; also various service awards; named disting. alumna of yr. U. Toledo, 1998. Mem. AAAS, Am. Assn. Higher Edn., Assn. Cath. Colls. and Univs. (exec. bd.), Internat. Assn. Sci. Edn., Nat. Assn. Ind. Colls. and Univs. (govt. rels. adv. com., bd. dirs. 1990-93, exec. com. 1991-93, treas. 1992-93), Nat. Assn. Biology Tchrs., Assn. Ind. Colls. and Univs. of Mass. (exec. com. 1981-96, vice chmn. 1985-86, chmn. 1986-87), Nat. Assn. Rsch. Sci. Tchg., Springfield C. of C. (bd. dirs.), Am. Assn. Univ. Adminstrs. (bd. dirs. 1989-92), Delta Kappa Gamma, Sigma Delta Epsilon. Office: 6713 County Road M Delta OH 43515-9778

MILLER, BONNIE SEWELL, marketing professional, writer; b. Junction City, Ky., July 24, 1932; d. William Andrew and Lillian Irene (McCowan) Sewell; m. William Gustave Tournade Jr., Nov. 5, 1950 (div. 1974); children: Bonnie Sue Tournade Zaner, William Gustave III, Sharon Irene Tournade Leach; m. Bruce George Miller, Nov. 15, 1981. BA, U. South Fla., 1968, MA, 1973. Cert. tchr., Fla. Chair dept. English Tampa (Fla.) Cath. H.S., 1972-78; tchr. Clearwater (Fla.) H.S., 1978-80; mgr. prodn. svcs. Paradyne Corp., Largo, Fla., 1980-83; freelance writer, cons. Tampa, 1983-84; mgr. product documentation PPS, Inc., Largo, 1984-86, mgr. mktg. comm., 1986-87; writer Nixdorf Computer Corp., Tampa, 1988-89; mktg. dir. Suncoast Schs. Fed. Credit Union, Tampa, 1989-98; co-owner, v.p., writer, cons. Need-A-Writer, Inc., Tampa, 1998—. Instr. English, Hillsborough C.C., Tampa, 1975—87; cons. bus. writing Coronet Instrnl. Media Writing Project, Tampa, 1976, Nat. Mgmt. Assn., Tampa, 1981—87; adj. instr. profl. writing U. South Fla., 1993; adj. instr. tech. writing U. Tampa, 2002, English instr., 2002—. Author: Youth Financial Literacy, 1999, Effective Business Writing for Credit Unions, 2000; contbr. articles to profl. jours. Bd. dirs. SERVE, Tampa, Credit Union Mktg. Assn. Coun., Sing Parent Displaced Homemakers Group; legis. chair Tampa PTA, 1965; judge speech contest Am. Legion, Tampa, 1976, vol. North Tampa Vol. Libr., 1988. NEH fellow, 1975. Mem. NAFE, Soc. Tech. Communicators, Am. Assn. Bus. Women, Kappa Delta Pi. Democrat. Baptist. Avocations: writing, sewing, gardening, exotic birds, travel, decorating. Home and Office: 516 2d Ave SE Lutz FL 33549

MILLER, BUFFY, dancer; b. Atlanta; Studies with, Patricia Bromley; student, New Ballet Sch. Mem. Feld Ballet Tech. Soc., 1986—97; with Ballet Tech., 1997—. Office: 108 High St #2 Portland ME 04101-3815

MILLER, CANDICE S. congresswoman; b. May 7, 1954; m. Donald G. Miller; 1 child, Wendy Nicole. Student, Macomb County C.C., Northwood U. Sec., treas. D.B. Snider, Inc., 1972-79; trustee Harrison Twp., 1979-80, supr., 1980-92; treas. Macomb County, 1992-95; sec. of state State of Mich., Lansing, 1995—2003; mem. U.S. Ho. Reps. from Mich. 10th dist., 2003—. Mem. Lake St. Clair Blue Ribbon Commn. Chair John Engler for Gov. campaign, Macomb County; del. Rep. Nat. Conv., 1996; co-chair Rep. Platform Com., 1996, Dole/Kemp Presdl. Campaign, Mich., 1996, Bush/Cheney Presdl. Campaign, Mich., 2000; mem. Carehouse-Macomb County Child Adv. Ctr., Selfridge Air Nat. Guard Base Cmty. Coun., Detroit Econ. Club; mem. adminstrv. bd. Mich. State, mem. safety commn. Republican. Avocations: boating, yacht racing. Office: 508 Cannon HOB Washington DC 20515

MILLER, CAROL LYNN, librarian; b. Kingsville, Tex., Mar. 31, 1961; d. Walter Edward, Jr. and Emma Lee (Nelson) Miller. BS in Early Childhood Edn., So. Nazerene U., 1985; M in Early Childhood Edn., Ala. A & M U., 1987; MLS, U. Ala., 1993. Office worker Salvation Army, Huntsville, Ala., 1979-83; libr. Madison (Ala.) Br. Libr., 1985, br. head, 1987-92; sub. tchr. Huntsville City and Madison County Sch. Sys., 1986-87; br. head Madison Sq. Mall Br. Libr., Huntsville, 1992-2000, head adult svcs./reference, asst. br. mgr. Madison Pub. Libr., 2000—02; libr. supr. Bold and Cool Satellite Librs. Ft. Worth Pub. Libr., 2002—. Methodist. Office: Ft Worth Pub Libr 1801 North/South Fwy Fort Worth TX 76102 Personal E-mail: carlyntx@sbcglobal.net.

MILLER, CAROLINE, editor-in-chief; Exec. editor Variety mag., N.Y.C., 1989—92; editor-in-chief Lear's mag., N.Y.C., 1992—94, Seventeen mag., N.Y.C., 1994—96, New York mag., N.Y.C., 1996—. Office: New York Mag 444 Madison Ave Fl 14 New York NY 10022-6999*

MILLER, CATHERINE LYNN, mental health services professional, writer; b. N.Y.C., Apr. 26, 1962; d. Paul Daniel Rosenberg and Isabel Joan Meisel Rosenberg. BA in Anthropology, SUNY, Stony Brook, 1984, MA in Psychology, 1986; MA in Anthropology, U. of Calif.-San Diego, La Jolla, 1988; PsychD, Calif. Coast U., Santa Ana, 2002. Lic. profl. counselor Tex., mental health counselor Wash. Mgr. intake ops. United Behavioral Health, San Francisco, 1997—99, psychiat. and substance abuse care mgr., 1999—2003, Managed Health Network, San Rafael, Calif., 2003—. Contbr. short stories,fictions and anthologies to jours. (2d prize, Reader's award The Storyteller lit. jour., 2001). Mem.: APA (assoc.). Avocations: scuba diving, horseback riding, international travel.

MILLER, CHERYL DEANN, former professional basketball coach, broadcaster; b. Riverside, Calif., Jan. 3, 1964; BA in Broadcast Journalism, U. So. Calif., 1985. Basketball player Jr. Nat. Team, 1981, U.S. Nat. Team, 1982, U.S. Olympics, 1984; commentator ABC Sports; head coach women's basketball U. So. Calif., 1993-94; commentator TNT Sports, Atlanta, 1996; gen. mgr., head coach Phoenix Mercury, 1997—2000. Player JC Penney All-Am. Team Five, U. So. Calif. Women's Basketball Team, World Championship Team, 1983. Recipient Sports Illustrated Player of Yr., 1986, Naismith Player of Yr. award, Kodak All-Am. award, more than 1,140 trophies and 125 plaques including Nat. Sports Festival, 1981, Pan Am. Games, 1983, FIBA World Championship, Goodwill Games, gold medal 1984 Olympic Games; elected to Naismith Basketball Hall of Fame, 1995.*

MILLER, CHERYL MARIE, special education educator, business owner; b. Syracuse, N.Y., Sept. 3, 1969; d. Lawrence J. and Georgia Ann (Smith) Gola; m. Wendell L. Miller, June 8, 1991; 1 child, Ian William. BS in Edn., SUNY, Geneseo, 1991; MS in Edn., SUNY, Oswego, 1995. Cert. spl. edn. tchr., reading tchr., N.Y. Spl. edn. tchr. South Jefferson Ctrl. Sch., Adams Center, N.Y., 1991-93; mental health case mgr. Oswego County Health Dept., Oswego, N.Y., 1994-98; spl. edn. aide Sandy Creek (N.Y.) Ctrl. Sch., 1998-99; spl. edn. tchr. Rehab Resources, Oswego, 1999—. Mem. Coun. for Exceptional Children, Internat. Reading Assn. Avocations: reading, archery. Home: 391 Kehoe Rd Sandy Creek NY 13145-2172

MILLER, CHRISTINE MARIE, marketing executive, public relations executive; b. Williamsport, Pa., Dec. 7, 1950; d. Frederick James and Mary (Wurster) M.; m. Robert M. Ancell, Mar. 30, 1985. BA, U. Kans., 1972; MA, Northwestern U., 1978, PhD, 1982. Pub. rels. asst. Bedford County Commr., Bedford, Pa., 1972-73; teaching asst. Northwestern U., Evanston, Ill., 1977-80; asst. prof. U. Ala., Tuscaloosa, 1980-82, Loyola U., New Orleans, 1982-85; vis. prof. Ind. U. Sch. Journalism, Bloomington, 1985-86; mktg. dir. Nat. Inst. Fitness & Sport, Indpls., 1986-88; program dir. Nat. Entrepreneurship Acad., Bloomington, 1986-88; mgmt. assoc. community and media rels. Subaru-Isuzu Automotive, Inc., Lafayette, Ind., 1988-91; dir. pub. rels. Giddings & Lewis, Fond Du Lac, Wis., 1991-93; v.p. comm. and enrollment mgmt. Milton Hershey (Pa.) Sch., 1993-94, dir. adminstrn., 1994-95; account mgr. WorldCom Govt. Markets, Vienna, Va., 1995—. Co-author: The Biographical Dictionary of World War II General and Flag Officers, 1996; contbr. articles to profl. jours. Bd. dirs. Indpls. Entrepreneurship Acad., 1988-91, Area IV Agy., Greater Lafayette Mus. Art, 1989-91. With USN, 1973-77, capt. USNR, 1977—. Mem. Armed Forces Comm. Electronics Assn., Pub. Rels. Soc. Am., Naval Order of the U.S. (nat. pub. affairs com.), U.S. Naval Pub. Affairs Alumnae Assn. (bd. dirs.), Naval Res. Assn., Res. Officers Assn. Presbyterian. Avocations: cooking, swimming, reading, travel, cycling. Home: 7406 Salford Ct Alexandria VA 22315-4728 Office: WorldCom Def Markets Ste 7055 1945 Old Gallows Rd Vienna VA 22182-3931 Office Phone: 703-343-6051. E-mail: christine.m.miller@mci.com.

MILLER, CHRISTINE ODELL COOK, judge; b. Oakland, Calif., Aug. 26, 1944; m. Dennis F. Miller; 2 children. BA in Polit. Sci., Stanford U., 1966; JD, U. Utah, 1969. Bar: D.C., Calif. Law clk. to Hon. David T. Lewis U.S. Ct. Appeals (10th cir.), Salt Lake City; trial atty. Dept. Justice, U.S. Ct. Claims; team leader atty. FTC; atty. Hogan & Hartson, Washington; spl. counsel Pension Benefit Guaranty Corp.; dep. gen. counsel U.S. Ry. Assn.; ptnr. Shack & Kimball, Washington; judge U.S. Ct. Fed. Claims, Washington, 1982—. Comment editor Utah law Rev. Scholar U. Utah Coll. Law. Mem. D.C. Bar Assn., Calif. State Bar, Order of Coif, Univ. Club, Cosmos Club. Avocation: geneology. Office: US Ct Fed Claims 717 Madison Pl NW Ste 716 Washington DC 20005-1011

MILLER, CLAIRE ELLEN, children's writer, editor, educator; b. Milw., July 17, 1936; d. Emil George Benjamin and Phyllis Dorothy (Rahn) Holtzen; m. Gerald Ray Miller, June 21, 1958; children: Karin, Russell. BS in Edn., Concordia U., 1961. Tchr. Grace Episcopal Day Sch., Silver Spring, Md., 1971-77, The Norwood Sch., Bethesda, Md., 1977-79; writer Media Materials, Balt., 1980; project editor Ednl. Challenges, Alexandria, Va., 1981; asst. mng. editor Ranger Rick Mag., Nat. Wildlife Fedn., Vienna, Va., 1981-87, mng. editor, 1988-2001, contbg. editor, 2002—; propr. Claire Ellen Miller, Writer and Editor, Rockville, Md., 2001—. Author numerous activity books for presch. thru jr. high, 1979-80; project editor 6 vocabulary books, 1981; author numerous children's mag. and newspaper stories and books, 1981—. Mem. Assn. Ednl. Pubs., Md. Ornithol. Soc. Democrat. Lutheran. Avocation: birding. Home and Office: 17501 Kirk Ln Rockville MD 20853-1033 E-mail: clairemiller@erols.com.

MILLER, CONNIE JOY, assistant real estate officer, broker; b. Martinez, Calif., May 7, 1949; d. Lee Issac James and Lela Martha (Carter) James Poe; m. Avery Jared Miller Oct. 22, 1967 (div. Mar. 1988); children: Elaine Paula Miller Bond, Alfred Saul Jacob Miller. AA, Contra Costa Coll., San Pablo; BA, St. Mary's Coll. Lic. real estate broker. Acct. AT&T, San Francisco, 1967; real estate broker, mgr. Berkeley and El Cerrito, Calif., 1979-93; CFO A.J. Miller & Assocs., Berkeley, Calif., 1978-87; auditor UCOP, Oakland, 1987-88, benefits acct., 1988, exec. asst. to assoc. v.p., 1988—94, sr. real estate analyst, 1994—2001, asst. real estate officer, 2001—. Chair Cmty. Resources for Children; past pres. El Cerrito Soccer, Tilden chpt. ORT; past v.p. Berkeley Hadassah. Mem. NAR, AAUW, Calif. Assn. Realtors, Berkeley Assn. Realtors, Am. Real Estate Assn. Avocations: gardening, travel, art, cooking. Home: 7300 Pomona Ct El Cerrito CA 94530 Office: UC Office of Pres 1111 Franklin St 6th Fl Oakland CA 94607-5200

MILLER, CONSTANCE JOHNSON, elementary school educator; b. Jacksonville, Fla., Mar. 16, 1948; d. Shepheard and Victoria (Fisher) Johnson; children: Rodney Johnson, Larry Miller. BS, Fla. Meml. Coll., 1972. Tchr., family planning educator Urban League of Greater Miami, Fla., 1972-73; recreation leader YMCA of Greater Miami, 1973-74; recreation therapist Dade County Corrections and Rehab., 1974-76; tchr. Broward County Sch. Bd., Ft. Lauderdale, Fla., 1976—, Hollywood Hills H.S., Hollywood, Fla., 1986—. Coach McNicol and Hallandale Middle Sch., Hollywood, Fla., 1976-87, Hollywood Hills Sr. H.S., 1992-97; asst. athletic dir. Hollywood Hills H.S., 1998—. Assoc. min. New Birth Bapt. Ch., Miami; mem. NAACP. Democrat. Avocations: cooking, collecting oldies, decorating, golfing, traveling. Home: 20680 NE 4th Ct Apt 202 Miami FL 33179-1880

MILLER, DAWN MARIE, retired meteorologist; b. Hartford, Conn., Sept. 17, 1963; d. Eugene E. Miller and Audrey E. (Flagg) Laurel; m. Dennis James Miller, Sept. 9, 1989; children: Zackarey, Amanda. BS in Meteorology, SUNY, Oneonta, 1985. Customer support specialist WSI Corp., Bedford, Mass., 1985-87, from media TV mktg. to product mktg. specialist-data svcs. Billerica, Mass., 1987-97, sr. meteorologist, product mktg. specialist, 1997-99, sr. meteorologist, assoc. product mgr., 1999—2001, sr. meteorologist, media mktg. and promotion, 2001—03, ret., 2004. Mem.: Nat. Weather Assn., Am. Meteorol. Soc., Am. Hort. Soc., Nature Conservancy, Nat. Audubon Soc., Nat. Arbor Day Found., Oneonta Alumni Assn. Republican. Episcopalian. Avocations: meteorology, astronomy, photography, gardening, bird watching, nascar (joe gibbs racing # 18 and # 20). Home: 37 Wren Dr Litchfield NH 03052-2540 E-mail: dmmiller17@hotmail.com.

MILLER, DENYCE KARLINA, tax specialist; b. Chgo., July 2, 1963; d. Sidney Miller, Vera Miller. BS in Commerce, DePaul U., 2001, M in Acctg., 2002. CPA Ill. Tax cons. Denyce Miller Tax Svc., Bellwood, Ill., 2001—; postal employee devel. tng. technician USPS, Chgo., 1985—. Mem. fin. com. Am. Postal Workers Union, Chgo., 2001—03. Author: Blind Love, 1996. Coord. hearing impaired Am. Postal Workers Union, Chgo., 1992—94, dir. clk. craft, 2001—03, coord. hearing impaired, 2001—03; combined fed. campaign key worker USPS, Chgo., 1989. Recipient Taekwondo First Dan award, Kukkiwon World Taekwondo Hdqs., 1996. Mem.: AICPA (Scholarship award 2001), Inst. Mgmt. Accts. (Scholarship award 2001), Ill. Cert. Pub. Accts. Soc. Democrat. Mem. Apostolic Ch. Avocation: Tae Kwon Do. Home: 1012 Marshall Bellwood IL 60104-2322 Office Phone: 708-268-1554. Home Fax: 708-544-8419. Personal E-mail: denyce@wans.net. E-mail: dmtaxes@hotmail.com.

MILLER, DIANE DORIS, executive search consultant; b. Sacramento, Jan. 18, 1954; d. George Campbell and Doris Lucille (Benninger) M. BA, U. Pacific, 1976, Golden Gate U., 1985, MBA, 1987. Mgr. A.G. Spanos, Sacramento, 1977-81, Lee Sammis, Sacramento, 1981-83; v.p. Consol. Capital, San Francisco, 1983-86; pres. Wilcox Miller & Nelson, Sacramento, 1986—. Bd. dirs. Sacramento Symphony En Corps, 1982-84, Sacramento Ballet, 1983-84, 86-92, Sacramento Symphony Assn., 1988-92, Oakland Ballet, Calif., 1984-85, Sacramento Symphony Found., 1994-98, Sacramento Reg. Found., 1996-99; chmn. bd. Sacramento Met. C. of C., 1998-2002; mem. Golden Gate U., 1995-97. Named Vol. of Yr., Jr. League, 1983; recipient award, Bus. Jour., 2002, Sacramento Bus. Woman of the Yr., 2003. Mem. U. Pacific Alumni Assn. (bd. dirs. 1978-85), Sacramento Metro. C. of C. (bd. dirs., Bus. Vol. in the Arts 1989); Calif. C. of C. (bd. dirs., 2004-); Humboldt Bancorp. (bd. dirs., 2004-) Republican. E-mail: dmiller@wilcoxcareer.com.

MILLER, DIANE WILMARTH, retired human resources director; b. Clarinda, Iowa, Mar. 12, 1940; d. Donald and Floy Pauline (Madden) W.; m. Robert Nolen Miller, Aug. 21, 1965; children: Robert Wilmarth, Anne Elizabeth. AA, Colo. Women's Coll., 1960; BBA, U. Iowa, 1962; MA, U. No. Colo., 1994. Cert. tchr., Colo.; vocat. credential, Colo.; cert. sr. profl. in human resources; lic. Colo. Ins. Prodr. Sec.-counselor U. S.C. Rep., Myrtle Beach AFB, 1968-69; instr. Coastal Carolina Campus U. S.C., Conway, 1967-69; tchr. bus. Poudre Sch. Dist. R-1, Ft. Collins, Colo., 1970-71; travel cons. United Bank Travel Svc., Greeley, Colo., 1972-74; dir. human resources Aims C.C., Greeley, 1984—2001, ret., 2001. Instr. part-time Aims Cmty. Coll., 1972—89. Active 1st Congl. Ch., Greeley. Mem.: Philanthropic Ednl. Orgn. (pres. 1988—89), Women's Panhellenic Assn. (pres. 1983—84), Questers (pres. 2002—), WTK Club, Scroll and Fan Club (pres. 1985—86). Home: 3530 Wagon Trail Pl Greeley CO 80631 3105

MILLER, DIXIE DAVIS, elementary school educator; b. Lubbock, Tex., June 3, 1940; d. Leroy and Sara Edna (Lightfoot) Davis; m. Greg Miller, Aug. 10, 1968; 1 child, Jason Davis. BS in Edn., Tex. Christian U., 1961, MEd, 1967; postgrad., Tex. Wesleyan U. Cert. elem., early childhood, secondary English tchr., Tex. Elem. tchr. Denver Pub. Schs., Ft. Worth Pub. Schs., Albuquerque Pub. Schs., Birmingham (Mich.) Pub. Schs., Aledo (Tex.) Ind. Sch. Dist., Gwinnett County Pub. Schs., Lawrenceville, Ga. Group leader Young Author's Conf.; insvc. leader creative writing; presenter in field. Active PTA, PTO. Named Tchr. of Yr., Dyer Elem. Sch., Lawrenceville, 1979, 82, Grayson Elem. Sch., 1986, Educator of Yr. award Lawrenceville Jaycees, 1981, Les Evans Chpt. award Tex. Assn. for Supervision and Curriculum Devel., 1989, Excellence in Tchg. award Tex. State Reading Assn., 1998. Mem. NEA, Internat. Reading Assn., Assn. Childhood Edn. Internat., Ga. Assn. Educators, Mich. Edn. Assn., Tex. Tchrs. Assn. Home: 113 Squaw Creek Rd Weatherford TX 76087-8240

MILLER, DONNA REED, city official; married; children: Tari McSween (dec.), Shakira. Mem. Dem. exec. com. 59th Ward, Phila., 1970-87; city councilwoman dist. 8 Phila., 1996—. Chair Parks and Recreation com., cultural com. Phila. City Coun., vice chair edn. com. Office: Room 312 City Hall Philadelphia PA 19107-3201 E-mail: donna.miller@phila.gov.

MILLER, DOROTHEA HELEN, librarian, educator; b. Macedonia, Iowa, Mar. 10, 1925; d. Carl Hamilton and Dorothy Marie (Wilson) Stempel; m. Ruben Roy Miller, Sept. 30, 1945 (dec. May 1987); children: Cecilia Rogge, Catherine Miller-King, Constance Miller. Student, U. Denver, 1942-45, State U. Iowa, 1960; BA with honors, Kearney (Nebr.) State Coll., 1966; ME, U. Nebr., 1970. Cert. media specialist Nebr. Libr. Oakland (Iowa) Pub. Libr., 1956-61; elem. libr. Grand Island (Nebr.) Pub. Schs., 1962-65, elem. libr. supr., 1965-78, media specialist, 1978-86; ret., 1986. Cons. Nat. Def. Edn. Act Inst. for Advanced Study in Ednl. Media Concordia Coll., 1967. Vol. Denver Mus. of Natural History, 1994-96, Nat. Def. Edn. Act Inst. Libr. Materials for Minority Students, Queens Coll., N.Y. Named Outstanding Educator in Am. Acad. of Am. Educators, 1973-74; rsch. grantee Howard Sch., 1966. Mem. AAUW, Cherry Creek Woman's Club, Nebr. Congress Parents and Tchrs. (hon. life), Order Ea. Star (assoc. matron). Democrat. Methodist. Avocations: genealogy, watercolors, calligraphy, poetry. Home: 13991 E Marina Dr Apt 303 Aurora CO 80014-3788 E-mail: TheaMil03@aol.com.

MILLER, DOROTHY ANNE SMITH, retired cytogenetics educator; b. N.Y.C., Oct. 20, 1931; d. John Philip and Anna Elizabeth (Hellberg) Smith; m. Orlando Jack Miller, July 10, 1954; children: Richard L., Cynthia K., Karen A. BA in Chemistry magna cum laude, Wilson Coll., Chambersburg, Pa., 1952; PhD in Biochemistry, Yale U., 1957. Rsch. assoc. dept. ob-gyn Columbia U., N.Y.C., 1964-72, from rsch. assoc. to asst. prof. dept. human genetics-devel., 1973-85; prof. dept. molecular biology and genetics Wayne State U., Detroit, 1985-94, prof. dept. pathology, 1985-96, prof. Ctr. for Molecular Medicine and Genetics, 1994-96. Vis. scientist clin. and population cytogenetics unit Med. Rsch. Coun., Edinburgh, Scotland, 1983-84; vis. prof. dept. genetics and molecular biology U. la Sapienza, Rome, 1988; vis. disting. fellow La Trobe U., Melbourne, Australia, 1992. Contbr. numerous articles to sci. jours. Grantee March of Dimes Birth Defects Found., 1974-93, NSF, 1983-84. Mem. Am. Soc. Human Genetics, Genetics Soc. Am., Genetics Soc. Australia, Phi Beta Kappa. Presbyterian. Home: 1915 Stonycroft Ln Bloomfield Hills MI 48304-2339

MILLER, DOROTHY ELOISE, education educator; b. Ft. Pierce, Fla., Apr. 13, 1944; d. Robert Foy and Aline (Mahon) Wilkes. BS in Edn., Bloomsburg U., 1966, MEd, 1969; MLA, Johns Hopkins U., 1978; EdD, Columbia U., 1991. Tchr. Cen. Dauphin East H.S., Harrisburg, Pa., 1966-68, Aberdeen (Md.) H.S., 1968-69; asst. dean of coll., prof. Harford C.C., Bel Air, Md., 1969—. Owner Ideas by Design, 1995—; mem. accreditation team Mid. States Commn., 1995— ; statewide writing skills assessment com., statewide English stds. com. Md. Higher Edn. Commn. 1997-2001, English composition com., 1997—, English alignment com., 2002—; adj. prof. U. Balt., 2001. Editor: Renewing the American Community Colleges, 1984; contbr. articles to profl. jours. Pres. Harlan Sq. Condominium Assn., Bel Air, 1982, 90-96, Md. internat. divsn. St. Petersburg Sister State Com., 1993-2001; edn. liaison AAUW, Harford County, Md., 1982-92; cen. com. mem. Rep. Party, Harford County, 1974-78; crusade co-chair Am. Cancer Soc., Harford County, 1976-78; mem. faculty adv. com. Md. Higher Edn. Commn., 1993-96; people's adv. coun. Harford County Coun., 1994-2003. Recipient Nat. Tchg. Excellence award Nat. Inst. for Staff and Orgn. Devel., U. Tex.-Austin, 1992. Mem. Nat. Mus. Women in the Arts (charter). Republican. Methodist. Avocations: skiing, swimming, golf, reading, image consulting. Office: Harford Community Coll 401 Thomas Run Rd Bel Air MD 21015-1627 E-mail: demiller@harford.cc.md.us.

MILLER, EDITH FISHER, special education educator; b. Pottsville, Pa., Aug. 9, 1946; d. Lewis Walter and Elsie Lu (Haas) Fisher; m. Charles Edward Miller, July 6, 1968; 1 child, Charmagne Elsie Miller Webb. BA, Gettysburg (Pa.) Coll., 1968; MEd, East Stroudsburg (Pa.) U., 1985; EdD, Temple U., Phila., 1994. Cert. English, spl. edn., reading, program specialist. Tchr. English Mifflin County Sch. Dist., Lewistown, Pa., 1968-69; substitute tchr. various dists., Monroe County, Pa., 1975-82; tchr. spl. edn. Intermediate Unit # 20, Nazareth, Pa., 1982-84, itinerant learning disabilities tchr., 1984-85, ednl. cons. Easton, Pa., 1985-90; Am. with Disabilities Act coord. East Stroudsburg U., 1992-98, disability svcs. coord., 1990—. Mem. adv. bd. LDA of Monroe County, Stroudsburg, Pa., 1994-97; cons. C & E Miller Assocs., Bethlehem, 1997—. Author: Effective Strategies for Tutoring Students and LD and ADHD, 1998. Presenter Vols. for Literacy, Jim Thrope, Pa., 1993, Parent Assn., Pine Grove, Pa., 1995, Higher Edn. & Disability, Innsbruck, Austria, 1995. Mem. Internat. Reading Assn., Assn. Higher Edn. and Disability, Nat. Tutoring Assn. (program chair 1993-94, Pres. award 1998), Phi Delta Kappa (pres. elect 1999-2000, Educator of Yr. Pocono chpt. 1995, C. of C. (ADA workshop organizer 1992). Democrat. Lutheran. Avocations: travel, snorkeling, reading medieval mysteries, cats. Home: 5540 Montauk Ln Bethlehem PA 18017-8909 Office: East Stroudsburg U 200 Prospect St East Stroudsburg PA 18301-2999 E-mail: emiller@po-box.esu.edu.

MILLER, EDNA RAE ATKINS, secondary school educator; b. Clarksville, Ark., Dec. 28, 1915; d. Sammie Lawrence and Dora May (Turner) Atkins; m. Oscar E. Miller, Feb. 27, 1936; children: Myrna Sue Miller Hanses, William Samuel. BE, Sacramento State Coll., 1966. Tchr. one rm. sch., Johnson County, Ark., 1933-35; tchr. elem. Placerville, Calif., 1953-61; tchr. spl. edn. and mentally retarded County of El Dorado, Placerville, Calif., 1961-74; ret. El Dorado (Calif.) County, 1974. Author: Mother Lode of Learning: One Room Schools of El Dorado County, 1990. Mem. Friends of the Libr. of El Dorado County, Placerville, 1974—; historian People-to-People Internat., 1975-90, Sister City Program, 1975-90. Recipient Cert. of Appreciation, Lung Assn. Sacramento and Emmagrant Trails, 1978, Cert. of Appreciation, Ret. Tchrs. of El Dorado County, 1984, 86, 88. Mem. El Dorado County Hist. Soc., Children's Home Soc. (assoc.), Epsilon Chi chpt. Delta Kappa Gamma (pres. Placerville chpt. 1966-68). Democrat. Baptist. Avocations: research, gardening, painting, cake decorating, quilting. Home: 4301 Golden Center Dr Placerville CA 95667-6260

MILLER, ELAINE WILSON, computer consultant; b. Ft. Worth, Sept. 16, 1944; d. Phillip Loren and Artie Inez (Neel) Wilson; m. Robert J. Copeland, Aug. 17, 1963 (div. 1983); children: Karen Kay Prince, Donna Lynn Copeland-Nay; m. Jared N. Miller Jr., Dec. 12, 1993 (div. 1995). BS in Bus., Info. Systems, U. Colo., Denver, 1984. Sec. Hartford Life Ins. Co., Dallas, 1964-66, St. George's Episcopal Ch., Dallas, 1976-77; technician data processing Manville Corp., Denver, 1980-81, assoc. analyst, 1984-85, analyst data processing, 1985-94; fin. technician 1st Interstate Bank, Denver, 1982-84; computer cons. Miller Cons., Lakewood, Colo., 1994—; bus. process analyst US WEST Comm., Inc., Denver, 1994-96; sys. specialist Trilogy Cons., Waukegan, Ill., 1996-99; cons. Telcordia Techs., 1999—. Dir. Denver SAS Users Group, 1994—. Chmn. precinct Rep. Party Tex., Dallas, 1970-76; clk. of the vestry St. Paul's Episcopal Ch., 2001—. Recipient Silver Spark award Camp Fire Girls, Denver, 1982. Mem. Home Based Bus. Connection, Assn. Info. Tech. Profls. (v.p. publicity 1986-88, 90-91, sec. 1989-90, asst. editor newsletter 1985-86, v.p. newsletter 1991-94, nat. liaison 2001—, pres., CEO 2002-03, Individual Performance award 1991, exec. v.p. 1994-95, pres. 1995-96, chmn. comms. task team 1996-97, events v.p. 1997-98, chpt. liason to nat. bd., 1998—), Jaycee-Ettes (hon. lifetime), Grand Prairie (Tex.) C. of C. (Newcomer of Yr. 1971), St. Paul's Ultreya Club (lay leader 1987-88). Episcopalian. Avocations: hiking, writing poetry.

MILLER, ELEANOR, English language and literature educator; b. Mill Valley, Calif. BA with honors, U. Nev., 1966, PhD in English with honors, 1970. Instr. English Valley Coll., San Bernardino, Calif., 1983-84, Crafton Hills Coll., Redlands, Calif., 1984-86, Coll. of the Desert, Palm Springs, Calif., 1986-90; prof. English Composition & Literature So. Nev. C.C., Las Vegas, 1990—. Chair teaching-learning excellence com. So. Nev. C.C., Las Vegas, 1991-94, new faculty mentor, 1995—. Author: English Placement Grading, 1991, CCSN Writing Across the Curriculum, 1994, New Faculty Mentoring, 1997, Teaching Excellence, 1998. Advisor/participant Women's Re-entry Ctr., Palm Springs/Las Vegas, 1989-94; vol. Womyn's Festival Com., U. Nev., Las Vegas, 1994—; mem. adv. bd. Collegiate Press, 1998—. Mem. AAUW, Nat. Coun. Tchrs. English, Nev. State Tchrs. English, Nev. Adult Edn. Assn., Nev. Humanities Com., Mountain Plains Adult Edn. Assn., U. Nev. Alumni Assn., Women in Comm., Phi Kappa Phi. Avocations: reading, travel. Office: So Nev CC 3200 E Cheyenne Ave North Las Vegas NV 89030-4228

MILLER, ELEANORA GENEVIEVE, freelance/self-employed poet; b. Gowrie, Iowa, Nov. 17, 1916; d. Alfred Theodore and Jennie Wilhelmina (Carlon) Liljegren; m. Chester Forest Miller, June 1, 1941; children: Carolin Miller Gibson, Loring. BA, Augustana Coll., Rock Island, Ill., 1938; MA, Drake U., 1983. Tchr. English and speech Keota (Iowa) High Sch., 1938-39, Moulton (Iowa) High Sch., 1940-41; reporter Des Moines Register, 1956—; bookkeeper Miller Ins. Ltd., Leon, Iowa, 1980—98; writer pvt. practice, Leon, 1938—. Author: (books of poetry) Poems in Iowa Annual of Lyrical Poetry, 1955, Interviewing the Ghosts, 2001, numerous poems published; winner of over 18 awards for poetry, (book) Interviewing the Ghosts, 2001; editor (newsletter) For Front, 1971-75. Vol. ARC, 1962-73; sec. South Ctrl. Iowa Theatre, Leon, 1978—; mem. Iowa Gov.'s Civil Rights Commn., 1961-65; state chmn. Iowa Citizens for Human Rights, 1965; mem. bd. ch. and society Iowa Conf., United Meth. Ch., 1985-90; lay speaker United Meth. Ch., Creston Dist., 1980—. Mem. VFW Aux. (Iowa state pres 1955-56), Nat, League of Am. Penwomen (br. pres. 1964-66, state pres. 1966-68, 1st pl. lyric poetry 1972), Iowa Poetry Assn. (state pres. 1972-74). Republican. Avocations: vocal music, book collecting. Home and Office: 208 SW Church St Leon IA 50144-1349

MILLER, ELIZABETH JEAN, geologist; b. Brookline, Mass., July 24, 1959; d. Steven Ralph Miller, Judith Reid Miller; m. David Robert Annis. BA in Geol. Sci., Case Western Res. U., 1982; MS Geology, Ariz. State U., 1987. Water resources supr. Ariz. Dept. Water Resources, Phoenix, 1990—90; water conservation specialist City of Mesa Utilities Dept., Ariz., 1990—93, water resource coordinator, 1993—2000; water resource advisor City of Scottsdale Water Resources Dept., Ariz., 2000—. Mem.: AAUW (program v.p. Scottsdale br. 1994—95), State Bar Ariz. (environ. and natural resources law sect.), Colo. River Water Users Assn., Am. Water Works Assn. Avocation: photography.

MILLER, ELIZABETH RODRIGUEZ, city official; b. Tucson, Feb. 22, 1954; d. Tony S. Martinez and Maria (Corral) Rodriguez; m. Marc Alan Miller, Nov. 5, 1972; children: Andrea Eve, Matthew Luke, Meredith C. BA in Spanish, U. Ariz., 1976, MLS, 1978. Unit mgr. S. Tucson Libr., 1978-80; activities coord. community cable com. City of Tucson, 1980; info./reference mgr. Tucson Pub. Libr., 1981-84, agy. mgr., 1984-85, regional mgr., 1985-87, asst. dir. pub. svcs., 1987-89; dep. exec. dir. divsn. ALA Libr. Adminstrn. & Mgmt. Assn., Chgo., 1990; dep. dir. Tucson Pima Libr., 1990-91, libr. dir., 1991-96; asst. city mgr. City of Tucson, 1996—. Co-editor: Great Library Promotion Ideas V, 1990; contbr. articles to profl. jours. Mem. adv. bd. libr. power grant Tucson Unified Sch. Dist., 1992-95; bd. dirs. Tucson area Literacy Coalition, 1992-95, YWCA, 1998—2001; active Hispanic Profl. Action Com., 1992—. Mem. ALA (mem. pres. program com. 1987, mem. nominating com. 1991-93), REFORMA (chair elections com. 1983-84, 85, chair conf. program 1987, pres. 1987-88), Libr. Adminstrn. and Mgmt. Assn. (mem. cultural diversity com. 1991-92, chair 1992-93, mem. nominating com. 1992-93), Pub. Libr. Assn. (mem. Pub. Libr. Assn.-Libr. Adminstrn. and Mgmt. Assn. cert. com. 1991-92, chair 1992-93, chair Allie Beth Martin Award com. 1987-88, mem. 1989), Ariz. Libr. Assn. (Libr. of Yr. 1995), Ariz. State Libr. Assn. (chair svcs. to Spanish-speaking Roundtable 1980-82, pres. pub. libr. divsn. 1984-85, chair ann. conf. 1986), Internat. City/County Mgmt. Assn. (assoc., participant Comparative Performance Measurement Consortium 1994-96, U. Ariz. Hispanic Alumni Assn., Women at the Top (mem. Carondelet health network fin. com). Office: City Mgrs Office City Hall 10th Fl West PO Box 27210 Tucson AZ 85726-7210

MILLER, ELLEN, advertising executive; Pres. health care mktg. svcs. Draft Worldwide (formerly DraftDirect Worldwide), Chgo. Office: Draft Worldwide 633 N Saint Clair St Chicago IL 60611-3234

MILLER, ELLEN S. marketing communications executive; b. Indpls., June 28, 1954; d. Harold Edward and Lilian (Gantner) M. BA, DePauw U., 1976; postgrad., Sch. Visual Arts, N.Y.C., 1981-82. Editorial asst. Daisy mag., N.Y.C., 1976-77; asst. dept. mgr., Christmas hiring mgr. Bloomingdale's, N.Y.C., 1978; sales rep. Rosenthal USA Ltd., N.Y.C., 1979, mktg. asst., 1980-81, dir. mktg. comms., 1982-90; mgr. consumer mktg. Creamer Dickson Basford, Providence, 1990, v.p., 1991-94; prin. E.S. Miller Comm., Providence, 1994—. Instr. Learning Connection. Editor Community Prep. Sch. newsletter, 1993. Trustee Cmty. Prep Sch., Providence, 1993—, mem. exec. com., 1997—. Recipient Bell Ringer award New Eng. Pub. Club, 1992, 93, Iris award N.J. chpt. Internat. Assn. Bus. Communicators, 1993, Silver Quill award Dist. I, 1993, Holland award Ctrl. Mass. Advt. Club, 1997. Mem. Pub. Rels. Soc. Am., Nat. Tabletop Assn. (com. chair 1989), Internat. Tabletop Awards (bd. dirs. 1989), Rotary Club. Republican. Presbyterian. E-mail: ellensmiller@att.net.

MILLER, EMILIE F. former state senator, consultant; b. Chgo., Aug. 11, 1936; d. Bruno C. and Etta M. (Senese) Feiza; m. Dean E. Miller; children: Desireé M., Edward C. BSBA, Drake U., 1958. Asst. buyer Jordan Marsh Co., Boston, 1958-60, Carson, Pirie, Scott & Co., Chgo., 1960-62; dept. mgr., asst. buyer Woodward & Lothrop, Washington, 1962-64; state labor coord. Robb Davis Daliles Joint Campaign; legis. aide Senator Adelard Brandt, Va., 1980-83; fin. dir. Saslaw for Congress, 1984; legis. cons. Va. Fedn. Bus. Profl. Women, 1986-87, 98-00; senator Va. Gen. Assembly, Richmond, 1988-92; cons. apptd. by Gov. Wilder to bd. dirs. Innovative Tech. Authority, 1992-94, Ctr. for Innovative Tech., 1992-94; cons., 1992—; sr. mgr. Thompson, Cobb, Bazilio & Assocs., 1998—. Bus. tng. seminars Moscow, Nizhny Novgorod, Russia, 1993, Novgorod, St. Petersburg, 1995; cons. in field. Guest editl. writer No. Va. Sun, 1981; host, prodr. weekly TV program, Channel 61. Mem. State Ctrl. Com. Dem. Party Va., Richmond, 1974—, steering com., 2000—, chair 11th congrl. dist., 2001—; mem. Fairfax County Dem. Com., 1968—, chair, 1976-80, 98-2000, Presdl. Inaugural Com., 1977, 1992 Dem. Nat. Platform Com., Va. mem. on temp. coms., Dem. Adv. Com. Robb-Spong Commn., 1978-79; chair 11th Congrl. Dist. Dem. Com., 2001—; founder, chair Va. Assoc. Dem. County and City Chmn., 1976-80, Fairfax County Dem. Com., 1976-80, 1998-00; security supr. 1980 Dem. Nat. Conv.; v.p. Va. Fedn. Dem. Women, 1992-94; bd. dirs. Stop Child Abuse Now, 1988, Ctr. Innovative Tech., 1992-94, Ct. Apptd. Spl. Advs., 1993-96; nat. alumni bd. J.A. Achievement, BRAVO adv. com. for the first Gov.'s Awards for Arts in Va., 1979-80; lay tchr. St. Ambrose Cath. Ch., 1963-80; del. to White House Conf. on Children, 1970; chair Va. Coalition for Mentally Disturbed, 1992-94; mem. com. of 100, Va. Opera Bd., 1994-99; bd. dirs. Social Action Linking Together. Recipient Disting. Grad. award Jr. Achievement, 1973, Woman of Achievement award Fairfax (Va.) Bd. Suprs. and Fairfax County Commn. for Women, 1982, Cmty. Svc. award Friends of Victims Assistance Network, 1988, Founders award Fairfax County Coun. of Arts, 1989, Mental Health Assn. of Northern Va. Warren Stambaugh award, 1991, Ann. Svc. award Va. Assn. for Marriage and Family Therapy, 1991, Psychology Soc. of Washington Cmty. Svc. award, 1993, pacesetter award So. Women in Pub. Leadership Conf., 1996. Mem. NOW, Nat. Mus. Women in the Arts, Va. Assn. Female Execs. (mem. adv. bd., bd. dirs., v.p. 1992-99), Va. Assn. Cmty. Svc. Bds. (chmn. 1980-82), North Va. Assn. Cmty. Bds. (chmn. 1978-79, 95-98), Fairfax County Coun. Arts (v.p. 1980—, mem. exec. com. internat. children's festival, Founders award 1989), Fairfax County C. of C. (mem. legis. com.), Greater Merrifield Bus. and Profl. Assn., Mental Health Assn. No.Va. (bd. dirs.), Ctrl. Fairfax C. of C., Falls Church C. of C., Bus. and Profl. Women's Fedn. Va., Mantua Citizens Assn. (exec. bd.), Bus. and Profl. Women's Club (pres. Falls Church chpt. 1994-96, Woman of Yr. award 1990), Women's Nat. Dem. Club (past v.p., mem. bd. govs.), Downtown Club (Richmond), Va. Assn. Female Execs. (bd. dirs. 1992-99), Phi Gamma Nu. Democrat. Roman Catholic. Avocations: cubs fan, tennis, art. Home: 8701 Duvall St Fairfax VA 22031-2711 Office: 8701 Duvall St Fairfax VA 22031 E-mail: EmilieMiller@cs.com.

MILLER, EMILY ELIZABETH, elementary school educator, editor; b. New York, NY, Nov. 7, 1919; d. Lewis Cooke and Helen Elizabeth Wechsler; m. Harry Miller, Jan. 20, 1952; children: Robert Lawrence, Roger David. BA, Hunter Coll., 1942; MA, Teacher's Coll., Columbia, 1958; MA in French Lit., Queens Coll., 1992. Cert. tchr. Calif., 1949. Tchr. San Francisco Pub. Sch., 1950—51, NY Bd. of Edn., Brooklyn, NY, 1962—87. Editor of Clarion newsletter Am. Assn. U. Women, New York, NY, 1975—2001. Del. Conv. AAUW, Ottawa, Canada, 2001—01; rep. UN, Org - Status of Women NGO, New York City, NY, 2001—02. Mem.: Columbia Club. Avocation: french conversation groups.

MILLER, ERIKA, on-air business news reporter; BA in Polit. Sci. with honors, UCLA; student, NYU. Field prodr., assignment editor Bus. News, CNBC, Ft. Lee, N.J.; prodr., reporter Nightly Bus. Report, N.Y.C.; corr. Morning Bus. Report, N.Y.C. Avocations: antiques, travel. Office: NBR 74 Trinity Pl New York NY 10006-2003

MILLER, EUNICE A. marriage and family therapist, sex therapist, foundation administrator; b. Phila., Mar. 29, 1940; d. Henry and Elizabeth Eisenberg; m. Melvin Norman Miller, May 12, 1963; children: Emily, Rachel, Deborah. BA, Adelphi U., 1961; MSW, U. Pa., 1965. Lic. social worker, Pa. Dir. Crossroads Counseling Ctr., Malvern, Pa., 1979—. Mem. Lower Merion Twp. (Pa.) Cable Adv. Com., 1985-97; pres. Melvin and Eunice A. Miller Found., Malvern, 1996—. Mem. Am. Assn. Sex Educators, Counselors and Therapists (cert. sex therapist, book and media reviewer), Am. Assn. Marriage and Family Therapists (clin. mem.).

MILLER, FRANCES SUZANNE, historic site curator; b. Defiance, Ohio, Apr. 17, 1950; d. Francis Bernard Johnson and Nellie Frances (Holder) Culp; m. James A. Batdorf, Aug. 7, 1970 (div. Aug. 1979); 1 child, Jennifer Christine Batdorf; m. Rodney Lyle Miller, Aug. 8, 1982 (div. Apr. 1987). BS in History/Museology, The Defiance Coll., 1990; AS in Bus. Mgmt., N.W. Tech. Coll., 1986. With accts. receivable dept. Ohio Art Co., Bryan, Ohio, 1984-87; leasing agent Williams Met. Housing Authority, Bryan, 1987-91; acting site mgr. James A. Garfield Nat. Historic Site, Mentor, Ohio, 1991—. Mem. AAUW (pres. 1993-95, treas. 1995-98), Nat. Trust Hist. Preservation, Ohio Mus. Assn., Ohio Assn. Host. Socs. and Mus., Cleve. Restoration Soc., Phi Alpha Theta. Avocations: needlework, reading. Office: Apt B14 8060 Deepwood Blvd Mentor OH 44060-7789

MILLER, FRANCIE LORADITCH, counseling administrator; b. Avilton, Md., Apr. 18, 1937; d. John William and Agnes Wilda (Broadwater) Loraditch; m. George Aloys Miller, Feb. 27, 1965; children: Peter Raymond, Sandra Patricia. Student, Kent State U., 1955-57; BA in English, Calif. State U., Dominguez Hills, 1978, Ma in English, 1980. Flight attendant Western Airlines, L.A., 1957-65; lectr. English Calif. State U., Carson, 1980—82, 1998—2002, asst. coord. learning assistance ctr., 1979-84, asst. dir. univ. outreach svcs., 1984-96, lectr., 1997—, asst. dean acad. affairs, 2001—. Dir. advisement & transfer svcs. Marymount Coll., Palos Verdes, Calif., 1996—2001; mem. L.A. Regional Intersegmental Adv. Bd., 1996. Editor: Campus Staff Newsletter, 1992—96. Vol. Olympic Games, L.A., 1984; participant Civic Chorale, Torrance, 1993—; campus rep. Statewide Alumni Coun., Sacramento, 1982—84; apptd. statewide campus adv. com. Project Assist, 1996. Scholar Acad., Kent State U., 1955. Mem.: Western Assn. Coll. Admission Counselors, Nat. Acad. Advising Assn., Calif. Intersegmental Articulation Coun. (newsleeter editor 1993—96, vice chair 1995—96), Palos Verdes C. of C. (bd. dirs. 1998), Phi Kappa Phi (chpt. pres. 1992—98, mem. comm. com. 1996). Republican. Roman Catholic. Avocations: singing, dance, golf. Office: Marymount Coll 30800 Palos Verdes Dr E Palos Verdes Peninsula CA 90275-6273 E-mail: fmiller@marymountpv.edu.

MILLER, FRANCINE KOSLOW, art history educator, art critic; b. Boston, Apr. 26, 1951; d. Myer and Lillian (Witten) Koslow; m. Mark Jay Miller, Oct. 6, 1991; 1 child, Rebecca. BA, Brandeis U., 1973; MA, U. Calif., Berkeley, 1976; PhD, Boston U., 1981. Asst. editor Worldwide Books, Allston, Mass., 1975-76; prof. art history McGill U., Montreal, Que., Can., 1981-83; guest curator De Cordova Mus., Lincoln, Mass., 1983-84; asst. prof. art history Pine Manor Coll., Chestnut Hill, Mass., 1984-86; prof. art history Mass. Coll. Art, Boston, 1986—. Author: Gaudier-Brzeska par Ezra Pound, 1992, (catalogs) Henry David Thoreau as a Source for Artistic Inspiration, 1984, David Brody Selected Works, 1995; contbg. writer, reviewer Artforum, 1988—; feature writer Print Collectors Newsletter, 1988—. Mem. Internat. Assn. of Art Critics, Phi Beta Kappa. Democrat. Jewish. Avocations: quilting, hiking, camping, doll collecting. Home and Office: 9 Woodhaven Dr Andover MA 01810-2822

MILLER, GAY DAVIS, lawyer; b. Florence, Ariz., Dec. 20, 1947; d. Franklin Theodore and Mary (Belshaw) Davis; 1 child, Katherine Alexandra. BA, U. Colo., 1969; JD, Am. U., 1975. Bar: D.C. 1975. Atty., spl. asst. to gen. counsel, sr. counsel corp. affairs Inter Am. Devel. Bank, Washington, 1975—78, 1983—2004; atty. Intelsat, Washington, 1978-80. Articles editor: Am. U. Law Rev., 1974—75, contbg. author: The Inspection Panel of the World Bank: A Different Complaints Procedure, 2001. Bd. dirs. Hist. Mt. Pleasant, Inc., Washington, 1985-86, Washington Bridle Trails Assn., 1992—. Mem.: ABA, Am. Soc. Internat. Law, Inter Am. Bar Assn.

MILLER, GENEVIEVE, retired medical historian; b. Butler, Pa., Oct. 15, 1914; d. Charles Russell and Genevieve (Wolford) M. AB, Goucher Coll., 1935; MA, Johns Hopkins U., 1939; PhD, Cornell U., 1955. 1944asst. in history medicine Johns Hopkins Inst. History of Medicine, Balt., 1943, 1948instr., 1945, rsch. assoc., 1979-94; asst. prof. history of sci. Case Western Res. U. Sch. Medicine, Cleve., 1953-67, assoc. prof., 1967-79, assoc. prof. emeritus, 1979—; rsch. assoc. med. history Clevel. Med. Libr. Assn., 1953-62; curator Howard Dittrick Mus. Hist. Medicine, 1962-67, dir., 1967-79. Corr. mem. fgn. socs. history of medicine. Author: William Beaumont's Formative Years: Two Early Notebooks 1811-1821, 1946; The Adoption of Inoculation for Smallpox in England and France, 1957 (William H. Welch medal Am. Assn. History Medicine 1962), Bibliography of the History of Medicine of the U.S. and Canada, 1939-1960, 1964, Bibliography of the Writings of Henry E. Sigerist, 1966, Letters of Edward Jenner and Other Documents Concerning the Early History of Vaccination, 1983; assoc. editor Bull. of History of Medicine, 1944-48, acting editor, 1948, mem. adv. editl. bd., 1960-92; mem. bd. editors Jour. History of Medicine & Allied Scis., 1948-65; editor Newsletter Am. Assn. History of Medicine, 1986-96; contbr. articles to profl. jours. Alumna trustee Goucher Coll., Balt., 1966-69; trustee Judson Retirement Cmty., Clevel., 1993-99, Am. Coun. Learned Socs. fellow, 1948-50, Dean Van Meter fellow, Goucher Coll., 1953-54. Fellow Cleve. Med. Libr. Assn. (hon.); mem. Am. Assn. History Medicine (pres. 1978-80, mem. coun. 1960-63, Lifetime Achievement award 1999), Am. Hist. Assn., Internat. Soc. History of Medicine, Soc. Archtl. Historians, Phi Beta Kappa. Democrat. Home and Office: Judson Manor Apt 616 1890 E 107th St Cleveland OH 44106-2251

MILLER, GERALDINE (TINCY), real estate company executive, educational association administrator; m. Vance Miller; 4 children. BS, So. Meth. U.; MS in Reading, Tex. A&M U. Vice chmn. Henry S. Miller Cos., 1994—. Tchr. reading lab. Tex. Scottish Rite HOsp. for Crippled Children, Highland Park Presbyn. Hillier Sch. for Dyslexia; bd. mem. Literacy Instrn. for Tex. Mem. Tex. State Bd. Edn., 1988—, pres., 2003—; chair fund-raising events United Cerebral Palsy Assn., Dallas Opera, Dallas Symphony Orch., TACA, Crystal Charity Ball; active I Have A Dream Found., Nat. Orton-Dyslexia Soc., Boy's and Girl's Club Greater Dallas, Dallas County Heritage Soc. Recipient Hall of State award for civic involvement, Dallas Hist. Soc., 1995, Tom Landry award of excellence in volunteerism, 1999. Mem.: Acad. Lang. Therapist Assn., Internat. Reading Assn., Kappa Delta Pi, Phi Delta Kappa. Republican. Address: 1100 Providence Tower West 5001 Spring Valley Rd Dallas TX 75244-3910

MILLER, GRETCHEN M. music educator; b. Roanoke, Va.Va., Oct. 14, 1950; d. Jeese Ward Moore and Mina Ray Munsey; m. Clarence Wilfred Miller, Nov. 6, 1982; 1 child, Brandon Hunter. BA in Music, Guilford Coll., 1972; MS in Counseling, Radford U., 1978; grad., Realtors Inst., 1987. Cert. profl. tchr. Va. Tchr. Bedford (Va.) County Pub. Sch., Va., 1973—77, The Achievement Group, Roanoke, 1979; ednl. mktg. Atalantis Group, Inc., Roanoke, 1980—83; realtor K.R. Recknor Real Estate Co., Roanoke, 1984—88; tchr. Cave Spring Meth. Pre-Sch., Roanoke, 1992—2000; pvt. music tchr., 1995—. Alto flutist: Bel Canto, 2000—, flutist: at various other events. Mem.: Nat. Flute Assn., Music Tchrs. Nat. Assn., United Daughters Confederacy (pres. 1998—2000, registrar 2001—02), DAR. Presbyterian. Home: 2301 Stallion Cir SW Roanoke VA 24018 E-mail: wghkm@cox.net.

MILLER, GWENDOLYN DORIS, special education educator, retired; b. N.Y.C., Oct. 22, 1933; d. Raymond Addison and Hattie Bryant; m. Leo Miller Jr., Oct. 22, 1955 (dec. Oct. 1999); children: Steven, Debra, Scott, Derek. BA, Hunter Coll., 1961; MS in Edn., L.I. U., 1978, profl. diploma, 1979. Cert. sch. adminstr., supr., N.Y. Tchr. trainer N.Y.C. Dept. of Edn., Divsn. Spl. Edn., 1978-80; supr. spl. edn. Sch. Dist. #22, Bklyn., 1980-92; owner, prin. Travel Network, Jamaica, N.Y., 1989-97; v.p., curator Ebony Treasures and Art Gallery Inc., Jamaica, 1997—. Mem. bd. examiners Bd. of Edn., Bklyn., 1986-92, cons., 1992-93; adj. profl St. John's U., Queens, N.Y., 1995-2001; edn. dir. UPK, 2001—. Bd. dirs. York Coll., Queens, N.Y., 1993-95, Hillside Eastern Queens Mental Health Coun., 1983-89; treas., bd. dirs. Jamaica Day Nursery Inc., 1993—; sec. bd. dirs. Reach Into Cultural Heights Inc., Queens, 1994—; mem. task force on South Africa, Presbytery of N.Y., 1993—; mem. N.Y. State jud. com., Queens Dem. Orgn., 1976, county com., 1975; active Boy Scouts Am., 1972, Girl Scouts of U.S., 1973; elder, Christian edn., Sunday Sch., Presbyn. Ch. Mem. Africa Travel Assn., Phi Delta Kappa, Protestant Tchrs. Assn. of N.Y.C., Rotary of South Eastern Queens (founding mem.). Avocations: collecting art from Africa, internat. travel, different cultures. Office: Ebony Treasures and Art Gallery 11335 Farmers Blvd Saint Albans NY 11412-2425

MILLER, GWENDOLYN M. councilman; b. Tampa, Fla., Aug. 2, 1934; d. Nathaniel Martin and Wilma Rivers; m. Lesley J. Jr. Miller. MEd, Fla. A&M U., 1966. Tchr. Hills County Sch. System, Tampa, Fla., 1957—67, human relations specialist, 1967—94; mem. Tampa City Coun., 1995—. Pres. Nat. Coalition of 100 Black Women Inc., Tampa, 2001—; nat. pres. The Charmettes, Inc., Tampa, 1997—2000; bd. dirs. Tampa-Hills Urban League, 1998. Recipient Hank Warren Meml. award, 1994, City of Tampa and Mayor's Challenge Fund award, 1997, USA Track and Field Florence Griffith Joyner Trailblazer Bus. award, 1998, Whitney Young Meml. award, Tampa-Hills Urban League, 1998, The Fla. A & M U. Disting. Alumni Award, 2003. Mem.: Alpha Kappa Alpha. Democrat. Baptist. Home: 2505 38th Ave Tampa FL 33610 Office: Office of City Council 315 E Kennedy Blvd Flr 3 Tampa FL 33602-5211

MILLER, HARRIET SANDERS, former art center director; b. Apr. 18, 1926; d. Herman and Dorothy (Silbert) S.; m. Milton H. Miller, June 27, 1948; children: Bruce, Jeffrey, Marcie. BA, Ind. U., 1947; MA, Columbia U., 1949; MS, U. Wis., 1962, MFA, 1967. Dir. art sch. Madison (Wis.) Art Ctr., 1963-72; acting dir. Ctr. for Contg. Edn., Vancouver, B.C., 1975-76; mem. fine arts faculty Douglas Coll., Vancouver, B.C., 1972-78; exec. dir. Palos Verdes (Calif.) Arts Ctr., 1978-84; dir. Jr. Arts Ctr., L.A., 1984-98. One woman exhibits at Gallery 7, Vancouver, 1978, Gallery 1, Toronto, Ont., 1977, Linda Farris Gallery, Seattle, 1975, Galerie Allen, Vancouver, 1973.

MILLER, HEIDI G. diversified financial company executive; b. 1951; married; 2 children. BA in History, Princeton U., 1974; PhD in History, Yale U., 1979. Various positions to mng. dir. emerging markets structured finance group Chemical Bank, 1979—92; joined as v.p. and asst. to the pres. Travelers Group, 1992, CFO, 1995—98, Citigroup (merger of Citibank and Travelers Group), N.Y.C., 1998—2000; CFO, sr. exec. v.p. strategic planning and adminstrn. Priceline.com, Norwalk, Conn., 2000; vice chmn. Marsh & McLennan Co., Inc., N.Y.C., 2001—02; exec. v.p. strategy and devel., CFO Bank One Corp., 2002—. Bd. dirs. Merck & Co., Inc., General Mills Inc. Trustee Princeton U., NYU Med. Sch. Office: Bank One Corp 1 Bank One Plaza Chicago IL 60670*

MILLER, HELEN, state representative, lawyer; b. Newark, Nov. 1945; BA, Howard U.; MS, Our Lady of the Lake U.; JD, Georgetown U. Bar: (D.C.), (Iowa). Atty.; state rep. dist. 49 Iowa Ho. of Reps., 2003—; mem. econ. growth com.; mem. human resources com.; mem. transp. com.; mem. justice sys. appropriations subcom. Vol. Cmty. Sch. Improvement Adv. Bd., Webster County Crime Stoppers, Leadership Iowa; exec. dir. Young At Art; bd. dirs. Youth Shelter Care N. Ctrl. Iowa, Blanden Meml. Art Mus. Democrat. Office: State Capitol East 12th and Grand Des Moines IA 50319

MILLER, HELEN F. music educator, musician; b. Lewistown, Mont., May 29, 1918; d. Otis Willard Freeman and Laura Olive Cowell; m. Paul Gilbert Miller, June 10, 1938; children: Don Paul, Barbara Helen. MusB, U. Wis., 1938; MusM in Edn., Immaculate Heart Coll., 1968. Mem. So. Symphony, Columbia, S.C., 1940, Music Under Stars Symphony, Milw., 1944-46; concert master Waukesha (Wis.) Symphony, 1948-51; mem. N.J. Symphony, Orange, 1952-54, Colonial Symphony, Madison, N.J., 1952-54; soloist U. Ariz. Symphony, Tucson, 1959; mem. Santa Monica (Calif.) Symphony, 1960-61. Pvt. violin tchr., 1938—; tchr. music Immaculate Heart Coll. Prep. Sch., L.A., 1960-67, Mt. Gleason Jr. High, Tujunga, Calif., 1961-62, Immaculate Heart Coll., L.A., 1963-66, Sch. Dist. #91, Idaho Falls, 1967-70, Rick's Coll. Music Camp, Rexburg, Idaho, summers 1968-69, Taipei (Taiwan) Am. Sch., 1970-71, Dept. Def., Secondary Schs., Seoul, 1972-73, U. Catolica, Valparaiso, Chile, 1973-80, Coll of the Desert, Palm Desert, Calif., 1982-88. Solo violin performances, Cheney, Wash., 1934-37, Clemson, S.C., 1939, Milw. Mus., 1947, Orange, N.J., 1955, U. Ariz. Symphony, Tucson, 1959, Immaculate Heart Coll., L.A., 1961-66, Idaho Falls Symphony, 1968, Taipei, 1971, Tsing Hwa U., Hsinchu, Taiwan, 1971, U. Law, Taipei, 1971, U. Catolica and U. Chile sede Valparaiso, 1973-80; violinist Westbrook Trio, N.J., N.Y., Conn., 1954-58, Angeles String Trio, L.A. Mus. Concert, 1961, Seoul Nat. U. Sch. Music, 1973; organizer, performer Twilight Festival of Music, Idaho Falls, summers 1967, 68, 69 Choir dir. Meth. Ch., Oconomowoc, Wis., 1958-61, Cmty. Meth. Ch., Tujunga, 1963-64, St. Philips Luth. Ch., Pacoima, Calif., 1964-67; organizer, founder Youth String Competition, Riverside, Calif., 1998, 99. Scholar U. Wis., U. Ariz.; tchg. fellow Immaculate Heart Coll. Home: 39517 Cedarwood Dr Murrieta CA 92563-5305

MILLER, HINDA, state senator, management consultant; b. Montreal, Can., Apr. 18, 1950; m. Joel Miller; 2 children. BA, Parson's Sch. Design, 1972; MFA, N.Y. U., 1976. Bus. cons.; senator State of Vt., 2003—. Mem. Vt. Bus. Social Responsibility; bd. trustees Champlain Coll. Commr. Burlington Internat. Airport. Mem.: Lake Champlain C. of C. Democrat. Office: 84 DeForest Heights Burlington VT 05401

MILLER, HOPE RIDINGS, author; b. Bonham, Tex. d. Alfred Lafayette and Grace (Dupree) Ridings; m. Clarence Lee Miller, Sept. 26, 1932 (dec. Jan. 1965). BA, U. Tex.; MA, Columbia; D.Litt., Austin Coll. Society editor Washington Post, 1938-45; Washington corr. Town and Country mag., 1944-46, The Argonaut mag., 1945-49; Washington columnist Promenade mag., 1945-51; syndicated column McNaught, 1945-50; asso. editor Diplomat mag., 1952-55, editor in chief, 1956-66; television prodn. staff Metromedia, Inc., 1966-70; Washington editor Antique Monthly, 1976-89. Mem. editorial adv. bd. Horizon mag., 1978-89. Author: Embassy Row: The Life and Times of Diplomatic Washington, 1969, Great Houses of Washington, 1969, Scandals In The Highest Office: Facts and Fictions in the Private Lives of Our Presidents, 1973; script for cassette tape Circling Lafayette Square, 1976. Mem. women's bd. Columbia Hosp., Friends of the Folger Library, Washington Heart Assn. Mem. Nat. Press Club, Hist. Soc. Washington, Friends of LBJ Libr., Am. News women's Club, The Circle of the Nat. Gallery of Art, Stephen F. Austin Soc., Am. Archives of Art, Smithsonian Assocs., Nat. Mus. Women in the Arts, Sulgrave Club. Home: 1868 Columbia Rd NW Washington DC 20009-5183

MILLER, IRIS ANN, landscape architect, urban designer, educator; b. Pitts., Jan. 6, 1938; d. Bernard and Sadye (Topel) Ress; m. Lawrence Alan Miller, Jan. 24, 1959; children: Bradley Stuart, Richard Lyle, Stefan Ress. BS cum laude, U. Pitts., 1959, MEd in Secondary Edn., 1961; postgrad. in psychology and counseling, U. Md., 1962-68; MArch, Cath. U. Am., 1979. Tchr. various pub. and pvt. schs., Pitts., Monroeville, Pa., Montgomery County, Md., 1959-61, 63-64; free lance landscape design Washington, 1965-81; architecture design and research O'Neil and Manion Architects, Bethesda, Md., 1979, 81; architecture design and drawing Frank Schlesinger Architects/Planners, Washington, 1979-80; prin. Iris Miller Urbanism and Landscape Design, 1982—; cons. architecture design Washington, 1982—. Vis. lectr. Cath. U. Am., Washington, 1983-86, vis. asst. prof., 1987-93, adj. asst. prof., 1993-96, adj. assoc. prof., 1997—, dir. landscape, arch. studies, 1986-89, dir. landscape studies, 1990—; urban design cons. Techworld, Washington, 1984-86; devel. dir. Tech. 2000 Mus., 1985-86; dir., presenter lectr. series resident assoc. program Smithsonian Instn., Washington, 1982, 83, 85, 87, 89, 98; dir., founder 7th, 8th and 9th Sts. Group Streetscape project, Washington, 1986-89, others; founder Charrette urban design seminar, Washington, Dallas, Alexandria, Va., St. Louis and Cleve., 1982-89; initiator, participant Sarasota (Fla.) Regional Urban Design Assistance R/UDAT Team, 1983, seminar Nat. Gallery Art, Washington, 1984, Nat. Arboretum, 1988, symposia Cath. U. Am., 1987—; invited jury panel, Fulbright Travel Awards, 1997-99; Lambda Alpha Internat. Hon. Soc., 1998—;facilitator/panel North Capital St./Fruxton Circle Charette, 2001; invited panel Japan Triennial Echigo-Tsumari, 1999, 2000; spkr., team leader McMillan Reservoir Charrette, Washington, 1999; apptd. mem. D.C. Downtown Partnership Streetscape subcom., 1989-91, D.C. Interactive Downtown Task Force Streetscape and Traffic subcom., 1996; D.C. Stakeholder Signage Subcommittee, 1997—, D.C. Stakeholder Traffic Subcommittee, 1998, D.C. Stakeholder Streetscape Subcom., 1999; co-founder, co-chmn. Brookland/CUA Neighborhood Improvement Partnership, 1999—; founder, co-dir. symposium. Libr. of Congress, 1995; dir. symposium D.C. Interagy. Task Force Seminar on Streetscape and Signage, 1995; dir., mem. steering com. numerous confs. in field; invited participant Congress for New Urbanism, 1994—; program spkr. U.S. Embassy Amman, Jordan, 1992, ICOMOS, 1992, 93, U. Va., 1993, Ecole Nationale Superieure du Paysage/Versailles, France, 1993, U. Osaka, Japan, 1993, 95, 96, 97 Tokyo Inst. Tech. U., 1993, Chiba Inst. Tech., Japan, 1998, SUNY, Buffalo, 1994, U. Colo., Denver, 1994, Mayors Inst. on City Design, St. Louis, 1994, Tongji U., Shanghai, China, 1995, 97, Tsinghua U., China, 1995, 98; jury critic Cath. U. Am., 1980-99, U. Puerto Rico, U. Va., 1993, Tsinghua U., China, 1998; instr. ceramics, Bethesda, Md., 1975-76. Author, co-editor: (book) Urban Design: Visions and Reflections, 1991, Capital Visions: Reflections on a Decade of Urban Design Charrettes and a Look Ahead, 1995, (map and text) Visions of Washington: Composite Plan of Urban Interventions, 1991; author: D.C. Streetscape & Signage Resource Manual, 1996; co-author: Retrospective Catalogue: Collegiate Exhibition for Excellence in Urban Design, 1997, Washington In Maps, 2002; contbr. articles to profl. jours.; landscape design featured in major landscape archtl. jours. in US and Japan, 1998, 2000; featured nationally in Assoc. Press articles on fragrant landscapes, 1999; curator, author exhbn. and catalogue on Washington Maps Sumner Sch. Mus., 1987, 92, U. Md., 1993, Embassy of France, 1993, SUNY Buffalo, 1994, U. Calif., Berkeley, 1994, U. Toronto, Can., 1995; curator, author exhbn. ACSA Ann. Meeting, Montreal, 1994; co-curator, author exhbn. and catalogue Octagon Mus., 1987; project dir., curator Paris-Washington Exhbn., 1987—; exhibitor, installation, Tokyo, Japan, 1997; recent residential and other landscape projects include Univ. Club. Wash., 1997-98, Salle de Fete Site Plan, Francheville, France, 1993, Kahn Residence, Arlington, Va., 1993-94, Marks Residence, Silver Spring, Md., 1993, Nesse, Lewis Residence, Silver Spring, 1992, Friedman Residence, Washington, 1992, Drysdale Hershon Residence, Washington, 1991, Miller Residence, Washington, 1990—, Sexton Residence, Kenwood, Chevy Chase, Md., 1990, 95, Romano Residence, Fairfax Station, Va., 1989, Mushinski Residence, Bethesda, Md., 1989, 8th St. Mall Washington, 1987-88, Mishkin, Jennis Residence, Bethesda, 1988, Cramer Residence, Bethesda, 1988; recent home design and renovations include Sexton Residence, Chevy Chase, 1994, Miller Jayapal Residence, San Francisco, 1993, Marks Residence, Silver Spring, 1993, Miller Residence, 1991, Washington, Mishkin Jennis Residence, Bethesda, 1988. Co-chmn. stamp com. Bicentennial Washington, 1987-90; founding mem. Washington Network, 1986-89; mem. adv. panel L'Enfant Forum, Washington, 1987-90, Hist. Georgetown Found., 1989-90; trustee John J. Sexton Fund for Local Govt. Studies, Sch. Pub. Affairs, U. Md., College Park, 1983-93; dir., founder Pub.-Pvt. Partnership and Univ. Scholarship Outreach Inner-City H.S. Program, Cath. U. Am., Washington Pub. Schs., 1985—; dir., founder Intern Exch. Program Landscape Architecture France-U.S.A., Cath. U. Am., U. Va., Friends of Vieilles Maisons Francaises, 1991-98, study-travel Asia Arch./Landscape Scholarship Fund, 1998—; dir., co-founder Intern Exch. Program Landscape Architecture China-U.S.A., Cath. U. Am., Tongji U., Shanghai, 1995—, Osaka U., Japan, 1996—, Chiba Inst. Tech., Japan, 1998-99; historic landscape com. U.S./Internat. Coun. on Monuments and Sites, 1990—; active Cultural Alliance Greater Washington, Nat. Trust Historic Preservation, Ikebana Internat., His. Soc. Washington, Nat. Mus. for Bldg. Arts; alumni coun. Sch. Architecture and Planning, Cath. U. Am., 1986—; mem. com. on environment Congress for New Urbanism, 1994—. Travel rsch. grantee Cath. U. Am., 1978, 79; grantee Govt. France, 1985, NEA (2), 1982, 92; recipient Program Devel. award Cath. U. Am., 1978. Mem. AIA (assoc., nat., regional and urban design exhbn. and panel, chmn. edn. subcom. 1987-96, sec. edn. subcom. 1997—, chmn., founder data base on design edn. and urban design, chmn. edn. conf. 1983, chmn. newsletter 1993, edn. com. D.C. chpt. 1981-83, Charrette co-chmn., program devel. award 1982), Assn. Collegiate Schs. Architecture (spkr. N.E. region conf. 1989, spkr. ann. meeting 1991-92, chmn. panel 1989—, chair Collegiate Exhbn. for Excellence in Urban Design 1990—, author conf. procs. 1991-93, Citation for Urban Design 1993, 95), Am. Soc. Landscape Architects (Potomac chpt. strategic planning com. 1994-95), Am. Planning Assn., U.S.-Internat. Coun. on Monuments and Sites (program spkr. 1987, 92, 93, hist. landscapes com.), Friends Vieilles Maisons Francaises (program spkr. 1987, 92), Friends of Vieilles Maisons Francaises, Congress for New Urbanism (com. on environment 1994—), Alpha Epsilon Phi (pres. D.C. alumni 1965-67). Avocations: photography, japanese flower arranging, tennis, jogging. Home: 3820 52nd St NW Washington DC 20016-1924

MILLER, JACQUELINE WINSLOW, library director; b. N.Y.C., Apr. 15, 1935; d. Lynward Roosevelt and Sarah Ellen (Grevious) W.; 1 child, Percy Scott. BA, Morgan State Coll., 1957; MLS, Pratt Inst., 1960; grad. profl. seminar, U. Md., 1973. Cert. profl. libr. With Bklyn. Pub. Libr., 1957-68; head ext. svcs. New Rochelle (N.Y.) Pub. Libr., 1969-70; br. adminstr. Grinton Will Yonkers (N.Y.) Pub. Libr., 1970-75; dir. Yonkers Pub. Libr., 1975-96. Mem. adj. faculty grad. libr. studies Queens Coll., CUNY, 1989, 90. Mem. commr.'s com. Statewide Libr. Devel., Albany, N.Y., 1980; mem. N.Y. Gov.'s Commn. on Librs., 1990, 91; bd. dirs. Cmty. Planning Coun., Yonkers, N.Y., 1987; mem. Yonkers Black Women's Polit. Caucus, 1987; pres. bd. Literacy Vols. of Westchester County, 1991-92; mem. fair campaign practices com. LWV, 1996—. Recipient Yonkers Citizen award Ch. of Our Saviour, 1980, 2d Ann. Mae Morgan Robinson award Yonkers chpt. Westchester Black Women's Polit. Caucus, 1992, 3d Ann. Equality Day award City of Yonkers, 1992, African-Am. Heritage 1st award YWCA, 1994; named Outstanding Profl. Woman Nat. Assn. Negro Bus. and Profl. Women's Clubs Inc., 1981. Mem. ALA (councilor 1987-91), N.Y. State Libr. Assn., Pub. Libr. Dirs. Assn. (exec. bd.), N.Y. State Pub. Libr. Dirs. Assn., Westchester Libr. Assn., Yonkers C. of C. (bd. dirs. 1992-95), Educate the Girls, Inc. (bd. dirs., 2003—) Rotary (Yonkers chpt.). E-mail: jacki@sprynet.com.

MILLER, JANEL HOWELL, psychologist; b. Boone, N.C., May 18, 1947; d. John Estle and Grace Louise (Hemberger) Howell; m. C. Rick Miller, Nov. 24, 1968; children: Kimberly, Brian, Audrey, Rachel. BA, DePauw U., 1969; postgrad., Rice U., 1969; MA, U. Houston, 1972; PhD, Tex. A&M U., 1979. Lic. clin. psychologist, sch. psychologist, Tex. Assoc. sch. psychologist Houston Ind. Sch. Dist., 1971-74; rsch. psychologist VA Hosp., Houston, 1972; assoc. sch. psychologist Clear Creek (Tex.) Ind. Sch. Dist., 1974-76; instr. psychology, counseling psychology intern Tex. A&M U., 1976-77; clin. psychology intern VA Hosp., Houston, 1977-78; coord. psychol. svcs. Clear Creek Ind. Sch. Dist., 1978-81, assoc. dir. psychol. svcs., 1981-82; pvt. practice Houston, 1982—. Faculty U. Houston-Clear Lake, 1984—; adolescent suicide cons., 1984—. DePauw U. Alumni scholar, 1965-69; NIMH fellow U. Houston, 1970-71. Mem. APA, Am. Assn. Marriage and Family Therapists, Soc. for Personality Assessment, Am. Coll. Forensic Examiners, Internat. Rorschach Soc., Tex. Psychol. Assn., Tex. Assn. Marriage and Family Therapists, Houston Psychol. Assn. (media rep. 1984-85), Houston Assn. Marriage and Family Therapists. Home: 806 Walbrook Dr Houston TX 77062-4030 Office: 16854 Royal Crest Dr Houston TX 77058-2529 E-mail: shrinkskate@sbcglobal.net.

MILLER, JANICE, electronics executive; B in Polit. Sci., U. Ariz.; MBA in Fin., Ariz. State U. With McDonnell Douglas; mng. dir. strategic planning Best Western Internat.; v.p. corp. strategic planning Avnet, Phoenix, 2001—02, v.p., dir. orgnl. devel., 2002. Mem. Gov.'s Ariz.-Mex. Commn. Bd., 2003; chmn. strategic planning com. United Way; bd. dirs. Centennial Village Housing Project, Strategic Leadership Forum. Office: Avnet Inc 2211 S 47th St Phoenix AZ 85034*

MILLER, JEAN PATRICIA SALMON, art educator; b. Little Falls, Minn., Sept. 28, 1920; d. Albert Michael and Wilma (Kaestner) Salmon; m. George Fricke Miller, Sept. 8, 1951 (dec. Apr. 1991); children: Victoria Jean, George Laurids. BS, St. Cloud State Tchrs. Coll., 1942; MS, U. Wis., Whitewater, 1976. Lic. cert. secondary English, art, Wis. Tchr. elem. and secondary art Pub. Schs. Sauk Center, Minn., 1943; tchr. secondary art Bd. Edn., Idaho, 1945; tchr. elem. and secondary art Elkhorn (Wis.) Area Schs., 1950-78; tchr. art adult edn. Kenosha Tech. Coll., Elkhorn, Wis., 1969; cooperating tchr., supr. art majors in edn. U. Wis., Whitewater, 1970-77. Coord. Art Train Project, Walworth County. Represented in permanent collections Irwin L. Young Auditorium, U. Wis., Whitewater. Sec. Walworth County Needs of Children and Youth, Williams Bay, Wis., 1956-57; co-chair, sponsor Senate Bill 161-art requirement for h.s. grad., 1988-89. Recipient Grand award painting Walworth County Fair, 1970, 3rd award painting Geneva Lake Art Assn., Lake Geneva, Wis., Acrylic Painting First award Badlants Art Assn., 1994. Mem. Nat. Art Edn. Assn., Wis. Women in Arts, Wis. Art Edn. Assn., Wis. Regional Artists Assn. (co-chmn. Wis. regional art program 1992, 93, corr. sec. 1992—), Walworth County Art Assn. (bd. dirs. 1979-94, pres. 1986-87), Badlands Art Assn., Kiwanis, Elks, Alpha Delta Kappa (pres. Theta chpt. Wis. 1968-70), Delta Kappa Gamma (Iota chpt.). Home and Office: PO Box 26 Taylor ND 58656-0026

MILLER, JEANNE-MARIE ANDERSON (MRS. NATHAN J. MILLER), English language educator, academic administrator; b. Washington, Feb. 18, 1937; d. William and Agnes Catherine (Johns) Anderson m. Nathan John Miller, Oct. 2, 1960. BA, Howard U., 1959, MA, 1963, PhD, 1976. Instr. dept. English Howard U., Washington, 1963-76, asst. prof., 1976-79, assoc. prof., 1979-92, prof., 1992-97, prof. emeritus, 1997—, asst. dir. Inst. Arts and Humanities, 1973-75, asst. acad. planning, office v.p. for acad. affairs, 1976-90. Cons. Am. Studies Assn., 1972-75, Silver Burdett Pub. Co., NEH, 1978—; mem. adv. bd. D.C. Libr. for Arts, 1973—. Editor, Black Theatre Bull., 1977-86; Realism to Ritual: Form and Style in Black Theatre, 1983; assoc. editor Theatre Jour., 1980-81; contbr. articles to profl. jours. and books. Mem. Washington Performing Arts Soc., 1971—, Friends of Sta. WETA-TV, 1971—, Mus. African Art, 1971—, Arena Stage Assocs., 1972—, Washington Opera Guild, 1982—, Wolf Trap Assocs., 1982—, Drama League N.Y., 1995, Shakespeare Theatre, 2001—, Met. Opera Guild, 2002—. Ford Found. fellow, 1970-72, So. Fellowships Fund fellow, 1973-74; Howard U. rsch. grant, 1975-76, 94-97, ACLS grant, 1978-79, NEH grant, 1981-84. Mem.: LWV (D.C. chpt.), MLA, ACLU, AAUP, Folger Shakespeare Libr., Acad. Am. Poets, Am. Theatre and Drama Soc., Studio Mus. Harlem, Nat. Mus. Women in Arts, Nat. Bldg. Mus., Winterthur Guild, Hist. Soc. Washington, D.C. Preservation League, Nat. Trust Historic Preservation, Zora Neale Hurston Soc., Langston Hughes Soc., Ibsen Soc., Friends of Kennedy Ctr. for Performing Arts, Am. Assn. Higher Edn., Coll. Lang. Assn., Common Cause, Am. Assn. Higher Edn., Am. Studies Assn., Coll. English Assn., Nat. Coun. Tchrs. English, Sierra Club, Pi Lambda Theta. Democrat. Episcopalian. Home: 504 24th St NE Washington DC 20002-4818

MILLER, JO CAROLYN DENDY, family and marriage counselor, educator; b. Gorman, Tex., Sept. 16, 1942; d. Leonard Lee and Vera Vertie (Robison) Dendy; m. Douglas Terry Barnes, June 1, 1963 (div. June 1975); children: Douglas Alan, Bradley Jason; m. Walton Sansom Miller, Sept. 19, 1982. BA, Tarleton State U., 1964; MEd, U. North State, 1977, PhD, Tex. Woman's U., 1993. Tchr. Mineral Wells (Tex.) High Sch., 1964-65, Weatherford (Tex.) Middle Sch., 1969-74; counselor, instr. psychology Tarrant County Jr. Coll., Hurst, Tex., 1977-82; pvt. practice family and marriage counseling Dallas, 1982—. Author: (with Velma Baker, Jeannene Ward) Becoming: A Human Relations Workbook, 1981. Mem. ACA, Tex. State Bd. Examiners Profl. Counselors, Tex. State Bd. Marriage and Family Therapists, Tex. Counseling Assn., North Ctrl. Tex. Counseling Assn., Dallas Symphony Orch. League, Nat. Coun. Family Rels., Tex. Mental Health Counselors Assn., Internat. Assn. for Marriage and Family Counselors. Methodist. Office: 8222 Douglas Ave Ste 777 Dallas TX 75225-5938 Office Phone: 214-691-0400.

MILLER, JO ELLEN, humanities educator; b. Berkeley, Calif., Dec. 28, 1957; d. Richard Charles Miller and Esther Elsie Cook; m. Larry Andrew Tosh, May 4, 1985; children: Emma Tosh, Dylan Tosh. BA, U. Oreg., 1980; MA, Colo. State U., 1983; PhD, U. Utah, 1993. Asst. prof. Grand Valley State U., Allendale, Mich., 1991—97, assoc. prof., 1997—, chair dept. English, 2000—. Contbr. articles to profl. jours. Leader 4-H Club, Ottawa County, Mich., 2001—03; pres. PTO, 2002—03; bd. dirs. Pigeon Creek Shakespeare Co., 2000—03. Office: Grand Valley State U Dept of English Allendale MI 49401

MILLER, JUDITH A. federal official; BA summa cum laude, Beloit Coll., 1972; JD, Yale U., 1975. Bar: U.S. Supreme Ct., U.S. Ct. Appeals (D.C. cir.), U.S. Ct. Appeals (armed forces cir.). Clk. to Judge Harold Leventhal, U.S. Ct of Appeals for D.C. cir., Washington; clk. to Assoc. Justice Potter Stewart Supreme Ct. of U.S., Washington; asst. to sec., dep. sec. of def. Office of Spl. Asst., Washington, 1977-79; assoc., ptnr. Williams & Connolly, Washington, 1979-94; adv. bd. on investigative capability Dept. Def., Washington, gen. counsel, 1994—. Civil justice reform act adv. group U.S. Dist. Ct. D.C.; mem. jud. conf. D.C. Cir. Recipient Vol. Recognition award Nat. Assn. of Attys. Gens.; DOD medal for Disting. Pub. Svc., 1997, Beloit Coll. Disting. Svc. Citation, 1997. Fellow Am. Bar Found.; mem. ABA, Am. Law Inst. Office: Office of Gen Counsel 1600 Defense Pentagon Washington DC 20301-1600

MILLER, KAREN, clinical psychologist, neuropsychologist; b. Tucson, Dec. 9, 1969; d. Keith Lee and Marlene Jean Miller. BS in Psychology, U. Ariz., 1992; MA in Theology, MA in Psychology, Fuller Sem., Pasadena, Calif., 1996, PhD in Clin. Psychology, 1998. Psychologist UCLA, 1994—, dir. neuropsychology externship tng. MPAC, 2003—; therapist VA West Los Angeles, Calif., 1996—2000; clin. facilty mem., supr. Fuller Psychol. and Family Svcs., Pasadena, Calif., 2000—. Dir. externship tng. for neuropsychology. Contbr. articles to profl. jours. John P. Schaeffer and Regents scholar, 1988-92. Mem.: APA, Calif. Psychol. Assn., Internat. Neuropsychol. Soc., Mortar Bd., Phi Beta Kappa. Home: 923 W Walnut Ave Monrovia CA 91016

MILLER, KAREN L. dean, nursing educator; BSN, Case Western Res. U.; MSN, PhD in Nursing, U. Colo. V.p. The Children's Hosp., Denver; assoc. prof. Coll. Nursing U. Colo. Health Scis. Ctr.; dean, prof. Sch. Nursing U. Kans., 1996—, dean Sch. Allied Health, 1998—. Mem. editl. bd. IMAGE: Jour. Nursing Scholarship. Grantee NIH, 1992. Fellow Am. Acad. Nursing; mem. ANA, ANA Coun. Nurse Rschrs., Am. Orgn. Nurse Execs., Coun. on Grad. Edn. for Nursing Adminstrn., Midwest Alliance in Nursing, Midwest Nursing Rsch. Soc., Sigma Theta Tau (collateral reviewer rsch. com.). Office: U Kans Sch Nursing 390 Rainbow Blvd Kansas City KS 66160-0001

MILLER, KAREN MARIE, county commissioner; b. Gary, Ind., Aug. 20, 1952; d. Donald Dean and Geraldine Joan (Inderski) Childress; m. Ronald Russell Miller, July 30, 1972 (div. July 1980); 1 child, Russell Dean (dec. Dec. 1975). Grad. H.S., Memphis, Mo. Lic. real estate broker Mo. Real Estate Commn. Counter staff Hi-Ho Drive Inn, Kirksville, Mo., 1971-72; bookkeeper Feese Automotive, Kirksville, 1972-74; waitress Gaspers Restaurant, Kingdom City, Mo., 1974-76; office mgr. Wulff Bros. Masonry, Columbia, Mo., 1976-79; lounge mgr. Holiday Inn West, Columbia, 1979-82; restauranteur The Establishment, Columbia, 1982-93; commr. Boone County, Columbia, 1993—. Pres. Columbia/Mid-Mo. Restaurant Assn., 1984; state dir. Mo. Restaurant Assn., Kansas City, 1985-92. Columnist Boone County Jour., 1993—. Dir. Columbia (Mo.) Quarterback Club, 1985-89, Cedar Creek Therapeutic Riding Ctr., Columbia, 1992-93; mem. Boone County Muleskinners/Ctrl. Com., Columbia, 1992—, Nat. Dem. County Ofcl., Columbia, 1993—; mem. rsch. tech. coordinating com. Fed. Hwy. Adminstrn., 2000—. Named Restauranteur of Yr., Columbia/Mid-Mo. Chpt. Restaurant Assn., 1985, Democrat of the Month, Boone County Muleskinners, Columbia, 1991. Mem. Nat. Assn. Counties (nat. bd. dirs. 1995—, pres. 2003-2004), Nat. Assn. Counties, Mo. Commn. on Intergovtl. Coop. (pres.), Mo. Assn. Counties (state dir. 1995—), County Commrs. Assn., State and Local Sr. Adv. Com. Dept. Homeland Security, Rsch. and Tech. Coordinating Com. Dept. Transp. Roman Catholic. Avocations: reading, golfing, traveling. Home: 2700 Northridge Dr Columbia MO 65202-2140 Office: Boone County Commn 801 E Walnut St Rm 245 Columbia MO 65201-4890

MILLER, KATHLEEN MAE, intermediate school administrator; b. Flint, Mich., Sept. 1, 1966; d. Joseph Casper and Karen Sue Shovels; m. James Stuart Miller, Mar. 30, 1991; children: Susan Marie, Rebecca Mae. BS in Edn. with honors, U. Mich., 1988; M in Ednl. Leadership, Ea. Mich. U., Michigan, 2002; grad., Leadership Shiawassee, 2002—03. Cert. tchg. K-8 Mich., 1988, tchg. 7-12 Mich., 1996. Assessment & tech. specialist Shiawassee Regional Svc. Dist., Corunna, Mich., 1999—2000; coord. of curriculum & assessment Shiawassee Regional Ednl. Svc. Dist., Corunna, Mich., 2000—03, dir. instrnl. svs., 2003—. Instr., office mgr., supr., program developer Learning Ctr. SW Flint, Mich., 1988—91; tchr. adult edn., program coord. Beecher Cmty. Schs., 1991—92, tchr. 3-4, 1992—95; tchr. 7-8 Swartz Creek Cmty. Schs., Swartz Creek, 1995—97; core curriculum support position Swartz Creek Cmty. Sch. Dist., 1997—99. Mem. Genesee County Queen Genesee County, Mich., 1987; co-dir. children's programs Chapin United Meth. Ch., Henderson, 2002; mem. Leadership Shiawassee, Ann Arbor, 1999. Recipient James B. Angell scholar, U. Mich., Branstorm Prize, Branstorm Assn.; grantee Regent's Alumni scholar, U. of Mich.; scholar Genesee Adminstrv. Tng. Acad. Mem.: Mich. Inst. for Ednl. Mgmt., Capital Quality Initiative, Assn. Supervision Curriculum Devel., Mich. Staff Devel. Coun. (assoc.), Mich. Ednl. Rsch. Assn. (assoc.), Am. Ednl. Rsch. Assn. (assoc.), Kappa Delta Phi, Phi Kappa Phi. Avocations: horseback riding, swimming, gardening, travel, fishing. Home: 8670 N Baldwin Rd Henderson MI 48841 Office: Shiawassee RESD 1025 N Shiawassee St Henderson MI 48817 E-mail: millerk@sresd.k12.mi.us.

MILLER, KATHLEEN S. management and accounting professional; b. Pitts., Nov. 6, 1958; d. Herbert Ellsworth and Elizabeth Lorraine (McKean) Shaffer; m. Richard Joseph Miller, Sept. 27, 1986; 1 child, Melissa Ann. AAS, Cmty. Coll. Beaver County, 1996; BA, Robert Morris Coll., 1998. Asst. project engr. Power Piping Co., Pitts., 1977-94; project engr. McCarl's Inc., 1997—. Home: 146 Irwin Rd Georgetown PA 15043-9521 Office: 1413 9th Ave Beaver Falls PA 15010-4106 E-mail: kmiller@mccarl.com.

MILLER, LA BRENDA, investment analyst, writer; b. Gary, Ind., Dec. 31, 1957; d. Earl Miller and Essie Birdsong Hill; m. Petion Michael Nemorin, Feb. 14, 1987 (div. Mar. 1987); 1 child, Chris. BA, Howard U., 1979; JD, U. West L.A., 1995. Domestic violence cert. adv. Haven Hills Shelter, 1999. 60 Minutes archives asst. CBS Broadcast Ctr., N.Y.C., 1970; mdse. supr. Universal Studio Tour, Universal City, Calif., 1981—83; employment liaison specialist Mayor's Office for the Disabled, L.A., 1984—86; ind. sales contractor various orgns., L.A., 1988—98; nutrition team mem. Whole Foods Market, Woodland Hills, Calif., 1999—2001; in-house security L.A. Family Housing Shelter, North Hollywood, 2002—04; Home Mag. staff writer Womens Care Cottage Shelter, North Hollywood, Calif., 2002—04; sr. investment analyst 1031 Commercial Exchange, Long Beach, Calif. Resident adv. com. mem. Haven Hills Shelter, Canoga Park, Calif.; mentor for youth prison Calif. Youth Authority, Camarillo; adv. for women's prison Calif. Instn. for Women, Corona. Author poetry. Pro-bono legal work San Fernando Valley Legal Aide, Pacorma, Calif., 1994; pub. rels. co-chair Lawyers for Human Rights, L.A., 1995; domestic abuse response team Haven Hills Shelter/L.A. Police Dept., Van Nuys, Calif., 1999; Joel S. Goldsmith meditation tape group leader, 1998—. Recipient Wiley M. Manuel for Pro Bono Legal Svc., State Bar Calif., 1994—95, Battered Women's Svc. award, Convicted Women Against Abuse, Calif. State Prison, 2000, Courageous Achievers award, Billy Blanks Found., 2001. Mem.: Alpha Kappa Alpha. Democrat. Christian Scientist. Home: 7727 Lankershim Blvd #142 North Hollywood CA 91605

MILLER, LAURA, mayor, journalist; b. Balt., Nov. 18, 1958; m. Steven Wolens; children: Alex, Lily, Maxwell. Grad., U. Wis., Madison. Mem. Dallas City Coun., 1998—2002; mayor City of Dallas, 2002—. Columnist, investigative reporter Dallas Observer, metro columnist Dallas Times Herald, New York Daily News, The Dallas Morning News, The Miami Herald. Recipient H.L. Mencken Writing award, Balt. Sun, 1995, 6 Katie awards, Dallas Press Club, 2 Tex. Headliner awards, 2 Philbin awards, Dallas Bar Assn., cert. of merit, ABA. Office: Dallas City Hall 1500 Marilla St Rm 5EN Dallas TX 75201-6390

MILLER, LAURA JEAN, medical center director; b. Louisville, Nov. 11, 1946; d. Arthur and Marion (Adams) M.; m. Garrett Van Koughnett; children: Michael J. Uhlik, Caroline E. Uhlik. BA, U. Mo., Columbia, 1970; MPA, U. Mo., Kansas City, 1978. Presdl. mgmt. intern U.S. Dept. Vets. Affairs, Topeka, 1978-79, Kansas City, Mo., 1979-80, asst. to chief of staff, 1980-86, regional quality assurance mgr. Grand Prairie, Tex., 1986-89, assoc. dir. trainee Dallas, 1989-90, asst. med. ctr. dir., 1990-91, assoc. med. ctr. dir. Salem, Va., 1991-94, med. ctr. dir. Pitts., 1994—. Mem. exec. planning coun. U. Pitts., Western Psychiat. Inst. and Clinic, 1995—; mem.adv. bd. Vietnam Vets. Leadership Program Western Pa., Pitts., 1995—. Mem. Am. Coll. Healthcare Execs., Health Exec. Forum of Southwestern Pa., Interagy. Healthcare Inst. Alummni. Office: VA Med Ctr 7180 Highland Dr Pittsburgh PA 15206-1206

MILLER, LENORE WOLF DANIELS, speech-language pathologist; b. N.Y.C., Mar. 9, 1937; d. Samuel D. and Sarah (Reisman) Wolf; m. Marshall Nelson Daniels, Mar. 30, 1958 (div. Jan. 1965); m. Macey I. Miller, Dec. 11, 1977; 1 child, Suzanne Hayley. BA, CUNY, 1958, MA, 1961; ScD, Boston U., 1983. Sr. speech pathologist L.I. Coll. Hosp., N.Y.C., 1959-68; supr. speech-lang. pathology Tufts-New England Med. Ctr., Boston, 1968-87, dir. speech-lang. pathology, 1987-95, co-dir dept. speech-lang. pathology, 1987-95; pvt. and cons. practice speech-lang. pathology, Newton, Mass., 1995—. Asst. prof. depts. otolaryngology and rehab. medicine Tufts U. Sch. Medicine, 1992—96, asst. prof. dept. child psychiatry, 1995—96; adj. faculty Emerson Coll., 1993, Northeastern U., 1994, Boston U., 1993—, Mass. Gen. Hosp. Inst. Health Professions, 1998, 2002; specialist in areas of cranio-facial anomalies, voice disorders, dysfluency, lang. and motor-speech disorders, pediat., adult and geriatric; presenter in field. Contbr. articles to profl. jours. Mem. Am. Fedn. Musicians, 1965—80; del. Mass. Health Coun., Boston, 1974, 1975; mem. Tanglewood Festival Chorus, 1971—75, Newton Singers, 2001—04, Newton Choral Soc., 2004—; former actor Ivy Tower Playhouse, Spring Lake, NJ, Bklyn. Heights Repertory Co. Theatre, Bklyn. Nat. Office Edn. grantee, 1980. Mem.: Boston Area Voice Interest Group, Mass. Speech-Lang.-Hearing Assn. (pres. elect 1976—77, pres. 1977—78, sr. chair govtl. affairs 1988—91, honors 1979), Am. Cleft Palate-Craniofacial Assn. (pub. rels. com. 1973—74, by-laws com. 1977—78), Am. Assn. Pvt. Practice Speech Pathology and Audiology, Am. Speech-Lang.-Hearing Assn. (legis. coun. 1973—75, chair com. spl. rules 1974—75). Avocations: singing, drama, gourmet cooking, biking, tennis.

MILLER, LESLIE ANNE, lawyer; b. Franklin, Ind., Nov. 4, 1951; d. G. Thomas and Anne (Gaines) Miller; m. Richard B. Worley, Feb. 14, 1987. AB cum laude, Mt. Holyoke Coll., 1973; MA in Polit. Sci., Rutgers U., 1974; JD, Dickinson Sch. Law, Carlisle, Pa., 1977; LLM with honors, Temple U., 1994; LLD (hon.), Thomas Jefferson U. Coll. Health Profls., 2002; HHD (hon.), Wilson Coll., 2001. Bar: Pa. 1977, U.S. Dist. Ct. (ea. dist.) Pa. 1977, U.S. Ct. Appeals (3d cir.) 1980, U.S. Dist. Ct. (ea. dist.) Pa. 1987. Assoc. LaBrum & Doak, Phila., 1977-81, ptnr., 1982-86, Goldfein & Joseph, Phila., 1986-95, McKissock & Hoffman, P.C., Phila., 1995—2003; gen. counsel Gov. Pa., 2003—. Bd. dirs. WHYY-TV, 1996-2003; del. Third Circuit Jud. Conf., 1981, 82, 85; mem. Jud. Inquiry and Rev. Bd., 1990-94, chair, 1993-94; mem. faculty trial advocacy program Dickinson Sch. Law, 1992, 94; mem. hearing com., disciplinary bd. Supreme Ct. Pa., 1996—; mem. faculty Acad. Advocacy Temple U., 1994—; judge pro tem Ct. of Common Pleas; interm pres. Kimmel Ctr. for the Performing Arts, 2001-02. Mem. acad. ball com. Phila. Orch., 1986-87, 89-91, 95-96, mem. acad. music com. 1998—; mem. Open Space Task Force Com., Lower Merion Twp., Pa., 1990, bd. dirs., 1990-94, mem. counsel, 1990, Lower Merion Conservancy, 1995-97, 2000—, others; bd. dirs. Med. Coll. Pa., 1985-96, sec., 1987-92, chair presdl. search com., 1993, chair presdl. inauguration, 1987, chair com. on acad. affairs, 1989-95, chair dean's search com., 1994-95, chair nomenclature com., 1996; bd. dirs. Med. Coll. Hosps., 1991-96, Allegheny Health Edn. and Rsch. Found., 1993-96, Hahnemann U. Med. Sch., 1994-96, Pa. Ballet, 1994—, St. Christopher's Hosp. for Children, 1991-94, vice chair, 1990-94; bd. dirs. Phila. Free Libr., 1997—, bd. dirs. Kimmel Ctr. for the Performing Arts, 1999—, interim pres., 2001-02, vice chair bd. dirs., 2002—; hon. chair Pa. Breast Cancer Coalition, 2003; trustee Mt. Holyoke Coll., 2000—; bd. govs. Dickinson Sch. Law, Pa. State U., 2001—. Recipient Mary Lyon award Mt. Holyoke Alumni Assn., 1985, Alumnae Medal of Honor, 1988, Hon. Alumnae award, 1989, Pres.'s award Med. Coll. Pa., 1993, Sylvia Rambo award Dickinson Sch. of Law, 1997, Star award Forum of Exec. Women, 1998, Ann Alpern award PBA Women in the Profession, 1999, Sandra Day O'Connor award Phila. Bar Assn., 1999, Outstanding Leadership in Support of Legal Svcs. award Pa. Legal Svcs., 1999, Women Making History Nat. Assn. of Women Bus. Owners, 2002, Women of Distinction award, Phila. Bus. Jour., 2001, Internat. Women's Forum "Women Who Make a Difference" award, 2003, Pink Ribbon award Pa. Breast Cancer Coalition, 2003, Woman One award Drexel U. Inst. for Women's Health and Leadership, 2004; named to Pa. Honor Roll of Women, 1996; named Disting. Dau. of Pa., Gov. of Pa., 1999. Fellow Am. Bar Found., Pa. Bar Found.; mem. ABA, Phila. Bar Assn. (mem. exec. com. divsn. young lawyers 1982-85, mem. bicentennial com 1986-87, bd. govs. 1990-93, mem. gender bias task force 1993-97, chair com. on jud. selection and retention 1987-89, vice chair 1985-87, investigative divsn. 1982-85, chair Andrew Hamilton Ball 1989, trustee Phila. Bar Found. 1990-97, co-chair century three commn. 1995-97, others), Pa. Bar Assn. (found. ho. dels. life fellow, bd. govs. 1980-83, 84-87, 91-93, chair young lawyers divsn. 1982-83, mem. long range planning com. 1985-87, mem. com. on professionalism, 1987-91, vice chmn. jud. inquiry and rev. bd. study com. 1989-91, sec. 1984-87, chair ho. dels. 1991-93, chair commn. on women in the profession 1993-95, v.p. 1996-97, pres. 1998-99, immediate past pres. 1999—, apptd. mem. ct. jud. discipline 1999), Pa. Bar Inst. (mem. faculty, course planner), Phila. Assn. Def. Counsel (mem. exec. coun. 1987-90, 94, mem. joint trial demonstration with Phila. Trial Lawyers Assn. 1993), Def. Rsch. Inst. (spkr. toxic torts seminar 1983), Phila. Bar Edn. Advocacy Women Litigators (course planner, mem. faculty 1993), Women's Assn. Women's Alternatives (bd. dirs. 1983-94, vice chair 1985-94), Phila. Forum Exec. Women, Pa. Women's Forum, Com. of Seventy, Mt. Holyoke Alumnae Assn. (bd. dirs. 1986-89, 1999—). Democrat. Lutheran. Avocations: collecting American antiques, gardening, running. Office: Governors Office of Gen Counsel 225 Main Capitol Bldg Harrisburg PA 17120 E-mail: millesq@aol.com.

MILLER, LINDA JEAN, music educator, writer; b. Morton, Wash., May 13, 1948; d. Roderick Hugh Scurlock and Phyllis Catherine Bolton; m. Robert Henry Provencio, Aug. 13, 1970 (div. Mar. 1988); children: Kristofer Douglas Provencio, Heather Noelle Provencio; m. Robert Wayne Miller, June 12, 1993. BA N.Mex. State U., 1970, MusM U. Idaho, 1992, PhD U. Idaho, 1997. Dir. clin. svcs. Rocky Mountain Foot Clinic, Denver, 1983—85; dir. music New Hope Cmty. Ch., Aurora, Colo., 1985—88; vocal/gen. music tchr. Boise (Idaho) Schs., 1988—91; choral dir. Meridian (Idaho) Schs., 1991—93; vocal/gen. music tchr. Lewiston (Idaho) Schs., 1993—94; adj. faculty U. Idaho, Moscow, 1995—98; chair music edn. Valdosta (Ga.) State U., 1998—99; gen. music specialist Puyallup (Wash.) Schs., 1999—2003; faculty edn. divsn. St. Martin's Coll., Lacey, Wash., 2003—. Mem. CHIME, Am. Guild of English Handbell Ringers, Dayton, Ohio, 1995—2000, edn. chair Area X, 1995—96. Author (curriculum materials): Chime Magic, 2002; contbr. articles to profl. jours. including Overtones, Idaho Music Notes. Music chair for Carol Ryrie Brink 100th Ann. Celebration, Latah County Hist. Soc., Moscow, Idaho, 1995; founder, dir. Puyallup Youth Chime Choir. Mem.: Music Educators Nat. Conf., Am. Guild of English Handbell Ringers, Phi Kappa Lambda, Phi Delta Kappa. Avocations: quilting, flower gardening, reading historical fiction. Home: 11313 Cemetery Rd E Eatonville WA 98328 Office: OM466 Lacey WA 98503-0297

MILLER, LINDA B. political scientist; b. Manchester, N.H., Aug. 7, 1937; d. Louis and Helene (Chase) M. AB cum laude, Radcliffe Coll., 1959; MA, Columbia U., 1961, PhD, 1965. Asst. prof. Barnard Coll., 1964-67; rsch. assoc. Princeton U., 1966-67, Harvard U., 1967-71, 76-81, lectr. polit. sci., 1968-69; assoc. prof. Wellesley (Mass.) Coll., 1969-75, prof. polit. sci., 1975—2004, chmn. dept., 1985-89. Vis. prof. rsch. Watson Inst., Brown U., 1997, adj. prof. internat. rels., 1998—2000, 2003—, sr. fellow, 2000—03; vis. prof. polit. sci. Brown U., 1997. Author: World Order and Local Disorder: The United Nations and Internal Conflicts, 1967, Dynamics of World Politics: Studies in the Resolution of Conflicts, 1968, Cyprus: The Law and Politics of Civil Strife, 1968; co-author, co-editor: Ideas and Ideals: Essays on Politics in Honor of Stanley Hoffmann, 1993; editor Internat. Studies Rev., 1999-2002; contbr. articles to profl. jours. Internat. Affairs fellow Coun. Fng. Rels., 1973-74, Rockefeller Found. fellow, 1976-77, Oceanographic Instn. sr. fellow, 1979-80, 82-83, NATO social sci. rsch. fellow, 1982-83. Mem. Inst. Strategic Studies, Internat. Studies Assn., Coun. Fgn. Rels., Phi Beta Kappa. Home: PO Box 415 South Wellfleet MA 02663-0415 Office: Wellesley Coll Dept Polit Sci Wellesley MA 02482 also: Watson Inst Brown U PO Box 1970 Providence RI 02912-1970 E-mail: Linda_Miller@brown.edu.

MILLER, LINDA B. administrator; Pres. Vol. Trustees Found., Washington. Office: Vol Trustees Found 818 18th St NW Ste 900 Washington DC 20006-3513

MILLER, LINDA KAREN, retired secondary school educator, social studies educator, law educator; b. Kansas City, Jan. 22, 1948; d. Bennie Chris and Thelma Jane (Richey) M. B of Secondary Edn., U. Kans., 1970; M of Secondary Edn., U. Va., 1978, EdD, 1991. Tchr. social studies Pierson Jr. High Sch., Kansas City, 1970-72; substitute tchr. Fairfax (Va.) Pub. Schs., 1972-73; reading aide Lake Braddock Secondary Sch., Burke, Va., 1973-74; tchr. social studies Mark Twain Intermediate Sch., Alexandria, Va., 1974-75, Herndon (Va.) Intermediate Sch., 1975-78, Fairfax High Sch., 1978—86, 1987—2002; ret., 2002. Cons. in field; instr. Sch. Law Cmty. Coll. So. Nev., Las Vegas, 2003. Named Pre-Collegiate Tchr. of Yr., Orgn. Am. Historians, 1996, Secondary Tchr. of Yr., Nat. Coun. for Social Studies, 1996, U. Va., 1997, Outstanding Secondary Tchr., Va. Hist. Soc., 1998, Va. Geography Tchr. of Yr., 1999, Global Technet Tchr. of Yr., Nat. Peace Corps Assn., 1999, Nat. Peace Educator, 2002; recipient George Washington medal, Valley Forge Freedom Found., 1988, Excellence in Tchg. award, U. Kans. Sch. Edn., 1999, Celebrating Tchg. Excellence award, Am. Coun. Tchrs. Russian, 1998, World History Tchg. prize, World History Assn., 2002, Humanities Leadership award, Nat. Endowment Humanities, 2003; fellow, Korean Soc., 2000, Am. Revolution fellow, N.Y. Hist. Soc., 2001. Mem. Nat. Coun. Social Studies (curriculum com. 1991-94), Am. Legal History Soc., Orgn. Am. Historians, Nev. Coun. Social Studies, U. Va. Alumni Assn. Republican. Episcopalian. Avocation: doll collecting.

MILLER, LISA FRIEDMAN, psychology educator; b. Iowa City, Iowa, July 25, 1966; m. Philip Roger Miller. BA, Yale U., 1988; PhD, U. Pa., 1994. Asst. prof. Tchrs. Coll. Columbia U., N.Y.C., NY, 1998—, asst. prof. Coll. Physicians and Surgeons, 1998—. Contbr. articles to profl. jours., chapters to books. Grantee, William T. Grant Found., N.Y.C., 1999—, NIMH, N.Y.C., 1999—. Mem.: APA (exec. com. divsn. 36 2001—02, WT Grant Faculty Scholars Award 1999-2003). Avocations: running, theater, museums. Office: Tchrs Coll Columbia U 525 W 120th St New York NY 10027 Business E-Mail: drlfm@yahoo.com.

MILLER, LORETTA MARIE, dispatcher, writer; b. Seattle, Jan. 15, 1957; d. Louis Joseph and Doreen Marie M.. Diploma, E. Detroit High Sch., Eastpointe, Mich., 1975. Sec. Grace Hosp., Detroit, 1975—77; 9-1-1 dispatcher City of Warren (Mich.) Police, 1977—. Chairperson adv. bd. Clemis, Pontiac, Mich., 1999—2001; intern Cable Channel 51 City of Troy, Mich.; camera and editing maching operator; EMD, CTO instr. Warren Police. Author: Whispers of the Wind, 1999, poems; performer (voice over): CD Demo, 2001. EMT vol. Richmond-Lenox (MIch.) EMS, 1977—81; vol. Royal Oak (Mich.) React, 1977. Recipient Civilian Citation, City of Warren. Avocations: short story and script writing, cross country skiing, music, tv, theater.

MILLER, LORRAINE, business owner; BA in History, U. Utah. Lab. technician U. Utah Med. Ctr., 1972-75; pres. Cactus & Tropicals, Inc., Salt Lake City, 1975—. Mem. adv. bd. Utah Securities Commn., 1994; panelist Am. Arbitration Assn., 1991; pres., bd. dirs. Phoenix Inst., 1986-87. Vol. VISTA, 1966-69; mem. Gov.'s Task Force Entrepreneurism, 1988, Gov.'s Task Force Work Force Devel., 1994; mentor Women's Network Entrepreneurial Tng., Small Bus. Adminstrn., 1990; mem. adv. bd. Utah Dem. Health Care Task Force, 1991, Women's Bus. Devel. Office State of Utah, 1990-92; employer Supportive Employment for the Handicapped, 1990-92. Recipient Pathfinder award Salt Lake C. of C., 1986, Women of Achievement award YWCA, 1992; named Nat. Small Bus. Person of Yr. by U.S. Small Bus. Adminstrn., 1994. Mem. Nat. Assn. Women's Bus. Owners (pres. Salt Lake chpt. 1992), Utah Assn. Women's Bus. Owners (pres. 1992, 1st v.p. 1991, bd. dirs. 1985, 89-90, named Woman Bus. Owner of Yr. 1987), Wasatch Cactus & Succulent Soc. (co-founder). Office: Cactus & Tropicals 2735 S 2000 E Salt Lake City UT 84109-1749

MILLER, LYNNE MARIE, environmental company executive; b. N.Y.C., Aug. 4, 1951; d. David Jr. and Evelyn (Gulbransen) M. AB, Wellesley Coll., 1973; MS, Rutgers U., 1976. Analyst Franklin Inst., Phila., 1976-78; dir. hazardous waste div. Clement Assocs., Washington, 1978-81; pres. Risk

Sci. Internat., Washington, 1981-86; CEO, Environ. Strategies Consulting, LLC, Reston, Va., 1986—. Bd. dirs. Scana Corp., Adams Nat. Bank. Editor: Insurance Claims for Environmental Damages, 1989, editor-in-chief Environ. Claims Jour.; contbr. chpts. to books. Named Ins. Woman of Yr. Assn. Profl. Ins. Women, 1983. Mem. Am. Cons. Engrs. Coun., Wellesley Bus. Leadership Coun. Office: Environ Strategies Consulting LLC 11911 Freedom Dr Ste 900 Reston VA 20190-5631 E-mail: lmiller@escva.com.

MILLER, MARCIA E. federal government official; married; 1 son. BA, Miami U., Oxford, Ohio, 1977; MA, Johns Hopkins U., 1981. With internat. trade divsn. Am. Textile Mfrs. Inst.; internat. economist Wilmer, Cutler & Pickering, 1985-87; profl. staff mem. Senate Com. on Fin., 1987-93, chief internat. trade counsellor, 1993-95, minority chief internat. trade counsellor, 1995-96; chmn. U.S. Internat. Trade Commn., Washington, 1996-98, vice chmn., 1998—, commr., 2000—. Office: US Internat Trade Commn USITC Bldg 500 E St SW Washington DC 20436

MILLER, MARGARET ALISON, education educator; b. L.A., Dec. 17, 1944; d. Richard Crump and Virginia Margaret (Dudley) M.; m. Spencer Hall, Aug. 21, 1967 (div. 1977); 1 child, Justin Robinson; m. Alan Blair Howard, Oct. 7, 1990. BA in English summa cum laude, UCLA, 1966; postgrad., Stanford U., 1966-67; PhD in English, U. Va., 1971. Instr. English U. Va., Charlottesville, 1971-72; from asst. prof. to assoc. prof. U. Mass., Dartmouth, 1972-83, prof. English, 1983-86, co-dir. women's studies program, 1981-83, asst. to dean arts and scis., 1983-85, asst. to pres., 1985-86; acad. affairs coord. State Coun. Higher Edn. for Va., Richmond, 1986-87, assoc. dir. for acad. affairs, 1987-97; pres. Am. Assn. for Higher Edn., Washington, 1997-2000; pres. emerita Am. Assn. Higher Edn., Washington, 2000—; prof. higher edn. policy U. Va., Charlottesville, 2001—. Head English sect. transitional summer program Brown U., 1976; instr. honors program Va. Commonwealth U., 1991-93; cons. Coun. Rectors, Budapest, 1993, Minn. State U. System, Mpls., 1992, U.S. Dept. Edn., Washington, 1990—, S.C. Higher Edn. Commn., 1989-90, Edn. Commn. States, Denver, 1994-2000; presenter in field; participant UNESCO World Conf. on Higher Edn., 1998; adv. commr. Edn. Commn. of the States, 1998-2000; chair steering com. Washington Higher Edn. Secretariat, 1997-2000; mem. Nat. Postsecondary Edn. Cooperative, 1997-2000; cons. Nat. Ctr. for Pub. Policy and Higher Edn., 1998—; bd. dirs. Nat. Ctr. for Edn. Mgmt. Sys., 2001—, Edn. Direct, participant Aspen Inst., 1998; exec. editor Change mag., 2000—; judge Tchrs. Ins. Annuity Assn./Coll. Retirement Equity Fund Hesburgh awards, 1999—. Contbr. articles to profl. jours. Mem. Am. Assn. Higher Edn. (leadership coun.), Am. Coun. on Edn. (exec. com. identification program in Va. 1988-97, participant nat. identification program's 41st nat. forum for women leaders in higher edn. 1989, adv. bd. Policy Inst.), Phi Beta Kappa. Avocations: reading, gardening, travel. Home: 2176 Lindsay Rd Gordonsville VA 22942-1620 Office: Curry Sch Edn U Va 405 Emmett St S Charlottesville VA 22903 E-mail: pmiller@virginia.edu.

MILLER, MARGERY, psychologist, speech pathologist, medical educator and administrator; b. May 7, 1951; m. Donald F. Moores; children: Kip Lee, Tige Justice. BA, Elmira Coll., 1971; MA, NYU, 1972; EdS, MS, SUNY-Albany, 1975; MA, Towson State U., 1987; PhD, Georgetown U., 1991. Lic. speech pathologist Md., lic. psychologist Md., cert. tchr. nursery-6th grades, spl. edn. N.Y., nationally cert. sch. psychologist. Speech and lang. pathologist Mental Retardation Inst. Flower and Fifth Ave. Hosp., N.Y.C., 1971—72; cmty. speech/lang. pathologist, dir. speech and hearing svc. N.Y. State Dept. Mental Hygiene, Troy, 1972—74; instr. comm. disorders dept. Coll. St. Rose, Albany, NY, 1975—77; clin. supr. U. Md., College Park, 1978; speech/lang. pathologist Md. Sch. for Deaf, Frederick, 1978—84; auditory devel. specialist Montgomery County Pub. Schs., Rockville, Md., 1984—87; coord. Family Life program Nat. Acad. Gallaudet U., Washington, 1987—88, interim dir., 1988—89; dir. Counseling & Devel. Ctr. N.W. Campus, Washington, 1989—93; prof. psychology, coord. psychology internship program Gallaudet U., Washington, 1993—; lic. practicing psychologist Bethesda, Md., 1998—. Instr. sign lang. program Frederick C.C.; dance instr. for deaf adolescents; diagnostic cons. on speech pathology. Author: It's O.K. To Be Angry, 1976; contbr. chpt. to Cognition, Education, and Deafness: Directions for Research and Instruction, 1985; mem. editl. rev. com. Gov.'s Devel. Disabilities Coun. Md., 1984; presenter at confs.; contbr. articles to profl. jours. Vol., choreographer Miss Deaf Am. Pageant, 1984. Office of Edn. Children's Bur. fellow, 1971. Mem.: Am. Assn. of Higher Edn., Am. Psychol. Assn., Nat. Assn. Sch. Psychologists, Nat. Assn. of Deaf, Am. Speech, Lang. and Hearing Assn. (cert. clin. competence in speech/lang. pathology). Office: Gallaudet U 800 Florida Ave NE Washington DC 20002-3660 E-mail: margery.miller@gallaudet.edu.

MILLER, MARIAN, professional society administrator; Grad., Ind. U. 3rd v.p., sec. Nat. Fedn. Rep. Women, Alexandria, Va., 1st v.p., mem. exec. com., also bd. dirs., pres. Chair program by-laws, sr. Am. and leadership coms., regent Nat. Fedn. Rep. Women. Advisor to Suellen Reed State Supt. Com., to Steve Goldsmith for Gov. Campaign; statewide vol. coord. for v.p. Dan Quayle's 1st U.S. Senate campaign, U.S. Senator Dan Coats, Gov. Otis Bowen, John Murtz for Gov. Campaigns; del. Rep. Nat. Convs., 1988, 92, 96; precinct committeewoman Tippecanoe County; pres. Tippecanoe County RWC; active Ind. Com. Humanities, Gov.'s Adv. Com. on Pub. Welfare, Pension Mgmt. Legis. Study Commn.; active gov. rels. com. Ind. Hosp. Assn.; bd. dirs. United Way Ind.; del. to White House Conf. on Aging; chmn. Ind. Commn. on Aging; del. to Nat. Forum on Excellence in Edn.; founder Hoosier Assocs., 1975—. Recipient Pres.'s award Ind. U. Alumni Assn., Sagamore of the Wabash award Gov. Ind. Office: Nat Fedn Rep Women 124 N Alfred St Alexandria VA 22314-3011 Fax: 703-548-9836.

MILLER, MARIE GELSINGER, music educator; b. Robesonia, PA, Mar. 3, 1959; d. Paul Norman Gelsinger and Edna June Merrell; m. Kelly Ray Miller, June 20, 1981; 1 child, Kathryn Ane. B Music Therapy, BMusEdn, Shenandoah U., 1981; MMus, Westminster Choir Coll., 1985; Kodaly cert., Westmininster Choir Coll., 1996; Orff Schulwerk cert., George Mason U., 2002. Cert. tchr. Pa. Piano tchr., Bethlehem, Pa., 1981—; music tchr. Centennial Sch., Bethlehem, 1985—88; dir. of music Olivet Presbyn. Ch., Easton, Pa., 1984—88; children's choir dir. First Presbyn. Ch., Bethlehem, 1981—84, 1988—; dir. of choruses Cmty. Music Sch., Allentown, Pa., 1985—2003; music tchr. Easton Area Schs., Easton, 1994—. Republican. Home: 1919 Kenmore Ave Bethlehem PA 18018 Office: Easton Area Sch Dist 723 Coal St Easton PA 18042

MILLER, MARILEE HEBERT, arts administrator, producer, director, consultant; b. Laredo, Tex., Feb. 25, 1949; d. Minos Joseph and Eulalie (Fisher) Hebert; m. Stewart E. Slater, Dec. 3, 1972 (div. July 1978); m. Robert K. Miller, Jan. 2, 1999. BA, Baylor U., 1970, MA, 1972. Cert. secondary sch. tchr., Tex. Actress, dir., assoc. producer Everyman Players, Ky. and La., 1972-80; community rels. dir. Actors Theatre of Louisville, 1973-74, dir. children's theatre, lunchtime & cabaret theatre, 1974-76, dir., apprentice intern program, 1974-77, new play festivals coord., 1979-81, mgr. internat. touring, 1980-98, assoc. dir., 1981-98; sr. v.p. external affairs Ky. Ctr. for the Arts, 1998—. Guest dir. Louisville Children's Theatre, 1978; grants panelist Ky. Arts Coun., La. Arts Coun.; conf. lectr. Ky. Arts Coun., Va. Arts Commn., Southeastern Theatre Conf., S.W. Theatre Conf., So. Arts Fedn. Author: (play) Hey Diddle Diddle!, 1976. Pres. Ky. Citizens for Arts, 1985-86, 90-92; co-chmn. subcom. on arts Edn. Workforce, 1990-93; grad. Leadership Louisville, 1989, bd. dirs., 1992-98; vice-chmn. Focus Louisville, 1994-96; chmn. nonprofit recruitment com., chmn. Louisville Downtown Mgmt. Dist., 1996-97, Leadership Ptnrs., 1996; chmn. Farm Works Coun., 1997-99; mem. Downtown Devel. Implementation com., Louisville, 1991-93; Louisville Forum adv. coun., 1995-96; bd. dirs. Louisville Ctrl. Area, 1996-98; pres. Park IV Condo Assn., 1989-91, sec. Main St. Assn., 1992-96, v.p., 1997—; staging dir., cons. Walnut St. Bapt. Ch., 1980-99, chmn. strategic planning, 1998, co-chair Phase II Facilities 2000, 1997-2000. Bingham fellow, 1995-96; recipient Ky. Commonwealth award 1996, NACL Disting. Leadership award, 1997. Democrat. Baptist. Avocations: travel, hiking, music. Office: Ky Ctr for Arts 501 W Main St Louisville KY 40202-2989 E-mail: mmiller@kca.org.

MILLER, MARILYN LEA, library science educator; AA, Graceland Coll., 1950; BS in English, U. Kans., 1952; AMLS, U. Mich., 1959, PhD of Librarianship and Higher Edn., 1976. Bldg.-level sch. libr. Wellsville HS, Kans., 1952-54; tchr.-libr. Arthur Capper Jr. HS, Topeka, 1954-56; head libr. Topeka HS, Topeka, 1956-62; sch. libr. cons. State of Kans. Dept. of Pub. Instrn., 1962-67; from asst. to assoc. prof. Sch. Librarianship Western Mich. U., Kalamazoo, 1967-77; assoc. prof. libr. sci. U. NC, Chapel Hill, 1977-87, prof., chair dept. libr. and info. studies Greensboro, 1987-95, prof. emeritus, 1996—. Vis. faculty Kans. State Tchrs., Emporia, 1960, 63, 64, 66, U. Minn., Mpls., 1971, U. Manitoba, Winnipeg, Can., 1971; vis. prof. Appalachian State U., Boone, NC, 1987; adv. bd. sch. libr. media program Nat. Ctr. for Ednl. Stats., 1989, user rev. panel, 1990; chair assoc. dean search com. Sch. Edn., 1988, coord. Piedmont young writers conf., 1989-94, 97-99, chair race and gender com., 1990-93, SACS planning and evaluation com., 1990-91, learning resources ctr. adv. com., 1991-93; hearing panel for honor code U. NC Greensboro, 1988-91, assn. women faculty and administrv. staff, 1987-95, faculty coun., 1987-95, chair, 1994-95, univ. libr. com., 1987-88, com. faculty devel. in race and gender scholarship, 1990-92; lectr. and cons. in field. Editor: Pioneers and Leaders in Library Service to Youth, 2003; mem. editl. bd. The Emergency Librarian, 1981-97, Collection Building: Studies in the Development and Effective Use of Library Resources, 1978-96; contbr. chpt. to books, articles to profl. jour. Children's libr. specialists to visit Russian sch. and pub. libr., book publs., Moscow, Leningrad, Tashkent, 1979; hon. del. White House Conf. on Libr. and Info. Svcs., Washington, 1991; head del. Romanian Summer Inst. on Librarianship in U.S., 1991; citizen amb. People to People Internat. Program, People's Republic of China, 1992, Russian and Poland, 1992, Russia, 1994, Barcelona, 1995; exec. bd. dirs. Friends of Greensboro Pub. Libr., 1996-99, chair gift shop and coffee shop adv. com., 1996-2002; chair Citizens Materials Adv. com., 1999—, Citizens Strategic Long Range Planning com., 1994-95, 2001-02, chair, 2002—, Sch. Pub. Libr. com., 2002-. Recipient Freedom Found. medal, 1962, Disting. Svc. to Sch. Librs. award Kans. Assn. Sch. Librs., 1982, Disting. Svc. award Graceland Coll., 1992, Disting. Alumnus award Sch. Libr. and Info. Studies, U. Mich., 1988, Contribution to Libr. Info. Sci. award Assn. Libr. Info. Sci., 1999; Delta Kappa Gamma scholar, 1972. Mem.: ALA (awards com. 1971—72, chair Chgo. conf. resolutions 1972, chair 1973—75, resolutions com. 1976—78, adv. com. Nat. Ctr. Ednl. Stats. 1984, standing com. libr. edn. 1987—91, yearbook adv. com. 1988—90, chair 1989—90, pres. 1992—93, exec. dir. 1994, chair rsch. com., chair search com., Disting. Svc. award Am. Assn. Sch. Librs. 1993), Friends of N.C. Pub. Librs. (bd. dirs. 2000—), So. Assn. Colls. and Schs. (accreditation team 1988), Southeastern Libr. Assn. (chair libr. educators sect. 1990—92), N.C. Assn. Sch. Librs., Assn. Libr Svc. to Children (bd. dirs. 1976—81, pres. 1979—80, rsch. com. 1982—85, chair 1984—85), Assn. Ednl. Comms. and Tech., Am. Assn. Sch. Librs. (nominating com. 1980, pub. com. 1981—82, chair search com. exec. dir. 1985, v.p., pres.-elect 1985—86, pres. 1986—87, coord. coms. nat. stds. vision and implementation 1995—98), N.C. Libr. Assn. (life; edn. libr. com. 1978—80, 1982—86, bd. dirs. 1987—99, exec. bd. status women roundtable 1989—, chmn.-elect 1995—97, chmn. 1997—99, commn. on status of sch. librs. 1999—2000).

MILLER, MARY HELEN, retired public administrator; b. Smiths Grove, KY, June 30, 1936; d. Walter Frank and Lottie Belle (Russell) Huddleston; m. George Ward Wilson, Sept. 12, 1958 (div. Sept. 1973); children: Ward Glenn, Amy Elizabeth Huddleston; m. Francis Guion Miller Jr., June 6, 1981. BA, Western Ky. U., 1958. Tchr. Fayette County Schs., Lexington, Ky., 1958-60, Seneca High Sch., Louisville, 1960-63, Shelby County High Sch., Shelbyville, Ky., 1963-69; rsch. analyst Legis. Rsch. Com., Frankfort, Ky., 1973-79, asst. dir., 1979-83, 90-91; chief exec. asst. Office Gov., Frankfort, 1983-87, 93-95, legis. liaison, 1991-93; cabinet sec. Natural Resources and Environ. Protection Cabinet, Frankfort, 1987-88; sales assoc. W. Wagner, Jr. Comml. Real Estate, Louisville, 1989-91; ret., 1996. Author: (constl. revision) Citizens Guide To/Perspective, 1978, (booklet) A Look at Kentucky General Assembly, 1979, A Guide to Education Reform, 1990, (handbook) Gubernatorial Transition in Kentucky, 1991. Active Leadershi Ky. Alumni, Frankfort, 1986, Waterfront Devel. Corp. Bd., Louisville, 1986—87, Greater Louis Partnership Econ. Devel., 1988—92, Shelbyville 2000 Found. Bd., 1991—92; mem., sec. Regional Airport Authority Bd., Louisville, 1986—89; pres. Shelby County Cmty. Theatre Bd., Shelbyville, 1989—90; mem. Ky. Long Term Policy Bd., 1992—99, chair, 1995; mem. Ky. Hist. Properties Commn., 1995—99; chair Shelby County Cmty. Found., 1995—2000; exec. com. Ky. Hist. Soc., 2002—; mem. Shelby Devel. Found., 2003—. Recipient Vic Hellard Jr. Pub. Svc. in Ky. award, 1999; named Shelbyville Citizen of Yr., 1998. Mem. Caryatid Book Club (pres. 1999), Women's Initiative Networking Groups (pres. 1998), Western Ky. U. Alumni Assn. (bd. dirs. 1992-95). Democrat. Episcopalian. Avocations: reading, theatre, gardening, antiques. Home: 1116 Main St Shelbyville KY 40065-1420

MILLER, MARY HOTCHKISS, lay worker; b. Washington, Dec. 4, 1936; d. Neil and Esther LeMoyne (Helfer) H.; m. Ronald Homer Miller, May 20, 1961; 1 child, Timothy Ronald. BA, Western Md. Coll., 1958; MRE, Union Theol. Sem, 1960; Cert., Windham House, N.Y.C., 1960. Dir. Christian Edn. Bruton Parish ch., Williamsburg, Va., 1960-61; dir. Christian Edn. (part-time) All Saints Episcopal Ch., Bklyn., 1961-62; adminstrv. and program asst., Christian Social Rels. Dept., Exec. Coun. Episcopal Ch. U.S.A. Episcopal Ch. Ctr., N.Y.C., 1967-72; nat. treas., mem. bd., chmn. Episcopal Peace Fellowship, Washington, N.Y.C. and Chgo., 1972-88, exec. sec. Washington, 1989-2001; mem. Standing Commn. on Anglican and Internat. Peace with Justice, Epis. Ch., 2001—; ret., 2001. Bd. dirs., exec. com. Nat. Campaign for Peace Tax Fund, Washington, 1989—91; bd. dirs. Ctr. on Conscience and War/Nat. Interreligious Svc. Bd. for Conscientious Objectors, Washington, 1989—96, Washington, 2001—; coord. The Consultation. Contbr. articles to Witness mag. and jours., newsletters in field; editl. bd. ISSUES of Gen. Convs. of Episcopal Ch., 1973-91; designer ch. vestments and banners. Democrat. Episcopalian. E-mail: mary.miller@ecunet.org.

MILLER, MARY JEANNETTE, office management specialist; b. Washinton, Sept. 24, 1912; d. John William and David Evengline (Hill) Sims; children: Sylvenia Delores Doby, Ferdi A., Cecil Jr.(dec.). Student, Howard U., 1929—30, U. Ill., 1940—42; student Dept. Agrl., U. Md.Grad. Sch., 1975; Cert. in Vocat. Photography, Prince George C.C., 1986. Chief mail processing unit Bur. Reclamation, Washington, 1940—57; records supr. AID, 1957—71; office engr. Bechtel Assocs., Washington, 1976—79; records mgmt. cons. AID, 1980—84; docent Mus. African Art Smithsonian Instn., Washington, 1986—89; circulation asst. Prince George County Libr. System, Hyattsville, Md., 1987—91; ret. Real estate assoc., tchr. English as Second lang. Ministry Edn., Seoul, Korea, Saint Helena, 1960—61; cons. Ministry Fin., Laos, 1968—70, Ministry Fin. Royal Lao Govt., 1971—74, AID Missions, Yemen, Sudan, Somalia, 1982; mem. Friends of Internat. Edn. Com., 1985—92; sec., treas., bd. dirs. Miller Transitional, Inc. Author Handbooks on Office Mgmt.; contbr. articles to travel books. Mem.: AARP, NAFE, Montgomery County Bd. Realtors, Am. Mgmt. Assn., Soc. Am. Archivists, Nat. Trust Hist. Preservation, Am. Fgn. Svc. Assn., Zeta Phi Beta. Roman Catholic. Home: 5601 Seminary Rd #602-N Falls Church VA 22041-3504

MILLER, MARY RITA, former college educator; b. Williamsburg, Iowa, Mar. 4, 1920; d. James Carl and Bernadette (O'Meara) Rush; m. Clarence Glenn Miller, June 2, 1947 (dec. Aug. 1987); 1 child, Ronald Rush; m. William J. Gibbons, July 14, 1992 (dec. June 2001). BA, U. Iowa, 1941; MA, Denver U., 1959; PhD, Georgetown U., 1969. From instr. to asst. prof. Regis Coll., Denver, 1962-65; from asst. prof. to prof. U. Md., College Park, 1968-91, prof. emeritus, 1991—. Author: Children of the Salt River, 1977, Place—Names of the Northern Neck of Virginia, 1983; contbr. numerous articles and revs. Avocations: research, travel, reading, farming. Home: 2825 29th Pl NW Washington DC 20008-3501

MILLER, MARY-EMILY, history educator; b. Wilmington, Del., Mar. 7, 1934; B.A. in History with distinction, U. Del., 1955; cert. Harvard-Radcliffe Program Bus. Adminstrn., 1956; M.A., Boston U., 1959, Ph.D., 1962. Sec. research com. Lemuel Shattuck Hosp., Harvard U., 1956-58; mem. staff registrar's office Radcliffe Coll., 1958-59; resident asst. Boston U., 1959-61; asst. prof. history, dean women Methodist Coll., Fayetteville, N.C., 1962-64, chmn. history dept. and social sci. area, 1963-64; asst. prof., dean women Park Coll., Parkville, Mo., 1964-66, acting chmn. dept., 1965; prof. history Salem (Mass.) State Coll., 1966-92, chmn. dept., liaison to Salem Partnership re Russia, 1989-92; part-time prof. history U. Del., 1992. Recipient Family Bus. Longevity award DESmall Bus. Bur., 2003. Contbr. numerous articles to profl. jours. Mem. Tercentennery Commn., Cumberland County, N.C., 1963, Kent County (Del.) Tricentennial Commn. and Exec. Bd., 1983; active Bicentennial and Bicentennial of Constn. activities in Mass. and Del.; mem. Fayetteville Symphony Orch., 1962-64, St. Joseph Symphony Orch., 1964-66, Hollis (N.H.) Town Band, 1970-83, Middlesex Wind Ensemble, 1978-81, U. Del. Alumni Band, Boston U. Alumni Band, 1978—; Mem. AAUP (chpt. pres. 1979-92), Am. Hist. Assn., Orgn. Am. Historians, Assn. Counseling and Devel., Am. Coll. Pers. Assn., New Eng. Hist. Assn., Soc. History Discoveries, N.Am. Oceanic History Assn., Peabody-Essex Mus., Blue Hen Power Squad. (treas. 1996—), Renaissance Assn., English-Speaking Union, Harvard Bus. Sch. Alumni Assn., Lewes Yacht Club, Phi Alpha Theta, Delta Tau Kappa, others. Home and Office: Box 287 113 S Market St Frederica DE 19946-0287

MILLER, MONICA JEANNE, educational association administrator; b. Laramie, Wyo., Mar. 18, 1948; d. R. Walt and Margaret Louise (Carroll) M.; m. Stephen Lee Spellman, June 3, 1973 (div. Aug. 1980); 1 child, Andrew M. French. BS cum laude in Journalism, U. Wyo., 1971. cert. food safety Nat. Restaurant Assn. Press officer Min. of Agr., Botswana, 1971-73; cmty. rels. officer Colo. Civil Rights Commn., Denver, 1973-80; chief info. officer Colo. Dept. Personnel, Denver, 1980-83, Colo. Divsn. Parks and Recreation, Denver, 1986-88; pub. rels. mgr. Unicover Corp., Cheyenne, Wyo., 1989-91, Taco John's Internat., Inc., Cheyenne, Wyo., 1991—; exec. dir. Wyo. Lodgine and Restaurant Assn. Edn. Found. Cons. The Promethean Corp., Denver, 1983-85. Author: (with others) Sexual Harassment in Public Employment, 1983. Dir. Children's Heritage Montessori Sch., Cheyenne, 1993-95, Wyo. Higher Edn. Assistance Authority, 1996—. Mem. Soc. Profl. Journalists, Pub. Rels. Soc. Am., Greater Cheyenne C. of C. (vice chair 1995—), Rotary (dir. 1996—). Democrat. Avocations: reading, vegetarian cooking, eastern philosophies and religions. Home and Office: 6840 Bomar Dr Cheyenne WY 82009-2632

MILLER, NANCY ANN, music educator; b. Bunham, Tex, Jan. 29, 1953; d. Charles H. Thompson and Stella L. Shimp; m. Robert Dale Miller, May 20, 1972; children: Jeff, Chad, Ingris, Micky. MusB, U. Tex., Arlington, 1979. Tchr. music Hurst Enles Bedford Ind. Sch. Dist., Tex., 1979—81; dir. choir Longview Ind. Sch. Dist., 1981—83; tchr. music Kilgore Ind. Sch. Dist., 1983—96, Lubboch Ind. Sch. Dist., 1996—99, Kenett Sch., Mo., 1999—2000, Jonesboro Pub. Schs., Ark., 2000—. Blood donor Red Cross, Jonesboro, Ark., 1997—2003; disaster relief team Cornerstone U.M.C., 2003. Mem.: Phila. Patriots, Ark. Choral Dirs., Music Educator's Nat. Coun. Methodist. Avocations: golf, reading, travel.

MILLER, NANCY ELLEN, computer consultant; b. Detroit, Aug. 30, 1956; d. George Jacob and Charlotte M. Miller. BS in Computer and Comm. Scis. with honors, U. Mich., 1978; MS in Computer Scis., U. Wis., 1981. Product engr. Ford Motor Co., Dearborn, Mich., 1977; computer programmer Unique Bus. Sys., Inc., Southfield, Mich., 1978; tchg. asst. computer scis. dept. U. Wis., Madison, 1978—82; computer scientist Lister Hill Nat. Ctr. Biomed. Commns., Nat. Libr. Medicine NIH, Bethesda, Md., 1984—88; pvt. practice West Bloomfield, Mich., 1993—. Active Nat. Abortion and Reproductive Rights Action League Pro-Choice Am., Washington, 1984—, Nat. Women's Polit. Caucus, Washington, 1984—, Planned Parenthood Fedn. Am., NY, 1986—, Jewish Fedn. Met. Detroit, Bloomfield Hills, 1991—, Dem. Nat. Com., Washington, 1984—, Hadassah: The Women's Zionist Org. of Am., Inc., N.Y., 1992—. Recipient Jour. of Am. Soc. for Info. Sci. Best Paper award, 1988. Mem. Assn. for Computing Machinery (sec. S.E. Mich. spl. interest group on artificial intelligence 1993-94), Am. Assn. for Artificial Intelligence, Assn. for Logic Programming, U. Wis. Alumni Assn. (life), U. Mich. Alumni Assn. (life), Am. Contract Bridge League. Home and Office: 6220 Village Park Dr Apt 104 West Bloomfield MI 48322-2146

MILLER, NANCY K. literature educator; PhD, Columbia U. Disting prof of Eng and comparative lit at Grad Ctr City U. N.Y., N.Y.C. Contbr. articles to profl. jours.; author: (books) Bequest and Betrayal: Memoirs of a Parent's Death, and, But Enough about Me: Why We Read Other People's Lives. Office: CUNY Grad Ctr PhD Program in Eng 365 5th Ave New York NY 10016-4309 E-mail: nmiller@gc.cuny.edu.

MILLER, NANCY SUZANNE, technology consultant, artist; b. Springfield, Mass., Nov. 8, 1946; d. Harry J. and Helen G. (Golden) Corwin; m. Daniel B. Morgan, May 26, 1983; children: Jillian Morgan, Bradley Morgan. BA, Columbia U., 1969; postgrad., NYU, 1972-74; MFA, CCNY, 1998. Tech. cons. J.P. Morgan, N.Y.C., 1986—; tchr. N.Y.C. Bd. Edn., 1996—. One-person shows include Ingrid Cusson Gallery, N.Y.C., 1989, Pines Gallery, 1990, Z Gallery, N.Y.C., 1991, New World Gallery, Boston, 1992, R.M. Bradley & Co., Boston, 1994, Mulberry Gallery, N.Y.C., 1995, Aquasource Gallery, N.Y.C., 1995; exhibited in group shows at Daniel Gallery, Ft. Lauderdale, Fla., 1988, Soha Open Studio Show, N.Y.C., 1988, Whitehall Gallery, Palm Springs, Calif., 1989, Peabody Gallery, Boston, 1989, AIR Gallery, N.Y.C., 1989, Tallahassee Gallery, 1990, Valerie Miller Gallery, Palm Springs, 1990, 91, Gallery Gaudi, Watermill, N.Y., 1991, Z Gallery, N.Y.C., 1992, C.W. Post Coll., 1993, Soha Art Gallery, 1993, New England Fine Arts Inst., Boston, 1993, Benton Gallery, Southampton, N.Y., 1993, Zimerlee Mus., Rutgers U., N.J., 1993, Viva Galeria, N.Y.C., 1994, Ann Harper Gallery, East Hampton, 1995, Bob Blackburn and CCNY Printmakers, NYC, 1996, Arthur Danzinger Gallery, Soho, 1996, AIR Galley, 25th Invitational Show, NYC, 1997, 27 West Gallery CCNY Alumni Show, 1998, Venezuelan Ctr., N.Y.C., 2003, Cork Gallery, N.Y.C., 2003, Queen's Coun. on Arts, 2003; represented in permanent collections Bankers Trust Co., N.Y., Morgan Stanley, Bryan Cave McPheeters & McRoberts, N.Y., Cellular One, Boston, Citibank, N.Y., Daiwa Am. Securities, N.Y., Equitable, N.Y., Gen. Instruments, N.Y., John Hancock, Boston, IBM, N.Y., Irving Trust, N.Y., others. Vol. fund raiser Pub. Sch. 87, 1990-92, vol. art tchr., 1995-96; dir. spring soccer Am. Youth Soccer Orgn., 1995; PTA treas., 2001-03. Mem.: Barnard Bus. and Profl. Women. Jewish. Avocations: scuba diving, skiing, soccer team parent, computer graphics. Home: 527 W 110th St New York NY 10025-2081

MILLER, NICOLE JACQUELINE, fashion designer; b. Ft. Worth, Tex., Mar. 20, 1951; d. Grier Bovey and Jacqueline (Mahieu) M. BFA, RISD, 1973; cert. de coursspeciale, École de la Chambre Syndicale de la Couture Parisienne, Paris, 1971. Opened boutique Gamine, Stockbridge, Mass., 1973—74; asst. designer Clovis Ruffin, N.Y.C., 1974; designer Raincheetahs, N.Y.C., 1974-75, P.J. Walsh, N.Y.C., 1975-82, Nicole Miller, N.Y.C., 1982—. Mem. Sports Commn. of N.Y., Commn. of Status of Women; bd. trustees R.I. Sch. of Design. Bd. dirs. Smith's Food and Drug. Recipient Dallas Fashion award, 1991, Earnie award for children's wear, Michael award for fashion. Mem. Fashion Group, Fashion Roundtable, Coun. of Fashion Designers of Am., N.Y. Athletic Club. Avocations: skiing, ice skating, waterskiing, wind surfing. Office: 525 7th Ave Fl 20 New York NY 10018-4901*

MILLER, PAMELA GUNDERSEN, mayor; b. Cambridge, Mass., Sept. 7, 1938; d. Sven M. and Harriet Adams Gundersen; m. Ralph E. Miller, July 7, 1962; children: Alexander, Erik, Karen. AB magna cum laude, Smith Coll., 1960. Feature writer Congl. Quar., Washington, 1962-65; dir. cable TV franchising Storer Broadcasting Co., Louisville, Lexington, Ky., 1978-80, 81-82; mem. 4th dist. Lexington Fayette County Urban Coun., 1973-77; councilwoman-at-large, 1982-93; vice mayor, 1984-86, 89-93; mayor, 1993—2003. Dep. commr. Ky. Dept. Local Govt., Frankfort, 1980-81; pres. Pam Miller, Inc., 1984-94, Cmty. Ventures Corp., 1985-95. Mem. Fayette County Bd. Health, 1975—77, Downtown Devel. Commn., 1975—77; bd. dirs. YMCA, Lexington, 1975—77, 1985—90, Fund for the Arts, 1984—93, Coun. of Arts, 1978—80, Sister Cities, 1978—80; vice chmn. Prichard Com. for Acad. Excellence, 1983—; alt. del. Dem. Nat. Com., 1976; chair Fund for Arts Campaign, 2003—04. Named woman of achievement YWCA, 1984, outstanding Woman of Blue Grass AAUW, 1984. Mem. LWV (dir. 1970-73), Profl. Women's Forum. Home: 140 Cherokee Park Lexington KY 40503-1304

MILLER, PATRICIA A. training services executive; b. Pa., Jan. 7, 1949; BA, Radford Coll., 1970; JD, George Mason U., 1992; cert., Harvard U., 1994. Proprietor Patricia A. Miller Real Estate Cons., 1975—; sr. v.p. The Gussie Group, 1988—89; pvt. practice law, 1992—; proprietor Patricia A. Miller ADR Cons., 1994—; pres. Nat. Inst. for Conflict Resolution, Inc., 1994—; dispute resolution faculty in field. Nat. Ams. with Disabilities Act panelist Dept. Justice, 1996—2000; commr. Md. Alt. Dispute Resolution Commn., 1998—2000; internat. panelist World Bank Mediation Program, 2000—; cons. and spkr. in field. Founder, chmn. bd. dirs., dir. Anne Arundel County Ct., Apptd. Spl. Advs., Inc., 1994—; dir., officer Hospice of the Chesapeake Found., Inc., 1999—; active Md. Promise Steering Com., 1998. Named to Md.'s Top 100 Women, The Daily Record, 2000; recipient commendation, Chief Judge Robert Bell, 1998—2000. Mem.: Md. State Bar Assn. (mem. leadership coun. ADR sect. 2000—). Office: Nat Inst for Conflict Resolution Inc 170 West St Annapolis MD 21401

MILLER, PATRICIA K. former state legislator; b. Lake Forest, Ill., Aug. 13, 1945; m. Robert C. Miller. Student, Oakton C.C. State legislator Miss. Ho. of Reps., Jackson, 1993-99. Vice chmn. apportionment and elections coms. Miss. Ho. of Reps., mem. local and pvt., municipalities, penitentiary, and pub. health coms. Former DeSoto County Planning Commr.; active Dem. Women's Club. Mem. BPW, NOWL. Roman Catholic. Home: 6608 Lake Forest Dr Walls MS 38680 Office: State Capitol Bldg Rm 400-E PO Box 1018 Jackson MS 39215-1018

MILLER, PATRICIA LOUISE, state legislator, nurse; b. Bellefontaine, Ohio, July 4, 1936; d. Richard William and Rachel Orpha (Williams) M.; m. Kenniteh Orlan Miller, July 3, 1960; children: Tamara Sue, Matthew Ivan. RN, Meth. Hosp. Sch. Nursing, Indpls., 1957; BS, Ind. U., 1960. Staff nurse Cmty. Hosp., Indpls., 1958, Meth. Hosp., Indpls., 1959; office nurse A.D. Dennison, MD, 1960-61; rep. State of Ind. Dist. 50, Indpls., 1982-83; senator State of Ind. Dist. 32, Indpls., 1983—; health welfare and aging com., 1983-90; mem. labor and pension com., 1983-94; mem. edn. com., 1984-90; legis. appt. and elections com., chmn. interim study com. pub. health and mental health Ind. Gen. Assembly, 1986; chair Senate Enfiron. Affairs, 1990-92; health and environ affairs, 1992—; mem. election com., 1992—; mem. budget subcom. Senate Fin. Com., 1995—. Mem. Bd. Edn. Met. Sch. Dist., Warren Twop., 1974-82, pres., 1979-80, 80-81; mem. Warren Twp. Citizens Screening Com. for Sch. Bd. Candidates, 1972-74, 84, Met. Zoning Bd. Appeals, Divsn. I, apptd. mem. City-County Coun. on Aging, Indpls. 1977-80; mem. State Bd. Vocat. and Tech. Edn., 1978-82, sec., 1980-82; mem. gov.'s Select Adv. Commn. for Primary and Secondary Edn., 1983; precinct committeeman Rep. Party, 1968-74, ward vice-chmn., 1975-78, ward chmn., 1978-85, twp. chmn., 1985-87; vice chmn. Marion County Rep., 1986—; del. Rep. State Copnv., 1968, 74, 76, 80, 84, 86, 88, 90, 92, 94, sgt. at arms, 1982, mem. platform com., 1984, 88, 90, 92, co-chmn. Ind. Rep. Platform Com., 1992; del. Rep. Nat. Conv., 1984, alternate del., 1988, Rep. Presdl. Elector Alternate, 1992; active various polit. campaigns; bd. dirs. PTA, 1967-81; pres. Grassy Creek PTA, 1971-72; state del. Ind. PTA, 1978; mem. child car adv. com. Walker Career Ctr., 1976-80, others; bd. dirs. Ch. Fedn. Greater Indpls., 1979-82, Christian Justice Ctr., Inc., 1983-85, Gideon Internat. Aux., 1977Y; mem. United Meth. Bd. Missions Aux. Indpls., 1974-80, v.p., 1974-76, mem. nominating com., 1977; bd. dirs. Lucille Raines Residence, Inc., 1977-80; exec. com. S. Ind. Conf. United Meth. Women, 1977-80, lay del. s. Ind. Conf. United Meth. Ch., 1977—, fin. and adminstrn. com., 1979-88, planning and rsch. com., 1980-88, co-chmn. law adv. com., chmn. health and welfare, conf. coun. ministries, also mem. task force, bd. ordained ministry, also panel, chmn. com. on dist. superintendency, dist. coun. on ministries; sec. Indpls. S.E. Dist. Council on Minstries, 1977-78, pres. 1982; chmn. council on ministries Cumberland United Meth. Ch., 1969-76; chmn. stewardship com. Old Bethal United Meth. Ch., 1982-85, fin. com., 1982-85, adminstrv. bd., mem. council on ministries, 1981-85; co-chair Evangelism Com., 1994—; jurisdictional del. United Meth. Ch., 1988, 92; alternate del. United Methodist Ch. Gen. Conf., 1988, del. 1992; mem. adv. com. Warren Fine Arts Found., 1991—; mem. adv. bd. St. Francis Hosp., 1992—; mem. health and human svcs. com. Midwest Legis. Conf., 1995. Recipient Lambda Theta Honor for Outstanding contbr. in fiedl of end., 1976; named Woman of Yr. Cumberland Bus. and Profl. Women, 1979; Ind. Vocat. Assn. citation award, 1984, others. Mem. Indpls. dist. Dental Soc. Women's Aux., Ind. Dental Assn. Women's Aux., Am. Dental Assn. Women's Aux., Coun. State Govt. (intergovtl. affairs com.), Nat. Conf. State Legis. (vice chmn. health com. 1994—), Warren Twp. Rep., Franklin Rep., Lawrence Rep., Center Twp. Rep., Fall Creek Valley Rep, Marion County Coun. Rep. Women (3rd v.p. 1986-89), Ind. Women's Rep. (legis. chair 1988-89), Nat. Fedn. rep. Women, Beech Grove Rep., Perry Twp. Rep., Indpls. Women's Rep. Club (3rd v.p. 1989—), Indpls. Press Club.

MILLER, PEGGY GORDON ELLIOTT, university president; b. Matewan, W.Va., May 27, 1937; d. Herbert Hunt and Mary Ann (Renfro) Gordon; m. Robert Lawrence Miller, Nov. 23, 2001; children from previous marriage: Scott Vandling Elliott III, Anne Gordon Elliott. BA, Transylvania Coll., 1959; MA, Northwestern U., 1964; EdD, Ind. U., 1975. Tchr. Horace Mann H.S., Gary, Ind., 1959-64; instr. English Am. Inst. Banking, Gary, 1969-70, Ind. U. N.W., Gary, 1965-69, lectr. Edn., 1973-74, asst. prof. edn., 1975-78, assoc. prof., 1978-80, supr. secondary student tchg., 1973-74, dir. student tchg., 1975-77, dir. Office Field Experiences, 1977-78, dir. profl. devel., 1978-80, spl. asst. to chancellor, 1981-83, asst. to chancellor, 1983-84, acting chancellor, 1983-84, chancellor, 1984-92; pres. U. Akron, Ohio, 1992-96, S.D. State U., 1998—. Sr. fellow Nat. Ctr. for Higher Edn., 1996-97; vis. prof. U. Ark., 1979-80, U. Alaska, 1982; bd. dirs. Lubrizol Corp., A. Schulman Corp., Commn. on Women in Higher Edn., Akron Tomorrow, Ohio Aerospace Consortium, Ohio Super Computer Com.; holder VA Harrington disting. chair in edn., 1994-96, Charles G. Herbrich chair in leadership mgmt., 1996—. Author: (with C. Smith) Reading Activities for Middle and Secondary Schools: A Handbook for Teachers, 1979, Reading Instruction for Secondary Schools, 1986, How to Improve Your Scores on Reading Competency Tests, 1981, (with C. Smith and G. Ingersoll) Trends in Educational Materials: Traditionals and the New Technologies, 1983, The Urban Campus: Educating a New Majority for a New Century, 1994, also numerous articles. Bd. dirs. Meth. Hosp., N.W. Ind. Forum, N.W. Ind. Symphony, S.D. Art Mus., Boys Club N.W. Ind., Akron Symphony, NBD Bank, John S. Knight Conv. Ctr., Inventure Pl., Akron Roundtable, Cleve. Com. Higher Edn., 4-H Found., S.D. Art Mus., S.D. Value. Recipient Disting. Alumni award Northwestern U., UA Disting. Alumni award, 1994, numerous grants; Am. Council on Edn. fellow in acad. adminstrn. Ind. U., Bloomington, 1980-81. Mem. Assn. Tchr. Educators (nat. pres. 1984-85, Disting. Mem. 1990), Ind. Assn. Tchr. Educators (past pres.), North Ctrl. Assn. (mem. commn. at large), Am. Assn. State Colls. and Univs. (acting v.p. divsn. acad. and internat. programs 1997, bd. dirs., treas., chmn. global priorities commn.), Am. Coun. Edn. (bd. dirs., exec. com.), Leadership Devel. Coun. ACE, Office Women Higher Edn., Ohio Inter Univ. Coun. (chairperson), Internat. Reading Assn., Akron Urban League (bd. dirs.), P.E.O., Cosmos Club, Phi Delta Kappa (Outstanding Young Educator award), Delta Kappa Gamma (Leadership/Mgmt. fellow 1980), Pi Lambda Theta, Pi Kappa Phi, Chi Omega. Episcopalian. Avocation: music. Home: 929 Harvey Dunn St Brookings SD 57006-1347 Office: South Dakota State Univ Office of the Pres Adminstrn Bldg 201 Brookings SD 57007-0001 E-mail: Peggy_Miller@sdstate.edu.

MILLER, PEGGY MCLAREN, retired management educator; b. Tomahawk, Wis., Jan. 12, 1931; d. Cecil Glenn and Gladys Lucille (Bame) McLaren; m. Richard Irwin Miller, June 25, 1955; children: Joan Marie, Diane Lee, Janine Louise. BS, Iowa State U., 1953; MA, Am. U., 1959; MBA, Rochester Inst. Tech., 1979; PhD, Ohio U., 1987. Instr. Beirut Coll. for Women, 1953-55, U. Ky., Lexington, 1964-66, S.W. Tex. State U., San Marcos, 1981-84; home economist Borden Co., N.Y.C., 1955-58; cons. Consumer Cons., Chgo., Springfield, Ill., 1972-77; sr. mktg. rep. N.Y. State Dept. Agr., Rochester, 1978-79; asst. prof., coord. bus. and mgmt. Keuka Coll., Keuka Park, N.Y., 1979-81; lectr. mgmt. Ohio U., Athens, 1984-2000; ret., 2000. Home: 17 Briarwood Dr Athens OH 45701-1302 E-mail: pmmiller@aol.com.

MILLER, REBECCA S. financial analyst; b. Troy, Ohio, Oct. 2, 1957; d. Lowell T. and Viola Wray Miller. A in Acctg., Middletown Bus. Coll., 1977; courses in computer programming, Edison State Comty. Coll., 1986—92. 1982billing clerk Hobart Corp., Troy, 1977; miscellaneous editor Premark Inc., Troy, 1982—89, supr. invoicing and commn., 1989—92; pricing analyst Ill. Tool Works, Troy, 1992—. Centennial Belle Tippecanoe Sesqui-Centennial, Tipp City, Ohio, 1990; first aid responder Premark Inc., Ill. Tool Works, Troy, 1992—; neighborhood collector March of Dimes Mother's March, Tipp City, 1994, Am. Inst. Cancer Rsch., Tipp City, 1998—99. Named Most Improved Bowler, Hobart Corp. Women's Bowling League, Troy, 1985—86. Mem.: Tipp City United Methodist Women (unit treas. 1999—2000), Ohio Soc. Daughters of Am. Revolution (Outstanding Jr. Mem. 1990, chpt. regent 1992—95, state page chmn. 1995—98, Piqua-Lewis Boyer chpt., state page chmn. 1995-98, outstanding jr. mem. 1990), Fort Pickawillany Soc. Children of Am. Revolution (sr.; sr. soc. pres. 1990—92, sr. regional marshall 1998—2001, Outstanding Sr. Mem. 1999—2000, nat. chaperone 2002, sr. state pres. 2002—, outstanding sr. mem. 1999—2000). Republican. Methodist. Avocations: cross stitch, reading. Home: 538 Linwood Dr Troy OH 45373-2125

MILLER, RITA, personnel consultant, diecasting company executive; b. Bklyn., Jan. 15, 1925; d. Joseph and Etta M.; BA, Bklyn. Coll., 1947; MA, Boston U., 1949; children: Erika Greenwald, Roy Barnet Glickman. Personnel officer, sec. to pres. Marine Elec. Corp., Bklyn., 1943-47; script writer Song Debut, Boston, 1949-50; dir. Writers' Workshops, interviewer pub. opinion surveys, New Rochelle, N.Y., 1962-64; mgr. employee relations Dynacast div. Coats & Clark, Inc., Yorktown Heights, 1966-89. Mem. Am. Soc. Personnel Adminstrn., Westchester Personnel Mgmt. Assn. (dir.), Personnel Council New Rochelle, Bus. and Profl. Women U.S.A., Nat. Sociology Hon. Soc. Editor: The Management Consultant (George Kenning), 1965; contbr. articles to profl. jours. Home: 16 Congress St New Rochelle NY 10801-1902

MILLER, ROBERTA DORIS, elementary school educator; b. Lynn, Mass., May 14, 1940; d. Morris and Lorraine Miller. BS in Edn. cum laude, Lesley Coll., Cambridge, Mass., 1961; M in Edn., Salem (Mass.) State Coll., 1964; postgrad., Boston U. Tchr. Brookline (Mass.) Pub. Schs., 1968—. Pilot math. programs Ednl. Devel. Corp., Newton, Mass., 1988-89; pilot sci. programs TV series 3! 2! 1! Contact!, 1991; developer curriculum materials in math. and lang. arts Brookline Pub. Schs., 1969—, presenter workshops math. for new tchrs., 1984—; faculty mem. Suffolk U., Boston, 2000—. Coord. presentation of programs to nursing homes and vets. hosps.; coord. fundraising victims and schs. of Hurricane Andrew, 1992; chair, coord. fundraising for victims of the Midwest floods, 1993. Mem.: MATSOL (Mass. Assn. Tchrs. of Speakers Other Langs., Inc.), NEA, Mass. Tchrs. Assn. Avocations: travel, reading, music. E-mail: bobdorrob@yahoo.com.

MILLER, RUBY SILLS, gerontologist; b. Montpelier, Ind., July 7, 1919; d. Elijah Bert and Alma (Beeks) Sills; m. Glenn Kenneth Miller, Mar. 26, 1966. BS in Edn., Ball State Tchrs. Coll., 1957; MBA, U. Wis., 1958; MPS, New Sch. Social Rsch., 1983; post-masters cert., Hunter Brookdale Ctr. on Aging, 1988. Reporter Montpelier Herald, 1937-41; soc. editor, reporter Hartford City (Ind.) News-Times, 1941-44, bus. office supr., 1945-57; asst. to dean, instr. U. Wis. Sch. Bus., 1958-60; exec. dir. Nat. Fedn. Bus. and Profl. Women's Clubs, 1960-64; asst. to nat. exec. dir. Girl Scouts U.S.A., N.Y.C., 1964-66, spl. asst. to nat. exec. dir., 1972-74; dir. exptl. project for adminstrv. trainees Camp Fire Girls, Inc. and Girl Scouts U.S.A., 1966-68; dir. regional confs. Nat. Assembly for Social Policy and Devel., Inc., 1968-71; project dir. Nat. Center for Vol. Action, 1971-72; cons. Nat. Council for Homemaker-Home Health Aide Service, Inc., 1972, 76; asst. dir. Gustavus Adolphus Community Lounge Sr. Center, 1977-78; Queens County community program officer N.Y.C. Dept. of Aging, 1978-89; gerontologist cons., 1989—. Sec. Hartford City Retailers Assn., 1951-54 Mem. bd.. life mem. Bellevue Day Care Ctr., 1979—, pres., 1980—82; bd. mem. Bellevue Hosp. Adv. Coun., 1978—82, 1991—97; region 1 field rep. N.Y. State Wide Sr. Action Coun., 1989—91, bd. trustees, 1992—2002, region 1 pres., 1993—95, state pres., 1996—98; coord. vol. nat. study guardianship system N.Y. OPlder Women's League and Ctr. Social Gerontology, Ann Arbor, Mich., 1990—91; Pres. Ind. Bapt. Youth Fellowship, 1944—46; supt. Sunday sch. 1st Bapt. Ch., 1949—51; bd. trustees Cmty Ch., Unitarian-Universalist, 1987—92, 1998—, vice chair, 1999—2002. Mem.: State Soc. Aging N.Y. Home: 165 E 32nd St Apt 5G New York NY 10016-6009

MILLER, SANDRA PERRY, middle school educator; b. Nashville, Aug. 3, 1951; d. James Ralph and Pauline (Williams) Perry; m. William Kerley Miller, June 22, 1974. BS, David Lipscomb U., 1973; MEd, Tenn. State U., 1983, cert. in spl. edn., reading splty., 1986. Cert. tchr., Tenn. Tchr. Clyde Riggs Elem. Sch., Portland, Tenn., 1973-86; tchr. social studies Portland Mid. Sch., 1986—. Adv. bd. tech. and comm. in edn. Sumner County Sch. Bd., Gallatin, Tenn., 1990—; co-dir., cons. Tenn. Students-at-Risk, Nashville, 1991—; assoc. edn. cons. Edn. Fgn. Inst. Cultural Exch., 1991-92; fellow World History Inst., Princeton (N.J.) U., 1992—; awards com. Tenn. Dept. Edn., Nashville, 1992; U.S. edn. amb. E.F. Ednl. Tours, Eng., France, Germany, Belgium, Holland, 1991; ednl. cons. HoughtonMifflin Co., Boston; apptd. Tenn. Mini-Grants award com., Tenn. 21st Century Tech. Com.; mem. Tenn. Textbook Com., 1995, Think-Tank on 21st Century Edn., Tenn. and Milliken Nat. Educator Found.; apptd. to Gov.'s Task Force Commn. on 21st Schs., Gov.'s Task Force for Anti-Drug and Alcohol Abuse Among Teens; mem. nat. com. for instnl. tech. devel. Milken Family Found. Nat. Edn. Conf., 1996; apptd. to Instrnl. Tech. Devel.-Project Strand, 1996 Milken Family Found., Nat. Edn. Conf.; appointed curriculum com. Bicentennial WW II Meml., 1996-97; developed State Model Drop-Out Prevent Program, 1996-97; U.S. tchr. amb. to Ukraine, Am. Coun. for Internat. Edn.; Sumner County music dir. Sumner Enrichment Program, 2001-02; mem. awards com. for U.S., Am. Couns. for Internat. Edn., Washington, 2002. Author curriculum materials; presenter creative crafts segment local TV sta., 1990-93; producer, dir. documentary on edn. PBS, Corona, Calif., 1990. Mem. nat. com. instnl. tech. devel. project Strand of the 1996 Milken Family Found. Nat. Edn. Conf., L.A., 1996; performer Nashville Symphony Orch., 1970—73; leader Sumner County 4-H Club, 1976—86; mem. Woodrow Wilson Nat. Fellowship Found. on Am. History, Princeton U., 1994; co-chair Inter Media Cable Commn.; apptd. tchr. mentoring program Midd Tenn. State U. and Tenn. State U. Dept. Edn.; chmn. Comcast Cable TV Commn., 2003—. Recipient Excellence in Tchg. award U. Tenn., 1992, 93, award for Outstanding Teaching in Humanities Tenn. Humanities Coun., 1994; named Tchr. of Yr. Upper Cumberland dist. Tenn. Dept. Edn., 1991-92, 92-93, Mid. Tenn. Educator of Yr. Tenn. Assn. Mid. Schs., 1991, Tenn. Tchr. of Yr. Tenn. Dept. Edn., 1992, Nat. Educator of Yr. Milken Family Found., 1992, U.S. Tchr. Ambassador to Ukraine, Am. Coun. Internat. Edn., Washington; grantee Tenn. Dept. Edn. for Devel. of Model Drop Out Prevention Program, 1996. Mem. NEA, ASCD, Sumner County Edn. Assn. (sch. rep. 1973—, Disting. Tchr. of Yr. 1992), Tenn. Edn. Assn. (rep. 1973—), Nat. Geographic Tenn. Alliance (rep. 1990—, grantee 1990), Tenn. Humanities Coun. (rep. 1990—), Nat. Coun. Social Studies, Internat. Platform Assn. Baptist. Avocations: crafts, doll collecting, reading, music, fashion modeling. Office: Portland Mid Sch 604 S Broadway Portland TN 37148-1624 Office Phone: 615-325-4146.

MILLER, SANDRA RITCHIE, artist, art therapist; b. Downers Grove, Ill., Aug. 15, 1940; d. Joseph Edgar and Ruby Irene (McAllister) Ritchie; m. David Martin Miller, Dec. 13, 1968; 1 child, Ritchie Wayne. Student, Cambridge (Eng.) U., 1975-76, U. Minn., 1971; AA in Art, Glendale Coll., 1979; BS in Psychology, Ariz. State U., 1982. Adminstrv. asst. Rand Corp., Santa Monica, Calif., 1959, System Devel. Corp., Santa Monica, Calif., 1965-69; art tchr. Wheelersburg, Ohio, 1983-85; artist, 1970—; art person, therapist Oak Meadow Nursing Home, Alexandria, Va., 1987—94, Woodbine Healthcare and Rehab., Alexandria, 1992—. Bd. dirs., v.p. Gallery West, Alexandria. One-woman shows Gallery West, Alexandria, Va., 1992, 93, 95, 96, Hamilton Gallery, Alexandria, 1991, Yarrow Gallery, Oundle, Eng., 1996; exhbns. include Women's Internat. League for Peace and Freedom Calendar, 1983, Nat. Mus. of Women in Arts archives, 1994—, Mus. Contemporary Art, Washington, 1996, Internat. Artists' Support Group, 1996, Amsterdam Whitney Gallery, N.Y.C. Vol. USAF Family Svcs., Duluth, Minn., 1970-72, RAF Alconbury, Eng., 1972-75, Friends of the Earth, San Francisco, 1980-81, Child Assault Prevention Program, Portsmouth, Ohio, 1983-85; bd. dirs. Art League/Torpedo Factory, Alexandria, 1989-91, Belle Haven on the Green, Alexandria, 1988-92, pres. 1991-92. Mem. Ward Nasse Gallery, Knickerbocker Artists, Washington Project for the Arts, Mus. Contemporary Art. Democrat. Avocations: travel, reading, study. Home: 5747 Blaine Rd Churchton MD 20733-9656 Office: 5747 Blaine Rd Churchton MD 20733-9656 Office Phone: 301-261-5045. E-mail: sdra@aol.com.

MILLER, SARABETH, secondary school educator; b. Apr. 6, 1927; d. Clayton Everett and Margaret (Noland) Reif; m. Lloyd Melvin Miller, Dec. 2, 1944; children: Virginia, Shirley, Judith, John, Nola, Steven. BA, Valparaiso U., 1972, MA in L.S., 1977; postgrad., Purdue U., 1983, Ind. U., 1986, postgrad., 1991, Art Inst. Ft. Lauderdale, Fla., 1992, Ind. State U., 1996, postgrad., 1997, St. Joseph U., 1998. Lic. tchr. Ind., cert. data processing. Office employee Porter County Herald, Hebron, Ind., 1954—55, Little Co. of Mary Hosp. and Home, San Pierre, Ind., 1960—65, Jasper County Co-op, Tefft, Ind., 1965—69, Hannon's, Valparaiso, 1969—72; tchr. art DeMotte (Ind.) elem. sch., 1972—76, Kankakee Valley High Sch., Wheatfield, Ind., 1976—. Participant Lilly Creative Tchr.'s Workshop. Participant (art and lit. mag.) Mirage; contbr. articles. Leader 4-H Club, Kouts; participant North Ctrl. Regional Forum, 1991, 1992, 1993; mem., elder Kouts Presbyn. Ch.; mem. adv. com. secondary sch. showcase Valparaiso U. Recipient various prizes, Lake Ctrl. (Ind.) Fair, 1975, 1980, photography award, Ind. Dept. Tourism, 1976, Porter County Fair, 1989, 1996, 1998, 2000, 2001, Gainer Bank Calendar award, 4-H Alumni award, 2002, 4-H 45 yr. leader tenure award, 1994; grantee, Nat. Gallery of Art, 1993; Lilly Endowment fellow, Lilly Extending Tchr. Creativity Inst., 1987, 1994, 1995, 1996, 2002, 2003. Mem.: NEA, North Ctrl. Assn. Secondary Schs. (mem. evaln. team), Kankakee Valley Tchrs. Assn., Ind. Art Edn. Assn., Ind. Tchrs. Assn., Nat. Art Edn. Assn. Presbyterian. Home: 1056 S Baums Bridge Rd Kouts IN 46347-9712 E-mail: smiller@kv.k12.in.us.

MILLER, SARAH PEARL, librarian; b. Wilkensburg, Pa., Aug. 31, 1938; d. Samuel Henry and Anna Deborah (Shirley) Lyons; m. Paul Victor Miller, Apr. 15, 1989; children: Cheryl, Michael, Daniel, Lorel. BS, Indiana U. of Pa., 1960; MREM, Denver Conservative Bapt. Sem., 1965; MA, U. Denver, 1966. Libr. Denver Conservative Bapt. Sem., 1966—. Mem. Am. Theol. Libr. Assn. (bd. dirs. 1978-81, 90-91, index bd. 1983-90). Home: 15707 E Grand Ave Aurora CO 80015-1708

MILLER, SARI ELIZABETH (SALLY DERBY), writer; b. Dayton, Ohio, July 1, 1934; d. Wallene Russell Derby and Hildred (Chester) Derby; m. Karl Stratton Miller, Dec. 10, 1955; children: David, Michael, Steven, Philip, Matthew, Sarah. BA, Western Coll., Oxford, Ohio, 1956. Author: (Juvenile fiction) My Steps, 1996, Taiko on a Windy Night, 2001, Hannah's Bookmobile Christmas, 2001, Two Fools and a Horse, 2003. Home: 770 Southmeadow Cir Cincinnati OH 45231 E-mail: derbymiller@fuse.net.

MILLER, SHANNON, Olympic athlete; b. Rolla, Mo., Mar. 10, 1977; Student, Boston Coll. MBA program at Carroll Sch. Gymnist U.S. National Gymnastic Team, 1990—97. Named Female Athlete of Yr., Nat. March of Dimes Found., 1993. Christian Scientist. Achievements include most decorated gymnast in U.S. history; won a total of 58 International and 49 National competition medals; won Silver Medal, all-around and balance beam, Barcelona Olympic Games, 1992; Bronze Medal, U.S. Gymnastic Team, Barcelona Olympic Games, 1992; Bronze Medal, floor exercise, Barcelona Olympic Games, 1992; Gold Medal, uneven bars, all-around, floor exercise, World Gymnastic Championships (Great Britan), 1993; Gold Medal, all-around, balance beam, World Gymnastic Championships (Australia), 1994; Gold Medal, U.S. Gymnastic Team, Atlanta Olympic Games, 1996; Gold Medal, balance beam, Atlanta Olympic Games, 1996. Address: 8 Easy Street Edmond OK 73003

MILLER, SHEILA, state legislator; d. Vernon and Mildred M.; m. Michael Miller; 1 child, Emilie C. BS cum laude, Pa. State U., 1974. Rep. dist. 129 State of Pa., 1993—. Bd. dirs. Berks County Farmland Preservation. Mem. Nat. Cattlemens Assn., Berks Farm Bur., Berks Cattlemens Assn., Pa. Cattlemens Assn., Heidelberg Heritage Soc., Berks County Rep. Women, Phi Kappa Phi, Gamma Sigma Delta Agrl. Alumni Soc. Republican. Office: Pa Ho of Reps B13 Main Capitol Bldg PO Box 202020 Harrisburg PA 17120-2020

MILLER, SHERRIE LYNN, artist; b. Richmond, Va., June 14, 1973; d. Eddie Roger and Cynthia Louise (Davis) M. BFA, Va. Commonwealth U., 1995; postgrad., U. Ga., 1997. Photog. finisher, 1995—98; graphic artist, 1999. Shows include Va. Commonwealth U., 1995. Dean's scholar Va. Commonwealth U., 1991-95. Mem. Va. Mus. Fine Arts, Golden Key, Phi Kappa Phi, Phi Eta Sigma. Avocations: painting, drawing, belly dancing, yoga. Studio: 2910 Floyd Ave Richmond VA 23221

MILLER, SUSAN ANN, school system administrator; b. Cleve., Nov. 24, 1947; d. Earl Wilbur and Marie Coletta (Hendershot) M. BS in Edn., Kent State U., 1969; MEd, Cleve. State U., 1975; PhD, Kent State U., 1993. Cert. supt.; cert. elem. prin., cert. elem. supervisor; cert. Learning Disabled/Behavior Disabled tchr.; cert. tchr. grades 1-8; cert. sch. counselor; lic. counselor. Tchr., guidance counselor, interim prin. North Royalton City Schs., Ohio, 1969-84; dir. elem. and spl. edn., acting supt., asst. supt. Ednl. Svc. Ctr. of Cuyahoga County, Valley View, Ohio, 1984—. Contbr. articles to profl. jours. Grantee Latchkey Program, State Dept. Edn., North Coast Leadership Forum, Peer Assistance and Rev., Entry Yr. Program, Alt. H.S. Mem. ASCD, Coun. Exceptional Children, Phi Delta Kappa. Office: ESC Cuyahoga County 5700 W Canal Rd Valley View OH 44125-3326 Home: 7236 Morning Star Trail Sagamore Hills OH 44067 E-mail: susan.a.miller@lnoca.org.

MILLER, SUSAN M. telecommunications industry executive; BA in English Lit. and Art History, Dickinson Coll., 1981; JD, Cath. U. Columbus Sch. Law, 1984. Counsel telecomm. Weil, Gotshal, & Manges, N.Y.C.; counsel GTE; v.p., gen. counsel ATIS, Washington, 1988—99, pres., CEO, 1999—. Rep. ATIS FCC, Am. Nat. Stds. Inst., N.Am. Numbering Coun., Network Reliability and Interoperability Coun., Internat. Engring. Consortium Adv. Coun. Office: ATIS 1200 G St NW Ste 500 Washington DC 20005

MILLER, THERESA L. library director; b. Port Huron, Mich., Apr. 2, 1959; d. David R. Miller and Mary Louise Preininger. AA, AS, St. Clair County C.C., Port Huron, Mich., 1990; BS, Wayne State U., 1992, MLIS, 1994. Support tutor St. Clair County C.C., 1988-89, master tutor, 1989-91; circulation supr. Baker Coll. of Port Huron, 1992-95, faculty math., 1998; pub. spkr. Mich., 1988—; investigative asst. Huffmaster Cos., Port Huron, 1998-2000; libr. dir. Baker Coll. of Pt. Huron, 1995—; judge Bus. Profs. of Am., St. Clair County, 1994—2000, 2003—04. Baker coll. rep. County Tech. Adv. Com., St. Clair County, 1997—; adv. bd. mem. Baker Coll. of PH Career Svcs., 1997—2003; judge Bus. Profs. of Am., St. Clair County, 2003, Port Huron H.S. Writing Competition, 1997—2001. Editor: (newsletter) Baker Beacon, 1997; author: (newsletter) LUC News, 1993-96; author: (book) A Reference Librarians User Guide to the Internet, 1993. Recorder for the blind, Libr. of Mich., Lansing, 1996—; mem. gov. bd. Seaway Cmty. Freenet, St. Clair County, 1995-96; pres., founding bd. First Night of Port Huron, 2001—. Mem.: ALA, Internat. Libr. Support Group (founder 1999—, chmn.), Librs. Using Computers/Mich. (chair 1994—96), Mich. Libr. Assn., Optimists (Port Huron bd. dirs. 1997—99, pres. Pt. Huron chpt. 2000—01, lt. gov. Mich. 2001—), Phi Theta Kappa (treas. 1989—90, founding alumni pres. St. Clair C.C. chpt. 1991). Avocations: profl. singing, jewelry collecting, auctions, theater, investing. Office: Baker Coll Port Huron Libr 3403 Lapeer Rd Port Huron MI 48060 Office Phone: 810-989-2122. Business E-Mail: theresa.miller@baker.edu.

MILLER, TONI M. ANDREWS, critical care nurse; b. Webb City, Mo., July 20, 1949; d. John F. and Gettius M. (Short) Henry; div.; children: Bradley Ardrey, Mischa Andrews, Paul Andrews. ADN, Mo. So. Coll., Joplin, 1973, BSN, 1995. Cert. ACLS, TNCC, PALS. Asst. insvc. dir. Kirksville (Mo.) Osteo. Hosp., 1975-76; charge nurse, unit program supr. St. Louis Devel. Disabilities Treatment Ctr., 1983-85; clin. supr. ICU Oak Hill Osteo. Hosp., Joplin, 1986-95; emergency room/ICU nurse Fitzgibbon Hosp., Marshall, Mo., 1997, house supr., 1998, 2000—, primary nurse utilization rev. and patient edn., 1998-2000; ICU nurse Bothwell Hosp., Sedalia, Mo. Recipient Joseph P. Kennedy award, 1966. Mem. AACN. Home: 900 Winchester Dr Apt A-9 Sedalia MO 65301

MILLER, VALERIE CAROL, journalist; b. Chgo. d. V. Heinz and Arlene Elizabeth Miller. A in Gen. Studies, C.C. So. Nev.; BA Comms., U. Nev., 1998. Travel coord. Great Escape Travel, Las Vegas, 1996—97; staff writer, reporter U. Nev. Las Vegas Rebel Yell Students Newspaper, 1997—98; travel coord. World Travel and Accessories, Las Vegas, 1998—2000; reporter, freelance writer, intern Las Vegas Sun Newspaper, 1998—2000; broadcaster, disk jockey Sta. KLAV AM 1230, Las Vegas, 1997—; reporter, staff writer Las Vegas Bus. Press Newspaper, 2000—. Vol. Shade Tree Shelter, Las Vegas, 2002; vol. writer Nev. Times Newspaper, Las Vegas, 1995, 1997. Nominee Journalist of Merit award, Nev. Press Assn., 2002, 2003, Small Bus. Journalist of Yr., Nev. Small Bus. Adminstrn., 2003; recipient Best Feature Story award, Nev. Press Assn., 2001, Best Bus. Story award, Nev. Press. Assn., 2002, Small Bus. Journalist of Yr. award for Nev., U.S. Small Bus. Assn., 2002, Merit award for news writing, Internat. Assn. Bus. Comm., 2003, Merit award for series writing, 2003, Best Bus. Story award, Nev. Press. Assn. Fellow: Soc. for the Advanced Placement of Materials, Working in Comms., Soc. Profl. Journalists, 3rd Wave Nev., Tortois Group; mem.: Phi Lambda Eta. Avocations: travel, writing poems and song lyrics, movies. Home: 613 Mosswood Dr Henderson NV 89015-8329 Office: Las Vegas Bus Press 1385 Pama Ln Ste 111 Las Vegas NV 89119

MILLER, VELVET G. healthcare administrator; b. Reading, Pa., Aug. 16, 1945; d. Louis L. and Pattee J. Miller; m. Calvin E. Davis, Sept. 14, 1991; 1 child, Toby L. C. BSN, Wagner Coll., 1967; MEd, Temple U., 1976; MPA, Harvard U., 1984; PhD, Boston U., 1997. RN. Assoc. commr. Mass. Dept. Pub. Welfare, Boston, 1988-89, Mass. Dept. Health, Boston, 1989-91; v.p. Wagner Coll., S.I., 1991-92; Medicaid dir. N.J. Dept. Human Svcs., Trenton, 1994-96, dep. commr., 1996-98; exec. dir. Children's Futures N.J., Princeton, 1998-99; ptnr. Davis Miller Group, Trenton, 1991—; pres., CEO Horizon/Mercy, Trenton, 2001—02, My Parent's Concierge, 1999—. Mem. adv. bd. Urban Inst., Washington, 1996—, Finding Common Ground, Columbia U., N.Y.C., 1997—2003. Co-author: (book) Renegotiating Healthcare, 1995 (ANA CPR inst. award, 1995, 1996); contbr. articles and reports to profl. jours. Bd. dirs. FAmilies USA, Washington, 1993—99. Recipient Pub. Svc. award, N.J. Pub. Policy Rsch. Inst., 1998, Carballo award for excellence in pub. svc., Commonwealth of Mass., 1988. Fellow: Am. Acad. Nursing; mem.: ANA, APHA. Democrat. Presbyterian. Home and Office: 219 Cornwall Ave Trenton NJ 08618-3321 E-mail: vmiller8529@comcast.net.

MILLER, VIDA O. state representative, art gallery owner; b. Travelers Rest, S.C., July 22, 1950; d. David William and Imogene Tankersley Osteen; m. James Dores Miller, Mar. 26, 1978; stepchildren: Jimmy, Allyson. Student, N. Greenville Coll., Bob Jones U. Owner Grayman Gallery; state rep. dist. 108 S.C. Legis., 1997—, mem. edn. and pub. works com., mem. invitations and meml. resolutions com., sec. agr. natural resources and environ. affairs. com., 1996—98, mem. environ. affairs I subcom. Sec. House Dem. Caucus. Mem. Georgetown County Sch. Bd., 1988—94, sec., 1992—94; past bd. dirs., organizer Georgetown County Human Rels. Coun.; bd. dirs. Five Rivers Commn. Develop. Corp.; mem. Georgetown County League Women Voters; bd. dirs. Rice Mus. Cultural Develop.; chmn. Georgetown County Legis. Del.; gen. assembly mem. S.C. Sch. Bds. Stratgic Planning Team; mem. S.C. Dept. Transp. Road Enhancement Com., S.C. Dept. Transp. Minority Bus. com.; bd. dirs. Waccamaw Regional Planning Commn.; vice chmn. Grand Strand Transp. Authority; mem. Gov,'s Med. Sch. Task Force, Palmetto Pride, Tourism Caucus and Arts Caucus; bd. dirs. First Steps; sec. House Dem. Caucus. Named Outstanding Legis. of Yr., S.C. Sch. Bds., 1999, 2000. Mem.: Georgetown County Bus. and Profl. Women, Georgetown County Wateroclor Soc. (bd. dirs.), S.C. Watercolor Soc. (regional dir. 1992—95), Waccamaw Arts & Craft Guild (bd. dirs. 1992—94), Pawleys Island-Litchfield Merchants Assn. (bd. dirs., organizer 1986—89), Nat. Found. Women Legislators (state co-chmn.). Democrat. Office: State Capitol 335D Blatt Bldg Columbia SC 29211 Home: PO Box 3157 Pawleys Island SC 29585 Address: 335 Westfield Dr Pawleys Island SC 29585 E-mail: VOM@scstatehouse.net.

MILLER, VINA ELIZABETH, music educator; b. Towanda, Pa., July 19, 1965; d. Donald Charles Miller and Roseanna Love Hardenstine. MusB in edn., Mansfield U., 1989; MS in edn., Elmira Coll., 1995. Cert. tchr. Pa. Dept. of Edn., 1989. Elementary gen. music tchr. Athens (Pa.) Area Sch. Dist., 1989—2000, dir. vocal music, 1989—, dir. orchestral music, 2000—, chmn. arts dept., 2001—. Dir. show choir reflections Athens (Pa.) Area HS, 1990—. Trumpet player for taps Miltown (Pa.) Firemen, 1996—2002; trumpet player Salvation Army, Sayre, Pa., 1995—2003; tchr. and youth dir. Saco Rd. Bapt. Ch., Ulster, Pa., 1983—89; tchr. Faith Bapt. Ch., Waverly, NY, 1990—99, treas., 2000—01; bd. dirs. youth Southren Teir Bapt. Assn., Owego, NY, 1999—2001; program dir. Laurel Lake Bapt. Camp, Corbin, Ky., 1990—93; co-dir. Spl. Needs Adaptive Program, Towanda, Pa. Scholar Governer Sch. scholarship, Pa. Dept. of Edn., 2003. Mem.: Bradford/Sullivan County Music Edn. Assn. (sec. 1994—2000), Nat. String Tchrs. Assn. (assoc.), Am. Choral Dirs. Assn. (assoc.), Pa. Music Educators Assn. (assoc.; sec., treas. dist. 8 2001—03), Music Educators Nat. Conf. (assoc.), Tau Beta Sigma (licentiate named Sister of Yr. 1986—87). Republican. Southern Baptist. Avocations: travel, landscaping, movies, music. Office: Athens Area School Distirct 401 W Frederick St Athens PA 18810 E-mail: vina@epix.net.

MILLER, WILMA HILDRUTH, education educator; b. Dixon, Ill., Mar. 8, 1936; d. William Alexander and Ruth Karin (Hanson) M. BS in Edn., No. Ill. U., DeKalb, 1958, MS in Edn., 1961; DEd, U. Ariz., 1967. Cert. reading specialist. Elem. tchr. Dist. 170, Dixon, Ill., 1958-63, Dist. 1, Tucson, Ariz., 1963-64; asst. prof. edn. Wis. State U., Whitewater, 1965-68; assoc. prof. edn. Ill. State U., Normal, 1968-72, prof., 1972-98, prof. emeritus, 1998—. Author: Diagnosing and Correcting Reading Difficulties in Children, 1988, Reading Comprehension, 1990, Complete Reading Disabilities Handbook, 1993, Alternative Assessment Techniques in Reading and Writing, 1995, Reading and Writing Remediation Kit, 1997, The Reading Teacher's Survival Kit, 2001, Reading Skills Problem Solver, 2002, Survival Reading Skills for Secondary School Students, 2003, 101 Ways for Developing Emergent Literacy, 2004, others; contbr. over 225 articles to profl. jours. Altar Guild, usher, greeter, communion asst. Our Saviour Luth. Ch., Normal, 1990—. Recipient Outstanding Contbn. to Edn. award No. Ill. U., 1998. Mem. Internat. Reading Assn. (parent and reading com. 1972-74, editl. adv. bd. 1995-98, Outstanding Dissertation award 1968), Mid-State Reading Coun. (editl. adv. bd. 1991-98), Alpha Upsilon Alpha (advisor Reading chpt. 1993-98), Pi Lambda Theta, Kappa Delta Pi, Phi Delta Kappa. Avocations: travel, writing, animals (particularly dogs), reading, antiques. Home: 302 N Coolidge St Normal IL 61761-2435 E-mail: whmiller@ilstu.edu.

MILLER, YOLANDA, publisher, writer; b. Chicago Heights, Ill., Aug. 5, 1957; m. Andrew Miller, Apr. 2, 1983. BS cum laude, U. Wis., Stout, 1978; MS in Rehab. Counseling, U. Wis., Milw., 1984. Pub. Victory Publs., Racine, Wis., 1996—. Author: (poetry) Ode to Precious, Priceless and Irreplaceable African-American Men, 1996. Avocation: reading. Home: 2526 Delaware Ave Racine WI 53403-3432

MILLER, YVETTE, lawyer, publishing executive; BA, Adelphi U.; JD, St. John's U., N.Y. Litig. assoc. Weil, Gotshal & Manges; gen. atty. pub. sect. CBS; v.p., dep. gen. counsel Hachette Filipacchi; with G + J USA, N.Y.C., 1993—2000, v.p., gen. counsel, 2000—. Office: G + J USA Pub Legal Dept 375 Lexington Ave New York NY 10017-5514

MILLER, YVONNE BOND, state legislator, educator; b. Edenton, N.C. d. John and Pency Bond. BS, Va. State Coll., Petersburg, 1956; postgrad., Va. State Coll., Norfolk, 1966; MA, Columbia U., 1962; PhD, U. Pitts., 1973; postgrad., CCNY, 1976. Tchr. Norfolk Pub. Schs., 1956-68; asst. prof. Norfolk State U., 1968-71, assoc. prof., 1971-74, prof., 1974-88, head dept. early childhood/elem. edn., 1984-87; mem. Va. Ho. Dels., Richmond, 1984-87, mem. edn. com., health, welfare and instns. com., militia and police com., 1983-87; mem. Va. Senate, Richmond, 1987—. Commerce and labor com., gen. laws com., transp. com., rehab. and social svcs. com. Va. Senate, HIV subcom., remediation subcom., unemployment compensation act subcom., infants and toddlers with disabilities subcom.; mem. intergovtl. coop. commn., youth commn., disability commn., Va. Coun. Coord. Prevention commn.; cons. in field. Commr. Ea. Va. Med. Authority; adv. bd. Va. Div. Children; active C.H. Mason Meml. Ch. of God in Christ. 1st black woman to be elected to Ho. of Dels. Legislature, 1983, 1st black woman to be elected to Va. Senate, 1987. Mem. Nat. Alliance Black Sch. Educators (bd. dirs.), Va. Assn. for Early Childhood Edn., Nat. Assn. Dem. Chairs, Zeta Phi Beta (past officer). Office: 2539 Corprew Ave Norfolk VA 23504-3909 also: Va Senate Gen Assembly Bldg Rm 318 Richmond VA 23219 Fax: 757-627-7203. E-mail: senatorybmiller@aol.com., ybmiller1@aol.com.

MILLER, ZOYA DICKINS (MRS. HILLIARD EVE MILLER JR.), civic worker; b. Washington, July 15, 1923; d. Randolph and Zoya Pavlovna (Klementinovska) Dickins; m. Hilliard Eve Miller, Jr., Dec. 6, 1943; children: Jeffrey Arnot, Hilliard Eve III. Grad., Stuart Sch. Costume Design, Washington, 1942; student, Cochran Galleries of Fine Arts, 1942, Sophie Newcomb Coll., 1944, New Eng. Conservatory Music, 1946, Colo. Coll., 1965; grad., Internat. Sch. Reading, 1969; student, Cochran Galleries of Fine Arts, 1942. Lic. pvt. pilot. Instr. Stuart Summer Sch. Costume Design, Washington, 1942; fashion coord. Julius Garfinckel, Washington, 1942-43; fashion coord., cons. Mademoiselle mag., 1942-44; star TV show Cowbelle Kitchen, 1957-58, Flair for Living, 1958-59; model mags. and comml. films, also nat. comml. recs., 1956-80; dir. rsch. devel. Webb-Waring Inst. for Cancer, Aging and Antioxidant Rsch., Denver, 1973—. Contbr. articles, lectrs. on health care sys. and fund raising. Mem. exec. com., bd. dirs. El Paso County chpt. Am. Lung Assn. Colo., 1965—84, bd. dirs., 1965—87, chmn. radio and TV coun., 1963—70, mem. med. affairs com., 1965—70, pres., 1965—66, procurer found. funds, 1965—70; developer nat. radio ednl. prodns. for internat. use Am. Lung Assn., 1963—70, coord. statewide pulmonary screening programs, other states, 1965—72; chmn. benefit fund raising El Paso County Cancer Soc., 1963; co-founder, coord. Colorado Springs Debutante Ball, 1967—; coord. Nat. Gov.'s Comprehensive Health Planning Coun., 1967—74, chmn., 1971—72, Colo. Chronic Care Com., 1969—73, chmn. fund raising, 1970—72, chmn. spl. com. conl. studies on nat. health bills, 1971—73; mem. Colo.-Wyo. Regional Med. Program Adv. Coun., 1969—73, Colo. Med. Found. Consumers Adv. Coun., 1972—78; mem. decorative arts com. Colorado Springs Fine Arts Ctr., 1972—75; founder, state coord. Nov. Noel Pediat. Benefit Am. Lung Assn., 1973—87; founder, chmn. bd. dirs. Newborn Hope, Inc., 1987—; mem. adv. bd. Beth-El Wagon Wheel Girl Scouts, 1991—94; mem. cmty. adv. coun. Beth-El Nursing Sch., 1998—; bd. dirs. Episcopal Columbarium Assn., 2001, The Family Attachment Ctr., Inc. Zoya Dickins Miller Vol. of Yr. award established Am. Lung Assn. of Colo., 1979; recipient James J. Waring award Colo. Conf. on Respiratory Disease Workers, 1963, Nat. Pub. Rels. award Am. Lung Assn., 1979, Gold Double Bar Cross award, 1980, 83, Jefferson award Am. Inst. Pub. Svc., 1991, Thousand Points of Light award The White House, 1992, Recognition award So. Colo. Women's C. of C., 1994, Silver Spur Cmty. award Pikes Peak Range Riders, 1994, Silver Bell award Assistance League Colorado Springs, 1996, Svc. to Mankind award Centennial Sertoma Club, 1997, Help Can't Wait award Pikes Peak chpt. ARC, 1997, Cmty. Weaver award The Independent News, 1997, Apgar award Colo. March of Dimes, 1998; named Humanitarian of Yr., Am. Lung Assn. of Colo., 1987, One of 50 Most Influential Women in Colorado Springs by Gazette Telegraph Newspaper, 1990, One of 5 Leading Ladies Colo. Homes & Lifestyles Mag., 1991. Mem.: Nat. Soc. Fund Raising Execs., Denver Round Table for Planned Giving, Colo. Assn. Fund Raisers, Nat. Soc. Colonial Dames, The Family Attachment Ctr., Nat. Cowbell Assn. (El Paso county pres. 1954, TV chmn., chmn. nat. Father of Yr. contest Colo. 1956—57), Broadmoor Garden Club, Garden of the Gods Club, Cheyenne Mountain Country Club. Home: 74 W Cheyenne Mountain Blvd Colorado Springs CO 80906-4336

MILLER-DUFFY, MERRITT, insurance agent, assistant camp director; b. Summit, N.J., July 16, 1966; d. Bertram B. and Lynne Clutsam Miller; m. James F. Duffy, Aug. 8, 1987; 1 child, Heather Ogden Duffy. BA, Cedar Crest Coll., 1988. Sr. underwriter St. Paul Fire & Marine Ins. Co., Iselin, N.J., 1988-93; v.p. B.B. Miller & Co., Elizabeth, N.J., 1993—. Asst. dir. Adirondack Camp, Putnam Sta., N.Y., 1999—, mem. adv. bd., 1996—. Vol. Jr. League of Summit, 1988-91; trustee CMI Cmty. Ctr., Inc., Elizabeth, 1999—; bd. dirs., vol. Jr. Achievement of Union County, N.J., Elizabeth, 1996—, Dir. of Distinction award, 1999. Recipient Vol. of Yr. award Jr. Achievement of Union County, 1996-97, Silver Life Card award Union County Conf. of PBA Dels., 1999. Mem. Ind. Ins. Agts., Nat. Assn. Ins. Women (cert. profl. ins. woman, sec. N.J. chpt. 1995-96, cert. ins. counselor), Young Agts. Coun. (county rep. 1996-97), 200 Club of Union County, Inc. (officer, trustee 1993—), N.J. State PBA (hon., life). Avocations: painting, gardening, community volunteer work. Office: BB Miller & Co 283 N Broad St Elizabeth NJ 07208-3791

MILLER-ENGEL, MARJORIE, foundation administrator, commissioner, small business owner; b. N.Y.C., Aug. 15, 1944; d. David Harry Siegel and Ruth Joan Gord; m. Robert Allan Engel, May 4, 1984; 1 child, Liana Laura Engel. BA, Syracuse U., 1966; cert. in interior design, N.Y. Sch. Interior Design, 1974. Assoc. dir. devel. Planned ParenthoodFedn., N.Y.C., 1967—69; account exec. Harold Oram Consulting, N.Y.C., 1969—72; pres., owner Marjorie Miller Pub. Rels., N.Y.C., 1975—81; founder, chmn. Life Ctr. Youth, Inc., Santa Fe, 1982—; pres., owner M. M. Designs, Inc., Santa Fe, 1989—. Co-owner Greenkey Property Mgmt., Santa Fe, 1989—. Commr. N.Mex Commn. Status Women, 2003—. Mem.: Intl. Women's Forum. Office: Life Ctr Youth Inc PO Box 8718 2725 Agua Fria St Santa Fe NM 87504 Office Phone: 505-986-0769.

MILLER(GORDON), MICHELLE RENEE, music educator; d. Gloria Jane and Frederick Russell Gordon; m. Charles Louis Miller, June 8, 2002. MusB, Bowling Green State U., Bowling Green, Ohio, 1993—97; MusM edn., The U. of Akron, Akron, Ohio, 2000—03. Pianist St. Paul Luth. Ch., Waynesburg, Ohio, 1993—; music intern Epworth United Meth. Ch., Toledo, 1996—98; music tchr. Louisville City Sch. Dist., Louisville, Ohio, 1998—99, Minerva Local Sch. Dist., Minerva, Ohio, 1999—2000, New Phila. City Sch. Dist., New Phila., Ohio, 2000—; piano instr. Pellegrino Music, North Canton, Ohio, 2003—. Accompanist Sandy Valley Coop. Chorus, Magnolia, Ohio, 2000—01. Musician St. Paul Luth. Ch., Waynesburg, Ohio, 1988—2003. Scholar Grad. Tchg. Assistantship, Kent State U., 2003. Mem.: Ohio Music Educators Assn. (con.). R-Consevative. Christian: Luth. Avocations: pilates, kickboxing, step aerobics, attending music concerts/recitals.

MILLERICK, JAYNE MARCUCCI, Republican party chairman; b. Boston, Mass, 1974; m. Shawn Mellerick. BA Polit. Sci., Univ. of New Hampshire, Durham, 1995. Dep. press sec. US Sen. Robert Smith; asst. sec. NH Rep. State Com. Exec. Bd., NH; intern for former Gov. Steve Merrill office State House, NH, 1995, scheduling dir.; dep. campaign mgr. Jay Lucas Rep. nominee for gov., NH, 1998; exec. dir. NH Rep. State Com., 1999—2000; ind. polit. cons. Rep. Nat. Com., 2002; chmn. New Hampshire Rep. State Com., 2003—; pres. Marcucci Consulting, 2003—. The first-ever recipient of the Ronald Reagan Young Rep. Award will be Jayne Marcucci. Office: 134 No Main St Concord NH 03301

MILLER-LANE, BARBARA See LANE, BARBARA

MILLER-LERMAN, LINDSEY, state supreme court justice; b. L.A., July 30, 1947; BA, Wellesley Coll., 1968; JD, Columbia U., 1973; LHD (hon.), Coll. of St. Mary, Omaha, 1993. Bar: N.Y. 1974, U.S. Dist. Ct. (so. dist.) N.Y. 1974, U.S. Ct. Appeals (2d cir.) 1974, Nebr. 1976, U.S. Dist. Ct. (ea. dist.) N.Y. 1975, U.S. Dist. Ct. Nebr. 1976, U.S. Ct. Appeals (8th cir.) 1979, U.S. Supreme Ct. 1982, U.S. Ct. Appeals (6th cir.) 1984, U.S. Ct. Appeals (10th cir.) 1987. Law clk. U.S. Dist. Ct., N.Y.C., 1973-75; from assoc. to ptnr. Kutak Rock, Omaha, 1975-92; judge Nebr. Ct. Appeals, Lincoln, 1992-98, chief judge, 1996-98; justice Nebr. Supreme Ct., 1998—. Contbr. articles to profl. jours. Bd. dirs. Tuesday Musical, Omaha, 1985—. Office: Nebr Supreme Ct State Capitol Rm 2222 Lincoln NE 68509

MILLER-PERRIN, CINDY LOU, psychology educator; b. McKeesport, Pa., Feb. 26, 1962; d. Emerson and Helen Francis (Beck) M.; m. Robin D. Perrin, Aug. 3, 1985; children: Jacob, Madison. BA, Pepperdine Univ., 1983; MS, Washington State Univ., 1987, PhD, 1991. Psychology intern Univ. Wash., Seattle, 1990-91, postdoctoral fellow, 1991-92; asst. prof. Pepperdine Univ., Malibu, Calif., 1992-96, assoc. prof., 1996—2002, prof. psychology, 2002—. Author: Preventing Child Sexual Abuse: Sharing..., 1992, Family Violence Across the Lifespan, 1997, 2d edit. 2004, Child Maltreatment, 1999; contbr. articles to profl. jours. Senator Grad. & Profl. Student Assn. Washington State U., 1988-89; guardian ad litem Whitman County, Wash., 1987-89. Mem. Am. Psychological Assn., Western Psychological Assn., Internat. Soc. Prevention of Child Abuse Neglect, Am. Profl. Soc. on the Abuse of Children, Sigma Xi, Psi Chi (faculty adv. 1992-95). Avocations: hiking, backpacking, golf, travel. Office: Pepperdine Univ Social Sci Div Malibu CA 90263

MILLER SCHEAR, ANNICE MARA, music educator; d. Trina C. and Herbert K Miller; 1 child, Ilana T. Schear. MusM, Cleve. State U., Cleve. Ohio, 1998—2002; MusB Edn., Kent State U., Kent, Ohio, 1990—93; BA in Comm. Arts, U. of Cin., Cin., Ohio, 1981—85. Orff Music Certification 1999, Kodaly Music Certification 2001. Music educator St. Ann Ch., Cleve. Heights, 1993—94, St. Joan of Arc Ch., Chagrin Falls, Ohio, 1993—94, Hebrew Acad. of Cleve., 1994—95; vocal music dir. Nathan Hale Mid. Sch., Cleve., 1995—. Dept. chairperson of fine arts Nathan Hale Mid. Sch., Cleveland, Ohio, 2000—, profl. devel. presenter, 2001—, acad. AAP facilitator, 2002—, acad. AAP team facilitator, 1996—2002; music dir. Beachwood Cmty. Theater, 2003—; asst. dir. jr. choir Anshe Chesed Fairmount Temple, 2003—. Author: (jour. article) OMEA - TRIAD Jour. Mem. Anshe Chesed - Fairmount Temple, Beachwood, Ohio, 1986—. Recipient Tchr. Recognition of the Yr., Nathan Hale Mid. Sch., 2002, PTA Reflections Chairperson Recognition, Southlyn Elem. Sch., 2003; grantee Monetary award for multicultural music materials, The Huntington Nat. Bank, 2002, Computer Lab, Cleve. Mcpl. Sch. Dist., 1999—2001, Monetary grant for Character Edn., City of Cleve. - Neighborhood Block Grant, 1996—98. Mem.: Ohio Music Educators Assn. (multicultural rep. 1999—), Ohio Music Educators Assn. (sec. 2002—), The Nat. Assn. of Music Educators, Anshe Chesed - Fairmount Temple Chorale, music com., Greenview Upper Elemenary PTA (pres. 2003), Southlyn Elem. PTA (v.p. 2000—02), Sigma Delta Tau Soc. Avocations: musical theater, board games, travel, inline skating, exercise. Home: 4102 Ellison Road South Euclid OH 44121 Personal E-mail: amschear@aol.com. E-mail: amschear@yahoo.com.

MILLER UDELL, BRONWYN, lawyer; b. Danbury, Conn., Aug. 7, 1972; BA, Barnard Coll., Columbia U., 1994; JD, U. Miami, 1997. Bar: (Fla.) 1997. Asst. state atty. State of Fla., 1997—; adj. prof. Fla. Internat. U., Miami, 2001—02. Mem. Witness Justice Adv. Bd. Mem. Cmtys. in Schs. Miami Mentoring Program, Coral Gables Sr. H.S. Parent Tchr. Assn.;

co-chair Expert Corps. Vol. Mem.: League of Prosecutors, Fla. Assn. Women Lawyers, Fla. Pros. Attys. Assn., Federalist Soc. Lawyer's Divsn., Elephant Forum, Phi Delta Phi. Office: Office of the State Atty 1350 NW 12th Ave Miami FL 33136

MILLETT, KATE (KATHERINE MURRAY MILLETT), political activist, sculptor, artist, writer; b. St. Paul, Sept. 14, 1934; m. Fumio Yoshimura, 1965. BA magna cum laude, U. Minn., 1956; postgrad. with 1st class honors, St. Hilda's Coll. Oxford, Eng., 1956-58; PhD with distinction, Columbia U., 1970. Instr. English U. N.C. at Greensboro, 1958; file clk. N.Y.C.; kindergarten tchr., 1960-61; sculptor, Tokyo, 1961-63; tchr. Barnard Coll., 1964-70; tchr. English Bryn Mawr (Pa.) Coll., 1970. Disting. vis. prof. Sacramento State Coll., 1972—73; adj. prof. NYU, N.Y.C.; founder Women's Art Colony Farm, Poughkeepsie, NY; rep. as non-govtl. orgn. on behalf of human rights UN. Author: Sexual Politics, 1970, The Prostitution Papers, 1973, Flying, 1974, Sita, 1977, The Basement, 1979, Going to Iran, 1982, The Loony Bin Trip, 1990, The Politics of Cruelty, 1994, A.D., 1995, Mother Millett, 2001; co-prodr., co-dir. film Three Lives, 1970; one-woman shows Minami Gallery, Tokyo, Judson Gallery, N.Y.C., 1967, Noho Gallery, N.Y.C., 1976, 79, 80, 82, 84, 86, 93, 99, 2001, Women's Bldg., L.A., 1977; drawings Andre Wanters Gallery, Berlin, 1980, Courtland Jessup Gallery, Provincetown, Mass., 1991, 92, 93, 94, 95, 98, 99, Retrospective Exhbn., U. Md., 1997, Hunter Coll., 1998, Northampton Ctr. for the Arts, 1998, John Jay Coll., N.Y.C., 1998, Nohs Gallery, 2002. Mem. Congress of Racial Equality; chmn. edn. com. NOW, 1966; active supporter gay and women's liberation groups, also mental patients liberation and political prisoners; UN rep. for polit. prisoners. Mem. Phi Beta Kappa. Office: 20 Old Overlook Rd Poughkeepsie NY 12603-6220

MILLIGAN, ANNETTE MARIE, secondary school educator; b. Pasadena, Texas, July 23, 1957; d. Anthony Vincent Nieves, Shirley Ruth and James Edward Trotter(Stepfather); m. Charles Edward Milligan, May 30, 1980; children: Jennifer Marisa, Alicia Gail, Sara Denise, Harry Edward. BA, U. Colo., Colorado Springs, 1999. Tchr. James Irwin Charter H.S., Colorado Springs, 2001—. Website design ArtQuest James Irwin Charter H.S., Colorado Springs, 1998—. Juried exhibition, Peacock Fantasy (Second Pl. cash award, (Air Force Worldwide Level), Textile Art, 2000 AIR FORCE ARTIST-CRAFTSMAN CONTEST, Randolph AFB, Tex., 2001), Abstraction to the Winds (STUDENT ART Exhbn., Gallery of Contemporary Art, U. of Colo., Colo. Springs, Colo., 1999), Peacock Fantasy (First Pl. , Textile Art, 2000 AIR FORCE ARTIST-CRAFTSMAN CONTEST, USAF Acad., Colo., 2000), Vase de Fleur (Flower Vase) (Second Pl. Maj. Command (MAJCOM) Level, Textile Art, 2000 AIR FORCE ARTIST-CRAFTSMAN CONTEST, USAF Acad., Colo., 2000), On Holiday (First Pl. , Digital Imaging and Enhancement, 2000 AIR FORCE PHOTOGRAPHY CONTEST, USAF Acad., Colo, 2000), Colorado Landscape (Second Pl. cash award, (Air Force Worldwide Level), Computer Imaging and Enhancement, 1999 AIR FORCE PHOTOGRAPHY CONTEST, Randolph AFB, T, 2000), (First Pl. , Textile Art, 1999 AIR FORCE ARTIST-CRAFTSMAN CONTEST, USAF Acad., Colo., 1999), juried for publication, (Publ. in riverrun, the student arts mag., 1999-2000 issue; U. of Colorado-Colorado Springs, 2000), juried competition, Lettuce (Painting included in Publicity Brochure for U. of Colorado-Colorado Springs, 1997), juried exhibition, Untitled (weaving with alternative materials) (STUDENT ART Exhbn., Gallery of Contemporary Art, U. of Colo., Colo. Springs, Colo., 1999). Co-comdr. varsity (high sch.) group AWANA Internat., Colorado Springs, 1986; co-leader H.S. youth group, Colorado Springs, 1999; 2nd v.p. Officers Spouses Club, Osan Air Base, 1994—96; sec. Protestant Women of the Chapel, Osan Air Base, Republic of, 1994—96; welfare treas. Officers Wives Club, Tyndall Air Force Base, Panama City, Fla., 1981—83. Recipient The Apple award (Vol. of the Yr.), Pacific Air Forces (PACAF), Am. Schs., 1996. Mem.: NOW in the Arts (assoc.), Nat. Art Educators Assn. (assoc.), Colo. Art Educators Assn. (assoc.). Republican. Avocations: swimming, travel, reading, painting. Office: James Irwin Charter High School 1626 South Murray Blvd Colorado Springs CO 80916 Office Fax: 1-719-576-8071. E-mail: annette.milligan@jamesirwinhigh.org.

MILLIGAN, SISTER MARY, theology educator, religious consultant; b. Los Angeles, Jan. 23, 1935; d. Bernard Joseph and Carolyn (Krebs) M. BA, Marymount Coll., 1956; Dr. de l'Univ., U. Paris, 1959; MA in Theology, St. Mary's Coll., Notre Dame, Ind., 1966; STD, Gregorian U., 1975; D. honoris causa, Marymount U., 1988. Tchr. Cours Marymount, Neuilly, France, 1956-59; asst. prof. Marymount Coll., Los Angeles, 1959-67; gen. councillor Religious of Sacred Heart of Mary, Rome, 1969-75, gen. superior, 1980-85; asst. prof. Loyola Marymount U., Los Angeles, 1977-78, provost, 1986-90, prof., 1990—, dean liberal arts, 1992-97, provincial superior, 1997—. Pres. bd. dirs. St. John's Sem., Camarillo, Calif., 1986-89; mem. exec. com. Internat. Union Superiors Gen., Rome, 1983-85; mem. planning bd. spiritual renewal program Loyola Marymount U., Los Angeles, 1976-78. Author: That They May Have Life, 1975; compiler analytical index Ways of Peace, 1986; contbr. articles to profl. jours. Vis. scholar Grad. Theol. Union, Berkeley, 1986. Mem. Calif. Women in Higher Edn., Coll. Theology Soc., Cath. Biblical Assn. Democrat. Roman Catholic. Home: 3216 Eagle St Los Angeles CA 90063-3121 E-mail: maryemilligan@earthlink.net.

MILLIKEN, MARY SUE, chef, television personality, writer; Former mem. staff Le Perroquet, Chgo., Restaurant d'Olympe, Paris; formerly chef, co-owner City Cafe, L.A.; chef, co-owner CITY, L.A., 1985—94, Border Grill, L.A., 1985—91, Santa Monica, 1990—. Co-host (TV series) Too Hot Tamales, 1995—, Tamales' World Tour, (radio show) Good Food; co-author: City Cuisine, 1989, Mesa Mexicana, 1994, Cantina, 1996, Cooking with Too Hot Tamales, 1997. Active Scleroderma Rsch. Found. Named Chef of Yr., Calif. Restaurant Writers, 1993. Mem.: Chef's Collaborative 2000, Women Chefs and Restaurateurs. Office: Border Grill 1445 4th St Santa Monica CA 90401

MILLIN, LAURA JEANNE, museum director; b. Elgin, Ill., June 11, 1954; d. Douglas Joseph and Patricia Ruth (Feragen) M. BA in Interdisciplinary Studies, The Evergreen State Coll., 1978. Dir. On The Boards, Seattle, 1979; art dir. City Fair Metrocenter YMCA, Seattle, 1980; dir. Ctr. on Contemporary Art, Seattle, 1981; co-owner Art in Form Bookstore, Seattle, 1981-89; co-dir. 3d internat festical of films by women dirs. Seattle Art Mus.. & 911 Contemporary Arts, 1988; auction coord. Allied Arts of Seattle, 1989; dir. Missoula (Mont.) Mus. of the Arts, 1990—. Dir. Visual AIDS Missoula Mus. of the Arts, 1989; curator Radio COCA, Ctr. on Contempoary Art, Seattle, 1986, co-curator, 1981, 83; lectr. in field. Co-editor: Another (ind. feminist newspaper), Seattle, 1989, editor: (exhibition catalog) James Turrell: Four Light Installations, 1981. Bd. dirs. Internat. Festival of Films by Women Dirs., Seattle, 1987, 89, Nine One One Comtemporary Arts Ctr., Seattle, 1981-87, bd. chmn. 1981-85; bd. advisors REFLEX (art mag.), Seattle, 1988-89, Ctr. on Contemporary Art, Seattle, 1983-86; state vis. Mont. Arts Coun., Missoula, 1991, NEA, Mpls., 1988, Chgo., 1987; ; panelist Mont. Arts Coun., Helena, 1990; cons. Seattle Arts Commn., 1989, juror, 1985. Home: 1721 S 9th St W Missoula MT 59801-3432 Office: Art Mus Missoula 335 N Pattee St Missoula MT 59802-4520

MILLMAN, AMY J. government official; b. Bklyn., June 12, 1954; m. Aug. 3, 1984; 2 children. BA in History, Carnegie Mellon U., 1976; MPA, George Washington U., 1978. Rschr. Congl. Quar., Inc., Washington, 1976-79; analyst OSHA, Dept. Labor, Washington, 1979-81; Washington rep. The Philip Morris Cos., Inc., 1981-91; dir. legis. affairs The Am. Trucking Assn., Inc., Washington, 1991-93; exec. dir. Nat. Women's Bus. Coun., Washington, 1993—2001; pres. Springboard Enterprises, 2001—. Adj. prof. George Washington U., Sch. Bus. and Public Mgmt., 2001—; bd. advisors Enterprising Woman Magazine, 2001—. Mem. Phi Kappa Phi.

MILLMAN, JOAN, state legislator; BA, Bklyn. Coll., 1962, MLS, 1974. Mem. 52nd Dist. N.Y. State Assembly, Albany, 1997—, mem. small bus. com., mem. aging com., mem. social svcs. com., mem. alcoholism and drug abuse com., mem. librs. and edn. tech. com.; elem. sch. tchr. Pub. Sch. 10, Bklyn., 1964-74, sch. libr., 1974-86. Ednl. cons. N.Y.C. Coun. Pres. Carol Bellamy and Senator Marty Connor, facilitator for comprehensive sch. devel. and planning. Mem. Ind. Neighborhood Dems., Bklyn. Heights Assn., Cadman Towers Assn.; bd. dirs. N.Y. State Bklyn. Devel. Zone; mem. South Bklyn. Enterprise Empowerment Zone, citywide adv. com. on mid. sch. initiatives; chairperson Kings County Dem. Com. Office: 341 Smith St Brooklyn NY 11231-4607

MILLMAN, MARILYN ESTELLE, elementary school educator; b. Lynn, MA, Nov. 28, 1936; d. Benjamin and Dora (Goldman) Millman. BS, Boston U., 1958. Elem. tchr. Beverly (Mass.) Sch. Dist., 1958—64, Lagunitas (Calif.) Sch. Dist., 1964—65, San Rafael (Calif.) City Schs., 1965—97; founder, pres. Marilyn Millman Scholarship Found., 1997—. Vol. chair and bd. dirs. Susan G. Komen Breast Cancer Found.

MILLS, ANNA M. realtor; b. Toledo, Aug. 27, 1949; d. George William and Ellen Louise (Eckert) Pethe; children: Lori Smotherman Derr, Jerry Donald II. Grad., Electronic Computer Programming Inst. Lic. real estate agt., Ohio, Mich., lic. builder Mich., Ohio. Realtor Century 21 Kasten, Toledo, 1977—. Owner Toledo properties; property mgr., Toledo, 1980—. Author: Landlord/Tenant Manual, 1994. Asst. leader Girl Scouts U.S., Toledo, 1979; leader Boy Scouts Am., Toledo, 1980; past pres. Elmhurst Sch. PTA, Toledo; adult advisor cheerleaders DeVeaux Jr. High Sch., Toledo, 1990-91, exec. sec., 1989—; dir. bd. trustees Housing Directions, 1993-96, exec. bd. dirs., 1996-98. Mem. Real Estate Investors Assn. (pres. 1996-99, state v.p. 1998, Ohio pres. 1999), Toledo Bd. Realtors, Monroe Bd. Realtors, Ohio Million Dollar Club, Million Dollar Club, Toastmasters (competent toastmaster, advanced toastmaster bronze, v.p., pres. 1998—), Women's Coun. of Realtors, Women's Entrepreneurial Network. Roman Catholic. Avocations: rental properties, cake decorating, travel. Home: 4741 Elmhurst Rd Toledo OH 43613-3036 Office: Century 21 Kasten 1421 S Reynolds Rd Toledo OH 43615-7413 Fax: 734-856-4745.

MILLS, CAROL MARGARET, business consultant, public relations consultant; b. Salt Lake City, Aug. 31, 1943; d. Samuel Lawrence and Beth (Neilson) M. BS magna cum laude, U. Utah, 1965. With W.S. Hatch Co., Woods Cross, Utah, 1965-87, corp. sec., 1970-87, traffic mgr., 1969-87, dir. publicity, 1974-87, cons. various orgns., 1988—. Bd. dirs. Intermountain Tariff Bur. Inc., 1978-88, chmn., 1981-82, 1986-87; bd. dirs. Mountainwest Venture Group. Fund raiser March of Dimes, Am. Cancer Soc., Am. Heart Assn.; active senatorial campaign, 1976, gubernatorial campaign, 1984, 88, congl. campaign, 1990, 92, 94, vice chair voting dist., 1988-90, congl. campaign, 1994, chmn. 1990-92, chmn. party caucus legis. dist.; witness transp. com. Utah State Legislature, 1984, 85; apptd. by gov. to bd. trustees Utah Tech. Fin. Corp., 1986—, corp. sec., mem. exec. com., 1988—; mem. expdn. to Antaractica, 1996, Titanic '96 expdn.; mem. Iceland and Greenland expdn., 2001; mem. Pioneer Theatre Guld, 1985--. Recipient Svc. awards W.S. Hatch Co., 1971, 80; VIP chpt. Easter Seal Telethon, 1989, 90, Outstanding Vol. Svc. award Easter Seal Soc. Utah, 1989, 90. Mem. Nat. Tank Truck Carriers, Transp. Club Salt Lake City, Am. Trucking Assn. (mem. pub. rels. coun.), Utah Motor Transport Assn. (bd. dirs. 1982-88), Internat. Platform Assn., Traveler's Century Club, Titanic Internat., Beta Gamma Sigma, Phi Kappa Phi, Phi Chi Theta. Home: HC 11 Box 329 Kamiah ID 83536-9410 Office: PO Box 1495 Kamiah ID 83536-1495

MILLS, CELESTE LOUISE, dog breeder, hypnotherapist, professional magician; b. LA, May 16, 1952; d. Emery John and Helen Louise (Bradbury) W.; m. Robert Richardson Feigel, Apr. 11, 1971 (div. 1973); m. Peter Alexander Mills, June 12, 1991. (div. 1992). BBA, Western State U., Doniphan, Mo., 1987; PhD in Religion, Universal Life Ch. Univ., 1987; grad., Hypnotism Tng. Inst., Glendale, Calif., 1990. Cert. hypnotherapist. Credit mgr. accounts receivable Gensler-Lee Diamonds, Santa Barbara, Calif., 1973-74, Terry Hinge and Hardware, Van Nuys, Calif., 1975-78; credit mgr., fin. analyst Peanut Butter Fashions, Chatsworth, Calif., 1978-82; personal mgr. Charter Mgmt. Co., Beverly Hills, Calif., 1982-83; co-owner, v.p. Noreen Jenney Communicates, Beverly Hills, 1983-85; corp. credit mgr., fin. analyst Ctrl. Diagnostic Lab., Tarzana, Calif., 1985-89; credit mgr., fin. analyst Metwest Clin. Lab., Inc., Tarzana, Calif., 1989-90; pvt. practice, clin. hypnotherapist Sherman Oaks, Calif., 1990—. Cons. Results Now, Inc., Tarzana, 1986-87; profl. magician Magic Castle, Hollywood, 1989—, Prodr., host (TV) Brainstorm, 1993—, Dances with Woofs, 2003. Media spokesperson Am. Cancer Soc., 1990—. Mem. NAFE, NOW, Nat. Humane Ednl. Found., Credit Mgrs. Assn. Trade Groups (bd. govs. 1988-89), Nat. Clin. Lab. Trade Group (chmn. 1988-89), Med. and Surg. Suppliers Trade Group (vice chmn. 1988-89, chmn. 1989-90), Soc. Am. Magicians, Acad. Magical Arts, Internat. Brotherhood of Magicians, Assn. Advanced Ethical Hypnosis, Am. Coun. Hypnotist Examiners, Golden Retriever Club of Am. (bd. dirs. LA chpt. 2002—). Avocations: scuba diving, sailing. Office Phone: 818-989-7999.

MILLS, DALE DOUGLAS, journalist; b. Seattle, Oct. 4, 1930; d. Donald Emery and Antoinette (Kinleyside) Douglas; m. William Russell Mills, Aug. 13, 1955; children: Lida Susan, William Tad Jr., Peter Donald, Jane Douglas. BA, U. Wash., 1952. Reporter Seattle Times, 1954-55, 74-83; asst. libr. Harvard U., 1955-56; editor Puget Soundings mag., 1968-71. Author: Deliver Us From Squid Roe, 1995. Mem. com. sign control Seattle City Coun., 1970-72; rsch. dir. City Coun. campaign; bd. mgrs. King County Juvenile Ct.; trustee Allied Arts Seattle; bd. dirs. King County Coun. for Prevention of Child Abuse and Neglect. Recipient awards for excellence in reporting Wash. Press Assn., Nat. Fedn. Press Women, Allied Daily Newspapers, C.B. Blethen Meml. award for disting. investigative reporting, Excellence award Soc. Profl. Journalists/Sigma Delta Chi. Mem.: Jr. League Seattle, Seattle Times Stars, Helen T. Bush Children's Hosp Guild., Sunset Club, Seattle Yacht Club, Kappa Kappa Gamma.

MILLS, DOLORES ELIZABETH, speech pathology/audiology services professional; d. José Gregorio Gutiérrez and María Ignacia C. de Baca; m. Nick Dean Mills, June 5, 1965; 1 child, Nikos Damian ; 1 child, Kyra Lois. BA, Highlands U., 1960; MA, U. Mo., 1962, U. N.Mex., 1966, Loyola Coll., 1997. Cert. clin. competence. Speech lang. pathologist Scottish Rite Children's Lang. Ctr., Balt., 1995—97, Gateway Sch., Balt., 1997—2000, Carlsbad Mcpl. Schs., N.Mex., 2000—03. Home: 1711 Loretta Ln Carlsbad NM 88220

MILLS, DOROTHY ALLEN, investor; b. New Brunswick, N.J., Dec. 14, 1920; d. James R. and Bertha Lovilla (Porter) Allen; m. George M. Mills, Apr. 21, 1945; children: Dianne Adele McKay, Dorothy Louise Sphatt. BA, Douglass Coll., New Brunswick, N.J., 1943. Investment reviewer Ctrl. Hanover Bank, N.Y.C., 1943-44; asst. to dir. of admissions and sec. undergrad. yrs. Douglass Coll., New Brunswick, 1944-45; sec., regional dir. O.P.A., Ventura, Calif., 1945-46; corp. sec. George M. Mills Inc., Highland Park, NJ, 1946-75; pvt. investor N. Brunswick, 1975—. Sr. v.p. Children Am. Revolution, N.J., 1965; active alumni com. Douglass Coll., 1990—. Recipient Douglass Alumni award, 1992. Mem. AAUW, New Brunswick Hist. Soc., DAR, English Speaking Union, Rutgers Alumni Faculty Club, Woman's League of Rutgers U., Princeton-Douglass Alumni Club, N. Brunswick Women's Club, Auxiliary Robert Wood Johnson Hosp. and Med. Sch. Republican. Mem. Dutch Reformed Ch. Avocations: travel, gardening, bridge. Home: 1054 Hoover Dr New Brunswick NJ 08902-3244

MILLS, DOROTHY JANE (DOROTHY Z. SEYMOUR), editor, consultant; b. Cleve., July 5, 1928; d. Henry Zander and Katherine Helen Reinert; m. Harold Seymour, May 21, 1949 (dec. Sept. 25, 1992); m. Roy Elburt Mills, Feb. 15, 1995. Student, Cleve. State U., 1946—49; BS, Case Western Res. U., 1950, MA, 19[illegible]. Cert. elem. and H.S. tchr. Ohio, N.Y. Tchr. Cleve. Pub. Schs., 1950—54, Parma Heights (Ohio) Pub. Schs., 1955—57, Pelham (N.Y.) Pub. Schs., 1957—63, Warwick (N.Y.) Pub. Schs., 1963—66; sr. editor Ginn & Co., Pubs., Boston, Lexington, Mass., 1967—73, Lexington, 1979—81; freelance writer, editor, cons., 1981—; owner Patrician Publs., Naples, Fla., 1998—. Cons. Stillpoint Pub., Walpole, NY, 1987—; freelance editor, 1987—95; lectr. in field. Author: (children's textbooks) Bill and the Fish, 1965, Brad and Nell, 1965, Stop Pretending, 1965, Ballerina Bess, 1965, Ann Likes Red, 1965, The Rabbit, 1965, The Tent, 1965, The Sandwich, 1965, Big Beds and Little Beds, 1965, (edn. text) Toad Charts, 1987, (novels) The Sceptre, 1998, 1999, The Labyrinth, 2003, (cookbook) Meatless Meat: A Book of Recipes for Meat Substitutes, 2001; co-author, editor: Fear Not to Sow Because of the Birds, 1988; ; co-author (with Harold Seymour): Baseball: The Early Years, 1960, Baseball: The Golden Age, 1971, Baseball: The People's Game, 1990; author: (autobiography) A Woman's Work: Writing Baseball History with Harold Seymour, 2004; co-author: (edn. text) Word Recognition, 1987, author short stories; contbr. articles to publs. Mem.: NASSH, SABR, AAUW. Avocations: piano playing, singing, traveling. Home and Office: Patrician Publs 300 Pier A Naples FL 34112 Office Phone: 239-775-2840.

MILLS, ELIZABETH JENNINGS, art educator; b. Baton Rouge, La., Feb. 19, 1947; d. Robert Bernard Jennings and Virginia Adelia (Lobdell) Jennings; m. Wilmer Riddle Millsm Dec. 28, 1967; children: Wilmer Hastings, Evelyn Kate, Virginia Young, John Jennings. BA in Art and English, La. State Univ., 1969. Agrl. missionary to Brazil S.Am. Presbyn. Ch. in U.S., La., 1972-80. Weaving demonstrator ch. and civic groups, St. Francisville, La., 1983—; guest lectr. James Madison U., Harrisonburg, Va., 1995. Dramatic monologue Fanny Mendlesolhm, 2004; exhbns. include Zeigler Mus., Jennings, La., 1993, La. State U., 1995, Cabaret Theater, 1995, La. Arts and Science Ctr. Mus., 1996; weaving exhibit Magnolia Mound Plantation, 2000; portrait show Eight First Ladies and Lecture, 2000; juried art show Grand Isle, La., 2003-04. Mem., officer, tchr. The Plains Presbyn. Ch., Zachary, La., 1980—; mem., officer Study Clubs/Book Clubs, Baton Rouge and Zachary, 1982—; vol. Baton Rouge Symphony, 1987-90; tour guide Plantation Homes St. Francisville Pilgrimage, West Feliciana, La., 1985—; mem. award grants panel, E.B.R. Parish, 2003, art com. Zachary Sch. Sys., 2004. Mem. Assoc. Women in the Arts (sec. 1991-93), Artist Guild of West Feliciana (bd. dirs. 1992—), The Weaving Group. Avocations: writing, poetry, weaving, book making, travelling to museums. Home: 22552 Old Scenic Hwy # 964 Zachary LA 70791-6222

MILLS, ELIZABETH SHOWN, genealogist, editor, writer; b. Cleve., Miss., Dec. 29, 1944; d. Floyd Finley Shown and Elizabeth Thulmar (Jeffcoat) Carver; m. Gary B. Mills, 1963; children: Clayton Bernard, Donna Rachal, Daniel Garland. BA, U. Ala., 1980. Cert. genealogist, geneal. lectr. Profl. geneal. writer, educator, 1972—; editor Nat. Geneal. Soc. Quar., Arlington, Va., 1987—2002. Faculty Samford U. Inst. of Genealogy and Hist. Rsch., Birmingham, Ala., 1980—; trustee Assn. for Promotion of Scholarship in Genealogy, N.Y., 1984-90; contract dir., cons. U. Ala., 1985-92; faculty Nat. Inst. of Geneal. Rsch., 1985-97. Author, editor, translator Cane River Creole Series, 6 vols.; author: Evidence: Citation and Analysis for the Family Historian, 1997, Professional Genealogy: A Manual for Researchers, Writers, Editors, Lecturers, and Librarians, 2001, Isle of Canes, 2004; contbr. articles to profl. jours. Trustee Nat. Bd. Certification Genealogists, 1984—, v.p., 1989-94, pres., 1994-96; trustee Assn. Profl. Genealogists, 1984-90, 92-94, regional v.p., 1988-89. Named Outstanding Young Women of Am. Jaycees, Gadsden, 1976, Outstanding Alumna award U. Ala. New Coll., Tuscaloosa, 1990. Fellow Am. Soc. Geneal. (sec. 1992-95, v.p. 1995-98, pres. 1998-2001), Nat. Geneal. Soc. (councilor 1987-92), Utah Geneal. Assn., Grady McWhiney Rsch. Found. (sr.); mem. Assn. Profl. Genealogists (Smallwood Svc. award, 1989). Republican. Roman Catholic.

MILLS, GLORIA ADAMS, energy service consultant; b. Chgo., Mar. 1, 1940; d. Edward Charles and Olive Margaret (McCarty) Adams; m. Peter Mills, Dec. 29, 1962 (div. July 1986). BA, Rosary Coll., River Forest, Ill., 1962, MALS, 1970; MBA, U. Chgo., 1976. Lit. chemist UOP, Inc., Des Plaines, Ill., 1962-70, supr. patent libr., 1970-77, mktg. engr., 1977-81, mgr. project devel., 1981-83; v.p. mktg. Covanta Waste to Energy, Inc., Fairfield, N.J., 1983-87, sr. v.p. mktg., 1987-89, exec. v.p. mktg., 1989-94, exec. v.p. bus. devel., 1994-01, ret., 2001. Chmn. of bd. Ambiente 2000 S.r.l., 1998-01, mem. indsl. adv. bd. So. Ill. U. Coll. Engring. and Tech., Carbondale, 1985-90, 2000—. Contbr. articles to profl. jours. Mem. ASME (solid waste processing div., medal of achievement 2001), Am. Chem. Soc. Avocations: travel, reading.

MILLS, HELENE AUDREY, education educator; b. Oct. 6, 1933; d. Paul Albert and Mabel Meister; m. Ray Mills, Apr. 17, 1954; children: Keith, Katherine (dec.), Kevin. BS in Family Life Edn., Wayne State U., 1954, MEd in Human Resources, 1965, EdD in Gen. Adminstrn., 1980. Supr., instr. Wayne State Coll. Edn., 1958-67; tchr. life studies, health edn. Seaholm H.S., Birmingham, Mich., 1967-72, 74-77, asst. to prin., 1974-77, asst. prin., 1978-79, prin., 1990-97, Derby Mid. Sch., Birmingham, 1980-90; asst. prof. Oakland U., Rochester Hills, Mich., 1997—. Adj. prof. Wayne State U., Detroit, 1989-91, Oakland U., Rochester, 1985-89, asst. prof., 1997—. Consulting editor Clearing Ho., 1985-97; contbr. articles to profl. jours. Mem. steering com. Meadowbrook Leadership Acad., 1984-87; mem. Detroit Strategic Planning Task Force, 1986-88; mem. exec. bd. Oakland County Youth Assistance, 1987-90; program chairperson women's group Northbrooke Ch., 1997-99, mem. adult ministries purpose com., 1998-99. Recipient PTSA Coun. Pres. award, 1982, Celebration of Women award Greater Detroit Coun. NA'AMAT USA, 1986, Exemplary Secondary Sch. award State Mich., 1991. Mem. NASCD, Nat. Staff Devel. Assn., Nat. Secondary Prins. Assn., Mich. Assn. Supervision and Curriculum Devel., Mich. Coun. Family Rels., Mich. Secondary Prins. Assn., Oakland County Secondary Prins. Assn. (pres. 1983-85, Prin. of the Yr. 1991), Phi Delta Kappa (chmn. mem. Oakland br. 1998—). Office: Oakland U 311 Odowd Hall Rochester Hills MI 48309-4423 E-mail: mills@oakland.edu.

MILLS, IANTHER MARIE, minister; b. Washington, Nov. 27, 1956; d. Jimmie Lee Williamson and Sarah Edna House; m. Hilton Earl Mills, Oct. 8, 1992. BS in math., Georgetown U., 1978; MS in computer sci., U. of NC, 1983; MBA, U. of Okla., 1987; MDiv summa cum laude, Wesley Theol. Sem., 1997, DMin, 2003. Ordained Elder United Meth. Ch., 2000, Ordained Deacon United Meth. Ch., 1997. Sr. software engr. TRW Inc, Hanover, Md., 1980—85; sr. cons. Booz, Allen, & Hamilton, Vienna, Va., 1986—87; sect. head/program mgr. TRW, Inc., Columbia, Md., 1987—90; dept./program mgr. GTE Govt. Systems, Rockville, Md., 1990—95; assoc. pastor Catonsville U.M. Ch., Md., 1997—2000; sr. pastor Good Hope Union U.M. Ch., Silver Spring, Md., 2000—. Mem. Black Clergywomen of the U.M.C., 1997—; mem., bd. of dirs. Suburban Pastoral Counseling Ctr., Catonsville, Md., 1997—2000. Mem. NAACP. Recipient Dalghren medal, Georgetown U., 1978; scholar Yokey award, U. of Okla., 1985—86; Pogue fellowship, U. of NC at Chapel Hill, 1978—79. Democrat-Npl. United Methodist. Avocations: golf, quilting. Office: Good Hope Union United Methodist Church 14680 Good Hope Rd Silver Spring MD 20905-6018

MILLS, KATHRYN, publishing executive, director; b. Nyack, N.Y., July 14, 1955; d. Charles Wright and Ruth (Harper) M.; m. Michael Moore, Aug. 25, 1984; 1 child, Eric Mills Moore. BS in Polit. Econs., Hampshire Coll., 1976. Facilitator housing and svcs. Mission Hill Planning Commn., Boston, 1978-81; from editl. asst. trade and reference divsn. to dir. contracts

Houghton Mifflin Co., Boston, 1982—2001, dir. contracts, trade and reference divsn., 2001—. Editor: C. Wright Mills: Letters and Autobiographical Writings, 2000. Mem. NOW, Audubon Soc., Pub. Citizen. Avocations: photography, patchwork quilting. Office: Houghton Mifflin Co 222 Berkeley St Fl 7 Boston MA 02116-3764

MILLS, KIM I. director; b. Rockville Centre, N.Y., Aug. 8, 1953; d. Donald L. and Genevieve Mills; life ptnr. Kimberly J. Smith. BA, Barnard Coll., 1975; MA, NYU, 1981. Publicity asst. Simon & Schuster, N.Y.C., 1975—76, Hawthorn Books, 1976—77; pub. rels. asst. dir. Am. Hotel & Motel Assn., 1977—80; reporter, editor The AP, 1981—95; comm. dep. dir. Human Rights Campaign, 1996—98, edn. dir., asst. v.p., 1998—. Mem. bd. advisors The Diversity Factor; equal opportunity advisor Monster.com; mem. nat. adv. bd. Out & Equal Workplace Advocates. Paul Miller Wash. Reporting fellow, Freedom Forum, 1989. Mem.: Nat. Lesbian and Gay Journalists Assn. Office: Human Rights Campaign 1640 Rhode Island Ave NW Washington DC 20036 E-mail: kim.mills@hrc.org.

MILLS, LINDA S. public relations executive; b. San Antonio, June 26, 1951; d. Frank M. and Betty A. (Young) M. BA, St. Mary's U., 1971. Asst. dir. Paseo Del Rio Assn., San Antonio, 1971-74; mktg. officer Frost Nat. Bank, San Antonio, 1974-79; account exec. Fleishman-Hillard Inc., St. Louis, 1979-81, v.p., sr. ptnr., 1981-85, exec. v.p., sr. ptnr., 1985-97, dir. corp. planning, 1986-97; sr. exec. v.p. comm. SBC Comm. Inc., San Antonio, 1997—. Mem. adv. bd. St. John's Mercy Med. Ctr.; bd. trustees St. Mary's U. Mem. Pub. Relations Soc. Am., Noonday Club. Office: SBC Comm Inc PO Box 2933 San Antonio TX 78299-2933

MILLS, LOIS JEAN, design company executive, retired education educator, aide; b. Chgo., Oct. 20, 1939; d. Martin J. and Annabelle M. (Hrabik) Rademacher; m. Frederick V. Mills, Dec. 1, 1974; children: Todd, Susan, Randal, Merre, Mollie, Michael, Mark (dec.). BS in Edn., Ill. State U., Normal, 1962, MS in Edn., 1969. Lectr. elem. curriculum Ill. State U., 1973-90; in-svc. advisor for elem., gifted, critical thinking and study skills, coop. learning Title I State Bd. Edn., Springfield, Ill., 1969-90; elem. tchr., supr. Metcalf Lab. Sch. Ill. State U., 1962-72; legis. aide to Asst. Majority Leader Senator John Maitland, Jr., Ill. Gen. Assembly, 1990-95; pres., ptnr. Mills Design Assocs., 1996—. Mem. state rep. Dan Rutherford's house task force for statute repeal, 1995—, adv. roundtable, 1995—, legis. task force for cmty. residential svcs. deaf adults, 1995—; campaign coord. Asst. Majority Leader Senator John Maitland, Jr., 1995—; county campaign coord. for Ill. Comptroller Loleta Didrickson, 1994-98. Contbr. articles to profl. jours. Pres. Leadership Ill., 1994—, pres.-elect, 1993-94; past pres. governing bd. Lake Bloomington Assn., v.p., 1993-94, pres., 1994-95; mem. mgmt. com. McLean County 21st Century commn., 1991-92, vice chair cmty. rels., 1991-92; commr. McLean County Regional Planning commn., vice chair 1994-95; charter bd. govs. Ill. Lincoln Excellence in Pub. Svc. Series, 1994—, charter bd. dirs., Save the Patient health edn. and resources orgn., other civic activities; mem. Ill. steering com. Beijing-UN Women's Conf. One Yr. Later, 1996; mem. gov.'s commn. on status of women, Econ. Opportunities Working Group, 1998-, State U. Annuitants Assn. and Found. Social Security Equity/Offset. Recipient Exemplary Tchr. awards Ill. State U. Student Elem. Edn. Bd., Women of Distinction award YWCA of McLean County, Ill. State Univ. Alumni Assn. Svc. Awd. Mem. NAFE, Ill. State U. Alumni Assn. (bd. dirs. 1982—, internat. pres. 1992-94, 1994—), McLean County Rep. Women's Club (v.p. 1986, pres. 1987, past pres. 1988), Ill. Rep. Committeewoman's Roundtable, Ill. Fedn. Rep. Women, Nat. Fedn. Rep. Women, Internat. Platform Assn. Home: K-162 Lake Bloomington 25306 Arrowhead Ln Hudson IL 61748-9414

MILLS, PATRICIA JAGENTOWICZ, political philosophy educator, writer; b. Newark, Mar. 18, 1944; d. Alexander A. and Louise A. (Breunig) Jagentowicz; 1 child, Holland. BA, Rutgers U., 1973; MA, SUNY, Stony Brook, 1975; PhD, York U., Toronto, Ont., Can., 1984. Lectr. U. Toronto, 1984—85, vis. scholar, 1985—86, asst. prof. philosophy, 1986—88; asst. prof. polit. theory U. Mass., Amherst, 1988—91, assoc. prof. polit. theory, 1991—. Vis. scholar Pembroke Ctr. for Tchg. and Rsch. on Women, Brown U., 1999-2000; lectr. philosophy dept. Smith Coll., spring 1992; manuscript referee Social Scis. and Humanities Rsch. Coun. Can., 1985-86, 87-88, 91-92, Polity: Jour. of Northeastern Polit. Sci. Assn., 1990, 91; invited spkr. New Sch. for Social Rsch., 1990, Coll. Holy Cross, 1991, NEH seminar, Mt. Holyoke Coll., 1992, U. Pitts., 1993, Antigone Conf., SUNY Buffalo, 1997; presenter paper 20th World Congress Philosophy, 1998. Author: Woman, Nature, and Psyche, 1987; editor: Feminist Interpretations of G.W.F. Hegel, 1996; author, contbr.: (book chpts.) The Sexism of Social and Political Theory: Women and Reproduction from Plato to Nietzsche, 1979, Ethnicity in a Technological Age, 1988, Taking Our Time: Feminist Perspectives on Temporality, 1989, Renewing the Earth: The Promise of Social Ecology, 1990, The Future of Continental Philosophy and the Politics of Difference, 1991, Ecological Feminist Philosophies, 1996, The Phenomenology of Spirit Reader, 1998, Hegel and Law, 2002; contbr. articles to profl. jours. Bd. dirs. Drop-In Ctr., Newark, 1972-73; mem. N.J. Abortion Project, 1971-73; mem. Fortune Soc., N.J., 1972; grassroots organizer against the war in Vietnam, N.J., 1970-71; grassroots organizer women's movement, N.J. and N.Y., 1971-73. Recipient Disting. Tchg. award Delta Lambda chpt. Pi Sigma Alpha Honor Soc., U. Mass., 1997; postdoctoral fellow Social Scis. and Humanities Rsch. Coun. Can., 1983-85; scholar York U., 1975; faculty grantee for tchg. U. Mass., 1991-92. Mem. Am. Philos. Assn. (conf. presenter 1995 meeting), Soc. for Phenomenology and Existential Philosophy (presenter conf. papers 1988, 91, 92), Hegel Soc., Ancient Philosophy Soc., Soc. for the Study of Women Philosophers. Office: U Mass Thompson Hall Dept Polit Sci Amherst MA 01003 E-mail: pjmills@polsci.umass.edu.

MILLS, PAULETTE EVERETT, human development educator, consultant; b. Anaconda, Mont., Sept. 4, 1944; d. Flora Marie Thoft Everett and Paul Joseph Everett, Jr.; m. Barry Davis Mills, Oct. 7, 1978. PhD, U. Wash., Seattle, 1994. Cert. aarly childhood tchr. Wash., 1989. Educator II, head tchr. Exptl. Edn. Unit, U. Wash., Seattle, 1969—73, educator III, supr., 1973—74, child study clinic educator, 1974—75; early childhood edn. specialist Bozeman Pub. Schs./Mont. Regional Svcs., Belgrade, 1975—76, Bozeman Pub. Schools, Mont., 1976—80; asst. prof. edn. Doane Coll., Crete, Nebr., 1980—84; pres. Parent & Child, Inc., Seattle, 1984—85; coord. rural svcs. providers, project testing coord. longitudinal curriculum comparison project Exptl. Edn. Unit, U. Wash., Seattle, 1985—88, follow-up rsch. coord. and testing coord., least restrictive environment model devel. project, 1988—90, follow-up rsch. coord. and testing coord., selected lang. intervention components evaluation rsch. project, 1990—94; asst. prof. of human devel. Wash. State U., Pullman, 1994—99, assoc. prof. of human devel., 1999—. Cons. Birth to Six planning project Dept. Social and Health Svcs., Olympia, Wash., 1989—90. Contbr. articles to profl. jours. Mem.: ASCD, Soc. for Rsch. in Child Devel., Nat. Assn. for Edn. of Young Children, Coun. for Exceptional Children, Am. Coun. on Rural Spl. Edn. (Mem. of Yr. 1991). Avocation: breeding, training and riding American Quarter Horses. Office: Wash State Univ PO Box 646236 Pullman WA 99164-6236

MILLS, REBECCA, national park administrator; BA, Swarthmore Coll., 1961; MSW, U. Calif., Berkeley, 1968. Cmty. and individual social work, 1963-69; adminstrv. analyst Statewide Pres.'s Office U. Calif., 1969-72; exec. dir. Advocates for Women Econ. Devel. Ctr., 1972-76; cons. in fundraising and tng. Stanford U., Girl Scouts USA, others, 1976-78; equal opportunity mgr., chief youth programs Western Regional Nat. Park Svc., 1978-95; supr. Gt. Basin Nat. Park, 1995—. Office: Great Basin Nat Pk Hwy 488 Baker NV 89311

MILLS, ROSIE ERICA, nursing educator; b. Dominica, Feb. 6, 1941; d. Leonard and Icilma Riviere; m. Rooseworth Mills, June 15, 1968 (div. Apr. 1977); 1 child, Rohan W. B in Profl. Studies, Audrey Cohen Coll., 1994; M in Adult Edn., Fordham U., 1996; postgrad., Walden U., 1998—. Cert. nursing asst. Med. Aid. Tngr. Sch., N.Y.C., 1991—96; exec. dir. William Hodson Cmty. Ctr. Inc., Bronx, NY, 1996—. Activities leader Laconia Nursing Home, Bronx, 1991—96; pres., CEO Wentworth & Assocs.; adj. prof. Met. Coll.N.Y. Exec. dir. William Hodson Sr. Ctr. Mem.: NAFE, Profl. Woman Spkrs. Bur., Profl. Woman Network. Home: 620 Batchester Ave 23J Bronx NY 10475 Office Phone: 718-538-1515.

MILLS, STEPHANIE ELLEN, writer; b. Berkeley, Calif., Sept. 11, 1948; d. Robert C. and Edith (Garrison) M.; m. Philip Thiel (div. 1990). BA, Mills Coll., 1969. Campus organizer Planned Parenthood, Alameda, San Francisco, Calif., 1969-70; editor in chief Earth Times, San Francisco, 1970; story editor Earth, San Francisco, 1971; conference facilitator Mills Coll., Oakland, 1973-74; writer family planning program Emory Univ., Atlanta, 1974; dir. outings program Friends of the Earth, San Francisco, 1975-76, dir. membership devel., 1976-78; fellow Found. for Nat. Progress, San Francisco, 1978-80; from asst. editor to editor CoEvolution Quar., Sausalito, Calif., 1980-82; editor in chief, rsch. dir. Calif. Tomorrow, San Francisco, 1982-83; dir. devel. World Coll. West, San Rafael, Calif., 1983-84; freelance writer, lectr., 1984—; adj. prof. Grand Valley State Univ., Traverse City, Mich., 2002. V.p. Earth First! Found., 1986-89; pres. No. Mich. Environ. Action Coun., 1987-88; mem. planning com. Great Lakes Bioregional Congress, 1991; pres. bd. dirs. Oryana Natural Foods Coop., 1992-93; mem. adv. coun. Earth Island Inst., mem. adv. bd. Orion Soc., mem. Am. for Maine Woods, Nat. Park Adv. com., Northwoods Wilderness Recovery. Author: In Service of the Wild: Restoring and Reinhabiting Damaged Land, 1995, Whatever Happened to Ecology?, 1989, Epicurean Simplicity, 2002; editor: Turning Away from Technology: A New Vision for the Twenty-first Century, 1997 (Utne Visionary award 1996); editor, contbr. In Praise of Nature, 1990; corr. Wild Earth; editor-in-chief Not Man Apart newsletter from Friends of the Earth, 1978; editl. adv. E; contbr. to Ency. Brit. Book of Yr., 1998; contbr. articles to popular mags. Bd. dirs. Planned Parenthood Fedn. Am., 1970-76. Recipient award Mademoiselle, 1969, Friends of UN Environ. Program, 1987; grantee Point Found., 1972, IRA-HITI Found., 1992; resident Blue Mountain Ctr., 1983, 86. Avocations: swimming, cooking. Office: care Katinka Matson Brockman Inc 5 E 59th St New York NY 10022-1027

MILLS, SUSAN W. music educator; b. Louisville, Ky., Nov. 12, 1962; BA, Rollins Coll., 1984; MA, U. Ctrl. Fla., 1991, Ed. D, 1999. Dir. sch. music St. Margaret Mary Sch., Winter Park, Fla., 1990—97; dir. children and youth music First Presbyn. Ch., Orlando, 1997—98; vis. asst. prof. U. Ctrl. Fla., Orlando, 1998—2000; asst. prof. Frostburg State U., Md., 2000—. Office: Frostburg State U PAC 104 Music Dept Frostburg MD 21532

MILMAN, DORIS HOPE, retired pediatrics educator, psychiatrist; b. N.Y.C., Nov. 17, 1917; d. Barnet S. and Rose (Smoleroff) Milman; m. Nathan Kreeger, June 15, 1941; 1 child, Elizabeth Kreeger Goldman. BA, Barnard Coll., 1938; MD, NYU, 1942. Diplomate Am. Bd. Pediat.; lic. physician, N.Y. Intern Jewish Hosp., Bklyn., 1942-43, resident, 1944-46, fellow in pediat., 1946-47; postgrad. extern in psychiatry Bellevue Hosp., N.Y.C., 1947-49; attending pediat. psychiatrist Jewish Hosp., Bklyn., 1950-56; asst. prof. pediat. Health Sci. Ctr. at Bklyn. SUNY, 1956-67, assoc. prof., 1967-73, prof., 1973 93, prof. emeritus, 1993—, acting chmn. dept. pediat., 1973-75, 82. Pvt. practice child and adolescent psychiatry, Bklyn., 1950-90; vis. prof. Ben Gurion U. of the Negev, Beersheva, Israel, 1977. Co-editor: AAP Adolescent Newsletter, 1993—; copyeditor: Bellevue Lit. Rev., 2001—. Mem. adv. bd. N.Y. Assn. for the Learning Disabled, N.Y.C., 1975-80. Recipient Disting. Alumna award Barnard Coll., 1986, Solomon R. Berson Achievement award NYU Sch. Medicine, 1991; Grace Potter Rice fellow Barnard Coll., 1938-39. Fellow Am. Acad. Pediat. (emeritus), Am. Psychiat. Assn. (disting. life fellow); mem. AAAS, Am. Orthopsychiat. Assn. (life), Am. Pediat. Soc. (emeritus), N.Y. Pediat. Soc. (emeritus), Phi Beta Kappa, Alpha Omega Alpha. Home: 2373 Broadway Apt 2028 New York NY 10024-2842

MILNE, LORNA, Canadian senator; b. Toronto, ON, Can., Dec. 13, 1934; BS in Agr., U. Guelph. Adminstr., lectr. Physics Dept. U. Guelph; senator The Senate of Can., Ottawa, 1995—. Trustee, vice-chair Peel County Bd. Edn. Bd. dirs. Peel County Mus., Brampton and Dist. YM-YWCA and Rapport House; former chair Brampton and Dist. Assn. for Mentally Retarded; former pres. Brampton and Dist. Univ. Women's Club. Mem.: Heart and Stroke Found. Ont. (residential coord.), Ont. Automobile Ins. Bd. Liberal. Office: 247 East Block The Senate of Canada Ottawa ON Canada K1A 0A4

MILNER, DEBBI ELISSA, computer company executive; m. John Milner; 2 children. BA in English Lit., History, SUNY, Binghamton, 1981. Prin., owner Jade Sys. Corp., Cold Spring, NY, 1984—. Office: Jade Systems Corp 3377 Rte 9 Cold Spring NY 10516

MILNER ANDERSON, KATHERINE, broadcast executive; BA in Edn., U. Miss., 1969. Dir., exec. sec. Dept. Transp., Washington, 1981-83; assoc. dir. Offive of Cabinet, White Ho., Washington, 1983-84; dir. Corp. Pub. Broadcasting, Washington; chief fin. officer Team Washington, Inc., Alexandria, Va., 1986—. Bd. dirs. Columbia Hosp. Women Found. Chair Am. Cancer Soc. Ball; sponsor Spl. Olympics, Barbados. Office: Corp Pub Broadcasting 901 E St NW Ste 300 Washington DC 20004-2012

MILNOR, HAZEL, nurse; b. Marble, Ark., Apr. 2, 1921; d. Andrew Jackson and Laura Jane (Davis) Spencer; m. John Champion Milnor, June 21, 1951 (dec. Aug. 1989); children: Mary Christine, Jean Ann Laura. RN, Calif., Hawaii. Nurse pvt. duty, Calif., 1942—; surg. nurse Queen's Hosp., Hawaii, 1944-46; flight attendant United Airlines, San Francisco, 1946-51. Author: Entertaining in Hawaii, 1977, (poetry) As Angels Watch, 1997. Founding pres. Spl. Angels Ministry, Hawaii; chair develop. com. Spl. Angels. Inducted Internat. Poetry Hall of Fame. Mem. Assn. Retarded Citizens, Angel Collector's Club Am., Clipped Wings (mem.-at-large, mem. coms.), Internat. Soc. Poets (disting.), Oahu Country Club. Republican. Episcopalian. Avocations: collecting angels, travel.

MILOY, LEATHA FAYE, university program director; b. Marlin, Tex., Mar. 12, 1936; d. J. D. and Leola Hazel (Rhudy) Hill; m. John Miloy, June 20, 1960; children: Tyler Hill, David Reed, Nancy Lee. BA, Sam Houston State U., 1957; MS, Tex. A&M U., 1967, PhD, 1978. Dir. pub. affairs Gulf Univs. Rsch. Corp., College Station, Tex., 1966-69; asst. dir. Ctr. for Marine Resources Tex. A&M U., College Station, 1974-76, dir. edn. svcs., 1974-78; dir. info. and spl. svcs. Tex. Woman's U., Denton, 1978-79; asst. v.p. univ. advancement S.W. Tex. State U., San Marcos, 1979-83, asst. to pres., 1983-84, v.p. student and instl. rels., 1984-90, v.p. univ. advancement, 1990-93, dir. capital campaign, 1993-98. Vis. lectr. humanities and sea U. Va., 1972-73; cons. Office Tech. Assessment, Washington, 1976-86, Tex. A&M U., Galveston, 1979-82, Bemidji State U., Glassboro State Coll., 1984; mem. Task Force on Edn. and Pub. Interest, 1987-88. Editor: The Ocean From Space, 1969; author, editor Sea Grant 70's, 1970-79 (Sea Grant award 1973-74); contbr. articles to profl. jours. Ad hoc mem. Marine Resources Coun. Tex., Austin, 1971-72, Tex. Energy Adv. Coun., 1974-75; chmn. United Way, Bryan, Tex., 1976; com. mem. various local elections, 1974-78. NSF grantee, 1970-78; recipient Marine Resources Info. award NSF, 1969-71, Tex. Energy Info. award Gov.'s Office, 1974-75, Tex. Water Info. award Dept. Interior, 1977-79. Mem. Nat. Soc. Fundraising Execs., Coun. for the Advancement and Support Edn. (bd. dirs. 1979-81, Disting. Achievement award 1998), Coun. Student Svcs. (v.p. Tex. 1988-90). Avocations: reading, painting, fishing. Home: PO Box 752 Buchanan Dam TX 78609-0752 E-mail: lmiloy@tstar.net.

MILSTED, AMY, biomedical educator; BSEd, Ohio State U., 1967; PhD, CUNY, 1977. Lectr. Hunter Coll./CUNY, 1970-76; instr. Carnegie-Mellon U., Pitts., 1976-77; postdoctoral fellow Muscular Dystrophy Assn./Carnegie-Mellon U., Pitts., 1978-79; rsch. assoc. Case Western Res. U., Cleve., 1979-82; rsch. chemist VA Med. Ctr., Cleve., 1982-87; project staff The Cleve. Clin. Found., 1987-89; asst. staff dept. brain and vascular rsch. Cleve. Clinic Found., 1989-93; grad. faculty Sch. Biomed. Scis. Kent (Ohio) State U., 1995—; assoc. prof. dept. biology U. Akron, Ohio, 1993-2000, prof. biology, 2000—. Contbr. articles to profl. jours. Fellow Am. Heart Assn.; mem. AAAS, Inter-Am. Soc. Hypertension, Am. Chem. Soc., Endocrine Soc., Assn. Women in Sci. Office: Univ Akron Dept Biology Asec 279 Akron OH 44325-3908 E-mail: milsted@uakron.edu.

MILTON, BARBARA ELLA, II, psychotherapist; b. Camden, NJ, May 13, 1959; d. Barbara Ella Milton Sr.; m. S.Kay Osborn, Jan. 8, 2002; children: Tania Kirkman, Ian Kirkman. BA, Seton Hill Coll., 1982; MSW, Rutgers U., 2001; postgrad., CUNY/Hunter Coll. Lic. social workder NJ. Lic. social worker State Bd. of Social Work Examiners, Trenton, NJ, 2001, cert. social worker, 1994—2001; school social worker Dept. Edn., Trenton, 2001. Pres. Imani Comms., Jersey City, 1995—. Mem. NAACP; workforce investment bd. YWCA of Central NJ, Hackensack, 1996—98; mem. Human Svcs. Adv. Coun., Hackensack, 1996—98; bd. dirs. YWCA of Central NJ, New Brunswick, 1992—95. Recipient Mark Foreman award, Rutgers U., 2001; fellow, CUNY Hunter Coll., 2001. Mem.: NASW, Juvenile Detention Assn., Avanta-Satir Network. Avocations: travel, sports. Office: Jersey City Med Ctr Liberty Health Sys 50 Baldwin St II-Ctr Bldg Jersey City NJ 07304

MILTON, CAROL LYNNE, artist; b. N.Y.C., June 23, 1947; d. August William Thiel and Ruth Elizabeth Gilbert; m. Thomas Macon Milton, Mar. 31, 1973; 1 child, Nicholas John. Sec. Herndon (Va.) Oldtown Gallery, 1989-90, treas., 1990-91; pres. Reston (Va.) Arts Gallery, 1991-92, treas., 1992-93; v.p. Vienna (Va.) Arts Soc. Inc., 1994-95, pres., 1995-98, bd. dirs., 1998-2001. Art program provider Gt. Falls. (Va.) Womens Club, Mobil Wife's Club; chair VAS Gallery, 2000-01, dir., 2001—. Watercolor painter, 1993—; exhbns. include Herndon (Va.) Old Town Gallery, 1988, Reston (Va.) Art Gallery, 1991, 92, Reston Health Club, 1992, Patrick Henry Libr., Vienna, Va., 1991, 97, 99, Reston Cmty. Art Ctr., 1992, Cameron Glenn Ctr., Reston, 1992, Vienna Town Hall, 1995, Hannabils Coffee House, Vienna, 1996, Thomas Jefferson Libr., Falls Church, Va., 1996. Art show provider Arts in Pub. Places, metro D.C. area, 1989—; mural painter Our Lady of Good Coun., Vienna, 1996; calendar artist Town of Vienna, 1998, mem. mural project com. Town of Vienna, 1999. Mem.: Vienna Art Soc. (chmn. bd. dirs. 2001, dir. gallery 2001—04, workshop coord. Vienna Art Ctr. 2004—). Avocations: gardening, gourmet cooking, antiquing, traveling. Studio: 10311 Yellow Pine Dr Vienna VA 22182-1344 E-mail: tmilton@cox.net., miltons22182@yahoo.com.

MILTON, CATHERINE HIGGS, social service entrepreneur; b. N.Y.C., Jan. 6, 1943; d. Edgar Homer and Josephine (Doughty) Higgs; m. A. Fenner Milton (div.); m. Thomas F. McBride, Aug. 25, 1974 (dec. Oct. 31, 2003); children: Raphael McBride, Luke McBride. BA, Mt. Holyoke Coll., 1964, PhD (hon.), 1992. Reporter, travel writer Boston Globe, 1964-68; with Internat. Assn. Chiefs Police, Washington, 1968-70; asst. dir. Police Found., Washington, 1970-75; spl. asst. U.S. Treasury Dept., Washington, 1977-80; project staff Spl. Com. Aging/Senate, Washington, 1980-81; spl. asst. to pres., founder/exec. dir. Stanford (Calif.) U. Haas Ctr. for Public, 1981-91; exec. dir. Commn. for Nat. and Cmty. Svc., Washington, 1991-93; v.p. Corp. for Nat. Svc., Washington, 1993-95; exec. dir. Presidio Leadership Ctr., 1995-96; exec. dir. U.S. Programs Save the Children, Westport, Conn., 1996—2002; pres. Friends of the Children, Portland, Oreg., 2002—. Mem. U.S. Atty. General's Task Force on Family Violence, 1981-82; chair nat. forum Kellogg Found., 1990. Author: Women in Policing, 1972, Police Use of Deadly Force, 1976; co-author: History of Black Americans, 1965, Team Policing, Little Sisters and the Law, 1970. Bd. mem. Youth Svc. Calif., L.A., 1986-91, Trauma Found., San Francisco, 1982-90; spl. advisor Campus Compact, 1986-91 Nat. Kellogg Found. fellow, Battle Creek, Mich., 1985-88; recipient Dedication and Outstanding Efforts award Bd. Suprs., Santa Clara, Calif., 1989, Outstanding Vol. Contbn. award Strive for Five, San Francisco, 1991, Dinkelspiel award Stanford U., 1991; named Outstanding Campus Adminstr. COOL, 1987. Avocations: backpacking, skiing, hiking, travel. Home: 3652 SE Oak St Portland OR 97214 Office: Friends of the Children 44 NE Morris St Portland OR 97214

MILTON-JONES, DELISHA, professional basketball player; b. Riceboro, Ga., Sept. 11, 1974; d. Beverly Milton; m. Roland Jones, June 30, 2003. BA in Sports Mgmt., U. Fla. Forward Portland Power, 1997—99, L.A. Sparks, 1999—; forward Ekaterinburg team/EuroLeague, Russia, 2002—; mem. USA Basketball Women's Sr. Nat. Team, 2004. Recipient gold medal, Olympic Games, 2000, World Championships, 1998, 2002, U.S. Olympic Cup, 1999, World Univ. Games, 1997, U.S. Olympic Festival, 1994. Office: Los Angeles Sparks 555 N Nash St El Segundo CA 90245*

MIMS, CLARICE ROBERTA, financial advisor; b. New York, Dec. 26, 1947; d. Clarence Robert Mims and Victoria Antoinette Tynes; 1 child, Dawn Imani Dawson. BS in Art Edn., Hampton Inst., 1969; MS in Urban Edn., Syracuse U., 1972; postgrad. in bus., NYU, 1972-74; Cert. Computer Techs., MIT, 1985; MEd in Supervision and Adminstrn., Bank St. Coll. Edn., 1995. Lic. securities, life and health ins.; cert. tchr. Acct. exec. 3M Corp., Caldwell, N.J., 1976-78; acct. exec., tech. cons. AT&T, New York, 1978-85; pres., cons. Mims Cons., New York, 1985-87; educator N.Y.C. Bd. Edn., Bklyn., 1987-95, cons. Chancellor's Dist., 1996-98; personal fin. adv. Am. Express Fin. Advs., Langhorne, Pa., 1999—. Pres., owner Loral Devel. Corp., N.Y.C., 1983-84, DSL Mortgage Co., N.Y.C., 1990-92. V.p. mktg. Black Edn. Network, N.Y.C., 1996-99; mem. adv. bd. African Am. Leadership Summit, Bklyn., 1995-97. Mem. Am. Bridge Assn., Alpha Kappa Alpha. Avocations: art, writing, bridge, guitar, piano.

MINARCZIK, JENNIFER ANN, communications company executive; b. Parma, Ohio, Oct. 23, 1973; d. Dennis Alan and Martha Lee (Mason) M. BS in Latin Am. and Leadership Studies, U. Richmond, Va., 1995. Coord. Joint Rep. Campaign, Richmond, 1995; legis. aide Senator Emmett Hanger, Richmond, 1996; dep. campaign mgr. Friends of Richard Cullen, Richmond, 1996; comm. coord. Dole/Kemp '96, Richmond, 1996; polit. affairs coord. GTE Corp., Washington, 1996-98, staff mgr. govt. advocacy planning, 1998—. Mem. Henrico County Rep. Com., Richmond, 1995-97, Arlington County (Va.) Rep. Com., 1997. Gov.'s fellow, Richmond, 1995. Mem. Women in Govt. Rels. Avocations: golf, running, swimming. Office: GTE 1850 M St NW Ste 1200 Washington DC 20036-5893 Home: 5270 Duke St Apt 210 Alexandria VA 22304-2944

MINARIK, ELSE HOLMELUND (BIGART MINARIK), author; b. Aarhus, Denmark, Sept. 13, 1920; d. Kaj Marius and Helga Holmelund; m. Walter Minarik, July 14, 1940 (dec.); 1 child, Brooke Ellen; m. Homer Bigart, Oct. 3, 1970 (dec.). BA, Queens Coll., 1942. Tchr. 1st grade, art Commack (N.Y.) Pub. Schs., 1950-54. Author children's books: Little Bear, 1957, Father Bear Comes Home, 1959, Little Bear's Friend, 1960, Little Bear's Visit, 1961, No Fighting, No Biting, 1958, Cat and Dog, 1960, The Winds That Come From Far Away, 1960, The Little Giant Girl and the Elf Boy, 1963, A Kiss for Little Bear, 1968, What If, 1987, Percy and the Five

Houses, 1988, It's Spring, 1989, The Little Girl and the Dragon, 1991, Am I Beautiful, 1992. Mem. PEN Club. Home: 30 Gebig Rd Nottingham NH 03290 Office: care Greenwillow Books 1350 Ave Americas New York NY 10019

MINATEE, STEFANIE RENEÉ, vocal educator; b. Newark, Apr. 14, 1957; d. Steven E. and Pearl T. Minatee. BA Music, Kean U., 1982; BS Religious Edn., United Bible Coll., 1990. Immigration officer U.S. Dept. Justice, Newark, 1980—83; arranger Savoy Recs., Elizabeth, 1984—86; A&R dir. Danbla Recs., Irvington, 1987; ch. organist various chs., 1980—97; tchr. vocal music Plainfield B.O.E., 1983—. Mem. N.J. Black Issues Conv., 1982—. Recipient Westry Horne Excellence in Edn. award, Frontiers, Internat., N.J., 1992. Mem.: Nat. Acad. Recording Arts and Sci., Music Educators Nat. Conf. Baptist. Avocations: basketball, movies, travel.

MINAULT, GAIL, history educator; b. Mpls., Mar. 25, 1939; d. Paul Adrien and Martha (McKim) M.; m. Thomas Graham, May 13, 1967 (div. 1973); 1 child, Mark Emlen (dec.); m. Leon W. Ellsworth, Apr. 11, 1992; children: Laila Minault, Alex Ellsworth. BA, Smith Coll., Northampton, Mass., 1961; MA, U. Pa., 1966, PhD, 1972. Trainee U.S. Info. Agy., Washington, 1961-62; jr. officer U.S. Info. Svc., Beirut, Lebanon, 1962-63, asst. cultural affairs officer Dacca, East Pakistan, 1963-64; asst. prof. U. Tex., Austin, 1972-79, assoc. prof., 1980-95, prof., 1996—. Author: The Khilafat Movement: Religious Symbolism and Plitical Mobilization Among Indian Muslims, 1982; editor: The Extended Family: Women's Political Participation in India and Pakistan, 1981, Abul Kalam Azad: An Intellectual and Religious Biography, 1988, Secluded Scholars: Women's Education and Muslim Social Reform in Colonial India, 1998; translator: Voices of Silence, 1986. Nat. Humanities Ctr. fellow, 1987-88, Social Sci. Rsch. Coun. fellow, 1993, NEH, 1994-95. Mem. Assn. for Asian Studies, Berkshire Conf. Women Historians, Am. Inst. Pakistan Studies (sec. 1994-96). Democrat. Avocations: swimming, singing, traveling, photography. Office: U Tex Dept History Austin TX 78712

MINDAS, MARY L. music educator, composer; b. Bogalusa, La., Nov. 4, 1952; d. Norman and Pebble (Montgomery) Lang; m. William Bruce Lipp, June 23, 1973 (div. 1981); m. Gary Donald Mindas, Jan. 14, 1989; 1 child, Analiese Mary. BA, St. Mary of Woods Coll., 1974; postgrad., Rutgers U., 1976—77, H.B. Studio, 1977—79, Kean Coll., 1981—82, Georgian Ct. Coll., 1991. Cert. music educator, spl. edn. tchr. Tchr. Eatontown Pre-Sch., NJ, 1981—86, Monmouth Regional H.S., Tinton Falls, NJ, 1988—. Dir. Club Bene Theatre, Sayreville, NJ, 1979—2000; artistic dir. Calliope Theatre Co., 1979—2000, Battleground Arts Ctr., Freehold, NJ, 1980—2001. Candlewood parent rep., 1997—. Recipient Svc. award, Battleground Arts Ctr., 2001, Borough of Eatontown, 1986, Candlewood Swim Team, 2002. Mem.: Monmouth Regional Edn. Assn. (pres. 1999—), N.J. Edn. Assn., N.J. Music Educator Conf., Music Educator Nat. Conf. Democrat. Roman Catholic.*

MINDES, GAYLE DEAN, education educator; b. Kansas City, Mo., Feb. 11, 1942; d. Elton Burnett and Juanita Maxine (Mangold) Taylor; m. Marvin William Mindes, June 20, 1969 (dec.); 1 child, Jonathan Seth; m. Matilde Delich-Funes Mindes Jun. 27, 2002. BS, U. Kans., 1964; MS, U. Wis., 1965; EdD, Loyola U., Chgo., 1979. Tchr. pub. schs., Newburgh, N.Y., 1965-67; spl. educator Ill. Dept. Mental Health, Chgo., 1967-69; spl. edn. supr. Evanston (Ill.) Dist. 65 Schs., 1969-74; lectr. Loyola U., Chgo., 1974-76, Coll. St. Francis, Joliet, Ill., 1976-79; asst. prof. edn. Oklahoma City U., 1979-80; prof. sch. edn. DePaul U., 1993-99, acting dean, 1998-99, prof. edn., 1999—, dir. EdD program, 2000—02, chair tchr. edn., 2003. Lectr. Northeastern Ill., U. Chgo, 1974, North Park Coll., Chgo., 1978; vis. asst. prof., rsch. assoc. Roosevelt U. Coll. Edn., Chgo, 1983-87, Albert A. Robin campus prof., dir. R&D dir. tchr. edn., dir. early childhood, dir. grad. edn. ctr., 1993; search com. multicultural student affairs, v.p. advancement, DePaul U., co-chair tcng., learning, tech. com, 2000—, mem. strategic planning univ. com., 2004; chair Roosevelt U. Senate, 1986-89; trustee Roosevelt U., 1987-93; co-chair ILAEYC Bldg. Bridges; faculty adv. com. to univ. plan. and info. tech. DePaul U. Sch. Edn., panel on grievances, 1995-99, comprehensive pers. devel. com., 1995-99; tng. sub-com. adv. Ill. Dept. Children & Family Svcs., 1993-95; panel of advisers comprehensive pers. devel. sys. Ill. State Bd. Edn., 1995-99; mentor, cons. to partnerships project tng. early intervention svcs. U. Ill., Champaign; panelist Ill. Initiative for Articulation between Ill. Bd. Higher Edn. and Ill. Cmty. Coll. Bd., Early Childhood Assessment Sys.; co-chair, panelist Bansenville Pub. Schs.; cons. in field; project evaluator Chgo. Tchr. Collaborative, Dept. Edn., 1999-2004; chair U. Tchg. Learning Tech. com., 2001-; mem. ISBE/NCATE Partnership Com., 2002, Ill. State Bd. Ednl. Content Expert panel, 2003. Author: Assessing Young Children, 1996, 2d edit., 2003; (with Marie Donovan) Building Character: Five Enduring Themes for a Stronger Early Childhood Curriculum PK-3, 2000; editor: DePaul U. Sch. Edn. Newsletter; co-author: Planning a Theme Based Curriculum for 4's or 5's, 1993, Assessing Young Children: 1996, Encyclopedia of Children's Play, 1997; mem. editl. bd. Ill. Sch. R&D, Ill. Divsn. Early Childhood Edn. Adv. Com. to Ill. Bd. Edn.; cons. editor: NAEYC, 2003; contbr. articles to profl. jours. Bd. dirs. North Side Family Day Care, 1981; northside affiliate Mus. Contemporary Art, 1991-96; active Gov's Task Force on Alternative Rts. to Cert., 1999; edn. adv. com. Okla. Dept. Edn., 1979-80; adv. bd. bilingual early childhood program Oakton C.C.; adv. bd. early childood tech. assistance project Chgo. Pub. Schs., Lake View Mental Health, 1986-90; planning com. Lake View Citizens Coun. Day Care Ctr., 1978-79; local planning coun. Ill. Dept. Child and Family Svcs.; childcare block grant tng. sub. com.; chair teen com. Florence G. Heller JCC, membership com.; adv. bd. Harold Washington Coll. Child Devel., regional tech. assistance grant LICA; mem. parents. com. Francis W. Parker Sch.; mem. assessment task force Dept. Human Svcs., City of Chgo., 2001-02; trustee Congregation Kol Ami., 2000-03. U. Kans. scholar, 1960, Cerebral Palsy Assn. scholar, 1965; U. Wis. fellow in mental retardation, 1964-65. Fellow: Am. Orthopsychiat. Assn.; mem.: ASCD, Found. for Excellence in Tchg. (selection com. Golden Apple 1989—94), Ill. Assn. for Edn. Young Children (co-chair bldg. bridges project), Ill. Coun. for Exceptional Children, Coun. for Exceptional Children, Am. Ednl. Rsch. Assn., Nat. Assn. for Edn. Young Children (tchr. edn. bd. 1990—94, editl. rev. bd., editl. panel 2003—), Pi Lambda Theta, Phi Delta Kappa, Alpha Sigma Nu. Office: DePaul Univ Sch Of Edn Chicago IL 60614 Office Phone: 773-325-7769. Business E-Mail: gmindes@depaul.edu.

MINDNICH, ELLEN, sales executive; b. Red Bank, N.J., Apr. 2, 1962; d. James Robert and Ann Marie M. BS in Bus. Mgmt., W. Chester U. Sales mgr. U.S. Healthcare, N.Y., 1991-96; sales recruiter Paragon Computer, N.Y., 1996-97; ins. agt., 1998—.

MINEAR, SARAH M. state legislator; b. Parsons, W.Va., Aug. 11, 1949; m. Robert W. Minear (dec.). Student, Fairmont State Coll., WVa. U., W.Va. Bus. Coll. Mem. W.Va. Senate, Charleston, 1995—. Mem. agr. com., edn. com., fin. com., govt. orgn. com., interstate cooperation com., natural resources com., rules com. Bd. dirs. Tucker County Arts Coun., Ohio-W.Va. YMCA Leadership Ctr.; charter mem. Tucker County Devel. Authority, Allegheny Front Regional Devel. Authority; founder Tucker Cmty. Endowment Found., W.Va. Grantmakers Assn. Mem. W.Va. Forestry Assn., Tucker County C. of C., W.Va. Farm Bur., Tucker County Farm Bur.; mem. W.Va. Rep. Com., Tucker County Rep. Exec. Com. Presbyterian. Office: WVa Senate 1900 Kanawha Blvd E Rm 441M Charleston WV 25305-0009 also: HC 70 Box 450 Davis WV 26260-9721 Fax: (304) 866-4880. E-mail: smminear@aol.com.

MINEHART, JEAN BESSE, tax accountant; b. Cleve., Nov. 8, 1937; d. Ralph and Augusta Besse; m. Ralph Conrad Minehart, Aug. 28, 1959; children: Patricia Minehart Miron, Deborah Minehart Rust, Elizabeth, Stephen. BA, Mass. Wellesley Coll., 1959; MEd, U. Va., 1971. Rsch. assoc. Age Ctr. of New Eng., Boston, 1959-61; substitute tchr. Charlottesville (Va.) Sch. System, 1976-81; tax acct. H&R Block, Charlottesville, 1982-94, Huey & Bjorn, Charlottesville, 1994—. Past pres. Ephphatha Village Housing for the Deaf, Charlottesville, 1984-87; bd. dirs. Tues. Evening Concert Series, Charlottesville, 1990-94; sec., bd. dirs. Family Svc., Inc., Charlottesville, 1987-91; bd. dirs. Westminster Organ Concert Series; elder Westminster Presbyn. Ch., 1979-81, 94-96. Scholar, Wellesley Coll. scholar. Mem. LWV (v.p., treas. 1991-95) Blue Ridge Wellesley Club (pres. Charlottesvillechpt. 1989-91, dorm rep. 1996—). Avocations: reading, music. Home: 1714 Yorktown Dr Charlottesville VA 22901-3034 Office: Huey & Bjorn 408 E Market St Ste 207 Charlottesville VA 22902-5261

MINEKA, SUSAN, psychology educator; b. Ithaca, N.Y., June 2, 1948; d. Francis Edward and Muriel Leota (McGregor) M. BA in Psychology magna cum laude, Cornell U., 1970; PhD, U. Pa., 1974. Lic. psychologist, Ill. Prof. psychology U. Wis., Madison, 1974-85, U. Tex., Austin, 1986-87; prof. Northwestern U., Evanston, Ill., 1987—. Co-dir. Panic Treatment Ctr., EvanstonHosp., 1988-99; mem. NIH Panic Consensus Panel, 1991. Editor Jour. Abnormal Psychology, 1990-94; contbr. articles to profl. jours. Grantee NSF and NIMH, 1988-97; fellow Ctr. for Advanced Study in the Behavioral Scis., Stanford, Calif., 1997-98. Fellow APA (bd. sci. affairs 1992-94, chair 1994, pres. divsn. 12, sect. 3 1995), Am. Psychol. Soc., Psychonomic Soc. (bd. dirs. 2001, 04); mem. Assn. for Advancement Behavior Therapy, Midwestern Psychol. Assn. (pres.-elect 1995-96, pres. 1996-97), Internat. Primatol. Soc., Internat. Soc. for Rsch. on Emotion, Soc. for Rsch. in Psychopathology (mem. exec. bd. 1992-94, 2000-03), Phi Beta Kappa, Sigma Xi. Democrat. Office: Northwestern U Psychology Dept Evanston IL 60208-0001

MINELLI, HELENE MARIE, artist; b. Sonoma, Calif., Sept. 26, 1918; d. Adolph Herman Trappe and Maria Barbara Hilzinger; m. Louie Minelli, Mar. 4, 1939 (dec. Aug. 1993); children: Ernest, Carol, Michael. Student, Santa Rosa Jr. Coll. Bd. trustees Calif. Exposition Adv. Coun., Sacramento, 1984—89; artistic treas. Cultural Fine Arts Commn., Sonoma Valley, 1989. Named one of 60 Pastel Artists of World, Internat. Pastel Mag. Mem.: Soc. We. Artists (bd. trustees 1988—), Nat. League Am. Pen Women (pres. 1995—96), Gen. Fedn. Women's Club (past state art chmn.), Sonoma Valley Art (past pres.). Home: 200 Malaga St Sonoma CA 95476

MINER, JACQUELINE, political consultant; b. Dec. 10, 1936; d. Ralph E. and Agnes (McGee) Mariani; m. Roger J. Miner, Aug. 11, 1975; children: Laurence, Ronald Carmichael, Ralph Carmichael, Mark. Ind. polit. cons., Hudson, NY; instr. history and polit. sci. SUNY, Hudson, 1974—79. Mem. nat. steering com. Fund for Am.'s Future, 2d cir. Hist. Com.; mem. White House Outreach Working Group on Central Am.; candidate for Rep. nomination U.S. Senate, 1982; co-chair N.Y. state steering com. George Bush for Pres. campaign, 1986—88; del. Rep. Conv., 1992, GOP Conv., 1992; Rep. county committeewoman, 1958—76; vice chmn. N.Y. State Ronald Reagan campaign, 1980, N.Y. State Rep. Com., 1991—93; co-chmn. N.Y. State Reagan Roundup Campaign, 1984—86; chmn. Coll. Consortium for Internat. Studies. Mem.: PEO, U.S. Supreme Ct. Hist. Soc. Address: 1 Merlins Way Hudson NY 12534-4157

MINER, VIRGINIA ANN, minister; b. Montrose, Pa., June 27, 1958; d. Robert Edmund and Eleanor Miner. BA, Wells Coll., 1980; MDiv, Princeton Theol. Sem., 1985. Ordained minister Presbyn. Ch., 1985. Pastor First Presbyn. Ch. Calvin United Presbyn., Peckville, Olyphant, Pa., 1985—. Moderator Camp Lackawanna Com., Scranton, Pa., 1995—2002; peace-making adv. com. Presbyn. Ch. USA, 1998—2000. Bd. dirs. Voluntary Action Ctr., Scranton, 1999, Stony Point (N.Y.) Retreat Ctr., 2002. 1st lt. USAR, 1982—87. Named N.E. Woman of the Week, Sunday Times, Scranton, 1992, Woman of Distinction, Girl Scout Coun., Scranton, 1998; recipient Pub. Svc. award, UN Assn., Scranton, 1988. Avocations: golf, skiing, hiking, canoeing, rock climbing. Home: 751 Main St Peckville PA 18452 Office: First Presbyn Ch 753 Main St Peckville PA 18452

MING, JENNY J. retail apparel company executive; married; 3 children. B.A. clothing merchandising, San Jose State U. Mdse. mgr. brand activewear Gap Inc., 1986, v.p., divsn. mdse. mgr., co-creator Old Navy subs., 1994—, sr. v.p. merchandising, Old Navy, 1994—96, exec. v.p. merchandising, Old Navy, 1996—99, pres., Old Navy, 1999—, mem., sr. oper. com., 1999—. Bd. dirs. E.piphany, Inc. Bd. dirs. Big Brothers Big Sisters, San Francisco; mem. Com. of 100. Office: Gap Inc 1 Harrison St San Francisco CA 94105-1602

MINGUS, JUDY ELLEN, special education educator, secondary school educator; b. Athens, Ohio, Sept. 27, 1955; d. John Andrew and Frieda Ellen Clifford; m. William Fredrick Mingus, July 30, 2002; m. Homer Dale Curry, June 9, 1979 (dec. Feb. 16, 1995); children: Heath Michael Curry, Paul Gene Curry, Heather Michelle Curry. BS in Spl. Edn., Ohio U., 1992; MEd, Rio Grande (Ohio) U., 2000. Patient svcs. asst. Planned Parenthood, Athens, Ohio, 1986—89; spl. edn. tchr. Tri-County Career Ctr., Nelsonville, Ohio, 1992—. Tutor Nelsonville-York (Ohio) HS, 1999—. Den mother Boy Scouts Am., Glouster, Ohio, 1984—89; daisy scout leader Girl Scouts Am., Glouster, 1986—87; coach, girl's teams mgr. Glouster (Ohio) Youth League, 1985—88; sunday sch. tchr. Bread of Life Full Gospel Ch., Jacksonville, Ohio. Avocations: expressive sign language, walking, enjoying nature. Office: Tri-County Career Center 15676 State Route 691 Nelsonville OH 45764

MINI, ANNE ALEXANDRA APOSTOLIDES, writer, educator; b. Oakland, Calif., Sept. 30, 1966; d. Norman and Kleo Varvara (Apostolides) M. AB, Harvard U., 1988; MA, U. Chgo., 1991; PhD, U. Wash., 1995. Freelance writer, Seattle, 1995—; pres. Thesisadvisor.com, 2000—; owner First Reader Editing, Seattle, 2002—. Lectr., tchg. asst. U. Wash., Seattle, 1991-95, Nancy Hartsock Rotating Chair, 1995. Author: The General Strike of 1934, 1988, Alexis de Tocqueville in Historical Context, 1991, An Expressive Revolution, 1995, Security Issues, 1996, Favorite Son, 1999, Background Noise, 2001, The Buddha in the Hot Tub, 2003. Precinct com. officer Seattle Dem. Com., 1996-2000; del. King County Dem. Ctrl. Com., Seattle, 1996-2000, mem. bylaws com., 1999; polit. campaign cons., 1998—; mem. Wash. State Dem. Platform Com., 1998, 2000; Wash. state del. Dem. Nat. Conv., 2000. Grantee, U. Wash., 1985, 1990, U. Chgo., 1989—91, Vt. Studio Ctr., 2004; Radcliffe scholar, 1984—88, Norcroft Writing fellow, 2002. Avocations: 18th and 19th century french liberalism, gourmandry, viticulture. Office: PO Box 27242 Seattle WA 98165 E-mail: authoress1@foxinternet.com.

MINIERI, JOAN, community organization director; b. Teaneck, NJ, Jan. 31, 1962; d. Mary and Alphonse Minieri; m. Francis Clarke Haberle, Dec. 13, 1998; children: Alin Rosina Haberle, Mariel Clarke Haberle. BA, Muhlenberg Coll., 1980—84; MS, Columbia U., 1984—86. Co-dir. NYC Organizing Support Ctr., NYC, 1998—2003; dir. of comm. Nat. Religious Partnership for the Environment, NYC, 1995—97. Bd. of directors Cmty. Voices Heard, NYC, 1992—. Author: (plays) Intertwine. Co-founder and current bd. mem. Cmty. Voices Heard, NYC, 1992—2003. Recipient Leadership for a Changing World award, Ford Found., 2001—03, Union Sq. award, Fund for the City of NY, 2002; Charles H. Revson Fellows Program for the Future of the City of NY, Charles H. Revson Found., 1991—92, Residence Grant in Fiction, Helene Wurlitzer Found., 1989. Avocations: creative writing, hiking, travel.

MINK, JO ANNA STEPHENS, humanities educator; b. Fort Wayne, Ind., Sept. 20, 1947; d. Jerald W. and Verda Albert Stephens. BS in English, Ill. State U., Normal, 1973, MS in English, 1975, DA, 1985. Instr. English, dir. of writing ctr. U. La., Lafayette, 1985—87; asst. prof. English, dir. of writing programs Barton Coll., Wilson, NC, 1987—90; prof. English Minn. State U., Mankato, 1990—. Editor: (scholarly anthology) Common Ground: Feminist Collaboration in the Academy, Communication and Women's Friendship: Parallels and Intersections in Literature and Life, The Significance of Sibling Relationships in Literature, Joinings and Disjoinings: The Significance of Marital Status in Literature; author: (bibliographical entries) Nineteenth-Century British Women Writers: A Bio-Bibliographical Critical Sourcebook, (book chapter) Heroines of Popular Culture; author: (photographer) (magazine article) Dorset Life; author: (biographical articles) Victorian Britain: An Encyclopedia. Found. fellowship, Ill. State U., 1984. Mem.: The Hypatia Trust, North Am. Victorian Studies Assn., Midwest Victorian Studies Assn., The Thomas Hardy Assn. (North Am.), Nat. Coun. of Tchrs. of English, Midwest MLA, The Thomas Hardy Soc. Avocations: photography, travel. Office: Dept English-AH 230 Minnesota State Univ Mankato MN 56001 E-mail: joanna.mink@mnsu.edu.

MINKOFF, HILDA BRESSLER, secondary and adult education educator; b. Havana, Cuba, Oct. 10, 1933; d. Isaac and Augustina (Draiman) Bressler; m. Paul Norman Minkoff, Nov. 24, 1957; children: David Jay, Debra Carol. BS in Indsl. Labor Rels., Cornell U., 1955; MEd in Counseling and Guidance, Temple U., 1969, EdD in Vocat. Edn. Adminstrn., 1983. Counselor various schs., Phila., 1967—74, King H.S., Phila., 1975—83; pres. Am. Sch. Counselor Assn., Alexandria, Va., 1983—84; counselor Washington H.S., Phila., 1984—85; supr. student support svcs. Sch. Dist. of Phila., 1984—94; counselor Cen. H.S., Phila., 1994—97. Adj. prof. Arcadia U., Glenside, Pa., 1990—2003.

MINKOFF, JILL S. business owner, entrepreneur, educator; b. July 12, 1953; d. Julius Burt and Eloise Joy (Shlensky) Minkoff; m. Barry Charles Goldman, Jan. 30, 1982 (div. Nov. 1995); children: Joshua Scott Goldman, Elise Lynn Goldman. Certificat d'Assiduite, U. Grenoble, France, 1968; BA, Pomona Coll., 1974. Cert. spiritual counselor Am. Bd. Hypnotherapy. Mktg. rep. IBM, Riverside, Calif., 1974-77, San Francisco, 1978-79; dir. store sys. Neiman Marcus, Dallas, 1979-81; dir. end-user computing svcs. Marion Labs., Kansas City, Mo., 1982-89, dir. info. sys. data and techs., 1989. Dir. corp. info. systems Marion Merrell Dow Inc., 1989-91; dir. Bus. Process Improvement, 1992-93; pres. Visions Connections, Inc., Kans., 1993-2000, Aleph Sys., 2000—. Sch. pres. ARC, Kansas City, Mo., 1966-67; v.p. chpt. B'nai B'rith Girls, Kansas City, 1968-69; mem. Nat. Coun. Jewish Women, 2001, bd. dirs. Kansas City chpt., 2002-03. Mem. Silicon Prairie Tech. Assn. (bd. dirs. 1992-99, adv. bd. creative courseware 1995-2002). Home and Office: 4404 W 62d Ter Fairway KS 66205 E-mail: mjsminkoff@aol.com.

MINNA, MARIA, member of Canadian Parliament; b. Pofi, Frosinone, Italy, Mar. 14, 1948; arrived in Can., 1957. Grad. in Sociology with honors, U. Toronto. Policy advisor to former Ont. Premier David Peterson; pres. COSTI-IIAS Immigrant Svcs.; v.p. pub. affairs cons. co., Toronto; M.P. from Beaches-Woodbine dist. Ho. of Commons, Toronto, 1993-97, MP from Beaches-East York dist. Ottawa, Ont., Can., 1997—; parliamentary sec. Min. Citizenship and Immigration, 1996—98; chmn. to social policy com. Nat. Liberal Caucus, 1998—99, min. for internat. cooperation, 1999—2002. Life-long liberal, mem. Nat. Platform Com., 1988; apptd. vice chair standing com. Human Resources Devel., 1994. Contbr. reports on cmty. devel. and provision of svcs. to immigrants and minority groups. Former mem. campaign cabinet United Way Gtr. Toronto; former dir. Nat. Coun. Welfare Recipient Premio Italia nel Mondo award, 2001, President's Award, Indo-Canada Chamber of Commerce, 2001, Outstanding Leadership Award, RESULTS Canada, 2002. Mem. Nat. Congress Italian-Canadians (former exec. dir. Toronto dist., former pres.). Liberal. Office: House of Commons 406 West Block Ottawa ON Canada K1A 0A6 also: 1912 Danforth Ave M4C1J4 Toronto ON Canada E-mail: Minna.M@parl.gc.ca.*

MINNELLI, LIZA, singer, actress; b. Los Angeles, Mar. 12, 1946; d. Vincente and Judy (Garland) M.; m. Peter Allen, 1967 (div. 1972); m. Jack Haley, Sept. 15, 1974 (div.); m. Mark Gero, Dec. 4, 1979 (div. 1992); m. David Gest, March 16, 2002 (div.). Appeared in Off-Broadway revival of Best Foot Forward, 1963; appeared with mother at London Palladium, 1964; nightclub debut at Shoreham Hotel, Washington, 1965; appeared in Flora, the Red Menace, 1965 (Tony award), The Act, 1977 (Tony award), The Rink, 1984, Victor Victoria; films include Charlie Bubbles, 1967, The Sterile Cuckoo, 1969, Tell Me That You Love Me, Junie Moon, 1970, Cabaret, 1972 (Oscar award), That's Entertainment, 1974, Lucky Lady, 1975, A Matter of Time, 1976, Silent Movie, 1976, New York, New York, 1977, Arthur, 1981, Rent A Cop, Arthur on the Rocks, 1988, Stepping Out, 1991; recorded You Are For Loving, 1963, Tropical Nights, 1977, Liza Minnelli at Carnegie Hall, 1987, Results, 1989, Maybe This Time, 1996, Gently, 1996, Minnelli on Minnelli, 2000, (with Herbie Hancock, Johnny Mathis, Donna Summer); (TV films) Parallel Lives, 1994, The West Side Waltz, 1995, Jackie's Back!, 1999; appeared on TV in own spl. Liza With a Z, 1972 (Recipient Emmy award); other TV appearances include Goldie and Liza Together, 1980, Baryshnikov on Broadway, 1980, The Princess and the Pea, Showtime, 1983, A Time to Live, 1985, Sam Found Out, 1988, Liza Minnelli Live from Radio City Music Hall, PBS (Emmy nomination, Music Program Performance, 1993), The West Side Waltz, 1990, The Wonderful World of Oz: 50 Years of Magic, 1990, A Century of Cinema, 1994, My Favorite Broadway: The Leading Ladies, 1999; internat. tour with Frank Sinatra, Sammy Davis Jr., 1988. Awarded the Brit. equivalent of the Oscar for Best Actress, 1972, Italy's David di Donatello award (twice), the Valentino award. Address: Capitol Records Inc 1750 Vine St Hollywood CA 90028-5209 also: Angel EMI Guardian Records 304 Park Ave S New York NY 10010-5339

MINNER, RUTH ANN, governor; b. Milford, Del., Jan. 17, 1935; m. Roger Minner (dec.). Student Del. Tech. and Community Coll. Office receptionist Gov. of Del., 1972-74; mem. Del. Ho. of Reps., 1974-82; mem. Del. Senate, 1982-92; lt. gov. State of Del., Dover, 1993-2001, gov., 2001—. Mem. Dem. Nat. Com., 1988. Office: Office Gov William Penn St Tatnall Bldg 3d Fl Dover DE 19901*

MINNEY, GLORIA JOAN, preschool and postsecondary school educator, massage therapist, holistic health practitioner, artist; b. Eugene, Oreg., Dec. 31, 1936; d. Arthur Benjamin Minney and Anna Lucille Hart Minney; m. Jack Junior Curtis, Dec. 20, 1958 (div. Jan. 1962); m. Michael Jacob Meils, June 19, 1965 (div. Nov. 4, 1980); children: Joanna Dianna Meils, Minney Sosa. BS, Univ. Oreg., 1959, MS, 1962; post grad., Ariz. State Univ., 1964. Cert. tchg., health, P.E., art, social studies Oreg., Ariz., New Mex., Tex., lic. massage therapist, instr. Tex., New Mex. Tchr. Lowell H.S., Oreg., 1959—62; instr. Colo. State Coll., Greley, Colo., 1962—64; tchr. Camelback H.S., Phoenix, 1964—67, White Mid. Sch., El Paso, Tex., 1968—70; instr. Jacksonville State Univ., Ala., 1970—73, El Paso C.C., 1973—; tchr. De Valle H.S., El Paso, Tex., 1989—. Instr. Univ. Tex., El Paso, Tex., 1979; curriculum devel. El Paso C.C.; message therapist; holistic health practitioner. Painting, printmaking, jewelry, (best show);, performer dance, drama; choreographer, tchr. (modern folk, square social). Sec., treas., pres., v.p. 4-H Clubs, 1945—55. Mem.: Nat. Edn. Assn., Am. Assn. for Health, Physical Edn. and Dance, Am. Massage Therapy Assn. Independent. Roman Cath. Avocations: painting, printmaking, travel, sewing, gardening. Home: Box 31143 El Paso TX 79931 Office: Del Valle H S 950 Bordeaux Dr El Paso TX 79907

MINNICH, DIANE KAY, legal association administrator; b. Iowa City, Feb. 17, 1956; d. Ralph Maynard Minnich and Kathryn Jane (Obye) Tompkins. BA in Behavioral Sci., San Jose State U., 1978. Tutorial program coord./instr. Operation SHARE/La Valley Coll., Van Nuys, Calif., 1979-81;

field exec. Silver Sage Girl Scout Coun., Boise, Idaho, 1981-85; continuing legal edn. dir. Idaho State Bar/Idaho Law Found. Inc., Boise, 1985-88, dep. dir., 1988-90, exec. dir., 1990—. Mem. adv. bd. legal asst. program Boise State U. Mem. Assn. CLE Adminstrs., Chgo., 1985-90; bd. dirs. Silver Sage coun. Girl Scouts, Boise, 1990-93, 99-2001, mem. nominating com., 1990-94, 97-2001, chair nominating com., 1991-92; mem. legal asst. program adv. bd. Boise State U. Named one of Outstanding Young Women in Am., 1991. Mem. Nat. Orgn. Bar Execs. (membership com. 1992-97, chair 1996-97), Zonta Club Boise (pres. 1991-92, bd. dirs. 1989-93), Rotary Club Boise (chair mem. com. 1994-97, bd. dirs. 1996-97, 99—). Avocations: softball, jogging, golf. Office: Idaho State Bar Idaho Law Found PO Box 895 525 W Jefferson St Boise ID 83702-5931 Home: 1118 Harrison Blvd Boise ID 83702-3448

MINNICK, MARY E. food products executive; MBA, Duke U. Exec. v.p., pres., CEO Asia The Coca-Cola Co., Atlanta, 2001—. Mem. Dean's Coun. John F. Kennedy Sch. Bus., Harvard U.; bd. visitors Fuqua Sch. Bus. Named one of most powerful women in the bus. world, Fortune mag. Office: The Coca-Cola Co PO Box 1734 Atlanta GA 30301

MINNIS, KAREN, state representative; b. Portland, Oreg., July 20, 1954; m. John Minnis, 1972; 3 children. Student, Clark C.C., 1978. Small bus. owner, 1995—97; legis. aide State Rep. John Minnis, 1987—; mem. Oreg. Ho. of Reps., 1998—; majority leader, 2001—03. Precinct committeeman, 1986—. Republican. Office: 900 Court St North East H-269 Salem OR 97301

MINNITI, MARTHA JEAN, home healthcare company executive; b. Shamokin, Pa., Dec. 13, 1951; d. Charles and Betty Minniti; m. James Hill, Apr. 19, 1986; 1 child, Katharine. Diploma, Bryn Mawr (Pa.) Hosp. Sch. Nursing, 1973; BS in Psychology magna cum laude, Rosemont Coll., 1979; postgrad., U. Pa., 1992—. RN, Pa. Staff nurse Chestnut Hill (Pa.) Hosp., 1973-76; staff-charge nurse Phila. Coll. Osteo. Medicine, 1976-78, Med. Staff, Phila., 1978-80; CEO The SNI Cos., Flourtown, Pa., 1980—. Contbr. articles to profl. jours. Mem. ANA, AACN, Am. Orgn. Nurse Execs., Am. Holistic Nurses Assn., Am. Hosp. Assn., Pa. Nurses Assn., Sigma Theta Tau (Kappa Chi chpt.). Office: Skilled Nursing Inc Ste 300 500 Office Center Dr Fort Washington PA 19034-3214

MINOR, ADDINE E. civic leader; b. Tupelo, Miss., June 22, 1919; d. George Bradley and Myrtle (Guyton) Jones; m. William Minor, Oct. 11, 1941; children: Ramona June Warhurst, Deborah Merle Ruff, William Bradley Minor, Bonnie Sue Shannon. Grad., Bandy's Secretarial Sch., Osceola, 1937; AA, So. Bapt. U., 1974; student, Parke Coll. Sec., bookkeeper Sinclair Refining Co., Osceola, Ark., 1948-53, Judge A.F. Barham, Osceola, 1953-59; sec., then welfare counselor State of Ark., Blytheville and Osceola, 1959-63, substitute tchr. Luxora and Osceola, 1983 86; sec., counselor U.S. Govt., Blytheville AFB, 1963-83; exec. sec. Calvary Bapt. Ch., Osceola, 1986—; substitute tchr. Rivercrest Jr. H.S., Wilson, 1994; tchr.'s asst. North Elem. Sch., Osceola, 1995; adminstrv. sec. Workforce Alliance, Blytheville, 1998—, asst. Class sec. bible study First Bapt. Ch., Osceola, 1985-86; mem. Calvary Bapt. Ch. 1971—, leader tng. union, 1986—, tng. union dir., 1988—, served baptismal com., 1986-88; ch. clk., 1988—. Mem. First Bapt. Ch., Miss. County Literacy Coun.; vol. AmeriCorps. Recipient English award State Miss., 1936, PMIT Golden Fingers award Hdqs. SAC Offutt AFB NE, 1978, 79, 80, Presdl. Cert. U.S. Govt., Washington, 1983. Mem. Explorer Bible First Bapt. Ch., Home Bible Study, Women's Missionary Union, Farm Bur., Nat. Assn. Female Execs., Homemaker's Extension Club (sec., treas. to 1987), Gen. Fedn. Women's Clubs, Profl. Women's Orgn. (sec.), Worldwide Communications. Republican. Avocations: reading, creative writing, needlepoint, croquet, golf.

MINOR, BEVERLY JUNE, retired social worker; b. Munhall, Pa., June 6, 1929; d. Edgar M. Sandberg and Marie Cahill; children: Betsy Sloan, Gary Minor, Gail Geer, Leslie Minor. BS in Chemistry, Chatham Coll., 1951; MSW, Barry U., 1993. LCSW. Rsch. chemist; chemist Jones & Laughlin Steel Corp., Pitts., 1951—; tel. counselor Crisis Line of Martin County, Stuart, Fla., 1980—; case mgr. Coun. on Aging of Martin County, Stuart, 1988—94; social worker Hospice of Treasure Coast, Ft. Pierce, Fla., 1994—2003; ret., 2003. Social worker Sr. Care Mgmt., Inc., Palm City, 2003—. Bd. dirs. Crisis Line of Martin County, Stuart, 1995—97. Office: Hospice of Treasure Coast Virginia Ave Fort Pierce FL 34982 Personal E-mail: beverly1644@aol.com.

MINOR, CLARA MAE, election judge; b. Altapass, N.C., Dec. 3, 1931; d. David Wilkerson Sullins and Carrie Mae Schism; m. Lawrence Alfred Minor, Oct. 27, 1950; children: Lawrence, Charles, Beverly, John. Grad. h.s., Canton, Ohio, 1949. Sales clk. JC Penney Co., Canton, 1973-80; presiding judge Stark County Election Bd., Canton, 1983—. Pres., mem. PTA, Hubbard, Ohio, 197-72. Mem. DAR, Daus. Am. Colonists, Daus. War of 1812. Republican. Methodist. Avocations: reading, collector ladies antique watches and compacts

MINOR, MARIAN THOMAS, elementary and secondary school educational consultant; b. Richmond, Va., Apr. 16, 1933; d. James Madison and Florence Elwood (Edwards) M. BS, U. Va., 1955; MEd, William and Mary Coll., 1968; postgrad., Va. Commonwealth U., 1987-88. Cert. guidance, health and phys. edn. Educator Richmond (Va.) Pub. Schs., 1955-90, ednl. cons., 1990—. Educator Sch. Nursing Med. Coll. Va., Richmond, 1958-68; camp dir. Manakin, Va., 1956-68; nat. basketball ofcl. Richmond (Va.) Bd. Ofcls., 1952-77; mem. faculty adv. com. Albert Hill Middle Sch., Richmond, 1965-90, dept. chmn., 1960-90, Tchr. of Yr., 1980; textbook adoption Richmond (Va.) Pub. Sch., 1975, 85, curriculum planner, 1978-79, 82-83, 84-85; PTA coord. Albert Hill Middle Sch., Richmond, 1985-89, chmn. self-study and accreditation team, 1987-88. Mem. Sherwood Park Civic Assn., Richmond, 1960-98; v.p. alumni weekend Mary Washington Alumni Assn., Fredericksburg, Va., 1965, 66, v.p. annual giving, 1967; chmn. basketball ofcl. examiners Richmond Bd. Women Ofcls., 1966-76; bd. dirs., homeowner adv., constrn. crewman, family svcs. com. Habitat for Humanity, 1994-2002, Blitz Build 2000 adv. chmn.; mem. exec. com. Northminster Bapt. Ch., 1991-94, 99-2002, deacon, clk., 97-99, worship team, 1999—, premises chair, 1991-94, mem. by-laws revision com., 1986, 98, 99, srs. task force chmn., v.p., sr. fellowship, regional Befriender Ministry adv. coun. Recipient J.C. Penney Golden Rule award, 1996, Outstanding Vol. award Habitat for Humanity, 1998, Outstanding Svc. award Albert Hill PTA, 1988. Mem. AAUW, AAHPERD, Va. Health Phys. Edn. Assn., Va. Ret. Tchrs. Assn., Train Collectors Assn., King and Queen Hist. Soc., Mortar Bd., Alpha Phi Sigma, Kappa Delta Pi. Republican. Avocations: genealogy, local history. Home and Office: 1507 Brookland Pky Richmond VA 23227-4707

MINOT, ELIZA, writer; b. Beverly, Mass., Apr. 8, 1970; d. George Richards Minot and Helen Ruth Hannon; m. Eric Burke Price, Sept. 11, 1999; children: Roan Price, Lila Price. BA, Barnard Coll., 1991. Author: The Tiny One (N.Y. Times Notable Book, 1999).

MINOW, JOSEPHINE BASKIN, civic volunteer; b. Chgo., Nov. 3, 1926; d. Salem N. and Bessie (Sampson) Baskin; m. Newton N. Minow, May 29, 1949; children: Nell, Martha, Mary. BS, Northwestern U., 1948. Asst. to advt. dir. Mandel Brothers Dept. Store, Chgo., 1948-49; tchr. Francis W. Parker Sch., Chgo., 1949-50; vol. in civil and charitable activities, 1950—; bd. dirs. Juvenile Protective Assn., Chgo., 1958—, pres., 1973-75. Bd. dirs. Parnham Trust, Beaminster, Dorset, Eng. Author: Marty the Broken Hearted Artichoke, 1997. Founder, coord. Children's divsn. Hospitality and Info. Svc., Washington, 1961-63; mem. Caucus Com., Glencoe, Ill., 1965-69; co-chmn. spl. study on juvenile justice Chgo. Cmty. Trust, 1978-80; chmn. Know Your Chgo., 1980-83; bd. dirs. Chgo. Coun. Fgn. Rels., 1977-2003, hon. life mem., 2003; trustee Chgo. Hist. Soc., Ravinia Festival Assn.; mem. women's bd. Field Mus., U. Chgo.; founding mem., v.p. women's bd. Northwestern U., 1978; bd. govs. Chgo. Symphony, 1966-73, 76[00bf] ; mem. Citizens Com. Juvenile Ct. of Cook County, 1985-96; exec. com. Northwestern U. Libr. Coun., 1974-96; co-chair grandparents' adv. com. Chgo. Children's Mus., 1999; bd. dirs. Jane Addams Juvenile Ct. Found. Recipient spl. award Chgo. Sch. and Workshop for Retarded, 1975, Children's Guardian award Juvenile Protective Assn., 1993. Mem. Hebrew Immigrant Aid Soc. (bd. dirs. 1977-98, award 1988), Friday Club, Northmoor Country Club, The Arts Club. Democrat. Jewish. Office: Chgo Hist Soc Clark St at North Ave Chicago IL 60614

MINSHALL, DOROTHY KATHLEEN, music educator; b. Bakersfield, Calif., Feb. 6, 1967; d. Donna Kathleen Bigler, Robert Lynn Bigler; m. Todd Allen Minshall; children: Eric, Rhett. BMus-flute and voice performance, Dallas Bapt. U., 1989. Owner, tchr. Dottie's Studio for Fine Arts, Snow, Okla., 1989—; guest artist, guest instr. drama, music and choreography Eastern Okla. State U., 2003. Cons. Music and Arts Okla. Task Force on Edn., 1991—92. Dir.(musical prodns.): For God and Country, 1992 (Outstanding Children's Prodn., 1992); musician: flute sub for two symphony orchestras; actor(musical theatre): My Fair Lady, 1989 (Best Actress, 1989); dir.(children's theatre): A Season of Giving, 2000 (Best Dir.--Best Overall Prodn.). Tchr. Sun. sch. Nashoba Valley Bapt. Ch., Nashoba, Okla., 1989—. Mem.: Okla. Music Tchrs. Assn. (cert. 1990), Music Tchrs. Nat. Assn. (cert. 1990). Baptist. Avocation: jewelry designer. Home: HC 69 Box 192 Snow OK 74567 Office: Dottie's Studio for Fine Arts HC 69 Box 191 Snow OK 74567 Personal E-mail: minshall@pisp.net.

MINSON, DIXIE L. legislative staff member; Student, Weber State U. Dir. dept. bus. regulation Utah's Divsn. Consumer Protection; dep. chief of staff Office of Gov. Norman H. Bangerter, Utah; commr. safety, health and indsl. accidents divsn. Indsl. Commn. Utah; state dir. Office of Senator Robert F. Bennett, Salt Lake City, 1993—. Active Utah Hearing Panel for Safety Auto and Inspection Stas., League Utah Consumers; Utah liaison U.S. Product Safety Commn.; v.p. Wester Assn. Worker's Compensation Bd. and Commn.; rep. Funeral Svc. Consumer Action Panel for Western States and Hawaii. Mem. Nat. Assn. Govtl. Labor Ofcls., Nat. Assn. Consumer Agy. Adminstrs., Nat. Assn. Unemployment Ins. Appellate Bds. Office: 125 S State St Fed Bldg Rm 4225 Salt Lake City UT 84138-1102

MINSON, MARY BETH, music educator, elementary school educator, musician; b. Cobleskill, N.Y., July 11, 1947; d. Lambertus Joseph and Helen Lorraine Schulte; m. Edward T. Minson, Jr., Aug. 14, 1971 (div. 1994); children: Elisabeth Danielle, Timothy Ford. B in Music Edn., Westminster Choir Coll., 1969. Cert. tchr. N.J. Elem. music tchr. Sayreville (N.J.) Bd. Edn., 1969—75, Dunellen (N.J.) Bd. Edn., 1983—; mezzo soprano soloist Presbyn. Ch. Westfield, NJ, 1979—2002, Temple Bnai Abraham, Livingston, NJ, 1991—. Mem., soloist Westminster Touring Choirs, Princeton, NJ, 1965—69, Choral Art Soc. N.J., Westfield, 1977—90. Mem.: NEA, Am. Choral Dirs. Assn., Music Educators Nat. Conf., Dunellen Edn. Assn., Middlesex County Educators Assn., N.J. Edn. Assn. Presbyterian. Avocations: reading, swimming, boating, antiques, concerts. Home: 351 Hickory Ave Garwood NJ 07027 Office: Faber Sch High and Lehigh Sts Dunellen NJ 08812

MINTER, JIMMIE RUTH, accountant; b. Greenville, S.C., Sept. 28, 1941; d. James C. and Lois (Williams) Jannino; m. Charles H. Minter, Nov. 3, 1972; children: Regina M. Laurie, Michael J. Minter; stepchildren: Rhonda, Julie, Gregg. BS in Acctg., U. S.C., 1962. Asst. controller Package Supply & Equipment Co., Greenville, 1964-70, Olympia Knitting Mills, Spartanburg, S.C., 1970-72; controller Diacou Knitting Mills, Spartanburg, 1972-74; adminstr. Atlanta Med. Specialists, P.C., Riverdale, Ga., 1974-79; adminstr., corp. sec. David L. Cooper, M.D., P.C., Riverdale, 1979-89; acct. Ted L. Griffin Enterprises, Jonesboro, Ga., 1988—; chief tax acct. Clayton County Tax Commn., Jonesboro, 1993—. Program chmn. 4th of July Celebration and Beauty Pageant, City of Riverdale; mem. exec. com. Clayton County Dem. Party, 1987—; Ga. State Dem. treas.; active Clinton Campaign Com.; active local and state election campaign fund raising; bd. dirs. Clayton County Human Rels. Coun., Clayton County Alzheimer's Support Svcs.; chairperson Gold Sword Annual Ball Am. Cancer Soc. Home: 1244 Branchfield Ct Riverdale GA 30296-2148

MINTON, TORRI, journalist; b. San Rafael, Calif., Oct. 7, 1956; d. John and Mary. BA in Ethnic Studies, U. Calif., Berkeley, 1983; M of Journalism, Columbia U., 1984. Reporter Associated Press, San Francisco, 1984, San Francisco Chronicle, 1986—, assigning editor, 2000—. Vice chmn. San Francisco Chronicle No. Calif. Newspaper Guild, 1992, 97, 2000; rep. assembly del., 1992, 93, 94, 95, 96; instr. newswriting U. Calif., Berkeley, 1995—; instr. journalism, lead advisor Golden Gater Newspaper, San Francisco State U., 2000; instr. journalism U. San Francisco, 2000—. Community devel. vol. Oper. Crossroads Africa, Tiriki, Kenya, 1979. Mem. Phi Beta Kappa. Office: San Francisco Chronicle 901 Mission St San Francisco CA 94103-2905 E-mail: tminton@sfchronicle.com.

MINTON, YVONNE FAY, mezzo-soprano; b. Sydney, Australia; d. Robert Thomas and Alice Violet M.; m. William Barclay, Aug. 24, 1965; children— Malcolm Alexander, Alison Elizabeth. Ed., Sydney Conservatorium of Music, 1960-61. Mezzo-soprano with all maj. orchs. in, Australia, 1958-61; moved to, London, 1961, joined, Royal Opera House, Covent Garden, 1965-70, guest artist, Cologne (Germany) Opera, 1969—, U.S. debut as Octavian in Der Rosenkavalier, 1970; appeared, with Lyric Opera, Chgo., 1970, Met. Opera, N.Y.C., 1973, San Francisco Opera, 1974, Paris Opera, 1974, Bayreuth, 1974, Salzburg, 1978; sings regularly with maj. symphony orchs. throughout world, 1968— ; recs. include The Knot Garden, 1970, Cosi Fan Tutte, 1971, Lulu, 1979; maj. vocal works include Mahler songs with, Chgo. Symphony. Comdr. Order Brit. Empire, 1980 Hon. mem. Royal Acad. Music. Office: care Ingpen & Williams 7 St Georges Ct 131 Putney Bridge Rd London SW15 2PA England

MINTY, JUDITH MAKINEN, poet, literature and creative writing educator; b. Detroit, Aug. 5, 1937; d. Karl Jalmer and Margaret (Hunt) Makinen; m. Edgar Sheldon Minty (dec. July 2002); children: Lora Ann, John Reed, Ann Sheldon. BS, Ithaca Coll., 1957; MA, Western Mich. U., 1973; PhD (hon.), Mich. Technol. U., 1997. Asst. prof., vis. poet-in-residence Ctrl. Mich. U., Mount Pleasant, Mich., 1977-78; assoc. prof., vis. poet-in-residence Syracuse U., N.Y., 1979; prof., poet-in-residence Humboldt State U., Arcata, Calif., 1982-93, prof. emerita English, 1993—. Guest lectr. English Grand Valley State U., Allendale, Mich., 1974-77; poet-in-prison pilot project Muskegon Correctional Facility, Mich., 1977; vis. poet-in-residence Interlochen Ctr. for Arts, Mich., 1980, U. Oreg., Eugene, 1983, U. Nebr., Lincoln, 1994, U. Alaska, Anchorage, 1999-2000; vis. lectr. English U. Calif., Santa Cruz, 1981-82. Author: (books of poetry) Lake Songs and Other Fears, 1974 (U.S. award 1973), Yellow Dog Journal, 1979, reprinted 1992, Letters to My Daughters, 1980, In the Presence of Mothers, 1981, Counting the Losses, 1986, Dancing the Fault, 1991, The Mad Painter Poems, 1996, 2d edit., 2003, Walking With the Bear: Selected and New Poems, 2000. John Atherton fellow in poetry Breadloaf Writers Conf., 1974, Yaddo fellow, 1978, 79, 82; recipient Eunice Tietjens award Poetry mag., 1974, Montalvo award for Excellence in Poetry, 1989, Mark Twain award Soc. for Study of Midwestern Lit., Mich. State U., 1998; Creative Artists grantee Mich. Coun. for Arts, 1981, 83, Found. for Women Residency grantee Hopscotch House, 1994; Charles H. Hackley Disting. lectr., Hackley Libr., Muskegon, Mich., 1996. Mem. PEN (syndicated fiction awards 1985, 86, Calif. fiction award 1987), Poetry Soc. Am., Acad. Am. Poets, Associated Writing Programs, Nat. Audubon Soc., Wilderness Soc., Sierra Club, Nature Conservancy. Avocations: birding, hiking, environmentalist. Home: 7113 S Scenic Dr New Era MI 49446-8005 E-mail: judminty@aol.com.

MINTZ, GWENDOLYN JOYCE, writer, educator; b. White Sands, N.Mex, July 23, 1961; BA with distinction, N.Mex State U., 1984. Lic. ednl. asst. N.Mex. Teddy bear artist, owner Teddy Hugs & Things, Las Cruces, N.Mex., 1983—; field rschr. Smithsonian Folklife Program, 1991—92; instr. Dona Ana Br. CC, Las Cruces, 1992—95, 2002; supr., activity asst. U. Ter. Good Samaritan Village, Las Cruces, 1997—99; news writer Las Cruces Bull., 1997—2000. Asst. fiction editor: Small Spiral Notebook, 2002—; editor: Scrivener's Pen Libr. Jour., 2003—; contbr. poetry, short stories, articles to publs. Vol. Univ. Hills Elem., Las Cruces, 1999—2002, Ctrl. Elem., Las Cruces, 2002—03. Named Outstanding Young Woman in Am., 1985, Flash Fiction Extraordinaire, Fiction Warehouse, 2004; recipient Hon. Mention, Writer's Digest Mag. Short Story Competition, 1981, 2001, 4th Ann. Mandy Poetry Contest, 2003, Black Scholar award, Office Black Programs N.Mex State U., 1986, 1990, 2001, 2d pl., The Ink/Border Book Festival Poetry Competition, 2001; scholar, Inst. Gerontol. Rsch. and Edn., 1986, Sarah Lawrence Coll., 2001; Crimson scholar, N.Mex State U., 1980—81. Personal E-mail: gwendolynjoycemintz@yahoo.com.

MINTZ, LENORE CHAICE (LEA MINTZ), consultant; b. N.Y.C., Aug. 6, 1925; d. Abraham and Dr. Eva (Kornblith) Chaice; m. Lewis R. Mintz, July 4, 1944 (dec. Aug. 1996); children: Richard Lewis, Alan Lee, Douglas Chaice. Student, U. Mich., 1942-44; BA magna cum laude, U. Bridgeport, 1976. Cert. personnel cons. Office mgr., personnel cons. Golden Door, Inc., Norwalk, Conn., 1970-78; v.p. permanent div. Aubrey Thomas, Inc., Stamford and Norwalk, 1978-84; sr. v.p. Aubrey Thomas Temps., N.Y., N.J., 1984-88; area v.p. Mid-Atlantic div. Talent Tree Personnel Svcs., 1988-89; v.p. bus. devel. Human Resources, Inc., Norwalk, Stamford, Statford and North Haven, 1989-90; prin. Lea Mintz & Assocs., Norwalk, 1990—. Spkr., panel mem., condr. workshop and seminars in field; justice of peace, Fairfield County, Conn., 1954—94; mem. adv. bd. Norwalk Savs. Soc., 1987—98, U.S. Surg. Corp. (now Tyco Corp.), 1991—; instl. animal care and use com. Bayer Corp., 2002—. Loaned exec. United Way of Norwalk & Wilton, Conn., 1991-92; mem. Norwalk Bd. Edn., 1966-72, chmn., 1969, Norwalk Planning and Zoning Commn., 1971-73, Conn. Edn. Coun., 1979-83, Conn. Small Bus. Adv. Coun., 1984-86; mem. regional adv. coun. Norwalk C.C., 1988-90; past pres. Norwalk Cmty. Tech. Coll. Found., 1988-90, bd. dirs. 1964-94, life hon. bd. dirs., 1995—; del. numerous Dem. state and county convs.; Clinton del. Dem. Nat. Conv., 1992; mem. adv. coun. displaced homemakers Bridgeport YWCA, 1988-90; v.p. Greater Norwalk Cmty. Coun., 1973-75; life mem. Women's Aux. Jewish Home for Aged in Conn.; cmty. rels. cons. Family & Children's Aid Mid-Fairfield County, Conn., 1992—; active numerous other orgns. Recipient numerous awards including Woman of Yr. award Norwalk Bus. and Profl. Womens Club, 1984, Outstanding Woman of Decade award UN Assn. Conn., 1987, Outstanding Svc. award Conn. Cmty. and Tech. Coll. Bd. Trustees, 1991 (1st honoree), Successful Aging award Conn. Cmty. Care Inc., 1999, Woman of Substance award Conn. Post Newspaper, 2000. Mem. Women in Mgmt. (pres. 1990, Ann. Recognition award Conn. and Met. N.Y. area 1988), Internat. Assn. Personnel Women, Greater Norwalk C. of C. (bd. dirs. 1980-84, 1st Athena award 1986), Nat. Coun. Jewish Women (life), LWV, Midday Club Stamford, B'nai B'rith (life), Alpha Sigma Lambda. Avocations: reading, knitting, travel, golf. Home and Office: Silvermine 4 May Dr Norwalk CT 06850-1033 Office Phone: 203-847-3824. E-mail: leamintz@optonline.net.

MINTZ, SUZANNE, association executive; b. Feb. 1946; m. Steven Mintz. BA, Queens Coll., City U. NY; MS, U. Md. Architect; pres., co-founder Nat. Family Caregivers Assn., Wash., DC, 1993—. Bd. dirs. Nat. Patient Safety Found.; adv. bd. Easter Seals, Nat. Assn. Hosp. Hospitality Houses. Author: Love, Honor and Value: A Family Caregiver Speaks Out About the Choices and Challenges of Caregiving, 2002; writer about caregiver issues. Recipient Lilly Welcome Back award for lifetime achievement, 2004. Achievements include has testified before Congress about caregiver issues. Office: Nat Family Caregivers Assn 10400 Conn Ave #500 Kensington MD 20895-3944 Office Phone: 800-896-3650. Office Fax: 301-942-2302.*

MINUDRI, REGINA URSULA, librarian, consultant; b. San Francisco, May 9, 1937; d. John C. and Molly (Halter) M. BA, San Francisco Coll. for Women, 1958; MLS, U. Calif., Berkeley, 1959. Reference libr. Menlo Park (Calif.) Pub. Libr., 1959-62; regional libr. Santa Clara County (Calif.) Libr., 1962-68; project coord. Fed. Young Adult Libr. Svcs. Project, Mountain View, Calif., 1968-71; dir. profl. svcs. Alameda County (Calif.) Libr., 1971, asst. county libr., 1972-77; libr. dir. Berkeley Pub. Libr., 1977-94; city libr. San Francisco Pub. Libr., 1997-2000. Lectr. U. San Francisco, 1970-72, U. Calif., Berkeley, 1977-81, 91-93, San Jose State U., 1994-97; cons., 1975-90; mem. adv. bd. Miles Cutter Ednl., 1992-98. Author: Getting It Together, A Young Adult Bibliography, 1970; contbr. articles to publs. including Sch. Libr. Jour., Wilson Libr. Bull. Bd. dirs. No. Calif. ACLU, 1994-96, Cmty. Memory, 1989-91, Berkeley Pub. Libr. Found., 1996-99; bd. dirs. Berkeley Cmty. Fund, 1995-99, chair youth com., 1994-96; mem. bd. mgrs. ctrl. br. Berkeley YMCA, 1988-93. Recipient proclamation Mayor of Berkeley, 1985, 86, 94, Citation of Merit, Calif. State Assembly, 1994; named Woman of Yr., Alameda County North chpt. Nat. Women's Polit. Caucus, 1985, Outstanding Alumna, U. Calif. Sch. Libr. and Info. Scis., Berkeley, 1987, Lifetime Achievement award Berkeley Cmty. Fund, 2001. Mem. ALA (pres. 1986-87, exec. bd. 1980-89, coun. 1979-88, 90-94, Grolier award 1974), Calif. Libr. Assn. (pres. 1981, coun. 1965-69, 79-82), LWV (dir. Berkeley chpt. 1980-81, v.p. comm. svcs. 1995-97). Office: Reality Mgmt 836 The Alameda Berkeley CA 94707-1916

MINYARD, LIZ, food products executive; BBA, Tex. Christian U., 1975. CEO Minyard Food Stores, Coppell, Tex., 1976—; dir. consumer affairs Minyard Food Stores Inc., Coppell, Tex., v.p. consumer affairs, 1980, v.p. corp. rels., 1983, also vice-chmn. bd. dirs., also co-chmn. bd. dirs. Trustee Boys and Girls Clubs of Am., 1995; chmn. United Way Dallas and Tarrant Counties, 1978, 1983—95; sect. chmn. United Way Tarrant County, 1983—84; chmn. mcht. divsn. United Way Dallas County, 1987, bd. dirs., 1995; bd. mem. Goodwill Industries of Dallas, Inc., 1981—94, mem. exec. com., 1987—88, 1993—95, vice chmn., 1992—94, chmn., 1995; mem. spring campaign drive YWCA, Dallas, 1982, chmn. campaign, 1983—85, co-chmn. capital campaign, 1995, co-chmn. mayor's summer youth employment commn., 1994, chmn. mayor's summer youth employment commn., 1995, bd. dirs., 1995; v.p. Dallas Urban League, 1989—91, bd. dirs., 1985—95, chmn. bd. dirs., 1992—93, chmn. bldg. com., 1995; mem. Dallas Citizens Coun., 1988—94, bd. dirs. exec. com., 1992—95; bd. dirs. Leukemia Assn. of North Ctrl. Tex., 1988—95; mem. Dallas Assembly, 1989—95; bd. dirs. Baylor Hosp. Found., 1989—95; mem. Dallas Summit, 1992—95, Dallas Together Forum, 1993—95, Dallas Women's Forum, 1994—95; bd. dirs. Zale Lipshy Hosp., 1993—95, Am. Heart Assn., 1991—94; chmn. City of Dallas Bond Program, 1995. Recipient Dallas/Ft. Worth Dist. Women in Bus. Adv. of Yr. award, U.S. Small Bus. Adminstrn., 1995, Tex. Family Bus. of Yr.-Cmty. Involvement award, Tex. Inst. Family Bus., 1995, Bus. award for Cmty. Involvement, Martin Luther King Jr. Cmty Ctr., 1995, Contbrs. award, Black State Employees Assn. of Tex., 1995, Art of Achievement award, Nat. Fedn. ow Women Bus. Owners, 1995. Mem.: North Tex. Commn. (bd. dirs. 1992—95), CIES The Food Bus. Forum (ann. congress com. mem. 1996), Tex. Food Mktg. Assn. (v.p. 1981—82, pres. 1982—84), Food Mktg. Inst. (consumer coun. 1977—88, steering com. 1982, pub. affairs com. 1989—90, bd. dirs. 1991—95), Greater Dallas C. of C. (leadership program 1982—83, bd. dirs. 1987—90, women's bus. issues exec. com. 1994—95, Women's Convenant Diamond Cutters award 1995), Second Harvest (Chgo. bd. dirs. 1992—95), North Tex. Food Bank (founding bd. mem., sec. 1981—83, bd. mem. 1982—95, pres. 1984, v.p. devel. 1987, chmn. hunger link program 1989—90). Office: Minyard Food Stores Inc PO Box 518 Coppell TX 75019-0518

MINZNER, PAMELA BURGY, state supreme court justice; b. Meridian, Miss., Nov. 19, 1943; BA cum laude, Miami U., 1965; LLB, Harvard U., 1968. Bar: Mass. 1968, N.Mex. 1972. Pvt. practice, Mass., 1968—71, Albuquerque, 1971—73; adj. prof. law U. N.Mex., Albuquerque, 1972—73, asst. prof., 1973—77, assoc. prof., 1977—80, prof. law, 1980—84; judge N.Mex. Ct. Appeals, Albuquerque, 1984—94, chief judge, 1993—94; justice N.Mex. Supreme Ct., Santa Fe, 1994—, chief justice, 1999—2001. Mem. faculty Inst. Preparativo Legal U., N.Mex. Sch. Law, 1975, 79; participant NEH Summer Seminars for Law Tchrs. Stanford Law Sch., 1982, U. Chgo. Law Sch., 1978. Author (with Robert T. Laurence): A Student's Guide to Estates in Land and Future Interests: Text, Examples, Problems & Answers, 1981, 2d edit., 1993. Mem.: ABA, State Bar N.Mex. (co-editor newsletter 1979—83, bd. dirs. 1978—79, 1983—84, sect. on women's legal rights and obligations), Gamma Phi Beta. Democrat. Avocations: reading, bridge, movies. Office: Supreme Ct Bldg 237 Don Gaspar Ave Santa Fe NM 87501-2178

MIQUELON, MIRIAM F. former prosecutor, lawyer; b. Elmhurst, Ill. children: Aaron, Rachel. Grad., U. Ariz., 1975, DePaul U., 1978; LLM in Taxation, Chgo.-Kent Coll. Law; postgrad. in Taxation, DePaul U.; postgrad. in History, Northwestern U. Lawyer, Houston, Stone, McGuire, Benjamin & Kocoras, Miquelon & Assocs., 1981—88, Keck, Mahin & Cate, Chgo., 1988—91; asst. U.S. atty. Ea. Dist. N.Y., Bklyn., 1991—93, So. Dist. Ill., 1993—99; asst. spl. counsel to Spl. Counsel John C. Danforth, 1999—2000; asst. U.S. atty. So. Dist. Ill., 2000—02, U.S. atty., 2002—03. Adj. prof. law Washington U. Sch. Law, St. Louis; adj. faculty Northwestern U. Coll. Law, Chgo. Recipient Chief Postal Inspector's award, U.S. Postal Inspection Svc., 2001, Spl. commendations, FBI, Drug Enforcement Adminstrn., U.S. Customs Svc., IRS. Avocations: volunteering, sports activities.

MIRACLE, DORIS JEAN, retired medical/surgical nurse; b. Louisville, Ky., July 23, 1931; d. Bernard Louis and Catherine Federle; m. Earl Miracle, Aug. 31, 1951; 1 child, David. Surg. nurse Norton Hosp., Louisville, Norton-Children's Hosp., Louisville. Contbr. poems to poetry anthologies, Theatre of the Mind, 2003, Internat. Libr. Poetry, 2003; poetry (albums) Sounds of Poetry, 2003; contbr. articles to profl. jours., poems to mags. Recipient Editors Choice award, 2003. Mem.: Gaslight Writers, Ky. Writer's Coalition, Internat. Soc. of Poets, Soc. Children's Book Writers and Illustrators. Avocations: reading, poetry, astronomy, art, music.

MIRANDA, MINDA, chemist, pharmacy technician; b. Alabat, Quezon, The Philippines, Apr. 7, 1955; came to U.S., 1990; d. Macario and Engracia (Malapajo) Felisco; m. Danilo E. Miranda, June 10, 1979; children: Mary Eisser, Dann Keoffer. BSChemE, Nat.U., Manila, The Philippines, 1977. Instr. Nat. U., Manila, 1977-90; pharm. technician Automated Pharm. Svcs., Moorestown, N.J., 1990-95; quality control lab. technician Marsam Pharms., Cherry Hill, N.J., 1995-96, assoc. stability chemist, 1996-97, stability chemist I, 1997—. Scholar Nat. U., 1972-75. Mem. Am. Chem. Soc. Home: 142 Cooper Ave Oaklyn NJ 08107-2246

MIRANDA-EVANS, VALETTA LEE, social worker, human services manager; d. Leland James and Mary Miranda; m. Bruce Claude Evans, Aug. 23, 1986; children: Darcel Lynette Murray, Adam Bruce Evans, Kristina L. Evans. BA, Boston U., 1977; MSW, Boston Coll., 1979. LCSW 1986, CEAP 1983, PHR 2000. Program specialist Nat. Clearinghouse for Alcohol/Drug Info., Rockville, Md., 1979—82; employee assistance counselor Prince George's County Health Dept., Beltsville, Md., 1982—84; substance abuse program coord. Social Security Adminstrn., Balt., 1984—88; dir. employee assistance program ARC, Washington, 1988—92; employee assistance cons. DuPont, Richmond, Va., 1992—96, human resource mgr., 1996—2002, employee assistance cons. Wilmington, Del., 2002—. Office: DuPont Rte 141 CRP 700/32 Wilmington DE 19808

MIRENDA, ROSALIE M. nursing educator, administrator; b. Phila., Sept. 22, 1937; d. Achille and Anna Pierotti; m. Anthony D. Mirenda, Sept. 9, 1961; children: Anthony D. Jr., John A., Rosalie A. BSN, Villanova U., 1959; MS in Nursing, U. Pa., 1978; DNSc, Widener U., 1992. Staff nurse, tchr. St. Agnes Med. Ctr., Phila., Mercy Cath. Med. Ctr., Darby, Pa.; prof., v.p. for acad. affairs Neumann Coll., Aston, Pa. Pres. Neuman Systems Model Trustee Group Inc. Contbr. articles to profl. jours. Chmn. Bd. trustees Sch. Holy Child, Drexel. Recipient Bronze medal; named Prof. of Yr. Coun. Adv. Support Edn., 1987, Outstanding Educator of Am., 1975, Outstanding Nurse award, 1990. Mem. ANA, NLN, AAUW, Sigma Theta Tau, Delta Tau. Office: Neumann Coll Libr 1 Neumann Dr Aston PA 19014-1277

MIRK, JUDY ANN, retired elementary school educator; b. Victorville, Calif., June 10, 1944; d. Richard Nesbit and Corrine (Berghoefer). BA in Social Sci., San Jose (Calif.) State U., 1966, cert. in teaching, 1967; MA in Edn., Calif. State U., Chico, 1980. Cert. elem. edn. tchr., Calif. Profl. psychology trainee John F. Kennedy U., Orinda, Calif., 1997—99; tchr. Cupertino (Calif.) Union Sch. Dist., 1967-95; lead tchr. lang. arts Dilworth Sch., San Jose, 1988-90, mem. supt.'s adv. team, 1986-90, mem. student study team, 1987-95; ret. Mem. student study team, 1987-95; mem. Dilworth Sch. Site Coun., 1981-95. Mem. The Commonwealth Club of Calif, Phi Mu. Green Party. Avocations: photography, natural history, watercolors. Home: 2075 Redwood Dr Santa Cruz CA 95060-1238

MIRRA, SUZANNE SAMUELS, neuropathologist, researcher; BA, Hunter Coll., 1962; MD, SUNY, Bklyn., 1967. Instr. pathology Yale U. Sch. Medicine, New Haven, 1971-73; staff pathologist Atlanta VA Med. Ctr., Decatur, Ga., 1973-97; asst. prof. pathology Emory U. Sch. Medicine, Atlanta, 1973-80, assoc. prof. pathology, 1981-93, prof. pathology, 1993-97; prof., chair dept. pathology SUNY Health Sci. Ctr., Bklyn., 1997—. Dir., prin. investor Emory Alzheimer's Disease Ctr., Atlanta, 1991—97. Mem. editl. bd. Arch Pathol. Lab. Med., 1988-2000, Jour. Neuropathology Exptl. Neurology, 1991-95, Brain Pathology, 1995-99, Alzheimer's Disease Reviews, 1995-2000. Recipient Albert E. Levy Sci. Faculty Rsch. award Emory U., 1987, Disting. Alumnus Achievement award SUNY, 1992; named to Hunter Coll. Hall of Fame, 1996. Fellow Coll. Am. Pathologists (Presdl. award 1987,89, Herbert Lansky award 1990, chair neuropathology commn. 1992-95); mem. Am. Assn. Neuropathologists (v.p. profl. affairs 1992-97, pres. 1999-2000), Alzheimer's Assn. (bd. dir. Atlanta chpt. 1987-97, nat. bd. dir. 1997—), Alpha Omega Alpha, mem., 2002. Office: SUNY Health Sci Ctr 450 Clarkson Ave Brooklyn NY 11203-2056 E-mail: suzanne.mirra@downstate.edu

MIRSKY, PHYLLIS SIMON, librarian; b. Petach Tikva, Israel, Dec. 18, 1940; d. Allan and Lea (Prizant) Simon; m. Edward Mirsky, Oct. 21, 1967; 1 child, Seth (dec.). BS in Social Welfare, Ohio State U., 1962; postgrad., Columbia U., 1962-63; AMLS, U. Mich., 1965. Caseworker field placement Children's Aid Soc., N.Y.C., 1962-63; hosp. libr. hosp. and instns. divsn. Cleve. Pub. Libr., 1963-64; reference libr. UCLA Biomed. Libr., 1965-68, reference/acquisitions libr., 1968-69, head cons./continuing edn. Pacific S.W. Regl. Med. Libr. Sv., 1969-71, asst. dir. Pacific S.W. Regl. Med. Libr. Sv., 1971-73, faculty coord. Biomed. Libr. program Cen. San Joaquin Valley Area Health Edn. Ctr., 1973-77, assoc. dir. Pacific S.W. Regl. Med. Libr. Sv., 1973-79; head reference sect., coord. libr. assoc. program Nat. Libr. of Medicine, Bethesda, Md., 1979-81; asst. univ. libr., scis. U. Calif.-San Diego, La Jolla, 1981-86, acting univ. libr., 1985, 92-93, 98-99, asst. univ. libr. adminstrv. and pub. svcs., 1986-87, assoc. univ. libr. adminstrv. and pub. svcs., 1987-92, assoc. univ. libr., 1993-95; dep. univ. libr., 1995—. Guest lectr. Libr. Schs. UCLA and U. So. Calif., 1967-78, Grad. Sch. Libr. Sci. Cath. U., Washington, 1980, Grad. Sch. Libr. and Info. Sci. UCLA, 1984; mem. task force on role of spl. libr. nationwide network and coop. programs Nat. Commn. on Libr. and Info. [illegible]/Spl. Libr. Assn., 1981-83; facilitator AASLD/MLA Guidelines Scenario Writing Session, L.A., 1984; mem. users coun. OCLC Online Computer Libr. Ctr., Inc., 1991-94; U. Calif.-San Diego rep. Coalition for Networked Info., 1992—; instr. Assn. Rsch. Librs., Office Mgmt. Studies, Mgmt. Inst., 1987; peer reviewer Coll. Libr. Tech. and Cooperation Grant Program U.S. Dept. Edn., 1988-94; cons. Nat. Libr. Medicine, Bethesda, Md., 1988, San Diego Mus. Contemporary Art Libr., La Jolla, Calif., 1993, Salk Inst., 1995; mem. Libr. of Congress Network Adv. Com., 1994-96, chair steering com., 1995-96. Contbr. articles to profl. jours. and bulls. Mem. fin. com. City of Del Mar, 1995-98, chair, 1997-98, facility adv. com., 2000—. NIH fellow Columbia U., 1962-63; sr. fellow UCLA/Coun. on Libr. Resources, 1987. Fellow Med. Libr. Assn. (bd. dirs. 1977-80); mem. ALA (site visitors panel com. on accreditation 1990-92, libr. adminstrn. and mgmt. assn. 1990-92), Med. Libr. Group So. Calif. and Ariz. (sec. 1970-71, v.p. 1971-72, pres. 1972-73), Documentation Abstracts, Inc. (bd. dirs. 1985-90, vice chair bd. dirs. 1988-90), Med. Libr. Assn. (pres. 1984-85), U. Mich. Sch. Libr. Sci. Alumni Assn. Office: U Calif San Diego U Libr 0175G 9500 Gilman Dr La Jolla CA 92093-0175

MIRVAHABI, FARIN, lawyer; b. Tehran, Iran; d. Ali and Azar Mirvahabi; children: Bobby Naemi, Jimmy Naemi. Degree in Law, Tehran U., Iran, 1968; M of Comparative Law, Georgetown U., 1972; LLM, George Washington U., 1976; JSD, NYU, 1978; diploma, The Hague Acad. Internat. Law, 1983. Bar: Va. 1989, U.S. Dist. Ct. (ea. and we. dists.) Va. 1990, D.C. 1990, U.S. Dist. Ct. D.C. 1990, U.S. Supreme Ct. 1997. With Gold & Cutner, N.Y.C., 1979-80; in-house counsel IRA Engring. and Constrn., Tehran, London, 1981-82; legal advisor Bank Markazi, Tehran, 1981-82; practiced law The Hague, The Netherlands, 1982-87; arbitrator Iran Air-Pan Am Arbitration Tribunal, Paris, 1984-87; legal cons. Rooney, Barry & Fogerty, Washington, 1987-88; atty. sole practice, 1989—. Law prof. No. Va. Law Sch., Alexandria, 1989-90; instr. Paralegal Inst., Arlington, Va., 1988-89; prof. Tehran U., 1982; panelist Am. Arbitration Assn.; guest speaker in field; life dep. gov. Am. Biog. Inst. Rsch. Assn., 19995—. Contbr. numerous articles to profl. jours. Named Maxplank fellow Maxplank Inst. of Internat. Law, 1986; recipient Clyde Eagleton award NYU, 1977, Woman of Yr. medallion honoring Cmty. Svc. and Profl. Achievement, 1995. Mem. ABA, Internat. Bar Assn., Arbitration Forum Inc., D.C. Bar Assn. (panelist client-atty. arbitration bd. 1990—), D.C. Bar & Lawyers Assn., Trial Lawyers Assn., Va. Bar Found., Am. Soc. Internat. Law, Am. Film Inst. The Kennedy Ctr. Avocations: reading, writing, Broadway shows, picnic, swimming. Office: 1730 K St NW Ste 304 Washington DC 20006-3839

MIRZA, LEONA LOUSIN, elementary school educator, director; b. Chgo., July 1, 1944; d. Max B. and Opal Lousin; m. David B. Mirza; children: Sara Anush, Elizabeth Ann. BA in Math., North Park Coll., Chgo., 1965; MA in Edn., Western Mich. U., Kalamazoo, 1967, EdD in Edn., 1972; cert. in computer studies, North Park Coll., 1983. Specialist in elem. curriculum and adminstrn. Tchr. Kalamazoo Pub. Schs., 1965-69; prof. math. edn. North Park U., Chgo., 1969-2001, asst. acad. dean, 1999—2001; dir. Inst. for Internat. and Cultural Studies, 2001—. Editor The Ill. Math. Tchr., 1992-95; contbr. articles to profl. jours. Chmn. adv. com. on edn. in Ill., 1975-77. Mem. Nat. Coun. Tchrs. Math., Ill. Coun. Tchrs. Math., Ill. Assn. Colls. of Tchr. Edn., Ill. Assn. Tchrs. Edn. in Pvt. Colls. (officer 1974-86). Home: 5241 N Sawyer Ave Chicago IL 60625-4715 Office: 3225 W Foster Ave Chicago IL 60625-4823

MISCELLA, MARIA DIANA, humanities educator; b. N.Y.C., July 11, 1929; d. Nicola and Giovanna (Tangorra) Torelli; m. Emilio Miscella, Feb. 27, 1954 (dec. Sept. 30, 1996); children: Delia, Marisa, Giuliana. Tchr. Degree, Istituto Magistrale, Lecce, Italy, 1946; postgrad., U. Naples, 1946-48; BA, Hunter Coll., 1954, MA, 1972. Cert. secondary educator, N.Y. state, N.Y.C. English corr. GE Co., Rome, 1950-51; corr. Spanish & French Pettinos Import & Export Co., N.Y.C., 1952-53; tchr. Italian Harrison (N.Y.) H.S., 1967-87, St. John's U., Queens, N.Y., 1987-89; lectr. Italian various orgsn., N.Y. State, 1987—; lectr. Italian lit. and history various colls. and univs., N.Y., 1987—. Moderator of club Harrison (N.Y.) H.S., 1967-87. Mem. Little Neck (N.Y.) Civic Assn., 1970-95, Am. Assn. Ret. People, Douglaston, N.Y., 1994—; founder, treas. Italian Am. Women's Ctr., 1997—. Recipient scholarship Columbia U., 1954, Letter of Commendation, Bd. Regents, Albany, N.Y., 1980; named Woman of Yr., Consortium of L.I. Italian Am. Orgns., 1992. Mem. AAUW (hostess, v.p. 1990-93, cert. of commendation 1996), Am. Assn. Tchrs. of Italian (sec. Societa Onoraria Italica 1979-91), Ams. of Italian Heritage (bd. mem. 1982—), Sons of Italy (John Marino Lodge cultural com. mem 1994—, Merit award 1995), Assn. Italian Am. Educators (dir./historian by-laws com. 2000), N.Y. State United Tchrs., Am. Fedn. Tchrs., Nat. Italian Am. Found., Douglaston Women Club, Retirees Club. Roman Catholic. Avocations: reading, writing, travel, going to theatre, playing bridge.

MISKILL, DEE SHELTON, design graphics executive; b. N.Y.C., Dec. 30, 1948; d. Nicholas T. and Estelle Shelton; m. Donald Keepers Miskill Jr., May 23, 1980; children: Nathan, Rachael, Justin, Colin. Student, Marymount Jr. Coll., 1966-67; BA in Sociology, Adelphi U., 1970. Naval reservist multiple units, Mass., Maine and Va., 1976-92; sr. advisor ARC, Sigonella, Sicily, Italy, 1992-94; subs. tchr. Stephen Decatur Sch., Sigonella, Sicily, Italy, 1993-94; pub. info. specialist Mid Coast Health Svcs., Brunswick, Maine, 1995-98; dir. devel. Mid Coast chpt. ARC, Brunswick, 1998-99; pres. Deesign Graphics, Orrs Island, Maine, 2000—. Co-chmn. ARC Annual Ball, Brunswick, 1995-97, chair adv. com. to Brunswick Naval Air Sta., 1987-92. Lt. USN, 1975-76. Mem. Naval Res. Assn. (life). Roman Catholic. Avocations: snowshoeing, cooking, hiking.

MISNER, CHARLOTTE BLANCHE RUCKMAN, retired community organization administrator; b. Gifford, Idaho, Aug. 30, 1937; d. Richard Steele and Arizona (Hill) Ruckman; m. G. Arthur Misner, Jr., Aug. 29, 1959; children: Michelle, Mary, Jennifer. BS in Psychology, U. Idaho, 1959. Vol. numerous orgns., India, Mexico, The Philippines, 1962-70; sec., v.p., pres., trustee St. Luke's Hosp., Manila, 1970-84; founding mem., 3d v.p., pres. Am. Women's Club of Philippines, 1980-84; exec. dir. Friends of Oakland (Calif.) Parks and Recreation, 1986-2000, ret., 2000. Active Lincoln Child Ctr., Oakland, 1984—. Recipient Vol. Svc. award Women's Bd. St. Luke's Hosp., 1977, Mid. Sch. Vol. award Internat. Sch.-Manila, 1980. Me. Alpha Gamma Delta (alumnae treas., pres. East Bay 1985-89, province dir. alumnae 1989-98, bd. dirs. alumni devel. 1998—, mem. steering com. centennial capital campaign 1999—), Cum Laude Soc. (hon.). Home: 5304 Woodgrove Ct Concord CA 94521-5422

MISNER, LORRAINE, laboratory technologist; b. Fitchburg, Mass., June 24, 1948; d. Cedric Winfield and Pearl Erma (Hallisey) M. BA in Biology, Fitchburg State Coll., 1971; MS in Med. Tech., Anna Maria Coll., 1983. Cert. Novell engr. Lab. technologist Leominster (Mass.) Hosp., 1971-87; rsch. asst. U. Lowell Rsch. Found. (now U. Mass. Lowell Rsch. Found.), 1987-99; sys. engr. TeleSpectrum Worldwide Inc., 1999—. Piccolo Townsend (Mass.) Mil. Band, 1964-93; mem. choir United Ch. of Christ, 1961—. Mem. Am. Soc. Clin. Pathologists (assoc., registrant). Avocations: bowling, music, travel, dance. E-mail: lorraine.misner@hp.com.

MISRACK, TANA MARIE, counselor, minister, writer; b. Toledo, July 25, 1954; d. Anthony James and Isabelle (Drinkhouse) Richards; m. Robert Aaron Misrack, June 30, 1996. AS in Interior Design, West Valley Coll., 1979. Ordained to ministry Universal Ch. of Master, 1986. Owner, designer Interiors by Tana Marie, Saratoga, Calif., 1979-88; min., profl. intuitive counselor Monterey, Calif., 1988—; CEO, cons. Strategies for Success, Monterey, Calif., 1994—; CEO, Tana Marie's Passion Island, 2002—. Lectr., seminar leader, Monterey, 1988—; radio personality Sta. KNRY-1240 Cannery Row, Monterey, 2000—; profl. intuitive counselor. Author: Isle of Fantasies, 1995, Mating Games:Stop Playing and Start Loving, 1999, Guy Code: Understand Your Man, 2000; contbr. articles to profl. jours. Amb. San Jose (Calif.) C. of C., 1993-2000; mem. Mountain View (Calif.) Chamber, 1994-98. Mem. Women's Fund (1st v.p. 1994-98, pres. 1998-2000), Monterey C. of C. Avocations: cycling, photography, writing. Office Phone: 831-646-1137.

MISSAKIAN, ILONA VIRGINIA, secondary school educator, bookkeeper; b. Huntington Park, Calif., July 16, 1968; d. Garo Garabed and Brigitte Renate Anne Marie (Kunkel) M. AA with honors, Mt. San Antonio Coll., 1991; BA with honors, Calif. State U., Fullerton, 1993, MA, 1997. Tchg. credential. Instr. Alexandra Ballet Acad., Hacienda Heights, Calif., 1985-92, Dellos Dance and Performing Arts Ctr., Walnut, Calif., 1989-91; apprentice Les Ballets Classiques, Montreal, Can., 1987-88; bookkeeper Garo's German Auto Repair, Walnut, 1986—; tchr. Brea (Calif.) Olinda H.S., 1994—. Instr. Dance En l'Air, Glendora, Calif., 1998—; tchr. Mt. San Antonio (Calif.) Coll., 1999—, Rio Hondo (Calif.) Coll., 2003—; assoc. dir. Calif. Classical Youth Ballet, 2001-; writing project fellow U. Calif., 2003. Mem. MLA, Calif. Lit. Project, Calif. State Fullerton Alumni, Alpha Gamma Sigma (sec., news editor 1988-91). Avocations: ballet, visual arts. Office: Brea Olinda HS 789 Wildcat Way Brea CA 92821-7402

MISSETT, JUDI SHEPPARD, dancer, jazzercise company executive; b. Iowa; BA in Theater, Radio/TV, Northwestern U., Chgo., 1966. Profl. dancer, Chgo., 1966-77; jazzercise instr., choreographer, tchr., 1977—; pres. worldwide dance-fitness franchise orgn. Jazzercise, Inc., Carlsbad, Calif.; prin. JM TV Prodns.; prin. mail-order catalog bus. Jazzertogs. Instr. convs., children's fitness progs. Author: (comprehensive nutrition prog.) The Jazzercise Know More Diet; author weekly fitness column for Los Angeles Times Syndicate; performer, prodr. home exercise videos. Mem. Calif. Gov.'s Coun. on Phys. Fitness & Sports; bd. dirs. San Diego Inner-City Games; contbr. millions of dollars for charities by leading spl., large-scale workout classes. Recognized for contbns. to growth and advancement of fitness industry by Pres. Reagan in his White House Conf. on Women in Bus., 1986, Aerobics and Fitness Assn. Am., Am. Coun. on Exercise, Pres.' Coun. on Phys. Fitness & Sports; named Entrepreneur of Year, Working Woman Mag., 1988; recipient Lifetime Achievement award Internat. Assn. Fitness Profls., 1991, Women Who Mean Bus. award San Diego Bus. Jour., 1995, A Woman of Accomplishment award Soroptimist Internat. of San Diego, 1996; inducted into Internat. Assn. Fitness Profls. Hall of Fame, 1992. Mem. Nat. Fitness Leaders Assn. (exec. dir., Charles Bucher Meml. award 1996). Office: Jazzercise Inc 2460 Impala Dr Carlsbad CA 92008-7226

MISTACCO, VICKI E. foreign language educator; b. Bklyn., Nov. 18, 1942; d. Anthony Sebastian and Lucia (Lalli) M. BA, NYU, 1963; MA, Middlebury Coll., 1964; M of Philosophy, Yale U., 1968, PhD, 1972. Instr. French Wellesley Coll., Mass., 1968-72, asst. prof. French, 1972-78, assoc. prof. French, 1978-84, prof. French, 1984—, chmn., 1978-81. Nat. adv. bd. Sweet Briar Jr. Yr. in France, Va., 1978—. Contbr. articles to profl. jours. Fulbright fellow, 1963-64, Woodrow Wilson fellow, 1964-67; NEH fellow, 1983-84, 94-95. Mem.: N.E. MLA, MLA, Soc. Internat. pour l'Etude des Femmes de l'Ancien Regime, Women in French, Am. Assn. Tchrs. French, Phi Beta Kappa. Democrat. Roman Catholic. Avocations: photography, travel. Office: Wellesley Coll Dept French 106 Central St Wellesley MA 02481-8268 Office Phone: 781-283-2406.

MITCHAM, CARLA J. utilities executive; BS in Indsl. Distbn., MS in Indsl. Tech., Tex. A&M U.; JD, U. Houston. Pres. Reliant Energy ERCOT Supply Reliant Resources, Inc., Houston. Office: Reliant Energy Exec Office PO Box 2286 Houston TX 77252-2286

MITCHARD, JACQUELYN, writer; b. 1953; H.S. English tchr., 1974—76; mng. editor, reporter Pioneer Press, Chgo., 1976—79; reporter The Capital Times, Madison, Wis., 1979—84; metro reporter, columnist Milw. Jour., 1984—88; speechwriter for Donna Shalala, 1989—93. Author: Mother Less Child, 1985, Jane Addams: Pioneer in Social Reform and Activist for World Peace, 1991, Jane Addams: Peace Activist, 1992, The Deep End of the Ocean, 1996, The Rest of Us: Dispatches from the Mothership, 1997, The Most Wanted, 1998, A Theory of Relativity, 2001, Twelve Times Blessed, 2003, Christmas Present, 2003, Starring Prima!, 2004. Office: c/o Jane Gelfman Gelfman Schneider Lit Agts Inc 250 W 57th St New York NY 10107

MITCHELL, ANDREA, journalist; b. N.Y.C., Oct. 30, 1946; d. Sydney and Cecile Mitchell; m. Alan Greenspan, Apr. 6, 1997. BA, U. Pa., 1967. Polit. reporter KYW Newsradio, Phila., 1967-76; polit. corr. Sta. KYW-TV, Phila., 1972-76; corr. Sta. WTOP-TV, Washington, 1977-78; gen. assignment and energy corr. NBC News, Washington, 1978-81, White House corr., 1981-88, chief congl. corr., 1989-92, chief White House corr., 1993-94, chief fgn. affairs corr., 1995—. Substitute anchor Meet the Press, 1988—; host MSNBC The Mitchell Report, Decision 2000. Trustee U. Pa., 1995—. Recipient award for pub. affairs reporting Am. Polit. Sci. Assn., 1969, Pub. Affairs Reporting award AP, 1976, AP Broadcast award, 1977; named Communicator of the Yr., Phila. chpt. Women in Comms., 1976, Woman of the Yr., Phila. chpt. Am. Women in Radio and TV, 1989, Lucretia Mott award Woman's Way, 1991. Office: NBC News 4001 Nebraska Ave NW Washington DC 20016-2733

MITCHELL, ANNA-MARIE RAJALA, quality/outcomes analyst; b. Detroit; d. Ruben Victor and Janie Elizabeth Rajala; m. Robert David Mitchell, Jan. 22, 1994; children: Kimberly, Andrew. BS in Med. Tech., U. Mich., 1986, M Health Svcs. Adminstrn., 1992. Cert. med. technologist Am. Soc. Clin. Pathologists. Med. technologist U. Mich. Med. Ctr., Ann Arbor, 1986-94; med. data analyst Blue Care Network, Southfield, Mich., 1994-98; quality/outcomes analyst M-CARE, Ann Arbor, 1998—. Mem. Jr. League of Ann Arbor, 1993-95. Mem. APHA, ACHE, S.E. Suburban Mothers of Twins Club (state rep., resale chairwoman 1997—). Office: M-CARE 2301 Commonwealth Blvd Fl 2 Ann Arbor MI 48105-2955 Fax: 734-747-7153. E-mail: armitch@umich.edu.

MITCHELL, BARBARA ANN, marketing professional; b. Washington, Oct. 27, 1954; d. Russell Anthony and Mary Rose Mitchell. BA, Cornell U., 1976; diploma in internat. rels., Inst. Social Studies, The Hague, The Netherlands, 1979; M in Mgmt., Northwestern U., 1983. Mktg. cons. Burson Marsteller, Kuala Lumpur, Malaysia, 1991—92; chief mktg. officer Trade Russia, Inc., Krasnedar, Russia, 1992—93; mgmt. cons. Mitchell & Assocs., Camp Springs, Md., 1994—98; sr. mktg. mgr. Metamor Techs., Alexandria, Va., 1998—99; sr. product mgr. Clear Blue Techs., Reston, Va., 1999—. Mem.: Women in Tech., Cornell Club Washington. Avocations: triathlons, American Revolutionary War history, travel, languages, art. Home: 21435 Falling Rock Terr Ashburn VA 20148

MITCHELL, BETTIE PHAENON, religious organization administrator; b. Colorado Springs, Colo., June 6, 1934; d. Roy William and Laura Lee (Costin) Roberts; m. Gerald Mitchell, May 3, 1952; children: Michelle Carter Smith, Laura Sweitz, Jennie Grenzer, Mohammad Bader. BS in Edn., Lewis & Clark Coll., 1954; postgrad., Portland State U., 1962-72; MA in Religion summa cum laude, Warner Pacific Coll., 1979. Cert. counselor, Oreg. Elem. tchr. Quincy Sch. Dist., Clatskanie, Oreg., 1955-56; substitute tchr. Beaverton (Oreg.) and Washington County Schs., 1956-77; tchr. of the Bible Portland (Oreg.) C.C., 1974-92; counseling and healing ministry, 1977-79; founder, exec. dir. Good Samaritan Ministries, Beaverton, 1979—2002, founder, internat. exec. dir., 1988—2002. Tchr. Christian Renewal Ctr. Workshops, 1977-2002; spkr., presenter in field; leader tours in the Mid. East; developing counselor edn. programs Spain, Ghana, Pakistan, Ukraine, Jordan, Egypt, Kenya, numerous other countries. Author: Who Is My Neighbor? A Parable, 1988, The Power of Conflict and Sacrifice, A Therapy Manual for Christian Marriage, 1988, Good Samaritan Training Handbook, 1989, Be Still and Listen to His Voice, The Story of Prayer and Faith, 1990, A Need for Understanding - International Counselor Training Manual, 1993, The Heros of Vietnam, The Children They Touched. Mem. Israel Task Force, Portland, 1974-80; Leader Camp Fire Internat., 1962-73, elem. sch. coord., 1962-68; asst. dir. Washington County Civil Def., 1961-63; precinct committeewoman Rep. Party, 1960; bd. dirs. Beaverton Fish, 1966-74; v.p. NCCJ, Portland, 1983-85; chmn., speaker's bur. Near East Task Force for Israel; chmn. fire bond issue campaign City of Beaverton, mgr. mayoral campaign, 1960; sunday sch. tchr., speaker, organizer Sharing and Caring program Bethel Ch., 1974-79. Mem. Am. Christian Counseling Assn., Christian Assn. for Psychol. Studies, Oreg. Counseling Assn. Republican. Avocations: historical research, writing, photography. Home: 6550 SW Imperial Dr Beaverton OR 97008-5311 Office: Good Samaritan Ministries 7929 SW Cirrus Dr Ste 23 Beaverton OR 97008-5973 Fax: 503-646-8898.

MITCHELL, BETTY LOU, state legislator, retired operations director; b. Hartford, Conn., Aug. 14, 1937; m. Don David Mitchell; 3 children. Grad., Ellsworth H.S. Various mgmt. positions NYNEX Bell Atlantic; ops. dir. State of Maine, Bell Atlantic, 1989-92; mem. Dist. 10 Maine Senate, Augusta, 1996—. Corporator Bangor Savs. Bank, Ea. Maine Health Care. Mem. bd. dirs., chair long range planning Bangor Brewer YWCA; bd. dirs., chair campaign, chair leadership United Way Ea. Maine; bd. dirs., chair leadership devel. Pine Tree chpt. ARC; mem. Better Bus. Womens Investment Club, Telephone Pioneers Am.; mem. SAD 38 and 48, sch. bd., 1975-85; mem. Bd. Environ. Protection, 1984—; mem. Low Level Radioactive Waste Authority, 1993-94; mem. planning bd. ETNA, 1994-95. Republican. Home: PO Box 6 Etna ME 04434-0006 Office: Maine State Senate 3 State House Sta Augusta ME 04333-0003

MITCHELL, BEVERLY SHRIVER, hematologist, oncologist, educator; b. Balt., May 14, 1944; m. John Robert Pringle; children: Robert Mitchell, Elizabeth Greene. AB summa cum laude in Biochemistry, Smith Coll., 1965; MD, Harvard U., 1969. Hematology fellow U. Mich., Ann Arbor, 1975-77, from instr. to asst. prof. internal medicine, 1977-81, assoc. prof., 1981-87, prof. internal medicine and pharmacology, 1987-91, U. N.C., Chapel Hill, 1991—, divsn. chief hematology/oncology, 1994—2003; assoc. dir. Lineberger Cancer Cu., Chapel Hill, 1994—. Vis. scientist Fred Hutchinson Cancer Ctr., Seattle, 1984; mem. bd. sci. counselors Cancer Treatment divsn. Nat. Cancer Inst. Recipient Stohlman award Leukemia Soc. Am., 1988. Mem. Am. Soc. Hematology (treas. 1991-96, v.p. 1998, pres. 2000), Phi Beta, Inst. Medicine. Achievements include research in nucleotide metabolism and the development of novel therapies for hematologic malignancies. Office: U NC at Chapel Hill CB # 7295 Lineberger Comprehensive Cancer Ctr Chapel Hill NC 27599-7295

MITCHELL, CARLENA MICHELLE, school system administrator; b. Miami, Fla., Feb. 16, 1972; d. Lola (Edge) and Carl Mitchell; 1 child, Paris Christopher Webb II. BJ broadcast journalism, Howard U., Washington, DC, 1990—94; MA human resource mgmt., Nova S.E. U., Ft. Lauderdale, Fla., 2001—02. Occupl. specialist Miami-Dade County Pub. Schools, Miami, Fla., 1996—98; mgr. II Miami Dade County Pub. Schools, Miami, Fla., 1998—. Coach and mentor inner city youth of Miami, Miami, Fla. Mem.: Sigma Beta Nat. Hon. Soc. (inducted for bus., mgmt., an admintrn.). D-Liberal. Baptist. Avocations: reading, exercising. Personal E-mail: lena216@bellsouth.net.

MITCHELL, CAROLYN COCHRAN, foundation administrator's executive assistant; b. Atlanta, Dec. 27, 1943; d. Clemern Covell and Agnes Emily (Veal) Cochran; m. W. Alan Mitchell, Aug. 30, 1964; 1 child, Teri Marie. AB magna cum laude, Mercer U., 1965, M in Svc. Mgmt., 1989. Caseworker Ga. Dept. Family & Children Svc., Macon, 1965-67, Covington, 1967-69; presch. dir. Southwestern Theol. Sem., Ft. Worth, 1969-70; presch. tchr., dir. Noah's Ark Day Care, Bowden, Ga., 1970-72, First Bapt. Ch., Bremen, Ga., 1972-75; preschool tchr., dir. Roebuck Pk. Bapt. Ch., Birmingham, Ala., 1975-79; freelance office mgr. and bookkeeper Macon, 1979-84; asst. to pres. Ga. Wesleyan Coll., Macon, 1984-98; asst. to pres., CEO Medcen Cmty. Health Found., Macon, 1998—. Exec. dir. Ga. Women of Achievement, 1991-95; dir. Macon Arts Alliance, 1987-91; mem. Cultural Plan Oversight Com., 1989-90. Active Get Out the Vote Task Force, Macon, 1981-95, Macon Symphony Guild, 1986-91; dep. registrar Bibb County Bd. Elections, Macon, 1981-95; asst. sec. Ronald McDonald House Ctrl. Ga., 1999-2000. Mem. AAUW (bd. dirs. Ga. chpt., v.p. 1991-93, chair coll.-univ. rels. com. 1993-94, bylaws com. 1991-92, v.p., sec., treas., historian, newsletter editor, Macon chpt., Named Gift Honoree 1988, 2000), NAFE, NOW, Women's Network for Change, Am. Mgmt. Assn., Presdl. Assts. in Higher Edn., Religious Coalition for Reproductive Choice, The Interfaith Alliance, Women's Polit. Orgn. Macon, Sigma Mu. Democrat. Baptist. E-mail: mitchell.carolyn@mccg.org.

MITCHELL, CAROLYN JOYCE, music educator; b. St. Louis Park, Minn., July 24, 1978; d. Carl David and Luana Blake Mitchell. MusB, Millikin U., 2000. Cert. K-12 music tchr. Ill. Tchr. music K-5 Blue Mound Macon Sch. Dist., Blue Mound and Macon, Ill., 2001; choral dir. Marquette H.S., Chesterfield, Mo., 2001—. Vocal cons. St. Louis Family Ch., Chesterfield, 2003—. Mem.: Music Educator's Nat. Conf., Am. Choral Dirs. Assn., Sigma Alpha Iota (treas. 1998—2000, Nat. Collegiate Treas. of Yr. 2000). Avocations: equestrian, singing, cello. Office: Marquette High School 2351 Clarkson Rd Chesterfield MO 63017

MITCHELL, CONNIE, director; m. George Mitchell, Sr.; children: Carlata, George Jr. Tchr. adv. Office Adminstrv./Instrnl. Pers. Detroit Pub. Schs. Dir. Ednll. Enrichment Acad. Active Meth. Children's Home Soc. Named Middle Sch. Tchr. of Yr., Newsweek Mag./WDIV-TV, 1994, Tchr. of Yr., Detroit Pub. Schs., 1994; recipient Golden Apple Tchr. award, Wayne County Regional Edn. Svc. Agy. Mem.: Nat. Bd. for Profl. Tchg. Stds. (bd. mem.), Alpha Kappa Alpha. Office: Detroit Pub Schs Schs Ctr Bldg 3031 W Grand Blvd Detroit MI 48202

MITCHELL, EDITH (BERTSCHE), secondary school educator; b. NYC, Oct. 1, 1924; d. Carl Victor and Hertha (Woelfler) Bertsche; m. Lee Carlyle Mitchell, June 22, 1946 (dec. May 1995); children: Lee Clark, Alan Wallace, Curtis Carl, Linda Claire, Ronald Bruce, Janet Susan. BA with honors, Swarthmore Coll., 1945; MS, Hofstra U., 1962. Cert. permanent tchr., NY; cert. for pvt. schs. profl. staff, cert. edn. profl., Hawaii. Dir. Head Start, Bay Shore, NY, 1967-68; organizer, dir. Windward Tutoring Project, Waimanalo, Hawaii, 1970-72; tchr. Title I Hawaii State Dept. Edn., 1975-78; tchr. Acad. of Pacific, Honolulu, 1979-87, 88-90, Fairhaven Sch., 1987-88, Hawaii State Dept. Edn., Kaneohe, 1990-96, Windward Sch. for Adults, Kailua, 1997—2003. Behavioral counselor Hawaii State Dept. Edn., Enchanted Lake, 1973-74; tchr. Assn. for Retarded Children, Bay Shore, N.Y., 1964-67. Sch. supt. United Meth. Ch., Bay Shore, 1953-55; co-founder United Meth. Action com., 1961; sch. supt. United Meth. Ch., Kailua, Hawaii, 1971-73, Stephen min., 1988-89; leader Cub Scout troop Boy Scouts Am., Bay Shore, 1956-58; leader Brownie troop Girl Scouts U.S., Bay Shore, 1959-61. Recipient tchr. of year, Windward Sch. for Adults, 2003. Mem. Religious Soc. of Friends. Avocations: swimming, reading, gardening, writing family memories, contacting friends and family.

MITCHELL, GINA LYNN, health facility administrator; b. Los Angeles, Calif., Nov. 10, 1968; d. Meredith B. and Lena C. Mitchell; m. Ramon L. Reyes, May 30, 2004. Cert., Am. U., Paris, 1989; BA in psychology, U. of Calif., 1992; D in Psychology, Alliant Internat. U., 2002. Conversational ptnr. program coord. English Lang. Program, UCSB Ext., Santa Barbara, Calif., 1990—92; english as a fgn. lang. instr. Four Seasons Lang. Sch., Hamamatsu-shi, Japan, 1993—95; pvt. practice cons. Hamamatsu/Handa, Japan, 1993—97; humanities specialist Nakano Vinegar Co., Handa-shi, Japan, 1996—97; psychology intern South Bay Child Guidance Clinic, Torrance, Calif., 2000—01; psychology intern/sch. counselor West County Counseling Ctr., Huntington Beach, Calif., 2001—02; dir. of clin. services Intercare Therapy, Inc., Los Angeles, Calif., 2003—. E-mail: gmitchell@intercaretherapy.com.

MITCHELL, JACQUELINE KEATON, English language educator; b. Jackson, Miss., Feb. 15, 1935; d. Randall Calvin and Leanna (Hayes) Anderson; m. William D. Keaton, July 27, 1958 (div. 1966); children: Leslie D., Linda D.. AB, Fisk U., 1958; MEd, Washington U., St. Louis, 1972; PhD, Iowa State U., 1984. Tchr. St. Louis Pub. Sch. System, 1963-73, head English Dept., 1972-73, asst. prin., 1972-82; research asst. Iowa State U., Ames, 1982-84; asst. prof. ednl. leadership Tex. Woman's U., Denton, 1984-89, mem. faculty senate, 1988-90; asst. prof. ednl. adminstrn. Iowa State U., Ames, 1989—. Cons. pvt. edn., Metroplex Area, Tex., 1984—, Effective Teaching, Tchr. Evalutation and Instrnl. Leasership; dir. Computer Assisted Tchr. Evaluation, Ames, 1983-84; instr. St. Louis U., 1983; guest lectr. various sch. dists., 1984—. Co-author: Computer Assisted Teacher Evaluation/Suprevision, 1986, Professinal Growth Plans for Texas Teachers: The Appraiser's Guide, 1986, A Compendium of Validated Professional Improvement Commitments, 1986, Writing Professional Growth Plans, 1987; contbr. articles to profl. jours. Washington U. fellow, 1971-72; scholar Iowa State U., 1982-84; recipient Outstanding Acad. Achievement award Minority Student Affairs, 1983, 84. Mem. Assn. for Supervision and Curriculum Devel., Tex. Profs. Ednl. Adminstrn., Assn. Black Journalists (faculty advisor), Tex. Woman's U. (faculty advisor), Phi Delta Kappa, Pi Lambda Theta (faculty advisor), Alpha Sigma. Methodist. Office: Iowa State U Coll Edn & Profl Studies 229N Lagomarcino Hall Ames IA 50010

MITCHELL, JANET ALDRICH, fund raising executive, reference materials publisher; b. Providence, Jan. 12, 1928; d. Norman Ackley and Janet Aldrich; m. Raymond Warren Mitchell, Jan. 9, 1954 (div. 1967); children: Lydia Aldrich, Polly Mitchell Ranson. AB, Smith Coll., 1949; MEd, Rutgers U., 1975. Engaged in devel. various non-profit orgns., 1954-72; dir. devel. Wilson Fellowship Found., Princeton, N.J., 1972-74; dir. spl. projects N.J. Dept. Higher Edn., Trenton, 1974-76; prin., owner Mitchell Guide, 1976—. Cons. numerous non-profit orgns., 1976-86; lectr. Adult Sch., Princeton, 1983-84. Editor: Directory of Woodrow Wilson Fellows, 1968, A Community of Scholars, 1980. Exec. officer Princeton Cmty. Dem. Orgn., 1984—86; elected Princeton Twp. Com., 1987—89; mem. NAACP Legal Def. Fund, 1980—86; trustee N.J. Hist. Soc., 1984—86, Smith Coll. Class of 1949, 1999—. Mem. Princeton Smith Coll. Club (fund agent 1964-69, pres. 1968-70), Princeton Dog Club (bd. dirs. 1962-68). Episcopalian. Avocation: breeding and showing standard poodles. Office: PO Box 626 Pennington NJ 08534 Address: 27 Woosamonsa Road Pennington NJ 08534 E-mail: grantsnj@aol.com.

MITCHELL, JANET BREW, health services researcher; b. N.Y.C., Oct. 20, 1949; d. Robert Moscrip Mitchell and Dorothy Brennan; m. Jerry Lee Cromwell, June 15, 1980; children: Alexander, Genevieve. BA with highest honors, U. Calif., San Diego, 1971; MSW, UCLA, 1973; PhD, Brandeis U., 1976. Rsch. asst. Brandeis U./Worcester Tng. Program in Social Rsch. & Psych., Waltham, Mass., 1973-75; sr. analyst Abt Assocs., Cambridge, Mass., 1975-77; asst. prof. Boston U. Sch. Medicine, 1977-80; pres. Ctr. for Health Econs. Rsch., Waltham, Mass., 1980—. Mem. com. on monitoring access to health care svcs. Inst. Medicine, 1989-92; mem. nat. adv. com. Robert Wood Johnson Health Care Fin. Fellows, 1988-93; cons. VA, 1982-85, NIH, 1983-85, Health Care Financing Adminstrn., 1979—; advisor Physician Reimbursement Study, Congl. Budget Office, 1984-85; mem. adv. panel on physicians & med. tech. Office of Tech. Assessment, 1984-85; mem. health care tech. study sect. Nat. Ctr. for Health Svcs. Rsch., 1984-88; psychiat. social worker UCLA Med. Ctr., 1971-72; med. social worker U. So. Calif., 1972-73, Univ. Hosp. San Diego, 1973. Author (with F.A. Sloan & J. Cromwell) Private Physicians and Public Programs, 1978; contbr. chpts. to 8 books; contbr. numerous articles to profl. jours. Thesis grantee VA, 1976-77. Office: Ctr for Hlth Econ Rsch 411 Waverly Oaks Rd Ste 330 Waltham MA 02452-8448 E-mail: jmitchell@her-cher.org.

MITCHELL, JO KATHRYN, retired hospital technical supervisor; b. Clarksville, Ark., Dec. 1, 1934; d. Vintris Franklin and Melissa Lucile (Edwards) Clark; m. James M. Mitchell, June 4, 1955 (dec. Feb. 1973); children: James, Karen Ann, Leslie Kay, Vicki Lynn. Student, U. Ark., Fayetteville, 1952-53; student, Coll. Ozarks, 1953-54, U. Ark., 1954-55, Little Rock U., 1958. Technologist clin. chemistry U. Hosp., Little Rock, 1956-57, asst. supr., 1957-59, rsch. technologist, 1960-62, asst. supr. clin. chemistry, 1979-82, supr. clin. chemistry, 1982—2003; technologist Conway County Hosp., Morrilton, Ark., 1959; office mgr., co-owner Medic Pharmacy, Little Rock, 1962-71; owner The Cheese Shop, Little Rock, 1977-80. Adult advisor Order Rainbow Girls local, Little Rock, 1970-84, state, Ark., 1977-84. Mem. Pharmacy Aux. (pres. 1967-69), Order Eastern Star. Methodist. Avocations: reading, needlework, genealogy, travel. Home: 6908 Lucerne Dr Little Rock AR 72205-5029

MITCHELL, JOAN LAVERNE, research scientist; b. Palo Alto, Calif., May 24, 1947; d. William Richardson and Doris LaVerne (Roddan) M. BS in Physics, Stanford U., 1969; MS in Physics, U. Ill., 1971, PhD in Physics, 1974. Rsch. staff mem. T.J. Watson Rsch. Ctr. IBM, Yorktown Heights, N.Y., 1974-88, 96-98, mgr. T.J. Watson Rsch. Ctr., 1979-88, image tech. cons. mktg. White Plains, N.Y., 1989-91, rsch. staff mem. T.J. Watson Rsch. Ctr. Hawthorne, N.Y., 1991-94, mgr. T.J. Watson Rsch. Ctr., 1992-94, supplemental employee Burlington, N.Y., 1994-96; vis. prof. U. Ill., Urbana, 1996; with IBM Printing Systems Divsn., Boulder, Colo., 1999—, IBM fellow, 2001—. Del. CCITT Study Group XIV, 1978-79, ISO JPEG Com., 1987-94. Co-author: JPEG Still Image Data Compression Standard, 1993, MPEG Video Compression Standard, 1997; contbr. articles to profl. jours. Xerox Indsl. fellow, 1970-71. Fellow IEEE, NAE (elected 2004); mem. Am. Phys. Soc., Soc. for Imaging Sci. and Tech., Sigma Xi (chpt. sec. 1976, v.p. 1977, pres. 1978). Democrat. Achievements include co-inventor on numerous patents. Home: 1172 Fall River Cir Longmont CO 80501 Office: IBM Printing Systems Divsn 6300 Diagonal Hwy MS004N Boulder CO 80301-9270 Office Phone: 303-924-4271.

MITCHELL, JOANN M. music educator; b. Phila., May 8, 1969; d. Caruso Peter and Florence Taddei; m. Brian Scott Mitchell, June 27. MusB in Edn. and Therapy, Immaculata U., 1991, MA in Arts in Music, 2000. Music therapist Little Sisters of Poor, Phila., 1991—2000, dir. activities, 1991—2000; tchr. Merion Mercy Acad., Merion Station, Pa., 2000—03, music dir., 2000—03; pvt. practice music tchr. Newtown Sq., Pa., 2003—. Home and Office: Merion Mercy Acad 511 Montgomery Ave Merion Station PA 19066

MITCHELL, JONI (ROBERTA JOAN ANDERSON), singer, songwriter; b. Ft. Macleod, Alta., Can., Nov. 7, 1943; d. William A. and Myrtle M. (McKee) Anderson; m. Chuck Mitchell (div.); m. Larry Klein, Nov. 21, 1982. Student, Alta. Coll. Albums Song to a Seagull, Clouds, Ladies of the Canyon, Blue, For the Roses, Court and Spark, 1974, Miles of Aisles, The Hissing of Summer Lawns, 1975, Hejira, 1976, Don Juan's Reckless Daughter, 1979, Mingus, 1979 (Jazz Album of Year and Rock-Blues Album of Year, Downbeat mag., 1979), Shadows and Light, 1980, Wild Things Run Fast, 1982, Dog Eat Dog, 1985, Chalk Mark in a Rainstorm, 1988, Night Ride Home, 1991, Turbulent Indigo, 1994, Hits, 1996, Taming the Tiger, 1998, Both Sides Now, 2000, Travelogue, 2002, screenwriter/actor (films) Love, 1982; contbr. album dog Eat Dog/Wild Things Run Fast, 1996. Named to Rock and Roll Hall of Fame, 1997; recipient Grammy award for Best Folk Performance, 1969, Grammy award for Best Arrangement Accompanying Vocalists (with Tom Scott), 1974. Address: care Reprise Records 3300 Warner Blvd Burbank CA 91505-4632

MITCHELL, KAREN FRANCES, artist, jewelry designer; b. Denver, Aug. 24, 1953; d. Harry Francis and Mary Jane Margrete (Jensen-Borg) Mitchell. BFA, U. Colo., 1975; postgrad., Gemological Inst. Am., 1986, Kulicke Jewelry Arts Inst., 1988, Cecilia Bauer Studio, 1992, Fashion Inst. of Tech., 1993, Nat. Acad. Design, 1994. Cert. tchr., art specialist. Jewelry designer, pres. Karen Mitchell Design, Aspen, Colo., 1978—; cultural rschr., cons. various Italian newspapers and mags., NY., Colo., 1992-94, Italian Consulate Cultural Inst., NY, 1992—94. Instr. workshops design and goldsmithing technique; apprentice Van der Schoot Disegno e Fabricazione, Milan, 1989—91. Co-designer, co-author (book) World Gold Coun. Jewelry Trend Book, 1991—95; exhibitions include World Gold Coun., Aaron Faber Gallery, N.Y.C., Yaw Gallery, Mich., SOFA, Chgo., J. Cotter Gallery, Cindy Griem Fine Jewels, Somerhill Gallery, N.C., Facere Gallery, Wash., Concepts Gallery, Calif., Greene & Greene Gallery, NJ. Vol. chmn. benefit com. Aspen Art Mus.; co-chmn. benefit com. Aspen Music Festival; mem. Les Dames d'Aspen; vol. Profl. Women's Orgn., Am. Craft Mus., NY, 1993, Coun. Fashion Designers Am., NY, Internat. Design Conf. of Aspen, Screening Com. Aspen Film Fest, Soprano, Aspen Choral Soc., Aspen Ski Club/U.S. Olympic Equestrian Team, 1995; trustee Aspen Snowmass Coun. Arts. Named Vol. of the Yr., Aspen Art Mus., 2001. Mem.: Jewelry Design Profl.'s Network, Am. Craft Coun., Soc. N.Am. Goldsmiths. Address: PO Box 4885 Aspen CO 81612-4885

MITCHELL, KATHERINE SARAH, not-for-profit developer; b. Atlanta, Ga., Aug. 5, 1962; d. Bernice Hindman and Bernard Mitchell; 1 child, Fiona Ashley Mitchell-McGroary. BA cum laude, Boston U., 1984; MA, Columbia U., 1987. Outreach coord., rschr. League of Conservation Voters, Portsmouth, NH, 1991—93; dir. devel. Hudson River Sloop Clearwater, Hudson River Valley, NY, 1993—95; membership dir. Bardavon Theatre, Poughkeepsie, NY, 1995—2000; dir. devel. Franklin and Eleanor Roosevelt Inst., Hyde Park, NY, 2001—03; freelance, cons. Poughkeepsie, NY, 2003—. Founding bd. mem. World Affairs Coun. of Dutchess County, Poughkeepsie, NY, 2003; dir. Environ. Fedn. N.Y., Albany, 1993—95; chair, grants distbn. panel Dutchess County Arts Coun., Poughkeepsie, NY, 1999—2001; mem. Leave a Legacy, Poughkeepsie, NY, 1996—; resource com. Hudson River Housing, Poughkeepsie, NY, 2001—. Author: (pamphlet) Greening the Debate: Environmental Nonprofits and the Elections. Activist Coalition for a Nuc. Free Harbor, New York, NY, 1987—88; family adv. Habitat for Humanity, Poughkeepsie, NY, 1999—2000; family support HIV/AIDS program Catharine St. Cmty. Ctr., Poughkeepsie, NY, 1994—96. Recipient scholarship for studies toward MPA, Marist Coll., 2002—03. Socialist. Congregationalist. Avocations: fibre arts, community agriculture, Latin American studies. Home: 13 Carroll St Poughkeepsie NY 12601 Personal E-mail: katesarahmitchell@msn.com.

MITCHELL, KIMBERLY JEANNE, psychologist, educator; b. Fort Meade, Md., Feb. 27, 1972; d. Thomas S. and Rita I. Mitchell; m. Lerna P. Dustin, Feb. 28, 2004. BA in Psychology magna cum laude, R.I. Coll., 1994, MA in Psychology, 1996; PhD in Exptl. Psychology, U. R.I., 1999. Rsch. asst. Cancer Prevention Rsch. Ctr. U. R.I., Kingston, 1995—96, cons. data analysis, 1996—98, rsch. asst. R.I. Dept. Correction, 1997—98; rsch. asst. prof. psychology Crimes against Children Rsch. Ctr., U. N.H, Durham, 2001—. Contbr. articles to profl. jours. Fellow, Crimes Against Children Rsch. Ctr., Family Rsch. Lab, 1999—2001. Mem.: APA, Internat. Soc. Prevention Child Abuse & Neglect, Am. Profl. Soc. Abuse Children. Achievements include research in youth and internet victimization. Avocations: irish step dancing, writing, physical fitness. Office: Crimes Against Children Rsch Ctr U NH 10 W Edge Dr Ste 106 Durham NH 03824 Business E-Mail: kimberly.mitchell@unh.edu.

MITCHELL, LILLIAN ADASSA, principal; b. Oct. 20, 1951; BS in Elem. Edn., W.I. Coll., 1982; MA, Andrew's U., 1987. Asst. prin. Bklyn. Sch., 1991-97; prin. Whispering Pines Sch., Old Westbury, N.Y., 1997—. Recipient Zappara Excellence in Tchg. award, 1992. Home: 3206 Bayswater Ct Far Rockaway NY 11691-1606

MITCHELL, LOUISE TYNDALL, special education educator; b. St. Louis, Oct. 25; d. Walter Eugene and Nellie May (Otey) Tyndall; m. Felix Mitchell Sr., Sept. 30, 1958; children: Felix Jr., Jeane Mitchell-Carr. AA, Stowe Tchrs. Coll., St. Louis, 1947; BA, Harris Tchrs. Coll., St. Louis, 1958; MA, St. Louis U., 1965. Cert. elem. tchr., secondary English and math., reading clinician. Tchr. math. Hadley High Sch., St. Louis, 1958-59; tchr. Emerson Elem. Sch., St. Louis, 1969-67; head dept. spl. edn. Laclede Elem. Sch., St. Louis, 1967-68, coord. curriculum, 1968-70; adminstrv. asst. Delmar High Sch., St. Louis, 1970-72; assoc. prof., reading clinician, mgr. apprentice tchrs. Harris Tchrs. Coll., 1972-78; chair dept. spl. edn. Cleveland High Sch., St. Louis, 1978-84, chmn. faculty, 1982-84; head dept. spl. edn. S.W. High Sch., St. Louis, 1984-87, tchr., mentor, 1987—. Mentor St. Louis Pub. Schs., 1988-89. Author: (handbook) Teachers Aide, 1987, curriculum guides, 1974, 78; co-author (curriculum guide) Fundamental Curriculum, 1990. Chair Rsch. and Status Black Women, St. Louis, 1974; charter mem. Triagle Club YWCA, 1970. Recipient Community Svc. award Top Ladies Distinction, St. Louis, 1981, 50 Yrs. Outstanding Svc. award A.M.E. Ch., St. Louis, 1987, Salute to Excellence in Edn. recognition St. Louis Am. Newspaper, 1991. Mem. NAACP, Am. Fedn. Tchrs., Nat. Coun. Negro Women, Colored Womens' Fed. Clubs, Women Achievement (coord. youth 1989), St. Louis U. Alumni Assn., (Svc. award 1986), Ch. Women United, Order Ea. Star (past Worthy Matron 1978), Sigma Gamma Rho (chaplain 1988-90), Phi Delta Kappa. Avocations: reading, writing, pub. speaking, drama, singing. Home: 4537 Fair Ave # A Saint Louis MO 63115-3054

MITCHELL, LUCILLE ANNE, retired elementary school educator; b. Dayton Corners, Ill., Oct. 19, 1928; d. Roy Rollin and Edna May (Whitehouse) Sheppard; m. Donald L. Mitchell; children: David, Diane, Barbara Rock, Patricia Reaves. BS in Edn., Augustana Coll., 1966; MS in Edn., Western Ill. U., 1972, Edn. Specialist, 1974. Tchr. Carbon Cliff (Ill.) Elem. Sch., 1962-65, Moline (Ill.) Bd. Edn., 1967-92. Mem. textbook selection com. Moline Bd. Edn., 1967-84; tchr. of gifted Moline Bd. Edn., 1985-87. Contbr. (poetry) Footprints Through the Forest, 2000, Best Poems and Poets of 2001, 2001. Counselor to pastor Cmty. of Christ, 2001—02, elder in priesthood. Named Ill. Master Tchr., State of Ill., 1984. Mem. Ill. Edn. Assn. (various coms.), Moline Edn. Assn. (various coms.), Delta Kappa Gamma (program chmn. 1978-79, recording sec. 1980-81). Avocations: organ, piano, oil and water color painting, writing poetry, teaching Bible study classes. Home: 3214 55th Street Ct Moline IL 61265-5740 E-mail: donnlucy@aol.com.

MITCHELL, MARCIA JEANNE, freelance/self-employed writer, events producer; b. San Jose, Calif., Feb. 20, 1932; d. Eugene Lewis Wilcox and Gladys Delphine Shoemaker; m. John Alexander Donnan (div. June 1, 1975); children: Alan James Donnan, Kristen Elizabeth Donnan; m. Thomas Francis Mitchell, June 29, 1985. Student, Colo. State U., 1965—67; BA, Norwich U., Vt. Coll., 1989. Writer, editor Rapid City (S.D.) Jour., 1968—73; cabinet officer, sec. labor S.D. State Govt., Pierre, SD, 1973—75; sr. exec. Corp. for Pub. Broadcasting, Washington, 1975—80; assoc. dir. Am. Film Inst., Washington & L.A., 1980—87; freelance writer, prodr., 1988—. Lectr., seminar leader mgmt. strategies for women, 1980—82; lectr. Crystal Cruise Lines, 1999, Cunard QE2, 2001; motivational sem. spkr. Prodr.: world premieres of maj. motion pictures, 1980—86, A Daughter's Tribute to Fred Astaire, 2001; author: Cosmetics from the Kitchen, 1972, Raindance to Research, 1977, Management Strategies for Women, 1980, 1981, The Spy Who Seduced America: Lies and Betrayal in the Heat of the Cold War, 2002. Past sec. Nat. Assns. Commns. on Women; vice chair Montserrat Found. for Charitable Giving, West Indies, 1995—2001; chair spl. events Hill City (S.D.) Arts Coun., 2001; mem. Montserrat Nat. Trust, Montserrat, 2001; past chair grants com. State Fine Arts Coun., SD; past mem. State Commn. on Status of Women, SD; mem., organizer S.D. Dem. Women, 2001—02; past bd. dirs. Women's Equity Action League, N.Y.C., NY; past chair TV broadcasting com. PBS Sta. WETA-TV, Washington. Recipient 1st pl. feature writing, S.D. Press Women, 1995, 1st pl., Non-fiction Books, 2003. Mem.: Nat. Fedn. Press Women (Top Press Woman of Yr. 1972—73). Roman Catholic.

MITCHELL, MARGARET YVONNE, forester; b. Niagara Falls, NY, June 4, 1963; d. Reece Graham and Judith Ann Mitchell. BS in Landscape Architecture, Colo. State U., 1986; MS in Forestry, U. Idaho, 1989. Landscape architect Wenatchee Nat. Forest, Wenatchee, Wash., 1982—87; tchg./rsch. asst. U. Idaho, Moscow, 1988—89; landscape architect Wenatchee Nat. Forest, Cle Elum, Wash., 1989—91, Tongass Nat. Forest, Wrangell, Ala., 1991—92, dist. planning staff officer, 1992—97, dist. ranger, 1997—2000, Wallowa-Whitman Nat. Forest/USDA Forest Svc., Enterprise, Oreg., 2000—.

MITCHELL, MARY ANN CARRICO, poet; b. Louisville, Aug. 1, 1937; d. Bernard and Catherine (Steinlockner) Carrico; m. William Ray Mitchell, Aug. 25, 1962; children: Michael, Anne Marie, Katherine. RN, St. Joseph Sch. Nursing, Louisville, 1958; BSN, U. Colo., 1962. Head nurse Our Lady of Peace Hosp., Louisville, 1960; mgr. collections Point Loma Credit Union, San Diego, 1974-77; charge nurse Mercy Hosp., San Diego, 1977-78; managerial sec. Gulf Oil, Denver, 1977-81; exec. sec. Phillips Petrol, Denver, 1981-82; adminstrv. asst. Reliance Petroleum, Denver, 1982-84. Author: (poems) Meeshak, 1997, My First Vertical, 1997, White Tail-a-Flyin', 1997, Friends, 1997. Mem. DAR, AAUW, Nat. League Am. Penwomen (founder, pres. Bluegrass of Ky. br.). Roman Catholic. Avocations: painting, sewing, quilting, gardening, poetry. Home: 494 Lea View Ave Campbellsburg KY 40011-7545 E-mail: macmky@aol.com.

MITCHELL, MARY LU, information researcher, civic volunteer, retired; b. Madisonville, Ky., June 8, 1938; d. John Walter and Augusta J. Wright; m. Wade Treutlen Mitchell, Aug. 18, 1966; children: Wade Wright, Catherine W. BA in Polit. Sci., Duke U., 1960. Dir. job placement libr. Harvard U. Bus. Sch., Cambridge, Mass., 1960-62; rschr., writer UN, N.Y.C., 1962-65; dir. pub. info. Econ. Opportunity Atlanta, 1965-69; rschr. N.Y. Times, Atlanta, 1984-91, ret. Cons. govtl. and social svc. agys., Atlanta, 1969-84. Trustee Atlanta Pub. Libr., 1979-97, chair, 1980-81; founding mem. Friends of Atlanta Pub. Libr., 1974-79, chair, 1976-79; pres. Ga. Libr. Trustees and Friends, Atlanta, 1981-85; bd. dirs. Friends of Libraries USA, Phila., 1981-85; bd. dirs., vol. other civic and ednl. programs, Atlanta, 1970—; bd. dirs. Davies Cmty. Health Libr., 1994—. Named Atlanta Woman of Yr. in the Profns., civic and profl. leaders of Atlanta, 1969; recipient Pres.' award Friends of Librs. USA, 1991; mem. Leadership Atlanta, 1974—. Avocations: reading, travel, family.

MITCHELL, MOZELLA GORDON, English language educator, minister; b. Starkville, Miss., Aug. 14, 1936; d. John Thomas and Odena Mae (Graham) Gordon; m. Edrick R. Woodson, Mar. 20, 1951 (div. 1974); children: Cynthia LaVern, Marcia Delores Woodson Miller. AB, LeMoyne Coll., 1959; MA in English, U. Mich., 1963; MA in Religious Studies, Colgate-Rochester Divinity Sch., 1973; PhD, Emory U., 1980. Instr. in English and Speech Alcorn A&M Coll., Lorman, Miss., 1960-61; instr. English, chmn. dept. Owen Jr. Coll., Memphis, 1961-65; asst. prof. English and religion Norfolk State Coll., U. Norfolk, Va., 1965-81; assoc. prof. U. South Fla., Tampa, 1981-93, prof., 1993—; pastor Mount Sinai AME Zion Ch., Tampa, 1982-89; presiding elder Tampa dist. AME Zion Ch., 1988—; pastor, founder Love of Christ AME Zion Tabernacle, Branden, Fla., 1993—; candidate for bishop AME Zion Ch., 2003—. Vis. assoc. prof. Hood Theol. Sem., Salisbury, N.C., 1979-80, St. Louis U., 1992-93; vis. asst. lectr. U. Rochester, N.Y., 1972-73; co-dir. Ghent VISTA Project, Norfolk, 1969-71; cons. Black Women and Ministry Interdenominational Theol. Ctr; lectr. Fla. Humanities Coun., 1994-95; Meml. lectr. Mordecai Johnson Inst., Colgate Rochester Div. Sch., 1997. Author: Spiritual Dynamics of Howard Thurman's Theology, 1985, Howard Thurman and the Quest for Freedom, Proc. 2d Ann. Howard Thurman Convocation (Peter Lang), 1992, African American Religious History in Tampa Bay, 1992;, New Africa in America: The Blending of African and American Religious and Social Traditions Among Black People in Meridian, Mississippi and Surrounding Counties (Peter Lang), 1994, also articles, essays in field; editor: Martin Luther King Meml. Series in Religion, Culture and Social Devel.; editorial bd. Cornucipia Reprint Series. Mem. Tampa-Hillsborough County Human Rels. Coun., 1987—; founder Women at the Well, Inc.; del. 7th assembly World Coun. Chs., Canberra, Australia, 1991, 17th World Meth. Coun., Rio de Janiero, 1996; del. 18th World Meth. Coun., Brighton, England, 2001; mem. connectional coun. A.M.E. Zion Ch., Charlotte, 1984—, staff writer Sunday sch. lit., 1981—, mem. jud. coun.; pres. Fla. Coun. Chs., Orlando, Fla., 1988—90, pres.-elect, 1998—, pres. exec. bd., 2000. Recipient ecumenical leadership citation Fla. Coun. Chs., 1990, Inaugural lectr. award Geddes Hanson Black Cultural Ctr. Princeton Theol. Sem., 1993; fellow Nat. Doctoral Fund, 1978-80; grantee NEH, 1981, Fla. Endowment for Humanities, 1990—, U. South Fla. Rsch. Coun., 1990—. Mem. Coll. Theology Soc., Am. Acad. Religion, Soc. for the Study of Black Religion (pres. 1992-96), Joint Ctr. for Polit. Studies, Black Women in Ch. and Soc., Alpha Kappa Alpha. Phi Kappa Phi. Democrat. Methodist. Avocations: piano, poetry, tennis, bicycling, Scrabble. Office: U South Fla 301 CPR Religious Studies Dept Tampa FL 33620 Office Phone: 813-974-1852. E-mail: mozellam@aol.com.

MITCHELL, PAMELA ANN, airline pilot; b. Otis AFB, Mass., May 6, 1955; d. Gene Thomas and Rose Margaret (Jones) Mitchell. BFA, Colo. State U., 1975; postgrad., Webster Coll., 1981. Lic. pilot Ill., comml. instr., airline transport pilot, jet rating, Boeing 747 and 727, Boeing 747-400, McDonnell Douglas DC-10. Flight attendant United Airlines, Chgo., 1976-80; owner, operator Deliverance, Unltd. Ferry Co., Aurora, Ill., 1978-81; flight test pilot Cessna Aircraft Co., Wichita, Kans., 1981-82, nat. spokeswoman, 1982-83; airline pilot Rep. Airlines, Mpls., 1983-84; airline pilot, captain Northwest Airlines, Mpls., 1985—; owner, pres. The Global Nomad LLC, 1997—. Mem. Safety Coun. Airline Pilots Assn., 99's Internat. Women Pilots Assn., Internat. Soc. Women Airline Pilots (bd. dirs. 1994-96), Nat. Aviation Club, N.W. Airline Ski Team (capt. 1989-94), Kappa Kappa Gamma. Republican. Presbyterian. Avocations: piano, snow skiing, tennis, travel, golf.

MITCHELL, PATRICIA EDENFIELD, television executive; b. Swainsboro, Ga., Jan. 20, 1943; d. James Otis and Bernice Tucker Edenfield; m. Jay Addison Mitchell, Aug. 20, 1964 (div. June 1970); 1 child, Mark Addison. BA magna cum laude, U. Ga., 1964, MA, 1965. English instr. U. Ga., Athens, 1965—69; English, drama instr. Va. Commonwealth U., Richmond, 1969—70; researcher, writer LOOK Mag., N.Y.C., 1970; cons., speech writer Garth Assocs., N.Y.C., 1970—71; TV prodr., reporter WB2-TV, Boston, 1971—77; anchor, talk show host WTTG-TV, Washington, 1977—79; corr. NBC-TV Today, N.Y.C., 1984—89, CBS-TV Sunday Morning, N.Y.C., 1989—90; exec. prodr., writer documentaries VU Prodns., L.A., 1990—; pres. CNN Prodns. and Time Inc. TV TBS, 1992—2000; pres. and CEO PBS, 2000—. Creator, prodr., host, owner Woman to Woman (nationally syndicated program), L.A., 1983—; spkr., conf. leader on women's issues, 1973—; bd. trustees Sundance Inst.; former mem. exec. com. TBS, Inc., CNN Exec. Com.; bd. mem. Internews, 2002—. Mem. adv. com. Nat. Coun. on Rsch. on Women, N.Y.C., 1990—92; mem. adv. bd. Schlesinger Libr. on History of Women, Radcliffe Coll., Cambridge, Mass., 1985—92; media com. Hollywood Women's Polit. Com., L.A., 1989—92, former trustee Metro Atlanta YMCA, High Mus. Art, Atlanta; mem. adv. bd. Santa Barbara Sch. Comm. U. Calif.; pres. Global Green USA (Am. affiliate Mikhail Gorbachev's worldwide conservation orgn.); nat. bd. mem. Girls Inc. Recipient Emmy for Best Daytime Program, TV Acad., 1984, Emmy for Best Host-Daytime, 1971, numerous film festival awards, 1989—92. Avocations: hiking, bicycling, horseback riding, reading. E-mail: pmitchell@pbs.org.

MITCHELL, PATSY MALIER, religious school founder and administrator; b. Greenwood, Miss., Aug. 28, 1948; d. William Lonal and Lillian (Walker) Malier; m. Charles E. Mitchell, Apr. 20, 1970; children: Christopher, Kara, Angela. BS in Edn., Delta State U., 1970, MEd, 1974, Edn. Specialist, 1979; MA in Ch. Ministries, Ch. of God Sch. Theology, 1990; PhD in Psychology and Counseling, La. Bapt. U., 1994; D in Edn. Christian Sch. Adminstrn., Baptist Christian U., 1992. Cert. sch. adminstr. Youth, Christian edn. dir. Ch. of God, Minter City, Miss., 1975—, teen talent dir., 1983—, missions rep., 1975—, dist. Christian edn. dir. Cleveland, Miss., 1983-85, sch. adminstr., 1985—. Del. Ch. of God Edn. Leadership, Cleveland, Tenn., 1990; del., spkr. Christian Sch. Internat., Chattanooga, 1991. Contbr. Dir. St. Jude Children's Hosp., Memphis, 1991; vol. 4-H Club, Greenwood, Miss., 1985—91. Named Outstanding Young Women of Am., 1983, Top 10 of 50 Leading Bus. Women in Miss., 2001, Internat. Educator of the Yr., Internat. Biographical Ctr., London, 2003; recipient Cmty. Pride award, Chevron, 1988, Internat. Woman of Yr. award, 1993. Mem.: NAFE, Ch. of God Edn. Assn., Christian Schs. Internat., Christian Sch. Adminstrs., Gospel Music Assn., Ch. of God Sch. of Theology Alumni assn., Delta State Alumni Assn. Republican. Home: 5642 County Rd 544 Minter City MS 38944 Office Phone: 662-299-4592.

MITCHELL, PAULA RAE, nursing educator, college dean; b. Independence, Mo., Jan. 10, 1951; d. Millard Henry and E. Lorene (Denton) Gates; m. Ralph William Mitchell, May 24, 1975. BS in Nursing, Graceland Coll., 1973; MS in Nursing, U. Tex., 1976; EdD in ednl. Adminstrn., N.Mex. State U., 1996. RN, Tex., Mo.; cert. childbirth educator. Instr. nursing El Paso (Tex.) C.C., 1979-85, dir. nursing, 1985—2003, acting divsn. chmn. health occupations, 1985-86, divsn. dean, 1998-99, dean health occupations, 1999-2000, curriculum facilitator, 1984-86, dean health occupations, math and sci., campus dean, 2000—. Ob-gyn. nurse practitioner Planned Parenthood, El Paso, 1981-86, med. com., 1986-98; cons. in field. Author: (with Grippando) Nursing Perspectives and Issues, 1989, 93; contbr. articles to profl. jours. Founder, bd. dirs. Health-CREST, El Paso, 1981—85; mem. pub. edn. com. Am. Cancer Soc., El Paso, 1983—84, mem. profl. activities com., 1992—93; mem. El-Paso City-County Bd. Health, 1989—91; mem. Govt. Applications Rev. Com. Rio Grande Coun. Govts., 1989—91; mem. collaborative coun. El Paso Magnet H.S. for Health Care Professions, 1992—94; co-chair health and human svcs. task force Unite El Paso Health, 1996—98, mem. steering com., 1999—2000; co-chair health taskforce El Paso Cmty. Legis. Agenda, 1997—99; mem. adv. com. Ctr. for Border Health Rsch., Paso del Norte Health Found., 1998—; mem. Leadership El Paso, 1999; mem. health profl. shortage task force Greater El Paso C. of C., 2001—, mem. health care coun., 2002—; bd. dirs. Border Health Inst., El Paso, 2001—, sec.-treas., 2003—. Capt. U.S. Army, 1972—78. Decorated Army Commendation medal, Meritorious Svc. medal. Named to Women's Hall of Fame, El Paso Commn., 1999, named Outstanding Alumni, N.Mex. State U., 2002-03. Mem. Nat. League Nursing (resolutions com. Assocs. Degree coun. 1987-89, accreditation site visitor, AD coun. 1990—, Tex. edn. com. 1991-92, Tex. 3d v.p. 1992-93, Tex. 1st v.p. 1997-99, nominating com. 1999-2000), Am. Soc. Psychoprophylaxis Obstetrics, Nurses Assn. Am. Coll. Ob-Gyn. (cert. in ambulatory women's healthcare, chpt. coord. 1979-83, nat. program rev. com. 1984-86, corr. 1987-89), Advanced Nurse Practitioner Group El Paso (coord. 1980-83, legis. com. 1984), Am. Phys. Therapist Assn. (commn. on accreditation, site visitor for phys. therapist asst. programs 1991—), Orgn. Assoc. Degree Nursing (Tex. membership chmn. 1985-89, chmn. goals com. 1989—, nat. bylaws com. 1990-95), Am. Vocat. Assn., Am. Assn. Women Cmty. and Jr. Colls., Tex. Orgn. Nurse Execs., Nat. Coun. Workforce Edn. (articulation task force 1986-89, program standards task force 1991-93), Nat. Coun. Instrnl. Adminstrs., Tex. Soc. Allied Health Profls., Tex. Nurses Assn. (pres.-elect dist. one 2002-2003, pres. 2003—2004), Nat. Soc. Allied Health Profls. (edn. com. 1993-96), El Paso C. of C. (healthcare coun. 2001—), Sigma Theta Tau, Phi Kappa Phi. Mem. Christian Ch. (Disciples Of Christ). Home: 4616 Cupid Dr El Paso TX 79924-1726 Office: El Paso C C PO Box 20500 El Paso TX 79998-0500 Business E-Mail: paulam@epcc.edu.

MITCHELL, SHARON, artist, designer; b. Elmira, N.Y., Dec. 5, 1944; d. Earl Arlington Mitchell and Mary Elizabeth Whitney; m. Chet F. Lunner, Aug. 2, 1966 (div. Feb. 1984); children: Kristina, Kimberly; m. John K. Craford, Dec. 3, 1994. Student, U. Maine, Augusta, 1989-91; BFA, RISD, 1994. Exec. dir., chmn. Maine State Housing Authority, Augusta, 1980-83; CEO Fin. Authority Maine, Augusta, 1983-84; v.p. pub. fin. Mossley, Boston, 1984-85; treas. Ctrl. Maine Power, Augusta, 1985-86; pres. Ariel Corp., Augusta, 1986-89; artist, cons. Saybrook, Conn., 1989—; pres., founder Emerald Tara Co., Saybrook, 1999—. Chair child abuse task force, Dept. Housing Svcs., 1983-84; chair Gov.'s Rural Devel. Commn., 1984-85; treas. Coun. State Fin. Agy., 1983-84. Exhibited at group shows a. Jain Maranouchi Gallery, N.Y.C., 1995—, Impact Woman's Gallery, Buffalo, 1996, N.Mex. Art League, Albuquerque, 1996, Assoc. Artists, Southport, N.C., 1999. Mem. Gov.'s Cost Mgmt. Task Force, 1983-84, Gov.'s Telecomms. Task Force, 1983-84, Future Maine Forests, 1984-85. Mem. Alliance for Art, Women Caucus for Art. Home: 463 W Gray St Elmira NY 14905-2527

MITCHELL, SHAWNE MAUREEN, author; b. Tacoma, Wash., Jan. 09; d. F. King and Nona Margaret Burnside (Hayes) M.; m. J.D. Cook, Spt. 4, 1982; children: Travis, Austin. BA, U. Wash., 1972; postgrad., U. Santa Monica, 1997—. CEO Adventures of the Spirit, Santa Barbara, Calif., 1994—; author, spkr. Soul Style, 1995—; columnist Feng Shui-Soul Style, Calif., 1996—. Cons. real estate, Wash., Calif., 1980—; dir. Small Luxury Hotels, L.A., 1986-87; internat. spkr., author on subject of higher consciousness; internat. spkr. on Feng Shui. Author: Soul Style, 1997, Exploring Feng Shui, Ancient Secrets and Modern Insights, 2001, Creating Home Sanctuaries with Feng Shui, 2002, Simple Feng Shui, 2004; editor: Home Sanctuaries mag.; contbr. articles to profl. jours. Bd. dirs. Montecito (Calif.) Ednl. Found., 1997-99, Los Positas Park Found., Santa Barbara, 1995. Mem. Womens Exec. Network, Seattle Tennis Club. Avocations: boating, hiking, traveling, music, art. Office: Adventures of the Spirit Inc PO Box 5765 Santa Barbara CA 93150-5765 Office Phone: 805-565-8885. E-mail: shawne@shawnemitchell.com.

MITCHELL, VIRGINIA ANN, investment company executive; b. El Dorado, Ark., June 1, 1951; d. Joseph Grover Mitchell and Wanda Frazier; m. Greg R. Hoban, Dec. 6, 1986 (div. July 5, 1995); children: Aimee Judy, Hunter Hoban. AA, Maui C.C., Hawaii, 1984; BS, Excelsior Coll., Albany, 2001. Owner, mgr. Vamm Enterprises, Miami, 1979—. Editor: Ho'oulu, 1998. Mem. Unity by the Sea; parent vol. Highland Oaks Middle Sch., 2001; parent vol. reading program Kamali'i Elem. Sch., 1998—99. Mem.: Forest Landowners Assn., Fed. Forest Farm Assn., Sigma Tau Delta. Avocations: hiking, scuba diving, boating. Home: # 139 16850-112 Collins Ave Miami FL 33160 Office: Vamm Enterprises 3741 Ne 163rd St # 139 Miami FL 33160 E-mail: vmitc1@aol.com.

MITCHELSON, MARY SUE, lawyer; b. Joplin, Mo., Mar. 17, 1951; d. L. R. and Mildred (Mathes) M. BA, U. Kans., 1973; JD, Georgetown U., 1976. Asst. dean Georgetown U. Law Ctr., Washington, 1976-78; law clk. to Hon. Harold Greene U.S. Dist. Ct. D.C., Washington, 1978-79; trial atty. civil div. comml. litigation br. U.S. Dept. Justice, Washington, 1979-86, asst. dir. civil div. comml. litigation br., 1986-89; asst. general counsel Clarke Cons. Group, 1989-90; asst. dir., dep. dir. comml. litigation br. Civil Div., Dept. of Justice, 1990-91, 1991-95; dep. general counsel Office of the General Counsel, Office of Pers. Mgt., Washington, 1995-2000; asst. inspector gen. U.S. Dept. Edn., Washington, 2000—. Office: US Dept Edn DIG 330 C St NW Washington DC 20415-0001

MITCHEM, CHERYL E. accounting educator; b. South Bend, Ind., June 24, 1947; d. Roy Francis and Marcella Evelyn (Chryst) Drake; m. Allen Pershing Mitchem, Jr., Nov. 28, 1969; children: Michael, Marlo, Megan, Melissa. BA, Tex. Christian U., 1969; MBA, San Diego State U., 1980; PhD, Va. Commonwealth U., 1990. CPA, Va.; cert. mgmt. acct. Vis. prof. acctg. Coll. William and Mary, Williamsburg, Va., 1986-88; adj. prof. acctg. Va. Commonwealth U., Richmond, 1988-89; asst. prof. acctg. Christopher Newport U., Newport News, Va., 1989-91; asst. prof. Va. State U., Petersburg, 1991-93, chair acctg., 1993—2003; assoc. prof. Va. State Univ., Petersburg, 1998—. Contbr. articles to profl. jours. Treas., Greenfield Dragons Athletic Assn., Richmond, 1988-95. Mem. AICPA, Am. Acctg. Assn., Inst. Mgmt. Accts. Mem. Christian Ch. (Disciples Of Christ). Avocations: travel, reading, family activities.

MITCHEM, MARY TERESA, publishing executive; b. Atlanta, Aug. 31, 1944; d. John Reese and Sara Letitia (Marable) Mitchem. BA in History, David Lipscomb Coll., 1966. Sch. and library sales mgr. Chilton Book Co., Phila., 1972-79; dir. market devel. Baker & Taylor Co. div. W.R. Grace, N.Y.C., 1979-81; dir. mktg. R.R. Bowker Co. div. Xerox Corp., N.Y.C, 1981-83, dir. mktg. research, 1983-85; mktg. mgr. W.B. Saunders Co. div. CBS, Inc., Phila., 1985-87; mktg. dir. Congl. Quarterly Inc., Washington, 1987-89; dir. mktg. rsch. and devel. Bur. Nat. Affairs, Inc., Washington, 1990-96; account exec. Hughes Rsch. Corp., Rockville, Md., 1996; vice pres., ptnr. The Psychological Advantage, Inc., Atlanta, 1997-2000; mktg. cons. Project Mgmt. Inst., Pub. Divsn., Newtown Square, Pa., 2000—. Mem. Book Industry Study Group, Inc. (chairperson stats. com. 1984-86), Mktg. Research Assn., Soc. Competitive Intelligence Profls. E-mail: TMitchem4mktg@aol.com.

MITCHUM, BETH, freelance/self-employed editor, writer; b. Logansport, Ind., Sept. 11, 1959; d. Normagene N. (Overmyer) M. BA, Southeastern Coll., Lakeland, Fla., 1981; MLA, U. N.C., Asheville, 1993. Childcare worker Fla. Bapt. Children's Home, Lakeland, 1981-85; asst. mgr. Walden Books, Seattle, 1993—2002. Journalist Comm. Connections, Asheville, N.C., 1992-93. Author: (books) The Diary of Allie Katz, 1993, Artemesian Artist, 1997, Driftwood, 1997, Higher Love, 1997; singer, songwriter, musician (CD) Driftwood the Music, 2002. Valedictorian Southeastern Coll., Lakeland, 1981. Mem. AAUW, NOW. Avocations: hiking, camping, travel, bicycling, drawing.

MITELMAN, BONNIE COSSMAN, editor, writer; b. Flint, Mich., Feb. 15, 1941; d. Maurice B. (dec.) and Frieda H. (Ragir) Cossman; m. Stanley D. Lelewer, Mar. 12, 1961 (div. 1969); children: Joanne, Stephen(dec.) ; m. Alan N. Mitelman, July 23, 1972; 1 child, Geoffrey. BA, Northwestern U., 1969; MA, Manhattanville Coll., 1977. Copywriter trainee Dancer-Fitzgerald-Sample, Inc., Chgo., 1956—60; advt. copywriter Spiegel, Inc., Chgo., 1961—63; freelance advt. and pub. rels. writer Chgo., N.Y.C., 1963—72; co-founder Mitelman & Assocs., Briarcliff Manor, NY, 1972—92, pub. rels. assoc., 1992—94, asst. dir. publ. rels., 1994—97; dir. internal comm. Anti-Defamation League, N.Y.C., 1997—. Adj. lectr., dept. history Mercy Coll., Dobbs Ferry, NY, 1979—85; contbr. articles N.Y. Times, Am. Experiences, Vol. II, Am. History Illustrated, Working Mother, Reform Judaism, 1977—. Author: Mothers Who Work: Stragtegies for Coping; mem. editl. bd.: Reform Judaism, 1977—. Mem.: Authors Guild, Women in Comm.

MITGANG, IRIS FELDMAN, retired lawyer; b. Chgo., Sept. 2, 1937; d. Harry and Leanore (Nelson) Feldman; m. Robert Newton Mitgang, Sept. 9, 1956 (div. Dec. 1974); children: Alix Susan, Steven Ross, Jennifer Lynn. AB, U. Chgo., 1958; MA, U. Rochester, 1967; JD, U. Calif., Davis, 1976. Bar: Calif. 1976, U.S. Dist. Ct. (no. and ea. dists.) Calif., cert.: (specialist family law). Ptnr. Dodge, Reyes, Brorby, Randall, Mitgang & Titmus, Walnut Creek, Calif., 1978-90; prin. Law Office Iris F. Mitgang, Walnut Creek, 1990—98; ret., 1998. Instr. legal writing Sch. Law U. Calif., Davis, 1975—76; adj. prof. family law Sch. Law John F. Kennedy U., Walnut Creek, 1977—87, Sch. Law Golden Gate U., San Francisco, 1987; mem. pro tempore judges panel Contra Costa Superior Ct.; spkr. in field. Mem. editl. bd. Law Rev. U. Calif., Davis Sch. Law, 1976; contbr. articles to profl. jours. Bd. dirs. Leadership Conf. Civil Rights, Washington, 1979—81, ACLU No. Calif.; founding mem. Rape Crisis Ctr. Contra Costa County. Recipient Woman of the Yr. award, Bus. and Profl. Women, 1979, Women's Leadership award, State of Calif., 1980. Mem.: Soc. Profls. in Dispute Resolution, Calif. Dispute Resolution Coun., Assn. Cert. Family Law Specialists, Assn. Family and Concilliation Cts., Alameda Contra Costa Trial Lawyers (bd. dirs. 1992—95, chair mentors program), Calif. Women Lawyers, Contra Costa Bar Assn. (co-chair family law mediation sect. 1992—), Am. Acad. Family Mediators, State Bar Assn. Calif., Nat. Women's Polit. Caucus (nat. chair 1979—81, nat. adv. bd. chair 1981—85, vice chair 1977—79, polit. action chair 1977—79). Democrat. Jewish. E-mail: irismitgang@hotmail.com.

MITHAUG, DEIRDRE KRISTEN, special education educator, researcher; d. Dennis Earl and Cathy Chouinard Mithaug. PhD, MPhil, Teachers Coll., Columbia U., New York, 1993—98, MA, 1992—93; BA, U. of Wash., Seattle, Washington, 1990—92. Cert. NYC Pub. Sch. Tchr. NYC/NY, 1997. Spl. edn. tchr. Babies Prep Sch., New York, NY, 1993—94, Herbert Birch Early Childhood Ctr., New York, NY, 1994—96, Herbert Birch Sch. for Exceptional Children, New York, NY, 1996—97, NY Bd. of Edn. PS 132, New York, NY, 1997—98; prof. Ea. Ill. U., Charleston, Ill., 1998—2000, St. John's U., Jamaica, NY, 2000—. Edn. evaluator Herbert Birch Early Childhood Ctr., New York, NY, 1994—96; program coord. St. John's U., New York, NY, 2001—; adj. instr. for online courses Teachers Coll., Columbia U., New York, NY, 2002—. Author (editor): (book- edn. (non fiction) Self-determined learning theory: Predictions, prescriptions, and practice.; author: (rsch. article) Jour. of Applied Behavior Analysis, (research article) Tchg. Exceptional Children; editor (author): (book- education) Self-Instrn. Pedagogy: How to Tchr. Self-determined Learning. Grantee Online Knowledge Transfer to Tobago, Columbia U., Tobago Ho. of Assembly, 2002-2004; Faculty Rsch. grant, Ea. Ill. U. Mem.: Quality Task For on Inclusive Schooling, Coun. for Exceptional Children. Office: St Johns University 306 Marillac Hall 8000 Utopia Parkway Jamaica NY 11439 E-mail: mithaugd@stjohns.edu.

MITRANY, DEVORA, writer, editor; b. Oak Park, Ill., Mar. 20, 1947; d. John Joseph and Frances Elizabeth (Kirke) Lang. BA cum laude, Beloit Coll., 1969; postgrad., Boston U., 1971-72. Elem. and presch. tchr., Boston, Oak Park, Ill., 1969-72; regional adminstr. TRW Fin. Sys., Wellesley, Mass., 1972-76; mgr. mktg. comm. Computer Sharing Svcs., Denver, 1976-82; dir. corp. comm. Corp. Mgmt. Sys., Denver, 1982-85; sr. copywriter On-Line Software Internat., Ft. Lee, NJ, 1985-86; mgr. corp. comm. Health Mgmt. Sys., N.Y.C., 1986-89; dir. pub. rels. Am. Sephardi Fedn., 1989-92; pres. Mitrell Group, 1992-94; U.S. mktg. dir. Best of Israel, 1994-95; publs. specialist PCS Health Sys., Inc., 1995—98; sci. publs. mgr. AdvancePCs, 1998—2002, consulting med. editor, 2002—. Press release chmn. Nassau Region Hadassah, 1992—94; bd. dirs. Chabad Women,

1995—98, Companion Animal Assn. Ariz., 1999—2000. Dir. pub. rels. Bus. Roundtable Nat. Security, Colo., 1983—84; bd. dirs. Talia Hadassah, 1986—94, co-pres., 1990—92; v.p. edn. Long Beach Hadassah, 1992—94. Named Woman of the Yr., Talia Hadassah, 1993; recipient Nat. Leadership award, Long Beach Hadassah, 1991—92, Talia Hadassah, 1993—94. Mem.: Am. Sephardi Fedn. (mem. edn. com. 1987—89), Colo. Conf. Communicators (Denver Advt. Fedn. liaison 1981—84), Denver Advt. Fedn. (bd. dirs. 1981—83, Alfie award 1984), Coun. Sci. Editors (mem. sponsorship com. 2000—, chmn. 2002—, mem. program com. 2001—), Am. Med. Writers Assn. (mem. biomedical communicators task force 2001—, chair 2003—, chmn. 2003—). Jewish.

MITSTIFER, DOROTHY IRWIN, honor society administrator; b. Gaines, Pa., Aug. 17, 1932; d. Leonard Robert and Laura Dorothy (Crane) Irwin; m. Robert Mitchell Mitsifer, June 17, 1956 (dec. Aug. 1984); children: Kurt Michael, Brett Robert. BS, Mansfield U., 1954; MEd, Pa. State U., 1972, PhD, 1976. Cert. home economist. Tchr. Tri-County High Sch., Canton, Pa., 1954-56, Loyalsock Twp. Sch. Dist., Williamsport, Pa., 1956-63; exec. dir. Kappa Omicron Phi, Williamsport, Pa., 1964-86, Kappa Omicron Phi, Omicron Nu, Haslett, Mich., 1986-90, Kappa Omicron Nu, East Lansing, Mich., 1990—. Prof. continuing edn. Pa. State U., University Park, 1976-80; prof. Mansfield (Pa.) U., 1980-86, pres.'s intern, 1984-86. Editor Kappa Omicron Nu Forum, 1986—; contbr. articles to profl. jours. Pres., bd. dirs. Profl. Devel. Ctr. Adv. Bd., Vocat. Edn., Pa. State U., 1980-86. Mem. ASCD, Am. Home Econs. Assn., Mich. Home Econs. Assn. (exec. dir. 1986-96), Am. Vocat. Assn., Am. Soc. Assn. Execs., Assn. Coll. Honor Socs. (sec.-treas. 1976—), Coll. Edn. Alumni Soc. Pa. State U. (pres. 1986-88, bd. dirs. 1980-90), Kappa Delta Pi. Avocations: sewing, camping, fishing. Home: 1425 Somerset Close St East Lansing MI 48823-2435 Office: Kappa Omicron Nu 4990 Northwind Dr Ste 140 East Lansing MI 48823-5031 E-mail: dmitstifer@kon.org.

MITTELSTAEDT, JANET RUGEN, music educator, composer; b. Port Washington, N.Y., Mar. 30, 1941; d. Chester Davis and Harriet Helen (Goodman) Rugen; m. Ronald Edward Mittelstaedt, Aug. 24, 1963; children: Edward D., Amy C. Leimbach, Thomas A. BS in Edn., Bucknell U., 1963; BA in Music, Marylhurst U., 1984; MM in Composition, U. Portland, 1993. Nat. cert. in piano and composition Music Tchrs. Nat. Assn. Tchr. 6th grade Spring Branch Sch. Dist., Houston, 1964-66; piano tchr. Houston, 1964-66, Pitts., 1967-74, Portland, Oreg., 1978—; composition tchr., 1988—. Composer: Solo Snips, 1991, Splashes of Color, 1992, Sonatina for Youth, 1993, Fabric and Frills, 1994, Beehive, 2002, Animal Antics, 2004. Pianist, music coord. Evergreen Presbyn. Ch., Portland, 1994—2000, dir. children's mus., 1996, 1997; youth choir accompanist First Presbyn. Ch., Portland, 2003—. Recipient award, Ernest Bloch Composers Symposium, 1993, spl. awards, ASCAP, 1994, 1995, 1997, 1998, 1999, 2000, 2001, 2002. Mem.: Oreg. Music Tchrs. Assn. (chair Portland program 1999—2001, Portland composition 1998—99, state composition 1992—95, chair Portland ensemble 1992—94, chair Pt. syllabus 1980s, music theory clinician 1980s, music composition clinician 1990—, composition adjudicator 1990—, syllabus adjudicator 2002—, Composer of Yr. 1994), Oreg. Fedn. Music Clubs (chair composition 1980s). Republican. Presbyterian. Avocations: reading, travel, writing poetry. Home: 4485 NW 187th Ave Portland OR 97229-2911 E-mail: JanRM@worldnet.att.net.

MITTLER, DIANA (DIANA MITTLER-BATTIPAGLIA), music educator, administrator, pianist; b. N.Y.C., Oct. 19, 1941; d. Franz and Regina (Schilling) Mittler; m. Victor Battipaglia, Sept. 5, 1965 (div. 1982). BS, Juilliard Sch., 1962, MS, 1963; DMA, Eastman Sch. Music, 1974. Choral dir. William Cowper Jr. H.S. and Springfield Gardens Jr. H.S., Queens, N.Y., 1963-68; coord. music Flushing H.S., Queens, 1968-79; asst. prin. music Bayside H.S., Queens, 1979-86; assoc. prof. music Lehman Coll., CUNY, 1986-87, prof., 1987—, choral dir., 1986—. Cons. ednl. projects New World Records, 1987—; ednl. cons. Flushing Coun. on Culture and the Arts; cons. Sta. WNET; assoc. condr. Queens Borough-Wide Chorus, 1964-70; pianist, founder Con Brio Chamber Ensemble, 1978; faculty So. Vt. Music Festival, 1979-83; soloist with N.Y. Philharmonic, 1956; solo and chamber music appearances; examiner N.Y.C. Bd. Edn. Bd. Exams., 1985—. Author: 57 Lessons for the High School Music Class, 1983, Franz Mittler: Austro-American Composer, Musician and Humorous Poet, 1993; contbr. articles to music publs.; performance Internat. Summer acad. Mozarteum, Salzburg, Austria, 1995, Weill Recital Hall, 1996, Merkin Hall, 1997, Herbert von Karajan Centrum, Vienna, Austria, 1998. Choral dir., accompanist various charitable, religious, mil., civic holiday functions. N.Y. State Regents scholar, 1958-62; scholarships Juilliard Sch. and Eastman Sch. Music; recipient Excellence in Tchg. award, 1993, Prism award, 1996. Mem. Am. Choral Dirs. Assn., Music Edn. Nat. Conf., Golden Key Soc. Democrat. Home: 10857 66th Ave Forest Hills NY 11375-2247 Office: Lehman Coll Music Dept Bedford Pk Blvd W Bronx NY 10468

MITTS, MARYBETH FRAZIER, real estate company executive, consultant; b. Hartford, Conn., Sept. 4, 1963; d. Robert Lee and Patricia Ann (Casey) Frazier. m. Kevin Garry Mitts, July 14, 1990; children: Margaret, Elizabeth, Katherine. BA, Mount Holyoke Coll., Mass., 1985; M in Pub. Mgmt., U. Md., 1987. Notary Pub., Calif., 1995-97. Rehab. mgmt. specialist U.S. Dept. Housing and Urban Devel., Washington, 1987-90; budget analyst Office of the Comptr., U.S. Dept. Navy, Crystal City, Va., 1990-91; fiscal officer MCAS, U.S. Dept. Navy, Camp Pendleton, Calif., 1991, dep. comptr. Tustin, Calif., 1991-92; sr. cons. Comprehensive Housing Svcs., Fountain Valley, Calif., 1992-95; prin. Affordable Housing Profls., San Diego, Calif., 1995-97. Treas. Naval Officers Spouses Club, Okinawa, 1999—2000; mem. Lenox Elem. Sch. Coun., 2001—. Mem. Mount Holyoke Club San Diego (chmn. pres. 1995-97). Republican. Roman Catholic. E-mail: kmbmitts@hotmail.com.

MITZEN, PHYLLIS BASS, social welfare administrator; b. Chgo., Mar. 27, 1942; d. Herbert and Eleanore (Goodman) Bass; m. Michael Allen Mitzen, Dec. 24, 1961; children: Matthew Gary, Jennifer Joy, Joshua Frederick. BA, Northeastern Ill. U., 1976; MA, U. Chgo., 1980; postgrad., Ill. Inst. Tech., 1990-92. Lic. social worker, Ill. Supr. family support Coun. for Jewish Elderly, Chgo., 1980-82, dir. social svcs., 1982-93, dir. home and cmty. based svcs., 1993—99, dir. devel., 1999—2003, dir. pub. affairs, 2003—. Co-chair adv. coun. Cmty. Care Program, Springfield, Ill., 1994-96. Mem. Gov.'s Cmty. Based Long Term Care Task Team, Springfield, 1995-96, Mayor's Commn. on Extreme Weather Conditions, Chgo., 1995; del. White House Conf. on Aging, Washington, 1995; chair Evanston (Ill.) Commn. on Aging, 1976-82; bd. dirs. Christian Home Missionary League, 2003—. Mem. NASW, Am. Soc. on Aging, Gerontol. Assn. Am., Am. Jewish Com. (v.p. 1992-95, bd. mem. 1995—), Ill. Assn. Cmty. Care Home Care Providers (pres. 1995-99). Democrat. Jewish. Avocations: race walking, crocheting, photography, travel. Office: Council for Jewish Elderly 3003 W Touhy Ave Chicago IL 60645-2833

MIYAMORI, KEIKO, artist, educator; b. Yokohama, Kanagawa, Japan, Jan. 14, 1964; arrived in U.S., 1998; d. Yukio and Yuriko Miyamori. BFA, U. Tsukuba, Japan, 1993, MFA, 1995. Adj. faculty Pa. Acad. Fine Arts, Phila., 2000—. Artist-in-residence U. Pa., Phila., 1998—99, Soc. Contemporary Craft, Pitts., 2003. Grantee, Leeway Found., 2003. Office: PO Box 11771 Philadelphia PA 19101 Personal E-mail: miyamorik@aol.com.

MIYAMOTO, ROBIN EMI SUGIHARA, psychologist, researcher, supervisor; b. Boston, Oct. 16, 1973; d. Jared Genji and Valerie Sugihara; m. Marc Masanori Miyamoto, Aug. 7, 1999; 1 child, Marley Mieko. BS, U. Wash., Seattle, 1991—95; PsyD, Am. Sch. of Profl. Psychology, Honolulu, 2000. Lic. clin. psychologist Hawaii, 2001. Post doctoral health fellow Tripler Army Med. Ctr., Honolulu, 2000—01; res. supr. Waimanalo Health Ctr., 2001—; clin. psychologist St. Francis Med. Ctr., Honolulu, 2001—. Adj. prof. Argosy U, Honolulu, 2002; psychologist and mem. St. Francis Inst. of Cancer, Honolulu, 2001. Grantee rsch., Clin. Rsch. Ctr., Honolulu, 1998, rsch. award, Hawaii Psychological Assn., 2001. Mem.: Am. Psychol. Assn., Soc. Behavioral Med., Am. Diabetes Assn. Avocations: hula, pilates. Office: #306 2226 Liliha St Honolulu HI 96817 E-mail: robinmiyamoto@hotmail.com.

MIYASAKI, NOLA, state agency administrator; BSl in Human Biology, Stanford U.; JD, U. Calif.; postgrad., Keio U., Tokyo, London Sch. Econs. Spl. asst. in tech. Gov. Benjamin Cayetano, Honolulu; exec. dir., CEO High Tech. Devel. Corp., Honolulu, 2000—. Office: Manoa Innovation Ctr 2800 Woodlawn Dr Honolulu HI 96822

MIZES, MARIA GABRIELA, cultural organization administrator, art historian; b. Buenos Aires, July 11, 1961; d. Jimmy M. and Beatriz Adot BA in art history magna cum laude, Columbia U., 1992. Asst. registrar Mus. Nacional de Bellas Artes, Buenos Aires, 1982-83, asst. curator, 1983-85, asst. dir., 1985-87, registrar, 1987-90; exhbn. asst. Lat. Am. Artists of the Twentieth Century Mus. Modern Art, N.Y.C., 1991-93; assoc. registrar Am. Fedn. Arts, N.Y.C., 1993-94, registrar, 1994-96, Trust for Mus. Exhbns., Washington, 1996—97; ind. registrar, 1998—; mgr. Racine Berkow Assoc., Alexandria, Va., 2003—. Mem. Am. Assn. Mus. (registrars com. 1990), Internat. Coun. Muss., Internat. Documentation Com., Phi Beta Kappa. Roman Catholic. Avocations: collecting magnets, collecting museum buildings' postcards, sunbathing, bird hunting with dogs. Home: 5500 Muncaster Mill Rd Derwood MD 20855-1825

MIZZI, CHARLOTTE H. city director; b. Malta, May 14, 1940; came to the U.S., 1950; d. Ely and Lily Mizzi; m. Robert Haley, May 27, 1961 (div. Feb. 1982); children: Mark, Alan, Audrey. Student, Montclair State Coll., 1958-60, Jersey City State Coll., 1974-79. Price analyst Kueffel & Esser Co., Hoboken, N.J., 1961-64; dir. divsn. tenant/landlord City of Jersey City, N.J., 1973-92, 94—, chief of staff, 1992-93, acting dir. pub. works, 1993-94. Debator League of Municipalities, 1974, 75, 76, 80, panelist, 1991; lectr. N.J. Property Owners Assnb., 1991. Co-editor Ch. Newsletter, 1997—. Elected mem. N.J. State Dem. Com., Trenton, 1974-78; mem. Electoral Coll., 1976, ethnic support coord. Com. to Elect Chris Whitman Gov., Hudson County, 1992-93; co-chairperson Election Com. for Mayor Schundler, Jersey City, 1993; Mayor's alt. to Hackensack Meadowlands Mcpl. Com., 1993—. Mem. N.Y. Tchg. Ctr. (pres., treas. 1997—), Rent Leveling Assn. N.J. (legis. com. 1996—, Presdl. award 1986-92), Rotary Club Jersey City. Avocations: bible studies, reading, horseback riding, hiking, world religions. Office: City of Jersey City 30 Montgomery St Jersey City NJ 07302-3821 E-mail: pwpo.charlotte@mail.cityofjerseycity.com.

MKRYAN, SONYA, geophysicist, educator, research scientist; b. Beyrouth, Lebanon, Mar. 1, 1935; arrived in U.S., 1979; d. Vahram and Marie (Topalian) Faradjian; m. Karapet Mkryan, Apr. 11, 1970; children: Marine, Anahit, Lusine. MS in Physics, Pedagogical Inst., 1956; PhD in Physics and Math., Tbilicy State U., 1970. Physics, math. tchr. HS, Ghaltakchi, 1956-57; libr. Ores Dept., Leninakan, Armenia, 1957-60; geophycist, rschr. Inst. Geophysics Enginrg. Seismology, Leninakan, 1960-70; assoc. prof. physics Polytech. Inst., Kirovakan, Armenia, 1970-79; mech. insp. Robertshaw Co., Anaheim, Calif., 1980-82; tchr. Pasadena (Calif.) Sch. Dist., 1983-86; eligibility worker, acting supr. Dept. of Pub. Svcs., Glendale, Calif., 1986-97; social worker home supportive svcs. Glendale, 1997-2001. Author: (poetry) Ups and Downs of Life, 1987, Incessant Melodies, 1992, Light and Darkness, 1997, (novels) Eternities Travelers, 1998; one-woman shows include Tekeyan Gallere, Pasadena, Calif., 1989, Pasadena Union of Marash Armenians Hall, 1982—95, exhibited in group shows at Altadena, Pasadena, Downey, Glendale, Ambassador Hotel, L.A. (2d prize, 1987), Wilshir Ebel, 1988. Bd. dirs. Sahag-Mesrob Armenian Christian Sch. Mem.: Armenian Radio and TV Com., Armenian Allied Arts Assn. (1st prize 1982, 1984, 1985, 1987, 1991), Nat. Libr. Poets, Internat. Soc. Poets, Armenian Writers Union Calif. Avocations: writing, walking, reading, cooking, dance. Home: 2723 N Lake Ave Altadena CA 91001-1903

MLAY, MARIAN, retired government official; b. Pitts., Sept. 11, 1935; AB, U. Pitts., 1957; postgrad., Princeton U., 1969-70; JD, Am. U., 1977. Mgmt. intern HEW, Washington, 1961-70, dep. dir. Chgo. region, 1971-72, dir. divsn. consol. funding, 1972-73; dep. dir. office policy devel. and planning USPHS, Washington, 1973-77; dir. program evaluation EPA, Washington, 1978-9, dep. dir. office of drinking water, 1979-84, dir. office of ground water protection, 1984-91, dir. oceans and coastal protection, 1991-95; sr. rsch. assoc. Nat. Acad. Pub. Adminstrn., 1995-97; ret., 1997. Contbr. articles to profl. jours., chpts. to books. Bd. dirs. D.C. United Fund, 1979-80, New Dominion Chorale, 2001--, Davis Meml. Goodwill Book Com., 1999-2002. Princeton U. fellow, 1969-70; recipient Career Edn. award Nat. Inst. Public Affairs, 1960. Mem. ABA, D.C. Bar Assn. (co-chair steering com. energy, environ. and natural resources sect.). Achievements include development of a ground-water protection strategy for EPA establishing a national program to support related state and local efforts and to define a common ground-water protection policy for EPA. Home: 3747 1/2 Kanawha St NW Washington DC 20015-1838 E-mail: mlayma@aol.com.

MLOCEK, SISTER FRANCES ANGELINE, financial executive; b. River Rouge, Mich., Aug. 4, 1934; d. Michael and Suzanna (Bloch) M. BBA, U. Detroit, 1958; MBA, U. Mich., 1971. CPA, Mich. Bookkeeper Allen Park (Mich.) Furniture, 1949-52, Gerson's Jewlery, Detroit, 1952-53; jr. acct. Meyer Dickman, CPA, Algaze, Staub & Bowman, CPAs, Detroit, 1953-58; acct., internal auditor Sisters, Servants of Immaculate Heart of Mary Congregation, Monroe, Mich., 1959-66, asst. gen. treas., 1966-73, gen. treas., 1973-76; internal auditor for parishes Archdiocese of Detroit, 1976-78; asst. to exec. dir. Leadership Conf. of Women, Silver Spring, Md., 1978-83; dir. of fin. Nat. Conf. of Cath. Bishops/U.S. Cath. Conf., Washington, 1989-94; CFO Sisters Servants of the Immaculate Heart of Mary, Monroe, Mich., 1994—. Trustee SSIHM Charitable Trust, Monroe, 1988—. Author: (manual) Leadership Conference of Women Religious/Confernce of Major Superiors of Men, 1981. Treas. Zonta Club of Washington Found., Washington, 1983-88, pres., 1992-93; bd. dirs. Our Lady of Good Counsel High Sch., Wheaton, Md., 1983-89. Mem. AICPA, D.C. Inst. CPAs (mem. not-for-profit com. 1992-94, CFOs com. 1990-94. Democrat. Roman Catholic. Office: Sisters Servants Immaculate Heart Mary 610 W Elm Ave Monroe MI 48162-7909

MOATES, BETTY CAROLYN, microbiologist, computer consultant; b. Rector, Ark., Sept. 27, 1937; d. Hubert E. and Edith R. (Robertson) Dawson; m. James J. Moates, Nov. 11, 1972 (dec.). BA, San Jose State U. Lic. clin. lab. scientist, Calif.; cert. med. technologist. Med. technologist O'Connor Hosp., San Jose, Calif., 1960, Vets. Hosp., Palo Alto, Calif., 1961; lab. supr. San Jose Med. Clinic, 1961-67; microbiology supr. Alexian Bros. Hosp., San Jose, 1967-74; microbiologist Good Samaritan Health Sys., San Jose, 1976-96, coord. clin. data sys., 1994-96; sr. microbiologist and microbiology system data coord. Columbia Good Samaritan Health System, Med. Ctr., San Jose, Calif., 1996—. Co-author, co-developer: (data users guide) Dogwood Information Management System for County Recorders, 1992, Dogwood Information Management System for Title Insurance Companies, 1992. Pres. Rebekah Assembly Calif., 1974-75, Internat. Assn. Rebekah Assemblies, 1988-89; rep. Internat. Coun. Ind. Order of Oddfellows, 1999—. Mem. Calif. Assn. Microbiologists, Calif. Assn. Med. Technologists (sec. 1960-75), Sunnyvale Rebekah Lodge (past presiding officer). Avocations: reading, computers, music. Home: 1975 Kobara Ln San Jose CA 95124-1517 E-mail: bmoates@packbell.net.

MOBERLY, BONNIE LOU, travel services executive; b. Ft. Wayne, Ind., Apr. 10, 1930; d. James Loyd and Rilla Elizabeth (Starner) Boyer; m. William Gregg Moberly, Oct. 26, 1952. Student, St. Francis Coll., 1971. Stock registrar Midwestern United Life Ins. Co., Ft. Wayne, 1956-59, adminstrv. asst., 1959-71; exec. sec. Zimmer, Inc., Warsaw, Ind., 1977-87; adminstrv. asst. Bristol-Myers Squibb, Warsaw, 1988-90, travel mgr., 1990-93; pres. Heritage Travel Svcs., 1994—2003.

MOBLEY, BARBARA JEAN, state legislator; b. Dec. 1, 1947; m. James L. Savage, Jr. BS, Savannah State Coll.; MSW, U. Ill.; JD, So. Meth. U. Atty.; mem. Ga. Ho. of Reps., 1992—, mem. higher edn. com., chair ethics com., mem. pub. safety com., mem. judiciary com., 1999. Democrat. Baptist. Home: 3009 Miriam Ct Decatur GA 30032 Office: Ga Ho of Reps 402 LO B Legis Office Bldg Atlanta GA 30334

MOBLEY, EMILY RUTH, library dean, educator; b. Valdosta, Ga., Oct. 1, 1942; d. Emmett and Ruth (Johnson) M. AB in Edn., U. Mich., 1964, AM in Libr. Sci., 1967, postgrad., 1973-76. Tchr. Ecorse (Mich.) Pub. Schs., 1964-65; adminstrv. trainee Chrysler Corp., Highland Park, Mich., 1965-66, engring. libr., 1966-69; libr. II Wayne State U., Detroit, 1969-72, libr. III, 1972-75; staff asst. GM Rsch. Labs. Libr., Warren, Mich., 1976-78, supr. reader svcs., 1978-81; libr. dir. GMI Engring. & Mgmt. Inst., Flint, Mich., 1982-86; assoc. dir. for pub. svcs. & collection devel., assoc. prof. libr. sci. Purdue U. Librs., West Lafayette, Ind., 1986-89, acting dir. librs., assoc. prof. libr. sci., 1989, dean librs., prof. libr. sci., 1989—; Esther Ellis Norton Disting. Prof. Libr. Sci. Purdue U., West Lafayette, Ind., 1997—. Adj. lectr. U. Mich. Sch. Libr. Sci., Ann Arbor, 1974-75, 83-86; grants reader Libr. of Mich., 1980-81; project dir. Mideastern Mich. Region Libr. Cooperation, 1984-86; cons. Libr. Coop. of Macomb, 1985-86, Clark-Atlanta U., 1990-91; search com. for new dir. of libr. Smithsonian Instn., 1988; mem. GM Pub. Affairs Subcom. on Introducing Minorities to Engring.; presenter in field. Author: Special Libraries at Work, 1984, numerous other publs.; mem. editl. bd. Reference Svcs. Rev., 1989—, Infomanage, 1993-97. Corp. vis. com. for librs. MIT, 1990—, Carnegie Mellon U., 1998—; mem. Ind. Statewide Libr. Automation Task Force, 1989-90; state tech. strategy subcom. on info. tech. and telecomms. Ind. Corp. for Sci. & Tech., 1989; nat. adv. com. Libr. of Congress, 1988; trustee Libr. of Mich., 1983-86, v.p., 1986, long range plan com., 1979-82, task force on document access and delivery, 1977-79; info. project mem. Rep. Nat. Conv., 1980; bd. dirs. Small Farms Assn., Southfield, Mich., Lafayette Symphony Orch., YWCA. Recipient Bausch & Lomb award, 1960, Cert. for Outstanding Performance in Acad. Achievement State of Mich. Ho. of Reps., 1976, Spl. Tribute for Outstanding Contbns. Libr. of Mich. Bd. Trustees, 1986, Disting. Alumnus award U. Mich. Sch. Info. & Libr. Studies, 1989; U. Mich. Regents Alumni scholar, 1960-64; CIC doctoral fellow in libr. sci., 1973-76. Mem. ALA (com. on accreditation, subcom. to rev. 1972, standards for accreditation 1988-89, OLOS minority internship com. 1988-89, nominating com. 1992-93, mem. coun. resolutions com. 1993-97), Assn. Coll. & Rsch. Librs. (task force on libr. sch. curriculum 1988-89, com. on profl. edn. 1990-92), Libr. Adminstrn. & Mgmt. Assn., Assn. Rsch. Librs. (bd. dirs. 1990-93), Spl. Librs. Assn. (pres. 1987-88, fellow 1991, com. mem.), Alpha Kappa Alpha, Phi Kappa Phi, Sigma Xi, Iron Key. Office: Purdue U Librs Stewart Ctr Lafayette IN 47907 Office Phone: 765-494-2900.

MOBLEY, KAREN RUTH, art gallery director; b. Cheyenne, Wyo., Aug. 26, 1961; d. David G. and Marlene G. (Franz) M. BFA, U. Wyo., 1983; MFA, U. Oka., 1987. Sales assoc. Morgan Gallery, Kansas City, Mo., 1984-85; grad. asst. U. Okla. Mus. Art, Norman, 1985-87; dir. Univ. Art Gallery N.Mex. State U., Las Cruces, 1988-93; exec. dir. Nicolaysen Art Mus., Casper, Wyo., 1993-96; dir. Spokane Arts Com., 1997—. Guest artist Okla. City Community Coll., 1986. Paintings exhibited in numerous exhbns. including Phoenix Triennial, 1990, New Am. Talent, Laguna Gloria Art Mus., Austin, Tex., 1992, Adair Margo Gallery, El Paso, 1992, 93, 94, Wyo. Arts Coun. Gallery and Casper Coll., 1995, Mont. State U., 1996. Wyo. Arts Coun. Individual Artist grantee 1994, Lit. fellow, 1995, 96; named Outstanding Young Women Am. Mem. Am. Assn. Mus., Mountain Plains Mus. Assn., N.Mex. Mus Assn., Coll. Art Assn., Phi Beta Kappa, Phi Kappa Phi. Office: Spokane Arts Com 808 W Spokane Falls Blvd Spokane WA 99203*

MOCEANU, DOMINIQUE, retired Olympic athlete; b. Hollywood, Calif., Sept. 30, 1981; Mem. Nat. Team, 1992—93, 1993—94, 1995—96, 1999; coach Gymnastics World, Ohio, 2002—. Competitions include U.S. Classic, 1991, 92, 93, U.S. Gymnastics Championships, 1992, Am. Classic, 1993, U.S. Olympic Festival, 1993, Coca-Cola Nat. Championships, 1993, 94, 95, 96, Am. Classic/World Championships, 1994, Am. Classic/Pan Am. Games, 1995, World Team Trials, 1995, U.S. Olympic Trials, 1996, John Hancock U.S. Gymnastics Championships, 1997, 98; mem. U.S. Olympic Team, Sydney, 2000. Named 1st pl. balance beam, U.S. Classic, Salt Lake City, 1991, 2d pl. in balanve beam jr. divsn., U.S. Gymnastics Championships, Columbus, 1992, 2d pl. in all around, 1st team vault, uneven bars and floor exercise, Jr. Pan Am. Games, 1992, 1st pl. in team and balance beam, 3d pl. in uneven bars, Internat. Tournament of Jr. Women's Gymnastics, Charleroi, Belgium, 1993, 1st pl. in all around, vault and team floor exercise, 3d in uneven bars and balance beam jr. divsn., Coca-Cola Nat. Championships, Nashville, 1994, 1st pl. in team all around, 1st pl. in vault, 3d pl. in balance beam and floor exercise, Am. Classic-Pan Am. Games Trials, Oakland, Calif., 1995, 1st pl. in all around, 2d pl. in floor exercise, 3d pl. in vault, Coca-Cola Nat. Championships, New Orleans, 1995, 1st pl. in all around, World Team Trials, Austin, 1995, 1st pl. in uneven bars, 3d pl. in balance beam, Reese's Internat. Gymnastics Cup, Portland, 1995, 1st pl. in all around, team and floor exercise, 3d pl. in vault and balance beam, 2d pl. in uneven bars, Visa Challenge, Fairfax, Va., 1995, 3d pl. all around for team, 2d pl. team balance beam, World Championships, Sabae, Japan, 1995, ISOC SportsWoman of Month (2), 1995, individual all-around finalist, World Championship Team, 1997; recipient Silver and Bronze medals, World Championships, 1995, Gold medal team competition, Atlanta Olympic Games, 1996, Gold medal, Goodwill Games, 1998. Avocations: swimming, reading, music. Office: Gymnastics World 6630 Harris Rd Cleveland OH 44147

MOCK, CHERRY L. marriage and family therapist, child therapist; b. Baytown, Tex., June 14, 1951; d. Jack Glenn and Joan Fay (Barry) Sawberger; m. Robert D. Mock, July 3, 1972; 1 child, Rhett Vaughn. BA in Edn., Southwestern Union Coll., Keene, Tex., 1973; MS in Marriage, Family and Child Therapy, Loma Linda U., 1976. Cert. in elem. edn.; lic. profl. counselor. Tchr. 5th grade Redlands (Calif.) Jr. Acad., 1973-75; dir. Meth. Home Svcs., Houston, 1976-79; pvt. practice marriage and family therapy The Mock Clinic, The Woodlands, Tex., 1979-88; Arabian horse breeder Almaz Aseel Arabians, The Woodlands, 1990—. Named Dir. of Yr., Meth. Home Svcs., 1979. Mem. Am. Assn. Marriage and Family Therapy. Republican. Seventh-day Adventist. Home: 10406 Treeridge Pl The Woodlands TX 77380-1338 Office: The Mock Clinic 1120 Medical Plaza Dr Ste 380 The Woodlands TX 77380-3243

MOCK, MELINDA SMITH, orthopedic nurse specialist, consultant; b. Austell, Ga., Nov. 15, 1947; d. Robert Jehu and Emily Dorris (Smith) Smith; m. David Thomas Mock, Oct. 20, 1969. ASN, DeKalb Coll., 1972. RN Ga., cert. orthop. nurse specialist, orthop. nurse, 1988; life care planner 2002. Nursing technician Ga. Bapt. Hosp., Atlanta, 1967, staff nurse, 1979; asst. corr. Harcourt, Brace & World Pub. Co., Atlanta, 1968-69; receptionist, sec. Goodbody & Co., Atlanta, 1969-70; nursing asst. DeKalb Gen. Hosp., Decatur, Ga., 1970-71; staff nurse Drs.' Meml. Hosp., Atlanta, 1972-73; staff nurse, relief charge nurse Shallowford Cmty. Hosp., Atlanta, 1973, charge nurse, 1973-76, head nurse, 1976-79, orthop. nurse specialist emergency rm., 1979; rehab. specialist, sr. rehab. specialist Internat. Rehab. Assocs., Inc., Norcross, Ga., 1981, rehab. supr., 1981-82; cons., founder, propr. Healthcare Cost Cons., Inc., Alpharetta, Ga., 1982-83, cons., founder, pres., 1983—. Legis. com. adv. coun. Ga. Bd. Nursing, Atlanta, 1984—85; adv. coun. Milton HS Coop. Bus. Edn., 1986—89; task force profl. liability ins. Nat. Fedn. Splty. Nursing Orgns., 1987—89; active Congressman Patrick Swindall Sr. Citizen Adv. Coun., 1988, Congressman Ben Jones Vets. Affairs Adv. Coun., 1989—92, White Ho Conf. Small Bus., 1995, spkr. Newt Gingrich Small Bus. Adv. Com., 1997—99, Congl. Small Bus. Summit, 1998. Atl. del.-at-large Nat. Rep. Conv., 1996; dep. voter registrar Fulton County, Ga., 1983—87; Rep. treas. 23d House Dist.; active various coms. and positions Fulton County Rep. Party, 1989—2001; Rep. treas. 41st House Dist., 1993—97; mem. state exec. com. Ga. Rep. State Com., 1997—99, mem., 1993—2002; 1st vice chairwoman Rep. 6th Congl. Dist., 1993—97, chmn., 1997—99; vice chair 7th Congl. Dist. Ga. Rep. Party, 2003—; del. various convs., 1993—; mem. Chattahoochee Rep. Women, 1989—2001, chmn. campaign com., 1992—94, rec. sec., 1995—2001; chmn. nominating com. House Dist. 23, 1990; mem. steering com. Re-Elect State Rep. Tom Campbell, 1990; mem. campaign staff Re-Elect State Senator Sallie Newbill, 1990, 1992, 1994; mem. health adv. campaign Elect Matt Towery for Lt. Gov., 1990, Elect Bob Barr U.S. Senate, 1991—92; mem. election com. Mark Burkhalter for State Rep.; vol. campaign staff Re-Elect Congressman Newt Gingrich, 1992, 1994, 1996, 1998; mem. campaign staff Elect Tom Price to State Senate, 1996, Cherokee County Reps., 2001—. Recipient Nat. Disting. Svc. Registry award, 1987; named Outstanding Young Women Am., 1984. Mem. Nat. Assn. Orthopedic Nurses (nat. policies com. 1981-82, chmn. govt. rels. com. 1987-90, nat. treas. 1991-95, nat. pres. elect 1998-99, pres. 1999-2000, Nurse in Washington intern 1987, 99, legis. contbr. editor news 1989, chmn. legis workshop 1989, co-chmn. legis. workshop 1990, guest editl. Orthop. Nursing Jour. 1988, Ann. Congress del. 1982, 91-94, 96, 98-2001, 03, Pres.'s award 1992, Outstanding Contbn. to NAON award 1996, chmn. budget and fin. com. 1991-95, nat. bylaws and policies com. 1995-98, bylaws and policies com. Atlanta chpt. 1994-96, pres-elect Atlanta chpt. 1996-97, pres. 1997-98, program dir. 2002-04), Orthop. Nurses Assn. (nat. bd. dirs. 1977-79, nat. treas. 1979-80), Coun. Splty. Nursing Orgns. Ga. (nominating com. 1976-77), Assn. Rehab. Nurses (bd. dirs. Ga. chpt. 1980-81, del. people-to-people program to China 1981), Nat. Fedn. Ind. Bus. (guardian 1988—, leadership coun. 1990—, healthcare task force chmn. 1992—, vice-chmn./fed. liaison Ga. adv. coun. 1995—), Am. Bd. Nursing Specialities (chmn. nominating com. 1993-95, chmn. com. on specialty bd. rev. 1993-95), Ga. Jaycees (dist. 4C rep. Ga. Jaycee Legis. 1984-85), Ga. Seatbelt Coalition, Orthop. Nurses Cert. Bd. (bd. dirs. 1991-96, pres. 1992-93, task force on advanced practice certification 1991-92), North Fulton C. of C. (vice chmn. health svc. effectiveness alliance 1984-85, chmn. 1985-86, co-chmn./editor periodical 1985, 3rd Quarter Workhorse award 1985), Alpharetta Jaycees (adminstrv. v.p. 1984-85, internal v.p. 1985-86), Alpharetta Jaycee Women (bd. dirs. 1983), Ga. Perimeter Coll. Nursing Alumni Assn. (bd. dirs. 2000—). Baptist. Avocations: scrapbooks, reading, community service activities. Office: Healthcare Cost Cons Inc PO Box 466 Alpharetta GA 30009-0466

MOCK, SUSAN E. pre-school educator, consultant; b. Hanover, NH, Sept. 27, 1946; d. Richard Howard and Louise Keane Mock; m. Daniel W. Freeman, Aug. 5, 1972; 1 child, Lee T.M. Freeman. BA, U. Vt., 1969; M in Early Childhood Edn., U. N.C., 1971; diploma in Am. Montessori, Chestnut Hill Coll., 1984. Kindergarten tchr. Cabot (Vt.) Pub. Schs., 1971—73; children's libr. Ilsley Pub. Libr., Middlebury, Vt., 1974—76; kindergarten tchr. New Orleans Pub. Schs., 1976—78; head tchr. head start Manna Bible Inst., Phila., 1978—80; pre-kindergarten head start tchr. Phila. Pub. Schs., 1980—86; presch. & kindergarten tchr. Ripton (Vt.) Pub. Schs., Vt., 1987—. Early childhood instr. Cmty. Coll. Vt., Middlebury, 1999—2002. Contbr. articles to profl. jours. Bd. dirs. Addison County United Way, 1994—96; cmty. rep. Head Start Policy Coun., Burlington, Vt., 1997—99; pres. League of Women Voters, Addison County, Vt., 1991—2001. Recipient Positive Tchg. award, Am. Family Inst., Pa., 1986; Charlotte Newcomb scholar, Chestnut Hill Coll., 1983. Mem.: Am. Montessori Soc., Vt. Assn. Edn. Young Children, N.E. Assn. Edn. Young Children (workshop presenter 1994—2002). Achievements include patents for rolling calendar. Avocations: reading, gardening, walking, tai chi. Home: 162 Butternut Ridge Dr Middlebury VT 05753 Office: Rolling Record 162 Butternut Ridge Dr Middlebury VT 05753

MOCKLER, ANNA, writer, ecologist; b. Mahopac, N.Y., Sept. 26, 1955; d. Nils Edward and Adele Rosen Mockler; m. Reuben D. Radding, Dec. 17, 2002. BA in Psychology, Antioch Coll., 1977; MA in Environ. Conservation, NYU, 1991. Cert. profl. wetland scientist. Wetland writer and scientist N.Y.C. Pks., 1990—92; proprietor Mockler Environ., Eugene, Oreg., 1992—96; mitigation specialist King County DDES, Renton, Wash., 1997—98; sr. wetland ecologist Cooke Sci. Svcs., Seattle, 1999—2000; proprietor Upstream Enterprises, Seattle, 2000—02; writer Bklyn., 2002—. Author: (booklet) Freshwater Wetlands of N.Y.C., 1990, Handbook of Sensitive Area Mitigation, 1998, (short stories) Burning Salt, 2003. Recipient Heintzelman Trophy award, Point No Point, 1999. Mem.: Bklyn. Bot. Gardens, Poets and Writers.

MOCKLER, ESTHER JAYNE, state senator; b. Jackson, Wyo., Sept. 21, 1957; d. Franklin and Nancy (Fisher) Mockler. BA in Polit. Sci., Wellesley Coll., 1980. Legal asst., 1981-84; legal adminstr., 1984-87; rschr., cons., 1987—; exec. dir. Wyo. Democratic Party, 1993-95; mem. from Dist. 44 Wyo. Ho., Cheyenne, 1992-96; mem. from Dist. 8 Wyo. Senate, Cheyenne, 1996—. Mem. Gov.'s Coun. on Devel. Disabilities, United Med. Ctr. Aux., Audobon Wyom. Bd. Office: PO Box 1857 Cheyenne WY 82003-1857

MODELAND, PHYLLIS JO, author; b. Carthage, Mo., Dec. 22, 1938; d. Howard Levi and Pauline (Crawford) Anderson; m. Dennis L. Rossiter, Mar. 30, 1968 (dec. Apr. 1992); 1 child, Eric Shawn; m. Vernon L. Modeland, May 29, 1996. Head libr. Trs. Regional Libr. Br., Odessa, Mo., 1979-83; editor, gen. mgr. Ozark County Times Newspaper, Gainesville, Mo., 1989. Adminstr. RunningRiver virtual village on World Wide Web; freelance writer, tchr., editor, lectr., photographer. Author: On the Scent of Danger, 1989, Moxie, 1990, A Living History of the Ozarks, 1992, Where Eagles Soar (e-book), 2000, On the Scent of Danger (e-book), 2000; editor, pub.: The Runningriver Reader; contbr. articles to profl. jours., periodicals, short story anthologies. Mem. Soc. Children's Book Writers, Women Writing the West, Ozarks Writers League (v.p. 1990, Dan Saults award 1988, 93), Mo. Writers Guild (Best Column. 1989, Best Book 1991, Best Major Work 1992). Avocations: photography, hand spinning, internet. Home: 462 Marion County 7045 Flippin AR 72634-8186 E-mail: phyllismodeland@runningriver.com.

MODEN, JOLEEN, communications executive; B in Bus. Adminstr. and Actg. CPA. Ptnr. Coopers & Lybrand; v.p., CFO, treas. Signature Home Care Group; dir. corp. audit PepsiCo Inc.; asst. contr. internal audit GTE, 1998—2000; sr. v.p. internal auditing Verizon Comms. Inc., N.Y.C., 2000—. Office: Verizon Comms Inc 1095 Avenue of the Americas New York NY 10036-6797

MODIE, CHRISTINE M. insurance company executive; BS, U. Vt., 1974. V.p. mutual fund info. svcs. State St. Bank and Trust Co., Quincy; chief info. officer Batterymarch Fin. Mgmt., Inc., Boston; verious sr. level positions Aetna Life Ins. Co., Hartford, Conn.; sr. v.p., chief info. officer Travelers Life & Annuity, 1997—99; exec. v.p., chief info. officer Mass. Life Ins. Co., Springfield, 1999—. Office: Mass Life Ins Co 1295 State St Springfield MA 01111-6001

MOE, JANET ANNE, elementary school educator, church organist; b. Sacramento, May 24, 1946; d. Joseph Robert and Virginia Lou (Jones) Mangan; m. Edward Earl Moe, Aug. 23, 1969 (dec. Aug. 2002); children: Erik John, Erin Jean Moe Mitchell. BA, Calif. Luth. U., 1968; std. secondary tchg. credential, Calif. State U., Sacramento, 1969, crosscultural, lang. and acad. devel. cert. (CLAD), 1996; cert. in Orff Schulwerk Levels I, II and III, U. Calif. Santa Cruz, 1987; MS, preliminary adminstrv. credential, Nat. U., Sacramento, 2001. Elem. tchr. Gloria Dei Luth. Sch., Sacramento, 1969—73; elem. music specialist Sacramento City Unified Sch. Dist., 1982—. All-city elem. choir coord. Sacramento City Unified Sch. Dist., 1999—2001; chorus dir. Sierra Mountain Music Camp, Sacramento, 2001. Touring choir Sacramento City Coll., Italy, 1998, 1998, 2002, 2002; touring choir So. Calif. and Hawaii Calif. Luth. U., 1967—68; task force to restore music and the fine arts Sacramento City Unified Sch. Dist., 1999—2000; organist Gloria Dei Luth. Ch., 1970—2002, Luth. Ch. of Good Shepherd, 2003—. Recipient Hon. Svc. award, PTA Bear Flag Sch., Sacramento, 1992. Mem.: NEA, Calif. Music Educators Assn. (elem. rep., mem. bd. Capitol Sect., Save the Music grant 2002, Outstanding Music Educator award 1996, 2003), Nat. Audubon Soc. Republican. Lutheran. Avocations: birdwatching, travel, yoga, reading, hiking. Home: PO Box 109 Elk Grove CA 95759-0109 Office Phone: 916-228-5880.

MOE-FISHBACK, BARBARA ANN, counseling administrator; b. Grand Forks, N.D., June 24, 1955; d. Robert Alan and Ruth Ann (Wang) Moe; m. William Martin Fishback; children: Kristen Ann Fishback, William Robert Fishback. BS in Psychology, U. N.D., 1977, MA in Counseling and Guidance, 1979, BS in Elem. Edn., 1984. Cert. elem. counselor Ill. Tchr. United Day Nursery, Grand Forks, 1977-78; social worker Cavalier County Social Svcs., Langdon, N.D., 1979-83; elem. sch. counselor Douglas Sch. Sys., Ellsworth AFB, S.D., 1984-87, Jacksonville (Ill.) Sch. Sys., 1987—. Vol. Big Sister program, Grand Forks, 1978—84; leader pine to prairie coun. Girls Scouts U.S., 1980—82; tchr. Head Start Program, Grand Forks, 1979. Mem.: AAUW (local br. newsletter editor 1980—81, br. sec. 1981—83), NEA, AACD, Am. Sch. Counselor Assn., Ill. Edn. Assn., Ill. Sch. Counselor Assn., Ill. Assn. Counseling and Devel., Jaycettes (bd. dirs. 1982—83), Kappa Alpha Theta (newsletter, mag. article editor 1976—77). Avocations: cooking, camping, curling, ceramics, creative writing. Home: 291 Sandusky St Jacksonville IL 62650-1844 Office: 310 N Clay Ct Jacksonville IL 62650

MOELHMAN, AMY JO, social worker; b. Lafayette, Ind., Mar. 18, 1954; d. Charles and Marian (Young) Moelhman. BS, Ball State U., 1976; MSW, U. Denver, 1979. Lic. clin. social worker, Ind. Social worker Adolescent Crisis Team, Adams County Social Svc., Denver; counselor adolescent boys prog. Pleasant Run Children's Home, Indpls.; group therapist Mothers of Victims of Sexual Abuse, Mid-Town Mental Health, Indpls.; supr. foster care and counseling prog. Children's Bur., Indpls.; mgr. Family Connection Ctr., 1989-90; dir. family programs Vis. Nurse Svc., Indpls., 1990-96; dir. Holy Family Svcs., Cath. Social Svcs., Indpls., 1996—2001; cons. Brown County Family Access Ctr., 1999—; supr. cmty. programs Indpls. Transition Ctr. Casey Family Programs, 2001—. Chair Ind. Coalition of Family-based Svcs., 1992-94; co-chair family preservation com. Marion County Stepahead; part-time faculty masters in social work program Ind. U.-Purdue U., Indpls. Contbr. articles to profl. jours. Mem. NASW, Acad. Cert. Social Workers. Home: 818 E 53rd St Indianapolis IN 46220-3104 E-mail: amoelhman@casey.org.

MOELLER, AUDREY CAROLYN, retired energy company executive, corporate secretary; b. Pitts., May 10, 1935; d. Nicholas William and Edith Tecla (Russman) M. Grad. high sch., Pitts. Legal sec. Equitable Resources Inc., Pitts., 1955-72, asst. corp. sec., 1972-80, corp. sec., 1980-86, v.p., corp. sec., 1986-99; also corp. sec. Equitable Resources Inc. subs.; ret., 1999. Com. mem. United Way Allegheny County, Pa., 1978, United Way Southwestern Pa., 1984. Mem.: Pa. Assn. Notaries, Am. Soc. Corp. Secs. (chmn. membership and asst. sec. Pitts. chpt. 1995, treas. 1996, v.p. and program chmn. 1997, pres. 1998), Loyal Christian Benefit Assn. (nat. coun. 1993, pres. br. 331 2000, nat. auditor 2001). Democrat. Roman Catholic. Avocations: choral singing, golf, travel. Home: 1003 Cherry Hill Dr Presto PA 15142

MOELLER, MARY ELLA, retired home economist, educator, radio commentator; b. Southampton, N.Y., Mar. 11, 1938; d. Harry Eugene and Edith Leone (Reeser) Parsons; m. James Myron Moeller, Aug. 5, 1961; 1 child, Mary Beth. BS in Home Econs., U. Nebr., 1960; MLS, SUNY, Stony Brook, 1977. Tchr. home econs. Port Jefferson Schs., N.Y., 1960-70; home econs. program asst. Suffolk County Coop. Extension of Cornell U., Riverhead, N.Y., 1972-82; tchr. home econs. Eastport (N.Y.) H.S., 1982-85, South County Schs., Bellport Middle Sch., N.Y., 1985-93; sch. coord. N.Y. state mentoring program Bellport Middle Sch., 1992-95. Host Ask Your Neighbor, Sta. WRIV, Riverhead, 1982-87; trainer Home Econs. Entrepreneurship N.Y. State Edn. Dept., 1986-95; mem. home and career skills regional team N.Y. State Edn. Dept., 1984-86; mem. consumer homemaking adv. bd. Bd. Coop. Edn.; friendly svc. chmn. N.Y. State Ret. Tchrs. L.I. Zone, 1995-2003. Contbr. monthly articles to consumer publs. Chairperson policy bd. South Country Tchrs. Ctr.; mem. East Hampton Town Citizens Adv. com., East Hampton Citizens Adv. Commn., East Hampton Sr. Citizen Adv. Com.; v.p. Friendly Svc., 2000-03. Mem.: DAR (historian 1985, parliamentarian East Hampton chpt.), East End Ret. Tchrs. Assn. (chmn. by laws com. 2003—), N.Y. State Ret. Tchrs. Assn. (v.p. Friendly Svc., L.I. Zone 2000—03, chmn. nominations Long Island zone 2003—, coord. health care 2003—), Suffolk County Home Econs. Assn., Am. Home Econs. Assn. (cert. home economist), N.Y. State Home Econs. Assn., East Hampton Ladies Village Improvement Soc. (bd. dirs.), Daus. of the Founders and Patriots of Am., Eastern Gate Garden Club, Eastern Star (matron 1970). Home: 161 Newtown Ln East Hampton NY 11937-2429 Office: Bellport Mid Sch Kreamer St Bellport NY 11713 E-mail: jasmoel@aol.com.

MOELLER, MARYANN, music educator; d. John George Moeller, Sr. and Anna Blasick Moeller. B in Music Edn., Northwestern U., 1955; M in Music Edn., Duquesne U., 1960; postgrad., Temple U., 1970, Hofstra U., 1971, Ariz. State U., 1971, SUNY, Stony Brook, 1974, Dowling Coll., 1978. Cert. tchr. N.Y., Pa. Music and chorus tchr. Mellon Jr. H.S., Mt. Lebanon, Pa., 1955—57, Sayville (N.Y.) Jr. H.S. and Cherry Ave. Elem., 1957—59, McMillan, Hillcrest and Meml. Elem. Schs., Bethel Park, Pa., 1959—62, Herricks Jr. H.S., New Hyde Park, NY, 1962—66, Garden City (N.Y.) Jr. H.S., 1966—72, Mt. Pleasant Elem., Smithtown (N.Y.) Elem. and Great Hollow Mid. Sch., 1974—88. Mem. curriculum com. Music Instrnl. Coun., Garden City, 1967, Garden City, 68; mem. chorus festival com. Nassau County Jr. H.S. Chorus Com., 1969; com. mem. Dist. Supt. Com., Garden City, 1971, Garden City, 72. Elsie Eckstein Music scholar, Northwestern U., 1951—55. Mem.: Pa. Music Educators Assn. (life), N.Y. State Sch. Music Assn. (life), Music Educators Nat. Conf. (life), Order Ea. Star, Sigma Alpha Iota. Republican. Avocations: sewing, gardening, singing, piano, walking. Home: 960 Buckingham Dr Allentown PA 18103

MOELLER, RACHEL NELSON, career development specialist; b. N.Y.C., N.Y., Sept. 22, 1965; d. Ralph Lowell and Ann Eileen Nelson; m. Timothy Alan Moeller, Oct. 26, 1991; children: Andrew Nelson, Lucy Brynn. BA in Econs. and Bus., Lafayette Coll., Easton, Pa., 1988; MS in Edn., U. of Pa., 1991. Cert. in career devel. 2002. Acad. advising specialist Northampton Cmty. Coll., Bethlehem, Pa., 1999—2002, career devel. specialist, 2002—. Dir. advising and retention Northampton C.C., Bethlehem, 1995—99. Mem.: Nat. Acad. Advising Assn. (mid-Atlantic regional bd. mem. 2002). Home: 3875 Dundee Rd Bethlehem PA 18020

MOELLER, SUSAN ELAINE, artist; b. Akron, Ohio, Jan. 27, 1949; d. Guy Raymond and June Elaine (Inherst) Walker; m. Robert Allen Moeller, Aug. 13, 1988. BFA, BA in Edn., Akron U., 1972. Art tchr., dept. head Manchester Sch. Sys., Akron, 1972-79; ad exec. The Repository, Canton, Ohio, 1979-81; art dir. Vic & Walt's, Akron, 1981-85; illustrator Collector's Marketplace Mag., Atwater, Ohio, 1983-85; freelance artist, graphic designer Akron, 1985-94; fine artist, co-owner Creative Images Studio, Cuyahoga Falls, Ohio, 1994-98, Nogal, N. Mex., 1998—; owner Paz de Nogal Gallery and Studio, Nogal, 1998—. Co-owner Creative Images Assocs., Cuyahoga Falls, 1986-98; Nogal, N. Mex., 1998—; graphic cons. Advanced Analytical and Computational Solutions, Inc., Cleve., 1996-97, Akron Chess Club, 1989-97; art juror Cuyahoga Falls H.S., 1997; owner, organizer Paz de Nogal Fine Art Shows, 1998—. Artist, designer: (bd. game) Barnes Publishing, 1984; contbr. poetry and drawing to Cat Fancy Mag., 1994; illustrator: (mag.) Collector's Marketplace, 1983-85, (newspaper) Canton Repository, 1979-81; exhibited N.E. Ohio Fine Art Guild shows, 1996-97. Donor of fine art to various charities, Akron, 1996-98. Recipient Hon. Mention award Kent (Ohio) Art-in-the-Park Com., 1996. Mem. ASPCA, Humane Soc. U.S., Humane Soc. Summit County, Pet Ptnrs. Rescue City (Pet Angel 1997), Lincoln County Humane Soc., Creative Connection, Ohio Arts and Crafts Guild, Cuyahoga Valley Soc. Fine Arts, Lincoln County Soc. Artists. Avocations: antiques, lapidary arts, gardening, writing. Studio: Paz de Nogal PO Box 190 Nogal NM 88341-0190

MOELLERING, CHARLOTTE LARESON, music educator; d. Charles Gene and LaGreta Stevens Reed; m. George Eric Moellering, Aug. 16, 1980; children: Laura Elizabeth, Jane Ann. BMus, Southwestern U., 1980; MEd, U. North Tex., 1996. Orchestra dir. Grand Prairie (Tex.) Ind. Sch. Dist., 1980—84, Irving (Tex.) Ind. Sch. Dist., 1985—86, Carrollton (Tex.) Farmers Br. Ind. Sch. Dist., 1986—. Dir. Nor'kirk Presbyterian Orch., Carrollton, Tex., 2001—. Recipient Cmty. Svc. award, DAR, 2003. Mem.: Am. String Tchrs. Assn. (state sec. 1992—94), Tex. Music Educators Assn., Music Educators Nat. Conf., Tex. Music Adjudicators Assn. (orchestra v.p. 2002—04), Tex. Orchestra Dirs. Assn. (pres. 1996—2001), Phi Delta Kappa, Mu Omicron. Presbyterian. Avocations: church activities, performing on violin, singing, reading. Home: 1020 Raleigh #1601 Carrollton TX 75007 Office: Blalack Middle Sch 1706 Peters Colony Carrollton TX 75007 Office Fax: 972-394-3140.

MOELY, BARBARA E. psychology researcher, educator; b. Prairie du Sac, Wis., July 17, 1940; d. John Arthur and Loretta Ruth (Giese) M.; children: John Jacob Moely Wiener, David Andrew Moely Wiener. Student, Carroll Coll., 1958-60; BA, U. Wis., 1962, MA, 1964; PhD, U. Minn., 1968. Asst. prof. U. Hawaii, Honolulu, 1967-71; rsch. psychologist UCLA, 1971-72; asst. prof. Tulane U., New Orleans, 1972-75, assoc. prof. psychology, 1975-85, prof., 1985—, dept. chmn., 1992-96, dir. Office of Svc. Learning, 1999—. Contbr. articles to profl. jours. Grantee U.S. Office Edn., Handicapped Pers. Preparation, 1977-80, Tulane U., 1973, 75, 77-78, 83-84, Inst. for Mental Hygiene, City of New Orleans, 1983-84, 2000, Nat. Inst. Edn., 1983-84, La. Edn. Quality Support Fund, 1988-89, 91-92, 96, HUD, 1997-2003, Annenberg, 1997, HHS, 1997-2002, US Dept. Edn., 1999-2002, Fund for Improvement Post-Secondary Edn., 2000-03, Corp. Nat. and Cmty. Svc., 2003-. Mem. AAUP (v.p. La. conf. 1992-93, sec. 1993-97, v.p. 1998-2000, pres. Tulane 1992-94), APA, Soc. Rsch. in Child Devel., Am. Ednl. Rsch. Assn., Southwestern Soc. for Rsch. in Human Devel. (pres. 1986-88), Phi Beta Kappa (pres. Alpha chpt. La. 1981-82, sec. 1995-99) Office: Tulane Univ Dept Psychology New Orleans LA 70118 Business E-Mail: moely@tulane.edu.

MOEN, MARGARET, print company editor; b. Tokyo, Apr. 2, 1951; arrived in U.S., 1951; d. Raymond Otis and Evelyn (Carr) M. BA in History summa cum laude, Seattle U., 1972; MA in English, U. Minn., 1980. Assoc. editor Wanderer Printing Co., St. Paul, Minn., 1973—. Contbr. articles to profl. jours. Mem.: Smithsonian Instn., Minn. Hist. Soc., U. Minn. Alumni Assn. Republican. Roman Catholic. Avocations: swing and ballroom dancing, photography, italian language, genealogy. E-mail: moeneditor@cs.com.

MOEVS, MARIA TERESA MARABINI, archaeologist; b. Rome, Jan. 31, 1926; came to U.S., 1955, naturalized, 1959; d. Giuseppe and Tosca (Toschi) Marabini; Laurea Lettere, U. Bologna, 1947; Ph.D. summa cum laude, U. Rome, 1951; postgrad. Italian Archaeol. Sch., Athens, 1950-51; m. Robert W. Moevs, Oct. 1, 1953; children— Marina F., Christian R. Insp. antiquities Ministry Edn., Italy, Syracuse, Padua, 1952-53; insp. Central Restoration Inst., Rome, 1953-55; instr. Italian, Harvard U., 1956-57, Douglass Coll., 1965-68, asst. prof. Italian, 1968-72, asso. prof., 1972-77, prof., 1977-81, prof. classics and archaeology, 1981— ; mem. Inst. Advanced Study, Princeton, N.J., 1977-78; mem. nat. screening com. Fulbright Am. Grad. Study Program, study in Italy, 1978-79, study in Italy-Greece, 1982-83. Recipient Goffredo Bellonci Spl. Prize, Rome Biennium, 1975-77; Italian Govt. fellow Italian Archaeol. Sch., Rome, 1947-50, Italian Archaeol. Sch. fellow, Athens, 1950-51, Fulbright fellow Am. Acad. Rome, 1952-53; Radcliffe Inst. Ind. Study asso. scholar, 1962-64, Am. Acad. Rome. fellow, 1963-64; NEH fellow, 1986-87. Mem. Archaeol. Inst. Am., Princeton Soc. of Archaeol. Inst. Am. (pres. 1986—), Rei Cretariae Romanae Favtores, Soc. Fellows, Am. Acad. Rome. Author: The Roman Thin Walled Pottery from Cosa, 1973; Gabriele D'Annunzio e le estetiche della fine del secolo, 1976; The Italo-Megarian ware from Cosa, 1980; Aco in Northern Etruria, 1980; Le Muse di Ambracia, 1981; Il Kalathos alessandrino di Bologna, 1983; Penteteris e le tre Horainella Pompe di Tolomeo Filadelfo, 1987. Contbr. articles on Roman pottery from excavations at Cosa, Italy to profl. jours, publs. Home: Blackwell's Mills Belle Mead NJ 08502

MOFFAT, MARYBETH, consulting company executive; b. Pitts., July 25, 1951; d. Herbert Franklin and Florence Grafe (Knerem) M.; m. Brian Francis Soulier, Nov. 30, 1974 (div.). BA, Carroll Coll., 1973. Indsl. engrng. technician Wis. Centrifugal Co., Waukesha, Wisc., 1976-77; indsl. engr. Utility Products, Inc., Milw., 1977-79; mgr. indsl. engrng. Bear Automotive (divsn. SPX Corp.), Bangor, Pa., 1980-90; program mgr. Toyota Johnson Controls, Inc. Automotive Systems Group, 1990-2001; pres., CEO Moffat Enterprises, Inc., 2001—. Group home house parent Headwaters Regional Achievement Ctr., Lake Tomahawk, Wis., 1974. Mem. Am. Inst. Indsl. Engrs., MTM Assn. for Standards Rsch., Indsl. Mgmt. Soc., Alpha Gamma Delta (standards chmn. 1971-72). Republican. Methodist. Avocations: skiing, horseback riding, swimming, reading. Office Phone: 859-272-0056. E-mail: mbmoffat123@cs.com.

MOFFAT SALANT, MARILYN, physical therapist, educator; d. Daniel and Georgina Thomson Moffat; m. Robert S. Salant, Sept. 12, 1970 (dec. Jan. 28, 1979); children: Susan Salant Wierdsma, Margaret Earle Vickery, Robert Stephen Salant. BS, Queens Coll., New York, 1962; MA, NY U., N.Y.C., 1964, PhD, 1973. Cert. physical therapy N.Y., 1963. Staff mem. to supr. phys. therapist Inst. of Rehab. Medicine, N.Y.C., 1963—71; pvt. practitioner Locust Valley and N.Y.C., 1964—; instr. Queens Coll., NY, 1967—67, co-dir. inst. devel. human resources, 1967—67; instr. to assoc. prof. N.Y. U., 1967—82; editor Jour. of the Am. Phys. Therapy Assn., 1968—70; adj. faculty U. of Del., Newark, Del., 1975—84; cons. phys. therapist Profl. Exam. Svc., N.Y.C., 1976—83, N.Y.C. Police Dept., 1980—85; prof. N.Y. U., 1982—. Mem. The Nat. Inst. of Social Scis., N.Y.C., 1993—2003; mem. benefit com. Helping Hands, Conn., 1998—98, Nassau County Mus. of Fine Arts, Roslyn, NY, 1980—80; mem. Howard A Rusk rehab. medicine campaign com. N.Y. U. Med. Ctr., N.Y.C., 1984—85; mem. benefit com. Planned Parenthood of LI, Hempstead, 1991—91; founding mem. and mem. of adv. bd. Women's Optimum Wellness Now - N.Y. U. Med. Ctr., N.Y.C., 1996—2003; mem. fund raising ball ARC (Nassau County chpt.), Locust Valley, 1998—2003; mem. bd. of directors and exec. com. World Rehab. Fund, N.Y.C., 1998—2003; mem. Four Oaks Found., Princeton, NJ, 1979—82; mem. bd. dirs. Children's Village, Dobbs Ferry, NY, 1983—93; mem. exercise rm. com. Piping Rock Club, Locust Valley, 2002—03. Recipient Founder's Day award, N.Y. U., 1973, Sawadi

Skulkai Lecture award, Mahidol U., Bangkok, 1986, commendation, Mahidol U., Bangkok Thailand, 1987, Phys. Therapy Assn. of the Republic of China, 1987, Barbara C. White Lecture award, U. of Fla., Gainesville, 1990, Howard A Rusk Humanitarian award, World Rehab. Fund, N.Y.C., 1998, Disting. Faculty award, Dept. of Phys. Therapy, N.Y. U., 2002, Amb. award, Nat. Strength and Conditioning Assn., 2003, Mildred Elson award for internat. leadership in phys. therapy, World Confederation for Phys. Therapy, 2003. Mem.: World Confederation for Phys. Therapy (exec. com. 2003), TriAlliance of Rehab. Professionals (chair 1996), Found. for Phys. Therapy (vice chair 1990—91, bd. trustees 1990—91, 2003—), N.Y. Phys. Therapy Assn. (pres. 1978—82, Disting. Svc. award 1994), Am. Phys. Therapy Assn. (exec. coun. sect. for edn. 1980—82, mem. bd. of directors 1983—89, pres. 1991—97, adv. panel on minority affairs, Highest Commendation bd. dirs. svc. 1986, 1989, Catherine Worthingham fellow 1990, Highest Commendation bd. dirs. svc. 1994, 1997, Diversity 2000 award 1999, R. Charles Harker Policy Maker award 2000, recipient first Marilyn Moffat Leadership award 2003, Mary McMillan Lectr. 2004), Kappa Delta Phi, Pi Lambda Theta. Avocations: travel, golf, reading, bridge, exercise. Home: Ludlam Lane Locust Valley NY 11560 Office: NY U Physical Therapy Dept 4th Floor 380 Second Ave New York NY 10010

MOFFATT, JOYCE ANNE, performing company executive; b. Grand Rapids, Mich., Jan. 3, 1936; d. John Barnard and Ruth Lillian (Pellow) M. BA in Lit., U. Mich., 1957, MA in Theatre, 1960; HHD (hon.), Profl. Sch. Psychology, San Francisco, 1991. Stage mgr., lighting designer Off-Broadway plays; costume, lighting and set designer, stage mgr. stock cos., 1954-62; nat. subscription mgr. Theatre Guild/Am. Theatre Soc., N.Y.C., 1965-67; subscription mgr. Theatre, Inc.-Phoenix Theatre, N.Y.C., 1963-67; cons. N.Y.C. Ballet and N.Y.C. Opera, 1967-70; asst. house mgr. N.Y. State Theater, 1970-72; dir. ticket sales City Ctr. of Music and Drama, Inc., N.Y.C., 1970-72; prodn. mgr. San Antonio's Symphony/Opera, 1973-75; gen. mgr. San Antonio Symphony/Opera, 1975-76, 55th St. Dance Theater Found., Inc., N.Y.C., 1976-77, Ballet Theatre Found., Inc./Am. Ballet Theatre, N.Y.C., 1977-81; v.p. prodn. Radio City Music Hall Prodns., Inc., N.Y.C., 1981-83; artist-in-residence CCNY, 1981—; propr. mgmt. cons. firm for performing arts N.Y.C., 1983—; exec. dir. San Francisco Ballet Assn., 1987-93; mng. dir. Houston Ballet Assoc., 1993-95; gen. mgr. Chgo. Music and Dance Theater, Inc., 1995—. Cons. Ford Found., N.Y. State Coun. on Arts, Kennedy Ctr. for Performing Arts., Lensic Performing Arts Ctr, Bloomington, Ill., Sheboygan (Wis.) Theater Found.; mem. dance panels N.Y. State Coun. on Arts, 1979-81; mem. panels for Support to Prominent Orgns. and Dance, Calif. Arts Coun., 1988-92. Appointee San Francisco Cultural Affairs Task Force, 1991; chmn. bd. dirs. Tex. Inst. for Arts in Edn., 1994—; trustee Internat. Alliance of Theatrical Stage Employees Local 16 Pension and Welfare Fund, 1991-94; bd. dirs. Rudolf Nureyev Dance Found., Chgo., 1998—. Mem. Assn. Theatrical Press Agts. and Mgrs., Actors Equity Assn., United Scenic Artists Local 829, San Francisco Visitors and Conv. Bur. (bd. dirs.), Argyle Club (San Antonio). Office: Chicago Music & Dance Theater 205 E Randolph Dr Chicago IL 60601-1210

MOFFATT, KATY (KATHERINE LOUELLA MOFFATT), musician, vocalist, songwriter; b. Ft. Worth, Nov. 19, 1950; d. Lester Huger and Sue-Jo (Jarrott) M. Student, Sophie Newcomb Coll., 1968, St. John's Coll., 1969-70. Rec. artist Columbia Records, 1975-79, Permian/MCA Records, 1982-84, Enigma Records, L.A., 1985, Wrestler Records, L.A., 1987-88, Red Moon Records, Switzerland, 1988-93, Philo/Rounder Records, 1989-96, Round Tower Music, U.K., Ireland, Europe, 1993-96, Watermelon Records, U.S., 1994-96, Panther City Records, New Zealand, 1998, Hightone/HMG Records, 1998-2001, Western Jubilee/Shanachie Records, 2001—, Demon/Westside Records, 2002. Folksinger, Ft. Worth, 1967-68; musician, vocalist, songwriter, rec. artist: (films) Billy Jack, 1970, Hard Country, 1981, The Thing Called Love, 1993; prodn. asst. film, Sta. KIII-TV, Corpus Christi, 1970, audio engr., Sta. KRIS-TV, Corpus Christi, 1970; musician, vocalist in blues band, Corpus Christi, 1970; receptionist, bookkeeping asst., copywriter, announcer, Sta. KFWT, Ft. Worth, 1971, musician, vocalist, songwriter, Denver, 1971-72, on tour, 1973, 75—, Denver, 1974, on tour, 1976-79, European tour, 1977, Can. tour, 1984-85, on tour in Europe, U.S., Can., Asia and Australia, 1985—; albums include Katy, 1976, Kissin' In The California Sun, Am. release, 1977, internat. release, 1978, A Town South of Bakersfield, 1985, Walkin' on the Moon, European release, 1988, U.S. release, 1989, Child Bride, 1990, (duet album with brother Hugh) Dance Me Outside, 1992, (Switzerland only) Indoor Fireworks, 1992, The Greatest Show On Earth A.K.A. The Evangeline Hotel, 1994, Hearts Gone Wild, 1994, Tulare Dust, 1995, (duet album with Kate Brislin) Sleepless Nights, 1996, Midnight Radio, 1996, Angel Town, 1998, Loose Diamond, 1999, Cowboy Girl, 2001, (reissue on CD) Katy/Kissin' in the California Sun, 2002; songs include The Magic Ring, 1971; Gerry's Song, 1973, Kansas City Morning, 1974, Take Me Back To Texas, 1975, (Waitin' For) The Real Thing, 1975, Didn't We Have Love, 1976, Kissin' in the California Sun, 1977, Walkin' on the Moon, 1989. Recipient Record World Album award, 1976; named one of 4 Top New Female Vocalists, Cashbox Singles Awards, 1976; nominee for Top New Female Vocalist, Acad. Country Music, 1985; winner best singer-songwriter category Ft. Worth Weekly Mag. Music awards, 1997. Mem. AFTRA, SAG, NARAS, Am. Fedn. Musicians.

MOFFATT, MINDY ANN, elementary school educator, educational training specialist; b. Mpls., Aug. 3, 1951; d. Ralph Theron and La Vone Muriel (Bergstrom) M. Student, UCLA, 1972-73; BA, Calif. State U., Fullerton, 1975, MS in Edn., 1991. Cert. elem. tchr., Calif. Tchr. early childhood edn. program Meadows Elem. Sch., Valencia, Calif., 1977—78; tchr. United Parents Against Forced Busing, Chatsworth, Calif., 1978—80; founding tchr. Gazebo Two Sch. for Young Gifted and Creative Children, Summerville, SC, 1980—81; tchr. Anaheim (Calif.) Union H.S. Dist., 1981—89, mentor, tchr., 1985—88; tchr. Greentree Elem. Sch., Irvine, Calif., 1989—90; with Thurston Mid. Sch., Laguna Beach, Calif., 1990—92; tng. specialist Scripps Clinics and Rsch. Found., LaJolla, Calif., 1993—94; tchr. White Hill Mid. Sch., Ross Valley Sch. Dist., San Anselmo, Calif., 1994—95, J.B. Davidson Mid. Sch., San Rafael, Calif., 1996—2000; asst. prin. Ventura (Calif.) H.S., 2000—01; lang. arts specialist in writing Ventura Unified Sch. Dist., 2001—. Cons. writing project U. Calif., Irvine, 1982—; textbook cons. McDougal, Littell & Co., Evanston, Ill., 1984-86; facilitator Summer Tech. Tng. Inst., Irvine, 1987. Co-author: Practical Ideas for Teaching Writing as a Process, 1986, 4th edit., 1997, Thinking/Writing: Fostering Critical Thinking Through Writing, 1991, Reading, Thinking, and Writing About Culturally Diverse Literature, 1995; contbr. articles to profl. jours. Mem. Our Ultimate Recreation (Orange County, Calif., chairperson social com. 1983, chairperson backpacking 1983, v.p. 1993-94). Avocations: whitewater rafting, canoeing, bicycling, skiing, backpacking. Office: Ventura Unified Sch Dist 120 E Santa Clara Ventura CA 93001 E-mail: mmoffatt@vtusd.k12.ca.us.

MOFFETT, PATRICIA LOU, music educator; b. Clarksburg, W.Va., July 20, 1953; d. Jack Moffett and Elnora Moffett Hanna, Glenn H. Hanna (Stepfather). MusB in Edn., W.Va. Wesleyan Coll., 1975; MusM in Edn., Ind. U., 1995. Choir dir. Spencer H.S., W.Va., 1975—77; dir. children's choir St. Marys United Meth. Ch., 1977—; music specialist Pleasants County Schs., St. Marys, 1977—; assoc. instr. Ind. U., Bloomington, 1992—93; asst. dir. and accompanist Ind. U. Children's Choirs, Bloomington, 1992—93; dir. River Valley Children's Choir, St. Marys, W.Va., 1995—. Pvt. piano instr., 1975—92; guest condr. Wood County Elem. Honors Choir, Parkersburg, 1996—; adj. instr. Glenville State Coll., Parkersburg, 1989—91, W.Va. U., Parkersburg, 1992—. Active St. Marys United Meth. Ch. Recipient Tchr. Achievement award, Arch Coal Co., 2001. Mem.: NEA, Am. Orff Schulwerk Assn., Orgn. Am. Kodaly Educators, Music Educators Nat. Conf., Am. Choral Dirs. Assn. (life; W.Va. pres. 1999—2001), Choristers Guild. Avocations: music, Bible study, reading, gardening. Home: 1210 Edgedale Dr St. Marys WV 26170 Office: St Marys Elementary School 315 Washington St St. Marys WV 26170 E-mail: pmoffett@alpha.wvup.wvnet.edu.

MOFFITT, CHRISTINE M. biologist, educator; PhD, U. Mass., 1978; BA, U. Calif., Santa Cruz, 1969; AM, Smith Coll., 1973. Instr. Smith Coll., Northampton, Mass., 1978—80; postdoctoral assoc. U. Mass., Amherst, 1980—81; asst. prof. U. Idaho, Moscow, 1982—88, assoc. prof., 1989—98, prof., 1999—. Asst. unit leader Idaho Coop. Fish and Wildlife Rsch. unit U.S. Geol. Survey. Contbr. articles to profl. jours. Named Outstanding Alumna, U. Mass. Natural Resources Coll., 1999. Mem.: Am. Fisheries Soc. (pres, pres. elect, 1st vp and 2 vp 1996—2000, Meritorious Svc. award 1994). Office: Dept Fish and Wildlife Resource Univ Idaho Moscow ID 83844-1136 E-mail: cmoffitt@uidaho.edu.

MOFFITT, KATHLEEN, marketing professional, writer, educator; b. Providence, Nov. 13, 1952; d. Raymond Edward and Doris Elaine Moffitt; m. Joseph Anthony Dilorenzo, Dec. 30, 1988. BA in English, Emmanuel Coll., 1974; MA in English, R.I. Coll., 1983; postgrad., U. R.I., 1992—2000. Dir. activities and social svcs. Cedar Crest Nursing Ctr., Cranston, RI, 1974—80; grad. tchg. asst. R.I. Coll., Providence, 1981—83; English instr. Fisher Coll., Attleboro, Mass., 1983—88, C.C. R.I., Warwick, 1986—90; writing instr. R.I. Coll., Providence, 1983—92; bus. mgr. Internal Medicine and Pediat., Cranston, 1992—. Contbr. articles to various publs.; author short stories. Sec. Bus. and Profl. Women's Club, Cranston, 1977—80; bd. dirs. Ret. Sr. Vol. Program, Cranston, 1977—80. Finalist Redbook Mags. Short Story Writing Contest for Young Writers, 1977; named Cranston's Young Career Woman, Bus. and Profl. Women's Club, 1977; recipient 2nd pl. in mystery writing, The Providence Jour., 2000. Mem.: Kappa Gamma Pi. Roman Catholic. Avocations: hiking, cross country skiing, swimming, kayaking, piano. Home: Box 341 Saunderstown RI 02874 Office: Internal Medicine and Pediat 1370 Cranston St Cranston RI 02920

MOGERMAN, SUSAN, state agency administrator; Dir. State of Ill. Historic Preservation Agy., Springfield. Office: State Ill Hist Preservation Agy 500 E Madison Springfield IL 62701-1028

MOGGIO, BARBARA JEAN, health education specialist; b. Bronx, N.Y., July 7, 1953; d. Thomas Francis and Barbara Margaret (Lang) O'Meara; m. Richard Albert Moggio, July 28, 1984; stepchildren: Samuel A., Jonathan F. ADN, Pace U., 1976; BS, Mercy Coll., Dobbs Ferry, N.Y., 1985; MPH, Yale U., 1987. RN, N.Y.; cert. health edn. specialist. Critical care nurse, nursing care coord. Westchester Med. Ctr., Valhalla, N.Y., 1974-85; adj. asst. prof. Iona Coll., New Rochelle, N.Y., 1988-94; proprietor, CEO Health Wave, Inc., Stamford, Conn., 1990—. Author health curriculum Health Promotion Wave, 1987, 88, 95, 96. Mem. APHA, AAUW, Am. Sch. Health Assn., Assn. Advancement of Health Edn. Avocations: opera, golf. Home: PO Box 120 446 Long Ridge Rd Pound Ridge NY 10576-2221 Office: Health Wave Inc 1084 Hope St Stamford CT 06907-1823

MOGUL, LESLIE ANNE, business development and marketing consultant; b. Balt., Mar. 9, 1948, d. Harry and Elaine Mogul; m. William Kasper. AS, Miami Dade Jr. Coll., 1969; BA, Temple U., 1976; MBA, U. Phoenix, 1996. Accredited pub. rels. Account exec. Gray & Rogers, Inc., Phila., 1976-80; pres. Leslie Mogul, Inc., Phila., 1980-84; v.p. McKinney, Inc., Phila., 1984-87; assoc. dir. comm. Scripps Meml. Hosps., San Diego, 1987-93; dir. pub. rels. Scripps Health, San Diego, 1993, dir. customer rels. and mktg., 1994-95; dir. bus. devel. Harborview Med. Ctr. Hosp., San Diego, 1995-96; cons. Projectworks, San Diego, 1996—, pres., 1996—. Recipient over 25 awards local and nat. pub. rels. and comm. orgns. Mem. Pub. Rels. Soc. Am. (dir.-at-large 1993-94), Alumni Leadership Calif. Office: Project Works PO Box 301395 Escondido CA 92030-1395 E-mail: leslie@projectworksmarketing.com.

MOHAJER, DINEH, cosmetics company executive; b. Bloomfield Hills, Mich., Sept. 2, 1972; d. Reza and Shahnaz Mohajer. Student, U. So. Calif. Founder, CEO Hard Candy, Inc., Beverly Hills, Calif., 1996—. Office: Hard Candy Inc Ste 208 661 N Harper Ave Los Angeles CA 90048-2253

MOHANTY, CHRISTINE ANN, retired language educator, actress; b. Coaldale, Pa., Jan. 4, 1945; d. Warren Russell and Helen Hargraves; m. Leonard Yehudi Seltzer; 1 child, Kasmira. BA, Queens Coll., Flushing, N.Y., MS Edn., 1972; PhD in English Lit., SUNY, Stony Brook, 1986. Tchr. fgn. langs. Three Village Ctrl. Sch. Dist., Setauket, NY, 1969—2000; asst. prof. Suffolk County C.C., Selden, NY, 1994—. Dir.: (plays) Deathtrap, 1992, Snow Queen, 1995; actor: Stepping Out, 1992, Prelude to a Kiss, 1998, Three Blind Mice, 1999, Social Security, 1999, Arsenic and Old Lace, 2000, Phantom of the Opera, 2000, Wuthering Heights, 2001, The Corn is Green, 2002, The Uninvited, 2002, Little Women, 2002, I Hate Hamlet, 2003, Noel Coward One Acts, 2003, Jekyll & Hyde, 2003, Dancing at Lughnasa, 2001; contbr. articles to profl. jours.; Exhibited in group shows at Bayport (NY) Pub. Libr., 2001—02. Recipient Educator of the Week award, NY55 WLNY-TV, 2000; U. Salamanca scholarship, N.Y. State Edn. Dept., 1990. Mem.: AAUW, Am. Assn. Tchrs. of French (pres. Suffolk county 1990—93, scholarship to France 1982), Long Island Lang. Tchrs., Phi Beta Kappa. Avocations: travel, tennis, creative writing, painting. Home: 109 Edgewater Ave Bayport NY 11705 Personal E-mail: christinemohanty@excite.com.

MOHLE, BRENDA SIMONSON, art appraiser; b. Dallas, May 9, 1959; d. Harold Lee and Lila Faye (Adair) Simonson; m. Robert F. Mohle, Mar. 28, 1981; children: Aaron, Alexandra. BA with high honors, U. Tex., 1980. Sales advisor Newman Gallery, Dallas, 1981-84; gallery mgr. Omni Art, Dallas, 1984-87; owner Signet Art, Carrollton, Tex., 1987—. Docent Dallas Mus. Art, 1985-95. Mem. Internat. Soc. Appraisers (cert. fine art appraiser, treas. North Tex. chpt. 1993-94, sec. North Tex. chpt. 1994-95, v.p. North Tex. chpt. 1995-96, pres. North Tex. chpt. 1996-97, nat. fine art chair 1996-97, chair nat. ethics com. 2001-03). Office: 2644 Newcastle Dr Carrollton TX 75007-1944

MOHLER, MARY GAIL, magazine editor; b. Milaca, Minn., Dec. 15, 1948; d. Albert and Deane (Vedders) M.; m. Paul Rodes Trautman, June 5, 1976 (div. 1994); children: Elizabeth Deane, David Albert Rodes, Theodore DeForest Lloyd. BA, U. Calif.-Davis, 1974; MA in Lit., SUNY-Stony Brook, 1976. Asst., then editor-reporter Family Circle Mag., N.Y.C., 1979-81; editorial coordinator Ladies' Home Jour., N.Y.C., 1981, assoc. articles editor, 1982, mng. editor, 1982-93, sr. editor, 1994-98; editor in chief Ladies' Home Jour. Parent's Digest; mng. editor Parents Mag., 1999—2001, editor at large, freelance writer, 2001—. Co-author: Those Who Can...Teach, 1999. Medieval philosophy fellow SUNY-Binghamton, 1978 Mem. MLA, Am. Soc. Mag. Editors, Phi Beta Kappa Clubs: Medieval; Overseas Press. Office: Parents Mag 375 Lexington Ave New York NY 10017-5514

MOHN, AMY ELIZABETH BRENNAN, special education educator, retail consultant; b. Manchester, Conn., June 7, 1969; d. William Francis and Judith Elizabeth Benz Brennan; m. Bryan Keith Mohn, Aug. 5, 1995. BA in Psychology, Coll. of William and Mary, 1991, MEd in Spl. Edn., 1992. Cert. tchr. learning disabled and emotionally disturbed K-12. Grade 6 disturbed children Chesterfield County Schs., Va., 1992-93; ednl. prescriptionist Dept. of Def., Republic of Panama, 1993-96; kindergarten tchr. Ft. McClellan (Ala.) Elem. Sch., 1996-97; tchr. exceptional children Devers Elem. Sch., Ft. Bragg, N.C., 1997-98; retail cons. The Gift Shop, Fayetteville, N.C., 1999—. Kindergarten summer camp advisor Jr. League of Fayetteville, 1999; tutor, homeless family advocate Highland Presbyn. Ch., Fayetteville, 1998—; vol. City Coun. Campaign, 1998—. Grantee State of Va., 1991. Mem. Coun. for Exceptional Children. Republican. Avocations: running, traveling, cooking, mountain biking, languages. Home: 64 Pinecrest Vlg Hopkinton MA 01748-2179 Office: The Gift Shop 1110 Hay St Fayetteville NC 28305-5318

MOHR, BARBARA JEANNE, secondary school educator; b. Santa Monica, Calif., Jan. 26, 1953; d. Edgar Kirchner and Beatrice Jeanne (Anderson) M. BA, Calif. State U., Fullerton, 1976; MS, Calif. State U., 1982. Multiple Subject Teaching Credential, 1977, Single Subject Tchr. Credential, 1977. Substitute tchr. Fullerton (Calif.) Sch. Dist., 1977-78, tchr., 1978—, mentor, 1984-96. Tchr. calligraphy Laguna Rd. Sch., 1985-92, student coun. advisor, 1988-92, advisor Just Say No Club, 1986-94. Named Tchr. of Yr. Fullerton Sch. Dist., 1989; recipient Hon. Svc. award Laguna Rd. Sch. PTA, 1989; Weingart fellow Nat. Gallery of Art Tchr. Inst., 1996. Mem. NEA, Calif. Tchrs. Assn., Fullerton Elem. Tchrs. Assn., Calif. State U. Alumni Assn., Phi Kappa Phi. Avocations: calligraphy, gardening, travel.

MOHR, CHRISTINA, retired economist; b. San Diego, Calif., June 1, 1949; d. Lloyd Crowell and Joan Watkins, Oliver Watkins (Stepfather); m. Peter Joseph Mohr, July 13, 1989; stepchildren: Robert, Tracie 1 child, Oliver Wise. BS in Polit. Sci, U. Pa., Phila., 1971; MA in Internat. Affairs, George Washington U., Washington, DC, 1979; PhD in Econs., U. Md., College Park, 1993. Cons. World Bank, Washington, 1982; analyst sci. resource Nat. Sci. Found., Washington, 1983—86, speech writer for dir., 1987—93; sci. diplomacy fellow US Agency for Internat. Devel., Washington, 1994—95; sr. analyst Nat. Sci. Found., Washington, 1996—2001; retired, 2001. Commr. People with Disabilities Commn., Montgomery County, Md., 1994—96. Home: 2932 Woodstock Ave Silver Spring MD 20910

MOHRAZ, JUDY JOLLEY, foundation administrator; b. Houston, Oct. 1, 1943; d. John Chesler and Mae (Jackson) Jolley; m. Bijan Mohraz; children: Andrew, Jonathan. BA, Baylor U., 1966, MA, 1968; PhD, U. Ill., 1974. Lectr. history Ill. Wesleyan U., 1972-74; asst. prof. history So. Meth. U., Dallas, 1974-80, coord. women's studies, 1977-81, assoc. prof. history, 1980-94, asst. provost, 1983-88, assoc. provost for student academics, 1988-94; pres. Goucher Coll., Towson, Md., 1994-2000, Virginia G. Piper Charitable Trust, Scottsdale, Ariz., 2000—. Cons. Ednl. Testing Svc., Princeton, N.J., 1984-93, Nat. Park Svcs., Seneca Falls, N.Y., 1992-93; bd. dirs. Balt. Equitable Soc., 1996-2000, The Assocs. First Capital, 1999-2000; bd. visitors U.S. Naval Acad., 1996-2001. Trustee The Lamplighter Sch., 1991-94, St. Mark's Sch. Tex., 1993-94; adv. bd. U. Tex. Southwestern Med. Sch., 1992-94; active Leadership Dallas, 1994; bd. dirs. Nat. Assn. Ind., The Balt. Cmty. Found.; pres. Ariz. Grantmakers Forum, 2003—; mem. Ariz. State Sch. Readiness Bd., 2003-. Recipient Disting. Alumni award Baylor U., 1993; named Woman of Merit, Omicron Delta Kappa, 1993. Office: Virgina G Piper Charitable Trust 6720 N Scottsdale Rd Ste 350 Scottsdale AZ 85253

MOHRMAN, KATHRYN J, academic administrator; BA, Grinnell Coll., 1967; MA, U. Wis., 1969; PhD, George Washington U., 1982. Dean undergrad. studies U. Md., College Park, 1988—93; pres. The Colo. Coll., Colorado Springs, 1993—2002; exec. dir. Hopkins-Nanjing Ctr. for Chinese and Am. Studies, Johns Hopkins U., 2003—. Office: 1619 Massachusetts Ave NW Washington DC 20036 Office Phone: 202-663-5801.

MOISTNER, MONA SUE, adult education educator; b. New Castle, Ind., Jan. 11, 1955; d. Kenneth Orlando Jr. and Mary Belle (Williams) M. AA in Liberal Studies/English, Ind. U. East, Richmond, 1997, BA in English, 1999; MLS, Ind. U., 2004. Cert. substitute tchr., Ind. Intern Huddleston Farmhouse Inn Mus., Cambridge City, Ind., 1998; disability accomodations asst. Ind. U. East, Richmond, 1999—2001; mgr. Foster Cmty. Learning and ResourceCtr. Ind. U., Bloomington, Ind., 2001—. Part-time faculty humanities dept. Ivy Tech. State Coll., Richmond, 2000—; staff photographer Huddleston Farmhouse Inn Mus., Hist. Landmarks Found. Ind., Cambridge City, 1998-99; instr. English Ivy Tech. State Coll., Richmond, Ind., 2000, Connersville, Ind., 2000; tutor Ind. U. East, Richmond, Ind., 1998. Dick and Joanne Reynolds scholar Ind. U. East, 1997-2000, Ruth Brown scholar, 1996, Judith Roman scholar, 1994. Mem. Ind. U. Alumni Assn., Hist. Landmarks Found. Ind., Am. Legion Aux. Methodist. Avocations: poetry, literature, travel, writing, promoting literacy. Office Phone: 812-856-4088. Business E-Mail: mmoistne@indiana.edu.

MOJICA, AGNES, academic administrator; Chancellor Inter Am. U. of PR, San German, P.R. Chair governing bd. Hispanic Assn. Colls. and Univs., 1995-96, co-chair leadership group; chair governing bd. Intercollegiate Athletic League, 2001-02. Pres., Consortium of Presidents and Chancellors for the Prevention of the Use and Abuse of Drugs and Alcohol, 1998-2002. Mem., Assn. Industrialists of P.R., Western C. of C., Am. Assn. Higher Edn., Assn. Profl. Women, Altrusa, Rotary (hon.), Alpha Delta Kappa, Phi Delta Kappa. Office: Inter Am U PO Box 5100 San German PR 00683-9801 E-mail: amojica@sg.inter.edu.

MOJTABAI, ANN GRACE, author, educator; b. N.Y.C., June 8, 1937; d. Robert and Naomi (Friedman) Alpher; m. Fathollah Mojtabai, Apr. 27, 1960 (div. 1966); children: Chitra, Ramin. BA in Philosophy, Antioch Coll., 1958; MA in Philosophy, Columbia U., 1968, MS in Libr. Sci., 1970. Lectr. philosophy Hunter Coll., CUNY, 1966-68; libr. CCNY, 1970-76; fellow Radcliffe Inst. Ind. Study, Cambridge, Mass., 1976-78; Briggs-Copeland lectr. on English Harvard U., 1978-83; writer-in-residence U. Tulsa, 1983—, Yaddo Found., Saratoga, NY, 1975, 76. Author: Mundome, 1974, The 400 Eels of Sigmund Freud, 1976, A Stopping Place, 1979, Autumn, 1982, Blessed Assurance, 1986, Ordinary Time, 1989, Called Out, 1994, Soon: Tales From Hospice, 1998. Recipient Richard and Hinda Rosenthal award Am. Acad. and Inst. Arts and Letters, 1983, Lillian Smith award So. Regional Coun., 1986, Lit. Acad. award AAAL, 1993; Guggenheim fellow, 1981-82 Mem. PEN, Mark Twain Soc., Tex. Inst. Letters, Phi Beta Kappa. Home: 2329 Woodside Drive Amarillo TX 79124-1036 Office: U Tulsa Dept English 600 S College Ave Tulsa OK 74104-3126 E-mail: ann-mojtabai@utulsa.edu., Agmojtabai@aol.com.

MOLDEN, A(NNA) JANE, counselor; b. Weeping Water, Nebr. BS, Schauffler Coll.; MA, Princeton (N.J.) Theol. Sem. Cert. adminstr., Iowa. Dir. outreach Chgo. City Union; dir. campus ministry Iowa State U., Ames; dir. Christian edn. 1st Congl. Ch., Ames; dir. community outreach Congl. Chs., Kansas City, Mo.; ctrl. regional dir. Am. Friends Svc., Des Moines; dir. acad. support counseling Grand View Coll., Des Moines; dir. Consortium of Higher Edn., Des Moines. Mem. Health Planing Coun. Ctrl. Iowa; mem. Gov.'s Vocat. Rehab. Adv. Coun., 1993—; mem. Protection and Adv. Pair Adv. Coun., 1993—; bd. dirs. Iowa Protection and Adv. Bd. Dir. Grand View Coll. Dems., 1971-93; active devel. com. for handicapped HUD, Des Moines; bd. dirs. Plymouth Pl.; mem. Dr. Martin Luther King Com., Des Moines, Internat. Black Children's Conf., Iowa Vocat. Rehab. Coun., Iowa Protection and Adv. Coun.; chair Des Moines Human Rights Commn.; mem. study com. LWV; past pres. Citizens Disability Coun.; mem. community adv. bd. McKinley Sch.; mem. George Washington Carver com. Simpson Coll.; bd. dirs. Bernie Lorenz House, Community Focus, Greater Des Moines YWCA, Christian Ednl. Plymouth Congl. Ch.; bd. dirs. Youth Incentives. Named Outstanding Educator Jack and Jill, Inc., Des Moines, Supporting Friend, Learning Disability Coun. Ctrl. Iowa. Mem.: AACD, Edmonds Acad. Fine Arts (mentor), Torch Club Internat. (pres.), Delta Kappa Gamma. Democrat. Mem. United Ch. of Christ.

MOLDENHAUER, JUDITH A. graphic design educator; b. Oak Park, Ill., Feb. 28, 1951; d. Raymond L. and Jean Marie (Carqueville) M. BFA, U. Ill., 1973; MA, Stanford U., 1974; MFA, U. Wis., 1977. Design supr. N.E. Mo. State U., Kirksville, Mo., 1977-79; asst. prof. design, design dept. Kans. City Art Inst., Mo., 1979-83; asst. prof. art, graphic design Sch. Art U. Mich., Ann Arbor, 1983-92; vis. lectr. Wayne State U., 1990-92, asst. prof. graphic design, 1992-98, assoc. prof. graphic design, 1998—, area coord. graphic design, 1992—. Free-lance designer The Detroit Inst. Arts, Toledo (Ohio) Mus. Art, Burroughs Corp. (Unisys) Detroit, Detroit Focus Gallery; vis. designer N.S. Coll. Art and Design, 1986; juror Ohio Mus. Assn., 1986, Collaborator Presdl. Initiative "Healthy Start": prenatal and pre-conceptional booklets and ednl. modules designs, 1992—; presenter Congress Women's Health Issues, 1997, 98, Internat. Inst. Info. Design, Schwarzenberg, Austria, 1998, Read Me exhbn., Bern, Switzerland, 1999, Expert Forum Manual Design, Malardalen U., Eskilstuna, Sweden, 2000, others; participant design confs. Contbr. articles to profl. jours. Recipient award of distinction, merit award Am. Assn. Museums, 1985, 86, Excellence Design award Beckett Paper Co., 1991, gold award for softcover books Printing & Pub. Competition, 1994, Am. Graphic Design award, 1996, 98; Rackham grantee U. Mich., 1987, grantee Nat. Endowment for Arts, 1988; US-EU FIPSE grantee U.S. Dept. Edn. student and faculty exch. info. design, 2003. Mem. Am. Ctr. Design, Univ. and Coll. Designers Assn. (merit award 1979, gold award 1979), Coll. Art Assn. (chmn. panel 1991), Women's Caucus for Art (panel chmn. 1987), Amnesty Internat., Women in Design (excellence award Chgo. 1985, Sierra Club, Audubon Soc., Organizing Group Health Info. Design Forum. Lutheran. Office: Wayne State U Dept Art and Art History 150 Art Bldg Detroit MI 48202 E-mail: FrogBoddg@aol.com.

MOLDENHAUER, NANCY A. social worker, educator; BSEd, Valparaiso U., 1976; MSW, cert. specialist in aging, U. Mich., 1984. Instr. Meiji Gakuin and Tokyo Med. and Dental U., 1977-81; corp. communication trainer Saito Internat., Inc., Tokyo, 1981-82; conf. coord. Ctr. for Japanese Studies U. Mich., Ann Arbor, 1982-84; gerontol. social worker Turner Geriatric Clinic U. Mich. Hosps., Ann Arbor, 1983-84; med. social worker Mo. Bapt. Med. Ctr., St Louis, 1985-88; geriatric social work specialist Program on Aging Jewish Hosp. Wash. U. Med. Ctr., St. Louis, 1988-92; dir. case mgmt. and corp. svcs. Aging Consult, St. Louis, 1993-95; libr. media specialist, ESL and elem. tchr. Michigan City Area Schs., Ind., 1999—. Adj. prof. Washington U., St. Louis, 1991-95; trainee in aging NIH, 1983-84; dir. Nat. Adult Day Svc. Assn., Nat. Coun. Aging, Washington, 1995-96; registration mgr. Landmark Edn. Corp., Alexandria, Va., 1997-98. Co-author: Positive Attitudes, Positive Aging: A Guide for Positive Actions in Later Life, NASDA Curriculum for Directors and Administrators, Adult Day Services - The Next Frontier, Handbook of Home Health Care Administration. Del. White House Conf. Aging, 1995. Named OWL Woman of Worth, 1993. Mem. NEA, ASCD, NASW, Acad. Cert. Social Workers, Gerontol. Soc. Am., Am. Soc. Aging, Nat. Coun. on Aging, Alzheimer's Assn., Older Women's League (local bd. dirs., pres. 1991-95, nat. bd. dirs., v.p. 1993-96), Challenge Metro (bd. dirs., pres. 1986-90). Avocations: gourmet cooking, restaurants, wine, foreign movies, travel. Office: 107 Kaye Ln Michigan City IN 46360-1730

MOLDOW, SUSAN, publishing executive; m. Bill Shinker. Various positions to exec. editor Avon Books, 1976—82; editor in chief Dell Books, 1982; editorial dir. Penguin Books, 1988—90; v.p. Viking Penguin Inc., 1988—90; editor in chief Doubleday Publishers, 1990—91; v.p. assoc. pub. and editor in chief, adult trade book div. HarperCollins, 1991—94; pub., v.p. Scribner (Simon & Shuster), N.Y.C., 1994—. Office: Scribner Simon & Shuster 1230 Ave Of The Americas New York NY 10020-1513

MOLER, ELIZABETH ANNE, lawyer; b. Salt Lake City, Jan. 24, 1949; d. Murray McClure and Eleanor Lorraine (Barry) M.; m. Thomas Blake Williams, Oct. 19, 1979; children: Blake Martin Williams, Eleanor Bliss Williams. BA, Am. U., 1971; postgrad., Johns Hopkins U., 1972; JD, George Wash. U., 1977. Bar: D.C. 1978. Chief legis. asst. Senator Floyd Haskell, Washington, 1973-75; law clk. Sharon, Pierson, Semmes, Crolius & Finley, Washington, 1975-76; profl. staff mem. com. on energy and natural resources U.S. Senate, Washington, 1976-77, counsel, 1977-86, sr. counsel, 1987-88; commr. FERC, Washington, 1988-93, chair, 1993-97; dep. sec. Dept. of Energy, Washington, 1997-98, acting sec., 1998; ptnr. Vinson & Elkins, Washington, 1998-99; sr. v.p. Exelon Corp., 2000—02, exec. v.p., 2002—. Mem. ABA, D.C. Bar Assn. Democrat. Office: Exelon Corp Suite 400 East 101 Constitution Ave NW Washington DC 20001 Home: 1537 Forest Ln Mc Lean VA 22101-3317

MOLINA, RICHELLE JULIETTA, music educator; b. Yankton, S.D., July 30, 1974; d. Ricardo A. and Edna Mae Molina. B in Music Studies, U. Tex., San Antonio, 1998, postgrad., 2000—. Cert. tchr. Tex. Edn. Agy., 1999. Asst. band dir. Anson Jones Mid. Sch., San Antonio, 1998—2003, head band dir., 2003—. Democrat. Roman Catholic. Avocations: performing, swimming, travel. Personal E-mail: richellemolina@earthlink.net.

MOLINA-GAVILAN, YOLANDA, language educator; b. Madrid, July 7, 1963; arrived in U.S.A., 1982, permanent resident; d. José Molina and Julia Gavilán. BA in English and French, U. Wis., Eau Claire, 1985; MA in Romance Langs., U. Oreg.; PhD in Spanish Lit., Ariz. State U., 1996. Grad. teaching fellow U. Oreg., Eugene, 1985—88; instr. U. Nev., Reno, Tokyo, 1989—91, Tokyo Advanced C.C., 1990—92; adj. instr. Spanish Phoenix (Ariz.) Coll., 1995—96; tchg. asst. Ariz. State Coll., Tempe, 1992—96; assoc. prof. Eckerd Coll., St. Petersburg, Fla., 1996—. Author: (book) Ciencia ficción en español; co-editor: (anthology) Cosmos Latinos, 2003; translator: (novels) The Delta Function; contbr. articles to jours. Mem.: MLA, Internat. Assn. of the Fantastic in the Arts. Office: Eckerd Coll 4200 54th Ave S Saint Petersburg FL 33711

MOLINARI, SUSAN, congresswoman; b. S.I., N.Y., Mar. 27, 1958; d. Guy V. and Marguerite (Wing) M. BA, SUNY, Albany, 1980, MA, 1982. Former intern for State Senator Christopher Mega; former rsch. analyst N.Y. State Senate Fin. Com.; former fin. asst. Nat. Rep. Gov.'s Assn.; ethnic community liaison Rep. Nat. Com., 1983-84; minority leader N.Y.C. Council, 1986-90; mem. 101st-104th Congresses from 14th (now 13th) N.Y. dist., 1990-97, vice-chair House Rep. Conf.; anchor CBS News Sat. Morning, N.Y.C., 1997-98; Chairman, CEO The Washington Group, 2001—. Author: (book) Representative Mom: Balancing Budgets, Bill and Baby in the U.S. Congress, 1998. Roman Catholic. Office: c/o The Washington Group 1401 K Street NW Washington DC 20005*

MOLINARO, VALERIE ANN, lawyer; b. N.Y.C, Oct. 21, 1956; d. Albert Anthony and Rosemary Rita (Zito) M.; m. Howard Robert Birnbach; 1 child, Michelle Annalise Birnbach. BA with honors, SUNY, 1978; JD, MPA, Syracuse U., 1980. Asst. counsel. New York State Housing Finance Agy., N.Y.C., 1980-82; assoc. counsel, asst. secy. N.Y. State Urban Devel. Corp., N.Y.C., 1982-85; assoc. Mudge Rose Guthrie Alexander & Ferdon, N.Y.C., 1985-87, Bower & Gardner, N.Y.C., 1988, Hawkins, Delafield & Wood, N.Y.C., 1988-91; of counsel McKenzie McGhee, N.Y.C., 1991-98; sr. assoc. Battle Fowler, N.Y.C., 1998-2000, Garfunkel Wild & Travis PC, Gt. Neck, NY, 2000—02; of counsel Emmet, Marvin & Martin, N.Y.C., 2002—. Author: Am. Bar Assn. Jour., 1981-1989 Mem. N.Y.C. Commn. on Status of Women, 1995-99. Mem. ABA, N.Y. State Bar Assn., (tax exempt fin. com.), Assn. Bar City of N.Y., Nat. Assn. Bond Lawyers, N.Y.C. Commn. on the Status of Women (legis. chmn.), 1995-99. E-mail: vmolinaro@emmetmarvin.com.

MOLINO, VIRGINIA LOUISE, lawyer; b. Jersey City, June 12, 1950; d. Nicholas and Jennie (Rocco) M.; m. Gregory S. Smith, June 1, 1985 BA cum laude, NYU, 1972, JD, 1976; MA, U. Wis., 1973. Bar: N.J. 1976, N.Y. 1984. Staff atty. Suburban Propane Gas Corp., Morristown, N.J., 1976-79, assoc. counsel, 1979-81, gen. counsel, 1982-85, McKinsey & Co., Inc., N.Y.C., 1985—. Mem. ABA, N.J. State Bar Assn., N.Y. State Bar Assn., Bar Assn. City of N.Y., Am. Corp. Counsel Assn., Phi Beta Kappa Office: McKinsey & Co Inc 55 E 52nd St Fl 27 New York NY 10055-0183

MOLL, DEBORAH ADELAIDE, lawyer; b. Wilmington, Del., Jan. 19, 1946; BA, St. John's Coll., Annapolis, Md., 1969; MA, U. Tex., 1972, JD, 1975. Bar: N.Mex 1977. Law clk. Tex. Ct. Criminal Appeals, Austin, 1975-76, U.S. Ct. Appeals (10th cir.), Santa Fe, 1977-78; asst. atty. gen. N.Mex Atty. Gen., Santa Fe, 1978-84; asst. appellate defender N.Mex Pub. Defender Dept., Santa Fe, 1984-87; staff atty. N.Mex Taxation and Revenue Dept., Santa Fe, 1987-92; shareholder Kemrer-Hayes & Moll, P.A., Albuquerque, 1992; gen. counsel N.Mex Gen. Svcs. Dept., Santa Fe, 1993—. Mem.: N.Mex. State Bar (bd. dirs. bankruptcy sect. 1992, adv. opinion com. 1993—96, bd. dirs. pub. law sect. 1996—, chair pub. law sect. 1997—98, bd. dirs. employment law sect. 1999—2003, chair ad hoc com. 2001, com. establish legal specialization constrn. and pub. contracts 2002—). Avocation: photography. Office: NMex Gen Svcs Dept 715 Alta Vista St Santa Fe NM 87505-4108 Office Phone: 505-827-2000. E-mail: Deborah.Moll@state.nm.us.

MOLL, SARA H. psychologist, volunteer; b. Oklahoma City, July 4, 1943; d. Virgil Blount and Kathryn (Holland) Hooks; m. Curtis Eric Moll, Nov. 29, 1963; children: Curtis David, Robert Theodore, Charles Merideth, Sara Frances. BA, Case Western Res. U., 1965, MA, 1990, PhD, 1992; MA, Cleve. State U., 1988. Postdoctoral fellow Univ. Hosp., Cleve., 1992-93; instr. Ursuline Coll., Pepper Pike, Ohio, 1994-95; clin. psychologist Ohio Dept. Mental Health, Medina, 1994—; mem. clin. faculty psychiatry Sch. Medicine Case Western Res. U., Cleve., 1994—. Contbr. articles to profl. jours. Mem. Coalition Against Domestic Violence, Cleve., 1993-94; psychotherapist, adult survivor group The City Mission, Cleve., 1994; mem. Clin. Oversight Coun., Medina, Ohio, 1999; chair expansion ministries for women and children The City Mission, Cleve., 1998—, trustee, bd. dirs., 1994—. Estab. Sara H. Moll Christian Youth Ctr., The City Mission, 1994. Mem. APA. Methodist. Avocations: bible study, book club, travel, choir, needlepoint. Office: Ohio Dept Mental Health 3076A Remsen Rd Medina OH 44256-9225

MOLLES, EMILY DEMARTINO, artist, real estate broker; b. Norwalk, Conn., Mar. 20, 1938; d. Frank DeMartino and Mary Louise (Perriffo) DeMartino; m. Eugene Joseph Molles, Dec. 1, 1956 (div. 1976); children: Deborah Lynn Molles Boy'er, Eugene Scott; m. Robert DiNardo Sr., June 9, 2000. Student, Sacred Heart U., 1973, U. Conn., 1975; cert. in real estate law, Fairfield U., 1976; BFA, Ringling Sch. Art and Design, 1995; MA, NYU, 2001; student, Venice, 1999—2001. Grad. Realtors Inst.; cert. residential specialist. Pres. PRM, Inc., Norwalk, 1976—; realtor June Scott's Assocs., Beverly Hills, Calif., 1980-82, Len Hoff Realty, Marina Del Rey, Calif., 1982-84; founder, owner Country Homes, Milford, Conn., 1984-89, Country Homes of Saugatuck Shores, Westport, Conn., 1989-91. Mem. Nat. Mus. Women in Arts (assoc.). Avocations: sailing, music. Home: 2425 Gulf Of Mexico Dr Unit 2B Longboat Key FL 34228-3282 Studio: Artist Studio & Gallery 1373 Main St Sarasota FL 34236 E-mail: emislands@aol.com.

MOLLOY, JEAN MARIE, psychologist, human services administrator; b. L.A., Apr. 20, 1964; d. Charles Sullivan and Ann (Ahern) M.; m. Edward Joseph Steinborn, Dec. 31, 1987 (div. Apr. 11, 2001); children: Lauren Steinborn, Ryne Steinborn, Matthew Steinborn. BA magna cum laude, Coll. Mt. St. Vincent, Bronx, N.Y., 1986; MA, Fordham U., Bronx, N.Y., 1987, PhD, 1994. Lic. psychologist Fla., 1996. Rehab. specialist Easter Seal Rehab. Ctr., Stamford, Conn., 1989—92; psychology intern James A. Haley V.A. Hosp., Tampa, Fla., 1993—94; clin. coord. ACTS/Juvenile Justice Program, Tampa, 1995—96; asst. prof. Fla. Sch. Profl. Psychology, Tampa, 1996—98; psychologist Rehab.Ctr., Stamford, 1998—99; pvt. practice Tampa, 1999—2003; exec. dir., bd. pres. Kathy's Place Ctr. Grieving Children, Tampa, 2000—. Presenter, CEO Feminist Family Therapy, 2003. Contbr. articles. Mem. West Shore Alliance, Tampa, 2001. Mem.: APA, Tampa Bay Assn. Women Psychotherapists (sec.), Fla. Psychol. Assn. Avocations: jetskiing, flower arranging, home design. Office: 2504 W Azeele St Tampa FL 33609

MOLLOY, SYLVIA, Latin American literature educator, writer; b. Buenos Aires, Aug. 29, 1938; came to U.S. 1967; d. Herbert Edward and Margarita Berta (Chasseing) M. Licence es Lettres, U. Paris, 1960, Diplome D'Etudes Superieures, 1961, Doctorat de U. Paris, 1967. Asst. prof. Spanish SUNY, Buffalo, 1967-69; asst. prof. Spanish Vassar Coll., Poughkeepsie, N.Y., 1969-70, Princeton U., Princeton, N.J., 1970-73, assoc. prof., 1973-81, Emory L. Ford prof., 1981-86; prof. Spanish Yale U., New Haven, 1986-90; Albert Schweitzer prof. of Humanities NYU, 1990—. Author: La Diffusion de la Litterature Hispanoamericaine en France, 1972, Las Letras de Borges, 1979, En Breve Carcel, 1981, At Face Value: Autobiographical Writing in Spanish America, 1991; co-author Women's Writing in Latin America, 1991, Hispanisms and Homosexualities, 1998, El Comun Olvido, 2002; author short stories and contbr. articles to profl. jours.; cons., editorial bd. Revista Iberoamericana, 1979-81, 1985-89, Latin Am. Literary Rev., 1985—, Revista de Filología, Buenos Aires, 1985— Fellow Am. Philos. Soc., 1970, NEH, 1976; Social Sci. Research Council grantee, 1983; Guggenheim Found. fellow, 1986-87 Mem. MLA (pres.), Asociacion Internacional de Hispanistas, Instituto Internacional de Literatura Iberoamericana

MOLNAR, KATHLEEN KAY, management information systems educator; b. El Paso, Sept. 25, 1958; d. Herbert Charles and Maureen MaryAnn (Wood) Finger; m. Jeffrey Allan Molnar, Sept. 22, 1984; children: Steven Charles, Alixandra MaryAnn. BS in Natural Sci. magna cum laude, Xavier U., 1979; MBA, U. Wis., Oshkosh, 1992; PhD in Bus. Adminstrn., Okla. State U., Stillwater, 1997. Air traffic control specialist FAA-Rockford (Ill.) Control Tower, 1979-81; programmer supr. St. Anthony Hosp., Rockford, 1983-84; programmer analyst, cons. Arthur Young, Milw., 1984-85; sys. analyst Columbia Hosp., Milw., 1985, St. Norbert Coll., DePere, Wis., 1986-92, dir. computer svcs., 1989-92, asst. prof., 1997—, U. Ctrl. Okla., Edmond, 1996-97. Contbr. chpts. to books, articles to profl. jours. Mem. AAUW, Decision Scis. Inst., N.E. Wis. Talented and Gifted Orgn. (v.p. 1998—), Phi Kappa Phi, Beta Gamma Sigma. Office: St Norbert Coll 100 Grant St De Pere WI 54115-2002

MOLNAR, VIOLET, mental health nurse; b. Budapest, Hungary; arrived in U.S., 1960; d. Janos Molnar and Erzsebeth Krekacs. ADN, Atlantic Union Coll., 1967; BSN, Walla Walla Coll., 1973. RN Mass., Calif. Staff nurse New Eng. Meml. Hosp., Stoneham, Mass., 1968—70; IV therapist Loma Linda (Calif.) U. Med. Hosp., 1970—72; psychiat. nurse St. Bernardines Med. Ctr., San Bernardino, Calif., 1974—89, Corona Regional Med. Ctr., San Bernardino, 1990—. Pub. spkr. Pres. Lady's Club Friendly Cir., Loma Linda, 1997—99; elder, deaconess, greeter Loma Linda U. SDA Ch., 1975—. Mem.: Rotary Club San Bernardino/Highland (Paul Harris fellow 2001). Avocations: travel, reading, church activities.

MOLNAU, CAROL, lieutenant governor; b. Sept. 17, 1949; m. Steven F. Molnau; 3 children. Attended, U. Minn. Mem. Minn. Ho. of Reps., 1992—2003; commr. Minn. Dept. Transportation; lt. gov. Minn., 2003—. Active Our Saviors Luth. Ch., 4-H, Chaska City Coun. Mem. Agrl. Com., Econ. Devel., Infrastructure & Regulation Fin.-Transportation Fin. Divsn., Fin. Inst. & Ins.: Internat. Trade & Economic Devel. Republican. Office: Office of the Governor 130 State Capitol Saint Paul MN 55155 Home: 49966 350th St Lafayette MN 56054-3161

MOLZ, REDMOND KATHLEEN, public administration educator; b. Balt., Mar. 5, 1928; d. Joseph T. and Regina (Barry) M. BS, Johns Hopkins U., 1949, MA, 1950; MALS, U. Mich., 1953; DLS, Columbia U., 1976. Librarian I and II Enoch Pratt Free Library, Balt., 1953-56; pub. relations officer Free Library of Phila., 1958-62; editor Wilson Library Bull. H.W. Wilson Co., Bronx, N.Y., 1962-68; chief planning staff Bur. Libraries and Learning Resources U.S. Office Edn., Washington, 1968-73; prof. library sci. Sch. Library Service Columbia U., N.Y.C., 1976-80, Melvil Dewey prof., 1980-93; prof. pub. affairs Sch. Internat. and Pub. Affairs, Columbia U., N.Y.C., 1993-99, prof. emeritus, 2000—. Cons. U.S. Nat. Commn. Librs. and Info. Sci., Washington, 1974-75, U.S. Adv. Commn. Intergovtl. Relations, Washington, 1979-80; mem. nat. adv. coun. The Sheridan Librs., Johns Hopkins U., 1997—. Author: Federal Policy and Library Support, 1976 (Ralph R. Shaw award 1977), National Planning for Library Service, 1935-75, 1984, Library Planning and Policy Making: The Legacy of the Public and Private Sector, 1990, The Federal Roles in Support of Public Library Services, 1990, The Federal Roles in Support of Academic and Research Libraries, 1991; co-author (with Phyllis Dain) Civic Space/Cyberspace: The American Public Library in the Information Age, 1999; co-editor: The Metropolitan Library (anthology), 1972; author TV script Portraits in Print, 1959. Recipient Leadership Tng. award Fund for Adult Edn., 1956-57; recipient Disting. Alumnus award Sch. Library Sci. U. Mich., 1969, George Virgil Fuller award Columbia U., 1975, Johns Hopkins U. scholar, 1949-50, Horace H. Rackham fellow U. Mich., 1952-53, Columbia U. scholar, 1974-76, Tangley Oaks fellow, 1975-76; Council Library Resources Inc. Officers' grantee, 1974 Mem. ALA (councilor 1972-74, 76-80, exec. bd. 1976-80, chmn. legis. com. 1985-86), Freedom to Read Found. (dir. 1972-79, pres. 1977-79) Office: Columbia U Sch Internat & Pub Affairs New York NY 10027 Business E-Mail: rkm2@columbia.edu.

MOMMSEN, KATHARINA, retired German language and literature educator; b. Berlin, Sept. 18, 1925; came to U.S., 1974, naturalized, 1980; d. Hermann and Anna (Johannsen) Zimmer; m. Momme Mommsen, Dec. 23, 1948. Dr.phil., U. Tübingen, 1956; Dr. habil., Berlin Free U., 1962. Collaborator Acad. Scis., Berlin, 1949-61; assoc. prof. Free U., Berlin, 1962-70; prof. German Carleton U., Ottawa, Can., 1970-74; Albert Guerard prof. lit. Stanford U., 1974-94, ret., 1995. Vis. prof. U. Giessen, Tech. U. Berlin, 1965, State U. N.Y., Buffalo, 1966, U. Calif., San Diego, 1973 Author over 150 publs. on 18th-20th century German and comparative lit.; editor: Germanic Studies in America. Mem. Goethe Soc., Schiller Soc. Home: 980 Palo Alto Ave Palo Alto CA 94301-2223 E-mail: k.mommsen@comcast.net.

MONAGHAN, EILEEN See WHITAKER, EILEEN

MONAGHAN, KATHLEEN M. art museum director; b. Waterville, Maine, Sept. 6, 1936; d. Russell Vernon and Gloria Beatrice (LeClair) M. BA in Art History, U. Calif.-Santa Barbara, 1979, MA in Art History, 1981. Curatorial fellow Whitney Mus., N.Y.C., 1979, dir. Equitable Br., 1985-93; asst. curator Santa Barbara Mus., Calif., 1980-81, curator of art, 1983-84; curator, dir. Akron Art Mus., Ohio, 1984-85; dir. The Hyde Collection, Glens Falls, N.Y., 1994; exec. dir. Fresno Metropolitan Museum, Fresno, Calif. Mem. Internat. Com. on Mus., Coll. Art Assn. Address: Fresno Met Museum 1515 Van Ness Ave Fresno CA 93721

MONAGHAN, M. PATRICIA, education educator, writer; b. Bklyn., Feb. 15, 1946; d. Edward Joseph and Mary Margaret (Gordon) M. BA in English, U. Minn., 1967, MA in English, 1971; MFA, U. Alaska, 1981; PhD, The Union Inst., 1995. News editor U. Alaska, Fairbanks, 1970-71; pub. rels. dir. Walker Art Ctr., Mpls., 1972; editor Minn. Monthly Minn. Pub. Radio, St. Paul, 1973-74; women's editor Daily News miner, Fairbanks, 1975; lectr., head English dept. Tanana Valley C.C., Fairbanks, 1976-87; instr. writing The Neighborhood Inst., Chgo., 1987-89; dir. cont. edn. St. Xavier U., Chgo., 1990—; assoc. prof. DePaul U. Sch. for New Learning, Chgo. Booklist reviewer ALA, Chgo., 1987—. Author: Book of Goddesses and Heroines, 1981, 90, Working Wisdom, 1994, O Mother Sun New View of Feminine, 1994, (poetry) Seasons of the Witch, 1992 (Friends of Lit. award 1992), (poems) Dancing with Chaos, 2002, The Red Haired Girl from the Bog, 2003, Meditation: The Complete Guide, 1999. Recipient Rsch. award NUCEA, 1993, Univ. Alaska, 1987. Mem. Am. Conf. on Irish Studies, Soc. Midland Authors, Authors Guild. Democrat. Mem. Soc. Of Friends. Office: DePaul Univ Sch for New Learning 16333 S Kilbourn Oak Forest IL 60452 Office Phone: 312-476-3073. E-mail: pmonagha@depaul.edu.

MONAHAN, DANIELLE JOAN, renal nutritionist; b. Tacoma, Feb. 22, 1952; d. Daniel Gustav and Bernice Elizabeth (Nordlund) Anderson; m. Jay Mitchell Littlefield, Nov. 13, 1976 (dec. 1997); children: David, Rachel, Paul; m. Aldrich B. Monahan, Jr., Oct. 30, 1999. BS, Va. Poly. Inst., 1974; MS, U. Md., 1975. Registered dietitian, Va. Therapeutic dietitian Samaritan Hosp., Troy, N.Y., 1976; renal dietitian BMA/Fresenius Med. Care (formerly Nat. Med. Care), Washington, 1977-85, Fairfax Dialysis (formerly BMA of Arlington), 1985—. Cons. Fairfax, 1985—; rep. network coordinating coun. Nat. Kidney Found., Chevy Chase, Md., 1980-84; chmn. BMA Dietitians Group, Washington, 1980-93. Contbr. articles to profl. jours., mags. Del. Va. Rep. Party, Vienna, 1982. Mem. Am. Dietetic Assn., No. Va. Dietetic Assn. Republican. Avocation: cooking. Office: Fairfax Dialysis 8316 Arlington Blvd #108 Fairfax VA 22031-5216 Office Phone: 703-698-8070.

MONAHAN, MARTHA J. psychologist; b. Salem, Mass., Aug. 8, 1956; d. Karl and Janis (Lee) Monahan; m. Barry F. Skoff, July 14, 1984; 1 child, Emily J. Skoff. MEd, Boston U., 1982, EdD, 1989. Lic. psychologist Mass. Psychologist Health & Edn. Svcs., Salem, 1993—99, Children's Friend and Family Svc., Salem, 1999—2003; pvt. practice, 2003—. Avocations: cooking, gardening, writing, reading, travel. Office: Northeast Psychol Assocs 70 Washington St Salem MA 01970*

MONCK, MAUREEN F. psychoanalyst; b. N.Y.C., Dec. 12, 1938; d. Lawrence Finnerty and Mary Henrietta Crean-Lynch; m. Robert A. Monck, June 16, 1962 (dec. Jan. 1983); children: Merritt Monck-Rowley, Erinna Monck Bernstein, Caitlin Monck-Marcellino. BS, Georgetown U., 1960; PhD, NYU, 1968; MA in Art History, Cooper Hewitt-New Sch., 1999; postdoctoral cert. in adult psychoanalysis, Derner Inst.; postdoctoral cert. in child and adolescent psychotherapy, Adelphi U. Pvt. practice psychoanalyst, Muttontown, NY, 1968—; guest curator Oyster Bay (N.Y.) Hist. Soc., 1997—; supr. of psychotherapy Metro. Ctr. for Mental Health, N.Y.C., 1997—; dir. psychotherapy tng. program L.I. Inst. for Psychoanalysis, East Meadow, NY, 1985—93; dir. nursing program C.W. Post - L.I. Univ., Brookville, NY, 1972—75.

MONCRIEF, WILLIAM ALVIN, JR., oil and gas producer; b. Little Rock, Mar. 27, 1920; d. William Alvin and Elizabeth (Bright) M.; m. Deborah Beggs, Jan. 30, 1947; children: William A. III, R.W., C.B., T.O. BS in Petroleum Engring., U. Tex., Austin, 1942. Registered profl. engr., Tex. Ptnr. Moncrief Oil, Ft. Worth, 1945—; dir. First Republic Bank, Dallas. Regent, U. Tex. system. Served to ensign USNR, 1944-45, PTO. Named Disting. Engring. Grad. U. Tex.-Austin, 1983 Mem.: Shady Oaks of Ft. Worth (pres.); Eldorado (Indian Wells, Calif.); Brookhollow (Dallas). Republican. Episcopalian. Office: Moncrief Oil Moncrief Bldg 9th And Commerce St Fort Worth TX 76102

MONCZEWSKI, MAUREEN R. secondary art educator, visual artist; b. Scranton, Pa., Jan. 14, 1957; d. Walter Albert and Ann Hedwig (Sawicki) M. BA in Profl. Art, Marywood U., 1978, MFA in Painting, 1987. Cert. art educator K-12. Art instr. Internat. Corr. Sch., Scranton, Pa., 1983-98; grad. asst. Marywood U., Scranton, 1985-86; art tchr. Moravian Acad., Bethlehem, Pa., 1989-90; adj. art instr. Penn State U., Lehman, Pa., 1990-91; art tchr. Notre Dame Jr./Sr. High Sch., East Stroudsburg, Pa., 1997—2001; secondary art tchr. Stroudsburg (Pa.) H.S., 2001—. Designer, painter of site specific murals Scranton Redevel. Authority, 1979, Scranton Sr. Activities Ctr., 1986, Carbondale (Pa.) Housing Authority, 1987, Teamsters Local 229, Scranton, 1990, Housing Authority of the County of Lackawanna-Dunmore (Pa.) Sr. Hi-Rise, 1994, The Artist's Studio, Scranton, 1995, Baird's County Kennel, Mehoopany, Pa., 1995, West Side Sr. Activities Ctr., Scranton, 1996, Wyo. Paint and Art Supply, Scranton, 1996, Suz's Marineland, Tunkhannock, Pa., 1996; represented in pvt. collections. Gen. Program grantee Boys & Girls Club, 1992, Housing Authority Mural grantee Lackawanna County, Dunmore, Pa., 1994, Arts to the People grantee Lackawanna County Commrs., Scranton, 1992, 95; recipient Cert. of Excellence award Dept. Labor, 1980. Mem. St. Luke's Art Soc., Kappa Pi. Democrat. Roman Catholic. Avocations: sculpture, writing, design, travel, drawing.

MONDALE, JOAN ADAMS, wife of former Vice President of United States; b. Eugene, Oreg., Aug. 8, 1930; d. John Maxwell and Eleanor Jane (Hall) Adams; m. Walter F. Mondale, Dec. 27, 1955; children— Theodore, Eleanor Jane, William Hall. BA, Macalester Coll., 1952. Asst. slide librarian Boston Mus. Fine Arts, 1952-53; asst. in edn. Mpls. Inst. of Arts, 1953-57; weekly tour guide Nat. Gallery of Art, Washington, 1965-74; hostess Washington Whirl-A-Round, 1975-76; ambassador to Japan, 1993-96. Author: Politics in Art, 1972, Letters from Japan, 1998. Mem. bd. govs. Women's Nat. Dem. Club; hon. chmn. Fed. Coun. on Arts and Humanities, 1978-80; bd. dirs. Associated Coun. of Arts, 1973-75, Reading Is Fundamental, Am. Craft Coun., N.Y.C., 1981-88, J.F.K. Ctr. Performing Arts, 1981-90, Walker Art Ctr., Mpls., 1987-93, Minn. Orch., Mpls., 1988-93, 97-2003, St. Paul Chamber Orch., 1988-90, Northern Clay Ctr., 1988-93, St. Paul, 1988-93, Nancy Hauser Dance Co., Mpls., 1989-93, Minn. Landmarks, 1991-93, Walker Art Ctr., Mpls., 1997-2003; trustee Macalester Coll., 1986—; mem. commn. Nat. Portrait Gallery, 1997—; chair Hiawatha Light Rail Transit Pub. Art and Design com., 2000— Walker Art Ctr., 2003-. Mem. Phi Beta Kappa Epsilon. Democrat. Presbyterian. Home: 2116 Irving Ave S Minneapolis MN 55405-2541 E-mail: joan.mondale@mac.com.

MONDRY, DIANE, secondary school educator; b. Reginas, Sask., Can. 3 children. Career and tech. edn. tchr. Cmty. H.S., Grand Forks, ND. Part-time instr. dept. info. sys. and bus. edn. U. N.D. Recipient Outstanding Tchr. award, Nat. Assn. Vocat. Edn. Spl. Needs Pers. Mem.: NEA, Assn. for Career and Tech. Edn. (immediate past pres. 2001—02), Nat. Bd. for Profl. Tchg. Stds. (bd. mem.). Office: Cmty High Sch 500 Stanford Rd Grand Forks ND 58203-2748

MONES, JOAN MICHELE, pathologist; b. Downey, Calif., Nov. 26, 1952; d. Joseph Morgan and Mary Kathryn (Crisp) Battersby; m. Harris Hal Mones, May 11, 1979 (div. Dec. 1987). BA, UCLA, 1975; DO, U. Osteo. Medicine, 1979. Diplomate Am. Bd. Pathology, Anatomic and Clin. Intern Drs. Gen. Hosp., Plantation, Fla., 1979-80; pvt. practice Coral Gables, Fla., 1980-81; resident in pathology Jackson Meml. Hosp., Miami, 1981-85, fellow in surg. pathology, 1985-86; instr. in pathology U. Miami, 1986-87; asst. lab. dir. North Miami Med. Ctr., 1987-90; attending pathologist Parkway Regional Med. Ctr., North Miami, 1990-97; fellow in dermatopathology Thomas Jefferson U., Phila., 1998-99; med. dir. Ackerman Acad. Dermatopathology, N.Y.C., 1999—. Clin. asst. prof. U. Miami, 1988—, Southeastern U. Osteo. Medicine, Miami, 1989—. Contbr. articles to profl. jours. Fellowship Nat. Cancer Soc., 1985. Fellow Coll. Am. Pathologists, Am. Soc. Clin. Pathologists; mem. U.S. and Canadian Acad. Pathology, Am. Osteo. Coll. Pathology, Am. Osteo. Assn. Office: Ackerman Acad Dermatopathology 145 E 32d St New York NY 10016

MONEY, RUTH ROWNTREE, infant development and care specialist, consultant; b. Brownwood, Tex. m. Lloyd Jean Money; children: Jeffrey, Meredith, Jeannette. BA in Biology, Rice U., 1944; MA in Devel. Psychology, Calif. State U., Long Beach, 1971; BA in Early Childhood Edn., U. D.C., 1979. Rsch. psychologist Early Edn. Project, Capitol Heights, Md., 1971-73; lectr. No. Va. C.C., Anandale, 1973-74; tchr. preschs. Calif. and Va., 1979-81; dir. various preschs., Washington and Va., 1981-85; instr. guided studies Pacific Oaks Coll., Pasadena, Calif., 1986-88; cons. parent/infant programs Resources for Infant Educarers, L.A., 1986—; founder, dir. South Bay Infant Ctr., Redondo Beach, Calif., 1988-92; instr. child devel. Harbor Coll., L.A., 1992-93. Bd. dirs. Resources for Infant Educarers, 1986—; pres. bd. dirs. South Bay Infant Ctr., Redondo Beach, 1988-94, treas., 1994-98. Producer (ednl. videos) Caring for Infants, 1988—. Mem. League of Women Voters, 1956—, v.p., 1972-76. Mem. Nat. Assn. for Edn. of Young Children, Assn. for Childhood Edn. Internat., Infant Devel. Assn. Calif. Avocations: traveling, hiking. Home: 904 21st St Hermosa Beach CA 90254-3105 Office: Resources for Infant Educarers 1550 Murray Cir Los Angeles CA 90026-1644 E-mail: ruthmoney@earthlink.net.

MONEYPENNY, NAOMI FELINA, research and development company executive; MSc in Astrophysics, U. of London, 1994; student, Northwestern U., 1998. Bus. mgr. Shell Internat., London, 1996—97; strategy and strategic relationships mgr. Royal Dutch/Shell, London, 1997—99; vp tech. ManyWorlds, Houston, 1999—2001; vp rsch., content & tech. ManyWorlds, Inc, Houston, 2001—. Editor: website, Signal Mag.e. Recipient Gold Medal award, London (Eng.) Acad. Music and Dramatic Art, 1990. Mem.: NAFE, SPCA (life), S.W. CEO Coun. Achievements include invention of fuzzy content network management & access. Office: ManyWorlds Inc 510 Bering Dr Suite 470 Houston TX 77057 E-mail: n.moneypenny@manyworlds.com.

MONFERRATO, ANGELA MARIA, investor, writer, designer; b. Wissembourg, Alsace-Loraine, France, July 19, 1948; came to U.S., 1950; d. Albert Carmen and Anna Maria (Vieri) M. Diplomate, Pensionnat Florissant, Lausanne, Switzerland, 1966-67; BS in Consumer Related Studies, Mktg., Pa. State U., 1971, postgrad. in speech and comm., 1971-72. Simultaneous translator fgn. langs. Inst. for Achievement of Human Potential, Phila., 1976-78; art dir. The Artworks, Sumneytown, Pa., 1975-76; asst. productionist Film Space, State College, Pa., 1976; real property mgr. Pla. 15 Condominium, Ft. Lauderdale, Fla., 1979-80; legal asst. Ft. Lauderdale, Fla., 1981-85; owner Rising Sun the Real Estate Corp. South Fla., Ft. Lauderdale, 1986—. Pres. Kideos Video Prodns., 1985—; owner, designer Monferrato Designs, 1988-99; designer homes, interiors, furniture and landscapes. Avocations: writing, designing, yoga, faux painting, restoration of antiques. Office: Monferrato Designs Telluride 200 Front St PO Box 2 Placerville CO 81430

MONG, MICHELLE DENISE, marriage and family therapist; b. Seattle, Nov. 17, 1972; d. Alvin and Joyce Mong; m. Sean Ryan, Sept. 7, 2002. BA in Psychology, U. of Wash., 1995; MA in Marriage and Family Therapy, Pacific Luth. U., Tacoma, 1997. Lic. marriage and family therapist Wash., 2002. Marriage and family therapist Kent Youth and Family Svcs., Kent, Wash., 1998—, counseling services coord., 1998—. Supr. in tng. Kent Youth and Family Services, Kent, Wash., 2003—. Co-chmn. Holiday Giving Program, Kent, 2002—02; grand marshall Kent holiday parade City of Kent, 2002; profl. tng. task force mem. Highline West Seattle Consortium, Seattle, 2003—; chmn. Kent Youth and Family Svcs. Staff Link Event and Tng. Com., 1999—; vol. Wash. State Dept. of Corrections, Seattle, 1998—99; rep. spkr. gradn programs Pacific Luth. U., Tacoma, 1996—97; presenter /educator to schools and cmty. groups Kent, 1999—; chmn. Holiday Giving program, 2003. Mem.: Am. Assn. of Marriage and Family Therapy (assoc.), Chi Omega (life; co-chairman of formal rush 1992—94). Methodist. Avocations: travel, photography, hosting events. Office: Kent Youth and Family Svcs 232 S 2nd Ave Ste 201 Kent WA 98032 Office Phone: 253-859-0300 3014.

MONGES, MIRIAM M. social studies educator; b. Phila., Feb. 1, 1950; d. Walter Holland and Ruth (Harris) Johnson; m. Pedro Chango Monges, Feb. 11, 1974 (div. June 1992); children: Taína Afaph, Caliph Caribe. BA cum laude, Bklyn. Coll., 1973; MSW, Temple U., 1979, PhD in African-Am. Studies, 1995. Project coord. Ctr. Social Policy and Cmty. Devel. Temple U., Phila., 1986-92, adj. prof., 1993-94; exec. dir. Spruce Adolescent Ctr., Phila., 1992-94; assoc. prof. Calif. State U., Chico, 1995—. Mem. adv. coun. Ctr. Multicultural & Gender Studies, Chico, 1995—; cultural resource specialist African Am. Culture XXVI Olympiad, Atlanta, 1996; multicultural cons. social work Bodo (Norway) Coll., 1997. Author: Kush: The Jewel of Nubia, 1997; mem. editl. bd. Jour. Black Studies, 1996—. Named for Disting. Scholarship and Mentoring, Internat. Assn. Women of Color Day, Sacramento, 1999. Mem. Nat. Assn. Black Social Workers, Nat. Assn. African Am. Studies, Nat. Coun. Black Studies. Avocations: spinning, making jewelry. Office: Calif State U Ctr Multicultural & Gender Studies Dept Sociology Social Work Chico CA 95929-0001 Home: 14 Wrangler CT Chico CA 95928-7611

MONHEIT, MOLLY JANE, artist; b. Yakima, Wash., Aug. 5, 1922; d. Laurel LaVergne and Edna (Bracewell) Lugar; m. John Palmer Ruckel (dec. 1952); children: Gail Ruckel, Andrew Ruckel; m. George Monheit, Dec. 7, 1952; 1 child, William. Student, Art Ctr. Sch., Calif., 1942; BA magna cum laude, Wash. State U., 1944; MA, Mills Coll., 1947. Clk., artist, cons. Papyrus, Lafayette, Calif., 1976-97; ret., 1997. Exhibited paintings in Wash., Tex., and Calif.; prin. works represented in permanent collections in pvt. homes and museums in 38 countries; contbr. articles to Bird Watchers Digest. Precinct chmn. Reps., Lafayette, 1954-70; social chmn. Valley View Estates, Lafayette, 1954-80. Recipient fellowship Aurelia Reinhart, 1945-47. Mem. Soc. Western Artists, Am. Women Artists, East Bay Watercolor Soc., Audubon Soc., Am. Field Svc. (pres. 1970), Diablo Art Assn. (pres.), Alpha Gamma Delta. Presbyterian. Avocations: travel on birding trips, track and field (Calif. sr. champion 100m for age group 1980-92). Home: 1107 Magnolia Ln Lafayette CA 94549-3118

MONIA, JOAN, retired management consultant; d. James Anthony and Anne Linden McCaffrey; m. Charles Anthony Monia, Dec. 30, 1961; 1 child, Clare Ann Woodman. BA, Ohio Dominican U., 1960. Info. specialist Battelle Meml. Inst., Columbus, Ohio, 1960-62; project leader Douglas Aircraft Corp., Huntington Beach, Calif., 1962-64; programmer analyst McDonnell Aircraft Corp., St. Louis, 1965-66; project mgr. Sanders Assocs., Nashua, N.H., 1968-70; database adminstrn. project leader Mass. Blue Cross, Boston, 1970-74; data strategist Factory Mut. Engring. Corp., Norwood, Mass., 1974-78; mgr. data resource planning Digital Equipment Corp., Maynard, Mass., 1978-84; sr. mem. tech. staff GTE Govt. Systems Corp., Needham, Mass., 1984-91; prin. DMR Group, Inc., Waltham, Mass., 1991-96; owner, mgr. Info-Driven Enterprise Structures, Marlborough, Mass., 1997, San Jose, Calif., 1998—2002; ret., 2002. Recipient Sci. medal, Bausch & Lomb, 1956. Avocation: painting. Home: 7553 Morevern Cir San Jose CA 95135-2106

MONIHAN, MARY ELIZABETH, lawyer; b. Cleve., Mar. 22, 1957; d. Michael Reilley and Donna (Warner) Monihan. BS in Econs., John Carroll U., 1979; JD, Cleve. State U., 1984. Bar: Ohio 1984, U.S. Dist. Ct. (no. dist.) Ohio 1985, U.S. Supreme Ct. 1989. Atty. in office of counsel Ameritrust Co. Nat. Assn., Cleve., 1984-85; assoc. Jones, Day, Reavis & Pogue, Cleve., 1985-89, Squire, Sanders & Dempsey, Cleve., 1989-95; ptnr. Spieth, Bell, McCurdy & Newell, Co., L.P.A., Cleve., 1995—. Pres. Estate Planning Coun. Cleve., 1994-95. Pres., vol. Coun. Cleve. Orch., 1998-2001; trustee Assn. Major Symphony Orch. Vols., 1997-99; trustee Women's Com. of the Cleveland Orch., 2000-2003. Mem.: ABA, Cleve. Cath. Lawyers Guild (exec. bd. 2001—), Cleve. Bar Assn., Ohio Bar Assn., Am. Coll. Trust and Estate Counsel, Jr. Com. Cleve. Orch. (pres. 1997—99). Office: Spieth Bell McCurdy & Newell Co LPA 925 Euclid Ave Ste 2000 Cleveland OH 44115-1407 E-mail: memonihan@spiethbell.com.

MONK, DIANA CHARLA, artist, stable owner; b. Visalia, Calif., Feb. 25, 1927; d. Charles Edward and Viola Genevieve (Shea) Williams; m. James Alfred Monk, Aug. 11, 1951; children: Kiloran, Sydney, Geoffrey, Anne, Eric. Student, U. Pacific, 1946-47, Sacramento Coll., 1947-48, Calif. Coll. Fine Arts, San Francisco, 1948-51, Calif. Coll. Arts & Crafts, Oakland, 1972. Art tchr. Mt. Diablo Sch. Dist., Concord, Calif., 1958-63; pvt. art tchr. Lafayette, Calif., 1963-70; gallery dir. Jason Aver Gallery, San Francisco, 1970-72; owner, mgr. Monk & Lee Assocs., Lafayette, 1973-80; stable owner, mgr. Longacre Tng. Stables, Santa Rosa, Calif., 1989—. One-person shows include John F. Kennedy U., Orinda, Calif., Civic Arts Gallery, Walnut Creek, Calif., Valley Art Gallery, Walnut Creek, Sea Ranch Gallery, Gualala, Calif., Jason Aver Gallery, San Francisco; exhibited in group shows at Oakland (Calif.) Art Mus., Crocker Nat. Art Gallery, Sacramento, Le Salon des Nations, Paris. Chair bd. dirs. Walnut Creek (Calif.) Civic Arts, 1972-74, advisor to dir., 1968-72; exhibit chmn. Valley Art Gallery, Walnut Creek, 1977-78; juror Women's Art Show, Walnut Creek, 1970, Oakland Calif. Art. Home and Office: Longacre Tng Stables 1702 Willowside Rd Santa Rosa CA 95401-3922 E-mail: longacrestables@msn.com.

MONK, MEREDITH JANE, artistic director, composer, choreographer, filmmaker, director; b. N.Y.C., Nov. 20, 1942; d. Theodore G. and Audrey Lois (Zellman) Monk. BA, Sarah Lawrence Coll., 1964; ArtsD (hon.), Bard Coll., 1988, U. of the Arts, 1989, Juilliard Sch. Music, 1997, San Francisco Art Inst., 1998, Boston Conservatory, 2001, Bennington Coll., 2002, Cornish Coll. Arts, 2002. Artistic dir., founder Ho. Found. Arts, N.Y.C., 1968—. Bd. dirs. Am. Music Ctr., The Kitchen. Prin. works include 16 Millimeter Earrings, 1966, Vessel, 1971, Quarry, 1976, Recent Ruins, 1979, Turtle Dreams, 1983, The Games, 1983, Book of Days, 1988, Facing North, 1990, Atlas, 1991, Three Heavens and Hells, 1992, Volcano Songs, 1994, American Archeology, 1994, The Politics of Quiet, 1996, Magic Frequencies, 1998, Mercy, 2001, Possible Sky, 2003, exhibitions include Libr. of Performing Arts, Lincoln Ctr., 1996, Walker Art Ctr., Mpls., 1998, Whitney Mus. Art, 2002, Exit Art, 2002. Recipient Obie award, Village Voice, 1972, 1976, 1985, Creative Arts award, Brandeis U., 1974, Villager award, 1980, 1983, Deutches Kritiker preis, 1981, 1986, Bessie award, 1985, Nat. Music Theatre award, 1986, Dance Mag. award, 1993, John D. and Catherine T. MacArthur award, 1995, Sarah Lawrence Disting. Alumna award, 1996, Samuel Scripps award, 1996, Sigma Phi Omega award, 1987; fellow Guggenheim, 1972, 1982, Norton Stevens, 1993—94, MacDowell Colony. Mem.: ASCAP (award 1980—2000). Office: House Found for Arts 131 Varick St New York NY 10013-1410

MONK, SUSAN MARIE, pediatrician, educator; b. York, Pa., May 7, 1945; d. John Spotz and Mary Elizabeth (Shelly) M.; m. Jaime Pacheco, June 5, 1971; children: Benjamin Joaquin, Maria Cristina. AB, Colby Coll., 1967; MD, Jefferson Med. Coll., 1971. Diplomate Am. Bd. Pediatrics. Pediatrician Children's Med. Ctr., Dayton, Ohio, 1975—; asst. clin. prof. pediat. Wright State U., Dayton, 1976—83, assoc. clin. prof. pediat., 1983—2000, asst. prof. pediatrics, 2000—. Mem. bd. dirs. Children's Med. Ctr., Dayton, 1991-96, chief-of-staff, 1992-94. Mem. Am. Acad. Pediatrics, We. Ohio Pediatric Soc., Pediatric Ambulatory Care Soc. Avocations: reading, gardening, travel, movies, theater. Office: Childrens Health Clinic 730 C Valley St Dayton OH 45404-1845 E-mail: monks@childrensdayton.org.

MONK KIDD, SUE, writer; m. Sandy Monk Kidd; 2 children. BS in Nursing, Tex. Christian U., 1970. Nurse St. Joseph's Hosp., Fort Worth, Tex., Med.Coll. Ga. Contbg. editor: Guideposts; author: God's Joyful Surprise, 1988, When the Heart Waits: Spiritual Direction for Life's Sacred Questions, 1990, The Dance of the Dissident Daughter: A Woman's Journey from Christian Tradition to the Sacred Feminine, 1996, The Secret Life of Bees, 2002 (SEBA Book of Yr. award, 2003); contbr. essays to mags. Recipient Katherine Anne Porter Second prize in fiction, Nimrod/Hardman Awards, 1993, S.C. Fiction Projectaward, S.C. Arts Commn., 1993, 1995, 1997, Isak Dineson Creative Non-Fiction award, 1994, Literal Latte Creative Non-Fiction Third prize, 1999, Bread Loaf scholar, Bread Loaf Writers Conf., 1995; fellow, S.C. Arts Commn., 1993—94, S.C. Acad. Authors, 1994, 1996. Office: c/o Carolyn Coleburn Viking Penguin 375 HudsonSt New York NY 10014*

MONKMAN, BETTY CLAIRE, curator; BA, U. N.D.; MA, George Washington U. Registrar Office of the Curator White House, Washington, 1967-80, assoc. curator, 1980-97, curator, 1997—2002. Lectr. on history, arch., changing interiors, decorative and fine arts collections, holiday traditions, archives and documentation of hist. properties in the White House. Author: (with others) Art in the White House: A Nation's Pride, 1992, Our Changing White House, 1995, The White House: Its Historic Furnishings and First Families, 2000, Treasures of the White House, 2001; contbr. articles to profl. jours. Bd. dirs. Mus. City of Washington, 1980-92, Heurich House Fedn., 2002—, N.D. Mus. Art Fedn., 2003—; bd. mgrs. Hist. Soc. Washington, 1980-92, D.C. Bicentennial Commn., 1987-92. Mem. Com. for Preservation White House, Am. Assn. Mus., Soc. for History in Fed. Govt., Cosmos Club.

MONPERE, LISA RENEE, budget and personnel administrator, entrepreneur; b. Pitts., June 8, 1965; d. Charles William and Leslie Jean Monpere. BA in Spanish, SUNY at Buffalo, Amherst, 1989. Graphic comms. Ednl. Opportunity Ctr. Constrn. and demolition worker M & M Rehab, Buffalo, 1978—83; model Barbizon Sch. of Modeling, Buffalo, 1983—87; pub. rels. Taizz DiscoTec, Cuernavaca, Mexico, 1986—87; student asst. SUNY at Buffalo, Amherst, 1986—89, budget and pers. adminstrator, 1989—; direct sales NuSkin Internat., Cooks Know How Cookware, Melissa Rice Interiors, Home Scentsations Candles, Mary Kay Cosmetics, Cell Tech Health Products, ACN Internat., Buffalo, 1991—. Editor layout and design Ctr. for Pub. Affairs Studies, SUNY-Buffalo, Amherst, 1988—94. Contbr. poetry to anthologies (Outstanding Achievement in Poetry, 2003). Deacon and singles ministry Harvest Tabernacle Ch., Buffalo, 2001—. Mem.: Swarovski Crystal Soc., United U. Profls. Avocations: collecting Swarovski crystal, travel, fishing, decorating, creating gift baskets and floral arrangements. Home: 69 Callodine Ave Amherst NY 14226 Personal E-mail: lmonpere@acninc.net.

MONRAD, ELIZABETH A. corporate financial executive; Grad., Wellesley Coll., 1976; MBA in Fin., MIT. Ptnr. Coopers & Lybrand, Boston; with Gen. RE, 1992—2003; chief fin. officer Gen. Re Corp., 2000—03; exec. v.p., chief fin. officer TIAA CREF, N.Y.C., 2003—. Mem.: AICPA (mem. fin. instns. expert panel), Reins. Assn. Am. (chmn. acctg. com.). Office: TIAA CREF 730 3d Ave New York NY 10017

MONRO, ELIZABETH (BETTY MONRO), federal agency administrator; m. Charles Monro. BA, U. Miss. Dir. fed. legis. Air Transport Assn. of Am.; spl. asst. aviation policy to Sec. Sam Skinner U.S. Dept. of Transp., Washington, 1989—91; chief of staff to adminstr. Gilbert Carmichael Fed. R.R. Adminstrn., 1991—93; chief of staff U.S. Congressman Mac Collins; dep. adminstr. Fed. R.R. Adminstrn., 2001—. Office: Fed RR Adminstrn 1120 Vermont Ave NW Washington DC 20590*

MONROE, BARBARA JEAN, writer, educator; b. Dillon, S.C., Oct. 19, 1948; d. James Arthur and Tina Thomasena Hines; m. William Monroe, Sept. 4, 1993; m. Eugene Bethea, Aug. 15, 1965 (dec. July 1, 1985); children: Timothy Eugene Bethea, Brian Avery Bethea, Regina Annette Solomon, Wendy Diane Markham. BS, Pembroke State U., 1981; MS, Fayetteville State U., 1987. Machine operator Acme Electric, Lumberton, NC, 1978—80; tchr. spl. edn. Robeson County Schs., 1982—89, Marion County Schs., Mullins, SC, 1989—90, Robeson County Schs., Lumberton, 1990—93; real estate salesperson N.C. Real Estate Commn., Fayetteville, 1995—97; tchr. spl. edn. Cumberland County Schs., 1994—. Owner J & M Pub., Fayetteville, 2000—. Author: Out of Death Came Life; contbr. articles to profl. jours. Scout leader Girl Scouts Am., Fayetteville, 1995—2003; com. mem. Ho. of Reps. Campaign, Lumberton, 1983—83; literacy coord. VISTA, Fairmont, 1976—79. Mem.: Nat. Tchr. Assn. (licentiate). Conservative. Baptist. Avocations: travel, crafts, writing. Personal E-mail: bamon3@aol.com. E-mail: bamon3@aol.com.

MONROE, BRENDA, priest; d. Martin Monroe and Carol Baillie. BS in Mgmt., Purdue U., 1981; MDiv, Episcopal Theol. Sem. of the S.W., Austin, Tex., 1998. Ordained priest Episcopal Ch., 2000. Asst. rector St. John's Episcopal Ch., Olney, Md., 1999—2000; rector St. James Episcopal Ch., Clayton, Ga., 2001—. V.p. Cmty. Partnership of Rabun County, Clayton, 2003. Avocations: reading, genealogy. Home: 242 Valley St Clayton GA 30525 Office: St James Episcopal Ch PO Box 69 Clayton GA 30525 E-mail: saintjames@alltel.net.

MONROE, DEBRA F. writer, educator; b. Aberdeen, S.D., July 15, 1958; d. Allen Louis and Arlene Louise (Tyman McElligott) Frigen; 1 adopted child, Marie. BA in English, U. Wis., Eau Claire, 1980; MA in English, Kans. State U., 1985; PhD in English, U. Utah, 1990. Prof. U. N.C., Greensboro, 1990—92, Tex. State U., San Marcos, 1992—. Presenter in field. Author: The Source of Trouble, 1990 (Flanney O'Connor award, 1990), A Wild, Cold State, 1995, Newfangled, 1998, short stories, articles. Recipient award Nat. Novella Competition, Quarterly West, U. Utah, 1993; John Gardner fellow, Breadloaf Writers Conf., Vt., 1994. Office: Tex State Univ 601 University Dr San Marcos TX 78666

MONROE, ERIN, psychiatric nurse practitioner; b. Topeka, Kans., Oct. 10, 1958; d. James Arthur and Virginia Marie Monroe. BA Psychology/Sociology magna cum laude, Bethany Coll., 1981; BSN magna cum laude, Washburn U., 1988; MSN summa cum laude, U. Kans., 1997. RN, Kans.; cert. addictions nurse, psychiatry/mental health nurse; cert. advanced nurse practitioner; cert. group psychotherapist. Lic. mental health technician Topeka State Hosp., 1982-87; staff psychiat. nurse Mennniger's, Topeka, 1988-98, advanced RN practitioner case mgr., 1998-99, primary clinician, 1999-2001, mem. quality assurance investigative com., 1999, Stormont-Vail Regional Health Ctr., Topeka, 2001—02; advanced practice nurse Cin. Children's Hosp. Med. Ctr., 2002—. Contbr. articles to profl. jours. Town rep. McPherson (Kans.) County Family Life Edn. Com., 1979. Mem. ANA, Am. Psychiat. Nurses Assn., Ohio Assn. Advanced Practice Nurses, Kans. State Nurses Assn., Psi Chi (pres., sec. 1979-81), Phi Kappa Phi, Sigma Theta Tau (Eta and Delta chpts.), Beta Tau Sigma. Democrat. Avocations: reading, films, psychoanalysis, art, walking. Office: Cincinnati Children's Hosp Med Ctr 3333 Burnet Cincinnati OH 45229 Home: 3781 Vineyard Woods Dr Cincinnati OH 45255-4699

MONROE, JANE D. federal agency administrator; Probation officer; police officer; spl. agt. FBI, Abuquerque, 1985, Tampa, Fla., Washington; spl. agt. criminal divsn. FBI Hdqs., Washington; spl. agt. behavioral sci. unit FBI Acad., Quantico, Va.; supr. white collar crime and pub. corruption squad FBI, San Diego, 1995, coord. hostage negotiation and evidence response teams, 1995—99, asst. spl. agt. in charge Denver, 1999, spl. agt. in charge L.A., 2002, asst. dir. cyber divsn. Washington, 2002—. Office: Fed Bur Investigation J Edgar Hoover Bldg 935 Penn Ave NW Washington DC 20535-0001*

MONROE, LEONORA, surgeon; b. Hazleton, Pa., Apr. 11, 1940; d. James and Ruth (Cuozzo) M.; 1 child, Franc. RN, U. Pa., 1960, BA, 1973; MD, Med. Coll. Pa., 1980. Bd. cert. in surgery Am. Bd. Surgery. Head nurse oper. rm. Columbia Presbyn. Hosp., N.Y.C., 1960-62; head nurse med.-surg. U. Pa. Grad. Hosp., Phila., 1963-68, head nurse emergency rm., 1972-75; head nurse labor and delivery Pa. Hosp., Phila., 1968-72; surg. resident Hahnemann U. Hosp., Phila., 1980-83, Polyclinic Med. Ctr., Harrisburg, Pa., 1983-86; attending surgeon Guiffré Med. Ctr., Phila., 1986-88; attending surgeon, instr. surgery Wyckoff Heights Med. Ctr., Bklyn., 1990—. Oper. rm. com. Wyckoff Heights Med. Ctr., Bklyn., 1992-96, med. records com., 1994-96, autopsy com., 1996. Fellow ACS; mem. Am. Soc. Gen. Surgeons, Soc. Laparoendoscopic Surgeons. Avocations: skiing, squash, racquetball. Office: Family Health Ctr Ridgewood 68-52 Fresh Pond Rd Ridgewood NY 11385

MONROE, MELROSE, retired bank executive; b. Flowery Branch, Ga., Apr. 13, 1919; d. Willis Jeptha and Leila Adell Cash; m. Lynn Austin, June 14, 1942. AB in Edn., Ga. State U., 1968. Negotiator Trust Co. Bank, Atlanta, 1962-89, ret., 1989. Mem. Nat. Women's C. of C. (pres. 1987-88), Atlanta Women's C. of C. (dir. 1965-66, pres. Fidelis SS class 1962-63), Nat. Am. Legion Aux. (so. divsn. chmn. aux. Americanism 1995-96, so. divsn. chmn. aux. emergency fund 1996-97, cmty. svc. com.), Am. Legion Aux. (pres. 5th dist. 1986-87, Ga. state chaplain 1989-90, state historian 1991-92, state 2d v.p. 1992-93, 1st v.p. 1993-94, pres. 1994-95, Americanism chmn. so. divsn. 1995-95, chmn. emergency fund 1996-97, mem. cmty. svc. com. 1997-98, nat. historian 1999-00, v. chmn. nat. poppy com. 2000-01), Order Ea. Star (worthy matron 1951-52). Democrat. Home and Office: 6243 Spout Springs Rd Flowery Branch GA 30542-5032

MONSEN, ELAINE RANKER, nutritionist, educator, editor; b. Oakland, Calif., June 6, 1935; d. Emery R. and Irene Stewart (Thorley) Ranker; m. Raymond Joseph Monsen, Jr., Jan. 21, 1959; 1 dau., Maren Ranker. BA, U. Utah, 1956; MS (Mead Johnson grad. scholar), U. Calif., Berkeley, 1959, PhD (NSF fellow), 1961; postgrad. NSF sci. faculty fellow, Harvard U., 1968-69. Dietetic intern Mass. Gen. Hosp., Boston, 1956-57; asst. prof. nutrition, lectr. biochemistry Brigham Young U., Provo, Utah, 1960-63; mem. faculty U. Wash., 1963—, prof. nutrition and medicine, 1984—, prof. nutrition, adj. prof. medicine, 1976-84, chmn. div. human nutrition, dietetics and foods, 1977-82, dir. grad. nutritional scis. program, 1994-99, mem. Council of Coll. Arts and Scis., 1974-78, mem. U. Wash. Press com., 1981—; chmn. Nutrition Studies Commn., 1969-83. Vis. scholar Stanford U., 1971-72; mem. sci. adv. com. food fortification Pan-Am. Health Orgn., São Paulo, Brazil, 1972; tng. grant coordinator NIH, 1976-97. Editor-in-chief Jour. Am. Dietetic Assn., 1983-2003; Editor Emeritus, Jour. Am. Dietetic Assn., 2003—; mem. editorial bd. Coun. Biology Editors, 1992-96; author rsch. papers on lipid metabolism, iron absorption. Bd. dirs. A Contemporary Theatre, Seattle, 1969-72; trustee, bd. dirs. Seattle Found., 1978-95, vice chmn., 1987-91, chmn., 1991-93; pres. Seattle bd. Santa Fe Chamber Music Festival, 1984-85; mem. Puget Sound Blood Ctr. Bd., 1996-99. Grantee Nutrition Found., 1965-68, Agrl. Rsch. Svc., 1969-84; recipient Disting. Alumnus award U. Utah, F. Fischer Meml. Nutrition Lectr. award, 1988, L.F. Cooper Meml. Lectr. award, 1991, L. Hatch Meml. Lectr. award, 1992, Goble Lectr. award Purdue U., 1997. Fellow: Am. Soc. Clin. Nutrition (sec. 1987—90), Am. Inst. Nutrition; mem.: Wash. Heart Assn. (nutrition coun. 1973—76), Am. Soc. Parenteral and Enteral Nutrition, Soc. Nutriton Edn., Am. Dietetic Assn. Office: U Wash PO Box 353410 Seattle WA 98195-3410

MONSON, ANGELA ZOE, state legislator; b. Oklahoma City, July 31, 1955; d. Epron Provo Monson. BS, Oklahoma City U., 1976; MPA, U. Okla., 1987. Probation and parole officer Okla. Dept. Corrections, 1976-77; cir. riding city mgr. East Ctrl. Rural Munic Area Coun., 1980-81; fiscal analyst Okla. State Legislature, 1981-84; sales rep. The Equitable, Oklahoma City, 1985-86; exec. dir. Okla. Health Care Project, 1986-90; mem. Okla. Ho. of Reps., 1990—. Mem. Okla. adv. com. U.S. Commn. on Civil Rights, 1984-89. Mem. editl. bd. Primary Care News. Past pres. Okla. chpt. NAACP; past bd. pres. Mary Mahoney Meml. Health Ctr., Neighborhood Svcs. Orgn., Tolliver Alt. Care Ctr.; nat. bd. dirs. State Alliance for Universal Health Care; mem. policy adv. bd. Ctr. for Health Care Access & Reform. Recipient Svc. to Achievement award Black Liberated Arts Ctr., 1981, Outstanding Achievement award Cmty. Health Ctrs. Inc., 1988. Mem. AAUW. Democrat. Baptist. Home: 720 NE 42nd St Oklahoma City OK 73105-7004 Office: Okla Senate State Capitol Oklahoma City OK 73105

MONSON, DIANNE LYNN, literacy educator; b. Minot, ND, Nov. 24, 1934; d. Albert Rachie and Iona Cordelia (Kirk) M. BS, U. Minn., 1956, MA, 1962, PhD, 1966. Tchr. Rochester (Minn.) Pub. Schs., 1956-59, U.S. Dept. Def., Schweinfurt, West Germany, 1959-61, St. Louis Park (Minn.) Schs., 1961-62; instr. U. Minn., Mpls., 1962-66; prof. U. Wash., Seattle, 1966-82; prof. literacy edn. U. Minn., Mpls., 1982-97, prof. emeritus, 1997—. Chmn. curriculum and instrn. U. Minn., 1986—89. Co-author: Scott Foresman Reading, 2000, New Horizons in the Language Arts, 1972, Children and Books, 6th edit., 1981, Experiencing Children's Literature, 1984, (monograph) Research in Children's Literature, 1976, Language Arts: Teaching and Learning Effective Use of Language, 1988, Reading Together: Helping Children Get A Good Start With Reading, 1991; assoc. editor: Dictionary of Literacy, 1995. Recipient Outstanding Educator award U. Minn. Alumni Assn., 1983, Alumni Faculty award U. Minn. Alumni Assn., 1991. Fellow Nat. Conf. Rsch. in English (pres. 1990-91); mem. ALA, Nat. Coun. Tchrs. English (exec. com. 1979-81), Internat. Reading Assn. (dir. 1980-83, Arbuthnot award 1993, Reading Hall of Fame 1997), U.S. Bd. Books for Young People (pres. 1988-90). Lutheran. Home: 515 S Lexington Pkwy # 604 Saint Paul MN 55116 Business E-Mail: monso001@tc.umn.edu.

MONTAGUE, DEBORAH MARIE, elementary school educator, music educator, consultant; b. Cin., July 2, 1953; d. Charles Jay and June Marie Henry; m. Steven A. Montague, Aug. 17, 1979; children: Sarah, Benjamin. BA in Music Edn., Ctrl. Wash. U., 1974; MA in Music Edn., U. Wash. Music educator grades 3-6 Northshore Sch. Dist., Bothell, Wash., 1974—79; music educator grades 5-9 Sumner (Wash.) Sch. Dist., 1979—88; freelance music educator/cons. Alta Loma, Calif., 1988—90; music educator grades 5-9 Northshore Sch. Dist., Kenmore, Wash., 1990—. Dist. honor band chair Northshore Sch. Dist., Bothell, 1990—; member-at-large Cascade Youth Orch. Symphony, Bothell, 1999—; performer N.W. Music Educator's Conf., 1993, 2001, 03, Nat. Music Educator's Conf., 2002. Mem.: NEA, West Ctrl. Music Educators Nat. Conf. (band rep. 1984—85), Music Educators Nat. Conf. Lutheran. Office: Kenmore Jr High 20323 66 Ave NE Kenmore WA 98028

MONTANARELLI, LISA, writer, researcher; d. Stephen and Jane Warrington Carr Montanarelli. BA summa cum laude, Yale U., 1989; PhD, U. Calif., 1998. Author: The First Year-Hepatitis C: An Essential Guide for the Newly Diagnosed, Forgotten Faces: A Window into Our Immigrant Past; contbr. articles to profl. jours. and mags. Mellon Dissertation fellow, Andrew Mellon Found., 1993—94, Regents-Intern fellow, U. Calif. Berkeley, 1989—93. Mem.: Phi Beta Kappa. Mailing: 593 Vanderbilt Ave #143 Brooklyn NY 11238 E-mail: surveyelf@yahoo.com.

MONTANE, FRAN, poet, film producer; b. Manhasset, N.Y., Aug. 1966; d. John Montagnino and Christine Miller. BFA in Comm. Arts summa cum laude, NY Inst. Tech., 1990. Program coord. N.Y. Open Ctr., N.Y.C., 1990—92; asst. dir. Fireball Films, N.Y.C., 1994; internat. segment prodr. In the Life Media, N.Y.C., 1995; exptl. film/video dir. Sarasvati Prodns. N.Y.C., 1996. Author: (collected poems) At the Grave's Mouth, 2001; prodr.: (stage play/video) The Owl Answers by Adrienne Kennedy, 1997. Scholar, U.S. Achievement Acad., 1987. Avocations: working out, reading, travel. Home: 502 Plandome Rd Manhasset NY 11030 Office: 502 Plandome Rd Manhasset NY 11030 Personal E-mail: sarasva@aol.com. E-mail: sarasva@aol.com.

MONTANEZ, CINDY, state representative; Student, UCLA. Legis. aide Former Councilmember Richare Alarcon; mem. Calif. Assembly, 2002—. Mem. City Coun., San Fernando, 1999—2001; mayor San Fernando, Calif., 2001—02. Democrat. Office: PO Box 942849 Rm 5144 Sacramento CA 94249 Address: 11541 Laurel Canyon Blvd Ste C Mission Hills CA 91345

MONTBERTRAND, LOIS SHINER, lawyer; b. Lakewood, N.J. d. Robert Lamont and Anne Shiner; children: Carine Montbertrand, Michelle Montbertrand; m. Alan Paul Poland, Feb. 18, 1996. Grad., Mt. Sinai Hosp. Sch. Nursing, N.Y.C.; diploma Prof. Francais a l'Etranger, U. Aix-Marseilles, France; BA, Wellesley Coll.; JD, Yale U., 1985. Bar: Conn. 1985, Wis. 1991, W.Va. 1997; RN, N.Y., Pa., Conn., Wis. Assoc. Wiggin & Dana, New Haven, 1985-87, Susman, Duffy & Segaloff, New Haven, 1988-89; atty. Aetna, Hartford, Conn., 1989-90; pvt. practice, Madison, Wis., 1990-91; gen. counsel Office Sec. of State, State of Wis., Madison, 1992-96, UCC counsel dept. fin. instns., 1996-98, on leave, 1998—. Supervising atty. Coll. Law, W.Va. U., 1997-2000. Mem. Wis. Bar Assn., W.Va. Bar Assn.

MONTE, BONNIE J. performing arts company executive, director, educator; b. Stamford, Conn., Nov. 27, 1954; d. Eugene N. and Ruth M. (Thompson) M. BA, Bethany Coll., 1976; diploma, Hartman Conservatory, Stamford, 1978. Assoc. artistic dir. Williamstown (Mass.) Theatre Festival, 1981-89; casting dir. Manhattan Theatre Club, N.Y.C., 1989-90; artistic dir. The Shakespeare Theatre of NJ, Madison, 1990—. Mem. faculty Drew U., 1991-96; guest artist-in-residence U. Notre Dame, The New Sch.-Eugene Lang. Coll., U. S.C. Recipient Nat. Soc. of Arts and Letters award, N.J., 1997, Alumni Achievement award for arts mgmt. Bethany Coll., 1999; grantee Lotte Crabtree Found., Boston, 1977. Democrat. Avocations: cycling, archery, writing, travel. Office: Shakespeare Theatre NJ 36 Madison Ave Madison NJ 07940-1434

MONTECEL, MARIA ROBLEDO (CUCA ROBLEDO MONTECEL), educational association administrator; b. Laredo, Tex., Jan. 14, 1953; d. Ismael and Paula (Benavides) Robledo; m. Lucas Montecel, Aug. 18, 1979; children: Ismael Gavino, Xavier Mario. BSSW magna cum laude, Our Lady of Lake U., 1972; MEd, Antioch U., 1975; PhD in Urban Edn., U. Wis., 1985. Rsch. asst. D.C. Devel. Assocs., Inc., San Antonio, 1973-75; test designer Dissemination and Assessment Ctr. for Bilingual Edn. U. Tex., San Antonio, 1975-76; grad. rsch. asst. office rsch. Sch. Edn. U. Wis., Milw., 1980-81, program dir. Midwest NODAC dept. cultural founds. Sch. Edn., 1985; evaluator Ctr. for Mgmt. Innovation in Multicultural Edn. Intercultural Devel. Rsch. Assn., San Antonio, 1976-77, dir. bilingual edn. cost analysis project, 1977-78, dir. divsn. rsch., devel. and evalutation, 1978-80, rsch. specialist, 1982-85, dir. Ctr. for Prevention and Recovery Dropouts, 1985-88, 90-92, dir. tng. and tech. assistance, 1988-89, dir. valued youth program, 1988-90, dep. dir., 1992, exec. dir., 1992—. Trustee Our Lady of Lake U. Mem. editorial bd. Tex. Rschr.; contbr. articles to profl. jours. Vol. advocate Alamo Area Rape Crisis Ctr.; mem. rsch. com. Hispanas Unidas; participant Leadership Tex. '85; invited mem. Tex. State Task Force Dropout Prevention; chmn. lifelong learning coun. San Antonio 2000; cons. edn. and immigrant students Mellon Found.; bd. dirs. Mex.-Am. Solidarity Found.; founding bd. dirs. CIVICUS World Alliance Citizen Participation; bd. dirs. community edn. leadership program Mott Found.; mem. nat. adv. coun. Race and Ethnic Studies Inst., Tex. A & M; mem. ednl. review bd. Tex. Ctr. Ednl. Rsch.; mem. nat. adv. bd. ERIC/CRESS, 1994. Recipient High Achievement Commendation, Antioch Coll., 1975, Peter F. Drucker award Coca-Cola Valued Youth Program; Women and Minority Rsch. fellow Nat. Inst. Edn., 1979, Title VII Doctoral fellow U. Wis., 1980-82; named to Top 100 Hispanic Influential, Hispanic Bus., 1997. Mem. Am. Edn. Rsch. Assn., Nat. Assn. Bilingual Edn., Nat. Dropout Prevention Network (charter), Alphi Chi. Roman Catholic. Avocations: reading, writing, fishing, golf. Office: Intercultural Devel Rsch Assn 5835 Callaghan Rd Ste 350 San Antonio TX 78228-1125

MONTEFERRANTE, JUDITH CATHERINE, cardiologist; b. N.Y., Jan. 27, 1949; d. Stanley and Monica (Vinckus) Sosaris; m. Ronald J. Monteferrante (div.); 1 child, Jason Paul ; m. Roger E. Salisbury, Mar. 3, 1990. BS, Adelphi U., Garden City, 1970; MS, SUNY, Buffalo, 1973; MD, Mt. Sinai, N.Y.C., 1978. Diplomate Cert. Coun. Nuc. Cardiology. Attending N.Y. Med. Coll., Valhalla, NY, 1983—; pvt. practice Primary Care and Cardiovasc. Assocs., divsn. Cardiology Cons. Westchester, White Plains, NY, 1994—. Mem. bd. White Plains Med. Ctr., 1997—2000; spkr. on women and heart disease. Contbr. articles to profl. jours. Past trustee Coll. Mt. St. Vincent, N.Y.C. Fellow: ACP, Am. Heart Assn. (past. pres. 1996—98), Am. Coll. Cardiology (councilor N.Y. state chpt.); mem.: Am. Soc. Nuc. Cardiology. Office: 15 N Broadway White Plains NY 10601-2225 Office Phone: 914-428-6000.

MONTEIRO, LOIS ANN, medical science educator; b. Central Falls, R.I., Mar. 22, 1934; d. William Henry and Martha Mae (Leach) Hodgins; m. George Monteiro, Aug. 14, 1958 (div. Feb. 1992); children: Katherine, Stephen, Emily. RN, Roger Williams Hosp., Providence, 1954; BA, Brown U., k1958, PhD, 1970; MS, Boston U., 1960. Asst. prof. Boston U., 1960-65, Brown U., Providence, R.I., 1971-77, assoc. prof., 1978-82, prof., 1983—, chmn. dept., 1985—, assoc. dean medicine, 1991—. Vis. prof. U. Va., 1990, U. Miss., 2002; bd. dirs. Harvard Cmty. Health Plan, 1990-95, Harvard Pilgrim Health Care Plan, New Eng., 1995—. Author: Montoring Health Status, 1976, Cardiac Rehabilitation, 1980; contbr. articles to profl. jours. Mem. Commn. State of R.I., Providence, 1989—. NSF grantee, 1969, Robert W. Johnson Found. grantee, Princeton, N.J., 1983, NIH grantee, 1987; Bunting Inst. fellow, Cambridge, Mass., 1981, Congrl. fellow House Vets. Affairs Commn., 1998; recipient Am. Sociol. Assn. Spivack award, 1998. Mem. Am. Sociol. Assn., R.I. State Nurses Assn. (pres. 1974-76), Women in Medicine/Assn. Am. Med. Colls. Democrat. Presbyterian. Avocation: collecting books on nursing history. Office: Brown U Dept Med Sci PO Box G-a413 Providence RI 02912-0001 E-mail: lois_monteiro@brown.edu.

MONTEIRO, PATRICIA M. clinical social worker; BSW, Western New Eng. Coll., Springfield, Mass., 1982; MSW, R.I. Coll., 1988. Cert. HIV counselor. Sr. social worker Dept. Social Svcs., New Bedford, 1982-89, clin. supr. social workers Cape Cod and Islands, 1989-90, clin. supr. social workders Fall River, 1990-94; med. social worker Staff Builders, New Bedford, 1997-98; clin. social worker Greater New Bedford Cmty. Health Ctr., 1998—2003; self-employed ct. investigator, guardian ad litem juvenile and probate cts., Bristol County, Mass., 1994—2003; pvt. practice social worker, 2002—. Mem. Mass. Coun. on Aging, 1996—99, ad hoc com. responsible for sr. ctr., 1995, New Bedford Adolescent Task Force, 1988—89; apptd. legal guardian for elderly in need Bristol County Probate Ct., 2002—. Daisy leader Girl Scouts U.S., 2000—01, Brownie leader, 2001—02; co-pres. PTA com. Mass., 2003—; founder, co-leader Drama Club Ctr. Sch., Mattaprisett, 2002—. Recipient Pride in Performance Recognition award Commr. Mass. Dept. Social Svc., 1992. Mem. NASW, Portuguese-Am. Leadership Coun. U.S.A. Avocations: reading, dinner parties, gardening, aerobics, travel. Office: PO Box 5322 New Bedford MA 02742-5322

MONTELEONE, PATRICIA, dean; MD, St. Louis U., 1961. Dean St. Louis U. Sch. Medicine, 1994—. Office: St Louis U Sch Medicine 1402 S Grand Blvd Saint Louis MO 63104-1004

MONTEVERDE, FRANCES ELAINE, social sciences educator; b. Connellsville, Pa., Feb. 19, 1938; d. Eugene Samuel and Alma Ruth Frankhouser; m. Eduardo Andres Montoverde; children: Dani Elaine, Susana Raquel. BS in Edn., Ind. U. of Pa., 1969; student in Latin Am. History, U. N.Mex., 1959—62; student in Psychology, U. Ams., 1975—79; MA, U. Ala., 1983; PhD, U. Tex., 1996. Lic. tchr. Tex., N.Mex. From tchr. to prin. The Am. Sch. Found., Mex. City, Mexico, 1974—93, prin. HS, 1993—94; tchg. asst. U. Tex., Austin, Tex., 1989—93, asst. instr., 1994—96, program coord., 2000—; asst. prof. Hanover (Ind.) Coll., 1996—99; ind. scholar Madison, Ind., 1999—2000. Mem. scholarship com. The Am. Sch. Found., 1984—89, 1993—94; mem. steering com. So. Assn. Colls. and Schs., Mex. City, 1979, 88. Editor: Qualitative Studies in Edn., 1995—96; mem. editl. bd.: Jour. Curriculum and Supr., 1998—2000; co-author: Women in Education: Onyx Dictionary of Educators, 1990, Current Mexican History: Issues in Social Education, 1999; contbr. articles to profl. jours. Bd. dirs. the Unitarian Universalist Fellowship, Mexico City, 1967—70. Mem.: Nat. Coun. Social Studies, So. Poverty Law Ctr., Am. Ednl. Rsch. Assn., Assn. Supr. and Curriculum Studies, Phi Kappa Phi, Kappa Delta Pi (treas. 1991—93). Avocations: writing, music, history, international cuisine. Home: 5935 Kevin Kelly Place Austin TX 78727 Office: The Univ Texas Coll Education University Station 1 Austin TX 78712-1294

MONTGOMERY, ANN D. federal judge, educator; b. Litchfield, Minn., May 9, 1949; m. Theodore Smetak; 2 children; 1 stepchild. BS, U. Kans., 1971; JD, U. Minn., 1974. Bar: Minn. 1974, U.S. Dist. Ct. Minn., U.S. Ct. Appeals (8th cir.), U.S. Supreme Ct. Law clk. D.C. Ct. Appeals, Washington, 1974-75; asst. U.S. atty. Dist. Minn., Mpls., 1976-83; mcpl. judge Hennepin County, 1983-85; judge Hennepin County Dist. Ct., 1985-94, U.S. Magistrate Ct., 1994-96; federal judge U.S. Dist. Ct., Mpls., 1996—. Adj. prof. U. Minn. Law Sch., Mpls., 1988—; steering com. mem., dir. criminal divsn. Minn. Jud. Coll., 1990-94. Recipient Trial Judge of Yr. award Am. Bd. Trial Advocates, 1996. Mem. FBA, Minn. Dist. Judges Assn., Minn. Bar Assn., Minn. Women Lawyers (Myra Bradwell award 2000), Hennepin County Bar Assn. (Professionalism award 1993). Office: US Dist Ct 300 S 4th St Minneapolis MN 55415-1320 Fax: 612-664-5097. E-mail: admontgomery@mnd.uscourts.gov.

MONTGOMERY, BETTY DEE, state auditor, former state attorney general, former state legislator; b. Apr. 3, 1948; BA, Bowling Green State U.; JD, Coll. Law U. Toledo, 1976. Former criminal clk. Lucas County Common Pleas Ct.; former asst. pros. atty. Wood County, Ohio, 1977—78, former pros. atty., 1980—88, City of Perrysburg, Ohio, 1978—81; former mem. Ohio Senate Dist. w, 1988—95; former atty. gen. State of Ohio, Columbus, 1994—2002, auditor, 2002—. Former mem. Econ. Devel. Tech. & Aerospace, Agr. & Ways & Means Com.; former vice-chmn. Judiciary Com. Mem. bd. dirs. Ohio Sch. Bd. Atty. Assn. Recipient Women of Achievement award, Toledo Women in Comms., 1984, Govt. Leaders Against Drunk Drivers, MADD, 1990, Senator of the Year, Ohio Hospice Assn., 1991, Disting. Svc. award, Ohio State Bar Assn., 1992, Ohio Women Hall of Fame award, 1996, Public Svc. award, Ohio Assn. of Big Brothers/Big Sisters, 1999, Advocacy award, Ohio Soc. Healthcare Consumer Advocacy, 1999, Child Adv. of the Year, Ohio Ct. Appointed Spl. Advs./Guardian Ad Litem Assn., 1999, Toledo YWCA Milestones award, Women in Govt., 2001, Presdl. award for Pro Bono Svc., The Ohio Legal Assistance Found., 2002, ABA Pro Bono award, to the Office of the Atty. Gen., 2002, Disting. Alumnus award, Bowling Green State Univ., 2003. Mem.: Ohio Prosecuting Atty. Assn. (mem. 1984), Legis. Com., Internat. Prosecutors Assn., Wood County Bar Assn., Alternative Edn. Adv. Com. (former chmn.), Wood County Child Abuse & Neglect Adv. Bd. (former vice-chmn., chmn.), Sexual Abuse Prevention Project, Wood County Sch. (mem. 1981—), Bowling Green C. of C. Republican. Office: Auditor of State 88 E Broad St 5th Fl Columbus OH 43215

MONTGOMERY, CHRISTINA LYNN, music educator; b. Oil City, Pa., July 30, 1951; d. Arthur Robert Montgomery and Joanne Guy (Heffernan) Wilson; children: Pamela Fellner, Michelle Kunkel. BSE in Music Edn., Clarion U., 1987; M in Secondary Guidance, Edinboro U., 1994. Cert. in music edn. Pa., 1993. Music educator Warren (Pa.) County Sch. Dist., 1988—. Named Tchr. of Yr., Philomel Club, 1993. Mem.: Warren County Educators Assn., Pa. Music Educators Assn. (exec. bd., CI/mid. sch. 2000—), Music Educators Nat. Conf. Avocations: reading, fishing, cooking, carpentry. Home: RD 1 Box 219H Youngsville PA 16371 Office: Youngsville Mid/Sr High Sch 227 College St Youngsville PA 16371

MONTGOMERY, DENISE KAREN, nurse; b. N.Y.C., Dec. 23, 1951; d. Thomas Cornell and Dorothy Marie (Castine) Simons; m. Timothy Bruce Montgomery, July 19, 1974 (div. Feb. 1981); m. Joseph Samuel Montgomery, Aug. 20, 1983. A in Nursing, San Jacinto Coll., 1971. RN, Tex. Charge nurse Aarons Womens Clinic, Houston, 1977; rsch. asst. dept. ob-gyn. Baylor Coll. Medicine, Houston, 1977-81, nursing supr., 1979-81, program coord. population control program, 1979-81; nurse Dr. Eric J. Haufrect, Houston, 1982-83; office mgr., supr. Dr. Samuel Law, Houston, 1983-84, Dr. J.S. Montgomery III, 1987—. Contbr. articles to profl. jours. Recipient Disting. Pub. Svc. award Am. Heart Assn., 1976; numerous rsch. grants. Mem. Nat. Assn. Coll. Ob-Gyn. Republican. Roman Catholic. Home: 8202 N Tahoe Dr Houston TX 77040-1256 Office Phone: 281-955-5300. E-mail: DenMnt@aol.com.

MONTGOMERY, DENISE LYNNE, librarian, researcher; b. Greenfield, Ind., Aug. 1, 1953; d. Herbert Walter and Virginia Lou Montgomery. AB, Sweet Briar Coll., 1975; MSLS, Fla. State U., 1981. Readers' svcs. libr. St. Leo Coll., St. Leo, Fla., 1983; assoc. prof., head of interlibr. loan Valdosta State U., Valdosta, Ga., 1984—. Contbr. articles to profl. jours. including Library Trends, Georgia Historical Quarterly, Jour. Interlibrary Loan and Information Supply; author (and webmaster): (web site) Princess Diana Shopping Arcade http://www.geocities.com/highgrove.geo/, 1999—; webmaster (web site) Princess Diana Shopping Arcade http://www.geocities.com/highgrove.geo/, 1999. Mem.: ALA (fee-based svcs. com. 2001—03, svcs. to adults com. 2003—), Ga. Libr. Assn. (chmn. interlibrary loan round table 1992—93). Liberal. Unitarian Universalist. Office: Odum Libr Valdosta State U 1500 N Patterson St Valdosta GA 31698 Office Phone: 229-333-5867.

MONTGOMERY, HELEN JANET, social worker; b. Washington, D.C., Jan. 17, 1972; d. G. Paul Montgomery, Jr. and Ilene J. (Nowicki) Montgomery; life ptnr. David L. McCarty, Jr.. BA, Kalamazoo Coll., 1993; MSW, Loyola U., Chgo., 2001; Advanced Cert. in Alcoholism and Substance Abuse Counseling, Harold Washington Coll., Chgo., 2002. LSW Ill., 2001. Adminstrv. asst. Northwestern Med. Faculty Found. Dept. Psychiatry, Chgo., 1997—99; rsch. asst. Northwestern U. Dept. of Psychiatry, Chgo., 1999—2001; social worker Aurora Chgo. Lakeshore Hosp., Chgo., 2001—. Crisis counselor / med. adv. Rape Victim Advocates, Chgo., 1993—2004. Contbr. articles to profl. jours. (Jimmy and Dorothy Fuerst Social Policy Paper award, 2001). Bd. mem. Phandemonium, Inc., Chgo., 2001—04. Mem.: NASW, Ill. Soc. for Clin. Social Work, Alpha Sigma Nu. Avocations: reading, pilates, theater, feminist activism.

MONTGOMERY, JUNE C. musician, composer; b. Columbia, S.C., Dec. 12, 1931; d. Joseph Watts Conyers and Justina Wylding; m. Edwin Fleming Montgomery, Dec. 28, 1954; children: Edwin Fleming III, Joseph Watts, James Leighton. BA in Piano with honors, Fla. State U., 1954; BS, U. Fla., 1968. Pvt. piano tchr., Jasper, Fla., 1954—63, Lake City, Fla., 1975—93; music tchr. Orange Park (Fla.) Elem., 1968—74; composer, author Music Encounters, Lake City, 1984—89, David C. Glover Method CPP/Belwin, Miami, Fla., 1988—90, Alfred Pub. Co., Van Nuys, Calif., 1990—. Carilloneur Stephen Foster Meml., White Springs, Fla., 1954—. Author, composer: FUNdamental Musicianship Skills, 1994, Theory Through the Year, 1995, author, composer with M. Mier: Musical Concepts, 1997, author, composer with M. Hinson: Meet the Great Composers, 1995, author, composer: Meet the Great Composers Repertoire Books, 1997, Stories of the Great Composers, 2000, Piano Camp, 1999, Musical Fantasies, 2001, Stories of the Great Hymns, 2002. Named Outstanding Elem. Tchr. Am., Orange Park, 1973. Mem.: Music Tchrs. Nat. Assn., Am. Coll. Musicians, Delta Kappa Gamma. Democrat. Presbyterian. Avocations: crafts, gardening. Home: Rt 8 Box 824 Lake City FL 32055

MONTGOMERY, KATHLEEN RAE, counselor; b. Bloomington, Ind., Aug. 15, 1950; d. Raymond Hershel and Helen Kathleen (Trent) Montgomery; m. Steven Myers, Oct. 2, 1970; children: Jason Paul, Lisa Dawn, Stephanie Kathleen. AS in Psychology, Vincennes U., 1970; BS in Social Svcs., Milligan Coll., 1974; MS in Counseling, Ind. U., 1992. Lic. school counselor, mental health counselor. Police dispatcher Ind. State Police, Bloomington, Ind., 1974-76; counselor Cookson Hills Christian Ministries, Kansas, Okla., 1976-78; social worker Health Svcs. Bur., Bloomington, 1982-88; tng. asst. The Associated Group, Indpls., 1990-91; ops. mgr. drug abuse prevention workshops Ind. U., Bloomington, 1991-92; outreach coord., counselor, testing coord. gender equity Ivy Tech. State Coll., Bloomington, 1992-99; counselor N. Putnam H.S., Roachdale, IN, 1999—. Counselor Upward Bound program, Vincennes, Ind., 1970; crisis counselor Matrix Lifeline, 1978-79; field instr. Ind. U. BSW program, Bloomington, 1983-88; support group leader Sherwood Oaks Christian Ch., 1991-92. Mem. adv. bd. Expectant Mother's Program, Bloomington, 1984-86, Parent's Group, Ellettsville, Ind., 1986-88, adv. bd. IMPACT, 1992-93; mem. retention com. Ivy Tech. Coll., 1993-98. Mem. AAUW, Ind. Coll. Counseling Assn., Ind. Counseling Assn., Ind. School Counselors Assn., Ind. Academic Advisors Network, Ind. Higher Edn. Assoc. for Disabilities. Republican. Avocations: biking, hiking, crafts. Home: 627 Bayberry Ct W Bloomington IN 47401-4673

MONTGOMERY, LINDA STROUPE, county official; b. Havaco, W.Va., Feb. 12, 1943; d. James Allen Stroupe and Opal Marie (Daugherty) Leif; m. James R. Sutliff, Aug. 9, 1960 (div. Feb. 1982); children: Mark S., Debra Lynn, Amy Sutliff Sweckard; m. Paul L. Montgomery, Apr. 23, 1983. Student, S.W. Mo. State U., 1979-93. Sec. Va. Poly. Inst., Blacksburg, 1961-64; office mgr., paralegal William H. Wendt, Springfield, Mo., 1973-84; office adminstr. Greene County Commn., Springfield, 1984-94; recorder of deeds Greene County, Springfield, 1995—. Mem. legis. com. Local Area Govt. Employees Retirement Sys., State of Mo., 1993—; dist. dir. Mo. Assn. Counties, 1997—. Bd. dirs. Springfield-Greene County Libr. Dist., 1991-97, also past pres.; committeewoman, legis. chmn. Greene County Rep. Ctrl. Com., 1987— Mem. Internat. Assn. Clks., Recorders, Election Ofcls. and Treas., Recorder's Assn. Mo., Springfield Area C. of C., Grand Order Pachyderms (past pres.), Phi Kappa Phi. Methodist. Avocations: reading, needlework, antiques. Home: 5209 S Shari Ln Rogersville MO 65742-9474 Office: Greene County Govt Recorder of Deeds 940 N Boonville Ave Springfield MO 65802-3802 Office Phone: 417-868-4068. E-mail: lmontgomery@gkeenecountymo.org.

MONTGOMERY, M. DARLENE, secondary education educator, English language educator; b. Muskogee, Okla., May 25, 1949; d. William Perry and Nemie Anne (Emery) Dunn; m. Rex Jay Montgomery, June 5, 1971; children: Emory Anne Lobb, April Marie. BA, Northeastern State U., 1971; M in Liberal Studies, U. Okla., 1994. Tchg. cert., Ark., Va., Okla. Journalism, speech, drama and English tchr. Virginia Beach (Va.) Pub. Schs., 1971-74; co-owner Taylor Rental Ctr., Ft. Smith, Ark., 1975-86; English tchr. Ft. Smith Pub. Sch., 1987—. Adj. English prof. Westark C.C., Ft. Smith, 1994-98. Editor (assn. newspaper) The Sounding Board, 1993-99. Choir/video technician Harvest Time Tabernacle, Ft. Smith, 1983-86. Recipient Lifetime PTA award Kimmons Jr. High, Ft. Smith, 1994, 1st place in state for assn. reporting Ark. Edn. Assn., Little Rock, 1996, 97. Mem. Ft. Smith Classroom Tchrs. Assn. (pres., 2000-02, faculty rep. 1992-93, bd. mem. 1993-99, publs. sec./editor 1993-99), Northside PTA, Phi Delta Kappa, Alpha Delta Kappa, Alpha Chi, Rho Theta. Avocations: reading, writing essays and short stories. Home: 3205 S 98th St Fort Smith AR 72903-5714 Office: Ft Smith Pub Schs 2301 N B St Fort Smith AR 72901-3433

MONTGOMERY, MARILYN RUTH, elementary school educator, consultant; d. William Maurice and Elsie Spencer Ely; children: Courtney Dawn, Erin Elizabeth. BA in Elem. Edn., Morehead State U., 1999, M in Elem. Sch. Counseling, M in Leadership K-12, Morehead State U. Cert. elem. tchr. Dept. Edn. Ky., 1989, elem. sch. counselor Dept. Edn. Ky., 1993, prin. grades K-12 Dept. Edn. Ky., 1999. Instrnl. asst. Magoffin Bd. Edn., Salyersville, Ky., 1973—78; elem. edn. tchr. Mid. Fork Elem., Salyersville, 1989—99, elem. sch. prin., 1999—2003; highly skilled educator Ky. Dept. Edn., Frankfort, 2003—. Prin. mentor Ky. Dept. Edn., Frankfort, 2003—. Recipient Prin. of Excellence award, Ky. Dept. Edn., 2001. Mem.: Ky. Leadership Acad. Avocations: drawing, decorating, dance, writing. Personal E-mail: marilyn08@alltel.net.

MONTGOMERY, PAULA KAY, publisher; b. Omaha, Sept. 23, 1946; d. Floyd Woodrow and Adelyn Ann (Peterson) M. BA in English, Fla. State U., 1967, MLS in Libr. Sci., 1968; PhD in Reading Edn., 1989. Sch. libr. Montgomery County Pub. Sch., Rockville, Md., 1969-72, libr. specialist, 1972-79; chief sch. libr. Md. State Dept. Edn., Balt., 1979-88; pub. Crinkles Children's Mag./Sch. Libr. Media Activities Monthly, Balt., 1984—. Del. Gov.'s Conf. on Librs., Balt., 1990. Author: Teaching Library Media Skills, 1983, Thematic Approaches to Literature, 1991, Subject Approaches to Literature, 1991, Subject Approaches to Literature, 1991, Literary Forms Approach to Literature, 1995, The Bookmark Book, 1995; editor: (book series) Library Media Skills, 1982—. Mem. ALA, Nat. Assn. State Ednl. Media Profls. (pres. 1987), Assn. Edn. Communication and Tech. Lutheran. Office: 17 E Henrietta St Baltimore MD 21230-3910 E-mail: paulam@crinkles.com.

MONTGOMERY, VELMANETTE, state senator; b. Tex. Student, U. Ghana; LLD (hon.), St. Joseph's Coll., 1991. Mem. N.Y.C. Dist. 13 Sch. Bd., 1977-80, pres., from 1977; former co-dir. advocacy group Child Care Inc.; mem. N.Y. Senate, Albany, 1984—. Mem. child care, consumer protection, health, fin. and housing, mental hygiene coms. Fellow Inst. Ednl. Leadership, 1981, Revson Found., 1984. Democrat. Office: 70 Lafayette Ave Brooklyn NY 11217-1520 also: NY State Senate 306 Legislative Office Bldg Albany NY 12247

MONTI, RENA MARIE, music educator; b. Portland, Maine, Apr. 22, 1958; d. Thomas James and Camille Massaro Caulfield; m. Mark Anthony Monti, Sept. 25, 1982; children: Kathryn Anne, Benjamin Caulfield, Emily Grace. MusB in Music Edn., SUNY, Fredonia, 1980; MusM in Opera and Voice Performance, U. Hartford, 1982. Cert. tchr. music K-12 N.Y., 2003. Music tchr. Webster Schroeder H.S., 1999—, Webster (NY) Ctrl. Schs., 1999—. Profl. classical singer. Worship leader Browncroft Cmty. Ch., Penfield, NY. Mem.: N.Y. State Sch. Music Assn. (assoc.; adjudicator 2003), Nat. Assn. Teachers of Singing (assoc.), Music Educators Nat. Conf. (assoc.). Republican. Avocations: scuba diving, gardening, cooking. Home: 35 Random Knolls Dr Penfield NY 14526-1958 Personal E-mail: mmonti1@rochester.rr.com. E-mail: rena_monti@penfield.monroe.edu.

MONTOYA, LEIALA, assistant principal; d. Michael J. and Virginia B. Chong; m. Michael S. Montoya, Aug. 31, 1974 (dec. Dec. 24, 1992); 1 child, Aaron. AA, Modesto (Calif.) Jr. Coll., 1963; BA, Calif. State U., Fresno, 1994; MEdn., Calif. State U., San Bernardino, 1996; postgrad. in EdD program, U. So. Calif., L.A., 1996—. Spl. edn. tchr. Cardozo Sch., Riverbank, Calif., 1971—74, Palm View Sch., Coachella, Calif., 1997—2001; asst. prin. John Kelley Sch., Thermal, Calif., 2001—. Mem.: AAUW (assoc.), Nat. Coun. Teachers of English, Internat. Reading Assn. (assoc.), Coun. for Exceptional Children (assoc.), Assn. for Supervison and Curriculum (assoc.), Phi Mu. Democrat. Roman Catholic. Avocations: mentoring teachers, exercise, travel, cooking. Office: John Kelley Elem Sch 87-163 Center St Thermal CA 92274

MONTOYA, PATRICIA T. federal agency administrator; b. Albuquerque; BSN, U. N.Mex., 1975, MA in Pub. Health Adminstrn., 1983. Asst. dir. ANA, Washington, 1987-89; exec. dir. N.Mex. Health Resources, 1989-93; practice mgr. Presbyn. Family Healthcare, Albuquerque, 1993-94; regional dir. HHS, Dallas, 1994-98, commr. adminstrn. children, youth and families Washington, 1998—2001; mem., board of dir. New Mexico Voices for Children, Albuquerque. Office: New Mexico Voices for Children 801 Encino NE Ste F21 Albuquerque NM 87102

MONTOYA, VELMA, economist, policy consultant; b. L.A., Apr. 9, 1938; d. Jose Gutierrez and Consuelo (Cavazos) Montoya; m. Earl A. Thompson; 1 child, Bret L. Thompson. BA in Diplomacy and World Affairs, Occidental Coll., 1959, MA in Internat. Rels., 1960; MS in Econs., Stanford U., 1965; PhD in Econs., UCLA, 1977. Asst. prof. econs. Calif. State U., L.A., 1965-68; vis. assoc. prof. U. So. Calif., 1979; instr. UCLA, 1981-82; staff economist The Rand Corp., Santa Monica, Calif., 1973-82; asst. dir. for strategy, White House Office of Policy Devel. Exec. Office of the Pres., 1982-83; expert economist Office Regulatory Analysis, OSHA, U.S. Dept. of Labor, 1983-85; dir. of Studies in Pub. Policy and Assoc. Prof. of Political Economy, Sch. of Bus. Mgmt. Chapman U., 1985-87; adj. prof. Sch. Bus. Mgmt. Pepperdine U., 1987-88; pres. Hispanic-Am. Pub. Policy Inst., 1984-90; assoc. prof. fin. Sch. Bus. Adminstrn., Calif. State Poly. U., Pomona, 1988-90; mem. Occupl. Safety and Health Rev. Commn., 1990-97; cons. on regulatory and econ. policy, 1997—. Cons. Urban Inst., 1974, Mexican-Am. Study Project UCLA, 1966, Grad. and Profl. Fellowships to the Office of Post Secondary Edn., U.S. Dept. Edn.; editl. referee Contemporary Policy Issues, Economic Inquiry, Policy Analysis, Jour. Econ. Lit.; discussion leader Am. Assembly on Rels. Between the U.S. and Mex.; pres. del. White House Conf. on Aging, 1981; reader of 1988 proposals for the U.S. Dept Edn. for the Improvement and Reform of Schs. and Tchg.; rsch. participant U.S. Dept. Edn. Delphi Assessment of Drug Policies for Use in Minority Neighborhoods, 1989; mem. Hispanic adv. panel Nat. Commn. for Employment Policy, 1981-82; lectr. Brookings Inst. Seminars for U.S. Bus. Leaders; bd. adv. Close-Up Found., 1982-83; discussant Western Econ. Assn. Meetings, 1985, 93; bd. adv. Nat. Rehab. Hosp., 1991-94; mem. nat. exec. adv. bd. Harvard Jour. Hispanic Policy, 1993-95; reader proposals for Hispanic Serving Instns., U.S. Dept. Edn., 2001; mem. regional panel to select White House Fellows, 2002-03. Mem. census adv. com. on hispanic population for 1990 census, 1988—93; mem. adv. com. Senate Rep. Conf. Task Force on Hispanic Affairs, Washington, 1991—; bd. regents U. Calif., 1994—; program rev. com. Los Alamos (N.Mex.) Nat. Lab.; mem. steering com. GetSmarter.org, 1998—99; mem. outreach adv. bd. U. Calif., 1998—; commr. Calif. Postsecondary Edn. Commn., 2000—01. Named One of the 100 U.S. Hispanic Influentials Hispanic Bus. Mag., 1982, 90, 97, Woman of the Yr. Mex.-Am. Oportunity Found., 1983, The East L.A. Com. Union, 1979, one of 80 Elite Hispanic Women, Hispanic Bus. Mag., 2002, 03; recipient Freedom Found. at Valley Forge Honor Econ. Edn. Excellence Cert., 1986, Profl. Achievement award S.E. L.A. Lincoln Club, 2002, Hispanic Leadership award Minorities in Bus. Mag., 2001; Univ. fellow Stanford U., Internat. Rels. fellow Calif. PTA, John Hay Whitney Opportunity fellow; Calif. State Univ. Found. Faculty Rsch. grantee; Marshall scholar, Fulbright scholar. Mem. ASTM (com. on rsch. and tech. planning 1985-87), Am. Econ. Assn. (session chair ann. meetings 1995), Nat. Coun. Hispanic Women (pres. 1997—), State Bar of Calif., Calif. State Bar Ct. (exec. com. 1987-89, disciplinary bd. 1986-89), Western Econ. Assn., Indsl. Rsch. Inst. for Pacific Nations (adv. bd. 1988-89), Salesian Boys and Girls Club (bd. dirs. 1989—), Vets. in Com. Svc. (adv. com. 1989-94), Phi Beta Kappa, Omicron Delta Epsilon, Phi Alpha Theta. Home: 6970 Los Tilos Rd Los Angeles CA 90068-3107

MONTY, GLORIA, former television producer, film executive; b. Union City, N.J. d. Joseph and Concetta M. (Mango) Montemuro; m. Robert Thomas O'Byrne, Jan. 8, 1952 BA, NYU; MA, Columbia U. Dir. New Sch. Social Rsch., N.Y.C., 1952-53; dir. Old Towne Theatres, Smithtown, N.Y., 1952-56, Abbey Theatre Workshop, N.Y.C., 1952-56; chmn. N.J. Motion Picture & TV Commn., Newark. Cons. ABC Dir. numerous TV programs, including Secret Storm, 1956-72, Bright Promise, numerous episodes ABC Wide World Entertainment; exec. prodr General Hospital, 1977-86, 90-92, The Hamptons, 1983-85; made-for-TV movies, including Confessions of a Married Man, 1982, The Imposter, 1984; exec. prodr. in devel. for primetime TV 20th Century Fox, 1987-90; head cons. daytime TV ABC, 1987-90; prin. Gloria Monty Prodns. for new ABC daytime drama devel.; co-exec. prodr. While My Pretty One Sleeps, 1994-95, CBS Remember Me, FAMILY CHANNEL, 1995-97, Let Me Call You Sweetheart, 1997—, Moonlight Becomes You, 1997—; made-for-TV movies in assn. with Grosso-Jacobson. Chair Film Commn., State of N.J. Recipient Emmy awards, 1982, 84, Am. Soc. Lighting Dirs. award, 1979, Most Successful TV Show in History of TV award ABC, 1982, Spl. Editors award Soap Opera Digest, 1984, numerous others; named Woman of Yr., Paulist Choristers So. Calif., 1986. Mem. Women in Film, Dirs. Guild Am. (mem. exec. com.), Stuntman's Assn. (hon.), Thunderbird Country Club (Rancho Mirage, Calif.), Bel Air Country Club (Calif.), Deal Country Club, Navesink Country Club. Office: NJ Motion Picture & TV Commn PO Box 47023 153 Halsey St 5th Fl Newark NJ 07101

MONTY, RUTHELAINE, musician, educator; b. Litchfield, Conn., Oct. 23, 1961; d. Jesse and Helen Irene Fisher; m. Michael Albert Monty, Dec. 27, 1986; children: Alexander Jesse, Zachary Eric. BA in Music Edn., Olivet Nazarene U., 1984; EdM in Music Edn., Ea. Nazarene Coll., 2001. Cert. tchr. Mass. Tchr. music 1-3 Wareham (Mass.) Pub. Schs., 1997—99; tchr. music 1-8 Sandwich (Mass.) Pub. Schs., 1999—2001; tchr. music 6-8 New Bedford (Mass.) Pub. Schs., 2001—03. Organist, choir dir. First Congl. Ch., Wareham, 1985—99; piano and voice tchr. Music Ctr., New Bedford, 1985—2000; organist, music dir. St. Patrick's Ch., Wareham, 2002—; soloist, mem. choir Ch. of Good Shepherd, Wareham, 2002; accompanist concert series, Wareham, 03. Mem.: Nat. Assn. Music Edn., Mass. Music Educators Assn. Avocations: swimming, hiking, bicycling, singing, playing piano and organ. Home: 537 Main Wareham MA 02571

MONZINGO, AGNES YVONNE, veterinary technician; b. Mangum, Okla., July 16, 1942; d. Ira Lee and Opal Alice (McAlexander) Mayfield; m. Monty Brent Monzingo, Dec. 19, 1959; children: Tara, Dawn, Michael, Kermit. AS, San Antonio Coll., 1969. Mgr. Tupperware Corp., Wichita Falls, Tex., 1966-69; with La Louisiane, San Antonio, 1974-79; counselor Diet Ctr., Duncanville, Tex., 1984-87; vet. technician DeSoto (Tex.) Animal Hosp., 1985-98, hosp. mgr., 1998—. Author: (weekly column) Happy Tracks, 1981. Commr. Boy Scouts Am., 1988—93, tng. chmn. Wisdom Trail Dist., 1991—98, dist. commr. Wisdom Trail commn., 1998—99; pres. Dallas Stake Primary, 1983—88. Recipient Wood badge Boy Scouts Am., 1987, Wisdom Trail Dist. award of merit, 1990, Silver Beaver award Boy Scouts Am., 1993. Mem. Tex. Assn. Registered Vet. Technicians (v.p. 1991), Tex. Assn. Animal Technicians (pres. 1988, com. chair 1990-92), Tex. Assn. Registered Technicians (pres. 1992), Am. Boxer Club, Dallas Boxers Club (sec. 1982-92), Metroplex Vet. Hosp. Mgr. Assn., mem. Tex. Vet. Medical Assn., 1980-present. Mem. Lds Ch. Avocations: dog show exhibitor, dog breeder.

MOODIE, JANICE, professional golfer; b. Glasgow, Scotland, May 31, 1973; Degree in psychology, San Jose State U., 1997. Winner Scottish Ladies title, 1992; mem. team Great Britain, 1994, Ireland Curtis Cup, 1996; turned profl., 1996. Avocations: fitness, movies. Office: PGA 100 International Golf Dr Daytona Beach FL 32124-1092

MOODY, FRANCES MARIE, former performing arts educator, musician; b. McComas, W.Va., May 15, 1922; d. Arthur and Della Virginia Moody. BA, Concord Coll., Athens, WV, 1944; MA, Columbia U., New York, NY, 1948. Choral dir. Princeton H.S., Princeton, W.Va., 1944—61; choir dir. Fairmont State Coll., Fairmont, W.Va., 1961—84, music edn. specialist, 1961—84, organ & piano specialist, 1961—84. Pres. W.Va. Am. Choral Directors, W.Va., 1967—68; guest dir. Choral Pl. Festivals, W.Va., 1968—75, accompanist, W.Va., 1968—75; emeritus prof. Fairmont State Coll., W.Va. Recipient Woman of the Yr., Gamma Chpt., Delta Kappa Gamma, 1970, Chosen for Choral Seminar, Phila. Coll. of Performing Arts, 1975. Mem.: Music Educators Nat. Conf., Am. Choral Directors Assn. D-Liberal. Methodist. Avocations: travel, reading, piano and organ performance, dining. Home: 221 College Avenue Princeton WV 24740

MOODY, MARIANNA S. dietician; b. Beverly, Mass., June 19, 1925; d. Roland C. and Helen (Cheever) Sears; m. Guy W. Moody, Sept. 14, 1969 (dec. 1993). BS in Food and Nutrition, Boston U., 1948. Registered dietitian, Mass. Chief dietitian Beverly (Mass.) Hosp., 1948-58, Crotty Bros. Food Svc., Boston, 1958-60, The Waltham (Mass.) Hosp., 1961-71; dietetic instr. Waltham Vocat. Sch., 1961-71; dietitian cons. Reservoir Nursing Home, Waltham, 1971-87, Swedish Home, Hopkins, Larchwood Lodge, Waltham, 1987-93; pvt. practice Manchester, Mass., 1993—. Cons. in field; dietitian for pilot study program HEW/Waltham Hosp. Sec. Manchester Hist. Soc., 1960-70, Manchester Hist. Dist. Commn., 1980-90; spkr. task force Nat. Rep. Com., 1996-97. Recipient Good Citizenship award DAR, 1943. Mem. Am. Dietetic Assn. Republican. Congregationalist. Avocations: interior decoration, flower arranging, party planning, theatre, music. Home: 14 Bridge St Manchester MA 01944-1408

MOODY, PATRICIA ANN, psychiatric nurse, artist, small business owner; b. Oceana County, Mich., Dec. 16, 1939; d. Herbert Ernest and Dorothy Marie (Allen) Baesch; m. Robert Edward Murray, Sept. 3, 1960 (div. Jan. 1992); children: Deanna Lee Cañas, Adam James Murray, Tara Michelle Murray, Danielle Marie Murray; m. Frank Alan Moody, Sept. 26, 1992. BSN, U. Mich., 1961; MSN, Washington U., St. Louis, 1966; student, Acad. of Art, San Francisco, 1975-78. RN; lic. coast guard, ocean operator. Psychiat. staff nurse U. Mich., Ann Arbor, 1961-62, Langley-Porter Neuro-Psychiat. Inst., San Francisco, 1962-63; instr. nursing Barnes Hosp. Sch. Nursing, St. Louis, 1963; psychiat. nursing instr. Washington U., St. Louis, 1966-68; psychiat. nurse instr. St. Francis Sch. Nursing, San Francisco, 1970-71; psychiat. staff nurse Calif. Pacific Med. Ctr., San Francisco, 1991-97. Psychiat. staff nurse Charter Heights Behavioral Health Sys., Albuquerque, 1996-97; owner, cruise cons. Cruise Holidays Albuquerque, 1995—. Oil and watercolors included in various group exhbns., 1982-93. V.p. Belles-Fundraising Orgn., St. Mary's Hosp., San Francisco, 1974; pres. PTO, Commodore Sloat Sch., 1982; docent Albuquerque Mus. Art and History, 1998—. Recipient Honor award Danforth Found., 1954, Freshman award Oreon Scott Found., 1958; merit scholar U. Mich., 1957. Mem. Nat. Alliance for Mental Illness (sec. bd. dirs. 2000), San Francisco Women Artists (Merit award for oil painting 1989), Artist's Equity (bd. dirs. No. Calif. chpt. 1987-89, pres. No. Calif. chpt. 1990), Met. Club. Republican. Lutheran. Avocations: cycling, hiking, sailing, photography, piano. Home: 219 Spring Creek Ln NE Albuquerque NM 87122-2013 Office: Cruise Holidays Albuquerque 11032 Montgomery Blvd NE Albuquerque NM 87111-3962 Business E-Mail: patmoody@goodmoodcruises.com.

MOODY, SUSAN S. bank executive; Exec. v.p. corp. banking NBD Bancorp Inc., Detroit; exec. v.p. corp & instl. banking 1st Chgo. NBD Corp., exec. v.p. cmml. banking mgmt. Office: First Chgo NBD Corp Ste 0184 9th Fl One First National Plz Chicago IL 60670

MOODY-LAWRENCE, BESSIE, state representative, education educator; b. Chester, S.C., Feb. 14, 1941; d. Robert Douglas Sr. Ayers and Bessie Lewis Akers; m. Lindberg Moody Sr., 1964 (dec.); children: Lindberg Jr., Katrina Joanne, Leah Bess; m. James Earl Lawrence, Feb. 9, 1991; 1 stepchild, Erick C. BS, S.C. State U., 1962; MEd, Winthrop U., 1971; EdD, U. S.C., 1981. Coll. marshal Winthrop U., 1983—97, program coord. elem. edn., 1985—88, assoc. prof. edn.; state rep. dist. 49 S.C. Legis., SC, 1993—, past mem. med., mil., pub. and mcpl. affairs com., mem. edn. and pub. works com. Pacesetter Stennis So. Women in Govt., 1997—98; mem. Joint com. Study Drug and Alcohol Abuse, 1993, Joint Legis. Com. Children and Families; clk. session Hermon United Presbyn. Ch., 1980—86. Fleming fellow. Mem.: S.C. Assn. Tchr. Educators (pres. 1982—83), NAACP (Laney award 2000), Ctrl. City Optimist (v.p. Rock Hill chpt. 1990—91). Democrat. Office: State Capitol 414C Blatt Bldg Columbia SC 29211 Home: 219 Bowser St Rock Hill SC 29730 E-mail: bam@scstatehouse.net.

MOOK, SARAH, retired chemist; b. Bklyn., Oct. 29, 1929; d. Wong and Lie Won (Woo) M. BA, Hunter Coll., 1952; postgrad., Columbia U., 1954-57, 62-65, U. Hartford, 1958-59. Cartographic aide U.S. Geol. Survey Dept. of Interior, Washington, 1952-54; rsch. asst. Mineral Beneficiation Lab. Columbia U., N.Y.C., 1954-57; analytical chemist nuclear divsn. Combustion Engring., Inc., Windsor, Conn., 1957-59; rsch. scientist Radiations Applications Inc., Long Island City, N.Y., 1959-62; chemist Marks Polarized Corp., Whitestone, N.Y., 1962-64; sr. chemist NRA Inc. subs. Nuclear Rsch. Assocs., Inc., New Hyde Park, N.Y., 1964-75; clin. chemist Coney Island Hosp., Bklyn., 1974-84, cmty. bd., 1978-80; assoc. chemist Bellevue Hosp. Ctr., 1984-89, prin. chemist, 1989-95; ret., 1995; instr. English as a second lang., 1999—. Contbr. articles to profl. jours. Mem. adv. com. to state assemblyman State of N.Y., 1970-72; trustee park Avenue Christian Ch., 1973-82, sec., 1973-80, vice-chair, 1980-81, chair bd. trustees, 1981-82, pres. Christian Women's Fellowship, 1962-65, elder, 1982—; mem. Neighborhood Adv. Bd. for Cmty. Devel., 1996—, sec., 1996-99, chair 2000-02; mem. Cmty. Bd., 2002—. Recipient Margaret M. McCord Woman of Yr. Meml. award, Sheepshead Bay Hist. Soc., 2004, Woman of Yr. Humanitarian award, N.Y. State Senate, 2004, Disting. Leadership in Cmty. award, N.Y.C. Office of Comptr. Mem. Am. Assn. Clin. Chemistry (sec. NY Met. sect. 1999—), AAAS, Am. Chem. Soc., NY Acad. Sci., Van Slyke Soc. Republican. Home: 2042 E 14th St Brooklyn NY 11229-3314

MOON, LINDA WALKER, music educator; b. Atlanta, May 22, 1949; d. Lawrence Oliver and Dorothy Warr Walker; m. John Larry Moon, July 11, 1970; children: Charlie, Chad. MusB, Ga. State U., 1971; M in Music Edn., U. S.C., 1986. 3d grade tchr. Newberry (S.C) Acad., 1974—76; music and civics tchr. Clinton (S.C) H.S., 1976—81; choral tchr. Newberry Jr. & H.S., 1981—87; choral dir. Batesburg-Leerville (S.C.) H.S., 1987—. Music coord. Lexington Dist. 3, Batesburg, 1987—89; mem. Atlanta Symphony Orch. Chorus1970, 1972; spkr. in field and workshops. Liason S.C. Gov.'s Sch. Arts Commn., Greenville, 1987—92; choral dir. various chs., Ga. and S.C., 1970—; dir. handbell choir First Bapt. Ch., College Park, Ga., 1970—72, Newberry, 1973—76, Batesburg, 1989—92. Mem.: Am. Choral Dirs. Assn., S.C. Music Educators Assn. (chmn. solo & ensemble festival

1987—90). Democrat. Baptist. Avocations: reading, sports, piano, singing. Home: 508 W Hartley St Batesburg SC 29006 Office: Batesburg-Leesville HS 600 Summerland Ave Batesburg SC 29006 E-mail: moonlinda99@hotmail.com.

MOONEY, MARILYN, lawyer; b. Pitts., July 29, 1952; d. James Russell and Mary Elizabeth (Cartwright) M. BA summa cum laude, U. Pa., 1973, JD, 1976. Bar: Mass. 1977, D.C. 1985, Pa. 1990, U.S. Dist. Ct. D.C. 1985, U.S. Ct. Appeals (D.C. cir.) 1985, U.S. Supreme Ct. 1986. Atty. E. I. du Pont de Nemours & Co., Wilmington, Del., 1976-84, Washington, 1985; assoc. Fulbright & Jaworski L.L.P., Washington, 1985-90, ptnr., 1990—. Contbr. articles to profl. jours. Mem.: ABA (fed. regulation securities com.), D.C. Bar (corp. fin. and securties law and internat. sections), Internat. Bar Assn. (issues and trading in securities com.), Am. Soc. Corp. Secs. (securities law com.). Office: Fulbright & Jaworski LLP 801 Pennsylvania Ave NW Washington DC 20004-2615 E-mail: mmooney@fulbright.com.

MOONEY, PATRICIA ANNE, secondary school educator; b. Bronx, N.Y., June 6, 1948; d. Peter Joseph and Helen (Houlihan) Mooney; m. Anthony John Grasso, Nov. 21, 1970 (div. 1977); 1 child, A. Benjamin Grasso. BA, Coll. New Rochelle, N.Y., 1970, MS, 1975. Tchr. Archdiocese of N.Y., Harrison, 1970-78; salesperson N.Y. Tel., N.Y.C., 1978-82; sales instr. AT&T, Aurora, Colo., 1983, sales mgr. N.Y.C., 1984, mgr. sales support dept., 1985, mgr. pricing and contract support dept. Morristown, NJ, 1986, mgr. new bus. support dept. Bridgewater, NJ, 1987, sales br. mgr. Englewood, Colo., 1988-92, sales change mgmt. orgn. Bridgewater, NJ, 1993, data networking customer svc. process mgmt. Bedminster, NJ, 1994, large bus. customer svc. strategy, 1995-97; bus. process improvement Nextel, McLean, Va., 1997-98; operational process improvement, retention, after-market sales and ordering exec. Aerial (now Voicestream), Tampa, Fla., 1998-2000; operational process improvement Intermedia (now Worldcom), Tampa, 2000—01; tchr. Belleville (N.J.) Sch. Dist., 2002—. Roman Catholic. Avocations: performing arts, travel, skiing. Home: 3 Tulip Ln Morristown NJ 07960-6768 E-mail: pamooney@att.net.

MOONEY, SARA, media specialist; b. Allentown, Pa., Dec. 26, 1976; d. Timothy and Barbara Mooney. BA in Comm. - Corp. Media, Elizabethtown Coll., Pa., 1998; AS in Show Prodn. and Touring, Full Sail Real World Edn., Winter Pk., Fla., 1999. Cert. SIM engr. Meyer Sound, Calif., 1999. Lab instr. Full Sail Real World Edn., Winter Pk., Fla., 1999—2000; stage technician Walt Disney World, Lake Buena Vista, Fla., 1999—. Mem.: IATSE, Fla. Writer's Assn. Personal E-mail: sara@stage-domain.com.

MOORE, ALECIA See PINK

MOORE, ALMA DONST, writer, lyricist; d. Albert Alfred and Mary M.; m. Robert Arthur Moore, Apr. 20, 1958 (dec. Feb. 12, 1995). Clk. domestic and juvenile ct., spl. dep. county clk. Warren County Bd. Freeholders Ct. Ho., Belvidere, NJ, 1948—58. Lectr. Sen. Garrett W. Hagedorn NJ State Hosp. Contbg. writer: Soul Food, 1999—; founder The Spotlight, 1948; editor: The Spotlight, 1948, Warren Jour., 1948; author: (lyrics) Lifetime. Coun. mem. Rambai Mukti Mission, Clinton, NJ, 1998—. Recipient Sliver Poet, World Poetry, 1989, Gold Poet, 1999, Homer Diamond, Famous Poets Soc., 1999, Outstanding Achievement in Poetry, Silver Cup, Internat. Soc. Poets, 2003. Mem.: Inter. Soc. of Poets. Home: 71 Grayrock Rd Clinton NJ 08809-1075

MOORE, ALMA MERLE, association executive; b. Webster Springs, W.Va., Aug. 8, 1937; d. Thomas Wayne and Edna Jane (Bullion) M. AB, Glenville (W.Va.) State Coll., 1960; MLS, U. Pitts., 1969; MPA, W.Va. U., 1977. Sch. libr. Webster County Bd. Edn., Webster Springs, 1959-65, Columbian County Bd. Edn., Lisbon, Ohio, 1965-66; libr. asst. W.Va. Libr. Commn., Charleston, 1966-68; libr. dir. Clarksburg (W.Va.)-Harrison Pub. Libr., 1969-89; dir. Lewis County C. of C., Weston, W.Va., 1990—. Pres. Back Fork Books, Inc., Webster Springs, 1979-90; library dir, chmn. Nat. Mine Health Safety Acad., Beaver, W.V., 1996-2002. ret. 2002. Mem. W.Va. Italian Heritage Festival, Clarksburg, 1979—; mem. W.Va. Humanities Coun., Charleston, 1980-86, v.p., 1985-86; mem. W.Va. Libr. Commn., Charleston, 1990—, chmn., 1995—; mem. vis. com. W.Va. U. Libr., 1987—; Bd. mem. W.V. Mus. Am. Glass, Weston, W.V., 1993-. Named Disting. West Virginian Gov. Gaston Caperton, Charleston, 1988, Hon. Italian, W.Va. Italian Heritage Festival, Clarksburg, 1989. Mem. ALA, W.Va. Libr. Assn. (Dora Ruth Parks award 1987), Sierra Club (treas. W.Va. chpt. 1974-75), W.Va. Highlands Conservancy. Democrat. Avocations: gardening, cooking, reading, hiking. Home: PO Box 752 Webster Springs WV 26288-0752

MOORE, AMANDA LEIGH See MOORE, MANDY

MOORE, AMY NORWOOD, lawyer; b. Durham, N.C., Sept. 24, 1953; AB summa cum laude, Mt. Holyoke Coll., 1976; MA, U. Va., 1978, JD, 1983. Bar: D.C. 1984, U.S. Ct. Appeals (D.C. and 6th cirs.) 1985, U.S. Tax Ct., 1998. Law clk. to Frank M. Coffin, U.S. Ct. Appeals (1st cir.), 1983-84; ptnr. Covington & Burling, Washington. Articles editor Va. Law Rev., 1982-83. Mem. Phi Beta Kappa. Office: Covington & Burling 1201 Pennsylvania Ave NW Washington DC 20004-2401

MOORE, ANDREA S. state legislator; b. Libertyville, Ill., Sept. 2, 1944; Attended, Drake U. m. William Moore; 3 children. Mem. Ill. Ho. of Reps., 1993—; mem. com. on elections and state govt.; mem. com. on aging; mem. cities and villages com.; mem. environ. and energy com.; mem. labor and commerce com.; mem. com. on healthcare; mem. revenue and commerce com. Republican. Home: 361 S Saint Marys Rd Libertyville IL 60048-9407 Office: Ill Ho of Reps State Capitol Springfield IL 62706-0001 also: 2014-h Stratton Bldg Springfield IL 62706-0001 also: 131 E Park Ave Libertyville IL 60048-2800

MOORE, ANN ROY, school system administrator; b. Florence, Ala. BA, Hampton (Va.) U.; MA, EdS, U. No. Ala.; EdD in Curriculum Leadership Pers. and Early Childhood Edn., Vanderbilt U., 1986; cert. in ednl. adminstrn., 1986, cert. in ednl. adminstrn., 1987; cert. supt., Ala. A&M, 1992. Former tchr. pre-sch. and elem. sch. Huntsville (Ala.) City Schs., curriculum specialist, 1978—80, former prin., mgr. elem. edn., dep. supt., 1999—2001, supt., 2001—; former asst. supt. Florence Sch. Sys. Office: Huntsville City Schs 200 White St Huntsville AL 35801

MOORE, ANN S. magazine executive; b. Biloxi, Miss., 1950; d. Monty and Bea Sommovigo; m. Donovan Moore; 1 son, Brendan. BA in Polit. Sci., Vanderbilt U., 1971; MBA, Harvard U., 1978. With Time, Inc., N.Y.C., 1978—; gen. mgr. Sports Illustrated, 1983—89; founding publisher Sports Illustrated for Kids, 1989-91; publisher People mag., 1991—93, pres., 1993—98, People Mag. Group (renamed People/In Style Mag. Group, 2001), 1998—2001; exec. v.p. Time, Inc., 2001—02, chmn., CEO, 2002—. Bd. dirs. Avon Products Inc., 1993; public spkr. bus. and women's issues. Hon. bd. mem. Gilda's Club, N.Y.C.; founder Time to Give Back. Named Pub. Exec. of Yr., Adweek, 1998, 2004 Bus. Statesman, Harvard Bus. Sch.; named one of The 50 Most Powerful Women in Am. Bus., Fortune Mag.; recipient AOL Time Warner Civic Leadership award, 2003. Achievements include guiding People magazine to spin off several popular titles including In Style (domestic and international), Teen People, People en Español, and Real Simple. Office: Time Inc Office of CEO 75 Rockefeller Plaza New York NY 10019*

MOORE, ANNE, physician; b. N.Y.C., Apr. 28, 1944; d. John D.J. and Mary Foote Moore; m. Arnold L. Lisio, Sept. 6, 1969; children: Philip Moore, Mary Foote. BA, Smith Coll., 1965; MD, Columbia U., 1969. Diplomate Am. Bd. Internal Medicine, Am. Bd. Hematology (chmn. 1996), Am. Bd. Oncology. Intern dept. medicine N.Y. Hosp., N.Y.C., 1969-73, assoc. attending physician, 1981-95, attending physician, 1996—; postdoctoral fellow Rockefeller U., 1972-73, hematology-oncology fellow, 1973-75; asst. prof. medicine Cornell U. Med. Coll., N.Y.C., 1975-91, assoc. prof. clin. medicine, 1981-91, prof. clin. medicine, 1996—; [illegible] Strang Cancer Prevention Ctr.; lectr., cons., in field. Author: Patient's Guide to Breast Cancer Treatment, 1992, rev. edit., 1997; ad hoc reviewer Am. Jour. Clin. Oncology, 1994, New Eng. Jour. Medicine, 1994, 96, 97; contbr. articles to profl. jours., chpts. to books. Trustee St. David's Sch., 1983-89, HealthCare Chaplaincy, Inc., 1991—; bd. dirs. Camilli Found., 1990—, Cure Myeloma Fund, 1988-98. Recipient award SHARE, 1992, Wholeness of Life award Hosp. Chaplaincy, 1992, Alumnae award Oak Knoll Sch., 1994, Eileen Dreyer Meml. Lectureship award Sass Found. for Med. Rsch., 1996, Commendation award Office of Exec. Nassau County, 1996, award Artists for Breast Cancer Survival, Inc., 2000. Mem. Am. Bd. Internal Medicine (bd. dirs. 1996—), Am. Soc. Hematology, Am. Soc. Clin. Oncology, N.Y. Acad. Scis., Soc. for Study of Blood (membership chmn. 1979-80), N.Y. Met. Breast Cancer Group (membership chmn. 1992-93, sec.-treas. 1993-95, v.p. 1995-96, pres. 1997—), Soc. for Study of Breast Disease, N.Y. Cancer Soc., N.Y. Acad. Medicine (trustee 1998—). Office: Weill-Cornell Med Ctr 428 E 72nd St New York NY 10021-4635

MOORE, ANNE FRANCES, arts administrator, consultant, educator, art appraiser; b. Jackson, Tenn., Jan. 6, 1946; d. William Clifton and Frances (Woods) Moore; m. Michael Mezzatesta, Mar. 14, 1970 (div. July 1987); children: Philip Moore Mezzatesta, Alexander Woods Mezzatesta, Marya Frances Mezzatesta; m. Ernest Watson Hutton, Jr., Apr. 20, 1996. BA, Columbia U., 1969, MFA, 1971; MA in History of Art, Hunter Coll., 1982; Cert. in Mus .Mgmt., Am. Fedn. of the Arts, Berkeley, Calif., 1993. Cert. appraiser fine and decorative arts N.Y., 2003. Lectr., rsch. assoc. Kimbell Art Mus., Ft. Worth, 1980-83; dir. outreach Dallas Mus. Art, 1986-88; curator edn. Allen Art Mus., Oberlin (Ohio) Coll., 1988-91, dir., 1991-96; lectr. NYU, N.Y.C., 1999—; project mgr. Peabody Essex Mus., Salem, Mass., 2000—02; owner Anne Frances Moore Fine Art Svcs., Bklyn., 2002—. V.p. bd. trustees Intermus. Conservation Assn., Oberlin, 1994-96, trustee, 1991-94. Editor Bull. of the Allen Meml. Art Mus., 1991-93. Mem.: Appraisers Assn. Am. Office: Fine Arts Svcs 172 Pacific St Brooklyn NY 11201-6214

MOORE, ANNETTE B. legislative staff member; b. Salt Lake City, Nov. 8, 1946; Sec., chief adminstrv. officer Utah State Senate, Salt Lake City, 1994—. Mem.: Am. Soc. Legislative Clks. and Secs. (chair mem. and comm. com. 2000—01, chair profl. com. 2001—02, editor Jour of Profl. Com. 2002—03, mem. exec. com. 2003). Office: Utah State Senate State Capitol Rm 319 Salt Lake City UT 84114

MOORE, BARBARA C. ambassador; b. Buffalo, N.Y. m. Spencer B. Moore; 1 child. BA, Coll. of New Rochelle, 1973. Tours as info. officer U.S. Info. Agy., Caracas, Venezuela, 1989—93; coun. pub. affairs Santiago, Chile, 1993—97; dep. dir. U.S. Info. Agy. Office of Western Hemisphere Affairs, 1997—98; dep. chief of mission U.S. Embassy, Bogota, Colombia, 1998—2002; amb. to Rep. of Nicaragua, 2002—. Office: US Embassy Managua Km 4 1/2 Carretera Sur PO Box 327 Nicaragua Fax: 011-(505)-2669943.*

MOORE, BEALER GWEN, transcription company executive; b. Roxboro, N.C., Sept. 16, 1944; d. Bealer William and Clara (Wilkins) M.; divorced; 1 child, Steven Todd. Cert., U. N.C., Greensboro, 1963; BSBA, U. S.C., Spartanburg, 1987; MS in Orgnl. Mgmt., Pfeiffer U., 2000. Exec. sec. Container Corp. Am., Greensboro, 1964-67; asst. dir. dept. med. record Spartanburg Regional Med. Ctr., 1986-88, mgr. dept. med. transcription, 1988—; owner Spartanburg Transcription Svc., 1986—. Instr. med. terminology Ctrl. Piedmont C.C., 2001—. Mem. adv. bd. Spartanburg Tech. Coll., 1984-95; mem. Matthews United Meth. Ch. Mem. Am. Med. Record Assn., Am. Med. Transcriptionist Assn. Avocations: tennis, painting. Office: Carolinas Healthcare Sys Dir Transcription Dept 1000 Blythe Blvd Charlotte NC 28203-5812 Home: 6807 Copernicus Cir Charlotte NC 28226-3923

MOORE, BEATRICE, religious organization administrator; b. Somerville, Mass., Oct. 6, 1928; d. George and Christina Turner; m. Wendell Moore, May 9, 1953; children: Karl C., Linda Moore Flewelling, Diane Pearl, Larry. BA in Theology and English, Berkshire Christian Coll., Lenox, Mass., 1950. Pres. The Woman's Home and Foreign Mission Soc., Loudon, N.H., past nat. pres. Charlotte, NC, 1987—96; chmn. Nat. Spiritual Life. Sunday sch. tchr., deaconess Loudon Ridge Family Bible Ch.; chair Concord Christian Women's Club, 2002-03; prayer coord. Concord Christian Women's Club, 2003-, Ladies Bible Study leader, 1998-; active Women's Home and Fgn. Mission Soc., Loudon, past pres. N.H. Soc., past pres. ea. region; hostess, contact chmn., prayer adv., Bible club guide Stonecroft Ministries, Friendship Bible Study Guide; past leader 4-H Club. Mem.: Concord Christian Womens Club (chair). Office: Woman's Home & Foreign Mission 845 Loudon Ridge Rd Loudon NH 03307-1712

MOORE, BETTY JEAN, retired education educator; b. L.A., Apr. 4, 1927; d. Ralph Gard and Dora Mae (Shinn) Bowman; m. James H. Moore, Nov. 25, 1944 (div. 1968); children: Barbara, Suzanne, Sandra; m. George W. Nichols, Oct. 15, 1983. BA, Pasadena Coll., 1957; MA, U. Nev., 1963; PhD, U. Ill., 1973. Tchr. Calif. Elem. Schs., 1951—63; sec. tchr. Calif. pub. schs., 1963-68; asst. prof. Ea. Ill. U., Charleston, 1968-71; grad. teaching asst. U. Ill., Champaign, 1971-73; asst. prof. to assoc. prof. S.W. Tex. State U., San Marcos, 1973-83, prof. edn., 1983-89, ret., 1989, prof. emeritus, 1995—. Sch. evaluator; cons. in field; reading clinic dir. S.W. Tex. State U., 1974-85; cons. Min. Edn., Rep. of Singapore, 1980, 97; citizen ambassador People to People, China, 1998. Contbr. articles to profl. jours.; author: Teaching Reading, 1984; producer/dir. 5 ednl. videos. Active fund raising various charitable orgns.; vol. reading cons., Ariz. pub. schs., 2000-03. Mem. Internat. Reading Assn. (chpt. pres. 1964-65), Nat. Coun. Tchrs. English, AAUP. Presbyterian. Avocations: reading, writing, swimming, cooking. Office: Tex State U-San Marcos C & I Dept San Marcos TX 78666

MOORE, BETTY JO, legal assistant; b. Medicine Lodge, Kans., July 10, 1921; d. Joseph Christy and Helen Blanche (Hubbell) Sims; m. Harold Frank Moore, June 19, 1941 (dec.); children: Terrance C., Harold Anthony, Trisha Jo. Cert., U. West L.A., 1978; student, Wichita (Kans.) U., 1940-41. Cert. legal asst./escrow officer. Sec. UCLA, 1949-59; escrow officer Security Pacific Nat. Bank, L.A., 1959-62, Empire Savs. & Loan Assn., Van Nuys, Calif., 1962-64; escrow supr. San Fernando Valley Bank, Van Nuys, 1964; escrow officer Heritage Bank, Westwood, Calif., 1964-66; escrow coord. Land Sys. Corp., Woodland Hills, Calif., 1966-67; escrow officer/asst. mgr., real estate lending officer Security Pacific Nat. Bank, L.A., 1967-80; real estate paralegal Pub. Storage, Pasadena, 1980-81; asst. mgr. escrow dept. First Beverly Bank, Century City, Calif., 1982-84; escrow trainer/officer Moore's Tng. Temps Inc., Canoga Park, Calif., 1984—92, legal asst., 1992—. Participant People to People Amb. Program/Women in Mgmt. to USSR, 1989; observer Internat. Fedn. Bus. and Profl. Women's Congress, Washington, 1965, 81, Nassau, Bahamas, 1989, Narobi, Kenya, 1991. Adv. bd. escrow edn. Pierce Coll., Woodland Hills, Calif., 1968-80. Recipient Cert. of Appreciation, Pierce Coll., 1979, Calif. Fedn. Bus. and Profl. Women, 1989, Nat. Women's History Project, 1995. Mem. Nat. Fedn. Bus. and Profl. Women's Clubs, Calif. Fedn. Bus. and Profl. Women (pres. dist. 1987-88, Calif. Found. chmn. 1988-89, internat. concerns chmn. 1996-97, 2003), Woodlands Hills Bus. and Profl. Women ((pres. 1991-92, 94-95), Valley/Sunset Dist. BPW (v.p. legislation/pub. policy 1997-98, 2001-02, Cert. of Appreciation 2002), Tri Valley Dist. Bus. and Profl. Women (legis. chair 1992-93, exec./corr. sec. 1993-94, 94-95), Internat. Fedn. Bus. and Profl. Women, Nat. Women's Polit. Caucus (coord., sec. San Fernando Valley caucus 1986-87, sec. 19990—, legis. co-chair 1991-93), Women's Orgn. Coalition San Fernando Valley (sec. 1992, exec. com. L.A. Women's Equality Day 1995, pres. 2002-03), San Fernando Valley Escrow Assn. (bd. dirs. 1962-64), L.A. Women's Family Equity Coalition, U. West L.A. Alumni Assn. Democrat. Methodist. Avocations: reading, musical theater.

MOORE, BILLIE JO, minister; b. Centerpoint, Ark., Aug. 15, 1929; d. Willie Corn Henry and Irene Ruby Bevill; m. Warner Conrad Moore, Aug. 14, 1948 (div. Sept. 1967); children: Mark Glenn, Janice Marie Baudat. Student, Maranatha Inst., Inc., Calif., 1995. Ordained minister Rhema Bible Tng. Ctr., Okla., 1984. Clk. City of Long Beach, Calif., 1968—79; missionary to Philippines Billie Moore Ministries, Cypress, Calif., 1984—85; self-employed Calif., 1982—2003; minister Rhema, Broken Arrow, Okla., 1984—2003; prayer coord. Ch. of Claremore, Okla., 1986—87. Area coord. Nat. Day of Prayer, Oakley, Antioch, Calif., 1990—99, Auburn, Calif., 2000—02; dir. jail ministry Billie Moore Ministries, Contra Costa County, Calif., 1995—; tchr./facilitator various chs., Calif., 1979—; chaplain Placer County Chaplaincy, Calif., 2000—. Area facilitator Traditional Values Coalition, Placer County, Calif., 2000—02; vol. Bread of Life Ministry, Antioch, 1990—94, Friendship Manor Ch. Svc., Antioch, 1993—99. Mem.: Foothill Christian Writers Group, Rhema Ministerial Assn. Internat., Christian Minsterial Assn. of the Foothills, Women's Aglow Internat. (spkr.), Christian Coalition Am. Republican. Avocations: writing, charity work. Office: Billie Moore Ministries Inc PO Box 71 Auburn CA 95604 Mailing: PO Box 71 Auburn CA 95604

MOORE, CAROL, state legislator; b. N.Y.C., Jan. 1, 1945; 1 child. BA, Boston U., 1967, MSW, 1971. Psychotherapist, 1968—; mem. dist. Merrimack 19 N.H. Ho. of Reps., 1993—; mem. children, youth and juvenile justice com.; mem. asst. to Dem. leaders. Mem. N.H. Assn. Social Workers, N.H. Women's Lobby (treas. 1983-84, chair 1984-89). Democrat. Avocations: singing, travelling, gardening. Home: 38 1/2 S Spring St Concord NH 03301-2427 Office: NH Ho of Reps State House Rm 307 Concord NH 03301

MOORE, CAROL A. academic administrator; b. Newark, N.J., Dec. 8, 1945; d. James Clifford and Helen Mohan Brierley; m. Thomas Eric Moore, Nov. 25, 1967; 1 child, Kimberly Ann. BS in Biology, Montclair St. Coll., N.J., 1967; MA in Biology, Monclair State Coll., N.J., 1972; PhD in Biology, Northeastern Univ., Boston, Mass., 1981. Sci. tchr. H.S. and Jr. H.S., 1967—71; asst. prof. biology Massasoit C.C., Brockton, Mass., 1972—83, divsn. chairperson sci. and tech., asst prof. biology, 1979—83, asst. dean academic affairs, asst. prof. biology, 1983—84; dean academic affairs, chief acadamic officer, prof. biology Lasell Coll., Newton, Mass., 1984—88; dean undergraduate sch., chief acadminc officer, prof. biology Lesley Coll., Cambridge, Mass., 1988—91; provost & v.p. academic affairs, chief academic officer, prof. biology Mercy Coll., Dobbs Ferry, NY, 1992—98; pres. Lyndon State Coll., Lyndonville, Vt., 1998—. Vis. scientist Marine Sci. Inst., Northeastern Univ., Nahant, Mass., 1991—. Contbr. scientific papers to numerous conf., chapters to books, articles to profl. jour. Mem., Vt. higher edn. coun. rep. New Eng. Higher Edn. Bd., 1991—; mem., adv. bd. Vt. Telecom Advancement Ctr. USDA Grant, 2002—, Office of Nursing Workforce Rsch., Planning and Develp., Univ. Vt., 2001—; mem., Vt. bd. dirs. Girl Scout Coun., 2001—; mem. Am. Coun. Edn. Commn. on Women in Higher Edn., 2002—03; mem. Vt. Higher Edn. Coun., 1998—; rep. New Eng. Bd. of Higher Edn., 2002—, pres., 2001—02, v.p., 2000—01, exec. com., 1999—, sec.-treas., 1999—2000, com. on cert. & accreditation, 1998—; bd. dirs. Northeastern Vt. Devel. Assn., 2000—, Northeast Kingdom Learning Svc., 2000—. Grantee Title III Retention Grant, 1995, AAC Cirriculm Devel. Grant, 1990, NSF, 1983. Mem.: Soc. of Devel. and Comparative Immunology, Soc. for Invertebrate Pathology, Nat. Shellfisheries Soc., Am. Soc. of Zoologists (travel award), New Eng. Estuarine Rsch. Soc., Nat/ Assn. for Women Deans, Adminstr., and Counselors, Assn. of Tchr. Educators, Am. Coun. of Edn./ Nat. Identification Program, Nat. Assn. of Academic Affairs Adminstr., Sigma Xi, Phi Sigma. Office: Lyndon State Coll 1001 Coll Rd Lyndonville VT 05851

MOORE, CAROL JEAN, music educator, musician; b. St. Louis, May 5, 1955; d. Heuby Estil and Dorothy Jean Moore. AA, Jefferson Coll., 1975; MusB Edn., Murray State U., 1977, MusM Edn., 1984. Band and choir dir. grades K-9, asst. to h.s. band dir. Marshall County Schs., Benton, Ky., 1977—78; band dir. grades 6-12 Fulton County Schs., Hickman, Ky., 1979—83; prof. music, dir. bands, chair dept. music Mineral Area Coll., Park Hills, Mo., 1984—. Organist Meml. United Meth. Ch., Farmington, Mo.; instr. various summer band camps; presenter in field. Accompanist: recitals, musical theater prodns., all-state choirs, performer with jazz artists including: Jim Widner, Gloria Cooper, Reggie Thomas, Bill Watrons, Byron Stripling, Clark Terry, Lou Marini, others. Mem. Mineral Area Coll. Coun. on the Arts, Park Hills, Mo., 1984—2003. Recipient Cultural Recognition award, Mineral Area Coun. Arts. Mem.: Internat. Assn. Jazz Educators, Mo. Music Educators Assn. (coll. v.p. E. Ctrl. dist.), Music Educators Nat. Conf., Phi Beta Mu, Sigma Alpha Iota. Avocations: travel, reading, cooking. Home: 225 Dakota Ct Farmington MO 63640 Office: Mineral Area College 5270 Flat River Rd Park Hills MO 63601 E-mail: carol@mineralarea.edu.

MOORE, CAROLE IRENE, librarian; b. Berkeley, Calif., Aug. 15, 1944; AB, Stanford U., 1966; MLS, Columbia U., 1967. Reference libr. Columbia U., N.Y.C., 1967-68, U. Toronto, Can., 1968-80, head cataloging, 1980-85, assoc. libr., 1985-86, chief libr., 1986—. Mem. nat. adv. bd. Nat. Libr. Can., Ottawa, 1991-94; bd. dirs. Rsch. Librs. Group. 1994-2000, U. Toronto Press, 1994—. Recipient Disting. Alumni award Columbia U., 1989. Mem. ALA, Can. Libr. Assn., Can. Assn. Rsch. Librs. (pres. 1989-91, bd. dirs. 1996-98). Avocation: gardening. Office: U Toronto Libr 130 Saint George St Toronto ON Canada M5S 1A5

MOORE, CAROLYN LANNIN, video specialist; b. Hammond, Ind., Aug. 14, 1945; d. William Wren and Julia Audrey (Mathews) Lannin; m. F. David Moore, Oct. 21, 1967; children: Jillian Winter Moore Mirise, Douglas Mathew, Owen Glen. BA, Ind. U., 1967; MA, Purdue U., 1991. Stockholders corr. Sears Roebuck and Co., Chgo., 1967-68; caseworker Lake County Dept. of Pub. Welfare, Hammond, Ind., 1968-71; field dir. Campfire Girls Inc., Highland, Ind., 1975-77; project dir. Northwest Ind. Pub. Broadcasting, Highland, 1984-85, interim exec. dir., 1985-87; cons. Telecom. and Grant Writing, Munster, Ind., 1981-85; prin. Carolyn Moore and Assocs.-Laughing Cat Prodns., Munster, Ind., 1987—. Instr. Purdue U.-Calumet, Ind., 1989-90, 99—; instr. Valparaiso (Ind.) U., 1990-91; lectr. in field. Prodr. TV series Visclosky Viewpoint, 1985-87; video prodr. A Kid's Eye View of the Symphony, 1987; vol. on-air talent Sta. WYIN Channel 56; co-host This Week in Munster, Just Around the Corner. Mem. Munster Cable TV Commn., 1984—; bd. dirs. N.W. Ind. Literacy Coalition, Inc., Lake County Master Gardeners. Recipient Telly award for Citizens Fin. Svcs. history, 1998. Mem. AAUW, NAFE, Alliance for Cmty. Media, Assn. Ind. Video and Filmakers Inc.(exec.'s coun.) Munster C. of C., Gary C. of C., Communicators N.W. Ind. (Edgar L. Mills a N.W. Ind. World Trade Coun. (pres. 2000, bd. dirs.), Ind. U. Alumni Assn., Purdue U. Alumni Assn., Scherwood Ladies Golf League, Wicker Park Ladies Golf League (pres.). Democrat. Roman Catholic. Avocations: golf, reading, sailing. Home and Office: Carolyn Moore & Assocs Laughing Cat Prodns 9604 Cypress Ave Munster IN 46321-3418 E-mail: laughingcat_98@yahoo.com.

MOORE, CASSANDRA CHRONES, real estate broker and policy analyst; b. Oneonta, N.Y., June 14, 1935; d. Constantine John and Antonia (Laskaris) Chrones; m. Thomas Gale Moore, Dec. 28, 1958; children: Charles Godwin, Antonia Laskaris. BA summa cum laude, Radcliffe Coll.,

Cambridge, Mass., 1956; MA, Harvard U., 1958; PhD, U. Mich., 1975. Lic. real estate broker, Calif. Lectr. Duquesne U., Pitts., 1962-65, Mich. State U., East Lansing, 1966-68; broker, owner Moore Assocs., Palo Alto, Calif., 1983-85; dir. state and mcpl. legislation Nat. Assn. Realtors, Washington, 1985-87; exec. dir. Fed. Interagy. Coun. on Homeless, Washington, 1987-89; adj. scholar Competitive Enterprise Inst., Washington, 1989—, mem. adv. bd., 1995—; adj. scholar Cato Inst., Washington, 1996—. Author: Haunted Housing, 1997. Co-chmn. Radcliffe Alumnae Lectureship Com., Palo Alto and San Francisco, 1984-2000; mem. nat. com. Radcliffe Alumnae Professorship Fund, 2001-02. Recipient Fulbright fellowship U.S. Govt., Washington, 1956-57. Mem.: Palo Alto Bd. Realtors (dir. 1984, 1985), Tsintzinian Soc. (bd. mem. 1999—, alt. bd. mem. 2001—02), Am. Assn. Small Property Owners (bd. mem. 1997—), Radcliffe Club Peninsula (pres. 1980—82), Phi Beta Kappa. Avocations: hiking, swimming, skiing. Office: 415 Cambridge Ave Palo Alto CA 94306 Business E-Mail: ccmassoc@pacbell.net.

MOORE, COLLEEN, piano and voice instructor; b. Austin, Tex., Oct. 2, 1928; d. Herbert D. and Alice (Heinen) Bohn; m. Doyle H. Moore, Feb. 2, 1949; children: Sherry, Frosty, Robin. Student, U. Tex., 1946-49. Piano and voice teacher pvt. studio; singer Austin Lyric Opera Chorus, Tex., Liz Carpenter's "Getting Better All the Time" Singers. Mem. exec. com. Austin Symphony, Art Guild (past pres.), Austin Lyric Opera Guild; choir mem., past dir. Westlake Hills Presbyterian Church. Named Tchr. of Yr., Austin Dist. Music Tchrs. Assn.; recipient Plaques of Recognition, Women's Symphony League, Austin Symphony Orch., Austin Lyric Opera Chorus. Mem. Womens Symphony League (past pres.), Wednesday Morning Music Club (past pres.), Austin Woman's Club (pres.), Nat. Piano Guild, Tex. Music Teachers Assn., Nat. Music Teachers Assn., Alpha Delta Pi Sorority, Austin District Music Teachers (past pres.). Republican. Presbyterian. Avocations: grandchildren, lake, ranch, family, friends. Home: 803 Westlake Dr Austin TX 78746-4507

MOORE, DARLA D. investment company executive; b. Lake City, S.C. d. Eugene and Lorraine Moore; m. Richard Rainwater, Dec. 13, 1991. BA, U. S.C.; MBA, George Washington U., 1981. Summer intern Sen. Strom Thurmond; rschr. Rep. Nat. Com., 1976; with Chem. Bank, N.Y.C.; pres., CEO Rainwater, Inc., Atlanta, 1994—. Office: Magellan Health Svcs 6666 Powers Ferry Rd NW Ste 110 Atlanta GA 30339-2915

MOORE, DEBORAH CHANTAY, protective services official, psychotherapist; b. Queens, NY, May 9, 1969; d. Charles Edward and Evelyn Elizabeth Moore. AA, LaGuardia C.C., 1989; BA, York Coll., 1994; MEd, Fordham U., 1997; PhD, Capella U., 2004. Police sgt., counselor N.Y.C. Police Dept., 1991—, founder, owner Personal Enrichment Svcs.; psychotherapist D.C. Moore & Assocs., Queens, 1998—; founder, owner Personal Enrichment Svcs. Cons. mcpl. law enforcement agys., NY, 2000—. Contbr. articles to profl. jours. Recipient Law Enforcement Appreciation award, Kings Dist. Atty. Office, 2001, Congl. Hearing Achievement award, 6th Dist. NY, U.S. Congress Ho. of Reps., 2003; scholar, NYC Police Dept., 2000. Mem.: Am. Acad. Experts in Traumatic Stress (diplomat), Internat. Assn. Marriage and Family Counselors, Am. Mental Health Counselors Assn., Am. Counseling Assn., Acad. Profl. Law Enforcement, Order Ea. Star. Democrat. Avocations: jogging, traveling, reading, soap-making, tennis. Office: Personal Enrichment Svcs DC Moore & Assn Counseling Svcs PO Box 130372 Springfield Gardens NY 11413 Office Phone: 718-288-8548. E-mail: chantay@mindspring.com.

MOORE, DEBRA, lawyer; Grad., U. Utah, 1983. Shareholder Watkiss & Saperstein; employment sect. chief litigation divsn. Utah Atty. Gen.'s Office, 1991—. Instr. legal writing U. Utah Coll. Law, 1993—96; rep. Utah Jud. Coun. Mem.: Utah State Bar (pres.-elect, commn. 1994—2000). Office: Atty Gens Office PO Box 140856 160 E 300 S Fl Salt Lake City UT 84114-0856

MOORE, DEMI (DEMI GUYNES), actress; b. Roswell, N.Mex., Nov. 11, 1962; d. Danny and Virginia Guynes; m. Bruce Willis, Nov. 21, 1987, div. 2000 ; 3 daughters: Rumer Glenn, Scout LaRue, Tallulah Belle. Studies with Zina Provendie. Actress: (feature films) Choices, 1981, Parasite, 1981, Young Doctors in Love, 1982, Blame it on Rio, 1984, No Small Affair, 1984, St. Elmo's Fire, 1985, About Last Night..., 1986, Wisdom, 1986, One Crazy Summer, 1987, The Seventh Sign, 1988, We're No Angels, 1989, Ghost, 1990, Mortal Thoughts, 1991 (also co-producer), The Butcher's Wife, 1991, Nothing But Trouble, 1991, A Few Good Men, 1992, Indecent Proposal, 1993, Disclosure, 1994, The Scarlet Letter, 1995, Now and Then, 1995 (also prodr.), Undisclosed, 1996, Striptease, 1996, The Juror, 1996, G.I. Jane, 1997, Deconstructing Harry, 1997, Passion of Mind, 2000, Charlie's Angels: Full Throttle, 2003 ; (TV series) General Hospital, 1982-83; (TV movies) If These Walls Could Talk, 1996 (also exec. prodr.); (voice) The Hunchback of Notre Dame, 1996, The Hunchback of Notre Dame II, 2002 ; Producer: Austin Powers: International Man of Mystery, 1997, Austin Powers: The Spy Who Shagged Me, 1999, Austin Powers in Goldmember, 2002. Office: Creative Artists Agy Inc 9830 Wilshire Blvd Beverly Hills CA 90212-1825

MOORE, ELVI, performing company executive; Mem. faculty U. Chgo.; dir. corp. and found. devel. Nat. Symphony Orch.; with Washington Ballet, 1983—, gen. dir., 1990—, mngng. dir., 1997—. Bd. dirs. Dance/USA; adv. panels Nat. Endowment for Arts, D.C. Commn. Arts and Humanities. Dancer, choreographer, prodr. numerous dance festivals. Office: The Washington Ballet 3515 Wisconsin Ave NW Washington DC 20016-3085

MOORE, EMILY ALLYN, pharmacologist; b. Evansville, Ind., Apr. 3, 1950; m. Robert Alan Yount, Nov. 25, 1972 (div. Feb. 1986); 1 child, Joseph Taylor; m. Robert E. Moore Jr., Aug. 11, 1990; 1 child, Alexander Allyn. AB in Chem. Biology, Ind. U., Bloomington, 1971; MS in Applied Computer Sci., Purdue U., Indpls., 1985; PhD in Pharmacology, Ind. U., Indpls., 1976. Vis. asst. prof. biology Ind. U., Bloomington, 1979, rsch. assoc. in biochemistry Indpls., 1979-81, rsch. assoc., 1982-83, computer programmer for med. genetics, 1983-85, asst. scientist med. genetics, 1985-87; tech. assessment specialist Boehringer Mannheim Corp., Indpls., 1987, mgr. sci. info., 1987-89; mgr. Tech. Assess, Indpls., 1989-93, quality process analyst, 1993-94. Contbr. articles to profl. jours. Officer or bd. dirs. LWV, Hendricks County, Ind., 1977-84; elder St. Luke's United Ch. of Christ, Speedway, Ind., 1983-85; mem. adv. bd. Operation SMART, Indpls., 1989-90. Achievements include participation in creation of first DNA bank for storage of DNA samples for future use in diagnosis of genetic diseases.

MOORE, ERICA, band director; b. Washington, Dec. 15, 1971; d. Harold Reginald and Shirley Armeda Moore. BA, Bowie State U., 1995, MEd, 2000. Cert. advanced profl. tchr., adminstrn. I. Band dir., gen. music instr. Thomas Johnson Mid. Sch., Lanham, Md., 1995—2001; asst. program coord. Prince George's County Workforce Svcs. Corp., Landover, Md., 1995—99. Musician: (Music MSPAP Curriculum Guide) Maryland State Performance Assessment Curriculum Guide Supplement, 2001. Recipient Cert. Appreciation, Mine, Safety, & Health Adminstrn., 2001, Oasis Program, P.G. County Pub. Schs., 1997, Cert. Recognition, Md. Music Educator's Assn., 2001; scholar Charlotte Bronte Robinson Meml. scholar, Nat. Alumni Assn. for Music Edn. Leadership, Bowie State U., 1984. Mem.: Prince George's County Assn., Md. Music Educators Assn. (Cert. Recognition 2001), Nat. Assn. for Music Educators, Phi Delta Kappa, Sigma Gamma Rho Sorority Inc. (Rhoer Club advisor 2000—02, Outstanding Svc. award (Phi Sigma Chapter) 2001, Youth Symposium Cert. of Appreciation (Eta Iota Sigma chpt. and Zeta Tau Sigma chpt.) 2001, Northeast Region Adv. of Yr. 2002, Nat. Adv. of Yr. 2002, named Rhoer Adv. of Yr. 2003, First Pl. Scrapbook and Exhibit award 2003, Advisor of Yr. N.E. Region 2002—03). African Methodist Episcopal. Avocations: teaching, learning, travel. Office: Thomas Johnson Mid Sch 5401 Barker Pl Lanham Seabrook MD 20706

MOORE, FAY LINDA, systems engineer; b. Houston, Apr. 7, 1942; d. Charlie Louis and Esther Mable (Banks) Moore; m. Noel Patrick Walker, Jan. 5, 1963 (div. 1967); 1 child, Trina Nicole Moore. Student, Prairie View Agrl. and Mech. Coll., 1960-61, Tex. So. U., 1961, Our Lady Lake U., 1993, Software Engring. Inst., 1995, U. Phoenix, 2003—. Cert. ISO 9000 Internal Auditor, 1994-97. Instr. Internat. Bus. Coll., Houston, 1965; keypunch operator IBM Corp., Houston, 1965-67, sr. keypunch operator, 1967-70, programmer technician, 1970-72, asst. programmer, 1972-73, assoc. programmer, 1973-74, sr. assoc. programmer, 1984-87, staff programmer, 1987-92, staff sys. analyst, 1992-96; sr. software quality engr. Loral Space Info. Sys., Houston, 1994—96; owner, pres. AFT Co., Houston, 1993—; sr. software quality engr. Lockheed Martin Corp., Houston, 1996-97; software quality engr. Motorola, Inc., Austin, 1998-2001, quality sys. rev. assessor, 1998-2001, info. tech. quality engr., 2000-2001; prin. sys. engr. Titan Corp., Houston, 2001—. Space shuttle flight support team IBM, 1985—92, mem. space sta. team, 1992—93. Recipient Apollo Achievement award, NASA, 1969, Quality and Productivity award, 1986, 1992, Cert. of Recognition, NASA Office of Space Flight, 2004. Mem. NAFE, Soc. Software Quality, Booker T. Washington Alumni Assn., Ms. Found. for Women, Inc. Democrat. Roman Catholic. Avocation: personal computing.

MOORE, FAYE ANNETTE, retired social services professional; b. Glasgow, Mont., Feb. 21, 1938; d. Chester Oliver and Viola Adelaide (Skalet) Baker; m. Russell Dale Guthrie, July 1, 1961 (div. Nov. 1975); children: Tamia Lee, Owen Bradley; m. William Bateman Moore, Jan. 6, 1979. BA Sociology, Mont. State U., 1959; MA Social Work, U. Chgo., 1961; MBA, N. Mex. State U., 1984, PhD Edn. Adminstrn., 1989. Social worker Ill. Childrens Home and Aid Soc., Chgo., 1961-63, Divsn. Social Svcs., Fairbanks, Alaska, 1964-72, supr. social worker, 1972-74, staff mgr., 1974-75; regl. mgr. Divsn. Family and Youth Svcs., Anchorage, Alaska, 1976-80, regl. adminstr., 1991-96; adminstr. Rsch. Ctr. N.Mex. State U. Coll. Bus., Las Cruces, 1984-86; instr. Golden Gate U., Holloman AFB/Alamogordo, N.Mex., 1989-91, Webster U., Ft. Bliss, El Paso, Tex., 1989-91; ret., 1996—. Presenter confs. in field. Contbr. articles to profl. jours. Recipient Supervisory Employee of the Year Commissioner's award Dept. of Health and Social Svcs., 1993. Mem. NASW, Realtor Assn. N.Mex. (state dir. 1990-91, chmn. state edn. com. 1991), Las Cruces Assn. Realtors (v.p. 1991), Am. Bus. Comm. Assn., Beta Gamma Sigma, Phi Kappa Phi. Avocations: gardening, walking, knitting, sewing. Home: PO Box 6162 Spring Hill FL 34611-6162

MOORE, HELEN LUCILLE, adult education educator, consultant; b. Watseka, Ill., July 24, 1930; d. John Kenneth and Thelma Mae (Wollschlaeger) Weidert; m. Harold Junior Gossett, June 24, 1948 (div. May 1971); children: Steven, Joyce, Gary, Ricky, Kenny, Jane; m. Herff Leo Moore, Jr., Nov. 24, 1991. AS in Mgmt., Kankakee (Ill.) Jr. Coll., 1969. Sr. sec. Nimz Transp., Watseka, 1948-57; tchg. aide Glenn Raymond H.S., Watseka, 1964-71; asst. pers. and safety mgr. Gt. Plains Bag Co., Jacksonville, Ark., 1971-81; sr. human resources rep. Maybelline Products Co., Inc. divsn. L'Oreal, North Little Rock, Ark., 1981-2000; recruiting dir. StaffMark, Little Rock, 2000—01; adult edn. cons. Dept. Workforce Edn., Little Rock, 2001—. Chmn. Ark. Human Resource Conf., Hot Springs, 1991-92. Contbr. articles to profl. publs. Bd. dirs. Ark. Urban League, Little Rock, 1985-93; co-founder, exec. bd. dirs. Workforce Alliance for Growth in Economy, 1993—; mem. Ark. Gov.'s Workforce Investment Bd. and Exec. Com., 1999—. Recipient Outstanding Ark. Human Resources Profl. award Ark. Human Resources Coun., 1994; named Sr. Inspirational Employee of Yr., ABLE (Ability Based on Long Experience), 1997. Mem.: Ctrl. Ark. Mfg. Pers. Assn. (chmn. 1990—99, co-founder), Ctrl. Ark. Human Resources Assn. (bd. dirs. 1988—90, profl.), Soc. for Human Resource Mgmt. (profl., Outstanding Profl. Mem. award 1989), Nat. Employer Coun. (Ark. chmn. local employer adv. couns. 1989—2000, sch.-to-work com., focus group 1998, Star Performer award 1999), Am. Legion Aux. (life). Office: Dept Workforce Edn Luther S Hardin Bldg Three Capitol Mall Rm 303 Little Rock AR 72034-3315

MOORE, JACQUELYN, art educator; b. Helena, Mont., July 31, 1949; d. John Winfield and Grace Genearl Oswalt Moore. BA in Art, Mont. State U., 1972, tchr. cert., 1980; MA in Art, U. Mont., 1979. Asst. claims adjuster Dept. Fish, Game and Wildlife, Helena, 1968; clk., auditor Dept. Revenue, Helena, 1972-79; instr. Carroll Coll., Helena, 1981-87, asst. dir. Guadalupe Hall, 1984-87; dispatcher Fire Tower Lookout Dept. State Lands, Helena, 1986; designer stained glass Shed Brand Studios, Charlotte, N.C., 1987; art tchr. Cedar Hill (Tex.) Ind. Sch. Dist., 1988—. Artist, co-planner Women's Commemorative Mural, Helena, 1979; artist, designer Carroll Coll., Helena, 1981-87; tchr. cmty. edn. Cedar Hill Ind. Sch. Dist., 1990-95, advisor/planner bldg. com., 1992-2001; asst. to Daniel Hillen, Carroll Coll. with various art exhbns./projects, 1981-2002. Numerous exhibits, including: Zula Bryant Wylie Libr., 1994, State Fair of Tex., 1992, Mont. Hist. Soc., Helena, 1982, Carroll Coll., Helena, 1984, Clay Gallery, Missoula, Mont., 1980, U. Mont., Missoula, 1978, others. Pres. libr. bd. Cedar Hill Zula Bryant Wylie Libr., Tex., 1999, v.p. libr. bd., 2002—03. Recipient 1st place watercolor award Zula Bryant Wylie Libr., 1994, hon. mention State Fair of Tex., "Hostage", a warvigil watercolor 1992, Vigil quilt, 2d pl., State Fair, Tex., 2003. Mem. Dallas Mus. Art, Dallas Symphony Soc., Kimball Mus./Ft. Worth. Avocations: painting, drawing, traveling, gardening, writing letters. Home: 707 Penn Pl Cedar Hill TX 75104-1747 Office: Beltline Intermediate Sch 504 Beltline Rd Cedar Hill TX 75104 E-mail: moorj@chisd.com., jacquelynmoore@sbcglobal.net.

MOORE, JACQUELYN CORNELIA, labor union official, editor; b. Dec. 25, 1929; d. James C. and Harriette I. Thomas; m. Clarence Carbin Moore, Jan. 19, 1947 (dec. Feb. 1970); children: Clarence Joseph, Janet Elizabeth Moore Marshall. Mail clk. U.S. P.O., Phila., 1966—93; editor Local 509 Newsletter Nat. Alliance of Postal and Fed. Employees, Washington, 1969—74, editl. newsletter chmn., 1969—74, sec. dist. 5, 1972—74, nat. editor Nat. Alliance, 1974—, mem. exec. bd., 1974—, union photographer, 1974—. Dir. 202 Housing for Elderly Corp. bds., Chattanooga, New Orleans, 1981—, Atlanta, 1988—; sec. supervisory com. Nat. Fed. Credit Union, 1977—82, 1984—94, chair, 1994—. Vol. D.C. Voting Rights Corp., Washington, 1979—; sustaining mem. Dem. Nat. Com., 1977—. Mem.: Nat. Press Club, Nat. Bus. and Profl. Women's Club. Roman Catholic. Home: 1102 R St NW Washington DC 20009-4364 Office: 1628 11th St NW Washington DC 20001-5086

MOORE, JANE ROSS, librarian, educator; b. Phila., Apr. 24, 1929; d. John William and Mary M. Ross; m. Cyril Howard Moore, Jr., June 1, 1956 (div. Mar. 1967). AB, Smith Coll., 1951; MLS, Drexel U., 1952; postgrad., Columbia U.; MBA with distinction, NYU, 1965; PhD, Case Western Res. U., 1974. Cataloguer Yale U. Libr., 1952-54; chief tech. processes libr. Lederle Labs., Am. Cyanamid Co., Pearl River, NY, 1954-58; chief serials catalog libr. Bklyn. Coll. Libr., 1958-65, asst. prof., chief catalog divsn., 1965-70, assoc. prof., chief catalog divsn., 1971-73, asso. profc., assoc. libr. adminstrv. svcs., 1973-76; prof., chief libr. Mina Rees Libr., Grad. Ctr., CUNY, 1976-91, prof., chief libr. emerita, 1991—. Lectr. Syracuse U. Grad. Sch. Libr. Sci., 1967, 69, Queens Coll. Grad. Sch. Libr. and Info. Studies, 1967—69, adj. assoc. prof., 1974—76, adj. prof., 1977—86; HEW Title IIB fellow Case Western Res. U. Sch. Libr. Sci., 1970—72; mem. chancellor's task force librs. CUNY, 1979—81; trustee N.Y. Met. Reference and Rsch. Libr. Agy., 1984—93, 2d v.p., 1985—88, v.p., 1988—90, treas., 1991—93. Elder Presbyn. Ch., clk. session, pres. corp.; bd. dirs. Vis. Nurse Assn. Bklyn., 1984—, mem. exec. com., 1987—, vice chmn., 2001—; bd. dirs., mem. exec. com., sec. Vis. Nurse Regional Health Care Sys., Inc., 2001—. Mem.: ALA (mem. membership com. 1967—71, chmn. coun. regional groups, resources and tech. svcs. divsn. 1968—69, dir. divsn. 1968—70, 1975—76, chmn. divsn. cataloging and classification sect. 1975—76), AAUW, AAUP, The Typophiles (sec.-treas. 1996—), N.Y. Tech. Svcs. Librs. (pres. 1963—64), Gt. Britain Spl. Librs. Assn., Chartered Inst. Libr. and Info. Profls. Eng., Am. Printing History Assn., OCLC Users Coun. (SUNY del. 1981—85), Assn. Coll. and Rsch. Librs. (chmn. univ. librs. sect. 1983—84), N.Y. Libr. Assn. (pres. resources and tech. svcs. sect. 1966—67, councilor 1966—67, sec.-treas. acad. and spl. librs. sect. 1973—75, councilor 1975—76, 1978—81, pres. 1979—80), NYU Grad. Sch. Bus. Adminstrn. Alumni Assn. (rec. sec. 1967—69, dir. 1969—70, 1975—79), Princeton Club N.Y., Smith Coll. Club Bklyn. (pres. 1966—67, 1967—68, class treas. 1976—81), N.Y. Libr. Club (sec. 1964—66, coun. 1966—70, 1973—77, 1979—82, pres. 1980—81), Smith Coll. Club N.Y., Archons of Colophon, Phi Kappa Phi. Home: 35 Schermerhorn St Brooklyn NY 11201-4826

MOORE, JANET L.S. music educator, dean; d. Roberta Lee and Wallace Milton Schulze, Wallace Milton and Roberta Lee Schulze; m. Marvin Lynn Moore; children: Gregory Scott, Kellia Lynne. MusB, Ea. Ky. U., 1974; MusM, U. N.C., Greensboro, 1977, EdD, 1984. Choral and keyboard instr. Rockingham County Sr. H.S., Wentworth, NC, 1977—80; fine arts supr., cultural arts coord. Rockingham County Schs., Wentworth, 1978—80; elem. music specialist Price Traditional Sch., Greensboro, 1984; asst. prof. music edn. Rutgers U., New Brunswick, NJ, 1985—88, Northwestern U., Evanston, Ill., 1988—89; asst. prof. music Sch. Music U. South Fla., Tampa, 1989—95, coord. music edn., 1995—98, assoc. prof. music, 1995—, assoc. dean Coll. Visual and Performing Arts, 1998—2003, assoc. dean undergrad. studies, 2003—. External evaluator Hillsborough County Sch. Sys., Tampa, 2002—; pres. faculty senate U. South Fla., 1997—99. Author: (music textbook) Understanding Music Through Sound Exploration and Experiments; contbr. music textbook On the Nature of Musical Experience; editor: (state curriculum guide) Introduction to Music Performance. Recipient Tchg. Incentive Program award, Fla. State Legislature and State U. Sys., 1994; grantee, U. South Fla. Rsch. Coun., 1990—97, U. South Fla. Ctr. Tchg. Enhancement, 1998; internat. travel grantee, Inst. on Black Life, U. South Fla., 1993, 1997, summer fellow, Rutgers U. Rsch. Coun., 1987. Mem.: Coun. Colls. Arts and Scis., Fla. Music Educators Assn. (Leadership award 1998), Am. Orff Schulwerk Assn., Internat. Soc. Music Edn. (nat. adv. bd. 1991—94, world conf. adv. bd. 1991—94), Soc. Gen. Music, Soc. Rsch. in Music Edn., Music Educators Nat. Conf. (editor Gen. Music Today jour., editl. bd. Soc. Gen. Music, nat. mem.-at-large Soc. Gen. Music 1997—99), Phi Kappa Phi (life), Pi Kappa Lambda (life; founding pres., Eta Lambda chpt. 1992—94). Office: U South Fla 4202 E Fowler Ave UGS SVC 2002 Tampa FL 33620-6920

MOORE, JEAN E. social worker, academic administrator, educator, radio personality; d. Hugh Huriel and Theodora H. Buchanan Campbell; m. Robert M. Moore, Jr.; children: Robert M. III, Doreen R. Moore Closson. BA, Hunter Coll., 1947; M of Social Svc., Bryn Mawr Coll., 1949; EdD, Temple U., 1978. Cert. social worker Acad. Cert. Social Workers. Social worker Children's Svc., Inc., Phila., 1949—52; asst. chief clin. social work svcs. Region 10 U.S. VA, Phila., 1952—60; social work specialist Ctrl. Relocation Bur., Phila. Redevel. Authority, 1962—67; social work/human svcs. adviser for Model Cities Region III U.S. Dept. Housing and Urban devel. for 6 states and D.C., Phila., 1967—69; assoc. prof., grad. faculty, dir. new career ladders Temple U., Phila., 1969—89, assoc. prof. emerita, 1989—; exec. asst. to pres. Cheyney U. of Pa., 1985—91; v.p. instnl. advancement U. Md. Ea. Shore, Princess Anne, Md., 1991—97; host, exec. prodr. Univ. Forum Temple U. Pub. Radio, Phila., 1997—. Mem. internat. bd. advisors Radio for Peace Internat.; bd. dirs., club dir. Gundaker Found., Inc., Darby Lansdowne Rotary Club; cons., spkr., presenter, lectr. in field. Contbr. articles to profl. publs. Past bd. trustees Lackawanna Jr. Coll., C.C. of Phila.; pres. Fair Housing Coun. Suburban Phila.; chair vis. accreditation teams Mid. States Assn. Colls. and Schs. Commn. on Higher Edn.; past bd. pres. Spectrum Health Svcs., Inc., State Bd. Pvt. Corresp. Schs.; active Lansdowne First Presbyn. Ch.; bd. dirs. Children's Svc., Inc. Named to Hall of Fame, Hunter Coll., 1999; recipient Crystal award of Excellence, The Communicator Awards, 1999, 2000, 2002, 2003, Documentary award, The Communicator Awrds, 1999, 1st pl. radio/ednl., Broadcast Edn. Assn., 2000, Documentary award, 2000, Achievement in Radio award, March of Dimes, 2000, Gold Cindy award, Internat. Assn. Audio Communicators, 2000, 2002, 2003, Media award, Kelly Anne Dolan Meml. Fund, 2003, Martin Luther King Jr. Humanitarian award, Upper Merion, 2004, Mayor's Fire Prevention medal, City of N.Y., Outstanding Contbn. in Edn. award, Theta Nu Sigma, Image award, Black Women in Sport Found. Mem.: NASW, Internat. Bd. Advisers for Radio Peace Internat., Broadcast Pioneers of Phila., Inc., Pa. Abolition Soc., Upper Darby-Lansdowne Club, Rotary Internat., Phi Delta Kappa, Alpha Chi Alpha, Phi Beta Kappa, Delta Sigma Theta. Avocation: international travel.

MOORE, JOANNE IWEITA, pharmacologist, educator; b. Greenville, Ohio, July 23, 1928; d. Clarence Jacob and Mary Edna (Klepinger) M. AB, U. Cin., 1950; PhD, U. Mich., 1959. Rsch. asst. Christ Hosp. Inst. Med. Rsch., Cin., 1950-55, U. Mich., Ann Arbor, 1955-57, teaching fellow, 1957-59; postdoctoral fellow in pharmacology Emory U., Atlanta, 1959-61; asst. prof. pharmacology U. Okla. Coll. Medicine, Oklahoma City, 1961-66, assoc. prof., 1966-71, acting chmn., 1969-71, prof., interim chmn., 1971-73, prof., chmn. dept., 1973-93, David Ross Boyd prof., chair, 1993, David Ross Boyd prof. emeritus, 1999. Mem. gen. rsch. support rev. com. NIH, 1975-79, mem. biomed. scis. study sect., 1986-90; mem. adv. bd. Fogarty Internat. Ctr., 1992-94. Contbr. articles to profl. jours. USPHS grantee, 1963-69, 72-74, 79-87. Mem. AAAS, Am. Soc. Pharmacology and Exptl. Therapeutics, Assn. Med. Sch. Pharmacology, Am. Heart Assn. (bd. dirs. Okla. affiliate 1973-88, pres. 1979-80, chmn. bd. 1983-85, bd. dirs. Oklahoma City div. 1988-91, pres. 1989-90), Sigma Xi. Office: U Okla Coll Medicine Dept Cell Biology 728 BMSB OUHSC Oklahoma City OK 73190-0001 E-mail: joanne-moore@ouhsc.edu.

MOORE, JUDITH MARIE, assistant principal; b. Swickely, Pa., Feb. 18, 1974; d. Frederick David and Maureen Elizabeth Halek; m. Michael Christopher Moore, June 8, 1996; children: Stephen Alexander, April Elizabeth. BA in History, N.C. State U., 1995; MA in Sch. Adminstrn., U. N.C., 2003. Lic. tchr. N.C., cert. principal N.C. Tchr. HS Wake County Pub. Schs., Raleigh, NC, 1996—98, Easton County Schs., Eastonia, NC, 1998—2000, asst. prin., 2002—. Cons. homeland security project U. N.C., Charlotte, NC, 2003. Mem.: ASCD, Nat. Assn. Secondary Sch. Prins., Runnymeade Homeowners Assn. (v.p. 2001—02, pres. 2002—03). Republican. Roman Cath. Avocations: gardening, volleyball, travel. Home: 165 West Walnut Ave Mount Holly NC 28120 Office: Easton County Schools Noah Easton HS 1133 Ratchford Rd Dallas NC 28034

MOORE, JULIANNE (JULIE ANNE SMITH), actress; b. Fayetteville, N.C., Dec. 3, 1960; BFA, Boston Univ. With The Guthrie Theater, 1988-89. Actress: (theater) Serious Money, 1987, Bone-the-Fish, 1988, Ice Cream with Hot Fudge, 1990, Uncle Vanya, (TV soap operas) As the World Turns (Emmy award outstanding ingenue in daytime drama series 1988), The Edge of Night, (TV movies) Money, Power, Murder, 1989, Lovecraft, 1991, (feature films) The Hand That Rocks the Cradle, 1992, The Gun in Betty Lou's Handbag, 1992, Body of Evidence, 1993, Benny & Joon, 1993, The Fugitive, 1993, Short Cuts, 1993, Vanya on 42nd Street, 1994, Roommates, 1995, Nine Months, 1995, Safe, 1995, Assassins, 1995, Surviving Picasso, 1996, The Myth of Fingerprints, 1997, The Lost World: Jurassic Park, 1997, Hellcab, 1997, Boogie Nights, 1997, Chicago Cab, 1998, The Big Lebowski, 1998, Psycho, 1998, Map of the World, 1999, Magnolia, 1999,

Cookie's Fortune, 1999, An Ideal Husband, 1999, The End of the Affair, 1999, Hannibal, 2001, Evolution, 2001, The Shipping News, 2001, Far From Heaven, 2002, The Hours, 2002, Marie and Bruce, 2004, Laws of Attraction, 2004. Office: Creative Artists Agy care Kevin Huvane 9830 Wilshire Blvd Beverly Hills CA 90212 1825

MOORE, KAREN NELSON, judge; b. Washington, Nov. 19, 1948; d. Roger S. and Myrtle Nelson; m. Kenneth Cameron Moore, June 22, 1974; children: Roger C., Kenneth N., Kristin K. AB magna cum laude, Radcliffe Coll., 1970; JD magna cum laude, Harvard U., 1973. Bar: DC 1973, Ohio 1976, U.S. Ct. Appeals (DC cir.) 1974, U.S. Supreme Ct. 1980, U.S. Ct. Appeals (6th cir.) 1984. Law clk. to Hon. Malcolm R. Wilkey U.S. Ct. Appeals (DC Cir.), Washington, 1973—74; law clk. to Hon. Harry A. Blackmun U.S. Supreme Ct., Washington, 1974—75; assoc. Jones, Day, Reavis & Pogue, Cleve., 1975—77; asst. prof. Case Western Res. Law Sch., Cleve., 1977—80, assoc. prof., 1980—82, prof., 1982—95; judge U.S. Ct. Appeals (6th cir.), Cleve., 1995—. Vis. prof. Harvard Law Sch., 1990—91. Mem. Harvard Law Rev., 1971—73; contbr. articles to profl. jours. Trustee Lakewood Hosp., Ohio, 1978—85, Radcliffe Coll., Cambridge, 1980—84. Fellow: Am. Bar Found.; mem.: Harvard U. Alumni Assn. (bd. dirs. 1984—87), Am. Law Inst., Phi Beta Kappa. Office: US Ct Appeals 6th Cir Carl B Stokes US Courthouse 801 W Superior Ave Cleveland OH 44113-1831

MOORE, LORI, information technology executive; BS in Polit. Sci., The Am. U. From mgr. to corp. v.p. Microsoft, Redmond, Wash., 1991—2000, corp. v.p. product support svc., 2000—. Office: One Microsoft Way Redmond WA 98052-6399

MOORE, LOUISE HILL, surgical technologist; b. Knoxville, Tenn., July 9, 1950; d. Mary Elizabeth Hill; m. David Oscar Moore; children: Kimberly Hill, Daveisha. Cert. surg. technologist; cosmetologist, aesthetician, first responder. Cosmetologist Millers Dept. Store, Knoxville, 1968—70, Austinian Beauty Shop, Knoxville, 1970—74, Hair Fashions E., Knoxville, 1974—78; gen. laborer Alcoa, Alcoa, Tenn., 1978—94; cert. surg. technologist St. Mary's Med. Ctr., Knoxville, 1995, Ft. Sanders Hosp., Knoxville, U. Tenn. Med. Ctr., Knoxville, 1997, safety coord., slip/pack/utility, 1997—; slip/pack/utillity Alcoa Inc., Alcoa, Tenn. Mem.: Knoxville Writers Guild, Assn. Surg. Technologists. Home: 225 Grata Rd Knoxville TN 37914

MOORE, MANDY (AMANDA LEIGH MOORE), singer, actress; b. Nashua, NH, Apr. 10, 1984; d. Don and Stacy Moore. Host MTV show, Mandy, 2000. Actor(voice): (films) Dr. Doolittle 2, 2001, The Princess Diaries, 2001, A Walk to Remember, 2002 (MTV Movie award breakthrough performance-female, 2002, Teen Choice awards choice breakout performance-actress, with Shane West Teen Choice awards choice chemistry, 2002), How to Deal, 2003, Chasing Liberty, 2004; singer: (albums) So Real, 1999, I Wanna Be With You, 2000, Mandy Moore, 2001, Coverage, 2003. Office: Epic Records 550 Madison Ave New York NY 10022-3211*

MOORE, MARCIA G. human resources specialist; b. Portland, Oreg., May 2, 1951; d. William Edmond Burns and Betty Ray Welch; children: Jason Michael, Amy. Student Portland State U., 1969—73. Dir. human resources Tomball Regional Hosp., Tex., 1980—89, 1996—; dir. internat. recruiting Healthfirst Mgmt. Svc., Tyler, Tex., 1989—93; v.p. ops. Maxwell Healthcare, Tulsa, 1993—96; v.p. H.R. Tomball Regional Hosp., 1996—. Guest spkr. U. the Philippines, Manila, 1994; mem. adv. bd. Angeles U., Angeles City, 1991—. Mem.: Internat. Recruitment of Healthcare Profls. Republican. Methodist. Avocations: gardening, travel, reading. Office: Tomball Regional Hosp 605 Holderrieth Tomball TX 77375 E-mail: mmoore@tomballhospital.org.

MOORE, MARGARET ANN, musician, composer; b. Portland, Oreg., Dec. 14, 1939; d. Neil Ray Kochendoerfer and Sophie Marie Blatnik; m. Richard Roy Moore, July 6, 1961 (div. Apr. 1967); children: Wire Matthew, Jordan Benjamin. Student, Portland State Coll., 1957—58, U. So. Calif., L.A., 1958—60, U. Wash., 1960—61. Piano and class tchr. Clark Coll., Vancouver, Wash., 1964; improvisor Portland Ballet Sch., 1967—72; composer in residence St. Francis of Assisi Cath. Ch., Portland, 1975—94; tchr. piano Portland, 1960—. Adj. piano tchr. Reed Coll., Portland, 1973—74, Portland State U., 1975—77; asst. dir. Cmty. Music Ctr., Portland, 1979—89; adjudicator student compositions Oreg. Music Tchrs. Assn., Portland, 1986—87. Composer (librettist): (Operas) (children's opera) Iver and the Mystical Fire, 1990; composer: various psalms, songs, parts of Mass, 1975—94, (piano solo) Exile in Residence: Alex Solzhenitsyn, 1975; A. Avsbalomov Piano Concerto on Chinese Themes. Vol. Vols. of the Gorge, Portland, 2000—01; bd. dirs. Christensen Found., Portland, 1982—88; bd. dirs., artistic dir. Oreg. Friends of C.G. Jung, Portland, 1984—89. Recipient Outstanding Vol. award, Oreg. State Police, 2001; Nellie Tholen scholar, 1978. Mem.: Oreg. Music Tchrs. Assn., Nat. Fedn. Music Clubs. Avocations: writing, gardening, grandchildren.

MOORE, MARGARET ANNE, retired civilian military employee; b. Birmingham, Ala., Nov. 9, 1937; d. Leonard Elgie Turner and Fannie Ellen Black-Turner; m. Robert Eugene Hunter, Jan. 6, 1956 (div. 1967); children: Desiree Hunter, Rita Hunter, Rico Hunter, Rennie Hunter; m. John Moore, Dec. 21, 1968; 1 child, Monica Anne 1 stepchild, Dirk Eugene. A in Procurement and Materials Mgmt., Sinclair C.C., 1982; BA in Mgmt., Antioch U., 1990. Cert. acquisition profl., level I Dept. of Air Force, 1991, acquisition profl., level II Dept. of Air Force, 1992. Clk. typist Def. Electronics Supply Ctr., Dayton, Ohio, 1955—56, 1959—60; clk. stenographer Wright Patterson AFB, Ohio, 1965—66, procurement asst., 1966—78; clk. asst. technician Arlington City, Va., 1978—80, Wright Patterson AFB, Ohio, 1985—95, configuration mgr., 1985—95, ret., 1995. Watercolor art, one-woman shows include Paul Lawrence Dunbar House, 2001. Corr. sec. Blacks in Govt., Wright Patterson AFB, 1980—90; mem. Fairborn Art Assn. Mem.: Iota Phi Lambda (pres. 1991—93). Baptist. Avocations: art, aerobics. Home: 298 Carpenter Dr Fairborn OH 45324

MOORE, MARGARET D. human resources specialist; b. New Haven, Conn., 1948; BA, Smith Coll., 1970; MBA, Columbia U., N.Y.C., 1974. Treasury analyst PepsiCo, 1973—77, asst. treas., 1977—87, v.p. investor rels., 1987—99, sr. v.p. human resources, 1999—; sr. v.p., treas. Pepsi Bottling Group, 1998—99, bd. dirs. Bd. dirs. Michael Foods; mem. corp. adv. coun. Fin. Acctg. Stds. Bd. Office: Pepsico Inc 700 Anderson Hill Rd Purchase NY 10577*

MOORE, MARIANNE, special education services professional, educator; b. Salt Lake City, Apr. 7, 1951; d. Andrew Lee and Margie Ellen Karavitis; m. David Robert Moore, Nov. 22, 1976; children: Nicholas Andrew, Margie Joanne. BA, Wash. State U., Pullman, 1973; MS, U. Oregon, Eugene, 1975; cert. advanced studies, Regent U., Va. Beach, Va., 2000. Spl. edn. tchr. Mead (Wash.) Pub. Sch., 1975—80; adult edn. tchr. Big Bend CC SHAPE, Belgium, 1984—85; spl. edn. tchr. Fairfax County Pub. Schs., Alexandria, Va., 1987—89, Newport News Pub. Schs., 1990—96, chair spl. edn. dept., 1996—99, transition specialist, 1999—2000; dir. Postsecondary Edn. Rehab. Transition Program, Fisherville, Va., 2002—. Sec. Va. Divsn. Career Devel. & Transition, 2000—; advisor Shenandoah Valley Regional Program - TP, Fisherville, 2003—; registration planner State Transition Forum, 2003; pres. registration planner Internat. Divn. on Career Development and Transition Conf., 2003; registration chair Internat. Div. on Career Development and Transition Conf., 2003—. Mem. Chamber Ballet, Williamsburg, Va., 1997—2002. Mem.: Coun. of Adminstrn. of Spl. Edn., Divsn. Career Devel. and Transition, Coun. Exceptional Children. Office: Woodrow Wilson Rehab Ctr PERT W 350 PO Box 1500 Fisherville VA 22939

MOORE, MARILYN, federal agency administrator; b. Md. B in Bus. Mgmt., Pers. and Labor Rels. magna cum laude, U. Md., 1990; M in Applied Mgmt., U. Coll. Md., 1997. Pers. staffing specialist U.S. Office Pers. Mgmt., Washington, 1990; mgmt. analyst U.S. Census Bur., chief corr. mgmt./info. mgmt. staff Policy Office, 1998, chief corr. quality assurance; exec. secretariat records mgmt. divsn. FBI, Washington, 2002—. With D.C. Air Nat. Guard, 1986—95. Office: FBI J Edgar Hoover Bldg 935 Pennsylvania Ave NW Washington DC 20535

MOORE, MARSHA LYNN, elementary school educator, counseling administrator; b. Washington, May 19, 1946; d. Marshall Alexander and Doris Virginia (Diggs) Moore. BA, Howard U., 1967; MEd, U. Md., 1973. Sch. counseling K-12, cert. tchr. grades 1-6, sci. resource tchr. grades 1-6. 1st grade demonstration tchr. Anne M. Goding Sch. D.C. Pub. Schs., 1967—72; counselor Balt. County Schs., Towson, Md., 1972—77; fashion coord., mgr. Wallach's Ladies' Store, Nanuet, NY and Livingston, NJ, 1977—80; adult edn. cons., counselor East Orange (N.J.) Adult High Sch., 1980—83; coord. lang. arts Faith Hope Christian Sch., 1983—84; minority counselor Essex County C.C., Newark, 1984—85; equal opportunity fund counselor, instr. Kean Coll., Union, NJ, 1985—87; tchr. 5th grade Randle Highlands Elem. Sch., 1987—90; tchr. 5th and 6th grade Brookland Sch., Washington, 1990—98; 5th grade tchr., math. and sci. resource tchr. Shepherd Elem. Sch., Washington, 1998—2000; tchr. 6th grade math and sci. Bertie Backus Mid. Sch., Washington, 2002—03; ret., 2003. Coord. counselor Summer Youth Program, East Orange, 1982; career fair coord. East Orange Adult H.S., 1981, Essex County C.C., 1985; mem. discipline com. PTA Shepherd Sch., Washington, 1998—2002; liaison, exec. bd., hospitality com., multicultural com. PTA, 2000—02; math.-a-thon coord. St. Jude's, 2000, coord. parent math. workshop, 2000—02, sci. resource tchr., United States, 2000—02; coord. Sci. Careers Expo and 1st Sci. Bee, 2001; co-sponsor Student Coun., 2001—02; facilitator DCACTS, 2001—02; math. tutor, 2000—01; sgt.-at-arms WT Union Sch. Orgn., 2002—03. Editor: Sci. newsletter. Chmn. Teen Lift, NJ, Delteens, Washington; 2d v.p. Washington Pan-Hellenic Coun., 1994—96, fin. sec., 1996—98, co-chair Greek Forum, 1996—98; mentor Best Friends, Inc. Mem.: NAACP, AFT, Nat. Mid. Sch. Assn., Nat. Sci. Tchrs. Assn., Washington Tchrs. Union, U.S. Tennis Assn., Howard U. Alumni Assn. (reunion planning com. 1967, N.J. coord. 1980—87, v.p. Washington 1989—91, pres. 1991—93, parliamentarian Washington chpt. 1999—2001, chairperson membership com. Wash. chpt. 2003—, life mem. Washington chpt.), Schomburg Rsch. Ctr. (N.Y.C.), Kennedy Ctr. for Performing Arts, Friends of Andrew Rankin Chapel (adj. sec. 1994—97, newsletter co-chair, fundraising and archives coms.), Delta Sigma Theta (Diamond Life mem.). Episcopalian. Avocations: tennis, gardening, landscape designing, swimming, travel.

MOORE, MARY FRENCH (MUFFY MOORE), potter, advocate; d. John and Rhoda French; m. Alan Baird Minier, 1982; children: Jonathan Corbet, Jennifer Corbet, Michael Corbet. BA cum laude, Colo. U., 1964. Ceramics mfg., Wilson, Wyo., 1969-82, Cheyenne, Wyo., 1982—. Commr. County Teton (Wyo.), 1976-83, chmn. bd. commrs., 1981, 83, mem. dept. pub. assistance and social svc., 1976-82, mem. recreation bd., 1978-81, water quality adv. bd., 1976-82. Bd. dirs. Teton Sci. Sch., 1968-83, vice chmn., 1979-81, chmn., 1982; bd. dirs. Grand Teton Music Festival, 1963-68, Teton Energy Coun., 1978-83, Whitney Gallery of Western Art, Cody, Wyo., 1995—, Opera Colo., 1998—; mem. water quality adv. bd. Wyo. Dept. Environ. Quality, 1979-83; Dem. precinct committeewoman, 1978-81; mem. Wyo. Dem. Ctrl. Com., 1981-83; vice chmn. Laramie County Dem. Ctrl. Com., 1983-84, Wyo. Dem. nat. committeewoman, 1984-87; chmn. Wyo. Dem. Party, 1987-89; del. Dem. Nat. Conv., 1984, 88, mem. fairness commn. Dem. Nat. Com., 1985, vice-chairwoman western caucus, 1986-89; chmn. platform com. Wyo. Dem. Conv., 1982; mem. Wyo. Dept. Environ. Quality Land Quality Adv. Bd., 1983-86; mem. Gov.'s Steering Com. on Troubled Youth, 1982, dem. nat. com. Compliance Assistance Commn., 1986-87; exec. com. Assn. of State Dem. Chairs, 1989; mem. Wyo. Coun. on the Arts, 1989-95, chmn., 1994-95, Dem. Nat. Com. Jud. Coun., 1989—; legis. aide for Gov. Wyo., 1985, 86; project coord. Gov.'s Com. on Childrens' Svcs., 1985-86; bd. dirs. Wyo. Outdoor Coun., 1984-85; polit. dir., dep. mgr. Schuster for Congress, 1994-95; adminstrv. dir. Freudenthal for Gov., 2002, personnel coord., 2002; mem. pres.' adv. com. on the performing arts John F. Kennedy Ctr. for the Performing Arts, 1999-2001. Recipient Woman of Yr. award Jackson Hole Bus. and Profl. Women, 1981, Dem. of Yr. Nellie Tayloe Ross award Wyo. Dems., 1990. Mem. Alden Kindred of Am., Jackson Hole Art Assn. (bd. dirs., vice chmn. 1981, chmn. 1982), Assn. State Dem. Chairs, Soc. Mayflower Descendents, Pi Sigma Alpha. Home: 8907 Cowpoke Rd Cheyenne WY 82009-1234 E-mail: muffy.moore@bresnan.net.

MOORE, MARY JOHNSON, nurse; b. West Point, N.Y., Feb. 8, 1940; d. Robert Phillip and Edith Virginia (Carr) Johnson; m. Prentis Monroe Moore, Dec. 28, 1960 (dec. Jan. 1990); children: Carol Edith, Tracey Marie. Diploma, Boston City Hosp. Sch. Nursing, 1960. RN. Clinic nurse in pediatrics and obstetrics Harris County Health Dept./Lyons Clinic, Houston, 1982-85; clinic nurse Tex. Sch. for the Deaf, Austin, 1986-87; staff nurse pediatrics Ben Taub Hosp., Houston, 1989-92; telephone triage nurse, ob-gyn. McGregor Clinic, Houston, 1992-93; staff nurse pediatrics Grant Hosp., Chgo., 1994-96; clinic nurse Columbus-Maryville Hosp., Chgo., 1996—2002; travel nurse Star-Med Profl. Staffing, 2002—03; case mgr. Brockton (Mass.) Neighborhood Health Ctr., 2003—. Mem. vol. choir St. Chrysostoms Episcopal Ch., 1997—2002. George Monks Meml. scholar, 1960. Democrat. Avocations: art, music, history, collecting unicorns, angels and lighthouses. Home: 72 Pine St Brockton MA 02302 Office Phone: 508-559-6699 613.

MOORE, MARY KATHRYN, psychologist; b. Douglas, Wyo., Jan. 8, 1947; d. John Richard and Hazel May (Slichter) Lewis; children: Kathryn Noelle Moore Huckins, Nicole Marie Feria. BS, Black Hills State U., 1970; MS, S.D. State U., 1993. Lic. prof. counselor; cert. sch. counselor; nat. cert. counselor. Tchr. Natrona Sch. Dist., Casper, Wyo., 1968-69, Rapid City (S.D.) Sch. Dist., 1969-70, Rapid City Christian H.S., 1982-93, counselor, 1992-93, Black Hills Childrens Home Soc., Rockerville, S.D., 1995-96, Meade Sch. Dist., Sturgis, S.D., 1993-96. Dir. Home Alone Program, Meade Sch. Dist., 1993-96; dir. Crisis Intervention Team, Sturgis Elem., 1993-96, Crook County Sch. Dist., 1996. Mem. Phi Delta Kappa. Republican. Avocations: reading, walking, crafts, traveling, music. Home: 2997 Connie Ct Rapid City SD 57703-6453 Office Phone: 605-347-4770. E-mail: mary.moore@meade.kr.sd.us.

MOORE, MARY TYLER, actress; b. Bklyn., Dec. 29, 1936; d. George and Marjorie Moore; m. Richard Meeker, 1955 (div. 1961); 1 child, Richard (dec.); m. Grant Tinker, 1963 (div. 1981); m. Robert Levine, 1983. Chmn. bd. MTM Enterprises, Inc., Studio City, Calif. Stage appearances include (Broadway debut) Breakfast at Tiffany's, 1966, Whose Life Is It, Anyway?, 1980, Sweet Sue, 1988, The Players Club Centennial Salute, 1989, Rose's Dilemma, 2003; appeared in TV series Richard Diamond, Private Eye, 1957-59, Dick Van Dyke Show, 1961-66, Mary Tyler Moore Show, 1970-77, Mary, 1978, Mary Tyler Moore Hour, 1979, Mary, 1985, Annie McGuire, 1988, New York News, 1995, Mary and Rhoda, 1998; miniseries Gore Vidal's Lincoln, 1988, New York News, 1995; in TV movies Love American Style, 1969, Run a Crooked Mile, 1969, First You Cry, 1978, Heartsounds, 1984, Finnegan Begin Again, 1984, The Last Best Year, 1990, Thanksgiving Day, 1990, Stolen Babies, 1993 (Emmy award, Outstanding Supporting Actress in a Miniseries or Special, 1993), Payback, 1997, Mary and Rhoda, 2000, Like Mother, Like Son: The Strange Story of Sante and Kenny Kimes, 2001, Miss Lettie & Me, 2002, The Gin Game, 2003, Blessings, 2003; films: X-15, 1961, Thoroughly Modern Millie, 1967, Don't Just Stand There, 1968, What's So Bad About Feeling Good?, 1968, Change of Habit, 1969, Ordinary People, 1980 (Acad. Award nominee for best actress 1981), Six Weeks, 1982, Just Between Friends, 1986, Keys to Tulsa, 1996, Flirting with Disaster, 1996, Reno Finds Her Mom, 1997, Labor Pains, 1999, appeared on Broadway in Whose Life Is It Anyway?, 1980, Sweet Sue, 1987, Labor Pains, 2000, Chaste, 2002; in TV spl. How to Survive the Seventies, 1978, How To Raise a Drug Free Child; author: After All, 1995. Chair Juvenile Diabetes Found., 1985—. Recipient Emmy award Nat. Acad. TV Arts and Scis. 1964-65, 73-74, 76, Golden Globe award 1965, 81, Star on the Hollywood Walk of Fame, 1992; named to TV Hall of Fame, 1985. Office: William Morris Agy care Betsy Berg 151 S El Camino Dr Beverly Hills CA 90212-2775*

MOORE, MATTIE H. clergy, folk artist, retired educator; b. Empire, Ga., Apr. 27, 1910; d. Joe and Pearlie (Oneal) Hodge; m. William A. Moore, 1934 (dec. Sept. 1948); chldren: Patricia M. Jones, Iris M., Pinkney, Robert D. Moore. BA in Psychology/Edn., Rutgers U., 1974; MA in Psychology/Edn., Columbia, 1980. Cert. elem. tchr., N.J. Tchr. Newark Pub. Schs., 1965-70; minister African Am. Mth. Episcopal Ch., Newark, 1960—. Adv. bd. Mount Carmel Guild Mental Health Ctr., 1979. Artist producing folk art. Candidate for mayor City of Newark, 1978. Recipient New Cmty. Corp. award, Newark, 1983, People Helping People award Essex County, 1976, Essex Plz. Choir Svc. award, 1976, Anheuser Busch Svc. award for Cmty. Svc., 1995, Outstanding Svc. for Religion award Tau Gamma Delta Sorority, 1995, Outstanding Cmty. Svc. award Urban League of Essex County, 1995, Svc. award Bur. Children Svcs. Day Care Program, Women of Influence award YWCA of Essex and West Hudson, 1999, others. Avocations: reading, painting, internet, writing, playing piano. Home: 1060 Broad St Apt 754 Newark NJ 07102-2333

MOORE, MELANIE RUTH, veterinary technician; b. San Jose, Calif., Nov. 21, 1955; d. Alan Claude and M. Laverne (Galeener) M. BS in Biol. Sci., U. Calif., Davis, 1977. Registered vet. technician; registered x-ray technician; registered vet. dermatologist. Head registered vet. technician Berryessa Animal Hosp., San Jose, Calif., 1977—. Cons. CARE, Animal Res. Orgn., San Jose, 1994-2000; behavioral study participant Primate Ctr., U. Calif., Davis, 1976-77. Editor, cons. (humor book) Collecting Dead Relatives, 1987, Further Undertakings, 1989. Mem. Human Soc.; petition circulator Three Strikes and You're Out Campaign, San Jose. Mem. ASPCA, Archaeol. Inst. Am., Soc. Expdns. Democrat. Avocations: archaeology, evolutionary biology, world travel, horticulture, reading. Office: Berryessa Animal Hosp 940 Berryessa Rd San Jose CA 95133-1001

MOORE, MELINDA, public health physician; MD, MPH, Harvard U., 1975. Diplomate Am. Bd. Pediat., Am. Bd. Preventive Medicine. With divsn. viral diseases Ctr. Disease Control, Atlanta, 1978-80, with divsn. nutrition, 1980-81, dep. dir. internat. health program office, 1991-96; assoc. dir. Global Health Ctr. Disease Control, Nat. Ctr. Environ. Health, Atlanta, 1998-2000; dep. dir. DHHS Office Global Health Affairs, Rockville, Md., 2000—. Cons. Africa Child Survival Project, Atlanta and Zaire, 1982-87, Zaire SPH, 1987-89, Ctr. for Disease Control HIV Policy Office, 1989-91; acting assoc. dir. Global Health, 1996-97. Office: DHHS Office Global Health Affairs Parklawn Bldg 5600 Fishers Ln Rm 18-105 Rockville MD 20857 E-mail: mmoore@osophs.dhhs.gov., Melinda.Moore@hhs.gov.

MOORE, MILDRED THORPE, dietician; b. St. Louis, July 11, 1924; d. Walter Proctor and Rose Frances (Fiala) Thorpe; m. John Austin Moore, June 7, 1947; children: John A. Jr., Frances Ann, Thomas Thorpe, Lynn Brownell. BS in Dietetics, U. Ala., 1945; postgrad., St. Louis U. Hosps., 1945-46. Registered dietitian. Clin. dietitian Jefferson-Hillman Hosp., Birmingham, Ala., 1946-47, VA Hosp., Tuscaloosa, Ala., 1947-48; teaching dietitian Riverside Hosp. Sch. Nursing, Newport News, Va., 1963-82; cons. registered dietitian Va. Bapt. Retirement Cmty., Newport News, 1975-90, Sarah Bonwell Hudgins Assn. Retarded Citizens, Hampton, Va., 1980—. Sec.-treas. Nutritionists in Nursing Edn., 1979—81; mem. Peninsula Nutrition Coun., 1983—, Gerontol. Nutrition Practice, 1982—. Spkr. in field. Den mother Boy Scouts Am., Newport News, 1963—64; vol. Am. Heart Assn., Am. Cancer Soc., Leukemia Assn., 1959—; pres. PTA, Newport News., 1965, 1968; vol. reading tutor 2d-4th grades, 1994—; elder Presbyn. Ch., 1986—89, 1999—2002, pres., hon. life mem. Presbyn. Women, 1999—2002. Mem.: AAUW, Cons. dietitians Health Care (pres. Hampton br. 1961—63), Tidewater Dietetic Assn. (pres. 1956, 1968), Va. Dietetic Assn. (pres. 1972—74, del. 1976—79, Dietitian of the Yr. 1978), Am. Dietetic Assn. (mem. by-laws com. 1977—79), Va. Peninsula Alumni Zeta Tau Alpha (sec. 1994), Zeta Tau Alpha (alumni pres. 1983, Cert. Merit award 1985, Order of the Shield 1992). Republican. Avocations: travel, walking, antiques, bridge. Home and Office: 152 Milstead Rd Newport News VA 23606-1118 E-mail: mtmjam@aol.com.

MOORE, MINVON, political organization worker; b. Chgo. Attended, U. Ill., Chgo. With Nat. Rainbow Coalition/DNC Voter Project, numerous presdl. campaigns; dep. asst. to Pres. and dep. dir. polit. affairs, 1997—98; asst. to Pres. Bill Clinton and dir. pub. liaison at White House, 1998—2001; COO Dem. Nat. Com. (DNC), 2001—02; co-founder Am. Coming Together, 2003—; prin. Dewey Square Group, 2002—; strategist, sr. advisor to DNC chmn. Terry McAuliffe, 2002—. Named one of 100 Most Powerful Women in Wash., Washingtonian mag., 2001. Office: Dewey Square Group 1001 G St NW Ste 300E Washington DC 20001 Office Phone: 202-638-5616. Office Fax: 202-638-5612. Business E-Mail: mmoore@deweysquare.com.*

MOORE, NEVALYN, music educator; b. Laurel, Miss., Mar. 12, 1948; d. Shelby Milburn Price Sr. and Neva Trapp; m. James W. Moore, Aug. 29, 1970; children: Christopher, Brian, Bonnie, Jenny K., Matthew. BA in Music, Judson Coll., 1969; MusM in Organ Perf., U. Miss., 1971. Music therapist Dyer County (Tenn.) Sch. System, 1979-80; instr. music Dyersburg (Tenn.) State C.C., 1975-80; asst. prof. music Campbellsville (Ky.) U., 1980—; staff organist Lexington Ave. Bapt., Danville, 1989-96; staff accompanist Danville (Ky.) Children's Choir, 1993-98; asst. music dir. Louisville Youth Choir, 1998-2000; staff organist St. Matthews Bapt. Ch., Louisville, 1998-2000. Keyboard specialist Ky. Bapt. Conv., Louisville, 1989-93; organ cons. Pleasant Hill Bapt. Ch., Campbellsville, 1984-85. Co-compiler: Organ Registration, 1991, Organ Techniques, 1992, Let's Get Back to Basics, 1992; co-compiler, author: The Expressive Organist, 1993. Mem. h.s. restructuring com. Campbellsville H.S., 1993-94, sch. improvement com., 1994-95. Nevalyn Moore scholarship Danville Children's Choir, 1998. Mem. Music Educators Nat. Conf., Ky. Music Educators Assn. (4th dist. Coll./U. Tchr. of Yr., 2000, 02, Coll./U. Tchr. of Yr. 2002), Music Tchrs. Nat. Assn. (cert.), Ky. Music Tchrs. Assn. (master tchr. 1988—), Am. Guild of Organists, Am. Guild of English Handbell Ringers. Baptist. Avocations: sewing and design, bicycle riding, hiking, folk music. Home: 316 N Columbia Ave Campbellsville KY 42718-2267 Office: Campbellsville U 1 University Dr Campbellsville KY 42718-2799 Office Phone: 270-789-5342.

MOORE, PAMELA RAE, elementary school educator; b. Paulding, Ohio, Feb. 22, 1959; d. Loren J. and Louella I. Thomas; m. Chet Moore, Dec. 10, 1977; children: Amy Renae, Cheryl Kae. BS, Defiance Coll., 1990; MS, St. Francis U., 1995. H.s. learning disabilities tchr., Paulding, 1991—99; mid. sch. reading tchr., 1999—. Home: 819 E Wayne St Paulding OH 45879

MOORE, PAMELA SUE, music educator; b. Wellsboro, Pa., Jan. 31, 1960; d. Richard William and Dorothy Mae Lawson; m. Douglas A. Moore, July 7, 1984. MusB, Ea. Ill. U., 1982; MEd in Spl. Edn., U. Utah, 1997. Cert. tchr. music K-12 Wyo. Band dir., computer tchr. Marissa (Ill.) Jr./Sr. H.S., 1982—85; gen. music tchr. K-6 Whittier Elem. Sch., Muskogee, Okla., 1985—87; gen. music tchr. K-5 Aspen Elem. Sch., Evanston, Wyo.,

1987—99; piano keyboarding tchr. grades 1-5 Sheridan (Wyo.) County Sch. Dist. #2, 1999—. Cons., instr. Brain Gym, Sheridan, 2000—03; internat. folkdance instr. YMCA, Sheridan, 1999—2003; facilitator implications of brain rsch. Sheridan County Sch. Dist. #2, Sheridan, 2001—03. Contbr. Strategies for Teaching: Pre-kindergarten Music, 1995, Strategies for Teaching: K-4 General Music, 1996, articles to profl. jours. Named Wyo. Tchr. of Yr., Coun. of Chief State Sch. Officers, Wyo. Dept. Edn., 1996, Educator of Yr., Uinta County Conservation Dist., 1995. Mem.: NEA, Wyo. Music Edn. Assn. (elem. v.p. 1991—95), Ednl. Kinesiology Found. (profl. mem., Tchg. Through Movement award 2000—01), Delta Kappa Gamma Soc. Internat. Home: 1631 Steffen Ct Sheridan WY 82801 Office: Sheridan County Sch Dist # 2 Box 919 Sheridan WY 82801

MOORE, PATRICIA KAY, investor, public relations director; b. Peoria, Ill., Jan. 20, 1947; d. David Harold and Mary Jane (Gregoryk) Jenkins. BBA, U. Mo., 1978; MBA, 1981. Planning analyst Emerson Electric Corp., St. Louis, 1972-79; mgr. mktg. adminstrn. Emerson Electric WED, Houston, 1979; dir. mktg. adminstrn. HBE Corp., St. Louis, 1979-82; mgr. market rsch. Emerson Electric ESD, St. Louis, 1982-92; dir., investor rels. ESCO Techs. Inc., St. Louis, 1992—. Mem. Nat. Investor Rels. Inst. (past pres. St. Louis chpt.), U. Mo. Alumni Assn. Home: 10335 Cable Ave Saint Louis MO 63131-2710 Office: ESCO Techs Inc 8888 Ladue Rd Ste 200 Saint Louis MO 63124-2056

MOORE, PATSY SITES, food service consultant; b. San Marcos, Tex., Mar. 29, 1939; d. Sam W. and Hilda (Wiede) Sites. BS in Home Econs. Edn., S.W. Tex. State U., 1970. Owner, operator Westoner Kindergarten and Nursery Sch., San Marcos, 1965-68; food svc. dir. San Marcos Consol. Ind. Sch. Dist., 1975-97; cons. to food svc. industry, San Marcos, 1997—. Cons. in field., 1997—. Mem. steering com. Play Scape/Children's Park, San Marcos, 1992; mem. Hays County Pks. Adv. Bd., City of San Marco Sr. Citizens Adv. Coun.; sr. adv. bd. City of San Marcos, 2000—; adv. bd. Hays County Parks, 1998—; vice chmn. Hays Rep. Club, 2001-2002, sec., 2003. Mem. Am. Sch. Food Svc. Assn., Tex. Sch. Food Svc. Assn., Ctrl. Tex. Sch. Food Svc. Dirs. Assn. (founder, past pres.), Heritage Assn. (mem. bd. dirs. 2003-), Order Eastern Star, San Marcos Fedn. Rep. Women (pres.), Spring Lake Garden Club (sec. 1999, 2000, pres. 2002-03). Lutheran. Avocations: gardening, oil painting, lapadary. Home and Office: 285 Hilliard Rd San Marcos TX 78666-8905

MOORE, PEARL B. nursing educator; b. Pitts., Aug. 25, 1936; d. Hyman and Ethel (Antis) Friedman; 1 child, Cheryl. BS in Nursing, U. Pitts., 1968, M Nursing, 1974. Staff nurse Allegheny Gen. Hosp., Pitts., 1957-60; instr. Liliane S. Kaufman Sch. Nursing, Pitts., 1960-70, asst. dir., 1970, dir., 1970-72; cancer nurse specialist Montefiore Hosp., Pitts., 1974-75; coord. Brain Tumor Study Group, Pitts., 1975-83; adj. asst. prof. U. Pitts., 1983 . Contbr. articles in field to profl. publs. Fellow Am. Acad. Nursing; mem. ANA, Oncology Nursing Soc. (exec. dir. 1983—, CEO 1999, Disting. Svc. award 1995), Am. Soc. Clin. Oncology, Am. Soc. Assn. Execs., Nurses Alumnae U. Pitts., Sigma Theta Tau. Home: 5701 Centre Ave Pittsburgh PA 15206 Office: 125 Enterprise Dr Pittsburgh PA 15275 E-mail: pearl@ons.org.

MOORE, PEGGY SUE, corporation executive; b. Wichita, Kans., June 16, 1942; d. George Alvin and Marie Aileene (Hoskinson) M. Student, Wichita State U., 1961-63, Wichita Bus. Coll., 1963-64. Contr. Mears Electric Co., Wichita, 1965-69; pres., CEO CPI Corp., Wichita, 1969—2001, also bd. dirs., pres., CEO, 1999—; dir. food svc. Bethel Coll., 2001—; dietary dir. food svcs. PMMA of Midwest U.S., 2002—. Trustee Fringe Benefits Co., Kansas City, Mo., 1984-85. Active Rep. Nat. Com., Washington, 1985-86, task force, 1986—; treas., bd. dirs. Good Shepherd Luth. Ch., Wichita, 1980-85, mem., 1977—; active Wichita Commn. on Status of Women, 1988. CPI Corp. recipient of Blue Chip Enterprise prize U.S. C. of C., 1996. Mem. NAFE, DAR, Nat. Assn. of Women Bus. Owners, Wichita C. of C., Women's Nat. Bowling Assn. (bd. dirs., pub. com. 1969-76), Internat. Platform Assn., Kans. Purveyors Assn. (bd. dirs. 1988-89), Women's Speakers Bur. Avocations: bowling, golf, fishing. Office: CPI Corp 816 E Funston St Wichita KS 67211-4398

MOORE, RACHEL SUZANNE, performing company executive, dancer; b. Davis, Calif., Feb. 19, 1965; d. Charles Vincent and Patricia (Dudley) M. BA, Brown U., 1992; MA, Columbia U., 1994. Dancer Am. Ballet Theatre II, N.Y.C., 1982-84, 1984—88; devel. officer Nat. Cultural Alliance, Wash., 1994—95; dir., coord. Center for Cmty. Devel. & Arts Americans for the Arts, Wash., 1995—97; mng. dir. Ballet Theater of Boston, Boston, 1998; exec. dir. Project STEP, Boston, 1998—2001; dir. Boston Ballet Center for Dance Ed., Boston, 2001—04; exec. dir. Amer. Ballet Theatre, NYC, 2004—. Adjunct dance prof. Emerson Coll., Boston U. Presidential scholar U.S. Dept. of Edn., Washington, 1982. Mem. Am. Guild of Mus. Artists. Democrat. Unitarian Universalist. Office: Am Ballet Theatre 890 Broadway Fl 3D New York NY 10003-1211

MOORE, ROSEMARY KUULEI, art gallery administrator; b. San Diego, Apr. 16, 1955; d. Edward James and Rina Larn (Young) M.; m. Lance Wesley Holter, June 16, 1994; children: Ian Everest Yannell, Jade River Holter, Sean Maru Yannell, Michael McKinley Yannell, Sarah Lehua Hotter. Student, U. So. Calif., L.A., 1975, U. Hawaii, Kahului, 1980. Project coord. Hawaiian Sea Village, Amfac Property Corp., Kaanapali, 1979-80; shopping ctr. mgr. Whalers Village, Amfac Property Corp., Kaanapali, 1980-83; comm. mgr., adminstrv. dir. Amfac Property Corp., Kaanapali, 1983, property mgr., 1983-85; v.p. Kahikinui (Hawaii) Homes Project, 1990-93; chair, com. rels. dir. Haleakala Waldorf Sch., Kula, Hawaii, 1991-92, headmaster, 1992-95; mgr. Viewpoints Gallery, Mokawao, Hawaii, 1999—; dir. Viewpoints Galleries, Maui, Hawaii, 1999—; pres. Merchants Assocs., 2000—. Author: Lightworker, 1990, Mikey & Cocoa are Friends, 1992; contbr. articles to profl. jours. Coord. hwy. beautification Dept. Transp., Maui, 1992—; mem. steering com. Valley Isle Voters Assn., Maui, 1994. Mem. Nat. Wildlife Soc., Cousteau Soc. Avocations: writing, surfing, skin diving, hiking, camping. Office: Viewpoints Gallery 3620 Baldwin Ave Ste 101 Makawao HI 96768-9500

MOORE, SALLY FALK, anthropology educator; b. N.Y.C., Jan. 18, 1924; d. Henry Charles and Mildred (Hymanson) Falk; m. Cresap Moore, July 14, 1951; children: Penelope, Nicola. BA, Barnard Coll., 1943; LL.B., Columbia U., 1945, PhD, 1957. Asst. prof. U. So. Calif., Los Angeles, 1963-65, assoc. prof., 1965-70, prof., 1970-77, UCLA, 1977-81; prof. anthropology Harvard U., Cambridge, Mass., 1981—, Victor Thomas prof. anthropology, 1991—, dean Grad. Sch. Arts and Scis., 1985-89. Author: Power and Property in Inca Peru, (Ansley Prize 1957), 1958, Law as Process, 1978, Social Facts and Fabrications, 1986, Moralizing States, 1993, Anthropology and Africa, 1994, Law and Anthropology, 2004. Trustee Barnard Coll., Columbia U., 1991-92; master Dunster House, 1984-89. Rsch. grantee Social Sci. Rsch. Coun., 1968-69, NSF, 1972-75, 79-80, Wenner Gren Found., 1983; Guggenheim fellow, 1995-96. Fellow Am. Acad. Arts & Scis., Am. Anthrop. Assn., Royal Anthrop. Inst. (Huxley medallist, lectr. for 1999); mem. Assn. Polit. and Legal Anthropology (pres. 1983), Am. Ethnological Soc. (pres. 1987-88), Assn. Africanist Anthropologists (pres.-elect 1995, pres. 1996-98). Democrat. Office: Harvard U 348 William James Hall Cambridge MA 02138

MOORE, SHANNA LA'VON, chemical company executive; b. Cleveland, Tenn., Oct. 25, 1963; d. Joel Thomas and Minnie Jean (Hall) M. AAS, Cleve. State Community Coll., 1984; BS, U. Tenn., 1988. Tech. svc. rep. Mobil Chem. Co., Pittsford, N.Y., 1990-93, nat. account tech. specialist, 1993-96; application devel. mgr. Latin Am. Mobile Chem. Co., Sao Paulo, Brazil, 1996—; comml. application devel. leader ExxonMobil Chem. Co., Macedon, N.Y., 2000—. Supr. product and application devel. with South Am. customers. Author: HFF & S Machine Conversions, 1991. Republican. Avocations: exercise, playing piano, sports. Address: Exxon Mobil Chem Co 729 Pittsford Palmyra Rd Macedon NY 14502-9179

MOORE, SHARON HELEN SCOTT, gerontological nurse; b. L.I., N.Y., Nov. 7, 1947; d. James G. and Bernice Virginia (Conklin) Scott; m. Richard A. Moore Sr., July 5, 1966; children: Brian Keith, Richard A. Jr., Kevin Scott, Shannon Nicole. AAS, Fayetteville (N.C.) Tech. Inst., 1979; BSN, Med. U. S.S., 1993. RN, N.C., S.C., N.Y., Conn.; lic. long term care adminstr.; cert. gerontol. nursing, legal nurse cons. DON Elizabethtown (N.C.) Nursing Home; head nurse VA Med. Ctr., Fayetteville; coord. patient care Hospice Charleston, S.C.; DON, dir. human resources Sea Island Health Care Corp., Johns Island, SC; v.p. Sea Island Comprehensive Health Care Corp.; salsa nurse Marriott Sr. Living Svcs., Stamford, Conn.; owner Moore's Legal Nurse Cons. Svcs. Spkr. in field; bd. dirs. Phoebe Taylor Family Clinic. Active St. Paul AME Ch., Rockville Ctr., N.Y.; pres. family support group S.C. Army NG; vol. ARC, Fayetteville; bd, dirs. CYDC Big Brothers/Big Sisters. Indian Nurse scholar Nat. Soc. Colonial Dames Am., 1992. Mem. Nat. League Nursing, N.C. Nurses Assn., S.C. Nurse Assn. Home: 428 Jefferson Ave Rockville Centre NY 11570 Office: Brighton Gardens Stamford by Marriott 69 Roxbury Rd Stamford CT 06902-1214

MOORE, SHIRLEY THROCKMORTON (MRS. ELMER LEE MOORE), accountant; b. Des Moines, July 4, 1918; d. John Carder and Jessie (Wright) Throckmorton; m. Elmer Lee Moore, Dec. 19, 1946; children: Fay, Lynn Dallas. Student, Iowa State Tchrs. Coll., 1937-38, Madison Coll., 1939-41; MCS, Banjamin Franklin U., 1944. CPA. Asst. bookkeeper Sibley Hosp., Washington, 1941-42, Alvord & Alvord, 1942-46, bookkeeper, 1946-49, chief acct., 1950-64, fin. advisor to sr. ptnr., 1957-64; dir. Allen Oil Co., 1958-74; pvt. practice acctg., 1964—. Contbr. articles to profl. jours. Mem. sch. bd. Takoma Acad., Takoma Park, Md., 1970—; mem. hosp. bd. Washington Adventist Hosp., 1974-85; chmn. worthy student fund Takoma Park Seven Day Adventist Ch., 1987-88; trustee Benson Found., 1963-99; vol. Am. Women's Vol. Svc., 1942-45. Recipient Disting. Grad. award Banjamin Franklin U., 1961. Mem. AICPA, D.C. Inst. CPAs (pub. rels. com. 1976—), Am. Women's Soc. CPAs, Am. Soc. Women Accts. (legis. chmn. 1960-62, nat. dir. 1952-53, nat. treas. 1953-54), Bus. and Profl. Women's Club (treas. D.C. 1967-68), Banjamin Franklin U. Alumni Assn. (Disting. Alumni award 1964, charter, past dir.), DAR, Md. Assn. CPAs (charter chmn. membership com. Montgomery Prince George County 1963-64, chmn. student rels. com. 1964-67, pres. 1968-69, mem. fed. tax com. 1971-73). Mem. Seventh Day Adventist Ch. Home and Office: 2401 Pine Lake Dr West Columbia SC 29169-3737

MOORE, STEPHANIE LAFAYE, advocate, director; d. Victor and Gwendolyn Hillman; m. Galloway Moore, III, June 7, 2003; children: Si'Eirria Di'Voushia Singleton Moore, A'Mira Masaun-Celeste, Galloway III. Student, Kalamazoo Valley C.C., 1990—92. Program coord. Northside Assn. for Cmty. Devel., Kalamazoo, 1993—95; legis. asst. U.S. Ho. Rep., Rep. Upton 6th Dist., Kalamazoo, 1995—96; exec. dir. Fannie Lou Hamer Project, Kalamazoo, 1999—; field organizing dir. Mich. Citizen Action, Kalamazoo, 1996—2001. Recipient Black Achiever award, Kalamazoo YMCA, 2002. Mem.: LWV (assoc.), NAACP (assoc.; polit. action chair 2003—04), Battle Creek Chpt. A. Phillip Randolph Inst. (assoc.). Avocation: reading. Office: Fannie Lou Hamer Project 729 Academy St Kalamazoo MI 49007 Office Phone: 269-349-9760. E-mail: smoore@flhp.org.

MOORE, SUSANNA, writer; b. Bryn Mawr, Pa., Dec. 9, 1948; d. Richard Dixon and Anne (Shields) M.; 1 child, Lulu Lenane Sylbert. Author: My Old Sweetheart, 1982 (Am. Book award nomination for best first novel 1983, Sue Kaufman prize for first fiction Am. Acad. Inst. Arts and Letters 1983), The Whiteness of Bones, 1989, Sleeping Beauties, 1993, In the Cut, 1995, One Last Look, 2004. Recipient Literary Lion award N.Y. Pub. Libr., 1993, PEN/Ernest Hemingway citation, Sue Kaugman prize, 1983.*

MOORE, TARA, secondary school educator; b. Rockville Centre, N.Y., Oct. 8, 1971; d. Michael Angelo Pantony and Constance Mary Gee; m. Edward Arthur Moore, Feb. 16, 2003. BA in History, Marist Coll., Poughkeepsie, N.Y., 1993; MS in Edn., Hofstra U., Hempstead, N.Y., 1995. Tchr. West Hempstead H.S., NY, 1995—96, Grand Ave. Mid. Sch., Bellmore, NY, 1996—. Mem.: Bellmore Merrick U.S. Tchrs. (new tchr. rep. 2000—), N.Y. State Congress of Parents and Tchrs. (life). Avocations: reading, travel. Office: Grand Ave Middle Sch 2301 Grand Ave Bellmore NY 11710

MOORE, TERRI KRAMER, information technology manager; d. Robert and Karen Kramer; m. John Jerrell Moore; children: Katren, Clayton. BS Orgnl. Mgmt., Colo. Christian U., 1996, MA in Curriculum and Instrn., 1997. Program adminstr. UNT Health Sci. Ctr., Fort Worth, Tex., 2000—; assoc. dir, curr and acad program mgmt UNTHSC/Tex. Coll. of Osteo. Medicine, Fort Worth, Tex., 1998—2000. Lead developer/spkr. tng. Pfizer Pharmaceuticals Nat. Hdqs., Manhattan, NY, 2000—01; lead developer/trainer ctr. for procedural excellence Am. Coll. of Osteo. Family Physicians, Chicago, Ill.; external reviewer Assn. Am. Med. Colls., Washington, 2002—03; peer rev. lead trainer Tex. Assn. of Local Health Officials, Austin, Tex., 2003—03; spkr. in field. Co-author articles to profl. jours. Recipient Distinguished Achievement award for Leadership and Academic Achievement, 1996. Mem.: Healthcare Businesswomen's Assn. (assoc.; rsch. com.). Office: UNT Health Sci Ctr 3500 Camp Bowie Blvd Fort Worth TX 76107 E-mail: tmoore@hsc.unt.edu.

MOORE, VERNA, county official; b. Belleville, Ill., June 26, 1926; d. Walter William and Stella Blomenkamp; m. Jay H. Moore, Apr. 5, 1952 (wid.); 1 child, Gail Moore Elmore. Classified advt. mgr., sales rep. The Item, Sumter, S.C., 1966-91; dep. coroner Sumter County, 1975-92, coroner, 1993—. Bd. mem. Elected Ofcls., Columbia. Active S.C. Dem. Party, Sumter, 1966—. Avocations: bowling, golfing. Home: 1814 W Oakland Ave Sumter SC 29150-5539 Office: Courthouse 141 N Main St Sumter SC 29150-4965

MOORE, VIRGINIA LEE SMITH, elementary school educator; b. Middletown, N.Y., May 13, 1943; d. James William and Anna Van Alst (Suydam) Smith; m. Thomas J. Moore, Oct. 16, 1965 (div. Apr. 1980); 1 child, Christian Thomas. AA in Liberal Arts, Orange County C.C., 1963; BA in Sociology magna cum laude, SUNY, Buffalo, 1965; MS in Edn., SUNY, New Paltz, 1980; MS in Edn. of Gifted, Coll. New Rochelle, 1990, cert. elem. edn., staff devel., 1994; cert. sch. adminstrn., 1994. Cert. elem. tchr., N.Y. Spl. edn. tchr. The Devereux Found., Glen Loch, Pa., 1965-66; elem. tchr. Harris Sch., Coatesville, Pa., 1967, Pine Bush (N.Y.) Cen. Schs., 1967-70, 78-00, substitute tchr., 1970-71; nursery sch. tchr. Olivet Meth. Nursery Sch., Coatesville, Pa., 1976-78; profl. devel. coord. Pine Bush Sch. Dsit., 1998. Presenter ednl. workshops Pine Bus Sch. Dist., Haldane Sch. Dist., Cold Spring, NY, Eldred Sch. Dist., Marlboro, NY, Middletown (N.Y.) Tchr. Ctr., N.Y. State Tech. Edn. Assn., Brookhaven Nat. Lab., NY, 1994, Nevele Conference Ctr., Ellenville, NY, 1995, Rochester (N.Y.) Inst. Tech., 1996, SUNY, Oswego, 1996, Rennselaer Poly. Inst., Troy, NY, 1997, Marriot Conf. Ctr., Syracuse, NY, 1999, Sci. Tchrs. Assn. N.Y. State, Nevele Conf. Ctr., Ellenville., 1995, Internat. Tech. Edn. Assn., Indpls., 1999; participant math., sci. and tech. on elem. level program NSF, 1997—2000. Contbr. articles to profl. jours., sci. and tech. articles to profl. publs. Pres. Redtown Residents' Assn., Middletown, 1988—; sec. Orange County C.C. Alumni Bd. Dirs. Recipient Dean's Acad. Excellence award Coll. of New Rochelle, 1991, Orange County Conservation Tchr. of Yr., 1993, N.Y.S. Conservation Tchr. of Yr., 1993, Presdl. award for excellence in math. and sci. tchg. N.Y. State, 1997; Partnership in Edn. grantee Area Fund Orange County, N.Y., 1991, Energy grantee Orange and Rockland Utilities, 1995, Tech. grantee Mid-Hudson Tchr. Ctr., 1997, 98, Energy grantee N.Y. State Electric and Gas, 1998. Mem. NSTA, Internat. Tech. Edn. Assn. (N.Y. State Elem. Sch. Tchr. Excellence award 1998-99), N.Y. State United Tchrs., Sci. Tchrs. Assn. N.Y. State (Outstanding Sci. Tchr. award 1992, Excellence in Sci. Tchg. award 1995), N.Y. State Tech. Edn. Assn. (Tech. grantee 1999), Phi Beta Kappa. Baptist. Avocations: piano, reading, local environmental issues, development of interactive science museum exhibits. Home: 1672 Route 211 E Middletown NY 10941-3718

MOORE, VIRGINIA LORRAINE, special education educator; b. Kingsville, Tex. d. Joseph Victor and Virginia O. Moore; m. Jerry Wayne Oakley, June 6, 1970 (div. June 6, 1980); children: Carolyn Oakley Hawkins, Cheryl Oakley, Catherine Ann Oakley. BA, Sul Ross U., 1971; MA, U. Tex. of Permian Basin, 2001. Cert. tchr. Spanish, history, bilingual, ESL, English spl. edn., elem. and secondary reading Tex. Sec. Adobe Oil & Gas Corp., Midland, Tex., 1981—85; Spanish tchr. Kermit (Tex.) Ind. Sch. Dist., 1985—86; bilingual tchr. Midland Ind. Sch. Dist., Midland, 1987—92, gen. edn. tchr., 1992—94; substitute tchr. Ector County Ind. Sch. Dist., Odessa, Tex., 1994—96, Spanish tchr., 1996—98, spl. edn. tchr., 1998—. Mem.: Tex. State Tchrs. Assn., Internat. Reading Assn., Coun. Exceptional Children, Phi Theta Kappa. Presbyterian. Avocation: reading historical fiction. Home: 2506 Fannin Ave Midland TX 79705 E-mail: moore2506@aol.com.

MOOREFIELD, CLAUDIA CANDYCE, confectionary marketing professional; b. Fresno, Calif., Nov. 24, 1949; d. Ernest Karl and Alice Vanoosh (Karoglanian) Hosepian; m. Kenneth Gene Moorefield, Dec. 9, 1978; 1 child, Kyle Zachary. BA summa cum laude, Calif. State U., Fresno, 1972, Cert. tchg., 1988. Assoc. editor Autoweek Mag., Reno, Nev., 1972-74; public rels. specialist Toyota Mtr. Sales, USA, Torrance, Calif., 1974-77; acct. exec. Bob Thomas & Assoc., Redondo Beach, Calif., 1977; sales rep. L'Oreal Cosmetics, Fresno, 1979-87; banking svcs. exec. Bank of Fresno, 1989; sales assoc. SRA Sch. Group, Fresno, 1989-95; sales rep. See's Candies, Fresno, 1995—. Author and editor: (book) 50 Years of Our Union, 1970. Mayoral appointee Meux Home Adv. Com., Fresno, 1976-78; mem. Friends of the Library, 1992—; mem. Fresno Conv. and Visitors Bur. Recipient Newswriting award William Randolph Hearst Found., 1969. Mem. Phi Kappa Phi, Kappa Alpha Theta. Avocations: reading, antiques, movies. Home: 2175 Morris Ave Clovis CA 93611-7408 Office: Sees Candies 380 W Shaw Ave Clovis CA 93612-3603

MOOREFIELD, SUSAN MORGAN, music educator; b. Greensboro, N.C., Aug. 26, 1953; d. Judson Jones and Frances (Loflin) Morgan; m. Perry Wayne Moorefield, Dec. 14, 1974; children: Lindsey Anne, Brandon Judson. MusB, U. N.C. Greensboro, 1974; MusM, U. Memphis, 1979. Cert. tchr. music, nat. bd. cert. tchr. Nat. Bd. Profl. Tchrs. Soc., 2002. Tchr. music Lithonia H.S., Ga., 1975, Whitehaven Presbyn. Sch., Tenn., 1976—78, Willow Oaks Sch., Memphis, 1978—81, Penn Christian Acad., Norristown, Pa., 1983—84, Thomasville Primary Sch., NC, 1995—. Mem.: N.C. Assn. Edn., Nat. Assn. Music Educators. Republican. Baptist. Home: 408 Wyndwood Dr Jamestown NC 27282*

MOORER, ANNETTE JOHNSON See WYNDEWICKE, KIONNE ANNETTE

MOORE SHAFFER, PATRICIA ANN, museum educator, art association administrator; b. Port Colborne, Ont., Can., June 22, 1965; arrived in U.S., 1996; d. Ronald Elgin Moore and Marion Anna Mills; m. Clifford Gordon Shaffer, Nov. 17, 1996; 1 child, Anna Rachel Shaffer. BA with honors, Brock U., St. Catharines, Ont., Can., 1988; MA, U. Toronto, Ont., Can., 2000. Cert. in mus. studies Ont. Museums Assn., 1991. Edn. officer Chatham (Ont.) Cultural Ctr., 1988—89; pub. program officer Art Gallery St. Thomas (Ont.)-Elgin, 1989—92, exhbn./program coord., 1992—93; coord. exhbn. enhancement and spl. projects McMichael Can. Art Collection, Kleinburg, 1993—94, head programs and interpretation, 1994—96; curator edn. Morris Mus. Art, Augusta, Ga., 1996—2002, curator edn., dep. dir., 2002—. Grant reviewer Inst. Mus. and Libr. Svcs., Washington, 1997—; adj. instr. Augusta State U., 2001—. Author (editor): (exhibition catalog) Expressions of Naturalism: Ronald Kingswood; contbr. chapters to books, articles to profl. jours. Named Ednl. Program of the Yr., Ga. Assn. Museums and Galleries, 2001. Mem.: Coalition for Arts and Edn. (steering com. mem. 1993—94), Ont. Assn. Art Galleries (bd. mem. 1995—96), Ga. Art Edn. Assn. (mus. edn. divsn. rep. 1997—99, sec. 1999—2003, Art Mus. Educator of the Yr. 2001, 2003), Am. Assn. Museums (southeastern rep. 1999—2003, com. for audience rsch. and evaluation). Methodist. Office: Morris Museum Art 1 Tenth St Augusta GA 30901 Office Phone: 706-724-7501. Business E-Mail: pmoore@themorris.org.

MOORHEAD, JENNIFER THERESA, art educator; b. Detroit, June 16, 1956; d. Arthur A. Jr. and Veronica W. (Popiela) DeB.; m. Jack David Moorhead, Aug. 4, 2000; children: Alison Mary Presley, Jacob Arthur Presley. Student, Banff Sch. Fine Arts, Alta., Can., 1974, U. No. Colo., 1974-75, U. Mich., 1977; BFA, Western Mich. U., 1978; MFA, U. Md., 1981. Mgr. Brush Gallery, Houston, 1981-82; adj. instr. North Harris Coll., Houston, 1982-84; program coord. art Kingwood (Tex.) Coll., 1984-94, divsn. chair, 1988-89, program coord. graphic design, 1992-93; assoc. prof. art U. Evansville, Ind., 1994—; program dir. graphic design and multimedia Westwood Coll. of Tech., Denver, 1997—, exec. dir., 2000. Tchg. asst. U. Md., College Park, 1979-81; adminstr. art after sch. program Kingwood Coll., 1984-86; owner DeBlock Design, Evansville, 1986-96; counselor European trips Cultural Heritage Alliance, Phila., 1992—; exec. dir. DeBlock Integrated Svcs., Alliance Tng. Sys., 2002—; prin., owner Furtography; presenter in field. One-woman shows at Fine Arts of Houston, 1982, 83, Ten Brooks Gallery, N.Y.C., 1986, Learning Resource Ctr. Gallery, Kingwood Coll., 1992, The Houstonian, 1993, Artswatch, 1997, Denver (Colo.) West Gallery, 2003; exhibited in group shows at Steers Gallery, Kalamazoo, Mich., 1978, Western Mich. U., Kalamazoo, 1978, Glen Oaks Country Club Auction, Birmingham, Mich., 1978, Fransic Scott Key Bldg., College Park, Md., 1980, U. Md. Gallery, 1981, Glassel Sch. Art, Houston, 1982, Ctr. for Art and Performance, Houston, 1982, Fine Arts of Houston Gallery, 1983, Chocolate Bayou Theater, Houston, 1983, McKowey Gallery, Houston, 1983, Cmty. Art Ctr., West Bend, Wis., 1985, Washington Ave. Gallery, N.Y.C., 1985, Diverse Works, Houston, 1988, Lawndale Annex, U. Houston, 1987, 88, 89, Rosenburg Gallery, Galveston, Tex., 1989, Archway Gallery, Houston, 1989, 90, North Harris Coll. Gallery, Houston, 1984, 85, 86, 89, 90, 91, 92, 93, Two Houston Ctr., 1987, 90, 91, 92, Sam Houston State U. Gallery, 1990, Baytown (Tex.) Civic Ctr., 1990, Transco Towers, Houston, 1991, Toni Jones Gallery, Houston, 1991, Brazosport (Tex.) Coll. Gallery, 1992, Art League Gallery, Houston, 1992, Shepherd Plz., Houston, 1993, Firehouse Gallery, Houston, 1993, West End Gallery, Houston, 1994, Dishman Gallery, Lamar U., Beaumont, Tex., 1994, 96, Krannert Gallery Art, U. Evansville, 1994, 95, San Francisco Women Artists Gallery, 1994, 96, Evansville Mus. Arts and Scis., 1994, 95, 96, Thorns Gallery Art, Ft. Hays State U., Hays, Kans., 1995, L.A. Conv. Ctr., 1995, Indpls. Marriott, 1995, Sawtooth Bldg. Galleries, 1995, S.W. Ind. Artists Collaborative, 1995, Indpls. Art Ctr., 1996, Art Pavilion, San Jose (Calif.) Conv. Ctr., 1997, Art Gallery, Marist Coll., Poughkeepsie, N.Y., 1997, A Boy & His Dog, Key West, Fla., 2003, Harrison Gallery, Key West, Fla., 2003, others. U. Md. scholar, 1979-81; recipient Hon. Mention award Tri-State Exhbn., Beaumont, 1986, Galveston Art League, 1988, 89, Top Artist award 4th Ann. East End Show, Lawndale Annex, 1988, 2d Pl. award YMCA Corp. Challenge, 1995, Southwestern Ind. Artists Collaborative, 1995. Mem. Univ. and Coll. Designers Assn., Coll. Art Assn., Founds. of Art and Theory in Edn., Amazing Space, Diverse Works, Founds. of Art and Theory in Edn., Houston Apple Users' Group, Houston Area Women's Ctr., Southwestern Ind. Artists Collaborative, Women's Caucus for Arts, Visual

Arts Alliance, Am. Inst. Graphic Arts. Avocations: airplane gliding, snow skiing, horseback riding, sail racing, dog training, parachute jumping. Home: 8337 Vivian St Arvada CO 80005-5277

MOORHEAD, ROLANDE ANNETTE REVERDY, artist, educator; b. Périgueux, France; d. RémyJean and Andrée Marcelle (Lavollée) Reverdy; m. [illegible] Moorhead, III, Sept. 30, 1960; children: Edward Marc, Roland Elliott, Rémy Bruce. Degree in liberal arts, Coll. Technique, Nice, France, 1954. Bi-lingual sec., France, 1957-58, French Embassy, Washington, 1959-60, 68-70; chmn. exhibit com. Lauderdale-By-The-Sea Art Guild, Ft. Lauderdale, Fla., 1972-75, v.p., 1972-74, founder group 5 Women Artists; exhibit com. Broward Art Guild, Ft. Lauderdale, Fla., 1976; treas., dir. Alliance Francaise, Miami, Fla., 1973-75. Juror, lectr. in field; invited guest artist Franco-Am. Art Show, Curemonte, France, 1996-97. One-woman shows include numerous galleries, Ft. Lauderdale area, 1971—, Ocean Club Art Gallery, Ft. Lauderdale, 1971-74, Pier 66 Gallery, Ft. Lauderdale, 1973, 75, 76, Ft. Lauderdale City Hall, 1974, 77-78, 81-88, 91-94, 95-2000, St. Basil Orthodox Ch., North Miami Beach, 1977, Galerie Vallombreuse, Biarritz, France, 1977, Gallerie Mooffe, Paris, 1978, Galerie du Palais des Fêtes, Périgueux, 1978, 88, Le Club Internat., Ft. Lauderdale, 1979, Leonard Gallery, Ft. Lauderdale, 1990-92, Tallahassee (Fla.) Capitol Bldg., 1990, Lighthouse Pt. (Fla.) Gallery, 1990, Hollywood (Fla.) Art and Cultural Ctr., 1987, 89, 90, 91, 93, 95, Ft. Lauderdale Arts Inst., 1991, 93-95, Dover Gallery, Boca Raton, Fla., 1992; Galerie Mouffe, Paris, 1978, Glass Gallery, Pembroke Pines, Fla., 2001; exhibited in group shows Gallery YES, Wilton Manors, Fla., 2001, Wave Gallery, Key west, Fla., Webber Art Center, Ocala, Fla., 2003; Broward Art Guild, 1971, 73, 74, Point of Am. Gallery, Ft. Lauderdale, 1971, 73, Internat. Festival, Miami, 1976, Internat. Salon, Biarritz, 1977, Internat. Summer Salon, Paris, 1977, Fine Art Gallery Show and Competition, Long Galleries, Ft. Lauderdale, 1979, Pembroke Pines (Fla.) City Hall, 1982, Hollywood City Libr., 1982, also area banks, ch. and libr., numerous local art festivals, Schacknow Mus. Plantation, Fla., 2000, Ft. Lauderdale Mus. Art, 2000; represented in permanent collections: Fr. Lauderdale City Hall, DAV Hdqrs., Washington, Associated Aircraft Co., March of Dimes Bldg. (both Ft. Lauderdale), Oakland Pk. Libr., Fla., St. Josephs Convent, St. Augustine, Fla., US Air Force Mus., Ohio, Main Line Fleets, Inc., Palm Beach, Fla., Creditreform, Dusseldorf, Germany, St. Front Cathedral, Périgueux, St. Sacerdoce Cathedral, Sarlat, France, Club Med, Fla. and Caribbean, also numerous pvt. collections US and Europe; author art manual for Broward Arts Coun., Fla., 1986. Recipient Best in Show award Internat. Salon, Biarritz, 1977; named artist in residence Broward County Sch., 1985. Mem. Am. Soc. Portrait Artists, Nat. Assn. Women Artists, Fla. Watercolor Soc., Palm Beach Watercolor Soc., Nat. League Am. Penwomen, Art 24, Périgueux, Internat. Soc. Marine Painters, Am. Watercolor Soc., Cathedral St. Sacerdoce, Nat. Mus. Women in Arts, Nat. Mus. Am. Indian, Gold Coast Water Color Soc. (pres. 1984-87), 2+3 The Artist Orgn., Union des Francais de l'Etranger. Office: PO Box 8692 Fort Lauderdale FL 33310-8692

MOORHOUSE, LINDA VIRGINIA, symphony orchestra administrator; b. June 26, 1945; d. William James and Mary Virginia (Wild) M. BA, Pa. State U., 1967. Sec. San Antonio Symphony, Tex., 1970-71, adminstrv. asst., 1971-75, asst. mgr., 1975-76; exec. dir. Canton (Ohio) Symphony, 1977—. Mem. Ohio Arts Coun. Music Panel, 1980-82, 87-89, Mich. Arts Coun. Music Panel, 1986. Bd. dirs. Stark County unit Arthritis Fedn., 1986-92, treas., 1989-91; bd. dirs. Canton Palace Theatre Assn., treas., 1994-96, pres., 1998-99; active Cen. Stark County United Way Allocations Panel, 1991-96. Mem. Met. Orch. Mgrs. Assn. (pres. 1983-85), Orgn. Ohio Orchs. (pres. 1985-86), Am. Symphony Orch. League (bd. dirs. 1983-85, nat. 1st ladies' site com. 1997—), Stark County Women's Hall of Fame (charter inductee), Soroptomist (Canton, Ohio, Women of Distinction 1992), Nat. First Ladies Libr. Office: Canton Symphony Orch 1001 Market Ave N Canton OH 44702-1024

MOOS, VERNA VIVIAN, special education educator; b. Jamestown, N.D., July 1, 1951; d. Philip and Violena (Schweitzer) M. BS in Edn., Valley City State U., 1973; MEd, U. So. Miss., 1983, EdS, 1988; AA, Minot State U., 1987; postgrad., East Tex. State U., U. Tex., N.D. State U., U. N.D., Kans. State U., McGill U. Supr. recreation Valley City (N.D.) Recreation Dept., 1969-73; tchr. Harvey (N.D.) Pub. Schs., 1973-75; tchr. spl. edn. Belfield (N.D.) Pub. Schs., 1975-77; edn. therapist N.D. Elks Assn., Dawson, 1976-77; tchr. spl. edn. Dickinson (N.D.) pub. Schs., 1977-87; ednl. technician ABLE, Inc., Dickinson, 1984-87; tchr. spl. edn. Pewitt Ind. Sch. Dist., Omaha and Naples, Tex., 1987—; tchr. adult edn. N.E. Tex. C.C., Mt. Pleasant, 1989—. Local and area dir. Tex. Spl. Olympics, Austin, 1988—; local, regional and state dir. N.D. Spl. Olympics, 1972-87; local coord. Very Spl. Arts Festival; mem. Am. Heart Assn., 1979-87, N.D. Heart Assn., 1979-87; mem. adminstrv. bd. First United Meth. Ch., Naples, Tex., 1994—; active Communities-In-Sch. program for at-risk students, 1995—. Named Dickinson Jaycees Outstanding Young Educator, 1979, Dickinson C. of C. Tchr. of Yr., 1985, Dallas area Coach of Yr., Tex. Spl. Olympics, 1993, Dir. of Yr., N.D. Spl. Olympics, 1985. Mem. NEA, Coun. Exceptional Children, Naples C. of C., Delta Kappa Gamma (scholar), Phi Delta Kappa, Kappa Delta Pi. Avocations: travel, reading, working, sports. Home: PO Box 788 Omaha TX 75571-0788 Office: Pewitt CISD PO Box 1106 Omaha TX 75571-1106

MOOSBRUGGER, SABINE ANDREA, education educator, writer; d. Lothar Gerhard and Christa Maria Moosbrugger. BA in English, U. So. Colo., 1993, BA in Spanish, 1994, BS in Liberal Studies and Elem. Edn., 2002. Provisional Tchr. Lic., Elem. Edn. Colo. Dept. of Edn., 2003, Provisional Vocat. Credential, Consumer/Family: Early Childhood Edn. Colo. State Bd. for C.C. and Occupl. Edn., 2003. Tchr. 3d grade Pueblo Sch. Dist. 60, Colo., 2003—; adj. instr., early childhood edn. Pueblo C.C., 2001—; child care group leader/site dir. YMCA of Pueblo, 1994—2001. Author: (poem) How To Write Free Verse (Hon. Mention, Poetry Contest, 2001). Mem.: Nat. Sci. Tchr. Assn., Nat. Coun. Tchrs. Math., Nat. Coun. Tchrs. English. Roman Catholic.

MORA, GABRIELA, language educator, researcher; b. Santiago, Chile; d. Carlos Mora and Rosario Cruz; m. Harold Fruchtbaum, June 20, 1972. PhD in Hispanic Lit., Smith Coll., 1971. Prof. de Castellano Santiago Coll., 1957—60; asst. prof. Spanish CUNY, N.Y.C., 1971—76; instr. Spanish U. Mass., Amherst, Mass., 1963—69; asst. prof. Spanish Columbia U., N.Y.C., 1977—80; assoc. prof. Spanish Rutgers U., New Brunswick, NJ, 1989—98, prof. II of Spanish, 1998—. Book evaluator U. Tex., Austin, Duke U., Durham, NC, 1996; cons. reader PMLA. Author: Hostos intimista: Introduccion a su Diario, 1976, Theory and Practice of Feminist Literary Criticism, 1982, Diario de Hostos Introduction, 1990, En Torno al Cuento, 1994, El Cuento Modernista, 1996, Clemente Palma: El Modernismo Decadente y Gótico, 2000. Mem.: MLA (chair divsn. L.Am. 1995—96), L.Am. Studies Assn. (Juror prize 1998). Home: 560 Riverside Dr 7K New York NY 10027 Office: Rutgers U 105 George St New Brunswick NJ 08901-1414

MORACA-SAWICKI, ANNE MARIE, oncology nurse; b. Niagara Falls, N.Y., Sept. 28, 1952; d. Joseph R. and Joan (Forgione) Moraca; m. Richard L. Sawicki, Sept. 15, 1979. BSN, D'Youville Coll., 1974; MS in Nursing, SUNY at Buffalo, 1977. Asst. prof. nursing D'Youville Coll., Buffalo, 1977-81; clin. editor Springhouse (Pa.) Corp., 1981-82; charge nurse Mt. St. Mary's Hosp., Lewiston, N.Y., 1982-84; surg. coord., adminstrv. asst. Dr. Richard L. Sawicki, Niagara Falls, N.Y., 1983—. Clin. cons., externship site supr. Niagara County C.C., Sanborn, N.Y.; bd. dirs. Health Assn. Niagara County, Inc., adult day care program Health Assn. Niagara County Inc. Contbr.: Nurses Legal Handbook, 1985, Pharmacotherapeutics: A Nursing Process Approach, 1986, 2d edit., 1990, 3rd edit., 1994, 4th edit., 1998; clin. editor, contbr. Nurses Ref. Libr. Series Vols. on Drugs, Definitions, Procedures and Practices; clin. reviewer Manual of Med./Sug. Nursing, 1995, contbr., 1996; clin. reviewer Critical Care Handbook and IV Drug Handbook, 1995; clin. cons. Critical Care Plans, 1987, Taber's Cyclopedic Med. Dictionary, 16th edit., 1989. Recipient Cert. of Appreciation Niagara County C.C., 1988, 91, 92, Cmty. Svc. award Am. Cancer Soc., 1978, Miss [illegible], Am. Cancer Soc. Nursing Fellowship Grant, 1977; Grad. fellow SUNY, Buffalo, 1976-77. Mem. AAUP, N.Y. State Nurse's Assn., Health Assn. Niagara County (chairperson 1995—, bd. dirs. adult day care program), Sigma Theta Tau. Home: 4658 Vrooman Dr Lewiston NY 14092-1049 E-mail: ams928@webtv.net.

MORAHAN-MARTIN, JANET MAY, psychologist, educator; b. N.Y.C., Jan. 13, 1944; d. William Timothy and May Rosalind (Tarangelo) Morahan; m. Curtis Harmon Martin, June 2, 1979; 1 child, Gwendolyn May. AB, Rosemont (Pa.) Coll., 1965; MEd, Tufts U., 1968; PhD, Boston Coll., 1978. Asst. mkt. rsch. analyst Compton Advt. Co., N.Y.C., 1965-67; mkt. rsch. analyst Ogilvy & Mather Advt., N.Y.C., 1967; ednl. rsch. asst. Tufts U., Medford, Mass., 1968-69; counselor Psychol. Inst. Bentley Coll., Waltham, Mass., 1971-72; dir. counseling svcs. Bryant Coll., Smithfield, R.I., 1972-75, psychology instr., 1972-76, asst. prof. psychology, 1976-81, assoc. prof. psychology, 1981-91, prof. psychology, 1991—. Bd. dirs. Multi-Svc. Ctr., Newton, Mass., 1980-82. Contbr. articles to profl. jours., chpts. to books; reviewer APA Conv., 1985—, Teaching of Psychology Jour., 1988—, Collegiate Micro-Computer Jour., 1991, 93, Nat. Soc. Sci. Jour., 1991; mem. editl. bd., spl. edit. editor Cyber Psychology and Behavior. Bd. dirs. Wellesley (Mass.) Community Children's Ctr., 1986-90, Coun. for Children, Newton, Mass., 1984-86. NIMH fellow, 1967-68; NSF grantee, 1974-76, U.S. Office Edn. grantee, 1980. Mem. APA, Mass. Audubon Soc., Internat. Soc. for Online Mental Health (founding mem.), Soc. for Tchg. of Psychology, Soc. Computers in Psychology. Avocations: photography, antiques, gardening, literature. Home: 17 Fuller Brook Rd Wellesley MA 02482-7108 Office: Bryant Coll 1150 Douglas Pike Smithfield RI 02917-1291 E-mail: jmorahan@bryant.edu.

MORALES, DIANE K. federal agency administrator; b. Houston, July 11, 1946; d. Arthur Clement and Helen Mary (Araiza) M. BA, U. Tex.-Austin, 1968. Account exec. Goodwin, Dannenbaum, Littman & Wingfield, Houston, 1968-70; pub. relations rep. Gittings, Inc., Dallas, 1970-71; asst. buyer, mgr. Neiman-Marcus, Dallas, 1971-80; sr. assoc., mktg. mgr. 3/D Internat., Houston, 1980-81; dep. asst. sec. policy U.S. Dept. Interior, Washington, 1981-83; bd. dirs. CAB, Washington, 1983-86; v.p. Earth Tech. Corp., Washington, 1986-88; pvt. practice cons. Washington, 1988-90; dep. asst. sec. def. for logistics Dep. Def., Washington, 1990—; dep. under secy. logistics material readiness U.S. Dept. Defense, Washington, 2001—. Mem. Def. Depot Maintenance Coun.; chmn. Def. Material Mgmt. Bd, Def Transp. Polic Coun., Def. Energy Policy Coun. Pres. Downtown Rep. Women's Club, Dallas, 1979-80, bd. dirs. Dallas County Men's Rep. Club, 1980, Dallas County Women's Rep. Club, 1980; mem. Rep. Women's Fed. Forum, Rep. Nat. Hispanic Assembly. Republican. Presbyterian. Office: US Dept Defense Logistics Material Readiness 3500 Defense Pentagon Washington DC 20301-3500

MORALES, MARCIA PAULETTE MERRY, language educator, archaeologist; b. Denver, Dec. 10, 1946; d. Paul Robert Merry and Berneice Roberta Lyddon; m. Jorge Bernardo Morales, Dec. 28, 1977; children: Marcia Paloma, Elisa Berenice, Andrea Paul-Etta. BA, U. Denver, 1969; MA cum laude, U. Am., 1975. Rsch. asst. dept. anthropology U. Ill., Puebla, Mexico, 1972—75; tchr. Eng., art history Escuela Preparatoria, Cuautla, Mexico, 1975—76; tchr., coord. Eng. Colegio Oquetza, Cuautla, 1982—91; tchr. anthropology, Eng. Centro Cultural Iberoamericano, Cuernavaca, Mexico, 1992—95; tchr. Spanish Aztec (N.Mex.) HS, 1996—. Instr. Spanish Fort Lewis Coll., Durango, Colo., 1997—. Contbr. chapters to books Ancient Chalcatzingo, 1987. Fellow: Durango Heartbeat (pres. 1997—), San Juan Audubon Soc. (treas. 1996—). Methodist. Avocations: hiking, birdwatching, travel.

MORALES, MARY E. social worker; b. Va., Jan. 14, 1972; d. Juan and Wanda I. Morales. BA in Psychology and BA in Environ. Studies, Yale U., 1994. Social worker Evergreen Children's Svcs., Det., 1994—96; child devel. specialist Klingberg Family Ctr., New Britain, 1998—99; resdl. supr. St. Agnes Family Ctr., West Hartford, Conn., 1997—99; high risk newborn social worker Dept. Children & Families, New Britain, 1999—. Mem. child protection team Bristol (Conn.) Hosp., 1999—. Vol. P.E.P. (Youth at Risk), Plainville, Conn., 1999—; mentor St. Agnes Family Ctr., West Hartford, 1999—. Recipient Conn. Cmty. Svc. award, Yale U., 1991—94, award for outstanding cmty. edn., U. Conn. Med. Sch. Home: 123 Stearns St Bristol CT 06010-5134

MORALES-HENDRY HOLGUIN, MARIA B. realtor, poet; b. Bogota, Colombia, Apr. 19, 1948;, U.S.1949; d. Alfredo L. Holguin and Beatrice Fairbanks Murray; m. Ricardo Alfonso Morales-Hendry, July 26, 1969 (div. Feb. 1992); children: Vanessa Isobel, Veronica Alexandra. Student, U. de los Andes, Colombia, 1980, Pratt Inst., 1972; AS in Data Processing, Palm Beach Jr. Coll., 1968. Computer programmer Estudios Tecnicos, Bogota, Colombia, 1968—69, PMI, N.Y.C., 1969—73; realtor assoc. VIP Realty, Wellington, Fla., 1988—93, Prestige Properties, Wellington, 1994—98, Gerald H. Grant, West Palm Beach, Fla., 1999—2000, Continental Properties, West Palm Beach, Fla., 2001, Linda A. Gary Real Estate, Palm Beach, Fla., 2002—03, Martinique II Realty, Wellington, Fla., 2003—. Author: Jewel of Verse, 2001, (poems) Love Lights, 2000, The Jewel of Verse II, 2003, La Joya del Verso, 2003, (poems) Dream of Love (Editor's Choice award, Internat. Libr. of Poetry, 1994), My Rainbow of Wishes (Editor's Choice award, Internat. Libr. of Poetry, 2000), (songs) Will You, Will I, 2000, tonight is Forever, 2001; contbg. author: Best Poems and Poets of the 20th Century. Republican. Roman Catholic. Avocations: photography, dance, art. Home: 1801 S Flagler Dr #208 West Palm Beach FL 33401 Office: Martinique II Realty 14765 Haymarket Ct Wellington FL 33414

MORALES-MARTIN, GISELA, interior designer; b. Miami, Fla., Mar. 14, 1959; d. Oscar and Silvia Morales; m. Richard Martin, Nov. 4, 1987 (div. Jan. 1997); children: Brittany Martin, Anthony Martin. B in Interior Design, Fla. Internat. U. Asst. designer Robison & Assocs., Coral Gables, Fla., 1980—81; sr. designer Dennis Jenkins Assocs., Coral Gables, 1981—85; head designer Blitstein Design Assocs., Coral Gables, 1985—89; owner, pres. Gisela Martin & Assocs., Coral Gables, 1989—. Critic student presentations Fla. Internat. U., Miami, 1993—96. Recipient 1st pl. Comml. Project, Interior Design Guild, 1998. Mem.: Nat. Trust of Historic Preservation, Am. Soc. Interior Design, Mercy Hosp. Aux.Program. Democrat. Roman Catholic. Avocation: Avocations: exercise, gardening, bird watching. Office: 285 Sevilla Ave Coral Gables FL 33134

MORAN, BARBARA BURNS, librarian, educator; b. Columbus, Miss., July 8, 1944; d. Robert Theron and Joan (Brown) Burns; m. Joseph J. Moran, Sept. 4, 1965; children: Joseph Michael, Brian Matthew. AB, Mount Holyoke Coll., S. Hadley, Mass., 1966; M in Librarianship, Emory U., Atlanta, 1973; PhD, SUNY, Buffalo, 1982. Head libr. The Park Sch. of Buffalo, Snyder, NY, 1974-78; prof. Sch. Info. and Libr. Sci. U. N.C., Chapel Hill, 1981—, asst. dean, 1987-90, dean, 1990-98, prof. and dir. internat. programs, 1999—. Participant various seminars; evaluator various edn. progs.; cons. in field; bd. govs. UNC Press, 1998—. Author: Academic Libraries, 1984; co-author: (with Robert D. Stueart) Library and Information Center Management, 6th edit., 2002; contbr. articles to profl. jours., chpts. to books; mem. editl. bd. Jour. Acad. Librarianship, 1992-94, Coll. and Rsch. Libraries, 1996-2002. Coun. Libr. Resources grantee, 1985, Univ. Rsch. Coun. grantee, 1983, 89, others. Mem. ALA, Assn. for Libr. and Info. Sci. Edn., Popular Culture Assn., N.C. Libr. Assn., Beta Phi Mu. Home: 1307 Leclair St Chapel Hill NC 27517-3034 Office: Univ NC Sch Info & Libr Sci Chapel Hill NC 27599-0001 E-mail: moran@ils.unc.edu.

MORAN, [illegible] AMES, library director; b. Camden, Maine, June 22, 1940; d. Robie Frank and Dorothy Dyer Ames; m. Andrew Jackson Moran, Dec. 3, 1966; children: Heather Elizabeth, Melissa Ames. BA, U. Maine, 1962; MA in Law & Diplomacy, Fletcher Sch. Law & Diplomacy, 1964; MLS, U. S.C., 1997. Intelligence officer CIA, Washington, 1964-68; sch. libr. Fairfax (Va.) County Schs., 1981-87; libr. Camden (Maine) Pub. Libr., 1988-90, libr. dir., 1990—. Bd. dirs. Camden Tech. Conf., 1997-98; chair Maine Libr. Commn., 2000—. Mem. ALA, Maine Libr. Assn. (pres. 1998-2000), Pub. Libr. Assn. Small Pub. Libr. Assn., Camden Garden Club, Phi Beta Kappa. Republican. Episcopalian. Avocations: sailing, needlework. Home: 32 Atlantic Hwy Northport ME 04849-3010 Office: Camden Pub Libr 55 Main St Camden ME 04843-1794

MORAN, JOAN JENSEN, physical education and health educator; b. Chgo., Sept. 25, 1952; d. Axel Fred and Mary J. (Maes) J.; m. Gregory Keith Moran. BS in Edn., Western Ill. U., 1974; MS in Edn., No. Ill. U., 1978. Cert. tchr., Ill. Tchr., coach East Coloma Sch., Rock Falls, Ill., 1974—. Part-time recreation specialist Woodhaven Lakes, Sublette, Ill., 1975-79; cons. Ill. State Bd. Edn., Springfield, 1984—; instr. NDEITA, Ill., 1988—; facilitator Project Wild, Ill., 1990—. Instr. ARC, Rock Falls, 1978—, Am. Heart Assn., Rock Falls, 1978—; exec. bd. East Coloma Cmty. Club; fitness del. to Russia and Hungary, 1992; cons. Alcohol Awareness & Occupant Restraint Ill. State Bd. Edn., Substance Abuse Guidance Edn. Com., Rock Falls Drug Free Cmty. Grant com., Whiteside County CPR Coord. com. Recipient Western Ill. U. Alumni Achievement award, 1993, Western Ill. Master Tchr. award, 1993, Svc. award Ill. Assn. Health, Phys. Edn., Recreation and Dance, 1991, 92, Outstanding Young Woman award, 1986, Phys. Educator of Yr. award, 1988; named Mid. Sch. Phys. Edn. Tchr. of Yr. Midwest AAHPERD, 1993, Ill. Assn. Health, Phys. Edn., Recreation and Dance, 1992, Gov.'s Coun. Health and Phys. Edn. award, 1991, Am. Tchr. of Yr. award Walt Disney Co., 1993, Excel award Ill. State Bd. Edn., 1995, finalist Ill. Tchr. of Yr., 1996, Milkin Nat. Educator award, 1997, Health Edn. award and Quarter Century award Ill. Assn. Health, Phys. Edn., Recreation and Dance, 1999, Presidential citation, 1998; named to USA Today Tchr. Team, 2000. Mem.: AAHPERD (Health Tchr. of Yr. midwest chpt. 2001), Environ. Edn. Assn. Ill., East Coloma Edn. Assn. (pres., pub. rels., v.p. 1993—94), Ill. Edn. Assn., No. Dist. Ill. Assn. Health, Phys. Edn., Recreation and Dance (newsletter editor 1984—85, exec. bd. 1985—90, treas. 1985—90), Ill. Assn. Health, Phys. Edn., Recreation and Dance (v.p. teenage youth 1988—90, pres. 1994, past pres., conv. coord. 1995, Honor Fellow award 1996). Democrat. Lutheran. Avocations: skiing, hiking, biking, reading, traveling. Home: 1903 E 41st St Sterling IL 61081-9449

MORAN, KATE, sculptor, photographer; b. Langhorne, Pa., Dec. 27, 1958; BA in Visual Arts, Antioch Coll., 1982; cert., Pa. Acad. Fine Arts, Phila., 1988; MFA, U. N.C., 1992. One-woman shows include Fleisher Art Meml., Phila., 1992, Westby Art Gallery, Rowan Coll. N.J., Glassboro, 1992, More Gallery, Phila., 1995, Lafayette Coll., Williams Ctr. for Arts, Easton, Pa., 1995, John Michael Kohler Arts Ctr., Shebyoyan, Wis., 1996, U. N.C., Chapel Hill, 1997 (also vis. artist, lectr.), Steinbaum Krauss Gallery, N.Y.C., 1997, 98, List Gallery, Swarthmore (Pa.) Coll., 1997, Mangel Gallery, Phila., 1998, Mus. Am. Art, Pa. Acad. Fine Arts, 1998, Bernice Steinbaum Gallery, Miami, Fla., 2000, Olin Gallery, Kenyon Coll., Gambier, Ohio, 2000; 2 woman shows SPACES, Cleve., 1996, Suzanne H. Arnold Art Gallery, Lebanon Valley Coll. Pa., Annville, 1996; exhibited in group shows, 1991—, including Del. Art Mus., Wilmington, 1991, 93, 96, Print Club, Phila., 1991, New Orleans Mus. Art, 1992, Phila. Art Alliance, 1992, 94, Nexus Gallery, Phila., 1993, Stuart Levy Gallery, N.Y.C., 1993, 94, More Gallery, 1993, 94, Beaver Coll., Glenside, Pa., 1994, Snug Harbor Cultural Ctr., S.I., N.Y., 1995, Woodmere Art Mus., Phila., 1996, Phila. Mus. Art, 1996, 98, Rosenwald-Wolf Gallery, U. Parts, Phila., 1996; represented in permanent collections Mus. Am. Art at Pa. Acad. Fine Arts, Phila. Mus. Art, Woodmore Art Mus., New Orleans Mus. Art, State Mus. Pa., Harrisburg, CIGNA Mus. an Art Collection, Phila., Bryn Mawr (Pa.) Coll. Library; work represented in various publs. Recipient award Friends of Beaver Coll., 1991, purchase award New Orleans Mus. Art, 1992; John Michael Kohler Arts-Industry Residency, 1997, Works on Paper award Pa. Coun. on the Arts, 2000; fellow Pa. Coun. on Arts, 1992-93, 95-96, photography fellow PEW Fellowships in Arts, 1993-94; grantee Leeway Found., 1996-97, 2000. Home: 357 Leverington Ave Philadelphia PA 19128 Office: The Bernice Steinbaum Gallery 3550 N Miami Ave Miami FL 33127 E-mail: kmor@erols.com.

MORAN, MARY SHANKS, hydrogeologist; b. Biloxi, Miss., Feb. 8, 1950; d. John William and Sara Lillie (Kirklin) Shanks; m. William Madison Moran, June 5, 1971; 1 child, Alice Janette. BS in Geology, Tenn. Tech. U., 1973; MS in Geology, Vanderbilt U., 1977; postgrad., Ohio U., 1979. Cert. and lic. profl. geologist. Hydrologist U.S. Geol. Survey, Nashville, 1974-77; hydrogeologist, rsch. assoc. Oak Ridge (Tenn.) Nat. Lab., 1977-80, hydrogeologist rsch. staff, 1981-85; sr. hydrogeologist Henningson, Durham & Richardson, Knoxville, 1980-81; hydrogeologist Birmingham, Ala., 1985-87; sr. hydrogeologist Sci. Applications Internat., Birmingham, 1987-89; environmental svcs. mgr. Atec Assocs., Birmingham, 1989; chief scientist, prin. Gallet & Assocs., Inc., Birmingham, 1989—. Geotech and environ. cons., 1989—; mem. adv. bd. Geoenviron. Cons., 1995—, Ala. State Drinking Water Act, 1998—; mem. Ala. Bd. Licensure Profl. Geologists, 1996—, Ala. Onsite Sewage Mgmt. Com., 1999—. Co-author: (book) Water Resources Investigations U.S. Geological Survey, 1977, Sourcebook of Hydrologic/Ecological Features Water Resouce Regions of the Conterminous U.S., 1980; contbr. articles to profl. jours. Named Outstanding Young Woman of Am. Mem.: ASCE (mem. geoinst. mem. com. 1999—), ASFE Profl. Firms Practicing Geoscis. (Svc. award 1998), Am. Inst. Profl. Geologists (sect. pres. 1993—95, Svc. award), Geol. Soc. Am., Assn. Groundwater Scientists and Engrs. (dir. 1995—97, Svc. award 1995), Rotary (pres. 1994—95), Sigma Xi. Avocations: horseback riding, needlepoint, field geology, drawing. Home: 913 Masters Ln Birmingham AL 35244-3262 Office: Gallet & Assocs Inc 320 Beacon Pkwy W Birmingham AL 35209-3171 E-mail: mmoran@gallet.com.

MORAN, PATRICIA, lawyer; b. Wilmington, Del., 1959; BS, U. Scranton, 1981; JD, Villanova U., 1984. Bar: Del. 1984. Atty. Skadden, Arps, Slate, Meagher & Flom LLP, N.Y., ptnr., 1994—. Office: Skadden Arps Slate Meagher & Flom LLP Four Times Square New York NY 10036*

MORAN, PATRICIA GENEVIEVE, corporate executive; b. Evanston, Ill., July 26, 1945; d. James Moran; children: Christine Coyle, Thomas Beddia, Donald Beddia. Student, Marquette U. Dir. corp. transp. JM Family Enterprises, Inc., 1984, corp. assoc. rels. dir., 1985, v.p., 1985-88; group v.p. sales Southeast Toyota, Deerfield Beach, Fla., 1988-89; pres., CEO JM Family Enterprises, Inc., Deerfield Beach, Fla., 1989—2000, chmn., 2000—. Bd. dirs. Am. Heritage Life Ins. Co. Bd. dirs. Take Stock in Children, Boca Raton Resort and Club. Named One of Top 50 Working Women by Working Woman's Mag. Mem. Nat. Assn. Automobile Dealers, Am. Internat. Automobile Dealers Assn., Fla. Council of 100, Com. of 200. Office: JM Family Enterprises 100 NW 12th Ave Deerfield Beach FL 33442

MORAN, RACHEL, lawyer, educator; b. Kansas City, Mo., June 27, 1956; d. Thomas Albert and Josephine (Portillo) Moran. AB, Stanford U., 1978; JD, Yale U., 1981. Bar: Calif. 1984. Assoc Heller, Ehrman, White & McAuliffe, San Francisco, 1982-83; prof. law U. Calif., Berkeley, 1984—, Robert D. and Leslie-Kay Raven prof. law, 1998—. Vis. prof. UCLA Sch. Law, 1988, 2002Stanford (Calif.) U. Law Sch., 1989, NYU Sch. Law, 1996, U. Miami Sch. Law, 1997, U. Tex. Law Sch., 2000; chair Chicano/Latino

Policy Project, 1993-96; dir. Inst. for Study Social Change, 2003—. Contbr. articles to profl. jours. Recipient Disting. Tchg. award, U. Calif. Mem.: ABA, Calif. Bar Assn., Am. Law Inst., Phi Beta Kappa. Democrat. Unitarian Universalist. Avocations: jogging, aerobics, reading, listening to music. Office: U Calif Sch Law Boalt Hall Berkeley CA 94720 Office Phone: 510-643-6351. E-mail: moran@law.berkeley.edu.

MORAN, SHARYN LEE, financial consulting company executive; b. Savannah, Ga., May 19, 1946; d. John J. and Sara Helen (Pritchett) M.; m. John Weisner, Feb. 28, 1973 (div. Aug. 1979). Grad. high sch., Marietta, Ga. Procider liaison, supr. Blue Cross/Blue Shield, Atlanta, 1970-77; acct. exec. Sta. WEEL Radio, Fairfax, Va., 1977-78; adminstrv. asst. Vis. Nurse Assn., Atlanta, 1978-80; ins. coord, supr. Ambulatory Svcs. Am. Inc., Atlanta, 1980-83; retail mgr. Interior Design Store, Atlanta, 1983-90; mgr. accounts receivable Robert H. Pogue & Assocs., Atlanta, 1990-92; mgr., ins. specialist So. Orthopedic Clinic PC, Atlanta, 1992-94; owner, mgr. Barrington Fin. Group, Inc., Atlanta and Lawrenceville, Ga., 1994—. Designer, writer procedure manuals related to ins., personal tng. and renal dialysis. Vice pres. Crown Park Homeowners Assn., 1996-97. Winner nat. contest Supervisory Mgmt. publ., 1973; featured in Atlanta Jour., 1973. Mem. NAFE. Democrat. Baptist. Avocations: interior design, antiques, snow skiing, publishing cookbook decated to her grandmother. Home: 102 Knotts Landing Dr Woodstock GA 30188-4559 Office: Barrington Fin Group Inc PO Box 1853 Lawrenceville GA 30046-1853

MORAN, SHEILA KATHLEEN, journalist; b. Norwalk, Conn. d. Edmond Joseph and Alice Marie (Laux) M.; m. John Joseph Reynolds, Apr. 2, 1987 (dec. Apr. 1993). BA in European History, Manhattanville Coll., Purchase, N.Y. Sportswriter, reporter AP, N.Y.C., N.Y. Post, N.Y.C., L.A. Times; actress, freelance writer L.A.; prodr. Evensong Assocs., N.Y.C. Vol. VA Hosp., L.A., Meml. Sloan Kettering Cancer Ctr., N.Y.C.; freelance reporter, USA Today. Mem.: AFTRA, Inner Circle, Prodrs. Group, N.Y.C., Actors' Equity Assn., Screen Actors Guild. Democrat. Episcopalian. E-mail: sheilamora@aol.com.

MORANG, DIANE JUDY, writer, television producer, business entrepreneur; b. Chgo., Apr. 28, 1942; d. Anthony Thomas Morang and Laura Ann Andrzejczak. Student, Stevens Finishing Sch., Chgo., 1956, Fox Bus. Coll., 1959-60, UCLA, 1967-69. Mem. staff Chgo. Sun Times, Daily News, 1957, Drury Ln. Theatre, Chgo., 1961-62, AM Show ABC-TV, Hollywood, Calif., 1970-71; creator, owner Internet store. Judge 2 categories regional Emmy Awards, 1985, chair, mem. judging panel, 89. Author: How to Get into the Movies, 1978; author, creator: The Rainbow Keyboard, 1991, The Translation of the Code of Music into Mathematics; creator: The Best Kids' Show in the World, The Best Dog Treats in the World; contbr. numerous articles to newspapers, mags. Bd. dirs., mem. scholarship com. Ariz. Bruins, UCLA Alumni Assn.; mem. Nat. Mus. Women in the Arts, Washington, D.C.; mem. Nat. Women's Hall of Fame, Seneca Falls, N.Y. Mem. NATAS (mem. Hollywood Emmy Award-winning team Hollywood, Calif. 1971), Ariz. Authors Assn. (bd. dirs.), Autry Mus. of Western Heritage, Amon Carter Mus. Roman Catholic.

MORANT, JOCELYN JUANITA JOHNSON, music educator; b. Smithfield, Va., Sept. 7, 1956; d. Paul Westover and Marie Hardy (Ford) Johnson; children: Natalie, La Sheena, Carlton, Mariana, Naomi, Stephanie, Paul. BS, Norfolk (Va.) State U., 1977. Lic. tchr. Va. Tchr. City of New Haven, 1978—81, Southampton Pub. Schs., Courtland, Va., 1986—87, Newport News (Va.) Pub. Schs., 1995—; assoc. min. Ch. of Jesus, Hampton, Va. Mem.: Music Educators Nat. Conf. Home: 219 S Curry St Hampton VA 23663 Office: Sedgefield Elementary School 804 Main St Newport News VA 23605

MORARIU, CORINA, professional tennis player; b. Detroit, Michigan, Jan. 26, 1978; d. Albin and Rodica Morariu; m. Andrew Turcinovich. Grad., St. Andrews H.S., 1996. Mem. U.S. Nat. Tennis team, 1996. Won Jr. Championship Australian, French and U.S. Opens, 1995, Australia, 1994, Wimbledon, doubles, 1999 (with Lindsay Davenport), Australian Open Mixed Doubles (with E. Ferreira), 2001; winner 1 Career Singles Title, 10 Career Doubles Titles, WTA Tour. Office: USTA 70 W Red Oak Ln White Plains NY 10604-3602 also: ATP Tour 201 Atp Tour Blvd Ponte Vedra Beach FL 32082-3211

MORAVEC, CHRISTINE D. SCHOMIS, medical educator; b. L.A., Apr. 26, 1957; BA, John Carroll U., 1978, MS, 1984; PhD, Cleve. State U., 1988. Tchr. Trinity H.S., Garfield Heights, Ohio, 1978-80; grad. teaching asst. dept. biology John Carroll U., Cleve., 1982-84; rsch. assoc. dept. cardiovascular biology Cleve. Clinic Found., 1990-93, project scientist dept. cardiovascular biology, 1990-93, asst. staff dept. cardiovascular biology, 1993-94; asst. prof. dept. physiology & biophys. Case Western Res. U. Sch. Medicine, Cleve., 1993—. Adj. asst. prof. Cleve. State U., 1994—; asst. staff Ctr. Anesthesiology Rsch. Cleve. Clinic Found., 1994—. Contbr. articles to profl. jours. Grad. fellow Cleve. Clinic Found., 1984-88, Postdoctoral fellow, 1988-89, recipient Tarazi fellow, 1989. Mem. Am. Physiol. Soc., Am. Heart Assn. (basic sci. coun. 1990—; Established Investigatorship award 1995), Ohio Physiol. Soc., Electron Microscopy Soc. Northeastern Ohio, Cardiac Muscle Soc. Office: Cleve Clin Found Ctr Anesthesiology Found 9500 Euclid Ave # FF40 Cleveland OH 44195-0001

MORAWETZ, CATHLEEN SYNGE, mathematician; b. Toronto, Ont., Can., May 5, 1923; arrived in U.S., 1945, naturalized, 1950; d. John Lighton and Elizabeth Eleanor Mabel (Allen) Synge; m. Herbert Morawetz, Oct. 28, 1945; children: Pegeen Morawetz Rubinstein, John Synge, Lida Morawetz Jeck, Nancy. BA, U. Toronto, 1945; SM, MIT, 1946; PhD, NYU, 1951; degree (hon.), Ea. Mich. U., 1980, Smith Coll., 1982, Brown U., 1982, Princeton U., 1986, Duke U., 1988, N.J. Inst. Tech., 1988, U. Waterloo, 1993, U. Dublin, 1996, U. Toronto, 1996. Research assoc. Courant Inst., NYU, 1952—57, asst. prof. math., 1957—60, assoc. prof., 1960—65, prof., 1965—, assoc. dir., 1978—84, dir., 1984—88. Chmn. bd. Sch. Theoretical Physics Dublin Inst. for Advanced Studies, 1995—2000. Former editor various math. jours., author articles in applications of partial differential equations, especially transonic flow and scattering theory. Trustee Princeton U ., 1973—78, Sloan Found., 1980—94. Recipient Nat. medal of Sci., NSF, 1998; fellow Guggenheim, 1967, 1979; grantee Office of Naval Rsch., 1990. Fellow: AAAS, Royal Soc. Can.; mem.: NAS, London Math. Soc., Royal Irish Acad., Soc. Indsl. and Applied Math., Am. Philos. Soc., Am. Acad. Arts and Scis., Am. Math. Soc. (term trustee 1975—85, pres. 1995—97). Office: CIMS 251 Mercer St New York NY 10012-1110

MORBY, JACQUELINE, venture capitalist; b. Sacramento, June 19, 1937; d. Junior Jennings and Bertha (Backer) Collins; m. Jeffrey L. Morby, June 21, 1959; children: Andrew Jennings, Michelle Lorraine. BA in Psychology, Stanford U., 1959; M in Mgmt., Simmons Grad. Mgmt. Sch., Boston, 1978. Assoc. TA Assocs., Boston, 1978-81, gen. ptnr., 1982-89, mng. dir., 1989—2002, prin., 2003—. Bd. dirs. HVL, Inc., Pitts., Softmed Sys. Inc., Bethesda, Md., Ansys, Inc., Canonsburg, Pa., Pacific Life Corp., Newport Beach, Calif., J&B Software, Inc., Bluebell, Pa. Trustee Simmons Coll., Pitts. Symphony. Mem. Nat. Venture Capital Orgn. Avocations: theatre, reading, art, skiing, travel. Office: TA Assocs 125 High St Boston MA 02110-2704 E-mail: jmorby@ta.com.

MOREHEAD, DEBORAH ELIZABETH BETTS, gifted and talented educator, music minister; b. Shreveport, La., Sept. 10, 1952; d. George Cornelius Betts, Jr. and Jackquelyn Shaw Bicknell; m. Lester Cox Morehead, Jr., Apr. 24, 1992; children: John, Les, Sam, Douglas Pearce, Kelli Pearce. BA in Speech and English, La. Tech. U., 1974; M in Religious Edn., Southwestern Theol. Sem., 1976; MEd in English and Gifted Edn., La. State U., Shreveport, 1993. Tchr. Chapel Trafton, Baton Rouge, 1984—86; asst. prin. Natalbany (La.) Bapt. Sch., 1986—89; libr. Natalbany Middle Sch., 1989—90; tchr. gifted and talented Caddo Magnet High, Shreveport, 1990—; min. music/edn. Parkview Bapt. Ch., Shreveport, 2000—. SS ch. growth specialist SBC, Nebr., 1980—, La., 1980—. Author: (biography) Don't Tell Me I Can't, 1995. Named Educator of Yr., Caddo Assn. of Educators and Shreveport Times, 1995; recipient Barbara Jordan award, La. Tex. Com. Disabilities, 1996. Mem.: Phi Kappa Phi. Home: 523 Applespice Dr Shreveport LA 71115

MOREHOUSE, SARAH MCCALLY, retired political science educator; b. Boston, Jan. 15, 1927; d. Ralph Dewey and Eugenia Whitehead (Norris) Powell; m. W. Bradley Morehouse, Nov. 8, 1969 (div. Nov. 1986); children: Richard, John, Catherine, David; m. Malcolm Edwin Jewell, Dec. 28, 1991. BA in Polit. Sci., Wellesley Coll., 1948; PhD in Polit. Sci., Yale U., 1964. Instr. Conn. Coll., New London, 1964-66; lectr. Hunter Coll., Bronx, N.Y., 1966-69; assoc. prof. Manhattanville Coll., Purchase, N.Y., 1969-75; prof. U. Conn., Stamford, 1976-92, prof. emerita, 1992—. Univ. senator U. Conn., 1982-85, assoc. dir., 1990-91. Author: State Politics, Parties and Policy, 1981, The Governor as Party Leader, 1998; contbr. various articles to profl. jours. Sec. Charter Revision Commn. Fairfield, Conn., 1960; chmn. Ethics Commn., Fairfield, 1984-88; pres. LWV, 1996-98; state LWV sec. bd. dirs. 1998-2001; political parties/elections, 2001. Vis. professorship for women NSF, 1991; fellow Danforth Found., 1960; rsch. grantee Russell Sage Found., 1983; vis. scholar U. Calif, Berkeley, 1991-92. Mem. Wellesley Club. Home: 242 Somerset Ave Fairfield CT 06430-4935

MOREHOUSE, VALERIE JEANNE, librarian; b. Taft, Calif., Jan. 30, 1947; d. Gordon Stanley and Cloe Ozelle (Reed) Hogue; m. Keith Herbert Morehouse, Aug. 22, 1968 (div. 1994); 1 child, Gordon. AA, Taft Coll., 1966; AB in English, U. Calif., Berkeley, 1968; MSLS, Simmons Grad. Sch. Libr. Sci., 1977. Cert. profl. librarian, Mass. Asst. libr. dir. Plymouth (Mass.) Pub. Librs., 1977—82; asst. exec. dir. Southeastern Librs. Coop., Rochester, Minn., 1982—84; libr. automation cons. N.D. State Libr., Bismarck, 1984—89; dist. libr. media dir. Bismarck Pub. Sch. Dist., 1989—97; sys. adminstr. MARINet, San Rafael, Calif., 1997—2000; libr. Temple Isaiah of Contra Costa County, Lafayette, 2001—. Adv. panelist for literature Mass. Coun. on Arts and Humanities, Boston, 1980-82. Editor, writer Libr. A Word to the Wise, 1995-97; author: Anthology: A Collection of Cape Cod Poets, 1974. Legis. chair, membership chair N.D. Libr. Assn., 1987-93; mem. N.D. Gov.'s Adv. Libr. Vision 2004 Com., Bismarck, 1995-96; mem. Ctrl. Dakota Libr. Network Bd., Bismarck, 1992—. Recipient Capewide 1st prize for poetry Provincetown Assn. for Living Arts, 1972, Spl. Recognition award COSMEP, 1977, Pres.' award for svc. to librs. N.D. Libr. Assn., 1994. Mem. ALA (chair publs. com. 1985-87, columnist, reviewer The Book List 1977-79), Calif. Libr. Assn., Beta Phi Mu. Avocations: gardening, travel. Office: Temple Isaiah Libr 3800 Mt Diablo Blvd Lafayette CA 94549 E-mail: valmorehouse@earthlink.net.

MORELAN, PAULA KAY, choreographer; b. Lafayette, Ind., Nov. 24, 1949; d. Dickie Booth and Marian Maxine (Fetterhoff) M.; m. Kerim Sayan, Aug. 10, 1974. Student, U. Utah, 1968-69; BFA, Tex. Christian U., 1972; postgrad., El Centro Coll., 1969-70. Tchr. Rosello Sch. Ballet, Dallas, 1972-74; mgr., tchr. Ballet Arts Ctr., Dallas, 1974-76; owner, tchr. Ballet Classique, Garland, Tex., 1976-87, Garland Ballet Acad., 1977-87; resident choreographer Garland Civic Theatre, 1988—, lifetime mem., 1998. Asst. to Mythra Rosello, Tex. Civic Ballet, Dallas, 1972-74; assoc. artistic dir. Dance Repertory Theatre Dallas, 1974-75; artistic dir. Dance Repertory Theatre Dallas, 1975-76, Garland (Tex.) Ballet Assn., 1977-90, Classical Ballet Acad., Performing Arts Sch., 1987-90. Bd. dirs. Garland Civic Theatre, 2000—. Recipient Leon Rabin award for Best Choreography, 1996, 98, 2000, 2001, Column award, Best Choreographer award 2003, Choreographer of the Yr., 2001, 2002. Personal E-mail: pkm@worldnet.att.net.

MORELAND, CHERYL, psychologist; d. Sidney and Jessie Moreland. PhD, U. So. Miss., 1999. Lic. psychologist Miss. Asst. prof. Tougaloo Coll., Miss., 1999; assoc. psychologist Oakley Tng. Sch., Raymond, Miss., 1999—2001; psychologist II Boswell Regional Ctr., Magee, Miss., 2001; correctional psychologist Dept. of Corrections, Pearl, Miss., 2001—. Mem.: APA. Avocations: dance, reading, travel, music. Personal E-mail: cdmoreland@hotmail.com. Business E-Mail: cmoreland@mdoc.state.ms.us.

MORELLA, CONSTANCE ALBANESE, ambassador, former congresswoman; b. Somerville, Mass., Feb. 12, 1931; d. Salvatore and Mary Christine (Fallette) Albanese; m. Anthony C. Morella, Aug. 21, 1954; children: Paul, Mark, Laura; guardians of: Christine, Catherine, Louise, Rachel, Paul, Ursula. AA, Boston U., 1950, AB, 1954; MA, Am. U., 1967, D of Pub. Svc. (hon.), 1988, Norwich U. and Dickinson Coll., 1989, Mt. Vernon Coll., 1995, U. Md. U. Coll., 1996, USUHS, 1997, U. Md., 1997, Elizabethtown Coll., 1999. Tchr. Montgomery County (Md.) Pub. Schs., 1956-60; instr. Am. U., 1968-70; prof. Montgomery Coll., Rockville, Md., 1970-86; mem. Md. Ho. Dels., Annapolis, 1979-86, U.S. Congress from 8th Md. dist., 1987—2003; mem. sci. com., tech. subcom., basic rsch. subcom., govt. reform com., chair D.C. subcom., mem. civil svc. subcom.; visiting fellow Kennedy School, Harvard, 2003; U.S. permanent rep. to Orgn. for Econ. Co-operation & Devel. U.S. Dept. State, Paris, 2003—. Mem. civil svc., adv. bd. Am. Univ., Washington; U.S. amb. Orgn. Econ. Coop. and Devel., 2003-. Mem. adv. coun. Montgomery County Hospice Soc.; hon. bd. mem. Nat. Kidney Found; active Human Rights Caucus; Congressional Women's Caucus, Older Ams. Caucus, Population and Devel. Caucus; mem. Bd. Cafritz Found. Named Glamour Woman of Yr. Glamour mag. 1995, Washingtonian of Yr. 1991; named to Md. Women's Hall of Fame, Md. Women's Hall of Fame, 1994. Republican. Avocations: theatre, tennis, reading. Home: USOECD PSC 116 APO AE 09777

MORELOCK, JASMINE CRAWFORD, artist; b. Boise, June 30, 1925; d. Graydon Clemson and Doris Cecile (Dinwiddie) Crawford; m. Max Maurice Morelock, Apr. 8, 1950; 1 child, Maurice Max. AA, Stephens Coll., 1945; BA, La. State U., 1948; MA, La. Sch. Tech., 1979; MFA cum laude, Inst. Allende, San Miguel Allende, Guanajuato, Mexico, 1978. Cert. tchr. speech and art, La. Advtsg. writer programming dept. KRMD Radio Sta., Shreveport, La., 1946—47; with Bozell and Jacobs Nat. Advt. Agy., 1949—50; with comml. design Glen Mason Advt. Agy.; asst. prof. fine arts La. State U., Baton Rouge, 1948-49; head art dept. Southfield Sch., Shreveport, La., 1972-74; tchr. portrait classes Bossier C. C., Bossier City, La., 1989-91; tchr. art Caddo Parish Sch. Bd., Shreveport, La., 1975-80; represented by Gallery on the Green, Lexington, Mass., Juleaux Gallery of Fine Arts, Kansas City, WLR Design Co., Shreveport, La., Lytle's, Shreveport, La., Riverwalk Gallery, New Orleans. Presenter workshops Barnwell Art Ctr., Shreveport, La., J&M Studio Groups, Shreveport, Women's Dept. Club, Shreveport, Springhill (La.) Art Assn., 1993. One woman exhbns. include La. State U. Shreveport Gallery, 1992, Cambridge Club, Shreveport, 1993, The Glen Gallery, Shreveport, 1995, Shreve Meml. Libr., Shreveport, 1995, numerous others; group exhbns. include Valerie Originals, KJ's Antiques and Silks, Hot Springs, Ark., 1986, Women Artists of La., Baton Rouge, 1987, Boots Pharmaceutical Co., Cambridge Club, Shreveport, La., 1988, 90, 92, Stoner Arts Ctr., Shreveport, 1989, 90, Gallery on the Green, Lexington, Mass., 1989, Simmers Gallery, Shreveport, 1989, La. Artist Group Show, 1990, Barksdale Air Base, 1990, Turner Art Ctr., 1990, Artport, Shreveport, 1990, 92, 93, 94, Riverside Galleries, Shreveport, Southwestern Watercolor Soc., 1992, 94, Nat. Mus. Art, Washington, 1993, Still River Artists, Danbury, Conn., 1993, Okla. 12th Annual Juried Show, 1995, numerous others; represented in pvt. and pub. collections La. State U. Ctr., St. Luke's Hosp., St. Vincent's Acad., U. Club, Seagull Cos., McGoldrick Oil Co., numerous others; featured in (cover) (Goodloe Stuck) The Shreveport Madam, 1986, Boots Pharm. Art Catalogue, 1990, Behold, I Make All Things New, 1991, Artists of La. Catalogue, 1991, (t.v. show) Focus on the Arts, The Shreveport Times, 1995. Recipient Special Selection award Ark. Arts Ctr., Little Rock, 1984, First Purchase Prize Izora and Thilo Steinschulte Meml. award First Meth. Ch. Alexandria (La.), 1984, First Place Ark-La-Tex-Okla Competition First Meth. Ch., Shreveport, 1984. Mem. Nat. Watercolor Soc., Nat. Assn. Women Artists, Southwestern Watercolor Soc. (Elizabeth Shanon Meml. award 1991), La. Watercolor Soc. Soc. Exptl. Artists, Hoover Watercolor Soc. (v.p., First Place 1984, H.M. award 1993), Registry of La. Artists, La. Artists, Inc., Southeastern Ctr. for Contemporary Art, Coalition of Women's Art (nat., Dallas). Home: 427 Monrovia St Shreveport LA 71106-1607

MORENCY, PAULA J. lawyer; b. Oak Park, Ill., Mar. 13, 1955; AB magna cum laude, Princeton U., 1977; JD, U. Va., 1980. Bar: Ill. 1980, U.S. Dist. Ct. (no. dist.) Ill. 1980, U.S. Ct. Appeals (7th cir.) 1981, U.S. Ct. Appeals (5th cir.) 1990, U.S. Dist. Ct. (ctrl. dist.) Ill. 1999, U.S. Dist. Ct. (ea. dist.) Wis. 2000. Assoc. Mayer, Brown & Platt, Chgo., 1980-86, ptnr., 1987-94, Schiff Hardin & Waite, Chgo., 1994—. Adj. prof. trial advocacy Northwestern U. Sch. Law, Chgo., 1997--; faculty Midwest Regional, Nat. Inst. for Trial Advocacy, 1988—; mem. pres.'s coun. Dominican U., 1998-2002. Author: Cross-Examination of a Franchise Executive, 1995, Insurance Coverage Issues in Franchise and Intellectual Property Litigation, 1996, Re-Emergence of Franchise Class Actions, 1997, Judicial and Legislative Update: ABA Forum on Franchising, 1999, How to Find, Use and Defend Against the Expert Witness, 2000, Dealing With System Change in a High-Tech World, 2001. Mem. ABA (forum franchising, governing com., litig. sect., intellectual property sect.), Chgo. Coun. of Lawyers (bd. govs. 1989-93), Constnl. Rights Found. Chgo. (chair 2001). Office: Schiff Hardin & Waite 7300 Sears Tower Chicago IL 60606

MORENO, DONNA MARIE, communications executive; b. Amesbury, Mass., July 25, 1957; d. Robert and Marie Doris (Lucier) Menzigian; m. Carlos Moreno, Nov. 17, 1999. BS in Math., U. Lowell, 1979, MBA in Ops., 1983. Material control analyst AVCO Corp., Wilmington, Mass., 1979-81; ops. analyst Blue Cross & Blue Shield, Boston, 1981-83, risk analyst, 1983-84; systems analyst Bell Atlantic Corp., Bethesda, Md., 1984-86, cons. internal, 1986-89, project mgr., 1989-91, new tech. strategic planning mgr., 1992-97, sr mgr. sales channel devel., 1997—2001, sr. mgr. mktg. Verizon, 2001—. Speaker FUSE Nat. and Regional Confs., 1988, 91 Inventor (software) User-assisted Adhoc Reporting, 1988, Natural English Report Access, 1988. Vol. Montgomery County Vol. Assn., Montgomery, Md., 1983—, PALS Montgomery County, 1984—; chair spl. events New Mem. Svcs. John F. Kennedy Ctr. Performing Arts, Washington, 1985—, mem. vol. adv. com., 1991, 92; chair vol. adv. com. Kennedy Ctr., 1992—; bd. dirs. Sister City Corp., Rockville, 1992—, v.p., 1993-95, pres.-elect, 1994-95, pres., 1995—; Geissenbier mem. Jr. Chamber Internat. Found., 1996—; Geissenbier mem. U.S. Jr. C. of C. Found., 1997— Recipient Internat Tng. Fellow, JCI, 2001— . Mem. NAFE, Ops. Rsch. Soc., Intelligent Computer Rsch. Inst., Focus User Group (co-chmn. artificial intelligence group 1989, leader, coord. spl. interest groups for Nat. Com., 1989, nat., regional spkr. 1988, 91), Rockville Jr. C. of C. (sec. 1992-93), Md. Jr. C. of C. (program mgr. internat. involvement 1992-93, dist. dir. 1993-94, cmty. devel. v.p. 1994-95, U.S. Jr. C. of C. internat. affairs commn. 1995-98, JCI individual devel. commn. 1996, spl. asst. to world pres. 1997—), Internat. Spkrs. Platform, Jr. C. of C. Republican. Roman Catholic. Avocations: photography, travel. Office: Verizon 13100 Columbia Pike Silver Spring MD 20902

MORENO, FIDELA LLORCA, physician, medical educator; b. San Fernando, The Philippines, May 22, 1949; came to the U.S., 1987; d. Florencio Manalon Moreno and Rosario Soliven Llorca; m. Arthur Moreno, May 21, 1991. BS, U. Santo Tomas, Manila, 1969, MD, 1973. Internal medicine resident VA Hosp., Quezon City, The Philippines, 1974-78; cardiology fellow Philippine Heart Ctr., Quezon City, 1978-81, U. Utah, Salt Lake City, 1981-83; cons., vis. staff Philippine Heart Ctr. for Asia and St. Luke's Hosp., Quezon City, 1984-86; chief hypertension sect. Philippine Heart Ctr. for Asia, Quezon City, 1985-86; rsch. assoc. physician LDS Hosp., Salt Lake City, 1987-93; assoc. dir. clin. rsch. Prizer Inc., Groton, Conn., 1993-96; sr. assoc. dir. for Asia, Pzifer Pharms. Group, N.Y.C., 1996-99; dir. internat. clin. rsch. group Pfizer Ind., N.Y.C., 1999—. V.p. clin. rsch. Pfizer India, 1999—; presenter in field.; instr. medicine U. Utah Med. Sch., Salt Lake City, 1990-91, asst. prof., 1991-93. Contbr. chpts. to books and articles to profl. jours. Fellow Philippine Heart Assn. (assoc.); mem. Assocs. Clin. Pharmacology, Am. Heart Assn. (Utah chpt.). Democrat. Roman Catholic. Avocations: reading, theatre, symphony, ballet. Office: Pfizer Inc 60 E 42d St PMB 1166 New York NY 10165-0006

MORENO, HELENA, newscaster; b. Xalapa, Veracruz, Mex. Grad. in Journalism, So. Meth. U., Dallas. Intern for Hillary Clinton White House, Washington; gen. assignment reporter, fill-in anchor WTOC-TV, Savannah, Ga.; reporter WDSU News Channel 6, New Orleans, 2000—. Office: WDSU News Channel 6 846 Howard Ave New Orleans LA 70113

MORENO, JUDITH WILSON, psychotherapist, consultant; d. Francis Melton Wilson and Ruth Evelyn Ingalls; children: Susan Ingalls, Melissa Wilcox Seiler, Judith Ainsley Romani-Haentze. MS in Nursing, U. Pa., 1968. RN Pa., NY. Dir. clin. svcs. Pa. Hosp. Hall-Mercer, Phila., 1968—80, psychotherapist, 1969—85; pvt. practice Phila., 1969—85; cons. surveyor Joint Commn. on Accreditation of Healthcare Orgns., Oakbrook Ter., Ill., 1980—; v.p. healthcare risk mgmt. Johnson & Higgins/Marsh McLennan Cos., Phila., 1987—98. Author: The Practice of Mental Health Nursing, 1973. Mem. Seabrook Health Svcs., NJ, 1991—99. Avocations: art history, travel, reading, politics. Home: 200 Locust Street # 27A Philadelphia PA 19106 Office: JCAHO One Renaissance Blvd Oakbrook Terrace IL 60181 Personal E-mail: jwm2030@aol.com.

MORENO, PATRICIA FRAZIER, lawyer; b. Lebanon, Pa. d. Joseph James and Cariella Agnes (Rothermel) Frazier; m. Camille Quijada Moreno, Dec. 4, 1982; children: William David, Helen Grace, Camille Fitzcarrado. Student, Millersville U., 1969-71, Cochise Coll., 1992-93; BA in Polit. Sci., U. Ariz., Sierra Vista, 1997; JD, U. Ariz., 2001. Cert.: Nat. Assn. Legal Secs. (profl. legal sec.), Nat. Assn. Legal Assts. (legal asst.). Law clerk John F. Kelliher, Jr. PC, Sierra Vista, Ariz., 1999-2001, assoc., 2002—. Assoc. faculty Cochise Coll., Sierra Vista, 1996—97, U. Ariz. S., 2003—. Mem. human rels. commn. City of Sierra Vista, 1982—83; mem. adv. bd. Salvation Army, Sierra Vista, 1988—92. Named Sec. of the Yr., S.E. Ariz. Legal Sex. Assn., 1993. Mem.: ACLU, Boderline Mensa (officer 1987—93, scholar 1992), Phi Kappa Phi. Democrat. Avocations: cyberculture, film history. Office: John F Kelliher Jr PC 500 E Fry Blvd L 12 Sierra Vista AZ 85635 Office Phone: 520-458-3633. E-mail: patricia.moreno@azbar.org.

MORENO, VERONICA, food products executive; m. Eduardo Moreno. Co-founder Olè Mexican Foods, Norcross, Ga., 1987—. Named Nat. Hispanic Businesswoman of Yr., U.S. Hispanic C. of C., 2001, Latina Entrepreneur of Yr., Hispanic Bus. Mag., 2004. Office: Ole Mexican Foods Inc 6585 Crescent Dr Norcross GA 30071*

MORENO, ZERKA TOEMAN, psychodrama educator; b. Amsterdam, The Netherlands, June 13, 1917; d. Joseph and Rosalia (Gutwirth) Toeman; m. Jacob L. Moreno, Dec.1949; 1 child, Jonathan D.; 1 stepchild, Regina. Student, Willesden Tech. Coll., 1937-38, NYU, 1948-49. Cert. trainer, educator, practitioner of psychodrama and group psychotherapy Am. Bd. Examiners. Rsch. asst. Psychodramatic and Sociometric Insts., N.Y.C.,

1942-51; pres. Moreno Inst., N.Y.C. and Beacon, N.Y., 1951-82; trainer in psychodrama Studiefrämjandet, Stockholm, 1976-83, Finnish Psychodrama Assn., Lahti, Finland, 1976-83. Lectr., trainer, Gt. Britain, Australia, China, New Zealand, Norway, Sweden, Italy, Germany, Japan, 1976-96, Argentina, Brazil, Greece, The Netherlands, Denmark, Belgium, Spain, Israel, Korea and Taiwan, 1977—; hon. pres. Internat. Zerka Moreno Inst., Nanjing, China; head advisor mental health Nanjing Brain Hosp., China, 1997. Co-author: Psychodrama, Surplus Reality, and the Art of Healing, (book of poetry) Love Songs to Life, 1971, 93; co-author: Psychodrama, Vol. II, 1967, Vol. III, 1969, The First Psychodramatic Family, 1964. Named hon. citizen Comune di Roma, Assessorato Alla Cultura, 1983, Municipalidad de la Ciudad de Buenos Aires, 1984, Hon. Mem. Federacao Brasiliero de Psicodrama, Sao Paulo, 1996; first recipient of prize from Astrid Badina Stiftung (Baden-Baden, Germany), 1999; nominated for Sigmund Freud award psychotherapy City of Vienna, 1999. Fellow Am. Soc. Group Psychotherapy and Psychodrama (pres. 1967-69, hon. pres. 1988—, sec.-treas. 1955-66); hon. mem. Internat. Assn. Group Psychotherapy (treas. 1974-76, bd. dirs. 1976-80), Soc. Psicodrama Sao Paulo (hon.), Sociedad Argentina Psicodrama (hon.). Home: The Colonnades C24 2600 Barracks Rd Charlottesville VA 22901-2198

MORENO-DUCHENY, DENISE, state senator; m. Al Moreno-Ducheny. Student, Univ. Lund (Sweden); BA in History, Pomona Coll.; JD, Southwestern U., 1979. Bar: Calif. Lawyer; trustee San Diego CC Dist. Governing Bd; mem. Calif. State Assembly, 1994—2000, Calif. State Senate, Sacramento, 2000—. Chair Housing and Cmty. Devel. Com.; mem. Agriculture and Water Resources Com., Banking, Commerce and Internat. Trade Com., Budget Com., Judiciary Com., Vets. Affairs, Calif. Border Environ. Cooperation Commn.; commr. San Diego County Regional Governance Efficiency Commn., State Commn. on the Califs.; mem. Latino Legis. Caucus, Women's Caucus; lectr. in field. Trustee Anza-Borrego State Park Found.; bd. dirs. San Diego Natural History Mus. Mem.: Calif. C.C. Trustees Assn. (bd. dirs.), Assn. Latino C.C. Trustees Calif. (chair, co-founder). Democrat. Mailing: State Capitol Rm 2062 Sacramento CA 95814 Office: 637 3rd Ave Ste C Chula Vista CA 91910

MORFORD, JOANN (JOANN MORFORD-BURG), state senator, investment company executive; b. Miller, S.D., Nov. 26, 1956; d. Darrell Keith Morford and Eleanor May (Fawcett) Morford-Steptoe. BS in Agrl.-Bus., Comml. Econs., S.D. State U., 1979; cert. in personal fin. planning, Am. Coll., 1992. Chartered fin. cons., Cert. Life Underwriter, Am. Coll., 2003. Agrl. loan officer 1st Bank System, Presho, S.D., 1980-82, Wessington Springs, S.D., 1982-86, Am. State Bank, Wessington Springs, 1986; registered investment rep. ARM Fin. Svcs. Inc., Wessington Springs, 1986-96; Miller, 1997—; mem. S.D. State Senate, Wessington Springs, 1990-96, majority whip, 1993-94, minority whip, 1995-96, mem., 1990-97, Miller, 1997-98; ins. agt. Western Fraternal Life Assn., 2001—. Mem. senate appropriations com. 1993-98; chair senate ops. and audit com. 1993, 94; mem. ops. and audit com., 1995-98; mem. Nat. Conf. State Legislators' Assembly of Fed. Issues Environ. Com., 1994-98, vice chair, 1996-97. Mem. Midwestern-Can. task force Midwest Conf., 1990-94; mem. transp. com., commerce com., taxation com. S.D. State Senate, Pierre, 1990-92; treas. twp. bd. Wessington Springs, 1990-92; mem. Wessington Springs Sch. Improvement Coun., 1992-95.; mem. fin. com. United Meth. Ch., Miller, S.D., 2001—. Fleming fellow Ctr. Policy Alternatives, 1996. Mem.: S.D. Farmers Union, Girl Scouts of Nyoda Council (bd. dirs.), Bus. and Profl. Women (2nd v.p. 2002), S.D. State U. 4-H Alumni Assn., Future Farmers Am. (adv. bd. Wessington Springs chpt. 1984—96), Alumni Coun. Young Polit. Leaders (China delegation 1996, host El Salvador delegation 1999), Order Ea. Star (various offices 1980—). Democrat. Home and Office: PO Box 21 Miller SD 57362-0021

MORFORD, LYNN ELLEN, state official; b. Peoria, Ill., June 17, 1953; d. Raymond Scott Jr. and Georgiana (Woodhall) M. BA, Millikin U., 1975; MA, U. Ill. was Sangamon State U., Springfield, Ill., 1984. News reporter Stas. WJBC-WBNQ, Bloomington, Ill., 1975-76, Sta. WSOY-AM-FM, Decatur, Ill., 1976-78, Stas. WXCL-WZRO-FM, Peoria, 1978, Sta. KACY-AM-FM, Ventura, Calif., 1978, Sta. WKAN, Kankakee, Ill., 1979-82; freelance news reporter Sta. WMAQ, Chgo., 1982; news dir. Stas. WXCL-WKQA-FM, Peoria, 1983; press sec. Ill. Ho. of Reps. Rep. Press Office, Springfield, 1984-85; chief Press Office, Ill. Dept. Commerce and Community Affairs, Springfield, 1986-95, comms. coord., 1995—. Mem. adv. bd. Ill. AP, 1983; radio news contest judge Okla. AP, 1983; bd. dirs. Ill. News Broadcasters Assn., 1980-84; mem. Gov.'s Conf. on Mgmt. of Illinois River, 1997—. Mem. adv. bd. Leadership Ill., 1992—, spring conf. chair, 1994; Springfield St. Patrick's Day Parade Com., 1991-99; chmn. pub. rels. film fund raiser Vachel Linds ay Assn., Springfield, 1989; mem. Springfield Jr. League, 1990-91; mem. Samaritans St. John's Hosp., Springfield, 1995—, Ill. River Econ. Devel. Action Team, 1996-97, Orlene Moore Scholarship Com., 1996—, Student of Yr. Selection Com., 1996; pres., bd. trustees Sherman Pub. Libr. Dist., 1995—; elder Buffalo Hart Presbyn. ch., 1998—; pres. Buffalo Hart Women's Assn., 1997—; mem. Town and Country Women's Assn., 1998—. Recipient Best Contbr. award Ill. AP, 1983; Robert Howard scholar Sangamon State U., 1983; named to Hon. Order of Ky. Cols., 1992. Mem. Order of Ea. Star. Presbyterian. Avocations: golf, competitive sewing and baking (state fair champion), vocal music, gardening, decorating. Home: 2 Willow Hill Dr Sherman IL 62684-9769 Office: Ill Dept Commerce and Community Affairs 620 E Adams St Springfield IL 62701-1615 E-mail: lmorford@commerce.state.il.us.

MORFORD, MARIE ARLENE, insurance company executive; b. Wichita, Oct. 21, 1929; d. George and Bertha (Wear) Bachman; divorced; children: Stephen, Cheryl, Phillip. Clk. McKesson Robbin Drug, Wichita, 1948-49, Safeway Offices, Wichita, 1952-55; ins. sec. Benfer Ins., Newton, Kans., 1955-70, Ctrl. Agy., Newton, 1970-87; patient admitting operator Halstead (Kans.) Hosp., 1988-90; ins. rep., office mgr., lic. rep. State Farm, Newton, Kans., 1990—. Dir. religious edn. St. Mary's Ch., Newton, 1988, advisor adult religious edn., 1996, eucharistic minister, 1982; rep. Mother to Mother Ministry, Newton, 1988, Harvey County Citizens for Life, Newton, 1989; regent Daughters of Isabella St. Joseph's Cir., Kans., 1993-97, treas., 1995—, state vice regent, 1999—; pres. Wichita Diocesan Coun. of Cath. Women, 1993-95; adv. bd. Wichita Diocesan Religious Edn. Mem. Daus. of Isabella (state vice regent 1999-2001, state auditor 2001, regent 2001—, state trustee, 2000—). Home: 1206 Harrison PO Box 135 Newton KS 67114-0135

MORGAN, ALEXIA BACA, psychologist; b. Albuquerque, Feb. 6, 1957; d. Eric and Jessie Baca; m. John Timothy Morgan, July 11, 1987; children: Marja, Johnny. BA, U. N.Mex., 1984; MA, Humboldt State U., 1989, Calif. Sch. Profl. Psychology, Fresno, 1992, PhD, 1994. Psychologist Benamor Inst., Arcata, Calif., 1986—89, Fresno City Coll., Calif., 1994—95, Calif. Dept. Corrections, Chowchilla, 1995—2001; pvt. practice Clovis, Calif., 2001—. Dir. EOP program Valley State Prison for Women, Chowchilla; presenter in field. Leader Girl Scouts USA, Clovis, 1994—2000; mem. Friends of Kathleen Kennedy Townsend, Gov. of Md., 1999—. Named Hon. Co-chmn. by U.S. Rep. Tom Delay, Pres. Bus. Coun., 2003. Mem.: APA, Jan Joquin Psychol. Assn., Calif. Psychol. Assn. Democrat. Achievements include research in stresses in incarcerated females. Home: 913 Ezie Ave Clovis CA 93611 Office: 106 Pollasky Clovis CA 93612 Office Phone: 559-298-9310. E-mail: AlexiaBacaMorgan@yahoo.com.

MORGAN, ALLYSON SUZANNE, elementary school educator; d. Robert L. and Janet L. Morgan. BA, Wesleyan U., 1983; MS, CUNY, 1992. Adminstrv. asst. Van Buren Buying Office, N.Y.C., 1983—88; classroom tchr. Bd. Edn., N.Y.C., 1988—. Mem.: Nat. Action Network, Kappa Delta Pi. Democrat. Baptist. Avocations: travel, music. Office: PS 76/A Philip Randolph Sch 220 W 121st St New York NY 10027

MORGAN, ANN M. artist, educator; b. Atlanta, July 27, 1918; d. Henry Marchman and Sallie Claude Holden; m. Robert Fleming Carter, July 6, 1952 (dec. Mar. 1955); 1 child, Robert Fleming Jr.; m. Cyril James Morgan, Mar. 13, 1989. BS, Ga. State Coll. Women, 1940, BA, 1941; postgrad., NYU, 1948-49. Cert. bus. edn., fine arts, English lit. and grammar tchr. Inst., Fulton County Pub. Schs., Atlanta; tchr. H.S. and jr. coll. Ramey AFB, P.R., 1939-40; tchr. girls H.S., Fulton County, Ga., 1940-41, S.W. H.S., Dade County Pub. Schs., Miami, Fla., 1957-58; instr. Dade Bus. Coll., Dade County; founder, instr. De Nova Art Sch., Miami. Exhibited in group shows at Lowe Mus., Horte Mus., others. Head blocks program Rockdale (Fla.) Civic Assn.; chmn. Wives of West Point Officers' Aux., 1945-59. Mem. Coral Gables Art Orgn. (membership chmn., various offices), Miami Watercolor Soc. (membership chmn., various offices), soc. Four Arts.

MORGAN, ANN MARIE, psychologist; b. Fresno, Calif., Mar. 8, 1949; d. Charles and Cassie Alvena (Armey) McMurray; m. Stephen Charles Morgan, Sept. 6, 1969; 1 child, Kesley Suzanne. BA, U. LaVerne, 1971, MEd, 1973; MS in Marriage and Family Counseling, U. Laverne, 1999; MA in Psychology, Calif. Sch. Profl. Psychology, 1999, PsyD in Clin. Psychology, 2001. Tchr. Ontario (Calif.)-Montclair Sch. Dist., 1971-78, Cabrillo Unf. Sch. Dist., Half Moon Bay, Calif., 1978-85; project coord. U. La Verne, Calif., 1986—94; dir. program Ctr. Aging Resources, 2004; pvt. practice, 2004. Mem. exec. com. Camp Fire Boys and Girls, Inc., Mount Baldy Region, Claremont, Calif., 1989—, bd. dirs., 1987—; mem. Children's Home Soc., Claremont, 1987—. Mem. Pi Gamma Mu. Mem. Ch. of the Brethren. Avocations: golf, reading, gardening, exercise, skiing. Office: Ctr for Aging Resources 447 N El Molino Ave Pasadena CA 91101-1403 Office Phone: 626-577-8480.

MORGAN, ANNE MARIE G. broadcast journalist, educator; b. Paducah, Ky., Apr. 23, 1955; d. Ralph Edward and Vera Christine Gill; m. Michael William Morgan, Nov. 19, 1977; children: Deborah, Jon, James. BA in Govt. and Psychology, Coll. William and Mary, 1976; MA in Polit. Sci., U. Richmond, 1997; postgrad. in Pub. Policy, Va. Commonwealth U., 1998. HS tchr. James-City County Sch., Williamsburg, Va., 1977, Colonial Hts. Sch., Va., 1977-79; TV and radio journalist Capitol News, Richmond, Va., 1984—, Va. Pub. Broadcasting, Richmond, Va., 1987—, WRIC-TV and WTVR-TV, Richmond, 1984—2000; broadcast news anchor Va. News Network, Richmond, Va., 2000—02; journalist WVTF Radio, Roanoke, 2002—. Asst. prof. polit. sci. U. Richmond, Va., 1998—. Author: (with others) Controversies in American Public Polity, 1999, Opposing Viewpoints Series, 1991. Sec. Parents' Guidance/Pupil Pers. Guidance Com., Powhatan, Va., 1996—98; bd. dirs. Va. Pub. Broadcasting, Richmond, 2000—02, Va. Adv. Coun. Adult Edn. and Literacy, Richmond, 1999—2002, Coun. Child Care and Early Childhood Devel., Richmond, 1995—96; chair bd. dirs. State Bd. for Cmty. Colls., Richmond, 1997—2002; chair Va. Coun. Status of Women, Richmond, 1994—2002. Recipient Gov. proclamation Anne Marie Morgan Day in Commonwealth Va., Gov. Va., 1997; Meritorious award Va. Assoc. Press Broadcasters, 2002; Univ. of richmond Faculty Svc. Award, 2003. Mem.: Soc. Profl. Journalists, Soc. Profl. Journalists (Va. profl. chpt.), Nat. Fedn. Press Women, Va. Press Women, Capitol Corrs. Assn., Am. Polit. Sci. Assn., Pi Sigma Alpha. Avocations: music, singing, mentoring.

MORGAN, ARLENE NOTORO, university administrator; b. Phila., July 27, 1945; d. James Vincent and Mary Rose (Actis-Grande) Notoro; m. David J. Morgan, Mar. 3, 1948; children: Elizabeth, Lauren. BS in Journalism, Temple U., 1967. Reporter Delaware County Daily Times, Chester, Pa., 1967-69, Phila. Inquirer, 1969—, dep. metro editor, 1990-91, sr. editor, asst. mng. editor, 1991-2000, reader advocate columnist, 1998-2000; asst. dean Columbia U. Grad. Sch. Journalism, N.Y.C., 2000—. Bd. dirs. Friends Hosp., Phila., 1978—; mem. adv. bd. Temple U., La. State U.; mem. Am. Soc. Newspaper Editors Journalism Credibility Project; dir. Columbia Race Project. Recipient Phila. Newspapers Inc. Employee Recognition award, 1987, Excellence in Diversity award Knight Ridder, 1995; Media Studies Ctr. fellow Freedom Forum, 1996-97. Mem. Soc. Profl. Journalists., Newspaper Assn. Am. (diversity com.). Roman Catholic. Avocations: ballet, travel, opera and art appreciation, advocate to the mentally ill. Office: Columbia Univ 2960 Broadway New York NY 10027-6900 E-mail: am494@columbia.edu.

MORGAN, BETSY STELLE, lawyer; b. Terre Haute, Ind., Mar. 15, 1963; BA, DePauw U., 1985; JD, John Marshall Law Sch., 1988. Bar: Ill. 1989. With Baker & McKenzie, Chgo., 1988—, counsel, 1997—2002, ptnr., 2002—. Co-chair N.Am. Pro Bono Initiative Baker & McKenzie, Chgo. Author: United States Business Immigration Manual, 2003. Office: Baker and McKenzie One Prudential Plz 130 E Randolph Dr Chicago IL 60601

MORGAN, BEVERLY CARVER, pediatrician, educator; b. N.Y.C., May 29, 1927; d. Jay and Florence (Newkamp) Carver; children— Nancy, Thomas E. III, John E. MD cum laude (Mosby Scholar), Duke U., 1955. Diplomate Am. Bd. Pediatrics (oral examiner 1984-90, mem. written examination com. 1990—), Nat. Bd. Med. Examiners. Intern, asst. resident Stanford U. Hosp., San Francisco, 1955-56; clin. fellow pediatrics, trainee pediatric cardiology Babies Hosp.-Columbia Presbyn. Med. Center, N.Y.C., 1956-59; research fellow cardiovascular diagnostic lab. Columbia-Presbyn. Med. Center, N.Y.C., 1959-60; instr. pediatrics Coll. Physicians and Surgeons, Columbia U., 1960; dir. heart sta. Robert B. Green Meml. Hosp., San Antonio, 1960-62; lectr. pediatrics U. Tex., 1960-62; spl. research fellow in pediatric cardiology Sch. Medicine, U. Wash., Seattle, 1962-64, from instr. to prof. pediatrics, 1962-73, chmn. dept. pediatrics, 1973-80; mem. staff U. Wash. Hosp., chief of staff, 1975-77; mem. staff Harborview Med. Ctr., Children's Orthopedic Hosp. and Med. Ctr., dir. dept. medicine, 1974-80; prof., chmn. dept. pediatrics U. Calif., Irvine, 1980-88, prof. pediat. and pediat. cardiology, 1980—; pediatrician in chief Children's Hosp. Orange County, 1988. Mem. pulmonary acad. awards panel Nat. Heart and Lung Inst., 1972-75; mem. grad. med. edn. nat. advisory com. to sec. HEW, 1977-80; mem. Coun. on Pediatric Practice; chmn. Task Force on Opportunities for Women in Pediatrics, 1982; mem. nursing rev. com. NIH, 1987-88. Contbr. articles to profl. jours.; mem. editorial bd. Clin. Pediatrics, Am. Jour. Diseases of Children, Jour. of Orange County Pediatric Soc., Jour. Am. Acad. Pediatrics, Los Angeles Pediatric Soc. Recipient Women of Achievement award Matrix Table, Seattle, 1974; Distinguished Alumnus award Duke U. Med. Sch., 1974; Ann. award Nat. Bd. Med. Coll. Pa., 1977; USPHS career devel. awardee, 1966-71 Mem. Am. Acad. Pediat. (chmn. com. on pediat. manpower 1984-86), Am. Coll. Cardiology, Soc. for Pediat. Rsch., Am. Fedn. Clin. Rsch., Am. Pediat. Soc., Assn. Med. Sch. Pediat. Dept. Chmn. (sec.-treas. 1981-87), Western Soc. for Pediat. Rsch., Alpha Omega Alpha. Office: U Calif Irvine Med Ctr Dept Pediatrics 101 The City Dr S Orange CA 92868-3201 E-mail: bcmorgan@uci.edu.

MORGAN, BRENDA GAYE, art educator; b. Cabool, Mo., Jan. 9, 1950; d. Harold David Clark and Ruth Lou Ellen Clark Sykes; m. Donald Clay Morgan; children: Feather Donelle, Fawn Janelle. BS in art edn., Drury U., 1994, MEd, 2000. Cert. art tchr. Mo. Sec., bookkeeper Success (Mo.) R-6 Sch., 1986; sec., teller Farmers State Bk., Houston, Mo., 1986—87; sales clk. Duff's Western Auto, Houston, 1988, Grand Appliance, Houston, 1989—91; substitue art tchr. Success (Mo.) R-6 Sch., 1991; substitute tchr. Houston, Success, Raymondville Schs., Mo., 1994—95; art tchr. Houston (Mo.) R-1 Elem. Sch., 1994—. Mem.: Mo. State Tchrs. Assn., SW Dist. Art Tchrs. Assn., Mo. Art Edn. Assn. Avocations: drawing, painting, crafts, reading, fishing. Office: Houston R1 Schs Elem 423 W Pine St Houston MO 65483

MORGAN, CHRISTINA, venture capital firm executive; Student, Am. U., Beirut; BS in Fin., MBA in Fin., Ariz. State U. With Memorex, Qume Corp., 1977-82; securities analyst Hambrecht & Quist LLC Investment Bankers, San Francisco, 1982-84, investment banking prin., 1984-90, mng. dir., 1990-94, mng. dir., co-head investment banking, 1994—, Chase H&Q, San Francisco. Bd. dirs. Visigenic Software. Office: Chase H&Q 1 Bush St San Francisco CA 94104-4475

MORGAN, DONNA EVENSEN, lawyer; b. Bklyn., Feb. 28, 1957; d. Edward Ivar and Judith (Larsen) Evensen; m. Charles S. Morgan, Sept. 3, 1988. BA, Colgate U., 1979; JD, U. Mich., 1984. Bar: Ill. 1985. Assoc. Chapman and Cutler, Chgo., 1985-86, Kirkland and Ellis, Chgo., 1987-89, Mayer Brown Rowe & Maw, Chgo., 1989—. Office: Mayer Brown Rowe & Maw 190 S La Salle St Ste 3100 Chicago IL 60603-3441

MORGAN, DONNA JEAN, psychotherapist; b. Edgerton, Wis., Nov. 16, 1955; d. Donald Edward and Pearl Elizabeth (Robinson) Garey. BA, U. Wis., Whitewater, 1983, MS, 1985. Cert. psychotherapist, Wis.; cert. mental health and alcohol and drug counselor; nat. cert. alcohol and drug abuse counselor; lic. marriage and family therapist, Wis.; lic. ind. social worker; lic. clin. ind. social worker; nat. cert. counselor; lic. profl. counselor; lic. advanced practice social worker. Clin. supr. Stoughton (Wis.) Hosp., 1985-88; pvt. practice Janesville, Wis., 1988-91; prin. Morgan and Assocs., Janesville, Wis., 1991-96; pvt. practice New Focus, Waukesha and Mukwonago, Wis., 1996-97, William N. Watson & Assocs., MD, S.C., Oconomowoc, Waukesha, Wis., 1997-98, Morgan Counseling, LLC, Janesville, Wis., 1998—. Mem. underaged drinking violation alternative program Rock County, 1986—96; co-chmn. task force on child sexual abuse, 1989—91; mem. Rock County Multi-disciplinary Team on Child Abuse, 1990—96; mem. spkrs. bur. Rock County C.A.R.E. House, 1990—; adv. bd. Parents Place, Waukesha County, Wis., 1997—99; active ARC, 2001—; vol. Red Cross, 2001—. Mem. APA, ACA., Am. Profl. Soc. on Abuse of Children, Wis. Profl. Soc. on Abuse of Children (bd. dirs. 1994-98, v.p. 1997-98), Am. Assn. Mental Health Counselors, Wis. Assn. Mental Health Counselors, Am. Assn. Marriage and Family Therapy (clin. mem.), Am. Assn. Christian Counselors, Wis. Counseling Assn., Am. Psycotherapy Assn., So. Wucks Unlted. (mem. com. 1980—). Office Phone: 608-757-1994.

MORGAN, ELAINE LUDLUM, minister; b. L.A., May 21, 1927; d. William Francis and Helen Katharine Ludlum; m. Robert Norman Morgan, Apr. 8, 1949; children: Robert Norman Jr., Lorene Elaine. AA, Pasadena C.C., 1947; BA, Pomona Coll., 1949; MA, U. So. Calif. L.A., 1953; postgrad., Diocesan Sch. Theology, Seattle, 1984. Ordained min. Episc. Ch.; cert. secondary tchr. Calif. Instr. English/Journalism Pasadena C.C., 1949—59; deacon All Saints Episc. Ch., Vancouver, Wash., 1984—89, St. Peters Episc. Ch., Carson City, Nev., 1989—95, Coventry Cross Episc. Ch., Minden, Nev., 1995—. Co-owner Crow's Nest Antiques, Greenford Farm, 1980—; chaplain Vancouver Meml. Hosp., 1984—89, Cason-Tahoe Hosp., Carson City, 1993—; chairperson Carson-Tahoe Rehab. Ctr., Carson City, 2001—. Editor: Pipes of Pan, 1947; editor: (cookbook) In the Kitchen With Women of Saint Marks, 1962, Not By Bread Alone, 1987, Coventry Cross Cuisine, 1998. Recipient scholarship, Pasadena Rotary Club, 1947. Mem.: Carson City Ministerial Assn., P.E.O. (chairperson ways and means com. 2003, pres. 1994—95), Phi Beta Kappa, Phi Lambda Theta. Republican. Avocations: reading, collecting communion tokens and conders. Home and Office: 402 W Robinson St Carson City NV 89703*

MORGAN, ELIZABETH SEYDEL, writer, educator, retired writer; b. Atlanta, Ga, Feb. 19, 1939; d. John Rutherford and Jane Reynolds Seydel; children: Matthew, John, Elizabeth Borkey. BA, Hollins College, Roanoke, Va, 1956—60; MFA, Virginia Commonwealth University, Richmond, Va, 1983—86. Teacher, english and creative writing St. Catherine's School, Richmond, Va., 1960—93. Author: (,poet,book,) Parties, 1988, (book) The Governor of Desire, 1993, On Long Mountain, 1998 (finalist, Lib. Va. prize, 1999); translator: (part of penn greek drama series) "Electra" by Euripides, 1998; author: (short fiction) "Economics", 1991 (Emily Clark Balch Prize, 1992); contbr. essay Wild In The City: the James River in Richmond, 1999; author: (screenplay) Queen Esther, 1993 (Govs. award, Fa. Film Fest., 1993), (short fiction anthologies) New Stories From The South, 1993. Bd. dir. Richmond Pub. Libr. Found., Richmond, 1999—. Mem.: Fellows Council, Virginia Center for the Creative Arts. Home: 504 Honaker Avenue Richmond VA 23226

MORGAN, EVELYN BUCK, retired nursing educator; b. Phila., Nov. 3, 1931; d. Kenneth Edward and Evelyn Louise (Rhineberg) Buck; m. John Allen McGeary, Aug. 15, 1958 (div. 1964); children: John Andrew, Jacquelyn Ann McGeary Keplinger; m. Kenneth Dean Morgan, June 26, 1965 (dec. 1975). Grad., Muhlenberg Hosp. Sch. Nursing, Plainfield, N.J., 1955; BSN summa cum laude, Ohio State U., 1972, MS, 1973; EdD, Nova U., 1978. RN, N.J., Ohio, Fla., Calif.; cert. clin. specialist ANCC; cert. advanced RN practitioner, Fla. Staff nurse Muhlenberg Hosp., 1955-57; indsl. nurse Western Electric Co., Columbus, Ohio, 195-59; supr. Mt. Carmel Hosp., Columbus, 1960-65; instr. Grant Hosp. Sch. Nursing, Columbus, 1965-72; cons. Ohio Dept. Health, Columbus, 1972-74; prof. nursing Miami (Fla.)-Dade C.C., 1974-96, prof. emerita, 1996—; pvt. practice family therapy, Ft. Lauderdale, Fla., 1982—. Family therapist Hollywood Pavilion Hosp., 1977-82; founder Elder Reach, Inc., care mgmt. co., 1998. Sustaining mem. Dem. Nat. Com., 1975— Mem. ANA, Nat. Guild Hypnotists, Am. Nurses Found., Am. Holistic Nurses Assn., Fla. Coun. Psychiat. and Mental Health Clin. Specialists, Sigma Theta Tau. Roman Catholic. E-mail: emorgan288@aol.com.

MORGAN, FLORENCE MURDINA, nurse; b. Northern Manchester, Jamaica, Mar. 1, 1936; came to U.S., 1967; d. James William and Juanita Agatha (Lorraine) M. RN, Wanstead Hosp., Hermon Hill London, 1962; State Cert. Midwife, Rochford Hosp., Essex, Eng., 1963; Queens Nurse, Queens Inst. Dist. Nursing, Eng., 1965; BSN cum laude, CUNY, 1989, MSN, 1992. Cert. Childbirth Educator. Staff nurse Toronto Gen. Hosp., 1964-65; jr. supr., queens nurse/midwife Surrey County Coun., Kingston-on-Thames, Eng., 1965-66; staff midwife St. Luke's Hosp., Guildford, Surrey, 1966-67; staff nurse No. Westchester Hosp., Mt. Kisco, N.Y., 1967-70, Vis. Nurse Svc., N.Y.C., 1970-71; pvt. duty med. surg. nurse N.Y.C., 1971-76; staff nurse divsn. substance abuse Beth Israel Med. Ctr., N.Y.C., 1976—. Tb coord., tchr. health, tb. prevention, AIDS prevention Beth Israel Med. Ctr., N.Y.C., 1993—; vol. nursing Spalding Hosp., Jamaica, 1955-57. Vol. Luth. Ch., N.Y.C., 1967-76; vol. 1199 Polit. Action., N.Y.C., 1989-95. Mem. N.Y. Acad. Scis., Hunter-Bellevue Alumni Assn., Sigma Theta Tau. Democrat. Avocations: swimming, tennis, arts and crafts, dance, unpublished poems. Home: 445 E 14th St Apt 3D New York NY 10009-2805

MORGAN, JANE HALE, retired library director; b. Dines, Wyo., May 11, 1926; d. Arthur Hale and Billie (Wood) Hale; m. Joseph Charles Morgan, Aug. 12, 1955; children: Joseph Hale, Jane Frances, Ann Michele. BA, Howard U., 1947; MA, U. Denver, 1954. Staff Detroit Pub. Libr., 1954-87, exec. asst. dir., 1973-75, dep. dir., 1975-78, dir., 1978-87; ret., 1987. Mem. Mich. Libr. Consortium Bd.; exec. bd. Southeastern Mich. Regional Film Libr.; vis. prof. Wayne State U., 1989—. Trustee New Detroit, Inc., Delta Dental Plan of Mich., v.p. Delta Dental Fund, Delta Dental Plan of Ohio; v.p. United Southwestern Mich.; pres. Univ.-Cultural Ctr. Assn.; bd. dirs. Rehab. Inst., YWCA, Met. Affairs Corp., Literacy Vols. Am., Detroit, Mich. Ctr. for the Book, Interfaith Coun.; bd. dirs., v.p. United Comty. Svcs. Met. Detroit; chmn. Detroiters for Adult Reading Excellence; chmn. adv. coun. libr. sci. U. Mich.; mem. adv. coun. libr. sci. U. Mich., mem. adv. coun. libr. sci. Wayne State U.; dir. Met. Detroit Youth Found.; chmn. Mich. LSCA adv. coun.; mem. UWA Literacy Com., Attys. Grievance Com., Women's Commn., Mich. Civil Svc. Rev. Com.; vice-chair Mich. Coun. for Humanities; v.p. Commn. for the Greening of Detroit; adv. com. Headstart; mem.

Detroit Women's Com., Detroit Women's Forum, Detroit Exec. Svc. Corps.; sec., treas. Delta Dental Fund, pres., 1999. Recipient Anthony Wayne award Wayne State U., 1981, Summit award Greater Detroit C. of C.; named Detroit Howardite of Year, 1983 Mem. ALA, AAUW, Mich. Libr. Assn., Women's Nat. Book Assn., Assn. Mcpl. Profl. Women, NAACP, LWV, Women's Econ. Club (bd. dirs.), Sorosis Club (v.p.), Alpha Kappa Alpha (pres.). Democrat. Episcopalian.

MORGAN, JOAN, financial planner; b. Key West, Fla., Dec. 4, 1953; d. Henry Sturgis Morgan and Fanny Gray Little Pratt. BA, Barnard Coll., 1975; MBA, Columbia U., 1977; postgrad., Adelphi U., 1983. CFP. Assoc., syndicate dept. Morgan Stanley & Co., N.Y.C., 1977-80; fin. planner, asst. v.p. Bankers Trust, N.Y.C., 1983-86; prin. Joan Morgan Adminstrv. Svcs., N.Y.C., 1986-93; fin. planner Am. Express Fin. Advisors, Inc., Washington, 1993-95, Dondero & Assocs., Ltd., Alexandria, Va., 1997-2000; prin. Joan Morgan Adminstrv. Svcs., 2001—. Bd. dirs. The Madeira Sch., McLean, Va., 1993—2003, pres., bd. dirs., 2000—03; bd. dirs. Ind. Sch. Chairpersons Assn., sec., 2003—. Mem.: Fin. Planning Assn. Avocations: skiing, rowing. Home: 3133 Connecticut Ave NW Washington DC 20008-5147

MORGAN, KATHRYN LAWSON, retired historian, educator; 1 child, Susan Morgan Crooks MA, Howard U., 1952, U. Pa., 1967, PhD, 1970. Asst. prof. U. Del., Newark, 1970-71; lectr. Swarthmore Coll., Pa., spring 1970, prof. history and folklore, 1972—95, Sara Lawrence Lightfoot Prof. History emerita, 1995. Vis. assoc. prof. Bryn Mawr Coll., 1972-75, Haverford Coll., 1972-74, U. Calif.-Berkeley, winter 1975; cons. Research for Better Schs., Phila., 1968-69, Black History Mus., Phila., 1966-76, Smithsonian Instn., 1974-76, Ednl. Film Service, 1977 Author: Children of Strangers; Stories of a Black Family, 1980, transl. Brazilian-Portuguese, 2002, Books Across the Seas, Selected for Youth, 1981; contbr. articles to profl. jours., mags. Grantee Smithsonian Instn.-Am. Philos. Soc., 1983; Danforth Found. fellow, 1968—70, sr. rsch. scholar, Swarthmore Coll., 2003. Avocations: traveling; storytelling; theatre; music. Office: Swarthmore Coll Dept Hist Swarthmore PA 19081

MORGAN, LINDA GAIL, producer; b. Tallahassee, May 14, 1952; d. Thomas Mitchell Morgan Sr. and Helen Frances (Rives) Stokes. BS, Fla. State U., 1974. Prodn. mgr. Valley Forge Ballet 5th World Peace Youth Culture Festival, Honolulu, 1985, Salute to Lady Liberty, Madison Square Gardens, 1986, U.S. Constn. 200 Yr. Anniversary Parade, Phila., 1986-89, Columbus Day Parade, N.Y.C., 1988, Gift of the White Bird Parade-Landmark Entertainment, Oita, Japan, 1990-91, 1996 Olympic Opening and Closing Ceremonies-Centenniel Events, Inc., Olympic Stadium, Atlanta, 1996, Super Bowl XXXI Half Time Show, New Orleans, 1997, N.Y. Jets Halftime Show, Meadowlands Stadium, N.J., 1997; prodn. state mgr. Walt Disney Bus. Prodns., 1998; coordinating prodr. (musical) This Is America, The New World, Freedom Music, Santa Monica, Calif., 1989, California Traditional Music Festival, Human Rights Lectr. Series, Soka U. Am., L.A., 1992-95, The Genius and the Great, L.A., 1993, Every Child Deserves a Chance, L.A., 1994, A Tribute to Burt Reynolds, L.A., 1994, Celebrate the Garnet and Gold IV Honoring Charles Nelson Reilly, L.A., 1995, Leisure Quest Internat./Entertainment Devel. Group, Burbank, Calif., 1997; artist agt., co. gen. mgr. Zoli Mgmt., Inc., N.Y.C., 1986-89; orch. prodn. mgr. All Am. Gen. Meeting, Spectrum, Phila., 1987; asst. prodn. mgr. 8th World Peace Culture Festival, Fukuoka, Japan, 1987, This Is America, Madison Square Gardens, 1988, 1991 Olympic Festival Opening Ceremonies Radio City Spl. Events, Dodger Stadium, L.A., 1991; prodn. staff Inauguration Mayor of Atlanta, Civic Ctr., Atlanta, 1998; event mgr. Coke on Ice World of Coca Cola, Atlanta, 1997-98, Disney Events Productions, 1998-2003; prodr. Anheuser-Bush Creative Svcs., 2001-. Mem. Soka Gakkai Internat. (arts divsn. culture dept. 1995-99), Fla. State U. So. Calif. Alumni Assn. (bd. dirs. 1991-95, Garnet/Gold award 1995), Internat. Spl. Event Soc., Alpha Chi Omega. Democrat. Buddhist. Avocations: arts, needlepoint, antiques, piano, gardening.

MORGAN, LINDA JOAN, former federal agency administrator; b. Chester County, Pa., May 19, 1952; m. Michael E. Karam; 1 child, Meredith Lyn. AB in Hispanic Studies, Vassar Coll., 1973; JD, Georgetown U., 1976; postgrad., Harvard U., 1991. Assoc. Welch & Morgan, Washington, 1976-78; staff counsel U.S. Senate Com. on Commerce, Sci. and Transp., 1978-86, gen. counsel, 1987-94; mem. ICC, Washington, 1994-96, chmn., 1995-96, Surface Transp. Bd., Washington, 1996—2003. Mem. D.C. Bar Assn., Bar of Supreme Ct. of U.S., Women's Bar Assn., Women's Transp. Seminar. Democrat.

MORGAN, LUCY WARE, journalist; b. Memphis, Oct. 11, 1940; d. Thomas Allin and Lucile (Sanders) Keen; m. Alton F. Ware, June 26, 1958 (div. Sept. 1967); children: Mary Kathleen, Andrew Allin; m. Richard Alan Morgan, Aug. 9, 1968; children: Lynn Elwell, Kent Morgan AA, Pasco Hernando C.C., New Port Richey, Fla., 1975; student, U. South Fla., 1976-80. Reporter Ocala Star Banner, Fla., 1965-68, St. Petersburg Times, Fla., 1967-86, capitol bur. chief, 1986—. Assoc. editor and bd. dirs. Times Pub. Co. Recipient Paul Hansel award Fla. Soc. Newspaper Editors, 1981, First in Pub. Service award Fla. Soc. Newspaper Editors, 1982, First Place award in pub. service Fla. Press Club, 1982, Pulitzer award for investigative reporting Columbia U., 1985, First Place award in investigative reporting Sigma Delta Chi, 1985; named to Kappa Tau Alpha Hall of Fame, 1992. Home: 7030 Spencer Dr Tallahassee FL 32312-3548 Office: St Petersburg Times 336 E College Ave Tallahassee FL 32301-1551

MORGAN, LYNN, sports association executive; BS in Mktg., U. Ga. Dir. sales devel., Olympic mktg. mgr. Cox Enterprises, Inc., Atlanta, 1991—2001; pres., CEO Women's United Soccer Assn., N.Y.C., 2001—03. Bd. dirs. Atlanta Sports Coun., Atlanta Thunder; gen. mgr. Atlanta Beat Women's United Soccer Assn. Bd. dirs. Salvation Army, Atlanta Ad Club, Atlanta Arts and Bus. Coun.*

MORGAN, M. JANE, computer systems consultant; b. Washington, July 21, 1945; d. Edmond John and Roberta (Livingstone) Dolphin (dec.); 1 child, Sheena Anne. Student, U. Md., 1963-66, Montgomery Coll., 1966-70; BA in Applied Behavioral Sci with honors, Nat.-Louis Univ., 1987, MS in Mgmt., 1991; postgrad. diploma in info. resource mgmt, Am. U., 1995; cert., USDA Grad. Sch., 2000; postgrad. diploma, State U. Calif., Northridge, 2002. With HUD, Washington, 1965-84, computer specialist, 1978-84; pres., CEO Systems and Mgmt. Assocs., 1983-91; dir. systems engring. Advanced Tech. Systems, Inc., Vienna, Va., 1984-86, sr. cons., 1989; chief tech. staff Tech. and Mgmt. Svcs., Inc., 1986-89; sr. computer scientist Integrated Systems divsn. Computer Scis. Corp., 1989-90; computer systems specialist gen. svcs. adminstrn. U.S. Govt., 1991—2001; divsn. dir. U.S. Gen. Svcs. Adminstrn., 2001—. Mgmt. cons. Author: Rapid Identification of Critical Staff, 1991. Bd. dirs. PL Active. Mem. Federally Employed Women (life, nat. exec. v.p. 1998-2000), Order Eastern Star. Episcopalian.

MORGAN, MARABEL, writer; b. Crestline, Ohio, June 25, 1937; d. Howard and Delsa (Smith) Hawk; m. Charles O. Morgan, Jr., June 25, 1964; children— Laura Lynn, Michelle Rene. Ed., Ohio State U. Pres. Total Woman, Inc., Miami, Fla., 1970—. Pub. speaker. Author: The Total Woman, 1973, Total Joy, 1976, The Total Woman Cookbook, 1980, The Electric Woman, 1985, The Home on the Range Cookbook, 1995. Office: c/o Total Woman Inc 1300 NW 167th St Ste 3 Miami FL 33169-5738

MORGAN, MARIANNE, corporate professional; b. Muncie, Ind., Oct. 13, 1940; d. Clarence Wilson and Mary Estle (Shafer) M. BA, Calif. State U., Long Beach, 1962; MS, U. So. Calif., 1968. Lic. real estate salesperson, Fla. Lab. technician Ball Meml. Hosp. Pathology Lab, Muncie, 1956-61; sr. libr. asst. Anaheim (Calif.) Pub. Libr., 1963-68; coll. libr. Orange Coast Coll., Costa Mesa, Calif., 1968-73; exec. v.p. Brady Products, Inc., Clearwater, Fla., 1973—. Bd. dirs. Brady Products, Inc., Clearwater, Suncoast Fluid Power, Inc., Clearwater. Fiction book reviewer, Libr. Jour., 1969-73; photography pub. in Irvine mag., 1973. Named Alice Miriam Kitselman Scholar, Kitselman Estate, Muncie, 1958. Mem. Nat. Water Well Assn., Boat Owners of the U.S., U.S. Tennis Assn., Sea Ray Boat Owners Club, RVing Women, Carefree Club, Sapphire Lakes Country Club, The Cliffs Country Club. Republican. Avocations: boating, tennis, photography, travel, raising akc bulldogs.

MORGAN, MARILYN, federal judge; b. 1947; m. James R. Grube; 1 child, Terrence M. Adamson. BA, Emory U., 1969, JD, 1976. Bar: Ga. 1976, Calif. 1977. Ptnr. Morgan & Towery, San Jose, Calif., 1979-88; bankruptcy judge U.S. Bankruptcy Ct. (no. dist.) Calif., 1988—. Mem. bankruptcy adv. com. U.S. Dist. Ct., 1984-88; law rep. 9th Cir. Jud. Conf., 1987-88. Mem. adv. bd. Downtown YMCA, 1984-88; dir. The Women's Fund, 1987-88; bd. dirs. Consumer Credit Counselors of San Francisco, 1999—, Cathedral Found., 2001—. Mem. Santa Clara County Bar Assn. (chmn. debtor and creditor and insolvency com. 1979, 81, treas. 1982, pres. 1985-86), Santa Clara County Bar Assn. Law Found. (trustee 1982, 86-88, pres. 1985, law related edn. trustee 1986-88), Nat. Assn. Bankruptcy Trustees (founding mem., v.p., sec. 1981-88), Rotary Club San Jose (bd. dirs. 1992-95), Nat. Assn. Bankruptcy Trustees (founder). Office: US Bankruptcy Ct 280 S 1st St Rm 3035 San Jose CA 95113-3010

MORGAN, MARY DAN, librarian; b. Tallulah, La., Nov. 30, 1943; d. Daniel Boone and Mary Louise (McLeod) M.; m. William Jefferson Day (div. Dec. 1995); 1 child, Forrest Jefferson Day. BA, La. Coll., 1965; MS in Libr. Sci., La. State U., 1968; MA in Edn., Murray State U., 1976; MS in Social Work, U. Louisville, 1992. Cert. social worker, Ky., Ind. Libr. Ascension Parish Schs., Donaldsonville, La., 1966-68, Jefferson County Schs., Louisville, 1968-75; tchr. Webster County Schs., Dixon, Ky., 1975-79, Hardin County Schs., Elizabethtown, Ky., 1979-82, dir. media ctr., 1982-87, tchr. day and residential juvenile facilities, 1987-91, tchr. mid. and sr. high alt. schs., 1991-93; social worker Hospice of Ctrl. Ky., Elizabethtown, 1993-2000, Gentiva Health Svcs., Louisville, 1995, Lincoln Trail Dist. Home Health, Elizabethtown, 1997-98; libr. Luther Luckett Correctional Complex, La Grange, Ky., 2000—. Pres. Webster County Tchrs. Assn., Dixon, Ky., 1977-78, sec. Ky. Libr. Network Bd., Frankfort, 1986-87. Mem. NEA (life), NASW, AAUW, ALA, Filson Club. Office: Luther Luckett Correctional Complex PO Box 6 La Grange KY 40031 Home: 4223 Garden Ridge Rd Crestwood KY 40014-7800

MORGAN, MARY E. publishing executive; married; 1 child. B, SUNY Binghamton. Adv. dir. Fitness Mag., 1992—94; assoc. group pub. Parents and Child Mag., 1994—95; assoc. pub. Ladies Home Journal, 1995—97; v.p., pub. Health Mag., 1997—2003, Redbook, 2003—. Mem. editl. bd. Pharmaceutical Executive Magazine. Mem.: Nat. Assn. of Chain Drug Stores, Cosmetic Exec. Women (philanthropy com.), Advt. Women of N.Y. (mem. bd. dirs.), Advt. Club of N.Y. Office: Redbooks 224 West 57th St New York NY 10019

MORGAN, MARY LOU, retired education educator, volunteer; b. Chgo., Mar. 5, 1938; d. William Nicholas and Esther Lucille (Galbraith) Wanmer; m. James Edward Morgan, May 30, 1963. BA in Bus. Edn. and Econs., Wichita State U., 1971, MEd in Student Pers. and Guidance, 1974; postgrad., Kans. State U., 1986. Cert. bus. tchr., Kans. Reservationist Braniff, Wichita, Kans., 1961-62; stenographer, fin. analyst, clk.-typist Boeing Co., Wichita, 1962-68, tng., pers. and records positions, 1979-93; pers. cons. Rita Pers. Svc., Wichita, 1974-75; adminstrv. aide, manpower specialist, job developer City of Wichita, 1975-76; account exec., employment counselor Mgmt. Recruiters, 1976-77; pers. mgr., patient cons. Women's Clinic, 1977; vocat. rehab. counselor State of Kans., Parsons, 1977-79; pvt. detective Investigation Svcs., Wichita, 1981-84; instr. career devel. Wichita State U., 1988-90. Paralegal asst. Turner & Hensley, Wichita, 1975. Coord. funding Women's Crisis Ctr., Wichita, 1975; docent Carver Mus., Hoover Mus.; vice chmn. Hist. Preservation Commn.; founder, coord. Ann. Women's Chautauqua; Precinct committeewoman Wichita Dem. Com., 1992—94; pres. Jasper County-Newton County Dems., 1998; mem. Grover Beach Dems., 2001—; bd. dirs. City of Wichita, Wichita Commn. on Status of Women, 1988—91. Mem.: NOW (founder, 1st pres., v.p. program chmn. Wichita chpt. 1969—93, asst. state coord. polit. action com. Wichita chpt. 1993—95, at-large state bd. Joplin com. 1994—95, 1997—98, 1999—2000, at-large state mem. Grover Beach chpt. 2001—), AARP, LWV (v.p. issues study Joplin area league 1998—2000, Grover Beach league 2001—, off board dir. 2002—03, bd. dirs. 2003—), AAUW (bd. dirs. edn., equity, women's issues Joplin br. 1999—2000, Grover Beach br. 2001—, pres. Grover Beach br. 2002—04, mem. state pub. policy com. 2003—04). Avocations: water skiing, boating, collecting victorian clothing, travel.

MORGAN, MARY LOUISE FITZSIMMONS, fund raising executive, lobbyist; b. N.Y.C., July 22, 1946; d. Robert John and Mary Louise (Gordon) Fitzsimmons; m. David William Morgan, Aug. 7, 1971; children: Mallory Siobhan, David William. BA, Marquette U., 1964; MA, Catholic U., Wash., 1966. Asst. prof. Monmouth U., West Long Branch, N.J., 1966-69; campaign dir. United Way, N.Y.C., 1969-80; pres. Morgan Communications, N.Y.C., 1980-82; capital campaign dir. YMCA of Greater N.Y., 1982-85; dir. devel. N.Y. Med. Coll., Valhalla, 1985-88; counsel Challenger Ctr., Va., 1988-89; v.p. Ctr. Molecular Medicine & Immunology, Newark, 1989-92, Garden State Cancer Ctr., Newark, 1989-92; chief devel. and pub. affairs officer Mental Health Assn., White Plains, N.Y., 1993-95; dir. external affairs St. Vincents Svcs., 1996—. Adj. prof. Iona Coll., New Rochelle, N.Y., 1994-95; dir. Meth Ch. Home for Aged, Riverdale, N.Y., Casita Maria Inc., N.Y.C., 1975-95; pres., founding dir. Achievement Rewards for Coll. Scientists Inc., 1978-80. Sec. Darien (Conn.) Dem. Town Com., 1984—, vice chmn. Darien nominating com. 1986—. Recipient 50th Anniversary award Casita Maria Inc., N.Y.C., 1984, Iris award Bus. Communicators of Am., 1991, Nat. Depression Awareness Campaign award NMHA, 1994, Am. Graphic Design award, 2002. Mem. Nat. Soc. Fund Raising Execs., Nat. Soc. Hosp. Adminstrn., Spring Lake (N.J.) Bath and Tennis Club. Democrat. Roman Catholic. Avocations: golf, gardening, tennis. Office: 66 Boerum Pl Brooklyn NY 11201-5705 E-mail: MaryL.Morgan@svs.org.

MORGAN, PAULETTE ELISE, state official, researcher; b. Fremont, Mich., Oct. 7, 1959; d. Walter and Janet Ann (Strzyz) M.; m. William Francis Howard, Sept. 17, 1988; 1 child, Katherine Eliza Howard. BA in English Lit. and Polit. Sci. summa cum laude, U. Cin., 1983; MA in Polit. Sci., Syracuse U., 1985. Rsch. assoc. N.Y. State Senate Rsch. Svc., Albany, N.Y., 1985-91, prin. analyst, 1991-95; rsch. assoc. Office Temporary and Disability Assistance, N.Y. State Dept. Family Assistance, Albany, 1995—. Mem. Tau Beta Sigma (lifetime). Avocations: collecting rookwood pottery, roycroft publications and rockwell kent illustrated books.

MORGAN, ROBIN EVONNE, poet, author, journalist, activist, editor; b. Lake Worth, Fla., Jan. 29, 1941; 1 child, Blake Ariel. Grad. with honors, The Wetter Sch., 1956; student, pvt. tutors, 1956-59, Columbia U.; DHL (hon.), U. Conn., 1992. Free-lance book editor, 1961-69; editor Grove Press, 1967-70; editor, columnist World column Ms. Mag., NYC, 1974-87, editor in chief, 1989-93, cons. editor, 1993—, columnist, 2003—. Vis. chair and guest prof. women's studies New Coll., Sarasota, Fla., 1973; disting. vis. scholar, lectr. Ctr. Critical Analysis of Contemporary Culture, Rutgers U., 1987, U. Canterbury, Christchurch, New Zealand, 1989, U. Denver Grad. Sch. Internat. Affairs, 1996-97; invited spl. cons. UN com. UN Conv. to End All Forms Discrimination Against Women, Sao Paulo and Brasilia, Brazil, 1987; mem. adv. bd. ISIS (internat. network women's internat. cross-cultural exch.); spl. advisor gen. assembly conf. on Gender UN Internat. Sch., 1985-86; free-lance journalist, lectr. cons., editor, 1969—; invited speaker numerous confs., orgns., acad. meetings, US and abroad. Author, compiler, editor: Sisterhood Is Powerful: An Anthology of Writings from the Women's Liberation Movement, 1970, Swedish edit., 1972, Sisterhood Is Global: The International Women's Movement Anthology, 1984, U.K. edit., 1985, Spanish edit., 1994, Feminist Press edit., 1996, Sisterhood Is Forever:The Women's Anthology for A New Millennium, 2003; author: (nonfiction) Going Too Far: The Personal Chronicle of a Feminist, 1978, German edit., 1978, The Anatomy of Freedom: Feminism, Physics and Global Politics, 1982, 2d edit., 1994, fgn. edits. UK, 1984, Germany, 1985, Argentina, 1986, Brazil, 1992, The Demon Lover: On the Sexuality of Terrorism, 1989, UK edit., 1989, Japanese edit., 1992, Italian edit., 1998, revised US edit., 2002, The Word of a Woman: Feminist Dispatches 1968-91, 1992, 2d edit., 1994, UK edit., 1992, Chinese edit., 1996, A Woman's Creed, English, Arabic, French, Italian, Sanskrit, Hindi, Russian, Spanish, Portuguese, Chinese and Persian edits., 1995, Saturday's Child: A Memoir, 2000, (fiction) Dry Your Smile: A Novel, 1987, U.K. edit., 1988, The Mer-Child: A New Legend, 1991, German edit., 1995, Korean edit., 2000, (poetry) Monster: Poems, 1972, Lady of the Beasts: Poems, 1976, Death Benefits: Poems, 1981, Depth Perception: New Poems and a Masque, 1982, Upstairs in the Garden: Selected and New Poems, 1968-88, 1990, A Hot January: Poems 1996-1999, 1999, (plays) In Another Country, 1960, The Duel, 1979; poetry editor: The New Woman: Anthology, 1969; contbr. numerous articles, essays, book revs., poems to various publs.; presenter poetry readings, univ., poetry ctr., radio, TV, others, 1970—. Mem. 1st women's liberation caucus CORE, 1965, Student Nonviolent Coordinating Com., 1966; organizer 1st feminist demonstration against Miss Am. Pageant, 1968; founder, pres. The Sisterhood is Powerful Fund, 1970; founder, pres. NY Women's Law Ctr., 1970; founder NY Women's Ctr., 1969; co-founder, bd. dir. Feminist Women's Health Network, Nat. Battered Women's Refuge Network, Nat. Network Rape Crisis Ctr.; bd. dir. Women's Fgn. Policy Coun.; adv. trustee Nat. Women's Inst. for Freedom of Press; founding mem. Nat. Mus. Women in Arts; founder Sisterhood is Global Inst. (internat. think-tank), 1984, officer, 1989-97, chair adv. bd., 1997—; co-organizer, US mem. official visit Coalition of Philippines Women's Movement, 1988; chair NY state com. Hands Across Am. Com. for Justice and Empowerment, 1988; mem. adv. bd. Global Fund for Women, Equality Now. Recipient Front Page award for disting. journalism, Wonder Woman award for internat. peace and understanding, 1982, Feminist of Yr. award Fund for Feminist Majority, 1990; Human Rights Activism Award from Equality NOW, 2002, Feminist Press award, 2003; writer-in-residence grantee Yaddo, 1980; grantee Nat. Endowment for Arts, 1979-80, Ford Found., 1982, 83, 84. Mem. Nat. Mus. Women in Arts, Feminist Writers' Guild, Media Women, N.Am. Feminist Coalition, Pan Arab Feminist Solidarity Assn. (hon.), Israeli Feminists Against Occupation (hon.). Office: c/o Edite Kroll Literary Agency 12 Grayhurst Park Portland ME 04102-3601

MORGAN, RUTH PROUSE, academic administrator, educator; b. Berkeley, Calif., Mar. 30, 1934; d. Ervin Joseph and Thelma Ruth (Prcesang) Prouse; m. Vernon Edward Morgan, June 3, 1956; children: Glenn Edward, Renée Ruth. BA summa cum laude, U. Tex., 1956; MA, La. State U., 1961, PhD, 1966. Asst. prof. Am. govt., politics and theory So. Meth. U., Dallas, 1966-70, assoc. prof., 1970-74, prof., 1974-95; prof. emeritus, 1995—; asst. provost So. Meth. U., Dallas, 1978-82, assoc. provost, 1982-86, provost ad interim, 1986-87, provost, 1987-93, provost emerita, 1993—; pres. RPM Assocs., 1993—; v.p. Chem. Abatement Tech., Inc., 1995—. Tex. state polit. analyst ABC, N.Y.C., 1972-84. Author: The President and Civil Rights, 1970, Governance By Decree: The Impact of the Voting Rights Act in Dallas, 2004; mem. editl. bd. Jour. of Politics, 1975-82, Presdl. Studies Quar., 1980—; contbr. articles to profl. jours. Active Internat. Women's Forum, 1987—, City of Dallas Redistricting Commn., 2001; trustee Hockaday Sch., 1988-94, The Kilby Awards Found., 1993-95; bd. dirs. United Way, Met. Dallas, 1993-99; adv. com. U.S. Army Command and Gen. Staff. Coll., 1994-97; founder Archives of Women of the Southwest, 1992, chmn. adv. com. 1995-99; mem. Women's Ctr. Dallas, Dallas Women's Found. Mem. Am. Polit. Sci. Assn., So. Polit. Sci. Assn. (mem. exec. coun. 1979-84), Southwestern Polit. Sci. Assn. (pres. 1982-83, mem. exec. coun. 1981-84), The Dallas Assembly, The Dallas Forum of Internat. Women's Forum (pres. 1996-97), Charter 100 Club (pres. 1991-92), Nat. Mus. for Women in the Arts (charter), The Women's Mus. (charter), Ctr. for the Study of the Presidency, Dallas Summit Club (pres. 1992-93), Phi Beta Kappa, Pi Sigma Alpha, Phi Kappa Phi, Theta Sigma Phi. Avocations: photography, travel.

MORGAN, SUSAN H. state representative; b. Nanaimo, Sept. 1, 1949; m. Kip Morgan; 3 children. AS, Lane C.C., 1977. Office mgr. Morgan Loggin, M&M Hardwoods, 1978—90; mgr. info. sys. Weyerhauser Pole Facility, 1990—93; sales rep. C&D Lumber Co., 1993—98; mem. Oreg. Ho. of Reps., 1998—. Mem. planning adv. com. South Umpqua County, 1980—98, mem. adv. bd. Myrtle Creek Pub. Libr., 1988—96 Mem.: Oreg. Lands Coalition (founding). Republican. Office: 900 Court St NE H-381 Salem OR 97301

MORGAN, SUSAN MCGRATH, Jungian analyst; b. New London, Jan. 11, 1937; d. Francis Foran and Helen Cuseck (Connolly) McGuire; m. Robert L. McGrath, Sept. 16, 1959 (div. May 1992); children: Robert L., Swithin, Charles Felix, William Ambrose. BA, Smith Coll., 1959, MSW, 1992; MA in Liberal Studies, Dartmouth Coll., 1982; diplomate, C.G. Jung Inst., 2001. Lic. social worker, Vt., Boston. Alcohol educator Dartmouth Med. Ctr., Hanover, N.H., 1972-77; program dir. Pub. Affairs Ctr. Dartmouty Coll., Hanover, 1978-82; cons. Alice Peck Day/Dartmouth Alcohol Program, Hanover, 1982-83; psychotherapist Orange County Mental Health Ctr., Randolph, Vt., 1993-97; pvt. practice Norwich, Vt., 1995—. Tchr. Inst. for Lifelong Edn. at Dartmouth, Dartmouth Coll., 1993—; spkr. in field. Contbr.: Understanding Alcohol, 1979, Loosening the Grip, Clinical Manual of Substance Abuse, 1996. Pres. Vt. Alcohol Counselors Assn., 1982-84; sec. Norwich Conservation Commn., 1972-82; bd. dirs. Upper Valley Found., 1997—. Mem. NASW, C.G. Jung Soc. of Vt., Cobb Hill Co-Housing (founding mem.), New Eng. Soc. Jungian Analysts, Internat. Assn. Analytical Psychology. Office: 2935 Dillon Rd Whitefish MT 59937-8295

MORGAN, VICTORIA, performing company executive, choreographer; BFA, U. Utah, 1973, MFA magna cum laude, 1976. Prin. dancer Ballet West, 1969-78, San Francisco Ballet, 1978-87; resident choreographer San Francisco Opera, 1987—97; artistic dir. Cin. Ballet, 1997—. Dancer with lead roles in numerous classical, neoclassical and modern ballets including works by George Balanchine, Forsythe, and Kudelka, lead roles for TV and films, choreographer creating over 40 works for 20 ballet and opera cos. across U.S. including Utah Ballet, Pacific Northwest Ballet, Glimmerglass Opera, N.Y.C. Opera and Cin. Opera. Office: Cincinnati Ballet 1555 Central Pkwy Cincinnati OH 45214-2863*

MORGAN, VIRGINIA MATTISON, magistrate judge; b. 1946; BS, Univ. of Mich., 1968; JD, Univ. of Toledo, 1975. Bar: Mich. 1975, Federal 1975, U.S. Ct. Appeals (6th cir.) 1979. Tchr. Dept. of Interior, Bur. of Indian Affairs, 1968-70, San Diego Unified Schs., 1970-72, Oregon, Ohio, 1972-74; asst. prosecutor Washtenaw County Prosecutor's Office, 1976-79; asst. U.S. atty. Detroit, 1979-85; magistrate judge U.S. Dist. Ct. (Mich. ea. dist.), 6th circuit, Detroit, 1985—. Mem. bd. Fed. Jud. Ctr., 1997-2001; mem. jud. conf. U.S. Com. on Long Range Planning, 1993-96. Recipient Spl. Achievement award Dept. of Justice, Disting. Alumni award U. Toledo,

1993. Fellow Mich. State Bar Found.; mem. FBA (chpt. pres. 1996-97), Fed. Magistrate Judges Assn. (pres. 1995-96). Office: US Courthouse 231 W Lafayette Blvd Detroit MI 48226-2700

MORGAN-PRAGER, KAROLE, lawyer, publishing executive; Assoc. Morrison & Foerster, L.A., 1987—92; assoc. gen. counsel Times Mirror Co., 1992—95; gen. counsel, corp. sec. McClatchy Co., Sacramento, 1995—, v.p., 1998—. Office: McClatchy Co Legal Dept 2100 Q St Sacramento CA 95818-6899

MORGART, MICHELE, psychologist, consultant; b. Phila., July 2, 1947; d. Robert Paul and Elizabeth (Byrne) M.; 1 child, Michael Paul. BA in Psychology and English, U. Akron, Ohio, 1981, MA in Clin. Psychology, 1984. Cert. tchr., Ohio; lic. profl. clin. counselor; cert. employee assistance profl. Counselor and edn. specialist Mercy Med. Ctr., Canton, Ohio, 1984—, dir., human resource cons., employee assistance program, 1992—2003, mgr. behavioral health svcs., 2003—. Cons. C.A.R.E. Cmty. Drug Edn., Cuy Falls, Ohio, 1984; cons., chair City Ethics Adv. Bd., 1994. Cons. Summit County Drug Bd., Akron, 1978-81. Mem. APA (cert.), Employee Asst. Profl. Assn., Psi Chi, Phi Sigma Alpha. Avocations: reading, fitness, film, theatre, music. Office: Mercy Med Ctr 1320 Mercy Dr NW Canton OH 44708-2614

MORGENSON, GRETCHEN C. reporter; b. State College, Pa., Jan. 2, 1956; BA in English and History, Saint Olaf Coll., 1976. Asst. editor Vogue Mag., 1976—81; stock broker Dean Witter Reynolds, N.Y.C., 1981—84; staff writer Money Mag., 1984—86; editor, investigative bus. writer Forbes Mag., 1986—93; exec. editor Worth Mag., 1993—95; mng. editor Forbes Mag., 1996—98; asst. bus. and fin. editor NY Times, 1998—. Author: Forbes Great Minds of Business, 1997; co-author: The Woman's Guide to the Stock Market, 1981; author: (with Campbell R. Harvey) The New York Times Dictionary of Money and Investing: The Essential A-to-Z Guide to the Language of the New Market, 2002; co-author: (with Allen R. Myerson (editor), Floyd Norris) The New Rules of Personal Investing: How to Prosper in a Changing Economy, 2001. Recipient Gerald Loeb award, 1998, 2002, Pulitzer Prize for beat reporting, 2002, TJFR Group/MasterCard Internat. Bus. News Luminaries award, 2003. Office: NY Times 229 W 43d St New York NY 10036*

MORI, MARIKO, artist; b. Tokyo, 1967; Student, Bunka Fashion Coll., Tokyo, 1986-88, Byam Shaw Sch. Art, London, 1988-89, Chelsea Coll. Art, 1989-92, Whitney Mus. Am. Art, 1992-93. One-woman shows include Geneva Project Room, N.Y.C., 1993, Shiseido Gallery, Tokyo, 1995, Am. Fine Arts Co., N.Y., 1995, Galerie Emmanuel Perrotin, Paris, 1996, Ctr. Nat. D'Art Contemporain Grenoble, Italy-Nordic Pavilion Venice Biennale, 1997, L.A. County Mus. Art, 1998, Mus. Contemporary Art, Cgo., 1998, Serpentine Gallery, London, 1998, Andy Warhol Mus., Paris, 1998, Bklyn. Mus. Art, Kunstmus. Wolfsburg, 1999, Fondazione Prada, Milan, 1999, Ctr. Pompidou, Paris, Ctr. Nat. Photography, 2000, Mus. Contemporary Art, 2002, Tokyo, 2004. Office: c/o Eyestorm 2nd Fl 547 W 27th St New York NY 10001*

MORI, TOSHIKO, architecture educator; Student, Cooper Union, 1970—71, BArch, 1976; AM (hon.), Harvard U., 1996. Registered Arch., Fla., Maine, N.Y., NCARB cert. Arch. Edward Larrabee Barnes and Assocs., 1976—81, Toshiko Mori Arch., 1981—; prof. architecture Grad. Sch. Design Harvard U., 1995—2001, Robert P. Hubbard prof. arch. Grad. Sch. Design, 2002—, chair dept. architecture Grad. Sch. Design, 2002—. Arch. Tod Williams and Assocs., 1972—73, ELS Design Group Urban Design, 1973—74; vis. critic Grad. Sch. Design Harvard U., 1989, 94; Eero Saarinen vis. prof. Sch. Architecture Yale U., 1992, vis. critic Sch. Architecture, 93, Columbia U., 1994; lectr. in field. Advisor Greenwich Village Soc. Historic Preservation; mem. adv. bd. Montreal Mus. Decorative Art McDonald Stewart Found. Recipient prize for urban design, Abraham Kazan Fund, 1976, Henry Adams Cert. of Achievement, AIA, 1976, The One Show Merit award, 1981, N.Y.C./AIA Design Award Citation Interior Architecture, 1988, N.Y.C./AIA Design award in interior architecture, Internat. Assn. Lighting Designers, 1989, 11th Ann. Interiors award for best retail design, Shinkenchiku/Crtl. Glass Internat., 1990, Renovation award, C. of C., Rockport, Rockland, Maine, 1995, Silver medal in exhbn. design at MOMA, Art Dirs. Club, 1999, N.Y.C./AIA Design award, 1998, 2000. Office: Harvard Design Sch 202 Gund Hall 48 Quincy St Cambridge MA 02138

MORIARTY, KAREN, state agency administrator; b. Mesa, Ariz., June 15, 1957; d. Glenn Federick and Rosalee Mae (Russell) Bowers; m. Brian Logan Moriarty, Aug. 15, 1981; children: Lisa Louise, Kimberly Ann. Cert. pub. mgr. Clk. typist State of Ariz. Indsl. Commn., Phoenix, 1978, acctg. clk., 1978-85, fiscal specialist svcs. I, 1985-96, fiscal speicalist svcs. II, 1996—2002, self-ins. administr., 2003—. Leader, trainer Ariz. Cactus Pine coun. Girl Scouts U.S., 1994—; active United Way, Phoenix, 1996, Big Bros./Big Sisters, Phoenix, 1987-91. Named Vol. of Yr., City of Chandler, 1995. Mem. NAFE, Nat. Assn. of the Deaf, Girl Scouts U.S. (life). Avocations: cross-stitch, swimming. Office: State of Ariz Indsl Commn 800 W Washington St Phoenix AZ 85007-2934

MORIARTY, MAUREEN C. marketing professional; b. Albany, N.Y., Nov. 4, 1946; d. Richard John and Margaret (Egan) Conners; m. James M. Moriarty, Feb. 1, 1969. BA in History, Coll. St. Rose, 1968; MBA in Mktg., U. Pa., 1976. Sch. tchr., Houston and San Francisco, 1969-74; from asst. product mgr. to group mktg. mgr. Gillette Co., Boston, 1977-86; mktg. dir. men's jean div. Levi Strauss & Co., San Francisco, 1986-92; sr. v.p. mktg. Mattel, Inc., 1992; pres. Global Bus. Group, Pebble Beach, Calif., 1992—. Bd. dirs. Bass Rocks Internat., San Francisco; cons., pub. speaker in field; instr. internat. mktg. Golden Gate U., U. Calif. Extension Program. Author: Goal 4 It, 1988. Bd. dirs. San Francisco Sr. Citizen's Ctr., 1986-89; mktg. adv. bd. United Way, San Francisco, 1990-91, Univ. of Calif. at Berkeley Ext. Prog., San Francisco, 1987-90. Home: PO Box 375 Pebble Beach CA 93953-0375

MORISATO, SUSAN CAY, actuary; b. Chgo., Feb. 11, 1955; d. George and Jessie (Fujita) M.; m. Thomas Michael Remec, Mar. 6, 1981. BS, U. Ill., 1975, MS, 1977. Actuarial student Aetna Life & Casualty, Hartford, Conn., 1977-79; actuarial asst. Bankers Life & Casualty Co., Chgo., 1979-80, asst. actuary, 1980-83, assoc. actuary, 1983-85, health product actuary, 1985-86, v.p., 1986-95, sr. v.p., 1996—, also bd. dirs. Participant individual forum Am.'s Health Ins. Plans, 1983; spkr. in field. Adv. panel on long term care financing Brookings' Inst. Fellow Soc. Actuaries (workshop leader 1990, 93, news editor health sect. news 1988-90, conf. spkr. 2001, 02); mem. Am. Acad. Actuaries, Am.'s Health Ins. Plans (long term care task force 1988—, chair 1993-95, tech. adv. com. 1991-93, legis. policy com. 1996-99, nominating com. 1996-98, other coms., policy coord. coun. 1999-2003, sr. mktg. task force chair 2000-01, chmn. task force on Medicare modernization 2002—, exec. com. 2004-, bd. dirs. 2004-, policy com. 2004-, Founders award 1996), Health Ins. Assn. Am. (conf. spkr. 2000), LIMRA Internat. (strategic mktg. ins. com. 2001—, bd. dirs. 2003—), Nat. Assn. Ins. Commrs. (ad hoc actuarial working group for long term care nonforfeiture benefits 1992), Am. Coun. Life Ins. (accelerated benefits/long term care com. 1997-2001), Chgo. Actuarial Assn. (sec. 1983-85, program com. 1987-89), Phi Beta Kappa, Kappa Delta Pi, Phi Kappa Phi. Office: Bankers Life & Casualty Co 222 Merchandise Mart Plz 19th Fl Chicago IL 60654 Office Phone: 312-396-6117. E-mail: s.morisato@banklife.com.

MORISSEAU, NAN KRUGER, television personality; b. Oklahoma City; d. Albert William and Lillie Mae (Kubala) K.; m. Fay Edwin Morisseau Esq., III, June 8, 1974; children: Katherine, Paul. BS, U. Okla., 1972; postgrad., U. Houston, 1986-90. Fashion designer Charm of Hollywood, L.A., 1972-74, Jackson Sq., New Orleans, 1974-75; buyer Federated Dept. Stores Foleys Houston, 1975-80; stockbroker Prudential Securities, Houston, 1980-86; pres. The Newport Beach (Calif.) Recital Series, 1995-99, also bd. dirs.; pres. Cachet' Prodns. Internatl., Newport Beach, 1994—, Golden Girl Jewelry, Newport Beach, 1997—; TV talk show host Rise & Shine with Nancy Morgan Pacific Family Entertainment, Fountain Valley, Calif., 1997—, also bd. dirs., 1996-97. Author (plays) White Russian, 1988, Meyerhold, 1990, (screenplay) Triumph of The Spirit, 1992; actor (situation comedy) Student Union, 1992, (play) Charon Unleashed, 1993. Hostess Chamber Music Salons, 1995-99; pres. Friends of Newport Beach Recital Series, 1995—; bd. dirs. Orange County Philharm. Soc., Big Canyon, Calif., 1996-97. Vol. Ctr. devel. grantee, 1996; recipient Bronze medal Nastar Downhill Skiing, 1996. Mem. AAUW (chair classical music sect. 1997), Womens Diversity Forum, North Orange County Computer Club, Arts Orange County. Avocations: skiing, surfing, computer graphics, music, ballet. Home and Office: Cachet Prodns Internatl 77 Montecito Dr Corona Del Mar CA 92625-1018

MORISSETTE, ALANIS, musician; b. Ottawa, ON, Canada, June 1, 1974; Singer: (albums) Alanis, 1991, Now is the Time, 1992, Jagged Little Pill, 1995, Supposed Former Infatuation Junkie, 1998, Under Rug Swept, 2002, Feast On Scraps, 2002, So-Called Chaos, 2004; actor: (films) Dogma, 1999, Jay and Silent Bob Strike Back, 2001. Recipient Grammy award for Album of Yr., Best Female Rock Vocal Performance, Best Rock Song, Best Rock Album, 1996. Address: Maverick Recording Co 9348 Civic Center Dr Ste 100 Beverly Hills CA 90210-3606*

MORITZ, JEAN LORIS, elementary school educator; b. San Leandro, Calif., July 28, 1934; d. Cyril Sidney and Annabel Alice (Nicholson) Humphrey; m. Arthur Lee Moritz, Oct. 18, 1957; children: Karen Ann Williams, Arthur Lee Moritz Jr., Michele Bird. AA, U. Calif., Berkeley, 1954; BA, Calif. State U., Fresno, 1976. Cert. tchr., Calif.; cert. lang. devel. specialist, Calif. Substitute tchr. Visalia (Calif.) Unified Sch. Dist., 1976-78; tchr. St. Paul's Sch., Visalia, 1978-85, Earlimart (Calif.) Mid. Sch., 1985—2000. Elder First Presbyn. Ch., Visalia, 1989-93. Mem. AAUW.

MORMAN, SHIRLEY H. director; d. Othello and Rheta Mae Hopkins; m. R.C. Morman, Aug. 27, 1977; children: Russell Christopher, Brandon LeRay. MSc, Fort Valley State U., Ga., 1975. Asst. dir. U. Md., College Park, 1974—87; dir. Coll. Gateway Programs U. of Md., College Park, 1987—. Co-dir. early intervention partnership project U. of Md., College Park, 1987—89; field reader cons. U.S. Dept. of Edn., Washington, 1988—2003; faculty-mentor Coun. for Opportunity in Edn., Washington, 1990—2003; rsch. cons. TERI Inst./U. Mass., Boston, 1992—93; grant cons. Gov.'s Commn. on Svc., Balt., 1995—96. Mem. bd. visitors Sch.-Univ. Coop. Programs, College Park, Md., 1998—2001; bd. dirs. Nyumburu Cultural Ctr., U. Md., College Park, 2000—03; bd. dirs. Seat Pleasant Partnership, Md., 2001—03. Recipient Coun. award, Prince George's County, 1987, Recognition award, I Have A Dream Found., 1994, Recognition of Svc. award, U.S. Dept. of Edn., 1999, 2001, Outstanding Svc. award, Gov. of State of Md., 2000. Mem.: Md. Exec. Coun. for Ednl. Opportunity (assoc.; pres. 1994—96, Hall of Fame award 1996), Mid-Eastern Assn. of Ednl. Opportunity Program Pers. (assoc.). Achievements include development of Project LINKS Digital Divide Online Tutoring. Office: Univ Md 3103 Turner Hall College Park MD

MOROI, KAZUE ELIZABETH, sculptor; b. Matsuyama, Saitama-ken, Japan, Aug. 5, 1930; arrived in U.S., 1959; d. Gunji and Kiku Sekiguchi; m. David Shuichi Moroi, Apr. 10, 1959; children: Sayoko E.A. Moroi-Fetters, Sigeyoshi Albert, Katsumi Karl. Master Degree, tchrs. cert., Koryu Flower Arrangement Sch., Tokyo, 1946; grad., Musashino Nutrition Coll., Tokyo, 1956; tchrs. lic., Koryu Flower Arrangement Sch., Tokyo, 1956; student, Tokyo Ningyo Gakuin, 1954—59; postgrad., Kent State U., 1974; pvt. tng., Nat. Inst. Am. Doll Artist, 1974; student, Portrait Doll. Sculpture, 2000. Instr. with tchrs. lic. Tokyo Ningyo Gakuin, 1959; Seeley's doll product tchr. Seeley Ceramic Co., Oneonta, NY, 1985. Instr. continuing edn. home econs. Kent (Ohio) State U., 1974—78; shop and studio owner Moroi Doll Boutique and Studio, Kent, 1988. Recipient Pres. Choice Rosettes, Region 12 Conv., 1986, Best of Show Rosettes, Great Lakes Doll Artists Assn., 1990, 2nd Pl. Rosettes, Santa Fe Doll Artist, 1995. Mem.: Original Doll Artists Coun. Am., Guild Ohio Dollmakers, United Fedn. Doll Clubs (workshop instr. 1989). Episcopalian. Avocations: sculpting, water color painting, gardening, fishing, travel. Home: 3759 Renwick Ln Columbus OH 43230

MORONEY, LINDA L.S. (MUFFIE), lawyer, educator; b. Washington, May 27, 1943; d. Robert Emmet and Jessie (Robinson) M.; m. Clarence Renshaw II, Mar. 28, 1967 (div. 1977); children: Robert Milnor, Justin W.R. BA, Randolph-Macon Woman's Coll., 1965; JD cum laude, U. Houston, 1982. Bar: Tex. 1982, U.S. Ct. Appeals (5th cir.) 1982, U.S. Dist. Ct. (so. dist.) Tex. 1982, U.S. Supreme Ct. 1988. Law clk. to assoc. justice 14th Ct. Appeals, Houston, 1982-83; assoc. Pannill and Reynolds, Houston, 1983-85, Gilpin, Pohl & Bennett, Houston, 1985-89, Vinson & Elkins, Houston, 1989-92. Adj. prof. law U. Houston, 1986-91, dir. legal rsch. and writing, 1992-96, civil trial and appellate litigation and mediation, 1996—. Mem. ABA, State Bar Tex., Houston Bar Assn., Assn. of Women Attys., Tex. Women Lawyers, Order of the Barons, Phi Delta Phi. Episcopalian. Home and Office: 4010 Whitman St Houston TX 77027-6334

MOROTO, NADINE B. secondary school educator; d. Robert Marcus and Estelle Glatman Barsky; m. Hirohi Moroto, July 21, 1981; children: Mariko, Robert. BA, UCLA, 1966; MA, La Verne (Calif.) U., 1978. Cert. tchr. lifetime credential Calif., LDS cert. Calif. Tchr. LA Unified Sch. Dist., 1967—, integration team leader, 1979, tchr. advisor, 1982; demonstration tchr. dept. edn. UCLA, 1971—75; curriculum advisor Instl. Objectives Exch., LA, 1971—72; master tng. tchr. UCLA and Pepperdine, 1972—76. Grantee scholarship, Delta Kappa Gamma, Calif., 2003, Smith Richardson Fellowship, LA, 1975. Mem.: Unified Tchrs. of LA (Platinum Apple award 2003), Delta Kappa Gamma (pres. 2002—, membership chair 1990—2000, co-pres. 2000—02). Avocations: swimming, camping, travel, reading, bicycling. Office: LA Unified Sch Dist 1403 Fairburn Ave Los Angeles CA 90024

MORPHEW, DOROTHY RICHARDS-BASSETT, artist, real estate broker; b. Cambridge, Mass., Aug. 4, 1918; d. George and Evangeline Booth (Richards) Richards; children: Jon Eric Bassett, Marc Alan Bassett, Dana Kimball Bassett. Grad., Boston Art Inst., 1949. Draftsman United Shoe Machinery Co., 1937—42; blueprinter, advt. artist A.C. Lawrence Leather Co., Peabody, Mass., 1949—51; propr. Studio Shop and Studio Potters, Beverly, Mass., 1951—53; tchr. ceramics and art Kingston, NH, 1953—; real estate broker, 1965—81; two-man exhbn. Topsfield (Mass.) Libr., 1960; owner, operator Ceramic Shop, West Stewartstown, NH. With USNR, 1942—44. Recipient Profl. award, New Eng. Ceramic Show, 1975, also numerous certs. in ceramics. Mem.: York (Maine) Art Assn., Englewood (Fla.) Art Guild. Studio: 24 Wanaque Rd Cape Neddick ME 00002-7130

MORREIM, E. HAAVI, medical ethics educator; b. Austin, Minn., July 21, 1950; d. Paul Eugene and Florence Adeline Morreim. BA in Philosophy, St. Olaf Coll., 1972; MA in Philosophy, U. Va., 1976, PhD, 1980. Med. philosopher program in human biology and soc. U. Va. Sch. Medicine, Charlottesville, 1980-82, asst. prof. philosophy in medicine, 1982-84; from asst. to assoc. prof. dept. human values and ethics U. Tenn. Coll. Medicine, Memphis, 1988—93, prof. dept. human values and ethics, 1993—. Adj. prof. philosophy Va. Commonwealth U., Richmond, 1980; vis. prof. philosophy St. Olaf Coll., Northfield, Minn., 1982; Andrew Mellon vis. asst. prof. humanities and medicine Georgetown U. Sch. Medicine, Washington, 1983; sr. vis. rsch. scholar Kennedy Inst. Ethics, Georgetown U., 1983; manuscript reviewer; presenter and lectr. in field. Author: Balancing Act: The New Medical Ethics of Medicine's New Economics, 1991, Holding Health Care Accountable: Law and the New Medical Marketplace, 2001; mem. editl. adv. bd. Jour. Medicine and Philosophy; bd. editors: Jour. Law, Medicine and Ethics, IRB: Ethics and Human Research; contbr. articles to profl. jours. Active Hastings Ctr. Mem. Am. Health Lawyers Assn., Am. Soc. Law, Medicine, and Ethics, Am. Soc. for Bioethics and Humanities, Phi Beta Kappa. Avocations: running, high-performance automobile driving, photography, skiing. Office: Univ Tenn Coll Medicine 956 Court Ave Ste B328 Memphis TN 38163-2814 E-mail: hmorreim@utmem.edu.

MORRELL, KAREN KAY, music educator; d. Robert Dee and Norma Jean (Ballin) Wade; m. Dale Lee Morrell, Mar. 30, 1968; children: Daylene Kay, Bryan Lee. MusB in Music Edn., Wichita State U., 1971, MusM in Edn., 2001, M in Music Performance, 2002. Tchr. Riverside Presch., Wichita, Kans., 1973—87, Wichita Pub. Schs., 1996—; pvt. music tchr. Maize, Kans., 1979—. Home: 702 Queen Maize KS 67101

MORRELL, RUTH ANN, speech pathology/audiology services professional; b. Washington, Ind., Apr. 28, 1953; d. Robert Verlin and Vera Chapman Dougherty; m. George Walter Morrell, Apr. 24, 1982; 1 child, Kenton Edward. BS in Audiology and Speech Scis., Purdue U., 1974, MS in Audiology and Speech Scis., 1978. Speech pathologist Indpls. Pub. Schs., 1975—. Mem.: Am. Speech-Lang.-Hearing Assn., Speech and Hearing Area Educators (pres. 1994—96), Ind. Speech and Hearing Assn. (continuing edn. adminstr. 2002—03). Methodist. Avocations: travel, skiing, mission work, reading. Home: 12373 Sunrise Dr Indianapolis IN 46229-9749 Office: Indpls Pub Schs 6550 E 42d St Indianapolis IN 46226 Personal E-mail: ramorrell@hotmail.com.

MORRELL, TANYA M. psychologist; b. Balt., Dec. 5, 1966; d. Robert Francis and Ilse Martin Moran; m. John Coats Morrel, July 31, 1993; children: Alexandra Baldwin, Jessica Moran. BS in Sys. Engring., U. Va., 1988; MA in Clin. Psychology, U. Md., 1995, PhD in Clin. Psychology, 1999. Lic. psychologist Bd. Examiners of Psychologists, Md. Sys. cons. KPMG Peat Marwick, N.Y.C., 1988—90, Coopers & Lybrand, Phila., 1990—92; fellow dept. pediats. U. Md., Balt., 2000; lead rsch. assoc. Ctr. for Promotion of Child Devel. through Primary Care, Balt., 2000—. Contbr. articles to profl. jours. Mem.: APA, Md. Psychol. Assn. Democrat. Presbyterian. Avocations: reading, yoga.

MORRILL, PENNY CHITTIM, art historian; b. San Antonio, Feb. 4, 1947; d. Jack Robert and Dorothy Born (Sutherland) Chittim; m. James Agrippa Morrill, July 12, 1969; children: Jackson Forrest, Julia Chiltipin. BA with honors, Tulane U., 1969; MA, U. Pa., 1971; PhD, U. Md., 2001. Program coord. Cancer Rsch. Found. Am., Alexandria, Va., 1990-95; adj. prof. Md. Inst. Coll. Art, Balt., 2000, Corcoran Coll. Art, Washington, 2003, Georgetown U., 2004. Curator and catalogue author for traveling exhbn. Maestros de Plata: William Spratling and the Mex. Silver Renaissance, San Antonio Mus. of Art., 1998-2004. Author: Silver Masters of Mexico, 1996, Mexican Silver, 1994; contbr. articles to profl. jours. Vol. teen pregnancy prevention Nat. ARC, Washington, 1986-98; participant Coro Women in Leadership, Washington, 1988; adv. com. Betty Ford Breast Health Ctr., Washington, 1997-98; adv. com. Nat. Rehab. Hosp., Washington, 1991—; mem., v.p. Newcomb Coll./Tulane U. Alumnae Bd., 1990-94; mem., pres. Lyceum Mus., Alexandria, 1992-97; mem., editor, pres. Hist. Alexandria Found., 1980-89; curator exhbn. Carlyle House Mus., Alexandria, 1980. Recipient Achievement award Jr. League of Phila., 1985, Award for RAP and AMAZE, Nat. ARC, 1988, Spirit of Volunteerism award Jr. League of Washington, 1992, Recognition award Nat. Rehab. Hosp., 1997. Mem. Coll. Art Assn., Am. Soc. Jewelry Historians. Episcopalian. Avocations: knitting, gardening.

MORRILL-CUMMINS, CAROLYN, social worker, consultant; b. Alexandria, Va., June 29, 1957; d. William Ashley and Lois (Birrell) Morrill; m. Joseph Paul Cummins, June 4, 1983; children: Katharine Jean, Cody William. BS in Psychology cum laude, Union Coll., Schenectady, N.Y., 1979; MSW, U. Albany, 1983. Cert. social worker, N.Y. Prin. Marion River Restaurant, Blue Mountain Lake, N.Y., 1979-82; home visitor Warren-Hamilton Counties Head Start, Indian Lake, N.Y., 1983-84; social worker, case mgr. Sunmount Devel. Disabilities Svc. Office, Tupper Lake, N.Y., 1984-86; social worker Wilton Devel. Disabilities Svc. Office, Indian Lake, 1986-93; tchr. asst. Indian Lake Ctrl. Sch., 1993-94; social worker Cmty. Workshop, Inc., Glens Falls, N.Y., 1994-95; clin. social worker Hamilton County Cmty. Svcs. Office, Indian Lake, 1995—. Social work cons. Mercy Healthcare Ctr., Tupper Lake, 1985-86, Warren-Washington ARC, Glens Falls, 1993, Eddy Home Care, Troy, N.Y., 1993-97. Bd. dirs. Hamilton County Cmty. Svcs. Bd., Indian Lake, 1983-84, Warren-Hamilton Counties Head Start, 1984-85, Hudson Headwaters Health Network, Warrensburg, N.Y., 1993-99, Indian Lake Ctrl. Sch. Bd. Edn., 1999—, pres. 2002—; co-pres. Indian Lake Ctrl. Sch. PTA, 1994-99, pastor parish rels. com. Blue Mountain Lake United Meth. Ch., 1993—. Home: PO Box 993 Sabael NY 12864-0993 Office Phone: 515-648-5355.

MORRIS, ANN HASELTINE JONES, social welfare administrator; b. Springfield, Mo., Feb. 3, 1941; d. Mansur King and Adelaide (Haseltine) Jones; m. Ronald D. Morris, Nov. 29, 1963 (div. 1990); children: David, Christopher. BA in Edn. and Art, Drury Coll., 1963. Art instr. Ash Grove (Mo.)/Bois D'Arc Pub. Sch. Dist., 1963-64; instr. Drury Coll., Springfield, 1966-67; tchr. Springfield R-12 Sch. Dist., 1974-86; exec. dir. S.W. Ctr. for Ind. Living, Springfield, 1986—. Adv. com. Springfield R-12 Spl. Edn., 1993—; tech. cons. and alternative dispute resolution mediator Ams. with Disabilities Act EEOC, Dept. of Justice Network, 1993—; peer reviewer Office Spl. Edn. and Rehabilitative Svcs. Bd. dirs. Ozark Greenways, 1991-93, Springfield Deaf Relay, 1988-90; adv. task force Allied Health Program Devel. S.W. Bapt Univ., 1988; mem. Drury Coll. Women's Aux., 1984-96, conservator of the peace, handicap parking enforcement action team, 1991—; bd. treas. Mo. Parent Act, 1989-91, Diversity Network of the Ozarks, 1990—; svc. coord. Youthnet, 1990—; community adv. bd. Rehab. Svcs., St. John's Regional Health Care Ctr., 1988-91; mem. Springfield Homeless Network, 1989—, others; apptd. to Mo. Gov.'s Coun. on Disability; pres. Statewide Ind. Living Coun; mem. Gov.'s Commn. on Home and Cmty. Based Svcs., 2000—. Mem. NOW (sec. 1991), P.E.O., Mo. Assn. of Ctrs. for Ind. Living (v.p. 1990-97), Mo. Assn. for Social Welfare (bd. treas. 1989-95), Nat. Assn. of Ind. Living Ctrs. (AIDS task force 1993-96), Assn. of Programs for Rural Ind. Living, Nat. Soc. of Fund Raising Execs., Mo. Rehab. Assn., C. of C. (healthcare divsn.), Zeta Tau Alpha. Home: 1748 E Arlington Rd Springfield MO 65804-7742

MORRIS, ARLENE MYERS, marketing professional; b. Washington, Pa., Dec. 29, 1951; d. Frank Hayes Myers and Lula Irene (Slusser) Kolcun; m. John L. Sullivan, Feb. 17, 1971 (div. July 1982); m. David Wellons Morris, July 27, 1984. BA, Carlow Coll., 1974; postgrad., Western New England Coll., 1981-82. Sales rep. Syntex Labs., Inc., Palo Alto, Calif., 1974-77; profl. sales rep. McNeil Pharm., Spring House, Pa., 1977-78, mental health rep., 1978-80, asst. product dir., 1981-82, dist. mgr., 1982-85, new product dir., 1985-87, exec. dir. new bus. devel., 1987-89, v.p. bus. devel., 1989-93, Scios Inc., Mountain View, Calif., 1993-96, Coulter Pharma., 1996—. Mem. Found. of Ind. Colls., Phila., 1989. Mem. Pharm.

Advt. Coun., Am. Diabetes Assn., Am. Acad. Sci., Healthcare Bus. Womens Assn., Lic. Execs. Soc. Home: 11701 Winding Way Los Altos CA 94024-6331 Office: Coulter Pharm 600 Gateway Blvd South San Francisco CA 94080-7014

MORRIS, DOROTHY KAY, writer; b. Charleston, S.C., Dec. 25, 1935; d. Robert Oliver and Desma Lee (Rudd) M.; m. Andre Maréchal, Aug. 20, 1955 (div. July 1965); children: Désireé Katherine Maréchal, Suzette Maréchal. Pvt. coach competitive horseback riding, 1972-92; credit professional Internat. Credit Unocal Corp., Brea, Calif., 1985-99; ret., 1999. Author: Secret Sins of the Mothers, 1999; contbr. articles to horsemanship mags. Vol. English tchr., tutor Thai Cmty., L.A., 1986-91; vol. book writing Allexperts.com. Mem.: Nat. Soc. DAR, Internat. Assn .Jungian Studies. Republican. Avocations: geneaology, languages. Office Phone: 661-513-9485. E-mail: dkm2001@msn.com.

MORRIS, ELIZABETH TREAT, physical therapist; b. Harford, Conn., Feb. 20, 1936; d. Charles Wells and Marion Louise (Case) Treat; m. David Breck Morris, July 10, 1961; children: Russell Charles, Jeffrey David. BS in Phys. Therapy, U. Conn., 1960. Phys. therapist Crippled Children's Clinic No. Va., Arlington, 1960-62, Shriners Hosp. Crippled Children, Salt Lake City, 1970-74; pvt. practice phys. therapy Salt Lake City, 1975—. Mem. nominating com. YMCA, Salt Lake City. Mem. AAHPERD, Am. Phys. Therapy Assn., Am. Congress Rehab. Medicine, Nat. Spkrs. Assn., Utah Spkrs. Assn., Salt Lake Area C. of C., Friendship Force Utah, U.S. Figure Skating Assn., Toastmasters Internat., Internat. Assn. for the Study Pain, Internat. Platform Assn., World Confederation Phys. Therapy, Medart Internat. Home: 4177 Mathews Way Salt Lake City UT 84124-4021 Office: PO Box 526186 Salt Lake City UT 84152-6186 Office Phone: 801-272-3118.

MORRIS, HARRIET R. elementary school educator; b. Springfield, Mass., July 4, 1923; d. Walter Dewitt and Ida Ann (Rome) Bearg; m. Samuel Morris, Oct. 14, 1945 (dec. 1993); children: Robert, Julia, Jonathan, Daniel. BS, Am. Internat. Coll., 1944; MS, Butler U., 1973, EdS, 1985. Cert. tchr. K-12 Ind., mentally retarded, emotionally disturbed, LD/neurol. impaired, reading tchr. Ind., lic. sch. psychologist Ind. Tchr. lang. arts, grades 1-6 Children's Ho., Indpls., 1971-72; tchr. Indpls. Pub. Schs., 1972-89; sch. psychologist Avon (Ind.) Sch. Sys., 1990. Leader cub scouts Boy Scouts Am., Schenectady, NY, 1955—56; leader brownies Girl Scouts U.S., Schenectady, 1957—58; Sunday sch. tchr. Indpls. Hebrew Congregation, 1964—66; bd. dirs. Indpls. chpt. Hadassah, 1990—; guardian ad litem Ind. Advs. for Children, 1994—95; docent Indpls. Children's Mus., 1996—97; vol. Older Adult Svc. and Info. Sys., 1996—98. Mem.: Mensa.

MORRIS, JILL CAROLE, psychotherapist; b. Phila., Sept. 15, 1965; d. Stephen M. and Deborah Sue (Moskovitz) Morris; m. Abraham Glickman, Feb. 14, 1987 (div. Sept. 1993); children: Deanna Justine, Jaisyn Rebecca. BFA in Fine Arts, Fla. Atlantic U., 1989, MEd in Mental Health Counseling, 1994; MS in Edn., Nova Southeastern U., 1992, PhD in Family Therapy, 1998. Lic. mental health counselor, Fla., marriage and family therapist, Fla.; nat. bd. cert. clin. hypnotherapist; diplomate Am. Bd. Child Mental Health Svc. Providers. Arts and crafts specialist Jewish Cmty. Ctr., Boca Raton, Fla., 1989—90, Congregation B'nai Israel, Boca Raton, 1991; head dept. art Ft. Lauderdale Prep. Sch., 1989—91; dir. edn., pub. affairs Planned Parenthood, Boca Raton, 1996—97; family therapist Dania, Fla., 1994—98; tchr. art, guidance counselor Grandview Prep. Sch., Boca Raton, 1997—98; pres., family therapist Every Woman's Place, Boca Raton, 1997—99; pres., family therapist in pvt. practice, 1999—; clin. supr., regional tng. ctr. Children's Aid Soc., Boca Raton, 2002—04. Exec. dir., founder Sage Inst. for Women and Families; family cons. Ann Stork Ctr., Ft. Lauderdale, 1996; pres., dir., founder Sage Inst. Women & Families, 1999—. Contbr. articles to profl. jours. Vol. counselor Compass, West Palm Beach, Fla., 1994; vol. Palm Beach County Mental Health Assn., 1994-95; sec. South Palm Beach County NOW, Boca Raton, 1997-99, v.p., 1999—. Mem. AAUW, ACLU, ACA, NOW (v.p. South Palm Beach County chpt. 1999—), Am. Mental Health Counselors Assn., Am. Assn. Marriage and Family Therapy, Internat. Assn. Marriage and Family Counselors, Phi Kappa Phi. Democrat. Jewish. Office: PO Box 970162 Boca Raton FL 33497

MORRIS, LISSA CAMILLE, music educator; d. Thomas Melvin Melot and Audrey Camille LaCroix; m. Randall Wyatt Morris, Mar. 15, 1986; children: Thomas Zachary, Linday Alissa, Jesse Randall. BA, Excelsior Coll., 1995. Music tchr. Village Pkwy. Sch., San Antonio, 1996—97; dir. music St. Michael's Ch., San Antonio, 1997—98, St. George Ch., San Antonio, 1998—99; co-owner WOW Sci. Lab., San Antonio, 2003—. Founder Little Mozarts Music Camp. Contbr. articles to profl. jours.; composer: On the Ledge, 2002. Mem.: Music Educators Nat. Conf., Nat. Piano Guild, San Antonio Music Tchr.'s Assn. (bd. dirs. 1997—98). Republican. Episcopalian. Avocations: reading, dance. Office: St George Episcopal Sch 6900 West Ave San Antonio TX 78213 Personal E-mail: mrsmorris2002@yahoo.com.

MORRIS, LOIS LAWSON, education educator; b. Antoine, Ark., Nov. 27, 1914; d. Oscar Moran and Dona Alice (Ward) Lawson; m. William D. Morris, July 2, 1932 (dec.); 1 child, Lavonne Morris Howell (dec.). BA, Henderson U., 1948; MS, U. Ark., 1951, MA, 1966; postgrad., U. Colo., 1954, Am. U., 1958, U. N.C., 1968. History tchr. Delight H.S., Ark., 1942-47; counselor Huntsville Vocat. Sch., 1947-48; guidance dir. Russellville Pub. Sch. Sys., Ark., 1948-55; asst. prof. edn. U. Ark., Fayetteville, 1955-82, prof. emeritus, 1982—. Ednl. cons. Ark. Pub. Schs., 1965-78. Author: Biographical Essays, 2000; contbr. 2 articles to profl. jours. including Ark. Biography, 2000. Mem. Hist. Preservation Alliance Ark.; pres. Washington County Hist. Soc., 1983-85, Pope County Hist. Assn.; mem. Ark. Symphony Guild; charter mem. Nat. Mus. in Arts; bd. dirs. Potts Inn Mus. Found. Named Ark. Coll. Tchr. of Yr., 1972; recipient Plaque for Outstanding Svcs. to Washington County Hist. Soc., 1984. Mem. LWV, AAUW, NEA, Washington County Hist., Soc. (exec. bd. 1977-80), Ark. Edn. Assn., Ark. Hist. Assn., Pope County Hist. Assn. (pres. 1991-92), The Ga. Hist. Soc., U. Ark. Alumni Assn., Sierra Club, Nature Conservancy, Ark. River Valley Arts Assn., Phi Delta Kappa, Kappa Delta Pi, Phi Alpha Theta. Democrat. Episcopalian. Address: 1601 W 3d St Russellville AR 72801-4725

MORRIS, MARGARET ELIZABETH, marketing professional; b. N.Y.C., Nov. 1, 1962; d. John Daniel and Jean Bingham (MacCollom) M. BA in English, Georgetown U., 1984. Cert. Rubenfeld Synergy Method, 1997; cert. scuba diver: openwater, rescue diver, divemaster, emergency first responder instr., PADI. Mem. staff mktg. programs AT&T Nat. Fed. Mktg., Arlington, Va., 1985; mktg. tech. cons. AT&T Nat. Fed. Systems, Washington, 1985-87; tech. cons. computer mktg. Cin. Bell Tel. Co., 1987-89, mktg. tech. cons., 1989-95; sr. acct. exec.-strategic accts., 1995—. Tutor (vol.) Ptnrs. in Edn. Editor: (newsletter) District Action Project RAP, 1981-82; contbr. chpt. to book. Intern Citizen's Complaint Ctr., Washington, 1981-82; asst. coach River City Volleyball Club; coach CYO Girls Volleyball; vol. tech. amb. Corryville Cath. Sch.; vol. coord. SPCA Cin.; participant Leukemia and Lymphoma Soc. Am. Team in Tng., Suzuki Rock n Roll Marathon, San Diego, 2000, Walt Disney World Marathon, Orlando, 2001, Flying Pig Marathon, Cin., 2001, Mayor's Midnight Sun Marathon, Anchorage, 2002, Las Vegas Internat. Marathon, 2003, Marine Corps Marathon, 2003. Named Salesperson of Yr., 1997, Corp. Vol. of Yr., SPCA Cin., 2001. Mem.: Telephone Pioneers Am. (Pioneer Vol. of Yr. 2000). Office: Cin Bell Tel Co 201 E 4th St Rm 102-1136 Cincinnati OH 45202-4122

MORRIS, MARGRETTA ELIZABETH, conservationist; b. Oakland, Calif., Sept. 14, 1950; d. Joseph Francis and Mildred Ruth Madeo; m. Dennis W. Morris, July 22, 1972; children: Matthew B., Roseanna A. BA in Geography, Radford U., 1972. Paralegal Law Office of Henry F. Zwack, Stephentown, N.Y., 1980-91; exec. dir. Ea. Rensselaer County Waste Mgmt. Authority, Stephentown, 1991-97; v.p., founder ERC Cmty. Warehouse, 1996—; mgr. govt. and cmty. rels. EnergyAnswers, Albany, N.Y., 1997—. Co-founder MDM Prodns., Stephentown, 1986—. Councilperson Town of Stephentown, 1987-92; treas. Stephentown Meml. Libr., 2002-03. Mem.: Fedn. N.Y. Solid Waste Assns. (chmn. 1997—), N.Y. State Assn. for Reduction, Reuse and Recycling (treas. 1992—), N.Y. State Assn. for Solid Waste Mgmt. (rec. sec. 1992—94), Nat. Recycling Coalition (bd. dirs. 1999—, pres.), Antilles H.S. Alumni Assn. (treas. 2002), Gamma Theta Upsilon. Republican. Roman Catholic. Avocations: cross-country skiing, hiking, biking. Office: EnergyAnswers 79 N Pearl St Albany NY 12207-2294

MORRIS, MARJORIE HALE, writer, artist; b. Chattanooga, Aug. 4, 1940; d. Laurie Everett and Marjorie (Hunt) H.; 2 children. Student El Camino Jr. Coll., 1958-60. Stewardess Am. Airlines, 1960-62, staff nat. advt. and publicity, 1961-62; mgr. Viking Ski Shop, Pacific Palisades, Calif., 1963-64; Pepsi Cola Corp. rep. to Republican Nat. Conv., 1964; co-owner, mgr. Ready Room Restaurant, L.A., 1967; architects adv., restaurant devel. and design, Honolulu, Dallas, Atlanta, L.A., 1967-73; mgr., buyer Great Things, Honolulu, 1972-74; mgr. Braille Inst. Thrift Shop, L.A., 1975-78, dir. 1978—, devel. officer, 1980-86; acct. exec. Alexanders Moving & Storage, Atlas Van Lines, 1981-86, interstate truckdriver, 1986-87; U.S. promotional cons. Kids Only Market, Granville Island, Vancouver, B.C., Can., 1985; owner Marjorie Morris, appraisers; freelance writer and photographer, 1974—; designer floats Pacific Palisades Parade, 1965, TransPace Race Com., Honolulu, 1972. Team mother Pacific Palisades Little League, 1974-76. Mem. Beverly Hills C. of C. (Outstanding Svc. to Cmty. award 1976-77). Originator, dir. Christmas Tree Project, Beverly Hills; cover editor Calif. Yacht Club Mag., 1976; founder, editor Waterlines, newsletter of Flotilla 12-7, USCG Aux., 1979. Mem. Am. Soc. Appraisers (panel speaker nat. conv. 1983), North Coast Vintage Aviation Soc. Address: PO Box 2651 Mckinleyville CA 95519-2651

MORRIS, MARTHA JOSEPHINE, information services administrator; b. LaPorte, Ind., Jan. 16, 1951; d. John J. and Pearl L. Gorski; m. Richard Dale Morris, Sept. 5, 1970; children: Valerie A., Marlene N. ASN, Purdue U., Westville, Ind., 1977; BSN, Nazareth (Mich.) Coll., 1989. Charge nurse alcoholism/med. surg. unit Borgess Med. Ctr., Kalamazoo, 1977-81, asst. clin. mgr. substance abuse, 1981-88, asst. clin. nurse mgr. nephrology, 1988-90, contingency and patient intensity coord., 1990-93, mgr. patient info. tech., 1993-98, clin. analyst, project leader info. svcs., 1998—2002, info. tech. dir. clin. sys. and web devel., 2002—. Test devel. com. for informatics nursing Am. Nurses Credentialing Ctr., Washington, 1994—. Mem. ANA, Mich. Nurses Assn. Roman Catholic. Avocations: painting, flower gardening. Office: Borgess Med Ctr 1521 Gull Rd Kalamazoo MI 49048-1666 E-mail: marthamorris@borgess.com.

MORRIS, MARTHA MARNEL, music educator; b. Trenton, NJ, Aug. 25, 1948; M Music, American Conservatory, 1977; B Music Edn., St Mary of the Woods Coll., 1972. Co-founder/dir. Flutes Unlimited, Chgo., 1997—; music exec. Saint Xavier U., Chgo., 1984—96; conductor St. Xavier U. Orch., Chgo., 1983—; assoc. prof. music St. Xavier U., 1977—. Recipient various grants, St. Xavier U.

MORRIS, MARY ANN, bookkeeper; b. Great Falls, Mont., Feb. 16, 1946; d. Francis Leonard and Dorothy Irene (Howe) De Lacey; m. Donald Edward Wermuth, June 29, 1968 (div. Jan. 1974); 1 child, Deborah Ann; m. Larry Dallas Morris, Apr. 23, 1977; stepchildren: Serena Jo, Bradley Dwayne, Brian Dale, Bruce Dean. Student, North Idaho Coll., 1985. Sales clk. Dundas Office Supply, Great Falls, 1964-68, Stationer's Office Supply, Tacoma, 1969-70; bookkeeper Miller's Office Supply, Puyallup, Wash., 1971-72, Judge Moving & Storage (Allied), Great Falls, 1973-74; bookkeeper, credit mgr. Meadow Gold Dairy, Great Falls, 1974; pro-rate clk. Builders Transport, Great Falls, 1975-77; bookkeeper C&S Glass, Coeur d'Alene, Idaho, 1978-81, Morris Trucking, Coeur d'Alene, 1977-82, LDM Transport, Hayden Lake, Idaho, 1982—2000, profl. truck driver (class A vehicle), 1988—, sec. and treas., 2000—; operator cons. svc. to small trucking bus. Mem. Women's Retail Credit Mgrs. Assn. Republican. Home and Office: PO Box 2350 Hayden ID 83835-2350

MORRIS, MARY ELIZABETH, pastor; b. Schenectady, N.Y. d. William and Kathryn Dilkes (Wilkins) Simpson; m. David John Stevens, Sept. 10, 1966 (dec. Dec. 1975); children: Jeffrey David, Wendy Elizabeth; m. Gerald Douglas Morris, Apr. 15, 1977; stepchildren: Laura Louise, Douglas Owen. BS with cert. in phys. therapy, Simmons Coll., 1966; MDiv, Boston U. Theology, 1988. Ordained min. 1993. Pvt. phys. therapist Muscular Dystrophy Assn., Dedham, Mass., 1971—93; vicar Holy Trinity Luth. Ch., North Easton, Mass., 1988—89; interim pastoral asst. Zion Luth. Ch., Plymouth, Mass., 1989—91; interim chaplain Symmes Hosp., Arlington, Mass., 1990—91; phys. therapist South shore Vis. Nurse Assn, Braintree, Mass., 1991—93; pastor Bethany Luth. Ch., Orange, Mass., 1993—98, St. Mark Evangelical Luth. Ch., Woonsocket, RI, 1999—. Dean R.I. Conf. of New Eng. Synod of Evangelical Luth. Ch. in Am., 2002—; ecumenical rep. R.I. State Coun. Chs., 2001—. Mem. Evangelical Luth. Ch. In Am. Office: St Mark Evangel Luth Ch 871 Harris Ave Woonsocket RI 02895 Office Phone: 401-769-8320.

MORRIS, MAUREEN SAUTER, bank officer; d. Harold J. and Mary Sauter; m. Jon P. Morris; 1 child, Jeffrey. BEd, U. Miami, 1969; MA, U. W. Fla., 2001. Tchr. Fairfax County Schs., Va., Okaloosa County Schs., Shalimar, Fla.; loan processor Eglin Fed. Credit Union, Ft. Walton Beach, Fla. Bd. dirs. Cmty. Band. Capt. USAF, 1969—74, maj. USAF Res., 1975—82. Mem.: Am. Soc. Mil. Comptrollers, Coun. Exceptional Children, Phi Lambda Theta. Avocations: reading, counted cross stitch, working out, bunko.

MORRIS, NANCY LOIS, elementary education educator; b. Oceanside, N.Y., Jan. 15, 1950; d. Maurice Morris and Sylvia Goodfriend. AAS, Sullivan County C.C., Lock Sheldrake, N.Y., 1970; BS in Elem. Edn., SUNY, Geneseo, 1971; MS in Spl. Edn., Hofstra U., 1975; postgrad., U. Ariz., 1979, Scranton (Pa.) U., 1978, 79, Bowie (Md.) State U., 1983, Nova U., Ft. Lauderdale, Fla., 1987. Lic. in elem. edn., spl. edn., N.Y., Md., D.C., Fla. Tchr. 2d and 3d grades Hempstead (N.Y.) Sch. Dist. 1, 1972-73; tchr., counselor Rhinebeck (N.Y.) Country Sch., 1976-77; tchr. 2d and 4th grades and ESL Bur. Indian Affairs, Phoenix, 1977-79; tchr. emotionally handicapped D.C. Children's Ctr., Laurel, Md., 1979-87, Sch. Bd. of Broward County, Ft. Lauderdale, 1987-88, Sch. Bd. of Palm Beach County, West Palm Beach, Fla., 1988-92; with HRS Divsn. Elder Abuse, Lake Worth, Fla., 1992-93, Am. Cancer Soc., West Palm Beach, 1993-94; substitute tchr. Sch. Bd. Palm Beach County, 1994, tchr. emotionally handicapped, 1994-96; with Ctr. for Info. and Crisis Svcs., Inc., Lantana, Fla., 1997-98; tchr. 6th grade Edison-Russell Sch., Palm Beach Gardens, 1998-2000; investigator The Fla. Dept. of Children and Family, West Palm Beach, Fla., 2001—. Mem. Phi Delta Kappa. Home: 10445 Boynton Place Cir Boynton Beach FL 33437-2627

MORRIS, NAOMI CAROLYN MINNER, clinical pediatrician, medical researcher, educator, health facility administrator; b. Chgo., June 8, 1931; d. Morris George and Carrie Ruth (Auslender) Minner; m. Charles Elliot Morris, June 28, 1951; children: Jonathan Edward, David Carlton. BA magna cum laude, U. Colo., 1952, MD, 1955; MPH magna cum laude, Harvard U., 1959. Diplomate Am. Bd. Preventive Medicine. Rotating intern LA County Gen. Hosp., 1955-56; clin. fellow in pediat. Mass. Gen. Hosp., Boston, 1957; pub health physician Mass. Dept. Health, Boston, 1957-58; clin. pediatrician Norfolk King's Daus. Hosp., Va., 1959-61; from rsch. assoc. to prof. dept. maternal/child health Sch. Pub. Health, U. NC, Chapel Hill, NC, 1962-70, 71-74, chair dept., 1975-77; prof., dir. cmty. pediat. U. Health Sci., Chgo. Med. Sch., Ill., 1977-80; prof. Sch. Pub. Health, U. Ill., Chgo., 1980—, dir. cmty. health sci. divsn., 1980-95. Advisor to chief pub.health officer, Guam, 1970-71; mem. liaison com. with Lake County Med. Soc. 1978-80; nursing divsn. adv. com. Lake County Health Dept., 1978-98; resource person Ill. 1980 White Ho. Conf. on Children, 1979-80; participant Enrich-A-Life series Chgo. Dept. Health, 1984-85, Ill. Health and Hazardous Substance Registry Pregnancy Outcome Task Force, 1984-86; mem. profl. adv. bd. Beethoven Project Ctr. Child Devel., 1986-96; mem. planning com. for action to reduce infant mortality Chgo. Inst. Medicine, 1986-89; founding mem. Westside Futures Infant Mortality Network, 1986; mem. Ill. vital stats. supplement Ill. Dept. Pub. Health, 1987; investigator and team leader Rev. Mo. Families Maternal and Child Health State Svcs., 1989; mem. children and youth 2000 task force MacArthur Found., 1992—; active Ill. Caucus on Teenage Pregnancies, 1978—, Chgo. Dept. Health Child Health Task Force, 1982-83, HSC Interprofessional Edn. Com., 1983-84, Med. Task Force Project Life, 1983-88, Women's Studies Curriculum Com., 1985-90, Com. Rsch. on Women, 1985-90, Mayor's Adv. Com. on Infant Mortality, 1986-2002, Coun. for Integrated Svc. Sys., 2001-02, Cmty. Access Program, 2002—, Gov. Adv. Coun. on Infant Mortality, 1988-96, Ctr. for Rsch. on Women Fellowship Com., 1993-98; cons. pediat. nursing resources group Ill. Dept. Pub. Health, 1983-84; cons. Cook County Hosp. Study of Preventive Childhood Obesity, 1983-84, Chgo. Dept. Pub. Health Coun. for an Integrated Svc. Sys., 2001-02. founder and dir. MCH training program, 1983-03 Contbr. chapters to books, articles to profl. jours. Mem. Ill. MCH Coalition, 1994—, Voices for Ill. Children, 1993—, Children and Youth 2000, 1992—. Recipient Jonas Salk Lifetime Achievement award, March of Dimes, 2003. Fellow APHA (task force on adolescence maternal and child health sect. 1977-85, sec. 1979-80, cons. manpower project 1982-83, publ. bd. 1985-87, coun. pediat. rsch. to Am. Acad. Pediats. 1985-92, APHA, Martha May Eliot award outstanding contbns. to field of maternal and child health 1999-, Am. Coll. Preventive Medicine, Am. Acad. Pediats. (Ill. chpt. com. on sch. health, 1992-94, and com. adolescent health 1993—)); mem. Ambulatory Pediat. Assn., Assn. Tchrs. Maternal and Child Health (exec. com. 1981-87, com. on tng. and continuing edn. needs of MCH/CCS dirs. 1982-83, liaison com. to fed. DCMH office 1983-87, pres. 1983-85), Chgo. Pediat. Soc. (Disting. Svc. award 2002), Phi Beta Kappa, Alpha Omega Alpha, Delta Omega, Sigma Xi. Avocations: photography, swimming, reading, classical music, travel. Office: U Ill Chgo Sch Pub Health 1603 W Taylor St Chicago IL 60612-4246

MORRIS, PHYLLIS, legislative staff member; b. Prague, Okla., June 27, 1951; d. Winford J. and Rosalie Magdalen Willoughby; m. Philip Joe Isaacs, June 19, 1976 (div. Oct. 1993); 1 child, Eric Joe; m. Danny Jay Morris, June 14, 1995. Student, S.W. Okla. Coll., 1971. Office mgr. Okla. Health Scis. Ctr., Oklahoma City, 1988-90; legis. asst. Okla. Ho. of Reps., Oklahoma City, 1991—. Fundraiser for numerous politicians Okla. Ho. of Reps., Okla. State Senate, 1991—. Democrat. Roman Catholic. Home: 8311 Blue Jay Rd Norman OK 73026-3762 Office: Okla Ho of Reps 328 State Capitol Oklahoma City OK 73026

MORRIS, SAMANTHA A. marketing professional, researcher; BA, Baylor U. Contracts mgr. Diamond Key Homes, Phoenix, Ariz., 1998—99; strategic mktg. mgr. Centex Homes-Phoenix Divsn., Scottsdale, Ariz., 1999—. Mem.: Am. Mktg. Assn. Office: Centex Homes-Phoenix Divsn 8665 East Hartford Dr # 200 Scottsdale AZ 85255

MORRIS, SANDRA JOAN, lawyer; b. Chgo., Oct. 13, 1944; d. Bernard and Helene (Davies) Aronson; m. Richard William Morris, May 30, 1965 (div. Jan. 1974); children: Tracy Michelle, Bretton Todd; m. William Mark Bandt, July 12, 1981; 1 child, Victoria Elizabeth. BA, U. Ariz., 1965; JD, Calif. Western U., 1969. Bar: Calif. 1970, U.S. Dist. Ct. (so. dist.) Calif. 1970; diplomate Am. Coll. Family Trial Lawyers. Ptnr. Morris & Morris, APC, San Diego, 1970-74; sole practice San Diego, 1974—. Mem. Adv. Commn. on Family Law, Calif. Senate, 1978-79. Contbr. articles to profl. jours. Pres. San Diego Cmty. Child Abuse Coordinating Coun., 1977; mem. human rsch. rev. bd. Children's Hosp., San Diego, 1977-92. Fellow: Internat. Acad. Matrimonial Lawyers, Am. Acad. Matrimonial Lawyers (chpt. pres. 1987—88, nat. bd. govs. 1987—89, parliamentarian 1989—91, nat. bd. govs. 1993—94, treas. 1994—97, v.p. 1997—2000, 1st v.p. 2000—01, pres. 2002—03); mem.: San Diego Cert. Family Law Specialists (chair 1995—96), State Bar Calif. (cert. family law specialist 1980—), ABA (family law sect. exec. com. marital property 1982—83, 1987—94, faculty mem. Trial Advocacy Inst. 2001—), Lawyers Club San Diego (bd. dirs. 1973). Republican. Jewish. Avocations: art, travel, skiing. Office: 3200 4th Ave Ste 101 San Diego CA 92103-5716 Office Phone: 619-296-6060.

MORRIS, SANDRA K. computer company executive; b. Paxtang, Pa., 1934, BS with honors and distinction, U. Del., 1976, MS, 1981; postgrad., U. Pa. Faculty mem. U. Del.; with RCA Corp. David Sarnoff Rsch. Ctr.; product mgr. Intel Corp., 1985, v.p. e-bus. group, 1999—. Co-author: Multimedia Application Development Using Indeo video and DVI Technology, 1982. Office: Intel Corp PO Box 58119 2200 Mission College Blvd Santa Clara CA 95052-8119

MORRIS, SCARLETT KAY, elementary school educator, music educator; b. Ozark, Ark., Dec. 7, 1963; d. Donald Wayne and Karen JoAnne Winfrey; m. David Wayne Morris, Sept. 1, 1984; children: Lacy, Jeromy. BA in Music, U. Ozarks, 1986; MA in Music, Stephen F. Austin State U., 1991. Chorale dir. LaTournea U., Longview, Tex., 1989—92, Jacksonville High and Mid. Sch., 1993—96, Trinity Sch. Tex., Longview, 1996—97, Kelly Mid. Sch., Springdale, 1997—2003. Dir. Crandell Handbell Ringers, 1996—2003; mem. Presbyn. Women, Springdale, 1996—2003. Mem.: Jacksonville Educators Assn. (pres. 1995—96), Music Educators Nat. Conf., Am. Guild Eng. Handbell Ringers, Am. Chorale Dirs. Assn. Presbyterian. Avocations: gardening, hiking, reading. Home: 1124 Quail Run Springdale AR 72764 Office: Kelly Mid Sch 1879 E Ribonson Springdale AR 72764

MORRIS, SHARON HUTSON, city manager; BA in Home Econs., Calif. State U., 1976; MA in Urban Planning, UCLA, 1979. Legislative analyst So. Calif. Gas Co., L.A., 1983-86, dist. mgr., 1986-90, cmty. outreach coord., 1990; dir. intergovt. affairs South Coast Air Quality Mgmt. Dist., Diamond Bar, Calif., 1990-94; commr. Bd. Pub. Works City of L.A., 1994-96, dep. mayor Office of Mayor Richard J. Riordan, 1996-97, gen. mgr. Dept. Animal Regulation, 1997-98, exec. dir. Dept. on Disability, 1998—; alt. pub. mem. South Coast Air Quality Hearing Bd., 1998—. Mem. KCET cmty. adv. bd. Hollywood Cmty. Housing Corp. Recipient Outstanding Alumna award Calif. State U., L.A., 1997. Mem. Am. Assn. Blacks in Energy, Nat. Forum for Black Pub. Adminstrn., The Ethnic Coalition (bd. dirs.), Women of Color, Inc. (past co-presiding officer), Calif. League Conservative Voters (bd. dirs.), Alpha Kappa Alpha, Phi Kappa Phi. Office: City Los Angeles Dept Disability 700 E Temple St Rm 380 Los Angeles CA 90012-4046

MORRIS, SHARON LOUISE STEWART, emergency medical technician, paramedic; b. Washington, Feb. 9, 1956; d. George Arthur Jr. and Shirley Ann (Dickinson) S. (dec.); m. Brian Stanley Morris, Feb. 9, 1979 (div.); children: Jessica Kristin, Krystle Maria. BS, Atlantic Christian Coll., Wilson, N.C., 1978; student, Wilson County Tech. Coll., 1998; paramedic stud., Nash Community Coll. Cert. tchr. elem. edn. and math., N.C., EMT paramedic, ACLS, Pediatric Advanced Life Support, pediat. edn. prehosp. profls., AHA CPR/BLS instr.; cert. pre-hosp. trauma life support (PHTLS); automatic external defibrilator (AED) instr.; basic trauma life support (BTLS); farm medic. Cashier Safeway Fin., Wilson, 1980-81, Provident Fin., Wilson, 1981-85; mktg. svc. mgr. Beneficial of N.C. Inc., Wilson, 1985-91, Ind. carrier Wilson Daily Times, 1991-94; child care provider Crestview Day Sch., Wilson, [illegible]; EMT [illegible] Elm City, N.C., [illegible]—, EMT paramedic Wilson County Emergency Med. Svcs., 1998—. Agt. Cen. Nat. Life Ins., Wilson, 1988-91, Olde Republic, 1990; EMT Elm City Emergency Svcs., 1996, attendant, driver Am. Med. Response, 1997; paramedic Sch. Nash Tech. C.C. Notary pub. State of N.C., 1986—; bd. dirs. Elm City, 1997, 99; paramedic for Johnston Ambulance Svc., 2002-, first responder instr. EMT, 2003. Democrat. Methodist. Avocations: crocheting, cross-stitch, needlepoint, plants, baking. Home: PO Box 9053 Wilson NC 27895

MORRIS, THERESA LINTHICUM, retired medical social worker; b. Wickliffe, Ky., Nov. 27, 1906; d. Charles Presley and Ruby Regal (Ives) Linthicum; m. Harrell H. Morris, Aug. 24, 1932. MSW, Washington U., 1947. Lic. social worker, Okla. Intake worker Okla. Emergency Relief, Oklahoma City, 1934-37; field supr. Works Progress Adminstrn., Oklahoma City, 1937-41; dir. med. social work Okla. Commn. Crippled Children, Oklahoma City, 1937-56, social work cons., 1956-57; med. social worker Okla. Dept. Pub. Welfare, Oklahoma City, 1957-58, Okla. Dept. Health, Oklahoma City, 1958-71; med. social worker otorhinolaryngology dept. U. Okla. Med. Ctr., Oklahoma City, 1971-90; ret., 1990. Past mem. bd. dirs. Salvation Army Sr. Citizens Ctr., Oklahoma City. Recipient spl. recognition U. Okla. Med. Ctr., 1989. Mem. Acad. Cert. Social Workers. Methodist. Home: 14901 N Pennsylvania Ave Oklahoma City OK 73134-6069

MORRIS, VALERIE, news correspondent; b. Phila. BA in journalism, San Jose State U.; M in broadcast journalism, Columbia U. Grad. Sch. Journalism. Morning drive anchor KCBS Radio, LA; anchor KCBS-TV, LA; researcher, gen. assignment reporter, anchor KRON-TV and KGO-TV, San Francisco; gen. assignment reporter, weekend anchor WPIX-TV, NY; joinged CNN, 1996; co-anchors CNNfn's The Flipside; anchor CNNfn's Smart Assets, 1996—. Recipient Three Calif. Emmy awards for breaking news events and special reports, Black Woman Yr. award, Outstanding Contbn. to Broadcasting award, Am. Women in Radio and TV, Award Courage, Nat. Orgn. Women. Mem.: Delta Sigma Theta. Office: CNN 5 Penn Plz Fl 20 New York NY 10001-1810 Office Phone: 212-714-7800.*

MORRIS-BLACKER, MARILYN EILEEN, librarian; b. Denver, Jan. 14, 1943; d. Lester Alfred and Edith May-Burnett Morris; m. Dennis Harold Blacker, Apr. 1, 1962; children: Denise Eileen Blacker Schupp, Wendy Sue Blacker Davis. Student, Kans. Wesleyan U., 1960-62; BA, U. Colo., 1983; MLS, Emporia State U., 1992. Cert. tchr., Colo. Tchr.'s aide Jefferson County Schs., Lakewood, Colo., 1979-84; tchr. St. John's Acad., Denver, 1984, Child Garden, Conifer, Colo., 1984-86; libr. asst. Auraria Libr., Denver, 1986-94; librarian Red Rocks C.C., Lakewood, 1994-98; dir. Idaho Springs Pub. Libr., Idaho Springs, 1998—2001. Sch. dist. adv. bd. Jefferson County Schs., 1971; monitor Westernaires, Lakewood, 1972-88; Sunday sch. tchr. Christ Congl., Denver, 1967, Rockland Cmty. Ch., Golden, Colo., 1996-99. Spl. Libr. Assn. scholar, Denver, 1990; recipient Colo. Scholar's award 1982. Mem. ALA, Colo. Libr. Assn. (various coms. 1989—). Avocations: reading, swimming, genealogy, hiking, water sports.

MORRISEY, MARENA GRANT, art museum administrator; b. Newport News, Va., May 28, 1945; BFA in Interior Design, Va. Commonwealth U., 1967, MA in Art History, 1970. With Orlando (Fla.) Mus. Art, 1970—, exec. dir., 1976—. Former v.p., chmn. mus. svcs. com., mem. ad hoc com. on collections sharing and long range planning com., past chmn. exhbns. and edn. com. Am. Fedn. Arts; former mem. nat. adv. coun. George Washington U. Clearinghouse on Mus. Edn.; former mem. accreditation com. Nat. Found. for Interior Design Edn. Rsch. Former mem. strategic planning adv. coun. Orange County Sch. Dist.; former mem. advt. rev. bd. BBB; former mem. Orlando Pub. Art Adv. Bd., Orlando Leadership Coun., Orlando Hist. Bldg. Commn.; mem. art selection com. Orlando Internat. Airport, former chmn.; former mem. bd. dirs. Sta. WMFE-TV; bd. dirs. New World Sch. of Arts; vol. Sister Cities of Orlando; mem. internat. arts and culture com. Metro Orlando Internat. Affairs Commn. Named Orlando's Outstanding Woman of Yr. in Field of Art; recipient Fla. State of Arts award. Mem. Am. Assn. Mus. (former mem. governing bd., accreditation commn., profl. stds. and practices com., internat. coun. of mus.), Assn. Art Mus. Dirs. (comm. and publs. com.), Southeastern Mus. Conf. (past pres.), Fla. Art Mus. Dirs. Assn. (past pres.), Fla. Assn. Mus. (former bd. dirs.), Greater Orlando C. of C. (past mem. steering com. Leadership Orlando), Jr. League Orlando-Winter Park, Rotary Club Orlando (program com. Orlando, membership com., chmn. found. com., Paul Harris fellow). Office: Orlando Museum of Art 2416 N Mills Ave Orlando FL 32803-1483 E-mail: mgmorrisey@omart.org.

MORRISON, ANN HESS, information technology specialist; b. Grants Pass, Oreg., Mar. 29, 1944; d. Wilbur Lill and Esther Elaine Groner; m. Robert Thornton Morrison, Apr. 14, 1996; children: David William Hess, William Albert Hess. BSEE, BS in Math., Oreg. State U., 1968; MBA in Info. Tech., Maryville U., St. Louis, 2001. Engr. Lawrence Livermore Lab., Livermore, Calif., 1968-69; owner RBR Scales, Inc., Anaheim, Calif., 1969-84; lead engr. Rockwell Internat., Seal Beach, Calif., 1984-86, '87-88; software engr. GM Hughes, Fullerton, Calif., 1986-87; sr. engr. Logican Eagle Tech., Inc., Eatontown, N.J., 1988-91; owner Holistic Eclectic Software Svc., Orange, Calif., 1991—92; sys. specialist Jacobs-Sverdrup Engring., 1993—2001; owner Homeland Def. 4U Inc., St. Louis, 2002—. Active Calif. Master Chorale, Santa Ana, 1990-92. Mem. Phi Kappa Phi, Eta Kappa Nu, Tau Beta Pi, Sigma Beta Delta. Lutheran. Avocations: singing, art, gardening. Office Phone: 314-727-0202. E-mail: ann@homeland-defense4u.com.

MORRISON, BARBARA SHEFFIELD, Japanese translator and interpreter, consultant, educator; b. Morristown, N.J., Dec. 22, 1958; d. Barclay Morrison and Pauline Morison O'Gorman; m. Michael Missiras, Nov. 2, 1991. BA, Wesleyan U., 1980; postgrad., Middlebury Coll., 1983; MA in Japanese Lit., Columbia U., 1998; postgrad., U. N.D., 2001—. Mem. Bklyn. Waterfront Coalition, N.Y. Group Shows, 1985-91; real estate salesperson Huberth & Peters, Inc., N.Y.C., 1986-88, Joseph Hilton & Assoc., N.Y.C., 1989; real estate systems rsch. cons. N.Y.C., 1989-92; pres. Redgate, Minn., 1990—. Tchr. The Bus. English Ctr., Tokyo, 1980-83; bilingual adminstrv. asst. The Chiba Bank, Ltd., N.Y.C., 1985-86; adj. instr. langs. dept. Minn. State U., 1999; instr. English Composition U. N.D., 2001--. One woman show, Soho, N.Y., 1992, The Pyramid Gallery, Rochester, N.Y., 1993, Spirit Rm. Gallery, Fargo, N.D., 1999; translator: Coltrane: A Player's Guide to His Harmony, 1994, American House Styles: A Concise Guide, 1997, Abstracts for the Proposed Shinto Dictionary, 1999. Mem. Fargo Moorhead Heritage Soc. (sec. 2001--). Avocations: painting, gardening. Home and Office: 703 5th St S Moorhead MN 56560-3403 E-mail: morrison@mnstate.edu.

MORRISON, BETH ANN, music educator, musician; d. Elizabeth and Chester Allen; m. John R. Morrison, June 28, 1998; 1 child, Kelsey. BA, Rowan U., 1982. Cert. tchr. Fla., 1995. Music educator King's Christian Sch., Haddon Heights, NJ, 1983—90, Charlotte County Pub. Schs., Port Charlotte, Fla., 1995—. Musician Venice (Fla.) Symphony, 1990—. Trio Unique, Nokomis, Fla., 1990—, Sarasota (Fla.) Concert Band, 1990—2000. Dir.: (children's choir) Swingsations (Walt Disney Magic Music Days Dir. Participant award, 2000);, author (dir., choreographer) various children's plays. Dir. The World's Largest Concert, Punta Gorda, Fla., 1997—99, TheWorld's Largest Concert, Rotonda West, Fla., 2001—03; vocal coach Lemon Bay Summer Theatre, Englewood, Fla., 2003. Office: Vineland Elem Sch 467 Boundary Blvd Rotonda West FL 33947-2002

MORRISON, DEBORAH JEAN, lawyer; b. Johnstown, Pa., Feb. 18, 1955; d. Ralph Wesley and Norma Jean (Kinsey) Morrison; m. Ricardo Daniel [illegible], [illegible] (div. Nov. 1991); children: Elena Raquel, Julia Rebecca. BA in Polit. Sci., Chatham Coll., 1977; postgrad., U. Miami, Fla., 1977-78; JD, U. Pitts., 1981. Bar: Pa. 1981, Ill. 1985. Legal asst. Klein Y Mairal, Buenos Aires, 1978-79; legal intern Neighborhood Legal Svcs., Aliquippa, Pa., 1980-81; law clk. Pa. Superior Ct., Pitts., 1981-84; atty. John Deere Credit Co., Moline, Ill., 1985-89; sr. atty. Deere & Co., Moline, Ill., 1989-96, sr. counsel, 1996—2003, asst. gen. counsel, 2003—. Mem. ABA, Pa. Bar Assn., Phi Beta Kappa, Order of the Coif. Democrat. Mem. United Church of Christ. Office: Deere & Co 1 John Deere Pl Moline IL 61265-8098

MORRISON, FRANCINE DARLENE, psychiatrist, massage therapist, herbal simplist; b. Newburgh, N.Y., Dec. 9, 1950; d. Frank Burke and Gladys (Morrison) Singleton. BA, Mt. St. Mary's Coll., Newburgh, 1980; MD, N.Y. Med. Coll., Valhalla, 1986; massage therapist, Blue Cliff Sch. Massage, Kenner, La., 1996. Resident, intern Lincoln Hosp., Bronx, N.Y., 1986-90; fellow in psychiatry Met. Hosp., N.Y.C., 1990-91; attending psychiatrist Med. Ctr. La., New Orleans, 1991-95; dir. neurobehavioral unit The Greenery, Slidell, La., 1992-94, cons. psychiatrist, 1994-95; attending psychiatrist East La. State Hosp., Jackson, 1995—. Reiki Master tchr. Contbr. articles to profl. jours. Mem. Am. Oriental Bodywork Therapists Assn. (nat. and La. chpts.), Am. Coll. Forensic Examiners, Bi-Parish Med. Soc.

MORRISON, GAIL, internist, nephrologist, educator; BA in Biology, Chemistry magna cum laude, Boston U., 1967; MD, U. Pa., 1971. Diplomate Am. Bd. Med. Examiners, Am. Bd. Internal Medicine, Am. Bd. Nephrology. Instr. dept. continuing edn. Boston U., 1966-67; clin. fellow Harvard U., Boston, 1971-72; intern Beth Israel Hosp., Boston, 1971-72; jr. asst. resident Georgetown U. Hosp., Washington, 1972-73; staff physician clin. ctr. NIH, Bethesda, Md., 1973-74, staff assoc. Nat. Heart & Lung Inst., 1973-74; fellow in nephrology renal electrolyte sect. U. Pa. Hosp., Phila., 1974-76, rsch. fellow in nephrology renal electrolyte sect. NIH, 1975-76, asst. prof. medicine, 1982-83; from asst. prof. to assoc. prof. medicine U. Pa. Sch. Medicine, Phila., 1976-94, prof. medicine, 1994—; attending Phila. Vets. Adminstrn. Med. Ctr., 1976-77, U. Pa. Health Sys., 1996—. Asst. dir. dialysis unit U. Pa. Hosp., Phila., 1976-77, assoc. dir., 1977-82, dir. renal outpatient prog., 1976-82, dir. outpatient dialysis unit, 1979-84, acting dir. dialysis prog. for inpatient and outpatient dialysis units, 1981-82, dir., 1982-86; acad. coord. dept. medicine U. Pa. Hosp., Phila., 1985-96; assoc. chmn. dept. medicine for student edn. U. Pa. Sch. Medicine, Phila., 1986-96, acting assoc. dean for clin. curriculum, 1991, assoc. dean for clin. curriculum, 1991-95, vice dean for edn., dir. acad. progs., 1995—, mem. numerous acad., search, planning, steering, alumni, budget, nutrition coms., others; cons., advisor in field; presenter, co-dir., tchr., leader workshops, symposiums, confs. Author: (with A. Goroll) Core Medicine Clerkship: A Curriculum Guide, Manual for Curriculum 2000, 1996; editor: (with others) Introduction to Clinical Medicine, 2d rev. edit., 1995, Concepts in Basic Science, 1995, Essentials of Nutrition: A Case-Based Approach, 1995; mem. editorial bd. Am. Jour. Medicine, 1996-99; author papers, reviews, abstracts, chpts. to books; contbr. articles to profl. jours. Grantee Pa. Sch. Nursing, 1989-90, Heinz Endowment Fund, 1990-95, U. Pa. Sch. Medicine, 1993-95, 93-96, 97-98. Fellow ACP, Coll. Physicians of Pa. (mem. sect. on pub. health and preventive medicine 1995—); mem. AAAS, Internat. Soc. Nephrology, Am. Soc. Nephrology, Am. Fedn. for Clin. Rsch., Am. Assn. Med. Colls. Women's Liaison Officer, Pa. Soc. Nephrology (coun. mem. network #24 federally funded end-stage renal disease orgn. 1978-83, mem. facility planning bd. 1979-80, chmn. 1980-82, mem. exec. com. 1980-82, ad-hoc mem. med. review bd. 1980-82, mem. nomination and credential com. 1982-83), Southeastern Nat. Kidney Found. (bd. dirs. 1984-88), Phi Beta Kappa, Sigma Xi, Alpha Omega Alpha. Home: 1040 Stony Ln Gladwyne PA 19035-1136 Fax: 215-573-4289.

MORRISON, JACQUELINE ANN, social worker, psychologist; b. Chattanooga, June 1, 1943; d. Curtis Matthew and Jacqueline Ann (Hurley) Hinsley; m. Randal Charles Morrison, Sept. 16, 1967; 1 child, Laura Jo. BS, Ohio State U., 1965, MSW, 1968, PhD, 1995. Cert. clin. social worker, lic., Ohio; lic. psychologist. Recreation dir., case worker United Meth. Children's Home, Worthington, Ohio, 1968-70; casefinding coord. The Nisonger Ctr./Ohio State, Columbus, 1972-74, social work faculty, 1978-79; project coord. cancer rehab. project Ohio State U. Cancer Ctr., 1974-77; social worker Cen. Ohio Dialysis Ctr., Columbus, 1978; asst. prof. Coll. of Social Work Ohio State U., 1979-81, grad. rsch. assoc., 1987-88; clinician, cons. Netcare, Inc., Columbus, 1986-87; social worker, pvt. practice Cancer and Chronic Illness Counseling, Columbus, 1980—. Adj. faculty Ohio State U., 1976-77, 84-85; cons. Harding Hosp., Columbus, 1994—, psychologist, 1998—; cons. Kids n' Kamp, Columbus, 1988—, Hospice of Columbus, 1983-85, Multiple Sclerosis Arthritis Prog., Columbus, 1982-85, Family Counseling/Crittenden Svcs., Columbus, 1982, Cystic Fibrosis Cen. Ohio, 1983. Author: To Find the Invisible Child; author/editor: Franklin County Community Cancer Resource Guide, 1975; designer/editor: (pamphlet) Make Today Count, 1979; developer breast cancer therapy support group prog., Woman to Woman, 1982-86. Chmn. unit mem. LWV, Columbus, 1972, 73; adv. com. Franklin County Unit Am. Cancer Soc., 1976-84; steering com. Make Today Count (cancer patient group), Columbus, 1977-83, others. Nominated for Jefferson award J.C. Penney, 1982; recipient Outstanding Human Svc. award Ohio State U., 1987. Diplomate Am. Bd. Examiners in Social Work; mem. NASW, Cen. Ohio Psychol. Assn. (membership chairperson), Ohio Psychological Assn., Golden Key. Democrat. Methodist. Avocations: tennis, swimming, cooking, reading, travel, writing poetry. Home and Office: 1260 Clubview Blvd S Columbus OH 43235-1632

MORRISON, K. JAYDENE, education counseling firm executive; b. Cherokee, Okla., Aug. 22, 1933; d. Jay Frank and Kathryn D. (Johnson) Walker; m. Michael H. Morrison, July 11, 1955 (dec. 1991); children: Jay, Mac. BS, Okla. State U., 1955, MS, 1957; postgrad., U. Colo., 1965, Ctrl. State U., Okla., 1967—70, postgrad., 1984, U. Denver, 1981—82. Lic. coun. Okla., marriage and family therapist, cert. sch. psychologist, counselor. Psychologist Cushing Pub. Schs., Okla., 1955—57, Indpls. Pub. Schs., 1958—59; counselor, tchr. spl. edn. Helena-Goltry Pub. Schs., Okla., 1965—73; psychometrist Okla. State Title III Program, Alva; sch. psychologist Okla. State Dept. Edn., Enid, 1977—85; pres., dir. Ventures in Learning, Inc., Helena, 1984—. Career counselor, Oklahoma City, 1985—86; rural specialist Okla. Conf. Chs. AG LINK, 1986—88; v.p., sec./treas. Okla. Made, Inc., Oklahoma City, 1988—89; sch. psychologist Okla. City Pub. Schs., 1988—93; therapist and pub. sch. liason Chisholm Trail Counseling Svc., 1993—95; coord. Statewide Farm Stress Program, 1994—95; therapist Greenleaf Drug/Alcohol Rehab., 1988—89; sec., treas. Okla. Pure; part-time counselor Clayton Clinic, 1987—89; cons. Okla. Family Inst., 1990—93; with Dept. Edn. Behavior Mgmt. Ctrl. Dist., Hawaii, 1995—. Author: Coping with ADD/ADHD, 1995; co-author: Coping With a Learning Disability, 1992. Chmn. Alfalfa County Excise and Equalization Bd., Cherokee, 1979—83; asst. state coord. Okla. Am. Agr. Movement, Oklahoma City, 1982—83; co-chmn. Alfalfa County Dem. Party, Cherokee, 1976—83; sec.-treas. 6th Dist. Okla. Dem. State Exec. Bd., 1983—87; counselor United Meth. Counseling Ctr., 1987—88; mem. Elder Christian Ch. Named Citizen of Yr., Okla. chpt. Nat. Assn. Social Workers, 1988; recipient Tchr. of Yr. award, Helena Masonic Lodge, 1967, Spl. award, Okla. Women for Agr., 1979. Mem.: Okla. Assn. Learning Disabilities, Garfield County Interagy. Task Force, Okla. Sch. Psychologists Assn., Nat. Assn. Sch. Psychologists, Okla. Soc. Advancement Biofeedback, Biofeedback Soc. Am., Chi Omega Alumni, Delta Kappa Gamma. Office: PO Box 917 Nederland CO 80466-0917 Office Phone: 303-258-3976. Business E-Mail: JaydeneMor@aol.com.

MORRISON, MARGARET [illegible], [illegible], educator, consultant; b. Atlanta, Oct. 06; d. Watson Russell Sr and Eva D. Morrison. BS in Edn., U. Ga., 1970. Cert. tchr., Ga. Supr. KPMG, Atlanta, 1971-97; art tchr. Decatur (Ga.) City Schs., Decatur, Ga., 1997-99; pvt. instr. in art and edn., 2000—. Pvt. practice cons. interior design, 1998—; consumer bd. AC Nielsen. Exhbns. include Coastal Ctr. for the Arts, St. Simons Island, Ga., Gallery One, St. Simons Island, Decatur Arts Alliance, Acad. Midi, Paris, The Glynn County Art Assn., Jekyll Island, Ga., L'Orangerie Mus., Paris. Royal patron Hutt River Province, Queensland, Australia, 1995; active High Mus. Art, Atlanta, 1989—; bd. govs. Internat. Biog. Ctr.; adv. bd. Am. Biog. Inst.; mem. consumer panel AC Nielsen. Fellow Acad. Midi (hon.); mem. DAR, NAFE, AAUW, Internat. Platform Assn., Nat. Mus. Women in Arts, Allied Artists of Ga., Pen and Ink, U. Ga. Alumni Soc., AC Nielsen Comsumer Bd. mem., Internat. Biographical Ctr., Bd. of Adv.

MORRISON, NANCY JANE, art educator; b. Hannibal, Mo., Oct. 29, 1953; d. Wiley Russell Morrison and Marguerite Grace Taylor; m. Stephen Mark Graboski. BFA, U. Kans., Lawrence, 1976; MFA, Md. Inst. Coll. Art, Balt., 1990. Art instr. Dundalk (Md.) C.C., 1990—91, Anne Arundel County Continuing Edn., Anne Arundel, Md., 1991; vis. artist St. Paul Sch. for Girls, Balt., 1991; art instr. Essex (Md.) C.C., 1991—94, Longview C.C., Lee's Summit, Mo., 1995—, Notre Dame de Sion, Kansas City, Mo., 1995—. Mem. Lee's Summit Arts Coun., 2002, 03; grad. student rep., Gallery Com. Md. Inst. Coll. Art, 1989—90; fine arts chair Student Union Activities Bd., Lawrence, 1974—75; grad. studies asst. to Dir. Mt. Royal Sch. Painting Maryland Inst. Coll. Art, 1989—90. Sitting In, 1973, exhibitions include Kans. Art Commn., Fox Gallery, MICA, Dundalk Gallery, New Eng. Fine Art Inst., Mulvane Art Mus., Spivia Art Ctr., Nelson-Atkins Mus. Art, Chatauqua Gallery Art, Bauhouse Gallery, Mus.. Contemporary Arts, Balt. Mem.: Mo. Art Edn. Assn., Nat. Art Edn. Assn., Lee's Summit Garden Club (treas. 2002—). Avocations: drawing, painting, gardening, genealogy.

MORRISON, PATRICE B. lawyer; b. St. Louis, July 8, 1948; d. Frank J. and Loretta (S.) Burgert; m. William Brian Morrison, Aug. 12, 1969; 1 child, W. Brett. AB, U. Miami, 1971, MA, 1972; JD, Am. U., 1975; LLM in Taxation, Georgetown U., 1978. Bar: Fla. 1975, D.C. 1977, N.Y. 1983. Atty. U.S. Dept. Treas., Washington, 1975-79; atty., ptnr. Nixon Hargrave Devans & Doyle, LLP, Palm Beach County, Fla., 1980-89, Nixon Peabody LLP (formerly Nixon, Hargrave, Devans & Doyle), Rochester, N.Y., 1989—. Bd. dirs. Rochester Friendly Sr. Svcs., Inc., 1996—. Bd. dirs. Alzheimer's Assn., Rochester, 1990-95, Nat. Women's Hall of Fame, 1990-92; mem. Rochester Women's Network; mem. exec. com. Estate Planning Coun. Rochester, 1992-95; dir. Cloverwood Sr. Living, Inc., 2000—. Mem. Am. Immigration Lawyers Assn. Republican. Office: Nixon Peabody LLP PO Box 31051 Rochester NY 14603-1051

MORRISON, PATRICIA B. retail executive; CIO GE Indsl. Sys. Gen. Electric; CIO Quaker Oats Co., Office Depot, Inc., Delray Beach, Fla., 2002—. Office: Office Depot Inc 2200 Old Germantown Rd Delray Beach FL 33445

MORRISON, PORTIA OWEN, lawyer; b. Charlotte, N.C., Apr. 1, 1944; d. Robert Hall Jr. and Josephine Currier (Hutchison) M.; m. Alan Peter Richmond, June 19, 1976; 1 child, Anne Morrison. BA in English, Agnes Scott Coll., 1966; MA, U. Wis., 1967; JD, U. Chgo., 1978. Bar: Ill. 1978. Ptnr. Piper Rudnick LLP, Chgo., 1978—. Lectr. in field. Pres. Girl Scouts of Chgo. Mem.: ABA, CREW Chgo., Chgo. Fin. Exch., Pension Real Estate Assn., Chgo. Bar Assn. (real property com., subcom. real property fin., alliance for women), Am. Coll. Real Estate Lawyers (pres.-elect, bd. govs.). Office: Piper Rudnick LLP 203 N La Salle St Ste 1800 Chicago IL 60601-1210 E-mail: portia.morrison@piperrudnick.com.

MORRISON, SARAH LYDDON, author; b. Rochester, N.Y., May 19, 1939; d. Paul William and Winifred (Cowles) Lyddon. BA, U. Vt., 1961. Sec. asst. Glamour mag., N.Y.C., 1961-63, Vogue mag., N.Y.C., 1963-65; asst. editor Venture mag., N.Y.C., 1966-71; dir. pub. rels. for tourism Commonwealth of P.R., N.Y.C., 1971-75; asst. Am. Legion, Washington, 1988-98; owner Sarah Lyddon Morrison Pub. Rels., Washington, 1999—. Author: The Modern Witch's Spellbook, 1971, Book II, 1983, The Modern Witch's Dream Book, 1985, The Modern Witch's Book of Home Remedies, 1988, The Modern Witch's Book of Healing, 1991, The Modern Witch's Book of Symbols, 1997, Modern Witch's Guide to Magic and Spells, 1998. Mem. Washington Club, DAR (dir. pub. rels. Emily Nelson chpt. 1999, 2000), Colonial Dames XVII. Avocations: travel, reading, swimming, rock music, cooking. E-mail: sarahlyd@aol.com.

MORRISON, SHELLEY, actress; b. N.Y.C., Oct. 26, 1936; d. Maurice Nissim and Hortense Mitrani; m. Walter R. Dominguez, Aug. 11, 1973. Student, L.A. City Coll., 1954—56. Presenter Alma awards, 2001—02, Imagan Awards, 2001, Nosotros Golden Eagle awards, 2002. Actress: (films) Interns, 1962, The Greatest Story Ever Told, 1964, Castle of Evil, 1965, Divorce, American Style, 1965, How to Save a Marriage, 1966, Funny Girl, 1967, Three Guns for Texas, 1969, Man and Boy, 1971, Blume in Love, 1972, McKenna's Gold, 1967, Breezy, 1973, People Toys, 1973, Rabbit Test, 1975, Max Dugan Returns, 1982, Troop Beverly Hills, 1988, Fools Rush In, 1996, others, (TV movies) The Girl Who Came Giftwrapped, Three's a Crowd, 1969, Once an Eagle, 1974, The Night That Panicked America, 1975, Kids Don't Tell, 1984, Cries From the Heart, 1994, Columbo: It's All In the Game, Lassie: A New Beginning, others, (TV series) Laredo, 1965-67, The Flying Nun, 1966-70, First and Ten, 1987, I'm Home, 1990, The Fanelli Boys, 1990, Love, Lies and Murder, 1990, Playhouse 90, Dr. Kildare, The Fugitive, Gunsmoke, Marcus Welby, General Hospital, and many others, 1960-70, Man of the People, Sisters, 1991, 92, Murder She Wrote, 1992, Johnny Bago, 1993, Columbo, 1993, L.A. Law, 1994, Live Shot, 1995, Courthouse, Home Improvement, 1997, Nothing Sacred, 1997, Prey, 1997, Nearly Yours, 1998; recurring role in Will & Grace, 1998—, series regular 1999—; TV guest appearances include Prey, Nothing Sacred, L.A. Law, Busting Loose, Marcus Welby, M.D., Occasional Wife, Between the Lines, Home Improvement, Murder, She Wrote, The Bold Ones, Divorce Court, Soap, The Streets of San Francisco, Dr. Kildare, Man of the People, The Partridge Family, My Favorite Martian, The Outer Limits, The Robert Taylor Show, numerous others; (voice over animated cartoon comml.) Handy Nanny, 2003, (A&E) Letters, 2003, numerous others, (stage prodns.) Pal Joey, 1956, Bus Stop, 1956, Only in America, 1960, Orpheus Descending, 1960, Spring's Awakening, 1962, over 65 other prodns., 1956-1970, also appeared in The Mikado, Pal Joey, Anastasia, Orpheus Descending, A Streetcar Named Desire, Sweet Bird of Youth, The Crucible, Zoo Story, Rashomon, Desk Set, Pygmalian, The Would-Be Gentleman, Comedy of Errors, Tiger at the Gates, The Rose Tattoo, Orpheus Descending, Come Back Little Sheba, The Odd Couple, Only in America, El Camino Real, Hamlet, Country Girl, Romeo and Juliet, Cotton Candy, Point of View, Coney Island of the Mind, Last of the Aztecs, numerous others; prodr., writer live shots, 1975—; prodr. (with husband Walter Dominguez) documentary Mexican culture, 2003. Condr. seminars (with husband Walter Dominquez) about Native Americans to keep traditions and ceremonies flourishing. Honored (with husband Walter Dominguez) for work with homeless City of L.A., 1985, for work during L.A. riots, 1992; nominated for Alma awards SAG, 2000, 2001, 2002; recipient SAG award for Will and Grace. Mem. SAG, AFTRA, Actors Equity Assn. Democrat.

MORRISON, TONI (CHLOE ANTHONY MORRISON), novelist; b. Lorain, Ohio, Feb. 18, 1931; d. George and Ella Ramah (Willis) Wofford; m. Harold Morrison, 1958 (div. 1964); children: Harold Ford, Slade Kevin. BA in English, Howard U., 1953; MA, Cornell U., 1955. Tchr. English and humanities Tex. So. U., 1955-57, Howard U., 1957-64; editor Random House, N.Y.C., 1965—; assoc. prof. English SUNY, Purchase, NY, 1971-72, Schweitzer Prof. of the Humanities Albany, NY, 1984-89; Robert F. Goheen Prof. of the Humanities Princeton Univ., Princeton, NJ, 1989—; chair, creative writing pgm. Princeton U. Visiting prof., Yale Univ., 1976-77, Bard Coll., 1986-88. Author: The Bluest Eye, 1969, Sula, 1973 (National Book award nomination 1975, Ohioana Book award 1975), Song of Solomon, 1977 (National Book Critics Circle award 1977, American Acad. and Inst. of Arts and Letters award 1977), Tar Baby, 1981, (play) Dreaming Emmett, 1986, Beloved, 1988 (Pulitzer Prize for fiction 1988, Robert F. Kennedy Book award 1988, Melcher Book award Unitarian Universalist Assn. 1988, National Book award nomination 1987, National Book Critics Circle award nomination 1987), Jazz, 1992, Playing in the Dark: Whiteness and the Literary Imagination, 1992, Nobel Prize Speech, 1994, Birth of a Nation'hood: Gaze, Script & Spectacle in the O.J. Simpson Trial, 1997, Paradise, 1998, The Big Box, 2002, The Book of Mean People, 2002, Love, 2003; editor: The Black Book, 1974, Race-ing Justice, En-Gendering Power: Essays on Anita Hill, Clarence Thomas, and the Construction of Social Reality, 1992; lyricist: Honey and Rue, 1992. Recipient New York State Governor's Art award, 1986; Washington College Literary award, 1987; Elizabeth Cady Stanton award National Organization for Women; Nobel prize in Literature Nobel Foundation, 1993. Mem. Author's Guild (council) Office: Princeton U Writing Program 305 Nassau St Princeton NJ 08544-2003*

MORRIS-ROGERS, CHERYL-ANN, daycare provider, director, educator; b. Chgo., Feb. 26, 1958; d. Richard Lee and Ruth Hortence (Davis) M. AA, Cen. YMCA Coll., 1979; BA, DePaul U., 1982. Cert. in child devel. Supr. C.E.T.A. Program, Chgo., 1979; asst. dir. WLS AM/FM Radio Pub. Affairs, Chgo., 1981-82; educator Auburn Pk. Day Care, Kindergarten, Chgo., 1982-83, pres., dir., 1983—; educator, pres., dir. Lakefront Children's Acad., Chgo., 1999—. Cons. in field. Mem. NAACP, Chgo., 1988—, United Negro Coll. Fund, Chgo., 1988—; com. mem. Election Judge Loretta Hall Morgan, Chgo., 1989; vol. Election Mayor Harold Washington, Chgo., 1987. Recipient Child Devel. award Love Drops Mag., 1987; named to Dean's List, 1980. Mem. Nat. Assn. Women-Bus. Owners, League Black Women, Preschool Owners Assn., Nat. Assn. for Edn. Young Children, Chgo. Assn. for Edn. Young Children. Avocations: reading, writing, swimming, camping, travel. Office: Auburn Pk Day Care 741 W 79th St Chicago IL 60620-2423 also: Lakefront Childrens Acad 400 E Randolph St Chicago IL 60601-7329

MORRIS SCHWEITZER, NANCY N. retired science educator, writer; b. La Place, La., Dec. 2, 1937; d. Gustave Joseph and Georgie Marie (Talbot) Naquin; m. James P. Schweitzer (dec.), June 8, 1975; children: Merlin James, Ricky John, m. John C. Morris, May 27, 2000. BS, Dominican Coll., 1963; MEd, La. State U., 1978. Sci. tchr. Orleans Parish, New Orleans, 1963-70, Jefferson Parish Pub. Sch. Sys., Harvey, La., 1970-75, E. Baton Rouge Parish, 1975-92; sci. tchr. Sch. Nursing So. U., Baton Rouge, 1991, 92; ret., 1992. Coord. marine sci. E. Baton Rouge Sch. Sys., 1981-82, phys. sci., 1991-92; chair sci. dept. Baton Rouge Magnet H.S., 1986-88, Scotlandville Magnet H.S., Baton Rouge, 1989-92. Contbr. articles to profl. jours. Mem. N.W. Fla. Symphony Chorus, 1998. Named La. State Outstanding Biology Tchr. Nat. Assn. Biology Tchrs., 1974, Disting. Sci. Tchr. La. Acad. Sci., 1987. Mem. AAUW (pres. Niceville/Valparaiso br. 1997-2000), Delta Kappa Gamma. Roman Catholic. Avocations: coaching soccer, painting. Home: 4457 Turnberry Pl Niceville FL 32578-3824

MORRISSEY, DOLORES JOSEPHINE, investment executive; b. N.Y.C., July 22; d. Joseph Lawrence and Madeleine Catherine (Curran) Morrissey. BS, NYU, 1963, MBA, 1968. Sr. v.p., treas. Bowery Savs. Bank, N.Y.C., 1958-87; exec. v.p. Mut. of Am., N.Y.C., 1987-94; pres., CEO Mut. of Am. Capital Mgmt., N.Y.C., 1994-96; CEO, chair Mut. of Am. Securities Corp., N.Y.C., 1996—. Pres., CEO, chair Mut. of Am. Investment Corp., 1989—; pres., CEO Mut. of Am. Instnl. Fund, 1996—; adv. commn. N.Y. State Comptroller Investment Adv. Com., N.Y.C., 1979-87. Past pres. Soroptimist Internat. N.Y., N.Y.C.; dir. Yorkville Common Pantry, Yorkville Christian-Jewish Coun., N.Y.C., 1978—. Mem. Money Marketeers of NYU, NYU Bus. Forum, Women's Bond Club, Women's Econ. Round Table, Dames of Malta, Order of Holy Sepulchre (Lady Comdr. with star), Alpha Kappa Delta Roman Catholic. Avocations: opera, photography, travel. Home: 180 East End Ave New York NY 10128-7763 Office: Mutual of America 320 Park Ave Fl 9 New York NY 10022-6839

MORRISSEY, JANE F. religious organization administrator; b. Holyoke, Mass., June 30, 1941; d. Richard Charles and Anna Joyce Morrissey. BA, Coll. of Our Lady of the Elms, Chicopee, Mass., 1962; MA, U. Mass., 1972, PhD, 1976. Prof. Coll. of Our Lady of the Elms, Chicopee, Mass., 1976—90; dir. Office of Justice and Peace, Holyoke, Mass., 1990—93; pastoral min. Blessed Sacrament Parish, Springfield, Mass., 1993—99; pres. Sisters St. Joseph of Springfield, Holyoke, Mass., 1999—. Bd. pres. The Gray Ho., Inc., Springfield, Mass., 1984—89, Springfield, 1994—99; co-chairperson U.S. Fedn., Srs. of St. Joseph, 2002—; chairperson PAX Christi Mass., 1994—97. Co-author: Gracias, Matiox, Thanks, Hermano Pedro; contbr. articles to profl. jours. Founder Police Chaplains-on-Call, Springfield, Mass., 1996; founding mem. Gray Ho., Inc., Springfield, Mass., 1982—; bd. mem. Mental Health Consortium, Springfield, Mass., 1980—83. Named Pioneer Valley Notre Dame Club Exemplar for svc. to Ch., 1997; recipient Pynchon award, Advt. Club of Western Mass., 2000, Disting. Grad. award, U. Mass., 2001. Mem.: Pax Christi (corr. 1994 Mass. Pax Christi Peacemaker 1994). Roman Catholic. Avocations: knitting, writing, reading, folding paper cranes, gardening. Office: Sisters of St Joseph of Springfield 34 Lower Westfield Rd - Ste 1 Holyoke MA 01040 Business E-Mail: jmorrissey@ssjspringfield.com.

MORRISSEY, MARY, state representative; b. Vennington, Vt., Mar. 26, 1957; State rep. Vt. Ho. Reps., 1996—. Bd. dirs. Southwestern Vt. Med. Ctr. Mem. Bennington Rep. Com., 1991—, Bennington County Rep. Com., 1992—; recording sec. Bennington Bd. Civil Authority; bd. dirs. Old Castle Theatre, 1986-89, exec. bd. 1989, guild 1985—); bd. dirs. Bennington County Choral Soc., 1985-88. Mem. Bennington Bus. and Profl. Women (pres. 1991-93), Bennington Crimestoppers (bd. dirs. 1992—, vice-chmn. 1996), Rotary, Cath. Daus. Am. Office: 228 Dewey St Bennington VT 05201-2222

MORRISSEY, MARY F. (FRAN), human resource consulting company executive; Cert. profl. employer specialist. Acctg., tax profl., small bus. cons., 10 yrs.; formre owner, mgr. profl. employer orgn.; co-founder, pres., CEO, Staff Mgmt., Inc., Rockford, Ill., 1983—. Part-owner John Morrissey, Accts., Rockford; presenter to state and fed. legislators, regulatory agys. and profl. orgns.; sec., mem. bd. Merc. Bank; bd. dirs. Inst. for Accreditation Profl. Employer Orgns. Bd. dirs. Swedish Am. Health Sys., Rockford; active numerous civic orgsn. Named One of Top 25 Women Bus. Owners, Crain's Chgo. Bus., 1993, 95, Connie Tremulis award for bus. owners YWCA, Rockford, 1998. Mem. Soc. for Human Resource Mgmt. (accredited sr. profl. in human resources), Nat. Assn. Profl. Employer Orgns. (past bd. dirs. and past pres.), former mem. profl. stds. com., also former chmn., past mem. comm. network, mgmt. performance, membership, govt. affairs, and edn. coms.), Midwest Assn. Profl. Employer Orgns. (past pres.), Nat. Assn. Women Bus. Owners (One of Top 25 Women Bus. Owners 1993, 95), Rockford Area C. of C. (coun. of 100, Woman Bus. Owner of Yr. 1998)), Rockford Women's Club, also others. Office: Staff Mgmt Inc 5919 Spring Creek Rd Rockford IL 61114-6447 Fax: 815-282-0515.

MORRISSEY, PATRICIA A. commissioner; PhD Spl. Edn., Pa. State U. Sr. assoc. Booz Allen Hamilton, McLean, Va.; commr. adminstrn. and devel. disabilities U.S. Health and Human Svcs. (HHS), 2001—. With Senate, Ho. of Reps., Pres. Ronald Regan; with Senate Ticket to Work and Work Incentives Improvement Act Wis. Gov. Thomson's Office; with Pres. George W. Bush's New Freedom Initiative. Republican. Office: 200 Independence Ave SW Washington DC 20201 Business E-Mail: pmorrissey@acf.dhhs.gov.

MORRIS-TYNDALL, LUCY, construction executive; married; 2 children. From sec. to cost engr. Swinerton & Walberg, San Francisco, 1977—92, asst. project mgr., 1992—94, with mgmt. and consulting br., 1994—97, v.p., ops. mgr., 1997—99; chief info. officer Swinerton Inc. (formerly Swinerton & Walberg), San Francisco, 1999—. Recipient Julia Morgan award, YWCA of Oakland, 1996, Medal of Excellence, Women at Work, 2002. Mem.: AGC of Calif. (info. tech. task force), Constrn. Info. Execs. Office: Swinerton Inc 260 Townsend St San Francisco CA 94107

MORROW, CONSTANCE PRESCOTT, music educator; b. Ann Arbor, Mich., May 3, 1951; d. Donald Paul and Ruth Clara Wesenberg; m. Wayne Shireman Morrow, Aug. 14, 1981; 1 child, Taylor Prescott. BA in Music Edn., Ea. Mich. U., 1973; M in Curriculum and Instrn., Memphis State U., 1987. Cert. tchr. Mo. Music tchr. k-5 Memphis City Sch. Sys., 1983—99, Columbia (Mo.) Pub. Schs., 1999—. Musician Opera Memphis, 1983—87, Memphis Symphony Chorus, 1984—86, Sarah Beth Causey Chorale, Memphis, 1986—88, Sarah Beth Causey Madrigal Ensemble, Memphis; muscian-paid sect. leader Lindenwood Christian Ch., Memphis, 1985—88. Dir.: (children's theater) Jammin' with Mama Goose, Under the Big Top, Gather Round and I'll Tell You a Story, (children's choir) Ring Around the World. Muscian Ch. of the Redeemer, Memphis, 1983—88; musician Kingsway Ch. of the Disciples, Memphis, 1984—87. Links for Learning grantee, Assistance League Mid-Mo., 2002. Mem.: Columbia Schs. Tchr. Assn., Mo. State Tchrs. Assn., Music Tchrs. Nat. Assn., Music Educators Nat. Conf., Orgn. Am. Kodaly Educators, Am. Orff Schulwerk Assn., Parent/Tchr. Assn. Am., Boy Scouts Am. (pack leader 1993—94). Luth. Ch.-Mo. Synod. Avocations: reading, musical performances of children's choirs, swimming, workshop facilitator for music education, the orff approach, travel. Home: 609 Hulen Dr Columbia MO 65203 Office: Shepard Boulevard Elementary School 2616 Shepard Blvd Columbia MO 65201 Business E-Mail: comorrow@columbia.k12.mo.us.

MORROW, DEBRA DEOLA, accountant; b. Louisville, Dec. 9, 1962; d. Ernest D. and Beatrice M. (Wallace) Watkins; m. Thomas E. Morrow, June 12, 1982; children: Michael T., Robert E. BS in Accountancy, No. Ky. U., 1996. Bookkeeper New Haven Moving Equipment, Louisville, 1984-96; acct., office mgr. Mackey McNeill Mohr, PSC, Ft. Mitchell, Ky., 1996-97; acct. C.A. Scribner Prodns., Cin., 1997—98; mem. Kenton County Airport Bd., 1998—2000; asst. contr. Kockner Desma, Hebron, Ky., 2000—. Bd. dirs., pres. YMCA. Recipient Bus. Merit award Nat. Collegiate Bd., 1995,, All Am. scholar Nat. Scholarship Found., 1995; scholar Becker Rev. Course, 1996. Mem. Inst. Mgmt. Accts., Cin. Profl. Women, Nu Kappa Alpha (bd. mem.). Republican. Avocations: swimming, coaching children's sports. Home: 21 Crystal Lake Dr Fort Mitchell KY 41017-9736 Office: Klockner Desma 2195 Arbor Tech Dr Hebron KY 41058

MORROW, ELIZABETH HOSTETTER, sculptress, museum administrator, farmer, educator; b. Sibley, Mo., Feb. 28, 1947; d. Elman A. and Lorine H. Morrow; married, 1970 (div. 1979); children: Jan Pawel, Lorentz Arthur. Student, William Jewell Coll., 1958-59, Colo. Coll., 1959-60, U. Okla., 1960-62; BFA, U. Kans., 1964, MFA, 1967; postgrad., U. Minn., 1965, U. Kans., 1968. Pres. E. Morrow Co., Kansas City, Mo., 1966-67; head dept. art U. Hawaii, Honolulu, 1968-69, Tarkio (Mo.) Coll., 1970-74; exec. dir. Pensacola (Fla.) Mus. Art, 1974-76; pres., owner Blair-Murrah Exhbns., Sibley, Mo., 1980—. Pres. bd. trustees, CEO Blair-Murrah, Inc., 1991—; sec.-treas. Coun. for Cultural Resources, 1995—. Del. White House Conf. on Small Bus., 1986. Lew Wentz scholar U. Okla., 1960-62. Mem. Internat. Coun. of Mus., Internat. Coun. Exhbn. Exch., Internat. Soc. Appraisers, Am. Assn. Mus., Canadian Assn. Mus., Internat. Trade Club of Greater Kansas City, Nat. Assn. Mus. Exhibitions, Ft. Osage Hist. Soc., Hist. Six MileCemetery Bd., Friends Art, Internat. Com. Fine Arts, Internat. Com. Conservation, Internat. Sculpture Ctr., DAR (regent Ft. Osage chpt.), Delta Phi Delta. Republican. Avocations: historical and cultural activities, antique cars, midwest farm auctions, genealogy. Home: RR # 1 Sibley MO 64088 Office: Blair-Murrah Vintage Hill Orch Sibley MO 64088 also: 7 rue Muzy PO Box Nr 554 1211 Geneva Switzerland Office Phone: 816-249-9400. E-mail: elizabethmorrow@blair-murrah.org., exhibits@blair-murrah.org.

MORROW, JENNIFER LEIGH See LEIGH, JENNIFER JASON

MORROW, LESLEY MANDEL, literacy and elementary education educator; BS, Syracuse U.; MA, N.J. City U.; PhD, Fordham U. Cert. early childhood tchr., elem. tchr., reading specialist K-12, supr., prin. Tchr. Bradford Elem. Sch., Montclair, NJ, 1964—68; demonstration tchr. Lab. Elem. Sch. William Paterson U., NJ, 1968—70; instr. edn. dept. Chapman Coll., Orange, Calif., 1970—71; instr. learning and tchg. dept. St. John's U., NY, 1971—74; instr. comm. scis. dept. and early childhood dept. Kean U., NJ, 1974—79; asst. prof. edn. dept. Douglas Coll. Rutgers U., New Brunswick, NJ, 1979—85, assoc. prof. Grad. Sch. Edn., 1986—91, chair dept. learning and tchg., 1991—93, 2000—02, prof. literacy and early childhood/elem. edn. Grad. Sch. Edn., 1991—. Coadjutant faculty N.J. City U., 1974—76, Fordham U., 1974—76, William Paterson U., 1974—76; cons. in field; author Scott Foresman Basal Reading Series, 1991—97; mem. adv. bd. Sesame Street PBS Children's TV Workshop, 1993—98; sr. author William H. Sadlier Reading Programs, 1998—; mem. adv. bd. Reading Rainbow PBS Program, 2002—. Recipient Disting. Achievement for Excellence in Ednl. Journalism award, Ednl. Press Assn. Am., 1989, Literacy award, N.J. Reading Assn., 1996, Spl. Svc. award, 2000, grants and scholarships in field. Fellow: Nat. Conf. on Rsch. in English; mem.: Nat. Assessment Ednl. Progress (adv. bd. 1992, 1994), Internat. Reading Assn. (pres. 2003—, Outstanding Tchr. Educator of Reading award 1995). Office: Rutgers The State U NJ Grad Sch Edn Rm 206A 10 Seminary Pl New Brunswick NJ 08901-1183

MORROW, MARTHA F. elementary school educator; d. Richard McGruder and Justine Vaughen Fry; m. John L. Morrow, Mar. 30, 1985; children: John IV, Christopher. BA in Elem. Edn., BA in Specific Learning Disabilities, Stetson U., 1984. Educators tng. cert. Fla. Tchr., spl. edn. coord. Osceola County Schs., Orange Park, Fla., 1985—89; tchr. grades pre-K to 5 Grace Episcopal Day Sch., Orange Park, 1995—. Coord. enrichment studies Grace Day Sch., Orange Park, 2003—. Corr. sec., vol. coord. Jr. League Jacksonville, Orange Park, 1989—2002, bd. dirs. Fla., 2000—02; bd. dirs., pres. Grace Parent Faculty League, Orange Park, 1995—97; bd. mem. Quigley House, Orange Park, 1990—93. Mem.: Coun. Exceptional Children.

MORROW, NENA RENEE, medical/surgical nurse; d. Evelyn Louise and Benjamin Morrow, Edward Richardson; 1 child, Jayla Nicole Talley. ADN, Washtenaw C.C., Ann Arbor, Mich., 2003. RN Mich., 2004. ATM fraud investigator Gt. Lakes Nat. Bank, Ann Arbor, 1990—98; outpatient clk. III U. Mich., Ann Arbor, 1999—2001. Children's ministry rep. Christian Love Fellowship Ministries Internat., Ypsilanti, Mich., 1992—2003. Grantee Mich. Ednl. Opportunity, Dept. Edn. State Mich., 1999—2004, Sex Equity Grant-Tuition, 2000—04; scholar Minnie Pearl Mitchell Meml., Washtenaw C.C. Found., 1999—2002. Democrat. Avocation: reading. Personal E-mail: nmorrow1@yahoo.com.

MORROW, SANDRA KAY, librarian; b. Levelland, Tex., Jan. 6, 1944; d. Oran Eiland and Martha Jane Johnson; m. Troy Leon Morrow; children: Paul, Kile. AA, Lubbock Christian U., 1964; BS in Edn., Abilene Christian U., 1966. Cert. libr. sci. U. Tex., 1973. Tchr. Andrews Sch. Dist., Andrews, Tex., 1966—68, New Deal Sch. Dist., New Deal, Tex., 1970—71, Ector County Sch., Odessa, Tex., 1971—72; libr. Austin Sch. Dist., Austin, Tex., 1974—77; tchr. Brentwood Christian Sch., Austin, 1984—. Originator Christian Librarians' Conf., Searcy, Ark., 1996—2003; presenter in field; dir. Yearly Booklist for primary, intermediate and Jr. H.S., 1992—. Creator Children's Crown award, 1992, Lamplighter award, 1996, Children's Crown Gallery award, 2000; ministry leader Westover Hills Ch. of Christ, Austin, 1977—2002, nursery dir., 1975—85. Recipient Disting. Alumni Award, Lubbock Christian U., 2002. Mem.: Nat. Christian Sch. Assn. (awards dir. 1996—, Christian Educator of Yr. award 2001), Tex. Christian Schools Assn. (Tchr. of Yr. award 2001), Tex. Libr. Assn. Republican. Mem.Church Of Christ. Avocations: reading, gardening, jogging, music. Home: 8308 Grayledge Drive Austin TX 78753 Office: National Christian School Association 11908 North Lamar Boulevard Austin TX 78753 Business E-Mail: smorrow@brentwoodchristian.org.

MORROW, SUSAN DAGMAR, psychic, medium educator, writer, consultant; b. Harrisburg, Pa., July 10, 1932; d. William Lime and Margaret Louise (Deckard) Brubaker; m. Henry Taylor Morrow, June 9, 1952 (div. Mar. 1984); children: Quenby Anne, Christopher Brian. Student, Carnegie Inst. Tech., 1950-52, U. Ariz., 1952-54, U. Calif., Berkeley Ext., 1960-72, Foothill Coll., 1980-81. Self-employed psychic, psychic tchr., Palo Alto, Calif., 1976-80, Mountain View, Calif., 1980—; medium, psychic, tchr Seekers Quest Profl. Ctr., San Jose, Calif., 1983—. Tchr. Sunnyvale Community Ctr., 1977-87; tchr. San Andreas Health Coun., Palo Alto, 1981-83; lectr. U. Calif., Berkeley, 1978, Foothill Coll., Los Altos, Calif., 1980; lectr. in field; medium, cons. in cases of mental disorientation to psychologists, Palo Alto and Mountain View, 1978—, to detectives and police in cases of missing persons, animals or property, 1983—, pvt. tutor, medium, cons. past lives, archeological information, 1990—. Contbr. articles on psychic awareness to various publs. Mem. Assn. Psychic Practitioners (co-founder, v.p. 1982-83, editor and writer newsletter 1982-83), Mountain View C. of C., Mind Being Found., Assn. Rsch. and Enlightenment, Inst. Noetic Sci., Friends of the Animals. Democrat. Episcopalian. Avocations: physical mediumship, painting, swimming, sailing.

MORROW, SYLVIA MARIE, councilwoman, volunteer; b. Natchitoches, La., Mar. 5, 1947; d. Willease Duncantell and Ethel Morrow. Student, Ctrl. Area Trade Sch., 1970; B in Elem. Edn. (hon.), Baptist Christian Coll., 1992. Tchr.'s aide Natchitoches Parish Sch. Bd., 1973—97. Ctr. dir. Happy Day and A.A. Frederick, Natchitoches, 1979—87; self-esteem cons. Parks Elem. Sch., Natchitoches, 1991—98, Ben. D. Johnson Found., Natchitoches, 1999—2000. Voter edn. registration Natchitoches Parish Voters League, 1970—2001; bd. mem. Natchitoches Parish Tourist Commn., 1990—97; 2nd v.p. Natchitoches Parish Voters & Civic League, 1996—; vol. Boys & Girls Club, Goins Christmas Tree Cmty. Outreach Program, 1969—; mem. Jackson Sq./Bailey Heights Cmty. Improvment Assn.; bd. dirs. Natchitoches Cmty. Improvement Bd., 1999—; dem. com. chairperson Parish of Natchitoches, 1987—99; mem. Mayor's Adv. Coun., Nachitoches, 1979—89; advisor Youth Vote Commn.; bd. dirs. Kasatchie Legal Svcs. Corp., 1984—98. Named one of Women of Excellence, Natchitoches Black Heritage Com., 1999; recipient Cmty. Svc. award, Nat. Coun. Women, 1995, Model of Excellence award, Martin Luther King Commn., 1997, Nat. cert. of Recognition, NEA Tchrs. and Paraprofessionals Forum. Mem.: NAACP (Woman of Yr. Natchitoches Br. 1985), Natchitoches Edn. Union (asst. rep. 1980), La. Assn. Educators (sec. 1992), La. Mcpl. Assn. (Cmty. Achievement award for Econ. Devel. 2002). Democrat. Avocations: child care consulting, gospel and jazz music, volunteering. Home: 1112 Lake St Natchitoches LA 71457 Office: 315 North St Natchitoches LA 71457-3949

MORSE, ANNE BERNADETTE, educational consultant; b. Bklyn., May 7, 1925; d. Salvatore and Lucia (Romano) Somma; m. George Morse, Oct. 14, 1951; children: Jonathan, David. BBA in Acctg., CCNY, 1950. Office mgr. Chesterfield Hat Corp., N.Y.C., 1947-54; spl. asst. edn. Office Borough Pres. Queens, N.Y.C., 1975-90; cons. Queensborough C.C. Fund, N.Y.C., 1991-95. Pres. PTA P.S. 188Q, Bayside, N.Y., 1967-69; founding mem., 1st chair Sch. Dist. 26 Pres. Coun., Queens, 1968-69; mem., v.p. Cmty. Sch. Bd. 26, 1969-75; apptd. mem. N.Y. State Task Force Edn., Albany, 1974-75; founding mem. Alley Pond Environ. Ctr., 1975—; mem. Queens Com. Childrens Svcs., 1976—; bd. dirs. Queens Child Guidance Ctr., 1982—, outreach com. chair; charter mem. Ams. Italian Heritage, 1982—; mem. adv. bd. Queensborough C.C. Holocaust Rsch. Ctr., 1983—, chair, 1999—. Recipient Girl Scouts Am. Cert. of Appreciation, 1975, Sonia Strumpf Humanitarian award, 2000. Mem. Coun. Suprs. and Adminstrs. (spl. edn. awards com.). Avocations: travel, opera, reading, walking, theatre.

MORSE, GLORIA JEANNE, executive secretary; d. Richard Banks Evans and Irene Mary Podgornik Evans; m. Julian Karl Morse, Apr. 17, 1971. AAS, Harper C.C., Palatine, Ill., 1986; BA in English, student, Loyola U., Chgo., 2003—. Cert. profl. sec. Adminstrv. asst. Time Inc., Chgo, 1963—82; exec. asst. to pres. Nat. Safety Coun., Itasca, Ill., 1982—97; edn. coord. Square D Co., Palatine, 1998—2001; receptionist LaSalle Bank Corp., Schaumburg, Ill., 2001—. Fundraiser Devan N. D'Silva Found., Arlington Heights, Ill., 1997—2002. Mem.: Phi Alpha Theta, Golden Key, Alpha Sigma Lambda. Presbyterian. Avocations: reading, history, poetry, collecting pigs, collecting crystal and jewelry. Office: LaSalle Bank 1805 E Golf Rd Schaumburg IL 60173

MORSE, JEAN AVNET, higher education administrator, lawyer; b. NYC, Jan. 2, 1947; d. Samuel and Helen Avnet; m. Stephen John Morse, Dec. 26, 1966; 1 child, Elisabeth Avnet Morse. BA in History with high honors, Wellesley Coll., 1968; JD cum laude, Harvard U., 1971. Bar: Mass. 1971, Calif. 1974. Law clk. Superior Ct. Commonwealth of Mass., Boston, 1971-72; atty. Palmer & Dodge, Boston, 1972-74; assoc. to ptnr. Kaplan, Livingston, Goodwin, Berkowitz & Selvin, Beverly Hills, Calif., 1974-81; ptnr. Hufstedler & Kaus, LA, 1981-87, of counsel, 1988; dep. assoc. dean, dir. coll. office, Sch. Arts and Sci. U. Pa., Phila., 1991-93; lectr. sociology, U. Pa. Sch. Arts and Sci., Phila., 1991; acting asst. provost U. Pa., Phila., 1991-92, dean's acad. planning cons., 1992-93; assoc. dean for admin. NYU Sch. Law, NYC, 1993—94; dep. to pres. U. Pa., 1994-95; exec. dir. Commn. on Higher Edn. Mid. States Assn. of Coll. and Sch., Phila., 1996—. Bd. dir. Women in Bus., 1985-88, The Women's Bldg., 1985-86; chair individual rights sect. LA County Bar Assn., 1985-86.

MORSE, KAREN WILLIAMS, academic administrator; b. Monroe, Mich., May 8, 1940; m. Joseph G. Morse; children: Robert G., Geoffrey E. BS, Denison U., 1962; MS, U. Mich., 1964, PhD, 1967; DSc (hon.), Denison U., 1990. Rsch. chemist Ballistic Rsch. Lab., Aberdeen Proving Ground, Md., 1966-68; lectr. chemistry dept. Utah State U., Logan, 1968-69, from asst. to assoc. prof. chemistry, 1969-83, prof. chemistry dept., 1983-93, dept. head Coll. Sci., 1981-88, dean Coll. Sci., 1988-89, univ. provost, 1989-93; pres. Western Wash. U., Bellingham, 1993—. Mem., chair Grad. Record Exam in chemistry com., Princeton, N.J., 1980-89, Gov.'s Sci. Coun., Salt Lake City, 1986-93, Gov.'s Coun. on Fusion, 1989-91, ACS Com. on Profl. Tng., 1984-92; cons. 1993; nat. ChemLinks adv. com. NSF, 1995; bd. advisor's orgn. com. 2008 summer Olympic Games, Seattle, 1995; faculty Am. Assn. State Colls. and Univs. Pres.'s Acad., 1995, 96; chair Wash. Coun. of Pres., 1995-96; bd. dirs. Whatcom State Bank; NCAA Divsn. II Pres.'s Coun., 1999—, CHEA bd., 2000—; Nat. Rsch. Coun. Chem. Svcs. Roundtable, 1999—. Contbr. articles to profl. jours. Mem. Cache County Sch. Dist. Found., Cache Valley, Logan, 1988-93; swim coach, soccer coach; trustee First United Presbyn.

Ch., Logan, 1979-81, 82-85; adv. bd. Sci. Discovery Ctr., Logan, 1993, KCTS-TV, Bellingham, 1996—, Seattle Opera Bd., 1999—; mem. bd. dirs. United Way, Whatcom County, 1993—; exec. com. Bellingham-Whatcom Econ. Devel. Com., 1993—. Recipient Disting. Alumni in Residence award U. Mich., 1989, Francis P. Garvan and John M. Olin medal, 1997. Fellow AAAS; mem. Am. Chem. Soc. (Utah award Salt Lake City and Cen. dists, 1988, Garvan Olin medal 1997), Am. Assn. State Colls. and Univs. (mem. policy and purposes com. 1995, chair 1996), Bus. and Profl. Women Club (pres. 1984-85), Philanthropic Edn. Orgn., Phi Beta Kappa, Sigma Xi, Phi Beta Kappa Assocs., Phi Kappa Phi, Beta Gamma Sigma. Avocations: skiing, biking, photography. Office: Western Washington U Office Pres 516 High St Bellingham WA 98225-5946

MORSE, KIMBERLY DEANE, artist; b. Fall River, Mass., Mar. 27, 1960; d. Alan Whitney and Elizabeth Mary Morse; 1 child, Alan Fredrick Koechlein. BFA cum laude, Va. Commonwealth Univ., 1978—82, student, 1983. Sub. tchr. Chesterfield County Schs., 1980—83; practicum tchg. Va. Mus. of Fine Arts Richmond City Sch. and Chesterfield County Schs., 1981—82; elem. art tchr. C.E. Curtis Elem., Chesterfield County Schs., 1983—90; art tchr. Dept. Def. Dependent Schs. Elem. and Middle Sch. Tchr., Panama, 1990—95, Woolridge Elem., Chesterfield County Schs., 1995—99; art instr. pvt. practice, Midlothian, Va., 2000—01; pvt. instr. Brandermill Retirement Cmty., 2000—01; art tchr. Mataco Middle Sch., Chesterfield County Schs., 2001—04. Mem. Supt. Comm. Task Force, Chesterfield County Schs., 1988—90; mentor Teachers Need Teachers, Chesterfield County Schs. Contbr. presenter and chairperson in field; one-woman shows include Jewlery Artisan, Vender Shockoe Slip and Cary Town, 1986—90, Jwelery Artisan, Painter and Theatre Prop and Set Designer, Panama, 1990—95, Water Colorist, Outdoor Canvas Painter and Muralist, 1995—2003. Recipient First Place in Panama Art Show for Jewelry, 1990, Nominee Walt Disney Tchr. of The Yr. award, 1994, Nominee, REB award, 1996. Master: The Nat. Art Edn. Assn.; mem.: Brandermill Artist and Writers Assn., Panama Artist and Theater Troupe, Overseas Art Edn. Assn., Parent Tchr. Assn., Va. Art Edn. Assn. Home: 3500 Seven Oaks Rd Midlothian VA 23112-4946

MORSE, TERRI FRASER, engineering administrator; d. James Howard and Bonnie Lou Fraser; m. Mark Harry Morse, Oct. 19, 1990. BA in Edn./Math. and Music, Ctrl. Wash. U., Ellensburg, 1978. Youth/Christian edn. dir. Kelso (Wash.) Presbyn. Ch., 1978-80; stability and flight controls engr. The Boeing Co., Seattle, 1980-82, avionics computer engr., 1982-85, flight sys. lab. engr. lead, 1985-86, engr. supr., 1986-89, rsch. engring. supr., 1989-90, mech./elec. supr., 1990-95, elec. processes/computing mgr., 1995—. Vol. mission team mem. Africa U., Zimbabwe, 1996; bd. dirs. Multifaith Works, Seattle, 1998—; mem. bishops coun. on children and poverty United Meth. Ch., Seattle, 1998—; loaned exec. Corp. Coun. for the Arts, Seattle, 1993-95, Leadership Tomorrow--Seattle Commerce/United Way, 1997-98. Mem. AIAA (sr.), Soc. Women Engrs. (life; bylaws chair, program chair). Avocations: hiking, camping, skiing, kite-flying, home improvement.

MORSE-MCNEELY, PATRICIA, poet, writer, retired middle school educator; b. Galveston, Tex., Apr. 2, 1923; d. Bleecker Lansing Sr. and Annie Maud (Pillow) Morse; m. Chalmers Rankin McNeely, Mar. 22, 1949 (div. Aug. 1959); children: David Lansing McNeely, Timothy Ann McNeely Caldwell, Patricia Grace McNeely Dragon, Abigail Rankin McNeely. BS in Edn., U. Tex., 1972; MA in Ednl. Psychology, Spl. Edn. LLD, U. Tex., San Antonio, 1976, MA in Ednl. Psychology Counseling, 1981. Cert. tchr. Tex., profl. counselor. Sec./adminstrv. sec. various cos., Galveston & Austin, Tex., 1945-49, 60-70; dep. clk. Ct. of Civil Appeals, Galveston, 1947-48; police stenographer Austin Police Dept., 1970-74; history and spl. edn. tchr. N.E. Ind. Sch. Dist., San Antonio, 1974-76; spl. edn. tchr. S.W. Ind. Sch. Dist., San Antonio, 1978-81; vocat. adjustment coord. East Ctrl. Ind. Sch. Dist., San Antonio, 1981-82; counselor, tchr. Stockdale (Tex.) Ind. Sch. Dist., 1982-84; clinic sec. Humana Hosp., Dallas, 1985-87; tchr. history and spl. edn. Dallas Ind. Sch. Dist., 1987-2000; ret., 2000. TSTA/NEA assn. rep. Hill Mid. Sch., Dallas, 1988—89, E.B. Comstock Mid. Sch., Dallas, 1991—2000. Author: (poetry) Texas City, 1947, A Gift of Love, 1978, The Key, 1991, The House, The Gull's Quill, 2001, Pat's Portfolio, 2002; contbr., articles to prof. newspapers and profl. jours. V.p. zone, sec., libr., com. mem. Parents Without Ptnrs., Inc., Austin, 1965—72, chmn. internat. ad hoc com. for writing leadership tng. program, 1968, newsletter editor, 1967—72. Mem.: AARP, NEA (life), San Gabriel Writers League, Writers League Tex., Soc. Children's Book Writers and Illustrators, Nat. Trust for Edn. (trustee), Tex. Writers' League (San Gabriel chpt.), U. Tex. Austin Alumni Assn. (First Bernice Milburn Moore scholarship award 1972), U. Tex. San Antonio Alumni (del. to Tex. State Tchrs. Assn. Conf. 1978—81, 1991—97), Internat. Libr. Poetry (Hall of Fame 1997), Assn. Am. Poets Nat. Edn. Assn., Tex. State Tchrs. Assn. (life), Internat. Soc. Poets (life). Episcopalian. Avocations: writing, reading, music, sewing/handcrafts, book collecting. E-mail: pmmcneely@prodigy.net.

MORSEY, SARA, actor, educator; d. William Joseph and Nellie Thompson Morsey. BS in Sci. and Dental Hygiene, U. Louisville, 1974, MEd, 1979, MFA in Acting, 1988. Co. mem. The Hippodrome State Theatre, Gainesville, Fla., 1992—. Free-lance actor regional theatres through the U.S., 1988—; adj. prof. Santa Fe C.C., Gainesville, Fla., 2000—; tchr. U. Louisville, 1980—87, U. Fla.; tchr. acting Horse Cave Theatre, Stage One, The Tenn. Govs. Sch. Arts, Ocala Civic Theatre, Am. Stage, Hippodrome State Theatre. Actor: (plays) An Enchanted Land (Pick of the Fringe, Edinburgh Festival Fringe, 1999). Recipient Best Actress award, Memphis Theatre Critics, 1998. Mem.: Actors' Equity Assn., Theatre Comm. Group. Liberal. Roman Catholic. Office: Hippodrome State Theatre 25 SE 2nd Pl Gainesville FL 32601-6567

MORTEN, ANN KEANE, nurse midwife; b. Portland, Oreg. d. Gordon Hunter and Georgia Miller Keane; m. John Adams Bright (div. 1972); children: Amy Elisabeth Bright-Thompson, Kathleen Ann Bright-Freer, Diana Sue Bright-Basye; m. Douglas Lynn Morten, 1981; stepchildren: Lise-Marie, Eric. Student, U. Colo.; BA in Social Scis., Maryhurst U., 1980; ADN, Portland (Oreg.) C.C., 1983; BSN, Oreg. Health Scis. U., 1985, MSN, 1989, cert. nurse midwife, 1991. RN, Wash.; ARNP, Wash., Oreg. Performance musician, 1970-86; counselor Juvenile Dept. Washington County, Hillsboro, Oreg., 1979-80, Boys & Girls Aide Soc., Portland, 1980-83; staff RN labor and delivery Emanuel Hosp., Portland, 1983-91; fullscope cert. nurse midwife Vancouver (Wash.) Clinic, 1991-98; pvt. pratice full scope cert. nurse midwife Portland, 1998—. Active Portland Art Mus., 1980—, Sierra Club and Nat. Pks. Orgn., 1980—, Zero Population, 1980—, Planned Parenthood, 1980—, Nature Conservancy, 1980—, Oreg. Pub. Broadcasting, 1980—. Mem. Am. Coll. Nurse Midwives, Ob-gyn. Jour. Club, Lake Oswego C. of C. Democrat. Episcopalian. Avocations: music (playing guitar and singing), golfing, skiing, sailing, tennis. Home: 3437 NE 31st Ave Portland OR 97212-2622

MORTENSEN-SAY, MARLYS, school system administrator; b. Yankton, SD, Mar. 11, 1924; d. Melvin A. and Edith L. (Fargo) Mortensen; m. John Theodore Say, June 21, 1951; children: Mary Louise, James Kenneth, John Melvin, Margaret Ann. BA, U. Colo., 1949, MEd, 1953; Adminstrv. Specialist, U. Nebr., 1973. Tchr. Huron (S.D.) Jr. H.S., 1944-48, Lamar (Colo.) Jr. H.S., 1950-52, Norfolk Pub. Sch., 1962-63; sch. supr. Madison County, Madison, Nebr., 1963-79. Mem. ASCD, NEA (life) AAUW, Am. Assn. Sch. Adminstrs., Dept. Rural Edn., Nebr. Assn. County Supts., N.E. Nebr. County Supts. Assn. Assn. Sch. Bus. Ofcls., Nat. Orgn. Legal Problems in Edn., Nebr. Edn. Assn., Nebr. Sch. Adminstrs. Assn. Republican. Methodist. Home: 1222 W S Airport Rd Norfolk NE 68701-1349

MORTHAM, SANDRA BARRINGER, former state official; b. Erie, Pa., Jan. 4, 1951; d. Norman Lyell and Ruth (Harer) Barringer; m. Allen Mortham, Aug. 21, 1950; children: Allen Jr., Jeffrey. AS, St. Petersburg Jr. Coll., 1971; BA, Eckerd Coll. Cons. Capital Formation Counselors, Inc., Bellair Bluffs, Fla., 1972-74; commr. City of Largo, Fla., 1982-86, vice mayor, 1985-86; mem. Fla. Ho. of Reps., 1986-94, Rep. leader pro tempore, 1990-92, Rep. leader, 1992-94; Sec. of State State of Fla., 1995-98; pub. affairs dir., CEO, exec. v.p. Fla. Med. Assn., 1999—. Bd. dirs. Performing Arts Ctr. & Theatre, Clearwater, Fla.; exec. com. Pinellas County Rep. Com., Rep. Nat. Com. Named Citizen of Yr., 1990; recipient Tax Watch Competitive Govt. award, 1994, Bus. and Profl. Women "Break the Glass Ceiling" award, 1995, Fla. League of Cities Quality Floridian award, 1995, also numerous outstanding legislator awards, achievement among women awards from civic and profl. orgns. Mem. Am. Legis. Exch. Coun., Nat. Rep. Legislators Assn., Largo C. of C. (bd. dirs. 1987—, pres.), Largo Jr. Woman's Club (pres., Woman of Yr. award 1979), Suncoast Community Woman's Club (pres., Outstanding Svc. award 1981, Woman of Yr. award 1986), Suncoast Tiger Bay, Greater Largo Rep., Belleair Rep. Woman's, Clearwater Rep. Woman's, Tallahassee Rep. Woman's Club (pres. 1999-2000), Fla. Fedn. Rep. Women (2d v.p.). Republican. Presbyterian. Home: 6675 Weeping Willow Way Tallahassee FL 32311-8795

MORTH-FRASER, GRACE M. social sciences educator; b. Fargo, N.D., Mar. 13, 1947; d. Ludwig John Morth and Leota Alzada Jones. BA, Univ. Utah, 1969; MA, Univ. Mass., 1971, PhD, 1979. Adj. lectr. Colby-Sawyer Coll., New London, NH, 1980—83; lectr. Plymouth (N.H.) State Coll., 1987—99, asst. prof., 1990—94, assoc. prof., 1994—. Asst. chair Dept. of Social Sci. PSC, 1994—2000, chair, 2000—03; pres. N.E. Anthro. Assn., NEAA-USY, Canada, 2002—. Contbr. to profl. jours. Mem. Hocal Historical Socs., NH; vol. Social Svc. & Pol. Campaigns, NH. Recipient Citizen of the Yr., Dorchester Grange, 1985; grantee Rsch. Grants, NIMH and Nat. Endowment for Humanities, Faculty Devel. grants, Plymouth State Univ. Mem.: Phi Kappa Phi, Delta Kappa Gamma (Post State Officer 1990—92). Avocations: gardening, antiques, travel, cooking. Office: Plymouth State Univ 17 High St Plymouth NH 03264

MORTIMER, ANITA LOUISE, minister; b. Jefferson City, Mo., July 2, 1950; m. Ross Maitland Snell and Viola Alice (Leigh) M.; children: Caleb Ross, Hannah Erin (dec.). BA, Graceland Coll., 1973; JD, Washburn U., 1976; MA in Religion with honors, Park Coll., 1992. Bar: Kans. 1976, U.S. Dist. Ct. Kans. 1976, Mo. 1980, U.S. Dist. Ct. (we. dist.) Mo. 1980, U.S. Ct. Appeals (8th cir.) 1980, U.S. Supreme Ct. 1980; ordained to ministry Reorganized Ch. of Jesus Christ of Latter-day Saints, 1993. Tng. cons. Orgn. to Counter Sexual Assault, Mo., Iowa, Kans., Ill., 1979-80; asst. dist. atty. Wyandotte County, Kansas City, Kans., 1976-80; asst. U.S. atty. U.S. Dept. Justice, Kansas City, Mo., 1980-97; min. Reorganized Ch. of Jesus Christ Latter-day Saints Ch., 1998—. Appointee Organized Crime and Drug Enforcement Task Force, 1988; cons. Govs. Task Force on Rape Prevention, Mo., 1979-80; instr. Nat. Coll. Dist. Attys., 1980, various camps and retreats, family-related topics, various seminars for fed. agts.; bd. dirs. SHARE, Inc. Contbr. articles to profl. jours. Bd. dirs. Met. Orgn. to Counter Sexual Assault, Kansas City, 1976-80, Outreach Internat., 1995-99, Graceland Ctr. for Profl. Devel., 1994—; apptd. to Presdl. Com. on Status of Women, 1979-80; trustee Independence (Mo.) Regional Health Ctr., 1990-94; mem. Ctr. Stake Strategic Planning Commn. RLDS, 1989-90; apptd. chair World Ch. Task Force on Singles' Ministry RLDS, 1990—; chair del. caucus RLDS World Conf., 1992, 94, 96, 98, 00; trustee Graceland Coll., 1994-2000, chair, 1998-2000; mem. Friends of the Zoo. Named to Honorable Order of Ky. Cols., Gov., 1980. Mem. ABA, Mo. Bar Assn., Assn. Women Lawyers, Kansas City Met. Bar Assn.; Alumni Assn. Graceland Coll. (bd. dirs. 1987, pres. 1988), John Whitmer Hist. Soc. Clubs: MOCSA (Kansas City), Friends of Art. Office: Peace and Justice Ministries Community of Christ PO Box 1059 Independence MO 64051-0559 E-mail: amortimer@cofchrist.org

MORTIMER, ANN O. executive secretary; b. Mt. Kisco, N.Y., Oct. 15, 1943; d. Owen A and Agnes (Brennan) O'Hare; m. Donald A. Mortimer, June 17, 1967. Degree in secretarial sci., Berkeley Sch.Westchester, White Plains, N.Y., 1962. Exec. sec. to CEO Gen. Foods Corp., White Plains, NY, 1967—81; adminstrv. asst. to CEO Avco Corp., Greenwich, Conn., 1981—86; exec. asst. to chmn./CEO Reader's Digest Assn., Inc., Pleasantville, NY, 1986—97; asst. to chmn./CEO IBM Corp., Armonk, NY, 1997—2002; adminstrv. asst. to David Rockefeller, N.Y.C., 2003—. Vice-chair Leonard Park Com., Mt. Kisco, NY, 1987—97. Mem.: Seraphic Soc. (pres. 1992—94). Office: 30 Rockefeller Pl Rm 5600 New York NY 10112

MORTIMER, PAMELA S. printing company executive; b. Oil City, Pa., May 17, 1966; d. Paul D. and Joan L. (Orszulak) M. Cert. graphic artist, Jeff Tech., 1984; student, R.I.T., 2001—. Gen. mgr. Premier Graphics, DuBois, Pa., 1989—; pub., editor-in-chief Poetic Justice, Penfield, Pa., 1990-95; owner, pub. Premier Pub., DuBois, Pa., 1991-94. Cons., pres. DuBois Area Coun. Arts, 1992-2002, exec. prodr. documentary, 2003—; lit. judge Nat. PTA, 1994-96. Author: Emma, 1992, Blue Jazz Moon, 1996, Emergence, 2002, A Document Design Primer, 2003; contbr. poetry to jours. Campaign fundraiser YMCA, DuBois, 1995, vice chair, sr. vol. Hope for Victims Violence, DuBois, 1989-94. Named Poet of Yr. World of Poetry, 1990-92; recipient Blue Ribbon award So. Poetry Assn., 1989, Merit award, 1990. Mem. Writers Revue (founder), Great Lakes Nordic Soc. Home: 415 E Scribner Ave Du Bois PA 15801-2264 Office: Pats Printing 309 W Long Ave Du Bois PA 15801-1885

MORTON, CYNTHIA C. geneticist; Geneticist Brigham & Women's Hosp., Boston. Recipient Warner-Lambert/Parke-Davis award Am. Soc. Investigative Pathology, 1997. Office: Brigham & Women's Hosp 75 Francis St Boston MA 02115-6106 E-mail: cmorton@partners.org.

MORTON, KATIE MARIE, special education educator; b. Grosse Pointe Woods, Mich., May 30, 1976; d. Richard James and Kathleen Marie (Kress) Morton. BS in Edn., Ctrl. Mich. U., Mt. Pleasant, 2001. Spl. edn. tchr. Macomb Ind. Sch. Dist., Warren, Mich., 2001—. Direct care worker Listening Ear C.C., Mt. Pleasant, Mich., 1999—2001; counselor Fowler Ctr., Mayville, Mich., 1999—. Mem. games com. Spl. Olympics, Mt. Pleasant, Mich., 1999—; respite provider People with Severe Cognitive Impairments. Mem.: Coun. Exceptional Children, Am. Assn. Mental Retardation, Autism Soc. Am. Home: 13741 McKinley Ave Warren MI 48089-3612 E-mail: KMorton@misd.net.

MORTON, MARILYN MILLER, retired genealogy and history educator, lecturer, researcher, travel executive, director; b. Water Valley, Miss, Dec. 2, 1929; d. Julius Brunner and Irma Faye (Magee) Miller; m. Perry Wilkes Morton Jr., July 2, 1958; children: Dent Miller Morton, Nancy Marilyn Morton Driggers, E. Perian Morton Dyar. BA in English, Miss. U. for Women, 1952; MS in History, Miss. State U., 1955. Cert. secondary tchr. Tchr. English, speech and history Starkville HS, Miss., 1952-58; part-time instr. Miss. State U., 1953-55; spl. collection staff Samford U. Libr., Birmingham, Ala., 1984-92; lectr. genealogy and history, instr. Inst. Genealogy & Hist. Rsch., Samford U., Birmingham, 1985-93, assoc. dir., 1985-88, exec. dir., 1988-93; founding dir. SU British and Irish Inst. Genealogy & Hist. Rsch. Samford U., Birmingham and British Isles, 1986-93; owner, dir. Marilyn Miller Morton Brit-Ire-U.S. Genealogy, Birmingham, 1994—95, 1994—95. Instr. genealogy classes Samford U. Metro Coll., 1986-94; former lectr. nat. conf. Fedn. of Geneal. Soc. Contbr. articles profl. jour. Miss. state pres. Future Homemakers Am., 1947-48; active Birmingham chpt. Salvation Army Aux., 1982-87. Named to Miss. U. for Women Hall of Fame, 1952. Fellow Irish Geneal. Rsch. Soc. London; mem. Nat. Geneal. Soc. (mem. nat. program com. 1988-92, lectr. nat. mtgs.), ex-mem., Assn. Profl. Genealogists, Soc. Genealogists London, mem., Antiquarian Soc. Birmingham (sec., 2d v.p. 1982-84), DAR (regent Cheaha chpt. 1977-78), Daus. Am. Colonists (regent Edward Waters chpt. 1978-79), Nat. League of Am. Penwomen, Phi Kappa Phi (charter mem. Samford U. chpt. 1972). Avocations: reading, research, travel, bridge, chess. Home: PO Box 660562 Birmingham AL 35266-0562

MORTON, NATALIE ELAINE, director; d. Clarence Leslie Morton and Priscilla Elaine Felton; m. Joel E. Britton, 1990 (div. 1994); 1 child, Racquel Morton Britton. BBA in Mktg., Loyola U., New Orleans, 1989; MA in Ednl. Leadership, We. Mich. U., 1995, postgrad. Weekend coll. coord., academic advisor We. Mich. U., Kalamazoo, 1994—96, acad. dir. Kalamazoo statewide program, 1996—. Bd. dirs. Kalamazoo Jr. Girls, 1999—, Mich. Festival Sacred Music, Kalamazoo, 2003—. Mem.: Am. Assn. Adult and Continuing Edn., Nat. Acad. Advising Assn., Univ. Continuing Edn. Assn. Avocation: singing. Office: We Mich U 1903 W Mich Ave Kalamazoo MI 49008 Business E-Mail: natalie.morton@wmich.edu.

MORTON, SAMANTHA, actress; b. Nottingham, Eng., May 13, 1977; d. Peter and Pamela; 1 child, Esme. Actor: (TV miniseries) Band of Gold, 1995, The History of Tom Jones, a Foundling, 1997; (TV series) Soldier Soldier, 1991, Max and Ruby, 2002; (TV films) The Token King, 1993, Emma, 1997, Jane Eyre, 1997; (films) The Future Lasts a Long Time, 1996, Under the Skin, 1997, This is the Sea, 1998, Sweet and Lowdown, 1999 (Acad. award nomination for best supporting actress, 2000), Jesus' Son, 1999, The Last Yellow, 1999, Eden, 2001, Morvern Callar, 2002, Minority Report, 2002, In America, 2002 (Acad. award nomination for best actress, 2004), Code 46, 2003. Mailing: c/o CAA 9830 Wilshire Blvd Beverly Hills CA 90212

MOSELEY, CAROL JUNE, security supervisor, small business owner; b. Portland, Oreg., Apr. 20, 1952; d. David Palmore Moseley and Patricia Ann (Goar) Craig. AS in Criminal Justice, Portland C.C., 1985; degree in psychology, Portland State U., 1985-88. Cert. in pvt. security Oreg. Bd. on Pub. Safety Stds. and Tng. Security supr. Burns Internat. Security Svcs., Portland, 1991—; owner Tomorrows Star Natural Health. Cons. on security Bethlehem Ch., Lake Oswego, 1993-94, Tech. Design and Constrn., Portland, 1996. Vol. case asst. Clackamas (Oreg.) Parole & Probation, 1984, State of Oreg. Parole & Probation, Portland, 1985-88; lifeguard, swim instr. City of Portland Pks. and Recreation, 1990-95; chief of peace officers Bethlehem Ch.-Coffeehouse, Lake Oswego, Oreg., 1992; deaconess Bethlehem Ch., Lake Oswego, 1990-94; supporter Right to Life, Portland, 1994—; 1st lt. CAP Aux., USAF, 1986-88. Named Outstanding Security Officer, Portland Trailblazers NBA, 1988. Mem. Internat. Platform Assn., Internat. Soc. of Poets (disting. mem., life mem.), Ofcl. Centennial Olympic Games Club, Elks (ladies aux.), Fraternal Order of Eagles (patron, ladies aux.). Avocations: swimming, crocheting, oil painting, beachcombing.

MOSELEY, CHRIS ROSSER, marketing executive; b. Balt., Apr. 13, 1950; d. Thomas Earl and Fern Elaine (Coleman) Rosser; m. Thomas Kenneth Moseley. BA with honors, The Coll. of Wooster, 1972. Asst. dir. advt. and promotion Sta. WBAL-TV, Balt., 1972-74; dir. pub. rels. Mintz & Hoke Advt. Inc., Hartford, Conn., 1974-75; promotion mgr. Sta. WFSB-TV, Hartford, 1975-77; audience promotion mgr. Sta. WTVJ-TV, Miami, Fla., 1977-78; pres. CMA Mktg. Cons., Hyde Park, N.Y., 1979-82; promotion mgr. Ind. Network News-Sta. WPIX-TV, N.Y.C., 1982-84; sr. v.p., mgmt. supr. Christopher Thomas Muller Jordan Weiss, N.Y.C., 1984-89, Earle Palmer Brown/N.Y., N.Y.C., 1989-90; sr. v.p. advt., promotion Discovery Networks, U.S., Bethesda, Md., 1990-99; exec. v.p. mktg. ABC, Inc., N.Y.C., 1999—2000; exec. v.p. worldwide mktg. and brand strategy Hallmark Channel, Studio City, Calif., 2000—. Recipient Best Bus.-to-Bus. award Art Direction mag., 1984, award of achievement in media rels. and edn. Nat. Resources Coun. Am., 1991, Best Editorial Excellence award Mag. Age, 1992, Best Overall Mktg. Campaign award MIP/MIPCOM, 1994, 1st Place Print award: Media Promotion, London Internat. Advt. awards, 1993, Gold award Broadcast Designers, 1993, Mktg. 100 award Ad Age, 1995, Cable Marketer of Yr. award Ad Age, 1995. Mem. CTAM (chair, Mark award 1995, 96, co-chair 1997, bd. dirs. 1997), NCTA (conv. com. 1995, 96, Vanguard award for mktg. 1996, named One of 2002 Multichannel News' Wonderwomen of Yr.), WIC, AWNY, PROMAX Internat. (chair 1996-97), CTPAA. Democrat. Avocations: horticulture, travel. Home: 5224 Los Encantos Way Los Angeles CA 90027 Office: Hallmark Channel 12700 Ventura Blvd Ste 100 Studio City CA 91604-6201

MOSELEY, JULIA W. music teacher, historic preservationist; b. Tampa, Fla., Mar. 21, 1919; d. Hallock Preston and Ruby Winifred Moseley. BA, Agnes Scott Coll., Decatur, Ga., 1940. Nat. cert. music tchr. Asst. food and fashion editor Atlanta Constn., 1940-41; credit report typist, publicist, fund raiser Mchts. Assn. Tampa, 1942-43; teletype operator, writer/editor, commodities marketer USDA, Atlanta, 1943-47; self-employed music tchr. Atlanta, 1945-47; hist. rschr. New Orleans, 1947—48; self-employed music tchr., 1948—; also cattle raiser, citrus grower; preservationist Moseley Homestead, Brandon, Fla., 1948—. Author, editor: Come to My Sunland, 1997; co-author: Internet Lake Atlas, 1999, Recipes and Remembrances, 1999; composer song Brandon, Brandon. Mem. Brandon Citizens Adv. Com.; established Timberly Trust, Inc., 1994; worked with Historic Tampa/Hillsborough Cunty Preservation Bd., 1983-92; spokesperson to Hillsborough County Bd. Commrs. on land use and preservation, 1966-99; mem. Brandon Task Force involved with county devel. issues; mem. hist. com. Brandon Centennial Celebration, 1990. Elizabeth Ordaway Dunn Found. grantee, 1998. Mem.: Fla. State Music Tchrs. Assn. (past officer), Limona Acad. Arts, Letters and Scis. (past officer and dir.), Art Pub. Soc. (Guild tchr.), Nat. Fedn. Music Clubs, Nat. Guild Piano Tchrs., Music Tchrs. Nat. Assn., Tampa Music Tchrs. Assn. (officer), Fla. Breeding Bird Atlas, Tampa Preservation, Inc., Nature Conservancy, Fla. Trust for Historic Preservation, Nat. Trust for Historic Preservation, Friday Morning Musicale Club. Avocations: bird watching, reading, walking, photography, star gazing. E-mail: ttland@hotmail.com.

MOSELEY, KAREN FRANCES FLANIGAN, educational consultant, retired school system administrator, educator; b. Oneonta, N.Y., Sept. 18, 1944; d. Albert Francis and Dorothy (Brown) Flanigan; m. David Michael McLaud, Sept. 8, 1962 (div. Dec. 1966); m. Harry R. Lasalle, Dec. 24, 1970 (dec. Feb. 1990); 1 child, Christopher Michael; m. Kel Moseley, Jan. 22, 1994. BA, SUNY, Oneonta, 1969; MS, SUNY and Hockerill Coll., Eng., 1970. Cert. secondary edn. tchr., Fla., Mass., N.Y. Tchr. Hanover (Mass.) Pub. Schs., 1970-80; lobbyist Mass. Fed. Nursing Homes, Boston, 1980-84; tchr., dept. chair Palm Beach County Schs., Jupiter, Fla., 1985-95; ret., 1996; chair of accredidation Jupiter H.S., 1990-91. Fulbright tchr., Denmark, 1994-95. Author: How to Teach About King, 1978, 10 Year Study, 1991. Del. Dem. Conv., Mass., 1976-84; campaign mgr. Kennedy for Senate, N.Y., 1966, Tsongas for Senate, Boston, 1978; dir. Plymouth County Dems., Marshfield, Mass., 1978-84; Sch. Accountability Com., 1991-95; polit. cons. Paul Tsongas U.S. Senate, Boston, 1978-84, Michael Dukakis for Gov., Boston, 1978-84; mem., spkr. PBC chpt. ARC; disaster team vol. Palm Beach County Red Cross. Mem. AAUW (North Palm Beach County, officer, Ednl. Found. Honor award 2003), NEA (life), Nat. Honor Soc. Polit. Scientists, Classroom Tchrs. Assn., Palm Beach County Classroom Tchrs. Assn., Mass. Coun. Social Studies (bd. dirs. Boston chpt. 1970-80), Mass. Tchrs. Assn. (chair human rels. com. Boston chpt. 1976-80), Plymouth County Social Studies (bd. dirs. 1970-80), Mass. Hosp. Assn. (bd. dirs. Boston chpt. 1980-84), Nat. Coun. for Social Studies, Fulbright Alumni Assn., Prologue Soc., Forum Club of the Palm Beaches, Fla. History Ctr., Marine Life Ctr., Norton Mus. Art. Roman Catholic. Avocations: reading, fishing, traveling, art collector, snorkeling. Home: 369 River Edge Rd Jupiter FL 33477-9350 Office Phone: 561-747-8706.

MOSELEY-BRAUN, CAROL, former senator, former ambassador; b. Chgo., Aug. 16, 1947; d. Joseph J. and Edna A. (Davie) Moseley; m. Michael Braun, 1973 (div. 1986); 1 child, Matthew. BA, U. Ill., Chgo., 1969; JD, U. Chgo., 1972. Asst. U.S. atty. U.S. Dist. Ct. (no. dist.) Ill., 1973-77; mem. Ill. Ho. of Reps., 1979-88; recorder of deeds Cook County, Ill., 1988-92; U.S. senator from Ill. Washington, 1993-99; Am. ambassador to New Zealand and Samoa U.S. Dept. State, 1999—2001; adj. prof., mgmt. DePaul U., 2002.

MOSELY, ELAINE W. school librarian; b. Tuscaloosa, Ala. d. Ollie and Minnie S. Washington; m. Willard Mosely, Dec. 29, 1973; children: Taimon, Erin. BA in Psychology, Coe Coll., 1973; postgrad., U. Mo., 1976—78; MS in Libr & Info. Sci., U. N.Tex., 2000. Cert. tchr. Iowa, Tex., libr. Tex. Tchr. Cedar Rapids (Iowa) Cmty. Schs., 1973—76; journalist various radio, TV and newspapers, Houston, 1979—85; pub. rels. practitioner City of Houston, 1985—88, Am. Heart Assn., Houston, 1988—89; pub. rels. cons. Coop. Ventures, Houston, 1989—91; tchr. Fort Bend Indep. Sch. Dist., Missouri City, Tex., libr. media specialist, 1994—2002. Adv. bd. Fort Bend County Librs., Richmond, Tex., 1999—2002. Mem. project blueprint United Way, Houston, 1990; charter mem. Fort Bend Lit. League, Sugar Land, Tex., 2000. Grantee, Viburnam Found. & ALA, 1992. Mem.: ALA, Tex. Libr. Assn., Houston Assn. Black Journalists (past bd. pres.), Alpha Kappa Alpha. Avocations: antiques, books.

MOSER, BARBARA JO, elementary school educator; b. Jacksonville, Fla., Jan. 12, 1947; d. Paul N. and Georgia J. Baldwin; m. Max L. Moser, Nov. 2, 1968; children: Max L. II, Robert P. Student, DePauw U., 1965—66; BS in Edn., Ball State U., 1969; MS in Edn., Ind. U., Indpls., 1974—74. English/journalism instr. Stonybrook Mid. Sch., Indpls., 1982—96, computer instr., 1996—. Tchr. leadership acad. Ctrl. Ind. Edn. Ctr., Indpls., 1998. Precinct worker Rep. Party, Indpls., 1969—2003. Recipient Golden Apple award, Indpls. Power and Light Co., 1998, Hon. Life Memebrship, Ind. PTA, Stonybrook PTA. Mem.: NEA (2nd vice-president 1993—98), Assn. for the Supervision of Curriculum Devel., Phi Delta Kappa. Avocations: reading, music, history. Home: 1625 Fogelson Dr Indianapolis IN 46229 Office: Stonybrook Middle Sch 11300 Stonybrook Dr Indianapolis IN 46229 Personal E-mail: barbmoser2@aol.com.

MOSER, DEBRA KAY, medical educator; BSN magna cum laude, Humboldt State U., Arcata, Calif., 1977; M in Nursing, UCLA, 1988, D in Nursing Sci., 1992. RN, Calif., Ohio; cert. pub. health nurse, Calif. Staff nurse, relief supr. med.-surg. fl. Mad River Cmty. Hosp., Arcata, 1977-78, staff/charge nurse intensive care/cardiac care unit, 1978-86; clin. nursing instr. Humboldt State U., Arcata, 1985-86; staff/charge nurse surg. ICU Santa Monica (Calif.) Hosp., 1987-88; spl. reader UCLA Sch. Nursing, 1990-91, rsch. assoc., 1986-91, clin. rsch. nurse, 1988-92, project dir., 1991-92, asst. prof., 1992-94; asst. prof. dept. adult health and illness Ohio State U. Coll. Nursing, Columbus, 1994-98, assoc. prof. dept. adult health and illness, 1998—. Mem. working group on ednl. strategies to Prevent Prehosp. Delay in Patients at High Risk for Acute Myocardial Infraction, Nat. Heart Attack Alert Program, NIH, Nat. Heart, Lung and Blood Inst., 1993-95; abstract grader sci. sessions program Am. Heart Assn., 66th Sci. Sessions, 1993, 96; grad. advisor Sigma Theta Tau-Gamma Tau chpt., 1993-94; mem. med. adv. com. Westside YMCA Cardiac Rehab. Program, 1993-94; mem. Task Force on Women, Behavior and Cardiovasc. Disease NIH, Nat. Heart, Lung and Blood Inst., 1991; coord. cont. care CHF cmty. case mgmt. Mt. Carmel Health Sys., Columbus, Ohio, 1997—; presenter in field. Reviewer Am. Jour. Critical Care, 1992—, Heart and Lung, 1991—, Progress in Cardiovasc. Nursing, 1993—, Heart Failure: Evaluation and Care of Patients With Left-Ventricular Systolic Function, 1993, Intensive Coronary Care, 5th edit., 1994, Rsch. in Nursing & Health, 1995—, Jour. Am. Coll. Cardiology, 1995; co-editor Jour. Cardiovasc. Nursing, 1997—; mem. editl. bd. Am. Jour. Critical Care, 1994—, Jour. Cardiovasc. Nursing, 1995—; contbr. articles to profl. jours., chpts. to books. Recipient scholarship UCLA, 1988-90, scholarship Kaiser Permanente Affiliate Schs., 1990, Ednl. Achievement award LA-AACN, 1990, Alumni rsch. award UCLA, 1990, rsch. abstract award AACN-IVAC, 1993, Heart Failure Rsch. prize AHA Coun. Cardiovascular Nursing/Otsuka Am. Pharm., Inc., 1995; grantee Sigma Theta Tau-Gamma Tau chpt., 1989-90, AACN, 1989-90, 92-93, NIH, Nat. Ctr. Nursing Rsch., 1990-92, UCLA Program in Psychneuroimmunology, 1992-93, UCLA Sch. Nursing, 1993, UCLA Acad. Senate, 1993-94, AACN/Sigma Theta Tau Internat., 1994-95, NIH, Nat. Inst. Nursing Rsch., 1991-96, Sigma Theta Tau Epsilon chpt., 1995, Ohio State U., 1995, Nat. Am. Heart Assn., 1995—. Mem. AACN (Critical Care Rsch. Abstract award 1995, 98), Am. Heart Assn. Coun. Cardiovasc. Nursing (New Investigator award 1995, Heart Failure Rsch. prize 1995), Am. Psychol. Soc., Heart Failure Soc. Am., AHA (fellow Coun. Cardiovascular Nursing), Sigma Theta Tau (mem. rsch. com. 1990-94, Excellence in Rsch. award Gamma Tau chpt. 1993). Office: Ohio State U Coll Nursing Dept Adult Health & Illness 1585 Neil Ave Columbus OH 43210-1216 Home: Apt 1010 4390 Clearwater Way Lexington KY 40515-6375

MOSER, DIANE, state agency administrator; AAS in Data Processing and BSBA in Acctg., U. So. Colo., 1978. CPA Colo. Auditor various acctg. firms, Denver, 1978—85; with Denver Technol. Ctr., 1985—95, acctg. mgr.; prin. acctg. Wyo. Dept. Agr., 1995—99; comptroller Wyo. Bus. Coun., Cheyenne, 1999—. Office: Wyoming Business Council 214 W 15th St Cheyenne WY 28002

MOSES, CYNTHIA GLASS, realtor; b. Kittery, Maine, Jan. 27, 1954; d. Park Roy Jr. and Mintie Jane (Eberhart) Glass; m. Robert William Moses, Nov. 26, 1983. BA, U. Md., 1975; MA, U. Va., 1976; postgrad., U. Conn., 1976-79. Cert. residential specialist; cert. relocation profl.; accredited buyer's rep. e-Pro, grad. Realtors Inst. Owner Cynthia Glass Antiques, Alexandria, Va., 1981-83; assoc. Shannon and Luchs, Bethesda, Md., 1983-89; assoc. broker Re/Max 2000, Rockville, Md., 1990-2000; broker Broker Residential Referrals Direct, 1994—; assoc. broker Keller Williams Md. Realtors, Gaithersburg, 2000—. Docent Nat. Mus. African Art, Washington, 1979-83. Recipient Rsch. grant U. Conn., Storrs, 1978. Mem. Nat. Assn. Realtors (gov. residential sales coun. 1993-96), Md./D.C. CRS Chpt. (pres. 1991-92, Diamond award 1992), Real Estate Buyers Agy. Coun., Montgomery County Assn. Realtors (life mem.). Avocations: snow skiing, roller blading, scuba diving. Home: 26301 Mullinix Mill Rd Mount Airy MD 21771-4301 Office: Keller Williams Md Realtors 11400 Rockville Pike Ste 110 Rockville MD 20852 E-mail: cindy@moseshometeam.com.

MOSES, KAREN, editor; B Journalism, U. N.Mex. Gen. assignment reporter Pioneer Press, Chgo., 1977; reporter, then regional editor Gallup Ind.; asst. city editor Albuquerque Jour., city editor, asst. mng. editor, 1994—2001, mng. editor, 2001—. Office: Albuquerque Jour 7777 Jefferson NE PO Drawer J Albuquerque NM 87103*

MOSES, MARCIA SWARTZ, artist; b. Canton, Ohio, Oct. 3, 1947; d. Elmer John Swartz and Marguerite Mary Welsh; m. Frederick Oscar Moses, June 7, 1969; children: Frederick, Angela Parker, John. Student, Kent State U., 1965—67, BFA, 1987; student, Ohio State U., 1984—86. Artist Watercolor Originals, Canton, 1991—. Author: (watercolor book) Untitled, 2002, Easy Watercolor, Learn to Express Yourself; prin. works include Vessels of Antiquity, 2000 (Best of Show award, 2000). Bd. dirs. Canton Artists League, 2001. Home and Office: Watercolor Originals 5101 Summitview Cir Canton OH 44708 E-mail: mosesart@neo.rr.com.

MOSHER, SALLY EKENBERG, lawyer, musician; b. N.Y.C., July 26, 1934; d. Leslie Joseph and Frances Josephine (McArdle) Ekenberg; m. James Kimberly Mosher, Aug. 13, 1960 (dec. Aug. 1982). MusB, Manhattanville Coll., 1956; postgrad., Hofstra U., 1958-60, U. So. Calif., 1971-73, JD, 1981. Bar: Calif., 1982. Musician, pianist, tchr., 1957-74; music critic Pasadena Star-News, 1967-72; mgr. Contrasts Concerts, Pasadena Art Mus., 1971-72; rep. Occidental Life Ins. Co., Pasadena, 1975-78; v.p. James K. Mosher Co., Pasadena, 1961-82, pres., 1982—, Oakhill Enterprises, Pasadena, 1984—; assoc. White-Howell, Inc., Pasadena, 1984-94; real estate broker, 1984-96. Harpsichordist, lectr., composer, 1994—; pub. Silver Wheels Pub., ASCAP. Musician (CD recs.) William Byrd: Songs, Dances, Battles, Games, 1995, From Now On: New Directions For Harpsichord, 1998; author: People and Their Contexts: A Chronology of the 16th Century World; contbr. articles to various publs. Bd. dirs. Jr. League Pasadena, 1966-67, Encounters Concerts, Pasadena, 1966-72, U. So. Calif. Friends of Music, L.A., 1973-76, Calif. Music Theatre, 1988-90, Pasadena Hist. Soc., 1989-91, I Cantori, 1989-91; bd. dirs. Pasadena Arts Coun., 1986-92, pres., 1989-92, chair adv. bd., 1992-93; v.p., bd. dirs. Pasadena Chamber Orch., 1986-88, pres., 1987-88; mem. Calif. 200 Coun. for Bicentennial of U.S. Constn., 1987-90; mem. Endowment Adv. Commn., Pasadena, 1988-90; bd. dirs. Foothill Area Cmty. Svcs., 1990-95, treas., 1991, vice chair, 1992-94, chair, 1994-95; sec., bd. dirs. Piano Spheres, 2001-02, pres., 2002—. Manhattanville Coll. hon. scholar, 1952-56. Mem. ABA, Calif. Bar Assn., Assocs. of Calif. Inst. Tech., Athenaeum, Kappa Gamma Pi, Mu Phi Epsilon, Phi Alpha Delta. Home: 1260 Rancheros Rd Pasadena CA 91103-2759 Fax: 626-795-3146. E-mail: sally@cyberverse.com.

MOSKOVITZ, ELISA MCMILLAN, music educator, musician; b. Columbia, S.C., Nov. 29, 1953; d. William Gooding and Elizabeth Anne McMillan; m. Barry L. Moskovitz, Apr. 5, 1980 (div. Dec. 1982); m. Finnbarr T. Dunphy, Nov. 19, 2000. B in Music Edn., Winthrop U., 1976, MMus, 1977; D in Musical Arts, U. S.C., 1989. Tchr. gen. music and chorus Lexington (S.C.) Sch. Dist. 1, 1977—89, program specialist for fine arts; tchr. music theory Lexington H.S., 1990—2002; choral dir. White Knoll H.S., 2002—. Organist, choirmaster St. Timothy's Episcopal Ch., Columbia, 1985—2002; pianist So. Arts Trio, Columbia, 1994—; adj. prof. U. S.C., Columbia, 1990—2004, Limestone Coll., Columbia, 1990, Columbia, 96; coord. of music Tri-Dist. Arts Consortium, Columbia, 1997—99; organist, choirmaster Columbia Presbyn. Ch., Columbia, 2004—. Author: Jour. Rsch. Music Edn., 1992. Coord. A Little Summer Music concert series St. Timothy's Ch., Columbia, 1995—. Fellow, NEH, 1992; grantee, Nat. Music Edn. Project, 1991. Mem.: S.C. Music Educators Assn., Am. Guild Organists, Pi Kappa Lambda, Delta Kappa Gamma. Episcopalian. Avocations: golf, poetry, literature. Office Phone: 803-996-4558. Office Fax: 803-996-4558.

MOSKOVITZ, NANCY SIEGEL, artist, elementary school educator; b. Boston, Massachusetts; d. Jack B. and Rosalie Siegel; m. Richard A. Moskowvitz, May 7, 1972; children: Adam, Cara, Dustin. Attended, Mass. Coll. of Art, 1969; BA in Elem. edn., art history (hon.), Simmons Coll., 1970; attended, Santa Fe Comm. Coll., Ctrl. Fla. Comm. Coll., 2003. Art tchr. Cornerstone Sch., Ocala, Fla., 1988—2003, ret. Demonstrator and tchr various art orgn., Fla., 1998—; portrait commn., 2003—. Two life size horses painted for pub. art, Horse Fever, 2002. V.p. Marion Art Educators Assn., Ocala, Fla., 1998; publicity chair Ocala Art Group, Inc., Fla., 1998—2000, web master, 1998—2003. Recipient Best of Show, Ocala Art Group, Inc., 2000, Honorarium, Marion Culture Alliance and Fla. Thoroughbred Breeders and Owners Assn., 2002, Best of Show, Nat. Assn. of Am. Pen Women, Nature Coast Branch, 2003. E-mail: nmoskovitz@aol.com.

MOSKOWITZ, DANIELLE MARA, art educator, artist; b. Bklyn., May 15, 1976; d. William and Francine Leight Moskowitz. BS, Lehigh U., 1998. Accredited jewelry profl. Gemological Inst. Am., 2002. Mktg. coord. GEM Comm., N.Y.C., 1998—99; mktg. assoc. Job Expo. Internat., 1999—2000; mktg. mgr. Gate42 Technologies, 2000—01; pvt. tutor NJ, 2001—02; substitute tchr. Marlboro Twp., 2001—03; tchr. art South Amboy Elem. Sch., 2003—03. Jewelry designer and creator, NJ, 2002—. Mem.: N.J. Art Educators Assn. Home: 52 Girard St Marlboro NJ 07746 Personal E-mail: danimaram@netscape.net.

MOSKOWITZ, RANDI ZUCKER, nurse; b. N.Y.C., Oct. 19, 1948; d. Seymour and Gertrude (Levy) Zucker; m. Marc N. Moskowitz, July 11, 1976. RN, Jewish Hosp. and Med. Ctr., 1969; BA, Marymount Manhattan Coll., 1975; MS, Hunter Coll., 1979; MBA, Columbia U., 1990. Gen. staff nurse neurosurgery unit N.Y. Hosp., N.Y.C., 1969-71, sr. staff nurse recovery rm., 1971-76, nurse coord. utilization rev., 1976-79; health educator Office of Cancer Comm., Meml. Sloan-Kettering Cancer Ctr., N.Y.C., 1979-81; adminstrv. nurse oncologist Bklyn. Cmty. Hosp. and Meth. Hosp., 1981-83, grants coord. radiotherapy dept., 1983-86; adminstr. Ambulatory Oncology Ctr., Columbia-Presbyn. Med. Ctr., N.Y.C., 1986-89; adminstr. Surg. Day Hosp., Meml. Sloan-Kettering Cancer Ctr., 1990-98; mgr. Oncology Svcs., St. Vincent Cath. Med. Ctrs., Jamaica, NY, 1999—. Masters prof. oncology Columbia U. Sch. Nursing. Co-editor Oncology Nursing: Advances, Treatments and Trends into the Twenty-first Century; contbr. articles to profl. jours. Mem. N.Y. Assn. Ambulatory Care, Oncology Nursing Soc. (sec. N.Y.C. chpt. 1983-87, pres. 1988-89). Home: 446 E 86th St Apt 5F New York NY 10028-6474 Office: Saint Vincent Cath Med Ctrs 15211 89th Ave Jamaica NY 11432-3730 Office Phone: 718-558-9308. E-mail: rmoskowitz@svcmcny.org.

MOSKOWITZ, REBECCA C. systems analyst; d. Stanley M. and Leah Z. Moskowitz; life ptnr. Erika Brown. BS in Psychology, No. Ky. U., 2003. Corp. trainer Micro Rental & Sales, Manalapan, NJ, 1994—96; helpdesk analyst Bessemer Trust Contractor, Woodbridge, NJ, 1996; info. tech. bus. analyst GE IT Solutions, Erlanger, Ky., 1996—. Interim v.p. Pride Ctr. of N.J., New Brunswick, NJ, 1996; publicity coord. Hillel Jewish Student Union, West Chester, Pa., 1994; co-chair Out There Outdoors Club, New Brunswick, 1997—98. Recipient Outstanding Undergrad. Scholarship award, Ford Motor Co. / Golden Key, 2003. Mem.: Golden Key, Pinnacle Nat. Honor Soc., Psi Chi, Alpha Psi Omega.

MOSLAK, JUDITH, retired music educator; b. New Kensington, Pa., Sept. 16, 1942; d. Michael B. and Edith V. Moslak. MusB, Marygrove College, Detroit, Mich., 1964; MA, University of Detroit, 1967; student internat. piano workshops, France, 1998, Austria, 2000, Norway, 2002. Cert. Orff-Schulwerk Levels 1, 2, 3 1973. Assistant organist Archdiocese of Detroit, Mich., 1957—67; organist/choir director Immaculate Heart of Mary Ch., Detroit, 1964—65; elem. vocal music tchr. Detroit Pub. Schs., 1964—69; elem. vocal music cons. Farmington (Mich.) Pub. Schs., 1969—97; pvt. piano tchr. Piano Studio of Judith Moslak, West Bloomfield, Mich., 1997—; adj. asst. prof. music Madonna Univ., Livonia, Mich., 2003—. Adj. asst. prof. music Madonna U., Livonia, Mich., 2003—. Mem.: Oakland Piano Tchrs. Forum, Mich. Assn. Calligraphers, Livonia Area Piano Tchrs. Forum, Music Tchrs. Nat. Assn., Am. Guild Organists (Detroit chpt.), Am. Orff-Schulwerk Assn. (treas. 1973—75), Friends of Four Hands (charter bd. mem. 1981), Delta Kappa Gamma (treas. 1994—96). Roman Catholic. Avocations: calligraphy, travel, ensemble piano performance, digital photography. Personal E-mail: J88am@aol.com.

MOSLEY, KAREN D. retired elementary school educator; b. St. Louis, Feb. 13, 1952; d. Leola Rollins Mason; m. Kem G. Mosley, July 22, 1978. BA, MacMurray Coll., 1974; ME, Washington U., St. Louis, 1979. Cert. tchr. Mo. Elem. vocal music tchr. Furguson-Florissant Sch. Dist., Florissant, Mo., 1974—2002, ret., 2002. Corp. sec. Mosley Constrn., Kirkwood, Mo., 1983—; adminstrv. dir. SPROG, Inc., Kirkwood, Mo., 1983—96, sec., 1989—, also bd. dirs. Contbr. articles to profl. jours. Min. music Kirkwood Ch. of God, 1990—. Church Of God. Avocations: theater productions, travel, computers, reading quotes. Home: 1319 Grant Rd Webster Groves MO 63119 Office: 11233 Manchester Rd Saint Louis MO 63122 E-mail: k_mosley@excite.com.

MOSLEY-MCCALL, JERALDINE, funeral director; b. Chgo., June 3, 1944; d. James and Artra Nell Mosley; m. John Sullivan McCall, Dec. 16, 1984. Cert. in Auto Mechanics, Wilson Tech. Coll., 1971; degree in Mortuary Sci., Worsham Coll. Mortuary Sci., 1971. Lic. embalmer Ill., 1971. Preparation mgr. Leak Funeral Home, Chgo., 1973—2004; co-owner Paradise Garden Funeral Home, Chgo., 2004—. Mem. adv. bd. So. Ill. U., Carbondale, Ill., 1995—, Worsham Coll., Wheeling, Ill., 1998—; ednl. dir. Ill. Selected Morticians, Chgo., 1990—92, 2002—. Mem. Ill. Rep. Committeewoman's Roundtable, 0858. Recipient Cert. of Achievement, Ill. Select Morticians. Mem.: Acad. Profl. Funeral Svc. Practice (cert. funeral svc. practitioner 2004), Epsilon Nu Delta (pres. 1987—88, treas. 2001—, Soldier award 2003). Republican. Baptist. Avocation: reading. Home: 8913 So Laflin St Chicago IL 60620 Office: 300 E 115th St Chicago IL 60628

MOSQUERA, ZOILA BIANCA, social worker; b. Rockland County, NY, Feb. 7, 1960; d. José M. and Cynthia M. Mosquera. BSW in Social Work with honors, LI U., 2003. Vol. St. Marks Sr. Ctr., Bklyn.; vol. adv. City Hall, Manhattan, 1980—91; adv. Altro Mentally Disabled, Manhattan, 1985—87. Recipient Adv. award, Fed. Employment Guidance Svs., 1991. Democrat. Methodist. Avocations: bowling, fencing, basketball, pottery, softball. Home: Apt D 2 611 Ocean Ave Brooklyn NY 11226

MOSS, DAVID, conductor; Cert., Musician's Inst. in Hollywood, 1985; B of commerce in mktg and fin., Concordia U., 1989. Dir., sch. of fine arts Saidye Bronfman Ctr. for the Arts, 1994—96, exec. dir., 1996—2002; gen. dir. Montreal Opera, 2003—. Founding mem., mem. exec. com. Culture Montreal; standing mem. Culture Montreal's Fin. Com.; apptd. to Groupe Conseil pour la Politique Culturelle de Montreal, 2002; appt. to bd. La Vitrine Culturelle de Montreal, 2003. Office: L'Opera de Montreal 260 Maisonneuve Blvd W Montreal Qu H2X 149 Canada

MOSS, ELIZABETH LUCILLE (BETTY MOSS), retired transportation executive; b. Ironton, Mo., Feb. 13, 1939; d. James Leon and Dorothy Lucille (Russell) Rollen; m. Elliott Theodore Moss, Nov. 10, 1963 (div. Jan. 1984); children: Robert Belmont, Wendy Rollen. BA in Econs. and Bus. Adminstrn., Drury Coll., 1960. Registrar, transp. mgr. Cheley Colo. Camps, Inc., Denver and Estes Park, 1960-61; office mgr. Washington Nat. Ins. Co., Denver, 1960-61; sec. White House Decorating, Denver, 1961-62; with Ringsby Truck Lines, Denver, Oakland, Calif., and L.A., 1962-67, System 99 Freight Lines, L.A., 1967-69, terminal mgr. Stockton, Calif., 1981-84; with Yellow Freight System, L.A., 1969-74, Hayward, Calif., 1974-77, ops. mgr. Urbana, Ill., 1977-80; sales rep. Calif. Motor Express, San Jose, 1981; regional sales mgr. Schneider Nat. Carriers, Inc., No. Calif., 1984-86; account exec. TNT-Can., Nev. and Cen. Calif., 1986-88; mgr. Interstate-Intermodal Divs. HVH Transp., Denver, 1988-89; regional sales mgr. MNX, Inc., Northern Calif., 1989-91; sales dir., nat. accts. mgr., terminal mgr. Mountain Valley Express, Manteca, Calif., 1992—2003; ret., 2003. Chmn. op. coun. for San Joaquin and Stanislaus Counties Calif. Trucking Assn., 1983-84, Truck Accident Reduction Projects, San Joaquin County, 1987-88. Mem. Econ. Devel. Coun. Stockton C. of C., 1985-86; active Edison High Sch. Boosters, 1982-88. Mem.: Calif. Trucking Assn. (tri county unit steering com. 2001—03), So. Calif. Round Table (bd. dirs. 1993—2001), Coun. Logistics Mgmt., Oakland Traffic Club, Ctrl. Valley Traffic Club, Stockton Traffic Club (bd. dirs. 1982—84, Trucker of Yr.), Nat. Def. Transp. Assn. (bd. dirs. 1986—87), Delta Nu Alpha (bd. dirs. Region 1 1982—84, v.p. chpt. 1984—85, pres. chpt. 1985—86, chmn. bd. 1985—87, regional sec. 1987—88, Outstanding Achievement award 1986, 1988). Methodist. Avocation: reading. Home: One Parkway Pl 2A 350 S John Q Hammons Pkwy Springfield MO 65806 E-mail: MossBetty@aol.com.

MOSS, MYRA ELLEN (MYRA MOSS ROLLE), philosophy educator; b. L.A., Mar. 22, 1937; m. Andrew Rolle, Nov. 5, 1983. BA, Pomona Coll., 1958; PhD, The Johns Hopkins U., 1965. Asst. prof. Santa Clara (Calif.) U., 1968-74; prof. Claremont McKenna Coll., 1975—, chmn. dept. philosophy, 1992-95. Assoc. dir. Gould Ctr. for Humanities, Claremont, Calif., 1993-94; adv. coun. Milton S. Eisenhower Libr./Johns Hopkins U., 1994-96, 2001—. Author: Benedetto Croce Reconsidered, 1987, Mussolini's Fascist Philosopher: Giovanni Gentile Reconsidered, 2004; translator: Benedetto Croce's Essays on Literature & Literary Criticism, 1990; co-author: Values and Education, 1998; assoc. editor Special Issues; Journal of Value Inquiry, 1990-95 (Honorable Mention, Phoenix award); cons. editor Jour. Social Philosophy, 1988—; assoc. editor: Value Enquiry Book Series, 1990-95; editor: The Philosophy of José Gaos, by Pio Colonnello, Value Inquiry Book Series, 1997. Bogliasco fellow, Liguria, Italy, 2000. Mem. Am. Philos. Assn., Am. and Internat. Soc. for Value Inquiry, Soc. for Aesthetics, Collingwood Soc. (life), Phi Beta Kappa (hon.). Avocations: gardening, horseback riding. Office: Claremont McKenna Coll 850 Columbia Ave Claremont CA 91711-3901

MOSS, PATRICIA L. bank executive; m. Greg Moss; children: Jennifer, Jeffrey. BS in bus. adminstrn., Linfield Coll., Oreg.; masters studies Portland State U.; certification ABA Comml. Banking Sch., U. Okla. From mem. staff to pres., CEO Cascade Bancorp, Bend, Oreg., 1977—99, pres., CEO, 1998—; CEO Bank of the Cascades, Bend, Oreg., 1998—. Bd. dirs. Cascade Bancorp, Bank of the Cascades, Aquilla Tax-Free Trust of Oreg., Ctrl. Oreg. Ind. Health Svcs., MDU Resources Group Inc., 2003—. Adv. bd. Oreg. State U. Cascade Campus. Named Disting. Citizen of Yr., Bend C. of C., Ctrl. Oreg. Bus. Woman of Yr. Mem.: Ind. Cmty. Bankers Assn. Am., Oreg. Bankers Assn. (bd. dir.), Oreg. Women's Forum. Office: Cascade Bancorp 1100 NW Wall St Bend OR 97701*

MOSS, SUSAN, nurse, retail store owner; b. Youngstown, Ohio, Aug. 17, 1940; d. Jarlath G. and Sara G. (Curley) Carney; divorced; children: John P., Jerri Ann Moss Winn. Lic. nurse, Choffin Sch., 1973; AS in Am. Bus. Mgmt., Youngstown State U., 1992. Surg. scrub nurse St. Elizabeth Hosp., Youngstown, 1972-78; office mgr. Moss Equipment Co., North Jackson, Ohio, 1978-83; pvt. duty nurse Salem, Ohio, 1979—; night nurse supr. Gateways for Better Living, Youngstown, 1982-84; owner Laura's Bride and Formal Wear, Salem, 1987—; CEO Strawberry Sunshine Svcs. Co., Salem, 1994—; co-owner McCollough Retirement Home for Ladies, 1998—. Cons. Edith R. Nolf, Inc., Salem. Author: (novelette) Turlaleen, (novels) The Document Box, Her Other Life. Water therapy aide Easter Seal Soc., Youngstown, 1970-75, bd. trustees, 1973-75; mem. Hear, Now, Denver, 1989; mem. regional bd. rev. Selective Svcs. Mem. LPN Assn. Ohio, Bus. and Profl. Women, Youngstown State U. Alumni Club, Short Hills Lit. Soc., Beta Sigma Phi (v.p., Silver Circle award 1986, Order of the Rose 1987). Democrat. Roman Catholic. Avocations: writing, painting, music, public speaking, traveling. Office: Lauras Bride & Formal Wear 1271 E Pidgeon Rd Salem OH 44460-4364

MOSS, SUSAN HECHT, artist, writer; b. Chgo., May 6, 1944; d. Benjamin Franklin and Amy (Hecht) Moss; m. Glen Galloway, Jan. 15, 1964 (div. Sept. 1974). BA in Art/Psychology with honors, U. Nev., 1966; MFA, Otis Art Inst., 1970. Spkr. breast cancer. Author: Keep Your Breasts! Preventing Breast Cancer the Natural Way, 1994, 7th edit., 2002; contbr. poetry to profl. publs.; exhibitions include David Findlay Gallery, N.Y., Albright-Knox Mus., Forum Gallery, N.Y., Represented in permanent collections L.A. County Mus. Art, Skirtball Mus., L.A., Laguna Mus. Art. Mem.: Cancer Ctrl. Soc. (spkr. 1996, 2002, 2003). Democrat. Jewish. Avocations: swimming, weight-lifting, hiking, booksigning, creating videos on breast cancer prevention. Studio: 4767 York Blvd Los Angeles CA 90042-1648 Home: 1879 Montiflora Ave Los Angeles CA 90041-2016

MOSSEL, PATRICIA L. retired opera executive; b. N.Y.C., Nov. 19, 1933; d. Burnet Thomas and Martha Camille (Leigh) Kraut; m. Allan A. Fleischer, Dec. 30, 1956 (div. 1987); children: Hillary Lee Fleischer, Jason Allan Fleischer; m. John W. Mossel, Sept. 4, 1993. BA, U. Rochester, 1955; MA, Yale U., 1956. Cert. fund raising exec. Tchr. Colby Coll., New London, N.H., 1956-57; editor Far Eastern Pub.-Yale U., New Haven, 1957-60; dir. devel. San Francisco Opera, 1979-84, dir. devel., mktg. and pub. relations The Wash. Opera, 1984-95, exec. dir., 1995—2000. Mem. bd. San Francisco Symphony and Opera; bd. chmn. Mt. Diablo Rehabilitation Ctr., exec. dir. ; co-founder Medi-Physics, Inc.; cons. D.C. Humanities Council, 1989. Editor: Western Lit. on China, 1959. Mem. adv. council Fund Raising Sch., Indpls.; v.p Nat. Soc. Fund Raising Exec. Found. bd. dirs, Washington, 1985—87. Named Fund Raising Exec. of Yr.; recipient Nat. Soc. Fund Raising Execs., 1986. Mem.: Yale Alumni (assoc.; del. 1988—91), Order of Rio Branco (officer), Yale Club, Phi Beta Kappa. Republican. Presbyterian. Avocations: writing, painting, piano. E-mail: patlm@aol.com.

MOSS-SALENTIJN, LETTY (ALEIDA MOSS-SALENTIJN), anatomist, educator; b. Amsterdam, The Netherlands, Apr. 14, 1943; came to U.S., 1968; d. Ewoud and Johanna Maria (Schoonhoven) Salentijn; m. Melvin Lionel Moss, Apr. 17, 1970. DDS, State U., Utrecht, The Netherlands, 1967, PhD, 1976. Asst. prof. histology State U., Utrecht, 1967-68; asst. prof. Columbia U., N.Y.C., 1968-74, assoc. prof., 1974-86, prof., 1986—, Edwin S. Robinson prof., 1999—, dir. dental radiology, 1980-86, dir. grad. program dental sci., 1986—, dir. postdoctoral affairs, 1987-90, asst. dean postdoctoral programs, 1990-94, assoc. dean acad. affairs, 1994—. Author: Orofacial Histology & Embryology, 1972; Dental and Oral Tissues, 1980, 2d edit., 1984, 3d edit., 1990; contbr. chpts. to books, articles to profl. jours. Fellow Royal Microscopical Soc., Am. Coll. Dentists; mem. Am. Assn. Anatomists, Internat. Assn. Dental Rsch., Am. Soc. Biomechs., Sigma Xi (chpt. sec. 1980-87, pres. 1987-89, 98-99), Omicron Kappa Upsilon (pres. local chpt. 1987). Avocation: stained glass art. Home: 560 Riverside Dr Apt 20K New York NY 10027-3239 Office: Columbia U/SDOS Assoc Dean Academic Affairs 630 W 168th St New York NY 10032-3702 E-mail: lm23@columbia.edu.

MOSTER, MARY CLARE, public relations executive; b. Morristown, N.J., Apr. 7, 1950; d. Clarence R. and Ruth M. Moster; m. Louis C. Williams, Jr., Oct. 4, 1987. BA in English with honors, Douglass Coll., 1972; MA in English Lit., Univ. Chgo., 1973. Accredited pub. rels. counselor. Editor No. Trust Bank, Chgo., 1973-75, advt. supr., 1975-77, communications officer, 1977-78; account exec. Hill & Knowlton, Inc., Chgo., 1978-80, v.p., 1980-83, sr. v.p., 1983-87, sr. v.p., mng. dir., 1987-88; staff v.p. comms. Navistar Internat. Corp., Chgo., 1988-93; v.p. corp. comms. Comdisco, Inc., Rosemont, Ill., 1993—2002; sr. v.p. L.C. Williams and Assocs., Chgo., 2002—. Bd. dirs. The Pegasus Players, 1993-2000. Author poetry, poetry translation. Bd. govs. Met. Planning Coun., Chgo., 1988-94; fellow Leadership Greater Chgo., 1989-90; bd. dirs. New City YMCA, Chgo., 1986-92; corp. devel. bd. Steppenwolf Theatre Co., Chgo., 1988-90; mem. The Chgo. Network, 1994—, bd. dirs., 1996-99. Mem. Nat. Investor Rels. Inst. (bd. dirs. 1988-89, 90-99, pres. Chgo. chpt. 1998-99), Arthur W. Page Soc., Pub. Rels. Soc. Am., Internat. Women's Forum. Avocations: sailing, cross-country skiing, book groups. Office: L C Williams & Assocs 150 N Michigan Ave Ste 3800 Chicago IL 60601

MOTEN, MARY ANNE, gifted and talented educator, small business owner; b. Birmingham, Ala., Sept. 04; d. Nathaniel H. and Lucille K. Moten. BS in Math., Wilberforce U., 1965; MS in Sch. Adminstrn., Cleve. State U., 1974; MS cert., U. Ala., Birmingham, 1982. Tchr. math. Pa. Sch. Sys., Pitts., 1965—67; tchr. Patrick Henry Jr. H.S. Cleve. Pub. Schs., 1967—73, 9th grade coord., 1967—73, asst. prin. Kennard Jr. H.S., 1973—74; tchr. gifted edn. EPIC Sch. Birmingham City Schs., 1978—2003. Owner Mary's Fashions, Birmingham, 1995—2001; tchr., trainer Ala. State Dept. Edn., 1995; lead math. tchr. B'ham Pub. Schs., 1990—2003; mem. com. Cleve. Pub. Schs., 2002, trainee for sci. for all program, 2001—02, mem. sci. com. for adopted sci. book, 2002. Editor: (books) Exaltation: A Poetic Black Experience, 1994. Chess coach EPIC, 1998—2003. Named to Honor Roll of Tchrs., Assn. Sci.-Tech., 1987; recipient Disting. Tchr. award, Birmingham Post-Herald, 1995, Chess Coord. of the Yr., 2003. Mem.: Alpha Kappa Alpha, Sorority Inc. (vender). Avocation: string bass instruments. Home: 920 Graymont Ave W Birmingham AL 35204-3926

MOTLEY, CHARLOTTE JUANITA, real estate company executive, consultant; b. Atlanta, Jan. 7, 1958; d. George and Charlotte Motley; m. Garey W. Burns; 1 child, Travis George Burns. BSBA in Fin., Auburn U., 1979; MBA, Ga. State U., 1980. Cert. comml. investment mem. V.p. real estate Racetrac Petroleum, Inc., Smyrna, Ga., 1981—92; pres. JMRE, Inc., Atlanta, 1992—. Mem. edn. adv. com. Ga. Real Estate Commn., 1998—. Author: (book) Commercial Real Estate, 1999, various commercial real estate training courses, 2003. Recipient Dedication of Svc. award, Clayton/Henry Bd. Realtors, 1994. Mem.: Metro South Assn. Realtors (mem. edn. com. 1992—), Ga. Real Estate Educators Assn. (pres. 2000—01, Program of the Yr. award 1999, Svc. award 2001). Avocations: running, flying. Office: JMRE Inc 1770 Old Spring House Ln Ste 114 Atlanta GA 30338

MOTLEY, CONSTANCE BAKER (MRS. JOEL WILSON MOTLEY), federal judge, former city official; b. New Haven, Sept. 14, 1921; d. Willoughby Alva and Rachel (Huggins) Baker; m. Joel Wilson Motley, Aug. 18, 1946; 1 son, Joel Wilson, III. AB, NYU, 1943; LLB, Columbia U., 1946. Bar: N.Y. 1948. Mem. Legal Def. and Ednl. Fund, NAACP, 1945-65; mem. N.Y. State Senate, 1964-65; pres. Manhattan Borough, 1965-66; U.S. dist. judge So. Dist. N.Y., 1966-82, chief judge, 1982-86, sr. judge, 1986—. Author: Equal Justice Under Law, 1998. Mem. N.Y. State Adv. Council Employment and Unemployment Ins., 1958-64. Mem. Assn. Bar City N.Y. Office: US Dist Ct US Courthouse 500 Pearl St New York NY 10007-1316 E-mail: constance_motley@nysd.uscourts.gov.

MOTT, MARY ELIZABETH, retired educational administrator; b. West Hartford, Conn., July 10, 1931; d. Marshall Amos and Mary Herman Mott. BA, Conn. Coll. for Women, 1953; MA, Western Res. U., 1963. Cert. tchr., Ohio; cert. computer tchr., Ohio. Mgr. sales promotion Cleve. Electric Illuminating Co., 1953-60; tchr. Newbury Bd. Edn., Ohio, 1960-67, West Geauga Bd. Edn., Chesterland, Ohio, 1967—97, ret., 1997. Chmn. state certification com. in computers ECCO, Mayfield, Ohio, 1983—, exec. bd., 1980—. Asst. dir. West Geauga Day Camp, Chesterland, 1968. Mem. Ednl. Computer Consortium Ohio, West Geauga Edn. Assn. (exec. bd. 1975-97), Delta Kappa Gamma. E-mail: pci238@aol.com.

MOTT, PEGGY LAVERNE, sociologist, educator; b. Stephenville, Tex., Mar. 23, 1930; d. Artemis Victor Dorris and Tempie Pearl (Price) Hickman; m. J.D. Mott, Sept. 11, 1947 (dec. Apr. 1988); children: Kelly A. Wilcoxson, Kimberly S. Mott. BA, Southwest Tex. State U., 1980, MA, 1982. Cert. instr. ceramic arts Nat. Ceramic Art Inst., 1972. Instr. ceramics Arts & Crafts Ctr. Lackland AFB, San Antonio, 1969-72, dir. sales Arts & Crafts Ctr., 1972-77; asst. instr. S.W. Tex. State U., San Marcos, 1980-82; instr. sociology Palo Alto Coll., San Antonio, 1991—. Author: Screaming Silences, 1994, (poem) Concho River Rev., 1993, Inkwell Echos, 1989-95, Lucidity, The T.O.P. Hwupp, 1994-95, Hwap, Patchwork Poems, 1995; co-author: Activities, Field Studies for Students. Vol. coord. Fisher Houses, Inc., Lackland AFB, 1992—; parliamentarian Artistic Expressions, 1996—. Named Vol. of Month, USAF, 1976, 77, 78, Vol. of Quarter, 1976, 77, 78, 84, Vol. of Yr., 1980. Mem. Internat. Soc. Poets, Clipper Ship Poets, San Antonio Poets Assn. (v.p. 1991-92, pres. 1992-93, Poet Laureate 1994-95), San Antonio Ethnic Arts Soc., San Antonio Poetry Festival. Avocations: reading, writing, needlework. Home: 1307 Canyon Ridge Dr San Antonio TX 78227-1727 E-mail: profpurple@msn.com.

MOTYKA, SUSANNE VICTORIA, music educator; b. Manhattan, N.Y., May 29, 1949; d. John Ozenher and Anna Victoria Galluccio; m. William Joseph Motyka, Aug. 29, 1976; children: Matthew, Caroline, Eric. B in Music Edn., Coll. Misericordia, 1971. Cert. secondary tchg. Tchr., Tunkhannock, Pa., 1971—73, 1976—80; head music dept. Wyoming Sem., Kingston, Pa., 1973—76; choral dir. Dallas (Pa.) H.S., 1990; tchr. Gate of Heaven Sch., Dallas, 1991—2002. Orch. dir. Bishop O'Reilly, Kingston, 2000—02; choir dir., organist Gate of Heaven Ch., Dallas, 2000—02; counselor Jr. Mozart, Wilkes-Barre, Pa., 1976—2002. Recipient Padereski award, Nat. Coll. Musicians, Washington, 1997—2001. Mem.: NCTA, Music Educators Nat. Conf., Nat. Guild Piano Tchrs. Home: 3 Laselle Ave Shavertown PA 18708

MOTZ, DIANA GRIBBON, judge; b. Washington, July 15, 1943; d. Daniel McNamara and Jane (Retzler) Gribbon; m. John Frederick Motz, Sept. 20, 1968; children: Catherine Jane, Daniel Gribbon. BA, Vassar Coll., 1965; LLB, U. Va., 1968. Bar: U.S. Dist. Ct. Md. 1969, U.S. Ct. Appeals (4th cir.) 1969, U.S. Supreme Ct. 1980. Assoc. Piper & Marbury, Balt., 1968—71; asst. atty. gen. State of Md., Balt., 1972—81, chief of litigation, 1981—86; ptnr. Frank, Bernstein, Conaway & Goldman, Balt., 1986—91; judge Md. Ct. of Special Appeals, 1991—94, U.S. Ct. Appeals (4th Cir.), 1994—. Mem.: ABA, Fed. Cts. Study Com., Lawyers Round Table, Md. Bar Found., Am. Bar Found., Am. Law Inst., Balt. City Bar Assn. (exec. com. 1988), Md. Bar Assn., Wranglers Law Club. Roman Catholic. Office: 920 US Courthouse 101 W Lombard St Ste 920 Baltimore MD 21201-2611

MOTZER, ROBIN LYNNE, interior designer, writer, artist, poet, singer; d. Louis Charles and Carolyn Sue Motzer. BS in Home Econs. and Allied Sci.(hon.), Miami U., Oxford, Ohio, 1987. Licensed Massage Therapist Massage Therapy/Calif., 1999, Energy Systems Practitioner The Biogeometrical Energy Systems Inst./CA, 2001, cert. healing touch practitioner Healing Touch Internat., Colo., 1999. Interior designer/project coord. Anthem Blue Cross and Blue Shield, Cin., 1992—96; interior designer/artist/writer Sacred Arts, Tucson, 1996—, San Diego, 1996—. Interior designer/sales, Cin., 1988—91; custom furniture and accessories designer. Author: (children's books) A Mouse in the House, The Heartist; custom greeting cards. Scholar European Design scholar, Miami U. Sch. of Interior Design, 1987. Mem.: Internat. Interior Design Assn., ASID (assoc.). Avocations: dance, singing, hiking, snorkeling. Personal E-mail: sacredarts@highstream.net. E-mail: sacredarts@highstream.net.

MOUDON, ANNE VERNEZ, urban design educator; b. Yverdon, Vaud, Switzerland, Dec. 24, 1945; came to U.S., 1966; d. Ernest Edouard and Mauricette Lina (Duc) M.; m. Dimitrios Constantine Seferis, Dec. 30, 1982; children: Louisa Moudon, Constantine Thomas. BArch with honors, U. Calif., Berkeley, 1969; DSc, Ecole Poly. Fed., Lausanne, Switzerland, 1987. Fed. Register of Swiss Archs. Rsch. assoc. Bldg. Sys. Devel., Inc., San Francisco, 1969-70; sr. project planner J.C. Warnecke and Assocs., N.Y.C., 1973-74; archtl. cons. McCue, Boone & Tomsick, San Francisco, 1974-76; asst. to assoc. prof. architecture MIT, Cambridge, Mass., 1975-81, Ford internat. career chair, 1977-79; sec. Assn. Collegiate Schs. Arch., 1978-80; assoc. prof. urban design U. Wash., Seattle, 1981-87, prof. architecture, landscape architecture, urban design and planning, 1987—, dir. urban design program, 1987-93, assoc. dean acad. affairs Coll. Arch. and Urban Planning, 1992-95; dir. Cascadia Cmty. and Environ. Inst., Seattle, 1993-98. Lectr. architecture U. Calif., Berkeley, 1973-75; sr. rschr. Kungl Tekniska Hogskolan, Sch. Architecture, Stockholm, 1989; faculty assoc. Lincoln Inst. Land Policy, 1997—; mem. adv. com. Robert Wood Johnson Found., 2002—. Author: Built for Change, 1986; editor: Public Streets for Public Use, 1987, 91, (monograph) Master-Planned Communities, 1990, Urban Design: Reshaping Our Cities, 1995, Land Supply Monitoring with Geographic Information Systems, 2000; contbr. articles to profl. jours. Recipient Applied Rsch. award, Progressive Architecture, 1983; fellow Nat. Endowment for the Arts, 1986—87, Urban Land Inst., 1999—; grantee Nat. Endowment for the Arts, 1976—89, Wash. State Dept. Transp., 1991—2003, NIH, 1995—2000, CDC, 2001—. Fellow: Inst. for Urban Design. Avocations: walking, gardening, skiing. Home: 3310 E Laurelhurst Dr NE Seattle WA 98105-5336 Office: U Wash Box 355740 PO Box Jo-40 Goul Seattle WA 98195-5740

MOUL, MAXINE BURNETT, state official; b. Oakland, Nebr., Jan. 26, 1947; d. Einer and Eva (Jacobson) Burnett; m. Francis Moul, Apr. 20, 1972; 1 child, Jeff. BS in Journalism, U. Nebr., 1969; DHL (hon.), Peru State Coll., 1993. Sunday feature writer, photographer Sioux City Iowa Jour., 1969-71; reporter, photographer, editor Maverick Media, Inc., Syracuse, Nebr., 1971-73, editor, pub., 1974-83, pres., 1983-90; grant writer, asst. coord. Nebr. Regional Med. Program, Lincoln, 1973-74; lt. gov. State of Nebr., Lincoln, 1991-93; dir. Dept. Econ. Devel., Lincoln, 1993-99; pres. Nebr. Cmty. Found., 1999—. Mem. Dem. Nat. Com., Washington, 1988-92, Nebr. Dem. State Ctrl. Com., Lincoln, 1974-88; del. Dem. Nat. Conf., 1972, 88, 92; mem. exec. com. Nebr. Dem. Party, Lincoln, 1988-93. Recipient Margaret Sanger award Planned Parenthood, Lincoln, 1991, Champion of Small Bus. award Nebr. Bus. Devel. Ctr., Omaha, 1991, Toll fellowship Coun. State Govts., Lexington, Ky., 1992. Mem. Bus. and Profl. Womem, Nebr. Mgmt. Assn. (Silver Knight award 1992), Nat. Conf. Lt. Govs. (bd. dirs. 1991-93), Nebr. Press Women, Women Execs. in State Govt., Cmty. Devel. Soc., U. Nebr.-Lincoln Journalism Alumni. Democrat. Avocations: reading, gardening. Office: Nebr Cmty Found 317 S 12th St Lincoln NE 68508-2108

MOULD, JOAN POWELL, social worker; b. Ellwood City, Pa., Jan. 18, 1940; d. William Edward and Catherine Hope (Boggs) P.; m. William Charles Mould, June 9, 1967; children: Catherine, Helen, Mary. BA in Theater, Allegheny Coll., 1961; MSW, Cath. U. Am., 1996. Lic. social worker, D.C., Va. Intern U.S. Probation Office, Alexandria, Va., 1994-95, Alexandria Mental Health Ctr., 1995-96. Recipient various awards for vol. svc.

MOULES, DEBORAH ANN, not-for-profit developer; b. Milton, Mass., Nov. 11, 1955; m. Brandon Thomas Boyd, Sept. 7, 1987; 1 child, Sienna Nicole Boyd. BFA, U. Mass., 1980; MFA cum laude, SUNY, New Paltz, 1984. Instr. Middlesex C.C., Burlington, Mass., 1988, North Shore C.C., Beverly, Mass., 1989; art program coord. Inst. Family, Danvers, Mass., 1985-96; art expressive cons. Women's Crisis Ctr., Newburyport, Mass., 1995-97, Cape Ann Families, Gloucester, Mass., 1998; founder, exec. dir., pres. S.A.F.E. Studio, Ipswich, Mass., 1993—. Mem. workshop com. North Shore Clay Works, Ipswich, 1989—96; art cons. Merrimack Sch., Chelmsford, Mass., 1990—96. Exhibitions include Harvard U., 1992, Ipswich, 1995, Radclift, Mass., 1995. Mem. adv. bd. Montessori Sch., Topsfield, Mass., 1997—99; mem. Cultural Coun., Ipswich, 1992—98; mem. edn. com. Domestic Violence Roundtable, Ipswich, 1998—99. Grantee Oper., McCarthy Family Found., 1996—98, Forest Found., 1997—98, Dolphin Trust, 1997. Mem.: Ipswich Bus. Assn., Assn. Granmakers Mass. Avocations: reading, dance, performance art, walking. Office: SAFE Studio Inc 2 Essex Rd Ipswich MA 01938

MOULTON, GRACE CHARBONNET, physics educator; b. New Orleans, Nov. 1, 1923; d. Wilfred J. and Louise A. (Hellmers) Charbonnet; m. William Gates Moulton, June 1, 1947; children: Paul Charbonnet Moulton, Nancy Gates Moulton. BA, Tulane U., 1944; MS, U. Ill., 1948; PhD, U. Ala., 1962. Asst. prof. physics U. Ala., Tuscaloosa, mem. 1962-65; asst. prof. physics Fla. State U., Tallahassee, 1965-74, assoc. prof. physics, 1974-80, prof. physics, 1980-91, prof. emerita, 1991. Cons. State Bd. Regents, Fla., 1985-90, Fla. Univ. System, 1985, 90. Referee jour. articles Jour. Chem. Physics, Radiation Rsch.; contbr. many sci. rsch. articles to profl. jours. Four Yr. Undergrad. scholar Tulane U., scholar U. Ill.; rsch. grantee NIH. Mem. Am. Phys. Soc. (mem. coun. southeastern sect. 1988-92). Avocations: gardening, music (classical and folk), birding. Office: Fla State U Dept Physics Tallahassee FL 32306

MOULTON, JENNIFER T. city official, architect; BA cum laude, Colo. Coll., 1971; MArch with honors, U. Colo., Denver, 1978. Registered arch., Colo. Corp. legal asst. Davis, Graham & Stubbs, Denver, 1972-75; mem. staff Ctr. for Cmty. Devel. and Design, Denver, 1976-77; assoc. Barker Rinker Seacat & Ptnrs., Archs., Denver, 1978-84; v.p., owner Anthony Pellecchia Archs., P.C., Denver, 1984-89; pres. Hist. Denver, Inc., 1989-91; dir. Denver Planning and Devel. Office, 1992—. Mem. master plan com. Colo. Coll., Colorado Springs, 1994-95, juror Ctrl. States Regional Awards of Excellence, 1995; team mem. Mayor's Inst. for City Design, Harvard U., 1996, Design Workshop for Oklahoma City, Nat. Endowment for Arts, 1995; mem. dean's search com. Sch. Architecture and Planning, U. Colo., Denver, 1986, mem. dean's adv. com., 1986-89, vis. lectr., 1979-81; instr. corp. paralegal courses U. Denver Coll. Law, Arapahoe C.C., C.C. Denver, 1973-75; lectr. Jr. League Denver, 1987-88, Colo. Coll. Alumni Assn., 1985. Prin. works include Grant Humphries Mansion restoration, Denver, also offices for Colo. Coun. on Arts and Humanities in carriage house therein, Washington Park Pavilion restoration, Denver, Goss Residence, Boulder, Colo., Georgetown (Colo.) Downtown Redevel. Project, Georgetown Loop R.R. Master Plan, Malo Mansion project, Denver. Founder, pres. Women for Downtown Housing, 1980-81; co-chmn. urban design and land use task force comprehensive plan adv. com. City of Denver, 1986-87, mem. parks and recreation adv. com., 1983-89; atrustee, chmn. preservation com. Hist. Denver, Inc., 1986-89; mem. Citizens for Denver's Future, 1989; vice chmn. Colo. Passenger Tramway Safety Bd., 1981-89; mem. design competition jury Denver Pub. Libr., 1990-91; chmn. design rev. com. Ctrl. Denver Pub. Libr., 1992-94; trustee Colo. Hist. Found., 1990—; mem. South Platte River Commn., 1995— Recipient Disting. Svc. award U. Colo. Sch. Architecture and Planning, 1987, Louis T. Benezet award for outstanding profl. achievements Colo. Coll., 1991. Mem. AIA (chmn. design awards program Denver chpt. 1983, bd. dirs. 1977-87, treas. 1982, sec. 1983, 2d v.p. 1984, pres.-elect 1985, pres. 1986), Colo. Soc. Archs. (chmn. design awards program 1980-82). Office: Denver Planning & Devel Office 200 W 14th Ave Ofc Ste 203 Denver CO 80204-2732

MOULTON, KATHERINE KLAUBER, hotel executive; b. Buffalo, Nov. 28, 1956; d. Murray Joseph and Joanna (Brown) Klauber; m. Michael Arthur Moulton, July, 10, 1982. BS, Cornell U., 1978. Hotel and restaurant designer Cini-Grissom Assoc., Potomac, Md., 1978-82; pres., gen. mgr. Colony Beach & Tennis Resort, Longboat Key, Fla., 1982—; owner Le Tennique, Longboat Key, 1982—; exec. v.p., cons., designer Total Environments, Longboat Key, 1982—. Contbr. articles to restaurant and hotel design mags. Mem. Coquille, Sarasota, Fla., 1982; organizer, fund raiser St. Jude's Children's Rsch. Hosp., 1982; mem. found. bd. Girls Inc.; mem. Sarasota County Tourist Devel. Coun. Recipient Region IV Advocacy award Girls Inc., 1993, She Knows Where She's Going award, Girls Inc., 2003, Women in Bus. award, Tampa Bay Bus. Jour., 2003, named Ind. Hotelier of the World, Hotels Mag., 2001. Mem. Am. Hotel Motel Assn.(resort com.), Fla. Hotel and Motel Assn.(bd. dirs., chair elect), Cornell Soc. Hotelmen, Sarasota C. of C. (bd. dirs., vice chmn., chmn.), So. Innkeepers Assn. Avocations: golf, skiing, tennis, reading. Office: Colony Beach & Tennis Resort 1620 Gulf Of Mexico Dr Longboat Key FL 34228-3403

MOULTON, SARA, chef, magazine editor; married; 2 children. Grad., U. Mich., 1974, Culinary Inst. Am., 1977; postgrad. stagaire with a master chef, Chartres, France, 1979. With Julia Child and More Co., 1979; mem. test kitchen Gourmet mag., 1984—88, exec. chef, 1988—; host Sara's Secrets, Food Network, Cooking Live, Food Network; exec. chef Good Morning Am., food corr., 1997, food editor; sous chef La Tulipe, NY; co-founder NY Women's Culinary Alliance; instr. Peter Kump's NY Cooking Sch. Author: Sara Moulton Cooks at Home, 2002; co-author (with Jean Anderson): Good Morning America Cut the Calories Cookbook, 2000. Office: Sara Moulton Enterprises Inc 130 W 24th St 3B New York NY 10011 Business E-Mail: sara@saramoulton.com.*

MOUNCE, CAROLYN P. school librarian; b. Ecru, Miss., Dec. 18, 1938; d. Walter Gerald and Mary Ozelle Mounce. BA, Blue Mountain Coll., 1960; MA in Libr. Sci., George Peabody Coll., 1963. Asst. libr. Guyton Libr. Blue Mountain (Miss.) Coll., 1960—70, head libr., 1971—. Libr. sci. instr. Blue Mountain Coll., 1967—87. Mem.: AAUW (officer, Branch Woman Achievement award 1990), Miss. Libr. Assn., Blue Mountain Coll. Alumnae Assn. (officer), Woodmen of World Lodge. Democrat. Baptist. Avocation: sports. Home: 785 North Rd Ecru MS 38841 Office: Guyton Libr Blue Mountain Coll PMB 173 Box 160 Blue Mountain MS 38610-0160 Office Phone: 662-685-4771 147.

MOUNT, WILLIE LANDRY, state legislator; b. Lake Charles, La., Aug. 25, 1949; d. Lee Robert and Willie Veatrice (McCullor) Landry; m. Benjamin Wakefield Mount, Aug. 19, 1976. BS, McNeese State U., 1971. Geophys. asst. La. Land and Exploration, Lake Charles, La., 1971-76; pharm. rep. Lederle, Lake Charles, 1976-80; realtor Mary Kay Hopkins, Lake Charles, 1976-87; co-owner Paper Place, Lake Charles, 1991-95; mayor City of Lake Charles, 1993—2000; mem. La. State Senate, 2000—, mem. select com. on consumer protection, mem. jud. C, health and welfare, legis. audit adv. commn., mem. state tech. adv. commn., joint juvenile justice commn., millennium port com., sch. fin. rev. commn., mem. edn. com., vice chair joint legis. com. on capital outlay, chmn. revenue and fiscal affairs com. Gov. Violent Crime & Homicide Task Force, Baton Rouge, 1993—95; mem. steering com. La. conf. Mayors bd. pres. La. Asset Mgmt. Pool Bd., 1997. Guest condr. Lake Charles Symphony, 1992; active La. Mcpl. Assn., Baton Rouge, 1995-98; pres. Jr. League of Lake Charles; mem. state interagy. coordinating coun. Dyslexia Study Com.; mem. adv. bd. S.W. La. Literacy Coalition; mem. adv. coun. Pet Overpopulation; active First United Meth. Ch., La. Meth. Conf., McNeese State U. Found., Prevent Child Abuse bd. Micro-Enterprise Devel. Alliance of La. Bd., United Way, Children's Miracle Network; exec. com. Coun. for a Better La. Recipient Spiritual Aims award Kiwanis Club, 1991, Cmty. Svc. award, 1995, Citizen of Yr. 1996-97, Dorthea Combre award NAACP, 1994, Patron Architecture, 2000; named Woman of Yr., Quota Club, 1991, Citizen of Yr., Women's com. S.W. La., 1992, Woman of Yr., Pub. Ofcl. of Yr. Msgr. Cramers KC, Pub. Ofcl. of Yr., NASW, 1997, La. Mcpl. Assn. Cmty. Achievement award, 1995-97, Disting. Citizen award Boy Scouts Am., 1999; Disting. Alumni award McNeese State U., 2000, Golden Apple award Delta Kappa Gamma, 2002, Spl. Friend of La. Mcpl. Assn. award, 2003, Disting. Svc. award La. Restaurant Assn., 2002. Mem. LWV, S.W. La. Mayor's Assn. (chmn. 1993-94). Home: 205 Shell Beach Dr Lake Charles LA 70601-5933 Office: PO Box 3004 Lake Charles LA 70602-3004 E-mail: lasen27@legis.state.la.us.

MOUNTJOY, HELEN W. educational association administrator; married; 3 children. Grad., Vanderbilt U. Mem. Ky. State Bd. Edn., 1991—, chairperson, 1998—. Mem. Ky. Literacy Partnership; mem. edn. adv. com. Coun. State Govts.; mem. Owensboro adv. bd. BB&T Bank. Chairwoman Daviess County Sch. Bd.; chair Owensboro Mercy Health Sys. Bd. Trustees. Leadership Owensboro Bd. Recipient Disting. Svc. award, Nat. Assn. State Bds. Edn., 2002. Mem.: Owensboro C. of C. (mem. edn. com., mem. citizens com. on edn.). Address: 449 Browns Valley Rd Utica KY 42376

MOUSSATOS, MARTHA ANN TYREE, librarian; b. Parris Island, S.C., Sept. 18, 1936; d. Frank La Prade and Vireen Florrie (Varn) Tyree; m. Apostolos Harilaos Moussatos, June 27, 1959; children— Vasiliana Vireen, Harilaos Apostolos. B.A., Columbia Coll., 1958; M.L.S., U. Ariz., 1974. Asst. reference librarian U. S.C., Columbia, 1958-59; librarian Fulton High Sch., Atlanta, 1962; substitute tchr. pub. schs., Sierra Vista, Ariz., 1967-68; librarian Naco Elem. Sch. (Ariz.), 1968-70, Benson High Sch. (Ariz.), 1970-75; head librarian Depot Library, Parris Island, S.C., 1975—99. Author: Young Eliza (play), 1958; Hagar (play), 1980; Marshgrass and Muscadines (poetry), 1980; Scuppernong Wine at Room Temperature (poetry), 1984, (cookbook) The Sandlappers' Salvation Cookbook, 1988; editor: No More Blues Now (poetry), 1990; editor, contbr.: Port Royal Sound (poetry), 1995; contbr. articles to profl. jours. and popular mags. Mem. Historic Port Royal Found. (S.C.), 1976—, bd. dirs., 1981—; active Carteret St. United Meth. Ch. Recipient award as head of outstanding single parent family Beaufort County Homebuilders Assn. (S.C.), 1980. Mem. ALA, Library Assn. Beaufort County, S.C. Library Assn. (editorial com. 1979—), Poetry Soc. S.C. (bd. dirs. 1980-83), Beaufort Writers, Parris Island Poets (founder), Grey Blades, Lydia McAfee Cir. Home: 3011 Hickory St Beaufort SC 29906-6831

MOUTTET, JANE ELIZABETH, librarian; b. Grand Rapids, Mich., Mar. 23, 1961; d. Roger Willis and Celia Driesens; m. David Frederick Mouttet, June 4, 1988; 3 children. BA, Calvin Coll., 1983. Cert. elem. tchr. ACSI. Tchr., libr. Hilltop Christian Sch., Window Rock, Ariz., 1983—. Contbr. column to Christian Libr. Jour., 2002. Mem.: ALA, Soc. Children's Book Writers and Illustrators, Nat. Coun. Tchrs. English, Taa Dine Libr. Assn., N.Mex. Libr. Assn. Office: Hilltop Christian School 02A Deerfield Gallup NM 87301 Mailing: PO Box 9090 Window Rock AZ 86515 E-mail: jane@mouttetfamily.com.

MOWATT, E. ANN, women's voluntary leader, lawyer; BA in History, Dalhousie U., Halifax, Nova Scotia, 1982, LLB, 1985. Barrister, solicitor Patterson Palmer, 1986—2001; small claims adjudicator Patterson Palmer Hunt Murphy, 1999-2001; dir. gen. survivors and high performance Income Security br. Human Resources Devel. Can., 2001—. Bd. dirs. YMCA-YWCA of Saint John N.B., Can., 1987-93; also mem. exec., fin., social action, and camp coms., pres., 1991; bd. dirs. YWCA of Can., 1989-98, chair constn. task force, mem.-at-large, treas., v.p., pres., 1995-97, past pres., 1997-98; bd. dirs. Coalition of Nat. Vol. Orgns., 1994-2001, chair; pres. Saint John chpt. Multiple Sclerosis Soc. Con., 1987-88, bd. dirs. Atlantic divsn., 1988-97, mem. nat. bd. dirs., 1992-95, 97-2001, pres. Atlantic divsn., 1993-95. Mem. Can. Bar Assn. (mem. N.B. coun. 1986-89), Law Soc. N.B. (mem. legal aid com. 1989-92), Eclectic Reading Club Avocations: reading, films, camping, canoeing, theatre. Home: 114 Orange St Saint John NB Canada E2L 1M4 also: Apt 1416 160 Chapel St Ottawa ON Canada K1N 8P5 E-mail: ann.mowatt@hrdc-drhc.gc.ca.

MOWERY, ANNA RENSHAW, state legislator; b. Decatur, Tex., Jan. 4, 1931; d. Lafayette William and Early Virginia (Bobo) Renshaw; m. Wesley Harold Mowery, June 2, 1951; children: Jeanette Mowery Hefferman, Mark William, Timothy Dean, Marianne Mowery Fichera. BA, Baylor U., 1951; MA, Ctrl. State U, 1967. Tchr. Ft. Hood (Tex.) Pub. Schs., 1951-52; petroleum landman Ft. Worth, 1979-82; dist. dir. U.S. Congl. Dist. 6 Joe Barton, Ft. Worth, 1985-86; polit. cons., pres. Trinity Assocs., Ft. Worth, 1987-88; state rep. Tex. House Reps., Ft. Worth, 1988—. Chmn. Tarrant County (Tex.) Rep. Party, 1975-77; mem. Tex. Rep. Exec. Com., Ft. Worth, 1980-84, Greater Ft. Worth Literacy Coun., 1990—; mem. adv. bd. Sr. Citizen Svcs./Tarrant County, Ft. Worth, 1988—. Recipient 4-H Clubs Am. Alumni award, 1990; nominee Newsmaker of Yr., Ft. Worth Press Club, 1974, 76. Mem. Tex. Women's Alliance, Women's Policy Forum. Republican. Baptist. Home: 4108 Hildring Dr W Fort Worth TX 76109-4722 Office: 6421 Camp Bowie Blvd Fort Worth TX 76116-5401 also: Tex House of Reps State Capitol Austin TX 78768-2910

MOWRER-REYNOLDS, ELIZABETH LOUISE, educational psychology educator; b. Camden, N.J., Jan. 5, 1955; d. Philip Aubrey and Louise Jamison (Koykka) M.; 1 child, Cali Jo., m. James O. Reynolds. BA, Trenton State U., 1977; MEd, Rutgers U., 1982, EdD, 1990. Rschr. assit. for dyslexia reading grant Rutgers U., New Brunswick, NJ, 1979-84; co-adj. prof. Rutgers Univ., New Brunswick, 1989—90; assoc. prof. U. Idaho, 1990—. Faculty in residence housemother for farmhouse Fraternity, Univ. of Idaho; progam coord. Univ. of Idaho Gifted & Talented. Author: (book) Study Guide for Good and Brophy, 1995, Contemporary Educational Psychology;Study Guides for Woolfolk, 1998, 2001; contbr. articles prof. jour. Recipient Evelyn Headley Award, Rutgers Univ., 1991, Coll. of End. tchg., public service, and advising award, Univ. of Idaho, 1993, Pi Beta Tchg. Excellance Award, 1995, Faculty Tchg. Excellance Award, Univ. of Idaho, 1994, 1995, 2001. Mem. Phi Delta Kappa (rsch. coord. 1991—, chmn. 1991—), Psi Chi, Am. edn. rsch. assoc., 1991—,Northwest Assoc. of Tchr. Educators, 1991—, (state rep., 1992), Am. Assoc. of Univ. Women, 1993, Acad. of Science, 1994—. Lutheran. Avocations: horseback riding, backpacking, camping, fishing, hunting.

MOY, AUDREY, retired retail buyer; b. Bronx, N.Y., May 6, 1942; d. Ferdinand Walter Melkert and Stella (Factorow) Schroff; m. Edward Moy, Aug. 16, 1974. BA in Biology, Hunter Coll., 1964, MA in Biology, 1966. Asst. buyer Bonwit Teller, N.Y.C., 1961-68; dept. mgr. Franklin Simon, N.Y.C., 1968; asst. buyer Saks Fifth Ave, N.Y.C., 1968-73; buyer Martins, Bklyn., 1973, Belk Store Svcs, N.Y.C., 1974-97. Mem.: AAUW. Avocations: cooking, antique collecting, gardening.

MOYA, ELIZABETH, language educator; b. El Paso, Tex., Nov. 8, 1970; d. Arnoldo Rojero and Ofelia Garcia; m. Arturo Moya, Apr. 15, 1998; children: Alexis, Lauren Brooke. BA in Psychology, U. Tex., El Paso, 1995. Asst. mgr. Payless-May Corp., El Paso, Tex., 1991—93; asset protection supr. Sears, Roebuck and Co., El Paso, Tex., 1993—99; sub. tchr. Ysleta Ind. Sch. Dist., El Paso, Tex., 1994—99; security officer Simon Mgmt. Co., El Paso, Tex., 1995—96; ABE/ESL instr. Ysleta Ind. Sch. Dist., El Paso, Tex., 1999—. Presenter in field. Blood dr. coord. United Blood Svcs., El Paso, Tex., 2000—03. Recipient Power of One award, United Blood Svcs., 2001—02, Achievement award, 2002—03, Cert. of Appreciation, Senator Eliot Shapleigh, Tex., 2002. Avocations: exercising, camping, learning about new cultures, flute, vacationing with family. Office: Ysleta Cmty Learning Ctr 121 Padres El Paso TX 79907

MOYARS-JOHNSON, MARY ANNIS, university official; b. Lafayette, Ind., July 19, 1938; d. Edward Raymond and Veronica Marie (Quigg) Moyars; m. Raymond Leon Molter, Aug. 1, 1959 (div. 1970); children: Marilyn Eileen Molter Davis, William Raymond Molter Johnson, Ann Marie Molter Guentert; m. Thomas Elmer Johnson, May 25, 1973 (div. 1989); children: Thomas Edward, John Alan, Barbara Suzanne. BS, Purdue U., 1960; MA, Purdue U., West Lafayette, Ind., 1991, postgrad., 1985—. Grader great issues Purdue U., West Lafayette, 1960-63, writer edni. films, 1962-65, publicity dir. convocations and lectures, 1969-74, devel. officer Sch. Humanities, 1979-88, asst. to dir. Optoelectronics Rsch. Ctr., 1989-90, mgr. indsl. rels. Sch. Elec. and Computer Engring., 1990—2002, assoc. v.p. for info. tech., for comm., 2002—; tchr. English and math. Benton Community Schs., Fowler, Ind., 1966-69; pub. rels. dir. Sycamore Girl Scout Coun., Lafayette, Ind., 1974-78; dir. pub. info. Ind. Senate, Majority Caucus, Indpls., 1977-78; sr. script writer Walters & Steinberg, Lafayette, 1988-89. Author: Colonial Potpourri, 1975, Ouiatanon--The French Post Among the Ouia, 2000; co-author: Historic Colonial French Dress, 1982, 2nd edit., 1998; contbr. articles to profl. jours. Bd. govs. Tippecanoe County Hist. Assn., Lafayette, 1981-97. Mem. Women in Comms., Inc. (v.p. program, Pres. award 1983), Ctr. for French Colonial Rsch. (dir. 1986-89, editor 1988-89), Palatines to Am., Ind. History Assn., Ind. Hist. Soc., French Colonial Hist. Soc. Roman Catholic. Avocations: history, genealogy, embroidery. Home: 924 Elm Dr West Lafayette IN 47906-2246 Office: Purdue Info Tech Young Hall West Lafayette IN 47906-3560 E-mail: mamoyars@indy.net.

MOYER, LINDA LEE, artist, educator, author; b. Niles, Mich, Feb. 11, 1942; d. Roy Delbert and Estelle Leona (Beaty) Moyer; m. Brock David Williams Dec. 3, 1994; 1 child from previous marriage, Metin Ata Gunsay. Student, Occidental Coll., 1959-61; BA, UCLA, 1964; MA, Calif. State U., Long Beach, 1977, MFA, 1980. Cert. tchr. secondary edn., cert. computer graphics, Calif. Instr. art. Huntington Beach Union HS, Calif., 1967-81, Calif. State U., Long Beach, 1981-85, Saddleback Coll., Mission Viejo, Calif., 1986-88, Fullerton Coll., Calif., 1990, 94, Goldenwest Coll., Huntington Beach, 1990. Artist-in-residence St. Margaret's Episc. Sch., San Juan Capistrano, 1993; lectr., workshop presenter Santa Barbara C.C., Calif., 1992; series lectr. Rancho Santiago Coll., 1985, 90; lectr. Cypress Coll., 1986, Watercolor West, 1987, others; methods and materials show instr. Am. Artist Mag., 1996, 97, 98, 99, 99, 2000, 01, 03; juror fine art exhbns; presenter workshops in field; website co-founder watercolor-online.com. Exhibited in group shows at Owensboro, Mus. Fine Arts, Ky., 1979, Newport Harbor Art Mus., Newport Beach, Calif., 1981, Burpee Art Mus., Rockford, Ill., 1981, one-woman shows include Orange County Ctr. Contemporary Art, 1982, 1985, exhibited in group shows at Nat. Acad. Galleries, NYC, 1982, one-woman shows include Laguna Beach Mus. Art, Calif., 1982, Orlando Gallery, Sherman Oaks, Calif., 1983, exhibited in group shows at Leslie Levy Gallery, Scottsdale, Ariz., 1983, Art Inst. So. Calif., 1984, one-woman shows include Orange County Ctr. Contemporary Art, 1985, Cerritos Coll., Norwalk, Calif., 1986, Louis Newman Galleries, Beverly Hills, 1986, exhibited in group shows at Saddleback Coll., Mission Viejo, Calif., 1988, one-woman shows include Louis Newman Galleries, Beverly Hills, 1988, exhibited in group shows at Ch. of Jesus Christ of LDS Mus. Art and History, Salt Lake City, 1988, Riverside (Calif.) Art Mus., 1989, one-woman shows include Louis Newman Galleries, Beverly Hills, 1990, exhibited in group shows at Ch. of Jesus Christ of LDS Mus. Art and History, Salt Lake City, 1991, one-woman shows include Westmont Coll., Santa Barbara, 1992, Maturango Mus., Ridgecrest, Calif., 1996, exhibited in group shows at Mt. San Antonio Coll., Calif., 1996, Springville Art Mus., Utah, 1999, Kimball Art Ctr., Park City, Utah, 2003, others, Represented in permanent collections Springville Mus. Art, Home Savs. Bank of Am., Nat. Bank of La Jolla, Greenburg Deposit Bank, Ashland, Ky., INMA Gallery, Saudi Arabia, exhibited in group shows at Springville Art Mus., Utah, 2000, Represented in permanent collections pvt. collectors; author: Light Up Your Watercolors Layer by Layer, 2003. Recipient Gold Medal of Honor, Am. Watercolor Soc., 1982, Walser S. Greathouse medal, 1988, Gold Medal of Honor for Watercolor Allied Artists Am., 1982, cash merit award Ch. of Jesus Christ Latter Day Saints Mus. Art and History, 1991, Best of Show award Utah Watercolor Soc., 2000, 2d award, Religious and Spiritual Art of Utah Exhbn., 2d award, 1998, 3d award, 1999, Best of Show, Challenge of Champions, Watercolor Art Soc. Houston, 2003. Signature mem. Nat. Watercolor Soc., Watercolor West (1st award 1984, N.W.S. award 1999, pres. 1999-2001), Watercolor West (life), Utah Watercolor Soc. Mem. Lds Ch. Avocations: reading, playing piano, genealogy. Home and Office: 22 Lakeview Stansbury Park UT 84074 E-mail: lindamoyer@watercolor-online.com.

MOYER, LOUISE EILEEN, lawyer; b. Reading, Pa., Feb. 22, 1967; d. Carson E. and Lillian R. (Dornmoyer) S.; m. Brian Keith Moyer, Sept. 30, 1995. BS summa cum laude, Drexel U., 1989; JD magna cum laude, Villanova U., 1992. Bar: Pa. 1992, U.S. Ct. Appeals (3rd cir.) 1994. Jud. law clk. U.S. Ct. Appeals for the Third Cir., Phila., 1992-94; assoc. Dechert LLP, Phila., 1994—. Mem. ABA, Pa. Bar Assn., Order of the Coif. Home: 23 Kurt Dr Mertztown PA 19539-9122 Office: Dechert LLP 4000 Bell Atlantic Tower 1717 Arch St Philadelphia PA 19103-2713

MOYER KLEMETSRUD, KANDACE MARIE, artist; b. Denver, Sept. 6, 1962; d. David Douglas and Evelyn Mavis Farr; m. Michael Earl Klemetsrud, 1990; m. Ron E. Moyer, 1980 (div. 1988). Artist Moyer Studio, N.D., Wash., 1987—. Artist N.D. Coun. of Arts, Bismarck, 1998—; trainer Child Care Resource and Referral, ND, 2000—02. Numerous grants, N.D. Coun. of Arts, 1998—. Mem.: Nat. Mus. Women in Arts. Methodist. Avocations: collecting primitive musical instruments, horseback riding, reading. Home and Office: Moyer Studio 512 Country Club Dr Devils Lake ND 58301

MOYERS, JUDITH DAVIDSON, television producer; b. Dallas, May 12, 1935; d. Henry Joseph and Eula E. (Dendy) Davidson; m. Bill D. Moyers; children: William Cope, Suzanne, John. BS, U. Tex., 1956; LittD (hon.), L.I. U., 1989, SUNY, 1990. Pres., exec. prodr. Pub. Affairs TV, N.Y.C., 1987—; exec. editor NOW, 2001—. Exec. prodr. TV documentaries (Emmy 1980, 93, 98, 2001, DuPont 1999, Christopher 1990, Parker 1992, Gold Hugo 1991, Humanitas prize 1995); exec. editor Now with Bill Moyers, 2001-; contbr. articles to profl. jours., newspapers, mags. Trustee SUNY, 1976-90; commr. U.S. Commn. UNESCO, Washington, 1977-80, White House commn. Internat. Yr. of Child, Washington, 1978-80; mem. jud. selection com. State N.Y., 1992-93; dir. Pub. Agenda Found. Recipient Christopher award, 2004. Mem. Acad. TV Arts and Scis., Century Club. Mem. Congregational Ch. Office: Pub Affairs TV Inc 450 W 33rd St Fl 7 New York NY 10001-2603

MOYERS, KELLI R. psychotherapist; b. Knoxville, Tenn., Sept. 8, 1961; d. Rayburn Neal and Vonnie Rae (Corley) M. BS in Edn., No. Tex. State U., 1988; MS in Edn., U. No. Tex., 1992. Lic. profl. counselor, Tex. Edn. cons. Adolescent Resource Corp., Kansas City, Mo., 1990-92; group home dir. Crittenton Ctr., Kansas City, Mo., 1992-94; adj. faculty Park Coll., Kansas City, Mo., 1994; program dir. STOP: Teen Outpatient Svc., Kansas City, 1994-96; supr. crisis ctr. Denton Co. MHMR, Denton, Tex., 1996-97; intake therapist Charter Hosp., Grapevine, Tex., 1997-98; psychotherapist pvt. practice, Grapevine, 1998—. Cons. and training, Devel. Sys., K.C., Mo., 1995-96. Vol. Kaufman Found., K.C., 1995-96; coord. Teen Pregnancy Coun., K.C., Mo., 1991-92. Recipient Outstanding Licensing Rep. award, State Tex. Dept. Human Resources, 1989. Mem. Tex. Counseling Assn. Democrat. Avocations: running, bicycling, home improvement.

MOYERS, SYLVIA DEAN, retired medical librarian; b. Independence, W.Va., Oct. 22, 1936; d. Wilkie Russell and Ina Laura (Watkins) Collins; m. Paul Franklin Moyers, June 29, 1957; children: Tammy Jeanne, Thomas Paul, Tara Sue. Student, Am. Med. Record Assn., 1977—79. Sec. Teets Lumber Co., Terra Alta, W.Va., 1954-58, Preston County News, Terra Alta, 1958-60; med. record clk. med. record dept. Hopemont (W.Va.) Hosp., 1960-75, dir., 1975-88; sec. The Terra Alta Bank, 1990-95; ret., 1995. Charter mem., past mother advisor Terra Alta Assembly No. 26, Order of Rainbow for Girls, past grand editor Mountain Echoes; vol. Preston Meml. Hosp., ARC, Salvation Army, Am. Cancer Soc., Boy Scouts Am., Muscular Dystrophy Assn.; active Kingwood Fire Dept. Aux. Mem.: Preston Meml. Hosp. Aux., Kingwood Civic Club. Republican. Methodist. Home: 120 Miller Rd Kingwood WV 26537-1321

MOYSEY, CAROL ANNE, investigator; b. Clifton Springs, N.Y., Jan. 29, 1940; d. John William Howard and Wilhelmina Wedman-Hildebrandt; adopted d. Charles Irving Sprong and Esther Florence Deweaver-Sprong; m. Robert Tellier, May 17, 1957 (deceased); 1 child, Michael Cloonan; m. Charles Karian, Feb. 7, 1958 (div. Oct. 1969); children: Terry Karian, Cathy Karian; m. Stanley P. Moysey, Nov. 1, 1969; children: Tom, Paul. BA in Bus. Law, Rochester (N.Y.) Bus. Inst., 1959. Birth family investigator Adoption and Birth Families of Am., N.Y., 1974—. Author: Me: An Adoption Story - Putting It All Together, 1989, Me - Book II, 1990, Wedman & Borau, 1990, Moysey-Hill, 1990, Me - An Adoption - Biological Genealogy Story, 1994, The Search is Over, 1995. Roman Catholic. Avocations: drawing, writing. Home and Office: 29 Carol Dr Poughkeepsie NY 12603-2603

MOZOSKI, DIANE MARIE, information technology executive; b. Paterson, N.J., Oct. 23, 1950; d. Joseph Thomas and Mary Winifred Barrett, Jenny Lou Barrett (Stepmother); m. Paul Anthony Mozoski Jr., June 7, 1970; children: Paul Anthony III, Christine Marie. AS in Computer Tech., Greenville (S.C.) Tech. Coll., 1991; BA in Computer Sci. and Bus., Furman U., 1993. CIO Dispoz-o Products, Inc., Fountain Inn, SC, 1993—. Fundraiser YMCA, Simpsonville, SC, 1988; fundraiser for local libr. Cmty. Civic Ctr., Fountain Inn, 2000; liaison officer Dispoz-o Products, Inc., 2000—03. Named Top Vocalist, Dreams Unlimited, 2002; recipient Mrs. Fountain Inn Internat. 2000, Mrs. SC. Internat., 2001—02; scholar, Nat. Leonardo DaVinci Soc., 1968. Roman Catholic. Avocations: singing, art, cooking, piano, lyric writing. Office: Dispoz-o Products Inc PO Box 766 Fountain Inn SC 29644

MTEGHA, DOROTHY MERCY, education educator; b. Africa, Mar. 8, 1950; arrived in U.S., 2001; d. Henry S. Chipeta and Ruth Nkhata; m. Hudson Dika Mtegha, Sept. 5, 1974; children: Lindizga, Chigomezgo, James. Diploma in edn., U. Malawi, 1974, EdB, 1982; M in Edn. Mgmt., Flinders U. South Australia, 1991. Cert. grad. tchr. Ministry Edn. Malawi. Secondary sch. tchr. Ministry Edn., Malawi, 1974—82, planning and adminstr., 1982—86; nat. tng. officer adult literacy Ministry Cmty. Svcs., Malawi, 1986—90; dep. prin. Marymount Girls Secondary Sch., Malawi, 1993—96; mng. dir. Newlands Edn Ctr., Malawi, 1996—97; lectr. Mzuzu U., Malawi, 1997—. Mem. univ. coun. U. Malawi, 1994—95; mem. Nat. Commn. on Gender and Devel. Malawi Govt., 1997—2001. Mem.: Assn. for the Study Higher Edn. Address: P179 Cardinal Ct Normal IL 61761-1584

MUCCI, LOUISE CATHERINE, family practice nurse practitioner, health care negotiator; b. Cornwall, N.Y., Nov. 15, 1951; d. James Eugene and Avis Ward Mucci; m. Richard Joseph Wilson (div. Sept. 6, 1989); children: Angela Christine Swink, James Eugene Wilson, Richard Wilson, Thomas William Wilson, Catherine Louise Borah. M in Pub. Svc., New Sch. Social Rsch., N.Y.C., 1989; MSN, Russell Sage, Troy, N.Y., 1999. Lic. family nurse practitioner, N.Y. Clin. nurse mgr. St. Luke's Cornwall Hosp., Newburgh, NY, 1979—; family nurse practitioner OMNI, Newburgh, 2001—. Democrat. Roman Catholic. Avocation: travel. Home: 515 Riley Rd New Windsor NY 12553 Office: St Luke's Cornwall Hosp 70 Dubois St Newburgh NY 12550 Personal E-mail: lmucci@slhospital.org. E-mail: lmucci@slh-tch.org.

MUEHL, LOIS BAKER, writer, retired language educator; b. Oak Park, Ill., Apr. 29, 1920; d. Arthur Franklin and Mary Hull Baker; m. Siegmar Muehl, Apr. 15, 1944; children: Erika, Sigrid, Torsten, Brian. BA in English, Oberlin Coll., 1941; MA in English Edn., U. Iowa, 1966. English tchr., drama coach Upper Sandusky (Ohio) H.S., 1941—42; TV sta. camera operator, actress W9XBK, Chgo., 1942—43; news anchor WIS Radio Sta., Columbia, SC, 1944, freelance writer, 1959—; dir. reading lab., assoc. prof. rhetoric U. Iowa, Iowa City, 1964—66, 1968—85; reading specialist Johnson C. Smith U., Charlotte, NC, 1966—68; English tchr. Hehei U., Nanjing, China, 1987—88. Tchr. creative writing, adult edn. Iowa City Pub. Schs., 1961—63; tchr. ESL adult edn. Merced (Calif.) Pub. Schs., 1984, 86, Kyungnam U., Masan, Republic of Korea, 1985. Author: My Name is _____, 1959 (Jr. Lit. Guild choice), Worst Room in the School, 1961 (N.Y. Times 100 Best List, 1961), The Hidden Year of Devlin Bates, 1967, Winter Holiday Brainteasers, 1979, A Reading Approach to Rhetoric, 1983, Talkable Tales, 1993; co-author: Trading Cultures in the Classroom, 1993; contbr. poetry to: New Adventures of Mother Goose, 1993, Golf, It's Just a Game, 1996, : Phonics Through Poetry, 1998; contbr. also numerous jours., mags. Vol. tchr. writing Sr. Ctr., Iowa City, 1991—93; co-founder, sustainer wild flower pk. Neighborhood Assn., Iowa City, 1998—2003; vol. tchr. refugee camps Internat. Rescue Com., Thailand, 1980, 1982. Recipient Cmty. Svc. commendation, Merced County, Calif., 1984, award, Lucidity, Midwest Poetry Rev., Grand prize, The Poetry Guild, 1997; fellow Old Gold Creative fellowship, U. Iowa, 1980. Mem.: Univ. Club Writers' Group, Iowa Poetry Assn. (area rep. 1990—, poetry prize), Nat. League Am. PEN Women (treas. 1990—2003, prizes for poetry and craft work), Phi Beta Kappa. Avocations: folk art, gardening, swimming, beachcombing, yoga.

MUEHLMEIER, RUTH EWART, painter, sculptor, art historian; b. Milwaukee, Wis., Oct. 13, 1925; d. William Gladstone Ewart and Maybel Elizabeth Anderson-Abrahamson; m. Peyton Albert Muehlmeier, Jan. 24, 1951; children: Christine Lou, Pamela Jean, Peyton Scot, Daniel Style. BFA, U. Chgo., 1948. Lectr. Milw. Art Ctr., 1958—67; art hist. U. of Wis., 1963—65; maj. founder and art hist. Inst. of Art and Design (formerly Milw. Sch. of the Arts), 1975—81. Designer Karl Brocker Assoc., 1949—50; textile designer, NYC, 1949—50; own gusiness design contract Comml. Interiors, 1975—85. Represented in permanent collections Milw. Art Ctr., private collections. Mem.: Wis. Painters and Sculptors (pres. 1966—67, 1970—72). Home: 2919 N Mill Rd Oconomowoc WI 53066

MUEHLNER, SUANNE WILSON, library director; b. Rochester, Minn., June 29, 1943; d. George T. and Rhoda (Westin) Wilson. Student Smith Coll., 1961-63; A.B., U. Calif.-Berkeley, 1965; M.L.S., Simmons Coll., 1968; M.B.A., Northeastern U., Boston, 1979. Librarian, Technische Univ. Berlin, Germany, 1970-71; earth and planetary scis. librarian MIT Libraries, Cambridge, 1968-70, 1971-73; personnel librarian, 1973-74, asst. dir. personnel services, 1974-76, asst. dir. pub. services, 1976-81; dir. libraries Colby Coll., Waterville, Maine, 1981—. Mem. ALA, New Eng. Assn. Coll. and Research Librarians (sec.-treas. 1983-85, pres. 1986-87), Maine Libr. Assn. (chmn. intellectual freedom com. 1984-88, OCLC Users Coun., 1988-95), Nelinet (bd. dirs. 1985-91, chair 1989-91). Office: Colby Coll Miller Libr Waterville ME 04901

MUELLER, ALICIA KAY, music educator; d. Howard Kenneth and Patricia Anne Brahmstedt; m. Kurt Patrick Mueller, May 20, 1989; children: Nicole Marie, Brenden Patrick. BS, Tenn. Technol. U., 1983; MS, U. Ill., 1984; EdD, Ariz. State U., 1993. Tchr. elem. music Prince William County Pub. Schools, Manassas, Va., 1984—87, Fairfax County Pub. Schools, 1987—89; assoc. prof. music Wash. State U., Pullman, 1993—2000, Towson U., Md., 2000—. Home: 918 Adana Rd Pikesville MD 21208 Office: Towson U Dept Music 8000 York Rd Towson MD 21252-0001

MUELLER, ANNE, legislator; b. Atlanta, Oct. 5, 1929; d. Howard Raymond O'Quin and Bessie Kate (Bell) Brace; m. Hans Kurt Mueller, June 22, 1953; children: Yvonne Marie Key, Heidi Spivey, Mark Jennings. BS in Zoology, U. Ga., 1951. Registered med. technologist. Med. technologist Grady Hosp., Atlanta, 1953—, St. Joseph Hosp., Atlanta, 1957, Meml. Hosp., Waycross, Ga., 1958-59; legislator Ga. Ho. of Reps., 1983—. Mem. Savannah (Ga.) area Rep. Women, sec., 1980-81, v.p., 1981-82, Ga. Fedn. of Rep. Women, Savannah, dist. dir., 1986—. Republican. Baptist. Home: 13013 Hermitage Rd Savannah GA 31419-2840 Office: GA House of Reps State Capitol Atlanta GA 30334-9003

MUELLER, BARBARA STEWART (BOBBIE MUELLER), youth drug use prevention specialist, volunteer; b. Weslaco, Tex., Oct. 5, 1934; d. Roy Wesley Stewart and Marjorie Eleanor (Crossley) Willis; m. Charles Paul Mueller, Sept. 5, 1957 (div. 1985); children: Kathryn Anne Bencomo, John Stewart. BA, U. Tex., 1957. Owner Kid Puppets and Co., San Antonio. Cons. Parent Music Resource Ctr., Washington, 1986; drug edn. prevention chmn. U.S. Attys. Office, San Antonio, 1989-90; prevention chmn. Mayor's

Alcohol and Drug Task Force, San Antonio, 1986-88. Author: (childrens TV): Henry Blue Shoe KONO-TV San Antonio, 1957; contbr. articles to profl. publs. Sec. Alamo Heights (Tex.) Recreation Coun., 1977-78; pres. San Antonio Petroleum Aux., 1978-79; founder, pres. Community Families in Action, 1980-89; trustee Youth Alternatives, Inc., 1983-85; mem. allocation panel United Way, 1988-90; mem. alcolol and drug adv. com N.E. Ind. Sch. Dist., 1986-91; mem. drug free schs. com. S.W. Ind. Sch. Dist., 1991-92; regional coord. Texans War on Drugs, 1988-92; vol. U.S. Dept. Justice, San Antonio, 1984-88; mem. proclamation com. Stop Tex. Epidemic, 1982 Recipient Yr. award Drug Awareness Ctr., San Antonio, 1984, Bexar Co. Med. Soc. Aux., San Antonio, 1984, Gov.'s Cert., Texans War on Drugs, Austin, 1982, Commendation U.S. Pres. Child Safety Partnership, Washington, 1986. Mem. Women in Communications, Inc. (hon.) (Pub. Awareness award 1984), Zeta Tau Alpha (sec., v.p., pres. San Antonio chpt. 1969-77, Nat. Merit award 1980). Avocations: genealogy, puppetry, hand embroidery, creative writing.

MUELLER, BETTY JEANNE, social work educator; b. Wichita, Kans., July 7, 1925; d. Bert C. and Clara A. (Pelton) Judkins; children— Michael J., Madelynn J. MSSW, U. Wis., Madison, 1964, PhD, 1969. Asst. prof. U. Wis., Madison, 1969-72; vis. asso. prof. Bryn Mawr (Pa.) Coll., 1971-72; asso. prof., dir. social work Cornell U., Ithaca, N.Y., 1972-78, prof. human svcs. studies, 1979-96, prof. policy and mgmt., 1996-98, prof. emeritus, 1998—. Nat. cons. Head Start, Follow Through, Appalachian Regional Commn., N.Y. State Office Planning Svcs., N.Y. State Dept. Social Svcs., N.Y. State Divsn. Mental Hygiene, Nat. Congress PTA, ILO; mem. internat. adv. com. Family Resources Tng. Ctr., Singapore, 1999—. Author: (with H. Morgan) Social Services in Early Education, 1974, (with R. Reinoehl) Computers in Human Service Education, 1989, Determinants of Human Behavior, 1995; contbr. articles to profl. jours. Recipient Fulbright Rsch. award, 1990; grantee, HEW, 1974—76, 1979—80, State of N.Y., 1975—95, Israeli Jewish Agy., 1985—87. Mem. Leadership Am., Chi Omega. Democrat. Unitarian Universalist. Home: 412 Highland Rd Ithaca NY 14850-2216 Office: Cornell U Policy and Mgmt 108 MVR Hall Ithaca NY 14853 Business E-Mail: bjm5@cornell.edu.

MUELLER, DIANE, hotel executive; m. Tim Mueller; children: Ethan, Erica. V.p., co-owner Okemo Mountain Resort, Ludlow, Vt., 1982—. Mem. Vt. State Bd. Edn., 1998—, chmn., 2003—; past mem. Green Mountain Union H.S. Bd., Chester; founder Okemo Cmty. Challenge. Named Citizen of the Yr., Vt. C. of C., 2001. Office: Okemo Mountain Resort 77 Okemo Ridge Rd Ludlow VT 05149

MUELLER, JEAN MARGARET, nursing consultant; b. Huntington, N.Y., June 3, 1951; Diploma in Nursing, Pilgrim State Hosp., 1973; BSN, SUNY, Stony Brook, 1979; M in Profl. Studies, New Sch. for Social Rsch., 1986. RN, N.Y. Nurses aide Huntington Hosp., N.Y., 1971, LPN, 1972, RN, charge ICU/CCU, MICU/SICU, telemetry, 1973-77; charge nurse, MICU North Shore U. Hosp, Manhasset, N.Y., 1977-78; private duty cases, Holter monitor scanning, 1978-84; dir. nursing svcs., assoc. dir. nursing svcs. Nesconset (N.Y.) Nursing Ctr., 1984-86; nursing edn. instr. St. Charles Hosp., Port Jefferson, N.Y.; labor and delivery nurse SUNY, Stony Brook; teaching and rsch. nurse II Diabetes Ctr., SUNY, Stony Brook; tchg. hosp. insvc. educator I SUNY, Stony Brook, 1990-94; hosp. nursing svcs. cons. Office Health Sys. Mgmt., N.Y. State Dept. Health, Hauppauge, N.Y., 1994—; team leader cross functional team pub. health edn. and info. N.Y. State Commr. Health, 1998—. Mem. adj. faculty Sch. of Nursing SUNY, Stony Brook, 1992—, St. Joseph's Coll., 1994; rsch. com. dept. family medicine with E. Stark, E.A.P.; hosp. nursing svcs. cons. office health sys. mgmt. N.Y. State Dept. Health, 1994—; lectr. Med., Emotional and Psychol. Indicators of Family Violence. Contbr. articles to profl. jours. Active Mothers Against Drunk Driving; mem. Suffolk County Family Violence Task Force. Recipient President's award for leadership tng. programs SUNY, 1993, for spl. needs of elderly tng. programs and humanistic approach to health care tng. programs, 1994. Mem. Nat. Nurses Assn., Sigma Theta Tau. Home: 234 Hallock Rd Stony Brook NY 11790-3026

MUELLER, JEANNE KAREN, music educator; b. Sheboygan, Wisc., Dec. 29, 1949; d. John Hoffmann and June Sutter; children: Branden, Tricia. AA, Lakeshore Tech. Coll., Cleve., Wis., 1971; BME, Silver Lake Coll., Manitowoc, Wis., 1991, MM, 2000—. Music educator Silver Lake Coll. (music for little people), Manitowoc, Wis., 1985—92, Sch. Dist. of Menomonee Falls, Wis., 1992—98, Sheboygan Area Sch. Dist., Sheboygan, Wis., 1998—. Music dir. Lakeshore Youth Chorale, Sheboygan, Wis., 1997—2003; asst. organist/youth music dir. First United Luth. Ch., Sheboygan, Wis., 1997—; pvt. piano tchr. home studio, Sheboygan, Wis., 1971—. Piloted a program for gifted music students Grant Elem., 2003; dir. Sheboygan Area Sch. Dist. Elem. Honors Chorus, 2003; bd. mem. Integrated Arts Coun. Sheboygan Area Sch. Dist., Wis., 1998—. Mem.: Wis. Choral Dir., Music Educators nat. Conf., Orgn. of Am. Kodaly Educators, Assn. of Wis. Area Kodaly Educators. Roman Cath. Avocations: gardening, bicycling. Home: 1507 S 22nd St Sheboygan WI 53081

MUELLER, LISA MARIA, chemical engineer; b. Macedonia, Ohio, Aug. 29, 1966; d. Dieter Hermann and Hannelore (Habeck) M. BSChemE, U. Akron, Ohio, 1988, postgrad., 1988-89, Kent State U., 1993; MEChemE, Lamar U., 1999. Newspaper delivery The Bull./Newsleader, 1979—80; dry cleaner Nordonia Dry Cleaners & Coin Laundromat, 1980—87; sys. adminstr. Engring. and Computer Graphics Facility, 1985—87; rschr. Process Engring. Computer Catalyst Controls, Akron, 1986-88; devel. engr. chem. divsn. Goodyear, Akron, 1988-90; engr. AcroMed Corp., Cleve., 1990; process design engr. NorPro, Akron, 1991-93; contract and assoc. engr. BF Goodrich Co., Akron, 1994-95; contract engr. BASF, Taco Bell, Kingfish Restaurant, Louisville, 1996; sr. process engr. ExxonMobil, Beaumont, Tex., 1996-97; contract engr. Matrix Engring., Beaumont, 1998. Co-author paper Food Engring. Ann. Nat. Meeting, Chgo., 1993. Mem.: Tau Beta Pi, Nat. Honor Soc. Avocations: music, Tae Kwon Do, computers. Home: 4025 Crow Rd Apt 12 Beaumont TX 77706-7032

MUELLER, LISEL, writer, poet; b. Hamburg, Germany, Feb. 8, 1924; BA in Sociology, U. Evansville; postgrad., Ind. U. Vis. faculty Goddard Coll., 1977-80, Warren Wilson Coll., 1983, 85-86; vis. lectr. U. Chgo., 1984; disting. writer-in-residence Wichita State U., 1981. Author: Dependencies, 1965, 2d edit. 1998, Life of a Queen, 1970, The Private Life, 1976, Voices from the Forest, 1977, The Need to Hold Still, 1980, Waving from Shore, 1989, Second Language, 1986, Learning to Play by Ear, 1990, Alive Together: New & Selected Poems, 1996 (Pulitzer prize). Recipient Pulitzer prize for poetry, Nat. Book award for poetry, Carl Sandburg award, Ruth Lilly Poetry prize, 2002, Jacob Glatstein Meml. prize, Eunice Tietjens Meml. prize; NEA fellow. Mem.: Poetry Ctr. Chgo. (founding mem.). Office: La State U Press PO Box 25053 Baton Rouge LA 10894-5053

MUELLER, LOIS M. psychologist; b. Milw., Nov. 30, 1943; d. Herman Gregor and Ora Emma (Dettmann) M. BS, U. Wis., Milw., 1965; MA, U. Tex., 1966, PhD, 1969. Cert. family mediator; lic. psychologist, Ill., Fla. Postdoctoral intern VA Hosp., Wood, Wis., 1969-71; counselor, asst. prof. So. Ill. U. Counseling Ctr. and dept. psychology, Carbondale, 1971-72, coord. personal counseling, asst. prof., 1972-74, counselor, asst. prof., 1974-76; individual practice clin. psychology Carbondale, 1972-76, Clearwater, Fla., 1977-90, Port Richey, Fla., 1990—. Family mediator, 1995—; mem. profl. adv. com. Mental Health Assn. Pinellas County, 1978, Alt. Human Services, 1979-80; cons. Face Learning Center, Hotline Crisis Phone Service, 1977-87; advice columnist Clearwater Sun newspaper, 1983-90; pub. speaker local TV and radio stas., 1978, 79; talk show host WPLP Radio Sta., Clearwater, 1980-83, WTKN Radio Sta., Tampa Bay, 1988-89, WPSO Radio Sta., New Port Richey, 1991. Contbr. articles to profl. jours. Campaign worker for Sen. George McGovern presdl. race, 1972; sec. bd. dirs. PACE Ctr. for Girls of Pasco; bd. dirs. Suncoast Girl Scout Coun. Mem. APA, Fla. Psychol. Assn., Pinellas Psychol. Assn. (founder, pres. 1978), Am. Soc. Clin. Hypnosis, Fla. Soc. Clin. Hypnosis, Calusa Bus. & Profl. Women (pres., Woman of Yr. 1999), West Pasco C. of C., Cmty. Svc. Coun., Office: 6709 Ridge Rd Ste 109 Port Richey FL 34668-6851

MUELLER, MARGARET S. musician, educator; b. Creston, Iowa, Dec. 3, 1924; d. Homer Cowan and Pearl Callahan Snodgrass; m. John Storm Mueller, June 10, 1958; 1 child, Laura Marjorie Mueller Woods. Student, Kans. U., 1943-46; MusB, Oberlin Conservatory, 1950, MusM, 1958. Instr. piano N.D. State Tchrs. Coll., Minot, 1950-51; instr. piano and organ Iowa State U., Ames, 1951-55, Randolph-Macon Woman's Coll., Lynchburg, Va., 1957-58; prof. organ and theory Salem Coll., Winston-Salem, N.C., 1958-95, prof. emerita, 1995—. Performing artist organ various concerts throughout the U.S. and Europe, 1953—; organist St. Paul's Episcopal Ch., Winston-Salem, 1963—2001; judge André Marchal Internat. Competition, Biarritz, France, 2001. Grantee Fulbright Assn., Frankfurt, Germany, 1955-56, Aeolian grantee, Paris, 1956-57. Mem.: Nat. Guild Piano Tchrs. (judge piano and organ), Winston-Salem Profl. Piano Tchrs. Assn., Music Tchrs. Nat. Assn. (judge piano and organ), Organ Hist. Soc., Am. Guild Organists (judge state, regional and nat. competitions 1965—, performing artist organ nat. and regional convs. 1973, 1976, 1987, 1993), Pi Kappa Lambda, Mu Phi Epsilon. Democrat. Episcopalian. Home: 1524 Sharon Rd Winston Salem NC 27103-4816 Office: Salem Coll Salem Square Winston Salem NC 27108

MUELLER, NANCY, food products executive; BS in chemistry, Russel Sage Coll., 1965. Founder, pres. Nancy's Specialty Foods, Newark, Calif., 1977—. Bd. trustees Rensselaer Polytechnic Inst., Palo Alto Med. Found.; bd. dirs. Sr. Coord. Coun. Palo Alto; mem. Com. 200; bus. adv. coun. Stanford Grad. Sch. Office: Nancys Specialty Foods 6500 Overlake Pl Newark CA 94560-1084

MUELLER, NANCY SCHNEIDER, retired biology educator; b. Wooster, Ohio, Mar. 8, 1933; d. Gilbert Daniel and Winifred (Porter) Schneider; m. Helmut Charles Mueller, Jan. 27, 1959; 1 child, Karl Gilbert. AB in Biology, Coll. of Wooster, 1955; MS in Zoology, U. Wis., 1957, PhD in Zoology, 1962. Instr. zoology U. Wis., Madison, 1966; asst. prof. poultry sci. and zoology N.C. State U., Raleigh, 1968-71; vis. prof. biology N.C. Ctrl. U., Durham, 1971-73, assoc. prof., 1973-79, prof., 1979-93; ret., 1993. Vis. scientist U. Vienna, Austria, 1975. Contbr. articles, abstracts to profl. publs. Mem. Am. Soc. Zoologists, Am. Ornithologists Union, Cooper Ornithol. Soc., Wilson Ornithol. Soc., Wis. Acad. Sci., Arts and Letters, N.C. Acad. Sci., LWV (bd. dirs. 1988—, natural resources com. 1988—), Sigma Xi. Avocations: bird migration, conservation and environmental issues. Home: 409 Moonridge Rd Chapel Hill NC 27516-5576

MUELLER, PAULA DEUTSCH, music educator; b. Chgo., Mar. 27, 1950; d. Zoltan (Bud) Robert Deutsch and Eleanor Esther Tomaszewski/Deutsch; m. Martin F. Mueller, May 5, 1973. MusB in Edn., VanderCook Coll. of Music, 1972. Cert. music tchr. Music Educators National Conference. Fine arts tchr. Elem. Sch. Dist. 2, Bensenville, Ill., 1973—. Handchime ensemble dir. Elem. Sch. Dist. 2, 1980—, fine arts dept. coord. gen. music, instrumental music, visual art, chorus, drama, 1993—; freelance handchime ensemble clinician, bassoon player, Ill., 1980—. Contbr.: gen. music chpt. Music Resource Manual for Curriculum Planning, 1993. Mem. fine arts content-area stds. panel Ill. State Bd. of Edn., Springfield, 1990, 2003—04; rep. Bensenville (Ill.) Arts Coun.; bd. dirs. Glen Ellyn (Ill.) Children's Chorus, 1993—2003, pres. bd. dirs., 1996—2002. Recipient Founder's Award for enduring contributions of exceptional quality and for sustained commitment to the educatiional well-being of the children in Bens, Elem. Sch. Dist. #2, 1990. Mem.: PTA (life), Chorus Am., Bensenville (Ill.) Edn. Assn. (pres. 1984—91, 1997—2004), Ill. Edn. Assn. (bd. dirs., chmn. region 58 1998—, exec. com. 2001—03), Ill. Music Educators Assn. (assoc.), Music Educators Nat. Conf. (assoc.; chmn., jr. h.s., elem. music coun. Dist. 9). Democrat. Presbyterian. Avocations: gardening, cooking, crafts. Home: 22 W 013 McCarron Road Glen Ellyn IL 60137 Office: Bensenville Elementary School District # 220 S Church Road Bensenville IL 60106 Office Phone: 630-766-2601 ext. 119. Personal E-mail: paula.mueller@ieanea.org. E-mail: paulamueller@bensenville2.k12.il.us.

MUELLER, PEGGY JEAN, dance educator, choreographer, rancher; b. Austin, Tex., June 14, 1952; d. Rudolph George Jr. and Margaret Jean (Locke) M.; m. John Yerby Tarlton, June 24, 1972 (div. June 1983). BS in Home Econs., Child Devel., U. Tex., Austin, 1974. Dance tchr. Shirley McPhail Sch. Dance, Austin, 1972-75, Jean Tarlton Sch. Dance, Alpine, Tex., 1975-77, College Station, Tex., 1977-80, Sul Ross State U., Alpine, 1975-77, Tex. A&M U., College Station, 1977-80, A&M Consol. Community Edn., Coll. Station, 1977-78, Jean Mueller Sch. Dance, Austin, 1980—, U. Tex., Austin, 1980—. Dancer, contest judge Gt. Tex. Dance-Off, Austin, 1985—86; mem. equestrian com. Austin Travis County Livestock Show and Rodeo, 1980—92, chmn. trail ride, 1986—, Star Tex. Fair and PRCA Rodeo, 2000—; trial boss, pres. Austin Founders Trail Ride, 1986—; trail boss Bandera Longhorn Cattle Dr. and Trail Ride, 1990, 91; choreographer, head cheerleader Austin Texans Pro Football Team, 1981; dance tchr. Austin Ballroom Dancers, 1988, the Austin Club, 1997, 98; dancer, agt. George Strait/Bud Light Comml. Auditions, 1990; head contest judge Am.'s Ultimate Dance Contest, Austin, 1994; contest judge Two-Stepping Across Am., Austin, 1994; hon. trial boss Dream Catcher Ranch Trail Ride, Franklin, Tex., 1995, 96, Grapevine/Housgon Country Donkey, Mule and Horse Trail Ride, 1997, 2000. Dancer Oklahoma, Austin, 1969, Kiss Me Kate, Austin, 1970; choreographer, lead role Cabaret, Alpine, 1976, (mini-series) True Women, 1997. Active Women's Symphony League Austin, 1972—, Settlement Club, Austin, 1987—; recreation chmn. St. Martin's Evang. Luth. Ch., Austin, 1972—; hon. trail boss St. Jude Children's Rsch. Hosp. Trail Ride, Austin and Kyle, Tex., 1991. Recipient Outstanding Trail Rider of Yr. award Wild Horse Trail Ride, Okla., 1984; named Tex. First Lady Trail Boss, Gov. Mark White, Mayor Frank Cooksey, Austin City Coun., 1986, Judge Bill Aleshire, Travis County Commrs., 1989, Outstanding Intramural Sports Team Mgr.-Player, Tex. A&M U., 1978-79. Mem. Tex Assn. Tchrs. of Dancing, Inc., U.S. Twirling and Gymnastics Assn., Univ. Tex. Ex-Students Assn., Tex. Execs. in Home Econs., Am. Vet. Med. Assn. Aux. (v.p. 1978-79, pres. 1979-80), Am. Horse Shows Assn., Internat. Arabian Horse Assn., Austin Women's Tennis Assn. (v.p. 1985-86, pres. 1986-90, spl. events chmn. 1990-92, advisor 1990—, winner 2d ann. Harriet Crosson Outstanding Player & Community Svc. award), Women's Team Tennis of Austin Assn. (pres.-elect 1992-93, pres. 1993-94), Capital Area Tennis Assn. (membership com. 1991, 92), Houston Salt Grass Trail Ride Assn., San Antonio Alamo Trail Ride Assn., Ft. Worth Chisholm Trail Ride Assn., U. Tex. Longhorn Alumni Band, Austin C. of C., Am. Bus. Women's Assn., Austin Alumnae Panhellenic Assn. (1st v.p. 1989-90, rush forum chmn. 1990, pres. 1990-91, parliamentarian 1991-92), Lone Grove Cmty. Club (treas. 199697, v.p. 1997-99, pres. 1999—, exec. trustee 1997-99, exec. dir. 1999-2000), Omicron Nu (v.p. 1973-74), Jr. Austin Woman's Club (historian 1990-91), Austin Country Club (team tennis captain 1994-95, player 1994—, dance tchr. 1993-96), Zeta Tau Alpha (Austin Alumnae Chpt., alumnae photographer, social advisor 1982-87, treas. 1987-89, publicity chmn. 1989, Easter Seals fundraiser, Honor Cup winner 1990, pres. 1991-92, internat. convention official del. 1988, 92, nominating chmn. 1992-93, mem. yearbook com. 1992-94, 2d v.p. 1993-94). Clubs: Cen. Tex. Arabian Horse, Capitol Area Quarter Horse Assn., Jr. Austin Woman's, Austin Country. Republican. Avocations: theatre, piano, drums, sports, travel. Home and Office: PO Box 5868 Austin TX 78763-5868 E-mail: aftr@USATrailRides.com.

MUELLER, ROBIN SUE, biology educator; b. Dubuque, Iowa, June 24, 1959; d. Louis Edward Hanson and Patricia Catherine Mills; m. Philip Wayne Clarkson, Jr., Apr. 21, 1979 (div. 1989); children: Tyler Louis Clarkson, Timothy Patrick Clarkson; m. Matthew James Mueller, Aug. 25, 1990. AAS, Hawkeye C.C., 1988; BS in Allied Health, U. Ala.-Birmingham, 1995, MEd, 1999. Cert. med. lab. technician Assn. Soc. Clin. Pathologists; profl. educator Ala., clin. lab. scientist Nat. Cert. Agy. Med. lab. technician ARC, Dubuque, Iowa, 1988—90; overnight technologist United Clin. Labs., Dubuque, 1990—91; med. technologist Lab. Corp. Am., Birmingham, 1991—96; rsch. asst. U. Ala., Birmingham, 1997—99; tchr. biology and marine biology Erwin H.S. Jefferson Ccounty Bd. Edn., Birmingham, 1999—. Com. mem. Textbook Com. Adv. Bd., Birmingham, 2001—02; sponsor Student Govt. Assn., Erwin H.S., Birmingham, 2000—02. Mem. Parent-Tchr. Assn., Birmingham, 1991—. Grantee grantee, Nat. Energy Coun., Erwin H.S., 2001. Avocations: travel, reading, music. Home: 5508 Spanish Trace Pinson AL 35126 Office: Erwin H S 532 23d Ave NW Birmingham AL 35215 E-mail: birdie0624@yahoo.com.

MUELLER, SHIRLEY ANNE, lawyer, real estate broker; b. Miami, Fla., Aug. 25, 1950; d. Robert Peter and Arvella Gertrude (Feldkamp) M.; divorced; children: Peter, Tybe, Samantha. AA in Journalism, Miami Dade Jr. Coll., 1970; BA in Philosophy, U. Calif., Berkeley, 1972; JD, Benjamin Cardozo Sch. Law, N.Y.C., 1982. Dir. children's advt. div. Coun. Better Bus. Bur., N.Y.C., 1973-79; assoc. Cutner & Rathkopf, N.Y.C., 1983-87; pres. Uncommon Properties, Inc., N.Y.C., 1990-94; pvt. practice N.Y.C., 1994—; assoc. broker Sotheby's Internat. Realty, N.Y.C., 2002—. Mem. fundraising com. Children's Air Ctr. N.Y. Hosp., N.Y.C., 1988—99, Nightingale Bamford Schl, N.Y.C., 1987—98; bd. dirs. Am. Symphony Orch., N.Y.C., 2003—. Roman Catholic. Avocations: reading, music, travel, dance. Home: Ste 18A 275 Central Park West New York NY 10024 Office: 379 W Broadway 2d Fl New York NY 10024 E-mail: smueller08@aol.com., shirley.mueller@sothebysrealty.com.

MUELLER-FITCH, HEATHER MAY, priest; b. Radford, Va., Apr. 28, 1942; d. Robert Rohn and Esther Helen (Schmidt) Selfridge; m. John Scott Mueller, Aug. 17, 1962 (div. May 1973); children: Anne Elizabeth, Heidi Michelle; m. Richard Keelor Fitch, Apr. 25, 1992. BS, Mich. State U., 1967; MDiv, Ch. Div. Sch. of the Pacific, Berkeley, 1978. Seminarian intern All Saints Episcopal Ch., Kapaa, Hawaii, 1976-77; chaplain Seabury Hall, Makawao, Hawaii, 1978-81; assoc. priest Holy Innocent's Episcopal Ch., Lahaina, Hawaii, 1981; rector St. John's Episcopal Ch., Kula, Hawaii, 1981—. Bd. mem. Episcopal Women's Caucus, N.Y.C., 1983-85. Founder Kula Cmty. Assn., 1985, Malama Makua Keiki, Wailuku, Hawaii, 1991; co-founder Hawaii Clergy Assn., Honolulu, 1993. Mem. Nat. Network Episcopal Clergy Assn. (bd. dirs. 1990-95), Hawaii Coun. Chs. (pres. 1992-96), Interfaith Clergy Assn. (pres., founder 1993-95), Rotary (Paul Harris fellow 1994). Democrat. Episcopalian. Home: St Johns Episcopal Ch 8992 Kula Hwy Kula HI 96790 E-mail: janetm@acha.net.

MUFSON, LAURIE ETHEL, theater educator, director, actress; b. New York City, NY, Nov. 11, 1953; d. Aleine Joan Austin Mufson Cohen and Abraham Isaac Mufson; m. James Nathan Applebaum, June 23, 1984; children: Julia Freda Cohen, Kenneth Hill Applebaum. BA, Beloit Coll., 1972—76; MFA, George Wash. U., 1980—83. Cert. Lessac Voice and Body Teacher Lessac Inst. of Voice and Body Tng., 2002. Fellow George Wash. U., 1981—82; dir. of theatre Bullis Sch., Potomac, Md., 1983—98; chair-theatre dept. Garrison Forest Sch., Garrison, Md., 1976—80; chair fine arts dept. and dir. of theatre Mercersburg Acad., Mercersburg, Pa., 1998—; adj. prof. The Am. U., Washington DC, 1996—98. Artistic dir. Potomac Theatre Co., Potomac, Md., 1994—98. Actor: (film) Washington Square; dir.(prodr. also creator of series): Chain Links an Evening of Original Plays, (producer): over 100 High School Plays And Musicals; actor: (plays) An Enemy of The People (by Ibsen adapted by Miller Silver), The Nerd (by Larry Shue), The Wise Woman; dir.: Woman Spends Year in Labor (by Leslie Milk), Burying Fiona (by Jeannie Marshall) (Best Dir. Wash. theatre festival, 1997), Deja Rondezvous (by Elliot Byrum), The Marie Antoinette Society (by Gary Bonnisorte), Cat on a Hot Tin Roof (by Tennesse Williams); prodr.: Out of Earshot (by Caleen Sennette Jennings) (No. Va. Theatre Assn. Festival Winner- Best Prodn. of an original play, 1995); actor: Stars in the Morning Sky (by Allexander Gallan), A Man With Connections (by Alexander Gellman). Elected mem. of the bd. of directors chair pers. com. The Wash. Ethical Soc., Washington, 1984—87; elected mem. - chair artistic com. / artistic dir. Potomac Theatre Co., Potomac, Md., 1994—98; elected mem. - play selection com. Caledonia Theatre Co. / Totem Pole Playhouse, Caledonia, Pa., 1999—2001; elected mem. The Actors Ctr., Washington, 1995—98; artistic liaison Garrison Playhouse, Garrison, Md., 1977—80. Recipient Ofcl. Citation Honoring Contributions to Potomac Theatre Co., Md. Ho. of Delegates, 1998, Paul Parady Meml. award for Outstanding Contributions to the U. Theatre, George Wash. U., 1982; Summer Study grant, Mercersburg Acad., 1999, 2000, 2003. Mem.: SAG, Am. Fedn. of TV and Radio Artists, Assn. for Theatre in Higher Edn., Assn. for Theatre in Higher Educaion (co-chair theatre edn. reform task force 1995—2000), Ednl. Theatre Assn., Theatre Comm. Group. D-Liberal. Ethical Culture. Avocations: travel, reading, singing, painting, collecting crafts. Home: 300 E Seminary St Mercersburg PA 17236 Office: Mercersburg Academy 300 E Seminary St Mercersburg PA 17236 E-mail: laurie_mufson@mercersburg.edu.

MUHAMMAD, CLAUDETTE MARIE, religious organization administrator; d. Travis and Ernestine Johnson; 1 child, Anthony L. Pinkins. Student, U. Abidjan, Ivory Coast, 1978—79; BA, Am. U., 1982; postgrad., UN, Geneva, Switzerland, 1982, U. Geneva, 1982, Johns Hopkins Sch. Advanced Internat. Studies, 1982. Tech. libr. Gen. Dynamics Astronautics, 1960—62; sec. to Congressman Lionel Van Deerlin U.S. Congress, Washington, 1963—68; spl. asst. to commrs. Pres.'s Commn. on Civil Disorders, Washington, 1968—69; dir. comty. affairs Fed. City Coll., Washington, 1973—75; dir. of mayor's call program Dep. Mayor Econ. Devel., Washington; mktg. dir. Manara Travel Agy., Washington, 1987—88; enrollment mgmt./recruitment counselor U. D.C., Washington, 1988; chief protocol to Hon. Min. Louis Farrakhan Nation of Islam. Contbr. articles to profl. jours. Model Ebony Fashion Model, 1963; pres. Jimmy Carter's Inauguration Com. Protocol; nat. dep. dir. Million Man March, Washington, 1995, Million Family March, Washington, 2000. Finalist 3d runner-up Miss Bronze California, 1958; recipient Women in History award, Urban League, 2002, Jerusalem 2000 Unity Day Conf. award, 2000, Jr. Achievement award, 1961—62.

MUHAMMAD, LATONJA WALKER, control engineer; b. Detroit, June 19, 1966; d. Harold Walker and Doris Barksdale Dandridge; m. Derick Muhammad, Nov. 24, 1994 (div.); children: Sultan A., Tariq L. BSME, Tuskegee U., 1989. Structural design engr. LTV Aircraft Products Group, Dallas, 1989—94; dimensional validation engr. Epcom (contracted to GM), Warren, Mich., 1999—2001; dimensional engring. project mgr. Craft Line Inc., Hazel Park, Mich., 2001—02; sr. dimensional control engr. Aerotek (contracted to Lear Corp.), Dearborn, Mich., 2002—. Site leader, VIS trainer Ford divsn. Dimensional Mgmt., Dearborn, 2002—03. Contbr. newsletter Future Leaders of Detroit, 2000—03. Campaign vol. Mich. Dem. Party, 2002, mem., 2002—; site mgr. Democratic Caucus Voting, 2004; precinct del. Wayne County, Mich., 2002—; vol. Detroit Exec. Svc. Corps., 2001—, Black Alliance for Ednl. Options, 2002—03, A.C.E.S. Mem.: Future Leaders of Detroit, Jim Dandy Ski Club (mentor). Democrat. Avocations: golf, skiing, writing, bowling, volunteer/community service.

MUHLENFELD, ELISABETH S. college president, educator, author; b. Washington, Nov. 12, 1944; d. Merle Roberts and Cornelia Elizabeth (Herring) Showalter; m. Edward F. Muhlenfeld, Sept. 10, 1966 (div. 1975); children: Allison Elisabeth, David Edward; m. Laurin A. Wollan, Jr., June

5, 1982; stepchildren: Ann Louise Wollan, Laurin A. Wollan III. BA in Philosophy, Goucher Coll., 1966; MA in English, U. Tex., Arlington, 1973; PhD, U. S.C., 1978. Rsch. asst., adminstrv. asst. So. Studies program U. S.C., Columbia, 1975-78; asst. prof. English Fla. State U., Tallahassee, 1978-82, assoc. prof., 1982-87, dir. undergrad and grad. studies, assoc. chmn. dept. English, 1987-96, prof. English, 1987-96, dean undergrad. studies, 1984-86; pres. Sweet Briar (Va.) Coll., 1996—. Mem. ABA Commn. on Coll. and Univ. Legal Studies, 1991-94. Author: Mary Boykin Chesnut: A Biography, 1981; editor: William Faulkner's Absolom, Absolom: A Critical Casebook, 1984, The Private Mary Chesnut: The Unpublished Civil War Diaries, 1984. Mem. Capital Women's Network. NEH Dir.'s grantee, 1983-84. Mem. MLA, St. George Tucker Soc. (charter fellow), So. Assn. Women Historians, William Faulkner Soc. (charter mem; sec.-treas. 1991-94), Phi Kappa Phi (exec. bd., pres. 1992-93). Office: Sweet Briar Coll Pres's Office Box C Sweet Briar VA 24595

MUHLERT, JAN KEENE, art museum director; b. Oak Park, Ill., Oct. 4, 1942; d. William Henry and Isabel Janette (Cole) Keene; m. Christopher Layton Muhlert, Jan. 1, 1966; 1 son, Michael Keene. BA in Art and French, Albion (Mich.) Coll., 1964; MA in Art History, Oberlin (Ohio) Coll., 1967; student, Neuchatel (Switzerland) U., Inst. European Studies, Paris, Inst. de Phonetique, Acad. Grande Chaumiere. Asst. curator Allen Meml. Art Mus., Oberlin, 1967-68; asst. curator 20th Century painting and sculpture Nat. Collection Fine Arts, Smithsonian Instn., Washington, 1968-73, assoc. curator, 1974-75; dir. U. Iowa Mus. Art, 1975-79, Amon Carter Mus., Ft. Worth, 1980-95, Palmer Museum of Art, University Park, Pa., 1996—. Author museum brochures, catalogues. Mem. Nat. Mus. Act. Adv. Coun., 1980—83; vis. com. Allen Meml. Art Mus. Oberlin Coll., Ohio, 1992—2003; chair adv. com. North Tex. Inst. Educators on the Visual Arts, U. North Tex., 1992—95. Grantee Nat. Endowment Arts-Donner Found., 1979; recipient Friend of Art Edn. award Tex. Art Edn. Assn., 1994. Mem. Assn. Art Mus. Dirs. (trustee 1981-82, 84-86, 92-93, chmn. govt. and art com. 1982-84, chmn. profl. practices com. 1990-92), Western Assn. Art Mus. (regional rep. 1978-79), Am. Assn. Mus. (commn. for new century 1981-84, gen. co-chair 1993 ann. meeting), Am. Arts Alliance (dir. 1980-86, vice-chmn. 1982-84). Office: Palmer Museum of Art Pa State U Curtin Rd University Park PA 16802-2507

MUHN, JUDY ANN, psychologist, genealogist; b. Detroit, Dec. 29, 1952; d. Wilbur William and Dolores Eleanor (Sutinen) Nimer; m. Dennis James Muhn, June 6, 1975. BS, Mich. State U., 1975; EdM, Boston U., 1992; MA in Counseling, U. San Francisco, 1997. Registered marriage, family and child counselor intern.; lic. psychologist, Mich. Legis. aide to Calif. state senator, 1982-84; dir. pub. rels. Tierra del Oro coun. Girl Scouts U.S., 1984-86, mgr. mem. devel. San Antonio area coun., 1986-90; counselor Yuba City Indian Health Ctr., 1997; intervention counselor Sutter-Yuba Mental Health, 1997-98; counselor, intern White Ho. Cmty. Counseling Ctr., 1998; pvt. practice Wixom, Mich., 1990—. Adj. faculty Henry Ford CC, 1998—2001, Oakland CC, 1998—2001; therapist Brighton Hosp., 2000—01, Advanced Counseling Svcs., Brighton, Mich., 2001—03; spkr. in field. Bd. dirs., chmn. pub. affairs com. Planned Parenthood Clinton County, N.Y., 1980-81; bd. dirs. Family Planning Advs., Albany, 1981, Planned Parenthood San Antonio, 1987-89; co-founder Womanspirit Rising, 1987-89; pres. Planned Parenthood Assn. Sacramento Valley, 1982-84; founder Women's Roundtable, Plattsburgh, 1981; sec. San Antonio Coun. Native Ams., 1986-89; dep. exec. dir. U. Santo Tomas Alumni Assn., 1998-2000; dir. adult devel. and vol. svcs. Girl Scouts of Met. Detroit, 2002—. Mem. Am. Soc. Tng. and Devel., Metro Detroit Vol. Adminstrs., San Antonio Women's C. of C. (bd. dirs. 1989), Fedn., Greenpeace, Amnesty Internat., Sierra Club. Office Phone: 313-972-4475 ext. 243.

MUIR, HELEN, journalist, author; b. Yonkers, N.Y., Feb. 9, 1911; d. Emmet A. and Helen T. (Flaherty) Lennehan; m. William Whalley Muir, Jan. 23, 1936; children: Mary Muir Burrell, William Torbert. With Yonkers Herald Statesman, 1929-30, 31-33, N.Y. Evening Post, 1930-31, N.Y. Evening Jour., 1933-34, Carl Byoir & Assocs., N.Y.C., Miami, 1934-35; syndicated columnist Universal Svc., Miami, 1935-38; columnist Miami Herald, 1941-42; children's book editor, 1949-56; women's editor Miami Daily News, 1943-44; freelance mag. writer numerous nat. mags., 1944—. Drama critic Miami News, 1960-65. Author: Miami, U.S.A., 1953, expanded edit., 2000, Biltmore: Beacon for Miami, 1987, 3d rev. edit., 1998, Frost in Florida: A Memoir, 1995. Trustee Coconut Grove Libr. Assn., Friends U. Miami Libr., Friends Miami-Dade Pub. Libr.; vis. com. U. Miami Librs.; bd. dirs. Miami-Dade County Pub. Libr. Sys., chmn. emeritus, 1999. Recipient award Delta Kappa Gamma, 1960, trustees and friends award Fla. Libr. Assn., 1973, award Coun. Fla. Librs., 1990, trustee citation ALA, 1984, spirit of excellence award, 1988; named to Fla. Women's Hall of Fame, 1984, Miami Centennial '96 Women's Hall of Fame; named chmn. emeritus Metro-Dade Libr. Sys., 1999. Mem.: ALA (named leading libr. adv. 20th Century), Authors' Guild, Soc. Women Geographers (meritorious svc. award 1996, Fla. Groups First Woman of World award 2000), Women in Comms. (Cmty. Headliner award 1973), Biscayne Bay Yacht Club, Cosmopolitan Club (N.Y.C.), Fla.Women's Press Club (award 1963). Home: 3855 Stewart Ave Miami FL 33133-6734

MUIR, PATRICIA ALLEN, professional association administrator; b. Dallas, Nov. 4, 1929; d. Jack Charleton Allen and Anna Patricia (Hovis) Allen Atchison; m. Lester Doyle Rader, Jr., Aug. 4, 1950 (dec. Sept. 1950); 1 child, Lester Doyle III; m. Perren James Muir, June 2, 1956 (div.); children: Edward John, Patricia Jane. Grad., Our Lady of Victory Coll., 1948; student, George Washington U., 1948-49, Washington Sch. for Sec., 1949-50. Traffic mgr. Am. Storage Co., Washington, 1960-69; asst. sec. Ind. Tele. Pioneer Assn., Washington, 1969-76; adminstrv. asst. ALA, Washington, 1977-98, staff liaison to Fed. Libr. Round Table, 1991-98, staff liaison to Armed Forces Libr. Round Table, 1991-98, staff liaison to Govt. Documents Round Table, 1991-98; office mgr. Fed. Documents Clearing House, Washington, 1998-2000; cons., 2000—. Columnist, contbr. The Ind. Pioneer, 1969-76. V.p. Friendship House Child Devel. Ctr. Parents, Washington, 1978, pres., 1979—83; mem. parish coun. St. Peter's Cath. Ch., 1987—91, mem. edn. and spiritual devel. com., 1986—, chair, 1988—91, coord. Bible study, 1999—2003; vol. St. Peter's Interparish Sch. Reading Program, 2001—02. Mem. Ladies Ancient Order of Hibernians (state pres. 1991-97, nat. budget com. 1996-98, nat. elections com. 1998—, nat. constn. com. 1998-02, nat. rules of order com. 2000-02). Avocations: travel, genealogy, reading, writing. Home: 343 11th St SE Washington DC 20003-2105

MUIR, RUTH BROOKS, counselor, substance abuse service coordinator; b. Washington, Nov. 27, 1924; d. Charles and Adelaide Chenery (Masters) B.; m. Robert Mathew Muir, Nov. 26, 1947 (dec. Feb. 20, 1996); children: Robert Brooks, Martha Louise, Heather Sue. BA in Art, Rollins Coll., Winter Park, Fla., 1947; MA in Rehab. Counseling, U. Iowa, 1979. Cert. substance abuse counselor, Iowa. Program advisor Iowa Meml. Union, Iowa City, 1959-66; counselor, coord. Mid Eastern Coun. on Chem. Abuse, Iowa City, 1976-81; patient rep. Univ. Hosp., Iowa City, 1982-85; rsch. project interviewer dept. psychiatry U. Iowa Coll. Medicine, 1985-88; pvt. practice family counselor, 1984—. Docent U. Iowa Mus. of Art, 1999—. Art exhibited at Iowa City Sr. Ctr., 1987, 92, Iowa City Art Ctr., 1989, U. Iowa Hosp., 1991, Great Midwestern Ice Cream Co., 1991, Summit St. Gallery, 1995, Iowa City C. of C., 2001, Iowa City's First Art Walk March, 2003; creator, coord. therapeutic series Taking Control, Iowa City Sr. Ctr., 1986-87, Art Walk Lorenz Boot Shop, 2003. Vol. coord. art exhibits Sr. Ctr., Iowa City, 1992-94, Iowa City Arts Exhbn. Com., 1996, Arrowmont Sch. Art, 1996—, Arrowmont Amb., 1996-98; treas. bd. dirs. Crisis Ctr., Iowa City, 1976-77; sec. coun. elders Sr. Citizens Ctr., Iowa City, 1976-78; pres. Unitarian-Universalist Iowa City Women's Fedn., 1985; friend U. Iowa Mus. Art, docent, 1999—; active Opera Supers, Iowa City Unitarian U.N. Envoy; fgn. rels. coun., bd. dirs. annual changing family conf. U. Iowa, 1986-92; non-govtl. rep. Earth Summit Global Forum, 1992; care review bd. Mental Health Homes, 1997-99; bd. dirs. Arts Iowa City, 2002—. Mem.: AAUW (state cultural rep. 1990—92, Iowa City chpt. co-chair for programs 1998—99), Nat. League Am. PEN Women (membership chair 2002), Iowa City Unitarian Soc. (adult program com. 1993—94, unitarian care com. 1993—, membership com.), Nat. Soc. Colonial Dames, U. Iowa Print and Drawing Study Club (bd. dirs. 2003—), Pi Beta Phi (pres. alumnae club 1995—97). Home and Office: 6 Glendale Ct Iowa City IA 52245-4430 Office Phone: 319-337-7287. E-mail: ruthmuir@inav.net.

MUJA, KATHLEEN ANN, state official, consultant; b. Denver, June 24, 1965; d. Thomas Raymond and Bridget Catherine (Hirschfeld) Cramer; m. Adrian Constantin Muja, June 4, 1988 (div. Apr. 1991); 1 child, Thomas Constantin. BBA, U. Denver, 1995. Employment specialist Dept. of Labor and Employment, Colo., 1991—98, 2000—02; office mgr. Colo. Dept. Labor, Denver, 1999-2000, bus. analyst, 2002—. Contbr. poems to various publs. Vol. Mus. Natural History, Denver, 1987—; home visitor Cmty. Caring Project, Denver, 1996-2001. Mem. AAUW, U. Denver Alumni Assn. Roman Catholic. Avocations: hiking, biking, canvas cross-stitch, writing, reading. Home: 460 Washington St Denver CO 80203-3810 Office: Colo Dept Labor 251 E 12th Ave Denver CO 80203-2272

MUKHERJEE, AMIYA K. metallurgy and materials science educator; PhD, Oxford (Eng.) U., 1962. Prof. U. Calif., Davis. Recipient Alexander von Humboldt award Fed. Republic Germany, 1988, Albert Easton White Disting. Tchr. award Am. Soc. Materials, 1992, Pfeil medal and prize Inst. Materials, 1993, U. Calif. prize and citation, 1993, Anatoly Bochvar medal U. Moscow, 1996, Inst. medal Max Planck Inst. for Metallforschung, 1997. Office: U Calif Davis Dept Chem Engring & Material Sci Davis CA 95616 E-mail: akmukherjee@ucdavis.edu.

MUKHOTI, BELA BANERJEE, economics educator; b. Vikrampur, Bengal, India, Mar. 1, 1932; came to U.S., 1965; d. Priyanath and Labanya (Ganguli) B.; m. Santi Ranjan Mukhoti, Dec. 14, 1957 (dec. 1988); children: Jayati, Mona. BA in Econs. with honors, Calcutta U., 1950, MA in Econs., 1953; PhD in Econs., London Sch. Econs., 1964. Rsch. specialist U. Ky., Lexington, 1965-66; assoc. prof. Memphis State U., 1966-68, U. No. Iowa, Cedar Falls, 1972-74; asst. prof. Lakehead U., Ont., Can., 1968-69; rsch. officer Planning Commn. Govt. of India, New Delhi, 1969-71; agrl. economist Econ. Rsch. Svc., USDA, Washington, 1979-86; prof. econs. Rowan U., Glassboro, N.J., 1987—. Author: Agriculture and Employment in Developing Countries--Strategy for Effective Rural Development, 1985; Measures of Development, 1986, International Monetary Fund and Low-Income Countries, 1986, Impact of Agricultural Growth Patterns on Import Demand for Food and Agricultural Commodities, 1983; contbr. articles to profl. jours. Recipient Rhoda Freeman recognition award N.J. Coll. and Univ. Coalition for Women's Edn., 1988, merit award Rowan U., 1989; Sir Ernest Cassels Trust grantee, 1962-63, Brit. Univ. and Coll. Tchr.'s Assn. grantee, 1964, also various univs. and colls., 1965—. Mem. Am. Econ. Assn., Ea. Econ. Assn., Internat. Assn. Agrl. Econs., Assn. Indian Econ. Studies (exec. com. 1990—), Congress Econ. and Polit. Democracy Internat. (program com. 1990), Am. Friends London Sch. Econs., Assn. Indians in Am., Sanskriti (exec. com. 1985, pres. 1990). Hindu. Avocations: horticulture, cooking, photography, travel. Home: 49 E Holly Ave Sewell NJ 08080-2603 Office: Rowan U Dept Econs Bunce Hall Glassboro NJ 08028 E-mail: mukhoti@rowan.edu.

MULCAHY, ANNE MARIE, printing company executive; b. Rockville Centre, N.Y., Oct. 21, 1952; BA in English and Journalism, Marymount Coll., 1974. Sales rep., various mgmt. positions Xerox Corp., 1976-91, v.p. human resources, 1992-95, v.p., staff officer customer ops., 1996-97, sr. v.p., chief staff officer, 1998, pres. gen. mkts. ops., 1999—2000, pres., COO, 2000—01, pres., CEO, 2001—02, chmn., CEO, 2002—. Bd. dirs. Target Corp., Fannie Mae, Fuji-Xerox Corp., Catalyst. Office: Xerox Corp 800 Long Ridge Rd Stamford CT 06904-1227

MULCAHY, JOANNE B. literature educator; d. Paul Nicholas and Jeanne Grace Mulcahy; m. Robert Dana Hazen. BA in Comparative Lit., U. Pa., 1977; MA in Anthropology, U. Wis., 1981; PhD in Folklore, U. Pa., 1988. Dir. Oreg. Folk Arts Program, Portland, 1988—91; asst. prof., dir. writing culture program, asst. prof. N.W. Writing Inst. Lewis & Clark Coll., 2002—. Vis. asst. prof. gender studies Lewis & Clark Coll., 1990—2002; adj. faculty The Union Inst., 1995—, Bard Coll., 1996—. Author: Brith & Death on an Alaskan Island, 2001. Mem. adv. bd. Island Inst., Sitka, Alaska, 1992—; tchr. Oreg. Dept. Corrections, Salem, 1998—. Fellow, Alaska Humanities Forum, Anchorage, 1991, Oreg. Humanities Coun., Portland, 1992, No. Ireland Brit. Coun., 1995. Mem.: Oral Hist. Assn., No. Ireland Partnership, Am. Folklore Soc. Democrat. Avocations: yoga, hiking, quilting.

MULCAHY, LUCILLE BURNETT, freelance writer; b. Albuquerque, Nov. 10, 1918; d. Harry Leland and Grace Ruth (Lomax) Burnett; m. Clemons David Mulcahy Jr., Sept. 1, 1939 (div. May 1957); children: Burnette Anne, DeeAnn Eileen. Student, N.Mex. State U., 1947, U. Albuquerque, 1975. Freelance writer, 1953—; procurement officer Albuquerque Pub. Libr., 1963-76. Storyteller various schs. Author: (childrens books) Dark Arrow, 1953, reprint 95, Pita, 1954, Magic Fingers, 1958, 95 (Jr. Lit. Guild award), Blue Marshmallow Mountains, 1959, Natoto, 1960, Fire on Big Lonesome, 1967, (under pseudonym) Dale Evans and Danger in Crooked Canyon, 1958. Recipient Zia award N.Mex. Press Women, 1967. Avocation: yoga. Home: 505 Doe Ln SE Albuquerque NM 87123-3530

MULDAUR, DIANA CHARLTON, actress; b. N.Y.C., Aug. 19, 1938; d. Charles Edward Arrowsmith and Alice Patricia (Jones) M.; m. James Mitchell Vickery, July 26, 1969 (dec. 1979); m. Robert J. Dozier, Oct. 11, 1981. BA, Sweet Briar Coll., 1960. Actress appearing in: Off-Broadway theatrical prodns., summer stock, Broadway plays including A Very Rich Woman, 1963-68; guest appearances on TV in maj. dramatic shows; appeared on: TV series Survivors, 1970-71, McCloud, 1971-73, Tony Randall Show, 1976, Black Beauty, 1978; star: TV series Born Free, 1974, Hizzoner, 1979, Fitz & Bones, 1980, Star Trek: The Next Generation, 1988-89; NBC miniseries and TV series A Year in the Life, 1986; TV movie Murder in Three Acts, The Return of Sam McCloud, 1989; TV series L.A. Law, 1989-91; motion picture credits include McQ, The Lawyer, The Other, One More Train to Rob, Mati, etc. Bd. dirs. Los Angeles chpt. Asthma and Allergy Found. Am.; bd. advisors Nat. Ctr. Film and Video Preservation, John F. Kennedy Ctr. Performing Arts, 1986. Recipient 13th Ann. Commendation award Am. Women in Radio and TV, 1988, Disting. Alumnae award Sweet Briar Coll., 1988. Mem. Acad. Motion Picture Arts and Scis., Screen Actors Guild (dir. 1978), Acad. TV Arts and Scis. (exec. bd., dir., pres. 1983-85), Conservation Soc. Martha's Vineyard Island. Office: Bauman Bedanty & Shaul 5757 Wilshire Blvd Ste 473 Los Angeles CA 90036

MULDER, ARLENE JOANN, mayor; b. Tulare, Calif., Oct. 13, 1944; d. Joseph R. and Anna W. (Lorenzo) Borges; m. Albert John Mulder, June 18, 1966; children: Michelle, Alison, Michael. BS, San Francisco State U., 1966, postgrad., 1967. Cert. secondary tchr., Calif., Ill. Tchr. pub. schs., Anaheim, Calif., 1967-69, Niles Twp. Dist. 219, Skokie, Ill., 1972-78, coach, 1973-78; mem. Arlington Heights (Ill.) Park Dist. Commn., 1979-91; village trustee Village of Arlington Heights, 1991-93, mayor, 1993—, first women mayor. Coach Sch. Dist. 25, Arlington Heights, 1990-92. Mem. Arlington Heights Centennial Commn., 1984-89. Avocations: music, golf, tennis. Office: Village Arlington Heights 33 S Arlington Heights Rd Arlington Heights IL 60005-1499

MULDER, PATRICIA MARIE, education educator; b. South Bend, Ind., Dec. 28, 1944; d. Ervin James and Carmen Virginia (Sheeley) Anderson; m. James R. Mulder, Dec. 27, 1964; children: Todd Alan, Scott Robert. BA, Western Mich. U., 1967. Freelance writer, photographer, Berrien Springs, Mich., 1980—; tchr. Eau Claire (Mich.) Pub. Schs., 1969-70; staff writer, sales rep. Jour. Era, Berrien Springs, 1979-81; sales rep. Berrien County Record, Buchana, Mich., 1981-82; account exec. WHFB Radio Palladium Pub. Co., St. Joseph, Mich., 1982-86; substitute tchr. Berrien County Intermediate Dist., 1986-89; instr. Southwestern Mich. Coll., Dowagiac, 1989-96, cons. Writing Ctr., 1996—; corp. trainer, 2000—. Editor The Positive Image newsletter, 1980—, The F Stop, 1982-90; author: Poetry Anthologies, 1989—; staff writer Decision Point, 1988-89; newsletter editor Fernwood Nature Photographers, 1980—. Ofcl. photographer Ind. and Internat. Spl. Olympics, Notre Dame, 1986. Named Emerging Artist Ind. Coun. for the Arts, 1989, Honor award Southwestern Coun. of Camera Clubs, 1988, Photographer of the Yr. Berrien County Photographic Artists, 1987, 90. Mem. AAUW, Nat. Authors Registry, Meth. Profl. Women (sec. 1990—), Berrien County Artists (v.p. 1986), Berrien County Photographic Artists (v.p. 1984), Southwestern Mich. Coun. Camera Clubs, Berrien Springs Camrea Club (v.p. 1980—). Methodist. Avocations: writing, photography, oil painting, watercolor painting. Home: 10252 Castner Dr Berrien Springs MI 49103-9602 Office: Southwestern Mich Coll 58900 Cherry Grove Rd # 316L Dowagiac MI 49047-9726

MULÉ, ANN C. oil industry executive; b. Phila., Pa., Oct. 22, 1956; BA magna cum laude, St. Joseph's U., 1978; JD cum laude, Villanova U., 1981. Bar: Pa. 1981, U.S. Supreme Ct./ 1988. From atty. to COO Sunoco Inc., Phila., 1980—2002, COO, 2002—. Bd. dir. Phila. (Pa.) Zoo. Mem.: ABA, Am. Corp. Counsel Assn. (vice chmn. exec. counsel, mem. corp. and securities law com.), Phila. (Pa.) Bar Assn., Pa. Bar Assn. (chmn. bus. law sect., mem. bd. govs., chmn. com. securities regulation, mem. title 15 task force), Am. Soc. Corp. Secs. (bd. dir., mem. exec. steering com., mem. nat. conf. com., mem. corp. practices com.), Alpha Sigma Mu (chmn. moot ct. bd.). Office: Sunoco Inc Ten Penn Center 1801 Market St Philadelphia PA 19103-1699*

MULERT, LYNNE CAROL, school counselor; b. Dubuque, Iowa, Jan. 30, 1949; d. Robert and Donna Meyer; m. Robert Ken Mulert, June 28, 1969; children: Troy, Travis. BS, U. So. Fla., 1993, MA, 1997. Guidance counselor Collier County Schs., Naples, Fla., 1997—. Mem.: ACA. Home: 2719 Wind Feather Trl Reno NV 89511

MULHALL, KIMBERLY A. marketing professional; b. Evanston, Ill., Dec. 26, 1967; d. Michael J. and Karen A. Mulhall, Mary M. Mulhall (Stepmother). B in Bus. Adminstrn., Roosevelt U., Chgo., 1990, MBA, 1996. Acct. Network Svcs. Co., Mount Prospect, Ill., 1990—95, sr. acct., 1995—97; asst. payroll supr. Underwriters Labs. Inc., Northbrook, Ill., 1997—98, payroll supr., 1998—2000, bus. analyst, 2000—01, sr. mktg. analyst, 2001—. Vol. Children's Advocacy Ctr. N.W. Cook County. Named Vol. of Yr., Children's Advocacy Ctr. N.W. Cook County, 2003. Mem.: Am. Mktg. Assn. Roman Catholic. Office: Underwriters Labs Inc 333 Pfingsten Rd Northbrook IL 60062 E-mail: kimberly.a.mulhall@us.ul.com.

MULKEY, SHARON RENEE, gerontology nurse; b. Miles City, Mont., Apr. 14, 1954; d. Otto and Elvera Marie (Haglof) Neuhardt; m. Monty W. Mulkey, Oct. 9, 1976; children: Levi, Candice, Shane. BS in Nursing, Mont. State U., 1976. RN, Calif.; nat. cert. gerontol. nursing. Staff nurse, charge nurse VA Hosp., Miles City, Mont., 1976-77; staff nurse obstetrics labor and delivery Munster (Ind.) Cmty. Hosp., 1982-83; nurse mgr. Thousand Oaks Health Care, 1986-88; unit mgr. rehab. Semi Valley (Calif.) Adventist Hosp., 1988-89, DON TCU, 1989-91; DON Pleasant Valley Hosp. Extended Care Vacility and Neuro Ctr., 1991-93, Victoria Care Ctr., Ventura, Calif., 1993—; clin. supr. Procare Home Health, Oxnard, Calif., 1996-97; staff nurse acute rehab. Los Robles East Campus Rehab. Unit, Westlake, Calif., 1998, clin. coord., 1998—2002; founder, CEO Internat. Womens Conf. Spkr. for Spiritual Growth and Devel., 2000—, Women of Distinction. Internat. conf. spkr. WCCD, 1991—. Mem. ANA, Nat. Gerontol. Nursing Assn., Internat. Platform Assn., Alpha Tau Delta (pres. 1973-75), Phi Kappa Phi. Home: 3461 Pembridge St Thousand Oaks CA 91360-4565

MULL, BETH A. counseling educator; b. Reading, Pa., Oct. 30, 1961; d. Edward William and Anna Catherine (Pazdrick) M. BA in Psychology, Alvernia Coll., 1994; MA in Counseling Psychology, Immaculata Coll., 1997, postgrad., 1998—. Therapist Progressions Health Sys., Reading, Pa., 1996—; adj. faculty Alvernia Coll., Reading, 1998. Psychology award for Clin. Excellence, Alvernia Coll., 1994. Mem. APA, ACA, Psi Chi, Chi Sigma Iota (past chpt. treas.). Roman Catholic. Avocations: aerobics, music.

MULLALLY, MEGAN, actress; b. LA, Nov. 12, 1958; d. Carter Mullally, Jr. and Martha Mullally; m. Michael Katcher (div.); m. Nick Offerman, Sept. 20, 2003. Student, Northwestern U. Actor: (TV films) Rainbow Drive, 1990, Winchell, 1998; (TV series) Ellen Burstyn Show, 1986; (TV films) Everything Put Together, 2000, Lifetime, The Pact, 2002; (TV series) My Life and Times, 1991, Fish Police, 1992, Rachel Gunn, RN, 1992, Will and Grace, 1998— (Emmy Award Supporting Actress in a Comedy, 2000, Outstanding Comedy Series award, 2000, Am. Comedy Award, 2001, Outstanding Female Actor Award, 2001, Screen Actors Guild award Outstanding Actress in a Comedy Series, 2001, 2002, 2003); (Broadway plays) Grease, 1994, How to Succeed in Business Without Really Trying, 1995—96; (films) Once Bitten, 1985, Last Resort, 1986, About Last Night, 1986, Anywhere But Here, 1999, Best Man in Grass Creek, 1999, Everything Put Together, 2000, Monkey Bone, 2001, Stealing Harvard, 2002; actor, actor: (films) Speaking of Sex, 2001, (voice) Teacher's Pet, 2004. Office: The Gersh Agency PO Box 5617 Beverly Hills CA 90210 also: Will and Grace KoMut Entertainment 4024 Radford Ave Studio City CA 91604*

MULLANE, JEANETTE LESLIE, artist, educator; b. Chgo., Oct. 7, 1938; d. Clarence Leslie and Marion Janet Shumaker; m. Richard Michael Mullane, Apr. 16, 1977. Degree, Am. Acad. Art, 1966; BS in Art Edn., U. Wis., 1973. Painting tchr. in Wis. & Oreg., Bergen, Norway. Exhibitions include Cider Painters Am. Ann. Internat. Miniature Art Exhbns. (Best of Show award, 1996, Judge's award, 1997, Excellence in Watercolor award, 1998, 2000, 2002, 2003, Leonards award, 2001, 1st pl. watercolor, 2002), Miniature Painters, Sculptors and Gravers Soc. Washington D.C. (3rd pl. still life, 1992, 2d pl. watermedia, 2002, Hon. Mention, 2003), exhibited in group shows at Miniature Art Soc. Fla. Ann. Internat. Miniature Art Show, 1990—2004 (7 awards transparent watercolor including 1st Pl. award, 2004, 3 awards human figure), Portland Audubon Soc. Wild Arts Festival, 1990—94, Rose Festival Art Show, 1990, 1991 (Portland Rose Soc. award), 1992, 1993, El Dorado Gallery, 1992 (1st pl. watercolor), exhibitions include Miniature Art Soc. N.J., 1993 (2nd pl. florals), Watercolor Soc. Oreg. Exhbn. 1993, 1997, 2001, World Fedn. Miniaturists Internat. Exhbn., London, Eng., 1995, one-woman shows include Trent Hughes Gallery, Portland, 1995, Artspace Gallery, Bay City, Oreg., 1995, 1996, exhibited in group shows at Irving Shapiro Meml. Nat. Watercolor Competition, Chgo., 1995, 1996, Antoinette Hatfield Gallery, Portland, Oreg., 1996—99, exhibitions include Paper Mill Playhouse Internat. Miniature Art Exhbn., 1996—2002, Snow Goose Gallery, Bethlehem, Pa., 1996, 1998, 2000, 2002, Watercolor Soc. Oreg. Exhbn., 1997, 2001, 1st Tone Internat. Miniature Exhbn., Dhaka, Bangladesh, 1998 (1st pl. florals), Hilliard Soc. Exhbn., Eng., 2000, World Fedn. Miniaturists Internat. Exhbn., Tasmania, 2000, Smithsonian Inst., 2004; curator (internat. minature art show) Lake Oswego Festival of Arts, Oreg., 2001—02; Exhibited in group shows at Hilliard Soc. Shows, Eng., 2000, 2002, Lawrence Gallery, Portland, Oreg., 2002. Mem.: Watercolor Soc. of Oreg., Miniature Painters, Sculptors and Gravers Soc., Miniature Art Soc. Fla., Miniature Artists Am. (signature mem.), Cider Painters Am. (signature mem.), Phi Kappa Phi. Home: 8240 SW Ridgeway Dr Portland OR 97225 E-mail: jmullane3@comcast.net.

MULLARKEY, MARY J. state supreme court chief justice; b. New London, Wis., Sept. 28, 1943; d. John Clifford and Isabelle A. (Steffes) M.; m. Thomas E. Korson, July 24, 1971; 1 child, Andrew Steffes Korson. BA, St. Norbert Coll., 1965; LLB, Harvard U., 1968; LLD (hon.), St. Norbert Coll., 1989. Bar: Wis. 1968, Colo. 1974. Atty.-advisor U.S. Dept. Interior, Washington, 1968-73; asst. regional atty. EEOC, Denver, 1973-75; 1st atty. gen. Colo. Dept. Law, Denver, 1975-79, solicitor gen., 1979-82; legal advisor to Gov. Lamm State of Colo., Denver, 1982-85; ptnr. Mullarkey & Seymour, Denver, 1985-87; justice Colo. Supreme Ct., Denver, 1987—, chief justice, 1998—. Fellow: Colo. Bar Found., ABA Found.; mem.: ABA, Denver Bar Assn. (Jud. Excellence award 2003), Thompson G. Marsh Inn of Ct. (pres. 1993—94), Colo. Women's Bar Assn. (Mary Lathrop award 2002), Colo. Bar Assn. Office: Supreme Ct Colo Judicial Bldg 2 E 14th Ave Denver CO 80203-2115

MULLEN, MARIE, actress; Founding mem., co-founder Druid Theatre Co., 1975. Appeared in numerous prodns. including the Beauty Queen of Leenane (Tony award, 1998, Obie award), The Loves of Cass McGuire, Silverlands, The Playboy of the Western World, Lovers' Meeting, the Colleen Bawn, The Shaughraun, A Doll's House, Much Ado About Nothing, 'Tis Pity She's a Whore, Famine, Drama at Inish, Conversations on a Homecoming, The Power of Darkness, The Plough and the Stars, the Cavalcaders, The Man of Mode, Love of the Nightingale, Man Who Came to Dinner, King Lear, Big Maggie, 2001 (Irish Theatre award nominee); TV/films appearances include The Butcher Boy, 1997, The Van, 1996, Snakes and Ladders, The Disappearance of Finbarr, 1996, Circle of Friends, Family, 1995, Dancing at Lughnasa, 1998, When Brendan Met Trudy, 2000, Disco Pigs, 2001. Address: Druid Theatre Co Chapel Ln Galway Ireland

MULLEN, MAUREEN ANN, social worker; b. Chgo., Mar. 22, 1949; d. Robert Vincent and Mary Geraldine M. BA, U. Ill., 1971; MEd, Coll. of William and Mary, 1974; MSW, Univ. Ill., 1990; postgrad., U. Chgo., 1985, 86. Programmer Computer Task Group, N.Y.C., 1980-81; analyst, programmer Guy Carpenter, N.Y.C., 1981-82; analyst C.N.A. Ins., Chgo., 1982-84; analyst, programmer Lakeshore Nat. Bank, Chgo., 1984-85; sales support Sterling Software, Chgo., 1986; owner Mullen Designs, Chgo., 1987; dir. of social svcs. Vista Health, Fayetteville, Ark., 2002—03; employee assistance counselor Ark. Employee Assistance Program, Fayetteville, 2003—. Prodr., host (TV show) Ozarks Live!. Vol. Samaritans hotline, Chgo., 1986; mem. adv. bd. Lakeview Mental Health Ctr., Chgo., 1986; mem. Chgo. Coun. on Fgn. Rels., 1986-87; chmn. fundraiser Habitat for Humanity, 1987; vol. Thomas Hynes Campaign, Chgo., 1987, Manic Depressive and Depressive Assn. and Nat. Alliance for Rsch. into Schizophrenia and Depression, 1988, Wilmette Sch. Bd., Caucus, 1997, mem. Endowment Fund Com., 1996, 97, Chgo. Bot. Garden, 1999, New Trier Democratic Orgn., 2000; bd. dirs. N.W. Ark. Mental Health Assn., 2002—, Cmty. Access TV, Fayetteville, 2003; spkrs. chmn. Fayetteville Freedom Festival, 2003; mem. ACLU, So. Poverty Law Ctr.; mem. Dem. Nat. Com. Ill. State scholar, 1971. Mem. NOW, Sierra Club. Avocations: painting, poetry, backpacking, photography, acting. Home: 3246 Autumn Ct Fayetteville AR 72703

MULLEN, REGINA MARIE, lawyer; b. Cambridge, Mass., Apr. 22, 1948; d. Robert G. and Elizabeth R. (McHugh) M. BA, Newton Coll. Sacred Heart, 1970; JD, U. Va., 1973. Bar: Pa., Del., U.S. Dist. Ct. Del., U.S. Ct. Appeals (3d cir.), U.S. Supreme Ct. Dep. atty. gen. State Del. Dept. Justice, Wilmington, 1973—79, state solicitor, 1979—83, chief fin. unit, 1983—88; v.p., counsel MBNA Am. Bank, N.A., Wilmington, Del., 1988—91, 1st v.p., sr. v.p., counsel, 1991—98, exec. v.p., sr. counsel, 1998—. Bd. profl. responsibility State of Del., 1996-99. Bd. dirs. Wilmington Music Festival, 1992-98, New Castle Hist. Soc., 1999—, World Affairs Coun. Wilmington, 2002—; fin. com. Chesapeake Bay coun. Girl Scouts Am., Wilmington, 1985-94, bd. dirs., 1988-94, v.p., 1990-94, cmty. devel. com., 1994-96, 99—2003, chair pers. com., 1996-99; bd. dirs. Cmty. Legal Aid Soc., 1994-99, treas., 1995-97. Mem. ABA, Del. State Bar Assn. (chair adminstrv. law sect. 1983-85), U. Va. Law Sch. Alumni Assn. (mem. alumni coun.). Democrat. Roman Catholic. Office: 1100 N King St Wilmington DE 19884-0001

MULLEN, TERRI ANN, retired special education educator; b. St. Louis, Apr. 01; d. William Earl and Sophia Kinniff; m. Thomas Patrick Mullen; children: David, Mark, Debi. BS in Edn., S.E. Mo. State U.; M in Sch. Adminstrn., Calif. State U., 1978, M in Spl. Edn., 1981; EdD in Institutional Mgmt., Pepperdine U., 1985. Cert. spl. edn., std. sec., std. elem., adminstrv. svc. K-12, cmty. coll. instr. Tchr. Irvine (Calif.) Unified Sch. Dist., 1972-84; lectr., spl. edn. Calif. State U., Fullerton, 1989-90; asst. prin. Moreno Valley (Calif.) Unified Sch. Dist., 1984-85; adminstr. of spl. svcs. Centralia Sch. Dist., Buena Park, Calif., 1984-89; elem. prin. Capistrano Unified Sch. Dist., San Juan Capistrano, 1989-93; spl. edn. tchr., dept. chair Moreno Valley (Calif.) Unified Sch. Dist., 1993—. Chair, cmty. staff ednl. planning com. Santiago Elem. Sch., Irvine Unified Sch. Dist., 1981; dir., staff devel. for spl. programs pers. Centralia Sch. Dist., Buena Park, 1984-89; workshop presenter Assn. of Calif. Sch. Adminstrs. Conf., San Francisco, 1983. Author: Resource Book of Classroom Interventions for the Collaborative Teaching Model, 1994, Tips of the Trade for the Classroom Aide, 1984; contbr. articles to profl. jours. Adv. bd. for sp. edn. Calif. State U. Fullerton, 1988-89. Recipient Cmty. Svc. award Disneyland, 1992, 93; named Outstanding Educator of Yr. Rotary Club, 1983. Mem. Coun. for Exceptional Children, Kappa Delta Pi, Phi Kappa Phi. Avocations: roller skating, fashion design, interior design, computer applications, writing. E-mail: tmullen@pacbell.net.

MULLENIX, LINDA SUSAN, lawyer, educator; b. N.Y.C., Oct. 16, 1950; d. Andrew Michael and Roslyn Marasco; children: Robert Bartholomew, John Theodore, William Joseph. BA, CCNY, 1971; M Philosophy, Columbia U., 1974; PhD Pres.'s fellow, 1977; JD, Georgetown U., 1980. Bar: D.C. 1981, U.S. Dist. Ct. D.C. 1981, U.S. Ct. Appeals (D.C. cir.) 1981, U.S. Supreme Ct. 1986, Tex. 1991, U.S. Ct. Appeals (5th cir.) 1995. U. Md. European divsn., Ramstein, Germany, 1974; instr. N.Y. Inst. Tech., N.Y.C., 1976; assoc. prof., lectr. George Washington U., Washington, 1977-80; asst. prof. Am. U., Washington, 1979; assoc. Pierson, Ball & Dowd, Washington, 1980-81; clin. prof. Loyola U. Law Sch., L.A., 1981-82; asst. prof. Cath. U. Law Sch., Washington, 1984-86; assoc. prof., 1986-90; prof., 1990; Reuschlein disting. vis. chair Villanova Law Sch., 2000. Vis. asst. prof. CCNY, 1977, Cooper Union Advancement Sci., Art, N.Y.C., 1977, Loyola U. Law Sch., L.A., 1982-83, Cath. U. Law Sch., Washington, 1983-84; jud. fellow U.S. Supreme ct. and fed. Jud. Ctr., 1989-90; Bernard J. Ward Centennial prof. U. Tex., 1991—; vis. prof. Harvard Law Sch., 1994-95, Mich. Law Sch., 1996; adj. instr. Fordham U., N.Y.C., 1975-76, adj. asst. prof., 1977. Author: ExamPro: Civil Procedure, 1998, Civil Procedure Roadmap, 1997, Casenotes: Federal Courts, 1997, Mass Tort Litigation: Cases and Materials, 1996; co-author: Understanding Fedeeral Courts, 1998, Federal Courts in the Twenty-First Century, 1996, 2d edit., 2002; Moore's Federal Practice and Procedure, 1991, 97; editor bibliographies Polit. Theory, A. Jour. Polit. Philosophy, 1972-74, The Tax Lawyer Jour., 1978-80; columnist The National Law Jour., 1998—; contbr. editor review of U.S. Supreme Ct. Cases; co-reporter Report and Plan of Civil Justice Reform Act Adv. Group, S.d., Tex., 1991; assoc. reporter ALI, Restatement of the Law Governing Lawyers; contbr. articles to profl. jours. Alt. del. Dem. State Conv., 1980. Fellow NDEA, 1971-74; N.Y. State Regents Scholar, 1967-71. Mem. ABA (reporter task force on class actions 1995-97), Am. Law Inst., D.C. Bar Assn. (com. on ethics, CLE and the Model Rules 1987), Am. Assn. Law Schs. (exec. com. sect. on civil proc. 1987-88, exec. com. sec. on conflicts of law 1991-92,chair prof. devel. com. 1991-93), Jour. Legal Edn. (editl. bd. 1997-1999), Phi Beta Kappa. Home: 722 Crystal Creek Dr Austin TX 78746-4730 Office: U Tex Sch Law 727 E Dean Keeton St Austin TX 78705-3224

MULLENS, SUSAN LYNN, psychologist, educator; b. Elkins, W.Va., Aug. 7, 1968; d. G. and B. Jackson; m. R. Mike Mullens, Mar. 17, 1999. BS in Psychology, Davis and Elkins Coll., Elkins, W.Va., 1990; MS in Psychology, Radford U., Va., 1991. Lic. psychologist W.Va., cert. counselor Nat. Bd. Cert. Counselors, 1994, lic. profl. counselor W.Va. Mental health profl. Youth Health Svc., Elkins, 1991—95; counselor E.A. Hawse Health Ctr., Baker, W.Va., 1996, W.Va. Bur. Employment Programs, Elkins, 1995—97; counselor, psychologist Appalachian Cmty. Health Ctr., Elkins, 1997—2001; psychologist Youth Health Svc., Elkins, 2002—. Part-time instr. Fairmont State Coll., Elkins, 1997—. Vol. Randolph County Cmty. Arts Ctr., Elkins, 2003—; Almost Heaven Golden Retriever Rescue, 2003—. Mem.: APA, W.Va. Counseling Assn. Avocations: pottery, basket weaving, Golden Retrievers. Home: PO Box 1848 Elkins WV 26241 Office: Youth Health Svc Inc 971 Harrison Ave Elkins WV 26241-3608 Office Phone: 304-636-9450. E-mail: susiemullens@sunlitsurf.com.

MULLER, CAROLYN BUE, physical therapist, volunteer; b. Crosby, N.D., Feb. 24; d. Sigurd Christian and Eleanor (Rushfeldt) Bue; m. Willard Chester Muller, Jan. 27, 1945; children: Marolyn Jean, Barbara Anne, Nancy Eleanor. BA, St. Olaf Coll., 1940; cert. in phys. therapy, Harvard U., 1944. Assoc. dir. younger girls and phys. edn. sect. YWCA, Syracuse, N.Y., 1940-43; phys. therapist Valley Forge Hosp., Phoenixville, Pa., 1944-45; med. records libr. Trust Territory of Pacific Islands, Truk, Caroline Islands, 1951-52. Founder, prin. organizer Am. Cmty. Sch., Truk, 1952, Lincoln Sch., Katmandu, Nepal, 1956, Am. Cmty. Sch., Mogadiscio, Somali Republic, 1958, Kampala, Uganda, 1966; panelist workshop Wash. Commn. for Humanities, Yakima, 1996. Author: Living in Uganda, 1967; cartographer: Maudie - An Oregon Trail Childhood, 1993. Charter registrar Clallam County Mus. and Hist. Soc., Port Angeles, Wash., 1977-87; vol. reading tutor Port Angeles Sch. Dist., 1980—; cmty. coord. UNICEF, Port Angeles, 1982-85; rep. Target Wash. Seminar, Seattle, 1984; rep. Asia-Can. Women in Mgmt. Conf., Victoria, B.C., Can., 1985; regional judge Wash. State Nat. History Day Contest, Port Angeles, 1985-2002; selection judge Wash. State Inquiring Mind Lecture Series, Seattle, 1989, 90, 96, organizer/coord., Inquiring Mind Lecture Series 1983-2002; Wash. state judge Nat. History Day Contest, Ellensburg, Wash., 1993-2003; bd. dirs. Wash. State Friends of the Humanities, 1991-94; trustee Wash. Commn. for the Humanities, 1995-97; pres. Am. Women's Club, Katmandu, 1957-58, Mogadiscio, 1959-60; v.p. Internat. Women's Club, Saigon, South Vietnam, 1971; mem. selection com. Evergreen State Soc. Awards, 1998, 99. Recipient Women Making a Difference award Soropimist Internat., 1984, Outstanding Vol. award Citizens' Ednl. Ctr. N.W., 1988, Evergreen award Evergreen State Soc., 1992. Mem. AAUW (br. pres. 1980-84, Edn. Found. scholarship in her name 1996). PEO (rec. sec. 1984-85, v.p. 1985-86, pres. 1987-89, chaplain 1994, Internat. Peace scholarship in her name 1990, state chmn. Internat. Peace scholarship 1989-90), Washington Athletic Club. Avocations: growing flowers, cross-country walking, oil painting, reading, travel. Home: 3624 S Mount Angeles Rd Port Angeles WA 98362-8910 E-mail: muller@tenforward.com.

MULLER, CHARLOTTE FELDMAN, economist, educator; b. N.Y.C., Feb. 19, 1921; d. Louis and Lillian (Drogin) Feldman; m. Jonas N. Muller, 1942 (dec.); m. Carl Schoenberg, 1970; children: Jeremy Lewis Muller, Sara Linda Muller. AB, Vassar Coll., 1941; A.M., Columbia U., 1942, PhD in Econs., 1946. Instr. econs. Bklyn. Coll., 1943; lectr. Barnard Coll., 1943-46; asst. prof. Occidental Coll., 1947; asst. study dir. Survey Rsch. Ctr., U. Mich., 1948; rsch. assoc. U. Calif., Berkeley, 1948-50; lectr. Yale U. Sch. Pub. Health, 1952-53; asst. prof. Columbia U. Sch. Pub. Health, 1957-67; assoc. dir. Ctr. for Social Rsch. CUNY, 1967-86, prof. econs., 1978-91, prof. emerita, 1991—, prof. sociology, 1982-91, prof. urban studies Ctr. for Social Rsch., 1967-78; v.p. CUNY Acad. for Humanities and Scis., 1985-88; prof. health econs. Mt. Sinai Sch. Medicine, 1986-91, prof. emerita, 1991—, dir. div. health econs., 1988-91, prof. dept. geriatrics, 1990-91, assoc. dir. Internat. Longevity Ctr.-USA, Ltd., 1991-97, sr. economist Internat. Longevity Ctr.-USA, Ltd., 1998—, co-dir. rsch. program Internat. Longevity Ctr.-USA, Ltd., 1999—. Cons. Health Care Financing Adminstrn., U.S. VA; disting. alumna speaker Vassar Centennial, 1971. Author: Health Care and Gender, 1990; mem. editorial bd. Am. Jour. Pub. Health, 1980-84, Women and Health, Rsch. on Aging; contbr. numerous articles on health econs. to profl. publs. Mem. N.Y.C. Mayor's Com. on Prescription Drug Abuse, 1970-73; bd. dirs. Alan Guttmacher Inst., 1972-81, CUNY Rsch. Found., 1985-91; vice chmn. Med. and Health Rsch. Assn., N.Y.C.; mem. health care tech. study sect. Nat. Ctr. Health Svcs. Rsch., 1976-79; mem. commn. on nat. policy Am. Jewish Congress, 1980-91. Ford/Rockefeller Founds. grantee, 1972-73, 75-76; Russell Sage Found. grantee, 1985-90. Mem.: APHA, Am. Econ. Assn. Jewish. Achievements include presenting report on Economic Status of Older Women to UN 2nd World Assembly on Aging., Madrid, 2002. Office: Internat Longevity Ctr-USA Ltd 60 E 86th St New York NY 10028-1009

MULLER, JENNIFER, choreographer, dancer; b. Yonkers, N.Y., Oct. 16, 1944; d. Don Medford and Lynette (Heldman) Muller. BS, Juilliard Sch. Music, 1967. Instr. in dance H.S. Performing Arts, 1967-72, Sarah Lawrence Coll., 1968-72, The Juilliard Sch., 1969-70, Nederlands Dans Theater, 1971-76, Utah rep., 1973-74, Centre Nat. de la Dance, Paris, 1998, Acad. Isola Danzo, Venice, 1999-2001, Atelier de Paris, 1999, Institut del Teatre de Barcelona, 2001, Centro Andaluz de Danza-Seville, 2003; commns.: Alvin Ailey Am. Dance Theatre, N.Y.C., 1977, 85, 2003, Festival d'Avignon, France, 1980, Lyon Opera Ballet, France, 1984, Aterballetto, 1988, Ballet Stagium, 1991, Dansgroep Krisztina de Chatel, 1992, Tanz-Forum Staatsoper Koln, Sachsische Staatopera-Dresden, ARTSCAPE-Balt., 1991, 95, Aterballetto, Italy, 1993, Les Ballet Jazz de Montreal, 1994, Ballet du Nord, France, 1995, White Wave Rising, 1996, Bat Dor Dance Co., Israel, Nederlands Dans Theatre 3, Ballet Contemporaneo, Argentina, Ohio Ballet, 2000, Dance Inst. U. Akron, 2003; cons. Met. Mus. Art, 1971-72, Mem. Pearl Lang Dance Co., N.Y.C, 1959-63, prin. dance, Jose Limon Dance Co., N.Y.C., 1963-71, assoc. dir., choreographer, prin. dancer, Louis Falco Dance Co., N.Y.C., 1968-74; founder, dir., choreographer: Jennifer Muller/The Works, N.Y.C., 1974[00bf] ; choreographic works include: Nostalgia, 1971, Rust, 1971, Cantata, 1972, Tub, 1973, An American Beauty Rose, 1974, Biography, 1974, Speeds, 1974, Winter Pieces, 1974, Clown, 1974, Four Chairs, 1974, Wyeth, 1974, White, 1975, Strangers, 1975, Beach, 1976, Crossword, 1977, Predicaments for Five, 1977, Mondriaan, 1977, Lovers, 1978, Solo, 1979, Conversations, 1979, Chant, 1980, Terrain, 1981, Shed, 1982, Kite, 1983, Souls, 1984, The Enigma, 1986, Fields, 1986, Couches, 1986, Life/Times, 1986, Darkness and Light, 1986, Interrupted River, 1987, Occasional Encounters, 1988, City, 1988, The Flight of a Predatory Bird, 1989, Refracted Light, 1990, RIGHTeous About Passing (on the LEFT), 1990, Woman with Visitors at 3am, 1991, Regards, 1991, arm in arm in arm..., 1991, Thesaurus, 1991, Glass Houses, 1991, 2-1-1/Attic, 1992, Momentary Gathering, 1992, The Waiting Room, 1993, The Politician/Peeling the Onion, 1993, Orbs, Spheres and Other Circular Bodies, 1993, HUMAN/NATURE-A Response to the Longhouse Gardens, 1993, Pierrot, 1993, Desire-That DNA Urge, 1994, Point of View (A Case of Persimmons and Picasso), 1994, The Spotted Owl, 1995, Some Days are Like That, 1995, Promontory, 1996, Fruit, 1996, The Dinner Party, 1996, A Broken Wing, 1996, Ricochet, 1997, Degas Revisited, 1998, Dialectics Part I, 1998, Spores, Solitude & Summer Humming, 1999, Beethoven-Not Four Naught, 2000, aSOlo, 2000, Hymn for Her, 2000, Time Treading, 2000, China Project: Sagone; Suk Road; Dancing Waves, 2001, The Door, 2001, Never in The Same Room, 2002, To Live Alone...., 2002, Moon, 2002, It's a c#!* City, 2002, Prayer, 2003, Bounce, 2003, Footprints, 2003, Flowers, 2004, Ecstatic Poems, 2004; choreographer for theatrical prodns.: Frimbo, 1980, The Death of von Richthofen..., 1982, Fame, The Musical, 1988, Up Against It, 1989, The Seven Deadly Sins, 1990, Signature, 1990, Esther, 1993, Once Around the City, 1998, 2001; dir. Le Jongleur, 2000. Recipient Best Performance award Berlin Festival, 1977, Acad. award Juilliard Sch. Music, 1967, Carbonell award, 1989; grantee Nat. Endowment for Arts, 1971-77, 80-85, 86-87, 87-88, Creative Artists Pub. Svc., 1976-77, N.Y. State Coun. on Arts, 1976-77, 78-79, 85-93, N.Y.C. Dept. Cultural Affairs, 1978-79, 94-2003, N.Y.C. Dept. Youth and Cmty. Devel., 2001-03. Mem. Am. Guild Mus. Artists, Soc. Stage Dirs. and Choreographers, World Arts Coun. Home and Office: The Muller/Works Found Inc 131 W 24th St New York NY 10011-1942 E-mail: jenniferm@compuserve.com., theworksnyc@compuserve.com.

MULLER, PATRICIA ANN, nursing administrator, educator; b. N.Y.C., July 22, 1943; d. Joseph H. and Rosanne (Bautz) Felter; m. David G. Smith, Mar. 19, 1988; children: Frank M. Muller III, Kimberly M. Muller. BSN, Georgetown U., 1965; MA, U. Tulsa, 1978, EdD, 1983. RN. Staff devel. coord. St. Francis Hosp., Tulsa, 1978-79, asst. dir. for nursing svc., nursing edn., 1979-82, dir. dept. edn., 1982-98, St. Francis Health Sys., 1998—2002, cons., 2002—. Mem. faculty Okla. U., Northeastern U., Tulsa U.; presenter at confs. and convs. Contbg. editor JOPAN, 1992-2001; contbr. articles to profl. jours. Mem. Leadership Tulsa, 1991; bd. dirs. Am. Heart Assn., Ronald McDonald House. Mem. ANA, Nat. League for Nursing, Am. Soc. for Nursing Svc. Adminstrs., Am. Soc. for Health Manpower Edn. and Tng., Okla. Nurses Assn., Okla. Orgn. of Nurse Execs. (pres. 1992-93), Sigma Theta Tau. Address: 6203 W Utica Ct Broken Arrow OK 74011 Office Phone: 918-671-7767. E-mail: mullsmi@aol.com.

MULLER, SUSAN MARIE, physician; b. Holyoke, Mass., Jan. 18, 1964; d. Robert Eugene and Antoinette Irene (Riccio) Muller. BS in Biology, SUNY, Albany, 1986; MD, Albany Med. Coll., 1991. Commd. ensign USN, 1988, advanced through grades to lt. comdr., 1997; internship Nat. Naval Med. Ctr., Bethesda, Md., 1992; gen. med. officer USS Emory S. Land, Norfolk, Va., 1992—94, Naval Air Sta. Oceana, Virginia Beach, Va., 1994—97, med. dir. acute care dept., 1994—97; family practice residency program Family Practice Med. Group, Inc., U. of Fla., 1997—99; family practitioner Benedict Family Health, Ballston Spa, NY, 1999—2001, Saratoga Family Health, Saratoga Springs, NY, 2001—. Med. dir. Saratoga Care Family Health Care Ctrs., Saratoga Springs, NY, 2000—. Recipient Achievement award, UpJohn, 1991, Physician's Recognition award, Am. Med. Assocs., 2002, Ams. Top Family Doctor's award, 2002—03. Avocations: equestrian sports, painting, photography, drawing, sculpting. Office: Saratoga Family Health 119 Lawrence St Saratoga Springs NY 12866

MULLETTE, JULIENNE PATRICIA, health facility administrator; b. Sydney, Australia, Nov. 19, 1940; came to U.S., 1953; d. Ronald Stanley Lewis and Sheila Rosalind Blunden (Phillips) M.; m. Fred Gillette Sturm, Nov. 24, 1964 (div. Dec. 1969); m. Kenneth Walter Gillman, Dec. 28, 1971 (div. Dec. 1978); children: Noah Khristoff Mullette-Gillman, D'Dhaniel Alexander Mullette-Gillman. BA, Western Coll. for Women, Oxford, Ohio, 1961; postgrad., Harvard U., 1964, U. Sao Paulo, Brazil, 1965, Inst. Philosophy, Sao Paulo, 1965, Miami U., Oxford, 1967-69. Tchr. English, High Mowing Sch., Wilton, N.H., 1962-64, Stoneleigh-Prospect Hill Sch., Greenfield, Mass., 1964; seminar dir. Western Coll. for Women, 1967-69; pres. Family Tree, Home U., Montclair, NJ, 1978—88; dir. Pleroma Holistic Health Ctr., Montclair, 1980—. Dir. Astrological Rsch. Ctr., Sydney, Australia, 1983; founder Spiritual Devel. Rsch. Group, 1986—; pvt. astrology counselor, 1962—; guest on radio & TV shows, 1962—; lectr. worldwide, 1963—; founder Pleroma Found. for Astrological Rsch. & Studies, 1990; breeder, trainer exotic animals; mem. Woodstock Pub. Access Com., 1993—. Author: The Moon-Understanding the Subconscious, 1973; contbr. articles to profl. jours.; editor (founding): KOSMOS Mag., 1968—78, Jour. Astrological Studies, 1970—; contbg. columnist: mags; hostess (radio talk shows) The Julienne Mullette Show, 1985—, others, —, (TV series) You and the Cosmos, Woodstock, NY, 1992—, The Julienne Mullette Show Connections TV, Newark, NJ, 1985—. Founder local chpt. La Leche League, Montclair, 1974; founding pres. The Internat. Astrology Forum, 2000. Mem. AAUW (chmn. cultural affairs Montclair chpt. 1987—), NAFE, Spiritual Devel. Group (founder), Internat. Soc. Astrological Rsch. (founding pres. 1968-78), Cosmos Hyperspace Astrological Origins and Supergravity Studies (founder), Am. Fedn. Astrologers (cert.), Belgian Soc. Astrology, Am. Assn. Humanistic Psychology, Internat. Llamas Assn., Internat. Soc. Astrological Studies and Rsch. (founder 2002). Avocations: tennis, local theatre, singing. E-mail: julienne@nep.net.

MULLIGAN, ELINOR PATTERSON, lawyer; d. Frank Clark and Agnes (Murphy) Patterson; m. John C. O'Connor; children: Christine Fulena, Valerie Clark, Amy O'Connor, Christopher Criffan O'Connor; m. William G. Mulligan, Dec. 6, 1975. BA, U. Mich.; JD, Seton Hall U., 1970. Bar: N.J. 1970. Assoc., Springfield and Newark, 1970-72; pvt. practice, Hackettstown, N.J., 1972; ptnr. Mulligan & Jacobson, N.Y.C., 1973-91, Mulligan & Mulligan, Hackettstown, 1976—. Atty. Hackettstown Planning Bd., 1973-86, Blairstown Bd. Adjustment, 1973-95; sec. Warren County Ethics Com., 1976-78, sec. Dist. X and XIII Fee Arbitration Com., 1979-87, mem. and chair, 1987-91, mem. dist. ethics com. XIII, 1992—; mem. spl. com. on atty. disciplinary structure N.J. Supreme Ct., 1981—; lectr. Nat. Assn. Women Judges, 1979, N.J. Inst. Continuing Legal Edn., 1988—. Contbr. articles to profl. jours. Named Vol. of Yr., Attys. Vols. in Parole Program, 1978. Fellow Am. Acad. Matrimonial Lawyers (1st woman pres. N.J. chpt. 1995-96); mem. ABA, Warren County Bar Assn. (1st woman pres. 1987-88), N.J. State Bar ASsn., N.J. Women Lawyers Assn. (v.p. 1985—), Am. Mensa Soc., Union League Club (N.Y.C.), Baltusrol Golf Club (Springfield, N.J.), Panther Valley Golf and Country Club (Allamuchy, N.J.), Kappa Alpha Theta. Republican. Home: 12 Goldfinch Way Hackettstown NJ 07840-3007 Office: 933 County Road 517 Hackettstown NJ 07840-4654 E-mail: llp-nj@mindspring.com.

MULLIGAN, ROSEMARY ELIZABETH, legislator; b. Chgo., July 8, 1941; d. Stephen Edward and Rose Anne (Sannasardo) Granzyk; children: Daniel R. Bonaguidi, Matthew S. Bonaguidi. AAS, Harper Coll., Palatine, Ill., 1982; student, Ill. State U., 1959-60. Paralegal Miller, Forest & Downing Ltd., Glenview, Ill., 1982-91; ind. contractor mcpl. law, 1991—. Paralegal seminar educator Harper Coll. Program chair White House Women's Econ. Leadership Summit, 1997. Pro-choice activist and mem. Ill. Ho. of Reps., 1993—, chmn. human svcs. appropriations com.; gov.'s workgroup on early childhood; gov.'s wokforce investment bd., 1999—. Recipient Disting. Alumnus award Ill. C.C. Trustee Assn., 1993, Legislator of Yr. award Ill. Assn. Cmty. Mental Health Agys., 1996, Heart Start award Nat. Ctr. Clin. Infant Programs, Legis. Leadership award Ill. Alcoholism and Drug dependence Assn., 1996, Cert. Appreciation Ill. Libr. Assn., Legis. cert. appreciation Delta Kappa Gamma Soc., 1997, Ida B. Wells-Barnett award, 1996; named Top 100 Women Making a Difference Today's Chgo. Woman, 1997; Flemming fellow Ctr. for Policy Alts., 1994. Mem. LWV, Nat. Women's Polit. Caucus, Ill. Fedn. Bus. and Profl. Women (Outstanding Working Woman of the Yr. 1997), Ill. Women in Govt., Chgo. Women in Govt. Rels., Ill. Fedn. Bus. and Profl. Women (nat. legis. platform rep. 1991-92, chair Outstanding Working Women of Ill. 1991-92, state membership chair 1989-90, state legis. co-chair, nat. platform rep. 1988-89, state legis. chair, nat. platform rep. 1987-88). Roman Catholic. Avocations: politics, tennis, reading. Home: 856 E Grant Dr Des Plaines IL 60016-6260 Office: Ill Ho of Reps State Capitol Springfield IL 62706-0001 also: 932 Lee St Ste 201 Des Plaines IL 60016-6594

MULLIKIN, SANDRA MARIE, music educator; b. Louisville, Ky., May 11, 1960; d. James Edward Stewart Sr. and Mary Angela Stewart; m. Douglas Lee Mullikin, June 15, 1991; children: Tiffany Marie Nicole,

Emily Elizabeth Ludmila. MusB in Ch. Music magna cum laude, MusB in Music Edn. with honors, Ky. Wesleyan Coll., 1982; MA in Elem. Edn. summa cum laude, Western Ky. U., 1986. Office asst. Dr. Alan Bornstein, Louisville, 1977—78; youth dir. Kirk Meml. United Meth., Owensboro, 1978—79; travel counselor Am. Auto. Assn., Owensboro, 1980—82; choir dir. Breckenridge St. United Meth., Owensboro, 1982—86; music tchr. Owensboro City Schs., 1982—85; sales mgr. Cottonwood Sales, Evansville, Ind., 1985—89; music tchr., band dir. Cloverport (Ky.) Ind. Schs., 1989—96; music tchr. Ohio County Bd. Edn., Hartford, Ky., 1996—. Realtor L. Steve Castlen Realtors, Owensboro, 1990—92; arts & humanities com. Fordsville (Ky.) and Wayland Alexander Elem., 1998—. Active Civitan, Owensboro, 1980; co-leader brownies Girl Scouts Am., Owensboro, 2001—02; precinct co-capt. Rep. Party, Owensboro, Ky., 1996, 2000, del. to state conv. Louisville, 1996; choir dir. Thruston United Meth. Ch., Maceo, Ky., 1986—94. Scholar, Kappa Kappa Iota, 2001, Ky. Orff-Schulwerk Assn., 1995. Mem.: Ky. Orff-Schulwerk Assn., Am. Orff-Schulwerk Assn., Ky. Music Educators Assn., Music Educators Nat. Conf., Gideons Aux. (pres.), Kappa Kappa Iota (state music chair), Delta Omicron (Outstanding Svc. award 1982). Republican. Methodist. Avocations: travel, reading, singing, photography. Home: 1621 Maple Ave Owensboro KY 42301 E-mail: smmullikin@yahoo.com.

MULLIN, PATRICIA JONES, banker; b. Long Branch, N.J., Oct. 27, 1955; d. George Edwin and JoAn Layden Jones; m. Peter William Mullin, Apr. 5, 1986; children: Ryan Peter, Connor Patrick. BBA, St. Mary's Coll., Notre Dame, Ind., 1977; MBA, Roosevelt U., 1982. Cert. cash mgr. Officer First Chicago, 1977-83; asst. v.p. Fidelity Bank, Phila., 1983-84; v.p. State St. Bank, Boston, 1984—99, Citizens Bank, Boston, 1999-2000; v.p., team leader Sovereign Bank, Boston, 2000—. Mem. Assn. Fin. Profls., Treasury Mgmt. Assn. New Eng. (pres., bd. dirs. 1994—), Boston Club, St. Mary's Club of Boston (bd. dirs. 1994-96). Roman Catholic. Avocations: quilting, needlework, hiking, swimming. Office: Sovereign Bank 75 State St Boston MA 02109-1829

MULLINS, BARBARA J. financial executive; b. Day, Fla., Aug. 29, 1938; d. James Eli and Bessie Geraldine (Johnson) Grantham; m. Mike B. Mullins, Dec. 20, 1956; children: Ronald Lee, Richard Bryan, Mikel Duane. Acctg. Cert., Longview C.C., Lee's Summit, Mo., 1978, AS, Johnson County C.C., Overland Park, Kans., 1980; student, Avila Coll., Kansas City, Mo., 1980-84. Contr., v.p. Bride Co., Leawood, Kans., 1970-82; mgr., cons. Price Waterhouse, Atlanta, 1984-92; owner, cons. Sys. Adv. Svcs., Kansas City, Mo., 1992—99; CFO Memphis Brooks Mus. Art, 1999—. Mem. Inst. Mgmt. Accts. (chpt. pres., nat. dir., regional dir.). Avocations: reading, interior decorating, sewing.

MULLINS, OBERA, retired microbiologist; b. Egypt, Miss., Feb. 15, 1927; d. Willie Ree and Maggie Sue (Orr) Gunn; m. Charles Leroy Mullins, Nov. 2, 1952; children: Mary Artavia, Arthur Curtis, Charles Leroy, Charlester Teresa, William Hellman. BS, Chgo. State U., 1974; MS in Health Sci. Edn., Governors State U., 1981. Med. technician, microbiologist Chgo. Health Dept., Chgo., 1976—, now pers. asst. III, to 1999; ret., 1999. Mem. AAUW, Am. Soc. Clin. Pathologists (cert. med. lab. technician), Ill. Soc. Lab. Technicians. Roman Catholic. Home: 9325 S Marquette Ave Chicago IL 60617-4131

MULLINS, RUTH GLADYS, nurse; b. Westville, N.S., Can., Aug. 25, 1943; came to U.S., 1949, naturalized, 1955; d. William G. and Gladys H.; m. Leonard E. Mullins, Aug. 27, 1963 (dec.); children: Deborah R. Jenkins, Catherine M., Leonard III. BS in Nursing, Calif. State U., Long Beach, 1966; MSN, UCLA, 1973; PhD, Columbia Pacific U. Cert. pediatric nurse practitioner. Pub. health nurse Los Angeles County Health Dept., 1967-68; nure Meml. Hosp. Med. Ctr., Long Beach, 1968-72; dir. pediatric nurse practitioner program Calif. State U., Long Beach, 1973-97, asst. prof., 1975-80, assoc. prof., 1980-85, prof., 1985—, coord. accelerated BSN program, 2003—. Health svc. credential coord. Sch. Nursing Calif. State U., Long Beach, chmn., 1979-81, coord. grad. programs, 1985-92; mem. Calif. Maternal, Child and Adolescent Health Bd., 1977-84; vice chair Long Beach/Orange County Health Consortium, 1984-85, chair 1985-86. Author: (with B. Nelms) Growth and Development: A Primary Health Care Approach; contbg. author: Quick Reference to Pediatric Nursing, 1984; assoc. editor Jour. Pediatric Health Care, 1985—. Tng. grantee HHS, Divsn. Nursing Calif. Dept. Health. Fellow Nat. Assn. Pediatric Nurse Assocs. and Practitioners (exec. bd., pres. 1990-91), Nat. Fedn. Nursing Splty. Orgns. (sec. 1991-93); mem. APHA, Nat. Alliance Nurse Practitioners (governing body 1990-92), Assn. Faculties Pediatric Nurse Practitioner Programs. L.A. and Orange County Assn. Pediatric Nurse Practitioners and Assocs. (treas. 1998—), Am. Assn. Univ. Faculty. Democrat. Methodist. Home: 6382 Heil Ave Huntington Beach CA 92647-4232 Office: Calif State U Dept Nursing 1250 N Bellflower Blvd Long Beach CA 90840-0001 Office Phone: 562-985-4476. E-mail: rgmullins@sprintmail.com., rmullins@csulb.edu.

MULRYAN, LENORE HOAG, art curator, author; b. Lompoc, Calif., Aug. 25, 1927; d. William Thomas and Lois Lorraine (Fratis) Hoag; m. Henry Trist Mulryan; children: Patricia Trist (dec.), James William, Carrie M. Neal. BA, UCLA, postgrad., 1979-81; Cert., Am. Inst. Fgn. Trade, Glendale, Ariz., 1949. Vis. art curator UCLA Fowler Mus. Cultural History, 1982—2004; art curator, editor, cons. Internat. Exec. Svc. Corps, 1998. Dir. fine art print calendars for Chapin Sch., Princeton, N.J., 1971-73; co-chair Fine Arts Tours, Princeton, 1973; cons. Internat. Exec. Svc. Corp., Zimbabwe, 1998, Romania, 1998; curator UCLA Fowler Mus. Nat. Hist. Author, curator, editor: (books/exhbns.) Mexican Figural Ceramists and Their Works, 1982, Nagual in the Garden: Fantastic Animals in Mexican Ceramics, 1996, Ceramic Trees of Life: Popular Art from Mexico, 2003, UCLA Fowler Mus. Cultural History, 2003—; curator Wilmot Collection of Mexican Art, 1982-91. Mem. Eisenhauer Disting. Fgn. Leader Program U. So. Calif. Mem. Delphians (pres. 1963-64), Westwood Village Rotary Club (chair Amb. Scholarship Selection com. 1996—). Avocations: music, art, yoga, travel.

MULTHAUP, MERREL KEYES, artist; b. Cedar Rapids, Iowa, Sept. 27, 1922; d. Stephen Dows and Edna Gertrude (Gard) Keyes; m. Robert Hansen Multhaup, Apr. 7, 1944; children: Eric Stephen, Robert Bruce. Student, State U. Iowa, 1942—43, Rice U., 1971. Tchg. faculty Summit (N.J.) Art Assn., 1956-60; art instr. studio classes Springfield, N.J., 1954-55, Bloomfield (N.J.) Art Group, 1955-56, Westport, Conn., 1962-63; tchg. faculty Hunterdon Art Ctr., Clinton, N.J., 1985-92. Numerous one-woman shows including most recently Coriell Gallery, 1995; exhibited in group shows at Nat. Assn. Women Artists, N.Y.C., 1957-2001 (awards in figure painting), Hartford (Conn.) Athanaeum Mus., 1961 (1st prize), Highgate Gallery, N.Y.C., Waverly Gallery, N.Y.C., Leicester Gallery, London, Silvermine Gallery, Conn., Pendut Gallery, Tex., Benedict Gallery, Sidney Rothman Gallery, N.J., Stamford (Conn.) Mus., Bridgeport (Conn.) Mus., Montclair (N.J.) Mus., Newark Mus., Coriell Gallery, Albuquerque; (traveling exhibit) Nat. Assn. Women Artists, 1996—, Travel USA, 1999, New World Art Ctr., N.Y.C., 1998-99, Gallery Art 54, N.Y.C., 1997, Atelier 14 Gallery, N.Y.C., 2000-2002; more that 30 commd. portraits. 1960--. Bd. dirs., exhbn. chmn. Summit Art Assn., 1950-60, Silvermine Guild of Art, New Canaan, Conn., 1960-64; bd. dirs. Artist's Equity of N.J., 1977-84, chmn. state-wide event, 1983, 86; artist's adv. coun. Hunterdon Art Ctr., Clinton, 1988-92; pres. Four Hills Neighbors, 1998-2000. Recipient awards in juried exhbns. in Iowa, Pa., N.J., Conn., N.Y.C. Mem. Nat. Mus. for Women in Arts (charter mem.), Nat. Assn. Women Artists Inc. (awards for figure painting 1957, 80-89), Silvermine Nat. Portrait Group of Artists. Avocations: entertaining, singing, dance, playing the piano, reading. Home: 1321 Stagecoach Rd SE Albuquerque NM 87123-4320

MULVANEY, MARY FREDERICA, systems analyst; b. N.Y., Nov. 27, 1945; d. Michael Joseph and Mary Catherine (Clapper) Mulvaney. BA, Marymount Coll., 1967; MA, U. Va., 1968; MS in Computer Sci., Marymount U., 1999. Cert. data processor Inst. Cert. of Computer Profls. Computer systems analyst Dept. of Def., Ft. Meade, Md., 1968-74; sr. programmer analyst Planning Rsch. Corp., McLean, Va., 1974-83; mem. tech. staff Fed. Systems Group TRW Inc., Fairfax, Va., 1983-90; sr. mem. tech. staff GTE Govt. Sys. Corp., Rockville, Md., 1990-94; engr., scientist TRW, Inc., Fairfax, Va., 1994—2002; software engr. Northrop Grumman, Fairfax, 2003—. Mem.: IEEE, Cath. Assn. Scientists and Engrs., Computer Measurement Group, Data Processing Mgmt. Assn. Roman Catholic. Office: Northrop Grumman Mission Sys 12900 Federal Sys Park Dr Fairfax VA 22033

MULVANEY, MARY JEAN, physical education educator, department chairman; b. Omaha, Jan. 6, 1927; d. Marion Fowler and Blanche Gibons (McKee) M. BS, U. Nebr., 1948; MS, Wellesley Coll., 1951; LHD (hon.), U. Nebr., 1986. Instr. Kans. State U., Manhattan, 1948-50, U. Nebr., Lincoln, 1951-57, asst. prof., 1957-62, U. Kans., Lawrence, 1962-66; assoc. prof. U. Chgo., 1966-76, prof., 1976-90, prof. emeritus, 1990—, chmn. women's divsn., 1966-76, chmn. dept. phys. edn. and athletics, 1976-90; mem. vis. com. on athletics MIT, 1978-81, Wellesley Coll., 1978-79. Dir. athletics U. Chgo., 2003—; mem. selection com. U. Chgo. Athletics Hall of Fame, 2004. Recipient Honor award Nebr. Assn. Health, Phys. Edn. and Recreation, 1962, U. Nebr. Alumni Achievement award, 1998; named to U. Chgo. Athletics Hall of Fame, 2003. Mem. AAHPERD, Nat. Collegiate Athletic Assn. (mem. coun. 1983-87), Collegiate Coun. Women Athletic Adminstrs., Midwest Assn. Intercollegiate Athletics for Women (chmn. 1979-81), Nat. Assn. Collegiate Dirs. of Athletics (mem. exec. com. 1976-80, Hall of Fame 1990), Ill. Assn. Intercollegiate Athletics for Women (chmn. 1978-80), Univ. Athletic Assn. (sec. 1986-90, mem. exec. com. 1986-90, mem. dels. com. 1986-90, chmn. athletic adminstr.'s com. 1986-88), Mortar Bd., Alpha Chi Omega. Home: 5821 Kennelley Ct Lincoln NE 68516-3799 E-mail: maryjeanmulvany@aol.com.

MULVANEY, MOLLY MARIE, women's health nurse practitioner; b. Dubuque, Iowa, June 13, 1976; d. Ronald John and Rose Ann Mulvaney. BSN, U. Iowa, 1998; cert. women's health care, Family Planning Coun. Iowa, Des Moines, 2001. RN Iowa, advanced registered ob-gyn nurse practitioner. Staff nurse U. Iowa Hosps. and Clinics, Iowa City, 1998—2000; head nurse Primary Care for Women, Iowa City, 2000—01; staff nurse Mercy Med. Ctr., Cedar Rapids, Iowa, 2001—02; nurse practitioner Linn County Ob-gyn, Cedar Rapids, 2002—. Vol. Proteus, Iowa City, 2001, Cmty. Health Free Clinic, Cedar Rapids, 2003. Mem.: Nurse Practitioner's Women's Health, Am. Coll. Nurse Practitioners. Republican. Roman Catholic. Avocations: exercising, cooking, gardening. Office: Linn County Ob-gyn 1260 3rd Ave SE Cedar Rapids IA 52403

MULVEY, MARY CROWLEY, retired adult education director, gerontologist, senior citizen association administrator; b. Bangor, Maine, Aug. 17, 1909; d. Michael J. and Ann Loretta (Higgins) Crowley; m. Gordon F. Mulvey, Jan. 25, 1940. BA, U. Maine, 1930; MA, Brown U., 1953; EdD, Harvard U., 1961; LHD (hon.), U. Maine, 1991. Chair R.I. Com. on Aging, 1953-65; dir. adminstrn. on aging State of R.I., 1960-63; co-founder Nat. Coun. Sr. Citizens, 1961; pres. Nat. Sr. Citizens Edn. and Rsch. Ctr., Washington, 1963—; 1st v.p. Nat. Coun. Sr. Citizens, 1976-2001; guidance counselor Providence Sch. Dept., 1963-65; dir. adult edn. City of Providence Sch. Dept., 1965-79; reg. prog. rep. Title V, Older Ams. Act, Nat. Coun. Sr. Citizens, Washington, 1980-94. Major role in enactment of Medicare and Older Americans Act, 1950-65; del., adv. com. White House Conf. on Aging, 1961, 71, 81, 95; cons. Fed. Housing for the Aging, Washington, 1963-65, tech. rev. com. Older Ams. Act Title IV, 1966-70; instr. preparing for retirement, developer women's program U. R.I., 1963-80; appt. by Pres. Carter to Fed. Coun. Aging, 1979, pres. R.I. State Coun. Sr. Citizens, 1982-98; charter mem. adv. bd. Coll. Arts and Humanities, U. Maine, 1992-96. Contbr. articles to profl. jours. Charter mem. U. Maine Friends of Mus. Art, 1997—; chair sr. citizen's rally Nat. Coun. Sr. Citizens, Washington, 1998. Recipient Cert. of award as Project Dir. of Sr. AIDES Employment Program, 1968-79, Medicare award R.I. State Coun. Sr. Citizens and Nat. Coun. Sr. Citizens, 1985, Disting. Achievement award U. Maine, 1980, Disting. Achievement award Berwick Acad., 1981, Justice for All award R.I. Bar Assn., 1981, Woman of Yr. award Nat. Sr. Pageant, 1982, R.I. Women 1st R.I. Sec. of State, 1991, citation Syracuse U., 1991, R.I. Dept. Elderly Affairs, 1993, 10th, 25th and 30th Anniversaries Title V Sr. Employment award Nat. Coun. Sr. Citizens, 1978, 93, 98, Lifetime Achievement award, 1994, Co-Founder and Continuing Bd. Mem. award, 1995, Svcs. for Sr. Citizens award, 1995, 30-yr. Sr. Aides award Nat. Sr. Citizens Edn. and Rsch. Ctr., 1999; named to R.I. Heritage Hall of Fame, 1993; Citation by Gov. Lincoln Almond for contbns. to R.I., 1996; Humanitarian award U. Maine Reunion, 2000; Soroptomists fellow in rsch. in gerontology Harvard U., 1955, 57, 59. Fellow Gerontol. Soc. Am.; mem. ACA, AAUW, Am. Assn. Adult and Continuing Edn., Harvard U. Alumni Assn. (Alumni award R.I. chpt. 1986), U. Maine Alumni Assn., Brown U. Alumni Assn., Harvard 1920 Club, Charles William Elliot Soc. (charter), Charles F. Allen Soc., Stillwater Soc. U. Maine (charter, Presdl. award for achievement), Paul Hamus Soc. Harvard, Pi Lambda Theta, Delta Delta Delta. Achievements include development of adult literacy program; has had 5 books published for teaching adult basic education and English as a second language. Home: 118 Evergreen Ln Windham ME 04062-4713

MUMTAZ, See GIFFORD, NANCY

MUND, GERALDINE, judge; b. L.A., July 7, 1943; d. Charles J. and Pearl M. BA, Brandeis U., 1965; MS, Smith Coll., 1967; JD, Loyola U., 1977. Bar: Calif. 1977. Bankruptcy judge U.S. Ctrl. Dist. Calif., 1984—, bankruptcy chief judge, 1997—2002. Past pres. Temple Israel, Hollywood, Calif.; past mem. Bd. Jewish Fedn. Coun. of Greater L.A. Mem. ABA, L.A. County Bar Assn. Office: 21041 Burbank Blvd Woodland Hills CA 91367-6606

MUNDINE, RACHEL QUINN, music educator; b. Newport, N.C., Aug. 14, 1935; d. Raymond Thomas and Ada Elizabeth (Quinn) M. Student, East Carolina U., Greenville, N.C., 1953-54. Music dir. Program Search For a Star WNCT-TV, Greenville, N.C., 1954-55, pianist various programs, 1954-55; soprano soloist Santa Monica (Calif.) Civic Opera, 1968-71; music tchr. piano, voice, organ Melody Haven Studio, Newport, N.C., 1972—; organist First United Meth. Ch., Morehead City, N.C., 1984—; guest piano soloist N.C. Symphony, Morehead City, 1981. Organist, pianist, vocalist various hotels and clubs throughout U.S., Can. and Thule, Greenland, 1958-71; pres., founder La Musique Club of Carteret County, N.C., 1975—; dir. Miss La Musique Pageant, Morehead City, 1993-2003; area and state chmn. music festivals N.C. Fedn. Music Clubs, Greenville and Chapel Hill, 1984-94. Composer: Our Majestic Mountains, 1986. Mem. Carteret County Social Svcs. Bd., 2002—; contbns. chmn. N.C. Symphony Carteret County chpt., Morehead City, 1993—2002, pres., 1981; entertainment chmn. Festival of the Trees, Hospice, Morehead City, 1997—2003; mem. adv. bd. Civic Ctr., Morehead City, 1999—2001. Named Woman of Yr. in Arts Carteret County Coun. Women, Morehead City, 1990, 92. Mem. Nat. Guild Piano Tchrs. (adjudicator 2003), N.C. Music Tchrs. Assn., Order Eastern Star (worthy matron 1977-78, grand organist 1981-82), N.C. Music Assn. (pres., founder 1995-2002), Lions. Methodist. Avocations: hiking, sailing, skiing, swimming. Home and Office: Melody Haven Studio 580 Lake Rd Newport NC 28570-6956 Office Phone: 252-223-4538.

MUNDINGER, MARY O'NEIL, nursing educator; b. Fredonia, N.Y., Apr. 27, 1937; d. Thomas Lewis and Dorothy (Hanselman) O'Neil; m. Paul C. Mundinger, Aug. 23, 1958; children: Paul Jr., Ann Mundinger Schimenti, Thomas, Elizabeth. BS, U. Mich., 1959; MA, Columbia U., 1974, PhD, 1981. Adminstr., instr. Tchrs. Coll. Columbia U., N.Y.C., 1975; adj. instr. Pace U., N.Y.C., 1975-77, asst. prof., 1977-82; asst. prof. nursing, dir. grad. program Columbia U. Sch. Nursing, N.Y.C., 1982-83, assoc. prof. nursing, dir. grad. program, 1983-84, assoc. prof., assoc. dean adminstrv. affairs, 1984-85, assoc. prof., asst. dean faculty of medicine, 1986—, dean, Centennial prof. health policy, 1986—. Bd. dirs. Conn. Hospice, Branford; adv. group steering com. N.Y. Acad. Medicine, N.Y.C., 1992—; regional adv. com. Nat. Network Librs. of Medicine, N.Y.C., 1992—; Robert Wood Johnson health policy fellows bd. Inst. Medicine, Washington, 1990—, Health Svcs. Improvement Fund, N.Y.C., 1992—, health policy adv. com. Sen. Edward Kennedy, Washington, 1985—, med. adv. bd. Walt Disney Imagineering (Wonders of Life), Orlando, Fla., 1988-89; charter mem. health care tech., Inst. Medicine, NAS, 1985—. Author: Home Care Controversy: Too Little, Too Late, Too Costly, 1983 (Book of Yr. 1984), Autonomy in Nursing, 1980 (Book of Yr. 1981). Recipient grant W.K. Kellogg Found., 1989, grant Katzenbach Found., 1986. Avocations: skiing, reading. Office: Office of Dean of Nursing 630 W 168th St Box 6 New York NY 10032-3702 Fax: (212) 305-1116.

MUNDORFF SHRESTHA, SHEILA ANN, cariologist; b. Rochester, N.Y., Dec. 14, 1945; d. Karl Mundorff and Elizabeth Mary (Braun) Ross; m. Buddhi Man Shrestha, June 18, 1988. BS in Biology, Nazareth Coll., Rochester, 1967; MS in Microbiology, U. Rochester, 1984. Lab. technician Eastman Dental Ctr. U. Rochester, 1967-69; rsch. asst. Eastman Dental Ctr., 1969-71, rsch. assoc., 1971-92, small animal expt. coord., 1984-92, sect. head animal/microbiol. rsch., 1987—, chmn. Instl. Animal Care and Use Com., 1990-97, vivarium dir., 1990-97, med. emergency program dir., 1991-92, asst. prof., 1992-97; assoc. prof. U. Rochester Eastman Dept. Dentistry, 1997—. Mem. univ. com. on animal resources U. Rochester, 1997—; mem. animal resource group ADA Health Found., Chgo., 1981-83; cons. working group Sci. Consensus Conf.-Assessment Cariogenic Potential of Foods, San Antonio, 1985; participant, reactor, co-chair animal caries models working groups Conf. on Clin. Aspects of Demineralization of Teeth, Rochester, N.Y., 1994; invited session chair symposium 2000, Univ. Leeds, 2000. Patentee in field. CPR instr. ARC, Rochester, 1978-94, cert. 1st responder, N.Y.S., 1992-95. NIH, Nat. Inst. Dental Rsch. grantee, 1986, 87, 88. Mem. Am. Assn. Dental Rsch. (sec.-treas. Rochester sect. 1977-92). Roman Catholic. Avocations: dance, sewing, swimming, flower arranging, painting on silk. E-mail: buddhis@msn.com.

MUNEIO, PATRICIA ANNE, public health nurse; b. Detroit, Oct. 7, 1949; d. Charles Eli and Mary Jane (Voletti) M. BSN, Wayne State U., 1973; MS, Calif. Coll. for Health Scis., San Diego, 1994. RN, Mich., Fla. Staff nurse to head nurse Detroit Osteo. Hosp., Highland Park, Mich., 1974-75; nurse emergency rm. Grace Hosp., Detroit, 1975-77; pub. health nurse, team leader Detroit VNA, Detroit, 1977-83; staff nurse, head nurse Comprehensive Health Svcs. of Detroit, 1983-85; pvt. duty nurse AbCare, Inc., Detroit, 1985; pub. health nurse, supr. Cmty. Home Care, Sterling Heights, Mich., 1985-88; home care supr. Med. Personnel Pool, Southfield, Mich., 1988-89; pub. health nurse III Macomb County Health Dept., Mt. Clemens, Mich., 1989-96; health care surveyor spl. svcs. sect. Mich. Dept. Consumer and Industry Svc., Lansing, 1996-97; owner The Pink Alligator Used Books and Consignment Store, Indian Rock Beach, Fla., 1998—2002; nurse mn. St. Anthony's Hosp., St. Petersburg, Fla., 2002—. Cons., 1999—; legal nurse cons., 1999; notary pub., Fla., 2000. Bd. dirs. Indian Rocks Beach Action 2000, 1998—, Indian Rock Beach Pks. and Recreatin Bd., 2003, City Indian Rock Beach Hist. Soc.; charter mem. N.Am. Inst. Smithsonian. Mem. ANA, Mich. Nurses Assn. (rep. 1992, Blue Water Dist. v.p. 1990-92, pres. 1992-96), Macomb County Health Dept. Staff Coun. (pres. 1990-94). Democrat. Roman Catholic. Avocations: knitting, embroidery, painting, travel, sports. Home and Office: 309 Bahia Vista Dr Indian Rocks Beach FL 33785

MUNGER, SHARON, market research firm executive; M. Robert Munger; 3 children: Shawn, Shane, Blair. Grad. Vanderbilt U. Sec., data processor, acct. exec. M/A/R/C, Inc., Irving, Tex., from 1973; now pres., chief operating officer Irving, Tex. Office: M-A-R-C Inc 7850 N Belt Line Rd Irving TX 75063-6098

MUNN, CAROL LOUISE, private school educator; d. Gene Lacoste and Mary Stroman Munn. BA, Baylor U., 1982; MFA, U. Mich., 1993. Cert. tchr. Tex., tchr. gifted and talented Tex. Tchr. Cypress Fairbanks Ind. Sch. Dist., Houston, 1978—90, U. Mich., Ann Arbor, 1991—93, Washtenaw C.C., Ann Arbor, 1993, Colegio Hispano-Norteamericano, Valencia, Spain, 1993—95, Cypress Fairbanks Ind. Sch. Dist., Houston, 1995—2003, St. Agnes Acad., Houston, 2003—. Jr. english team leader Cypress Fairbanks Ind. Sch. Dist., Houston, 1997—2003. Author: (literary criticism) Emily Dickinson's Religion of Defiance, (poetry) Christmas in the Pyrenees (Acad. of American Poets Prize, 1992), How To Grow Up Alive (Michael R. Gutterman award, 1991), Poetry, Naming the Miracles (Second Pl. in the Nat. Poetry Competition, 2002), Still Weather (pub. in Stories From Where We Live: The Gulf Coast, 2003), View of the Dead, 1994. English scholar, Baylor U., 1980—82; grantee, Nat. Endowment for the Humanities, 2000, Cowden fellow, U. Mich., 1990—91, Colby fellow, 1991—92. Mem.: Nat. Coun. of Teachers of English. D-Liberal. Protestant. Avocations: writing, reading, travel.

MUNN, JANET TERESA, lawyer; b. De Funiak Springs, Fla., Nov. 7, 1952; d. Willard Ernest and Olive Pauline (Wilkinson) M.; m. Michael E. Fass, Sept. 27, 1975. BA in Anthropology, Fla. State U., 1975, MA in Social Scis., 1977; JD with high honors, Nova U., 1985. Bar: Fla. 1985, U.S. Dist. Ct. (so. dist.) Fla. 1986, U.S. Dist. Ct. (mid. dist.) Fla. 1988, U.S. Ct. Appeals (11th cir.) 1989, U.S. Supreme Ct. 1990. Jud. clerk for Judge Jose A. Gonzalez Jr. U.S. Dist. Ct. (so. dist.) Fla., Ft. Lauderdale, 1985-87; litigation assoc. Steel Hector & Davis, Miami, Fla., 1987-91, litigation ptnr., 1992—. Editor: Southern District Digest, 1987-88. Leo S. Goodwin fellow Nova U., 1983-84. Mem. ABA (co-chmn. intellectual properties litigation com. litigation sect. 1991-94, chmn. trade regulation/intellectual property com. gen. practice sect. 1990-91, vice chmn. 1989-90), Fed. Bar Assn., Fla. Bar (Pro Bono award 1988), Phi Kappa Phi. Office: 200 S Biscayne Blvd Ste 4000 Miami FL 33131-2362

MUNNELL, ALICIA HAYDOCK, economist; b. N.Y.C., Dec. 6, 1942; d. Walter Howe Haydock and Alicia (Wildman) Haydock Roux; m. Thomas Clark Munnell (div.); children: Thomas Clark Jr., Hamilton Haydock; m. Henry Scanlon Healy, Feb. 2, 1980. BA in Econs., Wellesley, 1964; MA in Econs., Boston U., 1966; PhD in Econs., Harvard U., 1973. Staff asst. bus. rsch. div. New Eng. Tel. Co., Boston, 1964-65; teaching fellow econs. dept. Boston U., 1965-66; rsch. asst. for dir. econ. studies program Brookings Instn., Washington, 1966-68; teaching fellow Harvard U., Cambridge, Mass., 1971-73; asst. prof. econs. Wellesley Coll., Mass., 1974; economist Fed. Res. Bank Boston, 1973-76, asst. v.p., economist, 1976-78, v.p., economist, 1979-84, sr. v.p., dir. rsch., 1984-93; asst. sec. for econ. policy Dept. Treasury, Washington, 1993-95; mem. Coun. of Econ. Advisors, 1995—. Mem. Gov.'s Task Force on Unemployment Compensation, Mass., 1975; mem. spl. funding adv. com. for Mass. pensions, 1976; mem. Mass. Retirement Law Comm., 1976-82; staff dir. joint com. on pub. pensions Nat. Planning Assn., 1978; mem. adv. com. for urban inst. HUD grant on state-local pensions, 1978-81; mem. pension rsch. council Wharton Sch. Fin. and Commerce, U. Pa., 1979— ; mem. adv. group Nat. Commn. for Employment Policy, 1980-81; mem. adv. bd. Nat. Aging Policy Ctr. in Income Maintenance, Brandeis U., 1980-84; participant pvt. sector retirement security and U.S. tax policy roundtable discussions Govt. Rsch. Corp., 1984; mem. supervisory panel Forum Inst. of Villers Found., 1984; mem. Medicare working group, div. of health policy rsch. and edn. Harvard U.,

1984-87; mem. Commn. on Coll. Retirement, 1984-86; mem. com. to plan major study of nat. long term care policies Inst. Medicine, Nat. Acad. Scis., 1984-87; mem. steering com. Am. Assn. Ret. Persons, 1987—; mem. adv. council Am. Enterprise Inst., 1987—; com. mem. Inst. Medicine, Nat. Acad. Scis. Human Rights Com., 1987—; co-founder, pres. Nat. Acad. Social Ins., 1986—; bd. dirs. Pension Rights Ctr.; mem. program rev. com. Brigham and Women's Hosp., 1988—; mem. Commn. to Rev. Mass. Anti-Takeover Laws, 1988-89, econs. vis. com. MIT, 1989—. Author: The Impact of Social Security on Personal Saving, 1974, Future of Social Security, 1977 (various awards), Pensions for Public Employees, 1979, The Economics of Private Pensions, 1982; co-author: Options for Fiscal Structure Reform in Massachusetts, 1975; editor: Lessons from the Income Maintenance Experiments, 1987, Is There a Shortfall in Public Capital Investment?, 1991, (conf. proc.) Retirement and Public Policy, 1991, Pensions and the Economy: Sources, Uses, and Limitations of Data, 1992, co-editor: Pensions and the Economy: Sources, Uses, and Limitations of Data; contbr. articles to profl. jours., chpts. to books. Mem. Inst. Medicine of NAS, Nat. Acad. Pub. Adminstrn. Office: Council of Econ Advisers Old EOB Exec Office Of The Pres Washington DC 20502-0001

MUÑOZ DONES DE CARRASCAL, ELOISA, hospital administrator, pediatrician, consultant, educator; b. San Lorenzo, P.R., Oct. 25, 1922; d. Pedro and Maria (Dones) Muñoz; m. José D. Carrascal, Dec. 7, 1962; children: Lilia, Maria. BA in Edn. cum laude, BS in Chemistry cum laude, U. P.R., Rio Piedras, 1943; MD, Tulane U., 1948. Diplomate Am. Bd. Pediatrics. Intern Arecibo Charity Dist. Hosp., 1948-49; resident in pediatrics San Juan (P.R.) City Hosp., 1949-51, chief newborn svc., attending pediatrician, 1951—, dir. neonatal-perinatal medicine, 1965—, dir. fellowship tng. program, 1972—; from instr. to assoc. prof. clin. pediatrics sch. medicine U. P.R., 1951-89, prof., 1989—. Courtesy pediatrician neonatologist Tchrs. Hosp., Hato Rey, P.R., 1951-76, Ashford Presbyn. Drs. Hosp., Santurce, P.R., 1951-76, San Jorge H. H. Pavia Fernandez, Santurce, 1951-76; cons. pediatrician neonatologist Tchrs. H. Auxilio Mutuo H., Hato Rey, 1976—, Drs. H. San Jorge H. Ashford, San Juan, 1976—; mem. exec. com. San Juan City Hosp., 1976—, pres. med. faculty, 1976-77, 87-89, mem. instl. rev. bd., mem. ednl. rev. bd., mem. various coms.; lectr. in field. Contbr. articles to profl. jours. U.S. del. Care Orgn. Latin Am., 1962-63. Recipient Bronze medal Brazilian Acad. Human Scis., 1975, Hon. Cert. Internat. Yr. Women, City Mayor Lodo Carlos Romero Barceló, 1975, Hon. Cert. Disting. Svc. to Cmty., Julio Sellés Solá Elem. Sch., 1976, Pioneer Pediatrician award P.R. Pediat. Sect. Convention, 1993, Pioneer in Neonatology award P.R. Pediat. Sect. Convention, 1995, Pioneer Pidiat. Critical Care award Pediat. Critical Care Assn., 1996; grantee NIH, 1962. Fellow Am. Acad. Pediatrics (neonatal perinatal sect., mem. com. fetus and newborn P.R. chpt. 1956—, sec.-treas. 1962-64, mem. com. history perinatal sect. 1992—, Plaque in Recognition Disting. Pediatrician and Tchr. 1985), Pan Am. Pediatrics; mem. Am. Med. Women Assn., P.R. Med. Assn. (pediat. sect., mem. chamber of dels. 1962-63, Bronze plaque 1967, 91, Gold Pin 1980), P.R. Med. Women Assn. (sec.-treas. 1957-60, pres. 1960-64), Pan Am. Med. Women Assn. (pres. P.R. chpt. 1960-64, P.R. del. VIII Congress Manizales Colombia 1962), Pan Am. Med. Women Alliance (vis. lectr. 1962), Tulane Med. Alumni, London Royal Soc. Health, Colegio de Químicos, Soc. Dominicana de Pediatría (hon., vis. lectr. 1971), Dominican Rep. Soc. (hon.). Avocation: poetry.

MUÑOZ-SOLA, HAYDEÉ SOCORRO, library administrator; b. Caguas, P.R., Dec. 27, 1943; d. Gilberto Muñoz and Carmen Haydeé (Solá) de Muñoz; m. Juan M. Masini-Soler, Jan. 8, 1966 (div. 1979); children: Juan Martín Masini-Muñoz, Haydeé Milagros Masini-Muñoz. BA in Psychology, U. P.R., Río Piedras, 1965, MLS, 1970; D in Libr. Sci., Columbia U., 1985. Asst. libr. U. P.R., Río Piedras, 1964-67; dir. libr. Interam. U., Aguadilla, P.R., 1974-75; head svcs. to pub. U. P.R., Aguadilla, 1975-76; cataloguer Cath. U., Ponce, P.R., 1976-79, U. P.R., Río Piedras, 1982-84, head libr. and info. sci. libr., 1984-85, prof. grad. libr. sch., 1986, 99, dir. libr. sys., 1986-93, coord. external resources libr. sys., 1994-97, dir. of libr. Ponce, P.R., 1997, collection devel. officer Rio Piedras, 1998, sabbatical leave, 2000-01. Dir. P.R. Newspaper Project, Río Piedras, 1986-90; mem. Adv. Com. on Pub. Librs., San Juan, 1987-93; proposal reviewer NEH, 1990—; chmn. Puerto Rican Del. to Nat. White House Conf. on Libr. and Info. Svcs., 1991. Author: La Información y la Documentación Educativa/Informe Sobre la Situación Actual en Puerto Rico, 1991, Memorias: Segunda Pre-Conferencia de Casa Blanca Sobre Bibliotecas y Servicios de Información en Puerto Rico, 1991, Lineamientos para Colecciones Bibliograficas Nacionales, 1997, Premio por Excelencia en Investigación Aplicada y Publicación, 1997; compiler, editor ann. Puerto Rican Bibliography, 1999—; contbr. articles to profl. jours. Mem. Ponce Sport Club, 1976-83, ARC, Ponce, 1978. Recipient plaque White House Pre-Conf. on Libr. and Info. Sci., 1990, others, Leccion Magistral Josefina del Toro Fulladosa, 2002; French Alps Study Tour scholar Assn. Caribbean Univ. Rsch. and Instl. Libr., 1989, Germany Study Tour scholar Fgn. Rels. Office, Germany, 1991, coord. So. area 1974, Lauro award 1989, Leccion Magistral Josefina del Toro Fulladosa award, 2002. Mem. ALA, Am. Mgmt. Assn., Grad. Sch. Libr. and Info. Sci. Alumni Assn. (pres. 1988-90), Seminar for Acquisitions L.Am. Libr. Materials, Iberoamerican Nat. Libr. Assn. (pres. 1992-93), Puerto Rican Libr. Soc., Assn. Caribbean U. Rsch. and Instnl. Libr. (Parchment award 1988), Asoc. para las Comunicaciones y Tecnología Educativa, Mid. States Assn. Coll. and Sch. (collaborator), Am. Women Assn., Nat. Commn. P.R. Women, Phi Delta Kappa (chair P.R. com. 1988-90, Kappan of Yr. 1990), Eta Gamma Delta. Roman Catholic. Avocations: reading, crewel work, embroidery, knitting, movies. Office Phone: 787-764-0000 x2707. Personal E-mail: hmunoz@caribe.net. Business E-Mail: hmunoz@upracd.upr.clu.edu.

MUNRO, ALICE, author; b. Wingham, Ont., Can., July 10, 1931; d. Robert Eric and Anne Clarke (Chamney) Laidlaw; m. James Armstrong Munro, 1951 (div. 1976); children: Sheila, Jenny, Andrea; m. Gerald Fremlin, 1976 BA, U. Western Ont., 1952, DLitt (hon.), 1976. Established Munro Books, 1963; writer in residence U. of British Columbia & U. of Queensland, 1980. Author: (short stories) The Dimensions of a Shadow, 1950, Dance of the Happy Shades, 1968 (Gov.-Gen.'s Lit. award 1969), A Place for Everything, 1970, Lives of Girls and Women, 1971 (Can. Booksellers award, 1972), (short stories) Something I've Been Meaning To Tell You, 1974, Who Do You Think You Are?, 1979 (pub. in U.S. as Beggar Maid: Stories of Flo and Rose, 1984, Gov.-Gen.'s Lit. award 1978), The Moons of Jupiter, 1982, The Progress of Love, 1986 (Gov. Gens. Lit. award 1987), Friend of My Youth, 1990, (short stories) Open Secrets, 1994, A Wilderness Station, 1994, Selected Stories, 1996, The Love of a Good Woman, 1998 (Fiction prize Nat. Book Critics Circle 1999), Hateship, Friendship, Courtship, Loveship, Marriage, 2001; TV scripts: A Trip to the Coast, 1973, Thanks For The Ride, 1973, How I Met My Husband, 1974, 1847: The Irish, 1978. Recipient Can.-Australia Lit. Prize 1977, Marian Engel award, 1986, Governor General's award, 1968, 1978, 1986, Canadian Booksellers award, 1977, WH Smith award, 1995, Nat. Book Critics Circle award & Giller Prize, 1999, REA award for short story, 2001, O. Henry Prize for short stories, 2003. Office: William Morris Agy 16th Fl 1325 Avenue of the Americas New York NY 10019*

MUNRO, BARBARA HAZARD, nursing educator, dean, researcher; b. Wakefield, R.I., Nov. 28, 1938; d. Robert J. and Honore (Egan) Hazard; children: Karen Aimee, Craig Michael, Stephanie Anne. BS, MS, U. R.I., Kingston; PhD, U. Conn. RN, Conn. Asst. prof. U. of R.I. Coll. of Nursing, Kingston; assoc. prof., chmn. program in nursing rsch. Yale U., New Haven, Conn.; assoc. prof., asst. dir. Ctr. for Nursing Rsch. U. Pa., Phila.; dean, prof. Boston Coll. Sch. Nursing, 1991—. Presenter and workshop leader various nursing confs. and seminars in U.S. Contbr. articles and rsch. to profl. pubs. Trustee St. Elizabeth's Med. Ctr. Boston, 1994—. Recipient Nat. Rsch. Svc. award. Fellow Am. Acad. Nursing; mem. ANA, Golden Key, Sigma Theta Tau, Pi Lambda Theta, Phi Kappa Phi. Office: Boston Coll Sch Nursing Cushing Hall Chestnut Hill MA 02467-3812

MUNRO, ELEANOR, writer, lecturer; b. Bklyn., Mar. 28, 1928; d. Thomas and Lucile (Nadler) Munro; m. Alfred Frankfurter (dec. 1965); children: David, Alexander (dec.); m. E.J. Kahn, Jr. (dec.). BA, Smith Coll., 1949; MA, Columbia U., 1968. Staff writer, editor Art News Mag., N.Y.C., 1952-59; freelance writer, art critic, lectr. N.Y.C., 1960—. Vis. fellow Woodrow Wilson Nat. Fellowship Fedn., Princeton, N.J., 1990—; cons., juror Bush Fdn., St. Paul, 1994; resident fellow Bellagio Study Ctr., Lake Como, Italy, 1991, Yaddo, Saratoga Springs, N.Y., 1984. Author: Encyclopedia of Art, 1961, Through the Vermilion Gates, 1971, Originals: American Women Artists, 1979 (a N.Y. Times Notable Book of Yr.), Memoir of a Modernist's Daughter, 1988, On Glory Roads: A Pilgrim's Book about Pilgrimage, 1987 (named N.Y. Times Notable Book of Yr.); author articles, criticism, fiction and poetry. Bd. dirs. Truro (Mass.) Ctr. for Arts, 1979—, The Living Theater, N.Y.C., 1989—, Nat. Alliance Rsch. into Schizophrenia and Depression, N.Y.C., 1995-2000. Recipient Cleve. Arts prize, 1988, medal of honor Smith Coll., 1990, Nat. Lifetime Achievement award Women's Caucus for Art, 2003. Mem. PEN Am., Am. Internat. Assn. Art Critics, Authors Guild. Home: 176 E 71st St # 3B New York NY 10021-5159

MUNRO, ROXIE JEAN, artist, educator, illustrator, writer; b. Mineral Wells, Tex., Sept. 5, 1945; d. Robert Enoch and Margaret Bissey Munro; m. Bo I. Zaunders, May 17, 1986. Student, U. Md., 1963—65, Md. Inst. Coll. of Art, 1965—66; BFA, U. Hawaii, 1969; postgrad., Ohio U., 1969—70. Lectr. photography U. Hawaii, Honolulu, 1970—71; freelance editl. illustrator Washington, 1972—80; instr. painting Paint in Italy Workshops, Lake Como, 1995—. Author, illustrator The Inside-Outside Book of N.Y.C., 1985 (Best Illustration award N.Y. Times, 1985), Mazescapes, 2001; author: others; The New Yorker mag., 1981—93, solo and group shows, pvt. and pub. collections, mus. exhibitions, including solo at Zimmerli Mus., Rutgers U., N.J., 2004. Fellow, Yaddo Found., 1980. Mem.: Soc. Children's Book Writers and Illustrators, N.Y. Artists Equity. Office: Roxie Munro Studio 43-01 21st St Long Island City NY 11101 E-mail: rxstudio@aol.com.

MUNROE, SHIRLEY ANN, retired hospital association executive, health care consultant; b. Mar. 31, 1924; Pre-nursing cert., La Sierra Coll., Arlington, Calif., 1943; RN, Glendale Sanitarium and Hosp. Sch. Nursing, 1946; postgrad., UCLA Ext., 1953—55, L.A. City Coll., 1948—51; cert., U. Calif. Santa Cruz ext., 1971. Mgr. Roswell Symphony Orch., Roswell, N.Mex., 1998—. Asst. dir. pub. rels. alumni postgrad. assembly Loma Linda U., L.A., 1949—55; dir. pub. rels. world meeting Aerospace Med. Assn., L.A., 1953; chmn. re-edn. nursing com. Calif. Dept. Employment, 1962; cons. lectr. nurse aide edn., adult edn. Willits and Ukiah H.S., 1962; chmn. Career Project for Sr. HS Girls, 1962—64; mem. Mendocino-Lake adv. com. Regional Med. Program, 1969—73; mem. vocat. edn. adv. com. Ukiah Unified Sch. Dist., 1970—73. Co-chmn. edn. com. Mendocino County br. Am. Cancer Soc., 1961—62, bd. dirs., 1961—76, pres., 1963—65; chmn. trustees Tri-County Pre-Payment Medi-Cal Pilot Project State of Calif., 1969—71; trustee Nor Coa Health, 1967—76, 1st v.p., 1969—71, pres., 1971—72, chmn. South Planning Coun., 1972—74; mem. Mendocino-Lake counties Coun., 1966—76; leader, del. People to People Internat. U.S. Citizen Amb. Program, 1981; 2d v.p. Roswell Symphony Guild, 1993—95; supt. children's edn. Seventh-Day Adventist Ch., 1961—64, dir. pub. rels., 1967—78, chmn. fin. com., 1967—78, soloist, 1958—78, mem. ch. bd., 1967—78, mem. exec. com. Ill. conf., 1983—89; soloist Presbyn. Ch., Ukiah, 1956—69, Ukiah Oratorio Soc., 1958—65; mem. ch. bd. Seventh-Day Adventist Ch., Elmhurst, 1979—89, dir. music, mem. ch. bd. Roswell, 1989—, dir. ch. ministries, 1990—93, ch. elder, 1992—; mem. exec. com. Seventh Day Adventist Ch. Southwestern Union Conf., 1991—; N.Am. divsn. del. 56th World Session Gen. Conf. Seventh Day Adventists, Utrecht, Netherlands, 1995; choir dir. Westminster Presbyn. Ch., Roswell, 1993; mem. cmty. adv. bd. Ea. N.Mex. Med. Ctr., Roswell, 1998—; bd. dirs. Mendocino County chpt. ARC, 1968—70, Broadview Acad., Lafox, Ill., 1983—86, Roswell Symphony Orch., 1990—98, sec.-treas., 1991—93, 2d v.p., 1992—93, 1st v.p., 1993—95, pres., chmn. bd. dirs., 1995—98; mem. steering com. Am. Heart Assn., Mendocino County br. Calif. Heart Assn.; bd. dirs. Blue Cross No. Calif., 1971—78, exec. bd., 1973—78, hosp. provider rep., 1970—78; mem. bd. Adventist Health Sys./North, 1981—87, chmn. strategic planning com., 1983—87; mem. bd. Hinsdale Hosp., 1979—94, mem. joint conf. com., 1980—89, chmn. strategic planning com., 1983—88, bd. dirs. fin. com., 1989—94. Mem.: Am. Hosp. Assn. Address: 2614 N Pennsylvania Ave Roswell NM 88201-5871 E-mail: rso@dfn.com.

MUNSELL, ELSIE LOUISE, lawyer; b. N.Y.C., Feb. 15, 1939; d. Elmer Stanley and Eleanor Harriet (Dickinson) M.; m. George P. Williams, July 14, 1979. AB, Marietta Coll., 1960; JD, Marshall-Wythe Coll. William and Mary, 1972. Bar: Va. 1972, U.S. Dist. Ct. (ea. dist.) Va. 1974, U.S. Ct. Appeals (4th cir.) 1976, U.S. Supreme Ct. 1980. Tchr. Norview High Sch., Norfolk, Va., 1964-69; asst. Commonwealth atty. Commonwealth Atty.'s Office, Alexandria, Va., 1972-73; asst. U.S. atty. Alexandria, 1974-79; U.S. magistrate U.S. Dist. Ct. (ea. dist.) Va., Alexandria, 1979-81; U.S. atty. Dept. Justice, Alexandria, 1981-86; sr. trial atty. Office of Gen. Counsel, Dept. Navy, Washington, 1986-89, asst. gen. counsel installations and environ. law, 1989-91; dep. asst. environ. and safety Sec. Navy, 1991-2001, ret., 2001. Mem. USEPA Clean Air Act Adv. Com., 1997—; bd. dirs. BMT Designers & Planners. Active Va. Commn. on Status of Women, 1966-74; bd. vistors Coll. William and Mary, 1972-76; active Atty. Gen.'s Adv. Com. U.S. Attys., 1981-83; bd. dirs. Carpenter's Shelter, Inc., 1990-93; vestry St. Alban's Ch., Annandale, Va., 1996-99, 2003; fed. preservation officer Dept. of Navy, 1999. Presdl. Meritorious Exec., 1999; recipient Spl. Achievement awrd Nat. Mil. Fish and Wildlife Assn., 2001, Disting. Civilian Svc. award, 2001. Mem. Sr. Execs. Assn., Chi Omega. Episcopalian.

MUNSON, LUCILLE MARGUERITE (MRS. ARTHUR E. MUNSON), real estate broker; b. Norwood, Ohio, Mar. 26, 1914; d. Frank and Fairy (Wicks) Wirick; m. Arthur E. Munson, Dec. 24, 1937; children: Barbara Munson Papke, Judith Munson Andrews, Edmund Arthur. RN, Lafayette (Ind.) Home Hosp., 1937; AB, San Diego State U., 1963; student, Purdue U., Kans. Wesleyan U. Staff and pvt. nurse Lafayette Home Hosp., 1937-41; indsl. nurse Lakey Foundry & Machine Co., Muskegon, Mich., 1950-51, Continental Motors Corp., Muskegon, 1951-52; nurse Girl Scout Camp, Grand Haven, Mich., 1948-49; owner, ret. Munson Realty, San Diego, 1964—2002. Mem. San Diego County Grand Jury, 1975-76, 80-81, Calif. Grand Jurors Assn. (charter). Address: 3875-18 Vista Campana S Oceanside CA 92057-8151

MUNSON, LYNNE ANN, cultural critic; b. Heidelberg, Germany, Mar. 20, 1968; came to U.S., 1969; d. Gordon Carl and Linda Jean (Guidarini) M. BA in Art History, Northwestern U., Evanston, Ill., 1990. Spl. asst. to the chmn. NEH, Washington, 1990-93; rsch. assoc. Am. Enterprise Inst., Washington, 1993—; dir. domestic policy Dole for Pres., 1996. V.p. Orwell Inst.; bd. dirs. Nat. Alumni Forum. Contbr. articles to N.Y. Times., Wall St. Jour., Pub. Interest, also profl. jours. Republican.

MUNSON, NANCY K. lawyer; b. Huntington, N.Y., June 22, 1936; d. Howard H. and Edna M. (Keenan) Munson. Student, Hofstra U., 1959—62; JD, Bklyn. Law Sch., 1965. Bar: NY 1966, U.S. Dist. Ct. (ea. and so. dists.) NY 1968, U.S. Supreme Ct. 1970, U.S. Ct. Appeals (2d cir.) 1971. Law clk. to E. Merritt Weidner, Huntington, 1959-66; pvt. practice, 1966—. Mem. legal adv. bd. Chgo. Title Ins. Co., Riverhead, NY, 1981—; bd. dirs., legal officer Thomas Munson Found. Trustee Huntington Fire Dept. Death Benefit Fund; pres., trustee, chmn. bd. dirs. Bklyn. Home Aged Men Found.; bd. dirs. Elderly Day Svcs. sound, Huntington Rural Cemetery Assn., Inc. Mem.: DAR (trustee, treas. Ketewamoke chpt.), NRA, ABA, Bklyn. Bar Assn., Suffolk County Bar Assn., N.Y. State Bar Assn., Soroptimists (past pres.). Republican. Christian Scientist. Office: 197 New York Ave Huntington NY 11743-2711 Office Phone: 631-271-8161

MUNSON, SUSAN MARIE, special education educator; d. Earl Edwin and Shirley Jean Munson; m. Stephen James Bagnato, Mar. 21, 1987; children: Michael Stephen Bagnato, Mark Thomas Bagnato. BS in Education, Rock U., 1971, MS Edn. in Spl. Edn., 1974; PhD, Pa. State U., 1985. Asst. prof. spl. edn. U. Ga., Athens, 1985—87; assoc. prof., chair, dept. counseling, psychology and spl. edn. Duquesne U., Pitts., 1987—. Co-author: Linking Assessment and Early Intervention: An Authentic Curriculum-Based Approach, 2nd edit., 1989, Linking Assessment and Early Intervention: An Authentic Curriculum-Based Approach, 3d edit., 1997.

MUNSON, SYLVIA FRANCES FARRIS, energy company manager; b. Pensacola, Fla., Nov. 25, 1958; d. Earl Frances and Doris Marie (Bottoms) Farris; m. Terrance Everett Munson, Mar. 15, 1980 (div. Jan. 1996); children: Amanda Marie, Allison Hope. BS in Computer Sci., U. South Ala., 1980. Computer programmer M.W. Kellogg, Houston, 1980-81; programmer/analyst ANR Prodn. Co., Houston, 1981-83, Tenneco, Houston, 1983-87; computer cons. Natural Gas Industry Electronic Commerce, Houston, 1987—; advisor Natural Gas Industry Polit. and Regulatory Affairs, Houston, 1987—; cons. Natural Gas Industry Issues and Tech., Houston, 1987—; dir. Gas Industry Standards Bd., Houston, 1996-97; mgr. electronic commerce Altra Energy Tech., Houston, 1997—. Technical subcom. chair Gas Flow, Houston, 1994; advisor North Am. Adv. Com. Gas Standards, Houston, 1996—; instr. bus. and technical standards Gas Industry Standards Bd., Houston, 1996—, mem. exec. com., 1997—. Author: Gas Industry Standards Implementation Manuals for Nominations, Flowing Gas, Allocations, Electronic Delivery Mechanisms and Capacity Release, 1995, revised edits., 1996, 97. Founder, pres. Quality Extended Sch. Time, Houston, 1992-96; mem. Houston Ind. Sch. Dist. Parent Advisor Bd., 1997-98; pres. Hamilton Mid. Sch. PTA, Houston, 1997-98. Republican. Avocations: outdoor recreation, travel, collecting. Home: 1440 Harvard St Houston TX 77008-4247 Office: Altra Energy Tech 1221 Lamar St Ste 950 Houston TX 77010-3037

MUNSTERMAN, INGRID ANITA, assistant principal; b. The Hague, The Netherlands, Dec. 10, 1957; d. Theodorus and Hendrica Doesburg; m. Patrick Dean Munsterman. AA, Chaffey Coll., 1977; BA, Calif. State U., 1979; MA, Calif. State U., 1990. From elem. tchr. to asst. prin. Colton Joint Unified Sch. Dist., Calif., 1980—. Adj. faculty U. Redlands, Calif., 2000—, Nat. U., Calif., 2001—.

MUNT, JANET S. state legislator; b. N.Y.C., June 14, 1923; m. Plummer Coldwell Munt (dec.); 4 children. BA, Sweet Briar Coll., 1944; MS, Columbia U., 1948. Pvt. practice clin. social worker; mem., Chittenden County Vt. Senate, Montpelier, 1999—. Trustee Burlington Coll. Fellow Am. Orthopsychiat. Assn., Inc.; mem. NASW, Acad. Cert. Social Workers. Democrat. Office: Vt Legislative Coun 115 State St # 33 Montpelier VT 05633-0001

MÜNTER, LEILANI MAAJO, race car driver; b. Rochester, Minn. d. Manfred and Doris Munter. MS in Biology, U. Calif., San Diego; study, Sebring Internat. Raceway, Fla. Lic. stock car driver Nat. Assn. Stock Car Auto Racing. Former tchrs. asst. cellular biology U. Calif., San Diego; race car driver Nascar Dodge weekly series late model divsn., 2004—; competed in Panoz GT Series and ltd. schedule in Allison Legacy Series. Spl. corr. Nascar.com, 2004—. Photo double (for Catherine Zeta-Jones films) in Traffic and America's Sweethearts. Avocations: scuba diving, snowboarding. Office: Maia Motorsports PO Box 5497 Beverly Hills CA 90209 also: Christopher Biby Motor Sports Mgmt Internat 346 N Larchmont Blvd 90004 Home: #11-20 175 Carriage Club Dr Mooresville NC 28117-9003

MUNZ, DIANA, Olympic athlete; b. Cleve., Jan. 19, 1982; d. Robert and Carol Munz. Student, John Carroll U. Profl. swimmer, 2000—. Recipient Gold medal 4 x 200-meter freestyle Sydney Olympics, 2000, Silver medal 800-meter freestyle World Championships, 1998; winner 800-meter freestyle, non-Olympic 1500-meter freestyle nat. championships, spring and summer 1998, spring 1999, 400-meter freestyle nat. championships, spring 1999 Office: USA Swimming 1 Olympic Plz Colorado Springs CO 80909-5746 Address: 4820 Chagrin River Rd Chagrin Falls OH 44022-2407

MURAKAMI, GAEL BAXLEY, artist; b. Seattle, Nov. 26, 1946; d. William Milton and Grace Eleanor Baxley; m. Firmin Shinichi Murakami, Sept. 9, 1927. BA, U. Wash., 1969. One-woman shows include Site 250 Fine Art Gallery, 1998, Bear Gallery, Fairbanks Civic Ctr., 1998, 2000, Alaska House Gallery, Fairbanks, 2001, 2002. Office: PO Box 83406 Fairbanks AK 99708-3406 Personal E-mail: murakami@mosquitonet.com. E-mail: murakami@mosquitonet.com.

MURANO, ELSA A. federal agency administrator; b. Havana, Cuba; BS in Biol., Sci., Fla. Internat. U.; MS in Anaerobic Microbiology, Va. Polytechnic Inst.; PhD in Food Sci. and Tech., Va. State U. Asst. prof. Iowa State U., Ames, 1990—92, prof. in charge rsch. programs linear accelertor facility, 1992—95; various positions including dir. food safety A&M U., College Station, Tex., 1995—2001, assoc. prof. animal sci., 1995—2000, prof. dept. animal sci., 2000—01; undersec. food safety USDA, Washington, 2001—. Chair food safety state initiative com. Tex. Agr. Ext. Sta., 1999—2001; nat. adv. com. meat and poultry inspection USDA, 2001; mem. Nat. Alliance for Food Safety Ops. Com., 1998—2001, chair, 2000—01. Mem.: Intenat. Assn. Food Protection, Poultry Sci. Assn., Inst. Food Technologists, Assn. Meat Sci., Am. Soc. Microbiology. Office: USDA Food Safety 1400 Independence Ave Sw Washington DC 20250

MURDOCH, AMELIA CLARA, educational association administrator; d. Thomas Jerome and Viola Scanlan Murdoch. AB with honors, U. Pa., 1945, PhD, 1952. Instr. Juniata Coll., Huntingdon, Pa., 1950—51; linguist Nat. Security Agy., Ft. George, Md., 1951—82, Meade, Md., 1985—94; pres. and founder Nat. Mus. Lang., College Park, Md., 1998—. Mem. Tree and Landscape Bd., College Park, 1991—; chair Com. for a Better Environment, College Park, 1983—97, Vets. Meml. Improvement Com., College Park, 1991—2003. Josserand Travel fellow, U. Pa., 1948—49. Mem.: MLA, Medieval Acad. Am., Internat. Arthurian Soc., Phi Beta Kappa (Mary Isabel Sibley fellow 1947—48). Avocations: reading, gardening. Office: Nat Museum of Language 7100 Baltimore Ave Ste 202 College Park MD 20740

MURDOCK, DORIS DEAN, special education educator; b. Pacific Junction, Iowa, Feb. 7, 1913; m. Myron J. Murdock, June 28, 1933; 1 child, John Timothy. BS in Elem. Edn., So. Oreg. U., 1964; MS in Remedial Edn., U. Oreg., 1968. Primary tchr. Days Creek (Oreg.) Elem. Sch., 1962—68, Riddle Elem., Riddle, Oreg., 1968—71; founder, dir. Plowshare Sch., Rogue River, Oreg., 1972—78, Child Life Sanctuary, Rogue River, 1978—89, Ctr. for Habilitation Living, Grants Pass, 1989—2003. Author: (book) No Thank You! No Ritalin for Me Today!, 2003. Vol. Domestic Peace Corp., 1978—86. Mem.: Coun. for Exceptional Children (life). Republican. Adventist. Office: Ctr for Habilitative Living Inc 4493 Jerome Prairie Grants Pass OR 97527

MURDOCK, MARY-ELIZABETH, history educator; b. Boston, Jan. 4, 1930; d. Lester Joseph and Elizabeth Rowe (Collingwood) M. AB, Tufts U., 1952; A.M., Boston U., 1958; PhD, Brown U., 1962; S.M., Simmons Coll.,

1970; cert. mgmt. inst. women in higher edn., Wellesley Coll., 1985; cert. master gardener, U. Mass., 1988. Tchr. Nat. Cathedral Sch., Washington, 1954-57; assoc. prof. Trenton State Coll, N.J., 1962-66, U. R.I., Kingston, 1966-69; archivist, dir. Sophia Smith collection Smith Coll., Northampton, Mass., 1970-84, lectr. history, 1973-86, instr. Southeast Asian ESL program, 1986-88. Guest lectr. colls. and univs., 1986—; cons. N.Y.C. YWCA, 1974-75, HEN, 1976-86, Greenfield Cmty. Coll., Mass., 1983-86, Ednl. Testing Svc., Princeton, N.J., 1985—; faculty cons. Nat. Evaluation Sys., Amherst, Mass., 1984-92; bd. reviewers Hist. Jour. Mass., 1985-88; adv. bd. Ctr. Am. Studies, Concord, Mass., 1985-88; indexer Liberty Party newspaper (1845-48). Author articles, monographs, analytical catalogs. Mem. Am. Studies Assn., New Eng. Am. Studies Assn., Orgn. Am. Historians (state membership chmn. 1980-88), Am. Assn. State and Local History, Hist. Deerfield Inc., Hist. Northampton, Nat. Trust for Hist. Preservation, Phi Alpha Theta. Avocations: choral singing, piano, painting, photography, gardening. Mailing: PMB 261 4152 Meridian St Ste 105 Bellingham WA 98226-5589

MURDOCK, PAMELA ERVILLA, travel and advertising company executive; b. LA, Dec. 3, 1940; d. John James and Chloe Conger (Keefe) M.; children: Cheryl (dec.), Kim. BA, U. Colo., 1962. Pres. Dolphin Travel, Denver, 1972-87; owner, pres. Mile Hi Tours, Denver, 1973—, MH Internat., 1987—, Mile Hi Advt. Agy., 1986—. Bd. dirs. Rocky Mountain chpt. Juvenile Diabetes Found. Internat., 1994-2000; exec. bd. Rocky Mountain Father's Day Coun., 1998, 99. Named Wholesaler of Yr., Las Vegas Conv. and Visitors Authority, 1984; recipient Leadership award Nat. Multiple Sclerosis Soc., 1996. Mem.: NAFE, Nat. Fedn. Ind. Businessmen, Am. Soc. Travel Agts. Republican. Home: 5565 E Vassar Ave Denver CO 80222-6239 Office: Mile Hi Tours Inc 2160 S Clermont St Denver CO 80222-5007 E-mail: pamm@milehitours.com., pamelaemurdock@aol.com.

MURDOCK, TULLISSE ANTOINETTE (TONI MURDOCK), academic administrator; BS, MA, N. Mex. State U.; PhD, U. Ariz.; grad. HERS, Bryn Mawr Inst. Women in Higher Edn., 1988. Adminstr. Western Wyo. Coll., faculty; asst. dean coll. arts and scis. U. Ariz.; assoc. provost of programs Seattle U., 1989—97; pres. Antioch U., Seattle, 1997—. Office: Antioch U 2326 Sixth Ave Seattle WA 98121-1814*

MURE, BARBARA A. real estate property manager; b. Louisville, Apr. 27, 1940; BS in Bus., U. Ky., 1962. Escrow officer Minn. Title, Phoenix, 1963-1967; residential loan officer Southwest Savings, Prescott, Ariz., 1968-1987; property mgr. Atty. Gen. Office, Phoenix, 1988—. Vol. YWCA, Phoenix, 1998—, MS Zoo Walk Bd., Phoenix, 1996-1998. Mem. Ariz. Assn. Property and Evidence, (2nd v.p. 1994-96, 1997-99). Office: Atty Gen Office Property Mgr 1275 W Washington St Phoenix AZ 85007-2926 Fax: 602-542-5997.

MURILLO, CAROL ANN, secondary school educator; b. Portland, Oreg., Mar. 1, 1948; d. Carl Harvey and Frances Berniece Bryan; children: Michelle Frances, Adam Carlos Bryan. BA, Seattle Pacific U., 1970. Multiple subjects tchg. credential Calif., reading specialist credential Calif., secondary tchg. credential Calif. Exec. sec. Sybron Corp. - Heritage Laboratories, Inc., Seattle, 1971—72; elem. tchr. Highlands Acad., Daly City, Calif., 1973—74; dir. of childrens' ministries Resurrection City Ch., Berkeley and Oakland, Calif., 1980—82; interim prin. and tchr. Hilltop Christian Sch., Vallejo, Calif., 1982—93; cfo, ceo asst., event planner Mario Murillo Ministries, Inc., San Ramon, Calif., 1993—98; elem. sch. tchr. Vallejo City Unified Sch. Dist., Calif., 1998—2002. Mem. Falconette Academic Honors Club, Seattle, 1968—70. Editor (contributor): (book) Religious - Inspirational, 2000; editor: I'm the Christian the Devil Warned You About, 1996, Love Letters to Dangerous Christians, 1996; contbr. articles to religious magazines. Spkr. Lay Leadership conf.; worship leader religious retreats; corp. sec., trustee bd. mem. First Assembly of God, Inc., Ch. on the Hill, Vallejo, Calif., 1998—2002; mem. bd. dirs. Hilltop Christian Sch., Vallejo, 1997—2002. Mem.: Delta Kappa Gamma (grantee 1999). Avocation: travel. Home: 3008 Georgia St Vallejo CA 94591 Personal E-mail: carolannmurillo@msn.com.

MURILLO-ROHDE, ILDAURA MARIA, marriage and family therapist, consultant, educator, dean; b. Garachine, Panama; came to U.S., 1945; d. Amalio Murillo and Ana E. (Diaz) de Murillo; m. Erling Rohde, Sept. 19, 1959. BS, Columbia U., 1951, MA, 1953, MEd, 1969; PhD, NYU, 1971; hon. diploma, Escuela Nat. de Enfermeria, Guatemala, 1964; Naturopathia diploma, Centro Estudios Naturista, Barcelona, Spain, 1992. RN; lic. marriage and family therapist, N.J.; cert. mental health-psychiat. nursing, ANA; lic. sex. therapist, N.J. Instr., supr. Bellevue Psychiat. Hosp., N.Y.C., 1950-54; asst. dir., dir. psychiat. div. Wayne County Gen. Hosp., Eloise, Mich., 1954-56; chief nurse psychiat. div. Elmhurst Gen. Hosp., Queens, N.Y., 1956-58, Met. Hosp. Med. Ctr., N.Y.C., 1961-63; psychiat. cons. to govt. of Guatemala WHO, UN, Guatemala, 1963-64; assoc. prof., chmn. psychiat. dept. N.Y. Med. Coll. Grad. Sch. Nursing, N.Y.C., 1964-69; dir. mental health-psychiatry, asst. prof. NYU, N.Y.C., 1970-72; assoc. prof. Hostos Coll., CUNY, N.Y.C., 1972-76; assoc. dean. acad. affairs, prof. U. Wash., Seattle, 1976-81; prof., dean Coll. of Nursing SUNY, Downstate Med. Ctr., Bklyn., 1981-85; dean and prof. emeritus SUNY, Bklyn., 1985—. Bd. dirs. Puerto Rican Family Inst., N.Y.C., 1983—; dir. Latin Am. Oncological Nurses Fuld Fellowships, 1989-90; psychiat. cons. Sch. Nursing, U. Antioquia, Medellin, Colombia, 1972-73, WHO; psychiat./rsch. cons. for master program Sch. Nursing, U. Panama, Project Hope, 1986; dir., leader mental-psychiat. interdisciplinary group to study the Chinese family after 30 yrs. of communism People to People Amb. Program, 1985. Editor: National Directory of Hispanic Nurses, 1981, 2d edit., 1986, 3d edit., 1994; contbr. numerous articles to profl. nat. and internat. jours., chpts. to books in field. Bd. dirs. Nat. Coalition of Hispanic Mental Health and Human Svcs. Orgns., 1974-84, chmn. bd., 1980-84; mem. Wash. State adv. com. U.S. Commn. on Civil Rights, Seattle, 1971-81; nat. adv. com. White House Conf. on Families, Washington, D.C., 1979-81; pres. King County Health Planning Coun., Seattle, 1979-81; exec. com. Puget Sound Health Systems Agy., Seattle, 1979-81; mem. bd. advisors Marquis Who's Who, 1983-91; mem. Mosby Consumer Health's Hispanic adv. bd., 1996. Univ. Honors scholar NYU, 1972; named Citizen of the Day, Radio Sta. KIXI and N.W. Airlines, Seattle, 1979, Disting. lectr. Sigma Theta Tau, 1988-89, Woman of Yr., N.Y. Gotham Club Bus. and Profl. Women, 1989; recipient 1st Nat. Intercultural Nursing award Coun. of Intercultural Nursing, ANA, New Orleans, 1984, Women's Honors in Pub. Svc. award Minority Fellowship Programs and Cabinet Human Rights, ANA, 1986, Disting. Alumna award Divsn. Nursing, NYU Alumni Assn., 1989, 1st Nat. Dr. Hildegard Peplau award for outstanding svcs. in mental health, psychiat. nursing, edn., rsch. and practice, Las Vegas conv. ANA, 1992, Practice award Tchrs. Coll., Columbia U. Nursing Edn. Alumni, 1994; designated Living Legend for leadership in practice, edn. and rsch. Am. Acad. Nursing, 1994; inducted into Nursing Hall of Fame, Columbia U., 1999; bd. advisors Marquis Who's Who, 1991-99. Fellow Am. Assn. Marriage and Family Therapy; mem. ANA (affirmative action task force 1974-84, commn. human rights, cabinet human rights, rep. ANA at ICN Cong. Tokyo 1977, spokesperson Nat. Health Ins., conceived and designed Coun. Intercultural Nursing), Am. Orthopsychiat. Assn. (bd. dirs. 1976-79, treas. 1986-89, Presdl. nominee 1980, 93), N.Y. Assn. Marriage and Family Therapy (pres. 1973-76), Nat. Assn. Hispanic Nurses (founder, 1st pres. 1976-80), Internat. Fedn. Bus. and Profl. Women (UN rep. to UNICEF London, 1987—, del. to World UN Summit for Children N.Y.C. 1990, UN N.Y. Com. for Internat. Yr. of Family 1994, Hall of Fame for Outstanding Achievements in Field of Sci., Rsch., Mental Health-Psychiatry, 4th edit., 1995), Am. Rsch. Inst. (dep. govt. 1987), NYU Club, Gotham Bus. and Profl. Women's Club. Democrat. Avocations: travel, reading, music, stamp collecting, skiing. Home: 300 W 108th St Apt 12A New York NY 10025-2704 Office: SUNY Bklyn Coll Nursing Box 22 450 Clarkson Ave Brooklyn NY 11203-2056 Office Phone: 212-865-9795. E-mail: murillorohde@aol.com.

MURKOWSKI, LISA, senator; b. Ketchikan, Alaska, May 22, 1957; m. Verne Martell, Aug. 22, 1987; children: Nicholas, Matthew. BA, Georgetown U., 1980; JD, Willamette Coll., 1985. Dist. coun. atty., Anchorage, 1987-89; comml. atty. Hoge and Lekisch, 1989-96; atty. pvt. practice, 1997—; rep. Alaska Ho. Reps., Anchorage, 1998—2002; U.S. senator from Alaska, 2002—. Dir. First Bank; mem. Mayor's Task Force Homeless, 1990-91; state ctrl. com. Dist. 14 Rep. chair, 1993-98; commr. Anchorage Equal Rights Commn., 1997-2002; citizens adv. bd. Joint Com. Mil. Bases in Alaska, 1998—. Trustee Cath. Svcs.; pres. Govt. Hill Elem. PTA; dir. Alaskan Drug Free Youth; mem. YWCA, Arctic Power. Mem. Alaska Bar Assn., Anchorage Bar Assn., Alaska Fedn. Rep. Women (bd. dirs.), Anchorage Rep. Womens Club, Midnight Sun Rep. Women. Republican. Roman Catholic. Address: 510 L St # 550 Anchorage AK 99501 Mailing: US Senate 322 Hart Senate Off Bldg Washington DC 20510*

MURMAN, SANDRA L. state legislator, community activist; b. Indpls., Aug. 9, 1950; BS in Bus. and Mktg., Ind. U., 1972. Mem. Fla. Ho. of Reps., Tallahassee, 1996—. Mem. bus. devel. and internat. trade com., fin. and taxation com., juvenile justice com., children and family empowerment com., environ. protection com., edn. commn. reform and accountability; cmty. activist. Bd. trustees Children's Home Inc.; mem. steering com. United Way Mgmt. Assistance Program; troop leader Girl Scouts Am.; dir. devel. Tampa (Fla.) Children's Mus., 1991-95. Republican. Roman Catholic. Avocations: running, tennis, golf. Office: State Capitol Rm 1102 Tallahassee FL 32399-1300

MURNANE, MARGARET MARY, engineering and physics educator; b. Limerick, Ireland, Jan. 23, 1959; d. Matthew and Helen (Bourke) M.; m. Henry Cornelius Kapteyn, Mar. 26, 1987. MSc, U. Coll. Cork, Ireland, 1983; PhD, U. Calif., Berkeley, 1989. Postdoctoral researcher U. Calif., Berkeley, 1990; asst. prof. Wash. State U., Pullman, 1990-95; assoc. prof. U. Mich., Ann Arbor, 1995—. Presdl. Young Investigator awardee NSF, 1991, Sloan Found. fellow, 1992, Presdl. faculty fellow NSF, 1993. Mem. Am. Phys. Soc. (Simon Ramo award 1990, Maria Goeppert-Mayer award 1997), Optical Soc. Am., Soc. Photo-Optical Instrumentation Engrs., Assn. for Women in Sci. Office: U Mich Ctr for Ultrafast Optics 2200 Bonisteel Blvd Ann Arbor MI 48109-2099

MUROW, CHRISTINE, music educator; b. Chgo., Feb. 19, 1945; d. David R. and Dorothy B. Groth; m. Raymond J. Murow, Oct. 10, 1966. B, Susquehanna U., 1967. Budget analyst U.S. Dept. H.E.W., Washington, 1967-69, pub. info. specialist, 1969-72; tchr. piano Potomac, Md., 1972—; dir. KITS, Potomac, Md., 1985—. Author: KITS Music Theory Course, 1989 98; contbr. articles to profl. jours.; composer Sounds for One Hand, 1986, Voices of Invention, 1987; contbg. composer: Allison Contemporary Piano Collection, 1993, 96. Mem. Nat. Guild Piano Tchrs., Potomac Area Music Tchrs. (sec. 1989—). Avocations: gardening, bird watching. Office: KITS 9732 Corral Dr Potomac MD 20854-1510 E-mail: musictheory@earthlink.net.

MURPHEY, MARGARET JANICE, marriage and family therapist; b. Taft, Calif., July 24, 1939; d. Glen Roosevelt Wurster and Lucile Mildred (Holt) Lopez; m. Russell Warren Murphey, June 20, 1959; children: Lucinda Kalbfleisch, Rochelle Scott, Janice Sorenson. BA in Social Sci., Calif. State U., Chico, 1986, MA in Psychology, 1989; postgrad., La Salle U. Sec. Folson State Prison, Calif., 1963-66; tchr. Desert Sands Unified Schs., Indio, Calif., 1969-72; claims determiner Employment Development Dept., Redding, Calif., 1976-78; sec. Shasta County Pers., Redding, 1978-79; welfare worker Shasta County Welfare Office, Redding, 1979-85; therapy intern Counseling Ctr. Calif. State U., Chico, 1989-90; therapist Family Svc. Assn., Chico, 1987-90, Butte County Drug and Alcohol Abuse Ctr., Chico, 1989-90; mental halth counselor Cibecue (Ariz.) Indian Health Clinic, 1990-98; sch. counselor Cibecue Apache H.S. and Elem. Sch., 1998—. Mem. Kinisba Child Abuse Com., 1994—98. Vol. Pacheco Sch., Redding, 1972-76; Sunday sch. tchr., dir. vacation Bible sch. Nazarene Ch., Sacramento, Indio and Redding, 1958-85. Recipient Sch. Bell award Pacheco Sch., Indian Health Svc. Dirs. award excellence, 1997. Mem. ACA, Am. Assn. Christian Counselors, Am. Acad. Bereavement Facilitators, Ariz. Sch. Counselors Assn. Avocations: study of american indian history, sewing, crafts, travel, canoeing. Home: PO Box 1114 Show Low AZ 85902-1114 Office: Cibecue Apache HS PO Box 80068 Cibecue AZ 85911-0068

MURPHEY, SHEILA ANN, infectious diseases physician, educator, researcher; b. Phila., July 10, 1943; d. William Joseph and Sara Esther (Mallon) M. AB, Chestnut Hill Coll., 1965; MD, Women's Med. Coll. of Pa., 1969. Diplomate Am. Bd. Internal Medicine, Am. Bd. Infectious Diseases. Intern in internal medicine Mt. Sinai Hosp. of N.Y., 1969—70, resident in internal medicine, 1970—72, instr. internal medicine, 1971—72; fellow infectious diseases U. Pa. Sch. Medicine, Phila., 1972—74, instr. dept. medicine, 1974—75, asst. prof. dept. medicine, 1975—77; chief infectious diseases sect. Phila. Gen. Hosp., 1974—77; attending physician Hosp. U. Pa., Phila. Gen. Hosp., 1974—77; dir. divsn. infectious diseases, asst. prof. medicine Jefferson Med. Coll., Phila., 1977—80, clin. assoc. prof. medicine, 1980—2003; dir. divsn. infectious diseases Thomas Jefferson U., Phila., 1977—88; infection control officer, attending physician Thomas Jefferson U. Hosp., Phila., 1977—2003. Contbr. articles to profl. jours. Fellow Coll. Physicians Phila.; mem. ACP, Am. Soc. Microbiology, Soc. Healthcare Epidemiology of Am., Infectious Diseases Soc. Am., Alpha Omega Alpha. Democrat. Roman Catholic.

MURPHREY, ELIZABETH HOBGOOD, history educator, librarian; b. Rocky Mount, N.C., Mar. 22, 1947; d. Isaac Green and Ernestine Ragsdale (Hobgood) Murphrey. BA, U. N.C., Greensboro, 1969; MA, Duke U., 1971, PhD, 1976; postgrad., U. Fla., 1984; MLS, U. N.C., Chapel Hill, 1993. Vis. instr. history Wake Forest U., Winston-Salem, NC, 1976; asst. prof. history N.C. A&T State U., Greensboro, 1977—81; intelligence rsch. specialist U.S. Army, Fayetteville, NC, 1982—89; adj. prof. history Fayetteville State U., 1989—90; adj. instr. history Fla. Met. U. South Campus, Orlando, 2000—, asst. libr., 1998—. Vis. asst. prof. of history Elizabeth City State U., NC, 1993—96. Editor (guidebook): Socialist Party of America Papers, microfilm edit., 2 vols., 1973—77. Recipient award, NEH, 1994, 1996, 2000. Mem.: LWV (bd. dirs. Seminole County chpt. 2001—, bd. dirs. Guilford County chpt. 1978—82), ALA, Fla. Libr. Assn., Am. Hist. Assn. Home: 424 Windmeadows St Altamonte Springs FL 32701 Office: Fla Met U South Orlando Campus 9200 Southpark Center Loop Orlando FL 32819 E-mail: emurphrey@hotmail.com.

MURPHY, ANN MARIE, special education educator; b. Phila., Aug. 29, 1953; d. Daniel Joseph and Mary Ann Murphy. BA, Glassboro State Coll., 1975, MA, 1989. Cert. learning disabilities tchr. cons. Tchr. severly retarded Am. Inst. for Mental Studies, Vineland, N.J., 1975-79; tchr. emotionally disturbed and perceptually impaired Woodbury (N.J.) Sch. Dist., 1979-94, resource ctr. tchr., 1994—96, learning disabilities tchr. cons., 1994—, coord., child study team, 2001—. Asst. basketball coach Woodbury (N.J.) H.S., 1979-89, Glassboro State/Rowan Coll., 1989-94. Named to Glassboro State/Rowan Hall of Fame, Rowan Coll. N.J., Glassboro, 1989, South Jersey Basketball Hall of Fame, 1992, Gloucester County Sports Hall of Fame, 1996. Mem. Coun. for Exceptional Children, N.J. Edn. Assn. (bldg. rep. 1979-85), Women's Basketball Coaches Assn., Assn. Learning Cons., Delta Kappa Gamma. Office: Woodbury Pub Schs Walnut St Sch Woodbury NJ 08096

MURPHY, ANN PLESHETTE, magazine editor-in-chief; m. Steven Murphy; children: Madeleine, Nick. B.A. in psychology, Harvard U. Editor-in-chief Parents mag., N.Y.C., 1988—98, contributing editor, 1998—2002; parenting contributor, Am. Family segment Good Morning Am., 1998—; columnist, Mom Know How Family Circle mag. Author: The 7 Stages of Motherhood: Making the Most of Your Life as a Mom. Bd. dirs. Child Care Action Campaign, Parents as Teachers, Zero to Three; chair, bd. dirs. Greyston Family Inn. Recipient Academy of Women Achievers, YWCA, 1990.

MURPHY, BARBARA ANNE, emergency physician, surgery educator; b. Cin., Oct. 20, 1937; d. Harold August and Lorna Louise (Gabbard) Tiemeyer; m. D. Michael Murphy, Feb. 5, 1960; children: Michael Patrick, Douglas Andrew. BS cum laude, Ohio State U., 1959; MD magna cum laude, Med. Coll. Pa., 1975. Diplomate Am. Bd. Emergency Medicine. Resident in emergency medicine Geisinger Med. Ctr., Danville, Pa., 1978; staff physician Albemarle Hosp., Elizabeth City, N.C., 1978-79, Durham County Hosp., Durham, N.C., 1979-87; asst. prof. emergency medicine East Carolina U., Greenville, N.C., 1987-90; asst. prof. surgery-emergency medicine Duke U., Durham, 1990—. Dir. propsed residency emergency medicine Duke U., Durham, 1994—. Author: (book chpt.) Pediatric Emergency Medicine, rev. edit., 1992; editor: Micromedia Emergency Med. Abstracts, 1988—; book reviewer: Annals of Emergency Medicine, 1995—; contbr. articles to profl. jours. Fellow Am. Coll. Emergency Physicians (mem. clin. policies com. 1991—); mem. Soc. for Acad. Emergency Medicine, Alpha Omega Alpha, Phi Beta Kappa. Avocations: antique rose propagation, 18th-century american furniture collection, herbalism, needlework reproductions. Home: PO Box 837 Hillsborough NC 27278-0837 Office: Duke U Med Ctr PO Box 3096 Durham NC 27715-3096

MURPHY, BETTY JAGODA, small business owner; b. Washington, July 30, 1947; d. Harry Earl and Flory (Kabilio) Jagoda; m. Gregory James Murphy, Mar. 18, 1972; 1 child, Joshua. BA in Dance, Adelphi U., 1969. Cert. psychomotor therapy N.Y. Med. Ctr., 1970. Market research coord. Lee Creative Research, Fairfield, NJ, 1972-73; dir. new product test ctr. Lehn & Fink (Sterling Drug), Montvale, NJ, 1973-75; cons. new products Montclair, NJ, 1975-79; co-founder, pres. Creative Products Resource Assn., Fairfield, NJ, 1979—99; v.p. Jagoda Labs., Inc., Clifton, NJ, 1986—; pres., mng. mem. ReGenesis LLC, Montclair, NJ. Inventor, patentee household cleaning products and health & beauty aids. Adv. bd. Dress for Success, NY. Mem.: N.J. Assn. Women Bus. Owners, N.Y. Women in Comm. (membership com.). Democrat. Jewish. Avocation: performing ladino music in concert with family mems. Office: ReGenesis LLC 31 S Fullerton Ave Montclair NJ 07042*

MURPHY, BETTY SOUTHARD (MRS. CORNELIUS F. MURPHY), lawyer; b. East Orange, N.J. d. Floyd Theodore and Thelma (Casto) Southard; m. Cornelius F. Murphy, May 1, 1965; children: Ann Southard Hernly, Cornelius Francis Jr. AB, Ohio State U.; student, Alliance Française and U. Sorbonne, Paris; JD, Am. U.; LLD (hon.), Eastern Mich. U., 1975, Capital U., 1976, U. Puget Sound, 1986; LHD, Tusculum coll., 1987. Bar: D.C. Corr., free lance journalist, Europe and Asia, UPI, Washington; practiced in Washington, 1960—74; mem. firm McInnis, Wilson, Munson & Woods (and predecessor firm); dep. asst. sec., adminstr. Wage and Hour Divsn. Dept. Labor, 1974-75; chmn. and mem. NLRB, 1975-79, ptnr. firm Baker & Hostetler, LLP, 1980—. Adj. prof. law Am. U., 1972-80, 99—; mem. adv. com. on rights and responsibilities of women to Sec. HHS; mem. panel conciliators Internat. Ctr. Settlement Investment Disputes, 1974-85; mem. Adminstrv. Conf. U.S., 1976-80, Pub. Svc. Adv. Bd., 1976-79; mem. human resouces com. Nat. Ctr. for Productivity and Quality of Working Life, 1976-80; mem. Presdl. Commn. on Exec. Exch., 1981-85. Trustee Mary Baldwin Coll., 1977-85, Am. U., 1980-99, 2001—, George Mason U. Found., Inc., 1990-2000, George Mason U. Edn. Found., 1993-2000, 01—; nat. bd. dirs. Med. Coll. Pa., bd. corporators, 1976-85; bd. dirs. Ctr. for Women in Medicine, 1980-86; bd. govs. St. Agnes Sch., 1981-87; mem. exec. com. Commn. on Bicentennial of U.S. Constn., chmn. internat. adv. com., 1985-92; vice chmn. James Madison Meml. Fellowship Found., 1989-96; bd. dirs. Meridian Internat. Ctr., 1992-98; trustee Friends of Congl. Law Libr., 1992—, Friends of Dept. of Labor, 1984—; mediator World Intellectual Property Orgn., 1996—. Recipient Ohio Gov.'s award, 1980, fellow award, 1981, Outstanding Pub. Service award U.S. Info. Service, 1987; named Disting. Fellow John Sherman Myers Soc., 1986, 96; fellow Nat. Acad. Human Resources, 1998. Mem.: Am. U. Alumni Assn. (bd. dirs.), Supreme Ct. Hist. Soc., Union Internat. des Advocats (gov. bd. 1997—2000, 2003—), Rep. Nat. Lawyers Assn. (nat. v.p. 1990—95, nat. vice chmn. 1996—2000, 2001—03, co-chmn. 2003—, mem. bd. 2003—), Am. Arbitration Assn. (mem. editl. bd. 1992, mem. exec. com. 1995—2000, mem. internat. arbitration com. 1997—, steering com. lawyers for Bush 2000, bd. dirs. 1985-2000 2002—), Bar Assn. D.C., Inter-Am. Bar Assn. (co-chmn. labor law com. 1975—83, editor newsletter, Silver medal 1967), FBA, ABA (chmn. labor law com. 1980—83, chmn. internat. and comparative law adminstrv. law sect. 1983—88, chmn. customs, tariff and trade com. 1988—90, employment law sect. 1990, chmn. internat. com. dispute resolution sect. 1995—, adminstrv. law sect.), World Peace Through Law Ctr., Mortar Bd., Kappa Beta Pi. Republican. Office: Baker & Hostetler LLP Ste 1100 1050 Connecticut Ave NW Washington DC 20036-5304 Office Phone: 202-861-1500. E-mail: bsmurphy@bakerlaw.com.

MURPHY, CAROLYN, model; b. Walton Bch., Fla., Aug. 11, 1975; m. Jake Schroeder; 1 child. Model IMG Agy.; spokesperson Estee Lauder, 2001—. Actor: (films) Liberty Heights, 1999. Named Model Yr., VH1 Fashion Awards, 1998. Achievements include appeared on numerous mag. covers including Vogue, Harper's Bazaar, W, Elle, Marie Claire; one of the models to appear on the cover of Vogue's "Model of the Millennium" issue; starred in Calvin Klein's "Contradiction" comml. and print ads. Mailing: 420 W 45th ST New York NY 10036*

MURPHY, CARYLE MARIE, foreign correspondent; b. Hartford, Conn., Nov. 16, 1946; d. Thomas Joseph and Muriel Kathryn (McCarthy) Murphy. BA cum laude, Trinity Coll., 1968; M in Internat. Pub. Policy, Johns Hopkins U., 1987. Tchr. English, history St. Cecilia Tchr. Tng. Coll., Nyeri, Kenya, 1968—71; reporter Brockton (Mass.) Enterprise, 1972—73; freelance corr. Washington Post, Newsweek, Sunday Times of London, et al, Luanda, Angola, 1974—76; reporter Fairfax County Washington Post, 1976—77, fgn. corr. in South Africa, 1977—82, reporter immigration issues, 1982—85, bur. chief Alexandria, Va., 1985—89, fgn. corr. Mid. East, 1989—94. Vol. ARC, Washington, 1984, Whitman-Walker Found., Washington, 1988—89. Recipient Courage in Journalism award, Internat. Women's Media Found., 1990, George Polk award, L.I. U., 1991, Edward Weintal Journalism award, Sch. Fgn. Svc., Georgetown U., 1991, Pulitzer Prize for internat. reporting, 1991, Edward R. Murrow fellow, Coun. on Fgn. Rels., N.Y., 1994—95. Roman Catholic. Avocations: foreign languages, hiking. Office: Washington Post Fgn Desk 1150 15th St NW Washington DC 20071-0002

MURPHY, CATHY EMILY, photographer, educator, journalist; b. Bay City, Mich., Jan. 27, 1943; d. Douglas Patrick and Grace Anna Churchfield; m. Denis Michael Murphy, Mar. 1964 (div. 1974); 1 child, Paul. AA journalism, Diablo Valley Coll., Pleasant Hill, Calif., 1963; BA, Calif. State Univ.-Chico, Chico, Calif., 1992. ESL tchg. credential Univ. Zagreb, Yugoslavia, 1966, Brooks Inst. of Photo, Santa Barbara, Calif., 1975, Univ. Calif., 1964, tchg. credetial photography Ariz., Calif., Washington. Staff photographer Cesar Chavez and UFW, Keene, Calif., 1974—75, So. Ariz. Discovery, Tucson, 1977—78; photo instr. Clover Pk. Vocat. Tech Inst., Tacoma, 1980—84; photographic stringer US/Mex. Ariz. Rep., Phoenix, 1985—87; photo instr. Seattle Ctrl. C.C., 1989—90; photo journalist Bisbee

Observer, Bisbee news, Ariz., 1996—2000, Bisbee Daily News, Ariz., 2001—03. Photo instr. Butte Coll., Oroville, Calif., 1990—94, Cochise Coll., Douglas, Ariz., 1978, Douglas, 1980—87, Douglas, 1995—; photographer/tour guide Mex. Geronimo Ednl. Travel Studies, Bisbee, Ariz., 1997—2003; judge Profl. Photographers of Wash., Spokane, Wash., 1998. Author (photographer): (traveling photo essay) From the Califorina Fields, 1976, (photo documentary) Living on the Edge- The Tarahumara of Copper Canyon, 2000; photographer (exhibitions) Tang Gallery, Picture This, Bisbee, Ariz. Friends Copper Queen Libr., Bisbee, Ariz., 2002—03; mem. Nat. Mus. Women in Arts, Washington, 1998; bd. dirs. Cochise Fine Arts, Bisbee, Ariz., 1978. Grantee, Woody Guthrie Found., N.Y., 1976, Ariz. Arts. Commn., Phoenix, Ariz., 1978—79; scholarship award, Brooks Inst. of Photography, Santa Barbara, Calif., 1974. Mem.: Ariz. Newspaper Assn. (numerous state awards for photography and writing), Nat. Press Assn. Democrat. Achievements include photographs from Cesar Chavez days in PBS documentary 1999; Nat. merit awards from Profl. Photographers of Am. in fashion, fine art and archl. photography, state awards profl. photographers of Oreg. and Wash; 5 photographs of Tarahumara women in archives of th inst. nat. de las Mujeres, Mex. city, Mex. Avocations: photography, swimming, studying Spanish, documenting lifestyles native peoples of Mex.. Home: 31 Temby, PO Box 67 Bisbee AZ 85603 Office: Cochise Coll Art Dept 4190W Hwy 80 Douglas AZ 85607

MURPHY, CHRISTINE, medical facility administrator; b. Jan. 2, 1956; d. Mary. I. Jackson; m. Paul Murphy, June 19, 1976; children: Christie, Jannie-Kay. Diploma, Newport (R.I.) Hosp., 1977; BS, RWU, Bristol, R.I., 1994; MS, SRU, Newport, 1997. RN, R.I. Clin. educator Newport Hosp.; firm mgr. VAMC, Providence, R.I. Bd. dirs. Newport Hosp. Alumni, West House Housing Elderly. Mem. Assn. Oper. Rm. Nurse (cert.), Nat. Assn. Ambulatory Care Mgrs. Office: PVAMC 830 Chalkstone Ave Providence RI 02908-4734

MURPHY, DEBORAH MARGARET, mental health services professional, social worker; b. Monroe, La., Mar. 10, 1967; d. Ronald Gene and Billie Margaret Farmer; m. Larry Stevens Murphy, Dec. 20, 1992; children: Taylor Woodson, Macy Jean BA, Northeast La. State U., 1989. Admission clk. E.A. Conway Meml. Hosp., Monroe, La., 1986-87, 1988-90; soc. svcs. dir. Teh Oaks Nursing Home, Monroe, La., 1990-93; psychiatric technician St. Francis Hosp., Monroe, La., 1993-94; program dir. Ashley Meml. Hosp., Crossett, Ark., 1994—. Adv. bd. social workers U. Ark., Montcello, 1995—. Mem. ethics com. Ashley Meml. Hosp., Crossett, Ark., 1993. Democrat. Baptist. Avocations: table tennis, bowling. Home: 235 Morgan Hare Rd Monroe LA 71203-8442

MURPHY, DIANA E. federal judge; b. Faribault, Minn., Jan. 4, 1934; d. Albert W. and Adleyne (Heiker) Kuske; m. Joseph Murphy, July 24, 1958; children: Michael, John E. BA magna cum laude, U. Minn., 1954, JD magna cum laude, 1974; postgrad., Johannes Gutenberg U., Mainz, Germany, 1954—55, U. Minn., 1955—58; LLD, St. Johns U., 2003, U. St. Thomas, 2003. Bar: Minn. 1974, U.S. Supreme Ct. 1980. Assoc. Lindquist & Vennum, 1974—76; mcpl. judge Hennepin County, 1976—78, Minn. State dist. judge, 1978—80; judge U.S. Dist. Ct. for Minn., Mpls., 1980—94, chief judge, 1992—94; judge U.S. Ct. of Appeals (8th cir.), Mpls., 1994—. Chair U.S. Sentencing Commn., 1999—2004. Bd. editors: Minn. Law Rev., Georgetown U. Jour. on Cts., Health Scis. and the Law, 1989—92. Dir. Nat. Assn. Pub. Interest Law Fellowships for Equal Justice, 1992—95; Bd. dirs. Mpls. United Way, 1985—2001, treas., 1990—94, vice-chmn., 1996—97, chmn. bd. dirs., 1997—98; bd. dirs. Bush Found., 1982—, chmn. bd. dirs., 1986—91; organizer, 1st chmn. adv. coun. Amicus, bd. dirs., 1976—80; chair Mpls. Charter Commn., 1973—76; bd. dirs. Ops. De Novo, 1971—76, chmn. bd. dirs., 1974—75; mem., chmn. bill of rights com. Minn. Constl. Study Commn., 1971—73; regent St. Johns U., 1978—87, 1988—98, chmn. bd., 1985—98, bd. overseers sch. theology, 1998—2001; mem. Minn. Bicentennial Commn., 1987—88; trustee Twin Cities Pub. TV, 1985—94, chmn. bd., 1990—92; trustee U. Minn. Found., 1990—, chmn. of bd., 2003—; bd. dirs. Sci. Mus. Minn., 1988—94, vice-chmn., 1991—94; trustee U. St. Thomas, 1991—; vice chair Bd. of Gov. U. St. Thomas Law Sch., 2001—; Bd. dirs. Spring Hill Conf. Ctr., 1978—84. Recipient Amicus Founders' award, 1980, Outstanding Achievement award, U. Minn., 1983, YWCA, 1981, Disting. Citizen award, Alpha Gamma Delta, 1985, Devitt Disting. Svc. to Justice award, 2001, Disting. Alumnus award, U. Minn. Law Sch., 2002, Woman Who Makes a Difference award, Internat. Women's Forum, 2003; scholar Fulbright. Fellow: Am. Bar Found.; mem.: ABA (mem. ethics and profl. responsibility judges adv. com. 1981—88, standing com. on jud. selection, tenure and compensation 1991—94, mem. standing com. on fed. jud. improvements 1994—97, Appellate Judges conf. exec. com. 1996—99, chmn. ethics and profl. responsibility judges adv. com. 1997—2000), Fed. Jud. Ctr. (bd. dirs. 1990—94, 8th cir. jud. coun. 1992—94, convener task force 1993, mem. U.S. jud. conf. com. on ct. adminstrn. and case mgmt. 1994—99, chair gender fairness implementation com. 1997—98, 8th cir. jud. coun. 1997—), Hist. Soc. for 8th Cir. (bd. dirs. 1988—91), Fed. Judges Assn. (bd. dirs. 1982—2003, v.p. 1984—89, pres. 1989—91), U. Minn. Alumni Assn. (bd. dirs. 1975—83, nat. pres. 1981—82), Minn. Women Lawyers (Myra Bradwell award 1996), Nat. Assn. Women Judges (Leadership Judges Jud. Adminstrn. award 1998, Honoree of Yr. 2002), Nat. Assn. Governing Bds. Univs. Colls. (dir. 1998—), Am. Judicature Soc. (bd. dirs. 1982—93, v.p. 1985—88, treas. 1988—89, chmn. bd. 1989—91), Am. Law Inst., Hennepin County Bar Assn. (gov. coun. 1976—81), Minn. Bar Assn. (bd. govs. 1977—81), Order of Coif, Phi Beta Kappa. Office: 11 E US Courthouse 300 S 4th St Minneapolis MN 55415-1320

MURPHY, DONNA, actress; b. Corona, N.Y., Mar. 7, 1959; Student, NYU Sch. of the Arts. Actor: (Broadway plays) They're Playing Our Song, The Human Comedy, The Mystery of Edwin Drood, Passion (Tony award Best Actress in a Musical, 1994, Drama Desk award, Drama League award), The King and I, 1996 (Tony award Best Actress in a Musical, 1996, Drama League Award), Wonderful Town, 2003— (Tony nominee Best Actress in a Musical, 2004); (plays) Song of Singapore, Privates on Parade, Showing Off, Birds of Paradise, Little Shop of Horrors, A...My Name Is Alice, Twelve Dreams, 1995, Hello Again, 1994; (TV series) Murder One, 1995—96, Law & Order, 1993, 1997, 2000, The Practice, 1998, Ally McBeal, 1998, What About Joan, 2001, Hack, 2002; (TV miniseries) LIBERTY! The American Revolution, 1997; (TV films) Tales from the Hollywood Hills: A Table at Ciro's, 1987, Power, Passion and Murder, 1987, Passion, 1996, Someone Had to Be Benny, 1996, The Day Lincoln Was Shot, 1998, The Last Debate, 2000; (films) Jade, 1995, October 22, 1998, Star Trek: Insurrection, 1998, The Astronaut's Wife, 1999, Center Stage, 2000. Office: William Morris Agy 1325 Avenue Of The Americas New York NY 10019-6026*

MURPHY, EDRIE LEE, laboratory administrator; b. Redwood Falls, Minn., Dec. 4, 1953; d. Melvin Arthur and Betty Lou (Wenholz) Timm; m. David Joseph Murphy, July 28, 1984; children: Michael David, Scott Christopher. BS in Med. Tech. summa cum laude, Mankato State U., 1976; MBA, U. St. Thomas, 1984. Registered med. technologist. Med. technologist Children's Hosps. and Clinics, St. Paul, 1976-81, chemistry supr., 1981-85, lab. mgr., 1985-95, dir. lab. sys. Mpls., St. Paul's Campus, 1995-99; lab. mgr. Fairview Health Sys., Mpls., 2000—. Contbr. articles to profl. jours. Charles H. Cooper scholar, 1975. Mem.: Minn. Soc. Clin. Lab. Mgmt. Assn. (sec.-treas. Minn. chpt. 1994—96, bd. dirs. 1996—, pres.-elect 1998—2000, pres. 2000—02), Am. Soc. Clin. Lab. Scis., Elan Vital Ski Club (v.p. membership 1981—82), Phi Kappa Phi. Avocations: photography, sailing, skiing, tennis, travel. Office: Fairview Sys 2512 7th St S R300D Minneapolis MN 55454 E-mail: emurphy2@fairview.org.

MURPHY, ELISABETH MARIA, physical design engineer, consultant; b. Cleve., Nov. 9, 1956; d. Thomas Jerome and Dolores Dorothy (Bost) M. AAS, Ctrl. Ohio Tech. Coll., 1990; student, Ohio State U., 1991-92, Franklin U., 1992-94. Jewelry designer P.J. Rone Co., Reading, Pa., 1983-87; registrar Office Continuing Edn., Ctrl. Ohio Tech. Coll., Newark, 1987-88; civil engring. designer dist. 5, Ohio Dept. Transp., Newark, 1988-90; phys. design engr. Bell Labs./Lucent Techs., Columbus, Ohio, 1990—, safety coord., 1990-92, Ams. with Disabilities Act Disability adv. and archtl. cons., 1993—, edn. and resource developer, disability spokesperson, 1993—. Freelance writer, 1977—; portrait artist, 1983—; freelance math. tutor, Columbus, 1990-93, Ohio State U. and Ctrl. Ohio Tech. Coll., 1988-90; disability rights cons. Contbr. articles to profl. publs., poetry to newspaper. Mem. NOW, Instrument Soc. Am. (Outstanding Tech. Paper award 1989), Soc. Mfg. Engrs., Nat. Woodcarvers Assn., Nat. Mus. Women in Arts. Avocation: research on pre-modern women sculptors. E-mail: elisabethmurphy@lucent.com.

MURPHY, ELVA GLENN, executive assistant; b. Chickasha, Okla., Aug. 21, 1934; d. Elsie Lee (Murphy) Sommer and Maynard F. Glenn; m. Calvin E. Morgan, Mar. 11, 1972 (dec. Dec. 1976); m. C. Gordon Murphy, Oct. 17, 1981. Student, UCLA, 1954-55, Columbia U., 1973. Various secretarial positions, Calif., 1956-67; fgn. svc. sec. U.S. Dept. State, Paris, 1967-69; exec. asst. to Cyrus R. Vance Simpson Thacher & Bartlett, N.Y.C., 1969-77, 80-98, U.S. Dept. State, Washington, 1977-80; asst. to pres. Coun. on Fgn. Rels., Inc., N.Y.C., 1997—2003; asst. social medicine and pub. policy program Weill Med. Coll. Cornell U., N.Y.C., 2003—. Mem. Seraphic Soc. (pres. 1990-92), Women's City Club N.Y. Avocations: sailing, skiing, cooking, reading, theater. Home: 75 West End Ave # P30D New York NY 10023 Office: Weill Med Coll Cornell Univ 525 E 68th St Box 171 New York NY 10021 Business E-Mail: egm2003@med.cornell.edu.

MURPHY, EVELYN FRANCES, economist; b. Panama Canal Zone, Panama Canal Zone, May 14, 1940; d. Clement Bernard and Dorothy Eloise (Jackson) M. AB, Duke U., 1961, PhD, 1965; MA, Columbia U., 1963; hon. degrees, Regis Coll., 1978, Curry Coll., Northeastern U., Simmons Coll., Wheaton Coll., Anna Maria Coll., Bridgewater State Coll., Salem State Coll., Emmanuel Coll.; hon. degree, Suffolk U. Pres. Ancon Assocs., Boston, 1971-72; ptnr. Llewelyn-Davies, Weeks, Forrester-Walker & Bor, London, 1973-74; sec. environ. affairs Commonwealth of Mass., Boston, 1975-79, sec. econ. affairs, 1983-86, lt. gov., 1987-91; mng. dir. Brown Rudnick Freed and Gesmer, Boston, 1991-93; exec. v.p. Blue Cross/Blue Shield of Mass., Boston, 1994-98; also bd. dirs. Blue Cross Blue Shield Mass., Boston; resident scholar Brandeis U. Women's Studies Rsch. Ctr., 1999—; pres. The Wage Project, Inc., 2003—. Vis. pub. policy scholar Radcliffe Coll., 1991; vice chmn./chmn. Nat. Adv. Com. on Oceans and Atmosphere (Presdl. apptd.), 1979-80; bd. dirs. Citizens Energy Corp., SBLI USA Mut. Life Ins., The Commonwealth Inst.,, The Polaris Project, Nat. Ctr. on Women and Aging, chair; pres. Health Care and Policy Inst., 1997-98; resident scholar Brandeis U., 1998—; bd. trustees Regis Coll., 2003—. Recipient Dist. Svc. award New Eng. Coun., 1996, Nat. Sierra Club, 1978, Nat. Bd. Govs. Assn., 1978, Outstanding Citizen award Mass. Audobon Soc., 1978; Harvard U. fellow, 1979-80. Mem. Women Execs. in State Govt. (chair 1987), Internat. Women's Forum, 1993—. Democrat. Avocation: jogging. E-mail: EvMurphy1@aol.com.

MURPHY, FRANCES LOUISE, II, retired newspaper publisher; b. Balt., Oct. 8, 1922; d. Carl James and L. Vashti (Turley) M.; m. James E. Wood (div.); children: Frances Murphy Wood Draper, James E. Jr., Susan Wood Barnes, David Lloyd Campbell. BA, U. Wis., 1944; BS, Coppin State Coll., Balt., 1958; MEd, Johns Hopkins U., 1963. City editor Balt. Afro-Am., 1956-57; dir. News Bur., Morgan State Coll., Balt., 1964-71; chmn. bd. dirs. Afro-Am. Newspapers, Balt., 1971-74; assoc. prof. journalism State Univ. Coll., Buffalo, 1975-85, Howard U., Washington, 1985-91; editor Washington Afro-Am., 1951-56, pub., 1987-99; editl. page editor Afro-Am. Newspapers, Balt., 1999—. Treas. African Am. Civil War Meml. Freedom Found.; trustee State Colls. Md., 1971-76, U. D.C., 1994-99; bd. dirs. Delta Rsch. and Ednl. Found., 1993-95; nat. bd. dirs. NACCP, 1971-76; vestry St. James' Episcopal Ch. Named one of 100 Most Influential Black Ams., Ebony mag., 1973, 74, Disting. Marylander, Gov. State of Md., 1975; recipient Ida B. Wells award Congl. Black Caucus, 1989, Public Svc. award African Methodist Episcopal Ch., 1991, Invaluable Svc. award Martin L. King Jr. Found., 1992, Black Women of Courage award Nat. Fedn. Black Women Bus. Owners, 1993, Black Awareness Ach. award Holy Redeemer Catholic Ch., 1993, Bus. of the Yr. award Bus. and Profl. Women's League, 1993, Oustanding Svc. award Capital Press Club, 1993, Black Conscious Commitment trophy Unity Nation, 1993, Dedicated Cmty. Svc. award Ward I Cmty. and D.C. Pub. Schs., 1994, Women of Strength award Nat. Black Media Coalition, 1994, 95, Outstanding Woman of Yr. award Alpha Gamma chpt. Iota Phi Lambda, 1994, Art Carter Excellence award Capital Press Club, 1994, Excellence in Comm. award Washington Inter-Alumni Coun. United Negro Coll. Fund, 1994, 95, Disting. Cmty. Svc. award The Questers, Inc., 1995, Outstanding Journalist award Masons, 1995, Outstanding Achievement award Beta Zeta chpt. Zeta Phi Beta, 1996, award in recognition of outstanding contbns. made to youth The Soc., 1996, Disting. Black Women award BISA, 1996, Woman of 20th Century award Nat. Pol. Congress Black Women, 1999. Mem. Nat. Newspaper Pubs. Assn. (editl. com. 1987—, Merit award 1987, 89-97), Soc. Profl. Journalists (Disting. Svc. in local journalism award Washington chpt. 1994), Links (past v.p. Balt. chpt., pres. 2003—), Capital Press Club (exec. bd. 1987-98, Outstanding Svc. award 1993, Art Carter award 1994), Delta Sigma Theta (Frances L. Murphy II Comm. award Fed. City Alumnae chpt. 1993, Fortitude Image award Prince George's County chpt. 1994, Ethel L. Payne award 1996-97), Kiwanis Club (first woman hon. 1995). Democrat. Avocation: bridge. Home: 2406 Overland Ave Baltimore MD 21214-2440 Office: Baltimore 2519 N Charles St Baltimore MD 21218-4602 Address: 2406 Overland Ave Baltimore MD 21214-2440

MURPHY, FRANCES M. government agency administrator; MD with honors, Georgetown U., Washington, 1979; MPH, Uniformed Svcs. U. of the Health Scis., 1993. Diplomate Am. Coll. Psychiatry and Neurology. Resident in neurology Georgetown U., Washington; staff neurologist Andrews AFB, Md., 1983—87; chief cons. occupl. and environ. medicine Dept. Vet. Affairs, Washington, dep. under-sec. for health, 1999—2002, acting under sec. for health, 2002, dep. under sec. for health for health policy coord., 2002—. Adj. assoc. prof. neurology Uniformed Svcs. U. of the Health Scis. Contbr. articles to profl. jours. With USAF. Office: US Dept Vets Affairs 810 Vermont Ave NW Washington DC 20420*

MURPHY, GLORIA WALTER, novelist, screenwriter; b. Hartford, Conn., Feb. 22, 1940; d. Frank and Elizabeth (Lemkin) Walter; m. Joseph S. Murphy; children: William Gitelman, Laurie Gitelman, Daniel Gitelman, Julie Gitelman, Caitlin Fleck. Student, No. Essex Community Coll., Haverhill, Mass., 1979-81, Boston U., 1981-82. Columnist Pandora's Box The Peabody (Mass.) Times, 1975; columnist Murphy's Law The Methuen (Mass.) News, 1979. Author: Nightshade, 1986, Bloodties, 1987, Nightmare, 1987, The Playroom, 1987, Cry of the Mouse, 1991, Down Will Come Baby, 1991 (also movie 1999), A Whisper in the Attic, 1992, A Shadow on the Stair, 1993, Simon Says, 1994 (also movie 1997), A Stranger in the House, 1995, Til Death Do Us Part, 1997; contbr. publs to fgn. countries in various langs. Mem. Mystery Writers Am., Authors Guild. Office: PO Box 365 Ringwood NJ 07456-0365

MURPHY, HELEN, recording industry executive; b. Glasgow, Scotland, Oct. 2, 1962; came to U.S., 1990; d. Francis and Kathleen (Gallagher) M.; m. Michael Christopher Luksha, Apr. 1, 1989. BA in Econs. with honors, U. Guelph, Can., 1982; MBA, U. Western Ontario, Can., 1984. CFA. Asst. mgr. securities rsch. Confederation Life, Toronto, Can., 1984-86; sr. analyst entertainment & merchandising Prudential Bache Securities, Toronto, Can., 1986-89; v.p. rsch. Richardson Greenshields Can., Toronto, 1989-90; v.p. investor rels. Polygram Holding, Inc., N.Y.C., 1990-91; v.p., treas. Polygram Records Inc., N.Y.C., 1991-92, sr. v.p. corp. fin., treas., 1992-95; sr. v.p. investor rels. PolyGram Internat. Ltd., N.Y.C., 1995-97; sr. v.p. mergers and acquisitions PolyGram Holding, Inc., N.Y.C., 1995-97, CFO, 1997-99, Westvaco Corp., 1999; CFO & chief adminstrv. office Martha Stewart Living Omnimedia, Inc., N.Y.C., 1999—2001; exec. v.p., CFO Warner Music Group, 2001—. Lectr. U. Guelph, 1982-90. Fellow Nat. Investor Rels. Inst., N.Y. Soc. Security Analysts, N.Y. Treas. Group. Office: Warner Music Group 75 Rockefeller Plz New York NY 10019

MURPHY, IRENE HELEN, publishing executive; b. Boston; d. Charles Leo and Irene Muriel (Finney) M. BA, Regis Coll., 1958; MA, Boston Coll., 1963, Northeastern U., Boston, 1968, Manhattanville Coll., 1969. Tchr. elem. sch., Boston; high sch. dir. guidance; ednl. adminstr.; prof. master tchr. program, 1969—; prof. N.Y.C.; dir. sch. svcs. Glencoe/McGraw Hill Pub. Co., Woodland Hills, Calif., 1969—; v.p. Glencoe Pub. Co., Mission Hills, Calif. Vis. lectr. univs., including Boston Coll., Sacred Heart U., St. John, Nfld., Regis Coll., Teachers Coll., Sidney, Australia, Teachers Coll., Melbourne, Australia, McGill U., Mont., Providence (R.I.) Coll. Author series ednl. games for children. Recipient Gold Seal Recognition award Today's Cath. Tchr., 1987, Leadership award in religious edn., 1992. Mem. AAUW, Nat. Cath. Edn. Assn., Nat. Assn. Female Execs., Jordan Hosp. Club, St. Peter Cath. Women's Club, Adminstrs. Club, Passport Club, Admirals Club. Roman Catholic. Avocations: sports, music, art work, poetry, literature. Home: 59 Summer St Plymouth MA 02360-3462 also: 2677 SW Thunderbird Trl Stuart FL 34997-8944 Office: Benziger Pub Co 21600 Oxnard St Ste 500 Woodland Hills CA 91367-4947

MURPHY, JANET GORMAN, college president; b. Holyoke, Mass., Jan. 10, 1937; d. Edwin Daniel and Catherine Gertrude (Hennessey) Gorman. BA, U. Mass., 1958, postgrad., 1960-61, EdD, 1974, LLD (hon.), 1984; MEd, Boston U., 1961. Tchr. English and history John J. Lynch Jr. H.S., Holyoke, 1958-60; tchr. English Chestnut Jr. H.S., Springfield, Mass., 1961-63; instr. English and journalism Our Lady of Elms Coll., Chicopee, Mass., 1963-64; mem. staff Mass. State Coll., Lyndonville, Vt., 1977-83; pres. Mo. Western State Coll., St. Joseph, 1983—. Mem. campaign staff Robert F. Kennedy Presdl. Campaign, 1967. Recipient John Gunther Tchr. award NEA, 1961, award Women's Opportunity Com., Boston Fed. Exec. Bd., 1963, Phi Delta Kappa Educator of Yr. award NAACP, 1992; named one of 10 Outstanding Young Leaders of Greater Boston Area, Boston Jr. C. of C., 1973. Office: Mo Western State Coll Office of the President 4525 Downs Dr Saint Joseph MO 64507-2246

MURPHY, JEAN B. principal; b. Newton, Mass., Feb. 20, 1944; d. Francis T. Monahan and Katherine L. Ryan; m. Edward F. Murphy, Dec. 30, 1967; children: Edward F. III, Laura E. BA in edn., Mt. Saint Mary Coll., 1965; MEd, U. Mass., 1991. Tchr. Burlington (Mass.)Pub. Schs., 1965—67, Jackson Mann Alternative High, Allston, Mass., 1986—89, dir., 1989—94; prin. St. Mary IC Sch., Lawrence, Mass., 1994—99, St. Raphael Sch., Medford, Mass., 1999—. Adv. bd. Kristen Nolan Open, Burlington, Mass., 1997—. Mem.: Archdiocesan Prin. Assn., Assn. for Supr. and Curriculum, Nat. Cath. Edn. Assn. Avocations: reading, family, friends, exercise. E-mail: st.raphaelprincipal@hotmail.com.

MURPHY, JOANNE BECKER, writer; b. Detroit; d. Louis Norman and Gertrude Margaret (Kornmeier) Becker; m. Joseph A. Murphy, Jr., June 24, 1961; children: Michael Ellis, Joseph A. III. BA in Journalism, Mich. State U., 1958; MA in Humanities, Wayne State U., 1975. With pub. rels. dept. WBZ TV, Boston, 1958-60, The Jam Handy Orgn., Detroit, 1960-62, Detroit Symphony Orch., 1969-70; freelance writer, editor Detroit, 1978—90, Washington, 1990—. Contbg. writer: Affecting Change, 1986, Glass: State of the Art, 1989; editor: As Parents We Will, 1985 (1st Pl. award Pub. Svc. Nat. Found. for Alcoholism Comm.); writer, editor publs. for arts and human svcs. orgns.; contbr. articles to mags., newspapers. Program bd. Grosse Pointe (Mich.) War Meml., 1987—90; bd. dirs. Detroit Artists Market, 1982—90, Mich. Metro coun. Girl Scouts USA, 1971—78, Family Svcs. Detroit and Wayne County, 1970—76, All Hallows Guild Grounds Oversight Bd., Washington Nat. Cathedral, 1993—; bd. canvassers Grosse Pointe Sch. Sys., 1986—90; DC regional bd. Nat. Capital Area United Way, Washington, 1999—. Mem.: Washington Ind. Writers, Am. News Women's Club (Washington, bd. dirs. 1996—2001), Kappa Alpha Theta. Home and Office: 2717 O St NW Washington DC 20007-3128 Office Phone: 202-337-7856. E-mail: murphy.joanne@verizon.net.

MURPHY, JOANNE M. computer company executive; b. Holyoke, Mass., Dec. 31, 1957; d. LeRoy Paul and Rose Marie (Danehey) Miller; m. Dennis Francis Murphy III, June 2, 1979; 1 child, Dennis Francis IV. AS in Bus. Studies, Holyoke C.C., 1979; BS in Mktg., U. Mass., 1980; postgrad., U. Hartford. Account rep. Xerox Corp., Hartford, Conn., 1980-82; sr. account exec. Exxon Office Sys., Stamford, Conn., 1983-85; area sales cons. ShareTech, Hartford, 1985-86; sr. mktg. rep. Honeywell Info. Sys., Glastonbury, Conn., 1986-87; nat. account exec. Computer Horizons, Inc., 1987-93, dir. bus. devel., 1994-95; solutions mgr. IBM, 1995-97; engagement mgr. Horizons Cons., Inc. divsn. Computer Horizons Corp., Mountain Lakes, N.J., 1997—. Bus. devel. mgr. Oracle Corp., Waltham, Mass., 1997—98; nat. sales exec. Command Sys., Inc., Farmington, Conn., 1998—99; mgr. bus. devel., sales exec. Computer Assocs. Inc., East Windsor, Conn., 1999—2002; customer relationship mgr. The Hartford, 2002—. Editor shared tenant newsletter, 1985. Mem. NAFE, Data Processing Mgmt. Assn., Orgn. for Profls. in Telecom. Roman Catholic. Avocations: skiing, tennis, golf, personal computers. Home: 20 Partridge Ct Simsbury CT 06070-2342 Office: The Hartford 55 Farmington Ave Hartford CT Office Phone: 860-798-7840.

MURPHY, JUDITH CHISHOLM, trust company executive; b. Chippewa Falls, Wis., Jan. 26, 1942; d. John David and Bernice A. (Hartman) Chisholm. BA, Manhattanville Coll., 1964; postgrad., New Sch. for Social Research, 1965-68, Nat. Grad. Trust Sch., 1975. Asst. portfolio mgr. Chase Manhattan Bank, N.A., N.Y.C., 1964-68; trust investment officer Marshall & Ilsley Bank, Milw., 1968-72, asst. v.p., 1972-74, v.p., 1974-75; v.p., treas. Marshall & Ilsley Invesmtent Mgmt. Corp., Milw., 1975-94; v.p. Marshall & Ilsley Trust Co., Phoenix, 1982—, Marshall & Ilsley Trust Co. Fla., Naples, 1985—; v.p., dir. instnl. sales Marshall & Ilsley Trust Co., Milw., 1994-97, sr. v.p., 1997-98, M&I Investment Mgmt. Corp., 1998—. Coun. mem. Am. Bankers Assn., Washington, 1984-86; govt. relations com. Wis. Bankers Assn., Madison, 1982-88. Contbr. articles to Trusts & Estates Mag., 1980, ABA Banking Jour., 1981, Maricopa Lawyer, 1983. Chmn. Milw. City Plan Commn., 1986—97; commr. Milw. County Commn. on Handicapped, 1988—90; bd. dirs. Cardinal Stritch Coll., Milw., 1980—89, Children's Hosp. Wis., Milw., 1989—98, Milw. Ballet Co., 1996—2001, Milw. Ctr. for Independence, 1999—2004, Girl Scouts Milw. Area, 2002—, Milw. Symphony Orch., 2002—. Recipient Outstanding Achievement award YWCA Greater Milw., 1985, Sacajawea award Profl. Dimensions, Milw., 1988, Pro Urbe award Mt. Mary Coll., 1988, Vol. award Milw. Found., 1992; named Disting. Woman in Banking, Comml. West Mag., 1988. Mem. Milw. Analysts Soc. (sec. 1974-77, bd. dirs. 1977-80), Fin. Women Internat. (bd. dirs., v.p. 1976-80), Am. Inst. Banking (instr. 1975-78), TEMPO (charter), Profl. Dimensions (hon.), University Club, Woman's Club Wis., Rotary. Democrat. Roman Catholic. Home: 3622 N Lake Dr Milwaukee WI 53211-2644 Office: M&I Investment Mgmt Corp 1000 N Water St Milwaukee WI 53202-3197

MURPHY, KATHLEEN ANN, diversified manufacturing company executive; BS in Math., Syracuse U., 1972; MBA, U. Pa., 1976. Rsch. asst. Chase Econometrics, Bala Cynwyd, Pa., 1972-76; treasury assoc. IV

Internat., Phila., 1976-78, sr. treasury assoc., 1978-79, mgr. project fin., 1979-80; asst. treas. Fairchild Industries Inc., Chantilly, Va., 1980-86, dep. treas., 1985-86; v.p., treas. Connell Ltd. Partnership, 1986-93, v.p., CFO, 1993-2000, sr. v.p., CFO, 2000—. Dir. Entergy Corp., 2000. Office: Connell Ltd Partnership Ft Hill Sq 1 International Pl Boston MA 02110

MURPHY, KATHLEEN ANNE FOLEY, communications executive; b. Fresh Meadows, N.Y., Oct. 15, 1952; d. Thomas J. and Audrey L. Finn; m. Timothy Sean Murphy, Sept. 26, 1992; 1 child, G. David. BA, Marymount Coll., 1974; postgrad., Smith Coll., 1985. V.p. acct. supr., sr. v.p. mgmt. supr., sr. v.p. group dir. Ogilvy & Mather Inc., N.Y.C., 1974-90; sr. v.p., worldwide account dir. Young & Rubicam, San Francisco, 1990-92, sr. v.p., dir. account svcs., 1992-95, exec. v.p., dir. acct. svcs., 1995-97, exec. v.p., gen. mgr., 1997—2002; COO WPP, San Francisco, 2002—03, dir. network bus. devel. and integration, 2003—. Mem. Family Caregivers Alliance. Roman Catholic. Home: One Brookside Ave Berkeley CA 94705 Office: WPP 303 Second St S Tower 9th Fl San Francisco CA 94107 E-mail: kmurphy@wpp.com.

MURPHY, KATHLEEN MARY, former law firm executive, alternative healing professional; b. Bklyn., Dec. 16, 1945; d. Raymond Joseph and Catherine Elizabeth (Kearney) M. BA in Edn., Molloy Coll., 1971; MS in Edn., Bklyn. Coll., 1975. Ordained minister Ch. of the Loving Servant; cert. hypnotherapist; cert. elem. sch. tchr., N.Y. Elem. sch. tchr. various parochial schs., L.I., Bklyn., Queens, N.Y., 1969-80; from asst. prin. to prin. parochial sch. Queens, 1980-82; supr.-trainer Davis, Polk, Wardwell law firm, N.Y.C., 1982-88; mgr. Schulte Roth & Zabel, N.Y.C., 1988-95; Reiki master (alternative healing profl.), 1996—. Trainer program for new employees, 1984; speaker edn. topics, Bklyn., Queens, 1979-81. Mem. NAFE, Reiki Alliance. Democrat. Roman Catholic. Avocations: psychic phenomenon, workings of mind, ancient histories, crossword puzzles, museums. Office Phone: 718-381-7354.

MURPHY, KATHRYN MARGUERITE, archivist; b. Brockton, Mass. d. Thomas Francis and Helena (Fortier) M. AB in History, George Washington U., 1935, MA, 1939; MLS, Cath. U., 1950; postgrad., Am. U., 1961. With Nat. Archives and Records Svc., Washington, 1940-89, ret., supervisory archivist Ctrl. Rsch. br., 1958-62, archivist, 1962—. Mem. fed. women's com. Nat. Archives, 1974, rep. to fed. women's com. GSA, 1975; docent, 1989—; lectr. colls., socs. in U.S., 1950—; lectr. Am. ethnic history, 1978-79; free lance author and lectr. in field. Contbr. articles on Am. ethnic history to profl. publs. Founder, pres. Nat. Archives lodge Am. Fedn. Govt. Employees, 1965—, del. conv., 1976, 78, 80, recipient award for outstanding achievement in archives, 1980. Recipient commendation Okla. Civil War Centennial Commn., 1965; named hon. citizen Oklahoma City, Mayor, 1963. Mem. ALA, Soc. Am. Archivists (joint com. hosp. librs. 1965-70), Nat. League Am. Pen Women (corr. sec. Washington 1975-78, pres. chpt. 1978-80), Bus. and Profl. Womens' Club Washington, Phi Alpha Theta (hon.). Home: 1500 Massachusetts Ave NW Washington DC 20005-1821

MURPHY, LAURA, legal association administrator; b. Md. Grad., Wellesley Coll. Devel. dir. ACLU Found. So. Calif.; lobbyist ACLU, Washington, dir. D.C. office, 1993—. Mem.: ABA (mem. adv. commn. to the standing com. on election law 1998). Office: ACLU 122 Maryland Ave NE Washington DC 20002

MURPHY, LINDA S. community health nurse; b. Ft. Worth, Tex., Oct. 4, 1948; d. James Joseph and Wanda Margaret Murphy; life ptnr. Christopher Andrew Greagor. BSN, U. Tex., 1970; MS in Health Edn., Whitworth Coll., 1987. RN Tex., 1970. Staff nurse Brackenridge Hosp., Austin, Tex., 1970—72; sch. nurse, ho. parent Mary Lee Sch. Spl. Ed., 1972—74. Pub. health nurse Austin/Travis County Health Dept., Austin, 1973—75; nurse cons. Austin State Sch., 1975—78; wic coord. Coquille Co. Health Dept., Coos Bay, Oreg., 1978—80; home health nurse Jackson Co. Health Dept., Medford, 1980—82, Hillhaven Home Health Agy., Redding, Calif., 1982—84; nurse mgr. Spokane Co. Head Start, Spokane, Wash., 1984—93, Austin/Travis Co. Health Dept., Austin, 1993—97; pub. health nurse U. Tex. Sch. Nursing Children's Wellness Ctr., Del Valle, 1997—. Profl. mem. Cmty. Action Network, Austin, 1997; adv. Fair Budget Action Campaign, Spokane, 1989—93; mem. Citizens Health Care Network, Austin, 1994—2001; profl. rep. Spokane C. of C., Spokane, 1989—93; facilitator Austin Shambhala Meditation Ctr., 1995—2003; voting mem. South Rural Cmty. Ctr., Del Valle, Tex., 1997; co-chair Spokane Co. Birth to Six Interagency Coordinating Coun., 1992—93. Mem.: ANA (assoc.; chair cmty. rels. com. 1996—97), Tex. Nurses Assn. (assoc. dist. 6 Fabulous Five 1996), Tex. Soc. Pub. Health Educators (assoc.), Tex. Pub. Health Assoc. (assoc.). Liberal. Buddhist. Avocations: travel, reading, outdoor activities, dance. Home: 6934 Chinook Dr Austin TX 78736 Office: UTSON Children's Wellness Center 3311 FM 973 S Del Valle TX 78617 E-mail: lmurphy@mail.nur.utexas.edu.

MURPHY, MARGARET A. nursing educator, adult nurse practitioner; b. NYC, Apr. 4, 1934; d. William J. and Margaret (Burchill) Allen; m. Raymond L.H. Murphy, Jr., July 12, 1958; children: Raymond L.H. III, Michael W., Ann Murphy Postell, Maureen D. Murphy Olsen, Alice M., Matthew D. BSN, St. Joseph Coll., West Hartford, Conn., 1955; MS, NYU, 1957; PhD, Boston Coll., Chestnut Hill, Mass., 1987. RN Mass., cert. adult nurse practitioner. Instr. Boston U. Sch. Nursing, 1971-72; pulmonary clin. nurse specialist Pulmonary Assocs., Boston, 1972-73; pulmonary nurse clinician Tufts U., Medford, Mass., 1973-76; from instr. prof. nursing to assoc. prof. nursing Boston Coll., 1976—2001, assoc. prof. emeritus, 2001, chmn. adult health nursing, 1988-92, dir. adult nurse practitioner program, 1987—2001, dir. Kennedy Audio Visual Resource Ctr., 1991-95, coord. MBA-MSN program, 1993-99. Rschr. in lung sound patterns in health and disease, women's attitudes toward menopause. Co-editor: Pharmacotherapeutics and Advanced Nursing Practice, 1998; co-author: (CD-ROM) Learning Lung Sounds, 2002; contbr. articles to profl. jours. Fellow USPHS, 1957-58; grantee Uniformed Svcs. U. Health Scis., 1995-96. Fellow: Am. Coll. Nurse Practitioners; mem.: ANA, Mass. Thoracic Soc. (chmn. com. on nursing practice, counselor 1989—91), Am. Thoracic Soc., Mass. Nurses Assn. (co-chmn. cabinet on legis. 1985—88), Sigma Theta Tau (chmn. awards and scholarships com. Alpha Chi chpt. 1994—96, pres. 1996—98, newsletter editl. bd. 1998—2003, Alpha Chi chpt. Mentor award 2001). E-mail: murphy@bc.edu.

MURPHY, MARGARET HACKETT, US bankruptcy judge; b. Salisbury, N.C., 1948; BA, Queens Coll., Charlotte, N.C., 1970; JD, U. N.C., Chapel Hill, 1973. Bar: Ga. 1973, U.S. Dist. Ct. (no. dist.) Ga. 1973, U.S. Ct. Appeals (5th cir.) 1974, U.S. Ct. Appeals (11th cir.) 1982. Assoc. Smith, Cohen, Ringel, Kohler and Martin, Atlanta, 1973-79; ptnr. Smith, Gambrell & Russell (formerly Smith, Cohen, Ringel, Kohler and Martin), Atlanta, 1980-87; U.S. bankruptcy judge U.S. Dist. Ct. (no. dist.) Ga., Atlanta, 1987—. Office: 1290 US Courthouse 75 Spring St SW Atlanta GA 30303-3309

MURPHY, MARY C. state legislator; BA, Coll. St. Scholastica; postgrad., U. Wis., Superior, Am. U., Ind. U. H.s. tchr.; mem. Minn. Ho. of Reps., 1976—. Mem. judiciary fin. com., chair ethics com., mem. capital investments com., labor-mgmt. rels. com.; active del. Duluth Central Labor Body AFL-CIO; mem., lector St. Raphael's Parish; dir. State Democratic Farmer-Labor Party, 1972-74, chmn. 8th Dist. credentials com., 1974—, chmn. St. Louis County Legis. Delegation, 1985-86. Mem. Duluth Fedn. Tchrs. (1st v.p. 1976-77, various coms.), Minn. Fedn. Tchrs. (legis. com. 1972-75), Am. Fedn. Tchrs. (del. nat. convs.), Minn. Hist. Soc., Alpha Delta Kappa. Office: 100 Constitution Ave Saint Paul MN 55155-1232

MURPHY, MARY MARGUERITE, artist; b. S.I., N.Y., Mar. 29, 1958; d. Vincent Joseph and Teresa Marie (O'Connell) M.; m. James Thomas Primosch, Apr. 5, 1986. Student, Tyler Sch. Art, 1976—78; BA cum laude, Barnard Coll., 1981; student, NY Studio Sch., 1986—87; MFA in Painting, Tyler Sch. Art, 1991; student, Skowhegan Sch. Painting/Sculp., 1990. Panel mem. Coll. New Rochelle, NY, 1985, Phila. Art Alliance, 1997; tchg. fellow Tyler Sch. Art, Phila., 1989—91, instr., 1995, Fleisher Art Meml., Phila., 1992—98; vis. artist Ohio State U., Columbus, 1993, Columbus, 97; tchg. artist Inst. for Arts in Edn., Phila., 1994, Phila., 97; sr. lectr. U. of the Arts, Phila., 1996—98, adj. asst. prof., 2000—; lectr. Washington U., St. Louis, 1998—99; panel moderator Beaver Coll., Glenside, Pa., 1995, Nat. Mus. Jewish History, 1997; vis. artist lectr. Ohio State U., 1993, 97, Tyler Sch. Art, 1994, Pa. State U., 1997, U. Alaska, 2002. One person shows include S.P.A.C.E.S., Cleve., 1994, Fleisher Art Meml., Phila., 1995, Larry Becker Contemporary Art, Phila., 1995, Schmidt/Dean Gallery, Phila., 1998, 99, U. Alaska, 2002; exhibited in group shows 80 Washington Sq. East Galleries, N.Y.C., 1985, Va. Ctr. for Creative Arts, Sweet Briar, Va., 1986, The Drawing Ctr., N.Y.C., 1989, Larry Becker Gallery, Phila., 1991, 95, Temple Univ. Gallery, Phila., 1991, State Theatre Ctr. for the Arts, Easton, Pa., 1991, Momenta Art Alternatives, Phila., 1991, Beaver Coll., Glenside, Pa., 1992, 96, 99, White Columns, N.Y.C., 1992, Moore Coll. of Art and Design, Phila., Pa., 1992, 99, 1708 E Main St. Gallery, Richmond, Va., 1992, Ohio State U., Columbus, 1993, Main Line Ctr. of the Arts, Haverford, Pa., 1993, 55 Mercer St., N.Y.C., 1994, Vox Populi, Phila., 1994, 558 Broome St., N.Y.C., 1994, Tyler Sch. Art, Phila., 1994, Larry Becker Contemporary Art, Phila., 1995, Del. Art Mus., Wilmington, 1996, Borowsky Gallery, Phila., 1996, Ohio State U., Columbus, 1997, Del. Ctr. Contemporary Art, 1997, Abington Art Ctr., 1997, Phila. Art Alliance, 1997, Fleisher Art Meml., Phila., 1998, Margaret Thatcher Projects, N.Y.C., 1998, N.J. Ctr. Visual Arts, Summit, 1998, David Beitzel Gallery, N.Y., 1998, Schmidt/Dean Gallery, 1999, U. of the Arts, Phila., 2000; permanent collections Wilmington Trust, The Brooklyn Mus., Ark. Art Ctr., Am. Express; works included in publs. Richmond Times Dispatch, Phila. City Paper, New Art Examiner, The Phila. Inquirer, The Plain Dealer, Artnews, Eyelevel; contbr. to The New Art Examiner; contbr. articles to The New Art Examiner, lectr. in field. Mem. alumni bd. Tyler Sch. Art, Elkins Park, Pa., 1994-98. Resident Va. Ctr. for Creative Arts, 1985, 86; fellow Skowhegan Sch. Painting and Sculpture, 1990, Nat. Endowment for Arts fellow in painting, 1993-94; grantee Fleisher Art Meml., Phila., 1994, Venture Fund, U. of Arts, 2002, Pa. State Coun. on Arts, 2002; fellow Pa. State Coun. on the Arts, 1998; finalist Pew Fellowship in the Arts, 1994-95. Mem. Coll. Art Assn. Roman Catholic. Home: 20 Whitemarsh Ave Erdenheim PA 19038-8230 E-mail: mary.murphy52@verizon.net.

MURPHY, MELINDA, TV host, reporter; b. Midland, Tex., Dec. 10, 1963; d. James Palmer and Natalie (Harben) M. BA in Journalism, Tex. A&M U., 1986. Account exec. CBS Radio Rep., N.Y.C., 1986-88; dir. classical music mktg. Interep Radio Store, N.Y.C., 1988; entertainment stringer KOCO TV, 1995-97; co-host, EP, creator SCAM pilot for USA Network, 1996; info. specialist NewsTalk TV, 1995-96; host Global Shopping Network, 1996-97; reporter News 12 N.J., 1996—. Talent booker WWOR-TV, 1991-92; prodn. coord. CBS Tony awards, 1992, 93; prodn. exec. ABC, 1992; assoc. floor prodr. CNN Dem. Nat. Conv., 1992; talent coord. PBS Internat. Emmy Awards, 1992; prodr. Multimedia Entertainment, 1993-94; coordinating prodr. Buena Vista TV, 1994; sr. prodr. Dick Clark Prodns., 1994, New World Entertainment, 1994; on-air coach Columbia TriStar, 1994; prodn. mgr. PBS, 1996; writer, field prodr. WCBS-TV, 1990-97, contbg. writer Parents mag., 1996; judge Internat. TV Festival, 1995—. Recipient Emmy award, 1997. Mem. AFTRA, NATAS, Writer's Guild Am., Alpha Delta Pi. Avocations: animal rights, cooking and entertaining, traveling, outdoor sports. Home: 68 Lydia Dr West New York NJ 07093 8368

MURPHY, MICHELLE ZICK, special education educator; d. Christine Hayduk and Albert Adam Zick; m. John Michael Murphy, Aug. 17, 2002. BS in spl. edn., U. of Scranton, 1997—2003. Cert. Mental and/or Physical Handicapped, Bus. Computer Info. Tech. K-12 Commonwealth of PA, 2003. Tchr. Scranton Sch. Dist., Scranton, Pa., 2003—. Assistant editor (newsletter) The Theory and Practice Newsletter, Challenges. Recipient Academic Excellence in Spl. Edn., U. of Scranton, 2003, Outstanding Coop. Edn. Student, Lackawanna Trail H.S.; Lit. scholarship, Charlotte Newcomb, 2000—02, Peckville Profl. Women's Club, 2001—02, Scranton Profl. Women's Club, 2001—02. Mem.: Coun. for Exceptional Children, Kappa Delta Pi. D-Conservative. Roman Catholic. Avocations: kick boxing, power walking, travel, reading, fine dinning. Personal E-mail: zanderzk@aol.com.

MURPHY, MOLLY ANN, investment company executive; d. Charles William and Joan (Saul) Murphy. BS, Miami U., Oxford, Ohio, 1989; MBA, Xavier U., Cin., 1994. Chartered fin. analyst, Ohio. Mutual funds sales rep. Fidelity Investments, Cin., 1989—90; brokerage rep., fixed income specialist Fidelity Brokerage Svcs., Cin., 1990—93; portfolio mgr., officer Fifth Third Bank, Cin., 1993—2000; chief investment officer, v.p. Seasongood Asset Mgmt., Cin., 2000—. Bus. cons. Art League of Cin., 1999—2002; educator Ctr. for Pub. Investment Mgmt., Columbus, Ohio, 2000—02; presenter in field. Active Jr. League of Cin., 1998; com. mem. ann. workshop Ohio Assn. Sch. Bus. Ofcls., Columbus, 2000—. Mem.: Cin. Soc. Fin. Analysts, Assn. Investment Mgmt. and Rsch., Queen City Mcpl. Bond Club, Mensa. Office: Seasongood Asset Mgmt 414 Walnut St Cincinnati OH 45202-3910

MURPHY, PAMELA ANN, music educator; b. Cooperstown, N.Y., June 8, 1962; d. William John and Mary Kathryn Barrett; m. Michael Francis Murphy, II, July 11, 1987; children: Michael Francis III, Sean Patrick, Timothy Andrew. MusB, SUNY, Potsdam, 1984; MS, Western Conn. State U., 1990. Permanent tchg. lic. N.Y., cert. adjudicator NYSSMA. Music tchr. Valley Ctrl. Mid. Sch., Montgomery, NY, 1984—89, Valley Ctr. Mid. Sch., Montgomery, 1999—, Valley Ctrl. H.S., Montgomery, 1991—94, Kinry Rd. Elem. Sch., Poughkeepsie, NY, 1994—97. Guest condr. for all-county chorus Dutchess County (N.Y.) Music Educators Assn., 1994; pvt. music instr. Hudson Valley Conservatory Fine Arts, Walden, NY, 1995—, dir. musicals and plays, 1995—, sec., 1995—; profl. vocalist and keyboard player for various radio commls., weddings and bands. Composer: (songs) My Love, 2002. Facilitator fundraising activities Am. Heart Assn., Otego, NY, 1995; artistic dir. Hudson Valley Parents Performing Students, Walden, 1997—; fundraiser Muscular Dystrophy Assn., Newburgh, NY, 2003. Mem.: Orange County Music Educators Assn. (guest condr. for all-county chorus 1986, 1989, 2002), N.Y. State Sch. Assn., Music Educators Nat. Conf., Nat. Write Your Congressman. Roman Catholic. Avocations: singing, dance, acting, flute, painting. Home: 30 Browns Rd Walden NY 12586 Office: Hudson Valley Conservatory Fine Arts PO Box 704 35 E Main St Walden NY 12586

MURPHY, PATRICE ANN (PAT MURPHY), writer; b. Spokane, Wash., Mar. 9, 1955; m. Dave Wright, Feb. 14, 1999. BA in Biology, U. Calif., Santa Cruz, 1976. Sr. rsch. writer ednl. graphics dept. Sea World, 1978—82. Former instr. Clarion Speculative Fiction Workshop, Mich. State U.; former tchr. sci. fiction U. Calif., Santa Cruz; tchr. sci. fiction writing Creative Writing Program, Stanford U., 1995, 96, 97, 98. Author: The Shadow Hunter, 1982, The Falling Woman, 1987 (Nebula award 1987), Adventures in Time and Space with Max Merriwell, 2002, (novelette) Rachel in Love (Nebula award 1987, Isaac Asimov Reader's award 1987, Theodore Sturgeon Meml. award 1987), (short story collection) Points of Departure, 1990 (Philip K. Dick award 1990), (novella) Bones, 1991 (World Fantasy award 1991), (novelette) An American Childhood, Nadya-The Wolf Chronicles, There and Back Again, The City, Not Long After, 1984, By Nature's Design, The Color of Nature, 1996, The Science Explorer, 1996, Explorabook Bat Science, The Science Explorer, Out and About. Avocation: Karate. Office: care Tor Books 14th Fl 175 5th Ave Fl 14 New York NY 10010-7703 also: c/o Exploratorium 3601 Lyon St San Francisco CA 94123

MURPHY, PATRICIA ANN, physician, otolaryngologist; b. N.Y.C., Oct. 22, 1951; d. John Francis and Teresa (Whitney) M. BS, Wagner Coll., S.I., N.Y., 1974; MD, Virgen Milagrosa, The Philippines, 1981. Biochemist N.Y.C. Dept. Health, 1976-77; internist L.I. Coll. Hosp., Bklyn., 1981-82; surgeon St. Francis Hosp. and Med. Ctr., Trenton, N.J., 1982-83; clin. asst. instr., fellow otolaryngology SUNY Health Sci. Ctr. of Bklyn., 1984-87; fellow otolaryngology SUNY Health Sci. Ctr. of Bklyn., Brookdale Hosp. Med. Ctr., 1986-87; physician Family Health Plan, Fountain Valley, Calif., 1989-90; pvt. practice Santa Cruz, Calif., 1990-98, Elkins, W.Va., 1998—; clin. asst. instr. Otolaryngology dept. W.Va. U., 1998—. Bd. dirs. W.Va. Acad. Otolaryngology, 2000—; clin. instr. W.Va. U. Dept. Otolaryngology, 1999—; physician Hearing, Edn. and Awareness for Rockers, San Francisco; physician rock medicine Haight Ashbury Free Clin., San Francisco; clin. instr. W.Va. U., 1990—; bd. dir. W.Va. Otolaryngology Soc. Author: (with others) Ears, Nose, Throat Emergency Treatment, 1986. Fed. Rsch. grantee N.Y.C. Dept. Health, 1976-77. Mem. Am. Women's Med. Assn. (sec. 1990—), Women in Otolaryngology, Am. Acad. Otolaryngology, Am. Acad. Otolaryngic Allergy, Am. Acad. Facial Plastic and Reconstructive Surgery. Liberal. Roman Catholic. Avocations: reading, skiing, trekking. Office: 903 Gorman Ave Elkins WV 26241-3149

MURPHY, ROSEMARY, actress; b. Munich; came to U.S., 1939; d. Robert D. and Mildred (Taylor) M. Ed. in, Paris, France and Kansas City, Mo. Broadway appearances include Look Homeward Angel, 1958, Night of the Iguana, World premier at Spoleto (Italy) Festival of Two Worlds, 1959, Period of Adjustment, 1961, King Lear, 1963, Any Wednesday, 1964-66, Delicate Balance, 1966, Weekend, 1968, Butterflies are Free, 1970, Lady Macbeth, Stratford, Conn., 1973, Ladies of the Alamo, 1977, John Gabriel Borkman, 1980, Learned Ladies, 1982, Coastal Disturbances, 1987, The Devil's Disciple, 1988, A Delicate Balance, 1996, Waiting in the Wings, 1999; motion picture appearances include To Kill a Mockingbird, 1962, Any Wednesday, 1966, Ben, 1972, Walking Tall, 1972, You'll Like My Mother, 1972, Forty Carats, 1973, Julia, 1976, September, 1987, For the Boys, 1991, And The Band Played On, 1993, The Tuskegee Airmen, 1995, Message in a Bottle, 1998, Dust, 2001; TV appearance Eleanor and Franklin, 1975 (Emmy award for best supporting actress 1976), George Washington, 1983 (Tony award nominations 1961, 64, 67, award Motion Picture Arts Club 1966), E-Z Streets, 1996, The Unicorn's Secret, 1998, Frasier, 1997, 99. Recipient Variety Poll award, 1961, 67. Address: 220 E 73rd St New York NY 10021-4319

MURPHY, SANDRA ROBISON, lawyer; b. Detroit, July 28, 1949; m. Richard Robin. BA, Northwestern U., 1971; JD, Loyola U., Chgo., 1976. Bar: U.S. Dist. Ct. (no. dist.) Ill. 1976. Assoc. Notz, Craven, Mead, Maloney & Price, Chgo., 1976-78; ptnr. McDermott, Will & Emery, Chgo., 1978—. Mem. ABA (family law sect.), Ill. Bar Assn. (chair sect. family law coun. 1987-88), Chgo. Bar Assn. (chair matrimonial law com. 1985-86), Am. Acad. Matrimonial Lawyers (sec. 1990 91, v.p. 1991-92, pres. Ill. chpt. 1992-93, pres.-elect 1994-95, pres. 1995-96), Legal Club Chgo.

MURPHY, SHARON MARGARET, social studies educator; b. Milw., Aug. 2, 1940; d. Adolph Leonard and Margaret Ann (Hirtz) Feyen; m. James Emmett Murphy, June 28, 1969 (dec. May 1983); children: Shannon Lynn, Erin Ann; m. Bradley B. Niemcek, Aug. 7, 1999. BA, Marquette U., 1965; MA, U. Iowa, 1970, PhD, 1973. Cert. K-14 tchr., Iowa. Tchr. elem. and secondary schs., Wis., 1959-69; dir. publs. Kirkwood C.C., Cedar Rapids, Iowa, 1969-71; instr. journalism U. Iowa, Iowa City, 1971-73; asst. prof. U. Wis., Milw., 1973-79; assoc. prof. So. Ill. U., Carbondale, 1979-84; dean, prof. Marquette U., Milw., 1984-94; prof. Bradley U., Peoria, Ill., 1994—, provost, v.p. acad. affairs, 1994-97, pres. Cmty. Career and Tech. Ctr., 1997-98. Pub. rels. dir., editor Worldwide mag., Milw., 1965—68; reporter Milw. Sentinel, 1967; Fulbright sr. lectr. U. Nigeria, Nsukka, 1977—78; Fulbright sr. scholar U. Ljubljana, Slovenia, 2002. Author: Other Voices: Black, Chicano & American Indian Press, 1971; (with Wigal) Screen Experience: An Approach to Film, 1968; (with Murphy) Let My People Know: American Indian Journalism, 1981; (with Schilpp) Great Women of the Press, 1983; editor: (with others) International Perspectives on News, 1982. Mem. Peoria Riverfront Commn., 1995—2000; co-chair Peoria Race Rels. Com., 1999—2000; bd. dirs. Dirksen Congl. Leadership Ctr., 1994—2000, Dow Jones Newspaper Fund, NY, 1986—95, Peoria Symphony, 1996—2002. Recipient Medal of Merit, Journalism Edn. Assn., 1976, Amoco Award for Teaching Excellence, 1977, Outstanding Achievement award Greater Milw. YWCA, 1989; named Knight of Golden Quill, Milw. Press Club, 1977; Nat. headliner Women in Communication, Inc., 1985. Mem. Assn. Edn. in Journalism and Mass Comm. (pres. 1986-87), Soc. Profl. Journalists, Nat. Press Club, Accrediting Coun.on Edn. in Journalism and Mass Comm. (v.p. 1983-86). Democrat. Roman Catholic. Office: Bradley U Global Comm Ctr Peoria IL 61625-0001 Office Phone: 309-677-3621. E-mail: smm@bradley.edu.

MURPHY, SHEILA ANN, elementary school educator; b. N.Y.C., June 20, 1931; d. George A. Murphy and Martha F. Fairbrother. BA, Coll. New Rochelle, 1953; MFA, Cath. U. Am., 1958. Cert. elem. tchr. N.Y., art tchr. N.Y., prin. N.Y. Elem. sch. tchr. St. Jerome Parochial Sch., Bronx, NY, 1959—66, St. Philij Neri Sch., Bronx, 1966—68, prin., 1968—72; elem. sch. tchr. Our Lady of Mercy Sch., Bronx, 1973—82, prin., 1982—86; elem. sch. tchr. All Souls Parochial Sch., Sanford, Fla., 1987—97; tchr. ESL Regina Coeli Sch., Chieng Mai, Thailand, 1997—98; superior Ursuline Bedford Pk. Conv., Bronx, 1999—. Sec. Acad. Mt. St. Ursula Corp., Bronx, 1999—; mem. Ursuline Coun. Ea. Province of U.S., Bronx, 2000—03; mem. adv. bd. St. Philij Neri, Bronx, 2001—. Mem. social svcs. bd. Diocese of Orlando, Fla., 1993—95. Home: 2885 Marion Ave Bronx NY 10458

MURPHY, STACIA, health service association executive; BA, Talladega Coll. With Cmty. Service Soc., N.Y. City Mission Soc., N.Y. State Divsn. Youth, Alcoholism Coun. of N.Y.; exec. dir. N.Y.C. affiliate Nat. Coun. on Alcoholism and Drug Dependence, Inc., 1990-99, pres., 1999—. Office: Nat Coun Alcoholism & Drug Dependence 20 Exchange Pl Ste 2902 New York NY 10005

MURPHY, S(USAN) (JANE MURPHY), small business owner; b. Williamsport, Pa., Dec. 26, 1950; d. Jack W. and Edythe J. (Grier) M.; m. Michael J. Sanchez, Dec. 30, 1979. BBA, Pa. State U., 1978. Gen. mgr. Murphy Swift Homes, Hummelstown, Pa., 1970-75; owner, operator Murphy's Home Ctr., Hummelstown, 1975-79, 85-91; mgr. Builder's Emporium, San Diego, 1979-80; entrepreneur Castle in the Sand, San Diego, 1980-83; adminstr. Sohio Constrn., Prudhoe Bay, Alaska, 1983-85; fin. systems analyst Blue Shield, San Francisco, 1991-93; pres. San Francisco Mgmt. Svcs., Inc., San Francisco, 1993-99; entrepreneur Blue Skies Inn and Island Place of Olde Key West, Key West, Fla., 1999—. Cons. in field; dealer Servistar Home Ctrs. Photographs displayed at San Diego Art Inst. Vol. Hershey (Pa.) Free Ch. Donald MacIntyre scholar, 1979, Class of 1920 scholar, 1979, Congressman Kunkel scholar, 1979. Mem. Pa. Hardware Assn., Hummelstown C. of C., Better Bus. Bur. Evangelical Christian. Avocations: sailing, scuba diving, photography. Office: Blue Skies Inn 630 South St Key West FL 33045 E-mail: SuzyQQ@earthlink.net.

MURPHY, SYLVIA J. HARRIS, secondary school educator; b. Waverly, N.Y., Apr. 22, 1946; d. Eugene Kenneth and Alice Christine Harris; m. Malcolm LaRue Murphy, July 20, 1968; children: Teresa Marie, Annette Rae, Eileen Louise. BS in Home Econ., Mansfield U., 1968, M in Elem. Edn., 1971. Kindergarten tchr. Sayre (Pa.) Area Sch., 1968—69, 1st grade tchr., 1970—72; 4th grade tchr. Athens (Pa.) Area Sch., 1972—73, 6-8th grade home econ. tchr., 1974—80, 10-12th grade home econ. tchr., 1980—. Adv. bd. Bradford County Ext., Towonda, Pa., Bradford County 4H. Named Ext. Cooperator of Yr., Bradford County, 2000. Office: Athens Area Schs 401 W Frederick St Athens PA 18810 E-mail: smurphy@sobbs.com.

MURPHY, THELMA ARABELLA, elementary school educator, photographer; b. Cardston, Alta., Can., June 12, 1947; arrived in U.S., 1986; d. Raymond and Isabella (Many Feathers) King; m. Laurence Patrick Murphy, May 12, 1971. EdB, U. Lethbridge, Alta., 1976. Cert. tchr. Hawaii. Tchr. Dept. Indian Affairs, Edmonton, 1971—80, Edmonton Pub. Sch. Bd., 1980—86; tchr. spl. edn. Highlands Intermediate Sch., Pearl City, Hawaii, 1986—87; tchr. St. Theresa Sch., Honolulu, 1987—. Profl. wedding photographer, 1980—. Author poetry. Recipient scholarship, U. Lethbridge, 1967; scholar, Dept. Indian Affairs, 1967—71. Mem.: Nat. Cath. Edn. Assn., Indian Rights for Indian Women (sec. 1971—85). Roman Catholic. Avocations: photography, writing, reading, beading, sewing.

MURRAH, ANN RALLS FREEMAN, historical association executive; b. Gadsden, Ala., June 23, 1932; d. Oscar William Freeman, Sr. and Annie Collier (Ralls) Freeman; m. Robert Leland Murrah, Aug. 9, 1952; children: Frances Ralls Murrah Lovett, Robert Leland Murrah Jr. Grad., Brenau U., 1954. Pres. Gen. Descendants of the Signers of the Constn., Orlando, Fla., 1991—. Rep. Fla. 8th congl. dist. Congl. Sr. Intern Program, Wash., 1998; keynote spkr. Feminist Summit for Global Peace, Taipei, Taiwan, 1995; mem. protocol & hospitality coms. for equestrian events 1996 Olympics; mem. Am. com. Ball des Rosenkavaliers, Vienna, 1989—90; bd. dir. Arnold Palmer Hosp. Bd., Orlando, Fla.; founder Nat. Constn. Ctr., Phila., 2003—; spkr. in field. Mem. women's com. N.Y. U. Downtown Hosp., 1996—99; gala chmn. Winter Pk. Health Found., Winter Pk., Fla., 1996; ball chmn. Arnold Palmer Hosp. for Women & Children, Orlando, Fla., 1997—99, 2001; mem. Orlando Regional Healthcare Found., Orlando; active Coun. of 101-Orlando Mus. Art; v. chmn. dinner com. fundraiser March of Dimes, 1998. Named First Woman Knighted in her own right, Order of St. John of Jerusalem, 1992; named to Brenau U. Alumni Hall of Fame, 2001; recipient Meritorious Svc. award, Sons of the Am. Revolution, 1986, Martha Washington medal, 1988, The Rallye Saintogeais Hunt award, Foret De La Coubre, France, 1988. Mem.: Nat. Soc. So. Dames Am., Plantagenet Soc., Fla. Opera Guild, Met. Opera Guild, Washington Soc., Gavel Soc., Nat. Steeplechase Assn., Shakerag Hunt Club (awarded colors), Daughters of the Am. Revolution (first vice-regent), Sovereign Colonial Soc. Am. of Royal Descent, Magna Charta Dames (herald and courier), Colonial Order of the Crown, Daughters of the Cin., Colonial Dames of Am., Descendants of Knights of the Garter, Sons & Daughters of the Pilgrims (gov. in Ga. 1992—94, historian gen. of the U.S. 1994—97, first vice-gov.), Alpha Delta Pi (province pres., dir. ritual and paraphernalia). Home and Office: Soc of Descendants of Signers of Constitiution 903 Sussex Close Orlando FL 32804

MURRAY, ANNE, singer; b. Springhill, N.S., Can., June 20, 1945; d. Carson and Marion (Burke) M.; m. William M. Langstroth, June 20, 1975; children: William Stewart, Dawn Joanne. B.Phys. Edn., U. N.B., 1966, D.Litt. (hon.), 1978, St. Mary's U., 1982. Rec. artist for Arc Records, Canada, 1968, Capital/EMI Records, 1969—. Appeared on series of TV spls. CBC, 1970—81, 1988—93; star CBS spls., 1981—85; toured N. Am., Japan, Englan, Germany, Holland, Ireland, Sweden, Australia and New Zealand, 1977—82. Singer: (31 albums including) A Little Good News, 1984, (albums) As I Am, 1988, Greatest Hits, vol. I, 1981, vol. II, 1989, Harmony, 1987, You Will, 1990, Yes I Do, 1991, Croonin', 1993, The Best So Far, 1994, Now and Forever, Anne Murray, 1996, An Intimate Evening with Anne Murray-Live, 1997, What A Wonderful World, 1999, What A Wonderful Christmas, 2001, Country Croonin', 2002. Hon. chmn. Can. Save the Children Fund, 1978-80. Recipient Juno awards as Can.'s top female vocalist, 1970-81; Can.'s Top Country Female Vocalist, 1970-86; Grammy award as top female vocalist-country, 1974; Grammy award as top female vocalist-pop, 1978; Grammy award as top female vocalist-country, 1980, 83; Country Music Assn. awards, 1983-84; named Female Rec. Artist of Decade, Can. Rec. Industry Assn., 1980, Top Female Vocalist 1970-86; star inserted in Hollywood Walkway of Stars, 1980; Country Music Hall of Fame Nashville; decorated companion Order of Can.; inducted Juno Hall of Fame, 1993. Mem. AFTRA, Assn. Canadian TV and Radio Artists, Am. Fedn. Musicians. Office: Bruce Allen Talent No 500 425 Carrall St Vancouver BC Canada V6B6E3 also: EMI Music Distbn 21700 Oxnard St Ste 700 Woodland Hills CA 91367-3617

MURRAY, CATHERINE MARY MURPHY, accountant; b. Severn, Md., July 7, 1940; d. George William Murphy and Emma May Rodgers; m. Rudolph Chesley Stanley, Dec. 21, 1963 (dec. Oct. 31, 1978); children: Kenneth Michael Stanley, Mary Ellen Stanley Fahlstrom; m. Charles Edward Murray, Nov. 22, 1988 (dec. Dec. 13, 2001). Student in Early Childhood Edn., U. Maine, 1981. Classroom asst. to coord. Coastal Econ. Devel. Corp., Boothbay Harbor/Bath, Maine, 1969—81; acct. Pvt. Contractor Constrn., 1984—89; project acct. Chesapeake Sprinkler Co., Odenton, Md., 1990—. Proofreader, asst., editor David W. Webster FSA, Livingston, Scotland, 1998—; asst. to instr. Ancestry.com/myfamily.com, 2003—. Author: (non-fiction) Through the Generations, 1999, To Honor Thy Family, 1999; co-author: The Family True, 2001. Contbr. genealogy material Ch. of Jesus Christ of LDS, Salt Lake City; sponsor Anne Arundel County Scottish Festival, Inc., Crownsville, Md.; contbr. genealogy material Amesbury (Mass.) Pub. Libr. With USN, 1958—59. Avocations: genealogy, history, reading, travel, music. Office: Chesapeake Sprinkler Co 1913 B Betson Ct Odenton MD 21113 Personal E-mail: catherinemmurray@comcast.net.

MURRAY, CHERRY ANN, physicist, researcher; b. Ft. Riley, Kans., Feb. 6, 1952; d. John Lewis and Cherry Mary (Roberts) M.; m. Dirk Joachim Muehlner, Feb. 18, 1977; children: James Joachim, Sara Hester. BS in Physics, MIT, 1973, PhD in Physics, 1978. Rsch. asst. physics dept. MIT, Cambridge, 1969-78; rsch. assoc. Bell Labs., Murray Hill, N.J., 1976-77; mem. tech. staff AT&T Bell Labs., Murray Hill, 1978-85, disting. mem. tech. staff, 1985-87, dept. head low-temperature and solid-state physics rsch., 1987-90, dept. head condensed matter physics rsch., 1990-93, dept. head semicond. physics rsch., 1993-97, dir. phys. rsch. lab., 1997—. Co-chair Gordon Rsch., Wolfeboro, N.H., 1982, chair, 1984. Contbr. numerous articles to profl. jours. and chpts. to books. NSF fellow, 1969; IBM fellow MIT, 1974-76. Fellow AAAS, Am. Phys. Soc. (Maria Goeppart-Mayer award 1989), Nat. Acad. Scis., Sigma Xi. Office: Bell Labs Lucent Techs 700 Mountain Ave Rm Id-269 New Providence NJ 07974-1208

MURRAY, CONNIE WIBLE, state official, former state legislator; b. Tulsa, Oct. 13, 1943; d. Carl Prince Lattimore and Jimmie Bell Henry; m. Jarrett Holland Murray, May 4, 1995. Cert. of oral hygiene, Temple U., 1965; BA, Loyola Coll., 1975; JD, U. Md., 1980. Registered dental hygienist, Bethlehem, Pa., 1965-66, Joppa, Md., 1966-77; law clk. Hon. Albert P. Close, Belair, Md., 1980-81; atty., 1981-85; realtor, 1985-90; mem. Mo. Ho. of Reps., Jefferson City, 1990-96; pub. svc. commr. State of Mo., Jefferson City, 1997—. House mgr. Articles ot Impeachment of Judith Moriarty, Mo. Sec. of State, 1994; mem. budget com. Mo. Ho. of Reps., also mem. appropriations social svcs. and corrections com., judiciary and ethics com., civil and criminal law and accounts, opers. and fin. com., interim com. for fed. funds and block grants, commn. on intergovtl. affairs, commn. on mgmt. and productivity, legis. oversight com. for ct. automation, ho. automation com. Bd. dirs. North Springfield Betterment Assn., 1989; vocat. adv. bd., dir. house intern programs Nat. Conf. State Legislators. Named Outstanding Freshman Legis. on Health Care Issues, Mo. Rep. Caucus, 1992; recipient Jud. Conf. Legis. award Mo. Jud. Conf., 1994, Outstanding Woman Legis. award Assn. Probate and Assoc. Cir. Judges, 1995. Mem. LWV (bd. dirs. Springfield 1989, treas.), Nat. Order Women Legis., Nat. Conf. State Legis., Nat. Women's Polit. Caucus, Women Legis. Mo., Mo. Bar Assn. (Adminstr. for Justice award), Am. Legis. Exch. Counsel, Ctr. for Am. Women in Politics, Greene County Bar Assn., Forum-A Women's Network, Women in Govt. Avocations: golf, bicycling, jogging, travel. Home: 2118 S Catalina Ave Springfield MO 65804-2829 Office: Mo Gen Assembly State Capitol Office Bldg Jefferson City MO 65101-6806

MURRAY, DIANE ELIZABETH, librarian; b. Detroit, Oct. 15, 1942; d. Gordon Lisle and Dorothy Anne (Steketee) LaBoueff; m. Donald Edgar Murray, Apr. 22, 1968. AB, Hope Coll., 1964; postgrad., Mich. State U., East Lansing, 1964-66; MLS, Western Mich. U., 1968; MM, Aquinas Coll., 1982. Catalog libr., asst. head acquisitions sect. Mich. State U. Librs., East Lansing, 1968-77; libr. tech. and automated svcs. Hope Coll., Holland, Mich., 1977-88; dir. librs. DePauw U., Greencastle, Ind., 1988-91; acquisitions libr. Grand Valley State U., Allendale, Mich., 1991—. Sec., vice chair, chairperson bd. trustees Mich. Libr. Consortium, Lansing, 1981—85. V.p. Humane Soc. Putnam County, Greencastle, 1990—91; bd. dirs. Loutit Dist. Libr., 1999—. Mem.: ALA. Methodist. Avocations: dog breeding and showing, handbell ringing. Office: Grand Valley State U Zumberge Libr Allendale MI 49401 Business E-Mail: murrayd@gvsu.edu.

MURRAY, JULIA KAORU (MRS. JOSEPH E. MURRAY), occupational therapist; b. Wahiawa, Oahu, Hawaii, 1934; d. Gijun and Edna Tsuruko (Taba) Funakoshi; m. Joseph Edward Murray, 1961; children: Michael, Susan, Leslie. BA, U. Hawaii, 1956; cert. occupational therapy, U. Puget Sound, 1958. Therapist Inst. Logopedics, Wichita, Kans., 1958; sr. therapist Hawaii State Hosp., Kaneohe, 1959; part-time therapist Centre County Ctr. for Crippled Children and Adults, State College, Pa., 1963; vice chmn. adv. bd. Hosp. Improvement Program East Oreg. State Hosp., Pendleton, 1974; v.p. Ind. Living, Inc., 1976-79; job search instr.; mem. adv. com. Oreg. Ednl. Coordinating Commn., 1979-82; mem. Oreg. Bd. Engrng. Examiners, 1979-87; supr., occupational therapist Fairview Tng. Ctr., Salem, Oreg., 1984-94; occupational therapist U.S. Naval Hosp., Okinawa, Japan, 1994-99, Yokosuka, Japan, 1999—. Rep. from Umatilla County Commrs. to Blue Mountain Econ. Devel. Council, 1976-78; mem. Ashland Park and Recreation Bd., 1972-73; vice chmn. adv. bd. LINC, 1978; mem. exec. bd. Liberty-Boone Neighborhood Assn., 1979-83. Mem. Am. Occupational Therapy Assn., Oreg. Occupational Therapy Assn., Hawaii Occupational Therapy Assn. (sec. 1960, LWV (bd. dirs. Pendleton 1974, 77-78, pres. 1975-77; bd. dirs. Oreg. 1979-81, Ashland, Wis., 1967-71, Wis. v.p. 1970). Office: Ednl & Developmental Svcs US Naval Hosp APO AP Tokyo 96326 Japan also: Ednl & Develmntl Intervention Svcs Naval Hosp Yokosuka Japan E-mail: jkfmurray@hotmail.com.

MURRAY, JULIA KILLIN, art history educator; b. Washington, Dec. 14, 1951; d. Heslett Killin and Lucie Clark (Killin) M.; m. Andrew Michael Reschovsky, July 27, 1985; 1 child, Nina Michelle. BA, MA, Yale U., 1974, Princeton U., 1977, PhD, 1981. Researcher Asian art Met. Mus. Art, N.Y.C., 1977-79; mus. specialist Freer Gallery Art, Washington, 1979-83; curator Asian art Harvard U. Art Museums, Cambridge, Mass., 1983-86; vis. prof. Mt. Holyoke Coll., South Hadley, Mass., 1988-89; prof. art history U. Wis., Madison, 1989—. Cons. exhbn. N.C. Mus. Art, Raleigh, 1988-91; curatorial cons. East Asian legal studies Harvard Law Sch., Cambridge, 1988-89; founder, organizer New Eng. East Asian Art History Forum, Cambridge, 1987-89; assoc. Fairbank Ctr. for East Asian Rsch., Harvard U. Author: A Decade of Discovery, 1979, Last of the Mandarins, 1987, Ma Hezhi and the Illustration of the Book of Odes, 1993; art editor Jour. Sung-Yuan Studies, Albany, N.Y., 1986—. Wang Inst. Chinese Studies fellow, Lowell, Mass., 1986-87, Andrew Mellon fellow Met. Mus. Art, N.Y.C., 1979-80. Mem. Coll. Art Assn., Assn. Asian Studies. Avocation: squash. Office: Elvehjem Mus U Wis Dept Art History 800 University Ave Madison WI 53706-1414

MURRAY, KATHLEEN, municipal official; b. Phillipsburg, N.J., Nov. 1, 1960; d. Joseph A. and Joann P. (Sepple) M. BS, Rosemont Coll., 1983. Legis. asst. Office of Anna C. Verna, Phila., 1983-86, aide to fin. com., 1989-94, chief of staff, 1994—; head of circulation Haverford (Pa.) Coll., 1987-88; asst. dir. Outreach Coord. Ctr., Phila., 1988-89. Staff mem. select com. of fiscal stability, Phila., 1992-94; mem. pub. affairs com. Local Emergency Planning Commn., Phila., 1995-98; staff Mayor's Commn. of Phila. Naval Base, 1997; mem. Mayor's Commn. on Homelessness, Phila., 1993-96. Mem. Police Commrs. Gay and Lesbian Liaison Com., 1998—2001; bd. dirs. Southwest Task Force, Inc., Phila., 1983—86, Voyage House Inc., Phila., 1991—96, PrideFest Am., 1998—2001, Pride of Phila. Election Com., 1999—2001, Phila. Housing Devel. Corp., 2001—, Phila. Reinvestment Commn., 2001—, Eighteenth St. Devel. Corp., 2001—. Democrat. Episcopalian. Avocations: tennis, golf, reading, U.S. history. Office: Office of Pres 494 City Hall Philadelphia PA 19107-3201

MURRAY, MARY A. transportation executive; b. Savannah, Ga., June 17, 1950; d. James Buck and Dorothy Lee M.; m. Earnest Jackson Jr., Jan., 1978 (div. Jan. 1984); children: Chandra R. McKinney, Antony LaTroy Jackson, Earnesha J. Jackson. BS in Bus. Adminstrn., Savannah State U., 1968-71, 90-91. cert. key-punch, typing. Sales J.C. Pennys, Valdosta, Ga., 1973-75, Savannah, 1975-76; switchboard operator Savannah Fire Dept., 1976-80; a/c mechanic Gulfstream Aerospace, Savannah, 1982-94, engr. adminstr., 1994-95; exec. adminstr. Gulfstream Flight Test, Savannah, 1995—; resident mgr. Sihes Apt. Complex. Democrat. Avocations: bowling, photography. Office: Gulfstream Flight Test PO Box 2494 Savannah GA 31402-2494 Home: 105 S Robinhood Dr Savannah GA 31406-4135 E-mail: amurra11@bellsouth.net.

MURRAY, PATRICIA, electronics company executive; b. Detroit; BA, Michigan St. U.; BS, St. Louis U.; JD, U. Mich., 1986. Employment litigator Morrison & Foerster, Palo Alto, Calif., until 1990; atty. human resource's legal staff Intel Corp., 1990-91, mgr. human resoure's legal staff, 1992-95, dir., v.p. human resources, 1996—, sr. v.p., 1997—. Office: Intel Corp PO Box 58119 2200 Mission College Blvd Santa Clara CA 95052-8119 E-mail: patricia.murray@intel.com.

MURRAY, PATTY, senator; b. Bothell, Wash., Oct. 10, 1950; d. David L. and Beverly A. (McLaughlin) Johns; m. Robert R. Murray, June 2, 1972; children: Randy P., Sara A. BA, Wash. State U., 1972. Sec. various cos., Seattle, 1972-76; citizen lobbyist various ednl. groups, Seattle, 1983-88; legis. lobbyist Orgn. for Parent Edn., Seattle, 1977-84; instr. Shoreline Community Coll., Seattle, 1984-88; mem. Wash. State Senate, Seattle, 1989-92; U.S. senator from Wash., 1993—. Mem. Appropriations Com. ranking minority mem. subcom. mil. constrn.; vice chmn. Dem. Senatorial Campaign Com.; mem. Com. on Labor and Human Resources, Budget Com., Health, Edn., Labor and Pensions Com., Com. on Vets. Affairs. Mem. bd. Shoreline Sch., Seattle, 1985-89; mem. steering com. Demonstration for Edn., Seattle, 1987; founder, chmn. Orgn. for Parent Edn., Wash., 1981-85; lst Congl. rep. Wash. Women United, 1983-85. Recipient Recognition of Svc. to Children award Shoreline PTA Coun., 1986, Golden Acorn Svc. award, 1989; Outstanding Svc. award Wash. Women United, 1986, Outstanding Svc. to Pub. Edn. award Citizens Ednl. Ctr. NW, Seattle, 1987. Democrat. Office: US Senate 173 Russell Senate Office Bldg Washington DC 20510-0001*

MURRAY, SABINA, writer; BA, Mt. Holyoke Coll., Mass.; MA, U. of Tex. Writer-in-residence Phillips Acad., Andover, Mass., 2000—. Tchr. creative fiction and poetry. Author: (novels) Slow Burn, The Caprices, 2002 (PEN/Faulkner award for fiction, 2003). Address: Sabina Murray c/o Houghton Mifflin Co Trade Divsn Adult Editl 8th Fl 222 Berkeley St Boston MA 02116-3764 Office: Phillips Acad 180 Main St Andover MA 01810 E-mail: smurray@andover.edu.

MURRAY, THERESE, state legislator; one child. Student, El Camino Coll., Northeastern U., U. Mass., Midwest Acad., IL. Mitigation mgr. Mass. Hwy. Dept., 1984-91; mem. Mass. Senate, Boston, 1993—; chair. Joint Comm on Insurance, 2001—02; chair Ways and Means Com., 2003. Chmn. joint com. on human svcs. & elderly affairs Mass. State Senate, 1993-99, transp. com., 1993-2002; past market assoc. Coldwell Banker, Plymouth Port, Mass.; former cmty. rels. & coord. Am. Cablesys. Dir. Mcpl. Women's Project Inc., Boston; mem. Dem. State Com. Named among Ten Women Who Make Things Happen in Mass., Redbook Mag. Mem. Vis. Nurses Assn. (bd. dirs.), Women's Transp. Seminar, Plymouth County Dem. League, LWV. Democrat. Address: Rm 212 State House Boston MA 02133

MURRELL, DEBORAH ANNE, music educator, speaker, writer; b. Louisville, Ky., July 7, 1942; d. James Howard and Mayme Ruth (Manning) M. AB, Ea. Ky. U., 1964; MA, Western Ky. U., 1975; MACE, So. Bapt. Theol. Sem., Louisville, 1983; postgrad. in music, Ind. U. Band and choral dir. Hardin County Pub. Schs., Elizabethtown, Ky., 1964-66; dir. instrumental and vocal music Bullitt County Schs., Shepherdsville, Ky., 1966-74; band dir. Clark County Schs., Winchester, Ky., 1974-76; band and choral dir., head coach h.s. girls basketball Carroll County Schs., Carrollton, Ky., 1978-81; cons., speaker Nat. Single Adults, Louisville, 1981—; minister of single and sr. adults Temple Terr. First Bapt. Ch., Tampa, Fla., 1983-88; minister of adults First Bapt. Ch., Winston-Salem, N.C., 1988-91; minister of adults and evangelism Taylors (S.C.) First Bapt. Ch., 1991-93; music specialist Bullitt County Pub. Schs., Shepherdsville, Ky., 1993—2003; interim min. of music Bullitt Lick Bapt. Ch., Shepherdsville, Ky., 1999-2000; music specialist Pleasant Grove Elem. Sch., Mt. Washington, Ky., 2000—03, ret., 2003—; instrumental instr. Performing Arts Ctr., Mt. Washington, 2002—. Bd. dirs. Good News Clubs, Inc., Louisville, 1966-73; task force mem. single adults Bapt. Sunday Sch. Bd., Nashville, Tenn., 1991-93; Master's Men Orch., Inc., Louisville, 1993-99—; internat. spkr. to single adults, Eng. and Brazil, 1987-93, 2000; mentor Music Educators Nat. Conf., 2003—. Author: (with others) Single Adult Resource and Recipient, 1986, Single Adult Ministry, 1987; interviewee (video) Bapt. Sunday Sch. Bd., 1983-93; contbg. writer Christian Single Mag., 1980-93; prodr., dir.: PGE Sings the Music of America, 2002. Band hostess Ky. Derby Festival Commn., Louisville, 1980-83; internat. and nat. spkr. single adult ministries, 1981—; founder, organizer Bullitt County Music Festival, 1968—; mem. Louisville Bats Baseball Orgn., 2003-. Named Ky. Col. Commonwealth of Ky., Frankfort, 1978. Mem. NEA, Music Educators Nat. Conf., Ky. Edn. Assn., Ky. Music Educators Assn. (dist. officer 1964-81, 97-2001), Bullitt County Edn. Assn., Bullitt County Music Tchrs. Assn. (v.p. 1994-98, pres. 1998-99, sec. 2000-2001, v.p. 2002-2003), Religious Educators Assn., N.C. Religious Edn. Assn. (publicity, promotion com. 1990-91), Pilot Mt. Bapt. Assn. (mem. exec. com. N.C. 1989-91), Ea. Ky. U. Alumni Assn., Nat. Alumni Band (chmn. 1975-78), Tampa Bay Bapt. Assn. (con. 1983-88), Fern Creek High Sch. Alumni Assn., Phi Delta Kappa. Home and Office: 2805 Alice Ave Louisville KY 40220-1703 E-mail: dasailboat@msn.com.

MURRELL, SUSAN DEBRECHT, librarian; b. St. Louis, Aug. 10, 1951; d. Edward August and Edith (Keeney) DeB.; children: Brian, Katherine. BA in History, U. Ky., 1973; MLS, U. Mo., 1976. Children's libr. Louisville Free Pub. Libr., 1974-76, talking book libr. head, 1976-83; lower/mid. sch. libr. Ky. Country Day Sch., Louisville, 1983-84; children's libr. Emmet O'Neal Libr., Mountain Brook, Ala., 1984-86, asst. dir., 1986-89, dir., 1989—. Active Jefferson County Pub. Libr.; mem. allocations com. United Way, mem. admissions com.; bd. dirs. Mountain Brook Libr. Found., 1993—, Ala. Ctr. for Book. Mem. ALA, Ala. Libr. Assn. (mem. publicity com. 1992-93, pub. libr. chair 1995-96), Rotary Internat. Roman Catholic. Office: Emmet O'Neal Libr 50 Oak St Birmingham AL 35213-4295

MURTHA, PAMELA BERRY, secondary school educator; b. Oct. 24, 1941; d. Joseph Charles and Elenor (Kucharski) B.; 1 child, Katie Julia. BA, Western Mich. U., 1965; MA, U. Mich., 1975; Edn. Specialist, Wayne State U., 1985, postgrad. Lic. profl. tchr. Tchr. East Prairie Jr. H.S., Vicksburg, Mich., 1965-66, Allen Park (Mich.) H.S., 1966—, English dept. chair, 1969-81, tchr. English, 1993—. Rsch. asst. U. Mich., Ann Arbor, 1973-75, Wayne State U., Detroit, 1981-82, dir. politics in edn., 1981-82; spl. projects dir. Allen Park Pub. Schs., 1981-92; cons. Humanistic Mgmt. Sys., Columbus, Ohio, 1981-82; mem. Internat. Yr. of the Child, Wayne State U., Detroit, 1981-82; mem. std. setting com., (task force ensuring excellent educators, 2001) Mich. Dept. Edn., Lansing, 1998, content adv. com., 1998—, mem. task force State Bd. Edn., 2002; tech. liaison Allen Park Pub. Schs.; trainer Trainers County Mentoring Program. Pres. Young Dems., 1978-82; precinct dir. Dem. Party, del., 1985—. Nominee Phoebe Apperson award, Nat. PTA, 1985, Disney Tribute to Tchrs.; recipient Disting. Tchr. of Writing, Northwood U., 2001. Mem. Nat. Coun. Tchrs. English, Mich, (nominee Disney Tribute to tchr., Mich. Tchr. Yr.), Coun. Tchrs. English, Mich. Reading Assn., Phi Delta Kappa. Avocations: golf, reading, travel, theater, writing.

MUSACCHIO, LAURA R. planning and design educator; b. N.Y., Oct. 28, 1966; d. Bruce W. and Rose Marie E. Musacchio. Student, Le Moyne Coll., Syracuse, N.Y., 1984—86; B of Landscape Arch., 1989; M of Landscape Arch., SUNY, 1993; PhD in Urban and Regional Sci., Texas A&M U., College Station, 1999. Designer design and planning firms, Orange County, Calif., 1989—91; grad. asst. SUNY Coll. Environ. Sci. and Forestry, Syracuse, 1991—93; asst. prof. Utah State U., Logan, 1993—95; grad. asst. Tex. A&M U., College Station, 1995—96, asst. lectr., 1996—99; asst. prof. Ariz. State U., Tempe, 2000—03, U. Minn., Mpls., 2003—. Cons., intern Lower Colo. River Authority, Austin, 1996—98; coord. 16th ann. symposium program U.S. Regional Chapter, International Association of Landscape Ecology, Tempe, 1999—2001; rschr. Cen. Ariz. Phoenix Long-Term Ecol. Rsch. Project, 2000—. Contbr. articles to profl. jours. Mem. S.W. Riparian Mgmt. and Restoration Task Force, Phoenix, 2000—03. Named prin. investigator, Nat. Endowment of Arts, 2000, co-prin. investigator, S.W. Ctr. for Environ. Rsch. and Policy/EPA, 2000, 2001; recipient NASA/Mich. State U. Profl. Enhancement award, 1999. Mem.: Am. Soc. Landscape Archs. (mem.-at-large Utah chpt. 1994—95, Merit award 1989), Ecol. Soc. Am., Internat. Assn. Landscape Ecology (councillor-at-large U.S. Regional chpt. 2002—04), Sigma Lambda Alpha, Beta Beta Beta. Office: Dept Landscape Arch Univ Minn 89 Church St SE Minneapolis MN 55455 Business E-Mail: musacoo2@umn.edu.

MUSACCHIO, MARILYN JEAN, nurse midwife, educator; b. Louisville, Dec. 7, 1938; d. Robert William and Loretta C. (Liebert) Poulter; m. David Edward Musacchio, May 13, 1961; children: Richard Peter, Michelle Marie. BSN cum laude, Spalding Coll., 1968; MSN, U. Ky., 1972, cert. in nurse-midwifery, 1976; PhD, Case Western Res U., 1993. RN; cert. nurse-midwife; advanced registered nurse practitioner; registered nurse-midwife. Staff nurse gynecol. unit St. Joseph Infirmary, Louisville, 1959-60, staff nurse male gen. surgery unit, 1960; instr. St. Joseph Infirmary Sch. Nursing, Louisville, 1960-71; from asst. prof. to assoc. prof., dir. dept. nursing edn. Ky. State U., Frankfort, 1972-75; asst. prof. U. Ky. Coll. Nursing, Lexington, 1976-79, assoc. prof., coord., 1979-92, acting coordinator nurse-midwifery, 1982-84, coordinator for nurse-midwifery, 1987-92; assoc. prof., dir. nurse-midwifery U. Ala., Birmingham, 1992-96, assoc. prof., 1997-98; dean, prof. Tenn. Technol. U., Cookeville, 1998—. Cons. in field. Mem. editorial bd. Jour. Obstet., Gynecol. and Neonatal Nursing, 1976-82; author pamphlet; contbr. articles to profl. jours. Mem.Louisville Safety Coun., 1973-80. Brig. Gen. Army Nurse Corps, USAR, 1992-95. Recipient Disting. Citizen award City of Louisville, 1977, Jefferson Cup award Jefferson County, Ky., 1991; named Outstanding Alumna, Mercy

Acad., 1993; named to Hall of Disting. Alumni, U. Ky., 1995; recipient scholarships and fellowships, other awards. Fellow Am. Acad. Nursing; mem. AWHONN, NAFE, ANA, Nurse Assn. Am. Coll. Ob-Gyn. (charter; nat. sec. 1970-72, chmn. dist. V 1969), Am. Coll. Nurse-Midwives, Res. Officers Assn., Assn. Mil. Surgeons U.S., Sr. Army Res. Comdr. Assn., Assn. U.S. Army, Army Nurse Corps. Assn., Army War Coll. Alumni Assn. (life). Roman Catholic. Avocations: reading, candy making, cake decorating, cooking, sewing. Home: PO Box 5001 Cookeville TN 38505-0001 Fax: 931-372-6244. Office Phone: 931-372-3213. E-mail: mmusacchio@tntech.edu.

MUSANTE, PATRICIA W. library director; b. Pitts., June 15, 1944; d. Edward Anthony and Katherine (Webber) Wagner; m. Guido J. Musante, Ap4. BA, Carlow Coll., Pitts., 1967; MA, Carnegie Mellon U., 1970; MLS, U. Pitts., 1991. Tchr. Canevin H.S., Pitts., 1967-69; flight attendant Capitol Internat. Airways, Nashville, 1971-79; adj. prof. Carlow Coll., 1990-91; pub./editor Ft. Covington (N.Y.) Sun, 1982-89; asst. dir. Potsdam (N.Y.) Pub. Libr., 1991-99, dir., 1999—. Bd. dirs. North Country Dist. PTA, Potsdam, 1996—; founding trustee Ft. Covington Reading Ctr., 1984-89. Recipient Jos. Schubert Moving Toward Excellence award N.Y. State Libr., Albany, 1997, North Country Reference and Rsch. Resources award for excellence in libr. svcs., 2001. Mem. AAUW (chair book discussion group 1993—), Beta Phi Mu. Home: 871 River Rd Norwood NY 13668-3155

MUSGRAVE, MARILYN N. congresswoman; b. Greeley, Colo., Jan. 27, 1949; m. Steven Musgrave. BA, Colo. State U. Co-owner Musgrave Bale Stacking; mem. Colo. Ho. of Reps., 1994-98, Colo. Senate, Dist. 1, Denver, 1998—2002; chmn. transp. com.; mem. health, environment, welfare and instns. com.; mem. state, vets. and mil. affairs com.; mem. U.S. Ho. Reps. from 4th Colo. dist., 2003—. Past pres. Morgan County Rep. Women; former bd. mem. RE-3 Sch. Dist. Republican. Office: 1208 Longworth HOB Washington DC 20515-0604

MUSGRAVE, THEA, composer, conductor; b. Edinburgh, Scotland, May 27, 1928; m. Peter Mark, 1971. student, Mus D, Paris Conservatory. Composer: (opera) The Abbot of Drimock, 1955, The Decision, 1964-65, The Voice of Ariadne, 1972-73, Mary, Queen of Scots, 1975-77, (first performed Scottish Opera) A Christmas Carol, 1978-79 (first performed Va. Opera Assn., 1979), An Occurrence at Owl Creek Bridge, 1981, Harriet, The Woman Called Moses, 1981-84 (first performed Va. Opera 1985), Simon Bolivar, Pontalba, New Orleans Opera, 2001-03, (ballet) Beauty and the Beast, 1969, (symphony and orchestral music) Obliques, 1958, Nocturnes and Arias, 1966, Concerto for Orch., 1967, Clarinet Concerto, 1968, Night Music, 1969, Scottish Dance Suite, 1969, Memento Vitae, 1969-70, Orfeo II, 1975, Soliloquy II and III, 1980, From One to Another, 1980, Peripeteia, 1981, The Seasons, 1988, (marimba concerto) Journey through a Japanese Landscape, (bass-clarinet concerto) Autumn Sonata, (oboe concerto) Helios, Phoenix Rising, 1997, (orchestral work) Turbulent Landscapes, (chamber and instrumental music) String Quartet, 1958, Trio for flute, oboe and piano, 1960, Monologue, 1960, Serenade, 1961, Chamber concerto No. 1, 1962, Chamber Concerto No. 2, 1966, Chamber Concerto No. 3, 1966, Music for horn and piano, 1967, Impromptu No. 1, 1967, Soliloquy I, 1969, Elegy, 1970, Impromptu No. 2, 1970, Space Play, 1974, Orfeo I, 1975, Fanfare, 1982, Pierrot, 1985, Narcissus, 1987, Niobe, 1987, (vocal and choral music) Two Songs, 1951, Four Madrigals, 1953, Six Songs: Two Early English Poems, 1953, A Suite O'Bairnsangs, 1953, Cantata for a Summer's Day, 1954, Song of the Burn, 1954, Five Love Songs, 1955, Four Portraits, 1956, A Song for Christmas, 1958, Triptych, 1959, Sir Patrick Spens, 1961, Make Ye Merry for Him That Is to Come, 1962, Two Christmas Carols in Traditional Style, 1963, John Cook, 1963, Five Ages of Man, 1963-64, Memento Creatoris, 1967, Primavera, 1971, Rorate Coeli, 1973, Monologues of Mary, Queen of Scots, 1977-86, O Caro M'e Il Sonno, 1978, The Last Twilight, 1980, Black Tambourine, 1985, For the Time Being, 1986, Echoes Through Time, 1988, Wild Winter for Viols & Voices, 1993, On the Underground Sets 1, 2 & 3, 1994, 95, (Robert Burns' poems for soprano & orch.) Songs for a Winter's Evening, 1995, (for orch.) Phoenix Rising, 1996-97, (for 3 flutes and percussion) Voices from the Ancient World, 1998, (for chorus and orch.) Celebration Day, 1998-99, (for 8 instruments) Lamenting With Ariadne, 1999, (for orch.) Turbulent Landscapes, Boston Symphony, 2004. Office: VA Opera Assn PO Box 2580 Norfolk VA 23501-2580

MUSHINSKY, MARY M. state legislator; b. New Haven; m. Martin J. Waters; children: Martin Waters, Edward Waters. BA, So. Conn. State U., 1973; postgrad., Fla. Atlantic U.; MA, Wesleyan U., Middletown, Conn., 1993. Mem. Conn. Ho. of Reps., Hartford, 1981—, mem. environ., fin., revenue and bonding com., chmn., select com. on children. Democrat. Home: 188 S Cherry St Wallingford CT 06492-4016 Office: Conn House of Reps Capitol Ave Hartford CT 06106

MUSICK, MARILYN IRENE, secondary school educator; b. Springfield, Ill., Mar. 20, 1950; d. Kenneth Ray and Ida May Sampson; m. David Neil Musick, Aug. 19, 1972; children: John David, Allison Renee. B in Music Edn., Ill. Wesleyan U., 1972. Vocal music tchr. grades 5-12 El Paso (Ill.) C.U.D. # 375, 1972—. Music advisor Ill. Elem. Sch. Assn., Bloomington, 2000—03; music cons. Immanuel Bible Found., Bloomington, 1996—2001. Choir dir. Evang. Free Ch., Bloomington, 1984—. Recipient Those Who Excel award of recognition, Ill. State Bd. of Edn., Springfield, 1993. Mem.: Am. Choral Dirs. Assn., Music Educators Nat. Conf. Avocation: rose gardening. Home: 217 Reitan Rd Normal IL 61761 Office: El Paso CUD # 375 600 N Elm St El Paso IL 61738 E-mail: marilynim@yahoo.com.

MUSICK, PAT, artist; b. L.A., Sept. 14, 1926; d. Mark Melvin and Emma Lucille (Ferguson) Tapscott; m. John Elmore Musick, Aug. 18, 1946 (dec. Nov. 1977); children: Cathleen M. Goebel, Melinda M. King, Laura M. Wright; m. Gerald Paul Carr, Sept. 14, 1979. MA, Cornell U., 1972, PhD, 1974. Rsch. asst. Cornell U., Ithaca, N.Y., 1971-73; prof. SUNY, Oswego, 1974-76, U. Houston, 1976-85; postdoct. fellow Med. Sch. U. Tex., Galveston, 1978. Adj. prof. Syracuse (N.Y.) U., 1974-76, U. Ark., Fayetteville, 1986—; mem. bd, dirs. Alumni Cornell U., 1996-97; mem. com. site integrated art planning, art selection com. Walton Arts Ctr., Fayetteville, Ark., 1988-90; pres. CAMUS, Inc., Huntsville, Ark., 1995—. One-woman exhibns. Huntsville (Ala.) Mus. Art, 1992, Springfield (Mo.) Mus. Art, 1992, Ark. Arts Ctr., Little Rock, 1992, Walton Arts Ctr., Fayetteville, Ark., 1992, 95, Amarillo (Tex.) Mus. Art, 1995, Trail of Tears Traveling Exhibit to six Arkansas venues, 2002-2004,Charles B. Goddard Ctr., Ardmore, Okla., 1997, U. Ark., Little Rock, 1997, Albrecht Kemper Mus., 1998, tour of 7 Tex. museums, 1998—; group exhibns. include Senator David Pryor's Offices, Washington, 1991-93, Ark. Art Ctr., Little Rock, 1994, Walton Arts Ctr., 1994; permanent collections Jewish Theol. U., Ark. Aerospace Edn. ctr., Ark. Arts Ctr., Dartmouth Coll., Huntsville (Ala.) Mus. Art, Internat. Ctr. Transp. Studies, Promus Hotels, U. Houston, Springfield (Mo.) Art Mus., U. Ozarks, Walton Arts Ctr., U. Ark., Morrilton, Washington Regional Hosp., Fayetteville, Ark., Cornell U. Fine Arts scholar U. So. Calif., 1944; fellow in sculpture, Ark. Arts Coun. Touring grantee Ark. Arts Coun., NEA, 1987-88, Assistance grantee Ark. Arts Coun., 1997; Connemara Found. fellow, 1998; recipient Gold Medal Pizzo Calabro (Italy) Internat. Invitational, 1983, Gold Medal Southeastern Mus. Conf., 1993, Richard A. Florsheim Art Fund award, 1997; winner 9th Ann. Outdoor Sculpture Competition, Miami U., Ohio, 1998, Tour of Six Tex. Mus., 1998-99, Irving (Tex.) Art Ctr., 2000, Ozarks Woodland Sculpture Garden, 2000, Monarch Sculpture Garden, 2001, Buffalo Bayou Artpark, Houston, 2002, Ark. ARt Ctr., 2003. Avocations: cooking, swimming, reading, writing poetry. Home: 1655 Madison 1200 Huntsville AR 72740 Office: CAMUS Inc PO Box 919 Huntsville AR 72740-0919 Office Phone: 479-559-2966.

MUSILLI MESSANO, ESTER ANNA, music educator; b. Paterson, N.J, Nov. 25, 1969; d. Pompeo and AnnaMaria Messano; m. Paul Musilli, Oct. 18, 1998; 1 child, Julia Anna Musilli. MusB, William Paterson Coll., 1992; MA n Tchg., Marygrove Coll., 2002. Dir. mid. sch. band Parsippany-Troy Hills Bd. Edn., NJ, 1992—. Instr. colorguard Mt. Olive H.S., NJ, 1996—99, Basking Ridge H.S., 1993—95; dir. Crossmen Drum and Bugle Corps, Newark, 1993—94, instr. brass, Pa., 1992—93; dir. drama and musical Ctrl. Mid. Sch., Parsippany, NJ, 1995—, yearbook advisor, 1993—2000. Mem.: NEA, N.J. Music Assn., Music Educators Nat. Conf. (pres. student chpt. 1990—91). Personal E-mail: vienna20000@aol.com.

MUSKOPF, BETH A. curriculum consultant; b. Hicksville, Ohio, July 25, 1943; d. Claron Lavon Laub and Florence Elizabeth Laub; m. David Earl Muskopf, June 26, 1965; children: Richard, Stephen. BS in Edn., Miami U., Oxford, Ohio, 1965, MEd, 1973, PhD, 1998. Tchr. Mason (Ohio) Local Schs., 1967-68, Mason Local/City Schs., 1982-95; asst. prof. Cin. Bible Coll., 1996-98; supr. curriculum Clermont County Edn. Svc. Ctr., Batavia, Ohio, 1999—. Recipient Excellence in Tchg. award Warren County (Ohio) Area Progress Coun., 1990; Morrison scholar Dept. Edn. Leadership, Miami U., Oxford, 1997. Mem. ASCD, Internat. Reading Assn., Nat. Coun. Tchrs. English, Ohio Coun. Internat. Reading Assn., Phi Delta Kappa (rsch. chair 1999-2001, treas. 2001—). Avocations: reading, hiking, traveling. Home: 8060 Crest Acres Dr Mason OH 45040-9656 Office: Clermont County Ednl Svc Ctr 2400 Clermont Center Dr Batavia OH 45103-1957

MUSKOPF, MARGARET ROSE, elementary school educator; b. Saint Louis, July 18, 1942; d. George Oliver and Providence Pearl Knittel; m. Donald R. Muskopf, Mar. 29, 1969. AA, Chaffey Jr. Coll., Alta Loma, Calif., 1962; BA, San Diego State U., 1964; Qigong cert., Xiyuan Hosp., Beijing, China, 1999; Reiki master, 1991; cert., Holos Inst., 1998. Cert. elem. tchr., remedial reading K-12. Elem. tchr. LaMesa-Spring Valley Sch., 1964-70; jr. h.s. tchr. state operated schs., Adak, Alaska, 1970-73; remedial reading tchr. Ritnour Dist., Overland, Mo., 1973-77; dir. Sch. Metaphysics, 1978-79; Tai Chi tchr. Rockhaven, House Springs, Mo., 1988—2000; energy tchr. Sisters of St. Benedict Kordes, Ferdinand, Ind., 1998-99. Co-owner Passport to Wellness, Webster Groves, Mo., 2001—. Foster parent Bur. Indian Affairs, Alaska, 1970-73; hospice vol. St. Anthony's Hosp., St. Louis, 1989-92; vol. tchr. Maria Ctr. Sch. Sisters Notre Dame, St. Louis, 1987-91; vol. Mercy Ctr., Sisters of Mercy, St. Louis. Mem. Greenpeace, Amnesty Internat., Children Internat., Women's Connection Network. Avocations: tai chi, qigong, volunteering, reading.

MUSSER, GLORIA J. retired composer; b. Endicott, NY; d. Anna Hvizdos, Andrew Hvizdos; m. Willard I. Musser. BS, SUNY, Potsdam, 1967. Dir. instrumental music St. Regis Falls (N.Y.) Ctrl. Sch., 1967—71; ednl. cons. Greentown, Pa., 1971—99; adj. instr. Marywood U., Scranton, Pa., 1999—. Composer: (instrumental music) International Method for Band, 2001, numerous instrumental music publs. Bd. dir. Lake Wallenpompack Watershed Mgmt. Dist. Recipient cert., Nat. Found. for Advancement in the Arts. Mem.: Assn. Concert Bands, NY State Sch. Music Assn., Music Educators Nat. Conf. (life). Avocations: swimming, travel, carpentry. Home: 10569 Quebec Head Ln Clayton NY 13624 Personal E-mail: gmusser@northnet.org.

MUSTAKOVA-POSSARDT, ELENA M. social sciences educator, counselor; b. Sofia, Bulgaria, Mar. 8, 1960; d. Michail Mustakov and Roza Mustakova; m. Earl E. Possardt, June 25, 1994; children: Alipi Naydenov, Rose Elizabeth, Jacqueline Marie Possardt. EdD, U. of Mass., 1990—96. Lic. counselor Ga., 2000. Instr. Fgn. Lang. Ctr., Sofia, Bulgaria, 1985—89; lectr. Hillside Tchr. Tng. Coll., Bulawayo, Zimbabwe, 1989—90; asst. prof. Psychology Dept., State U. of West Ga., 1997—; assoc. prof. Landegg Internat. U., Wienacht, Switzerland, 2002—. Founder Latinos United of Carroll County, Carrolton, Ga., 2000—. Founder Latinos United of Carroll County, Ga., 2000. Mott grant, Nat. Coun. of La Raza, 1991. Mem.: APA. Democrat-Npl. Baha'I. Achievements include research in ontogenesis of critical consciousness. Avocation: travel. Office: State University of West Georgia 1600 Maple St Carrollton GA 30118 Personal E-mail: emustakova@earthlink.net. E-mail: elenam@westga.edu.

MUSTARD, CINDY SINGLETON, social worker, administrator; b. St. Louis, Oct. 29, 1943; d. George Conley and Elizabeth Ann (Nye) Miller; m. Marvin Eugene Mustard, Aug. 9, 1969; 1 child, Katherine Conley. Ba, U. Mo., 1965. Caseworker II Jackson Co. Divsn. Divsn. Family Svcs., Kansas City, Mo., 1965-68; program & tng. dir. Camp Fire Inc., Kansas City, 1969-88; field rep. Am. Cancer Soc., Columbia, Mo., 1988-91; exec. dir. Voluntary Action Ctr., Columbia, 1991—. Bd. dirs. Rusk Rehab. Ctr., Columbia, 1993—. Fin. advisor Kappa Kappa Gamma, 1988—, mem. census com.; elder, mission com. mem. 1st Presbyn. Ch., Columbia, 1989-93; sec. bd. dirs. Mo. Vols., 1994—; chair United Way Exec. Dirs. Coun., 1993; co-chair City Bd. Election Proposition I, Columbia, 1994; chair Commn. Cultural Affairs, Columbia, 1994-95, commn. mem., 1994—; bd. dirs. Boys and Girls Club, 1996—. Mem. Boone County Related Agys. (v.p. 1993-94), Caring Cmtys. Partnership, Interfaith Coun., Downtown Rotary (bd. dirs. 1992-97), Columbia C. of C. (bd. dirs. 1991-94). Democrat. Avocations: reading, volunteer work, cooking, travel. Home: 600 S Greenwood Ave Columbia MO 65203-2769 Office: Voluntary Action Ctr 800 N Providence Rd Columbia MO 65203-4300

MUSTARD, MARY CAROLYN, financial executive; b. North Bend, Nebr., Sept. 21, 1948; d. Joseph Louis and Rosalie Margaret (Emanuel) Smaus; m. Ronald L. Mustard, Apr. 19, 1969 (div. 1988); children: Joel Jonathan, Dana Marie. Student, Creighton U., 1966-67, C.E. Sch. Commerce, 1967-68, Coll. of St. Mary, 1983-84, Met. C.C., Omaha, 1988-90, Bellevue U., 1991-92. With Platte County Dept. Pub. Welfare, Columbus, Nebr., 1968-69; sec. to plant mgr. B.L. Montague Steel Co., Sumter, S.C., 1969-70; property disposal technician Property Disposal Office, Shaw AFB, S.C., 1970-71; libr. technician Hdqs. Strategic Air Command Libr., Offutt AFB, Nebr., 1971-76; sec.-steno Hdqs. Strategic Air Command Comm./Frequency Mgmt., Offutt AFB, 1976-79; security specialist/program analyst Hdqs. Strategic Air Command Security Police, Offutt AFB, 1979-88; budget analyst Hdqs. Strategic Air Command Fin. Mgmt., Offutt AFB, 1988-92; funds control analyst Hdqs. Air Mobility Command, Scott AFB, Ill., 1992-93, chief hdqs. and comm. account, 1993-94, chief hdqs. relocation, transition assistance/comm. programs, 1994-95; chief base realignment and closure program Air Mobility Command, Scott AFB, 1995-96; sys. adminstr. Def. Fin. and Acctg. Svc., Kansas City, Mo., 1996-2000, fin. sys. mgmt., 2000—02, fin. ops. analyst, bus. mgmt. office, 2002—. Mem. Am. Soc. Mil. Comptrollers (SAC Budget Analyst of Yr. 1990). Democrat. Roman Catholic. Avocations: walking, reading, biking. Office: DFAS-KC/ADB 1500 E Bannister Rd Kansas City MO 64197-0001 E-mail: mmustard1@msn.com.

MUSTOKOFF, HENRIETTA M. music educator; b. Phila., Feb. 28, 1946; d. Simon and Goldye (Love) Mustokoff. MusB in Bassoon, U. of the Arts, Phila., 1968. Cert. tchr. Pa., N.J. Elem. music tchr. Atlantic City Bd. Edn., 1968—69; elem. vocal and instrumental music tchr. Willingboro Bd. Edn., NJ, 1969—2001; pvt. music tchr. Burlington, NJ, 1965—. Workshop leader New Sch. Am. Music, Paradise, Calif., 2001—; mem. Wind Symphony So. N.J., Golden Eagle Band, Pastorial Woodwind Quintet, Warminster Symphony Orch. Mem.: Double Reed Soc., Phila. Musicians Union, Music Educators Nat. Conf. Home and Office: 1139 Kaye Ct Burlington NJ 08016

MUSTOVIC, FAITHANN MARIAN (FAITHANN GRIGALUNAS), pharmacist; b. Pottsville, Pa., Apr. 29, 1964; d. Anthony Frederick and Nancy (Wortyla) Grigalunas. BA in Biology, Susquehanna U., 1986; BS in Pharmacy, Temple U., 1989. Registered pharmacist, Pa. Staff pharmacist Rite Aid Corp., Inc., various cities, Pa., 1989-95, pharmacy mgr. Lansford, White Haven, Pa., 1991-93; staff pharmacist Morris Drugs, Mahanoy City, Pa., 1995-96, Miners Meml. Med. Ctr., Coaldale, Pa., 1995-96, RXD Pharmacies, Inc., Minersville, Pottsville, Shenandoah, Pa., 1996—, The Milton S. Hershey Med. Ctr., Hershey, Pa., 1996-97. Profl. mem. Am. Diabetes Assn., 1996—. Vol. Am. Cancer Soc., 1996—, Children's Miracle Network Pa. State U. Children's Hosp., Hershey, 1997; mem. Asthma and Allergy Found. Am., 1996-97. Named to 200 list of pharmacists selected for Diabetes Cert. program, Miami, Fla., 1996. Mem. Am. Pharm. Assn. (selected for young leadership conf. 1997), Pa. Pharmacists Assn. (del. 1995-98, vice spkr. house of dels. 1998—, profl. practice com. 1997—, com. edn. 1997—, Disting. Young Pharmacist award 1997), Schuykill Pharm. Assn. (2d v.p., 1994, 95, 97, pres. 1996), Capital Area Pharm Assn. (mem.-at-large exec. com. 1997), Am. Soc. Health System Pharmacists, Am. Soc. Parenteral and Enteral Nutrition. Avocations: reading, sewing, skiing, tennis, cooking. Home: 140 N Washington St Evans City PA 16033-1076 Office: Evans City Pharmacy & Gift Shoppe Med Arts Bldg 201 E Main St Evans City PA 16033-1219 also: The Medicine Shoppe 220 W Main St Grove City PA 16127-1224

MUSZYNSKA, AGNIESZKA (AGNES MUSZYNSKA), mechanical engineering researcher, consultant; b. Warsaw, Oct. 10, 1935; came to U.S., 1980; d. Zdzislaw E. and Wida-Wanda (Jellinek) Galinowski; m. Jerzy Muszynski, Dec. 2, 1954 (div. July 1974); 1 child, Roman. MSME, Warsaw Tech. U., Poland, 1960; PhD in Tech. Scis., Polish Acad. Scis., Warsaw, 1966, habilitation, 1977; prof. tech. scis., Poland, 1998. Designer Machine Tool Design Co., Warsaw, 1960-61; asst. prof. Inst. Fundamental Tech. Rsch., Polish Acad. Scis., Warsaw, 1961-78, assoc. prof., 1978-82; sr. rsch. scientist Bently Nev. Corp., Minden, Nev., 1981-82; rsch. mgr. Bently Rotor Dynamics Rsch. Corp., Minden, 1982-99; cons. A.M. Cons., Minden, 1999—. Vis. prof. Inst. Nat. Scis., Lyon, France, Swiss Fed. Inst. Tech., Zurich, 2000—01, U. Franche Comte, Besancon, France, 2001; vis. rsch. scientist U. Dayton, Ohio, 1980—81; fac. mem. U. Nev., Reno, 1984—89. Editor 5 books; sci. editor: Dynamics of Machines (in Polish), 1974, Dynamics of Machines: Vibration Control in Machines (in Polish and English), 1978, (with D. E. Bently, R.C. Hendricks) Instability of Rotating Machinery, 1985, (with J.C. Simonis) Rotating Machinery Dynamics, 1987, Don Bently Through the Eyes of Others, 1995, Procs. of 7th Internat. Symposium on Transport Phenomena and Dynamics of Rotating Machinery, 1998, other procs.; regional editor Internat. Jour. Rotating Machines, 1994—; contbr. articles to profl. jours. Recipient Gold Cross of Merit Polish Acad. Scis., 1975, Innovation award NASA, 1990, Outstanding Rsch. award Pacific Ctr. Thermal Fluids Engring., 1996; titled Prof. of Tech. Scis., Pres. of Poland, 1998. Fellow ASME (assoc. editor Transactions of the ASME 1988-94); mem. NAFE, Am. Acad. Scis. Achievements include contributions to the new discipline of mechanical engineering; vibrational diagnostics of rotating machines. Office Phone: 775-782-7229. Business E-Mail: agnes@gbis.com.

MUSZYNSKI, STACY, editor, writer; d. Robert and Elaine Muszynski, Barbara Muszynski (Stepmother). BA magna cum laude, Wayne State U., 1990—94, post grad, 2001—03. Ednl. aid, english dept. Wayne State U. Writing Ctr., Detroit, 1993—95; editl. asst. Wayne State U. Press, Detroit, 1994—96; interim editor, staff writer, copy editor Corp. Detroit Mag., 1995—97; freelance writer, editor, cons. St. Clair Shores, 1997—; print and online editor Visteon Automotive Systems, Dearborn, Mich., 1999; interim editor, writer, copywriter J. Walter Thompson, Detroit, 2000—01; website editor and asst. pr dir. Wayne State U., WDET 101.9 FM, Detroit, 2001—; freelance editor, writer, cons. St. Clair Shores, Mich., 1997—. Coord. Writing/Life, St. Clair Shores, Mich., 2003—; cons., writer and editor, spec issue of kick! youth soccer publ., Campbell Ewald Comm., Warren, Mich., 1998; creative lead and writer, ad Gt. Lakes Women's Soccer League, Livonia, Mich., 1998—98; staff mentor Living, Learning Communities, Wayne State U., Detroit, 2003—. Author: (short stories) Breathe (Thompkins award for Fiction, Grad., 2003), (poetry) A Poem on Rent; editor (writer, reporter): (newsletter) Inside Sheldon Road Plant. Co-founder APLAUDD (Art for Pub. Life and Urban Devel. in Detroit), Detroit, 2003—03. Recipient All-American Scholar award, US' Achievement Acad., 1994; Merit scholarship, Wayne State U., 1990—94. Mem.: Golden Key Honor Society, Phi Beta Kappa. Achievements include research in Research-in-progress for a work of translation, Italian to English. Office: WDET 1019FM Detroit Public Radio 4600 Cass Avenue Detroit MI 48201 E-mail: smuszynski@wdetfm.org.

MUTO, SUSAN ANNETTE, religion educator, academic administrator; b. Pitts., Dec. 11, 1942; d. Frank and Helen (Scardamalia) M. BA in Journalism and English, Duquesne U., 1964; MA, U. Pitts., 1967, PhD in English Lit., 1970. Asst. dir. Inst. of Formative Spirituality Duquesne U., Pitts., 1965—80, dir., 1980—88, faculty coord. grad. programs in foundational formation, 1979—88, prof., 1981—. Guest lectr. formative reading various colls. and cmty. orgns., 1970—. Author: Catholic Spirituality from A to Z: An Inspirational Dictionary, 2000, Deep Into the Thicket: Soul Searching Meditations Inspirited by the Spiritual Canticle of Saint John of the Cross, Praying the Lord's Prayer with Mary. Mem.: Ephinany Acad. of Formative Spirituality (dean), Epiphany Assn. (exec. dir. 1998—), Soc. for Sci. Study of Religion, Phi Kappa Phi. Home: 820 Crane Ave Pittsburgh PA 15216-3050 E-mail: samuto@epiphanyassociation.org.

MUZYKA-MCGUIRE, AMY, marketing professional, nutrition consultant; b. Chgo., Sept. 24, 1953; d. Basil Bohdan and Amelia (Rand) Muzyka; m. Patrick J. McGuire, June 3, 1977; children: Jonathan, Elizabeth. BS, Iowa State U., 1975, postgrad., 1978—; registered dietitian, St. Louis U., 1980. Cert. dietitian. Home economist Nat. Livestock and Meat Bd., Chgo., 1975-77; dietary cons. various hosps. and nursing homes, Iowa, 1978-79; supr. foodsvc. Am. Egg Bd., Park Ridge, Ill., 1980-83; assoc. dir., mgr. foodsvc. Cole & Weber Advt., Seattle, 1984-85; prin., owner Food and Nutrition Comms., Federal Way, Wash., 1986—. Co-author: Turkey Foodservice Manual, 1987; editor: (newsletter) Home Economists in Business, 1975-77, Dietitians in Business and Industry, 1982-85; Food Net on Internet, 1995, Food and Culinary Profls. Newsletter, 1999-2001; contbr. articles to profl. jours. Named Outstanding Dietitian of Yr. North Suburban Dietetic Assn., 1983, Tastemaker of the Month, 2001, 02, 03. Mem. Am. Dietetic Assn., Internat. Foodsvc. Editl. Coun., Cons. Nutritionists, Internat. Assn. Culinary Profls. Avocations: gardening, travel, music, food and beverage tastings. Home: 5340 SW 315th St Federal Way WA 98023-2034

MYATT, SUE HENSHAW, nursing home administrator; b. Little Rock, Aug. 16, 1956; d. Bobby Eugene and Janett Lanell (Ahart) Henshaw; m. Tommy Wayne Myatt; children: James Andrew, Thomas Ryan. BS in Psychology, Old Dominion U., 1978, MS in Ednl. Counseling, 1982. Cert. activity cons. Nat. Cert. Coun. of Activity Profls., gerontol. activity therapy cons., Va. Dir. activity Manning Convalescent, Portsmouth, Va., 1983—84, Camelot Hall, Norfolk, Va., 1984—86; coord. activities Beverly Manor, Portsmouth, 1986—87, Georgian Manor Assisted Living Facility, 1989—90; dir. activities Huntington Convalescent Ctr., Newsport News, Va., 1990—91; nursing home adminstr.-in-tng. Bayview Healthcare Ctr., Newport News, 1991—92; adminstr. Evangeline of Gates, Gatesville, NC, 1992—95, Mary Washington Health Ctr., Colonial Beach, Va., 1993—95, Brian Ctr. Health & Rehab., Lawrenceville, Va., 1995—97; social worker, admissions/mktg. dir. Thornton Hall Nursing Home, 1997—98; adminstr. Arcadia Nursing and Rehab. Ctr., 2000—. Instr. Tidewater Community Coll., 1990. Mem. Nat. Assn. Activity Profl. (cert. legis. com.), Va. Assn. Activity Profl. (v.p. 1986-87, creator logo), Hampton Roads Activity Profls. Assn. (sec. 1985-86, pres. 1986-87, v.p. 1987-88). Avocations: crafts, aerobics. Home: 100 North Tree Williamsburg VA 23188-1667

MYERBERG, MARCIA, investment banker; b. Boston, Mar. 25, 1945; d. George and Evelyn (Lewis) Katz; m. Jonathan Gene Myerberg, June 4, 1967 (div. Mar. 1994); 1 child, Gillian Michelle. BS, U. Wis., 1966. Corp. trust adminstr. Chase Manhattan Bank, N.Y.C., 1966-67; asst. cashier Glore Forgan, Wm. R. Staats, Phoenix, 1967-68; bond portfolio analyst Trust Co. of Ga., Atlanta, 1969-72; asst. v.p. 1st Union Nat. Bank, Charlotte, N.C., 1973-78; dir. cash mgmt. Carolina Power & Light Co., Raleigh, N.C., 1978-79; sr. v.p., treas. Fed Home Loan Mortgage Corp., Washington, 1979-85; dir. Salomon Bros. Inc., N.Y.C., 1985-89; sr. mng. dir. Bear, Stearns & Co. Inc., N.Y.C., 1989-93; mng. dir. Bear, Stearns Home Loans, London, 1989-93; chief exec. Myerberg & Co., L.P., N.Y.C., 1994—. Home: 37 W 12th St Apt 6K New York NY 10011-3205 Office: 780 3rd Ave New York NY 10017-2024

MYERS, ADELE ANNA, artist, educator, nun; b. Bklyn., Oct. 4, 1925; d. Everett Ecil and Anna Maria (Menig) M. Student, U. Notre Dame; BS in Edn., Fordham U., 1956; MA in Fine Arts, Villa Schifanoia, Florence, Italy, 1962; postgrad., NYU, Pratt Graphics Ctr., Columbia U. Cert. permanent tchr. art, grades K-12, N.Y.; joined Sparkill Dominican Sisters, Roman Cath. Ch., 1944. Tchr. art Monsignor Scanlon H.S., Bronx, N.Y., 1956-60, Albertus Magnus H.S., Bardonia, N.Y., 1961-62; founder, dir. Thorpe Intermedia Gallery, Sparkill, N.Y., 1976-91; prof., chairperson art dept. St. Thomas Aquinas Coll., Sparkill, 1962-78, adj. prof., 1978-99. Design cons. sr. housing devels. Thorpe Village and Dowling Gardens, Sparkill, N.Y., 1981—; mem. adv. bd. Bogliasco Found., N.Y.C. and Italy, 1997—; freelance curator contemporary art exhbns., 1986—. Commd. works include cross in fresco and cement St. Peter's Ch., Yonkers, N.Y., 1990, outdoor sidewalk mosaic Thorpe Village, 1997, stained glass windows for meditation rm. Dowling Gardens, 1996, outdoor mosaic, meditation garden Dominican Sisters, Sparkill, 2001, stained glass windows Our Lady of Rosary Chapel, Dominican Convent, 2001, Way of the Cross in fresco and cement, Chapel at St. Thomas Aquinas Coll., Sparkill, N.Y., 2002; exhibited sculpture in fresco and cement, most recently at ArtBldrs. Gallery, Jersey City, 1994-95, Rockland Ctr. for Arts, 1995, 96, 99, St. John's Chapel Gallery, Newark, 1996, Piermont Flywheel Gallery, N.Y., 2002, Azarian-McCullough Gallery, Sparkill, N.Y., 2001, Visions Gallery, Albany, N.Y., 2001; one-woman shows include Hopper Ho. Art Ctr., Nyack, 1992, Piermont Flywheel Gallery, 1996, 98, 2000, 01, 02, ArtBuilders Gallery, 1996, 2003, Old Ch. Cultural Ctr. Gallery, Demarest, N.J., 1997; represented in pub. and pvt. collections; works and exhibits reviewed in various publs., including N.Y. Times, Star Ledger, Suburban People, Arts Happenings; featured on cable TV program, N.J., 1988. Apptd. art in pub. places com. Rockland County, 1987-92; founding bd. dirs. Arts Fund Rockland, 1989-91. Villa Schifanoia scholar, 1960; Sister Adele Myers Scholarship established in her name St. Thomas Aquinas Coll., 1986; recipient award for Outstanding Contbn. in Field of Art, Rockland County Women's Network, Rockland C.C., Suffern, N.Y., 1980, 1st Ann. Arts award Rockland County Execs., 1987. Mem. Nat. Mus. Women in Arts, Internat. Sculpture Ctr., Christians in Visual Arts. Democrat. Avocations: reading, travel, visiting places of historical interest. Home: Dominican Convent 175 Route 340 Sparkill NY 10976-1041

MYERS, BARBARA ANN, lawyer; b. Pitts., Mar. 27, 1960; d. Donald Joseph and Elizabeth Ann Myers; m. Ronald Farson Karp, Dec. 28, 1998; 1 child, Allison Lauren Karp. Honors BA in History summa cum laude with highest distinction, Pa. State U., 1982; JD, U. Calif., San Francisco, 1991. Bar: (Calif.) 1992. Spl. projects coord. mktg. Provident Ctrl. Credit Union, Burlingame, Calif., 1982—83; editor and ops. adminstr. Banana Republic Hdqs. The Gap, Inc., San Francisco, 1983—86; publs. editor Calif. Casualty Mgmt. Co., San Mateo, 1986—88; contract atty. various law firms, San Francisco, 1992—96; mktg. and mgmt. cons. Ctrl. Pt., Oreg., 1996—99. Adj. prof. So. Oreg. U., Ashland, 1998—99; law clk. Law Offices Lois Glanby, McMurray, Pa., 2000—; tutor, instr. ESL, Rogue C.C., Medford, Oreg., 1998—99. Articles editor: Hastings Internat. and Comparative Law Rev., 1990—91. Tutor SMART reading program Patrick Elem. Sch., Gold Hill, Oreg., 1999; dir. Family Race Festival, Providence Hosp. and Mail Tribune, Medford, 1997—98. Mem.: Phi Beta Kappa. Democrat. Avocations: cooking, gardening, swimming, walking. Home: 1449 Trance Dr Pittsburgh PA 15234

MYERS, CAROL MCCLARY, retired sales administrator, editor; b. Dawson, N.Mex. d. Joseph Franklin and Alberta Lenore (McGarvey) McClary; m. Dwight Andrew Myers, Sept. 16, 1950 (dec. Sept. 1995); children: Robert Andrew, Debra Ann, James Allen. MusB, U. Redlands, 1950. Cert. tchr., Calif. Tchr. music Barstow (Calif.) Pub. Schs., 1950-52; sec., acct. U.S. Army, Columbus, Ga., 1952-54; part-time sec. Robert Lafollette, Atty., Albuquerque, 1954-57; sec., acct. Midland Specialty Co., Albuquerque, 1957-60; pvt. tchr. piano Oakland, N.J., 1960-70; organist, choir dir., ch. sec. Ramapo Valley Bapt., Oakland, N.J., 1965-70; order fulfillment/invoicing U. N.Mex. Press, Albuquerque, 1974-76, sales mgr., 1976-88, ret., 1988. Editor (mag.) Book Talk, 1971-2001; (7 books) In Celebration of the Book: Literary New Mexico, 1982, Literary New Mexico: Essays From Book Talk, 1998. Recipient Edgar Lee Hewett award Hist. Soc. N.Mex., 1985, Paso Por Aquí award Rio Grande Hist. Collections, 1990. Mem. N.Mex. Libr. Assn. (hon. life, treas. 1989-91, bd. dirs. 1992-94), Rocky Mountain Book Pubs. Assn. (Jack D. Rittenhouse award 1994), Mountains and Plains Booksellers Assn. Republican. Avocations: piano playing, New Mexico Book League (vol. editor). Home: 8632 Horacio Pl NE Albuquerque NM 87111-3218

MYERS, CHARLOTTE WILL, biology educator; b. Harbor Beach, Mich., Jan. 5, 1930; d. Louis John and Ruth (Sageman) Wills; m. John Jay Myers, Dec. 27, 1958; children: Sandra, Andrew, Susan Ruth. BA in Biology, U. Mich., 1951, MS in Edn., 1952. Tchr. biology Birmingham (Mich.) Pub. Schs., 1952-59; tchr. art pvt. practice, Birmingham, 1962-78, Santa Fe, 1979—. Instr. Oakland U., Pontiac, Mich., 1975-77; demonstrator, coord. Internat. Porcelain Art Teaching, Birmingham and Santa Fe, 1972—. V.p. PTA, Birmingham, 1957; founder Future Tchrs., Birmingham, 1956; area chmn. Muscular Dystrophy, Birmingham, 1963-64; leader Girl Scouts Am., Birmingham, 1969-71. Mem. N.Mex. State Fedn. Porcelain Artists (sec. 1986—), Mich. China Painting Tchrs. Orgn. (pres. 1973-77), Rocky Mountain Outdoor Writers and Photographers (bd. dirs. 1995—), N.Mex. Outdoor Writers and Photographers (v.p. 2002-03), Internat. Porcelain Arts Tchrs., Artists Equity (treas. 1981-83), Porcelain Arts Club (pres. 1979-81, treas. 1987-89). Democrat. Presbyterian. Avocations: gardening, needlework, travel. Home and Office: 9 Cibola Cir Santa Fe NM 87505-9006

MYERS, CONNIE, assemblywoman; b. Staten Island, N.Y., Nov. 14, 1944; BA in English, Montclair State Coll.; MA in Pub. Adminstrn., Rider Coll. Alt. del. Rep. Nat. Conv., 1988; mem. Hunterdon County Bd. of Elections, 1989—95, Hunterdon County Planning Bd., 1992—97; county coord., local media coord. Whitman for Gov., 1993; county coord. Haytaian for U.S. Senate, 1994; assemblywoman N.J. Gen. Assembly, 1996—. Mem. Holland Twp. Rep. Com.; mem., vice chair Hunterdon County Rep. Com. Mem. Moravian Coll. Parents Coun. Mem.: N.J. Hist. Soc., Descendants of the Founders of N.J. (scholarship chair), N.J. Farm Bureau, N.J. Daughters of the Am. Revolution (geneal. records chair), North East Organic Farmers Assn. Republican. Office: 124 W Washington Ave Washington NJ 07882 E-mail: AswMyers@njleg.org.

MYERS, DEBRA ANNELLA, speech pathology/audiology services professional; d. Gordon Everett and Jo Ann Schiber Bogle; m. Alan G. Myers; children: Jennifer, Mark, Adrianne, Jeffrey. BS, Fontbonne Coll., 1992, MS, 1993. Speech lang. pathologist Spl. Sch. Dist., St. Louis, 1994—2000, Fox C-6 Sch. Dist., St. Louis, 2000—; co-owner and speech lang. pathologist Creve Coeur Speech Lang. Learning Ctr., Mo., 2000—. Mem.: Am. Speech Lang. Hearing Assn. Office: Creve Coeur Speech Lang Learning Ctr 711 Old Ballas Rd Ste 211 Creve Coeur MO 63141

MYERS, DEBRA TAYLOR, elementary school educator, writer; b. Balt., Feb. 5, 1953; d. James Zachary and Gene Elizabeth (Blubaugh) Taylor; m. Kenneth Lee Myers Jr., June 18, 1977; children: Kenneth Andrew, Katherine Elizabeth. BS in Elem. Edn., Towson State U., 1975, MEd, 1983. Cert. tchr., Md. 5th grade tchr. N.W. Mid. Sch., Taneytown, Md., 1975-80; home and hosp. sch. tchr. Balt. County Schs., 1992-93; tchr. educator in elem. edn. dept. Towson (Md.) State U., 1993—94; 2d grade tchr. Balt. County Pub. Schs., 1994—. Tchr. Dept. Elem. Edn. Towson (Md.) U.; workshop leader in field; lectr. in field. Contbr. articles to children's mags. and jours. Mem. Fieldstone Hist. Com., A Randallstown Cmty. Group Assn., Balt., 1993—; bd. dirs. Child Devel. Ctr., Milford Mill United Meth. Ch., 1992—; coord. Jr. Fieldstone Garden Club. Recipient Outstanding Vol. award Balt. County PTA, 1992, 93, 94; named N.W. Area Educator of Yr., 1999. Mem. Kappa Delta Pi. Avocations: travel, reading, writing for children, volunteering, spending time with family. Home: 3607 Blackstone Rd Randallstown MD 21133-4213 Office: Office of Gifted and Talented Edn and Magnet Programs 6019 Charles St Towson MD 21204

MYERS, ELISSA MATULIS, publisher, association executive; b. Munich, Aug. 4, 1950; (parents Am. citizens); d. Raymond George and Anne Constance (Moley) Matulis; m. John Wake Myers, Sept. 13, 1967 (div. 1972); 1 child, Jennifer Anne Myers Bick. BA in English Lit., George Mason U., 1972, MA in English Lit., 1982. Dir. rsch. and info. Am. Soc. Assn. Execs., Washington, 1972-80, dir. mem. svcs., 1980-88, v.p., pub. Assn. Mgmt. mag., 1988-97; pres., CEO Nat. Informercial Mktg. Assn., Washington, 1997—, Electronic Retailing Assn., Washington, 1998—. Pub. Principles of Association Management, 1976, 3d edit., 1996; columnist Footnotes, 1988-97. Bd. dirs. Ethics Resource Ctr., Washington, 1982-86; mem. Universal Postal Union Adv. Group 2000-; mem. Fed. Adv. Commn. on e-commerce; appointee DofC 1fac-4 Ecommerce, 2001-. Mem. Am. Soc. Assn. Execs. (cert.), Assn. Conv. Mktg. Execs., Greater Washington Soc. Assn. Execs. (bd. dirs. 2000—), Nat. Assn. Hispanic Mktg. Profls. (adv. bd.), Soc. Nat. Assn. Publs., Com. of 100 U.S. C. of C., Soc. Scholarly Pubs. Roman Catholic. Avocations: running, scuba diving. Home: 5315 Moultrie Rd Springfield VA 22151-1915 Office: Electronic Retailing Assn 2101 Wilson Blvd Arlington VA 22201-3062 E-mail: elissa@elissamyers.com.

MYERS, HELEN MARIE, education educator, choreographer; d. Robert Allen and Helen Mae Myers; m. Paul Murphy, Aug. 11, 2000. MFA, Ohio State U., Columbus, Ohio, 1992. Cert. Pilates Tchr. IMX Pilates Corp./N.Y.C., 2003. Asst. prof. of dance N. Mex. State U., Las Cruces, N.Mex., 1996—2001, SUNY at Geneseo, Geneseo, NY, 2001—. State grant panelist N. Mex Arts Divsn., Santa Fe, 1994—98. Dancer eMOTIONalogic (Presentation at Joyce Soho, N.Y.C.); contbr. chapters to books (ALA Outstanding Reference Source, 2000). Recipient Nat. Grad. Rsch. Award, Congress on Rsch. in Dance, 1992; grantee Numerous grants received from pvt., state, and academic sources, 1987-2003. Fellow: Assn. for Theatre in Higher Edn. (exec. officer 2000—03). Office: Sch of Performing Arts 1 Coll Cir Geneseo NY 14454 Personal E-mail: 585-245-5826. E-mail: 585-245-5826.

MYERS, IONA RAYMER, real estate property manager; b. Guymon, Okla., Sept. 18, 1931; m. Harold Rudolph Myers, Mar. 28, 1953 (dec. Apr. 13, 2003); children: Richard Galen, Sandra Dawn, Paula Colleen. BS magna cum laude, So. Nazarene U., 1952; MEd, U. Okla., 1959; postgrad., McNeese State U., 1970. Tchr. home econs. Can. County Pub. Schs., Mustang, Okla., 1952-53; tchr. elem. Oklahoma City Pub. Schs., 1955-61, Transylvania County Pub. Schs., Brevard, N.C., 1961-67; elem. tchr., student tchr. supr. Allen Parish Pub. Schs., Oakdale, La., 1967-71; mgr. DeRidder Tracts and Comml. Property, Metairie, 1968-94; tchr. elem. and jr. high history Lafourche Parish Pub. Schs., Raceland and Lockport, La., 1974-76; tchr. elem. sci. Jefferson Parish Pub. Schs., Metairie, 1976-80; treas. Harold R. Myers Engring. (divsn. Harold R. Myers, Inc.), Metairie, 1993—2003; mgr. Harion Properties, L.L.C., Metairie, 1980—. Vol. founding bd. dirs. Jefferson Performing Arts Soc., Metairie, 1977-83; vol. founding mem. community adv. coun. East Jefferson Gen. Hosp., Metairie, 1980-87. Vol. scout leader S.E. La. Girl Scouts U.S. coun., Metairie, 1977-89, fund raising com., 1992-93; vol. tchr. music Harold Keller Elem. Sch., Metairie, 1981-83; life mem. Rep. Nat. Com., Washington, 1980-91, mem. fin. com., 1988; jubilee chmn., fundraiser Jefferson Performing Arts Soc., Metairie, 1987; candidate La. Ho. of Reps. Dist. 88, Baton Rouge, 1991; com. YWCA New Orleans Role Model Luncheon, 1994-95; financier Bus. and Profl. Women USA Found., 1990-95, Golden Circle donor, 1996-2001; sec. East Jefferson Rep. Parish Coun., 1998-99; parliamentarian Nat. Women's Polit. Caucus Greater New Orleans Region, 1998-99. New Orleans Mus. of Art fellow, 1984-94, So. Nazarene U. fellow, 1985-94; recipient Rice in the Ear award S.E. La. Girl Scouts U.S., 1982, Great Lady/Great Gentleman award Ladies Aux. East Jefferson Gen. Hosp., 1987, Commendation award Jefferson Performing Arts Soc., 1988, Women as Winners award YWCA New Orleans, 1993; honoree City Business Woman of the Year, 2001. Mem. AAUW (pres. 1988-90, vol. coord. Metairie chpt. 1990-91, del. 5 nat. and 5 regional convs. 1987-94, 98, 99, corr. sec. La. chpt. 1989-91, scholar and grantee 1989, Magnolia editor 1991-96, Magnolia co-editor 1996-97, chair nominating com. 1992-93, 98-99, sec. 1998-2000, state parliamentarian 2000-01, state pres. elect 2001-02, state pres. 2002-04, state sec. 2004—, grant honoree La. 1994, program v.p. Metairie br. 1997-99, Parliamentarian br. 1999-2000, chmn. fin. 2000-2001, br. pres. 2002-04), Jefferson Hist. Soc. (life), La. Landmarks Soc. (life), Nat. Assn. Parliamentarians (pres. Metairie unit 1996-97, 98-99, del. nat. conv., 1997-99, v.p. program chair, 1999-2000, parliamentarian 2000-2001, pres. 2002-03, sec. 2003-04), La. Assn. Parliamentarians (2d v.p., edn. chair 1997-2001, state 1st v.p. 2001—), La. Fedn. Bus. Profl. Women's Clubs, Inc., La. Fedn. Bus. Profl. Women's Clubs, Inc. (auditor, legis. chmn. 1990-91, rec. sec. 1991-92, membership v.p. 1992-93, state newsletter Pelican editor 1995-2000 (pres. Jefferson Parish chpt. 1980-82, 1st v.p. 1993-94, state pres. 1995-96, pres.-elect 1994-95, state historian, 2001—, program v.p. 1993-94, mem. v.p. 1992-93, rec. sec. 1991-92, auditor and legis. chmn. 1990-91, Vision editor 1993-96, Jefferson Parish Voice editor 1993—, sec. 1998-99, parliamentarian 1999-2001, pres. 2001-02, Outstanding Dist. Dir. award 1985, Nike award 1991, Highest Mem. honor 1992-93, Best Membership Recruiter 1993-94), Metairie Woman's Club (corr. sec. 1994-96, parliamentarian 2002-03); New Orleans Mus. Art (fellow 1984-94), E. Jefferson Parish Republican Coun., 1998-99, Nat. Women's Political Caucus (New Orleans region pres. 1999-2000, v.p. polit. activity, 2000-2001, del. nat. conv., 1997, 99), Jefferson Twenty-five bd. (sec. 2003—, Patty Strong award 1997). Methodist. Avocations: plate collector, gardening, lobbyist. Home: 4701 Chastant St Metairie LA 70006-2059

MYERS, JULIE L. federal agency administrator; b. Shawnee, KS; BA, Baylor U.; JD, Cornell U. Assoc. Mayer, Brown & Platt, Chgo., 1993—97; assoc. ind. counsel Office of Ind. Counsel Kenneth Starr, Washington, 1998—99; asst. U.S. atty. U.S. Atty.'s Office, Ea. Dist. N.Y., Bklyn., 1999—2001; dept. asst. sec. for money laundering and fin. crimes Office of Enforcement, Dept. Treasury, Washington, 2001—03; chief of staff to asst. atty. gen. criminal divsn. U.S. Dept. Justice, Washington, 2003; asst. sec. for export enforcement U.S. Dept. Commerce, Washington, 2003—. Office: Herbert Clark Hoover Bldg Rm 3721 14th St and Constitution Ave NW Washington DC 20230*

MYERS, KANDY KAY, music educator; b. Oklahoma City, May 4, 1961; d. William Baird Whetstone and Gail Berneice Andrews; m. Michael Gene Myers, Mar. 20, 1982; children: Gerrod Michael, Zachary. BS in Early Childhood Edn. magna cum laude, B of Music Edn., U. Cen. Okla., 1996. Cert. Nat. Bd. Profl. Tchg. Stds., 2003. Comml. loan sec. Yukon (Okla.) Nat. Bank, 1977—79, Lakeshore Bank, Oklahoma City, 1980—81; new accounts, CD clk. Founders Bank, Oklahoma City, 1981—82, loan officer, exec. sec. Guaranty Bank, Oklahoma City, 1982—85; substitute tchr. Mustang Valley Elem., Mustang, Okla., 1991—96; pvt. piano and voice tchr. Skyview Elem., 1993—; music tchr. Yukon Pub. Schs., 1996—. Accompanist Yukon Pub. Schs., Yukon, 1997—, Mustang Pub. Schs., 1997—2000, 1st Bapt. Ch., Mustang, 2000—03. Grantee, Yukon Found. Excellence, 2000, 2001, 2003, Yukon Art League, 2003. Mem.: NEA, Okla. Educators' Assn., Yukon Profl. Educators' Assn. Republican. Baptist. Avocations: singing, playing piano. Home: 1433 E Persimmon Ln Mustang OK 73064 Office: Skyview Elem Sch 2800 N Mustang Rd Yukon OK 73099

MYERS, LEAH LYNNETTE, military officer; b. Charlotte, N.C., Sept. 24, 1977; d. Michael M. and Kathleen Cogswell, Mary Cogswell (Stepmother). Student, U. Alaska, Anchorage, 2000—. With USAF, 1999—. Mem.: Golden Key Hon. Soc. (assoc.; n/a). Avocations: reading, travel, writing, sewing, cross stitch. Home: PO Box 201823 Anchorage AK 99520-1823

MYERS, LIBBY ANN, retired medical/surgical nurse; b. Hutchinson, Kans., July 22, 1936; d. Edwin Eugene and Verna Maxine (Craig) Schroëder; m. William Wayne Osborne, Apr. 1950 (div. 1960); m. William Andrew Myers III, June 21, 1962; children: Linda Kay, Lloyd Lee, Diana Gaye, Joe Lyle, Delbert Matthew. MSN, Okla. Bapt. U., 1958. RN, Okla. Nurse Bapt. Meml. Hosp., Oklahoma City, 1967-70, Doctors Gen. Hosp., Oklahoma City, 1970-73, Mercy Hosp., Oklahoma City, 1973-79; nurse, team leader PICU Hutchinson (Kans.) Hosp., 1979-87; pvt. practice pvt. duty nurse Oklahoma City, 1987-93; ret., 1993. Owner, operator Day Care Facility, Oklahoma City, 1977-79. Precinct poll inspector Precinct 238 Oklahoma City Election Bd., 1988-96, precinct com. chair Precinct 238 Oklahoma City Rep., 1992-96; exec. com. Oklahoma County Rep. Hdqrs., Oklahoma City, 1994-96; pres., former block capt. Epworth Neighborhood Assn., Oklahoma City, 1991-96; counselor Homicide Survivors Support Group, Oklahoma City, 1991-96, lobbyist for victims bills, 1992-96; Sunday sch. tchr., Bible sch. tchr. Crestwood Bapt. Ch., Oklahoma City; rescue worker during Oklahoma City bombing aftermath, also mem. survivor notifcation team, 1st Christian Ch., and victim advocate, Save Haven, Oklahoma City, during trials; candidate for Okla. Ho. of Reps., Dist. 88, 1998. Mem. Tri-City Rep. Women, Bapt. Women. Avocations: reading, poetry writing, watching ball games, cooking, crafts.

MYERS, LINDA K. retired editor, state representative; b. Nanty Glo, Pa., Aug. 18, 1940; m. Martin J. Myers (dec.); children: Robyn, Kasey. B in Journalism, B in Polit. Sci., Kent State U. Cert. safety certifier cheerleading coaches, Vt., certified cheerleading judge Vt., N.Y., N.H. Ret. newspaper editor; state rep. State of Vt., 2001—, mem. loint legis. oversight com. corrections, 2002—. Mem. Essex Selectboard, Essex Bd. Civil Authority; justice of peace; bd. dirs. Essex Town Rep. Com. Named Contbr. of Yr., Vt. Cheerleading Coaches Assn., 2003. Mem.: Nat. Fedn. Intersch. Spirit Assn., Nat. Assn. Female Exec. (adv. bd.), Women in Comm. Inc., Am. Assn. Cheerleading Coaches and Advisors (founding mem.), Vt. Prin. Assn. Cheerleading Com. (adv. mem.). Republican. Office: 51 Forest Rd Essex Junction VT 05452 E-mail: themyers@attglobal.net., lmyers@leg.state.vt.us.

MYERS, LINDA M. writer; b. Boston, Mass., May 29, 1948; d. Beatrice Catherine Kovacev; m. Lewis Brown, May 2, 2003; children: Stacey Anne, Danielle Bernadette. BA in Psychology, Framingham (Mass.) State Coll., 1981. Salesperson, assoc. Horne Realty, Framingham, 1983—85; caterer/banquet waitress Hillcrest, Waltham, Mass., 1986—87; staff asst. I, staff asst. II Harvard U. Office of Univ. Pubs., Cambridge, Mass., 1986—89; auditor, sec. RGIS Inventory Specialists, Cambridge, 1989—92; customer sales/svc. rep. Electrolux, West Newton, Mass., 1992—93; v.p. Nature Stone Art Gallery, South Easton, Mass., 1998—; pres., owner, CEO Lillemoor Ent., South Easton, 1994—; atty. pro se Supreme Ct., Mass., 1995—96, 1995—96. Prodr. Lewis Brown Nature Stone Art Pub. Access Broadband/AT&T, South Easton, Mass., 1996—; trustee Nature Stone Art Bus. Trust, South Easton, 1997—. Author: Lewis Brown's National Register's Who's Who Biography, 2001—02; prodr.: 10 documentaries, Linda & Lewis Diversity Radio Talk Show, 2002—03, cyberstationusa-.com. Mem. Nat. Trust for Hist. Preservation, Nat. Fedn. for the Blind. Recipient 3 Certs. of Merit, Easton Film Festival, 2002. Mem.: Nat. Mus. of Women in the Arts. Roman Catholic. Avocations: dancing, photography, biking, drawing, design. Home and Office: Lillemoor Enterprise 305 Turnpike St 14B South Easton MA 02375

MYERS, LINDA SHAFER, secondary educator; b. Lebanon, Tenn., Apr. 12, 1943; d. Odie and Nellie Irene Shafer; m. C. Bruce Myers (div.); children: James B., Joseph C. BA, Berea Coll., 1965; MA, Austin Peay State U., 1972, postgrad., 1993. Cert. tchr., Tenn. English tchr. Montgomery County Schs., Clarksville, Tenn., 1985—; chair dept. English Clarksville H.S., 2001—. Mem. Nat. Tenn. Edn. Assn., Nat. Tenn. Coun. of Tchrs. of English, Delta Kappa Gamma Soc. Internat. Avocation: genealogy. Office: Clarksville H S 151 Richview Rd Clarksville TN 37043-4723

MYERS, MARGARET ALICE, music educator; b. Des Arc, Ark., Jan. 14, 1937; d. Cecil Ernest and Juneidabeth Letsch Myers. BSE, U. Ark., 1958, MEd, 1963. Cert. tchr. Kans. Music and string tchr. El Dorado (Ark.) Dist. # 15, 1958—77; string tchr. Parsons (Kans.) Schs. Unified Sch. Dist. # 503, 1977—. Viola player South Ark. Symphony, El Dorado, 1958—77, S.E. Kans. Symphony, Pittsburg, 1979—, Labette C.C. Orch., Parsons, 2000—. Recipient commendation, Ark. Senate, 1971. Mem.: Suzuki Assn. of Ams., Music Educators Nat. Conf., Ark. Elem. Music Assn. (sec.-treas. 1968—77). Republican. Lutheran. Avocations: cats, knitting, travel. Home: 3105 Dirr Parsons KS 67357 Office: Parsons Unified Sch Dist 503 2900 Southern Parsons KS 67357 E-mail: mmyers@vikingnet.net.

MYERS, MARGARET JANE (DEE DEE MYERS), television personality, editor; b. Quonset Pt., R.I., Sept. 1, 1961; d. Stephen George and Judith Ann (Burleigh) M. BS, U. Santa Clara, 1983. Press asst. Mondale for Pres., L.A., 1984; deputy Senator Art Torres, L.A., 1985; dep. press sec. to press sec. Mayor Tom Bradley, L.A., 1985-87; deputy press sec. Tom Bradley For Gov., L.A., 1986; Calif. press sec. Dukakis for Pres., L.A., 1988; press sec. Feinstein for Gov., L.A. and San Francisco, 1989-90; campaign dir. Jordan for Mayor, San Francisco, 1991; comm. cons. DeeDee Myers Assocs., Valencia, Calif., 1991—; press sec. Clinton for Pres., Little Rock, 1991-92, White House, Washington, 1993-94; co-host Equal Time, CNBC, Washington, 1995-97; contbg. editor Vanity Fair, Washington, 1995—. Mem. bd. of trustees, Calif. State U.,1999— Recipient Robert F. Kennedy award Emerson Coll., Boston, 1993. Democrat. Roman Catholic. Avocations: running, cycling, music, major league baseball.

MYERS, MARILYN GLADYS, pediatric hematologist and oncologist; b. Lyons, Nebr., July 17, 1930; d. Leonard Clarence and Marian N. (Manning) M.; m. Paul Frederick Motzkus, July 24, 1957 (dec. Aug. 1982). BA cum laude, U. Omaha, 1954; MD, U. Nebr., 1959. Diplomate Am. Bd. Pediatrics. Intern Orange County Gen. Hosp., Orange, Calif., 1959-60, resident, 1960-62; fellow in hematology/oncology Orange County Gen. Hosp./Children's Hosp. L.A., 1962-64; assoc. in rsch., chief dept. hematology/oncology Children's Hosp., Orange, 1964-80, dir. outpatient dept., 1964-73, assoc. dir. leukapheresis unit, 1971-80; clin. practice hematology, oncology, rheumatology Orange, 1964-80; instr. Coll. Medicine U. Calif., Irvine, 1968-71, asst. clin. prof. pediatrics, 1971—; pvt.

practice hematology, oncology, rheumatology Santa Ana, Calif., 1980—. Clin. rschr. exptl. drugs. Contbr. articles to med. jours. Mem. med. adv. com. Orange County Blood Bank Hemophiliac Found. Grantee Am. Leukemia Soc., 1963, Am. Heart Assn., 1964. Fellow Am. Acad. Pediatrics; mem. AMA, Calif. Med. Assn., L.A. County Med. Assn., Orange County Med. Assn., Orange County Pediatric Soc., Southwestern Pediatric Soc., L.A. Pediatric Soc., Internat. Coll. Pediatrics, Orange County Oncologic Soc., Am. Heart Assn. (Cardiopulmonary Coun.). Republican. Methodist. Avocation: reading. Office: 2220 E Fruit St Ste 217 Santa Ana CA 92701-4459 Office Phone: 714-541-3393.

MYERS, MARY ELIZABETH, police officer; b. Akron, Ohio, Aug. 5, 1953; d. Robert A. and Helen M. (Cassidy) M. BA in Edn., BA in Arts and Sci., U. Akron, 1975; MA in Counseling, Kent State U., 1990, postgrad., 1994. Lic. practical clin. counselor, Ohio, social worker, Ohio; cert. fgn. lang. instr.; cert. peace officer instr., Ohio. Tchr. Spanish and French Triway Local High Sch., Wooster, Ohio, 1976-77; with Akron Police Dept., 1977—2001, police sgt., homicide detective supr., 1991-95, police lt., 1995—2000, police capt., 2000—01. Instr. U. Akron, 1983—, prof., 1993—; counselor trainee supr. Kent (Ohio) State U., 1992-93; speaker and presenter in field. Contbr. articles to profl. jours. Mem. Summit Medina Regional Critical Incident Stress Debriefing Team, Akron Police Peer Support Program. Recipient numerous shooting awards, 1980-87; named Gov.'s Top Twenty Shooters Team, Gov. of Ohio, 1986, 87. Mem. NRA, ACA, Internat. Assn. Women Police, Nat. Law Enforcement Trainers Assn., Fraternal Order of Police, Chi Sigma Iota. Avocation: martial arts. Home: 1871-6th St Cuyahoga Falls OH 44221 Office: U Akron Polsky Bldg 166K Akron OH 44325-4304

MYERS, MARY KATHLEEN, publishing executive; b. Cedar Rapids, Iowa, Aug. 19, 1945; d. Joseph Bernard and Marjorie Helen (Huntsman) Weaver; m. David F. Myers, Dec. 30, 1967; children: Mindy, James. BA in English and Psychology, U. Iowa, 1967. Tchr. Lincoln H.S., Des Moines, 1967-80; editor Perfection Learning Corp., Des Moines, 1980-87, v.p., editor-in-chief, 1987-93; pres., founding ptnr. orgn. to promote Edward de Bono Advanced Practical Thinking Tng., Des Moines, 1992—; founder Myers House LLC, 2002. Pres. Innova Tng. & Cons., Inc., 2000—. Editor: Six Thinking Hats, 1991, Lateral Thinking, 1993, Direct Attention Thinking Tools, 1997, Total Creativity, 1997. Adv. bd. Sch. Bus., Econs. and Acctg., Simpson Coll., 1998—. Mem. ASTD, Am. Creativity Assn. (bd. dirs. 1997—, pres. 1999), Instrnl. Systems Assn. (v.p. mem. svcs. 2002-3, v.p. nominations 2003-04). Home: 813 56th St West Des Moines IA 50266-6314 Office: APTT 2882 106th St # 200 Des Moines IA 50322-3771 Office Phone: 515-334-2687. E-mail: kymers@aptt.com.

MYERS, MICHELE TOLELA, academic administrator; b. Rabat, Morocco, Sept. 25, 1941; arrived in U.S., 1964; d. Albert and Lillie (Abecassis) Tolela; m. Pierre Vajda, Sept. 12, 1962 (div. Jan. 1965); m. Gail E. Myers, Dec. 20, 1968 (div. Oct. 2003); children: Erika, David. Diploma, Inst. Polit. Studies, U. Paris, 1962; MA, U. Denver, 1966, PhD, 1967; MA, Trinity U., 1977; LHD, Wittenberg U., 1994, Denison U., 1998, U. Denver, 1999. Asst. prof. speech Manchester Coll., North Manchester, Ind., 1967—68; asst. prof. speech and sociology Monticello Coll., Godfrey, Ill., 1968—71; asst. prof. communication Trinity U., San Antonio, 1975—80, assoc. prof., 1980—86, asst. v.p. for acad. affairs, 1982—85, assoc. v.p., 1985—86; assoc. prof. sociology, dean Undergrad. Coll. Bryn Mawr Coll., Pa., 1986—89; pres. Denison U., Granville, Ohio, 1989—98, Sarah Lawrence Coll., Bronxville, NY, 1998—. Comm. analyst Psychology and Commn., San Antonio, 1974—83; bd. dirs. Sherman Fairchild Found., 1992—; mem. Fed. Res. Bank Cleve., 1995—98; pres.'s commn. Nat. Collegiate Athletic Assn., 1993—97, JSTOR, 1999—, ARTSTOR, 2003—. Co-author (with Gail Myers): The Dynamics of Human Communication, 1973, The Dynamics of Human Communication, 6th and internat. edits., 1992, The Dynamics of Human Communication, French transl., 1984, Communicating When We Speak, 1975, Communicating When We Speak, 2d edit., 1978, Communication for the Urban Professional, 1977, Managing by Communicaton: An Organizational Approach, 1982, Managing by Communicaton: An Organizational Approach, Spanish transl., 1983, Managing by Communicaton: An Organizational Approach, internat. edit., 1982. Trustee Phila. Child Guidance Clinic, 1988—89; trustee assoc. The Bryn Mawr Sch., Balt., 1987—89; v.p., bd. dirs. San Antonio Cmty. Guidance Ctr., 1979—83. Fellow Bank 1 Columbus, 1990—94; fellow in acad. adminstrn., Am. Coun. Edn., 1981—82. Mem.: Am. Coun. Edn. (commn. on women in higher edn. 1990—92, bd. dirs. 1993—99, chmn. 1997—98). Home: 935 Kimball Ave Bronxville NY 10708-5507 Office: Sarah Lawrence Coll One Mead Way Bronxville NY 10708 E-mail: mmyers@sarahlawrence.edu.

MYERS, PRISCILLA A. insurance company executive; BS in Polit. Sci. and Econs., U. Mass., 1973; MBA, Suffolk U., 1978. Staff auditor The Prudential Ins. Co. Am., Boston, 1976-95, sr. v.p. and auditor, 1995-98, sr. v.p. demutualization, 1998—2002; sr. v.p., chief mktg. officer Prudential Fin., Inc., Newark, 2002—. Mem. Auditing Com. Mcpl. Excess Liability Joint Ins. Fund; trustee Inst. Internal Auditors Profl. Rsch. Found. Trustee St. Peter's Coll. Office: Prudential Fin Inc Chief Mktg Officer 213 Washington St 18th Fl Newark NJ 07102-2992

MYERS, SHARON DIANE, auditor; b. Lawrence, Kans., Sept. 18, 1955; d. Richard Paul and Helen Carol (Overbey) M. AA, Mt. San Antonio Coll., Walnut, Calif., 1981; BSBA, Calif. State U., Pomona, 1983, MBA, 1986. Cert. fraud examiner; cert. govt. fin. mgr. Revenue agt. IRS, Glendale, Calif., 1984-85; auditor Def. Contract Audit Agy., L.A., 1985-92; auditor Office Inspector Gen. FDIC, Newport Beach, 1992—2002; auditor officer Inspector Gen., USPS, Portland, Oreg., 2002—. Instr. Azusa (Calif.) Pacific U., 1987, 88, West Coast U., San Diego, 1992. Musician, Sunday sch. supt. Covina (Calif.) Bapt. Temple, 1975-95, Liberty Bapt. Ch., Irvine, Calif., 1995-2002, Landmark Bapt. Ch., Olympia, Wash., 2002—. Mem. Assn. Govt. Accts. Republican. Avocations: piano, traveling. Home: 2702 44th Ave NW Olympia WA 98502-3692

MYERS, SHEILA JOHN, artist; b. Garrett, Ind., Aug. 9, 1957; d. John Leo and Jane Cecilia (Schooley) Foley; m. Kevin Reynold Myers, Aug. 2, 1980; children: Brittany Katherine, Shawn Elizabeth. BFA Art and Graphic Design, Western Mich. U., 1981. Graphic designer The Design Ctr. Holt Enterprises, Greensboro, NC, 1981—82; freelance graphic designer, art dir. Dimension Mktg. Inc., Greensboro, NC, 1982—85; advt. artist Barnes, Dennis & Assocs., Greensboro, NC, 1985—86, asst. art dir., 1986, art dir., 1986—87; freelance artist, designer Conyers, Ga., 1988—95; pvt. art instr., artist, designer, 1995—. Asst. artist Conyers/Rockdale Coun. for the Arts, Conyers, Ga., 2000, Conyers, 01, watercolor instr., 2002—. One-woman shows include Conyers-Rockdale Ctr. for the Arts, Conyers, Ga., 2001, Conyers Welcome Ctr., 2001. Gov. awards judge visual arts Rockdale County Schs., Conyers, Ga., 2001, PTA Reflections contest judge visual arts, 2001, 2002; Christmas contest judge Human Resources Office, Conyers, Ga., 2000, 2001. Mem.: Nat. Mus. Women in the Arts, Conyers-Rockdale Coun. for the Arts. Avocations: reading, piano, gardening. Home: 1630 Spaniel Ct Conyers GA 30094-4071

MYERS, SUE BARTLEY, artist; b. Norfolk, Va., Aug. 22, 1930; d. Louis and Rena M. Bartley; m. Bertram J. Myers, Nov. 24, 1949; children: Beth R., Mark F., Alyson S. Student, Stephens Coll., Va. Wesleyan. V.p. Jamson Realty Inc., Myers Realty Inc. Ltd. ptnr. Downtown Plaza Shopping Ctr., Warwick Village Shopping Ctr., Suburban Park Assocs. Solo shows at Village Gallery, Newport News, 1988, Artist at Work Gallery, Virginia Beach, Va., 1991, Va. Wesleyan U., Virginia Beach, 1991, 92, Will Richardson Gallery, Norfolk, Va., 1993, 94, Ctrl. Fidelity Bank, Norfolk, Va., 1995. Pres. adv. coun. Va. Wesleyan U., 1982-94; mayor's del. Sister Cities, Norwich, Eng., 1984, Kidikushu, Japan, 1982, Edinburgh, Scotland, 1991, Toulon, France, 1992; mem. entertainment com. Azalea Festival Norfolk, 1984; founder art scholarship Va. Wesleyan; bd. dirs. corp. campaign Va. Zool. Soc., 1996; trustee Guardian Angels, Jackson Meml. Hosp., Miami. Mem. Tidewater Artists Assn., Art Odyssey, Harbor Club, Bayville Golf Club. Jewish. Avocations: travel, physical fitness, reading, golf.

MYERS, VIRGINIA LOU, education educator; b. Indpls., July 18, 1940; d. John Rentschler and Bonnie Mae (Powell) Jones; m. James W. Rose Jr., Aug. 2, 1966 (div. Nov. 1986); m. Byron P. Myers, Sept. 11, 1987. BS in Edn., U. Indpls., 1966; MS in Edn., Butler U., 1971; PhD in Edn. Psychology, U. South Fla., 1991. Cert. elem. tchr., reading specialist and prin., Ind. Tchr. Indpls. Pub. Schs., 1966-72; pvt. tutor Self, Indpls., 1972-74; tchr.'s tchr. Urban/Rural Sch. Devel. Project, Indpls, 1974-77; reading techr. Met. sch. dist. Pike Twp., Indpls., 1977-80; curriculum specialist Met. sch. Dist. Washington Twp., Indpls., 1980-82; tchr. chpt. I Noblesville (Ind.) Pub. Schs., 1982-83; instr. social scis. Manatee C.C., Venice, Fla., 1983-87; asst. prof. edn. Mo. So. State Coll., Joplin, 1990-91, East Carolina U., Greenville, N.C., 1992-96; ednl. cons. Cath. Diocese of Venice, Fla., 1996-99; program mgr. child devel. and edn. Manatee Cmty. Coll., 1999—2001; sr. rsch. assoc. Fla. Inst. Edn., 2001—02; indep. early childhood cons., 2002—. Cons. Bertie County Schs., Windsor, NC, 1994—96; program mgr. early childhood and edn. Manatee C.C., 1999—2001, mem. early childhood adv. bd., 1996—2001; lead coach early literacy and learning model project Fla. Inst. Edn., 1990—2001; cons. Early Learning Accelerates Total Edn. Treas. Smart Start Initiative, Greenville, 1993—96; chair Birth Through Kindergarten Higher Edn. Consortium, 1994—96; mem. Fla. C.C. Early Childhood Network, 1999—, Manatee County Early Childhood Trainers Adv. Coun., 2000—, Lakewood Ranch H.S. Child Devel. Lab. Sch. Adv. Bd., 2000—, Sch. Readiness Coalition of Sarasota County, Inc., 2001—, exec. dir., 2002. Mem. ASCD, Nat. Assn. for Edn. Young Children, Orton Dyslexia Soc., Assn. Childhood Edn., Internat., Venice Area C. of C. (edn. com. 2001-02), Phi Theta Kappa (advisor 2000-01). Presbyterian. Avocations: needle work, reading. Home: 334 Woodvale Dr Venice FL 34293-4161 E-mail: drvmyers@comcast.net.

MYERS BROWN, JOAN, dance company executive, consultant; b. Phila., Dec. 25, 1931; d. Julius Thomas Myers and Nellie (Woods) Lewis Myers; m. Frederick Johnson, 1951 (div.); m. Max Brown, Nov. 18, 1967 (div.); children— Dannielle C. Brown, Marlisa J. Brown. D (hon.) U. Arts, 1994. Dancer various prodns. U.S., Can., Caribbean, 1950-61, Pearl Bailey Prodns., nat. tour, 1961-66; choreographer Harlem Prodns., Atlantic City, N.J., 1958-67; dir., choreographer, tchr. Phila. Sch. of Dance Arts, 1960—; exec. dir. Phila. Dance Co., 1970—; cons. Nat. Endowment for Arts, 1970-84, panelist, 1970-82; panelist Ohio State Arts Council, 1981-84, Mich. State Arts Council, 1981-84; dance panel Pa. State Arts Council, 1987, Md. State Arts Coun., 1990, Arts Presenters, 1995, NJ/Del. State Coun. on The Arts, 1994, The Kennedy Ctr. AAEP, 1996; dir. Wade Communications, 1983— . Bd. dirs. Spruce Family Planning Clinic; mem. Mayor's Cultural Adv. Council, 1984 ; bd. dirs. Greater Phila. Cultural Alliance; bd. dirs. Dance/USA, Citizens for Arts in Pa., Coalition of African-Am. Culture Inst. Recipient awards Nat. Council Negro Women, 1983, Award of Merit, West Phila. C. of C., 1983, Arts and Humanities Cultural award Phila. chpt. Continentals Socs., 1979, Philadelphians for Pub. Awareness award, 1984, Nat. Endowment Arts Choreographic fellow, 1979, Womens Way award, 1986, Theodore L. Hazlett Meml. award for excellence in the arts in Pa., 1986, Kool Achiever award, 1989, Black United Fund Arts award, 1989, Phila. Arts and Cultural award, 1989, Stella Moore Dance award, 1990, Black Unite Fund award, 1990, UNCF award, 1990, YWCA-Pioneer award, 1990, Excellence in Arts award, 1995, 50 Most Influential Women award, 1995, Arts and Business Coun. award, 1996, Chisolm award NPCBW, 1996, Democrat. Office: Phila Dance Co 9 N Preston St Philadelphia PA 19104-2299

MYERS-MORRISON, CYNTHIA JEAN, marriage and family therapist, educator; b. Bozeman, Mont., Dec. 22, 1946; d. Robert Evan and Norma Jean (Nicholas) Myers; m. Peter Keith Morrison, Sept. 26, 1999; m. John Charles Adams (div.); m. Bradford Harmon (div.). AB in English, UCLA, 1969, MEd in Reading, 1975; MA in Spl. Edn., Calif. State U., 1987; EdD in Leadership, UCLA, 1998. Cert. marriage and family therapist Calif., Pa. Tchr. LA (Calif.) Unified Sch. Dist., 1971—76, Wissahickon Sch. Dist., Ambler, Pa., 1976—78, LA (Calif.) Unified Sch. Dist., 1978—99. Pres. English Coun. LA; english specialist LA (Calif.) Unified Sch. Dist., 1986—88. Recipient award, San Fernando (Calif.) Valley Gifted Children's Assn., 1981; grantee Nat. Gifted and Talented grant. Avocations: genealogy, writing, skiing, nutrition.

MYERS-RAMI, MASEQUA, theatrical company executive, theater producer; m. Pemon Rami, 1975. CEO, founder Masequa Myers & Assoc., 1992; co-founder Lamont Zeno Theatre and Cultural Arts Program, Chgo., 1973; appeared in, provided casting svcs. for 14 films and TV movies including Mahogany, The Spook Who Sat By the Door, 1975; co-prodr., co-dir., co-host series of radio dramas A Taste of Culture, WBMX Radio, Chgo., 1980; co-mgr. Phoenix Black Theatre Troupe, 1982; acad. dir., acting instr. Maria Gibbs' Crossroads Nat. Edn. and Arts. Ctr. of L.A., 1990. Prodr.: (romantic comedy) Miss Dessa (9 Beverly Hills/Hollywood NAACP Theatre awards), (recruitment video) Take a Close Look; dir.: (TV talk shows for series) Getting It Right; prodr., dir., creative cons., costume designer : (video) It's OK to Say No Way; Follow Your Dream; cons., prodr., dir., co-writer (touring prodn. and video) Give Life a Chance. Named one of Top 100 Prodrs. in Nation, AV Video Multimedia Prodr. mag.; recipient award, Joseph Jefferson Com. Chgo., Chgo. Black Theatre Alliance, Ariz. Commn. on Arts, Ariz. Health Edn. Media Makers award, award, Am. Advt. Fedn., Nat. Assn. Audio Visual Communicators, Key to City of Detroit. Mem.: SAG, Women in Entertainment, Phoenix Arts Commn. (mem. grant panel), Ill. Arts Coun. (mem. grant panel), Ariz. Commn. on Arts (mem. grant panel), Women in Film. Office: Masequa Myers & Assocs 6100 S Dorchester 1 West Chicago IL 60637

MYHAND, CHERYL, minister, educator; d. Jack and Ora Williams; children: Kenyana children: Anjela, Patrick, Bernadette, Nikita. DD(hon.), Solomon's Temple of The World, 1984. Licensed Pastor United Meth. Ch., Mich., 1990; Certified Prevention Specialist Detroit Pub. Schools, Mich., 2000. Pres. Myhand & Associates Pub. Rels. Co., Detroit, 1977—89; site coord. Detroit Coun. of the Arts, Detroit, 1987—89; pastor North Detroit United Meth. Ch., Detroit, 1990—94; adminstrator Non-Profit Sector, Detroit, 1989—2001; prevention specialist Detroit Pub. Schools, 2000—; pastor John Wesley United Meth. Ch., River Rouge, Mich., 2000—. Youth commr. Detroit City Coun., 1987—90; mem. bio ethics com. Aurora Youth & Adolescent Hosp., Detroit, 1994—99; mem. exec. team Faith Base Initiative, Wayne County, Detroit, 2000—02; mem. bd. of global ministries United Meth. Detroit Ann. Conf., 2000—. Prodr.: (plays) What You Believe You Can Achieve - The Ron Milner; prodn. asst. (films) One In A Million - The Ron LeFleur Story, 1980, associate producer (albums) Lord We Need A Miracle, 1983, production assistant (TV films) United Negro College Fund - Lou Rawls Telethon, mng. editor Detroit Life Magazine, assoc. editor-writer (newspaper) For My People, contributing editor (magazine) Tribe Magazine. Mem. of the inaugural planning com. Gov. Jennifer Granholm Inaugural, Detroit, 2002—03, Mayor Dennis Archer Inaugural, Detroit, 1994, 1998; mem. of the transition team Mayor Kilpartick, Detroit, 2000; chairperson Hunger Action Coalition, Detroit, 1994; mem. bd. of directors Empowerment Zone, Detroit, 1998; mem. of the cmty. adv. panel Pub. TV TV-56, Detroit, 1999. Recipient Crescent award - Outstanding Spiritual Leadership, Nation of Islam, 1998, Outstanding Leadership - Detroit 300, Detroit 300 Com., 2001, Peace award, Denby H.S., Detroit, 2003, Outstanding Clergy Leadership, Wayne County Commn., 1997, Proclamation for Outstanding Leadership, United State Congl., 2000, Outstanding Cmty. Leadership and Spirit of Detroit, Mayor of the City of Detroit, 1994, Disting. Citizen, Detroit City Clerk's Office, 1981, Cmty. Leader, Wayne County C.C., 1992, Outstanding Svc., Wayne County Commn. and NAACP - Detroit Br. Prison Program, 2002, Human Svc., Nat. Assn. for Advancement of Colored People, 2002; fellowship, Eureka Communities, 1994, fellowship, Interreligious Dialogue, Golden Inst. for Internat. Partnership and Peace - Hosted by The Coun. for a Parliament of the Worlds Religions, 2002. Mem.: Inkster Ministerial Alliance (polit. action chairperson 1999), Nat. Assn. for Advancement of Colored People (life). Democrat-Npl. Methodist. Avocations: travel, writing, reading, collecting dolls. Office: John Wesley United Methodist Church 555 Beechwood River Rouge MI 48218

MYKLEBY, KATHY, newscaster, reporter; Degree, U. Iowa, 1976. With KRNA-FM Radio, Iowa City, 1976, WKY-Radio, Oklahoma City, 1976—80, WVTV-TV Channel 18, Milw., 1980; reporter, anchor WISN, Milw., 1980—. Active telethon Children's Miracle Network; co-chmn. Briggs and Stratton Run/Walk for Children's Hosp. of Wis. Recipient Regional award for best TV feature, UP Internat., 1984, Best Single Report Contbg. to Cmty. Welfare award, Milw. Press Club, 1987, Press Club award, 1992, Best Spot News award, Wis. Broadcasters Assn., 1997. Office: WISN PO Box 402 Milwaukee WI 53201-0402

MYLES, MARGARET JEAN, real estate appraiser; b. Detroit, Oct. 26, 1952; d. William Thompson and Patricia M.; 1 child, Tessa Marie. Student, Western Mich. U., 1973, Oakland U., 1974; AA, Coastline C.C., 1986. Unit sec. Hoag Meml. Hosp., Newport Beach, Calif., 1976-80, buyer, 1981-86; real estate appraiser P.M. Myles & Assocs., Irvine, Calif., 1986—, MJM Appraisal Svc., Irvine, Calif. Home: 4531 Wyngate Cir Irvine CA 92604-2345 Office: E Trade Financial Irvine CA 92612

MYLROIE, WILLA WILCOX, transportation engineer, regional planner; b. Seattle, May 30, 1917; d. Elgin Roscoe and Ruth B. (Begg) Wilcox; m. John Ellis Mylroie (dec. 1947); children: Steven Wilcox Mylroie, Jo Mylroie Sohneronne; m. Donald Gile Fassett, Dec. 30, 1966. BS in Civil Engring., U. Wash., 1940, MS in Regional Planning, 1953. Lic. profl. civil engr. Civil engr. U.S. Engring. Dept. C.E., Seattle, 1941-46; affiliate prof. civil engring. U. Wash., Seattle, 1948-51, research asst. prof. civil engring., 1951-56; assoc. prof. civil engring. Purdue U., Lafayette, Ind., 1956-58; research engr. and planner Wash. State Dept. Hwys., Olympia, 1958-69; head research and spl. assignment div. Wash. State Dept. Transp., Olympia, 1969-81; adv. cons. civil engring. and regional planning Thurston County, Wash., 1981-97. Cons. King County Design Commn., Seattle, 1981-89; advisor Coll. Engring. U. Wash., 1978-86, affiliate prof. civil engring., 1981-84; advisor Wash. State U. Coll. Engring., Pullman, 1977-85. Active Girls Scouts county coun., Boy Scouts Am., Olympia, Renton, 1950-56; pres. high sch. PTA, Olympia; commr. Thurston County Planning Commn., Olympia; U.S. Coast Guard Auxilliary, 1982-89, U.S. Power Squadron, 1967—; citizen amb. People to People Trip, Moscow, St. Petersburg, Russia and Muensk, Bolarus. Recipient Profl. Recognition award Women's Transp., Spokane, Spl. Svc. award Transp. Rsch. Bd. Coun., Washington, U. Wash. Coll. Engring. Alumni Achievement award, 1993. Fellow ASCE (ad hoc vis. com. engring. coun. for profl. devel., Edmund Friedman Profl. Recognition award 1978), Inst. Transp. Engrs. (hon. mem., internat. bd. dirs., Tech. Coun. award 1982); mem. Planning Assn. Wash. (bd. dirs.), Sigma Xi. Avocations: sailing, gardening, travel, music, vol. community activities. Home and Office: 7501 Boston Harbor Rd NE Olympia WA 98506-9720

MYRDAL, ROSEMARIE CARYLE, state official, former state legislator; b. Minot, North Dakota, May 20, 1929; d. Harry Dirk and Olga Jean (Dragge) Lohse; m. B. John Myrdal, (dec.) June 21, 1952; children: Jan, Mark, Harold, Paul, Amy. BS, N.D. State U., 1951. first grade tchr., N.D. Tchr., ND, 1951-71; bus. mgr. Edinburg Sch. Dist., ND, 1974-81; mem. N.D. Ho. of Reps., Bismarck, ND, 1984-92, mem. appropriations com., 1991-92; lt. gov. State of N.D., Bismarck, 1993—2001. Sch. evaluator Walsh County Sch. Bd. Assn., Grafton, N.D., 1983-84; evaluator, work presenter N.D. Sch. Bd. Assn., Bismarck, 1983-84; mem. sch. bd. Edinburg Sch. Dist., 1981-90; adv. com. Red River Trade Corridor, Inc., 1989-2001. Co-editor: Heritage '76, 1976, Heritage '89, 1989. Precinct committeewoman Gardar Twp. Rep. Com., 1980-86; leader Hummingbirds 4-H Club, Edinburg, 1980-83; bd. dir. Camp Sioux Diabetic Children, Grand Forks, N.D., 1980-90; N.D. affiliate Am. Diabetes Assn., Families First-Child Welfare Reform Initiative, Region IV, 1989-92; dir. N.D. Diabetes Assn., 1989-91; chmn. N.D. Ednl. Telecom. Coun., 1989-90; vice chmn. N.D. Legis. Interim Jobs Devel. Commn., 1989-90. Mem. AAUW (pres. 1982-84 Pembina County area), Pembina County Hist. Soc. (historian 1976-84); Northeastern N.D. Heritage Assn. (pres. 1986-92), Red River Valley Heritage Soc. (bd. dir. 1985-92); N.D. Sch. to Work Mgmt. Team chairperson Clubs: Agassiz Garden (Park River) (pres. 1968-69). Republican. Lutheran. Avocations: gardening, architecture, ethnic foods, history, cultural preservation. Home: 12987 80th St NE Edinburg ND 58227-9635*

MYRICK, KATHERINE JULIA, minister; b. Hancock, N.Y., Aug. 11, 1947; d. Floyd Daniel and Frances Eleanor Myrick; adopted children: Julia, Victoria. Degree, Northeast Bible Coll., 1969. Ordained minister Gen. Coun. Assemblies of God, 1975. Pastor Maple Lane Assembly of God, Deposit, NY, 1971—; prin. Deposit (N.Y.) Christian Acad., 1979—2000. Evangelist Assembly of God Chs. Bd. dirs. Deposit's (N.Y.) Closet, 2002—03. Mem.: Delta Epsilon Chi. Republican. Avocations: gardening, woodworking, bicycling, hiking. Home: 5 Monument Street Deposit NY 13754 Office: Assembly of God 1 Maple Lane Deposit NY 13754-1211

MYRICK, SUE, congresswoman, former mayor; b. Tiffin, Ohio, Aug. 1, 1941; d. William Henry and Margaret Ellen (Roby) Wilkins; m. Jim Forest (div.); children: Greg, Dan; m. Wilbur Edward Myrick Jr., Sept. 11, 1977. Student, Heidelberg Coll., 1959-60, LLD (hon.), 1995. Exec. sec. to mayor and city mgr. City of Alliance, Ohio, 1962-63; dir. br. office Stark County Ct. of Juvenile and Domestic Rels., Alliance, 1963-65; pres. Myrick Agy., Charlotte, N.C., 1971-95; mayor City of Charlotte, 1987-91; pres. Myrick Enterprises, 1992—94; mem. 104th-108th Congress from 9th N.C. Dist., Washington, 1995—. Candidate for U.S. Senate from N.C., 1992. Active Heart Fund, Multiple Sclerosis, March of Dimes, Arts and Scis. Fund Dr.; past mem. adv. bd. Uptown Shelter, Uptown Homeless Task Force, bd. dirs. N.C. Inst. Politics; v.p. Sister Cities Internat.; mem. Pres. Bush's Affordable Housing Commn.; founder, coord. Charlotte vol. tornado relief effort; former bd. dirs. Learning How; former mem. adv. bd. U.S. Conf. Mayors; mem.-at-large Charlotte City Coun., 1983-85, Strengthening Am. Commn.; lay leader, Sunday sch. tchr. 1st United Meth. Ch.; treas. Mecklenburg Ministries; former trustee U.S. Conf. of Mayors. Recipient Woman of Yr. award Harrisonburg, Va., 1968; named one of Outstanding Young Women of Am., 1968. Mem. Women's Polit. Caucus, Beta Sigma Phi. Republican. Home and Office: Myrick Enterprises 9169 Bonnie Briar Cir Charlotte NC 28277-1576 also: US House Reps 230 Cannon Hob Washington DC 20515-0001

MYRTIS-GARCIA, CARMEN RUTH, social sciences educator; b. Fort Hood, Tex., Oct. 14, 1952; m. Michael Grimes, June 7, 1997; children: J. L. Thompson, M. R. Thompson. BA in Sociology, Colo. State U., Ft. Collins, 1994, MS in Student Affairs in Higher Edn., M in Women's Studies, Colo. State U., Ft. Collins, 1997. Asst. women's studies program developer U. Coll. of Belize, Belize City, Belize, 1996; women's studies instr., curriculum developer Front Range C.C., Ft. Collins, Colo., 1999—. Founder/dir., presenter motivational seminars DreamAchiever Prodns., Ft. Collins, 1997—; founder/dir., workshop presenter, lectr. Sophia's Tree of Life, Ft. Collins, 1997—. Author: (textbook) The Other Half of the World: Goddesses and Women in Prehistory, Antiquity, and the Middle Ages, 2003

(Kendall/Hunt Pub. Co., 2003); contbr. articles to mags. and profl. publs. Recipient Nat. Excellence in Tchg. and Leadership award, Nat. Inst. of Svc. and Orgnl. Devel., 2002. Office: Front Range Cmty Coll 4616 S Shields Fort Collins CO 80526 Personal E-mail: dreamacheiver@hotmail.com. E-mail: carmen.myrtis-garcia@frontrange.edu.

NABEL, ELIZABETH G., medical researcher, cardiologist; BA summa cum laude, St. Olaf Coll., 1974; postgrad., Union Theol. Sem., 1974-75, Columbia U., 1975-77; MD, Cornell U., 1981; DHC (hon.), Katholik U. Leuven, 2001. Diplomate Am. Bd. Internal Medicine and cardiovascular diseases. Intern & resident in internal medicine Brigham and Women's Hosp.-Harvard Med. Sch., Boston, 1981—84, clin. and rsch. fellow cardiovasc. divsn., 1984-87; asst. prof. internal medicine U. Mich., Ann Arbor, 1987-91, assoc. prof. internal medicine, 1991-94, prof. internal medicine, 1994—, dir. Cardiovasc. Rsch. Ctr., 1992—, prof. physiology, 1995—, chief divsn. cardiology, 1997-99; sci. dir. clin. rsch. NIH/NHLBI, Bethesda, Md., 1999—. Mem. sci. adv. bd. Vical Inc., San Diego, 1992—; mem. arteriosclerosis, hypertension, and lipid metabolism adv. com. NHLBI, NIH, 1991-93, parent program project grant rev. com., 1995—, mem. task force on human gene therapy, 1992, mem. cardiology adv. com., 1993-94, mem. spl. emphasis panel arterial thrombosis, 1996; chair sci. pub. com. Am. Heart Assn., 1996-98, bd. of dir, 1996-98; chair Atherosluosis Thrombosis and Vascular Biology Coun., 2002—, Gordon Conf. on Vascular Cell Biology, 1996; pres. N.Am. Vascular Biology Orgn., 1996-97; sci. adv.bd. Keystone Symposia, 1999—, bd. of dir. 2001—; mem. com. on space medicine Inst. of Medicine, 1991-2001; councilor and sec.-treas. Am. Soc. of Clin. Investigation, 2001—; lectr. Mayo Clinic, 1996, Yale Univ., 1997, Univ. of Texas, 1997, Womens Hosp., 1997, 2001, Univ. of Hawaii, 1980, Temple Univ., 1999, John Hopkins, 1999, 2000, 2002, Am. Heart Assn., 1999, Univ. of Mich., 2001, Vanderbilt Univ., 2001, Univ, of Va., 2002, among many others. Assoc. editor Jour. of Clin. Investigation, 1997—2002, mem. editl. bd., 2002—, mem. bd. reviewing editors Science, 1998—, mem. editl. bd. New Eng. Jour. Medicine, 2001—; editor: Trends in Cardiovascular Medicine, 2001; cons. editor Circulation, Circulation Rsch., Atherial Thrombosis and Vascular Biology, 2000—. Fellow Am. Coll. Cardiology, Am. Heart Assn. (basic sci. coun., clin. cardiology coun., circulation coun., atherosclerosis coun., bd. dirs. 1996-97, sci. adv. and coord. com. 1996-97, chair sci. pub. com. 1996-97, sci. pub. com. 1994-96, sci. sessions program com. 1994-95; rsch. fellowship com. Mich. chpt. 1993-95, rsch. grant-in-aid com. 1994-96, vice chair rsch. grant-in-aid com. 1995-96, rsch. exec. com. 1995-96, rsch. com. 1995-96, chair peer rev. rsch. com. 1996-97); mem. AAAS, ACP, Am. Soc. for Biochemistry and Molecular Biology (Amgen Sci. award 1996), Am. Fedn. Clin. Rsch., Am. Soc. Investigative Pathology, Am. Soc. Clin. Investigation, N.Y. Acad. Scis., Am. Soc. Gene Therapy (bd. dirs. 1996), Assn. Am. Physicians, N.Am. Vascular Biology Orgn. (councillor 1994-95, sec., treas. 1994-95, pres. 1996-97), Inst. of Medicine, Ctrl. Soc. Clin. Rsch., Phi Beta Kappa, Alpha Omega Alpha. Office: NIH/NHLBI Bldg 10 Rm 8C103 10 Center Dr Bethesda MD 20892

NACHTIGAL, PATRICIA, lawyer; b. 1946; BA, Montclair State U.; JD, Rutgers U.; LLM, NYU. Tax atty. Ingersoll-Rand Co., Ltd., Hamilton, Bermuda, 1979—83, dir. taxes and legal, 1983—88, sec., mng. atty., 1988—91, v.p., gen. counsel, 1991—2000, sr. v.p., gen. counsel, 2000—, bd. dirs., 2002—. Trustee Rutgers, State U. N.J., 1996—, chair, 2003—04. Office: Ingersoll-Rand Co Ltd 200 Chestnut Ridge Rd Woodcliff Lake NJ 07677

NACK, CLAIRE DURANI, artist, author; b. N.Y.C., NY, Dec. 02; d. Myron Irving and Rachel Rita Adele (Feldman) N. Student, NYU, 1975, Sculpture Ctr., N.Y.C., 1975, Arts Student League. Pres., owner, founder Claire Durani Nack Corp. subs. Princess Enterprs./Durani Co., N.Y.C., 1993; pres. Books of Poetry by Claire Durani Nack, Mystery Stories by Claire Durani Nack, Books of Science Fiction by Claire Durani Nack, Works of Art by Claire Durani Nack, C.D.N. Co. Prof. N.Y. State Mus., Albany, 1992, Hudson Valley C.C., 1986-92, Schenectady (N.Y.) Mus.; lectr. Troy Arts League, 1989. Artist sketchbooks; author (plays for theater); author/artist: Something Happened in the Kitchen, 1981, European Journey, Book II, 1981, Cat Book, 1994, Diary, 2, 1980, Diary, Vol. 4, 1994, Vol. 5, 1994, The Journals of Claire Durani Nack, 1994, Art Book 1, 1982, Art Book 2, 1982, My World, 1999, Blue Book, Upwards Bent (books 1-5), 1993-94, Spiders Web Unspun, 1994, An Unfamiliar Place, 1993, The Adventures of Cora, 1994 (books 1-5), Cahiers de Dessins de Paris, 1994, Big City Lights, 1991, Something Happened in the Bathroom, 1981, Something Happened in the Living Room, 1981, Children's Coloring Books, 1995, Animal Book, 1995, The Adventures of Cora, Plot, Counterplot, Plot, 1997, All About Life, Sorrow and Joy, Essays and Soliliquies, Stoolie the Ghoulie, The Small Book of Art, The Gold Book, 1997, The Book of Art, 1997, Conversations with Myself, 2003, Facts, Fools and Ghools, 1997, All About Life, 1997, Sorrow and Joy, 1997, The Silver Book, 1997, A Light's Work, 1997, (play) The Agenda, 1997, 2003, Being C, 1997, (play) Not the Marrying Kind, Liz Muller, Alive, 1998, The Cheerful Book, 1998, Essays and Soliloquies, 1998, Questions and Answers, 1998, The Prosecuting Lawyer, 1998, Life's a Theatre, 1999, (short story)The Cheetah, 1999, Toulouse Lautrec and Claire Durani Nack, 1999, The Scrapbook of Claire Durani Nack, 1998, The Album of Claire Durani Nack, 1999, Life's a Theatre, 1999, The Portfolio of Claire Durani Nack in Paris, 1999, Conversations with Myself, Garden of the Orient, 2001, Dating, Waiting & Mating, The Orange Book, Excavations and Illuminations, Elizabeth Getty, The BroRon Doll and Elizabeth Getty Repaired. Recipient poetry award Nat. Libr. of Poetry, Calif., 1991; scholar Art Students League, 1985. Mem. Nat. Mus. of Women in the Arts (charter mem.), Art Students League (life), N.Y. State Mus. Avocations: travel, collecting model airplanes, collecting hats, art and art books, Am. and European real estate. Office: 416 East St Rensselaer NY 12144-2303

NACOL, MAE, lawyer; b. Beaumont, Tex., June 15, 1944; d. William Samuel and Ethel (Bowman) N.; children: Shawn Alexander Nacol, Catherine Regina Nacol. BA, Rice U., 1965; postgrad., South Tex. Coll. Law, 1966. Bar: Tex. 1969, U.S. Dist. Ct. (so. dist.) Tex. 1969. Pvt. practice law, Houston, 1969—; escrow officer Commonwealth Land Title Co., Houston; mem. bd. devel. Prosperity Bank, Houston. Author, editor ednl. materials on multiple sclerosis, 1981-85. Nat. dir. A.R.M.S. of Am. Ltd., Houston, 1984-85. Recipient Mayor's Recognition award City of Houston, 1972. Mem. Fed. Bar Assn., Houston Bar Assn. (chmn. candidate com. 1970, membership com. 1971, chmn. lawyers referral com. 1972), Assn. Trial Lawyers Am., Tex. Trial Lawyers Assn., Am. Judicature Soc. (sustaining), Houston Fin. Coun. Women, Houston Trial Lawyers Assn. Presbyterian. Office: 600 Jefferson St Ste 750 Houston TX 77002 also: 8401 Westheimer Ste 104 Houston TX 77063

NADELMAN, CYNTHIA J. writer, editor; b. Naples, Italy, Aug. 2, 1953; (parents Am. citizens); d. E. Jan and Joyce V. (Cavanah) N. AB, Bryn Mawr Coll., 1975. Editl. asst. ARTnews mag., N.Y.C., 1978-80, asst. editor, 1980-81, assoc. editor, 1981-83, sr. editor, 1983-84, freelance writer, editor, 1984—. Assoc. editor Drawing mag., 1984-86, contbg. editor ARTnews mag., 1984—; oral-history interviewer Archives of Am. Art, 1987-91; contbr. articles, reviews, poems to mags. and jours. Fellow Ingram Merrill Found., 1990, N.Y. Found. for the Arts, 1993. Mem. Internat. Art Critics Assn., Authors Guild. Home and Office: 205 W 91st St Apt 5B New York NY 10024-1316

NADELSON, CAROL COOPERMAN, psychiatrist, educator; b. Bklyn., Oct. 13, 1936; m. Theodore Nadelson, July 16, 1965; children: Robert, Jennifer. BA magna cum laude, Bklyn. Coll., 1957; MD with honors, U. Rochester, N.Y., 1961. Dir. med. student edn. Beth Israel Hosp., Boston, 1974-79, psychiatrist, 1977; assoc. prof. psychiatry Harvard U. Med. Sch., Boston, 1976-79; rsch. scholar Radcliffe Coll., Cambridge, Mass., 1979-80; prof. psychiatry Tufts Med. Sch., Boston, 1979-95; vice-chmn., dir. tng. and edn. dept. psychiatry Tufts-New Eng. Med. Ctr., Boston, 1979-93; clin. prof. psychiatry Harvard Med. Sch., Boston, 1995—; psychiatrist dept. medicine, divsn. psychiatry Brigham and Women's Hosp., Boston, 1998, [illegible] office for [illegible], 1998. Cons. Peace Corps, 2000. Editor: The Woman Patient, Vols. 1, 2 and 3, 1978, 82; Treatment Interventions in Human Sexuality, 1983; Marriage and Divorce: A Contemporary Perspective, 1984, Women Physicians in Leadership Roles, 1986, Training Psychiatrists for the '90s, 1987, Treating Chronically Mentally Ill Women, 1988, Family Violence, 1988, Women and Men: New Perspectives on Gender Differences, 1990, International Review of Psychiatry Vols. 1 & 2, 1993, 96, Major Psychiatric Disorders, 1982, The Challenge of Change: Perspectives on Family, Work and Education, 1983; editor-in-chief Am. Psychiatric Press, Inc., 1986—, pres., CEO, 1995—; contbr. over 217 articles to profl. jours. Trustee Menninger Found., 1988—. Recipient Gold Medal award Mt. Airy Psychiat. Ctr., 1981, award Case Western Res. U., 1983, Elizabeth Blackwell award Am. Med. Women's Assn., 1985, Women in Medicine Leadership Devel. award Am. Assn. Med. Colls., 1999, Alexandra Symonds award 2002; Picker Found. grant, 1982-83. Fellow: Am. Psychiat. Assn. (pres. 1985—86, Seymour D. Vestermark award 1992, Disting. Svc. award 1995), Ctr. Advanced Study Behavioral Scos.; mem.: AMA (impaired physicians com. 1984, Sidney Cohen award 1988), Group for Advancement of Psychiatry (bd. dirs. 1984), Am. Coll. Psychiatrists (bd. regents 1991—94, Disting. Svc. award 1989), Phi Beta Kappa, Alpha Omega Alpha. Avocation: travel. Office: Brigham and Women's Hosp 75 Francis St PB502 Boston MA 02119- Home: 30 Amory St Brookline MA 02446 E-mail: carol_nadelson@hms.harvard.edu.

NADER, LAURA, anthropology educator; b. Winsted, Conn., Sept. 30, 1930; m. Norman Milleron, Sept. 1, 1962; 3 children BA, Wells Coll., 1952; PhD, Radcliffe Coll., 1962. Mem. faculty U. Calif.-Berkeley, 1960—, now prof. anthropology; vis. prof. Yale Law Sch., New Haven, fall 1971; Henry R. Luce prof. Wellesley Coll., Mass., 1983-84; Henry R. Luce prof. Sch. Law Harvard U., 1987-89, Stanford U., 1987-89. Field work in Mex., Lebanon, Morocco; mem. adv. com. NSF, 1971-75; mem. cultural anthropology com. NIMH, 1968—, chmn. to 1971, chmn. social scis. research tng. rev. com., 1976-78; mem. NAS-NRC assembly behavioral and social scis., 1969-71, 73-75, 75—; mem. com. Nuclear and Alternative Energy Forms, NAS, 1976-77. Editor: Law in Culture and Society, 1969, The Disputing Process, 1978, No Access to Law-Alternatives to the American Judicial System, 1980, Harmony Ideology, 1990, Naked Science, 1996, The Life of the Law, 2002; contbr. articles to profl. jours.; author ednl. films, mem. editl. com. Law and Soc. Rev., 1967—. Mem. Calif. Council for the Humanities, 1975-79; mem. Carnegie Council on Children, 1972-77; active Coun. Librs. at Libr. of Congress, Washington, 1988—. Radcliffe Coll. grantee, 1954-59; Thaw fellow Harvard U., 1955-56, 58-59; Peabody Mus. grantee, 1954-59; Am. Philos. Assn. grantee, 1955; Mexican Govt. grantee, 1957-58; Milton Fund grantee, 1959-60, Wellness Found. grantee, 1993-96; fellow Ctr. Advanced Study in Behavioral Scis., Stanford, Calif., 1963-64; NSF grantee, 1966-68; Wenner Gren Found. grantee, 1964, 66, 73; Carnegie Corp. grantee, 1975; Woodrow Wilson fellow, 1979-80; Wells Coll. Alumnae award, 1980; Radcliffe Coll. Alumnae award, 1984 Mem.: AAAS, Soc. Women Geographers, Am. Acad. Arts and Scis., Ctr. for Study of Responsive Law (trustee 1968—), Law and Soc. Assn. (trustee 1967—72), Social Sci. Rsch. Coun., Am. Anthrop. Assn. (planning and devel. com. 1968—71, 1975—76), Am. Acad. Arts and Scis. Office: U Calif Dept Anthropology 313 Kroeber Hl Berkeley CA 94720-0001

NADLER-HURVICH, HEDDA CAROL, public relations executive; b. Bronx, N.Y., June 15, 1944; d. Julius Louis and Julia Cohen; m. David George Nadler, Oct. 3, 1965 (div. 1979); 1 child, Laura Lee Nadler ; m. Burton Earl Hurvich, Dec. 8, 1984. BBA, Baruch Coll., 1965. V.p., sec. Irving L. Straus Assocs., Inc., N.Y.C., 1965-80; pres. Mount & Nadler Inc., N.Y.C., 1999—. Avocations: aerobics, yoga. Office: Mount & Nadler 425 Madison Ave New York NY 10017-1110 E-mail: Hedda615@aol.com.

NADROTOSKA, BARBARA ANNA, art educator; b. Stamford, Conn., Aug. 25, 1938; d. Michael and Gladys Nadrotoski. BFA, Pratt Inst., 1960; M in Liberal Arts, U. South Fla., 1989. Art dir. Heim Advt., Sarasota, Fla., 1979—83, Hunt-Wilde, Tampa, Fla., 1983—84; freelance designer Tampa, 1984—85; graphic designer Hillsboro Printing, Tampa, 1985—88; art dir. AAA Auto Clubs, Tampa, 1988—91; instr. art Remington Coll., Tampa, 1991—2003. Adj. prof. humanities U. South Fla., Tampa, 1995—2003. Exhibitions include Warde-Nasse Gallery, N.Y.C., 1975—76, Lever House Gallery, 1976, Woman's Art Ctr. Gallery, Sarasota, 1979—82, Fla. Ctr. for Contemporary Art, Tampa, 1987, 1991, Lee Scarfone Gallery, 1989—99, Art Ctr. Sarasota, 1990, St. Petersburg (Fla.) Art Ctr., 1998—2001, J.J. Watts Studio Gallery, Tampa, 1999—2000, Gold Dragon Gallery, 2001—02. Scholar Pratt Inst., Scholastic Mag., N.Y.C., 1956, U. South Fla., Tampa, 1988. Mem.: Friday Morning Musicale, Women Artists Rising, Nat. Mus. Women in the Arts, St. Petersburg Arts Ctr., Tampa Mus. Art. Home: 8730 N Himes Ave #1010 Tampa FL 33614

NAEGLE, MADELINE ANNE, mental health nurse, educator; b. Penn Yan, N.Y., Feb. 2, 1942; d. Lester Lawrence and Nona Caroline (Muir) N.; m. James Michael McGowan, Aug. 6, 1966 (div. 1984); children: Amanda Allen, Benjamin Logan. BS, Nazareth Coll. Rochester, 1964; MA, NYU, 1967, PhD, 1980. Staff nurse Syracuse (N.Y.) Meml. Hosp., summer 1964; staff nurse, asst. head nurse Payne Whitney Clinic, N.Y.C., 1964-65; instr. nursing Herbert H. Lehman Coll., Bronx, N.Y., 1972-75, part-time instr. nursing, 1975-78; asst. clin. prof. Sch. Nursing U. Pa., Phila., 1979-83; pvt. practice N.Y.C., 1980—; assoc. prof. Leinhard Sch. Nursing Pace U., Pleasantville, N.Y., 1983-85; prof. div. nursing NYU, N.Y.C., 1985—2003, prof., 2003—. Cons. The Day Sch., 1980-84; mem. N.Y. State Gov.'s Health Care Adv. Bd., 1991-94. Author: Nursing Process with Clients Using Drugs, 1993, Patterns of Substance Abuse, 1996; author, editor: (model curriculum) Substance Abuse Education in Nursing, 1991; editor Addictions Nursing, 1988-98, Addictions and Substance Abuse: Stratgies for Advanced Nursing Practice, 2000; contbr. articles to profl. jours. Recipient Presdl. Citation award N.Y. County RN Assn., 1986, Amanda Silver Disting. Svc. award N.Y. County RN Assn., 1994; named Outstanding Alumna, Nazareth Coll. of Rochester, 2000; inducted into Acad. Women Achievers, YWCA, 1991; USPHS fellow, 1978-79, Pres.'s award Nat. Nurses Soc. on Addiction; grantee Nat. Inst. Alcohol Abuse and Alcoholism, Nat. Inst. Drug Abuse, 1989-90, Ctr. for Substance Abuse Prevention, 1990-95, U.S. Human Resources Adminstrn., 1999; Fulbright scholar U. Malta, 1995. Fellow: Am. Acad. Nursing; mem.: ANA (com. chair 1987—89, com. on addiction 1999, nominating com. 1996—2000, pres.-elect 1987—89, pres. 1989—91, Hildegard Peplau award 2002), Assn. Med. Educators and Rschrs. in Substance Abuse, N.Y. State Nurses Assn. (chair com. on impaired nursing practice 1986—88), Sigma Theta Tau. Democrat. Avocations: hiking, running, dance, theatre, music. Office: NYU Div Nursing 246 Greene St New York NY 10003-6677 Business E-Mail: MAN1@nyu.edu.

NAESER, NANCY DEARIEN, geologist, researcher; b. Morgantown, W.Va., Apr. 15, 1944; d. William Harold and Katherine Elizabeth (Dearien) Cozad; m. Charles Wilbur Naeser, Feb. 6, 1982. BS, U. Ariz., 1966; PhD, Victoria U., Wellington, New Zealand, 1973. Geol. field asst. U.S. Geol. Survey, Flagstaff, Ariz., 1966; sci. editor New Zealand Jour. Geology and Geophysics, New Zealand Dept. Sci. and Indsl. Rsch., Wellington, 1974-76; postdoctoral rsch. assoc. U. Toronto, 1976-79, U.S. Geol. Survey, Denver, 1979-81, geologist, 1981—. Adj. prof. Dartmouth Coll., Hanover, NH, 1985—97, U. Wyo., Laramie, 1984—91. Editor: Thermal History of Sedimentary Basins--Methods and Case Histories, 1989, Debris-Flow Hazards - Mechanics, Prediction and Assessment, 2000; contbr. articles on fission-track analysis to profl. jours. Docent, Denver Zoo, 1991-99. Fulbright fellow, New Zealand, 1967-68. Fellow Geol. Soc. Am.; mem. Am. Assn. Petroleum Geologists, Geol. Soc. New Zealand, Mortar Board, Phi Kappa Phi. Methodist. Office: US Geol Survey Mail Stop 926 A 12201 Sunrise Valley Dr Reston VA [illegible] E-mail: [illegible]

NAEVE, CATHERINE ANN, secondary school educator; b. Long Beach, Calif., Aug. 20, 1946; d. Harry Naeve, Jr. and Rae Catherine (Sieler) Coyle. AA, Long Beach City Coll., 1966; BA, Calif. State U., Long Beach, 1969, Tchg. Credential, 1970, MA, 1972; Spl. Edn. Credential, Calif. State U., Turlock, 1981. Lectr. Calif. State U., Long Beach, 1972-75; tchr. Locke H.S., L.A., 1975-78, Mark Twain Jr. H.S., Modesto, Calif., 1980-84, Beyer H.S., Modesto, Calif., 1984-93, Johansen H.S., Modesto, Calif., 1993—. Chair student sect. Calif. Assn. for Health, Physical Edn., Recreation & Dance, Long Beach, 1968-70, publ. chair, 1978-82; chair women's coaches L.A. City Schs., 1978-80; chairperson spl. edn. curriculum Modesto City Sch., 1987—, chair elem. spl. edn. curriculum, 1997—. Trustee First Bapt. Ch., Linden, Calif., 1989-97, sound technician, 1983—; mentor tchr. Modesto City Sch., 1986-88; sound technician No. Calif. Youth Choir (So. Bapt. Chs.). Recipient Hall of Fame award Coaches L.A. Women's Coaches, 1989, Disting. Svc. award Calif. Girls and Women in Sports, 1989, Cert. of Appreciation and Recognition Modesto City Schs.-Project Workability, 1990, 91, CIF Pioneer award. Mem. Computer Using Educators, Coun. for Exceptional Children. Home: PO Box 22 21596 E Acampo Rd Clements CA 95227 Office: Johansen HS 641 Norseman Dr Modesto CA 95357-0405

NAGLE, CAROL ANN, elementary school educator; b. Chgo., July 20, 1956; d. Edward O'Brien and Barbara Ann Martin; m. Walter David Nagle, Nov. 28, 1980; children: Kelly Lynn, Mackenzie Kate. AA, Moraine Valley C.C., Palos Hills, Ill., 1979; BA in Edn., Gov. State U., 1989; EdM, U. Ill., 1997. Substitute tchr. South Suburban Chgo. Sch. Dist., 1989—93; tchr. grade 4 Kirby Dist. 140, Tinley Park, Ill., 1993—94, title I tchr., 1994—98, lang. specialist, 1998—. Mem.: Ill. ASCD (curriculum cons. 2001—). Avocations: reading, yoga, walking, camping, bicycling. Office: Helen Keller Elem Sch 7846 163rd St Tinley Park IL 60477-1299

NAGLE, JEAN SUSAN KARABACZ, sociologist, psychologist; b. Detroit, 1936; d. Peter and Hedy (Grusczynski) Karabacz; m. Robert D. Nagle, Nov. 20, 1956; children: Carl A., Sonya L., Paula E. BS in Sociology, Wayne State U., 1956; postgrad., U. Chgo., 1953-55; MA, N.Mex. Highlands U., 1960; PhD, Union Grad. Sch., 1977; postgrad., Bryn Mawr. Inst., 1981. Diagnostic technician Vocat. Counseling Inst., Detroit, 1952; rsch. technician United Auto Workers-CIO, Detroit, 1958; clin. psychology intern N.Mex. State Hosp., Las Vegas, 1962-63; clin. psychology trainee VA Hosp., Omah and Lincoln, Nebr., 1963-64; instr. sociology N.W. Mo. State U., Maryville, 1965-70, prof. sociology and psychology, 1971-92, ret., 1992. Bd. dirs. Inst. Discourse. Grantee N.W. Mo. State U., 1981, 82. Mem. APA, Am. Sociol. Assn., Am. Psychol. Soc., Midwest Sociol. Soc., Psychology/Sociology Club, Mo. Psychol. Assn., World Federalists, Psi Chi, Pi Gamma Mu. also: 3106 E 80th St Kansas City MO 64132-3638

NAGRA, PARMINDER, actress; b. Leicester, England, Oct. 5, 1975; Actor: (films) Bend It Like Bechham, 2002, Ella Enchanted, 2004; (TV series) Turning World, 1996, Always and Everyone, 1999, ER, 2003—; (TV films) King Girl, 1996, Donovan Quick, 1999, Twelfth Night, 2003, Second Generation, 2003. Office: NBC/ER 4000 Warner Blvd Burbank CA 91522*

NAGTALON-MILLER, HELEN ROSETE, humanities educator; b. Honolulu, June 27, 1928; d. Dionicio Reyes and Fausta Dumrigue (Rosete) Nagtalon-Miller; m. Robert Lee Ruley Miller, June 15, 1952. BEd, U. Hawaii, 1951; Diplôme, The Sorbonne, Paris, 1962; MA, U. Hawaii, 1967; PhD, Ohio State U., 1972. Cert. secondary education educator. Tchr. humanities Hawaii State Dept. Edn., Honolulu, 1951-63; supr. student tchrs. French lab. sch. Coll. of Edn. U. Hawaii, Honolulu, 1963-66, instr. French, coord. French courses Coll. Arts and Scis., 1966-69; teaching asst. Coll. Edn. Ohio State U., Columbus, 1970-72; instr. French lab. sch. Coll. Edn. U. Hawaii, Honolulu, 1974-76; adminstr. bilingual-bicultural edn. project Hawaii State Dept. Edn., Honolulu, 1975—76; coord. disadvantaged minority recruitment program Sch. Social Work, U. Hawaii, Honolulu, 1976—83; coord. tutor tng. program U. Hawaii, Honolulu, 1983—85; program dir. Multicultural Multifunctional Resource Ctr., Honolulu, 1985—86; vis. prof. Sch. Pub. Health, ret. U. Hawaii, Honolulu, 1986—91. Bd. dirs. Hawaii Assn. Lang. Tchrs., Honolulu, 1963-66, Hawaii Com. for the Humanities, 1977-83; mem. statewide adv. coun. State Mental Health Adv. Com., Honolulu, 1977-82; task force mem. Underrepresentation of Filipinos in Higher Edn., Honolulu, 1984-86. Author: (with others) Notable Women in Hawaii, 1984; contbr. articles to profl. jours. Chairperson edn. and counseling subcom. First Gov.'s Commn. on Status of Women, Honolulu, 1964; vice chairperson Honolulu County Com. on the Status of Women, 1975—76, Hawaii State Dr. Martin Luther King Jr. Commn., Honolulu, 1982—85; pres. Filipino-Am. Hist. Soc. of Hawaii, 1980—2000; mem. Hawaii State Adv. Com. to U.S. Commn. on Civil Rights, 1981—, chairperson, 1982—85; bd. dirs. Japanese Am. Citizens League Honolulu chpt., 1990—2001, mem. Hawaiian Sovereignty com., 1994—98, Protect Our Constitution; mem. Pro-Choice Polit. Action Com., 1989—92. Women of Distinction, Honolulu County Com. on Status of Women, 1982; recipient Nat. Edn. Assn. award for Leadership in Asian and Pacific Island Affairs, NEA, 1985, Alan F. Saunders award ACLU in Hawaii, 1986, Disting. Alumni award U. Hawaii Alumni Affairs Office, 1994. Mem. Filipino Am. Nat. Hist. Soc., Filipino Coalition for Solidarity, Gabriela Network (Hawaii chpt.), Filipino Cmty. Ctr., Philippine Centennial Coordinating Com./Hawaii, NOW, Alliance Française of Hawaii, Rainbow Peace Fund. Democrat. Avocations: social-political advocacy, reading, classical music, theater, literary presentations. Home and Office: 47-543 Halemanu St Kaneohe HI 96744-4604 E-mail: rlrmiller@earthlink.net.

NAGY, CHRISTA FIEDLER, biochemist; b. Marienbad, Czech Republic, July 8, 1943; d. Herbert A. Fiedler and Anna C. (Gluth) Rathmann; m. Bela Imre Nagy, Aug. 22, 1969; 1 child, Byron. BS in Biology, Fairleigh Dickinson U., 1967, MS in Biochemistry, 1974; PhD in Biochemistry, Rutgers U., 1981. Sr. scientist Hoffmann-La Roche Inc., Nutley, N.J., 1981-88, assoc. rsch. investigator, 1988-95; asst. dir. preclin. rsch. Eisai Inc., Teaneck, N.J., 1997-98, assoc. dir. clin. pharmacology, 1998—. Mem.: AAAS, Am. Soc. Clin. Pharmacology and Therapeutics, Drug Info. Assn., Am. Soc. Biol. Chemists, N.Y. Acad. Scis. Roman Catholic. Avocations: travel, skiing, tennis, hiking. Office: Eisai Inc Glenpointe Ctr E 300 Franklin Burr Blvd Teaneck NJ 07666-6741 Personal E-mail: nagychrista@excite.com.

NAGYS, ELIZABETH ANN, environmental issues educator; b. St. Louis; d. Dallas and Miriam (Miller) Nichols; m. Sigi Nagys, Feb. 7, 1970; children: Eric M., Jennifer R., Alex E. BS., So. Ill. U. Extenstion, Edwardsville, 1970. Cert. tchr., Mo., Ill. Announcer Sta. KMTY, Clovis, N.Mex., 1970-71; substitue tchr. Ritneour Sch. Dist., Overland, Mo., 1977-78; instr. biology, environ. issues Southwestern Mich. Coll., Dowagiac, Mich., 1988-92; exec. v.p. Profl. Sound Designers, Goshen, Ind., 1994-96; customer svc. coord. Meijer, Inc., 1995-96; constrn. adminstr. Trans Eastern Homes, Weston, Fla., 1997—98, Trafalger Assocs., 1998—99. Reviewer textbooks Harcourt, Brace & Co., 1993; notary pub. State of Fla., 1999—. Active Nat. Arbor Day Found.; hazardous waste com. Elkhart County, Ind., 1991—94; asst. dir. South Fla. Folk Festival, 1998—2003, dir., 2003—; bd. dirs. United Meth. Ch., Marvin Park, 1979—84; coord. United Meth. Women, 1980—87; bd. dirs., corr. sec. Broward Folk Club, 1998—2003; charter mem. Holocaust Meml. Mus.; assoc. mem. Art Inst. Chgo. Mem. AAUW (v.p. Goshen 1994-96), Nat.

Audubon Soc., Nat. Women's History Mus. (charter mem.), Sierra Club, Welcome Wagon Club. Avocations: reading, gardening.

NAHUMCK, NADIA CHILKOVSKY, performer, dance educator, choreographer, author; b. Kiev, Ukraine, Jan. 8, 1908; came to U.S., 1914; d. Moiseiy Nicholas and Bela (Segalova) Chilkovsky; m. Nicholas Nahumck, Mar. 1940 (dec. Nov. 1994). BS in Edn., Temple U., 1928; MusD, Combs Coll. Music, 1971; postgrad., U. Pa., 1973-74; D Dance (hon.), Phila. Coll. Performing Arts, 1979. Founder, dir. Phila. Dance Acad., 1946-77; dean sch. dance Phila. Coll. Performing Arts (now Univ. Arts), 1977-79, dean emeritus, 1979—. Instr. Curtis Inst. Music, Phila., 1946-68, Acad. Vocal Arts, Phila., 1958-78; vis. lectr. Temple U., Phila., 1944-45, 67, 69, Swarthmore (Pa.) Coll., 1958-60, Thomas Jefferson U., 1976; lectr. in dance ethnology U. Pa. Mus., 1973-76; vis. rsch. scholar Rhodes U., 1977; founder Performing Arts Sch. for combined arts and acad. edn., 1962. Author: Three R's for Dancing, book I, 1953, book II, 1956, book III, 1960, My First Dance Book, 1954, Isadora Duncan: The Dances, 1994, Ten Dances in Labanotation, 1955, Three R's for Dancing, 1955, 3d edit., 1960, Short Modern Dances in Labanotation, 1957, American Bandstand Dances, 1959, Introduction to Dance Literacy, 1978, Dance Curriculum Resource Guide, 1980, Interpretation of the Labanotated Duncan Dance Scores, 2000; contbr. articles to profl. jours.; choreographer 75 works including 5 with Phila. Orch., 1947-50; prodr. 17 dance films for classroom use. Mary Wigman Profl. Dance Sch./Steinway Hall scholar, 1931-32; grantee U.S. Office of Edn., 1965-67, Wenner-Gren Found., 1965, 73. Fellow Internat. Coun. Kinetography Laban; mem. Internat. Isadora Duncan Inst. Coun., Soc. Ethnomusicology (coun. 1958-63, Svc. award 1976, master notator 1965—), Nat. Mus. Women in the Arts (charter mem.). Avocations: language studies, music, gardening, mentoring young students, reading.

NAIDU, JENNY, principal; b. Durban, South Africa, July 21, 1949; arrived in U.S., 1987; d. Krishnasamy and Bangaramma Naidoo, m. Gona Naidu, Jan. 7, 1972; children: Kershini, Loushaana, Latasha. BA, U. South Africa, 1976, BEd, 1980; MEd, U. Akron, 1989; D, Kent State U., 2000. Tchr. Indian Edn. Dept., Durban, 1970—73, dept. head, 1973—88; prof. Kent State U., Ohio, 1988—90; supr. Early Childhood Head Start, Akron, 1990—95; asst. prin. Akron Pub. Schs., 1996—. Prof. U. Akron, 1990—; adv. bd. mem. Coming Together Project, Akron, 1999—2002; bd. mem. Internat. Inst., Akron, 1999—2001; mem. fed. rev. Nat. Head Start, Chgo., 1990—. Mediator Common Ground, Akron, 1990; reviewer Coun. for Devel. Early Childhood, Washington, 2000. Recipient Merit award, Ohio Dept. Edn., 1993, Outstanding award, Nat. Multicultural Inst., 1995. Mem.: Nat. assn. Secondary Prins., Law Against Poverty. Avocations: photography, reading, gardening, art, home decorating.*

NAJIMY, KATHY, actress; Actress theater The Kathy and Mo Show, 1985 89 (also writer)(Obie award, 1989), Afterbirth: Kathy and Mo's Greatest Hits, 2004; Broadway shows Dirty Blonde, 2001; films Topsy and Bunker, Other People's Money, 1991, The Hard Way, 1991, The Fisher King, 1991, Soapdish, 1991, This Is My Life, 1992, Sister Act, 1992, Hocus Pocus, 1993, Sister Act 2: Back in the Habit, 1993, It's Pat, 1994, Jeffrey, 1995, Cats Dont' Dance, 1997, Nevada, 1997, Woman Without Implants, 1997, Hope Floats, 1998, Zack and Reba, 1998, Bride of Chucky, 1998, Attention Shoppers, 2000, Leaving Peoria, 2000, The Wedding Planner, 2001, Rat Race, 2001; TV: King of the Hill (voice), 1997-, Veronica's Closet, 1997-2001, TV movies: If These Walls Could Talk II, 2000, The Scream Team, 2002. Office: Creative Arts Agy 9830 Wilshire Blvd Beverly Hills CA 90212-1804*

NAKAJIMA, YASUKO, medical educator; b. Osaka, Japan, Jan. 8, 1932; came to U.S., 1962, 69; m. Shigehiro Nakajima; children: Hikeko H., Gene A. MD, U. Tokyo, 1955, PhD, 1962. Intern U. Tokyo Sch. Medicine, 1955-56, resident, 1956-57, instr., 1962-67; assoc. prof. Purdue U., West Lafayette, Ind., 1969-76, prof., 1976-88; prof. anatomy and cell biology U. Ill. Coll. Medicine, Chgo., 1988—. Vis. rsch. fellow Coll. Physicians and Surgeons, Columbia U., N.Y.C., 1962-64; asst. rsch. anatomist UCLA Sch. Medicine, 1964-65; vis. rsch. fellow Cambridge U., 1967-69; mem. study sect. NIH, 1996-98. Contbr. articles to sci. jours. Fulbright travel grantee, 1962-65; Univ. scholar U. Ill., 1997—. Mem. AAAS, Am. Physiol. Soc., Soc. Neurosci., Am. Soc. Cell Biology, Am. Assn. Anatomists, Biophys. Soc., Marine Biol. Lab. Corp. Office: U Ill Coll Medicine Dept Anatomy m/c 512 808 S Wood St Chicago IL 60612-7300

NAKAMURA, KIMIKO, language educator; b. Fukui-Ken, Japan, Feb. 11, 1945; arrived in USA, 1966; d. Toshiji and Emiko Matsumura; m. Takamitsu Nakamura, Jan. 22, 1966; children: Takashi, Yoko. BM, Osaka Coll. Music, Japan, 1966; MusB, DePaul U., 1993; MusM, Valparaiso U., 1996. Japanese tchr. Inland/EastPack Co., Ea. Chgo., 1987—. Piano instr. O'Day Music Sch., Highland, Ind., 1999—. Mem.: Nat. Guild Piano Tchrs., Japan-Am. Soc. (Japanese lang. tchr. 1996—). Office: Japan America Soc Chgo 20 N Clark St Ste 750 Chicago IL 60602

NAKANISHI, YUKO JULIE, engineering educator, consultant; b. Westland, Mich. d. Ukyo Stanley and Tatsuko Ann Nakanishi; life ptnr. Larry Lifschultz. BA in English Lit., Harvard U., 1987; MBA, Columbia U., 1993; MSCE, CCNY, 1997; PhD in Civil Engring., Polytech U., 2004. Chair NY Area Data Coun., NYC, 1997-99; sr. tchg. assoc., cons. Rensselaer Poly. Inst., Troy, NY, 1999-2000; program mgr. Urban ITS Ctr. Poly. U., Bklyn., 2000—; chair subcommittee on tng., ed., and tech. transfer, 2003—. Chair Freight and Intermodal Transp. Data Com., NY, 1997-2000; asst. dir. Univ. Transp. Rsch. Ctr., NYC, 1996-99; info. svc. com. Transp. Rsch. Bd., 1998—, critical transp. infrastructure protection com., chair edn., tng. and tech. transfer subcom. Contbr. articles to profl. jours. Fellow Eisenhower fellow, 1997—2000, Eno fellow, 2001. Mem. IEEE, ASCE, Inst. Transp. Engr., Intelligent Transp. Soc. NY (bd. dir.), NY Data Coun. Bd. of Dir. Office: Poly U 6 Metrotech Ctr Brooklyn NY 11201 Home: 93-40 Queens Blvd 6A Rego Park NY 11374 E-mail: ynakanis@poly.edu., ynakan@aol.com.

NAKAYAMA, PAULA AIKO, state supreme court justice; b. Honolulu, Oct. 19, 1953; m. Charles W. Totto; children: Elizabeth Murakami, Alexander Totto. BS, U. Calif., Davis, 1975; JD, U. Calif., 1979. Bar: Hawaii 1979. Dep. pros. atty. City and County of Honolulu, 1979-82; ptnr. Shim, Tam & Kirimitsu, Honolulu, 1982-92; judge 1st Cir. Ct. State of Hawaii, Oahu, 1992-93; justice State of Hawaii Supreme Ct., Honolulu, 1993—. Mem. Am. Judicature Soc., Hawaii Bar Assn., Sons and Daughters of 442. Office: Hawaii Supreme Ct Ali'iolani Hale 417 S King St Honolulu HI 96813-2902*

NAKER, MARY LESLIE, legal firm executive; b. Elgin, Ill., July 6, 1954; d. Robert George and Marilyn Jane (Swain). BS in Edn., No. Ill. U., 1976, MS in Edn., 1978, postgrad., 1980, Coll. Fin. Planning, 1990. Cert. tchr., Ill., fin. paraplanner. Retail sales clk. Fin'n Feather Farm, Dundee, Ill., 1972-75; pvt. practice tchr. South Elgin, Ill., 1974-78; tchg. asst. Sch. Dist #13, Bloomingdale, Ill., 1976-78, substitute tchr.; office mgr. Tempo 21, Carol Stream, Ill., 1978-82, LaGrange, Ill., 1982-85; sales coord. K&R Delivery, Hinsdale, Ill., 1986-89; fin. planner coord. Elite Adv. Svcs., Inc., Schaumburg, Ill., 1989-90; adminstrv. coord. Export Transports, Inc., Elk Grove Village, Ill., 1990-98; adminstrn. mgr. SBS Worldwide Chgo. Inc., Bensenville, Ill., 1998-99; office adminstr. DiMonte & Lizak, Attys. at Law, Park Ridge, Ill., 2000—. Leader Girl Scouts U.S.A., 1972—77, camp counselor, 1972—79; Sunday sch. tchr., 1999—. Music Scholar PTA, U. Wis., 1967, PTA, U. Iowa, 1968-69. Mem. Nat. Geographic Soc., Smithsonian Assn. Lutheran. Avocations: ceramics, bowling, knitting, camping, sewing. Home: 2020 Clearwater Way Elgin IL 60123-2588 Office: DiMonte & Lizak 216 Higgins Rd Park Ridge IL 60068-5706

NAKHLE, DJENANE, psychologist; b. Cairo, Oct. 9, 1945; came to U.S., 1981; children: Joëlle, Sabrina. BA in Psychology cum laude, NYU, 1988, MA in Psychology, 1992, PhD in Child and Sch. Psychology, 1995. Lic. psychologist, N.Y.; cert. sch. psychologist, N.Y. Staff psychologist Special Needs Clinic Columbia-Presbyn. Med. Ctr., 1994-95, supervising staff psychologist Special Needs Clinic, 1995-97, dir. therapeutics, 1997-98, supervising psychologist dept. pediatric psychiatry, 1998, 1998—; supervising psychologist N.Y. Hosp.-Cornell Med. Ctr., 1998; cons. St. Luke's-Roosevelt Hosp. Ctr., Global Comm. Svcs., Inc., N.Y. Devel. Cons.; asst. clin. prof. med. psychology in psychiatry Columbia U. Coll. of Physicians and Surgeons. Adj. asst. clin. prof. applied psychology NYU Sch. of Edn. Contbr. articles to profl. jours. Rsch. fellowship Dept. of Health and Human Svcs., 1992. Mem. Soc. of Practitioners of the Columbia-Presbyn. Med. Ctr., Am. Psychol. Assn., Nat. Assn. of Sch. Psychologists, N.Y. Assn. of Sch. Psychologists, Internat. Soc. for Prevention of Child Abuse and Neglect, Am. Profl. Soc. on the Abuse of Children. Office: 815 Park Ave New York NY 10021-3276 E-mail: NakhleD@aol.com.

NALLEY, ELIZABETH ANN, chemistry educator; b. Catron, Mo., July 8, 1942; d. Arthur E. and Thelma L. (King) Frazier; m. Robert L. Mullican, Jan. 2, 1986; 1 child, George L. BS, Northeastern Okla. State U., 1965; MS, Okla. State U., 1969; PhD, Tex. Woman's U., 1975. High sch. tchr. Muskogee (Okla.) Ctrl. High Sch., 1964-65; instr. Cameron U., Lawton, Okla., 1969-72, asst. prof., 1972-75, assoc. prof., 1975-78, prof., 1978—. Contbr. articles to profl. jours. Recipient Disting. Svc. award Cameron U., 1995, Alumni Hall of Fame award, 1996; named Okla. Sci. Tchr. of Yr., Okla. Sci. Tchrs. Assn., 1999, S.W. Tech. Disting. Rsch. award, 2001, Disting. Alumnus Tex. Woman's U., 2001. Mem. AAAS, Assn. for Advancement of Computers in Edn., Am. Chem. Soc. (councilor 1980-97, sec. div. profl. rels. 1987-, sec. divsn. profl. rel. 1987-96, chair-elect divsn. profl. rels. 1996, chair divsn. profl. rels. 1997, nat. bd. dirs. 1997-2003, Okla. Chemist award 1992, divsn. profl. rels. Henry Hill award, 1996), Am. Inst. Chemists (nat. bd. dirs.), Phi Kappa Phi (regent 1981-89, nat. v.p. 1989-92, nat. pres.-elect 1992-95, nat. pres. 1995-98, Disting. Faculty award 1978), Sigma Xi, Sigma Pi Sigma, Iota Sigma Pi. Home: RR 3 Box 176-1 Chickasha OK 73018-9544 Office: Cameron U Dept of Chemistry 2800 W Gore Blvd Lawton OK 73505-6320 E-mail: annn@cameron.edu.

NANAGAS, MARIA TERESITA CRUZ, pediatrician, educator; b. Manila, Jan. 21, 1946; came to U.S., 1970; d. Ambrosio and Maria (Pasamonte) Cruz; m. Victor N. Nanagas, Jr.; children: Victor III, Valerie, Vivian. BS, U. of the Philippines, 1965, MD, 1970. Diplomate Am. Bd. Pediat. Intern, resident St. Elizabeth's Hosp., Boston, 1971-74; fellow in ambulatory pediat. North Shore Children's Hosp., Salem, Mass., 1974-75; active staff medicine Children's Med. Ctr., Dayton, Ohio, 1976—, head divsn. gen. pediat., 1988-90, 95-97, co-interim head ambulatory pediat., 1989-90, med. dir. ambulatory pediat., 1990—. Clin. asst. prof. pediat. Wright State U., Dayton, 1977-83, clin. assoc. prof. pediat., 1983—, selective dir., 1989—, assoc. prof. pediat., 2000—; clin. asst. prof. family practice Wright State U., Dayton, 1999—; dir., preceptor Wright State U. residents continuing clinic Children's Med. Ctr., 1989—, attending physician family practice programs, 1978—. Active Miami Valley Lead Poisoning Prevention Coalition, 19926. Fellow Am. Acad. Pediat.; mem. Western Ohio Pediat. Soc., Ambulatory Pediat. Assn. Office: Children's Med Ctr Health Clinic 1 Childrens Plz Dayton OH 45404-1898

NANCE, BETTY LOVE, librarian; b. Nashville, Oct. 29, 1923; d. Granville Scott and Clara (Mills) N. BA in English magna cum laude, Trinity U., 1957; MLS, U. Mich., 1958. Head dept. acquisitions Stephen F Austin U. Libr., Nacogdoches, Tex., 1958-59; libr. 1st Nat. Bank, Ft. Worth, 1959-61; head catalog dept. Trinity U., San Antonio, 1961-63; head tech. processes U. Tex. Law Libr., Austin, 1963-66; head catalog dept. Tex. A&M U. Libr., College Station, 1966-69; chief bibliographic svcs. Washington U. Libr., St. Louis, 1970; head dept. acquisitions Va. Commonwealth U. Libr., Richmond, 1971-73; head tech. processes Howard Payne U. Libr., Brownwood, Tex., 1974-79; libr. dir. Edinburg (Tex.) Pub. Libr., 1980-91. Pres. Edinburg Com. Salvation Army. Mem. ALA, Pub. Libr. Assn., Tex. Libr. Assn., Hidalgo County Libr. Assn. (v.p. 1980-81, pres. 1981-82), Pan Am. Round Table Edinburg (corr. sec. 1986-88, assoc. dir. 1989 90), Edinburg Bus. and Profl. Womens Club (founding bd. dirs., pres. 1986-87, bd. dirs. 1987-88), Zonta (bd. dirs. West Hidalgo Club, 1986-88, San Antonio 1996-97), Alpha Lambda Delta, Alpha Chi. Methodist. Home: 5359 Fredericksburg Rd # 806 San Antonio TX 78229-3549 E-mail: bettynance@webtv.net.

NANCE, SUSAN I. sociologist, educator; d. Oscar H. and Ann L.; m. George S. Nance, Nov. 9, 1968 (div.). BA, U. Hawaii, 1989; MA, Bowling Green (Ohio) State U., 1990; PhD, U. N.Mex., 1994. Instr. Bowling Green (Ohio) State U., 1989—90, U. N.Mex., Albuquerque, 1991—94; tchr. U. Hawaii, Honolulu, 1995—97, Acad. of the Pacific, Honolulu, 2001—. Lectr. Hawaii Film Festival, Honolulu, 1985—; documentarian Com. on Status Women, Honolulu, 1976. Co-author: Popular Culture: An Introduction, 1993, She Wields A Pen, 1998. Pres. REACH, Honolulu. Recipient Constl. Forum award, U.S. Dept. Edn., 2003; scholar Presdl. scholarship, U. Hawaii, 1989. Mem.: NOW, ACLU, Pop Culture Assn., Phi Beta Kappa. Avocations: activism, films, reading, music. Home: 6489 Hawaii Kai Drive Honolulu HI 96825 Office: Academy of the Pacific 913 Alewa Drive Honolulu HI 96817 E-mail: snance@aop.net.

NAND, SUCHA, medical educator; b. Thiriewal, Punjab, India, Feb. 3, 1948; d. Narsingh Dass and Swaran Devi; m. Surinder S. Nand, June 15, 1973; children: Ranveer, Rahul. Pre-med. student, Dayanand Ayur Vedic Coll., Amritsar, India, 1966; MB, BChir, Med. Coll., Amritsar, India, 1971. Diplomate Am. Bd. Internal Medicine, Am. Bd. Hemotology, Am. Bd. Med. Oncology. Asst. prof. Stritch Sch. Medicine Loyola U., Maywood, Ill., 1981-88, assoc. prof. Stritch Sch. Medicine, 1989-95; prof. medicine, 1996—. Editor Jour. of Med. Coll., 1969-71; contbr. articles to profl. jours. Clin. fellow Am. Cancer Soc., 1981; Brilliant Student scholarships, 1962-71. Mem. ACP, Am. Fedn. Clin. Rsch., Am. Soc. Hematology, Am. Soc. Clin. Oncology, S.W. Oncology Group (mem. leukemia com. 1988—). Avocations: chess, reading, swimming. Office: Loyola Univ Med Ctr 2160 S 1st Ave Maywood IL 60153-3304

NANKERVIS, MEDORA B. artist; b. L.A., Oct. 5, 1925; d. Granville Harrison and Sylvia (Tolman) Pierson; m. William Melvin Nankervis, May 9, 1957 (dec. 1995); children: Craig Melvin, Sylvia Kay, Michael Scott. Grad. high sch., Ashland, Oreg. Bookkeeper Pierson Prodn., Lynwood, South Gate, Calif., 1940-50's, Map Brass Products, Lynwood, South Gate, 1940-50's; co-operator Pierson Brass Foundry, South Gate, 1950's, Sunset Beach Airport, Huntington Beach, Calif., 1955-57; bookkeeper Wm. Nankervis Bldg. Contractors, Garden Grove, Calif., 1958-67; operator, owner Sunnyside Cattle and Guest Ranch, Rogue River, Oreg., 1968-76, May Hill Tree and Art Farm, Rogue River, 1987—2000. Workshop instr., so. Oreg., 1970's-80's. Founder Woodville Fine Arts Assn. and Gallery, Rogue River, 1968-88; mem. founding bd. Grants Pass (Oreg.) Mus. Art, 1979—, chair bd., 2001—; founder Women Artists Cascades, Oreg., 1982—, Hillary Rodham Clinton Fan Club, 1995-2000, Great We Artists Retreats. Mem. Inst. Noetic Scis., Watercolor Soc. Oreg. Independent. Mem. Soc. Of Friends. Avocation: wildlife preservation. Office: # B 229 SW G St Grants Pass OR 97526-2415

NAPADENSKY, HYLA SARANE, engineering consultant; b. Chgo., Nov. 12, 1929; d. Morris and Minnie (Litz) Siegel; m. Arnaldo I. Napadensky; children: Lita, Yafa. BS in Math., MS in Math., U. Chgo. Design analysis engineer Internat. Harvester Co., Chgo., 1952-57; dir. rsch. Ill. Inst. Tech. Rsch. Inst., Chgo., 1957-88; v.p. Napadensky Energetics Inc., Evanston, Ill., 1988-94; engring. cons., Lutsen, Minn., 1994-98. Contbr. numerous articles to profl. jours. Bd. overseers Armour Coll. Engring. Ill. Inst. Tech., 1988-93. Mem. NAE, Sigma Xi. Home and Office: 3284 W Highway 61 Grand Marais MN 55604-7537

NAPIER, CAMERON MAYSON FREEMAN, historic preservationist; b. Shanghai, Dec. 5, 1931; d. Hamner Garland and Cameron Middleton (Brame) Freeman; m. John Hawkins Napier III, Sept. 11, 1964. Student, L'Ecole des Artes Municipale, Paris, 1950-51; BA, U. Ala., 1955. Photographer's asst. Scott, Demott & Perry, Montgomery, Ala., 1951; art dir. WCOV-TV, Montgomery, 1955; self-employed graphic designer Dallas, 1956-64; self-employed designer Alexandria, Va., 1965-71; restoration chmn. White House Assn. Ala., Montgomery, 1973-76, 1st vice regent, 1976-80, regent, 1980—. Co-founder Friends of Stratford Hall for No. Va., Alexandria, late 1960s; docent chmn. Lee's Boyhood Home, Alexandria, late 1960s; bd. dirs. Landmarks Found., Montgomery, 1971-75; advisor Conde Charlotte House, Mobile, Ala., 1994-95. Author, designer booklet: The First White House of the Confederacy, 1978 (nat. printers award 1979). Bd. dirs. English Speaking Union, Montgomery, 1980-83. Named Hon. First Lady, by the Gov.'s wife, Montgomery, Ala., 1985; recipient Awards of Excellence, Advt. Artists Assn., Dallas, 1960, 1961, 1962, disting. svc. award, Ala. Hist. Commn., Montgomery, 1977, Cert. of Commendation, Gov. Ala., 1986, So. Patriot award, 1997, Lifetime Achievement award, Ala. Preservation Alliance, 2001, Jefferson Davis award, 1984, Winnie Davis award, United Daus. of Confederacy, 1985. Mem.: Antiquarian Soc. (pres. 1981—82), Sojourners Lit. Club (pres.), Order of the Crown in Am., Soc. Desc. of Colonial Clergy, Sovereign Mil. Order Temple of Jerusalem (aumoniere 1995, dame comdr. 1996), Nat. Soc. Colonial Dames in Am. (hist. properties com. 1994—95, state bd. mgrs. 1998—2000, ctr. vice chmn. 1998—2000), Am. Soc. Most Venerable Order of the Hosp. of St. John of Jerusalem (assoc. officer sister 1995—2002, named Comdr. Sister 2002), Daus. of Barons Runnymede, Militi Templi Scotia (dame 1993), Kappa Delta. Episcopalian. Avocations: jumbles, cryptoquotes, crossword puzzles, afternoon tea. Office: First White House Confed 644 Washington St Montgomery AL 36130-3057

NAPLES, MARY CECILIA, mental health services professional, health facility administrator; b. Ocana, Colombia, Oct. 31, 1954; d. Efrain and Olga (Rodriguez) Pineres; m. Anthony Louis Naples Jr., May 30, 1981; children: Marina Nicole, Alysia Marie. BA, Coll. of Comm. and Fine Arts, 1992, MEd in Counselor Edn., 1994; PhD in Family Therapy, Nova Southeastern U., 2003. Lic. mental health counselor; bd. cert. clin. hypnotherapist; bd. cert sex therapist. Owner, CEO Every Woman's Place, Boca Raton, Fla., 1997-99, Family Life Counseling Ctr., Boca Raton, Fla., 1999—. Mem. ACA (profl.). Roman Catholic. Avocations: movies, connecting with family and friends. Office: Family Life Counseling Ctr 400 S Dixie Hwy Ste 100 Boca Raton FL 33432 E-mail: napleslmhc@aol.com.

NAPOLES, VERONICA, graphic designer, consultant; b. N.Y.C., July 9, 1951; d. Florencio Andres and Elena (Colomar) N.; 1 child, Samuel Andres. BA, U. Miami, 1972; BArch, U. Calif., Berkeley, 1979. Account supr. Marsh & McLennan, Miami, Fla., 1974-76; designer Mus. of Anthropology, San Francisco, 1977-79; project dir. Landor & Assocs., San Francisco, 1979-81; prin. Communications Planning, Kentfield, Calif., 1981—. Bd. dirs. Mind Fitness, Mill Valley, Calif., Main Arts Coun., Mykytyn Cons. Group; instr. U. Calif.-Berkeley, San Francisco, 1983—, Sonoma State U., Santa Rosa, Calif., 1983-84; tchr. Dynamic Graphics Ednl. Found., San Francisco. Author: Corporate Identity Design, 1987; exhibited at San Francisco Airport, 1992. Bd. dirs. Marin Arts Coun. Recipient Bay Area Hispanic Bus. Achiever award, 1988, Design award PRINT, 1990, Excellence award Am. Corp. Identity, 1989, 90, 91, 92, 93, 94, 95, 96, Excellence award N.Y. Art Dirs. Show, 1989; finalist Sundance Inst., 1991. Mem. Am. Inst. Graphic Arts, Women in Communications. Avocations: painting, writing. Office: Napoles Design 189 Madrone Ave Larkspur CA 94939-2113

NAPOLITANO, GRACE F. congresswoman; b. Brownsville, Tex., Dec. 4, 1936; d. Miguel and Maria Alicia Ledezma Flores; m. Frank Napolitano, 1982; 1 child, Yolando M., Fred Musquiz Jr., Edward M., Michael M., Cynthia M. Student, Cerritos Coll., L.A. Trade Tech, Tec Southwest Coll. Mem. Calif. Assembly, 1993-98, U.S. Congress from 38th Calif. dist., Washington, 1999—; mem. resources com., sml. bus. com. U.S. Ho. Reps.; mem. Ho. Com. on Internat. Relations. Councilwoman City of Norwalk, Calif., 1986-92, mayor, 1989-90; active Cmty. Family Guidance. Mem. Cerritos Coll. Found., Lions Club. Democrat. Roman Catholic. Office: US Ho Reps 1609 Longworth Ho Office Bldg Washington DC 20515-0001 also: PO Box 408 Sacramento CA 95812-0408*

NAPOLITANO, JANET ANN, governor; b. N.Y.C., Nov. 29, 1957; d. Leonard Michael and Jane Marie (Winer) Napolitano. BS summa cum laude, U. Santa Clara, Calif., 1979; JD, U. Va., 1983. Bar: Ariz. 1984, U.S. Dist. Ct. Ariz. 1984, U.S. Ct. Appeals (9th cir.) 1984, U.S. Ct. Appeals (10th cir.) 1988, U.S. Ct. Appeals (5th cir.), U.S. Ct. Appeals, U.S. Ct. Appeals (7th cir.), U.S. Ct. Appeals (8th cir.). Law clk. to Hon. Mary Schroeder U.S Ct. Appeals 9th Cir., 1983—84; assoc. Lewis & Roca, Phoenix, 1984—89, ptnr., 1989—93; U.S. atty. Dist. Ariz., Phoenix, 1993—97; atty Lewis and Roca, Phoenix, 1997—98; atty. gen. State of Ariz., Phoenix, 1999—2002, gov., 2003—. Mem. Atty. Gen.'s Adv. Com., 1983—, chair, 1995—96; chair victims rights subcom. Ariz. Criminal Justice Commn.; chair Ariz. High Intensity Drug Traficking Area; mem. Ariz. Peace Officer Stds. and Tng. Bd., Ariz. Pros. Attys.' Adv. Coun.; past com. to study civil litigation abuse, cost and delay Ariz. Supreme Ct.; past pres. Ariz. Cmty. Legal Svcs. Corp.; past judge pro tem Ariz. Ct. Appeals. Contbr. articles to profl. jours. Chmn. Nucleus, 1989—91; active Phoenix Design Stds. Rev. Com., 1989—91, Ariz. Women's Forum, Charter 100; hon. chmn. Camp Fire Boys and Girls, 1999; 1st vice-chmn. Ariz. Dem. Com., 1990—92; active Dem. Nat. Com., 1990—92; chmn. Ariz. del. Dem. Nat. Conv., 1992, chmn., 2000; active Ariz. Bd. Tech. Registration, 1989—92; bd. dirs. Ariz. Fire Fighters and Emergency Paramedics Meml., Phoenix Children's Hosp., Actors' Lab Ariz., Inc., Ariz. Peace Officers Meml.; bd. regents Santa Clara U., 1992—. Named Ariz. Dem. of Yr., 1989; recipient Leader of Distinction award, Anti-Defamation League, Human Betterment award, Roots and Wings, Golden Apple award, West Valley NOW, Nat. Network To End Domestic Violence award, Woman of Distinction award, Crohns and Colitis Disease Found., Women Making History award, Nat. Mus. Women's History, Tribute to Women award, YWCA; fellow Dillard fellow; scholar, Truman Scholarship Found, 1977. Fellow: Ariz. Bar Found.; mem.: ABA, Raven Soc., Sandra Day O'Connor Inn of Ct. (barrister), Ariz. Women Lawyers Assn., Ariz. State Bar (chmn. civil practice and procedure com. 1991—92), Am. Judicature Soc., Maricopa County Bar Assn. (past long range planning com.), Ariz. Bar Assn. (past com. on minorities in law, past chmn. civil practice and procedure com.), Nat. Assn. Attys. Gen. (exec. com., tobacco bankruptcy working group, health care fraud group, co-chmn. civil rights com., stop underage smoking com., exec. working group on prosecutorial rels.), Am. Law Inst., Alpha Sigma Nu, Phi Beta Kappa. Democrat. Avocations: hiking, walking, travel, reading, film. Office: Office of Gov 1700 W Washington Phoenix AZ 85007*

NAPP, GUDRUN F. artist; b. Kiel, Germany, Aug. 14, 1929; arrived in U.S., 1986; d. Walter Alexander and Erika Elisabeth (Burchard) Rode; m. Edmund Carl Napp, Dec. 29, 1951 (dec. Dec. 2001); children: Helenita F., Johann Christian, Anneke J., Florian D. Student, Art Sch., Kiel, 1949, Escuela Artes Plastias, Caracas, Venezuela, 1950, Toronto (Can.) Coll. Art, 1950-51. Assoc. dir. One Ear Soc., 1999—2001. Exhibited in group shows at Miami Beach Conv. Ctr., 1997, Art Expo L.A., 1997, 98, Art Expo N.Y., 1998, Art Expo Fla., 2000, FIA Caracas Internat. Art Fair, 2003; one-woman shows include Art Am., 1997. Recipient cert. of excellence Art Horizon, N.Y.C., 1988, hon. mention Royal Poinciana Fiesta, Miami, 1993, The Fla.

Mus. of Hispanic and L.Am. Art, Miami, 1994, Miami Watercolor Soc. exhibit, 1999, One Ear Soc. exhibit. Mem. Nat. Collage Soc., Internat. Soc. Exptl. Artists (signature mem.), Miami Watercolor Soc. (signature mem., pres. 1995-96, trustee 1997, publicity chair 1998-99, 3rd place 1990), Art Expo Fla. Lutheran. Avocation: painting. Home: 1586 Passion Vine Cir Weston FL 33326 Studio: Studio Gallery Napp Inc 1388 Weston Rd Weston FL 33326 Office Phone: 945-217-1777. E-mail: art1100@aol.com.

NAPPIER, DENISE L. state official; BA, Va. State U., 1973; MA in Cmty. Planning, U. Cin., 1975. Analyst Office Hartford (Conn.) City Mgr.; cons. Conn. Office of Policy and Mgmt.; dir. instnl. rels. U. Conn. Health Ctr.; city treas. City of Hartford, 1989—98; treas. State of Conn., Hartford, 1999—. Exec. dir. Riverfront Recapture, Inc. Office: Office of State Treas 55 Elm St Hartford CT 06106-1746*

NAQUIN, DEBORAH ANN, humanities educator; d. William Clarence and Elizabeth Beshada Stewart; m. Douglas Joseph Naquin, Dec. 18, 1976; children: Kaely Maria, Julie Vanessa. EdB edn., Old Dominion U., Norfolk, Va., 1972—76; EdM edn., U. So. Calif., Los Angeles, Calif., 1980—82; MA applied linguistics, Nova/Southeastern U., Ft. Lauderdale, Fla., 1988—93; EdD higher edn. adminstrn./tech., The George Wash. U., Washington, DC, 1998—2001. Assoc. prof. English/reading No. Va. C.C., Sterling, Va., 1976—; English tchr. Fairfax County Pub. Schools, Fairfax, Va., 1976—80; English instr. U. Md., Okinawa, Japan, 1980—82; English as a second lang. instr. Thammasat U., Bangkok, 1982—84, Panama Canal Coll., Panama, Panama, 1987—89; ednl. counselor Fulbright Commn., Nicosia, Cyprus, 1991—92; writing program dir. Fgn. Broadcast Info. Services, Reston, Va., 1995—2001. Webmaster No. Va. C.C., Sterling, Va., 1997—99, chair, tchg. and learning tech. roundtable, 2000—, English dept. coord., 2001—02, tech. applications ctr. liaison, Annandale, Va., 2001—. Grantee Funded devel. of a web-based course, The Sloan Found., 1998, Funded web publ. of a faculty tech. manual, Va. C.C. Sys., 1999, Funded rsch. into the diffusion of ednl. tech., No. Va. C.C., 2000. Mem.: Va. Assn. Devel. Educators. Home: 21240 Rosetta Place Ashburn VA 20147 Office: No Virginia Cmty Coll 1000 Harry Byrd Highway Sterling VA 20164 Office Phone: 703-450-2519. E-mail: dnaquin@nvcc.edu.

NAQVI, TASNEEM ZEHRA, cardiologist, researcher, consultant; b. Karachi, Sind, Pakistan, Jan. 19, 1960; came to U.S., 1991; d. Shaiq Hussain and Laila (Rajabali) Zaidi; m. Syed Shujat A. Naqvi, June 30, 1985; children: Ali A., Kazim A. BS, St. Joseph's Coll., Karachi, 1976; MBBS, Dow Med. Coll., Karachi, 1984. Diplomate Am. Bd. Internal Medicine, Am. Bd. Cardoivasc Disease, Nat. Bd. Echocardiography, Am. Bd. Vascular Tech., registered vascular technologist. House officer internal medicine & gen. surgery Civil Hosp., Karachi, 1984—85; resident med. officer internal medicine Aga Khan U. Hosp., Karachi, 1985—86; registrar, instr. Civil Hosp., Karachi, 1986—87; sr. house officer Lister Hosp., Stevenage, England, 1988—89; registrar Queen Elizabeth U. Hosp., Birmingham, England, 1989—91; asst. clin. instr. in medicine Stony Brook U. Hosp., NY, 1991—93; fellow in clin. cardiology Cedars Sinai Med. Ctr., L.A., Calif., 1993—96, staff cardiologist, 1996—, assoc. dir. cardiac non-invasive lab, 1996—, dir. interventional echocardiography, 2003. Asst. prof. medicine UCLA Sch. Medicine, 1997-2004, assoc. prof. cardiology, 2004-; mem. instl. review bd. Cedars-Sinai Med. Ctr.; spkr. in field. Reviewer Jour. Am. Coll. Cardiology, Am. Jour. Cardiology, Jour. Am. Soc. Echocardiography, Am. Jour. Med. Scis., Archives of Internal Medicine, Echocardiography. Co-recipient Young Investigator award Am. Heart Assn., 1995; recipient Laverna Titus Young Investigators award Am. Heart Assn., 1995; fellow Am. Coll. Cardiology/Merck, 1996-97, L.A.Echo Soc., 1997. Fellow Am. Coll. Cardiology (cardiovasc. imaging com. 2003-, edn. com. 2003-, Merck Rsch. Fellowship award 1996-97, Jr. Faculty award), Am. Soc. Echocardiography (vascular task force, women's health adv. group 2003-), L.A. Soc. Echocardiography (bd. dirs. 1997-, mem. adv. bd.); mem. Royal Coll. Physicians U.K., Am. Heart Assn., Pakistan Med. and Dental Coun. Office: Cedars Sinai Med Ctr 8700 Beverly Blvd Rm 5341 Los Angeles CA 90048 Office Phone: 310-423-6889. E-mail: tasneem.naqvi@cchs.org.

NARANG, DEBORAH LYNN, education educator; b. Columbus, Ohio, Aug. 31, 1961; d. Gerald R. and Alice M. Haas; m. Kamal Narang, Sept. 14, 1985; 1 child, Maya Noelle. BA in Math., Capital U., 1983; MS in Math., Ohio State U., 1987; PhD in Math., U. N.H., 1994. Vis. asst. prof. SUNY, Potsdam, 1994—95, U. of Alaska, Anchorage, 1995—2001, assoc. prof., 2001—. Pres. faculty senate U. Alaska, Anchorage, 2002—. Mem.: Math. Edn. Reform Forum, Assn. Women in Math., Am. Math. Soc., Math. Assn. Am. Avocations: oriental brush painting, water aerobics, birdwatching. Office: U Alaska Anchorage 3211 Providence Dr Anchorage AK 99508 E-mail: afdln@uaa.alaska.edu.

NARASIMHAN, PADMA MANDYAM, physician; b. Bangalore, India; came to U.S., 1976; d. Alasingracher Mandyam and Alamela Mandyam Narasimhan; 1 child, Ravi. MD, Maulana Azad Med. Coll., New Delhi, 1970. Diplomate Am. Bd. Internal Medicine. Intern in internal medicine Flushing Hosp., N.Y.C., 1976-77; resident in internal medicine Luth. Med. Ctr., N.Y.C., 1977-79; fellow hematology, oncology Beth-Israel Med. Ctr., N.Y.C., 1979-81; asst. prof. King Drew Med. Ctr., L.A., 1983-87, Harbor UCLA, Torrance, 1987—. Mem. editorial bd. Jour. Internal Medicine, 1986—. Mem. ACP, AAPI, Am. Soc. Clin. Oncology, So. Calif. Acad. Clin. Oncology. Hindu. Avocations: travel, reading, meeting people, music, walking. Home: 6604 Madeline Cove Dr Palos Verdes Peninsula CA 90275-4608 Personal E-mail: padmanarasim@yahoo.com.

NARDELLI-OLKOWSKA, KRYSTYNA MARIA, ophthalmologist, educator; b. Myslowice, Poland, June 23, 1939; d. Walerian and Stefania (Jasinska) Nardelli; m. Zbigniew L. Olkowski, Apr. 15, 1963. MD, Silesian U. Med. Sch., 1964. Diplomate: Am. Bd. Ophthalmology; 1983. Intern, resident ophthalmology Emory U. Med. Sch., Atlanta, 1977-80, fellow in glaucoma, 1980-81, asst. prof. dept. ophthalmology, 1972—; pvt. practice ophthalmology, 1982—. Postdoctoral fellow Fight for Sight, 1974-75. Fellow Am. Soc. Research in Ophthalmology; mem. AMA, Royal Micros. Soc. (Eng.). Home: Villa Sadyba 1018 McConnell Dr Decatur GA 30033-3402 Office: 724 Holcomb Bridge Rd Bldg 4 Norcross GA 30071-1325

NARDI RIDDLE, CLARINE, legislative staff member; b. Clinton, Ind., Apr. 23, 1949; d. Frank Jr. and Alice (Mattioda) Nardi; children: Carl Nardi, Julia Nardi. AB in Math with honors, Ind. U., 1971, JD, 1974; LHD (hon.), St. Joseph Coll., 1991. Bar: Ind. 1974, U.S. Dist. Ct. (so. dist.) Ind. 1974, Conn. 1979, Fed. Dist. Ct. Conn. 1980, U.S. Supreme Ct. 1980, U.S. Ct. Appeals (2d cir.) 1986, U.S. Ct. Appeals (D.C. cir.) 1994. Staff atty. Ind. Legis. Svc. Agy., Indpls., 1974-78, legal counsel, 1978-79; dep. corp. counsel City of New Haven, 1980-83; counsel to atty. gen. State of Conn., Hartford, 1983-86, dep. atty. gen., 1986-89, acting atty. gen., 1989, atty. gen., 1989-91, judge Superior Ct., 1991-93; assn. exec., sr. v.p., gen. counsel Nat. Multi-Housing Coun., Nat. Apartment Assn., 1995—2003; chief of staff Senator Joseph I. Lieberman, Washington, 2003—. Asst. counsel state majority Conn. Gen. Assembly, Hartford, 1979, legal rsch. asst. to prof. Yale U., New Haven, 1979; legal counsel com. on law revision Indpls. State Bar Assn., 1979; mem. Chief Justice's Task Force on Gender Bias, Hartford, 1988-90; mem. ethics and values com. Ind. Sector, Washington, 1988-90; co-organizer Ind. Continuing Legal Edn. Forum Inst. Legal Drafting Legislature and Pvt. Practice; Internat. Women's Yr. panelist Credit Laws and Their Enforcement; mem. Atty. Gen.'s Blue Ribbon Commn., Chief Justice's Com. Study Publs. Policy Conn. Law. Jour., Law Revision Commn. Adminstrv. Law Study, Chief Justice's Task Force Gender, Justice and Cts., Gov.'s Task Force Fed. Revenue Enhancements; mem. exec. com. Jud. Dept.; mem. panel arbitrators Am. Arbitration Assn., 1994; gen. counsel Nat. Multi Housing Coun.; lectr. in field. Author: (with F.R. Rembusch) Drafting Manual for the Indiana General Assembly, 1976; sr. editor Ind. U. Law Sch. Interdisciplinary Law Jour.; contbr. articles to profl. jours. Bd. visitors Ind. U., Bloomington, 1974-92; mem. Gov.'s Missing Children Com., Hartford, Conn, Child Support Guidelines Com., Gov.'s Task Force on Justice for Abused Children, Hartford, 1988-90, mem. Mayor's City of New Haven Task Force Reorganization Corp. Counsel's Office, Gov.'s Child Support Commn., Mayor of New Haven's Blue Ribbon Commn.; former bd. dirs. New Haven Neighborhood Music Sch.; bd. dirs., mem. youth adv. com. Gov.'s Partnership Prevent Substance Abuse Workforce-Drugs Don't Work. Recipient Women in Leadership Recognition award Hartford Region YWCA, 1986, Award of Merit, Women & Law Sect. Conn. Bar Assn., 1989, Fellowship award South End Ladies Dem. Club, 1989, Woman of Yr. award Greater Hartford Fedn. of Bus. & Profl. Women's Clubs, 1990, Conn. Original award Somers-Mabelle B. Avery Sch., 1990, Cert. of Recognition, Consortium Law-Related Edn., 1990, Citizen award Conn. Task Force Children's Constl. Rights, 1991, Ann. award Hartford Assn. Women Attys., 1993; named Conn. History Maker, U.S. Dept. Labor, Women's Bur. & Permanent Commn. Status Women, 1989, Impact Player, The Conn. Law Tribune, 1992; inductee Ind. U. Sch. Law Alumni Acad. Fellow, 1999. Mem. ABA, Conn. Bar Assn. (chair com. on gender bias, Citation of Merit women and law sect. 1989), Nat. Assn. Attys. Gen. (chair charitable trusts and solicitation 1988-90), New Haven Neighborhood Music Sch. (bd. dirs.), Am. Arbitration Assn. (arbitration panel 1994), Ind. Bar Assn., Conn. Bar Assn. (chair com. gender bias legal profession), Indpls. Bar Assn., Ind. Civil Liberties Union (bd. dirs., mem. exec. com., chair long range planning com., mem. women's rights project, membership v.p., Disting. Svc. award), Conn. Consortium Law and Citizenship Edn., Inc. (bd. dirs.), Conn. Judges Assn. (mem. legislation com.), Ind. U. Law Sch. Alumni Assn. (bd. dirs.), Enomene Hon. Soc., Pleiades Hon. Soc., Mortar Bd. (nat. fellow), Alpha Lambda Delta. Democrat. Presbyterian. Office: Nat Multi Housing Coun 1850 M St NW Ste 450 Washington DC 20036-5803

NARVAEZ, BERNICE WILLIAMS, financial consultant; b. Houston, June 7, 1956; d. Ella Mae Williams; 1 child, Alexis Appollonia; m. Raymond Narvaez, June 5, 1999. BS in Mech. Engring., MIT, 1978; MS-MIS, George Washington U., 1994. Engr. Shell Oil Co., Houston, Sacramento, 1977-81; programmer U. Tex., Houston, 1985-89; cons. Ciber/MCI, Arlington, Tyson's Corner, Va., 1989-90; system analyst MCI Comm., Arlington, 1990-94; sr. cons. Comsys. Tech. Svcs. Network MCI, Arlington, 1994-97; tech. staff IBM Global Svcs., Tampa, 1997-99; sr. cons. Comsys/Metamor Tech. Svcs., 1999-2000; sr. bus. process cons. Sci. Applications Internat. Corp., Balt., 2000—04, prin. sys. engr., 2003—. Cons. various inhouse publs. Sci. Applications Internat. Corp., Shell Oil, MCI; pres. ALEXIS Enterprises, Tampa, 1994—; co-founder of All4Less distbr. w/Raymond Narvaez, Md., July 2001. Vol. industry adv. bd. Pub. Schs., Balt.; mem. process improvement com. Childreach, Covenant House, SAIC, Orlando. Avocations: tennis, piano, parenting, art collecting, travel. Office: 7125 Columbia Gateway Dr Ste 300 Columbia MD 21046 Business E-Mail: bernice.w.narvaez@saic.com.

NASCIMENTO, ANA PAULA, entrepreneur, food service executive; b. Brasilia, Brazil, July 11, 1970; arrived in U.S., 1989; d. Eliseu Botani and Elizete de Freitas Nascimento; m. Christopher Noel Kellon, Feb. 7, 1993 (div. Sept. 27, 1997). Student, Brasilia U., No. Va. Coll. Au parir, Arlington, Va., 1989—91; flyer girl Focaccia Fiorentina, N.Y.C., 1991, hostess, gen. mgr., 1999; owner Nascimento Restaurant, N.Y.C., 1999; entrepreneur Nascimento Sauces and Dressings, N.Y.C., 2001—. Contbr. Kennedy Child Study Ctr., March of Dimes, Parents Assn. Internat. Pre-Schs., Joey di Poglo AIDS Found., Art of Am., Ricardo O'Gorman Garden Sch., City Harvest, Meals-on-Wheels, QSAC-Autism, Share our Strength, The Charles Dickens Found., Builders of a Better World. Mem.: Nat. Restaurant Assn. (Outstanding Cmty. Involvement award 2001), Jewish Found., Holocaust Found. Avocations: volunteering, reading, running marathons, traveling, inspirational speaking. Office: 1068 1st Ave New York NY 10022-2202

NASH, ALICIA, computer programmer, physicist; b. San Salvador, Jan. 1, 1933; came to U.S., 1944; d. Carlos Roberto and Alicia (Lopez-Harrison) Larde; m. John Forbes Nash, Jr., Feb. 16, 1957; children: John Charles Martin. BS in Physics, MIT, 1955, postgrad., 1959. Physicist Nuclear Devel. Corp. of Am., White Plains, N.Y., 1956-57, Tech. Ops., Burlington, Mass., 1957-58; rsch. assoc. MIT Computation Ctr., Cambridge, Mass., 1958-59; physicist, aerospace engr. R.C.A. Astro Divsn., Hightstown, N.J., 1960-66; programmer, analyst Mgmt. Data Processing, N.Y.C., 1972-74, Con Edison, N.Y.C., 1974-80, Blue Cross Blue Shield of N.Y., N.Y.C., 1980-82; systems/analyst programmer specialist N.J. Transit, Newark, 1983—. Mem. AAUW, MIT Club of Princeton (past pres., bd. dirs.), Soc. of Women Engring. Home: 932 Alexander Rd Princeton Junction NJ 08550-1002 Office: NJ Transit One Penn Plaza East Newark NJ 07105

NASH, CYNTHIA JEANNE, journalist; b. Detroit, Dec. 24, 1947; d. Frederick Copp and Carolyn (Coffin) N.; 1 child, Lydia Anne Maza; m. Richard Zahler, July 22, 1994. BA, U. Mich., 1969. Reporter Detroit News, 1970-75, sports columnist, 1975-77, Life Style columnist, Life Style editor, 1979-82; news features editor Seattle Times, 1983; asst. mng. editor Sunday Seattle Times, 1983-86, assoc. mng. editor, 1986-97, dir. content devel., 1986-2000, dir., brand and content devel., 2000—. Mem. Harbor Sq. Club. Office: Seattle Times PO Box 70 Fairview Ave N & John St Seattle WA 98111-0070 E-mail: cnash@seattletimes.com.

NASH, DONNA CECILE, county official; b. St. Joseph, Mo., June 21, 1938; d. Cecil Noah and Georgia Lorraine (Younger) Green; m. Karlton B. Nash, Aug. 14, 1962; children: Karlton Scott, Timothy Joseph. Student, Plat Coll., 1957-59, St. Joseph Jr. Coll., 1956-57. Acct. Westab, Inc., St. Joseph, Mo., 1958-62; acct., data processing TWA, Inc., Kansas City, Mo., 1970-73; dep. collector Platte County, Platte City, Mo., 1978-82, collector of revenue, 1982—. Owner Nash Gas Co., Inc. Dir. women conv. activities MidWest Propane Conv., St. Louis, 1990; charter mem. Women's Exch., Kansas City, Mo., 1985—; committeewoman Platte County Rep. Com., 1981—. Recipient Svc. award Northland Career Ctr., 1986, Award of Excellence Mo. County Collectors Assn., 1994. Mem. Kansas City C. of C., Mo. Assn. of Counties (dist. 3 dir. 1995—), Mo. State Collectors Assn. (1st woman pres. 1990), DAR (treas. St. Joseph chpt. 1998—). Methodist. Avocations: geneaology, oil painting. Home: 23585 Highway 371 Dearborn MO 64439-9118 Office: Platte County Collector PO Box 40 Platte City MO 64079-0040

NASH, JUNE CAPRICE, anthropology educator; b. Salem, Mass, May 30, 1927; d. Joseph and M. Josephine Bousley; m. Manning Nash, 1952 (dec. 1999); children: Eric, Laura; m. Herbert Menzel, July 1, 1972 (dec. Jan. 1987); m. Frank Reynolds, 1997. BA, CUNY, 1948; MA, U. Chgo., 1953, PhD, 1960. Asst. prof. Chgo. Tchr. Coll., Chgo., 1960-63, Yale U. New Haven, Conn., 1963-68; assoc. prof. NYU, NY, 1968-72; prof. CUNY, 1972—90; disting. vis. prof. Am. U., Cairo, 1978, U. Colo., Boulder, 1988—; vis. prof. SUNY, Albany, 1988-89; disting. prof. CUNY, NYC, 1990—98; Neilson prof. Smith Coll., 1996; disting. prof., emerita CUNY, NYC, 1998. Author: In the Eyes of the Ancestor, 1970, We Eat the Mines and the Mines Eat Us: Dependency and Exploitation in Bolivian Mining Communities, 1979, From Tank Town to High Tech: The Clash of Cmty. and Industrial Cycles, 1989; Mayan Visions: the Quest for Autonomy in an Age of Globalization, 2001; editor: Crafts in the World Market: The Impact of Global Exchange on Middle American Artisans, 1993, La explosíon de comunidades en chiapas, México, 1995, Social Movements A Reader, 2004; co-editor: (with Helen I. Safa) Sex and Class in Latin America, 1976, Women and Change in Latin America, 1986, (with Juan Corradi and Hobard Spalding) Ideology and Change in Latin America, 1976, (with Jorge Dandler and Nicholas Hopkins) Popular Participation in Change: Cooperatives, Collectives and Self-Management, 1976. Mem. Soc. for the Anthropology of Work (pres. 1988—), Assn. Polit. and Legal Activities (pres. 1983, 2003), Am. Anthropology Assn. (Disting. Svc. award 1995), Am. Ethnographic Soc., Assn. for Feminist Anthropology (pres. 1990-93). Avocations: skiing, hiking. Home: 68 Prospect St Plainfield MA 01070

NASH, MILDRED JEAN, English educator, poet; b. Sharon, Pa., Aug. 3, 1938; d. Merrill G. and Mary (Dallas) Leonard; m. James A. Nash, Aug. 14, 1960; children: Noreen Elizabeth, Rebecca Anne. AB, Grove City (Pa.) Coll., 1960; EdM, Harvard U., 1977. Tchr. English Rockport (Mass.) H.S., 1960-61, Burlington (Mass.) H.S., 1979-84; dir. BEAM (Burlington's Extended Acad. Model) Marshall Simonds Mid. Sch., 1984—. Author: (poetry) Beyond Their Dreams, 1989; contbr. numerous poems to mags., jours. and anthologies. Rep. Town Meeting, Burlington, 1975—. Recipient awards World Order of Narrative Poets, 1994. Mem. Poetry Soc. Am. (Emily Dickinson award 1979), New Eng. Poetry Club (sec. 1978-89, Power Dalton Meml. award 1980, Leighton Rollins Meml. award 1980). Avocations: biking, piano, recorder. Home: 39 Sunset Dr Burlington MA 01803-4119 Office: Marshall Simonds Mid Sch Winn St Burlington MA 01803

NASH, RUTH S. foundation administrator; b. Westfield, Mass., May 7, 1916; d. George Whitney and Marguerite (Mueller) Searle; m. Clayton Richmond Nash, Sept. 7, 1940 (dec. 1990); children: Roberta Marie, Marguerite Louise, Gail Winifred; m. Charles Williams, Mar. 13, 2002. Student, Simmons Coll., 1935-37; Diploma, Sch. Handicraft and Occupl. Therapy, 1937-39; B in Liberal Studies, Fla. So. Coll., 1996. Leader Girl Scouts, Winthrop, Mass., 1934-40, field dir., exec. dir. Greater Lynn (Mass.), 1940-43; leader, bd. mem. Reading, Mass., 1940-60; field dir., exec. dir. Naumkeag Area Girl Scouts, Salem, Mass., 1949-56, field dir., tng. dir. Greater Lawrence (Mass.), 1958-63; leader Mystick Side Medford, Mass., 1960-63; field dir., pub. rels., tng. dir., camping svcs. dir. Merrimack River Coun., Andover, Mass., 1963-78. Author: High Seas to High Stakes, 2000, Tales & Tails From Stagecoach Lodge, 2002; editor: Monthly Civic Newspaper Beacon, 1984-99; contbr. articles to profl. jours. Vol. Meals on Wheels, 1991-96, Cmty. Svc., 1978-98; sec., mem. choir, handbell ringer Harbour Heights (Fla.) United Meth. Ch., 1991—; mem., founder H.H. Kitchen Band, 1990—; trail guide Charotte Harbor Environ. Ctr., Punta Gorda, Fla., 1997—; leader disadvantaged girls Girl Scouts USA, 1998—, study ptnr. for disadvantaged children, 1998—. Mem. AAUW (sec. 1998-), Learning in Retirement (sec. bd.), Alzheimers Assn. (support leader, bd. dirs. 1992-97). Republican. Methodist. Avocations: writing, watercolors, canoeing, golf, camping. Home: 3524 Peace River Dr Punta Gorda FL 33983-3523 also: RR 1 Box 70A Alton NH 03809-9719

NASH, SYLVIA DOTSETH, consultant; b. Montevedio, Minn., Apr. 25, 1945; d. Owen Donald and Selma A. (Tollefson) Dotseth; married; 1 child, Elizabeth Louise. Grad., Calif. Luth. Bible Sch., 1965; doctorate (hon.), Pilgrims Theol. Seminary, 1994. Office mgr. First Congl. Ch., Pasadena, Calif., 1968-75; pastoral asst. Pasadena Presbyn. Ch., 1975-78; dir. adminstrv. svcs. Fuller Theol. Sem., Pasadena, 1978-81; CEO Christian Mgmt. Assn., Diamond Bar, Calif., 1981-94; pres. Christian Healthcare Network, La Mirada, Calif., 1994-95; sr. cons. Lillestrand and Assocs., Chino Hills, Calif., 1996—. Cons. various orgns., 1985—. Author: Inspirational Management, 1992 (Your Church Mag. award 1992); editor: The Clarion, 1975-78, The Christian Mgmt. Report, 1981-94; mem. editl./adv. bd. Your Church Mag.; mem. editl. bd. Jour. Ministry Mktg. and Mtmg.; contbr. articles to profl. jours. Bd. dirs. Nat. Network of Youth Ministries, The Mustard Seed, Inc., Nat. Assn. of Ch. Bus. Adminstrn., Found. for His Ministry, Lamb's Players, Gospel Lit. Internat., Evang. Coun. for Fin. Accountability, Campus Crusade for Christ Internat. Sch. Theology. Mem. NAFE, Nat. Assn. Ch. Adminstrs. (sec. 1979-81), Am. Soc. Assn. Execs., So. Calif. Soc. Assn. Execs. Office: Lillestrand & Assocs 2729 Brookside Drive Chino Hills CA 91709

NASON, NICOLE, federal agency administrator; married; 1 child, Alexandra. Grad., Am. U., Washington, 1992; JD, Case Western Res. U., Cleve. Counsel House Judiciary Subcom. on Crime, Washington; govt. affairs counsel Met. Life Ins. Co., 1999—2000; comm. dir., counsel U.S. Rep. Porter J. Goss, 2000—02; asst. commr. Office of Congl. Affairs, U.S. Customs Svc., Washington, 2002—03; asst. sec. for govtl. affairs U.S. Dept. Transp., Washington, 2003—. Office: US Dept Transportation 400 7th St Washington DC 20590*

NASON, ROCHELLE, conservation organization administrator; b. Oakland, Calif., May 21, 1959; d. Milton and Ann Frances (Reed) Nason. BA, U. Calif., Berkeley, 1984; JD, U. Calif., San Francisco, 1987. Bar: Calif. 1987. Law clk. to Chief Justice Malcolm Lucas Supreme Ct. of Calif., San Francisco, 1987-88; litigation assoc. Morrison & Foerster, San Francisco, 1988-92; staff lawyer League to Save Lake Tahoe, South Lake Tahoe, Calif., 1992-93, exec. dir., 1993—. Adj. instr. Sierra Nev. Coll., Incline Village, 1992—94, Lake Tahoe C.C., 1992—96. Editor: The Traynor Reader, 1987; sr. rev. editor: Hastings Law Jour., 1986—87; editor: (jour.) Keep Tahoe Blue, 1992—; columnist: newspaper Tahoe Daily Tribune; contbr. articles to profl. jours. Mem. leadership coun. Tahoe-Truckee Regional Econ. Coalition, Stateline, Nev., 1992—94; v.p., bd. dirs. Jewish Cmty. South Lake Tahoe/Temple Bat Yam, 1992—99; bd. dirs. Tahoe Ctr. Sustainable Future, Glenbrook, Nev., 1995—98, Earthshare Calif., 2002—. Mem.: Thurston Soc., Order of Coif. Jewish. Avocations: backpacking, skiing. Office: League to Save Lake Tahoe 955 Emerald Bay Rd South Lake Tahoe CA 96150-6410

NASRALLAH, JUNE, plant pathologist, department chairman; PhD in Genetics, Cornell U. Prof. plant biology, chair plant genomics Cornell U., Ithaca, NY. Contbr. articles to profl. jours. Mem.: NAS. Office: Cornell U 218 Plant Sciences Ithaca NY 14853 Business E-Mail: jbn2@cornell.edu.

NASS, CONNIE KAY, state auditor; m. Alan Nass; 3 children. V.p. Nass & Son, Inc., 1974—; auditor State of Ind., 1999—. Bd. Senator Richard Lugar's Excellence in Pub. Svc. Program. Bd. mem. Huntingburg Utility Bd., 1975—; city coun. mem., Huntingburg, 1979-88, mayor, 1988-96; mgr. municipally owned utility cos., Huntingburg, 1988-96; candidate for lt. gov. State of Ind., 1995-96; mem. GOP Platform Com., 1992; del. Rep. Nat. Conv., 1996; bd. dirs. Welborn Found. Evansville, S.W. Ind. Regional Health Care Ctr., Inc.; adv. bd. AAA, Evansville, 1990—; mem. fin. com. and emergency svcs. com. ARC Greater Indpls., 1999—; nat. gen. synod del. Ind.-Ky. Conf. United Ch. of Christ, 1981, com. on planning and evaluation, 1990—, bd. dirs., 1996—; Sunday sch. tchr., music dir. Salem United Ch. of Christ. Recipient Protect Our Woods Environtl. award, 1995; named Outstanding Rep. Woman Ind. Reps Mayor's Assn., 1995. Mem. Nat. Automated Clearing House Assn. (internet coun., electronic benefits coun., strategic expansion bd.), Nat. Assn. State Auditors, Comptrs. and Treas., Network Women in Bus., Women Execs. in State Govt., Ind. State Auditor Adv. Coun., Ind. Farm Bur., Ind. Assn. of Cities and Towns (bd. dirs.), Dubois County GOP Women's Club (pres. 1996-98), Marion County GOP Women's Club, Huntingburg C. of C. Republican. Office: State House Rm 240 200 W Washington St Indianapolis IN 46204-2728

NAST, DIANNE MARTHA, lawyer; b. Mount Holly, N.J., Jan. 30, 1948; d. Henry Daniel and Anastasia (Lovenduski) N.; m. Joseph Francis Roda, Aug. 23, 1980; children: Michael, Daniel, Joseph, Joshua, Anastasia. BA, Pa. State U.; JD, Rutgers U., 1976. Bar: Pa. 1976, U.S. Dist. Ct. Pa. 1976, N.J. 1976, U.S. Dist. Ct. N.J. 1976, U.S. Ct. Appeals (3d, 5th, 6th, 7th, 8th and 11th cirs.) 1976, U.S. Supreme Ct. 1982, U.S. Dist. Ct. Ariz. 1985. Dir., v.p. Kohn, Nast & Graf, P.C., Phila., 1976-95, Roda & Nast, P.C., Lancaster, Pa., 1995—. Mem. lawyers adv. com. U.S. Ct. Appeals (3d cir.), 1982-84, chmn., 1983-84, mem. com. on revision jud. conf. conduct rules, 1982-84; mem. Third Cir. Task Force on Selection of Class Clunsel, 2001-02mem. U.S. Ct. Appeals for the 3d Cir. Jud. Conf. Permanent Planning Com., 1983-90; bd. dirs. 3d Cir. Hist. Soc., Phila. Pub. Def., 1980-89, Fed. Jud. Ctr. Found., 1992-2002, chmn. 1997-2002; chmn. lawyers adv. com. U.S. Dist. Ct. (ea. dist.) Pa., 1982-90. Pres. Hist. Soc., 1988-91. Fellow ABA (coun. litigation sect. 1986-89, co-chmn. anti-trust com. litigation sect. 1984-86, div. dir. 1990-91, practical litigation editl. bd. 1989—, ho. of dels. 1992-94, mem. task force state justice initiatives, mem. task force state of justice system, 1993, mem. task force long range planning com. 1994), Am. Law Inst. (chair internat. professionalism com. 1991-94, civil justice task force 1993-95), Am. Arbitration Assn. (bd. dirs., mem. alt. dispute resolution and mass torts task force), Am. Judicature Soc., Pa. Bar Assn. (bd. of dels. 1983-95), N.J. Bar Assn., Pa. Trial Lawyers Assn., Phila. Bar Assn. (bd. govs. 1985-87, chmn., bicentennial com. 1986-87, chmn. bench bar conf. 1988-89), Lancaster Bar Assn. (co-chair civil litigation and rules com. trial law sect.), Rutgers Law Sch. Alumni Assn. Home: 1059 Sylvan Rd Lancaster PA 17601-1923 Office: Roda & Nast PC 801 Estelle Dr Lancaster PA 17601-2130 E-mail: dnast@rodanast.com.

NASTASI, LISA R. psychologist; b. S.I., N.Y., Aug. 27, 1964; d. Anthony and Mary Jo Nastasi; m. David A. Feinburg, Sept. 5, 1993; children: Samuel Wyatt Feinburg, Sascha Belle Feinburg. BA in Polit. Sci., U. Wyo., 1986; MA in Gen. Psychology, NYU, 1993; PhD in Clin. Psychology, Adelphi U., Garden City, N.Y., 1997. Lic. clin. psychologist N.Y. Pres. L&L Wellness-Corp. Wellness Svc., N.Y.C., 1999—; clin. instr. psychology in psychiatry N.Y. Presbyn. Hosp., N.Y.C., 2003—. Author: Mindfulness Based Cognitive Initiative, 1999. Mem.: APA, Assn. Spirituality in Psychotherapy. Democrat. Achievements include patents for nail product. Avocations: yoga, writing, meditation. Home: 118 W 79th St #10B New York NY 10024 Office: 21 W 86th St Ste 301 New York NY 10024

NATALE, DIANE THERESA, communications executive; b. Winchester, Mass., Sept. 15, 1956; d. Charles Joseph and Catherine Anne Natale; m. Paul Robert LaRoche, Nov. 14, 1982 (div. July 8, 1993); children: Olivia Rachel, Isabel Marysa. BA in English magna cum laude, Salem State Coll., 1986. Tech. writer, mgr. Kodak, Bedford, Mass., 1984—95; comm., prin. Words That Work, Danvers, Mass., 1995—98; mgr. Engage a CMGI Co., Andover, Mass., 1998—2000, !Hey, Inc., North Andover, Mass., 2000—01; v.p. comms. Void Automation, Inc., Westford, Mass., 2002—. Editor-in-chief: Sounding East Mag., 1983, 1984. Recipient Judge award, Boston chpt. Soc. Tech. Comms., 1993. Avocations: dance, knitting. Home: 27 Lockwood Ln Topsfield MA 01983

NATALE, FERNANDA MARIA MADDALENA, conservator, artist; b. Pietramelara, Caserta, Italy, Mar. 21, 1951; d. Pasquale and Anna Gina Natale; m. Robert Carl Hertz, June 13, 1972 (div. July 13, 2001); children: Angela Marie Phalen, Diana Marie Hertz, Carla Marie Hertz, Robert William Hertz, Tanya Marie Hertz. Diploma, Raggioneria, Teano, Italy, 1968. Conservator/ restoration of hist. landmark Ho. of Hospitality of Balboa Pk., San Diego, 1996—97; conservator The Wanda Gag Ho., New Ulm, Minn., 1997—98; artisan and restoration Minn. Masonic Home, Mpls., 1998; artist of classically inspired realism Fernanda's Studio, Watertown, SD, 1995—; co-owner, founder and dir. of exhibits and hospitality Signature Art Gallery, Watertown, SD, 2001—; conservator of oil painting and canvas First Dawson Convenant Ch., Dawson, Minn., 2003—. Orgnl. dir. and mem. Valley Ctr. Art Assn., Valley Center, Calif., 1992—95; co-founder The S.D. NE Artists Assn., Watertown, SD, 1996—; tchr. and dir. Artist Network Workshop, Watertown, SD, 2000—. Exhibitions include Signature Gallery, exhibited in group shows at Collection of Works Show, exhibitions include Park Bench, South Dakota Made, Contemporary Women, Classic Art. Recipient 1st prize, San Diego Art Critics, 1995; grantee, S.D. Art Alliance, 2001. Independent. Avocations: travel, cultural events. Home: 26 S Broadway St Watertown SD 57201 Office: Signature Art Gallery 17 East Kemp St Watertown SD 57201 Personal E-mail: fernanda@aol.com.

NATALICIO, DIANA SIEDHOFF, academic administrator; b. St. Louis, Aug. 25, 1939; d. William and Eleanor J. (Biermann) Siedhoff. BS in Spanish summa cum laude, St. Louis U., 1961; MA in Portuguese lang., U. Tex., 1964, PhD in Linguistics, 1969. Chmn. dept. modern langs. U. Tex., El Paso, 1973-77, assoc. dean liberal arts, 1977-79; acting dean liberal arts, 1979-80; dean Coll. Liberal Arts U. Tex., El Paso, 1980-84, v.p. acad. affairs, 1984-88, pres., 1988—. Bd. dirs. El Paso br. Fed. Res. Bd. Dallas, chmn., 1989; mem. Presdl. Adv. Commn. on Ednl. Excellence for Hispanic Ams., 1991; bd. dirs. Sandia Corp., Trinity Industries; bd. dirs. Nat. Action Coun. for Minorities in Engring., 1993—; mem. Nat. Sci. Bd. 1994-2000; mem. NASA Adv. Coun., 1994-96; bd. mem. Fund for Improvement of Post-Secondary Edn., 1993-97; bd. dirs. Fogarty Internat. Ctr. of NIH, 1993-96; bd. chair Am. Assn. Higher Edn., 1995-96; bd. dirs. U.S.-Mexico Commn. for Ednl. and Cultural Exch., 1994—. Co-author: Sounds of Children, 1977; contbr. articles to profl. jours. Bd. dirs. United Way El Paso, 1990-93, chmn. needs survey com., 1990-91, chmn. edn. divsn., 1989; chmn. Quality Edn. for Minorities Network in Math. Sci. and Engring., 1991-92; chairperson Leadership El Paso, Class 12, 1989-90, mem. adv. coun., 1987-90, participant, 1980-81; mem. Historically Black Colls. and Univs./Minority Instns. Consortium on Environ. Tech. chairperson, 1991-93. Recipient Harold W. McGraw. Jr. prize in edn., 1997, Torch of Liberty award Anti-Defamation League B'nai B'rith, 1991, Conquistador award City of El Paso, 1990, Humanitarian award El Paso chpt. NCCJ, 1990; mem. El Paso Women's Hall of Fame, 1990. Mem. Philos. Soc. Tex. Avocations: hiking, bicycling, skiing, skating. Home: 711 Cincinnati Ave El Paso TX 79902-2616 Office: U Tex at El Paso Office Of President El Paso TX 79968-0001*

NATHANSON, LINDA SUE, publisher, author, technical writer; b. Washington, Aug. 11, 1946; d. Nat and Edith (Weinstein) N.; m. James F. Barrett. BS, U. Md., 1969; MA, UCLA, 1970, PhD, 1975. Tng. dir. Rockland Research Inst., Orangeburg, N.Y., 1975-77; asst. prof. psychology SUNY, 1978-79; pres. Cabri Prodns., Inc., Ft. Lee, N.J., 1979-81; rsch. supr. Darcy, McManus & Masius, St. Louis, 1981-83; mgr. software tng., documentation On-Line Software Internat., Ft. Lee, 1983-85; pvt. practice Ft. Lee, 1985-87; founder, exec. dir. The Edin. Group, Inc., Gillette, N.J., 1987-98; founder, pres. Edin Books, Inc., Gillette, N.J., 1994—. Author: (with others) Psychological Testing: An Introduction to Tests and Measurements, 1988; (with S.J. Thayer) Interview with an Angel, 1997; (with S.J. Thayer) The Heart of Interview with an Angel, 1998; publ. A Funny Thing Happened at the Interview (G.F. Farrell), 1996, Angel Talk (R. Crystal), 1996; (audiobook with W. Barnes) I Built the Titanic: Past-Life Memories of a Master Shipbuilder, 1999, Thomas Andrews, Voyage into History, 2000; (audio book with W. Barnes and F. Baranowski) A Past-Life Interview with Titanic's Designer, 1999. Recipient Rsch. Svc. award 1978; Albert Einstein Coll. Medicine Research fellow, 1978-79. Jewish. Home and Office: 102 Sunrise Dr Gillette NJ 07933-1944 Office Phone: 908-361-3535. E-mail: edinbooks@patmedia.net.

NATIONS, JANICE MCKINNEY, music educator; b. Bakersville, N.C., July 20, 1954; d. Glenn Lee and Ruth McQuire McKinney; m. Robert Samuel Nations, Jan. 14, 1950; 1 child, Robert Brian. BS in Edn., Western Carolina U., Cullowhee, N.C., 1987. Cert. tchr. S.C. Ch. organist, choir dir. Moncks Corner Meth. Ch., SC, 1998—; choral dir. West Ashley Mid. Sch., Charleston, SC, 2002—. Choral dir. Drayton Hall Mid. Sch., Charleston, SC, 2001—02. Vol. Hollings Cancer Ctr., Charleston, SC, 2001—03. Mem.: Music Educators Nat. Conf. R-Liberal. Methodist. Achievements include Activist for Breast Cancer Awareness. Avocations: playing the piano, reading good novels, walking, going to the beach. Home: 107 Mainridge Blvd Goose Creek SC 29445 Office: West Ashley Mid Sch 1776 William Kennerty Dr Charleston SC 29417 Personal E-mail: jansambri@msn.com. E-mail: janice_nations@charleston.k12.sc.us.

NATIVIDAD, LISALINDA SALAS, family advocacy outreach manager; b. AAFB, Guam, Mar. 31, 1971; d. Paul Castillo and Concepcion Quichocho Natividad; 1 child, Atdao-mami Paul. BA, U. Hawaii, 1993, MSW, 1996. Cert. marriage and family therapist Guam. Caseworker Sanctuary, Inc., Mangilao, 1993—94, cons., 1993—, dep. dir., 1998—2001; outreach counselor Key Project, Kahaluu, Hawaii, 1995; clinician Waianae (Hawaii) Mental Health Ctr., 1996; adj. prof. U. Guam, Mangilao, 1998—; individual marriage and family therapist Marianas Clinic, Tamuning, 2001—. Contbr. chpt. Culturally Competitent Practice with Pacific Islanders, 1998. Recipient Pulama Project award, State of Hawaii, 1994—96, Women's Studies scholarship, U. Hawaii, 1993. Mem.: NASW (pres. bd. dirs. Guam chpt. 2001—), Guam Assn. Social Workers (v.p. 1999—2000). Avocations: hiking, the beach.

NATORI, JOSIE CRUZ, apparel executive; b. Manila, May 9, 1947; came to U.S., 1964; d. Felipe F. and Angelita A. (Almeda) Cruz; m. Kenneth R. Natori, May 20, 1972; 1 child, Kenneth E.F. BA in Econs., Manhattanville Coll., 1968; Degree (hon.), Acad. Art Coll., San Francisco, 2003. With Bache Securities, N.Y.C.; joined Merrill-Lynch Co. as an investment banker, 1971; v.p., 1976—77; owner, CEO The Natori Co., N.Y.C., 1977—. Bd. dirs. The Alltel Corp., 1995—. Bd. dirs. Philippine Am. Found., Jr. Achievement, Inc., 1992, Ednl. Found. for Fashion Industries; trustee Manhattanville Coll., Asian Cultural Coun.; commr. White House Conf. on Small Bus., 1993. Recipient Human Relations award Am. Jewish Com., N.Y.C., 1986, Harriet Alger award Working Woman, N.Y., 1987, Castle award Manhattanville Coll., Purchase, 1988, Galleon award Pres. Philippines, 1988, N.Y.C. Asian-Am. award, Friendship award Philippine-Am. Found., Hall of Fame award Mega Mags., Salute to Am. Fashion Designers award Dept. of Commerce, Ellis Island medal of Honor, 1994, Presdl. Awards for Filipino Individuals and Orgns. Overseas, Pamana ng Pilipino award Philippine Consulate Gen., 2002; named Bus. Woman of Yr. N.Y.C. Partnership and C. of C., 1998. Mem. CFDA, Young Pres.'s Orgn., Fashion Group, Com. of 200. Avocations: pianist, tennis player. Home: 45 E 62nd St New York NY 10021-0025 Office: Natori Co 40 E 34th St Fl 18 New York NY 10016-4563*

NATSUME, KAORI TAKAMI, artist, small business owner; b. Machida, Japan, Sept. 26, 1967; arrived in U.S., 1986; d. Tshihiro Tom and Shinko Alice Takami; m. Shigeru Gary Natsume, May 28, 1999; 1 child, Takumi Shou. BFA in Studio Art and Asian Studies, St. Olaf Coll., 1991; MFA in Fiber, Cranbrook Acad. Art, 1998. Asst. to dir. Asian Rural Inst., Nishinasuno, Japan, 1991—93; rschr. batik Japan and Indonesia Batik Design Rsch. Group, Tokyo, 1993—94; freelance translator Nishinasuno, 1995—96; prin., owner Fiber Zero Assocs., Nishinasuno, 1998—, Fiber Zero Assns., Inc., Bklyn., 2001—. North Light Book, 1995, exhibitions include Palos Verdes Art Ctr., Rancho Palos Verdes, Calif., 1993 (Silk Painting award, 93); contbr. artwork to jours. Grantee, Toyota Found., 1995—96, Ctr. Global Partnership, 1998, Japan Arts Found., 1999, 2001—03. Home: 138 Broadway 1B Brooklyn NY 11211

NATSUYAMA, HARRIET HATSUNE KAGIWADA, mathematician, educator; b. Honolulu, Sept. 2, 1937; d. Kenjiro and Yakue Natsuyama; children: Julia, Conan. BA, U. Hawaii, 1959, MS, 1960; PhD, Kyoto U., 1965. Math. Rand Corp., Santa Monica, Calif., 1961—68, cons., 1968-77; adj. assoc. prof. U. So. Calif., L.A., 1974-79; sr. scientist Hughes Aircraft Co., El Segundo, 1979-87; chief engr. Infotec Devel. Inc., Camarillo, 1987-89; prof. systems engring. Calif. State U., Fullerton, 1990-96; v.p. Advanced Indsl. Materials, 1996-97; co-founder Planet Aura, Inc., 2002—. Fgn. spl. vis. prof. Oita U., 1995, Kyoto Sch. of Computer Sci., 1997—; vis. prof. Sci. U. Tokyo, 1998; co-founder PlanetAura, Inc., L.A., 2002. Author: Invariant Imbedding and Time-Dependent Transport Processes, 1963, System Identification: Methods and Applications, 1974, Integral Equations via Imbedding Methods, 1974, Multiple Scattering Processes: Inverse and Direct, 1975, Numerical Derivatives and Nonlinear Analysis, 1986, Terrestrial Radiative Transfer: Modeling, Computation, Data Analysis, 1998. Mem. Grad. Women in Sci. (pres. 1990-91), Phi Beta Kappa, Phi Kappa Phi.

NATZKE, PAULETTE ANN, manufacturing executive; b. Wausau, Wis., Oct. 23, 1943; d. Milton L. and Geraldine J. (Henrichs) Marth; m. Kenneth A. Natzke, June 29, 1963; children: Jerome E., Julie J. Cert. ceramic tchr. Sec. Marth Wood Shavings Supply, Marathon, Wis., 1973—85, pres., 1985—; v.p. Marth Transp. Inc., Marathon, 1984—; adminstr. Marth Found., Marathon, 1982—; owner Privacy Point on Lake Nokomis, Tomahawk, Wis., 1992—97; treas. Marth Mfg., Inc., 2000. Dir. Marathon Area Credit Union, 1985-87. Republican. Lutheran. Avocations: decorating chicken eggs, framing. Home: 6752 State Highway 107 Marathon WI 54448-9444 Office: Marth Wood Shavings Supply Inc Marathon WI 54448-9802

NAUDZIUS, ALDONA KANAUKA, pianist, music educator; b. Kaunas, Lithuania, Sept. 18, 1933; came to U.S., 1949; d. Vincas and Ona Kanauka; m. Victor K. Naudzius, Dec. 1961; children: Ingrid Aldona, Renata Victoria. BA, Bennington Coll., 1955; MA, Columbia U., 1957; EdD, U. Ill., 1983; studied piano with, C. Friedberg, J. DeGray, C. Frank, V. Bacevicius, T. Richner, A. Forte, R. McDowell, S. Dorfman, S. Stravinsky, V. Leyetchkiss. Cert. music tchr. Ill., Ind., N.Y., M ass., social studies tchg. cert. Ill., N.Y. Tchr. music Pub. Schs., N.Y., 1958-59, 1959-62, East Chicago, Ind., 1963-67; tchr. piano Morton East H.S., Cicero, Ill., 1985-86; tchr. music De Lourdes Coll., Des Plaines, Ill., 1986, Chgo. Pub. Elem. Schs., 1989-94, Near North Metro H.S., Chgo., 1994-96, William Taft H.S., Chgo., 1996-98; pvt. piano tchr., 1998—. Participant internat. piano seminars, Graz, Austria, 1992, Lyon, France. Musician: Nelita True's Master Class, Dmitry Paperno's Master Class, 2000, C. Kiraly's piano master class, 2003. Mem. Am.-Lithuanian Cmty., Lithuanian Scouts Assn. (collegiate divsn.), Am.-Lithuanian Music Soc., Wagner Music Soc. Roman Catholic. Home: 5733 N Sheridan Rd Apt 29C Chicago IL 60660-8767 E-mail: aldona_n@yahoo.com.

NAUGHTON, MARIE ANN, corporate executive; b. Boston, Feb. 19, 1954; d. Robert J. and Beatrice T. (McDonald) N. BS in Speech magna cum laude, Emerson Coll., 1976; MA, Ind. U., 1977; cert. spl. studies bus. and adminstrn., Harvard U., 1989. Speech-lang. pathologist Dedham (Mass.) Pub. Schs., 1977-79, Mass. Gen. Hosp., Boston, 1979-81; speech pathologist Mt. Auburn Hosp., Cambridge, Mass., 1982-84; v.p. Curtis-Newton Corp., Dedham, 1984—. Author: A Coarticulation Manual for the Remediation of /S/, 1979. Elected mem. Dedham Sch. Com., 1993-96. Mem. Am. Speech, Lang. and Hearing Assn. (cert. clin. competence), Northeastern Retail Lumber Assn. (bd. dir.), Mass. Retail Lumber Assn. (bd. dirs. 1996-2002), Mass. Bldg. Materials Higher Edn. Consortium, Zeta Phi Eta. Home: 77 Circuit Rd Dedham MA 02026-3605 Office: 41 River St Dedham MA 02026-2935

NAUGLE, CHARLOTTE JUNE, principal, educator; b. Long Beach, Calif., June 1, 1938; d. Robert F. and Florence A. (Smith) Ballenger; children: Roberta Lynn, Marina Rae. AA, San Bernardino Valley Coll., 1959; BA, Calif. State U., 1966, MA, 1978. Tchr. Barstow (Calif.) Sch. Dist., 1966, U.S. Dependent Sch., Kenitra, Morocco, 1967-69; tchr., bilingual coord., state demonstration tchr. Colton (Calif.) Sch. Dist., 1970-81, state compensation project dir., 1981-83; prin. Smith Demonstration Sch., Bloomington, Calif., 1984-87, Walter Zimmerman Sch., Bloomington, 1987-94, Wilson Elem. Sch., Colton, Calif., 1994-97; tech. dir. PeaceBuilders, Inland Agy., Riverside, Calif., 1998—. Ednl. cons.; extension instr. U. Calif., Riverside, 1975-77. Pub. edn. chmn. San Bernardino-Riverside Counties, Am. Cancer Soc., 1979-81; bd. dirs. Cedar House Rehab. Ctr. Mem. steering com. Island Empire Quality Improvement Network. Recipient Able Toastmasters award, 1982; named Outstanding Tchr. of Writing award Inland Area Writing Project, U. Calif., Riverside, 1980. Mem. ASCD, Nat. Assn. Exec. Women, Mgmt. Assn. Colton Educators (pres. 1990), Assn. Calif. Sch. Adminstrs. (sec. region 12 1992-93), Toastmasters (internat. pres. 1980, div. ednl. v.p. 1981), Phi Delta Kappa. Republican. Home: 25590 Prospect Ave Apt 41E Loma Linda CA 92354-3154 Office: Inland Agy 6235 River Crest Dr Ste P Riverside CA 92507-0758

NAULTY, SUSAN LOUISE, archivist; b. Abington, Pa., May 28, 1944; d. Charles J. and Ruth E. (Schick) N. BA, Whittier Coll., 1967; MA, Loyola U., L.A., 1972. Tchr. history and English, Whittier (Calif.) H.S., 1968-70; from libr. asst. to asst. curator Huntington Libr., San Marino, Calif., 1972-91; archivist Richard Nixon Libr. and Birthplace, Yorba Linda, Calif., 1991—. Office: Richard Nixon Libr and Birthplace 18001 Yorba Linda Blvd Yorba Linda CA 92886-3903

NAUMIK, MARIA CHARLENE, academic administrator, educator; b. Perth Amboy, N.J., Aug. 20, 1952; d. John Louis Oliva and Gloria Maria Guarnieri; m. Stephen Peter Naumik, Aug. 29, 1990; m. Albert Robert Benaquista, Apr. 10, 1976 (div. Apr. 27, 1987); children: Gina Maria Benaquista, Laura Maryann Benaquista. BFA in Art Edn. cum laude, Ohio U., Athens, 1973; EdM in Adminstrn. Supervision and Curriculum, Georgian Ct. Coll., Lakewood, N.J., 1990. Tchr. fine arts Matawan (N.J.) Regional Sch. Dist., 1973—76, Middletown (N.J.) Sch. Dist., 1976—77; basic skills program asst. Middlesex County Supt., New Brunswick, NJ, 1980—83; arts and crafts program dir. Mill Rd. Day Camp, North Brunswick, NJ, 1985—91; internat. del. leader People to People Student Amb. Program, Spokane, Wash., 1992—2000; tchr. fine arts Monroe Twp. (N.J.) Sch. Dist., 1983—, asst. dir. adult edn. program, 1994—. Bd. trustees, sec. Art and Edn. Ctr., New Brunswick, 1985—, Seasons Multigenerational Orchs., Trenton, 1999—. Pres. Monroe Twp. Cmty. Theater Mighty Oak Players, 1990—; chairwoman Monroe Twp. Cultural Arts Commn., 1998—; bd. trustees Monroe Twp. Patrons of Arts, 2002—. Recipient Tchr. of Yr., Applegarth Mid. Sch., 2003. Mem.: Art Educators of N.J., N.J. Edn. Assn., Assn. Supervision and Curriculum Devel. (assoc.). Avocations: travel, gardening. Home: One Polonia Ct Monroe Township NJ 08831

NAVA, CARMEN P. communications executive; Degree in Bus. Adminstrn., U. So. Calif., 1984. Joined gen. mgmt. devel. program Pacific Bell, 1984, v.p., gen. mgr. Diverse Markets Group; regional pres. L.A. SBC Comm., L.A., 1997—99, pres. SBC Ctr. for Learning, 1999, pres. SBC West Consumer Markets, 1999—. Bd. govs. U. So. Calif. Alumni Assn. Office: SBC Comm Inc 175 E Houston San Antonio TX 78205-2233*

NAVA, CYNTHIA L. state legislator; b. Dona Ana, N. Mex., 1953; BS, Western Ill. U.; MA, Ea. Ill. U. Dep. supt. Gadsden Schools; mem. N.Mex. Senate, Dist. 31, Santa Fe, 1992—; mem. rules com., fin. com. N.Mex. Senate, chair legis. edn. study com., excellence in higher edn. com., health & human svcs. com., 1997—. Home: 3002 Broadmoor Dr Las Cruces NM 88001-7501 Office: N Mex Senate State Capitol Rm 301 Santa Fe NM 87503-0001

NAVARRA, TOVA, writer; b. Newark, July 10, 1948; d. Joe and Rose Leslie Treihart; m. John G. Navarra Jr., Aug. 26, 1967 (div. 1998); children: Yolanda, John G. III. BA magna cum laude, Seton Hall Univ., 1974; AAS with honors, Brookdale C.C., Lincroft, N.J., 1984; postgrad., Fairleigh Dickinson U. Elem. sch. tchr., Jersey City, 1967-69; corr. Village Times, Long Island, N.Y., 1974-75; tchr. music, humanities, German, art, art history Seton Hall Prep. Sch., South Orange, N.J., 1975-78; entertainment, feature writer, press corr. Asbury Park Press, Neptune, N.J., 1978-85, feature writer, art critic, family writer, 1985-92; feature writer, art columnist Two River Times, Red Bank, N.J., 1993-94. Psychiatric charge nurse, 1985; supr. grant rsch. Vis. Nurse Assn. Ctrl. Jersey, Red Bank, N.J., 1993-94; lectr. at writing confs. Author: The New Jersey Shore: A Vanishing Splendor, 1985, Jim Gary: His Life and Art, 1987, Your Body: Highlights of Human Anatomy, 1990, Playing It Smart: What to Do When You're on Your Own, 1989, also, pub. On My Own: Helping Kids Help Themselves, (translated into Italian, Portuguese and Hebrew) 1994, An Insider's Guide to Home Health Care: An Interdisciplinary Approach (with Margaret Lundrigan), 1995, Wisdom for Caregivers, 1995; (staged readings) Through the Kunai Grass with Dad, 1988, Don't Cry, Pandora, 1989; (with Myron A. Lipkowitz and John G. Navarra) Therapeutic Communication: A Guide to Effective Interpersonal Skills for Health Care Professionals, 1990, Encyclopedia of Vitamins, Minerals, and Supplements, 1995; (with Lipkowitz), Allergies A-Z, 1994; Images of America: Howell and Farmingdale 1996; (with Lundrigan) Image of America: Levittown: The First Fifty Years, 1997, Staten Island, 1997, Staten Island II, 1998, Levittown II, 1998; Toward Painless Writing, 1998; The American Century: Staten Island (with Lundrigan), 1999; Seton Hall University: A Photographic History, 1999; illustrator Drugs and Man, 1973; editor in chief Shore Affinity, 1979-81; contbg. editor Am. Jour. Nursing, 1990-94; staff writer, illustrator, photographer N.J. Music and Arts, 1978-81; editor Associated Univ. Presses, 1981-82; copywriter, photographer Jersey Shore Med. Ctr., 1985; feature writer, columnist Copley News Svc., 1988 93; health trend columnist Personal Fitness, 1989-90; assoc. editor The Courier, Middletown, N.J., May-Dec. 1998; lifestyle editor The Two River Times, Red Bank, N.G. May 1999—; contr. to Nursing Spectrum Magazine; photography exhbns. in N.Y., N.J., Pa.; guest various radio and TV programs; contbr. photographs to books, articles and photogs. to mags., newspapers; solo exhibits include Atlantic City Art Ctr., 1982, O.K. Harris Works of Art, N.Y.C., 1990, Gallery Axiom, Phila., 1991, Monmouth U., 1991, M. Thomson Kravetz Gallery, Bay Head, N.J.; group shows at Moravian Coll., Bethlehem, Pa., 1992, Art Forms, Red Bank, 1991. Mem. Gov.'s Coun. on Alcoholism and Drug Abuse Prevention, co-chair Later Childhood subcom., 1992 Mem. N.J. Playwrights Workshop (charter), N.J. State Nurses Assn. Avocations: singing, guitar, piano, belly dancing, crafts. Office: Sanford J Greenburger Assocs care Faith H Hamlin 55 5th Ave New York NY 10003-4301*

NAVARRO, JANYTE JANINE, real estate executive; b. LaJara, Colo., Apr. 14, 1935; d. John Charles Blissard and Mary Margaret (Mathias) Tedesco; m. Daniel David Myers (div. 1968); children: Kelli Myers, Keith Myers, Kim Myers; m. Rafael Fowler Navarro (div. July 31, 2003); children: Eric, Marshall, Laura Lynne, Mitchell; m. Jac Blackman, Sept. 21, 2003. Student, Colo. U., 1954-55, U. N.Mex. Owner Poodle Breeding Bus., Albuquerque, 1964-67, Jan-Knits, Albuquerque, 1973-74, Sharing Is Caring, Albuquerque, 1980—; mng. ptnr. Land-Ho Enterprises, 1988—. Regional dir. EXCEL Telecoms., 1996; bd. dirs. Fieseta de Shaklee, Albuquerque. Producer: (video) The Sponsoring Process, 1981; articles, newsletters in field. Bd. dirs. Sandia Ch. Religious Sci.; social dir. High Desert Ch. Religious Sci., 2000—. Mem. Rio Grande Sales Leaders Assn. (pres. 1984, 86). Avocations: walking, metaphysical research, teaching self-image classes, environ. issues. Home and Office: 1505 Gretta St NE Albuquerque NM 87112-4319 Office Phone: 505-292-0773. E-mail: blacjacjan@aol.com.

NAVARRO, LYDIA, language educator; b. Yabucoa, P.R., Oct. 20, 1949; d. José Navarro and Juana Crespo; m. Arnaldo Rivera; children: Arnaldo Jr., Miguel Angel, Jorge Luis, José Antonio. BA in english, U. P.R., 1986; MS in TESOL, Nova Southeastern U., 1997; D in edn., U. Ctrl. Fla., 2004. Cert. profl. educator in english, TESOL. Tchr. P.R. Pub. Schs., Mayaguez, PR, 1986—90, Volusia County Schs., Deltona, Fla., 1990—2000, dist. translator, 2000—02, tchr. on assignment, 2002—. Foreign lang. dept. chmn. Deltona (Fla.) HS, 1996—2000; dist. ESOL trainer ESOL Program, Deland, Fla., 1996—; clin. edn. Volusia County Schs., 1997—. Mem.: Assn. TESOL, Assn. Supr. and Curriculum Devel., Leadership West Volusia, C of C West Volusia, Nat. Rep. Party, Kappa Delta Pi. Avocations: dance, gardening, swimming, landscaping, interior decorating. Home: 1640 Humphrey Ct Deltona FL [illegible] Office: Volusia County Schs 200 N Clara Ave Deland FL 32720

NAVARRO-STEINEL, CATHERINE A. municipal official; Degree in Bus. Mgmt., ICS Newport Pacific, 1995; BSc in Criminal Justice Mgmt., La Salle U., 1997; student, Rutgers U., Thomas Edison State Coll. Cert. Pub. Supr. Mgmt. N.J. Dept. Personnel, 99, registered Mpl. Clk. State Dept. Cmty. Affairs, cert. pub.mgr. 2003. Supr. fire dispatcher N. Hudson Regional Comm. Ctr., West N.Y., NJ, 1985—91; prin. tech. aid to supt. Twp. Teaneck, Teaneck, NJ, 1992; fire comm. dispatcher N. Hudson Regional Comm. Ctr., 1992—94; police records clk. Twp. Teaneck, 1994—95, fire dept. sr. clk., 1995—99; dep. mcpl. clk. City of Orange, Orange, NJ, 1999—2000; mcpl. clk. Borough of Fairview, NJ, 2000—02; borough adminstr. Borough of Little Ferry, NJ, 2002—. Mem.: Internat. Inst. Mcpl. Clk., Am. Soc. Notary Pub., Internat. Soc. Cert. Employee Benefits Assn., Am. Acaed. Cert. Pub. Mgrs., Cert. Pub. Mgr. Soc. N.J., Bergen County Clk. Assn., Mcpl. Clk. Assn. N.J. Home: 16 Ann Street Bergenfield NJ 07621-1602 Office: Borough of Little Ferry 215-217 Liberty St Little Ferry NJ 07643

NAVRATILOVA, MARTINA, professional tennis player; b. Prague, Czech Republic, Oct. 18, 1956; came to U.S., 1975, naturalized, 1981; d. Miroslav Navratil and Jana Navratilova. Student, schs. in Czechoslovakia; Hon. doctorate, George Washington U., 1996. Tennis commentator/broadcaster HBO Sports, 1995-99; Profl. tennis player, 1973-94, 2003—. Player U.S. Fed Cup Team, 1982—86, 1989, 95, 2003; mem. World Team Tennis, 1990—. Author: (with George Vecsey) Martina, 1985, (with Liz Nickles) The Total Zone, 1995, (with Liz Nickels) The Breaking Point, (with Liz Nickles) 1996, Killer Instinct, 1997; columnist. Co-founder Rainbow Card. Winner Czechoslovak Nat. singles, 1972-74, U.S. Open singles, 1983, 84, 86, 87, U.S. Open doubles, 1977, 78, 80, 83, 84, 87, 90, U.S. Open mixed doubles, 1987, Va. Slims Tournament, 1978, 83, 84, 85, 86, Va. Slims doubles, 1991, Wimbledon singles, 1978, 79, 82, 83, 84, 85, 86, 87, 90, Wimbledon women's doubles, 1976, 79, 81, 82, 83, 84, 86, Wimbledon mixed doubles, 1985, 93, 95, 2003, French Open singles, 1982, 84, Australian Open singles, 1981, 83, 85, Australian Doubles (with Nagelsen) 1980, (with Shriver), 1982, 84, 85, 87, 88, 89, Australian Mixed Doubles, 2003, Roland Garros (with Shriver), 1985, 87, 89, Italian Open doubles (with Sabatini), 1987, (with Shriver) COREL WTA Tour doubles team of yr., 1981-89, triple Crown at U.S. Open, 1987; recipient Women's Sports Found. Flo Hyman award, 1987; named Female Athlete of the Decade (1980s) The Nat. Sports Review, UPI, and AP, WTA Player of Yr., 1978-79, 82-86, Women's Sports Found. Sportswoman of Yr., 1982-84, Hon. Citizen of Dallas, AP Female Athlete of Yr., 1983, Chgo. Hall of Fame, 1994; Martina Navratilova Day proclaimed in Chgo., 1992; recipient BBC Lifetime Achievement Award, 2003. Mem. Women's Tennis Assn. (dir., exec. com., pres.), Women's Tennis Assn. Tour Player's Assn. (pres. 1979-80, 83-84, 94-95). Achievements include being the holder of 167 singles titles and 173 doubles titles; holder of record of singles-match wins (1,309), 1991; holds record for 109 consecutive doubles matches won; 3rd women in history to win singles, doubles and mixed doubles titles at all four Grand Slam Tournaments; oldest women (43 years) to become a Wimbledon Champion (mixed doubles, 2003).

NAWROCKI, SUSAN JEAN, librarian; b. Aurora, Ill., Mar. 3, 1942; d. David John and Sarah (Willoughby) Calvert; m. Thomas Dennis Nawrocki, June 25, 1966; children: Selena, Steffan. BA, Coe Coll., Cedar Rapids, Iowa, 1964; MS in Art, Milw., 1965. Cert. Tchr. Iowa, 1966, Wis., 1967. Libr. Milw. Pub. Libr. Main Br., 1966—67; reference libr. Columbus/Lowndes County Libr., Columbus, Miss., 1986—. Exhibitions include 57 competitive : Watercolor Wis., Weston Mus. Fine Arts, Milw., 1966, exhibitions include Ann. San Antonio Artists' Exhbn., 1968 ($200 award, 1969), Witte Meml. Mus., San Antonio, 1969, Exhbn. Southwest Prints and Drawings, Dallas Mus. Fine Arts, 1969 (award, 1969), Ann. Festival of Arts 8-State Exhbn. Paintings and Graphics, Fort Smith Art Ctr., Ark., 1971 (award, 1971), Ann. Print and Drawing Competition, 1972, Ann. U. Wis. Art Competition, U. Wis., Milw., 1976, 1977, 1979, 1982, Bi-State Competition, Meridian (Miss.) Mus. of Art, 1976 (purchase award, 1987), 1978, 1980, 1987, Nat. Arts Festival, Tupelo, Miss., 1980 (Purchase award, 1980, 2 Purchase awards, Top Graphics award, 1981, Purchase award and Graphics award, 1983), 1981, 1983, Ann, Miss. Arts Exhbn., Univ. So. Miss., Hattiesburg, 1982, Ann, Miss. Arts Exhbn. Juried, 1987, 1988 (Purchase award, 1987); contbg. editor (art editor): (Coll. Mag.) Acorn, 1962—64; co-editor, 1964; contbg. editor: Caravan Literary Mag., 1963—64. Home: 147 Shane Cir Columbus MS 39702 E-mail: refer@lowndes.lib.ms.us.

NAYER, JO ANN ELIZABETH, executive, multimedia producer; b. Rome, N.Y., May 28, 1954; d. Veto Philip and Josephine Spohn; children: Tracy, Matthew. BA, SUNY, Binghamton, 1976; MLS, U. Md., 1978; student in Nursing, Phillips Beth Israel U., 2003—. Media libr. Langston Hughes Libr., Corona, N.Y., 1978-80; prodn. mgr. Showtime Networks, N.Y.C., 1980-87; dir. post prodn. Lifetime TV, N.Y.C., 1987-94; owner, multimedia producer Tama Interactive Design, Inc., Bklyn., 1995—2003, co-owner, 2003—. Office: Tama Interactive Design 230 11th St Brooklyn NY 11215-3916

NAYLOR, ILLANA, pediatrics nurse; b. Denver, May 13, 1954; d. Kurtis Friend and Gladys Shank Naylor; m. Richard David Barrett, June 27, 1981; children: Rianna, Benjamin, Alisa. BA in Theology, The Colo. Coll., 1976; BSN-RN, George Mason U., 1985, grad. student in Nursing Adminstrn., 2000—. Lic. practical nurse, Prince William County, 1980, RN Va., 1985. Pediat. nurse Prince William (Va.) Health Sys., 1980—. Instr. Prince William (Va.) Health Sys., 1986—, mem. nurse devel. coun., 1998—99, mem. ednl. com., 2003—, facilitator ednl. task force, 2003—; presenter in field. Vol. literacy program Baldwin Elem. Sch., 1999—; founder Unity in Cmty., 1995—, treas.; beautification chmn. Baldwin Elem. Sch. PTA, 1992—99; Mid-Atlantic dist. rep. Decade to Overcome Violence Citizens Adv. Com. Solid Waste Man; active Virginians Alternative to Death Penalty, 1993—; mem. various coms. Manassas (Va.) Ch. Brethren, 1976—; mem. citizens adv. com. solid waste mgmt. Manassas, Va., 1991—. Named one of Ten People of Yr., Manassas Jour. Messenger, 2001; recipient Cmty. Svc. award, Prince William County Human Rights Commn., 1997, award, Baldwin Elem. Sch., 1999, Golden Rule award, J.C. Penney, 2000. Mem.: Sigma Theta Tau, Golden Key, Alpha Lambda Delta. Democrat. Avocations: reading, singing, dance, family and friends, hiking. Home: 10294 South Grant Ave Manassas VA 20110-6135 Office: Prince William Health Sys 8700 Sudley Rd Manassas VA 20110

NAYLOR, PHYLLIS REYNOLDS, writer; b. Anderson, Ind., Jan. 4, 1933; d. Eugene Spencer and Lura Mae (Schield) Reynolds; m. Thomas A. Tedesco, Jr., Sept. 9, 1951 (div. 1960); m. Rex V. Naylor, May 26, 1960; children: Jeffrey, Michael. Diploma, Joliet Jr. Coll., 1953; BA, Am. U., 1963. Author more than 118 books including Crazy Love: An Autobiographical Account of Marriage and Madness, 1977, Revelations, 1979, A String of Chances, 1982 (ALA notable book), The Agony of Alice, 1985 (ALA notable book), The Keeper, 1986 (ALA notable book), Unexpected Pleasures, 1986, Send No Blessings, 1990 (YASD best book for young adults), Shiloh, 1991 (ALA notable book, John Newbery medal 1992), The Fear of Place, 1994, Sang Spell, 1998, Walker's Crossing, 1999, Blizzard's Wake, 2002, After, 2003. Recipient Golden Kite award Soc. Children's Book Writers Am., 1985, Child Study award Bank St. Coll., 1983, Edgar Allan Poe award Mystery Writers Am., 1985, Internat. book award Soc. Sch. Librs., 1988, Christopher award, 1989, Newbery award ALA, 1992, Nat. Endowment of Arts Creative Writing fellow, 1987. Mem. Children's Book Guild of Washington (pres. 1974-75, 83-84), Soc. Children's Book Writers, Authors Guild, PEN, Council for a Livable World, Physicians for Social Responsibility, Amnesty Internat. Unitarian Universalist. Avocations: theater, swimming. Home and Office: 9910 Holmhurst Rd Bethesda MD 20817-1618

NAYLOR, SUSAN EMBRY, music educator; b. Huntington Park, California, Feb. 21, 1951; d. Hollie J. and Sara Mozelle (Maddox) E. MusB in piano performance, Converse Coll., 1973; MusM, Ga. State U., 1975. Cert. music tchr. Ga. Prof. piano and music theory Reinhardt Coll., Waleska, Ga., 1975—, music program coord., 1995-2000. Pvt. piano tchr. Waleska, Marietta, and Kennesaw, Ga., 1973—. Performer solo piano and ensemble recitals colls., chs. and profl. orgns., 1973—; pianist Spartanburg (S.C.) Symphony Orch., 1970-73, featured soloist, 1972; guest pianist Nat. Pub. Radio, 1988. Ch. pianist Bapt., Meth. Churches in Marietta, Dallas, and Kennesaw, 1973—. Recipient Cobb County Young Artist Award; Cobb County Arts Coun. Parks and Recreation and Jr. League, 1983, 86. Mem. Ga. Music Tchr. Assn., adjudicator 1976—, coll. faculty chair 1996-98, cert. credentials chair 1997-99, pres. elect 1998-2000, pres. 2000-2002, Finance/Advisory Comm., 2000-, Ga. Fedn. Music Clubs adjudicator 1976—, Cherokee Music Tchr. Assn. pres. 1988-91, 1st v.p. program 1997-99, Cherokee County Arts Coun. exec. bd., v.p. 1993-95, Music Tchr. Nat. Assn., Nat. coll. faculty cert., nat. cert. evaluation team 1993-96, ho. dels. 2000-2002. Baptist. Avocations: antiques, reading. Home: 109 Myrtle Ct Waleska GA 30183-4202 Office: Reinhardt Coll 7300 Reinhardt Coll Cir Waleska GA 30183-2981 E-mail: sen@reinhardt.edu.

NAZARIO, SONIA, reporter; b. Madison, Wis., Sept. 8, 1960; m. William Regensburger. BA in History, Williams Coll., Williamstown, Mass., 1982; MA in Latin Am. Studies, U. Calif., Berkeley, 1988. Freelance reporter El Pais, Madrid, 1980; staff reporter Wall St. Jour., Atlanta, 1982—84, Miami, 1984—86, LA, 1988—93; urban affairs writer L.A. Times, 1993—94, projects and urban affairs reporter, 1994—. Recipient Pulitzer prize for feature writing, 2003, Pulitzer prize finalist for pub. svc., 1998, Nat. Coun. on Crime and Delinquency PASS award, 1998, Commendation for outstanding reporting on psychiat. issues, Am. Psychiat. Assn., 1998, Life-Time award, Inst. for Suicide Prevention, 1997, Guillermo Martinez-Marquez award for overall excellence, Nat. Assn. Hispanic Journalists, 1995, George Polk award for local reporting, 1994, Cameron R. Duncan World Hunger Media award, 1994, George Polk award for internat. reporting, 2003, Robert F. Kennedy Journalism award, 2003, Overseas Press Club award, 2003, award, Nat. Assn. Hispanic Journalists Guillermo Martinez-Marquez, 2003. Office: LA Times 202 W 1st St Los Angeles CA 90012*

NAZIR, TABINDA, physician; b. Rawalpindi, Punjab, Pakistan, Mar. 15, 1961; d. Nazir Ahmed Sheikh and Khalida Adib (Khanum) N. MBBS, Rawalpindi Med. Coll., Pakistan, 1985. Intern in internal medicine, gen. surgery Fauji Found. Med. Ctr., Rawalpindi, Pakistan, 1985-86, 86, resident coronary care unit, 1986-89; resident in medicine, surgery, pediats. Ali Med. Ctr., Islamabad, Pakistan, 1989; observer, clin. clerkship Beth Israel Med. Ctr., N.Y.C., 1989-90; pvt. practice Islamabad, 1990-93; resident in transitional medicine Elmhurst (N.Y.) Hosp. Ctr./Mount Sinai Svcs., 1994-95, resident in primary care internal medicine, 1995-97; mem. blood utilization rev. com., 1996-97; fellow in infectious diseases The Mount Sinai Hosp., N.Y.C., 1997-99. Author: Clinical Obstetrics and Gynecology, 1996, Rakel-Conns Current Therapy, 1997. Mem. AMA, ACP (assoc.). Avocations: stamp collecting/philately, reading, walking. Home: 555 Kappock St #21B Bronx NY 10463 Office: The Mount Sinai Hosp One Gustave L Levy Pl New York NY 10029

NEAL, ALAINE (DIANN NEAL), nursing administrator; b. Seaside, Oreg., Jan. 25, 1942; d. Alan Welch Jr. and Beatrice June (Wisdom) Smith; m. Kelly Sayre Neal Jr., July 31, 1965; children: Kelly III, Karter B. BS, U. Portland, 1964; MS, U. Ariz., 1970. RNC in in-patient obstetrics, nursing adminstrn. advanced. Head nurse Family Childbirth Ctr. St. Joseph's Hosp. and Med. Ctr., Phoenix, 1982-87, nurse mgr. maternal-newborn svcs., 1987-90, dir. nursing women's and children's svcs., 1990-95; dir. pediatrics and nursery, pediatric intensive care Desert Samaritan Med. Ctr., Mesa, Ariz., 1995-2000; dir. women and infants svcs. St. Joseph's Hosp., Carondelet Health Network, Tucson, 2000—. Author: (with others) High-Risk Intrapartum Nursing, 1992. Capt. Nurse Corps, U.S. Army, 1964-67. Mem. Sigma Theta Tau. Episcopalian. Avocations: equestrian, genealogy, cooking. Office: 225 W Spring Valley Dr Tucson AZ 85737-6745 E-mail: dneal@carondelet.org.

NEAL, CYNTHIA ANN, elementary school educator, composer; b. High Point, N.C., Apr. 10, 1968; d. Larry Edward Overcash and Donna Ann Cashatt; m. Jerry Dolan Neal, II., Sept. 15, 1990; children: Catrina Ann, Charles Alexander, Zachary Edward. BA in Mid. Grades Edn., High Point U., 1990. Cert. mid. grades edn. lang. arts/social studies N.C., 1990. Tchr. Randolph County Schs., Trinity, NC, 1997—. Workshop cons. Randolph County Schs., Asheboro, NC, 1998—2001, mem. literacy team, 2002—. Composer: (contemporary Christian songs, collection of works) The Blessing, (songs) Eyes of a Child. Ch. pianist; children's ministry activities Hopewell United Meth. Ch., Trinity, 2002—03, co-chair worship com., 2002—03. Literacy grantee, Randolph County Schs., N.C., 1999. Mem.: N.C. Assn. Educators. R-Conservative. United Methodist. Avocations: reading, music/songwriting, gardening, fishing. Personal E-mail: cneal@randloph.k12.nc.us.

NEAL, DARWINA LEE, government official; b. Mansfield, Pa., Mar. 31, 1942; d. Darwin Leonard and Ina Belle (Cooke) N. BS, Pa. State U., 1965; postgrad., Cath. U, 1968-70. Registered landscape architect. Landscape architect nat. capital region Nat. Pk. Svc., 1965-69, office of White House liaison, 1969-71, office of profl. services, 1971-74, div. design svcs., 1974-89, chief design svcs., 1989-95, chief landscape arch. office of stewardship and partnership, 1996-98, chief cultural resource preservation svcs. nat. capital reg., 1998—. Judge numerous award juries. Contbr. articles to profl. jours.; co-author sects. of profl. bull., mag.; author introduction to book Women, Design and the Cambridge School; columnist: Land monthly, 1975-79. Recipient Merit award Landscape Contractors Met. Washington; recipient hon. mention Les Floralies Internat. Montreal, 1980 Alumni Achievement award Pa. State U. Arts and Architecture Alumni Soc., 1981 Fellow Am. Soc. Landscape Architects (v.p. 1979-81, pres. elect 1982-83, pres. 1983-84, trustee 1976-77, nat. treas. 1977-79, legis. coord. 1975-79, sec. Coun. Fellows 1988-90, del. to Internat. Fedn. Landscape Architects 1989-92, 2000-03, ex-officio rep. to U.S./internat. coun. on monuments and sites 1985-98, liaison to historically black coll. and univ. program Dept. Interior, chair internat. task force 1999-2000, Pres.' medal 1987); Treas. U.S. Internat. coun. on Monuments and Sites, 1998-2004, sec. Internat. Fed. Landscape Architects, W. Region, 2003-; mem. Landscape Archtl. Accreditation Bd. (roster vis. evaluators), Nat. Recreation and Parks Assn., Nat. Soc. Park Resources (bd. dirs. 1978-80), Nat. Trust Hist. Preservation, Pa. State U. Alumni Assn. (Washington met. chpt. trustee 1972-74), Am. Arbitration Assn. (nat. panel arbitrators), Com. 100 for the Fed. City, Preservation Action, Nat. Assn. Olmsted Parks, Beekman Pl. Condominium Assn. (bd. dirs. 1985-91, archtl. control com. 1977-2000, landscape com. 2000-02), Alliance for Historic Preservation, Garden Conservancy, Scenic Am., Preservation Action, Preservation Roundtable, Hist. Soc. Washington. Office: Nat Park Svc/Nat Capital Region Off Lands Resources & Plan 1100 Ohio Dr SW Washington DC 20242-0001

NEAL, IRENE COLLINS, artist, educator; b. Greensburg, Pa., May 14, 1936; d. Oliver Shupe and Betsey Cowap (Mann) Collins; m. Paul Whitaker Neal, Nov. 24, 1960; children: Paul Collins Gordon, Betsey Whitaker. BA, Wilson Coll., 1958; student, Sch. Visual Arts, Rio de Janeiro, 1976-77, Memphis State U., 1979-80, U. Bridgeport, 1982-83, participant, Triangle Art Workshop, Pine Plains, N.Y., 1985. Guest spkr. Coll. Santa Fe, Albuquerque, N.Mex., 1994. One-woman shows include Allied Chem. Corp., Morristown, N.J., 1975, Planetarium Rio de Janeiro, 1977, Pat Ackerman Gallery, Memphis, 1980, Westmoreland Mus. Art, Greensburg, 1986, Wilson Coll., 1993, Cooper Classics Collections, N.Y.C., 2001, 02, Trans-Lux Cocteau Corp., Irene Neal Recent Paintings, Santa Fe, N.M., 2003; group exhbns. include Jersey City Mus., 1975, N.J. State Mus., 1975, Somerset (N.J.) Tri-State Mus., 1975, Nat. Arts Club, N.Y.C., 1975, Garden State Watercolor Soc., 1975, Salao de Marinhas, Rio de Janeiro, 1977, Stamford Mus., 1984, 85, 89, Branchville Soho Gallery, Ridgefield, Conn., 1984, Silvermine Guild, New Canaan, Conn., 1984, Stamford Libr., 1985, Shippee Gallery, N.Y.C., 1986, 110 Greene St., N.Y.C., 1986, Wilton (Conn.) Libr., 1986, Aldrich Mus. Contemporary Art, Ridgefield, 1987, Visual Arts Festival, Edmonton, Alta., Can., 1989, Mus. Art., Ft. Lauderdale, Fla., 1991-92, Salander-O'Reilly Galleries, Inc., N.Y., 1994, Vanderleelie Gallery, Edmonton, 1996, Galerie Piltzer, Paris, 1996, Fine Art 2000 Gallery, Stamford, 1996, 97, York Coll., Queens, N.Y., 1997, Ctr. for Performing Arts, Stamford, 1997, Mus. Contemporary Art, Palm Beach, Fla., 1997, Griffis Art Ctr., New London, 1997, Vero Beach (Fla.) Mus., 1998, Flint (Mich.) Inst. Art, 1999, Mus. Contemporary Art, Denver, 1999, Gelabert Studios Gallery, N.Y.C., 2000, Hotel de Ville, Brussels, 2000, 69th Regiment Armory, N.Y.C., New New Painters, The Real Avant Garde, 2000, Nat. Gallery, Prague, The Czech Repub., 2001, 2002 Galerie Anne-Lettrie, Paris, 2001, The Durst Orgn., N.Y.C., 2002, 03, Musee du Bas-Saint Laurant Riviere de Lupe, Que., Can., 2002-03, Scope N.Y. Stevenson Fine Art, Dylan Hotel, N.Y.C., 2003, Mus. au Bus, St. Laurant, Quebec, 2003, Elfsar Collection, Ltd., Vancouver, BC, 2003, Juten Gallery, Toronto, Ont., 2003; represented in permanent collections Planetarium Rio de Janeiro, Internat. Paper, N.Y.C., Westmoreland Mus. Art, Greensburg, Pepperdine U., Malibu, Calif., Newport Harbor Art Mus., Newport Beach, Calif., Hoover Instn. Stanford U., St. Matthew's Episcopal Ch., Wilton, Columbia U., Ctr. Arts, Vero Beach, Fla., Mus. Art, Ft. Lauderdale, Alamo Rent A Car, Ft. Lauderdale, Denver Ctr. Performing Arts, Flint (Mich.) Inst. Art, The Nat. Gallery, Prague, The Czech Rep., Wilson Coll., Chambersburg, Pa., The Appleton Mus. of Art, Ocala, Fla.; pub., contbr. art to book New New Painting, 1996, catalog, 2000, Cooper Classics Collection, 2001, 2002. Recipient Tift award, Wilson Coll., Chambersburg, Pa., 2003. Republican. Episcopalian. Avocations: ocean diving, tennis, golf, gardening. Home: 700 River Rd Cos Cob CT 06807-1907

NEAL, LEORA LOUISE HASKETT, social services administrator; b. N.Y.C., Feb. 23, 1943; d. Melvin Elias and Miriam Emily (Johnson) Haskett; m. Robert A. Neal, Apr. 23, 1966; children: Marla Patrice, Johnathan Robert. BA in Psychology and Sociology, City Coll. N.Y., 1965; MS in Social Work, Columbia U., 1970, cert. adoption specialist, 1977; IBM cert. community exec. tng. program, N.Y., 1982. Cert. social worker N.Y. Caseworker N.Y.C. Dept. Social Service, 1965-67, Windham Child Care, N.Y.C., 1967-73; exec. dir., founder Assn. Black Social Workers Child Adoption Counseling and Referral Service, N.Y.C., 1975-96; adoption tng. specialist Ctr. for Devel. Human Svcs., SUNY-N.Y. State Office Children and Family Svcs., Yonkers, N.Y., 1996—. Cons. in field; founder Haskett-Neal Publs., Bronx, N.Y., 1993. Co-author: Transracial Adoptive Parenting: A Black/White Community Issue, 1993; contbr. articles to profl. jours. Pres. bd. dirs. Fountain Ave. Cmty. Devel. Corp. Child Welfare League Am. fellow, 1976; recipient cert. No Time to Lose cert. N.Y. State Dept. Social Svcs., 1989. Mem. NAFE, Nat. Assn. Black Social Workers, Columbia U. Alumni Assn., CCNY Alumni Assn., Missionary Com. Revival Team (outreach chair 1982-88). Democrat. Avocations: writing, history and religious studies, travel, cultural activities. Office: NY State Office of Children and Family Svcs SUNY 525 Nepperhan Ave Yonkers NY 10703-2857

NEAL, MO (P. MAUREEN NEAL), sculptor; b. Houston, Oct. 26, 1950; d. Gordon Taft and Mary Louise (O'Connor) N.; m. Thomas Alan Buttars, Jan. 2, 1984. BA cum laude, Wash. State U., 1988; MFA, Va. Commonwealth U., 1991. Assoc. prof. art and art history U. Nebr., Lincoln, 1994—. Adj. faculty dept. fine arts U. S.D., Vermillion, 1991-92. Grantee S.D. Arts Coun., 1992, 94, Nat. Endowment for Arts, 1994; fellow Nebr. Arts Coun., 1998. Mem. Mid Am. Coll. Art Assn. (bd. dirs. 1997, pres. 2000-02), Phi Beta Kappa. Democrat. Office: U Nebr Dept Art & Art History Rm 120 Richards Hall Lincoln NE 68588-0114 E-mail: moneal@unl.edu.

NEAL, TARA-JANE, director, educator; b. Toronto, Ont., Can., Mar. 25, 1970; d. John Paul and Kerry Diane Federspiel. BA, S.W. Tex. State U., 1992, MEd, 1996; PhD, U. Tex., Dallas, 2001. Sr. grad. asst. U. Tex., Dallas, 1996—2001; prof. history Paul Quinn Coll., Dallas, 1997—98; lectr. history Richland Coll., Richardson, Tex., 1999—2001; dir. acad. affairs U. Phoenix, Dallas, 2001—. Conf. presenter Brit. Assn. Am. Studies, Swansea, Wales, 2000, Gorgias Nat. Conf., U. Tex., Dallas, 2000. Contbr. book revs. to profl. publs. Mem.: Rotary Club Dallas. Avocation: triathlons. Office: U Phoenix Ste 200 12400 Coit Rd Dallas TX 75251 Home: 12530 Daimler Dr Frisco TX 75034-5233

NEAL, TERESA SCHREIBEIS, secondary school educator; b. Wheatland, Wyo., Mar. 19, 1956; d. Gene L. and Bonnie Marie (Reed) Schreibeis; m. Michael R. Neal, Apr. 7, 1990; 1 child, Rianna Michele. BA in Am. Studies and English Edn., U. Wyo., 1978; MA in History, U. So. Calif., 1989, PhD, 1994, Cert. Studies of Women/Men in Soc., 1995. Cert. secondary edn. tchr., Wyo., Colo. Tchr. lang. arts and social studies, asst. coach Carbon County Sch. Dist. 1, Rawlins, Wyo., 1978-86; asst. lectr. freshmen writing program U. So. Calif., L.A., 1986-90; adj. prof. history Palomar (Calif.) C.C., San Diego, 1991; software support specialist Dynamic Data Systems, Westminster, Colo., 1992-93; tchr. humanities gifted and talented classes Arvada (Colo.) West H.S., 1993-98; tchr., program developer New Montessori Mid. Sch., 1998-00, Mountain Shadows Mid. Sch., Boulder, Colo., 1998-2000; adj. prof. history, humanities and English composition Red Rocks C.C., Lakewood and Arvada, Calif., 2002—. Participant critical thinking and humanities secondary edn. project NEH, Wyo., 1985-86; adj. prof. English Composition, Front Range C.C., Westminster, Colo., 2000-03. Mem., chmn. Reading Is Fundamental Program, Rawlins, 1983-85, Women of the West Mus., 2001—; tchr., sponsor Denver-Metro YMCA Youth and Govt., 1994-97, Close Up, Washington, 1984-86, 97; tchr., advisor Nat. History Day Contest, 1995—; tchr., sponsor World Affairs Challenge, Denver U., 1998; vol. math. tutor Foothills Acad., Wheat Ridge, Colo., 2001-02. Mem. AAUW (Project Renew fellow 1987-88), Western Assn. Women Historians, G. Autrey Mus. Western Art, Phi Beta Kappa. Avocations: travel, fine arts, baseball, reading. E-mail: tneal@javakats.com.

NEAL, YOLANDA KIMBERLY TABB, small business owner; b. Chgo., Oct. 18, 1964; d. Albert H. Jourdan and Hattie Lee Jackson; m. Orlandus Neal Jr., Apr. 1, 1987 (div. Aug. 1990); 1 child, Marquel Antonio ; children: Maurice M. Macklin, Kenyata L. Macklin, Shaquele Macklin. Cert. manicurist, Emily Griffith Oppt., 1983, cert. office mgr. legal svcs., 1982. Conservator San Bernadino County, Barstow, Calif.; care giver Sr. Foster Grandparent, Denver; food server Lowry AFB, Denver, Fitzmons Army Med. Ctr., Denver, Denver Pub. Sch.; foster home Kimberly's, Sacramento, guardian Apple Valley, Calif. Republican. Roman Catholic. Avocations: crafts, poetry, cooking, drawing. Home: 14031 Pawnee Rd Apple Valley CA 92307 Office: Kimberly's PO Box 2853 Apple Valley CA 92307*

NEALE, DIANE YUNCK, artist; b. Olney, Ill., Dec. 1, 1944; d. George Feick and Dorothy (Phillips) Yunck; m. Latimer Ford Neale, June 14, 1967; children: Georgia Ford, Jules Arthur. BA in Art, French, Coll. Wooster, 1966; postgrad., Pratt Inst., 1967. Presch. and elem. art tchr. So. Calif. Sch. Dists., 1966-78. One-woman shows include Helen Drue Gallery, 1989, Arabesque-Stearns & Black Gallery, 1990, Rose Cafe Gallery, 1990, 92, 94, Valentine Owens Gallery, 1992, Nemiroff Deutsch Gallery, 1995, Gallery Cafe, Bergamot Station, Santa Monica, Calif., 1996, Z-2 Gallery, L.A., 1996, Indigo Cafe, Santa Monica, 1998, Viva Gallery, Northridge, Calif., 1999; group exhibitions include Brushworks Gallery, San Diego, 1994-95, Gallery Viva, Kawasaki City, Japan, 1994, C.G Rein Gallery, Scottsdale, Ariz., 1993-94, Gallery Milieu, 1992, Diane Nelson Gallery, 1995, Gloria Delson Contemporary Art, L.A., 1997; juried exhbns. include Malibu Art Assn., 1999, Wiseman Mus. Art, Malibu, 1999 (2d Pl. prize for oil painting 2002), Celebration Fine Art, Scottsdale, 2001. Bd. trustees Malibu (Calif.) United Meth., 1990, Sunday sch. tchr., choir mem., 1983-90. Methodist. Avocations: running, dance, backpacking.

NEAL-PARKER, SHIRLEY ANITA, obstetrician, gynecologist; b. Washington, Aug. 28, 1949; d. Leon Walker and Pearl Anita (Shelton) Neal; m. Andre Cowan Dasent, June 21, 1971 (div. Feb. 1978); 1 child, Erika Michelle Dasent; m. James Carl Parker, Feb. 11, 1979; 1 child, Amirah Nabeehah. BS in Biology, Am. U., 1971; MD, Hahnemann U., 1979. Lic. Md., Calif., Wash. Intern Howard U. Hosp., 1979-80, resident, 1980-84; physician Nat. Health Svc. Corp., Charleston, W. Va., 1984-86; clin. instr. W. Va. U., Charleston, 1985-86; pvt. practice ob./gyn. Sacramento, 1986-95; pvt. practice Chehalis, Wash., 1995—; chair dept. perinatology Providence Centralia Hosp., 1999-2000. Bd. dirs. Ruth Rosenberg Dance Ensemble, Sacramento, 1992-95, Human Response Network, Chehalis, 1995-97. Mem.: Wash. State Obstet. Assn., Lewis County Med. Soc., Wash. State Med. Assn., Am. Med. Women's Assn. (comty. svc. award Mother Hale br. 1994), Nat. Med. Assn., Am. Reproductive Health Profls., Am. Assn. Gynecologic Laparoscopists, Soroptomist Internat. Avocations: traveling, reading, crocheting, collecting ethnic dolls, magnets. Office: PO Box 997 171 S Market Blvd Chehalis WA 98532 Home: 4440 W Orchard Ave Visalia CA 93277-6964 E-mail: drsanp@earthlink.net.

NEAR, TIMOTHY, theater director; Grad., San Francisco State U., Acad. Music and Dramatic Art, London. Artistic dir. San Jose Repertory Theatre, 1987—. Past actress, dir. with numerous prestigious theaters including The Guthrie Theatre, Berkeley (Calif.) Repertory Theater, La Jolla (Calif.) Playhouse, The Alliance Theatre, Atlanta, The Mark Taper Forum, L.A., Ford's Theatre, Washington, Repertory Theatre of St. Louis, N.Y. Shakespeare Festival, Stage West, Mass., A.C.T., Seattle. Dir. Ghosts on Fire, La Jolla Playhouse (Drama League award), Singer in the Storm, Mark Taper Forum (Drama League award), Thunder Knocking on the Door (Drama League award). Recipient 1997 Woman of Achievement in the Arts, San Jose Mercury News and The Woman's Fund. Office: San Jose Repertory Theatre 101 Paseo De San Antonio San Jose CA 95113-2603

NEARING, VIVIENNE W. lawyer; b. N.Y.C. d. Abraham M. and Edith Eunice (Webster) N. BA, Queens Coll.; MA, JD, Columbia U. Bar: N.Y., D.C., U.S. Dist. Ct. (so. and ea. dists.) N.Y., U.S. Ct. Appeals (2d cir.), U.S. Claims Ct. Ptnr. Stroock & Stroock & Lavan, N.Y.C. Gen. counsel Plays for Living, 1998—2002, gen. co-counsel, 2002—. Mem. editorial bd. Communications and the Law, 1978-82, adv. bd. 1982—; mem. editorial bd. U.S. Trademark Reporter, 1982-86. Bd. dirs. Light Opera of Manhattan, 1981-82, Lyric Opera N.Y., 1984-90, Concert Artists Guild, 1989-91, Plays for Living, 1998—. Mem. ABA, Fed. Bar Coun., N.Y. State Bar Assn., U.S. Trademark Assn., Copyright Soc. U.S.A., N.Y. Lawyers for Pub. Interest (bd. dirs. 1983-87), Am. Arbitration Assn., Commn. for Law and Social Justice, Carnegie Coun., Women's City Club, Respect for Law Alliance. Office: Stroock Stroock & Lavan 180 Maiden Ln New York NY 10038-4982 E-mail: vnearing@stroock.com.

NEARY, PATRICIA ELINOR, ballet director; b. Miami; d. James Elliott and Elinor (Mitsitz) N. Corps de ballet Nat. Ballet of Can., Toronto, Ont., 1957-60; prin. dancer N.Y.C. Ballet, 1960-68; ballerina Geneva Ballet, Switzerland, 1968-70, ballet dir., 1973-78; guest artist Stuttgart Ballet, Germany, 1968-70; asst. ballet dir., ballerina West Berlin Ballet, 1970-73; ballet dir. Zurich Ballet, Switzerland, 1978-86, La Scala di Milano ballet co., Italy, 1986-88; tchr. Balanchine ballets, Balanchine Trust, 1987—.

NEAS, SHERRY LEE, purchasing agent, procurement manager; b. Elgin, N.D., July 18, 1967; d. William Lee and Irene Kathryn (Schutz) Vogel; m. Allen Darrell Neas, Apr. 4, 1987; children: Alexis, Braxton. BA in Interdisciplinary Studies, U. S.C., 1993. Adminstrv. specialist USAR, 1994—95; med. clk. Beaufort (S.C.) Naval Hosp., 1988—89; procurement clk. USMC Air Sta., Beaufort, 1990—91; purchasing agt. Beaufort Naval Hosp., 1991—94, N.D. Dept. Transp., Bismarck, 1995—2000; state procurement mgr. N.D. State Procurement Office, Bismarck, 2000—; State emergency preparedness liaison adminstr. non-commd. officer USAR, Bismarck, ND, 1998—. With USAR, 1985—. Mem.: Nat. Assn. Purchasing Mgmt. (edn. chair No. Plains-North Dakota Inc. 1998—). Pentecostal. Avocations: singing, piano. Office: ND State Procurement Office 600 E Boulevard Ave Bismarck ND 58505

NEASE, JUDITH ALLGOOD, marriage and family therapist; b. Arlington, Mass., Nov. 15, 1930; d. Dwight Maurice Allgood and Sophie (Wolf) Allgood Morris; m. Theron Stanford Nease, Sept. 1, 1962; children: Susan Elizabeth, Alison Allgood. Student, Rockford Coll., 1949-50; BA, NYU, 1953, MA, 1954; MS, Columbia U. Sch. Social Work, 1956. Psychiat. social worker Bellevue Psychiat. Hosp., N.Y.C., 1956-59, St. Luke's Hosp., N.Y.C., 1959-62; asst. psychiat. social work supr. N.J. Neuropsychiat. Inst., Princeton, 1962-64; group co-leader Ctr. for Advancement of Personal and Social Growth, Atlanta, 1973-76; asst. dir., social work supr., group co-leader Druid Hills Counseling Ctr., Columbia Theol. Sem., 1973-82; marriage and family therapist Cath. Social Svcs., Atlanta, 1978-87; chief Cmty. Mental Health Svc., Ft. McPherson, Atlanta, 1987-92; master's level clinician Ctr. for Psychiatry, Smyrna, Ga., 1990-92; pvt. practice Grayson, Ga., 1992—. Democrat. Episcopalian. Home and Office: 1557 Bennett Rd Grayson GA 30017-1046

NEBLETT, CAROL, soprano; b. Modesto, Calif., Feb. 1, 1946; m. Philip R. Akre; 3 children. Studies with William Vennard, Roger Wagner, Esther Andreas, Ernest St. John Metz, Lotte Lehmann, Pierre Bernac, Rosa Ponselle, George London, Jascha Heifetz, Norman Treigle, Sol Hurak, Dorothy Kirsten, Maestros Julius Rudel, Claudio Abbado, Daniel Barenboin, Erich Leinsdorf, James Levine, others. Soloist with Roger Wagner Chorale; performed in U.S. and abroad with various symphonies; debut with Carnegie Hall, 1966, N.Y.C. Opera, 1969, Met. Opera, 1979; sung with maj. opera cos. including Met. Opera, N.Y.C., Lyric Opera Chgo., Balt. Opera, Pitts. Opera, Houston Grand Opera, San Francisco Opera, Boston Opera Co., Milw. Florentine Opera, Washington Opera Soc., Covent Garden, Cologne Opera, Vienna (Austria) Staatsoper, Paris Opera, Teatro Regio, Turin, Italy, Teatro San Carlo, Naples, Italy, Teatro Massimo, Palermo, Italy, Gran Teatro del Liceo, Barcelona, Spain, Kirov Opera Theatre, Leningrad, USSR, Dubrovnik (Yugoslavia) Summer Festival, Salzberg Festival, others; rec. artist RCA, DGG, EMI; appearances with symphony orchs., also solo recitals, (film) La Clemenza di Tito; filmed and recorded live performance with Placido Domingo, La Fancuilla del West; numerous TV appearances. Office: 622 Glorietta Blvd Coronado CA 92118-2304

NEBLETT, MARCIA AMELIA, artist, educator; b. N.Y., Dec. 8, 1970; d. Colin Neblett and Sandra Lynn. BFA, Purchase Coll., 1995; MFA, SUNY, 1998. Lectr. art Cazenovia (N.Y.) Coll., 1999—2001, Baruch Coll., N.Y.C., 2001, SUNY, Farmingdale, NY, 2001; prof. art Savannah (Ga.) Coll. Art and Design, 2002—. Mem. adv. bd. Children's Art League, N.Y.C., 2000—. Prin. works include The Chase, 1996, Hanzel & Gretel, 2000. Fellow MacDowell fellowship, 96, 2000. Mem.: Soc. Am. Graphic Artists, Coll. Art Assn. Avocations: exercise, animals, crafts, reading. Home: 25 Parkview Ave 2A Bronxville NY 10708

NECCO, E(DNA) JOANNE, school psychologist; b. Klamath Falls, Oreg., June 23, 1941; d. Joseph Rogers and Lillian Laura (Owings) Painter; m. Jon F. Puryear, Aug. 25, 1963 (div. Oct. 1987); children: Laura L., Douglas F.; m. A. David Necco, July 1, 1989. BS, Cen. State U., 1978, MEd, 1985; PhD in Applied Behavioral Studies, Okla. State U., 1993. Med.-surg. asst. Oklahoma City Clinic, 1961-68; spl. edn. tchr. Oklahoma City Pub. Schs., 1978-79, Edmond (Okla.) Pub. Schs., 1979-83; co-founder, owner Learning Devel. Clinic, Edmond, 1983-93; asst. prof. profl. tchr. edn. U. Ctrl. Okla., Edmond, 1993-97; assoc. prof. U. Ctr. Okla., Edmond, 1998—2001, prof. profl. tchr. edn., 2002—. Adj. instr. Ctrl. State U., Edmond, 1989-93, Oklahoma City U., 1991-93; mem. rsch. group Okla. State U., Stillwater, 1991-93; faculty senator U. Ctrl. Okla., 1998-2000; Coll. Edn. rep. AAUP, 2000-01; presenter in field. Contbr. articles to profl. jours. Com. mem. Boy Scouts Am., SCUBA Post 604, Oklahoma City, 1981-86; mem. Edmon TAsk Force for Youth, 1983-87, Edmond C. of C., 1984-87; presenter internat. conf. Okla. Ctr. for Neurosci., 1996; evaluator for Even Start Literacy Program, 1994-96, reviewer Okla. Even Start applicants, 1997, presenter internat. conf., Singapore, 1996, Alta., Can., 1996, 98; tri-coord. Univ. Cntrl. Okla. Am. Demcoracy Project, 2003—. Named to, State of Okla. Outstanding Profs.' Acad., 2003, Am. Registry of Outstanding Prof., 2001—02. Mem. AAUP, ASCD, PEO, Am. Psychol. Soc., Nat. Assn. for Sch. Psychologists, Am. Bus Women's Assn., Coun. for Exceptional Children, Learning Disabilities Assn., Am. Assn. for Gifted Underachieving Students, Am. Tchr. Educators, Okla. Learning Disabilities Assn., Okla. Ctr. Neurosci., Okla. Assn. for Counseling and Devel., Okla. Psychol. Soc., U. Ctrl. Okla. Golden Key Nat. Honor Soc., Internat. Soc. for Sci. Study of Subjectivity, Am. Coun. on Rural Spl. Edn., Ctrl State U. (Okla., life), Phi Delta Kappa. Republican. Avocations: scuba diving, underwater photography, water skiing, travel, golf. Home: 3624 Equestrian Ct Edmond OK 73034 5871 Office: U Ctrl Okla Coll Edn 100 N University Dr Edmond OK 73034-5207 E-mail: jnecco@ucok.edu.

NEDDER, JANET MARIE, elementary school educator; b. Lowell, Mass., June 17, 1943; d. Arthur T. and Mary M. (Kennedy) DeAngelo; m. Robert S. Nedder, Apr. 23, 1966; children: Joseph A., Robert S. Jr., Arthur P. BA in Math., Regis Coll., 1965, MA, cert. elem., 1973, MA, cert. reading, 1983, MA, cert. math., 1991. Cert. in elem. edn., reading, math., Mass. Mathematician Regis Coll. Math. Project, Weston, Mass., 1962-65; rsch. mathematician Air Force Cambridge Labs., Waltham, Mass., summer 1964; math. analyst Rust Craft Greeting Cards, Dedham, Mass., summer 1965, elem. tchr. St. Pius X Sch., Milton, Mass., 1965-66; mathematician Space Physics Lab., Hanscom AFB, Bedford, Mass., 1966-67; Title I tchr. Dedham Pub. Schs., 1978—. Campaign aide local rep., Hyde Park, 1961, Selectman, Dedham, 1989. Grantee in biostats. Lemuel Shattuck Hosp./Harvard U., 1965. Mem. Internat. Reading Assn., Exec. Female, Mass. Reading Tchrs. Assn., Dedham Title I Tchrs. Assn. (bargaining com. 1989, treas. 1989-90, v.p. 1990—, sec. 2000—), Dartmouth Women's Club. Democrat. Roman Catholic. Avocations: reading, travel, writing, piano. Home: 43 High St Medfield MA 02052-3119

NEDERVELD, RUTH ELIZABETH, retired real estate executive; b. Hudsonville, Mich., Oct. 29, 1933; d. Ralph and Hattie (Ploeg) Schut; m. Terrill Lee Nederveld, June 6, 1952; children: Courtland Lee, Valerie Lynn Nederveld Heisey, Darwin Frederic. Degree in Real Estate, U. Mich., 1979; student, Pa. State U., Centre Hall, 1973, Aquinas Coll., Grand Rapids, Mich., 1974; degree, Grad. Realtors Inst., 1979. Cert. residential specialist; registered securities agt. With sales dept. Field Enterprises, Lancaster, Pa., 1962-72; sales assoc. E. James Hogan, Lancaster, 1972-74, C-21 Packard, Grand Rapids, Mich., 1974-80; assoc. broker comml. divsn. Markland Devel., Inc., Grand Rapids, 1980-86, Am. Acquest Realty, Inc., Grand Rapids, 1986-89; broker, owner R.E. Nederveld Realtors, Ada, Mich., 1989-94; ret., 1994. Pres. Civic Nucomers of Grand Rapids, 1978; trustee, elder Forest Hills Presbyn. Ch., Cascade, Mich., 1983-86. Named Laureate, 2002. Mem. Nat. Assn. Realtors (mem. comml. dept. 1973—), Mich. Assn. Realtors, Grand Rapids Real Estate Bd., Woman's Council Realtors (corr. sec. 1986-87), Nat. Assn. Female Execs., Assn. Sales and Mktg. Execs. (exec. dir. internat. chpt. 1977-84, pres. Grand Rapids chpt. 1986-87). Republican. Avocations: poetry, hammered dulcimer and banjo, sailing, art, author.

NEDZA, SANDRA LOUISE, manufacturing executive; b. Chgo., Aug. 20, 1951; d. Thomas and Ina Louise (Wilson) Ingle; m. James Owen Earnest, May 5, 1973 (div. Nov. 1984); m. Ronald Edward Nedza, Nov. 22, 1986; 1 child, Thomas Edward. Student acctg., Met. Sch. Bus., Chgo., 1970. Acctg. clk. Gane Bros. & Lane, Inc., Chgo., 1967-72; advanced from expeditor to buyer Hammond Organ Co., Chgo., 1972-84; purchasing/prodn. control supr. IRP-Profl. Sound Products, Addison, Ill., 1984-2000; purchasing agt. ANI Safety and Supply, Inc., Lincolnwood, Ill., 2000; adminstrv. asst. to v.p. mktg. svcs. and mktg. The Willy Wonka Candy Factory divsn. Nestle, Itasca, Ill., 2001—03. Mem. Jobs Daughters, 1967—. Mem. Lions (pres. 2000—), Alpha Iota (scholarship key 1970). Clubs: Juke Box Sno-Riders (sec. 1986-87) (Fox Lake, Ill.), Lakeview Sno-Riders. Lodges: Lioness (pres. 1988-89) (Chgo.). Lutheran. E-mail: buzzylion@juno.com.

NEE, SISTER MARY COLEMAN, college president emeritus; b. Taylor, Pa., Nov. 14, 1917; d. Coleman James and Nora Ann (Hopkins) N. AB, Marywood Coll., 1939, MA, 1943; MS, Notre Dame U., 1959; DHL (hon.), U. Scranton; Dr.Humanities (hon.), King's Coll.; DHL (hon.), Marywood U., 2003. Joined Order of Sisters, Servants of Immaculate Heart of Mary, 1941; assoc. prof. math. Marywood Coll., Scranton, Pa., 1959-68, pres., 1970-88, pres. emerita, 1988—. Apostolic coord. Sisters, Servants Immaculate Heart of Mary, Scranton, Pa., 1968-70. Home and Office: Cathedral Convent 333 Wyoming Ave Scranton PA 18503-1223

NEECE, OLIVIA HELENE ERNST, investment company executive, consultant; b. LA, Jan. 3, 1948; d. Robert and Beatrice Pearl Ernst; m. Huntley Lee Bluestein, 1967 (div. 1974); children: Melissa Dawn, Brendon Wade; m. Anthony Ray Neece, Mar. 20, 1976. Cert. interior design, UCLA, 1972-75; BSBA, U. So. Calif., 1990; MBA, UCLA, 1993; postgrad., Claremont U., 1998—. Cert. interior designer Calif. Coun. for Interior Design; lic. gen. contractor, real estate broker, Calif. Staff designer Frances Lux Designs, LA, 1974; project designer Yates Silverman Inc., LA, 1974-77; owner Olivia Neece Planning & Design, Tarzana, Calif., 1977-86; v.p. project devel. Design Svc. /Acoa, Englewood, Colo., 1986-87; v.p. project adminstrn. Hirsch-Bedner Assoc., Santa Monica, Calif., 1987-88; treas.-sec. EON Corp., LA, 1980—; owner Olivia Neece Planning & Design, Tarzana, 1988-93; dir. ops. The Ernst Group, LA, 1980—85. Instr. ext. program UCLA, 1981—83; part-time prof. Calif. State U., Northridge, 1994—99; acad. rschr. Jet Propulsion Lab., 2000—02; spkr. in field. Co-author: A Step by Step Approach to Hotel Devel., 1988; contbr. chapters to books, articles to profl. jours. Co-chair LA Master Chorale Gala; mem. Hollywood Bowl Soc.; charter mem. L.A. County Mus. Art; vol. restoration of San Diego R.R. Mus., 1985—92; patron LA Philharm.; gold patron LA Opera Soc.; Found. of Music Ctr. of Los Angels; fellow circle Ctr. Theatre Group; Patron and charter mem. of LA Country Mus. of Art; bd. dir.,historian Master Choral Assoc. Recipient Holiday Inn Devel. award, Foster City, Calif., 1986, Warwick, R.I., 1988, 1st and 2d pl. awards, Lodging Hospitality Designers Cir., 1987, Gold Key award, Russell St. Inn, 1986, Best Paper award, Am. Conf. on Info. Systems, 2002. Mem. Am. Soc. Interior Designers (1st pl. portfolio competition 1974), Acad. of Mgmt. (Best Paper award 2002), Fin. Mgmt. Assn., Internat. Inst. Designers & Arch. (profl., v.p., bd. dir.), We. Acad. Mgmt., Assn. Info. Sys., Inst. Ops. Rsch. and Mgmt. Sci, Beta Gamma Sigma. Office: Neece Assoc 18200 Rosita St Tarzana CA 91356-4622

NEEDHAM, TRACY LEE, marketing professional, consultant; d. Thomas Edward and Linda Anne Needham. BA, Coll. William & Mary, 1991; MS, Boston U., 1995; postgrad., Coach U., Park City, Kans., 2002—. CFP. Retirement products dir. Ind. Ins. Agts. Am., Alexandria, Va., 1996—98; fin. svcs. writer NRECA, Arlington, Va., 1998—99; competitive affairs mgr. Calvert Group, Bethesda, Md., 1999—2003; founder, profl. life & bus. coach Adventure to Success, LLC, 2003—. Vol. Reading Connection, Arlington, 2002—03; fin. vol. Bill Clinton for Pres., Washington, 1992. Mem.: Fin. Planning Assn., Am. Mktg. Assn., Internat. Coach Fedn., Soc. Competitive Intelligence Profls. Avocations: writing, travel. Personal E-mail: tneedham55@comcast.net.

NEEDLEMAN, BARBARA, newspaper executive; BS in Eng., Northwestern Univ., 1994. V.p. Tribune Media Svcs., Chgo., 1993—. Office: Tribune Media Svcs 435 N Michigan Ave Ste 1500 Chicago IL 60611-4012

NEEL, JUDY MURPHY, association executive; b. Rhome, Tex. d. James W. and Linna B. (Vess) Neel; m. Ellis F. Murphy, Jr., Dec. 30, 1975; children from previous marriage: Mary B. Schmidt, Janet E. Hollingsworth, Susan E. Salinas. BS, Northwestern U., 1977; MBA, Roosevelt U., 1983. V.p. Murphy, Tashjian & Assocs., Chgo., 1960-73; exec. dir. Automotive Affiliated Rep. Assn., Chgo., 1973-78; mgr. Automotive Svc. Ind. Assn., Chgo., 1978-80; exec. dir. Am. Soc. Safety Engrs., Des Plaines, Ill., 1980-98, Am. Assn. Diabetes Educators, 1999—2003. Recipient Assn. Leadership Award Bus. Women's Network/Assn. Trends Mag., 1998. Mem. Chgo. Soc. Assn. Execs. (bd. dirs. 1979—, pres. 1985—, Shapiro award 1991), Am. Soc. Assn. Execs. (sec.-treas. 1994, found. dir. 1986-90, bd. dirs. 1990-95, Key award 1986). Republican.

NEEL, NANCEE R. counselor; b. Marianna, Fla., Feb. 16, 1954; d. Henry Clay Neel, Elmetta Flora Messer; m. C. Kirk Avent; 1 child, Clayton Avent. BSN, Emory U., 1977; MSN in Nurse Mid-Midwifery, U. Miami, 1980; MPH, U. Ala., 1986, DrPH, 1989, MA in Counseling, 1999. Lic. profl. counselor, CNM Am Coll. Nurse-Midwives. Asst. prof. nursing U. Ala. Sch. Medicine, Birmingham, 1982—86, nurse midwife dept of ob-gyn., 1989—92; co-founder Well Women's Clinic Cooper Green Hosp., Birmingham, 1994—99; profl. counselor Magnolia Ctr. Counseling & Wellness, Birmingham, Ala., 2000—01. Cons. Kamuzu Coll. Nursing, Lilongwe, Malawi, 1983; adj. asst. prof. internat. health U. Ala. Sch. Pub. Health, Birmingham, 1995—99. Office: Mangnolia Ctr Counseling & Wellness 1025 23rd St S Birmingham AL 35205 Office Phone: 205-322-8002.

NEELEY, ABIGAIL ENGLISH, music educator; b. Batavia, N.Y., Sept. 18, 1974; d. Gordon Leigh and Mary Brinkman English; m. Anthony Wayne Neeley, June 27, 2003. Bachelor's of Music, SUNY, Potsdam, 1996; MS in Edn. with a concentration in adminstrn., SUNY, Brockport, 2000. Tchr. gen. and choral music Frederick Douglass Mid. Sch., Rochester, NY, 1996—98; tchr. choral, art and gen. music Southampton County Schs., Cortland, Va., 1998—2001; tchr. choral music Lafayette H.S., Williamsburg, Va., 2001—. Festival host Music in the Pks., Williamsburg, 2001—.

NEELEY, BEVERLY EVON, sociologist, consultant; b. Oakland, Calif., June 14, 1947; d. Chester Arthur Neeley Jr. and Thalia Evon Littlefield; m. Niles Bruce, Sept. 13, 1970 (div. Aug. 1977); children: Autumn Yvonne, Bruce Curd, Thalia Evon Neeley-Littlefield. BA, U. Calif., Berkeley, 1970, MPH, 1972; PhD, U. Calif., San Diego, 1983. Eligibility supr. W. Oakland Health Ctr., 1970-72; health edn. supr. San Diego County Drug Edn., 1972-74; proposal writer, cons. Cmty. Crisis Ctr., San Diego, 1974-77; sociologist, dir., sec., treas. Image Mind, Inc., Oakland, 1993—. Instr. Calif. State U., San Diego, 1976; health planner Health Sys. Agy., San Diego, 1978; mem. adv. bd. Help Other People Evole Inst., Oakland, 2000—; sr. acad. cons. Hercules NAACP Saturday Sch., 2002; tchrs., rschr. Oakland Pub. Schs., 1983—. Author: The Ethiopian Grail, 1994, Ancient Ethiopian Egyptian Cultural Excellence, 2003. Founder S.E. Drug Coalition, San Diego, 1974, Nu-Way Youth Svc. Ctr., San Diego, 1976. Mem. NAACP, Sojourner Truth Tenants Assn. Avocations: reading, walking, cooking. Home and Office: 5915 Martin Luther King Jr Way B10 Oakland CA 94609 E-mail: drbneeley3@hotmail.com.

NEELY, EVELYN HOPE (EVELYN HOPE GILLESPIE), humanities educator, archaeologist; b. N.Y.C. d. Charles Batcheller Neely and Evelyn Leak; m. William Stephen Bokus (div.); 1 child, Hunter Sabin Bokus ; m. Roderick B. Gillespie (div.). BA in English, U. Montevallo, 1960; postgrad., U. So. Ala., 1971—74, U. Ala., Tuscaloosa, 1978—79; archaeology accreditation, U.S. Dept. of Interior and Soc. Profl. Archaeologists 1978. Cert. historic resources coord., qualified archaeologist. Tchr. art, speech, and English Theodore H.S., Ala., 1964—65; prof. English Faulkner Jr. Coll., Bay Minette, Ala., 1965—66; archivist, mem. archaeology crew Excavation of Ft. Mims, Baldwin County, Ala., 1973; prin. investigator Pre-Columbian village, Islas Tortugas, Costa Rica, 1973; dir. archaeology Ft. Condé, Mobile, Ala., 1979—81; archivist, photography archaeologist Mid-Continental Rsch., Ark., 1983—84; field dir. search for route of DeSoto Ala.-Tombigbee Regional Commn., Clarke County, Ala., 1989—90; founder, owner, dir. Mobile Delta Writers Workshop, Mobile, 1997—; field supr. office archeol. rsch. U. Ala., 1976—79. Adj. prof. English Faulkner State Coll., Bay Minette, 1992—94; adj. prof. intensive English lang. Spring Hill Coll., Mobile, 1996—98; adj. prof. English and creative writing U. S. Ala., Mobile, 1993—; cons. Mobile Historic Devel. Commn., Mobile, 1989—; spkr. in field. Author: (book) History of Fort Mims, Alabama, 1973, History of Alabama Dept. Interior, 1978; author, photographer (book) History of Mississippi County Arkansas, 1984; contbr. articles to profl. jours.; author novella. Active Amnesty Internat., Habitat for Humanity; charter mem. Nat. Mus. Women in Arts, Washington; active Dem. Party; mem. exec. com. Sierra Club, Ala., 1985; bd. dirs. Audubon Soc., Mobile Bay Area, Ala., 1985. Recipient Honors scholarship, U. Montevallo, 1956, Spl. Recognition Gold award, Robert F. Kennedy Meml., 1991; grantee, PEN Am. Ctr., 1992, 1995. Mem.: Southeastern Archaeol. Conf., Soc. Profl. Archaeologists, U. Montevallo Alumni Daughters. Democrat. Episcopalian. Office: U Montevallo Alumni Office Station 6215 Montevallo AL 35115

NEELY, SALLY SCHULTZ, lawyer; b. L.A., Mar. 2, 1948; BA, Stanford U., 1970, JD, 1971. Bar: Ariz. 1972, Calif. 1977. Law clk. to judge U.S. Ct. Appeals (9th cir.), Phoenix, 1971-72; assoc. Lewis and Roca, Phoenix, 1972-75; asst. prof. Law Sch. Harvard U., Cambridge, Mass., 1975-77; assoc. Shutan & Trost, P.C., L.A., 1977-79; ptnr., sr. counsel Sidley & Austin, L.A., 1980—. Mem. faculty Am. Law Inst.-ABA Chpt. 11 Bus. Reorgns., 1989-95, 97—, Banking and Comml. Lending Law, 1997-99, Nat. Conf. Bankruptcy Judges, 1988, 90, 95, 96, 97, 99, 2002, Fed. Jud. Ctr., 1989, 90, 94-95, Southeast Bankruptcy Law Inst., 2002, Workshop Bankruptcy and Bus. Reorgn. NYU, 1992—; rep. 9th cir. jud. conf., 1989-91; mem. Nat. Bankruptcy Conf., 1993—, chair com. on legislation, 2001--. Chair Stanford U. Law Sch. Reunion Giving, 1996; bd. vis. Stanford U. Law Sch., 1990-92. Mem.: ABA, Calif. Bar Assn., Am. Coll. Bankruptcy (mem. bd. regents 1998—2003, trustee 2003—, chair edn. programs com. 2003—). Office: Sidley Austin Brown & Wood LLP 555 W 5th St Ste 4000 Los Angeles CA 90013-3000 E-mail: sneely@sidley.com.

NEESE, KRISTAL ANN, comptroller; b. Milton, Fla., June 29, 1968; d. Arthur Bill and Helen Margaret Bailey; m. Edward Terrell Neese, Jr., June 25, 2000; children: John Leamon Jr., Shawn Michael. BS cum laude in Acct., U. South Ala., 1996. CPA. Tax acct. Sirmon, Frankel & Pawlowski, CPA, Mobile, Ala., 1995—96; cost acct. So. Aluminum Casting Co., Bayminette, Ala., 1996—97; staff mgr. Gulf States Airgas, Mobile, 1997; comptroller, asst. mgr., fin. adm. Lake Forest Property Owner's Assn. Inc., Daphne, Ala., 1997—; also bd. dirs. Mem.: Ala. State Bd. Acct., Daphne H.S. Quarterback Club. Methodist. Avocations: reading, football, raising children. Home: 30529 Pine Ct Daphne AL 36527 Office: Lake Forest POA Inc One Golf Place Terr Daphne AL 36527 Office Phone: 251-626-0788.

NEFF, BONITA DOSTAL, communication development facilitator; b. Grinnell, Iowa, Aug. 16, 1942; d. Lester Ernest and Mary Margaret (Hudnut) Dostal; m. Gregory Pall Neff, Apr. 27, 1974; 1 child, Kristiana. BA, U. N. Iowa, 1964, MA, 1966; PhD, U. Mich., 1973; AA cum laude, Lansing (Mich.) C.C., 1980. Edn. leadership fellow George Washington U., Washington, 1976-77; specialist Mich. State U., East Lansing, 1977-80, co-investigator family and child inst. energy rsch. team, 1980-82; asst. prof. comm. Purdue U., Hammond, Ind., 1982-87; pres. Pub. Comm. Assocs., Munster, Ind., 1986—; assoc. prof. comm. Valparaiso (Ind.) U., 1991—. Co-organizer European Comm. Conf., Dubrovnik, Croatia, 2002—; vis. prof. grad. comm. program U. Kadar, Croatia, 2003; co-founding mem. Internat. Interdisciplinary and Intercultural Annual Conf. in Pub. Rels.; presenter, cons. in field. Mem. adv. bd., reviewer Jour. Applied Comm. Rsch.; mem. editl. bd. Jour. Promotional Mgmt., Jour. Pub. Rels. Rsch., on-line jour. multicultural comm. from Cyprus; reviewer Mgmt. Comm. Quar.: An Internat. Jour.; editor procs. on accreditation for nat. conf.; contbr. chpts. in books, profl. articles and poetry to jours. Mem. Nat. Steering Commn. for Revision of Pub. Rels. Curriculum, 1996—; chair nat. benchmark study on pub. rels. edn.; mem. Nat. Task Force Pub. Rels. Conf. 1998; mem. Lake County (Ind.) Cmty. Devel. Bd., 1984—; bd. dirs. Big Bros. and Big Sisters N.W. Ind., 1984, 87; pres., chmn. bd. dirs. N.W. Ind. Youth Chorus, 1985—; bd. dirs., mem. mktg. com. N.W. Ind. Symphony, bd. dirs. PBS56-Ind., sec. exec. com., 2000—. Faculty rsch. grantee U. Mich., 1971, Consumer Product Safety Coun. grantee, 1976-77, Ind. Arts Commn./Nat. Endowment for Arts grantee, 1990-92, Valparaiso U. Diversity grantee, 1996; recipient top rsch. honors regional confs. Mem.: Nat. Commn. on Undergrad. and Grad. Pub. Rels. Curriculum (nat. task force for conf. 1998), Pub. Rels. Soc. Am. (advisor 2001, established student chpt.), Internat. Acad. Bus. Disciplines (co-chair pub. rels. divsn.), World Comm. Assn., Assn. Educators in Journalism Mass Comm. (chair internat. com. 1994—96, scholarly liaison com. 1995—), Ctrl. States Comm. Assn. (founder and chmn. 1988—89, pub. rels. officer 1989—92), Nat. Comm. Assn. (founder and twice chair of pub. rels. divsn. 1988, chmn. nat. Pub. Rels. Rsch. awards com. PRIDE 1988, nat. legis. coun. rep. 1993—, nat. com. on convs. allied orgns., task force on nat. policy), Internat. Pub. Rels. Assn., Internat. Comm. Assn. (chmn. task force on accreditation 1988, newsletter editor 1997, chair planning pub. rels. divsn. internat. conf. South Korea, chair dissertation thesis award com. pub. rels. divsn.), Assn. Women in Comm. (assoc.; pres. Calumet chpt. 1985—90, advisor Valparaiso Student AWC, Inc. 1994—, Outstanding Communicator 1990, Nat. Outstanding chpt. advisor 1999). Democrat. Roman Catholic. Avocations: ballet, tap, piano, reading, professional clown. Home: 8320 Greenwood Ave Munster IN 46321-1813 Office: Pub Comm Assocs 8320 Greenwood Ave Munster IN 46321-1813 Office Phone: 219-464-6827. E-mail: bonita.neff@valpo.edu.

NEFF, DIANE IRENE, university administrator; b. Cedar Rapids, Iowa, Apr. 26, 1954; d. Robert Mariner and Adeline Emma (Zach) N. BA in Psychology and Home Econs., U. Iowa, 1976; MA in Sociology, U. Mo., 1978; MEd in Ednl. Leadership, U. West Fla., 1990; EdD in Ednl. Leadership, U. Ctrl. Fla., 2003. Contract compliance officer, dir. EEO, City of Cedar Rapids, 1979-81; commd. ensign USN, 1981, advanced through grades to lt. comdr.; asst. legal officer Naval Comm. Area Master Sta., Guam, 1982-83; comm. security plans and requirements officer Comdr.-in-Chief US Naval Forces in Europe, London, 1983-85; dir. standards and evaluation dept. Recruit Tng. Command, Orlando, Fla., 1985-89; rsch. and analysis officer Naval Res. Officers Tng. Corps Office Chief Naval Edn. and Tng., Pensacola, Fla., 1989-91; tech. tng. officer Recruit Tng. Command, Great Lakes, Ill., 1991-92, mil. tng. officer, 1992-93, dir. apprentice tng., 1993-95; coord. ednl. and tng. programs U. Ctrl. Fla., Orlando, 1995—. Founding mem. Unity of Gulf Breeze, Fla., 1990; performer various benefits for chs., mus., others, Orlando, 1988, 91, 95, 96, 97. Fellow Adminstrn. on Aging, 1977. Mem. ASTD. Unitarian Universalist. Avocation: piano. E-mail: dneff@mail.ucf.edu.

NEFF, JEANNE HENRY, academic administrator; b. Fairmont, W. Va., Oct. 5, 1942; d. Percy Byron Henry and Rebecca Jacqueline Ridgely; m. Richard E. Kammer, Aug. 6, 1966 (div. July 1978); 1 child, Brian S. Kammer; m. Edward W.S. Neff II, Dec. 19, 1982; stepchildren: Larrie A., Edward W.S. III. BA, Wheeling Coll., 1964; MA, Rice U., 1966; ArtsD, Carnegie-Mellon U., 1976; postdoct., Harvard U., 1984. Instr. English Carlow Coll., Pitts., 1966-69; from asst. prof. to assoc. prof. English Wheeling (W. Va.) Coll., 1970-77, from assoc. dean to dean, 1977-80, academic v.p., 1980-86; v.p. academic affairs Susquehanna U., Selingsgrove, Pa., 1986-95; pres. The Sage Colls., Troy and Albany, N.Y., 1995—. Bd. dirs. Capital Bank & Trust Co., Albany. Trustee Albany Acad., 1996—; mem. Waterfront Commn., Troy, N.Y., 1996—; dir., v.p. Troy Redevel. Found., 1996—. Mem. Am. Coun. Edn. (fellow 1978-79, mem. commn. leadership devel. 1995—), Assn. New Am. Colls. (mem. pres.'s coun. 1997—), Assn. Am. Colls. and Univs. (dir. 1984-88, chair Am. Conf. Academic Deans, 1987), Univ. Heights Assn. (dir., v.p. 1996—). Home: 46 1st St Troy NY 12180-3811 Office: The Sage Colls 45 Ferry St Troy NY 12180-4115

NEFF, JENNIFER ELLEN, painter, artist; b. Kingston, NY, July 16, 1973; d. Wilfred Henry Neff and Susan Jean Foster. BFA, SUNY, New Paltz, NY. Sr. support staff and analysis Philliber Rsch. Assocs., Accord, NY, 1989—; freelance artist Jennifer Neff Studios, Kingston, 1999—; pres., owner Off the Wall Studios, Inc., Kingston, 1999—2001. E-mail: jnefferart@yahoo.com.

NEFF, MARIE TAYLOR, museum director, artist; d. James Arthur Taylor and Pearl Jackson; m. Edward Lewis Neff, June 24, 1946 (dec. July 1, 1994); children: Edward James, Charles Lewis. Degree in art and photography, Western Tex. Coll., 1985. Studio artist, Post, 1943—; art instr. Neff Art Sch., Post, 1963—78; co-owner retail bus. Post, 1963—88; art instr. Post Art Guild, Kids n Art, Post, 1975—85; dir. OS Ranch Found. Mus., Post, 1991—. Represented in permanent collections, pvt. collections. Pres., bd. dirs. Post Commerce and Tourism Bur., 1994—2002; dir., coord. Tex. Heritage Plains Trail, 2002—. Named Queen Panhandle South Plains, Mrs. Tex. Sr. Pageant, 1999. Mem.: North Tex. Mus. Assn. (pres. 2001—04), Tex. Assn. Mus. (planning bd. state conv. 1997—2001, trustee-sec. 2000—04), Post C. of C. (designer commemorative coin 1976, Woman of Yr. 1972), Post Art Guild (pres., founding mem. 1974—2003), Rotary. Avocations: archaeology, photography, reading, travel. Office: OS Ranch Found Mus Ste 3 201 E Main St Post TX 79356 E-mail: mtneff@caprock-spur.com.

NEFF, MARILYN LEE, nursing consultant; b. Lancaster, Pa., Nov. 12, 1942; d. Norman Booth and F. Irene (Fridy) N. RN, U. Pa., 1963, BA, 1974; MBA, Widener U., 1988. Cert. nephrology nurse, nurse adminstr. advanced. Staff nurse Hosp. of U. Pa., Phila., 1963-64, asst. head nurse, 1964-68, staff nurse, 1968-71, asst. head nurse, 1971-75, head nurse, 1975-77, nursing supr., 1977-84; adminstr. Out-patient Dialysis Unit U. Pa., Phila., 1984-86; v.p. ops. Renal Care Cts. Corp., Wilmington, Del., 1986-88, Renal Treatment Ctrs., Inc., Berwyn, Pa., 1988-91; cons. MLN Cons., Wallingford, Pa., 1991-92; v.p. bus. devel. Healthdyne Home Nutritional Svcs., Inc., Marietta, Ga., 1992-94; cons. MLN Enterprises, Marietta, Ga., 1994—. Contbr. articles to profl. jours. Pres. Women's Fellowship, Calvary Presbyn. Ch., Media, Pa., 1982-86. Mem. ANA, Nat. Renal Adminstrs. Assn., Nat. Kidney Found. (del. 1990-91, Disting. Vol. Svc. award, 1990), Am. Nephrology Nurses Assn. (pres. 1991-92, Shiley Mgmt. award 1988, rsch. grant 1989). Avocations: Sunday sch. tchr., choir mem., reading, motorsports spectator. Home and Office: 5222 Pikes Peak Ct Marietta GA 30062-6550

NEGA, NANCY KAWECKI, middle school science educator; b. Chgo., Mar. 16, 1946; d. John Sebastian and Irene M. (Wantuch) Kawecki; m. Lance J. Nega, Feb. 24, 1968 (div. 1997); children: Sandi Kawecka Nenga, Todd J. BA in Biology, Ill. Coll., 1968; MS Tchg. in Elem. Math., U. Ill., Chgo., 1991. Cert. early adolescent sci. tchr. 1999. Rschr. Morton-Norwich, Inc., Woodstock, Ill., 1968-72; tchr. Elmhurst (Ill.) Unit Dist. 205, 1986—; master tchr. Dept. Energy pre-service tchr. program Argonne Nat. Lab., Ill., 2001—. Trainer Globe Program, Washington, 1995-99; Internet trainer Argonne (Ill.) Nat. Lab., 1996-2000. Recipient Presdl. award of excellence in sci. and math. tchg. NSF, 1995, Paul DeHart Hurd award, NMLSTA, 1999 Mem. Nat. Sci. Tchrs. Assn., Ill. Sci. Tchrs. Assn. (award of excellence 1994), Nat. Mid Level Sci. Tchrs. Assn., Mid Level Sci. Tchrs. Network. Office: Churchville Mid Sch 155 Victory Pkwy Elmhurst IL 60126-1215 Office Phone: 630-832-8682. E-mail: n.nega@comcast.net.

NEGRETE MCLEOD, GLORIA, state official; married. Pres., mem. governing bd. Chaffey C.C., 1995—2000; candidate Dist. 61 Calif. State Assembly, 1998, state assembly mem. Dist. 61, 2000—. Mem. appropriations com.; mem. govtl. orgn. com.; mem. health com.; mem. higher edn. com.; mem. labor and employment com.; chair pub. employees, retirement and social security com. Democrat. Mailing: Rm 5016 PO Box 942849 Sacramento CA 95814 Office: Ste 100B 4959 Palo Verde St Montclair CA 91763

NEIHARDT, HILDA, lawyer, foundation administrator, writer, educator, lawyer; b. Bancroft, Nebr., Dec. 6, 1916; d. John Gneisenau and Mona (Martinsen) N.; m. Albert Joseph Petri, Apr. 18, 1942 (div. Oct. 1963); children; Gail Petri Toedebusch, Robin, Coralie Joyce Hughes. AB, U. Nebr., 1937; postgrad., Letitia Barnum Sch. Theatre, Chgo., 1943-44; JD, U. Mo., 1963. Bar: Mo. 1963. Adminstrv. asst. Consulate of Switzerland, St. Louis, 1937-42; pvt. practice Columbia, Mo., 1963-85, Lake Ozark, Mo., 1985-88; pres. John G. Neihardt Found., Bancroft, 1987—2000. Lectr. in field. Author: Black Elk and Flaming Rainbow, 1995, Black Elk Lives, 2000; editor: The Giving Earth, 1991, The End of The Dream, 1991, The Ancient Memory, 1991. Trustee John G. Neihardt Trust, Columbia and Tekamah, Nebr., 1973-99; chmn. bd. dirs. John G. Neihardt Found., 2000-02; with USN, 1944-45. Mem. AAUW, Westerners, Internat. P.E.O. Avocations: boating, camping, horses. Home: PO Box 358 504 Pennsylvania Ave Bancroft NE 68004 also: 15019 W Monterey Way Goodyear AZ 85338 Office: John G Neihardt Found PO Box 344 Bancroft NE 68004-0344

NEILL, VE, make-up artist; b. Riverside, Calif., May 13, 1951; d. Charles and Eileen Anne (Bernasco) Flores. Grad., Louisville H.S., Woodland Hills, Calif. Credits include (TV movies) Cry for Help, 1978, The London Affair, 1978, Sultan and the Rock Star, 1979, Muppets Go to the Movies, 1981, First Lady of the World, 1982, Money on the Side, 1982, Jane Doe, 1986; (TV Spls.) Sold Out-Lily Tomlin, 1981, Lily for President, 1982, Comedy Store 15th Yr. Reunion, 1988; (TV pilots) One Night Band, 1981, T.J. Hooker, 1981, Madeline (Madeline Kahn), 1982, Girls Life, 1982, A-Team, 1982, Rock & Roll Mom, 1987, Kowalski Loves, 1987, Stephen King's The Shining, 1996 (Emmy award Best Make Up), From the Earth to the Moon, 1997 (Emmy award nomination); (TV show) Pee Wee's Playhouse (Emmy award 1988, Emmy award nominee 1989); (feature films) Star Trek: The Motion Picture (Saturn award 1981), The Incredible Shrinking Woman, 9 to 5, Monty Python at the Hollywood Bowl, Sword and the Sorcerer, The Last Star Fighter, All of Me, The Lost Boys, 1986 (Saturn award 1987), Beetlejuice, 1987 (Acad. award 1987, Saturn award 1988, Brit. Acad. award nominee 1988), Cocoon II, 1988, Big Top Pee Wee, 1988, Dick Tracy, 1989, Flatliners, 1989, Edward Scissorhands, 1990 (Acad. award nominee 1989, Brit. Acad. award nominee 1990), Curly Sue, 1990, Hook, 1991, Batman Returns, 1991 (Saturn award 1992, Acad. award nominee 1992, Brit. Acad. award nominee 1992), Hoffa, 1992 (Acad. award nominee 1992), Rising Sun, 1992, Mrs. Doubtfire, 1993 (Acad. award 1993), Ed Wood, 1993 (Acad. award 1994), Cobb, 1994, Junior, 1994, Batman Forever, 1995, Matilda, 1995, Evening Star, 1996, Mars Attack, 1996, Gattaca, 1996, Batman and Robin, 1996, Amistad, 1997, Stigmata, 1998, Man on the Moon, 1998, Galaxy Quest, 1999, How the Grinch Stole Christmas, 1999, Blow, 2000, A.I., 2000, Death to Smochy, 2001, Duplex, 2002, Blackout, 2002, Pirates of the Caribbean, 2002, (commercial) Sony Mini Disc, 1997, (mag.) Vanity Fair Hollywood Issue, 1998. Mem.: Brit. Acad. Film and TV, Acad. Motion Picture Arts and Scis. Avocations: collecting antiques, beading with antique Am. trade beads, hiking, traveling the U.S. Office: IATSE Local 706 828 N Hollywood Way Burbank CA 91505

NEILSON, JANE SCOTT, mathematics educator; b. Oakland, Calif., July 29, 1919; d. George Robert and Ethel Genevive (Smith) Scott; m. James Drake Neilson II, Sept. 24, 1955 (dec.). Student in engring., U. Mich., 1937, student in lit. and art, 1938-40; BA in Elem Edn., Calif. State U., Northridge, 1960; postgrad. in secondary edn., UCLA, 1966-67. Process engr. Brigs Mfg. Co., Detroit, 1941-43; mathematician dept. purchasing Detroit GM, 1943-44; mathematician Chrysler Corp., Highland Pk., Mich., 1944-45; dir. recreation ARC, Europe and Korea, 1945-54; assoc. engr. Dr. Betando, Santa Monica, Calif., 1954-56; tchr. math. Las Virgines Unified Sch. Dist., Calabasas, Calif., 1961-79, subs. tchr., 1984-93. Docent Getty Mus., Malibu, Calif., 1982-94. Avocations: sno-skiing, biking, painting, piano, photography. Home: 4624 Eastbourne Bay Oxnard CA 93035-3703

NEIMAN, DEBORAH L. physician; b. Ithaca, N.Y., May 4, 1958; d. Alan and Rhoda Wolin; m. Jeffrey Neiman, Apr. 26, 1983; children: Erica, Nicole, Brian. BA, Barnard Coll., N.Y.C., 1980; MD, N.Y. Med. Coll., 1984. Cert. Am. Bd. Internal Medicine. Physician Internal Medicine Assn., Hillsborough, NJ, 1990—. Adv. bd. People's Care Ctr., Somerville, NJ, 2000—. Mem.: Somerset County Med. Soc., Am. Med. Women's Assn., AMA. Avocations: running, basketball, travel. Office: Internal Medicine Assocs of Somerset 309 Omni Dr Hillsborough NJ 08844

NEJIB, PERRI UMID-RASHID, electrical engineer; b. Pitts., Nov. 30, 1964; d. Umid Rashid Nejib and Mary Margaret (Grubb) Swaback. BSEE, Wilkes U., 1986; MSEE, Johns Hopkins U., 1989. Electronics engr. Harry Diamond Labs, Adelphi, Md., 1986-90; project officer Army Rsch. Lab., Adelphi, 1990-95, project leader, 1995—2002; prin. mem. tech. staff Litton/TASC, Annapolis Junction, Md., 1997—2002; sect. mgr. Northrop Grumman-TASC, Annapolis Junction, 2002—. Mem. women's advisory coun. Harry Diamond Labs., Adelphi, 1989-93; tech. recruiter HDL/ARL, Adelphi, 1990—; cons. Macintosh Systems, Adelphi, 1989—; mediator Mid-Level Employee Com., Adelphia, 1991—. Contbr. articles to profl. jours. Asst. coach Howard County Youth Soccer, Columbia, Md., 1994—; registrar Md. Soccer Assn., Balt., 1993—, team mem. Strike-Hers Soccer Club, capt. 1988—; mem. Chesapeake Bay Lightning Women's Hockey Club; asst. sci. instr. Prince George's Schs., Md., 1986-90; mem. N.E. Pa. Assn. of Arab Ams., Wilkes-Barre, Pa., 1982—. Recipient Disting. Alumnus award, Wilkes U., 2001. Mem. Mac Sci. Tech., Md. State Soccer Assn. (women's program coord., del. 1993-95). Republican. Moslem. Avocations: soccer, music, ice hockey, shopping, travel. Home: 2810 S Haven Rd Annapolis MD 21401-7124 Office: Northrop Grumman TASC Ste 120 2701 Technology Dr Annapolis Junction MD 20701

NEKRITZ, ELAINE, state representative; b. Wichita, Kan., Dec. 11, 1957; m. Barry Nekritz. BA, Trinity Univ., 1979; JD, Univ. of Mich., 1982. State Rep. House of Rep., Dist. 57, 2002—; atty., 1982—; former ptnr. Altheimer & Gray Law Firm. Mem.: Local Gov. Comm., Judiciary I - Civil Law Comm., Housing & Urban Develop. Comm., Elections & Campaign Reform Comm., Appropriations Comm.- pub. health, Trail Users Rights Found. Bd. Mem.-1995-present, Chgo. Bar Assoc.-1982-1989, Am. Bar Assoc.-1982-1989, Ill. State Bar Assoc., 1982-present, Comty. Rels. Commn. (chair), Chgo. and Bicycle Fed. Democrat. Office: Capitol 244-W Stratton Office Bldg Springfield IL 62706 also: District 24 So Des Plaines River Suite 200 Des Plaines IL 60016

NELKIN, DOROTHY, sociology and science policy educator; b. Boston, July 30, 1933; d. Henry and Helen (Fine) Wolfers; m. Mark Nelkin, Aug. 31, 1952; children: Lisa, Laurie. BA, Cornell U., 1954. Research assoc. Cornell U., Ithaca, 1963-69, sr. research assoc., 1970-72, assoc. prof., 1972-76, prof. sci. tech. sociology program, 1976-90, prof. sociology, 1977-90; univ. prof., prof. sociology, affiliate prof. law NYU, 1990—2003, Clare Boothe Luce vis. prof., 1988-90. Cons. OECD, Paris, 1975-76, Inst. Environ., Berlin, 1978-79; maitre de conference U. Paris, 1975-76; maitre de recherche Ecole Polytechnique, Paris, 1980-81. Author: The Atom Besieged, 1981, The Creation Controversy, 1982, Science as Intellectual Property, 1983, Workers at Risk, 1984, Selling Science: How the Press Covers Science and Technology, 1987, 2d edit., 1995, Dangerous Diagnostics: The Social Power of Biological Information, 1989, 2d edit., 1994, A Disease of Society: Cultural Impact ofAIDS, 1991, The Animal Rights Crusade, 1991, Controversy: Politics of Technical Decision, 3d edit., 1992, The DNA Mystique: The Gene as Cultural Icon, 1995, Body Bazaar: The Market for Body Tissue in the Biotechnology Age, 2001. Adviser Office Tech. Assessment, 1977-79, 82-83; expert witness ACLU, Ark., 1982; mem. Nat. Adv. Coun. to NIH Human Genome Project, 1991-95; mem. exec. com. NIH Ethical, Legal and Social Issues Working Group, Commn. on Embryo Rsch., 1998-99; mem. Working Group for Nat. Commn. on Future of DNA Evidence, 1998-2000. Vis. scholar Resources for the Futures, 1980-81; vis. scholar Russell Sage Found., N.Y.C., 1983; Guggenheim fellow, 1983-84. Fellow AAAS (bd. dirs.), Hastings Inst. Soc. Ethics and Life Scis.; mem. NAS Inst. of Medicine, Soc. for Social Studies Sci. (pres. 1978-79). Home: New York, NY. Died May 28, 2003.

NELLERMOE, LESLIE CAROL, lawyer; b. Oakland, Calif., Jan. 26, 1954; d. Carrol Wandell and Nora Ann (Conway) N.; m. Darrell Ray McKissic, Aug. 9, 1986; 1 child, Devin Anne. BS cum laude, Wash. State U., 1975; JD cum laude, Willamette U., 1978. Bar: Wash. 1978, U.S. Dist. Ct. (ea. dist.) Wash. 1979, U.S. Dist. Ct. (we. dist.) Wash. 1983. Staff atty. Wash. Ct. Appeals, Spokane, 1978-79; asst. atty. gen. Wash. Atty. Gen. Office, Spokane, 1979-83, Olympia, 1983-85; assoc. Syrdal, Danelo, Klein, Myre & Woods, Seattle, 1985-88; ptnr. Heller Ehrman White & McAuliffe, Seattle, 1990—. Bd. dirs. N.W. Environ. Bus. Coun., 1996—, Campfire Boys & Girls, Seattle, 1991-97. Mem. ABA, Wash. State Bar Assn., King County Bar Assn., Wash. Environ. Industry Assn. (bd. dirs.). Office: Heller Ehrman White & McAuliffe 701 5th Ave 6100 Columbia Ctr Seattle WA 98104-7043

NELLIGAN, ANNETTE FRANCES, clinical coordinator; b. Bangor, Maine, Sept. 20, 1954; d. Paul James and Laura Jenny (Sumner) N.; m. Peter Jamie Smith, June 22, 1985 (dec. June, 1997); children: Angelica Grace Nelligan-Smith, Acatia Faith Nelligan-Smith. AA, U. Maine, Bangor, 1974; BS, U. Maine, 1977, MEd, 1978, EdD, 1995. Lic. clin. profl. counselor; lic. marriage and family counselor; lic. social worker; cert. secondary sch. tchr., Maine, sch. counselor, Maine. Tchr. Bangor H.S., 1978, Etna (Maine)-Dixmont Sch., 1979-80; residential advisor Penobscot Job Corps, Bangor, 1980-84; group life worker St. Andre's Home, Bangor, 1984; caseworker, supr. Maine Dept. Human Svcs., Bangor, 1984-96; clin. coord. Old Town Regional Program, Bangor, 1996—. Mem. Homeless Edn. Adv. Bd., Bangor, 1992-95; instr. counselor edn. U. Maine, 1996—. Mem. ACA, Assn. for Specialists in Group Work. Roman Catholic. Avocations: doll collecting, camping, downhill skiing, sailing. Home: 14 Albert Lane GL Enburn ME 04401-5505 Office: Main St Old Town ME 04468

NELLIGAN, KATE (PATRICIA COLLEEN NELLIGAN), actress; b. London, Ont., Can., Mar. 16, 1951; d. Patrick Joseph and Alice (Dier) N. Attended, York U., Toronto, Ctrl. Sch. Speech and Drama, London. Appeared in plays in Bristol, London, and New York: Barefoot in the Park, 1972, Misalliance, A Streetcar Named Desire, The Playboy of the Western World, London Assurance, Lulu, Private Lives, Knuckle, 1974, Heartbreak House, 1975, Plenty, 1975, As You Like It, A Moon for the Misbegotten, 1984, Virginia, 1985, Serious Money, 1988, Spoils of War, 1988, Bad Habits; films include: The Count of Monte Cristo, 1979, The Romantic Englishwoman, 1979, Dracula, 1979, Mr. Patman, 1980, Eye of the Needle, 1980, Agent, 1980, Without a Trace, 1983, Eleni, 1985, White Room, 1990, Bethune: The Making of a Hero, 1990, Frankie and Johnnie, 1991 (BAFTA Film award, 1992), The Prince of Tides, 1991, Shadows and Fog, 1992, Fatal Instinct, 1993, Wolf, 1994, Into the Deep, 1994, How to Make an American Quilt, 1995, Margaret's Museum, 1995, Up Close and Personal, 1996, U.S. Marshals, 1998, (voice) Stolen Moments, 1998 Boy Meets Girl, 1998, The Cider House Rules, 1999; TV appearances include: The Arcata Promise, 1974, The Onedin Line, The Lady of the Camellias, Licking Hitler, Measure for Measure, Therese Raquin, 1980, Forgive Our Foolish Ways, 1980, Kojak: The Price of Justice, 1987, Control, 1987, Love and Hate: A Marriage Made in Hell, 1990, Terror Strikes the Class Reunion, 1992, The Diamond Fleece, 1992, Liar Liar, 1993, Shattered Trust: The Shari Karney Story, 1993, Spoils of War, 1994, Million Dollar Babies, 1994, A Mother's Prayer, 1995, Captive Heart: The James Mink Story, 1996, Calm at Sunset, Calm at Dawn, 1996, Love Is Strange, 1998, Swing Vote, 1999, Blessed Stranger: After Flight 111, 2000, Walter and Henry, 2001, A Wrinkle in Time, 2002; TV guest appearance Road to Avonlea, 1990. Recipient Best Actress award Evening Standard, 1978. Avocations: reading, cooking. Office: Innovative Artists Ste 2850 1999 Avenue Of The Stars Los Angeles CA 90067-4612

NELLIS, NORA LAJOY, special education educator, writer; b. Glens Falls, NY, July 2, 1938; d. William Thomas LaJoy and Pauline Elizabeth LaPlanche; m. Robert Selmser Nellis, June 7, 1980 (dec.); m. Warren Merritt Cole, Sept. 11, 1964 (div. Apr. 30, 1970); 1 child, Stephen Merritt Cole. AA in English, Adirondack C.C., Queensbury, N.Y., 1987; BA in English, Skidmore Coll., Saratoga Springs, N.Y., 1990; MA in Creative Writing and Women's Studies, Vt. Coll. of Norwich U., Montpelier, 1993. Editor internat. trade mag. Glens Falls Continental Ins., Glens Falls, NY, 1958—62; advt. mktg. specialist Radio Sta. WSET, Glens Falls, 1962—63; libr. Bklyn. Pub. Libr. Ft. Hamilton, Bklyn., 1964—66; Title I instr. spl. needs Glens Falls City Schs., 1971—97; freelance writer and workshop leader, 1998—. Mentor - facilitator children's writing Bd. of Coop. Ednl. Svcs., Saratoga Springs, 1998—2000; founding com. mem. and tchr. Intergenerational Writing, Glens Falls, 1995—2000. Contbr. Linking Roots, 1993, Unbearable Uncertainty, 2000; author and co-editor: From the Listening Pl., 1999. Founder Nat. Cystic Fibrosis Found. (Adirondack chpt.), Glens Falls, 1990, Support Group Single Parents, Glens Falls, 1995. Grantee DfSCA SPOKES, 1997, Troy Arts Coun., 1999; Golub Found. scholarship, 1991. Mem.: Nat. Assn. of Poetry Therapy, Am. Cancer Soc. (breast cancer resource), Wiawaka Women's Creative Orgn. (founding com. mem., facilitator 1995—). Liberal. Lutheran. Avocations: photography, recitation, health and fitness. Home: PO Box 564 Lake George NY 12845 Office: Poemweavers at Mohawk Mountain 2204 Luzerne Rd Lake George NY 12845 E-mail: nnellis@capital.net.

NELSON, ALICE CARLSTEDT, retired nursing educator; b. Strandquist, Minn., May 25, 1921; d. Peter Gustaf and Florence Olivia (Berg) Carlstedt; m. Armour Halstead Nelson June 5, 1954 (dec. Dec. 1993). RN, Bethesda Hospital, St. Paul, 1944; BS, Augustana Coll., Rock Island, Ill., 1948; MA, U. Chgo., 1954. RN, Minn., Ill., N.D., Iowa, Calif.; cert. lactation educator, cert. lifetime cmty. coll. tchr. Asst. night supr. Bethesda Hosp., St. Paul, 1944-45; with Army Nurse Corps, 1945-46; jr. grade nurse Wadsworth VA Hosp., L.A., 1947-48, intermediate grade nurse, 1967-68; head nurse Crippled Children's Sch., Jamestown, N.D., 1948-50, Sch. for Handicapped Children U. Iowa, Iowa City, 1950-51; clin. instr. Chgo. Lying-In Hosp., 1951-54, St. Luke's Hosp., Fargo, N.D., 1954-60; tchr., supr. lab. pre-sch. N.D. State U., Fargo, 1962-64; coll. health svc. Calif. Luth. U., Thousand Oaks, 1968-74, faculty dept. nursing, 1982-85; private duty nurse Thousand Oaks, 1976-81; retired, 1990. Obstetric nurse Moline (Ill.) Luth. Hosp., Miller Hosp., St. Paul, 1947-48; state sec. League for Nursing, N.D., 1956-64; team mem. preparation Nat. Achievement Test in Nursing of Children, N.Y., 1959. Author: Post-War Europe Through The Eyes of Youth, 2002; editor: The Conquest of Chicago, 2004; contbr. articles to profl. jours. Various offices including Ch. Coun. Holy Trinity Luth. Ch., Thousand Oaks, 1964-90; founding bd. dirs. Honey Tree Pre-Sch., Thousand Oaks, 1972; mem. task force on aging S.W. Pacific Luth. Synod Office, L.A., 1979; parent-aide, hotline, etc. Child Abuse & Neglect, Ventura County, Calif., 1979-82; bd. dirs. La Serena Retirement Ctr., Thousand Oaks, 1985-88; mem. ch. choir Salemsborg Luth. Ch., Smolan, Kans., 1990—, mem. ch. coun., 1996—, tchr. adult classes, 1996—. Recipient award Am. Jour. Nursing, 1969, Calif. Nurse, 1987, Outstanding Vol. award Ventura County Child Abuse & Neglect, 1982. Mem. Am. Assn. Univ. Women, Bethany Bibliophiles Book Club, Writer's Cramp Group. Democrat. Avocations: travel, reading, writing.

NELSON, ANN BRYAN, religious studies educator; b. Grand Rapids, Mich., Nov. 7, 1949; d. John William and Alice May Gieseler; m. Ross E. Bryan III, Jan. 30, 1971 (div. Aug. 1995); children: Ross E. Bryan IV, Adam John Bryan; m. Gerald Keith Nelson, Mar. 23, 1996. BA, Albion (Mich.) Coll., 1971; MLS, Western Mich. U., 1977; student computer tech., Mich. State U., 1996—98; student pastoral studies, Loyola U., Chgo., 2000—01. Tchr. English and Sci. Union City (Mich.) Middle Sch., 1971—73; tchr. English and Sci. Homer (Mich.) Middle Sch., 1973—75; libr. media dir. Homer Pub. Schs., 1975—89; dir. elementary libr. media svcs. Marshall (Mich.) Pub. Schs., 1989—2001; dir. Christian Edn. Presbyn. Ch. and Ctr. for Childen, Marshall, 2001—03. Moderator Justice for Women Presbyn. Ch. Great Lakes Presbytery, Portage, Mich.; workshop presenter various women and ch. groups, libr. coops and childrens' librs., 1988—; ednl. cons., reviewer Libr. Media Connection; mem. staff Kids N' Stuff Interactive Mus., Albion, Mich., 2003—; session ednl. chair 1st Presbyn. Ch., Marshall, Mich., 2003—. Contbr. columns in newspapers articles to media jours., 1987—2000. Sec. Homer (Mich.) Edn. Assn., 1987—89; session mem. 1st Presbyn. Ch., Albion, 1973—74, 1993—96, 2003—; bd. dirs. Marshall (Mich.) Edn. Assn., 1998—2000. Named Outstanding Tchr., Homer Ednl. Boosters, 1987. Mem.: AAUW (Grant award 2001), Nat. Storytelling Network, Mich. Assn. for Media Edn. (founder Multi Assignment Interest Group 1983). Avocations: cross country skiing, hiking, knitting, reading, cooking. Home: 502 Linden Ave Albion MI 49224 Office: Presbyn Ch & Ctr for Children 200 W Mansion Ave Marshall MI 49068 also: Kids N' Stuff Interactive Mus 301 S Superior St Albion MI 49224 E-mail: agbnelson@hotmail.com.

NELSON, ANTONYA, writer; b. Wichita, Kans., 1961; m. Robert Boswell; children: Jade, Noah. BA, U. Kans., 1984; MFA, U. Ariz., 1986. Prof. Warren Wilson MFA program, N.Mex. State U. Author: The Expendables (Flannery O'Connor award, 1990), In the Land of Men, Family Terrorists, Talking in Bed (Heartland award, 1996), Nobody's Girl, Living to Tell; contbr. stories to mags. Named one of N.Y. Times Notable Books, 1992, 1996, 1998, 2000; fellow, Guggenheim Found., 2000—01; grantee, NEA, 2000—01. Office: New Mexico State Univ Dept English Dept 3E Las Cruces NM 88003

NELSON, ARLEEN BRUCE, social worker; b. Loma Linda, California, Oct. 25, 1926; d. Delbert Francis and Sarah Enns Bruce; m. A. Gordon Nelson, Oct. 29, 1948 (dec. Sept. 1976); children: Gregory Bruce, Mark Andrew, Heidi, Scott Bradford. BA, UCLA, 1948; MSW, U. Wash., 1975. Cert. ACSW 1979, BCSW 1987, MSW Wash., 1989, LCSW Wash., 2001. Case worker L.A. County DPSS, L.A., 1949—50, 1958—61, child protective Svc. Supr., 1966—69; dir. Manson Migrant Daycare Ctr., Manson, Wash., 1970—72; I and A coord. Sr. Svc., Seattle, 1975—78; co-dir., psychotherapist Soc. Workers N. W., Seattle, 1979—95; coord., HIV-AIDS Seattle Counseling Svc. for Sexual Minorities, 1986—94, psychotherapist, supr., 1991—2000, intern supr., 1993—96; aux. faculty U. Wash., 1995—2001; intern supr. Seattle Counseling Svc. for Sexual Minorities, 2002—. Edn. com. Wash. Soc. of Clin. Soc. Work, Seattle, 1986. Co-founder Nat. Parents and Friends of Gays and Lesbians; dir. PNU / Mountain Region Nat. PFLAG, multi states, 1981—83, v.p., 1983—89; gay and lesbian advocate multiple T.V. appearances, 1978—85; task force for gays and lesbians Ch. Coun. of Greater Seattle, 1977—80; bd. mem. The Dorian Group, Seattle, 1980; co-founder Seattle Chap. Parents and Friends of Lesbians and Gays, Seattle, 1979; pres. Seattle Chap. PFLAG, 1993—94; Bd. Ch. and soc. PNW Conf. United Meth. Ch., Wash., 1970—82, commn. of race and religion, 1982—88. Recipient The Dorian Award, Dorian Group, 1982, 1998 Cmty. Leadership Award, Greater Seattle Bus. Assn., 1999, Founders Award, Seattle PFLAG, 1989, Nat. PFLAG, 1991, Award for Dedication and Svc., Seattle Gay Clinic, 1994, Award of Merit for long Svc. to the Trans - gendered Cmty., The Trans-gendered Group, 2000. Mem.: Nat Assn. of Soc. Workers, Wash. Chap. NASW. Democrat. Methodist. Avocations: nat., internat. travel, reading, grandchildren. Office: Seattle Counseling Svc 112 Broadyway E Seattle WA 98102 Office Phone: 206-323-1768.

NELSON, BARBARA ANNE, judge; b. Mineola, N.Y., Jan. 16, 1951; d. Richard William and Dorothee Helen (Thorne) N. BA, Inter Am. U. P.R., 1972; JD, New Eng. Sch. Law, 1975. Legal editor Prentice Hall Pub. Co., Englewood Cliffs, N.J., 1976-77; assoc. Antonio C. Martinez Law Firm, N.Y.C., 1977-79, Pollack & Kramer, N.Y.C., 1979-83; pvt. practice N.Y.C., 1983-95; immigration judge U.S., N.Y.C., 1995—. Author, spkr., tng. film. Mem. ACLU, Legal Aid Soc. N.Y., Amnesty Internat., Asia Soc., Internat. Assn. Refugee Judges. Avocations: travel, yoga, foreign languages. Home: 324 W 14th St Apt 5A New York NY 10014-5003 Office: 26 Federal Plz New York NY 10278-0004 E-mail: nelsonferrets@yahoo.com.

NELSON, BARBARA J. dean; b. Ohio; d. Bernard James and Betty-Jane (James) N. BA in Polit. Sci., Ohio State U., 1971, MA in Polit. Sci., 1975, PhD in Polit. Sci., 1976. Policy rsch. assoc. Mershon Ctr. Pub. Policy, Columbus, Ohio, 1974-76; asst. prof. Princeton (N.J.) U., 1976-83; assoc. prof. Hubert H. Humphrey Inst. U. Minn., Mpls., 1983-89, program dir. MA program, 1987-90, dir. ctr. women & pub. policy, 1984-94, prof. Hubert H.Humphrey Inst., 1983-94; v.p., disting. prof. Radcliffe Coll., Cambridge, Mass., 1994-96; dean UCLA Sch. Pub. Policy & Social Rsch., L.A., 1996—. Bd. trustees Ctr. Women in Pub., Mpls., 1984-98. Author: Making an Issue of Child Abuse, 1984, American Women in Politics, 1984; co-editor: Wage Justice, 1989, Women and Politics Worldwide, 1995. Bd. trustees Radcliffe Coll., 1994-96; mem. Minn. Supreme Ct.'s Commn., 1987-88; advisor Govt. of Sweden Parliamentary Commn. Women & Democracy. W.K. Kellogg Found. grantee, 1994-97, Ford Found. grantee, 1993-97, Hewlett Ctr. Conflict Resolution grantee, 1988, 93. Mem. Am. Polit. Sci. Assn. (bd. trustees 1988-98), Assn. Pub. Policy Analysis & Mgmt. Office: UCLA Sch Pub Policy/Social Rsch 3284 Pub Policy Bldg Los Angeles CA 90095-0001

NELSON, BETH CARLSON, educational consultant; b. Crofton, Nebr., Dec. 31, 1926; d. Harold and Alta Iona (Jones) Carlson; m. Sidney Hascue Nelson, Apr. 8, 1946; children: Judith Nelson, Jeanie Anderson, Betty Whitley. BS, Radford (Va.) U., 1958; MS, Va. Poly. Inst. and State U., 1964; EdD, U. Va., 1972. Cert. tchr., adminstr., supr., supt., Va. Classrm. tchr. Radford City Schs., 1958-66; supr. reading Pulaski County Schs., Pulaski, Va., 1966-69, supr. elem. edn., 1969-74; pres. Va. Edn. Assn., Richmond, 1975-76; prof. edn. Radford U., 1974-91; ednl. cons., 1991—. Pres. U. Va. Edn. Found., Charlottesville; instr., cons. Am. Schs., Sao Paulo, Brazil, 1977-79; dir. Region 1, Beginning Tchrs. Assn. Program, Va. State Dept. Edn., 1985-91. Sch. bd. Pulaski County, 1996—; bd. dirs. Fine Arts Ctr. for NRV, Pulaski, 1978—; vice chair Pulaski County Dem. Com., 1994-96. Recipient Outstanding Svc. award Radford U., 1985. Mem. NEA (bd. dirs. 1977-83, Outstanding Woman Educator award 1976), Va. Congress PTA (hon.), Delta Kappa Gamma (chpt. pres.). Methodist. Avocations: gardening, travel, reading. Home: 6800 Viscoe Rd Radford VA 24141-6906

NELSON, CAROL KOBUKE, bank executive; m. Ken Nelson; 2 children. BA in fin. magna cum laude, Seattle U., Wash., 1978, MBA, 1984; attended grad. sch. Credit & Fin. Mgmt., Santa Clara U., Calif. With SeaFirst Bank (now Bank of Am.); sr. v.p., No. regional consumer exec. Bank of Am.; pres., COO Cascade Fin. Corp., Everett, Wash., 2001—02, pres., CEO, 2002—, Cascade Bank, Everett, Wash., 2001—. Exec. adv. bd. Albers Sch. Bus. and Economics Seattle U. Chair bd. dirs. United Way, Snohomish County; bd. dirs. Boys and Girls Club, Snohomish County, Econ. Devel. Coun., Snohomish County; adv. bd. Leadership Snohomish County. Named One of 25 Women to Watch, U.S. Banker Mag., 2003. Mem.: Wash. Bankers Assn. (bd. dirs.), Wash. Fin. League (bd. dirs.). Office: Cascade Financial Corp 2828 Colby Ave Everett WA 98201*

NELSON, CAROLYN, state legislator; b. Madison, Wis., Oct. 8, 1937; m. Gilbert W. Nelson; children: Paul, John, Karla. BS, N.D. State U., 1959, MS, 1960. Sr. lectr. emeritus N.D. State U., 1968—; mem. N.D. Ho. of Reps., 1986-88, 92-94, N.D. Senate from 21st dist., 1994—; mem. judiciary com., vet. affairs com. N.D. Senate, minority caucus leader, 2000—. Mem. N.D. State Investment Bd., 1989-92. Mem. Bd. Edn., Fargo, N.D., 1985-91, pres., 1989-90; trustee N.D. Tchrs. Fund for Retirement, 1985-92, pres., 1990-92; mem. N.D. PTA, pres., 1978-81, N.D. Women's and Children's Caucus. Recipient Merit Svc. award Gamma Phi Beta, 1978, 90, Legis. Voices award Children's Caucus, 1995; named Legislator of Yr., N.D. Bar Assn., 2000, N.D. Student Assn., 2001. Mem. LWV, Am. Guild English Handbell Ringers (area chmn. 1982-84, nat. bd. dirs. 1982-90), N.D. Fedn. Music Clubs (life; pres. 1997-2001, Rose Fay Thomas fellow 2001), Gamma Phi Beta, Phi Kappa Phi, Sigma Alpha Iota. Address: 1125 College St Fargo ND 58102-3433 Office: ND Senate State Capitol Bismarck ND 58505

NELSON, CHARLENE DESS, elementary school educator; b. Akron, Ohio, June 11, 1963; d. Roy Jefferson and Judith Charlene (Bittinger) N.; m. Robert Scott Forbes, May 20, 1989. BA in Elem. Edn., U. Akron, 1987, MA in Edn. Founds., 1989. Cert. elem. and music tchr., Ohio. Media specialist U. Akron, 1989; from tchr. elem. music and band to tchr. 5th grade Akron (Ohio) Pub. Schs., Ohio, 1991—2001, tchr. 5th grade, 2001—; audio visual coord. Crosby Elem. Sch., Akron, 1994-95; video news dir. Crosby Elem./Akron Pub. Sch., 1994-95; newspaper editor Akron Pub. Schs., 1993-95, sponsor Astronomy Club, 1996-99, Newspaper Club, 1996-99. Dir. bell choir Firestone Park United Meth. Ch., Akron, 1993-95; Ambassador to Solar Sys., 1996—. Mem. ASCD, Nat. Coun. Tchrs. Math., Ohio Ednl. Libr. and Media Assn. (internship 1986), Phi Delta Kappa (v.p. membership 1996-98, foundation officer 1998-99, pres. 2001-03). Avocations: computers, video production.

NELSON, CHARLOTTE BOWERS, public administrator; b. Bristol, Va., June 28, 1931; d. Thaddeus Ray and Ruth Nelson (Moore) Bowers; m. Gustav Carl Nelson, June 1, 1957; children: Ruth Elizabeth, David Carl, Thomas Gustav. BA summa cum laude, Duke U., 1954; MA, Columbia U., 1961; MPA, Drake U., 1983. Instr. Beaver Coll., 1957-58, Drake U., Des Moines, 1975-82; office mgr. LWV of Iowa, Des Moines, 1975-82; exec. asst. Iowa Dept. Human Svcs., Des Moines, 1983-85; exec. dir. Iowa Commn. on Status of Women Dept. Human Rights, Des Moines, 1985—. Bd. dirs., pres. LWV, Beloit, Wis., 1960-74; bd. dirs. LWV, Des Moines, 1974-82, Westminster House, Des Moines, 1988-97, pres. 1996-97. Recipient Gov.'s Golden Dome award as Leader of the Yr., 2002; named Visionary Woman, Young Women's Resource Ctr., 1994. Mem. Am. Soc. Pub. Adminstrn. (mem. exec. coun. 1984-92, 98-99, past pres., Mem. of Yr. 1993), Phi Beta Kappa, Pi Alpha Alpha. Home: 1141 Cummins Cir Des Moines IA 50311-2113 Office: Human Rights Dept Lucas State Office Bldg Des Moines IA 50319-0001 E-mail: charlotte.nelson@iowa.gov., nelson514@aol.com.

NELSON, CLARA SINGLETON, human resources consultant; b. Union Ridge, Tenn., Apr. 10, 1935; d. Ernest Caldwell and Willie Emma (Hord) Singleton; m. Joe Edward Nelson, July 26, 1953; children: Drexel Edward, Dorissia Lynett. Student, Tenn. State U., 1961-62, Middle Tenn. State U., 1984; AS, Motlow Coll., 1978; BS in Edn. with highest honors, U. Tenn., Knoxville, 1991. Sec., adminstrv. asst. Bedford County Sch., Shelbyville, Tenn., 1957-64; sec., personnel asst. Aro, Inc., Arnold Air Force Sta., Tenn., 1964-71; mem. pub. rels. staff, job interviewer Employment Security, Shelbyville, 1971-81; mgr. employment EEO Calspan Corp., Arnold Air Force Sta., 1981-94; with Micro Craft Tech., 1994-95; employment and recruiting mgr. Sverdrup Tech., 1995-97; pvt. practice human resource cons., 1998—. Cons. dir. Career Devel. Workshops, Shelbyville. Mem. adv. bd. Tenn. Area Vocat. Sch., Shelbyville, 1979-2001; chmn. adv. commn. Equal Employment Opportunity, 1983—, chmn. employer com. Tullahoma Job Svc., Tenn., 1985—; mem. Patrons Coun. Argie Cooper Libr., Shelbyville; trustee Motlow Coll. Found.; former mem. Shelbyville Regional Planning Commn.; mem. Shelbyville Power, Water and Sewerage Bd. Recipient cert. of appreciation ARC, 1985. Mem.: Soc. of Human Resource Mgmt. (state diversity chair 2000—, cert.), Nat. Assn. Bus. and Profl. Women's Clubs, Inc. (chair membership 1991—93, charter mem.), Nat. Mgmt. Assn., Nat. Assn. Female Execs. (network dir. 1985, charter mem.), Highland Rim Human Resources Mgmt. Assn. (treas. 1983—84, 1987, sec. 1988, chair program com. 1989, sec. 1994, SHRM affiliate), Am. Mgmt. Assn. (chair program com. 1994—, pres. 1998—2000), Am. Assn. Affirmative Action Tenn. State U. Cluster (chmn. 1984—2000), Better Homes and Gardens Shelbyville Club. Methodist. Avocations: reading, gardening, writing. Home and Office: 105 Sun Cir Shelbyville TN 37160-2519

NELSON, CYNTHIA KAYE, infrastructure security engineer; b. Kearney, Nebr., May 8, 1949; d. LeRoy J. and W. Eileen (Schmidt) Wacker; m. James C. Nelson (div. 1987); children: Alexis Ann, Whitney Eileen. BA, U. No. Iowa, 1971; postgrad., No. Ill. U., 1973. Cert. tchr., Ill., Mo. Tchr. Dixon (Ill.) Pub. Schs., 1972-74, Maplewood (Mo.)-Richmond Heights Sch. Dist., 1974-75; counselor Mo. Bus. Men's Clearing House, St. Louis, 1975-76; dir. edn. Deltex Co., Naperville, Ill., 1982-84; trainer Electronic Data Systems Co., LaGrange, Ill., 1985-86; learning technologist Bellcore Tng. and Edn. Ctr., Lisle, Ill., 1988-90; sr. tech. tng. engr. Fujitsu Network Comm., Raleigh, N.C., 1990-98; sr. network engr. Signal Corp., Raleigh, 1998-2000; network design engr. Nortel Networks, Raleigh, 2000—01; infrastructure security engr. Nat. Info. Sys. Support Ctr., Raleigh, NC, 2002—. Mem. ASTD, AAUW, Internat. Soc. of Performance and Improvement, Alpha Chi Omega, Beta Sigma Phi. Republican. Lutheran. Home: 7404 Rainwater Rd Raleigh NC 27615-3743 Office: 4200 Wake Forest Rd Raleigh NC 27668-9700 Personal E-mail: cknelson@aol.com. E-mail: cnelson7@email.usps.gov.

NELSON, DEBRA JEAN, journalist, public relations executive, consultant; b. Birmingham, Ala., Nov. 12; BA, U. Ala., Tuscaloosa, 1980. Dir. pub. affairs Sta. WSGN Radio, Birmingham, 1980-84, news anchor, reporter, 1982-84; dir. community affairs Sta. WBRC-TV, Birmingham, 1984-88, producer, anchor, 1986-88; instr. spl. studies U. Ala., Birmingham, 1988—; dir. media rels. U. Ala. System, Tuscaloosa, 1991-94; mgr. external affairs Mercedes-Benz U.S. Internat., Inc., Tuscaloosa, 1994-2000; mgr. corp. diversity Mercedes-Benz USA, Inc., Montvale, NJ; sr. mgr. group mktg., diversity, N.Am. Regional Comm. Daimler Chrysler Corp., Auburn Hills, Mich., 2000—02; sr, mgr. comms., human rels., labor, mfg. and govt. affairs Chrysler Group, 2002—. Pub. affairs prodr./host Sta. WUAL-FM/WQPR, Tuscaloosa, 1991—. Mem. U.S. libr. literacy rev. panel Dept. Edn., Washington, 1987—92; pres.-elect Found. Women's Health in Ala., Inc., 1993—; mem. Leadership Birmingham, 1991—92, U.S. Mil. Rev. Panel for 6th Congl. Dist., 1987; mem. gen. campaign com. Ala. campaign United Negro Coll. Fund, 1992, chair Pres.'s Gala; chair Edward Davis Found., 2003—; bd. dirs., mem. exec. com. Ala. affiliate Am. Heart Assn., 1986—91; bd. dirs. Am. Cancer Soc., United Cerebral Palsy, Birmingham Urban League, Woman of Distinction, Cahaba coun. Girl Scouts, William Patterson U. Found. Recipient award of distinction Internat. Assn. Bus. Communicators, 1985, Disting. Leadership award United Negro Coll. Fund, 1985, 87, 88, Outstanding Achievement award Delta Sigma Theta, 1986, Outstanding Vol. Svc. award ARC, Birmingham, 1987, Woman of Distinction award Iota Phi Lambda, 1987, Human Rights award So. Christian Leadership Conf., Outstanding Corp. & Cmth. Rels. award Human Resources Devel. Inst., 2000, Woman Yr. African Ams. Wheels Mag., 2001, Corp. Woman of the Yr. N.J. Hispanic C. of C., 2001; Named one of the Top Twenty -five Influential Woman in Bus. Network Jour. Mag., 2001. Mem. Assn. Black Women in Higher Edn. (bd. dirs. 1993—, chair com. on pub. rels.), Am.-Japan Soc., Coun. for Advancement and Support of Edn. Avocations: writing fiction, travel. Home: 1228 Rock Valley Dr Rochester MI 48307-2739 Office: Daimler Chrysler Corp 1000 Chrysler Dr Auburn Hills MI 48326-0100

NELSON, DEBRA L. consultant for non-profit organizations; b. Williston, N.D., Sept. 14, 1953; d. Duane Robert Leroy and Ida M. (Lester) Evanson; m. Kenneth E. Nelson, Nov. 8, 1975; children: Brian Paul, Brent Allen. BS in Secondary Edn., Minot State U., 1975. Classroom instr. Donnybrook (N.D.) H.S., 1976-82, Dickinson (N.D.) H.S., 1982-83; mgr. B. Dalton Bookseller, Dickinson, 1983-88; traffic safety coord. City of Dickinson, 1988-93; prevention and traffic safety coord. Cmty. Action and Devel., Dickinson, 1993-98; state and fed. hwy. safety cons. State N.D. Dept. Transp./Nat. Hwy. Traffic Safety Adminstrn., Bismarck, N.D. and Denver, 1998—; owner, mgr. DLN Consulting, Inc., Dickinson, N.D. Editor: (manuals) N.D. Cmty. Traffic Safety Program Manual, 1996, N.D. Safe Cmtys. Coords. Handbook, 1998, 2000. Adult coord. Teen Action Group, 1990-2000; bd. dirs. children's svcs. coord. com., Dickinson, 1993-99, Sunrise Youth Bur., Dickinson, 1998-99; mem. City of Dickinson Traffic Commn., 1994-97, N.D. Safety Belt Coalition, 1989-93, N.D. Children's Caucus, 1996—. Recipient N.D. Gov.'s Hwy. Safety award, Bismarck, 1998, Gold Belt award N.D. Safety Belt Coalition, 1993. Mem. AAUW, Roughrider Country Kiwanis (fellow, bd. dirs. 1992-97, pres. 2001, chmn. orientation com. 1989-2001, Builders award 1996). Avocations: volunteering with Boy Scouts Am., reading, gardening, concerts, plays, sporting events. Home: 130 7th Ave W Dickinson ND 58601-3013 Office: 2493 4th Ave W Ste G Dickinson ND 58601 E-mail: deb@dlnconsulting.com.

NELSON, DENISE GRAU, special education educator, consultant; b. Elkader, Grau, Apr. 16, 1957; d. Robert Bodholdt and Ruth Button Grau; m. Daniel K. Nelson, Aug. 4, 1984; children: Anders Grau, Marit Gjevre. BA summa cum laude, Luther Coll., Decorah, Iowa, 1979; MEd, Ill. State Univ., Normal Ill., 1989. Tchr. deaf/hard of hearing John Hersey H.S., Arlington Heights, Ill., 1982—84; coord. program for the deaf and hard of hearing Rochester Pub. Sch., Rochester, Minn., 1984—94; tchr. deaf and hard of hearing BOCES #1, Fairport, NY, 1994—98; lead tchr. deaf and hard of hearing Durham Sch. of the Arts/Durham Pub. Sch., Durham, NC, 1998—. Contbr. articles to profl. jour. Den leader Cub Scouts, Pittsford, NY; girl scout leader Girl Scouts, Pittsford, NY. Mem.: Nat. Edn. Assn., Convention of Am. Instr. of the Deaf, Minn. State Criteria Com., Minn. Region 10 tchrs. of the Deaf, Minn. State Coord. Group. Avocations: music, reading, swimming. Office: Durham Sch of Arts 400 N Duke St Durham NC 27701

NELSON, DONNA GAYLE, state representative, aviation executive, business owner, educator, writer, journalist; b. Paducah, Tex., June 13, 1943; d. Jack Harold Williams and Hazel Louise (Cooper Moss) Stephens; m. Douglas Caldwell Nelson, June 24, 1966 (div. 1976); children: Kellye Lou Fetters, Robert Kreg Nelson, J. Graigory. AB, South Plains Coll., Levelland, Tex., 1963; BBA, West Tex. State U., Canyon, 1965, MBA, 1967. Founder Evergreen Mut., McMinnville, Oreg., 1975; co-founder Evergreen Life Line, McMinnville, 1970—; founder, corp. dir. AAA Profl. Promotions, McMinnville, 1977—; pres. Evergreen Bus. Mgmt. Co., McMinnville, 1978—; sr. v.p. Evergreen Helicopters, Inc., McMinnville, 1978—, Evergreen Internat. Aviation, Inc., McMinnville, 1978—; Oreg. State Rep., 2000—04. Dir. Evergreen Air Ctr., Inc., Marana, Ariz., Evergreen Aircraft Sales & Leasing Co., Evergreen Aviation Ground Logistics Enterprises, Inc., Evergreen Internat. Aviation, Inc., McMinnville; speaker Nat. Speakers' Assn., Phoenix, 1986—; mem. adv. bd. Chemeketa Community Coll., McMinnville, 1984-85; owner 3N & Assocs. Inc., Donna G. Nelson Auctions, LLC; founder Yamhill Co. Market; teacher Tex., Calif., and Oregon; author, journalist. Poet World's Most Beloved Poetry, 1985 (Silver poet); composer Beta Sigma Phi, 1973; writer Aviation/Space Writers' Assn., 1989-90 Mem. Team 100 Rep. party, Washington, 1989; co-founder Poyama Land Treatment Ctr., Independence, Oreg., 1973; den mother, sustained membership chmn. Boy Scouts Am., McMinnville, 1977-79; dr. mem. March of Dimes, Heart Fund, McMinnville, 1973-75; sr. transportation com., Yamhill Co. Budget Parks, Elks Lions, Red Cross, NRA, N1IB Farm Bureau; founder Newcomers Club, Fund for Hope; bd. dirs. Humane Soc., Linfield Chamber Orch., Salvation Army. Named Woman of Excellence, Portland, Oreg., 1985. Mem. DAR, C. of C., Soroptimists Club, Beta Sigma Phi (pres. 1974-75). Republican. Baptist. Avocations: music, sports, bridge, writing, poetry, speaking, travel, fishing, computers, charity auctioneer. Home and Office: 2150 St Andrews Dr # 1252 Mcminnville OR 97128-2436

NELSON, DONNA JEAN, chemistry educator, researcher; b. Eufaula, Okla., Aug. 29, 1952; d. John Howard Jr. and Dorotha (Eckelkamp) Baker; 1 child, Christopher Brammer. BS in Chemistry, U. Okla., 1974; postgrad., Auburn (Ala.) U., 1974-76; PhD, U. Tex., 1979; postgrad., Purdue U., 1980-83. Robert A. Welch pre-doctoral fellow, 1977, 78, 79; Robert A. Welch postdoctoral fellow, 1980; asst. prof. U. Okla., Norman, 1983-89, assoc. prof., faculty adminstrv. fellow Provost's Office, 1989—. Jr. faculty rsch. fellow Okla. U., 1984, assocs. disting. lectr., 1985-86; vis. prof. MIT, 2003. Asst. editor: Progress Mag., 2002—, assoc editor: AWIS Mag., 2002—03. Recipient Sooner Spotlight award U. Okla., 1986, Sequoyah medal Am. Indians in Sci. and Engring. Soc., 2003; named Woman of Achievement, USBE and Info. Tech. Mag., 2003; Robert A. Welch grantee, 1979; A.P. Sloan Found. travel awardee, 2003; Ford Found. fellow, 2003-04; Guggenheim awardee, 2003-04. Mem. Am. Chem. Soc. (women chemists com. 1988—, James Flack award com. 1987-90), Phi Lambda Upsilon, Alpha Chi Sigma, Iota Sigma Pi, Sigma Xi (nat. diversity com. 2001—). Home: 1700 Winding Ridge Rd Norman OK 73072-3149 Office: U Okla Dept of Chemistry Norman OK 73072 E-mail: djnelson@ou.edu.

NELSON, DOREEN KAE, mental health counselor, educator, reserve military officer; b. Duluth, Minn., Oct. 18, 1957; d. Norman G. Nelson and Carola Gerene (Sunneli) Cooper. B Applied Scis., U. Minn., 1983; MS in Human Resources Mgmt. Devel., Chapman U., 1988; MAEd in Mental Health Counseling, Western Ky. U., 1995. Commd. 2nd lt. U.S. Army, 1983, advanced through grades to lt. col., 2001, pers. officer 62nd Med. Group, 1987—88, med. pers. officer Acad. Health Scis. Ft. Sam Houston, Tex., 1989, chief adminstrv. svcs. div. Med. Dept. Ctr. and Sch., 1989—92; med. advisor Readiness Group Knox, Ft. Knox, Ky., 1992—94; counselor intern Ireland Army Hosp., Ft. Knox, 1995; mental health counselor IV Meridian Behavioral HealthCare, Inc., Gainesville, Fla., 1995—97; substitute tchr. Ind. Sch. Dist. #381, Silver Bay, Minn., 1997—2001, Title I tchr., 2001—. Lutheran. Avocation: family genealogy.

NELSON, DOROTHY WRIGHT (MRS. JAMES F. NELSON), federal judge; b. San Pedro, Calif., Sept. 30, 1928; d. Harry Earl and Lorna Amy Wright; m. James Frank Nelson, Dec. 27, 1950; children: Franklin Wright, Lorna Jean. BA, UCLA, 1950, JD, 1953; LLM, U. So. Calif., 1956; LLD (hon.), U. San Diego, 1997, U. So. Calif., 1983, Georgetown U., 1988, Whittier U., 1989, U. Santa Clara, 1990, Whittier U., 1989, Pepperdine U. Sch. of Law, 2003. Bar: Calif. 1954. Rsch. assoc. fellow U. So. Calif., 1953—56, instr., 1957, asst. prof., 1958—61, assoc. prof., 1961—67, prof., 1967—, assoc. dean., 1965—67, dean., 1967—80; judge U.S. Ct. Appeals 9th Cir., 1979—95, sr. judge, 1995—. Com. to consider stds. for admission to practice in fed. cts. Jud. Conf. U.S., 1976—79; cons. project STAR Law Enforcement Assistance Adminstrn.; select com. on internal procedures Calif. Supreme Ct., 1987—; co-chair Sino-Am. Seminar on Mediation and Arbitration, Beijing, 1992. Contbr. articles to profl. jours.; author: Judicial Adminstration and The Administration of Justice, 1973; author: (with Christopher Goelz and Meredith Watts) Federal Ninth Circuit Civil Appellate Practice, 1995. Co-chair Confronting Myths in Edn. for Pres. Nixon's White House Conf. on Children, Pres. Carter's Commn. for Pension Policy, 1974—80; pres. Reagon's Madison Trust; mem. Nat. Spiritual Assembly of Bahais of U.S., 1967—; bd. dirs. Dialogue on Transition to a Global Soc., Weinacht, Switzerland, 1992; bd. vis. U.S. Air Force Acad., 1978; bd. dirs. Coun. on Legal Edn. for Profl. Responsibility, 1971—80, Constl. Right Found., Am. Nat. Inst. for Social Advancement; adv. bd. Nat. Ctr. for State Cts., 1971—76; adv. com. to promote equality for woman and men in cts. Nat. Jud. Edn. Program; bd. dirs. Pacific Oaks Coll., Childrens Sch. & Rsch. Ctr., 1996—98; adv. bd. World Law Inst., 1997—, Tahirih Justice Inst., Washington, 1998—; chmn. bd. Western Justice Ctr., 1986—; chair 9th Cir. Standing Com. on Alternative Dispute Resolution, 1998—. Named Law Alumnus of Yr., UCLA, 1967, Woman of Yr., Times, 1968, Disting. Jurist, Ind. U. Law, 1994; recipient Profl. Achievement award, 1969, AWARE Internat. award, 1970, Humanitarian award, U. Judaism, 1973, Ernestine Stalhut Outstanding Woman Lawyer award, 1972, Pub. Svc. award, Coro Found., 1978, Pax Orbis ex Jure medal, World Peace thru Law Ctr., 1975, Hollzer Human Rights award, Jewish Fedn. Coun., 1988, Medal of Honor, UCLA, 1993, Emil Gumpert Jud. ADR Recognition award, L.A. County Bar Assn., 1996, Julia Morgan award, YWCA, 1997, Samuel E. Gates Litigation award, Am. Coll. Trial Lawyers, 1999, Bernard E. Witkin award, State Bar Assn. Calif., 2000, Judge of the Year award, Pasadena Bar Assn., 2002; fellow, Davenport Coll.; Lustman fellow, Yale U., 1977. Fellow: Davenport Coll., Am. Bar Found.; mem.: ABA (sect. on jud. adminstrn., chmn. com. on edn. in jud. adminstrn. 1973—89, D'Alemberte/Raven award 2000), Assn. Am. Law Schs. (chmn. com. edn. in jud. adminstrn.), Am. Judicature Soc. (bd. dirs., Justice award 1985), Bar Calif. (bd. dirs. continuing edn. bar commn. 1967—74), Order of Coif (nat. v.p. 1974—76), Phi Beta Kappa. Office: US Ct Appeals Cir 125 S Grand Ave Ste 303 Pasadena CA 91105-1621

NELSON, ELAINE EDWARDS, lawyer; b. Waco, Tex., Sept. 16, 1947; d. Bedford Duncan and Joyce (Harlan) Edwards; m. David A. Nelson, Apr. 12, 1969; children: Carol Christine, Harlan Claire. BA, Baylor U., 1969, JD, 1978. Bar: Tex. 1978. Gen. counsel Austin Industries, Inc., Dallas, 1978—. Office: Austin Industries Inc 3535 Travis St Ste 300 Dallas TX 75204-1466 also: PO Box 2879 Dallas TX 75221-2879*

NELSON, ESTHER, dance educator; b. N.Y.C., Sept. 9, 1928; d. Rubin and Freda (Seligman) N.; m. Leon Sokolsky, Nov. 18, 1949 (dec. May 1992); children: Mara, Risa. BA in psychology, Bklyn. Coll., 1949; MA in dance edn., N.Y. Univ., 1950. Dance and music educator Horace Mann Preschool, N.Y.C., 1992—2000; founder, ptnr. Granny Press, Tappan, NJ, 2003—. Adj. prof. music and dance Bklyn. Coll., 1982-85, workshop and speaker Libr. Conf., 1981-2003; workshop presenter in field. Author: Everybody Sing and Dance!, 1989, The World's Best Funny Songs, 1988, The Fun-to-Sing Songbook, 1986, The Great Rounds Songbook, 1985, The Funny Songbook, 1984, The Silly Songbook, 1981, Holiday Singing & Dancing Games, 1980, Singing and Dancing Games for the Very Young, 1977, Musical Games for Children of All Ages, 1976, Movement Games for Children, 1975, Dancing Games for Children of All Ages, 1973, Riggeldy Jiggeldy Joggeldy Jam...Can You Guess What I Am?, Riggeldy Jiggeldy Joggeldy Roo...Can You Guess What I Do?; produced numerous cassette tapes. Avocations: visiting my children and grandchildren, travel. Home: 3605 Sedgwick Ave Apt A32 Bronx NY 10463-6041 Office: Dimension 5 PO Box 403 Bronx NY 10463-0403 Office Phone: 718-548-6112. E-mail: estnelson@aol.com.

NELSON, ETHELYN BARNETT, civic worker; b. Bessemer, Ala., Jan. 16, 1925; d. Laurence McBride and Ethel Victoria Fortesque (King) Barnett; student Huntingdon Coll., 1943, U. Ala., 1948, George Washington U., 1948-49, 74; m. Stuart David Nelson, May 6, 1949; children— Terryl Lynn, Cynthia Dianne, Jacqueline Margo. Sec., U.S. Air Force, Montgomery, Ala. and Panama Canal Zone, 1944-49; sec. to dep. undersec. U.S. Dept. State, Washington, 1951-53, U.S. Ho. of Reps. and U.S. Senate, 1959-60; adminstrv. asst. editorial div. Nat. Geog. Soc., Washington, 1962-65; rec. sec. Dist. IV, Nat. Capital Area Fedn. Garden Clubs, Inc., Washington, 1981-83. Mem. Women's Com. Nat. Symphony Orch. Mem. Nat. Trust for Historic Preservation, Salvation Army Aux., Am. Scandinavian Assn., Landon Woods Garden Club (pres. 1978-80), Congl Country Club. Patentee. Republican. Methodist. Home: 6410 Maiden Ln Bethesda MD 20817-5612

NELSON, FREDA NELL HEIN, librarian; b. Trenton, Mo., Dec. 16, 1929; d. Fred Albert and Mable Carman (Doan) Hein; m. Robert John Nelson, Nov. 1, 1957 (div. Apr. 1984); children: Thor, Hope. Nursing diploma, Trinity Luth. Hosp., Kansas City, Mo., 1950; B. Philosophy, Northwestern U., 1961; MS in Info. and Libr. Sci., U. Ill., 1986. RN. Operating rm. nurse Trinity Luth. Hosp., Kansas City, Mo., 1950-52, Johns Hopkins Hosp., Balt., 1952, Wesley Meml. Hosp., Chgo., 1952-58, Tacoma Gen. Hosp., 1958-59, Chgo. Wesley Hosp., 1959-61; libr. asst. Maple Woods Campus Met. Community Colls., Kansas City, 1987-89, libr., libr. mgr. Blue Springs Campus, 1989-96; ret., 1996. Co-founder Coll. for Kids, Knox Coll., Galesburg, Ill., 1982. Nurses scholar Edgar Bergen Found., 1947; recipient Award of Merit, Chgo. Bd. Health, 1952. Avocations: swimming, walking, cross-word puzzles. Home: 7000 N Elm St Pleasant Valley MO 64068-9571

NELSON, HEDWIG POTOK, marketing executive; b. Detroit, Oct. 6, 1954; m. Richard Alan Nelson. BA with honors, U. Mich., 1976; MBA, Am. U., 1980. Fin. asst. antitrust divsn. U.S. Dept. Justice, Washington, 1979—80; fin. analyst corp. treasury Martin Marietta Corp., Bethesda, Md., 1980—81, fin. adminstr. aggregates div., 1981—83, sr. fin. adminstr. bus. devel. data systems div., 1983, mgr. fin. planning and analysis, 1983—85; mgr. mergers and acquistions M/A-COM Devel. Corp., Rockville, Md., 1985—88; sr. analyst group fin. Marriott Corp., Bethesda, 1988—89, mgr. bus. planning, hotel divsn., 1989—90; mgr. planning and analysis, geon vinyl divsn. BF Goodrich, Cleve., 1990—91, bus. contr. molding, geon vinyl divsn., 1991—93; bus. mgr. extrusions The GEON Co., Cleve., 1993—96; dir. planning and analysis Elsag Bailey, Inc., Wickliffe, Ohio, 1996—98; product mgr. Saint-Gobain, Aurora, Ohio, 1998—2001, mktg. mgr., 2001—. Mem.: NAFE (treas. Montgomery County chpt. 1987—88). Home: 325 Middlebush Cir Akron OH 44321-2778 Office: Saint-Gobain Performance Plastics Corp 1395 Danner Dr Aurora OH 44202 E-mail: hedwig.p.nelson@saint-gobain.com.

NELSON, HOPE LINDA, pilot; b. Plainfield, N.J., Nov. 25, 1964; d. Ralston J. and Eileen M. (Creed) N. BS in Aviation Mgmt., Fla. Inst. Tech., 1986. Capt. Am. Eagle, Raleigh, N.C., 1990-95, Nashville, 1995-96; fist officer Northwest Airlines, Mpls., 1996—. Mem. Airlines Pilots Assn., Aircraft Owners Pilots Assn. Avocations: sailing, traveling, diving, golf, jogging.

NELSON, JANE GRAY, state legislator, small business owner, educator; b. Hamilton, Ohio, Oct. 5, 1951; d. Robert Allen and Edna Mae (Allen) Gray; m. James Michael Nelson, Sept. 27, 1978; children: Brian, Elizabeth, Christina, Michelle, Jennifer. Student, U. Tex., Arlington, 1969-70; BS in Edn. and Linguistics, N. Tex. State U., 1972, postgrad., 1973-75, So. Meth. U., 1973-75. Cert. tchr. Tchr. Arlington (Tex.) Ind. Sch. Dist., 1973-78; instr. community edn. Lewisville (Tex.) Ind. Sch. Dist., 1980—; owner, pres. Connections, Lewisville, 1987-92; owner Mayday Mfg., 1992—; mem. Tex. State Senate, 1993—. Chmn. Lewisville Community Edn. Adv. Coun., 1986-89; mem. steering com. Tex. Community Edn. Counel of Couns., 1986; pres. Tex. Community Edn. Adv. Coun. Assn., 1986-88; bd. dirs., founder INFOHELP, Lewisville; mem. Tex. Bd. Edn., 1988-90; mem. adv. com. Tex. Ctr. for Ednl. Rsch.; mem. Nat. Com. for Tech. Edn. Excellence; vice chmn. TPC Task Force on Family; chmn. Tex. Rep. Women Leaders Forum Author: Drill Team, 1985; mem. editorial adv. bd. Tex. Researcher. Chmn. cultural arts Lewisville Ind. Sch. Dist. Community Edn. Adv. Council, 1984-89, ticket sales fundraiser, 1984-85, nominating com., 1986, sci. fair, 1985, ednl. com. Congressman Armey's Drug Abuse Task Force, Denton County, Tex., 1986-89, communications Lewisville Bond Election Steering Com., 1986, talent com. Red Stockings Follies Prodn., Lewisville, 1985, student com. Tex. State Bd. Edn., 1988-90; adv. com. Tex. Ctr. Ednl. Rsch.; nat. com. Tech. Edn. Excellence; editorial adv. bd. Tex. Researcher; founder, charter mem. Community Against Substance Abuse, Lewisville, 1987-89; mem. Lewiston Ind. Sch. Dist. Drug and Alcohol Abuse Task Force, 1986-89, Community Action League Lewisville, 1979—, v.p., 1980-81; active Lewisville Ind. Sch. Dist. Council PTA's, Highland Village Elem. PTA, (PTA Tex. Life Membership award 1987), Am. Cancer Soc.; bd. dirs. Dist.-Wide Drill Team and Baton Twirling Corps, 1980-86, edn. work com. 1st United Meth. Ch., Parent Support, Friends of Hospice, Denton, Tex., 1986—; mem. Tex. Cancer Coun., 1995—, Tex. Conservative Coalition Bd., 1993-96. Mem. Nat. Community Edn. Assn. (Citizen Leadership award 1986), Tex. Community Edn. Assn. (Citizen Leadership award 1987), Tex. Community Edn. Adv. Coun. Assn. (pres. 1986-88), Tex. Tchrs. Assn. (chmn. textbook adoption com. 1975-76), North Tex. State U. Alumnae Assn., Delta Zeta (founder Lewisville-Lake Cities chpt., bd. dirs. Province XVII 1975-81). Republican. Avocations: reading, travel. Office: 900 Parker Sq Ste 200 Flower Mound TX 75028 also: PO Box 12068 Capitol Sta Austin TX 75028-7871

NELSON, JOANN, secondary school educator, educational consultant; b. Little Rock, Arkansas, July 11, 1943; d. Lucinda Nelson. BA cum laude(hon.), Philander Smith Coll., Little Rock, 1962—66; EdM, Cleveland State U., 1977—79. Cert. tchg. Ark., 1966; Ohio, 1966, 1987. English tchr. Cleve. Pub. Sch., 1966—78, dept. chmn., English, reading, and language arts, 1978—96. Cons., Cleve., 1996—. Rec. sec. Neighborhood St. Club, Cleve., 1978—96. Mem.: Greater Cleve. Roundtable, Metro Cleve. Alliance of Black Sch. Educators, Nat. Coun. of Negro Women, Nat. Coun. of Teachers of English. Democrat. Baptist. Achievements include city wide lesson plans, Cleve. Pub. Sch., 1982; students' performance and reading tests, Cleve. Pub. Sch., 1986; proficiency test coord.,Cleve. Pub. Sch., 1994. Avocations: reading, theater, photography, travel, collecting brass and crystal. E-mail: njoann1@aol.com.

NELSON, K. BONITA, literary agent; b. Austin, Minn., July 5, 1945; d. Wallace Arthur and Opal Rebecca (Lastine) N. BA, Hunter Coll., 1969; B in laws, LaSalle U., 1982. Lit. agt. Am. Play Co., Inc., N.Y.C., 1970-75; legal sec., reviewer Eastman & DaSilva, Esqs., N.Y.C., 1975-79; founder, pres. BK Nelson Literary Agy., N.Y.C., 1983—, BK Nelson Lect. Bureau, N.Y.C., 1988—, BK Nelson Wordprocessing, Pleasantville, NY, 1994—; pres., publ. Internat. Media Comm., Inc., 1998. Bd. dirs. Dynaray, N.Y.; founder BK Nelson, Inc., 1995; founder Literacy Inst. for Edn. (Life) Inc., 1996. Collaborator: Looking for Canterbury, 1994; author: My Literary Agent, 1998; co-prodr. (movie) Beyond Forever, 2003. Mem. Authors Guild (assoc.), NAFE (assoc.), Nat. Assn. Campus Activities (assoc.), AAUW, (assoc.), Dramatists Guild (assoc.), Minority and Woman Owned Businesses. Avocations: aerobics, yoga, needlepoint, stamp collecting. Home and Office: 1565 Paseo Vida Palm Springs CA 92264 Office: NY Office 84 Woodland Rd Pleasantville NY 10570 E-mail: bknelson4@cs.com.

NELSON, KARI J. psychologist, educator; b. Aberdeen, S.D., July 10, 1964; d. Martin Martell Mack and Barbara Jane Schreiber; m. Daniel Ray Nelson, May 26, 1984; children: Ryan Michael, Danielle Marie. BS, North Ctrl. U., 1986; MA, St. Mary's U., Mpls., 1989; D in Psychology, U. St. Thomas, 1999. Lic. psychologist Minn. Behavioral specialist Mpls. Pub. Schs., 1986—89; lic. psychologist Minn. Psychol. Resources, Plymouth, 1989—. Adj. prof. North Ctrl. U., Mpls., 1986—98, prof., 1999—. Exec. sec. Parent Tchr. Orgn., M.W. Savage Elem., 1999—2002, exec. pres., 2002—03. Mem.: APA. Mem. Assemblies Of God Church. Avocations: gardening, reading, exercising, travel. Office: North Ctrl Univ 910 Elliot Ave So Minneapolis MN 55404

NELSON, KAY ELLEN, speech and language pathologist; b. Milw., Apr. 14, 1947; d. John A. and Magaret B. (Janke) Strobel; m. Dale Kuglitisch, Mar. 2, 1974 (div. Dec. 1981); 1 child, Ashley Lara ; m. Ronald P. Anderson, Sept. 7, 2002. BA with distinction, U. Wis., Madison, 1969; MA, U. Wis., Milw., 1972. Speech and lang. pathologist Sch. Dist. 146, Dolton, Ill., 1970-71, Waukesha County Handicapped Children's Edn. Bd., Waukesha, Wis., 1972-77, 79-80, Kettle Moraine Area Schs., Wales, Wis., 1980-94; dir. speech/lang. pathology MJ Care, Inc., Fond du Lac, Wis., 1994-96; speech-lang. pathologist, team leader NovaCare, Inc., New Berlin, Wis., 1996-97, clin. specialist, 1996-98, Prism Rehab Systems, Glendale, Wis., 1998-99, Mariner Health Care, Greenfield, Wis., 1999—2003; clin. supr., instr. U. Wis.-Whitewater, 2000—03, ret., 2003; with Aegis Therapies & Mariner Healthcare, 2003—. Pvt. practice, Dousman, Wis., summers 1991-93. Fellow Herb Kohl Found., 1993. Mem.: NC Speech, Hearing and Lang. Assn., Internat. Soc. for Augmentative and Alternative Comm., U.S. Soc. for Augmentative and Alternative Comm., Wis. Soc. for Augmentative and Alternative Comm. (sec. 1990—92, membership chmn. 1990—93, v.p. profl. affairs 1993), Wis. Speech, Lang. and Hearing Assn. (sch. rep. dist. VII 1991—94, chmn. sch. svcs. com. 1992—94, v.p. sch. svcs. 1994—95, rep.-at-large 1995—96, v.p. healthcare 1998—99), Am. Speech, Lang. and Hearing Assn. (ACE award 1990, 1991, 1992, 1994, 1995, 1996, 1997, cert. of clin. competence, ACE award 2001). Unitarian Universalist. Avocations: sewing, computers, nature activities, travel. E-mail: snrslp@hotmail.com.

NELSON, KIMBERLY TERESE, federal agency administrator; B, Shippensburg U.; M, U. Pa. Spl. asst. to sec., spl. asst. to deputy sec. adminstrn., spl. asst. deputy sec. field ops. Pa. Dept. Environ. Resources, 1987—95; dir. program integration and effectiveness then chief info. officer Pa. Dept. Environ. Protection, 1999—2001; asst. adminstr. environ. info. EPA, Washington, 2001—. Office: EPA 1200 Pennsylvania Ave NW MC 2810A Washington DC 20460

NELSON, LA VONNE ARLENE, music educator; d. Turnell Joshua and Joycelyn Augustina Nelson. Bachelor of Music in Vocal Performance cum laude, Temple U., 1989, Master of Music in Music Edn., 1993. Instr. children's musical devel. Temple U., Phila., 1987—95; tchr. music Phila. Pub. Sch., 1993—95; music min. Christian Joy Ctr., El Paso, Tex., 1993—, music dir., 1995—; tchr. music Christian Joy Ctr. Acad., El Paso, 1998—; piano and voice instr. El Paso C.C., 2002—. Founder, pvt. voice and piano instr. Zamar Sch. of Music/Performing Arts, 1995—. Author: (rsch. study) The Investigation of Musical Aptitude Among Primary-aged Trinidadian Students, 1993. Avocations: hiking, bicycling, cooking, interior decorating. Home: 12024 Kings Crest Dr El Paso TX 79936 Office: Christian Joy Ctr 1208 Sumac El Paso TX 79925

NELSON, LEANN LINDBECK, small business owner; b. McCook, Nebr., Jan. 27, 1937; d. Clifford Roy Lindbeck and Elizabeth J. (Downs) Rollstin; m. Lawrence L. Nelson, June 21, 1958; children: Glen Lindbeck, Todd Alan. BS in Dietetics, U. Tex., 1960. Dietitian Parkview Bapt. Hosp., Yuma, Ariz., 1960-61; instr. foods and nutrition Jefferson County Schs., Lakewood, Colo., 1969-71; dir. education and consumer programs, cons. nutrition Dairy Coun., Inc., Denver, 1971-74; coord. low-income foods and nutrition programs Emily Griffith Opportunity Sch., Denver, 1974-76; dir., asst. dir. edn./info. and product publicity Am. Sheep Prodrs. Coun., Denver, 1976-83; pres. Natural Accents, Denver, 1983-90; pres., owner LeAnn Nelson Presents, Denver, 1988—; sales mgr. Weekenders, U.S.A., Inc., 2001—. Cons. fixed income counseling program City of Denver, Denver County, 1975-76, comm. cons., 1989—; co-chairperson Home Econs. Nat. Task Force on Profl. Unity and Identity, 1992-93; prof. home econs., mem. adv. com. Coll. Applied Human Scis., Colo. State U., 1994-96. Author: Accessories... What a Finish!, 1988. Chmn. home econs. adv. com. U. No. Colo., 1980-82; v.p. Clock Tower Mchts. Assn., Denver, 1983-85; chmn., buyer Denver Symphony Guild Gift Shop, 1984-87; mem. adv. bd. State Bd. Cmty. Colls. Occupational Edn., Home Econ. Tech. Adv. Com., 1986-95, Coll. Applied Human Scis. Colo. State U., Ft. Collins, 1986-87; mem. consumer & family studies adv. com. Emily griffith Opportunity Sch., 1993—, chair profl. sewing adv. com., 1996—. Named Colo. Home Economist of Yr. Colo. Home Econs. Assn., 1979, Colo. Bus. Home Economist of Yr. Colo. Home Econs. Assn., 1980; recipient Leadership award Colo. Home Econs. Assn. Mem. Nat. Assn. Women Bus. Owners, Home Economists in Bus. (nat. chmn.-elect 1981-82, nat. chmn. 1982-83, Nat. Bus. Home Economist of Yr. 1986), Colo. Assn. of Profl. Saleswomen, Profl. Aux. Assistance League of Denver (corr. sec. 1994-96), Denver Fashion Group (regional dir. 1984-86), Am. Women in Radio & TV (treas. Denver chpt. 1978-79), Sales Profl. Internat. Clubs: Penrose, Executive, PEO. Home and Office: 1250 Humboldt St Apt 1001 Denver CO 80218-2416

NELSON, LINDA J. state legislator; b. Plentywood, Mont., June 12, 1942; m. Roger Nelson. Grad., Medicine Lake H.S. Farmer, rancher; mem. Mont. Ho. of Reps., 1989-94, Mont. Senate, Dist. 49, Helena, 1994—2004; mem. ethics com., mem. rules com., mem. fin. and claims com.; mem. agr., livestock and irrigation com.; mem. jt. appropriations subcom. natural resources/commerce; minority whip Mont. Senate, 1999—2002, dean of senate, 2003—04. Mem. Medicine Lake (Mont.) Sch. Bd., 1981-88, chair, 1984-88; active Mont. Dem. Party. Mem. Women Involved in Farm Econs., Nat. Order Legis. Women, N.E. Mont. Land and Mineral Owners Assn., Mont. Grain Growers, Sheridan County Dem. Women. Democrat. Lutheran. Home: 469 Griffin Medicine Lake MT 59247-9708

NELSON, MARCELLA MAY, volunteer; b. Schaunavon, Sask., Can., Oct. 11, 1928; d. Ilmer Alexander and Zylpha May (Geier) Madson; m. William Robert Nelson, June 12, 1951 (dec. Nov. 2000). Stenographer Idaho Employment Security, Bonners Ferry, 1947-50, interviewer, 1950-51, mgr., 1951-63; supr., asst. mgr. Employment Security Agy., Sandpoint, Idaho, 1963-83, program supr. Coeur d'Alene, Idaho, 1983-84; ret., 1984. Tutor illiteracy program NIC Coll., Coeur d'Alene, 1985-91; v.p. solicitations Festival at Sandpoint, 1988—. Campaign mgr. state rep. candidate for Vi Sims, Sandpoint and Bonners Ferry, 1984; pres. Pend Oreille Arts Coun., 1993-95, bd. dirs.; bd. dirs. Clean Air Coalition; bd. dirs. fundraising com. Panida Theatre; mem. Cmty. Assistance League, 1994—; mem. Sandpoint Centennial Commn., 2001; chmn. fundraising auction Sandpoint C. of C., 2001-02, 2002, One Festival, Sandpoint, 2002, Winter Carnival, Sandpoint C. of C., 2003, The Festival at Sandpoint, 2003; v.p. bd. dirs. The Festival at Sandpoint, 2003; bd. dirs. Nat. Festival of Wooden Boats, 2003; mem. Ponderay (Idaho) Cmty. Devel. Corp., 2003—; citizens adv. mem. Com. on Hwy Bypass in Sandpoint, 2000—; mem. com. Leadership Sandpoint, 2000—; mem. com. Ponderay Cmty. Devel. Corp., 2003—. Named Vol. of the Month, Sandpoint C. of C., 1987, 2000, Citizen of Yr., 1990, Retiree of Yr. Idaho chpt. 1985, Internat. Assn. Personel in Employment Security, Woman of Wisdom Women Honoring Women, 2000; recipient Woman of Distinction award, sr. category, Women's Forum Inc. of N. Idaho, 1999. Mem. Employment Security Agy. Rets., Internat. Pers. in Employment Security (sec., treas. 1970, Retiree of Yr. award 2003), Idaho State Employees Assn. (v.p. 1977, pres. elect 1978, pres. 1979, Employee of the Yr. 1968), Sandpoint C. of C. (events asst. 1984—, membership coord. 1984—, chmn. auction fundraiser 2001, 02, chmn. winter carnival 2003, v.p. bd. dirs. 2003, leadership com. 2000—). Republican. Avocations: dressmaking, skiing, swimming, aerobics, reading. Home: PO Box 54 Sandpoint ID 83864-0054 Office: Sandpoint C of C PO Box 928 Sandpoint ID 83864-0887

NELSON, MARCIA Z. writer, educator; b. Chgo., Mar. 10, 1953; d. Adolph A. and Lillian (Pietras) Zdun; m. William D. Nelson, Sept. 8, 1984; children: Margaret, Andrew. BA, Shimer Coll., 1975; MA, U. Chgo., 1977; MS in Journalism, Northwestern U., 1984. Mem. faculty Shimer Coll., Mt. Carroll, Ill., 1978—80; bus. and promotion mgr. Lawrence Ragan Comm., Chgo., 1980—83; reporter and editor Pioneer Press, Barrington, Ill., 1985—90, Beacon News, Aurora, Ill., 1990—98; adj. faculty Waubonsee C.C., Sugar Grove, Ill., 1998—2000; freelance writer Aurora, 1998—; adj. faculty Aurora U., Aurora, 2001—02, 2004. Author: Th God of Second Chances: Stories of Lives Transformed by Faith, 2001, Come and Sit: A Week Inside Meditation Centers, 2002. Bd. trustees Hesed House, Aurora, 2000—; bd. dirs. Aurora Cmty. Study Cirs., 1998; pres. and bd. dirs. YWCA of Aurora, 2002—03. Mem.: Religion Newswriters Assn. (Cassels Meml. award 1996).

NELSON, MARGUERITE HANSEN, special education educator; b. S.I., N.Y., June 23, 1947; d. Arthur Clayton and Marguerite Mary (Hansen) Nelson. AB magna cum laude, Boston Coll., 1969; MS in Edn., SUNY, Plattsburgh, 1973; cert. in gerontology, Yeshiva U., 1982; PhD, Fordham U., N.Y.C., 1995. Cert. elem. and spl. edn. tchr. N.Y. Pre-primary tchr. Pub. Sch. 22R S.I., N.Y.C. Bd. Edn., 1969—70; primary tchr. Oak Street Sch., Plattsburgh, NY, 1971—73, Laurel Plains Sch., Clarkstown Ctrl. Schs., New City, NY, 1973—78, Resource Rm. Lakewood Sch., Congers, NY, 1978—2002; assoc. prof. St. Thomas Aquinas Coll., Sparkill, NY, 2002—. Adj. faculty St. Thomas Aquinas Coll., Sparkill, 1985—89, 1995—2002, Fordham U., N.Y.C., 1990; presenter in field. Author: (book) Teacher Stories, 1993, Research on Teacher Thinking, 1993, Metaphor as a Mode of Instruction, 1995; contbr. articles to profl. jours. Recipient Impact II Tchr. Recognition award, 1984; grantee, Chpt. II, 1983—84, Clarkstown Ctrl. Schs., 1986—91, Office Spl. Edn., 1992, 1995, N.Y. Assn. Comprehensive Edn., 1997. Mem.: APA, AAUW, Coun. for Exceptional Children, Am. Ednl. Rsch. Assn., N.Y. State Congress Parents and Tchrs. (hon.). Avocations: reading, poetry, ballet, gardening, flower arranging. Home: PO Box 395 Valley Cottage NY 10989-0395 Office: Saint Thomas Aquinas Coll Rt 340 Sparkill NY 10976 E-mail: mnelson@stac.edu.

NELSON, MARILYN C. hotel executive, travel company executive, food service executive, marketing professional; b. Mpls. m. Glen Nelson; children: Diana, Curtis C., Wendy. Student, U. Sorbonne, Paris, Inst. Hautes Etudes Econ., Geneva; degree in internat. econs. with honors, Smith Coll., 1961; DBA (hon.), Johnson & Wales U.; DHL (hon.), Coll. St. Catherine, Gustavus Adolphus Coll. Securities analyst Paine Webber, Mpls.; pres., COO Carlson Cos., Inc., Mpls., 1997—2003, CEO, 1998—, chmn., 1999—, also bd. dirs. Co-chair Carlson Holdings, Inc., 1991—; dep. chair Thomas Cook Holdings; co-chair Carlson Wagonlit Travel, 1994—; disting. vis. prof. Johnson & Wales U.; bd. dirs. Exxonmobil Corp.; chmn. Nat. Women's Bus. Coun., 2002— Pres. United Way Mpls., campaign chair, 1984; bd. dirs. United Way Am., 1988-90, U.S. Nat. Tourism Orgn., 1996-98, Ctr. for Internat. Leadership, 1990—; mem. Internat. Adv. Coun., 1996—; mem. disting. adv. coun. Coll. of St. Catherine, 1989—; mem. Bretton Woods Com., 1986—; hon. bd. dirs. Svenska Inst., Stockholm, 1993—; mem. adv. bd. Hubert H. Humphrey Inst. Pub. Affairs, 1992-96; co-founder Minn. Women's Econ. Roundtable, 1974—; chair Minn. Super Bowl Task Force, 1984-92; chair, founder Midsummer Internat. Festival of Music; co-chair New Sweden '88; past bd. dirs. Guthrie Theatre, Greater Mpls. Girl Scout Coun., Jr. Achievement, Jr. League Mpls., KTCA Pub. TV, Minn. Congl. Award, Minn. Opera Co., Women's' Assn. Minn. Symphony Orch.; trustee Smith Coll., Northampton, Mass., 1980-85, Macalester Coll., St. Paul, 1974-80. Named Woman of Yr., Minn. Exec. Women in Tourism, Sales Exec. of Yr., Sales and Mktg. Exec. of Mpls., Woman of Yr. Roundtable for Women in Foodsvc., 1995, Outstanding Individual in Tourism, Minn. Office of Tourism, 1992, Woman of Yr., Minn. Exec. Women in Tourism, 1991-92, The Top 25 Execs. Yr. Bus. Week, 1999, Exec. Yr. Corp. Report Minn., 1999; recipient Minn. Congl. award for initiative and svc. to cmty., cert. of commendation State of Minn., Cmty. Svc. award YWCA, Independence award Vinland Nat. Ctr., Cmty. Svc. award Park-Nicollet Med. Ctr., Outstanding Mktg. Exec. of Yr. award, Minn. Distributive Edn. Club Am., Career Achievement award Sales and Mktg. Execs. Mpls., Outstanding Achievement award United Way Mpls., Extraordinary Leadership award Greater Mpls. C. of C., Disting. Svc. award United Way of Am., 1984-90, Nat. Caring award Caring Inst., 1995, Outstanding Bus. Leader award Northwood U., 1995, The 50 Most Powerful Women award in Am. Bus. Fortune, 1998-2003, United Way Minn. Disting. Svc. award United Way's highest vol. honor, 1998, Good Neighbor award WCCO Radio, 1999, Caring Heart award charitable contbns. by Larry King Cardiac Found., 1999, Am.'s 100 Most Important Women award Ladies' Home Jr., 1999, The 50 Most Powerful Women in Bus. Fortune 1999-2001, The Most Powerful Women in Travel #1 Travel Agent Mag., 1997-2003, Svc. Above Self award The Rotary Club Downtown, Minn., 1999, The Top 500 Women-Owned Bus.'s award Working Woman, 1999-2001, The 25 Most Influential Executives award Leisure Travel News, 2000, Northwest Airlines Disting. World Traveler award Hospitality Sales and Mktg. Assn. Internat., 2000, Responsible Capitalism award FIRST mag., 2001, Businesswoman of World, Bus. Women's Network, 2001, Glass Ceiling award Minn. Women's Consortium, 2001, Great Swedish Heritage award Swedish Coun. Am., 2002, Lifetime Achievement award Internat. Investment Forum, 2002; named Swedish Am. of Yr., 2003, Minnesotan of Yr., 2003; named to Sales and Mktg. Execs. Hall of Fame, 2003, Lifetime Achievement award Hospitality Sales and Mktg. Assn. Internat., 2004. Mem. Hennepin County Med. Soc. Aux., Jr. League Mpls., Minn. Meetings, Smith Coll. Alumni Assn., Smith Club Mpls., Woodhill Country Club, Mpls. Club, N.W. Tennis Club, Nat. Ctr. Social Entrepreneurs, Com. of 200, Hospitality Sales and Mktg. Assn. Internat. (Lifetime Achievement award 2004), Minn. Orchestral Assn., Orphei Dranger, Alpha Kappa Psi. Office: Carlson Cos Inc Carlson Parkway Minneapolis MN 55459-8212

NELSON, MARTHA JANE, magazine editor; b. Pierre, SD, Aug. 13, 1952; d. Bernard Anton and Pauline Isabel (Noren) Nelson. BA, Barnard Coll., 1976. Mng. editor Signs: Jour. of Women in Culture, N.Y.C., 1976—80; staff editor Ms. Mag., N.Y.C., 1980—85; editor-in-chief Women's Sports and Fitness Mag., San Francisco, 1985—87; exec. editor Savvy, N.Y.C., 1988—89, editor-in-chief, 1989—91; asst. mng. editor People, 1993; founding editor In Style Mag., N.Y.C., 1993—2002, exec. prodr. TV program Celebrity Weddings, 1997—2002, exec. prodr. TV programs Celebrity Moms, Celebrity Homes, 2001; mng. editor People Mag., N.Y.C., 2002—. Editor: Women in the American City, 1980; editor: (cons. editor) Who Weekly, 1992; contbr. articles to profl. jours. Bd. dirs. Painting Space 122, N.Y.C., 1982—85, 1995—96, Urban Athletic Assn., 1986, ACRIA, Comm. Rsch. Inst. on AIDS, Am. Soc. Mag Editors; adv. bd. Accessories Coun., 1999—2001, NYU Grad. Sch., 2000—03. Mem.: N.Y. Women in Comm., Women in Film, Am. Soc. Mag. Editors, Athletic and Swim Club (bd. dirs. 2000—).

NELSON, MARY CARROLL, artist, writer, b. Bryan, Tex., Apr. 24, 1929; d. James Vincent and Mary Elizabeth (Langton) Carroll; m. Edwin Blakeley Nelson, June 27, 1950; children: Patricia Ann, Edwin Blakely. BA in Fine Arts, Barnard Coll., 1950; MA, U. N.Mex., 1963. Juror Am. Artist Golden Anniversary Competition, 1987. Guest instr. continuing edn. U. N.Mex., 1991; conf. co-organizer Affirming Wholeness, The Art and Healing Experience, San Antonio, 1992, Artists of the Spirit Symposium, 1994. Group shows include N.Mex. Mus., 1987, Art is for Healing, The Universal Link, San Antonio, 1992, Fuller Lodge Art Ctr. Los Alamos, N.Mex., 1993, Layering, Albuquerque, 1993, Crossings, Bradford, Mass., 1994, The Layered Perspective, Fayetteville, Ark., 1994, Tree of Life, San Miguel de Allende, Mex., 1996, (honoree Magnifico, Albuquerque, 1997, Bravo award Excellence in Arts 2004), Guardian Spirits, Marlborough, Eng., 1997, Memories in Multi-Media, Columbus, Ohio, 1998, Agora Gallery, N.Y.C., 1998, Celtic Connections, Mass., 1998, Bridging Time and Space, Calif., 1999, Musings on the Millennium, Ohio, 2000, Layerists in Multi-Media/Affirming Wholeness, Albuquerque, 2000, The Birth of Wisdom, N. Mand Gordes, France, 2000, Tides of Change, Tex., 2001, EarthSpirit, Ohio, 2001, Shadow & Light, Albuquerque, 2001, Landscape and Memory, Sedona, Ariz., 2002, dsg Gallery, Albuquerque, 2002, Albuquerque (N.Mex.) Mus., 2003, Fire in the Heart, Ashland, Oreg., 2003, Layered Images, Albuquerque, 2003, others; represented in pvt. collections in U.S., Germany, Eng. and Australia; author: American Indian Biography Series, 1971-76, (with Robert E. Wood) Watercolor Workshop, 1974; (with Ramon Kelley) Ramon Kelley Paints Portraits and Figures, 1977, The Legendary Artists of Taos, 1980, (catalog) American Art in Peking, 1981, Masters of Western Art, 1982, Connecting, The Art of Beth Ames Swartz, 1984, Artists of the Spirit, 1994, Doris Steider, A Vision of Silence, 1997, Beyond Fear, A Toltec's Guide to Freedom and Joy, 1997, Layering, An Art of Time and Space, 1985, (catalog) Layering/Connecting, 1987; contbg. editor Am. Artist, 1976-91, Southwestern Art, 1987-91; editor (video) Layering, 1990; arts correspondent Albuquerque Jour., 1991-93; contbr. One Source Sacred Journeys, 1997, Bridging Time and Space, Essays on Layered Art, 1998, Lightstream, 2003; co-author: Bridging Time and Space, Essays on Layered Art, 1998, Toltec Prophecies of Don Miguel Ruiz, 2003; co-editor The Art of Layering: Making Connections, 2004. Mem. Albuquerque Arts Bd., 1984-88. Mem. Soc. Layerists in Multi-Media (founder 1982). Home: 1408 Georgia St NE Albuquerque NM 87110-6861 E-mail: mcn50@comcast.net.

NELSON, MARY KATHRYN, bilingual counselor, artist, singer, comedienne; b. Chgo., May 28, 1954; d. James C. Nelson and Leila R. Cooke. BS in Social Work, So. Ill. U., 1978; MS in Rehab. Counseling, U. Ariz., 1982. Cert. rehab. counselor, substance abuse counselor, profl. counselor, Ariz.; nat. cert. counselor; lic. real estate agt., Ariz. Bilingual counselor Ill. Migrant Council, 1975-76; social worker Child Protective Svcs., 1980-85; bilingual clinician pvt. nonprofit agys., 1985-96; bilingual counselor contractor, counselor Suprme Ct. Ariz., Phoenix, 1995—; owner, mgr. Bilingual Svcs., LLC, Phoenix, 1985—; actress, comedienne, singer, 1995—; real estate agt. ERA Artizan Realty. Exhibited in group shows at Franciscan Renewal Ctr., Scottsdale, 2001, exhibitions include Artareas.com, 2001—; performer: Talent Show at Crossroads, 1999—2001; singer: Franciscan Renewal Ctr., 2000—01; exhibitions include Fountain Hills Ariz. Art Exhibit, 1995, Channel 22 Phoenix Cable Amateur Hr., Spanish Songs, 1996, Iberoamericana Internat. Art Exhibit, Miami, Fla., 1997, Phoenix K Lite Radio TV Commn., 1997, Peoria Sportscomplex Art Fair, Ariz., 1998, Franciscan Renewal Ctr. Art Fair, Scottsdale, Ariz., 1999, 2001, ArtAreas.com. Vol. Big Bros.-Big Sisters, Tucson, 1999; family advocate Cesar Chavez Farmworkers Union Labor Movement; art donor Ariz. Foster Care Assn., Paradise Valley, Ariz., 2001, donor original oil painting with World Trade Ctr. motif, 2001; vol. campaign worker Jon Kyle for Senator, Phoenix, 1996—99; fundraiser John Shadeg for Congressman, Ariz., 2002; choir mem. Franciscan Renewal Ctr., Paradise Valley, Ariz., 1999—2002. Recipient humanitarian award Inst. Arts Plastiques, 1997. Mem. Drama Beat Acting Club. Republican. Avocations: singing, comedy, acting. Home and Office: PO Box 3435 Scottsdale AZ 85271-3435

NELSON, NEVIN MARY, interior designer; b. Cleve., Nov. 5, 1941; d. Arthur George Reinker and Barbara Phyllis (Gunn) Parks; m. Wayne Nelson (div. 1969); children: Doug, Brian. BA in Interior Design, U. Colo., 1964. Prin. Nevin Nelson Design, Boulder, Colo., 1966-70, Vail, Colo., 1970—, Denver, 2002—. Program chmn. Questers Antique Study Group, Boulder, 1969. Coord. Bob Kirscht for Gov. campaign, Eagle County, Colo., 1986; state del. Rep. Nat. Conv., 1986-88; county coord. George Bush for U.S. Pres. campaign, 1988, 92; chmn. Eagle County Reps., 1989-93; v.p. bd. dirs. Park Lane Condo Assn., Denver, 1995-96; pres. Save Our Imperiled Land, Vail, 1998. Mem. Am. Soc. Interior Designers, City Club of Denver, Chaine des Rotisseurs; Fndr. Denver Dollies Red Hat Soc., 2001. Episcopalian. Avocations: gardening, party planning, cooking, reading, travel. Home: 1440 S Dahlia St Denver CO 80222

NELSON, NORMA RANDY DEKADT, psychotherapist, consultant; b. Irvington, N.J., Nov. 10, 1930; d. Ralph Joseph and Irma Marie (Richardson) Miele; m. Pieter Pim deKadt, Sept. 15, 1956 (div. 1984); children: Sharon, David, John; m. Ronald Prescott Nelson, July 27, 1985. BS, Northwestern U., Evanston, Ill., 1953; MS, Bridgeport U., 1974; cert. therapist, Found. Religion & Mental Heath, 1980; M in Neuro Linguistics, U. Calif., Santa Cruz, 1996. Pers. trainer B. Altman & Co., N.Y.C., 1953-54, asst. to merchandise mgr., 1954-55; dir. promotion Operation Home Improvement U.S. C of C and Time Inc., N.Y.C., 1955-57; counselor Stamford Counseling Ctr., Conn., 1975-80; trainer cons. N.Y.C., 1980-95; psychotherapist, cons. Stamford (Conn.) Counseling Ctr., 1976-82; pvt. practice Old Greenwich, Conn., 1980—. Condr. positive parenting programs; keynote spkr. on raising self-esteem, development of motiviation, personal and spirit in the work place; seminar leader personality profile styles and teamwork, work and family life, motivation and mental attitude, Open to Spirit seminars; founder, pres. Positive Parenting Program, Ctr. Well-Being, 1995; founder Family Re-entry Fathers Helping Fathers Program, 1995. Author: Magic of Attitude, 1995; contbr. articles to profl. jours. Pres. Old Greenwich (Conn.) Riverside Community Ctr., 1960; bd. dirs. YWCA, Greenwich, 1968-76, Greenwich Women's Club, Parents Together, Greenwich, 1980-86; chmn. Women Together, Christ Ch., Greenwich, 1989-90; speaker PTAs, Greenwich, 1980-93, vol. Jr. League, 1956-75; founder KCC Confs., 1994; creator Eden Rising Seminars, 1999, a Continuous Awakening Program. Recipient Environ. Beautification award Old Greenwich, Conn., 1975. Mem. Assn. Carlton Learning Systems, Capr. Assn. Bus. Orgn. Colls., Transactional Analysis Assn., Trains Values Realization Inst., Kripalu Cons. Collaborative. Episcopalian. Avocations: teaching meditation and yoga, skiing, art, painting, tennis. Home and Office: 8 Middle Way Old Greenwich CT 06870-2405

NELSON, PATRICIA JOAN PINGENOT, retired educator; b. Boulder, Colo., Nov. 12, 1930; d. Elmer Louis and Elizabeth Isabelle (Madden) Pingenot; children: Gail Jo Gardner, Marvin D. Jr., Stephen Michael. BA, Hastings Coll., 1962; MA in English, U. Nebr., 1964; postgrad., U. Minn. Cert. elem. tchr. 1-6, english/language arts 7-12, devel./remedial reading 7-12, reading specialist/cons. K-12. Freshman composition writing lab instr. Hastings (Nebr.) Coll.; tchr. Edina (Minn.) Schs.; English tchr., reading specialist Woodbury (Minn.) High Sch., South Washington County Schs.; ret., 1991. Mem. South Washington Edn. Assn. (v.p., treas., IPD co-chair), Capitol Uniserv, (v.p., communications chair), Minn. Edn. Assn., NEA, Minn. Coun. Tchrs. English, Nat. Coun. Tchrs. English, Twin City Area Reading Coun., Minn. Reading Assn. (chair publications com., editor MRA Highlights, newspaper in edn. com.), Minn. Acad. for Reading (pres., v.p.), ASCD, Minn. ASCD, Delta Kappa Gamma (Alpha Omega chpt.). Home: 5524 Warden Ave Edina MN 55436-2241

NELSON, PAULA MORRISON BRONSON, gifted and talented educator, consultant; b. Memphis, Mar. 26, 1944; d. Fred Ford and Julia (Morrison) Bronson: m. Jack Marvin Nelson, July 13, 1968; children: Eric Allen, Kelly Susan. BS, U. N.Mex., 1967; MA, U. Colo., Denver, 1985. Physical edn. tchr. Grant Union Sch. Dist., Sacramento, 1967-68, Denver Pub. Schs., 1968-74, with program for pupil assistance, 1974-80; tchr. ESL Douglas County Pub. Schs., Parker, Colo., 1982-83; chpt. 1 reading specialist Denver Pub. Schs., 1983-96, computer/reading specialist, 1996-98, reading specialist, gifted and talented tchr., 1998-99, lead tchr. in charge instrn., 1999-2001, edn. cons., 2001—02. Demonstration tchr. Colo. Edn. Assn., 1970-72; mem. curriculum com. Denver Pub. Schs., 1970-72; mem. Douglas County Accountability Com., Castle Rock, Colo., 1986-92; mem. educators rev. panel Edn. for Freedom; computer trainer Denver Pub. Schs. Tech. Team, 1992-02. Co-author: Gymnastics Teacher's Guide Elementary Physical Education, 1973, Applauding Our Constitution, 1989; editorial reviewer G is for Geography, Children's Literature and the Five Themes. 1993; producer slide shows Brotherhood, 1986, We the People...Our Dream Lives On, 1987, Celebration of Cultures, 1988. Named Pub. Edn. Coalition grantee, Denver, 1987, 88, 89, 90, grantee Rocky Mountain Global Edn. Project, 1987, Wake Forest Law Sch., Winston-Salem, N.C., 1988, 89, 90, 92, Read to Achieve grantee Colo. State Dept. Edn., 2000; recipient chpt. II grant, 1991, Tech. grant, 1993, Title VI Reading grant, 1999, 2000, Three R's of Freedom award State Dept. Edn., 1987, Nat. Recognition award Commn. on Bicentennial of Constitution., 1987, Distinguished Tchr. award City of Denver, 1994. Mem.: Denver Fedn. Tchrs., Am. Fedn. Tchrs., Tech. in Edn. Republican. Methodist. Avocations: snow and water skiing, tennis. Home: 18 Covewood Dr Norwalk CT 06853

NELSON, SARAH MILLEDGE, archaeology educator; b. Miami, Fla., Nov. 29, 1931; d. Stanley and Sarah Woodman (Franklin) M.; m. Harold Stanley Nelson, July 25, 1953; children: Erik Harold, Mark Milledge, Stanley Franklin. BA, Wellesley Coll., 1953; MA, U. Mich., 1969, PhD, 1973. Instr. archaeology U. Md. extension, Seoul, Republic Korea, 1970-71; asst. prof. U. Denver, 1974-79, assoc. prof., 1979-85, prof. archaeology, 1985—, chair dept. anthropology, 1985-95, dir. women's studies program, 1985-87, John Evans prof., dir. Asian studies, 1996, vice provost for rsch., 1998—2002, interim vice provost grad. studies and rsch., 2001—02. Vis. asst. prof. U. Colo., Boulder, 1974; resident Rockefeller Ctr. in Bellagio, Italy, 1996. Co-editor: Powers of Observation, 1990, Equity Issues for Women in Archaeology, 1994; author: Archaeology of Korea, 1993, Gender in Archaeology: Analyzing Power and Prestige, 1997, 2d revised edit., 2004, (novel) Spirit Bird Journey, 1999; co-author: Denver: An Archaeological History, 2001; editor: The Archaeology of Northeast China, 1995, Ancestors for the Pigs: Pigs in Prehistory, 1998; co-editor: In Pursuit of Gender: Worldwide Archaeological Perspectives, 2001, Ancient Queens: Archaelogical Perspectives, 2003. Active Earthwatch, 1989. Recipient Outstanding Scholar award U. Denver, 1989; grantee S.W. Inst. Rsch. on Women, 1981, Acad. Korean Studies, Seoul, 1983, Internat. Cultural Soc. Korea, 1986, Colo. Hist. Fund, 1995-97, Rockefeller Found. Residency, Bellagio, Italy, Wenner-Gren Found., 2000-02, Nat. Geographic Soc., 2000—. Fellow Am. Anthrop. Assn.; mem. Soc. Am. Archaeology, Assn. Asian Studies, Royal Asiatic Soc., Sigma Xi (sec.-treas. 1978-79), Phi Beta Kappa. Democrat. Avocations: skiing, gardening. Home: 5878 S Dry Creek Ct Littleton CO 80121-1709 Office: U Denver Dept Anthropology Denver CO 80208-0001 Business E-Mail: snelson@du.edu.

NELSON, SHIRLEY W. bank executive; From jr. teller to v.p., sr. mgr. Ctrl. Bank Med. Ctr. branch, Oakland, Calif., 1966—82; founder, chmn., CEO, pres. Summit Bank, Oakland, Calif., 1982—90, chmn., CEO, 1982—, Summit Bancshares Inc. Chmn. bd. Summit Bank Found., 1998—, No. Calif. Women's Leadership Forum. Co-chmn. No. Calif. Women's League Coun.; bd. dirs. Cal State Hayward Ednl. Found. Named One of 25 Most Powerful Women in Banking, U.S. Banker Mag., 2003. Office: Summit Bancshares Inc 2969 Broadway Oakland CA 94611-5710*

NELSON, SUE GRODSKY, humanities educator, consultant; b. Bklyn., Apr. 1, 1943; d. Juliette Dorfman and Louis Grodsky; m. Michael R. Nelson, Nov. 23, 1968; children: Andrew Robert, John Samuel. BA, Allegheny Coll., Meadville, Pa., 1964; EdM, John Carroll U., University Heights, Ohio, 1995. Cert. tchr. Ohio, 1988. Asst. prodn. mgr. CBS, N.Y.C., 1964—65; tchr./dept. chair of English, honors English, reading, journalism, French Cleve. Bd. of Edn., 1965—71; group home foster parent Jewish Children's Bur., Shaker Heights, Ohio, 1971—75; tchr. of English, inclusion English/learning cmty., career edn., journalism East Cleve. Bd. of Edn., 1972—98; adj. instr., reading cons. Cuyahoga C.C., Cleve. Mem. tchr. rev. panel McDougal, Littell & Co., Evanston, Ill., 1990—92; presenter Cons. - Multiple Intelligences Workshops, Ohio, 1994—99; mem. adv. com. John Carroll U., University Heights, Ohio, 1995—97; mem. Newbury Bd. of Edn., Ohio, 2000—04, past pres. Author: (instruction manual) Getting Elected to Public Office; contbr. anthology Humanities Programs Today; co-author/editor (instruction manual) Multiple Intelligences at Work!; editor: (inspirational lessons) Zen Shin Talks. Pres. East Cleve. Edn. Assn., 1982—83; chairperson Ohio Edn. Assn. Svc. Coun., Cuyahoga County, Ohio, 1980—81, People for Polensek, Cleve., 1977—90; vice chairperson and sec. Cuyahoga County Dem. Party, Cuyahoga County, Ohio, 1982—89, vol. coord. Boyle for Senate, Cleveland, Ohio, 1997—98. Recipient Ashland Achievement award, Ashland Oil, Inc., 1992; Coach of State Champion - Oratorical Interpretation, Ohio H.S. Speech League, 1986. Mem.: NEA (life), Ohio Sch. Bd. Assn., Ohio Edn. Assn. (life). Democrat-Npl. Jewish. Avocations: reading, exercising, interior decorating, political activism, traveling. Home: 10450 Bell St Newbury OH 44065 Office: Cuyahoga CC 2900 Community College Avenue Cleveland OH 44114 Personal E mail: m.s.nelson@juno.com.

NELSON, THERESA VERONICA, medical technologist, small business owner; b. Rosebud, S.D., Nov. 10, 1940, d. Narcisse and Ethel Marie (YellowRobe) White; m. Timothy D. Wise, July 20, 1968 (div. May 1974); children: Dawn Marie, James, Stephen, Narcissa, Kimberly, Linda Morgan; foster daughter: Linda Morgan; m. Woodrow D. Nelson, Feb. 28, 1975 (dec. Nov. 1996). Grad., Mercy H.S., Chgo. Med. technician Indian Health Svc., Rosebud, S.D., 1961-62, Rapid City, S.D., 1967-71, med. technologist Shiprock, N.Mex., 1971-94, Dzithnao dithle Health Bloomfield Clin., Bloomfield, N.Mex., 1995-96. Union pres. Nat. Assn. Govt. Employees, Shiprock, 1988-94; EEO counselor Shiprock Svc. Unit, 1977-81; pres. employees assn. Dhithnoodithle Clinic, Bloomfield, N.Mex., 1995-96; pres., owner A Lakota Woman's Enterprise, Kirtland, N.Mex., 1997—. Mem. NOW (pres.), Bus. and Profl. Womans Club, Am. Bus. Women's Assn., N.Mex. Indian C. of C. (bd. mem. 1997). Democrat. Roman Catholic. Avocations: Scrabble, travel, bowling. Home and Office: PO Box 1271 Kirtland NM 87417-1271

NELSON, VIRGINIA SIMSON, pediatrician, educator, physiatrist; b. L.A. d. Jerome and Virginia (Kuppler) Simson; children: Eric, Paul. AB, Stanford U., 1963, MD, 1970; MPH, U. Mich., 1974. Diplomate Am. Bd. Pediatrics, Am. Bd. Phys. Medicine and Rehab. Pediatrician Inst. Study Mental Retardation and Related Disabilities, U. Mich., Ann Arbor, 1973-80; mem. faculty phys. medicine and rehab. dept. U. Mich. Med. Ctr., Ann Arbor, 1980-83, 85—, resident in phys. medicine and rehab., 1983-85, chief pediatric phys. medicine and rehab. physician, 1985—. Contbr. articles to profl. jours. Office: Univ Mich Med Ctr F7822 Mott Hospital Ann Arbor MI 48109-0230 also: Pediat Phys Medicine and Rehab 325 E Eisenhower Dr Ste 100 U Mich Campus Zip 0744 Ann Arbor MI 48108

NELSON-SMALL, KATHY ANN, foundation administrator; b. Williamsport, Pa., Sept. 21, 1954; d. Dan LeRoy and Shirley Joann (Klein) Hoover; m. Robert Joseph Small, Feb. 14, 1996. BS in German Edn., Ind. U. of Pa., 1976; postgrad., Pa. State U., 1978 83. Tchr. German Hollidaysburg (Pa.) Area Sch. Dist., 1977-85; adminstr. Carlisle (Pa.) Project, 1985; dir. fin. devel. and pub. rels. Am. Lung Assn., York, Pa., 1986; chief profl. officer Adams County United Way, Gettysburg, Pa., 1987—. Press sec. Nancy Kulp's campaign for 9th Congl. Dist., Pa., 1984; mem. Main Street Gettysburg, 1987—, mem. pub. rels. com., 1996-98, 125th Battle of Gettysburg Anniversary Commn., 1988; treas. Adams County Coun. Cmty. Svcs., 1987-89, sec. 1995-99, Pa. State Club of Adams County, 1989—; mem. adv. bd. Adams County Job Ctr., 1989-91, Minority Youth Ednl. Inst., 1988-91, Intercultural Resource Ctr., Gettysburg Coll., 1989-91; mem. Adams Area Postal Customer Coun., 1987-89; dir. Adams Cmty. TV, 1988-89; mem. profl. adv. coun., chmn. small cities task force United Way Pa., 1990—, mem. network com., 1992-94, now mem. pub. sector impact com. and pers. com.; mem. planning com. United Way Leaders' Conf., 1995, also participant; mem. collaborative bd. Family Svc. Sys. Reform Initiative; bd. dirs. Adams County Interfaith Housing Corp., Adams County Coop. Ext., bd. dirs., 1996—, v.p., 2001—, sec., 1999-2000, strategic planning com. chair, 1999—; bd. dirs. Adams County Partnership for Cmty. Health, 1996—. Fulbright/Goethe Haus scholar, Stuttgart, Germany, 1982; named citizen of yr. Gettysburg-Adams County Area C. of C., 2000. Mem. Ctrl. Pa. Assn. Women Execs. (charter), Kiwanis (pres. Hist. Gettysburg chpt. 1989-95, chmn. dist. conv. Pa. chpt. 1992, dist. maj. emphasis program chairperson 1992-93), Gettysburg Rotary (club svc. chair 1998-2000, sec. 2000—), Pa. State Alumni Assn. (life), Gettysburg-Adams County Area C. of C. (pub. rels. com. 1989-98, strategic planning com. 1998—), Alpha Omicron Pi (endowment com. 1993—). Democrat. Lutheran. Avocations: traveling, skiing, antiquing, sewing, gardening. Home: 2566 Old Route 30 Orrtanna PA 17353-9417 Office: Adams County United Way PO Box 3545 Gettysburg PA 17325-0545 Office Phone: 717-334-5809. E-mail: uwaccares@planetcable.net.

NEMAN, EILEEN, not-for-profit organization executive; 1 child. Exec. dir. Film/Video Arts, N.Y.C., 1998—. Program officer New Visions for Pub. Schs. Mem.: The N.Y. Film/Video Coun. (bd. dirs.), N.Y. Women in Film and TV (bd. dirs., past v.p.), Educators for Social Responsibility (v.p.). Office: Film/Video Arts 462 Broadway Ste 520 New York NY 10013*

NEMCOVA, EVA, professional basketball player; b. Czech Republic, Dec. 3, 1972; arrived in U.S., 1997; Guard A.S. Montferrand, France, 1993—96, Bourges, France, 1996—97, Cleveland Rockers, (WNBA), 1997—. Named Best Player European Championship, 1995, 1996. Avocations: volleyball, handball, football, mountain biking. Office: Cleve Rockers Gund Arena 1 Center Ct Cleveland OH 44115-4001

NEMECEK, GEORGINA MARIE, molecular pharmacologist; b. Mineola, N.Y., Aug. 27, 1946; d. George and Frances Valerie (Masaryk) N. AB, Mt. Holyoke Coll., 1968; PhD, U. Pa., 1972. Rsch. assoc. dept. biochemistry U. Mass. Med. Sch., Worcester, 1972-73, postdoctoral fellow of Am. Heart Assn., dept. biochemistry, 1974, asst. prof., 1974-80, assoc. prof., 1981-83, sr. scientist platelet dept. Sandoz Pharm. Corp., East Hanover, N.J., 1983-87, mem. sr. sci. staff, platelet dept., 1986, fellow, sect. head molecular biology, 1987-91, fellow diabetes, 1991-93, study dir. regulatory toxicology, 1993-96; internat. project mgr. preclin. safety Novartis Pharm. Corp., East Hanover, 1997, assoc. dir. project mgmt., 1997-2000, dir. project mgmt., 2000—02, dir. integrative compound and product profiling, 2002—03, dir. project review, biomarker devel., 2003—. Vis. scientist dept. molecular biology, Princeton (N.J.) U., 1987, Sea Pharm. Inc., 1985, NATO, U. Libre, Brussels, 1979, biotechnology dept. Sandoz AG, Basel, Switzerland, 1988. Contbr. articles to profl. jours. Named Nat. Heart, Lung, and Blood Inst. Young Investigator, NIH, 1977-81. Mem. Am. Soc. Pharmacol. Exptl. Therapeutics, N.Y. Acad. Scis. (chmn. biochem. sect. 1992-94), Tissue Culture Assn., Soc. Toxicology, Soc. Toxicol. Pathologists, Sigma Xi. Avocations: boating, gardening, riding, needlework. Office: Novartis Pharm Corp 1 Health Plz East Hanover NJ 07936-1005

NEMEC-KESSEL, CHARLENE, artist, educator; b. Milw., Apr. 2, 1970; m. P. Kessel. BFA, Sch. of Art Inst. Chgo., 1993; MFA, Sch. of Art Inst. of Chgo., 1997. Assoc. lectr. fiber art Concordia U., Mequon, Wis., 1997—, U. Wis., Milw., 1997—98; represented by Thirteen Moons. Represented by Thirteen Moons Gallery, Santa Fe. One-woman shows include Lyons Wier Gallery, Chgo., 1999, Evanston (Ill.) Art Ctr., 1999, art work featured in, Art Textiles of the World, 2000, Surface Design mag., Fiberarts. Recipient Award of Excellence, Coalition of Creative Orgns., 1993, Expressions of Culture, 1997; fellow James Nelson Raymond fellow, 1997.

NEMEROFF, ROBIN KIM, psychologist, educator, researcher; b. N.Y.C., Mar. 19, 1969; d. Stanley and Sandy Nemeroff. BA cum laude, Amherst Coll., 1991; MPhil in Clin. Psychology, MS in Psychology, Columbia U., 1998, PhD in Clin. Psychology, 1999. Lic. psychologist N.Y., 2000. Asst. dir. Ctr. for the Advancement of Children's Mental Health Columbia U., N.Y.C., 2000—, instr. clin. psychology Coll. Physicians and Surgeons, 2001—, adj. asst. prof. psychology and edn. Tchrs. Coll., 2002—; asst. prof. psychology William Paterson U., Wayne, NJ, 2003—. Pvt. practice, N.Y.C., 2000—; rsch. cons. Barnard Coll. Health Svcs., N.Y.C., 2002—. Contbr. chapters to books, articles to profl. jours. Grantee, Lowenstein Found., 2002—; Postdoctoral Rsch. fellow, Weill Med. Coll., Cornell U., 1999—2000. Achievements include first to organized a community-wide effort to use an evidence-based diagnostic assessment tool to assess children for potential mental health problems in 25+schools located in the Midwest. Avocations: yoga, meditation, theater. E-mail: rkn6@columbia.edu.

NEMEROWICZ, GLORIA, academic administrator; 2 children. BA, MA, PhD in Sociology, Rutgers U. Assoc. prof. sociology Monmouth Coll., NJ, provost; exec. dir. Women's Leadership Inst. Wells Coll., Aurora, NY, 1993—96; pres. Pine Manor Coll., Chestnut Hill, Mass., 1996—. Author: (books) Children's Perceptions of Gender and Work Roles; co-author (with Eugene Rosi): Professionalism in Unpaid Work; contbr. op-ed pieces to newspapers. Office: Pine Manor Coll 400 Health St Chestnut Hill MA 02467*

NEMETH, DIAN JEAN, secondary school educator; b. Lakewood, Ohio, Mar. 5, 1949; d. Alex Ray and Doris Jean (Sakach) N.; 1 child, Kymberlee Marie. BS, Kent State U., 1971, MEd, 1994. Cert. home econs. tchr., vocat. consumer-homemaking tchr., Ohio. Tchr. vocat. family and consumer scis. Cleve. Bd. Edn., 1972—2002. Piloted modern design fine arts course Cleve. Bd. Edn., 1989-90; writer course of study for hospitality and facility care svcs. Active Tchrs.-Leader Inst., 1994-97, Urban Task Force. Mem. Greater Cleve. Assn. Family and Consumer Sci. (auditor 1994-95, treas. 1995-98, 2002-), Ohio Hotel and Motel Assn., Sigma Sigma Sigma (chpt. adv. bd. 1992, chpt. housing coord. 1992), Omicron Tau Theta. Democrat. Roman Catholic. Home: 9505 N Church Dr Apt 122 Cleveland OH 44130-4773

NEMETZ MILLS, PATRICIA LOUISE, engineer, educator; b. Bethlehem, Pa., June 10, 1956; d. Stephen Andrew N. and Anna Julia Schadl; m. Alyn James Mills, June 18, 1983; 1 child, Andrea. BS in Mech. Engring., Pa. State U., 1979; MBA, Gonzaga U., 1985; PhD in Bus. Adminstrn., U. Wash., 1989. Project engr. Air Products and Chems., Trexlertown, Pa., 1979-83; instr. Gonzaga U., Spokane, Wash., 1984-85; prof. Ea. Washington U., Spokane, 1989—. Cons. Spokane Auto Transport, Auburn, Wash., 1985-95, Boeing, Seatle, 1988-89, Eldec, Seattle, 1988; instr., seminar leader Bulgaria, 1990, EWU/Montenegro U., 1991. Contbr. articles to profl. jours. Office: Ea Washington U 668 N Riverpoint Blvd Ste A Spokane WA 99202-1677

NEMIRO, BEVERLY MIRIUM ANDERSON, author, educator; b. St. Paul, May 29, 1925; d. Martin and Anna Mae Anderson; m. Jerome Morton Nemiro, Feb. 10, 1951-75; children: Guy Samuel, Lee Anna, Dee Martin. Student, Reed Coll., 1943-44; BA, U. Colo., 1947; postgrad., U. Denver. Tchr. Seattle Pub. Sch., 1945-46; fashion coord., dir. Denver Dry Goods Co., 1948-51; fashion dir. Denver Market Week Assn., 1952-53; free-lance writer Denver, 1958—. Moderator TV program Your Presch. Child, Denver, 1955-56; instr. writing and comm. U. Colo. Denver Ctr., 1970—, U. Calif., San Diego, 1976-78, Met. State Coll., 1985; dir. pub. rels. Fairmont Hotel, Denver, 1979-80; freelance fashion and TV model. Author, co-author: The Complete Book of High Altitude Baking, 1961, Colorado a la Carte, 1963, Colorado a la Carte, Series II, 1966, (with Donna Hamilton) The High Altitude Cookbook, 1969, The Busy People's Cookbook, 1971 (Better Homes and Gardens Book Club selection 1971), Where to Eat in Colorado, 1967, Lunch Box Cookbook, 1965, Complete Book of High Altitude Baking, 1961, (under name Beverly Anderson) Single After 50, 1978, The New High Altitude Cookbook, 1980. Co-founder, pres. Jr. Symphony Guild, Denver, 1959-60; active Friends of Denver Libr., Opera Colo.; mem. Friends of Painting and Sculpture, Denver Art Mus. Recipient Top Hand award Colo. Authors' League, 1969, 72, 79-82, 100 Best Books of Yr. award NY Times, 1969, 71; named one of Colo. Women of Yr., Denver Post, 1964. Mem. Am. Soc. Journalists and Authors, Colo. Authors League (dir. 1969-79), Authors Guild, Authors League Am., Friends Denver Libr., Opera Colo. Guild, Denver Women's Press Club, Rotary, Kappa Alpha Theta. Address: Park Towers 1299 Gilpin St Apt 15W Denver CO 80218-2556

NEMIROFF, MAXINE CELIA, art educator, gallery owner, consultant; b. Chgo., Feb. 11, 1935; d. Oscar Bernard and Martha (Mann) Kessler; m. Paul Rubenstein, June 26, 1955 (div. 1974); children: Daniel, Peter, Anthony; m. Allan Nemiroff, Dec. 24, 1979. BA, U. So. Calif., 1955; MA, UCLA, 1974. Sr. instr. UCLA, 1974-92; dir., curator art gallery Doolittle Theater, Los Angeles, 1985-86; owner Nemiroff Deutsch Fine Art, Santa Monica, Calif. Leader of worldwide art tours; cons. L'Ermitage Hotel Group, Beverly Hills, Calif., 1982—, Broadway Dept. Stores, So. Calif., 1979—, Security Pacific Bank, Calif., 1978—, Am. Airlines, Calif. Pizza Kitchen Restaurants; art chmn. UCLA Thieves Market, Century City, 1960—, L.A. Music Ctr. Mercado, 1982—; lectr. in field. Apptd. bd. dirs. Dublin (Calif.) Fine Arts Found., 1989; mem. Calif. Govs. Adv. Coun. for Women, 1992; mem. art selection com. Calif. State Office Bldgs., 1997—. Named Woman of Yr. UCLA Panhellenic Council, 1982, Instr. of Yr. UCLA Dept. Arts, 1984; recipient Woman of Achievement award Friends of Sheba Med. Ctr., 2003; elected to Fashion Circle of the Costume Coun., L.A. County Mus. Art, 1997—; honoree L.A. Art Core 15th Ann. Awards Benefit, 2003. Mem. L.A. County Mus. Art Coun., UCLA Art Coun., UCLA Art Coun. Docents, Alpha Epsilon Phi (alumnus of yr. 1983). Avocations: tennis, horseback riding, skiing, piano and guitar. E-mail: mumseyart@aol.com.

NEMYIER, MARGARET GERTRUDE, sales executive; b. Herkimer, N.Y., Dec. 23, 1930; d. Franklin Clark and Reba Louise (Jones) Culver; m. Charles Henry Nemyier, July 22, 1978. BS, Oneonta (N.Y.) State Coll., 1953; MS in Edn., Geneseo (N.Y.) State U., 1973. Cert. elem. tchr. N.Y. Elem. tchr. Richfield Springs (N.Y.) Ctrl. Sch., 1953—54, Ilion (N.Y.) Ctrl. Sch., 1954—57, Wester (N.Y.) Ctrl. Sch., 1957—76; sales rep. Equitable Ins. Co., Perfield, NY, 1976—77; sales clk. Fuelihan's Dress Store, East Rochester, NY, 1977—79; with Projansky Furier & Dress Shop, Victor, NY, 1979—81; sales rep. Avon Products, 1977—. Sec.-treas. Webster (N.Y.) Plank North PTA, 1959; vol. cemetery tours Mt. Hope Cemetery Orgn., Rochester, NY, 1978—83; vol. fundraiser at various PBA's, 1977—79; reach for recovery vol. Am. Cancer Soc., Rochester, 1981—86; election insp. Monroe & Herkimer Counties, NY, 1990—2003; coord. Ilion HS Mega Reunion Com., 2002. Recipient Cert. of Appreciation, Dept. of Recreation and Parks, Rochester, 1980. Mem.: NEA (life). Democrat. Methodist. Avocations: latch hook rugs, embroidery, traveling to hist. places, collectibles. Home: 236 E Main St Ilion NY 13357

NENGUDI, SENGA, artist, educator; b. Chgo., Ill., Sept. 18, 1943; d. Elois Lillian and Samuel Allen Irons; m. Elliott Fittz, Dec. 29, 1976; children: Sanza Azizi Fittz, Oji Azizi Fittz. BA in Art, Calif. State U., L.A., 1966, MA in Sculpture, 1971; fgn. study, Waseda U., Tokyo, 1966—67. Art instr. Pasadena Art Mus., Pasadena, Calif., 1969—71; art instr. & resources mgr. Children's Art Carnival (est. by Mus. Modern Art), N.Y.C., NY, 1971—74; developer, coord. arts programs L.A. Sch. Dist. and other cmty. based organizations, L.A., Calif., 1982—88, Colorado Springs Sch. Dist. and other cmty. based organizations, Colo., 1991—; lectr./instr. U. of Colo., Colorado Springs, Colo., 1998—. Bd. mem. Tutmose Acad. Charter HS, Colorado Springs, Colo., 1998—2003, Performing Arts for Youth Orgn., Colorado Springs, Colo., 1990—94; mem. curatorial com.-performance art The Women's Bldg., Los Angeles, Calif., 1984—85. Exhibitions include Mus. Contemporary Art, Chgo., L.A., Thomas Erben Gallery. Resources vol. Urban Peak (Art Program for Homeless Teens), Colorado Springs, Colo., 2003. Recipient Best Website of the Week award, Artwomen.org, 2002; Creative Artists Pub. Svc. grantee, N.Y. Coun. on the Arts, 1972. Mem.: Negro Hist. Assn. of Colo. Springs (assoc.), Toni Morrison Soc. (assoc.). African Methodist Episcopal Church. Achievements include Founding Member Sankofa African Dance and Cultural Organization; development of Developed Art Gallery for Colorado Springs Hillside Community Center; Curated Whisper! Stomp! Shout! A Festival of African-American Performance Art documentation -1st everin Colorado Springs Fine Arts Center. Avocations: dance, walking, travel, American history. Office: Thomas Erben Gallery 516 W 20th St New York NY 10011 Personal E-mail: sfittz@uccs.edu. E-mail: www.thomaserbengallery.com.

NENSTIEL, SUSAN KISTHART, fundraising professional; b. Hazleton, Pa., Aug. 21, 1951; d. Frank W. and Mary A. (Price) Kisthart. BS, Pa. State U., 1973; MBA, Wilkes (Pa.) Coll., 1982. Cert. fund raising exec. Control mgr. Barrett, Haentjens & Co., Hazleton, 1973-79, export mgr., 1979-86; exec. dir. Leadership Hazleton, 1986-87; devel. officer Planned Parenthood of NE Pa., Wilkes-Barre, 1986-87; ins. broker, office mgr. Nenstiel & Nenstiel, West Hazleton, Pa., 1988-96; assoc. dir. devel. Hospice St. John, 1996-97; devel. assoc. Luth. Svcs. N.E., 1997-98, reg. dir. devel., 1998-2000; exec. dir. LWV of Pa., 2000-01; sr. v.p. devel. Easter Seals Ea. Pa., 2001—03; dir. major gifts Albright Coll., 2003—. Pres. YWCA, Hazleton, 1983-85, Women's Coalition of Greater Hazleton, 1987-91; sec. Govt. Study Commn., Hazleton, 1986; trustee Hazleton Area Pub. Libr., sec., 1987-89, v.p., 1990-91, pres., 1991-93; chmn. Luzerne County Commn. for Women, 1988-91; mem., chmn. Hazleton City Zoning Bd., 1988-92; treas. Pa. Women's Campaign Fund, 1987-91, pres., 1991-92; mem. Leadership Hazleton Adv. Coun., 1988-92; mem. Pa. Pub. Libr. Project, 1992-94; bd. dirs. Hazleton Health Care Found., 1992-2000, chairperson, 1994-99, Cmty. Banks, Inc., 1996-2001; mem. Greater Hazleton Health Alliance Bd., 1995-2000, sec., 2000; mem. Luzerne County Regional Bd. Cmty. Banks, N.A., 1993-2000, YWCA adv. coun., 1998-2000. Named one of Outstanding Women Penns Woods Coun. Girl Scouts USA, 1977, Outstanding Young Women in Am., 1985, Woman of Yr. Soroptimist Internat., 1984, Greater Hazleton Jaycee Disting. Svc. award, 1990; recipient Luzerne County Pathfinder's award, 1990, Hon. P.E.A.R.L. award YWCA, 1996; named to Pa. Honor Roll of Women, 1996. Mem. AAUW (br. pres. 1977-79, 97-2000, state sec. 1981-83, state treas. 1983-85, state pres. 1992-96, Br. Outstanding Woman of Yr. 1980, assn. program com. 1995-97, ednl. found. bd. dirs. 1999—2003, ednl. found. devel. v.p. 2001-2003), Assn. Fund Raising Profls., Assn. Luth. Devel. Execs., Greater Hazleton C. of C. (bd. dirs. 1995-2000, treas. 1998-2000), Kiwanis Club. Home: 318 Oxford Pl Macungie PA 18062-1817 E-mail: s.nenstiel@worldnet.att.net.

NESBIT, LYNN, literary agent; BA in speech, Northwestern U. Asst. to agent Sterling Lord; head literary dept. Internat. Creative Mgmt.; ptnr. Janklow & Nesbit Assocs., N.Y.C., 1989—. Achievements include representing leading authors, among others, Tom Wolfe, Toni Morrison. John LeCarre, Jimmy and Rosalynn Carter, Anne Rice, Nora Ephron, Michael Crichton and Gail Sheehy. Office: Janklow & Nesbit Assocs 598 Madison Ave New York NY 10023*

NESBITT, ELEANOR TROUTMAN, elementary school educator, music educator; b. Burlington, N.C., June 17, 1955; d. Hanson DeVaux and Lois Holt Troutman; m. Richard Winford Nesbitt, Aug. 11, 1979; children: Annah Ruth, Daniel Winford, Gregory James. MusB in Music Edn., U. N.C., Greensboro, 1977. Cert. tchr. Nat. Bd. Profl. Standards., 2003. Band and choral tchr. Benvenue Mid. Sch., Rocky Mount, NC, 1977—79; tchr. asst. Alderman Elem., Greensboro, 1979—82; elem. music tchr. Pleasant Garden (N.C.) Elem., 1982—85, Nathanael Greene Elem. Sch., Julian, NC, 1982—85, Nathaniel Green Elem., Julian, NC, 1987—88, Rena Bullock Elem., Greensboro, 1982—85, Allen Jay Elem., High Point, 1982—85, Union Hill Elem., High Point, 1982—85; gen. music and choral tchr. Sumner Mid. Sch., Greensboro, 1985—88, Alamance Elem., Greensboro, 1987—. Contbr. N.C. Symphony edn. materials, 1981. Mem. chancel choir 1st Luth. Ch., Greensboro, 1981—. Mem.: N.C. Music Educators Assn. (elem. bd. dist. rep. 2000—02, honors chorus chair-elect 2002—03, honors chorus chair 2003—), Music Educators Nat. Conf. Avocations: sewing, sports. Home: 4402 Oakcliffe Rd Greensboro NC 27406 Office: Alamance Elem Sch 3600 Williams Dairy Rd Greensboro NC 27406

NESBITT, VERONICA A. management executive; b. Henderson, Tenn., June 10, 1959; d. Hiawatha Daniel and Laura Mae (Green) Thompson; divorced; children: Shemenya A. Davis, Maleka L. Cert. stenographer, Miller-Hawkins B. Coll., 1979; Cert. data transcriber, IRS, Memphis, Tenn., 1981; Cert. computer operator, U.S. Army, Newport News, Va., 1985, Cert. computer programmer, 1987; postgrad., Columbia Coll., 1990. Cert. computer opr. Stenographer Memphis & Shelby County Health Dept., Memphis, 1979-80; cash clk./data transcriber IRS, Memphis, 1980-82; data transcriber U.S. Army, Fort Sheridan, Ill., 1982-83, work order clk., 1984-85, quality control clk., 1985-89; mgmt. asst. HQ USAREC, Fort Sheridan, Ill., 1989-92; data transcriber Selective Svc., North Chicago, Ill., 1983-84; telemarketer Allstate Ins. Co., Northbrook, Ill., 1986-88, unit supr. Glenview, Ill., 1988-92; employee coun., 1994; total quality facilitator Allstate Ins. Co., Glenview, Ill., 1992; mgmt. asst. Hdqs. US Army Recruiting Command, Ft. Knox, Ky., 1992-94, 233d Base Support Bn., Darmstadt, Germany, 1994-97; staffing specialist Snelling Staffing Network, Columbia, Md., 1997-99; exec. adminstrv. asst. GSE Sys., Inc., Columbia, Md., 1999; mgmt. analyst Navy Internat. Programs/INS, Inc., 1999-2001; internat. jr. analyst/adminstr. Jil Info. Sys., Inc., 2001—03; program support analyst AT&T Govt. Solutions, 2003—. Mgmt. analyst, INS, Inc., Washington, 1999-2001—; chmn. task force Allstate, Glenview, 1990; interviewer Mathematica Policy Rsch., Inc., Columbia, Md., 1998-99, supr., 1999. Mem. Am. Heart Disease Found., 1991-92, Easter Seal Soc., 1991-92, March of Dimes, 1991—, Nat. Heart Rsch., 1991-95; mem. Nat. Cancer Rsch., 1991-95, fed. women's program mgr., 1995-97; treas. Second Glance Thrift Store, 1996-97; welfare com., continuing edn. grants Darmstadt Women's Club, 1995-96, chmn. Second Glance Thrift Store; counselor Equal Employment Opportunity, 1995-97; mem. Equal Opportunity Adv. Action Team, 1995-97; asst. supt. ch. schs. Asbury Town Neck United Meth. Ch., Severna Park, Md. Mem. NAFE, Am. Cancer Soc., Am. Heart Disease Prevention Found., Jack Anderson Internat. Platform Assn., Order Ea. Star (assoc. matron 1997). Baptist. Avocations: reading, knitting, drama, bicycling, sewing. Office: Naval Sea Systems Command 1333 Isaac Hull Ave Washington DC 20376 E-mail: vnesbittself@marykay.com.

NESBITT, WANDA L. ambassador; b. Phila., Dec. 1956; married. BA in Internat. Rels. and French, U. Pa., 1978; postgrad., Nat. War Coll., 1996—97. Vice-consul Dept. State, Port-au-Prince, Haiti, 1982—83, Paris, 1983—85, with Bur. L.Am., 1986—88, regional consular officer, 1990—92, with consular affairs Kinshasa, Zaire, 1992—93, with legis. affairs, 1995—96, dep. chief of mission, 1997—99, Dar es Salaam, Tanzania, 1999—2001, U.S. amb. to Madagascar, 2002—. Office: DOS Amb 2040 Antananarivo Pl Washington DC 20521 E-mail: nesbittwl@state.gov.

NESS, SUSAN, federal official; married; 2 children. BA, Douglass Coll., Rutgers U., 1970; JD cum laude, Boston Coll.; MBA, U. Pa. Asst. counsel com. banking, currency and housing U.S. House of Reps.; founder, dir. jud. appointments project Nat. Women's Polit. Caucus; commr. FCC, Washington, 1994—2001. Chair Charter Rev. Commn., Montgomery County, Md.; vice chair Montgomery County Task Force on Cmty. Access TV; pres. Montgomery County Commn. for Women. Named one of 12 to Watch, Electronic Media, 1997. Mem. Nat. Assn. Regulatory Utility Commrs. (com. comm.), Leadership Washington, Fed. Comm. Bar Assn. Office: FCC 1919 M St NW Washington DC 20554-0001

NESTERUK, JULIA ANN, marriage and family counselor; b. Hartford, Conn., Aug. 3, 1955; d. Jacob and Maria (Laszczuk) N. AA, Becker Jr. Coll., Worcester, Mass., 1975; BA magna cum laude, Cen. Conn. State U., 1985, MS, 1991. Lic. marriage and family therapist. Ct. recording monitor judicial dept. State of Conn., Hartford, 1975-88; clin. therapist Children's Ctr., 1992-96, clin. supr., 1996-99, dir. day programs, 1999—. Chmn. Profl. Staff Orgn., 1994—; workshop lectr. Ukrainian Catholic. Avocations: tennis, floral arranging, party/theme decorating, comedy, dance. Home: 65 Marmor Ct Wethersfield CT 06109-3353

NESTOR CASTELLANO, BRENDA DIANA, real estate company executive; b. Palm Beach, Fla., Nov. 10, 1948; d. John Joseph and Marion O'Connor Nestor; m. Robert Castellano. Student, U. Miami, Fla., 1978. Lic. real estate broker, Fla. Salesman Oscar E Dooley, Inc., Miami, Fla., 1978-80; prin. Brenda Nestor Assocs, Inc., Miami Beach, Fla., 1980—. Exec. v.p., bd. dirs. D.W.G. Corp., 1988-94, N.V.F. Corp., Salem Corp., 1988-97, Southeastern Pub. Svc., Graniteville Corp., 1988-94, Essex Ins., Chesapeake Ins.; exec. v.p., dir. Security Mgmt. Bd. dirs. Vizcayan Mus.; dir. Miami's Jackson Meml. Found. Named Ms. Charity, City of Miami, 1985, Lady Comdr., State of Fla. Mem. Miami Beach Bd. Realtors (bd. dirs. 1984—), Real Estate Securities and Exch. Com., Knights of Malta, Doubles Club (N.Y.C.), La Gorce Country Club, Fisher Island Club, Surf Club. Espicopal. Avocations: golf, tennis, boating. Home and Office: 39 Palm Ave Miami FL 33139-3263

NETTELS, ELSA, English language educator; b. Madison, Wis., May 25, 1931; d. Curtis Putnam and Elsie (Patterson) N. BA, Cornell U., 1953; MA, U. Wis., 1955, PhD, 1960. From instr. to asst. prof. English Mt. Holyoke Coll., South Hadley, Mass., 1959-67; from asst. prof. to prof. English Coll. William and Mary, Williamsburg, Va., 1967-97, prof. emeritus, 1997—. Author: James and Conrad, 1977 (South Atlantic Modern Lang. Assn. award 1975), Language, Race and Social Class in Howells' America, 1988, Language and Gender in American Fiction: Howells, James, Wharton, and Cather, 1997; contbr. articles to profl. jours. NEH fellow, 1984-85. Mem. MLA, South Atlantic MLA (edit. bd. 1977-83), Henry James Soc. (editl. bd. 1983—). Office: Coll William and Mary Dept English Williamsburg VA 23187 E-mail: exnett@wm.edu.

NEU, JENNIFER ELIZABETH, music educator; b. Los Gatos, Calif., Mar. 27, 1972; d. Gerald Dean and Elizabeth Ann Goetsch; m. Gregg Eugene Neu, Aug. 11, 2000; 1 child, Nathan Eugene. B in Music Edn., No. State U., 1995. Pvt. vocal/piano instr., 1995—; mid. sch. music and drama tchr. Huron (S.D.) Pub. Schs., 1996—99; H.S. vocal tchr., musical dir. Aberdeen (S.D.) Pub. Schs., 1999—2001; mid. sch. vocal tchr. St. Michael (Minn.)-Albertville Schs., 2001—; ch. choral dir. Immaculate Conception Ch., Becker, Minn., 2002—. Showchoir/jazz dir. Aberdeen Pub. Schs., 1999—2001. Mem. cmty. builders St. Michael Mid. Sch., 2001—. Mem.: NEA (student coun. advisor 1997—99), Music Educators Nat. Conf., Am. Choral Dirs. Assn., Kappa Delta Phi (life), Sigma Alpha Iota (life Nat. scholar 1992). Republican. Roman Catholic. Avocations: going to church, music, fishing, theater, scrapbooks.

NEUBURGER, KAREN, apparel executive; Retail buyer Maurice's, Emporium, San Francisco; v.p. merchandising Eber Internat., 1980-91; founder, pres., design dir. Karen Neuburger Sleepwear, San Rafael, Calif., 1991—. Guest appearence Oprah Winfrey TV show. Office: Karen Neuburger Sleepwear 3100 Ferner Blvd Ste J San Rafael CA 94901

NEUERBURG-DENZER, URSULA, theater director, educator, actress; b. Bonn, Germany, May 18, 1962;, U.S., 1990; d. Helmut Neuerburg, Doris Neuerburg-Heusler; m. Ralph Denzer; children: Clara Louise Denzer, Emil Jakob Denzer. Acting cert., Arne Baur-Worch Acting Sch., Berlin, 1987; BA, Freie U. Berlin, 1990; MA, NYU, 1992. Cert. midwife. Vis. asst. prof. U. Calif., Santa Cruz, Calif., 1996—99; resident dir. Swarthmore (Pa.) Coll., 1999—. V.p. Theater Zerbrochene Fenster, Berlin, 1985—90; pres. East Coast Artists, N.Y.C., 1992—96. Dir.: (Shakespeare) Macbeth, 1995, (Seneca) Trojan Women, 1997, (Brecht) Mother Courage, 1998, (Tretyakov) I Want a Baby, 2002. Named Outstanding Artist Visa, Internal Naturalization Svs., 1994, 1995; grantee, Arts Internat., 1992, Goethe Inst., 1992—94. Mem.: Theatre Comm. Group.

NEUFELD, ELIZABETH FONDAL, biochemist, educator; b. Paris, Sept. 27, 1928; married, 1951. PhD, U. Calif., Berkeley, 1956; DHc (hon.), U. Rene Descartes, Paris, 1978; DSc (hon.), Russell Sage Coll., Troy, N.Y., 1981; DSc (hon.), Hahnemann U. Sch. Medicine, 1984; DSc (hon.), Queens Coll., 1996. Asst. rsch. biochemist U. Calif., Berkeley, 1957—63; with Nat. Inst. Arthritis, Metabolism and Digestive Diseases, Bethesda, Md., 1963—84, research biochemist, 1963—73, chief sect. human biochem. genetics, 1973—79, chief genetics and biochem. br., 1979—84; prof., chmn. dept. biol. chemistry UCLA Sch. Medicine, 1984—. Named Passano Found. sr. laureate, 1982, Calif. Scientist of Yr., 1990; recipient Dickson prize, U. Pitts., 1974, Hillenbrand award, 1975, Gairdner Found. award, 1981, Albert Lasker Clin. Med. Rsch. award, 1982, William Allan award, 1982, Elliott Cresson medal, 1984, Wolf Found. prize, 1988, Christopher Columbus Discovery award for biomed. rsch., 1992, Nat. Medal of Sci., 1994. Fellow: Fellow AAAS; mem.: NAS, Am. Soc. Gene Therapy, Am. Soc. Clin. Investigation, Am. Soc. Cell Biology, Am. Soc. Biochemistry and Molecular Biology (pres. 1992—93), Am. Chem. Soc., Am. Soc. Human

Genetics, Am. Philos. Soc., Am. Acad. Arts and Scis, Inst. Medicine of NAS. Office: UCLA David Geffen Sch Medicine Dept Biol Chemistry Los Angeles CA 90095-1737 E-mail: eneufeld@mednet.ucla.edu.

NEUFELD, FRANCES FOSS, sculptor; b. Buenos Aires, Mar. 1, 1939; d. Joseph Weldon and Pearl Lee (Bristow) F.; m. Peter L. Blake, Oct. 1966 (div. 1973); 1 child, Christopher Oakley Blake; m. Harold L. Neufeld, Apr. 19, 1986. Student, Skidmore Coll., 1957-60, NYU, 1960-61, U. Akron, 1978-79. Cert. bi-lingual, spl. edn. tchr., Fla. Artist, sculptor Turquoise Flamingo Gallery, Albuquerque, 1989-90, Brandywine Gallery, Albuquerque, 1990-93, Chimayo Trading and Mercantile Gallery, Chimayo, N.Mex., 1993-97, Blankley Gallery, Albuquerque, 1994, Bardean Gallery, Albuquerque, 1995—. Presenter workshops Bardean Gallery, 1996—. Exhibited in group shows at Mantou Springs, Colo., 1994 (People's Choice award), St. Paul, 1997 (Best of Show), Loveland, Colol., Sedona, Ariz. V.p. Akron (Ohio) Assn. for Gifted Children, 1978-79. Mem. Layerist Soc. Avocations: study with sculptors, dance, reading, raising keeshounds. Home: 1804 Pedregoso Ct SE Albuquerque NM 87123-4415

NEUGEBAUER, MARCIA, physicist, administrator; b. N.Y.C., Sept. 27, 1932; d. Howard Graeme MacDonald and Frances (Townsend) Marshall; m. Gerry Neugebauer, Aug. 25, 1956; children: Carol, Lee. BS, Cornell U., 1954; MS, U. Ill., 1956; D of Physics (hon.), U. New Hampshire, 1998. Grad. asst. U. Ill., Urbana, 1954-56; vis. fellow Clare Hall Coll., Cambridge, Eng., 1975; sr. research scientist Jet Propulsion Lab. Calif. Inst. Tech., Pasadena, 1956-96, disting. vis. scientist, 1996—2003; vis. prof. planetary sci. Calif. Inst. Tech., Pasadena, 1986-87. Mem. com. NASA, Washington, 1960-96, NAS, Washington, 1981-94; Regents lectr. UCLA, 1990-91; adj. sr. rsch. sci. Lunar & Planetary Lab., U. Ariz., 2002-. Contbr. numerous articles on physics to profl. jours. Named Calif. Woman Scientist of Yr. Calif., Mus. Sci. and Industry, 1967, to Women in Tech. Internat. Hall of Fame, 1997; recipient Exceptional Sci. Achievement medal NASA, 1970, Outstanding Leadership medal NASA, 1993, Disting. Svc. medal NASA, 1997, COSPAR award for space sci., 1998. Fellow Am. Geophys. Union (sec., pres. solar planetary relationships sect. 1979-84, editor-in-chief Rev. Geophysics 1988-92, pres.-elect 1992-94, pres. 1994-96) mem. governing bd. Amer. Inst. Physics, 1995-97. Democrat. Home: 7519 S Eliot Ln Tucson AZ 85747-9627 Office: U Ariz Lunar & Planetary Lab 1629 E Univ Blvd Tucson AZ 85721

NEUHAUS, JOAN T. finance company executive, private investigator; b. Houston, Oct. 28, 1958; d. Philip Ross and Lacey (Thompson) N.; m. Daniel J. Schaan. BA, Williams Coll., 1980; MBA, Rice U., 1987. Registered rep., SEC. Mem. fixed income dept. Goldman, Sachs, N.Y.C., 1986; dir. tech. transfer Houston Area Rsch. Ctr., The Woodlands, 1988-89; v.p. Instl. Equity Sales Underwood, Neuhaus & Co., Inc., Houston, 1981-85, mem. corp. fin. dept., 1989; mktg. mgr. energy and fin. div. Westinghouse Credit Corp., Houston, 1989-91; pres. Neuhaus Capital Corp., Houston, 1991-93; pres., prin. Confidential Adv. Svcs., Inc., Houston, 1993—. Appointee Tex. Commn. on Pvt. Security by Gov. George Bush, 1999—. Bd. dirs., treas. St. Joseph's Meca, Tex. Lyceum Assn., 1988-93; founding mem. Charity Players, Houston, 1982-89; bd. dirs., treas. Julia C. Hester House, 1994—; adv. bd. Southwest Bank Tex., Univ. Houston Sch. Architecture. With USNR, 1993—; apptd. Tex. Commn. on Pvt. Security by Gov. George W. Bush, 1999. Mem. Tex. Assn. Lic. Investigators, World Affairs Coun., Tex. Tech. Transfer Assn. (profl.), Williams Coll. Alumni Assn. (bd. dirs. 1984-86). Republican. Episcopalian. Address: Confidential Advisory Serv Inc 5615 Morningside Dr Houston TX 77005-3218

NEUMAN, LINDA KINNEY, retired state supreme court justice, lawyer; b. Chgo., June 18, 1948; d. Harold S. and Mary E. Kinney; m. Henry G. Neuman; children: Emily, Lindsey. BA, U. Colo., 1970, JD, 1973; LLM, U. Va., 1998. Ptnr. Betty, Neuman, McMahon, Hellstrom & Bittner, 1973-79; v.p., trust officer Bettendorf Bank & Trust Co., 1979-80; dist. ct. judge, 1982-86; supreme ct. justice State of Iowa, 1986—2003; ptnr. Betty Neuman & McMahon. L.L.P., Davenport, Iowa. Mem. adj. faculty U. Iowa Grad. Sch. of Social Work, 1981, part-time jud. magistrate Scott County, 1980-82; mem. Supreme Ct. continuing legal edn. commn.; chair Iowa Supreme Ct. commn. planning 21st Century; mem. bd. counselors Drake Law Sch., time on appeal adv. com. Nat. Ctr. State Cts.; mem. adj. faculty U. Iowa Sch. Law. Trustee St. Ambrose U. Recipient Regents scholarship, U. Colo. award for disting. svc. Fellow ABA (life; chair appellate judges conf., mem. appellate standards com., JAD exec. coun.); mem. Am. Judicature Soc., Iowa Bar Assn., Iowa Judges Assn., Scott County Bar Assn., Nat. Assn. Woman Judges (bd. dirs.), Dillon Am. Inn of Ct. (pres. 2003-04), U.S. Assn. Constl. Law, Am. Acad. ADR Attys. E-mail: lkn@bettylawfirm.com.

NEUMAN, NANCY ADAMS MOSSHAMMER, civic leader; b. Greenwich, Conn., July 24, 1936; d. Alden Smith and Margaret (Mevis) Mosshammer; m. Mark Donald Neuman, Dec. 23, 1958; children: Deborah Adams, Jennifer Fuller, Jeffrey Abbott. BA, Pomona Coll., 1957; LLD, 1983; MA, U. Calif., Berkeley, 1961; LHD, Westminster Coll., 1987. Disting. lectr. Am. govt. Pomona Coll., 1990; disting. vis. prof. Washington and Jefferson Coll., 1991, 94, Bucknell U., 1992. Editor: A Voice of Our Own: Leading American Women Celebrate the Right to Vote, 1996, True to Ourselves: A Celebration of Women Making a Difference, 1998. Pres. Lewisburg (Pa.) LWV, 1967-70; bd. dirs. LWV Pa., 1970-77, pres., 1975-77; bd. dirs. LWV U.S., 1977-90, 2nd v.p., 1978-80, 1st v.p., 1982-84, pres., 1986-90; mem. Pa. Gov.'s Commn. on Mortgage and Interest Rates, 1973, Pa. Commonwealth Child Devel. com., 1974-75, Nat. Commn. on Pub. Svc., 1987-90; bd. dirs. Housing Assistance Coun., Inc., Washington, 1974—, pres., 1978-80; bd. dirs. Nat. Coun. Agrl. Life and Labor, 1974-79, Nat. Rural Housing Coalition, 1975-95, Pa. Housing Fin. Agy., 1975-80, Jud. Inquiry and Rev. Bd. Pa., 1989-93; disciplinary bd. Supreme Ct. Pa., 1980-85; mem. Pa. Gov.'s Task Force on Voter Registration, 1975-76, Nat. Task Force for Implementation Equal Rights Amendment, 1975-77; mem. adv. com. Pa. Gov.'s Interdepartmental Coun. on Seasonal Farmworkers, 1975-77; mem. Appellate Ct. Nominating Commn. Pa., 1976-79; mem. Fed. Jud. Nominating Commn. Pa., 1977-85, chmn., 1978-81, 82-83; mem. Pa. Gov.'s Study Commn. on Pub. Employee rels., 1976-78; del. Internat. Women's Yr. Conf., 1977; bd. dirs. ERAmerica, Inc., 1st v.p., 1977-79, Nat. Low Income Housing Coalition, 1979-82; Rural Am., 1979-81, Fed. Home Loan Bank Pitts., 1979-82; mem. Nat. adv. Com. Women, 1978-79; mem. nat. adv. com. Pa. Neighborhood Preservation Support Sys., 1976-77; bd. dirs. Pa. Women's Campaign fund, 1984-86, 92-2002, pres., 1992-96, 2001-02, Rural coalition, Washington, 1984-90, Com. on the Constitutional Sys., 1988-90, Am. Judicature Soc., 1989-93; exec. com. Leadership Conf. Civil Rights, 1986-90; bd. dirs. Pennsylvanians for Modern Cts., 1986—; trustee Citizen's Rsch. Found., 1989-99; mem. mid. dist. Pa. adv. com. judicial and U.S. atty. nominations, 1993-94; bd. dirs. Pathmakers, 1993-97, pres. 1993-95; bd. dirs. Capital Concerts, 1997—. Virginia Travis lectureship Bucknell U., 1982; Woodrow Wilson vis. fellow, 1993-2000; recipient Disting. Alumna Award MacDuffie Sch. Girls, 1979, Liberty Bell award Pa. Bar Assn., 1983, Barrows Alumni Award Pomona Coll., 1987, Thomas P. O'Neill Jr. award for Exemplary Pub. Svc., 1989; Disting. Daughter of Pa., 1987. Mem. ABA (com. election law and voter participation 1986-90, accreditation com. 1990-96, coun. sect. of legal edn. 1997-2003, sec. 2000-03), Cosmos Club. Home: 190 Verna Rd Lewisburg PA 17837-8747

NEUMAN, PAULA ANNE YOUNG, cultural organization administrator; b. Tiffin, Ohio, Sept. 15, 1960; d. Paul Everett and Mary Virginia (Brocious) Young; children: Nichole Adele, Jessica Theresa, Samantha Rebekah, Mary Elizabeth; m. Russell M. Neuman, Aug. 19, 2000. BS in Psychology, Heidelberg Coll., 1982; MA in Polit. Sci., Bowling Green (Ohio) State U., 1987; MA in Adult Edn., Ball State U., 1996; EdD, Nova Southeastern U., Ft. Lauderdale, Fla., 2000; cert. in fundraising mgmt., Ind. U., 1997. Cert. tng. cons. CTC; fundraising exec. Ball State U., 2003, tng. cons. Ball State U., 2003, human performance improvement FUPUI, 2004. Child therapist Sandusky (Ohio) Youth Referral Svc., 1982-83; parole officer State of Ohio, Columbus, 1983-86; dep. dir. Seneca, Sandusky and Wyandot Commn. Mental Health Bd., Tiffin, 1987-88; program dir. WSOS Cmty. Action Commn., Fremont, Ohio, 1988-90; exec. dir. Tiffin Area C. of C./Seneca Indsl. & Econ. Devel. Corp., Tiffin, 1988-90; pres. Chapman Cmty. Devel. Cons., Tiffin, 1990—93; dir. devel. St. Francis Health Care Ctr., Green Springs, Ohio, 1993-94, St. Francis Coll., Fort Wayne, Ind., 1994-95; dir. of fund devel. Girl Scout Coun., Inc., Fort Wayne, 1995-97; exec. dir., CEO McMillen Ctr. for Health Edn., Fort Wayne, 1997-2000; pres., owner edn. and devel. cons., 2000—. Adj. prof. econs. Tiffin U., 1987—94; adj. prof. non-profit mgmt. Ivy Tech. State Coll., 1999—2000; mem. ednl. adv. bd. Vanguard/Sentinel Vocat Sch., Fremont, 1989—90; chmn. Tiffin Fair Housing Bd., 1985—90; bd. dirs. Ohio Indsl. Tng. Program, Sandusky, 1988—90, Pvt. Industry Coun., Fremont, Seneca County Revolving Loan Fund, Tiffin; chair adv. bd. WSOS; cons. in field. Candidate Seneca County Commr., 1992; mem. Grad. Ft. Wayne Leadership Works, 1994; bd. dirs. Purdue U. Ext., 2000-02; founder, bd. dirs. Children of Divorce & Broken Relationships. Mem. Nat. Soc. Fundraising Execs. (bd. dirs. Ind. chpt. 1999-2002), Bus. and Profl. Women's Assn. (Young Career Woman of Yr. 1987, 89), Glens of Liberty Mills Assn. (bd. dirs., sec., 2002-03, pres. 2003-2004). Avocation: philanthropic studies. Home: 6217 Spy Glass Run Fort Wayne IN 46804 Office Phone: 260-436-7137. E-mail: neumans2000@yahoo.com.

NEUMAN, SUSAN B. federal agency administrator; Grad., Am. U.; master's, Calif. State U., Hayward; doctorate, U. Pacific. Reading specialist; tchr. elem. sch.; instr. Boston Coll., U. Mass., Yale U.; prof. Temple U., Phila.; dir. Ctr. Improvement Early Reading Achievement U. Mich., Ann Arbor, prof.; asst. sec. elem. and secondary edn. Dept. Edn., Washington, 2001—. Office: Dept Edn Office Elem and Secondary Edn 400 Maryland Ave SW FOB 6 Washington DC 20202-6100

NEUMAN, SUSAN CATHERINE, public relations and marketing consultant; b. Detroit, Jan. 29, 1942; d. Paul Edmund and Elsie (Goetz) N. AB, U. Miami, Fla., 1964; MBA, Barry U., Miami Shores, Fla., 1985. Journalist, writer The Miami Herald, 1962-65; editor Miamian Mag., 1965-69; pres. Susan Neuman Inc., Miami, 1969—; ptnr. Neuman Enterprises Unltd., 1994—. Mem. Fla. Gov.'s Pub. Rels. Adv. Coun., 1978-86. Mem. Pub. Rels. Soc. Am. (accredited, past officer, bd. dirs.), Miami C. of C., Counselors Acad., Miami City Club (founder, bd. govs.), Miami Internat. Press Club (charter, founder, pres. 1985-86), Com. of One Hundred (bd. dirs., sec.). Democrat. Roman Catholic. Home: 13540 NE Miami Ct Miami FL 33161-2739 Office: Susan Neuman Inc Venetia 25th Fl 555 NE 15th St Ste 25K Miami FL 33132-1404 E-mail: s_neuman@hotmail.com.

NEUMANN, IRMA WANDA, musician, educator; b. L.A., Apr. 9, 1916; d. William and Wanda Gisella Neumann. Studied with, Carmon Luboviski and Felix Slatkin. First violin Hancock Ensemble, L.A., 1943, L.A. Philharm. Orch., 1944—45, 20th Century Fox film Orch., L.A., 1946—58; free lance musician L.A., 1958—. Tchr. violin, L.A.*

NEUMANN, LISELOTTE, professional golfer; b. Finspang, Sweden, May 20, 1966; With LPGA, 1987—. Mem. European Solheim Cup Team, 1990, 92, 94, 96, 98. Named Golf Digest Rolex Rookie of Year, 1988, Swedish Golfer of Year, 1994, GolfWorld's Most Improved Golfer, 1994. Achievements in LPGA victories include: U.S. Women's Open, 1988, Mazda Japan Classic, 1991, Minn. LPGA Classic, 1994, Weetabix Women's Brit. Open, 1994, GHP Heartland Classic, 1994, Chrysler-Plymouth Tournament of Champions, 1996, PING/Welch's Championship, 1996, First Bank-Edina Realty Classic, 1996, Welch's Champsionship, 1997, Toray Japan Queens Cup, 1997, Standard Register Ping, 1998, Chick-fil-A Charity Championship, 1998; other victories include: European Open, 1985, German Open, 1986-88, French Open, 1987, Solheim Cup, 1998. Office: LPGA 100 International Golf Dr Daytona Beach FL 32124-1092

NEUMANN, STEPHANIE TOWER, retired librarian; b. N.Y.C., Jan. 26, 1947; d. George Francis and Mary Corbet Neumann; m. Charles Donald Dukes, Mar. 21, 1994; 1 stepchild, Jonathan Andrew Dukes. BA, Ea. Wash. U., 1973; MLS, Western Mich. U., 1975. Svc. rep. Mountain Bell (now U.S. West), Albuquerque, 1970—74; reference libr. City of Littleton, Colo., 1977—90, econ. intelligence specialist, 1990—98. Mem.: Rocky Mountain Spl. Libr. Assn., Spl. Libr. Assn. (presenter 1991, 1995), Beta Phi Mu. Home: 53 W Ranch Trl Morrison CO 80465 E-mail: stnm@earthlink.net.

NEUMANN, TAMMY LEIGH, speech pathology/audiology services professional; d. Scott Andrew Neumann and Jacqueline Louise Schwartz. BA in Musical Arts, U. Mich., 1993; MA in Speech Lang. Pathology, Hoftsra U., 1996. Cert. tchr. speech and hearing handicapped N.Y., 2002. Speech-lang. pathologist Oceanside (N.Y.) Pub. Schs., 1996—97, Sch. Lang. and Comm. Disorders, Bellmore, NY, 1997, Lawrence (N.Y.) Pub. Schs., 1997—. Spkr., presenter in field. Musician (french horn): South Shore Symphony Orch., (plays) Man of La Mancha; actor: (plays) Blood Brothers, Annie Warbucks. Coach, mentor Leukemia and Lymphoma Soc., Melville, NY, 1999—2002. Mem.: Am. Speech-Lang. and Hearing Assn. (licentiate cert.). Jewish. Avocations: marathons, travel, philanthropy. Home: 666 Shore Rd Apt 5K Long Beach NY 11561 Office: Lawrence Pub Sch #4 Wanser Ave Inwood NY 11096 Personal E-mail: mgoblu93@aol.com.

NEUSTEIN, ROBIN, investment company executive; Attended, Mt. Holyoke Coll., 1971—73; AB in anthropology, Brown U., 1975; JD, MBA, Northwestern U., 1979. Atty. Altheimer & Gray, Chgo.; with Goldman Sachs & Co., N.Y.C., 1982—, ptnr. Investment Banking Divsn., 1990-95, chief of staff to sr. ptnrs., 1992—99, mng. dir., 1996—, co-head Pvt. Equity Group, 1999—, past mem. mgmt. com. Trustee Rockefeller U., Brown U., Mount Holyoke U., Mount Sinai Med. Ctr.; pres. bd. trustees Am. Ballet Theatre, 2002—. Mem.: Am. Women's Econ. Devel. Corp. (bd. mem., vice chmn.). Office: Goldman Sachs & Co 85 Broad St New York NY 10004-2456*

NEUWIRTH, BEBE (BEATRICE NEUWIRTH), dancer, actress, actress; b. Newark, Dec. 31, 1958; d. Lee Paul and Sydney Anne Neuwirth; m. Paul Dorman, 1984 (div.); m. Michael Danek. Student, Juilliard Sch., 1976-77. Appeared: (on Broadway) A Chorus Line (as Sheila), 1975-90, Dancin', 1978-82, Little Me, 1982, Sweet Charity, 1986-87 (Tony award for best featured actress in a musical, 1986), Damn Yankees, 1994-95, Chicago, 1996 (Tony award for best actress in a musical, 1997, Outer Critics Circle award for best actress in a musical, 1997, Drama League Award for disting. performance, 1997, Drama Desk Award for outstanding actress in a musical, 1997, Astaire Award for best female dancer, 1997), Fosse, 1999-2001, Funny Girl, 2002; (off Broadway) include West Side Story, 1981, Upstairs at O'Neal's, 1982-83, The Road to Hollywood, 1984, Just So, 1985, Waiting in the Wings: The Night the Understudies Take the Stage, 1986, Showing Off, 1989, Kiss of the Spider Woman (London), 1993, Pal Joey, 1995, Here Lies Jenny, 2004. Prin. dancer on Broadway Dancin', 1982; leading dance role Kicks, 1984. Actor: (TV series) The Edge of Night, 1981, Cheers, 1986-93 (Emmy award for Best Supporting Actress in a Comedy Series 1990, 91), (voice) Aladdin, 1993, (voice) All Dogs Go to Heaven: The Series, 1996, Deadline, 2000-01; (TV series guest appearances) Frasier, 1994-2003; (TV miniseries) Wild Palms, 1993; (TV films) Without Her Consent, 1990, Unspeakable Acts, 1990, Dash and Lilly, 1999, Cupid & Cate, 2000, Sounds From a Town I Love, 2001; (films) Say Anything, 1989, Green Card, 1990, Bugsy, 1991, The Paint Job, 1992, Malice, 1993, Jumanji, 1995, (voice) All Dogs Go to Heaven 2, 1996, The Adventures of Pinocchio, 1996, The Associate, 1996, Dear Diary, 1996, Celebrity, 1998, The Faculty, 1998, (voice) An All Dogs Christmas Carol, 1998, Summer of Sam, 1999, Liberty Heights, 1999, Getting to Know You, 1999, Tadpole, 2002, How to Lose a Guy in 10 Days, 2003, Le Divorce, 2003, The Big Bounce, 2004. Vol. performances for March of Dimes Telethon, 1986, Cystic Fibrosis Benefit Children's Ball, 1986, Ensemble Studio Theater Benefit, 1986, Circle Repertory Co. Benefit, 1986, all in N.Y.C. Democrat. Office: Internat Creative Mgmt 8942 Wilshire Blvd Beverly Hills CA 90211-1934

NEVANS, LAUREL S. rehabilitation counselor; b. N.Y.C., Aug. 1, 1964; d. Roy N. and Virginia (Place) Nevans; m. Russell Baird Palmer III, Oct. 12, 1991 (div. Jan. 2001). BA in English, Secondary Edn. cum laude, U. Richmond, 1986, postgrad., 1989-92; MA in Edn. and Human Devel., George Washington U., 1991, cert. in job devel. and placement, 1992. Group leader S.E. Consortium for Spl. Svcs., Larchmont, NY, 1980—85; vocat. instr. Assn. for Retarded Citizens Montgomery County, Rockville, Md., 1986—89; edn. specialist George Washington U. Out of Sch. Work Experience Program, Washington, 1989—90; rsch. asst. George Washington U. Dept. Tchr. Prep. & Spl. Edn., Washington, 1989—91; employability skills tchr., rsch. intern Nat. Rehab. Hosp. Rehab. Engring. Dept., Washington, 1991; vocat./ind. living skills specialist The Independence Ctr., Rockville, Md., 1991—93; leadership team mgr. Career Choice project The Endependence Ctr. of No. Va., Arlington, 1993—94; program dir. United Cerebral Palsy of D.C. and No. Va., Washington, 1994—97; sr. assistive tech. specialist Tech., Automation & Mgmt., Inc., Greenbelt, Md., 1997—98; owner WebLaurels Designs, Silver Spring, Md., 1998—, Artist-Crafts, 2001—, Clayers with Disabilities Listserv (electronic discussion list), 2002—, Artist Crafts, Silver Spring, 2001—. Teaching asst. Rehab. Counseling Program, George Washington U., 1991; moderator FPList Electronic Discussion List, 2000—; owner Clayers with Disabilities Electronic Discussion List, 2002- . Bd. mem., newsletter editor Cameron Hill Owners Assn., 2002—. Recipient traineeship GWU Counseling Dept., 1990, 91. Mem. Nat. Rehab. Assn., Nat. Rehab. Counselors Assn., D.C. Met. Area Assn. Person's in Supported Employment (editor newsletter 1995-97), Nat. Career Devel. Assn., Nat. Employment Counseling Assn., Nat. Assn. Ind. Living, Am. Assn. Counseling and Devel., Am. Rehab. Counseling Assn., Nat. Polymer Clay Guild. Democrat. Avocations: writing, photography, music, travel, jewelry making. Home: 8501 Cameron St Silver Spring MD 20910-3466 E-mail: laurel@artistcrafts.com

NEVELLS, KIMBERLY A, medical/surgical nurse, educator; b. Lincoln, Maine, June 7, 1961; d. Carroll and Shirley Worcester; m. Ralph Nevells, Oct. 9, 1982 (div. Mar. 1995); children: Leigh, Ian, Nathan. ADN, Stratham Tech. Coll., Stratham, NH, 1991—93; MSN anticipated May, 2004, U. of Maine, Orono, Maine, 2001—. Cert. Diabetes Educator Nat. Bd. of Diabetes Educators, 2000; registered Nurse, NH, 1993, State Bd. of Nursing/Maine, 1993, cert. Family Nurse Practitioner(Anticipated Spring 2004), Maine, 2004. RN Portsmouth Regional Hosp., Portsmouth, NH, 1993—93; RN, (intensive care unit and med-surg) Penobscot Valley Hosp., Lincoln, Maine, 1993—96; diabetes educator PVH, Lincoln, Maine, 1994—2001; RN, (intensive care unit) York Hosp., York, Maine, 1995; RN, (nurse mgr.) Penobscot Valley Hosp., Lincoln, Maine, 1996—. Icu nurse practice com. chairperson Penobscot Valley Hosp., Lincoln, Maine, 1996—2001, diabetes adv. bd. chairperson, 1994—2001. Author: (journal article) Advance for Nurse Practitioners; organizer (diabetes education) Several cmty. edn. programs including,"A Night Out for Diabetes", "Diabetes Info. Day", "Walk for Diabetes" (Nomination for Am. Diabetes Assn. Reaching People Award, 1998), organization and implementation (cmty. edn. program, diabetes education) Shop and Save Food Labeling Project (Grant from Diabetes Control Project(Maine), 1996). Scholar Nurse Traineeship Award, U. of Maine, 2002-2004 Mem.: Patient Care Mgmt. Com., Sigma Theta Tau. R-Liberal. Avocations: vacationing at the beach, horseback riding, watching children participate in sports, gardening, theatre. Office: Penobscot Valley Hospital Transalpine Road Lincoln ME 04457

NEVILLE, CARA LEE T. judge; JD, William Mitchell Coll. Law, 1975. Lawyer felony divsn. Hennepin County Attys. Office, 1972; asst. pub. defender Hennepin County, 1978; judge Hennepin County Mcpl. Ct., 1983, Hennepin County Dist. Ct., 1986; dist. ct. judge 4th Jud. Dist., Mpls., 1986—. Mem.: ABA (bd. govs. 9th dist. 2000—03). Office: Hennepin County Dist Ct 1859-C Govt Ctr 300 S 6th St Minneapolis MN 55487-0999

NEVILLE, PHOEBE, choreographer, dancer, educator; b. Swarthmore, Pa., Sept. 28, 1941; d. Kennith R. and Marion (Eberbach) Balsley; m. Philip E. Hipwell, June 21, 1969 (dissolved Sept. 1978); m. Philip Corner, Nov. 3, 1996. Student, Wilson Coll., 1959-61. Cert. practitioner body mind centering, registered somatic movement therapist. Instr. Bennington (Vt.) Coll., 1981-84, 87-88; vis. lectr. UCLA, 1984-86. Dancer, choreographer Judson Meml. Ch., N.Y.C., 1966—70, Dance Uptown Series, 1969, Cubiculo Theatre, 1972—75, Delacorte Dance Festival, 1976, Dance Umbrella Series, 1977, Riverside Dance Festival, 1976, 1978, N.Y. Seasons, 1979—, dancer, artistic dir. Phoebe Neville Dance Co., N.Y.C., 1975—, Jacob's Pillow Splash! Festival, 1988 , Dance Theater Workshop Winter Events, 1988—, performances with Philip Corner: Venice, Genoa San Michele al' Adige, 1966—, BBB Festival, Thailand, Genoa, Salso Maggiore, Terme, 1997—, Seoul NY Max Festival, N.Y.C., 1998, Malpartida de Caseras, Spain, Caserano, Italy, 1998, Besancon, France, 1998, Paris, Lyon, 1999, Saluggia, Italy, 1999, Performance Festival, Odense, Denmark, 1999, 2001, Bassano del Grappa, Genoa, Italy, 2000, 2001, 2002, Novarra, Italy, 2002—; performances with, Ghent, Belgium, 2002—; performances with : Castelvetro di Modena, 2003; Argos Festival; performances with Castelvetro di Modena, Naples, Belgium, 2003. Recipient Creative Artist Public Svc. award, 1975; Nat. Endowment for Arts fellow, 1975, 79, 80, 85-87, 92-94, Choreographic fellow N.Y. Found. for Arts, 1989. Mem.: Internat. Assn. Healthcare Practitioners, Internat. Movement Edn. and Therapy Assn. (registered), Body-Mind Centering Assn. (cert. practitioner and tchr.). Buddhist.

NEVILLE, REGINA FRANCES LICKTEIG, performing arts company executive, educator; b. Algona, Iowa, Apr. 29, 1962; d. Charles Joseph Lickteig and Helen Marion Gimzo; m. Thomas Joseph Neville, Aug. 6, 1988; children: Kathryn Mary, James Patrick, Emily Rose. BA magna cum laude, U. No. Iowa, 1985; MFA, Yale U. Sch. of Drama, 1988. Cert. tchr. State of Iowa Bd. of Pub. Instrn., 1985, Minn. Dept. Edn., 2003. Lectr. U. NC, Chapel Hill, 1989—91; mng. dir. PlayMakers Repertory Co., Chapel Hill, 1989—91, Marin Theatre Co., Mill Valley, Calif., 1992—99; arts mgmt. cons. Corte Madera, Calif., 1999—2000; substitute tchr. Edina Pub. Schs., Edina, Minn., 2002—. Asst. stage mgr. (Broadway run and Soviet tour) A Walk In The Woods, (Broadway prodn.) Ah, Wilderness!, prodn. stage mgr. (regional theatre) PlayMakers Repertory Co. Mem. Our Lady of Grace Faith Formation Bd., Edina, 2003—; v.p. Ring Mountain Day Sch., Tiburon, Calif., 1997—99; pres. Countryside Elem. Parent-Tchr. Orgn., Edina, 2002—03; co-chair Parent Leadership Coun., Edina, 2003—. Mem.: Theatre Comm. Group, Theta Alpha Phi (life; pres. 1984—85).

NEVIN, JEAN SHAW, artist; b. Bklyn., Dec. 21, 1934; d. Marshall Robert and Dorothy Frances (Brown) Shaw; m. Robert Stephen Nevin, Dec. 9, 1955. BA in English, SUNY, Albany, 1956. Textbook and freelance editor, 1959—74; printmaker, papermaker Jean Nevin Graphics, Indpls., 1969—84; owner, mgr., knitwear designer Chameleon, Indpls., 1985—88; pres., knitwear designer Knitting Machine Shop, Inc., Indpls., 1988—91; owner Knitwearables, Albuquerque, 1991—97; painter Albuquerque, 1995—. Instr. print and paper making Indpls. Art League, 1974-83, exhibits coord., 1969, 73, edn. coord., 1979-80, editor Artifacts, 1968-69, 72-73; editor, pub. Swatchnotes, 1987-91; owner, gallery dir. Kokopelli Gallery,

2000-01. Exhibited to nat. group shows and galleries prints and handmade paper, 1970-84, garments and jewelry, 1992-97, Florence Biennale, Florence, Italy, 2003; painter, sculptor, mixed media artist, 1998-2001; digital painter, 2001—. Mem.: Digital Fine Art Soc. N.Mex. (co-founder), Soc. Layerists in MultiMedia. (signature mem.). Home and Studio: 9641 Mendoza Ave NE Albuquerque NM 87109-6614 Office Phone: 505-288-2044. E-mail: [illegible]@nevinart.com

NEVINS, FRANCES (FRANKIE) RUSH, tourism professional; b. Kansas City, Mo., Dec. 15, 1932; d. George Herbert and Bertha Emmaline (Hyne) Rush; m. Warren Griffith Nevins, Feb. 17, 1952 (div. Mar. 2002); children: Ronald Douglas(dec.), Deborah Lynn, Philip Rush. Grad., Baker U., 1954; cert. tourism industry specialist, Ind. U.-Purdue U., 1990. Personnel adminstr. Man-Wood, 1974—81; relocation dir. Gallery of Homes, 1982—84; tourism develop. mgr. N.J. Divsn. Tourism, Trenton, 1984—98; ret., 1998. Co-editor: N.J. State Guide, 1984—98. Mem. Somerset County (N.J.) Hist. Commn., 1987—98; active various civic and charity coms., Augusta, Ga.; mem. Daus. of the King, Episcopal Ch. Women. Mem.: DAR, Am. Bus. Assn. (panel mem. 1984—98, conf. planning com., edn./scholarship com.), Nat. Tour Assn. (panel mem. 1984—98, conf. planning com.), Federated Women's Club (past pres.), Delta Delta Delta (past pres.). Republican. Episcopalian. Home: 3753 Boulder Tr Augusta GA 30907-5124

NEVINS, LYN (CAROLYN A. NEVINS), educational supervisor, trainer, consultant; b. Chelsea, Mass., June 9, 1948; d. Samuel Joseph and Stella Theresa (Maronski) N.; m. John Edward Herbert, Jr., May 1, 1979; children: Chrissy, Johnny. BA in Sociology, Edn., U. Mass., 1970; MA in Women's Studies, George Washington U., 1975. Cert. tchr., trainer. Tchr. social studies Greenwich (Conn.) Pub. Schs., 1970-74; rschr. career/vocat. edn. Conn. State Dept. Edn., Hartford, 1975-76; rschr., career/vocat. edn. Area Coop. Edn. Svcs., Hamden, Conn., 1976-77; program mgr., trainer career edn. and gender equity Coop. Ednl. Svcs., Norwalk, Conn., 1977-83, trainer, mgr., devel., Beginning Educator Support and Tng. program Fairfield, Conn., 1987—; state coord. career edn. Conn. State Dept. Edn., Hartford, 1982-83; supr. Sacred Heart U., Fairfield, 1992—. Bias com. Conn. State Dept. Edn., Hartford, 1981—; vision com. Middlesex Mid. Sch., Darien, Conn., 1993-95; mem. ednl. quality and diversity com. Town of Darien, 1993-95; cons., trainer career devel./pre-retirement planning Cohen and Assocs., Fairfield, 1981—, Farren Assocs., Annandale, Va., 1992—, Tracey Robert Assocs., Fairfield, 1994—; freelance cons., trainer, Darien, 1983-87; presenter Nat. Conf. GE, 1980, Career Edn., 1983, Am. Edn. Rsch. Assn., 1991; lectr. in field. Tennis coach Spl. Olympics, 1993—, Darien (Conn.) Girls' Softball League, 1992-96, tennis coord. Spl. Olympics Summer Games, 1997—; mem. bldg. com. Darien (Conn.) High Sch., 1999—. Mem. NOW (founder, state coord. edn. 1972-74), ASCD. Avocations: tennis, running, walking, golf, travel. Home: 4 Hollister Ln Darien CT 06820-5404 Office: Coop Ednl Svcs 40 Lindeman Drive Trumbull CT 06611-4723

NEVINS, SHEILA, television programmer and producer; b. N.Y.C. d. Benjamin and Stella Nevins; m. Sidney Koch; 1 child, David Andrew. BA, Barnard Coll.; MFA, Yale U. TV prodr. Great Am. Dream Machine, NET, 1971-73, The Reasoner Report, ABC, 1973, Feeling Good, Children's TV Workshop, 1975-76, Who's Who, CBS, 1977-78; dir. documentary and family programming HBO, N.Y.C., 1978-82; v.p. documentary programming Home Box Office, N.Y.C., 1986-95, sr. v.p. original programming, 1998-99; exec. v.p. original programming HBO, N.Y.C., 1999—2003, pres. documentary and family, 2004—. Bd. dirs. Film Forum, Creative Capital, Ind. Feature Project. Bd. dirs. Women's Action Alliance. Named Woman of Achievement YMCA, 1991, Top 25 Women in TV, Emmy mag., 1996, Top 25 Smartest Women Am., Mirabella Mag., 1999; named one of Top 50 Women in TV, Hollywood Reporter Mag.; named to Broadcasting and Cable Hall of Fame, 2000; recipient Peabody award, 1986, 1992, 1995, 1996, 1997, 1999, 2000, Acad. Award for Documentary, 1993, 1996, 1998, 1999, 2000, 2001, 2003, Emmy award, 1994, 95, 96, 97, 98, 99, 2000, Glaad Media award, 1989, Media award Mental Health Assn. N.Y.C., 1996, Three Arts award, Personal Peabody award, 1999, Wellness Cmty. award, 2001, NATAS Silver Cir., 2000, Humanitarian award, Nat. Bd. Rev., 2002, Lucy award, Women in Film, 2003. Mem.: Internt. Documentary Assn. (Vision award 1998), N.Y. Women in Film (Muse award 1998), Writers Guild Am.

NEVIUS, JANET DRYDEN, real estate company executive, government agency administrator; b. Verona, Nj, Jan. 17, 1926; d. Harold Clifford and Marian Longstreth Dryden; m. Robert Foster Nevius, Oct. 11, 1958; children: Janet, Carolyn. BA, Barnard Coll., 1949; MA, Seton Hall U., 1970; PHD, NYU, 1975. Cert. tchr. in French, Spanish and secondary edn. NJ. Liaison officer-interpreter U.S. Dept., Washington, 1955—61; secondary sch. tchr. Montclair H.S., Montclair, NJ, 1961—68; dir. Am. Inst. for Fgn. Study, Greenwich, Conn., 1968—76; mgr. Citibank, New York, NY, 1977—82; v.p. dir. of mktg. J. Henry Schroder bank & Trust Co., New York, NY, 1982—87; real estate exec. UN, New York, NY, 2002—. Trustee NJ Hist. Soc., Newark; exec. v.p. UN Delegations Hospitality Com., New York, NY; sponsor Orpheus Chamber Orch., NY. Mem.: The Met. Club, The Mus. of Natural History, The Met. Opera Guild, The Met. Mus. of Art, The Essex Fells Country Club, President's Cir. R-Consevative. Episcopalian. Avocations: music, golf, book club discussions, theatre, literary history. Home: PO box 175 Essex Fells NJ 07021 Office: PO box 175 Essex Fells NJ 07021

NEW, ANNE LATROBE, public relations, fund raising executive; b. Evanston, Ill., May 10, 1910; d. Charles Edward and Agnes (Bateman) N.; m. John C. Timmerman, Sept. 30, 1933; 1 child, Jan LaTrobe. AB, U. S.C., 1930; postgrad., Hunter Coll., 1930-31, NYU, 1932-33. APR (Accredited Pub. Relations Practitioner). Editl. asst. Pictorial Review Mag., N.Y.C., 1930—32; copy asst. J. Walter Thompson Co., N.Y.C., 1932—33; sub editor Cosmopolitan Mag., N.Y.C., 1933—37; with Girl Scouts of the U.S., N.Y.C., 1937—57, chief pub. rels. officer, 1945—57; dir. pub. info. edn. Nat. Recreation and Park Assn., 1957—66; special asst. gen. dir. Internat. Social Svc. Am. Branch, N.Y.C., 1966—68; dir. devel. Nat. Accreditation Coun. for Agys. Serving Blind and Visually Handicapped, N.Y.C., 1969—78; pres. Timmerman & New Inc., Mamaroneck, NY, 1980—2001; ret., 2001. Cons. dept. pub. adminstrn. Baruch Coll., CUNY, 1987-94, Sch. Pub. Affairs, 1994-99. Author: Service For Givers, The Story of the National Information Bureau, 1983, Raise More Money for Your Nonprofit Organization, 1991; contbr. articles to profl. jours. Bd. dirs. Mamaroneck (N.Y.) United Fund, 1963-64; chair nominating com. LWV, Mamaroneck, 1988; warden emerita St. Thomas' Episc. Ch., Mamaroneck. Recipient Marzella Garland award for outstanding achievement in promotion of improved housing conditions in Mamaroneck Village, 1995. Mem. Pub. Rels. Soc. Am. (bd. dirs. N.Y. chpt. 1958-72), Women Execs. Pub. Rels. (sec. 1962-63), Assn. Fundraising Profls. (bd. dirs. Greater N.Y. chpt. 1978-84), Phi Beta Kappa. Democrat.

NEW, MARGARET ANN, educational consultant; b. Stevens Point, Wis., Jan. 26, 1940; d. Robert Byron and Millicent (Coombs) Freed; m. William New Jr., Oct. 1, 1966 (div. 1982); 1 child, Catherine Ann. BS, U. Wis., 1962; MA, Stanford U., 1966; EdD, UCLA, 1972. Asst. dean housing UCLA, 1969-72; dean students Marlborough Sch., L.A., 1972-73; head counselor Half Moon Bay (Calif.) H.S., 1973-85; real estate profl. Calif., D.C., Va., 1975-85; dir. devel. Foxcroft Sch., Middleburg, Va., 1985-87, Youth Svc. Am., Washington, 1987-89; cons. Middleburg Group, 1989-93; mktg., devel. mgr. Am. Soc. Naval Engrs., 1993-95; career cons. Middleburg (Va.) Group, 1987—. Bd. dirs. Stanford (Calif.) U. Eastern Coun.; adj. prof. George Washington U., Marymount U., Strayer Online. Vice chair Middleburg Planning Commn., 1994—, Action on Smoking & Health, Washington, 1993—; mem. gov.'s club Alexander for Pres., Nashville, 1995—; pres. Meadowbrook Homeowners Assn., Middleburg, 1995—; mem. Middleburg Town Coun., 2002—. Mem. Am. Counseling Assn., Met. Area Career/Life Planners Network, Internat. Assn. Career Mgmt. Profls., Stanford Assocs., Colonial Dames Am., Met. Club. Episcopalian. Avocations: tennis, travel, cooking. Office: Middleburg Group LLC PO Box 933 Middleburg VA 20118 0933

NEW, MARIA IANDOLO, pediatrician, educator; b. N.Y.C. d. Loris J. and Esther B. (Giglio) Iandolo; m. Bertrand L. New, 1949 (dec. 1990); children: Erica, Daniel, Antonia. BA, Cornell U., 1950; MD, U. Pa., 1954; degree in medicine (hon.), U. di Parma, Italy, 2000, U. degli Studi di Roma, Rome, 1999. Diplomate Am. Bd. Pediatrics. Med. intern Bellevue Hosp., N.Y.C., 1954-55; resident pediatrics N.Y. Hosp., 1955-57; fellow NIH, 1957-58, 61-64; practice medicine specializing in pediatrics N.Y.C., 1955—; mem. staff N.Y. Hosp., N.Y.C., dir. Pediatric Endocrine and Metabolism Clinic, 1964—, attending pediatrician, 1971-80; pediatrician-in-chief N.Y.-Presbyn. Hosp., 1980—2002, dir. pediatric endocrinology, 1998—2002. Asst. prof. dept. pediat. Joan and Sanford Weill Med. Coll. of Cornell U., N.Y.C., 1963-68, assoc. prof., 1968-71, prof., 1971—, Harold and Percy Uris prof. pediatric endocrinology, 1978—, prof., 1980—, chmn. dept. pediat., 1980-2002; program dir. Childrens Clin. Rsch. Ctr., 1996-2000; assoc. dir. Pediatric Clin. Rsch. Ctr., 1980-88; adj. faculty prof. Rockefeller U., 1981—; career scientist N.Y.C. Health Rsch. Coun., 1966-75; adj. attending pedatrician dept. pediat. Meml. Sloan-Kettering Cancer Ctr., 1979-93; cons. United Hosp., Port Chester, N.Y., 1977—, North Shore Univ. Hosp., 1982-97, dept. pediat. Cath. Med. Ctr. Bklyn. and Queens, N.Y., 1987—; vis. physician Rockefeller U. Hosp., N.Y.C., 1973-87; mem. endocrine study sect. NIH, 1977-80, Gen. Clin. Rsch. Ctrs. Adv. Com.; chmn. Divsn. Rsch. Resources Gen. Clin. Rsch. Ctrs. Com. NIH, 1987-88; bd. dirs. Robert Wood Johnson Clin. Scholars Program; mem. N.Y. State Gov.'s Task Force on Life and Law, 1985—; mem. NIH Reviewers Res.; mem. FDA endocrinology and metabolism drug adv. com., 1994—; panelist ACGME bd. appeals, 1994—; cons. Meml. Sloan-Kettering Cancer Ctr., 1993—, Meml. Hosp. for the Cancer and Allied Diseases, 1993—; hon. mem. pediat. dept. Blythedale Children's Hosp., Valhalla, N.Y., 1992—; mem. rsch. adv. com. Population Coun. Ctr. for Biomed. Rsch., 1991-97. Editor-in-chief Jour. Clin. Endocrinology and Metabolism, 1994-99; mem. editorial adv. coun. Jour. Endocrinol. Investigation, 1995—; mem. editorial bd. Jour. Women's Health, 1993; corr. editor Jour. Steroid Biochemistry, 1985; mem. adv. bd. pediatric anns., assoc. editor Metabolism. Trustee Irma T. Hirschl Trust. Recipient Mary Jane Kugel award Juvenile Diabetes Found., 1977, Katharine D. McCormick Disting. Lectureship, 1981, Robert H. Williams Disting. Leadership award, 1988, Albion O. Bernstein award Med. Soc. State N.Y., 1988, medal N.Y. Acad. Medicine, 1991, Disting. Grad. award U. Pa. Sch. Medicine, 1991, Optimate Recognition award Assn. Student-Profl. Italian-Ams., 1991, Outstanding Woman Scientist award N.Y. chpt. Am. Women in Sci., 1986, Maurice R. Greenberg Disting. Svc. award, 1994, Humanitarian award Juvenile Diabetes Found., 1994, Rhône Poulenc Rorer Clinical Investigator Lecture award, 1994, Dale medal Brit. Endocrine Soc., 1996, Merit award USPHS, NIHCHD, 1998, 11th Ann. award for excellence in clin. rsch. USPHS, NIH, 1998; grantee; named to Hall of HOnor, NICHD. Fellow AAAS, Italian Soc. Endocrinology (hon.); mem. NAS (sr. mem. Inst. Medicine), AAAS, APHA, Am. Soc. Human Genetics, Am. Acad. Pediatrics, Soc. for Pediatric Research, Harvey Soc., Endocrine Soc. (mem. coun. 1981-84, pres. 1991-92, Fred Conrad Koch award), Lawson Wilkins Pediatric Endocrine Soc. (pres. 1985-86), Am. Soc. Nephrology, Am. Soc. Pediatric Nephrology, Am. Pediatric Soc., Am. Fedn. Clin. Research, Am. Diabetes Assn., European Soc. Pediatric Endocrinology, Soc. for the Advancement of Women's Health Rsch. (basic sci. award 1996), Am. Coll. Clin. Pharmacology, Am. Clin. and Climatol. Assn., N.Y. Acad. Scis., Pan Am. Med. Assn., Assn. Am. Physicians, Am. Fertility Soc., U.S. Pharmacopeial Conv. (elected), Am. Acad. of Arts and Scis. (elected 1992), Alpha Omega Alpha. Office: N Y-Presbyn Hosp Dept Pediatrics 525 E 68th St New York NY 10021-4870

NEW, ROSETTA HOLBROCK, home economics educator, nutrition consultant; b. Hamilton, Ohio, Aug. 26, 1921; d. Edward F. and Mabel (Kohler) Holbrock; m. John Lorton New, Sept. 3, 1943; 1 child, John Lorton Jr. BS, Miami U., Oxford, Ohio, 1943; MA, U. No. Colo., 1971; PhD, Ohio State U., 1974; student Kantcentrum, Brugge, Belgium, 1992, Lesage Sch. Embroidery, Paris, 1995, Kent State U., 1998. Cert. tchr., Colo. Tchr. English and sci. Monahans (Tex.) HS, 1943-45; emergency war food asst. U.S. Dept. Agr., College Station, Tex., 1945-46; dept. chmn. home econs., adult edn. Hamilton (Ohio) Pub. Schs., 1946-47; tchr., dept. chmn. home econs. East HS, Denver, 1948-59, Thomas Jefferson HS, Denver, 1959-83; exec. bd. Denver Pub. Schs.; lectr. in field; exec. dir. Ctr. Nutrition Info. U.S. Office Edn. grantee Ohio State U., 1971-73. Mem. Cin. Art Mus., Nat. Trust for Historic Preservation. Mem. Am. Home Econs. Assn., Am. Vocat. Assn., Embroiders Guild Am., Hamilton Hist. Soc., Internat. Old Lacers, Ohio State U. Assn., Ohio State Home Econs. Alumni Assn., Fairfield (Ohio) Hist. Soc., Republican Club of Denver, Internat. Platform Assn., Phi Upsilon Omicron. Presbyterian. Lodges: Masons, Daughters of the Nile, Order of Eastern Star, Order White Shrine of Jerusalem. Home and Office: 615 Crescent Rd Hamilton OH 45013-3432

NEWBERG, DOROTHY BECK (MRS. WILLIAM C. NEWBERG), portrait artist; b. Detroit, May 30, 1919; d. Charles William and Mary (Labedz) Beck; student Detroit Conservatory Music, 1938; m. William C. Newberg, Nov. 3, 1939; children: Judith Bookwalter Bracken, Robert Charles, James William, William Charles. Trustee Detroit Adventure, 1967-71, originator A Drop in Bucket Program for artistically talented inner-city children. Cmty. outreach coord. Reno Police Dept.; bd. dirs. Bloomfield Art Assn., 1960-62, trustee 1965-67; bd. dirs. Your Heritage House, 1972-75, Franklin Wright Settlement, 1972-75, Meadowbrook Art Gallery, Oakland U., 1973-75, Sierra Nevada Mus. Art, 1978-80, NCCJ; mem. adv. bd. Gang Alternatives Partnership Adv. Bd. Recipient Heart of Gold award, 1969; Mich. vol. leadership award, 1969, Outstanding Vol. award City of Reno, 1989-90. Mem. Nevada Mus. Art, No. Nev. Black Cultural Awareness Soc. (bd. dirs.), Hispanic 500 C. of C. No. Nev. Roman Catholic. Home: PO Box 18527 Reno NV 89511-0527

NEWBERG, ESTHER, literary agent; d. Marion Newberg. MA, Wheaton Coll., Norton, Mass., 1963, hon. degree, 2003. Worked with Gov. Ella Grasso, Conn., Robert F. Kennedy, Bella Abzug, Morris Udall Presdl. Campaign, 1976; joined Internat. Creative Mgmt., N.Y.C., 1976, v.p., co-dir. lit. dept., 1988, sr. v.p., co-dir. lit. dept. Recipient Matrix Award, N.Y. Women in Comm., 1997. Office: Internat Creative Mgmt 40 W 57th St New York NY 10019*

NEWBERN WILLIAMS, MARY RUTH, minister; b. Cleve., Nov. 27, 1951; d. Philip Newbern and Mary Christian Horne; children from previous marriage: Joy Chandra, Philip Newbern, Stultz Robert III. BA, Baldwin-Wallace, 1973; MA, Princeton Seminary, 1986, MDiv, 1988; LHD (hon.), Mary Holmes Coll., 1999. Tchr. BOE, Cleve., 1978—79; sales asst. USSteel Corp., Cleve., 1979—81; rsch. assoc. Murtis Taylor Ctr., Cleve., 1981—85; assoc. pastor Westminster Presbyn. Ch., Pasadena, Calif., 1989—91; coord. spl. programs L.A. Urban League, 1993—96; pastor Redeemer Presbyn. Ch., L.A., 1994—96; assoc. higher edn. PCUSA-Gen. Assembly Coun., Louisville, 1996—99; assoc. exe. presbyter PCUSA-Presbytery of Sheppards and Lapsley, Birmingham, Ala., 2000—. Contbr. articles various profl. jours., chapters to books Women of Color Study Bible, 2002, Hunger by Bread for World, 2004. Mem.: Cmty. Presbyn. Ctr., Presbyn. Children's Home, First Light, Inc., So. Poverty Law Ctr. Achievements include appointed PCUSA Gen. Assembly delegate to Phana 2004 for world alliance of reformed churches. Avocations: writing, singing, travel, swimming, music. Office: Presbytery of Sheppards and Lapsley 3603 Lorna Rdg Dr Birmingham AL 35216 E-mail: marynw@pcusa.org.

NEWBURGE, IDELLE BLOCK, psychotherapist; b. Bklyn., [illegible] G. Newburge; children: Geri, Scott. AB magna cum laude, U. Miami, 1972, MEd, 1973. Lic. mental health counselor; nat. cert. counselor. Acting supr., lead counselor Office Vocat. Rehab., Miami, 1973-79, supr. mental health unit, 1985-87; vocat., edn. specialist Spectrum Programs, Inc., Miami, 1979-81, outpatient supr., 1981-85; psychotherapist Alan Jaffe, PhD and Assoc., Lauderhill, Fla., 1985-88, A.C.S. Pvt. Counseling, Plantation, Fla., 1988-91, KPK Counseling Svcs., Plantation, 1992—. Community adv. bd. Fellowship House, Miami, 1985-87; chmn., com. mem. Parent Resource Ctr., Miami, 1979-82. Active Nat. Mus. for Women in the Arts (charter), Washington, 1991—, U.S. Holocaust Meml. Mus. (charter), Washington, 1991—, Greenpeace, Humane Soc. Fellow Am. Bd. Cert. Managed Care Providers (master addiction counselor, cert. criminal justice specialist, bd. cert. expert in traumatic stress); mem. NASW, ACA, NOW, Am. Mental Health Counselors Assn., Am. Soc. Clin. Hypnosis, Mental Health Assn. Broward County (Listen to Children Programs cons., trainer 1988—), Mental Health Assn. Broward County (profl. mem., bd. dirs., treas., vice-chair, chair), South Fla. Soc. for Trauma Based Disorders, Fla. Soc. Clin. Hypnosis, Lauderhill C. of C. (charter), Plantation C. of C., Women's Forum (charter). Office: KPK Counseling Services 8030 Peters Rd # D106 Plantation FL 33324-4038

NEWCOMB, JOAN LESLIE, elementary school educator; b. Castro Valley, Calif., Jan. 6, 1960; d. Blanchard Dean and Frances Jeanette (Carpenter) N.; m. James Brian Cameron, July 2, 1983 (div. Apr. 21, 1995). BA in History, Calif. State U., Hayward, 1982. Cert. K-12 tchr., Calif. Tchr. John Reed Sch., Rohnert Park, Calif., 1987-90, Monte Vista Sch., Rohnert Park, Calif., 1990—; integrated tchr./project based coach Cotati-Rohnert Park Unified Sch. Dist., 1997—. Pres. Sch. Site Coun., Rohnert Park, 1990-92, 95-97; leadership team Monte Vista Sch., Rohnert Park, 1990-96; lead tchr. North Coast Beginning Tchr. Project, Santa Rosa, Calif., 1995-96; coord. 4/5 lang. arts task force Cotati-Rohnert Park Unified Sch. Dist., 1996-97; spkr. in field. Soprano United Ch. of Christ, Petaluma, Calif., 1995—, mem. bd. Christian edn., 1996—. Recipient Fulbright award, Japan, 1997, Edn. Found. grant Rohnert Park Edn. Found., 1989, 90, 97. Mem. NEA, NSF, Internat. Tech. Educator's Assn., New Eng. Hist. Geneal. Soc. Democrat. Avocations: travel, writing, reading, needlework, history. Office: Monte Vista Elem Sch 1400 Magnolia Ave Rohnert Park CA 94928-8129

NEWELL, BARBARA ANN, coatings company executive; b. Portland, Oreg., Mar. 20, 1945; d. John Wesley and Marion Josephine (Hill) Clausen; children: Shamaz, Hukam (dec.), Mardana. BA, Lindenwood Coll. for Women, 1968; MA, Portland State U., 1972; PhD, Summit U., 2000. Owner Shamaz Trading Co., Ukiah, Calif., 1974-77; mgr. small bus. dept. Ernst & Ernst, Portland, 1977-78; CFO All Heart Lumber Co., Ukiah, 1978-83; CFO, CEO Performance Coatings Inc., Ukiah, 1983—, chmn. bd. dirs., 1992—. Chmn. bd. dirs. Rural Visions Found.; treas. chmn. fin. com. Mendocino County Health Clinic, chmn. bd. dirs., 2001—; CEO, chmn. bd. dirs. Dusky Rose & Assoc., Botanics of Calif.; founder Potter Valley Cafe, 2000. Founder, chair Penofin Jazz Festival; chmn. bd. dirs. Mendocino Ballet Co.; bd. dirs. Potter Valley Youth and Cmty. Ctr. Mem. Nat. Paint and Coatings Assn., Golden State Paint and Coatings Assn., Ukiah C. of C. (mem. econ. devel. com. 1993-94), Women in Coatings (Leadership award 1994), Leadership Mendocino. Avocations: raising Arabian horses, reading, children, organic gardening, dance. Office: Penofin-Performance Coatings Inc PO Box 1569 Ukiah CA 95482-1569 E-mail: ceo@penofin.com.

NEWELL, CHARLDEAN, public administration educator; b. Ft. Worth, Oct. 14, 1939; d. Charles Thurlow and Mildren Dean (Looney) Newell. BA, U. North Tex., 1960, MA, 1962; PhD, U. Tex., 1968; cert., Harvard U., 1988. Instr. U. North Tex., Denton, 1965-68, asst. prof., 1968-72; assoc. prof., dir. Fedn. North Tex. Area Univs., Denton, Dallas, 1972-74; assoc. prof., assoc. v.p. acad. affairs U. North Tex., Denton, 1974-76, assoc. prof., chair dept. polit. sci., 1976-80, prof. polit. sci., 1980-92, assoc. v.p., spl. asst. to chancellor, 1982-92, regents prof. pub. adminstrn., 1992—2002, prof. emeritas, 2002—. Cons. Miss. Bd. Trustees State Instns. Higher Learning, Jackson, 1983—84, Ednl. Testing Svc., Princeton, NJ, 1980, Princeton, 82, Princeton, 85, Spear Down & Judin, Dallas, 1994—95, North Tex. Inst. Edn. Visual Arts, Denton, 1993—94; bd. regents Internat. City/County Mgmt. Assn., Washington, 1994—98, vol. credentialing adv. bd., 2002—. Author (with others): (book) City Executives: Leadership Roles, Work Characteristics and Time Management, 1989, Texas Politics, 2002, The Effective Local Govt. Mgr., 2004, Essentials of Tex. Politics, 2004; contbr. articles to profl. jours. Chmn. Denton Charter Rev. Com., 1978—79; mem. Denton CSC, 1989—97, chmn., 1992—97; active Denton Blue Ribbon Capital Improvements Com., 1995—96; mem. Denton Devel. Plan Com., 1996—97, Denton Pub. Utilities Bd., 1997—, chmn., 2002—; v.p. Denton Christian Pre-Sch. Bd., 2001—02, pres., 2002—; mem. Cit Council Ethics Com., 2004; mem. exec. coun. Episcopal Diocese Dallas, 1985—88. Recipient Elmer Staats Career Pub. Svc. award, Nat. Assn. Sch. Pub. Affairs Adminstrn., 1993. Fellow: Nat. Acad. Pub. Adminstrn.; mem.: Soc. for Indsl. and Applied Math., Internat. City/County Mgmt. Assn. (hon.), Am. Soc. for Pub. Adminstrn. (sect. chmn. 1982—83, mem. editl. bd. 1985—88, Donald C. Stone award), Pi Alpha Alpha (exec. coun. 1995—99), Pi Sigma Alpha (exec. coun. 1988—92). Democrat. Avocations: spectator sports, reading. Home: 2008 Tremont Cir Denton TX 76205-7408 Business E-Mail: cn0003@unt.edu.

NEWELL, ELLEN ELIZABETH, landscape manager; b. Montclair, N.J., July 13, 1955; d. Harry Edmond Newell and Elizabeth May Howes; m. Glenn Craig Doster, Dec. 4, 1976 (div. Aug. 13, 1983). BS cum laude, Utah State U., 1976. Landscape mgr. Utah State U., Logan, 1977—. Leader 4-H Horse Program, Richmond, Utah, 1984—99; mem. Richmond City Planning and Zoning Commn., 1994—97. Mem.: Profl. Grounds Mgmt. Soc. (far west dir. 1999—2002, cert. grounds mgr., treas. 2003, Grand award U. Landscape Maintenance 1994). Avocation: dressage. Office: Utah State U Facilities 6600 Old Main Hill Logan UT 84322

NEWELL, JANE ANN, retired elementary school educator; b. Joplin, Mo., May 23, 1938; d. Earnest and Ruth Madge (Turner) Kirkpatrick; m. Max G. Newell, Nov. 7, 1957(dec.); children: Terry, Tamera, Shari, David. BA in Edn., Wichita State U., 1975; MS in Edn., Pittsburg (Kans.) State U., 1981. Cert. elem. tchr., Kans., Mo. Elem. sch. tchr. Galena (Kans.) Unified Sch. Dist. 499, 1976—2003; ret., 2003. Piano and organ tchr. Organist Meth. Ch. Mem. NEA, Kans. Edn. Assn., Retired NEA Kans. Edn. Assn., Epsilon Sigma Alpha, Beta Sigma Phi. Democrat. Avocations: reading, travel, quilting, music.

NEWELL, KARIN BARNES, bank executive; b. Oklahoma City, Okla., June 24, 1951; d. Lynn Carl Barnes and Donna-Jean Berry; m. Michael Roy Jackson, Dec. 30, 1970 (div. Sept. 1988); children: Micah Roy Jackson, Aaron Lynn Jackson; m. Gary Lynn Newell, Nov. 26, 1994. A in Bus., Tarrant County Jr. Coll., Ft. Worth, 1983. Group One ins. lic.; Series 6 and 63 securities lic. Mktg. officer Bank of Arlington, Tex., 1984-90; event coord. March of Dimes, Ft. Worth, 1990-91; bank mgr. Bank One Tex., Arlington, 1991-96; personal banking officer Compass Bank, Dallas, 1996-97; br. mgr., v.p. Bank of Commerce, Southlake, Tex., 1997-99; v.p. Frost Nat. Bank, Southlake, 1999—2001; with Administaff, Dallas, 2002—. Mem. city coun. City of Bedford, Tex., 1998-2001, mayor pro-tem, 1999-2001; liaison Bedford Hotel/Motel Assn., 1999-2000, Regional Transp. Authority, 2000-2001, North Tex. Coun. Govts., 2000-2001; bd. dirs. Arts Coun. of N.E. Tarrant County, gala chair, 1998, Am. Heart Assn.,

Childrens Ctr. for Self Esteem, ARK Program, Am. Cancer Soc.; bd. sec. Supporters of the Shelter, 2003; mem. Leadership Colleyville, 2001. Mem. Bedford Citizens Police Acad. Alumni Assn., Bedford Citizens Fire Acad. Alumni Assn., N.E. Leadership Forum, Southlake C. of C. (chair Southlake bus. expo 1999), Hurst-Euless-Beford C. of C. (chair HEB econ. devel. found. 1999-2000), Grapevine C. of C., Irving (Tex.) C. of C., N.E. Tarrant County Women in Govt., Rotary, North Tex. USAFA Acad. Parents Club (publicity chair 2000-01, sgt. at arms 2001—02. pres. 2002-03). Avocations: volunteering, public speaking, travelling. Office: PO Box 211792 Bedford TX 76095-8792 E-mail: karinnewell@hotmail.com.

NEWGENT, REBECCA ANN, counselor, educator; b. Ohio; BA in Psychology, Kent (Ohio) State U., Kent, OH, 1986; MEd in Cmty. Counseling, Kent (Ohio) State U., 1993; PhD in Guidance and Counseling, U. Akron, 2001. Cert. family and divorce mediator. Case mgr. II/counselor trainee Cmty. Support Svcs., Inc., Akron, Ohio, 1988—93; counselor, family life edn. coord., vol. coord., divorce mediator Jewish Family Svc., Akron, 1993—95; counselor Cath. Svc. League, Akron, 1995—96; divorce mediator Domestic Rels. Divsn. Summit County Ct. Common Pleas, Akron, 1995—99; pvt. practice counselor, divorce mediator Akron Psychol. Assocs., 1995—98; counselor, sch.-based counselor, divorce mediator Cath. Social Svcs. of Summit County, Inc., Akron, 1997—99; emergency clinician Portage Path Behavioral Health-Psychiat. Emergency Svcs., Akron, 1997—2000; grad. asst. dept. counseling and spl. edn. U. Akron, 1998—2000, mem. adj. faculty dept. ednl. founds. and leadership, 2000, mem. ad hoc temporary grad. faculty, doctoral intern dept. counseling and spl. edn., 2000—01; asst. prof. counselor edn. U. Ark., Fayetteville, 2001—. Bd. advisors The Clinic for Child Study and Family Therapy U. Akron, 1998—2001. Mem. mental health trauma action team Summit County Red Cross Disaster Svcs., Akron, 1998—2000. Mem.: ACA, AAUP, S.W. Ednl. Rsch. Assn., Ark. Assn. Assessment in Counseling, Ark. Assn. Counselor Edn. and Supervision, Ark. Counseling Assn., Assn. for Advancement of Ednl. Rsch., Assn. Counselor Edn. and Supervision, Chi Sigma Iota (Outstanding Doctoral Student award 2001). Office: U Ark 236 Graduate Education Bldg Fayetteville AR 72701 Office Phone: 479-575-7311. Business E-Mail: rnewgent@uark.edu.

NEWHALL, EDITH ALLERTON, writer; b. Phila., Feb. 13, 1951; d. John Allerton and Dorothy (Todd) N.; m. David Walters, May 29, 1988. BA in Art History, Moore Coll., 1973; MFA, Art Inst. Chgo., 1979. Asst. editor Phila. Bulletin, 1974-76, Harry N. Abrams Publ., N.Y.C., 1979-81; writer N.Y. Mag., N.Y.C., 1981—.

NEWHOUSE, NANCY RILEY, newspaper editor; b. Bellingham, Wash. d. Fenwick Charles and Elizabeth (Grace) Riley; m. John Newhouse, Sept. 27, 1961 (div. 1970); m. Michael Iovenko, Mar. 6, 1983. BA, Vassar Coll., 1958. Sr. editor N.Y. Mag., N.Y.C., 1970-75, House & Garden Mag., N.Y.C., 1976; successively home editor, style editor and travel editor N.Y. Times, N.Y.C., 1976—. Editor: Hers: Through Women's Eyes, 1985; editor Hers column N.Y. Times, 1976-92; mem. adv. bd. Vassar Quar., Poughkeepsie, N.Y., 1985—. Decorated chevalier Nat. Order Merit; recipient Penney-Mo. Newspaper award U. Mo. Sch. Journalism, 1982-83. Mem. The Century Assn., Women's Forum N.Y. Office: NY Times Co 229 W 43rd St New York NY 10036-3959

NEWLAND, RUTH LAURA, small business owner; b. Ellensburg, Wash., June 4, 1949; d. George J. and Ruth Marjorie (Porter) N. BA, Cen. Wash. State Coll., 1970, MEd, 1972; EdS, Vanderbilt U., 1973; PhD, Columbia Pacific U., 1981. Tchr. Union Gap (Wash.) Sch., 1970-71; owner Newland Ranch Gravel Co., Yakima, Wash., 1998; ptnr. Arnold Artificial Limb, Yakima, 1981-86, owner, pres. Yakima and Richland, Wash., 1986—. Owner Newland Ranch, Yakima, 1969—. Contbg. mem. Nat. Dem. Com., Irish Nat. Caucus Found.; mem. Pub. Citizen, We The People, Nat. Humane Edn. Soc.; charter mem. Nat. Mus. Am. Indian. George Washington scholar Masons, Yakima, 1967. Mem. NAFE, NOW, Am. Orthotic and Prosthetic Assn., Internat. Platform Assn., Nat. Antivisection Soc. (life), Vanderbilt U. Alumni Assn., Peabody Coll. Alumni Assn., Columbia Pacific U. Alumni Assn., World Wildlife Fund, Nat. Audubon Soc., Greenpeace, Mus. Fine Arts, Humane Soc. U.S., Wilderness Soc., Nature Conservancy, People for Ethical Treatment of Animals, Amnesty Internat., The Windstar Found., Rodale Inst., Sierra Club (life), Emily's List. Democrat. Avocations: reading, gardening, sewing, handcrafts, people. Home: 2004 Riverside Rd Yakima WA 98901-8540 Office: Arnold Artificial Limb 9 S 12th Ave Yakima WA 98902-3106

NEWLIN, YVONNE ANN, adult education educator; b. Robinson, Illinois, Mar. 2, 1950; d. Leo Jr. and Leola Mae (Gurley) Guyer; m. J. Douglas Newlin, Jan. 15, 1994; children: Rodney C., Jodi Y., Jesse M., William D. AS, Lincoln Trail Cmty. Coll., 1987; MusB, Ea. Ill. U., Charleston, Ill., 1989, MA, 1990. Music tchr. Lincoln Trail Cmty. Coll., Robinson, Ill., 1991—, performing arts coord., 1999—. Chair mem. performing arts Crawford County Arts, Robinson, Ill., 1995—97. Mem.: Music Educators Nat. Conf., Ill. Music Educators Assn., Humanities and Fine Arts panel, Ill Bd. Higher Edn., Crawford County Arts, Internat. Assn. Jazz Educators. Protestant. Avocations: family, ch., golf. Office: Lincoln Trail Cmty Coll 11220 State Hwy 1 Robinson IL 62454-5707

NEWMAN, ANDREA FISCHER, air transportation executive; AB, U. Mich., 1979; JD, George Washington U., 1983. Sr. v.p. govt. affairs Northwest Airlines, Detroit. Bd. regents U. Mich., Ann Arbor, 1994—; vice chmn. George W. Bush for Pres. Campaign, co-chmn. fin. com., 2000; bd. dirs. Mich. Econ. Devel. Corp. Found., Mich. Thanskgiving Day Parade Found., Isiah Thomas Found. Mem.: Detroit Econ. Club (v.p.). Office: Northwest Airlines Detroit Met Airport North Terminal Mezzanine Level Detroit MI 48242

NEWMAN, BARBARA MILLER, psychologist, educator; b. Chgo., Sept. 6, 1944; d. Irving George and Florence (Levy) Miller; m. Philip r. Newman, June 12, 1966; children: Samuel Asher, Abraham Levy, Rachel Florence. Student, Bryn Mawr Coll.; AB with honors in Psychology, U. Mich., 1966, PhD in Devel. Psychology, 1971. Undergrad. research asst. in psychology U. Mich., 1963-64, research asst. in psychology, 1964-69, teaching fellow, 1965-71, asst. project dir. Inst. for Social Research, 1971-72, univ. lectr. in psychology and research assoc., 1971-72; asst. prof. psychology Russell Sage Coll., 1972-76, assoc. prof., 1977-78; assoc. prof. and chair dept. family rels. and human devel. Ohio State U., 1978-83, prof. and chair, 1983-86, assoc. provost for faculty recruitment and devel., 1987-92, prof., 1992-2000; prof. and chair dept. human devel. and family studies U. R.I., 2000—. Author: Development Through Life, 1975, 8th edit., 2003; author: (with P. Newman) Living: The Process of Adjustment, 1981, Understanding Adulthood, 1983; author: Adolescent Development, 1986, When Kids Go to College, 1992, Childhood and Adolescence, 1997; author: (with P. Newman, L. Landry-Meyer and B. Lohman) Life Span Development: A Case Book, 2003; contbr. articles to profl. jours. Mem. AAAS, APA, Soc. Rsch. in Child Devel., Am. Psychol. Soc., Nat. Coun. Family Rels., Groves Conf. on Marriage and Family, Soc. for Rsch. on Adolescence. Office: U RI Human Devel and Family Studies 112 Transition Ctr Kingston RI 02881 E-mail: bnewman@uri.edu.

NEWMAN, CONSTANCE BERRY, federal agency administrator; b. Chgo., July 8, 1935; d. Joseph Alonzo and Ernestine (Siggers) B.; m. Theodore Roosevelt Newman, July 25, 1959 (div. 1980). AB, Bates Coll., 1956; BSL, U. Minn., 1959; JD (hon.), Bates Coll., 1972, Amherst Coll., 1980; LHD (hon.), Central State U., 1991. Dir. VISTA, Washington, 1971-73; commr. Consumer Product Safety Commn., Washington, 1973-76; asst. sec. U.S. HUD, Washington, 1976-77; pres. The Newman & Hermanson Co., Washington, 1977-82; cons. Govt. of Lesotho, 1987-88; dir. nat. voter coalition Bush-Quayle '88, Washington, 1988; dir. Office Pers. Mgmt., Washington, 1989-92; under sec. Smithsonian Instn., Washington, 1992-2000; vice chair D.C. Fin. Responsiblity and Mgmt. Assistance Authority, 1995—; ptnr. Upstart Ptnrs., 2000—; asst. adminr. bur. for africa USAID, Washington, 2001—. Mem. adj. faculty John F. Kennedy Sch. Govt., Harvard U., Cambridge, Mass., 1979-82. Contbr. articles to profl. jours. Mem. Adminstrn. Conf. U.S., Washington, 1973-76, 1989—; commr. M.L. King Fed. Holiday Commn., Washington, 1989; chmn. Def. Adv. Com. on Women in the Svcs., Washington, 1985-86; trustee Community Coll. Balt., 1985-89; adv. to chmn. 1988 Rep. Nat. Conv., New Orleans, 1988; bd. overseers Morehouse Coll. Sch. Medicine, Atlanta, 1976-77; bd. dirs. Brookings Instn., Aspen Inst., Coun. for Excellence in Govt. Recipient Pub. Svc. award Ohio State U., 1991. Mem. NAACP, Exec. Women in Govt. (founding mem.). Republican. Avocation: photography. Office: US-AID Bur for Africa RRB 1300 Pennsylvania Ave NW Washington DC 20523-4600 E-mail: cnewman@usaid.gov.

NEWMAN, DIANA S. development consultant; b. Toledo, June 15, 1943; d. Fred Andrew and Thelma Elizabeth (Hewitt) Smith; m. Dennis Ryan Newman, Feb. 15, 1964; children: Barbara Lynn Newman LaBine, John Ryan, Elizabeth Anne. Student, Oberlin Coll., 1961-64. Asst. treas. Marble Cliff Quarries Co., 1964-68; cmty. vol., 1968-83; dir. Ohio Hist. Found., Columbus, 1983-90; v.p. advancement The Columbus (Ohio) Found., 1990-95; pres. Philanthropic Resource Group, Columbus, 1995—. Author: Opening Doors: Pathways to Diverse Donors, 2002 (AFP/Skystone Ryan prize for rsch., 2003). Bd. dirs. Leader Inst., Inc., 2001-04; mem. governing bd. First Cmty. Ch., 1983-88, chair, 1987-88; bd. dirs. LWV Ctrl. Ohio, 1968-72, Ohio Mus. Assn., 1985-90, Crittenton Family Svcs., Columbus, 1992-95; founder Franklin County Com. on Criminal Justice, Columbus, 1972; pres. Jr. League Columbus, 1980-81. Recipient Skystone Ryan Prize, AFP, 2003, Ryan Prize for Rsch. on Funraising and Philanthropy, AFP, Skystone, 2003. Mem. Assn. Fundraising Profls. (bd. dirs. Ctrl. Ohio chpt. 1985-88, 2004-, nat. rsch. coun. 2003—), Ctrl. Ohio Planned Giving Coun. (bd. dirs. 1990-2001, pres. 1998), Columbus Female Benevolent Soc. (bd. dirs. 1984—). Home: 1944 Chatfield Rd Columbus OH 43221-3702 Office: Philanthropic Resource Group 1944 Chatfield Rd Columbus OH 43221-3702

NEWMAN, FRANCINE M. healthcare company executive; BA, St. Lawrence U. With group ins. ops. CIGNA Co., 1970-73, with human res., mgmt. svcs., 1973-81, dir. underwriting for life and health reinsurance ops., 1981-82; 2d v.p. CIGNA Reinsurance, 1982-84, pres., 1984—. Bd. dirs. Lyme Borelleosis Found. Mem. Greater Hartford C. of C. Edn. Task Force on Strategic Planning (mem. women execs. subcom.). Named among America's Top 50 Women Executives Business Week Magazine, 1987; co-recipient Partners in Leadership award Soc. of Info. Mgmt. Mem. Home Office Life Underwriters Assn. (exec. com.), Health Ins. Assn. Am. (group ins. com.), Am. Coun. Life Ins. (reinsurance subcom.). Office: CIGNA Corp CIGNA Reinsurance 1 Liberty Pl Philadelphia PA 19192-0001

NEWMAN, GERALDINE ANNE, advertising executive, inventor; b. Boston, Apr. 01; d. Joseph M. and Clara (Bistry) N. BS, UCLA; postgrad., Alliance Francaise, Paris, Los Angeles Sch. Fine Arts, NYU. Writer Tinker Dodge and Delano, N.Y.C., 1970-72, Ketchum Advt., N.Y.C., 1972-75, Advt. to Women, N.Y.C., 1975-78; v.p., creative supr. Young and Rubicam, N.Y.C., 1978-83; v.p., assoc. creative dir. Backer Spielvogel Bates Worldwide Internat. Div., N.Y.C., 1983-90; pres. Geraldine Newman Comm., Inc., N.Y.C., 1990—. County committeewoman Dem. Party, N.Y.C., 1972; advt. adviser Youth at Risk, Breakthrough Found., Food Bank, Food for All, Gifts that Give Back. Featured in Adweek mag., 1986; winner Andy award 1975, 78, 82, 84, Clio award 1982, ERA award, 1998, Astrid award Mercomm Internat., 2002, numerous others. Mem.: Ad Club N.Y., Electronic Retailing Assn., Ad-net (bd. dirs. 1984—89, creative dir. 1986—89, Pres.'s award 1988). Avocations: travel, painting. Home and Office: 315 E 72nd St New York NY 10021-4625

NEWMAN, JOAN MESKIEL, lawyer; b. Youngstown, Ohio, Dec. 12, 1947; d. John F. and Rosemary (Scarmuzzi) Meskiel; children: Anne R., Elyse S. BA in Polit. Sci., Case-Western Reserve U., 1969; JD, Washington U., St. Louis, 1972, LLM in Taxation, 1973. Bar: Mo. 1972. Assoc. Lewis & Rice, St. Louis, 1973-80, ptnr., 1981-90, Thompson Coburn, St. Louis, 1990—. Adj. prof. law Washington U. Sch. Law, St. Louis, 1975-92; past pres. St. Louis chpt., mem. Midwest Pension Conf. Mem. nat. coun. Washington U. Sch. Law, 1988—91; chmn. bd. dir. Great St. Louis coun. Girl Scouts USA, 1975—92, officer, 1978—92; mem. cmty. wide youth svcs. panel United Way Greater St. Louis, 1992—96; fin. futures task force Kiwanis Camp Wyman, 1992—93; chmn. staff blue ribbon fin. com. Sch. Dist., Clayton, 1986—87; vol. Women's Self Help Ctr.; bd. dirs. Parents as Teachers, 2001—; bd. dir., exec. com. Girl Scouts USA, 1993—99, nat. treas., 1996—99; bd. dirs. Met. Employment and Rehab. Svcs., 1980—2001, chmn. bd. dir., 1994—96; bd. dirs. Jewish Ctr. Aged, 1990—92, bd. dir., 1999—2001, Jewish Fedn. St. Louis, 1991—96, City Mus. 1998—2001, Parents as Tchrs., 2000—; chmn. bd. dir. Women of Achievement, 1993—96; bd. dir. United Way Greater St. Louis, 2000—, Oasis, 1999—2001; bd. dirs. MERS/Goodwill Industries, 2001—, Walker Scottish Rite Ctr., 2002—. Named Woman of Achievement St. Louis, 1991. Mem. Mo. Bar Assn. (staff pension and benefits com. 1991—), Bar Met. St. Louis (past chmn. taxation sect.), St. Louis Forum, Order of Coif (hon.). Office: Thompson Coburn LLP Ste 3300 One US Bank Plz Saint Louis MO 63101-1643

NEWMAN, JUDITH YORK, real estate developer, curator; b. N.Y., Aug. 11, 1934; d. Joseph and Jean (Goldman) York; m. Richard Newman, Sept. 20, 1958 (div. Mar. 1979); children: Alexander, Roberta Newman-Hernandez. BArch, Cornell Univ., Ithaca, N.Y., 1957. Registered architect, NY, 1962. Draftsperson, N.Y., 1957—60; assoc. editor of arch. Living Mag./House and Garden, N.Y., 1960—68; prin. Newman & Newman, N.Y., 1967—72, Judith York Newman, Arch., N.Y., 1972—83; asst. prof. Pratt Inst./NYU continuing Edn., N.Y., 1964—76; dir. founder Spaced: Gallery of Arch., N.Y., 1975—; real estate devel. various pvt., N.Y., 1962—. Adv. coun. friends Cornell Univ. Arch., Ithaca, NY, 1990—; lectr. in field, 1991—. Designs featured in profl. pub. Recipient citation for residence westside urban renewal, NYC Planning Bd., 1972, Record House Archtl. Record, 1975, spl. citation, N.Y. Chpt. Am. Inst. of Arch., 1982. Avocation: sports cars. Home: 39 W 67th St New York NY 10023

NEWMAN, MALANE L. digital designer, cartoonist, illustrator, computer graphics designer, educator, small business owner; b. San Diego, Aug. 6, 1955; d. Charles L. and Marlene A. (Walker) Newman. Cert., Art Instrn. Schs., Mpls., 1972; BA, U.S. Internat. U., San Diego, 1975. Graphic artist La Jolla (Calif.) Advt., 1972; lead illustrator PS Mag., Perspective Corp., San Diego, 1983; art dir. CBT Courseware, Inc., San Diego, 1986; owner, creator animated cards Imagination Enterprises, San Diego, 1986; creative dir., lead designer websites, WBT, electronic design Accenture Corp., 1989; owner Malane Newman Designs, Ramona, Calif., 2001; tchr. computer applications, computer art and design, multimedia Ramona H.S., 2004. Guest lectr. cartooning, self pub., copyright, mail order; cons. corp. graphics, bus. presentations. Mem.: So. Calif. Cartoonist Soc., Nat. Computer Graphics Assn., Nat. Cartoon Soc. Home: 16765 Daza Dr Ramona CA 92065-4613 E-mail: malanenewman@cox.net.

NEWMAN, MARJORIE YOSPIN, psychiatrist; b. N.Y.C., July 8, 1945; d. Toby and Audrey (Kreinik) Yospin; children: Eric, David. Student, Smith Coll., 1963-64; AB, Barnard Coll./Columbia U., 1967; MD, Med. Coll. Pa., 1971. Diplomate Am. Bd. Psychiatry and Neurology. Psychiatry intern, resident Albert Einstein Coll. Medicine, N.Y.C., 1971-75; asst. prof. psychiatry U. Tex. Health Sci. Ctr., San Antonio, 1975-77, UCLA Sch. Medicine, 1977-80; dir. residency tng. in psychiatry Harbor-UCLA Med. Ctr., 1977-79; asst. clin. prof. psychiatry UCLA Sch. Medicine, 1980—; pvt. practice Pasadena, Calif., 1983—. Mem. admissions com. UCLA Med. Sch., 1995—. NSF grantee, London, Eng., 1969; Am. Field Svc. Internat. scholar, Argentina, 63. Fellow L.A. Acad. Medicine (bd. govs. 2000, sec. 2002—, v.p., pres.-elect 2003—); mem. Am. Psychiat. Assn., So. Calif. Psychiat. Soc. (regional councillor 2001—), Smith Coll. Alumna Assn., Barnard Coll. Alumna Assn., Columbia U. Alumni Assn., Ivy League Assn. So. Calif. Avocations: travel, music, art, swimming, cycling. Office: Cotton Med Ctr South 50 Alessandro Pl Ste 340 Pasadena CA 91105-3149

NEWMAN, MIRIAM See **DEHORITY, MIRIAM**

NEWMAN, NANCY, publishing executive; Sr. v.p. & publ. dir. Ziff Davis Pub. Co., N.Y.C. Office: Ziff Davis Pub Co 28 E 28th St Fl 12 New York NY 10016-7930

NEWMAN, NANCY MARILYN, ophthalmologist, educator; b. San Francisco, Mar. 16, 1941; BA in Psychology magna cum laude, Stanford U., 1962, MD, 1967. Diplomate Am. Bd. Ophthalmology. NIH trainee neurophysiology Inst. Visual Scis., San Francisco, 1964-65; clin. clk. Nat. Hosp. for Nervous and Mental Disease, London, 1966-67; intern Mount Auburn Hosp., Cambridge, Mass., 1967-68; NIH trainee neuro-ophthalmology, from jr. asst. resident to sr. asst. resident to assoc. resident dept. ophthalmology sch. medicine Washington U., St. Louis, 1968-71; NIH spl. fellow in neuro-ophthalmology depts. ophthalmology and neurol. surgery sch. medicine U. Calif., San Francisco, 1971-72, clin. asst. prof. ophthalmology sch. medicine, 1972; asst. prof., chief divsn. neuro-ophthalmology Pacific Med. Ctr., San Francisco, 1972-73, assoc. prof., chief, 1973-88; physician, cons. dept. neurology sch. medicine U. Calif., VA Med. Ctr., Martinez, Calif., 1978—. Prof. dept. spl. edn. Calif. State U., San Francisco, 1974-79; vis. prof. Centre Nat. D'Ophtalmologie des Quinze-Vingts, Paris, 1980; clin. assoc. prof. sch. optometry U. Calif., Berkeley, 1990—; bd. dirs., adv. bd. Frank B. Walsh Soc., 1974-91, Rose Resnick Ctr. for the Blind and Handicapped, 1988-92, Fifer St. Fitness, Larkspur, 1990-92; Internat. Soc. for Orbital Disorders, 1983—, North Calif. Soc. Prevention of Blindness, 1978-88, North African Ctr. for Sight, Tunis, Tunisia, 1988—; pres., CEO Minerva Medica; cons. in field. Author: Eye Movement Disorders; Neuro-ophthalmology: A Practical Text, 1992; mem. editoral bd. Jour. of Clin. Neuro-ophthalmology, Am. Jour. Opthalmology, 1980-92, Soc. Francaise d'Ophtalmogie, Ophthalmology Practice, 1993—; contbr. numerous articles to profl. jours. Recipient NSPI award Self Instrnl. Materials Ophthalmology, Merit award Internat. Eye Found., fellow 1971; Smith-Kettlewell Inst. Vis. Scis. fellow, 1971-72. Mem. AMA (leader Calif. del. continuing med. edn. 1982, 83), San Francisco Med. Soc., Calif. Med. Assn. (sub com. med. policy coms. 1984—, chair com. on accreditation continuing med. edn. 1981-88, chair quality care rev. commn. 1984), Assn. for Rsch. in Vision and Ophthalmology, Pan Am. Assn. of Ophthalmology, Soc. of Heed Fellows, Pacific Coast Oto-Ophthalmology Soc., Lane Medical Soc. (v.p. 1975-76), Internat. Soc. of Neuro-Ophthalmology (founder), Cordes Soc., Am. Soc. Ophthalmic Ultrasound (charter), Orbital Soc. (founder), West Bay Health Systems Agy., Oxford Opthalmology Soc., Pacific Physician Assocs., Soc. Francaise D'Ophtalmologie (mem. editorial bd. jour.). Home: 819 Spring Dr Mill Valley CA 94941-3924

NEWMAN, NELLIE YVONNIE, nurse; b. St. Ann's Bay, Jamaica, May 31, 1934; came to U.S., 1969; d. William and Violet Stevens; m. Delmar Warrington, Mar. 29, 1965 (div. 1982); 1 child, Delmarie Avonnie Newman Butler. Diploma in nursing, Tunbridge Wells Sch. Nursing, Kent, England, 1964; degree in midwifery, Victoria Jubilee Hosp., Kingston, Jamaica, 1967; degree in pub. health, West Indies Sch. Pub. Health, Kingston, Jamaica, 1968. Staff nurse Port Maria Hosp., St. Mary, Jamaica, 1964-66, Linstead Hosp., St. Mary, Jamaica, 1966-67; pub. health field nurse St. Mary, 1967-68; staff nurse Mt. Sinai Hosp., Cleve., 1969-70; pvt. duty nurse Catalanos Nurses Registry, Hialeah, Fla., 1970-93; home health field nurse Best Care, Miami, 1991-97. Staff nurse Hospice Care, Miami, 1991. Democrat. Avocations: gardening, reading, crocheting, piano playing, travel. Home: 16857 Murcott Blvd Loxahatchee FL 33470-2760

NEWMAN, PAULINE, federal judge; b. N.Y.C., N.Y., June 20, 1927; d. Maxwell Henry and Rosella Newman. BA, Vassar Coll., 1947; MA, Columbia U., 1948; PhD, Yale U., 1952; LLB, NYU, 1958. Bar: N.Y. 1958, U.S. Supreme Ct. 1972, U.S. Ct. Customs and Patent Appeals 1978, Pa. 1979, U.S. Ct. Appeals (3d cir.) 1981, U.S. Ct. Appeals (fed. cir.) 1982. Research chemist Am. Cyanamid Co., Bound Brook, NJ, 1951—54; mem. patent staff FMC Corp., N.Y.C., 1954—75, Phila., 1975—84, dir. dept. patent and licensing, 1969—84; judge U.S. Ct. Appeals (fed. cir.), Washington, 1984—; Disting. prof. George Mason Law Sch., 1995—. Program specialist Dept. Natural Scis. UNESCO, Paris, 1961—62; mem. State Dept. Adv. Com. on Internat. Indsl. Property, 1974—84; lectr. in field. Contbr. articles to profl. jours. Trustee Phila. Coll. Pharmacy and Sci., 1983—84; bd. dirs. Med. Coll. Pa., 1975—84, Midgard Found., 1973—84. Mem.: ABA (coun. sect. patent trademark and copyright 1983—84), Coun. Fgn. Rels., U.S. Trademark Assn. (bd. dirs. 1975—79, v.p. 1978—79), Pacific Indsl. Property Assn. (pres. 1979—80), Am. Inst. Chemists (bd. dirs. 1960—66, 1970—76), Am. Chem. Soc. (bd. dirs. 1972—81), Am. Patent Law Assn. (bd. dirs. 1981—84), Yale Club, Vassar Club, Cosmos Club. Office: US Ct Appeals Nat Cts Bldg 717 Madison Pl Washington DC 20439-0002*

NEWMAN, RACHEL, editor; b. Malden, Mass., May 1, 1938; d. Maurice and Edythe Brenda (Tichell) Newman; m. Herbert Bleiweiss, Apr. 6, 1973 (div. Apr. 1989); m. Michael Lucas, Feb. 24, 2004. BA, Pa. State U., 1960; cert., N.Y. Sch. Interior Design, 1963. Accessories editor Women's Wear Daily, N.Y.C., 1964—65; designer, publicist Grandoe Glove Corp., N.Y.C., 1965—67; assoc. editor McCall's Sportswear and Dress Merchandiser mag., N.Y.C., 1967; mng. editor McCall's You-Do-It Home Decorating, 1968—70, Ladies Home Jour. Needle and Craft mag., N.Y.C., 1970—72; editor-in-chief Am. Home Crafts mag., N.Y.C., 1972—77; fashion dir. Good Housekeeping mag., N.Y.C., 1977—78, home bldg. and decorating dir., 1978—82; editor-in-chief Country Living mag., N.Y.C., 1978—98; founding editor Country Cooking mag., 1985—90, Dream Homes mag., 1989—2000, Country Kitchens mag., 1990—93, Country Living Gardener Mag., 1993—2000, Healthy Living mag., 1996—2000. Bd. dirs. Mothers and Others for a Livable Planet. Named Disting. Alumna, Pa. State U., 1988; recipient Cir. of Excellence award, Internat. Furnishings and Design Assn., 1992, YMCA Hall of Fame, 1992; Pa. State U. Alumni fellow, 1986. Mem.: Am. Soc. Mag. Editors, Am. Soc. Interior Designers, Nat. Home Fashions League, N.Y. Fashion Group. E-mail: Rachelsfree@aol.com.

NEWMAN, REBECCA K. principal; BA, Mich. State U., 1968; MEd, U. Kans., 1975, EdD, 1978. Cert. spl. edn. grades K-12 Md., secondary prin. and supr. Md., supt. Md., elem. edn. K-8 Mich., spl. edn. K-12 Mich., English 9-12 Mich., social studies 7-9 Mich. Head tchr. adolescent unit Lafayette Clinic, Detroit, 1968—70; asst. prin., tchr. Island View Adolescent Ctr., Detroit, 1970—71; head tchr. children's unit Lafayette Clinic, Detroit, 1971—73; ednl. dir. Mid-Continent Psychiat. Hosp., Olathe, Kans., 1973—75; program mgr. Severe Personal Adjustment Program, Kansas City, Kans., 1975—78; asst. prin. Rock Terrace H.S. Montgomery County Pub. Schs., 1978—80, prin. Regional Inst. for Children and Adolescents, 1980—86, prin. Mark Twain Mid.-Sr. H.S., 1986—90, supr. secondary instrn. Area 3, 1990—91, acting asst. prin. Wootton H.S., 1991—92, prin. Paint Branch H.S., 1992—95, prin. Wootton H.S., 1995—. Mem. Corp. Partnerships Task Force, Montgomery County, 1996; participant prin.'s view Montgomery County Pub. Schs. Pub. TV, 1989; mem. adv. bd. multidisciplinary master's degree tng. program for tchrs. of the behaviorally disordered/emotionally disturbed U. Md., College Park, 1985—86. Mem. editl. bd.: Focus on Autistic Behavior, 1990—91. Mem.: Montgomery County Assn. Adminstrv. and Supr. Pers. (mem. negotiations team 1993—96).

NEWMAN, ROBIN GORMAN, communications executive, writer; b. Bklyn., Aug. 11, 1960; d. Aaron and Sylvia Gorman; m. Marc Newman, Sept. 13, 1992; 1 child, Seth Loren. BS in Econs., Hofstra U., Hempstead, N.Y., 1981; MBA in Mktg., St. John's U., Jamaica, N.Y., 1987. Package devel. assoc. Warner Cosmetics, N.Y.C., NY, 1981—82; mktg. comm. specialist Eastman Kodak Co., N.Y.C., 1982—86; account supr. Delibes Comm., N.Y.C., 1986—88; v.p. KCSA Pub. Rels., N.Y.C., 1988—94; pres. RGN Comm., Great Neck, NY, 1994—. Creator www.LoveCoach.com, 1999—. Author: How to Meet a Mensch in New York, 1996; contbr. articles to New York mag. Mem.: Am. Soc. Journalists and Authors, Ind. Bus. Women's Cir. (founder, exec. dir. 1999—). Avocations: tennis, travel, theater, crafts. Office Phone: 516-773-0911.

NEWMAN, SANDRA SCHULTZ, state supreme court justice; BS, Drexel U., 1959; MA, Temple U., 1969; JD, Villanova U., 1972; D (hon.) (hon.), Gannon U., 1996, Widener U., 1996, Clarion U., 2000. Bar: Pa., U.S. Dist. Ct. (ea. dist.) Pa., U.S. Ct. Appeals (3d cir.), U.S. Supreme Ct. Asst. dist. atty. Montgomery County, Pa.; pvt. practice; judge Commonwealth Ct. of Pa., 1993—95; justice Supreme Ct. of Pa., 1995—. Past chair bd. consultors Villanova U. Law Sch.; mem. jud. coun. Supreme Ct. of Pa., liaison to the 3rd cir. task force on mgmt. of death penalty litigation, liaison to Pa. lawyers fund for client security bd., liaison to domestic rels. procedural rules com.; liaison Pa. Bar Inst.; jud. work group HHS; mem. adv. com. Nat. Ctr. for State Cts., Am. Law Inst.; mem. Drexel U. Coll. Bus. and Adminstrn.; lectr. and spkr. in field. Author: Alimony, Child Support and Counsel Fees, 1988; contbr. articles to profl. jours. Named named Disting. Daughter of Pa.; recipient Phila. award for Super Achiever, Pediatric Juvenile Colitis Found. Jefferson Med. Coll. and Hosp, 1979, award for Dedicated Leadership and Outstanding Contbns. to the Cmty. and Law Employment, Drexel 100 award, Police Chiefs Assn. of Southeastern Pa., 1993, Medallion of Achievement award, Villanova U., 1993, Susan B. Anthony award, Women's Bar Assn. Western Pa., 1996, award, Justinian Soc., 1996, Tau Epsilon Law Soc., 1996, Legion of Honor Gold Medallion award, Chapel of Four Chaplain, 1997, honored by, Women of Greater Phila., 1996. Fellow: Pa. Bar Found., Am. Bar Found.; mem.: Montgomery Bar Assn., Nat. Assn. Women Judges, Am. Law Inst. Office: Supreme Ct Pa Ste 400 100 Four Falls Corporate Ctr West Conshohocken PA 19428-2950*

NEWMAN, SHERRYL A. HOBBS, secretary of the district; BA in Chemistry, Rutgers Coll.-Rutgers Univ., New Brunswick, NJ, 1986; BA in Economics, Rutgers Coll.-Rutgers Univ., 1986; MBA in Management, Lubin Graduate Sch. of Bus. Pace Univ., White Plains, NY, 1992. Exec. sec.-Tax Operation Bureau NYC-Dept. of Finance, 1986, special projects coordinator-Program Devel. Divsn., 1986—87, special property coordinator-Program Devel. Divsn., 1986—87, asst. to dir.-Taxpayer Assistance Divsn., 1987—89, unit mgr.-Taxpayer Corr., 1989—90, unit mgr.-Real Estate Tax Assistance, 1990—92, acting dep. dir.-Taxpayer Assistance Divsn., 1992—93, city collector-Property Bureau, 1993—96; dir. Customer Svc. Adminstrn.-Office of Tax and Revenue, DC, 1997—99, Citywide Customer Svc. Adminstrn.-Office of the City Adminstr., DC, 1999, Dept. of Motor Vehicles, DC, 1999—2003; sec. of dist. DC Govt., 2003—. Office: John A Wilson Bldg 1350 Pennsylvania Ave NW Rm 419 Washington DC 20004

NEWMAN, STACEY CLARFIELD, artist, curator; b. N.Y.C., July 21, 1956; d. Wallace J. Clarfield and Elinor (Kandel) Clarfield-Toberoff; m. Fredric Alan Newman, Nov. 27, 1983; children: Benjamin Clarfield, Marissa Paige, Alexandra Brooke. Student, Franklin & Marshall, 1974-76; BS in Labor Rels. and Mgmt., U. Bridgeport, 1978. Dir. ops. Nat. Rec. and Video Studios, N.Y.C., 1978-80; dir. tech. ops. VCA/Teletronics, N.Y.C., 1980-82, cons., client rep./MTV, 1981-83, exec. prodr., 1982-85; artist, art curator Stacey Clarfield Newman Studios, Scarsdale, N.Y., 1986—; mem. faculty Young at Art, Scarsdale Art Enrichment Ctr., 2002—; dir. tech ops. prodr. VCA/Teletronics, N.Y.C. Merchandise dir. Tahari Fashions, N.Y.C., 1985-86; artist mem., jury com. You Gotta Have Art program White Plains Hosp. Ctr., 1990-92; art tchr. collage Scarsdale (N.Y.) Adult Edn. Program, 1993-95; artist in residence Scarsdale Elem. Schs., 1995-97; art cons., curator Manhattan Transfer, Inc., N.Y.C., 1997-2000; faculty mem. Young at Art Enrichment Sch., Scarsdale, 2002-03; artist in residence Scarsdale Elem. Sch., 1995-2003; juror The Figure & Form, Edward Hopper House Mus., N.Y., 2004 One-person shows include Quogue (N.Y.) Gallery, 1986, Piermont (N.Y.) Fine Arts Gallery, 1997-98, Manhattan Transfer, Inc., 1997, Piermont Fine Arts Gallery, 2001, J&W Gallery, New Hope, Pa., 1999, Studio 4 West, 1999, 93 South Gallery, 2000, Adele Greenberg Salon, Cambridge, Mass., 2000, Amb. Galleries, Palm Beach, Fla., 2001, Viridian Gallery, N.Y.C., 2001, Piermont Fine Arts Gallery, 2001, Viridian Gallery @ Chelsea, 2002, Viridian Gallery, N.Y.C., 2002; exhibited in juried group shows: Piermont Fine Art Gallery, 1995, 96, 98, 2000, 01, Anaya Gallery, Scarsdale, 1986, Katonah (N.Y.) Gallery, 1986, Gallery at Jamaica, Stratton Mountain, Vt., 1987, CDS Contemporary Art, Albuquerque, 1989, Mari Galleries, Mamaroneck, N.Y., 1992, Manhattan Transfer, Inc., 1993, 98, 93 South Gallery, Nyack, N.Y., 1998-99, Bibro Fine Arts Gallery, Chelsea, N.Y., 1998, Weber Fine Art, Scarsdale, N.Y., 1998, 2000, 93 South Gallery, Nyack, N.Y., 1998, J&W Gallery, New Hope, Pa., 1998, 99, 2001, Studio 4 West, Piermont, N.Y., 1999, Hewlett Mus., 2000, Ambassador Gallery, Palm Beach, Fla., 2000, Viridian Gallery, N.Y.C., 2000, 01, 02, 03, Hewlett Mus., 2000, Adele Greenberg Salon, 2000, 01, A Pirate Space, Denver, 2001, Contemporary Art Oasis, Denver, 2001, J&W Gallery, 2001, 2002, Manhattanville Coll. Gallery, 2002, Nat. Assn. Women Artists, N.Y.C., 2003, Chgo. (Ill.) Fine Arts Bldg. Gallery, 2003, Viridian @ Chelsea, 2003, Chgo. Fine Arts Bldg. Gallery, 2003; commd. Am. Soc. Plastic and Reconstructive Surgeons, L.A. Conv. Ctr., 1988, White Plains Hosp. Ctr., 1989, 90, Cystic Fibrosis Found., N.Y.C., 1990, Joan Kroc Found., Calif., 1989-91. 1st v.p., bd. dirs. Internat. Coll. Surgeons aux., Chgo., 1988—90; mem. Juvenile Diabetes Found., Gala, 2000; Regional v.p. Am. Cancer soc., White Plains, 1986—88; bd. dirs. White Plains Hosp. Ctr. Aux., 1995—; fund raiser, event planner Holocaust Commn., N.Y.C., 1998; mem. J&W Gallery, 2000—, Viridian Artists, Inc., 2001—; active Scarsdale Tremont Synagogue Gala, 2001, 2002; mem. Nat. Assn. Women Artists; fund-raiser Larson-Alternative Arts and Music Events, Scarsdale Teen Ctr., 2003—; laison Scarsdale HS PTA, Alternative Art and Music Events, Scarsdale Teen Ctr., 2003—05. Mem. Internat. Platform Assn., Nat. Mus. Women in Contemporary Arts, Nat. Assn. Women Artists, Inc., Katonah Mus., Nat. Mus. Women in the Arts (artist mem.), Nat. Arts Club. Avocations: piano, photography, tennis, kayaking, skiing. Studio: 21 Wayside Ln Scarsdale NY 10583-2911 E-mail: StaceySCN21@aol.com.

NEWMAN, SUZANNE DINKES, web site development executive; b. Bklyn., Apr. 28, 1949; d. Philip and Natalie (Hollander) Dinkes; m. Ralph Michael Newman, Mar. 9, 1975. Student, Cooper Union, 1967-71, Sch. Visual Arts, N.Y.C., 1971-72. Asst. art dir. Lincoln Ctr. Art Progs., N.Y.C., 1973-74; art dir. BimBamBoom Mag., Yonkers, NY, 1974; with Fairfax Advtg., N.Y.C., 1974-75; dir. ops. TBE Advtg., N.Y.C., 1975-87, ceo Yonkers, NY, 1987-94; art dir. Timer Barrier Express, Yonkers, NY, 1975-80; CEO R.S. Newman Assocs., Yonkers, NY, 1994-98; ptnr. WWW.Dott-Comm.com, 1997—. Concert coord. Classic Harmony Prodns., N.Y.C., 1975; apl. event planner, The Left Bank, Mt. Vernon, N.Y., 1980-81; apl. event cons. Glen Island Casino, New Rochelle, N.Y., 1984-85; event coord., Top Brass, Yonkers, 1986-87; art dir., cons. various music publs., 1974-80, dir. comms., Yonkers C. of C., 1998—. Editor: Rockin' in the Fourth Estate, 1979-80, Chamber News, 1998—. Art dir.: White and Still All Right!, 1977, Sun Records, 1980, The Buddy Holly Story, 1979. Mem. Yonkers Citizen's Adv. Grp., Yonkers Mayorial Transition Com., 1991-92, Alliance Devel. Com., Yonkers Sch. and Bus. Alliance, 1991-94, prog. com., 1991-94; mem. Yonkers Coun. Pres.'s Citizens Adv, Grp., 1992, Yonkers Dem. Com., dist. leader, 1991-93; jour. chair gala com, Hudson River Mus., 1992; mem. Yonkers Local Bus. Adv. Coun., 1992-94; mem. Yonkers Pvt. Industry Coun., 1992-94, sec. 1993-94; promotion chair Yonkers Hudson Riverfest, 1992-93; bus. adv. com. Yonkers Econ. Devel. Zone, 1993-94; active Yonkers Waterfront Task Force, 1993-94; bd. dirs. Youth Theater Interaction, 1994—; bd. dirs. Westchester divsn. Jewish Guild for Blind, 1994-97, gala chair, 1994; events coord. Mayor's Inaugural Ball, 1996; leader Jr. Girl Scouts, Southwest Yonkers, 1996—. Recipient Disting. Leadership and Svc. Awd., Westchester County C. of C., 1985, Westchester Awd., Westchester Small Bus. Counc., 1989, Outstanding Leader award Girl Scouts U.S., 2000. Mem. Westchester Small Bus. COun. (comms. chmn. 1984-85, Westchester winner, 1989), Yonkers C. of C. (bd. dirs. 1996—, comm. chair 1996-97), Coun. for Arts Westchester. Democrat. Jewish. Avocations: reading, antiques, gardening. E-mail: snewman@dott-comm.com.

NEWMAN-GORDON, PAULINE, French language and literature educator; b. N.Y.C., Aug. 5, 1925; d. Bernard and Eva Newman; m. Sydney A. Gordon, Sept. 13, 1959 (dec.); m. Richard Yellin, Feb. 9, 1997. BA, Hunter Coll., 1947; MA, Columbia U., 1948; PhD, Sorbonne U., Paris, 1951. Instr. French Wellesley (Mass.) Coll., 1952-53; mem. faculty Stanford (Calif.) U., 1953—, prof. French lit., 1969-93, prof. emerita, 1994—. Author: Marcel Proust, 1953, Eugene Le Roy, 1957, Corbiere, Laforgue and Apollinaire, 1964, Helen of Troy Myth, 1968, (poetry) Mooring to France, (prose poem) Sydney: editor: Dictionary of Ideas in Marcel Proust, 1968, also articles in field; contbr. articles to profl. jours. Scholar Internat. Inst. Edn., 1948-51, MLA, 1956-57, AAUW, 1962-63, Am. Philos. Soc., 1970-71, NEH, 1989; elected to Hall of Fame, Alumni Assn. Hunter Coll. of CUNY, 1990 Mem. MLA, Am. Assn. Tchrs. French, Soc. Friends Marcel Proust. Office: Stanford U Dept French Italian Stanford CA 94305

NEWMAR, JULIE CHALANE, actress, dancer, real estate businesswoman; b. Hollywood, Calif. d. Donald Charles and Helene (Jesmer) Newmeyer; m. J. Holt Smith, Aug. 5, 1977 (div. Apr. 1986); 1 child, John Jewl Smith. Student, UCLA. Actress TV series, plays, movies. Mem. Actors Studio, N.Y. and Los Angeles. Appeared on Broadway in Marriage Go Round (Tony award), Damn Yankees, Guys and Dolls, Irma La Douce, Stop the World, L'il Abner, Dames At Sea; films: Seven Brides for Seven Brothers, Marriage Go Round, Mackenna's Gold, The Maltese Bippy, Streetwalkin', 1985, Dance Academy, 1987, Ghosts Can't Do It, Oblivion I and II, To Wong Foo, Thanks for Everything, Julie Newmar; TV: Rhoda the Robot in My Living Doll, Catwoman on Batman, guest starred on Get Smart, The Monkees, Bewitched, Route 66, Hart to Hart, Love American Style, Star Trek, Twilight Zone, Beverly Hillbillies, Columbo, Fantasy Island, Melrose Place, Hope & Gloria, The Making of Seven Brides for Seven Brothers, 1997; prima ballerina with L.A. Opera Co.; video: Too Funky (George Michael); Thierry Mugler high fashion shows, Paris. Recipient Antoinette Perry award. Avocations: gardening, piano.

NEWMARK, MARILYN, sculptor; b. N.Y.C., July 20, 1928; d. Edward Ellis and Mabel (Davies) Newmark; m. Leonard J. Meiselman, Mar. 15, 1952. Student, Adelphi Coll., 1945-47, Alfred U., 1949. Sculpture specializing in horses, equestrian figures, dogs, foxes. Exhibited in group shows; sculpture exhbn. Ky. Derby Mus., Fleischer Mus., Scottsdale, Leigh Yawkey Woodson Art Mus., Wis., Bennington Ctr. for Arts, Vt., NAD, N.Y.C., Nat. Arts Club, N.Y.C., Smithsonian Instn., Washington, Mus. of Horse, Ky., Port of History Mus., Pa., Marietta/Cobb Mus. Art, Wildlife Experience, Denver, Brookgreen Gardens, S.C., Nat. Geog. Soc., Washington, Allegheny Colls. Galleries, Butler Inst. Am. Art; represented in permanent collections Nat. Mus. Racing, Saratoga, N.Y., Internat. Mus. Horse, Ky. Horse Park, also in pvt. collections. Recipient Anna Hyatt Huntington award, 1970, 71, 72, 75, 78, 80, 81, 82, 83, 86, 88, 90, 97, 2002, Gold medal, 1973, award Coun. Am. Artists Socs., 1972, 73, 79, 80, Hudson Valley John Newington award, 1973, 77, Gold medal, 1979, Elliot Liskin Meml. award, 1989, 96, Academician NAD Ellin P. Speyer award, 1974, 93, 99, Artist Fund award, 1982. Fellow Nat. Sculpture Soc. (coun. 1973-75, rec. sec. 1976, sec. 1977-79, coun. 1981-83, 92-97, Bronze medal 1986, Mildred Victor Meml. award 1996, Leonard Meiselman Meml. award 2003), Audubon Artists (Elliott Liskin Meml. award 2000, 02), Am. Artists Profl. League (Gold medal 1974, 77, medal of hon. 1987), Allied Artists Am. (Gold medal 1981, 93, In Memorium award 1994), Pen & Brush Club (Gold medal 1977, Salmagundi Club award 1982, 83, 91, C. Dunwiddie Meml. award 1999), Soc. Animal Artists (jury of admissions 1972-75, 90—, bd. dirs. 1991—, v.p. 1998—, Legacy award 2002), Am. Acad. Equine Art (founding mem., dir. sculpture 1980—), Nassau Suffolk Horsemans Assn. (dir. 1968-82), Catherine Lorillard Wolfe Art Club, Smithtown Hunt Club, Meadowbrook Hunt Club. Address: 22 Woodhollow Rd Roslyn Heights NY 11577-2217 Office Phone: 516-621-5914.

NEWPORT, L. JOAN, clinical social worker, retired psychotherapist; b. Newkirk, Okla., July 5, 1932; d. Crawford Earl and Lillian Pearl (Peden) Irvine; m. Don E. Newport, July 9, 1954 (div. 1971, dec. 1999); children: Alan Keith, Lili Kim. BA cum laude, Wichita State U., 1955; MSW, U. Okla., 1977. Bd. cert. diplomate in clin. social work Acad. Cert. Social Workers; lic. social worker, Okla. Dir. children's work Wesley United Meth. Ch., Oklahoma City, 1969-71; social worker Dept. Human Svcs., Newkirk, Okla., 1972-77; in-sch. suspension counselor Kay County Youth Svcs., Ponca City, Okla., 1977; med. social worker St. Joseph Med. Ctr., Ponca City, 1977-78, dir. social work, 1978-83; pvt. practice, Ponca City, 1979-97; med. social worker Healthcare Svcs., Ponca City, 1983-84; pvt. practice home studies, cons., supervision, Newkirk, 1997—. Cons. Blackwell, Perry, Pawhuska, O'Keene Hosps., 1978-85; cons. social work Bass Meml. Hosp., Enid, Okla., 1985; sponsor, organizer Kay County Parents Anonymous, Ponca City, 1976-83; vice chair Okla. State Bd. Lic. Social Workers, Oklahoma City, 1988-90; presentor, lectr. in field; supr. students Okla. U. Sch. Social Work, Okla. State U., No. Okla. Coll., Okla. Christian Coll., 1977-85; supr. for clin. social workers working toward lic. in Okla., 1985—. Mem. Okla. Women's Network, 1989-96; mem. adv. bd. Displaced Homemakers, Ponca City, 1985-89; mem. adv. bd. Kay County Home Health, 1979-83, chair, 1979-81; Sunday sch. tchr. Newkirk United Meth. Ch.; mem. Newkirk Main St., 1999-2000. Named Hon. State Life Mem. Burbank PTA, Oklahoma City, 1971; scholar Wichita (Kans.) Press and Radio Women, 1953, Conoco, Inc., Houston, 1951-54. Mem. NASW (Okla. del. Del. Assembly Washington 1987, chmn. vendorship com. 1985-87, pres. Okla. chpt. 1988-90, Social Worker of Yr. 1987), Child Abuse Prevention Task Force (pres. dist. 17 1986-88, mem. grant evaluation com. 1986-96), Zeta Phi Eta. Democrat. Methodist. Home: 109 N Walnut Ave Newkirk OK 74647-2036 Office: PO Box 74 Newkirk OK 74647-0074

NEWSOM, CAROLYN CARDALL, management consultant; b. South Weymouth, Mass., Feb. 27, 1941; d. Alfred James and Bertha Virginia (Roy) Cardall; m. John Harlan Newsom, Feb. 4, 1967; children: John Cardall, James Harlan. AB, Brown U., 1962; MBA, Wharton Sch., 1978; PhD, U. Pa., 1985. Systems engr. IBM, Seattle, 1964-70, Newsom S.E. Services, Seattle, 1970-76; instr. U. Pa. Wharton Sch., Phila., 1978-81; v.p., prin. sr. cons. PA Cons. Group, Princeton, N.J., 1981-88; pres. Newsom Assocs., Yardley, Pa., 1988; ptnr. Bus. Strategy Implementation, Princeton, N.J., 1989-90; pres. Strategy Implementation Solutions, Yardley, Pa., 1990—. Examiner N.J. Gov.'s Performance Excellence Award, 1993, sr. examiner, 1994—2002; judge N.J. Gov.'s Performance Excellence award, 2003—04; examiner Malcolm Baldrige Nat. Quality award, 2003. Bd. dirs. Chandler Hall, 1980-87; trustee St. Mary Hosp., Langhorne, Pa., 1986-94; sec. bd. dirs. Gordonstown Am. Found., 1999—. Mem.: Quality N.J. (vice chair 1998—99), Am. Soc. for Quality, Am. Acad. Mgmt., Brown Alumni Assn. (pres.-elect 1993—95, pres. 1995—97). Office: Strategy Implementation Solutions 1588 Woodside Rd Yardley PA 19067-2611

NEWSOME, KATHY NOEL, accountant; b. Lexington Park, Md., Mar. 29, 1941; d. William Clement Sr. and Myrtle Sarah (Harris) Butler; m. Walter Burch Noel Jr., July 13, 1957 (div.); 1 child, Walter B. Noel III; m. Billy Gene Newsome, Oct. 30, 1966 (div.); 1 child, Adrienne Y. BS in Acctg. magna cum laude, Meyers Coll., 1984. Cert. govt. fin. mgr., cert. dept. of def. logistics auditor. Agt. IRS, 1984-85; auditor Navy Internal Rev., Patuxent River, Md., 1985-87, AF Audit Agy., Wright-Patterson AFB, Ohio, 1987-88; fin. ops. supr. 375 Combat-Support Group, Scott AFB, Ill., 1988-90; NAF fin. mgmt. officer AFE 7276 AB6, Crete, Greece, 1990-92; auditor AF Audit Agy., Eglin AFB, Fla., 1992-94, audit mgr. Wright Patterson AFB, 1994—. Mem. Am. Soc. Mil. Contrs., Federally Employed Women. Democrat. Avocations: music, movies, games, exercise, fashion. Office: Air Force Audit Agy 4170 Hebble Creek Rd Ste 1 Wright Patterson Afb OH 45433-5653

NEWSOME, LEE ANN, anthropologist, educator; BA, U. of Fla., 1982, MA, 1986, PhD, 1993. Curator of collections So. Ill. U. Ctr. for Archaeological Investigations, Carbondale, 1993—2001; assoc. prof. Pa. State U., U. Pk., 2002—. Contbr. articles in Jour. of Ethnobiology, Am. Antiquity, Southeastern Geology. Office: Dept of Anthropology Pa State U 316 Carpenter Bldg University Park PA 16802-3404

NEWTON, CHERYL KAY, music educator; b. Arlington, Va., May 16, 1953; d. Andren Earl and Alberta Christine Newton. B in Music Edn., E. Carolina U., 1975; MS, U. Ill., 1981; EdD, Va. Tech, 1988. Lic. K-12 music Va., secondary prin. Va. Dir. band Fairmont (N.C.) City Schs., 1975—80, Thomas Jefferson HS, Alexandria, Va., 1980—84, Oakton HS, Vienna, Va., 1984—. Democrat. Presbyterian. Avocations: sailing, gardening. Home: 67 McPherson Cir Sterling VA 20165 Personal E-mail: NEWT53@aol.com.

NEWTON, ELIZABETH PURCELL, counselor, consultant, author; b. Madison, N.C., June 3, 1925; d. Charles Augustus and Anna Meta (Buchanan) P.; m. William Edward Newton, June 11, 1949; children— James Purcell, Betsy Newton Hein, Christina Newton Harwood. A.A., Peace Coll., 1944; B.A., U. N.C., 1946; M.Ed., Ga. State U., 1969; Ed.S., West Ga. Coll., 1981. Tchr., counselor S. Cobb High Sch., Austell, Ga., 1965-69; counselor, dept. head Wheeler High Sch., Marietta, Ga., 1969-76; counselor, div. head guidance services Walton High Sch., Marietta, Ga., 1976—90; ret., 1990; sch. rep. Coll. Bd., Princeton, N.J., 1981—90, panelist, presenter S.E. region, Atlanta, 1983-85; presenter Ga. Sch. Counselors Assn., Atlanta, 1980—90; cons. Panhandle Area Edn. Coop., Chipley, Fla., 1985. Author: Steps to College Admissions, 1978; Student's Guide to College Admissions, 1981; Student's Guide to Career Preparation, 1982. Sch. rep. Citizens Adv. Council, Marietta, 1981, 82, 85. Ga. Dept. Edn. grantee, 1981; named Outstanding Woman in Edn., Atlanta Jour., 1985. Mem. Cobb Counselor Assn. (organizer, chmn. nominations com. 1985), Ga. Sch. Counselors Assn. (Secondary Counselor of Yr. 1983), Am. Sch. Counselors Assn. (Nat. Secondary Counselor of Yr. 1984), Phi Delta Kappa. Presbyterian.

NEWTON, ESTHER MARY, anthropologist, educator; b. N.Y.C., Nov. 28, 1940; d. Saul B. and Virginia Newton. BA, U. Mich., 1962; MA, U. Chgo., 1964, PhD, 1968. Asst. prof. CUNY, Queens, 1968-71; from asst. prof. to assoc. prof. anthropology SUNY, Purchase, 1971-92, prof. anthropology, 1992—, Kempner disting. professorship, 1999. Coord. women's studies program SUNY, Purchase, 1984-86; vis. prof. Yale U., 1970, U. Amsterdam, 1993; affiliated scholar CUNY, 1992-93; scholar in residence U. Calif., Santa Cruz, 1993; curator exhbn. Gay and Lesbian Cmty. Svcs. Ctr., 1993. Author: Mother Camp: Female Impersonators in America, 1972, reprinted with new introduction, 1979, Cherry Grove, Fire Island: Sixty years in America's First Gay and Lesbian Town, 1993, Margaret Meade May Me Gay, 2000; co-author: (with Shirley Walton) Womanfriends, 1976; contbr. to anthologies including The Lesbian Issue: Essays from Signs, 1985, Hidden from History: Reclaiming the Gay and Lesbian Past, 1989, International Gay Studies: The Amsterdam Conference, 1994, History of Homosexuality in Europe and America, 1994, Writing Lesbian and Gay Culture, 1995; mem. editl. bd. The Cutting Edge: Lesbian Life and Literature Series, Between men, Between Women: Lesbian and Gay Studies Series, GLQ: Jour. of Queer Studies, Jour. of Homosexuality, Jour. Sexuality in History; contbr. to books including Amazon Expedition, 1973, Anthropology and American Life, 1974, Symbolic Anthropology: A Reader in the Study of Symbols and Meaning, 1977, Strategies des femmes, 1984, Pleasure and Danger: Exploring Female Sexuality, 1984, Homosexuality, Which Homosexuality? Vol. 2, 1987, The Lesbian and Gay Studies Reader, 1993; contbr. articles to mags. and jours. La Verne Noyes scholar U. Chgo., 1962-63; training grantee NIH, 1963-65, faculty support grantee SUNY, Purchase, 1987, 92; pre-doctoral fellow NIMH, 1965-67; recipient experienced faculty travel award SUNY, 1987, 91; Rockefeller Humanities fellow, 1999. Mem. Am. Anthrop. Assn. (cochair commn. lesbian and gay issues, 1994-96). Avocation: dog training. Office: Divsn Social Sci SUNY Purchase NY 10577

NEWTON, GLORIA JONES, accountant, feminist activist; b. Gary, Tex., Feb. 3, 1960; d. Jessie Wyatt and Vera Mae (Jackson) Jones; m. Larry Donell Newton, Aug. 20, 1979 (div. Oct. 1988); 1 child, Jasmine Tiffany. Student, Kilgore (Tex.) Jr. Coll., 1978-79; BBA, Jarvis Christian Coll., 1982; postgrad., U. Houston, 1983-85. Lic. ins. agt., Tex. Database rschr. GTE, Baytown, Tex., summer 1981; clerical asst. Social Security Adminstrn., Tyler, Tex., summer 1982; sales mgr. Revelation Shoes, Baytown, 1982; warehouse acct. Universal Terminal Warehouse, Houston, 1982-83; sr. acct. Bayer, Houston, 1984-90, fixed asset acct., 1990-95. Author: (autobiography) In My Father's House. Mem. Tex. Dem. Caucus, Houston, 1995; vol., mem. spkr.'s bur., hotline advocate Houston Area Women Ctr., 1994—; lobbyist Planned Parenthood; pres., chmn. Jr. Achievement, Tex., 1993. Mem. NOW (activist 1994—). Democrat. Avocations: traveling, reading, singing, writing, gardening. Home: PO Box 300812 Houston TX 77230-0812

NEWTON, JUANITA, social worker, educator; b. LaGrange, Ga., Sept. 16, 1931; d. Limus Lee Newton and Lillia Bertha Baugh; children: Marcellette A. Reynolds, Lymus Dannerro(dec.), De'Juan, Sharold Lynn, Lydia. AA, Wayne County C.C., 1976; B in Social Work, Wayne State U., 1978, MA in Social Work, 1979. Cert. in elem.edn. 1988. Social worker local ctrs. and schs., Hamtramck, Mich., 1979—80; dir. social work Brent Gen. Hosp., 1980—81, Sidney A. Sumby Hosp., 1981—83; tchr. Detroit Pub. Schs., 1985—91; v.p. Detroit Gen. Hosp., 1972—81; chair proposal rev. com. Detroit Wayne County Mental Health Bd., 1972—75; adminstr. The Haven Mission 138, 1990—93; instr. genealogy rsch. Wayne County C.C., 1994—97; ret. Mem. exec. com. 4th precinct Police Cmty. Rels. Coun., 1998—; cmty. rels. chairperson Friends of Duffield Br. Pub. Libr., 2001; pres. concerned Citizens of N.W. Goldberg Cmty., Inc., 1995—; urban coord. 4H, 1995—; del. county rels. Citywide Police. Named Angel for Children, Blue Cross/Blue Shield Network, 2002—03; recipient 8th Spirit of Detroit award for Cmty. Svcs., Gov.'s award for Cmty. Svcs., Gov. William Milligen. Mem.: NASW, SCLC, NAACP (life), FH Williams Geneaol. Soc. Democrat.

NEWTON, LISA HAENLEIN, philosopher, educator; b. Orange, N.J., Sept. 17, 1939; d. Wallen Joseph and Carol Bigelow (Cypiot) Haenlein; m. Victor Joseph Newton, June 3, 1972; children: Tracey, Kit, Cynthia Perkins, Daniel Perkins, Laura Perkins. Student, Swarthmore Coll., 1957-59; BS in Philosophy with honors, Columbia U., 1962, PhD, 1967. Asst. prof.

philosophy Hofstra U., Hempstead, NY, 1967-69; from asst. prof. to assoc. prof. Fairfield (Conn.) U., 1969—78, prof., 1978—, dir. program applied ethics, 1983—, dir. program environ. studies, 1986—; lectr. in medicine Yale U., 1984—. Lectr., cons. in field. Author: (book) Ethics and Sustainability, 2002, Ethics in Am., Study Guide, 2d edit. (2 vols.), 2003, Ethics in Am. Source Reader, 2d edit., 2003; co-author: Watersheds, 1994, 3d edit., 2001, Wake-Up Calls, 2d edit., 2003; co-editor: Taking Sides: Controversial Issues Bus. Ethics, 8th edit., 2004; contbr. articles to profl. jours. Mem. exec. bd. Conn. Humanities Coun., 1979—83. Mem.: Internat. Soc. Environ. Ethics (mem. exec. bd.), Assn. Practical Prof. Ethics (exec. bd.), Soc. Bus. Ethics (past pres.), Am. Soc. Bioethics and Humanities, Soc. Ethics Across Curriculum (exec. bd.), Am. Soc. Polit. and Legal Philosophy, Am. Philos. Assn., Am. Soc. Value Inquiry (past pres.), Phi Beta Kappa (local sec.). Home: 4042 Congress St Fairfield CT 06824 Office: Fairfield U Program Applied Ethics Fairfield CT 06824 E-mail: ihnewton@mail.fairfield.edu.

NEWTON, LORETTA JEAN, insurance agent; b. Chambersburg, Pa., Oct. 31, 1942; d. Edmund Koontz and Pearl May (Corbin) Helwig; m. Neil Edward Newton, June 20, 1964 (dec. Sept. 1982); children: Betsy A. Tauraso, Scott E. BA, Gettysburg Coll., 1964. Tchr. math and gen. sci. Mid. Sch., Hagerstown, Md., 1964-65; tchr. biology south Hagerstown H.S., Hagerstown, 1965-67, Stuart (Fla.) H.S., 1980-84; ins. agt. The Prudential, Hagerstown, 1985—. Tchr. classes for Life Underwriters Tng. Coun., Frederick, Md., 1995-96. Program chair Luth. Ch. Women, Boonsboro, Md., 1968-72; mem. exec. bd. Md. Luth. Ch. Women, Balt., 1976-79; organizer, mgr. ch. libr. St. Timothy's Luth. Ch., Balt., 1975-79, tchr. Sunday sch., 1975-79. Recipient Nat. Quality award Nat. Assn. Life Underwriters Tng. Coun., 1994, 95, 96, 97, Sales Achievement award, 1988, 89, 90. Mem. Life Underwriters of Frederick County (v.p. 1996-97, past membership chair). Avocations: reading, symphony music. Home: 131 Albany Ave E Walkersville MD 21793-9142

NEWTON, MICHELLE MARIE, sales executive; b. Orange, Calif., May 27, 1971; d. Wayne Clair and Maria Palmar Newton; 1 child, Jazmyn Victoria Wallington. BA in Comm., Calif. State U., Fullerton, 1994; MBA, Pepperdine U., 2000. Mktg. adminstr. Ingram Micro, Santa Ana, Calif., 1994—96, internat. mktg. adminstr., 1995; sales support rep. APL, Ltd., Costa Mesa, Calif., 1996—97, inside sales rep., 1997—98, acct. exec., 1998—2000, sr. acct. exec., 2000—02; child care owner Michelle's Child Care, Rancho Santa Margarita, Calif., 2002—03; internat. sales Oakley, Inc., Foothill Ranch, Calif., 2003—. Roman Catholic. Avocations: motorcycling, skiing, rollerblading, walking, shopping. Home: 1 Spinel Ct Rancho Santa Margarita CA 92688

NEWTON, NELL JESSUP, dean, law educator; b. St. Louis, Apr. 30, 1944; d. Robert Edward and Marcella (Boehm) Mier. BA, U. Calif., Berkeley, 1973; JD, U. Calif., Hastings, 1976. Bar: Calif., Washington, U.S. Ct. Appeals (9th cir.), U.S. Supreme Ct. Prof. Cath. U. Sch. Law, 1976-92; prof. Washington Coll. Law Am. U., Washington, 1992—98; dean U. Denver Law Sch., 1998—2000, U. Conn. Sch. Law, Hartford, 2000—. Lectr. Internat. Law Inst., Washington, 1984-89; prof. Pre-Law Summer Inst. for Native Am. Students, U. N.Mex. Law Sch., Albuquerque, 1990, 91, 93; panelist, speaker NEH, 1991; presenter S.W. Intertribal Ct. of Appeals, 1990; panelist Orgn. Am. Historians, 1991. Co-author: American Indian Law, 3d edit., 1991; contbr. articles to profl. jours. NEH fellow Harvard Law Sch., 1980. Mem. Assn. Am. Law Schs. (Native Am. rights sect., mem. exec. com. 1987—, chair 1987-88, oral argument newsletter editor 1987—, mem. women in legal edn. sect. 1987—, chair profl. devel. workshop com. 1992, sec. 1993), Balt.-Washington-Va. Women Law Tchrs. Group (planning com. Symposium on Scholarship I 1985, II 1986), Thurston Soc., Order of Coif. Office: U Conn Sch Law Hartranft 103 55 Elizabeth St Hartford CT 06105

NEWTON, RHONWEN LEONARD, writer, microcomputer consultant, data processing executive, consultant; b. Lexington, N.C., Nov. 13, 1940; d. Jacob Calvin and Mary Louise (Moffitt) Leonard; children: Blair Armistead Newton Jones, Allison Page, William Brockenbrough III. AB, Duke U., 1962; MS in Edn., Old Dominion U., 1968. French tchr. Hampton (Va.) Pub. Schs., 1962-65, Va. Beach (Va.) Pub. Schs., 1965-66; instr. foreign lang. various colls. and univs., 1967-75; foreign lang. cons. Portsmouth (Va.) Pub. Schs., 1973-75; dir. The Computer Inst., Inc., Columbia, S.C., 1983; pres., founder The Computer Experience, Inc., Columbia, 1983-88, RN Enterprises, Columbia, 1991—. Author: WordPerfect, 1988, All About Computers, 1989, Microsoft Excel for the Mac, 1989, Introduction to the Mac, 1989, Introduction to DOS, 1989, Introduction to Lotus 1-2-3, 1989, Advanced Lotus 1-2-3, 1989, Introduction to WordPerfect, 1989, Advanced WordPerfect, 1989, Introduction to Display/Write 4, 1989, WordPerfect for the Mac, 1989, Introduction to Microsoft Works for the Mac, 1990, Accountant, Inc for the Mac, 1992, Introduction to Filemaker Pro, 1992, Quicken for the MAC, 1993, Quicken for Windows, 1993, WordPerfect for Windows, 1993, Advanced WordPerfect for Windows, 1993, Lotus 1-2-3 for Windows, 1993, Introduction to Quick Books, 1994, Quick Book for Windows, 1994, Introduction to Word for Windows, 1995, Introduction to File Maker Pro 4.0, 1998, Introduction to Microsoft Word, 1999, Introduction to Microsoft Excel, 1999, Introduction to AOL, 1999, Introduction to Excel, 1999, Using America OnLine, 1999. Mem. Columbia Planning Commn., 1980-87; bd. dirs. United Way Midlands, Columbia, 1983-86, Assn. Jr. Leagues, N.Y.C., 1980-82, S.C. Wildlife Fedn., 1997-98 ; trustee Heathwood Hall Episcopal Sch., Columbia, 1979-85; mem. S.C. Episcopal Home Bd., 1999—, chmn., 2001-2003; vestry Trinity Cathedral, 1999-02; mem. S.C. Real Estate Appraisers Bd., 2000, sec., 2002—. Mem. Investment Club (pres. 1995-97, regional coun.), Nat. Assn. Investors Corp. (dir. S.C. Midlands regional coun. 1998-02). Republican. Episcopalian. Avocations: golf, walking. Home and Office: 1635 Kathwood Dr Columbia SC 29206-4509 E-mail: rnewton@sc.rr.com.

NEWTON, VIRGINIA, archivist, historian, librarian; d. John Walter and Reba Catherine Newton. Student, Inst. Tecnológico y de Estudios Superiores de Monterrey, Nuevo Leon, Mex., 1957; AA in Bus. Adminstrn., Stephens Coll., 1958; BA in History, Okla. State U., 1960; M of Librarianship, U. Wash., 1963; cert. in libr. sci., U. Tex., 1968, MA in History Archives and Libr. Sci., 1975, PhD in History, Archives and Libr. Sci., 1983. Libr. Inst. Pub. Affairs U. Tex., Austin, 1963-65, libr. Art Libr., 1965-67; coord. Sr. Cmty. Svcs. Program Econ. Opportunities Devel. Corp., San Antonio, 1968-69; archivist, spl. collections libr. Trinity U., San Antonio, 1969-73; spl. collections and reference libr. Pan Am. U., Edinburg, Tex., 1974-77; archivist, records analyst Alaska State Archives and Records Svc., 1983-84, dep. state archivist, 1984-87; state archivist Alaska State Archives & Records Mgmt. Svcs., 1988-93; dir. Columbus Meml. Libr. OAS, Washington, 1993—. Archives cons. Ford Found. for Brazilian Archivists Assn., 1976, Soc. for Ibero-Latin Thought, 1980, Project for a Notarial Archives Computerized Guide, 1980; chair Alaska State Hist. Records Adv. Bd., 1988-93, coords. steering com., 1991-93; cons. Puerto Rican Hist. Records Adv. Bd., 1997-99. Author: An Archivists' Guide to the Catholic Church in Mexico, 1979; contbr. articles to profl. publs. Founder jail libr. Bexar County Jail, San Antonio; hon. dep. sheriff Bexar County, 1972-75; mem. dem. party; chair Dems. Abroad in Mex., 1979-81; mem. Dems. Abroad Del. The Dem. Nat. Conv., N.Y., 1980; vice- chair Bill Egan Forum Greater Juneau Dem. Precinct, 1986-88 Recipient Commendation award Gov. of Alaska William Sheffield, 1985, Disting. Alumnae award U. Tex. Sch. Libr. and Info. Sci., 1998; Masonic Scholarship for internat. rels. George Washington U., 1960-61; univ. fellow U. Tex.-Austin, 1982-83, post masters fellow U.S. Dept. Edn.-U. Tex., Austin, 1967-68; scholar Orgn. Am. States, 1980, 81, Fulbright-Hays scholar, 1979, 80, scholar Nat. Def. Fgn. Lang.-U. Tex., Austin, 1978-79, scholar Calif. State Libr., 1962-63. Mem. AAUW (bd. dirs. 1983-86, scholar 1983), Nat. Assn. Govt. Archives and Records Adminstrs. (bd. dirs. 1989-93, chair membership com. 1989-93), Alaska Hist. Soc. (bd. treas. 1988-94), Alaska Libr. Assn., Acad. Cert. Archivists (cert. 1989), Rotary, Phi Kappa Phi. Democrat. Unitarian Universalist. Avocations: skiing, dance, researching, reading, hiking. Office: 206 Laurel Heights Place San Antonio TX 78212

NEZIRI, MARIA G. DE LUCIA, elementary school educator; b. Mineola, N.Y., Dec. 27, 1967; d. Salvatore and Alfonsina DeL.; m. Lulzim Neziri, Aug. 20, 1995; 1 child, Noah. BS Edn., Adelphi U., 1990; MS in Edn., Queens U., 1994; MS in Reading and Spl. Edn., Hofstra U., 1999. Cert. tchr. reading, spl. edn. K-12. Elem. tchr. Westbury (N.Y.) Pub. Schs., 1990—. Creator, coord The Write View, The Writing Club after school club; creator, instr. inservice courses Reading and Writing Workshop; mentor for new tchrs. Mem. Nat. Coun. Tchrs. Maths., Nat. Coun. Tchrs. English, Internat. Reading Assn. Avocations: gardening, cooking, reading. Home: 37 S Fulton St Westbury NY 11590-5205

NG, BETTY, electronics executive; Pres. Reliance Tech Svcs., Sunnyvale, Calif., 1981—. Office: Reliance Tech Svcs 895 Kifer Rd Sunnyvale CA 94086-5205 Fax: 408-720-0838. E-mail: info@RTSII.com.

NGUYEN, HUONG TRAN, English language professional, federal agency official; b. Haiphong, Vietnam, Nov. 16, 1953; came to the U.S., 1971; d. Joe (Quang) Trong Tran and Therese (Nguyet-Anh) (Do) Dotran; m. Tony (Phu) The Nguyen; children: Long Tran Nguyen, Ty Tran Nguyen. B in Liberal Studies, San Diego State U., 1976, tchg. credential grades K-12, 1977; M in Curriculum Devel., Point Loma Coll., 1984; lang. devel. specialist cert., Calif. Commn. Credentialing, 1991. ESL tchr. San Diego (Calif.) Job Corps, 1978-80; resource tchr. grades K-12 San Diego (Calif.) Unified Sch. Dist., 1980-82; resource tchr. SEAL project grades K-12 Long Beach (Calif.) Unified Sch. Dist., 1982-83, ESL specialist, 1983-85, 85-92, English lang. devel. tchr., chair, 1992-95; adminstr., 1996-98; sr. fellow officer U.S. Dept. Edn., Office Bilingual & Minority Lang. Affairs, Washington, 1995-96; disting. tchr.-in-residence Calif. State U., Long Beach, 1998—. Named Outstanding Tchr. of 1994, Disney Co. Am. Tchr. Awards, Washington, 1994, Outstanding Tchr. in Fgn. Lang./ESL, Disney Co. Am. Tchr. Awards, Washington, 1994. Mem. NEA, TESOL, Calif. Lang. Tchrs. Assn., Calif. Tchr. Assn., Calif. Assn. for Bilingual Edn., Tchr. Assn. Long Beach, Assn. Curriculum and Supervision. Avocations: reading, traveling, gardening, visiting museums. Home: 6262 Cherokee Dr Westminster CA 92683-2004 Office: Calif State U Coll Edn Dept Tchr Edn 1250 N Bellflower Blvd Long Beach CA 90840-0001

NGUYEN, LAN THI HOANG, physician, educator; b. Hai-Duong, Vietnam, July 18, 1950; came to U.S., 1975; d. Thua Nang and Niem Thi (Do) N.; m. Khanh Vinh Quoc, Oct. 15, 1981. MD, U. Kans., 1983. Intern St. Mary Med. Ctr./UCLA, Long Beach, Calif., 1983-84; resident City of Faith Med. Rsch. Ctr.-Oral Roberts Sch. Medicine, Tulsa, 1986-88; fellow VA Med. Ctr.-Wadsworth-UCLA, 1988-90; physician Santa Ana (Calif.) Med. Ctr., Doctors Hosp. Santa Ana, Fountain Valley (Calif.) Regional Med. Ctr. Clin. assoc. prof. family medicine Keck Sch. Medicine U. So. Calif., L.A., 2002—. Contbr. articles to profl. jours. V.p. Vietnamese Am. Med. Rsch. Found. Kans. Med. scholar, 1979-81. Fellow: ACP, Am. Coll. Endocrinology, Am. Coll. Nutrition; mem.: Am. Assn. Clin. Endocrinologists (charter). Office: 14971 Brookhurst St Westminster CA 92683-5556

NGUYEN, MAI (MAI TUYET NGUYEN), writer; b. Saigon, Vietnam, Nov. 18, 1936; arrived in U.S.A., 1983; d. Tu Van Mai and Hiep Thi Doan; m. Tony Tung Quoc, Sept. 30, 1967; 1 child, Kevin Duy. Degree, Dai Hoc Van Khoa, Saigon, Vietnam, 1960. Sec. Soc. Gen. de Surveillance, Belgium Consulate, Saigon, Vietnam, 1954—57; adminstrv. mgr. Connell Bros. Co., Saigon, 1959—75; adminstrv. asst. Tandon Corp., Calif., 1983—86; freelance writer Calif., 1986—. Author: God's Will, 1996, Little Daisy, 1998, 10 books, 1996—2001, Shadow of Hapiness, 2002. Mem.: Independent Scholars Asia, Nat. Writers Assn. Avocations: reading, art, music, travel, landscaping.

NICASTRO, TRACEY A. lawyer; b. 1969; BA, U. Ill., 1991; JD, Valparaiso U., 1994. Bar: Ill. 1994. With Sidley Austin Brown & Wood, Chgo., 1996—, ptnr., 2002—. Mem.: ABA, Chgo. Bar Assn. Office: Sidley Austin Brown and Wood Bank One Plz 10 S Dearborn St Chicago IL 60603*

NICCOLINI, DIANORA, photographer; b. Florence, Italy, Oct. 3, 1936; arrived in U.S., 1945, naturalized, 1960; d. George and Elaine (Augsbury) N. Student, Hunter Coll., 1955-62, Art Students League, 1960, Germain Sch. Photography, 1962; BA magna cum laude, Marymount Manhattan Coll., 1995. Med. photographer Manhattan Eye, Ear and Throat Hosp., 1963-65; organizer med. photography dept. Lenox Hill Hosp., 1965-67, 1st chief med. photographer, 1965-67; organizer, head dept. med. and audio visual edn. St. Clare's Hosp., N.Y.C., 1967-76; mem. Third Eye Gallery, N.Y.C., 1974-76; owner Dianora Niccolini Creations, 1976—. Instr. photography Camera Club N.Y., 1978-79, Germain Sch. Photography, 1978-79, N.Y. Inst. Photography, 1981-83; instr. comml. photography N.Y. Inst. Tech., 1996-97. One-woman shows include 209 Photo Gallery, Top of the Stairs Gallery, Third Eye Gallery, 1974, 75, 77, Photographics Unltd. Gallery, N.Y.C., 1981, West Broadway Gallery, N.Y.C., 1981, Camera Club N.Y., 1982, Overseas Press Club, N.Y.C., 1983, Impulse Gallery, Provincetown, Mass., 1983, Throckmorton Fine Art Gallery, N.Y.C., 1998, 2001; exhibited in group shows at Photography Over 65, N.Y.C., 1978, Jacob Javits Fed. Bldg., N.Y.C., 1992, Neikrug Gallery, N.Y.C., 1993, Ward-Nasse Gallery, N.Y.C., 1996, Internat. Salon, N.Y.C., 1996, Curcio-Spector Gallery, N.Y.C., 1996, Throckmorton Fine Art, Inc., 1997, 2001; pub. portfolios; author: Women of Vision, 1982, Men in Focus, 1983, Big Fun with Billy, 2001; editor: P.W.P. Times, 1981-82; contbr. to photog. books, 1979-2001; designer greeting cards Flashcards, Inc., 1988-90; contbg. editor Functional Photography, 1979-80, N.Y. Photo Dist. News, 1980; listed in numerous anthologies. Mem. Women Photographers N.Y. (founder 1974), Biol. Photog. Assn., Internat. Ctr. Photography, Am. Soc. Mag. Photographers, Am. Soc. Picture Profls., Profl. Women Photographers (pres. 1980-84). Home: 356 E 78th St New York NY 10021-2239 E-mail: dianoran@aol.com.

NICHOL, ALICE J. state legislator; b. Denver, Feb. 6, 1939; m. Ron Nichol; 4 children. Grad. H.S. Ret. sch. sec.; beauty cons. Mary Kay; mem. Colo. Ho. of Reps., 1992-98, Colo. Senate, Dist. 24, Denver, 1998—. Active Tri-City Bd. Health, Grassroots Adams City Dem. Party. Democrat. Roman Catholic. Office: State Capitol 200 E Colfax Ave Ste 274 Denver CO 80203-1716 also: 891 E 71st Ave Denver CO 80229-6806 Fax: 303-287-7742.

NICHOLAS, CLAUDIA JO, music educator; b. Idaho Falls, Idaho, Sept. 27, 1942; d. Winston James Soelberg and Josephine (Soelberg) Stokes; m. Peter Rodney Nicholas, Mar. 9, 1970. BA in Elem. Edn., Idaho State U., Pocatello, 1991. Profl. vocalist, Torrance, Calif., 1966—79; tchr. elem. music Johnson Elem. Sch., Firth, Idaho, 1985—88; choir tchr. Rocky Mountain Mid. Sch., Idaho Falls, Idaho, 1992—94; elem. music specialist Bonneville Sch. Dist. # 93, Idaho Falls, Idaho, 1994—. Pvt. voice tchr., Idaho Falls, Idaho, 1985—. Singer: dedication of Palasades (Idaho) Dam, 1952, nat. anthem at Dodger, Cubs game, 1961; singer: (lead) Funny Girl, Utah Valley Opera Prodn., 1966. Vocal performer USO. Fellow: NEA, Music Educators Nat. Conf., Idaho Edn. Assn., Bonneville Edn. Assn. Republican. Mem. Lds Ch. Avocations: drama, swimming, cooking, reading, aerobics. Home: 3275 April Dr Idaho Falls ID 83402 Office: Bonneville Joint Sch Dist # 93 3497 N Ammon Rd Idaho Falls ID 83402

NICHOLAS, LYNN HOLMAN, historian, researcher, writer; b. New London, Conn., Nov. 11, 1939; d. William Grizzard Holman and Carol (Ackiss) Wakelin; m. Robert Carter Nicholas III, Dec. 20, 1965; children: William C., R. Carter, Philip H. Student, Radcliffe Coll., 1957-59; diploma, U. Madrid, 1960; BA, Oxford (Eng.) U., 1964. Mem. adv. panel Presdl. Commn. on Holocaust Assets in the U.S., 1999. Author: The Rape of Europa, 1994 (Nat. Book Critics Circle award 1995). Recipient Chevalier Légion d'Honneur, France, 1999, Amicus Poloniae, 2003. E-mail: lynnick105@aol.com.

NICHOLS, ALICE MARSHALL, manufacturing executive; b. Phila., Aug. 19, 1947; d. Thomas John and Elizabeth (Morris) Marshall; m. John Slocum Nichols, Jan. 5, 1970; children: James Treadwell, Christopher Grosvenor. BA, Wheaton Coll., 1969; MA, Brown U., 1977. Tchr. Gordon Sch., East Providence, R.I., 1978-82, head middle sch., 1980-82; founder, pres. Up Country, Inc., Rumford, R.I., 1982—. Mem. mission com. Gen. Congl. Ch. Mem. Agawan Hunt Club (mem. squash team. Avocations: squash, tennis, golf, jogging, swimming. Home: 94 Congdon St Providence RI 02906-1413 Office: Up Country Inc 9 Newman Ave Rumford RI 02916-1939

NICHOLS, ALLENE RASMUSSEN, writer, educator; b. Paxton, Ill., Oct. 14, 1962; m. David Eugene Nichols, June 14, 1997; 1 child, Maxwell Clark. BS in Drama, Tex. Woman's U., 1987; MA, U. Tex., Dallas, 2002. Prof. North Lake C.C., Irving, Tex., 2002—; vol. tchr. The Writer's Garrett/Writers in the Schools, Dallas, 2003—; tchr. Gateway Sch., Arlington, Tex., 2003—. Author plays and poems. Big sister Big Bros./Big Sisters, Arlington, Tex. Mem.: The Writer's Garrett, DFW Playwrights, Austin ScriptWorks, The Dramatists Guild (assoc.). Avocations: travel, drawing, painting, tennis, gardening.

NICHOLS, AVIS B. state legislator; b. Waterbury, Vt. married; 3 children. Student, Burdett Bus. Coll., U. N.H. Mem. dist. 2 N.H. Ho. of Reps.; fin. com., adminstrv. rules com.; tchr. Burdett Bus. Coll.; pvt. sec. Mem. Merrimack County Rep. com. and exec. com., Rep. state com., state boiler adv. coun., Kearsarge Regional Sch. Bd., 1976-89, Warner budget com., 1977-83; co-chair Warner br. ARC, 1972-82, dir. swimming program; former marshal and fin. chair Rebekah Assembly N.H.; mem. Girl Scouts U.S. Mem. Welcome Rebekah Lodge (former noble grand). Avocations: oil painting, photography. Home: PO Box 306 Main St Warner NH 03278 Office: NH Ho of Reps State House Concord NH 03301

NICHOLS, BRENDA SUE, nursing educator; b. Henderson, Ky., Dec. 6, 1950; d. Marvin Elam and Cleona Jane (Bentley) Ashby; m. Harry David Nichols, Nov. 13, 1967; children: David Allen, Christopher Lynn, Thomas Andrew. AS in Nursing, U. Evansville, 1972, BSN, 1976, MA, 1978; DSc in Nursing, Ind. U., 1983. Staff nurse Community Meth. Hosp., Henderson, 1972-76, 81, 83; sch. nurse Evansville (Ind.)-Vandeburg Sch. Corp., 1977-78; nursing instr. Ky. Wesleyan Coll., Owensboro, 1978; asst. prof. U. Evansville, Ind., 1978-84; assoc. prof., dir. rsch. U. So. Miss., Hattiesburg, 1984-87; prof. nursing, dean sch. health sci. U. New Eng., N.Rivers, Lismore, Australia, 1987-90; assoc. prof., chair sch. nursing Old Dominion U., Norfolk, Va., 1990-97, prof., 1997—. Bd. dirs. Norfolk Neighborhood Clinic, pres., 1997-98; statis. cons. Dr. James Crumbaugh and R. Henrion, Biloxi, Miss., 1984-85; cons. Gold Coast Coll., Queensland, Australia, 1988-89, Mitchell Coll., Bathurst, Australia, 1988, Children's Hosp. of the Kings Daus., 1990-94; WHO cons. to U. Indonesia, 1995; cons. distance edn. Dept. Def., VA, Uniformed Svcs. U. Health Sci., 1995—; mem. peer evaln. bd. Coun. Baccalaureate and Higher Degrees Nat. League Nursing Accredition Commn., 1996-98. Author: Nursing Theories, 1989; contbr. chpts. to book, articles to profl. jours.; NCLEX item writer, 1993—. Vol. Am. Cancer Soc., 1983—, Drug and Alcohol Prevention, Virginia Beach, Va., 1990-92. Fellow Am. Pain Soc., Royal Coll. Nursing; mem. ANA, Nat. League for Nursing (program evaluator 1991—), Va. Assn. Colls. Nursing (sec. 1991), Va. League for Nursing (bd. dirs. 1996—), Am. Assn. Colls. Nursing (bd. dirs. 2000—). Democrat. Episcopalian. Avocations: swimming, crafts, reading. Office: Old Dominion U Sch Nursing Norfolk VA 23529-0500 Home: 5315 Greenbriar Ln Beaumont TX 77706-7348

NICHOLS, CAROL D. real estate professional; BA, U. Pitts., 1964; cert. in advanced mgmt., U. Chgo. From mgmt. trainee to buyer May Dept. Stores Co., Pitts., 1964-70; various mgmt. positions, then mng. dir. mortgage/real estate Tchrs. Ins. and Annuity Assn. Am., N.Y.C., 1970-97; sr. mng. dir. Insignia/ESG Capital Advisors, N.Y.C., 1997—. Instr. real estate div. continuing edn. Marymount Manhattan Coll., N.Y.C., 1975-76, Woman's Sch. Adult Edn. Ctr., N.Y.C., 1976-77; Real Estate Bd. N.Y., past chmn. fin. com. Recipient Nat. Humanitarian award, Arthur B. Lorber award Nat. Jewish Med. and Rsch. Ctr., Nat. Brotherhood award NCCJ. Mem. Assn. Real Estate Women (past pres.), Urban Land Inst. (trustee, past chmn. urban devel. and mixed use coun., past chmn. awards for excellence jury). Home: 165 Winfield St Norwalk CT 06855-1622 Office: Insignia/ESG Capital Advisors 200 Park Ave New York NY 10166-0005 E-mail: carol.nichols@iesg.com.

NICHOLS, CAROL-LEE, real estate broker, property manager; b. Middletown, N.Y., Aug. 1, 1964; d. Donald Larry Powell and Malia Kaipolani Gullette; m. Albert Emile Nichols, Mar. 21, 2003; children: Gerry Donald Pinson, David Bradford Powell, Sean Paul Clarke King. Diploma, Framingham (Mass.) Tech. Ctr., 1984; cert. in bookkeeping, CCD Tech. Ctr., Denver, 1991. Real estate brokers lic. J. Y. Monk. Dancer Dandy Dans, Denver, 1986—97; asst. deli mgr. Safeway, Denver, 1997—99; salesperson, broker Bob Vurno Real Estate, Fayetteville, NC, 1999—2002; broker N.C. Properties Unlimited, Fayetteville, 2002, Abode Real Estate, Fayetteville, 2002; owner CL's Real Estate, Fayetteville, 2002—. Realtor Fayetteville Assoc. Realtors, 2002—. Deacon Mountain Christian Ch., Lakewood, Colo., 1997; svc. dir. 1st Christian Ch., Fayetteville, 2002—. Home: 6958 Brockwood St Fayetteville NC 28314 Office: CLs Real Estate PO Box 71357 Fort Bragg NC 28307 Personal E-mail: CLsRE64@aol.com.

NICHOLS, CHERIE L. publishing executive, composer; b. Portsmouth, Va., Apr. 4, 1955; d. Conley Ray and Ann Lanease (Holderfield) Edwards; m. Harold Eugene Nichols, 1971 (div. 1975); life partner Chloe S. Burke. Art sales Poster Art-N-Graphics, Tarzana, Calif., 82-84; art cons. Martin Lawrence Galleries, L.A., 1984-86; print rm. mgr. Circle Fine Art Corp., L.A., 1986-93; driver United Cerebral Palsy, Sacramento, 1997-98; owner Morning Dove Pub., Sacramento, 1997—. Art dir. Lavender Libr., Archives and Cultural Exch., Sacramento, 1999-2002; artist, rep. and product devel. plush toys Milk Buds, 1999; assoc. Frames Unlimited, Mich., Ohio, Ind. Songwriter Time Doesn't Play, 2003, Reckless, 2003, If Only, 2004, What's There To Say, 2004. Avocations: music, guitar, drums, golf. Personal E-mail: cnik55@yahoo.com.

NICHOLS, DEBRA, bank executive; Sr. v.p. and dir. women's fin. adv. svcs. Wachovia Bank, Charlotte, NC, 1997—. Office: Wachovia Corp 301 South College St Charlotte NC 28288-0570*

NICHOLS, DIANE COLLEEN, municipal official; b. Oconto, Wis., Apr. 4, 1943; d. Earl Frank and Betty Florence (Ingram) Kamke; m. Lyle Richard Nichols, Aug. 14, 1965; children: Lara Jeanne, Brett William. BS, U. Wis., Madison, 1965; MS, U. Wis., Green Bay, 1976. Tchr. Ashwaubenon H.S., Green BaY, Wis., 1965—69; advsor U. Without Walls, Green Bay, 1977—79; small bus. owner A Nichol's Worth, Oconto, Wis., 1985—2000; devel. coord. Oconto Hosp. Found., 1999—2000; program mgr. Revitalize Gillett, Wis., 2002—. Pres. Oconto County Hist. Soc., 1994—2000. Editor:

(Book) John and Almira Volk, 1996, From the McCauslin to Jabswitch, 1998, The Oconto River Sackers, 2000. Methodist. Home: 4295 County J Oconto WI 54153 Office: Revitalize Gillett 117 E Main PO Box 304 Gillett WI 54124

NICHOLS, DONNA MARDELL, nurse anesthetist; b. Mpls., Mar. 24, 1936; d. Donald Burma and Lucille Elvera Nichols. Diploma, Northwestern Hosp. Sch. Nursing, Mpls., 1957, Mpls. Sch. Anesthesia, 1959; BS in Nurse Anesthesia, U. Minn., 1977. RN Minn., 1957. Nurse anesthetist Hennepin County Med. Ctr., Mpls., 1959—60, Eden Twp. Hosp., Castro Valley, Calif., 1960—63, Bethesda Hosp., St. Paul, 1963—64, Meml. Bapt. Hosp., Houston, 1964—67, St. Joseph's Hosp., St. Paul, 1967—95; ret., 1995. Mem.: Minn. Assn. Nurse Anesthetists (bd. dirs. 1975—77), Am. Assn. Nurse Anesthetists (emeritus, cert. anesthetists). Avocations: golf, gardening, antiques. Home: 10427 Upton Ave S Bloomington MN 55431

NICHOLS, EDIE DIANE, executive recruiter; b. Grahamstown, Eastern Cape Province, Republic of South Africa, Mar. 28, 1939; arrived in U.S., 1963; d. Cyril Doughtry and Dorothy Ethel (Nottingham) Tyson; m. John F. Nichols, Dec. 16, 1962 (div. Dec. 1978); 1 child, Ian Tyson. Adminstrv. asst. Am. Acad. Medicine, N.Y.C., 1963-64, Jack Lenor Larsen, Inc., N.Y.C., 1964-70; v.p. John Scott Fones, Inc., N.Y.C., 1971-76, Howard J. Rubenstein Assocs. Inc., N.Y.C., 1976-80; dir. comm. Carl Byoir & Assocs., N.Y.C., 1981-83; account supr. Hill and Knowlton, N.Y.C., 1983-85; broker Cross & Brown Co., N.Y.C., 1986-88; v.p. Marc Nichols Assocs., Inc., N.Y.C., 1989-95; mng. ptnr. Nichols Brown Internat., N.Y.C., 1995—. Trustee Ctrl. Pk. Hist. Soc., N.Y.C., 1978-80. Mem. NOW, Internat. Assn. Corp. and Profl. Recruitment, N.Y. Women in Comm. (pub. rels. chair 1980-81, v.p., programs bd. dirs. 1985-87), Fin. Women's Assn. of N.Y. (bd. dirs. 1997-98), City Club of N.Y. (trustee, v.p., fin. and devel. 1987-89). Democrat. Episcopalian. Office: Nichols Brown Internat 155 W 20th Ste 2J New York NY 10011-3612 Home: 16 Stuyvesant Oval Apt 10F New York NY 10009

NICHOLS, ELIZABETH GRACE, nursing educator, dean; b. Feb. 1, 1943; d. Terence and Eleanor Denny (Payne) Quilliam; m. Gerald Ray Nichols, Nov. 20, 1965; children: Tina Lynn, Jeffrey David. BSN, San Francisco State U., 1969; MS, U. Calif., San Francisco, 1970, D of Nursing Sci., 1974; MA, Idaho State U., 1989. Staff nurse Peninsula Hosp., Burlingame, Calif., 1966-72; asst. prof. U. Calif.-San Francisco Sch. Nursing, 1974-82; chmn. dept. nursing Idaho State U., Pocatello, 1982-85; assoc. dean Coll. Health Scis. Sch. Nursing U. Wyo., Laramie, 1985-91, asst. to pres. for program revs., 1991-95; dean Coll. Nursing U. N.D., 1995—. Cons. U. Rochester, NY, 1979, Carroll Coll., Mont., 1980, divsn. Nursing Dept. HHS, Washington, U. Maine, Ft. Kent, 1992, Stanford Hosp. Nursing Svc., Calif., 1981—82, Ea. N.Mex. U., 1988, Met. State U., Minn., 1998, U. Nev.-Reno, 2003; cons. evaluator Higher Learning Commn., 1993—; site visitor CCNE, 1998—; mem. accreditation review com. The Higher Learning Commn., 2001—. Contbr. articles to profl. jours. Mem. adv. bd. dir. Ombudsman Svc. of Contra Costa Calif., 1979—82, U. Calif. Home Care Svc., San Francisco, 1975—82, Free Clin. of Pocatello, 1984; mem. bd. of rev. coun. baccalaureate & higher degree programs, 1990—92. Fellow ACE, U. Maine Sys., 1990—91. Fellow: Am. Acad. Nursing, Gerontol. Soc. Am. (chmn. clin. medicine sect. 1987, sec. 1990—93); mem.: ANA, Western Inst. Nursing (chmn. 1990—92, bd. govs., bd. dir. mid-west alliance), Idaho Nurses Assn. (dist. 51 adv. bd. dir. 1982—84), ND Nurses Assn. (pres. 2003—), Oakland Ski Club. (1st v.p. 1981—82), Sigma Theta Tau. Office Phone: 701-777-4555. E-mail: elizabeth.nichols@mail.und.nodak.edu.

NICHOLS, ELIZABETH LITTERER, real estate developer; b. Nashville, Sept. 24, 1953; d. William and Jean (Gray) Litterer; m. J. Donald Nichols, Dec. 7, 1985; 1 child, Mary Britt. BS, U. Tenn. Mgmt. trainee First Am. Nat. Bank, Nashville, 1975-76; mortgage loan officer Dobson's Johnson, Nashville, 1976-81; v.p. fin. JDN Ent., Nashville/Atlanta, 1981-89; pres. JDN Realty Corp., 1989—. Treas. bd. Cumberland Mus. of Sci. Ctr.; bd. dirs., exec. com. Nashville Ballet; bd. dirs. Tenn. Repertory Theatre, Mercedes Benz of Nashville; chmn. Swan Ball Auction Com.; active Jr. League of Nashville. Mem. Internat. Coun. Shopping Ctrs. Republican. Episcopalian. Avocations: snow skiing, tennis, reading, swimming. Home: 416 Jackson Blvd Nashville TN 37205-3426 Office: JDN Realty Corp Ste 400 359 E Paces Ferry Rd NE Atlanta GA 30305-2373

NICHOLS, FREDA CAROL, elementary school educator, artist; d. Clinton Euel Austin and Rowena Maddeline Boyd; m. Carl Daniel Nichols; children: Adam Bradly, Amy Loren. BA magna cum laude, Ferrum Coll., 1998. Teller, bookkeeper 1st Nat. Bank Ferrum, Va., 1979—84; gen. clk. Ctrl. Tel. Co., Martinsville, Va., 1990—91; asst. mgr. print shop Ferrum Coll., 1991—96, acad. counselor, 1998—99; specialized reading tutor Henry (Va.) Elem., 1998—99; audit clk. Atlanta Mut. Ins. Co., Roanoke, Va., 1999—2000; art educator Benjamin Franklin Mid. Sch., Rocky Mountain, Va., 2000—. CSIP Benjamin Franklin Mid. Sch., Rocky Mountain, mem. pub. rels. com. Editor: (yearbook) The Spectacle, 2002. Children's ch. instr. Evangelistic Ho. Prayer, Ferrum, 1995—2003. Mem.: Piedmont Arts Assn., Nat. Art Edn. Assn., Alpha Chi. Avocations: painting, photography, travel, collecting art, walking. Office: Benjamin Franklin Mid Sch 375 Middle School Rd Rocky Mount VA 24151

NICHOLS, GRACE A. retail executive; b. 1946; married; 2 children. Degree, UCLA. With Weinstock's, Sacramento, 1971—78; mgr. gen. merchandise The Broadway, Calif., 1978—86; v.p., mgr. gen. merchandise Victoria's Secret Stores, 1986—88, exec. v.p., mgr. gen. merchandise, 1989—91, pres., CEO, 1991—. Office: Victorias Secret Stores Inc Four Ltd Pkwy Reynoldsburg OH 43068*

NICHOLS, IRIS JEAN, illustrator; b. Yakima, Wash., Aug. 2, 1938; d. Charles Frederick and Velma Irene (Hacker) Beisner; (div. June 1963); children: Reid William, Amy Jo; m. David Gary Nichols, Sept. 21, 1966. BFA in Art, U. Wash., 1978. Freelance illustrator, graphic designer, Seattle, 1966—2004; med. illustrator, head dept. illustration Swedish Hosp. Med. Ctr., Seattle, 1981-86; owner, med. and sci. illustrator Art for Medicine, Seattle, 1986—2003. Med. illustrator U. Wash., Seattle, 1966-67; part-time med. illustrator, graphic coord. dept. art The Mason Clinic, 1968-78; instr. advanced illustration Cornish Coll. Arts, Seattle, 1988-90; organized, coordinated and gifted the artwork of Prof. Glen E. Alps of U. Wash. after his death in 1966. Illustrator various books including Bryophytes of Pacific Northwest, 1966, Microbiology, 1973, 78, 82, 94, 98, Introduction to Human Physiology, 1980, Understanding Human Anatomy and Physiology, 1983, Human Anatomy, 1984 Regional Anesthesia, 1990, many other med. and sci. books, and children's books on various subjects; exhibited in group shows at Seattle Pacific Sci. Ctr., summer 1979, 82, Am. Coll. Surgeons (1st prize 1974), N.W. Urology Conf. (1st prize 1974, 76, 2d prize 1975); pub. illustrations Constellation Pk. and Marine Res., City Seattle Pk., 1999. Pres. ArtsWest (formerly West Seattle Arts Coun.), 1983; active Seattle Art Mus.; chmn. West Seattle (Wash.) H.S. Art Acquisition Com., 2003—. Named to West Seattle H.S. Alumni Hall of Fame, 1986, Matrix Table, 1986-96. Mem. Assn. Med. Illustrators (Murial McLatchie Fine Arts award 1981), Nat. Mus. Women in the Arts (Wash. state com., bd. dirs. 1987-95, pres. 1993-94), Women Painters of Wash. (pres. 1987-89), U. Wash. Alumni Assn., Lambda Rho (pres. alumni assn. 1995-98, treas. 2002-04) Avocations: artwork, printmaking, small books. E-mail: artformed@aol.com.

NICHOLS, JOANN EDITH HESELTON, retired legal secretary; b. Tinmouth, Vt., Dec. 1, 1930; d. Ward McKinley and Gladys (Gilman) Heselton; m. Alaric George Nichols, Oct. 6, 1973 (dec. May 1991). Office worker Holstein-Friesian Assn., Brattleboro, Vt., 1948-53; bookkeeper Brattleboro Trust Co., 1953-60; sec. Gates Ins. Agy., Brattleboro, 1960-71; from admissions sec. to sec. to pres. Marlboro (Vt.) Coll., 1971-84; legal sec. various law offices, Brattleboro, 1984-87; sec., paralegal John A. Rocray, Brattleboro, 1987-95. Author: Descendants Giles Roberts, Scarborough, Maine, 1994, Index Known Cemetery Listings in Vermont, 1995. Historian Centre Congl. Ch., Brattleboro, 1990—; treas. Blind Artisans of Vt., 1991—. Mem. Nat. Geneal. Soc., Geneal. Soc. Vt. (sec. 1971-75, pres. 1975-93), N.H. Soc. Genealogists, NE Hist. Geneal. Soc. Avocations: genealogy, history, research. Home: 110 Chestnut St Brattleboro VT 05301-6579

NICHOLS, KAREN, academic administrator; b. Ind. m. Jim Nichols. DO, U. Health Scis., Coll. Osteo. Medicine, Kansas City. Intern and resident in internal medicine Okla. Osteo. Hosp., Tulsa; asst. dean grad. med. edn. Ariz. Coll. Osteo. Medicine; dean Chgo. Coll. Osteo. Medicine, 2002—. Contbr. articles to profl. jours. Bd. trustees Mut. Ins. Co. of Ariz.; with Mesa Symphony, Mesa United Way, Central Christian Ch. Recipient Physician of Yr., Ariz. Osteo. Med. Assn., 1996, Educator of Yr., Mesa Gen. Hosp. Mem.: Am. Osteo. Assn. (chair bur. state and govt. affairs, mem. health related and fed. health policies coms., chair adv. com. of end-of-life care). Office: Chgo Coll Osteo Medicine Midwestern U 555 31st St Downers Grove IL 60515

NICHOLS, KAREN, architect; Grad., Smith Coll., MIT. Prin. Michael Graves & Assocs., Princeton, NJ, 1977—. Fellow: AIA. Office: 341 Nassau St Princeton NJ 08540

NICHOLS, KATHIE S. psychologist; b. Bonner Springs, Kans., Aug. 30, 1952; d. Bailey Bennett and Helen Francis Wiles; m. Patrick Raymond Nichols, Feb. 14, 1985; m. William Todd Hyten, Sept. 0, 1975 (div. July 0, 1983); children: Sarah Francis, Ami Hyten, Lisa Hyten. BA, Washburn U., 1992, Masters, 1994; PhD, U. Kans., 2000. Lic. psychologist Kans. Behavioral Sci. Regulatory Bd., 2000. Rschr. psychophysiological lab Menninger Found., Topeka, 1996—2002; therapist Family Svc. and Guidance Ctr., Topeka, 1999—2000; clin. dir. Prison Health Svcs., Topeka, 2000—01; pvt. practice Bldg. Bridges, Lawrence, Kans., 2000—. Vol. Battered Women's Task Force, Topeka, 1990—92; sch. violence task force FBI, Va., 2000—00; presenter in field. Author: (children's book) Sarah, a story of love and Adoption; contbr. articles to publs. Precinct com. person Dem. Party, Lawrence & Topeka, 1985—2003; officer Achievement Pl. for Boys, Lawrence, Kans., 2001—03. Mem.: APA, Kans. Psychol. Assn. Achievements include research in effects of media violence on children. Office: Building Bridges Ste G 10 E 9th Lawrence KS 66044 E-mail: drknichols@sunflower.com.

NICHOLS, LEE ANN, library media specialist; b. Denver, Apr. 27, 1946; d. Bernard Anthony and Margaret Mary (Pughes) Wilhelm; m. Robert Joseph Nichols, July 12, 1975; children: Rachel, Steven, Sarah. BS in Edn., St. Mary of the Plains, Dodge City, Kans., 1968; MA in Edn., Colo. U., 1978. Cert. type B profl. tchr., Colo. Tchr. So. Tama Sch. Dist. Montour, Iowa, Iowa, 1968-70, Strasburg (Colo.) Sch. Dist., 1970-73; svc. rep. Montain Bell, Denver, 1973-75; libr., tchr. Simla (Colo). Sch. Dist., 1976-78; dir. Simla Br. Libr., 1978-81; dir. Christian edn. St. Anthony's Ch/, Sterling, Colo., 1983-84; libr. cons. Rel Valley Sch., Iliff, Colo., 1984-98, Plateau Sch. Dist., Peetz, Colo., 1986-99; dir. Fleming Cmty. Libr., Colo., 1997—. Mem. Colo. Coun. for Libr. Devel., Denver, 1986-92, chmn. 1991; instr. Northeastern Jr. Coll., Sterling; del. Gov.'s Conf. on Libr. and Info. Scis., 1990. Author: Computers 101. . .in a Nutshell, 2002; contbr. articles to profl. jours. Active Sterling Arts Coun., sec., 1982-85, v.p., 1985, pres., 1986-87; chair Northeastern Jr. Coll. Found., Sterling, 1983-87, mem. 1981-91; mem. community adv. coun. Northeastern Jr. Coll., 1991-93, chair, 1993; bd. dirs. Wagon Wheel chpt. Girl Scouts Am., 1975-78. Mem. ALA, Am. Assn. Sch. Librs., Assn. Libr. Svcs. to Children, Colo. Ednl. Media Assn., Colo. Libr. Coun., Internat. Reading Assn. (Colo. Coun.). Avocations: reading, sewing. Home: 12288 County Road 370 Sterling CO 80751-8494 Office: Fleming Cmty Libr 506 N Fremont Ave Fleming CO 80728-9520

NICHOLS, MARGARET IRBY, librarian, educator, library and information scientist; b. Maud, Tex., July 9, 1924; d. James Rainwater and Winnie (Pride) Irby; m. Irby Coghill Nichols Jr., Apr. 18, 1953 (div. Jan. 1992); children: Nina Nichols Austin, Irby C. Nichols III. BA, U. North Tex., 1945; MLS, U. Tex., 1957. Libr. Mercedes (Tex.) H.S., 1945-46; cataloger Bethany (W.Va.) Coll., 1946; chief reference libr. Tex. Tech U., Lubbock, 1946-48; ref. libr. El Paso Pl., 1949-51; chief reference libr. N.Mex. Mil. Inst., Roswell, 1951-53; sch. libr. South Jr. H.S., Roswell, 1954-55; acad. dean Selwyn Sch., Denton, Tex., 1965-67; prof. Sch. Libr. and Info. Scis. U. North Tex., Denton, 1968-91, assoc. dean Sch. Libr. and Info. Scis., 1989-91, emeritus prof., 1996. Cons. in field, 1991—; exec. bd. North Tex. Regional Libr. Sys., 1996—, chair, 1997-99; chmn. exec. bd. Libr. Ptnrs., 2003— Author: Core Reference Collections, 1986, 2d edit., 1993, Guide to Reference Sources, 4th edit., 1992, Reference Sources for Small and Medium Libraries, 1988, 2d edit., 1994, Texas Information Sources, 1996, Building And Using A Core Reference Collection, 4th edit., 2004; contbr. articles to profl. jours. Mem. ALA (mem. coun. 1988-92), Tex. Libr. Assn. (exec. bd. 1983-86, 88-92, pres. 1984-85, Disting. Svc. award 1990, Lois Bebout Outstanding Svc. award Ref. Roundtable 1995, recipient Elizabeth Crabb Disting. Svc. award 2003). Home: 2514 Royal Ln Denton TX 76209-2244

NICHOLS, NATALIE REGA, development consultant; b. Mount Pleasant, Pa., July 21, 1970; d. John Michael and Paula Jean Rega; m. Edward Charles Nichols, June 10, 1964; 1 child, Adam Richard. BA, Washington and Jefferson Coll., Washington, Pa., 1992. Pers. asst. Adelphoi Inc., Latrobe, Pa., 1991; feature writer Daily Courier, Connellsville, Pa., 1992; devel. cons. Teeter Assocs., Inc., Greensburg, Pa., 1992—. Bd. sec. Nichols Electronics, Inc., Pitts., 1999—. Mem.: Phi Beta Kappa.

NICHOLS, SANDRA B. public health service officer; b. Little Rock, Mar. 27, 1958; m. Ronnie A. Nichols, 1985; 1 child, Marquise. BA in Chemistry, Columbia Coll., Mo., 1980; student, Meharry Med. Coll., 1979-80; MS in Biology, Tenn. State U., 1982; MD, U. Ark., 1988. With dept. physiology U. Ark. Med. Scis., Little Rock, 1984-85, with microbiology lab., 1985-88, resident dept. family and community medicine, 1988-91, chief resident dept. family and community medicine, 1990-91, fellow dept. family and community medicine, occupational and environ. medicine, 1991-92; dir. Ark. Dept. of Health, Little Rock, 1994—; med. dir. United Health Care Corp. of Ark., 1998-2000; sr. med. dir. United Healthcare Ala., Inc., 2000. Adj. prof. health adminstrn. U. Ark., Little Rock; officer dept. health and human svcs. FDA; physician Mid Delta Health Clinic, 1992-94, interim med. dir., 1993-94; med. educator Delta Area Health Agy., U. Ark. Med. Scis., 1992—; dir. Merc. Bank; bd. dirs. Nat. Cancer Policy Bd., Nat. Mamography Quality Assurance Adv. Com. Author: (with others) Family Medicine Principles and Practice, 1994, 95; contbr. articles to profl. jours. Officer HHS, FDA; mem. Pine Bluff Arsenal Citizen's Adv. Com.; chmn. Gov.'s Partnership Coun. for Children and Families, Women Execs. in State Govt.; conf. participant Am. Swiss Found. Young Leaders Conf., 1995; mem. Ark. chpt. Internat. Women's Forum, Ark. Arts Ctr., Nat. Cancer Policy Bd., Nat. Mammography Quality Assurance Assessment Com.; bd. dirs. Mercantile Bank; spkr. Career Day, local schs.; vol. physician high schs. Recipient Nat. FBI Comty. Leadership award, 1996; named one of Ark. Bus. Top 100 Women in Ark., 1996-97, Top 10 Women in Ark., 1995, Top 100 Women in Ark., 1998, 1999, one of Outstanding Young Women in Am., 1981; Nat. Med. fellow, 1984-85; Pub. Health Leadership Inst. scholar, 1996, scholar Columbia Coll., 1976-80. Mem. AMA, Ark. Med. Assn., Am. Acad. Family Physicians, Ark. Acad. Family Physicians, Pulaski County Med. Soc., Assn. State and Territorial Health Officers (sec.-treas.), Zeta Phi Beta. Avocations: tennis, reading, speaking, cycling, travel. Office: 3700 Colonnade Pkwy Birmingham AL 35243-2361

NICHOLS, SANDRA JEAN, secondary school educator, coach; b. Robinson, Jan. 11, 1947; d. Chester Lyle and Effie Anna (Hickox) Bailey. BS in Edn., Ea. Ill. U., 1969, MA, 1989. Music tchr. Jasper County Schs., Newton, Ill., 1961—69; band dir. Dieterich (Ill.) Schs., 1969—72; music and English tchr. Newton H.S., 1972—99; music tchr. Hutsonville (Ill.) Schs., 1999—2003; coach softball Newton H.S., 1977—2001; choir dir., English tchr. Robinson (Ill.) H.S., 2003—. Named Hutsonville (Ill.) Hall of Fame. Mem.: NEA, Ill. Edn. Assn., Ill. Music Educators Assn., Music Educators Nat. Conf.

NICHOLS, VICKI ANNE, financial consultant, librarian; b. Denver, June 10, 1949; d. Glenn Warner and Loretta Irene (Chalender) Adams; m. Robert H. Nichols, Oct. 28, 1972 (div.); children: Christopher Travis, Lindsay Meredith. BA, Colo. Coll., 1972; postgrad., U. Denver, 1976-77. Treas., controller, dir. Polaris Resources, Inc., Denver, 1972-86; controller InterCap Devel. Corp., 1986-87; treas., controller, dir. Transnat. Cons., Ltd., 1986-91; web coord. Jefferson County (Colo.) Pub. Libr., 1986—. Dir., owner Nichols Bus. Services. Home: 4305 Brentwood St Wheat Ridge CO 80033-4412 Office: 10200 W 20th Ave Lakewood CO 80215 E-mail: vnichols@jefferson.lib.co.us.

NICHOLS, VIRGINIA VIOLET, independent insurance agent, accountant; b. Monroe County, Mo., Oct. 26, 1928; d. Elmer W. and Frances L. (McKinney) N. Student, Belleville (Ill.) Jr. Coll., 1959-60, Rockhurst Coll., 1964-65, Avila Coll., Kansas City, Mo., 1981-84. Sec. Panhandle Eastern Pipeline Co., Kansas City, Mo., 1964-65, St. Louis County Dept. Revenue, 1965-69, Forest Park Community Coll., 1969-71, Nooney Co., St. Louis, 1971-77, J. A. Baer Enterprises, St. Louis, 1979; acct. Panhandle Eastern Pipe Line Co., Kansas City, Mo., 1979-85. Vol. ARC, 1965—. Mem. Profl. Secs. Internat. (Sec. of Year 1979, sec. Mo. div. 1975-76), Jr. Women's C. of C. (Girl of Yr. 1975, pres. 1974-75), Soroptimist's Internat. (treas. Kansas City chpt. 1990-91), Desk and Derrick Club Kansas City (pres. 1999). Republican. Mem. United Ch. of Christ. Home: PO Box 33076 Kansas City MO 64114-0076 Office Phone: 816-941-8328.

NICHOLSON, ELLEN ELLIS, clinical social worker; b. Boston, Apr. 1, 1940; d. George Letham and Mary Stirling (Money) McIver; divorced; 1 child, Matthew Norman Ellis. Dental Hygienist, Forsyth Coll., 1959; BS, Northeastern U., 1973, MEd in Counseling, 1974; MSW, Boston U., 1984. Registered dental hygienist, Mass. Dental hygienist, 1959-66; clin. coord., pvt. dental practice Forsyth Dental Ctr., Boston, 1966-70; dir. vol. counseling Solomon Mental Health Ctr., Lowell, Mass., 1974-75; social worker East Boston Social Ctrs., Inc., 1976-77, dir. youth family counseling, 1977-79; supr. family svc. Boston Housing Authority, 1979-81; social worker Mass. Soc. Prevention Cruelty to Children, Hyannis, 1984-86, supr., 1986-93, clinic dir., 1993-95; dir. profl. svcs. Child and Family Svc. of Cape Cod, Hyannis, 1995-98, dir., 1998—, dir. Abuse Prevention Svcs., 1995-96, dir., 1995—. Psychotherapist Riverview Sch., Sandwich, Mass., 1989-93. Advisor youth group Christ Episcopal Ch., Needham, Mass., 1960-64, St. Paul's Ch., Newburyport, Mass., 1964-65; vol. counselor Solomon Mental Health Ctr., Lowell, 1972-74; chair Barnstable County Children's Task Force, 1994-96; chmn. adv. com. Barnstable County Sexual Abuse Intervention Network, 1994-96; mem. task force Barnstable County Juvenile Firesetters, 1995-96, mem. steering com., 1996—; mem. adv. bd. Cape and Islands Child Advocacy Ctr.; mem. Cape & Islands Domestic Violence Coun. Bd., 1998—. Mem. NASW, Am. Profl. Soc. on Abuse of Children, Assn. for Treatment of Sexual Abusers, Sigma Phi Alpha, Sigma Epsilon Rho, Kappa Delta Pi. Avocations: travel, ballroom dancing, skiing. Office: Child and Family Svc Cape Cod 1019 Rt 132 Hyannis MA 02601-1839

NICHOLSON, FRANCES MARY BAUM, secondary school educator, writer; b. Pasadena, Calif., Nov. 30, 1956; d. William Frank Baum and Mary Bryce Cogswell; m. Paul Michael Nicholson, June 27, 1981; children: Bryce Clinton, Mary Katherine. BA, U. of the Pacific, 1978; MFA, Spalding U., 2002—. Ryan single subject tchg. credential Calif. Tchr. history and govt. Blair H.S., Altadena, Calif., 1984—. Theater critic San Gabriel Valley News Group, West Covina, Calif., 1982—. Author: (book of poetry) The Song Inside, On Becoming Human. Ordained elder and deacon Pasadena (Calif.) Presbyn. Ch., 1974—2003. Named Tchr. of Excellence, Pasadena Rotary Club, 2001; named one of L.A. County's Most Inspiring Tchrs., Sta. KRTH - FM, 2002; recipient Excellence in Edn. award, West Covina Optimist Club, 1994, 1st Pl. and 3rd Pl. Grad. Poetry award, Metroversity, Inc. of Louisville, 2003. Mem.: Delta Kappa Gamma, Phi Delta Kappa. Independent. Presbyterian. Home: 1810 Morada Pl Altadena CA 91001 Office: Blair H S 1201 S Marengo Ave Pasadena CA 91106 Personal E-mail: mznick311@aol.com.

NICHOLSON, FREDA HYAMS, museum executive, medical educator; b. Asheville, N.C., Sept. 10, 1934; d. John Fred and Thelma (Lewis) Hyams; m. Henry Hale Nicholson Jr., Sept. 24, 1956; children: Henry Hale III, T.D. Miller, J. Christie, Michael Witherspoon, Freda Amanda, Stuart. RN, St. Joseph's Hosp., 1955; BS in Nursing and Biology, Queens Coll., 1959, LHD (hon.), 1982; MEd, U. N.C., Charlotte, 1976. Surg. nurse Ochesner Clinic, New Orleans, 1955-56; nursing adminstr. Presbyn. Hosp., Charlotte, 1956-59; part-time instr. biology and nursing Ctrl. Piedmont Coll., Charlotte, 1976-81; health educator, edn. curator Discover Place, Inc. (formerly Charlotte Nature Mus.), 1971-80, pres., CEO, 1981—. Acting dir. Discovery Place, Charlotte, 1981; cons. health Health Adventure, Asheville, 1968; mem. mus. planning com. Sci. Mus. Project, Little rock, 1984; in internat. partnership NEA, Washington, 1983; mem. U.S. Cultural Commn./India, participant in seminar in India, 1984; mem. adv. panel NSF, 1988—; bd. dirs. First Union Nat. Bank N.C. Bd. dirs. United Way, Charlotte, 11983, March of Dimes, Charlotte, 1978-83, Jr. Achievement, 1983—, Mission Air, 1984—; cons. Gov.'s Com. for Econ. Growth throuth Edn., 1984; mem. exec. bd. N.C. Sch. of Math. and Sci., 1986—; active mem. local, state and nat. med. auxs., 1956—; mem. bd. visitors J.C. Smith U., Charlotte, 1983—; mem. adv. panel NSF, 1988—. Recipient Gov.'s N.C. award, 1994; named Woman of Yr., City of charlotte, 1982, Nat. Outstanding Alumna Alpha Chi Omega, 1983, Outstanding Alumna Queens Coll., 1982. Mem. AAUW, Women Execs., Assoc. Sci./Tech. Ctrs. (sec. 1984-90, pres. 1990), Internat. Coun. Mus. Execs. (commr. Semocet-Sci. 1988—), Am. Assn. Mus. (commr. for accreditation, at-large coun., mem. 1989—), S.E. Mus. Coun., Greater Charlotte C. of C. (advt. com.), Jr. Women, Guild of Nature Mus. Office: Discovery Place 301 N Tryon St Charlotte NC 28202-2138

NICHOLSON, JENNIFER DENISE, workers' compensation claims administrator; b. Redlands, Calif., Apr. 30, 1968; d. Jimmie Douglas Crow and Kathleen Ann (Gasponi) Hartman; m. Steven Edgar Nicholson, Dec. 17, 1994. BS in Math., Azusa Pacific U., 1990. Cert. workers' compensation claims profl. Ins. Ednl. Assn., Calif. Workers' compensation adjuster GAB Bus. Svcs., San Bernardino, Calif., 1990-92, Alexsis Risk Mgmt., West Covina, Calif., 1992; workers' compensation sr. adjuster Utica Mut. Ins. Co., Glendora, Calif., 1992-94; workers' compensation claims supr. May Dept. Stores Co., Redondo Beach, Calif., 1994-95, workers' compensation claims mgr., 1995-97; worker's compensation supr. Keenan & Assoc., Torrance, Calif., 1997-98, worker's compensation mgr., 1998—99; asst. svc. ctr. mgr. AIG Claim Svcs. South Coast Metro., Calif., 2000—. Mem. NAFE.

NICHOLSON, JUNE C. DANIELS, retired speech pathologist; b. Augusta, Maine, Dec. 28, 1938; d. Sumner T. and Bernadette (Dulac) Daniels; m. Kenneth E. Nicholson, June 27, 1964; children: Jeffrey Scott, Daren

Patrick. BS, Abilene Christian U., 1963; MS, U. Vt., 1980. Cert. ASHA CCC, Vt. Dept. Edn.; cert. tchr., Vt. Speech pathologist grades K-12 Arlington (Vt.) Pub. Sch., ret., 1996. Vol. Peace Corp., Shumen, Bulgaria, 2001—03, St. Lucia, West Indies, 1971—73. Mem. NEA, Ret. Tchrs. Assn. of NEA, Am. Speech/Hearing Assn., Vt. Speech/Hearing Assn., Vt. Edn. Assn., Vt. Ret. Tchrs. Assn., Delta Kappa Gamma.

NICHOLSON, MARILYN LEE, arts administrator; b. San Jose, Calif., Feb. 7, 1949; d. John Hart Nicholson and Betty Ann (Price) Shepardson; m. Neal Luit Evenhuis. BA in English and History, U. Ariz., 1972; BFA in Studio, MA in English, U. Hawaii-Manoa, Honolulu, 1977, AS, 1984. Edn. coord., dir. Bishop Mus. Arts and Crafts Sch., Honolulu, 1977-79; owner Fiber Arts Store, Kailua, Hawaii, 1978-82; field coord. Hawaii State Found. on Culture and Arts, Honolulu, 1981-85; exec. dir. Sedona (Ariz.) Arts Ctr., 1986-92, Volcano (Hawaii) Art Ctr., 1992—. Mem. bd. artist selection com. Ariz. Indian Living Treasures, 1988-92; bd. dirs., treas. Sedona Cultural Arts Ctr., 1987-92; conf. speaker Nat. Assembly Arts Agys., 1988. Founding Chmn. Sedona Gallery Assn., 1990-92; mem. com. Sedona Acad., 1986-92; mem. steering com. community plan City of Sedona, 1989-91; commr. Arts & Cultural Ctr., Sedona, 1989-91; mem. exec. com. planning Volcano Community Assn., 1993-96. Recipient Mayor's award for Disting. Svc., Sedona City Coun., 1992. Mem. Hawaii Mus. Assn. (bd. dirs. 1995-00), Cooper Ctr. Coun. (bd. dirs. 1992—), Aloha Festivals-Hawaii Island (bd. dirs. 1992-99). Office: Volcano Art Ctr PO Box 129 Volcano HI 96785

NICHOLSON, PAMELA D. school librarian; b. Norwich, Conn., Sept. 5, 1972; d. William H. Nicholson, III and Nancy S. Nicholson. Degree in Libr. Tech. Assistance, Three Rivers CTC, Norwich, Conn., 1994; AS in Liberal Arts, Three Rivers CTC, 1994; BA in Psychology, Ctrl. Conn. State U., 1997; MLS, So. Conn. State U., 2001. Lic. sch. media Conn., 2001. Children's libr. Raymond Libr., Oakdale, Conn., 1990—94; children's libr. asst. Bristol Pub. Libr., Bristol, Conn., 1995—96; children's libr. Cragin Meml. Libr., Colchester, Conn., 1997—99; school-pub. libr. program coord. Killingly Pub. Schs., Danielson, Conn., 1999—2001; sch. media specialist Killingly Ctrl. Sch., Dayville, Conn., 2001—. Chairperson Nutmeg Children's Book Award, Conn., 1999—2001. Home: 41 Estabrook Rd Hampton CT 06247 Office: Killingly Central Elementary School 60 Soap St Dayville CT 06241 Office Phone: 860-779-6759. Business E-Mail: pnicholson@killingly.k12.ct.us.

NICKEL, JANET MARLENE MILTON, geriatrics nurse; b. Manitowoc, Wis., June 9, 1940; d. Ashley and Pearl Milton; m. Curtis A. Nickel, July 29, 1961; children: Cassie, Debra, Susan. Diploma, Milw. Inst., 1961; ADN, N.D. State U., 1988. Nurse Milw. VA, Wood, Wis., 1961-62; supervising nurse Park Lawn Convalescent Hosp., Manitowoc, 1964-65; newsletter editor Fargo (N.D.) Model Cities Program, 1970-73, supervising night nurse Rosewood on Broadway, Luth. Hosps. and Homes, Fargo, 1973-92; assoc. dir. nursing Elim Care Ctr., Fargo, 1992-94, night nurse, 1994—. Mem. Phi Eta Sigma. Office: 3534 S University Dr Fargo ND 58104-6228

NICKELS, ELIZABETH ANNE, office furniture manufacturing executive; 2 children. BSBA in Acctg., Econs. and Bus. Admin., Aquinas Coll., 1983. CPA. CFO, mem. exec. and ops. coms. Universal Forest Products, Grand Rapids, Mich., 1993-2000; CFO Herman Miller, Inc., Zeeland, Mich., 2000—. Office: Herman Miller Inc 855 E Main Ave Zeeland MI 49464-0302

NICKELS, RUTH ELIZABETH, band director; b. Warsaw, Ind., Nov. 21, 1955; d. Marjorie Jane Shipley; m. David Brent Nickels, July 7, 2001. MusB in Performance, DePauw U., 1978; MusM in Performance, Ithaca Coll., 1980; cert. in edn., Grace Coll., 1986; post-master credits, Ind. U., 1986. Profl. tchg. lic. music edn. Dir. bands Fairfield Jr.-Sr. H.S., Goshen, Ind., 1986—92; H.S. band dir. Yorktown (Ind.) H.S., 1992—93; dir. bands Orleans (Ind.) Jr.-Sr. H.S., 1993—97, Southwestern Jr.-Sr. H.S., Hanover, Ind., 1997—. Music judge Ind. State Music Assn., Indpls. Mem.: NEA, Ind. State Tchrs. Assn., Ind. Bandmasters Assn., Music Educator's Nat. Conf., Women Band Dirs. Assn., Nat. Band Assn. Avocations: reading, travel, cooking, walking. Home: PO Box 337 Hanover IN 47243 Office: Southwestern Jr-Sr HS 167 S Main Cross St Hanover IN 47243 Personal E-mail: renickels@msn.com. Business E-Mail: rnickels@swjcs.k12.in.us.

NICKELSON, KIM RENÉ, internist; b. Chgo., Feb. 13, 1956; d. Robert William and Carolynn Lucille (Marts) N.; m. Louis Peter Sguros; children: Brian Louis, Justin Robert Peter. BS in Chemistry, U. Ill., 1978; MD, Loyola U., Maywood, Ill., 1981. Diplomate Am. Bd. Internal Medicine. Intern and resident in internal medicine Luth. Gen. Hosp., Park Ridge, Ill., 1981-84; pvt. practice Oakbrook, Ill., 1984-87, Plantation, Fla., 1987—. Adj. attending staff Rush-Presbyn. St. Luke's Med. Ctr., Chgo., 1984-87; assoc. attending staff Hinsdale (Ill.) Hosp., 1984-87, Westside Regional Med. Ctr., Plantation, Plantation Gen. Hosp., Fla. Med. Ctr., Lauderhill, Fla. Musician Elk Grove (Ill.) Community Band, 1978-87, Hollywood (Fla.) Symphony Orch., 1987—, Sunrise (Fla.) Pops Symphony, 1987—, Deerfield (Fla.) Community Band, 1987—. Mem. ACP, Internat. Horn Soc. Office: Internal Medicine Assocs 499 NW 70th Ave Ste 200 Plantation FL 33317-7578

NICKENS, PAULA, political organization administrator; b. Washington; BA, U. D.C., 1975. Chair Dem. State Com., Washington, 1998—. Mem. Assn. of State Dem. Chairs. Office: Dem State Com 499 S Capitol St SW Ste 100 Washington DC 20003-4001

NICKLAS, THERESA ANN, nutritionist, educator, researcher; b. Elsworth, S.D., Sept. 29, 1956; d. James and Muriel (Schard) N. BS in Dietetics and Nutritional Care, Roch. Inst. Tech., 1979; MPH in Maternal and Child Health, Tulane U., 1980, DrPH in Nutrition, 1987. Lic. dietitian and nutritionist, La. Nutritionist Dept. Family and Children's Svcs., Atlanta, 1974-75; adminstrv. asst., head nutritionist Haitian Bur. Nutrition, Port-au-Prince, 1975-76; dietary technician Glen Cove (N.Y.) Community Hosp., 1977-78; instr. nutrition dept. medicine La. State U. Med. Ctr., New Orleans, 1984-87, asst. prof. sect. cardiology, 1987—, sr. rsch. nutritionist Bogalusa Heart Study, 1984-87, head nutrition Bogalusa Heart Study, 1987—. Prin. nutrition investigator Ft. Polk Heart Smart Project, 1988-91; adj. instr. nutrition sect. dept. applied health scis. Tulane U. Sch. Pub. Health and Tropical Medicine, New Orleans, 1988-97; prof., chmn. dept. food and nutrition N. D. State U., Fargo, 1997-99; prof. pediats. Children's Nutrition Rsch. Ctr., Baylor Coll. of Medicine, Houston, 1999—; presenter numerous profl. meetings, workshops and seminars for health profls.; vis. prof. Wyeth-Ayerst Labs., 1990—; referee Jour. Am. Coll. Nutrition, Preventive Medicine, Health Edn. Quar., Jour. Clin. Nutrition. Contbr. articles to sci. jours., also chpts. to books, monographs. Vol. La. Am. Heart Assn., New Orleans, 1980—, bd. dirs., 1989—, mem. tassk force com. on women and heart disease, 1990—, sec. New Orleans div. 1989-90, coord. physicians' cholesterol edn. program, 1988-91. Grantee Nestle's, Kelloggs Co., 1981, 91, Nat. Heart, Lung and Blood Inst., 1984—, AID, 1981, U.S. Army Rsch. Inst. for Environ. Medicine, 1988—, Nat. Cancer Inst., 1993, also FDA. Mem. Am. Dietetic Assn. (nutrition dietetic rsch. practice group 1987—, co-editor Digest 1989—), Am. Soc. Clin. Nutrition, Am. Inst. Nutrition, Am. Heart Assn. (fellow coun. on epidemiology), N.Y. Dietetic Assn., La. Dietetic Assn. (bd. dirs. 1989—, chmn. fundraising 1989-90), New Orleans Dietetic Assn. (pres. 1990—), La. Heart Assn., Sigma Xi (assoc.), Delta Omega. Roman Catholic. Avocations: tennis, gardening, cooking, collecting antique cookbooks, fishing. Office: Children's Nutrition Rsch Ctr Baylor Coll Medicine 1100 Bates Ave Houston TX 77030-2600

NICKLESS, BARBARA A. primary school educator; b. Clark AFB, Philippines, 1960; d. Anthony and Ruby Borzymowski; m. Geoffrey G. Nickless, Jan. 1999. BA in Social Work and Criminal Justice, Colo. State U., Ft. Collins, 1983; postgrad. in MA in Edn. program, Calif. State U., Sacramento, 2003. Cert. tchr. Calif. Mid. sch. educator Winters (Calif.) Mid. Sch., 1994—98; h.s. educator Natomas H.S., Sacramento, 1998—99; mid. sch. educator Leroy F. Greene Mid. Sch., Sacramento, 1999—2002; primary sch. educator Two Rivers Elem. Sch., Sacramento, 2002—. Ind. contractor The Coll. Bd., Western Regional Office, San Jose, Calif., 2002—; master tchr. Intel Teach to the Future Program, Sacramento, 2000—03; tchr.-cons. Area 3 Writing Project U. Calif., Davis, 1996—. Mem.: Calif. Teachers Assn., Nat. Teachers Assn., Porsche Club Am. (sec. SVR region 1996—97, v.p. 1997—98), Italian Cultural Soc. Roman Catholic. Avocations: travel, competitive go-cart racing, Italian. Office: Natomas Unified Sch Dist TR 1901 Arena Blvd Sacramento CA 95834

NICKS, STEVIE (STEPHANIE LYNN NICKS), singer, songwriter; b. Phoenix, May 26, 1948; Joined Fleetwood Mac, 1974. Albums include: (with Lindsey Buckingham) Buckingham Nicks, 1973, (with Fleetwood Mac) Fleetwood Mac, 1975, Rumours, 1977 (co-winner, Billboard award for Album of the Year, Group of Year 1977), Tusk, 1979, Fleetwood Mac Live, 1980, Mirage, 1982, Tango in the Night, 1987, Greatest Hits, 1989, Behind The Mask, 1990, 25 Years-The Chain, 1992, The Dance, 1997, Say You Will, 2004; (solo) Bella Donna, 1981, The Wild Heart, 1983, Rock a Little, 1985, The Other Side of the Mirror, 1989, Time Space, 1991, Street Angel, 1994, Enchanted: The Works of Stevie Nicks, 1998, Trouble in Shangri-La, 2001, The Divine, 2001; composer songs Rhiannon, 1975, Landslide, 1975 (Most Performed Country Song of the Year, BMI Awards 2003), Leather and Lace, 1975, Dreams, 1977, Sara, 1979, Edge of Seventeen, 1981, If Anyone Falls (with Sandy Stewart), 1982, Stand Back (with Prince Rogers Nelson), 1983, I Can't Wait (with others), 1985, Seven Wonders (with Sandy Stewart), and others.*

NICOLAÏ, JUDITHE, international business executive; b. Lawrence, Mass., Dec. 15, 1945; d. Victor and Evelyn (Otash) Abisalih. Student in photography, L.A. City Coll., 1967, UCLA, 1971; AA in Fgn. Langs., Coll. of Marin, 1983; hon. degree, Culinary Inst., San Francisco, 1981; AS in Photography with honors, San Francisco City Coll., 2002, AS in Culinary Arts with honors, 2003. Photographer Scott Paper Co., N.Y.C., 1975; owner, operator restaurant The Raincheck Room, West Hollywood, Calif., 1976; prin., pres., CEO, photographer fashion Photographie sub. Nicolaï Internat. Svcs., Nice, France, 1977—; prin., pres., CEO, instr. catering and cooking Back to Basics sub. Nicolaï Internat. Svcs., San Francisco, 1980—; chief photographer exhibit and trade show, chief of staff food div. Agri-Bus. U.S.A., Moscow and Washington, 1983; head transp. U.S. Summer Olympics, L.A., 1984, interpreter for Spanish, French, Portuguese, and Italian, 1985; prin., pres.,CEO, interpreter Intertrans subs. (Nicolaï Internat. Svcs.), San Francisco, 1985—; founder, pres. Nicolaï Internat. Svcs., San Francisco, 1985—; pres., CEO Cyprus Personal Care Products, Inc., 1994—. Mem. Internat. Diplomacy Coun., 1997—; founder, creator Sweettooth Baking & Pastry Concern. Contbr. column on food and nutrition to jour., 1983-84. Mem. NAFE, Internat. Diplomacy Coun., Alpha Gamma Sigma. Avocations: cooking, fencing, archery, golf, photography. Office: Nicolai Internat Svcs 2269 Chestnut St # 237 San Francisco CA 94123-2600 Address: 2269 Chestnut St PMB 237 San Francisco CA 94123-2600 E mail: nis@worldscope.net.

NICOLAIDES, MARY, lawyer; b. N.Y.C., June 7, 1927; d. George and Dorothy Nicolaides. BCE, CUNY, 1947; MBA with distinction, DePaul U., 1975, JD, 1981. Bar: Ill. 1982, U.S. Dist. Ct. (no. dist.) Ill. 1982, U.S. Patent Office 1983. Sr. design engr. cement subs. U.S. Steel Corp., N.Y.C., then Pitts., 1948-71; sole practice Chgo., 1982—. Republican. Greek Orthodox. Address: 233 E Erie St Apt 1804 Chicago IL 60611-2903

NICOLL, GAYLE, chemistry educator; b. Ind., Aug. 23, 1973; d. James D and Linda R Wozniewski; m. Alex Nicoll, Aug. 13, 1994; children: Serena, Lyta. BS in chemistry, BS in physics, Ind. U., 1991—94; MS, Purdue U., 1994—97, PhD, 1994—2000. Asst. prof. Tex. Tech U., Lubbock, 1999—2000; lectr. U. of Nebraska-Lincoln, 2000—. Contbr. articles to profl. jours. Sci. fair judge Internat. Sci. & Engring. Fair, 1999—2003; judge 4-H, Omaha, Nebr., 2000—01; host of chemistry edn. workshop NSF, Lincoln, Nebr., 2003—03. Nebr. Women in Sci., EPSCoR Small Grant Program, 2003. Mem.: Nat. Assn. of Rsch. in Sci. Tchg., AAAS, Iota Sigma Pi (outreach coord. 1997—99), Am. Chem. Soc., Phi Lambda Upsilon. Office: University of Nebraska-Lincoln Dept of Chemistry Hamilton Hall Lincoln NE 68583

NICOLODI, THERESA ANNE, speech pathologist; b. Hazelton, Pennsylvania, Nov. 8, 1954; d. Gerald Lawrence and Doris (Sherwood) Nicolodi; m. Billy Legrce Gibson, Aug. 16, 1980 (div. Mar. 1990). AS, Hillsbourgh Cmty. Coll., 1973—75; BS, Fla. State U., 1975—77, MS, 1977—78. Cert. Am. Speech, Lang., and Hearing Assn. Speech pathologist Harambee Head Start, Albany, Ga., 1978—80, Duval County Sch., Jacksonville, Fla., 1980—91, Clay County Sch., Middleburg, Fla., 1991—

NICOLOSI, GIANNA RUTH, marketing professional; b. Birmingham, Ala., July 3, 1977; d. Robert Joseph and Karen Bristley Nicolosi. Degree in Mktg., U. Ky., 1999. From field mktg. rep. to acct. exec. Black and Decker, NJ, 1999—2002, acct. exec., 2002—03, mgr. comml. ter., 2004—. Recruiter Black and Decker, N.Y.C., NY, 1999—, Tampa, 1999—, mem. mentor com., 1999—, N.Y.C., 1999—. Office: Black and Decker 701 E Joppa Rd Towson MD 21286

NICOLS, ANGELA C. software engineer, computer consultant; b. Jamaica, N.Y., Apr. 15, 1940; d. Henry Ralph and Josephine Sadie (Zarcone) Grieco; m. Otto John Nicols, May 21, 1960; children: Annemarie Nicols-Grinenko, Elizabeth Marie, John Joseph, William Joseph, Richard Joseph. BS in Math., Hofstra U., 1979; MS in Math. and Computer Sci., Adelphi U., 1985. Supr. programs/project leader Book Clubs Info. Sys. Doubleday and Co. Inc., Garden City, N.Y., 1979-87; mgr. software engring. Martin Marietta Info. Sys., Orlando, Fla., 1987-94; chmn. tech. and grants Mus. of the Apopkans Apopka (Fla.) Hist. Soc., 1994—2002, v.p. Mus. of the Apopkans, 2002—; computer cons. and trainer, owner Nicols Cons., Apopka, 1995—. Vol. Apopka H.S. Adv. Coun., 1994-97; sec. Bd. Edn.: Bishop Moore H.S., Orlando, 1995-98. Mem. St. Francis Disabilities Com., 1995—; mem. pastoral coun. St. Francis of Assisi Ch., mem. social action commn., 2000—. Mem. AAUW, IEEE Computer Soc., Assn. for Computing Machinery, Math. Assn. Am., Nat. Assn. Women in Computing, Am. Math. Soc., Apopka Hist. Soc., Coun. Cath. Women, Gray Panthers, Foliage Garden Club of Apopka (2d v.p. 1996-2001), Errol Estates Country Club (comms. com. 1998-2000), Golfside Village Homeowners Assn. (exec. v.p. 1999-2000), Kappa Mu Epsilon. E-mail: angenic@cfl.rr.com.

NICOTRA, MARY, healthcare consultant; b. Evanston, Ill., June 29, 1966; d. William Thomas and Mary Louise (Jackson) Hofstetter; m. Paul Anthony Nicotra, July 4, 1993; 1 child, Jacob Arthur. BA in Bus., Columbia Coll., Chgo., 1990. Acct. terr. rep. injectable pharms. Bristol Meyers, Downers Grove, Ill., 1991-93; acct. mgr. outsourcing OME equipment mgmt. Universal Hosp. Svcs., 1993-96; acct. exec. Matria Healthcare, 1996—99; acct. mgr. Accredo Therapeutics. Regional trainer Matria Healthcare Inc. Avocations: gardening, aerobics, boating, scuba diving. Home: 2957 Stockton Ct Naperville IL 60564-8423

NIEBYL, JENNIFER ROBINSON, obstetrician, gynecologist, educator; b. Montreal, Que., Can., Dec. 5, 1942; BSc, McGill U., Mont., 1963; MD, Yale U., 1967. Diplomate Am. Bd. Ob-Gyn., Am. Bd. Maternal and Fetal Medicine. Intern in Internal Medicine N.Y. Hosp.-Cornell Med. Ctr., 1967-68, resident in ob-gyn., 1968-70, Johns Hopkins Hosp., Balt., 1970-73, fellow in maternal and fetal medicine, 1976-78, mem. staff, 1973—88, U. Iowa Hosps. and Clinics, Iowa City, 1988—; prof., head ob-gyn. dept. U. Iowa Sch. Medicine, Iowa City, 1988—. Mem. ACOG, Am. Gynecol. and Obstetrical Soc., Soc. Gynecol. Investigation, Soc. Maternal Fetal Medicine, Inst. Medicine of NAS. Office: U Iowa Hosps & Clinics 200 Hawkins Dr Iowa City IA 52242 Office Phone: 319-356-1976.

NIEDERBERGER, JANE, information technology executive; m. Mark Niederberger; children: Amy, Sarah. BS in nutrition, Simmons Coll., 1982; MBA in health care adminstrn., Northeastern U. With Pilgrim Health Care, Boston, 1983—96; with IT divsn. Anthem, Inc., Indpls., 1997, acting CIO, 1998—99, CIO, 1999—. Bd. mem. Jr. Achievement, Indpls. Recipient Women and Hi Tech Leading Light award, 2002. Office: Anthem Inc 120 Monument Cir Indianapolis IN 46204*

NIEDERMEIER, MARY B. retired nutritionist; b. Webster Groves, Mo., Oct. 20, 1914; d. Albertus and Daisey May (Christman) Wickersham; m. Walter H. Neidermeier, Sept. 9, 1939; children: Gail Santarelli, Bart Neidermeier. BS, Mich. State U., 1937; MA, Columbia U., 1957, profl. diploma, 1959. Cert. in dietetics Ohio. Dist. nutritionist N.J. State Dept. of Health, Newark; instr. nutrition edn. Sch. of Dentistry Fairleigh Dickinson U., Teaneck, NJ; instr. nutrition edn. Sch. of Nursing St. Louis U. Pres. Oradell (N.J.) Pub. Sch. PTA, 1954—57; bd. dirs. Rancho Bernardo (Calif.) Oaks N. Cmty. Ctr., 1974—76; treas. PEO-TV chpt., Rancho Bernardo, 1990; bd. deacons Rancho Bernardo Presbyn. Ch., 1975—76. Grace McCloud fellow, Columbia U., 1957—59. Mem.: AAUP, AAUW, N.J. Dietetic Assn., Calif. Dietetic Assn., Am. Dietetic Assn., Alpha Omicron Pi. Republican. Avocations: electronic organ music, painting, golf, lawn and indoor bowling. Home: 17411 Plaza De La Rosa San Diego CA 92128-2223

NIEHAUS, MARY C. C. lawyer; b. 1961; BA with honors, Grinnell Coll., 1985; JD cum laude, Northwestern U., 1988. Bar: Ill. 1988, U.S. Dist. Ct. (no. dist.) Ill. 1988, U.S. Tax Ct. 1989. With Sidley & Austin, Chgo., 1988—, ptnr., 1996—. Mem. editl. staff Northwestern U. Law Rev., 1987-88. Mem. Order of Coif, Phi Beta Kappa. Office: Sidley & Austin Bank One Plz 10 S Dearborn St Chicago IL 60603 Fax: 312-83-7036. E-mail: mniehaus@sidley.com.*

NIELSEN, BARBARA STOCK, state educational administrator; State supt. S.C. Dept. Edn., Columbia, 1991—99; vis. prof. sch. edn. Coll. at Charleston; sr. fellow Strom Thurmond Inst. Clemson U., 2000—; dir. Schs. Around the World. Office: Strom Thurmond Inst Govt and Pub Affairs Clemson U Perimeter Rd Clemson SC 29634-0125

NIELSEN, GWYN ENGLISH, writer, illustrator, publishing executive; b. Plainfield, N.J., Dec. 12, 1958; d. Richard English and Valerie Victoria Youtkus; m. Christian Anthony Nielsen, June 22, 1986 (div. Nov. 1996); 1 child, Saxony Annin. BA in English/Comm. cum laude, Bucknell U., 1981. Cert. English tchr. NJ.J. Dept. Edn. State Bd. Examiners. Adminstrv. coord. Group W Satellite Comm., N.Y.C., 1981—83; dir. drama Ctrl. Bucks H.S. East, Buckingham, Pa., 1983—84; English tchr. Rahway (N.J.) H.S., 1984—85; English and drama tchr. Mother Seton Regional H.S., Clark, NJ, 1985—89; English tchr. Connackamack Sch., Piscataway, NJ, 1989—90; pres. Video Sta. CGS Inc./Overlook Video, Summit, NJ, 1990—2002, CGS Press, Scotch Plains, NJ, 1997—. English tutor Mentor Learning Group, Summit, 1989; substitute tchr. Bd. Edn., Scotch Plains, Westfield, 2000—; playwright, dir. Performing Arts Studio, Scotch Plains, 2001; tchr. Summit Cmty. Ctr., Summit, NJ, 2002—03. Author, illustrator: children's book Torey the Turkey Goes Skiing, 1998, author, pub.: poetry Teaching Love Life, 2000, children's book Serendipity and the Dream Catcher, 2003. HEART grantee, Union County Arts Coun. bd. freeholders, 2002. Mem.: Soc. Children's Book Writers and Illustrators, Acad. Am. Poets, Publishers Mktg. Assn., Bucknell Univ. Assn. of the Arts, Alpha Lambda Delta. Presbyterian. Avocations: singing, acting. Office: CGS Press PO Box 1394 Mountainside NJ 07092

NIELSEN, JACQUELINE ANNE, music specialist; b. Sandusky, Ohio, Feb. 15, 1977; d. Betty J. and David J. Nielsen. MusB Edn., Heidelberg Coll., Tiffin, OH, 1995—99. Music K-12 Teaching License Ohio Dept. of Edn., 2000. Elem. music specialist Benton-Carroll-Salem Schools, Oak Harbor, Ohio, 2002—; prep. dept. instr. Heidelberg Coll., Tiffin, Ohio, 1996—. Triad editl. bd. mem. Ohio Music Edn. Assn., Ohio, 2001—; profl. accompanist Heidelberg Coll. Concert Choir and Chamber Singers, Tiffin, Ohio, 1997—; pres. elect Dist. I Ohio Music Edn. Assn., 2003—. Sunday sch. instr. Trinity United Ch. of Christ, Tiffin, Ohio, 2000—. Recipient Dorothy and Ferris Ohl Prize, Heidelberg Coll. Dept. of Music, 1999, Triad Club Award, Heidelberg Coll., 1997; scholar Mildred P. McCrystal Award, Mildred P. McCrystal Scholarship Com., 1998. Mem.: Ohio Music Edn. Assn. (pres.-elect 2003), Omicron Delta Kappa Leadership Honor Soc. (life), Alpha Lambda Delta Academic Honor Soc. (life), Kappa Delta Pi Edn. Honor Soc. (life), Tau Mu Sigma Music Honor Soc. (life).

NIELSEN, LINDA MILLER, city councilwoman; b. Cedar Falls, Iowa, Apr. 13, 1948; d. Donald Hugh and Mary I. (Hansen) Miller; m. Kenneth Andrew Nielsen, Aug. 22, 1970; children: Annette Marie, Kirsten Viola. BS in Home Econs., Iowa State U., 1970, MS in Food Sci., 1972. Rsch. asst. Iowa State U., Ames, 1970-72, rsch. assoc., 1972-74, instr., 1975-76; city councilwoman City of Charleston, W.Va., 1988—; minority leader Charleston City Coun., 2003—; asst. dir. continuing edn. and cmty. svc. W.Va. State Cmty. and Tech. Coll., 1998—. Leader Girl Scouts U.S.A., 1978-96; chair environ. and recycling com. of Charleston, 1991-2003, realignment com. of Charleston, 1992-94, 2002, mcpl. planning com., 1988—, fin. com., 1995—, storm water com., 1997-99, 2003—, parks and recreation com., 1988-95; classroom vol. Kanawha County Schs., Charleston, 1978-90; mem., officer Forest Hills Comm. Assn., Charleston, 1983-87. Contbr. articles to profl. publs. Mem. Nat. Inst. for Chem. Studies (bd. dirs. 1994—), Sigma Xi, Iota Sigma Pi, Omicron Nu. Republican. Avocations: hiking, camping, reading, sewing, cooking. E-mail: nielsen413@charter.net.

NIELSEN, LOUISA AUGUSTA, broadcast association executive; b. Balt., Dec. 14, 1950; d. William Alexander and Louisa Augusta N. BA, Coll. Notre Dame Md., Balt., 1972; MA, Antioch U., 1975. Coord. Assn. Ind. Md. Schools, 1972-75; chair theater dept. Maryvale Coll. Prep. Sch., 1972-75; coord. Balt. Cable Planning Ctr., 1974-75; proj. founder/dir. Mayor's Office Manpower Resources Sidewalk Theater, Balt., 1975; documentary dir. Wash. Cmty. Video Access Ctr., D.C., 1975; adj. asst. prof. Antioch Coll., Balt. and D.C., 1976-79; asst. prof. Howard U., D.C., 1976-77; dir. ednl. programming svcs. Nat. Publ. Radio, D.C., 1976-79; humanities adminstr. media programs Nat. Endowment Humanities, D.C., 1979-82; dir. cable TV, asst. dir. broadcast TV Nat. Captioning Inst., D.C., 1982-83; vis. asst. prof. George Wash. U., D.C., 1983-1985, dir., prodr. ednl. programming, 1985-87; exec. dir., CEO Broadcast Edn. Assn., D.C., 1987-96; pub. Jour. Broadcasting & Electronic Media, Feedback mag., Jour. Radio Studies, others. Spl. invitee/fellow, Harvard Law Sch., 1987—; trustee, Brit. Broadcasting Corp., Nat. Univ., 1999—; bd. dirs. George Foster Peabody Awards, Ohio State Awards; bd. advisors, FCC; video conf. moderator, Nat. U.; judge, ACE Awards, NCTA, Corp. Publ. Broadcasting Programming Awards; presenter, AT&T, Publ. Svc. Satellite Consortium; invited panelist, Internat. Inst. Astronautics, Annenberg Wash. HDTV workshop; reviewer, Annenberg/CPB Project prog. Editl. advisory bd. Simon & Schuster Communications Dictionary; appeared as guest, PBS Nat. Narrowcast Svc. Telecommunication and Distance Learning. Chair,

Soc. Satellite Profls. Internat., mid-atlantic region. Office: Broadcast Education Assn World Hdqs 1771 N St NW Washington DC 20036-2812 Home: 604 Gittings Ave Baltimore MD 21212-2603 E-mail: lnielsen@nab.org.

NIELSEN, NANCY, publishing executive; b. Jeffersonville, Ind., 1950, BA, Univ. Calif., Berkeley, 1975; MBA, Yale U., 1979. Asst. city editor, weekend mag. editor Dallas Times Herald, 1975-77, cons. McKinsey & Co. Inc.; dir. office of comm. Capital Cities/ABC Inc., N.Y.C., 1984-86; deputy dir. corp. rels. The N.Y. Times Co., N.Y.C., 1986-88, dir. corp. rels./Pa., 1987-93, v.p. corp. comm., 1992-2000; dir. bus. and media devel. Harvard U., 2000—. Bd. dirs. Berkeley Div. Sch. Yale U. Recipient Alumni Assn. award for outstanding performance in journalism Univ. Calif. Berkeley. Mem. Coun. Fgn. Rels. Office: The New York Times Co 229 W 43rd St New York NY 10036-3959

NIELSEN, NANCY H. health organization executive; m. Don Nielsen; 5 children. BA, W.Va. U., 1964; MS in Microbiology, Cath. U., 1967, PhD in Microbiology, 1969; MD, SUNY, Buffalo, 1967. Past chief med. officer N.Y. State Dept. Health Western Region; former pres. med. staff Buffalo Gen. Hosp.; asst. dean med. edn., clin. prof. medicine U. Buffalo Sch. Medicine and Biomed. Sci., Buffalo; spkr. ho. dels. Med. Soc. State of N.Y., 1995—2000; 3-term vice-spkr. AMA Ho. of Dels., 2000—03, spkr., 2003—. Former pres. Erie County (N.Y.) Med. Soc.; mem. AMA Coun. on Sci. Affairs; bd. dirs. Med. Liability Mut. Ins. Co.; assoc. med. dir. for quality Ind. Health Assn. N.Y. Bd. dirs. Nat. Patient Safety Found. Recipient Samuel P. Capen award, U. Buffalo Alumni Assn., 1996. Fellow: ACP. Office: AMA 515 N State St Chicago IL 60610 Business E-Mail: nielse@buffalo.edu.*

NIELSON, ALYCE MAE, poet; b. Saugerties, N.Y., Feb. 27, 1943; d. George John Wodischeck and Martha Elizabeth Casler; m. David Bruce Nielson, Oct. 5, 1963; children: Kenneth David, Nancy Lynn Nielson Nowicki. AS in Food, SUNY, Cobleskill, N.Y., 1963. Sch. lunch mgr. Bklyn. Pub. Sch. #61, 1963-64; clk. stock and bond dividend dept. First Nat. City Bank, N.Y.C., 1966—69; lectr., trainee, group leader, ctr. mgr. Weight Watchers, N.Y.C., Bklyn., S.I., 1979—. Contbr. poetry to anthologies. Vol. Warm up Am., Kingston, N.Y., 1999-2002. Named to Internat. Poetry Hall of Fame, 1996—; recipient numerous Editors Choice awards, 1995—2003. Mem. Internat. Soc. of Poets. Avocations: tae kwon do (2d degree black belt), tai chi, music, needlework, cooking.

NIELSON, KRISTY ANN, psychology educator, researcher; b. Inglewood, Calif., Dec. 11, 1964; d. Alfred M. Nielson Jr. and Dolores M. (Gattuso) Hetland. BA, Calif. State U., Long Beach, 1987; MA in Exptl. Psychology, So. Ill. U., 1990, PhD in Biopsychology, 1992. Instr. Learning Ctr., Santa Ana, Calif., 1985-86; rsch. asst. psychology So. Ill. U., Carbondale, 1988-92, lectr. in psychology, 1991-92; neuropsychology intern U. Calif., Irvine, 1992-95, postdoctoral rsch. fellow, 1992-96, lectr. in psychobiology, 1996; asst. prof. psychology Marquette U., Milw., 1996—2002, assoc. prof. psychology, 2002—; asst. clin. prof. psychiatry Med. Coll. Wis., Milw., 1998—, dir. Foley Ctr. for Aging and Devel., 1998—. Mem. sci. adv. com. Alzheimer's Assn. S.E. Wis., Milw., 1996—; bd. dirs., vice chair Clement Manor, Inc., Greenfield, Wis. Contbr. articles to profl. jours. Block watch capt. City of Wauwatosa, Wis., 1996—; sci. adv. bd. Alzheimer's Assn. S.E. Wis., Milw., 1996- Grantee Nat. Inst. Aging, 1995-96, 2003-08, Med. Coll. Wis., 1998—, Epilepsy Found. Am., 1999. Mem. APA, AAAS, Am. Psychol. Soc., Soc. for Neurosci., AAUP, Sigma Xi. Avocations: volleyball, softball, golf. Office: Marquette U Dept Psychology PO Box 1881 Milwaukee WI 53201-1881 E-mail: kristy.nielson@marquette.edu.

NIEMAN, VALERIE GAIL, editor; b. Jamestown, N.Y., July 6, 1955; d. Warner Ernest and Eleanor A. (Aiken); m. Jack Hobbs Student, Jamestown C.C., 1975-76; BS in Journalism, W.Va. U., 1978; postgrad., Queens U. of Charlotte. Staff writer W.Va. U News Svc., Morgantown, W.Va., 1978; reporter Dominion Post, Morgantown, 1978, Times West Virginian, Fairmont, W.Va., 1979-92, city editor, 1992-95, exec. editor, 1995-97; asst. city/state editor News & Record, Greensboro, NC, 1997—. Tchr. basic newswriting W.Va. U., Morgantown, 1990, tchr. sci. fiction writing, 1995; instr. dept. journalism and mass comm. N.C. A&T State U., 2000—; lectr., vis. writer tri-state area, 1988-1997; founding co-editor Kestrel lit. jour., Fairmont, 1992-1997; co-founder, co-dir. Kestrel Writers Conf., Fairmont, 1993-1997. Author: (novel) Neena Gathering, 1988, Survivors, 2000, (poetry chpts.) How We Live, 1996, Slipping Out of Old Eve, 1988. W.Va. cir. writer W.Va. Humanities Commn., 1994; mem. Leadership Marion, Fairmont, 1995-96. Recipient award in letters Fairmont Arts and Humanities, 1988, 94, Elizabeth Simpson Smith prize, 1998, 2002, Greg Grummer award in poetry George Mason U., 1999, others; fellow in poetry NEA, 1991, fellow in fiction Ky. Found. for Women, 1991, fellow in fiction W.Va. Commn. on Arts, 1992. Democrat. Lutheran. Avocations: gardening, hiking, fishing, travel. Office: News & Record 200 E Market St Greensboro NC 27401

NIEMANN, LINDA GRANT, railroad conductor; b. Pasadena, Calif., Sept. 22, 1946; d. Carl George and Mary Grant (Parkhurst) N. BA, U. Calif., Santa Cruz, 1968; PhD, U. Calif., Berkeley, 1975. Brakeman, condr. Union Pacific, 1979—2001; assoc. prof. Kennesaw (Ga.) State U., 2001—. Author: Boomer: Railroad Memoirs, 1990, Railroad Voices, 1998. Mem. Nat. Writers Union. Address: PO Box 4412 Marietta GA 30061-4412

NIEMANN, PATRICIA, nurse; b. Montrose, S.D., June 30, 1941; d. Alfred Hagen and Alvina Margaret Johnson; m. Marvin Carl Niemann, July 2, 1960; children: Charlotte Niemann Crisp, Paula Niemann Nussbaum, John, Jill Niemann Brown, Julie (dec.). LPN, S.E. Area Sch. Practical, 1977; student, U. Sioux Falls, 1989-91. Nurse Good Samaritan Ctr., Sioux Falls, 1977, VA, Sioux Falls, 1977—2002. Bd. dirs. ARC, Sioux Falls, 1987-88; union pres. Orgn. Grievance Negotiations Local Contract, 1981. Mem. NOW, AIC, Am. Inst. Cancer Rsch., Am. Fedn. Govt. Employees (local union pres.), LPN Assn. (local). Democrat. Lutheran. Avocations: reading, swimming, music, snowmobiling. Home: 5605 W 14th St Sioux Falls SD 57106-0207

NIEMEYER, ERIN JANICE, pharmaceutical sales consultant, journalist, editor; b. Torrance, Calif., July 5, 1974; d. Robert Frederick and Patricia Ann Niemeyer. BA magna cum laude, U. Nev., Las Vegas, 1998. Freelance writer-editor, Las Vegas, 1997—; substitute tchr. Clark County Sch. Dist., Las Vegas, 1998—; individual ins. sales rep. UNUMProvident, Las Vegas, 1998—. Vol. Juvenile Diabetes Found., Las Vegas, 1992-95, Big Bros. and Big Sisters, Las Vegas, 1996-97. Mem. Soc. Profl. Journalists, Phi Kappa Phi, Phi Alpha Delta, Alpha Gamma Delta. Republican. Christian. Avocations: writing, reading nonfiction, exercising, teaching, motivational speaking. Home and Office: 944 Osterville St Unit B Hendersonville NV 89052 E-mail: erin.j.niemeyer@pharmacia.com.

NIEMI, BEATRICE NEAL, social services professional; b. Fitchburg, Mass., July 23, 1923; d. Albert G. and Florence E. (Copeland) Neal; m. Walter V. Niemi, Oct. 21, 1944 (div. 1970); children: Karen Smith-Gary, Gail Niemi Shaw. AS, Colby-Sawyer Coll., 1942; BS in Psychology, Northeastern U., 1972; MA in Counseling Psychology, Assumption Coll., 1974. Diplomate in psychotherapy Am. Psychotherapy Assn. Dir. homemaker svcs. Children's Aid and Family Svcs., Inc., Fitchburg, 1965-73; founder, exec. dir. Home Health Aide Svc. of North Cen. Mass., Inc., Fitchburg, 1973-85, Ctr. for Well Being, Inc., Fitchburg, 1985—; instr. Touch for Health Found., Pasadena, Calif., 1977—; tchr., 7th degree master The Radiance Technique Assn. Internat., St. Petersburg, Fla., 1986—; Outreach trainer The Monroe Inst., Faber, Va., 1990—. V.p. Mass. Coun. for Homemaker-Home Health Aide Svcs., Inc., 1973-81. Pres. Children's Aid and Family Svcs., Inc., Fitchburg, 1964-65; bd. dirs. United Way of Greater Fitchburg, Inc., 1964-70, Leominster (Mass.) Vis. Nursing Assn, 1972-78; chmn. adv. bd. Salvation Army, Fitchburg, 1970-72; v.p. Fitchburg Coun. of Girl Scouts. Mem. ACA, Am. Psychotherapy Assn. (diplomate), Assn. Comprehensive Energy Psychology, Am. Mental Health Counselors Assn., Am. Holistic Health Assn., Am. Holistic Med. Found., Mass. Assn. Cmty. Health Agys. (bd. dirs. 1970-83), Mass. Mental Health Counselors Assn., Assn. for Transpersonal Psychology, Nat. Guild Hypnotists, N.E. Holistic Counselors Assn., Touch For Health Kinesiology Assn., others. Avocations: yoga, meditation, travel. Office: Ctr for Well Being Inc 70 Bond St Fitchburg MA 01420-2251 Office Phone: 978-345-5964.

NIEMI, JANICE, retired lawyer, retired state legislator; b. Flint, Mich., Sept. 18, 1928; d. Richard Jesse and Norma (Bell) Bailey; m. Preston Niemi, Feb. 4, 1953 (div. 1987); children: Ries, Patricia. BA, U. Wash., 1950, LLB, 1967; postgrad., U. Mich., 1950-52; cert., Hague Acad. Internat. Law, The Netherlands, 1954. Bar: Wash. 1968. Assoc. firm Powell, Livengood, Dunlap & Silverdale, Kirkland, Wash., 1968; staff atty. Legal Svc. Ctr., Seattle, 1968-70; judge Seattle Dist. Ct., 1971-72, King County Superior Ct., Seattle, 1973-78; acting gen. counsel, dep. gen. counsel SBA, Washington, 1979-81; mem. Wash. State Ho. of Reps., Olympia, 1983-87, chmn. com. on state govt., 1984; mem. Wash. State Senate, 1987-95; sole practice Seattle, 1981-94; superior ct. judge King County, 1995-2000; chief criminal judge, 1997-2000; ret., 2000; mem. Wash. State Gambling Commn., 2002—. Mem. White Ho. Fellows Regional Selection Panel, Seattle, 1974—77, chmn., 1976, 77; incorporator Soudn Savs. & Loan, Seattle, 1975; bd. dirs. Artists Trust; mem. panel Am. Arbitration Assn., 2003—. Bd. visitors dept. psychology U. Wash., Seattle, 1983—87, bd. visitors dept. sociology, 1988—98; mem. adv. bd. Tacoma Art Mus., 1987—; mem. Wash. State Gender and Justice Commn., 1987—89; Bd. dirs. Allied Arts, Seattle, 1971—78, Ctr. Contemporary Art, Seattle, 1981—83, Women's Network, Seattle, 1981—84, Pub. Defender Assn., Seattle, 1982—84, Artist's Trust, 2002—. Named Woman of Yr. in Law, Past Pres.'s Assn., Seattle, 1971, Woman of Yr., Matrix Table, Seattle, 1973, Capitol Hill Bus. and Profl. Women, 1975. Mem. Wash. State Bar Assn., Wash. Women Lawyers, Am. Arbitration Assn. (panel 2003—). Democrat. Home: PO Box 20516 Seattle WA 98102-1516

NIENOW, BETH MARIE, librarian; b. Rochester, Minn., Jan. 22, 1961; d. Duane Reuben and Elaine Nienow. BA, Hamline U., St. Paul, 1983; MLS, U. Wis., 1984; MA, Mankato (Minn.) State U., 1998. Libr. U. N.D., Grand Forks, 1984-89, U. Tenn., Chattanooga, 1989-91; grad. asst. Mankato State U., 1991—93; libr. Rochester Pub. Libr., 1994—. Lutheran. Home: 2303 Fisher Ct NW Rochester MN 55901-8084 Office: Rochester Pub Libr 101 2d St SE Rochester MN 55904

NIERMAN, MEREDITH ALISA, multimedia producer; b. Boston, Mass., Apr. 29, 1970; d. Elaine Barbara Goldman and Lewis Gerald Nierman. ALB, Harvard U., Divsn. of Continuing Edn., Cambridge, Mass., 1993; MEd, Harvard Grad. Sch. of Edn., Cambridge, MA, 1994. Health edn. multimedia prodr. WGBH Ednl. Found., Boston, Mass., 1999—, children's ednl. multimedia prodr., 1999—; multimedia cons. to health and mental health care organizations Boston, Mass., 2001—; consulting dir. of social services The Commonwealth Housing and Land Trust, Boston, Mass., 1998—99; rsch. assoc. Fenway Cmty. Health Ctr., Boston, Mass., 1998—98; program coord. Trauma and Dissociative Disorders Partial Hosp. Program - McLean Hosp., Belmont, Mass., 1994—98; rsch. asst. Judge Baker Media Ctr. - Children's Hosp., Boston, Mass., 1994—94, Dept. of Psychology - Harvard U., Cambridge, Mass., 1991—94, WGBH Ednl. Found., Boston, Mass., 1991—94. Vol. Internat. Vol. Svc./Volunteers for Peace, Bristol, England, 1992—92. Prodr.(content producer & writer): (children's educational web site) ZOOM (companion site to PBS Children's TV series), (health education web site) Struggling to Learn, Understanding NF1 (Neurofibromatosis 1); contbr. educational web site Misunderstood Minds (companion site to PBS TV spl. on Learning Disabilities); prodr-.(content producer): (educational web site) Discovering Psychology; contbr. children's educational web site Between the Lions (companion site to the PBS children's TV series). Jury mem. Prix Jeunesse Internat. Media Festival, 2004. Nominee Best Children's Web Site, Mass. Interactive Media Coun., 1999; recipient Japan Prize Second Web Prize, NHK Broadcasting Corp., Tokyo, Japan, 2002, Prix Jeunesse Internat. Web Prize for Children's Media, Prix Jeunesse, 2000, Best Web Site, Mass. Interactive Media Coun., 2002, Silver Award for Kids Entertainment Web Site, NewMedia Mag., 1999, Finalist, New Media Award, The Worldfest-Flagstaff Internat. Film and Video Festival, 1999, Cool Site of the Week, Yahooligans (Yahoo.com), 2003. Mem.: APA (assoc.). Office: WGBH Educational Foundation 125 Western Avenue Boston MA 02134

NIEWIAROSKI, TRUDI OSMERS (GERTRUDE NIEWIAROSKI), social studies educator; b. Jersey City, Apr. 30, 1935; d. Albert John and Margaret (Niemeyer) Osmers; m. Donald H. Niewiaroski, June 8, 1957; children: Donald H., Donna, Margaret Anne, Nancy Noel. AB in History and German, Upsala Coll., East Orange, N.J., 1957; MEd, Montgomery County Pub. Schs., Rockville, Md., 1992. Cert. tchr., Md. Tchr. geography Colego Americano, Quito, Ecuador, 1964-66; bd. dirs. Cotopaxi Acad., Quito, 1964-65; tchr. speed reading Escuela Lincoln, Buenos Aires, Argentina, 1966-67; substitute thcr. Montgomery County Pub. Schs., Rockville, 1978-83, tchr. social studies, 1984—. Del. Eisenhower People to People Educators' Del. Vietnam, 1993; pres. Fulbright Meml. Fund Program, 1997; resident tchg. fellow Russia-Ukraine Excellence in Tchg. Program, 1997; resident scholar in Korea, The Korea Soc., 1999. Author curricula; contbr. chpts. to books, articles to profl. jours.; lectr. at workshops. Bd. dirs. Cotopaxi Acad., Quito, 1964-65; pres. Citizens Assn., Potomac, Md., 1977-81; leader Girl Scouts U.S., 1975-76; adv. coun. Milken Found; pres. Fulbright Meml. Fund Program Japan Alumni, 1999—. Recipient Md. Tchr. of Yr. award State of Md. Edn. Dept., 1993, finalist nat. Tchr. of Yr., 1993, Disting. Alumni award Upsala Coll., 1993, Nat. Educator award Milken Found., 1994, Summer Fellowship Korean Studies Program, 1999, Joseph Malone fellowship Sultanate of Oman, 2003, Goethe Inst. fellowship, Germany, 2003; Fulbright fellow, India, 1985, China, 1990, Japan Keizai Koho Ctr. fellow, 1992, Fulbright Meml. Fund Tchr. Program fellow, Japan, 1997, Fulbright fellow, South Africa, 2001, Malone fellow, Oman, 2003; UMBC-U. Mex. Art and Culture scholar, 1995. Mem. AAUW, ASCD, Nat. Coun. Social Studies, Md. Coun. for Social Studies, Asia Soc., Smithsonian Instn., Montgomery County Hist. Soc., Spl. Interest Groups-China, Japan and Korea, Md. Bus. Roundtable for Edn., Nat. Social Studies Suprs. Assn., Kappa Delta Pi. Avocations: cake and cookie decorating, travel. Office: R Montgomery High Sch Rockville MD 20852 E-mail: trudi_niewiaroski@fc.mcps.k12.md.us.

NIGHTINGALE, DEBORAH SEIFERT, systems engineer, consultant; b. Dayton, Ohio, Sept. 10, 1949; m. Tom Seifert, 1971; children: Jessica, Danielle, Jordan. BS, U. Dayton, 1970; MS, Ohio State U., 1975, PhD, 1979. Programmer U. Dayton Rsch. Inst., 1968-71; sr. engrng. scientist Wright Patterson AFB, 1971-79; project leader Allied Signal Engines, 1979-80; mgr. facility planning, factory modernization, Corp CIM Com., 1980-84, mfg. sys. engr., indsl. engr., ops. support, chmn., 1984-87, sr. project mgr. mktg. svc., dir. strategic planning, 1987-96; cons. Paradise Valley, Ariz., 1996—; prof., focus lead, Lean Enterprise Team & Lean Aerospace Initiative Dept. of Aerospace & Aeronautics, MIT, Cambridge, Mass., 1997—. Contbr. articles to profl. jour. Mem. NAE (4th decade com. 1993—), Inst. Indsl. Engr. (pres. elect 1994—), Soc. Mfg. Engr., Computer and Automated Sys. Assn. Home: 43 Canterbury St Andover MA 01810-2850 Office: Dept Aerospace & Aeronautics MIT Rm 33-312 77 Mass Ave Cambridge MA 02139

NIGHTINGALE, ELENA OTTOLENGHI, geneticist, pediatrician, academic administrator, educator; b. Livorno, Italy, Nov. 1, 1932; arrived in U.S., 1939, naturalized; d. Mario Lazzaro and Elisa Vittoria (Levi) Ottolenghi; m. Stuart L. Nightingale, July 1, 1965; children: Elizabeth, Marisa. AB summa cum laude, Barnard Coll., 1954; PhD, Rockefeller U., 1961; MD, NYU, 1964. Asst. prof. Cornell U. Med. Coll., N.Y.C., 1965-70, Johns Hopkins U., Balt., 1970-73; fellow in clin. genetics and pediat. Georgetown U. Hosp., Washington, 1973-74; sr. staff officer NAS, Washington, 1975-79, sr. program officer Inst. Medicine, 1979-82, sr. scholar-in-residence, 1982-83; spl. advisor to pres. Carnegie Corp. N.Y., N.Y.C., 1983-94, sr. program officer, 1989-94; scholar-in-residence NAS, Washington, 1995—. Vis. assoc. prof. Harvard Med. Sch., Boston, 1980—84, vis. lectr., 1984—95; adj. prof. pediat. Georgetown U. Med. Ctr., 1984—, George Washington U. Med. Ctr., 1994—; mem. recombinant DNA adv. com. NIH, Bethesda, Md., 1979—83. Editor: The Breaking of Bodies and Minds: Torture, Psychiatric Abuses and the Health Professions, 1985, Prenatal Screening, Policies and Values: The Example of Neural Tube Defects, 1987, Promoting the Health of Adolescents: New Directions for the 21st Century, 1993, Adolescent Risk and Vulnerability: Concepts and Measurement, 2001; co-author: Before Birth: Prenatal Screening for Genetic Disease, 1990; contbr. numerous sci. articles to profl. publs. Bd. dirs. Amnesty Internat., U.S.A., Washington, 1989—91, Ctr. for Youth Svcs., Washington, 1980—84, Sci. Svc., Inc., Washington, 1985—96. Fellow: AAAS (chmn. com. on sci. freedom and responsibility 1985—88), Royal Soc. Medicine, N.Y. Acad. Scis.; mem.: Inst. Medicine of NAS (chmn. com. on health and human rights 1987—90), Genetics Soc. Am., Am. Soc. Human Genetics (social issues com. 1982—85), Am. Soc. Microbiology, Harvey Soc., Sigma Xi, Phi Beta Kappa. Office: NAS 2101 Constitution Ave NW Washington DC 20418-0007

NIGHTINGALE, SUSIE, librarian; b. Reno, Nev., May 10, 1945; d. Herbert Larned and Jeanne Gates Dorrance; m. James Alan Bridson, June 23, 1973 (div. Sept. 1997); children: Christopher Kenneth Bridson, Rebecca Noelle Bridson. BA in English, Fla. State U., 1967; MA in English, U. Ariz., 1972; MLS, Emporia State U., 1983. Tchr. Thomas Jefferson Jr. H.S., Arlington, Va., 1967—68, Jacksonville (Fla.) Episcopal H.S., 1968—70, Amphitheater H.S., Tucson, 1972—74, Seaman H.S., Topeka, 1980—82; libr. media specialist Hayden H.S., Topeka, 1982—87, Olathe (Kans.) South H.S., 1987—88, Santa Fe Trail Jr. H.S., Olathe, 1988—. Mem.: Kans. Assn. Sch. Libr. (sec.), US Assn. Triathletes, US Masters Swim Club, Lawrence Multisport Club (bd. dirs.), Lawrence Masters Swim Club (sec.). Democrat. Episcopalian. Avocations: swimming, bicycling, running, gardening, sewing. Office: Santa Fe Trail Jr HS 1100 N Ridgeview Rd Olathe KS 66061

NIGUIDULA, KATHLEEN ANN, music educator, musician; b. Upper Darby, Pa., Apr. 5, 1972; d. Faustino Nazario Niguidula and Brenda Marie Maybury. B in Music Edn., Eastman Sch. Music, 1994; MusM in Piano Performance, Boston Conservatory, 1998. Cert. K-12 music tchr. N.Y., Tex., Mass. Music tchr., choir dir. grades 6-8 Aldine Ind. Sch. Dist., Houston, 1994—95; music tchr., choir dir. grades 7-8 Norwood Pub. Schs., Mass., 1998—99; music tchr. K-8 Music On The Move, Chelsea, Mass., 1999—2001; piano tchr. Timeline Music, Wakefield, Mass., 1998—2001; music tchr. Wolf Sch., Providence, 2001—; piano tchr. Music Sch. R.I. Philharm., Providence, 2001—. Freelance accompanist, Boston, 1996—; choir dir. K-5 after-school programs, Providence, 2001—; early childhood music coord. Music Sch. R.I. Philharmonic, 2002—. Music dir., organist Islington Cmty. Ch., Westwood, Mass., 1999—. Finalist piano, Florida Concerto Competition, 1989; recipient Excellence in Music award, Sarasota Visual and Performing Arts, 1990, 1st prize Composition, Women's Soc. Sarasota, 1990, 1st prize Music Performance, Shriner's Club, 1990; scholar, Eastman Sch. Music, 1990—94. Mem.: Orff-Schuwerk Assn., Music Educators Nat. Conf., Music Tchrs. Nat. Assn., New Eng. Piano Tchrs. Assn., Chopin Club. Personal E-mail: Kathleen-n@netzero.net.

NIJINSKY, TAMARA, actress, puppeteer, author, librarian, educator; b. Vienna; came to U.S., 1961; d. Waslaw and Romola (de Pulszky) N.; widowed; 1 child, Kinga Maria Szakats-Gaspers. ed. in Europe, postgrad. studies in U.S. Mem., actress Nat. Theater of Budapest; owner, tchr. Tamara Nijinsky Performing Art Studio, Montreal; tchr. speech/drama, French and German, libr. Cath. H.S., Phoenix; established non-profit internat. orgn. The Waslaw and Romola Nijinsky Found., Inc., 1991, exec. dir., 1991—. Lectr. on Nijinsky, U.S., Can. and Europe. Author: Nijinsky and Romola, 1991. Decorated chevalier de l'Ordre des Arts et des Lettres, officier de l'Ordre des Arts et des Lettres (France); recipient Nijinsky medal, Pagart, Poland, Polish Order of Arts and Letters, 1997, La Medaille Vermeil de Paris, 2000. Roman Catholic. Avocations: reading, computer, swimming. Office: Nijinsky Foundation Inc PO Box # 15981 Phoenix AZ 85060-5981 Fax: (602) 952-7149, 602-840-9605.

NIKODINOV, ANGELA, professional figure skater, Olympic athlete; b. Spartanburg, S.C., May 9, 1980; Competitive history includes 2nd place Pacific Coast Jr., 1994, 3rd place Southwest Pacific Jr., 1994, 5th place U.S. Championships Jr., 1994, 2nd place Pacific Coast Jr., 1995, 3rd place Southwest Pacific Jr., 1995, 5th place U.S. Championships Jr., 1995, 6th place World Jr. Selections Competition, 1996, 2d place Pacific Coast Sr., 1996, 5th place U.S. Olympic Festival, 1995, 1st place Southwest Pacific Sr., 1996, 3rd place O. Nepela Meml., 1996, 1st place Pacific Coast Sr., 1997, 3rd place World Jr. Selection Competition, 1997, 2nd place Pokal Der Blauen Scwerter, 1996, 4th place U.S. Championships, 1997, 4th place Skate America, 1997, 5th place U.S. Championships, 1998, 11th place World Jr. Championships, 1998, 4th place Goodwill Games, 1998, 2nd place Keri Lotion Figure Skating Classic, 1998, 3rd place Four Continents Championships, 1999, 3rd place Skate America, 1998, 3d place U.S. Championships, 1999, 12th place World Championships, 1999, 7th place Skate America, 1999, 5th place Keri Lotion Figure Skating Classic, 1999, 4th place Cup of Russia, 1999, 4th place U.S. Championships, 2000, 1st place Four Continents, 2000, 9th place World Championships, 2000, 3d place Cup of Russia, 2001, 3rd place Nations Cup, 2001, 3rd place, U.S. Championships, 2001, 2nd place, Great American Figure Skating Challenge, 2001, 5th place Workd Championships, 2001, 4th place, U.S. Championships, 2002, 1st place, Pacific Coast Sectionals, 2004, 5th place, U.S. Championships, 2004. Avocations: water skiing, snow skiing, rollerblading, jet skiing. Office: USFSA 20 1st St Colorado Springs CO 80906-3624*

NILES, BARBARA ELLIOTT, psychoanalyst; b. Boston, Jan. 31, 1939; d. Byron Kauffman and Helen Alice (Heissler) Elliott; m. John Denison, June 25, 1960 (div. 1981); children: Catherine Elliott, Andrew Elliott. AA, Briarcliff Coll., 1958; BA, SUNY, 1984; MSW, Hunter Coll., 1986. Cert. psychotherapy and psychoanalysis Inst. Contemporary Psychotherapy; social worker N.Y. Exec. com. Legal Aid Soc. Women's Aux., N.Y.C., 1965-67; sec. Water Quality Task Force Scientists' Com. for Pub. Info., N.Y.C., 1973-74; founding dir., sec. Consumer Action Now Inc., N.Y.C., 1970-77; dir. devel. Consumer Action Now's Council Environ., N.Y.C., 1976-77; dir. 170 Tenants Corp., N.Y.C., 1979-81; mem. pub. interest com. Cosmopolitan Club, N.Y.C., 1979-82; dir. INFORM Inc., N.Y.C., 1978-84; pvt. practice psychotherapy and psychoanalysis N.Y.C., 1986—. Mem. adj. faculty metro ctr. Empire State Coll., N.Y.C., NY, 1987—97. Editor: (biography) Off the Beaten Track, 1984. Bd. trustees Salisbury Assn., 2001—; active Land Trust Bd., 2001—; bd. dirs. Salisbury Housing Trust, 2001—, Salisbury Vis. Nurse Assn., 2001—. Mem.: NASW, St Botolph Club (Boston), Vincent Club (Boston), Cosmopolitan Club (N.Y.C.). Avocations: wilderness camping, travel, literature. Office: c/o Arnold Rosen MD 200 E 78th St New York NY 10021-2004

NILES, JUDITH F. librarian; b. Temple, Tex., Mar. 18, 1944; d. Fern Fredrickson Niles, John Loraine Niles. BA, U. N.D., 1966; MA, U. Wis., 1968; MLS, Ind. U., 1973. Serials libr. U. Tex., San Antonio, 1974—77; head tech. svcs. Laredo (Tex.) State U., 1977—81; head acquisitions Rice U., Houston, 1981—85; dir. libr. tech. svcs. U. Louisville, 1986—91, dir. libr. collection mgmt., 1991—2003, libr. spl. collections, 2004—. Contbr. articles to profl. jours. Grantee Fulbright Grant, U.S. Dept. State, 1966—67. Mem.: AAUP, ALA, N.Am. Serials Interest Group, Assn. for Libr. Collections and Tech. Svcs. (chair budget and fin. com. 2001—02), Beta Phi Mu, Phi Beta Kappa. Presbyterian. Avocation: travel. Office: Univ Louisville Ekstrom Libr LL05 2301 S 3rd St Louisville KY 40292

NILES, KATHRYN M. artist, art educator; b. Sidney, NY, July 10, 1956; d. Margaret Mae Sibley and William Lewis Niles; 1 child, Damian C. Jennings. MFA, Colo. State U., 1996. Adj. instr. Colo. State U., Ft. Collins, 1996—96; adj. lectr. SUNY, Binghamton, 1997—. Co-treas. Cooperative Gallery 213, Binghamton, 1999—, founding mem., 1999—. Pastel and mixed media painting intaglio, Tracks at Sunset, 1992, 1992, lithographic and monotype prints, Landscape Conversations, 1998, exhibitions include The Finer Side Gallery, Washington, DC, 1998—99, Blue Pony Gallery & Press, Charlotte, NC, 1999—, Cooperative Gallery 213, Binghamton, NY, 1999—, Contemporary Am. Printmakers Renaissance Exhbn., Atlanta, GA, 1995—, Schoharie County Arts Coun. Nat. Small Works Exhbn., Cobleskill, NY, 1995—, Armory Art Ctr. 5th Ann. Figurative Small Works Exhbn., West Palm Beach, Fla., 1996, Abstraction, Banana Factory, Bethlehem, PA, 2000, Pressed & Pulled VI, Ga. Coll. & State U., Milledgeville, 1997, Pressed & Pulled IX, 2000, Internat. Miniature Print Exhbn., Conn. Graphic Arts Ctr., Norwalk, 2001, Works on Paper, Perkins Ctr. for the Arts, Moorestown, NJ, 1999, 2001, Faculty Exhbns., Binghamton U., SUNY, 2000—01, Sixty Square Inches, Purdue U., West Lafayette, Ind., 2002, East of Ithaca 8 Printmakers, The Ink Shop, Ithaca, NY, 2002, Rude and Bold Women, Binghamton, NY, 2001, 2002. Recipient Carolyn Giffuni Marcellino Meml. award, Grand Gallery, Nat. Arts Club, 1998. Mem.: Coll. Art Assn. Avocations: swimming, travel. Home: 213 State St # 4 Binghamton NY 13901 Office: SUNY Binghamton PO Box 6000 Binghamton NY 13902 Business E-Mail: kniles@binghamton.edu.

NILSON, PATRICIA, clinical psychologist; b. Boulder, Colo., Oct. 22, 1929; d. James William and Vera Maude (Peacock) Broxon; m. Eric Walter Nilson, Dec. 23, 1950; children: Stephen Daniel, Eric Jon, Christopher Lawrence. Registered Phys. Therapist, Med. Coll. Va., 1951; MA in Clin. Psychology, L.I. U., 1972, PhD, 1973. Cert. psychologist N.Y. Clin. psychologist Court Cons. Unit, Hauppauge, N.Y., 1972-92, Three Village Counseling Svc., Setauket, N.Y., 1974-75, Farmingville (N.Y.) Mental Health Ctr., N.Y., 1992-95; pvt. practice Commack, N.Y., 1975— Adj. asst. prof. C.W. Post Coll., Brookdale, 1974-80; cons., supr. psychologist Wayside Sch. for Girls, Valley Stream, 1975-85; cons. L.I. Lighting Co., 1980; lectr. in field. Author children's therapeutic stories; author therapeutic games: The Road to Problem Mastery; contbr. articles to profl. jours. Mem. APA, Suffolk County Psychol. Assn., Nat. Register Health Svc. Providers in Psychology, Soc. for Clin. and Exptl. Hypnosis (life). Office: 11 Montrose Dr Commack NY 11725-1312 E-mail: drpat11@netzero.net.

NILSSON, MARY ANN, music educator; b. N.Y.C., Jan. 5, 1944, d. Gerhard Eugene and Selma Christine (Landy) N.; m. June 19, 1988. BS with honors, New Paltz State U., 1965; MA, NYU, 1983; MM, Meredith Coll., 2000; student, The Christian U., 2003. LPN, N.Y. Piano tchr. New Paltz (N.Y.) State U. Coll., 1983-85, Ulster County C.C., Stone Ridge, N.Y., 1983-85; music instr. Piedmont C.C., Roxboro, N.C., 1999, Durham Tech. Coll., 1999, Durham (N.C.) C.C., 2000—02; coll. instr. Vance-Granville C.C., Henderson, NC, 2002, Mt. Olive Coll., Research Triangle Park, NC, 2002—. Music history tchr. Family of Ellenville, N.Y., 1990-91; tchr. music appreciation Long Meml. Music Acad., Roxboro, N.C., 2001, tchr. music course continuing edn., 2001; music instr. Mt. Olive Coll., Research Triangle Park, N.C., 2002. Musician (Performances): New Paltz State U., 1992, Town of Lumberland, N.Y., 1993, Lunch & Listen series, 1994, Hudson Valley Sr. Residence, 1995, South Winds Sr. Residence, 1995, Forest at Duke, 1997, Long Meml. Ch., 1997; musician: (pianist competition) Meredith Coll., 1999; musician: (master class) Walter Hautzig Meredith Coll., 1999; musician: (recital) Meredith Coll., Durham Regents, 2001, Forest at Duke, Carolina House, 2001, Carol Woods, Croasdale, Chapel Heill Sr. Ctr., 2003; contbr. articles to profl. jours. Choir dir., organist First Presbyn. Ch., Monticello, N.Y., 1985-86; vol. Durham (N.C.) Hosp., 1996—. Named one of 12 winners, Van Cliburn Tchrs. program, Ft. Worth Tex., 2003; grantee, Ulster County Office of Aging, 1983, Sullivan County Office of Aging, Nat. Music Tchrs. Assn., 2001, Music Tchrs. Nat. Assn., 2001. Mem. Nat. Guild Piano Tchrs. (adjudicator 1983—, chmn. piano audition ctr. 1988-95), Durham Music Tchrs. Assn., Pi Kappa Lambda. Avocations: reading german, walking, fitness. Home and Office: 214 Equestrian Chase Rougemont NC 27572-9351

NIMEROFF, PHYLLIS RUTH, electronic engineer, visual artist; b. Washington, Apr. 22, 1951; d. Isadore and Anne (Schultz) N. BFA, Md. Inst. Coll. Art, 1973; BS in Electronic Engring. Tech., Capitol Coll., 1988. Exhibiting vis. artist East Coast, 1968—; art tchr. D.C. Schs., Washington, 1974-75; ops. tech. TV Stas., Mont., Nebr., Md., Washington, 1978-85; engr. PRC, Inc., Suitland, Md., 1988-1997; multimedia communicator Lockheed Martin, Washington, 1998—. Mem. Alpha Chi, Tau Alpha Pi. Avocation: gardening. Home: 6505 Greentree Rd Bethesda MD 20817-3325 E-mail: primeroff@zdnetonebox.com.

NIMMO, CHARLENE, minister; b. Hamilton, Ontario, Can., May 21, 1938; d. Robert Ernst and Marie Esther LeMon; m. Del Wayne Roy Nimmo, May 27, 1960; children: Christina Brooke Clapp, Charity Anne Chapman. BS, Evangel U., 1960; MDiv, Denver (Colo.) Sem., 1986; D cum laude in Ministry, Fuller Sem., 2002. Ordained minister Disciples of Christ, Rocky Mountain Region, 1986. Min. Disciples of Christ, Colo.; sr. min. Park Hill Christian Ch., Pueblo, Colo. Instr. Disciples of Christ, Rocky Mountain Region, Denver, 1998—2002. Chmn. Larimer County Colorado Citizen's Budget Com., Ft. Collins, Colo., 1982—85. Mem.: Colo. 14rs. Avocation: high altitude climbing. Home: 245 S Montecito Drive Pueblo West CO 81007 Office: Park Hill Christian Church 1401 E 7th Street Pueblo CO 81001 Personal E-mail: revdoc@aculink.net.

NIMS, KELLY MICHELLE, literature educator, researcher; b. Bridgeport, Conn., Nov. 1, 1970; d. Albert Nims and Charletta Johnson. BA in English Lang. and Lit., U. Va., 1999; MA in Internat. Edn., Columbia U., N.Y.C., 2002; MA in African Studies, postgrad., Columbia U., 2002—. Tchr. Mercy Learning Ctr., Bridgeport, Conn., 1998—99; libr., program facilitator Matabo Dist. Cmty. Resource Ctr. Libr., Zimbabwe, 1999—2000; tchr. Peace Corps, Zimbabwe, 1999—2000; asst. editor Disney Pub. Worldwide, N.Y.C., NY, 2000—01; user svcs. cons. Columbia U., N.Y.C., 2002; cons. S.W. Cmty. Health Ctr., Bridgeport, 2002; lectr. Baruch Coll., CUNY, 2002—03, Rutgers U., Newark, 2003—. Editor: Be Boy Buzz, Grump Groan Growl, Homemade Love, This Girl Say, Chip Wants a Dog, Wegmanology, Fly, Little Tree; editor: (and founder) Word lit. mag., 2001—; contbr. articles to profl. jours. Scholar Alice Munro scholar for acad. excellence, 1995. Mem.: MLA, Inst. for Rsch. in African-Am. Studies, Africa Studies Assn., Am. Anthrop. Assn., Kappa Delta Pi. Buddhist. Avocations: reading, tennis, painting. Office: City Univ of New York 1 Bernard Barveh Way New York NY 10010 Home: 119 Eagle St Bridgeport CT 06607-1619

NIPERT, DONNA ANN See BARRETT, JESSICA

NIPPERT, CAROLYN COCHRANE, college official, information scientist; b. Bklyn., Mar. 14, 1946; d. Fredrick and Astrid (Bergh) Cochrane; m. Charles Raymond Nippert Jr., Nov. 11, 1972; children: Andrew, Philip, Collin, Corinne. BA, Adelphi Suffolk Coll. (now Dowling Coll.), 1968; MLS, U. Pitts., 1971. Sci. and engring. cataloger Lehigh U., Bethlehem, Pa., 1971-74; dir. libr. Lehigh Valley Hosp. Ctr., Allentown, Pa., 1974-88; reference libr. Cedar Crest Coll., Allentown, Pa., 1988-93, head info. and instrnl. svcs., 1994—. Conf. presenter Nat. Online Meeting, 1985. Mem. Cooperating Hosp. Lehigh Valley, 1974-88, mem. adv. bd., 1979-85. Mem. Med. Libr. Assn., Acad. Health Profls. (sr.). Home: 222 Pleasantview Rd Pottstown PA 19464 Office: Cedar Crest Coll Cressman Libr 100 College Dr Allentown PA 18104-6132

NIQUETTE, GERALDINE NORMA, marriage and family therapist; b. Kansas City, Mo., Apr. 27, 1924; d. Glenn Nesbit Niquette and Naomi Ruth Wilson-Niquette; m. Brigham Julius Lundquist, Feb. 28, 1946 (div. June 1, 1966); children: Gerre Niquette Lundquist, Lorenn Ruth Lundquist, Philip Julian Lundquist, John Brigg Lundquist. AA, Contra Costa Coll., San Pablo, Calif., 1966; BA, Calif. State U. Sonoma, Cotati, 1976; MPH, Loma Linda U., Calif., 1978; PhD in Counseling Psychology, Prof. Sch. Psychol. Studies, San Diego, 1984. RN Calif., 1966; cert. Marriage Family Therapist Calif. Bd. Behavioral Sci., 1987. Clin. dir./program mgr. Dual Diagnosis Extended Care, San Marcos and Palm Springs, Calif., 1987—93; pvt. practice therapist, supr., educator Rancho Mirage, Del., 1988—93; cons. Splty. Hosp., Redding, Calif., 1994—94; clinician/treatment planner Consol. Tribal Health, Ukiah, Calif., 1996—99; clinician/childrens' team leader Lake County Mental Health, Lakeport, Calif., 2000—03; pvt. clinician Lakeport, Calif., 2001—. Pub. health extern WHO, Geneva, 1977; continuing edn. provider Ca Bd. Registered Nursing, Sacramento, 1990—94; adv. bd. Canyon Springs Psychiat. Hosp., Cathedral City, Calif., 1992—93; lectr. and mem. Nat. Coun. of Alcoholism, San Diego, 1984—93. Vol./developmentally delayed Los Lomas Sch., Lafayette, Calif., 1958—60; nursing aux. Seattle Well Baby Clinics, Seattle, 1953—57; vol. support person various drug and alcohol programs, Calif., 1972—. Mem.: Am. Assn. Family Therapists (licentiate), Calif. Assn. Marriage Family Therapists (licentiate), Lake County Women's Club. Avocations: acquiring new knowledge, travel, gardening, needlecrafts. Home: 83 Lafferty Rd Lakeport CA 95453 Office: Gerre Niquette Ph D MFT 906 C S Main St Lakeport CA 95453

NISCE, LOURDES, radiologist; b. Manila, Apr. 13, 1925; m. Francisa N. and Elena (Zandueta) N. MD, U. Santo Tomas, Manila, 1946. Diplomate Am. Bd. Radiology. Intern Holy Name Hosp., Teaneck, N.J., 1952-53; resident N.Y. Hosp.-Cornell Med. Coll., N.Y.C., 1957-61; fellow Meml. Hosp. Sloan-Kettering Ctr., N.Y.C., 1961-62, attending radiation oncologist, 1965-86; prof. radiology N.Y. Hosp., 1965—, Cornell Med. Coll., 1965—. Contbr. articles to med. jours. Fellow Am Coll. Radiology; mem. Am. Coll. Radiologists, Radiol. Soc. N.Am., RADIUM, Am. Soc. Therapeutic Radiology and Oncology. Address: 525 E 68th St Box 575 New York NY 10021-4870

NISCHKE, ANN M. state legislator; b. Jan. 19, 1951; BS, U. Wis., Eau Claire, 1977. Real estate marketer; exec. dir. C. of C.; mem. Wis. State Assembly, Madison, 2002—, vice chair econ. devel. com., mem. aging and long-term care com., mem. edn. reform com., mem. energy and utilities com., mem. fin. instns. com., mem. small bus. com. Republican. Office: State Capitol Rm 8 N PO Box 8953 Madison WI 53708-8953 Address: 246 N Racine Ave Waukesha WI 53186

NISKALA APPS, JENNIFER A. pediatric neuropsychologist, researcher, educator; d. Jan and Tom Niskala. BS, Tex. Christian U., 1994; PhD, U. Tex. Southwestern Med. Ctr., 1998. Registrant Nat. Register of Health Svc. Providers in Psychology, 2003. Pediatric neuropsychologist Assurred Behavioral Health, Dallas, 2000—02; pediatric neuropsychologist, asst. prof. U Tex. Southwestern Med. Ctr., Dallas, 2002—03; pediatric neuropsychologist,/ asst. prof. Med. Coll. Wis., Milw., 2003—. Postdoctoral intern in pediatric neuropsychology Children's Med. Ctr., Dallas, 1998—2000; cons. NHL Concussion Program, Dallas, 1997—2003; spkr. on pediat. mental health issues. Departmental scholar in Psychology, Tex. Christian U., 1994. Mem.: Nat. Acad. Neuropsychology, APA, Psi Chi (pres. chpt. 1993—94). Achievements include research in bipolar disorder in children and adolescents; pediatric neuropsychology. Avocation: ice hockey. Office: Med Coll of Wis 9000 W Wisconsin Ave MS #750 Milwaukee WI 53201-1997 Personal E-mail: jnf414@sbcglobal.net. E-mail: JNiskala@chw.org.

NISSON, MARY, elementary school educator; b. Berkeley, Calif., May 19, 1960; d. Peter Fenn Samuelson and Jeanne Francis Mulligan. BA in Econs., U. Calif., Davis, 1984; multiple subjects credential, Calif. State U., 1994. ESL/parent literacy tchr. Old Marshall Sch., Susan B. Anthony Elem. Sch., Sacramento, 1996—; bus. English educator Blue Diamond Almond Co., Sacramento, 1998; reading remediation instr. River Oaks Elem. Sch., Galt, Calif., 1999. Co-founding adult educator Twilight Program, Elk Grove Sch. Dist. Prairie Elem. Site, Sacramento, 1995-97; elem. tchr. Feickert Elem., Elk Grove, Calif., 1995. Co-author: (ESL handbook) Curricular Reference, 1996; editor (cookbook) The Melting Pot, 1999; contbr. articles to profl. jours. Founding coord. Natomas Mothers Group, Sacramento, Calif., 1988; co-founder, mem. AUTASTICS, San Francisco, 1996—; mem. Graffiti Busters, Autism Soc. Am. Recipient Recognition certificate Natomas Mothers Group, Sacramento, 1998. Mem. Calif. Tchrs. Assn., Calif. Tchrs. of English to Speakers of Other Langs. Roman Catholic. Avocations: reading, birdwatching, bicycling, cross-country skiing. Office: Old Marshall Adult Edn Ctr 2718 G St Sacramento CA 95816-3720 E-mail: mdsong@earthlink.net.

NITKA, ALICE W. social services administrator, state representative; b. Little Falls, N.Y., Dec. 13, 1944; m. Martin Nitka; children: Abigail, Molly. Ba, Russell Sage Coll., 1967. Social worker; with Vt. Achievement Ctr., Inc.; rep. Vt. State Ho. Reps., 1999—. Justice of the peace; mem. Ludlow Planning Commn., Zoning Bd. Adjustment; bd. dir. Ludlow Bd. Civil Authority; chmn. bd. Rutland Regional Bd. Family Svcs. Mem.: Vt. Foster and Adoptive Families Assn., Black River Valley Rod and Gun Club. Democrat. Home: North Hill PO Box 136 Ludlow VT 05149

NITKIN, REBECCA A. lawyer; d. Lewis and Judith Nitkin; m. Paul Saltzman; 1 child, Cydney Paige Saltzman. BS, Skidmore Coll., 1980; MSW, Boston U., 1984; JD, Cath. U., 1991. Bar: U.S. Ct. Appeals Md. 1992, U.S. Ct. Appeals D.C. 1995, U.S. Dist. Ct. Md. 1995, U.S. Dist. Ct. D.C. 2002. Child protective svc. investigator Prince George's County Dept. of Social Svcs., 1987—93; ptnr. Futrovsky, Nitkin & Scherr, Chartered, Rockville, Md., 1993—. Spkr. in field. Vol. legal callback program Commn. for Women, 1999—. Mem.: Women's Bar Assn. Montgomery County (mem. prepare for success planning com. 2001—), Nat. Assn. Criminal Def. Atty.'s Assn., Md. Criminal Def. Atty.'s Assn. (bd. dirs. 2003), Md. State Bar Assn., Prince George's County Bar Assn., Montgomery County Bar Assn. (co-chair criminal sect. 1999—2001, mem. exec. com. 2003, judicial selections com. 2000—02, chmn. nominations and elections 2002). Democrat. Jewish. Avocations: dance, camping, working out. Office: Futrovsky Nitkin & Scherr 77 S Washington St Fl 1 Rockville MD 20850

NITSCH, BRENDA SUE, music educator; b. Nanticoke, Pa., June 8, 1966; d. Donald Russell and Beth Iris Nelson; m. Kevin Robert Nitsch, Aug. 1, 1992; children: Daniel Kevin, David Robert, Samuel Douglas. BS in Music Edn., Marywood U., Scranton, Pa., 1988; MS in Music Edn., Mansfield U., 1990; MusM in Vocal Performance, Eastman Sch. of Music, 1991. Cert. tchr. NY, 1988. Vocal music tchr. Eastridge HS, East Irondequoit, NY, 1991—2001, Webster Thomas HS, Webster, NY, 2001—. Music dir. Bapt. Temple, Rochester, NY, 1991—2001, youth dir., 1991—. Dir.: (opera) Amahl and the Night Visitors, 2002, (music theater) Jesus Christ Superstar, 1996, 2001, Joseph and the Amazing Technicolor Dreamcoat, 2003. Vol. Bapt. Temple, Rochester, NY. Mem.: Nat. Assn. Tchrs. of Singers (1st place award 1986), N.Y. State Schs. Music Assn., Music Educators Nat. Conf., Pi Kappa Lambda, Kappa Gamma Pi. United Methodist. Avocations: running, singing, reading. Home: 142 Hampton Way Penfield NY 14526 Office: Webster Thomas High Sch 800 Five Mile Line Rd Webster NY 14580 Personal E-mail: bnvocal@rochester.rr.com. E-mail: brenda_nitsch@websterschools.org.

NIX, BARBARA LOIS, real estate broker; b. Sept. 25, 1929; d. Martin Clayton and Norma (Gunter) Westfield; m. B. H. Nix, July 12, 1968; children: William Martin Dahl, Theresa Irene Dahl; stepchildren: Dennis Leon, Denise Lynn. Student, St. Elizabeths Sch. Nursing, Yakima, Wash., 1949-50; AA, Sierra Coll., 1978; student, Calif. State U., Sacramento, 1984. Bookkeeper, office mgr. Lakeport (Calif.) Tire Svc., 1966-69, Dr. K. J. Absher, Grass Valley, Calif., 1972-75; real estate sales and office mgr. Rough and Ready Land Co., Penn Valley, Calif., 1976-77, co-owner, v.p., sec., 1978—, Wildwood West Real Estate, Gateway Real Estate. Co-owner Nix's Antiques, 1996—. Youth and welfare chmn. Yakima Federated Jr. Women's Club, 1957; den mother Cub Scouts, 1959-60; leader Girl Scouts, 1961-62; mem. Friends of Hospice; mem. Sierra, Nev. Meml. Hosp. Found.; adv. bd. dirs., v.p. Roots and Wings Ednl. Found., 1991-95; mem. Nevada County Sch. Dist. Redistricting Bd. Recipient Pres.'s award Sierra Coll., 1973, others. Mem. Lake Wildwood Women's Club, Penn Valley (founder, pres. 1978), Sierra Nevada Meml. Hosp. Aux., Job's Daus. (life). Republican. Roman Catholic. Home: 19365 Wildflower Dr Penn Valley CA 95946-9735 Office: POBox 191 Penn Valley CA 95946

NIX, KATHERINE JEAN, medical case manager; d. Samuel Watson and Dorothy Lee (Woods) Lewis; m. Robert Milton Nix, May 5, 1963 (div. Feb. 1988); children: Araina Catrice, Cynthia Lathier. AA in Safety and Health, Merritt Coll., 1976; AA in Nursing, Chabot Coll., 1974, BSN, U. San Francisco, 1979. RN Calif. Staff nurse Highland Hosp., Oakland, Calif., 1961-73; nurse cmty. health Alameda County, Oakland, Calif., 1973-75; nurse occupational health Caterpiller Tractor Co., San Leandro, Calif., 1975-77, inspector safety hygiene, 1981-84; nurse cons. occupational health Intel Corp., Livermore, Calif., 1981-84; cons. health & safety Quaker Oats Co., Oakland, 1984-86; nurse cons. occupational health Rawson Drug & Sundry Co., San Leandro, 1986-89; rehab. nurse Continental Rehab. Resources, Pleasanton, Calif., 1989-91; rehab. nurse cons. GAB, Campbell, Calif., 1991-93; med. case mgr. Conservco Travelers Ins. Co., Walnut Creek, Calif., 1993-95, Olsten Kimberly Quality Care, San Leandro, Calif., 1995—. Health advisor Black Women Organized for Polit. Action, Oakland, 1979—, Alemeda (Calif.) Coll., 1982-86. Fellow Nat. Safety Coun., Rehab. Nurses Group. Democrat. Avocations: skiing, reading, stage plays. Home: PO Box 5834 Oakland CA 94605-0834 Office: St Marys Hosp 450 Stanyan St San Francisco CA 94117-1079

NIX, LINDA ANNE BEAN, public relations executive; b. Sept. 20, 1943; d. Norman Arthur and Gladys Mae (Charlton) Bean, Jr.; m. Henry Taylor Betts, Jr., Sept. 5, 1964 (div. 1970); m. John Asa Nix, Nov. 24, 1971 (div. 1990). Student, Syracuse U., 1961-64; BA, Scarritt Coll., 1965; postgrad., Middle Tenn. State U., 9171 73. Mobile coord. Children's Mus., Nashville, 1967-69; promotion dir. Sta. WDCN-TV/8, Nashville, 1969-82; dir. pub. info. Sta. WYES-TV/12, New Orleans, 1982—; mktg. dir. Sta. KOFY-TV Radio San Francisco, 1989-91, Sta. KUSI-TV, San Diego, 1992-93; self-employed in pub. rels., 1992—. Mem. pub. info. adv. com. Pub. Broadcasting Service, Washington, 1977-80, chmn. 1979-80, mem. festival task force, 1979-80. Author, editor: (tchr. workbook) Yellow Submarine, 1968; contbr. Great Chefs, 2001—; contbr. articles to profl. jours. Bd. dirs. Nashville League for Hearing Impaired, 1973-76, Tennessee Williams/New Orleans Literacy Festival, 1995--; chmn. membership com. Coun. Cmty. Svcs., Nashville, 1978-80; mem. allocation panel United Way Greater Nashville, 1979-81, United Way Greater New Orleans, 1982-86. Mem. Pub. Rels. Soc. Am. (chmn. accreditation com. 1985, pres. New Orleans chpt. 1988), Broadcast Promotion and Mktg. Execs., Inc. (Promax) (bd. dirs. 1982-91, pres. 1989-90). Avocations: flying (multi-engine, commercial), sewing. Home and Office: PO Box 7068 Metairie LA 70010-7068 E-mail: lagator@mindspring.com.

NIXON, AGNES ECKHARDT, television writer, producer; m. Robert Nixon (dec.); 4 children. Student, Sch. Speech, Northwestern U. Writer for radio and TV; freelance writer for: TV programs Hallmark Hall of Fame, Robert Montgomery Presents, Studio One; creator, packager, head writer: daytime TV series All My Children; creator nightime mini-series The Manions of America; creator, packager daytime TV series One Life to Live; creator, packager: daytime TV series Loving; co-creator: daytime TV series As The World Turns; formerly head writer, The Guiding Light, daytime TV series Another World; creator, story cons. The City. Recipient Trustees award Nat. Acad. TV Arts and Sci., 1981, Super Achiever award Jr. Diabetes Found., 1981, Wilmer Eye Inst. award, 1981, Communicator award Am. Women in Radio & TV, 1984, Gold Plate award Am. Acad. Achievement, 1993, Popular Culture Lifetime Achievement award Popular Culture Assn., 1995, Pub. Svc. award Johns Hopkins Hosp., 1995, Humanitarian award Nat. Osteoporosis Found., 1996; inducted into TV Hall of Fame, 1993. Mem. Internat. Radio and TV Soc. Nat. Acad. TV Arts and Scis., Harvard Found. (bd. dirs.), Mus. TV and Radio (bd. dirs.), The Friars Club. Address: All My Children 320 W 66th St New York NY 10023-6304

NIXON, CAROL HOLLADAY, retired park and recreation director; b. Salt Lake City, Dec. 25, 1937; m. William L. Nixon; children: William H., Joan, Michael, Jennifer, Jacqueline, John. From dep. chief of staff to chief of staff to gov. State of Utah, Salt Lake City, 1991-93, dir. Cmty. Devel. Divsn., 1993-96; pres., CEO This Is the Place Heritage Park, Salt Lake City, 1996—2001, ret., 2001. Fax: 801-584-8325.

NIXON, CYNTHIA, actress; b. New York, Apr. 9, 1966; d. Walter and Anne Nixon. BA in English, Barnard Coll., 1988. Founding member The Drama Dept., 1996. Actor: (plays) The Philadelphia Story, 1980 (Theatre World Award, 1981), Indiscretions, 1996 (Tony Award nom., 1996); (films) Little Darlings, 1980, Prince of the City, 1981, Tattoo, 1981, I Am the Cheese, 1983, Amadeus, 1984, The Manhattan Project, 1986, O.C. and Stiggs, 1987, Let It Ride, 1989, Through an Open Window, 1992, The Pelican Brief, 1993, Addams Family Values, 1993, Baby's Day OUt, 1994, The Cottonwood, 1996, 'M' Word, 1996, Marvin's Room, 1996, Advice From a Caterpillar, 1999, The Out-of-Towners, 1999, Igby Goes Down, 2002, The Paper Mache Chase, 2003; (TV series) Sex and the City, 1998—2004 (Emmy nom. for Outstanding Supporting Actress in a comedy series, 2002); (TV miniseries) Tanner '88, 1988; (TV films) The Seven Wishes of a Rich Kid, 1979, The Private History of a Campaign That Failed, 1981, Rascals and Robbers: The Secret Adventures of Tom Sawyer and Huck Finn, 1982, My Body, My Child, 1982, Fifth of July, 1982, The Murder of Mary Phagan, 1988, Women & Wallace, 1990, Love She Sought, The, 1990, Face of a Stranger, 1991, Love, Lies and Murder, 1991, Kiss-Kiss, Dahlings!, 1992, Sex and the Matrix, 2000, Papa's Angels, 2000, Stage on Screen: The Women, 2002. Office: William Morris Agency One William Morris Place Beverly Hills CA 90212

NIXON, JUDITH MAY, librarian; b. Gary, Ind., June 14, 1945; d. Louis Robert Sr. and Mable Sophia (Reiner) Vician; m. Cleon Robert Nixon III, Aug. 20, 1967; 1 child, Elizabeth Marie. BS in Edn., Valparaiso U., 1967; MA in LS, U. Iowa, 1974. Tchr. U.S. Peace Corps, Kingdom of Tonga, 1968-69; popular books libr. Lincoln Libr., Springfield, Ill., 1971-73; reference libr. Cedar Rapids (Iowa) Pub. Libr., 1974-76; reference coord. U.

Wis., Platteville, 1976-82; bus. libr. U. Ariz., Tucson, 1982-84; consumer and family sci. libr. Purdue U., West Lafayette, La., 1984-93, Krannert mgmt. and econs. libr., 1993—. Editor: Industry and Company Information, 1991, Organization Charts, 1992, 2d edit., 1996, Hotel and Restaurant Industries, 1993; editor quar. serial Lodging and Restaurant Index, 1985 93. Leader Girl Scouts U.S., Lafayette, 1985—. Recipient John H. Moriarty award Purdue U. Librs., 1989. Mem. ALA (chairperson bus. reference and svcs. sect. 1995-96, GALE Rsch. award for excellence in bus. librarianship 1994). Home: 2375 N 23rd St Lafayette IN 47904-1242 Office: Purdue U Libraries KRAN Mgmt and Econs Libr 504 W State St West Lafayette IN 47907-2058 Office Phone: 765-494-2922. E-mail: jnixon@purdue.edu.

NIXON, MARNI, singer; b. Altadena, Calif., Feb. 22, 1930; d. Charles and Margaret (Wittke) McEathron; m. Ernest Gold, May 22, 1950 (div. 1969); children: Andrew Maurice, Martha Alice, Melani Christine; m. Lajos Frederick Fenster, July 23, 1971 (div. July 1975); m. Albert David Block, Apr. 11, 1983. Student, L.A. City Coll., UCLA, U. So. Calif., Tanglewood, Mass. Dir. vocal faculty Calif. Inst. Arts, Valencia, 1970-72; pvt. tchr., vocal coacn, condr. master classes, 1970—; pvt. voice tchr., coach, condr. master classes, 1970—; head apprentice divsn. Santa Barbara Music Acad. of West, 1980; formerly dir. opera workshop Cornish Inst. Arts, Seattle. Tchr. in field; judge Met. Opera Internat. Am. Music Awards, Nat. Inst. Music Theatre, 1984-87; panelist New Music, Nat. Assn. Tchrs. Singing, pres., N.Y. chpt., 1994—; dialect dir., opera recs. Actress Pasadena (Calif.) Playhouse, 1940-45, soloist Roger Wagner chorale, 1947-53, appeared with New Eng. Opera Co., L.A. Opera Co., Ford Found. TV Opera, 1948-63, San Francisco Spring Opera, 1966, Seattle Opera, 1971-73; classical recitals and appearances with symphony orchs. throughout U.S., Can., also Eng., Israel, Ireland; in motion pictures as Sister Sophia in Sound of Music, 1964, Aunt Alice in I Think I Do, 1996; appeared on (TV) Boomerang, from 1975; Broadway and off-Broadway shows: Eliza Doolittle in My Fair Lady, 1964, Edna in Taking My Turn, 1983, Sadie in Opal, 1992-94, Fraulein Schneider in Cabaret, 1998, Mrs. Willson in Ballymore, 1999, Heidi Schiller in Follies, 2001, Aunt Kate in James Joyce's The Dead, 1999-2001, Mamma in Nine, 2003; taped for Great Performances PBS-TV Role of Edna, 1994; voice dubbed for film My Fair Lady, The King and I, An Affair to Remember, West Side Story, Disney's Mulan, others; rec. artist for Columbia, Mus. Heritage Records, Capital, RCA Victor, Ednl. Records, Reference Recs., Varese-Sarabande, Nonesuch. Recipient 4 Emmy awards for best actress, 2 Action for Childrens TV awards, 1977; nominee Drama Desk award; recipient Chgo. Film Festival award, 1977, 2 Gold Records for Songs from Mary Poppins and Mulan, 2 time Grammy award nominee Nat. Acad. Rec. Arts and Scis. (1st rec. Cabaret Songs and Early Songs by Arnold Schoenberg, RCA, 1977 and 1st rec. Emily Dickinson Songs by Aaron Copland, Reference Recs., 1988). Mem. Nat. Assn. Tchrs. Singing (pres. N.Y. chpt. 1994-97). Personal E-mail: singermarnix@aol.com.

NIXON, SHIRNETTE, pharmaceutical company administrator; b. N.Y.C. BA in English, Bklyn. Coll., 1969. Pers. asst. Mut. N.Y., N.Y.C., 1969-73; editorial asst. Franklin Watts Inc., N.Y.C., 1973-76; adminstrv. sec. for pers. Pfizer, Inc., N.Y.C., 1976-82, adminstrv. sec. for tax, 1982—, instr. to execs. secs., 1988, 89, Mabel Dean Bacon H.S., 1990; mem. tax support staff team, 1998—. Mem. Pfizer Support Staff Tng. Coun., 1996—. Mem. YWCA Helpline; spkr. Pfizer Town Meeting, 1996; participant Pfizer Fin. Town Meeting, 1999; mem. CSMTI Team, 1999. Recipient Spl. Recognition Letter Mayor David Dinkins. Mem.: AAUW, Internat. Tng. in Communication, Bklyn. Coll. Alumni Assn., Pfree Speech Toastmasters Club. Avocations: creative writing, teaching communication skills, speaking.

NIZNIK, CAROL ANN, electrical engineer, educator, consultant; b. Saratoga Springs, N.Y., Nov. 10, 1942; d. John Arthur Niznik and Rosalia Sopko; m. Donald H. Walter, Jan. 11, 1964. AAS in Engring. Sci., Alfred (N.Y.) State Coll., 1962; BSEE, U. Rochester, N.Y., 1969, MSEE, 1972; PhD in Elec. Engring., SUNY, Buffalo, 1978. Technician Taylor Instrument Corp., Rochester, 1962-64; sr. technician IBM Corp., Poughkeepsie, N.Y., 1964-68; rsch. scientist Eastman Kodak Corp., Rochester, 1969-70; sr. engr. Xerox Corp., Webster, N.Y., 1971-74; rsch. ast. prof. SUNY, buffalo, 1979-80; assoc. prof. elec. engring. U. Pitts., 1980-83; pres., cons. NW Systems, Rochester, 1975—. Adj. prof. math. Rochester Inst. Tech., 1993-94; vis. assoc. prof. Ctr. for Brain Rsch., Sch. Medicine, U. Rochester, 1983-84. Author tech. monograph on cerebellum prosthesis component; contbr. some 70 articles to profl. jours.; patentee in field. Recipient fellowships, grants and U.S. govt. contracts. Mem. IEEE (sr.), Sigma Xi, Eta Kappa Nu, Tau Beta Pi. Roman Catholic. Avocations: doll collecting, care of pets, gardening. Office: NW Sys PO Box 18133 Rochester NY 14618-0133

NJIE, VERONICA P.S. clinical nurse, educator; d. Edward G. Njie and Grace B.S. Daniels-Njie. BSN, Howard U., Washington, 1992; MSN, The Cath. U. Am., Washington, 1996. RN Washington, clin. specialist in med.-surg. nursing. Tchr. Dept. Edn., Banjul, The Gambia, 1980—82; state registered nurse (SRN) Royal Victoria Hosp., Banjul, 1985—86; rsch./field asst. Med. Rsch. Coun., Fajara, 1986—87; nurse technician Howard U. Hosp., Washington, 1988—90, clin. nurse II, 1990—96; clin. nurse N.W. Health Care Ctr. Beverly Enterprise, 1990—98; clin. instr. Montgomery Coll., Tacoma Park, Md., 1996; asst. prof. nursing Balt. City C. C., Balt., 1997. Contbr. articles to profl. jours. Recipient Intramural Rsch. Tng. award, NIH, 2000. Mem.: Md. Assn. Higher Edn., ANA, Nat. League Nursing, Sigma Theta Tau. Democrat. Roman Catholic. Avocations: reading, travel, theater, dance, movies. Office: Cath U Am Michigan Ave NE Washington DC 20064 E-mail: vpnjie@aol.com.

NNADI, EUCHARIA E. academic administrator; BS in Pharmacy, Creighton U., 1977; MS in Hosp. Pharmacy, U. Minn., 1978, PhD in Social and Adminstrv. Pharmacy, 1982; JD with high honors, Fla. State U., 1993. Lic. pharmacist. Asst. prof. pharmacy adminstrn. Coll. Pharmacy and Pharm. Scis. Fla. A&M U., Tallahassee, 1981—89, prof., 1989—94, dean, 1994; former dean Coll. Pharmacy and Pharm. Scis. Howard U.; v.p. acad. affairs U. Md. Ea. Shore, Princess Anne. Reviewer health affairs divsn. Tex. Higher Edn. Coordinating Bd. Contbr. articles to profl. jours., chpts. to books. Recipient Pharmacist award, Md. Pharm. Soc., 1996. Mem.: Nat. Assn. Bds. Pharmacy (item writer), Am. Coun. on Pharm. Edn. (accreditation site visits team for colls. and schs. pharmacy), Nat. Assn. State Univs. and Land-Grant Colls. (coun. acad. affairs), Order of Coif, Rho Chi. Office: U Md Ea Shore Office VP Acad Affairs Princess Anne MD 21853

NNAEMEKA, OBIOMA GRACE, French language and women's studies educator, consultant, researcher; b. Agulu, Anambra, Nigeria; came to U.S., 1974; d. Christopher Egbunike and Jessie Ifemelue (Ogbuefi) Obidiegwu; children: Ike, Uchenna. BA with honors, U. Nigeria, Nsukka, 1972; MA, U. Minn., 1977, PhD with distinction, 1989. Rsch. fellow U. Nigeria, 1972-74, lectr., 1982-87; asst. prof. Concordia Coll., Minn., 1988-89, Coll. Wooster, Ohio, 1989-91; assoc. prof. Ind. U., Indpls., 1991—. Cons. Govt. Senegal, Dakar, 1990-92; commentator Internat. Svc. Radio Netherlands, Hilversum, 1990—; Edith Kreeger Wolf Disting. prof. Northwestern U., 1992. Author: Agrippa d'Aubigné: The Poetics of Power and Change, 1998; editor: The Politics of Mothering, 1996, Sisterhood, Feminisms, & Power, 1997; contbr. articles to profl. jours. Founder, pres. Assn. African Women's Scholars, 1995; convener, organizer First Internat. Conf. Women in Africa & African Diaspora, 1992. Named Achiever of Yr. Leadership Nigeria Network, 1994; grantee from McArthur Found, Rockefeller Found., Swedish Internat. Devel. Agy., Swedish Agy. for Rsch. Cooperation with Developing Countries, 1991-92. Mem. Am. Assn. Tchrs. French, Ind. Fgn. Lang. Tchrs. Assn., Modern Langs. Assn., African Studies Assn., African Lit. Assn. Avocations: reading, travel. Office: Ind U Dept Fgn Langs Cultrs 425 University Blvd Indianapolis IN 46202-5148 E-mail: waad@iupui.edu.

NOAH, JULIA JEANINE, retired librarian; b. Craig, Mo., July 14, 1932; d. Hiram Curtis and Eloise Julia (Puckett) True; m. Raymond Laverne Noah, Sept. 5, 1954; children: David Scott, Danny Ray, Deborah Jill, Douglas True. BS, U. Ill., 1953; MA in Library Sci., U. South Fla., 1983. Asst. rsch. librarian Parke, Davis & Co., Detroit, 1953-55; cataloging librarian U. Mo., Columbia, 1955-57; sch. librarian High Point Elem. Sch., Clearwater, Fla., 1968; library aide Clearwater High Sch., 1973-78; reference asst. Dunedin (Fla.) Pub. Library, 1978-84, dir. info. svcs., 1984-88, library dir., 1988-94; ret. Mem. DAR, Fla. Libr. Assn., Pinellas Genealogy Soc., Questers, Nat. Soc. Colonial Dames XVII Century, Daus. of Union Vets. of the Civil War 1861-1865, Nat. Soc. Magna Charta Dames, Phi Kappa Phi, Beta Phi Mu. Republican. Presbyterian. Avocations: antiques, genealogy.

NOAKES, BETTY LAVONNE, retired elementary school educator; b. Oklahoma City, Okla., Aug. 28, 1938; d. Webster L. and Willie Ruth (Johnson) Hawkins; m. Richard E. Noakes, Apr. 22, 1962 (dec.); 1 child, Michele Monique. Student, Oklahoma City U., MEd, 1971; BS, Cen. State U., 1962; postgrad., Cen. State U., Okla. State U. Elem. tchr. Merced (Calif.) Pub. Schs., 1966-67, Oklahoma City Schs., 1971-73, Mid-Del Schs., Midwest City, Okla., 1973-95; founder, owner Noakes-I Care Day Care, 1995—2002. 2d v.p. PTA, Pleasant Hill, 1991, cert. recognition, 1992-93; active Nat. PTA, 1991-92; charter mem. Nat. Mus. of Am. Indian-Smithsonian Instn.; chmn. stewardship com. Quayle U. Meth. Ch., 1997—; mem. Wesley Found. bd. Langston U.; mem. Urban League, Urban League Guild, YWCA. Recipient Cert. Appreciation YMCA, 1992-92, Disting. Svc. award Mid-Del PTA, 1992. Mem. NEA, AAUW, NAACP, NAFE, LWV, Okla. Edn. Assn., Nat. Ret. Tchrs. Assn., Okla. Ret. Tchrs. Assn., Smithsonian Instn., Oklahoma City U. Alumni Assn., United Meth. Women Assn., Ctrl. State U. Alumni Assn., Okla. Order Ea. Star, Order of the Golden Cir. (aux. of Great We. Consistory # 34 Dorcas-LL Golden Ci. assembly # 41, Standard Bearer), Daus. of Isis- Outside Spy, Phi Delta Kappa (Dean of Pledges), Zeta Phi Beta (1st v.p.). Avocations: aerobics, singing, piano, clarinet, folk dancing. Home: 5956 N Coltrane Rd Oklahoma City OK 73121-3409 E-mail: nblnzeta@sbcglobal.net.

NOBERT, FRANCES, music educator; b. Winston-Salem, N.C., Dec. 12, 1936; d. Henry Carrington and Frances Mozelle (Harrison) Cuningham; m. Jon Marshall Nobert (div. Jan. 1980). BM in Music Edn., Salem Coll., 1959; Fulbright Cert. in Organ, Conservatory of Music, Frankfurt am Main, Germany, 1961; MM in Organ, Syracuse U., 1963; DMA in Choral Music, U. So. Calif., 1980. Organist, choir dir. United Ch., Fayetteville, N.Y., 1961-67; choral an gen. music tchr. Fayetteville Manlius Sch. Dist., 1963-67; vocal music tchr. U.S. Grant H.S., Van Nuys, Calif., 1967-80; organist United Ch. of Christ Congregational, Claremont, Calif., 1981-83; organist, choir dir. St. Matthias Episcopal Ch., Whittier, Calif., 1983-94; organist First United Meth. Ch., Pasadena, Calif., 2000—03; prof. music, coll. organist Whittier Coll., 1982-98, coord. women's studies, 1995-98, Disting. Svc. prof. music, 1998—99, prof. emeritus, 1999—. Choral singer L.A. Master Chorale, 1972-86; vis. instr. of key bd. theory, L.A. Valley Coll., Van Nuys, Calif., 1980-81, spring 1982; bd. dirs., program chair, sub-dean, dean Pasadena chpt. Am. Guild of Organists, Pasadena, Calif., 1991-95, dean, 1998-99, convenor, 1999—; resident dir. for Denmark's Internat. Study Program, Whittier Coll., 1994. Faculty Rsch. grantee Whittier Coll., 1984, devel. grantee, 1986, 88, 90, 91, 93. 96, 97, Irvine grantee, 1995. Mem. NOW, Internat. Alliance for Women in Music (treas. 1997-2000, v.p. 2000-03), Am. Guild Organists, Organ Hist. Soc., Rio Hondo Symphony Guild, Whittier Cultural Arts Found., Mader Corp., Feminist Majority, Pi Kappa Lambda, Mu Phi Epsilon. Episcopalian. Avocations: travel, fine dining, languages.

NOBLE, SUNNY A. business owner; b. Moorhead, Minn., May 22, 1940; m. Eric Scott Noble, Apr. 11, 1980. MBA, U. Calif., Berkeley, 1960; qualified parapsychologist, U. Minn., 1979. Mgr. Spear & Hill Attys., N.Y.C., 1969-70; mgr. exec. property mgmt. May Co. Dept. Stores, La Jolla, Calif., 1981-82; owner, pres. The Computer Tutor, L.A., 1984—94. Columnist: That Computes, 1984-88, The Storyteller, 1987-91, Chit-Chat, The Westside Examiner, 1996-97; author stage plays: The Garlic Eater (Writer's Digest Mag. nat. writing competition award 1998), Mother's Day (Writer's Digest Mag. nat. writing competition award 1998); (screen play) The Tangled Web; editor: From Book Signing to Best Seller. Mem.: Internat. Platform Assn., Safe Harbor Writers Workshop, Mensa, Toastmasters Internat. (ednl. v.p. 1988), Beta Sigma Phi. Home and Office: PO Box 4427 Lancaster CA 93539-4427

NOBLES, SUSANNE LEE, language educator; d. William Bura and Constance Cummings Nobles; m. Kevin Michael Perry, Dec. 31, 1995. Med, Va. Commonwealth U., 1999; BA, Duke U., 1993. H.S. Tchr. Va., 2003. Chair English dept. Fredericksburg Acad., Va., 1995—, dir. coll. counseling, 2000—; tchr. English Broad Run H.S., Ashburn, Va., 1993—95. Author: (poetry) Virginia Writing, (article) The ALAN Review, The English Journal. Mem.: PCACAC. Avocations: travel, reading, remodeling and renovation, exercise, gardening. Office: Fredericksburg Academy 132 Falcon Drive Fredericksburg VA 22408 E-mail: snobles@fredericksburgacademy.org.

NOBLITT, NANCY ANNE, aerospace engineer; b. Roanoke, Va., Aug. 14, 1959; d. Jerry Spencer and Mary Louise (Jerrell) N. BA, Mills Coll., Oakland, Calif., 1982; MS in Indsl. Engring., Northeastern U., 1990; JD, Coll. William and Mary, 2003. Data red specialist Universal Energy Sys., Beaver Creek, Ohio, 1981; aerospace engr. turbine engine divsn. components br. turbine group aero-propulsion lab. Wright-Patterson AFB, Ohio, 1982-84, engine assessment br. spl. engines group, 1984-87; lead analyst cycle methods computer aided engr. GE, Lynn, Mass., 1987-90, Lynn PACES project coord., 1990-91; software sys. analyst Sci. Applications Internat. Corp., with artificial intelligence, 1991-92, software engring. mgr., intelligence applications integration Hampton, Va., 1992-93, mgr. test engring. and sys. support, 1993-94, mgr. configuration mgmt., 1994, mgmt. asst. to TBMCS program mgr., 1994-95; sr. simulation engr. Chem Demil, 1995-98; supervisory engr. Analytical Mechanics Assocs., Hampton, 1998-99; sr. project engr. Newport News (Va.) Shipbuilding Inc., 1999-00. Tutor math. and sci. Centerville Sch. Bd., Ohio, 1982-86; tutor math. and physics Marblehead Sch. Bd., Mass., 1988-90; tutor math., chemistry and physics Poquoson Sch. Bd., Va., 1994—; rep. alumnae admissions Boston area Mills Coll., 1987-91, trustee, bd. govs., 1995-98; mem. Citizens for Hilton Area Revitalization, 1994—. Math. and sci. tutor Centerville Sch. Bd., Ohio, 1982-86, math. and physics tutor Marblehead (Mass.) Sch. Bd., 1988-90; tutor math., chemistry and physics Poquoson Sch. Bd., Va., 1994—; rep. alumnae admissions Mills Coll., Boston area, 1987-91, trustee/bd. govs., 1995-98; mem. Citizens for Hilton Area Revitalization, 1994—. Recipient Notable Achievement award USAF, 1984, Spl. award Fed. Lab. Consortium, 1987. Mem. Soc. Mfg. Engrs., Sports and Entertainment Law Soc., Phi Alpha Delta. Avocation: book collecting. Home: 58 Hopkins St Newport News VA 23601-4034 Office: Newport News Shipbuilding Newport News VA 23607

NOBUMOTO, KAREN S. prosecutor; BA, U. Hartford, 1973; JD Southwestern U., 1989. Dep. dist. atty. County of L.A. Mem.: Assn. Dep. Dist. Attys., Black Women Lawyers L.A., Women Lawyers Assn. L.A., John M. Langston Bar Assn., State Bar Calif. (pres. 2001—02). Office: LA Dist Attys Office 210 W Temple St Ste 18000 Los Angeles CA 90012-3210

NOCHMAN, LOIS WOOD KIVI (MRS. MARVIN NOCHMAN), retired educator; b. Detroit, Nov. 5, 1924; d. Peter K. and Annetta Lois (Wood) Kivi; m. Harold I. Pitchford, Sept. 6, 1944 (div. May 1949); children: Jean Wood Pitchford Scott, Joyce Lynn Pitchford Undiano; m. Marvin A. Nochman, Aug. 15, 1953; 1 child, Joseph Asa. AB, U. Mich., 1946, AM, 1949. Tchr. adult edn., Honolulu, 1947, Ypsilanti (Mich.) H.S., 1951-52; spl. instr. English Wayne State U., Detroit, 1953, 54; tchr. Highland Park (Mich.) Coll., 1950-51, instr. English, 1954-83, ret., 1983. Mem. exec. bd. Highland Park Fedn. Tchrs., 1963 66, 1973, del. to nat conv., 64, 1971—74; rep. higher edn. Mich. Fedn. Tchrs. Exec. Com., 1972—76; mem. faculty adv. com. Gov's Commn. Higher Edn., 1973—. Contbr. articles to profl. jours. Tchr. Baha'i Schs., Davison, Mich., 1954—55, 1958—59, 1963—66, Beaulac, Canada, 1960, Greenacre, Maine, 1965; sec. local spiritual assembly Baha'is, Ann Arbor, Mich., 1953, sec. Detroit, 1954, chmn., 1955; mem. nat. com. Baha'is U.S., 1955—58; sec. com. and coun. Baha'i Schs., Davison, Mich., 1956, 1958, 1963—68; Baha'i lectr. subject of local TV show Senior Focus, 1992. Named one of 10 Best of 1995, Swim Mag., 2000; recipient Women's Movement plaque, Women Lawyers Assn. Mich., 1975, Lawrence award, Mich. Masters Swimming, 1991, 6 World Master Records in Age Group short course meters, 1994—95, 5 records in Long Course Meters, 1995, 23 Nat. Masters Records, 1994—96, 6 Nat. YMCA records, 1995, 2 U.S. Nat. Sr. Sports Classic Records, 1995, 2 World Sr. Games Records, 1993, All-Am. award, 1990—2003, U.S. Long Distance All Star, 1995—2002, U.S. MS Finals All Star, 1995, 2000, 8 Huntsman World Sr. Games Records, 1998, 5 Huntsman Masters World Records short course meters, 1999, 9 Huntsman World Games Records in age group 75-79, 1999. Mem.: MLA, NOW, Nat. Soc. Lit. and Arts, Am. Fedn. Tchrs., Mich. Coll. English Assn., Nat. Coun. Tchrs. English, Women's Equity and Action League (sec. Mich. chpt. 1975—79), Alpha Gamma Delta, Alpha Lambda Delta. Avocation: U.S. Swimming Master Champion.

NOCKLER, LINDA A. corporate financial executive; d. Erich Nockler and Sandra Anne Griffith. B in Commerce, U. Cape Town, South Africa, 1987, U. Cape Town, 1988; MPhil in Internat. Rels. (Internat. Econs.), Cambridge (Eng.) U., 1992. CFA Level 1. Analyst Union Bank of Switzerland, Zurich, 1989—91; mgmt. program Anglo Am. Corp., Johannesburg, 1993—95; product devel. cons. Phillips, Hager & North, Vancouver, Canada, 1995—97; v.p., dir. content mgmt. and mktg. Greenwich Assocs., Greenwich, Conn., 1998—. Scholar, Std. Bank South Africa, 1985, IBM Corp., 1987. Buddhist. Avocations: art, theater, travel, yoga. Office: Greenwich Assocs 8 Greenwich Office Park Greenwich CT 06831-5195

NODDINGS, NEL, education educator, writer; b. Irvington, N.J., Jan. 19, 1929; d. Edward A. Rieth and Nellie A. (Connors) Walter; m. James A. Noddings, Aug. 20, 1949; children: Chris, Howard, Laurie, James, Nancy, William, Sharon, Edward, Vicky, Timothy. BA in Math., Montclair State Coll., 1949; MA in Math., Rutgers U., 1964; PhD in Edn., Stanford U., 1973; PhD (hon.), Columbia Coll., S.C., 1995. Cert. tchr., Calif., N.J. Tchr. Woodbury (N.J.) Publ Schs., 1949-52; tchr. math. dept. Matawan (N.J.) High Sch., 1958-62, chair, asst. prin., 1964-69; curriculum supr. Montgomery Twp. Pub. Schs., Skillman, N.J., 1970-72; dir. precollegiate edn. U. Chgo., 1975-76; asst. prof. Pa. State U., State College, 1973; from asst. prof. to assoc. prof. Stanford (Calif.) U., 1977-86, prof., 1986—, assoc. dean, 1990-92, acting dean, 1992-94, Lee L. Jacks prof. child edn., 1992-98, prof. emeritus, 1998—; prof. philosophy and edn. Columbia U., N.Y.C., 1998—. Bd. dirs. Ctr. for Human Caring Sch. Nursing, Denver, 1986-92; cons. NIE, NSF and various other sch. dists. Author: Caring: A Feminine Approach to Ethics and Moral Education, 1984, Women and Evil, 1989; author: (with W. Paul Shore) Awakening the Inner Eye: Intuition in Education, 1984; author: (with Carol Witherell) Stories Lives Tell, 1991; author: The Challenge to Care in Schools, 1992, Educating for Intelligent Belief or Unbelief, 1993, Philosophy of Education, 1995; author: (with Suzanne Gordon and Patricia Benner) Caregiving, 1996; author: (with Michael Katz and Kenneth Strike) Justice and Caring, 1999; author: Starting at Home: Caring and Social Policy, 2002, Educating Moral People, 2002, Happiness and Education, 2003. Mem. disting. women's adv. bd. Coll. St. Catherine. Recipient Anne Roe award for Contbns. to Profl. devel. of Women, Harvard Grad. Sch. Edn., 1993, medal for disting. svc. Tchrs. Coll. Columbia, 1994, Willystine Goodsell award, 1997, Laureate chpt. Kappa Delta Pi, Pi Lambda Theta award, 1999; Spencer Mentor grantee, Spencer Found., 1995-97. Fellow Philosophy of Edn. Soc. (pres. 1991-92); mem. Am. Ednl. Rsch. Assn. (Div B, 2000, Lifetime achievment award), Am. Philos. Assn., Nat. Acad. Edn. (pres. 2001—), John Dewey Soc. (pres. 1994-96), Phi Beta Kappa (vis. scholar). Avocation: gardening. E-mail: noddings@stanford.edu.

NODDINGS, SARAH ELLEN, lawyer; b. Matawan, N.J. d. William Clayton and Sarah Stephenson (Cox) Noddings; children: Christopher, Aaron. BA in Math., Rutgers U., New Brunswick, N.J., 1965, MSW, 1968; JD cum laude, Seton Hall U., Newark, 1975; postgrad., UCLA, 1979. Bar: Calif. 1976, Nev. 1976, N.J. 1975, U.S. Dist. Ct. (ctrl. dist.) Calif. 1976, U.S. Dist. Ct. N.J. 1975. Social worker Carteret (N.J.) Bd. Edn., 1970-75; law clk. Hon. Howard W. Babcock, 8th Jud. Dist. Ct., Las Vegas, Nev., 1975-76; assoc. O'Melveny & Myers, L.A., 1976-78; atty. Internat. Creative Mgmt., Beverly Hills, Calif., 1978-81, Russell & Glickman, Century City, Calif., 1981-83, Lorimar Prodns., Culver City and Burbank, Calif., 1983-87, v.p., 1987-93; atty. Warner Bros. TV, Burbank, Calif., 1993-2001, v.p., 1993-2001, sr. atty., 1999-2001; pvt. practice, 2001—. Dir. county youth program, rsch. analyst Sonoma County People for Econ. Opportunity, Santa Rosa, Calif., 1968-69; VISTA vol. Kings County Cmty. Action Orgn., Hanford, Calif., 1965-66; officer, PTA bd. West H.S., Casimir Mid. Sch. and Arlington Elem. Sch. Mem. Acad. TV Arts and Scis. (nat. awards com. 1994-96), L.A. Copyright Soc. (trustee 1990-91), Women in Film, L.A. County Bar Assn. (intellectual property sect.), Women Entertainment Lawyers, Media Marine League Bd. Dist. Intellectual Propr. Bar Assn. (bd. dirs. 1999-2001), South Bay Marine League Bd. (B-2 rep.). Avocations: travel, tennis, skiing, bicycling, swimming.

NODEEN, JANEY PRICE, company executive; b. Scotland Neck, N.C., Nov. 7, 1959; d. Wade Hampton and Joyce Ann (Councill) P.; m. Thomas Nodeen. BS in Info. Sci., Christopher Newport Coll., 1987; grad., Def. Sys. Mgmt. Coll., 1994; grad. advanced mgmt. program, Nat. Def. U., 1995. Engring. analyst Newport News (Va.) Shipbldg., 1978-86; mgr. submarine info. resources and computer ops. Dept. of the Navy, Washington, 1986-93, mem. exec. devel. program, 1993-96, sr. staff Navy Acquisition Reform Exec., 1995, dep. program exec. officer Submarines for Acquisition, 1996-97; prin. Burke Consortium, Inc., Springfield, Va., 1997—. Mil. legis. fellow for Congressman Sam Gejdenson, 1994; sr. exec. fellow John F. Kennedy Sch. Govt. Harvard U., class officer, 1994. Home: 6915 Ashbury Dr Springfield VA 22152-3221 Office: Burke Consortium Inc Ste 510 5500 Cherokee Ave Alexandria VA 22312

NODELMAN, NANCY ZIEGLER, sculptor, designer; b. Scranton, Pa., Apr. 23, 1937; d. Alvin and Gertrude (Friedman) Ziegler; m. Jared Nodelman, Aug. 31, 1958 (div. Dec. 17, 1993); children: Seth, Ilisa. BS, Ohio State U., 1957, postgrad., 1958; sculpture student, San Francisco Art Inst., 1986-87. Founder Fiber Dimensions, Kentfield, Calif., 1990; co-dir. Atrium Gallery, Greenbrae, Calif., 1992—. Exhbns. include Regional Ctr. Arts Biennials, 1991, 93, Convergence Internat. Biennial, 1992 (Hon. Mention), Calif. Contemporary Design Biennial, 1992, Md. Park Commn. and Catalog, 1994, Internat. Miniature Textiles Biennial, Catalog, 1996, Gallery Strasse Hyogo, Japan, 1997, SOFA98NYC, 1998, Calif. Design 2000, Fiberarts Design Book Six; work featured in Fiber Arts mag., 1992; represented in permanent collections Szombathely Keptár Mus., Bank of Am. Marathon Plaza, Marin Gen. Hosp. Mem. humanities coun. bd. Marin Gen. Hosp., Greenbrae, Calif., 1992—; trustee Isaac Ziegler Trust, Scranton, Pa., 1996—. Recipient Hon. Mention Handweavers Am., 1992. Mem. Internat. Wine and Food Soc., Fiber Art Internat., Soc. Encouragement of Contemporary Art. Avocations: architectural, landscape and furniture design, paper toy collecting, consulting.

NOE, ADRIANNE, museum administrator; PhD in History, U. Del. Assoc. dir. Armed Forces Inst. Pathology; dir. Nat. Mus. Health and Medicine, Washington. Adj. prof. computational biosciences George Mason U., Fairfax County, Va.; v.p. bd. dirs. Nat. Health Sci. Consortium. Fellow, Guggenheim Found.; History fellow, USAF. Mem.: Med. Mus. Assn. (past pres.), Washington Soc. for the History of Medicine (pres.), Acad. Medicine. Office: Nat Mus Health and Medicine Bldg 54 6825 16th St NW Washington DC 20306-6000*

NOE, CINDY J. state representative; b. St. Louis, Mo., Aug. 23, 1947; m. John Noe; 2 children. BS, Ind. U., 1969. Budget analyst Atlantic-Richfield, 1970—71; dir. recruiting and placement Louisville Vocat./Tech. Sch., 1971—72; former corp. sec.-treas., v.p. IHM Facility Svcs., Inc., Hamilton County, Ind., CEO, majority owner; state rep. dist. 87 Ind. Ho. of Reps., Indpls., 2001. Precinct committeeman Washington Twp. Dist. 87, Ind., 1996—; del. Ind. Rep. State Conv., 1998, 2000, 2001; v.p. bd. Character Coun. of Ind., late 1990s. Mem.: Sales and Mktg. Execs. (sec. 1994—96), Nat. Fedn. Ind. Bus. (leadership coun. 1990—), Ind. C. of C. (mem. com. 1998—2002). Republican. Office: Ind Ho of Reps 200 W Washington St Indianapolis IN 46204-2786

NOE, ELNORA (ELLIE NOE), retired chemicals executive; b. Evansville, Ind., Aug. 23, 1928; d. Thomas Noe and Evelyn (West) Dieter. Student, Ind. U.-Purdue U., Indpls. Sec. Pitman Moore Co., Indpls., 1946—60; with Dow Chem. Co., Indpls., 1960-90, pub. rels. asst. then mgr. employee comm., 1970-87, mgr. cmty. rels., 1987-90, DowBrands, Inc., Indpls., 1986-90, vice chmn. Indpls. C. of C. corp. affairs discussion group, 1988—89, chmn., 1989-90; mem. steering com. Learn About Bus. Recipient 2d pl. award as Businesswoman of Yr., Indpls. Bus. and Profl. Women's Assn., 1980, Indpls. Profl. Woman of Yr. award Zonta, Altrusa, Soroptomist & Pilot Svc. Clubs, 1985, DowBrands Great Things Cmty. Svc. award, 1991. Mem. Am. Bus. Women Assn. (Woman of Yr. award 1965, past pres.), Ind. Assn. Bus. Communicators (hon., Communicator of Yr. 1977), Assn. Women in Comm. (Louise Eleanor Kleinhenz award 1984), Zonta (dist. pub. rels. chmn. 1978-80, area dir. 1980-82, pres. Indpls. chpt. 1977-79, bd. dirs. 1993-95, 2000-02, 2004—), Dow Indpls. Retiree Group (pres. 1995—). E-mail: elenoe@aol.com.

NOEL, BARBARA HUGHES MCMURTRY, retired music educator; b. Mt. Vernon, Wash., Feb. 27, 1929; d. Lowell Robinson and Mary Evelyn (Hayton) Hughes; children: Sarah Kathleen, Martha Elizabeth. BM, U. Ky., 1951, MM, 1952; PhD, U. Ill., 1972; student, Oberlin Conservatory, 1947-49. Instr. music Union Coll., Barbourville, Ky., 1952-54; instr. music and fine arts Annie Wright Sem., Tacoma, 1957-63; organist, choirmaster Episc. churches, Calif., Wash., 1954-66; chmn. music dept. U. Richmond (Va.), 1971-76, Mankato (Minn.) State U., 1976-78; dean coll. humanities and fine arts Tex. Woman's U., Denton, 1978-81; dean coll. visual and performing arts U. Mass. Dartmouth, North Dartmouth, 1981-89; prof. music U. Mass., Dartmouth, 1990—96, ret., 1996. Cons. for various music orgns. and univs., 1976—, textbook pubs., 1980—; reviewer Nat. Endowment for the Humanities. Book reviewer Providence Sunday Jour., 1984—; contbr. articles to music jours.; contbr. New Grove Dictionary of Music, 1974. Bd. dirs. Community Symphony Orchs., Mankato, 1976-78, New Bedford, Mass., 1981-87. Grad. fellow Danforth Found., U. Ill., 1966-71. Mem. Coll. Music Soc. (treas. 1983-87, v.p. 1979-83, coun. mem.), Nat. Assn. Schs. Music (undergrad. commr. 1978-81). Episcopalian. Avocations: reading, traveling, hiking. Home: 73 Tucker Ln North Dartmouth MA 02747-3529

NOEL, CHERYL ELAINE, artist, poet; b. Syracuse, N.Y., Oct. 1, 1954; d. Arthur Raymond and Alice Thane N.. BA in Philosophy, Randolph-Macon Women's Coll., 1978; postgrad., Lynchburg Coll. Rehab. counselor Hudson House, Lynchburg, Va.; waitress The Ground Round, Lynchburg; tchr. modern dance Campbell County Dept. Recreation, Lynchburg, asst. mgr. Burgerette, Inc., Lynchburg; staff counselor Camp Zarahemela, Clintwood, Va.; inventory counter GE, Lynchburg, copper plating processor. Author: poems; dancer traveling dance theater, Randolph-Macon; exhibitions include Leagett at Randolph-Macon, featured, Randolph-Macon Alumnae Bull., 1978.

NOETH, CAROLYN FRANCES, speech and language pathologist; b. Cleve., July 21, 1924; d. Sam Falco and Barbara Serafina (Loparo) Armaro; m. Lawrence Andrew Noeth Sr., June 29, 1946; children: Lawrence Andrew Jr. (dec.), Barbara Marie. AB magna cum laude, Case Western Res. U., 1963; MEd, U. Ill., 1972; postgrad., Nat. Coll. Edn., 1975—. Lic. speech and lang. pathologist, Ill. Speech therapist Chgo. Pub. Schs., 1965; speech, lang. and hearing clinician J. Sterling Morton High Schs., Cicero and Berwyn, Ill., 1965-82, tchr. learning disabilities/behavior disorders, 1982, dist. ednl. diagnostician, 1982-84, Title I Project tchr., summers 1966-67, lang. disabilities cons., summers 1968-69, in-svc. tng. cons., summer 1970, dir. Title I Project, summers 1973-74; learning disabilities tchr. West Campus of Morton, 1971-75; chmn. Educable-Mentally Handicapped Opportunities Tchrs. Com., 1967-68; spl. edn. area and in-sch. tchrs. workshops, 1967—. Chmn. in compiling and publishing Student Handbook, Cleve. Coll., 1962; contbr. lyric parodies and music programs J. Sterling Morton H.S. West Retirement Teas, 1972-83. Precinct elections judge, 1953-55; block capt. Mothers March of Dimes and Heart Fund, 1949-60; St. Agatha's rep. Nat. Cath. Women's League, 1952-53; collector various charities, 1967, 93-94, 98, 99, 2000, 2001, 2002; mem. exec. bd. Morton Scholarship League, 1981-84, corr. sec., 1981-83; vol. Am. Cancer Soc., 1985—; vol. judge Ill. Acad. Decathlon, 1988—. First recipient Virda L. Stewart award for Speech, Western Res. U., 1963, Outstanding Sr. award, 1963. Mem. Am. Speech, Lang. and Hearing Assn. (life, cert.), Ill. Speech, Lang. and Hearing Assn. (life), Coun. Exceptional Children (divsn. for learning disabilities, pioneers divsn., chpt. spl. projects chmn., exec. bd. 1976-81, chpt. pres. 1979-80), Coun. for Learning Disabilities, Profls. in Learning Disabilities, Kappa Delta Pi, Delta Kappa Gamma (chmn., co-chmn. chpt. music com. 1979—, state program com. 1981-83, chpt. music rep. to state 1982—, chmn. chpt. promotion com. 1993-94, 96—), St. Norbert's Women's Club (Northbrook, Ill.), Case-Western Res. U., U. Ill. Alumni Assns., Lions (vol. Northbrook 1966-93). Roman Catholic. Home and Office: 1849 Walnut Cir Northbrook IL 60062-1245

NOGUERE, SUZANNE, publishing manager, poet; b. Bklyn., Dec. 1, 1947; d. Eugene R. and Virginia Helene (Braun) N.; m. Henry Grinberg, June 5, 1983. BA in Philosophy magna cum laude with honors, Columbia U., 1969. Classified ad. mgr. Printing News, Melville, N.Y., 1973—, sr. acct. exec., 1999—. Author: (children's books) Little Koala, 1979, Little Raccoon, 1981, (poetry collection) Whirling Round the Sun, 1996; poet (with artist Miriam Adams): (exhibitions) Leaf Lines, 1998, poet (with artist Lesley Nishigawara): (exhibitions) Left Out, 2003; co-author (with James V. Hatch): The Stone House, A Blues Legend, 2000; co-author: (plays) Klub Ka, The Blues Legend, U. Iowa, 2002, La MaMa E.T.C., 2004. Recipient Discovery award The 92nd St. Y Unterberg Poetry Ctr. and The Nation mag., 1996. Mem. Acad. Am. Poets, Poetry Soc. Am. (Gertrude B. Claytor Meml. award 1989), Poets House, Dramatists Guild Am. Home: 27 W 96th St Apt 12B New York NY 10025-6515 Office: Printing News 445 Broad Hollow Rd Melville NY 11747-3669 E-mail: snoguere@eclipse.net.

NOHNER, SHARON, nun, minister; b. Watkins, Minn., Jan. 2, 1949; d. Fabian Peter and Bernice Nohner. BA, St. Benedict's Coll., St. Joseph, Minn., 1972; MM, Creighton U., 1987. Entered St. Benedict's Monastery, 1967. Tchr. elem. edn. St. Anastacia's Sch., Hutchinson, Minn., 1972—76; religious edn. dir. St. Mary's Indian Mission, Red Lake, Minn., 1976—82; pastoral min. Holy Rosary Cath. Ch., Mpls., 1982—85; pastoral assoc. St. Edward's Cath. Ch., Princeton, Minn., 1985—92; pastoral adminstr. St. John's Cath. Ch., Hector, Minn., 1992—2001, St. Paul's Cath. Ch., Comfrey, Minn., 2001—. Chaplain Renville County Hospice, Olivia, Minn., 1997—2001; mem. evangelization com. New Ulm (Minn.) Diocese, 1998—, mem. fin. coun., 2002—. Recipient Bishop's medal of svc., Diocese of New Ulm, 2000. Office: St Pauls 209 Field St N Comfrey MN 56019

NOLAN, CATHERINE T. state legislator; m. Gerard Marsicano. Grad. cum laude, NYU. Apptd. ombudsman Dept. of State; mem. N.Y. State Assembly, Albany, 1984—, chmn. real property taxation com., mem. vets. com., ins. com., corps., authorities and commns. com., commerce, industry and econ. devel. com., chmn. mass transit subcom., women vets. subcom. Chair N.Y. State Legis. Women's Caucus; mem. Assembly's Hispanic task force Somos Uno; mem. capital planning rev. bd. MTA. Co-founder Queens Displaced Homemakers Program; bd. dirs. Ridgewood Property Owners and Civic Assn.; bd. trustees Wyckoff Heights Hosp.; active supporter United Forties Civic Assn., Dutch Kills Civic Assn., Farmer's Oval Civic Assn., Hunter's Point Cmty. Coun., Queensbridge Tenant Assn., Youth Patrol and Tenant Patrol, Ravenswood Tenant Assn., Lincoln Block Assn., 56th Street Block Assn., 68th Rd. Block Assn., Cornelia Street Block Assn., Queens Spl. Olympics, Vol. Ambulance Corps., Queens Outreach Project, Ridgewood Vol. Ambulance Corps., Irish Immigration Reform Movement; adv. bd. Borden Ave. Vets. Shelter; Conrad Weiser post Steuben Soc.; mem. Queens Coalition for Political Alternatives; del. Dem. Nat. Conv., 1988; bd. dirs. Ridgeoow Dem. Club. Recipient Pres.' medal LaGuardia C.C., 1989. Mem. NAACP, Sunnyside C. of C., Astoria Kehillah, Sunnyside Kiwanis, Irish-Am. Legis. Club, Italian-Am. Legis. Club. Home: 879 Woodward Ave Ridgewood NY 11385-4465 Office: NY State Assembly 522 Legislative Office Bldg Albany NY 12248-0001

NOLAN, JOAN T. elementary school educator; b. Bklyn., Jan. 31, 1942; d. Thomas Louis and Vivian LaForte; m. Gerard Thomas Nolan, Nov. 19, 1996 (div. Oct. 1994); children: Kenneth, Andrew. BA, Bklyn. Coll., 1963; MS, Hunter Coll., 1968. Classrm. tchr. Bd. Edn., City of N.Y., Bklyn., 1963-68, Richardson (Tex.) Ind. Sch. Dist., 1981—. Cooperating tchr. for student tchrs. Forestridge Elem. Sch., Richardson, 1993, 97, sci. fair coord., 1995-99, initiator sci. club, 1999—. Mem. AAUW (cultural rep., Ednl. Found. Gift given in her name 1999), Assn. Tex. Profl. Educators, Sci. Tchrs. Assn. Tex., Sierra Club. Roman Catholic. Avocations: reading, needlework, exercising, travel, cooking.

NOLAN, MARILYN ANN, health facility administrator; b. Brighton, Mass., July 17, 1935; d. Anthony Henry and Anne Claire Nikiel; m. George Francis Nolan; 2 children. BA, Trinity Coll., Washington, 1957; MSS in Social Wk., Boston U., 1959. Diplomate Am. Inst. of Hypnotherapy; LCSW. Med. social worker Peter Bent Brigham Hosp., Boston, 1959—60; geriatric and psychiat. social worker Modesto State Hosp., Calif., 1960—63; psychiat. social worker, visual impairment svc. coord. VA Med. Ctr., Bedford, Mass., 1966—87, psychiat. social worker, substance abuse therapist, 1989—91, visual impairment svc. team coord. Long Beach, Calif., 1987—89, St. Petersburg, Fla., 1991—. Chmn. disabled people's program Bay Pines VA Med. Ctr., St. Petersburg, 1991—94; field work instr. Boston Coll., 1972—86, Boston U., 1972—86. Recipient Outstanding Contrbn. award, Am. Legion, 1990, Tampa Bay Fed. Equal Employment Opportunity, 1993, Blinded Vets. Assn., 2002. Mem.: NASW (bd. cert. diplomate), Nat. Guild of Hypnotists (cert.), Acad. Cert. Social Workers. Roman Catholic. Avocations: reading, piano, accordion. Office: VA Med Ctr PO Box 5005 Bay Pines FL 33744 Office Phone: 727-398-6661 4516.

NOLAN, MARY, state representative; Attended, Dartmouth Coll. State rep., dist. 36 Oreg. House Rep., Salem, 2001—; pres. Avrotec, Inc., Aurora, Oreg., 1990—. Mem. Agr. and Forestry Com., Student Achievement and Sch. Accountability Com., Wayns and Means Com., Natural Resources sub com. Democrat. Office: 900 Court St NE H-375 Salem OR 97301 Address: Avrotec Inc 22781 Airport Rd NE Aurora OR 97002

NOLAN, PATRICIA ANN, public health officer; MD, McGill U., Montreal, Que., Can., 1969; MPH, Columbia U., 1973. Cert. in pub. health Am. Bd. Prevention Medicine. Local pub. health adminstr., N.Y.C., 1971-75, Tucson, Ariz., 1981-88; med. adminstr. Ariz. Health Care Cost Containment Sys., 1988-92; state pub. health adminstr. Ill., 1975-81; exec. dir. Colo. Dept. Pub. Health and Environ., 1992-95; dir. R.I. Health Dept., 1995—. Adj. prof. Brown U. Mem. APHA. Office: RI Health Dept 3 Capitol Hl Providence RI 02908-5034

NOLAN, VICTORIA, theater director; b. Portland, Maine, June 15, 1952; d. Herbert Wallace and Diane Katharine (Kremm) N.; m. Clarkson Newell Crolius, Aug. 30, 1980; children: Covey Emmeline, Wilhelmina Adams. BA magna cum laude, U. Maine, 1976. Publicity asst. Loeb Drama Ctr. Harvard U., Cambridge, Mass., 1975; pub. rels. asst. to dir. Sch. for Arts Boston U., 1975-76; mgmt. asst. TAG Found., N.Y.C., 1976-77; mng. dir. Ram Island Dance Co., Portland, 1977-78; dir. devel. Ctr. Stage, Balt., 1979-81, assoc. mng. dir., 1981-87; mng. dir. Ind. Repertory Theatre, Indpls., 1988-93; dep. dean, mng. dir., prof. Yale Sch. Drama, Yale Repertory Theatre, New Haven, 1993—. Program evaluator Nat. Endowment for Arts, Washington, 1988—, panelist, 1991—; mem. Indpls. Cultural Consortium, v.p., 1991-93; bd. dirs. Greater Indpls. Progress Com., Indpls. Urban League, Arts Coun. Indpls.; mem. nat. bd. Theatre Comm. Group, N.Y.C., treas., 1995-99; bd. dirs. New Haven Arts Industry Coalition, co-chair, 1997-99, treas., 1999-2002. Mem. exec. com. League Resident Profl. Theatres. Nat. Performing Arts Mgmt. fellow Exxon, Doner Fedn. and NEA, 1978; Elizabeth L. Mahaffey arts adminstrn. fellow Conn. Commn. on the Arts, 2000. Home: 120 Rimmon Rd Woodbridge CT 06525-1915 Office: Yale Repertory Theater PO Box 208244 Yale Station 222 York St New Haven CT 06520-8244

NOLAN-CONNERS, ELIZABETH ANN, director, educator; b. South Kingston, R.I., Apr. 19, 1966; d. James P. and Gloria L. Nolan; m. James J. Conners, Sept. 1, 2002; 1 child, Anne Elizabeth Conners. BA, U. Calif., Davis, 1988; MEd, Harvard U., Cambridge, Mass., 1989; PhD, Boston Coll., Chestnut Hill, Mass., 2001. Dir. student support The Meadowbrook Sch., Weston, Mass., 1989—; adj. faculty Lesley U., Cambridge, Mass., 2001—. Internat. spkr. Internat. Reading Assn., USA, Europe, Can., 1993—2001. Author: (book) Learning Differences in the Classroom; contbr. articles to profl. jours. Sch. coun. Bolton Pub. Sch., Mass., 2003—; mem. Theatre III, Acton, Mass., 2000—03. Recipient Young Alumna of Yr., U. Calif., Davis, 1998. Mem.: APA, Internat. Reading Assn. Office: The Meadowbrook Sch 10 Farm Rd Weston MA 02493 Personal E-mail: drbethnolan@hotmail.com. Business E-Mail: bnolan@meadowbrook-ma.org.

NOLAND, CHRISTINE A. magistrate judge; b. 1945; BA, JD, La. State Univ. Law clk. to Hon. John V. Parker U.S. Dist. Ct. (La. mid. dist.), 5th circuit, magistrate judge, 1987—. Mem. ABA, La. State Bar, La. trial Lawyers Assn., Baton Rouge Bar Assn., Dean Henry George McMahon Inn of Ct. (counselor 1995-97). Office: Russell B Long Fed Bldg & Courthouse 777 Florida St Rm 278 Baton Rouge LA 70801-1717

NOLAND, LINDA M, music educator; b. Red Bud, Ill., Mar. 26, 1954; m. Robert L Noland, Aug. 14, 1976; children: Katie, Leanne. BA, McKendree Coll., 1972—76; Med, Olivet Nazarene U., 2000—02. Music edn. specialist Holy Childhood Sch., Mascoutah, Ill., 1976—78, Freeburg Elem. Sch., Dist #70, Ill., 1978—81, Scott Elem. Sch., Scott Air Force Base, Ill., 1989—. Fundraising chairperson Lebanon H.S., Ill., 1998—2003; musical theater prodr. Lebanon H.S. drama dept, Ill., 2000—03; ch. musician O'Fallon United Meth. Ch., Ill., 1981—2003. Recipient St. Clair County Golden Apple Tchg. award, St. Clair County, 1997, Outstanding Cmty. Support award, Lebanon Sch. Dist. #9, 1998. Mem.: Nat. Educators Assn., Ill. Music Educators Assn., Music Educators Nat. Conf., Delta Kappa Gamma. United Methodist. Avocations: travel, entertaining, reading. Home: 315 W Center St Lebanon IL 62254 Office: Scott Elementary School 4732 Patriots Dr Scott Air Force Base IL 62225

NOLAND, MARIAM CHARL, foundation executive; b. Parkersburg, W.Va., Mar. 29, 1947; d. Lloyd Henry and Ethel May (Beare) Noland; m. James Arthur Kelly, June 13, 1981. BS, Case Western Res. U., 1969; M in Edn., Harvard U., 1975. Asst. dir admissions, fin. aid Baldwin-Wallace Coll., Berea, Ohio, 1969-72; asst. dir. admissions Davidson (N.C.) Coll., 1972-74; case writer Inst. Edn. Mgmt., Cambridge, Mass., 1975; sec., treas., program officer The Cleve. Found., 1975-81; v.p. The St. Paul Found., 1981-85; pres. Community Found. for S.E. Mich., 1985—. Trustee Coun. Mich. Founds., 1988-98, Coun. on Founds., 1994-99, Henry Ford Health System, 1994-2002, 04— Alma Coll., 1994—, John S. and James L. Knight Found., 2002—; commr. Detroit 300, 2000-01. Office: Community Found Southeastern Mich 333 W Fort St Ste 2010 Detroit MI 48226-3134 Business E-Mail: mnoland@cfsem.org.

NOLAN-PITERI, DAWN C. state legislator; b. McKees Rocks, Pa. m. David Piteri; 3 children. Mem. N.H. Ho. of Reps. (dist. 34), Concord, 1996—, mem. local and regulated rev. com., 1996—. Mem. Nashua Rep. City Com., 1996—. Home: 14 Lockness Dr Nashua NH 03062-3010

NOLD, AURORA RAMIREZ, business and economics educator; b. Honolulu, Apr. 21, 1958; m. Allan Jeffrey Nold, Aug. 1, 1995. BSBA cum laude, St. Louis U., 1969, MS in Bus. Adminstrn. magna cum laude, 1975, PhD summa cum laude, 1986. Exch. prof., dept. chairperson mgmt. St. Louis U., Baguio City, Philippines, 1980-86, dean Coll. Bus., 1980—86; rsch. asst. East/West Ctr. for Am. Studies, Honolulu, 1986-87; dir. Am. studies USIS, Washington, 1987-89; fin. cons. Shadow Hill Samaritan, Long Beach, Calif., 1989-93; dir. A&A Edu Care Consultancy Programs, Inc., Las Vegas, Nev., 1993—. Bd. advisors Am. Biog. Inst., Raleigh, N.C., 1995—, Internat. Biog. Ctr., Cambridge, Eng., 1995—; rschr. S.H.S. Inc., Las Vegas, 1995—; prof. econs., bus and mgmt. C.C. So. Nev.; prof. stats. U. Nev., Las Vegas; tutor C.C. So. Nev. Author: Business Education in the Philippines, 1986; contbr. articles to profl. jours. Pres. Rep. Presdl. Task Force, Las Vegas, 1995—. Cultural Exch. grant Fulbright Am. Studies, 1987, scholarship grant St. Louis U., 1979-86; recipient Appreciation award Nat. Humane Edn. Soc., 1996, Nat. Park Trust, 1996, Nat. Law Enforcement Officers Meml. Fund, 1997, Oustanding Cmty. and Profl. Achievement Commemorative medal Am. Biog. Inst., 1997, internat. cultural diploma of honor, 2000. Mem. AAUW, NAFE, Asian Am. Studies Assn., U.S. Profl. Bookkeepers Assn., Nev. Faculty Alliance. Republican. Mem. Lds Ch. Avocations: collecting rare coins, writing, reading, music and coin collecting. Office: A&A Edu Care Consultancy Programs Unit 657-10 7812 Clarkdale Dr Las Vegas NV 89128-3866 Office Phone: 702-242-6020. Personal E-mail: auroranold@aol.com.

NOLEN, DARLENE ELIZABETH, small business owner; b. Beaumont, Tex., Aug. 7, 1947; d. Louis Joseph and Audrey Elizabeth Wheeler; m. C. E. Page, Aug. 1965 (div. 1976); children: Dwayne Edward, Brett Louis stepchildren: Rochelle, Mark; m. E. E. "Butch" Nolen, Feb. 14, 1977. H.s. grad., Sour Lake, Tex., 1965. Acct. Beaumont Coca-Cola Bottling Co., Beaumont, Tex., 1974—76, Beaumont 7-Up Bottling Co., Beaumont, Tex., 1976—77, Kirby Forest Industries, Silsbee, Tex., 1978—82; substitute tchr aide Silsbee Sch. Dist., Silsbee, Tex., 1982—84; owner, mgr. Klothes Kloset Inc., Jasper, Tex., 1987—. CEO Cir. of Peace Found., Jasper, Tex., 2000—; bd. dirs. Mayor's Task Force on the Arts, Jasper, Tex., 2001—, Mayor's Task Force on Cmty. Businesses, Jasper, Tex., 1999—, Jasper/Lake Sam Rayburn C. of C., Jasper, Tex., 1996—, Jasper Main St., Jasper, Tex., 1993—, Jasper Walk of Hope-Breast Cancer Awareness, Jasper, Tex., 2001— Mem.: Nat. Trust Hist. Preservation, Jasper Lion Club (cmty. activities com.). Avocation: community fundraisers. Office: Klothes Kloset Inc 115 N Peachtree St Jasper TX 75951-4016 Business E-Mail: darlene@klotheskloset.com.

NOLL, JEANNE C. retired music educator; b. Reading, Pa., Aug. 12, 1935; d. Carl Foreman and Barbara Rebecca (Mengel) Winter; m. Clair W. Noll; children: Eric W., Douglas C. BS in Music Edn., Lebanon Valley Coll., Annville, Pa., 1957; music student, West Chester U., Milligan U., Lehigh U., MIT. Cert. tchr. Pa., 1961. Elem. music Tchr. N. Coventry Elem. Sch., Chester County, Pa., Yokohama (Japan) Army Sch., 1957—58; jr. HS vocal tchr. Reading (Pa.) Sch. Dist., 1959—61; organist, choir dir. St. Paul's United Ch. of Christ, Fleetwood, Pa., 1967—2001, organist/choir dir. emerita, 2002—; vocal music tchr., elem., jr. and sr. HS Kutztown (Pa.) Area Sch. Dist., Kutztown, 1981—94. Accompanist Kutztown Cmty. Choir, 1999—2001; dir. award-winning show choir Kutztown Area Sch. Dist., 1981—94. Del. Rep. Nat. Conv. Pa. 6th Congl. Dist., Phila., 2000—00; committeewoman Berk County Rep. Party, Fleetwood, 1982—; state Rep. committeewoman Pa. Rep. state com., Harrisburg, 1998—; mem. Berks Area Muhlenberg Coun. of Rep. Women, 1996, 2d v.p., 2003—. Mem.: East Penn Valley Kiwanis Club (Director, Key Club Advisor 1994—, Kiwanian of the Year 2000). United Ch. Of Christ. Avocations: travel, singing, reading, politics.

NOLL, LAURIE JANE, secondary school educator; b. Alton, Ill., Aug. 27, 1961; d. David Richard and Shirley Ann Bliven; m. Tim Joseph Noll, Mar. 22, 1982; children: Emily, Ian, Eileen. BA, MacMurry Coll., Jacksonville, Ill., 1982; MA, Western Ill. U., 1994. Cert. elem. tchr., nat. bd. cert. tchr. Tchr. Davenport Schs., Iowa, 1982—85, AEA, Bettendorf, Iowa, 1985—92; spl. svc. tchr., dept. chmn. Burlington Cmty. Schs., Iowa, 1992—, dept. chmn., 1997—, interpreter, 1984—92. Bd. dirs. Players Workshop, 2000—, interpreter, 1999—, City of Burlington, 1998—. Named Local Tchr. of Yr., Wal-Mart, 2002. Mem.: PEO, Pi Lambda Theta. Home: 1639 Madison Ave Burlington IA 52601 Office: Burlington Community Schs 421 Terrace Dr Burlington IA 52601

NOOLAN, JULIE ANNE CARROLL, management consultant; b. Adelaide, South Australia, Australia, June 14, 1944; came to U.S., 1966; d. Archibald Henry and Norma Mae (Gillett) Noolan; m. Daniel Thuering Carroll, Aug. 20, 1977. MA, U. Chgo., 1968, PhD, 1974, Exec. MBA, 1983. With State Library of South Australia, 1962-63, Repatriation Dept. South Australia, 1962-66; asst. librarian U. Chgo. Libraries, 1966-68; dir. edn. Med. Library Assn., Chgo., 1972-77; exec. dir. Assn. Coll. and Research Libraries, Chgo., 1977-84; COO Carroll Group, Inc., Chgo., 1984-95; pres. COO Carroll Group, Inc., Chgo., 1995—. Mem. faculty U. Chgo., 1968-89, Am. U., 1995—. Author: Libraries and Accreditation in Higher Education; contbr. articles to jours. U. Chgo. fellow, 1967-68, Higher Edn. Act fellow, 1969-72; Nat. Library of Medicine grantee, 1967-69; named Outstanding Young U.S. Leader 1985 Coun. on the U.S., Mem. ALA, Am. Soc. Assn. Execs., Am. Mgmt. Assn., Spol. Librs. Assn., Am. Soc. for Info. Scis. (past pres., doctoral award, Watson Davis award), ASTD, Nat. Tng. Labs. (bd. dirs. 1990-94), Orgn. Devel. Network, Internat. Assn. Neuro-Linguistic Programming (bd.dirs. 1990-93), Internat. Plant Genetic Resources Inst. (Rome, bd. dirs. 1991-98), Internat. Ctr. Agrl. Rsch. in Dry Areas (Syris, bd. dirs. 1992-98), Planning Forum, Beta Phi Mu.

NOONAN, JACQUELINE ANNE, pediatrics educator; b. Burlington, Vt., Oct. 28, 1928; BA, Albertus Magnus Coll., 1950; MD, U. Vt., 1954, DSc (hon.), 1980. Diplomate Am. Bd. Pediatrics, Am. Bd. Pediatric Cardiology. Intern N.C. Meml. Hosp., Chapel Hill, 1954-55; resident in pediatrics Children's Hosp., Cin., 1955-57; rsch. fellow Children's Med. Ctr., Boston, 1957-59; asst. prof. pediatrics State U. Iowa Sch. Medicine, 1959-61; asst. prof. pediatrics cardiology U. Ky. Coll. Medicine, Lexington, 1961-64, assoc. prof., 1964-69, prof., 1969-99, chmn. dept. pediatrics, 1974-92, emeritus prof., 1999—. Mem. embryology and human devel. study sect. NIH, 1973-78; mem. U.S.-USSR Symposium on Congenital Heart Disease, 1975; mem. sub. bd. pediatric cardiology Am. Bd. Pediatrics, 1977-82; examiner, mem. test. com. Nat. Bd. Med. Examiners, 1984-90, exec. com., 1991-95, participant various confs. in field; vis. prof. Vanderbilt U., Nashville, 1987; spkr. in field. Contbr. articles to med. publs., mem. editl. bd. Am. Jour. Diseases Children, 1970-80, Am. Jour. Med. Edn., 1975-78, Pediatric Cardiology, 1978-90, Am. Heart Jour., 1994-96, Clin. Pediatrics, 1990-99. Mem.: AMA, So. Soc. Pediat. Rsch. (pres. 1972), Soc. Pediat. Rsch., NIH Alumni Assn., Ky. State Med. Assn., Irish-Am. Pediat. Soc. (pres. 1999—2001), Fayette County Pediat. Soc., Am. Pediat. Soc., Assn. Med. Sch. Pediatrics (dept. chmn. exec. com. 1978—81), Am. Coll. Cardiology (gov. Ky. chpt. 1989—92), Am. Acad. Pediatrics (chmn. cardiol. sect. 1972—74). Office: U Ky Coll Medicine MN 117 Lexington KY 40536-0001

NOONAN, JEAN, lawyer; BA with highest honors, Okla. State U.; JD, U. Tex., Austin. Staff atty. FTC, McLean, Va., 1977-80, mgr. Equal Credit Opportunity Act Enforcement Program, 1980-83, asst. dir. div. credit practices, 1983-86, assoc. dir. credit practices, 1986-91; gen. counsel Farm Credit Adminstrn., 1991—. Office: Farm Credit Adminstrn 1501 Farm Credit Dr Mc Lean VA 22102-5004

NOONAN, MELINDA DUNHAM, nursing administrator; b. Peoria, Ill., Feb. 19, 1954; d. Emmett Maxwell Dunham and Dixie Maurine (De-Counter) Widner; m. Robert Joseph Noonan; children: Alissa, Meris. Diploma, Ravenswood Hosp. Sch. Nursing, 1977; BSN cum laude, U. Ill., Chgo., 1989; MS, North Park Coll., 1995. Med. asst. James J. Hines, M.D., S.C., Chgo., 1973-76; staff nurse Northwestern Meml. Hosp., Chgo., 1978-79, asst. head nurse, 1979-80, staff nurse, 1980-86, perinatal and women's health educator, 1983-92, coord. Health Learning Ctr., 1989-92; coord. Women's Ctr., Prentice Women's Hosp., Chgo., 1992-94; dir. women's programs Columbus Hosp., Chgo., 1994-96; dir. women's and family svcs. Swedish Convenant Hosp., Chgo., 1996-99; sr. cons. Phillips & Fenwick, Inc., Scotts Valley, Calif., 1999-2000; pres. M. D. Noonan, Inc., Chgo., 2000—02; dir., women and infant svcs. Advocate Christ Med. Ctr., 2002—. Founder, bd. dirs. Mothers Organized for Mut. Support, Chgo., 1981-89; creator, coord. Beyond The Birth Experience Program, Chgo., 1983-91. Contbg. author: Drugs, Alcohol, Pregnancy and Parenting, 1988, Clinical Issues of Perinatal and Women's Health Nursing, 1991, Jour. Obstetrical, Gynecological and Neonatal Nursing, 1996. Bd. dirs. Mothers Organized for mut. Support, 1981-88; troop leader Girl Scouts U.S., Chgo., 1991-93. Mem. Assn. Women's Health, Obstetrics and Neonatal Nurses (consumer edn. com. 1992-93, edn. com. 1994-95), Nat. Assn. Women's (bd. dirs. 1998—, pres. 2000—)2003, Rebekah (vice grand 1981-82, noble grand 1982-83), Sigma Theta Tau. Democrat. Roman Catholic. Home: 7632 Arguilla Dr 1B Palos Heights IL 60463-3420 Office: 4440 W 95th St 244N Oak Lawn IL 60453

NOONAN, PEGGY, writer; b. Brooklyn, N.Y., Sept. 7, 1950; d. Jim and Mary Jane (Byrne) N.; m. Richard Kahn, Nov. 27, 1985 (div. 1990); 1 child, Will. BA in English Literature & Journalism, Fairleigh Dickinson U., Rutherford, N.J., 1974, PhD in Humane Letters (hon.), 1990. Premium adjuster Aetna Ins. Co., Newark, 1968-70; student Antiwar Protester of Vietnam; temp. agency sec. N.Y.C., 1974; news staffer WEEI Radio (CBS station), Boston, 1974, editl. dir., 1975-77; writer, editor CBS News, N.Y.C., 1977-80, commentary for Walter Cronkite and Dan Rather, 1980-81, full time commentary writer for Dan Rather, 1981-84; White House speech writing tech. Ronald Reagan, Washington, 1984-86; White House speech writer George Bush, Washington, 1988-89; contbg. editor The Wall St. Jour., Time, Good Housekeeping. Bd. dir. The Manhattan Inst. Author: What I Saw at the Revolution: A Political Life in the Reagan Era, 1990, Life, Liberty, & the Pursuit of Happiness, 1995, Simply Speaking: How to Communicate Your Ideas With Style, Substance, and Clarity, 1998, The Case Against Hillary Clinton, 2000, When Character was King: A Story of Ronald Reagan, 2001, A Heart, a Cross and a Flag, 2003; contbr. articles to Forbes, Mirabella, Newsweek, N.Y. Times, O Mag., Time, Wash. Post. Coll. Guest Editor Mademoiselle, 1990; Mother of Yr. award, 1990; Nat. Mother's Day Com., 1990. Mem. Judson Welliver Soc. Republican. Roman Catholic. also: ICM 40 W 57th St Fl 16 New York NY 10019-4001*

NOONAN, SHAUNA GAY, petroleum engineer; b. Edmonton, Alta., Apr. 11, 1969; came to U.S., 1997; d. Duane Thomas and Edna Irene (Carlson) Freeman; m. Michael James Noonan, Aug. 3, 1996; children: Heather Gwendolyn, Lisa Danielle. BS in Petroleum Engring., U. Alta., Edmonton, 1993. Prodn. engr. Chevron Can. Resources, Edmonton, 1993-94, Fox Creek, Alta., 1994-96, petroleum engr. Calgary, Alta., 1996-97; prodn. engr. artificial lift Chevron Petroleum Tech. Co., Houston, 1997—. Mem. adv. panel La. State U. Downhole Water Separation Initiative, Baton Rouge, 1998, Baton Rouge, 2001, U. Tulsa Sand Monitoring Project, 1998; chmn. working group Am. Petroleum Inst., Houston, 1998—; mem. ISO task force group on Gas Lift Equipment Specifications, 1999—. Mem.: ASME (chmn. gast lift workshop 2003), Soc. Petroleum Engrs. (electric submersible pump adv. panel 1997—, mem. progressive cavity pump steering com. 2002, chmn. electric submersible pump adv. panel 2003—, Outstanding Achievement award 1998—2002), Montgomery County Alumnae Delta Gamma Sorority (publicity officer 2000—02). E-mail: snoonan@chevrontexaco.com.

NOONAN, SHEILA M. energy consulting company executive; BA in Bus. Adminstrn., U. St. Thomas; postgrad., Harvard U., Boston U. Numerous positions including dir. security & fire alarm bus. Honeywell; v.p. sales Cadence Networks, Cin. Office: Cadence Networks 105 E 4th St Ste 250 Cincinnati OH 45202-4006

NOONAN, SUSAN ABERT, public relations executive; b. Lancaster, Pa., May 10, 1960; d. James Goodear and Carole (Althouse) Abert; m. David Lindsay Noonan, July 28, 1986; children: Caroline du Pont, Elizabeth Augusta. BA, Mt. Holyoke Coll., 1982. Account exec. Merill Lynch, N.Y.C., 1982-83; sr. v.p. Cameron Assocs., N.Y.C., 1983-88; pres., founder Noonan/Russo Comm. (now Euro RSCG Life NRP), N.Y.C., 1988—. Mem. Nat. Investor Rels. Inst. Office: Noonan Russo Comm Inc 220 5th Ave New York NY 10001-7708*

NOONE, PALMER, academic administrator; Doctorate in higher edn. adminstrn., Union Insit.; JD, MBA, U. Iowa; BBA, U. Dubuque. Pres. U. Phoenix, 2002—, provost, sr. v.p. acad. affairs, dir. acad affairs, faculty; atty gen. civil practice Iowa; judge City of Chandler, Ariz. Office: U Phoenix 3201 E Elwood St Phoenix AZ 85034

NOOYI, INDRA K. food products company executive; BS, Madras (India) Christian Coll.; MBA, Indian Inst. Mgmt., Calcutta; M Pub. and Pvt. Mgmt., Yale U. Product mgr. Johnson & Johnson, India, Mettur Beardsell, Ltd., India; dir. internat. corp. strategy projects Boston Cons. Group; bus. devel. exec. Motorola, v.p., dir. corp. strategy and planning; sr. v.p. strategy, planning and strategic mktg. Asea Brown Boveri; sr. v.p. strategic planning PepsiCo, Purchase, N.Y., 1994-2000, sr. v.p., CFO, 2000-01, pres., CFO, 2001—. Bd. dirs. Phoenix Home Life Mut. Ins. Co. Bd. dirs. PepsiCo Found.; trustee Convent of Sacred Heart Sch., Greenwich, Conn. Office: Pepsico Inc 700 Anderson Hill Rd Purchase NY 10577-1444*

NORA, AUDREY HART, physician; b. Picayune, Miss., Dec. 5, 1936; d. Allen Joshua and Vera Lee (Ballard) H.; m. James Jackson Nora, Apr. 9, 1966; children: James Jackson Jr., Elizabeth Hart. BS, U. Miss., 1958, MD, 1961; MPH, U. Calif., 1978. Diplomate Am. Bd. Pediat., Am. Bd. Hematology and Oncology. Resident in pediat. U. Wis. Hosp., Madison, 1961-64; fellow in hematology/oncology Baylor U., Tex. Childrens Hosp., Houston, 1964-66, asst. prof. pediat., 1966-70; assoc. clin. prof. pediat. U. Colo. Sch. Medicine, Denver, 1970—; dir. genetics Denver Childrens Hosp., 1970-78; commd. med. officer USPHS, 1978, advanced through grades to asst. surgeon gen., 1983 cons. maternal and child health 1978-83, asst. surgeon gen. regional health adminstr., 1983-92, dir. maternal & child health bur., health resources and svc. adminstrn., 1992-99. Mem. adv. com. NIH, Bethesda, 1975-77; mem. adv. bd. Metronet Health, Inc., Denver, 1986—, pres., 2004—; mem. adv. bd. Colo. Assn. Commerce and Industry, Denver, 1985—, WIC program USDA, 1989-99; mem. adv. coun. NICHD, 1992-909; pres. bd. dirs. RMC for Health Promotion and Edn., 2004-. Author: (with J.J. Nora) Genetics and Counseling in Cardiovascular Diseases, 1978, (with others) Blakiston's Medical Dictionary, 1980, Birth Defects Encyclopedia, 1990, (with J.J. Nora and K. Berg) Cardiovascular Diseases: Genetics, Epidemiology and Prevention, 1991; contbr. articles to profl. jours. Recipient Virginia Apgar award Nat. Found., 1976. Fellow Am. Acad. Pediat.; mem. Am. Pub. Health Assn. (governing coun. 1990-92, coun. mem. maternal and child health 1990—), Commd. Officers Assn., Am. Soc. Human Genetics, Teratology Soc., Western Soc. Pediatric Rsch. Presbyterian. Avocations: quilting, cooking, hiking. Office: 1973 S Kenton Ct Aurora CO 80014-4709

NORA, LOIS MARGARET, neurologist, educator, academic administrator, dean; BS in Biology with honors, U. Ill., 1976; MD, Rush Med. Coll., Chgo., 1979; JD, U. Chgo., 1987; MBA, U. Ky., 2002. Fellow Am. Bd. Neurology, Am. Bd. Electrodiagnostic Medicine; bar: Ill. 1988, D.C. 1988. Intern in family medicine Cmty. Meml. Gen. Hosp., LaGrange, Ill., 1980; resident in neurology Rush-Presbyn.-St. Luke's Med. Ctr., Chgo., 1981-84, chief resident in neurology, 1983-84, fellow electromyography and neuromuscular disease, 1984-85; asst. prof. dept. neurology, asst. dean clin. curriculum Rush Med. Coll., Chgo., 1987-94, assoc. prof. dept. neurology, 1994-95; fellow Ctr. for Clin. Med. Ethics U. Chgo., 1993-95; assoc. dean acad. affairs, assoc. prof. dept. neurology U. Ky. Coll. Medicine, 1995—2002; prof. neurology U. Ky. Coll. Law, 1996—2002; pres. Northeastern Ohio Univ. Coll. of Med., 2002—, dean, 2002—. Spkr. in field. Contbr. articles to profl. jours., chpts. to books. Vice chair Epilepsy Found. of Greater Chgo., 1988-90, chair, 1991, chair strategic planning com. 1990-91, bd. dirs., 1987-94; bd. dirs. Epilepsy Found. of Am., 1992-95, co-chair quality standards com. 1992-94; mem. needs assessment com. United Way of Chgo., 1989-90; camp physician children's summer camp program Muscular Dystrophy Assn., 1984-86; vol. tchr. Christ the King Elem. Sch., 1996—2002. Mem. AMA (mem. dean's com. on family violence curriculum 1993, mem. report and resolutions subcom. for reference com. C 1997), Am. Acad. Neurology (mem. ethics com. 1997—2002), Am. Assn. Electrodiagnostic Medicine (chair profl. practice com. 1991—97, sec., treas., 1999-2002, pres.-elect, 2002-03, pres. 2003-04), Soc. Clin. Neurologists. Office: Northeastern U Coll Med PO Box 95 4209 St Rt 44 Rootstown OH 44272

NORAAS, DIANE RICE, computer scientist, educator; b. Kansas City, Mo., Feb. 20, 1948; d. Ray R. and Nellie Lu (Clark) Rice; m. Dennis P. Tihansky, Feb. 20, 1971 (div. June 1983); children: Suzanne Marie Clement, John Raymond Tihansky; m. William C. Noraas, May 25, 2001. BS, Marygrove Coll., Detroit, 1969; MS, Harvard U., 1972. Computer programmer I City of Alexandria, Va., 1972; computer programmer U.S. Dept. Treasury, Washington, 1972—74; computer specialist, rsch. asst. Resources for the Future, Washington, 1976; instr. Fla. Internat. U., Miami, 1977—78; asst. prof. and chair dept. math. and computer sci. St. Mary's Coll., Orchard Lake, Mich., 1983—89; infrastructure analyst EDS, Troy, Mich., 1989—99; adj. faculty Baker Coll., Clinton Twp., Mich., 2001—. Asst. leader Girl Scouts U.S., Cambridge, Mass., 1981—82; treas. PTA, Miami, Fla., 1980—81. Mem.: Ridgedale Players (bd. dirs. 1997—99), Avon Players (Stoney award 1999, 2001), Kappa Gamma Pi. Republican. Roman Catholic. Avocations: reading, needlecrafts, puzzles, community theater. Home: 23375 Crystal Dr Clinton Township MI 48036-1285

NORBECK, JANE S. retired nursing educator; b. Redfield, S.D., Feb. 20, 1942; d. Sterling M. and Helen L. (Williamson) N.; m. Paul J. Gorman, June 28, 1970. BA in Psychology, BSN, U. Minn., 1965; MS, U. Calif., San Francisco, 1971, DSN, 1975. Psychiat. nurse Colo. Psychiat. Hosp., Denver, 1965-66, Langley Porter Hosp., San Francisco, 1966-67; pub. health nurse San Francisco Health Dept., 1968-69; prof. U. Calif. Sch. of Nursing, San Francisco, 1975—2003, dean, 1989-99, dept. chair, 1984-89, prof. and dean emeritus, 2003. Chair study sect. Nat. Inst. of Nursing Rsch., 1990-93, mem. editl. bd. Archives of Psychiat. Nursing, 1985-95, Rsch. in Nursing and Health, 1987-2003. Co-editor: Annual Review of Nursing Research, 1996-97; contbr. articles to profl. jours. Mem. ANA, Am. Acad. Nursing, Inst. of Medicine, Sigma Theta Tau.

NORBERG, DEBORAH DORSEY, museum administrator; b. New Haven, Conn., Jan. 31, 1950; d. Gray Lankford and Jeanne (DeVall) Dorsey; m. Henry F. Norberg, Sept. 11, 1971; children: Sarah E., Daniel G. BA, Stanford U., 1968; M in Mus. Practice, U. Mich., 1974; JD, Stanford U., 1980. Rsch. asst. San Jose (Calif.) Mus. Art, 1975, asst. to curator, 1975-76, exhibition coord., 1987-88, asst. curator, 1988-89, assoc. registrar, assoc. permanent collection curator, 1989-90, registrar, assoc. permanent collection curator, 1990—91, registrar, permanent collection curator, 1991—92, dep. dir., 1992—; assoc. Hopkins and Carley, San Jose, 1980-82. Ford Found. fellow, 1972. Mem. Phi Beta Kappa. Office: San Jose Mus Art 110 S Market St San Jose CA 95113-2383

NORCEL, JACQUELINE JOYCE CASALE, educational administrator; b. Nov. 19, 1940; d. Frederick and Josephine Jeanette (Bestafka) Casale; m. Edward John Norcel, Feb. 24, 1962. BS, Fordham U., 1961; MS, Bklyn. Coll., 1966; 6th yr. cert., So. Conn. State U., 1980; postgrad., Bridgeport U. Elem. tchr. pub. schs., N.Y.C., 1961-80; prin. Coventry (Conn.) Schs., 1980-84, Trumbull (Conn.) Schs., 1984—2003, Frenchtown Elem. Sch., 2003—. Guest lectr. So. Conn. State U., 1980; cons. Monson (Mass.) Schs., 1984; mem. Conn. State Prin. Acad. Adv. Bd., 1986-88; mem. adj. faculty Sacred Heart U., Fairfield, Conn., 1985—, So. Conn. State U., summer 1991; fed. rels. coord. Nat. Assn. Elem. Sch. Prins., Conn., 1999-2002. Editor: Best of the Decade, 1980; mem. editl. adv. bd. Principal Matters; contbr. articles to profl. jours. Chmn. bldg. com. Trumbull Bd. Edn., 1978-80; chmn. Sch. Benefit Com., Trumbull, 1985-86; catechist Bridgeport Diocese, Roman Cath. Ch., Conn., 1975-85, youth min., 1979-84, coord., evaluator leadership tng. workshops for teens and adults, 1979-84; mem. St. Stephen's Parish Coun., 1993-97, trustee, 1997—, Eucharist minister, 1999—, lector, 1990—; com. mem. New Sch. Bldg. Town of Trumbull, 2001-04. Recipient Town of Trumbull Svc. award, 1982, Nat. Disting. Prin. award, 1988, Joseph Formica Disting. Svc. award EMSPAC, 1994. Mem.: ASCD, Assoc. Tchrs. Math. in Conn., New Eng. Coalition Edn. Leaders, Ea. Conn. Coun. Internat. Reading Assn., Conn. Assn. Elem. Sch. Prins., Trumbull Adminstrs. Assn. (pres.-elect 1989—91, pres. 1991—93, 2002—), Conn. Assn. Supervision and Curriculum Devel., Nat. Assn. Elem. Sch. Prins. (del. to gen. assemblies 1984—90, zone I dir. 1987—90, del. to gen. assemblies 1999—), Hartford Area Prins. and Suprs. Assn. (local pres. 1981—82), Conn. Assn. Schs. (bd. mem. 2000—), Adminstrn. and Supervision Assn. (sec. 1980—81, pres. 1981—82, exec. bd. 1982—93), Elem. Mid. Sch. Prins. Assn. (pres. 1985—86, state elected rep. 1989—90, fed. rels. coord. 1990—94, dists. 1, 2 and 3 dir. 1995—98, commr. 1997—2000, fed. rels. coord. 1999—2002, Citizen of Yr. award 1991, Pres.'s award 1981—85), N.E. Regional Elem. Prins. Assn. (rep. 1984—86, sec. 1986—87), Delta Kappa Gamma (v.p. 1996—2000), Pi Lambda Theta, Phi Delta Kappa (v.p. rsch. and projects 1993—95, Disting. Fellow award 1992). Home: 5240 Madison Ave Trumbull CT 06611-1016 Office: Frenchtown Elem Sch 30 Frenchtown Rd Trumbull CT 06611 Office Phone: 203-452-4227. Personal E-mail: norcelJ98@Yahoo.com.

NORDEN, MELISSA SHARI, lawyer; b. Bklyn., Oct. 7, 1972; BA, Tufts U., 1994; JD, Bklyn. Law Sch., 1999. Bar: NY 2000. Atty. Madison Sq. Garden Cheering for Children Found., NYC, 2000; staff coun. ASPCA, NYC, 2000—. Editor: Jour. Law Policy, 1997—99. Mem.: ABA, Am. Corp. Counsel, Assn. Bar City NY (non-profit com. 2000—), Tufts Lawyers Assn. Office: ASPCA 424 E 92d St New York NY 10128

NORDGREN, MARY KATHLEEN, secondary school educator; b. Minn. d. Robert J. and Ihla L. Ellingson; m. Richard B. Nordgren; children: Stephanie, Erik. BS in Home Econ., U. Minn., Mpls., 1973, MEd, 1987. Home econ. educator Lake Superior Sch. Dist., Silver Bay, Minn., 1973—82; banker Union State Bank, Hazen, ND, 1982—92; family & consumer sci. educator Golden Valley (N.D.) H.S., 1992—. Del. leader People to People Student Ambassadors, 2001. Advisor Kids on the Block; bd. dirs. English Luth., fin. sec. Recipient Prevention Through Edn. award, Mental Health Assn., 2001, 2002. Mem.: Hazen Lions Club, Jaycees, Lioness Club (charter pres.), Phi Upsilon Omicron, Alpha Delta Kappa. Office: Golden Valley High Sch 10 3rd St NW Golden Valley ND 58541

NORDGREN, SHARON L. state legislator; b. Chgo., Oct. 21, 1943; m. Richard Nordgren; 2 children. Student, U. Minn. N.H. state senator; mem. appropriations com.; mem. dist. 10 N.H. Ho. of Reps., 1998—. Mem. Hanover Bd. Selectman, 1979-88, chmn., 1982-88. Trustee Montshire Mus. Sci., 1984-92, chair, 1991-92; chmn. Cmty. Substance Abuse Com., 1989—; bd. dirs. N.H. Women's Lobby, 1992—; mem. Children's Trust Fund, 1990—, State Leadership Team Abuse and Neglect, 1991—, Hanover H.S. Coun., 1983—; cmty. mem. Hanover Inn Bd. Overseers, 1985—. Named Citizen of Yr., Hanover C. of C., 1992. Mem. Ch. of Christ. Avocations: fishing, hiking, sports. Home: 23 Rope Ferry Rd Hanover NH 03755-1404 Office: NH Ho Rep House of Reps Concord NH 03301

NORDHAGEN, HALLIE HUERTH, nursing home administrator; b. Apr. 2, 1914; d. Mathias James and Ethel Elizabeth (Fann) Huerth; m. Carl E. Nordhagen, May 24, 1947; children: Bruce Carl, Brian Keith. EdD, U. Wis., Superior, 1938, MA, 1949. Prin. tchr. Wis. Pub. Schs., 1932—46; supervising tchr. Wis. C.C., 1946—48; nursing home adminstr. Trempealeau County Health Care Ctr., Whitehall, Wis., 1959—. Mem. Wis. Nursing Home Adminstrs. Examining Bd.; fellow Menninger Clinic, Topeka, 1979—81. Author: Wisconsin Indians, 1966. Chmn. BRAD Assn./Alcohol and Drug Abuse; mem. Trampealeau County Alliance Drug Free Youth; mem. com. cons. to bishop Evang. Luth. Ch. Am., 1995—96. Recipient Disting. Svc. award in edn. and hosp. adminstrn., London, 1967, award for svcs. to human svcs. programs, Wis. Assn. Human Svcs., 1972, award for outstanding svcs. to exceptional children, Assn. Retarded Children, 1978, award for accomplishments in human resources, Trempealeau County Conservation Svc., 1981, citation, Wis. State Senate, 1983, Wis. Gov., 1984, Wis. State Assembly, 1989, Women of Leadership, Delta Kappa Gamma Alpha Kappa chpt. Jackson Counties, Wis., 2000. Mem.: Internat. Platform Assn., Wis. Assn. Human Svcs. Programs, Wis. Edn. Assn., Wis. Assn. County Homes, Am. Lutheran Ch. Women, Women's Club, Whitehall Country Club. Home: 35681 Claire St Whitehall WI 54773-8430

NORDIN, PHYLLIS ECK, sculptor, painter, consultant; b. Chgo. Student, Beloit Coll., Wayne State U.; BS, U. Toledo, 1963, BA cum laude, 1972, MLS, 1992. Instr. Lourdes Coll., Sylvania, Ohio, 1986-89, U. Toledo, 1986-89. Prin. works include large bronze sculptures Lucas County Main Libr., Toledo, Christ figure St. Joan of Arc Ch., Maumee, Ohio, Ronald McDonald House, Toledo, First English Evangel. Luth. Ch., Grosse Pointe Woods, Mich., Christ Presbyn. Ch., Covenant Presbyn. Ch., Toledo, Toledo Hosp., Reynolds Br. Libr., Toledo, Port Clinton and Defiance (Ohio) Librs., stone wall mural Epworth United Meth. Ch., Toledo, Beloit Coll., Wis., bronze fountain U. Toledo, bronze life-size children Treasure Coast Mall, Stuart, Fla., Kingston, Tenn. Pub. Libr., welded steel sculpture Town Ctr. Mall, Port Charlotte, Fla., Carey (Ohio) Bank, Toledo Bank, Bi-Centennial Park, Toledo, wood wall carvings 1st Meth. Ch., LaGrange, Ill., ferrocement abstract Flower Hosp., Sylvania, Ohio, Rossford (Ohio) Meth. Ch., 12 stained glass windows Lucas County Courthouse, Toledo, 2 stained glass panels 1st Bapt. Ch., Holland, Ohio; numerous others; exhibited Butler Inst. Am. Art, U.S. Embassies Program, Yalta Mus., Allied Artists Am., Salmagundi Club, Audubon artists, Ohio Watercolor Soc., N.Am. Sculpture exhibit, numerous others; represented by Collectors Corner Toledo Mus. Art, 1970—, Am. Gallery, Sylvania. Recipient Alpha award Foothills Art Ctr., 1983, 1st prize Ann. Nat. Art Exhbn., 1978, numerous others; named to Lyons Twp. H.S. Hall of Fame, 1996. Mem. N.W. Ohio Watercolor Soc., Athena Art Soc., Toledo Artists Club (bd. dirs.), Phi Kappa Phi (hon.). Home: 4035 Tan Tara Dr Toledo OH 43623-3311

NORDQUIST, SONYA LYNN, information technology executive; b. Syracuse, N.Y., Nov. 7, 1969; d. Fred James and Mary Jo Nordquist; m. Hans F. Altenbach, Apr. 20, 2003. Student, Geneva Coll., 1987—89; BS in Bus. Adminstrn., SUNY, Oswego, 1989—91. Mortgage credit processor Commonwealth Info. Svcs., Charleston, SC, 1992—93; asst. to v.p. mktg. Dynapower/Stratopower, Charleston, 1993—95; telecom. cons. TTE, Inc., Charleston, 1995—96; sales mgr. Enterprise Network Svcs., Charleston, 1996—2002; CEO, tech. cons. C3 Technology, Inc., Charleston, 2002—. Fundraiser Happy Days and Spl. Times, Charleston, 1996—2002, Girl Scouts Carolina Low Country, Charleston, 2003—. Mem.: C. of C. (CEO Roundtable 2003—), Trident Bus. Assn., Young Profl. Kiwanis Club Charleston, Top Informed Profl. Sales Club (pres. 1995—2000), Toastmasters Daniel Island Club (v.p. pub. rels. 2003—). Republican. Achievements include patents pending in field. Avocations: tennis, running, travel. Home and Office: C3 Tech Inc PO Box 22081 Charleston SC 29413

NORDSIECK, KAREN ANN, custom apparel company executive; b. Ft. Campbell, Ky., Nov. 2, 1955; d. Reuben James and Shirley Jean (Walters) Simpson; m. Kenneth M. Farber, Mar. 5, 1977 (div. July 1982); children: Carissa Ann, Laurie Jean; m. Derrell E. Hiett, May 10, 1985 (div. May 1989); m. Michael Louis Nordsieck, June 2, 1989. Student, El Paso Community Coll., 1976, 84. Sales clk. Busy B Gift Shop, El Paso, Tex., 1973; svc. rep. Bell System, El Paso and Seattle, 1974-85; substitute tchr. Cleburne County Elem. Sch., Heflin, Ala., 1986; credit clk. Wakefields, Anniston, Ala., 1986-87; svc. rep. Ala. Power, Anniston, 1986-88; beauty cons. May Kay Cosmetics, El Paso and Heflin, Ala., 1983-88; mgr. Rock's T-Shirts & Screen Printing, El Paso, 1988-92; owner Custom Designs and Promotions, Richmond, Mo., 1992-96; svc. rep. Southwestern Bell Telephone Co., Kansas City, Mo., 1993—; owner Kreations by Karen, Richmond, 1996—. Liaison for ptnrs. in edn. El Paso Ind. Sch. Dist., Rock's T-Shirts and Screen Print, El Paso, 1990-1992; co-chairperson quality of work life com. Southwestern Bell, El Paso, 1984; union steward Communication Workers Am., El Paso, 1974-75. Troop leaders Brownies, Girl Scouts U.S.A., troop # 126, Heflin, 1985-88, mag. chairperson, 1986; v.p. Clendenin Elem. PTA, El Paso, 1989-90, pres., 1990-92; family support leader Ft. Bliss Family Support, El Paso, 1990-91; mem. El Paso Ind. Sch. Dist. Strategic Planning Com., 1990-91; mem. campus improvement com. Clendenin Elem., 1991-92, vol. pub. schs., 1989-92; mem. parent adv. com. ctrl. area El Paso Ind. Sch. Dist., 1989-92; mem. Richmond PTA, 1992-1998; mem. com. Richmond A-Plus Sch. Planning, 1994-95; co-chairperson Jr. Class Parents After Prom/Project Graduation, 1995-96; mem. Battlefield Piece Makers Quilt Guild, 1995—; chmn., editor CWA Local 6327 newsletter, The Localizer, 1997-98, union steward, 1996-98; mem. Southwestern Bell/CWA United Way com., 1997-98; chair office improvement com. Southwestern Bell Kansas City Soc., 1997-98. Recipient Outstanding Troop Leader award Girl Scouts U.S.A., Anniston, 1987, cert.

outstanding svc. Clendenin PTA, El Paso, 1990, 91, 92; cert. of honor Clendenin Elem. Sch., 1990, 91, 92, Cert. of Appreciation, 1991, 92; Cert. of Appreciation, Ft. Bliss Army Family Support, 1991, plaque Vols. in Pub. Sch., El Paso, 1991, 92, Ptnrs. in Edn., El Paso Ind. Sch. Dist., 1991, 92, Desert Storm vol. pin Ptnrs. in Edn., 1991, Pres. Appreciation award S.W. Bell, 1997. Mem. Battlefield Piecemakers Quilt Guild (sec. 2000-01, chair newsletter 2000-2001), Order Ea. Star, Telephone Pioneers. Mem. Assembly of God. Avocations: sewing, painting, quilting, reading, sailing. Office: Kreations by Karen 15601 E 3rd Street Ct S Independence MO 64050-1970 E-mail: mknordsk@swbell.net.

NORDSTRAND, NATHALIE ELIZABETH JOHNSON, artist; b. Woburn, Mass., Nov. 6, 1932; d. Edward N. and Ruth Peterson Johnson; m. Robert I. Nordstrand, Jan. 12, 1962. AA, Bradford Jr. Coll., 1952; BA, Barnard Coll., Columbia, 1954; studies with Jay Connaway, Don Stone, Roger Curtis. Rsch. assoc. Gerontology Age Ctr. of New Eng., Boston, 1955-64; clk. corp. dir. Johnson Bros. Greenhouses, Inc., Woburn, 1958-84; owner Nordstrand Gallery, Rockport, Mass., 1970-99. Artist oils and watercolor works exhibited at Nat. Acad. Galleries, N.Y.C., Springfield Mus. Fine Arts, Hammond Mus., North Salem, N.Y.C., Bhulabha Meml. Inst., Bombay, India, Copley Soc. at Boston Symphony Hall, Hermann Fine Arts Ctr., Marietta, Ohio, Am. C. of C., Hong Kong, 1975, 76, Silvermine Guild, Conn., 1976, Wall of Fame, Balt. Watercolor Soc., 1976, Ann. Copley Masters Exhbn. Boston, others; one woman shows include Rockport (Mass.) Art Assn., 1969, Laura Knotts Art Gallery, Bradford Coll., 1982, Reading Pub. Libr. Found., 1997; paintings in Nat. Mus. Am. Art, Smithsonian Inst., 1994, Best of Watercolors, 1995, Best of Oil Painting, 1996, Landscape Inspirations, 1997, Gallery of Marine Art, 1998. Mem. planning bd. North Suburban Art Festival, 1963—68; chair. planned giving Barnard Coll., N.Y.C., 2003—. Named Citizen of Yr., Reading chpt. Am. Cancer Soc., 1983; recipient Excellence in Watercolor award, Rockport Art Assn., 1997, Philip Isenberg Meml. award, Salmagundi Club, 1997, 179 awards in nat. and regional competition, 1960—. Fellow Am. Artist Profl League (Gold medal 1971, 75, award 1978, 79); mem. Acad. Artists Assn. (Watercolor awards 1973, 74, 76, 77, New Eng. Heritage award 1993), Copley Soc. Boston (master artist), Hudson Valley, North Shore (bd. dirs. 1964-67, 86—), Rockport Art Assn. (Lifetime Dedication to Promotion of Art award 1999), Affiliated Art Assn. Mass. (v.p. 1980), Reading Art Assn. (charter, program chmn. 1960-86, Pres.'s awards 1973-80), Am. Watercolor Soc. (juror 125th Ann. Internat. Exhbn., 1992), Allied Artists Am. (Watercolor award 1973, 74), New Eng. Watercolor Soc. (2d v.p. 1984-90), Boston Watercolor Soc. (award 1975), Guild Boston Artists (bd. dirs. 1986-99, A. Lassall Ripley award 1993), Reading Assn. Fine and Performing Arts (charter, bd. dirs. 1993), Nat. Mus. Women in Arts (charter mem.), Salmagundi Club (40 awards including MacGowin Tuttle Meml. award 1976, 78, 79, Elliot Liskin Meml. award 1988, Steven Blackman award 1988, Joseph Hartley award 1989, 2001, 2002, Mortimer Freehof Meml. award 1991, Bruce Crane award 1994, Rita Duis Meml. award 2001, Margery Saroka Meml. award 2003, Thomas Moran award 2004). Methodist. Address: 384 Franklin St Reading MA 01867-1036 E-mail: nordstrands@aol.com.

NORDYKE, ELEANOR COLE, population researcher, public health nurse; b. Los Angeles, June 15, 1927; d. Ralph G. and Louise Noble (Carter) Cole; m. Robert Allan Nordyke, June 18, 1950; children: Mary Ellen Nordyke-Grace, Carolyn Nordyke Cozzette, Thomas J., Susan Nordyke Bell., Gretchen Nordyke Worthington. BS, Stanford U., 1950; P.H.N. accreditation, U. Calif.-Berkeley, 1952; MPH, U. Hawaii, 1969. RN. Pub. health nurse San Francisco Dept. Health, 1950-52; nurse-tchr. Punahou Sch., Honolulu, 1966-67; clinic coordinator East-West Population Inst., East-West Ctr., Honolulu, 1969-75, population rschr., 1975-82, rsch. fellow, 1982-92. Cons. Hawaii Commn. on Population, Honolulu, 1970-83; mem. Hawaii Policy Action Group for Family Planning, Honolulu, 1971-89, chmn., 1976-77; nurse-cons. vol. Straub Clinic and Hosp., 2001 . Author: The Peopling of Hawaii, 1977, 2d rev. edit., 1989, A Profile of Hawaii's Elderly Population, 1984; author: (with Robert Gardner) The Demographic Situation in Hawaii, 1974; author: Pacific Images-Views from Captain Cook's Third Voyage, 1999, I'm Third-An American Boy of Depression Years - Memoirs of Robert A. Nordyke, MD, 2003; mem. editl. bd. Hawaiian Jour. History, 1980—; contbr. articles to profl. jours. Bd. dirs. YMCA, Honolulu, 1970-85, YMCA Camp Erdman Br., 1985—, vice-chmn. 1978-79, chmn. YMCA Camp Erdman, 1989-92; bd. dirs. Hawaii Planned Parenthood, 1974-78, Friends of Libr. of Hawaii, 1985-87, 2002—; trustee Hawaiian Hist. Soc., 1978-82, Arcadia Retirement Residence, Honolulu, 1978-87; mem. liberal arts coun. Hawaii Pacific U., 1988—. Mem. Population Reference Bur., Am. Statis. Assn., Hawaii Econ. Assn., Hawaiian Hist. Soc., Friends of East-West Ctr., Friends of Univ. Hawaii Sch. Medicine, Stanford Nurses Alumni Assn., Stanford Alumni Assn. (bd. dirs. Hawaii chpt.), U. Hawaii Sch. Pub. Health Alumni Assn. (life), Honolulu County Geneal. Soc., Gen. Fed. Women's History Club, Adventure Club of Honolulu, Book Reading Club, Outrigger Canoe Club, Morning Music Club, Caledonian Soc., NAIC Wiki Kala Investment Club, Phi Beta Kappa. Democrat. Congregationalist. Avocations: music, art, swimming, birds, travel. Home: 2013 Kakela Dr Honolulu HI 96822-2158 E-mail: rnordyke@aol.com.

NORELL, JUDITH REGINA, small business owner, musician, political administrator; b. N.Y.C. d. Sandor and Sylvia (Duchin) Hirsch; m. Ian Strasfogel, Feb. 15, 1973; children: Daniella, Gabirelle. MM, Juilliard Sch., 1971. Artistic dir. Bach Gesselschaft N.Y., N.Y.C., 1984-86, Opera Antica, Palm Beach, Fla., 1987-93; exec. dir. Women's Campaign Sch. Yale U., New Haven, 1996—; prin., owner Silver Moon Bakery, N.Y.C., 2000—. Ford Found. fellow, 1970; recipient medal Mayor of City of N.Y., 1995. Mem. LWV, NWPC (legis. dir. N.Y. state chpt. 1995—). Office: Silver Moon Bakery 2740 Broadway New York NY 10021

NORELLI, TERIE THOMPSON, state legislator; b. Orange, N.J., July 7, 1952; d. George Russell and Iverna C. (Weber) Thompson; m. Allen M. Norelli, Dec. 31, 1973; children: Gina Marie, Daniel Thompson. BS in Math., U. N.H., 1985. Tchr. math. Winnacunnet H.S., Hampton, N.H., 1985-95; mem. N.H. Ho. of Reps., Concord, 1996—, sci., tech. and energy com., 1996—, telecomm. oversight com., 1997—2992, ho. Dem. leadership, 1998—, asst. Dem. whip, 2002—, chair clean air subcom., 1998—, electric utility restructuring oversight com., 1998—2002, co-chair reproductive rights caucus, 1996—2002, mem. legis. caucus for children, 1997—. Participant in devel. series geometry insvc. workshops U. N.H., 1986-89. Aarea team Nat. Abortion Rights Action League of N.H., Portsmouth, 1990-94, bd. dirs., Concord, 1996—2002; chair Naral-Prochoice N.H. Pac; bd. dirs. Sexual Assault Support Svcs., Portsmouth, 1992-96, pres. bd., 1993-95; del. to Joint U.S.-China Conf. on Women's Issues, Beijing, 1995; organizing com. Bringing Back Beijing '95, Statewide Women's Conf., Concord, 1996, Beijing +5 Tri-State Preperation Conf., 1999; adv. bd. Feminist Health Ctr. Ports, Portsmouth, 1996-97; active Leadership Seacoast, 1995. Mem. Phi Beta Kappa, Phi Kappa Phi, Pi Mu Epsilon. Avocations: travel, arts and culture, running. Office: Rm 201 LOB State St Concord NH 03301

NORKIN, CYNTHIA CLAIR, retired physical therapist; b. Boston, May 6, 1932; d. Miles Nelson and Carolyn (Green) Clair; m. Stanislav A Norkin, Feb. 19, 1955 (dec. 1970); 1 child, Alexandra. BS in Edn., Tufts U., 1954; cert. phys. therapist, Bouve Boston Coll., 1954; MS, Boston U., 1973, EdD, 1984. Instr. Bouve Boston Coll., 1954-55; staff phys. therapist New Eng. Med. Ctr., Boston, 1954-55, Abington (Pa.) Meml. Hosp., 1965-70, Ea. Montgomery County Vis. Nurse Assn., 1970-72; asst. prof. phys. therapy Sargent Coll./Boston U., 1973-84; assoc. prof. phys. therapy, dir., founder Ohio U. Sch. Phys. Therapy, Athens, 1984-95, ret., 1995. Consult Boston Ctr Independent Living, Cambridge Vis Nurse Asn, Mass Medicaid Cost Effectiveness Project, 1978; secy Health Planning Coun Greater Boston, 1976—78; book, manuscript reviewer F A Davis Co, 1986—; arthritis adv comt Ohio Dept Health. Author (with P Levangie and C Norkin): Joint Structure and Function: A Comprehensive Analysis, 1983, 3d edit., 2001; author: (with D J White) Joint Measurement: A Guide to Goniometry, 1985, 3d edit., 2003. Trustee Brimmer and May Sch, 1980. Mem.: APHA, AAAS, Athens County Vis Nurse Asn (secy adv coun 1984—95), Mass Asn Mental health, Mass Physical Therapy Asn (chair quality assurance comt 1980—83), Am Physical Therapy Asn (on site evaluator comn on accreditation 1986—95). Episcopalian.

NORMAN, ALLINE L. health facility administrator; b. Homerville, Ga., Dec. 20, 1938; d. John F. and Alline D. N. BS, Ga. Coll., 1960; cert. Sch. for Med. Records, U.S. Pub. Health Svc., 1961. U.S. pub. svc. offcr. U. Cin., 1961-65; asst. chief and chief med. records U.S. Pub. Health Svc. Hosps., New Orleans, Chgo., Norfolk, 1965-70; chief med. info. section, Med. Adminstrn. Svc. VA Med. Ctr., N.Y., 1970-72, Miami, 1972-75, asst. chief Med. Adminstrn. Svc. East Orange, N.J., 1975-80, Miami, 1980-83, chief Med. Adminstrn. Svc. Augusta, Ga., 1983-85, chief field ops. divsn., Med. Adminstrn. Svc. Atlanta, 1988-89, from dep. dir. to dir. Med. Adminstrn. Svc., 1990-93, dir. Adminstrn. Svc. Office, 1993-94, dir. Lake City, Fla., 1994-97, ret., 1997, acting dir., 1998-99. Chmn. combined fed. campaign Vets. Health Adminstrn., 1991, co-chmn. chief med. dir.'s adv. com. on diversity, 1992-96, mem. task force subcom. on recommendations of commn. on future structure of vets. health car, 1992; mem. White House Nat. Health Care Task Force on Integration Govt. Sys., 1993, Sec.'s Adv. Group on Sexual Harassment, 1993-96, Interagy. Inst., 1993-94. Bd. dirs. Suwanee United Way, 1994-95, Lake City C.C. Found., 1995-96, Am. Cancer Soc., Lake City, 1995-96. Recipient Fed. Leadership award, 1992, cert. achievement Fed. Women's Interagency Bd., 1993, Sec. Meritorious Svc. award, 1994, Under Sec. Health Honor award, 1994. Mem. VA Sr. Execs. Assn. (bd. dirs. 1994). Methodist. Office: VA Med Ctr 801 S Marion St Lake City FL 32025-5827

NORMAN, CHRISTINA, broadcast executive; b. July 30, 1963; m. Charles Hunt; children: Zoe, Asha. BA, Boston U. Freelance prodn. coord MTV, 1986—91, prodn. mgr., 1991—93, supervising prodr., on-air promotions, 1993—94, dir., on-air promotions, 1994—95, v.p., on-air promotions, 1995—97, sr. v.p., on-air promotions, 1997—99, sr. v.p., mktg. and on-air promotion, 1999—2002; exec. v.p. and gen. mgr. VH1, 2002—04, pres., 2004—. Named one of 10 Most Powerful Blacks in TV, Ebony mag., 2002; named to 100 Most Powerful Women in Hollywood list, Hollywood Reporter, 2003, 40 under 40 list, Crain's N.Y. Bus., 2003. Office: VH1 20th Fl 1515 Broadway New York NY 10036*

NORMAN, E. GLADYS, retired business computer educator, consultant; b. Oklahoma City, June 13, 1933; d. Joseph Eldon and Mildred Lou (Truitt) Biggs; m. Joseph R.R. Radeck, Mar. 1, 1953 (div. Aug. 1962); children: Jody Norman, Ray Norman, Warren Norman (dec. May 1993), Dana Norman; m. Leslie P. Norman, Aug. 26, 1963 (dec. Feb. 1994); 1 child, Elayne Pearce. Student, Fresno (Calif.) State Coll., 1951-52, UCLA, 1956-59, Linfield Coll., 1986 95. Math. aid U.S. Naval Weapons Ctr., China Lake, Calif., 1952-56, computing systems specialist, 1957-68; systems programmer Oreg. Motor Vehicles Dept., Salem, 1968-69; instr. in data processing, dir. Computer Programming Ctr., Salem, 1969-72; instr. in data processing Merritt-Davis Bus. Coll., Salem, 1972-73; sr. programmer, analyst Teledyne Wah Chang, Albany, Oreg., 1973-79; sr. systems analyst Oreg. Dept. Vets. Affairs, Albany, 1979-80; instr. in bus. computers Linn-Benton C.C., Albany, 1980-95; ret., 1995. Computer cons. for LBCC Ret. Sr. Vol. Program, 1995-2002; presenter computer software seminars State of Oreg., 1991-93, Oreg. Credit Assoc. Conf., 1991, Oreg. Regional Users Group Conf., 1992; computer tchr. Linn-Benton C.C., 1999-2001; computer cons. Oremet-Wah Chang, 1996-2002, Oreg. State Yr. 2000 Project, 1997-98; adj. prof. Cheneketa C.C., 2000-02; computer cons. in field. Mem.: Assn. Info. Tech. Profls. (region treas. 1999, region sec. 2000—02), Data Processing Mgmt. Assn. (bd. dirs. 1977—84, 1989—95, region sec. 1995—96, assoc. v.p. 1988, Diamond Individual Performance award 1985). Democrat. Avocations: drawing, painting, sewing. E-mail: gladys33@quik.com.

NORMAN, JEAN REID, journalist; b. Phoenix, Feb. 13, 1957; d. James August and V. Janice (Radford) R.; m. James E. Norman, Jr., Dec. 30, 1982; children: James R., Janiece C. BS in Journalism, Northwestern U., 1979. Reporter Fallon (Nev.) Eagle-Standard, 1979-80; reporter, spl. sections editor North Las Vegas Valley Times, 1980-81; mng. editor Good Times, Santa Cruz, Calif., 1981-83; copy editor Daily Review, Hayward, Calif., 1983-85, Journal-Bulletin, Providence, R.I., 1986-89, Contra Costa Times, Walnut Creek, Calif., 1989, The Washington Post, 1990, USA Today Money Sect., Rosslyn, Va., 1990-93; mng. editor Navy Times, Springfield, Va., 1993-98; asst. metro editor Las Vegas Sun, 1998—. Vestry mem. St. Mark's Episcopal Ch., 1996-98. Democrat. Office: Las Vegas Sun 2275 Corporate Cir Ste 300 Las Vegas NV 89074 E-mail: jeanrnorman@earthlink.net.

NORMAN, JESSYE, soprano; b. Augusta, Ga., Sept. 15, 1945; d. Silas Sr. and Janie (King) N. B.M. cum laude, Howard U., 1967; postgrad., Peabody Conservatory, 1967; M.Mus., U. Mich., 1968; MusD (hon.), U. South, 1984, Boston Conservatory, 1984, U. Mich., 1987, U. Edinburgh, 1989, Cambridge U., 1989. Debut, Deutsche Oper, Berlin, 1969, Italy, 1970; appeared: in operas Die Walküre, Idomeneo, L'Africaine, Marriage of Figaro, Aida, Don Giovanni, Tannhauser, Gotterdammerung, Ariadne auf Naxos, Les Troyens, Dido and Aeneas, Oedipus Rex, Hérodiade, Les Contes d'Hoffmann; debut in operas, La Scala, Milan, Italy, 1972, Salzburg Festival, 1977, U.S. debut, Hollywood Bowl, 1972, appeared with, Tanglewood Festival, Mass., also Edinburgh (Scotland) Festival, debut, Covent Garden, 1972; appeared in 1st Great Performers recital, Lincoln Center, N.Y.C., 1973—; other guest performances include, L.A. Philharm. Orch., Boston Symphony Orch., Am. Symphony Orch., Chgo. Symphony Orch., San Francisco Symphony Orch., Cleve. Orch., Detroit Symphony, N.Y. Philharm. Orch., London Symphony Orch., London Philharm. Orch., BBC Orch., Israel Philharm. Orch., Orchestre de Paris, Nat. Symphony Orch., English Chamber Orch., Royal Philharm., London Phila. Orch., Milw. Symphony Orch., Stockholm Philharm. Orch., Vienna Philharm. Orch., Berlin Philharm. Orch.; tours, Europe, S. Am., Australia, numerous recs., Columbia, EMI, Philips Records; PBS TV spcls. include Kathleen Battle and Jessye Norman Sing Spirituals, 1991, Concert at Avery Fisher Hall, 1994; recordings include Amazing Grace, Brava, Jessye!, Jessye Norman at Notre Dame, Lucky to Be Me, Sacred Songs, With a Song in My Heart, In The Spirit. Recipient 1st prize Bavarian Radio Corp. Internat. Music Competition, 1968, Grand Prix du Disque, Acad. du Disque Francais, 1973, 76, 77, 82, 84, Deutsche Schallplatten, Preis, 1975, 81, Alumni award U. Mich., 1982, Outstanding Musician of Yr. award Musical Am., 1982, Grand Prix du Disque Academie Charles Cros, 1983, Commandeur de l'Ordre des Arts et des Lettres, France, 1984, Grammy awards, 1980, 82, 85, numerous other awards; named hon. life mem. Girl Scouts U.S., 1987. Mem. Royal Acad. Music (hon.), Alpha Kappa Alpha, Gamma Sigma Sigma, Sigma Alpha Iota, Pi Kappa Lambda. Clubs: Friday Morning Music (Washington). Office: L'Orchidee PO Box S Crugers NY 10521-0710

NORMAN, MARY MARSHALL, alcohol/drug abuse services professional; b. Auburn, N.Y., Jan. 10, 1937; d. Anthony John and Zita Norman. BS cum laude, LeMoyne Coll., 1958; MA, Marquette U., 1960; EdD, Pa. State U., 1971. Cert. alcoholism counselor. Tchr. St. Cecilia's Elem. Sch., Theinsville, Wis., 1959-60; vocat. counselor Marquette U., Milw., 1959-60; dir. testing and counseling U. Rochester (N.Y.), N.Y., 1960-62; dir. testing and counseling, dean women, assoc. dean coll. Corning (N.Y.) C.C., Corning (N.Y.) C.C., 1962-68, asst. dean students, dir. student activities, asst. prof. ps University Park, 1962-68; rsch. asst. Ctr. for Study Higher Edn. Pa. State U., University Park, Pa., 1969-71; dean faculty South Campus C.C. Allegheny County, West Mifflin, Pa., 1971-72, campus pres., coll. v.p., 1972-82; pres. Orange County C.C., 1982-86; alcohol counselor Sullivan County Alcohol Drug Abuse Svc., 1985-90; sr. counselor Horton Family Program, 1990-96, ednl. cons., writer, 1996—. Cons. Boricua Coll., N.Y.C., 1976-77; reader NSF, 1977-78; mem. govtl. commn. com. Am. Assn. Cmty. and Jr. Colls., 1976-79, bd. dirs., 1982—; mem. and chmn. various middle state accreditation teams. Contbr. articles to profl. jours. Mem. Econ. Devel. Seneca County, Seneca County Tourism Bd.; active St. Patrick's Ch.; bd. dirs. Orange County United Way; bd. dirs. Orange County Alcoholism and Drug Abuse Coun., 1993—96; bd. dirs. Seneca County Hist. Soc., 1997—, Guild and Altar Soc., 1999. Mem. Nat. Women's Hall of Fame. Mem.: Pa. Coun. on Higher Edn., Nat. Am. Coun. on Edn. (Pa. rep. identification women for adminstrn. 1978—82, bd. dirs., pres. 1980—96), Pitts. Coun. Women Execs. (charter), Pa. Assn. Acad. Deans, Pa. Assn. Two-Yr. Colls., Am. Assn. Women in Cmty. and Jr. Colls. (charter, Woman of the Yr. 1981), Nat. Assn. Women Deans and Counselors, Am. Assn. Higher Edn., Seneca County C. of C. (bd. dirs., mem. tourism com.), Orange County C. of C. (bd. dirs.), Amnesty Internat. (charter mem. women's coun. 2000—), Concerned Citizens for Good Govt. (charter), Kiwanis (bd. dirs. Seneca Falls), Gamma Pi Epsilon. Home: 9 S Park St Seneca Falls NY 13148-1423

NORMAN, PAMELA KAY, special education educator, director; b. Cuba City, Wis., Mar. 28, 1959; d. Ivan Adams and Velma Ruth Bingham-Adams; m. Gary Thomas Norman, Aug. 8, 1981; children: Heather Layne, Landon Thomas. BS in Learning/Behavior Disorders, Murray (Ky.) State U., 1981, MA in Elem. Edn., 1985, MA in Adminstrn., 1999—2001. Cert. tchr. Ky., 1981, dir. spl. edn. Ky., 1999. Tchr. Crittenden County Bd. of Edn., Marion, Ky., 1981—98, Lyon County Bd. of Edn., Eddyville, 1998—99; dir. spl. edn. Lyon County Schs., Eddyville, Ky., 1999—. Mem. Ky. Dept. Edn. Stakeholder Group, Frankfort, Ky., 2003—. Composer musical works. Charter mem. Lyon County Interagency Coun., Eddyville, Ky., 2003. Mem.: Ky. Coun. Adminstrs. Spl. Edn. (bd. dirs. 2002—), Ky. Assn. Sch. Adminstrs., Coun. for Exceptional Children. Office: Lyon County Schs 217 Jenkins Rd Eddyville KY 42038 E-mail: pnorman@lyon.k12.ky.us.

NORMAND, BEVERLY ANN, counseling administrator; d. Vernon Lee and Rejoyner Elizabeth Ross; children: Niama, Jerusha, Davida. BA in Psychology, Roosevelt U., Chgo., 1970; MA, DePaul U., 1984; MEd in Sch. Adminstrn., Chgo. State U., 1999; LittD (hon.), Grant Coll., 1992. Cert. adminstrn. Ill., social-emotional Ill., learning disabilities Ill., tchg. Ill. Resource tchr. Chgo. Pub. Schs., Horace Mann Sch., 1972—92; citywide specialist Chgo. Pub. Schs., Ctrl. Office, 1993—2000; psychology facilitator Chgo. Pub. Sch., 2001—. Founder, pres. RALD Inst., Chgo., 1988—. Contbr. articles to profl. jours.;, author poems. Asst. dir. theater City of Chgo. Model Cities, 1969—71; commn. religion & race South Shore United Meth. Ch., Chgo., 1983—99, fine arts, 1985—. Grantee Ednl. Rsch., Oppenheimer Found., 1993, 1994, 1995, Akarama Found., Chgo., 1998. Mem.: Ctr. Black Music Rsch., Poetry Found. (assoc.). Methodist. Office: Chgo Pub Sch 125 S Clark 8th Flr Chicago IL 60603

NORMANN, MARGARET ELLA, deacon, educator; b. Providence, Jan. 13, 1931; d. Parker Edward and Margaret Millard (McDowell) Monroe; m. Conrad Neil Normann, July 17, 1953; children: Andrea Kristin Mudge, Margaret Ingrid Wierdsma, Conrad Neil, Parker Monroe. BA in Drama, Vassar Coll., 1952; MA in English, NYU, 1966; MS in Recreation and Leisure, So. Conn. State U., 1978. Ordained deacon Protestant Episcopal Ch., 1993. Human svc. officer, dir. recreation programs Town of Bedford, NY, 1975—83; cmty. edn. coord., writer, cons. Cmty. Residences Info. Svc. Program, White Plains, NY, 1983—91; initiator, exec. dir. Apropes Housing Opportunities and Mgmt. Enterprises, Inc., Bedford/Mount Kisco, NY, 1985—93; deacon Ch. of the Holy Communion, Mahopac, NY, 1993—; chaplain Four Winds Hosp., Cross River, NY, 1993—. Writing instr., tutor, evaluator SUNY Empire State Coll., Hartsdale, NY, 1984—. Recipient Disting. Svc. Alumnae award, Lincoln Sch., Providence, 1988, Cert. of Merit, State of N.Y., Albany, 1991, Mickey Leland Home for the Homless award, 1991. Republican. Home (Summer): Margaret House Box 591 Route 107 Bridgton ME 04009 Home (Winter): #511-513 1 Hamilton Heights Dr West Hartford CT 06119-6320

NORMENT, RACHEL GOBBEL, artist, educator, writer; b. Durham, NC, Apr. 3, 1934; d. Luther Lafayette and Marcia (Russell) Gobbel; m. Owen Lennon Norment, Jr., Dec. 21, 1957; children: Marcia Lynnette, Russell Owen. AB in English, Rhodes Coll., 1955; MA in Art Edn., Vanderbilt U., 1956. Arts and crafts tchr. Baibridge Jr. High Sch., Richmond, Va., 1956—57; grade tchr. E.S.H. Greene Sch., Chesterfield County, Va., 1957—59; third grade/second grade tchr. Cameron Park Sch., Hillsborough, NC, 1962—64; art instr. Southside Va. C.C., Keysville, Va., 1972—82; self-employed artist, 1972—; art instr., 1982—. Workshop instr. area arts groups in Va., 1985—; lectr. in field. Exhibitions include numerous one-woman shows and invitational exhbns., Va. and N.C., 1973—, numerous juried group shows in Va., W.Va., Colo., Ala., Calif., N.Y. and others., Represented in permanent collections Hampden-Sydney Coll., Longwood U., Greensboro Coll., Va. Episc. Sch., Westtown Sch., Ethyl Corp.; contbr. columns in newspapers on dreamwork in newspapers, 2000. Group facilitator Dreamwork, 1994—. Mem.: Ctrl. Va. Watercolor Guild, Miss. Watercolor Soc., So. Watercolor Soc., Ky. Watercolor Soc., Va. Watercolor Soc. (v.p. 1994—95, pres. 1996—97), Assn. Study of Dreams. Home: 1247 Courtyard Dr Charlottesville VA 22903-7881

NORMINGTON, NORMA SHOTWELL, secretary; b. Lakewood, Ohio, Apr. 7, 1924; d. Phillip Bassett and Alice Mae (Teed) Shotwell; m. Joshua James Normington, July 18, 1944; children: Peter Jay, Patricia Jean Normington Zieher. BS in English, U. Wis., 1948. Cert. tchr., Wis. Tchr. Madison (Wis.) East High Sch., 1948-50, Belmont (Calif.) Primary Grades, 1951; sec.-treas., now CEO Saddle Mound Cranberry Co., Inc., City Point, Wis., 1975—. Mem. AAUW (sec. 1953, pres. 1954), Marshfield Women's Club (v.p.), Wood County Rep. Women's Club, Sigma Alpha Iota, Kappa Delta. Avocations: travel, cooking, playing organ, needlepoint, reading. Home and Office: 7848 Shotwell Rd Pittsville WI 54466

NORMORE, LORRAINE FRANCES, information systems researcher; b. Regina, Sask., Can., Aug. 13, 1946; came to U.S., 1975; d. John Charles and Jean Dorothy (Werstiuk) Dombrowski; m. Calvin G. Normore, May 18, 1969 (div. May 1983); 1 child, Christina. BA in Psychology with honors, McGill U., Montreal, 1967; MLS, U. Toronto, 1975; PhD in Experimental Psychology, Ohio State U., 1986. Rschr. Chem. Abstracts Svc., Columbus, Ohio, 1983-97, Online Computer Libr. Ctr., Dublin, Ohio, 1997—2003; cons., 2004—. Troop leader Girl Scouts Am., Columbus, Ohio, 1988-96. Mem. APA, Am. Soc. Info. Sci., Human Factors and Ergonomics Soc. (TG sec., treas. 1990-91, pres. ctrl. Ohio chpt. 1986-87, newsletter editor 1991—), Assn. for Computing Machinery Spl. Interest Group on Computer-Human Interaction. Avocation: gardening.

NORRINGTON, EILEEN O'HICKEY, military officer, chaplain; b. Boston, Aug. 10, 1947; d. James William and Doris Violet (Smith) Hickey; m. Dennis Bartley Kelly, Sept. 4, 1965 (div. Apr. 1971); children: Sean Patrick, Brian Scott; m. Giles Roderick Norrington, July 9, 1988; stepchildren: Keeley Norrington Hunt, Giles Roderick Jr. BA magna cum laude, U. N.H., 1974; MDiv, Andover Newton Theol. Sch., 1978. Commd. lt. (j.g.) USN, 1978, advanced through grades to capt., 1996; chaplain Naval Tng. Ctr., Orlando, Fla., 1978-80; chaplain, retreat facilitator Chaplains Religious Enrichment Devel. Orgn., Norfolk, Va., 1980-82; pastoral counseling resident Portsmouth (Va.) Naval Hosp., 1982-83; chaplain Naval Air Sta., Norfolk, 1983-85, Naval Support Facility, Diego Garcia, 1985-86, Marine Corps Base, Camp Pendleton, Calif., 1986-88; command chaplain Naval

Submarine Sch., Groton, Conn., 1989-92, USS Emory S. Land, 1992-94; policy br. head chief chaplains office Bus. Naval Pers., Washington, 1994-96; staff chaplain Naval Security Group Command, Ft. Meade, Md., 1996-98; dep. claimant chaplain Comdr. Naval Res. Forces, 1998—2001; mem. nat. staff, min. for authorization and endorsement United Ch. Christ, 2001—. Named Outstanding Young Women of Am., 1982, Mil. Woman of the Yr. Naval Air Sta., Norfolk, 1983, Marine Corps Base Camp Pendleton, Oceanside, Calif., 1987, Mil. Mem. of Yr., Naval Submarine Base, Groton, 1990. Mem. AAUW, LWV, NOW, Women in Mil. Svc., Mil. Chaplain Assn., Internat. Assn. Women Mins. (life, trustee 2003), Women Officers Profl. Assn. Democrat. Mem. United Ch. of Christ. Avocations: jogging, reading, needlework, motorcycle travel, ballroom dance. Office: United Church Christ 700 Prospect Ave Cleveland OH 44115-1100 Home: 32560 Bridgestone Dr N Ridgeville OH 44039-4398

NORRIS, ANDREA, government agency administrator; Dep. chief info. officer NASA, Washington. Office: NASA Headquarters Washington DC 20546

NORRIS, ANDREA SPAULDING, art museum director; b. Apr. 2, 1945; d. Edwin Baker and Mary Gretchen (Brendle) Spaulding. BA, Wellesley Coll., 1967; MA, NYU, 1969, PhD, 1977. Intern dept. western European arts Met. Mus. Art, N.Y.C., 1970, 72; rsch. and editorial asst. Inst. Fine Arts NYU, 1971, lectr. Washington Sq. Coll., 1976-77; lectr. Queens Coll. CUNY, 1973-74; asst. to dir. Art Gallery Yale U., New Haven, 1977-80, lectr. art history, 1979-80; chief curator Archer M. Huntington Art Gallery, Austin, Tex., 1980-88; lectr. art history Dept. Art U. Tex., Austin, 1984-88; dir. Spencer Mus. Art U. Kans., Lawrence, 1988—. Co-author: (catalogue) Medals and Plaquettes from the Molinari Collection at Bowdoin College, 1976; author: (exhbn. catalogues) Jackson Pollock: New-Found Works, 1978; exhbn. The Sforza Court: Milan in the Renaissance 1450-1535, 1988-89, Am. Indian Traditions Transformed, 2000. Mem.: Mus. Loan Network (adv. bd. 2003—), Assn. Art Mus. Dir., Coll. Art Assn. (bd. dir. 2000—, v.p. for coms. 2002—04), Renaissance Soc. Am., Phi Beta Kappa. Office: Spencer Mus Art U Kans 1301 Mississippi St Lawrence KS 66045-7500

NORRIS, JEAN MARIE, director; b. Chgo., Mar. 3, 1965; d. Joseph John Miller and Marlene Dorothy Carroll, James Carroll (Stepfather); m. Vincent E. Norton, Nov. 2, 1999; 1 child, Michael Joseph. BA in Mgmt., Nat.-Louis U., 1995; MA in Communication and Tng., Governor's State U., 1997; EdD, U. Sarasota, 2003. CEO Norton Norris, Inc., Tinley Park, Ill., 1998—; v.p. admissions and enrollment svcs. U. St. Francis, Joliet, 2001—. Cons. Norton Norris, Inc., 1998—; presenter in field. Recipient Admissions Advt. awards, Admission Mktg. Report, 1998, 1999, 2001, 2002. Mem.: AAUW (assoc.), Ill. Assn. Coll. Admission Counselors (assoc.), Nat. Assn. Grad. Admission Profls. (assoc.), Nat. Assn. Coll. Admissions Counselors (assoc.), Am. Mktg. Assn. (assoc.), Am. Bus. Women's Assn. (assoc.). Roman Catholic. Achievements include Tactical Enrollment Management (trade mark). Avocations: golf, sailing, reading, softball, walking. Office: U St Francis 500 Wilcox St Joliet IL 60435 E-mail: jnorris@stfrancis.edu.

NORRIS, JOAN CLAFETTE HAGOOD, retired assistant principal; b. Pelzer, SC, June 26, 1951; d. William Emerson and Sarah (Thompson) Hagood; divorced; 1 child, Javiere Sajorah. BA in History and Secondary Edn., Spelman Coll., 1973; MA in Teaching in Edn., Northwestern U., 1974; MA in Adminstrn. and Supervision, Furman U., 1984. Cert. elem. edn. tchr., elem. prin., social studies tchr., elem. supr., S.C.; notary pub., S.C. Clk. typist Fiber Industry, Greenville, SC, 1970, Spelman Coll. Alumni Office, Atlanta, 1970-73; tchr. Chgo. Bd. Edn., 1973-74, Greenville County Pub. Schs., Greenville, S.C., 1974-97, Hollis Acad., Greenville, S.C., 1996-97; asst. prin. Nevitt Forest Elem. Sch., Anderson, SC, 1997—2002; ret., 2002. Dir. elem. summer sch. Anderson Sch. Dist. 5, 1998, asst. prin. acad., 2001—02; mem. steering com. N.W. area Greenville County Sch. Dist., 1994—95, chmn. elem. steering com., 1996, participant Curriculum Leadership I, 96, participant potential adminstrs. internship program, 1997—; participant Asst. Prins. Inst. Furman U., summer, 1999; flagship status application reader S.C. Sch., 2000. Contbr. articles to profl. jours. Staff devel. com. summer sch. program Anderson County Elem. Sch. Dist. 5, 2000—02; mem. NEA; bd. dirs. Girl Scouts of Old 96 Coun. Inc., 2001—; sec. Webette's Temple 1312, Greenville, 1985, parliamentarian, 1986; bus. ptnr. contact person Nevitt Forest Elem. Sch., 1997—2000, comm. contact person, 1997—2000, after-sch. site dir., 2000—01. Selected to Potential Adminstrs. Acad., Furman U., 1991; named Tchr. of Yr., Armstrong Elem. Sch., 1982, 91; grantee Alliance of Quality Edn., 1989-90, 97-98, Chick-A-Fil-A extended day program in math and reading, 1998; grantee Publix Charities Media Ctr. Books, 2000. Mem. AAUW (exec. bd. cmty. rep. Greenville br. 1993-94, v.p. programs 1994-96, pres.-elect. 1996-97, pres. 1997-98, nominating com., gift honoree, 5 Star Recognition award 1998), S.C. Edn. Assn., S.C. Assn. Sch. Adminstrs. (nom. Disting. Asst. Prin. 2000, Sch. of Promise application reader 2000), S.C. Coun. Sci., S.C. Assn. Curriculum Devel. (nat. mem.), Spelman Alumni Assn., Northwestern Alumni Assn., S.C. Coun. Sci., Am. Assn. Ret. Persons, S.C. Educator's Ret. Assn., Phi Delta Kappa (chpt. alt. del. 1992-93, sec. chpt. 1993-94, v.p. membership 1996-97). Democrat. Baptist. Avocations: reading, talking to older people, listening to blues music, travel, watching old black and white movies. Home: 219 Barrett Dr Mauldin SC 29662-2030 E-mail: jhagoodnorris@hotmail.com.

NORRIS, KAREN W. grants specialist; b. Washington, Mar. 5, 1950; d. Jerome J. and Lillian (Pittle) N.; children: Elysa, Mindy. BA, George Washington U., 1972; MBA, Hood Coll., 1994. Tchr. journalism, TV and English Montgomery County Pub. Schs., Rockville, Md., 1972-80; broadcast engr. CBS TV-WDVM-TV, Washington, 1980-83; pvt. practice comm. cons. Washington, 1983-88; grants specialist Prince George's County Pub. Schs., Upper Marlboro, Md., 1988—. Mem. cultural arts adv. com. Montgomery County Govt., Rockville, 1975; mem. performing arts adv. com. Prince George's County Pub. Schs., Upper Marlboro, 1994-98; panel chair U.S. Dept. Edn. 21st Century Sch., 2001 Bd. dirs. Journalism Edn. Assn., Balt., 1972-75. Recipient Excellence in H.S. Journalism award Montgomery County C. of C., Rockville, 1978; named Md. Journalism Tchr. of Yr., Md. Journalism Edn. Assn., Rockville, 1972. Mem. AAUW (mem. pub. policy com. 1998). Office: Baltimore City Pub Sch Grants Adminstrn 200 E North Ave Baltimore MD 21202

NORRIS, LOIS ANN, elementary school educator; b. Detroit, May 13, 1937; d. Joseph Peter and Marguerite Iola (Gourley) Giroux; m. Max Norris, Feb. 9, 1962 (div. 1981); children: John Henry, Jeanne Marie, Joseph Peter. BS in Social Sci., MA, Ea. Mich. U., 1960; cert. adminstr., Calif. State U., Bakersfield, 1983. Kindergarten tchr. Norwalk-LaMirada Unified Sch. Dist., 1960-62; tchr. various grades Rialto Unified Sch. Dist., 1962-66; kindergarten tchr. Inyokern (Calif.) Sch., 1969-82; 1st grade tchr. Vieweg Basic Sch, 1982-92, kindergarten tchr., 1992-96; retired, 1996. Head tchr. Sierra Sands Elem. Summer Sch.; adminstrv. intern Sierra Sands Adult Sch., master tchr., head tchr., counselor. Ofcl. scorekeeper, team mother, snack bar coord. China Lake Little League; team mother, statistician Indian Wells Valley Youth Football; bd. mem. PTA; pres. Sch. Site Coun.; treas. Inyokern Parents Club; run coord. City of Hope; timekeeper, coord. Jr. Olympics; mem. planning com. Sunshine Festival; active Burros Booster Club; docent Maturango Mus.; mem. Pink Lady orgn., mem. hosp. corp. bd. Ridgecrest Regional Hosp.; mem. Women's Aux. for Commd. Officers Mess. Recipient Hon. Svc. award PTA, 1994. Mem. NEA, AAUW, Calif. Tchr. Assn., Desert Area Tchr. Assn., Assn. Calif. Sch. Adminstr., Inyokern C. of C. (sec.), Am. Motorcycle Assn., NRA, AOPA, Bakersfield Coll. Diamond Club, Inyokern Rotary, Beta Sigma Phi. Republican. Mem. Lds Ch. Avocations: swimming, physical fitness, music, American history, gardening. Home: PO Box 163 201 N Brown Rd Inyokern CA 93527 E-mail: anorris@iwvisp.com.

NORRIS, MILDRED ELEANOR, consultant; b. Melbourne, Fla., Dec. 25, 1940; d. Byron Edgar and Mildred Eleanor (Raymond) Steele; m. Raymond E. Norris Sr., June 16, 1959; children: Amy, Ray Jr., Mike, Jarrod. AS, St. Petersburg Jr. Coll. Med. record technician/coding specialist Tampa (Fla.) Gen. Hosp.; coding/DRG coord. Fla. Med. Quality Assurance Inc., Tampa; clin. coding technician Code Plus, Inc., West Palm Beach, Fla.; supr. med. records James A. Haley VA Hosp., Tampa, Fla.; coder III Naples (Fla.) Cmty. Hosp.; cons., co-owner Norris Coding/Billing Svcs.; coding supr. H. Lee Moffitt Cancer Ctr., Tampa, 2000—. Coding editor A.R.T. Examination Rev. Book, 1997; adj. instr. St. Petersburg Jr. Coll., Hillsborough C.C., 1997, Edison C.C., 1997—. Mem. NAFE, Soc. for Clin. Coding, Am. Acad. Profl. Coders, Am. Health Info. Mgmt. Assn., Phi Theta Kappa. Avocations: sewing, cooking, boating, fishing, writing. Home: 23 Lois Ave Inglis FL 34449-9582

NORRIS, RUTH ANN, social worker; b. Leavenworth, Kans., Oct. 29, 1955; d. Ival Eugene and Maxine Barbara (Ripper) Scholtz; m. V.W. Rusty Norris, May 21, 1977. BA, Graceland Coll., 1978; MSW, U. Kans., 1988. Lic. clin. social worker. Social worker Okla. Dept. Human Svcs., Miami, 1979-82, Mo. Div. Family Svcs., Kansas City, Mo., 1982-87; clin. social worker Western Mo. Mental Health Ctr., Kansas City, 1988-97; exec. dir., pres. Ctr. for Wholeness Concepts, Independence, Mo., 1992-93; with Norris Counseling Svcs., Independence, 1993—2001; sr. social worker Truman Behavioral Health Network, Kansas City, Mo., 1997—2001; group home dir. Western Mo. Mental Health Ctr., Kansas City, Mo., 2001—. Named one of Outstanding Young Women Am., 1991. Mem. NASW, Acad. Cert. Social Workers. Avocations: volunteer counseling, reading, camping. Office: Western Mo Mental Health Ctr Esperanza House 600 E 22nd St Kansas City MO 64108 Business E-Mail: munorrr@mail.dmh.state.mo.us.

NORRIS, SANDRA LOVE, occupational therapist; b. East St. Louis, Ill., Jan. 6, 1956; d. Morrison Love and Sarah (Cameron) Miller; m. Frank Rex Norris, Aug. 15, 1987. AAS, Ill. Ctrl. Coll., 1979. Lic. occupl. therapy asst. Ill. Tchr. asst. Mamie O Stookey Sch., Belleville, Ill., 1980—83; activity therapy asst. Belleville Meml. Hosp., 1983—90, occupl. therapy asst., 1990—95, Good Samaritan Hosp., Mt. Vernon, Ill., 1995—97, Eden Village Therapy Ctr., Glen Carbon, Ill., 1997—2001, Select Therapies, Lebanon Greenville, Highland, Ill., 2002—, So. Ill. Specialized Healthcare Assocs./Anderson Hosp., Maryville, Ill., 2003—. Clin. instr. Eden Village Therapy Ctr., Glen Carbon, 1997—99. Radio reader for blind Radio Info. Svc. Shrine Lady Snows, Belleville, 1984—; vol., Buddy Program Bethany Pl. AIDS Svc. Orgn., Belleville, 1995—96. Avocations: reading, Bingo. Home: 814 N Douglas Ave Belleville IL 62220 Office: Cedar Ridge Nursing Home 1 Perryman Lebanon IL 62254

NORSTRAND, IRIS FLETCHER, psychiatrist, neurologist, educator; b. Bklyn., Nov. 21, 1915; d. Matthew Emerson and Violet Marie (Anderson) Fletcher; m. Severin Anton Norstrand, May 20, 1941; children: Virginia Helene Norstrand Villano, Thomas Fletcher, Lucille Joyce. BA, Bklyn. Coll., 1937, MA in Biochemistry, 1965, PhD in Biochemistry, 1972; MD, L.I. Coll. Medicine, 1941. Diplomate Am. Bd. Psychiatry and Neurology, cert. geriat. psychiatry. Intern Montefiore Hosp., Bronx, N.Y., 1941-42; asst. resident in neurology N.Y. Neurol. Inst.-Columbia-Presbyn. Med. Ctr., N.Y.C., 1944-45; pvt. practice Bklyn., 1947-52; resident in psychiatry Bklyn. VA Med. Ctr., 1952-54, resident in neurology, 1954-55, staff neurologist, 1955-81, asst. chief neurol. svc., 1981-91, staff psychiatrist, 1991-95. Neurol. cons. Indsl. Home for Blind, Bklyn., 1948-51; clin. prof. neurology SUNY Health Sci. Ctr., Bklyn., 1981—; attending neurologist Kings County Hosp., Bklyn., State U. Hosp., Bklyn.; cons. in field. Contbr. articles to profl. jours. Mem. Nat. Rep. Congl. Com., Rep. Senatorial Inner Circle. Recipient Spl. plaque Mil. Order Purple Heart, 1986, Spl. Achievement award PhD Alumni Assn. of CUNY, 1993, Lifetime Achievement award Bklyn. Coll., 1995, others. Fellow Am. Psychiat. Assn., Am. Acad. Neurology, Internat. Soc. Neurochemistry, Am. Assn. U. Profs. Neurology, Am. Med. EEG Soc. (pres. 1987-88), Nat. Assn. VA Physicians (pres. 1989-91, James O'Connor award 1987), N.Y. Acad. Scis., Sigma Xi. Republican. Presbyterian. Avocations: writing, piano, travel, reading. Home: 7624 10th Ave Brooklyn NY 11228-2309

NORTH, ANITA, secondary school educator; b. Chgo., Apr. 21, 1963; d. William Denson and Carol (Linden) N. BA, Ind. U., 1985; MS in Edn., Northwestern U., 1987. Cert. tchr., Ill. Social studies and English tchr. Lake Pk. High Sch., Roselle, Ill., 1987-89; social studies tchr. West Leyden High Sch., Northlake, Ill., 1989—2003, Oak Pk. River Forest High Sch., Ill., 2003—. Exch. program coord. West Leyden H.S., 1989-98, head coach boys' tennis team, 1989-97, asst. coach girls' tennis team, 1994-2000, asst. speech coach, 1992-93; adj. prof. Orgnl. Mgmt. program Concordia U., River Forest, Ill., 2000—. Docent, Chgo. Architecture Found., 2000—. Humanities fellow Nat. Coun. Humanities, 1995; recipient Fern Fine Tchg. award West Leyden H.S., 1992. Mem. Nat. Coun. for Social Studies, Ill. Coun. for Social Studies, Orgn. Am. Historians, Ill. Tennis Coaches Assn., Phi Delta Kappa. Christian. Avocations: tennis, gardening, antique books and maps, photography, architecture.

NORTH, CAROL SUE, psychiatrist, educator; b. Keokuk, Iowa, May 6, 1954; d. Ray Stemen and Doris Ethelyn (Wood) N. BS in Gen. Sci., U. Iowa, 1976; MD, Washington U., St. Louis, 1983, M in Psychiat. Epidemiology, 1993. Resident in psychiatry Barnes Hosp., Washington U. Med. Sch., St. Louis, 1983—87; rsch. fellow dept psychiatry Washington U., St. Louis, 1987-90, instr. dept. psychiatry, 1987-89, asst. prof. dept. psychiatry, 1989-97, assoc. prof. psychiatry, 1997-2001, prof., 2001—; staff psychiatrist Grace Hill Neighborhood Health Ctr., St. Louis, 1987-96, Midwest Psychiatry, 1993-95, Adapt of Am., 1995—. Author: Welcome, Silence, 1987, Multiple Personalities, Multiple Disorders: Psychiatric Classification and Media Influence, 1993; contbr. articles to profl. jours. Bd. Dirs. St. Louis Met. Alliance for the Mentally Ill, 1992-2000; trustee Rosati Stblzn. Ctr. for Homeless and Mentally Ill, 1992-94; bd. med. advisors Grace Hill Neighborhood Health Ctr., 1997—. Nat. Inst. Alcoholism and Alcohol Abuse grantee, 1988-93, Nat. Hazards Rsch. Applications Info. Ctr. grantee, 1987-88, NIMH grantee, 1991-95, 97-99, 2002-2008, Ctr. Substance Abuse Treatment grantee, 1997-2002, Nat. Inst. on Drug Abuse grantee, 1998-2003. Fellow Am. Psychiat. Assn., Am. Psychopathol. Assn.; mem. AMA, Life History Rsch. Soc., Ea. Mo. Psychiat. Soc. (exec. coun. and pres. 1996-98), Internat. Soc. Traumatic Stress Studies, Am. Acad. Clin. Psychiatrists (bd. dirs. 1999-2003), Nat. Alliance for Mentally Ill, Am. Assn. Cmty. Psychiatrists, St. Louis Track Club. Presbyterian. Avocations: distance running, oil painting, historic home rehabilitation. Office: Washington U Sch Medicine Dept Psychiatry Campus Box 8134 660 S Euclid Saint Louis MO 63110-1002

NORTH, HELEN FLORENCE, classicist, educator; b. Utica, NY; d. James H. and Catherine (Debbold) N. AB, Cornell U., 1942, MA, 1943, PhD, 1945; LLD (hon.), Rosary Coll., 1982; DLitt (hon.), Trinity Coll., Dublin, 1984, Fordham U., 1999; LHD (hon.), La Salle U., 1985, Yale U., 1986. Instr. classical lang. Rosary Coll., River Forest, Ill., 1946-48; faculty Swarthmore Coll., 1948—61, prof. classics, 1961-91, chmn. dept., 1959-91, emerita, 1991—, Centennial prof. classics, 1966-73, 78-91, Kenan prof., 1973-78, sr. rsch. scholar, 2003—. Vis. asst. prof. Cornell U., 1952—; vis. assoc. prof. Barnard Coll., 1954-55; vis. prof. LaSalle Coll., Phila., 1965, Am. Sch. Classical Studies, Athens, 1975, 87; Blegen disting. vis. rsch. prof. Vassar Coll., 1979. Author: Sophrosyne: Self-Knowledge and Self-Restraint in Greek Literature, 1966, From Myth to Icon: Reflections of Greek Ethical Doctrine in Literature and Art, 1979, (with Mary C. North) The West of Ireland: A Megalithic Primer, 1999, Cork and the Rest of Ireland: A Megalithic Primer II, 2003; translator: John Milton's Second Defense of the English People, 1966; editor: Interpretations of Plato. A Swarthmore Symposium, 1977; co-editor: Of Eloquence, 1970; editor Jour. History of Ideas; mem. editl. bd. Catalogus Translationum et Commentariorum, 1979[00bf] . Bd. dirs. Am. Coun. Learned Socs., 1977-85; trustee LaSalle U., 1972-2003, chmn. bd. trustees, 1991-93; trustee King's Coll., Am. Acad. in Rome; chmn. com. on Classical Sch. Recipient Harbison prize Danforth Found., 1969, Centennial medal Am. Acad. Rome, 1995; named Distinguished Daughter of Pa., 1989, del. of Am. Philological Assn. to Am. Coun. Learned Socs., 1991-95; grantee Am. Coun. Learned Socs., 1943-45, 73, fellow, 1971-72, 87-88; Mary Isabel Sibley fellow Phi Beta Kappa Found., 1945-46, Ford Fund Advancement Edn. fellow, Fulbright fellow Rome, 1953-54, Guggenheim fellow, 1958-59, 75-76, AAUW, 1963-64; grantee Danforth Found., 1962, Lindbach Found., 1966; Sr. fellow NEH, 1967-68; NEH Coll. Tchrs. fellow, 1983-84; Martin classical lectr. Oberlin Coll., 1972. Mem. Am. Philol. Assn. (dir. 1968—, pres. 1976—, Charles J. Goodwin award 1969, Disting. Svc. medal 1996), Classical Assn. Atlantic States, Cath. Commn. Intellectual and Cultural Affairs (chmn. 1968-69), Am. Acad. Arts and Scis., Am. Philos. Soc., Soc. Religion Higher Edn., Phi Beta Kappa (bd. vis. scholars 1975-76, senate 1991—2003), Phi Kappa Phi. Home: 604 Ogden Ave Swarthmore PA 19081-1131 E-mail: hnorth1@swarthmore.edu.

NORTH, KATHRYN E. KEESEY (MRS. EUGENE C. NORTH), retired educator; b. Columbia, Pa., Jan. 25, 1916; d. Isaac and Elizabeth (French) Keesey; B.S., Ithaca Coll., 1938; M.A., N.Y. U., 1950; m. Eugene C. North, Aug. 18, 1938. Dir. music Cairo (N.Y.) Central Sch. Dist., 1938; music edn. cons. Argyle (N.Y.) Central Sch. Dist., 1939; dir. gen. music curriculum Hartford (N.Y.) Central Sch. Dist., 1939; mem. staff Del. Dept. Pub. Instrn., Dover, 1943; dir. music edn. Herricks (N.Y.) Pub. Schs., 1944-71; ret., 1971. Vis. lectr. Ithaca Coll., summers 1959, 60, 62-65, Fairleigh-Dickinson U., Rutherford, N.J., summer 1966, Albertus Magnus Coll., New Haven, summer 1968; instr. Adelphi Coll., 1954-55, Sch.. Edn., N.Y.U., 1964-65. Mem. Music Educators Nat. Conf., N.E.A., N.Y. State Sch. Music Assn., N.Y. State Tchrs. Assn., Nassau Music Educators Assn. (exec. bd. 1947-58), N.Y. State Council Adminstrs. Music Edn. (chpt. v.p. 1967-68), Herricks Tchrs. Assn. (pres. 1948), Sigma Alpha Iota. Mem. Order Eastern Star. Home: 1645 Calle Camille La Jolla CA 92037-7107

NORTH, MARJORIE MARY, columnist; b. Mt. Clemens, Mich., Oct. 21, 1945; d. Robert Haller and Hilla Beryl (Willard) Wright; m. William B. Hirons; children: Laura, Christina, Angela. Student, Wayne State U., 1963—66. Features editor Elizabeth City (N.C.) Daily Advance, 1966-69; news/mng. editor Brandon (Fla.) News, 1977-78; city editor Leesburg (Fla.) Comml., 1978-79; metro editor Sarasota (Fla.) Herald Tribune, 1979-80, Fla. West editor, 1980-85, daily columnist, 1985—. Host Weekly Interview Show, SNN-TV, 1997—. Author: Sarasota: A City For All Seasons, 1994, (plays) With the Best Intentions, 1994, Back in the Game, 1998. Recipient Layout, Creativity and Overall Publ. awards Fla. Press Assn., numerous comty. awards and citations; winner Fla. shorts competition Fla. Studio Theater New Play Festival, 1994, 98; Paul Harris fellow. Avocations: tennis, entertaining, theater. Office: Sarasota Herald-Tribune PO Box 1719 Sarasota FL 34230-1719 E-mail: mnorth10@comcast.net.

NORTHERN, ERNESTINE, gifted and talented educator; d. Ella and Ernest Northern; children: Imoni Unique, Dana Ferron. M in ednl. adminstrn., U. of So., 2002—03. Tchr. Atlanta Pub. Schools, Atlanta, Ga., 1994—; site leader Ga. Reading Challenge, Atlanta, Ga., 2000—01. Author: Language Arts Handbook Strategy for Success, 2000. Recipient Coun. for Exceptional Children Classroom award, Coun. for Exceptional Children, 2001—02. Mem.: Coun. for Exceptional Children (assoc.). Non-Denominational. Achievements include development of Project Friends, an intergenerational group of students and community residents.

NORTHUP, ANNE MEAGHER, congresswoman; b. Louisville, Ky., Jan. 22, 1948; d. James L. and Floy Gates (Terstegge) Meagher; m. Robert Wood Northup, Apr. 12, 1969; children: David, Katherine, Joshua, Kevin, Erin, Mark. BA in Econs. and Bus., St. Mary's Coll. Notre Dame, South Bend, Ind., 1970. Mem. Ky. Ho. of Reps., Frankfort, 1987-96, U.S. Congress from 3d Ky. Dist., 1997—; mem. house appropriations com.; founder House Reading Caucus, 1998; mem. speaker's drug free task force, 1998; chair speaker's task force on education, 1998; mem. World Trade Org. congl. advisory group, 1999, free trade working group, 2000, comm. on educational accountability, 1993—95, economic development task force, 1991—92, task force to study highway needs, 1990—91, state debt capacity task force. Mem. fin. adv. bd. EPA, 1989-93; mem. home econs. adv. bd. U. Ky. Coll. Agr., 1992— Appeared on Meet the Press, Fox News Sunday, Larry King Live, CNN & Co., Hardball with Chris Matthews. Mem. exec. com. Partnership Ky. Sch. Reform, 1990—; bd. dirs. Greater Louisville Pub. Radio, 1993—, Hospice Louisville, 1994—, Ky. Cancer Consortium, 1992—; mem. cmty. adv. bd. Jr. League Louisville, 1993—; active Holy Spirit Cath. Ch. Named Outstanding Woman of Achievement St. Matthews BPW, 1990; recipient Cath. Schs. Disting. Alumni award, 1991, U. Notre Dame award of the yr. Ky. Alumni Assn., 1991, Clearing the Air award Am. Lung Assn. of Ky., 1991, Svc. Above Self award St. Matthews Rotary Club, 1992, Pub. Svc. award Am. Heart Assn., 1992, Sacred Heart Acad. Alumna award, 1994, Nat. Fedn. of Ind. Bus./Guardian of Small Bus. award, 1996, 97, 98, Legislator of Yr. award Environ. Industry Assn., 1997, Outstanding Freshman Mem. of Congress award Nat. Industries for Blind, 1997, Spirit of Enterprise award U.S. C. of C., 1997, Bulldog award Watchdogs of Treasury, 1998, Jefferson award Citizens for Sound Economy, 1998, Outstanding Support award Am. Printing House for Blind, 1998, Legislator of Yr. award Assn. Equipment Distbrs., 1999, Cmty. Healthcare Champion award Nat. Assn. Cmty. Health Ctrs., Inc., 1999, Spirit of Enterprise award C. of C., 1999, Susan B. Anthony Congl. award, 1999, Pub. Policy Adv. of Yr. award Nat. Assn. Women Bus. Owners, 1999, Honor Roll of Legis. Achievement in Econ. Devel. award So. Econ. Devel. Coun., Inc., 1999, Legislator of Yr. award Nat. Beer Whoesalers Assn., 1999. Mem. Nat. Order Women Legislators, Nat. Conf. State Legislators, Nat. Rep. Legis. Conf., Inst. Rep. Women, So. Legis. Conf. (alternate from Ky. to fiscal affairs and govtl. com.), Nat. Fedn. Ind. Bus. Republican. Roman Catholic. Office: US Ho Reps 1004 Longworth House Office Bl Washington DC 20515-1703*

NORTHWAY, WANDA I. real estate company executive; b. Columbia, Mo., July 11, 1942; d. Herman W. and Goldie M. (Wood) Proctor; m. Donald H. Northway, June 12, 1965; 1 child, Michelle D. RN, U. Mo. Lic. real estate agt. Mo., grad. Realtors Inst. Realtor, 1970—81; co-owner, pres., realtor, ptnr. House of Brokers Realty, Inc., Columbia, 1981—. Pres., organizer Realtor-Assoc. Sales Club, Columbia, 1975; pres. Columbia Bd. Realtors, 1982. Contbr. articles to realty mags. Vol. ARS, local hosp.; mem. allocation com. United Way; active vol. Am. Cancer Soc. and Heart Assn.; campaign worker for various legislators; Sunday sch. tchr., girls' aux. leader Bapt. Ch. Named Realtor Assoc. of Yr., Columbia Bd. Realtors, 1974, Realtor of Yr., 1980. Mem.: Nat. Assn. Realtors (nat. dir. 1977), Realtors Nat. Mktg. Inst. (cert. residential specialist 1978), Mo. Assn. Realtors (state dir. 1974—77, Realtor Assoc. of Yr. 1977), Epsilon Sigma Alpha (state corr. sec., local pres.). Baptist. Office: House of Brokers Realty Inc 1515 Chapel Hill Rd Columbia MO 65203-5457

NORTON, ELEANOR HOLMES, congresswoman, lawyer, educator; b. Washington, June 13, 1937; d. Coleman and Vela (Lynch) Holmes; m. Edward W. Norton (div.); children: Katherine Felicia, John Holmes. BA, Antioch Coll., 1960; MA in Am. Studies, Yale U., 1963, LLB, 1964. Bar: Pa., 1965, U.S. Supreme Ct., 1968. Law clk. to Judge A. Leon Higgonbotham Fed. Dist. Ct., 1964-65; asst. legal dir. ACLU, 1965-70; exec. asst. to mayor City of N.Y., 1971-74; chmn. N.Y.C. Commn. on Human Rights, 1970-77, EEOC, Washington, 1977-81; sr. fellow Urban Inst., Washington, 1981-82; prof. law Georgetown U., Washington, 1982—; del. (at large) U.S. Congress from D.C., 1990—; mem. coms. on govt. reform and transp./infrastructure. Democrat. Office: US Ho of Reps 2136 RayburnHo Office Bldg Washington DC 20515-0001*

NORTON, ELIZABETH WYCHGEL, lawyer; b. Cleve., Mar. 25, 1933; d. James Nicolas and Ruth Elizabeth (Cannell) Wychgel; m. Henry Wacks Norton Jr., July 16, 1954 (div. 1971); children: James, Henry, Peter, Fred; m. James Cory Ferguson, Dec. 14, 1985 (div. Apr. 1988). BA in Math., Wellesley Coll., 1954; JD cum laude, U. Minn., 1974. Bar: Minn. 1974. Summer intern Minn. Atty. Gen.'s Office, St. Paul, 1972; with U.S. Dept. Treasury, St. Paul, 1973; assoc. Gray, Plant, Mooty, Mooty & Bennett, P.A., Mpls., 1974-79, prin., 1980-94, of counsel, 1995-96. Mem. Minn. Lawyers Bd. Profl. Responsibility, 1984-89; mem. U. Minn. Law Sch. Bd. Visitors, 1987-92. Trustee YWCA, Mpls., 1979-84, 89-91, co-chmn. deferred giving com., 1980-81, chmn. by-laws com., bd. dirs., 1976-77, lectr.; treas. Minn. Women's Campaign Fund, 1985, guarantor, 1982-83, budget and fin. com. bd. dirs., 1984-87; trustee Ripley Meml. Found., 1980-84; treas. Jones-Harrison Home, 1967, bd. dirs., 1962-69, 2d v.p., chmn. fin., 1968-69; mem. Sen. David Durenberger's Women's Network, 1983-88. Durant scholar. Fellow Am. Bar Found.; mem. ABA (mediation task force family law sect. 1983-84), Minn. Bar Assn. (human rights com. family law sect., task force uniform marital property act 1984-85), Minn. Bar Found. (dir. 1991-94), Hennepin County Bar Assn. (pres. 1987-88, chmn. task force on pub. edn. 1984, chmn., mem. exec. com. family law sect. 1979-94), Minn. Inst. Legal Edn., Minn. Women's Lawyers (exec. com.), Hemlock Soc. of S.W. Fla. (co-chmn. 1999-2001), U. Minn. Law Sch. Alumni Assn. (dir. 1975-81, exec. com. 1981-83), Wellesley Club (Naples, pres. 2002-04), Phi Beta Kappa. Home: 26 Water Oaks Way Naples FL 34105-7157

NORTON, FRAN, parks and recreation director; b. July 5, 1950; m. Richard Spitz, Jr. BFA, Rochester Inst. Tech., 1972. Park technician Frederick Douglass NHS Nat. Parks-East, Washington, 1972-75; supr. park technician John F. Kennedy Ctr. Performing Arts, Washington, 1975-80; supr. park ranger Klingle Resource Ctr. Nat. Capital Region, Washington, 1980-81, regional vol., grants mgr., 1982-84, supr. park ranger Career Conservation Devel. Corp., 1990; self employed Annapolis, Md., 1984-90; site mgr. Arlington House, Robert E. Lee Meml. George Washington Meml. Pkwy., McLean, Va., 1993-94; unit mgr. cultural resources, site mgr. Arlington House Clara Barton NHS, Glen Echo Park, Women in Mil. Svc. Am., McLean, 1994-98; chief ranger, divsn. interpretation Ft. Sumter, Sullivan's Is., S.C., 1998—. Office: 1214 Middle St Sullivans Island SC 29482-9717 Fax: 843-883-3910.

NORTON, GALE ANN, secretary of interior; b. Wichita, Mar. 11, 1954; d. Dale Bentsen and Anna Jacqueline (Lansdowne) N.; m. John Goethe Hughes, Mar. 26, 1990. BA, U. Denver, 1975, JD, 1978. Bar: Colo. 1978, U.S. Supreme Ct. 1981. Jud. clk. Colo. Ct. of Appeals, Denver, 1978-79; sr. atty. Mountain States Legal Found., Denver, 1979-83; nat. fellow Hoover Instn. Stanford (Calif.) U., 1983-84; asst. to dep. sec. USDA, Washington, 1984-85; assoc. solicitor U.S. Dept. of Interior, Washington, 1985-87; pvt. practice law Denver, 1987-90; atty. gen. State of Colo., Denver, 1991—99; sr. counsel Brownstein, Hyatt & Farber, P.C., 1999—2000; sec. U.S. Dept. Interior, Washington, 2001—. Lectr. U. Denver Law Sch., 1989; transp. law program dir. U. Denver, 1978-79. Contbr. chpts. to books, articles to profl. jours. Past chair Nat. Assn. Attys. Gen. Environ. Com.; co-chair Nat. Policy Forum Environ. Coun.; candidate for 1996 election to U.S. Senate; chair environ. commn. Rep. Nat. Lawyers Assn. Named Young Career Woman Bus. and Profl. Women, 1981, Young Lawyer of Yr., 1991, Mary Lathrop Trailblazer award Colo. Women's Bar Assn., 1999. Mem. Federalist Soc., Colo. Women's Forum, Order of St. Ives. Republican. Methodist. Avocation: skiing. Office: Dept of the Interior Office of the Sec 1849 C St NW Washington DC 20240

NORTON, JANE E. lieutenant governor; b. Grand Junction, Colo. d. Bus and Elinor Bergman; m. Mike Norton; children: Lacee, Tyler. BS, Colo. State U., 1976; MS in Mgmt., Regis U. With Med. Group Mgmt. Assn., Englewood, Colo.; mem. Colo. Ho. Reps., 1986—87; regional dir. U.S. Dept. Health and Human Svcs.; exec. dir. Colo. Dept. Pub. Health Environment, 1999—2002; lt. gov. Colo., 2003—. Chair Colo. Commn. on Indian Affairs. Republican. Office: 130 State Capitol Denver CO 80203

NORTON, KAREN ANN, accountant; b. Nov. 1, 1950; d. Dale Francis and Ruby Grace (Gehlhar) N. BA, U. Minn., 1972; postgrad., U. Md., 1978; MBA, Calif. State Poly. U., Pomona, 1989. CPA, Md. Securities transactions analyst Bur. of Pub. Debt, Washington, 1972-79, internal auditor, 1979-81, IRS, Washington, 1981; sr. acct. World Vision Internat., Monrovia, Calif., 1981-83, acctg. supr., 1983-87; sr. sys. liaison coord. Home Savs. Am. (name changed to Washington Mut.), 1987-97, sys. auditor, 1997-2000, sect. mgr., 2000—02, group mgr., v.p., 2003—. Author: (poetry) Ode to Joyce, 1985 (Golden Poet award 1985). 2d v.p. chpt. Nat. Treasury Employees Union, Washington, 1978, editor chpt. newsletter; mem. M-2 Prisoners Sponsorship Program, Chino, Calif., 1984-86. Recipient Spl. Achievement award Dept. Treasury, 1976, Superior Performance award Dept. Treasury, 1977-78; Charles and Ellora Alliss scholar, 1968. Mem. Angel Flight, Flying Samaritans. Avocations: flying, chess, racquetball, whitewater rafting.

NORTON, LINDA LEE, pharmacist, educator; b. Vallejo, Calif., Aug. 12, 1953; d. Don Leroy and Pearl Etta (Cain) Hartzell; m. Lawrence Henry Norton, Aug. 19, 1972; children: Joshua David, Gabriel Aaron. PharmD, U. Pacific, 1991. Lic. pharmacist, Calif., Nev. Pharmacy resident St. Joseph's Med. Ctr., Stockton, Calif., 1991-92, U. Ariz., Tucson, 1992-93; fellow in pain rsch. and drug info. U. of Pacific and Am. Acad. Pain Mgmt., Stockton, 1993-95; asst. prof. pharmacy practice U. of Pacific, Stockton, 1995-99, assoc. coord. postgrad. profl. edn., 1995-99, assoc. prof., dir. postgrad. profl. edn., 1999—. Mng. editor Enjoying Good Health, 1997-99; contbr. articles to profl. jours. Mem. shared governance com. Liberty Union H.S., Brentwood, Calif., 1995-97, health careers acad. com., 1995-97; bd. dirs. SMART Coalition, Sacramento, 1998-2000. Recipient Award for outstanding article in pain mgmt. Am. Jour. Pain Mgmt., 1997; grantee Valley Mountain Reg. Ctr., 1998-2000, Diagnostek, 1994; Thomas J. Long Faculty fellow, 1997, 98, 2000-03. Mem. Am. Assn. Colls. Pharmacy (chmn. CPE sect. 2001-2003), Am. Soc. Health-Sys. Pharmacists, Calif. Soc. Health-Sys. Pharmacists (co-chair C.E. Focus '98), Rho Chi. Avocations: small-scale farming and ranching, horse shoe pitching, fishing. Office: Univ Pacific Sch Pharmacy 751 Brookside Rd Stockton CA 95211-0001

NORTON, MARY BETH, history educator, writer; b. Ann Arbor, Mich., Mar. 25, 1943; d. Clark Frederic and Mary Elizabeth (Lunny) N. BA, U. Mich., 1964; MA, Harvard U., 1965, PhD, 1969; DHL (hon.), Siena Coll., 1983, Marymount Manhattan Coll., 1984, De Pauw U., 1989; DLitt (hon.), Ill. Wesleyan U., 1992. Asst. prof. history U. Conn., Storrs, 1969-71; from asst. prof. to prof. Cornell U., Ithaca, NY, 1971-87, Mary Donlon Alger prof. Am. history, 1987—. Author: The British-Americans: The Loyalist Exiles in England, 1774-1789, 1972, Liberty's Daughters: The Revolutionary Experience of American Women, 1750-1800, 1980 (Berkshire prize for Best Book Woman Historian 1980), Founding Mothers and Fathers: Gendered Power and the Forming of American Society, 1996 (finalist Pulitzer prize in history 1997), In the Devil's Snare: The Salem Witchcraft Crisis of 1692, 2002 (Amb. Book award of English-Speaking Union 2003); co-author: A People and A Nation, 1982, 7th rev. edit., 2004; editor: AHA Guide to Hist. Literature, 3d rev. edit., 1995; co-editor: Women of America: A History, 1979, To Toil the Livelong Day: America's Women at Work, 1790-1980, 1987, Major Problems in American Women's History, 1989, 3d rev. edit., 2003; contbr. articles to profl. jours. Trustee Cornell U., 1973-75, 83-88; mem. Nat. Coun. Humanities, Washington, 1979-84. Woodrow Wilson Found. fellow, 1964-65, NEH fellow, 1974-75, Shelby Cullom Davis Ctr. fellow Princeton U., 1977-78, Rockefeller Found. fellow, 1986-87, Soc. for Humanities fellow Cornell U., 1989-90, John Simon Guggenheim Meml. Found. fellow, 1993-94, Starr Found. fellow Lady Margaret Hall, Oxford U., 2000, Mellon postdoctoral fellow Huntington Libr., 2001. Fellow Soc. Am. Hist. (exec. bd. 1974-87, 2003—, Allan Nevins prize 1970); mem. Am. Hist. Assn. (v.p. for rsch. 1985-87), Am. Acad. Arts and Sci., Orgn. Am. Hist. (exec. bd. 1983-86), Berkshire Conf. Women Hist. (pres. 1983-85) Democrat. Methodist. Office: Cornell U Dept History 325 Mcgraw Hall Ithaca NY 14853-4601 E-mail: mbn1@cornell.edu.

NORTWEN, PATRICIA HARMAN, music educator; b. New Ulm, Minn., Mar. 6, 1930; d. Joseph Absolom and Viola Maureen (Stroud) Harman; m. Dallas Ernest Andrew Nortwen, Dec. 22, 1956; children: Laura Lee, Daniel Harman. BA magna cum laude, U. Minn., 1952, BS in Edn., MA, U. Minn., 1956. Tchr. music N.W. Sch., U. Minn., Crookston, 1952-54; instr. music S.D. State U., Brookings, 1954-56; tchr. music Robbinsdale (Minn.) Jr. H.S., 1956-57; music dir. Bethlehem Luth. Ch., Mpls., 1957-67; instr. music Golden Valley Luth. Coll., Mpls., 1967-85; ind. music tchr., Mpls., 1957—. Performer Early Music Consort, also others; prodr. (cable TV series) Women/Music, 1984-85; author, mng. editor: Music Theory Workbook, Vols. 1-6, 1993-96. Bd. dirs., sec., pres. Civic Orch. Mpls., 1989-94; cmty. adv. bd. U. Minn. Sch. Music, 1998—. Mem.: Thursday Mus. (pres. 1988—92, various offices 1992—97, devel. chair 1997—, treas. 2004—), Young Peoples Symphony Concert Assn. (v.p. 1992—2000), U. Minn. Sch. Music Alumni Coun. (chair 1997—99), Minn. Music Tchrs. Assn. (chair edn. found. 1995—97, pres.-elect 1997—99, pres. 1999—2001, found. bd. dirs. 2000—02, found. treas. 2002), Frederic Chopin Soc. (sec. 1992—96, bd. dirs. 1992—), Music Tchrs. Nat. Assn., Phi Beta Kappa, Sigma Alpha Iota (province officer 1975—85, nat. dir. 1975—89, 1998—, Nat. Leadership award 1952, Ring of Excellence award 1990). Avocations: reading, singing, hiking, fishing, knitting. Home: 210 W Grant St Apt 313 Minneapolis MN 55403-2244 E-mail: pdnortwen@juno.com.

NORVILLE, DEBORAH ANNE, news correspondent; b. Aug. 8, 1958; d. Zachary S. and Merle Olson Norville; m. Karl G. Wellner Dec. 12, 1987; children: Karl Nikolai, Kyle Maximilian, Mikaela Katharina. BJ, U. Ga., 1979. Reporter Sta. WAGA-TV, Atlanta, 1978-79, anchor, reporter, 1979-81, Sta. WMAQ-TV, Chgo., 1982-86; anchor NBC News, N.Y.C., 1987-89; news anchor Today Show, NBC, N.Y.C., 1989, co-anchor, 1990-92; corr. Street Stories, CBS, N.Y.C., 1992-94; co-anchor America Tonight, CBS, N.Y.C., 1994; anchor Inside Edition, King World Produs., 1994—; contbg. editor McCall's, N.Y.C.; host Deborah Norville Tonight MSNBC, N.Y.C., 2004—. Author: Back on Track: How to Straighten Out Your Life When it Throws You a Curve, 1997, I Don't Want To Sleep Tonight, 1999, I Can Fly, 2001. Bd. dirs. Greater N.Y. coun. Girl Scouts U.S., 1989-, Broadcaster's Found.; mem. steering com. Rita Hayworth Gala Alzheimer's Assn; nat. celebrity spokesperson Mother's March of Dimes, 2001, 02. Recipient Outstanding Young Alumni award Sch. Journalism, U. Ga., Emmy award, 1985-86, 89, Gracie Award, Am. Women in Radio and TV; named Person of Yr., Chgo. Broadcast Advt. Club, 1989, 91, Anchor of Yr. 2000, Washington Journalism Rev., 1989. Mem. Soc. Profl. Journalists. Office: Inside Edition King World Prod 515 W 57th St New York NY 10019-2901*

NORWALK, KELLI CURRAN, retail executive, entrepreneur; b. Cleve., Sept. 25, 1949; d. Paul Joseph and Ella (Eylar) Curran; m. Keith Otto Norwalk, Apr. 3, 1970; children: Keith Curran, Alyssa Barr. BA, Butler U., 1978. Exec. dir. Heritage Place, Indpls., 1975-77; social worker Americana Health Care, Indpls., 1978-81; pres., prin. Down By the Ducks, Inc., Indpls., 1982-85; chief exec. officer, prin. The Tarkington Tweed, Inc., Indpls., 1985—. Chmn. Spotlight, 2001, 02. Mem. Butler Tarkington Neithborhood Assn., Indpls., 1978—, Arts, Ind. Finalist Entrepreneur of Yr. award Ernst and Young Ind. Heartland, 1998. Mem. 500 Festival Assocs., Indpls. C. of C. Democrat. Roman Catholic. Avocations: painting, theatre, travel. Home: 5534 Bay Landing Ct Indianapolis IN 46254-9564 Office: The Tarkington Tweed Inc 5631 N Illinois St Indianapolis IN 46208-1554

NORWOOD, BRANDY, singer, actress; b. McComb, Miss., Feb. 11, 1979; d. Willie and Sonia Norwood. Student, Pepperdine U. Actress (sitcoms TV series) Thea, 1996, Moesha, 1995—2001, rec. artist (albums) Brandy, 1994, Never S-A-Y Never, 1998, Full Moon, 2002; actor: (films) I Still Know What You Did Last Summer, 1998; voice Osmosis Jones, 2001. Named Favorite New Artist, Am. Music Awards, 1996; recipient Grammy award, 1996. Office: 15030 Ventura Blvd 710 Sherman Oaks CA 91403

NORWOOD, CAROLYN VIRGINIA, business educator; b. Florence, S.C., Dec. 11; d. James Henry and Mildred (Jones) N. BS, N.C. A&T State U., 1956; MA, Columbia U., 1959; postgrad., Seton Hall U., Temple U.; cert. scholarly distinction, Nat. Acad. Paralegal Studies, 1991. Instr. Gibbs Jr. Coll., St. Petersburg, Fla., Fayetteville State U., N.C.; asst. prof. C.C. Phila.; prof. Essex County Coll., Newark, 1968—. Cons. Mercer County Coll., Trenton, N.J.; mem. assessment team Lehman Coll., Bronx, N.Y., Mid.-States Commn., Phila., 1980—; vol. tutor Newark Literacy Campaign, 1998—. Co-author: Alphabetic Indexing, 6th edit., 1999. Mem. Nat. Coun. on Black Am. Affairs, AACC; vol. tutor Newark Literacy Campaign. Recipient EDDY award Gregg/McGraw-Hill Co., N.Y.C., 1986, cert. of recognition of outstanding and dedicated svc. Mid. States Assn. Colls. and Schs., Commn. on Higher Edn., 1994; profiled in NBEA Yearbook chpt. on Leadership in Bus. Edn., 1993; postdoctoral fellow Temple U., 1977-78. Mem. AAUW, NAACP, Nat. Coun. Black Am. Affairs, Nat. Bus. Edn. Assn. (bd. dirs. 1982-85), Ea. Bus. Edn. Assn. (pres. 1986-87, membership dir. 1976-85, Educator of the Yr. 1994), Nat. Coun. Negro Women, N.J. Bus. Edn. Assn., Alpha Kappa Alpha, Phi Delta Kappa, Delta Pi Epsilon. Avocations: bowling, photography. Office: Essex County Coll 303 University Ave Newark NJ 07102-1719

NORWOOD, CECILIA STUBBS, communications executive; b. Kansas City, Mo. married. BBA cum laude, MBA in Mktg. summa cum laude, U. North Tex. Analyst Exxon Co. U.S., 1978, sales rep. for dealer operated stores in North Tex. region, mkt. devel. analyst; v.p. corp. comms. Southland Corp., until 1996; corp. v.p. global comms. Electronic Data Sys. Corp., Plano, Tex., 1996—. Chair Conf. Bd. Coun. Corp. Comms. Strategy; pres. Dallas chpt. Nat. Investor Rels. Inst., So. Meth. U. Coll. Comms. Adv. Bd.; active U. North Tex. Pres.'s Coun.; bd. dirs. Planned Parenthood Dallas, Planned Parenthood Northeast Tex., Dallas Women's Found. Recipient Clarion award. Office: Electronic Data Sys Corp 5400 Legacy Dr Plano TX 75024-3199 Fax: 972-605-2643.

NORWOOD, DEBORAH ANNE, law librarian; b. Honolulu, Nov. 12, 1950; d. Alfred Freeman and Helen G. (Papsch) N.; 1 child, Nicholas. BA, U. Wash., 1972, M in Law Librarianship, 1979; JD, Willamette U., 1974. Bar: Wash., U.S. Dist. Ct. (we. dist.) 1975, U.S. Ct. Appeals (9th cir.) 1980. Ptnr. Evans and Norwood, Seattle, 1975-79; law libr. U.S. Courts Libr., Seattle, 1980-89; state law libr. Wash. State Law Libr., Olympia, 1989—2002, reporter of decisions, 1994-2001; asst. dir. pub. svcs. Jacob Burns Law Libr. George Washington U., Washington, 2002—. Mem. Freedom to Read Found. Mem. Am. Assn. Law Librs. (chmn. state, ct. and county spl. interest sect. 1995-96, chair legal info. svcs. to pub. spl. interest sect. 2001-02). Office: Jacob Burns Law Libr George Washington U 716-20th St NW Washington DC 20052 Office Phone: 202-994-7338. E-mail: dnorwood@law.gwu.edu.

NORWOOD, JANET LIPPE, economist; b. Newark, Dec. 11, 1923; d. M. Turner and Thelma (Levinson) Lippe; m. Bernard Norwood, June 25, 1943; children: Stephen Harlan, Peter Carlton. BA, Douglass Coll., 1945; MA, Tufts U., 1946; PhD, Fletcher Sch. Law and Diplomacy, 1949; LLD (hon.), Fla. Internat. U., 1979, Carnegie Mellon U., 1984, Harvard U., 1997, Rutgers U., 2003. Instr. Wellesley Coll., 1948-49; economist William L. Clayton Ctr., Tufts U., 1953-58; with Bur. Labor Stats., U.S. Dept. Labor, Washington, 1963-91; dep. commr., then acting commr. Bur. Labor Stats. Dept. Labor, Washington, 1975-79, commr. labor stats., 1979-92; sr. fellow The Urban Inst., Washington, 1992-99; counselor, sr. fellow N.Y. Conf. Bd., 2001—. Dir. Nat. Opinion Rsch. Ctr., chair adv. coun. unemployment compensation, 1993—96; dir. Inst. Global Ethics; chair panel to rev. 2000 census NAS; mem. adv. bd. Bur. Transp. Stats.; pres. COSSA, 2001—02. Author: Organizing to Count: Change in the Federal Statistical System, 1995; contbr. Named Hall Disting. Alumni, Rutgers U., 1987; recipient Disting. Achievement award, Dept. Labor, 1972, Spl. Commendation award, 1977, Philip Arnow award, 1979, Elmer Staats award, 1982, Pub. Svc. award, 1984, Presdl. Disting. Exec. Rank, 1988, Elizabeth Scott award, Com. Pres.'s Statis. Assns., 2002. Fellow: AAAS, Nat. Assn. Bus. Economists, Royal Statis. Soc., Am. Statis. Assn. (pres. 1989, Founder's award 1997); mem.: Nat. Inst. Statis. Sci. (bd. trustees 1991—2000), Nat. Acad. Pub. Adminstrn., Am. Econ. Assn., Internat. Assn. Ofcls. Stats., Internat. Statis. Inst., Douglass Coll. Soc. Disting. Achievement, Cosmos Club (pres. 1995—96). Home: 5610 Wisconsin Ave Ph 21-d Chevy Chase MD 20815-4444 E-mail: janetnor@aol.com.

NORWOOD, PHYLLIS KATHERENE, director, educator; d. E. Terrell Holloway and Emily Jane Gray; m. John M. Norwood (div. May 26, 1984); children: Gregory, Denetra. BS, Jackson State U., 1964; MA in English, Calif. State U., Dominguez Hills, 1981. English tchr. Burgland H.S., McComb, Miss., 1963—64; libr. J.E. Johnson H.S., Prentis, Miss., 1964—66; English prof. L.A. C.C. Dist., 1966—; dir. workforce edn. L.A. C.C., 1987—. Bd. mem. Eureka Arts Soc., L.A., 1989—95, NETWORK, Washington, 1992—96. Recipient Commendation/Citation, Excellence for Econ. Devel. Excellence, L.A. County Excellence in Welfare to Work Program. Mem.: Nat. Coun. English (assoc.), Top Ladies Distinction (assoc.), Alpha Kappa Alpha (assoc. Honored by Mu Bega Omega Chpt. for establishing Partnership in Math and Sci. for disadvantaged youth). Office: Los Angeles Cmty Coll Dist 1600 West Imperial Hwy Los Angeles CA 90047 Personal E-mail: norwoopk@lasc.cc.ca.us E-mail: norwoopk@lasc.cc.ca.us.

NORWOOD, VIRGINIA TOWER, retired engineer; b. Ft. Totten, N.Y., Jan. 8, 1927; d. John Vogler and Eleanor (Monroe) Tower; m. Lawrence Norwood, June 5, 1947; children: Naomi, Peter, David; m. Maurice Schaeffer, Dec. 29, 1982. BS, MIT, 1947. Physicist Signal Corps Engring. Labs., Belmar, N.J., 1948-53; sr. engr. Sylvania Electronic Def. Lab., Sunnyvale, Calif., 1953-54; lab. scientist Hughes Aircraft Co., Culver City, Calif., 1954-90; cons. Aerospace Corp., El Segundo, Calif., 1992-93; ret., 1993. Patentee in field; contbr. articles to profl. publs., chpt. to book. Mem. corp. vis. com. MIT, Cambridge, 1976-78. Recipient WIlliam Pecora award U.S. Dept. Interior and NASA, 1979, Woman of Yr. in Sci. award YWCA, L.A., 1980. Mem. IEEE (life, sr., profl. group sec.), Sigma Xi (emeritus). Avocation: antique clock repair and restoration. Home: 1289 Old Topanga Canyon Rd Topanga CA 90290-3829

NOSANOW, BARBARA SHISSLER, art association administrator; b. Roanoke, Va. d. Willis Morton and Kathryn Sabin (Bradford) Johnson; m. John Lewis Shissler Jr., July 28, 1957 (dec. May 1972); children: John Lewis Shissler III, Ada Holland Shissler; m. Lewis Harold Nosanow, Oct. 15, 1973. AB, Smith Coll., 1957; MA, Case Western Res. U., 1958. Asst. mng. editor Jour. Aesthetics and Art Criticism, Cleve. Mus. Art, 1958-63; dir. publs. and rsch. Mpls. Inst. Arts, 1963-72; dir. U. Minn. Art Mus., Mpls., 1972-76; dir. exhbns. and edn. Nat. Archives, Washington, 1976-79; curator Smithsonian Instn., Washington, 1979-82; asst. dir. Nat. Mus. Am. Art, Smithsonian Instn., 1982-88; dir. Portland (Maine) Mus. Art, 1988-93, Art Spaces, 1993—; study leader, lecturer Smithsonian Study Tours of France and Russia, 1997—. Lectr. art history, also author. Past mem. various rev. panels NEH, Washington. Bd. dirs. Md. Com. for Humanities, Balt., 1980-83. Mem. Internat. Women's Forum. Avocation: travel. Office: Art Spaces 3386 Piperfife Ct Keswick VA 22947-9142

NOSSAMAN, MARIAN ALECIA, manufacturing engineering executive; b. Kansas City, Mo., Apr. 26, 1961; d. M.A. and Ellen Ardena (Hume) Nossaman; m. Michael Keith Taylor, July 26, 1986 (div.); children: Alecia Ellen, Nathaniel Alexander. AA, Johnson County C.C., 1989; BSME, BS in Bus., U. Kans., 1993. Dental asst. SE Brotherson DDS, Kansas City, Kans., 1983-85; dental instr. Kansas City Coll. of Med. and Dental Careers, Overland Park, 1985-86; math tutor Overland Park, 1988-91; tech. writer ArComm, Lenexa, Kans., 1991-92; total quality mgmt. rschr. U. Kans., Lawrence, 1992-93; process engr. Symbios Logic Inc., Ft. Collins, Colo., 1993-95; mfg. devel. engr. Hewlett Packard, Loveland, Colo., 1995-97, mech. engring. mgr., 1998-99, support engring. sect. mgr., 1999—2001, strategic support program mgr. Houston, 2001—02, customer adv., mktg., 2002—; owner Alyse Sagen, Houston. Sec. Hilltop Child Devel. Ctr., Lawrence, 1991-93. Contbr. articles to profl. jours. Student senator U. Kans. Student Senate, Lawrence, 1992-93; com. mem. Kans. U. Child Care Com., Lawrence, 1991-93, work and family com., 1991-92; mem. libr. bd. City of Loveland, 1999—. Recipient U. Kans. Hilltopper award, 1993. Mem. ASME (treas. 1992-93), Oaks Nontraditional Students Orgn. (pres. 1991-92, treas. 1990-91, editor 1990-92), Tau Beta Pi, Pi Tau Sigma. Avocations: reading, sports events, music, hiking, puzzles. Office: Hewlett Packard Loveland Mfg Ctr 815 14th St SW Loveland CO 80537-6330 Home: 12906 Oakwood Manor Dr Cypress TX 77429-4900

NOTLEY, THELMA A. retired librarian, educator; b. Ogbomosho, Nigeria, Feb. 7, 1928; came to U.S., 1931; d. John Spurgeon and Della (Black) Richardson; m. Loren Spencer Notley, June 16, 1946 (dec.); children: Dan, Kathleen, R. Steven, Laura. BS in Lang. Arts, Okla. State U., Stillwater, 1961; MS in LS, Okla. U., 1972. Tchr. English, Helena (Okla.) Pub. Schs., 1962-64, Skiatook (Okla.) Pub. Schs., 1964-66, Tulsa Pub. Schs., 1966-67, sch. libr., 1967-86; tchr. ESL Dongbi U. Fin. and Edn., Dalian, China, 1988-90; tchr. English, libr. Anglican Internat. Sch., Jerusalem, Israel, 1994-96. Author: China Bound, 1999; contbr. articles to profl. jours. Republican. Episcopalian. Avocations: writing, quilting, travel. Home: RR 2 Box 1920 Adair OK 74330-9438 E-mail: tnotley@rectec.net.

NOTT, TARA LEE, Olympic athlete; b. Stilwell, Kans., May 10, 1972; Student, Colo. Began competing in weightlifting, 1995; Am. Open Gold medallist, 1996; Sr. Nat. Championships Gold medallist, 1996; Silver Dragon Team mem. Silver Medallist, 1997; World Team Trials Gold medallist, 1997; Am. Open Silver medallist, 1997; Sr. Nat. Championships Gold medallist, 1997; Sr. World Championships Gold medallist, 1997; Sr. World Championships 10th place, 1997; NACACI Team Mem. Gold medallist, 1997; Sr. Nat. Championships Bronze medallist, 1998; World Team Trials Silver medallist, 1998; Sr. World Championships 6th place, 1998; Sr. Nat. Championships Gold medallist, 1999; NACACI Team Mem. Gold medallist, 1999; Pan Am Games Gold medallist, 1999; Sr. World Championships 9th place, 1999; Sr. Nat. Championships Gold medallist, 2000; Olympic Gold medallist, 2000; Am. Open Gold medallist, 2001; Mermet Cup Team mem. Gold medallist, 2002; Am. record holder 48 kg. Snatch-82.5 kg., 48 kg. Clean and Jerk-102.5 kg., 48 kg. Total-185 kg.; 53 kg. Snatch-85.5 kg. Mem. several USA Soccer teams. Named to Colo. Coll. Hall of Fame. Achievements include only athlete to train at the U.S. Olympic Training Center in 3 different sports; only American Women's Olympic Gold Medallist in Weightlifting.

NOTTI, DONNA BETTS, special education educator; b. Manassas, Va., Sept. 4, 1968; d. William Jackson and Christine Joan (Fant) B.; m. David L. Notti, Oct. 14, 1995. BS in Spl. Edn., Old Dominion U., 1990. Tchr., counselor Southeastern Cooperative Ednl. Programs, Norfolk, Va., 1991—; vol. tutor Tonelson Teaching and Learning Ctr., Norfolk, Va., 1989. Mem. Coun. for Exceptional Children (v.p. 1989-90), Coun. for Children With Behavior Disorders, Coun. for Exceptional Children-Mental Retardation, Am. Re-ED Assn., Va. State Reading Assn., Chesapeake Reading Coun. Lutheran. Office: 861 Glenrock Rd Norfolk VA 23502-3720 Office Phone: 757-485-4735.

NOUR, NAWAL M. obstetrician, gynecologist, health facility administrator; arrived in U.S.A., 80; BA, Brown U, 1984; MD, Harvard U., 1994; MPH, Harvard U, 1999. Chief residency Brigham and Women's Hosp., Boston, 1998; instr. dept of Obstetrics, Gynecology and Reproductive Biology Harvard Sch. of Medicine; dir. obstetric resident practice Brigham and Women's Hosp., Boston; founder African Women's Health Practice, 1999—. Recipient Commonwealth Fund Harvard U., 1999; fellow H. Rchard Nesson Fellowship, Brigham and Women's Hosp., 1999, MacArthur Found., 2003. Office: Brigham and Women's Hosp 75 Francis St Boston MA 02115

NOVACK, BARBARA, writer, educator; BA, CCNY, 1967; MA, U. Mich., 1968. Instr. Adelphi U., Garden City, NY, Nassau C.C., Garden City, Hofstra U., Hempstead, NY, Molloy Coll., Rockville Ctr., NY, 1993—. Lectr., instr. workshops and artistic devel. programs in field; co-founder Mendicant Order of Poets (mendicantorderofpoets.org). Contbr. poetry and short stories to jours., anthologies, websites, books; poetry exhbn. Molloy Coll. Art Gallery, 2002. Recipient Tchrs. USA award, Tchrs. as Writers, 1988, Nassau Rev. Poetry prize, 1989, Alms Ho. Press Honors, 1992, In Other Words Honors, 1998, 1st pl. in 7th ann. poetry competition, Cultural Arts Ctr. Mid-Island YJCC/N.Y. State Coun. Arts, Plainview, N.Y., 2003, Editor's Choice Awards, Poetry.com, Internat. Libr. of Poetry, 2003. Mem.: The Authors League, The Authors Guild, Lambda Iota Tau.

NOVAK, BARBARA, art history educator; b. N.Y.C. d. Joseph and Sadie (Kaufman) N.; m. Brian O'Doherty, July 5, 1960. BA, Barnard Coll., 1951; MA, Radcliffe Coll., 1953, PhD, 1957. TV instr. Mus. Fine Arts, Boston, 1957-58; mem. faculty Barnard Coll., Columbia U., N.Y.C., 1958-98, prof. art history, 1970—, Helen G. Altschul prof., 1984-98, prof. emeritus, 1998—. Adv. council Archives of Am. Art, NAD Author: American Painting of the 19th Century, 1969, Nature and Culture, 1980, rev. edit., 1995, The Thyssen-Bornemisza Collection 19th Century American Painting, 1986, Alice's Neck, 1987, (novels) The Margaret-Ghost, 2003, The Ape and the Whale, 1995, (play) The Ape and the Whale: Darwin and Melville in Their Own Words, 1987 (performed at Symphony Space 1987), Dreams and Shadows: Thomas H. Hotchkiss in 19th Century Italy, 1993; co-editor: Next to Nature, 1980; mem. editorial bd. Am. Art Jour. Commn. Chair commn. Nat. Portrait Gallery. Fulbright fellow Belgium, 1953-54; Guggenheim fellow, 1974; Nat. Book Critics nominee, 1980; L.A. Times Book Award nominee, 1980; Am. Book Award paperback nominee, 1981; recipient disting. tchg. award Coll. Art Assn., 1997, Lawrence Fleishman award for outstanding scholarship Archives Am. Art, 1999, medal of distinction, Barnard Coll., 2002. Fellow Soc. Am. Historians, Phila. Atheneum; mem. Soc. Am. Historians, Am. Antiquarian Soc., Coll. Art Assn. (dir. 1974-77, Disting. Tchg. of Art History award 1997), PEN.

NOVAK, JOYCE KEEN, artist, secondary school educator; d. Clifford Patrick and Mildred Ella Keen; m. Jack Janis, Dec. 15, 1950 (div. July 16, 1954); m. William John Moore, Oct. 28, 1955 (div. Feb. 26, 1965); children: Robert John, William Keen, Marilyn Joyce, James Clifford; m. Robert Novak, May 7, 1966; stepchildren: Susan Grace, Nina Louise. BS of Bus. Edn., U. Mich., 1954, MS of Bus. Edn., 1950. Tchr. H.S. Southfield H.S., Highland Pk., Mich., 1950, Wayne Meml. H. S., 1955—57, Dist. 214, Wheeling, Ill., 1964—66; profl. fine artist Arlington Heights, 1968—89, Platine, 1989—95, Nokomis, Fla., 1995—. Pres. Contemporary Art Ctr., Arlington Heights, Ill., 1984—86; adv. bd. Space 900, Chgo., 1992—95. Pres. N.W. Suburban Panhellenis Assn., Chgo.; sister city emissary Village Arlington Heights, Zoazhuang, China, 1989. Mem.: Digital Fine Arts Assn. (v.p. 2000—), Fla. Artists Group (v.p. 2003—), Chi Omega Alumni Assn. (chpt. advisor 1970—73, White Carnation 2002). Presbyterian. Avocations: swimming, golf, bicycling, hiking. Home: 1066 Truman St Nokomis FL 34275 E-mail: jnart@comcast.net.

NOVAK, JULIE COWAN, nursing educator, researcher, clinician; b. Peoria, Ill., Oct. 2, 1950; m. Robert E. Novak, 1972; children: Andrew, Christopher, Nicholas. BS in Nursing, U. Iowa, 1972, MA in Nursing of Children, 1976; DNSc, U. San Diego, 1989. RN, Va., Calif.; pediat. nurse practitioner. Charge nurse surg. and med. ICU U. Iowa Hosp. and Clinics, 1972-73; instr. med. sur. nursing St. Luke's Sch. Nursing, Cedar Rapids, Iowa, 1973-74; instr. family and cmty. health U. Iowa Coll. of Nursing, 1974-75; perinatal nurse clinician U. Iowa Hosps., 1976-77; pediatric nurse practitioner Chicano Cmty. Health Ctr., 1978-80; lectr., asst. prof. child health nursing and physical assessment San Diego State U., 1977-79; child health nurse practitioner program coord. U. Calif., San Diego, 1978-82; pediatric nurse practitioner San Diego City Schs., 1980-82; coord. infant spl. care ctr. follow-up program U. Calif., San Diego, 1982-83, assoc. clin. prof. intercampus grad. studies, 1983-90, dir. health promotion divsn. cmty. and family medicine, 1985-90; assoc. clin. prof. dept. cmty. family medicine U. Calif. Divsn. Health Care Sci., San Diego, 1990-94; assoc. prof. San Diego State U. Sch. Nursing, 1990-94, Calif. Nursing Students Assn. faculty advisor, 1992-94; pediatric nurse practitioner Naval Hosp., 1990-92, Comp. Health Clinic, 1990-94; prof. (Theresa A. Thomas Endowed), dir. Master's in Primary Health Care/Primary Care Nurse Practitioner, Pediatric Nurse Practitioner Progs. U. Va. Schs., Charlottesville, 1994-2000; sch. hlth. coordinator Alb. County Schs. Clin. Prac. U. Va. Dept. Fam. Med.; assoc. head grad. studies, prof.. practice and cmty. collaboration Sch. of Nursing Purdue U., 2000—; pvt. practice Family Health Clinic, Carroll County, 2000—. Cons. child health San Diego State U. Child Study Ctr.; mem. accident prevention com. Am. Acad. Pediats.; chair adv. bd. Albemarle County Sch Health, 1995-2000, Camp Holiday Trails, 1995-99; mem. adv. bd. Am. Lung Assn., 1998-99; sch. health coord. Albemarle County Schs.; clin. practice U. Va. Dept. Family Medicine. Contbr. numerous articles to profl. jours. and book chpts. to 12 texts; co-author: Ingall's & Salerno's Maternal Child Nursing, 1995, 99, Mosby Year Book; mem. editl. bd. Jour. Perinatal and Neonatal Nursing, 1986-2001, Children's Nurse, 1982-2001, ; mem. editl. bd., reviewer Jour. Pediatric Health Care, 1987-93, Clin. Letters for Nurse Practitioners, 1999-2001—, Advance for Nurse Practitioners, 1998—; speaker in field. Chair Ann. Refugee Clothing Drive, East San Diego, ESL Program, Car Seat Roundup U. Calif., San Diego, 1983-85; mem. telethon March of Dimes; mem. steering com. Healthy Mothers/ Healthy Babies Coalition; chair ways and means com. Benchley-Weinberger Elem. Sch. PTA, 1985-87, pres., 1988-90; v.p., pres. Friends Jamul Schs. Found.; co-chair teen outreach program Jr. League San Diego, 1987-88, chair, 1989-90, bd. dirs., 1990-92; educator presch. health San Carlos Meth. Ch.; mem. Head Start Policy Coun., 1992-94, San Diego County Dropout Prevention Roundtable, 1991-93, Western Albemarle H.S. Planning Team, 1994—; citizen amb./peace educator Mothers Embracing Nuclear Disarmament, Russia and Estonia; project co-dir. San Luis Xochimilco Health Clinic, Mex. Recipient Svc. award Benchley-Weinberger Elem. Sch. PTA, 1988, Hon. Youth Svc. award Calif. Congress Parents and Tchrs., Loretta C. Ford Award for excellence as an nurse practitioner in edn. U. Colo., 1990, March of Dimes Svc. commendation, 1983, Project Hope Svc. commendation, 1983, Hon. Svc. award Calif. Congress of Parents, Tchrs. & Students, 1988, Doctoral Student fellowship U. San Diego, 1986, 2020 Internat. Commn. commendation, 2000, and numerous others. Mem. ANA (mem. ANCC rsch. coalition on credentialing 1997-99, rep. nat. coalition sch. health, AAP com. sch. health), Nat. Certification Bd. Pediatric Nurse Practitioners and Nurses (pres.), Nat. Assn. Pediat. Nurse Practioners Assoc. (chpt. pres., program com., coord. legis. field, nat. cert. chair 1992-98, nat. pres. 2001-2002), Va. Nurse Assn., Rotary Internat., Pi Lambda Theta, Sigma Theta Tau (mem. nominations com. 1990-91, pres. elect Gamma Gamma chpt. 1993-94, Beta Kappa 1995-2000, Delta Omicron 2000—, Media award 1992). Home: 603 Kossuth St Lafayette IN 47905-1444 E-mail: jnovak@nursing.purdue.edu.

NOVAK, KIM (MARILYN NOVAK), actress; b. Chgo., Feb. 13, 1933; d. Joseph A. and Blanche (Kral) N.; m. Richard Johnson, April 1965 (div. 1966); m. Robert Malloy, Jan. 1977. Student, Wright Jr. College, Chgo.; AA, Los Angeles City College, 1958. Appeared in: (films) The French Line, 1953, Pushover, 1954, Phffft, 1954, Five Against the House, 1955, Son of Sinbad, 1955, Picnic, 1955, The Man with the Golden Arm, 1956, The Eddie Duchin Story, 1956, Jeanne Eagles, 1957, Pal Joey, 1958, Vertigo, 1958, Bell, Book and Candle, 1958, Middle of the Night, 1959, Strangers When We Meet, 1960, Pépé, 1960, Boys' Night Out, 1962, The Notorious Landlady, 1962, Of Human Bondage, 1964, Kiss Me Stupid, 1964, The Amorous Adventures of Moll Flanders, 1965, The Legend of Lylah Clare, 1968, The Great Bank Robbery, 1969, Tales That Witness Madness, 1973, The White Buffalo, 1977, Just a Gigolo, 1979, The Mirror Crack'd, 1980, The Children, 1990, Liebestraum, 1991; (TV movies) Third Girl from the Left, 1974, Satan's Triangle, 1975, Malibu, 1983, Obsessed with Vertigo, 1997; (TV series) Falcon Crest, 1986-87, Alfred Hitchcock Presents, 1985, Liebestraum, 1989; (TV appearances) Cleopatra: The Film that Changed Hollywood, 2001. Named one of 10 most popular movie stars by Box-Office mag. 1956, All-Am. Favorite 1961, Brussels World Fair poll as favorite all-time actress in world 1958. Office: William Morris Agency care Norman Brokaw 151 S El Camino Dr Beverly Hills CA 90212-2775*

NOVAK, RANDI RUTH, engineer, computer scientist; b. Chgo., July 10, 1954; d. Bernard Richard and Shirley Ann (Fiedorczyk) Novak; children: Rona Rachel Reich, Bonnie Shaina Reich. BS in Math., BA in Econs. with honors, U. Calif., Santa Cruz, 1976; postgrad., U. Rochester, 1976-78. Rsch. asst. U. Calif., Santa Cruz, 1974-76; Russian translator U. Chgo., 1977—78; intern economist Congl. Budget Office, Washington, 1977; engr. Lockheed MSC, Sunnyvale, Calif., 1978-82; software engr. contractor Silicon Valley Systems, Belmont, Calif., 1982, 83-84, Data Encore (subs. of Verbatim), Sunnyvale, 1982-83; systems programmer CompuPro/Viasyn Corp., Hayward, Calif., 1984-87; mem. tech. staff Network Equipment Techs., Redwood City, Calif., 1987-89; v.p. engring., founder Segue Setups, Burlingame, Calif., 1989-92, ptnr., 1992—; sr. tech. staff NEC Am., San Jose, Calif., 1992—94; sr. systems engr. Hitachi Computer Products, Santa Clara, Calif., 1994-96; prin. engr. Rapid-City Comms./Bay Networks/Nortel Networks, Santa Clara, Calif., 1996—2002, Trapeze Networks, Pleasanton, Calif., 2002—04; prin. engr. tech. staff Foundry Networks, San Jose, 2004—. Fellow Dept. Treasury, 1974-76, NSF, 1977-78, U. Rochester, Rush Rhees fellow. Mem. IEEE Computer Soc., Am. Math. Assn., Computer Profls. for Social Responsibility, Soc. for Computing and Info. Processing, Internat. Platform Assn., Calif. Scholarship Fedn. (life). Avocations: piano, oboe, music, photography, mathematics. Home: 4166 School St Pleasanton CA 94566-6218

NOVAK, VICKI ANN, human resources specialist; Bachelor's, U. Tenn., 1973. Various positions in human resources Dept. of Commerce, Washington, Dept. of Housing and Urban Devel., Washington, Dept. of Transp., Washington; spl. asst. to dir. of personnel NASA, Washington, chief of agy. personnel policy br.; personnel officer NASA Hqrs., Washington; dir. personnel NASA, assoc. adminstr. for human resources and edn. Mem. Internat. Personnel Mgmt. Assn., Sr. Exec. Assn., Phi Beta Kappa. Office: NASA Human Resources and Edn 300 E St SW Washington DC 20546-0005

NOVELLO, ANTONIA COELLO, state health commissioner, former surgeon general, pediatric nephrologist, educator, retired federal agency administrator; b. Fajardo, P.R., Aug. 23, 1944; d. Antonio and Ana D. (Flores) Coello; m. Joseph R. Novello, May 30, 1970. BS, U. P.R., Rio Piedras, 1965; MD, U. P.R., San Juan, 1970; MPH, Johns Hopkins Sch. Hygiene, 1982; DrPh (hon.), Johns Hopkins U., 2000; DSc (hon.), Med. Coll. Ohio, 1990, U. Ctrl. Caribe, Cayey, P.R., 1990, Lehigh U., 1992, Hood Coll., 1992, U. Notre Dame, Ind., 1991, N.Y. Med. Coll., 1992, U. Mass., 1992, Fla. Internat. U., 1992, Cath. U., 1993, Washington Coll., 1993, St. Mary's Coll., 1993, Ea. Va. Med. Sch., 1993, Ctrl. Conn. State U., 1993, Georgetown U., 1993, U. Mich., 1994, Mt. Sinai Sch. Medicine, 1995; LHD (hon.), Alvernia Coll., 1996; HHD (hon.), Kings Coll., 1996; D in Health Sci. (hon.), Ponce Sch. of Medicine, 1996; D in Law (hon.), Gannon U., 1997; LHD (hon.), Loyola U., 1997; DSc (hon.), U. North Tex., Ft. Worth, 2002, Howard U., 2003, NYU, 2003, Pace U., 2003, others. Diplomate Am. Bd. Pediatrics. Intern in pediatrics U. Mich. Med. Ctr., Ann Arbor, 1970-71, resident in pediatrics, 1971-73, pediatric nephrology fellow, 1973-74, Georgetown U. Hosp., Washington, 1974-75; project officer Nat. Inst. Arthritis, Metabolism and Digestive Diseases NIH, Bethesda, Md., 1978-79, staff physician, 1979-80; exec. sec. gen. medicine B study sect., div. of rsch. grants NIH, Bethesda, 1981-86; dep. dir. Nat. Inst. Child Health & Human Devel., NIH, Bethesda, 1986-90; surgeon gen. USPHS-HHS, Washington, 1990-93; spl. rep. for health and nutrition UNICEF, N.Y.C., 1993—96; vis. prof. health policy and mgmt. Johns Hopkins U. Sch. of Hygiene and Pub. Health, 1996—99; commr. of health New York, 1999—. Clin. prof. pediatrics Georgetown U. Hosp., Washington, 1986, 89, Uniformed Svcs. U. of Health Scis., 1989; adj. prof. pediatrics and communicable diseases U. Mich. Med. Sch., 1993; adj. prof. internat. health Sch. Hygiene and Pub. Health, Johns Hopkins U., Balt.; prof. dept. health policy mgmt. and behavior SUNY, 1999—; clin. prof. pediats. U. Rochester, N.Y., 1999—; mem. Georgetown Med. Ctr. Interdepartmental Rsch. Group, 1984—; legis. fellow U.S. Senate Com. on Labor and Human Resources, Washington, 1982-83; mem. Com. on Rsch. in Pediatric Nephrology, Washington, 1981—; participant grants assoc. program seminars Nat. Inst. Arthritis, Diabetes and Digestive and Kidney Diseases, NIH, Bethesda, 1980-81; pediatric cons. Adolescent Medicine Svc., Psychiat. Inst., Washington, 1979-83; nephrology cons. Met. Washington Renal Dialysis Ctr. affiliate Georgetown U. Hosp., Washington, 1975-78; phys. diagnosis class instr. U. Mich. Med. Ctr., Ann Arbor, 1973-74; chair Sec.'s Work Group on Pediatric HIV Infection and Diseases, DHHS, 1988; cons. WHO, Geneva, 1989; mem. Johns Hopkins Soc. Scholars, 1991. Contbr. numerous articles to profl. jours. and chpts. to books in field; mem. editorial bd. Internat. Jour. Artificial Organs, Jour. Mexican Nephrology. Served in USPHS, 1978-99. Recipient Intern of Yr. award U. Mich. Dept. Pediatrics, 1971, Woman of Yr. award Disting. Grads. Pub. Sch. Systems, San Juan, 1980, PHS Commendation medal HHS, 1983, PHS Citation award HHS, 1984, Cert. of Recognition, Divsn. Rsch. Grants, NIH, 1985, PHS Outstanding medal HHS, 1988, PHS Unit Commendation, 1988, PHS Surgeon Gen.'s Exemplary Svc. medal, 1989, PHS Outstanding Unit citation, 1989, DHHS Asst. Sec. for Health Cert. of Commendation, 1989, Surgeon Gen. Medallion award, 1990, Alumni award U. Mich. Med. Ctr., 1991, Elizabeth Blackwell award, 1991, Woodrow Wilson award for disting. govt. svc., 1991, Congl. Hispanic Caucus medal, 1991, Order of Mil. Med. Merit, 1992, Washington Times Freedom award, 1992, Charles C. Shepard Sci. award, 1992, Golden Plate award, 1992, Elizabeth Ann Seton award, 1992, Ellis Island Congl. Medal of Honor, 1993, Legion of Merit medal, 1993, Athena award Alumnae Coun., 1993, Nat. Citation award Mortar Bd., 1993, Disting. Pub. Svc. award, 1993, Healthy Am. Fitness Leaders award, 1994, Pub. Leadership Edn. Network Mentor award, 1994, Disting. Svc. award Nat. Coun. Cath. Women, 1995, James E. Van Zandt Citizenship award, 1995, Ronald McDonald Children's Charities Excellence award, 1995, Hispanic Heritage Leadership award, 1998, Disting. Alumnus award Am. Assn. of State Colls. and Univs., 1997, Humanitarian award Am. Cancer Soc., 2001, James Smithson Bicentenial medal Smithsonian Inst., 2002; named Health Leader of Yr., COA, 1992; inductee Nat. Women's Hall of Fame, 1994, Internat. Pediatric Hall of Fame Miami Children's Hosp., 1996, Am. Med. Women Assn. Hall of Fame, 2002. Fellow Am. Acad. Pediatrics (Excellence Pub. Svc. award 1993); mem. AMA (Nathan Davis award 1993, Meritorious Svc. award 1993, Luther L. Terry award, 2000), Inst. Medicine, Internat. Soc. Nephrology, Am. Soc. Nephrology, Latin Am. Soc. Nephrology, Soc. for Pediatric Rsch., Am. Pediatric Soc., Assn. Mil. Surgeons U.S., Am. Soc. Pediatric Nephrology, Pan Am. Med. and Dental Soc. (pres.-elect, sec. 1984), D.C. Med. Soc. (assoc.), Johns Hopkins U. Soc. Scholars, Alpha Omega Alpha. Avocation: collecting antique furniture. Office: NY State Health Commr Corning Tower Empire State Plz Albany NY 12237

NOVETZKE, SALLY JOHNSON, former ambassador; b. Stillwater, Minn, Jan. 12, 1932; married; 4 children. Student, Carleton Coll., 1950-52; PhD (hon.), Mt. Mercy Coll., 1991. Amb. to Malta, Am. Embassy, Valletta, 1989-93. Past mem., legis. rep. Nat. Coun. on Vocat. Edn.; past mem. adv. coun. for career edn., past mem. planning coun. Kirkwood C.C.; bd. dir., life trustee Cedar Rapids Cmty. Theater, Cedar Rapids; past bd. dir. James Baker III Pub. Policy Inst., Rice U.; past trustee, v.p. bd. dir. Shattuck-St. Mary's Sch., Faribault, Minn., Mt. Mercy Coll., Cedar Rapids; vice chmn., life trustee, mem. exec. com. Hoover Presdl. Libr., 1982—, v.p. Hoover trustees; mem. Coun. Am. Amb.; trustee 4-Oaks Juvenile Facility; chmn. Nat. Coun. Youth Leadership; adv. coun. Shattuck-St. Mary's Sch., Faribault, Minn.; state chmn.. Iowa Rep. Ctrl. Com., 1984—86; co-chair rep. Ctrl. Com.; chmn. Linn County Rep. Com., 1980—83; mem. adv. bd. Nat. Rep. Women, 1987—89; co-chmn. V.P. Bush Inauguration, 1980; Iowa co-chmn. George Bush for Pres.; trustee Am. U. in Rome, 2001—; bd. dir. Amb. Forum. Decorated dame Order of Knights of Malta; recipient Disting. Alumnus award Stillwater High Sch., 1991; Disting. Alumni award for outstanding achievement Carleton Coll., 1994. Republican. Home: 4747 Mount Vernon Rd SE Cedar Rapids IA 52403-3941

NOVOGROD, NANCY GERSTEIN, editor; b. N.Y.C., Jan. 30, 1949; d. Max and Hilda (Kirschbaum) Gerstein; m. John Campner Novogrod, Nov. 7, 1976; children: James Campner, Caroline Anne. AB, Mt. Holyoke Coll., 1971. Sec. fiction dept. The New Yorker, N.Y.C., 1971-73, reader, 1973-76; asst. editor Clarkson Potter/Pubs., N.Y.C., 1977-78, assoc. editor, 1978-80, editor, 1980-83, sr. editor, 1984-86, exec. editor, 1987; sr. editor HG (House & Garden mag.), N.Y.C., 1987-88, editor-in-chief, 1988-93, Travel & Leisure, N.Y.C., 1993—; editl. dir. Am. Express Pub., N.Y.C., 2000—. Bd. dirs. N.Y. Bot. Garden, 1991—; exec. com., bd. dirs. Mount Holyoke Coll., 1992—97; adv. bd. Breast Cancer Rsch. Found., 1993; bd. dirs. Children's Advocacy Ctr. of Manhattan, 2003. Mem.: Am. Soc. Mag. Editors (bd. dir.). Office: Travel & Leisure 1120 Avenue Of The Americas New York NY 10036-6700 E-mail: nnovogrod@travelandleisure.com.

NOVOTNY, DEBORAH A. management consultant; d. Russell Anthony and Barbara J. Novotny. BA in Econs., Northwestern U., 1986; postgrad., U. Minn., 1988-91; masters cert. in project mgmt., George Washington U., 2000. Series 7 lic., mutual fund mktg. analyst, cert. project mgr., QMS coord., auditor, PowerBuilder developer-profl., instr., PowerSoft divsn. Sybase, Inc. Mgr. lab., cons. Northwestern U., Evanston, Ill., 1983-86; asst. mgr. microcomputer services Sara Lee Corp., Chgo., 1986; sr. cons. Lante Corp., Chgo., 1987-88; fin. exec., Series 7 lic. mutual fund mktg. analyst, nat. non-bank banking sys. coord., credit dept. mgr. IDS Fin. Svcs., Inc., Mpls., 1988-91; fin. system coord. Met. Water Reclamation Dist. of Greater Chgo., Chgo., 1991-92; mgmt. systems cons., pres., CEO Deborah A. Novotny, Inc., Chgo., 1992—; various consulting, mgmt. positions Sybase, Inc., 1993—2003, area project mgmt. office mgr., 1999—2003; dir. process and portfolio mgmt. global program office LexisNexis, Dayton, Ohio, 2003—. Invited spkr., instr. Ann. Powersoft User Conf., Comdex Trade Show, homeless and underprivileged families Christmas gift program, 1994—. Vol. Cath. Charities, 1990—, Greater Chgo. Food Repository, 1997—; vice chmn., chair fin. com. Mt. Assisi Acad. Bd. Dirs., 1997—99; active teen retreat team St. Michael's Ch., Orland Park, Ill., 1978—84. Ill. State scholar. Mem.: Macintosh Users Group, Chi Omega Rho (charter, chmn. housing assn. 1986—91). Avocations: piloting aircraft, photography, travel, reading, writing.

NOWAK, CAROL ANN, city official; b. Buffalo, Mar. 5, 1950; d. Walter S. and Stella M. (Gurowski) N. AAS in Bus. Adminstrn., Erie Community Coll., Buffalo, 1986; BS in Bus. Mgmt., SUNY, Buffalo, 1991. With Liberty Nat. Bank/Norstar, Buffalo, 1968-70, City of Buffalo, 1970-74, asst. adminstrn. and fin., 1974-82, pension clk., adminstr. city police and fire pension fund, city clk., 1982-90, sr. coun. clk., city clk., 1990—. Artist, designer holiday greeting cards, 1984—. Mem. Nat. Notary Assn., SUNY Alumni Assn., Golden Key, Alpha Sigma Lambda. Avocations: fashion design, art, writing. Home: 422 Dingens St Buffalo NY 14206-2321

NOWAK, CAROL LEE, art educator; b. Bryan, Ohio, Aug. 31, 1946; d. Otho Byron and Martha Lee (Hall) Stockman; children: Lisa Michelle Dickey, Travis Christian, Matthew Jay. BS in Art Edn., Bowling Green State U., 1968. Spl. cert. in art, K-12, Ohio. Art tchr. North Central (N.Y.) H.S., 1968-69, Hilltop H.S., West Unity, Ohio, 1972-74, Bryan (Ohio) City Schs., 1987—2003; adminstr., head tchr. Headstart, Bryan, 1970-71; LD tutor Bryan City Schs., 1974-75, LD tutor, tchr. K-5, 1975-77; tchr. Edgerton (Ohio) Elem. Schs., 1977-83, Edgerton and Bryan City Schs., 1984-87. Hot glass asst. Sauder FarmCraft Village, Archbold, Ohio, 1989—98; insight facilitator Williams County Probation Schs., Bryan, 1988-94; adv. Hi Art Assn., 1987—. V.p. Tri State Artists Club, Angola, Ind., 1994—; mem. Assn. Recognizing Talented Students (ARTS). Jennings scholar, 1991; recipient Art Appreciation award Northwest State Cmty. Coll., 2001. Mem. NEA, Ohio Edn. Assn., Bryan Edn. Assn., Ohio Art Edn. Assn., Art to Art, Tri State Artists Assn., Toledo Glass Collectors Club, Toledo Sculptors Guild, Toledo Art Mus. Avocations: art history, reading, travel, writing, collecting art. Home: 315 N Walnut St Bryan OH 43506-1355

NOWAK, JUDITH ANN, psychiatrist; b. Albany, N.Y., Feb. 18, 1948; d. Jacob Frank and Anne Patricia Nowak. BA, Cornell U., 1970, MD, 1974. Diplomate in psychiatry Am. Bd. Psychiatry and Neurology. Resident U. Va. Hosp., Charlottesville, 1974-77; fellow in psychiatry Westchester divsn. Cornell U. Med. Coll. Westchester Div., White Plains, N.Y., 1977-78; clin. affiliate Cornell U. Med. Coll., White Plains, N.Y., 1978-79; staff psychiatrist Chestnut Lodge Hosp., Rockville, Md., 1979-81; med. officer in psychiatry St. Elizabeths Hosp., Washington, 1981; pvt. practice Washington, 1981—. Clin. asst. prof. of psychiatry, George Washington U., Washington, 1981-89; clin. assoc. prof. psychiatry, George Washington U. 1989-94, clin. prof. psychiatry, 1994—. Mem. Am. Psychiat. Soc. (pub. affairs rep. 1995), Am. Psychoanalytic Soc., Washington Psychiat. Soc. (sec. 1989-90, 2001-2003, pres. 1991-92), D.C. Med. Soc. (speaker ho. of dels. 1996-98, chair coun. med. specialty socs. 1998-2000). Office: 908 New Hampshire Ave NW Washington DC 20037-2049 Office Phone: 202-887-5495.

NOWAK, NANCY STEIN, judge; b. Des Moines, Sept. 17, 1952; d. Russell D. and Christine (Evanoka) Stein; m. Raymond A. Nowak, May 26, 1973. BA, Drake Univ., Iowa, 1974, MA, 1976; JD, George Washington Univ., D.C., 1980. Bar: D.C. 1980, Iowa 1982, Tex. 1986. Briefing atty. Judge Jamie Boyd, 1983-84, Judge Edward Prado, 1984-87; asst. U.S. atty., 1987-88; asst. U.S. trustee, 1988-89; magistrate judge U.S. Dist. Ct. (Tex. we. dist.), 5th circuit, San Antonio, 1989—. Office: US Courthouse 655 E Durango Blvd San Antonio TX 78206-1100

NOWATZKI, MELODEE, psychologist; d. Peter and Susan Nowatzki; m. Chris Kunszt; children: Alexandra Nowatzki-Kunszt, Nickolas Nowatzki-Kunszt. BS in Psychology, BS in Sociology, ND State U., Fargo, 1989; MS in Sch. Psychology, Moorhead State U., 1994. Cert. sch. psychologist Ariz. Owner Nowatzki Psychol. Svcs., Inc., Phoenix, 1996—, sch. psychologist Mesa, Ariz., 2001—03. Child instr. Dayspring Meth. Ch., Tempe, Ariz., 2000—02. Recipient Lifesaving award, Phoenix Police Dept. Mem.: APA, Ariz. Assn. Sch. Psychologists, Nat. Assn. Sch. Psychologists. Office: Nowatzki Psychological Services Inc 4168 E Patrick St Higley AZ 85236

NOWELL, GLENNA GREELY, librarian, consultant, city manager; b. Gardiner, Maine, Apr. 15, 1937; d. Bion Mellon and Faith Louise (Hutchings) Greely; m. Dana Richard Nowell, Sept. 1, 1956 (div. 1971); children: Dana A., Mark R., Dean E. BA in English, U. Maine, 1986. Dir. Gardiner Pub. Libr., 1974-97; city mgr. Gardiner, 1997-00. Bd. dirs. Gardiner Bd. Trade; mem. Maine Libr. Commn., 1980-88, Gov.'s Commn. Employment of Handicapped, 1978-81; mem. adv. bd. Gardiner Savs. Bank, 1986—; trustee J. Walter Robinson Welfare Trust, 1986—. Creator, editor Who Reads What publ., 1988—. Mem. Gardiner Econ. Devel. Com., 1989-98; interim city mgr. City of Gardiner, 1991; bd. dirs. Kennebec Valley Mental Health, 1995-97; trustee Maine Criminal Justice Acad., 1998-99; mem. State Ct. Libr. Com., 1996-99; mem. Maine Real Estate Commn., 2000—. Recipient Hugh Hefner 1st Amendment award Playboy Found., 1987, Outstanding Libr. award Maine Libr. Assn., 1993, Cmty. Svc. award Kennebec Valley C. of C., 1993. Mem. Rotary (pres. Gardiner chpt. 1993-94). Office: RR 5 Box 1910 Gardiner ME 04345-9738 E-mail: nowell@adelphia.net.

NOWELL, LINDA GAIL, organization executive; b. Ft. Worth, Apr. 24, 1949; d. Jesse Wade and Bennie Dale (Flint) Stallings. BA in English, North Tex. State U., 1970. Cert. secondary edn. tchr. Tex. Ind. sales rep. Jostens Printing & Pub. Div., Owatona, Minn., 1980-84; v.p. Nowell Equipment Co., Cranfils Gap, Tex., 1984-89; edn. coord. Tex. Farm Bur., Waco, Tex., 1987-90; account exec. MAC Printing, Las Vegas, 1991-94; mgr. frontier health outreach program Nev. Rural Health Ctrs., Inc., 1994-97; state coord. Nev. 5-A-Day Coalition, 1995-96; exec. dir. No To Abuse, Pahrump, Nev., 1999—. Exec. dir. Landmark Edn., Inc.; vol. sexual assault advocate CASA; bd. dirs. United Way Pioneer Territory. Mem.: NAFE. Home: PO Box 790 Pahrump NV 89041-0790 Office Phone: 775-751-1118.

NOWIK, DOROTHY ADAM, medical equipment company executive; b. Chgo., July 25, 1944; d. Adam Harry and Helen (Kichkaylo) Wanaski; m. Eugene Nicholas Nowik, Aug. 9, 1978; children: George Eugene, Helen Eugene. A.A., Columbia Coll., 1980. Cert. lactation counselor, lactation educator, lactation cons. Sec., adminstrv. asst. to pres. Zenco Engrng Corp., Chgo., 1970-71; sales rep. Medizenco USA Ltd., Chgo., 1971-73; ptnr. Pacific Med. Systems, Inc., Bellevue, Wash., 1973 76, pres., 1976— Mem. NAFE, Pacific Mothers Support, Inc. (pres. 1991), Wash. Assn. Lactation Cons. (treas. 1994—). Mem. Orthodox Ch. Am. Home: 303 126th Ave NE Bellevue WA 98005-3217 Office: 1407 132nd Ave NE # 10 Bellevue WA 98005-2259

NOWLAND-CURRY, BETSY, state official; m. David Curry. Grad., U. Ky. Dir. Tng. and Leadership Ctr. Ky. League of Cities; dir. comm. and tng. Gov. Paul E. Patton, 1998—2000; exec. dir. Ky. Women's Leadership Network, Lexington YWCA; dir. cmty. edn. Transylvania U.; exec. dir. Ky. Commn. on Women, Frankfort, 2000—. Wrote grant to establish YWCA Spouse Abuse Ctr., 1976. Named Outstanding Bus. Woman of Frankfort, 1979, Outstanding Kentuckian, Gov. Martha Layne Collins, 1982; named one of Outstanding Young Women of Am., 1978; recipient Lexington Outstanding Young Woman of Yr. award, 1981. Office: Ky Commn on Women 312 W Main St Frankfort KY 40601

NOYES, JUDITH MITCHELL, sales executive; b. New Haven, Nov. 29, 1931; d. Albert William Mitchell and Olive Annamay Branch; m. Richard Hall Noyes, Oct. 10, 1953; children: Catherine N. Boddington, Stephanie N. Kane, Matthew Hall. BA, Vassar Coll., 1953. Columnist, reporter Ocean Beach Reporter, Jacksonville Beach, Fla., 1944—49; reporter, movie reviewer Jacksonville Jour., 1950; broadcaster, writer Radio Sta. WJVB, Jacksonville Beach, 1948—50; mil. history writer Dept. of Army, Tokyo, 1953—54; co-founder, co-owner The Chinook Bookshop, Inc., Colorado Springs, Colo., 1959—; city coun. mem. City of Colo. Springs, Colorado Springs, 2000—03; commr. Colo. Springs Urban Renewal Authority, 2003—. Office Phone: 719-635-1195.

NOZIGLIA, CARLA MILLER, forensic scientist, consultant; b. Erie, Pa., Oct. 11, 1941; d. Earnest Carl and Eileen (Murphy) Miller; m. Keith William Noziglia, Nov. 21, 1969; children: Pama Noziglia Cook, Kathryn Noziglia Volpi. BS, Villa Maria Coll., 1963; MS, Lindenwood Coll., 1984. Registered med. technologist, Am. Soc. Clin. Pathologists. Med. technologist Monmouth (N.J.) Gen. Hosp., 1963-64; spl. chem. med. technologist Hamot Hosp. Med. Ctr., Erie, Pa., 1965-69; pathologists' assoc. Galion (Ohio) Comm. Hosp., 1969-75; dir. crime lab. Mansfield (Ohio) Police Dept., Richland County Crime Lab., 1978-81; crime lab. supr. St. Louis County Police, Clayton, Mo., 1981-84; dir. crime lab. Las Vegas (Nev.) Met. Police, 1984-88, dir. lab. svcs., 1988-93, dir., cons. forensic scis., 1993-95; dir. Tulsa Police Dept. Forensic Lab., 1995-2000, cons. Forensic Sci., 2000—; forensic advisor U.S. Dept. of Justice/Internat. Criminal Investigative Tng. Assistance Program, Tbilisi, Georgia, 2002, sr. forensic advisor, 2002—. Tech. abstracts editor Jour. Police Sci. and Adminstrn., 1983-91; mem. editl. bd. Jour. Forensic Identification, 1988—; editor chpt. in Drug Facilitated Sexual Assault: A Forensic Handbook, 2001; contbg author: Journal of Police Science, 1989, Encyclopedia of Police Science, 1989. Mem. Gov.'s Com. on Testing for Intoxication, Las Vegas, 1984-93; mem. adv. bd. Nev. Bd. Pharmacy, 1988-93; recruiter United Blood Svcs., Las Vegas, 1986-93; bd. dirs., pres. Cmty. Action Against Rape, Las Vegas, 1987-94; co-founder So. Nev. Sexual Assault Protocol, 1986; adv. bd. Tulsa C.C., 1999-2000, Tulsa Tech. Ctr., 1997-2000; chmn. bd. trustees Forensic Sci. Found., 2000—. Named Outstanding Cath. Erie Diocese N.W. Pa., 1988, Woman of Achievement, Las Vegas C. of C., 1989, Outstanding Alumni, Villa Maria Acad., 2001, Disting. Alumna Sci., Gannon U., 2004; recipient award, Ohio Ho. of Reps., 1981, Alumni of Yr. award, Villa Maria Coll., 1981. Fellow Am. Acad. Forensic Scis. (disting. fellow, 2003, bd. dirs. 1988-91, sec. Criminalistics sect. 1986, sect. chmn. 1987, Outstanding Svc. award 1995, Paul L. Kirk award 1998); mem. Am. Coll. Emergency Physicians (nat. sexual assault task force 1999), Am. Soc. Crime Lab Dirs. (emeritus, bd. dirs. 1980-87, treas. 1981-82, 88-91, pres. 1986-87), Internat. Homicide Investigator's Assn.(charter), Internat. Police Assn., Internat. Assn. for Identification, S.W. Assn. Forensic Scientists (emeritus), Am. Bus. Women's Assn. (Woman of Yr. 1988, one of Nat. Top Bus. Women 1993), Alzheimer's Assn. (Okla. chpt. bd. dirs. 1997-2000, exec. bd. sec. 1999). Republican. Roman Catholic. Avocations: avid reader, knitting, sewing, needlepoint, swimming. E-mail: skipncar@aol.com.

NUBEL, MARIANNE KUNZ, cultural administrator, writer, composer; b. Cin., Sept. 14, 1966; d. Walter Charles and Marjorie (Larson) Kunz; m. Christopher Robert Nubel, Aug. 12, 1989. BS in Cmty. Arts Mgmt., East Carolina U., 1989. Exec. dir. Cmty. Arts Ctr., Wilmington, N.C., 1989-94; dir. film and media svcs. and cultural arts coord. City of Wilmington, 1994—. Founding mem., v.p. 5 & Dime Cultural Prodns., Wilmington, 1992-96,Big Dawg Productions, 1995; bd. dirs. Arts Coun. of the Lower Cape Fear, Wilmington, 1991-95, sec., 1994-95; pres. prodn. bd. Cape Fear Shakespeare, Wilmington, 1994—, music dir., coord., 1994—; pres. adv. bd. Journey Prodn. Performance Edn. Theatre, 2000—; mem. adv. bd. Big Dawg Theatre Co, 2001—. Composer for children's theatre. Music dir. Pied Piper Theatre, Jr. League, Wilmington, 1989-95; mem. co. Bessie's Underground Mole Players, Wilmington, 1995-99; mem. Arts Coun. Lower Cape Fear, Opera House Theatre Co. Recipient Arts and Humanities award N.C. Recreation and Parks Soc., 1993, 94, Cmty. Svc. award Thalian Assn. Cmty. Theatre, 1993, 94. Mem. Theatre N.O.W., Blues Soc. of the Lower Cape Fear (bd. dirs. 1990-92, 1st woman dir.), Big Dawg Theatre Co., Lower Cape Fear Hist. Soc., Opera House Theater Co., Wilmington Choral Soc. Avocations: writing, composing, community theatre, children's theatre, travel. Office: City of Wilmington Pub Svcs and Facilities PO Box 1810 Wilmington NC 28402-1810 E-mail: Marianne.Nubel@ci.wilmington.nc.us.

NUCKLOS, SHIRLEY, health facility administrator, consultant; b. Canton, Ohio, Aug. 30, 1949; D. Boyd Alexander and Julia Lillian (Hood) Curtis; m. William W. Nucklos, Mar. 11, 1972; children: Tuere Tene, Tiombé Nigina, Khari Oji-Lee. BS in Edn., Cen. State U., Wilberforce, Ohio, 1970; MA, Ohio State U., 1971. Cert. elem. tchr., guidance counselor. Guidance counselor Scioto Village High Sch., Powell, Ohio, 1973-78; acad. advisor Franklin U., Columbus, Ohio, 1980-82, acting asst. dir. records, 1982-83, asst. registrar, 1983-90; registrar Ohio Dominican Coll., Columbus, 1990-93; dir. human resources Mid-Am. Phys. Medicine & Exec. Med., Inc., Columbus, Ohio, 1994—; adminstr. Woodland Med. Arts Ctr., Columbus, 1998—. Adminstrv. advisor to Black Student Union, Franklin U., 1982-85; human resource cons. Exec. Med., Inc., Westerville, Ohio, 1989-93, dir. human resources, bus. mgr., 1994—. Vol. tchr. Umoja Sasa Shule, Columbus, 1971-74; booster Mid-west Gymnastic and Cheerleading, Dublin, Ohio, 1988-93; active various com. for minority concerns. Mem. Ohio Assn. Collegiate Registrars and Admissions Officers (sec. 1991-93, Cert. Appreciation 1985, 93), Am. Assn. Collegiate Registrars and Admissions Officers, Nat. Assn. Coll. Deans, Registrars and Admissions Officers, Ohio Assn. Women Deans, Adminstrs. and Counselors, Nat. Assn. Women Deans, Adminstrs. and Counselors, Am. Assn. Univ. Adminstrn., Va. Admissions Counselors for Black Concerns, Ohio Health Info. Mgmt. Assn. Democrat. Mem. Church of God in Christ. Avocations: weight training, cycling, reading. Office: William W Nucklos MD Inc 254 Woodland Ave Ste 105 Columbus OH 43203-1782

NUESKE-PEREZ, BARBARA ALLEN, art educator; b. Chgo., Aug. 7, 1957; d. Robert Albert and Barbara Maire (Batchelder) Nueske; m. Alphonse Lara Perez, Mar. 15, 1980 (div. 2004); 1 child, Maryah Michelle. BA in Arts, Loyola U., 1979. Cert. State Bd. Edn., 1990. Art tchr. St. Athanasius, Evanston, Ill., 1990—. Art educator, grant cons., publicity chair St. Athanasius, Evanston, 1990—; Internet cons. art edn.; cons. in field. Author textbooks on curriculum devel.; contbr. author: Introducing Art, 2d edit., Exploring Art, 2d edit., Understanding Art, 2d edit.; contbr. articles to profl. jours. Beat rep. Chgo. Police Dept., 1990—; judge Dick Blicks Speedball Contest, 2003; liason St. Athanasius Sch. Recipient Dean Goldberg award, Chgo. (Ill.) Park Dist., 1994, Tchr. award, Ill. Art Alliance, 1998, Spl. Recognition Power Art Competition award, U.S. Dept. Energy, 2000; grantee, Artsonia. Mem. ASCD (comm. com.), Nat. Arts Edn. Assn., Nat. Cath. Edn. Assn., Ill. Art Edn. Assn., Ill. art Alliance for Edn., Am. Craft. Roman Catholic. Avocations: arts, crafts, gardening, dogs, cooking. Office: St Athanasius Sch 2510 Ashland Ave Evanston IL 60201-2319

NUGENT, JANE KAY, retired utilities executive; b. Detroit, Aug. 31, 1925; d. Albert A. and Celia (Betzing) Kay; m. Robert L. Nugent, Apr. 3, 1991. BS, U. Detroit, 1948; MA, Wayne State U., 1952; MBA, U. Mich., 1963. Sr. personnel interviewer employment Detroit Edison Co., 1948-60, personnel coord. for women, 1960-65, office employment adminstr., 1965-70, gen. employment adminstr., 1970-71, dir. personnel svcs., 1971-72, mgr. employee rels., 1972-77, asst. v.p. employee rels., 1977-78, v.p. employee rels., 1978-82, v.p. adminstrn., 1982-90, ret., 1990. Tchr. U. Detroit Evening Coll. Bus. and Adminstrn., 1963-75; seminar leader div. mgmt. edn. U. Mich., 1968-74, Waterloo Mgmt. Edn. Ctr., 1972-77. Mem. Mich. Employment Security Adv. Coun., 1967-81; chmn. bd. dirs. Detroit Inst. Commerce, 1976-79; exec. bd. NCCJ, 1980-91, nat. trustee, 1984-88; bd. dirs. Childrens Home Detroit, 1991-2001, 1st v.p. 1994-96, pres. 1996-98; bd. dirs. St. John Hosp. and Med. Ctr., 2000—, St. John Health Care System Found., 2000—, St. John Sr. Svcs., 1998—. Recipient Alumni Tower award U. Detroit, 1967, Headliner award Women Wayne State U., 1970, Wayne State U. Alumni Achievement award, 1974, Career Achievement award Profl. Panhellenic Assn., 1973, Bus. Achievement award Assn. Bus. Deans, 1989, Svcs. Older Citizens All Star Award, 1996; named one of Top Ten Working Women of Detroit, 1970, Alumnus of Yr., U. Detroit, 1981, Woman of Yr. Am. Lung Assn., 1991, Sr. Profl. in Human Resources Soc. Human Resource Mgmt.; cert. Adminstrv. Mgr. Am. Mgmt. Soc.; inducted in Mich. Women's Hall of Fame, 1988. Mem. Internat. Assn. Personnel Women (pres. 1969-70), Women's Econ. Club (v.p. 1971-72, pres. 1972-73), Am. Soc. Employees (bd. dirs. 1979-90), Personnel Women Detroit (pres. 1960-61), U. Detroit Alumni Assn. (pres. 1964-66), Phi Gamma Nu (nat. v.p. 1955-57), Boys and Girls Club S.E. Mich. (pres. 1987-89), Econ. Club Detroit (v.p. 1981-90), Internat. Womens Forum.

NUGENT, NELLE, theater, film and television producer; b. Jersey City, May 24, 1939; d. John Patrick and Evelyn Adelaide (Stern) N.; m. Donald G. Baker, June 6, 1960 (div. 1962); m. Benjamin Janney, June 22, 1969 (div. Apr., 1980); m. Jolyon Fox Stern, Apr. 7, 1982; 1 child, Alexandra Fox Stern. BS, Skidmore Coll., 1960, DHL (hon.), 1981. Chmn. bd. McCann & Nugent, Prodns. Inc., N.Y.C., 1976-86; pres. Foxboro Prodns., Inc., N.Y.C., 1985-94; pres., CEO Foxboro Entertainment, 1990-94; pres. The Foxboro Co., Inc.; co-prin. Golden Fox Films, Inc. Stage mgr. various off-Broadway shows, 1960-64; prodn. asst.: Broadways plays Any Wednesday, 1963-64, Dylan, 1964, Ben Franklin in Paris, 1964-65; stage mgr. Broadway shows, 1964-68; prodn. supr., then gen. mgr., 1969-76, assoc. mng. dir. Nederlander Corp., operating theaters and producing plays in, N.Y.C. and on tour, 1970-76; prodr.: Dracula, 1977 (Tony award), The Gin Game (Tony nom.), The Elephant Man, 1978 (Tony award, Drama Critics award), Morning's at Seven, 1980 (Tony award), Home, 1980 (Tony nomination), Amadeus, 1981 (Tony award); also produced: Rose and Piaf, 1980, Otherwise Engaged, The Life and Adventures of Nicholas Nickleby, 1981 (Tony award, Drama Critics award), The Dresser (Tony award nominee), 1981, Mass Appeal, 1981; The Lady & The Clarinet, 1982; The Glass Menagerie (revival), 1983; Painting Churches (Obie award), 1983; Total Abandon, 1983; All's Well That End's Well, 1983 (Tony nominee); Pilobolus Dance Company, 1983; Pacific Overtures (revival), 1984; Much Ado about Nothing/Cyrano de Bergerac (repertory) (Tony award nominees), 1984; Leader of the Pack (Tony award nominee), 1985, The Life and Adventures of Nicholas Nickleby (revival) (Tony award nominee), 1986; prodr.: TV spls.; Morning's At Seven, Piaf; Pilobolus; prodr. A Fighting Choice, 1986-88, A Conspiracy of Love, 1987, The Final Verdict, 1990 (Cable Ace award nominee Best Picture); exec. prodr. (TV pilot) Morning Maggie, 1987, Dick Clark Prodns., 1988-90, (feature films) Student Body, 1993, Getting In, 1994, Jane Doe, 1996; (TV films) In the Presence of Mine Enemies, 1995-96 (Houston Festival Silver Star award), A Town Has Turned to Dust, 1997 (World Festival Silver medal 1998), After the Storm (Best Feature Film N.Y. Internat. Independent Film & Video Festival, 2000), Angelciti Festival (Best Feature 2001), Houston Worldfest (Platinum award, Best Film Made for TV 2001), (Broadway prodn.) The Smell of the Kill, 2002, Sly Fox, 2004. Mem.: League Am. Theaters, Prodrs. Guild Am. (exec. com.), Am. Women's Econ. Devel. Corp. (bd. dirs.). Office: Foxboro Co Inc 133 E 58th St Ste 301 New York NY 10022-1236

NUGENT, S. GEORGIA, academic administrator; m. Thomas J Scherer. B cum laude, Princeton U., 1973; PhD in classics, Cornell U. Instr. Swarthmore Coll.; assoc. prof. Brown U., 1985; asst. prof. Princeton U., 1979, dean, Harold McGraw Jr. Ctr. for tchg. and learning, asst. to pres., 1992—95; assoc. provost, 1995; pres. Kenyon Coll., 2003—. Author books. Recipient Wriston award for excellence in tchg. Office: President Ransom Hall Kenyon Coll Gambier OH 43022

NULL, ELISABETH HIGGINS, librarian, writer; b. Worcester, Mass., Dec. 1, 1942; d. Carter Chapin Higgins and Katharine Huntington (Bigelow) Doman; m. Henry Harrison Null IV, July 13, 1963 (div. 1970); children: John Higgins, Jacob Van Vechten. BA, Sarah Lawrence Coll., Bronxville, N.Y., 1983; MA, Yale U., 1985, MPhil in Am. History, 1989; MA in Folklore, U. Pa., 1987; M Libr. and Info. Sci., Cath. U. Am., 1995. V.p. Abington Pub. Co., Clark's Summit, Pa., 1966-70; CEO Green Linnet Records, Danbury, Conn., 1971-81; vis. lectr. Am. Musical Life, Georgetown U., 1991-98; libr. and conversion specialist nat. digital libr. program Libr. of Congress, Washington, 1996-98, expert cons., 1995; writer on edn. issues Rural Sch. and Cmty. Trust, 1999—2003; rsch. coord. congl. campaign Janine Selendy (Dem.) N.Y. Dist. 17, 2002—. Bd. dirs. Maine Folklife Ctr.; Horizon Internat., New Haven; program co-chair Washington Folk Festival, 1999-2000; program chair Folklore Soc. Greater Washington, 1993-94; humanities scholar-in-residence Conn. Coun. for Humanities and Conn. Dept. for the Arts, Waterbury, Conn., 1986-87; fieldworker in folklore Waterbury Ethnic Music Project, 1986-87; rsch. coord. Selendy for Congress Campaign, 2002. Singer 2 recordings: The Feathered Maiden, 1977, American Primitive, 1981; performance career with guitarist Bill Shute included 6 appearances with Garrison Keillor's A Prairie Home Companion; major venues include Phila. Folk Festival, Bklyn. Mus., Mus. Natural History. Incorporator John Woodman Higgins Armory, Worcester, Mass., 1966—; sec. Stanton Park Neighborhood Assn., Washington, 1990; bd. dirs. John and Clara Higgins Found., 1999—; rsch. coord. Selendy for Congress, 2002. Folger Shakespeare Libr. Seminar fellow, 1989-91. Mem. ALA, Am. Folklore Soc., Soc. for History of Early Am. Rep. Democrat. Episcopalian. Avocations: folk music performer, song writer. Home and Office: 706 Bonifant St Silver Spring MD 20910-5534 E-mail: elisabeth.null@tcs.wap.org.

NUMANN, PATRICIA JOY, surgeon, educator; b. Bronx, N.Y., Apr. 6, 1941; BA, U. Rochester, 1962; MD, SUNY Health Sci. Ctr., Syracuse, 1965. Intern, resident SUNY Health Sci. Ctr., Syracuse, 1970, from asst. prof. to assoc. prof. surgery, 1970-89, assoc. dean Coll. Medicine, 1978-84, assoc. dean Coll. Medicine Clin. Affairs, prof. surgery, 1989—, Lloyd S. Rogers prof. of surgery, med. dir., 1997—. Dir. breast care program SUNY Health Sci. Ctr., Syracuse, 1986—; presenter in field. Contbr. chpts. to books, articles to profl. jours. Found. bd. dirs. Vera House, Syracuse, 1993-94; hon. bd. dirs. F.A.C.T., Syracuse, 1994. Named one of Women of Distinction, N.Y. State Gov. Mario Cuomo, 1994, Disting. Tchg. Prof. SUNY, 1991, Disting. Svc. Prof.; recipient Disting. Surgeon award Assn. Women Surgeons, 1991. Mem. AMA (coun. sci. affairs), ACS (com. on cancer grad. med. edn. com., 2nd v.p. 1999, 2d v.p. 1999-2000), Am. Bd. Surgeons (bd. dirs. 1994—, chair 2001), Am. Assn. Endocrine Surgeons (v.p. 1992), Assn. for Surg. Edn. (pres. 1985), Corinthian Club. Office: SUNY Health Sci Ctr 750 E Adams St Syracuse NY 13210-1834

NUNES, PRICILLA O. special education educator, artist; b. Acushnet, Mass., Aug. 6, 1928; d. George Mendall and Rose Blanche (Pepin) Nunes; m. Joseph Nunes, Apr. 19, 1949; children: Jay Joseph, Tod Albert, Marc Truman. BA, U. Mass., Dartmouth, 1977; MEd, Worcester State Coll., 1981. Advisor spl. edn. New Bedford, Mass., 1993—. Exhibited works with Bierstadt Art Soc., 1993; exhibited at Davoll Country Store, 1997-98. Active in various charity events. Mem. AAUW, Mass. Ret. Tchrs. Assn., Ret. State, County and Mcpl. Employees Assn., Internat. Porcelain Artists and Tchrs. Inc., New Bedford Art Mus., Friends of Free Pub. Libr., Friends of Zeitarian Theater, Coll. Club of New Bedford. Avocation: china and porcelain painting. Home: 37 Lawrence St New Bedford MA 02745-5521

NUNLEY, CYNTHIA ANN, special education educator; b. Sheridan, Wyo., June 26, 1953; d. John Franklin, Jr. and Virginia Houx Nunley. BA in Elem. Edn./Spl. Edn., U. Wyo., 1977; MEd in Ednl. Tech., Lesley U., 2000. Cert. administrv. endorsement Wyo. Profl. Tchg. Stds. Bd. Spl. edn. tchr. Fremont County Sch. Dist. #1, Lander, Wyo., 1977—. Chair agrl. com. Lander 2020 Visioning Group, 1995—98; mem. Lander Econ. Devel. Assn., 1992—2000; mem. state bd., sec. Wyo. Very Spl. Arts, 2002—; Fremont County state comitteewoman Wyo. State Dems., 1994—2003; mem. rsch., rev. and priorities com. U. Wyo., Water Resources Ctr., Laramie, 1995—97. Named Wyo. Dem. Partybuilder of the Yr., Wyo. Dems., 1996; Mid-Career, Spl. Edn. scholar, Wyo. Assn. Spl. Edn. Dirs., 2003. Mem.: ASCD, Wyo. Schools Univ. Partnership (chair staff devel. task force 1999—2002), Wyo. Edn. Assn. Avocation: music. Home: 864 N 4th Lander WY 82520 Office: Fremont County Sch Dist #1 400 Baldwin Creek Rd Lander WY 82520 Personal E-mail: cnunle@hotmail.com.

NUNN, PATARICA DIAN, poet, telephone directory operator; b. Arkadelphia, Ark., Aug. 10, 1951; m. Freddie Lee Nunn, Mar. 16, 1979; children: Katarica Lakisha, Roshonda Lanae, Ophelia Lorraine, Opal Laverne. Student, Ouachita Bapt. U., 1971—72. Dir. assistance operator Southwestern Bell Tel. Co., Hot Springs, Ark., 1978—2003; ret., 2003. Songwriter My Moment of Miles, Time, 1998, Mellow Drifting, 2002, Sassy Sassy Lady, 2003; author: (poetry) Sacred Memories, 1996, A True Mother's Love, 1997, A True Father's Love, 1998 (Hon. Mention Nat. Authors Registry), Out in Left Field, 1998, A Breathe of Fresh Air, 2002. Bd. dirs., mem. adv. com. Nat. Libr. Poetry. Named to Internat. Poetry Hall of Fame, 1997; recipient elected into the Internat. Poetry Hall of Fame, 1997, elected into the Internat. Hall of Fames's Mus. on the Internet's World Wide Web., http:/www.poets.com, Bd. of Dir. and Adv. Com. of The Nat. Libr. of Poetry, mentioned "A True Fathers Love", Iliad Press, 1998, hon. mention "Contemporary Verse From Around the World Edit.", The Nat. Authors Registry, 1997, hon. mention,"Sacred Memories", Whispers In The Garden edit., The Poetry Guild, 1997. Mem.: Poetry Guild, Nat. Author's Registry. Democrat. Home: 4 Stillman Dr Little Rock AR 72209

NUNNELLEY, CAROL FISHBURNE, editor newspaper; b. Montgomery, Ala., Dec. 25, 1942; m. William A. Nunnelley; 1 child, Meg. BA, Samford U., 1965; postgrad., U. Ky., 1965-66. Reporter The Birmingham (Ala.) News, 1966-78, city editor, 1978-92, mng. editor, 1992—. Recipient reporting and writing awards Ala. Soc. Porfl. Journalists, Ala. Press Assn., Ala. Associated Press, Journalist of the Yr. award Troy State U., Achievement award Birmingham Emancipation Assn. Mem. Soc. Profl. Journalists, Leadership Birmingham, The Women's Network. Office: The Birmingham News 2200 4th Ave N Birmingham AL 35203-3840

NUOVO, BETTY A. state representative; b. Englewood, N.J., Dec. 10, 1931; m. Victor L. Nuovo, 1953; two children. BS, Bucknell U., 1953. State rep. Vt. Ho. of Reps., Middleury, 1981-90, 96—; pvt. law practice Middleury, 1974—94. Jud. com. Ho. of Reps., 1981-88, chmn. 1985-88, chmn. jud. rules com. 1985-86, adminstrv. rules com. 1985-88, vice-chmn. 1987-88, ways and means com. 1989-90, Middlebury natural resources and energy com., 1996-2000, jud. com., 2001-02, agr. com., 2003—. Chair Vt. State Dem. Platform Com., Middlebury Charter Comn., Vt., Addison County Dem. Com.; bd. dirs., exec. bd. Addison County Regional Planning Com; bd. selectmen Middlebury; bd. dirs. Vt. YMCA; mem. Middlebury LWV. Office: PO Box 347 Middlebury VT 05753-0347

NURIK, CINDY BUNIN, educational consultant, marriage and family therapist; b. Bronx, N.Y., May 24, 1952; d. Murray and Kitty Bunin; m. Marc Steven Nurik, Sept. 16, 1978; 1 child, Kacey Leigh. D of Early Childhood and Devel., Nova Southeastern U., 1981; MusM in Therapy and Edn., U. Miami, 1977; BA, Ithaca Coll., 1975. Lic. marriage and family therapist Fla. Dept. of Health, 2003, registered Music Therapist Nat. Assn. of Music Therapy, 1977. Music therapist Seagull Sch. For The Handicapped, Ft. Lauderdale, Fla., 1978—80; founder, child devel. specialist, chairwoman bd. Mommy and Me Enterprises, Inc., Ft. Lauderdale, 1993—2004; child devel. cons., dir. of content Mommy and Me Co., Burbank, Calif., 2002—; founder, dir. of edn., tchr. Parent Child Enrichment

Ctr., Coral Springs, Fla., 1980—87; founder, dir. of progarm, clinician Cancer Wellness Program, Ft. Lauderdale, 1988—90; marriage and family therapist, crisis counselor Cimineo and Assocs., Miami and Ft. Lauderdale, 1991—97. V.p. Y-Me Breast Cancer Program, Ft. Lauderdale, 1987—92; child devel. specialist Moms Online/Oxygen Media, New York, 1997—2001. Author: (book) Fun With Mommy and Me; contbr. children's videos Fun and Friends, Splish Splash, and Lullabye and Goodnight (Dr. Toy Award for best activity product in 2001); author and ednl. cons.: Mommy and Me Playgroup Favorites and More Playgroup Favorites, 2003. Chairwoman Mommy and Me Holding Co., Ft. Lauderdale, 1998—. Recipient Hall of Gt. Grads., Lindenhurst H.S. Student Coun., 2002, Discovery Award of Excellence for Fun With Mommy and Me, Discovery Channel, 2001, Best Parenting Book, Parents Choice Awards, 2001, Top 10 Parenting Books, Amazon.com, 2001, Editor's Choice award, Parenting Publ. Am. award, 2001. Fellow: Am. Assn. Of Marriage and Family Therapists. Achievements include first to A pioneer of the Mommy and Me class movement. Created her unique curriculum and has taught thousands of families throughout the years. Avocations: singing, painting, animal advocate. Office: Mommy and Me Company 4100 W Alameda Ave Burbank CA 91505 Office Phone: 954-472-2052.

NUROK, ZITA, elementary school educator; arrived in U.S., 1976; d. Abram Berkowitz and Tamara Sacks; m. David Nurok, Nov. 2, 1969; children: Michael, Saul. Tchr.'s diploma, Johannesburg Coll. Edn., South Africa, 1962; BA, U. South Africa, 1967. Tchr. I. H. Harris Primary Sch., Johannesburg, 1963—70, Bellair Primary Sch., Durban, 1971, Jewish Comty. Ctr., Indpls., 1980—85, Hasten Hebrew Acad., Indpls., 1985—. Mem.: Nat. League Am. Pen Women (sec. Indpls. br. 1996—2000, v.p. Indpls. br. 2001—02, pres. Indpls. br. 2002—04). Avocations: book clubs, writing, music, gardening. Home: 1545 Trace Ln Indianapolis IN 46260 Office: Hasten Hebrew Acad 6602 Hoover Rd Indianapolis IN 46260 Office Phone: 317-251-1261.

NUSBACHER, GLORIA WEINBERG, lawyer; b. N.Y.C., July 22, 1951; d. Murray and Doris (Togman) Weinberg; m. Burton Nusbacher, Aug. 4, 1974; 1 child, Shoshana. BA magna cum laude, Barnard Coll., 1972; JD, Columbia U., 1975. Bar: N.Y. 1976. Assoc. Hughes Hubbard & Reed LLP, N.Y.C., 1975-83, counsel, 1983-91, ptnr., 1991—. Lectr. in field. Mem. Columbia Law Rev.; contbr. articles to profl. jours. Troop leader, leader trainer Girl Scouts USA, 1991-97. Mem. ABA (employee benefits and exec. compensation com. 1987—, fed. regulation securities com., subcom. employee benefits, exec. compensation and sect. 16, 1983—, task force Sect. 16, 1991-97, vice-chair com. employee benefits and exec. compensation 2001—03, chair subcom. fed. and state securities laws of com. employee benefits and exec. compensation 1994-2001, 03—, mem. task force exec. compensation 1992-94). Office: Hughes Hubbard & Reed LLP 1 Battery Park Plz New York NY 10004-1482 Office Phone: 212-837-6719.

NUSIM, ROBERTA, publisher; b. N.Y.C., Dec. 1, 1943; BA in English, CCNY, 1964; MA, CUNY, 1966. Tchr. N.Y.C. Bd. Edn., 1964-73; v.p. program devel. Mind, Inc., Westport, Conn., 1973-76; pres. Mind Media, 1976-78; founder, pres. Lifetime Learning Systems, Fairfield, Conn., 1978-90; founder dir. The Film Study Guild, 1979-90; founder, pres. The Work & Family Publishing Group, Inc., 1991-94; founder, pres. Youth Mktg. Internat., Ltd., 1995—. Editor: Let's Talk About Health, 1980. Mem. ASCD, NAFE, Am. Film Inst., Women in Comm., Ednl. Press Assn. Am., Ptnrs. for Global Edn. (founder). Avocations: reading, painting. Mailing: 400 E 56th St New York NY 10022

NUSS, BARBARA GOUGH, artist; b. Washington, Apr. 11, 1939; d. Gaines Homer Gough and Edwerta Barbara (Beyer) Barber; m. Frederick A. Johnson, Sept. 30, 1968 (div. 1975); 1 child, Mark Eugene; m. Fred Dean Nuss, Dec. 18, 1982. BFA, Syracuse U., 1960; postgrad., Schuler Sch. Fine Arts, Balt., 1986—87. Art dir. Chappell's Dept. Store, Syracuse, NY, 1960-62, 66; mgr., illustrator Holman Anderson & Moore, Washington, 1967-70; art dir., advt. mgr. Ad-Media & Howard Advt. Assocs., Columbia, Md., 1970-75; acct. exec. Graphic Arts Inc., Alexandria, Va., 1975-77; sales mgr. The Jour. Newspapers, Washington, 1977-82; tchr., adult edn. Montgomery Coll., Rockville, Md., 1984-85; pvt. tchr. fine arts, Woodbine, Md., 1982-96; instr. Plein air painting workshop, 1998—. Chmn. Montgomery County Juried Art Exhibit, Rockville, 1988, Mid-Atlantic Regional Watercolor Exhibit, 1998—99; pres. Nuss Fine Arts, Inc., 1992—; judge Am. Landscape Show Art League Torpedo Factory, Alexandria, Va., 2002; judge Mountain State Forest Festival Fine Art Exhibition, Elkins, W.Va., 2002, Potomac Valley Watercolorists Ann. Juried Show, 2004. One-woman shows include Pa. State U., 1986, NIH, Bethesda, Md., 1989—90, Md. Nat. Capital Pk. and Planning Commn., 1991, Art League Gallery, Alexandria, 1992, Bendann Art Galleries, Towson, Md., 1999—2000, Troika Gallery, Easton, Md., 2004, Strathmore Hall Art Ctr., Bethesda, Md., 2004, Washington County Arts Coun. Gallery, Hagerstown, Md., 2004, Grand Style Gallery, Balt., 2004, exhibited in group shows at Art League at the Torpedo Factory, 1987—92, 2002, Mid-Atlantic Regional Watercolor Exhbn., 1989—90 (Holbein award), Heritage Gallery Classical Realism, 1989—90, Art Barn Gallery, Washington, 1990, Carmen's Gallery, 1991—2000, Art Showcase 100 Md. Artists, 1991—92, Assn. pour la Promotion du Patrimoine Artistique Francais, Galerie Jean Lammelin, Argenteuil, France, 1991, Salmagundi Club 14th Ann. Exhbn., 1991, Atrium Gallery Georgetown U., Washington, 1991, 18th Ann. Exhbn., 1995, Mid-Atlantic Regional Watercolor Exhbn., 1996, State House, Annapolis, 1996, World Trade Ctr., Balt., 1996, Bendann's Art Gallery, Towson, 1997—2002, Principle Gallery, Alexandria, 1998—2004, Miniature Painters, Sculptors and Gravers Soc. Washington, 1999, Addison/Ripley Fine Art Gallery, Washington, 1999, Rock Creek Gallery, 1999, Main St. Gallery, Annapolis, 1999—2000, Miniature Art Soc. Fla., 2000, Oil Painters Am., 2000—01, Rock Creek Gallery, Washington, 2001, Troika Gallery, Easton, 2001—04, Washington County Arts Coun. Gallery, Hagerstown, 2001—04, Brazier Fine Art, Richmond, Va., 2002, Grand Style Gallery, Balt., 2002—04, Black Rock Ctr. for the Arts, Germantown, Md., 2003—04, Kushnir Taylor Gallery, Ellicott City, Md., 2003—04, Represented in permanent collections Am. Coun. Edn., NIH, Bell Atlantic, Kiplinger Washington Editors, Fairhaven Retirement Cmty., Md. State Treas.'s Office, NIH; work represented in: Art from the Parks, How Did You Paint That?, 2000, How Did You Paint That? 100 Ways to Paint Landscapes, 2004; author: 14 Formulas for Painting Fabulous Landscapes, 2003. Finalist still life competition, Artist's mag., 1996, landscape competition, 2003; recipient 1st prize for watercolor, C&O Canal Show, 1987, 1st prize for oil painting, Rockville Art League, 1987, Montgomery County Art Assn., 1983, 1989, Gaithersburg Fine Arts Assn., 1983, 1989, grand champion award for oil painting, Howard County Fair, 1989, one of Top 100 award for oil painting, Nat. Arts for Parks, 1989, 1991, 1992, 2001, Top 200, 1990, 1993, 1996, Best in Show award, Nat. League Am. Pen Women, Md. Biennial Conv., 1999, 1st prize watercolor, 1st prize oils, Best in Show award, 2003. Mem. Nat. League Am. Pen Women (sec. Bethesda, Md. 1989, treas. 2000-03), Balt. Watercolor Soc. (bd. dirs. 1997-99), Washington Soc. Landscape Painters (sec. 1999, pres. 2000-03, Baustian award for Excellence 1999), Salmagundi Club (NYC), Oil Painters Am. Avocations: quilting, crossword puzzles. Home: 3132 Cabin Run Woodbine MD 21797-7933 Office Phone: 301-854-6447.

NUSS, JOANNE RUTH, sculptor, artist; b. Gt. Bend, Kans., May 2, 1951; d. Melvin Oliver and Ruth Helen (Brauer) N. Student, Valparaiso U., 1969-71, U. Kans., 1972-73, U. Copenhagen, 1974; BA, Ft. Hays State U., 1975; MFA, Santa Fe Inst. Fine Arts, 1991. Lectr. Noon Edition Sta. KCMO-TV, Kansas City, 1981, Menoriah Hosp., Brookridge Elem. Sch., The Jill Shurin Show Telecable 10, Kansas City, 1982, Barton County C.C., Gt. Bend, Nelson-Atkins Mus., Kansas City, Mo., 1984; artist-in-residence Helen Wurlitzer Found., Taos, N.Mex., 1984, 90. One-woman shows include Bette Moses Gallery, Great Bend, 1980, Art Expo Ctr., San Francisco, 1981, Univ. Gall., Ft. Hays State U., 1985, Am. Legation Mus., Tangiers, Morocco, 1986, Inma Gallery, Dhahran, Saudi Arabia, 1994, Bab Rouah Gallery, Rabat, Morocco, 1996, Agora Gallery, Soho, New York, 2001, Amsterdam Whitney Internat. Fine Art Gallery, N.Y.C., 2003, others, exhibited in group shows at Second Internat. Sculpture Fair, Boston, 1980, Joan Cooke Gallery, Kansas City, Mo., 1983, The Batz Lawrence Gallery, Kansas City, 1984, Galerie de Rond Point des Champs Elyssees, Paris, 1989, Tetouan & La Kabila Gallery, Tetouan, Morocco, 1991, N.Mex. Sculptors Guild, Fuller Lodge Art Gallery, Los Alamos, 1992, Hermosas Fine Arts Gallery, Durango, Colo., 1995, Tanjah Flandria Art Gallery, Tangiers, 1997—99, Shidoni Gallery, Tesuque, N.Mex., 1999—2002, Birger Sandzen Gallery, Lindsborg, Kans., 2000, Nat. Assn. Women Artists, Sarasota Visual Arts Ctr., 2000, U. No. Iowa, Cedar Falls, 2001 (1st pl., 2001), Coplan Gallery, Boca Raton, Fla., 2002, Attleboro (Mass.) Mus., 2002, Jeanette Hare Art Gallery, West Palm Beach, Fla., 2002, Twelfth Ann. Benefit Auction, Attleboro (Mass.) Mus., 2003, 114th Ann. Exhbn. Nat. Assn. Women Artists Fifth Ave. Gallery, N.Y.C., 2003, Attleboro Mus., Mass., 2003, Baker Arts Ctr. 7th Nat. Juried Art Exhbn., 2004; featured artist Artist Spectrum Mag.; exhibitions include Nat. Assn. Women Artists, 2003. Recipient 1st Kans. Artist Purchast award Ft. Hays State U., 1985, Best 3-D Works award Wichita Art Assn., 1983; 1st female fgn. artist commd. for archtl. major project, Tangiers, 1988-90. Mem. Nat. Assn. Women Artists, Nat. Sculpture Soc., Nat. Mus. of Women in the Arts, Internat. Sculpture Ctr., Kans. Sculptor's Assn., Internat. Platform Assn. Avocations: traveling, working with other artists, gardening.

NUSS, SHIRLEY ANN, computer coordinator, educator; b. Madison, Minn., Oct. 22, 1946; d. Woodland Henry and Aileen Thelma (Mattox) Cover; divorced; 1 child, Melissa Ann. BEd, Trinity U., Washburn U., 1969; MA, Mich. State U., 1982, PhD, 1990. 3d grade tchr. Topeka Pub. Schs. System, 1969-70; 6th grade tchr. McCune (Kans.) Middle Sch., 1970-72; 7th grade English tchr. Muskego (Wis.) Norway Sch. Dist., 1972-78; intermediate level. tchr. Gibson Sch. for Gifted Children, Redford, Mich., 1979-82; 3d grade tchr. Cranbrook Edn. Community, Bloomfield Hills, Mich., 1982-89, multi media/computer coord., instr., 1989—. Adj. prof. ednl. tech. cert. program and master's degree in tech. edn. Mich. State U., 2000-01. tchr. Space Pioneer Learning Adventure design camp, 2003; ednl. adv. bd. Henry Ford Mus. and Greenfield Village, Dearborn, 1988-91; Renaissance Outreach for Detroit Area Schs; task force Mich. Coun. for the Humanities, Lansing, 1991-92; speaker, presenter on tech. Mich. Sci. Tchr. Assn., Lansing, 1992-96, Mich. Assn. Computer Users in Learning, Ind. Sch. Assn. Ctrl. States; tchr. adv. bd. Teaching and Computer Magazine, 1988-90; developer grades 1-5 multimedia/computer curriculum Brookside Sch., Cranbrook, 1995-96. Author: (museum activities) Henry Ford Museum, Greenfield Village, 1991. Space camp fellowship Mary Bramson award Huntsville, Ala., 1992; Detroit Edison Conservation grantee Detroit Edison, 1992, ROADS Mimi grant Mich. Coun. for Humanities, Lansing, 1993. Mem. Cranbrook Schs. Faculty Coun. (pres., v.p. 1993-95). Republican. Presbyterian. Avocations: antique collecting, reading, gardening, computers and technology. Home: 1715 Shankin Dr Walled Lake MI 48390-2446 Office: Cranbrook Schs Brookside 550 Cranbrook Rd # 801 Bloomfield Hills MI 48301 E-mail: snuss@cranbrook.edu., drnuss@aol.com.

NUSSBAUM, MARTHA CRAVEN, philosophy and classics educator; b. N.Y.C., May 6, 1947; d. George and Betty (Warren) Craven; m. Alan Jeffrey Nussbaum, Aug., 1969 (div. 1987); 1 child, Rachel Emily. BA, NYU, 1969; MA, Harvard U., 1971, PhD, 1975; LHD (hon.), Kalamazoo Coll., 1988, Grinnell Coll., 1993. Asst. prof. philosophy and classics Harvard U., Cambridge, 1975-80, assoc. prof., 1980-83; vis. prof. philosophy, Greek and Latin Wellesley (Mass.) Coll., 1983-84; assoc. prof. philosophy and classics Brown U., Providence, R.I., 1984-85, prof. philosophy, classics and comparative lit., 1985-87, David Benedict prof. philosophy, classics and comparative lit., 1987-89, prof., 1989-95; prof. law and ethics U. Chgo., 1995-96, prof. philosophy dept., 1995—, prof. Divinity Sch., 1995—, Ernst Freund prof. law and ethics Law Sch./Divinity Sch., 1996-99, assoc. mem. classics dept., 1996—. Rsch. advisor World Inst. Devel. Econs. Rsch., Helsinki, Finland, 1986-93; vis. prof. law U. Chgo., 1994. Author: Aristotle's De Motu Animalium, 1978, The Fragility of Goodness, 1986, Loe's Knowledge, 1990, The Therapy of Desire, 1994, Poetic Justice: The Literary Imagination and Public Life, 1996, For Love of Country, 1996; editor: Language and Logos, 1983; (with A. Rorty) Essays on Aristotle's De Anima, 1992, (with A. Sen) The Quality of Life, 1993, (with J. Brunschwig) Passions & Perceptions, 1993, (with J. Glover) Women, Culture and Development, 1995, Poetic Justice, 1996, Cultivating Humanity, 1997, Sex and Social Justice, 1998. Soc. Fellows Harvard U. jr. fellow, 1972-75, Humanities fellow Princeton U., 1977-78, Guggenheim Found. fellow, 1983, NIH fellow, vis. fellow All Souls Coll., Oxford, Eng., 1986-87; recipient Brandeis Creative Arts award, 1990, Spielvogel-Diamondstein award, 1991; Gifford lectr. U. Edinburgh, 1993. Fellow Am. Acad. Arts and Scis. (membership com. 1991-93, coun. 1992-96), Am. Philos. Soc.; mem. Am. Philos. Assn. (exec. com. Ea. divsn. 1985-87, chair com. internat. coop., ex-officio mem. nat. bd. 1989-92, chair com. on status of women 1994-97), Am. Philol. Assn., PEN. Office: U Chicago The Law Sch 1111 E 60th St Chicago IL 60637-2776

NUSZ, PHYLLIS JANE, not-for-profit fundraiser, consultant, educational consultant; b. Lodi, Calif., Dec. 16, 1941; d. Fred Henry and Esther Emma (Enzminger) Nusz. BA, U. Pacific, 1963, MA, 1965; EdD, Nova Southeastern U., 1987. Cert. fund raising exec. Prof. speech comm. Bakersfield (Calif.) Coll., 1965-86; from asst. dir. student activites to found. exec. dir. Bakersfield (Calif) Coll., 1965-86; mgmt. seminar dir. Delta Kappa Gamma Soc. Internat., Austin, 1983-86; loaned exec. United Way San Joaquin County, Stockton, Calif., 1990; fundraising and edn. cons. PJ Enterprises, Lodi, 1987—. Bd. dirs. U. Calif. Sch. Medicine Surg. Found., San Francisco, 1989—92; mem. Heritage Cir. and Chancellor's Assn. U. Calif., San Francisco, 1987—. Recipient Archives award of merit, Evang. Luth Ch. Am., 1988; fellow, Calif. Luth. U., 1985—. Mem.: NEA, World Affairs N. Am. Coun., Nat. Assn. Parliamentarians, Nat. Soc. Fund Raising Execs. (bd. dir. 1988—91, chmn. mentor program Calif. Capital chpt. 1991, chmn. acad. fund raising 1991, chmn. mentor program Golden Gate chpt. 1991, founding pres. San Joaquin chpt. 1992—93, Pres.'s award for Meritorious Svc., Golden Gate chpt. 1991), Rotary Internat. (North Stockton bd. dir. 1993—99, treas. 1994—96, pres.-elect 1996—97, pres. 1997—98, dist. 5220 membership devel. com. 1997—98, immediate past pres. 1998—99, membership task force 1998—99, dist. membership chmn. 1999—2000, dist. gov. elect 2000—01, dist. gov. 2001—02, mem. Internat. Afghan refugee relief com. 2001—02, chair Zone Inst. Prog. 2003, TRF Permanent Fund nat. adv. 2003—, Internat. Alleviation of Poverty Task Force 2003—04, coord. zone 24 chmn. 2004 Far West PETS, multiple Paul Harris fellow, RI Found. Bequest Soc., RI Found. major donor benefactor), U. Pacific Alumni Assn. (bd. dir. 1974—82), Delta Kappa Gamma (chpt. pres. 1976—78, Chi State parliamentarian 1979—81, chair Internat. Golden Gift Fund 1982—86, sec. 1985—87). Republican. Lutheran. Avocations: photography, travel, swimming, walking, fishing. Office: PJ Enterprises 1300 W Lodi Ave Ste A11 Lodi CA 95242-3000 E-mail: pjnursz@aol.com.

NUTT, SANDRA MARIA, actress, writer; d. Ambrose Benjamin and V. Elaine Nutt. BA in Theatre and Drama, U. Mich., 1986. Owner, pres., founder Riprap Entertainment, North Hollywood, Calif., 1999—. Prodr., writer, actress Riprap Entertainment, North Hollywood, Calif., 1999—2003. Author: (screenplay) Prevarications, Little White Lies (Kodak's Champagne Celebration Award for First and Second Time Filmmakers, 1996). Office: Riprap Studio Theatre 59 Seat Equity Waiver 5755 Lankershim Blvd North Hollywood CA 91601 Office Phone: 818-990-7498. Personal E-mail: sandy@riprapentertain.com.

NUTTELMAN, DORIS GRAVES, nursing administrator; b. Mass., Apr. 20, 1930; Student, Lynn (Mass.) Hosp., 1951; MS, U. Mass., 1975, MA in Teaching, 1973; EdD, Vanderbilt U., 1989. RN, Mass., N.H. Dir. nursing div. Am. Internat. Coll., Springfield, Mass., 1975-77; chair dept. nursing Colby-Sawyer Coll., New London, N.H., 1980-84, exec. dir. N.H. Bd. of Nursing, Concord, 1990—. Mem. ANA, APHA, Nat. League of Nursing, Sigma Theta Tau.

NUTTER, ZOE DELL LANTIS, retired public relations executive; b. Yamhill, Oreg., June 14, 1915; d. Arthur Lee Lantis and Olive Adelaide (Reed) Lantis-Hilton; m. Richard S. West, Apr. 30, 1941 (div. Nov. 1964); m. Ervin John Nutter, Dec. 30, 1965. Assoc. in Bus., Santa Ana Jr. Coll., 1944. Cert. spl. emergency secondary tchr., Calif.; FAA cert. lic. commercial, instrument, single/multi engine land airplanes pilot. Promoter World's Fair & Comml. Airlines Golden Gate Internat. Expn., San Francisco, 1937-39; pirate theme girl, official hostess Treasure Island's World Fair, San Francisco, 1939-40; prin. dancer San Francisco Ballet, 1937-41; artist, 1941-45; program dir. Glenn County H.S., Willows, Calif., 1952-58; pub. rels. Monarch Piper Aviation Co., Monterey, Calif., 1963-65; pilot, pub. rels. Elano Corp., Xenia, Ohio, 1968-85. Bd. dirs. Nat. Aviation Hall of Fame, Dayton, Ohio, pres., chmn., 1989-92, bd. trustees, 1976—, chmn. bd. nominations, 1992—; bd. trustees Ford's Theatre, Washington, Treasure Island Mus., San Francisco; charter mem. Friends of First Ladies, Smithsonian, Washington, 1990-93. Assoc. editor KYH mag. of Shikar Safari Internat., 1985-87; contbg. columnist Scripps Howard San Francisco News, 1938. Bd. dirs. Cin. May Festival, 1976-80, San Francisco Aero. Soc., 1997-; cen. com. Glenn County Rep. Party, Willows, 1960-64; state cen. com. Rep. Party, 1962-64; adv. bd. Women's Air & Space Mus., Dayton, 1987-94. Warrant officer, Civil Air Patrol, 1967-69. Recipient Civic Contbn. Honor award Big Brothers/Big Sisters, 1991, John Collier Nat. award Camp Fire Girls & Boys, 1988, Tambourine award Salvation Army, 1982, State of Ohio Gov.'s award for Volunteerism, 1992, Spirit of Innovation award Wright State U., 2001, Amb. award Wright Bros. Heritage Benefit, 2001, East Ann. Zoe Dell Nutter Dayton Air Show award, 2003, In grateful appreciation of contbn. 1909 Wright Flyer Monument award INVENTING FLIGHT, 2003; named Most Photographed Girl in World, News Burs. & Clipping Svcs., 1938-39. Mem., founder Dancers Over 40, NYC; Fellow Pres.'s Club U. Ky., Ohio State U., Wright State U.; mem. 99's Internat. Women Pilots Orgn. (life, hospitality chmn. 1968), San Francisco Aeronaut. Soc. (bd. dirs. 1997—), Monterey Bay Chapter 99's (mem. chmn. 1964-65), Walnut Grove Country Club, Rotary (Paul Harris fellow 1987), Shikar Safari Internat. (host com. 1976), Country Club of the North. Achievements include established ann. Zoe Dell Nutter Dayton Air Show award, 2003. Avocations: aviation, flying, horseback riding, hunting, shooting, fashion. Home: 986 Trebein Rd Xenia OH 45385-9534

NUXOLL, CARLA, federal official; m. Jim Braukmann. Degree in polit. sci. and history, Gonzaga U. English tchr. Mead H.S., Spokane, 1972; pres. Wash. Edn. Assn., 1989-93; apptd. sec.'s regional rep. U.S. Dept. Edn. Region X, Seattle, 1994—. Avocations: avid fly fisherwoman, bridge player, reader of detective novels. Office: US Dept Edn Region X Jackson Fed Bldg 915 2nd Ave Seattle WA 98174-1009

NWAFOR, BERNADETTE EGO, educational psychologist, educator; arrived in US, 1970; d. Philip Uchegbu and Martha Ugochi Opara-Nadi; 5 children. BA, Rust Coll.; MEd, EdD, Loyola U. Sr. edn. officer Chgo. City Coll., 1980—83; sr. lectr. Fed. Govt. of Nigeria, 1983—91; with Brit. Commonwealth U. Jos, Saint Lucia, 1992—94; prof. Chaflin U., Orangeburg, SC, West Indies, 1994—. Grad. asst., Schmidt fellow Loyola U., 1988—99. Contbr. articles to profl. jours., chapters to books. Mem.: S.C. Assoc. Tchr. Edn., Am. Psychol. Assn., Am. Psychol. Soc. Achievements include discovery of the relationship of authoritorianism and dogmatism to cognitive style among American and third world foriegn students. Avocations: sewing, cooking, reading, gardening, walking. Office: Claflin U 400 Magnolia St Orangeburg SC 29115

NYBORG, VANESSA MARIE, psychologist, researcher, educator; b. San Francisco, Mar. 1, 1972; d. Milton and Beatrice Nyborg. BA, UCLA, 1995; PhD, Duke U., 2001. Postdoctoral rsch. fellow Brown Med. Sch., Providence, 2001—03; rschr. Ctr. for Sch. Based Youth Devel., U. Calif., Santa Barbara, 2003, asst. rschr., adj. prof. Gevirtz Sch. Edn., 2003—. Grantee, NIH, 2003—. Mem.: APA, Psi Chi. Office: Gevirtz Grad Sch Edn U Calif Santa Barbara Santa Barbara CA 93106

NYCE, DOROTHY YODER, writer, retired religious studies educator; b. Kalona, Iowa, Nov. 10, 1937; d. Herman M. and Bessie King Yoder; m. John David Nyce, Aug. 5, 1961; children: Lynda D., Gretchen L. BA, Goshen (Ind.) Coll., 1960; MDiv, Associated Mennonite Biblical, 1981; D of Ministry, Western Theol. Sem., Holland, Mich., 1997. Campus ministry, sec., residence hall dir. Goshen Coll., 1961—62, 1966—68, 1975—76, adj./asst. prof. Bible and religion, 1981—96; tchr., residence hall dir. Woodstock Sch., Mussoorie, India, 1962—65; part-time pastoral counselor, tchr. Associated Mennonite Biblical Sem., Elkhart, Ind., 1980—82; preaching elder Assembly Mennonite Ch., Goshen, 1989—90; faculty theol. coll. Evang. Luth. Ch. in Am., Chennai, India, 1998. Bd. dirs., exec. com. Kodaikanal Woodstock Internat., Inc., Atlanta, 1987—96; bd. dirs., overseas com. chair Mennonite Bd. of Mission, Elkhart, 1985—91; peace sect. bd. Mennonite Ctrl. Com., Akron, Pa., 1972—75, peace sect. task force on women, 1973—76. Author: (script, slide set, video) Women of Strength: Ancient & Modern, 1987, (books) Strength, Struggle and Solidarity: India's Women, 1989, Jesus's Clear Call to Justice, 1990, Different Drummers, 2001; editor: (books) To See Each Other's Good, 1996, Rooted and Branching Women Worldwide, 1998; contbr. numerous articles to books and profl. jours.; compiler, editor: Bessie Lucie King (Yoder) Kansas Years 1906-1931, 2001; prodr.: (videos) Holy Respect, No Less, 1996, India Kaleidoscope, 1996; co-editor: Mission Today Challenges and Concerns, 1998. Grantee Fulbright Study Tour, U.S. Ednl. Found. India, 1988, C. Henry Smith Peace Lectureship, 1988—89, ecumenical events/resources, Calvin Inst. of Christian Worship, Grand Rapids, Mich., 2001. Democrat. Avocations: photography, gardening, hospitality, reading, research. Home: 1603 S 15th St Goshen IN 46526

NYCUM, SUSAN HUBBELL, lawyer; BA, Ohio Wesleyan U., 1956; JD, Duquesne U., 1960; postgrad., Stanford U. Bar: Pa. 1962, U.S. Supreme Ct. 1967, Calif. 1974. Sole practice law, Pitts., 1962-65; designer, adminstr. legal rsch. sys. U. Pitts., Aspen Sys. Corp., Pitts., 1965-68; mgr. ops. Computer Ctr., Carnegie Mellon U., Pitts., 1968-69; dir. computer facility Computer Ctr., Stanford U., Calif., 1969-72, Stanford Law and Computer fellow, 1972-73; cons. in computers and law, 1973-74; sr. assoc. MacLeod, Fuller, Muir & Godwin, Los Altos, Los Angeles and London, 1974-75; ptnr. Chickering & Gregory, San Francisco, 1975-80; ptnr.-in-charge high tech. group Gaston Snow & Ely Bartlett, Boston, NYC, Phoenix, San Francisco, Calif., 1980-86; mng. ptnr. Palo Alto office Kadison, Pfaelzer, Woodard, Quinn & Rossi, Los Angeles, Washington, Newport Beach, Palo Alto, Calif., 1986-87; sr. ptnr., chmn. U.S. intellectual property/info. tech. practice group Baker & McKenzie, Palo Alto, 1987—, mem. U.S. leadership team, 1987-97, mem. Asia Pacific regional coun., 1995—. Founder Tech. Disputes Resolution Svcs., Inc., 2002—; trustee EDUCOM, 1978-81; mem. adv. com. for high tech. Ariz. State U. Law Sch., Santa Clara U. Law Sch., Stanford Law Sch., U. So. Calif. Law Ctr., law sch. Harvard U., U. Calif.; U.S. State Dept. del. OECD Conf. on Nat. Vulnerabilities, Spain, 1981; invited speaker Telecom, Geneva, 1983; lectr. N.Y. Law Jour., 1975—, Law & Bus., 1975—, Practicing Law Inst., 1975—; chmn. Office of Tech. Assessment Task Force on Nat. Info. Sys., 1979-80. Author:(with Bigelow) Your Computer and the Law, 1975, (with Bosworth) Legal Protection for Software, 1985, (with Collins and Gilbert) Women Leading, 1987; contbr. monographs, articles to profl. publs. Fellow Am. Bar Found.;

mem. Town of Portola Valley Open Space Acquisition Com., Calif., 1977; mem. Jr. League of Palo Alto, chmn. evening div., 1975-76 NSF and Dept. Justice grantee for studies on computer abuse, 1972— Fellow Am. Bar Found., Assn. Computer Machinery (mem. at large of coun. 1976-80, nat. lectr. 1977—, chmn. standing com. on legal issues 1975—, mem. blue ribbon com. on rationalization of internat. propr. rights protection on info. processing devel. in the '90s 1990—), Coll. Law Practice Mgmt. (trustee 2002—); mem. ABA (chmn. sect. on sci. and tech. 1979-80), Computer Law Assn. (v.p. 1983-85, pres. 1986—, bd. dirs. 1975—), Calif. State Bar Assn. (founder first chmn. econs. of law sect., vice chmn. law and computers com.), Internat. Bar Assn. (U.S. mem. computer com. of corps. sect.), Nat. Conf. Lawyers and Scientists (rep. ABA), Strategic Forum on Intellectual Property Issues in Software of NAS, Internat. Coun. for Computer Comm. (gov. 1998). Office: 35 Granada Ct Portola Valley CA 94028-7736 Office Phone: 650-851-3304. E-mail: susan@nycum.net.

NYIEN, PATRICIA, music educator; b. Kenosha, Wis., May 16, 1953; d. David Arne and Sarah Viola (Molgaard) Dissmore; m. Phillip Dwayne Nelson, Aug. 16, 1973 (div. Oct. 1995); children: Phillip Kirk Nelson, Kindra Lynn Nelson; m. Harvey David Nyien, Apr. 20, 1996; 1 child, Kevin Patrick Nelson. Student, LaSalle Extension U., 1971; B Music Edn., Belmont U., 1977. Pvt. piano tchr., Avilla, Mo., 1973—75, Hendersonville, Tenn., 1975—77, Clarksville, Tenn., 1977—79, Hinsdale, Ill., 1979—86, Westmont, Ill., 1986—; choral dir. Greenwood Annex/Jr. H.S., Clarksville, 1977—79; presch. music/jr. choir dir. Oak Brook (Ill.) Christian Sch., 1981—95. Mem.: The Internat. Cat Assn., Am. Choral Dirs. Assn., Music Tchrs. Nat. Assn. (theory chmn. 2001—03, cert.), Salt Creek Music Tchrs. Assn. (publicity com. 1990—94, membership com. 1994—98, treas. 1998—2000, theory chmn. 2001—, pres. 2003—), Internat. Bengal Cat Assn., Ill. state music tchr. assoc. (treas. 1998—2000). Republican. Mem. Assemblies Of God. Avocations: needlepoint, skiing, singing, knitting, breeding Bengal cats. Home: 830 Franklin St Westmont IL 60559

NYLANDER, JANE LOUISE, museum director, lecturer, writer; b. Cleve., Jan. 27, 1938; d. James Merritt and Jeannette Cayford; m. Daniel Harris Giffen, 1963 (div. 1970); children: Sarah Louise, Thomas Harris; m. Richard Conrad Nylander, 1972: 1 child, Timothy Frost. AB, Brown U., 1959; MA, U. Del., 1961; postgrad., Attingham (Eng.) Summer Sch., 1970; PhD (hon.), New Eng. Coll., 1994. Curator Hist. Soc. York (Pa.) County, 1961-62, N.H. Hist. Soc., Concord, 1962-69; instr. New Eng. Coll., Henniker, NH, 1964-65, Monadnock C.C., Peterborough, NH, 1966-69; curator of textiles and ceramics Old Sturbridge (Mass.) Village, 1969-85; adj. assoc. prof. Boston U., 1978-85; sr. curator Old Sturbridge Village, 1985-86; dir. Strawbery Banke Mus., Portsmouth, NH, 1986-92, Soc. for Preservation of New Eng. Antiquities, Boston, 1992-93, pres., 1993—2002, pres. emerita, 2002—. Adj. prof. art history and Am. studies Boston U., 1993-96; trustee Worcester (Mass.) Hist. Mus., 1978-84, trustee Hist. Deerfield (Mass.), Inc., 1981-94, 2003—, hon. trustee, 1994-2003, chmn. strategic planning com., 2003—, trustee Hist. Mass. Inc., 1991-93, Portsmouth Athenaeum, 1988-90, Japan Soc. N.H., 1988-92, Fort Ticonderoga, 2000-02; bd. govs. Decorative Arts Trust, 1991—; mem. adv. bd. Concord (Mass.) Mus., 1986-94, Wentworth-Coolidge Commn., 1991-96, John Nicholas Brown Ctr. for Am. Studies, Providence, 1995—; mem. adv. com. Wentworth-Coolidge, 1996—; mem. adv. bd. dept. Am. decorative arts Mus. Fine Arts, Boston, 1971-99, Art of the Ams., 1999-2000; mem. adv. com. Lakes Region Conservation Trust, 2002-03; mem. coun. Colonial Soc. Mass., 1993-96; advisor, house com. Moffatt Ladd House, 1973—; mem. interpretation com. N.H. Hist. Soc., 2003—; bd. dirs. Castle Preservation Soc., 2003—; cons. in field. Author: Fabrics for Historic Buildings, 4th edit., 1990, Our Own Snug Fireside: Images of the New England Home 1760-1860, 1993, paperback edit., 1994, Windows on the Past, 2000, The Art of Family, 2002; mem. editl. bd.: Hist. N.H., 1993—2000, The Dublin Seminar, 1984—; contbr. numerous articles to profl. jours. Mem. adv. bd. New Eng. Heritage Ctr., 1993-2002; active State House Adv. Com., Boston, 1984-85, Gov.'s Coun. for Wentworth Coolidge Mansion, Concord, 1964-66; mem. Com. for Preservation of N.H. State Flags, 1989-92; mem. H.F. duPont award com. Winterthur Mus., 1993—, Mt. Vernon adv. com. for 1999, 1996-99, collections com. N.J. Hist. Soc., 1994-96; designator The Henderson Found., 1992-2004. Recipient Charles F. Montgomery prize Decorative Arts Soc., 1985, (with Richard C. Nylander) The Anne and Roger Webb award Hist. Mass., Inc., 1996, John F. Ayer award Bay State Hist. League, 2002, Boston History award Bostonian Soc., 2003. Mem.: N.H. Hist. Soc. (interpretation com. 2003—), Costume Soc. Am. (bd. dirs. 1977—83), New Eng. Hist. Geneal. Soc., N.H. Humanities Coun., Soc. Preservation of N.H. Forests, Soc. Winterthur Fellows, Mass. Hist. Soc., Portsmouth Athenaeum, Royal Oak Assn., Nat. Trust for Hist. Preservation, Am. Assn. for State and Local History (Cert. of Commendation 2001), Am. Antiquarian Soc., Friends of the Moffatt Ladd Huse., Colonial Soc. Mass., Nat. Soc. Colonial Dames in N.H. (bd. dirs. 1967—73, program chair 2002—), Friends of Hist. Deerfield, Lakes Region Conservation Trust, St. Botolph Club, Brown Club N.H. (trustee 1988—93). Episcopalian. Home: 17 Franklin St Portsmouth NH 03801-4501 E-mail: jane.nylander@verizon.net.

NYLANDER, PATRICIA MARIE, pilot; d. Mary Ellen Weise and Lawrence William Schweitzer; m. Ryan George Nylander, Mar. 18, 2000; 1 child, Madeline Marie. BS, No. Ariz. U., 1987. Cert. airline transport pilot FAA, 1992, flight instr. FAA, 1993, sea plane pilot FAA, 1993, flight engr. rating FAA, 1998. Pilot Grand Canyon Airlines, Ariz., 1992—93, Doss Aviation, Hondo, Tex., 1993—94, Minn. Air N.G., St. Paul, 1994—2001, N.W. Airlines, St. Paul, 1998—. Mem. Christ's Ch. Of The Valley, Phoenix, 1996—2003. Decorated Commendation Medal USAF, Achievement Medal. Mem.: Airline Pilots Assn. (licentiate), Delta Delta Delta (life; panhellenic v.p. 1986—87, highest sorority mem. grade point average 1985, 1986, 1987). R-Consevative. Avocations: running, travel, snow skiing, hiking, water-skiing. Office: Northwest Airlines 5101 Northwest Dr Saint Paul MN 55111 Home: 6603 Falstaff Rd Woodbury MN 55125

OAKAR, MARY ROSE, congresswoman; b. Cleve., Mar. 5, 1940; d. Joseph M. and Margaret Mary (Ellison) O. BA in English, Speech and Drama, Ursuline Coll., Cleve., 1962, LHD (hon.); MA in Fine Arts, John Carroll U., Cleve., 1966; LLD (hon.), Ashland U., 1978, Ursuine Coll., 1984, St. Mary's Notre Dame, 1989, Baldwin Wallace Coll., 1988; LHD (hon.), Trinity Coll., 1987. Instr. English and drama Lourdes Acad., Cleve., 1963-70; asst. prof. English, speech and drama Cuyahoga Community Coll., Cleve., 1968-75; mem. Cleve. City Council from 8th Ward, 1973-76, 95th-102nd Congresses from 20th Dist. Ohio, 1977-92; mem. Pepper Commn. on Long Term Health Care, chair subcom. internat. devel., fin., trade and monetary policy; chair task force on social security, elderly, women; chair subcom. on personnel and police; mem. banking, fin. and urban affairs com., select com. on aging, post office and civil service com., com. on house adminstrn., also numerous subcoms.; ptnr. Mary Rose Oakar and Assocs. Apptd. to Sec. Conf. to Establish Nat. Action Plan on Breast Cancer, 1994, by Pres. Clinton to bd. dirs. Bldrs., For Peace, 1994, to policy to White House Conf. on Aging. Founder, vol.-dir. Near West Side Civic Arts Center, Cleve., 1970; ward leader Cuyahoga County Democratic Party, 1972-76; mem. Ohio Dem. Central Com. from 20th Dist., 1974; trustee Fedn. Community Planning, Cleve., Health and Planning Commn. Cleve., Community Info. Service Cleve., Cleve. Soc. Crippled Children, Public Services Occupational Group Adv. Com., Cuyahoga Community Coll., Cleve. Ballet, Cleve. YWCA. Recipient Outstanding Service awards OEO, 1973-78, Community Service award Am. Indian Center, Cleve., 1973, Community Service award Nationalities Service Center, 1974, Community Service award Club San Lorenzo, Cleve., 1976, Cuyahoga County Dem. Woman of Yr., 1977, Ursuline Coll. Alumna of Yr. award, 1977, awards Irish Nat. Caucus, awards West Side Community Mental Health Center, awards Am. Lebanese League, awards Cleve. Fedn. Am.-Syrian Lebanese Clubs, Breast Cancer Awareness award Nat. Women's Health Resource Ctr., 1989, 1st lay recipient Barbara Bohen-Pfeiffer award Italian-Am. Found. Cancer Rsch., 1989, Disting. Svc. award Am. Cancer Soc., 1989, Myrl H. Shoemaker award Ohio Dem. Party, 1992, Philip Hart award Consumer Fedn. Am., 1987; cert. appreciation City of Cleve.; Woman of Yr. award Cuyahoga County Women's Polit. Caucus, 1983; decorated Knight of Order of St. Ladislaus of Hungary, Women in Aerospace Outstanding Ach. award, Black Focus Woman of the Decade award. Office: 1888 W 30th St Cleveland OH 44113-3447

OAKES, CLAUDIA, museum administrator; Asst. dir. pub. programs Utah Mus. Nat. History, Salt Lake City; asst. dir. exhibits & ops. Utah Mus. Natural History & Hansen Planetarium, Salt Lake City, assoc. dir. mus. affairs; v.p. pub. programs Milw. Pub. Mus., Milw.; assoc. curator, acting aeronautics dept. chmn. Smithsonian Inst. Nat. Air & Space Mus., Washington. MAP III surveyor; reviewer IMLS-GOS. Mem.: Am. Assn. Mus. (v.chmn.), Nat Assn. Mus. Exhib. (bd. dir.), We. Mus. Assn. (bd. dir.). Office: Utah Museum Natural History 1390 E Presidents Circle Salt Lake City UT 84112-0050

OAKES, ELLEN RUTH, psychotherapist, health institute administrator; b. Bartlesville, Okla., Aug. 19, 1919; d. John Isaac and Eva Ruth (Engle) Harboldt; m. Paul Otis Oakes Sr., June 12, 1937 (div. April 1974); children: Paul Otis Jr., Deborah Ellen, Nancy Elaine Masters; m. Siegmar Johann Knopp, Nov. 24, 1975 (div. Feb. 1998). BA in Sociology, Psychology summa cum laude, Oklahoma City U., 1961; MS in Clin. Psychology, U. Okla., 1963, PhD, 1967. Lic. clin. psychologist, Okla. Chief psychometrist Okla. U. Guidance Ctr., Norman, 1962; psychology trainee VA Hosp., Oklahoma City, 1962-64, Cerebral Palsy Ctr., Norman, Okla., 1964-65; psychology intern Guidance Service, Norman, 1965-66, staff psychologist, 1966-67; asst. prof. psychology Okla. U. Med. Sch., Oklahoma City, 1967-70; supr. psychology interns Okla. Univ. Health Scis. Ctr., 1967-80; founder, dir. Timberridge Inst., Oklahoma City, 1970-90, pres., 1980-90; pvt. practice clin. psychologist Oklahoma City, 1970-92. Instr. Okla. U. extension course, Tinker AFB, Oklahoma City, 1963, U. Okla., 1965-66; discussion leader Inst. for Tchrs. of Disadvantaged Child Oklahoma City Sch. System, 1966; leader group therapy sessions Asbury Meth. and Westminster Presbyn. Chs., Oklahoma City, 1966; mem. psychology team confs. for hearing disorders, Okla. U. Med. Sch., 1967-70; cons. Oklahoma City Pub. Schs., 1970-72, cons., group leader halfway house, 1972; mem. Okla. State Bd. Examiners Psychologist, 1974, 75; lectr. chs., PTAs, hosps.; reviewer Am. Psychol. Assn. Civilian Health and Med. Program of the Uniformed Svcs., 1978-89. Workshop conductor on Shame & Sexuality, Zurick Jungian Inst. winter seminar, 1992; attended Européen Congrés de Gestalt Thérapie in Paris, 1992; contbr. articles to profl. jours. Speaker Okla. County Mental Health Assn. Annual Worry Clinic, St. Luke's Ch., Oklahoma City, 1968-92, psychology dept. Sorosis Club, St. Luke's Ch.; charter mem. English spkg. Christian Congregation mission outreach Pauluskirche, Bochum, Germany, 1993-97, exec. coun., 1996-97. Mem. APA (peer rev. project with CHAMPUS, 1978-89), Okla. Psychol. Assn. (life, pres. 1975-76, named Pioneer Psychologist of Okla. by exec. com. 1998). Avocations: art, travel, poetry, photography, walking.

OAKES, JUDY DIANNE, real estate broker; b. Charleston, W.Va., Aug. 14, 1950; d. William E. and Betty A. Hager; m. Gary H. Oakes, Dec. 21, 1968; children: Scott E., Christina D. McDaniel, Brian M. Real estate sales Bishop Realtors, Cleve., 1973-82, Armstrong Realty, Riverside, Calif., 1986-88; real estate broker Remax All Stars, Riverside, Calif., 1988-94, Realty Exec., Riverside, Calif., 1994—2001. Named #1 Agt. in Co., Real Estate Sales, 1994—2002. Mem. Cert. Residential Specialist, Magnolia Ave. Bapt. Ch., Inland Valley Assn. Realtors (bd. dirs. 1995). Avocations: reading, rose garden, ocean. Office: Judy Oakes Real Estate Group 3742 Tibbetts St #101 Riverside CA 92506 E-mail: judy@judyoakes.com.

OAKES, LAURA, radio personality; Grad. Comms. and History, U. Minn.; postgrad., Brown Inst. With radio, Fergus Falls, Minn.; with radio and TV Duluth; news reporter, morning news anchor Sta. KDLH-TV; co-anchor 5 pm Sta. WCCO News Hour. Mem.: Minn. AP Broadcasters Assn. (bd. dirs.). Avocations: competitive figure skater, music, theater, sports. Office: WCCO 625 2nd Ave S Minneapolis MN 55402

OAKES, NANCY, chef, restaurant owner; Student, San Francisco Art Inst. Formerly chef Alexis, San Francisco; formerly chef, co-owner Barnacle, San Francisco, L'Avenue, San Francisco; chef, co-owner Boulevard, San Francisco, 1993—. Named Best Chef in Calif., James Beard Found., 2001. Office: Boulevard 1 Mission St San Francisco CA 94105

OAKES, SHARON LORRAINE, elementary school educator, researcher; b. San Francisco, July 20, 1962; d. James Langdon Rodak and Florence Nerona Hunt; 1 child, Samuel Joseph. AA, MiraCosta C.C., Oceanside, Calif., 1984; BA, San Diego State U., 1988; postgrad., Ind. U., 2002. Tchg. credential Calif., 1990, Ind., 1994, cert. ESL instr. Calif. Cmty. Colleges, MiraCosta C.C., 1989. ESL educator Mira Costa C.C., Oceanside, 1989—92; elem. educator Murrieta (Calif.) Valley Unified Sch. Dist., 1990—93, mid. sch. educator, 1993—95, Carlsbad (Calif.) Unified Sch. Dist., 1991—; ESL educator Vista (Calif.) Unified Sch. Dist., 1993—94; gifted and talented educator Met. Sch. Dist. Martinsville, Ind., 1997—99; tchr. educator assoc. instr. Ind. U. Sch. Edn., Bloomington, 1999—2001. Gifted and talented site coord. E. Hale Curran Elem. Sch., Murrieta, 1991—92; doctoral dissertation participant Ind. U. Sch. Edn., Bloomington, 2000—01; site coun. mem. Aviara Oaks Mid. Sch., Carlsbad, Calif., 2001—; presenter in field. MiraCosta Spartan scholar, MiraCosta C.C., 1980, Mildred R. Lowel scholar, Ind. U. Sch. Edn., 1999, 2000, 2001. Mem.: Nat. Educators Assn., Calif. Tchrs.' Union, Nat. Art Edn. Assn., Am. Ednl. Rsch. Assn., Pi Lambda Theta. Democrat. Roman Catholic. Achievements include development of Vocational English As A Second Language Curriculum and Instruction; research in arts integration curriculum and instruction. Avocations: reading, exercise, art. Home: 1351 Enchante Way Oceanside CA 92056 Office: Carlsbad Unified Sch Dist 6225 El Camino Real Carlsbad CA 92008 Personal E-mail: sharonrodakoakes@hotmail.com.

OAKLEY, CAROLYN LE, state legislator, small business owner; b. Portland, Oreg., June 28, 1942; d. George Thomas and Ruth Alveta Victoria (Engberg) Penketh; children: Christine, Michelle. BS in Edn., Oreg. State U., 1965. Educator Linn County (Oreg.) Schs., 1965-76; owner Linn County Tractor, 1965-90; mem. Oreg. Legis. Assembly, Salem, 1989—, asst. majority leader, 1993—, majority whip, 1994; apptd. regional dir. region 10 Dept. Health and Human Svcs., Seattle, 2002—. Mem. exec. bd. Oreg. Retail Coun., 1987-90. Chmn. Linn County Rep. Ctrl. Com., 1982-84; chmn. bd. dirs. North Albany Svc. Dist., 1988-90; chair Salvation Army, Linn and Benton Counties, 1987—; vice chmn. bd. trustees Linn-Benton C.C. Found., 1987—; pres. Women for Agr., Linn and Benton Counties, 1984-86; mem. STRIDE Leadership Round Table, 1991—; state chair Am. Legis. Exch. Coun., 1991-96; nat. bd. dirs., 199-99, exec. com., 1995, 1st vice chair, 1998; mem. Edn. Commn. of the States, 1991—, com. policies and priorities, 1993—, steering com., 1998—, exec. com., 1998; mem. Leadership Coun. on Higher Edn., 1995—; mem. nat. policy bd. Danforth Found., 1995—; state dir., Women in Govt., 1996—; state dir., Nat. Order Women Legislators, 1993—; hon. mem. Linn-Benton Compact Bd., 1993—; active Linn County Criminal Justice Coun., 1994—. Named Woman of Yr. Albany chpt. Beta Sigma Phi, 1970. Mem. Nat Conf. State Legislators (chmn. edn. com. 1992—), Albany C. of C. (bd. dirs. 1986-93, 96—), Linn County Rep. women (legis. chmn. 1982-91). Republican. Methodist. Avocations: gardening, camping. Home: 10047 Main St Unit 216 Bellevue WA 98004 Office: 2201 6th Ave RX-01 Seattle WA 98121-0001

OAKLEY, DEBORAH JANE, researcher, educator; b. Jan. 31, 1937; d. George F. and Kathryn (Willson) Hacker; m. Bruce Oakley, June 16, 1958; children: Ingrid Andrea, Brian Benjamin. BA, Swarthmore Coll., 1958; MA, Brown U., 1960; MPH, U. Mich., 1969, PhD, 1977. Dir. teenage and adult programs YWCA, Providence, 1959-63; editl. asst. Stockholm U., 1963-64; rsch. investigator, lectr. dept. population planning U. Mich., 1971-77, asst. prof. cmty. health programs, 1977-79, asst. prof. nursing rsch., 1979-81, assoc. prof., 1981-89, prof., 1989—2002, interim dir. Ctr. Nursing Rsch., 1988-90, acting dir. Ctr. Nursing Rsch., 1998, prof. emeritus, 2002. Vis. prof. Beijing Med. U., 1996—; prin. investigator NIH, CDC and pvt. found. funded rsch. grants and contracts on family planning, women's health and health care in China, mem. nat. adv. com. nursing rsch., 1993-97; mem. adv. workshop on Nat. Survey on Family Growth, 1994-97; co-chair Mich. Initiative for Women's Health, 1993-95. Author: (with Leslie Corsa) Population Planning, 1979; contbr. articles to profl. jours. Bd. dirs. Planned Parenthood Fedn. Am., 1975-80. Recipient Margaret Sanger award Washtenaw County Planned Parenthood, 1975, Outstanding Young Woman of Ann Arbor award Jaycees, 1970, Dist. Faculty award Mich. Assn. Gov. Bds., 1992, Blue Cross Blue Shield Found. of Mich. award for Excellence in Health Policy, 1996. Mem. APHA (chmn. population sect. coun.), Internat. Union Sci. Study Population, Midwest Nursing Rsch. Soc., Population Assn. Am., Delta Omega, Sigma Theta Tau (hon.). Democrat. Home: 5200 S Lake Dr Chelsea MI 48118-9481 Office: U Mich Sch Nursing Ann Arbor MI 48109-0482

OAKLEY, DIANE, insurance executive, benefit consultant; b. Teaneck, N.J., Dec. 27, 1953; d. Geard Joseph and Joan B. (Peterson) O. BS, Fairfield U., 1975; MBA, Fordham U., 1984. Actuarial asst. TIAA-CREF, N.Y.C., 1975-79, benefit plan counselor, 1979-82, adv. officer, 1982-85, branch mgr., 2nd v.p. Bethesda, Md., 1985-89, v.p., assns. & govt. rels., 1989-95, v.p., 1995—2002, v.p for spl. cons. svcs., 2002—. Bd. dirs. Nat. Assn. Coll. and Univ. Bus. Officers, 1995-2000; bd. trustees Fairfield U. Mem. Am. Assn. Higher Edn., Am. Assn. Women in C.C.'s, Women in Govt. Rels., Working in Employee Benefits, Secure Retirement Coalition (treas.). Roman Catholic. Home: 4400 E West Hwy Apt 432 Bethesda MD 20814-4504 Office: TIAA-CREF Ste 800 1101 Pennsylvania Ave NW Washington DC 20004-2526

OAKLEY, MARY ANN BRYANT, lawyer; b. Buckhannon, W.Va., June 22, 1940; d. Hubert Herndon and Mary F. (Deeds) Bryant; m. Godfrey P. Oakley, Jr., Sept. 2, 1961; children: Martha, Susan, Robert. AB, Duke U., 1962; MA, Emory U., 1970, JD, 1974. Tchr. Winston-Salem/Forsyth County Schs., N.C., 1961-65; assoc. Margie Pitts Hames, Atlanta, 1974-80; ptnr. Stagg Hoy & Oakley, Atlanta, 1980-83, Oakley & Bonner, Atlanta, 1984-90; pvt. practice, 1990-96; ptnr. Holland & Knight LLP, Atlanta, 1996—. Adj. prof. trial practice Ga. State U., 1986-95; adj. prof. pretrial Emory U. Law Sch., 1991, 95; bd. dirs. Nat. Employment Lawyers Assn., 1989-94; founding coord. NELA, Ga.; mem. Ga. Supreme Ct. Commn. on Racial and Ethnic Bias, 1994-95; mem. Ga. Bd. Bar Examiners, 1990-94, chmn., 1994. Author: Elizabeth Cady Stanton, 1972; mem. editl. rev. bd.: The Ga. Labor Letter, 1997—2001, notes and comments editor: Emory Law Jour., 1973—74; contbr. articles to law jours. Bd. dirs. Atlanta Met. YWCA, 1975-79, 1st v.p., 1978-79; mem. Leadership Atlanta, 1979; bd. dirs. Ga. chpt. ACLU, 1981-83, Holland & Knight Charitable Found. Bd., 2002—, Ga. Legal Svcs. Program, 1991-98; trustee Unitarian Universalist Congregation Atlanta, 1977-80, pres., 1979-80, mem. Unitarian Universalist Commn. Appraisal, 1980-85; bd. dirs. Unitarian Universalist Service Com., 1984-90, v.p., 1986-88, pres., 1988-90. Nat. Merit scholar, 1958. Fellow: Ga. Bar Found., Am. Bar Found.; mem.: ABA, Gate City Bar Assn., Ga. State Bar Disciplinary Bd. (investigative panel 1985—88, chmn. 1987—88), Ga. Assn. Women Lawyers (Kathleen Kessler award 1998), Lawyers Club Atlanta, Atlanta Bar Assn., State Bar Ga. (chmn. individual rights sect. 1979—81, Disting. Svc. award 1998, H. Sol Clark Pro Bono award 1996), Am. Judicature Soc., Order of Coif, Phi Beta Kappa, Bleckley Inn of Ct. (pres. 1996—99). Home: 2224 Kodiak Dr NE Atlanta GA 30345-4152 Office: 1201 W Peachtree St One Atlantic Ctr Ste 2000 Atlanta GA 30309-3400

OAKLEY, PHYLLIS ELLIOTT, retired diplomat; b. Omaha, Nov. 23, 1934; d. Thomas Myron Elliott and Elsa (Kerkow) Elliott Garabedian; m. Robert Bigger Oakley, June 8, 1958; children: Mary Oakley Kress, Thomas Elliott. BA, Northwestern U., 1956; MA, Fletcher Sch. Law & Diplomacy, 1957. Commd. fgn. svc. officer Dept. State, 1957-58, 74-99, ret., 1999. Asst. cultural affairs officer, Kinshasa, Zaire, 1979-82, desk officer, Afghanistan, 1982-85, Pearson Exchange officer Senator Mathias, 1985-86; dep. spokesman, 1986-89, AID Afghan Humanitarian Assistance program, Islamabad, 1989-91, dep. asst. sec. INR Bur., 1991-93, sr. dep. PRM, 1993-94, asst. sec. PRM, 1994-97, INR Bur., 1997—. Mem. Coun. Fgn. Rels., Cosmos Club, Phi Beta Kappa. Office: Dept of State INR Bur 2201 C St NW Washington DC 20520-0001

OAKS, LUCY MOBERLEY, retired social worker; b. Lexington, Ky., May 10, 1935; d. Shelton Neville Moberley and Jane Emison (Roberts) Meadors; m. William Bryant Oaks, Nov. 10, 1956; children: Bryant, Michael, Kevin, Richard, Deborah. BA in Social Work, U. Ky., 1957; MA in Counseling Psychology, Bowie (Md.) State Coll., 1979. Lic. mental health counselor, Wash. Youth dir. Calvary Bapt. Ch., Renton, Wash., 1960-64, ch. tng. dir., 1980-87; youth dir. Temple Bapt. Ch., Redlands, Calif., 1965-68, Calvary Bapt. Ch., Morgantown, W.Va., 1971-73; cmty. coll. parent educator Bellevue (Wash.) Cmty. Coll., 1980-89; pvt. counselor Renton, 1980-90; Christians social svcs. dir. Puget Sound Bapt. Assn., Federal Way, Wash., 1984-87; therapeutic program dir. ACAP Child and Family Svcs., Auburn, Wash., 1984—94, assoc. dir., 1994—96; retired, 1996. Parent instr. APPLE Parenting, Auburn, 1990-92; seminar presenter, Puget Sound, Wash., 1980-95; dir. social svc. ministries ACAP Child and Family Svcs., 1996-98; cons. Mary Kay Cosmetics, 1996—; file supr. Year 2000 Dept. of Commerce/Census Bur., Bellevue (Wash.) br., 1999-2000; product advisor Advocare, 2003—04. Bd. trustees Valley Cmty. Players, Renton, 1995; featured spkr. parent edn. Puget Sound Area, 1988—96; bd. dirs. Calvary Bapt. Ch., Renton, 1981—87. Mem. Puget Sound Adlerian Soc. (bd. dirs. 1981-83), Kiwanis (chmn. interclub com., membership chmn. 1994-95). Democrat. Avocations: drama, reading, walking, traveling, bowling. Home: 2218 177th Pl NE Redmond WA 98052-6071

OATES, JOYCE CAROL, author; b. Lockport, N.Y., June 16, 1938; d. Frederic James and Caroline (Bush) O.; m. Raymond Joseph Smith, Jan. 23, 1961. BA, Syracuse U., 1960; MA, U. Wis., 1961. Instr. English U. Detroit, 1961-65, asst. prof., 1965-67; prof. English U. Windsor, Ont., Can., 1967-87; writer-in-residence Princeton (N.J.) U., 1978-81, prof., 1987—. Author: (short story collections) By the North Gate, 1963, Upon the Sweeping Flood, 1966, The Wheel of Love, 1970, Marriages and Infidelities, 1972, The Hungry Ghosts, 1974, The Goddess and Other Women, 1974, Where Are You Going, Where Have You Been?: Stories of Young America, 1974, The Poisoned Kiss and Other Stories From the Portuguese, 1975, The Seduction and Other Stories, 1975, Crossing the Border, 1976, Night-Side, 1977, All the Good People I've Left Behind, 1978, The Lamb of Abyssalia, 1980, A Sentimental Education: Stories, 1981, Last Days: Stories, 1984, Wild Nights, 1985, Raven's Wing: Stories, 1986, The Assignation, 1988, Heat: And Other Stories, 1991, Where is Here?, 1992, Haunted: Tales of the Grotesque, 1994, Will You Always Love Me? and Other Stories, 1995; (novels) With Shuddering Fall, 1964, A Garden of Earthly Delights, 1967 (Nat. Book award nomination 1968), Expensive People, 1967 (Nat. Book award nomination 1969), them, 1969 (Nat. Book award for fiction 1970), Wonderland, 1971, Do With Me What You Will, 1973, The Assassins, 1975, Childwold, 1976, The Triumph of the Spider Monkey, 1976, Son of the Morning, 1978, Unholy Loves, 1979, Cybele, 1979, Bellefleur, 1980 (L.A. Times Book award nomination 1980), A

Sentimental Education, 1981, Angel of Light, 1981, A Bloodsmoor Romance, 1982, Mysteries of Winterthorn, 1984, Solstice, 1985, Marya, 1986, You Must Remember This, 1987, (as Rosamond Smith) The Lives of the Twins, 1987, American Appetites, 1989, (as Rosamond Smith) Soul-Mate, 1989, Because It Is Bitter, and Because It Is My Heart, 1990, (as Rosamond Smith) Nemesis, 1990, I Lock My Door Upon Myself, 1990, The Rise of Life on Earth, 1991, Black Water, 1992, (as Rosamond Smith) Snake Eyes, 1992, Foxfire: Confessions of a Girl Gang, 1993, What I Lived For, 1994 (PEN/Faulkner award nomination 1995) The Barrens, 2001, Faithless: Tails of Transgression, 2001, Middle Age: A Romance, 2001, Big Mouth and Ugly Girl, 2002; (non-fiction) The Faith of a Writer: Life, Craft, Art, 2003; (poetry collections) Women in Love, 1968, Expensive People, 1968, Anonymous Sins, 1969, Love and Its Derangements, 1970, Angel Fire, 1973, Dreaming America, 1973, The Fabulous Beasts, 1975, Season of Peril, 1977, Women Whose Lives are Food, Men Whose Lives are Money: Poems, 1978, The Stepfather, 1978, Celestial Timepiece, 1981, Invisible Women: New and Selected Poems, 1970-1972, 1982, Luxury of Sin, 1983, The Time Traveller, 1987; (plays) The Sweet Enemy, 1965, Sunday Dinner, 1970, Ontological Proof of My Existence, 1970, Miracle Play, 1974, Three Plays, 1980, Daisy, 1980, Presque Isle, 1984, Triumph of the Spider Monkey, 1985, In Darkest America, 1990, I Stand Before You Naked, 1990, The Perfectionist and Other Plays, 1995; (essays) The Edge of Impossibility, 1972, The Hostile Sun: The Poetry of D.H. Lawrence, 1973, New Heaven, New Earth, 1974, Contraries: Essays, 1981, The Profane Art, 1984, On Boxing, 1987, (Woman) Writer: Occasions and Opportunities, 1988; editor, compiler: Scenes from American Life: Contemporary Short Fiction, 1973, (with Shannon Ravenel) Best American Short Stories of 1979, 1979, Night Walks, 1982, First Person Singular: Writer's on Their Craft, 1983, (with Boyd Litzinger) Story: Fictions Past and Present, 1985, (with Daniel Halpern) Reading and Fights, 1988, The Oxford Book of American Short Stories, 1992, The Sophisticated Cat: An Anthology, 1992; editor (with Raymond Smith) Ontario Rev.; contbr. to nat. mags. including N.Y. Times Book Rev., Mich. Quarterly Rev., Mademoiselle, Vogue, North Am. Rev., Hudson Rev., Paris Rev., Grand Street, Atlantic, Poetry, Esquire. Recipient O. Henry award, 1967, 73, Rosenthal award Nat. Inst. Arts and Letters, 1968, O. Henry Spl. award continuing achievement, 1970, 86, Award of Merit Lotos Club, 1975, St. Louis Lit. award, 1988, Rea award for the Short Story, 1990, Alan Swallow award for fiction, 1990, Nobel Prize in Lit. nomination, 1993; Guggenheim fellow, 1967-68, Nat. Endowment for the Arts grantee, 1966, 68. Mem. Am. Acad. and Inst. Arts and Letters. Office: care John Hawkins 71 W 23rd St Ste 1600 New York NY 10010-4102 also: Princeton U Dept Creative Writing 117 185 Nassau St Princeton NJ 08544-0001*

OATES, SHERRY CHARLENE, portraitist, artist, photographer; b. Houston, Sept. 11, 1946; d. Charles Emil and Berniece Faye (Lohse) O. Student, North Tex. State U., 1965-66; student under Martin Kellogg; BA in English, Health and Phys. Edn., Houston Bapt. U., 1968. Cert. art tchr., Tex. Tchr. Jackson Jr. High Sch., Houston, 1968-69, Percy Priest Sch., Nashville, 1969-70, Franklin (Tenn.) High Sch., 1970-84; freelance illustrator Bapt. Sunday Sch. Bd., Nashville, 1978-85, United Meth. Pub. House, Nashville, 1980-85; portraitist in oils, owner Portraits, Ltd., Nashville, 1984—. Portraits include corp. leaders, educators, politicians, hist. and equestrian subjects, society figures and children; participated in various exhbns. at Bapt. Sunday Sch. Bd. and All State and Ctr. South Exhibits at the Parthenon. Recipient 3d place in graphics Ctrl. South Exhbn. at The Parthenon-Tenn. Art League, 1986. Mem. Tenn. Art League. Republican. Baptist. Avocation: antiques. Studio: 816 Kirkwood Ave Nashville TN 37204-2602

OATLEY, NINA KAREN, music educator; b. NYC, Apr. 5, 1958; d. Henry Clay Oatley and Tove Halvorsen; m. Billy S. Anderson, Aug. 25, 1979 (div. Oct. 25, 1990); children: Peter, Adam. Diploma in music edn., U. So. Maine, 2000. Cert. tchr. Maine. Spl. edn. tchr. Lake and Peninsula Schs., Chiguik, 1981—83; city clk. City of Chignik, 1984—87; town clk. Town of Falmouth, Maine, 1988—97, asst. town mgr., 1997—99; instrumental dir. Freeport (Maine) Mid. Sch., 2001—. Music dir. Italian Heritage Concert Band, Portland, 1997—; pvt. tchr., Westbrook, Maine, 2003—. City councilor Chignik City Coun., 1986—87. Mem.: Maine Music Educators Assn., Music Educators Nat. Conf. Avocations: contradancing, cross country skiing, reading, walking. Home: 25 E Bridge St #37 Westbrook ME 04092 E-mail: ninaoatley@netscape.net.

OBAID, THORAYA AHMED, international organization official; b. Baghdad, Iraq, Mar. 2, 1945; married; 2 children. BA, Mills Coll., Oakland, Calif., 1966; MA, Wayne State U., Detroit, 1968, PhD, 1974. Asst./assoc. social affairs officer Econ. and Social Commn. Western Asia, 1975—81, women and devel. prog. mgr., 1981—92, chief, social devel. and population divsn., 1992—93, dep. exec. sec., 1993—98; dir. divsn. arab states and Europe UN Population Fund, 1998—2000, exec. dir., 2000—; under-sec. gen. UN, 2001—. Coord. group on women Econ. and Social Commn. for Western Asia, 1989—90, v.p. staff coun., 1980—82; chair Inter-agy. Task Force on Gender, Amman, Jordan, 1996. Mem. editl. bd. Jour. Arab Women, 1984—90. Mem.: Assn. Working Mothers, Al Nadha Women's Assn. Office: 220 E 42nd St New York NY 10017

O'BAIRE, MARIKA, community health nurse, writer; b. Manila, Oct. 3, 1947; d. Gerald John and Giovanna (BelForti) Barry; children: Matthew, Alexei, Rita, D. Patrick. Student, U. Conn., 1964-65; diploma, Ellis Hosp. Sch. Nursing, 1977; BSN, Russell Sage Coll., 1980, postgrad., 1983, 94; grad. ontological design, Logonet Inc. ODC-J, 1993; postgrad. in humanities, Calif. State U., Dominguez Hills, 1995—; postgrad., Univ. Dundee, 2000—. RN N.Y.; lic. avatar master/wizard Star's Edge Internat., 1999. English tchr. Lang. Inst., Taipei, Taiwan, 1971-73; team leader, staff nurse in acute psychiatry Samaritan Hosp., Troy, N.Y., 1978-80; staff nurse, pediatric ICU Albany (N.Y.) Med. Ctr., 1980-84, 97—; rsch. nurse Commn. on Quality Care for Mentally Disabled, Albany, 1984; staff nurse Columbia-Greene Med. Ctr., Catskill, N.Y., 1984-89; night charge nurse Conifer Park, Scotia, N.Y., 1991-92; nursing educator St. Clare's Hosp., Schenectady, N.Y., 1992-96; adjunct clin. educator Albany Med. Ctr. So. Vt. Coll., Bennington, 1997—2001. Philosophy coaching Cmty. Hospice Saratoga, N.Y., 1998—; founder Future Design: Create What You Prefer, Avatar Tech. & Skills, 2000; Favorite Nurses, Colonie, N.Y., 2002—. Contbr. Echo Mag.; author: (screenplays) Dragon, 2002, About Love, (novels) Future Joyous, 2002, (screenplays) Syin. Vol. curriculum designer in gifted and talented programs; mem. Red Cross Disaster Team. Mem. Amnesty Internat. Childreach Plan Internat., Upstate Independent Filmakers/Screenwriters, Thorobred Toastmasters. Home and Office: 90 Lincoln Ave Saratoga Springs NY 12866-4536 E-mail: mobaire@nycap.rr.com.

OBAMOGIE, MERCY A. physician; b. Lagos, Nigeria, Jan. 18, 1954; d. Godwin I and Janet E. (Amiolemen) O.; m. Abiodun O. Odunmbaku, June 20, 1980 (div. 1995); children: Abisola, Adenike, Abiodun. BS, Columbia U., 1980; MD, U. Medicine and Dentistry N.J., Piscataway, 1984; MPH, Johns Hopkins U., 1987; MBA, U. Calif., Irvine, 2000. Diplomate Am. Bd. Family Practice, Nat. Bd. Med. Examiners. Intern in internal medicine Muhlenberg Hosp., Plainfield, N.J., 1984-85; resident in gen. preventive medicine Johns Hopkins U., Balt., 1985-86; resident in family practice Georgetown U./Providence Hosp., Washington, 1986-89; pvt. practice Washington, Greenbelt, Md., 1989—; med. dir. Doctors Slim and Fitness Ctr., Greenbelt, 1996-98. Med. adv. bd. Metra Health Ins. Co., 1992-94; utilization com. Aetna Ins. Co., 1993-95, credentialing com., 1996; med. adv. com. United HealthCare, 1997; mem. planning com. Providence Hosp., Washington, 1996-98; with Prince George's Hosp. Ctr., Cheverly, Md., Howard U. Hosp., Washington, Doctors Cmty. Hosp., Lanham, Md., Providence Hosp., Washington; pres., med. dir. Mercy Med. Ctr., Benin City, Nigeria, 1996—; pres., CEO ASAKI Corp., Greenbelt, Md., 2000—. Contbr. articles to profl. jours. Home: 25 Atwood Ct Silver Spring MD 20906-2089 Office: 7323 Hanover Pkwy Ste A Greenbelt MD 20770-3617 E-mail: aimmercy@aol.com.

O'DANNION, MINDY MARTHA MARTIN, nurse; b. Cushing, Okla., Aug. 19, 1953; d. John William and Martha Florence (Vineyard) Martin; children: Mindi Martha Mae, William Neale Aaron. Student, Okla. State U., 1971-73, Oscar Rose Jr. Coll., 1973; grad., St. Anthony Sch. Nursing, 1975. RN, Tex. Med. clk. Martin Clinic, Cushing, Okla., 1968-72; nursing asst. Cushing Mcpl. Hosp., 1973-75, head nurse surg. fl., 1975-76, charge nurse med. unit, 1978-79, 82-83; staff nurse Met. Hosp., Dallas, 1985; staff nurse med. unit Mesquite (Tex.) Cmty. Hosp., 1985-87; nurse post partum unit, breastfeeding and discharge educator post partum unit Trinity Med. Ctr. Tenet Healthcare System, Carrollton, Tex., 1987—. Ind. beauty cons. Mary Kay Cosmetics, Dallas, Tex., 1993-99. Social com. Royal Haven Bapt. Ch. Women's Missionary Union, Dallas, 1977-78; mem. extension dept. nursery First Bapt. Ch., Cushing, 1979-82, extension dept. presch., 1982-84; mem. extension dept. presch. Royal Haven Bapt. Ch., Dallas, 1986-87; mem. Montgomery Elem. Sch. PTA, Farmers Branch, Tex., 1986-94, Vivian Field Jr. H.S. PTA, Farmers Branch, 1993-97, Valwood Park Bapt. Ch., Farmers Branch, 1994-2002, R.L. Turner H.S. PTA, R.L. Turner H.S. Orch. Booster Club, 1995-2001, Farmers Branch/Carrollton, 1995-2001, Prestonwood Bapt. Ch., Plano, Tex., 2002-; treas., nominating com. Joyce Harms group Women's Missionary Union; clk., charter mem. Brookhaven Bapt. Ch., Farmers Branch, 1989-92. Mem. Am., Tex., Okla. State Nurses Assns., St. Anthony Hosp. Sch. Nursing Alumnae, Bluebonnet Shelties (founder), Tau Beta Sigma (Alpha chpt.), Alpha Xi Delta (epsilon Omicron chpts. corr. sec. 1973). Baptist. Home: 13505 Onyx Ln Dallas TX 75234-4912

OBED, LEONORA RITA VILLEGAS, writer; b. Manila, Philippines, May 22, 1971; d. Reynaldo Nera and Josefina Kalaw (Villegas) Obed. BA, St. Joseph's U., 1993; MA, U. Toronto, 1994; PhD in English Lit., U. Edinburgh. Spkr. in field. Author: The Invention of Candles, 2001, I Won't Send Roses, 2001, (plays) Epitome, 2003; contbr. articles to profl. jours. Mem.: Hopkins Soc., Yeats Soc., Oscar Wilde Soc. Home: 10 Michelle Ct Trenton NJ 08628-2924

OBERLY, KATHRYN ANNE, lawyer, diversified financial services company executive; b. Chgo., May 22, 1950; d. James Richard and Lucille Mary (Kraus) Oberly; 1 child, Michael W. Goelzer ; m. Haynes B. Johnson, June 29, 2002. Student, Vassar Coll., 1967—69; BA, U. Wis., 1971, JD, 1973. Bar: Wis. 1973, D.C. 1981, N.Y. 1995. Law clk. U.S. Ct. Appeals, Omaha, 1973-74; trial atty. U.S. Dept. Justice, Washington, 1974-77, spl. asst., 1977-81, spl. litig. counsel, 1981-82, asst. to Solicitor Gen., 1982-86; ptnr. Mayer, Brown & Platt, Washington, 1986-91; assoc. gen. counsel Ernst & Young LLP, Washington, 1991-94, vice-chair, gen. counsel N.Y.C., 1994—. Bd. dirs. CPR Ctr. for Dispute Resolution. Bd. dirs. Appleseed Found., 2003—. Named one of 50 Most Influential Women Lawyers in Am., Nat. Law Jour., 1998. Mem. ABA, Am. Law Inst. (coun. mem.), Am. Acad. Appellate Lawyers, Wis. Bar Assn., D.C. Bar Assn. Democrat. Office: Ernst & Young LLP 5 Times Sq New York NY 10036 E-mail: kathryn.oberly@ey.com.

OBERMEYER, THERESA NANGLE, sociology educator; b. St. Louis, July 25, 1945; d. James Francis and Harriet Clare (Shafer) Nangle; m. Thomas S. Obermeyer, Dec. 23, 1977; children: Thomas Jr., James, Margaret, Matthew. BA, Maryville U., St. Louis, 1967; MEd, St. Louis U., 1970, PhD, 1975. Lic. real estate broker Alaska, 1979, cert. Type A teacher Alaska, 1979. Dir. student activities Lindenwood Univ., St. Charles, Mo., 1969-70; asst. dean of students Loyola Coll., Balt., 1972-73; asst. dir. student activities St. Louis C.C., 1973-78; dir. student activities U. Alaska, Anchorage, 1978-79; instr. sociology Chapman U., Anchorage, 1981-93; secondary tchr. McLaughlin Youth Ctr. for Juvenile Delinquents, 1984-90. Mem Anchorage Munic Health Commn., 1980—81; elected alt. coun. urban bd edn. Nat Sch. Bds. Assn., 1994; maj. party nominee US Senate Gen. Election, 1996; founder, mem. Alaska Women's Polit. Caucus, 1979—; elected Anchorage Sch. Bd., 1990—94, treas., 1993. Recipient Fed Women's Equity Act, US Dept Educ Univ Alaska, 1978—79; fellow Fulbright, Project India, 1974, Project Jordan, 1977; grantee Title I, Univ Md and Loyola Col, 1972—73; scholar NDEA, 1968—70. Mem.: AAUW (bd. dirs. Anchorage br. 1980—81), DAR (regent col. John Mitchell chpt. 1992—94), Am. Soc. Pub. Adminstrn. (pres., bd. dirs. south ctrl. chpt. 1981). Avocations: athletics, swimming, horseback riding, skiing, running. Home: 3000 Dartmouth Dr Anchorage AK 99508-4413 Fax: 907-278-9455. Office Phone: 907-278-9455. E-mail: tobermeyer@gci.net.

OBERNDORF, MEYERA E. mayor; m. Roger L. Oberndorf; children: Marcie, Heide. BS in Elem. Edn., Old Dominion U., 1964. Broadcaster Sta. WNIS, Norfolk, Va.; mem. city coun. City of Virginia Beach, Va., 1976—, vice-mayor, 1986, mayor, 1988—. Mem. exec. bd. Tidewater coun. Boys Scouts Am.; bd. dirs. Virginia Beach Pub. Libr., 1966-76, chmn. bd., 1967-76. Mem. AAUW, U.S. Conf. Mayors, Va. Mcpl. League (exec. bd.), Nat. League Cities (vice-chmn.), Princess Anne Women's Club. Jewish. Home: 5404 Challedon Dr Virginia Beach VA 23462-4112 Office: 2401 Courthouse Drive City Hall Bldg 1 Municipal Ctr Virginia Beach VA 23456*

OBERSTAR, HELEN ELIZABETH, retired cosmetics company executive; b. Ottawa, Ill. d. Milton Edward and Helen (Herrick) Weiss; m. Edward Charles Oberstar, Feb. 3, 1945 (dec. 1984). BS in Chemistry, Monmouth (Ill.) Coll., 1943; postgrad., Northwestern U., Chgo., 1947-49; LLD (hon.), Monmouth Coll., 1987. Asst. food technologist Standard Brands, Inc., Bklyn., 1943-45; chemist Miner Labs., Midwest div., Arthur D. Little, Chgo., 1946-50; rsch. chemist/rsch. supr. Toni Co., div. Gillette Co., Chgo., 1951-65; group leader rsch. and devel. Shulton, Inc., Clifton, N.J., 1965-72; sect. leader rsch. and devel. Am. Cyanamid, Clifton, 1972-75; mgr. rsch. and devel. Clairol Bristol Myers Internat., Stamford, Conn., 1975-82; dir. tech. Clairol Bristol Myers Squibb Consumer Products Group Internat., Stamford, 1982-93; dir. technology internat. group Clairol, Inc. divsn. Bristol-Myers Squibb, Stamford, 1993-95; ret. Wilton, Conn., 1995. Patentee in field. Recipient Disting. Alumni award Monmouth Coll., 1986, Hall of Achievement award Monmouth Coll., 1995. Mem. Soc. Cosmetic Chemists (house chmn. 1963-64), Cosmetic Toiletries Fragrance Assn. (internat. com. 1985-95). Episcopalian. Avocations: rughooking, gardening, travel. Home and Office: 512 Belden Hill Rd Wilton CT 06897-4221

OBOLENSKY, MARILYN WALL (MRS. SERGE OBOLENSKY), metals company executive; b. Detroit, Aug. 13, 1929; d. Albert Fraser and Christine (Frischkorn) Wall; m. Serge Obolensky, June 3, 1971. Student, Duschesne Jr. Coll., 1947. Chmn. bd. Wall-Colmondy Corp., Detroit, 1959-61, exec. sec., 1961—. Chmn. bd. Wall-Gases Inc., Morrisville, Pa., 1959-61; pres. Serge Obolensky Assocs. Bd. dirs. Heart and Lung Assn. N.Y.C., 1963— . Mem.: Bathing Corp. (Southampton, N.Y.), Southampton. Republican. Roman Catholic. Address: 45 Preston Pl Grosse Pointe Farms MI 48236-3035

O'BOYLE, MAUREEN, television show host; News prodr., anchor Sta. KREM-TV, Spokane, Wash.; reporter, prodr., writer, co-anchor Sta. WMAZ-TV, Macon, Ga.; nightside reporter, anchor Sta. WECT-TV, Wilmington, N.C.; morning news anchor Sta. WITN-TV, Washington, N.C.; anchor A Current Affair; anchor, sr. corr. Extra, Glendale, Calif., 1995-96, co-host, 1997—; host In Person With Maureen O'Boyle, 1996-97. Office: PO Box 509 Hurley NY 12443-0509

OBRAMS, GUNTA IRIS, medical officer; b. Düsseldorf, Germany, Sept. 2, 1953; came to U.S., 1961; d. Robert and Olga (Baltins) O.; m. Malcolm DeWitt Patterson, Dec. 22, 1975; 1 child, Andrew McDougal Patterson. BS in Biology cum laude, Rensselaer Poly. Inst., 1977; MD, Union U., Albany, N.Y., 1977; MPH, Johns Hopkins U., 1982, PhD, 1988. Resident in obstetrics and gynecology Ea. Va. Grad. Sch. Medicine, Norfolk, 1977-78; community physician Southampton Meml. Hosp., Franklin, Va., 1978-81; resident in gen. preventive medicine sch. hygiene and pub. health Johns Hopkins U., Balt., 1981-84, project dir., 1983-85, med. dir., 1985-86; med. officer divsn. cancer etiology Nat. Cancer Inst., Bethesda, Md., 1986-89, dep. chief, 1989-90, chief, 1990-96, dir. extramural epidemiology & genetics program, 1996-2001; mgmt. US Coast Guard Health Svcs., 2001—. Editor: (with M. Potter): The Epidemiology and Biology of Multiple Myeloma, 1991; contbr. articles to profl. jours. With USPHS, 1987—. Recipient Nat. Cancer Inst. Nat. Rsch. Svc. award, 1981, Rsch. Career award Nat. Inst. Occupational Safety & Health; scholar Am. Med. Women's Assn., 1977. Mem. Phi Beta Kappa, Delta Omega, Alpha Omega Alpha. Office: Health Svcs Mgmt Dvsn US Coast Guard Hdqts G-WKH-3 2100 Second St SW Washington DC 20593

OBRECHT, MARGARET M. H. cultural organization administrator; b. June 12, 1938; married; 3 children. AB in Religion, Goucher Coll., 1960; MA in Theology, St. Mary's Sem. Ecumen. Inst., 1978; cert. in hosp. chaplaincy, Archdioc. Balt. Health Affairs, 1979; postgrad., St. Mary's Sem. Ecumen. Inst., 1987-88. Admissions counselor admissions office Goucher Coll., Towson, Md., 1965-70; cons. Sevynmor Farm, Inc., Kennett Square, Pa., 1986-87; dir. ch. rels. U.S. Holocaust Meml. Mus., Washington, 1989—. Lectr. in field. Chairperson residential gifts divsn. United Way, 1975, chairperson individual spl. gifts divsn., 1980-81; bd. dirs. Anne Frank Inst. of Phila., 1978-89, pres. pro tem, 1985; adj. chaplain Johns Hopkins Hosp., 1979—; chairperson adv. com. Women's Detention Ctr., 1987-93; foster parent Balt. City Dept. Social Svcs., 1987—; bd. dirs. St. Mary's Sem. and U. Alumni Assn., 1982-84, 87—, Ecumenical Inst. of St. Mary's Sem., 1982-87, Red Cross Holocaust and War Victims Tracing and Info. Ctr., 1990-97. Recipient Disting. Alumnae award Bryn Mawr Sch., 1996, Chevra Ahavas Chesed, Inc., Humanitarian award, 1994, Benemerenti Papel award 2000; Holywell Trust Grant lectr., No. Ireland, 1995; fellow Shalom Hartman Inst. for Advanced Judaic Studies, Jerusalem, 1984. Office: US Holocaust Meml Mus Dept Ch Rels 100 Raoul Wallenberg Pl SW Washington DC 20024-2126

O'BRIEN, AMY V. apparel designer; b. Santa Rosa, Calif., Nov. 30, 1961; d. Kenneth and Arleen Elizabeth (Hill) O'B.; divorced. AA, Fashion Inst. Design and Merchandise, L.A., 1983. Designer Faris Bros., L.A., 1983-86, Tosca, L.A., 1986-92; tech. product mgr. MAST, Andover, Mass., 1992-95; quality control Nap, N.Y.C., 1995-96; designer Deena, L.A., 1994-96, Jezebel, L.A., 1996-99, On Gossamer, Miami, Fla., 1999—. Owner Marvelous Mayhem, L.A., 1996-2000. Mem. Underfashion Club, Ultimate Apparel Sq. Club. Democrat. Home: PMB # 212 11762 N Kendall Dr Miami FL 33186-2102

O'BRIEN, ANNE THERESE, chemist; b. N.Y.C., Apr. 11, 1936; d. Charles Daniel O'Brien, Margaret Mary FitzGerald; m. Ronald P. Tedesco, Dec. 28, 1974. BS, Marymount Coll., Tarrytown, N.Y., 1957; PhD, Fordham U., Bronx, 1964. Tchr. Marymount Secondary Sch., Tarrytown, 1957—59; instr. to assoc. prof. Marymount Coll., Tarrytown, 1962—72; assoc. prof. U. Waterloo, Canada, 1973—76; sr. rsch. info. chemist Am. Cyanamid, Pearl River, NY, 1976—86, group leader, 1986—91, mgr. libr. svcs., 1991—94, Am. Home Products (formerly Am. Cyanamid), Pearl River, NY, 1994—2002, Wyeth (formerly Am. Home Products), Pearl River, NY, 2001—02; ret., 2002. Mem. Westchester Environ. Coun., Westchester County, NY, 1985—, Tarrytown Environ. Adv. Com., 1980—2001. Mem.: Am. Chem. Soc. (councilor 1984—, bd. dirs. 2001—, dir. 2001—, mem. budget and fin. com., chmn. bd. com. profl. and mem. rels.). Roman Catholic. Home: 15 Crest Dr Tarrytown NY 10591-4305

O'BRIEN, BEA JAE, artist; b. Oshkosh, Wis., Dec. 4, 1940; d. Harry A. and Mammie Anna (Smith) Mac Farlane; m. John Walsh O'Brien, July 27, 1965; 1 child, John Christian. BA, U. Wis. Profl. artist B.J.'s Fine Arts, Moraga, Calif. Publs. include The Best of Watercolor, 1996, Painting Texture, 1997, Best of Drawing and Sketching, 1999, Collective Best of Watercolor, 2002; art included in various art publs.; represented in archives at Women in the Arts Mus., Washington, 1997; exhib. include Dennos Mus., Calif. Art & Wine Festival, 2001, Internat. Art Show, 2001, Valley Art Gallery, Calif., 2001-03 Calif. Art (3 awards); Included in Internat. Art Show, Chicgo. Ill., one-woman shows include: Moraga, Calif., 1996, 97, 98, 99, 2000, 2001. Vol. children's art publ. Moraga Sch. Sys., local sch. projects, Calif. open art exhibits, 2003; vol. organizer Cmty. Art Gallery, Moraga Gallery, 2000, 01, donated, vol., Outreach Art for Funds and Scholarships, Calif. Recipient 1st place award, Calif. Art and Wine Festival, 1999, Bay Area Art Festival, 1999, 2000; Nat. Coll. award, Nat. Coll. Soc., 1999, 98, 97. Mem.: Digital Image Art Career, Women in the Arts Mus. (honor roll), Intuitive Layering Art Group, Valley Arts Ctr., Collage Artists Am., Nat. Collage Soc. (signature), Internat. Soc. Exptl. Artists (signature, Nautilus award 2003), Lamorinda Arts Alliance, Coll. Art Am. Avocations: reading, volunteering. Office: BJs Fine Arts 34 Sea Pines Moraga CA 94556-1029

O'BRIEN, CATHERINE LOUISE, museum administrator; b. N.Y.C., July 21, 1930; d. Edward Denmark and Cathrine Louise (Browne) O'B.; m. Philip R. James (div.); m. Sterling Noel (div.). BA, Finch Coll., 1952; postgrad, Williams Coll., 1954, Marymount Coll., 1954. Reprodn. mgr. Met. Mus. Art, N.Y.C., 1975—; dir. sales Simon Pearce Gallery, N.Y.C. Exhibited in group shows at Parrish Art Mus., Southampton, N.Y., 1965-70, Met. Mus. Art, N.Y.C., 1975-85, Guild Hall Exhibit, East Hampton, N.Y., 1965-85; founding mem. Parrish Art Mus. Players, Southampton, 1958, Williamstown (Mass.) Theater, 1955; mem. John Drew Theater Co., Guild Hall, 1956-59. Mem. aux. Southampton Hosp., 1970-85; founder East Hampton Horse Show, Ladies Village Improvement Soc., East Hampton, 1970—; mem. fair coms. St. James Ch., N.Y.C., St. Luke's Ch., East Hampton, 1970-85; mem. alumnae adv. bd. Marymount Coll., N.Y.C., 1984-86, chmn. alumnae event, 1994; mem. Women's Nat. Rep. Club, N.Y.C.; chmn. Landmark and Tree Planting Com. for Madison Ave. Assn., N.Y.C., 1994—; mem. founding com. Internat. Debutante Ball, Waldorf Astoria, N.Y.C., 1955; founding mem. Williamstown (Mass.) Theater, 1955; founder Parrish Art Mus. Players, Southampton, N.Y., 1955. Mem. DAR (founding; vice regent East Hampton chpt. 1974-85), Colonial Dames Am. (archives com. 1980-85), Daus. Brit. Empire (historian 1978-85), United Daus. Confederacy (state historian 1970-85), Daus. Colonial Wars (corr. sec. 1983-85), Sons and Daus. of Pilgrims (corr. sec. 1983-85), Victorian Soc., Soc. Mayflower Descs. (life), English Speaking Union, New Eng. Soc. (mem. ball com. 1983-86), Daus. of Cin. (historian 1979-85), Squadron "A", Devon Yacht, Maidstone, Southampton Yacht, Metropolitan Club (women's com., chmn. debutante ball 1980-84), Reciprocal/India House, St. Anthony Union League. Republican. Episopalian. Avocations: show horses, dogs. Home: 605 Park Ave New York NY 10021-7016 also: Seacote PO Box 1488 East Hampton NY 11937-0711 Office: Met Mus of Art 5th Ave New York NY 10028 also: Simon Pierce Gallery 500 Park Ave New York NY 10022-1606

O'BRIEN, CHRISTINE LEDUC, art educator; b. Southbridge, Mass., June 12, 1930; d. Arthur Wilfred and Doris Blanche (Archambeault) Leduc; m. Thomas Joseph O'Brien, Sept. 1, 1951; children: Thomas Arthur, James Mark. Social worker Dept. Pub. Welfare, Southbridge, Mass., 1948—57; tchr. Diocese of Worcester, Mass., 1962—71; pvt. instr., artist, owner L'atelier de Christine, Southbridge, 1971—. Vol. Apostolate of Divine

Mercy and Healing, Worcester, 2000—, Southbridge Hospitality Interfaith Network, Southbridge, 2001—. Roman Catholic. Avocations: gardening, music. Office: L'atelier de Christine Southbridge MA 01550

O'BRIEN, JANE, special education educator; b. Garfield Heights, Ohio, June 24, 1954; d. Harry Edward and Helen Lena Sykora; m. Fred Eugene Yoak, Oct. 3, 1981 (div. Oct. 1998); children: Helen Alexis Yoak, Evan Edward Yoak, Trevor Franklin Yoak; m. Russell O'Brien, Aug. 31, 2002. BS in Edn., Bowling Green State U., 1976; MS in Edn., U. Akron, 1981; postgrad., Kent State U., 1994-96. Cert. tchr. Ohio. Spl. edn. tchr. Cleve. Pub. Schs., 1976, Marshall (Ill.) Schs., 1976-78, Stow (Ohio) City Schs., 1978-94, Ravenna (Ohio) City Schs., 1996—. Instr. childbirth Childbirth Edn. Assn., Akron, 1984—86; instr. parenting Cath. Svc. League, 1994; student tchr. supr., grad. asst. Kent (Ohio) State U., 1994—96; rep. Ravenna City Schs. Portage County Tchr. Adv. Coun., 1997—99; workshop presenter, 1996—99. Mem. PTA, Stow Players Theater Group. Recipient Apple Tchr. award, Ashland Oil, 1997, Friend of Children award, 1995; Martha Holden Jennings scholar, 2000. Mem.: NEA, Coun. Exceptional Children, Ravenna Edn. Assn., Ohio Edn. Assn. Avocations: storytelling, vocal and instrumental music, gardening, acting. Office: Ravenna City Schs West Park 1076 Jones Ave Ravenna OH 44266-3558

O'BRIEN, JOAN SUSAN, lawyer, educator; b. New York, Apr. 14, 1946; d. Edward Vincent O'Brien and Joan Therese (Kramer) Quinn; m. Michael P. Wilpan, May 27, 1979; children: Edward B. Wilpan, Anabel T. Wilpan. BA, NYU, 1967; JD, Georgetown U., 1970. Bar: N.Y. 1971, Mass. 1971, U.S. Dist. Ct. (so. and ea. dist.) N.Y. 1972, U.S. Ct. Appeals (2d cir.) 1971. Law clk. to Hon. Frank J. Murray U.S. Dist. Ct. Mass., Boston, 1970-71; asst. U.S. atty. Office of U.S. Atty. U.S. Dist. Ct. (ea. dist.) N.Y., Bklyn., 1972-76; pvt. practice N.Y.C., 1976-79; trial atty. Mendes & Mount, N.Y.C., 1979-84; asst. prof. St. Johns U., Jamaica, N.Y., 1984-90; adminstrv. law judge N Y State Workers Compensation Bd., Hempstead, N.Y., 1990-93; appellate atty. Scheine, Fusco, Brandenstein & Rada, Woodbury, N.Y., 1993-97; trial atty. Grey & Grey, L.L.P., Farmingdale, N.Y., 1997—. Editor: Georgetown Law Jour., 1968-70. Pres. Nassau County Dem. Com. Women's Caucus, Westbury, N.Y., 1988-90; leader Girl Scouts Nassau County, 1990-93. Unitarian-Universalist. Office: Grey & Grey LLP 360 Main St Farmingdale NY 11735-3592

O'BRIEN, JULIA FRANCES, architect; b. Dallas, Tex., Dec. 20, 1946; d. Robert David O'Brien and Frances Buster. BArch, U. Tex., Arlington, 1970; MArch, M in City Planning, U. Pa., Phila., 1977. V.p. / regional mgr., Devel. Svcs. Group Coldwell Banker, Chgo., 1981—85; pres., CEO RESCORP Devel. Corp., Chgo., 1985—87; owner Briar Devel. Group, Chgo., 1987—93; dir., design & constrn. group Mid-Peninsula Housing Coalition, Redwood City, Calif., 1998—2002; sr. constrn. specialist San Francisco Redevelopment Agy., 2002—. Office: San Francisco Redevelopment Agency 770 Golden Gate Ave San Francisco CA 94102 E-mail: jill.obrien@sfgov.org

O'BRIEN, K. PATRICIA, product development engineer; b. Cin., Feb. 13, 1970; d. John Edward and Carolyn Ann (Hufler) O'Brien; m. Robert J. Novak, JUly 1, 1995. BS in Mech. Engring., U. Cin., 1993. Grad. Ford Coll. Ford Motor Co., Livonia, Mich., 1993-95, product devel. engr., 1995—. Bus. mentor Jr. Achievement, Livonia, 1994; mem. adv. bd. Univ. Cinn.-Detroit. Mem. Soc. Women Engrs. (chair golf outing, fundraising and publicity 1993—). Avocations: scrapbooking, reading, biking, hiking traveling.

O'BRIEN, KATHY MOSDAL, director, educator; b. Billings, Mont., Nov. 10, 1951; d. Thelmer and Grace Ruth (McCaskie) Mosdal; m. Wayne Robert Moist, June 16, 1979 (div. May 1981); m. Curtis Charles O'Brien, Oct. 19, 1985. BA, Wartburg Coll., 1974; MA, Western Wash. U., 1992. Tchr. Dawson County Sch. Dist., Glendive, Mont., 1974—75, Crook County Sch. Dist., Sundance, Wyo., 1975—87, Albany County Sch. Dist., Laramie, Wyo., 1987—90; tchg. asst. Western Wash. U., Bellingham, 1990—92; English instr. Bellingham Tech. Coll., Whatcom C.C., Bellingham, Wash., 1992—94, Skagit Valley Coll., Mt. Vernon, Wash., 1992—94, Miles C.C., Miles City, Mont., 1994—99; curator of edn. Western Heritage Ctr., Billings, Mont., 2000—01; asst. dir. Acad. Support Ctr. Mont. State U., Billings, 2001—. Mem. State Hist. Records Adv. Bd., Helena, Mont., 2000—02, Mont. Com. for the Humanities, Missoula, 2001—04. Contbr. articles to profl. jours. Recipient Celebrate Literacy award, Internat. Reading Assn., Laramie, 1989. Democrat. Avocations: quilting, reading.

O'BRIEN, MARY DEVON, communications executive, consultant; b. Buenos Aires, Feb. 13, 1944; came to U.S., 1949, naturalized, 1962; d. George Earle and Margaret Frances (Richards) Owen; m. Gordon Covert O'Brien, Feb. 16, 1962 (div. Aug. 1982); children: Christopher Covert, Devon Elizabeth; m. Christopher Gerard Smith, May 28, 1983 BA, Rutgers U., 1975, MBA, 1976. Project mgmt. cert., 1989. Contr. manpower Def. Comm. divsn. ITT, Nutley, N.J., 1977-80, adminstr. program, 1977-78, mgr. cost, schedule control, 1978 79, voice processing project, 1979-80; mgr. project Avionics divsn. ITT, Nutley, 1980-81, sr. mgr. projects, 1981-93, cons. strategic planning, 1983-95; pres. Anamex, Inc., 1995—. Bd. trustees South Mountain Counseling Ctr., 1987-98, chmn. bd. trustees, 1994—; bd. dirs. N.J. Eye Inst.; session leader Internet Conf., Florence, Italy, 1992; session moderator, panel mem. MES Conf., Cairo, Egypt, 1993, spkr., session leader Vancouver, 1994, keynote spkr. New Zealand, 1995; lectr. in field Author: Pace: System Manual, 1979, Voices, 1982; contbr. articles to profl. jours. and Maplewood Community calendar. Chmn. Citizens Budget Adv. Com., Maplewood, N.J., 1984-87, chmn. recreation, libr., pub. svcs., 1982-83, 94-96, chmn. pub. safety, emergency svcs., 1983-84, chmn. schs. and edn., 1984-85, chmn. gen. gov. and fin., 1998-2000; first v.p. Maplewood Civic Assn., 1987-89, pres., 1989-91, 2000—, sec. 1993-94, bd. dirs., officer, 1984—; chmn. Maple Leaf Svc. award Com., 1987-89, 94—, Community Svc. Coun. of Oranges and Maplewood Homelessness, Affordable Housing, Shelter Com., 1988—; chmn. speaker's bur. United Way, 1989-93; bd. trustees United Way Essex and West Hudson Cmty. Svc. Coun., 1988—; v.p. mktg. United Way Community Svc. Coun. of Oranges and Maplewood, 1990-93, v.p. 1994; mem. Maplewood Zoning Bd. of Adjustment, 1983-95; officer, mem. exec. bd. N.J. Project Mgmt. Inst., 1985—, pres., 1987-88, 95-2000, v.p. adminstrn., 1994-95; bd. dirs. Performance Mgmt. Assn.; chmn. Charter Com.; chmn. Internat. Project Mgmt. Inst. Jour. and Membership survey, 1986-87, mktg. com., 1986-89, long range planning and steering com., 1987—; bd. dirs., vice chmn. Coun. Chpt. Pres. Interaction Com., 1986-90, chmn., 1991—, pres. Internat. Project Mgmt. Inst., 1991, chmn., 1992, v.p. Region II, 1989-90; adv. bd. Project Mgmt. Jour., 1987-90, N.J. PMI Ednl., 1987—; liaison officer, PMI internat. liaison to Australian Inst. of Project Mgmt. and Western Australia Project Mgmt. Assn.; apptd. fellow Leadership N.J., 1993—, Internat. Project Mgmt. Inst. and Performance Mgmt. Assocs.; mem. MCA/N.J. Blood Bank Drive; chmn. Maplewood Community Calendar, 1990-98; trustee community svc. coun. and edn. program United Way Essex and West Hudson, 1988—, also, chmn. leadership div., chmn. speakers bur., 1991— and mem. communications com.; pres. N.J. Project Mgmt. Inst., 1995—; chmn. Maplewood Rep. County Com., 1996—; chair, sec. Essex County Rep. County Com. Recipient Spl. commendation for Community Svc. Twp. Maplewood, 1987; First Place award Anti-Shoplifting Program for Distributive Edn. Club Am., 1981, N.J. Fedn. of Women's Clubs, 1981, 82, Retail Mchts. Assn., 1981, 82; Commendation and Merit awards Air Force Inst. Tech., 1981; Pres.'s Safety award ITT, 1983; State award 1st Pl. N.J. Fedn. of Women's Clubs Garden Show, 1982, Outstanding Pres. award Internat. Project Mgmt. Inst., 1988, Outstanding Svc. and Contbrn. award 1986-87; Cert. Spl. Merit award N.J. Fedn. of Women's Clubs, 1982, Disting. Contbn. award United Way, 1990, Pursuit of Exellence Cost Savings Achievement award ITT Avionics, 1990, Meritorious Svc. Recognition award Internat. Project Mgmt. Inst., 1989-90, Maple Leaf award for outstanding community svc., 1992, Phoebe and Benjamin Shackelford award United Way, 1992, U.S. Ho. Reps. citation, 1992, N.H. Gen. Assembly Senate resolution for Community Leadership and Svc., 1992, resolution of Appreciation Township of Maplewood; N.J. Leadership fellow, 1993, awarded fellow of Internat. Project Mgmt. Inst., 1995. Mem. Internat. Platform Speakers Assn., Grand Jury Assn., Telecommunications Group and Aerospace Industries Assn., Women's Career Network Assn., Nat. Security Indsl. Assn., Assn. for Info. and Image Mgmt., Internat. Project Mgmt. Inst. (liaison officer pres. 1991—), Performance Mgmt. Assn, Indsl. Rels. Rsch. Assn., ITT Mgmt. Assn., NAFE, Rutger's Grad. Sch. Bus. Mgmt. Alumni Assn., Maplewood LWV (chair women and family issues com., voter registration bd. dirs.), Maplewood Women's Evening Membership Div. (pres. 1980-82), Lions (Maplewood dir. 1992-95, program chmn. 1991-92, treas. 1994-95, N.J. dist. 16E zone gov., chmn. 1992-93, 95-96, cabinet sec. internat. dist., region chmn. 1993-94, 96—, trustee Eye Bank N.J., internat. dist. 16-E cabinet sec. 1994-95, dist. 16-E chmn. peace poster contest 1995-99, pres. Newark 1995-97, sec. 1997—, N.J. State chmn. youth outreach and quest 1995-98, internat. dist. 16-E gov., 1999—, dist. MD16 treas., 1999—). Home: 594 Valley St Maplewood NJ 07040-2616 Office: 21 Madison Plz Ste 152 Madison NJ 07940-2354

O'BRIEN, MARY KATHLEEN, state representative, lawyer; b. Kankakee, Ill., June 4, 1965; d. Donald Lawrence and Norma Margaret O'Brien. BS, Western Ill. U., 1986; JD, U. Ill., 1994. Bar: Ill. 1994. Asst., advocate Ill. Atty. Gens. Office, Kankakee, 1987-91; asst. state's atty. Grundy County State's Atty., Morris, Ill., 1993-94; lawyer Cortina, Mueller & O'Brien, Coal City, Ill., 1994-99; pvt. practice Coal City, 1999—; state rep. Ill. Gen. Assembly, Coal City, 1997—. Bd. dirs. Trailways Girl Scouts, Joliet, 1998—, Breaking Award Domestic Violence, Morris, 1997—, Ill. Valley Ctr. for Ind. Living, LaSalle, Ill., 1998—; precinct com. Kankakee County Dems., 1988-90, Grundy County Dems., Morris, 1996—. Named Legis. of Yr. Advocates United, 1999, Cmty. Behavioral Assn. of Ill., 1998; recipient William Morgan Meml. award Kankakee County Mental Health Coun., 1998, Activator award Ill. Farm Bur., 1998. Mem. Kiwanis Club of Ill. Roman Catholic. Avocations: gardening, reading, cooking. Office: 760 E Division St Coal City IL 60416-1367

O'BRIEN, NANCY A. youth counselor; b. Watertown, Minn., July 4, 1945; d. Julius Vitus and Viola Frances (Rieland) Hardt; m. Robert S. O'Brien, June 8, 1968; children: Sean, Scott. BS, Coll. St. Teresa, Winona, Minn., 1967; MS, Iowa State U., 1978. Lic. tchr., counselor, Iowa. Tchr. Colorado Springs (Colo.) Community Schs., 1967-68; counselor Title 1 Des Moines Pub. Schs., 1978-79, Waukee (Iowa) Community Schs., 1980-85; guidance cons. Heartland Area Edn. Agy., Johnston, Iowa, 1985-88; counselor Des Moines (Iowa) Pub. Schs., 1988—. Conf. coord., trainer, cons. Children's Health Market. Active Honolulu Symphony, Hawaii Assistance League. Mem. Iowa Assn. For Counseling and Devel. (editor newsletter 1981-83, editorial bd. jour. 1983-85, pres. local chpt. 1985, pub. relations com. 1986, sec. 1987-95), Iowa Sch. Counselors Assn. (sen. 1985, del. to nat. conv. 1987), Am. Assn. for Counseling and Devel., Am. Sch. Counselors Assn. Roman Catholic. Avocation: reading. Home: 13591 Village Court Clive IA 50325

O'BRIEN, NANCY LYNN, bank executive; b. Norfolk, Nebr., Sept. 6, 1951; d. Robert Sammie and Betty Ann (Petersen) Auten; m. Leo E. O'Brien, Aug. 3, 1984. BSE, U. Nebr.-Lincoln, 1972, U. Nebr.-Omaha, 1975; PhD, U. Nebr.-Lincoln, 1979. Tchr. spl. edn. Omaha Pub. Schs., 1973—79; devel. studies specialist Metro Tech. Community Coll., Omaha, 1979—80; mgr. tng. Omaha Nat. Bank, 1981—84, mgr. employment and tng. 1984—. Area rep/travel cons. Am. Leadership Study Groups, Worcester, Mass., 1977—; grant mgr. Coun. Exceptional Children, 1978; adj. faculty Coll. St. Mary's, Omaha, 1983—. Active United Way, Omaha; pres. Child Abuse Coun., Omaha, 1982—83, Coun. for Exceptional Children, 1981. Grantee, Coun. for Exceptional Children, 1978. Mem.: ASTD (dir.). Democrat. Lutheran. Home: 22627 Wilson Ave Waterloo NE 68069-9797

O'BRIEN, NANCY PATRICIA, librarian, educator; b. Galesburg, Ill., Mar. 17, 1955; d. Leo Frederick O'Brien and Yvonne Blanche (Uhlmann) O'Brien Tabb; 1 child, Nicole Pamela. AB in English, U. Ill., 1976, MS in LS, 1977. Vis. instr. U. Ill., Urbana, 1977-78, asst. prof. libr. adminstrn., 1978-84, assoc. prof., 1984-91, prof., 1991—, serials bibliographer, 1977-78, social sci. bibliographer collection devel. div., 1979-81, project dir. Title II-C grant, 1987-88, acting libr. and info. sci. libr., 1989-90, head Edn. and Social Sci. Libr., 1994—, coord. social scis. divsn., 1996—2003, edn. subject specialist, 1981—. Discussion leader Ill. White House Conf. on Libr. and Info. svcs., 1990; mem. nat. adv. bd. Office Ednl. Rsch. and Improvement, U.S. Dept. Edn., 1989-91; grant proposal reviewer NEH, 1991; mem. adv. bd. Ctr. for Children's Books, 1992-97; cons. Ark. Coll., 1989; chmn. rev. team Instrnl. Materials Ctr., U. Wis., Madison, 1989; chair exec. com. Nat. Edn. Network Nat. Libr. Edn. U.S. Dept. Edn., 1998—2002; presenter in field. Author: Test Construction: A Bibliography of Resources, 1988, (with Emily Fabiano) Core List of Books and Journals in Education, 1991; Education: A Guide to Reference and Information Sources, 2d edit., 2000, (with John Collins III) Greenwood Dictionary of Edn., 2003; co-editor Media/Microforms column Serials Rev., 1979-82; mem. editl. bd. Bull. Bibliography, 1982-90; asst. editor Libr. Hi Tech., 1983-85; editor EBSS Newsletter, 1990-91; contbr. articles to profl. jours., chpts. to books. Mem. ALA (Whitney-Carnegie grantee 1990-91), Am. Ednl. Rsch. Assn. (spl. interest group on libr. resources and info. tech.), Assn. Coll. and Rsch. Librs. (access policy guidelines task force 1990-95, vice chmn., chmn.-elect edn. and behavioral scis. sect. 1993-94, chmn. 1994-95, acad. status com. 1996—2000, Disting. Edn. and Behavioral Scis. Libr. 1997), Libr. Adminstrn. and Mgmt. Assn. (edn. and tng. com. pub. rels. sect. 1990-95), Resources and Tech. Svcs. Divsn.(micropub. com. 1982-85, chmn. 1983-85, cons. 1985-87). Office: U Ill Edn & Social Sci Libr 100 Main Libr 1408 W Gregory Dr Urbana IL 61801-3607 E-mail: npobrien@uiuc.edu.

O'BRIEN, ODESSA LOUISE, protective services official; m. John Daniels O'Brien, May 30, 1964; children: James John, Jeanne Jacqueline, Kevin Raymond. B.Elective Studies, St. Cloud State U., 1975. Lic. pilot. Stewardess Northwest Airlines, St. Paul; adminstrv. officer Minn. Wing Civil Air Patrol, St. Paul, 2001—. Area rep. Youth for Understanding, Brainerd, Minn., 1979—82; v.p. Christian Women's Club, Brainerd, 1976—80; chmn. St. Francis Ch. Women's Guild, Brainerd, Minn., 1978—79, St. Francis Parochial Sch. Bd., Brainerd, Minn., 1979—80; mem. coun. St. Francis Ch., Brainerd, Minn., 1979—80; adv. bd. Pine County Vo-Tech Sch., Pine City, Minn., 1967—71. Recipient Outstanding Woman of Collier County, Am. Bus. Women's Assn., 1983—85, Comdrs. Commendation, Naples Sr. Squadron, Civil Air Patrol, 1983, Grover Loening award, Minn. Wing Civil Air Patrol, Air Force Aux., Paul E. Garber award, Civil Air Patrol, 2003, Gill Robb Wilson award, 2004. Mem.: AAUW (life; pres. 1983—85), USAF Aux., Civil Air Patrol, Collier Automotive Mus. (sec. of vol. docents), Naples Woman's Club (internat. chmn.). Roman Catholic. Avocations: bridge (Bronze Life Master), flying, travel, tennis, reading. Office: Minn Wing Civil Air Patrol PO Box 11230 Saint Paul MN 55111-0230 also: 5861 Paradise Cir Naples FL 34110

O'BRIEN, ORIN YNEZ, musician, educator; b. Hollywood, Calif., June 7, 1935; d. George Joseph and Marguerite Graham (Churchill) O'Brien. Studied with Frederick Zimmermann, Milton Kestenbaum and Herman Reinshagen; diploma, The Juilliard Sch., 1957. Double bassist N.Y.C. Ballet Orch., 1956—66, Saidenberg Little Symphony, Music Aeterna, Am. Symphony (with Stokowski), N.Y. Philharm., N.Y.C., 1966—; faculty Manhattan Sch. Music, N.Y.C., 1969—, Mannes Coll. Music, N.Y.C., 1988—, The Julliard Sch., N.Y.C., 1990—, co-chair double bass dept., 1992—2002. Participant numerous chamber music festivals, including Marlboro; featured in 1st performances of Gunther Schuller Quartet for 4 double basses; artist for GM, CBS and RCA Recording cos. Mem.: Internat. Soc. Bassists, Am. Fedn. Musicians, The Bohemians. Avocations: reading, writing, cooking.

O'BRIEN, ROSANNE P. corporate financial executive; d. Rosalie Theresa O'Brien; m. Donald Anderson, May 20, 1985. BS in Bus. Adminstrn., U. Redlands, Calif., 1972. Dir. corp. comm. Tiger Internat./Flying Tiger, 1972—83; sr. v.p., dir. corp. comm. Glendale Fed. Bank, 1983—92; v.p., corp. rels. Teledyne, Inc./Allegheny Teledyne, 1993—99; corp. v.p., comm. Northrop Grumman Corp., L.A., 1999—. Bd. mem. Calif. Sci. Ctr., L.A., L.A. Ednl. Partnership; trustee San Francisco Acad. Mem.: Nat. Investor Rels. Inst. Office: Northrop Grumman Corp 1840 Century Park E Los Angeles CA 90067 Business E-Mail: rosanne.obrien@ngc.com.

O'BRIEN, SHANNON PATRICIA, state treasurer; b. Boston, Apr. 30, 1959; m. Emmet Hayes; 1 child, Regan Ann; 1 stepchild: Jill. BA, Yale U., 1981; JD, Boston U., 1985. State rep., 1987-93; state senator, 1993-95; health care exec., 1995-97; lectr. Boston U., 1997-98; treas. State of Mass., Boston, 1999—. Office: State House Rm 227 Office Of Treasurer Boston MA 02133

O'BRIEN, SHEILA MARIE, judge; b. Nov. 8, 1955; BA, U. Notre Dame, 1977, JD, 1980. Bar: Ill., Mo., U.S. Supreme Ct. Asst. pub. defender, 1980—81; atty. Brown & James, 1981—82, Moser & Marsalek, 1982—85; judge St. Clair County, Ill., 1985—91, Cook County, Chgo., 1991—94; justice Ill. Appellate Ct., 1st Jud. Dist., Chgo., 1994—. Adj. prof. law St. Louis U. Sch. Law, 1989—90. Past assoc. judge seminar coord. com.; past Juvenile Task Force-Solovy Commn.; apptd. Ill. Juvenile Justice Commn., Drug Task Force for East St. Louis, Child Fatality Task Force; supplemental mem. Chgo. Symphony Chorus; former mem. St. Louis Symphony Chorus; past bd. dirs. Children First, Inc. Recipient Women of Achievement award, Belleville (Ill.) News-Dem. Mem.: Women's Bar Assn., Ill. State Bar Assn., Chgo. Bar Assn., Notre Dame Club of Chgo., Irish Fellowship Club.

O'BRIEN, SOLEDAD, newscaster, news anchor; Student, Harvard U. Prodr. Second Opinion, reporter Health Week in Review Sta. KISS-FM, Boston; assoc. prodr., newswriter Sta. WBZ-TV, Boston; prodr. NBC News, 1991—93, co-host The Know Zone Discovery Channel; chief East Bay bur. Sta. KRON-TV, San Francisco, reporter, 1993—96; co-host The Site, Nightly News, Weekend Today MSNBC, 1996—99; anchor, Weekend Today NBC, 1999—2003; co-anchor, American Morning CNN, 2003—. Recipient Emmy. Office: CNN 820 1st St NE Washington DC 20002-4243

O'BRYANT, CATHY, retired social worker, evangelist; b. Camden, N.J., Jan. 5, 1941; d. James Hearl and Ruth Virginia Jackson; children: Wendell, Penny, Terence, George, Ramona. AA Liberal Arts, Camden County Coll., Blackwood, N.J., 1972; BA in Psychology, Glassboro State Coll., N.J., 1976. Dir. Nat. Congress of Neighborhoods, Washington, 1980—82; social worker Dept. Human Svcs., Phila., 1989—94; ret., 1994. Internat. housing conf. coord. Alternatives for Women and UN, Camden, 1987; workshop leader Black Women's Health Project, Nairobi, Kenya, 1985; welfare caucuse leader Women, Work and Welfare, Houston, 1978; motivational spkr.; workshop developer Welfare, IWY Conf., Houston, 1978. Author: (book) If My People, 1996; editor: (newsletters) Christian Voices, 2002—, (newletters) Grassroots Women Speak, 1980—82. Asst. state chairperson N.J. Welfare Rights Orgn., Camden, 1971—77; mem. D.C. Women's Polit. Caucus, 1981—82, cert. mem. Juvenile Conf. Com. of Camden County, NJ, 1976—77. Recipient Bronze Star Outstanding Achievement award, Nat. Hook-Up of Black Women, 1992. Mem.: Poetic Ministries (founder, dir. 1998—), Parade of Poets (founder, coord. 1996—), Sketches of Christian Life (founder, pres. 2001—). Democrat. Seventh Day Adventist. Avocations: travel, nature walks, logic puzzles. Home: 231 N Evergreen Ave Apt 34B Woodbury NJ 08096

O'BRYON, LINDA ELIZABETH, television station executive; b. Washington, Sept. 1, 1949; d. Walter Mason Ormes and Iva Genevieve (Batrus) Ranney; m. Dennis Michael O'Bryon, Sept. 8, 1973; 1 child, Jennifer Elizabeth. BA in Journalism cum laude, U. Miami. News reporter Sta. KCPX (now KTVX), Salt Lake City, 1971-73; documentary and pub. affairs prodr. Sta. WPLG-TV, Miami, Fla., 1974-76; producer, reporter, anchor, news dir. then v.p. for news and pub. affairs, exec. editor, sr. v.p. Nightly Business Report Sta. WPBT (PBS), Miami, 1976—. Recipient award Fla. Bar, Tallahasse, 1977, 2 awards Ohio State U., 1976, 79, award Corp. for Pub. Broadcasting, 1978, Econ. Understanding award Dartmouth Coll., 1980, award Fla. AP, 1981, 1st prize Nat. Assn. Realtors, 1986, Bus. News Luminary award TJFR, 1990, Am. Women in Radio and TV award, 1995, 98; named Most Influential Woman Bus. News Exec., TJFR, 2001. Mem. NATAS (past bd. dirs. So. Fla. chpt., local Emmy award So. Fla. chpt. 1978), Radio-TV News Dirs. Assn., Am. Pub. TV (trustee). Republican. Roman Catholic. Avocations: aerobics, tennis, golf. Office: Sta WPBT 14901 NE 20th Ave Miami FL 33181-1121

O'BYRNE, ELIZABETH MILIKIN, pharmacologist, researcher; b. Miami, Fla., May 19, 1944; d. Richard Mershon and Anne (Smith) Milikin; m. Brian Kenneth O'Byrne, July 1, 1972; children: Lucy Milikin, Kenneth Daniel. AB in Chemistry, Emory U., 1965, MS in Biochemistry, 1968; PhD in Biochemistry, N.Y. Med. Coll., 1985. Assoc. scientist Eli Lilly Rsch. Labs., Indpls., 1968-70; sr. rsch. scientist CIBA-GEIGY Pharms., Summit, N.J., 1970-96; rsch. fellow Novartis Pharms., East Hanover, NJ, 1997—. Contbr. articles to profl. jours. Mem. AAAS, N.Y. Acad. Sci., Inflammation Rsch. Assn., Osteoarthritis Rsch. Soc. Achievements include isolation, characterization and development of radioimmunoassay for hormone relaxin to monitor production and secretion, of assays of cytokine and enzyme degradation of cartilage in vitro and in vivo, of proton and sodium magnetic resonance properties of cartilage; demonstration of therapeutic efficacy of matrix metalloprotease inhibitors to retard tissue damage in animal models of diseases; investigation of autologous bone marrow-derived mesechymal stem cells to repair osteoarthritic lesions in cartilage and bone, co-founder of CIBA-GEIGY Partnership in Sci. in which scientists work with teachers to bring hands-on experiences in laboratory investigation to high school students. Home: 234 Sagamore Rd Millburn NJ 07041-2136 Office: Novartis Pharms One Health Plaza East Hanover NJ 07936-1080 E-mail: elizabeth.obyrne@pharma.novartis.com.

OCCHETTI, DIANNE, psychologist, writer; b. Henderson, N.C., Aug. 27, 1951; d. Archie W. and Lillie J. Reavis; m. Armand Occhettti, June 10, 1979. MSW, Univ. N.C., Chapel Hill, N.C., 1974; PhD, Fielding Grad. Inst., Santa Barbara, Calif., 1988. AAMFT approved Supr. and Clin. Mem. Am. Assn. for Marriage & Family Therapy, cert. Group Psychotherapists. Pres., ptnr. Pembroke Psychological Svc. L.L.P., Raleigh, NC, 1983—. Author: Do I Stay or Do I Go? How To Make a Wise Decision About Your Relationship, 2000, transl. into Spanish, 2002; contbr. articles to profl. jour. Human svc. bd. appt. by Wake County Commr., Raleigh, NC, 1996—; bd. mem. Good Shepard Pre-Sch., Raleigh, NC, 2000—. Mem.: Raliegh Profl. Women's Forum. Office: Pembroke Psychol Svc LLP 6512 Six Forks Rd Ste 202A Raleigh NC 27615

OCCHIPINTI, LISA, artist; b. Mass., Oct. 30, 1970; d. Samuel Occhipinti and Barbara Urbanek. BA summa cum laude, Notre Dame Coll., 1992. Painter and designer, Portsmouth, NH, 1992—; faculty mem. N.H. Inst. Art, Manchester, 1997—2001; faculty and coord. Summer Abroad Burren Coll. Art, Ballyvaughan, Ireland, 2001. Artist resident Vt. Studio Ctr., Johnson, 1997; set designer New Art Theater, Manchester, 1999—2001. Exhibitions include Regis Coll., Tremont Gallery at the Internat. Soc., Thoreau Gallery,

Franklin Pierce Coll., Fitchburg Art Mus., Bristol Art Mus. Grantee Alfred T Granger Art Fund, N.H. State Coun. on the Arts, 1998; Clowes Fund fellow, Vt. Studio Ctr., 1997. Mem.: Copley Soc. Art. Personal E-mail: paintedi@hotmail.com.

OCHELTREE, CAROLYN DONINE, minister, religious studies educator; b. Bklyn., Apr. 20, 19[illegible]; d. Ritchie Don Ocheltree and Elizabeth Boyer-Ocheltree; children: Richard Don, Robert Dean, Randall David. BA, UCLA, 1976; MA, Loyola-Marymount U., 1982; PhD, Drew U., 1996. Ordained min. United Meth. Ch., 1991. Tchr. Divine Saviour Sch., LA, 1984—87; preceptor Hagadorn Psychiat. Hosp., Glen Gardner, NJ, 1988—91; min. Grace United Meth. Ch., Dover, NJ, 1992—98, First United Meth. Ch., Fremont, Calif., 1999—2003. Adj. prof. Caldwell (N.J.) Coll., 1996—98. Contbr. articles to religious jours. Home: 459 37th Street Apt 2 Oakland CA 94609

OCHOA, ELLEN, astronaut; b. L.A., May 10, 1958; d. Roseanne Ochoa; m. Coe Fulmer Miles; one son. BS in Physics, San Diego State U., 1980; MSEE, Stanford U., 1981, PhD in EE, 1985. Rsch. engr. Sandia Nat. Labs., Livermore, Calif., 1985—88; chief intelligent systems tech. br. NASA/Ames Rsch. Ctr./Moffet Field Naval Air Sta., Mountain View, Calif.; Astronaut NASA, Houston, 1991—, dep. dir., flight crew ops. Recipient two Space Act Tech Brief Awards, 1992, Space Flight Medals 1993, 1994, 1999, 2002; Outstanding Leadership Medal, 1995, Exceptional Svc. Medal, 1997, Women in Aerospace Outstanding Achievement Award, the Hispanic Engr. Albert Baez Award for Outstanding Tech. Contribution to Humanity, the Hispanic Heritage Leadership Award, San Diego State U. Alumna of the Year. Mem. Optical Soc. Am., Am. Inst. Aeronautics and Astronautics, Phi Beta Kappa, Sigma Xi, Pres. Commn. on the Celebration of Women in Am. History. Achievements include being the first female Hispanic astronaut chosen for Space Shuttle program. Office: NASA Johnson Space Ctr Astronaut Office Houston TX 77058*

OCHOA-BRILLEMBOURG, HILDA MARGARITA, investment banker; b. July 8, 1946; BS in econs., Universidad Catolica Andres Bello, Caracas, Venezuela; MPA John F. Kennedy Sch., Harvard U.; doctoral candidate in fin., Harvard Bus. Sch. Chief investment officer, pension investment div. World Bank, 1976—87; mng. dir. Emerging Markets Investment Corp.; founder, pres., CEO Strategic Investment Group, 1987—. Bd. dirs. USAir Group, Harvard Mgmt. Co., World Bank / Internat. Monetary Fund Credit Union; treas. C.A. Luz Electrica de Venezuela, Caracas, Venezuela; lectr. Universidad Catolica Andres Bello; bd. dirs. General Mills, Inc., 2002—; ind. cons. in econs. and fin. Published articles in Fin. Analyst Jour. and Pensions & Investments. Bd. dirs. Nat. Symphony Orchestra, Washington Opera; chmn, bd. dirs. Youth Orchestra of the Americas; mem. investment com. Rockefeller Family Fund; vice chair, Group of 50 Carnegie Endowment for Internat. Peace; adv. com. Rockefeller Ctr. for Latin Am. Studies, The Hauser Ctr. at Harvard U., Sun Trust / Asset Mgmt. Advs.; exec. com. Small Enterprise Asst. Funds. Named Top 50 Hispanic Women in Bus., Hispanic Mag., Top 50 Smartest Women in Bus., Money Mag., 2000; grantee Fulbright-Hays Fellow. Office: 1001 19th St N 16th Fl Arlington VA 22209-1722 Office Phone: 703-243-4433. Office Fax: 703-236-1798.*

OCHS, CAROL REBECCA, theologian, philosophy and religion educator; b. N.Y.C., May 7, 1939; d. Herman and Clara Florence (Michaels) Blumenthal; m. Michael Ochs, Sept. 27, 1959; children: Elisabeth Amy, Miriam Adina. BA, CUNY, 1960, MA, 1964; PhD, Brandeis U., 1968. Philosophy lectr. CUNY, 1964-65; from asst. prof. to prof. philosophy Simmons Coll., Boston, 1967-92, prof. emerita, 1992—. Adj. faculty Grad. Sch. Union Inst., Cin., 1992—97, Hebrew Union Coll.-Jewish Inst. Religion, N.Y.C., 1994—97, dir. grad. studies, vis. prof. philosophy, 1997—2001, dir. grad. studies, adj. assoc. prof. Jewish Religious Thought, 2001—; cons. Inst. for Svc. to Higher Edn., Chestnut Hill, Mass., 1972, St. Mary's Coll., South Bend, Ind., 1980; scholar-in-residence Hollins Coll., Roanoke, Va., 1987, numerous temples and synagogues; mem. selection com. Kent Postdoctoral Fellowships Bunting Inst., Radcliffe Coll.; lectr. in field. Author: Behind the Sex of God: Toward a New Consciousness Transcending Matriarchy and Patriarchy, 1977, Women and Spirituality, 1983, 2d edit., 1997, An Ascent to Joy: Transforming Deadness of Spirit, 1989, The Noah Paradox: Time as Burden, Time as Blessing, 1991, Song of the Self: Biblical Spirituality and Human Holiness, 1994, Jewish Spiritual Guidance, 1997, Our Lives as Torah: Finding God in Our Own Stories, 2001, Reaching Godward: Voices from Jewish Spiritual Guidance, 2004; contbr. articles to profl. jours. Mem. Jewish-Cath. Dialogue, Boston, 1989-93; mem. Cath.-Jewish com. Archdiocese of Boston, 1989-93. Fellow NEH, 1976, 88, Nat. Humanities Inst., U. Chgo., 1978-79, Danforth Found., 1981-86, Coolidge Rsch., Colloquium, 1985, Resource Theologian, 1995-99. Fellow Soc. for Values in Higher Edn. (bd. dirs. 1982-88, 2003—, v.p. 2004, chair ctrl. com. 1985-87), Assn. for Religion and Intellectual Life (mem. editl. bd. 1986—). Office: Hebrew Union Coll 1 W 4th St New York NY 10012

OCHS, ELINOR, linguistics educator; Prof. dept. TESL and applied linguistics UCLA. Co-editor: Developmental Pragmatics, 1979, Language Socialization Across Cultures, 1986, Interaction with Grammar, 1996; author: Culture and Language Development: Language Acquisition and Language Socialization in a Samoan Village, 1988, (with L. Capps) Constructing Panic, The Discourse of Agoraphobia, 1995; contbr. articles to profl. publs. MacArthur fellow J.D. and C.T. MacArthur Found.; grantee NSF, 1986-89, Nat. Inst. Child Health and Devel., 1986-89, Spencer Found., 1990-93, 94-97, U.S. Dept. Edn., 1993-96 Achievements include research on discourse structures, grammar in context, language and affect, spoken and written language, cross-cultural communication. Office: UCLA Dept Applied Linguistics TESL 330 Rolfe Hall Room 3326 PO Box 951531 Los Angeles CA 90095-1531

OCKO, STEPHANIE, writer, journalist; b. Newport, R.I. d. Howard Webster and Irma Coffin (Richardson) Goss; m. Stephen Ocko (div. 1993); 1 child, Peter Jeffrey. BA in Anthropology, Boston U., 1972; grad. diploma in comm., Simmons Coll., 1978; MA in Fine Arts, Harvard U., 1986. English instr. Inst. Pedagogique Nat., Kinshasa, Zaire, 1965-66, Stonehill Coll., North Easton, Mass., 1985-89. Author: Environmental Vacations, 1990, 2d edit., 1991 (Best Travel Book, Am. Book Assn. 1990-91), Water, Almost Enough for Everyone, 1995, Adventure Vacations, 1995, Doomsday Denied, 1997, Spiritual Adventures, 2003, Fantasy Vacations, 2003. Mem. Nat. Writers Union, Soc. Environ. Journalists. Avocations: photography, sailing. Home: PO Box 51959 Boston MA 02205-1959 E-mail: ocko2000@att.net.

O'CONNELL, CARMELA DIGRISTINA, appraisal executive, consultant; b. Johnstown, Pa., Nov. 8, 1925; d. Salvatore and Josephine (Riggio) Digristina; m. Maurice F. O'Connell, Sept. 21, 1974 (dec. Feb. 1984); children: Geraldine, John, Bernard. Diploma, Eastern Secretarial Sch., N.Y.C., Sch. Interior Design. From typist to sec.-treas. Philip P. Masterson Co., N.Y.C., 1942-72; exec. v.p., bd. dirs. Masterson & O'Connell Inc., N.Y.C., 1972-80, cons., 1981—; founder, pres. N.Y. Appraisal Corp., N.Y.C., 1971-80; co-founder, pres. Park Ave. Appraisal, N.Y.C., 1981—. Mem. N.Y. Rep. Com., 1974—, Met. Opera Guild, N.Y.C., 1986; chmn. Ch. of Our Saviour, N.Y.C., 1986; mem. Ladies of Charity, Cath. Charities Archdiocese of N.Y., 1990; bd. dirs. 80 Park Avenue Condominiums, 1997—. Recipient Amita award for Bus. Woman of Yr., 1977, Lena Madesin Phillips award N.Y. League/Fortune 500 Bus. and Profl. Women, 1989. Mem. Nat. Fedn. Bus. and Profl. Women's Clubs Inc. (2d v.p. 1964, 1st v.p. 1966). Roman Catholic. Home: 2421 Old Collier Rd Land O Lakes FL 34639

O'CONNELL, MARUEEN C. state legislator, lawyer; m. Don O'Connell; 1 child, Don. BS in Health Care Adminstrn., St. Josephs Coll.; JD, St. John's U.; RN, Flushing Hosp. Med. Ctr. Mem. adv. bd. Nassau Cmty. Coll., Molloy Coll. Sch. of Nuring. Recipient Am. Jurisprudence award. Mem.: Oncology Nursing Soc., Nassau Co. Bar Assn., Am. Cancer Soc. Democrat. Office: 1600 Stewart Ave Ste 315 Westbury NY 11590

O'CONNELL, MARY ANN, state legislator, small business owner; b. Albuquerque, Aug. 3, 1934; d. James Aubrey and Dorothy Nell (Batsel) Gray; m. Robert Emmett O'Connell, Feb. 21, 1977; children: Jeffery Crampton, Gray Crampton. Student, U. N.Mex., Internat. Coun. Shopping Ctrs. Exec. dir. Blvd. Shopping Ctr., Las Vegas, Nev., 1968-76, Citizen Pvt. Enterprise, Las Vegas, 1976; media supr. Southwest Advt., Las Vegas, 1977—; owner, operator Meadows Inn, Las Vegas, 1985—99, 3 Christian bookstores, Las Vegas, 1985-99; mem. Nev. State Senate, 1985—, chmn. govtl. affairs com., vice chmn. commerce and labor com. Vice chmn. Legis. Commn., 1985—86, 1995—96, mem. edn. com. to rewrite standards; mem. Edn. Commn. of the States, 1997—; rep. Nat. Conf. State Legislators; past vice chair State Mental Hygiene and Mental Retardation Adv. Bd. Pres. explorer div. Boulder Dam Area coun. Boy Scouts Am., Las Vegas, 1979-80, former mem. exec. bd. mem. adv. bd. Boulder Dam chpt.; pres., bd. dirs. Citizens Pvt. Enterprise, Las Vegas, 1982-84, Secret Witness, Las Vegas, 1981-82; vice chmn. Gov.'s Mental Health-Mental Retardation, Nev., 1983-; past mem. community adv. bd. Care Unit Hosp., Las Vegas; past mem. adv. bd. Kidney Found., Milligan Coll., Charter Hosp.; tchr. Young Adult Sunday Sch.; 1st vice chmn. Clark County Rep. Party, 2001-03. Recipient Commendation award Mayor O. Grayson, Las Vegas, 1975, Outstanding Citizenship award Bd. Realtors, 1975, Silver Beaver award Boy Scouts Am., 1980, Free Enterprise award Greater Las Vegas C. of C., Federated Employers Assn., Downtown Breakfast Exch., 1988, Award of Excellence Women in Politics, 1989, Legislator Yr. award Bldg. and Trades, 1991, Legislator Yr. award Nat. ASA Trade Assn., 1991, 94, Guardian Liberty award Nev. Coalition Conservative Citizens, 1991, Internat. Maxi Awards Promotional Excellence, Guardian Small Bus. award Nat. Fedn. Ind. Bus., 1995-96, Legislator Yr. award Nev. Med. Polit. Com., 1999, Assoc. Builders and Contractors, New Mortgage Brokers, 2000, Nev. Ind. Check Cashing Assn., 2001, Nev. Phys. Therapists, 2002, Atty. Gen. award Women's Role Model, 2002, Nicholas J. Horn award Nev. State Med. Assn., 2003; named Nev. Public Health Assoc. Legislator Yr., Nev. Retail Assn., 1992, New Assn. Bldg. Contractors, 1999, Nev Polit. Med. Action Com., 1999; inducted into Nev. Vets. Citizens Hall Fame, 1999; named one of 25 Notable Las Vegas Women, 2004. Mem. Retail Mchts. Assn. (former pres., bd. dirs.), Taxpayers Assn. (bd. dirs.), Greater Las Vegas C. of C. (past pres., bd. dirs., Woman of Achievement Politics women's coun. 1988). Republican. Mem. Christian Ch. Avocations: china painting, reading. Office: Nev Legislature Senate 401 S Carson St Carson City NV 89701-4747

O'CONNELL, MARY ITA, psychotherapist; b. Balt., July 3, 1929; d. Richard Charles and Ona (Buchness) O'C.; m. Leon Jack Greenbaum, Dec. 28, 1962 (div. Jan. 1986); children: Jessie A., Elizabeth K. BA, U. Md., 1956; postgrad., Am. U., 1960—; M in Creative Arts in Therapy, Hahnemann Med. Coll., 1978. Registered Acad. Dance Therapists. Tchr. Robert Cohan Sch. Dance, Boston, 1958-61; instr., choreographer Wheaton Coll., Norton, Mass., 1959-60, Harvard/Radcliffe Colls., Boston, 1960-62; tchr., performer, choreographer Profl. Studios, Washington, 1962-69; asst. prof., adminstr. Fed. City Coll., Washington, 1969-74; movement psychotherapist Woodburn Ctr. for Community Mental Health, Fairfax, Va., 1975-76, Gundry Hosp., Balt., 1976-77, Prince Georges' Community Mental Health Dept., Capitol Heights, Md., 1978-80; lectr. George Washington U., D.C., 1981-85; pvt. practice psychotherapy Silver Spring, Md., 1977—. Sr. movement psychotherapist Regional Inst. for Children and Adolescents, Rockville, Md., 1980-82; movement cons. Ctr. for Youth Svcs., Washington, 1981-83; movement psychotherapist D.C. Mental Health Ctrs., Washington, 1985-87, 90-99, Community for Creative Non-Violence Women's Shelter, Washington, 1986, LICSW, Washington, 1989. Choreographer, soloist (dance performance) The Artist: A Theatre Happening, 1963; choreographer, co-dir. (outdoor dance event) Tree Sculpting, 1974; choreographer (dance performance) Excitations, 1967, A Dance Event, 1974; soloist, New England Opera, 1961; performer, choreographer WGBM TV/Laboratory Concert Series, 1961; performer, CBS-TV/Erika Thimey Dance Theatre, 1965; guest artist, Harford Coll. Art Festival, 1967. U. Md. scholar, 1955-56. Mem. Dance Circle of Boston (life, pres. 1959-61), Modern Dance Council of Washington (exec. bd dirs., editor 1965-69), Am. Dance Therapy Assn. (treas. metro chpt. 1977-81), Assn. Humanistic Psychology, Family Therapy Network, Am. Dance Guild, NIH (movement specialist 1978-79). Democrat. Avocations: sailing, lacrosse, stone collecting, collage making. Home and Office: 16 Sussex Rd Silver Spring MD 20910-5435

O'CONNELL, TAAFFE CANNON, actress, publishing executive; b. Providence; d. Joseph Ceril and Edith Ethelyn (Dent) O'C. BA, MFA, U. Miss. Regional supr. Gloria Marshall Figure Salons, S.C.; v.p., co-founder Doc Sox Inc., Pacific Palisades, Calif., 1988-90; pres., founder Canoco Pub., L.A., 1991—, 1-800-266-DYNE, L.A., 1992-93. Founder Rising Star Distbn., Yes I Can Actor's Workshops, 2001—, Get Inside the Agent's Head Seminars, 2003; exec. prodr. Beanie/Twigg 1999-, Canoco Prodn. Appeared in films, including Men Without Dates, Dangerous, Hot Chili, Cheech & Chong Nice Dreams, Rocky II, Galaxy of Terror, New Years Evil, Rich Man Poor Man Book I, Caged Fury; TV appearances include Malubu Branch, General Hospital, Dangerous Women, Dallas, Knight and Daye, The New Gidget, Knight Rider, Three's Company, Dr. Joyce Brothers Show, Blansky's Beauties, Peter Lupus Show, Fix-It City, Happy Days, Laverne & Shirley, Wonder Woman, The Incredible Hulk; theater appearances include Too True to be Good, Damn Yankees, Anastasia, Star Spangled Girl, The Beaux Stratagem, The Canterbury Tales; founder, pub. Astrocaster, 1991, Power Agent, 1993; Jan. founder Rising Star Distbn. and Canoco Prodns., 1999—, Get Inside the Agents' Head Seminars, Yes I Can Actors Workshops; exec prodr.: Beanie & Twigg, Paranormal Private Eyes, Inside the Industry, 2000; founder Get Inside the Agents Head, 2003. Mem. Screen Actors' Guild, Am. Fedn. TV Radio Artists, Actor's Equity, Actor's Forum (bd. dirs. 1985-94). Avocations: singing, spinning, sailing, travel. Office: Canoco Pub 11611 Chenault St Ste 118 Los Angeles CA 90049-4574 E-mail: industryedge@earthlink.net.

O'CONNELL, SISTER VIRGINIA M. school librarian; b. Boston, Apr. 26, 1930; d. John Joseph and Katherine Walsh O'Connell. BS, Boston Coll., 1962; postgrad., Framingham State U. Tchr., libr. Marian High Sch., Framingham, Mass., 1969—84; tchr., bus mgr. Newton Cath. High Sch., 1984—88; pastoral assoc. St. Rose Parish, Chelsea, 1988—92; libr. Matignon High Sch., Cambridge, 1993—. Mem. adv. bd. Boston Coll. Advancement Studies, Chestnut Hill, 1993—; mem. adv. group Marian High Sch., 1994—96. Named Woman of Excellence, Mt. St. Joseph Acad., 1999. Mem.: LWV, Sisters St. Joseph Chorus, Mt. St. Joseph Acad. Roman Catholic. Avocations: travel, walking, reading. Home: 106 Waban St Newton MA 02458 E-mail: oconnell2001@hotmail.com.

O'CONNOR, BETTY LOU, hotel executive, food service executive; b. Phoenix, Oct. 29, 1927; d. Georg Eliot and Tillie Edith Miller; m. William Spoeri O'Connor, Oct. 10, 1948 (dec. Feb. 1994); children: Thomas W., William K., Kelli Anne. Student, U. So. Calif., 1946-48, Calif. State U., Los Angeles, 1949-50. V.p. O'Connor Food Svcs., Inc., Jack in the Box Restaurants, Granada Hills, Calif., 1983-93; pres. O'Connor Food Svcs., Inc., Granada Hills, Calif., 1994—, Western Restaurant Mgmt. Co., Granada Hills, 1986—, C.E.O. Foods, Inc., Victorville, Calif., City Snippers, Inc., Santa Clarita, Calif. Mem. adv. bd. Bank of Granada Hills; bd. dirs. Nat. Franchise Purchasing Coop., nc. Recipient Frannie award Foodmaker, Inc., Northridge, Calif., 1984, First Rate award, 1992. Mem. Jack in the Box Franchisee Assn., Spurs Hon. (sec. U. So. Calif. 1947-48), Associated Women Students (sec. U. So. Calif. 1946-47), Gamma Alpha Chi (v.p. 1947-48), Chi Omega. Republican. Roman Catholic. Avocation: rowing. Office: O'Connor Food Svcs Inc 17545 Chatsworth St Granada Hills CA 91344-5720

O'CONNOR, CATHERINE MARIE, music educator; b. Oakland, Calif., Dec. 26, 1959; d. Jack Wilbur and Arlene Mary O'Connor. BA, Calif. State U., Hayward, 1982. Pvt. piano instr., Hayward, Calif., 1982—. Musician: (chamber music /accompanist /performances) Solo and ensemble performances, 2000—. Mem.: Music Tchrs. Nat. Assn., Chamber Musicians of No. Calif., Music Tchrs. Assn. Calif. (pres. 1996—98, chmn. Friends of Today's Music Project 2001). Avocation: golf. Personal E-mail: cathoc@aol.com.

O'CONNOR, DENISE LYNN, marketing communications executive; b. West Palm Beach, Fla., Oct. 29, 1958; d. Joseph John and Ada Colleen (Doyle) Fields; m. William York O'Connor, May 31, 1985; 2 children. BS in Bus., Fla. State U., 1979; MBA, Fla. Inst. Tech., 1983, postgrad. in elec. engring., 1984-86. Cons. Small Bus. Inst., Tallahassee, 1979; mgr. select accts. Burroughs, West Palm Beach, 1980-81; mgr. mktg. communications Harris-Satellite Communications, Melbourne, Fla., 1981-84; sect. mgr. mktg. communications Gen. Electric Info. Svcs., Rockville, Md., 1984-86; mgr. pub. rels. Mgmt. Sci. Am., Atlanta, 1986-88; pres., owner Mktg. Comms. Cons., Atlanta, 1988—, Saddle River, N.J., 1995—. Cons. Sci.-Atlanta (Ga.), Inc., 1988—. Author (brochure) Genie, 1986 (Disting. award Soc. for Tech. Communications); editor (brochure) Electronic Data Interchange, 1986 (Excellence Soc. for Tech. Communications). Vol. Atlanta (Ga.) Humane Soc., 1988, (mem. auxiliary, 1989—). Recipient Ross Systems Pres. award, 1991. Mem. AAUW, PEO (v.p. reciprocity 1990-91, pres. evening and weekend reciprocity coun. 1991-92, chmn. Internat. Peace scholarship 1990), Soc. Tech. Comm., Atlanta Lawn and Tennis Assn.(pres. B-5 team 1989), Country Club South, Delta Zeta. Republican. Methodist. Avocations: tennis, golf, swimming, boating, water and snow skiing. Home and Office: Telcom HDQ Saddle River NJ 07458-2807

O'CONNOR, DORIS JULIA, non-profit fundraiser, consultant; b. Apr. 30, 1930; 1 dau., Kim C. BA cum laude in Econs., U. Houston, 1975. Adminstrv. asst. Shell Cos. Found. Inc., N.Y.C., 1966-71, asst. sec. Houston, 1971-73, sec., 1973-76, sr. v.p., dir., mem. exec. com., 1976-93; prin. Doris O'Connor & Co., 1993—. Corp. assoc. United Way of Am., Washington, 1976-93; corp. advisor Bus. Com. of Arts, N.Y.C., 1976-91, del., 1982-87; dir. Ind. Sector, Washington, 1981-89, vice chmn., 1983-87; mem. contbns. coun. Conf. Bd., N.Y.C., 1976-93; advisor Coun. of Better Bus. Burs., Washington, 1975-94, vice chmn., 1983-87; commr. adv. commn. on work-based learning, Dept. Labor, 1991-93; mem. Houston/Harris County Arts Task Force, 1991-93, Houston Ind. Sch. Dist. Task Force, 1991-93; trustee Houston Grand Opera, 1993-99, Houston Symphony Soc., 1993-99, Soc. Performing Arts, 1993-99, Cultural Arts Coun., 1993-96, Greater Houston Coalition Edn. Excellence, 1993-96; mem. adv. bd. Houston Zool. Soc., 1993-99; mem. New Orleans Mus. of Art, Opera Assn. Mem. Houston Com. Fgn. Rels., Houston Philos.Soc., Plaza Club (bd. givs. 1987-89), Omicron Delta Epsilon.

O'CONNOR, EILEEN J. federal agency administrator; Grad., Columbus State U., Cath. U. Ptnr. Office Fed. Tax Svcs. Grant Thornton, 1984—99; officer for tax svcs. Aronson, Fetridge and Weigle; asst. atty. gen. tax divsn. U.S. Dept. Justice, Washington, 2001—. Adj. prof. law George Mason Law Sch., Georgetown U. Law Sch. Office: US Dept Justice Tax Divsn 950 Pennsylvania Ave NW Washington DC 20530-0001

O'CONNOR, GENEVIEVE, pharmaceutical executive; b. Cortland, N.Y., Mar. 5, 1975; d. Sean Gary and Sharon Anne O'Connor. BS, Villanova U., 1997; postgrad., Fordham U. Events coord. Rainbow Pormotions, Landsdowne, Pa., 1993—95, World Class Promotions, Balt., 1994—95; fgn. exch. traders asst. The Asahi Bank, Ltd., N.Y.C., 1998—99; pharm. sales rep. 3M Pharm., St. Paul, 1999—2000, profl. instl. sales rep., 2000—01, sr. profl. instl. sales rep., 2001—. Regional trainer 3M Pharm., St. Paul, 2002—, intranet adv. bd., West Coldwell, NJ, 2001—02, computer trainer, 2002—. Mem.: Alpha Chi Omega (chi connections coord. 1994—96). Avocations: skiing, tennis, travel, art, writing. Home: 11 N Marwood Rd Port Washington NY 11050 Office: 3M Pharm PO Box 33275 3M Ctr Bldg 0275-03-W-01 Saint Paul MN 55133 E-mail: geoconnor@mmm.com.

O'CONNOR, SISTER GEORGE AQUIN (MARGARET M. O'CONNOR), academic administrator, sociology educator; b. Astoria, N.Y., Mar. 5, 1921; d. George M. and Joana T. (Loughlin) O'C. BA, Hunter Coll., 1943; MA, Catholic U. Am., 1947; PhD (NIMH fellow), NYU, 1964; LL.D. Manhattan Coll., 1983; D of Pedagogy (hon.), Dowling Coll., 1997; DHL, St. Francis Coll., 1997, St. Joseph's Coll., 1997. Mem. faculty St. Joseph's Coll., Bklyn., 1946—, prof. sociology and anthropology, 1966—, chmn. social sci. dept., 1966-69, pres., 1969-97; pres. emeritus. Fellow African Studies Assn., Am. Anthrop. Assn.; Bklyn. C. of C. (dir. 1973-97), Alpha Kappa Delta, Delta Epsilon Sigma. Author: The Status and Role of West African Women: A Study in Cultural Change, 1964. Named one of N.Y. State Senate's Women of Distinction. Office: Saint Joseph's Coll 245 Clinton Ave Brooklyn NY 11205-3602

O'CONNOR, JENNIFER, lawyer; b. Somerville, Mass., Feb. 12, 1966; m. Paul J. Meyer, Nov. 13, 1993. BA in Govt. magna cum laude, Harvard U., 1987; MPA, Columbia U., 1993; JD magna cum laude, Georgetown U., 1997. Dep. press sec., econ. devel. assoc. Office of Manhattan Borough Pres Ruth Messinger, N.Y.C., 1990-92; budget specialist, N.E. regional polit. dir. Presdl. Transition Office, Little Rock, 1992-93; dep. dir. Office of Mgmt. and Adminstrn. The White House, Washington, 1993, spl. asst. to Pres. for Cabinet affairs, 1993-95, spl. asst. to Pres. Office Dep. Chief of Staff, 1995-96; dep. asst. sec. policy U.S. Dept. Labor, Washington, 1997; law clk. to judge U.S. Ct. Appeals/D.C. Cir., 1997-98; assoc. Miller, Cassidy, Larroca & Lewin/ Baker Botts (merged), Washington, 1998—2002; counsel Wilmer, Cutler and Pickering, 2002—. Field. dir. N.Y. primary campaign, polit. dir. N.J. primary campaign, dep. mgr. at Dem. Nat. Conv., state dir. Vt. gen. election campaign Clinton for Pres./Clinton-Gore '92, 1992. Democrat. Office: Wilmer Cutlre Pickering LLP 2445 M St NW Washington DC 20037

O'CONNOR, KAREN LENDE, Olympic athlete; b. Feb. 17, 1958; m. David O'Connor, 1993. Mem. US Equestrian Olympic Team, Seoul, Korea, 1988, Atlanta, 1996, U.S. Equestrian Team, 2000. Winner CCI, Boekelo (Holland), 1984, CCI, Chesterland (Pa.), 1985, placed 1st Role/Kentucky Internat. CCI Three Day Event, 1991, 1st Tetbury (Eng.) Horse Trials, 1991, 1st Fair Hill (Md.) Horse Trials, 1991, 3rd Burghley Three Day Event CCI (Eng.), 1991, 6th World Three Day Event Rider Rankings L'Annee Hippique, 1991, 3rd CCI, Loughanmore (Ireland), 1992, 6th Blenheim Audi Internat. Horse Trials (Eng.), 1993, 1st CCI, Punchestown (Ireland), 1993, 10th CCI Internat. de Saumur, 1994; recipient Silver medal, Olympic Games, Atlanta, 1996; named U.S. Combined Tng. Assn. Lady Rider of the Year, 1989, 90, 91, 95, 96, 97, 98, Female Equestrian Athlete of the Year Olympic Com., 1993, USET spring champion, winning Kentucky CCI, USET FAll Reserve champion, 2nd Fair Hill, 1999, World Equestrian Games Bronze Medal Team, 1998, USET spring champion, winner Kentucky CCI, 1997; grantee USET, 1991. Office: care US Equestrian Team Inc PO Box 355 Gladstone NJ 07934-0355

O'CONNOR, KATHLEEN MARY, lawyer; b. Camden, Jan. 14, 1949; d. John A. and Marie V. (Flynn) O'C. BA, U. Fla., 1971, JD, 1981. Bar: Fla. 1981, U.S. Ct. Appeals (11th cir.) 1982, U.S. Supreme Ct. 1987. Atty. Walton, Lantaff, Schroeder & Carson, Miami, Fla., 1981-84, Thornton, Davis & Murray PA, Miami, 1984-98, Thornton, Davis & Fein, P.A., Miami, 2002—. Exec. editor U. Fla. Law Rev., 1981; contbr. articles to profl. jours. Legal advocate Miami Project to Cure Paralysis, 1992-97. Mem. ABA, Dade County Bar Assn. (vice-chair appellate cts. com. 1981, 2003), Def. Rsch. Inst., Fla. Def. Lawyers Assn., Fla. Assn. for Women Lawyers (bd. dirs. Miami-Dade County chpt. 2002—), Fla. Bar (mem. appellate rules com. 2002—). Office: Thornton Davis & Fein PA 80 SW 8th St Ste 2900 Miami FL 33130 E-mail: oconnor@tdflaw.com.

O'CONNOR, KAY F. state legislator; b. Everett, Wash., Nov. 28, 1941; d. Ernest S. and Dena (Lampers) Wells; m. Arthur J. O'Connor, Sept. 1, 1959; 6 children. Diploma, Lathrop H.S., Fairbanks, Alaska, 1959. Office mgr. Blaylock Chemicals, Bucyrus, Kans., 1981-84; store mgr. Copies Plus, Olathe, Kans., 1984-86; acct. Advance Concrete Inc., Spring Hill, Kans., 1986-92; mem. Kans. Ho. of Reps. from 14th dist., 1993-2000, Kans. Senate from 9th dist., 2001—. Exec. dir. Parents in Control, Inc.; bd. dirs. Hometel Ltd.; author sch. voucher legis. State of Kans., 1994-2002; corrections and juvenile justice oversight com., judiciary com., fed. and state affairs com., vice chair elections and local govt. com. Kans. Senate, 2001—. Republican. Roman Catholic. Avocations: choir directing, statue renovations, speaking on school vouchers. Home: 1101 N Curtis St Olathe KS 66061-2709 Office: PO Box 2232 Olathe KS 66051-2232 E-mail: kayoisok@comcast.net.

O'CONNOR, KIM CLAIRE, chemical engineering and biotechnology educator, researcher, inventor; BS magna cum laude, Rice U., Houston, 1982; PhD, Calif. Inst. Tech., Pasadena, 1987. Postdoctoral rsch. fellow chemistry dept. Calif. Inst. Tech., Pasadena, 1987-88; postdoctoral rsch. fellow chem. engring., biochemistry, molecular biology, and cell biology depts. Northwestern U., Evanston, Ill., 1988-90; asst. prof. chem. engring. Tulane U., New Orleans, 1990-96, assoc. prof. chem. engring., 1996—2002, prof. chem. engring., 2002—03, prof. chem. and biomolecular engring., 2003—, faculty molecular and cellular biology grad. program, Newcomb fellow, 1991—, co-dir. molecular and cellular biology grad. program, 1996-99, interim dir. molecular and cellular biology grad. program, 1997. Mem. Tulane Cancer Ctr., 1994—; adj. assoc. prof. dept. surgery Tulane U. Sch. Medicine, 1999—; cons., inventor in field. Contbr. articles and revs. to profl. jours. and orgns. including NASA, NSF, NRC, European Space Agy., pvt. founds. and univs.; patentee in field. Recipient NASA Space Act award, 1994, 95, 96, Outstanding Engring. Student award Tex. Soc. Profl. Engrs., 1982, Tulane award for excellence in undergrad. tchg., 1999, Lee H. Johnson award for excellence in tchg., 2001, Tulane Interdisciplinary Tchg. award, 2001; Robert A. Welch Merit scholar, 1978-82, Brown Engring. Merit scholar, 1980-82, Roy Merit scholar, 1981-82; Weyerhaeuser Co. Found. fellow, 1982-83. Mem.: AIChE, Tissue Engring. Soc., Soc. Women Engrs., Soc. In Vitro Biology, European Soc. Animal Cell Tech., Am. Chem. Soc., Am. Assn. for Cancer Rsch., Phi Lambda Upsilon, Tau Beta Pi, Sigma Xi. Achievements include interdisciplinary research in engineering and the biological sciences; patents. Office: Tulane U Dept Chem Engring Lindy Boggs Ctr Rm 300 New Orleans LA 70118 E-mail: koc@tulane.edu.

O'CONNOR, MAUREEN, judge; b. Washington, Aug. 7, 1951; d. Patrick and Mary E. O'Connor; children: Alex, Ed. BA, Seton Hill Coll., 1973; postgrad., SUNY, 1975-76; JD, Cleve. State U., 1980. Pvt. practice, 1981-85; referee Probate Ct., 1985-93; judge Common Pleas, 1993-95; prosecutor Summit County, 1995-99; lt. gov., dir. Dept. Pub. Safety State of Ohio, 1999—2003; Supreme Ct. Ohio Supreme Ct. Justice, Ohio, 2003. Dir. Summit County Child Support Enforcement Agy.; spkr. in field. Parishioner St. Vincent's Ch.; vol. Comty. Drug Bd., Am. Cancer Soc., bd. dirs.; bd. dirs. Victim Assistance, St. Edward Home, Fairlawn, Furnace St. Mission. Recipient MADD Law Enforcement award, 1997, Cleve. State Disting. Alumnae award for Civic Achievement, 1997. Mem. MADD, Nat. Dist. Attys. Assn., Nat. Child Support Enforcement Assn., Nat. Coll. Dist. Attys. Assn., Ohio Prosecuting Attys. Assn. (exec. com.), Ohio Family Support Assn., Atty. Gen.'s Prosecutor Liaison Com., Summit County Police Chiefs Assn., Summit Forum, Summit County Child Mortality. Republican. Office: Ohio Supreme Ct 30 E Broad St Fl 3 Columbus OH 43215*

O'CONNOR, PATRICIA ERYL, telecommunications consultant; b. Kansas City, Mo., Oct. 16, 1945; d. Jesse Edwin O'Connor and Olive Mae (Geagan) Brooks; m. James Harrie Reed, Dec. 18, 1964 (div. July 1972); 1 child, Jana Diann Reed; m. John Robert Morgan, Sept. 27, 1985. AAS, Pima Community Coll., Tucson, 1982. Cert. Nat. Assn. Broadcast Engrs. Radio, radio-telephone lic. gen. class FCC. Comm. technician AT&T, Kansas City, Mo., 1972-79, Tucson, 1979-85, San Francisco, 1985-92, Denver, 1992-99, Conyers, Ga., 1999—; CEO, cons. Profl. Forum Mgmt./MacCircles, Tucson, 1985, Pleasanton, Calif., 1985-92, Denver, 1992-96. Co-adminstr. Mac Symposium, Cupertino, Calif., 1987-93. Editor: (electronic mag.) Handshake, 1985-96. Election judge, Tucson, 1979-81; area v.p. CWA Local 8150, Ariz., N.Mex., 1984-84, exec. v.p., 1984-85, deptmental rep. local 3250, Conyers, Ga., 2003. Mem.: Kansas City Cactus and Succulent Soc. (founding mem.). Avocation: property management. Home: 45 Surrey Chase Dr Social Circle GA 30025-4912 E-mail: patoconnor@aol.com.

O'CONNOR, PEGGY LEE, communications manager; b. Chgo., Apr. 20, 1953; BS in Biology, Northeastern Ill. U., 1982; MBA, No. Ill. U., 1985. Emergency med. technologist, 1976-82; instr. Chgo. City Wide Colls., 1976-81; program dir. U. Ill. Hosp., 1979-81, Fermilab, Roselle, Ill., 1978-81; dist. mgr. Decision Data Svc., Schaumburg, Ill., 1981-89; gen. mgr. sales svc. Putnam Pub., 1989-91; mgr. fin. and adminstrn. Weyerhaeuser, 1991-93; ops. mgr. Ameritech Cellular, 1993-96, telesales mgr., 1996-98, customer care mgr., 1999; program mgr. ops. mgmt. Verizon Wireless (formerly Ameritech Cellular), 2000—. Program dir. Am. Cellular Women's Adv. Panel. Recipient awrd Summit Club, 1987, 88, 89. Mem. NAFE, NWAAR, Women in Bus., Pres.'s Club, BPA (chmn. bd. dirs.), Chgo. Credit Mgrs. Assn. Avocation: computers. Office: Verizon Wireless 777 Big Timber Rd Elgin IL E-mail: peggy.oconnor@verizonwireless.com.

O'CONNOR, SANDRA DAY, United States Supreme Court Justice; b. El Paso, Tex., Mar. 26, 1930; d. Harry A. and Ada Mae (Wilkey) Day; m. John Jay O'Connor, III, Dec. 1952; children: Scott, Brian, Jay. AB in Econs. with great distinction, Stanford U., 1950, LLB, 1952. Bar: Calif., Ariz. Dep. county atty., San Mateo, Calif., 1952—53; civilian atty. Q.M. Market Ctr., Frankfurt am Main, Germany, 1954—57; pvt. practice Phoenix, 1958—65; asst. atty. gen. State of Ariz., 1965—69; state senator Ariz., 1969—75; chmn. com. on state, county and mcpl. affairs, 1972—73; majority leader, 1973—74; judge Maricopa County Superior Ct., 1975—79, Ariz. Ct. Appeals, 1979—81; assoc. justice U.S. Supreme Ct., 1981—. Referee juvenile ct. Maricopa County, 1962—64; chmn. vis. bd. Maricopa County Juvenile Detention Home, 1963—64; mem. Maricopa County Bd. Adjustments and Appeals, 1963—64, Anglo-Am. Legal Exchange, 1980, Maricopa County Superior Ct. Judges Tng. and Edn. Com., 1977—79, Maricopa Ct. Study Com.; chair com. to reorganize lower cts. Ariz. Supreme Ct., 1974—75; faculty Robert A. Taft Inst. Govt.; mem. Ariz. Criminal Code Commn., 1974—76; bd. visitors Ariz. State U. Law Sch., 1981, liaison com. on med. edn., 81. Mem. bd. editors: Stanford (Calif.) U. Law Rev. Mem. Ariz. Pers. Commn., 1968—69, Nat. Def. Adv. Com. on Women in Svcs., 1974—76; trustee Heard Mus., Phoenix, 1968—74, 1976—81, pres., 1980—81; mem. adv. bd. Phoenix Salvation Army, 1975—81; trustee Stanford U., 1976—81, Phoenix County Day Sch.; mem. citizens adv. bd. Blood Svcs., 1975—77; nat. bd. dirs. Smithsonian Assocs., 1981—, Colonial Williamsburg Found., 1988—2000; exec. bd. Ctrl. Eastern European Law Initiative, 1990—; adv. bd., v.p. NCCJ, Maricopa County, 1977—81; bd. dirs., sec. Ariz. Acad, 1969—75, Cathedral chpt. Washington Nat. Cathedral, 1991—99; past Rep. dist. chmn.; bd. dirs. Phoenix Cmty. Coun., 1969—75, Jr. Achievement Ariz., 1975—79, Blue Cross/Blue Shield Ariz., 1975—79, Channel 8, 1975—79, Phoenix Hist. Soc., 1974—78, Maricopa County YMCA, 1978—81, Golden Gate Settlement. Named Woman of Yr., Phoenix Advt. Club, 1972, National Women's Hall of Fame, 1995; recipient Ann. award, NCCJ, 1975, Disting. Achievement award, Ariz. State U., 1980, Sara Lee Frontrunner award, 1997, ABA medal, 1997. Mem.: ABA (select law enforcement revision commn. vice chair 1979—80), Maricopa County Bar Assn. (referral svc. chair 1960—62), Calif. Bar Assn., Ariz. Bar Assn. (legal edn., pub. rels. com., lower ct. reorgn. com.), Soroptimist Club (Phoenix). Office: US Supreme Ct Supreme Ct Bldg 1 First St NE Washington DC 20543*

O'CONNOR TAYLOR, SHERYL ANN, medical services administrator; b. Rome, Ga., Jan. 26, 1951; d. Robert W. and Phyllis M. (Lambert) Nippler; 1 child, Ashley. BS, Ea. Mich. U., 1972; LPN, Washtenaw Community Coll., Ann Arbor, Mich., 1976; RN, Santa Ana Coll., 1980; MA Bus. Mgmt., U. Redlands, 1983. Cert. RN, cert. pub. health nurse, lic. healthcare risk mgr., cert. case mgr., cert. quality assurance/utilization mgmt., cert. med. staff coord., cert. provider credentialing specialist, cert. legal nurse cons., registered health information tech. Med.-surg./oncology nurse Western Med. Ctr., Santa Ana, Calif.; community health nurse Vis. Nurse Assn., Orange, Calif.; hosp. adminstr. USNR Med. Svcs. Corps., Jacksonville, Fla., 1985-88; ins. coord. Blue Cross/Blue Shield Fla., Pensacola, Fla., 1988-90; ctr. dir. Singleday Surgery, Jacksonville, 1990-91; dir. quality mgmt. Humana Hosp., Orange Park, Fla., 1991—93; dir. quality and med. affairs Humana Health Plans, Maitland, Fla., 1991—93; dir. health svcs. PCA/Century Med. Health Plans, Inc., Orlando, Fla., 1993-94; dir. nursing Nations Healthcare Inc., Jacksonville, Fla., 1994-95; dir. central credentials and privileging dept. USN Healthcare Support Office, Jacksonville, Fla., 1995-99; corp. risk mgr. Universal Health Svcs. Inc., King of Prussia, Pa., 1999-2001; dir. risk mgmt. Children's Nat. Med. Ctr., Washington, 2001—02; v.p. clin. effectiveness, quality improvement, patient safety Main Line Health Sys., Bryn Mawr, Pa., 2002—04; dir. quality resource mgmt. Parrish Med. Ctr., Titusville, Fla., 2004—. Mem. Am. Coll. Healthcare Execs., Am. Bd. Quality Assurance and Utilization Physicians, Naval Res. Assn., Nat. Assn. Med. Staff Svcs., Am. Soc. Healthcare Risk Mgmt., Am. Health Info. Mgmt. Assn. Personal E-mail: soconn@bellsouth.net.

O'DAY, ANITA BELLE COLTON, entertainer, musician, vocalist; b. Chgo., Dec. 18, 1919; d. James and Gladys (Gill) C. Student, Chgo. public schs. Singer and entertainer various Chgo. Music Clubs, 1939-41; singer with Gene Krupa's Orch., 1941-45, Stan Kenton Orch., 1944, Woody Herman Orch., 1945, Benny Goodman Orch., 1959; singing tours in U.S. and abroad, 1947—; rec. artist Polygram, Capitol, Emily Records, Verve, GNP Crescendo, Columbia, London, Signature, DRG, Pablo; million-seller songs include Let Me Off Uptown, 1941, And Her Tears Flowed Like Wine, 1944, Boogie Blues, 1945; appeared in films Gene Krupa Story, 1959, Jazz on a Summer's Day, 1960, Zigzag, 1970, Outfit, 1974; TV shows 60 Minutes, 1980; Tonight Show, Dick Cavett Show, Today Show, Big Band Bash, CBS Sunday Morning, CNN Showbiz Today; inductee Jazz Hall of Fame, Tampa, 1997, Nat. Endowment Fellowship. Author: High Times, Hard Times, 1981, rev. edit., 1989; performed 50 yr. anniversary concert Carnegie Hall, 1985, Avery Fisher Hall, 1989, Tanglewood, 1990, JVC Festival Town Hall, 1993, Rainbow and Stars, 1995, JVC Festival Carnegie Hall, 1996, JVC Festival Avery Fisher Hall, 1999, Hollywood Palladium, 1999, Blue Note, N.Y.C., 2000, Atlas Supper Club, Los Angeles, 2000, Fez, N.Y.C., 2001, Plush Room, San Francisco, 2002, Iridium, N.Y.C., 2003, Blue Note, N.Y.C., Jazz Alley, Seattle, 2003; currently touring worldwide; albums include Drummer Man, Kenton Era, Anita, Anita Sings The Most, Pick Yourself Up, Lady is a Tramp, An Evening with Anita O'Day, At Mr. Kelly's, Swings Cole Porter, Travelin' Light, All the Sad Young Men, Waiter Make Mine Blues, With the Three Sounds, I Told Ya I Love Ya Now Get Out, Uptown, My Ship, Live in Tokyo, Anita Sings the Winners, Incomparable, Anita 1975, Live at Mingos, Anita O'Day/The Big Band Sessions, Swings Rodgers and Hart, Time for Two, Tea for Two, In a Mellowtone (Grammy nomination 1990), At Vine St. Live, Mello'Day, Live at the City, Angel Eyes, The Night Has a Thousand Eyes, The Rules of the Road, Jazz Masters, Skylark, Swingtime in Hawaii, SS 'Wonderful (Carnegie Hall), Jazz Past Midnight, Compact Jazz, Let Me Off Uptown, The Complete Verve/Cleff Sessions, Ultimate Anita O'Day, After Midnight, Hi-Ho Trailus Bootwhip, Legends of the Swing Era, The Legacy Lives On, Finest Hour, complete Signature and London Recordings, The Young Anita. Jazz Masters fellow Nat. Endowment for the Arts, 1997. Mem. AFTRA, Screen Actors Guild, BMI. Office: Alan Eichler 6064 Selma Ave Los Angeles CA 90028-6415

O'DAY, KATHLEEN M. federal official; Assoc. gen. counsel bd. mems. office Fed. Res. Sys., Washington. Office: Fed Res Sys Bd Mems Office 20th & C Sts NW Ofc Washington DC 20551-0001

ODEGAARD, CYNTHIA, sales executive; b. Somerset, Pa., May 18, 1956; d. Joseph and Irene (Segedy) Kubas; m. Roger W. Hackett, June 6, 1984 (div. Jan. 1993); m. Barry Odegaard Jan. 1999. BS, Cornell U., 1978; MBA, Pepperdine U., 1990. Lab. technician Cornell U., Ithaca, N.Y., 1978-80; pharm. salesperson Stuart Pharms., Jamestown, N.Y., 1980-83, Adria Labs., Ithaca, 1983-85, T.A.P. Pharms., L.A., 1985-86, Schering Corp., L.A., 1986-89, Ortho Biotech, Honolulu, 1989—2000, AstraZeneca, Honolulu, 2001—. Bd. dirs. The Life Found., Honolulu, 1994—2003; mem. "Race for the Cure" Com., Honolulu, 1995; chairperson 1995 AIDS Walk, Honolulu. Mem. Cornell U. Alumni Assn.(pres. Cornell Club of Hawaii) Avocations: kayaking, running.

ODEH, KRISTIN S. information technology executive; b. DeKalb, Ill., Dec. 7, 1960; d. Richard Edmund Nelson, Sr. and Shelby Jean Nelson; m. Sam E. Odeh, Mar. 16, 1991; children: Nicholas, Brandon. BS in Retail Mgmt., Bradley U., 1982. Mgr. ops. The Signature Group, Chgo., 1985—87; dir. Infoctr. Svcs. Platinum Tech., Chgo., 1987—88; dir. ops. Whitehall Jewelers, Marks Bros., Chgo., 1988—89, asst. v.p., client svcs. ops., 1990—92; sys. mgr. Sears, Roebuck and Co., Chgo., 1992—94, sr. sys. dir., 1995—99; dir. global consumer sys. info. tech. Ford Motor Co., Dearborn, Mich., 1999—. Named one of 100 Leading Women in Automotive, Crain's Bus., 2000. Mem.: Mich. Coun. Women in Tech. (sponsorship chairperson 2002—). Avocations: family, cooking, boating, entertaining, reading. Office: Ford Motor Co 16800 Executive Plaza Dr Dearborn MI 48126

O'DELL, ELIZABETH ANN, controller; b. Jersey City, Apr. 27, 1960; d. William P. and Madeline M. (Conheeney) O'D.; m. Dennis Polizzi, Sept. 7, 1985. BBA, MBA, Pace U., 1982. CPA, N.J. Sr. auditor Touche Ross & Co., Newark, 1982-85; supr. Coopers & Lybrand, Newark, 1985-87; controller/dir. internal ops. Kratos Analytical Inc., Ramsey, N.J., 1987-91; controller Radiodetection Corp., Mahwah, N.J., 1991—. Mem. AICPA, N.J. State Soc. CPA's, NAFE, Am. Woman's Soc. CPA's. Office: Alteon Inc 170 Williams Dr Ramsey NJ 00746

O'DELL, JANE, automotive company executive; Co-owner Westfall GMC Truck Inc., Kansas City, Mo. Office: Westfall GMC Truck Inc 3915 Randolph Rd Kansas City MO 64161-9383

O'DELL, JOAN ELIZABETH, lawyer, mediator, business executive, educator; b. East Dubuque, Ill., May 3, 1932; d. Peter Emerson and Olive (Bonnet) O'D.; children: Dominique R., Nicole L. BA cum laude, U. Miami, 1956, JD, 1958. Bar: Fla. 1958, DC 1974, Ill. 1978, Va. 1987, U.S. Supreme Ct. 1972; lic. real estate broker Ill., Va., W.Va. Trial atty. SEC, Washington, 1959-60; asst. state atty. Office State Atty., Miami, Fla., 1960-64; asst. county atty. Dade County Atty.'s Office, Miami, 1964-70; county atty. Palm Beach County Atty.'s Office, West Palm Beach, Fla., 1970-71; regional gen. counsel Region IV EPA, Atlanta, 1971-73, assoc. gen. counsel Washington, 1973-77; sr. counsel Nalco Chem. Co., Oakbrook, Ill., 1977-78; v.p., gen. counsel Angel Mining, Washington and Tenn., 1979-96; pres. S.W. Land Investments, Miami, 1979-88; v.p. Events U.S.A., Washington, 1990—. Mem. Exec. Women's Coun., Tucson, 1982—85; co-chmn. sch. improvement com. Harpers Ferry Jr. H.S., 2000—; bd. dirs. Tucson Women's Found., 1982—84, U. Ariz. Bus. and Profl. Women's Club, Tucson, 1981—85, LWV, Tucson, 1981—85, pres., 1984—85; bd. dirs. LWV Ariz., 1984—85, chmn. nat. security study; bd. dirs. LWV, Palm Beach County, Fla., 1990—92, Jefferson County Visitors and Conv. Bur., Harpers Ferry, W.Va., 2001—. Mem. Fla. Bar Assn., D.C. Bar Assn., Va. State Bar Assn., Ill. Bar Assn. Avocations: camping, hiking, skiing. E-mail: treetopsjodell@yahoo.com.

O'DELL, LISA A. special education educator; b. Galesburg, Ill., May 10, 1961; d. Edward Andrew and Una Arillis Bowman; m. Craig Warren O'Dell, July 5, 1986; 1 child, Michael Craig. BS in Edn., Ill. State U., Normal, 1983, MS in Ednl. Adminstrn., 2003. Spl. edn. tchr., K-12 Lee Ctr. Dist. 271, Paw Paw, Ill., 1983—86; mid. sch. spl. edn. tchr. Dimmick Dist. # 175, Peru, Ill., 1986—90; elem. spl. edn. tchr. McLean County Unit # 5, Normal, Ill., 1992—. Co-chmn. sch. inclusion com., Normal, 2001—; mem. sch. dist. evaluation com., Normal, 1998—2001; mem. spl. edn. assessment com., Normal, 2000—; presenter workshops, 1998—2001; chmn. sch. edn. com. McLean County Unit #5, 2002—. Grantee Beyond the Books Found., Normal, 1996, 1997, 2000. Mem.: NEA, Coun. for Exceptional Children (treas., founding mem. 1998—2002). Office: Oakdale Elem Sch 601 S Adelaide Normal IL 61761 E-mail: odellla@unit5.org.

O'DELL, LYNN MARIE LUEGGE (MRS. NORMAN D. O'DELL), librarian; b. Berwyn, Ill., Feb. 24, 1938; d. George Emil and Helen Marie (Pesek) Luegge; m. Norman D. O'Dell, Dec. 14, 1957; children: Jeffrey, Jerry. Student, Lyons Twp. Jr. Coll., La Grange, Ill., 1957, No. Ill., Coll. of Dupage. Sec. Martin Co., Chgo., 1957-59; dir. Carol Stream (Ill.) Pub. Libr., 1964—. Chmn. automation governing com. DuPage Library System, v.p., 1982-85, pres. exec. com. adminstrv. librarians, 1985-86, chair automation search com., 1991-92. Named Woman of Yr., Wheaton Bus. and Profl. Woman's Club, 1968. Mem. ALA, Ill. Libr. Assn., Libr. Adminstrs. Conf. No. Ill., Pub. Libr. Assn. Lutheran. Home: 182 Yuma Ln Carol Stream IL 60188-1917 Office: 616 Hiawatha Dr Carol Stream IL 60188-1634 E-mail: lodell@cslibrary.org.

ODEM, JOYCE MARIE, human resources specialist; b. Des Moines, Mar. 21, 1936; d. Robert Gibson and Minnie Anna (Godown) Hague; m. Phillip Wayne Odem, May 23, 1954; children: Vickie, Phillip, Beth, Amy, Keith. Student, Merced C.C., 1976-78. Legal sec. C. Ray Robinson, Merced, Calif., 1959-60; office mgr., legal aid Kane & Canelo, Merced, Calif., 1960-65; recorder disciplinary control bd. U.S. Army Civil Svc., Okinawa, Japan, 1965-69; legal aid, office mgr. Courtney & Sharrow, Merced, 1969-72; adminstr. USAF Civil Svc., Okinawa, 1972-75; asst. indsl. rels. mgr. Maracay Mills Divsn. Mohasco, Merced, 1975-78; safety dir., personnel mgr. Keller Industries, Merced, 1978-83; mgr. employee rels. McLane Pacific, Merced, 1983-85; corp. dir. human resources McLane Co., Inc., Temple, Tex., 1983—2002; v.p. people dept. McLane Foodservice, Carrollton, Tex., 2002—. Mem. adv. bd. Pvt. Industry Coun., Merced, 1980-85. Mem. Cen. Tex. Human Resource Mgrs. Assn. (adv. coun.), Soc. Human Resource Mgrs. Avocations: sporting clays, golf, hunting. Office: McLane Foodservice Inc 2085 Midway Rd Carrollton TX 75006

ODEN, GLORIA, English educator, poet; b. Yonkers, N.Y., Oct. 30, 1923; d. Redmond Stanley and Ethel (Kincaid) Oden. BA in History, Howard U., 1944, JD, 1948. Faculty New Sch. for Social Rsch., N.Y.C., 1966; vis. lectr. dept. English SUNY, Stony Brook, 1969-70; asst. prof. English U. Md., Balt., 1971-75, assoc. prof., 1975-83, prof., 1983—96. Sr. editor IEEE Proc. and tech. mags., 1966-67; supr. math./sci. books Appleton-Century-Crofts, 1967-68; project dir. lang. arts books Holt, Rinehart and Winston, 1968-72, sr. editor coll. dept., 1968-71; editor Am. Inst. Physics/Am. Jour. Physics, 1961-66; lectr. in field; condr. numerous poetry readings; juror fiction panel Mass. Cultural Coun., 1994, poetry panel N.J. State Coun., 1993, 94, numerous others; cons. Reel Deal Prodns. Co., NEH, 1984, 87. Author: (books of poetry) Resurrections, 1978, The Tie that Binds, 1980, Appearances, 2003; contbr. numerous poetry to mags., newspapers, audio, anthologies; contbr. numerous articles to profl. jours. Recipient Disting. Black women's award Towson U., 1984; NEH summer stipend, 1974; Breadloaf Writers scholar, 1960; John Hay Whitney Found. Creative Writing fellow, 1955-56; Yaddo fellow, 1956. Mem. Poetry Soc.. Am. (bd. govs. 1981-82, v.p. 1983-84), PEN Am. Ctr. Home: Apt 8119 707 Maiden Choice Ln Catonsville MD 21228-4185 Office: U Md Baltimore County Dept English Baltimore MD 21228-5398

O'DOHERTY, KATHLEEN MARIE, library director; b. May 25, 1950; d. Thomas and Elizabeth Theresa (Keleher) O'D; m. Shaheen Mozaffar, Dec. 7, 1991. BA, Northeastern U., 1973; MS, Simmons Coll., 1979. Asst. reference libr., asst. cataloguer Woburn Pub. Libr., 1977-79; cataloguer Bradford (Mass.) Coll., 1979-81, libr. dir., 1981-83, Brooks Sch., North Andover, Mass., 1983-85, Woburn Pub. Libr., 1986—. Vol. mem. Woburn Mcpl. Fed. Credit Union, 1996—. Author: Images of America, 2000. Mem. Cable Adv. Com. Woburn, 1997—, Violence Prevention Task Force, Woburn, 1994—; judge Pub. Speaking contest, Woburn H.S., 1987-95. Mem. ALA, Minuteman Libr. Network (sec. 1996-97, exec. bd. 1998-99), Friends of Woburn Pub. Libr. (founder), Rotary Club of Woburn (sec. 1996-99). Home: 3 Lewis Rd Apt 5 Winchester MA 01890-2533 Office: Woburn Pub Libr 45 Pleasant St Woburn MA 01801-4135

ODOM, JUDY, software company executive; b. 1952; BBA in Acctg., Tex. Tech. U., 1974. CPA. With Coopers & Lybrand, Dallas, 1974-76, Grant Thornton, Dallas, 1976-85; co-founder, owner Software Spectrum, 1983—2002, CEO, 1988—2002. Bd. dirs. Storage Tek, Leggett & Platt Inc., Harte-Hanks Inc. Named to, Computer Reseller News Industry Hall of Fame, 2003.*

ODOM, MARY E. (LIBBY ODOM), musician, educator; b. Mobile, Ala., Dec. 18, 1928; d. Frederick and Bertha (Summers) Yost; m. Gerald Stuart Odom, Sept. 3, 1947 (dec. Oct. 1997); 1 child, Maria Renee. BS cum laude, U. Ala., 1980, MA in Edn., 1982. Voice tchr., accompanist Madame Rose Palmai Studio, Mobile, Ala., 1944-50; voice and piano tchr. Birmingham, Ala., 1954-64; music therapist State Sch. for Girls, Springville, Ala., 1951-57; voice and theory tchr. Meridian (Miss.) Jr. Coll., 1964-68; voice and piano tchr. Birmingham, 1968-88. Performer Mobile Opera Guild, Mobile Opera Workshop, 1943-53, Carnegie Hall, 1947, Met. Opera, N.Y.C., 1950-52, Boris Goldovsky Opera, W.Va., 1952-53, Town and Gown Little Theatre, Birmingham, 1953-73. Co-founder Mobile Opera Guild, 1943, Birmingham Civic Opera, 1955, Birmingham Civic Chorus, 1964; choir soloist Govt. St. Meth. Ch., Ctrl. Presbyn. Ch., Mobile, 1943-49, choir soloist, children's choir Ind. Presbyn. Ch., Birmingham, 1953-64; soloist, youth choir dir. Mountain Brook Presbyn. Ch., Birmingham, 1968-78; ch. organist Riverchase Presbyn. Ch., Birmingham, 1980-84, co-founder Active Elders, 1983; chmn., v.p. Birmingham Opera Guild, 1958—; mem. Salvation Army Women's Aux., 1989—; chorus dir. Shades Valley Music Club, 1980—. Recipient Cert. Appreciation Presbytery of Sheppards and Lapsley, Presbyn. Ch. USA, 1991, Riverchase Presbyn. Ch., 1999. Mem. AAUW, Ala. Fedn. Music Club (officer 1953—, Odom scholarship 1999, parliamentarian, past state pres.), Shades Valley Music Club (2d v.p. for programs), Birmingham Music Club Guild (publicity chmn., bd. dirs. 1964-68, guest artist 1953—), Delta Omicron, Kappa Delta Pi. Avocations: gardening, reading, programs for senior citizens, cooking. Home: 3804 Briar Oak Dr Birmingham AL 35243-4834

O'DONELL, ROSA ELIA, assistant principal, educator; b. Amherst, Tex., Apr. 3, 1959; d. Rosendo, Jr. and Maria Eulalia Reyes; m. David John O'Donnell, Apr. 24, 1993 (div. Dec. 1998); children: Ilea, Paul. BS, Boise State U., Idaho, 1984; MS, Cardinal Stritch Coll., Brownsville, Minn., 1994. Cert. principalship-mid. mgmt. Tex., 2001. Dispatcher San Juan (Tex.) Police Dept., 1973—77; teller Security State Bank, Pharr, Tex., 1977—79; tchr. Pharr - San Juan - Alamo ISD, Pharr, 1994—2001, asst. prin., 2002—. Advisor Pharr - San Juan - Alamo Dist. DEIC. Capt. U.S. Army, 1985—94. Mem.: Am. Fedn. Tchrs. Avocations: jogging, aerobics, watercolor painting, reading. E-mail: odrosel@msn.com.

ODONER, ELLEN J. lawyer; b. N.Y.C., Jan. 23, 1952; BA magna cum laude, Yale U., 1973; JD, Harvard U., 1977. Bar: N.Y. 1978. Mem. Weil, Gotshal & Manges, N.Y.C. Mem. Assn. of Bar of City of N.Y. (com. on mergers, acquisitions and corp. control contests). Office: Weil Gotshal & Manges LLP 767 Fifth Ave New York NY 10153-0119

O'DONNELL, DENISE ELLEN, lawyer; BS in Polit. Sci., Canisius Coll., 1968; MSW, SUNY, Buffalo, 1973, JD summa cum laude, 1982. Bar: NY 1983, U.S. Dist. Ct. (we., no., ea. and so. dists.) NY, U.S. Ct. Appeals (2d cir.), U.S. Supreme Ct. Law clk. Hon. M. Dolores Denman NY Appellate Divsn. 4th Dept., Buffalo, 1982-85; asst. U.S. atty. Western Dist. N.Y., Buffalo, 1985-90, appellate chief, 1990-93, 1st asst. U.S. atty., 1993—97, U.S. atty., 1997-2001; ptnr. Gen. Litigation Practice Group, Hodgson, Russ, LLP, Buffalo, 2001—. Part-time instr. trial technique program SUNY, 1990—; lectr. ethics, evidence and trial practice Office Legal Edn.U.S. Dept. Justice, 1988—2000; lectr. NITA seminar Western NY Trial Acad., 1994, 98; mem. Atty. Gen.'s Adv. Com., 1999—2001, vice-chair, 2000—01. Mem. Vol. Lawyers Program, 1997—2001; bd. dirs. NCCJ, 2000—; sec. Nat. Women's Hall of Fame, 2001—, bd. dirs., 2001—. Mem.: ABA, Nat. Assn. Former U.S. Attys. (bd. dirs.), Western NY Trial Lawyers Assn., Women's Bar Assn. State NY (founding mem. Western NY chpt. 1985), Bar Assn. Erie County (dep. treas. 1992—93, treas. 1993—94), West Side Rowing Club. Office: Hodgson Russ LLP One M&T Plz Ste 2000 Buffalo NY 14203-2931 Office Phone: 716-848-1314. E-mail: dodonnel@hodgsonruss.com.

O'DONNELL, KATHLEEN C. artist; b. Clifton, N.J., Nov. 15, 1919; d. George Francis and Alvina Rose (Munzell) Denzel; m. John Joseph O'Donnell, Feb. 17, 1942; children: John Joseph, Sharon Rose. BA cum laude, Montclair (N.J.) State Coll. Designer Denzell Mfg. Co., Passaic, NJ, 1937—38, clk., 1939—41; sec. Marschalk Ins., Clifton, NJ, 1941—42; clk. The Fair, Passaic, 1968—69; designer Arise Ministry, Lakewood, NJ, 1983—91; assoc. N.J. Bell, Clifton & Totowa, NJ, 1969—85. One-woman shows include Dwight Eisenhower Libr., Totowa, 1982, No. Lights Art Gallery, Clifton, 1985, YWHA, 1988, Fine Arts Ctr., Passaic, 1988, Denville Libr., 2003, exhibited in group shows at Fine Arts Ctr., Passaic, 1983, 1988, Willowbrook Mall, Wayne, N.J., 1984, YWHA, Clifton, 1985, Clifton Libr., 1988, The Nathan's Art Gallery, West Paterson, N.J., 1994, Montclair Country Club, 1994, Montclair State U., 1995, 1998, Westbeth Gallery, N.Y.C., 1996, Caldwell (N.J.) Women's Club, 1999, Botto House, Haledon, N.J., 1999, Clifton (NJ) Arts Ctr., 2001, Hamilton House, Clifton, 2002, Clifton Arts Ctr., 2003, 2004, represented in numerous pvt. collections, exhibited in group shows at Denville Lib., 2003. Mem.: Clifton Assn. Artists, Bell Atlantic Pioneers. Roman Catholic.

O'DONNELL, KATHLEEN MARIE, lawyer; b. San Diego, Jan. 2, 1952; d. James Joseph and Patricia Ann (Dunne) O'D. AB, Boston Coll., 1974; JD, U. Miami, 1977. Bar: Mass. 1978. Title atty. Lawyers Title Ins. Corp., Boston, 1979-85; assoc. Hay & Dailey, Boston, 1985-86, DiCara, Selig, Sawyer & Holt, Boston, 1986-87, Ropes & Gray, Boston, 1987-92; ptnr. Dillingham & O'Donnell, Boston, 1992-97, Kopelman & Paige, P.C., Boston, 1997—. Adj. prof. Boston U., 1995-97. Editor: Handling Residential Real Estate In Mass., 1996. Mem., bd. dirs., Dedham (Mass.) Choral Soc. Mem. New Eng. Women in Real Estate, Real Estate Bar Assn. Mass. (bd. dirs. 1995—), Larchmont Yacht Club, The Abstract Club, Cohasset Yacht Club. Republican. Roman Catholic. Home: 12 Belcher Cir Milton MA 02186-5105 Office: Kopelman & Paige PC 31 Saint James Ave Boston MA 02116-4101

O'DONNELL, PAT A. state representative; b. Holyoke, Mass., Oct. 15, 1954; m. Robert J. O'Donnell; 4 children. Degree, Holyoke (Vt.) C.C. Salesperson; rep. Vt. State Ho. Reps., 1999—. Clk. Vernon (Vt.) Selectboard; mem. Vernon (Vt.) PTC, Vernon (Vt.) ELF; chmn. Vernon (Vt.) Sch. Bd. Roman Catholic. Home: PO Box 355 Vernon VT 05354

O'DONNELL, ROSIE, television personality, actress, comedienne; b. Commack, N.Y., Mar. 21, 1962; m. Kelli Carpenter, Feb. 26, 2004; children: Parker Jaren, Chelsea Belle, Blake Christopher. Attended, Dickinson Coll., Boston Univ. Appearances include (TV series) Gimme A Break, 1986-87, Stand By Your Man, 1992, Women Aloud, 1992, Stand-up Spotlight, VH-1 (American Comedy award nomination best female performer in a TV special 1994, Cable ACE award nomination best entertainment host 1994), (TV) host The Rosie O'Donnell Show, 1995-2002 (Daytime Emmy awards 1997, 98, 99, 2000, 2001), (TV movie) The Twilight of the Golds, 1997; (films) A League of Their Own, 1992, Sleepless in Seattle, 1993 (American Comedy award nomination best supporting female in a motion picture 1994), Another Stakeout, 1993 (American Comedy award nomination best actress in a motion picture 1994), Car 54, Where Are You?, 1994, I'll Do Anything, 1994, The Flintstones, 1994, Exit to Eden, 1994, Now and Then, 1995, Beautiful Girls, 1996, Harriet the Spy, 1996, A Very Brady Sequel, 1996 (uncredited), Wide Awake, 1996, Get Bruce, 1999, Jackie's Back, 1999, Tarzan, 1999 (voice), Flintstones in Viva Rock Vegas, 2000; Broadway shows include Grease, 1994, Seussical the Musical, 2001; author: Find Me, 2002; editor: Rosie mag., 2000-2002, prodr.: Taboo (Broadway) 2003-2004. Office: ICM 8942 Wilshire Blvd Beverly Hills CA 90211*

O'DONNELL, SUSAN LYNEE, psychologist, educator; b. Lafayette, Ind., Nov. 17, 1961; d. Charles Bruce Hatcher and Catherine Swartley Wooledge; m. Sam C. O'Donnell, June 28, 1992; children: Elizabeth Catherine, Michael James, David Paul. BS, U. Minn., Mpls., 1996, MA, 2000, PhD, 2002. Asst. prof. George Fox U., Newberg, Oreg., 2001—. Chair dept. psychology George Fox U., Newberg, Oreg., 2002—03. Com. mem. Newberg First Bapt. Ch., Newberg, Oreg., 2002. Grad. rsch. fellow, NSF, 1996—2000. Mem.: APA, Soc. for Personality and Social Psychology, Tchg. of Psychology, Nat. Coun. on Family Rels., Soc. for Rsch. on Adolescence, Soc. for Rsch. in Child Devel., Phi Beta Phi. Evangelical Christian. Avocations: reading, camping, hiking, bicycling, photography. Home: 1630 Lilly Ct Newberg OR 97132 Office: George Fox U 414 N Meridian St # 6155 Newberg OR 97132 E-mail: sodonnell@georgefox.edu.

O'DONNELL, TERESA HOHOL, application developer, electrical engineer; b. Springfield, Mass., Nov. 25, 1963; d. Marion and Lena Hohol; m. Patrick Alan O'Donnell; children: Kelly Marie, Tracy Alana. BS in Computer Engring., BSEE, MIT, 1985, MSEE, 1986, MS in Computer Sci., 1986. Rsch. asst. MIT Rsch. Lab Electronics, Cambridge, 1985-86; lead VHSIC insertion engr. USAF Electronic Sys. Divsn., Hanscom AFB, Mass., 1986-88; intelligent antennas engr. USAF Rome Lab., Hanscom AFB, 1988-91; sr. scientist ARCON Corp., Waltham, Mass., 1991—. Composer: (choral mass setting) Mass of Rejoicing, 1989. Performer Zbeide's Harem, Tewksbury, Mass., 1986—93; organist, composer St. Theresa's Chour, Billerica, Mass., 1987—95. Lt. col. USAFR. Decorated Commendation medal (2), Joint Svc. Achievement medal, Meritorious Svc. medal (2). Mem.: IEEE, Assn. Computing Machinery, Am. Guild Organists, Nat. Assn. Pastoral Musicians, Res. Officers Assn., Eta Kappa Nu (v.p. 1985—86), Sigma Xi. Roman Catholic. Achievements include patents for cab to cap gap filler; weather seal strip; infant stimulus toy. Avocations: music, dance, theater, composing, rollerskating. Office: ARCON Corp 260 Bear Hill Rd Ste 5 Waltham MA 02451-1000

O'DONNELL RICH, DOROTHY JUANITA, small business owner; b. Midland, Pa., Aug. 31, 1934; d. William Theodore and Jennie Cecilia (Forrest) Verzella; m. Hugh Terrence O'Donnell, Aug. 9, 1958 (dec. Jan. 1987); children: Kathleen Denise, Suzanne Lynn; m. Hugh B. Rich IV, Nov. 12, 1988. Ch. organist Blessed Virgin Mary Ch., Midland, 1948-59; sec. E.W. Bliss Co., Midland, 1952-59; tchr. piano Beaver, Pa., 1962-81; owner, bus. mgr. H.B. Rich, Drexel Hill, Pa., 1988—. Counselor Cath. Daughters of Am., Midland, 1952-54; pianist Midland Rotary Club, 1952-58; program chmn. Sr. Cath. Daughters of Am., Beaver, 1958-68; mem. ways and means com. Jr. Women's Club, Midland, 1954-56; mem. Midland Cath. Sodality; mem. Italian Sons and Daughters of Am., Sewickley, Pa., 1954-60. Named Jr. of the Yr., Jr. Cath. Daus., 1948. Mem. NAFE. Roman Catholic. Avocations: piano, walking, reading, chess, bicycling.

ODORIZZI, MICHELE L. lawyer; b. Chgo., July 12, 1952; BA, Northwestern U., 1973; JD cum laude, U. Chgo., 1976. Bar: Ill. 1976, U.S. Ct. Appeals (7th cir.) 1976, U.S. Dist. Ct. (no. dist.) Ill. 1977, U.S. Supreme Ct. 1980, U.S. Ct. Appeals (4th, 9th, 10th cirs.). Ptnr. Mayer, Brown & Platt, Chgo. Office: Mayer Brown & Platt 190 S La Salle St Ste 3100 Chicago IL 60603-3441

ODUM, FELICIA SELLERS, art educator; b. Blackshear, Ga., Nov. 2, 1965; d. Troy Randall Sellers and Connie Gene Johnson, Donna Diane Sellers (Stepmother); m. William Brian Odum, Oct. 21, 1985; children: Sidney Martha, Whitney Rachael, Courtney Elyse. BS in Edn., Ga. So. U., 1999. Cert. T4 art educator Ga. Salesperson J & K Sporting Goods, Claxton, Ga., 1982—84; cashier The Claxton Bank, 1984—86; shipping clk. Mincey's Dept. Store, Claxton, 1986—88; self employed Odum Farms, Claxton, 1988—96; art educator William James Mid. Sch., Statesboro, Ga., 1999—2001, Evans County Sch. Sys., Claxton, 2001—. Tchg. children in poverty trainee Bulloch County Sch. Sys., Statesboro, 1999, mem. career edn. planning com., 2000, mem. Title 9 planning com., 01; yearbook coord. William James Mid. Sch., Statesboro, 2000—01. Sr. Exhbn., Juried Student Exhbn. (Hon. Mention, 1998), Musing on Mona. Youth arts festival coord. Ga. So. U., Statesboro, 1999; asst. coach girls fastpitch softball William James Mid. Sch., 2000—01; art coord. Tattnall Camp Meeting Day Camp, Manassas, Ga., 1992—98. Scholar Rosalind D. Ragans scholar, 1999—2000; Robert J. Focht Meml. Scholarship, 1999. Mem.: NEA (assoc.), Ga. Edn. Assn., Nat. Art Edn. Assn. (assoc.), Ga. Art Edn. Assn. (assoc.; student rep. 1997—99, leadership workshop 1998, divsn. meeting presenter 2001—03, mid. grades divsn. chair 2001—03, 1st dist. pres. 2003—, Fall profl. devel. chairperson 2004, Youth Art award 2000, Mid. Grades Art Educator of Yr. 2003), Omicron Delta Kappa (life; charter mem.), Golden Key (life). Republican. Methodist. Avocations: travel, reading, fine art. Home: 245 Sam Green Rd Claxton GA 30417 Office: Claxton Mid Sch 4 N College St Claxton GA 30417 E-mail: feliciaodum@evans.k12.ga.us.

O'DWYER, JOAN, judge; b. N.Y.C., Sept. 26, 1926; d. James and Mildred (Gantz) O'D.; m. John P. O'Neill, Nov. 24, 1959 (div. July 1973); children: Shane O'Neill, Liam O'Neill, Kelly O'Neill; m. Anthony P. Savarese, Aug. 24, 1973. BA, Beaver Coll., Jenkintown, Pa., 1947; LLB, Columbia U., 1950. Atty. O'Dwyer and Bernstein, N.Y.C., 1950-60; magistrate City of N.Y., 1960-96, criminal ct. judge, 1960-96; acting Supreme Ct. judge State of N.Y., N.Y.C., 1960-96, judge Ct. of Claims, 1996—. Pres. Bronx Womens Bar Assn., 1960. Home: 59 Kenwood Rd Garden City NY 11530-3137

O'DWYER, MARY ANN, automotive executive; BS, DePaul U.; MS, Benedictine U. CPA. With Ernst and Young, McDonald's Corp.; various positions CC Industries (a Henry Crown Co.); sr. v.p. fin. ops., CFO Wheels, 1991—; sr. v.p. fin & ops., CFO Frank Consol. Enterprises. Office: Frank Consol Enterprises 666 Garland Pl Des Plaines IL 60016

OEHRLEIN, MARY LOU, architect; b. Clinton, Iowa, Dec. 7, 1950; d. Gilbert Joseph and Virginia Marie (Thrun) O.; m. David Evans Heacock, Jan. 16, 1979. BArch, Iowa State U., 1973. Registered architect, D.C., Md., Va. Staff architect Hist. Am. Bldgs. Survey U.S. Nat. Parks Service, Washington, 1972-74; archtl. conservator Universal Restoration, Inc., Washington, 1975; v.p. Bldg. Conservation Tech., Washington, 1975-83; sr. assoc., dir. Washington office The Ehrenkrantz Group, 1978-83; prin. Oehrlein & Assocs., Washington, 1984—. Reviewer State of Va. Div. Hist. Landmarks, Richmond, 1985-96; commn. fine arts Old Georgetown Bd., 1996—; bd. dirs. Cosmos Club Hist. Preservation Found., Washington, 1987-95. Author handbooks on hist. property and maintenance. Bd. dirs. D.C. Preservation League, 1987-96. Recipient Cert. Appreciation Town of Leesburg, Va., 1987. Fellow AIA (v.p. Washington chpt. 1987, pres. 1988—, numerous awards 1983-99); mem. Assn. Preservation Tech., Constrn. Specifications Inst. (bd. dirs. Washington chpt. 1983-85), Preservation Round Table, Cosmos Club. Office: Oehrlein & Assocs 1350 Connecticut Ave NW Washington DC 20036-1722

OELKE, ANITA JEAN, special education educator; b. Beloit, Kans., July 6, 1948; d. John William and Virginia Lee Severance; m. Jimmie Dean Oelke, Mar. 16, 1997; 1 child, Eva Lee Gavin. B.S. in Elem. Edn., Ft. Hays State U., 1970. Cert. early childhood spl. educator Kans. Tchr. USD 291, Grinnell, Kans., 1970—76, USD 412, Hoxie, Kans., 1976—2002; tchr. early childhood spl. edn. USD 602, Oakley, Kans., 2002—, tchr., 2002—. Mem.: NEA (assoc.; uniserv-resolutions commr. 2000—03), Kans. Reading Assn. (assoc.), Coun. for Exceptional Children (assoc.), Phi Delta Kappa (assoc.; treas. 1986—90). Avocation: reading. Home: 1425 15th PO Box 751 Hoxie KS 67740 Office: Nkesc 703 W 2nd Oakley KS 67748

OERTEL, YOLANDA CASTILLO, pathologist, educator, diagnostician; b. Lima, Peru, Dec. 14, 1938; came to U.S., 1966; d. Leonardo A. and Dalila (Ramirez) C.; m. James E. Oertel, Sept. 24, 1969. MD, Cayetano Heredia, Lima, 1964; Dr. honoris causa, U. Peruana Cayetano Heredia, 1999. Diplomate Am. Bd. Pathology (mem. test com. for cytopathology 1988-94). Internat. postdoctoral fellowship NIH, Bethesda, Md., 1966-68; asst. prof. pathology Sch. Medicine George Washington U., Washington, 1975-78, assoc. prof., 1978-84, prof., 1984-98, prof. emerita, 1998—. Adj. prof. pathology and lab. medicine MCP Hahnemann U. Sch. Medicine; cons. Registry Cytology Armed Forces Inst. Pathology, Washington, 1981—. Author: Fine Needle Aspiration of the Breast, 1987; contbr. chpts. to books and articles to profl. jours. Decorated comendador de la Orden Cayetano Heredia, 1999; recipient Francisco A. Camino prize Peruvian Med. Assn., 1965, cert. Meritorious Svc. Armed Forces Inst. Pathology, 1974; named Disting. Alumna Cayetano Heredia Med. Sch., 1989. Mem. Assn. Mil. Surgeons (hon), Colombian Soc. Pathology (hon.), Argentinian Soc. Pathology (hon.), Peruvian Soc. Pathologists (hon.), Argentinian Soc. Cytopathology, (hon.), Am. Soc. Cytopathology, Internat. Acad. Pathology, Soc. Latinoamericana Patologia, Am. Soc. Clin. Pathologists (coun. on cytopathology 1982-88), Coll. Am. Pathologists, Arthur Purdy Stout Soc. Surg. Pathologists, Am. Thyroid Assn., L.Am. Thyroid Soc. Avocations: reading, opera. Office: Washington Hosp Ctr Pathology Dept Washington Cancer Inst 110 Irving St NW Washington DC 20010-2975 Fax: (202) 877-0197. Office Phone: 202-877-2740. E-mail: Yolanda.C.Oertel@medstar.net.

OESTMANN, MARY JANE, retired senior radiation specialist; b. Chgo., May 22, 1924; d. Charles Edward and Harriet Evelyn (Stoltenberg) O. BA in Math, Chemistry with honors, Denison U., 1946; MS, U. Wis., 1948, PhD, 1954; DSc., Denison U., 1975. Research chemist Inst. for Atom Energy, Oslo, 1954—55; vis. scientist AB Atom Energy, Stockholm, 1955—56; vis. prof. chem. dept. U. Iowa, Iowa City, 1957; sr. scientist Battelle Meml. Inst., Columbus, Ohio, 1957—61; assoc. chemist Argonne Nat. Lab, Ill., 1961—71; environ. project mgr. U.S. AEC, Washington, 1971—75; sr. radiation specialist U.S. Nuclear Regulatory Commn., Glen Ellyn, Ill., 1975—87; ret. Bd. dirs. U. Wis.-Madison Alumni Assn. of the So. Lakes, 1992—. Contbr. numerous articles to scientific jours. Mem. planning and zoning commn. Town of Burlington, 1992--; bd. trustees Plymouth Congl. UCC Ch. Burlington, 1993-96. Recipient Internat. Women's Yr. award Nuclear Regulatory Commn., 1975, Dist. Alumni citation Denison U., 1971. Fellow Am. Inst. Chemists, Am. Nuclear Soc. (bd. dirs. 1983-86); mem. Am. Chem. Soc., Inst. Environ. Sci. and Tech. (sr. mem.), Health Physics Soc. (sec.-treas. Midwest chpt. 1978, exec. com. 1983-86), N.Y. Acad. Scis., Wis. Acad. Scis., Arts and Letters, Wis. Fedn. Rep. Women (1st Congl. Dist.), Nat. Parks Conservation Assn., Burlington Woman's Club (treas., chair scholarship com. 1993—), Browns Lake Yacht Club (Burlington), Rep. Women Racine County-West Club (v.p. 1992-93, pres. 1994—, Anita Hunt award, Bovay award), Sigma Xi, Phi Beta Kappa, Sigma Delta Epsilon, Iota Sigma Pi. Home: 2520 Cedar Dr Burlington WI 53105-9174

OETTINGER, KATHLEEN LINDA, artist; b. Jan. 16, 1943; d. Herbert Irving and Aura Orvokki (Lehto) Johnson; m. Frank Frederic Oettinger, Aug. 24, 1963; children: Meredith Laura, Melanie Beth, Megan Michelle. BFA, Pratt Inst., 1965; MA, Regis Coll., 1984; MFA, Catholic U., 1987. Art instr. Dept. Recreation Montgomery County (Md.), 1971-75; adj. faculty Washington Internat. Coll., 1974-82; writer, editor Nat. Inst. for the Family, Washington, 1981-84; mag. columnist, contbg. editor Abbey Press, St. Meinrad, Ind., 1982-84; studio artist Oettinger Studio, Rockville, Md., 1984-96; art editor Visions Internat. Mag., Fredericksburg, Va., 1994-98; adj. faculty Polk C.C., Winter Haven, Fla., 1998—. Nat. Bd. Outline Com. Catholic Engaged Encounter, Del., 1978-79; Nat. bd. mem. Women's Caucus Art, Phila., 1994-97; guest curator, bd. govs. Fed. Res. Bank, Washington, 1995. One-man shows include Window Gallery, Kotka, Finland, 1995; exhibited in group shows at World Trade Ctr., Beijing, 1995, Elite Gallery, Moscow, 1996, Nat. Mus. Women Arts, Washington, 1996. Family Ministry Commn. Archdiocese Washington, 1979-80; rep. NGO Forum 4th UN World Conf. Women, Beijing, 1995; exhbn. designer Explorations V Children's Mus., Lakeland, Fla., 1997-98. Recipient Creativity Svc. Ams. Children award Every Child by Two, Inc., Washington, 1994; named Feature Artist Finnish- Am. Heritage Ctr., Hancock, Mich., 1993, named artist-in-residence Rockville (Md.) Arts Palace, 1993-96. Mem. So. Graphics Coun., Arts on the Park, Lakeland, Women's Caucus Art (chpt. pres. 1994-96), Fla. Printmakers (bd. dirs.). Roman Catholic. Avocations: family ministry, singing, water sports. Home: 5209 Mantua Ct Las Vegas NV 89130-7075

O'FALLON, KATHY, psychologist, writer; b. Hanover, N.H., Dec. 3, 1949; d. Richard Jay and Marion Skelly Wilcox; m. Bruce Edward Walton, Apr. 27, 1974 (div. Dec. 1985); children: Harmony Jain Walton, Kameron Skelly Walton. BA, Arcadia U., 1971; MA, Chapman Coll., 1981; PsyD, U.S. Internat. U., 1988. Pvt. practice lic. psychologist Peace Builders, Lake Arrowhead, Calif., 1991—, Solana Beach, Calif., 1991—. Program dir. Island Muse, Cook Island, Fla., 2003; tchr. U. Calif. San Diego, La Jolla, 1993, 95; trainer Stanford U., Palo Alto, Calif., 2002. Author poetry, (books) When the Moon Spills Her Milk, Underbelly. Finalist, Glimmer Train Poetry Open, 2000; recipient 1st pl. short stories, Voices, 1996, 3rd pl. short stories, No. Tex. Profl. Writers, 1999, 3rd pl., N.Am. Open Poetry Contest, 2000, Runner-up Best Unpublished Manuscript, San Diego Book Awards, 1999. Mem.: Rotary Club. Avocations: reading, writing, tennis, swimming, yoga. Office: PO Box 614 Lake Arrowhead CA 92352

OFFEN, KAREN MARIE, historian, educator; b. Pocatello, Idaho, Oct. 10, 1939; d. Norman V. and Ella Mae (McAlister) Stedtfeld; m. George R. Offen, Dec. 30, 1965; children: Catherine, Stephanie. BA, U. Idaho, 1961; AM, Stanford U., 1963, PhD, 1971. Lectr. History U. Santa Clara, Calif., 1973, U. San Francisco, 1975-76, Stanford (Calif.) U., 1978, 1982, 1984, 1986, 1989, 1992, 2002, Ctrl. European U., Budapest, 1999, U. of Konstanz, 2000. Ind. scholar affiliated with Inst. Rsch. Women & Gender, Stanford U., 1978—; dir. summer seminar NEH, 1984, 86, 89, 92, 2002; founding mem., sec. treas. Internat. Fedn. Rsch. Women's History, 1987-95; pres. Western Assn. Women Historians, 1991-93. Mem. editl. adv. bd. French Hist. Studies, Arenal, L'Homme, Jour. Women's History, European Legacy, Hist. Reflections; contbr. articles to profl. jours. Bd. dirs. Internat. Mus. Women, San Francisco, 1999—. Recipient Disting. Alumni Achievement award U. Idaho, 1994, Sr. Scholar award, 1995, Internat. Mus. of Women (bd. dirs., 1999—); NEH Ind. Study & Rsch. fellow, 1980-81, Rockefeller Found. Humanities fellow, 1985-86, J.S. Guggenheim fellow, 1995-96. Mem. AAUW, Am. Hist. Assn. (com. women historians 1983-86, chair com. internat. hist. activities 1986-90), Soc. French Hist. Studies (exec. com. 1983-86), P.E.O., Kappa Kappa Gamma. Democrat. Avocations: skiing, travel, hiking. Office: Stanford U Inst Rsch Women & Gender Stanford CA 94305-8640

OFFUTT, REBECCA SUE, business and sales executive; b. Wheeling, W.Va., Jan. 20, 1951; d. John Howard and Mary Concetta (Lanzuisi) Warden; m. Denver C. Offutt, Apr. 13, 1970 (div. 1990); children: Kimberly Dawn, Jody Monroe. Student, W.Va. U., 1968-70, W.Va. State Coll., 1973-75; grad., Real Estate Career Ctr., Huntington, W.Va., 1988. Lic. realtor, W.Va. Founder, pres. Marabec Designs, Inc., Charleston, W.Va., 1980-82; realtor, sales assoc. McQuire Realty Co., Huntington, 1988-89; sales assoc. Focus Mktg. Consultants, Charleston, 1987-90; ter. mgr. Quorum Corp., Hurricane, W.Va., 1990—96; network sales specialist Danka Office Imaging, Charleston, 1996—99; founding ptnr. Komax Bus. Sys., LLC, South Charleston, W.Va., 1999—. Developer five-yr. plan Jr. League, Charleston and Huntington, 1984; dist. coord. Huntington Galleries; pres. Pea Ridge Elem. PTA, Huntington, 1986-87; del.-at-large Ohio Valley Tennis Assn., 1986-87. Recipient Local, Dist. and Regional winner Ricoh Corp., 1993, finalist, 1994. Mem.: South Charleston Area Devel. Coun. (U.S. Congl. bus. adv. chmn. 2004, W.Va. Businessman of Yr. 2004), South Charleston Conv. and Visitors Bur. (sec./treas. 2000—02, bd. dirs. 2004), Putnam County Rotary (charter mem.). Home: 318 Southpointe Dr Charleston WV 25314 Office Phone: 304-744-7440.

OFFUTT, SUSAN ELIZABETH, economist; b. Newport, R.I., Apr. 17, 1954; d. William Franklin and Carol Dorothy (Chieves) O. BS, Allegheny Coll., 1976; MS, Cornell U., 1980, PhD, 1982. Asst. prof. agrl. econs. U. Ill., Urbana, 1982-87; sect. leader Econ. Rsch. Svc. USDA, Washington, 1987-88; chief agr. br. U.S. Office Mgmt. and Budget, Washington, 1988-92; exec. dir., bd. agr. Nat. Rsch. Coun., Washington, 1992-96; adminstr. U.S. Dept. Agrl./Econ. Rsch. Svc., Washington, 1996—. Office: Econ Rsch Svc 1800 M St NW Rm 4145 Washington DC 20036-5802

OFSTAD, EVELYN LARSEN BOYL, retired primary school educator, radio personality, film producer; b. Laurel, Oreg., Sept. 11, 1918; d. Walter Winfred and Nellie Lyle (Gellatly) Larsen; m. Robert Morris Boyl (dec.); children: Kathleen Roberta Boyl, Robert Morris Boyl Jr., Shannon Gae Boyl, Brian Larsen Boyl; m. Olaf Ofstad, Nov. 15, 1988. BS, Oreg. State U., 1940; MS in Tchg., Portland State U., 1968. Cert. learning specialist.

Radio announcer Sta. KOAC, Corvallis, Oreg., 1939-40; announcer, script writer Sta. KWIL, Albany, Oreg., 1940-42, operator, announcer, 1941-42; sec. Higgins Ship Bldg., New Orleans, 1943-44; elem. tchr. Portland Pub. Schs., 1968-71; learning specialist North Clackamas Schs., Milw., Ore., 1972-85, home instr. Milwaukie, Oreg., 1985-86. Prodr., actor (video travelogues) Portland Cable Access, 1987—; actor: Oreg. Sr. Theater, 1987—95, Plz. Players, 1999—. Co-leader Girl Scouts Am., Oak Grove, Oreg., 1954—55, Webelos Boy Scouts Am., 1956—57, 1970—71; videographer Ptnrs. Ams., Oreg., 1990—91; head video prodn. Channel 29 In-House TV Ret.; prodr. biweekly travel show, weekly activities show; mem. synchronized swim team Holladay Park Plz., head video prodn. Mem.: AAUW (pres. Albany chpt.). Avocations: painting, video production, bell playing, travel, synchronized swimming.

OGBURN, NANCY WRENN, civic volunteer; b. Honolulu, Sept. 16, 1926; d. Heaton Luse and Carolene (Cooke) Wrenn; m. Hugh Gerhard Petersen Jr., July 1, 1948 (div. 1972); children: Hugh G. Petersen III, Suzanne Elise Petersen, Monte Cooke Petersen, Alexander Wrenn Petersen; m. Hugh Bell Ogburn, Sept. 5, 1974. BA, Wellesley Coll., 1948. With outside sales dept. Harris Travel, Greenwich, Conn., 1974-78. Guide Hawaiian Mission Children's Soc., Honolulu, 1978-81, Lyon Arboretum; treas. Rep. precinct, Honolulu, 1993. Recipient Carey E. Quinn award Am. Daffodil Soc., 1964, Roberta C. Watrous award, Medal of Merit Garden Club Am., 1966, Corning medal, 1991. Fellow Honolulu Acad. Arts; mem. Greenwich Garden Club (non-resident, Horticultural Com. award (2)), Garden Club Honolulu (chmn. various coms., Horticultural Com. award). Republican. Episcopalian. Avocations: bridge, traveling, grandchildren, hiking. Home: 4340 Pahoa Ave Apt 16A Honolulu HI 96816-5032

OGDEN, ANITA BUSHEY, nursing educator; b. Malone, N.Y., May 23, 1938; d. John Richard and Eleanor Miriam (Wright) Bushey; m. William Alan Ogden, Dec. 27, 1972. Nursing diploma, N.Y. Med. Coll., 1959; BSN, Columbia U., 1962; MS in Adult Health, SUNY, Buffalo, 1968; PhD, Cornell U., 1984. Faculty Flower-Fifth Ave. Sch. Nursing, N.Y.C., 1959-62, Meth. Hosp., Bklyn. Sch. Nursing, N.Y.C., 1962-66, Hartwick Coll., Oneonta, N.Y., 1968-73; faculty, chair divsn. nursing edn. Corning (N.Y.) C.C., 1973-89; faculty Alfed U., Alfed Station, N.Y., 1984-88; prof., dir. nurse edn. Elmira (N.Y.) Coll., 1989—; clin. staff nurse various orgns., 1959—. Cons. curriculum devel., 1978—. Mem. adv. coun. Alfed U., Alfed Station, 1984-87; mem. bd. dirs. Cmty. Health Svcs. for Elderly, Elmira, 1992—; nursing cons. St. Kitts/Nevis U.S. Aid Ptnrs. Ams., 1986-87. Mem. ANA (various offices), N.Y. State and Dist. Nurses Assn. (various offices), Internat. Resources Instructional Svcs. (faculty 1990—), Nat. League for Nursing (regional bd. dirs. 1973—, ednl. cons. 1982—), LWV (regional coord.), Order Ea. Star (various offices), Delta Kappa Gamma (scholarship award 1981, 83), Delta Kappa Gamma (pres., bd. dirs. 1970), Sigma Theta Tau. Republican. Avocations: bicycling, hand crafts, cats. Home: 104 Fairview Ave Painted Post NY 14870-1215

OGDEN, ANN, writer; b. Kansas City, Mo. d. Audley W. and Leona R. (Locke) Porter; m. Alvin C. Ogden, Apr. 20, 1954; 1 child, Karen. BS in Tech. Journalism, Kans. State U., 1954; MA in Sec. Edn., U. Mo., Kansas City, 1968. Society editor Lyons (Kans.) Daily News, 1954-56; asst. editor Rose Pubs., Shawnee Mission, Kans., 1962-63; instr. developmental reading U. Mo., Kansas City, 1964-67; journalism tchr. Bishop Miege High Sch., Shawnee Mission, 1966-67; asst. editor Kans. Alumni, Lawrence, 1967-68, Vol. Leader and Trustee of Am. Hosp. Assn., Chgo., 1969-72; asst. editor, directory editor Barks Pubs., Chgo., 1975-81; adj. instr. bus. English Triton Coll., River Grove, Ill., 1981-84; freelance writer, editor, 1973-94. Contbr. chapters to books. Bd. dirs. Overland Park (Kans.) Heritage Found., 1991—; mem. Strang hist. display com., 1991—, sec. 1998-99, pres. 2000-02; trustee Shawnee Mission Indian Hist. Soc., Inc. Johnson County, 1993—, 1st v.p., 1996-97, pres. 1998-99; mem. bd. Hospitalized Vets. Writing Project, 1979-80, 89—, v.p., 1996-99, pres., 1999-2003. U. Mo. Kansas City fellow, 1964-65, 65-66. Mem. Overland Pk. Hist. Soc., Alpha Chi Omega (editor Lyre chpt. 1989-91, historian 1991-93, chaplain 1993-95).

OGDEN, LYDIA LEE, government agency administrator; b. Murfreesboro, Tenn., July 17, 1960; d. Alfred Edwin and June (McCarter) O.; m. Kenneth Roland Askew, Nov. 15, 1986 (div. Dec. 1994); m. James Walter Buehler, Mar. 27, 1997; children: Philip, Lauren, Branch, Guthrie. BS summa cum laude, Middle Tenn. State U., 1981; MA, Vanderbilt U., 1984; MPP, Harvard U., 1998. Editor Am. Health Cons., Atlanta, 1984-86; strategic comms. cons. Words' Worth, Atlanta, 1986-89; account exec. Pringle Dixon Pringle, Atlanta, 1988; cmty. liaison Agy. for Toxic Substances & Disease Registry, Atlanta, 1989-92; comms. specialist Divsn. of HIV/AIDS Prevention Ctrs. for Disease Control & Prevention, Atlanta, 1992—96; sr. policy analyst Nat. Ctr. HIV, STD and TB Prevention, 1998—2001, dir. policy and planning Global AIDS Program, 2001—04; dep. chief of staff Ctrs. Disease Ctrl. and Prevention, 2004—. Mem. Atlanta Episcopal Diocese Commn. on AIDS, 1995—. Author: Applying Prevention Marketing, 1995; editor: Hosp. Risk Mgmt., 1984-86, The Public Health Implications of Medical Waste: A Report to Congress, 1989. Democrat. Episcopalian. Office: Ctrs for Disease Control & Prevention 1600 Clifton Rd NE # E7 Atlanta GA 30329-4018

OGDEN, MAUREEN BLACK, retired state legislator; b. Vancouver, B.C., Nov. 1, 1928; came to U.S., 1930; d. William Moore and Margaret Hunter (Leitch) Black; m. Robert Moore Ogden, June 23, 1956; children: Thomas, Henry, Peter. BA, Smith Coll., 1950; MA, Columbia U., 1963; M in City and Regional Planning, Rutgers U., 1977. Researcher, staff asst. Ford Found., N.Y.C., 1951-56; staff assoc. Fgn. Policy Assn., N.Y.C., 1956-58; mem. Millburn (N.J.) Twp. Com., 1976-81; mayor Twp. of Millburn, N.J., 1979-81; mem. N.J. Gen. Assembly, Trenton, 1982-96. Chmn. Assembly Environment Com., N.J. Gen. Assembly; chmn. Energy and Pub. Utilities Com., Coun. State Govts., 1991-92; mem. adv. bd. Sch. Policy and Planning, Rutgers Univ., New Brunswick, N.J., 1992-96. Author: Natural Resources Inventory, Township of Millburn, 1974. Bd. govs. N.J. Hist. Soc., Newark, 1992-2000; trustee N.J. chpt. The Nature Conservancy, 1994-99; hon. trustee Paper Mill Playhouse, Millburn, 1990—; former trustee St. Barnabas Med. Ctr., Livingston, N.J.; former pres. N.J. Drug Abuse Adv. Coun.; chair Gov.'s Coun. on N.J. Outdoors, 1996-99; mem. Palisades Interstate Park Commn., 1996-99; chair Garden State Preservation Trust, 1999—; mem. policy com. N.J. Conservation Found., 2000—. Recipient citation Nat. Assn. State Outdoors Recreation Liaison Officers, 1987, cert. appreciation John F. Kennedy Ctr. for the Performing Arts, The Alliance for Art Edn., 1987, disting. svc. award Art Educators N.J., 1987, ann. environ. quality award EPA Region II, 1988, citation Humane Soc. U.S., 1989, award N.J. Hist. Sites Coun., 1989, N.J. Sch. Conservation, 1990, pres.'s award The Nature Conservancy, 1995, pub. policy award Nat. Trust for Hist. Preservation, 1995. Republican. Episcopalian. Home: 59 Lakeview Ave Short Hills NJ 07078-2240 E-mail: mrogden@worldnet.att.net.

OGDEN, PEGGY A. retired personnel director; b. N.Y.C., Mar. 21, 1932; d. Stephen Arnold and Margaret (Stern) O. BA with honors, Brown U., 1953; MA, Trinity Coll., Hartford, Conn., 1955. Asst. dir. YMCA Counseling Svc., Hartford, 1953-55; employment interviewer R.H. Macy & Co., N.Y.C., 1955; asst. pers. dir. Inst. Internat. Edn., N.Y.C., 1956-59; pers. advisor Girl Scouts U.S.A., N.Y.C., 1959-61; store and pers. mgr. Ohrbachs, Inc., N.Y.C., 1961-74; dir. pers. N.Y.C. Coll. Tech., CUNY, Bkyn., 1974-2000, ret., 2000. Arbitrator, mediator Better Bus. Bur., N.Y.C., 1988—; cons. Girl Scout Coun. N.Y., N.Y.C., 1988-89. Advocate Am. Diabetes Assn., 1999—. Mem APA, AAAS, Am. Assn. U. Adminstrs., Women in Human Resources, N.Y. Pers. Mgmt. Assn. Home: 1100 Park Ave New York NY 10128-1202

OGDEN, VALERIA MUNSON, management consultant, state representative; b. Okanogan, Wash., Feb. 11, 1924; d. Ivan Bodwell and Pearle (Wilson) Munson; m. Daniel Miller Ogden Jr., Dec. 28, 1946; children: Janeth Lee Ogden Martin, Patricia Jo Ogden Hunter, Daniel Munson Ogden. BA magna cum laude, Wash. State U., 1946. Exec. dir. Potomac Coun. Camp Fire, Washington, 1964-68, Ft. Collins (Colo.) United Way, 1969-73, Designing Tomorrow Today, Ft. Collins, 1973-74, Poudre Valley Community Edn. Assn., Ft. Collins, 1977-78; pres. Valeria M. Ogden, Inc., Kensington, Md., 1978-81; nat. field cons. Camp Fire, Inc., Kansas City, Mo., 1980-81; exec. dir. Nat. Capital Area YWCA, Washington, 1981-84, Clark County YWCA, Vancouver, Wash., 1985-89; pvt. practice mgmt. cons. Vancouver, 1989—; mem. Wash. Ho. of Reps., 1991—2002, spkr. pro tempore, 1999—2002. Mem. adj. faculty pub. adminstrn. program Lewis and Clark Coll., Portland (Oreg.) State U., 1979-94; mem. Pvt. Industry Coun., Vancouver, 1986-95; mem. regional Svcs. Network Bd. Mental Health, 1993—2003. Author: Camp Fire Membership, 1980. County vice-chair Larimer County Dems., Ft. Collins, 1974-75; mem. precinct com. Clark County Dems., Vancouver, 1986-88; mem. Wash. State Coun. Vol. Action, Olympia, 1986-90; treas. Mortar Bd. Nat. Found., Vancouver, 1987-96; bd. dirs. Clark County Coun. for Homeless, Vancouver, 1989—2004, chmn., 1994; bd. dirs. Wash. Wild Life and Recreation Coalition, 1995-2002, Human Svcs. Coun., 1996-02, State Legis. Leaders Found., 2001-02; mem. adv. bd. Wash. State U., Vancouver, 2002—; chair arts and tourism com. Nat. Conf. State Legis., 1996-97, exec. com., 2000-02; bd. dirs. Wash. State Hist. Soc., 1996—, Affordable Cmty. Environments, 1998—, Clark County Skill Ctr. Found., 2003—; spkr. pro tem Wash. Ho. of Reps., 1999-2002; pres. Nat. Order of Women Legislators, 1999-2001; chair Wash. State Interagy. Com. for Outdoor Recreation, 2003, Wash. State Historic Preservation Fund; mem. Columbia Springs Edn. Ctr. Found.; co-chair SW. Wash. Ctr. for the Arts. Named Citizen of Yr. Ft. Collins Bd. of Realtors, 1975, State Legislator of Yr., Wash. State Labor Coun., 2000; recipient Gulick award Camp Fire Inc., 1956, Alumna Achievement award Wash. State U. Alumni Assn., 1988; named YWCA Woman of Achievement, 1991; named Citizen of Yr., Vancouver, Wash., 2002. Mem. Internat. Assn. Vol. Adminstrs. (pres. Boulder 1989-90), Nat. Assn. YWCA Exec. Dirs. (nat. bd. nominating com. 1988-90), Sci. and Soc. Assn. (bd. dirs. 1993-97), Women in Action, Philanthropic and Ednl. Orgn., Phi Beta Kappa. Democrat. Avocations: hiking, travel. Home: 3118 NE Royal Oak Dr Vancouver WA 98662-7435 E-mail: repval@comcast.net.

OGE, MARGO TSIRIGOTIS, environmentalist; b. Athens, Greece, Feb. 20, 1949; came to U.S., 1968; d. John Tsirigotis and Joana Lambrinakos; m. Cuneyt Oge, Aug. 24, 1975; children: Nicole, Marisa. Degree in Plastic Tech., Lowell U., 1972, degree in Plastic Engring., 1975. Chem. engr. EPA, Washington, 1980-83, sect. chief, 1983-85, dep. dir. toxic substances office, 1986-88, dir. radon divsn., 1988—; legis. asst. to Sen. Chafee U.S. Senate, Washington, 1985; dir. transp. air quality EPA, Washington, 1994—. Avocations: reading, tennis, skiing, travel. Office: EPA Ariel Rios Blvd N MC6401A 1200 Pennsylvania Ave NW Washington DC 20460-0001

OGLE, ROBBIN SUE, criminal justice educator; b. North Kansas City, Mo., Aug. 28, 1960; d. Robert Lee and Carol Sue (Gray) O. BS, Ctrl. Mo. State U., 1982; MS, U. Mo., 1990; PhD, Pa. State U., 1995. State probation and parole officer Mo. Dept. Corrections, Kansas City, 1982-92; collector J.C. Penney Co., Mission, Kans., 1990-92; instr. U. Mo., Kansas City, 1990-92; grad. lectr. Pa. State U., University Park, 1992-95; prof. criminal justice dept. U. Nebr., Omaha, 1995—. Author: Battered Women Who Kill: A New Framework, 2002; contbr. articles to profl. jours. Athletic scholar Ctrl. Mo. State U., Warrensburg, 1978-82. Mem. AAUW, ACLU, NOW, Am. Soc. Criminology, Acad. Criminal Justice Scis., Am. Correctional Assn., Phi Kappa Phi. Avocations: reading, watching basketball, walking dog. Office: U Nebr Dept Criminal Justice 1100 Neihardt Lincoln NE 68588-0630 Home: 2410 N 99th St Omaha NE 68134-5642 E-mail: RSOgle@webtv.net.

OGLE-BREWER, PAULA BETH, music educator; d. Thomas Paul and Glynna Beth Knight; m. Dave Brewer, Dec. 22, 2001; children: Eden Brewer, Deana Ogle, Darryl Ogle, Sarah Ogle. MusB magna cum laude, U. Tex., 1980; MusM magna cum laude, Baylor U., 1996. Choral dir. Round Rock (Tex.) Ind. Sch. Dist., 1989—2002, Veterans Meml. H.S., Mission, Tex., 2002—. Accompanist: concert Texas All-State Treble Chorus. Vacation bible sch. tchr. First Bapt. Ch., Round Rock, Tex., 1989—99. Recipient Golden Apple award, Round Rock Leader, 1996. Mem.: Tex. Music Adjudicators Assn. (assoc.), Am. Choral Dirs. Assn. (assoc.), Tex. Choral Dirs. Assn. (assoc.), Tex. Music Educators Assn. (assoc.; hospitality com. 1998—99, election com. 1999—2000). Republican. Avocations: travel, stitching, reading, swimming, snorkeling. Office: Veterans Memorial High School 700 E 2 Mile Mission TX 78574

OGLESBY, JERRI BURDETTE, elementary school educator; b. Olney, Md., Oct. 13, 1953; d. Herbert M. and Ellen (Miller) Burdette; m. Albert C. Oglesby Jr., Nov. 18, 1978; children: Matthew Jacob, Nathan Bryan. BA in Elem. Edn., Shepherd Coll., 1975; MEd, Johns Hopkins U., 1995, cert. adminstrn., 1999. Cert. elem. tchr., Md.; cert. adminstrn. and supervision, Md. Tchr. elem. Montgomery County Pub. Schs., Rockville, Md., 1976-97, asst. prin., 1997-99, prin., 1999—; assoc. faculty mem. Johns Hopkins U., 1995—. Deacon Boyds (Md.) Presbyn. Ch., 1980—. Mem. NEA, ASCD, Nat. Coun. Tchrs. Math., Montgomery County Edn. Assn., Elem. Prins. Assn., Nat. Reading Assn., Tchrs. of English, Montgomery County Adminstrs. Assn.

O'GRADY, BEVERLY TROXLER, investment executive, counselor; d. Robert Andrew and Beverly Beam (Barrier) Troxler; m. Robert Edward O'Grady, Aug. 6, 1966. BA, St. Mary's Coll., 1963; MA, Columbia U., 1965. Exec. v.p. Wilkinson & Hottinger Inc., N.Y.C., 1973-94, Helvetia Capital Corp., N.Y.C., 1987-94; pres. Wilkinson O'Grady & Co., Inc., N.Y.C., 1994—. Mem. adv. bd. Charles Schwab Fin., San Francisco, 1991-93. Active Women's Nat. Rep. Club, N.Y.C., 1991-94; trustee St. Mary's Coll., Notre Dame, Ind., 2002--. Mem. Assn. Investment Mgrs., N.Y. Soc. Security Analysts, Women's Bond Club (pres. 1992-94), Univ. Club. Roman Catholic. Office: Wilkinson O'Grady & Co Inc 520 Madison Ave New York NY 10022-4213

OH, ANGELA E. lawyer; b. L.A., Sept. 8, 1955; BA, UCLA, 1977, MPH, 1981; JD, U. Calif., Davis, 1986. Bar: Calif. 1986. With Beck, DeCorso, Daly, Barrera & Oh, Redondo Beach, Calif., 1987—. Lawyer del. 9th Cir. Jud. Conf., 1995-96, lawyer rep.; mem. Senator Boxer's Jud. Noms. Com. for Ctrl. Dist. Calif., 1994-95; bd. mem. Calif. Women's Law Ctr., Lawyers Mutual Ins. Co., Lawyer Representive to the 9th Cir. Judicial Conf. Contbr. articles to profl. jours. and newspapers such as L.A. Times, L.A. Sentinel; spkr. in field including Dartmouth Coll., Hastings Sch. Law, Columbia Univ., Harvard Law Sch., Princeton Theology Seminary. Spl. counsel to the Assembly Spl. Com. on the L.A. Crisis; active Lawyers' Mutual Ins. Co.; active cmty. adv. bd. First Interstate Bank Calif.; bd. dirs. Calif. Women's Law Ctr. Mem. ABA, State Bar Calif., Korean-Am. Bar Assn. So. Calif. (pres.), L.A. County Bar Assn. Office: Beck DeCorso Daly Barrera & Oh PO Box 7000 639 Redondo Beach CA 90277

O'HANLON, CAROL ANN, minister; b. Jacksonville, Fla. d. Oscar Lee Miller and Elsie (Beecher) Simpson; m. Arthur Francis, July 16, 1963; 1 child, Arthur Patrick. BA, Montreat, 1956; M of Religious Edn., Union Sem., 1959, MDiv, 1963; MS in Counseling, L.I. U., 1977, Profl. Diploma, 1980. Ordained to ministry United Meth. Ch., 1965; cert. Christian edn. min., expert in traumatic stress; nat. cert. counselor; cert. hypnotherapist; registered behavioral therapist. Asst. pastor, minister edn. Kings Hwy. United Meth. Ch., Bklyn., 1961-63; asst. pastor Bellmore (L.I.) United Meth. Ch., 1964-66; assoc. pastor Farmingdale (L.I.) United Meth. Ch., 1966-80; assoc. pastor, coord. food pantry Babylon (N.Y.) United Meth. Ch., 1980-95; pastor United Meth. Ch., Bellmore, NY, 1995—98; interim pastor Bridgehampton United Ch., 1999; counselor Mental Health Faculty Mercy Haven Inc., 2000—. Coord. children's work United Meth. Ch., L.I., 1966-78, chmn. dist. edn., 1978-85, 87-91, dist. dir. Sch. Faith and Life, 1980—, coord. adult ministries, 1983-85, founder dist. edn. com, 1979—, dist. bd. ministry, 1990-95, dist. nominating com., 1983-91, dist. coun. on ministries, 1966-93. Author: The Knockout Punch - Facets and Ways of Coping with a Sudden Death, 1999. Mem.: Am. Acad. ExpertsTraumatic Stress, Am. Assn. Profl. Hypnotherapists, N.Y. Mental Health Counselors Assn., Suffolk Coalition. Home: 25 Barry Rd Amity Harbor NY 11701-4001

O'HARA, CATHERINE, actress, comedienne; b. Toronto, Mar. 4, 1954; m. Bo Welch, 1992. Actress, writer with Second City, Toronto, 1974; co-founder of SCTV, 1976 (Emmy award); films include After Hours, 1985, Heartburn, 1986, Beetlejuice, 1988, Dick Tracy, 1990, Betsy's Wedding, 1990, Home Alone, 1990, Little Vegas, 1990, There Goes The Neighborhood, 1992, Home Alone II: Lost In New York, 1992, (voice) The Nightmare Before Christmas, 1993, The Paper, 1994, Wyatt Earp, 1994, A Simple Twist of Fate, 1994, Tall Tale, 1995, Waiting for Guffman, 1996, The Last of the high Kings, 1996, (voice) Pippi Longstocking, 1997, Home Fries, 1998, The Life Before This, 1999, (voice) Bartok the Magnificient, 1999; TV, SCTV, Comic Relief, Dream On (dir.), Hope, 1997; co-writer SCTV, Cinemax, 1984, Really Weird Tales, HBO, 1986; dir. (TV series) Dream On, 1990; writer Really Weird Tales, 1987; TV guest appearances The Simpsons Show, The Larry Sanders Show, 1992, The Outer Limits, 1995.

O'HARA, CYNTHIA O'CONNOR, writer, columnist, food consultant; b. New Hartford, N.Y., Sept. 17, 1963; d. Miles Joseph and Janice Louise O'Connor; m. Michael Timothy O'Hara, June 17, 1989; children: Colleen Meghan, Kelly O'Connor. Grad., Utica Sch. Commerce, 1984. Culinary instr. Bd. of Coop. Ednl. Svcs., New Hartford, 1996—; newspaper columnist Observer-Dispatch (Gannett News Svc.), Utica, N.Y., 1997—; TV personality numerous TV stas., 1997—. Spkr. N.Y.C. pub. librs., orgns., bus.; food demonstrator various stores, N.Y.C. Author: The Harried Housewife's Cookbooks, 1997; contbr. articles to mags. Leader Girl Scouts Am., Utica, N.Y., 1996-97. Mem. Internat. Assn. Culinary Profls., Mohawk Valley Businesswomen's Network. Roman Catholic. Avocations: cooking, gardening, reading. Office: The Harried Housewife PO Box 16 Whitesboro NY 13492-0016 Fax: 315-768-2714. E-mail: harried@borg.com.

O'HARA, DELIA IGLAUER, family nurse practitioner; b. Cin., Feb. 5, 1942; d. Arnold and Virginia Iglauer; children: Robert, Matthew, William; m. Herbert G. Johnson, Sept. 23, 2000. BS, Simmons Coll., 1965; Cert. Nurse Practitioner, George Washington U., 1975; JD, Howard U., 1987. Bar: D.C.; cert. family nurse practitioner. Dir. home care program for cancer patients George Washington U. Med. Ctr., 1975-79; occupational health nurse practitioner Libr. of Congress, Washington, 1979-84; lawyer FTC, Washington, 1987-89; dir. student health svcs. Presdl. Classroom for Young Ams., 1987-98; health svcs. mgr. Time-Life Books, Inc., Alexandria, Va., 1990-92; pvt. practice law Washington, 1990-99; occupational health nurse practitioner Washington Hosp. Ctr., 1993-96, nurse practitioner Admissions Testing Ctr., 1996-98; nurse practitioner dept. pre-surgery Kaiser Permanente Med. Ctr., Oakland, Calif., 1998—; quality liason nurse practitioners East Bay Kaiser Permanente, Oakland, Calif., 2003—. Chmn. D.C. Home Care Task Force; vol. Winterhaven Shelter for Homeless Women; active Bd. Nursing, Washington; vestrywoman St. John's Episcopal Ch., Montclair, 1999—2001; mentor edn. ministry EFM Ministries, Montclair, 2001—03. Recipient Trustee's scholarship Howard U. Fellow Am. Acad. Nurse Practitioners (bd. dirs. region 3 rep. 1991-94, rec. sec. 1994-96, treas. 1996-97), Am. Acad. Nurse Practitioners Found. (bd. dirs. 1996-2004, pres. 2001), Nurse Practitioner Assn. of D.C. (pres. 1992-95), Capitol Area Network of Nurse Attys. (v.p. 1992-93), Simmons Coll. Alumnae Assn. (class sec. Class of 1964, 1989-94). Home: 2525 Alida St Oakland CA 94602-2503 Office: Kaiser Permanente Med Ctr 280 W Macarthur Blvd Oakland CA 94611-5642

O'HARA, PATRICIA A. dean, law educator; BA summa cum laude, Santa Clara U., 1971; JD summa cum laude, Notre Dame, 1974. Bar: Calif. 1974. Assoc. Brobeck, Phleger & Harrison, 1974—79, 1980—81; assoc. prof. law Notre Dame Law Sch., 1981, prof., 1990, v.p. student affairs, 1990—99, dean, law educator, 2001—. Contbr. chapters to books, articles to law jours. Office: U Notre Dame 203 Law Sch PO Box R Notre Dame IN 46556 E-mail: Patricia.A.O'Hara.3@nd.edu.

O'HARE, VIRGINIA LEWIS, human resources administrator; b. Pitts., May 2, 1951; d. Robert Edward and Ellen Marie (Saylor) Lewis; m. John Francis O'Hare, Sept. 17, 1994; 1 child, Merit Elisabeth. BS in Edn., U. Pitts., 1973; MS in Human Resources Mgmt., Laroche Coll., 1984. Legal asst. Meyer, Darragh, Buckler, Bebenek & Eck, Pitts., 1973-85; legal office mgr. Rockwell Internat., Pitts., 1985-86; pers. mgr. Rose, Schmidt, Hasley & DiSalle, Pitts., 1986-88; legal adminstr. Duquesne Light Co., Pitts., 1988-99; mgr. human resources Klett Lieber Rooney & Schorling, Pitts., 1999—. Mem. Assn. Legal Adminstrs., Pitts. Legal Adminstrn. Assn. (sec. 1989-93, membership chair 1993-97, edn. chair 1997-2000, pres.-elect 2000-2001), Pa. Bar Assn., Allegheny Bar Assn., Pitts. Human Resources Assn. Republican. Avocations: horseback riding, target shooting, walking, biking. Office: Klett Lieber Rooney Lieber & Schorling 40th Fl 1 Oxford Ct Pittsburgh PA 15219-1407

O'HEARN, JANE E. state legislator; b. Gardner, Mass., Feb. 20, 1949; m. Robert O'Hearn; children: Megan, Matthew. BA, Anna Maria Coll., 1971; student, Fitchburg State Coll., Worcester State Coll. Tchr. Lunenburg Sch. Sys., 1971-77; tutor, 1979-92; mem. N.H. No. of Reps. from 26th Dist., Concord, 1993-2000, N.H. Senate from 12th Dist., Concord, 2001—, mem. edn., enrolled bills, interstate coop. coms., 2001—, mem. pub. instns., health and human svcs. coms., 2001—. Vol. coord. Birch Hall Sch./Nashua Sch. Dist., 1986-90; vice chair N.H. House Edn., 1996-97, chair, 1997-2000; adv. bd. CHADD; vol. Am. Cancer Soc., Heart Fund, Devel. Disabilities Coun., PTO; dir. Sch. Vol. Program, After Sch. Ski Program; mem. N.H. Fedn. Rep. Women; mem. Commn. on Adequate Edn. and Adequate Fin., 1999-2000; chair Pub. Higher Edn. Study Commn., 1999-2000; mem. Spl. Edn. Adv. Commn., 1999-2000; mem. Commn. on Deaf Studies, 1996; mem. steering com. Office of Spl. Edn. Programs, 2000; mem. N.H. Edn. Improvement Assessment Program, 1997-2000; mem. nominating com. N.H. Higher Edn. Assistance Found., 2000. Home: 7 Pope Cir Nashua NH 03063-3307 Office: State House 107 N Main St Concord NH 03301 Fax: (603) 886-6728.

OHIRA, AKEMI, art educator; b. Tokyo, May 7, 1967; came to U.S., 1980; d. Takeo and Michi Ohira. BFA, Cornell U., 1990; MFA, Carnegie Mellon U., 1992. Asst. prof. art U. Va., Charlottesville, 1993—99, assoc. prof., 1999—. Sesquicentennial assoc. U. Va., Charlottesville, 1997. One-woman shows include Galerie Voyage, San Francisco, 1990, 97, Santensho Gallery, Kumamoto, Japan, 1990, Collective Ctr. for the Arts, Jackson, Mich., 1994, St. Mary's Coll., Notre Dame, Ind., 1995, Piedmont Va. C.C., Charlottesville, 1995, Western Mich. U., Kalamazoo, 1996; exhibited in group show at Laguna Gloria Art Mus., Austin, Tex., 1994, U. Ala., Tuscaloosa, 1995, Ohio State U., Mansfield, 1995. Admissions amb. Cornell U., 1992-93. Recipient prize and grants John Kip Brady Found., Annapolis, Md., 1989, Francis Weatherspoon Printmakers award, Dome Gallery, 1991, Purchase award Rembrandt Graphics/Print Club, 1994;

Visual Arts grantee Southeastern Coll. Arts Conf. Mem. Soc. Am. Graphic Artists, Coll. Art Assn. Avocations: fitness, gardening. Office: U Va McIntire Dept Art Fayerweather Hall PO Box 400130 Charlottesville VA 22904

OHL, JOAN E. federal agency administrator; b. Harrisburg, Pa.; m. Ronald E. Ohl. Grad., U. Del., 1967; [illegible], SUNY, Buffalo, 1969; post grad., Pa. State U. Commr. Adminstrn. on Children, Youth and Families Dept. HSS, Washington, 2002—; W.Va. cabinet sec., chief adminstr. Dept. Health and Human Resources, 1997—2001; cons. CE "Jim" Compton of FIVE-J Energy & Grafton Coal Co., 1984—93. Asst. to v.p. Fairleigh Dickson Univ., Rutherford, NJ, 1975—82. Recipient Disting. West Virginian award, 2000, Joan E. Ohl Rural Health Leadership award, W.Va. Rural Health Assn., 2000, Leadership Award, Multi-CAP, Inc., 2000, Bateman Award, WV Hosp. Assoc., 2000, Leadership Award, WV Pub. Health Assoc., 2000. Mem.: Ind. Coll. Fund of NJ & the Assoc. of Ind. Coll. & Univ. in NJ (v.p. 1982—83), WV Health Care Cost Review Authority (bd. mem. 1993—97). Office: Dept HHS Adminstrn on Children Youth and Families 330 C St SW Rm 2134 Washington DC 20447

OHMAN, DIANA J. government agency administrator, former state official; b. Sheridan, Wyo., Oct. 3, 1950; d. Arden and Doris Marie (Carstens) Mahin. AA, Casper Coll., 1970; BA, U. Wyo., 1972, MEd, 1977, postgrad., 1979—. Tchr. kindergarten Natrona County Sch. Dist., Casper, Wyo., 1971-72; tchr. rural sch. K-8 Campbell County Sch. Dist., Gillette, Wyo., 1972-80, rural prin. K-8, 1980-82, prin. K-6, 1982-84, assoc. dir. instrn., 1984-87; dir. K-12 Goshen County Migrant Program, Torrington, Wyo., 1988-89; prin. K-2 Goshen County Sch. Dist., Torrington, Wyo., 1987-90; state supt. pub. instrn. State of Wyo., Cheyenne, 1991-94, secretary of state, 1995-98; dir. Dept. Def. Dep. Schs., 2002—. Chmn. Campbell County Mental Health Task Force, 1986-87; mem. Legis. Task Force on Edn. of Handicapped 3-5 Yr. Olds, 1988-89. State Committeewoman Wyo. Rep. Party, 1985-88. Recipient Wyo. Elem. Prin. of Yr. award, 1990; named Campbell County Tchr. of Yr. 1980, Campbell County Profl. Bus. Woman of Yr. 1984, Outstanding Young Woman in Am., 1983. Mem. Coun. of Chief of State Sch. Officers (Washington chpt.), Internat. Reading Assn., Wyo. Assn. of Sch. Adminstrs., N.Am. Securities Adminstrs. Assn., Kappa Delta Pi, Phi Kappa Phi, Phi Delta Kappa. Republican. Lutheran. Office: CMR 443 Box 111 APO AE 09096-9111

OHMANN, ELIZABETH J. advocate; b. Greenwald, Minn., Mar. 9, 1933; d. John and Elizabeth Ohmann. BA, Coll. St. Catherine, 1963; MA, Maryknoll Sch. Theology, N.Y., 1983. Fgn. and Native Am. missionary Cath. Ch., Peru, 1967—76; religious edn. Cath. Ch., Ariz. & Minn., 1976—81; adminstr. Franciscan Sisters, Little Falls, Minn., 1983—85; educator and coord. BorderLinks, Tucson, 1995—2001, 1995—2001; social justice activist Humane Borders, Tucson, 2001—. Pres. Tucson Diocese Sisters Coun., 1990—92; women's adv. and chaplain Kairos Outside Ariz., Tucson, 1998—2002. Roman Catholic. Avocations: reading, travel, camping, crocheting, crafts. Home: 116 8th Ave SE Little Falls MN 56345-3597 Office: Humane Borders 740 E Speedway Blvd Tucson AZ 85719 Office Phone: 520-628-7753.

OHST, WENDY JOAN, government agency administrator, educator; b. Muskegon, Mich., Feb. 20, 1949; d. Edward John Barron, Jr. and Mable Barron; m. Terrence Duane Ohst, Oct. 21, 1972; children: Heather Lynn Reyes, Holly Ann Garratt. AA, Muskegon (Mich.)C.C., 1969; BS, Calif. Coast U., 1994; BBA, Baker Coll., 1998; MPA, Grand Valley State U., 2001. Contract asst. Teledyne Continental Motors, Muskegon, 1968; bookkeeper, teller FMB Lumberman's Bank, Muskegon, 1969—72; adminstrv. svcs. supr. Muskegon (Mich.) County Dept. of Employment & Tng., 1972—94, dep. dir., 1994—. Adj. prof. Baker Coll., Muskegon, Mich., 2002—; cons., presenter in field. Pres. local chpt. Nat. Fedn. of Bus. & Profl. Woman, Muskegon, 1990—91; campaign coord. United Way, 1990—2001; bd. dir. Muskegon (Mich.) Schs. Health & Human Svcs. Adv. Bd., 2002—03, Baker Corp. Svcs. Adv. Bd., 1999—2003. Mem.: Muskegon (Mich.) C.of C., Mich. Works Assn., Nat. Assn. Workforce Devel. Profls., Pi Alpha Alpha, Phi Kappa Phi, Delta Mu Delta. Lutheran. Avocations: travel, reading. Office: Department of Employment & Training 1611 Oak Avenue Muskegon MI 49442

OJINNAKA, BECKY, publishing executive; b. Orlu, Nigeria, July 27, 1956; d. Kevin and Felicia Anasott. BSBA, Southeastern U., Washington, 1978, MBA, 1980; PhD, Fell Sem., Calif., 1996; DBA, Calif. Coast U., 1999. Youth svc. ACB-Bank, Lagos, Nigeria, 1981-82; with Fin. Merchant Bank, Lagos, 1982-86; sr. mgr. CCB Bank, Lagos, 1986-92; asst. gen. mgr. Winggold Savings, Lagos, 1992-96; pres. World Achievers, Lagos, 1994—, Jireh Shammah, Lagos, 1998—. Author: Be You Own Cosmetics, 1985, Cosmetician, 1990, Part 1 and 2. Cons. to First Lady of Nigeria, 1996-98. Mem. DBA Execs., Nigerian Assn. Female Execs. (cons. 1994). Home: 6703 Kerman Ct Lanham Seabrook MD 20706-2186

O'KANE, MARGARET E. non-profit organization executive; children: Katie, Beth. BA in French, Fordham U., 1969; MHS in Health Adminstrn. and Planning, Johns Hopkins U. Sch. Hygiene and Public Health. Second grade tchr. St. Ambrose Sch., Bklyn., 1970-72; neurology rsch. asst. Children's Hosp., Boston, 1972-73; respiratory therapist St. Elizabeth's Hosp., Boston, U. Va. Med. Ctr., Charlottesville, Va., Children's Hosp., Washington, DC, 1973-78; program analyst office of planning, evaluation, legislation health svcs. adminstrn. U.S. Dept. Health and Human Svcs., Washington, 1979-81; rsch. assoc. intergovernmental health policy project (IHPP) The George Washington U., Washington, 1981-83; public health svc. fellow U.S. Dept. Health and Human Svcs. Nat. Ctr. for Health Svcs. Rsch., Washington, 1983-84, special asst. to dir., 1985-86; dir. med. dirs. divsn. Am. Assn. Health Plans (formerly Group Health Assn. of Am., Inc.), Washington, 1986-89; dir. quality mgmt. Group Health Assn., Inc., Washington, 1989-90; pres. Nat. Com. Quality Assurance, Washington, 1990—. Elected mem. Inst. of Medicine, 1999. Named Health Person of Yr. Medicine & Health Jour., 1996; recipient Founder's award Am. Coll. Med. Quality, 1997. Office: Nat Com for Quality Assurance 2000 L St NW Ste 500 Washington DC 20036-4918*

O'KEEFE, BEVERLY DISBROW, state official, federal official; b. Wilton, Conn., Sept. 1, 1946; d. Harry Harbs and Jane Corrine (Young) Disbrow; children: Marcia Corrine, Jennifer Lynn; m. John Patrick O'Keefe, Aug. 1981 (div. 1985). AA, Berkshire Community Coll., 1973; BA in Psychology, U. Mass., 1975; MPA, U. S.C., 1979; cert. master gardener, U. R.I., 1999. Lic. social worker, S.C. Statis. clk. U. S.C., Columbia, 1976-78; pub. adminstr. employment and tng. Office of Gov., State of S.C., Columbia, 1976-78, 88—; project coord. Trident Tech. Coll., Charleston, S.C., 1981-82; office mgr. Med. U. S.C., Charleston, 1983-85; coord. bus. svcs. AMI East Cooper Community Hosp., Mt. Pleasant, S.C., 1985-87; mktg. rep. R.L. Bryan Co., Columbia, 1987; pub. adminstr. S.C. Dept. Social Svcs., Columbia, 1988; pub. adminstr., employment and tng. Office Gov. State S.C., Columbia, 1988-89; mem. employment and tng. staff City of Norfolk (Va.) Div. Soc. Svcs., 1990-91; social sci. analyst Naval Edn. and Tng. Ctr. Family Svc. Ctr., Newport, R.I., 1992-96; program coord. Naval Edn. and Tng. Ctr. Family Svc. Ctr., Newport, R.I., 1996—; rsch. assoc. U. R.I., Kingston, 1999; project dir. U. R.I. Family Resource Partnership, Providence, 1999; marine rsch. specialist Sea Grant Coll. Program, U. R.I. Narragansett Bay Campus, 2002—03; supervisory planner RI Water Resources Bd., Providence, 2003—. Editor newsletter Friends of Library, 1982-84. Sec. Friends of Charleston County Libr., 1981-82, pres. 1982-84; bd. dirs. Wando High Sch. Local Adv. Coun., Mt. Pleasant, 1981-84, Newport Armed Svcs. YMCA, 1996-98; pres. Wando High Sch. PTA, 1982-83, editor newsletter, 1982-85; vol. Navy-Marine Corps Relief Soc., 1993-96; mem. Newport County Coun. Cmty. Svcs., 1996-98; publicity chmn. Navy-Marine Corps Relief Soc., Newport, 1993-94; asst. dir., fin. U. R.I. Sea Grant Program, 2002; supr. planner R.I. Water Resources Bd., Providence, 2003—. Grantee Marine Rsch. Specialist Sea Grant Coll. Program, U. R.I., Narragansett, 2002—03. Mem. Am. Soc. Pub. Adminstrs.,R.I. Orchid Soc. (sec. 2000), Ocean State Orchid Soc. (sec. 2003), Nat. Marine Educators Assn. Democrat. Roman Catholic. Avocations: writing fiction, water colors, gardening. Home: 472 Gardiner Rd West Kingston RI 02892-1068 Office: RI Water Resources Bd 100 N Main St 5th Flr Providence RI 02903 E-mail: ladyslip1@mindspring.com.

O'KEEFE, ELLEN MARGARET, special education educator; b. Newburyport, Mass., Sept. 19, 1954; d. Richard James and Ellen Honora O'Keefe. BA in Elem. and Spl. Edn., Rivier Coll., Nashua, N.H., 1976; MA in Learning Disabilities, U. No. Colo., Greeley, 1979. Spl. edn. tchr. Brown Sch., Newburyport, Mass., 1976—78, Twin Spruce Jr. High Sch., Gillette, Wyo., 1980—84, West HS, Waterloo, Iowa, 1984—87; tchr. Carroll Sch., Lincoln, Mass., 1987—89; spl. edn. tchr. Springville (Iowa) Cmty. Schs., 1989—98; asst. prof. Mt. Mercy Coll., Cedar Rapids, Iowa, 1998—. Author: Tools for Conflict Resolution: A Practical K-12 Program based on Peter Senge's 5th discipline. Parish coun. Sacred Heart Ch., Walker, Iowa, 1999—2002. SCRIPT Family Interagency grantee, SCRIPT of Iowa, 2001—03. Mem.: Assn. for Curriculum and Supervision, Learning Disabilities Assn., Coun. for Exceptional Children. Independent. Roman Catholic. Avocations: reading, travel, cooking, needlepoint. Home: 612 Sunrise Ct Center Point IA 52213 Office: Mount Mercy Coll 1330 Elmhurst Dr NE Cedar Rapids IA 52402 E-mail: eokeefe@mtmercy.edu.

O'KEEFE, KATHERINE PATRICIA, elementary school educator; b. Long Beach, N.Y., Mar. 6, 1971; d. Raymond John and Therese Marie (Lederman) O'K. Student, U. Fribourg (Switzerland), 1991-92; BA, Providence College, 1993. Lic. FCC.; provisional cert. tchr., N.Y., 2003. Journalist Merrick (N.Y.) Life, 1993; adminstrv. asst. Grey Entertainment, N.Y.C., 1994-95, acct. coord., 1995-97; acct. exec. Rabasca & Co., Melville, NY, 1997—98; elem. sch. tchr. in art Pub. Sch. 151, Bklyn., 1998—2001, tchr. 2d grade, 2001—. Prodn., script and continuity asst. Piccioli and Piccioli Prodns., N.Y.C., 1995. Roman Catholic. Avocations: guitar, piano, scuba diving, art, songwriting. Home: 1992 Debra Ct North Merrick NY 11566-1732 Office: PS 151 763 Knickerbocker Ave Brooklyn NY 11207

O'KEEFE, KATHLEEN MARY, state government official; b. Butte, Mont., Mar. 25, 1933; d. Hugh I. and Kathleen Mary (Harris) O'Keefe; m. Nick M. Baker, Sept. 18, 1954 (div. 1970); children: Patrick, Susan, Michael, Cynthia, Hugh, Mardeen. BA in Comm., St. Mary Coll., Xavier, Kans., 1954. Profl. singer, mem. Kathie Baker Quartet, 1962-72; rsch. cons. Wash. Ho. of Reps., Olympia, 1972-73; info. officer Wash. Employment Security Commn., Seattle, 1973-81, dir .pub. affairs, 1981-90, video dir., 1990-95, ret., 1995. Freelance writer, composer, producer, 1973—. Author: Job Finding In the Nineties, The Third Alternative, handbook on TV prodn., (children: So You Want to be President, 1995; composer numerous songs, also writer, dir., prodr. numerous spots. Founder, pres. bd. Eden, Inc., visual and performing arts, 1975—; pub. rels. chmn. Nat. Women's Dem. Conv., Seattle, 1979, Wash. Dem. Women, 1976-85; bd. dirs., composer, prodr., dir. N.Y. Film Festival, 1979; Dem. candidate Wash. State Senate, 1968. Recipient Silver medal Seattle Creative Awards Show for composing, directing and producing Rent A Kid, TV Pub. Svc. spot, 1979. Mem. Wash. Press Women. Roman Catholic. Home: 4426 147th Pl NE # A12 Bellevue WA 98007-7191 Office Phone: 425-881-7800. E-mail: kathie@nwrain.com.

O'KEEFE, NANCY JEAN, retired real estate company executive; b. Mpls., Jan. 26, 1926; d. Dana Charles and Bonnie Theresa (Lane) Eckenbeck; m. John Robert O'Keefe, Sept. 11, 1946 (div. June 1977); children: Teresa O'Keefe Ankeny, J. Patrick, Leslie O'Keefe Kelly, Bridget O'Keefe Gidley, Elizabeth, Peter. BS in Social Welfare, U. Minn., 1973. Cert. real estate specialist, Minn., real estate appraiser, Minn.; grad. Real Estate Inst. Sales agt. Harvey Hansen Realty, Edina, Minn., 1976-87; pres., mgr., agt. lst Mpls. Realty, Edina, 1987-92; agt. Great. Mpls. Real Estate, 1992-99; ret., 1999—. Mem. 5th Dist. Rep. Com., Mpls., 1951-52, Minn. Rep. Ctrl. Com., 1951-52; dist. chmn. fund drive ARC, Mpls., 1956; city chmn. fund drive March of Dimes, Mpls., 1957, 58; bd. dirs. St. Barnabas Hosp., Mpls., 1960-61; pres. Mpls. League Cath. Women, 1974-75. Mem. Minn. Assn. Realtors (bd. dirs. 1990-92), Greater Mpls. Assn. Realtors (bd. dirs. 1986-89, chmn. arbitration bd. 1988, Super Sales Agt. award 1982), Profl. Women's Appraisal Assn., Am. Arbitration Assn. (panel), Pi Beta Phi. Roman Catholic. Avocations: writing, poetry, watercolors, bridge, reading. Home: 6400 York Ave S Apt 602 Minneapolis MN 55435-2352 E-mail: nokeefen@aol.com.

O'KEEFE, PATRICIA M. state legislator; b. Methuen, Mass., Feb. 28, 1955; BA in Psychology, U. N.H. Commr. Seabrook Beach Village Dist., 1989-91; mem. dist. 21 N.H. Ho. of Reps., Concord, mem. health, human svcs. and elderly affairs com. Bd. dirs. Seacoast Vis. Nurses, 1992—, Granite State AIDS consortium, 1995-97; mem. Seabrook Budget Com., 1989-90, 96-97; trustee Seabrook Town Libr., 1995-97. Democrat. Roman Catholic. Home: PO Box 145 Seabrook NH 03874-0145 Office: NH Ho of Reps State Capitol Concord NH 03301

O'KELLEY, WINNIE, editor; m. Patrick McGeehan; 2 children. Grad., Northwestern U., 1984. Asst. copy desk chief Adv. Age, 1985; with Am. Banker, 1988; mng. editor Banking Week; dep. bus. editor NY Times, NYC, 1993—. Recipient Best in Bus. for Overall Excellence Cert. Merit, Am. Bus. Editors and Writers, 2003. Office: NY Times Bus Section 229 W 43rd St New York NY 10036 Office Phone: 646-728-9200.*

OKERLUND, ARLENE NAYLOR, university official; b. Emmitsburg, Md., Oct. 13, 1938; d. George Wilbur and Ruth Opal (Sensenbaugh) Naylor; m. Michael Dennis Okerlund, June 6, 1959 (div. Apr. 1983); 1 dau., Linda Susan. BA, U. Md., 1960; PhD, U. Calif.-San Diego, 1969. Instr. sci. Mercy Hosp. Nursing Sch., Balt., 1959-63; prof. English San Jose (Calif.) State U., 1969-80, 94—, dean humanities and arts, 1980-86, acad. v.p., 1986-93. Cons. Ednl. Testing Svc., Berkeley, Calif., 1976-80 Editor: San Jose Studies, 1975-80; contbr. articles on the humanities to profl. jours. Bd. dirs. World Forum Silicon Valley; mem. Peninsula Banjo Band. Grantee NEH, 1979; grantee San Jose State U., 1971-72. Mem. Philol. Assn. Pacific Coast (sec.-treas. 1975-78), MLA (del. to assembly, west coast rep. 1976-77), Internat. Coun. Fine Arts Deans, Calif. Coun. Fine Arts Deans (pres. 1984-86), Am. Beethoven Soc. (bd. dirs., vice-chair). Democrat. Office: San Jose State U Dept English Washington Sq San Jose CA 95192-0001 E-mail: okerlund@email.sjsu.edu.

OKERSON, ANN SHUMELDA LILLIAN, librarian; d. Jacob and Alexandra Tereshtshenko Shumelda. MLS, U. Calif. Libr. Simon Fraser U., Vancouver, Canada, 1970—85; dir. libr. svcs. Jerry Alper Inc., Eastchester, N.Y., 1985-90; sr. program officer Assn. of Rsch. Librs., Washington, 1990-95; assoc. dir. librs. Yale U., New Haven, 1995—. Adv. bd. Britannica Online, 1995-98, Acad. Press, 1995-98, Serials Rev., 1995—. Editor numerous books; contbr. articles to profl. publs. Named Alumni of Yr. Mt. View Acad., 1995; recipient Best Article Am. Libr. Assn., 1988, 93, Excellence in Libr. Tech., 1998. Avocations: chocolate, traveling, reading. Office: Yale U Libr PO Box 208240 New Haven CT 06520-8240

OKOLSKI, CYNTHIA ANTONIA, psychotherapist, social worker; b. N.Y.C., July 26, 1954; d. Augusto and Valerie (Toffolo) Zaccari; m. Andrzej L. Okolski, Jan. 8, 1983; children: Gabriel, Christian. BA, Hofstra U., 1976; MA, Columbia U., 1978, MSW, 1983; cert. psychoanalytic psychotherapy, Advanced Ctr. Analytic Therapy, 1986. Counselor, instr. Hofstra U., Hempstead, N.Y., 1975-76; recreational dir. Residence for Young Adults Hostel, Hempstead, 1976-78; rsch. asst. Ctr. Policy Rsch., N.Y.C., 1978-79, Ctr. Psychosocial Studies, N.Y.C., 1979-81; group leader Fidel Sch., Glen Cove, N.Y., 1981; rsch. asst. Assn. of Jr. League, N.Y.C., 1982; social worker Children's Aid Soc., N.Y.C., 1983-84, Manhattan Psychiat. Ctr. N.Y.C., 1984-85, psychotherapist Advanced Inst. Analytic Psychotherapy, Jamaica, N.Y., 1986—. Supervising psychotherapist in therapeutic foster care program St. Christopher-Ottillie, 1994—. Mem. NASW, Acad. Cert. Social Workers, Alpha Kappa Delta.

OKOS, MILDRED, city manager; b. L.I., N.Y., July 17, 1913; d. William Fohs and Estelle Solomon; 1 child. Grad. H.S., N.Y.; student, Birds Bus. Sch. Model, sec., sales and mktg. staff Macy's Dept. Stores & Lord & Taylor, N.Y.C., 1940-44; with Floyd Bennett Airport, Bklyn., 1944-48; mgr. sales boutique L.I., N.Y., 1994; exec. dir. Town Village Aircraft Safety & Noise Abatement Gov. Town of Hempstead, N.Y., 1985-99. Office: Town Village Aircraft Safety & Noise Abatement Com 196 Central Ave Lawrence NY 11559-1438

OKOSHI-MUKAI, SUMIYE, artist; b. Seattle; One-woman shows include Gallery Internat., N.Y.C., 1970, Miami Mus. Modern Art, 1972, Galerie Saison, Tokyo, 1982, St. Peter's Ch., Living Room Gallery, N.Y.C., 1987, Viridian Gallery, 1987, 1992, 1996, 1999, Port Washington (N.Y.) Pub. Libr., 1985, NAS, Washington, 1991—92, exhibited in group shows at Bergen Mus. Art and Scis., 1983, Am. Acad. Arts and Scis., 1984, Port Washington Pub. Libr., 1985, Hudson River Mus., 1985, Sao Paulo and N.Y. Culture Exch., 1988, Hyundai Gallery, Pusan, Korea, 1988, Gary Snyder Fine Art, N.Y.C., 2002, Represented in permanent collections The Mitsui & Co., N.Y., Hotel Nikko, Atlanta, Bank of Nagoya, N.Y., Palace Hotel, Guam Island, Port Washington Pub. Libr., Lowe Gallery-U. Miami, Miami Mus. Modern Art, Nat. Women's Edn. Ctr., Saitama-ken, Japan, NAS, Hammond Mus., North Salem, N.Y., The Jane Voorhees Zimmerli Art Mus., N.J., Asian Traditions Modern Expressions; included in Collage-Techniques, 1994. Mem. Nat. Women Artists Assn. (Belle Cramer award Zluta and Joseph Fund award, Ralph Mayer Meml. award, Doris Kreindler Meml. award 2002), Nat. Mus. Women in the Arts (charter mem. 1994).

OKTAVEC, EILEEN M. anthropologist, artist; b. Apr. 9, 1942; d. Albert W. and Margaret (O'Reilley) O. Student, Cooper Union, N.Y.C., 1960-61; BA in Anthropology, SUNY, Stony Brook, 1973; MA in Anthropology, U. Ariz., 1975. Instr. anthropology White Pines Coll., Chester, N.H., 1975-76; art dir. Great Walks, Inc., Goffstown, N.H., 1989—. Author: Answered Prayers: Miracles and Milagros Along the Border, 1995; photographs in: Great Walks of Acadia National Park and Mount Desert, 1990, Great Walks of Southern Arizona, 1991, Great Walks of Big Bend National Park, 1991, Great Walks of the Great Smokies, 1992, Great Walks of Yosemite National Park, 1993, Great Walks of Sequoia and Kings Canyon National Parks, 1994, Great Walks of Acadia National Park and Mount Desert Island, 1994, Great Walks of the Olympic Peninsula, 1999, The Woodland Garden, 1996; exhibited in group shows at Rockport (Mass.) Art Festival, 1977, 78, Berkshire Art Assn., Pittsfield, Mass., 1979, The Ogunquit (Maine) Art Ctr., 1982, 83, N.H. Art Assn., Manchester, 1985, Concord (Mass.) Art Assn., 1988, 91, 92, 96-98, Sharon (N.H.) Art Ctr., 1998. Winner Southwest Book award for Answered Prayers, 1997. Mem. Concord Art Assn., Sharon Arts Ctr. Office: Great Walks Inc PO Box 410 Goffstown NH 03045-0410 Home: PO Box 410 Goffstown NH 03045-0410

OKUN, DEANNA T. government agency administrator; BA in Political Science, Utah State U.; JD, Duke U. Sch. of Law. Research assoc. Competitive Enterprise Inst., Washington; assoc. attorney and mem. of Internat. Trade Group Hogan & Hartson law firm, Washington; legislative asst. to Senator Frank Murkowski; counsel for internat. affairs to Sen. Frank Murkowski, 1993—99; chmn U.S. Internat. Trade Comm., 2002—. Office: US Internat Trade Commission 500 E Street SW Washington DC 20436

O'LAUGHLIN, JOANIE, broadcast executive; b. Pasadena, Calif. Student, San Diego St. Sales rep. Blair TV, 1961-63, nat. sales coord., traffic mgr., 1963-75, ops. mgr., 1975-82, sta. mgr., 1982-95; v.p., gen. mgr. Sta. XETV-TV, San Diego, 1996—. Adv. bd. Shared Vision Found.; bd. trustees San Diego Lions Club Welfare Found. Office: Sta XETV TV 8253 Ronson Rd San Diego CA 92111-2004

OLBRICK, VALERIE LYN, management consultant, information technologist; b. Pitts., Feb. 9, 1959; d. Kenneth Donald and LaVerne Estelle (Aiken) O. BS, Grove City Coll., 1981. Sr. telecomm. analyst Timken Co., Canton, Ohio, 1981-85; network planning mgr. Leaseway Transp. Inc., Cleve., 1985-87; group mgr. Network Strategies, Fairfax, Va., 1987-88; sr. mgr. Ernst & Young, L.A., 1988-95, prin. N.Y.C., 1995, dir. tech. planning and deployment Internat. divsn., 1995—. Avocations: sailing, skiing, bicycling, gardening, reading. Office: Ernst & Young Internat 787 7th Ave Fl 14 New York NY 10019-6085

OLD, MARNIE LORRAINE, sommelier, consultant; b. Evanston, Ill., Dec. 10, 1969; d. Daniel James Old and Margaret Doreen Phimister. Cert. advanced sommelier Ct. of Master Sommeliers. Sommelier, capt. Chanterelles Restaurant, Phila., 1994—96; sommelier Striped Bass Restaurant, Phila., 1996—98; beverage dir. Meal Ticket Inc., Phila., 1996—2001; wine educator, cons. Old Wines LLC, Phila., 2001—. Author: (wine column) Phila. (Pa.) Mag., 2001. Named Best Sommelier, Phila. Mag., 2001. Office: Old Wines 710 Chestnut St #3 Philadelphia PA 19106

OLDHAM, MAXINE JERNIGAN, real estate broker; b. Whittier, Calif., Oct. 13, 1923; d. John K. and Lela Hessie (Mears) Jernigan; m. Laurance Montgomery Oldham, Oct. 28, 1941; 1 child, John Laurence. AA, San Diego City Coll., 1973; student Western State U. Law, San Diego, 1976-77, LaSalle U., 1977-78; grad. Realtors Inst., Sacramento, 1978. Mgr. Edin Harig Realty, LaMesa, Calif., 1966-70; tchr. Bd. Edn., San Diego, 1959-66; mgr. Julia Cave Real Estate, San Diego, 1970-73; salesman Computer Realty, San Diego, 1973-74; owner Shelter Island Realty, San Diego, 1974—. Author: Jernigan History, 1982, Mears Geneology, 1985, Fustons of Colonial America, 1988, Sissoms. Mem. Civil Svc. Commn., San Diego, 1957-58. Recipient Outstanding Speaker award Dale Carnegie. Mem. Nat. Assn. Realtors, Calif. Assn. Realtors, San Diego Bd. Realtors, San Diego Apt. Assn., Internationale des Professions Immobilieres (internat. platform speaker), DAR (vice regent Linares chpt.), Colonial Dames 17th Century, Internat. Fedn. Univ. Women. Republican. Roman Catholic. Avocations: music, theater, painting, genealogy, continuing edn. Home: 3348 Lowell St San Diego CA 92106-1713 Office: Shelter Island Realty 2810 Lytton St San Diego CA 92110-4810

OLDHAM, PHYLLIS VIRGINIA KIDD, retired librarian; b. Mar. 19, 1926; d. Hulbert Haven and Grace Ellene (Doup) Kidd; 1 child, Stephen Kidd. BS, Purdue U., 1948; MS, Butler U., 1966. Tchr. English Jefferson H.S., Lafayette, 1950—51; tchr., libr. Tudor Hall Sch., Indpls., 1954—70; libr. Park Tudor Sch., 1970—91; ret., 1991. Mem. exec. bd. Central Ind. Area Library Svcs. Authority, sec., 1983—85. Mem. People-to-People Internat., dist. dir. Student Ambassador Program, 1970—80; chmn. bd. Cen. Christian Ch., Indpls., 1979—81, 1989—90, bd. trustees, 1991; mem. vol. council Indpls. Zool. Soc. Mem.: Assn. Ind. Sch. Librs., Pi Beta Phi, Delta Kappa Gamma (treas. Alpha Eta chpt. 1974—80), Kappa Delta Pi. Home: 7015 Warwick Rd Indianapolis IN 46220-1050

OLDS, JACQUELINE, psychiatrist, educator; b. Springfield, Mass., Jan. 4, 1947; d. James and Marianne (Ejier) O.; m. Richard Stanton Schwartz, Aug. 26, 1978; children: Nathaniel Leland, Sarah Elizabeth. BA, Radcliffe Coll., 1967; MD, Tufts U., 1971. Diplomate Am. Bd. Psychiatry and

Neurology. Resident in adult psychiatry Mass. Mental Health Ctr., Boston, 1974; resident in child psychiatry McLean Hosp., Belmont, Mass., 1976, assoc. attending child psychiatrist, 1979—; psychiatrist-in-charge inpatient unit McLean Hall-Mercer Children's Ctr., Belmont, 1976-79; assoc. child psychiatry Beth Israel Hosp., Boston, 1979—; cons. in child psychiatry Mass. Gen. Hosp., Boston, 1994—. Instr. psychiatry Harvard U. Med. Sch, Boston, 1976-86; asst. prof. clin. psychiatry, 1986-2000, assoc. clin. prof. psychiatry, 2000—; cons. North Shore Mental Health Ctr., Salem, 1981-82. Author: Overcoming Loneliness in Every Day Life, 1996, Marriage in Motion, 2000, editor Clin. Challenges column in Harvard Rev. of Psychiatry; contbr. articles to profl. jours.; author (translator into Spanish): Matrimonio in Moviemento. Recipient Mentoring award Mass. Gen. Hosp. Dept. Child Psychiatry, 1998. Disting. fellow, Am. Psychiat. Assn.; mem. Mass. Psychiat. Soc. (ethics com. 1988-93, mem. pub. affairs com. 1992—), Am. Acad. Child Psychiatry, Am. Psychoanalytic Assn., New England Coun. Child and Adolescent Psychiatry (bd. dirs.). Democrat. Avocations: piano, writing, cooking, watercolors.

OLDSON, JO, state representative, lawyer; b. Ft. Dodge, Iowa, May 15, 1956; BA, JD, Drake U. First dep. ins. commr., 1994—99; policy advisor to Gov. Tom Vilsack, 1999—2000; state rep. dist. 61 Iowa Ho. of Reps., 2003—; mem. commerce, regulation and labor com.; mem. govt. oversight com.; mem. state govt. com.; mem. ways and means com.; mem. oversight appropriations subcom. Vol. Young Women's Resource Ctr. Democrat. Office: State Capitol East 12th and Grand Des Moines IA 50319

O'LEARY, KATHLEEN ANN, writer; b. Washington, Dec. 17, 1946; d. Patrick Christopher and Hilda Elizabeth (Gobrecht) O'Leary; children: Kara Ann Topper, Scott Patrick Thompson, Ryan Arthur Thompson, Kelly Marie Shifflett. Student, Montgomery Jr. Coll., 1964-66, Colo. State U., 1973-74; BS in Bus. Adminstrn., U. Md., 1975. Acct. exec. Sta. WSBT-AM-FM-TV, South Bend, Ind., 1972-74; mgr. advt. and promotion Sta. WGHP-TV, High Point, N.C., 1978-83; acct. exec. Wheat, First Securities, Greensboro, N.C., 1983-85; investment broker Legg Mason Wood Walker, Greensboro, 1985-88; investment exec. Ferris, Baker Watts, Inc., Bethesda, Md., 1988-90. Legal sec., paralegal complex civil and criminal investigation and def. practice Washington, 1988-94; legal staffer Morgan, Lewis & Bockius LLP, Washington; lectr. in investment field, 1996-2002. Exec. prodr. TV documentary Classic Memories, 1985. Founder, 1st pres., bd. dirs. Big Brothers/Big Sisters of High Point, 1981-85; founder, sec.-treas. Furniture City Classic, Inc., High Point, 1981-88; founder, bd. dirs. Henredon Classic LPGA Golf Tourament, High Point, 1981-88; mem. Leadership High Point, 1987-89; Challenge: High Point grad. and steering com. mem. High Point C. of C., 1984-85; bd. dirs. met. bd. YMCA of High Point, 1981. 82, Adams Meml. YWCA, High Point, 1985-87, Salvation Army Boys Club, 1980-81, Vols. to Ct., Guilford County, 1980-81; Sunday sch. tchr. Immaculate Heart of Mary Ch., High Point, 1980-87, exec. bd. mem. Greater Washington Open LPGA Golf Tourament, 1980-90. Democrat. Roman Catholic. Avocations: creative writing, classical piano. Office Phone: 301-549-3114. E-mail: kathleenoleary@msn.com.

O'LEARY, PRENTICE LEE, lawyer; b. L.A., May 6, 1942; BA, UCLA, 1965, JD, 1968. Bar: Calif. 1969. Ptnr. Sheppard, Mullin, Richter & Hampton, L.A., 1974—. Bd. dirs. Legal Aide Found. L.A., 1987—93, 2000—. Mem. ABA (bus. bankruptcy com.), State Bar Calif., Los Angeles County Bar Assn. (chmn. bankruptcy com., chmn. comml. law and bankrupt sect. 1985-86), Am. Coll. Bankruptcy Profls., Order of Coif. Office: Sheppard Mullin Richter & Hampton 333 S Hope St Fl 48 Los Angeles CA 90071-1406

OLEEN, LANA, state legislator; b. Kirksville, Mo., Apr. 26, 1949; d. Robert James and Frances (Primm) Scrimsher; m. Kent E. Oleen; children: Brooke, Bentson. BS in Edn., Ks. State Tchrs. Coll., 1972; MS in Curriculum, Emporia State U., 1977. Tchr., Council Grove, Kans., 1972-74, St. George, Kans., from 1978; communications coord. Woodward-Clyde Cons., San Francisco, 1974-75; dir. communication Kans. Dept. Human Resources; mem. Kans. State Senate, 1988—. Mem. Rep. Precinct Com., 1978—. Active Kans. Rep. Women, Riley County Rep. Women. Mem. NEA, Nat. Coun. Tchrs. of English. Lutheran. Office: Kansas Senate State Capitol Rm 136-N Topeka KS 66612 Address: 1619 Poyntz Ave Manhattan KS 66502-4148

OLENYIK, DEBRA ANN, minister; b. Danville, Pa., Oct. 24, 1955; d. Richard Rawlings and Agnes Mae (Leiby) Bichner; m. John Robert Olenyik, July 15, 1978; children: Christopher, Kelly. BA, Valparaiso U., 1976; MDiv, Iliff Sch. Theology, 1982. Ordained elder Rocky Mountain Conf., United Meth. Ch. Assoc. min. Christ United Meth. Ch., Ft. Wayne, Ind., 1980—81; chaplain Sch. Mines, Golden, Colo., 1981—82; assoc. min. St. Matthew United Meth. Ch., Frankfort, Ind., 1982—83, Newcastle (Wyo.) United Meth. Ch., 1984—88; min. Montrose/Olathe/Paonia United Meth. Chs., Colo., 1988—94, Wilson United Meth. Ch., Colorado Springs, Colo., 1994—97, Torrington (Wyo.) United Meth. Ch., 1998—. Mem. alumni bd. Iliff Sch. Theology, Denver, 1980—93; mem. bd. global ministry Rocky Mt. Conf., Denver, 2002—; mem. bd. ordained ministry, Colo., 2000—. Mem. adv. bd. H.S. and mid. sch., Torrington, 1999—; convener Goshen County Emergency Housing Bd., Torrington, 2001—; leader overseas mission trips, camp and retreat dir. Mem.: Goshen County Ministerial Assn. (pres. 2002—03), P.E.O. Sisterhood (sec. 2003—), Rotary Internat. Democrat. Avocations: travel, jazz, movies, outdoor activities, tennis. Office: United Meth Ch 2702 Main St Torrington WY 82240

OLESEN, CAROLYN MCDONALD, dance educator, choreographer; b. Blytheville, Ark., Aug. 27, 1963; d. Travis Eugene and Barbara Jean (Myers) McDonald; m. Donald John Olesen Jr., Nov. 3, 2001. BA in Dance, U. Calif., Irvine, 1987; MA in Edn., U. Iowa, 1998; choreographer, Coe Coll., 1998. Instr. dance Kirkwood C.C., Cedar Rapids, Iowa, 1987-90, choreographer, 1987—2001, artistic dir., 1990—2001; owner, pres. McDonald Arts Ctr., Marion, Iowa, 1988—2001; instr. dance Coe Coll., Cedar Rapids, 1989—2001; choreographer show choir All Saints Mid. Sch., Marion, Iowa, 1998-2000; choreographer color guard dance ensemble Washington H.S., Cedar Rapids, 1996-97; instr. fitness, gourmet cooking S.E. C.C., Lincoln, Nebr., 2002—, instr., 2002—; choreographer The Lofte Theatre, Manley, Nebr., 2002. Cons. Jane Boyd Cmty. House, Cedar Rapids, 1993—94; dir. Auburn Dance Team, 2003—. Singer/songwriter Rockit Science, 2000-01, Split Decision, 2001, Dark Horse, 2001--. Avocations: wine tasting, gourmet cooking, gardening, song writing.

OLESKOWICZ, JEANETTE, physician; b. N.Y.C., Oct. 10, 1956; d. John Francis and Helen (Zielinski) Oleskowicz. BA, NYU, 1977; D Chiropractic, N.Y. Chiropractic Coll., 1982; MS, U. Bridgeport, 1984; MD, U. Medicine and Dentistry N.J., 1990. Diplomate Am. Bd. Psychiatry and Neurology, cert. in addiction psychiatry. U.S. immigration officer U.S. Dept. Justice, N.Y.C., 1977; commd. med. officer USAR, 1983, advanced through grades to maj., 1990; resident and intern Eisenhower Army Med. Ctr., Ft. Gordon, Ga., 1990-94; chief psychiatry U.S. Army Hosp., Vicenza, Italy, 1994-95; cons.-liaison psychiatrist Brooke Army Med. Ctr., Tex., 1995-98; staff psychiatrist Value Options, Phoenix, 1998—2001; hospitalist VA Med. Ctr., Roseburg, Oreg., 2001—. Supporter Am. Leprosy Missions, India, Children Internat. Mem.: AMA, Am. Psychiat. Assn. Home: 2515 NW Edenbower 20 Roseburg OR 97470 Office: Dept VA Affairs 913 Garden Valley Blvd Roseburg OR 97470

OLEVSKY, KATHY KILMARTIN, owner, instructor karate school; b. Utica, N.Y., Nov. 17, 1957; d. Arthur F. and Mary Ellen (Benson) Kilmartin; m. Albert Robinson Olevsky, Sep. 27, 1980; children: Joshua, Casey. Grad. H. S., Raleigh, N.C., 1975; student, E. Carolina U., 1975-79; A in mgmt., Am. Martial Arts Inst., 1983. Instr., gen. mgr. Karate Internat., Raleigh, 1979—; physical edn. instr. Meredith Coll., Raleigh, 1990—; dist. mgr. Nature's Sunshine Products, 1993-96. Dir. karate divsn. N.C. Amateur Sports, Raleigh, 1987-92, dir. Am. Martial Arts Assn., Raleigh, 1988—. Author: Practical Self Defense Awareness, 1989, Real Estate Self Protection, 1994, Healthy People/Fit Kid 2000, 1995; editor: Essentials of American Karate Work Book, 1991. Chair Wake County Coun. on Fitness & Health, Raleigh, 1993—, bd. mem. Wake County Sch. Health Advisory Coun., 1995, 96, Youth Fitness Task Force, Raleigh, 1995, 96. Recipient Gold medals (3) N.C. Amateur Sports, Durham, N.C., 1993, award of Excellence Gov. Coun. Fitness & Health, 1994. Roman Catholic. Avocation: 7th degree black belt karate, 2d degree black belt ju jitsu, brown belt judo. Office: Ste 140 4720 Hargrove Rd Raleigh NC 27616-2809

OLEY, NANCY H. psychobiologist, educator; b. Manhattan, NY, Jan. 21, 1946; d. Arthur and Elizabeth Franklin Hurwich; m. Jordan Richard Pola, July 5, 1986; 1 child, Loren Pola ; m. James Leonard Kirkland (div.); m. Robert Carter Oley (div.). Student, Brandeis U., Waltham, Mass., 1963—65; Bachelors, Barnard Coll., 1967; Doctorate, Columbia U., 1973. Postdoctoral fellow in neurophysiology Fla. State U., Tallahassee, 1972—74; asst. prof. psychology Augustana Coll., Rock Island, Ill., 1974—76, Trinity Coll., Hartford, Conn., 1976—83; dir. neurodiagnostic lab. Zuckerman & Zuckerman, MD, Bklyn., 1983—87; postdoctoral fellow neuropsychology Columbia U., N.Y.C., 1983—85; prof. psychology Medgar Evers Coll./CUNY, Bklyn., 1988—. Vis. asst. prof. Columbia U., N.Y.C., 1984, 87; adj. asst. prof. psychology Touro Coll., NY, 1987; chair rev. panel for the undergrad. course and curriculum devel. grants program NSF, Washington, 1992—94; software cons. PSYCH SOFT, Inc. Pres. Barnard Club of Hartford County, Hartford, Conn.; cons. Bklyn. AIDS Task Force, 1989; com. mem. Nassau County Dem. Com., NY. Recipient Presdl. Rsch. award, Medgar Evers Coll., 2000; faculty fellow, Columbia U., 1967—71, postdoctoral fellow, NIMH, 1972—74, Faculty Rsch. award, PSC/CUNY, 1991—92, Instrumentation & Lab. Improvement grantee, NSF, 1991—93, Rsch. grantee, CUNY Office Acad. Affairs, 1994, Software Devel. grantee, Title III, 1994, Faculty Devel. grantee, Medgar Evers Coll., 1994, 1995. Mem.: Soc. for Neurosci., N.Y. Neuropsychology Group (bd. dirs., webmaster 1987), Coun. on Undergrad. Rsch. (psychology councilor 2000—), Ea. Psychol. Assn. (liaison from Medgar Evers Coll. 1992), Am. Psychol. Soc., Psi Chi. Avocations: organic gardening, weaving. Home: 10 Arlington Pl Sea Cliff NY 11579 Office: Medgar Evers Coll/CUNY 1650 Bedford Ave Brooklyn NY 11225 E-mail: oley@mec.cuny.edu.

OLIAN, JOANNE CONSTANCE, curator, art historian; b. N.Y.C. d. Richard Edward and Dorothy (Singer) Wahrman; m. Howard Olian; children: Jane Wendy, Patricia Ann Student, Syracuse U.; BA, Hofstra U., 1969; MA, NYU/Inst. Fine Arts, 1972. Grad. internship Met. Mus., N.Y.C., 1973; asst. curator Mus. of City of N.Y., 1974, curator costume collection, 1975-91; cons. curator Costume Collection, 1992-95, curator emeritus, 1995—. Lectr. Parsons Sch. Design; vis. lectr. Musée des Arts Decoratifs, Paris, summer 1983, 84, 85. Author: The House of Worth: The Gilded Age, 1860-1918, 1982; editor: Authentic French Fashions of the Twenties, 1990, Everyday Fashions of the Forties, 1992, Children's Fashions from Mode Illustrée 1860-1914, 1994, Wedding Fashions, 1862-1912, 1994, Everyday Fashions, 1909-1920, 1995, La Mode Illustrée, 1997, Victorian and Edwardian Fashions, 1998, 80 Godey's Full-Color Fashions Plates, 1838-1880, 1998, Full-Color Victorian Fashion, 1870-1893, 1999, Everyday Fashions of the Sixties, 1999, Parisian Fashions of the Teens, 2002, Everyday Fashions of the Fifties, 2002, Children's Fashions, 1900-1950, 2003; contbr. articles to profl. jours., chpts. to books. Mem. Internat. Council Mus. (costume com.), Costume Soc. Am. (dir. 1976-79, 83 86), Fashion Group (bd. dirs. 1985-86), Centre Internat. d'Etude des Textiles Anciens. Clubs: Cosmopolitan (N.Y.C.). Home and Office: Shepherds Ln Sands Point NY 11050 E-mail: olianhojo@aol.com.

OLIM, DOROTHY, theater administrator; b. Bronx, N.Y., Oct. 14, 1933; divorced Student, Julliard Sch. Music, 1949-50; BFA, Columbia Univ., 1955, MFA, 1956. Owner, operator, pres. Dorothy Olim Assocs., Inc., 1960-87; pres. Krone-Olim Advt. Inc., 1967-87. Founding mem. B'Way-N.Y. Entertainment Industry Wellness Program, 1992—; adv. com. Riverside Stage Co., 1996—. Produced 6 plays; managed over 80 productions. Spl. drama adv. com. to pres. Carnegie-Mellon Univ., Pitts., 1992—. Mem. Assn. Theatrical Press Agents and Mgrs. (bd. govs. 1978-87, sec.-treas. 1987-91), League of Broadway Theatres and Producers (sec./treas. 1961-86), League of Advtsg. Agys. (pres. 1975), League of Profl. Theatre Women (bd. dirs. 1993—, Lee Reynolds award 1997), N.Y. Coalition of Profl. Women in the Arts (spl. adv. 1993—, mem. Tony Awards nom. com. 1996-97). Office: 588 W End Ave New York NY 10024-1732

OLIN, MARILYN, secondary school educator; b. Rochester, N.Y. BA in English, Nazareth Coll. Rochester, 1965; MS in English Edn., SUNY, Brockport, 1971. Nat. bd. cert. tchr. 1999. Tchr. Rochester Diocese Cath. Schs., 1965—68, Rochester Pub. Schs., Duval County (Fla.) Pub. Schs., 1972—, Paxon Sch. for Advanced Studies, Jacksonville, Fla., 1996—. Mem.: Nat. Forensic League, Nat. Bd. for Profl. Tchg. Stds. (bd. mem.). Office: Paxon Sch for Advanced Studies 3239 Norman E Thagard Blvd Jacksonville FL 32254 Office Phone: 904-693-7583 ext 161.

OLINGER, CARLA D(RAGAN), medical advertising executive; b. Cin., Oct. 8, 1947; d. Carl Edward and Selene Ethel (Neal) Dragan; m. Chauncey Greene Olinger, Jr., May 30, 1981. BA, Douglass Coll., 1975. Mgr. info. retrieval services Frank J. Corbett, Inc., N.Y.C., 1976—77; editor, proofreader, prodn. asst. Rolf W. Rosenthal, Inc., N.Y.C., 1977—78, copywriter, 1978—80, copy supr., 1980—82, v.p. copy dept., 1982—83; v.p., group copy supr., adminstrv. copy supr. Rolf W. Rosenthal, Inc., divsn. Ogilvy & Mather, 1984—89; v.p., assoc. creative dir. RWR Advt., 1989; v.p., copy supr. Barnum & Souza, N.Y.C., 1990—92, Botto, Roessner, Horne & Messinger, Ketchum Comm., N.Y.C., 1992—95, Lyons Lavey Nickel Swift, N.Y.C., 1995—. Editor: Antimicrobial Prescribing (Harold Neu), 1979. Mem.: St. George's Soc. N.Y., Ch. Club N.Y. Office: Lyons Lavey Nickel Swift 220 E 42nd St New York NY 10017-5806

OLIPHANT, MARTHA CARMICHAEL, civic worker; b. Providence, Sept. 17, 1935; d. Leonard and Pearl (Kidston) Carmichael; m. S. Parker Oliphant, June 2, 1962 (dec. Jan. 2001); children: Leonard Carmichael, Samuel Duncan. BA, Wellesley Coll., 1957. Lab. asst. NIMH, Bethesda, Md., 1957-63. Bd. govs. Washington Home and Hospice, 1976—. Bd. dirs., past pres. All Hallows Guild, Washington Cathedral, 1971-93; mem. bd. lady visitors Childrens Nat. Med. Ctr., 1971-93, Children's Hosp. Found., 1974-90; mem. Com. of 100 of Fed. City, 1977-86; bd. dirs. Washington Home and Hospice, 1976—, also past pres.; past bd. dirs., v.p. Jr. League Washington; mem. Smithsonian Women's Com., Washington, 1993—. Recipient voluntarism award Jr. League Washington, 1988. Mem. Sulgrave Club (bd. dirs. 1985-88), Evergreen Garden Club (pres. 1989-91). Republican. Episcopalian. Avocation: golf. Home: 4977 Glenbrook Rd NW Washington DC 20016-3222

OLIVEIRA, THERESA RAZZANO, secondary school educator; b. Queens, N.Y., Apr. 3, 1952; d. Pasquale A. and Agnes M. Razzano; m. Antonio M. Oliveira, Aug. 6, 1978; children: Antonio Razzano, Francesca Razzano. BA magna cum laude, Ladycliff Coll., 1973; MA, William Paterson State Coll., 1978. Cert. secondary edn. teaching, student personnel svcs., N.J. High sch. math. tchr. Randolph (N.J.) Twp. Bd Edn. Recipient Non Art Educator award Art Educators N.J., 1989, mini grant N.J. State, 1979-80. Mem. Randolph Edn. Assn. (pres. 2002-, negotiations chair, 1990-2002), N.J. Edn. Assn. (state budget com. 2002-), Nat. Edn. Assn. Rep. Assembly (delegate NEA-RA 1999-), Phi Delta Kappa. Home: 64 Lawrence Rd Randolph NJ 07869-3105

OLIVER, BARBARA ANN, retired apparel executive; b. Coffeeville, Miss., July 1, 1936; d. Raymond Victor Branum, Georgia Rae Caver; m. Collie Oliver, July 17, 1956 (dec. Jan. 1994); children: Mitchell Caver, Susan Annelle. Student, Memphis Art Acad. Cutting supr. Normandie Mills, Coffeeville, 1960—63, FormFit Rogers, McMinnville, Tenn., 1963—91, Alamo Mills, Alamo, Tenn., 1991—93, FormFit Apparel, Lafayette, Tenn., 1993—2001; ret., 2001. Owner gift shop, McMinnville, Tenn., 1993—94; owner antique mall, McMinnville, 1994—98; cons. in field. Active various charitable orgns. Named Congeniality Winner, Ms. Sr. Macon County, 2002; recipient 4-Star award, Tenn. Divsn. Am. Cancer Soc., 1990, Award of Appreciation for Cmty. Svc., WalMart, 2002, numerous other cmty. svc. awards. Mem.: AARP, Am. Legion, Nat. Garden Club, Women of Moose, Ladies Aux. of VFW (nat. info. com. chmn. 89th conv. 2001—02, sec. and treas. 2002—03, pres. 2003—, Mary B. Cochran award Dept. Tenn. 2001—02, Bronze medallion Outstanding Pres. 2001—02). Methodist. Avocations: painting, fishing, dance, gardening, cooking. Home: 1003 Ellington Dr Lafayette TN 37083

OLIVER, DONNA H. secondary school educator; AB, Elon Coll.; MEd, U. N.C.; MS, N.C. State U.; PhD, U. N.C. Tchr. biology Hugh M. Cummings High Sch., Burlington, NC; v.p. academic affairs Bennett Coll., Greensboro, NC, 1989—. Office: Bennett College 900 E Washington St Greensboro NC 27401

OLIVER, ELIZABETH KIMBALL, writer; b. Saginaw, Mich., May 21, 1918; d. Chester Benjamin and Margaret Eva (Allison) Kimball; m. James Arthur Oliver, May 3, 1941 (div. July 1967); children: Patricia Allison (dec.), Dexter Kimball. BA, U. Mich., 1940. Tchr. Dexter (Mich.) High Sch., 1940-41; libr. Sherman (Conn.) Libr. Assn., 1966-75; pres. Sherman (Conn.) Libr. Assn., 1983-84; writer, historian, 1976—. Reporter Sherman Sentinel, 1965-70; editor newsletter Sherman Hist. Soc., 1977-78; columnist Citizen News, Fairfield County, Conn., 1981-83. Author: History of Staff Wives-AMNH, 1961, Background and History of the Palisades Nature Association, 1964, History and Architecture of Grace United Methodist Church, 1990, Legacy to St. Augustine, 1993, Franklin W. Smith and His Casa Monica Hotel, 2000; guest columnist Mandarin News, 1995-97; columnist St. Augustine Record, 1998—, Viewpoint of St. Augustine, 2004. Vol. N.Y. Hist. Soc., N.Y.C., 1961-65; treas. Coburn Cemetery Assn., Sherman, 1976-82; historian Greenbrook-Palisades Nature Assn., Tenafly, N.J., 1962-64; mem. St. Augustine Hist. Soc., Naromi Land Trust (life), Cedar Key Hist. Soc.; adv. bd. IBC (Eng.). Mem. AAUW, Friends of Libr. (life), Inst. Am. Indian Studies, Marjorie Kinnan Rawlings Soc. (charter), St. Augustine Woman's Club (archivist, cert. of appreciation 1990), Sherman Hist. Soc., Mandarin Hist. Soc., Smithsonian Nat. Mus. of the Am. Indian (charter). Republican. Congregationalist. Avocations: sacred choral music, research, reading, piano and dulcimer playing, botany. Home: 2292 Commodores Club Blvd Saint Augustine FL 32080-9161

OLIVER, HEATHER A. See KOT, HEATHER

OLIVER, KATHERINE C. museum director, Exec. dir. Mid Ga. Hist. Soc. Inc., Macon. Office: Mid Ga Hist Soc Inc 935 High St Macon GA 31201-2034

OLIVER, MARY, poet; b. Maple Heights, Ohio, Sept. 10, 1935; d. Edward William and Helen Mary (Vlasak) O. Student, Ohio State U., 1955—56, Vassar Coll., 1956—57. Chmn. writing dept. Fine Arts Work Ctr., Provincetown, Mass., 1972-73, mem. writing com., 1984; Banister poet-in-residence Sweet Briar Coll., 1991-95 William Blackburn vis. prof. creative writing Duke U., 1995; Catharine Osgood Foster prof. Bennington Coll., 1996-2001. Author: No Voyage and Other Poems, 1963, enlarged edit., 1965, The River Styx, Ohio, 1972, The Night Traveler, 1978, Twelve Moons, 1979, American Primitive, 1983, Dream Work, 1986, House of Light, 1990, New and Selected Poems, 1992, A Poetry Handbook, 1994, White Pine, 1994, Blue Pastures, 1995, West Wind, 1997, Rules for the Dance, 1998, Winter Hours, 1999, The Leaf and the Cloud, 2000, What Do We Know, 2002, Owls and Other Fantasies, 2003, Why I Wake Early, 2004, Long Life, 2004; contbr. to Yale U. Rev., Kenyon Rev., Poetry, Atlantic, Harvard mag., others. Recipient Shelley Meml. award, 1970, Alice Fay di Castagnola award, 1973, Cleve. Arts prize for lits., 1979, Achievement award Am. Acad. and Inst. Arts and Letters, 1983, Pulitzer prize for poetry, 1984, Christopher award, 1991, L.L. Winship award, 1991, Nat. Book award, 1992, Lannan award, 1998; Nat. Endowment fellow, 1972-73; Guggenheim fellow, 1980-81. Mem. PEN. Home: care Molly Malone Cook Lit Agy PO Box 619 Provincetown MA 02657-0619

OLIVER, MARY MARGARET, state legislator; BA, Vanderbilt U.; degree in law, Emory U. Bar: Ga., chair individual rights sect., mem. letgis. correctional facilities, servicing coms. Staff atty., mng. atty. Ga. Legal Svcs. Program; former mem. Ho. of Reps., former mem. judiciary, transp., indsl. rels. coms.; mem. Ga. Senate, Atlanta, 1992—, chmn. judiciary com., vice chmn. edn. com., mem. appropriations, ethics, rules coms. Mem. task force Commn. Mental Health, Retardation and Substance Abuse Delivery; adj. prof. Emory U.; asst. prof. law Boston Coll.; former hearing officer Sec. of State Joint Examining Bd., Ga. Dept. Med. Assistance, past assoc. magistrate DeKalb County Magistrate Ct. Past pres. Coun. for Children, Inc.; v.p. bd. dirs. CHARLEE Homes; bd. dirs. Ga. Legal Svc. Program. Honors received Ga. Mcpl. Assn., Parents Support Network, Ga. Psychol. Assn., Mental Health Assn. Metro Atlanta, NASW, Ga. Hosp. Assn., Ga. Coun. on Aging, Ga. Assn. Gifted Children; recipient Disting. Svc. award Ga. Bar Assn., 1996. Mem. Lawyers Club Atlanta. Democrat. Office: State Capitol Rm 421 Atlanta GA 30334 also: Ste 480 150 East Ponce Deleon Ave Decatur GA 30030

OLIVER, NANCY LEBKICHER, artist, retired elementary education educator; b. Stockton, Calif., 1939; d. John B. and Marjorie Lebkicher; m. Douglas C. Oliver, 1963; children: Charles, Elaine. BA with honors, San Jose State U., 1961. Summer playground dir. Recreation Dept., Redwood City, Calif., 1956-61; 1st grade tchr. Redwood City (Calif.) Elem. Sch. Dist., 1961-63; kindergarten tchr. Ukiah (Calif.) Unified Sch. Dist., 1963-67; assoc. tchr. kindergarten San Carlos (Calif.) Elem. Sch. Dist., 1976-81. Shopper for dept. store Macy's, San Francisco, 1975-82; asst. in hist. rsch., 2000—. Sunday sch. dir. St. Peter's Episcopal Ch., Redwood City, 1973-78; active White Oaks PTA, San Carlos, 1973-81, newsletter editor, 1978-81; leader Girl Scouts U.S.A., San Carlos, 1978-81; bd. mem. Sequoia H.S. Ednl. Found., co-chmn., 2000-2002, chmn. 2002—; bd. dirs. San Mateo County Hist. Resources Adv. Bd., 2000-. Mem. AAUW (San Carlos br. newsletter editor 1972-74, editor historic tour booklet 1981, editor historic resources booklet 1989, chmn. historic preservation sect. 1979—, pres. Willits br. 1966-67, co-pres. San Carlos br. 2002—, Named Gift honoree 1976), San Carlos Heritage Assn. (founder, dir. 1995—), Sequoia H.S. Alumni Assn. (founding sec., membership chmn. 1985—, centennial coord. 1992-95, pres. 1996-98, sec. 2oo2-, newsletter editor, 2003-, Unsung Hero award 1998), Internat. Order Rainbow Girls (grand officer Calif. 1957-58, mother advisor Redwood City 1987-89), SeriPrinters (serigrapher 1986—). Democrat. Episcopalian. Avocations: needlework, historic preservation activities, walking, calligraphy, classical music. Home: 147 Belvedere Ave San Carlos CA 94070-4818

OLIVER, PATRICIA, medical assistant; b. Atwater, Calif., July 30, 1954; d. Robert and Helen Raye Wilson; m. Alonzo Charles Oliver, May 1, 1974. AA in Social Sci., Coll. of Sequoias, Visalia, Calif., 1996, AS in Math., Sci. and Engring., 1997, AS in Nursing, 1999. RN, Calif. Supr. data entry Huntington Computing, Corcoran, Calif., 1980-83; data enterer, biller Hillman Health Ctr., Tulare, Calif., 1983-85, lab. asst., 1995—; dep. sheriff, bailiff Tulare County Sheriff's Office, Visalia, 1985-95; med. asst. Visalia

Walk-In Med. Clinic, 1995—. Rschr. chemistry dept. Coll. of Sequoias, 1997—; sci. nursing tutor, 1995—. Mem. NAFE, Am. Chem. Soc., Math., Sci. and Engring. Achievement Assn. Avocations: aerobics, softball, reading, Karate, relating at home. Home: 23434 5 l/2 Ave Corcoran CA 93212

OLIVER, ROSEANN, lawyer; b. Chgo., Oct. 7, 1947; BA, Northwestern U., 1969, JD, Loyola U., 1972. Bar: Ill. 1972, U.S. Dist. Ct. (no. dist.) Ill. 1974, U.S. Ct. Appeals (7th cir.) 1974. Legal writing instr. I.I.T. Chicago-Kent Coll. Law, 1973-74, Loyola U., 1974-75; mem. Cook County Bd. Ethics. Articles editor Loyola Law Jour., 1971-72; contbr. articles to profl. jour. Mem. Ill. State Bar Assn., Chgo. Bar Assn. (spl. counsel 1981-82, chmn. standing com. on litigation 1985-88, amicus curiae com. 1989-95), 7th Cir. Bar Assn., Inns of Ct. Office: Cahill Christian & Kunkle 224 S Michigan Ave Ste 1300 Chicago IL 60604-2583

OLIVER, SUSAN M. air transportation executive; b. Des Moines, Iowa, July 6, 1947; married; 3 children. BS, George Washington U., 1970; JD, U. Denver, 1980. Atty. Kempell, Huffman and Ginder, 1983—84; asst. counsel Wein Airlines, 1984—85; labor rels. cons. City of Reno, 1985—86; counsel employee rels. Am. Airlines, 1986—90, mng. dir. flight svcs., 1990—96, mng. dir. strategic planning, 1996—97, v.p. employee rels., 1997—2000, sr. v.p. human resources, 2000—. Office: AMR Corp 4333 Amon Carter Blvd Fort Worth TX 76155*

OLIVER-SIMON, GLORIA CRAIG, human resources advisor, consultant, lawyer; b. Chester, Pa., Sept. 19, 1947; d. Jesse Harper and Lavinia Craig Cuff; m. James Russell Norwood, Sept. 1970 (div.); 1 child, James Russell Jr.; m. Joseph M. Simon, Jan. 1993. BS, U. Md., 1987; JD, Am. U., 1990, MS, 1992. Bar: Pa. 1991, U.S. Ct. Appeals (fed. cir.) 1994, D.C. 1997. Pers. specialist VA Med. Ctr., Phila., 1974-80; pers./human resources specialist VA Ctrl. Office, Washington, 1980-90, human resources mgr., 1990-97; atty./adviser human resource mgmt./sr. human resources cons. VACO. Mem. VA Work Group on Minority Initiatives, 1990, 93—; VA coord., rep. Coun. for Excellence in Govts. Spkrs. Bur. Project, 1991-92, Pub. Employees Roundtable for Pub. Svc. Recognition Week, 1991-92; subcom. chair Student Employee Programs, Office of Pers. Mgmt. Work Group, 1993; coord. VA Caring and Courtesy Campaign Focus Group, 1993; mem. VA Veterans Health Adminstrn. Nursing Shortage Task Group, 1987, 93, VA Work Group on the Nat. and Cmty. Svc. Program, 1993-94, 95-96, Veterans Health Adminstrn. Healthcare Reform Work Group on Customer Svc., 1993-94; VA's Nat. Com. on Employment of Disabled Vets. and People with Disabilities, 1992-93; VA Office Human Resources Mgmt. coord. Pres.'s Com. on Employment of Persons with Disabilities/Dept. of Def. Student Employment Initiative, 1994-95; VA Office of Human Resources Mgmt. steering com. 1994-96; mem. Dept. of Energy Student Employment Task Group, 1994-96; VACO coord. Welfare to Work Initiative, 1997—; VACO coun. mem. VA Early Mediation Program, 1999—; mem. VACO Workgroup on Position Sensitivity and Suitability Adjudication, 1999—; mentor VA VACO Fed. Women's Program, 1999—. Bd. dirs. So. PG County Cmty. Charities, Inc., 1999—, pres., CEO, 2000. Mem. ABA, Fed. Bar Assn., Nat. Bar Assn., Fed. Cir. Bar Assn., D.C. Bar Assn., Bar Assn. of D.C., Phi Delta Phi, U. Md. Alumni Assn. (mentor program), Am. U. Alumni Assn. (admissions com., mentor program for grad. and law students), Leadership VA Alumni Assn. (chair promotions com. 1997-2000), AKA Sorority Inc., DAV Aux. (fed. unit 1), Zonta Internat., Am. Legion Aux. Avocations: reading, traveling. Home: 809 Braeburn Dr Fort Washington MD 20744-6022 Office: Dept Vets Affairs 810 Vermont Ave NW Washington DC 20420-0001

OLIVER-WARREN, MARY ELIZABETH, retired library science educator; b. Hamlet, N.C., Feb. 23, 1924; d. Washington and Carolyn Belle (Middlebrooks) Terry; m. David Oliver, 1947 (div. 1971); children: Donald D., Carolyn L.; m. Arthur Warren, Sept. 14, 1990 (dec. Feb. 1995). BS, Bluefield State U., 1948; MS, South Conn. State U., 1958; student, U. Conn., 1977. Cert. tchr., adminstr. and supr., Conn.; cert. pub. sch. substitute tchr., K-12, N.J. Media specialist Hartford (Conn.) Pub. Schs., 1952-86; with So. Conn. State U., New Haven, 1972—, asst. prof. Sch. Libr. Sci. and Instructional Tech., 1987-95, ret., 1995; substitute tchr. K-12 Windsor, Conn., 1999—. Mem. dept. curriculum com. So. Conn. State U., 1987-95, adj. prof., 1995—; cert. substitute tchr. Somerset County Pub. Schs., 1997—; cert. substitute tchr. Windsor, Conn. Sch. Sys., 1999-. Author: My Golden Moments, 1988, The Elementary School Media Center, 1990, Text Book Elementary School Media Center, 1991, I Must Fight Alone, 1991, (textbook) I Must Fight Alone, 1994. Mem. ALA, Conn. Ednl. Media Assn., Black Librs. Network N.J. Inc., Assn. Ret. Tchrs. Conn., Black and Hispanic Consortium, So. Conn. State U. Women's Assn., Cicuso Club (v.p.), Friends Club (v.p.), Delta Kappa Gamma, Alpha Kappa Alpha. Avocations: reading, music, piano, walking. Home: 224 High Path Rd Windsor CT 06095-4103 Office: So Conn State U 501 Crescent St New Haven CT 06515-1330

OLIVIER, KATHY, college basketball coach; b. Placentia, Calif. 1 child, Alexis. Student, Calif. State U., Fullerton; grad., U. Nev., 1982. Various coaching positions U. Nev., U. Calif.-Irvine, U. So. Calif., 1981-86; asst. coach UCLA Bruins, 1986; reached NCAA Sweet 16, 1991-92; head coach UCLA Bruins, 1993—; finished 2d in conf. (sch. record), 1997-98; ranked 14th in NCAA, 1998-99. Office: c/o Athletic Dept UCLA Women's Basketball PO Box 951361 Los Angeles CA 90095-1361

OLLIE, PEARL LYNN, artist, singer, songwriter; b. Highland Park, Mich., Oct. 15, 1953; d. Sam and Estelle Theresa Ollie; m. Christopher John Keyes, Nov. 29, 1975 (div. Nov. 1978); 1 child, Shane Michael Fiondella. Student, Henry Ford C.C., Dearborn, Mich., 1988-89, Soc. Arts and Crafts Coll., 1971-74, Ctr. for Creative Study, 1980-81. Tchr. ceramics Detroit Head Start, Mt. Zion, Mich., 1973; logo designer, platemaker, printer and painter Island Art Ctr., St. Simons Island, Ga., 1976-79; sec., receptionist High Performance Tube Inc., St. Simons Island, 1976-79; personal legal sec. State Senator Bill Littlefield, St. Simons Island, 1979; art coord., booking agt. Club Savoy Tivoli, San Francisco, 1979; tchr. art Redmond Hall, Skamokawa, Wash., 1980; artist Hollywood Costumes, Dearborn, 1980-90; account mgr. ins. Dr. Sheryl A. Ollie, Lynn, Mass., 1990; staff artist, acting, costumes Creative Currents, Ferndale, Mich., 1990—; art tchr. Art in Nahant, Mass., 1991-97. Make-up artist Paramount Costumes (was Hollywood Costumes), Dearborn; art tchr. music St. Lukes Montessori Sch., Detroit; artist Mich. Art and Design, Detroit, Dearborn Awnings, Lincoln Park, Mich.; instr. Aups, Provence, France, 1997. Make-up artist TV commls. and shows, movies; commd. portrait artist, illustrator; guest TV program All Star Kids. Co-pres. Nahant PTO, Johnson Sch., 1991-92; tchr. 8th grade religious edn.; vocalist area ch. chorus; choir dir. St. Anselms; vocal instr. Axis Music Musicians Inst.; instr. art, music and drama Hope of Detroit Acad. Roman Catholic. Avocations: paint, sculpting, singing, writing, piano. Home and Office: 805 Switchgrass Cocoa FL 32926

OLMSTEAD, MARJORIE ANN, physics educator; b. Glen Ridge, N.J., Aug. 18, 1958; d. Blair E. and Elizabeth (Dempwolf) Olmstead. BA in Physics, Swarthmore Coll., 1979; MA in Physics, U. Calif., Berkeley, 1982, PhD, 1985. Rsch. staff Palo Alto (Calif.) Rsch. Ctr. Xerox Corp., 1985-86; asst. prof. physics U. Calif., Berkeley, 1986-90, U. Wash., Seattle, 1991-93, assoc. prof., 1993-97, prof., 1997—. Prin. investigator sci. materials divsn. Lawrence Berkeley Lab., 1988—93. Contbr. articles to profl. jours. Named Presdl. Young Investigator, NSF, 1987; recipient Devel. award, IBM, 1986, 1987, Rsch. award, A. von Humboldt Found., 2000. Fellow: Am. Phys. Soc. (chair com. on status of women in physics 1999, Maria Goeppart-Mayer award 1996), Am. Vacuum Soc. (Peter Mark Meml. award 1994); mem.: Assn. Women in Sci., Am. Assn. Physics Tchrs., Sigma Xi, Phi Beta Kappa. Office: U Washington Dept Physics PO Box 351560 Seattle WA 98195-1560

OLMSTED, AUDREY JUNE, communications educator, department chairman; b. Sioux Falls, S.D., June 5, 1940; d. Leslie Thomas and Dorothy Lucille (Else) Perryman; m. Richard Raymond Olmsted; 1 child, Quenby Anne. BA, U. No. Iowa, 1961, MA, 1963; PhD, Ind. U., 1971. Comm. instr. Boston U., 1964-71, acting chair comm., 1972-73, asst. prof. comm., 1971-74; debate coach R.I. Coll., Providence, 1978-92, asst. prof. comm., 1987—, chmn. dept. of comm., 1999—, internat. student advisor, 1980—. Text editor Prentice-Hall Pub., 1986-88. Recipient Faculty award R.I. Coll. Alumni Assn., 1987. Mem. Nat. Assn. Fgn. Student Advisors, Eastern Comm. Assn., Nat. Comm. Assn. Democrat. Office: RI Coll Dept Comm 600 Mount Pleasant Ave Providence RI 02908-1924

OLMSTED, RUTH MARTIN, humanities educator; b. Albany, N.Y., Oct. 26, 1950; d. Sterling Pitkin and Barbara (Starr) O.; m. Lawrence Daniel Syzdek, Oct. 27, 1990. Student, Oberlin Coll., 1968-69; AB in Lit. and Lang./History and Govt., Wilmington Coll., 1972; MA in Comparative Lit., U. Wis., 1973, PhD in Comparative Lit., 1976. Cert. tchr., Iowa, N.Y. Adj. faculty mem. in sociology Chatfield Coll., St. Martin, Ohio, 1974-75; adj. faculty mem. in writing and phys. edn. Wilmington (Ohio) Coll., 1975-77; adj. faculty mem. in writing, speech and adult basic edn. So. State Coll., Wilmington, 1975-77; asst. prof. English, drama and speech William Penn Coll., Oskaloosa, Iowa, 1977-82; substitute tchr. 10 sch. dists., So. Iowa, 1982-83; instr. in English and humanities Emma Willard Sch., Troy, N.Y., 1983-89; asst. prof. speech Sage Jr. Coll. of Albany, N.Y., 1989-93; mng. editor assessment Regents Coll./Excelsior Coll., Albany, 1993—, asst. dean for test development, 1999—. Mem. workshops in medieval music-drama NEH, 1979, 81. Editor, desktop music pub. Theatre Wagon, 1994—; editor, translator: (plays) Crown Light Editions: Ordo Prophetarum, 1982, Iconia Sancti Nicolai, 1986. Life mem. Girl Scouts U.S., 1959—; mem. policy, pers. com., ann. meeting and gen. coms. Friends Com. on Nat. Legislation, Washington, 1979—. Ind. Study in Humanities fellow NEH, 1988. Mem. MLA, Nat. Coun. Tchrs. English, Soc. Tech. Comm., Tchrs. and Writers Collaborative, Country Dance and Song Soc. Am., Internat. Boethius Soc., Pokingbrook Morris Dancers (squire, foreman, treas. 1984—). Avocations: music, dance, raising sheep, camping, hiking, swimming. Office: Excelsior Coll Assessment 7 Columbia Cir Albany NY 12203-5159

OLNESS, KAREN NORMA, pediatrics and international health educator; b. Rushford, Minn., Aug. 28, 1936; d. Norman Theodore and Karen Agnes (Gunderson) O.; m. Hakon Daniel Torjesen, 1962. BA, U. Minn., 1958, BS, MD, 1961. Diplomate Am. Bd. Pediat., Am. Bd. Med. Hypnosis. Intern Harbor Gen. Hosp., Torrance, Calif.; resident Nat. Children's Hosp. Med. Ctr., Washington; asst. prof. George Washington U., Washington, 1970-74; assoc. prof. U. Minn., Mpls., 1974-87; prof. pediat., family medicine and internat. health Case Western Res. U., Cleve., 1987—. Named Outstanding Woman Physician, Minn. Assn. Women Physicians, 1987; recipient Christopherson award Am. Acad. Pediat., 1998, Aldrich award, Am. Acad. Pediat., 1999, Ann. award Soc. Devel. and Behavioral Pediat., 2003; named to Cleve. Med. Hall of Fame, 2000. Fellow Am. Acad. Pediat. (chair internat. health sect. 2001), Am. Acad. Family Physicians, Am. Soc. Clin. Hypnosis (pres. 1984-86), Soc. Clin. and Exptl. Hypnosis (pres. 1991-93); mem. Soc. for Behavioral Pediat. (pres. 1991-92), Northwestern Pediat. Soc. (pres. 1977), Internat. Hypnosis Soc. (pres. 2003—). Office: Case Western Res U 11100 Euclid Ave Cleveland OH 44106-1736 Office Phone: 216-368-0072. E-mail: kno@cwru.edu.

OLNEY, NANCY HELEN, secondary school educator; b. Montgomery, Ala., Jan. 1, 1954; d. George W. and Virginia E. Olney. BS in Edn., Auburn (Ala.) U. Cert. tchr. Ga. Tchr. Troup County Sch. Sys., La Grange, Ga.; tchr., fine arts chair La Grange H.S. Tchr. Chattahoochee Valley Art Mus., La Grange; artist in residence Ga. Nat. Fair, Perry, 1997. Exhibited in group shows at LaGrange City Sch. Tchrs.' Exhibit, 1993, Jasper Fine Arts Festival, 1994—2001, Breneau U., 1995, 1998, Wesleyan U., 1996, 1998, Gov.'s Show, 1996—98, 2000—03, Kennesaw State U., 1997, Chattahoochee Valley Art Mus. Exhibit of Art Educators, 1997—99, Chattahoochee Valley Exhibit, 1998, Moultrie Traveling Exhibit, 1999—2000, Artist in Residence Invitational, 2001, Electronic Gallery, N.Y., 2001, Miami, 2002. Bd. dirs., art dir. Miss Troup County, La Grange, 1993—96; bd. dirs. Lafayette Soc. Performing Arts, La Grange. Mem.: Ga. Art Educators Assn., Nat. Art Educators Assn. Home: 213 Junewood Dr Lagrange GA 30241 E-mail: nolney@troup.org.

O'LOONEY, PATRICIA ANNE, medical program administrator; b. Bridgeport, Conn., Dec. 2, 1954; d. John Joseph and Marjorie Ellen (Curran) O'L. BA in Molecular Biology, Regis Coll., 1976; MS in Biochemistry, George Washington U., 1978, PhD in Biochemistry, 1982. Rsch. asst. biochemistry dept. George Washington Med. Sch., Washington, 1976-82, teaching asst., 1978-81, rsch. assoc., 1982-84, sr. rsch. scientist, 1984-86, asst. prof. medicine and biochemistry, 1986-88; asst. dir. The Nat. Multiple Sclerosis Soc., N.Y.C., 1988-90, assoc. dir. rsch. and med. programs, 1990-91, dir. rsch. and med. programs, 1991—. Vis. lectr. George Washington Med. Sch., 1988—. Author: Lipoprotein Lipase, 1987; contbr. articles to profl. jours. Recipient New Investigator Rsch. award NIH, 1985. Mem. Am. Soc. for Biochemistry and Molecular Biology, N.Y. Acad. Scis., Assn. for Women in Sci., The Mid-Atlantic Lipid Soc., Sigma Xi, Beta Beta Beta. Republican. Roman Catholic. Avocations: tennis, golf. Office: Nat Multiple Sclerosis Soc 733 3rd Ave New York NY 10017-3204 Office Phone: 212-476-0413. E-mail: patricia.olooney@nmss.org.

O'LOUGHLIN, JUDITH BERYL, elementary and special education educator; b. N.Y.C., July 4, 1944; d. Sol and Mary (Testa) Bernstein; m. Joseph John O'Loughlin; children: Jennifer, Amy. BA, Montclair State U., 1966; MEd, William Paterson U., 1990; post-masters certs., Montclair State U., 1995, 97. Cert. tchr., N.J., English 7-12, 1966, ESL K-12, 1990, elem. edn. K-8, 1990, handicapped K-12, 1995, learning disabilities tchr. cons., 1997. English tchr. grades 9-12 Kearny (N.J.) H.S., 1966-67; English tchr. grade 9 West Brook Jr. H.S., Paramus, N.J., 1967-73; ESL adult educator Evening Sch. for the Fgn. Born, Hackensack, N.J., 1977-95; ESL tchr. Spl. Svcs. Sch. Dist., Ridgewood, N.J., 1986-88; ESL and spl. edn. tchr. Ho-Ho-Kus (N.J.) Pub. Sch., 1988—. Workshop coord. Fall ESL/Bilingual Ann. Conf., William Paterson U., Wayne, N.J., 1990—. Cons. writing process books for ESL students; presenter workshops and demonstrations in field, various regional and nat. confs. ESL trainer Lit. Vols. of Am., Englewood, N.J., 1990. Title VII Bilingual-ESL Tchr. Tng. grantee Fed. Govt., Washington, 1986-90. Mem. NEA, N.J. Edn. Assn., TESOL (awards com. coord. 1995-97, chair 1999—, bd. dirs. 2003), N.J. Tchrs. English to Spkrs. Other Langs.-N.J. Bilingual Educators (sec. exec. bd. 1992-96, v.p. 1997-99, pres. 1999-2001, past pres. 2001-03, sec. Perth Amboy chpt. 1992-96, co-founder, past chair North Region Paramus 1989—), Internat. Reading Assn., Coun. for Exceptional Children, Kappa Delta Pi, Pi Lambda Theta (Excellence in Tchg. Multicultural Edn. award 2003). Office: Ho-Ho-Kus Pub Sch 70 Lloyd Rd Ho Ho Kus NJ 07423-1550 Home: 420 Ustilago Ct San Ramon CA 94583-3069

O'LOUGHLIN, KATIE EILEEN BRIDGET, poet; m. Scott Koblish, July 26, 2003. AA in Theater and Early Childhood Edn., Palomar Coll., San Marcos, Calif., 1984; BS in Computer and Info. Sci., Coleman Coll., La Mesa, Calif., 1986. Poetic License Poetry Slam Inc., 2001. Ind. creator, prodr., host, Hollywood, Calif., 1999—2000. Poet in the schs. mid. sch. and HS, East Los Angeles, Calif., 2001—. Author: (book of poetry) I Can't Pull it Together Enough to Look Like My Poster; author: (performer) (spoken word poetry slam performance) Unknown Man with Soft, Soft skin (1st Pl. (tie) BBC Radio Scotland Internat. Poetry Slam, Edinburgh/Glasgow, Scotland, 2002), They Always Said You're Gonna be Like Your Momma When You Grow Up (3rd Pl. Bristol Poetry Festival 2002 Internat. Poetry Slam in Bristol, Eng., 2002), Skinny be Damned, Concave Bellies Don't Bear Babies, Compassion, Being Tempted to Fall from Grace (3rd Pl. Bristol Internat. Poetry 2000 Slam, 2000), They Always Said You're Gonna be Like Your Momma, Snow Globe, Compassion (2nd Pl. Urban Grind San Diego Poetry Slam, 2003), Snow Globe, They Always Said Your Gonna be Like Your Momma, Being Tempted to Fall from Grace (1st Pl. Orange County Big Damn Poetry Slam, 2003), Compassion, Exact Shade, Skinny be Damned, Concave Bellies Don't Bear Babies (1st Pl. Long Beach Big Damn Poetry Slam, 2002), Being Tempted to Fall From Grace, Exact Shade, Skinny be Damned, Concave Bellies Don't Bear Babies (1st Pl. Urban Grind San Diego Poetry Slam, 2002), Exact Shade, Compassion, Being Tempted to Fall from Grace (2nd Pl. Los Feliz Pig Slam, 2002), Being Tempted to Fall from Grace, Compassion, Exact Shade (1st Pl. Long Beach Big Damn Poetry Slam, 2001); author: (book of poetry) For My Sisters; author: (performer) (spoken word poetry slam performance) Skinny be Damned, Concave Bellies Don't Bear Babies, Compassion, Being Tempted to Fall From Grace (2nd Pl. Urban Grind San Diego Poetry Slam, 2001), (spoken word poetry performance) A Woman Revealed (Acceptance into the LA Women's Theatre Festival 2001, 2001). Performer for benefit show Sojourner Ho. for Abused Women and Children, L.A., Calif., 2001. Mem.: Poetry Slam Inc. Avocations: travel, scuba diving. Personal E-mail: katieo@performancekatieo.com.

O'LOUGHLIN, SANDRA S. lawyer; b. Buffalo, Jan. 15, 1942; BA summa cum laude, Rosary Hill Coll., 1973; JD cum laude, U. Buffalo, 1978. Bar: N.Y. 1979. Atty. Hiscock & Barclay, LLP, Buffalo, 1978-79, ptnr., 1990—. Chmn. character and fitness com. appellate divsn. 4th dept. 8th jud. dist. N.Y. Supreme Ct., 1986—; adj. prof. SUNY Law Sch., Buffalo. Note editor Buffalo Law Rev., 1977-78. Mem. Erie County Legis. Task Force Mental Health, 1979-81; mem. adv. bd. Congregation of Sisters of St. Joseph, 1987—. Mem. ABA (bus. law com. on securities), Nat. Assn. Bond Lawyers, N.Y. State Bar Assn. (ethics com. 1984-94, 2000-03, vice chmn. 1987-92, unauthorized practice of law com. 1998-2002, mem. com. on securities regulation 1999—, com. standards atty. conduct 2004—), Erie County Bar Assn. (ethics com. 1984-87, chmn. 1987-89, corp. law com. 1984, grievance com. 1993—). Office: Hiscock & Barclay LLP 1100 M&T Ctr 3 Fountain Plaza Buffalo NY 14203-1486 Business E-Mail: soloughlin@hiscockbarclay.com.

OLSEN, ASHLEY FULLER, actress; b. Sherman Oaks, Calif., June 13, 1986; d. David and Jarnette Olsen, Mackenzie Olsen (Stepmother). Co-founder, prin. Dualstar Entertainment, Calif., 1993—. To Grandmother's House We Go, 1992, Double, Double, Toil and Trouble, 1993, The Little Rascals, 1994, How the West Was Fun, 1994, It Takes Two, 1995, The Challenge, 2003, Charlie's Angles: Full Throttle, 2003; (TV films) Billboard Dad, 1998; (TV series) Full House, 1987—95, Two of a Kind, 1998; actor, prodr. : So Little Time, 2001; Mary-Kate and Ashley in Action!, 2001; actor, actor, prodr.: (films) Switching Goals, 1999; Passport to Paris, 1999; Our Lips are Sealed, 2000; Winning London, 2001; Holiday in the Sun, 2001; Getting There, 2002; When In Rome, 2002; New York Minute, 2004; (video series) The Adventures of Mary-Kate and Ashley; You're Invited to Mary-Kate and Ashleys; prodr.: (TV series) Tough Cookie, 2002, Fashion Forward: Spring 2001, 2001. Named one of 100 Most Powerful Women in Hollywood, Hollywood (Calif.) Reporter, 2003. Office: Dualstar Publications c/o Thorac and Co 1801 Century Park East Los Angeles CA 90067*

OLSEN, FRANCES ELISABETH, law educator, theorist; b. Chgo., Feb. 4, 1945; d. Holger and Ruth Mathilda (Pfeifer) O.; m. Harold Irving Porter, June 8, 1984. Cert., Roskilde (Denmark) Højskole, 1967; BA, Goddard Coll., 1968; JD, U. Colo., 1971; SJD, Harvard U., 1984. Bar: Colo. 1972, U.S. Dist. Ct. Colo. 1972. Law clk. hon. Arraj U.S. Dist. Ct. Colo., Denver, 1972; lawyer Am. Indian Movement, Wounded Knee, S.D., 1973; pvt. practice Denver, 1973-74; law prof. U. Puget Sound, Tacoma, Wash., 1975-79, St. John's U., Jamaica, N.Y., 1982-83, UCLA, 1984—. Vis. fellow New Coll., Oxford (Eng.) U., 1987; vis. prof. U. Mich., Ann Arbor, 1988, Harvard U., Cambridge, Mass., 1990-91, U. Berlin, Germany, 1995, Ochanomizu U., Tokyo, 1997, U. Tokyo, 1997, Cornell U., 1997, French U. Reunion, 2000, Hebrew U. Jerusalem, 2001, Haifa U., 2001, Tel Aviv U., 2001, 2002, Addis Ababa U., 2002, Bar Ilan U., 2002, Alberto Hurtado, Santiago, Chile; sr. Fulbright prof. U. Frankfurt, Germany, 1991-92; overseas fellow Churchill Coll., Cambridge, Eng., 1997-99; mem. faculty law Cambridge U., 1997-99; del. UN 4th World Conf. on Women, Beijing, China, 1995, NGO Forum, Huairou, China, 1995. Co-author: Cases and Materials on Family Law: Legal Concepts and Changing Human Relationships, 1994; editor: Feminist Legal Theory I: Foundations and Outlooks, 1995, Feminist Legal Theory II: Positioning Feminist Theory Within the Law, 1995; contbr. articles to law revs. Named Outstanding Alumnus U. Colo., 1989. Mem. Assn. Am. Law Schs. (chair jurisprudence sect. 1987-88, chair women in law tchg. sect. 1995-96), Conf. on Critical Legal Studies, European Conf. Critical Legal Studies, Internat. Bar Assn. Avocations: scuba diving, kayaking, long distance hiking. Office: UCLA Sch Law 405 Hilgard Ave Los Angeles CA 90095-1476 Office Phone: 310-825-6083. E-mail: olsen@law.ucla.edu.

OLSEN, JOSEPHINE K. federal agency administrator; B, U. Utah; MSW, PhD, U. Md. Vol. Peace Corps, Tunisia, 1966—68, various positions incuding chief of staff, regional dir. North Africa, Near East, Asia and the Pacific, country dir. Togo, 1979—84, 1989—92; exed. dir. Coun. Internat. Exch. of Scholars, 1992—97; sr. v.p., dir. Peace Corps, 1997—2002, deputy dir., 2002—. Office: Peace Corps 1111 20th St NW Washington DC 20526-0001

OLSEN, JUDITH JOHNSON, reference librarian; b. Manitowoc, Wis., May 13, 1948; d. Gordon Frank Johnson and Ellen Jeanette Knutson; m. Axel K. Olsen (div. 1999); children: Maren, Kristina. BA, Luther Coll., 1970; ML, U. S.C., 1976; MA, Villanova (Pa.) U., 1996. Reader's svcs. libr. Cabrini Coll., Radnor, Pa., 1977-88; ref. and publs. libr. Villanova (Pa.) U., 1988—. Mem. MLA, ALA, Assn. of Colls. and Rsch. Librs. Democrat. Office: Villanova U 800 Lancaster Ave Villanova PA 19085 E-mail: judith.olsen@villanova.edu.

OLSEN, KATHIE LYNN, federal agency administrator; b. Portland, Oreg., Aug. 3, 1952; d. Roland Berg and Gladys Elizabeth (Eldreth) O. BS, Chatham Coll., 1974; PhD, U. Calif., Irvine, 1979. Postdoct. fellow Harvard Med. Sch., Boston, 1979-80; rsch. scientist Long Island Rsch. Inst., Stony Brook, N.Y., 1980-83; rsch. asst. prof. SUNY, Stony Brook, 1982-85, asst. prof., 1985-89; assoc. program dir. NSF, Washington, 1984-86, program dir., 1988, leader neurosci., 1991; assoc. director, tech. Off. Science and Tech. Policy, Washington, 1999—. Adj. assoc. prof. George Washington U., Washington, 1989—; cons. editor Hormones and Behavior, 1988—. Contbr. articles to profl. jours, chapters to books. Mem. Soc. Neurosci., Endocrine Soc., Women in Neurosci., Sod. Study of Reproduction, Internat. Acad. Sex Rsch. Office: Exec Off of the Pres Off Science and Tech Policy EEOB, 17th & Pennsylvania Ave NW Washington DC 20502

OLSEN, MARY-KATE, actress; b. Sherman Oaks, Calif., June 13, 1986; d. David and Jarnette Olsen, Mackenzie Olsen (Stepmother). Co-founder, prin. Dualstar Entertainment, LA, 1993—. Actor: (films) To Grandmother's House We Go, 1992, Double, Double, Toil and Trouble, 1993, The Little Rascals, 1994, How the West Was Fun, 1994, It Takes Two, 1995, The Challenge, 2003; (TV films) Billboard Dad, 1998; (TV series) Full House, 1987—95, Two of a Kind, 1998; actor, prodr. : (films) Switching Goals, 1999; Passport to Paris, 1999; Our Lips are Sealed, 2000; Winning London, 2001; Holiday in the Sun, 2001; Getting There, 2002; When In Rome, 2002; actor: Charlie's Angels: Full Throttle, 2003; actor, prodr. : New York Minute, 2004; (TV series) So Little Time, 2001; Mary-Kate and Ashley in Action!, 2001; (video series) The Adventures of Mary-Kate and Ashley; You're Invited to Mary-Kate and Ashley's; prodr.: (TV series) Tough Cookie, 2002, Fashion Forward: Spring 2001, 2001. Named one of 100

Most Powerful Women in Hollywood, Hollywood (Calif.) Reporter, 2003. Office: Dualstar Publications c/o Thorne and Co 1801 Century Park East Los Angeles CA 90007*

OLSEN, TAVA MARYANNE LENNON, industrial and operations engineering educator; b. Aarhus, Denmark, Dec. 20, 1969; came to U.S., 1990; d. Michael James and Jennifer Anne Lennon; m. Timothy Robert Olsen, Dec. 30, 1995. BSc in Math. with honors, U. Auckland, New Zealand, 1989; MS in Stats., Stanford (Calif.) U., 1992, PhD in Ops. Rsch., 1994. Asst. prof. indsl. and ops. engring. U. Mich., Ann Arbor, 1994—2001; assoc. prof. Olin Sch. Bus., Wash. U. in St. Louis, 2001—. Mem. Inst. Ops. Rsch. and Mgmt. Sci., Sigma Xi. Office: Campus Box 1133 PO Box 1133 Saint Louis MO 63188-1133

OLSEN, TILLIE, author; b. Omaha, Nebr., Jan. 14, 1912; d. Samuel and Ida (Beber) Lerner; m. Jack Olsen; children: Karla, Julie, Kathie, Laurie. LittD (hon.), U. Nebr., 1979, Knox Coll., 1982, Hobart and William Smith Coll., 1984, Clark U., 1985, Albright Coll., 1986, Wooster Coll., 1991, Mills Coll., 1995, Amherst Coll., 1998. Writer-in-residence Amherst Coll., 1969-70; vis. faculty Stanford U., 1972; Writer-in-residence, vis. faculty English M.I.T., 1973-74, U. Mass., Boston, 1974; internat. vis. scholar Norway, 1980; Hill prof. U. Minn., spring 1986; writer-in-residence Kenyon Coll., 1987—. Regents lectr. U. Calif. at San Diego, 1977—, UCLA, 1987; commencement spkr. English dept. U. Calif., Berkeley, 1983, Hobart and William Smith Coll., 1984 Bennington Coll., 1986. Author: Tell Me A Riddle, 1961 (title story received First prize O'Henry award 1961), Rebecca Harding Davis: Life in the Iron Mills, 1972, Yonnondio: From the Thirties, 1974, Silences, 1978, The Word Made Flesh, 1984; editor: Mother to Daughter, Daughter to Mother, 1984; Preface Mothers and Daughters, That Special Quality: A Exploration in Photographs, 1987, 95, Essay Afterword: Saxton's Bright Web in the Darkness, 1998; short fiction published in over 200 anthologies; books translated in 11 langs. Pres. women's aux. Calif. CIO, 1941-43, dir. war relief, 1944-45. Recipient Am. Acad. and Nat. Inst. of Arts and Letters award, 1975, Ministry to Women award Unitarian Universalist Fedn., 1980, Brit. Post Office and B.P.W. award, 1980, Mari Sandoz award Nebr. Libr. Assn., 1991, REA award Dungannon Found., 1994, Disting. Achievement award Western Lit. Assn., 1996; Grantee Ford Found., 1959, NEA, 1968; Stanford Univ. Creative Writing fellow, 1962-64, Guggenheim fellow, 1975-76, Bunting Inst. Radcliffe Coll. fellow, 1985; Tillie Olsen Day designated in San Francisco, 1981. Mem. Authors Guild, PEN, Writers Union. Address: c/o Elaine Markson Agency 44 Greenwich Ave New York NY 10011-8347

OLSEN, VIRGINIA, human services manager; b. L.A., Mar. 6, 1920; d. Alva Millard and Pearl Ann Smith; m. Ralph Orlando Olsen, Feb. 22, 1941; children: Bonnie Lee, Greg Millard. AA, Orange Coast Coll., 1962; MPH, Loma Linda U., 1993. RN. Nurse Co. Hosp., Orange, Calif., 1962-64; nurse supr. Palm Harbor Hosp., Garden Grove, Calif., 1964-68; pediatric nurse Childrens Hosp., Orange, 1968-75; pediatric supr. Cmty. Hosp., Huntington Beach, 1976-80; head nurse pediat. John F. Kennedy Hosp., 1982—84; med. surg. Eisenhower Med. Ctr., Rancho Mirage, Calif., 1984—88; case mgr. Hemet Hosp., Hemet, Calif., 1988-96. Author: (book) Weethee Withee, 1977. Nurse bd. Cmty. Hosp., Huntington Beach; circle leader Congregational Ch., Hemet; regent Daughters Am. Revolution, 1976—; mem. Womens Republican Party, 1979-82. Mem. Calif. Nurses Assn. Avocation: genealogy.

OLSEN-ESTIE, JEANNE LINDELL, golf course owner; b. Everett, Wash., July 17, 1946; d. Carmen David Lindell and Violet Louise (Harrison) Johnson; m. Wayne William Olsen, Dec. 22, 1984 (dec. Apr. 1993); children: Kenda, Justin; m. John Gary Estie, Nov. 5, 1994. Grad. Lee Sch. Cosmetology, 1966, Everett Beauty Sch., 1968, Everett Plz. Sch. Cosmetology, 1987. With Marysville (Wash.) Police Dept., 1967-72, Durham Transp., 1979-87; owner, mgr. Olsen's Riverside Golf Course and Olsen's Golf Equipment, 1979—. Author of poems. Active Maryfest, Marysville, 1976-78. Recipent Editors Choice award for outstanding achievement in poetry, 1999. Mem. Nat. Granite Ware Collectors, Everett Antique Club, Hummel Club Collectors,Everett Elks (officer lodge #479). Avocations: golfing, collecting and restoring antiques, singing. Home and Office: PO Box 5609 Everett WA 98206-5609

OLSHAN, REGINA, lawyer; b. Kiev, Ukraine, 1964; m. Yves Cantin; children: Maxime, Gabrielle. AB cum laude, Harvard U., 1985; cert. in European Studies, Coll. d'Europe, 1986; JD, Yale U., 1989. Bar: Conn. 1991, N.Y. 1994. Law clk. Hon. José Cabranes U.S. Dist. Ct. Conn., 1989—90; atty. Skadden, Arps, Slate, Meagher & Flom LLP, N.Y., 1990—98, ptnr., 1998—. Scholar, Fulbright Found. Office: Skadden Arps Slate Meagher & Flom LLP Four Times Square New York NY 10036

OLSON, BARBARA FORD, physician; b. Iowa City, June 15, 1935; d. Leonard A. and Anne (Swanson) Ford; m. Robert Eric Olson, 1959 (div. 1973); children: Katherine Gee, Eric Ford, Julie Marie. BA, Gustavus Adolphus Coll., 1956; MD, U. Minn., 1960. Diplomate Am. Bd. Family Practice, Am. Bd. Geriat. Medicine, added qualification geriat. medicine. Intern St. Paul-Ramsy Med. Ctr., 1960-61; resident in anesthesiology U. Hosp. Cleve., 1961-62, U. Minn. Hosp., Mpls., 1962-63; pvt. practice anesthesiology St. Johns Hosp. and Devine Redeemer Hosp., St. Paul, 1963-67, Mercy Hosp., Coon Rapids, Minn., 1967-74; staff physician Oak Terrace Nursing Home, Minnetonka, Minn., 1974-88; staff physician, med. dir. geriatric evaluation clinic VA Med. Ctr., St. Cloud, Minn., 1988—. Pres. Alpha Epsilon Iota Med. Found., Mpls., 1980—86, bd.dirs., 1980—86, 2003—. Mem. Minn. Med. Assn., Minn. Women Physicians (pres. 1981-82), Minn. Nursing Home Med. Dirs. Home: PO Box 7306 Saint Cloud MN 56302-7306 Office: VA Med Ctr 4801 8th St N Saint Cloud MN 56303-2015 E-mail: Barbara.Olson@med.va.gov.

OLSON, BETTYE JOHNSON, artist, retired educator; b. Mpls., Jan. 16, 1923; d. Emil Antonious and Irene Irina (Wandtke) J.; m. Howard Einar Olson, July 16, 1949; children: Martha, Jeffrey, Barbara, Virginia. BS in Art Edn., U. Minn., 1945, MEd in Art Edn., 1949; student, U. N.Mex., Taos, 1947; student summer sch., Cranbrook Summer Art, Mich., 1948. Tchr. art grades 3-12 Summit Sch. for Girls, St. Paul, 1945-47; instr. art U. Minn., Mpls., 1947-49; instr. painting and design Concordia U., St. Paul, 1975-78, 83-84; instr. painting summer sch. Augsburg Coll., Mpls., 1983—89, instr. painting prints, 1988—89; lectr. art Augsburg Coll. of 3rd Age, Mpls., 1984—2003, dir., 1992—98; ret.; instr. painting Elder Learning Inst. U. Minn., 2000—04. Mem. staff Walker Art Ctr., summer 1947; instr. Grunewald Guild, Wash., summer 1990; lectr. women in liturgical arts Luther Northwestern Sem., 1985, lectr. theology and the arts, 1987, 89; lectr. art and lit. series AAUW, 1986-89; artist-in-residence Holden Village Luth. Retreat Ctr., Chelan, Wash., summers 1967-68, 70-71, 73, 78-79, 86-90, 94-97; curriculum bd. Elder Learning Inst., U. Minn. One-woman shows include Met. Med. Ctr., Mpls., 1974, Concordia Coll., St. Paul, 1975, St. Olaf Coll., Northfield, Minn., 1977, West Lake Gallery, 1964, 67, 71, 75, 78, 82, Inver Hills Coll., Inver Grove Heights, Minn., 1978-, House of Hope Ch., St. Paul, 1978, 1998, Plymouth Congl. Ch., Mpls., 1978-97, Jerome Gallery, Aspen, Colo., 1978, Osborn Gallery, St. Paul, 1979, Augsburg Coll., 1979, 96, Luther Coll., Decorah, Iowa, 1980, Wilson Libr., U. Minn., 1981, St. Paul Campus Gallery, U. Minn., 1981, Am. Swedish Inst., 1978, 1982, Smaland Mus., Vaxjo, Sweden, 1982, Luth. Brotherhood Co., 1983, Phipps Gallery, Hudson, Wis., 1985, Luther Sem., St. Paul, 1998, Berge Gallery, Stillwater, Minn., 1995, 2000, Augsburg Coll., 1978, 1996, Luther Sem., St. Paul, 1998, Johnson Heritage Gallery, Grand Marias, Minn., 2002, Heritage; participant juried exhbns., including Walker Art Ctr., 1947, Mpls. Art Inst., 1947, St. Paul Gallery, 1961, Sky Gallery, 1975, Minn. Arts Assn., 1975 (Merit award 1975, 76), 76, Minn. Mus. Art, 1976, Watercolor U.S.A., Springfield, Mo., 1977, Minn. State Fair, 1947, 64, 66-68, 74-79, 90, 93 (Merit award 1976, 3rd prize 1977, 93), Lakewood Coll., White Bear Lake, Minn., 1974-79, 81 (Grand prize 1977, Purchase prize 1977), Butler Inst. Am. Art, Youngstown, Ohio, 1977, W.A.R.M. Gallery, Mpls., 1977, Calif. Women's Conf., Pasadena, Calif., 1978, AAUW, 1981; exhibited in group shows at Friends of Art Inst., 1979, West Lake Gallery, 1964-83, Kuopio Art Mus., Finland, 1982, St. Paul Co., 1983, Augsburg Coll., 1988, 89, Minn. Mus. Art, 1988, Nash Gallery, U. Minn., 1994, Hill Mansion-History Soc., 1995, 96, Sosin and Sosin Gallery, Mpls., 2002, Stillwater Print Show, 2002; others; represented in permanent collections: 3M Co., Minn. History Soc., Minn. Mus. Am. Art, Employers Ins. Co. of Wausau, Concordia Coll., Nothern States Power Co., Cray Rsch., Pillsbury World Headquaters, Luther Coll., Kuopio Art Mus. Finland, Am. Swedish Inst., Smaland Mus. Sweden, Augsburg Coll., Luther Sem., St. Paul, and many others. Mem. bd. congl. life Evang. Luth. Ch. Am., St. Paul, 1989-91; coop. mem. West Lake Gallery, Mpls., 1963-83; mem. Mpls. Art Inst., 1945—, Minn. Mus. Am. Art, Walker Art Ctr.; juror, Minn. State Fair, 2001. Mentor tchg. scholar Met. Arts Coun. to Woman's Art Registry Minn., St. Paul, 1990-94; grantee liberal arts programs Minn. Humanities Commn., Augsburo Coll Third Age, St. Paul, 1995-96, 97-98. Mem. AAUW (bd. dirs. 1992-94), Woman's Art Registry Minn. (bd. dirs. 1992-95). Avocations: attending concerts, theater, skiing, hiking, reading. Home: 1721 Fulham St Apt H Saint Paul MN 55113-5251

OLSON, BETTY-JEAN, retired elementary education educator; b. Camas, Wash., Apr. 26, 1934; d. Earl Raymond and Mabel Anna (Burden) Clemons; m. Arthur H. Geda, Dec. 31, 1957; children: Ann C. Geda, Scott A. Geda; m. Conrad A. Olson, June 14, 1980. AA, Clark Coll., 1954; BA in Edn., Cen. Wash. Coll. Edn., 1956; MEd, No. Monn. Coll., 1975. Cert. elem. tchr. class I, Mont., supr. K-9 class III. Supervising tchr., demo. teaching No. Mont. Coll.; kindergarten, 1st grade instr. Glasgow, Mont.; supervisor, head tchr. Reading Lab, Glasgow AFB, Mont.; 1st grade instr., kindergarten tchr., elem. adminstr. K-7 Medicine Lake (Mont.) Dist. 7; now ret. Certification stds. and practices Adv. Coun. to the State Bd. Pub. Edn.; mem. bd. examiners Nat. Coun. for Accred. of Tchr. Edn., adv. com. Western Mont. Coll., U. Mont.; grad. spkr. Medicine Lake, 1998; v.i.p. Day Spkr., Plentywood; workshop leader and presenter in field. Mem. Sheridan County Cmty. Protective Svcs. Com., Med-Lake Scholarship Com.; mem. Treasure State coun. Girl Scouts U.S.A., 1998, Mo. River Tourism bd.; trustee Sheridan County Meml. Scholarship Com.; bd. dirs. Glenwood Inc. Vol. Mus. Recipient Golden Key Profl. award Glasgow Edn. Assn., Outstanding Svc. award NE Mont. Reading Coun., State Merit Award Tchr. Nat. Coun. of Geographic Tchrs., Outstanding Svc. award Fort Peck Fine Arts Coun.; named Tchr. of Mo. KUMV-TV Channel 8, 1998. Mem. NEA, ASCD, Internat. Reading Assn., Nat. Coun. Social Studies, Nat. Elem. Prin. Assn., Medicine Lake Edn. Assn. (past pres.), Mont. Edn. Assn. (rev. bd., officerships), Mont. Elem. Prin., N.E. Mont. Reading Coun. (v.p.), Delta Kappa Gamma (state pres., chpt. pres., exec. bd., committeeships, mem. internat. exec. bd., inspirational spkr.). Home: 108 E Antelope Antelope MT 59211-9607

OLSON, CANDY, school system administrator; b. Glen Ridge, N.J., Sept. 3, 1947; d. George Francis and Elizabeth Ehlers Sullivan; m. John Karl Olson, June 26, 1974; children: Elizabeth Ann, Katherine Louise. BA, Newton (Mass.) Coll., 1969; MBA, U. South Fla., Tampa, 1976. Staff Exec. Office Transp. and Constrn., Boston, 1972; registered rep. Josephthal & Co. and Estabrook & Co., Boston, 1972-73; analyst, adminstrv. asst. Endowment Mgmt. & Rsch., Boston, 1973-75; trust investment resource officer Exch. Bank, Tampa, 1976-77; dir. fin. and planning Drug Abuse Comprehensive Coord. Office, Tampa, 1977-80; freelance writer Tampa, 1981-95. Mem. adv. bd. Child Abuse Coun., Tampa, 1990-99, Sch. Enrichment Resource Vols., T ampa, 1994-2000; mem. Hillsborough County Sch. Bd. 1994—, chair 1998-99; bd. dirs. United Way, Tampa, 1994-99, mem. fin. com., 1996—; bd. dirs. Tampa Bay Performing Arts Ctr., 1998—, chair edn. com., 1999—; mem. parent bd. U. Del., 1998-2002, co-pres., 2000-2002. Mem. Jr. League Tampa, Athena Soc., Tiger Bay Club. Roman Catholic. Avocations: gardening, reading. Office: Hillsborough County Sch Bd 901 E Kennedy Blvd Tampa FL 33602-3507 E-mail: candy.olson@sdhc.k12.fl.us.

OLSON, CAROL JOAN, foundation administrator, consultant; b. Cleve., Mar. 3, 1937; d. Edward Andrew Olson and Mildred Mary (Robejsek) Olson. BA in Psychology, Baldwin Wallace Coll., 1975. Adminstrv. asst. United Appeal/Cmty. Fund, Cleve., 1960—71; exec. asst. United Way Svcs., Cleve., 1971—81; cons. George M. Keith and Assocs., Cleve., 1981; exec. dir., sec. Cleve. Zool. Soc., 1982—96, cons., 1997; cons., pres. Carol J. Olson, Inc., Lakewood, Ohio, 1997—. Publ. dir. Exec. Women Internat., Cleve., 1980—81; chmn., resource fund devel. com. Eliza Jennings Corp., Cleve., 1984—86; mem. bd., chmn. com. Samaritan Counseling Ctr., Cleve., 1988—90. Editor: (quar. publ.) Zoo News, 1997 (Merit, 1997), (ann. report) Cleveland Zoological Soc. A.R., 1997 (Gold, 1997); advisor (manuscript by Ralph Brody, PhD and Marcie Goodman) Fund-Raising Events, Strategies and Programs for Success, 1988, (manuscript by Ralph Brody, PhD) Effectively Managing Human Service Organizations, 1993. Recipient Printing Industry Assn. award, North Coast Print Competition, No. Ohio, 1996, Resolution of Appreciation award, Bd. Park Commrs. Cleve. Metroparks, 1996, Comm. Awards Competition, 1997. Mem.: Ohio Coun. Fundraising Execs., Lakewood C. of C., Am. Zoo and Aquarium Assn., Assn. Fundraising Profls., Press Club Cleve. Republican. Lutheran. Avocations: cross country skiing, biking, yoga, antiques, alpine skiing. Home and Office: Carol J Olson Inc Consulting 1478 Bunts Rd Lakewood OH 44107-4518 E-mail: cjo@bge.net.

OLSON, CAROL LEA, lithographer, educator; b. Anderson, Ind., June 10, 1929; d. Daniel Ackerman and Marguerite Louise Olson. AB, Anderson Coll., 1952; MA, Ball State U., 1976. Pasteup artist Warner Press, Inc., Anderson, 1952-53, apprentice lithographer stripper, 1953-57, journeyman, 1957-63, lithographic dot etcher, color corrector, 1959-73, prepres coord. art dept., 1973-81, prepres tech. specialist, 1981-83, color film assembler, 1983-96. Part-time photography instr. Anderson Univ.; tchr. photography Anderson Fine Arts Ctr., 1976-79; instr. photography, photographics Anderson U., 1979-2003, Ind. U. East, 2003-054 mag. photographer Bd. Christian Edn. of Ch. of God, Anderson, 1973-86; freelance photographer. One person show Anderson U., 1979; exhibited in group shows Anderson U., 1980—, Purdue U., 1982. Instr. 1st aide ARC, Anderson, 1969-79; sec. volleyball Anderson Sunday Sch. Athletic Assn., 1973-2000. Recipient Hon. mention, Ann Arbor, Mich., 1977, Anderson Fine Arts Ctr., 1977, 78, 83, 1st Pl., 1983, Hon. Mention, 1983, 2d Pl., 1988, Hon. Mention, 1988, 93, Best of Show, 1983, 91, 92, Best Nature Catagory Anderson Fine Arts Ctr., 1994. Mem. AAUW, Associated Photographer Internat., Nat. Inst. Exploration, Profl. Photographers Am. Mem. Ch. of God. Avocations: camping, travel, canoeing. Home: 2604 E 6th St Anderson IN 46012-3725

OLSON, DIANA CRAFT, image and etiquette consultant; b. Langley, Va., May 5, 1941; d. Winfred O. and Joyce (Clark) Craft; m. Robert J. Olson, May 30, 1976; stepchildren: Stacey, Kirsten Lowry. BA, U. Tex., 1963; MA, San Francisco State U., 1970; cert. image cons., Fashion Acad., Costa Mesa, Calif., 1980; cert., Protocol Sch. Washington, 1988. Cert. image profl. Assn. Image Consultants Internat., 2002. Tchr. USAF, P.R., 1963-64, Long Beach (Calif.) Unified Sch. Dist., 1964-68, South San Francisco (Calif.) Unified Sch. Dist., 1968-79; founder Diana's Color Collage & Color Collage Inst., Pasadena, Calif., 1979—. Etiquette affiliates Dorthea Johnson and Marjabelle Stewart, Washington, 1988—; cons. Weight Watchers Internat., L.A., Ventura, Calif., 1987-90, Marriott Hotels, Long Beach, 1989, 1st Interstate Bank, L.A., 1990, Ritz Carlton Hotels, 1995. Designer: The Compassionate Friends nat. meml. pin, 1998; prodr. (book, CD and tape) The Secrets of Color and Style, 2001; contbr. articles to mags. Mem.: Assn. Image Consultants Internat. (sec. 1989—90, v.p. 1990—92, 2000—01, v.p. programs 2001—02, pres. So. Calif. chpt. 2002—04). Republican. Presbyterian. Avocations: swimming, skiing. Studio: Diana's Color Collage 465 E Union St Ste 100 Pasadena CA 91101-1783 Fax: 626-584-1856. Office Phone: 626-584-9761. E-mail: olsonco465@aol.com.

OLSON, DIANE DOWD, lawyer; b. San Francisco, Calif., Mar. 11, 1953; d. Harry J. and Dorothy B. (Taylor) Dowd; m. Gary Albert Olson, Jan. 25, 1972. JD, Pepperdine U., Malibu, CA, 1984. Bar: D.C. 1986. Atty. Diane Dowd, Washington, 1985—; prodr. ABC, CBS, CNN, NBC, Los Angeles, Calif., 1976—79. Cons. New Tech., Chicago, Ill., 1983—84. Editor: (lawyers securities) Young Lawers Edition. Mem. The Shrine of Immaculate Conception, Washington, 1985. Achievements include Arizona Press Club. Office: Diane Dowd Attorney at Law 3220 N Street NW Washington DC 20007 E-mail: dianedowdatty1@yahoo.com.

OLSON, GEN, state legislator; b. May 20, 1938; BS in Edn. with distinction, EdD, U. Minn. Mayor, Minnetrista, Minn., 1981-82; mem. Minn. Senate from 34th dist., St. Paul, 1983—. Former mem. Park and Recreation Commn., Planning and Zoning Commn., Police Commn., City Council. Republican. Office: Minn State Senate State Capitol Building Saint Paul MN 55155-0001

OLSON, JEAN A. psychotherapist; b. Homewood, Ill., Sept. 9, 1956; d. John W. and Florence Mae (Anderson) Olson; m. Paul Duncan, May 27, 1990. ASN, Cuyahoga C.C., Parma Heights, Ohio, 1977; BSN, Case Western Res. U., 1980; MSN, Kent State U., 1985. Lic. profl. clin. mental health counselor, N.Mex.; approved clin. cons. in hypnosis; clin. specialist adult psychiat. nursing. Staff nurse critical care various hosps., Tucson, Cleve., 1977-80; nursing supr., staff devel. St. Alexis Hosp., Cleve., 1980-83; staff devel., clin. specialist Akron (Ohio) Gen. Med. Ctr., 1983-85; tchr.-practitioner Rush-Presbyn. St. Luke's Hosp., Chgo., 1985-88; psychotherapist, clin. coord. Assoc. Mental Health Svcs., Chgo., 1986-90; facult, program cons. Coll. Nursing, Divsn. Continuing Edn., U. N.Mex., Albuquerque, 1990—96; psychotherapist, cons., educator Catalyst...Facilitating Change, Albuquerque, 1990—. Coord. S.W. regional conf. on dissociative disorders Divsn. Continuing Edn., U. N.Mex., 1991-95; lectr. in field. Contbr. articles to profl. jours., chpts. to books. Recipient Linnea Henderson award for scholastic excellence Delta Xi chpt. Sigma Theta Tau, 1985. Fellow Am. Soc. Clin. Hypnosis (workshop and ann. meeting faculty 1992—, exec. com. 1992-94, 2003—, Presdl. award 1996); mem. ANA, N.Mex. Nurses Assn. (clin. nurse specialist coun.). Avocations: writing, gardening, baking, reading. Office: 1300 Lomas Blvd NW Albuquerque NM 87104-1234

OLSON, JEANNE INNIS, technology and technical management executive; b. South Bend, Ind., May 10, 1960; d. Francis Bedford and Mary Ann Innis; m. Thomas Hilton Olson, Apr. 12, 1992; 1 child, Walter Samuel. Student, Purdue U., 1978-80; BS in Tech. & Mgmt. summa cum laude, U. Md., 1986; MS in Sys. Mgmt. with honors, U. So. Calif., 1991. Analyst Potomac Rsch., Inc., Alexandria, Va., 1980-82; staff specialist SWL, Inc., McLean, Va., 1982-87; sr. staff Advanced Tech., Inc., El Segundo, Calif., 1987-89; prin. staff/section mgr. PRC, Inc., El Segundo, Calif., 1989-95, dep. dir. space sys. acquisition support, 1995-96, dir. space sys. acquisition support and LA operations, 1997-98; v.p., mgr. ANSWER program Litton PRC, 1998—2001; mgr. ANSWER program Northrop Grumman Info. Tech., 2002—. Mem. South Bay Friends Planned Parenthood, Calif., 1992—, v.p. fund raising, 1994. Recipient Vol. Recognition award Planned Parenthood L.A., 1994, 96. Mem. Innes Clan Soc. (v.p. 1984-91, pres. 1991-92), Innes Clan Ctr. Assn. (bd. dirs. 1993—), Nat. Def. Indsl. Assn. (bd. dirs. Greater L.A. chpt., disbursements chair 2002-04), So. Calif. Aerospace Profl. Rep.(SCAPR) (activities chair 2004), Phi Kappa Phi. Avocations: skiing, music, travel, scottish heritage, family planning edn. Office: Northrop Grumman Info Tech Ste 1310 222 N Sepulveda Blvd El Segundo CA 90245-5648

OLSON, JEANNE M. real estate broker; m. Harlen C. Olson; children; Kara, Ryan. BS, Stout State U., 1970. Tchr. Cudahy (Wis.) Schs., 1970, West Bend (Wis.) Schs., 1970-80, Madison Area Tech Schs., Reedsburg, Wis., 1980-85; realtor, broker Check Realty, Reedsburg, 1986-89; realtor, broker, owner Evergreen Realty, Reedsburg, 1989—. Adv. bd. Madison Area Tech. Coll. Chmn. residental United Way, Reedsburg, 1989; mem. Positive Experiences and Activities for Kids, 1990-94. Mem. Saul/Columbia Bd. Realtors (treas. 1994-95), Wis. Realtors Assn., Nat. Realtors Assn., Mid-Wis. Builders Assn., Reedsburg C. of C. (bd. dirs., pres. 1989-94). Office: Evergreen Realty Inc 2350 E Main St Reedsburg WI 53959-9438

OLSON, JOANNE J. artist, art educator; b. Morristown, N.J., July 11, 1942; d. Eads Johnson Jr. and Jane Cook Johnson; m. Robert F. Rogel, Apr. 30, 1966 (div.); children: Tyler, Tori, Dan, Mac; m. Eric A. Olson, Oct. 18, 1996. AA, Colby Sawyer Coll., 1962. Part-time art dir. The Whitney Shop, New Canaan, Conn., 1960—64; asst. mgr. Johnny Seesaws, Peru, Utah, 1963—64; ski instr. Star Skiers, Crystal Mountain, Wash., 1978—84; clk., creative dir. Lindon Bookstore, Enumclaw, Wash., 1984—94; owner, dir. Apple Hill Art Sch., Enumclaw, 1992—96, itinerant art tchr., 1996—2003. Sec., v.p. Maple Valley (Wash.) Co-op Presch., 1973—75. Sec. Maple Valley Arts Commn., 1975—77; arts coord. Westwood PTSA, Enumclaw, 1979—83. Recipient Golden Acorn award, Nat. PTSA, 1986, Excellence in Cmty. Svc. award, Enumclaw Arts Commn., 1993. Episcopalian. Avocations: skiing, hiking, reading, creative activities.

OLSON, JUDITH MARY REEDY, retired public information officer, former state senator; b. Mitchell, S.D., June 24, 1939; d. John Marvin and Camille (Murphy) Reedy; m. Robert George Olson, Aug. 5, 1961; children: Jeffrey, Jennifer, Jon, Jaime, Jason, Jeremy. EdB, U. Tucson, 1961; MEd, S.D. State U., 1984; postgrad., U. S.D., 1985—. Cert. secondary tchr., edn. adminstrn. Tchr. jr. high sch. Mpls. Pub. Schs., 1961-63; mem. State Bd. Edn., S.D., 1972-83, pres., 1975-78; dir. S.D. Edn. Policy Seminar, 1975-79; substitute tchr. Rapid City (S.D.) Schs., 1979-81, tchr. adult basic edn., 1979-81, supr. community relations, 1981-88, supr. community edn., pub. info., 1988—95; senator S.D. Legis. (dist. 33), Pierre, SD, 1989—95; edn. dir. Career Learning Center of the Black Hills. Speaker, cons. sch. bds., adminstrs., tchrs., sch. dists., pub. relations, various states, 1972—. Bd. dirs. Black Hills Symphony, 1987—; chair, S.D. State Democratic Party, 1998—. Mem. AAUW (Women of Worth award), Rotary, PEO, Delta Kappa Gamma. Democrat. Roman Catholic. Avocations: reading, spectator sports. Home: 4603 Ridgewood St Rapid City SD 57702-2063 Office: South Dakota Democratic Party 207 East Capitol Pierre SD 57501-2724

OLSON, JULIE ANN, systems consultant, educator; b. Oklahoma City, May 14, 1957; d. Willard Alton and Ruth Harriet (Ehlers) O.; m. Kevin Peter McAuliffe, Oct. 12, 1985; children: Scott Andrew, Shannon Elizabeth, Kathryn Victoria, Ryan Douglas. BA in History, Augustana Coll., 1979; MBA, Keller Grad. Sch. Mgmt., Chgo., 1989. Sys. analyst Continental Bank, Chgo., 1979-82; prin., staff mgr. west regional tng. mgr., profl. devel. mgr Computer Scis. Corp. (formerly Computer Ptnrs.), San Bruno, Calif., 1982—, chmn. nat. orgn. change mgmt. SIG, 1982—. Instr. data processing Oakton C.C., Des Plaines, 1982-96, faculty coord. accelerated data processing cert. program, 1983-92. Exec. dir., chmn. scholarship Miss N.W. Cmtys. Inc., Des Plaines, 1984-88; bd. dirs. Mt. Prospect Hist. Soc., 1994-96, Mt. Prospect chpt. Am. Cancer Soc., Peninsula Quilt Guild; pres. women's group Hope Luth. Ch., 1999; bd. dirs., registrar Am. Youth Soccer Orgn. Recipient Grand prize for quilt, San Mateo County Fir, 2002. Mem. ASTD, NAFE, IAF, Data Processing Mgmt. Assn. (asst. faculty coord. Student chpt. 1985-87). Lutheran. Avocations: classical pianist, reading, flamenco dancing, scrapbooking, quilting. Home: 409 Castilian Way San Mateo CA 94402-2327 Office: Computer Sci Corp 1111 Bayhill Dr Ste 250 San Bruno CA 94066-3041 E-mail: mcaulke_409@yahoo.com.

OLSON, KRISTINE, prosecutor; b. N.Y.C., Aug. 9, 1947; d. Harold John and Arline (Schneider) Olson; children: Karin, Tyler. B.A., Wellesley Coll., 1969, J.D., Yale U., 1972. Bar: Oreg. 1973, U.S. Dist. Ct. Oreg. 1974, U.S. Ct. Appeals (9th cir.) 1975. Asst. U.S. atty. Dept. Justice, Portland, Oreg., 1974-84; vice chair State Indigent Def. Bd., Salem, Oreg., 1985-87; assoc. dean, prof. law Lewis & Clark Coll., 1989-94; U.S. atty. Dept. Justice, Dist. Oreg., Portland, 1994—; adj. prof. Lewis and Clark Coll. Northwestern Sch. Law, 1975-89, U. Oreg. Law Ctr., 1984—; mem. 9th Cir. Task Force on Tribal Cts. Contbr. articles to profl. jours. Bd. dirs., chmn. bd. Oreg. Council on Crime and Delinquency, 1981-87; bd. dirs. State Bd. Police Standards and Tng., 1976-80; chmn. Community Corrections Adv. Bd. Multnomah County, Portland, 1978-80; chmn. women's rights project ACLU Oreg., 1977; mem. World Affairs Council Oreg.; commr., mem. exec. com. Met. Human Relations Commn., mayor's appointee, 1986—. Root Tilden fellow, 1969. Mem. Soc. Am. Archaeology Native Am. Rights Fund, Earthwatch, 1000 Friends of Oreg., Archaeol. Conservancy, Nature Conservancy. Democrat. Clubs: Early Keyboard Soc., City Club of Portland (bd. govs. 1984—, pres.-elect 1995), Multnomah Athletic (Portland). Home: 900 SW 83rd Ave Portland OR 97225-6308

OLSON, LINDA ANN SALMONSON, minister; b. Charleston, Ill., Apr. 12, 1951; d. Kenneth Emmett Salmonson; m. Sheldon Ellis Olson, Sept. 18, 1971; children: Jeffery Ellis, Steven Eric, Ingrid Ann Olson Douglas, Karin Melinda. BSN, Oreg. Health Scis. U., 1973; MDiv, Pacific Luth. Theol. Sem., Berkeley, Calif., 1997. RN Calif., cert. diplomate, Am. Bd. Quality Assurance and Utilization Rev.; ordained Evang. Luth. Ch. in Am., 1997. Intensive care charge nurse St. Vincent Hosp. and Med. Ctr., Portland, Oreg., 1973—75; med. rev. specialist Multnomah Found. Med. Care, Portland, 1975—77; rehab. specialist Internat. Rehab. Assocs., Portland, 1979—81; nursing cons. SAIF Corp., Eugene, Oreg., 1981; med. rev. analyst Blue Cross/Blue Shield of Oreg., Portland, 1981—83; quality assurance mgr. Good Samaritan Hosp. and Med. Ctr., Portland, 1983—84; unit mgr., dist. mgr., nat. product dir. Intracorp, Wayne, Pa., 1984—91; dir. quality svcs. Golden State Rehab. Hosp., San Ramon, Calif., 1991—93; parish pastor Our Savior's Luth. Ch., Ferndale, Calif., 1997—2002; hospice chaplain VITAS Healthcare Corp. of Calif., San Diego, 2002—. Spkr. in field. Contbr. articles to profl. jours. Bd. dirs. Luth. Home for Aging of Humboldt County, Fortuna, Calif., 1998—2002, Newburg Retirement Ctr., Fortuna, 1998—2002, Mt. View Village, Fortuna, 1998—2002, mem. Chaplaincy Svcs. Bd. of John Muir Hosp. and Med. Ctr., Walnut Creek, Calif., 1993—97; chair social concerns com. Resurrection Luth. Ch., Dublin, Calif., 1992—94. Recipient 2d pl. nat. photography contest, Luth. Brotherhood, 1986, 1st pl. photography contest, Cat Fanciers Assn., Bend, Oreg., 1991; scholar, Luth. Brotherhood, 1993—97, Aid Assn. for Luths., 1993—97. Republican. Avocations: photography, tennis, poetry. Office: VITAS Healthcare Corp of California 9655 Granite Ridge Ste 300 San Diego CA 92123 Office Fax: 858-503-4785.

OLSON, LYNN, editor; m. Steve Olson; 2 children. Grad., Yale U. Sr. editor Edn. Week, 1990—. Author: The School to Work Revolution: How Employers and Educators Are Joining Forces to Prepare Tomorrow's Skilled Workforce, 1997. Recipient award, Edn. Writers Assn., Nat. Assn. Secondary Sch. Prins., Internat. Reading Assn.; grantee, Alfred P. Sloan Found., N.Y., 1995. Mem.: Carnegie Found. for Advancement Tchg. (bd. mem.). Office: Editl Projects in Edn Inc Ste 100 6935 Arlington Rd Bethesda MD 20814-5233

OLSON, LYNN ANN, psychologist, educator; d. Donald Claire and Jane Ann Olson. PhD, U. S.C., 2000; MA, Mankato State U., 1996; BA summa cum laude, Augustana Coll., 1993. Licensed Psychologist N.C. State Bd. of Psychology, 2002. Pediat. psychologist Pitt County Meml. Hosp., Greenville, NC, 2001—; lectr. East Carolina U., Greenville, NC, 2002—; clin. faculty Brody Sch. of Medicine, Greenville, 2001—; postdoctoral fellow, predoctoral intern Children's Hosp. of Orange County, Orange, Calif., 1999—2001; practicum student Mayo Clinic, Rochester, Minn., 1995. Reviewer Jour. Pediat. Psychology, 2003—. Contbr. articles to profl. jours. Mem. quality improvement com. Pitt County Meml. Hosp., Greenville, 2002. Mem.: APA (assoc.), Divsn. Devel. Psychology (assoc.), Divsn. Pediat. Psychology (assoc.), Children's Oncology Group (assoc.).

OLSON, MARGARET SMITH, program director, hospitality professional; b. Niagara Falls, N.Y. d. Andrew Maule and Mary Elizabeth (Hurst) Smith; m. Lou Fletcher Mathews (div.); m. Richard Carlson Stevens (div.); m. Richard C. Olson, July 19, 1985; children: Kimberly Ann Mathews, Christopher Scott Mathews, Andrea Carlson Stevens. BA cum laude, Niagara U., 1972, MA cum laude, 1977. Instr. Niagara U., Niagara Falls, 1972-79; supr. mfg. Harrison Radiator divsn. GM, Lockport, N.Y., 1979-85; owner, mgr. Town House Restaurant, Ligonier, Pa., 1985-91; dir. restaurant mgmt., dir. acad. affairs Pa. Inst. Culinary Art, Pitts., 1992-97; sr. mgr. Gen. Cinema, Bridgewater, N.J., 1997-2001; dir. Ctr. for Workforce Excellence in Info. Tech. Middlesex Coll., Edison, NJ, 2001—. Advisor: (videos) Food Service Security, 1992, Sexual Harassment, 1994. Bd. dirs., treas. Hist. Soc. Ligonier, 1987-90; com. mem. Ligonier Libr. Arts, 1988-90; bd. dirs. Christian Charities, Ligonier, 1997—; mem. adv. bd. Goodwill Industries, Pitts., 1984-97. Named Hospitality Profl. of Yr., Allegheny County C.C., 1991. Mem. Nat. Restaurant Assn. (cert. food svc. mgmt. profl., cert. ServSafe serving safe food instr., instr. in sanitation 1992-97), Pa. Restaurant Assn. (state bd. dirs. 1988-95, bd. dirs. Western chpt. 1988-95, treas. Western chpt. 1990, pres. 1991, chmn. bd. 1992-93, lectr. 1992-95), Coun. Hotel, Restaurant & Instnl. Edn. Avocations: reading, cross-stitch, crossword puzzles, theater, music. E-mail: margaret_olson@middlesexcc.edu.

OLSON, MARIAN EDNA, nursing consultant, social psychologist; b. Newman Grove, Nebr., July 20, 1923; d. Edward and Ethel Thelma (Hougland) O. Diploma, U. Nebr., 1944, BSN, 1953; MA, State U. Iowa, 1961, MA in Psychology, 1962; PhD in Psychology, UCLA, 1966. Staff nurse, supr. U. Tex. Med. Br., Galveston, 1944-49; with U. Iowa, Iowa City, 1949-53, from supr. to asst. dir., 1953-59; asst. prof. nursing UCLA, 1965-67; prof. nursing U. Hawaii, 1967-70, 78-82; DON Wilcox Hosp. and Health Ctr., Lihue, 1970-77; chmn. Hawaii Bd. Nursing, 1974-80; prof. nursing No. Mich. U., 1984-88; ret., 1988; cons. nursing svcs. adminstr. practice and curriculum, 1988-2000; ret., 1988. Bd. dirs. Bay de Noc C.C. Home and Office: 6223 County 513 T Rd Rapid River MI 49878-9595

OLSON, MARIAN KATHERINE, management executive, consultant, publisher; b. Tulsa, Oct. 15, 1933; d. Sherwood Joseph and Katherine M. (Miller) Lahman; m. Ronald Keith Olson, Oct. 27, 1956 (dec. May 1991). BA in Polit. Sci., U. Colo., 1954, MA in Elem. Edn., 1962; EdD in Ednl. Adminstrn., U. Tulsa, 1969. Tchr. pub. schs., Wyo., Colo., Mont., 1956-67; tchg. fellow, adj. instr. edn. U. Tulsa, 1968-69; asst. prof. edn. Eastern Mont. State Coll., 1970; program assoc. rsch. adminstrn. Mont. State U., 1970-75; on leave with Energy Policy Office of White House then with Fed. Energy Adminstrn., 1973-74; with Dept. Energy and predecessor, 1975—, program analyst, 1975-79, chief planning and environ. compliance br., 1979-83; regional dir. Region VIII Fed. Emergency Mgmt. Agy., 1987-93; exec. dir. Search and Rescue Dogs of the U.S., 1993—. Pres. Marian Olson Assocs., Bannack Pub. Co Contbr. articles in field. Bd. dirs. Disaster Preparedness and Emergency Response Assn. Internat. Grantee Okla. Consortium Higher Edn., 1969, NIMH, 1974. Mem. Internat. Assn. Emergency Mgrs., Am. Soc. for Info. Sci., Am. Assn. Budget and Program Analysis, Assn. of Contingency Planners, Nat. Inst. Urban Search and Rescue (bd. dirs.), Nat. Assn. for Search and Rescue, Colo. Search and Rescue, Search and Rescue Dogs of U.S., Colo. Emergency Mgmt. Assn., Front Range Rescue Dogs, Kappa Delta Pi, Phi Alpha Theta, Kappa Alpha Theta. Republican. Home: 203 Iowa Dr Golden CO 80403-1337 Office: Marian Olson Assocs 203 Iowa Dr Ste B Golden CO 80403-1337 E-mail: mlolson@ix.netcom.com.

OLSON, PAMELA FAITH, lawyer; b. Fargo, N.D., July 6, 1954; d. Norman Clifford and Inga (Larson) O.; m. Grant Douglas Aldonas, Apr. 12, 1980; children: Nicole Helen, Kirsten Inga, Noah Grant. BA magna cum laude, U. Minn., 1976, JD, 1980, MBA, 1984. Bar: D.C. 1981. Instr. U. Minn., Coll. Bus. Adminstrn., Mpls., 1979; atty., advisor Office of Chief Counsel, IRS, Washington, 1981-84, spl. asst. to chief counsel, 1984-86; assoc. Skadden, Arps, Slate, Meagher & Flom, Washington, 1986-90, ptnr., 1990—. Precinct chair-woman Ind.-Rep. Party, 1980; coun. mem. Holy Trinity Luth. Ch., Falls Church, Va., 1988-91, pres., 1990; bd. dirs. Arlington (Va.) Forest Club, Inc., 1990-92; trustee Millenium Inst., 1993—. Mem. ABA (vice chmn. employment taxes com. 1988-90, chmn. 1990-92, com. on govt. rels. 1992—, com. on coms. 1992—, com. on women and minorities 1993—, com. on membership and mktg. 1993—, coun. dir. sect. on taxation 1993—), Equipment Leasing Assn., D.C. Bar Assn. (chmn. legis. and regulations com.), U. Minn. Law Sch. Alumi Assn. (bd. dirs. 1992—). Avocations: children, volunteering, cooking, softball, skiing. Office: Skadden Arps Slate Meagher & Flom 1440 New York Ave NW Ste 600 Washington DC 20005-6000

OLSON, RUE EILEEN, retired librarian; b. Chgo., Nov. 1, 1928; d. Paul H. and Martha M. (Fick) Meyers; m. Richard L. Olson, July 18, 1964; children: Catherine, Karen. Student, Herzl Coll., 1946-48, Northwestern U., 1948-50, Ill. State U., 1960-64, Middle Mgmt. Inst. Spl. Librs. Assn., 1985-87. Acct. Ill. Farm Supply Co., Chgo., 1948-59; asst. libr. Ill. Agrl. Assn., Bloomington, 1960-66, libr., 1966-86, dir. libr. svcs., 1986-96, ret., 1996. Bd. dirs. Corn Belt Libr. Sys., 1989-94, sec., 1991-94; mem. area com. Nat. Libr. Week, 1971, area steering com., 1972; mem. steering com. Illinet/OCLC, 1985-87; mem. adv. coun. of librs. Grad. Sch. Libr. Sci. U., Ill., 1976-79; mem. Ill. State Libr. Adv. Com. for Interlibr. Cooperation, 1979-80; del. Ill. White Ho. Conf. on Libr. and Info. Svcs., 1978; coord. Vita Income Tax Assistance, Bloomington, Ill., 1986-89, 95-99, preparer, 1978—; sec. Hawthorn Village Homeowner's Assn., 1995-2002, v.p., 2002—; congl. sec. Good Shepherd Luth. Ch., 1999-2001, newsletter editor, 1994-96. Mem. Am., Ill., McLean County (pres. 1970-71), Libr. Assns., Spl. Librs. Assn. (pres. Ill. chpt. 1977-78, first to be named Disting. Mem. food, agr. and nutrition divsn. 1989), Ill. OCLC Users Group (treas. 1988-90, bd. dirs. 1991-92), Internat. Assn. Agrl. Librs. and Documentalists, Am. Soc. Info. Sci., Am. Mgmt. Assn., USIN, Mended Hearts, Inc. (sec. Ill. chpt. 250, 1994-95, v.p. 1995-96, pres. 1996-98), Zonta (pres. 1987-89), Bloomington Club, Am. Heart Assn. (McLean County divsn., midwest affiliate, sec. 1998-2000). Home: 8 Aspen Ct Bloomington IL 61704-2781

OLSON, SANDRA, aerospace engineer; BSChE, U. Pitts.; MS in Mech. and Aerospace Engring., PhD, Case We. Res. U. Aerospace engr. Glenn Rsch. Ctr. NASA, Cleve. Avocations: Karate, horseback riding, ice skating, singing, scuba diving. Office: NASA Glenn Rsch Ctr MS 77-5 Cleveland OH 44135

OLSON, SANDRA FORBES, neurologist; b. East Chicago, Ind., Jan. 8, 1938; MD, Northwestern U., 1963. Diplomate Am. Bd. Psychiatry and Neurology. Intern Chgo. Wesley Meml. Hosp., 1963—64, resident in internal medicine, 1964—65; resident in neurology Northwestern Med. Sch., Chgo., 1965—68, fellow in electroencheplograph, 1968—69; pvt. practice neurology Chgo., 1969—; prof. clin. neurology Northwestern U., Chgo. Attending neurologist Northwestern Meml. Hosp., Chgo., 1969—75, attending physician, 1975—. Mem.: AMA, CNS, AE, Am. Acad. Neurology (pres.-elect 2002—). Mailing: 710 N Lake Shore Dr #1419 Chicago IL 60611-4542

OLSSON, ANN-MARGRET See ANN-MARGRET

OLVER, RUTH CAROL, social worker, retired; b. Allentown, Pa., Feb. 16, 1918; d. Isadore and Sarah (Wexler) Prosky; m. John Appley Olver, Dec. 12, 1944; children: Richard, Amy. BS, Hunter Coll., 1939; MSW, Fordham U., 1970. Sr. psychiat. social worker St. Joseph's Hosp., Yonkers, N.Y.; social worker Graham Home for Children, Hastings on Hudson, N.Y., Cath. Charities, Yonkers, Abbott House, Irvington, N.Y.; founder, coord. Women's Justice Coun. Westchester, 1986—95; ret., 1995. Co-founder My Sister's Place Shelter, Westchester; adj. prof. Sch. of Social Svcs. Fordham U., 1988—90; caseworker numerous orgns. in field. Vol. founding com. UN Internat. Sch., N.Y.C., 1948; vol. refugee camp/A Women's Sch. Clothing and Ednl. Materials Depot, Tripoli, Libya, 1951; past bd. dirs. Westchester County Commrs. Mental Health Advs., Yonkers Cmty. Mental Health Adv. Bd. Mem.: LWV, NASW (Westchester Social Worker of Yr. 1990), Mental Health Assn., Acad. Am. Social Workers, Am. Orthopsychiat. Assn., UN Women's Guild (founder Westchester chpt.), Sierra Club. Home: 4208 Thiell Rd Rye NY 10580

OLZEROWICZ, SHARON, information technology executive; Founder Matrix, Rochelle Park, NJ, 1986—. Office: Matrix Info Consulting Inc 365 W Passaic St Rochelle Park NJ 07662

O'MALIA, MARY FRANCES, special education educator; d. Horace Emmett Fansler and Frances Fansler Kittle, Robert Blair Kittle (Stepfather); m. William Biff O'Malia, Nov. 8, 1980; children: Nohealani Marie, Shanice Francine. BA, Dominican U. of Calif., San Rafael, 1977; postgrad., Dominican U., 1977—83; postgrad. in Sch. Counseling, U. Nev., 1998—. Lic. tchr. Nev., 1979, cert. alcohol and drug abuse counselor Nev., 1999. Tchg. prin. Mineral County Sch. Dist., Hawthorne, Nev., 1986—88; spl. edn. tchr. Hawaii State Dept. of Edn., Holualoa, 1989—91; HIV/AIDS instr./trainer ARC: Hawaii State Chpt., Honolulu, 1992—97; substance abuse counselor Ctr. for Behavioral Health, Reno, 1999—99; grad. tchg. asst. U. of Nev., Reno, 1999—2001; spl. edn. diagnostician Washoe County Sch. Dist., Reno, 2001—03; spl. edn. tchr. Silver Stage Mid. Sch., Silver Springs, Nev., 2003—. Contbr. articles to profl. jours. Recipient Vol. of the Quarter, ARC, 1995, Distinquished Svc. award, Mineral County Sch. Dist., 1988. Mem.: Coun. for Exeptional Children. Catholic. Avocations: scuba diving, travel, computers, reading. Office: Silver Spring Mid Sch Silver Springs NV Personal E-mail: maryo@unr.edu. E-mail: momalia@lyon.k12.nv.us.

O'MALLEY, KATHLEEN M. federal judge; b. 1956; AB magna cum laude, Kenyon Coll., 1979; JD, Case Western Reserve, 1982. Law clk. to Hon. Nathaniel R. Jones U.S. Ct. of Appeals, 6th circuit, 1982-83; with Jones, Day, Reavis & Pogue, Cleve., 1983-84, Porter, Wright, Morris & Arthur, Cleve., 1985-91; chief counsel, first asst. atty. gen., chief of staff Office of Atty. Gen., Columbus, 1991-94; district judge U.S. Dist. Ct. (Ohio no. dist.), 6th circuit, Cleve., 1994—. Mem. ABA, FBA, Anthony J. Celebrezze Inn of Ct., Order of Coif, Phi Beta Kappa. Office: US District Courts 801 W Superior Ave Cleveland OH 44113-1629

O'MALLEY, KIMBERLY JOY, psychometrician, researcher; b. Baytown, Tex., Sept. 10, 1965; d. Harry Jan and Phyllis Joy Wristers; m. Christopher Sean O'Malley, Sept. 1, 2001; 1 child, Jace Christopher. BS in Edn., U. Houston, 1989, BS in Math., 1991; MS, U. Houston-Clear Lake, 1994; PhD, U. Houston, 1999. Cert. tchr. Tex. Asst. prof. Baylor Coll. Medicine, Houston, 1999—; psychometrician Houston Ctr. for Quality of Care, 1999—; dir. measurement excellence initiative VA Med. Ctr., Houston, 2000—. Contbr. articles to profl. jours. Grantee, VA Health Svcs. Rsch. Svc., 2000, 2003, Agy. for Healthcare Rsch. and Quality, 2001. Avocations: sand volleyball, flag football, softball, skiing. Office: VA Med Ctr 2002 Holcombe Blvd Houston TX 77057 Home: 2504 Dartford Bnd Cedar Park TX 78613-4323

O'MALLEY, MARGARET PARLIN, marketing administrator; b. Cin., Jan. 20, 1940; d. John Andrew and Agnes Sophia (Tietig) Parlin; m. Daniel L. Hutchinson, Nov. 6, 1965 (div. 1986); children: Daniel L., Jr., Agnes Alexina; m. John Patrick O'Malley, June 24, 1989. AB, Bryn Mawr Coll., 1961, postgrad., 1963-65; MBA, Villanova U., 1989. Tchr. The Shipley Sch., Bryn Mawr, Pa., 1961-63; adminstrv. asst. Bryn Mawr Coll., 1963-67, Villanova (Pa.) U., 1976—90; v.p. Winsor Assocs., 1990-91; mgr. mktg. and support svcs. Normandeau Assocs., Inc., 1992—. Mem. women's commn. Univ. Mus., U. Pa., Phila., 1969—76; trustee The Old Eagle Sch., Wayne, Pa., 1997—99; v.p. Phoenixville Area C. of C., 1998—99, commerce bd., 1997—99; bd. trustees The Norfolk Libr., 2001—; bd. dirs. Normandeau Assocs., 2001—02, Phila. Child Guidance Clinic, 1970—76, The Agnes Irwin Sch., 1982—85, Strings for Schs., 1982—89, The West Hill Sch., 1970—87, The Schuylkill River Greenway, Assn., 1993—96. Mem. The Weeders Club, Norfolk Libr. Assocs. Republican. Congregationalist. Office: Normandeau Assocs Inc PO Box 586 Norfolk CT 06058-0586

O'MALLEY, MARIE KIERNAN, healthcare products company professional; b. Sayre, Pa., May 1, 1964; d. James Joseph and Karin Margreta (Ottergren) Kiernan; m. James Sean O'Malley, Apr. 25, 1992. BS in Fin. summa cum laude, SUNY, Binghamton, 1990; MBA, Bentley Coll., 1992. Cert. mgmt. acct., Mass. Corp. staff acct. M/A-Com, Inc., Burlington, Mass., 1986-89; fin. analyst Bull Worldwide Info. Sys., Billerica, Mass., 1989-91, sr. fin. and operational auditor, 1991-93, sr. fin. planning analyst, 1993-94; sr. fin. analyst Bard Vascular Sys. divsn. C.R. Bard, Haverhill, Mass., 1994—99, mgr. sales and contracts adminstrn., 1995—99; dir. Supply Chain Mgmt. Medtronic, Danvers, Mass., 1999—. Mem. strategic planning com. Town of North Andover, Mass., 1994—. Mem. Inst. Cert. Mgmt. Accts. (cert., Robert Beyer silver medal 1994). Avocations: skiing, swimming, aerobics. Home: 18 Lacy St North Andover MA 01845-3307 Office: Supply Chain Mgmt Medtronic 37A Cherry Hill Drive Danvers MA 01932

O'MALLEY, PATRICIA, critical care nurse; b. Boston, May 13, 1955; d. Peter and Catherine (Dwyer) O'M. BSN, Coll. Mt. St. Joseph, Cin., 1977; MS, Ohio State U., 1984, PhD, 2000. Cert. critical care nurse. Clin. nurse specialist cardiology svcs. and palliative care svcs. Miami Valley Hosp., Dayton, Ohio, nurse educator, cons. Adj. faculty Wright State U., Dayton, Ind. U. East. Contbr. articles to profl. jours., textbooks. Recipient honors Dayton Area Heart Assn., Ohio Ho. of Reps., 1994, Ohio Dept. Health, 1996. Mem. AACN, Soc. Critical Care Medicine, Midwest Nursing Rsch. Soc., Nat. Assn. Clin. Nurse Specialists, Assn. for Death Edn. and Counseling, Sigma Theta Tau. Office: Miami Valley Hosp 1 Wyoming St Dayton OH 45409-2722 Office Phone: 937-208-4518. E-mail: paomalley@mvh.org.

O'MALLEY, SUSAN, professional basketball team executive; Degree in Bus. and Finance, Mt. St. Mary's, 1983. Dir. advt. Washington Bullets, 1986-87, dir. mktg., 1987-88, exec. v.p., 1988-91, pres., 1991-96, Washington Wizards, 1996—. Achievements include becoming 1st women ever to become a president of an NBA franchise. Avocations: tennis, vacations. Office: Washington Wizards 718 7th St NW Washington DC 20001-3716*

OMAN, DEBORAH SUE, health science facility administrator; b. North Platte, Nebr., Aug. 26, 1948; d. Rex Ardell and Opale Louise (Smith) O. BS, Kearney State Coll., 1970; MA in Journalism and Mass Comm., U. Nebr., 1993. Med. technologist Physicians Pathology Labs., Lincoln, Nebr., 1970-71; med. technologist student health Colo. State U., Ft. Collins, 1971-72; supr. hematology lab. Bryan Meml. Hosp., Lincoln, 1972-76; sect. supr. hematology, hemostasis QUEST Diagnostics, Inc., 1976—. Hemostasis cons. Dade-Behring, Inc., Miami Fla., 1998-2000; clin. cons. Med. Lab. Automation, Inc., Pleasantville, N.Y., 1990-97; adj. prof. Sch. Med. Tech., Nebr. Wesleyan U., Lincoln, 1979-85; clin. instr. Sch. Med. Tech., U. Nebr. Med. Ctr., Omaha, 1990-95. Contbr. articles to profl. jours. Mem. Am. Soc. Clin. Pathologists (cert., affiliate, recognition award 1986), Lancaster Soc. Med. Technologists, Fastbreaker's for Nebr. Women's Basketball (sec. 1995-98), UNL Touchdown Club, Cornhusker Ski Club (pres. 1982-83), Kappa Tau Alpha. Republican. Mem. Christian Ch. Avocations: snow skiing, golf, tennis, spectator college football and basketball. Office: Quest Diagnostics Inc Ste 100 5925 Adams St Lincoln NE 68507-2229

O'MEARA, ANNA M. lawyer; b. Chgo., Aug. 11, 1947; BS cum laude, Loyola U., 1969, JD cum laude, 1984. Bar: Ill. 1984, U.S. Dist. Ct. (no. dist.) Ill. 1984. Ptnr. Mayer, Brown & Platt, Chgo., 1984—. Mem. ABA, Ill. Bar Assn. Office: Mayer Brown & Platt 190 S La Salle St Ste 3100 Chicago IL 60603-3441

O'MEARA, SARA, nonprofit organization executive; b. Knoxville, Tenn., Sept. 09; m. Robert O'Meara (dec.); children: John Hopkins, Charles Hopkins (dec.); m. Robert Sigholtz, Nov. 1986; stepchildren: Taryn, Whitney. Attended, Briarcliff Jr. Coll.; BA, The Sorbonne, Paris; D (hon.), Endicott Coll. Co-founder, chmn. bd., CEO CHILDHELP USA (formerly Children's Village USA), Scottsdale, Ariz., 1960—. Bd. dirs. Nat. Soc. for Prevention of Child Abuse and Neglect of Gt. Britain, Children to Children, Inc.; hon. com. mem. The Dyslexia Found., Inc.; mem. Mayor's adv. bd., Defense for Children Internat., Nat. Soc. Prevention Cruelty to Children, World Affairs Coun., Ariz. Found. Women Charter 100; bd. dirs. Internat. Alliance on Child Abuse and Neglect; sustaining mem. Spastic Children's League, past pres.; mem., past recording sec. Assistance League So. Calif. Recipient Cross of Merit, Knightly Order of St. Brigitte, 1967, Victor M. Carter Diamond award Japan-Am. Soc., 1970, Dame Cross of Merit of Order of St. John of Denmark, 1980, Official Seal of 34th Gov. Calif., 1981, Woman of Achievement award Career Guild, 1982, Women Making History award Nat. Fedn. Bus. Profl. Women's Clubs, 1983, Disting. Am. award for svc., 1984, Humanitarian award Nat. Frat. Eagles, 1984, Nat. Recognition award outstanding leadership Am. Heritage Found., 1986, Notable Am. award svc. to Calif., 1986, Dove of Peace award Pacific Southwest and Ctrl. Pacific Regions B'nai B'rith, 1987, Paul Harris fellow award Rotary Found., 1989, Internat. Collaboration to Prevention Child Abuse award HRH Queen of Eng., 1989, Living Legacy award Women's Internat. Ctr., 1989, Love and Help the Children award, 1990, Presdl. award, 1990, Kiwanis World Svc. medal, 1991, Women Who Make a Difference award Family Circle Mag., 1992, Outstanding Woman from Tenn. award Nat. Mus. Women in Arts, 1993, Nat. Caring award Nat. Caring Inst., 1993, Hubert Humphrey award Touchdown Club Washington, 1993, Lifetime Achievement award Nat. Charity Awards Com., 2001, Champions of Children award Nat. Children's Alliance, numerous others. Mem. SAG, AFTRA, Victory Awards (exec. com.), Am. Biographical Inst. (nat. bd. advisors), Alpha Delta Kappa (hon.). Office: Childhelp USA 15757 N 78th St Scottsdale AZ 85260-1629

O'MEARA, VICKI A. lawyer; b. Mpls., May 13, 1957; d. James Michael and Joan Kathleen (Shepers) O'M.; children: Joseph O'Meara Masterman, Nicolas James Reisinger O'Meara. BA in Polit. Sci., Cornell U., 1979; JD, Northwestern U., Chgo., 1982; MA in Environment & Natural Resource, George Washington U., Washington, 1987. Bar: Minn. 1982, D.C. 1983, Ill. 1989. Asst. to Army gen. counsel U.S. Army-Pentagon, Washington, 1982-86; spl. asst. to White House Counsel The White House Fellows Program, Washington, 1986-87; dep. exec. sec., domestic policy counsel, cabinent affairs The White House, Washington, 1987; dep. gen. counsel litigation and regional ops. U.S. EPA, Washington, 1987; ptnr. Jones, Day,

Reavis & Pogue, Chgo., 1988-92, 93—; asst. atty. gen. U.S. Dept. Justice, 1992; exec. vice-pres., gen. counsel Ryder Systems Inc., Miami, FL. Hon. mem. faculty U.S. Army Logistics Mgmt. Sch., Ft. Lee, Va., 1982-85; adj. prof. The Union Inst., Cin., 1989-92. Author rev. Nat. Wetlands Newsletter, 1990; contbr. articles to profl. jours. Bd. dirs. Northwestern U. Alumni Assn., Chgo., 1988-90; mem. com. Chgo. Coun. Fgn. Rels. Mem. Chgo. Econ. Club Chgo. (com. fgn. affairs). Office: Ryder Stystem Inc 3600 NW 82nd Ave Miami FL 33166-6623

OMLAND, JACQUELINE LEIGH-KNUTE, secondary school educator, small business owner; b. Grand Forks, ND, Nov. 19, 1955; d. Denora Muriel and Jerry John Knute; m. Thomas Jay Omland, May 17, 1985; 1 child, Brian. BS in Natural Scis., U. N.D., 1978; MS in Edn., No. State U., 1985. Sci. tchr. Thief River Falls (Minn.) Pub. Schs., 1978—79, Alvarado (Minn.) Pub. Schs., 1979—83; sci. instr. Aberdeen (S.D.) Pub. Schs., 1984—2002; adj. physics instr. Presentation Coll., Aberdeen, 1995—; Matster E-Learning physics tchr. No. State U. Statewide E-learning Ctr., Aberdeen, 2002—. Adj. physics instr. No. State U., Aberdeen, 1994. Police and fire commr. City of Aberdeen, 2001—. Named S.D. Tchr. of Yr. award, Coun. of Chief Sch. Officers, 1996; recipient Presdl. award for Excellence in Sci. and Math. Tchg., NSF, 1995, Walt Disney Am. Tchr. award, The Disney Corp., 1998. Mem.: Nat. Sci. Tchrs. Assn., Aberdeen Edn. Assn. (sec. 1984—85), NEA, Phi Delta Kappa, Am. Legion Auxiliary (pres. 1995—99, 2002—, Legionette of Yr. 2001, Legionette of Yr. 2002), Zonta (pres. 1997—99, Silver Plate), Delta Kappa Gamma (pres. 1996—98). Lutheran. Avocation: travel. Home: Box 1177 Aberdeen SD 57402-1177

OMOREGIE, IRENE O. accountant; b. Benin, Nigeria, Mar. 30, 1960; arrived in U.S., 81; d. Festus U. and Grace S. Okungbowa; m. Charles E. Sr. Omoregie; children: Charles O.(dec.), Jeffrey O. BS in Acctg., So. U., 1984, M Profl. Acctg., 1986, Grad. asst. So. U., Baton Rouge, 1986—87; asst. mgr. KFC, Inc., Newark, 1987—88, Crownwell Inc., Irvington, NJ, 1988—89; fiscal analyst County of Essex, East Orange, NJ, 1989—93, prin. acct., 1994—. Counselor AARP, Irvington, 1999—. Recipient Cert. of Appreciation, AARP, 1999, 2000, NJ4A-Retreat, 1999. Avocations: travel, dance, cooking, reading. Office: County of Essex DOA 50 S Clinton St East Orange NJ 07018

O'NEAL, NELL SELF, retired principal; b. Glenwood, Ark., Feb. 19, 1925; d. Jewell Calvin and Nannie May (Bankston) Self; m. Billie Kenneth O'Neal, Apr. 1, 1943 (div. Jan. 1976); children: Kenneth Dan O'Neal, Rikki Devin O'Neal, Teresa Lynn Severson Gordon. BA, Little Rock U., 1964; MS in Edn., Ark. State Tchrs. Coll., 1965. Cert. tchr. mentally retarded, blind; cert. elem. sch. prin. Spl. edn. tchr. Little Rock Pub. Schs., 1961-65; prin. exceptional unit Ark. Sch. for the Blind, Little Rock, 1965-95; retired, 1995. Mem. LWV, AARP, NOW, NEA, AAUW, Assn. for the Edn., and Rehab. of Blind and Visually Impaired (J. Max Woolly Superior Svc. award 1990), Ark. Edn. Assn., Ark. Retired Tchrs. Assn., Sierra Club, Alpha Delta Kappa. Democrat. Methodist. Avocations: dance, swimming, gardening, reading, writing. Home: 6513 Cantrell Rd Little Rock AR 72207-4218

O'NEAL, PATRICIA JANE, human resources specialist; b. Bayard, Nebr., Sept. 8, 1937; d. William B. and Freda (Ebel) Barrett; m. Ralph L. O'Neal, Feb. 4, 1955 (div. Dec. 1978); children: Michael, Douglas (dec. Dec. 1995), Steven, Darla, Kerry O'Neal. AA, Golden West Coll., 1975; BA in Mgmt., U. Phoenix, 1987. Cert. adminstrn. mgr.; cert. profl. sec. Pers. adminstr. Elec. Equipment Co., Phoenix, 1976-81; exec. asst. ITT Courier, Phoenix, 1980-81; pers. adminstr. Valley Seed Co., Phoenix, 1981-82; mgr. pers. and adminstrn. Kurta Corp., Phoenix, 1982-92; sole proprietor All Ink, Phoenix, 1992-96, pres. All Ink Corp., Phoenix, 1992-96; adminstrv. svcs. mgr. Superior Cos, Phoenix, 1995-97; dir. human resources Soc. St. Vincent de Paul, 1998—2003; ret., 2003; master tchr. Mahatma Reiki, 1999—. Instr. Rio Salado CC, Phoenix, 1988—, Phoenix Coll., 1984—87; spkr. in field. Mem. Adminstrv. Mgmt. Soc. (pres. 1984-86, Mem. of Yr. 1986), Cert. Profl. Sec. Soc. Ariz. (bd. dirs. 1980-90, founding chmn.), Metro Phoenix Human Resources Assn. (dir. 1992). Republican. Avocations: mentoring, travel, volunteerism, music.

O'NEIL BIDWELL, KATHARINE THOMAS, fine arts association executive, performing arts executive; b. Dayton, Ohio, Mar. 23, 1937; d. Charles Allen and Margaret Stoddard (Talbott) Thomas; children: Margaret, Stephen, Thomas; m. J. Truman Bidwell. BA, Sarah Lawrence Coll., Bronxville, N.Y., 1959. Mng. dir. Met. Opera Assn., 1977-86, v.p., 1979-86; first v.p. Met. Opera Guild, N.Y.C., 1978-79, pres., chief exec. officer, 1979-86; dir. spl. projects Lincoln Ctr., N.Y.C., 1986-96. Bd. dirs. Norlin Corp.; exec. cons. N.Y.C. Opera, 1997—. Bd. dirs. Lincoln Ctr. for Performing Arts, N.Y.C., Assn. of Mentally Ill Children, 1975-76, Valerie Bettis Sch. of Theater/Dance, 1976-79, Salisbury Sch., Conn., 1982-84; trustee Sarah Lawrence Coll., 1977-86; Westminster Choir Coll., 1986-91, Greenwall Found., 1986, Vol. Cons. Group, 1986; chmn. hon. mems. of chmn. coun. N.Y.C. Opera-Lincoln Ctr. Mem. Assn. Sarah Lawrence Coll. (pres. 1975-77), Chamber Music Soc. Lincoln Ctr. (bd. dirs. 1996—). Republican. Episcopalian. Home: 455 E 57th St New York NY 10022-3065

O'NEILL, BEVERLY LEWIS, mayor, former college president; b. Long Beach, Calif., Sept. 8, 1930; d. Clarence John and Flossie Rachel (Nicholson) Lewis; m. William F. O'Neill, Dec. 21, 1952 AA, Long Beach City Coll., 1950; BA, Calif. State U., Long Beach, 1952, MA, 1956; EdD, U. So. Calif., 1977. Elem. tchr. Long Beach Unified Sch. Dist., 1952-57; instr., counsellor Compton (Calif.) Coll., 1957-60; curriculum supr. Little Lake Sch. Dist., Santa Fe Springs, Calif., 1960-62; women's advisor, campus dean Long Beach City Coll., 1962-71, dir. Continuing Edn. Ctr. for Women, 1969-75, dean student affairs, 1971-77, v.p. student svcs., 1977-88, supt.-pres., 1988—93, exec. dir. LBCC, 1983—; mayor City of Long Beach, Calif., 1994—. Advisor Jr. League, Long Beach, 1976—, Nat. Coun. on Alcoholism, Long Beach, 1979—, Assistance League, Long Beach, 1982—; bd. dirs. NCCJ, Long Beach, 1976—, Meml. Hosp. Found., Long Beach, 1984-92, Met. YMCA, Long Beach, 1986-92, United Way, Long Beach, 1986-92. Named Woman of Yr., Long Beach Human Rels. Commn., 1976, to Hall of Fame, Long Beach City Coll., 1977, Disting. Alumni of Yr., Calif. State U., Long Beach, 1985, Long Beach Woman of Yr. Rick Rackers, 1987, Assistance League Aux., 1987, Woman of Yr., Calif. Legislature 54th Dist., 1995; recipient Hannah Solomon award Nat. Coun. Jewish Women, 1984, Outstanding Colleague award Long Beach City Coll., 1985, NCCJ Humanitarian award, 1991, Woman of Excellence award YWCA, 1990, Community Svc. award Community Svcs. Devel. Corp., 1991, Citizen of Yr. award Exch. Club, 1992, Pacific Regional CEO award Assn. Community Coll. Trustees, 1992, EDDY award, 1999, Long Beach Excellence in Leadership, 1999. Mem. Assn. Calif. Community Coll. Adminstrs. (pres. 1988-90, Harry Buttimer award 1991), Calif. Community Colls. Chief Exec. Officers Assn., Rotary, Soroptomists (Women Helping Women award 1981, Hall of Fame award 1984), U.S. Conf. Mayors (trustee, 2001-), League Calif. Cities (pres. 2002-). Democrat. Office: Office Mayor Civic Ctr Plz 333 W Ocean Blvd Fl 14 Long Beach CA 90802-4604*

O'NEILL, BRIDGET R. lawyer; b. 1963; BSBA, Georgetown U., 1985; JD, U. Wis., 1988. Bar: Wis. 1988, Ill. 1988, N.Y. 1992. With Sidley Austin Brown & Wood, Chgo., ptnr., 1996—. Office: Sidley Austin Brown & Wood Bank One Plz 10 S Dearborn St Chicago IL 60603*

O'NEILL, CATHERINE, cultural organization administrator; m. Richard Reeves; children: Colin, Conor, Fiona O'Neill Reeves. BA in History, St. Joseph's Coll., Bklyn.; MS in Social Welfare, Howard U.; MS in Internat. Rels., Columbia U., N.Y.C. Editl. writer KFWB Radio, L.A.; pub. affairs officer Internat. Monetary Fund, Internat. Herald Tribune, Atlantic Inst. for Internat. Affairs, Fgn. Policy Assn. of the U.S.; pub. affairs dir. RCA; dir. UN Info. Ctr., Washington, 1999—. Co-founder Women's Commn. for Refugee Women and Children, chair emeritae. Office: UN Info Ctr 1775 K St NW Ste 400 Washington DC 20006*

O'NEILL, ELIZABETH STERLING, trade association administrator; b. NYC, May 30, 1938; d. Theodore and Pauline (Green) Sterling: m. W.B. Smith, June 18, 1968 (div. Aug., 1978); 1 child, Elizabeth S. Kroese; m. Francis James O'Neill, May 19, 1984. BA, Cornell U., 1958; postgrad. studies, Northwestern U., 1959-60. Social sec. Perle Mesta Ambassador Luxembourg, N.Y.C.; spl. asst. Vivian Beaumont Allen, philanthropist, N.Y.C.; rep. Prentice-Hall Pub. Co., Eastern Europe; exec. dir. New Caanan (Conn.) C. of C., 1985-97. Apptd. Commn. Small Bus. State of Conn., 1996; spkr. in field. Pres. Newcomers, New Caanan, Conn.; pub. rels. rep. Girl Scouts of U.S., Fairfield County; bd. dirs. Young Women's Rep. Club; mem. Gov. Weicker's Com. for Curriculum Reform; mem. community bd. Waveny Care Ctr., New Caanan; apptd. mem. Gov. John Roland's Commn. on Small Bus., Conn., 1996—; bd. dirs., trustee Clinton (N.J.) Mus. Art; bd. trustees, Hunterdon Mus. Art, 2000, Tewksbury Women's Club (program chair). Recipient Service awards New Caanan YMCA, N.Y. ASPCA, certs. of appreciation New Caanan Lions Club, President Bush. Mem. AAUW (bd. dirs. New Caanan chpt.), Kiwanis, Woman's Club of Twekesbury Twp. (pres. 2002-03, 2003-04). Christian Scientist. Avocations: tennis, horses, travel. Home: 17 Lance Rd Lebanon NJ 08833-5007

O'NEILL, HARRIET, state supreme court justice; Undergrad. degree with honors, Converse Coll.; JD, U. S.C., 1982. Practice law, Houston; with Porter & Clements, Morris & Campbell; pvt. practice, 1982-92; judge 152d Dist. Ct., Houston, 1992; justice 14th Ct. Appeals, Houston, 1995, Tex. Supreme Ct., 1998—. Lectr. continuing edn. courses; adv. bd. CLE Inst., 1996; panelist Tex. Ctr. Advanced Jud. Studies., Austin, 1993. Contbr. articles to profl. publs. Mem. U. S.C. academic honors soc.; law sch. rep. ABA. Office: Supreme Ct PO Box 12248 Austin TX 78711-2248

O'NEILL, JUDITH JONES, insurance agent; b. Cin., Dec. 24, 1935; d. Charles Haddon Jones and Adelle Geagan; m. Howard Tiel O'Neill, Mar. 27, 1965; children: Samantha Lee, Rebecca Tiel. BA in Polit. Sci., Duke U., 1958. Registered agt. property, casualty, accident and health Pa. Staff asst. ITT&C, Inc., Phila., 1959—66, Martin Ins. Agy., Jenkintown, Pa., 1980—90; account mgr. Posse-Walsh, Inc., Blue Bell, Pa., 1990—92, Ryers Agy./Gembridge, Jenkintown, 1992—98; account exec. Oxford Ins. Agy. Group, Jenkintown, 1998—. Bd. dirs. Jenkintown Urban Mobilization Program, 1985—90; elected mem. Jenkintown Borough Coun., 1978—94, v.p., 1980—85, pres., 1986—90; lay vol. Episcopal Ch. of Our Saviour, vestry mem., 1997—2003, sr. warden, 1998—2002, people's warden, 2002—03. Recipient Cmty. Svc. award, Greater Jenkintown C. of C., 1991, citation, Commonwealth Pa. Ho. Reps., 1994. Republican. Episcopalian. Office: Oxford Ins Agy Ste 823-A 261 Old York Rd Jenkintown PA 19046

O'NEILL, MARGARET E. psychological counselor; b. Youngstown, Ohio, Jan. 23, 1935; d. Julius and Anna (Zakel) Huegel; children: Paul McCann, Kathleen McCann, Kevin McCann; m. Thomas B. O'Neill, Oct. 21, 1971 (div. 1979). BSN, UCLA, 1961, MSN, 1963; MA in Counseling, Calif. Luth. Coll., Thousand Oaks, 1974; PhD in Psychology, U.S. Internat. U., San Diego, 1986. Cert. hypnotherapist Calif., critical incident stress mgmt., trauma specialist. Instr. Ventura (Calif.) Coll., 1965-69, dept. chair, 1969-74, coord. Women's Ctr., 1974-79, counselor, 1979-91; marriage, family and child psychologist Ventura, 1981-92, Morro Bay/San Luis Obispo, 1992—. Trainer; cons. County of Ventura, 1984—90, County of San Luis Obispo, 1991—98. Mem. commn. on the status of women San Luis Obispo County Bd. Suprs. Mem.: Coast Psychol. Assn., Rotary Morro Bay, Morro Bay C.of C. Democrat. Avocations: reading, dance, hiking, walking, traveling. Office: 1203 Main St Morro Bay CA 93442-1945

O'NEILL, MARY JANE, not-for-profit administrator, consultant; b. Detroit, Feb. 24, 1923; d. Frank Roger and Kathryn (Rice) Kilcoyne; m. Michael James O'Neill, May 31, 1948; children: Michael, Maureen, Kevin, John(dec.), Kathryn. PhB summa cum laude, U. Detroit, 1944; postgrad., U. Wis., 1949—50. Editor East Side Shopper, Detroit, 1939—45; club editor Detroit Free Press, 1945—48; reporter UP, Milw. and Madison, Wis., 1949; dir. pub. rels. Fairfax-Falls Church (Va.) Cmty. Chest, 1955—60; copy editor Falls Church Sun-Echo, 1958—60; freelance writer Washington, 1960—63; assoc. editor Med. World News, Washington, 1963—66; dir. publ. rels. Westchester Lighthouse, N.Y. Assn. for Blind, 1967—71; dir. pub. edn. The Lighthouse, N.Y.C., 1971—73, dir. pub. rels., 1973—80; exec. dir., CEO Eye-Bank for Sight Restoration, Inc., 1980—2000; ret., 2000. Mem. N.Y. State Transplant Coun., 1991—2002; mem. instl. rsch. rev. bd. Manhattan Eye, Ear and Throat Hosp., 1981—; bd. dirs. N.Y. Organ Donor Network, 1997—2003, Pro Mujer, 1997—2003, Found. of Women Execs. in Pub. Rels., 2000—, Pan Am. Eye Bank Assn., 1997—. Named to Top 100 Irish Ams., Irish Am. Mag., 1999. Mem.: Pan Am. Eye Bank Assn. (bd. dirs. 1997—), Women Execs. in Pub. Rels. (dir. 1982—88, pres. 1986—87), Eye Bank Assn. Am. (lay adv. bd. 1981—83, dir. 1983—86, pres. N.E. Region 1993—96, exec. com. 1994—96, EBAA Heise award 1997), N.Y. Acad. Scis., Women in Comm. (pres. N.Y. chpt. 1980—81), Cosmopolitan Club.

O'NEILL, SHEILA, principal; Prin. Cor Jesu Acad., St. Louis. Recipient Blue Ribbon award U.S. Dept. Edn., 1990-91. Office: Cor Jesu Acad 10230 Gravois Rd Saint Louis MO 63123-4099

O'NEILL MCGIVERN, DIANE, nursing educator, educator; PhD, NYU, 1972. RN. Head divsn. nursing NYU, N.Y.C., Erline Perkins McGriff prof. nursing, head divsn. nursing, vice chancellor Bd. Regents, 1999—. Fellow AAN. Office: NYU Sch Edn Divsn Nursing 50 W 4th St Rm 429 New York NY 10012-1156

O'NEILL TATE, FRANCES, construction executive; b. Memphis, Aug. 16, 1957; d. Mark Alexander and Luanne (Davis) Harris; m. Keith J. O'Neill, Nov. 21, 1987 (div. Feb. 1990); 1 child, Sean Patrick; m. Charles Daniel Tate, June 15, 1997 (div. June 1999); 1 child, Charles Alexander. BFA in Product Design, Memphis State U., 1980. Lic. contractor, Tenn.; lic. real estate broker N.C. Interior designer J.M. Walton's, Phila., 1982; rsch. asst. Larry King Show, Washington, 1981; space designer, office Desks & Furnishings, Washington, 1983-84; lic. contractor Residential Home Builder, Tenn. and N.C., 1985—; lic. real estate broker Tenn. and N.C., 1987—. Address: 4893 Walnut Grove Rd Memphis TN 38117-2623

O'NEILL WOTANOWSKI, EILEEN MARY, special education educator; b. Livingston, NJ, Dec. 9, 1975; d. Eugene Lawrence and Mary Teresa O'Neill; m. Wotanowski Matthew Thomas, Aug. 9, 2002. BA in sociology, Rutgers U., 1996; MEd in counseling, William Patterson U., 2004. Cert. tchr. of handicapped, sch. counselor, elem. educator U. NC, 2000. Support counselor Options, Wilmington, NC, 1998—2000; special edn. tchr. New Hanover County BOE, Wilmington, 1998—2000; spl. edn. tchr. East Orange (NJ) BOE, 2001—02; cmty. support coord. Easterseals, Somerset, NJ, 2000—; behavior cons. ARC of Morris County, Morristown, NJ, 2002—; sch. counselor Lebanon Twp. (NJ) BOE, 2002—; spl. edn. tchr. Lebanon Twp. BOE, 2002—. Nat. cons. First Step Cons., Livingston, NJ, 2003—; autistic behavior cons. pvt. instr., Hunterton, Morris Counties, NJ, 2000—. Recipient Loyal Heart award for Assisting Disabled Persons, NJ Coalition on Women and Disabilities, 2003. Mem.: Coun. for Exceptional Children, Phi Lambda Theta (Lillian Barry award 2003). Roman Cath. Avocations: running, cooking, gardening, interior decorating, woodcarving.

ONG, LAUREEN E. broadcast executive; b. Sept. 24, 1952; m. Richard Ong. BA in math. and speech theatre arts, Montclair State Coll., N.J., 1974; MA in comm., Columbia U., N.Y.C., 1977. Mgr. sales MTM TV Distbn. Group; acct. exec. WPVI-TV, Phila.; sales mgr. KRON-TV, San Francisco; sr. exec. Rainbow Programming, 1994—96; v.p. and gen. mgr. KSAZ-TV, Phoenix, 1997—98, WTTG-TV, Washington, 1998—2000; pres. and CEO Nat. Geog. Channel, Washington, 2000—. Office: Nat Geog Channel 1145 17th St NW Washington DC 20036*

ONGAS, SHARON, elementary school educator; b. Franklin, N.J., Mar. 6, 1948; d. Joseph J. and Maria (Lacika) Regavich; m. Kaljo Ongas, July 26, 1980. BA, William Paterson Coll., Wayne, N.J., 1972, MA in Spl. Edn., 1981. Tchr. Vernon (N.J.) Bd. Edn., 1972—. Learning disability tchr. cons. William Paterson Coll., 1981; commissioner's symposium for outstanding tchrs. Trenton State Coll., 1988; child study team liasion, 1984—86; intermediate area coord. for grades 3 and 4, 1989—; ski club advisor for grades 3 and 4, 1972—; superintendent's faculty senate, 1993—95; tchr. of yr. com., 1984—95. Named Vernon Twp. Tchr. of Yr., Vernon Bd. Edn., 1982—83; recipient Tchr. Scholar award, 1982, Governor's Recognition award, 1988. Avocations: alpine skiing, walking for exercise, cross country skiing, travel, golf.

ONISHI, ANNA TOKIKO, financial analyst; b. Richland, Wash., July 28, 1975; d. Yasuo and Esther Anna Onishi. BA, Smith Coll., 1997. CFA. Sr. rsch. assoc. Fidelity Investments, Merrimack, NH, 1997—2000; sr. analyst Digitas, Boston, 2000—04; exec. dir. rsch. and mktg. strategy Legal Sea Foods, 2004—. Mem. at large N.H. bd. dirs. Girls Inc., Nashua, 1999—2000; asst. fund agt. class of 1997 Smith Coll. Alumnae, Northampton, Mass., 1999—2002, spl. gifts chair class of 1997, 2002—. Mem.: Assn. Investment Mgmt. and Rsch. Avocations: crew, running, sailing, skiing, volunteering. Home: 22 Endicott Ave Marblehead MA 01945 Business E-Mail: aonishi@legalseafood.com. E-mail: aonishi2003@yahoo.com.

ONLEY, SISTER FRANCESCA, academic administrator; Prin. Nazareth Acad. H.S.; asst. to pres. Holy Family U., Phila., 1980—81, pres., 1981—. Chair Internat. Assn. of U. Pres., UN Commn. on Disarmament Edn., Conflict Resolution and Peace. Office: Holy Family U Grant and Franklin Aves Philadelphia PA 19114*

ONO, YOKO, conceptual artist, singer, recording artist; b. Tokyo, Feb. 18, 1933; U.S. citizen; m. Toshi Ichiyanagi, 1957 (div.); m. Tony Cox, 1964 (div.), children: Kyoko Chan; m. John Ono Lennon, Mar. 20, 1969 (dec. Dec. 8, 1980); children: Sean Taro. Student, Peers' Sch., Gakushuin U., Tokyo, Sarah Lawrence Coll., Harvard U.; PhD (hon.), Art Inst. Of Chicago, 1997, Liverpool U., 2001, Bard College, 2002. One-woman shows include Alchemical Wedding, Albert Hall, London, 1967, Evening with Yoko Ono, Birmingham, 1968, Event, U. Wales, 1969, Everson Mus., Syracuse, N.Y., 1971, Yoko Ono: Objects, Films, Whitney Museum of Amer. Art, 1989, Yoko Ono: A Piece of Sky, Galleria Stefania Miscetti, Rome, 1993, Endangered Species, Wacoal Art Center/Spiral Garden, Tokyo, 1993, Yoko Ono and Fluxus, Royal Festival Hall, South Bank Centre, London, 1997, Have You Seen The Horizon Lately?, Museum Of Modern Art, Oxford, 1997, Open Window, Umm El-Fahem, Israel, 2000, YES Yoko Ono, Japan Society, 2001, My Mommy Was Beautiful, Shoshana Wayne Gallery, Santa Monica, 2002, Yoko Ono Women's Room, Musée d'Art moderne de la Ville de Paris, 2003, Yoko Ono: Odyssey of a Cockroach, Institute of Contemporary Arts, London, 2004; recorded albums: (with John Ono Lennon) Two Virgins, 1968, Life With Lions, 1969, Wedding Album, 1970, Live Peace in Toronto (1969), 1970, Some Time in New York City, 1972, Double Fantasy, 1980 (Grammy award Album of Yr., 1982), Milk and Honey, 1984; solo albums include Yoko Ono Plastic Ono Band, 1970, Fly, 1971, Approximately Infinite Universe, 1973, Feeling the Space, 1973, Welcome: The Many Sides Of Yoko Ono, 1973, Season of Glass, 1981, It's Alright (I See Rainbows), 1982, Every Man Has A Woman, 1984, Starpeace, 1985, Walking On Thin Ice, 1992, Rising, 1995, New York Rock, 1995, Rising Mixes, 1996, Blueprint For A Sunrise, 2001; co-prodr. Gimme Some Truth - The Making Of John Lennon's Imagine Album, 2001 (Grammy award best long form music video, 2001); exec. prodr. Come Together: A Night for John Lennon's Words & Music, 2001; composer numerous songs including Don't Worry Kyoko, Mummy's Only Looking for her Hand in the Snow, Walking on Thin Ice (Grammy award nomination Best Female Rock Performance on Single 1981), Don't Be Sad; author: Grapefruit, 1964, A Hole to See the Sky Through, 1971, Just Me! (Tada No Atashi), 1986, Sometime In New York City, 1995, Acorns, 1996, ; author 6 film scripts, Tokyo, 1964, 13 film scores, London, 1967, John & Yoko Calendar, 1970. Recipient Helen Caldicott leadership award, 1987, Skowhegan award, 2002, Lifespire award, 2002, MOCA award, 2003. Office: c/o John Hendricks 488 Greenwich St New York NY 10013-1313*

ONTON, ANN LOUISE REUTHER, chemist; b. Bridgeport, Conn., Sept. 29, 1943; m. Aare Onton, 1965; children: Alan David, Daryl John, Julie Ann. BS in Chemistry, Purdue U., 1965. Lab. chemist Great Lakes Chem. Corp., 1965-67; rsch. asst. Geigy Chem. Corp., 1967-70; abstractor Chem. Abstracts Svc., 1970-72; rschr. Cancer Prevention II Study, 1980-90; chemist Prototek Enzyme Sys. Products, 1992-93; rsch. assoc. Applied Biotech Concepts, Inc., 1995-98, Genaissance Pharms., 1999-2000; mgr. rsch. devel. and prodn. AllExcel, Inc., 2000—. NIH grantee, 1996, 97. Mem. NAFE, AAUW, Am. Chem. Soc., Assn. for Women in Sci. Achievements include development of novel materials and methods for improved electrophoresis and DNA sequencing technologies, development of methodologies for purification and testing of enzymes, U.S.A. Nat. and world medalist in Masters and Senior Olympic Swimming. Office: AllExcel Inc 135 Wood St West Haven CT 06516-3700 E-mail: ontonalr69@yahoo.com.

ONYSHKEVYCH, LARISSA M. L. ZALESKA, theater educator, editor; b. Stryi, Ukraine; arrived in the U.S., 1961; d. Thaddeus and Maria W. (Shankovska) Zalesky; m. Lubomyr S. Onyshkevych, June 3, 1961; children: Vsevolod, Boyan, Lada. Cert., Ryerson Poly. Inst., Toronto, Can., 1954, Royal Can. Conservatory Music, 1958; BA, U. Toronto, 1962; MA, U. Pa., 1966, PhD, 1973. Vis. asst. prof. Rutgers U., New Brunswick, NJ, 1974-78, 90; rschr. Gwball Inst., Princeton, N.J., 1979-81; acad. rschr. Inst. for Advanced Study, Princeton, 1981-82; editor, dir. PRF Editl. Assocs., Princeton, 1986-97. Pres. Princeton Rsch. Forum, 1992-96; prof. Lviv U., Ukraine, 1997. Editor: Kontrasty, 1970, Svity Shevchenka, vol. 1, 1991, vol. 2, 2001, Lytsar Neabsurdnykh Idei: Borys Antonenko-Davydovych, 1993, The Twins Shall Meet Again: An Anthology of Ukrainian Drama in the Diaspora, 1997, Anthology of Modern Ukrainian Drama, 1998. Exec. Plast-Ukrainian Youth Orgn., Can., 1959-61; editor Plast-Ukrainian Youth Orgn. Internat., 1968-92, exec. bd. mem., 1980—; bd. gifted and talented programs Lawrence Twp. Schs., 1980-83; com. woman GOP, Lawrenceville, 1984-86. Grantee Internat. Rsch. and Exch. Bd., 1992, 94-95; Fulbright sr. scholar, 1997. Mem. Ukrainian Acad. Arts and Scis. in the U.S. (dep. chair Vynnychenko com. 1986—), Shevchenko Sci. Soc. (v.p. and learned sec. 1989-96, exec. v.p. 1996-2000, pres. 2000—). Home: 9 Dogwood Dr Lawrenceville NJ 08648-3259

OPARIL, SUZANNE, cardiologist, educator, cardiologist, researcher; b. Elmira, N.Y., Apr. 10, 1941; d. Stanley and Anna (Penkova) Oparil. AB, Cornell U., 1961; MD, Columbia U., 1965. Diplomate Am. Bd. Internal Medicine. Intern in medicine Presbyn. Hosp., N.Y.C., 1965—66; sr. asst. resident in medicine Mass. Gen. Hosp., Boston, 1967—68, clin. and rsch. fellow in medicine, cardiac unit, 1968—71; asst. prof. medicine Med. Sch., U. Chgo., 1971—75, assoc. prof., 1975—77; assoc. prof. dept. medicine U. Ala., Birmingham, 1977—81, asst. prof. physiology and biophysics, 1980—81, assoc. prof., 1981—, prof. medicine, 1981—, dir. vascular biology and hypertension program, 1985—, prof. med. physiology and biophysics, 1993—. Mem. vis. faculty Nat. High Blood Pressure Edn.

Program, 1974—, Joint Nat. Com. on Detection, Evaluation and Treatment High Blood Pressure, 1991; mem. bd. sci. advisors Sterling Drug, Inc., 1988—91; lectr. in field; Selkurt lectr. Ind. U. Sch. Medicine, 1994; hon. prof. Peking Union Med. Coll., 1994; Louis Gross-Harold Segall lectr. Jewish Gen. Hosp., Montreal, Que., 1995; Joy Goodwin Disting. lectr. Auburn U., 1996, A Ross McIntyre award U. Nebr., 1996. Author books on hypertension; editor: Am. Jour. Med. [illegible] 1981 [illegible]; assoc. editor: Hypertension, 1979—83, mem. editl. bd.:, 1984—, assoc. editor: Am. Jour. Physiology-Renal, 1989—91, mem. editl. bd.: Jour. Hypertension, 1989—98; contbr. over 450 articles to profl. jours., chapters to books. Recipient Young Investigator award, Internat. Soc. Hypertension, 1979, ann. award, Med. Coll. Pa., 1984; fellow, Am. Coll. Cardiology, 1992. Fellow: Am. Coll. Cardiology; mem.: AAAS, Am. Fedn. for Clin. Rsch. (midwest councillor 1974—75, nat. councillor 1975—78, sec.-treas. 1978—80, pres. 1981—82), Assn. Am. Physicians, So. Soc. for Clin. Investigation (Founder's award 1995), Soc. Exptl. Biology and Medicine (councillor 1993—), Am. Soc. for Clin. Investigation (sec.-treas. 1983—86), Am. Physiol. Soc. (clin. physiology advd. com. 1992—, Carl Ludwig disting. lectr. 2002), Am. Heart Assn. (coun. for high blood pressure rsch. 1973—, coun. on basic scis. 1978—, mem.-at-large, exec. com. 1979—81, chmn. Louis B. Katz Prize com. 1984—86, exec. com. 1985—90, vice chmn. 1986, v.p. Ala. affiliate 1986—87, pres.-elect Ala. affiliate 1987—88, pres. Ala. affiliate 1988—89, chmn. 1988—90, chmn. budget com. 1990—91, mem.-at-large bd. dirs. 1992, Lewis K. Dahl Meml. lectr. 1993, pres.-elect Ala. affiliate 1993—94, nat. pres.-elect 1993—94, nat. pres. 1994—, Arthur C. Corcoran Meml. lectr. 1998, Irving Page-Alva Bradley Lifetime Achievement award 2002), Assn. for Women in Sci., Am. Soc. Hypertension (sci. program com. 1990—92, pub. policy com. 1990—), Inter-Am. Soc. Hypertension, Endocrine Soc., Inst. Medicine of NAS (corr. com. on human rights 1992, chmn. com. adviser Dept. Def. 1993 Breast Cancer Rsch. Program), Phi Kappa Phi, Alpha Omega Alpha (mem. nat. bd. dirs., dir.-at-large 1991, treas. 1993), Sigma Xi, Phi Beta Kappa. Avocations: horseback riding, tennis, hiking, travel. Office: U Ala 703 S 19th St ZRB 1034 Birmingham AL 35294-0007 E-mail: soparil@uab.edu.

OPENSHAW, JENNIFER, finance company executive; BA in comm. studies, MBA in comm. studies, UCLA. Press sec. Calif. State Treas.; dir. media rels. ICN Pharm., 1995; sr. v.p. Bank One; v.p. investment mgmt. svcs. group Bank Am.; dir. investment svcs. Wilshire Assoc., 1999; founder, chmn., CEO, pres. Women's Fin. Network, 1999—2000; vice chmn. Women's Fin. Network at Siebert, 2000—. Fin. commentator Wise Women, Lifetime TV; corr. Money Expert, CBS-TV, LA; columnist Women & Money, CBS MarketWatch; featured on CNBC; featured in Bus. Week publ., Wash. Times publ.; adv. bd. Wyndham Hotels, MuchoInfo. Author: What's Your Net Worth? Click Your Way to Wealth, 2001. Commr. Little Hoover Commn., Calif. Recipient Tribute to Women and Industry award, YWCA, 2001. Mem.: Young Entrepreneurs Orgn. Office: WFN at Seibert 885 Third Ave Ste 1720 New York NY 10022*

OPIE, CATHERINE, photographer; b. Sandusky, Ohio, 1961; BFA, San Francisco Art Inst., 1985; MFA, CalArts, Valencia, 1988. One-woman shows include Mills Coll., Oakland, Calif., 1989, 494 Gallery, N.Y.C., 1991, Kiki Gallery, San Francisco, 1994, Jack Hanley Gallery, San Francisco, 1994, Galeria Massimo de Carlo, Milan, 1995, Parco, Tokyo, 1995, Richard Fonke Galerie, Ghent, Belgium, 1995, Richard Feigen Gallery, Chgo., 1996, Ginza Art Space, Tokyo, 1997, Suzanne Hilberry Gallery, Birmingham, Mich., 1997, Mus. Contemporary Art, L.A., 1997, Jay Gorney Modern Art, N.Y.C., 1998, Wood St. Gallery, Pittsburgh, 1999, Thread Waxing Space, NY, 2000; exhibited in numerous group shows, 1985—, latest being Santa Monica (Calif.) Mus. Art, 1992, 94, 95, Inst. Contermporary Art, Boston, 1993, Long Beach (Calif.) Mus. Art, 1994, Mus. Modern Art at Heide, Melbourne, Australia, 1994, Nat. Mus. Modern Art, Paris, 1995, Los Angeles County Mus. Art, 1995, Whitney Mus. Am. Art, N.Y.C., 1995, UCLA Armand Hammer Mus. Art and Cultural Ctr., 1996, Mus. Contemporary Art, Miami, Fla., 1996, Gröninger Mus., Gröningen, The Netherlands, 1996,, Galerie Rodolphe Janssen, Brussels, 1996, Nat. Gallery, Athens, 1996, Guggenheim Mus., N.Y.C., 1997, St. Louis Art Mus., 1997, Milw. Art Mus., 1997, Mus. Contemporary Art, L.A., 1998, Stedelijk Mus., Amsterdam, The Netherlands, 1998; represented in permanent collections Whitney Mus. Am. Art, Mus. Modern Art, San Francisco, Mus. Fine Arts, Boston, Mus. Contemporary Art, L.A., Los Angeles County Mus. Art, Long Beach Mus. Art, Gröninger Mus., Centro Cultural Arte Contemporaneo, Mexico City, Ctr. for Creative Photography, U. Ariz., Tucson; work represented in numerous publs. Address: c/o Gorney Bravin & Lee 534 W 26th St New York NY 10001-5515

OPPELT, MAREN JOYCE, secondary school educator; d. K. Gordon and Joyce Vivian Egertson; m. Michael John Oppelt, Aug. 30, 1980; children: Monicza Joyce, macKenzie Jae. BA cum laude, Pacific Luth. U., Tacoma, Wash., 1979, 5th Yr. Certification - Edn., 1981; MEd, U. Idaho, 2002. Cert. Adolescent/Young Adult English/Language Arts Nat. Bd. for Profl. Tchg. Stds., 2001. Tchr. Minidoka County Sch. Dist., Rupert, Idaho, 1984—; English/music adj. Coll. of So. Idaho, Twin Falls, Idaho, 1999—. Team leader Minico HS, Rupert, Idaho, 2001—; dept. chair Minico HS English Dept., Rupert, Idaho, 2001—; lang. arts coord. Minidoka County Sch. Dist., Rupert, Idaho, 2002—. Substitute organist local chs., Idaho, 1985—2003. Grantee NBPTS certification, J.A. and Kathryn Albertson Found., 2000; Whittenberger Fellow, Whittenberger Found., 1989. Independent. Evangelical Lutheran. Avocations: crafts, gardening, swimming, reading, writing. Office: Minico High Sch 292 West 100 South Rupert ID 83350 Office Phone: 208-436-5355 313. E-mail: moppelt@sd331.k12.id.us.

OPPENHEIM, MARTHA KUNKEL, pianist, educator; b. Port Arthur, Tex., June 25, 1935; d. Samuel Adam and Grace (Moncure) Kunkel; m. Russell Edward Oppenheim, June 18, 1960; children: Lauren Susan, Kristin Lee Oppenheim Mortenson. MusB with honors, U. Tex., 1957, MusM, 1959; diploma in piano, Juilliard Sch. Music, 1960; student, Am. Conservatory, Fontainebleau, France, 1956, student, 1958. Soloist Amarillo (Tex.) Symphony, Austin (Tex.) Symphony, U. Tex. Orch., San Antonio Symphony, Dallas Symphony, Heilbronner Kammer Orch., Heilbron, Germany. Solo and chamber music recitals in Tex., N.Y., France; mem. Halcyon Trio, 1974—77; tchg. asst. U. Tex., 1957—59, 1968—69; pvt. piano tchr., San Antonio, 1962—; pianist in duo with cellist Dan Zollars, 1991—. Recipient 1st place award, Internat. Piano Rec. Festival, Nat. Guild Piano Tchrs., 1956, 1956, Tuesday Mus. Club Young Artist Competition, 1956, 1st place award Young Artist Competition, Amarillo Symphony, 1959, 1st place award G.B. Dealey competition, Dallas Symphony and Dallas Morning News, 1959; scholar, U. Tex., Juilliard Sch. Music. Mem.: San Antonio Music Tchrs. Assn., Tex. Music Tchrs. Assn., Music Tchrs. Nat. Assn., Tuesday Musical Club (San Antonio, bd. dirs.), Pi Kappa Lambda, Sigma Alpha Iota. Presbyterian. Home and Office: 9118 E Valley View Ln San Antonio TX 78217-5160 E-mail: moppenheim@satx.rr.com.

OPPENHEIM, SARA E. psychologist; b. N.Y.C., Feb. 7, 1958; d. David and Ellen (Adler) Oppenheim; m. Alfred Boland; children: Julian David Boland, Theodore James Boland. ABL in Psychology, Harvard U., 1984; PhD in Psychology, NYU, 1996. Rsch. scientist dept. neuroscience N.Y. State Psychiat. Inst., 1995—2001; asst. adj. prof. John Jay Coll. of Criminal Justice, 1999—2002; pvt. practice, 1997—. Mem.: APA. Democrat. Jewish. Avocation: flute. Home: Apt 3G 165 Pinchurst Ave New York NY 10033-1814 Office: 159 W 53d St # 33H New York NY 10019 Office Phone: 212-765-7948. E-mail: saraoppenheim@yahoo.com.

OPPENHEIMER, DEANNA WATSON, bank executive; Degree cum laude in Polit. Sci. and Urban Affairs, U. Puget Sound. From mktg. and govt. rels. officer to pres. Washington Mutual Bus. Banking, Seattle, 1985—99, pres. Banking and Fin. Svcs. Group, 1999—, overseer corp. R&D and corp. rels., 1999—. Bd. dir. Catellus Devel. Corp., U. Puget Sound. Pres. Seattle (Wash.) Children's Theatre Bd.; bd. dir. Corp. Coun. Arts, Greater Seattle (Wash.) YMCA. Named Person of Yr., Media Inc.; recipient Double Halo award, Seattle (Wash.) Advt. Fedn. Mem.: Mktg. Comm. Execs. Internat. (pres.). Office: Washington Mutual Business Banking 1201 3rd Ave Seattle WA 98101

OPPENHEIMER, SONYA, advertising executive, graphics designer; b. Linden, N.J., Sept. 4, 1936; d. George and Lydia (Clark) Wein; m. Alfred Oppenheimer, Nov. 21, 1965; children: John Jacob, Simone Ayna. Student, Boston U., 1954-56; BA in Humanities, Thomas Edison State Coll., 1996. Disc jockey, copywriter Sta. WAUG, Augusta, Ga., 1956-57; copy and continuity writer Sta. WQXI, Atlanta, 1957-58; columnist, feature writer Fair Lawn (N.J.) News Beacon, 1962-63; copy and pub. rels. writer Park Advt., Elizabeth, N.J., 1963-65; copy chief Botany Industries, N.Y.C., 1965-67; freelance feature and copy writer A&S, Boston Globe, Cranford Chronicle, 1967-69; pres. Sonya Oppenheimer Advt., Randolph, N.J., 1969—. Editor: Conscious Living, 2000—; contbr. articles to mags. Mem. Sisterhood Morristown Jewish Cmty. Ctr.; bd. dirs. Holistic Alliance Internat., Denville, NJ, 1991—. Recipient Gold award, Advt. and Pub. Rels. Assn. N.J., 1991, 1992, Hon. Mention award, Writer's Digest, 1999. Mem.: NOW, Hadassah. Avocations: fashion design, cooking, reading, gardening. Home and Office: 100 Radtke Rd Randolph NJ 07869-3815 Office Phone: 973-366-1441. E-mail: oppyalso@aol.com.

OPPENHEIMER, SUZI, state legislator; b. N.Y.C., Dec. 13, 1934; d. Alfred Elihu Rosenhirsch and Blanche (Schoen) O.; m. Martin J. Oppenheimer, July 3, 1960; children: Marcy, Evan, Josh, Alexandra. BA in Econs., Conn. Coll. for Women, 1956; MBA, Columbia U., 1958. Security analyst McDonnell & Co., N.Y.C., 1958-60, L.F. Rothschild Co., N.Y.C., 1960-63; mayor Village of Mamaroneck, N.Y., 1977-85; mem. N.Y. State Senate, Albany, 1985—. Ranking mem. edn., mem. fin., transp., water resources, health, ethics, environ. conservation and banking com., chmn. N.Y. State Women Legislators' Lobby, chmn. Senate Dem. Task Force on Women's Issues, treas. Legis. Women's Caucus, pres. Senate Club. Former pres. Mamaroneck LWV, Westchester County Mcpl. Ofcls. Assn., Westchester Mcpl. Planning Fedn. Recipient Humanitarian Svc. award Am. Jewish Com., 1988, Legis. Leadership award Young Adult Inst., 1988, Legis. award Westchester Irish Com., 1988, Hon. Svc. award Vis. Nurses Svcs., 1989, Humanitarian Svc. award Project Family, 1990, Meritorious Svc. award N.Y. State Assn. Counties, 1990, Friend of Edn. award N.Y. State United Tchrs., 1991, Assn. Health Care Providers award, 1993, Govtl. award Cmty. Opportunity Program, 1994, Spl. Recognition award Open Door Family Med. Group, 1995, Appreciation award, Careers for People with Disabilities, 1996, Dominican Sisters Family Health Svcs., 1996, Vets. Svc. award JWV, 1997; honoree Windward Sch. Ann. Dinner, 1992, Leadership award Westchester Dem. Com., 2003, Citizen of Yr. award NASW, 2003, others; named Legislator of Yr., N.Y. State Women's Press Club, Woman of Yr., Westchester ORT, 1990, Woman of Yr., Woman of the Yr. bus. and profl. women's club, 2001, Pub. Svc. award cmty. housing, 2002, honoree, Wash. housing alliance dinner, 2002, Hope Cmty. Svcs. Club, 2002, Westchester Fedn. Women's Clubs, 2002. Democrat. Jewish. Office: 222 Grace Church St Port Chester NY 10573-5168

OPPENHEIM-SCHREINER, ELISSA, composer; b. N.Y.C., July 12, 1934; d. Gustave Denny and Birdie (Horn) Oppenheim; m. Leslie Marvin Schreiner, Jan. 22, 1956; children: Gary Nevin Schreiner, Robin Schreiner-Kroll. BS in Music, Hunter Coll.-CUNY, 1956. Pvt. music tchr., Crestwood, N.Y., 1960—; judge editing and music Emmy Awards, 2003; accompanist, jazz pianist. Composer: (TV spl.) Sneakers, 1987-88 (Emmy award 1988), (musical score) Once Upon A Vine, 2000; composer, producer: Let's Celebrate Hanukkah, 1991, Let's Celebrate Passover, 1993, Let's Celebrate Christmas, 1993; author: C for Two, 1997; author: 2 By Two, 1988, Playland, 2002. Mem. ASCAP (awards 1978-95), NARAS, NATAS (judge for children's programming Emmy 1994, 95, 96, 97, 98, 2004), Dramatists Guild. Avocations: cooking, gardening.

OPPERMAN, ROSANNA RESENDEZ, adult education educator; b. LA, Apr. 06; d. Victor Thomas and Dolores Resendez Mendez; m. Daniel Charles Opperman, Aug. 3, 1974; children: Joshua Mendez, Timothy Mendez, Laura Mendez. BA in Exptl. Psychology, U. Calif., Santa Barbara, Calif., 1976; degree in Multiple Subject Tchg., Azusa Pacific Coll., 1979; MA in Ednl. Leadership, Calif. State U., 2004. Admin. Svcs. Credential 2003. From instr. to coord. ESL Program Fremont Sch. for Adults, Sacramento, 1989—2002, coord. ESL Program, 2002—, wasc accreditation co-chair, 2002—. Awards chmn. No. Sect. Calif. Coun. Adult Edn., Sacramento, 1997—99, pres. No. Sect., 1999—2000, v.p. No. Sect., 1999—2000. Cmty. adv. co-chair Fremont Sch. for Adults, Sacramento, 1999—2000; caravans dir. Nazarene Ch., Sacramento, 1988—94. Recipient Outstanding Leadership award, Calif. Coun. Adult Edn., 1997—2001, Excellence in Tchg. award, 1998. Mem.: Adult Basic Educators (assoc.), Calif. Assn. Tchrs. English to Spkrs. Other Langs. (assoc.). Office: Fremont School for Adults 2420 N Street Sacramento CA 95816 E-mail: rosanna-opperman@sac-city.k12.ca.us., rropperman@cs.com.

O'QUINN, APRIL GALE, obstetrician, gynecologist, educator; b. Columbia, Miss., Apr. 21, 1936; d. R.V. and Anna Pauline (Cook) O'Q. Diploma, Scott and White Sch. Nursing, 1965; AA, Temple Jr. Coll., 1965; BS with honors, Baylor U., 1968; MD, U. Tex. Med. Br., 1971. Diplomate Am. Bd. Ob-Gyn. Intern U. Tex. Med. Br., Galveston, 1971-72, resident ob-gyn., 1972-75; fellow in oncology M.D. Anderson Hosp., Houston, 1976-78; practice medicine specializing in ob-gyn. Galveston, 1978-81, New Orleans, 1981—. Asst. prof. dept. ob-gyn. U. Tex. Med. Br., Galveston, 1975—81; mem. staff John Sealy Hosp., St. Mary's Hosp., Galveston, Tulane Med. Ctr., New Orleans Charity Hosp., Touro Infirmary, New Orleans; assoc. prof., dir. div. gynecol. oncology dept. ob-gyn. Tulane U. Sch. Medicine, New Orleans, 1981—85, prof., 1985—89, prof., chair dept. ob-gyn., 1989—. Fellow: ACOG, Willard R. Cooke Obstet. and Gynecol. Soc.; mem.: AMA, La. Med. Assn., Assn. Profs. in Ob-Gyn., Coun. Univ. Chmn. in Ob-Gyn., Soc. Gynecologic Oncologists, Felix Rutledge Soc. Orleans Parish. Republican. Baptist. Home: 5100 Bancroft Dr New Orleans LA 70122-1218 Office: Tulane U Sch Medicine Dept Ob Gyn New Orleans LA 70112 E-mail: aoquinn@tulane.edu.

ORAN, ELAINE SURICK, physicist, engineer; b. Rome, Ga., Apr. 16, 1946; d. Herman E. and Bessye R. (Kolker) Surick; m. Daniel Hirsh Oran, Feb. 1, 1969. AB, Bryn Mawr Coll., 1966; MPh, Yale U., 1968, PhD, 1972. Rsch. physicist Naval Rsch. Lab., Washington, 1972-76, supervisory rsch. physicist, 1976-88, sr. scientist reactive flow physics, 1988—. Head Ctr. for Reactive Flow and Dynamical Systems, 1985-87; mem. adv. bd. NSF; cons. to U.S. govt., agys., NATO.; mem. Aero. Adv. Coun. NASA, 1995-97. Author: Numerical Simulation of Reactive Flow, 1987, 2d edit., 2001, Numerical Approaches to Combustion Modeling, 1991; assoc. editor Jour. Computational Physics; mem. editl. bd. Prog. Ener. Comb. Sci.; mng. editor Shock Waves, 1992-2002; contbr. numerous articles to profl. jours., chpts. to books. Named hon. prof., U. Wales, 2001—; named to Hall of Fame, Women in Tech. Internat., 2002; recipient Arthur S. Flemming award, 1979, Women in Sci. and Engring. award, 1988, Oppenheim prize, 1999, Zeldovich Gold medal, 2000; grantee, USN, NASA, USAF, Def. Advanced Rsch. Projects Agy. Fellow AIAA (publs. com. 1986—2002, v.p. publs. 1993-97, Dryden Disting. lectr. 2002, editor-in-chief AIAA Jour.), Nat. Acad. Engring., Am. Phys. Soc. (exec. com. fluid dynamics divsn. 1986, 96, exec. com. computational physics 1989—, chair 1991-92); mem. Am. Geophys. Union, Combustion Inst. (bd. dirs. 1990-2002), Inst. Dynamics of Energetic Sys. (bd. dirs. 1989—, pres.), Soc. Indsl. and Applied Math., Soc. Women Engrs., Sigma Xi. Office: Naval Rsch Lab Code 6404 # 6004 Washington DC 20011 E-mail: oran@lcp.nrl.navy.mil.

ORCHARD, OLGA SOKOLICH, music educator; b. Bklyn., N.Y., Nov. 19, 1948; d. Peter Sokolich, Anna (Rotko) Sokolich; m. Lauren Ward Orchard, July 25, 1980; 1 child, William David Andrew. B in Music Edn., Evangel U., 1972; M in Music Edn., Tex. Christian U., 1977. Cert. Pub. sch. music tchr. Ind., 1998. [illegible] William Floyd Mid. Sch., Mastic Beach, NY, 1972—73, Edison Pub. Schs., Edison, NJ, 1973—75; music faculty North Ctrl. U., Mpls., 1978—80; dir. band and choral Sundance H.S., Sundance, Wyo., 1981—84; music faculty Evangel U., Springfield, Mo., 1985—88; editor broadcasting Gospel Publ. House, Springfield, 1990—98; dir. choral, tchr. music Rensselaer Mid. and H.S., Rensselaer, Ind., 1998—. Contbr. articles to profl. jours. Named Outstanding Women of Am., 1979. Mem.: Music Educators Nat. Conf., Am. Choral Dirs. Assn., Mu Phi Epsilon (dist. dir. 1973—75, Sr. Achievement award 1972). Avocations: painting, writing, composing. Home: PO Box 66 Rensselaer IN 47978

ORCUTT, BEN AVIS, retired social work educator; b. Falco, Ala., Oct. 17, 1914; d. Benjamin A. and Emily Olive Adams; m. Harry P. Orcutt, 1946 (dec.). AB, U. Ala., 1936; MA, Tulane U., 1939, MSW, 1942; DSW, Columbia U., 1962. Social worker ARC, Lagarde Gen. Hosp., New Orleans; social worker, acting field dir. Fort Benning (Ga.) Regional Hosp., 1942-46; chief social work svc. VA Regional Office, Phoenix, 1946—51; chief social work svc. unit outpatient office VA, Birmingham, Ala., 1954-57, 58; rsch. asst. Rsch. Ctr. Sch. Social Work, Columbia U., N.Y.C., 1960-62, field advisor social work, 1962, assoc. prof. social work, 1965-76, La. State U., Baton Rouge, 1962-65; prof. social work, dir. doctoral program U. Ala., University, 1976-84; ret. Rsch. cons. Tavistock Centre, London, 1972; cons. sch. social work U. Houston, 1990, Troy State System, 1992. Author: Science and Inquiry in Social Work Practice, 1990, (with Harry P. Orcutt) America's Riding Horses, 1958, (with Elizabeth R. Prichard, Jean Collard, Austin H. Kutscher, Irene Seeland, Nathan Lefkowitz) Social Work with the Dying Patient and the Family, 1977, (with others) Social Work and Thanatology, 1980; editor: Poverty and Social Casework Services, 1974; mem. editl. bd. Jour. Social Work, 1982-84; contbr. articles to profl. books and jours. Mem. alumni bd. Sch. Social Work Columbia U., 1985—88, 1991—94. Recipient Centennial award for edn. Columbia U. Sch. Social Work, 1998; named to Ala. Social Work Hall of Fame, 1999; NIMH fellow, 1957-60; Ben Avis Adams Orcutt doctoral scholar in social work named in his honor, U. Ala. Mem. NASW, Ala. Conf. Social Welfare, Group for Advancement Doctoral Edn. (steering com., editor newsletter 1980-83), Zonta, others. Episcopalian. Home: 222 Fox Run Tuscaloosa AL 35406 Office: PO Box 870314 Tuscaloosa AL 35487-0314

ORD, LINDA BANKS, artist; b. Provo, Utah, May 24, 1947; d. Willis Merrill and Phyllis (Clark) Banks; m. Kenneth Stephen Ord, Sept. 3, 1971; children: Jason, Justin, Kristin. BS, Brigham Young U., 1970; BFA, U. Mich., 1987; MA, Wayne State U., 1990. Asst. prof. Sch. Art U. Mich., Ann Arbor, 1994—. Juror Southeastern Mich. Scholastic Art Award Competition, Pontiac, 1992, Scarab Club Watercolor Exhbn., Detroit, 1991, Women in Art Nat. Exhbn., Farmington Hills, Mich., 1991, U. Mich. Alumni Exhbn., 1989-90; mem. dean's adv. coun. U. Mich. Sch. Art and Design, 2001—. One-woman shows Atrium Gallery, Mich., 1990, 91; group shows include Am. Coll., Bryn Mawr, Pa., Riverside (Calif.) Art Mus., Kirkpatrick Mus., Oklahoma City, Montgomery (Ala.) Mus. Fine Arts, Columbus (Ga.) Mus., Brigham Young U., Provo, Utah, Kresge Art Mus., Lansing, Mich., U. Mich., Ann Arbor, Detroit Inst. Arts, Kirkpatrick Ctr. Mus. Complex, Oklahoma City, 1994, Riverside (Calif.) Art Mus., 1995, San Bernadino County Mus., Redlands, Calif., 1996, Neville Mus., Green Bya, Wis., 1996, Downey Mus. Art, Calif., 1996, Detroit Inst. Arts, 1996, Gallery Contemporary Art, U. Colo., Colorado Springs, 1996, Saginaw (Mich.) Art Mus., 1998, Springfield (Mo.) Art Mus., 1998, Art Inst. So. Calif., Laguna Beach, 1998, San Diego Art Inst., 1998, U. Mich., Dearborn, 1998. Hillsdale (Mich.) Coll., 1998, Ferris State U., Big Rapids, Mich., 1998, Sangre de Cristo Arts Ctr., Pueblo, Colo., 1999; works in many pvt. and pub. collections including Kelly Svcs., Troy, Mich., FHP Internat., Fountain Valley, Calif., Swords Into Plowshares Gallery, Detroit; work included in: (books) The Artistic Touch, 1995, Artistic Touch 2, 1996, Best of Watercolor-Painting Color, 1997, Best of Watercolor-Painting Light; Shadow, 1997, Artistic Touch 3, 1999; (mag.) Watercolor, An Am. Artist, 1996; subject of articles. Chairperson nat. giving fund Sch. Art U. Mich., 1993, Sch. art rep. Coun. Alumni Svcs., 1992—, mem. dean's adv. coun. Sch. Art and Design, 2001—. Recipient 1st Pl. award Swords Into Plowshares Internat. Exhbn., Detroit, 1989, Silver award Ga. Watercolor Soc. Internat. Exhbn., 1991, Pres.'s award Watercolor Okla. Nat. Exhbn., Oklahoma City, 1992, Flint Jour. award Buckham Gallery Nat. Exhbn., 1993, Ochs Meml. award N.E. Watercolor Soc. Nat. Exhbn., Goshen, N.Y., 1993, Color Q award Ga. Watercolor Soc., 1994, St. Cuthberts award Tex. Watercolor Soc., 1996, Daler-Rowney award San Diego Watercolor Soc. Internat. Exhbn., 1998, Hon. Mention award Nat. Watercolor Okla. Exhbn., 1998, Winsor:Newton award N.e. Watercolor Soc., 22d Annual Nat. Exhbn., 1998; many state and nat. painting awards. Mem. U. Mich. Alumni Assn. (bd. dirs. 1992—, Sch. Art rep.), U. Mich. Sch. Art Alumni Soc. (bd. dirs. 1989-91, pres.), Mich. Watercolor Soc. (chairperson 1992-93, bd. dirs. adv. 1993-94). Avocations: music, theatre, tennis, golf, reading. E-mail: lbanksord@cox.net.

ORDIN, ANDREA SHERIDAN, lawyer; m. Robert Ordin; 1 child, M. Victoria; stepchildren: Allison, Richard. AB, UCLA, 1962, LLB, 1965. Bar: Calif. 1966. Dep. atty. gen. Calif., 1965-72; So. Calif. legal counsel Fair Employment Practices Commn., 1972-73; asst. dist. atty. L.A. County, 1975-77; U.S. atty. Central Dist. Calif., 1977-81; adj. prof. UCLA Law Sch., 1982; chief asst. atty. gen. Calif. L.A., 1983-90; ptnr. Morgan, Lewis & Bockius, L.A., 1993—. Mem. L.A. County Bar Assn. (past pres., past exec. dir.). Office: Morgan Lewis & Bockius 300 S Grand Ave Ste 2200 Los Angeles CA 90071-3109 E-mail: aordin@morganlewis.com.

ORDWAY, ELLEN, biologist, educator, entomologist, researcher; b. N.Y.C., Nov. 8, 1927; d. Samuel Hanson and Anna (Wheatland) Ordway. BA, Wheaton Coll., Mass., 1950; MS, Cornell U., 1955; PhD, U. Kans., 1965. Field asst. N.Y. Zool. Soc., N.Y.C., 1950-52; rsch. asst. Am. Mus. Natural History, N.Y.C., 1955-57; tchg. asst. U. Kans., Lawrence, 1957-61, rsch. asst., 1959-65; asst. prof. U. Minn., Morris, 1965-70, assoc. prof. biology, 1970-85, prof., 1986-97, prof. emeritus, 1997, acad. advisor, 1997—. Cooperator, cons. USDA Bee Rsch. Lab., Tucson, 1971, Tucson, 83. Contbr. articles to profl. jours. Lectr. Morris area svc. clubs, 1972—; mgr. preserves Nature Conservancy, Mpls., 1975—; bd. dirs. county chpt. ARC, 1998—2003; bd. dirs. U. Minn. Morris Retirees Assn., 1997—2003, sec., treas., 1998—2003. Mem.: AAUP, AAAS, Ecol. Soc. Am., Internat. Bee Rsch. Assn., Kans. Entomol. Soc., Sigma Xi. Episcopalian. Avocations: travel, photography, exploring natural environments, wilderness, areas. Office: U Minn Div Sci And Math Morris MN 56267 E-mail: ordwaye@mrs.umn.edu.

O'REGAN, DEBORAH, association executive, lawyer; b. New Prague, Minn., Aug. 30, 1953; d. Timothy A. and Ermalinda (Brinkman) O'R.; m. Ron Kahlenbeck, Sept. 29, 1984; children: Katherine, Ryan. BA, Coll. of St. Catherine, 1975; JD, William Mitchell Coll. of Law, 1980. Bar: Ala. 1982, Minn. 1980. Asst. city atty. City of Bloomington, Minn., 1978-81, asst. city mgr., 1981-82; CLE dir. Alaska Bar Assn., Anchorage, 1982-84, exec. dir., 1985—. Mem. task force on gender equality State Fed. Joint Commn., Anchorage, 1991—; mem. selection com. U.S. Magistrate Judge, U.S. Dist of Ala., 1992; mem. adv. bd. Anchorage Daily News, 1991-93. Mem. Nat. Assn. Bar Execs. (exec. com. 1993-97). Avocations: travel, outdoors, rollerblading. Office: Alaska Bar Assn 510 L St Ste 602 Anchorage AK 99501-1959

ORESKES, NAOMI, science historian; b. N.Y.C., Nov. 25, 1958; d. Irwin Oreskes and Susan Eileen Nagin Oreskes; m. Kenneth Belitz, Sept. 28, 1986; children: Hannah Oreskes Belitz, Clara Oreskes Belitz. BSc with honors, Imperial Coll., London, 1981; PhD, Stanford U., 1990. Geologist Western Mining Corp., Adelaide, Australia, 1981-84; rsch. and tng. asst. Stanford (Calif.) U., 1984-89; vis. asst. prof. Dartmouth Coll., Hanover, N.H., 1990-91, asst. prof., 1991-96; assoc. prof. Gallatin Sch. NYU, 1996-98, U. Calif., San Diego, 1998—. Consulting geologist Western Mining Corp., 1984-90; consulting historian Am. Inst. Physics, N.Y.C., 1990-96. Author: The Rejection of Continental Drift, 1999, Theory and Method in American Earth Science, 1999; editor: Plate Tectonics: An Insider's History of the Modern Theory of the Earth, 2001; contbr. articles to profl. jours. Recipient Lindgren prize Soc. Econ. Geologists, 1993, Young Investigator award NSF, 1994-99, George Sarton Lectr. award AAAS, 2004; fellow NEH, 1993. Mem. Geol. Soc. Am., History Sci. Soc. Jewish. Home: 14174 Bahama Cv Del Mar CA 92014-2901 Office: U Calif San Diego 9500 Gilman Dr La Jolla CA 92093-0104 Office Phone: 858-534-4695. Business E-Mail: noreskes@ucsd.edu.

ORGEBIN-CRIST, MARIE-CLAIRE, biology educator; b. Vannes, France, Mar. 20, 1936; License Natural Scis., License Biology, Sorbonne, U. Paris, 1957; D. Scis., Lyons U., France, 1961. Stagiaire dept. biochemistry faculty medicine, Paris, France, 1957-58; stagiaire Centre Nat. de la Recherche Scientifique, Paris, 1958-60, attachee de recherche, 1960-62; research assoc. Population Council (Med. Div.), N.Y.C., 1962-63; research assoc. dept. ob/gyn Vanderbilt Sch. Medicine, 1963-64, research instr., 1964-66, asst. prof., 1966-70, assoc. prof., 1970-73, Lucius E. Burch prof. reproductive biology, 1973—, prof. dept. anatomy, 1975—; dir. Vanderbilt Sch. Medicine (Center Reproductive Biology Research.), 1973—. Editor-in-Chief Jour. Andrology, 1983-89. Recipient Career Devel. award NIH, 1968-73, NIH Merit award, 1986,; Fogarty Internat. sr. fellow, 1977; Disting. Scientist award Am. Soc. Reproductive Medicine, 1996. Mem. Am. Assn. Anatomists, Am. Soc. Cell Biology, Am. Soc. Andrology (v.p. 1994-95, pres. 1995-96, Disting. Svc. award 1997, Disting. Andrologist award 1990), Internat. Com. on Andrology, Endoccrine Soc., Soc. for Study Fertility (Eng.), Soc. for Study Reprodn., N.Y. Acad . Scis. Office: Vanderbilt U Sch Med Ctr Reproductive Biology Rsch Rm C-3306 MCN Nashville TN 37232-0001 E-mail: m-c.orgebin-crist@mcmail.vanderbilt.edu

O'RILEY, KAREN E. principal; b. L.A. BA, Loyola Marymount U., L.A., 1981; MPA, Calif. State U., 1983. Home: PO Box 261005 Encino CA 91426-1005

ORITSKY, MIMI, artist, educator; b. Reading, Pa., Aug. 14, 1950; d. Herbert and Marcia (Sarna) O. Student, Phila. Coll. Art, 1968-70; BFA, Md. Inst. Coll. Art, 1975; MFA, U. Pa., 1979. Artist, supr. subway mural projects Crisis Intervention Network, Phila., 1978-83; instr. painting U. Arts, 1984, 1989—93, Abington Art Ctr., Jenkintown, 1989—, Main Line Art Ctr., Haverford, 1993—. One-woman shows include Gross McCleaf Gallery, 1980-82, Callowhill Art Gallery, Reading, Pa., Amos Eno Gallery, NYC, 1986, 89, 91, 94, 96, 98, 2001, 03, Hahnemann U. Gallery, Phila., 1988, Kauffman Gallery, Shippensburg, Pa., 1989, 97, Kimberton (Pa.) Gallery, 1990, Rittenhouse Galleries, Phila., 1992-94, A.I.R. Gallery, NYC, 2003; exhibited in group shows at Current Representational Painting in Phila., 1980, Gross McCleaf Gallery, 1980-82, Yearsley Spring Gallery, Phila., 1998, Phila. Art Alliance, 1998, Coll. Art Gallery, Trenton, NJ, 1996, 98, 2000, Abington Art Ctr., 1999, Brattleboro Mus., TW Wood Mus., Montshire Mus., Phila. Art Alliance, Florence Griswold Mus., 2002-04; pub. in NewAmerican Paintings, 2000. Recipient Purchase award Pa. Coun. Arts and Arcadia Coll., 1983, Reading Pub. Mus., 1984, Best of Show award Abington Art Ctr. Juried Annual, 1998; fellow Environment Found., 1980, Millay Colony for Arts, 1983. Mem. Coll. Art Assn. E-mail: gill1313@aol.com.

ORLAND, RACHEL JANE, elementary school educator, musician; b. Belvidere, Ill., May 15, 1970; d. Peter Scott Edwards and Janey Frances Frost; m. Stephen Patrick Orland, Nov. 26, 1993; 1 child, Jackson Thomas. AA, Rock Valley Jr. Coll., Rockford, Ill., 1990; B in Music Edn., Ill. State U., Normal, 1993; M in Music Edn., U. Ill., Champaign, 1997; MA in Ednl. Leadership, Aurora U., 2003. Cert. music edn. Ill., 1993, adminstrn. Ill. Elem. tchr. W. Aurora Sch. Dist., 1993—95; middle sch. tchr. Oswego (Ill.) Sch. Dist., 1995—; adj. music edn. faculty N. Ctrl. Coll., Naperville, Ill., 2000—. Guest condr. Jr. Band Camp, Normal, Ill., 1999, Indian Prairie Sch. Dist., Naperville, Ill., 2002, Ill. Youth Music, Champaign, 2002. Named Outstanding Music Educator, Quinlan & Fabish Co., 1999. Mem.: Music Educators Nat. Conf., Nat. Band Assn. (Citation of Excellence 1998), Am. Sch. Band. Dir. Assn. (Outstanding Jr. Band Dir. North Ctrl. Region 2000). Avocation: American saddlebred horses. Office: Traughber Jr High Sch 61 Franklin St Oswego IL 60543 E-mail: rorland_308@yahoo.com.

ORLANDO, VALERIA, music educator, musician, artist; d. Ross and Mary Orlando. MusB magna cum laude, Hartt Sch. Music, Hartford, Conn., 1972; MA in Music, CUNY, 1974. Tchg. credential K-12 Calif., c.c. instr. credential Calif. Music educator Santa Monica (Calif.) C.C., 1986—96, El Camino C.C., Torrance, Calif., 1986—96, L.A. Valley Coll., Van Nuys, Calif., 1987—95, U. of Redlands, Calif., 1995—97, Moreno Valley (Calif.) Unified Sch. Dist., 1997—2000, Anaheim (Calif.) Union H.S. Dist., 2000—. Bd. dirs. Nat. Assn. Tchrs. of Singing, L.A., 1992—94; music adjudicator numerous orgns.; music cons. YMCA, Anaheim, 2002—. Mem., vol. Anaheim Arts Coun., 2000—. Named winner, Viotti Internat. Voice Competition, Italy, nat. finalist, Lyric Opera of Chgo. Ctr. for Am. Artists, semi-finalist, Young Concert Artists Internat., N.Y.C.; recipient Tchr. Recognition and Talent Search award, Nat. Found. for Advancement of Arts, 1997; Disneyland Arts Partnership Enabling grantee, 2001. Mem.: Tech. Inst. for Music Educators, So. Calif. Vocal Assn., Calif. Music Educators Assn. (bd. dirs., 2d v.p. 2001—), Zurich Opernhaus Studio, Mu Phi Epsilon. Avocations: genealogy, gourmet cooking, reading, gardening. Office: Ball Jr HS 1500 W Ball Rd Anaheim CA 92802

ORLANDO-SPINELLI, JOSEPHINE, gifted and talented educator, educational consultant; b. Philadelphia, New Jersey, Mar. 15, 1958; d. Frank and Rita Orlando; m. Paul F. Spinelli, June 20, 1992; 1 stepchild, Paul A. Spinelli. EdB, Coll. St. Elizabeth, Convent Sta., N.J., 1976—80; M in Holocaust and genocide studies, Stockton Coll., Pomona, N.J., 2000—. Cert. tchg. N.J., 1980. Tchr. of lang. arts, gifted and talented Atlantic City Bd. of Edn., Atlantic City, 1980—95; tchr. of gifted and talented Brigantine Pub. Sch., Brigantine, NJ, 1995—2002, Upper Twp. Pub. Sch., Petersburg, NJ, 2002—. Attended Lest We Forget Study Tour du Europe, 2003. Founding mem. Red and Gray Gridiron Club, Vineland, NJ, 1999—2003; com. mem. SITE, Upper Twp. Pub. Sch., Petersburg, NJ, 2002—03, Impact, Upper Twp. Pub. Sch., Petersburg, NJ, 2001—03. Recipient to attend Stamm Found., Phila., N.J., 2001. Mem.: N.J. Assn. for Gifted Children, mem., pres. Alpha Delta Kappa, Gamma Chap. Achievements include establishing the Frank Orlando Meml. Gifted Awards in Brigantine Pub. Schools. Avocations: theater, singing, dance, singing the Nat. Anthem at the Atlantic City Surf games, 1999. Home: 2284 Baywood Dr Vineland NJ 08361-6682 Office: Upper Twp Pub Sch 525 Perry Rd Petersburg NJ E-mail: JosieCatLover@comcast.net.

ORLOSKI, SHARON, secondary school educator; b. Taylor, Pa., Aug. 15, 1943; d. Leo Paul and Sophie Ann O. BS, Ctrl. Conn. State U., New Britain, 1965; MS, U. Conn., Storrs, 1970; CAS, Wesleyan U., Middletown, Conn., 1972. Cert. tchr. biology, chemistry and gen. sci., Conn. Gen. sci. tchr. Bridgeport (Conn.) Adult Edn., 1966-68; homebound tchr. Bridgeport Bd. Edn., 1966-67; tchr. biology Ctrl. H.S., Bridgeport Bd. Edn., 1965-82, Ctrl. Magnet H.S., Bridgeport Bd. Edn., 1982—. Master tchr. Bridgeport Bd. Edn., 1974, 2002, tchr. mentor vertical curriculum devel., 2002; leader citywide workshops. Bd. dirs., pres., sec. Madison Gardens Condominium Assn. NSF grantee, 1967-71. Mem. NEA, Nat. Assn. Biology Tchrs., U. Conn. Alumni Assn. (life), Ctrl. Conn. State Alumni Assn. (life), Conn. Edn. Assn., Bridgeport Edn. Assn., Lladro Soc., U.S. Humane Soc. Avocations: N.Y. Yankees, stocks, gardening. Office: Ctrl Magnet HS One Lincoln Blvd Bridgeport CT 06606

ORLOWSKA-WARREN, LENORE ALEXANDRIA, art educator, fiber artist; b. Detroit, May 22, 1951; d. William Leonard and Aloisa Clara (Hrapkiewicz) Orlowski; m. Donald Edward Warren, May 11, 1990. AA, Henry Ford C.C., 1972; BS in Art Edn., Wayne State U., 1974, M in Spl. Edn., 1978; BFA, Ctr. for Creative Studies, 2000. Tchr. arts and crafts Detroit Pub. Schs., 1974—2002; fiber artist Detroit Inst. Arts. Cons. Arts Detroit Cmty. Plan, TRIACO Arts & Crafts, 1996—; instr., demonstrator weaving Detroit Inst. Arts; represented by Gallery Five, Tequesta, Fla., Ann Arbor Art Ctr. One-woman show at Dearborn C. of C., Ctr. for Creative Studies, 2000; exhibited in group shows, including alumni exhibit Henry Ford C.C., 1989, Detroit Artist Market, 1995-2000, Scarab Club, 1996, Lansing Art Gallery, 1997, Ctr. for Creative Studies, 1997, Yr. of the Woman Exhibit, 1998, Tom Thompson Meml. Art Gallery Juried Ontario Artists Exhibit, 1998, 2001, One Focus, Two Worlds Exhibit, 1999, Fashion Exhibit and Felt the Feeling of Fiber, U.245 Gallery, 1999, Ctr. Creative Studies, 2000, Ann Arbor Art Ctr., 2001, Downriver Coun. for the Arts, 2001, Alumni Fiber Artist exhibit Coll. Creative Studies, 2002, Ann Arbor Art Ctr. All Media Exhbn., 2002 (Barbara Dorr Meml. award), Outside The Lines Gallery, 2001, 02, Padziewski Gallery, 2003, Scarab Club, 2003; contbr. to Sch. Arts Mag.; represented in permanent collections Gallery Five, Tequesta, Fla., Ann Arbor Art Ctr. Mem. exec. bd. Springwells Pk. Assn., 1989-99, pres., 1994-96, chairperson youth act workshops; com. mem. Dearborn cmty. art coun. Art on the Ave., 1993-99, Gallery Crawl chairperson, 1998; chair Nat. Woman's History Month workshop, 1995. Mem.: Cranbrook Acad. Art, Am. Tapestry Alliance, Art Inst. of Chgo., Downriver Coun. for Arts, Surface Design Assn., The Textile Mus., The Nat. Mus. Women in Art Williamsburg Burgesses, Met. Mus. Art, Norton Mus. Art (Williamsburg assoc.), Mich. Surface Design, Friends of Fiber Art Internat. Assn., Coll. Art Assn., Birmingham Bloomfield Art Assn., Detroit Inst. Arts-Founders Soc., Am. Craft Coun., Mich. Art Edn. Assn. (presenter art advocacy workshop), Nat. Art Edn. Assn. (electronic gallery coord 1992—99). Avocations: fiber art, travel, colonial gardening, reading colonial history and biographies. Home: 10 Berwick Ln Dearborn MI 48120-1102

ORMAI-BUZA, ILDIKO, soprano, composer, organist, music educator; b. Budapest, Hungary, Dec. 21, 1927; came to U.S., 1949, naturalized, 1955; d. Janos and Margit Ormai; m. George Buza, Oct. 28, 1950; children: George F., Paul L. Student in piano and theory, Hannig Conservatory, Budapest, 1938-44; student, Ecole D'Arts Coll., Freiburg, Germany, 1947-49; studied voice with Carmela Cafarelli; studied composition and orchestration, Janos Kiss. Cert. pvt. voice, piano and organ tchr., Ohio. Organist, soloist St. Raphael Cath. Ch., Bay Village, Ohio, 1957-72; concert soprano Cafarelli Opera Co., Cleve., 1957-67; organist, soloist Holy Spirit Ch., Avon Lake, Ohio, 1972-97, Our Lady of Angels Ch., Cleve., 1998-99; frequent guest, organist, soloist St. Emeric Ch., Cleve. Choir dir. Midnszenty Chamber Choir, Cleve., 1981-84; guest soloist Fatima World Congress, Germany, 1985, Portugal, 1992; guest concert soloist, U.S. and Can., 1960—. Composer: (organ and chorus) Mass of Adoration (Silver medal 1975), (choir and organ) Berzsenyi Poem: Supplication (Gold medal 1986), Piano Solos, 1996; performed solo concert Perpetual Adoration Ch., Budapest, 1989; soprano guest soloist West Suburban Philharm. Orch., Ann. Opera Concert, Cleve., 1980, 82, in concert record, 1981; commd. composer Hymn of Worldwide St. Ladislaus Order, 1989; prodr., announcer NBN weekly classical Hungarian Concert Hall Radio Hour, 1977-85; performer voice and piano Hungarian Assn., 1955—. Recipient Papal Blessing for composition Ave Maria, Pope John Paul II, 1987. Mem. Music Tchrs. Nat. Assn., Am. Guild Organists, Ohio Music Tchrs. Assn. (winner composition contest 1989, publicity com. 1981-97), St. Ladislaus Order (knighted Dame 1983, Cross of Honor 1987), Arpad Acad., Cleve. Piano Tchrs. Club. Avocations: painting, portrait drawing, sewing, dance, poetry.

ORNDOFF, ELIZABETH CARLSON, retired junior college librarian, educator; b. Spearville, Kans., Mar. 28, 1918; d. Carl Edward and Laura Rebecca (Pine) Carlson; m. John Delbert Orndoff, Dec. 26, 1942; children: Barbara Kay Orndoff Fazal, David Keith, Richard Lee. BA in Sociology, BEd, U. Colo., 1940; postgrad., U. So. Calif., 1941. Lic. pvt. pilot, 1941; cert. tchr. sociology. Physics dept. libr., sec. U. Colo., Boulder, 1937-40; head coll. librarian Trinidad (Colo.) State Jr. Coll., 1940-42, tchr. sociology, 1941-42; reference librarian Los Alamos (N.Mex.) Pub. Libr., 1963-73. Editor: (non-fiction book) All of These Things, 1974. Tchr. Sunday sch. Meth. Ch., Trinidad, 1940-41; den mother Boy Scouts Am., Los Alamos, 1953-55; leader Girl Scouts U.S.A., Los Alamos, 1955-56; charter mem. United Ch. Los Alamos, 1947—, historian, 1994, 95; mem. Friends Los Alamos Pub. Libr., 1989-90, 94—, Habitat for Humanity, 1994—; active Los Alamos Retirement Ctr., Inc., Blood Mobile, Svcs. and Aid for the Relief of the Poor, Inc., India, 1993—, Meals on Wheels, 1993-99. Mem. AAUW (life), United Ostomy Assn., U. Colo. Alumni Assn., Sr. Citizens. Democrat. Avocations: playing piano, writing, skiing, dance, teaching english grammar to foreigners upon request. Home: 1010 Sombrillo Ct 107 Los Alamos NM 87544-4200

ORNE, EMILY CAROTA, psychologist, researcher; b. Boston, Sept. 7, 1938; d. Emil and Ruth (Farrell) Carota; m. Martin T. Orne, Feb. 3, 1962; children: Franklin Theodore, Tracy Meredith. BA, Bennington Coll., 1959. Rsch. assoc. Mass. Mental Health Ctr., Boston, 1963-64; rsch. psychologist Unit. for Exptl. Psychiatry, Phila., 1964-79, sr. rsch. psychologist, 1979-83, co-dir., 1982—; rsch. assoc. psychology U. Pa. Sch. Medicine, Phila., 1983—. Trustee Inst. Exptl. Psychiatry Rsch. Found., Mass., 1964—, assoc. co-dir., 1987-97, exec. dir., 1998—; bd. dirs. False Memory Syndrome Found., 1995—. Contbr. articles to profl. jours.; assoc. editor Internat. Jour. Clin. and Exptl. Hypnosis, 1977—. Recipient Benjamin Franklin Gold medal Internat. Soc. Hypnosis, 1982, Roy M. Dorcus award Soc. Clin. and Exptl. Hypnosis, 1985, Bernard B. Raginsky award, 1993, Morton Prince award Soc. Clin. and Exptl. Hypnosis and APA, 1994. Avocations: fishing, swimming, reading. Office: U Pa Sch Medicine 1013 Blockley Hall 423 Guardian Dr Philadelphia PA 19104-6021

ORNER, LINDA PRICE, family therapist, counselor; b. Gettysburg, Pa., June 27, 1943; d. John Robert and Ruby Pearl (Vines) Price; m. Ted Arnold Orner, Mar. 29, 1963; children: Penni Ann, Jennifer Arianna. AA, North Harris Coll., 1991; BA summa cum laude, U. St. Thomas, 1994; MEd in Counseling Psychology, U. Houston, 1997, postgrad.; MA in Family Therapy, U. Houston, Clear Lake, 1999. Lic. profl. counselor. Therapist Houston VA Hosp./Trauma Recovery Program, 1996, U. Houston Counseling and Testing Svcs., 1997, U. Houston-Clear Lake Psychol. Svcs., 1998—99; intern/assoc., family therapist Houston Galveston Inst., 1998—2000; pvt. practice counselor Family Life Svcs., Colorado Springs, 2001—. Vol. Women's Ctr.; vol. seminar instr., counselor Tex. Prison; keynote spkr. Christian Women's Clubs Internat. Mem.: APA, ACA, Am. Assn. of Christian Counselors, Am. Psychotherapy Assn., Tex. Counseling Assn., Tex. Assn. for Marriage and Family Therapy, Am. Assn. for Marriage and Family Therapy. Presbyterian. Avocations: travel, scuba diving, hiking, antiques, art. Home: 4684 Stone Manor Hts Colorado Springs CO 80906-8605 Address: 2210 W Dallas # 942 Houston TX 77019 Office Phone: 719-632-4661.

ORNER, PATRICIA ANN, desktop publishing administrator, writer; d. John Felmy Shaffer and Helen Mae Royer Shaffer; m. Ray A. Orner, Jr., Aug. 27, 1988; children: Rebecca Ann, Amy Elizabeth, Samuel Ray. BA in Journalism, Shippensburg U. Pa., 1987. Membership coord. Greater Harrisburg Assn. Realtors, Camp Hill, Pa., 1989—97; adminstr., desktop pub. Cmty. Bapt. Ch., Carlisle, Pa., 2001—. Newsletter editor Cmty. Bapt. Ch., Carlisle, Pa., 1998—; rschr., Shippensburg, Pa., 2002—. Author: First in the First - A History of the 474th AAA Battalion; contbr. articles to profl. jours. Coord. GHAR - Thanksgiving Food Dr., Camp Hill, Pa., 1992—97; sec. Awana clubs Cmty. Bapt. Ch., Carlisle, Pa., 1999—2003, publicity coord. vacation Bible sch., 1998—2003. Mem.: Nat. Geog. Soc., Rep. Nat. Com., Nat. WWII Meml. Soc. Conservative. Baptist. Avocations: reading, travel, photography.

ORNT, JEANINE ARDEN, lawyer; b. Apr. 29, 1955; BA, SUNY, 1977; JD, Union U., 1980. Ptnr. Greisberger, Zicari, Rochester, N.Y., 1985-89; gen. counsel med. ctr. U. Rochester, 1989—. Office: U Rochester Med Ctr 601 Elmwood Ave Rochester NY 14642-0001

OROPEZA, JENNY, state official; b. Long Beach, Calif., Sept. 27, 1957; m. Tom Mullins. BSBA, Calif. State U. Mem. Long Beach Unified Sch. Dist. Bd. Edn., 1988—94; coun. mem. Long Beach City Coun., 1994—2000; state assembly mem. Dist. 55 Calif. State Assembly, 2000—. Mem. Latino Caucus. Democrat. Mailing: Rm 6026 PO Box 942849 Sacramento CA 94249 Office: Ste 320 One Civic Plaza Dr Carson CA 90745

O'ROURKE, ANN MARIE CECILIA, social worker; b. Teaneck, Nj, Sept. 17, 1977; d. Thomas Patrick O'Rourke and Patricia Ann Jones-O'Rourke. BA in Criminal Justice and English, Caldwell Coll., N.J., 1999; MSW, NYU, 2002. Social work intern Day Care Coun. of N.Y., Harlem/Washington Heights, NY; acctg. and file clk. Brach, Eichler, Rosenberg, Silver, et al, Roseland, NJ, 1997—99; white collar fraud intern Morris County Prosecutor's Office, Morristown, NJ, 1998—99; spl. asst. to dir. Children's Futures N.J., Princeton, NJ, 1998—99; social work intern Essex Jr. Acad., Cedar Grove, NJ, 2000—01; psychiatric social worker Meadowview Psychiat. Hosp., Secaucus, NJ, 2001—. Editor: Caldwell Coll. Lit. Jour.; contbr. to lit. jours. Union del. 1199 J, Secaucus, NJ, 2003. Recipient L. McMurray award, NASW, 2002. Mem.: NASW, Amnesty Internat. (women's coun.), Alpha Phi Sigma, Sigma Tau Delta. Democrat. Roman Catholic. Avocations: reading, travel, Latin dancing, cooking, fitness, acting. Office: County of Hudson Meadowview Hospital 595 County Ave Bldg 10 Secaucus NJ 07094 Personal E-mail: orourkenj@aol.com.

O'ROURKE, JOAN B. DOTY WERTHMAN, retired school system administrator; b. N.Y.C., June 7, 1933; d. George E. Doty and Lillian G. Bergen; 10 children. BA summa cum laude, Marymount Manhattan Coll., 1953, MA, Columbia U., 1958; PhD, St. John's U., 1971. Tchr. history Marymount HS, N.Y.C., 1953-55; instr. history Marymount Manhattan Coll., 1957-59; acting chmn. history dept. Nassau C.C., Mineola, NY, 1959-60; dir., writer Sta. WFAS, White Plains, NY, 1963—64; prof. history Westchester CC, Valhalla, NY, 1963-74; prin. Pius X Sch., Scarsdale, NY, 1974-77; assoc. dir. alumni rels. Fordham U., N.Y.C., 1980-84; co-founder, dir. Assn. for Profl. Psychol. and Ednl. Counseling, Wilmette, Ill., 1987-91; ptnr., pres. O'Rourke and Assocs., 1993-97; ret., 1997. Adj. prof. social sci. Fordham U., N.Y.C., 1974—76. Mem. resident bd. Del Webb, Sun City, Calif., 2001—03; mem. fin. com. St. Francis of Assisi Ch., LaQuinta, Calif., 2001—; bd. dirs. Cath. Charities Diocese of San Bernardino, 2001—04, Sun City, Palm Desert, 2001—03, Cath. Charities of San Bernardino, Calif., 1999—. Recipient Alumni award, Marymount Coll., 2003, Mother Raymunde McKay Cmty. Svc. award, Marymount Manhattan Coll., 2003; Tchg. fellow, St. John's U., Jamaica, N.Y., 1968. Mem.: Mich. Shores Club, Order of Holy Sepulchre (lady), Soc. Mayflowers Descs. Ill. Democrat. Roman Catholic. E-mail: doctorjoan@web.tv.net.

OROZCO, EDITH DELL, counselor; b. Stanton, Tex., June 11, 1940; d. Oran Rivers and L. Juanita Nichols; m. Luis Arturo Orozco, Jan. 26, 1963; children: Julia M., Daniel Luis, David Arturo. BS, U. North Tex., 1962, MEd, 1967; ASN, San Antonio Coll., 1984. Lic. profl. counselor, Tex.; cert. sch. counselor, Tex.; cert. spl. edn. counselor, Tex.; cert. bilingual/ESL tchr., Tex.; cert. faith based therapon Belief Therapist, 2000. Elem. tchr. Midland (Tex.) Ind. Sch. Dist., 1962-63, Irving (Tex.) Ind. Sch. Dist., 1963-67, South San Antonio Ind. Sch. Dist., 1975-82, 84-93, sch. counselor, 1993-99, spl. edn. counselor, 1999—. Counselor South Tex. Counseling Svcs., San Antonio, 1998—; co-leader support group Project Heart, Olivares Elem. Sch., San Antonio, 1993-99. Family/sch. coord. counseling Families & Schs. Together, Olivares Elem. Sch., San Antonio, 1997-99; counseling vol. Palo Alto Coll. Returning Adult Ctr., San Antonio, 1996-97; screening vol. Nat. Depression Screening, Palo Alto Coll., San Antonio, 1995, 96. Mem.: Christian Counselors Tex., Am. Assn. Christian Counselors, Tex. Counseling Assn. Baptist. E-mail: eoro@earthlink.net.

ORPHANIDES, NORA CHARLOTTE, ballet educator; b. N.Y.C., June 4, 1951; d. M.T. and Mary Elsie (Tilly) Feffer; m. James Mark Orphanides, July 1, 1972; children: Mark, Elaine Orphanides Mastrosimone, Jennine. BA, CUNY, 1973; student, Joffrey Ballet Sch., N.Y.C., 1970-75; postgrad., Princeton Ballet Sch., 1976-86. Cert. speech and hearing handicapped tchr. With membership dept. M.M.A., N.Y.C., 1987—2002; mem. faculty Princeton (N.J.) Ballet Sch., 1983—, trustee emeritus, 1992—. Mem. cast Princeton Ballet ann. Nutcracker, 1985-90, now Am. Repertory Ballet Co., 1993—; appeared in Romeo & Juliet, 1995-96, 2000. Fundraising gala chmn. Princeton Ballet, 1985, 86, 91-92, chmn. spl. events, 1987—, trustee, 1986—, chmn. Nutcracker benefit, 1990—, Dracula benefit, 1991, honoree, 1999; dept. chmn. June Fete to benefit Princeton Hosp., 1988, 90-91, 92, 96, 2000, trustee, 1995-99; vol. Nat. Hdqrs. Recording for the Blind, 1991-93; dinner chmn. Nassau Ch. Music Festival, 1992, Handel Festival, Nassau Ch., 1993, Princeton Chamber Symphony, 1993; hon. chmn. Princeton Ballet Gala, 1993; chmn. Christmas Boutique, Princeton Med. Ctr., 1993; trustee, Princeton Med. Ctr. Aux. Bd., 1992-2002, trustee 1995—, pres., 1997-99, past pres., 2000-2002; found. bd. dirs. U. Med. Ctr. Princeton, 2004—; choreographer Stuart Country Day Sch., Princeton, 1996-99, 2001; chmn. benefit dinner Eden Inst., 2000. Named honoree Princeton Ballet, 1999, recipient Edward R. and Irene D. Farley Cmty. Stewardship award, Eden Inst. Found., 2003. Democrat. Avocations: piano, skiing, tennis. Office: 301 N Harrison St Princeton NJ 08540-3512

ORR, ADRIANA PANNEVIS, retired librarian; b. Albertson, N.Y., Sept. 30, 1923; d. Adrian Jacobus and Clara (Edgar) Pannevis; m. Oliver Hamilton Orr Jr., Feb. 15, 1956. AB, Elmira Coll., 1944; MSLS, U. N.C., 1958; postgrad., U Md., 1967-68. Tchr. Wisner (Nebr.) H.S., 1944-45; tchr., libr. Downsville (N.Y.) Ctrl. H.S., 1945-48, Lago Cmty. Sch., Aruba, 1948-53; reference libr. U. N.C., Chapel Hill, 1953-58; Latin tchr. Josephus Daniels Jr. H.S., Raleigh, N.C., 1958-59; textiles libr. N.C. State U., Raleigh, 1959-65; reference libr. U.S. Dept. Transportation, Washington, 1966-70; libr. rschr. Oxford English Dictionary, Washington, 1966-90; ret. Active Chapel Hill Hist. Soc., 1991—, Chapel Hill Preservation Soc., 1991—. Methodist. Avocations: reading, letter writing, cooking. Home: 750 Weaver Dairy Rd Apt 172 Chapel Hill NC 27514-1441

ORR, AMY J. sociologist, educator; d. Jody Ann Klute; m. A. Erik Svec, July 5, 1996; 1 child, Hunter Phoenix. BS with highest distinction, Nebr. Wesleyan U., Lincoln, 1993; MA, U. Notre Dame, 1996, PhD, 2000. Vis. asst. prof. sociology U. Notre Dame, Notre Dame, Ind., 2000—01; asst. prof. sociology Linfield Coll., McMinnville, Oreg., 2001—. Bd. mem. Multicultural Adoption Adv. Program, Inc., McMinnville, Oreg., 2003—.

Contbr. articles to profl. jours. and encys., chapters to books. Founding mem. Nat. Campaign for Tolerance (So. Poverty Law Ctr.), Montgomery, Ala., 2001—03; friend of the Ctr. So. Poverty Law Ctr., Montgomery, Ala., 2003—. Rsch. Found. grantee, Carnegie Scholarship of Tchg. Program and the Kaneb Ctr. for Tchg. and Learning, 2000, Nat. Coun. Teachers English, 2001. Mem.: AAUW, NOW, NAACP, ACLU, Pacific Sociol. Assn. (program com. mem. 2003—), Am. Sociol. Assn. (soc nominations com. 1996—97), Nat. Women's History Mus. (charter). Achievements include research on the effects of wealth (net worth) on academic achievement (especially with regard to the black-white test score gap and marital status). Business E-Mail: aorr@linfield.edu.

ORR, BOBETTE KAY, diplomat; b. Oak Park, Ill., Oct. 28, 1941; d. Robert Jay and Neta (Hoobler) Pottle; m. William Rucker Orr, Oct. 11, 1974; step children: Bridgette, Brietta, Alyson, William Jr. BA in Econs., Conn. Coll. for Women, 1963; student auditor Internat. Econs., London Sch. of Econs., 1964; postgrad. studies in Internat. Econs., George Washington U., 1964-65. Rsch. asst. C. of C. USA, Washington, 1965-66; country desk officer for Scandanavia U.S. Dept. Commerce, Washington, 1966-69, country desk officer for France, 1970-72, 79-81, country desk officer for Belgium, Netherlands, Luxembourg, 1974-77, country desk officer for Japan, 1981-82; mkt. rsch. officer United States Trade Ctr., Stockholm, 1973, trade promotion officer London, 1977-78; asst. comml. attache Am. Embassy, Paris, 1982-87; comml. attache Am. Consulate Gen., Auckland, New Zealand, 1988-92, consul gen. Edinburgh, Scotland, 1992-95; comml. counselor Am. Embassy, London, 1995-99, Cairo, 1999—2002; regional dir. Africa, Near East and South Asia U.S. Dept. Commerce, Washington, 2002—. Mem. bd. dirs. U.S. Dept. Commerce Fed. Credit Union, Washington, D.C., 1972-77, pres., 1976-77, mem. supervisory com., 1979-81; equal employment opportunity counselor for Greater Washington Met. Area, 1972-75; mission dir. for USDOC's Concrete Constrn. Techniques Seminar Mission to Hong Kong, Singapore, Malaysia, 1980; detailed to Office of Dir. Fgn. Comml. Svc. as evaluator of candidates for Fgn. Comml. Svc., 1981. Author: (with others) 10 pamphlet series, on free enterprise, The Power of Choice, 1966; contbr. to Bus. Am., 1966-81, Overseas Bus. Reports 1966-76 (Dept. Commerce publs.). Mem. Am. Women's Club of Edinburgh, (hon. pres.), The English Speaking Union. Avocations: skiing, bicycle riding. Home: PO Box 63 Great Falls VA 22066-0063 Office: ANESA/USFCS/ITA Dept Commerce 14th and Constitution Ave NW Rm 1223 Washington DC 20230 Office Phone: 202-482-4836.

ORR, CAROLE, artist; b. Alexandria, Ind., June 10, 1933; d. Carl Victor and Marian Martha (Long) Coonse; m. Larry D. Ribble (dec. July 1953); m. Thomas LeRoy Orr, Nov. 10, 1950 (div. Oct. 1979); children: Karen Sue, Terri Ribble, David Thomas; m. Lev C. Hamblet Jr., Feb. 5, 1982 (div. Oct. 1998); stepchildren: James, Jean, Laura, Anne. Cert., Famous Artist Sch., Westport, Conn., 1956, Art Instrn. Schs., Mpls., 1962. Asst. art dir. La Gallerie du Mall, Houston, 1975—78; freelance fine artist Lantern Ln. Gallery, Houston, 1968—81, asst. mgr., design cons., 1979—81; artist Artist Showroom, Houston, 1982—. Participating artist Assistance Guild, Houston, 1968, Beaux Arts, Houston, 1968-70, Houston Gamma Phi Gallery, 1971-72, Houston Delta Gamma Found., 1978-81, Glassell Sch. of Art Houston, 1983; art instr. children's art Houston Park and Recreational Programs, 1964-68. One-woman shows include Nobler Gallery, Houston, 1967, Art Gallery, Pasadena, Tex., 1968, Gallarie La Rue, Austin, Tex., 1971, Gallery 12, Houston, 1972, Main St., Houston, 1974, La Galerie de Mall, Houston, 1976-78, Triumvirate Gallery, Santa Fe, N.Mex., 1980, Houshang's Gallery, Dallas, 1980-82, Battle Horn Galleries Ltd., Santa Fe, 1984, New Trends Inc., Santa Fe, 1985-88, Horizons Galleries, Houston, 1990-93, Houston C.C., 1992, Heinen Theatre, 1992, Windsor Gallery, Ft. Lauderdale, Fla., 1994; exhibited in group shows at Motorola Invitational, Houston, 1964, Assistance Guild Houston, 1968, Am. Gen. Bldg., Houston, 1968, Beaux Arts, Houston, 1968-70, Gamma Phi Gallery, Houston, 1971-72, Lantern Ln. Gallery, Houston, 1971-72, Delta Gamma Found., Houston, 1978-81, Glassell Sch. Art, Houston, 1983, New Trends Gallery Inc., Santa Fe, 1985-88, Pasadena (Tex.) Art Invitational, 1988, Double Tree Hotel, Houston, 1990, Horizons Gallery, Houston, 1990-93, Windsors Gallery, Dania, Fla., 1993, 2003, Magnolias Art Gallery, Town and Country Ctr., Houston, 2003-04. Art instr. adults Ch. of the Advent, Houston, 1968-70; adult edn. instr. arts Ch. Sch. Conf., Dept. Christian Edn., Trinity Ch., Diocese of Tex., Houston, 1969. Recipient Profl. Best Ann. Competition Art Instrn. Schs., Mpls., 1965; named Best-Selling Artist of Yr., 2001, Paintings DIRECT, N.Y.C., 2001, 03. Avocations: self-study in psychology, music, dance. Home and Office: Artist Showroom DBA 880 Tully Rd Apt 29 Houston TX 77079-5418

ORR, MARGARET, newscaster; b. New Orleans; married; 3 children. Grad. in English, La. State U.; grad. in Broadcast Meteorology, Miss. State U. Photographer, editor, prodr., reporter, anchor, weathercaster WCIV-TV, Charleston, SC; weathercaster WBRZ-TV, Baton Rouge; from assignment reporter to meteorologist WDSU News Channel 6, New Orleans, 1979—. Mem.: Am. Meteorol. Soc. Avocations: gardening, painting. Office: WDSU News Channel 6 846 Howard Ave New Orleans LA 70113

ORR, MARJORIE, poet, dancer, publishing executive; d. William F. and Winifred M. Yeatts; m. Marshall Hugh Orr, Aug. 22, 1964; children: Michael S., Matthew W. children: Marshall H. Jr. BS, U. R.I., Kingston, 1964. Cert. editor Md. Substitute tchr. math Madison (Conn.) HS, 1964—65, Guilford (Conn.) HS, 1964—65; pres. Pointe Press, Bryantown, Md., 1999—. Author, editor: poems Blue Willow, 1999; dancer Arlington (Va.) Ctr. Dance. Campaign aid, Gibsonia, Pa. Mem.: Am. Jour. Poetry (assoc.). Office Phone: N/A.

ORR, SUSAN PACKARD, business owner; BA in Econs., Stanford U., 1968, MBA, 1970; MS in Computer Sci., N.Mex. Inst. Mining and Tech., 1984. Chmn. David and Lucile Packard Found., Los Altos, Calif.; CEO Tech. Resource Assistance Ctr., Palo Alto, Calif., 1986—. Bd. dirs. Hewlett-Packard Co. Trustee Stanford U., 1998—. Office: The Packard Found 300 2nd St Ste 200 Los Altos CA 94022-3643

ORR, ZELLIE, entrepreneur, educator, writer, researcher; b. Holly Ridge, May 12, 1951; d. Leonard and Lucille Rainey; m. Foster G. Orr Jr., Feb. 28, 1976 (div. July 14, 1998); children: Kai A., Nia Haley. Student, L.A. City Coll., 1970—71, U. Calif., Northridge, 1971—73; cert., Airline Schs. Pacific, 1974, CMLS Inst., 1979; MA in Human Letters, U. Metaphysics, 1983. Cert. real estate salesperson, Ga., 1979, pub. notary, Ga, 1985. Personal lines underwriter Kemper Ins. Co., L.A., 1976—78, Comml. Union Ins. Co., Atlanta, 1980—82, Moore Group ins. Co., Atlanta, 1982—85; lic. real estate agent Wofford Realty, Riverdale, Ga., 1979—81; owner Traffic Jam Lounge and Restaurant, Sunflower, 1986—89; documentation specialist Windsor Group, Atlanta, 1989—2001; pres., founder Comm. Unltd., Austell, Ga., 1995—. Mem. rsch. bd. advisors Am. Biog. Inst., Raleigh, NC, 1992—93. Co-author: Treasured Poems of America, 1989 (Editor's Choice award, 1989), The Best Poems & Poets of the 20th Century, 2000 (Editor's Choice award, 2000), Theatre of The Mind, 2003; contbr. poetry to mags. Organizer Sunflower Co. Civil Rights and Cmty. Reunion, Indianola, 1999; founder Charles E. Scattergood Meml. Found., Marietta, Ga., 2000. Recipient Cert. Appreciation, Superior Ct., Calif., 1976, Cert. Recognition, CME Ch., Indianola, 1999, award, Columbus AFB, 2004. Mem.: NAACP, Nat. Assn. Female Execs., Nat. Trust Hist. Preservation, Nat. Mus. Women in Arts, Nat. Black MBA Assn. Achievements include naming of Cox Park after 1st black Postmistress of U.S.A. (Minnie Cox); obtaining 5 posthumous medals from the military and recognition as inductee in Alcorn U. Hall of Fame for Tuskeegee Airman Lt. Quitman C. Walker. Avocations: stamp collecting/philately, reading, coin collecting/numismatics, antiques, chess. Home: 3285 Doyle Ln Marietta GA 30060 Office: Comm Unltd 3999 Austell Rd Ste 303 #158 Austell GA 30106 E-mail: zellie@artsonwheels.com.

ORR-CAHALL, CHRISTINA, art museum director, art historian; b. Wilkes-Barre, Pa., June 12, 1947; d. William R.A. and Anona (Snyder) Boben; m. Richard Cahall. BA magna cum laude, Mt. Holyoke Coll., 1969; MA, Yale U., 1974, MPhil, 1975, PhD, 1979. Curator of collections Norton Gallery Art, West Palm Beach, Fla., 1975-77; asst. prof. Calif. Poly. State U., San Luis Obispo, 1978-81, Disting. prof., 1981; dir. art div., chief curator Oakland (Calif.) Mus., 1981-88; chief exec. officer Corcoran Gallery Art, Washington, 1988-90; dir. Norton Mus. Art, West Palm Beach, 1990—. Author: Addison Mizner: Architect of Dreams and Realities, 1974, 2d printing, 1993, Gordon Cook, 1987, Claude Monet: Am Impression, 1993; editor: The Art of California, 1984, The American Collection at the Norton Museum of Art, 1995. Office: Norton Museum of Art 1451 S Olive Ave West Palm Beach FL 33401-7162 Fax: 561-832-6529.

ORROCK, NAN, state legislator; children: Jesse, Daniel. BA, U. Va. Mem. Ga. State Ho. of Reps., Atlanta, 1986—. Mem. Indsl. Rels. Com., Appropriations Com.; vice chmn. Health and Ecology Com. Exec. dir. Fund for So. Cmties. Mem. Unitarian Ch. Home: 1070 Delaware Ave SE Atlanta GA 30316-2470 Office: State Capitol 401 Rm 109 Capitol Square Atlanta GA 30334

ORSON, BARBARA TUSCHNER, actress; b. N.Y.C., May 19, 1929; d. Jonah Tuschner and Rebecca Traceman; m. Jay M. Orson, June 24, 1956; children: Beth-Diane, Theodore. Student, Dramatic Workshop, N.Y.C., 1948-50. Leading soubrette Am. Savoyards, N.Y.C., 1950-51, 53-55; actress Trinity Repertory, Providence, 1964—2001. Founding mem. Trinity Sq. Repertory Co., Providence, 1964—2001. Actress Edinburgh Festival, Scotland, 1968, Am. Repertory Theatre, Cambridge, Mass., 1981-85, Williamstown (Mass.) Theatre, 1985-89, Dallas Theatre Ctr., 1985, Yale Repertory Co., New Haven, Conn., 1991; appeared in: (films) Mission Hill, Code of Ethics, My One and Only, Swimming Upstream, Mr. North, Strangers in Transit (TV) Theatre in America, Feasting with Panthers, Life Among the Lowly, House of Mirth, Camera Three, RI Demon Murder, Miller's Court, Conflict of Interest (Am. premiere) The Suicide, 1980, (world premiere) Grown Ups, 1981, God's Heart, 1995; founding mem., appeared in over 100 prodns. Trinity Sq. Repertory Co., Providence, 1964—; (radio) House of Mirth, Masterpiece Radio Theatre with Jane Alexander; guest artist (Lady Macbeth), Brown U. Recipient Adrian Hall award, Trinity Repertory Co., RI, 2002. Mem. Am. Fedn. Radio and TV Artists, Screen Actors Guild, Actor's Equity Assn., Trinity Rep. Co. (founder). Home: 281 Hillside Ave Pawtucket RI 02860-6119

ORTEGA, LORRAINE G. state land office executive; b. Santa Fe, Apr. 4, 1940; d. Lorin A. and Aurelia (Rodriguez) Gonzales; m. Cecil R. Ortega, Jr., June 17, 1961; children: Carl Michael, Nadine Ortega Wells, Carolyn L. Martinez. Student in bus. adminstrn., Coll. of Santa Fe, 1959, Santa Fe Bus. Coll., 1966. Various positions State of N.Mex. Health and Edn. Depts., 1958-78; dep. state dir. gov.'s svc. ctrs. Gov. King's Office, Santa Fe, 1978-82; personnel bur. chief N.Mex. State Land Office, Santa Fe, 1983-87; constituent svc. dir. Gov. King's Office, 1990-93; exec. asst. commr. N.Mex. State Land Office, 1993-96. Dep. registrar voter registration Santa Fe County, 1975—; state coord. N.Mex. Queen's Pageant Am. GI Forum, 1985; mem. Santa Fe County steering com. for Bruce King for Gov., 1989—90; mgr. Santa Fe County office King Campaign, 1989—90; Santa Fe County Dem. ctrl. com. mem., 1976—; State of N.Mex. Dem. ctrl. com. mem., 1976—91; Santa Fe County Dem. ward chmn., Ward 48-A, precincts 24, 25, 27, 3d congrl. dist.; mem. Gov. Bruce King Inauguration Ceremonies com., 1978, 1991; del. N.Mex. State Dem. Convs., 1976—; alt. del. Nat. Dem. Conv., N.Y.C., 1980; eucharistic min., religious edn. tchr.; N.Mex. State sec./treas. Nat. League of Postmasters Aux., 1990—93. Recognized top-level position Hispanic employee in gov.'s adminstrn. by Albuquerque Hispano C. of C. and Hispanic Mag., 1991. Mem.: VFW, Am. Legion, Eagles, Elks. Democrat. Roman Catholic. Avocations: baking, boating, fishing.

ORTENBERG, ELISABETH CLAIBORNE See CLAIBORNE, LIZ

ORTHMANN, ROSEMARY ANN, editor; b. Ridgewood, N.J., Oct. 10, 1952; BA, Washington Coll., 1974; MA, U. Minn., 1977; PhD, Ind. U., 1987. Editl. asst. Am. Historical Review, Bloomington, Ind., 1977-80; asst. book editor 21st Century Books, Frederick, Md., 1987-88; mng. editor U. Publ. of Am., Frederick, Md., 1987-88, editor, 1988-2000; mng. editor LexisNexis Acad. and Libr. Solutions, Bethesda, Md., 2000—. Author: Out of Necessity, 1991; contbr. articles to profl. jours. Mem. steering com. Commn. for Women, Frederick, 1991-92; mem. Frederick County Commn. for Women, 1992-97; mem. Frederick County Election Judges, 2002—; mem. Walters Art Gallery, Planned Parenthood, U.S. Holocaust Meml. Mus. Internat. Rsch. and Exch. Bd. fellow, 1980-81, Social Sci. Rsch. Coun. fellow, 1981-82; Fulbright-Hays scholar, 1981-82, German Acad. Exch. Svc. scholar, 1974-75. Mem. AAUW, ACLU, Nat. Mus. Women in Arts, Nat. Abortion Rights Action League, LWV, Planned Parenthood, U.S. Holocaust Meml. Mus., Walters Art Gallery, Whitman Walker Clinic, Vietnam Vets. Meml. Funds. Democrat. Avocations: reading, soccer, basketball, listening to music, science fiction. Office: LexisNexis Acad and Libr Solutions 4520 E West Hwy Bethesda MD 20814-3389

ORTIZ, DEBORAH V. state legislator; b. Sacramento, Mar. 19, 1957; Student, U. Calif., Davis, 1975-81; JD, U. of the Pacific, 1987. Mem. Calif. State Assembly, 1996-98, chair select com. on taxpayer's rights; mem. Calif. State Senate, 1998—. Mem. Sacramento City Coun., 1993-96; chair ad hoc com. Neighborhood Svcs. Dept., 1993. Recipent Sacramento Housing Alliance award. Democrat. Roman Catholic. Office: State Capital Rm 4032 Sacramento CA 95814 also: 1020 N St Ste 576 Sacramento CA 95814-5606 also: 5975 Birdcage Centre Ln # 145 Citrus Heights CA 95610-8001

ORTIZ, KATHLEEN LUCILLE, travel consultant; b. Las Vegas, N.Mex., Feb. 8, 1942; d. Arthur L. and Anna (Lopez) O. BA, Loretto Hghts. Coll., 1963; MA, Georgetown U., 1966; cert. in tchg., Highlands U., 1980; cert. in travel, ABQ Travel Sch., 1984. Mgr. Montezuma Sq., Las Vegas, 1966—70; office mgr. Arts Food Market, Las Vegas, 1971-75; tchr. Robertson HS, Las Vegas, 1976-80; registered rep. IDS Fin. Svcs., N.Mex., 1980-84; travel cons. VIP Travel & Tours, Albuquerque, 1985-86, New Horizons Travel, Albuquerque, 1986-87, All World Travel, Albuquerque, 1987-90, Premium Travel Svcs., Albuquerque, 1990-91; travel cons., group tours Going Places Travel, Albuquerque, 1991—2003, All World Travel, Albuquerque, 2003—. Contbr. 100 articles to newspapers. Founding mem. Citizens Com. for Hist. Preservation, Las Vegas, 1977-79; fund raiser St. Anthony's Hosp., Las Vegas, 1969-75; mem. Hispanic Geneol. Rsch. Ctr., N.Mex., 1996—. Mem. LWV (numerous positions), N.Mex. Hispanic Cultural Ctr. (inaugural mem. 1998), Georgetown Club of N.Mex. (bd. dirs. at large 1991-94). Avocations: tennis, langs., photography, writing. Home: 7600 Adele Pl NE Albuquerque NM 87109-5362 Office: All World Travel 5200 Eubank Blvd NE Ste C1 Albuquerque NM 87111 Office Phone: 505-294-5031.

ORTIZ-BUTTON, OLGA, social worker; b. Chgo., July 12, 1953; d. Luis Antonio and Pura (Acevedo) Ortiz; m. Dennis Vesley, Aug. 11, 1973 (div. 1976); m. Randall Russell Button, Nov. 3, 1984 (div. Oct. 1993); children: Josh, Jordan, Eli. BA, U. Ill., 1975; MSW, Western Mich. U., 1981. Cert. social worker, sch. social worker. Social svcs. dir. Champaign County Nursing Home, Urbana, Ill., 1976; social svcs. and activity dir. Lawton (Mich.) Nursing Home, 1977; job developer Southwestern Mich. Indian Ctr., Watervliet, 1977-78; staff asst. New Directions Alcohol Treatment Ctr., Kalamazoo, 1978; counselor, instr. Alcohol Hwy. Safety, Kalamazoo, 1978-79; clin. social worker Mecosta County Community Mental Health, Big Rapids, Mich., 1981-84, program dir. substance abuse Sr. Svcs., Inc., Kalamazoo, 1984-85; sch. social worker Martin (Mich.) Pub. Schs., 1985-96, J.C. Huizenga Charter Schs., Grand Rapids, Mich., 1996—; owner, therapist Plainwell (Mich.) Counseling Ctr., 1989-98; co-dir. Everlasting Covenant Ministry, Kalamazoo, 1997—; owner Christian Counseling Ctr., 2003. S.W. cons. Med. Pers. Pool, 1993-94; founder, owner Christian Coun. Ctr., 2003—. Vol. social worker Hospice-Wings of Hope, Plainwell, 1984-85; mem. Hospice Quality Rev. Bd., 1993-96; supporter Students Against Aparteid South Africa, Kalamazoo, 1979-81; mem. World Vision and Countertop Ptnr., 1984-90; mem., vol. Christian Life Ctr., Kalamazoo, 1996; sponsor, vol. People for Ethical Treatment of Animals, 1986-91; vol. helper Sparkies for Awana Club Ch., 1989-95; consortium mem. Mich. Post Adoption Svc. System, 1994-97; co-founder Everlasting Covenant Ministry, Kalamazoo, 1997; sch. social worker Nat. Heritage Acads., 1997—. NIMH Rural Mental Health grantee, 1979-81. Mem.: NASW, Nat. Assn. Christian Social Workers, Am. Assn. Christian Counselors, Mich. Assn. Sch. Social Workers. Avocations: jogging, plants, cross country skiing. Home: 1339 Cadet Ln Kalamazoo MI 49009-1838 Office Phone: 269-760-1999. E-mail: obutton@ureach.com.

ORTIZ - ROBLEDO, CINDA AURELIA, music educator; b. Ft. Jackson, S.C., Jan. 18, 1964; d. Agustin Ortiz-Perez and Lelis Marina Robledo Ramos; 1 child, Marisol Imani Dothard - Ortiz. MusB, Ga. So. Coll., 1986. PBT4 tchg. cert. Ga., 1986. Music tchr. Ctrl. Jr. H.S., Springfield, Ga., 1986—87; band dir. Miller Mid. Sch., Macon, Ga., 1990—. Co-prin. trumpet Statesboro (Ga.)- GSC Symphony, 1986—87; trumpet player Minot (N.D.) Symphony Orch., 1988—90, Amb. Brass, 1988—90, Tara Winds, Jonesboro, Ga., 1993—97; flag instr. Ctrl. H.S. Band, Macon, 2001—. Leader Girl Scouts, Minot, 1988—90, Macon, 2001—02. Recipient Outstanding Vol. award, North West N.D. Girl Scout Coun., 1990. Mem.: Ga. Music Educators Assn. Avocations: cross stitch, travel.

ORTNER, TONI, English language educator; b. Bklyn., Mar. 11, 1941; d. Melvin and Sylvia (Klein) O.; m. Stephen Michael Zimmerman, May 27, 1962 (div. 1988); 1 child, Lisa Lampe. BA, Hofstra U., 1962; MA in English, Western Conn. State Coll., 1979. Tchr. English dept. Monroe Coll., Bronx. Tchr. Mercy Coll., Bronx C.C., Coll. New Rochelle, U. Conn., Norwalk C.C. Author: Woman in Search of Herself, 1971, To an Imaginary Lover, 1975, Never Stop Dancing, 1976, Entering Another Country, 1976, I Dream Now of the Sun, 1976, Stones, 1976, As If Anything Could Grow Back Perfect, 1979, Requiem, 1991, Real Stories, 2003; contbr. to anthologies and jours. Mem. Poets and Writers, The Authors Guild, Nat. Coun. Tchrs. English. Avocations: reading, hiking, traveling. Home: 20 Sherwood Rd Stamford CT 06905-3601

ORTOLANO, MARY KAY, music educator; b. Dunkirk, N.Y., July 15, 1959; d. George Joseph and Beatrice (Sowinski) Ortolano; m. John Richard Valby, Dec. 3, 1983 (div. July 1993); 1 child, Rose Katherine Valby. MusB, Hartt Sch. Music, Hartford, Conn., 1981; MusM, New Eng. Conservatory, Boston, 1983. Cert. tchr. N.Y. N.Y. state cert. all-state adjuntor N.Y. State Sch. Music Assn., Rochester, 1994; tchr. instrumental music Clarence Ctrl. Schs., NY, 1995, Gates Chili Ctrl. Schs., Rochester, NY, 1996—2002, Frontier Ctrl. Schs., Hamburg, NY, 2002—. Clinician N.Y. State Bd. Dirs. Symposium, Syracuse, 2001. Chamber Music grantee, Hamburg Youth Found., 2002—03, Buffalo Bills Youth Found., 2003—04. Mem.: Nat. Band Assn., Music Educators Nat. Conf., N.Y. State Sch. Music Assn. Home: Box 196 6055 Elm St Clarence Center NY 14032 Office: Frontier Ctrl Schs 4432 Bayview Rd Hamburg NY 14075

ORTON, EVA DOROTHY, civic worker; b. San Jose, Calif., Aug. 21, 1921; d. George Alfred and Marguerite Carolyn (Del Ponte) Prudhomme. AB in Dietitics, San Jose State Coll., 1943. Intern Highland-Alameda Hosp., Oakland, Calif., 1944; dietitian Providence Hosp., Oakland, 1944-46; relief dietitian Santa Clara Valley Med. Ctr., San Jose, 1949-51, 52-53, sr. dietitian, 1953-63; food adminstr., dir. nutrition and food svc. Santa Clara Valley Ctr., San Jose, 1963-86; ret., 1986—. Bd. dirs., vol. YWCA, San Jose, 1984-93; adv. legis. com. chair Adv. Coun. to Coun. on Agy., San Jose, 1987-95, 97—; mem. adv. com., bd. dirs. Cmty. Kids to Camp, San Jose, 1987-93; active Hunger Coalition, 1992-99; mem. bd. suprs. Santa Clara County Sr. Care Commn., 1998—; advocate Cmty. Health Com., 1998—2001; mem. Voting Rights Adv. Com., 1990—, San Jose Hosp. Coalition, 1998—. Named Disting. Alumni, San Jose State U., 1982, Vol. of Yr. Silicon Valley Charity Ball Found., 1991-92; recipient disting. citizen award Exch. Club and City Coun. San José, Cert. of Appreciation Calif. Sr. Legislature, 1996. Mem. AARP (legis. chair 1990—,cmty. team fed. affairs specialist, 2003—), LWV (exec. com., v.p., pres. 1993-95, bd. dirs. 1989-96, exec. chmn. 1997-98), Am. Dietitic Assn. (registered dietitian), State and Local Dietitic Assn. (chmn. various coms.), Interagency Nutrition Coun. (various coms.), Ret. Pub. Employees Assn. (bd. dirs. Santa Clara County chpt. 31), Congress Calif. Srs. (bd. dirs. 1997—), AARP (dist. coord. congl. dist. 15 1990-96, 98—). Roman Catholic. Avocations: gardening, hiking, reading. Home: 4925 Bel Escou Dr San Jose CA 95124-5441

ORULLIAN, B. LARAE, bank executive; b. Salt Lake City, May 15, 1933; d. Alma and Bessie (Bacon) O. Cert., Am. Inst. Banking, 1961, 63, 67; grad. Nat. Mortgage Sch., Ohio State U., 1969-71. With Tracy Collins Trust Co., Salt Lake City, 1951-54, Union Nat. Bank, Denver, 1954-57; exec. sec. Guaranty Bank, Denver, 1957-64, asst. cashier, 1964-67, asst. v.p., 1967-70, v.p., 1970-75, exec. v.p., 1975-77, also bd. dirs.; chair, CEO, pres. The Women's Bank N.A., Denver, 1977-97, Colo. Bus. Bankshares, Inc., 1980-97; vice chmn. Guaranty Bank and Trust Co., Denver, 1998—. Pres., bd. dirs. Guaranty Corp., Lange Golf Co., Holladay (Utah) Bank; vice-chmn. bd. dirs. Frontier Airlines. Treas. Girl Scouts U.S., 1981-87, 1st nat. v.p., chair exec. com., 1987-90, nat. pres., 1990-96; 1st vice chair world bd. World Assn. Girl Guides Girl Scouts, London. Recipient Woman Who Made a Difference award Internat. Women's Forum, 1994; named to Colo. Women Hall of Fame, 1988; named Colo. Entrepreneur of Yr., Inc. Mag. and Arthyr Young and Co., 1989, Woman of Yr., YWCA, 1989, Citizen of Yr., EMC Lions Club, 1995, laureate Colo. Bus. Hall of Fame, 1999. Mem. Bus. and Profl. Women Colo. (3d Century award 1977), Internat. Women's Forum, Am. Bankers Assn. (adv. bd. edn. found.), Com. of 200. Independent. Mem. L.D.S. Ch. Home: 6650 W 10th Pl Denver CO 80214 Office Phone: 303-296-9600.

ORY, MARCIA GAIL, social science researcher; b. Dallas, Feb. 8, 1950; d. Marvin Gilbert and Esther (Levine) O.; m. Raymond James Carroll, Aug. 13, 1972. BA magna cum laude, U. Tex., 1971; MA, Ind. U., 1972; PhD, Purdue U., 1976; MPH, Johns Hopkins U., 1981. Rsch. asst. prof. U. N.C., Chapel Hill, 1976-77, from adj. asst. prof. to assoc. prof. sch. pub. health, 1978-88; rsch. fellow U. Minn., Mpls., 1977-78; asst. prof. Sch. Pub. Health U. Ala., Birmingham, 1978-80; program dir. biosocial aging and health Nat. Inst. on Aging, Bethesda, Md., 1981-86, chief social sci. rsch. on aging, 1987—2001; prof. Sch. Rural Pub. Health Tex A&M U. Sys., College Station, 2001—. Dir. RWJF Nat. Program Office on Increasing Phys. Activity in the 50 Plus, 2001—; coord. Program on Aging and Health Promotion. Contbr. articles, editor vols. to profl. jours. Mem. several nat. task forces on aging and health issues; bd. dirs. Ctr. for Health Improvement. Named Disting. Alumna, Purdue U.; named one of 5 Industry Innovators in Active Aging, Internat. Coun. on Active Aging, 2003; named to McKnights Long Term Care News 100, 1997; recipient Dept. Health and Human Svcs. award, 1984, 1985, 1988, Am. Men and Women of Sci., 1989—90, NIH Dir.'s award, 1995, NIH Dir's Lifetime Achievement award, 2000, NIH award of merit, 1999, Polisher award, Gerontol. Soc. Am., 2001, award of merit, NIH, 2001. Fellow: Soc. Behavioral Medicine (program chmn. pub. health track 1988—89, program com. 1991—92, program chair lifespan/devel. track 2001—02), Acad. for Behavioral Medicine Rsch., Gerontol. Soc. Am.; mem.: APHA (program chmn. 1986, gov. coun. 1986—88, chmn.-elect 1989—91, chmn. 1992—93, leadership group 1996—, chair older women's interest group), Am. Acad. Health Behavior, Am. Sociol. Assn. (regional reporter 1984—94, program com. 1986, nominations com. 1987, councilor-at-large 1992—93), Omicron Nu, Phi Kappa Phi. Avocations: walking, birding, travel. Office: Dept Soc & Behav Health-Sch of Rural Pub Health Tex A&M U Sys Health Scis Ctr Univ Pk Plz 1103 Univ Dr Ste 100 College Station TX 77840 Business E-Mail: mory@srph.tamu.edu.

ORZECK, SUSAN BETH STERN, psychologist, consultant; b. Brooklyn, NY, June 10, 1965; d. Madeline Sandra and Harvey Gerald Stern; m. Neil Michael Orzeck, Apr. 18, 1999; 1 child, Morgan Isabelle. BA, Am. U., 1983—87; MA, PhD, Calif. Sch. of Profl. Psychology, 1988—95. Master Black Belt JP Morgan Chase, NY, 1999. V.p. JP Morgan Chase, NYC, 1998—; mgmt. cons./health care cons. Ernst & Young, NYC, 1996—98. Vol. JP Morgan Chase: Global Days of Svc., NYC, 1998—2003. Mem.: APA, Soc. of Indsl./Orgnl. Psychologists, Womens Initiative Network. Office: JP Morgan Chase 246 Park Ave New York NY 10167 E-mail: susan.orzeck@jpmchase.com.

OSBORN, JUNE ELAINE, pediatrician, microbiologist, educator, foundation administrator; b. Endicott, N.Y., May 28, 1937; d. Leslie A. and Dora W. (Wright) Osborn; children: Philip I. Levy, Ellen D. Levy, Laura A. Jana. BA, Oberlin (Ohio) Coll., 1957; MD, Western Res. U., 1961; DSc (hon.), U. Med. Dental Sch. N.J., 1990; DMS (hon.), Yale U., 1992; DSc (hon.), Emory U., 1993, Oberlin Coll., 1993; LHD (hon.), Med. Coll. Pa., 1994; DSc (hon.), Rutgers U., 1994, Case Western Res. U., 1997, SUNY, Stony Brook, 1999. Intern, resident in pediatrics Harvard U. Hosp., 1961—64; fellow Johns Hopkins, 1964—65, U. Pitts., 1965—66; prof. med. microbiology and pediat. U. Wis. Med. Sch., Madison, Wis., 1966—84, prof. pediat. and microbiology, 1974—84, assoc. dean Grad. Sch., 1975—84; dean Sch. Pub. Health U. Mich. Sch. Pub. Health, 1984—93; prof. epidemiology, pediat. and communicable diseases U. Mich. Sch. Pub. Health and Med. Sch., 1984—96, prof. emeritus, 1997—. Pres. Josiah Macy, Jr. Found., 1997—; mem. rev. panel viral vaccine efficacy FDA, 1973—79, mem. vaccines and related biol. products adv. com., 1981—85; mem. exptl. virology study sect. Divsn. Rsch. Grants, NIH, 1975—79; mem. med. affairs com. Yale U. Coun., 1981—86; chmn. life scis. associateships rev. panel NRC, 1981—84; mem. U.S. Army Med. R&D Adv. Com., 1983—85; chmn. working group on AIDS and the Nation's Blood Supply NHLBI, 1984—89; chmn. WHO Planning Group on AIDS and the Internat. Blood Supply, 1985—86. Contbr. articles to profl. jours.; mem. editl. bd.: Jour. AMA, 2002—. Active task force in AIDS, Inst. of Medicine, 1986; mem. adv. com. Robert Wood Johnson Found. AIDS Health Svcs. Program, 1986—91; mem. nat. adv. com. on health of pub. program Pew and Rockefeller Founds.; mem. health promotion and disease prevention bd. Inst. Medicine, 1987—90; mem. Global Commn. on AIDS, WHO, 1988—92; chmn. Nat. Commn. on AIDS, 1989—93; trustee Kaiser Found., 1990—98, Case Western Reserve U., Cleve., 1993—97; mem. coun. Inst. Medicine, 1995—2000; mem. Nat. Vaccine Adv. Cte., HHS, 1995—98; mem. adv. coun. Nat. Inst. on Drug Abuse, 1995—98; mem. internat adv. bd. Nat. Acads., 2002—; bd. dirs. Legal Action Ctr., 1994—2001, Ctr. for Health Care Strategies, 1998—2003, The Mind Inst., 2003—. Recipient NIH Pub. Svc. award, 2000, Scientific Freedom and Responsibility award, AAAS, 1994; grantee NIH, 1969, 1972, 1974—75, Nat. Multiple Sclerosis Soc., 1971. Fellow: Infectious Diseases Soc. Am., Am. Acad. Microbiology, Am. Acad. Arts and Scis., Am. Acad. Pediat.; mem.: Inst. Medicine, Soc. Pediat. Rsch., Am. Assn. Immunologists. Office: Josiah Macy Jr Found 44 E 64th St New York NY 10021-7306

OSBORN, LA DONNA CAROL, clergywoman; b. Portland, Oreg., Mar. 13, 1947; d. T.L. and Daisy (Washburn) O.; m. Cory A. Nickerson, Dec. 11, 1981; children: Tommy O'Dell, LaVona Thomas, Daneesa Dolan, Donald O'Dell. Student, Assemblies of God Coll., 1963; BA, Okla. City U., 1994; DD, Bethel Coll., 1995; Doctor of Humane Letters (hon.), Wesley Synod, 1998; MA, Oral Roberts U., 2000; D in Ministry, Am. Christian Coll. and Sem., 2001; DD, Zoe Univ., 2001. Fgn. mission corr., purchaser, personnel agt. Osborn Found., Tulsa, 1969-75, exec. asst., 1975-76, internat. gen. mgr., 1976-81, internat. editor-in-chief, 1981-86, corp. pres., 1986-93; assoc. pastor Internat. Gospel Ctr., Tulsa, 1986-89, sr. pastor, 1989-94, sr. pastor, overseer, 1994-97; founder, presiding bishop Internat. Gospel Ctr. (IGC) Chs. and Mins., Tulsa, Okla., 1997—; mem. Coll. of Bishops Internat. Communion of Charismatic Chs., 1998—; v.p., CEO OSFO Internat. 1998—. Internat. minister, religious tchr., and motivational spkr. Nigeria, Kenya, Uganda, Colombia, Papua New Guinea, France, Russia, Belarus, Kazakhstan, Kyrgyzstan, Ukraine, Russia, Sweden, Eng., Holland, Can., India, Zambia, Guatemala, Ecuador, China, U.S.; internat. spiritual advisor Christian Women's Fellowship Internat. Nigeria; founder Believers' Network Internat., Women's Internat. Network. Author: (book) Jesus & Women, 2000, God's Big Picture, 2001; author, editor Bible tng. courses. Republican. Avocations: jewish biblical history, interracial issues, biblical equality, women's issues. Home: 3111 E 89th St Tulsa OK 74137-3362 Office Phone: 918-743-0872. E-mail: revldo@aol.com.

OSBORN, LYNDA PAUWELS, social worker; b. Amarillo, Tex., May 30, 1951; d. Edward Louis and Virginia Lorena Pauwels; m. George Steven Osborn, Sept. 2, 1999; 1 child, Steven Sean ; m. James O. Hendricks, Dec. 31, 1970 (div. June 1998); children: Andrea Lyn Hendricks, James Adams Hendricks. BA, U. Ctrl. Okla., 1985; MSW, Va. Commonwealth U., 1992. LCSW. Tinker AFB coord. ARC, Oklahoma City, 1985—87, dir. emergency svcs. Arlington, Va., 1987—92, program assoc. Washington, 1992—93; project coord. Parks and Recreation Dept., Arlington, 1993—94; coord. Info. and Referral Ctr. Am. Parkinson Disease Assn., Fairfax, Va., 1995—98; dialysis social worker Fosrenius Med. Care, Alexandria, Sterling, Va., 1996—99; oncology social worker Integris Southwest Med. Ctr., Oklahoma City, 1999—. Mem.: NASW, Assn. Oncology Social Workers. Baptist. Office: Integris Southwest Med Ctr 4401 S Western Ave Oklahoma City OK 73109*

OSBORN, MARY JANE MERTEN, biochemist, educator; b. Colorado Springs, Colo., Sept. 24, 1927; d. Arthur John and Vivien Naomi (Morgan) Merten; m. Ralph Kenneth Osborn, Oct. 26, 1950. BA, U. Calif., Berkeley, 1948; PhD, U. Wash., 1958. Postdoctoral fellow, dept. microbiology NYU Sch. Medicine, N.Y.C., 1959-61, instr., 1961-62, asst. prof., 1962-63; asst. prof. dept. molecular biology Albert Einstein Coll. Medicine, Bronx, N.Y., 1963-66, asso. prof., 1966-68; prof. dept. microbiology U. Conn. Health Ctr., Farmington, 1968—, dept. head, 1980—2002. Mem. bd. sci. counselors Nat. Heart, Lung and Blood Inst., 1975-79; mem. Nat. Sci. Bd., 1980-86; adv. coun. Nat. Inst. Gen. Med. Sci., 1983-86, divsn. rsch. grants NIH, 1989-94, chair, 1992-94; trustee Biosci. Info. Systems, 1986-91, chair, 1990-91; mem. German Am. Acad. Coun., 1994-97; mem. space scis. bd. NRC, 1994-2000, chair com. space biology and medicine, 1994-2000; cochair com. on indications for waterborne pathogens, 2002-03. Assoc. editor Jour. Biol. Chemistry, 1978-80; contbr. articles in field of biochemistry and molecular biology to profl. jours. Mem. rsch. com. Am. Heart Assn., 1972-77, chair, 1976-77. NIH fellow, 1959-61; NIH grantee, 1962-95 ; NSF grantee, 1965-68; Am. Heart Assn. grantee, 1968-71 Fellow Am. Acad. Arts and Scis. (coun. 1988-91), NAS (coun. 1990-93, com. sci. engrng. and pub. policy 1993-96); mem. Am. Acad. Microbiology (bd. govs. 1994-2000), Am. Fedn. Soc. Exptl. Biology (pres. 1982-83), Am. Soc. Biol. Chemists (pres. 1981-82), Am. Soc. Microbiology. Democrat. Office: U Conn Health Ctr Dept Microbiology Ctr Farmington CT 06030-0001

OSBORN, SUSAN CHANEY, writer, educator; b. Ft. Campbell, Ky., Jan. 7, 1953; d. Lawrence Elvie and Wilma Barbara (Powell) Howard; m. Nicholas Lourick, Aug. 1, 1976 (div. Oct. 1981); m. Steve Osborn, Mar. 20, 1993; 1 child. BS, Ga. State U., 1989; MS, U. Colo., 1997. Lic. tchr., Colo, pvt. occupational tchr., Colo. Owner, photographer Creative Assistance, Atlanta, 1979-89; educator St. Mary's Acad., Cherry Hills Village, Colo., 1989-90, Denver Pub. Schs., 1990-92; internet resource coord. Nat. Renewable Energy Lab., Golden, Colo., 1993-95; writer Diners Club Internat., Englewood, Colo., 1995-96; owner, writer, coord. Publs. Resolution, Denver, 1996—. Website advisor Colo. Dept. Pub. Health and Environment, Denver, 1998-99; advisor Houghton-Miffilin Co., Boston, 1992; mem. math. text seclection com. Denver Pub. Schs., 1991; cons. Hauser Chem. Co., Boulder, Colo., 1994. Author: Public Service Company Classroom Connection, 1992, photography manual. Art/photography dir. Boy's Club, Marietta, GA., 1987; art show sect. organizer Girl's Club, Atlanta, 1988; implementor Bear Creek Blvd. Civic Assn., Lakewood, Colo., 1995; pub. rels. coord. Resolve Rocky Mountain Assn., Denver, 1996. Fellow Colo. Writing Project; mem. NEA, Golden Key. Avocations: creative writing, creative photography, theatre, hiking, mountain biking. Office: Publs Resolution PO Box 37263 Denver CO 80237

OSBORN, SUSAN TITUS, editor; b. Fresno, Calif., July 11, 1944; d. Clifford Leland Feldt and Jane (Taylor) Cousins; m. Richard G. Titus, Aug. 28, 1965 (div. Dec. 1990); children: Richard David, Michael Craig; m. Richard A. Osborn, Aug. 22, 1992. BA in Religious Studies, Calif. State U., Fullerton, 1988, MA in Comm., 1993. Svc. rep. Mountain Bell Tel., Colorado Springs, Colo., 1965-67; freelance writer Fullerton, Calif., 1978—; assoc. dir. Biola U. Writers Inst., La Mirada, Calif., 1986-92; co-dir. Christian Communicators Conf. The Master's Coll., Santa Clarita, Calif., 1993-95, adj. prof., 1993-96, Pacific Christian Coll., 1996—. Mem. adv. bd. Christian Writers Fellowship, Huntington Beach, Calif., 1987-93; mem. adv. bd. Christian Communicator, San Juan Capistrano, Calif., 1989-94, mng. editor, 1991-92, editor, 1992-98, contbg. editor, 1998—; pub. cons. Ednl. Ministries, Brea, Calif., 1989- 91; conf. spkr. numerous cities, 1987—; tchr. India Comm. Inst., Bombay; bd. dirs. Moscow Christian Sch. Psychology, 1992-95; mem. adv. bd. Am. Christian Writers, 1996—. Author: Parables for Young Teens, 1986, You Start With One, 1990, Meeting Jesus, 1990, Eyes Beyond the Horizon, 1991, Children Around the World Celebrate Christmas, 1993, The Complete Guide to Christian Writing and Speaking, 1994, Rest Stops for Single Mothers, 1995, Potpourri of Praise, 1997, The Complete Guide to Writing for Publication, 1999, Beanie Baby Stories, 1999, Parables in Action series, 2000, Just Write!, 2000, Heartlifters for Sisters, 2001, Ten Friends Together, 2002, Rest Stops for Busy Moms, 2003, Rest Stops for Teachers, 2003, A Special Kind of Love, 2004. Bd. dirs. Jr. Ebell Club, Fullerton, 1969-75, Youth Sci. Ctr., Fullerton, 1970-75, YMCA Swim Club, Fullerton, 1976-82; pres. Troy Swim Boosters, Fullerton, 1982-88, Moscow Christian Sch. Psychology, 1992-95. Recipient Spl. Recognition award Troy Swim Boosters, 1986. Mem. Presbyn. Writers Guild., Spiritual Overseers Svc. Republican. Evangelical. Avocations: writing, reading, gardening, theatre, beach.

OSBORNE, CARRIE LYNN, special education educator; d. Marvin Earl and Karen Marie Osborne. BS in Edn., Baldwin Wallace Coll., Berea, Ohio, 1997; MS in Edn., Ga. State U., Atlanta, 2000. Cert. exceptional needs specialist Nat. Bd. for Profl. Tchg. Standards, 2001. Spl. edn. tchr. Turner Mid. Sch., Lithia Springs, Ga., 1997—2003, Abbotsford Cmty. Sch., Burgess Hill, England, 2003—. Recipient Turner Mid. Sch. Tchr. of the Yr., Douglas County Sch. Sys., 2001, Honor Tchr., Atlanta Jour. and Constn., 2003. Mem.: Coun. for Exceptional Children (pres. 2001—03, v.p. 2001—03, Professionally Recognized Spl. Educator 2000). Personal E-mail: osbornecarrie@hotmail.com.

OSBORNE, GLENNA JEAN, health services administrator, social services administrator; b. East Rainelle, W.Va., Jan. 5, 1945; d. B.J. and Jean Ann (Haranac) Osborne; m. Thomas Joseph Ferrante Jr., June 11, 1966 (div. Nov. 1987); 1 child, Thomas Joseph Osborne; m. Brian Mark Popp, Aug. 13, 1988 (div. Oct. 1999). BA cum laude, U. Tampa, 1966; MA, Fairleigh Dickinson U., 1982; cert., Kean Coll., 1983. Cert. English, speech, dramatic arts tchr., prin./supr.; cert. nursing child assessment feeding scale and nursing child assessment tchg. scale, DENVER II cert., HOME cert. Tchr. Raritan H.S., Hazlet, N.J., 1966, Keyport (N.J.) Pub. Schs., 1968-86, coord. elem. reading and lang. arts, 1980-84, supr. curriculum and instrn., 1984-86; prin. Weston Sch., Manville, N.J., 1986-88, The Bartle Sch., Highland Park, N.J., 1988-91, Orange Ave. Sch., Cranford, N.J., 1991-92; dir. The Open Door Youth Shelter, Binghamton, N.Y., 1992-94; child protective investigator supr. Dept. Health and Rehab. Svcs., Orlando, Fla., 1994-95; program supr. Children's Home Soc., Sanford, Fla., 1995; clin. supr. Healthy Families-Orange, Orlando, Fla., 1995-98; dir. program ops. Children's Home Soc., Tavares, Fla., 1998—. Regional trainer Individualized Lang. Arts, Weehawken, N.J., 1976-86; cons. McDougal/Littel Pubs., Evanston, Ill., 1982-83; chair adv. bd. women's residential program Ctr. for Drug Free Living, Orlando, 1996. Contbr. chpt.: A Resource Guide of Differentiated Learning Experiences for Gifted Elementary Students, 1981. V.p. Sch. Readiness Coalition for Lake County, 1999; mem. adv. coun. Lake Cmty. Action Agy., Head Start, 1999; bd. dir. Mt. Dora Cmty. Trust, 2002—04, Leadership Lake County, 2004; bd. dir., sec. Ctrl. Healthy Start Coalition, 1999—2004; Sunday sch. tchr. Reformed Ch., Keyport, 1975—80, supt. Sunday sch., 1982—84. Mem.: Elks, Order Ea. Star, Mt. Dora Kiwanis (bd. dirs. 2000, pres. 2002—03, 2002—03, internat. Hixson fellow 2003, Divsn. 9 Lt. Gov.'s award outstanding svc. to club and cmty. 2003), Phi Delta Kappa. Republican. Methodist. Avocation: writing. Office: Children's Home Soc 1300 S Duncan Dr Bldg D Tavares FL 32778-4223

OSBORNE, JOAN (ELIZABETH), singer, songwriter; b. Anchorage, Ky., July 8, 1962; d. Jerry and Ruth (Yunker) O. Student, NYU. Singer various blues clubs, N.Y.C. Albums include Soul Show, 1991, Blue Million Miles, 1993, Relish (includes One of Us), 1995 (7 Grammy nominations 1996, named No. 1 album Entertainment Weekly), Early Recordings, 1996. Office: care Mercury Records Worldwide Plz 825 8th Ave New York NY 10019-7416

OSBORNE, JUDITH BARBOUR, artist; b. Winnipeg, Man., Can., Oct. 14, 1950; came to U.S., 1952; d. John Anderson and Laura May (Jones) Barbour; m. Frederick Spring Osborne Jr., Feb. 15, 1986; 1 child, Sheila. BFA, Univ. of Arts, Phila., 1974; student, Vt. Studio Ctr., 1984-89; MFA, Pa. Acad. Fine Arts, Phila., 1997. Prin. Barbour CalliGraphics, Phila., 1976—2002; dir. publs. and publicity Phila. Conf. on Calligraphic Arts, Phila., 1982; mem. faculty Phila. Coll. Art (now Univ. of Arts), 1982-85, 92, 00, Drexel U., Phila., 1991—2002; faculty Innovations Internat. Calligraphy Conf., N.Y., 1987; exhbns. coord. Calleidoscope Internat. Calligraphy Conf., Trenton, NJ, 1993. Guest curator Kamin Gallery, U. Pa., Phila., 1993, 95; exhbn. juror Phila. Calligraphers' Soc., 1989, 91, 94-95, 98, Phila. Sketch Club, 2002; spkr. 19th Internat. Calligraphy Conf., Guilford, Conn., 1999. One-woman shows include Rourke Art Gallery, Moorhead, Minn., 1999, Phila. Art Alliance, 1999, Artists' House, 1998, 2000, 02, Living Arts, Tulsa, Okla., 2000, Shipley Sch., Bryn Mawr, Pa., 2000; exhibited in group shows at Nat. Arts Club, N.Y.C., 1990, Pa. State Mus., Harrisburg, 1994, 2000-01, Am. Coll., Bryn Mawr, Pa., 1996, Nexus Found. for Today's Art, Phila., 1997, Del. Ctr. for Contemporary Art, 2002, Parallels Gallery, Phila., 2002, Tenri Cultural Inst., N.Y.C., 2002; Shanxi Art Mus., Xian, China, 2003, Ice House Gallery, Berkeley Springs, W.Va., 2004; represented in permanent collections at Fed. Res. Bank Phila., Blue Cross, Rourke Art Gallery Mus., Moorhead, Barbour/Ladouceur Archs., Mpls.; also pvt. collections; collaborator Sophia Osborne Dance Assocs., 1999-2001; contbr. articles to mags. and newspapers including Art Matters, 1997-2001, Letter Arts Rev., 2003. Recipient Best of Show Abington (Pa.) Art Ctr., 1990; Pa. Acad. Fine Arts fellow, Phila., 1997, Independence Found. fellow, 2001. Mem. Coll. Art Assn., Phila. Calligraphers' Soc. (bd. mem., publs. editor 1980-85), Inst. Noetic Scis. Avocation: metaphysics. Home: 11 Mitchel Terr Ivoryton CT 06442-1042

OSBORNE, MARGERY DIANE, education educator; b. New Milford, Conn., Sept. 9, 1955; d. John Frost and Mary Simons Osborne; children: Larkin Kennedy, Cornelia. AB, Wellesley Coll., 1977; PhD, U. Western Ont., London, Ont., Can., 1983, Mich. State U., 1993. Assoc. prof. U. Ill., Champaign, 1993—. Author: (book) Constructing Knowledge in the Elementary School Classroom, 1999, Teaching science in diverse settings: Marginalized discourses and classroom practice, 2001, The Love We Call Science: Constructing A Womanist Science from Observations of Practice, 2002, Teaching Science for Social Justice, 2003. Office: U Ill 1310 S 6th St Champaign IL 61820

OSBORNE, MARY POPE, writer; b. Ft. Sill, Okla., May 20, 1949; d. William Perkins and Barnette (Dickens) Pope; m. William R. Osborne, May 16, 1976. BA in Religion, U. N.C., 1971. Author: Run, Run, As Fast As You Can, 1982, Love Always, Blue, 1983, Best Wishes, Joe Brady, 1984, Mo to the Rescue, 1985, Last One Home, 1986, Beauty and the Beast, 1987, Favorite Greek Myths, 1988, American Tall Tales, 1990, The Many Lives of Benjamin Franklin, 1990, Moon Horse, 1991, George Washington, Leader of a New Nation, 1991, Spider Kane Mystery Series, 1992, 1993, Magic Tree House Series, 1992—2002, Haunted Waters, 1994, Molly and the Prince, 1994, Favorite Norse Myths, 1996, One World, Many Religions, 1996, Rocking Horse Christmas, 1997, Favorite Medieval Tales, 1998, Standing in the Light, 1998, The Life of Jesus, 1998, Adaline Falling Star, 2000, My Brothers Keeper, 2000, My Secret War, 2000, Kate and the Beanstalk, 2000, The Brave Little Seamstress, 2002, After the Rain, 2002, The One-Eyed Giant, 2002, The Land of the Dead, 2002, New York's Bravest, 2002, Tales from the Odyssey, 2002, Happy Birthday, America, 2003. Recipient Disting. Alumna award, U. N.C., Chapel Hill, 1994, Distinctive Contbn. to Arts award, N.Y. Carolina Club. Mem.: PEN, Authors League Fund (bd. dirs.), Authors Guild (pres. 1993—97). Office: Brandt & Brandt Lit Agy 1501 Broadway Ste 2310 New York NY 10036-5689

OSBOURNE, KELLY LEE, television personality, singer; b. London, Oct. 27, 1984; d. Ozzy and Sharon Osbourne. Singer: (albums) Shut Up, 2002, Changes, 2003, (songs) Papa Don't Preach, 2002, (concert DVD) Live at the Electric Ballroom, 2004; co-star (TV series) The Osbournes, 2002—, creative cons., 2002—. Office: Sanctuary Records Group Sanctuary House 45-53 Sinclair Rd London W14 ONS England*

OSBOURNE, SHARON ARDEN, music manager, actress, talk show host; b. London, Oct. 9, 1952; d. Don and Hope Arden; m. Ozzy Osbourne; children: Aimee, Kelly, Jack; 2 stepchildren. Mgr. Ozzy Osbourne, 1980—; founder & organizer OzzFest, 1995—; co-star The Osbournes, MTV, 2002—; host The Sharon Osbourne Show, 2003—04. Named One of People Magazine's 50 most beautiful people, 2002. Office: The Osbournes MTV Networks 2600 Colorado Ave Santa Monica CA 90404

OSBURN, ELLA KATHERINE, elementary school educator; b. Waycross, Ga., Nov. 25, 1961; d. William Daniel and Mabelle Irene (Tatum) O. BS in Home and Consumer Econs., Freed-Hardeman Coll., Henderson, Tenn., 1984, MEd in Curriculum and Instrn., 1992. Cert. in elem. edn. K-8, Ga. Tchr. 1st grade South Ga. Christian Acad., Albany, 1986-88; substitute tchr. Gwinnett County Schs., Lawrenceville, Ga., 1988-89; childcare worker The Children's Home, Valdosta, Ga., 1989-90; sec. Ga. Christian, Valdosta, 1990-91; tchr. 1st grade S.W. Elem.-Hancock County Schs., 1994-96. Author: (curriculum guide) Log of Intervention and Curriculum Guides for Reading Difficulties, 1991-92. Mem. NEA, ASCD, Ga. Assn. Educators, Smithsonian Inst. Mem. Ch. of Christ. Avocations: collecting and saving pennies, travel, collecting antiques, playing putt-putt golf. Home: PO Box 575 Hoschton GA 30548-0575

OSEGUERA, PALMA MARIE, retired career officer; b. Kansas City, Mo., Dec. 29, 1946; d. Joseph Edmund and Palma Louise (Utke) O'Donnell; m. Alfonso Oseguera, Jan. 1, 1977; stepchildren: Kristie M. Daniels, Michelle L. Nielson, Lori A. Kelley. BA in Phys. Edn., Marycrest Coll., 1969. Commd. 2d lt. USMC, 1969, advanced through grades to col., 1991; asst. Marine Corps exch. officer Hdqs. and Hdqs. Squadron, Marine Corps Air Sta., Beaufort, S.C., 1969-71; classified material control officer Hdqs. and Svcs. Battalion, Camp S.D. Butler, Okinawa, 1971-73; adminstrv. officer, asst. Marine Corps exch. officer Marine Corps Air Sta., El Toro, Santa Ana, Calif., 1973-76, Marine Corps exch. officer Yuma, Ariz., 1976-77; asst. Marine Corps exch. officer Hdqrs. and Support Bn., Marine Corps Devel. and Edn. Command, Quantico, Va., 1977-79; Marine Corps exch. officer Hqrs. Marine Corps, Washington, 1979-80; adminstrv. officer Marine Air Base Squadon 46, Marine Air Group 46, Marine Corps Air Sta., El Toro, Santa Ana, 1981-83, Hdqs. and Maintanence Squadron 46, Marine Air Group 46, Marine Corps Air Sta., El Toro, Santa Ana, 1983-85, Mobilization Tng. Unit Calif. 53, Landing Force Tng. Command, Pacific, San Diego, 1985-89, 3d Civil Affairs Group, L.A., 1989; dep. asst. chief of staff G-1 I Marine Expeditionary Force, Individual Mobilization Augmentee Detachment, Camp Pendleton, Calif., 1990-91; assoc. mem. Mobilization Tng. Unit Del. 01, Del., 1992-94; adminstrn. officer Mobilization Tng. Unit, CA-53, EWTG Pac, NAB, Coronado, San Diego, 1994-96; exch. officer MWRSPT ACT IMA Det MCB, Camp Pendleton, Calif., 1996-99; ret. from 30 yrs. commissioned svc. USMCR, 1999. Mem. choir St. Elizabeth Seaton, Woodbridge, Va., 1978-80, St. Patricks, Arroyo Grande, Calif., 1990-94; vol. Hospice, San Luis Obispo, 1995—; mem. Los Osos (Calif.) veteran's events com., 1994-2000. Mem. AAUW (past libr.), Marine Corps Assn., Marine Corps Res. Officer Assn., Marine Corps Aviation Assn. (12 dist. dir. 1987), Women in Mil. Svc. for Am., Woman Marine Assn., Marine Corps League. Republican. Roman Catholic. Avocations: skiing, gardening, reading, pet care/sitting, horseback riding. Home: 728 Scenic Cir Arroyo Grande CA 93420-1617

OSGOOD, VIRGINIA M. vocational educator; b. Oklahoma City, Okla., Dec. 9, 1942; d. John Allen Jr. and Christena Hazel (Grove) Simon; m. O. Emmet Osgood Jr., Jan. 19, 1963; children: Christopher J., Steven J. BS in Edn., Ctrl. State U., Edmond, Okla., 1989; MSEd, U. Ctrl. Okla., 1991; EdD, Okla. State U., 1999. Prodn. artist Lowe Runkle Advert, Oklahoma City, 1960-63; graphic designer Comm. Pub., Oklahoma City, 1963-70; owner, graphic designer Osgood Co., Oklahoma City, 1970-86; instr. Can. Valley Area Tech. Sch., El Reno, Okla., 1986-94; asst. prof. U. Ctrl. Okla., Edmond, 1994—. Rschr. in field. Contbg. editor (CD-rom) Advisor Survivor Kit: ASK, 1999. Com. chair St. Monica Parish, Edmond, 1993-99. Named Woman of Achievement, St. Monica Parish, 2000. Mem. Am. Vocat. Assn. (Region IV Trade & Indsl. Instr. of Yr. 1992, Nat. Trade & Indsl. Instr. of Yr. 1993), Okla. Vocat. Assn. (Okla. Vocat. Tchr. of Yr. 1991), Vocat. Indsl. Clubs of Am. (Nat. Advisor of Yr. 1993). Roman Catholic. Avocations: calligraphy, woodworking, crossword puzzles. Office: U Ctrl Okla 100 N University Dr Edmond OK 73034-5207

O'SHAUGHNESSY, ELLEN HODGSON, elementary school educator; b. Richmond, Va., Mar. 7, 1945; d. David Sherman and Margaret Elizabeth (McCrann) Hodgson; m. John Nelson O'Shaughnessy, July 7, 1966; children: John Nelson, Jennifer Leitrim, James Ryan. BM in Theory and Composition cum laude, U. Conn., Storrs, 1966, MA, 1971, postgraduate, 1986—87, Calif. State U., Sacramento, 1972—74. Cert. tchr. math and music Calif., Conn. Prof. musician Sacramento Symphony and other groups, 1971—; tchr. grades 7-12 San Juan Unified Sch. Dist., Carmichael, Calif., 1971—78; advtsg. sales rep. Local Yellow Pages/Sr. Citizen Publ., Springfield and Brighton, Mass., 1981—83; tchr. gen. music, choral

Stafford (Conn.) Middle Sch., 1987—93, tchr. music and choral ensembles, 1994—2001; edn. specialist, trainer TRO Learning/Plato, Farmington, Conn., 1993—94; tchr. math., algebra Tolland (Conn.) Middle Sch., 2001—; 7. Beginning Educator Support Tng. (B.E.S.T.) mentor tchr. Conn. Dept. Edn., Tolland and Stafford, 1999—; ch. choir dir. St. Luke's Ch., Ellington, Conn., 1984—97. Author: poems. Mem. Cultural Arts Commn., Ellington, Conn., 1980—83, vol. blood donor Conn. region ARC, Farmington, 1980—. Nominee Disney Am. Tchr., Disney Co., 2002. Mem.: Music Educators Nat. Conf. (ret.), Conn. Edn. Assn., Nat. Coun. Tchrs. Math., Jr. Women's Club (mem. publicity chmn. 1984—87, Rookie of Yr. 1984), Tau Beta Sigma (founder, pres. Gamma Kappa chpt. 1964). Roman Catholic. Avocations: crossword puzzles, gardening, reading, crafts. Office: Tolland Middle Sch 96 Old Post Rd Tolland CT 06084

O'SHAUGHNESSY, ROSEMARIE ISABELLE RAO, clinical nutritionist; b. N.Y.C., Sept. 25, 1940; d. Dr. John O. and Maria Wellmann (Larranaga) Rao; m. John Michael O'Shaughnessy, 1961 (div. 1976); children: Michelle Marie, Chevonne Eileen, Melany Rose; m. Louis L. Feldman, May 3, 1980. BA, St. Mary's Coll., Notre Dame, Ind., 1961; MS, Donsbach U., 1978, PhD, 1979; postdoctoral, Union for Experimenting Colls. and Univs., Cin., 1987. Cert. clin. nutritionist, 1991. Pvt. practice clin. nutrition, Orlando, Fla., 1979-92, Kissimmee, Fla., 1992—; dir. Beauticontrol Cosmetics Inc., Orlando, Fla., 1992-94, 1992—, RAO Properties, Kissimmee, Fla., 2000. Expert witness for clin. nutritionists and nutritional cons. testimony before state legis. coms. State of Fla., Tallahassee, 1983-88; speaker in field. Interviewee numerous TV and radio programs. Fellow Am. Coun. Applied Clin. Nutrition; mem. Internat. and Am. Assn. Clin. Nutritionists (founder 1987, bd. dirs. 1987-91, co-founder Fla. chpt. 1983, bd. dirs. 1986-91, exec. dir. 1986-90, pres. 1991; founding dir. life), Internat. Acad. Nutrition and Preventive Medicine (bd. dirs. 1987-89), N.Am. Acad. Nutrition and Preventive Medicine. Republican. Roman Catholic. Avocation: public speaking. Home: 4430 S Orange Blossom Trail Kissimmee FL 34746

O'SHEA, CATHERINE LARGE, marketing and public relations consultant; b. Asheville, N.C., Feb. 27, 1944; d. Edwin Kirk Jr. and Mary Mitchell (Westall) Large; m. Roger Dean Lower, Dec. 19, 1970 (dec. Sept. 1977); children: Thaddeus Kirk Lower and David Alexander Lower (twins, dec.); m. Michael Joseph O'Shea, Dec. 29, 1980 (div. 2001). BA in History magna cum laude, Emory U., 1966. Mktg. staff mem. Time Inc., N.Y.C., 1966-69; mktg. adminstr. Collier-Macmillan Internat., N.Y.C., 1970-71; circulation mgr. Coll. Entrance Exam. Bd., N.Y.C., 1971-73; spl. asst. to pres. Wayne Dressel Assocs. Exec. Search, N.Y.C., 1973-75; freelance writer, editor, pub. rels. Princeton, N.J., 1975-78; dir. constituency rels. Emory U., Atlanta, 1978-80; devel. assoc. U. Del., Newark, 1981-83; asst. to pres. Elizabethtown (Pa.) Coll., 1983-85; assoc. v.p. Beaver Coll., Glenside, Pa., 1985; cons. mktg. and pub. rels. Phila., S.C., Ga., 1985—. Co-author: 50 Secrets of Highly Successful Cats, 1994 (trans. German edit. Schnurrende Tyrannen by Manfred Sommer, 1996); editor Elizabethtown mag., 1983-85; contbr. articles to nat. mags. and profl. jours. Founder Helping Hands Internat.; trustee Large Found.; founding trustee Newberry Opera House Found.; mem. founding com. Rachel Longstreet Found., Jessye Norman Sch. of Arts. Mem. Pub. Rels. Soc. Am. (accredited), Augusta Choral Soc. (bd. dirs.), Mortar Bd., Phi Beta Kappa, Phi Mu.

O'SHEA, KAREN, public relations executive; V.p. comm., pub. rels. Lennox Internat., Richardson, Tex. Office: Lennox Internat PO Box 799900 Dallas TX 75379-9900

O'SHEA, LYNNE EDEEN, management consultant, educator; b. Chgo., Oct. 18, 1950; d. Edward Fisk and Mildred (Lessner) O'S. BA, BJ in Polit. Sci. and Journalism, U. Mo., MA in Info. Theory, 1971; PhD in Consumer Cultures, Northwestern U., 1978; postgrad., Sch. Mgmt. and Strategic Studies, U. Calif., 1988. Congl. asst., Washington, 1969-70; brand mgr. Procter & Gamble Co., Cin., 1971-73; v.p. Foote, Cone & Belding, Inc., Chgo., 1973-79; v.p. corp. comms. Internat. Harvester Co., Chgo., 1979-82; dir. mktg. and comms. Arthur Andersen & Co., Chgo., 1983-86; v.p. bus. devel. Gannett Co., Inc., Chgo., 1987-94; pres., chief oper. officer Shalit Place L.L.C., 1995—98; exec. v.p. Mus. Broadcast Comm., Chgo., 1996-97; cons. A.T. Kearney, Chgo., 1998—; pres. Ill. Women's Forum, 2003—. Prof. mktg. U. Chgo. Grad. Sch. Bus., 1979—80, Kellogg Grad. Sch. Mgmt., 1983—84, 1994—95; exec.-in-residence, prof. Kellstadt Grad. Sch. Bus., DePaul U., 2000—03; bd. dirs. AskRex.com, Clark/Bardes Inc., Motown Snacks, Robison Securities/Fleet Bank, Advocate Healthcare, Internat. Leadership Forum. Bd. dirs. Off-the-Street Club, Chgo., 1977-86; mem. adv. bd. U. Ill. Coll. Commerce, 1980-2000, Chgo. Crime Commn., 1987-90, DePaul U., 1989-95, Roosevelt U., 1994-2000, St. Mary's U., 1995-98. Recipient numerous Eagle Fin. Advt. awards, Silver medalist Am. Advt. Fedn., 1989; named Advt. Woman of Yr. Chgo. Advt. Club, 1989; named Fed. Glass Ceiling Commn., 1991-95, Com. 21st Century, 1992—; named One of Top 100 in Tech., 2003. Mem. Internat. Women's Forum (v.p. devel., v.p. comms., exec. com., bd. dirs.), Chgo. Network, Women's Forum Chgo., Women's Forum Mich., Women's Forum Ill. (pres.), Tarrytown Group, Social Venture Network, Execs. Club Chgo., Mid-Am. Club (bd. govs. 1990-92), Women's Athletic Club Chgo. Cleve. Yachting Club. Office: AT Kearney Inc 222 W Adams St Fl 25 Chicago IL 60606-5227 E-mail: lynne.o'shea@atkearney.com.

OSHEROW, JACQUELINE SUE, poet, English language educator; b. Phila., Aug. 15, 1956; d. Aaron and Hilda (Victor) Osherow; m. Saul Korewa, June 16, 1965 (div. 2003); children: Magda, Dora, Mollie. AB Magna cum laude, Radcliffe Coll., Harvard U., 1978; postgrad., Trinity Coll., Cambridge U., 1978-79; PhD in English and Am. Lit., Princeton U., 1990. Prof. English C. Utah, Salt Lake City, 1989—. Author: (poetry) Looking for Angels in New York, 1988, Conversations with Survivors, 1994, With a Moon in Transit, 1996, Dead Men's Praise, 1999. Recipient Witter Bynner prize Am. Acad. and Inst. Arts and Letters, 1990; Ingram Merrill Found. grantee, 1990; Guggenheim fellow, 1997-98, Nat. Endowment for the Arts fellow, 1999—. Mem. Poetry Soc. Am. (John Masefield Meml. award 1993, Lucille Medwick Meml. award 1995, Cecil Hemley Meml. award 1997). Jewish. Office: U Utah Dept English 255 S Central Campus Dr Rm 3500 Salt Lake City UT 84112-0494

OSHIN, DIANE, publisher; married; two children. BA in Polit. Sci. and French, Tufts U.; MBA in Mktg. and Fin., Columbia U. Formerly with Woman's Day, Conde Nast Traveler, Ogilvy & Mather, others; former advt. dir. Vogue; v.p., group pub. The Parenting Group AOL Time Warner, N.Y.C., 1994—. Office: Time Inc The Parenting Grp 530 Fifth Ave New York NY 10036

OSHMAN, MARILYN, retail executive; Chmn. bd. dirs. Oshman's Sporting Goods, Inc., Houston. Office: Oshman's Sporting Goods Inc 1050 W Hampden Ave Englewood CO 80110-2118

OSKIN, JOELLEN ROSS, special education educator, school librarian; b. McKeesport, Pa., Apr. 26, 1943; d. Clarence Melvin Ross and Ada Mae Oliver; m. David William Oskin, Sept. 5, 1964; children: David William, Steven Ross. BS in Spl. Edn. magna cum laude, 1980, MLS So. Conn. U., 1987. Spl. edn. tchr. Greenwich (Conn.) Bd. Edn., 1980—89, Darien (Conn.) Bd. Edn., 1989—91; libr. Automated Kings Coll. Libr., Kings Coll., Auckland, New Zealand, 1992—94. Bd. dirs. Vis. Nurse/VNC Network, Wilton, Conn.; mem. adv. bd. Kids In Crisis, Greenwich, 2001—02. Mem.: AAUW. Avocations: golf, reading, travel.

OSMAN, EDITH GABRIELLA, lawyer; b. N.Y.C., Mar. 18, 1949; d. Arthur Abraham and Judith (Goldman) Udem; children: Jacqueline, Daniel. BA in Spanish, SUNY, Stony Brook, 1970; JD cum laude, U. Miami, 1983. Bar: Fla. 1983, U.S. Dist. Ct. (so. dist.) Fla. 1984, U.S. Dist. Ct. (mid. dist.) Fla. 1988, U.S. Ct. Appeals (11th cir.) 1985, U.S. Supreme Ct. 1987, U.S. Ct. Mil. Appeals 1990; cert. family law mediator, civil mediator Fla. Supreme Ct. Assoc. Kimbrell & Hamann, PA, Miami, 1984-90, Dunn & Lodish, PA, Miami, 1990-93; pvt. practice Miami, 1993-98; shareholder Carlton Fields, Miami, 1998—, practice group leader, family law divsn. Bd. dirs. Miami City Cab; spkr. in field. Adv. com. for Implementation of the Victor Posner Judgement to Aid the Homeless, 1986-89. Recipient Breaking the Glass Ceiling award Ziff Mus., 2000, In the Company of Women award Dade County, 2000, Judge Mattie Belle Davis award, 2000, FAWL's Rosemary Barkett Achievement award, 1997, Outstanding Past Vol. Bar Pres.'s award, 1996; selected for photographic exhibit Florida Women of Achievement, 2000, South Fla.'s Top 250 Lawyers South Fla. Legal Guide, 2001, 02, 03, 04; named 100 Women to Watch MIA Metro Mag., 2000. Fellow Am. Bar Found., Fla. Bar Found.; mem. ABA (family law, Ho. of Dels. 1998—, standing com. on independence of judiciary 2000-2003, standing com. bar svs. 2003-), The Fla. Bar (budget com. 1989-92, 97-98, voluntary bar liaison com. 1989-90, spl. com. on formation of All-Bar Conf. 1988-89, chair mid-yr. conv. 1989, long range planning com. 1988-90, bd. govs. 1991-98, spl. commn. on delivery of legal svcs. to the indigent 1990-92, bus. law cert. com. 1995-96, practice law mgmt. com. 1995-96, chair program evaluation com., 1993-94, exec. com. 1992-93, 96-2000, rules and bylaws com., 1993-94, vice-chair disciplinary rev. com. 1994-95, investment com. 1994-95, vice-chair rules com. 1994-95, All-Bar Conf. chair 1997, chair grievance mediation com. 1997-99, pres.-elect 1998-99, pres. 1999-2000, exec. coun. family law sect. 2001—, vice-chair legis. 2001-2002, co-chair alternative dispute resolution com. 2003—, chair commn. legal needs of children), Dade County Bar Assn. (fed. ct. rules com. 1985-86, chmn. program com. 1988-91, 96-97, exec. com. 1987-88), Fla. Assn. Women's Lawyers Assn. (Dade County chpt. bd. dirs. 1984-85, treas. 1985-86, v.p. 1986-87, pres. 1987-88), Fla. Assn. Women Lawyers (v.p. 1988-89, pres. 1989-90), Fla. Bar Found. (dir. 1998-2001), Nat. Conf. Women's Bar Assn. (dir. nat. conf. 1990-91), Cuban Am. Bar Assn., Fla. Acad. Trial Lawyers, Dade County Trial Lawyers Assn., Nat. Conf. Bar Pres., So. Conf. Bar Pres., Leading Attys. (bd. dirs. 2000—), Iron Arrow Honor Soc. Office: Carlton Fields PA 100 SE 2nd St Ste 4000 Miami FL 33131-2148 Office Phone: 305-539-7258. E-mail: eosman@carltonfields.com.

OSMOND, MARIE, singer; b. Ogden, Utah, Oct. 13, 1959; d. George and Olive O.; m. Stephen Craig, 1982 (div.) m. Brian Blosil, 1986; children: Stephen James, Jessica Marie, Rachel. Ed. pub. schs., pvt. tutors. Appeared with The Osmond family singing group from age 7, solo act, 1973— ;(TV co-star): Donny & Marie TV show, 1976-79, Donny & Marie Christmas Spl, 1979, Osmond Family Show, 1979, Osmond Family Christmas Show, 1980, Donny & Marie, 1998; (star TV spl.) Marie, 1981; appeared in TV series Maybe This Time, 1995, video Buster & Chauncey's Silent Night, 1998; (record albums) include (with Donny Osmond): Make the World Go Away, I'm Leaving It All Up To You; songs from their TV Show Goin Coconuts; (solo albums) include: Paper Roses, In My Little Corner of the World, Who's Sorry Now?, This Is The Way That I Feel, There's No Stopping Your Heart, 1985, I Only Wanted You, 1987, All In Love, 1988, Steppin' Stone, 1989, Twenty Five Hits-Special Collection, 1995; (#1 singles) include Meet Me in Montana (Best Country Duo of Yr. award with Dan Seals), 1986, You're Still New to Me, 1986, There's No Stoppin' Your Heart, 1986, I Only Wanted You, 1987, The Best Of, 1990; toured with Bob Hope, Persian Gulf, 1991; (co-author): Fun, Fame, and Family, 1973; Marie Osmond's Guide to Beauty, Health, and Style, 1980. Recipient (with Donny Osmond) Georgie award for best vocal team Am. Guild Variety Artists, 1978 Mem. Lds Ch.

OSMUNDSEN, BARBARA ANN, sculptor; b. Jacksonville, N.C., Apr. 21, 1945; d. Robert Nygaärd and Catherine Ann (Wilent) Osmundsen; m. Baxter Smith Rains III, Sept. 20, 1986; 1 child, Holly Christine Delaney. Student, Vanderbilt U., 1963-64; BS, U. Tenn., Chattanooga, 1967; postgrad., U. Tenn., Knoxville, 1969-70, Va. Mus. of Fine Arts, Richmond, 1988-89. Fashion, accessory designer, Atlanta, 1972—85; ptnr. Bara Designs, Richmond, 1987—88; art instr. Mus. Art and Sci., Melbourne, Fla., 1998—2002, Vero Beach Mus. of Arts, 2000—03; artist in residence Brevard Cultural Alliance, Viera, Fla., 1999—. V.p., cons. artist Hope Dragon Found., Indian Harbour Beach, Fla., 1996. Exhibitions include Arlington Arts Ctr., 1991, Raleigh Gallery, Boca Raton, 1992—97, Gaier Contemporary Gallery, Orlando, 1994—96, Renee Foosaner Ctr., Mus. Art and Sci., Melbourne, 1998—2002, Marine Resources Coun. East Fla., Rockledge, 1999, Ctr. for the Arts, Vero Beach, Fla., 2000—02, Brevard Mus. of Arts and Sci., Melbourne, 2001, one-woman shows include Melbourne Internat. Airport, 2001, Represented in permanent collections Freedom 7 Cmty. Ctr., Wuesthoff Health Sys. Found., Caron Wills Collection, Killaloe/Bullina, Ireland, Mort Harris Collection, Detroit, Sch. Dist. Brevard County, Viera, Fla., Edgar and Alberta Holtz Collection, Vero Beach, Fla., Price Collection, Oilville, Va., pvt. collections, Brevard Mus. Art and Sci.; one-woman shows include Brevard County Govt. Complex, Viera, Fla., 2001—03, exhibited in group shows at Brevard Mus. Art and Sci., 2003; co-editor, author: Studio Link newsletter, 1994. Adv. bd. Women's Shelter, Valdosta, Ga., 1987; co-founder bd. govs. Vector Arts Endowment, 1997-2000. Mem.: Internat. Sculpture Assn., Nat. League Am. Pen Women (pres. Cape Canaveral Br., Fla. 2000—02). Avocations: organic gardening, gourmet cooking. Office: PO Box 372628 Satellite Beach FL 32937-0628 E-mail: barbaraosm@yahoo.com.

OSNES, PAMELA GRACE, behavior analyst; b. Burke, S.D., Sept. 10, 1955; d. John Ruben and Dortha Grace (Wilson) O.; children: Jocelyn Fern, Logan John. BS in Spl. Edn., BS in Elem. Edn., U. S.D., 1977; MA in Clin. Psychology, W.Va. U., 1981; PhD in Spl. Edn., 1998. Spl. edn. tchr. Sioux Falls (S.D.) Sch. Dist., 1977-79; instr. psychology dept. W.Va. U., Morgantown, 1982-85; dir. Carousel Preschool Program, Morgantown, 1982-85; assoc. prof. U. South Fla., Tampa, 1986-93, adminstrv. coord. advanced grad. programs dept. spl. edn., 1994-97, instr. dept. spl. edn., 1997-98, assoc. prof., 1999—2003, coord. Master's Program in Applied Behavior Analysis, 2000—03; asst. prof. spl. edn. Ohio State U., 2003—. Mem. Assn. for Behavior Analysis, Coun. for Exceptional Children (div. early childhood, div. rsch., tchr. edn. div.), Coun. Adminstrs. Spl. Edn., Coun. for Children with Behavior Disorders. Home: 927 Grandon Ave Bexley OH 43209-2529

OSOWIEC, DARLENE ANN, clinical psychologist, educator, consultant; b. Chgo., Feb. 16, 1951; d. Stephen Raymond and Estelle Marie Osowiec; m. Barry A. Leska. BS, Loyola U., Chgo., 1973; MA with honors, Roosevelt U., 1980; postgrad. in psychology, Saybrook Inst., San Francisco, 1985-88; PhD in Clin. Psychology, Calif. Inst. Integral Studies, 1992. Lic. clin. psychologist, Mo., Ill., Calif. Mental health therapist Ridgeway Hosp., Chgo., 1978; mem. faculty psychology dept. Coll. Lake County, Grayslake, Ill., 1981; counselor, supr. MA-level interns, chmn. pub. rels. com. Integral Counseling Ctr., San Francisco, 1983-84; clin. psychology intern Chgo.-Read Mental Health Ctr. Ill. Dept. Mental Health, 1985-86; mem. faculty dept. psychology Moraine Valley C.C., Palos Hills, Ill., 1988-89; lectr. psychology Daley Coll., Chgo., 1988-90; cons. Gordon & Assocs., Oak Lawn, Ill., 1989; adolescent, child and family therapist Orland Twp. Youth Svcs., Orland Park, Ill., 1993; psychology fellow Sch. Medicine, St. Louis U., 1994-95; pvt. practice Geneva and St. Charles, Ill., 1996—; founder Maximum Potential, Chgo., 1996—. Contbr., author: Transpersonal Hypnosis, 1999. Ill. State scholar, 1969-73; Calif. Inst. Integral Studies scholar, 1983. Mem. APA (chair edn. and tng. com. divsn. 30 1998-2000, chair mem. svcs. 2001—), Am. Psychol. Soc., Am. Women in Psychology, Ill. Psychol. Assn., Calif. Psychol. Assn., Mo. Psychol. Assn., Fla. Psychol. Assn., Am. Soc. Clin. Hypnosis, Chgo. Soc. Clin. Hypnosis, NOW (chair legal adv. corps, Chgo. 1974-76), Lincoln Park Bus. Devel. Inst. (chair program com. 2003—). Avocations: playing piano, gardening, reading, backpacking, writing. Office; 2210 Dean St Ste E-1 Saint Charles IL 60175

OSSENBERG, HELLA SVETLANA, psychoanalyst; b. June 10, 1930; came to U.S., 1957, naturalized, 1964; d. Anatole E. and Tatiana N. (Dombrovski) Donath; m. Carl H. Ossenberg, June 7, 1958. Diploma langs. and psychology, U. Heidelberg, Germany, 1953; MS, Columbia U., 1968. cert. Nat. Psychol. Assn. Psychoanalysis, 1977; diplomate Am. Bd. Examiners. Sr. psychiat.. social worker VA Mental Hygiene Clinic, N.Y.C., 1975-88. Mem. Theodor Reik Cons. Center 1978—; field instr. Columbia U., Fordham U. schs. social work. Mem. NASW, Acad. Cert. Social Workers, Nat. Psychol. Assn. Psychoanalysis, Nat. Assn. Advancement Psychoanalysis (Am. Bds. Accreditation and Certification), Coun. Psychoanalytic Psychotherapists. Office: 345 W 58th St New York NY 10019

OSSENFORT, STEPHANIE HELEN, music educator, secondary school educator, special education educator; d. Leo Michael and Helen Julie Podolec; divorced; children: Matthew, Victoria. B in Music Edn., SUNY, Fredonia, 1979; MS in Spl. Edn., Coll. St. Rose, 1986. Elem. music tchr. Greater Amsterdam Sch. Dist., 1979—81; choral tchr. Greater Amsterdam Sch. Dist.-Lynch Middle Sch., 1983—95; band dir., curriculum leader Greater Amsterdam Sch. Dist.-Amsterdam H.S., 1995—. Pvt. clarinet instr. Bd. dirs. Amsterdam Cmty. Concerts, Montgomery County, 1996—2003; dir. variety show Rotary Club, 2000, 2002, 2003; musician for local cmty. bands. Named Citizen of the Yr., Rotary Club, 2003, Montgomery County Tchr. of the Yr., Walmart Corp., 2003, Educator of the Week, WNYT/N.Y. State Lottery, 2003. Mem.: N.Y. State United Tchrs. (com. mem. on subject area for the arts 2002—03), N.Y. State Band Dirs. Assn., N.Y. State Sch. Music Assn. Democrat. Roman Catholic. Office: Amsterdam High Sch 104 Saratoga Ave Amsterdam NY 12010

OSSEWAARDE, ANNE WINKLER, real estate company executive; b. Dallas, June 2, 1957; d. Lowell Graves and Ruth Lenore (Lind) Winkler; m. Kirk L Ossewaarde, Apr. 27, 1991. BBA in Fin. with honors, Emory U., 1979; MBA in Acctg. and Fin. with honors, U. Tex., 1983; MS in Real Estate Devel., MIT, 1988. Cert. comml. investment mem., Comml. Investment Real Estate Inst. Mgmt. trainee Citizens & So. Nat. Bank, Atlanta, 1979-81; banking assoc. Continental Ill. Nat. Bank, Chgo. and Dallas, 1983-85; asst. v.p., devel. assoc. Trammell Crow Residential, Dallas, 1985-87, Seattle, 1988-91; devel. mgr. Blackhawk Port Blakeley Cmtys., Seattle, 1991-93; v.p., real estate portfolio mgr. Aegon U.S.A. Realty, Atlanta, 1994-98; exec. dir. asset mgmt. Morgan Stanley (formerly Lend Lease Real Estate Investments, Inc.), Atlanta, 2000—. Dir. UBS Brinson Realty Investors (formerly Allegis Realty Investors), Dallas, 1998-2000. Charles Harritt Jr. Presdl. scholar U. Tex., 1982, Alexander Grant scholar, 1982. Mem. Comml. Real Estate Women, MIT Ctr. for Real Estate Alumni Assn., Alpha Epsilon Upsilon. Methodist. Avocations: singing, photography, bicycling, reading. Home: 3170 Windsor Lake Dr Atlanta GA 30319

OSTBY, KAREN JEAN, speech pathology/audiology services professional; d. Walter Norman and Marguerite Larsen Ostby. BS, Ithaca Coll., 1968; MA, We. Ill. U., 1969. Cert. Am. Speech and Hearing Assn. Speech-lang. pathologist Ctrl. Ct. Rehab. Ctr., Meriden, Conn., 1969—71, Regional Sch. Dist. 13, Middlefield-Durham, Conn., 1971—2003. Mem. Christian edn. com. Immanuel Luth. Ch., Meriden, 2002—03, mem. ch. coun., 2002—03. Mem.: NEA, Conn. Speech-Hearing and Lang. Assn., Am. Speech-Hearing Assn., Region 13 Edn. Assn. (v.p. 1981—82, pres. 1982—85, sec. 1998—2003), Conn. Edn. Assn. (vice chmn. Middlesex county 1986—91). Democrat. Evang. Luth. Avocations: reading, history, needlecrafts. Office: RegionalSchool Dist 13 Brewster School Tuttle Rd Durham CT 06422

OSTENDORF, JOAN DONAHUE, fund raiser, volunteer; b. Boston, Dec. 9, 1933; d. John Stanley and Genevieve Catherine (Morrissey) Donahue; m. Edgar Louis Ostendorf, Feb. 10, 1962; 1 child, Mary Elizabeth. BA, Marymount Coll., Tarrytown, N.Y., 1956; postgrad., Boston U., 1956. Tchr. Boston pub. schs., 1956-57, Waltham (Mass.) pub. schs., l957-62. Trustee Cleve. Inst. Music, 1984—, mem. trustees coordianting coun., 1989; mem. Jr. League Cleve., 1964, 1st v.p. 1972-73; founder adv. coun. pub. rels. com. Cleve. Orch., 1974, 1st v.p., 1975-76; mem. del. assembly United Way, 1977-87; chmn. benefits Vis. Nurse Assn., 1987-88, March Dimes, 1982; trustee women's com. U. Hosps. Case Western Res. U. Med. Sch., 1974—; mem. nominating com. Inst. Music, 1990-91; 2d v.p. Music and Drama Club, 1991-93 (pres. 2001-2003), corresponding sec., 1993-95; chair Lyric Opera, 1992, Platform Assn., 1992—; pres. bd. trustees Cleve. Inst. Music, 1980-82, pres. women's com., 1980-82; mem. adv. bd. Women's Community Found., 1991—; v.p. Cleve. Inst. Piano Competition, 1994—; women's coun. Cleve. Mus., 1996. Mem. Internat. Platform Assn., Longwood Cricket Club, Intown Club, Chagrin Valley Hunt Club. Republican. Roman Catholic. Address: 3425 Roundwood Rd Chagrin Falls OH 44022-6634

OSTER, ROSE MARIE GUNHILD, foreign language professional, educator; b. Stockholm, Feb. 26, 1934; came to U.S., 1958; d. Herbert Jonas and Emma Wilhelmina (Johnson) Hagetorn; m. Ludwig F. Oster, May 17, 1956; children: Ulrika, Mattias. Fil. mag., U. Stockholm, 1956; PhD, Kiel (Germany) U., 1958. Postdoctoral rsch. fellow linguistics Yale U., 1958-60, rsch. fellow Germanic langs., 1960-64, lectr. Swedish, 1964-66; mem. faculty U. Colo., Boulder, 1966-80, assoc. prof. Germanic langs. and lits., 1970-77, prof., 1977-80, chmn. dept., 1972-75, assoc. dean Grad. Sch., 1975-79, assoc. vice chancellor for grad. affairs Grad. Sch., 1979-80; dean for grad. studies and rsch. U. Md., College Park, 1980-83, prof. Germanic langs. and lits., 1980—, acting chair dept., 1997—2001. Mem. Fulbright Nat. Screening Com., Scandinavia, 1973, 83-87, chair, 1986-87; mem. selection com. Scandinavia Internat. Exch. of Scholars, 1982-86; cons. panelist Nat. Endowment for Humanities, 1975—, mem. bd. cons., 1980—; state coord. Am. Coun. on Edn., Colo., 1978-80, Md., 1981-83, dir. dept. leadership program, 1986-91; mem. exec. com. Assn. Grad. Schs., 1980-83; mem. dean's exec. com. African-Am. Inst., 1981-85; interim dir. Washington Sch. Psychiatry, 1994-95; cons. in field. Contbr. articles and revs. to profl. publs. Bd. dirs. Washington Sch. Psychiatry, Am.-Swedish Hist. Mus., Phila., Open Theatre, Washington; mem. nat. fellowship com. Am.-Scandinavian Found., 1997—, bd. trustees, 2001—. Carnegie fellow, 1974; grantee Swedish Govt., Am. Scandinavian Found., German Acad. Exch. Svc.; recipient Translation prize Am.-Scandinavian Found., 1997. Mem. NOW, MLA (mem. Del. Assembly 1995—), AAUP, Soc. Advancement Scandinavian Studies (pres. 1979-80), Am. Scandinavian Assn. of Nat. Capital Area (pres. 1983-86, 96—), Am.-Scandinavian Found., Am. Assn. Higher Edn., Modern Lang. Assn. (mem. del. assembly). Home: 4977 Battery Ln Bethesda MD 20814-4931 Office: U Md Dept Germanic Studies College Park MD 20742-0001 E-mail: ro8@umail.umd.edu.

OSTERGAARD, JONI HAMMERSLA, lawyer; b. Seattle, May 26, 1950; d. William Dudley and Carol Mae (Gillett) Hammersla; m. Gregory Lance Ostergaard, May 22, 1976 (div. 1985); 1 child, Bennett Gillett; m. William Howard Patton, Jan. 1, 1988; 1 child, Morgan Hollis; stepchildren: Colin W., Benjamin C. BS, U. Wash., 1972; MS, Purdue U., 1974; JD, U. Wash., 1980. Bar: Wash. 1980, U.S. Dist. Ct. (we. dist.) Wash. 1980, U.S. Ct. Appeals (9th cir.) 1981, U. S. Ct. Claims 1983. Clin. psychol. intern Yale Med. Sch., 1976-77; law clk. U.S. Ct. Appeals (9th cir.), Seattle, 1980-81; assoc. Roberts & Shefelman, Seattle, 1982-86, ptnr., 1987, Foster Pepper & Shefelman, Seattle, 1988-92; sole practitioner Seattle, 1996—2003; dep. pros. atty. Snohomish County, Everett, Wash., 2004—. Contbr. articles to profl. jours.; notes and comments editor Wash. Law Rev., 1979-80.

Recipient Sophia and Wilbur Albright scholarship U. Wash. Law Sch., 1979-80, law sch. alumni scholarship U. Wash. Law Sch., 1978-79; fellow NIMH. Avocations: gardening, reading. Office: Snohomish County Prosecuting Attys Office Civil Divsn 2918 Colby Ave Ste 203 Everett WA 98201 Office Phone: 425-388-6370. Office Fax: 425-388-6333. Personal E-mail: jostergaard@att.net. Business E-Mail: jostergaard@co.snohomish.wa.us.

OSTERKAMP, DALENE MAY, psychology educator, artist; b. Davenport, Iowa, Dec. 1, 1932; d. James Hiram and Bernice Grace Simmons; m. Donald Edwin Osterkamp, Feb. 11, 1951 (dec. Sept. 1951). BA, San Jose State U., 1959, MA, 1962; PhD, Saybrook Inst., 1989. Lectr. San Jose (Calif.) State U., 1960—65, U. Santa Barbara (Calif.) Ext., 1970-76; prof. Bakersfield (Calif.) Coll., 1961-87, prof. emerita, 1987—; adj. faculty, counselor Calif. State U., Bakersfield, 1990—95. Gallery dir. Bakersfield Coll., 1964-72. Juried group shows include Berkeley (Calif.) Art, Ctr., 1975, Libr. of Congress, 1961, Seattle Art Mus., 1962. Founder Kern Art Edn. Assn., Bakersfield, 1962, Bakersfield Printmakers, 1976. Staff sgt. USAF, 1952-55. Recipient 1st Ann. Svc. to Women award Am. Assn. Women in C.C., 1989. Mem. APA, Assn. for Women in Psychology, Assn. for Humanistic Psychology, Calif. Soc. Printmakers. Home: PO Box 387 Glennville CA 93226-0387 Office: Calif State Univ Stockdale Ave Bakersfield CA 93309

OSTERMANN, GRACE GENTILE, librarian, media specialist; b. Bklyn., N.Y., Oct. 20, 1948; d. Thomas James and Nancy Pittari Gentile; m. John E. Ostermann, Aug. 8, 1970; children: L. Susan, Sharon L. BA, Molloy Coll., Rockville Ctr., N.Y., 1970; MLS, Queens Coll., N.Y., 1974. Cert. tchg. N.Y., libr. media specialist N.Y. Tchr. lang. arts St. Elizabeth Sch., Ozone Pk., NY, 1970—74; libr. media specialist Washingtonville Jr. High, NY, 1974—84, Somers Inst. Sch., NY, 1989—. Bldg. rep. Somers Faculty Assn., NY, 2003—; editor Brookside pub. ctr. Brookside Elem. Sch., Yorktown, NY, 1986—88. Mem. Croton Heights Cmty. Assn., Yorktown Heights, NY, 1975—. Mem.: Sch. Libr. Media Specialist of Southeastern N.Y. Avocations: travel, theater, reading.

OSTERYOUNG, JANET GRETCHEN, chemistry educator; b. Pitts., Mar. 1, 1939; d. Arthur Roberts and Elizabeth Jane (Peebles) Jones; m. Bruce Ulrich, Aug. 16, 1967 (div. 1968); m. Robert Allen Osteryoung, Aug. 17, 1969; children: Anne Elizabeth, Adam Armstrong. BA, Swarthmore Coll., 1961; PhD, Calif. Inst. Tech., 1967. Asst. prof. chemistry Mont. State U., Bozeman, 1967-68; fellow Colo. State U., Ft. Collins, 1968-73, asst. prof. civil engring., 1969-73, asst. prof. civil engring., microbiology, 1972-73, assoc. prof., 1973-78, assoc. prof. civil engring., rsch. chemist, 1978-79; assoc. prof. chemistry SUNY, Buffalo, 1979-82, prof., 1982-92, faculty exch. scholar, 1987-92; head dept. chemistry N.C. State U., 1992-94; prof. NSF, 1992—, dir. chemistry divsn., 1994—. Vis. prof. Colo. Coll., 1972, Calif. Inst. Tech., 1985, Guggenheim fellow, vis. prof. U. Southampton (Eng.), 1985-86; cons. Colo. State U., Ft. Collins, 1970-72, EG&G Princeton (N.J.) Applied, 1983—; dir. program chem. analysis NSF, Washington, 1977-78, mem. ad hoc rev. panel 1988. Co-author: Models in Chemical Science, 1971; assoc. editor Electrochemica Acta, 1986—; contbr. over 180 articles to profl. jours.; patentee controlled-growth mercury drop electrode. Hon. Fulbright fellow, 1986; recipient Anachem award Soc. Analytical Chemists of Detroit, 1990, Schoellkopf medalist WNY-Am. Chem. Soc., 1992, ACS award in Electrochemistry-Electrochem. Soc., 1996. Fellow AAAS; mem., Internat. Soc. Electrochemistry (mem. divsn. 3 1985-88), Soc. Electroanalytical Chemistry (founding mem., pres. 1986-87, chmn. 1987-88), Am. Chem. Soc. (Garvan medal 1987, western N.Y. chpt., chmn. exec. com. 1981-89, Disting. Svc. award 1988), Soc. Applied Spectroscopy (Disting. Svc. award Niagara Frontier chpt. 1988), N.Y. Acad. Scis., Electrochem. Soc. (pres. Rocky Mountain sect. 1976-77), Fedn. Am. Scientists, Phi Beta Kappa, Sigma Xi, Iota Sigma Pi (Triennial Hon. mem.). Democrat. Episcopalian. Home: 4201 Wilson Blvd Ste 110 Arlington VA 22203-1859 Office: NC State U Dept of Chemistry PO Box 8204 Raleigh NC 27695-0001

OSTMANN, CINDY, state legislator; BS, Lindenwood Coll. Tchr. Ft. Zumwalt Sch. Dist., 1958-62, 64-67, Fayetteville Sch. Sys., 1963-64; owner, mgr. residential property; mem. Mo. State Ho. of Reps. Dist. 14, 1992—, mem. children, youth and families com., mem. energy and environ. com., mem. local govt. and related matters com. Recipient Outstanding Contbr. to Edn. award Phi Delta Kappa, 1988. Mem. Coun. of Chambers Charter Govt. Com., St. Charles County Arts Coun., Grand Order of Pachyderm, Friends of St. Louis Symphony, Mo. Fedn. Rep. Women, First Capitol Rep. Club. Home: 445 Knaust Rd Saint Peters MO 63376-1713 Office: Mo Ho of Reps State Capitol Building Jefferson City MO 65101-1556

OSTOLAZA, YVETTE, lawyer; b. Miami, Fla., 1964; d. Oscar J. and Carmen O.; m. Peter B. Dewar, Nov. 10, 1991; children: Aidan S., Alec P., Elena I. BA, U. Miami, 1985, JD, 1992. Bar: Tex. 1992. Various mktg. positions Ea. Airlines, Ft. Lauderdale, Fla., Gainesville, Fla., Continental Airlines, Orlando, Fla.; internat. sales mgr. Continental/Ea. Sales, Inc., Miami; assoc., comml. litig. arbitration and employment law Weil, Gotshal & Manges LLP, Dallas, 1992—. Mem. U. Miami Law Rev., 1991-92; articles and comments editor Bus. Law Jour., 1991-92. Mem. Jr. League Dallas. Mem. ABA, Attys. Serving Cmty., Soc. Bar and Gavel, Golden Key, Dallas (Tex.) C. of C. (internat. adv. coun.). Avocations: snow skiing, foreign travel, theatre. Office: Weil Gotshal & Manges LLP 200 Crescent Ct Ste 300 Dallas TX 75201-7821 Office Phone: 214-746-7805.

OSTRIKER, ALICIA SUSKIN, poet; b. N.Y.C., Nov. 11, 1937; d. David and Beatrice (Linnick) Suskin; m. Jeremiah P. Ostriker, 1958; children: Rebecca, Eve, Gabriel. BA, Brandeis U., 1959; MA, U. Wis., 1961, PhD, 1964. Asst. prof. Rutgers U., New Brunswick, N.J., 1965-68, assoc. prof., 1968-72, prof. English, 1972—. Author: Vision and Verse in William Blake, 1965, Songs, 1969, Once More Out of Darkness, and Other Poems, 1974, A Dream of Springtime, 1979, The Mother/Child Papers, 1980, A Woman Under the Surface: Poems and Prose Poems, 1982, Writing Like a Woman, 1983, The Imaginary Lover, 1986 (William Carlos Williams prize Poetry Soc. Am. 1986), Stealing the Language: The Emergence of Women's Poetry in America, 1986, Green Age, 1989, Feminist Revision and the Bible, 1993, The Nakedness of the Fathers: Biblical Vision and Revisions, 1994, The Crack in Everything, 1996 (Nat. Book award finalist 1996, Paterson Poetry prize 1996, San Francisco State Poetry Ctr. award 1997), The Little Space: Selected and New Poems, 1998 (Nat. Book award finalist 1998), Dancing at the Devil's Party: Essays on Poetry, Politics, and the Erotic, 2000, The Volcano Sequence, 2002; editor: William Blake: Complete Poems, 1977. Nat. Coun. on Humanities grantee, 1968; NEA fellow, 1976-77, N.J. Arts Coun. fellow, 1982, Guggenheim Found. fellow, 1984-85, faculty fellow Rutgers Ctr. for Hist. Analysis, 1995-96, Rockefeller Found. fellow, 1982; recipient Strousse Poetry prize Prairie Schooner, 1986, Edward Stanley award Prairie Schooner, 1994, Anna David Rosenberg Poetry award, 1994, Best American Poetry award, 1996, Paterson prize, 1997, San Francisco State Poetry Ctr. award, 1997, Pushcart prize, 1999, Larry Levis prize 2001. Office: Rutgers Univ Dept of English New Brunswick NJ 08903 E-mail: ostriker@rci.rutgers.edu.

OSTROFSKY, ANNA, music educator, violinist; b. NYC, June 27, 1953; d. Joseph and Lena (Cipollone) Simeone; m. Frederick Ostrofsky, May 26, 1975; 1 child, Jacqueline. MusB, Manhattan Sch. Music, 1974, MusM, 1975; profl. diploma, Fordham U., 1990. Orch. dir., tchr. Harlem Sch. Arts, NYC, 1975-76; first violinist NJ Symphony Orch., Newark, 1975-76; string instr. Hoff-Barthelson Sch. Music, Scarsdale, NY, 1976-79; concertmaster Chappaqua Chamber Orch., NY, 1976-89; orch. dir./string instr. City Sch. Dist. New Rochelle, NY, 1978-83; first violinist Hudson Valley Philharm. Orch., Poughkeepsie, NY, 1981-89; 1st violinist Ea. Philharm. Orch., Greensboro, NC, 1982-83; orch. dir. Briarcliff Union Free Sch. Dist., Briarcliff Manor, NY, 1983—; 1st violinist Concert Soc. Putnam and No. Westchester, 1982—; first violinist New Rochelle Opera, NY, 1997, 98; adj. prof. violin/viola King's Coll., Briarcliff Manor, 1989-94. Coord. employment opportunities Westchester County (NY) Sch. Music Assn., Dist. coord. for Performing Arts, 2002-. Debut Carnegie Recital Hall, 1976; conductor Westchester Elem. All-County Orch., 1997. Recipient First prize Artists' Internat. Mgmt., 1975, Excellence in Chamber Music Teaching award Chamber Music Am., 1991. Mem. NY State Acad. Teaching and Learning. Democrat. Roman Catholic. Avocations: writing music composition and orchestration, reading, swimming, walking, cooking. Home: PO Box 396 Somers NY 10589-0396 Office: 444 Pleasantville Rd Briarcliff Manor NY 10510-1922 Fax: 914-769-2509.

OSTROM, KATHERINE ELMA, retired educator; b. L.A., Dec. 30, 1928; d. Charles W. and Mabel M. (Christensen) Shults; m. Carl R. Ostrom, Jan. 29, 1949 (dec.); children: Margaret K. Larson, Carl R. Jr. BA cum laude, U. Wash., 1966, MA in Tchg. English, 1973, EdD, 1994. Std. tchg. cert. grades K-12, Wash.; continuing prin. cert.-secondary, Wash. Substitute tchr. Renton, Kent & South Ctrl. Sch. Dist., 1966; tchr. Foster HS, Tukwila, Wash., 1966-67, 75-76, Showalter Mid.Sch., Tukwila, 1967-79; dept. chair Showalter Mid. Sch., Tukwila, 1968-87, vice prin., 1979-87; tchr., supr. student tchr. U. Wash., Seattle, 1989-91; subs. tchr. Tukwila Sch. Dist., 1999—. Tchr. Western Wash. State Coll., Bellingham, 1967-68; liaison, supr. Jr. Achievement, Seattle, 1988-89; cons., trainer Nat. Assn. Elem. Sch. Prins., 1992-98; vol. tchr. Immigrant and Refugee Resources Ctr., Seattle, 1996-2003; dir. Forum on Edn., PDK, Seattle, 1997; mem. Citizen Adv. Com. in Curriculum, Renton, S.D., 2001—, chair, 2002-03. Host del., mem. Tukwila-Ikawa (Japan) Sister Cities, 1980—88, 1997—, chair, 1999—2002; block-watch organizer King County, Wash., 1994—2001; key communicator Renton (Wash.) Sch. Dist., 1996—2003; tutor Skyway Meth. Ch., Seattle, 1997—2000, staff parish com., 1996—2003. Named Vol. of Yr., BPW, Tukwila, Wash., 1990; Coll. scholar U. Puget Sound, Tacoma, Wash., 1946; PBK Pathfinder award, 1997. Mem. Assn. Wash. Sch. Prin. (chair state vice prin. conf. 1986, regional dir. 1986-88), Wash. Physicians for Social Responsibility (del. to Mid. East 1994), Key Players Prosser Piano and Organ, Phi Delta Kappa (pres. chpt. 1991-95, newsletter editor 1988-90, 1995-2003, area coord. 1995-2001), Phi Beta Kappa (bd. dirs., trustee Puget Sound Assn., 2000—, pres. Puget Sound Assn., 2003—). Democrat. Home: 12817 80th Ave S Seattle WA 98178-4911 E-mail: kateostrom@aol.com.

OSTROW, RONA LYNN, librarian, educator; b. N.Y.C., Oct. 21, 1948; d. Morty and Jeane Goldberg; m. Steven A. Ostrow, June 25, 1972; 1 child, Ciné Justine. BA, CCNY, 1969; MS in LS, Columbia U., 1970; MA, Hunter Coll., 1975; PhD., Rutgers U., 1998. Cert. libr., N.Y. Br. adult and reference libr. N.Y. Pub. Libr., N.Y.C., 1970-73, rsch. libr., 1973-78; asst. libr. Fashion Inst. Tech., N.Y.C., 1978-80; assoc. dir. Grad. Bus. Resource Ctr., Baruch Coll., CUNY, 1980-90, assoc. prof.; assoc. dean of librs. for pub. svcs. Adelphi U., Garden City, N.Y., 1990-94; chief libr. Marymount Manhattan Coll., N.Y.C., 1994-98; asst. provost Fairleigh Dickinson U., Teaneck, N.J., 1998-2000; chief libr. Lehman Coll. CUNY, Bronx, 2000—. Author: Dictionary of Retailing, 1984, Dictionary of Marketing, 1987; co-author: Cross Reference Index, 1989. Mem.: ALA, Assn. Coll. and Rsch. Librs. Office: CUNY Lehman Coll Libr 250 Bedford Park Blvd W Bronx NY 10468-1589 E-mail: rostrow@lehman.cuny.edu.

OSTRY, SYLVIA, academic administrator, economist; b. Winnipeg, Man., Can. d. Morris J. and B. (Stoller) Knelman; m. Bernard Ostry; children: Adam, Jonathan. BA in Econs., McGill U., 1948, MA, 1950; PhD in Econs., Cambridge U. and McGill U., 1954; also 18 hon. degrees. Lectr., asst. prof. econs. McGill U.; rsch. officer Inst. Stats., U. Oxford, Eng.; assoc. prof. U. Montreal, Can.; with dept. stats. Econ. Coun. Can., Ottawa, 1964-72, chmn., 1978-79; chief statistician Stats. Can., Ottawa, 1972-75; dep. minister consumer and corp. affairs Govt. Can., Ottawa, 1975-78, dep. minister internat. trade, coordinator internat. econ. relations, 1984-85, ambassador for multilateral trade negotiations, personal rep. of Prime Minister for Econ. Summit, 1985-88; chancellor U. Waterloo, 1991-96; head dept. econs. and stats. OECD, Paris, 1979-83; chmn. Ctr. for Internat. Studies U. Toronto, Ont., Can., 1990-97, disting. rsch. fellow Munk Ctr. for Internat. Studies, 1997—. Lectr. Per Jacobssen Found., 1987; chmn. nat. coun. Can. Inst. Internat. Affairs, 1990-95; western co-chmn. Blue Ribbon Commn. for Hungary's Econ. Recovery, 1990-94; mem. adv. bd. Inst. Internat. Econs., Washington; founding mem. Pacific Coun. on Internat. Policy; Volvo Disting. vis. fellow Coun. on Fgn. Rels., N.Y.C., 1989. Author: Governments and Corporations in a Shrinking World: The Search for Stability, 1990, The Threat of Managed Trade to Transforming Economies, 1993; co-author: (with Richard Nelson) Technonationalism and Technoglobalism: Conflict and Cooperation, 1995; co-editor: (with Karen Knop, Richard Simeon, Katherine Swinton) Rethinking Federalism: Citizens, Markets and Governments in a Changing World, 1995; New Dimensions of Market Access, 1995, (with Gilbert R. Winham) The Halifax G-7 Summit: Issues on the Table, 1995, Who's on First: The Post-Cold War Trading System, 1997, APEC and Regime Creation in the Asia-Pacific: The OECD Model?, 1998, Technology, Productivity and Multinational Enterprise, 1998, Intellectual Property Protection in the World Trade Organization: Major Issues in the Millennium Round, 1999, Globalization Implications for Industrial Relations, 1999, The Future of the World Trading System, 1999, Convergence and Sovereignty: Policy Scope for Compromise?, 2000, Regional Versus Multilateral Trade Strategies, 2000, Making Sense of it All: A Post Mortem on the Meaning of Seattle, 2000; The Uruguay Round North-South Grand Bargain: Implications for Future Negotiations, 2000, Regional Dominos and the WTO: Building Blocks or Boomerang?, 2000, Business, Trade and the Environment, 2000, The Changing Scenario in International Governance, 2000, Looking Back to Look Forward: The Multilateral Trading System after 50 Years, 2000, The WTO: Post Seattle and Chinese Accession, 2001, The WTO and International Governance, 2001, The WTO After Seattle: Something's Happening Here, What It Is Ain't Exactly Clear, 2001, WTO Membership for China: To Be & Not To Be. Is That The Answer?, 2001, The Question of the Q's: What Cue Should Quebec Send to Qatar?, 2001, The WTO and Internat. Governance, 2001, WTO Membership for China: To Be & Not To Be, Is That the Answer?, 2001, The Question of The Q's: What Cue Should Quebec Send to Qatar?, 2001, Global Integration: Currents and Counter-Currents, 2002; contbg. author: China and the Long March to Global Trade, 2003; contbr. articles on empirical and policy-analytic subjects to more than 90 profl. publs. Decorated companion Order of Can., 1990; recipient Outstanding Achievement award Govt. of Can., 1987, Hon. Assoc. award Conf. Bd. of Can., 1992; Disting. vis. fellow Volvo, 1989-90. Fellow Royal Soc. Can., Am. Statis. Assn.; mem. Am. Econ. Assn., Can. Econ. Assn., Royal Econ. Soc. (founding), Ctr. for European Policy Studies (internat. adv. coun.), Group of Thirty, Inst. for Internat. Econs. (adv. bd.). Avocations: films, theatre, contemporary reading. Office: Munk Ctr Internat Studies U Toronto 1 Devonshire Pl Toronto ON Canada M5S 3K7 E-mail: sylvia.ostry@utoronto.ca.

O'SULLIVAN, CHRISTINE, retired executive director social service agency, consultant; b. Washington, July 5, 1947; d. George Albert and Mary Ruth (Stalcup) Markward; m. Donald Phillip O'Sullivan, June 27, 1985. Sec. Gas Distributors Info. Svc., Washington, 1966-70; adminstr. asst. Nat. Airlines, Washington, 1970-71; office mgr. Tire Industry Safety Coun., Washington, 1971-75; pres. Type-Right Exec. Sec. Svc., Washington, Pitts., 1976-91; exec. dir. Eastside Cmty. Ministry, Zanesville, Ohio, 1991—2001. Chair FEMA Emergency Bd., Muskingum, Morgan and Perry Counties, Ohio, 1994-97, 99-2000; chair United Way Exec. Dirs. Coun., 1994-97, United Way agy. relations com. 2000-03, allocations com. 2002-03; v.p. Muskingum County Hunger Network, Zanesville, 1993-99. Author: Write a Good Resume, 1976. Mem. task force Literacy Coun., 1993—2000; mem. steering com. Muskingum County Operation Feed, 1992—99; trustee Disability Network of Ohio-Solidarity, 2001—; mem Zanesville City Sch. Bldg. Adv. Coun., Ohio, 2001—02; v.p. Muskingum County Women's Rep. Club, 1994, sec., 1995; mem. Downtown Clergy Assn., 1992—, pres., 1995—96; bd. dirs. Human Care Ministry, Ohio dist. Luth. Ch., Mo. Synod, PRO-Muskingum, 1995—2000; commr. Mo. Synod Luths. to Commn. on Religion in Appalachia, 1996—98; chair human care bd. Trinity Evang. Luth. Ch., 2003—; bd. dirs. Muskingum County Women's Coalition, 1994—97, Families and Children First Coun., 1995—2000, Interfaith Response to Ohio Disaster, 1988—91, Luth. Social Svcs. Emergency Assistance Com., 1998—99, Muskingum County Family Adv. Team, 2000—01. Recipient Cert. of Achievement for Mil. Family Support, U.S. Army, 1991, Excellence in Cmty. Svc. award Aid Assn. Luths., 1993, Excellence in Cmty. Svc. award Muskingum County DAR, 1994, Positive Action award, NOW, 1997, YWCA Woman of Achievement award, 1997, Americanism award VFW, 1992, Cmty. Involvement award Richvale Grange, 1997, Cmty. Citizen award State of Ohio Grange, 2000; named Outstanding Cmty. Vol. Zanesville Daybreak Rotary Club, 1997. Mem.: Nat. Multiple Sclerosis Soc. (program com. Buckeye chpt. 2001—03), Muskingum County Respiratory Assn. (bd. dirs. 2001—, sec., bd. dirs. 2003—), Disability Network Ohio Solidarity (trustee 2001—), Richvale Grange, Kiwanis (Zanesville chpt. bd. dirs. 1997—99, spiritual aims com. chair Dist. 18 of Ohio 1998—99). Avocations: creative writing, music. Office: Eastside Cmty Ministry 221 Stillwell St PO Box 965 Zanesville OH 43702-0965 Home: 62 N 3rd St Apt 201 Zanesville OH 43701 E-mail: chrissyduck@hotmail.com.

O'SULLIVAN, JUDITH ROBERTA, lawyer, author, artist; b. Pitts., Jan. 6, 1942; d. Robert Howard and Mary Olive (O'Donnell) Gallick; m. James Paul O'Sullivan, Feb. 1, 1964; children: Kathryn, James. BA, Carlow Coll., 1963; MA, U. Md., 1969, PhD, 1976; JD, Georgetown U., 1996. Editor Am. Film Inst., Washington, 1974—77; assoc. program coord. Smithsonian Resident Assocs., Washington, 1977—78; dir. instl. devel. Nat. Archives, Washington, 1978—79; exec. dir. Md. State Humanities Coun., Balt., 1979—81, 1982—84, Ctr. for the Book, Libr. of Congress, Washington, 1981—82; dep. asst. dir. Nat. Mus. Am. Art, Washington, 1984—87, acting asst. dir., 1987—89; pres., CEO The Mus. at Stony Brook, NY, 1989—92; exec. dir. Nat. Assn. Women Judges, Washington, 1993; clk. Office Legal Adviser U.S. Dept. State, Washington, 1994—96; trial atty. Atty. Gen.'s honors program U.S. Dept. Justice, 1996—, trial atty. Criminal divsn., Domestic Security sect., 2002—; spl. asst. U.S. atty. U.S. Dist. (ea. dist.) Va., 1998—2002; asst. U.S. atty. U.S. Dist. Ariz., Tucson, 1999—2000. Summer assoc. Piper & Marbury, Balt., 1995; chair Smithsonian Women's Coun., Washington, 1988-89. Author: The Art of the Comic Strip, 1971 (Gen. Excellence award Printing Industry Am.); Workers and Allies, 1975; (with Alan Fern) The Complete Prints of Leonard Baskin, 1984, The Great American Comic Strip, 1991; editor Am. Film Inst. Catalogue: Feature Films, 1961-70, 1974-77; mem. editl. bd. Am. Film Inst. Catalog, 1979-1990. Trustee Child Life Ctr., U. Md., College Pk., 1971-74; chair Smithsonian Women's Coun., 1988-89. Univ. fellow U. Md., 1967-70, Mus. fellow, 1970-71, Smithsonian fellow Nat. Collection Fine Arts, Washington, 1972-73. Mem.: Mystery Writers of Am., D.C. Bar Assn., Md. Bar Assn. Avocations: landscape painting, mystery writing. Home: The Edgemoor 4821 Montgomery Ln # 803 Bethesda MD 20814 Office: US Dept Justice Domestic Security Sect Criminal Divsn Washington DC 20530 E-mail: Judith.O'Sullivan@usdoj.gov.

O'SULLIVAN, LYNDA TROUTMAN, lawyer; b. Oil City, Pa., Aug. 30, 1952; d. Perry John and Vivian Dorothy (Schreffler) Troutman; m. P. Kevin O'Sullivan, Dec. 15, 1979; children: John Perry, Michael Patrick. BA, Am. U., 1974; JD, Georgetown U., 1978, postgrad., 1982-83. Bar: D.C. 1978. Ptnr. Perkins Coie, Washington, 1985-92, Fried, Frank, Harris, Shriver & Jacobson, Washington, 1993-97, Miller & Chevalier, Washington, 1997—. Mem. adv. bd. Fed. Contracts Report, 1991-97, Govt. Contract Costs, Pricing & Acctg. Report, 1997-99; mem. faculty govt. contracts program George Washington U., 1993-99; lectr. in field. Contbr. articles to profl. jours. Fellow Am. Bar Found.; mem. ABA (chair truth in negotiations com. 1991-94, chair acctg., cost and pricing com. 1996-2000, coun. sect. pub. contract law 1993-95). Office: Miller & Chevalier 655 15th St NW Ste 900 Washington DC 20005-5799 E-mail: losullivan@milchev.com.

O'SULLIVAN, MARY J. physician, maternal fetal medicine educator; b. Bklyn., Mar. 22, 1938; d. Michael and Annie (O'Donnell) Sullivan. BS, St. John's U., Bklyn., 1959; MD, Women's Med. Coll., Phila., 1963. Intern St. Vincent's Hosp., N.Y.C., 1963-64; resident in ob-gyn. Hosp. Women's Med. Ctr., Phila., 1964-68; instr. ob-gyn. N.Y. Med. Coll., 1968-73, asst. prof., 1973-77, chief obstetrics and maternal fetal medicine, 1973-77, assoc. dean, 1975-77; assoc. prof. ob-gyn. U. Miami, Fla., 1977-80, prof., 1980—, chief obstetrics svcs. and perinatology, dept. ob-gyn., 1982—, chief maternal fetal medicine, 1987—. Mem. exec. bd. Am. Bd. Ob-Gyn., 1990-96. Col. USAF, 1981-93. Fellow Am. Coll. Ob-Gyn. (sec. 1989-91); mem. Soc. Perinatal Obstetricians, So. Atlantic Ob-Gyn. Soc. (membership com. 1988-90), Miami Ob-Gyn. Soc. (sec. 1988-90). Roman Catholic. Avocations: cooking, sewing, gardening, skiing. Office: U Miami Dept Ob-Gyn PO Box 16960 R-136 Miami FL 33101-6960

OSWALD, EVA SUE ADEN, retired insurance company executive; b. Ft. Dodge, Iowa, Feb. 2, 1949; d. Warren Dale Aden and Alice Rae (Gingerich) Aspeslet; m. Bruce Elliott Oswald, Nov. 27, 1976. BBS, U. Iowa, 1972. With Great Am. Ins. Co., 1975—, v.p. mktg. div., 1987, v.p. profit ctr., 1988-90; pres. Garden of Eva, Inc., 1990—. Mem. Snelling-Selby Bus. Coun. Mem. Nat. Assn. Ins. Women, State Guarantee Fund (bd. dirs. 1986-87), Exec. Women St. Paul, Midway C. of C. Methodist. Office: 1585 Marshall Ave Saint Paul MN 55104-6222

OSWALT, SALLY HUNDT, small business owner; b. Bangor, Wis., Apr. 17, 1917; d. Peter A. Hundt and Mary Ann Zanter-Hundt; divorced; children: David, Mary Ellen, Jeffrey, Nancy. BS in Polit. Sci., U. Wis., La Crosse, 1991. Owner, mgr. Coiffures by Sally, La Crosse, 1941—. Bd. dirs. Diocese of La Crosse Cemetery Assn., 1995—; pres. Ridge History Pk., Inc., 2001—, treas., 2001—. Bd. dir. La Crosse County, 1974-76, 84-90, 92-94, bd. health, 1986—, mem. regional planning com., 1998—, vice chmn. rep. women, 2003.. Mem.: Bus. and Profl. Women (pres. 1987—89). Republican. Roman Catholic. Avocations: politics, gardening, golf, bridge, singing. Home and Office: Coiffures by Sally 2116 Pine St La Crosse WI 54601-3811

OSWELL, AUDREY S. casino executive; b. Phila. m. Marc Oswell. BA, Temple U.; MBA, Drexel U. With fin. dept. Caesars Atlantic City, from 1979; various fin., mktg. and hotel ops. positions Caesars Atlantic City and Caesars World Corp.; sr. v.p. mktg. Caesars Atlantic City Hotel/Casino; gen. mgr., exec. v.p. Caesars Atlantic City, 1996-99, pres., COO, 1999—. Also involved with Sheraton Atlantic City and Dower Downs slot machines. Bd. dirs. Miss America Orgn., N.J. State Aquarium, Atlantic County Spl. Svcs. Edn. Found.; chmn. governance bd. Success By 6; chmn. ann. F.D.R. cmty. svc. award March of Dimes. Inducted into Class of 1997, Acad. Women Achievers, YWCA, 1997; recipient honor Exec. Women N.J., Woman of Achievement award Englewood and Cliffs chpt. Women's Am. ORT; named Businesswoman of Yr., Greater Atlantic City C. of C., 1998. Mem. South Jersey C. of C. (bd. dirs.). Office: Caesars Atlantic City Atlantic City NJ 08401

OTERO, LETTICE MARGARITA, lawyer; b. May 7, 1952; JD, Ind. U., Bloomington, 1977; LLM, U. Calif., Berkeley, 1986. Bar: Ind. 1978, Calif. 1989. Sole practice, Gary, Ind., 1978-85; estate and gift tax atty. IRS, San Jose, Calif., 1988-93; chief legal counsel Ind. Dept. Revenue, Indpls.,

1993—, inheritance tax adminstr., 1997—. Vol. Girl Scouts Am., Indpls., 1998; chairwoman Hispanic caucus Ind. Dem. Party, Indpls., 1999; mem. adv. coun. Office of Women's Affairs Ind. U., 1996; mem. Gov.'s Task Force on Election Integrity, 2001. Mem. Calif. Bar Assn. (mem. exec. com. 1992). Office: Ind Dept Revenue 100 N Senate Ave Rm N248 Indianapolis IN 46204-2217

OTERO-SMART, INGRID AMARILLYS, advertising executive; b. Santurce, P.R., Jan. 9, 1959; d. Angel Miguel and Carmen (Prann) Otero; m. Dean Edward Smart, May 4, 1991; 1 child, Jordan. BA in Comm., U. P.R., 1981. Traffic mgr. McCann-Erickson Corp., San Juan, P.R., 1981-82, media analyst, 1982, asst. account exec., 1982-83, account exec., 1983-84, sr. account exec., 1984-85, account dir., 1985-87; account supr. Mendoza-Dillon & Assocs., Newport Beach, Calif., 1987-89, sr. v.p. client svcs., 1989-96, exec. v.p., dir. client svcs., 1996—99; Pres. & COO Mendoza-Dillon & Assoc., Aliso Viejo, Calif., 1999—. Mem. Youth Motivation Task Force, Santa Ana, Calif., 1989—; bd. dirs. Orange County Hispanic C. of C., Santa Ana, 1989-90, U.S. Hispanic Family of Yr.; mem. Santa Ana Project P.R.I.D.E., 1993. Mem. Assn. Hispanic Advt. Agys. (bd. dirs. 1998—, pres. 2002-03). Avocations: reading, writing, antiques, music, theater. Office: Mendoza-Dillon 65 Enterprise, Ste 420 Aliso Viejo CA 92656

OTHELLO, MARYANN CECILIA, quality assurance professional; b. N.Y.C., Oct. 23, 1946; d. Alphonse Reasum and Edith (Atwater) O. BS, St. Paul's Coll., Lawrenceville, Va., 1968; MS, Columbia U., 1972. Cert. adoption specialist. Family therapist crisis intervention Dept. Social Svcs., N.Y.C., 1968-72; dir. treatment team Abbott House, Irvington, N.Y., 1972-73; unit chief Manhattan State Psychiat. Facility, N.Y.C., 1973-75; asst. dir., dir. social svcs. St. Peter's Sch., Peekskill, N.Y., 1975-77; dir. Patchwork Svcs. for Children, Santa Ana, Calif., 1977-78; dir. adult and geriatric svcs. Cen. City Community Mental Health, L.A., 1978-79; trainer, facilitator Lifespring, Inc., San Rafael, Calif., 1978-80; sr. mgmt. cons. Nelson Cons. Group, Inc., Mpls., 1980-92; dep. dir. Div. Family Svcs. Dept. of Svcs. to Children, Youth and Their Families, Wilmington, Del., 1992-93; dir. planning and quality assurance Episcopal Cmty./Diocese of Pa., Phila., 1993-94; dep. exec. dir. Episcopal Cmty. Svcs./Diocese of Pa., Phila., 1994-97; CEO, MCO Cons. Ltd., Wilmington, Del., 1997-99; field svc. mgr. N.Am. Ctr. Consultation and Profl. Devel. Child Welfare League of Am., 1999—. Cons. Calif. Dept. Edn., 1977; field instr. casework Hunter Coll. Sch. Social Work, N.Y.C., 1975-77; adj. instr. U. So. Calif., L.A., 1977-78; specialist career devel. Goal for It, L.A., 1977-82; mgmt. devel. cons. Mgmt. Dynamics, Irvine, Calif., 1980-82; treas. Images of Sisterhood, Crofton, Md., 1994. Contbr. articles to profl. jours.; was interviewed twice on radio talk show As It Is, U. Calif., Irvine. Bd. dirs., presenter humanitarian awards L.A. Commn. on Assaults Against Women, 1985-87, Lettye's Sisters In Session, Wilmington, 1993—; facilitator Ch. of Religious Scis., Huntington Beach, Calif., 1981-83, NAACP, Urban League; founding mem. Kinship Alliance, Pacific Grove and Tustin, Calif., 1992—; mem. Afro-Am. Mus., Phila., 1993—; mem. nat. adv. com. on managed care Child Welfare League Am., 1995—; mem. adv. bd. Nat. Leadership Inst., 1996. Named one of Outstanding Young Women of Am., 1976, 81; N.Y. State Regent scholar, 1968; Marie Antoinette Canon fellow Columbia U., 1972. Fellow Child Welfare League Am. (Adoption Specialist plaque 1976); mem. NAFE, Smithsonian Instn., Nat. Soc. for Historic Preservation, Wadsworth Antheneum, Nat. Trust for Hist. Preservation, Assn. for Female Execs. Avocations: caligraphy, photography, bicycling, photography, traveling. Office: Nat Ctr for Consultation and Profl Devel CWLA 440 1st St NW Ste 3 Washington DC 20001-2028

OTHERSEN-KHALIFA, CHERYL LEE, insurance agent, realtor; b. Bay City, Mich., Aug. 17, 1948; d. Andrew Julius and Ruth Emma (Jacoby) Houthoofd; m. Wayne Korte Othersen, Sept. 5, 1964 (div.); 1 child, Angela Othersen ; m. Imed M. B. Salah Khalifa, Sept. 27, 1997 (div.). Lic. ins., Mich. State U., 1980, lic. realtor, 1981. Owner, operator Glad Rags Boutique, Unionville, Mich., 1976-79; dept. mgr. Gantos, Saginaw, Mich., 1979-80; agt., bookkeeper Othersen Ins. Agy., Inc., Unionville, 1979-81, v.p., 1981—; realtor Osentoski Realty Corp., Unionville, 1981—; benefits specialist AFLAC Ins. Co., 1995—. Active Mich. chpt. Nat. Head Injury Found., Crohn's and Colitis Found. Am., Inc.; active Nat. Mus. in Arts, Nat. Trust Hist. Preservation; assoc. mem. Am. Mus. Natural History; charter supporter U.S. Holocaust Meml. Mus.; vol. local Rep. campaigns, 1982, 1984, 1986, 2001. Fellow: John F. Kennedy Libr. Found. (hon.); mem.: Saginaw County Homebuilders Assn., Nat. Mus. Women in the Arts, Profl. Ins. Agts., Saginaw Christian Women's Assn., Saginaw County C. of C., Saginaw Twp. Bus. Assn. (bd. dirs. 2002, 2003). Avocations: sports, painting, travel, gardening, reading. Home: 2575 Ranier St Saginaw MI 48603-3325 Office: Cheri Othersen Agy 2575 Ranier St Saginaw MI 48603

OTIS, GERTRUDE MAXINE, home economist; b. Hobson, Mont., Oct. 29, 1917; d. Vernon Edward Watson and Leota Edna Barrick; m. Clayton Leonard Otis, Oct. 18, 1947; children: Jacqueline Elaine, Larry Edward, Donald Earl, Clayton Max. BS, Mont. State Coll., 1940; MS, Iowa State Coll., 1943. Mgr. women's co-op Mont. State Coll., Bozeman, Mont., 1938—40; tchr. home econs. Mussell Shell (Mont.) HS, 1940—41; home mgmt. adv. Iowa State Coll., Ames, Iowa, 1942—43; head Dept. Home Econs. Macalester Coll., St. Paul, 1943—45; ext. agt. U.S. Dept. Agr., Redding, Calif., 1945—47; home svc. adv. Great Falls (Mont.) Gas Co., 1962—76; mgr. Watson Ltd. Partnership, Hobson, Mont., 1994—. Fellow: Judith River Sr. Citizens (sec. 1996—); mem.: Hobson (Mont.) Federated Women's Club (sec. 1985—), Ea. Star (sec. 1990—). Home: HC 81 Box 11 Hobson MT 59452

OTIS, LEE LIBERMAN, lawyer, educator; b. N.Y.C., Aug. 19, 1956; d. James Benjamin and Deen (Freed) L.; m. William Graham Otis, Oct. 24, 1993. BA, Yale U., 1979; JD, U. Chgo., 1983. Bar: N.Y. 1985, D.C. 1994. Law clk. U.S. Ct. Appeals (D.C. cir.), Washington, 1983-84; spl. asst. to asst. atty. gen., civil div. U.S. Dept. Justice, Washington, 1984-86, dep. assoc. atty. gen., 1986, assoc. dep. atty. gen., 1986; law clk. to Justice Antonin Scalia U.S. Supreme Ct., Washington, 1986-87; asst. prof. law George Mason U., Arlington, Va., 1987-89; assoc. counsel to the Pres. Exec. Office of the Pres., Washington, 1989-92; assoc. Jones, Day, Reavis & Pogue, Washington, 1993-94; chief judiciary coun. U.S. Sen. Spence Abraham, 1995-96; chief counsel subcom. on immigration Com. on the Judiciary, U.S. Senate, 1997-2000; gen. counsel U.S. Dept. Energy, 2001—. Adj. prof. law Georgetown Law Sch., 1995, 96. Mem. Federalist Soc. for Law and Pub. Policy (founder). Republican. Jewish. Avocations: sailing, computers.

O'TOOLE, KATHLEEN M. police commissioner; m. Dan O'Toole; 1 child. BA, Boston Coll.; JD, New Eng. Sch. Law. Bar: Mass. 1982. Officer Boston Police Dept., 1979-86; officer, supt. Met. Police Dept., 1986-90; security mgmt. Digital Equipment Corp., 1990-92; lt. col. Mass. State Police, 1992-94; sec. Office Pub. Safety, Boston, 1994—98; commr. Boston Police Dept., 2004—. Office: Boston Police Hdqs One Schroeder Plz Boston MA 02120-2014*

OTREMBA, GERALDINE MARIE, congressional and international relations executive; b. N.Y.C., Apr. 13, 1946; d. Frank Stanley and Beatrice Gloria (O'Malley) O.; m. Stanley F. Turesky, Oct. 26, 1975; children: Sarah, Catherine. BA, St. John's U., 1967; MA, U. N.C., 1969, PhD, 1979. Dep. dir. ops. John F. Kennedy Ctr. for the Performing Arts, Washington, 1984-87, dir. planning, 1987-90, dir. ops., 1990-91, dir. govt. liaison, 1991-92, assoc. mng. dir., 1991-94; dir. of congrl. rels. Libr. Congress, Washington, 1994—99; exec. dir. Open World Leadership Ctr., 1999—. Chmn. Nat. Conf. Performing Arts Ctrs., 1990-93. Roman Catholic. Office: Open World Leadership Ctr Library of Congress 101 Independence Ave SE Washington DC 20540-9980

OTT, DELVA JOLEEN, former state legislator; b. Wichita, Kans., June 3, 1940; d. Kenneth Theodore and Vera Esther (Harvey) Massey; m. Harold Arthur Ott, 1959; children: Teresa Dawn, Bruce Kenton. Mem. from dist. 92 Kans. State Ho. of Reps., 1977-82, 95-97, chmn. ho. election com., 1979-82. Mem. Women's Polit. Caucus; med. sec. Mid-Am. Heart Assn., Pa., 1977-81; mem. Kans. Fedn. Rep. Women; precinct committeewoman Sedgwick County Rep. Party, 1972—, ward chmn., 1973—; del. 4th Dist. Rep. Party Conv., 1976—; alt. del. Kans. State Rep. Conv., 1976. Mem. LWV, Am. Coun. Young Polit. Leaders, Sedgwick County Rep. Women's Club. Address: 821 Litchfield St Wichita KS 67203-3106

OTT, DORIS ANN, librarian; b. Elgin, N.D., Sept. 24, 1942; d. Oscar Edward Hirning and Lorraine Wilhelmina Gruebele; m. Richard Donald Ott, Nov. 21, 1998; m. Bernnett Gordon Reinke, Sept. 1961 (div.); 1 child, Scott Bernnett Reinke; m. James Lee Daugherty, June 1974 (div.). BS, Dickinson State U., 1964; MLS, George Peabody Coll., 1965. Lic. Ind. life tchr. Elem. tchr. Mott (N.D.) Pub. Schs., 1963-64; asst. prof. Dickinson (N.D.) State U., 1965-73; media specialist Minot (N.D.) Pub. Schs., 1973-74; head tech. svcs. Bartholomew County Libr., Columbus, Ind., 1974-75; media specialist Rushville (Ind.) Pub. Schs., 1975-86; head interlibr. loan N.D. State Libr., Bismarck, 1986-87, asst. state libr., 1987—2001, state libr., 2001—. Image cons. Beauty For All Seasons, 1984—. Mem. Humane Soc. Mem. ALA, N.D. Libr. Assn., Mountain Plains Libr. Assn. Avocation: image consulting. Office: ND State Libr 604 E Boulevard Ave Dept 250 Bismarck ND 58505-0800 E-mail: dott@state.nd.us.

OTT, MARY DIEDERICH, artist; b. Cleve., Aug. 31, 1944; d. Norman Frank and Agnes Marie (Gaertner) Diederich; m. Edward Ott, Jan. 5, 1974; children: William Louis, Miles. BA in Physics, Seton Hill Coll., 1965; SM in Physics, U. Chgo., 1967, PhD in Edn., 1971; student, U. Md., 1991-96, Art League Sch., Alexandria, Va., 1991-95. Lectr. Sch. Applied & Engring. Physics Cornell U., Ithaca, N.Y., 1971-74, rsch. assoc. Ctr. Improvement Undergrad. Edn., 1973-74, lectr. dept. physics, 1974-75, rsch. assoc. Coll. Engring., 1974-78, rsch. assoc. Inst. Occupl. Edn., 1978-79; statistician Nat. Ctr. Edn. Stats. HEW, Washington, 1976; sr. rsch. analyst Office Instnl. Studies U. Md., College Park, 1982-91; artist Silver Spring, Md., 1995—. Resident artist Montpelier Cultural Arts Ctr., Laurel, Md.; ednl. cons., Silver Spring, 1980-82, 91-94. Contbr. articles to profl. jours. Chair Women's Caucus Cornell U., 1978. Recipient Disting. Alumna award Seton Hill Coll., 1995; NSF fellow, 1965-66, U. Chgo. fellow, 1968-71; Nat. Merit scholar, 1961-65. Mem. Touchstone Gallery (Washington). Home: 12421 Borges Ave Silver Spring MD 20904-2940

OTT, SABINA, art educator; b. N.Y.C., Oct. 8, 1955; d. Aaron and Rita (Schwartz) O.; m. Bruce Robert Gluck, Dec. 16, 1978 (div. Apr. 1982). BFA, San Francisco Art Inst., 1979, MFA, 1981. Assoc. prof. Calif. State U., L.A., 1990-94; mem. grad. faculty Art Ctr. Coll. of Design, Pasadena, Calif., 1985-95; assoc. prof., dir. grad. program Washington U., St. Louis, 1996—. Bd.. dirs. L.A. Contemporary Exhbns.; mem. bd. advisors Found. for Art Resources, L.A., 1991—. Solo exhbns. include San Francisco Mus. Art, 1988, The Corcoran Gallery of ARt, 1990, L.A. County Museum of Art, 1992, 200 Gertrude St., Melbourne, Australia, 1996, Forum for Contemporary Art, 1997. Mem. fundraisng com. Coalition for Freedom of Expression, 1989-90; activist WAC, L.A., 1989-91. Grantee NEA, 1990; recipient New Talent award L.A. County Museum of ARt, 1986. Mem. Coll. Art Assn., Forum for Contemporary Art, Critical Mass (bd. dirs. 1997—, St. Louis). Office: Washington U Sch Art Room 100 CB1031 One Brookings Dr Saint Louis MO 63130 Home: 17 Costa St San Francisco CA 94110-5305

OTT, SHARON, artistic director; Theatre dir.: The Wash, Yankee Dawy You Die; artistic dir.:Berkeley Repertory Theatre; now artistic dir. Seattle Repertory Theatre. Former bd. dirs. Theatre Comms. Group, v.p. Recipient Obie award, numerous others awards. Office: Seattle Repertory Theatre 199 Mercer St Seattle WA 98109-4639

OTTAVIANO, DORIS BAGINSKI, librarian; b. Middletown, Conn., June 14, 1938; d. Edward Francis and Genevieve M. (Recko) Baginski; m. Thomas J., April 16, 1983. BA, U. Conn., Storrs, 1960; MSLS, Syracuse (N.Y.) U., 1963. Gen. asst. Hartford Pub. Library, Conn., 1960-61; grad. asst. Syracuse U., N.Y., 1961-63; reference libr. Enoch Pratt Free Libr., Balt., 1963-64, sr. reference libr., 1964-65, subject specialist, 1965-69; suject cataloger Yale U. Libr., New Haven, 1969-70; head reference libr. U.S. Naval War Coll., Newport, R.I., 1970—. Contbr. articles to profl. jours. Mem. Spl. Libr. Assn.(pres. 1988-89, R.I. chpt.), Am. Libr. Assn., New Eng. Libr. Assn., R.I. Libr. Assn., Coalition of Libr. Advs., Beta Phi Mu (Libr. Sci. Honor Soc.), Bus. & Profl. Women's Assn. Home: 11 Admiralty Dr Apt 3 Middletown RI 02842-6254

OTTE, DEBRA BERGSMA, designer, educator, art administrator; b. Lansing, Mich., Jan. 24, 1951; d. Stuart Kenneth Bergsma and Eleanor De Graaf; m. Michael Otte, Aug. 26, 1972; children: Elizabeth, David. BA, Calvin Coll., 1972; MFA in Design, NYU, 1978. Costume shop mgr. NYU, N.Y.C., 1987—89; program dir. theatre and arts mgmt. L.I. U., Brookville, NY, 1994—. Freelance designer, N.Y.C., 1978—; resident designer Post Theatre Co., Brookville, 1989—. Region II chair Kennedy Ctr. Am. Coll. Theatre Festival, 2002—. Recipient Gold Medallion for Excellence in Arts Edn., Kennedy Ctr., 2001. Mem.: Alliance for Media Literacy, Assn. Theatre Higher Edn., USITT. Office: Long Island Univ 720 Northern Blvd Brookville NY 11548 E-mail: dotte@liu.edu.

OTTEN, ROBIN DOZIER, state agency administrator; Supt. regulation and licensing dept. State of N. Mex., Santa Fe. Office: Off Supt Reg Licensing Dept 725 Saint Michaels Dr Santa Fe NM 87505-7605

OTTO, CHARLOTTE R. consumer products company executive; b. Duluth, Minn., Aug. 15, 1953; BS, Purdue U., 1974, MS in Mgmt., 1976. With Procter & Gamble, 1976—, from asst. brand mgr. to brand mgr. various products, 1977-83, assoc. advt. mgr. paper products divsn., 1984-87, assoc. advt. mgr. toilet tissue/towels, paper products div., 1987-89, dir. issues mgmt., pub. affairs divsn., 1989-90, dir. pub. rels., pub. affairs divsn., 1990-91; v.p. pub. rels. Procter & Gamble USA, 1991-93; v.p. corp. comms. Procter & Gamble Worldwide, 1993-95, v.p. pub. affairs, 1995-96; sr. v.p. pub. affairs The Procter & Gamble Co., 1996-99, global pub. affairs officer, 1999—2000, global external rels. officer, 2000—. Dir. Royal Bank Fin. Grou, Canada; adv. bd. Jour. Corp. Pub. Rels., The Medill Sch. Journalism, Northwestern Univ. Mem. nat. bd. Boys & Girls Club Am.; mem. YWCA Acad. Career Women of Acheivement; chair (past pres.) Cin. Playhouse in the Park; chair exec. com. Downtown Cin., Inc.; mem. Riverfront Advisors Commn.; v.p. exec. com. Joy Outdoor Edn. Ctr.; trustee Arts & Cultural Coun. Greater Loveland; bd. mem. Am. Red Cross, Cin. Chpt.; bd. selectors, The Jefferson Awards Am. Inst. Pub. Svc.; vice-chmn. exec. com. Greater Cin. C. of C.; bd. mem. The Port of Greater Cin. Devel. Authority, Good Samaritan Hosp., Cin. Fire Mus.; mem. Leadership Cin. - Class XIV. Recipient YWCA Career Woman of Achievement award, 1993, Woman of Distinction award Gt. Rivers Girl Scouts Coun., Inc., 1998, Purdue "Old Master", 1996; recipient Disting. Alumni, Purdue U., Krannert Sch. Mgmt. Mem. Ctr. Quality Leadership Founders, Vice Pres.'s Forum, Commonwealth Club, Women's Capital Club, Queen City Club (bd. govs.), Club at Harper's Point, Arthur Page Soc., PR Seminar Com., Kenwood Country Club. Office: Procter & Gamble Co 1 Procter And Gamble Plz Cincinnati OH 45202-3393

OTTO, JEAN HAMMOND, journalist; b. Kenosha, Wis., Aug. 27, 1925; d. Laurence Cyril and Beatrice Jane (Slater) Hammond; m. John A. Otto, Aug. 22, 1946; children: Jane L. Rahman, Mary Ellen Takayama, Peter J. Otto; m. Lee W. Baker, Nov. 23, 1973. Student, Ripon Coll., 1944-46. Women's editor Appleton (Wis.) Post-Crescent, 1960-68; reporter Milw. Jour., 1968-72, editorial writer, 1972-77, editor Op Ed page, 1977-83; editorial page editor Rocky Mountain News, Denver, 1983-89, assoc. editor, 1989-92, reader rep., 1992-99; endowed chair U. Denver, 1992-97. Founder, chmn. bd. trustees First Amendment Congress, 1979-85, chmn. exec. com., 1985-88, 89-91, pres. 1991-96, mem. bd. trustees, 1979-96; founding mem. Wis. Freedom of Info. Council. Recipient Headliner award Wis. Women in Communications, 1974; Outstanding Woman in Journalism award YWCA, Milw., 1977; Knight of Golden Quill Milw. Press Club, 1979; spl. citation in Journalism Ball State U., 1980; James Madison award Nat. Broadcast Editorial Assn., 1981; spl. citation for contbn. to journalism Nat. Press Photographers Assn., 1981; Ralph D. Casey award U. Minn., 1984; U. Colo. Regents award, 1985; John Peter Zenger award U. Ariz., 1988; Paul Miller Medallion award Okla. State U., 1990; Colo. SPJ Lowell Thomas award, 1990, Disting. Alumna award Ripon Coll., 1992, Hugh M. Hefner First Amendment Lifetime Achievement award Playboy Found., 1994; named to Milw. Press Club Hall of Fame, 1993, Freedom of Info. Hall of Fame, 1996. Mem. Colo. Press Assn. (chmn. freedom of info. com. 1983-89), Assn. Edn. in Journalism and Mass Communications (Disting. Svc. award 1984), Am. Soc. Newspaper Editors (bd. dirs. 1987-92), Soc. Profl. Journalists (nat. treas. 1975, nat. sec. 1977, pres.-elect 1978, pres. 1979-80, First Amendment award 1981, Wells Key 1984, pres. Sigma Delta Chi Found. 1989-92, chair Found. 1992-94), Milw. Press Club (mem. Hall of Fame 1993). E-mail: jottofirst@aol.com.

OTTO, MARGARET AMELIA, librarian; b. Boston, Oct. 22, 1937; d. Henry Earlen and Mary (McLennan) O.; children— Christopher, Peter. AB, Boston U., 1960; MS, Simmons Coll., 1963, MA, 1970; MA (hon.), Dartmouth Coll., 1981. Asst. sci. librarian M.I.T., Cambridge, 1963, Lindgren librarian, 1964-67, acting sci. librarian, 1967-69, asst. dir., 1969-75, asso. dir., 1976-79; librarian of coll. Dartmouth Coll., Hanover, N.H., 1979—. Pres., chmn. bd. Universal Serials and Book Exch., Inc., 1980-81; bd. dirs. Rsch. Libr. Group; trustee Howe Libr., Hanover, 1988—, chmn., 1992—; mem. Brown Libr. Com., rsch. lbirs. adv. com. OCLC, 1991—, ARL; editl. com. Univ. Press New Eng., 1993—. Council on Library Resources fellow, 1974; elected to Collegium of Disting. Alumnus Boston U., 1980 Mem. ALA (task force on assn. membership issues 1993—, ad hoc working group on copyright issues), Assn. Rsch. Librs. (chair preservation com. 1983-85, bd. dirs. 1985-88, mem. stats. com., chair membership com. 1992—), Coun. on Libr. Resources (proposal rev. com. 1992—), Dartmouth Club (N.Y.C.), St. Botolph Club (Boston), Sloane Club (London). Home: 2 Berrill Farms Ln Hanover NH 03755-3205 Office: Dartmouth Coll 115 Baker Meml Libr Hanover NH 03755

OTUS, SIMONE, public relations executive; b. Walnut Creek, Calif., Jan. 10, 1960; d. Mahmut and Alexa (Artemenko) O. BA, U. Calif., Berkeley, 1981. Account exec. Marx-David Advt., San Francisco, 1981-82; freelance writer Mpls. and San Francisco, 1982-83; account exec. D'Arcy, MacManus & Masius, San Francisco, 1983; account supr. Ralph Silver Assocs., San Francisco, 1984-85; ptnr., co-founder Blanc & Otus Pub. Relations, San Francisco, 1985—. Address: Blanc & Otus Pub Rels 444 Castro St Fl 6 Mountain View CA 94041-2017

OTWELL, DONNA SHARON, history educator; b. Hot Springs, Ark., June 3, 1951; d. Woodrow James and Elsie (Randolph) O. BSE, Ouachita Bapt. U., Arkadelphia, Ark., 1973, MSE, 1977; EdD, U. Memphis, 1994. Tchr. devel. reading, geography, Am. history and psychology North Little Rock (Ark.) Sch. Dist., 1979—. Recipient Educator of the Yr. award, 1987, PTA Lifetime award 1988; named All-Am. scholar Nat. Coll. award U.S. Achievement Acad., 1995. Mem. Phi Delta Kappa (past pres.), Alpha Delta Kappa, Delta Kappa Gamma, Alpha Delta Kappa (v.p.).

OUELLETTE, DEBRA LEE, administrative assistant, consultant; b. Butte, Mont., Aug. 1, 1962; d. Eugene George and Avonne Gail (Smeltzer) O.; m. Anthony Lee Jaeger, Aug. 27, 1994 (div.). BA in Soc. and Tech., Mont. Coll. Mineral Sci. and Tech., 1985. Photographer, trainer Mountain States Energy, Butte, 1984-85; lab. asst. Western Energy, Butte, 1985-86, receptionist, 1986; acctg. data entry clk. N.Am. Resources, Butte, 1986, lease and oil data entry clk., 1986-87; data entry clk. Spl. Resource Mgmt., Butte, 1987-89; adminstrv. asst. N.Am. Indian Alliance, Butte, 1989-97, asst. dir., 1998-99; dir. Butte Parent-Aide Program, 1999; adminstrv. asst. Human Resources Coun. Dist. XII, 2000—01; site coord. Continental Gardens Housing Corp., 1999—. Designer chem. dependency forms. Mem.-at-large Vol. Ctr., Butte, 1995-96; vol. CPR first aid instr. ARC, 1999. Outstanding Pub. Svc. award Soc. Security Adminstrn., Proctective Payee Program.Personnal Invitation to Pres. Inauguration. Mem. VFW Ladies Aux. (sr. v.p. 1994-96, jr. vice trustee 1998—, 3 yr. trustee dist. 4 State of Mont. 1999—, pres. dist. 4 2001-02). Avocations: reading, assisting urban indian programs with policy and procedures, traveling. Office: Continental Gardens 100 Gardens Way Butte MT 59701-2840

OUTHWAITE, LUCILLE CONRAD, ballerina, educator; b. Peoria, Ill., Feb. 26, 1909; d. Frederick ALbert and Della (Cornett) C.; m. Leonard Outhwaite, Mar. 1, 1936 (dec. 1978); children: Ann Outhwaite Maurer, Lynn Outhwaite Pulsifer. Student, U. Nebr., 1929-30, Mills Coll., 1931-32; student piano, Paris, 1933-35, Legat Sch., London, 1934, N.Y.C. Ballet, 1936-41, Royal Ballet Sch., London, 1957-59. Tchr. ballet Perry Mansfield, Steamboat Springs, Colo., 1932; toured with Am. Amb. Ballet, Europe and S.Am., 1933-35; tchr. ballet Cape Playhouse, Dennis, Mass., 1937-41, Jr. League, N.Y.C., 1937-41, King Coit Sch., N.Y.C., 1937-41; owner, tchr. dance sch. Oyster Bay, N.Y., 1949-57. Prodr., choreographer ballets Alice in Wonderland, 1951, Pied Piper of Hamlin, 1952. Author: Birds in Flight, 1992, Flowers in the Wind, 1994, To the Ends of the Earth, 1997, Night Wind Whispers (A Glimpse Down Memory Lane), 1999, Far Suns and Open Seas, 2001, The Spice of Life, 2003. Mem. English Speaking Union, Preservation Soc., Alliance Française, Mill Coll. Club, Spouting Rock Beach Club, Clambake Club, Delta Gamma. Republican. Methodist. Office: 26 Elm St Topsham ME 04086-1426

OVADIAH, JANICE, non-profit organization consultant, cultural institute executive; m. Isaac Ovadiah; children: Meir Benjamin, Simha Victoria Miriam. BA, Washington U., St. Louis, 1965; MA, Columbia U., 1967, PhD, 1978. Dir. profl. study tours Am. Odysseys, Inc., 1973-84; escort, interpreter in French U.S. Dept. State, 1978-84; asst. to exec. dir. Meml. Found. for Jewish Culture, 1984-87; exec. dir. Congregation Shearith Israel/The Spanish & Portuguese Syn., N.Y.C., 1987—, Sephardic House, N.Y.C., 1987—2003; freelance cons., 2003—. Instr. French Rutgers U., New Brunswick, N.J., 1978-79; asst. to dir. of The Maison Franclase, Columbia U., 1970-72; instr. French Columbia U., 1968-70; lectr. in field. Author: (books) Toward a Concept of Cinematic Literature: An Analysis of Hiroshima, Mon Amour, 1983, The Far Away Island of the Grey Lady, 1979, others; contbr. articles to profl. jours. E-mail: jovadiah@aol.com.

OVEJERO, GRACIELA, artist; d. Antonio Serafin Ovejero and Magdalena Postigo; life ptnr. Hamid Dayani. MFA, U. of Calif., San Diego, 1996; Prof. of Classical Dance, Provincial Sch. of Classical Dance, San Miguel de Tucumán., 1973; Lic. in Fine Arts, Nat. U. of Tucumán,

Argentina, 1993. Founder-owner and main author www.ArtOrchard.com, Davis, Calif., 2002—; founder-owner and state contr. Artists At Work, Comprehensive Paint & Artistic Services, Davis, Calif.; solo dancer Provincial Ballet, San Miguel de Tucumán, Argentina, 1973—85; co-founder, dir. and main choreographer Alrededor del Movimiento, San Miguel de Tucumán, Argentina, 1977—78; co-founder and mem. of interdisciplinary artists group Crónica, San Miguel de Tucumán, Argentina, 1983—85; artist mem. Border Arts Workshop, San Diego, 1990—91, Las Comadres, San Diego, 1991—93. Commr. Arts Adv. Com., San Diego, 1989—96; juror for st. sites, art in pub. places program Sushi Performance, San Diego, 1991; invited workshop creator and presenter MOCA/L.A. Mus. of Contemporary Art, 1998; invited workshop creator and presenter in collaboration with poets Leroy Quintana and Diego Davalos San Diego Mus. of Contemporary Art, 1998; key spkr./artist presenter WELL/Women Educators & Lang. Learners Conf., Saitama, Gumna Prefecture, Japan, 2000; invited presenter III Encounter of Ibero-Am. Women in the Dramatic Arts, Cadiz, Andalucia, Spain, 1999; juror, VIII salon Carlos Maria Navarro Nat. U., San Miguel de Tucumán. 1998., Argentina; invited panelist for chicano/a, latino/a film and video forum San Diego State U., 1997; video presenter Grad. Women Conf., U. of Calif., L.A., Calif., 1996; featured videographer Cine Estudiantil (future Chicano Latino Film & Video Festival), San Diego, 1996; featured videograper Cine Estudiil, San Diego, 1994; invited artist presenter Nat. U., San Miguel de Tucumán, Argentina, 1992. Author, curator-dir. (ongoing internat. installation series) Souvenir of Tucumán-Nomadic Anthology of Objects; author (performer and video editor): (video diptych) Apacheta; author: (artist page for collective arts book.) Librarte. Ed. by Institute of Art, Ethic & Human Rights. UNT, Argentina; author: (performer-editor) (video-performance) Naturalization; primary dancer (experimental dance concert) Two Solos & Two Duets; editor: (collected writings for book-catalogue) Souvenir of Tucumán - Nomadic Anthology of Objects; author: (critical, creative & autobiog. article) Beyond Self portrait, The Body as Discoursive Instrument; 30 solo exhibits & major installations., numerous collective exhibitions, ballet and contemporary dance performer. Recipient Proposal Award for St. Sites, Sushy Gallery. San Diego, 1988, Nat. Contest Jury's Mension award (painting), Centro Cultural La Recoleta. Buenos Aires, Argentina., 1985, Provincial Contest Jury's Mension award (painting), Salon Spilimbergo, Universidad Nacional de Tucumán. Argentina, 1984, Provincial Contest Jury's Mension award (engraving), Salon Primavera, Peña El Cardón. Tucumán. Argentina, Installation award for InSite 94, Installation Gallery and Centro Cultural de la Raza in San Diego., 1994, Installation award, Installation Gallery and Centro Cultural de la Raza. San Diego, 1992, Installation award for ArtWalk, temp. pub. art projects., Installation Gallery. San Diego, 1990; fellow, U. of Calif. in San Diego, 1993—96; grantee Catalogue Pub. award, Comm. for Arts and Culture, 1990, For Collaborative Interdisciplinary Project, Nat. Endowment of the Arts, 1988. Mem.: Coll. Art Assn., Bay Area Video Coallition. Office: ArtOrchard PO Box 72044 Davis CA 95617 E-mail: graciela@artorchard.com.

OVERBECK, CARLA WERDEN, soccer player, coach; b. Pasadena, Calif., May 9, 1969; m. Greg Overbeck, Dec. 5, 1992; 1 child, Jackson. BS in Psychology, U. N.C., 1990. Asst. women's soccer coach Duke U., Durham, NC. Mem. U.S. Nat. Women's Soccer Team, 1988—, including world championship FIFA Women's World Cup team, 1991, FIFA Women's World Cup team, 95, gold medal U.S. Olympic Team, 96. Named 3-time NSCAA All Am.; named to Soccer Am. All-Freshman team. Achievements include played 63 consecutive international games, a record for any U.S. national team player. Office: US Soccer Fedn 1801 S Prairie Ave Chicago IL 60616-1319

OVERMYER, JANET ELAINE, counselor; b. Allentown, Pa., July 3, 1951; d. Harold Romig and Amanda Babb Fegely; m. Warren Reichert, June 9, 1973 (div. Sept. 1987); children: Nathan, Rebekah, Matthew; m. Michael Steven Overmyer, May 23, 1997. BA in Psychology, Muhlenberg Coll., 1973; MA in Clin. Counseling, Heidelberg Coll., 2000. Lic. Profl. Clin. Counselor Ohio, cert. Chemical Dependency Counselor Ohio. Dir. social svc. Glanzman Colonial Nursing Home, Toledo, 1994—98; cmty. svc. provider Zepf Cmty. Mental Health Ctr., Toledo, 1999—2001; primary therapist Focus Healthcare of Ohio, Maumee, Ohio, 2000—01; dir. women's outpatient program Behavioral Connections of Wood County, Perrysburg, Ohio, 2001—02; clin. svc. dir. Vol. of Am., N.W. Ohio, Toledo, 2002—03; assessment clinician Behavioral Connections of Wood County, Perrysburg, 2003—. Bd. trustees Huntingdon Cmty. Ctr., Sylvania, Ohio, 1992. Mem.: Nat. Coun. Alcoholism & Drug Dependency (intervention specialist 2001—), Mental Health Counselors Assn., Am. Counseling Assn. Lutheran. Avocations: reading, piano, travel, family. Home: 4501 Luann Ave Toledo OH 43623

OVERSTREET, KAREN A. federal bankruptcy judge; BA cum laude, Univ. of Wash., 1977; JD, Univ. of Oregon, 1982. Assoc. Duane, Morris & Heckscher, Phila., 1983-86; ptnr. Davis Wright Tremaine, Seattle, 1986-93; bankruptcy judge U.S. Bankruptcy Ct. (we. dist.) Wash., Seattle, 1994—. Assoc. editor Oregon Law Review; dir. People's Law Sch.; mem. advisory com. U.S. Bankruptcy Ct. (we. dist.) Wash. Mem. Nat. Conf. of Bankruptcy Judges, Wash. State Bar Assn. (creditor-debtor sec.), Seattle-King County Bar Assn. (bankruptcy sec.), Am. Bar Assn., Wash. Women Lawyers Assn. Office: US Bankruptcy Ct Park Place Bldg 1200 6th Ave Ste 315 Seattle WA 98101-3130

OVERTON, NICOLE YOLANDA, program analyst; b. Buffalo, Feb. 24, 1973; d. Dewitt David and Mary Lee Overton. BS, Buffalo State Coll., 1996. EDI programmer, analyst Ingram Micro, Buffalo, 1996—; cashier supr. Quality Markets, Buffalo, 1991-96. Tchg. asst., tutor for computers Buffalo State Coll., application designer, career dept. Troop leader Girl Scouts Buffalo and Erie County, 1996—, trip dir., treas., axcct., 1999—. Gir Scout Coun. Delegate 2002-. Democrat. Baptist. Avocations: drawing, dance, reading novels, music, movies. Office: Ingram Micro 1759 Wehrle Dr Buffalo NY 14221-7032

OVERTON, ROSILYN GAY HOFFMAN, financial services executive; b. Corsicana, Tex., July 10, 1942; d. Billy Clarence and Ima Elise (Gay) Hoffman; m. Aaron Lewis Overton, Jr., July 2, 1960 (div. Mar. 1975); children: Aaron Lewis III, Adam Jerome; m. Mardiros Hatsakorzian, 1991. BS in Math., Wright State U., Dayton, Ohio, 1972, MS in Applied Econs. (fellow), 1973; postgrad. N.Y. U. Grad. Sch. Bus., 1974-76; Cert. Coll. Fin. Planning, 1987. CFP. Research analyst Nat. Security Agy., Dept. Def., 1962-67; bus. reporter Dayton Jour.-Herald, 1973-74; economist First Nat. City Bank, N.Y.C., 1974, A.T. & T. Co., 1974-75; broker Merrill Lynch, N.Y.C., 1975-80; asst. v.p. E.F. Hutton & Co., N.Y.C., 1980-84; v.p., nat. mktg. dir. investment products Manhattan Nat. Corp., 1984-86; pres. R.H. Overton Co., N.Y.C., 1986—; ptnr. Brown & Overton Fin. Svcs., 1987—. Named Businesswoman of Yr., N.Y.C., 1976. Mem. Inst. Cert. Planners, Internat. Assn. Fin. Planning (pres. N.Y. chpt.), Gotham Bus. and Profl. Womens Club, Rotary Internat., Wright State U. Alumni Assn., Mensa, Zonta. Methodist. Office: 25418 Northern Blvd Ste 5 Little Neck NY 11362-1451

OVERTON, SHARON FAYE, elementary school educator; b. Tell City, Ind., Oct. 20, 1949; d. Albert John Dauby and Anna Catherine Harpenau; m. Ron Overton, Apr. 14, 1973; children: Jennifer, Jeff. BS cum laude, Ind. State U., 1970, MS, 1972. Cert. elem. tchr., middle sch. endorsement math. 3d grade tchr. Tell City-Troy Twp. Sch. Corp., 1970-73; 2d grade tchr. E.V.S.C., Evansville, Ind., 1973-74, math. tchr., 1974-84, tchr. 5th grade, 1984—. Sunday sch. tchr. St. Benedict's Ch., Evansville, 1989—, mem.; debate judge North H.S. Debate Team, Evansville, 1994—; mem. PTA. Mem. Gamma Phi Beta (rituals chairperson). Roman Catholic. Avocations: traveling, sewing, golf. Home: 3725 Aspen Dr Evansville IN 47711-3011 Office: Scott School 14 940 Old State Rd Evansville IN 47711

OVREBO, JUDITH, retired physical education educator; b. Wausau, Wis., Mar. 28, 1950; d. Donald Irving and Rozella Eileen (Boggs) O.; m. Harold Marvin Oberg, July 5, 1975 (div.); children: Jessica Kristine, Deborah Elisabeth. BS, U. Conn., 1972; MS in Phys. Edn., U. R.I., 1978; grad., So. Conn. State U., 1986, postgrad., 1992. Tchr. phys. edn. Fitch Jr. High Sch., Groton, Conn., 1972-79, Fitch Sr. High Sch., Groton, Conn., 1979-97. Mentor co-op. tchr. State of Conn., Groton, 1988—; evaluator New Eng. Assn. Schs. and Colls., 1993. Chairperson phys. edn. sub-com. New Eng. Assn. of Schs. and Colls., Groton, Conn., 1988-90; bd. dirs. Ledyard (Conn.) Girls Softball League, 1989—, mgr., coach, 1989—; coach Ledyard Youth Basketball League, 1991—; mentor Take Stock in Children, Ocala, Fla.; organizer Connections, 2000—; vol. Hospice Marion County, Gerla, Fla., 2002-. Mem. AAHPERD, NEA, Am. Softball Assn., Conn. Assn. Health, Phys. Edn., Recreation and Dance, Conn. Edn. Assn., Groton Edn. Assn., Nat. Assn. Sports and Phys. Edn., Nat. Assn. Girls and Women Sports, Phi Kappa Phi. Avocations: swimming, organ. church involvement, reading. Home: 7598 SW 81st Pl Ocala FL 34476-6924 E-mail: jovrebo@cs.com.

OWADES, RUTH MARKOWITZ, marketing company executive; b. Los Angeles, Sept. 2, 1944; d. David and Yonina (Graf) Markowitz; m. Joseph L. Owades, Sept. 7, 1969. BA with honors, Scripps Coll., Claremont, Calif., 1966; MBA, Harvard U., 1975; postgrad. U. Strasbourg (France), 1966-67. Exec. asst. Los Angeles Econ. Devel. Bd., N.Y.C., 1968-69; copywriter D'Arcy Advt. Co., St. Louis, 1970-71; asst. program dir. KMOX-AM Radio, St. Louis, 1971-72; assoc. producer WCVB-TV, Boston, 1972-73; mktg. project mgr. United Brands Co., Boston, 1975; mktg. dir. CML Group Inc., Concord, Mass., 1975-78; founder, pres. Gardener's Eden Inc., Boston, 1978-82; pres. Gardener's Eden, div. Williams-Sonoma Inc., Emeryville, Calif., 1982-87; founder, pres. Calyx & Carolla, Inc., 1988—; bd. dirs. Hellenic Breweries S.A., Athens, Greece. Bd. of advisors An Income of Her Own; trustee Scripps Coll. Recipient Bausch & Lomb award, 1962, Disting. Alumna award Scripps Coll., 1989, Woman of Achievement award Woman's City Club Cleve., 1991, Woman Who Has Made a Difference award Internat. Women's Forum, 1991, Woman of the Yr. award Woman's Direct Response Group N.Y., 1992, Catalogur of Yr. award Target Marketing Mag., 1992, Direct Marketer of Yr. award, No. Calif. Direct Mktg. Club, 1993; Fulbright scholar, 1966; named student Goodwill Ambassador to Nagoya, Japan, 1960. Mem. Direct Mktg. Assn., Phi Beta Kappa. Club: Harvard (N.Y.C.), Women's Forum West (v.p. and treas.), Com. of 200. Home: 2164 Hyde St San Francisco CA 94109-1788 Office: 185 Berry St Ste 6200 San Francisco CA 94107-1750

OWEN, AMY, library director; b. Brigham City, Utah, June 26, 1944; d. John Wallace and Bertha (Jensen) Owen. BA, Brigham Young U., 1966, MLS, 1968. Sys. libr. Utah State Libr., Salt Lake City, 1968—72, dir. reference svcs., 1972—74, dir. tech. svcs., 1974—81, dep. dir., 1981—87, dir., 1987—. Serials com. chmn. Utah Coll. Libr. Coun., Salt Lake City, 1975—77, exec. sec., 1978—84, mem. coun., 1987—; mem. staff Gov.'s Utah Sys. Planning Task Force, Salt Lake City, 1982; staff liaison Utah Gov.'s Conf. on Libr. and Info. Svcs., 1977—79, chmn. exec. planning com., 1990—91; mem. pres.'s adv. panel Baker & Taylor Co., Somerville, NJ, 1977—78; panelist U.S. Dept. Edn., 1992; mem. rsch. project adv. com. U. Wis. Sch. Libr. and Info., Madison, 1992—94; mem. adv. panel Nat. Commn. Libr. and INfo. Svcs., 1985; Alumni Honor lectr. Coll. Humanities Brigham Young U., 1990; cons., trainer in field. Contbr. chpts. to books; contbg. author: various manuals. Mem. coun. Utah Endowment for Humanities, 1986—91, vice chmn., 1987—88, chmn., 1988—90; trustee Bibliographic Ctr. for Rsch., 1987—, mem. pers. com., 1988—89, chmn. person com., 1989—90, mem. nominating com., 1984, v.p. bd. trustees, 1989—91, pres., 1991—93; active Chief Officers of State Libr. Agys., 1987—, mem. stats. com., 1988—93, mem. network com., 1993—, mem. state info. policy workshop com., 1988, bd. dirs., 1992—; mem. conf. program com. Fedn. of State Humanities Couns., 1988; mem. coop. pub. libr. data sys. task force Nat. Commn. on Libr. and Info. Svcs., 1988—90; grant rev. panelist NEH, 1988, 1992, panel mem. reading and discussion groups, 1988; regional project mgmt. bd. mem. Intermountain Cmty. Learning and INfo. Ctr. Project, 1987—90; mem. midcontinental regional adv. com. Nat. Libr. Medicine, 1991—94; mem. adv. com. Brigham Young U. Sch. Libr. and Info. Svcs. Named Libr. of Yr., Libr. Jour., 1990. Mem.: ALA (planning, orgn. and bylaws com. 1981—85, LITA divsn. Satellite Conf. Task Force mem. 1982, bd. dirs. ASCLA divsn. 1984—86, fin. com. 1984—86, clene roundtable mem. com. 1984—86, SLAS program com. 1984—86, ALA Office for Rsch. coop. pub. libr. data sys. adv. com. 1985—89, pres. program com. 1986, nominations com. 1986—87, PLA divsn. editor column 1987—89, PLA divsn. goals, guidelines and stds. com. 1987—90, nat. adv. bd. office comms. svcs., voices and visions project 1988—89, exec. bd. mem. 1988—90, PLA pub. libr. data svc. adv. com. 1988—91, fin. com. 1989—92, chair 1990—91, PLA non MLS involvement com. 1990—91, PLA Kellogg Phase III EIC project adv. com. chmn. 1990—92, PLA strategic issues and directions com. 1991—92, exec. bd. mem. 1993—94, bd. dirs. ASCLA divsn. 1993—96, fin. com. 1993—96, pres. ASCLA divsn. 1994—95), Utah Partnership Edn. and Econ. Devel. (rsch. com. 1995—), Utah Edn. Network (steering com. 1996—), Dynix Snowbird Leadership Inst. (nat. adv. bd. 1990—), Mountain Plains Libr. Assn. (rec. sec. 1979—80, fin. com. 1982—84, Disting. Svc. award 1989), Utah Libr. Assn. (exec. bd. 1976—80, pres. 1978—79, Spl. Svc. award 1989), Alpha Lambda Alpha, Phi Kappa Phi. Home: 4786 Naniloa Dr Salt Lake City UT 84117-5547 Office: Utah State Libr 250 N 1950 W Ste A Salt Lake City UT 84116-7901

OWEN, CAROL THOMPSON, artist, educator, writer; b. Pasadena, Calif., May 10, 1944; d. Sumner Comer and Cordelia (Whittemore) Thompson; m. James Eugene Owen, July 19, 1975; children: Kevin Christopher, Christine Celese. Student, Pasadena City Coll., 1963; BA with distinction, U. Redlands, 1966; MA, Calif. State U., L.A., 1967; MFA, Claremont Grad. Sch., 1969. Cert. cmty. coll. instr., Calif. Head resident Pitzer Coll., Claremont, Calif., 1967-70; instr. art Mt. San Antonio Coll., Walnut, Calif., 1968-96, prof. art, 1996—, 1996-97, prof. emeritus, 1997, dir. coll. art gallery, 1972-73. Group shows include Covina Pub. Libr., 1971, U. Redlands, 1964, 65, 66, 70, 78, 88, 92, Am. Ceramic Soc., 1969, 97, 99, 2000, Mt. San Antonio Coll., 1991, The Aesthetic Process, 1993, Separate Realities, 1995, Sequence 1, 2001, San Bernardino County Mus., 1996, 97, 98, 99, Tampa Fla. Black, White & Gray, Artists Unltd., 1998, Current Clay VII, La Jolla, Calif., 1998, Westmoreland Art Nat., 1998, 99, Riverside Art Mus., 1998, Fine Art Inst. Juried Show, San Bernardino, 1998, 99, 2000, Parham Gallery, L.A., 1998, 99, Angels Gate Cultural Ctr., San Pedro, Calif., 1998, Los Angeles County Fair, Pomona, Calif., 1998, Monrovia, Arts Festival, 1998, Art for Heavens Sake Festival, 1998, 99, Riverside Art Mus., 1998, 99, 2000, Birger Sandzen Meml.Gallery McPherson, Kans., 1998, 2000, Earthen Art Works Gallery, LA, 1999, State Polytechnic U., Pomona, 1999, 2001, Mo. State U., Warrensburg, 1999, City, of Brea Gallery, 1999, 2000, All Media Exhibit, Chico, Calif.. 1999, Period Gallery, Omaha, 1999, 2000, 01, 02, Mixed Media, Period Gallery, 2002, Franklin Square Gallery, Southpoet, NC, 1999, 2000, Judson Gallery, LA, 1999, San Angelo (Tex.) Mus. Fine Arts, 2000, So. Calif. Juried Art Exhbn., San Bernardino, Calif., 2000, Gallery 212, Ann Arbor, Mich., 2000, Judson Gallery, LA, 2000, Artists Unltd., Inc., Tampa, Fla., 2000, Urban Inst. Contemporary Arts, Grand Rapids, Mich., 2000, Tri-Lakes Ctr. for Arts, Palmer Lake, Colo., 2000, Santa Cruz Art League, Calif., 2000. Fine Arts Inst., San Bernardino County Mus., Redlands Calif. 2000, Vermont Artisan Designs, Brattleboro, 2000, USA Craft '99, New Caanan, Cons., 1999, Keith Gallery, Dexter, Mich., 1999, Claremont Forum Gallery, 1999, Parham Gallery, Santa Monica, Calif., 1999 (Grand prize 1999), City of Brea Galleries, Calif., 2000, 01, Chiarosouro Galleries, Chgo., 2000, TLD Design Ctr. and Gallery, Westmont, Ill., 2000, 2001, North Tahoe Art Ctr., Calif., 2000, Palos Verdes Art Ctr., Rancho Palos Verdes, Calif., 2000, Peck Gallery, Providence, 2000, Alder Gallery, Oreg., 2001, Rocky Mt. Arts Ctr., NC, 2001, Esmay Fine Art Gallery, Rochester NY, 2001, Hillcrest Festival, 2001, Dysfunctional, Business of Art Ctr., Manitou Springs, Colo., 2001, Nat. Juried Exhbn., Gallery 214, Montclair, NJ, 2002, Mt. San Antonio Coll., Walnut, Calif., 2001, Gallery Mia Tyson, Wilmington, NC, 2002, Millard Sheets Gallery, Pomona, Calif., 2002 (Honorable mention), Period Gallery, "Abstraction", Omaha, 2002, Rocky Mount Art Ctrs., Rocky Mount, NC, 2003, Ink & Clay 29 Exhbn., Kellogg U. Art Gallery, Calif. State Poly. U., Pomona, 2003, Period Gallery, Omaha, 2003, Feats of Clay XVI Lincoln (Calif.) Arts, 2003, Sanchez Art Ctr., Pacifica, Calif., 2003, "Containment", SKH, Great Barrington, Mass., 2003, numerous others; ceramic mural commd. U. Redlands, 1991; represented in permanent collections Redlands Art Assn Gallery, Redlands; artwork in (book) Collectible Teapots, 2000; Group Internat. Exhbn. Internationale Wertbewerb Salzbrand Keramic, 2002, der Handwerks Kammer Koblenz, Galerie Handwerk, Germany, 2002. Recipient San Bernardino County Mus., 1996, Hon. Mention, 1998, 1999,; Past Pres. Monetary award, 1997, Jack L. Conte Design Cons. Purchase award Westmoreland Art Nat., 1998, 3rd Pl. Monetary award All Calif. City of Brea Galleries, 2000, Honorarium for teapots Urban Inst. Contemporary Arts, Grand Rapids, Mich., 2000. Mem. Am. Ceramic Soc. (design divsn., Design chpt. monetary award 1999), Calif. Scholarship Fedn., Coll. Art Assn. Am., Friends of Huntington Library, L.A. County Mus. Art, Redlands Art Assn., Heard Mus. Assn., Riverside Art Mus., Fine Arts Inst., Sigma Tau Delta. Republican. Presbyterian.

OWEN, CYNTHIA CAROL, sales executive; b. Ft. Worth, Oct. 16, 1943; d. Charlie Bounds and Bernice Vera (Nunley) Rhoads; m. Franklin Earl Owen, Oct. 20, 1961 (div. Jan. 1987); children: Jeffrey Wayne, Valeria Ann, Carol Darlena, Pamela Kay; m. John Edward White, Jan. 1, 1988 (div. Sept. 1991). Cert. Keypuncher, Comml. Coll., 1963; student, Tarrant County Jr. Coll., 1974-77; BBA in Mgmt., U. Tex., Arlington, 1981. Keypunch operator Can-Tex. Industries, Mineral-Wells, 1966-67; sec. Electro-Midland Corp., Mineral-Wells, 1967-68; exec. sec. to v.p. sales Pangburn Co., Inc., Ft. Worth, 1972-78; bookkeeper, sec. CB Svc., Ft. Worth, 1978-82; project mgr. Square D Co., Ft. Worth, 1982—. Mem. NAFE, NOW, AAUW. Baptist. Avocations: miniature golf, volleyball. Home: 1221 Pine Ridge Rd Roanoke TX 76262 Office: Square D Co 204 Airline Dr Ste 300 Coppell TX 75019-4663 E-mail: cindy.owen@us.schneider-electric.com.

OWEN, DIAN GRAVE, investment corporation executive; b. 1940; Pres. Owen Healthcare, Houston, 1970-96; chmn. Mansefeldt Investment Corp., Abilene, Tex., 1997— Office: Mansefeldt Investment Corp 400 Pine St Ste 1000 Abilene TX 79601-5142

OWEN, PRISCILLA RICHMAN, state supreme court justice; BA, Baylor U., JD, 1977. Bar: Tex. 1978, U.S. Ct. Appeals (4th, 5th, 8th and 11th cirs.). Former ptnr. Andrews & Kurth, L.L.P., Houston; justice Supreme Ct. Tex., Austin, 1995—. Liaison to Tex. Legal Svcs. for Poor Spl. Supreme Ct. Tex., Supreme Ct. Adv. Com. on Ct.-Annexed Mediations. Named Young Lawyer of Yr., Baylor U., Outstanding Young Alumna. Office: Supreme Ct Tex PO Box 12248 Austin TX 78711-2248*

OWEN, SUE ANN, poet; b. Clarinda, Iowa, Sept. 5, 1942; d. Theodore Reynold and Elizabeth (Roderick) Matthews; m. Thomas Charles Owen, Aug. 29, 1964. BA in English, U. Wis., 1964; MFA in Writing, Goddard Coll., 1978. Poet in schs. Arts and Humanities Coun., Baton Rouge, 1980—92; artist fellowship La. Divsn. of Arts, 1993, 2001; instr. La. State U., 1992—98, poet-in-residence, 1998—. Author: Nursery Rhymes for the Dead, 1980, The Book of Winter, 1988 (Ohio State Univ. Press/The Jour. award, 1988), My Doomsday Sampler, 1999; contbr.: poems to mags., anthologies, including Harvard Mag., Iowa Rev., The Nation, Poetry, Ploughshares, So. Rev., The Best of Intro, The Poetry Anthology: 1912-2002, USA Poetry (Sweden), readings in: Boston, N.Y.C., Washington, San Francisco, New Orleans, Moscow, London. Named Profl. Artist of Yr., La. State Arts Coun., 1998. Mem.: Poets and Writers, Arts and Humanities Coun., Associated Writing Programs, Poetry Soc. Am. Home: 7825 Rue Cache Baton Rouge LA 70808

OWEN, SUZANNE, retired savings and loan association executive; b. Lincoln, Nebr., Oct. 6, 1926; d. Arthur C. and Hazel E. (Edwards) O. BSBA, U. Nebr., Lincoln, 1948. With G. F. Lessenhop & Sons, Inc., Lincoln, 1948-57, First Fed., Lincoln, 1963-91, v.p., dir. pers., 1975-81, 1st v.p., 1981-87, sr. v.p., 1987-91; ret., 1991. Mem. pers. bd. City of Lincoln, 1989-96. Mem. Lincoln Human Resources Mgmt. Assn., Wooden Spoon Club, Exec. Women's Breakfast Group, Thursday Morning Lecture Cir., Cmty. Women's Club, Lincoln Symphony Guild, Pi Beta Phi Alumnae, Order of Ea. Star, Phi Chi Theta. Republican. Christian Scientist.

OWENS, CAROL, state legislator; b. Aug. 8, 1931; Town clk, Neklml, 1977—93; bd supvr Winnebago Cty, 1980—92; State assemblywoman, Dist 53 Wis., 1992—. Recipient Friend of Agri, 1994 & 1996. Republican. Lutheran. Office: Wis Assembly PO Box 8952 Madison WI 53708-8952

OWENS, DANA See QUEEN LATIFAH

OWENS, DEBORAH, artist, writer; b. Columbus, Ga., Mar. 10, 1951; d. Donald Owens and Diane Stewart Hobbs; m. Jon Gordon Graber, Mar. 24, 1990; children: Edith Hall, Renee Peete. BS, Columbus State U., 1982; postgrad., U. Ga., 1982-83, Auburn U., 1993. Tchr. kindergarten, Columbus; substitute elem. tchr. Fayetteville, N.C.; coll. recruiter Fla. Inst. Sci. and Tech.; self-employed writer and painter Columbus. Tchr. liquid acrylics. Author: (novel) Sacred Cypress, 1995, Between Light and Shadow, 1997, Stonegate of the Braveheart, 1998, Chocolate Secrets to a Dear Friend, Chattahoochee Chicken, Muffin Mallarkey and Wee Bitty Cakes; contbr. to fine art mags.; paintings, drawings, pen and inks are represented in pvt. collections. Women's counsleor, counselor Crisis Intervention Ctr.; hosp. and ARC vol. Recipient award Nat. Mus. of Women in Arts, 1999. Mem. Nat. Watercolor Soc. (assoc.), Am. Watercolor Soc., So. Watercolor Soc., Ga. Watercolor Soc., Watercolor Soc. Ala., N.C. Watercolor Soc. Methodist. Avocations: gardening, painting, drawing, sculpting, photography. Home: 6843 Lorna Dr Columbus GA 31909-3162 E-mail: deborahowens2000@aol.com.

OWENS, DEBRA ANN, chiropractor; b. Poplar Bluff, Mo., Dec. 21, 1953; d. James Alva and Veleta Frances (Pierce) Stutts; 1 child from previous marriage, Jacqueline. BS in Edn., S.E. Mo. State U., 1975; DC, Logan Coll. Chiropractic, 1991; fellow, Internat. Acad. Clin. Acupunct, 1996. Chiropractor Albers Chiropractic, Washington, Mo., 1991-92, Owens Chiropractic Ctr., P.C., Dexter, Mo., 1992—. Mem. Chiropractors Restoring Energy Worldwide. Mem. Humanitarian Chiropractic Mission to Panama, 1997, Humanitarian Chiropractic Mission to South Africa, 1999, Humanitarian Chiropractic Mission to Costa Rica, 2000, Humanitarian Chiropractic Mission to Dominican Republic, 2002. Mem. Am. Chiropractic Assn., Internat. Chiropractors Assn., Mo. Chiropractors Assn., World Congress of Women Chiropractors, Logan Coll. Alumni Assn. (Alumni Rsch. award 1991), Dexter C. of C. (2nd v.p. 1993, 1st v.p. 1994, pres. 1995, sec. devel. corp. 1996, v.p. devel. corp. 1997, pres. devel. corp. 1998, 99, econ. devel. com. 1996), Kiwanis (bd. dirs. 1994-98, 2nd v.p. 1997-98. Avocations: swimming, boating, patchwork quilting, flying. Office: Owens Chiropractic Ctr PC 907 N Harris Dr Ste B PO Box 678 Dexter MO 63841-0678

OWENS, DIANE DOBRAY, music educator; b. Galveston, Tex., Mar. 7, 1948; d. Irving Leslie and Sylvia Marie Dobray; m. Ronald Wayne Owens, May 3, 1969. BS in Edn., U. North Tex., 1976; MEd, Tex. A&M, Commerce, 1987. Cert. tchr. Sec. Philco-Ford Corp. - NASA, Houston, 1966—69; piano tchr. First Bapt. Ch. Sch., Carrollton, Tex., 1971—76; substitute tchr. Richardson (Tex.) Ind. Sch. Dist., 1976—77; pre-sch. dir. First Bapt. Ch. North, Carrollton, 1977—79; pvt. practice Richardson, 1979—92, Coleman, Tex., 1994—99; music instr. City of Richardson, 1988—92; adj. faculty, pre-coll. music dir. Howard Payne U., Brownwood, Tex., 1994—2000, piano instr., pre-coll. music dir., 2001—. Active Coleman County Hist. Hist. Commn., Coleman, 1994—; bd. dirs. Cmty. Concert Series, Brownwood, Tex., 2000—03. Mem.: Am. Coll. Musicians, Kindermusik Internat., Heart of Tex. Music Tchrs. Assn., Tex. Music Tchrs. Assn., Music Tchrs. Nat. Assn., Nat. Fedn. Music Clubs (chmn. dist. 7-A jr. festival). Republican. Baptist. Avocations: cooking, travel, reading. Home: 213 West Pecan St Coleman TX 76834-4005 Office: Howard Payne Univ 1000 Fisk Ave Brownwood TX 76801-2794 Business E-Mail: dowens@hputx.edu.

OWENS, GEORGIA KATHERINE, human resources specialist, consultant; d. Kenneth Boyd Chapman and Leila Katherine Zollner; children: Lena Gwynn Anderson, Colin Stuart. BS in hist. and polit. sci., Portland State U., 1976—79. Civil rights staff asst. City of Portland/Multnomah County, Portland, Oreg., 1989—90; asst. dir. affirmative action Portland State U., 1990—96; human resources diversity profl. PacifiCorp, Portland; nat. employment & compensation mgr. AmeriCold Logistics, Atlanta, 1999—2002; recruiter PNM, Albuquerque, 2003—. Nw adv. bd. mem. Ctr. for Dem. Renewal, Seattle, 1989—92; chair Bias Crimes Alert Network, Portland, 1992—93; cons. Ga. Owens Diversity Cons. Facilitator Trainer, Albuquerque, 1990—2003. Civil rights adv., sch. events organizer Met. Human Rights Commn., Portland, 1990—96; civil rights commn. employee Youth Gangs Task Force, Portland, 1990—94; nw adv. bd. Ctr. for Dem. Renewal, Seattle, 1989—92; co-chair, sec., bd. mem. Refugee Immigrant Consortium of Oreg. and SW Wash., Portland, 1990—2003. Mem.: Am. Ex-Prisoners of War, Dept. of N.Mex, Bataan Veterans Orgn. Next of Kin (life). Democrat-Npl. Episcopalian. Avocations: art, painting, ceramics. Home: 611 Lead Ave SW #921 Albuquerque NM 87102 Office: Pnm Alvarado Square Albuquerque NM 87158-2130 Personal E-mail: owensgk@hotmail.com.

OWENS, JANA JAE, entertainer; b. Great Falls, Mont., Aug. 30, 1943; d. Jacob G. Meyer and Bette P. (Sprague) Hopper; m. Sidney Greif (div.); children: Matthew N., Sydni C.; m. Buck Owens. Student, Interlochen Music Camp, 1959, Internat. String Congress, 1960, Vienna (Austria) Acad. Music, 1963-64; BA magna cum laude, MusB magna cum laude, Colo. Womens Coll., 1965. Tchr. music Ontario (Oreg.) Pub. Schs., 1965-67, Redding (Calif.) Pub. Schs., 1969-74; entertainer Buck Owens Enterprises, Bakersfield, Calif., 1974-78, Tulsa, 1979—. Concertmistress Boise (Idaho) Philharm., 1965—67, Shasta Symphony, Redding, Calif., 1969—74; founder Grand Lake Festivals, Inc., Redding, 1996—. Rec. artist (violinist, vocalist) Lark Records, 1978—. Avocations: skiing, tennis, swimming. Office: Jana Jae Enterprises Lark Record Prodns Inc PO Box 35726 Tulsa OK 74153-0726

OWENS, JUDITH L(YNN), lawyer; b. Benkelman, Nebr., Oct. 17, 1942; d. Daniel E. and Estelle M. (Carlin) O. BA in History, MA in History, Creighton U., 1967, JD, 1978. Bar: Nebr. 1978. Adminstrv. asst. Creighton U., Omaha, 1968; grad. asst. Am. U., Washington, 1972; tchr. Omaha Pub. Schs., 1972-75; atty. Owens and Owens, Benkelman, 1979-82; legal counsel Nebr. Legislature, Lincoln, 1982-87; pvt. practice Benkelman, 1987—. Mem. delinquency prevention bd. City of Benkelman, 1995—; mem. juvenile delinquency prevention com. State of Nebr., Nebr. Crime Commn., Lincoln, 1994—; mem. cert. of need bd. State of Nebr. Health Dept., Lincoln, 1993—. Elected county atty. Dundy County, Benkelman, 1995—; del. Dem. Nat. Conv., San Francisci, 1984; bd. dirs., chair Cmty. Family Ctr., Benkelman, 1991-95. Mem. Internat. PEO (local pres. 1982—), Nebr. State Bar Assn. Avocations: reading, political and election work, theater, choral singing. Office: Box 316 508 Chief St Benkelman NE 69021

OWENS, KATHLEEN C. academic administrator; married; 2 children. BS in Biology, Loyola U., Chgo.; MS in Edn. Biol. Scis., DePaul U., Chgo.; EdD in Curriculum and Instr., Loyola U., Chgo. Dean Lewis U., Romeoville, Ill., 1986—92; v.p. academic affairs St. Francis U., Loretta, Pa., 1992—2002; pres. Gwynedd-Mercy Coll., Gwynedd Valley, Pa., 2002—. Office: Gwynedd-Mercy Coll PO Box 901 1325 Sumneytown Pike Gwynedd Valley PA 19437-0901*

OWENS, LUVIE MOORE, association consultant; b. Cleve., July 26, 1933; d. Dan Tyler and Elizabeth (Oakes) Moore; m. Lloyd Owens, Jan. 1, 1955 (dec. July 18, 2002); children: Luvie Owens Myers, Elizabeth, Lloyd H. Student, Smith Coll., Northampton, Mass., 1956. Tchr. Howard Jr. High Sch., Wilmette, Ill., 1971-75; U.S. ops. mgr. Frank T. Ross & Co., Evanston, Ill., 1976-86; CEO Internat. Platform Assn., Winnetka, Ill., 1986—99, dir., 1972—99; ret., 1999. Mem. jr. league Cleve. Mus. Art, 1954—98; mem. Cleve. Mus. of Art, 1954—2003, women's coun., Jr. League, 2004, treas., 1960—61; treas., mem. jr. coun. Cleve. Mus. Art, 1964—65; mem. alumnae bd. Madeira Sch., Greenway, Va., 1984—88; commr. Police and Fire Commn., Winnetka, 1986—87; chmn. bd. Lake Shore Unitarian Ch., Winnetka, 1986—87. Mem.: Univ. Club of Chgo., Winnetka Women's Club, Rotary.

OWENS, MARGARET ALMA, educational administrator; b. Houston, Mar. 10, 1938; d. Leon Edgar and Velma Rotha (Miller) Owen; m. Robert Harvey Owens, May 28, 1958 (div. 1975); children: Robert Stephen, Keith Randall. BS, Mary-Hardin Baylor U., 1960; MEd, Tex. Woman's U., 1972; supervision cert., 1975; postgrad., 1979-82. Cert. mid-mgmt. adminstr. Tex. Vocat., Trinity Coll. Nat. Health, ND, 2001, home economist Tex. A&M U., Bryan, Tex., 1960-64; substitute tchr. Dallas Ind. Sch. Dist., 1965-67, permanent substitute tchr. in home econs. and sci., 1968-69, tchr. spl. edn., 1969-71; jr. acct. Burgess Manning Co., Dallas, 1967-68; asst. dir. Camp Nerby, Oak Cliff YMCA, Dallas, 1968; tchr. spl. edn. Austin Ind. Sch. Dist., Tex., 1972-74, supr. secondary spl. edn., 1974—; adminstrv. intern SW Tex. State U., San Marcos, 1973; owner Allergy Elimination Clin., Naturopathic Physician, cons. San Marcos Bapt. Acad., Tex., 1976; mem. student tchr. adv. com. U. Tex., Austin, 1984-1994; citizen ambassador of edn. to China, 1986. Author, editor, advisor various profl. tng. materials. Active various Tex. councils Boy Scouts Am., 1968—; mem. Pres.'s Com. on Employment of People with Disabilities, 1987—. Recipient The Golden Measure Achievement award Grand Prairie YMCA, 1968, Haskew award for outstanding contbn. to edn., 1990, Outstanding Leadership award Boy Scouts Am., 1971; Fed. edn. grantee, 1971-72. Mem. AAUW, Nat. Coun. for Exceptional Children (mem. pioneer div., v.p. 1971), NARF, Tex. Edn. Agy. (com. to revise EXCET test), Austin Assn. Pub. Sch. Adminstrs. (chmn. task force, pres. cen. div. 1989-90), Paramount Theatre Club, World-Wide Vacation Club, Candlelight Dance Club, Demolay (pres. Mother's Aux. 1977-78), Alpha Delta Kappa (former officer), Phi Delta Kappa (sec. Austin 1987-89, found. rep. 1989-91), Pi Lambda Theta. Baptist. Avocations: reading, travel, art collecting, theatre, gourmet cooking. Home: 1777 Cricket Hollow Dr Austin TX 78758-4254 Office: Allergy Elimination Clin 4105 Med Pky 202 Austin TX 78756

OWENS, ROCHELLE, poet, playwright; b. Bklyn., Apr. 2, 1936; d. Max and Molly (Adler) Bass; m. George Economou, June 17, 1962. Writer-in-residence, Brown U., 1989; tchr. U. Calif. 1982, U. Okla., 1985, 87, 88, U. Southwestern La., 1998, Tex. A&M Univ. Author: (plays) The String Game, 1965, Istanboul, 1965 (Obie award 1966), Futz, 1967, Homo, 1966, Beclch, 1966, Futz and What Came After, 1968, He Wants Shih, 1969, Farmers Almanac, 1969, The Queen of Greece, 1969, Kontraption, 1970, The Karl Marx Play, 1971, O.K. Certaldo, 1975, Emma Instigated Me, 1976, The Widow and the Colonel, 1977, Mountain Rites, 1977, Who Do You Want, Peire Vidal, 1978, Chucky's Hunch, 1981 (Obie award 1982), Who Do You Want, Peire Vidal, 1982, Plays by Rochelle Owens, 2000, (poetry) Not be Essence That Cannot Be, 1961, Salt and Core, 1968, I am the Babe of Joseph Stalin's Daughter, Poems from Joe's Garage, The Joe 82 Creation Poems, The Karl Marx Play & Others, The Joe Chronicles, Part 2, Four Young Lady Poets, 1962, Shemuel, 1979, French Light, 1984, Constructs, 1985, Anthropologists at a Dinner Party, 1985, Who Do You Want Peire Vidal, 1986, W.C. Fields in French Light, 1986, How Much Paint Does the Painting Need, 1988, Black Chalk, 1995, New and Selected Poems: 1961-1996, Rubbed Stones: Poems from 1960-1992, 1994, The Passersby, 1993, Wild River, Poems, 1999, Luca: Discourse on Life and Death, 2001, (radio play) Sweet Potatoes, 1979 (Obie award 1982); The Passerby by Liliane Atlan (translation); (feature film) Futz, 1969 (Obie award); North American Women's Drama From Colonial Times to Present, 2004; editor: (plays) Spontaneous Combustion (Obie award 1967); recs. include: From a Shaman's Notebook, 1968, The Karl Marx Play, 1974, Totally Corrupt, 1976, Black Box 17, 1979, (play) Three Front, 1990, (radio play) Guerre a'Trois, 1991; reading performances at St. Mark's Poetry Project, Mus. Modern Art, Guggenheim, Whitney Mus., Oxford U., Am. Coll., Paris, Kelly Writer's House, Pa.; host of The Writer's Mind; prodr. radio show, U. Okla.; (video) Oklahoma Too, 1987, How Much Paint Does the Painting Need, Black Chalk, 1995; prodr.: (CD ROM) N.Am. Women's Drama, 2004; reading performance: Am. Coll. Athens, Greece. Founding mem. N.Y. Theatre Strategy, Women's Theatre Coun. Ford Found. grantee, 1965, Creative Arts Pub. Svc. grantee, 1973, Nat. Endowment for Arts grantee, 1974, Rockefeller Found. grantee, 1974; Yale Sch. Drama fellow, 1968, Guggenheim fellow, 1971; honors N.Y. Drama Critics Cir.; Rockefeller Found. Bellagio resident, 1993; recipient Nomination in poetry Okla. Ctr. for the Book, 1995. Mem. Dramatists Guild, ASCAP. Achievements include being in anthologies. Address: 226 W Rittenhouse Sq Apt 1001 Philadelphia PA 19103

OWENS, SUSAN, state supreme court justice; b. Kinston, N.C., Aug. 19, 1949; BA, Duke U., 1971; JD, U. N.C., Chapel Hill, 1975. Bar: Oreg. 1975, Wash. 1976. Judge Dist. Ct., Western Clallam County, 1981—2001; justice Wash. State Supreme Ct., 2001—. Mem.: Dist. and Mcpl. Ct. Judges' Assn. (bd. dirs., sec.-treas., v.p., pres.-elect). Office: PO Box 40929 Olympia WA 98504-0929

OWENS, SUSAN ELIZABETH, realtor; b. Providence, Nov. 22, 1957; d. Lee Edward and Nancy Elizabeth Norton; m. George Ray Bunch Jr., Aug. 15, 1980 (div. Jan. 1986); children: Michael, Melissa, George Ray III; m. Joseph Craig Owens, Oct. 16, 1987. Cert. ct. reporter, Reporting Acad. Va., 1993; study real estate, Tidewater C.C., Chesapeake, Va., 2001. Sec. capital campaign United Way, Norfolk, Va., 1985—86; med. transcriptionist Humana Hosp. Bayside, Virginia Beach, Va., 1986—90; property mgr. Kamla Condominium Assn., Virginia Beach, 1990—93; ct. reporter Adams, Harris & Martin, Norfolk, 1993—94; office mgr. Slone Chiropractic Clinic, Norfolk, 1994—99, Riddle Assoc. Inc., Chesapeake, Va., 1999—2003, comml. real estate agt., 2001—. Pres. So. Bass'n Gal, 1998—2003; sec. Va. Bassmasters, Inc., 1997—2003. Avocations: bass fishing, bowling, writing children's stories. Office: Riddle Assoc Inc 1736 S Park Ct Ste 101 Chesapeake VA 23320 E-mail: sowens@riddleassociates.com.

OWENS-DWYER, DINA, utilities executive; b. 1963; With Dwyer Real Estate and Devel., Inc., Waco, Tex., 1981—, sec., 1989-98, dir., 1989—, co-chair bd. dirs., 1994-95, v.p. ops., 1995—, pres., CEO, 1999—; dir. Rainbow, Mr. Rooter; dir., pres. Nat. Accts. Office: The Dwyer Group Inc 1010 N University Parks Dr Waco TX 76707

OWENS-HICKS, SHIRLEY, state legislator; 2 children. Grad., Boston U., Harvard U. Adminstrv. asst. Mass. State Sen. Bill Owens; mem. Mass. Ho. of Reps., 1987—, chair fed. fin. asst. com. Pres., CEO Urban League Eastern Mass. Mem. Phi Delta Kappa, Delta Sigma Theta. Office: State Ho Rm 156 Boston MA 02133

OXELL, LOIE GWENDOLYN, fashion and beauty educator, consultant, columnist; b. Sioux City, Iowa, Nov. 17, 1917; d. Lyman Stanley and Loie Erma (Crill) Barton; m. Eugene Edwin Eschenbrenner, Aug. 8, 1936 (dec. 1954); children: Patricia Gene, Eugene Edward (dec. Feb. 1994); m. Henry J. Oxell, Nov. 3, 1956 (dec. July 1994). AS in Fashion Merchandising, Broward C.C., Davie, Fla., 1978. Fashion rep. Crestmoor Suit & Coat Co., St. Louis, 1951-56; appeared on "To the Ladies" weekly TV show KSD-TV, St. Louis, 1950s; cons./instr. Miami-Herald Newspaper Glamor Clinic, Miami, Fla., 1957-71; pres./owner Loie's (Loy's) Inc., Miami, Fla., 1958-71; pres., owner West Coast East Talent Agy.; instr./lectr. Charron-Williams Coll., Miami, 1973-77; instr. Fashion Inst. Ft. Lauderdale, Fla., 1977-86; pres./owner Image Power Unltd., Plantation, Fla., 1992—. Lectr. in field; columnist Sr. Life and Boomer Times, Fla., 1993-97, Sr. Life, 1997-98, The Entertainer, 1997-98 Author: I'd Like You to Meet My Wife, 1964, Executive Wives, A.C. Sparkplug Co., So! We're in Our 60's, 70's, 80's Plus; regularly appeared in comedy skits, fashion segments, commentary, and TV commls. Del Russo Beauty Show, 1960s; actress Red Skelton TV show, Miami, Fla., also fashion show prodns., TV commls. Lectr., instr. Work Force, AARP Sr. Cmty. Svc. Employment Program, Ft. Lauderdale and Hollywood, Fla., 1987—, keynote spkr. nat. conv., Charlestown, S.C., 1986; life mem. women's com. Miami Children's Hosp. Aux.; faculty adv. Nu Tau Sigma Charron Williams Coll., 1973-77; pres. Venice of Am. chpt. Am. Bus. Women's Assn., 1975-76. Recipient Cert. of Appreciation Dade County Welfare Dept. Youth Hall, Miami, 1966, Community TV Found., Miami, 1966, 71, Woman of the Yr. award Am. Bus. Women's Assn. (Venice of Am. chpt.), 1976-77, Award for Svc. AARP Sr. Community Svc. Program, 1993. Mem. The Fashion Group Internat. Avocations: bridge, golf.

OXENREIDER, LAURA ELIZABETH, elementary guidance counselor; b. Bronx, N.Y., Dec. 18, 1964; d. Salvatore Emile and Mary Ellen (Giglio) Sorrillo; m. David Alan Oxenreider, Oct. 16, 1993. BS in Psychology cum laude, East Stroudsburg U., 1990; MA in Sch. Counseling, U. Ctrl. Fla., 1996. Mental health tech. Meadows Psychiat. Ctr., Centre Hall, Pa., 1990-91; case mgr. Osceola County Mental Health, Kissimmee, Fla., 1991-93; tchr. emotionally handicapped Orange County Schs., Orlando, Fla., 1993-96; guidance counselor Orange County Pub. Schs., 1996; elem. guidance counselor West Shore Sch. Dist., Pa., 1997—99; counselor elem. sch. Carlisle (Pa.) Area Sch. Dist., 1999—. Mem. ACA, Orange County Counseling Assn. Home: 1275 Sandy Ln Boiling Springs PA 17007-9647

OXLEY, ANN, television executive; b. Canton, Ohio, Aug. 3, 1924; d. Edward and Dorothy (Duffy) Adang; m. Jack Raymond Oxley, Aug. 10, 1946 (dec.); children: Kathleen Oxley Wiggins, Maureen Oxley Gaff, Joseph, Jeffrey, Christeen Oxley Rhodes, Daniel (dec.), Sister Julie Marie Oxley, Jamie, Kevin, Valerie Oxley Fouch, Amy. BA with distinction, Ind. U., 1974, MPA, 1982. Advt. account salesperson Ft. Wayne (Ind.) Jour. Gazette, 1945-47; office mgr. Ind. Equestrian Assn., Ft. Wayne, 1971-73; rsch. dir. Taxpayers Rsch. Assn., Ft. Wayne, 1974-76; exec. dir. Ft. Wayne Pub. TV Inc., 1976-86. Active Bicentennial Com., 1976; adviser Media Arts Panel Ind. Arts Commn.; pres. Allen County Coun. on Aging. Found., 1995-98. Mem. AAUW, Svc. Corps Ret. Execs. (publicity chair 1986, nat. mktg. dir. 1989-90), Mensa Internat. (nat. coord. Project Inkslinger Mensa Ednl. Rsch. Found. 1998-2000), C. of C. (cultural com.), Phi Alpha Alpha. Roman Catholic. Home: 4305 Arlington Ave Fort Wayne IN 46807-2635 Office: SCORE 1300 S Harrison Federal Bldg Fort Wayne IN 46807

OXLEY, MARGARET CAROLYN STEWART, elementary school educator; b. Petaluma, Calif., Apr. 1, 1930; d. James Calhoun Stewart and Clara Thornton (Whiting) Bomboy; m. Joseph Hubbard Oxley, Aug. 25, 1951; children: Linda Margaret, Carolyn Blair Oxley Greiner, Joan Claire Oxley Willis, Joseph Stewart, James Harmon, Laura Marie Oxley Brechbill. Student, U. Calif., Berkeley, 1949—51; BS summa cum laude, Ohio State U., 1973, MA, 1984, postgrad., 1985, postgrad., 1988, postgrad., 1992, Ohio State U, 2003. Cert. tchr., Ohio. 2d grade tchr. St. Paul Sch., Westerville, Ohio, 1973—. Presenter in field. Mem. editl. bd. Reading Tchr., vol. 47-48, 1993-94, Jour. Children's Lit., 1996—; co-author: Reading and Writing, Where it All Begins, 1991, Teaching with Children's Books: Path to Literature-Based Instruction, 1995, Adventuring With Books, vol. 12, 2000, vol. 13, 2002, Children's Literature Remembered: Issues, Trends, and Favorite Books, 2004. Active Akita Child Conservation League, Columbus, Ohio, 1968-70. Named Columbus Diocesan Tchr. of Yr., 1988; Phoebe A. Hearst scholar, 1951, Rose Sterheim Meml. scholar, 1951; recipient Mary Karrer award Ohio State U., 1994. Mem. Nat. Coun. Tchrs. English (Notable Children's Books in the Lang. Arts com. 1993-94, chair 1995-96, treas. Children's Literature Assembly bd. dirs. 1996-99, co-chair fall breakfast children's lit. assembly, 2000-03, co-chair excellence in poetry for children com. 2003—), Internat. Reading Assn. (Exemplary Svc. in Promotion of Literacy award 1991), Literacy Connection (pres.), Children's Lit. Assembly, Ohio Coun. Tchrs. English Lang. Arts (Outstanding Educator 1990), Phi Kappa Phi, Pi Lambda Theta (hon., Outstanding Work in Literacy Edn. citation 2004). Democrat. Roman Catholic. Avocations: reading, writing, travel, gardening, working with children. Home: 298 Brevoort Rd Columbus OH 43214-3826

OZAKI, NANCY JUNKO, performance artist, performing arts educator; b. Denver, Feb. 14, 1951; d. Joe Motoichi and Tamiye (Saki) O.; m. Gary Steven Tsujimoto, Nov. 12, 1989. BS in Edn., U. Colo., 1973; postgrad., U. Colo., Denver, 1977, Metro State Coll., 1982, Red Rocks C.C., 1982-83, U. No. Colo., 1982, U. N.Mex., 1985, U. No. Colo., 1988. Elem. tchr. Bur. Indian Affairs, Bloomfield, N.Mex., 1973—75, Aurora Pub. Schs., Colo., 1977—83, Albuquerque Pub. Schs., 1983—84, Denver Pub. Schs., 1984—87, Oak Grove Sch. Dist., San Jose, Calif., 1988—89, San Mateo City Elem. Dist., Calif., 1990—92; performing artist Japanese drums Young Audiences, San Francisco, 1992—93, Denver, 1994—97; performing artist Japanese drums Epcot Ctr. Walt Disney World, Orlando, Fla., 1993—97; co-dir., mgr., performer One World Taiko Japanese Drum Troupe, Denver, 1997—2001, Seattle, 2001—; artist-in-residence Washington States Arts Commn., 2003—. Mem. Touring Arts Roster, King County. Vol. worker with young Navajo children; co-sponsor girl's sewing and camping groups. Mem. Kappa Delta Pi (Theta chpt.). Avocations: reading, sewing, skiing, hiking, snorkeling. Office: PO Box 80158 Seattle WA 98108 E-mail: oneworldtaiko@earthlink.net.

OZANICH, RUTH SHULTZ, artist, poet, retired elementary educator; b. Calif., Feb. 12, 1915; d. Charles Andrew Shultz and Martha Viola Boring; m. Anton M. Ozanich, Nov. 1931; children: Antom M., Saralen Elaine, Marc Charles Dee. BEd, Fresno (Calif.) State U., 1956. Life cert. tchr. credential, Calif. Tchr. Bardsley Elem. Sch., Oildale, Calif., 1954-65, Sierra Vista Elem. Sch., Arvin, Calif., 1965-70; ret., 1970. Exhibited in group shows Bakersfield Art Assn. Gallery, Cunningham Gallery, Bakersfield, Kern County Fair, Calif. (numerous blue ribbons); contbr. poetry to anthologies. Elder Paiute Coun., Lake Isabella Calif.; treas. Mexican Am. Srs. Mem. Internat. Poetry Hall of Fame (life), Calif. Tchrs. Assn., Kern River Valley Poets and Writers Club (founder, past pres.), Bakersfield Art Assn. (founder, past treas.), Ladies Moose. Avocations: arts and crafts, reading, poetry, writing. Home: PO Box 1396 Lake Isabella CA 93240-1396

OZAWA, MARTHA NAOKO, social work educator; b. Ashikaga, Tochigi, Japan, Sept. 30, 1933; came to U.S., 1963; d. Tokuichi and Fumi (Kawashima) O.; m. May 1959 (div. May 1966). BA in Econs., Aoyama Gakuin U., 1956; MS in Social Work, U. Wis., 1966, PhD in Social Welfare, 1969. Asst. prof. social work Portland (Oreg.) State U., 1969-70, assoc. prof. social work, 1970-72; assoc. rsch. prof. social work NYU, 1972-75; assoc. prof. social work Portland State U., 1975-76; prof. social work Washington U., St. Louis, 1976-85, Bettie Bofinger Brown prof. social policy, 1985—2003, Bettie Bofinger Brown Disting. prof. social policy, 2003—. Author: Income Maintenance and Work Incentives, 1982; editor: Women's Life Cycle: Japan-U.S. Comparison in Income Maintenance, 1989, Women's Life Cycle and Economic Insecurity: Problems and Proposals, 1989; editl. bd. Social Work, Silver Spring, Md., 1972-75, 85-88, New Eng. Jour. Human Svcs., Boston, 1987-95, Ency. of Social Work, Silver Spring, 1974-77, 91-95, 99-2003, Jour. Social Svc. Rsch., 1977-97, 2004—, Children and Youth Svcs. Rev., 1991—, Social Work Rsch., 1994-97, 2004—, Jour. Poverty, 1997—. Grantee Adminstrn. on Aging, Washington, 1979, 84, NIMH, 1990-93. Mem. Nat. Assn. Social Workers (presdl. award 1999), Nat. Acad. Social Ins., Nat. Conf. on Social Welfare (bd. dirs. 1981-87), The Gerontol. Soc. Am., Coun. Social Work Edn., Soc. for Social Work and Rsch., Washington U. Faculty Club (bd. dirs. 1986-91). Avocations: photography, tennis, swimming, gardening. Home: 13018 Tiger Lily Ct Saint Louis MO 63146-4339 Office: PO Box 1196 Saint Louis MO 63188-1196 Office Phone: 314-935-6615. E-mail: ozawa@wustl.edu.

OZER, MARTHA ROSS, psychologist, counselor; b. Richmond, Ky., Sept. 4, 1932; d. Robert Lee and Virginia Eudelle (Hurst) Ross; m. John Dudley Redden, Dec. 27, 1953 (dec. June 1969); children: Mary, Patricia, Robert, Mark; m. Mark N. Ozer, Aug. 12, 1979. BA in Elem. Edn., Georgetown Coll., 1954; MA in Counseling, Murray State U., 1966, MS in Psychology, 1968; EdD in Edn. Adminstrn., U. Ky., 1976; LLD (hon.), Georgetown Coll., 1995; postdoctoral cert. in infant and young child mental health program, Wash. Sch. Psychiatry, 1995-96. Cert. sch. psychologist with autonomous functioning Ky. Bd. Psychology, lic. sch. psychologist Va. Dept. Edn., D.C. Pub. Schs., profl. counselor D.C., nat. cert. sch. psychologist Nat. Assn. Sch. Psychologists, lic. psychologist Bd. of Psychology, D.C. Elem. tchr. Jefferson County Pub. Schs., Louisville, 1954-58, Hickman County Pub. Schs., Campbellsburg, Ky., 1960-62; tchr. emotional disturbed, dir. psychol. svcs. Paducah (Ky.) Pub. Schs., 1965-70; psychologist, program dir. Louisville Pub. Schs., 1970-74; doctoral intern Bur. Edn. for Handicapped U.S. Dept. Edn., Washington, 1974-75; program dir. project sci. tech. and disability AAAS, Washington, 1986—87; postdoctoral fellowship NYU Brain Trauma Program NYU Med. Ctr., N.Y.C., 1986-87; program dir., adminstr., asst. prof. dept. rehab. medicine Med. Coll. Va., Richmond, 1987-89; psychologist MCV Pediatric Devel. Ctr., Richmond, 1989; sch. psychologist Fairfax (Va.) County Pub. Schs., 1989-98; pvt. practice, 1998—; dir. Project Link, William Wendt Ctr. for Loss and Healing, Washington, 2000—03; psychologist Ednl. Diagnostics Inst., Inc., 1998—. Cons. Am. Coun. on Edn., Washington, 1976-97; project coord. Higher Edn. and the Handicapped Am. Coun. on Edn., 1976-86; cons. rehab. and spl. edn., Brazil, Saudi Arabia, Qatar, Turkey; numerous other profl. and disability orgns. Authored more than 20 books and contbr. articles to profl. jours. on access for persons with disabilities to sci. edn. and careers, contbn. of sci./tech. to persons with disabilities. Advisor Disability Rights, 1975—86; vol. William & Wendy Ctr. for Loss and Healing, Washington Hebrew Congreagation. Recipient U.S. Presdl. Pvt. Sector award, award Am. Coalition Citizens with Disabilities, 1980, Alumni award Geotgetown Coll., 1985, Disting. Alumni award Murray St. U., 1996; grantee U.S. Dept. Edn., 1975-86, U.S. Dept. Civil Rights, 1975-82, Grant Found., 1975-77, Exxon Found., 1976, IBM, 1976, NSF, 1977-86, Nat. Inst. for Rehab. Rsch., 1978-84. Mem.: APA (bd. dirs. rehab. sect.), NSTA (award), Am. Mental Health Assn., Am. Assn. of Mental Health Counsellors, Am. Counseling Assn., Va. Psychol. Assn., Nat. Assn. of Sch. Psychologists (nat. cert.). Avocations: photography, pottery, travel. Home: 3420 38th St NW Apt A-415 Washington DC 20016-3032

OZICK, CYNTHIA, writer; b. N.Y.C., Apr. 17, 1928; d. William and Celia (Regelson) O.; m. Bernard Hallote, Sept. 7, 1952; 1 dau., Rachel Sarah. BA cum laude with honors in English, NYU, 1949; MA, Ohio State U., 1950; LHD (hon.), Yeshiva U., 1984, Hebrew Union Coll., 1984, Williams Coll., 1986, Hunter Coll., 1987, Jewish Theol. Sem. Am., 1988, Adelphi U., 1988, SUNY, 1989, Brandeis U., 1990, Bard Coll., 1991, Spertus Coll., 1991, Skidmore Coll., 1992, Seton Hall U., 1999, Rutgers U., 1999, U. N.C., Asheville, 2000, NYU, 2001, Bar-Ilan U., Israel, 2002, Balt Hebrew U., 2004. Author: Trust, 1966, reissued, 2004, The Pagan Rabbi and Other Stories, 1971, Bloodshed and Three Novellas, 1976, Levitation: Five Fictions, 1982, Art and Ardor: Essays, 1983, The Cannibal Galaxy, 1983, The Messiah of Stockholm, 1987, Metaphor & Memory: Essays, 1989, The Shawl, 1989, Epodes: First Poems, 1992, What Henry James Knew, and Other Essays on Writers, 1994, Portrait of the Artist as a Bad Character, 1996, The Cynthia Ozick Reader, 1996, Fame & Folly, 1996, The Puttermesser Papers, 1997, (novel) Heir to the Glimmering World, 2004; (plays) Blue Light, 1994, The Shawl, 1996; guest editor Best Am. Essays, 1998, Quarrel & Quandary: Essays, 2000; also poetry, criticism, revs., translations, essays and fictions in numerous periodicals and anthologies. Phi Beta Kappa orator, Harvard U., 1985. Recipient Mildred and Harold Strauss Living award Am. Acad. Arts and Letters, 1983, Rea award for short story, 1986, PEN/Spiegel-Diamonstein award for the Art of the Essay, 1997, Harold Washington Literary award City of Chgo., 1997, John Cheever award, 1999, Lannan Found. award for fiction, 2000, Koret Found. award for lit. studies, 2001, Nat. Book Critics Circle award for nonfiction, 2001; Lucy Martin Donnelly fellow, Bryn Mawr Coll., 1992, Guggenheim fellow, 1982. Mem. PEN, Authors League, Am. Acad. of Arts and Scis., Am. Acad. of Arts and Letters, Dramatists Guild, Académie Universelle des Cultures (Paris), Phi Beta Kappa.

OZOG, DIANE L. allergist; b. Chgo., July 28, 1955; MD, U. Health Scis., Chgo. Med. Sch., 1982. Cert. allergy and immunology 1987, pediat. 1987. Resident Cook County Hosp., Ill., 1982—85; fellowship Children's Meml. Hosp., Ill., 1985—87; allergist Good Samaritan Hosp. Mem.: Children's Comm. Physicians Assn. Office: 3825 Highland Ave Tower 2 Ste 204 Downers Grove IL 60515 Address: 636 Raymond Naperville IL 60563

PACE, SALLY MAE, student services dean; b. Tehachappi, Calif., Mar 22, 1946; d. Ben Franklin Jr. and Mary Elizabeth (Miller) Stinson; m. Michael D. Pace, June 15, 1969; children: Ryan Seth, Natalie Michelle. BA in Home Econs., San Jose State U., 1969; MEd, Fresno Pacific, 1990. Home econs. tchr. Homestead H.S., San Jose, Calif., 1970, Visalia (Calif.) Unified, 1970-71, Woodlake (Calif.) H.S., 1971-86, counselor, 1986-90, dean student svcs., 1990—. Active Woodlake Meml. Dist., 1986-89. Named Calif. Home Econs. Tchr. of Yr., Calif. Home Econs. Assn., 1983, Woodlake Woman of the Yr., Woodlake C. of C., 1994. Mem. Woodlake Kiwanis (charter sec./treas. 1989-92, Kiwanian of Yr. 1995). Avocations: travel, crafts. Home: 19524 Avenue 364 Woodlake CA 93286-9526 Office: Woodlake HS 400 W Whitney Ave Woodlake CA 93286-1240 E-mail: sallywh@woodlake.k12.ca.us.

PACHAN, MARY JUDE KATHRYN DOROTHY, guidance counselor; b. East Otto, N.Y., Jan. 29, 1933; d. Nicholas and Mary (Podolinsky) P. BS in Edn., Medaille Coll., 1964; MS in Edn., St. Bonaventure U., 1972. Cert. guidance counseling, N.Y., elem. edn. tchr., N.Y. 3d grade tchr. Holy Cross Sch., Buffalo, 1955-56; 3d and 4th grade tchr. Immaculata Heart of Mary Sch., Buffalo, 1956-60; 8th grade tchr. Our Lady of Loretta Sch., Buffalo, 1960-64; tchr. English DeSales High Sch., Lockport, N.Y., 1964-68; counselor campus ministry SUNY, Buffalo, 1968-72; counselor St. Joseph's Collegiate Inst., Buffalo, 1973—99; ret., 1999. Dir. guidance svcs. St. Joseph's Collegiate Inst., Buffalo, 1989-96. Grantee in English, Nazareth Coll., Rochester, N.Y., 1965, journalism grantee Wall St., Boston U., 1966. Mem. N.Y. State Pers. and Guidance Assn., Counseling and Devel. Hospice Tng., AACD. Avocations: cross country skiing, horseback riding, concerts. Home: 557 Burroughs Dr Amherst NY 14226-3900

PACHECO, SUSAN, automotive executive; d. Jorge Pacheco; married; children: Alex, Adam. MBA, U. Detroit, 1989. Ford grad. tng. program Ford Motor Co., 1984—86, product design engr., 1986—89, supr. steering column and shiftsystem design and devel., 1989—92, program mgr. Ford Explorer special studies, 1992, chief program engr., pres. Ford Unlimited, dir. Mercury programs. Named one of 50 Most Important Hispanics in Bus. and Tech., Hispanic Engr. & Info. Tech. mag., 2003. Office: Ford Motor Co 1 American Rd Dearborn MI 48126-2798 Office Phone: 313-322-3000. Office Fax: 313-845-5259.*

PACHER, NANCY A. real estate company executive; Grad. cum laude, Georgetown U.; JD, Northwestern U. Atty. Katten, Muchin, Gitles, Zavis, Pearl & Galler (now Katten Muchin Zavis Rosenman), Chgo., 1975; sr. v.p., prin. Howard Ecker & Co.; pres., COO US Equities Realty, Chgo., 1993—. Bd. mem. Access Living Met. Chgo.; commr. City of Chgo. Plan Commn., mem. aux. bd. Sch. Art Inst. Chgo. Mem. editl. adv. bd.: Ill. Real Estate Jour. Named Broker of the Yr., Chgo. Sun-Times; named one of 100 Most Influential Women in Chgo., Crain's Chgo. Bus., 1996; named to Who's Who in Chgo. Bus., 2002, 20th Ann. Hall of Fame, Today's Chgo. Women. Mem.: ABA, Comml. Real Estate Orgn., Comml. Real Estate Exec. Women, Chgo. Network (bd. mem.), Chgo. Bar Assn., Econ. Club Chgo., Phi Beta Kappa. Office: US Equities Realty Ste 400 20 N Michigan Ave Chicago IL 60602

PACI, RUTH A. freelance/self-employed writer; b. West New York, N.J., Mar. 7, 1928; d. Joseph Frederick and Theresa Becker Paci. BA in History and Polit. Sci., Fordham U., 1984; MA in Journalism, NYU, 1987. Adminstrv. officer, press officer U.S. Info. Agy., Washington and N.Y.C., 1951—86, dep. dir. Fgn. Press Ctr. N.Y.C., 1985—86; ret., 1986; freelance writer. Author: Down By the River and Under the Cliff, 1994, Dearest Friends, 2004, short stories and essays. Trustee Edgewater Pub. Libr., 1995—; mem., founder, chair Cultural and Hist. Commn. Edgewater, 2000—; mem. Bergen County com. Dem. Party, Hackensack, NJ, 2000—; hist. preservation advisory bd. Bergen County, 2004. Recipient Cert. of Commendation, Bergen County Bd. Chosen Freeholders, 2003, Hist. Preservation resolution, NJ Gen. Assembly, 2003. Roman Catholic. Avocations: travel, gardening, reading. Home: 24 Valley Pl Edgewater NJ 07020

PACIELLO, LINDA KATHERINE, psychologist; b. Utica, N.Y., Mar. 1, 1943; d. William John and Frances Ellen Kenefick; m. Michael Anthony Paciello, May 30, 1964; children: Michael Anthony Paciello III, Krista Lynn Plenn. BA, Coll. of the Univ. of the State of N.Y., 1995; MSEd, Coll. of St. Rose, Albany, 1997; PhD, Capella U., Mpls., 2003. Cert. sch. psychologist N.Y. Exec. sec. Indium Corp., Utica, NY, 1983—88, PAR Tech. Corp., New Hartford, NY, 1988—92; sch. psychologist BOCES, New Hartford, NY, 1997—99, Westmoreland Ctrl. Sch. Dist., NY, 1999—. Mem.: APA, NASP, N.Y. State United Tchrs., N.Y. State Assn. Sch. Psychologists. Home: 6 Croft Rd New Hartford NY 13413

PACINI, RENEE ANNETTE, software company executive; b. Phila., Apr. 12, 1960; d. Joseph Leonard and Joanna Sarah (Fedele) P.; m. Bruce D. Walter, Feb. 14, 1994; children: Andrew Joseph Walters, David Leon Walters. BS in Spl. Edn., West Chester U., 1982, MSA in Tng. and Devel., 1994. Cert. tchr., Pa. Tchr. Devereaux Found., West Chester, 1982-85; application trainer Applied Bus. Technologies, Newtown Square, Pa., 1985-87, mgr., client svcs., 1987-94, v.p., client rels., 1994-96; v.p. Premier Bus. Advisors, Swarthmore, Pa., 1996-98; v.p. client mgmt. Applied Bus. Tech., 1998—. Bd. dirs. ABT, Newtown Square. Mem. AAUW. Democrat. Roman Catholic. Avocations: athletics, reading, cooking. Home: 310 Stump Rd North Wales PA 19454-1909 Office: ABT 4631 W Chester Pike Newtown Square PA 19073-2225

PACK, BOBIGENE, minister, writer; b. Sumter, S.C., Mar. 3, 1949; d. Altomount Pack and Maybelle Farmer Thompson; m. Albert Alonzo Turner (div.); children: Kwind, Emory Harrison Turner; m. Jesse Miller (div.). Student, U. S.C., 1974; cert., Forsyth Tech., 1983; diploma, Rhema Bible Tng. Ctr., 2000. Owner, adminstr. New Beginnings Assisted Living, Winston-Salem, NC, 1983—97; founder, pres. Love in Action Outreach, Ellenwood, Ga., 1998—; founder, radio personality Your Dreams Can Come True, Tulsa, Okla., 2000—01; founder, motivational spkr. Bringing Success to the Surface, 2000. Author, pub.: God Made Me Beautiful from the Inside Out, 1998. Active The Salvation Army Child Devel. Ctrs., Tulsa, 1998—99. Office: Love in Action Outreach PO Box 766 Ellenwood GA 30294

PACK, NANCY J. special education educator, speech therapist; b. Santa Monica, Calif., May 28, 1952; d. James Neil and Muriel Elaine (Stone) Hess; m. Albert Richard Pack, Mar. 22, 1986; children: Ember, Andrea, Galen. BA in Speech/Drama, Chico State U., 1975, MA in Speech Pathology, 1977. Cert. in early childhood spl. edn., Wash. Lang. disorders specialist Shasta County Office of Edn., Redding, Calif., 1977-80; tchr. hearing impaired Tehama County Dept. Edn., Red Bluff, Calif., 1983-89, speech and lang. pathologist, 1983-89, spl. edn. tchr., 1989-94, North Kitsap Sch. Dist., Poulsbo, Wash., 1994—. Mem. adv. bd. Spl. Edn. Steering Com., Poulsbo, 1996-97, Spl. Edn. Tech. Com., Poulsbo, 1997-98; presenter in field. Tchr. adult edn. Tehama County Dept. Edn., Red Bluff, 1980-82. Recipient Tchr. of Yr. award Tehama County Edn. Found., 1992-93, Exemplary Educator award Calif. Coun. for Edn. Exceptional Children, 1993-94."Who" award Redd ing Svc. Ctr. Coun. of Calif. Tchrs. Assn., 1993. Mem. Am. Speech and Lang. Assn. (cert. clin. competence), Tehama County Cert. Employees Assn. (pres. 1988-94), Coun. for Exceptional Children, Nat. Assn. Edn. of Young Children, Wash. Educators Assn. Avocations: backpacking, mountain climbing, cross country skiing, windsurfing, camping. Home: 2255 Dalarna Ct NE Poulsbo WA 98370-7590

PACK, SUSAN JOAN, art consultant; b. N.Y.C., June 15, 1951; d. Howard Meade and Nancy (Buckley) P. BA summa cum laude, Princeton U., 1973. Copywriter Laurence Charles & Free, N.Y.C., 1978-83, Warwick Advt., N.Y.C., 1983-85; sr. copywriter Saatchi & Saatchi Compton, N.Y.C., 1985-88; pres. The Pack Collection, 1989—. Author: Film Posters of the Russian Avant-Garde, 1995. Mem. Princeton (N.J.) U. Libr. Coun., 1985-93; trustee Pack Found. for Med. Rsch., N.Y., 1983—; bd. dirs. The Poster Soc., N.Y., 1985-87. Recipient 4 Clio awards, 1981, 1 Clio award, 1982; named one of top art collectors under 40 Art and Antiques Mag., 1985, one of top 100 collectors in U.S., 1996. Mem. Phi Beta Kappa. E-mail: spdesign@pacbell.net.

PACKARD, BONNIE BENNETT, former state legislator; b. Concord, N.H., Nov. 9, 1946; d. James Oliver and Caro Lucia (Arsenault) Bennett; m. David Bartlett Packard, Oct. 1, 1983. Mem. N.H. Ho. of Reps., Concord, 1981-82, 85-96, vice chair ho. econ. devel. com., 1992, chair ho. commerce com., 1993-96; v.p., treas. Dodd Ins. Agy., Contoocook, N.H., 1984-85; dir. govt. rels. Roussos & Hage, P.A., Attys. at Law, 1996-97, Orr & Reno, P.A., Concord, N.H., 1998—. Bd. dirs. Bus. Fin. Authority, 1994-96. State pres. N.H. Fedn. Rep. Women, 1982-83; chmn. Merrimack County (N.H.) Rep. Com., 1979-80; mem. Hillsborough County Rep. Com., 1995, chair Hillsborough County Del., 1995-96; mem. Bd. Selectmen, New Ipswich, N.H., 1989-90; nat. del. trustee Nat. Kidney Found., 1990-91, 1st v.p. N.H. chpt., 1990-91. Recipient Spirit of Independence award N.H. Health Underwriters Assn., 1996, Chmn.'s award Bus. Fin. Authority of State of N.H., 1996. Mem. New Ipswich Hist. Soc. Episcopalian. Avocations: sketching, antiques, political campaigns. Home: 6 Joy Ln New Ipswich NH 03071-3610 Office: 1 Eagle Sq Concord NH 03301-4903

PACKARD, JULIE, aquarium administrator; d. David and Lucile P. Co-founder & exec. dir. Monterey Bay Aquarium, Monterey, Calif., 1984—, vice chair, bd of trustees, 1984—. Recipient Edward H. Bean Awd., Am. Assn. Zoological Parks and Aquariums, 1993, Audubon Medal for Conservation, 1998. Mem.: bd. David and Lucile Packard Found., Monterey Bay Aquarium Research Inst., Calif. Nature Conservancy. Office: Monterey Bay Aquarium 886 Cannery Row Monterey CA 93940-1023

PACKARD, ROCHELLE SYBIL, elementary school educator; b. June 25, 1951; d. Dave Wallace and Jeanette (Goddy) P. BA in Early Childhood Edn., Point Park Coll., 1973; MEd in Elem. Edn., U. Pitts., 1975. Instrnl. II permanent tchg. cert., Pa. Substitute tchr. Pitts. Pub. Bd. Edn., 1973-77, tchr. kindergarted, 1st grade, 2d grade, 1977—92, tchr. kingergarten, 1992—. Chair Israel Day Parade, Pitts., 1981; mem. Hadassah, Pitts., 1983—, Pioneer Women, Pitts., 1982—, ORT, Pitts., 1975—. Mem. Pitts. Fedn. Tchrs., Pitts. State Edn. Agy. Democrat. Jewish. Home: 4100 Lydia St Pittsburgh PA 15207 1126

PACKARD, SANDRA PODOLIN, education educator, consultant; b. Buffalo, Sept. 13, 1942; d. Mathew and Ethel (Zolte) P.; m. Martin Packard, Aug. 2, 1964; children: Dawn Esther, Shana Fanny BFA, Syracuse U., 1964; MSEd, Ind. U., 1966, EdD, 1973. Cert. tchr. art K-12, N.Y. Asst. prof. art SUNY-Buffalo, 1972-74; assoc. prof. art Miami U., Oxford, Ohio, 1974-81, spl. asst. to provost, 1979-80, assoc. provost, spl. programs, 1980-81; dean Coll. Edn. Bowling Green State U., Ohio, 1981-85; provost and vice chancellor for acad. affairs U. Tenn., Chattanooga, 1985-92; pres. Oakland U., Rochester, Mich., 1992-95, prof. edn., 1995—, dir. higher edn. doc. cognate; sr. fellow, dir. tech. in edn. Am. Assn. State Colls. and Univs., 1995; coord. Nat. Coun. for Accreditation of Tchr. Edn., Washington, 1995—2001; acting dir. PhD program in end. leadership Oakland U., 2003—04. Cons. Butler County Health Ctr., Hamilton, Ohio, 1976-78; vis. prof. art therapy Simmons Coll., 1979, Mary Mount Coll., Milw., 1981; bd. dirs. SE Ctr. for Arts in Edn., 1994-96; mem. corp. adv. com. Corp. Detroit Mag., 1994-95; cons. Univ. of the North, South Africa Project of the Am. Coun. on Edn., 1995; bd. mem. Fellows Coun. Am. Coun. on Edn., 1994-96. Sr. editor Studies in Art Edn. jour., 1979-81; mem. editl. adv. bd. Jour. Aesthetic Edn., 1984-90; editor: The Leading Edge, 1986; contbr. articles to profl. jours., chpts. to conf. papers Chmn. com. Commn. on Edn. Excellence, Ohio, 1982-83, Tenn. State Peformance Funding Task Force, 1988, Tenn. State Task Force on Minority Tchrs., 1988; reviewer art curriculum N.Y. Bd. Edn., 1985; mem. supt. search com. Chattanooga Pub. Schs., 1987-88; mem. Chattanooga Met. Coun., 1987-88, Chattanooga Ballet Bd., 1986-88, Fund for Excellence in Pub. Edn., 1986-90, Tenn. Aquarium Bd. Advisors, 1989-92, Team Evaluation Ctr. Bd., 1988-90; mem. Strategic Planning Action Team, Chattanooga City Schs., 1987-88, Siskin Hosp. Bd., 1989-92, Blue Ribbon Task Force Pontiac 2010: A New Reality, City of Pontiac Planning Divsn., 1992—; steering com., cultural action bd. Chattanooga, planning com United Way, 1987; Jewish Fedn. Bd., 1986-91; mem. coun. for policy studies Art Edn. Adv. Bd., 1982-91; ex-officio mem. Meadow Brook Theatre Guild, 1992-95; bd. chair Meadow Brook Performing Arts Co., 1992-95; chair World Cup Soccer Edn. Com./Mich. Host Com. 1993-95; bd. dirs. Ptnrs. for Preferred Future, Rochester Cmty. Schs., 1992-95, Traffic Improvement Assn. Oakland County, 1992-95, Oakland County Bus. Roundtable, 1993-95; Rochester C. of C. host com. chair on edn. World Cup, 1992-95; mem. fin. adv. com. Jewish Fedn. Detroit, 1995-97; bd. dirs. United Way Southeastern Mich., 1992-95; bd. dirs. United Way Oakland County, 1992-95, Pontiac 2010: A New Reality, mayor's transition team city/sch. rels. task force: team evaluation leader Dept. of State Am. Univ. Bulgaria, 1995; bd. trustees Cohn's & Colitis Found., 1996-97. Am. Coun. on Edn. and Mellon fellow Miami U., 1978-79; recipient Cracking the Glass Ceiling award Pontiac Area Urban League, 1992. Fellow Nat. Art Edn. Assn. (disting.); mem. Nat. Coun. Profs. of Ednl. Adminstrn. (technology com., 2000-03), Am. Assn. Colls. for Tchr. Edn. (com. chair 1982-85), Am. Art Therapy Assn. (registered), Nat. Art Edn. Assn. Women's Caucus (founder, pres. 1976-78, McFee award 1986), Am. Assn. State Colls. and Univs. (com. profl. devel. 1993-95, state rep. 1994-95), Econ. Club Detroit (bd. dirs. 1992-95), Rotary Club, Great Lakes Yacht Club (social chmn. 1996-97, ground chmn., bd. dirs. 1997-98), Phi Delta Kappa (Leadership award 1985), Nat. Assn. Profs. of Edn. Adminstrn. (com. chair 1998-), Great Lakes Yacht Club, 1995 (bd. dir. 1996-1998). Avocation: sailing. Home: 10471 Scout Trail White Lake MI 48386 Office: Oakland U 475 Education Bldg Rochester MI 48309-4423 Office Phone: 248-370-3059. E-mail: packard@oakland.edu.

PACKER, DIANA, retired reference librarian; b. Cleve., Sept. 04; d. Herman and Sabina (Hochman) Reich; m. Herbert Packer, June 21, 1964 (dec.); children: Cynthia, Jeremy, Todd. BA, Case Western Res. U., 1951, MLS, 1952. Libr. Horizons Rsch. Inc., Cleve., 1952-64, Cleveland Heights (Ohio) University Heights Pub. Libr., 1969-98, ret., 1998. Officer Cleveland Heights PTA, 1971-84; bd. dirs. LWV, Cleveland Heights, 1974—; officer Spl. Librs. Assn., 1952-64. Mem. Ohio Libr. Assn. Avocations: travel, theater, art, music, reading. Home: 2201 Acacia Park Dr Apt 522 Lyndhurst OH 44124-3841

PACKER, REKHA DESAI, lawyer; b. N.Y.C., Apr. 20, 1955; d. Rajanikant C. and Santosh (Nagpaul) Desai; m. Michael Benjamin Packer, Aug. 11, 1979. AB magna cum laude, Harvard U., 1976, JD, 1979. Bar: Mass. 1979, U.S. Dist. Ct. Mass. 1979, U.S. Tax. Ct. 1980. Assoc. Gaston & Snow, Boston, 1979-87, ptnr., 1987-91; sr. ptnr. Hale and Dorr, Boston, 1991-96; tax dir. Pricewaterhouse Coopers LLP, 1997-99; ptnr. Stradley, Ronon, Stevens & Young, LLP, Phila., 1999—. Speaker Fed. Tax Inst., 1987—, World Trade Inst., 1986—. Mem. Internat. Bar Assn. (mem. com. on investment cos., funds and trusts 1989—), ABA (mem. com. on regulated investment cos., labor law sect. 1986—, com. on U.S. activities of foreigners 1988—), Boston Bar Assn. (labor law sect. 1987—, co-chmn. internat. tax. com. 1987-89), Phi Beta Kappa. Office: Stradley Ronon Stevens & Young LLP 2600 1 Commerce Sq Philadelphia PA 19103-7098

PACKER, ZZ (ZUWENA), writer, literature educator; b. Chgo., Jan. 12, 1973; d. Robert; m. Michael Boros, 2001. BA, Yale U., 1994; MA in Creative Writing, Johns Hopkins U., 1995; MFA, U. Iowa, 1999. Tchr. various pub. schs., Balt.; Jones lectr. Stanford U.; vis. asst. prof. Writers' Workshop U. Iowa, 2003—04. Author: (short stories) Drinking Coffee Elsewhere, 2003. Recipient Ms. Giles Whiting award, 1999, Bellingham Rev. award, 1999; grantee, Rona Jaffe Writers Found., 1997; Wallace Stegner and Truman Capote fellow, Stanford U. Office: Univ Iowa Writers Workshop 102 Dey House 507 N Clinton St Iowa City IA 52242-1000

PACKERT, G(AYLA) BETH, retired lawyer; b. Corpus Christi, Tex., Sept. 25, 1953; d. Gilbert Norris and Virginia Elizabeth (Pearce) P.; m. James Michael Hall, Jan. 1, 1974 (div. 1985); m. Richard Christopher Burke, July 18, 1987; children: Christopher Geoffrey Makepeace Burke Packert, Jeremy Eliot Marvell Packert Burke. BA, La. Tech. U., 1973; MA, U. Ark., 1976; postgrad., U. Ill., 1975-81, JD, 1985. Bar: Ill. 1985, U.S. Dist. Ct. (no. dist.) Ill. 1985, U.S. Ct. Appeals (7th cir.) 1987, Va. 1988, U.S. Dist. Ct. (we. dist.) Va. 1989. Assoc. Jenner & Block, Chgo., 1985-88; law clk. U.S. Dist. Ct. Va. (we. dist.), Danville, 1988-89; asst. commonwealth atty. Commonwealth of Va., Lynchburg, Va., 1989-95; pvt. practice Lynchburg, 1995—2002; ret., 2002. Notes and comments editor U. Ill. Law Rev., 1984-85. Mem. Phi Beta Kappa. Home: 3900 Faculty Dr Lynchburg VA 24501-3110

PACKHAM, MARIAN AITCHISON, biochemistry educator; b. Toronto, Ont., Can., Dec. 13, 1927; d. James and Clara Louise (Campbell) A.; m. James Lennox Packham, June 25, 1949; children: Neil Lennox, Janet Melissa. BA, U. Toronto, 1949, PhD, 1954; DSc honoris causa, Ryerson Poly. U., 1997. Sr. fellow dept. biochemistry U. Toronto, 1954-58, lectr. dept. biochemistry, 1958-63, 66-67; rsch. assoc. dept. physiol. scis. Ont. Vet. Coll., U. Guelph, 1963-65; rsch. assoc. blood and cardiovascular disease rsch. unit U. Toronto, 1965-66, asst. prof. dept. biochemistry, 1967-72, assoc. prof., 1972-75, prof., 1975—, acting chmn. dept. biochemistry, 1983. Contbr. articles to profl. jours. Royal Soc. Can. fellow, 1991; recipient Lt. Govs. Silver medal Victoria Coll., 1949; co-recipient J. Allyn Taylor Internat. prize in Medicine, 1988. Mem.: Can. Soc. Biochemistry and Molecular and Cellular Biology, Can. Atherosclerosis Soc., Internat. Soc. Thrombosis and Haemostasis, Can. Soc. Clin. Investigation, Can. Soc. Hematology, Am. Soc. Hematology. Office: U Toronto Dept Biochemistry Toronto ON Canada M5S 1A8

PADBERG, HARRIET ANN, mathematics educator; b. St. Louis, Nov. 13, 1922; d. Harry J. and Marie L. (Kilgen) P. AB with honors, Maryville Coll., St. Louis, 1943; MMus, U. Cin., 1949; MA, St. Louis U., 1956, PhD, 1964. Registered music therapist; cert. tchr. math. and music, La., Mo. Tchr. elem. math. and music Kenwood Acad., Albany, N.Y., 1944-46; tchr. secondary math. Acad. of Sacred Heart, Cin., 1946-47; instr. math. and music Acad. and Coll. of Sacred Heart, Grand Coteau, La., 1947-48; secondary tchr. music Acad. Sacred Heart, St. Charles, Mo., 1948-50; instr. math. and music Acad. and Coll. Sacred Heart, Grand Coteau, 1950-55, Maryville Coll., St. Louis, 1955-56; tchr. elem. and secondary math. and music Acad. Sacred Heart, St. Louis, 1956-57; asst. prof. Maryville Coll., St. Louis, 1957-64, assoc. prof., 1964-68, prof. math., 1968-92, prof. emeritus, 1992—; music therapist Emmaus Homes, Marthasville, Mo., 1992—. Recipient Alumni Centennial award Maryville Coll., St. Louis, 1986; grantee Danforth Found., Colorado Springs, 1970, Tallahassee, 1970, Edn. Devel. Ctr., Mass., 1975, U. Kans., 1980. Mem. Assn. Women in Math., Am. Math. Soc., Math. Assn. Am., Nat. Coun. Tchr. Math., Mo. Acad. Sci., Delta Epsilon Sigma (sec. local chpt. 1962), Pi Mu Epsilon (sec. local chpt. 1958), Sigma Xi. Avocations: computer music, organist, knitting. E-mail: hpadberg@rscj.org.

PADDOCK, SANDRA CONSTANCE, music educator; b. Buffalo, Sept. 20, 1972; d. Walter Robert and Susan Elizabeth Wloch; m. Darren Ennis Paddock, July 20, 1996; children: Leanne Kristine, Robert Duane. B in Music Edn. cum laude, SUNY, Buffalo, 1994, M in Arts and Humanities, 1997. Cert. tchr. N.Y. Music tchr. Niagara Wheatfield (N.Y.) Schs., 1995—96; orchestra dir. Kenmore-Tonawanda Schs., 1996—2000; orch. dir., string tchr. Orchard Park (N.Y.) Mid. Sch., 2000—. String adjudicator Erie County Elem. and Jr. High Festivals, 1998, 2002; co-chairperson Erie County (N.Y.) Jr. High Music Festivals, 2001, 02. Musician (solo violinist): faculty recital, 2001. 1st violin Amherst Symphony Orch., 1997—. Mem.: Erie County Music Educator's Assn., Music Educator's Nat. Conf. Avocations: reading, attending concerts.

PADELFORD, NICOLE, accountant; b. Manhattan, Kans., Feb. 3, 1977; d. George Joseph and Janie Laverne Hieger. BS in Acctg., Kans. State U., 1998. Corp. tax intern UMB Fin. Corp., Kansas City, Mo., 1998; tax intern Baird Kurtz & Dobson CPAs, Kansas City, 1999; tax acct. Transport Corp. of Am., Inc., Eagan, Minn., 1999—2001; tax analyst 3M, St. Paul, 2001—. Mem.: AICPAs, Beta Alpha Psi. Home: 3216 200th St W Farmington MN 55024-1199 Office: 3M Center Tax Dept Bldg 224-5N-40 Saint Paul MN 55144

PADEN, MARY GRACE NUCKOLS, humanities educator; d. William Bryan and Nancy Hodnett (Moore) Nuckols; m. John M. Paden, July 30, 1996. BA, Coll. William and Mary, 1982; MA in English and Arts and Scis., Georgetown U., 1988. Prodn. editor Bd. Govs. Fed. Res. Sys., Washington,

1983—85; assoc. editor Sci. & Children, Nat. Sci. Tchrs., Washington, 1985—88; tchr. Severn Sch., Severna Park, Md., 1988—90; instr. English Duke U., Durham, NC, 1990; editor publs. Durham Tech. C.C., 1991—93, coord. arts and humanities, 1993—95; prof. English Rappahannock C.C., Glenns, Va., 1995—2000, John Tyler C.C., Chester, Va., 2000—. Editl. cons. Nat. Endowment Democracy, Washington, 1987. Editor: Inquiry, 2001—. Mem.: MLA, Va. Assn. Mus., Nat. Coun. Tchrs. English, Va. Mus. Fine Arts. Office: John Tyler Cmty Coll 13101 Jefferson Davis Hwy 11 Chester VA 23236

PADGETT, CYNTHIA S. artist; b. Kansas City, Mo., Mar. 4, 1948; m. Charles Allen Padgett, June 10, 1967; children: Claire Elise, Charles Alexander. BA, Goucher Coll., 1972; MA in Liberal Arts, Johns Hopkins U., 1983. Docent The Walters Art Gallery, Balt., 1986-89; alumni bd. mem. Goucher Coll., Balt., 1993-95. One-woman show: A. Jain Marunouchi Gallery, NY, 1998, 99, 2000, 01, 03; works exhibited at A. Jain Marunouchi Gallery, NYC, 1993—, Artshowcase, Balt., 1993, Internat. Contemporary Art Festival (NICAF), Yokohama, Japan, 1995, Tokyo, 1997, LINEART, Gent, Belgium, 2000, 01, Europ'art, Geneva, 2001, Art Phil., 2003; slide registries: Maryland Art Place, State Dept., Nat. Mus. of Women in the Arts. Bd. mem. LWV, St. Petersburg, Fla., 1980-81, Balt., 1981-83; guide Nat. Aquarium, Balt., 1995—; bd. mem., pres. women's com. Historic Hampton, Inc., Towson, Md., 1995-97; chmn. Dulaney Valley, Md. Ho. and Garden Pilgrimage, 1996, 99; Mission Ch., 1992-95. Mem. Johns Hopkins Club, Goucher Club, Hamilton St. Club. Republican. Episc. Avocations: certified pilot, sailing, tennis.

PADGETT, GAIL BLANCHARD, lawyer; b. Douglasville, Ga., Aug. 20, 1949; d. William David and Dorothy Rose (Bennett) P. BA, Ga. State U., 1971, MEd, 1974; JD, Georgetown U., 1981. Bar: Va., Ga., D.C., U.S. Supreme Ct. Tchr. Clayton Co. Bd. Edn., Jonesboro, Ga., 1971-77; spl. asst. to dir. Community Rels Svc., Chevy Chase, Md., 1977-81, gen. counsel, 1981-89, assoc. dir., 1989-96; asst. chief immigration judge U.S. Dept. Justice, Falls Church, Va., 1996—. Recipient Disting. Svc. award Atty. Gen. of the U.S., 1992. Home: 2165 Astoria Cir # 108 Herndon VA 20170 Office: Exec Office Immigration Rev 5709 Leesburg Pike Falls Church VA 22041-2904

PADGETT, NANCY WEEKS, law librarian, consultant, lawyer; b. Newberry, S.C., June 3, 1932; d. Price John and Caroline (Weeks) P.; m. David Lazar, Aug. 6, 1953 (div. Feb. 1994). BS, Northwestern U., 1953; MLS, U. Md., 1972; JD, Georgetown U., 1977. Bar: D.C. 1977. Asst. law libr. U.S. Ct. Appeals for D.C., Washington, 1972—74, supervisory law libr., 1974—84, circuit libr., 1984—. Mem. ALA, D.C. Bar Assn., Am. Assn. Law Librs. Home: 5301 Duvall Dr Bethesda MD 20816-1873 Office: US Ct Appeals for DC Cir Judges' Libr 5518 US Court House Washington DC 20001-5618 Office Phone: 202-216-7396.

PADILLA, SANDRA LYNN, counselor, consultant; b. Denison, Tex., July 19, 1965; d. Daniel Webster Jenks and Anita Louise Nuñez Jenks; m. Bobby Joe McNatt, June 18, 1984 (div. Dec. 10, 1999); 1 child, Sara Ann McNatt ; m. Salvador Padilla, Apr. 15, 2000; 1 child, Shannon Kern. B in Bus. Adminstrn., Ea. N.Mex. U., 1983, B in Clin. Psychology, 2002. Adminstrv. asst. Credit Cons., Dallas, 1990—95; caregiver State of N.Mex., Picacho, 1995—96; chmn. Head Start of Lincoln County, Ruidoso, 1996—2000; dir. Children, Youth and Families Daycare, Ruidoso, 2000—02; CEO, owner, founder Trinity Group, Roswell, N.Mex., 2002—. Adviser Am. Med. Adv. Bd., Roswell, 2000—; legal cons. Prepaid Legal Svcs. Inc., Roswell, 2001—. Activist So. Poverty Law Ctr., Roswell, 2001—02; adviser Roswell Hispanic Chamber, 2001—02. Republican. Avocations: volunteer work, painting, sculpting, reading, puzzles. Home: 601 S Missouri Roswell NM 88203 Office: Trinity Group 209 B N Main Roswell NM 88201 E-mail: sspadilla2000@yahoo.com.

PADRICK, KERRY BRIDGES, elementary school educator; d. Dale Eugene and Dolly Rader Bridges; m. Will E. Padrick, Jr., June 15, 1985; children: Jacob Eugene, Nicholas Alexander. AA, Indian River C.C., 1983; BS in Pub. Rels., U. Fla., 1985; student in Ednl. Leadership, Fla. Atlantic U. Tchr. Sch. Bd. St. Lucie County, Ft. Pierce, Fla., 1989—, learning resource specialist, 1995—98, curriculum specialist, 1998—2002. Mem.: St. Lucie County Reading Assn., Fla. Reading Assn., Assn. Supr. and Curriculum Devel., Delta Kappa Gamma (2d v.p. 2000, pres. 2002—). Republican. Baptist. Office: Dan McCarty Middle School 1201 Mississippi Ave Fort Pierce FL 34950

PAEGLE, JULIE SOPHIA, writer, editor, educator; b. Salt Lake City, Dec. 3, 1971; d. Jan and Julia Elvira Paegle; m. Stephen Lehigh, Sept. 22, 2002; 1 child, Jan Connor Lehigh. BS, U. Utah, 1990, BA, 1997, MFA, postgrad., U. Utah, 2000—. Rsch. asst. Lamont Doherty Geol. Inst., Palisades, NY, 1992, Geophys. Inst., Fairbanks, Alaska, 1994; tchg. fellow dept. English U. Utah, Salt Lake City, 1998—; tchg. fellow Writing Program, Salt Lake City, 1998—; writer in residence Wasatch Elem., Salt Lake City, 1999—2002; English tchr. Upward Bound, Fairbanks, 1999; poetry editor Quar. West, Salt Lake City, 2001—. Author: That Other Sky; contbr. poetry to various publs. Pres. Amnesty Internat., Salt Lake City, 1988—92. Mem.: Acad. Am. Writers.

PAETZOLD, MARY E. agricultural products supplier; b. 1950; BA in Math., Montclair State U. CPA. Audit ptnr. KPMG Peat Marwick LLP, 1973; v.p., CFO Ecogen Inc., Langhorne, Pa., 1994—, bd. dirs., 1996—. Mem. bus. adv. coun. Montclair State U. Mem. AICPA, N.J. Soc. CPA's. Office: Ecogen Inc 2000 W Cabot Blvd # 170 Langhorne PA 19047

PAGANO, MICHELINA OLIMPIA, art director, writer; d. Domenico and Mary Pagano; m. Anthony Jude Parente, Sept. 17, 1960. Grad. h.s., Floral Pk., N.Y. Art dir. Lintas Worldwide Advt., N.Y.C., 1986—88; sr. art dir. Wells, Rich, Greene, N.Y.C., 1988—93, N.W. Ayer & Ptnrs. Advt., N.Y.C., 1993—95; sr. v.p., group creative dir. D'Arcy Worldwide Advt., N.Y.C., 1996—2000; freelance creative dir. & creative cons. Virgo Comm. LLC, N.Y.C., 2002—. Instr. advt. Sch. Visual Arts, N.Y.C., 1989—90; freelance creative dir. & cons. various advt. agencies and advertisers, N.Y.C., 2000—. Author: (novel) The Road To Jude, 2004, Grace of the Clouds, 2002, (children's book) The Magic Paint Box, 1991; writer and co-prodr. (short film) Two Shoes, dir., co-writer and co-prodr. Wishful Thinking, co-creator, dir., writer and co-prodr. Return of the Masterminds, dir., co-prodr. Mini Happy Returns, co-dir., co-writer, co-prodr. (music video) Suit for Jesus. Design and mktg. Fourth Universalist Soc., N.Y.C., 2003—. Recipient Cannes Bronze Lion, Cannes Internat. Festival, 1988, Bronze medal, N.Y. Festivals Internat., 1991, Bronze Effie, Effie Awards, 1994, Golden Trailer award, 1999, Internat. Advt. award, London, 1991. Mem.: Ind. Film Project (assoc.), N.Y. Friar's Club (assoc.). E-mail: mickipagano@yahoo.com.

PAGE, ANNE RUTH, gifted education educator, education specialist; b. Norfolk, Va., Apr. 13, 1949; d. Amos Purnell and Ruth Martin (Hill) Bailey; m. Peter Smith Page, Apr. 24, 1971; children: Edgar Bailey, Emmett McBrannon. BA, N.C. Wesleyan Coll.; student, Fgn. Lang. League; postgrad., N.C. State U.; student, Overseas Linguistic Studies, France, Spain, Eng., 1978, 85, 86. Cert. tchr., N.C. Tchr. Cary (N.C.) Sr. High Sch., 1971-72; tchr., head dept. Daniels Mid. Sch., Raleigh, N.C., 1978-83; chmn. fgn. lang. dept. Martin Mid. Gifted and Talented, Raleigh, N.C., 1983—. Leadership team Senate Bill 2 Core co-chair; dir. student group Overseas Studies, Am. Coun. for Internat. Studies, France, Spain, Eng., 1982, 84, 86, 88; bd. dirs. N.T.H., Inc., Washington; cert. mentor tchr. Wake County Pub. Schs., 1989; dir. student exchs. between Martin Mid. Sch. and Sevigné Inst. of Compiegne, France. Sunday sch. tchr. Fairmont United Meth. Ch., Raleigh, 1983-85. Mem. Alpha Delta Kappa. Democrat. Home: 349 Wilmot Dr Raleigh NC 27606-1232 Office: Martin Mid Sch GT 1701 Ridge Rd Raleigh NC 27607-6737

PAGE, BERNADETTE RYAN, emergency physician; b. Chgo., Feb. 10, 1946; d. Frank James and Bernadette Rosamund (Halm) Ryan; m. Jack R. Page, Dec. 23, 1967; children: Jeremy, Sara, Alex, Rachel. MD, Loyola U., 1970. Diplomate Am. Bd. Emergency Medicine. Rotating O intern San Bernardino (Calif.) Hosp., 1970-71; resident in pediat. Orange County Med. Ctr., Anaheim, Calif., 1971-72; staff physician emergency rm. Kaiser Permanente, Bellflower, Calif., 1972-73, St. Mary's Hosp./Long Beach (Calif.) Cmty., 1973-76, Appalachian Regional Hosp., Beckley, W.Va., 1976-78, Charleston (W.Va.) Area Med. Ctr., 1978-82; staff physician, owner Doctors Urgent Care, Charleston, 1982-88; staff physician Orange Chatham Comp. Health, Carrboro, N.C., 1988-91; attending physician emergency dept. Duke U. Med. Ctr., Durham, N.C., 1991—. Chair violence prevention com. Am. Assn. Women Emergency Physicians, Durham, 1994-98; mem. adv. coun. family violence AMA, 1994-98; mem. nat. faculty ACLS Am. Heart Assn., 1976-82. Active Durham City-County Violence Prevention Com., 1993-98; co-chair Religious Coalition for a Nonviolent Durham, 1997—. Fellow Am. Coll. Emergency Physicians (mem. violence prevention com. 1997-99). Democrat. Roman Catholic. Office: Duke U Med Ctr PO Box 3096 Durham NC 27715-3096

PAGE, CHERYL MILLER, elementary school educator; BS in Social Sciences, Calif. Polytechnic State Univ., San Luis Obispo, Calif., 1975. Cert. health edn. specialist Nat. Commn. for Health Edn. Credentialing, Edn. Certification Program Calif. Polytechnic State Univ., San Luis Obispo, Calif., 1976. Elem. educator Dalles Pub. Schs., Dalles, Oreg., 1980—86, Salem-Keizer Pub. Schs., Salem, Oreg., 1986—95, middle sch. health educator, 1995—2002, health educator; prevention curriculum resource specialist Salem-Keizer Pub. Schs. Mid Valley. Named Oreg. Outstanding Elementary Health Educator, 1991, Nat. Health Edn. Profl. Yr., Oreg. Outstanding Secondary Health Educator of Yr., Vol. of Yr., Am. Cancer Soc.; recipient Tambrands award, Am. Assn. Health Edn., 1996, Health and Safety Educator of Year, NW Div. AAHPERD, 1996; Partnership Safe Sch. Healthy Students Grant, Salem, Oreg., 2002—. Mem.: Oreg. Alliance Health, Phys. Edn., Recreation and Dance (treas. 1992—96, pres. 2001—02), Oreg. Assn. for the Advancement of Health Edn. (sec./treas. 1990—92), Nat. Bd. for Profl. Tchg. Stds. (bd. mem.). Avocations: running, reading. Office: Salem-Keizer Sch Dist PO Box 12024 Salem OR 97309

PAGE, LINDA ANN, special education educator, language educator; b. Port Arthur, Tex., June 9, 1947; d. Edward Ernest and Pearl (Martin) Kubitz; m. Donny Roy Page, Dec. 27, 1969; 1 child, Adrian Nicole. BA, U. Ga., 1969; MEd, U. Houston, 1977. Cert. tchr. spl. edn. Tex., tchr. ESL. Tchr. spl. edn. Burke County Bd. Edn., Waynesboro, Ga., 1973—75, Houston Ind. Sch. Dist., 1975—76, Ft. Bend Ind. Sch. Dist., Stafford, Tex., 1976—81, Tomball (Tex.) Ind. Sch. Dist., 1981—82, 1985—88, Conroe (Tex.) Ind. Sch. Dist., 1983—85; tchr. spl. edn., tchr. ESL Klein (Tex.) Ind. Sch. Dist., 1988—. Mem.: NEA, Alliance Francaise-Houston, Tex. State French Symposium, Am. Assn. Tchrs. French, Am. Assn. Ret. Persons. Democrat. Lutheran. Avocations: travel, reading, gardening, exercise. Home: 15 Mallard Glen Pl The Woodlands TX 77381 Personal E-mail: dpage@houston.rr.com.

PAGE, LINDA KAY, bank executive; b. Wadsworth, Ohio, Oct. 4, 1943; d. Frederick Meredith and Martha Irene (Vance) P. Student, Ohio U., 1976-77; grad. banking program, U. Wis., 1982-84; BA, Capital U. cert. in pers. Am. Bankers Assn. Asst. v.p., gen. mgr. Bancohio Corp., Columbus, 1975-78, v.p., dist. mgr., 1979-80, v.p., mgr. employee rels., 1980-81, v.p., divsn. mgr., 1982-83; commr. of banks State of Ohio, Columbus, 1983-87, dir. Dept. Commerce, 1988-90; pres., CEO Star Bank Ctrl. Ohio, Columbus, 1990-92; state dir. Rural Devel/USDA, 1993-2000; pub. svc. dir. City of Columbus, 2000—04. Bd. dirs. Clark County Mental Health Bd., Springfield, Ohio, 1982-83, Springfield Met. Housing, 1982-83, Pvt. Industry Coun. Franklin County, 1990-2000—, Ohio Highe Edn. Facilities Commn., 1990-93, Ohio Devel. Corp., 1995—; bd. advisers Orgn. Indsl. Standards, Springfield, 1982-83; trustee League Against Child Abuse, 1986-90; treas. Ohio Housing Fin. Agy., 1980-90; vice chair Fed. Res. Bd. Consumer Adv. Coun., 1989-91; trustee, treas. Columbus State C.C. Found., 1990-2000, pres., 1997-99; bd. dirs. Columbus Urban league, 1992-98; mem. Comp-Drug Bd., 1998-2000; mem. Mid Ohio Regional Planning Commn., 2000-04. Recipient Leadership Columbus award Sta. WTVN and Columbus Leadership Program, 1975, 82, Outstanding Svc. award Clark County Mental Health Bd., 1983, Giles Mitchell Housing award, 1996. Mem.: LWV (treas. edn. fund 1992—2000), Women in Transp., Risk Mgmt. Assn., Women in Transp. (bd. trustees Ohio chpt. 2000, bd. dirs. 2002), Internat. Womens Forum, Am. Pub. Works Assn. (treas. Ohio chpt. 2000—03, treas. 2002, govt. affairs com. 2002—03), Ohio Mortgage Bankers Assn. (legis. commn. 1998), Ohio Devel. Assn., Ohio Bankers Assn. (bd. dirs. 1982—83, 1991—92), Conf. State Bank Suprs. (dist. chmn. 1984—85, sec.-treas. 1985—90, bd. dirs.), Women Execs. in State Govt., Am. Bankers Assn. (govt. rels. coun. 1990—92), Nat. Assn. Bank Women (pres. 1980—81). Democrat. Avocations: animal protection, reading, cultural arts, travel. Home: 1477 Sedgefield Dr New Albany OH 43054-9431 E-mail: lpage@insight.rr.com.

PAGE, MARY STANCILL, insurance agency executive; b. Greenville, N.C., July 8, 1958; d. William Samuel and Viola (Sutton) Stancill; children: Andrew, Rusty, Derrick. Grad., high sch., 1976. CPCU; cert. profl. ins. woman, ins. counselor, assoc. in underwriting, accredited advisor in ins. Bookkeeper The Fixture House, Greenville, NC, 1979; ins. agt., officer mgr. Bill Clifton Agy., 1979—83; personal and comml. lines agt. Mid-Atlantic Ins., 1983—84; clk., personal lines agt. Tadlock Ins. Agy., Inc., 1971—79, personal and comml. lines agt., 1984—88, mgr. comml. lines, 1988—91, v.p. ops., 1991—95; acct. mgr. BB&T Ins. Svs., 1995—2003, asst. v.p., 2003—. Recipient several scholarships. Mem. Nat. Assn. Ins. Women, N.C. Assn. Ins. Women (v.p. 1990-91, pres.-elect 1991-92, pres. 1992-93), Soc. CPCU's (continuing profl. devel. program 1993, pres. Downeast subchpt. N.C. chpt. 1989—), Carolina Assn. Profl. Ins. Agts., Ind. Ins. Agts. N.C., Soc. Cert. Ins. Counselors, Pitt County Assn. Ins. Profls. (sec. 1987-88, pres. 1988-89, com. chmn.). Democrat. Baptist. Avocations: reading, piano, aerobics, biking. Office: BB&T Ins Svcs Inc 543 S Evans St Greenville NC 27858

PAGE, PATRICIA (PATTY) NEWTON, real estate broker, real estate company executive; b. Nashville, Tenn., May 16, 1963; d. James Kelton and Alice (Clement) Cuff; m. Larry Jim Page. Grad., Realtor Inst., 1999. Cert. affiliate broker North Ctrl. Inst., 1993, accredited credit buyer rep. Nat. Assn. Realtors, 2001, lic. real estate broker, cert. residential specialist. Sr. customer svc. rep. Comdata Corp., Brentwood, Tenn., 1981—92; realtor Century 21 ABC, Clarksville, Tenn., 1993—94, Lakeland Properties, Dover, Tenn., 1994—96; designated realtor Cherry Properties, Dover, Tenn., 1996—2003; owner, broker Patty Page Properties, LLC, 2004—. Mem.: Nat. Assn. Realtors (coun. residential specialist 2002). Methodist. Avocations: Continued Education, travel. Office: Patty Page Properties LLC 620 Donelson Pkwy Ste B Dover TN 37058 Office Phone: 931-232-5082. Personal E-mail: PattyPageProp@aol.com.

PAGE, PATTI (CLARA ANN FOWLER), vocalist; b. Claremore, Okla., Nov. 8, 1927; m. Jerry Filiciotto, 1990. Country singer Sta. KTUL-AM, Tulsa; with Art Klauser and his Ok 1ahomans Tulsa; with Meet Patti Page Show Sta. KTUL-AM, Tulsa; vocalist Breakfast Club, Chgo., 1948, Benny Goodman Septet, 1948; recording artist, 1950—. Appeared extensively on TV during the '50s on shows such as the Scott Music Hall, the Big Record variety show and her own shows for NBC and CBS; made several movies including "Elmer Gantry", 1960, "Dondi", 1961, and "Boys Night Out", 1962; prodr. Patti Page Pure Maple Syrup and Pancake Mix. First hit record "Confess", 1949, first million-seller "With My Eyes Wide Open I'm Dreaming", hits throughout the '50s included "I Don't Care If the Sun Don't Shine", "All My Love" (U.S. #1), "The Tennessee Waltz", "Mockin' Bird Hill", "I Went to Your Wedding", "Once in a While", "You Belong to Me", "Why Don't You Believe Me", (How Much Is) "That Doggie in the Window", "Let Me Go, Lover", "Allegheny Moon", "Old Cape Cod." Records continued to sell well into the 1960s; last U.S. Top 10 entry 1965 title song from Bette Davis-Olivia De Havilland movie "Hush, Hush, Sweet Charlotte." In 1970s recorded mainly country material; in the '80s signed with Nashville-based Plantation Records. In 1988 gained excellent reviews when she played the Ballroom in N.Y.C., her first appearance in that city in nearly 20 years; albums: Patti Page Live at Carnegie Hall, 1999, Cocktail Hour, 2000, Brand New Tennessee Waltz, 2001, Sweet Sounds of Christmas, 2002, Child of Mine, 2002; host (radio show) Patti Page Show. Winner Grammy award for Best Traditional Popular Vocal Performance, 1999; Living Legend award Okla. Jazz Hall of Fame, 2002. Office: Filiciottos Hilltop Farm Inc 484 Lang Rd Bath NH 03740

PAGE, POLLY E. state agency administrator; b. Fairmont, W. Va. children: Larry, Paul. Student, Fairmont State Coll. Mem. Aurora City Coun., Aurora, Colo., 1987—95; commr. Arapahoe County, Colo., 1995—2000, Pub. Utilities Commn., Denver, 2000—. Chmn. Arapahoe County Pub. Airport Authority, Arapahoe Water & Wastewater Authority; bd. dir. Aurora Econ. Devel. Coun.; chmn. Denver Regional Coun. of Gov.; bd. dir. E-470 Pub. Hwy. Authority, Metro Wastewater Reclamation Dist.; chmn. S.E. Trans. Advocacy Group; bd. trustees S.W. Bus. Partnership. Auxilliary mem. Salvation Army; den mother Cub Scouts; home rm. mother; bd. dir. YMCA, Comitis Crisis Ctr. Recipient Vol. of Yr. award, Arapahoe Rep. Party. Office: Colorado Dept Regulatory Agencies PUC 158 Logan St 022 Denver CO 80203

PAGE, SALLY JACQUELYN, university official, management educator; b. Saginaw, Mich., 1943; d. William Henry and Doris Effie (Knippel) P. BA, U. Iowa, 1965; MBA, So. Ill. U., 1973. Copy editor C.V. Mosby Co., St. Louis, 1965-69; editl. cons. Editl. Assocs., Edwardsville, Ill., 1969-70; rsch. adminstr. So. Ill. U., 1970-74, asst. to pres., affirmative action officer, 1974-77; officer of instn. U. N.D., Grand Forks, 1977—, lectr. mgmt., 1978—. Polit. comentator Sta. KFJM, Nat. Public Radio affiliate, 1981-90; mem. mayor's com. Employment of People With Disabilities, 1980-97. Contbr. articles to profl. jours. Chmn. N.D. Equal Opportunity Affirmative Action Officers, 1987-2003; chmn. NDUS Diversity Coun.; pres. Pine to Prairie coun. Girl Scouts U.S., 1980-85; mem. employment com. Ill. Commn. on Status of Women, 1976-77; mem. Bicentennial Com., Edwardsville, 1976, Bikeway Task Force, Edwardsville, 1975-77, Bus. Leadership Network, ARC Upper Valley; bd. dirs. Grand Forks Homes, 1985—2003, pres., 1996-2001; mem. Civil Svc. Rev. Task Force, Grand Forks, 1982, civil svc. commr., 1983-98, chmn., 1984, 86, 88, 92, 96; ruling elder 1st Presbyn.; mem. Grand Forks Mayor's Adv. Cabinet, 1998-2000. Mem. AAUW (dir. Ill. 1975-77), PEO, Coll. and Univ. Pers. Assn. (rsch. and publs. bd. 1982-84), Soc. Human Resource Mgmt., Am. Assn. Affirmative Action, ADA Coords. Democrat. Presbyterian. Home: 3121 Cherry St Grand Forks ND 58201-7461 Office: U ND Grand Forks ND 58202 E-mail: Sally-Page@mail.und.nodak.edu.

PAGEL, INGA ANN, accountant; b. Silver City, N.Mex., Sept. 30, 1949; d. Lester Richard and Claudia Marcella (Huckaby) Lee; m. Russell Joseph Cortright, June 25, 1986 (dec. Jan. 2000), m. Jürgen Pagel, Sept. 6, 2003. BS in Acctg., Ariz. State U., 1976, MBA, 1978; postgrad., Walden U., 1995. CPA, Ariz., Tex. Sole practice cert. pub. acctg., Ariz., 1981—. Cons. in field. Mem. AICPA. Republican. Episcopalian. Avocation: travel. E-mail: icortright@aol.com.

PAGLIA, CAMILLE, writer, humanities educator; b. Endicott, N.Y., 1947; d. Pasquale John and Lydia (Colapietro) P. BA in English summa cum laude with highest honors, SUNY, Binghamton, 1968; MPhil, Yale U., 1971, PhD in English, 1974. Mem. faculty Bennington (Vt.) Coll., 1972-80; vis. lectr. Wesleyan U., 1980, Yale U., New Haven, 1980-84; prof. humanities U. Arts, Phila., 1984-2000, univ. prof. and prof. humanities and media studies, 2000—. Author: Sexual Personae: Art and Decadence from Nefertiti to Emily Dickinson, 1990, Sex, Art, and American Culture, 1992, Vamps and Tramps: New Essays, 1994, Alfred Hitchcock's "The Birds", 1998; columnist: Salon.com, 1995—2001; contbg. editor: Interview Magazine, 2001—. Office: Univ Arts 320 S Broad St Philadelphia PA 19102-4994

PAGON, ROBERTA ANDERSON, pediatrics educator; b. Boston, Oct. 4, 1945; d. Donald Grigg and Erna Louise (Goettsch) Anderson; m. Garrett Dunn Pagon Jr., July 1, 1967; children: Katharine Blye, Garrett Dunn III, Alyssa Grigg, Alexander Goettsch. BA, Stanford U., 1967; MD, Harvard U., 1972. Diplomate Am. Bd. Pediatrics, Am. Bd. Med. Genetics. Pediatric intern U. Wash. Affiliated Hosp., Seattle, 1972-73, resident in pediatrics, 1973-75; fellow in med. genetics U. Wash. Sch. Medicine, Seattle, 1976-79, asst. prof. pediatrics, 1979-84, assoc. prof., 1984-92, prof., 1992—. Prin. investigator, editor in chief GeneTests (www.genetests.org), Seattle, 1992—; pres. Am. Bd. Med. Genetics, 2002, 03; bd. sci. counselors Nat. Human Genome Rsch. Inst., NIH, 2000—04. Sponsor N.W. region U.S. Pony Club, 1985-94. Mem. Am. Soc. Human Genetics, Am. Coll. Med. Genetics, Western Soc. Pedat. Rsch., Phi Beta Kappa. Avocations: hiking, backpacking, horseback riding. Office: Children's Hosp & Reg Med Ctr Divsn Genetics & Devel M2-9 4800 Sand Point Way NE Seattle WA 98105-0371 Office Phone: 206-987-2056.

PAGOTTO, LOUISE, English language educator; b. Montreal, June 22, 1950; came to U.S., 1980; d. Albert and Elena (Tibi) P. BA, Marianopolis Coll., Montreal, 1971; TESL Diploma, U. Papua New Guinea, 1975; MA, McGill U., 1980; PhD, U. Hawaii at Manoa, Honolulu, 1987. Tchr. Yarapos H.S., Wewak, Papua New Guinea, 1971-73, Electricity Commn. Tng. Coll., Port Moresby, Papua New Guinea, 1975-76, Coll. of Marshall Islands, Majuro, summers 1983-91, Leeward C.C., Pearl City, Hawaii, 1988-89, Kapiolani C.C., Honolulu, 1989—, interim asst. dean instrn., 1996-98, chair dept. lang. arts, 1998—2000, interim asst. dean of arts and scis., 2000—02, acting dean arts and scis., 2002—. Presenter in field. Contbr. articles to profl. jours. McConnell fellow McGill U., 1979, Can. Coun. fellow, 1980-83; recipient Excellence in Teaching award Bd. of Regents, 1993. Mem. AAUW, Linguistic Soc. Am., Nat. Coun. Tchrs. English, Hawaii Coun. Tchrs. English. Avocations: water sports (swimming, bodyboarding), walking. Office: Kapiolani CC 4303 Diamond Head Rd Honolulu HI 96816-4421 E-mail: pagotto@hawaii.edu.

PAIGE, KATHLEEN K. naval officer; b. Schenectady, N.Y., Aug. 31, 1948; m. David Tuma. BS, U. N.H., 1970; MS, Naval Postgrad. Sch., 1976; grad., Def. Sys. Mgmt. Coll.; grad. program for execs., Cornell U. Commd. USN, advanced through grades to rear admiral; acquisition mgr. Navy's Std. Embedded Computer Resource Office; AEGIS C3 warfare officer USN; baseline mgr. combat sys. divsn. AEGIS Shipbuilding Program; chief engr. Naval Surface Warfare Ctr., Port Hueneme; tech. dir. AEGIS Program Office; comdr. Naval Surface Warfare Ctr., Arlington, Va., 1996-98, admiral, 1998—. Decorated Legion of Merit. Office: Naval Sea Systems Command SE#1100 1333 Isaac Hull Ave Washington DC 20376-1100

PAIN, BETSY M. lawyer; b. Albertville, Ala., Aug. 29, 1950; d. Charles Riley and Jean Faye (Rains) Stone; m. William F. Pain, Nov. 18, 1977; children: Taylor Holland, Emily Anne Pain. AA, Northeastern Okla. A&M, Miami, 1970; BA, U. Okla., 1974, JD, 1976. Bar: Okla. 1977; U.S. Dist. Ct.

(we. dist.) 1979. Staff atty. Okla. Dept. Corrections, Oklahoma City, 1978-79; gen. counsel Okla. Pardon and Parole Bd., Oklahoma City, 1979-84, exec. dir., 1983—88; corp. counsel Roberts, Schornick & Assocs., Inc., Norman, Okla., 1990-2000, Atkins Benham, Inc., 2002; chief legal officer The Benham Cos., Inc., Oklahoma City, 2002—. Editor: (newsletter) RSA Environ. Report, 1991—. With extended family program Juvenile Svcs., Inc. Cleveland County, Okla., 1983-91. Mem. NAFE, Okla. Bar Assn. Democrat. Methodist. Avocations: reading, needlework, church activities. Office: The Benham Cos Inc 9400 N Broadway Oklahoma City OK 73114 Office Phone: 405-478-5353. E-mail: betsy.pain@benham.com.

PAINE, KATHARINE DELAHAYE, communications research company executive; Journalist Washington Post.; later for Boston Herald, San Jose Mercury News-San Francisco Chronicle; dir. corp. comm. Lotus Devel. Corp.; owner, The Delahaye Group, pub. rels. and mktg. comm. rsch., until 1999; pres. Delahaye Medialink Comm. Rsch., Medialink Inc., N.Y.C., 1999—. Co-chmn. U.S. Pub. Rels. Task Force; U.S. liaison to European Stds. Task Force; spkr. in field. Contbr. numerous articles to profl. publs. Office: Delahaye Medialink Comm Rsch Medialink Inc 708 3rd Ave Fl Dave9 New York NY 10017-4201

PAINE, LYNN, academic administrator; m. Tom Paine; 3 children. Grad Summa Cum Laude, Smith Coll.; PhD in moral philosophy, Oxford U.; law degree, Harvard Law Sch. Lawyer Hill & Barlow, Boston; asst. prof. Georgetown U. Bus. Sch; prof. U. Va., Darden Sch., Nat. Cheng Chi U., Taiwan; John G. McLean prof. Harvard Bus. Sch., course head, MBA ethics module Leadership, Values, and Decision Making, 1996—2002, co-leader, MBA course: Leadership and Corporate Accountability, 2004—. Permanent mem. Luce Scholar Selection Panel, 1987—. Author: Leadership, Ethics, and Organizational Integrity, 1997, Value Shift: Why Companies Must Merge Social and Financial Imperatives to Achieve Superior Performance, 2002 (Best Bus. Books, 2002, Library Journal, 2002). Mem. adv. bd. Leadership Forum Internat.; mem. Conference Bd. Blue-Ribbon Commn. on Public Trust and Private Enterprise. Named Luce Scholar, 1976—77. Mem.: Mass. Bar Assn, Phi Beta Kappa. Office: Harvard Bus Sch Soldiers Field Boston MA 02163*

PAINTER, ELIZABETH MARIE, insurance agent, financial consultant; b. Lexington, Ky., Apr. 11, 1972; d. Lloyd E. and Bobbie Painter. BS in Econ., Centre Coll., Danville, Ky., 1990—94; MBA in Internat. Mgmt., Am. Grad. Sch. Internat. Mgmt., Glendale, Ariz., 1994—96. Long-term care profl. Health Ins. Assn. Am., 2003; cert. fin. advisor Inst. of Bus. and Fin., 1999, Assn. Investment Mgmt. and Rsch., 2000. Sr. fin. analyst Brown Forman Corp., Louisville, 1996—98; mgmt. cons. Balance - Klyb, Dnipropetrovsk, Ukraine, 1998—99; v.p. Painter Fin., Louisville, 1999—. Bd. dirs. Centre Coll. Alumni Assn., Danville, Ky.; v.p. fundraising Jr. League of Louisville, 2002—03; new mem. chair Actors Theatre Devel. Bd. Exec. Com., Louisville. Named one of Top 40 under 40, Bus. First, 2002. Mem.: Fin. Planning Assn., Louisville Soc. Fin. Analysts, Louisville Com. on Fgn. Rels., Omicron Delta Kappa. Roman Catholic. Avocations: travel, running, sailing. Office: Painter Fin PO Box 385 Greenville KY 42345 Office Phone: 502-893-9927. E-mail: epainter@painterfinancial.com.

PAINTER, NELL IRVIN, historian, educator, writer; b. Houston, Aug. 2, 1942; BA, U. Calif., Berkeley, 1964; student, U. Bordeaux, France, 1962-63, U. Ghana, 1965-66; MA, UCLA, 1967; PhD, Harvard U., 1974. Teaching fellow Harvard U., Cambridge, Mass., 1969-70, 72-74; asst. prof. history U. Pa., Phila., 1974-77, assoc. prof., 1977-80; prof. history U. N.C., Chapel Hill, 1980-88, Princeton (N.J.) U., 1988-91, acting dir. Afro-Am. Studies Program, 1990-91, Edwards Prof. Am. History, 1991—. Russell Sage vis. prof. history Hunter Coll., CUNY, N.Y.C., 1985-86. Author: Exodusters: Black Migration to Kansas After Reconstruction, 1976, The Narrative of Hosea Hudson: His Life as a Negro Communist in the South, 1979, Standing at Armageddon: The United States 1877-1919, 1987, Sojourner Truth: A Life, A Symbol, 1996, Southern History Across the Color Line, 2002; editor: Gender and Am. Culture Series; mem. editl. bd. Jour. Women's History, Ency. Americana; contbr. articles to profl. jours. Ford Found. fellow, 1971-72, Am. Coun. Learned Soc. fellow, 1976-77, Charles Warren Ctr. Studies in Am. History fellow, 1976-77, Radcliffe/Bunting Inst. fellow, 1976-77, Nat. Humanities Ctr. fellow, 1978-79, Guggenheim fellow, 1982-83, Ctr. Advanced Study in Behavioral Scis. fellow, 1988-89, Kate B. and Hall J. Peterson fellow Am. Antiquarian Soc., 1991, NEH fellow, 1992-93; recipient Ccoretta Scott King award AAUW, 1969-70, Grad. Soc. medal Radcliffe Coll. Alumnae, 1984, Candace award Nat. Coalition One Hundred Black Women, 1986; named U. Calif. at Berkeley Alumnae of Yr., 1989. Mem. Am. Coun. Learned Soc., Am. Antiquarian Soc., Am. Hist. Assn. (mem. program com. 1976-78, J. Franklin Jameson fellowship com. 1978-79, Beveridge and Dunning prizes com. 1985-87, mem. coun. 1991-93), Am. Studies Assn. (mem. internat. com. 1983-88, mem. nat. coun. 1989-92, mem. adv. coun. 1991-92), Assn. Study Afro-Am. Life and History (mem. program com. 1976), Assn. Black Women Historians (mem. rsch. com. 1980—, nat. dir. 1982-84, chair Brown pub. prize com. 1983-86, 88 91), Berkshire Conf. Women Historians (mem. program com. 1976), Inst. So. Studies (mem. exec. com. 1987-88), Orgn. Am. Historians (mem. com. status women 1975-77, mem. program com. 1977-79, 83-85, Frederick Jackson Turner award com. 1983, mem. exec. bd. 1984-87, chair ad hoc com. on minority historians 1985-87, chair Avery O. Craven award 1994-95), Nat. Book Found. (chair non-fiction jury, Nat. Book awards 1994), Social Sci. Rsch. Coun. (mem. com. social sci. pers. 1977-78), So. Hist. Assn. (chair Syndor prize com. 1991-92), So. Regional Coun. (mem. Lillian Smith Book prize com. 1986, mem. exec. com. 1987), Soc. Am. Historians (chair Parkman prize com. 1993—). Office: Princeton U History Dept Princeton NJ 08544-0001

PAINTER, VANESSA L. music educator; d. Donald L. and Trudi A. Whaley; m. Michael S. Painter, July 29, 2000. B in Music Edn., U. Toledo, 1998; MusM, Kent State U., 2003. Vocal music dir. Tallmadge (Ohio) City Schs., 1998—2002, Minerva (Ohio) Local Schs., 2002—. Mem.: Ohio Music Educators Assn., Music Educators Nat. Conf., Nat. Assn. Music Educators. Avocations: scrapbooks, piano, musical theatre, bicycling, boating.

PAITICH, OLIVIA, project coordinator, office manager; b. Bucharest, Romania, May 29, 1965; came to U.S., 1987; d. Lucian and Floarea (Dragan) Dragulinescu; m. Srgian Paitich, June 20, 1992; children: Ashley Gordana, Justin Eric. AA, Northeastern U., Chgo., 1990. Legal sec. Casualty Ins. Co., Chgo., 1990-91, legal asst., 1991-95; exec. asst. Fremont Compensation, Chgo., 1995-2001; tech. exec. asst. ABN AMRO, Chgo., 2001—. Mem. NAFE, Chgo. Coun. Fgn. Affairs. Eastern Orthodox. Avocations: reading, jogging, travel. Home: 4844 N Nordica Ave Chicago IL 60656-3821 Office: ABN AMRO 540 W Madison Ave #2012 Chicago IL 60661 E-mail: olivia.paitich@abnamro.com.

PAIVA-WEED, M. TERESA, state legislator; b. Newport, R.I., Nov. 5, 1959; m. Mark Weed. BA, magna cum laude, Providence Coll., 1981; JD, Catholic Univ. of America, 1984. Bar: R.I., 1984. Asst. city solicitor city of Newport; mem. R.I. Senate, Dist. 49, Providence, 1992—; chairwoman senate com. on judiciary R.I. State Senate, 1997-98. Mem. Newport County Bar Assn., Rhode Island Bar Assn., ABA. Office: RI State Senate State House Rm 312 Providence RI 02903

PAJUNEN, GRAZYNA ANNA, electrical engineer, educator; b. Warsaw, Dec. 15, 1951; d. Romuald and Danuta (Trzaskowska) Pyffel; m. Veikko J. Pajunen (div. 1990); children: Tony, Thomas, Sebastian. MSc, Warsaw Tech. U., 1975; PhD in Elec. Engring., Helsinki (Finland) U., 1984. Grad. engr. Oy Stromberg Ab, Helsinki, 1974, design engr., 1975-79; teaching/rsch. asst. Helsinki U. Tech., 1979-85; vis. asst. prof. dept. elec. and computer engring. Fla. Atlantic U., 1985-86, asst. prof. elec. and computer engring., 1986-90, assoc. prof. elec. engring., 1990—; vis. asst. prof. dept elec. engring. UCLA, 1988-89. Cons. Motorola; lectr. in field. Author: Adaptive Systems - Identification and Control, 1986; contbr. articles to profl. jours.; holder 14 patents in field. Grantee Found. Tech. in Finland, Ahlstrom Found., 1982, Wihuri Found., 1982, Foun.d Tech. in Finland, 1983, Acad. Finland, 1984, EIES Seed grantee, 1986, Finnish Ministry Edn., 1985, NSF, 1988-89, 93-94, State of Fla. High Tech. and Industry Coun., 1989. Mem. IEEE, Control Sys. Soci., N.Y. Acad. Sci., AAUW, SIAM, Control and Sys. Theory Group. Roman Catholic. Avocations: jazz, ballet, piano, jogging, skiing. Office: Fla Atlantic U Dept Elec Engring Boca Raton FL 33431

PAK, SE RI, professional golfer; b. Daejeon, Korea, Sept. 28, 1977; Professional golfer LPGA Tour, 1997—. Mem. KLPGA, 1996, 97. Recipient Rolex Rookie of Yr. award. Winner Seoul Ladies Open, 1997, Jamie Farr Kroger Classic, 1998, 99; Giant Eagle LPGA Classic, 1998, McDonald's LPGA Championship, 1998, U.S. Women's Open, 1998, Shop-Rite LPGA Classic, 1999; qualified for 14 events, winning 6 times and placing 2d 7 times. Address: LPGA 100 International Golf Dr Daytona Beach FL 32124-1082

PAK, SUCHIN, newscaster; b. Korea; Degree in polit. sci., U. Calif., Berkeley. Corres. MTV News, N.Y.C., 2001—. Office: MTV Networks 1515 Broadway New York NY 10036

PAKENHAM, ROSALIE MULLER WRIGHT, magazine and newspaper editor; b. Newark, June 20, 1942; d. Charles and Angela (Fortunata) Muller; m. Lynn Wright, Jan. 13, 1962; children: James Anthony Meador, Geoffrey Shepard; m. E. Michael Pakenham, Sept. 29, 2001. BA in English, Temple U., 1965. Mng. editor Suburban Life mag., Orange, N.J., 1960-62; assoc. editor Phila. mag., 1962-64, mng. editor, 1969-73; founding editor Womensports mag., San Mateo, Calif., 1973-75; editor scene sect. San Francisco Examiner, 1975-77; exec. editor New West mag., San Francisco and Beverly Hills, Calif., 1977-81; features and Sunday editor San Francisco Chronicle, 1981-87, asst. mng. editor features, 1987-96; v.p. and editor-in-chief Sunset Mag, Menlo Park, Calif., 1996—2001. Editl. cons., 2002 ; tchr. mag. writing U. Calif., Berkeley, 1975—76; participant pub. procs. course Stanford U., 1977—79; chmn. mag. judges at conf. Coun. Advancement and Support of Edn., 1980, judge, 84. Contbr. numerous mag. articles, critiques, revs., Compton's Ency. Mem.: Internat. Assn. Culinary Profls., Am. Soc. Mag. Editors, Am. Newspaper Pubs. Assn. (pub. task force on minorities in newspaper bus. 1988—89, Chronicle minority recruiter 1987—94), Am. Assn. Sunday and Feature Editors (treas. 1984, sec. 1985, 1st v.p. 1986, pres. 1987, Hall of Fame 1999), Washington D.C. Women's Forum, Women's Forum West (bd. dirs. 1993—, sec. 1994), Internat. Women's Forum. E-mail: RosalieMpakenham@aol.com.

PAKTER, JEAN, maternal and child health consultant; b. N.Y.C., Jan. 1, 1911; d. David and Lillian (Kunitz) P.; m. Arnold L. Bachman, MD, Sept. 17, 1939 (dec. Dec. 1992); children: Ellen Bachman Mendelson, MD, Donald M. Bachman, MD. BS, NYU, 1931, MD, 1934; MPH, Columbia U., 1955. Diplomate Am. Bd. Pediat. Intern Mt. Sinai Hosp., N.Y.C., 1934-36, resident in pediat., 1937-39; pvt. practice, N.Y.C., 1939-43; dir. Bur. Dept. Health, Maternity, Newborn and Family Planning, N.Y.C., 1950-82; cons., lectr. maternity, child health Columbia U. Sch. Pub. Health, N.Y.C., 1984—, dep. dir. maternal and child health program, 1984-94, lectr. maternity, child health, 1970—. Contbr. numerous articles to profl. med. jours. Advisor March of Dimes, N.Y.C., 1975—. Recipient Fund for City of N.Y. Pub. Svc. award, 1974, Jacobi medal Mt. Sinai Hosp., 1975. Fellow APHA (Martha May Eliot award 1990), Am. Acad. Pediatrics, N.Y. Acad. Medicine (trustee 1979-83), N.Y. Obstet. Soc. (assoc.); mem. Pub. Health Assn. N.Y.C. (bd. dirs. 1992-96), Women's City Club, Alpha Omega Alpha. Avocations: concerts, opera, theatre, reading. Home: 1175 Park Ave New York NY 10128-1211

PAKULA, ANITA SUSAN, dermatologist; b. L.A., Nov. 20, 1961; BA, Pomona Coll., 1983; BS, Calif. Luth. Coll., 1985; MD, U. Calif., Irvine, 1988. Diplomat Am. Bd. Dermatology, NAt. Bd. Med. Examiners. Intern Evanston (Ill.) Hosp., 1988-89; resident Northwestern U. Med. Sch., Chgo., 1989-92; asst. clin. prof. dermatology UCLA MEd. Ctr., 1993—. Presenter in field. Contbr. articles to profl. jours. Fellow Am. Acad. Dermatology; mem. Soc. Pediatric Dermatology. Office: 267 W Hillcrest Dr Thousand Oaks CA 91360-4923

PAL, CHERYL LYNN, music teacher; b. Punxsutawney, Pa., July 11, 1954; d. Elvin Dale and Lois Jeanne (Geist) Depp; m. Dulal Pal, Mar. 11, 1978; children: Timothy Ranjan, Monica Suniti. BS in Music Edn., Rutgers U., 1976; MS, L.I. U., 1983. Cert. music educator K-12, N.J., N.Y. Music tchr. Island Park (N.Y.) Union Free Sch. Dist., 1976—. Mem. site-based team Lincoln Orens Mid. Sch., 1996-98; leader Altar Guild, St. Peter's Luth. Ch., 1994-98, 2002—, mem. ch. choir, 1980—, mem. congl. coun., 2001—. Mem. Am. String Tchrs. Assn., Music Educators Nat. Conf., L.I. String Festival Assn. (mem. exec. bd. 1985—, membership chair, libr.), Nassau Music Educators Assn. Republican. Lutheran. Avocations: violoncello, reading. Home: 680 Lakeside Dr Baldwin NY 11510-3507 Office: Island Park UFSD Trafalgar Blvd Island Park NY 11558

PALAC, JUDITH ANN, music educator; b. Evanston, Ill., Feb. 8, 1954; d. Kazimir and Phyllis Josephine (Bochat) P.; m. James Edward Lorenz, July 25, 1992; 1 child, Matthew Palac Lorenz. MusB, U. Mich., 1976, MusM, 1977; DMA, U. Tex., 1987. Acad. staff specialist U. Wis., Oshkosh, 1977-81; asst. dir. U. Tex. String Project, Austin, 1983-85; lectr. violin S.W. Tex. State U., San Marcos, 1983-85; assoc. prof. music edn. Mich. State U., East Lansing, 1985—. 2d violinist Collegium String Quartet, Oshkosh, 1977-80; violinist Austin Symphony, 1981-85, Lansing (Mich.) Symphony Orch., 1985—. Editor: (booklet) Community Resources and School Orchestras, 1992; author: (jours.) Am. String Tchr., 1995, 2d edit., 1999, Med. Problems of Performing Arts, 1992, (periodical) Suzuki World, 1986. All-Univ. rsch. grantee Mich. State U., 1995. Mem. Performing Arts Medicine Assn., Am. String Tchrs. Assn. (pres. Mich. unit 1996-98, mem. nat. bd., 2000-02, named Tchr. of Yr. Mich. unit, 2003), Music Educators Nat. Conf., Suzuki Assn. of the Ams. Avocations: skiing, hiking, films, arts medicine, folk music. Office: Mich State U Sch of Music East Lansing MI 48823

PALACIO, JUNE ROSE PAYNE, nutritional science educator; b. Hove, Sussex, Eng., June 14, 1940; came to U.S., 1949; d. Alfred and Doris Winifred (Payne) P.; m. Moki Moses Palacio, Nov. 30, 1968 (wid. June 1999); m. Cliff Duboff, Dec. 22, 2003. AA, Orange Coast Coll., Costa Mesa, Calif., 1960; BS, U. Calif., Berkeley, 1963; PhD, Kans. State U., 1984. Registered dietitian. Asst. dir. food svc. and res. halls Mills Coll., Oakland, Calif., 1964-66; staff dietitian Servomation Bay Cities, Oakland, 1966-67; commissary mgr. Host Internat., Inc., Honolulu, 1967-73; dir. dietetics Straub Clinic and Hosp., Honolulu, 1973-80; instr. Kans. State U., Manhattan, 1980-84; prof. and program dir. Calif. State U., L.A., 1984-85; prof., asst. dean Pepperdine U., Malibu, Calif., 1985—. Instr. Kapiolani C.C., Honolulu, 1973-79, U. Hawaii, Honolulu, 1975-80, Ctr. for Dietetic Edn., Woodland Hills, Calif., 1986—; cons. Clevenger Nutritional Svcs., Calabasas, Calif., 1985—, Calif. Mus. Sci. and Industry, L.A., 1989—, Calif. State Dept. Edn., Sacramento, 1985—. Author: Foodservice in Institutions, 1988, Introduction to Foodservice, 1992, 97, 2001, The Profession of Dietetics, 1996, 2000. Mem. Am. Dietetic Assn. (del. 1977-80, 86-89, commr. Commn. for Accreditation of Dietic Edn. 1997—), Calif. Dietetic Assn. (pres. 1992-93), L.A. Dist. Dietetic Assn., Foodsvc. Systems Mgmt. Edn. Coun., Dietetic Educators of Practitioners, Gamma Sigma Delta, Omicron Nu, Phi Upsilon Omicron. Republican. Episcopalian. Avocations: tennis, running, reading, traveling. Office: Pepperdine U 24255 Pacific Coast Hwy Malibu CA 90263-0002 Home: 1500 E Ocean Blvd Unit 612 Long Beach CA 90802-6931 E-mail: june.palacio@pepperdine.edu.

PALACIOS, CHRISTINA, academic administrator; With S.W. Gas, 1984—, former mgr. human resources, adminstrn., customer rels., ops. and support, v.p. So. Nev. divsn., 1995—97, v.p. in charge of So. Ariz. divsn., 1997—; mem., asst. sec. Ariz. Bd. Regents, Phoenix. Mem. Sch. Facilities Bd., Ariz. Office: Ariz Bd Regents Ste 230 2020 N Central Ave Phoenix AZ 85004

PALAST, GERI DEBORAH, federal agency administrator, Lawyer; b. L.A., Dec. 27, 1950; BA in Polit. Sci., Stanford U., 1972; JD, NYU, 1976. Bar: Calif. 1977, D.C. 1980. Atty., legis. program analyst Am. Fedn. State County and Mcpl. Employees, Washington, 1976-77; legal counsel, field rep. Nat. Treasury Employers Union, Washington, 1977-79; dir., supervising atty. Nat. Employment Law Project, Washington, 1979-81; dir. politics and legislation Svc. Employees Internat. Union, AFL-CIO, Washington, 1981-93; asst. sec. congrl. and intergovtl. affairs Dept. Labor, Washington, 1993-2000; exec. dir. justice at stake campaign Georgetown U., Washington, 2000. Home: 2737 Devonshire Pl NW Apt 402 Washington DC 20008-3475 Office: 50 F St NW #1050 Washington DC 20001

PALCHIK, ANNA, book designer, writer; b. Oceanside, N.Y., July 12, 1951; d. Walter and Helen Palchik; m. John Post, June 1, 1975 (div. Nov. 1981); m. Herbert George, Sept. 11, 1988 (div. Dec. 2003). BFA cum laude, Syracuse U., 1973. Art tchr. Braintree (Mass.) Pub. Schs., 1973—74; pasteup layout artist Sport Eye Inc. Newspapers, Great Neck, NY, 1975; art dir. Patriot Profile Newspaper, Dedham, Mass., 1975—76; book designer Little Brown & Co., Boston, 1976—80; owner book design bus. Boston, 1980—86, Chgo., 1986—92, Shores, Ind., 1992—2003; art dir. Bedford Books/St. Martin's Press, Boston, 2003—. Catalogue designer Cultural Ctr., Chgo., 1990, Muskegon (Mich.) News Art, 1992, Blank Ctr. for Arts, Michigan City, Ind., 1999. Exhibitions include Beverly Shores (Ind.) Depot Gallery, 1998—99; author: Picturing Texts, 2003. Recipient Excellence in Book Design, New England Bookbuilders, 1982, 1997, 2001, 2002, 2003, Cert. Merit, Bookbuilders West, 1989, 1991, 1992, 1993, Cert. Merit for Printing Design, Arcada Graphics Book Group, 1991, Cert. Excellence, Bookbuilders West, 1996, 1997, 1998, 2nd Pl. Design award, N.Y. Bookbuilders, 2002. Mem.: Phi Lambda Theta, Phi Kappa Phi. Russian Orthodox. Avocations: painting, gardening, tai chi.

PALESKY, CAROL EAST, tax accountant; b. Orange, N.J., May 13, 1940; d. Neil Norell and Marie R. Reiss; m. Jacob Palesky; children: Donna, Lewis. AB, Am. Inst., Pleasantville, N.J., 1973; postgrad., Am. Inst., Portland, Maine, 1980; student, Atlantic C.C., Mays Landing, N.J., 1971-73. With mgmt. First Nat. Bank of South Jersey (now First Fidelity), Pleasantville, N.J., 1967-74; loan officer Maine Savs. Bank, Portland, 1980-81; acct., owner East Acctg. Assocs., Topsham, Maine, 1985—. Pres. Sensible Tax Limits Coalition, 1995—. Treas., bd. dirs. Congl. Term Limits Coalition, Topsham, 1993—; bd. dirs. Maine Citizens Rev. Bd., Portland, 1993—. Scholar Nat. Taxpayer Union, 1992, 94; recipient United to Serve Am. award, 1992. Mem. Nat. Assn. Small Business Owners, Maine Taxpayers Action Network (pres. 1990—), Topsham Taxpayer Assn. (pres. 1991—). Roman Catholic. Home and Office: 24 Sokokis Cir Topsham ME 04086-1615 E-mail: cep@mtan.org.

PALEY, GRACE, author, educator; b. N.Y.C., Dec. 11, 1922; d. Isaac and Mary (Ridnyik) Goodside; m. Jess Paley, June 20, 1942; children: Nora, Dan.; m. Robert Nichols, 1972. Ed., Hunter Coll., NYU. Formerly tchr. Columbia, Syracuse U.; ret. mem. lit. faculty Sarah Lawrence Coll., Stanford, Johns Hopkins, Dartmouth, CUNY. Author: The Little Disturbances of Man, 1959, Enormous Changes at the Last Minute, 1974, Learning Forward, 1985, Later the Same Day, 1985, Long Walks and Intimate Talks, 1991, New and Collected Poems, 1992, The Collected Stories, 1994 (Nat. Book award nomination, 1994), Just As I Thought, 1998, Begin Again Collected Poems, 2000; contbr. stories to Atlantic, New Yorker, Ikon, Genesis West, others. Sec. N.Y. Greenwich Village Peace Center. Recipient Literary award for short story writing Nat. Inst. Arts and Letters, 1970, Edith Wharton award N.Y. State, 1988, 89, Rea award for short story, 1993, Vt. Gov.'s award for Excellence in the Arts, 1993, award for contbn. to Jewish culture Nat. Found. Jewish Culture; Guggenheim fellow; apptd. Vt. Poet Laureate, 2003—. Mem. Am. Acad. and Inst. Arts and Letters, Am. Acad. Arts and Scis. Office: PO Box 620 Thetford VT 05074-0620

PALEY, MAGGIE, writer, editor; b. N.Y.C., Dec. 29, 1939; d. David and Sylvia (Leichtling) P. BA magna cum laude, Brandeis U., 1960. Assoc. editor The Paris Rev., N.Y.C., 1963-66; mng. editor Status, N.Y.C., 1966-67; assoc. editor The Saturday Evening Post, N.Y.C., 1967-69; asst. editor Life, N.Y.C., 1969-71; writer Time, N.Y.C., 1971-72; contbg. editor Vogue, N.Y.C., 1984-85, Elle, N.Y.C., 1988-89, Mirabella, N.Y.C., 1990-94; adv. editor The Paris Rev., N.Y.C., 1967—. Author: (novel) Bad Manners, 1986, (chapbook) Elephant, 1990, (play) In One Door, 1985, The Book of Penis, 1999; co-author and prodr.: (radio play) The President's Big Day, 2003; contbr. articles and book revs. to N.Y. Times Book Rev., Bookforum, Mirabella, Elle, Vogue, Harper's Bazaar, Connoisser, others. Mem. PEN, Authors Guild, Nat. Writers Union. Office: Gelfman Schneider care Jane Gelfman 250 W 57th St Ste 2515 New York NY 10107-2595

PALIGA-TANZOLA, RHONDA, special education educator; b. Hackensack, N.J., July 5, 1948; d. Walter and Adele Paliga; m. Matthew Tanzola; children: Terri Tanzola, Jennifer Tanzola. BA, N.J. City U., 1970, MA, 1990. Cert. tchr. of handicapped, tchr. elem. edn. Tchr. Title I, N.I., P.I., LLD, resource ctr. Ringwood Bd. Edn., NJ, 1970—. CEO Tutoring Svcs., Sparta, NJ, 2001—. Foster parent N.J. Foster Parents Assn., 1986—95. Recipient Professionally Recognized Spl. Educator, Coun. Exceptional Children, 1999, N.J. Gov.'s Recognition award, 1985. Mem.: N.J. Dyslexic Assn. (tutor 2001—). Avocations: movies, decorating, shopping. Office: Peter Cooper Sch Roger Ct Ringwood NJ 07456*

PALKO, LORRI M. automotive company executive; BS in Acctg., Indiana U. Pa. With Ernst & Whinney; pres., CEO Morgan Corp. subs. J.B. Poindexter & Co., Inc., Morgantown, Pa.; various fin. and materials mgmt. positions Dorsey Trailers, Inc., Atlanta, 1994—, pres., COO, 1997—. Office: Dorsey Trailers Inc Bldg 1 Ste 1700 2727 Paces Ferry Rd Atlanta GA 30339

PALL, ELLEN JANE, writer; b. N.Y.C., Mar. 28, 1952; d. David B. and Josephine H. (Blatt) P.; m. Richard Holmes Dicker, July 12, 1986; 1 child, Benjamin. BA, U. Calif., Santa Barbara, 1973. Freelance writer for several jours., 1987—. Staff assoc. Bread Loaf Writers Conf., Middlebury, Vt., 1986; instr. UCLA-Ext., 1980-83; adj. asst. prof. Fordham U./Coll. at Lincoln Ctr., N.Y.C., 1990-93. Author (under pen name Fiona Hill): The Trellised Lane, The Wedding Portrait, The Practical Heart, Love in a Major Key, Sweet's Folly, The Autumn Rose, The Love Child, The Stanbroke Girls, 1981, The Country Gentleman, 1987; author: (as Ellen Pall) Back East, 1983, Among the Ginzburgs, 1996, Corpse de Ballet, 2001, Slightly Abridged, 2003; contbr. articles to N.Y.Times Mag., N.Y. Times Arts & Leisure, New Yorker mag., Chgo. Tribune, Washington Post; book reviewer. Shane Stevens fellow Bread Loaf Writer's Conf., Vt., 1983. Mem. Am. PEN (freedom to write com.). Office: care Mary Evans Inc 242 E 5th St New York NY 10003-8501

PALLADINO-CRAIG, ALLYS, museum director; b. Pontiac, Mich., Mar. 23, 1947; d. Stephan Vincent and Mary (Anderson) Palladino; m. Malcolm Arnold Craig, Aug. 20, 1967; children— Ansel, Reed, Nicholas. BA in English, Fla. State U., 1967; grad., U. Toronto, Ont., Can., 1969; MFA, Fla. State U., 1978, PhD in Humanities, 1996. Editorial asst. project U. Va Press, Charlottesville, 1970-76; instr. English Inst. Franco Americain, Rennes, France, 1974, adj. instr. Fla. State U., Tallahassee, 1970-79, dir. Four Arts Ctr., 1979-82, dir. U. Mus. of Fine Arts, 1982—, prof. mus. studies. Mem. grad faculty Mus. Studies Cert. Program Fla. State U. Curator, contbg. editor: Nocturnes and Nightmares, Monochrome/Polychrome, Chroma; contbg. editor: Body Language; guest curator, author: Mark Messersmith: New Mythologies, Terrestrial Forces; curator, editor Albert Paley--Sculpture, Drawings, Graphics and Decorative Arts, Trevor Bell: A British Painter in America, and Trial by Fire: Contemporary Glass; curator, author: The Abridged Walmsley--Selections from the Career of William Aubrey Walmsley; author: Jack Nichelson: Micro-Theatres, Alexa Kleinbard: Talking Leaves, Jake Fernandez--Ethereal Journeyman, Jim Roche-Sense of Place; editor: Athanor I-XXIII, 1980—; Represented in permanent collections Fla. Ho. of Reps., Barnett Bank, IBM. Individual artist fellow Fla. Arts Coun., 1979 Mem. Am. Assn. Mus., Fla. Art Mus. Dirs. Assn. (sec. 1989-91), Phi Beta Kappa. Democrat. Avocation: antique american fountain pen collecting. Home: 1410 Grape St Tallahassee FL 32303-5636 Office: Fla State U Mus of Fine Arts 250 Fine Arts Bldg Tallahassee FL 32306-1140 E-mail: apcraig@mailer.fsu.edu.

PALLARES, ANNETTE MARIE, dietician; b. Lake Charles, La., Sept. 5, 1944; d. Vincent and Marjorie Mary (Chapman) Rivera; m. Mariano Pallares, July 31, 1965; children: Michelle, Eduardo. BS in dietetics and food svc. mgmt., Madonna U., 1992. Registered clinical dietetic technician, Mich. Cmty. nutrition worker WIC program Detroit Dept. of Health, 1979-81; registered dietetic technician mgr. Marriott Corp.-Botsford Hosp., Farmington Hills, Mich., 1981—. Active Latinos De Livonia, Mich., 1992-97. Mem. Am. Dietetic Assn., Planetary Soc. Democrat. Roman Catholic. Avocations: reading, art, anthropology, astronomy. Home: 22411 Foxton Dr Novi MI 48375-3931 Office: Marriott Corp Botsford Hosp Farmington Hills MI 48334

PALLART, CHERYL, literature educator, writer; b. N.Y.C., Jan. 8, 1960; d. Emanuel and Joan; m. Kevin Hefferman. BA, L.I. U., 1982, MA, 1983. Tchr. Va. Commonwealth U., Richmond, 1985—2001, U. Richmond, 2001—03. Tchr. Ottawa U., Kans., 1996—98. Editor: Contact Qtr., 2003—; author: Spontaneities, 2001, Uncommon Grammar Cloth, 2001, Into Stillness, 2003.

PALLASCH, MAGDALENA HELENA (MRS. BERNHARD MICHAEL PALLASCH), artist; b. Chgo., Sept. 6, 1908; d. Frank and Anna (Meier) Fixari; m. Bernhard Pallasch, Nov. 26, 1931 (dec. Nov. 1977); children: Bernhard Michael, Diana Pallasch Miller Student, Chgo. Acad. Fine Arts, 1922-26, Am. Acad. Fine Arts, 1926-30, U. Chgo., 1960, Art Inst. Chgo.; pvt. study with Joseph Allworthy, 1935-38, hon. doctorate, 1985. Contbr. two murals and ten life size figures for Woman's World Fair, Chgo., 1928, Century of Progress Exhbn., Chgo., 1933-34; portrait artist, subjects include Cardinal Cody, Chgo., 1980—, Cardinal Francis George, Chgo., 1998, Carlotta Ames, Boston, Mrs. Timothy Kingston, Arlington Heights, Ill., Dr. Neal Coleman, Hinsdale, Ill., Catherine Eardley Murphy, Lake Forest, Ill., Anita Mangels, Sao Paulo, Brazil; mural St. Mary of the Lake Ch., Chgo., 1987; exhbn. at Montifiori Estate, 1992, 93, 94, Hinsdale Art Ctr., 1995, 96, 97; represented in pvt. and pub. collections Loyola U., Chgo., Barat Coll., Lake Forest, Ill., Internat. Coll. Surgeons, Chgo., Med. Library, Columbus Hosp and others. Recipient first award for still life Arts Club, N.Y.C., 1960, First award Nat. League Am. Pen Women, 1972, 1st place and best of show State Exhibit, Springfield, Ill., 1973, 1st award Chgo. Woman's Club, 1978, hon. mention for portrait Italian Cultural Ctr., hon. alumna award Loyola U., Chgo., 1983, award of excellence for portrait of author Gail Brook Burket, Wheaton Hist. Mus., 1987, Gold Medal of Honor for disting. lifelong achievements, 1987, award of honor for portrait of sculptor Lisa Gengler, 1989, medallion from Archduke Markus Habsburg of Austria, 2003; named Dame Commandeur with Starbust, 1997, with second Starburst, 2003, Sovereign Mil. Order Temple of Jerusalem, 1995. Mem. Presentation Ball Aux.; mem. President's Club, Loyola U., also mem. women's bd. Nat. League Am. Pen Women (v.p. Chgo. br. 1966-68, art chmn. 1978-80, Margaret Dingle Meml. award 1979), Mcpl. Art League Chgo., Nat. Soc. Arts and Letters (art chmn. chgo. chpt. 1982—, apptd. nat. chmn. 1997—), Friends of Austria, Friends of D'Arcy Gallery of Medieval and Renaissance Art., Ill. Cath. Women Club (gov. 1979[00bf]), Cuneo Mus. (Vernon Hills, Ill.). Home: 723 W Junior Ter Chicago IL 60613-1512

PALLMEYER, REBECCA RUTH, judge; b. Tokyo, Sept. 13, 1954; arrived in U.S., 1957; d. Paul Henry and Ruth (Schrieber) Pallmeyer; m. Dan P. McAdams, Aug. 20, 1977; 2 children. BA, Valparaiso U., Ind., 1976; JD, U. Ill., Chgo., 1979. Bar: Ill. 1980, U.S. Ct. Appeals (7th cir.) 1980, U.S. Ct. Appeals (11th and 5th cir.) 1982. Judge clk. Minn. Supreme Ct., St. Paul, 1979-80; assoc. Hopkins and Sutter, Chgo., 1980-85; judge, administrv. law Ill. Human Rights Commn., Chgo., 1985-91; magistrate judge U.S. Dist. Ct. (No. Dist.), Chgo., 1991-98, dist. judge, 1998—. Mem. jud. resources com. Jud. Conf. U.S., 1994—2000. Nat. adv. coun. Christ Coll., Valparaiso U., 2001—; bd. dirs. Augustana Ctr., 1990—91. Recipient Profl. Achievement award, Chgo.-Kent Coll. of Law, 2002, President's Award for Disting. Svc., N.W. Suburban Bar Assn., 2003. Mem.: FBA (bd. mgrs. Chgo. chpt. 1995—99), Chgo. Bar Assn. (chair devel. law com. 1992—93, David C. Hilliard award 1990—91), Fed. Magistrate Judges Assn. (bd. dirs. 1994—97), Womens Bar Assn. Ill. (bd. mgrs. 1995—98), Valparaiso U. Alumni Assn. (bd. dirs. 1992—94). Lutheran. Avocations: choral music, sewing, running. Office: US Dist Ct 219 S Dearborn St Ste 2178 Chicago IL 60604-1877

PALLOTTA, JOHANNA ANTONIA (JOHANNA STEPHEN), physician, educator, researcher; b. Boston, May 7, 1937; d. John and Antonia (Lanni) P.; m. Michael John Stephen, Aug. 13, 1966; children: Jacqueline, Antonia, Michael, Andrew. BS in Chemistry magna cum laude, Boston Coll., 1958; MD, N.Y. Med. Coll., 1962. Diplomate Am. Bds. Internal Medicine, Endocrinolgoy and Metabolism; lic. N.Y., Mass., Calif. Intern St. Elizabeth's Hosp., Boston, 1962-63; resident in medicine N.Y. Med. Coll. Metro. Hosp., N.Y.C., 1963-64; resident in medicine, fellow radioisotope svc. VA Hosp., Bronx, 1964—66; fellow metabolism and endocrinology Yale U. Sch. Medicine, 1966-67; instr. medicine Harvard Med. Sch., 1967-69, Beth Israel Deaconess Hosp. Harvard Med. Sch., Boston, 1969-70; asst. prof. medicine Harvard Med. Sch., Boston, 1970—2003, assoc. prof. medicine, 2004—. Tutor med. scis. Harvard Med. Sch., 1972-73; dir. endocrinology clinic Beth Israel Deaconess Hosp., Boston, 1967—, dir. radioimmunoassay lab., 1972-83, clin. cons., 1984—, asst. in medicine, 1967-69, assoc. in medicine, 1969-70, asst. physician, 1970-79, assoc. physician, 1979-87, sr. physician, 1987—, dir. clin. rsch. ctr. core radioimmunoassay lab., 1984-93; cons. staff Mount Auburn Hosp., Cambridge, 1974-90; mem. numerous other coms., 1969—. Researcher in field; contbr. articles to profl. jours. Named Carl Shapiro scholar, BIDMC-Harvard Med. Sch., 2000—; recipient S. Robert Stone Harvard Med. Sch.-BIDMC tchg. award, 1998. Fellow: ACP, Am. Assn. Clin. Endocrinologists; mem.: Am. Fedn. Clin. Rsch., Am. Thyroid Assn., Am. Assn. Clin. Endocrinology, Endocrine Soc., Harvard Aesculapian Club, Alpha Omega Alpha. Roman Catholic. Home: 16 Fresh Pond Ln Cambridge MA 02138-4616 Office: Beth Israel Hosp Harvard Med Sch 330 Brookline Ave Boston MA 02215-5491 Office Phone: 617-667-4016. E-mail: jpallott@BIDMC.harvard.edu.

PALLOTTI, MARIANNE MARGUERITE, foundation administrator; b. Hartford, Conn., Apr. 23, 1937; d. Rocco D. and Marguerite (Long) P. BA, NYU, 1968, MA, 1972. Asst. to pres. Wilson, Haight & Welch, Hartford, 1964-65; exec. asst. Ford Found., N.Y.C., 1965-77; corp. sec. Hewlett Found., Menlo Park, Calif., 1977-84, v.p., 1985—. Bd. dirs. N.Y. Theatre Ballet, N.Y.C., 1986-90, Austin Montessori Sch., 1993, Djerassi Resident Artists Program, 1998—, Mexican Mus., 1999—; mem. women's adv. com., nat. coun.World Wildlife Fund, 1997—; mem. program com. Ind. Sector, Washington, 1998—. Mem. Women in Founds., No. Calif. Grantmakers. Office: William & Flora Hewlett Found 525 Middlefield Rd Ste 200 Menlo Park CA 94025-3448

PALLOZOLA, CHRISTINE, non-profit administrator; b. St. Louis, Mar. 28, 1952; BS, U. Mo., 1974. Purchasing and sales mgmt. computer industry, Mo., 1984-92; exec. dir. Cahokia Mounds Mus. Soc., Collinsville, Ill., 1993—2001, dir. spl. events, mktg. Arts and Edn. Coun., 2001—04; exec. dir. Am. Acad. Physician and Patient, St. Louis, 2004—. Mem. Assn. Fundraising Profls. Home: 150 Burtonwood Ballwin MO 63011

PALL-PALLANT, TERI, paleontologist, inventor, behavioral scientist, design engineer, advertising agency executive; b. Somerville, N.J., Jan. 6, 1921; d. Stanley and Milicent P.-P. BA, Imperial Coll., London, 1948; MS, Imperial Coll., 1949; postgrad., Warren Sch. Aero., L.A., 1950, Calif. Inst. Tech., 1951; PhD, London U., 1954, 66; student, UCLA, 1955; PhD, Columbia U., 1963; ScD, London Inst. Applied Rsch., 1973; cert. rehab. counselor, U. So. Calif., 1975. Design engr. Simmonds Aerocessories Ltd., London, 1949, dir. vocat. rehab., 1950; founder, owner Teri Pall Advt. Agy., L.A., 1951—, Pall Indsl. Surveys, Pasadena, Calif., 1952—. Pall Tech. Industries, Tarzana, Calif., 1979—. Chmn. bd. Pall Industries, Ltd., Taipei, Taiwan and Tarzana, Calif., 1980—; vertebrate paleontologist Am. Mus. Natural History, N.Y.C., 1965-69; leader Teri Pall Trio, L.A., 1951-69; exec. dir. Hoffman House, Long Beach, Calif., 1970-72; sr. adminstrv. analyst Econ. and Youth Opportunities, L.A. County, 1973-74; dep. dir. Head Start Program L.A. County, 1974-75; assoc. dir. Casa del las Amigas, Pasadena, dir. rsch. and evaluation projects Nat. Inst. Alcohol Abuse and Alcoholism, Washington, 1977; pvt. practice vocat. rehab. counseling, Beverly Hills, Calif., 1977; exec. dir. Little House L.A. County, 1978; robotics cons. Jet Propulsion Lab., Pasadena, 1974-95, NASA, 1990—. Author: (play) El Rancho Verde, 1951, (novel) With Banners Flying, 1953, Chinese and Western Worlds from 1800 B.C. to Modern Times, 1950, 4000 Years of Egyptian History, 1950, The Integrating Power Meter, 1956, About the Mammoth, 1962, Look, a Travelogue in Time, 1967, The History of Our Calendar, 1977; designer robotics exhibit Calif. Mus. of Sci. and Industry, L.A., 1990; inventor proximity warning device for aircraft. Fossil exhibit contbr. L.A. County Mus., 1968-77; chmn. Mayor's Commn. on Barrier-Free Arch., 1978—; vice chmn. rsch. and coordinating com. Gov.'s Commn. on Safe Energy Alternatives, 1979—; mem. Cancer Rsch. Coordinating Com., 1979—; lectr. Long Beach Hosp., 1978; office bd. Inventor's Workshop Internat. Edn. Found., 1980—, Am. Guild of Inventors, 1990—; bd. dirs. Commn. Conserve Chinese Culture. Recipient Spl. Contbns. award Engring. and Grading Constructors Assn., 1968, Interkamera Gold award Cannes Art Festival, 1969, Spkr. of Yr. award Toastmasters Calif., 1971, Woman of Yr. for Civil Leadership award Long Beach, 1971, Outstanding Achievement award Am. Cancer Soc., 1979, others. Mem. AAUW, Statis. Quality Control Engrs. (sec. 1951—), Assn. Bus. Publs., Nat. Rehab. Counseling Assn., Archs. and Engrs. Inst., Nat. Soc. Vertebrate Paleontologists, Phi Beta Kappa. Republican. Episcopalian. Achievements include developer 2-mile cordless telephone, 1978, wrist chronograph calculator, 1979, Etch-A-Sketch, 1962, AC-DC multimeters, 1954, Miniaturized transcutaneous nerve stimulator, 1969, Electronic remote control system, 1972, proximity warning device for aircraft 1986.

PALM, LINDA J. psychology educator; b. Abington, Pa., Jan. 28, 1949; d. Arthur W. Palm and M. Jean (Stucky) P. BA, Rollins Coll., 1970; MA, Wake Forest U., 1972; PhD, U. South Fla., 1980. Planner, evaluator Fla. Mental Health Inst., Tampa, 1980-83; asst. prof. psychology U. Wis., Platteville, 1983-88; prof. psychology Edison C.C., Fort Myers, Fla., 1988-92; assoc. prof. psychology Coastal Carolina U., Conway, SC, 1992—2001, prof. psychology, 2001—. Contbr. articles to profl. jours. Bd. dirs. Tara Hall, Georgetown, S.C., 1996—. Mem. APA, S.C. Psychol. Assn., Phi Kappa Phi. Office: Coastal Carolina U Dept Psychology PO Box 261954 Conway SC 29528

PALM, MARY EGDAHL, mycologist; b. Mpls., Jan. 27, 1954; d. Lauren and Mary E.; children: Natalie Elizabeth, Christopher Steven. BA in Biology, St. Olaf Coll., 1976; MSc in Plant Pathology (mycology), U. Minn., 1979, PhD in Plant Pathology (mycology), 1983. Lab. asst. St. Olaf Coll. Biology Dept., Northfield, Minn., 1974, tchg. asst., 1975-76; rsch. asst. U. Minn. plant pathology dept., Mpls., 1976-83, post doctoral rsch. assoc., 1983-84; mycologist (botanist GS12) USDA/APHIS biol. assessment and support staff, Beltsville, Md., 1984-91; mycologist scientific svcs. USDA/Animal and Plant Health Inspection Svc., Beltsville, 1991—. Instr., coord. seminars and tng. sessions for USDA and ednl. sci. group, 1982—; adj. assoc. prof. plant pathology Pa. State U., State College, 1995. Co-author: Deuteromycetes and Selected Ascomycetes That Occur On or In Wood: An Indexed Bibliography, 1979, An Indexed Bibliography and Guide to Taxonomic Literature, 1988, A Literature Guide for the Identification of Plant Pathogenic Fungi, 1987, Fungi on Rhododendron: A World Reference, 1996, Mycology in Sustainable Development: Expanding concepts, Vanishing Borders, 1997; contbr. articles to profl. jours. including Mycologia, Plant Disease, Can. Jour. Botany, Mycotaxon. Recipient St. Olaf Coll. Hon. Biology scholarship, 1976, Disting. Alumnus Dept. Plant Pathology U. Minn., 1999; grantee U. Minn. Computer Ctr. 1979, 80, 81, 82. Mem. Am. Phytopathol. Soc. (chairperson mycology com. 1988, 89, vice chairperson 1987, mem. 1985, 86, regulatory plant pathology com. 1993—, organizer, moderator colloquim on systematics of plant pathogenic fungi 1987), Mycol. Soc. Am. (sec. 1991-94, Am. Inst. Biol. Scis. rep. 1994—, v.p. 1995-96, pres.-elect 1996-97, pres. 1997-98, other coms.), L.Am. Mycol. Assn. (U.S. liaison), Internat. Assn. Plant Taxonomy (subcom. C of com. on fungi and lichens 1986, 87, 88). Office: USDA Rm 329 B-011A 10300 Baltimore Ave Beltsville MD 20705-2350

PALMER, ADA MARGARET, systems analyst, consultant; b. Feb. 8, 1940; d. Mark Lloyd Palmer and Eunice Elizabeth (Thompson) Palmer Schnitzer. AA, Colo. Woman's Coll., 1960; BA, George Washington U., 1962. Programmer, analyst U.S. Navy Dept., Washington, 1962-66, Schroder Trust, N.Y.C., 1967-68; v.p. EDP Learning Systems, N.Y.C., 1968-69; cons. JWI Assoc. Tech. Group, N.Y.C., 1969; adv. sr. programmer Merrill Lynch, N.Y.C., 1969-72; sys. analyst Tchrs. Ins. & Annuity, N.Y.C., 1972-77; sys. specialist N.Y. Times, N.Y.C., 1977-81; computer cons. Applied Sys. Resources, Inc., N.Y.C., 1981-82; asst. sec. Chase Bank, N.Y.C., 1982-94; computer cons. A.Z. Software Shop Inc., Garden City, N.Y., 1994-95; sys. acct. UN, N.Y.C., 1995-99; computer cons. AMP Consulting, Inc., 1999—. Mem. Women's Assn. of the Wichita Symphony, Allegro Movement Soc. of the Wichita Symphony. Recipient George Washington U. Alumni Svc. award, 1992. Mem. AAUW, Archeol. Inst. Am., Colo. Woman's Coll. Alumni Club, George Washington U. Alumni Club of N.Y.C. (past pres.), Am. Overseas Schs. Hist. Soc. (bd. dirs. 2002—). Republican. Presbyterian. Home and Office: Apt 1707 550 W Central Wichita KS 67203-4238

PALMER, ANN THERESE DARIN, lawyer; b. Detroit, Apr. 25, 1951; d. Americo and Theresa (Del Favero) Darin; m. Robert Towne Palmer, Nov. 9, 1974; children: Justin Darin, Christian Darin. BA, U. Notre Dame, 1973, MBA, 1975; JD, Loyola U., Chgo., 1978. Bar: Ill. 1978, U.S. Supreme Ct. 1981. Intern Wall Street Jour., Detroit, 1974; freelancer Time Inc. Fin. Publs., Chgo., 1975—77; extern, Midwest regional solicitor U.S. Dept. Labor, 1976—78; tax atty. Esmark Inc., 1978; counsel Chgo. United, 1978—81; ind. contractor Legal Tax Rsch., 1981—89; fin. and legal news contbr. The Chgo. Tribune, 1991—, Bus. Week, 1991—, Automotive News, 1993—97, Crain's Chgo. Bus., 1994—2000, contbg. editor Registered Rep, 2002—. Mem.: Woman's Athletic Club Chgo. Home: 1570 Christina Ln Lake Forest IL 60045

PALMER, BEVERLY BLAZEY, psychologist, educator; b. Cleve., Nov. 22, 1945; d. Lawrence E. and Mildred M. Blazey; m. Richard C. Palmer, June 24, 1967; 1 child, Ryan Richard. PhD in Counseling Psychology, Ohio State U., 1972. Lic. clin. psychologist, Calif. Adminstrv. assoc. Ohio State U., Columbus, 1969-70; rsch. psychologist Health Svcs. Rsch. Ctr. UCLA, 1971-77; commr. pub. health L.A. County, 1978-81; pvt. practice clin. psychology Torrance, Calif., 1985—; prof. psychology Calif. State U., Dominguez Hills, 1973—. Reviewer manuscripts for numerous textbook pubs; contbr. numerous articles to profl. jours. Recipient Proclamation, County of Los Angeles, 1972, 1981, Fulbright scholar, Malaysia, 2001, 2004; Fulbright sr. specialist, 2002—. Mem. APA. Office: Calif State U Dominguez Hills Dept Psychology Carson CA 90747-0001

PALMER, CHRISTINE (CLELIA ROSE VENDITTI), operatic singer, pianist, vocal educator; b. Hartford, Conn., Apr. 02; d. John Marion and Immacolata (Morcaldo) Venditti; m. Raymond Smith, Oct. 5, 1949 (div. June 1950); m. Arthur James Whitlock, Feb. 25, 1953. Student, Mt. Holyoke Coll., 1937-38, New Eng. Conservatory of Music, 1941-42; pvt. studies, Boston, Hartford, N.Y.C., Florence and Naples, Italy; RN with honors, Hartford Hosp. Sch. Nursing, 1941. Artist-in-residence El Centro Coll., Dallas, 1966-71. Pvt. vocal instr.-coach, specializing in vocal technique for opera, mus. comedy, supper club acts, auditions, Dallas, 1962-94; voice adjudicator San Francisco Opera Co., 1969-72, Tex. Music Tchrs. Assn., 1964-75, others; lectr. in field; appearances with S.M. Chartocks' Gilbert and Sullivan Co.; now performing lecture/entertainment circuit. Leading operatic soprano N.Y.C. Opera, Chgo., San Francisco, San Carlo, other cities, 1944-62; presented concert N.Y. Town Hall, 1951; soloist with symphony orchs. maj. U.S. Cities, 1948-62; soloist Marble Collegiate Ch., Holy Trinity Ch.; coast-to-coast concert tour, 1948; numerous appearances including St. Louis MUNY Opera, Indpls. Starlight Theatre, Lambertville Music Circus; soloist Holiday on Ice, 1949-50; TV performer, including Home Show on NBC, Telephone Hour on NBC, Holiday Hotel; performer various supper clubs, N.Y.C., Atlanta, Bermuda, Catskills, others, including Number One Fifth Avenue, The Embers, The Carriage Club, Viennese Lantern. Hon. mem. women's bd. Dallas Opera Assn.; mem. adv. bd. Tex. Opera News; mem. Tex. Music Tchrs. Cert. Bd., Collegiate Chorale, Don Craig Singers, The Vikings; mem. women's bd., Dallas Bapt. Univ. Oliver Ditson scholar, 1942; recipient Phi Xi Delta prize in Italian, 1937; named Victor Herbert Girl, ASCAP; Spl. Recognition Gold book of Dallas Soc. Mem. Nat. Assn. Tchrs. of Singing (pres. Dallas chpt. 1972-74), Nat. Fedn. Music Clubs, Tex. Fedn. Music Clubs, Dallas Fedn. Music Clubs (pres. 1972-74), Dallas Symphony League, Dallas Music Tchrs. Assn. (pres. 1971-72, Tchr. of Yr. 1974), Thesaurus Book Club (pres. 1990-91, 97-98), Friday Forum (Dallas, bd. dirs.), Dallas Women's C. of C., Eagle Forum, Pub. Affairs Luncheon Club, Dallas Fedn. Music Club, Pro Am., Wednesday Morning Choral Club, Dallas Knife and Fork Club, Prestoncrest Rep. Club. Presbyterian. Home: 6232 Pemberton Dr Dallas TX 75230-4036

PALMER, DEBORAH JEAN, lawyer; b. Williston, N.D., Oct. 25, 1947; d. Everett Edwin and Doris Irene (Harberg) P.; m. Kenneth L. Rich, Mar. 29, 1980; children: Andrew, Stephanie. BA, Carleton Coll., 1969; JD cum laude, Northwestern U., 1973. Bar: Minn. 1973, U.S. Dist. Ct. Minn. 1973, U.S. Ct. Appeals (8th cir.) 1975, U.S. Supreme Ct. 1978, U.S. Ct. Appeals (11th cir.) 1999. Econ. analyst Harris Trust & Savs. Bank, Chgo., 1969-70; assoc. Robins, Kaplan, Miller & Ciresi LLP, Mpls., 1973-79, ptnr., 1979—. Trustee Carleton Coll., 1984-88; mem. bd. religious edn. Plymouth Congl. Ch., 1992-95; bd. dirs. Mpls. YWCA, 1996-99; mem. Dist. Minn. Civil Justice Reform Act Adv. Group, 1990-93; bd. dirs. RKM&C Found. Edn., Pub. Health & Social Justice, 1999—. Mem. ABA, Minn. Bar Assn., Minn. Women Lawyers Assn. (sec. 1976-78), Minn. Fed. Bar Assn. (chpt. bd. dirs. 1996-98), Hennepin County Bar Assn., Hennepin County Bar Found. (bd. dirs. 1978-81), Carleton Coll. Alumni Assn. (bd. dirs. 1978-82, sec. 1980-82), Women's Assn. of Minn. Orch. (bd. dirs. 1980-85, treas. 1981-83). Home: 1787 Colfax Ave S Minneapolis MN 55403-3008 Office: Robins Kaplan Miller & Ciresi LLP 800 Lasalle Ave Ste 2800 Minneapolis MN 55402-2015 E-mail: djpalmer@rkmc.com.

PALMER, DENISE, publishing executive; m. Gregory G. Palmer. BA, U. Dayton, 1977; MS in Mgmt., N.W. U. Sr. auditor Coopers & Lybrand, Dayton, Ohio, 1977—80; corp. auditor Tribune, 1980—86, planning analyst, 1983—86, mgr. planning, 1986—88; dir. fin. WGN Radio, Chgo., 1988—93, sta. mgr., 1993; dir. fin. Chgo. Tribune, 1994—2000, v.p. devel., strategy, fin., 1998—2000; pres., CEO CLTV, Oakbrook, Ill., 2000—02; pres., pub., CEO Balt. Sun, 2002—. Office: Baltimore Sun 501 N Calvert St Baltimore MD 21278*

PALMER, FAYE DIANE, music educator; b. Oberlin, Kans., Nov. 22, 1955; d. Robert Guy and Dorothy Irene Bemis; m. Scott Vincent Palmer, May 25, 1979; children: Raymond Matthew, Carl Michael. MusM, Wichita State U., 1978—80. Cert. Instrumental Music Tchr. Kans., 1993. Sect. violinist Wichita Symphony, Wichita, Kans., 1978—80; pvt. violin tchr. Wichita, Kans., 1978—; strings tchr. Bethel Life Sch., Wichita, Kans., 1993—2003, libr., 1994—2001; strings tchr. Wichita Pub. Schools, Wichita, Kans., 2001—. Ch. musician Bethel Life Ctr., Wichita, Kans., 1994—2003. Mem.: Am. String Teachers Assn.

PALMER, IRENE SABELBERG, university dean and educator emeritus, nurse, researcher, historian, genealogist; b. Franklin, N.J., May 28, 1923; d. John Joseph and May (Heiser) Sabelberg. BS, N.J. State Tchrs. Coll., 1945; diploma, Jersey City Med. Center Sch. Nursing, 1945; MA, NYU, 1951, PhD, 1963. Edn. dir. Diploma Schs. Nursing, N.J., Mass., 1948-52; ednl. dir. Glenn Dale (Md.) Hosp., D.C. Dept. Pub. Health, 1956, dir. nursing svc. and edn., 1956-61; assoc. clin. prof. nursing Georgetown U., 1960-61; USPHS trainee, 1961-62; assoc. chief nursing svc. for rsch. VA Hosp., San Francisco, 1963-64; rsch. nurse cons. HEW, USPHS, Div. Nursing, Nursing Rsch. Field Center, San Francisco, 1964-66; asst. dean, assoc. prof. nursing U. Colo. Sch. Nursing, Denver, 1966-68; dean, prof. nursing Boston U. Sch. Nursing, 1968-74; prof. Hahn Sch. Nursing, U. San Diego, 1974-91, prof. emeritus, 1991—, dean, 1974-87, dean emeritus, 1988—. Lectr. Classical Alliance of the western States, Uskudar, Turkey, 1994, Italy, 1995. Editor: Nursing Clinics of North America, 1970; Contbr. articles to profl. jours. Served to capt. Nurse Corps U.S. Army, 1953-56. Internat. Nightingale scholar; Nat. Health Svc. fellow; recipient Excellence in Nursing Scholarship award Orgn. Nurse Execs., 1993. Fellow Nat. League Nursing (bd. visitors 1977-87), Am Acad. Nursing; mem. ANA, Am. Assn. History Nursing, Am. Assn. Colls. Nursing (hon.), Boston U. Nursing Archives, German Rsch. Assn. (pres. 1995), Sigma Theta Tau (Leadership award Zeta Mu chpt. 1986, Excellence in Nursing award 1991).

PALMER, JOCELYN BETH, volunteer; b. Salina, Kans., Dec. 19, 1927; d. Paul Franklin and Josie Murtle (Schultz) Swartz; m. Gerald Keith Palmer, Dec. 28, 1952; children: David, Paula, Brian, April. AA, Christian Coll., Columbia, Mo., 1947; BS with honors, Kans. State U., 1949; MA, U. Iowa, 1951. Grad. asst. presch. U. Iowa, Iowa City, 1949-51; instr. U. Ill., Urbana, 1951-52; co-dir. child devel. ctr. Long Beach (Calif.) City Coll., 1954-56. Mem. task force Early Childhood Edu., 2000-01. Tchr. trainer, presch. tchr., cons., chmn. nursery com., elder, deacon Presbyn. Ch.; mem. Com. to Develop Stds. for Presch. Handicapped, Salina, 1981-83; pres., bd. dirs. # 305 Salina Sch. Dist., 1975-87; com. chair, bd. dirs. St. Francis Boyd Home,

Salina, Ellsworth, 1984-87; bd. dirs. YWCA, 1993-97; bd. dirs. Asburg Hosp. Aux., 1993-96, sec. 1994-96; mem. com. planning early childhood edn. USD 305. Mem. Clippership Mariners (chaplain 1991-93, logkeeper 1994-95, 2000-01, skipper 1997, chaplain, 2002-03), Saline County Med. Alliance (bd. dirs. 1992-96, 98-2000), Twentieth Century Forum (courtesy chmn. 1989-93, 2000—), PEO (pres. 1989-91, 94-95, treas. 1993-95), Salina Downtown Lioness (bd. dirs. 1988-89, 91-93, program chair 1997, pres. 2000-03), Phi Kappa Phi, Omicron Nu. Republican. Avocations: sewing, reading, music, swimming.

PALMER, LYNNE, writer, astrologer; b. El Centro, Calif., Dec. 14, 1932; d. Clarence Lee and Paquita Mae (Hartley) Hafer; m. Bruno Cazzaniga, Mar. 13, 1964 (div. 1965); m. Sidney Latter, Nov. 29, 1997. Student, Ch. of Light, 1957-62, Calif. Sch. Escrows, L.A., 1960; theatre mgmt. degree, Mus. Arenas Theatres Assn., N.Y.C., 1963. Asst. teller Western Mortgage, L.A., 1957-58; head teller Sutro Mortgage Svc., L.A., 1958-61; freelance astrologer N.Y.C., 1961-92, Las Vegas, Nev., 1962—; owner, operator, tchr. astrology sch. N.Y.C., 1970-72; owner Star Bright Pubs., Las Vegas, 1996—. Spkr. in field; interviewed in N.Y. Post and other major newspapers and mags. including Life and Oggi (Italy), Veja (Brazil), Wall St. Jour., People Mag., Globe, Die Welt am Sonntag (West Germany), New Woman Mag., Forbes. Author: Prosperity, Nixon's Horoscope, Astrological Almanac, Astrological Compatibility (Profl. Astrologers award 1976), Horoscope of Billy Rose, ABC Basic Chart Reading, ABC Major Progressions, ABC Chart Erection, Pluto Ephemeris (1900-2000), Daily Positions, Is Your Name Lucky For You?, Do-It-Yourself Publicity Directory, Your Lucky Days and Numbers, Money Magic, Astro-Guide to Nutrition and Vitamins, Gambling to Win, The Astrological Treasure Map, Dear Sun Signs, Are You Compatible With Your Boss, Partner, Coworkers, Employee, Client?, Bet to Win, Special Report: USA Under Attack; columnist: Self, House Beautiful, Gold; record album: Cast and Read Your Horoscope; TV appearances include The Johnny Carson Tonight Show, What's My Line, 60 Minutes, CBS News Night Watch, Cosmos (BBC), Sci. Series (Italian TV), Fantastico (Brazilian TV), Japan TV, News (Nippon), Do We Really Need It? (ASAHI), The World is Calling (Uranai); contbr. articles to mags. and newspapers. Mem. AFTRA, Am. Fedn. Astrologers (cert.). Avocation: travel. Home: 850 E Desert Inn Rd Apt 912 Las Vegas NV 89109-2100 Office: Star Bright Pubs 1155 E Twain Ave Ste 108-248 Las Vegas NV 89109 Office Phone: 702-894-9919. E-mail: lynnepalmer@lynnepalmer.com.

PALMER, MARCELLA, reporter; b. Edison, N.J. B, Rutgers U. News anchor Sta. WBGE-FM, Peoria; reporter Sta. WEEK, Peoria, 1993—97, Sta. WKEF-TV, Dayton, Ohio, Sta. WCBS-TV, N.Y.C., 1997—. Office: CBS 524 W 57th St New York NY 10019

PALMER, MARY ANN, videoconference product manager, sales engineer; b. South Montrose, Pa., July 31, 1950; d. Glenn Earl and Doris Lorraine (Allen) P.; 3 children. Student in computer programming, Oglethorpe U., 1983. Completed videoteleconferencing systems program, Compression Labs, Inc., San Jose, Calif.; cert. VTEL systems engrng.; Adtran product cert.; Ascend cert. tech. tng. Asst. mgr. Sears Catalog Store, Montrose, 1968-78; exec. sec. Douglas Foods, N.Y., Ga., 1978-80, Kimberly-Clark Corp., Roswell, Ga., 1980-90, videoconf. specialist, 1990-96; videoconf. product mgr. Kans. Comm., Lenexa, Kans., 1996-97; ind. cons. videoconf./telemedicine Lenexa, Kans., 1996-97. Cons. videoconf./telemedicine, Atlanta, Kansas City, Mo., 1996-97. Avocations: culinary, reading, computers, camping, fishing.

PALMER, NOREEN E. psychotherapist; b. Columbus, Ohio, Nov. 24, 1960; d. Alfred and Lurlena White; m. Charles Edwin Palmer, Apr. 18, 1991; children: Charles Jr., Arianna. BS, Ohio U., 1983; MA, Ohio State U., 1986, MSW, 1988. Lic. ind. social worker. Grad. asst. Ohio State U., Columbus, 1986-88, program coord., 1989—92; social worker Nat. Med. Care, Columbus, 1992-96; profl. liaison Grant/Riverside Hosp., Columbus, 2000—; pvt. practice psychotherapist Pickerington, Ohio, 1995—. Pvt. practice grant writing cons., Columbus, 1990-99; vol. clin. dir. Homeless Families Found., Columbus, 1996-99, v.p., 1997-99; bd. mem. Am. Diabetes Assn.-Heartland Chpt., Columbus. Co-author: Going Off: A Guide for Black Women Who've Just About Had Enough, 2001, Going Off: A Black Woman's Guide for Dealing with Anger and Stress, 2002; guest contbr. Heart and Soul, Black Expressions Mag. Founder Blackboard Literacy Initiative, exec. dir., 1995-97. Recipient Commendation, Canton (Ohio) City Coun., 1988, Appreciation award Pathways Mentors, Columbus, 1989, Vol. award Homeless Families Found., Columbus, 1999, commendation Ohio Ho. of Reps., 2002. Mem. Nat. Coalition of 100 Balck Women (Appreciation award 1997). Avocations: reading, cooking, walking, freelance writing. Office: Grant/Riverside Health Ctr 697B Hill Rd N Pickerington OH 43147-1157 also: 5554 Isaac Rd Canal Winchester OH 43110

PALMER, PAMELA S. lawyer; BA, U. Calif., Irvine, 1978; JD, U. So. Calif., 1982. Bar: Calif. 1982. Jud. clk. to Hon. Walter Ely, U.S. Ct. Appeals (9th cir.); with Heller, Ehrman, White & McAuliffe, L.A., ptnr., 1992—96, Latham & Watkins, L.A., 1996—. Office: Latham and Watkins LLP 633 W Fifth St Ste 4000 Los Angeles CA 90071*

PALMER, ROSE, humanities educator, writer; b. London, Eng., Feb. 11, 1914; arrived in U.S., 1929; d. Harris Schneider and Rebecca Albeitman; m. Frank Palmer, Apr. 12, 1941 (div. Sept. 1988); children: Diane, Richard, Pamela, Kenneth. Lit. tutor, Chgo., 1985—. Achievements include development of simplified phonics method for tutoring adults and teens. Home: 3009 N Harlam Ave Chicago IL 60634-4752*

PALMER, ROSE ANN, television producer, writer, educator; b. Bklyn. BA, St. Joseph's Coll.; MA, Bklyn. Coll.; PhD, N.Y. U., 1997. Lic. H.S. English tchr., H.S. speech tchr., tchr. of deaf, ednl. evaluator, N.Y.C. English tchr. N.Y.C. Bd. Edn., Bklyn., 1957-63; tchr., radio and TV broadcaster WNYE-FM-TV, Bur. Radio and TV, Bklyn., 1963-82; tchr. deaf, lang. coord., edn. edr. N.Y.C. Bd. Edn., 1982-90; producer Telecare TV, Uniondale, N.Y., 1992—; novelist, 1990—. Grad. asst. NYU, 1990; tchr. Bklyn. Coll., 1969, Evelyn Wood Reading Dynamics, 1968. Author: A History of the NY League for the Hard of Hearing in the Context of the Progressive (1900-1918) and Neo-Progressive Eras, 1997. Mem. AAUW, United Fedn. Tchrs., Mystery Writers Am. Avocations: reading, theatre going.

PALMER, SHARON-JOY, agricultural research company executive; b. S.I., N.Y., Oct. 16, 1947; d. James Murdock Palmer and Lillian Elinore (Nelson) Daniels; 1 child, Cameron Nelson Polland. Student, Wayne U., Chgo., 1966-68; student in real estate, Dade Jr. Coll., 1969-73; BS in Edn./Ch. Ministries, Liberty U., 1989, ThM, MAR/Counseling, 1994. Dental asst. Francis J. Byron Jr., DDS, S.I., N.Y., 1966-69; flight attendant Delta Airlines, Miami, 1969-77; realtor D.W. Hyder and Assocs., Albuquerque, 1976-78; sales rep. Postique of Colo., Denver, 1976-78; dir. Combanc Internat., Inc., Albuquerque, 1976-80; mfr.'s rep. Innovative Mktg. Concepts, Albuquerque, 1977-79, owner; developer, owner Angel Skye Investments, Ltd., Angel Fire, N.Mex., 1979—; econ. adv. Am. S.S.T. Corp., Parkersburg, W.Va., 1982-85; founder, pres., CEO Sci. Econ. Environ. Devel. Internat., Inc., Albuquerque, 1981—. Ptnr. Angel Skye Investments, 1980—; bd. dirs. Asia Enterprise Ltd., Tokyo, Condoc-Paraguay Ltd., Asuncion, Victory Internat. Inc., Panama City, Republic of Panama, Sci Econ. Environ. Devel. Kenya Ltd., Nairobi, 1980—, Sci. Econ. Environ. Devel. Internat. Del., Mountains Herbs and Spices, Albuquerque, 1980—; pres. World Solar Seed, 1999-, Native Seed Internat., Native Am. Nations, 2000, Mighty Seed Internat., CEO, 1999, Mighty Seed Corp., 1998-. Inventor agrl. energy efficient units, 1982; inventor, designer above ground and underground "mighty seed" units for food prodn., seed programmable environ. controller and modular housing, disaster hurricane enclosures. Active Embassy Kenya, Washington for Agrl. Devel., Nairobi, Kenya, East Africa, 1982; mem. various childrens' hosps., Miami, 1973, Westside Assn., Coralles, N.Mex., 1980, various children's hosps. Mem. Am. Dental Assts. Assn., Better Bus. Bur., Bd. Realtors, NAFE (nat. dir.), Nat. Platform Assn., Entrepreneur's Assn. Clubs: Angel Fire Country, Rio Rancho (N.Mex.) Country. Republican. Baptist. Home: 3208 Sue Cir Albuquerque NM 87124

PALMER, STACY ELLA, periodical editor; b. Middletown, Conn., Oct. 25, 1960; d. Marvin Jerome Palmer and Eileen Sondra (Cohen) Palmer Burke. B in Liberal Arts and Internat. Rels., Brown U., 1982. Asst. editor Chronicle of Higher Edn., Washington, 1982-86, sr. editor, 1986-88; news editor Chronicle of Philanthropy, Washington, 1988-93, mng. editor, 1993-98, editor, 1998—. Bd. dirs. Brown Alumni Monthly, Providence, 1988-91, vice chmn., 1991-93, mem. 1996—. Mem. Comm. Network in Philanthropy, Investigative Reporters and Editors, Brown Club Washington (bd. dirs. 1993—, pres. 1994-99), Brown U. Alumni Assn. (bd. govs. 1997—). Avocations: swimming, bicycling, travel. Home: 2301 Connecticut Ave NW Apt 7C Washington DC 20008-1730 Office: Chronicle of Philanthropy 1255 23rd St NW Washington DC 20037-1125

PALMER, SUE, former state legislator, oil industry executive; b. Jan. 31, 1942; m. Duke Palmer. Pres. Lucky Lady Oil, Fort Worth, Tex.; rep. dist. 89 Tex. House Reps., Austin, 1997—2001. Republican. also: PO Box 4590 Fort Worth TX 76164-0590

PALMER, THERESA JOAN GRIFFIN, restaurant owner executive; d. Sidney Lawrence Griffin and Sybil Theresa Arnold; 1 child, Damon Shawn. BA in psychology, sociology, U. W. Ga., 1972. Concept founder, v.p., sec.-treas., CFO T.J. Applebee's Edibles and Elixirs, Inc. (now Applebee's Neighborhood Bar & Grill), Lawrenceville, Ga., 1980—83; sec.-treas., CFO Cafe Ventures Inc., Lilburn, Ga., 1985—96; v.p., sec.-treas. Apple Restaurants Inc., Lilburn, 1988—98, Apple Restaurants Mgmt. Co. Inc., Duluth, Ga., 1991—98; ret., 1999; cons., 1999—. Mem.: Ga. Walking Horse Assoc., Gwinnett County Hist. Soc., Atlanta Hist. Soc., The Carl Jung Soc. Atlanta, Atlanta Kennel Club, Am. Kennel Club. Achievements include founding and opening of first Applebee's restaurant in 1980 in Decatur, Ga. Home: 8205 Dogwood Trail Cumming GA 30041 Office: Apple Rio Inc 8205 Dogwood Trail Cumming GA 30041 E-mail: tj@applebees.us.

PALMER, VICKI R. food products executive; b. Memphis; m. John E. Palmer; 1 child, Alexandria. B in Econs. and Bus. Adminstrn., Rhodes Coll., 1975; MBA in Fin., U. Memphis, 1980. Corp. loan officer First Tenn. Bank.; head pension investment FedEx, mgr. corp. fin.; mgr. pension investments Coca-Cola Co., 1983—86; asst. treas. Coca-Cola Enterprises Inc., 1986—93, v.p., 1993—99, treas., 1993—, sr. v.p., spl. asst. to CEO, 1999—, bd. dirs., 2001—. Bd. dirs. Spelman Coll., Rhodes Coll., Woodward Acad., First Tenn. Nat. Corp. Named one of 20 Women of Power and Influence in Corp. Am., Black Enterprise Mag., 100 Black Women of Influence, Atlanta Bus. League, 1998; recipient Disting. Alumni award, U. Memphis Alumni Assn. Office: Coca-Cola Enterprises 2500 Windy Ridge Pkwy Atlanta GA 30339*

PALMER, WENDY, professional basketball player; b. Aug. 12, 1974; BA in History, U. Va., 1996. Forward Oviedo, Spain, 1996—97, WMBA - Utah Starzz, Salt Lake City, 1997—99, Detroit Shock, 1999—. Named to, All-Am., 1995, 1996. Avocations: horseback riding, music. Office: 2 Championship Auburn Hills MI 48326

PALMERIO, ELVIRA CASTANO, art gallery director, art historian; b. Cin., July 23, 1929; d. John and Josephine Castano; m. Carlo Palmerio, June 1, 1958 (dec.); 1 child, Marina. B Lit. Interpretation, Emerson Coll., 1950; postgrad., Pius XII Inst., Florence, Italy, 1954-55; student opera with Cesare Sturani. Curator Castano Art Gallery, Boston, 1965-78, dir. Needham, Mass., 1978-98; rschr. for Archivies of Am. Art Smithsonian Instn., Boston, 1988-89; performed voiceover in Italian for Nova PBS TV Series, Nova, Italy, 1997; gov. adv. com., 1997. Vatican translator; interpreter Italian art specializing in Macchiaioli art; Italian interpreter Ritz Carlton Internat. Festival, (Italian) Mayor's Office Sister Cities Internat. Conv.; appointed sec. World Affairs Coun., Boston; tchr. Emmanuel Coll. Boston, 1953. Mem. Rep. Presdl. Task Force, Nat. Rep. Senatorial Com., Presdl. Inner Circle; active Boston chpt. UN; bd. dirs. Needham Hist. Soc., Boston U. Women's Coun.; vol. Sail Boston, 1992; del. Presdl. Trust, 1992; apptd. Gov.'s Com. on Women's Issues; del. to Nat. Fedn. of Rep. Womens Conv., 1999, 2002; vol. WGBH. Cardinal Spellman scholar; recipient Pirandello Lyceum award, I Migliori, 1997, Vol. award Nat. Fedn. Commns. Women, 1999, Nat. Assn. Commissions for Women, 1999. Mem. UN, Boston U. Women's Coun., Boston Browning Soc., Fogg Art Mus. of Harvard U., Friends of Needham Libr., Archives Am. Art Boston, World Boston, World Affairs Coun. Boston (sec.), Nat. Mus. Women in Arts, Needham Hist. Soc. (bd. dirs.), Wellesley Hist. Soc., Nat. Italian Am. Found., French Libr., World Boston. Avocations: current events, internat. affairs, writing, travel, music. Address: 50 Grove St Wellesley MA 02482-7713

PALMIERI, PATRICIA J. elementary school educator; b. McKees Rocks, Pa., Jan. 4, 1954; d. George Alfred and Annette Marie Fuze; m. Michael Louis Palmieri, Aug. 2, 1975 (div. Apr. 1993); 1 child, Kathryn Veronica. BS in Music Edn., Geneva Coll., 1975; BS in Elem. Edn., Cabrini Coll., 1977; EdM, Arcadia Coll., 1980. Tchr. William Penn Sch. Dist., Yeadon, Pa., 1975—90, Jacaranda Sch., Plantation, Fla., 1990—93, Am. Heritage Sch., Plantation, Fla., 1993—. Avocations: piano, tennis, reading, interior decorating. Home: 7876 Dixie Beach Cir Tamarac FL 33321-8892

PALMORE, CAROL M. state official; b. Owensboro, Ky., Jan. 13, 1949; d. P.J. and Carrie Alice (Leonard) Pate; m. John Stanley Palmore Jr., Jan. 1, 1982. BS in History and Polit. Sci., Murray State U., 1971; JD, U. Ky., 1977. Social worker Dept. Human Resources, Frankfort, Ky., 1971-74; assoc. Rummage, Kamuf, Yewell & Pace, Owensboro, 1977-81; hearing officer Ky. Bd. Claims, Frankfort, 1980-81; gen. counsel Ky. Labor Cabinet, Frankfort, 1982-83, dep. sec. labor, 1984, 1986-87, sec. labor, 1987-90, 91-94; ptnr. Palmore & Sheffer Attys., Henderson, Ky., 1984-86; dep. sec. Ky. Pers. Cabinet, Frankfort, 1996-98, acting sec., 1998, sec., 1998—. Bd. dirs. Ky. Employer's Mutual Ins., Ky. Retirement Sys., Ky. Pub. Employees Deferred Comp. Authority, Govtl. Svcs. Ctr. Authority, Gov.'s Collective Bargaining Task Force, Gov.'s Minority Mgmt. Trainee Program Task Force, State Parks Commn., Ky. Group Health Ins. Bd.; chmn. Ky. Safety & Health Stds. Bd., Frankfort, 1987-90, 91-94; co-chmn. Ky. Labor Mgmt. Adv. Coun., Frankfort, 1987-90, 91-94; bd. dirs. Ky. Workers' Comp Funding Commn., Frankfort, 1987-90, 91-94, Community Svc. Commn., Frankfort, 1993-94, Ky. Info. Resources Mgmt. Commn., Frankfort, 1994, Sch.-to-Work Partnership Coun., Frankfort, 1994; ex-officio bd. dirs. Pub. Employees Collective Bargaining Task Force, Frankfort, 1994, Ky. Workforce Partnership Coun., Frankfort, 1994. Labor liaison Jones for Gov., Lexington, 1990-91; del. Dem. Nat. Conv., N.Y.C., 1992; mem. inaugural class Ky. Women's Leadership Network, Frankfort, 1993; bd. dirs. Alliant Health Systems Adult Oper. Bd., Louisville, 1992-96, Ky. Commn. Homeless, Frankfort, 1993-94; candidate for Sec. State Commonwealth Ky., 1995; chair Dem. Women's Think Tank, 1995. Mem. Ky. Bar Assn. (del. ho. dels. 1985-86, chair law day/spkr. bur. 1985-86, mem. 1986-90), Ky. Bar Found. (bd. dirs. 1985-92, sec. 1986-89, pres. elect 1989-90, pres. 1990-91), Rotary (program chair Frankfort chpt. 1993-94). Democrat. Episcopalian. Avocations: antiques, reading, vintage jewelry, walking. Home: 2310 Peaks Mill Rd Frankfort KY 40601-9437 Office: Personnel Cabinet 200 Fair Oaks Ln Frankfort KY 40601-1134

PALOMBO, LISA, artist; b. Providence, Mar. 1, 1965; d. Joseph Christopher Palombo and Catherine Ann Walsh. BFA, R.I. Sch. Design, 1987. Featured artist: (books) The Best of Oil Painting, 1996, Exploring Color, 1998. Recipient honors recognition Artist's Mag., 2003, 2004. Mem.: Oil Painters of Am., N.J. Am. Artists Profl. League. Office: Palombo Studios 55 Mountain Ave Caldwell NJ 07006 E-mail: art@lisapalombo.com.

PALSER, BARBARA F. botany researcher, retired educator; b. Worcester, Mass., June 2, 1916; d. G. Norman and Cora A. (Munson) P. AB, Mt. Holyoke Coll., 1938, A.M., 1940, D.Sc. (hon.), 1978; PhD, U. Chgo., 1942. From instr. to prof. botany U. Chgo., 1942-65; from assoc. prof. to prof. botany Rutgers U., New Brunswick, N.J., 1965-83, dir. grad. program in botany, 1973-80; adj. prof. botany U. Mass., Amherst, 1991—. Erskine fellow U. Canterbury, Christchurch, N.Z. 1969; vis. prof. Duke U., Durham, N.C., fall 1962; vis. research fellow U. Melbourne, Parkville, Victoria, Australia, fall 1984-85 Author lab. manual Principles of Botany, 1973, also numerous research papers in bot. jours.; bot. adviser Ency. Brit., Chgo., 1958-59; editor Bot. Gazette, Chgo., 1960-65 Named Outstanding Tchr., Rutgers Coll., 1977 Mem. Bot. Soc. Am. (sec. 1970-74, v.p. 1975, pres. 1976, Merit award 1985), Torrey Bot. Club (pres. 1968), Internat. Soc. Plant Morphologists, N.J. Acad. Scis. (pres. elect 1987-88, pres. 1988-89, Outstanding Svc. award 1985, 90). Avocations: hiking, stamp collecting, photography. Home: 330 Spencer Dr Amherst MA 01002-3367

PALSHO, DOROTHEA COCCOLI, information services executive; b. Philadelphia, Pennsylvania, June 9, 1947; d. John Charles and Dorothy Lucille (Decker) Coccoli; m. Edward Robert Palsho; children: Christopher, Ryan, and Erica (stepchild). BS, Villanova Univ., 1976; MBA, Temple Univ., 1977. V.p. info. svc. Dow Jones and Co., Princeton, NJ, 1977-97, pres. bus. info. svc., 1995-97, v.p. interactive pub. N.Y.C., 1997—2002, v.p. electronic pub., 2000—02, v.p. stragetic mktg., 2002—. Named to Class of Women Achievers, YWCA Acad. of Women Achievers, 1985. Avocation: sports with the boys. Office: Dow Jones and Co Inc 200 Liberty St New York NY 10281

PALTROW, GWYNETH, actress; b. L.A., Sept. 28, 1972; d. prodr. Bruce Paltrow and actress Blythe Danner; m. Chris Martin, Dec. 2003. Grad. Spence Sch., N.Y.C., 1990. Appeared in films: Shout, 1991, Hook, 1991, Malice, 1993, Flesh and Bone, 1993, Mrs. Parker and the Vicious Circle, 1994, Jefferson in Paris, 1995, Moonlight and Valentino, 1995, Seven, 1995, The Pallbearer, 1996, Emma, 1996, Hard Eight, 1996, Sliding Doors, 1998, Out of the Past, 1998 (voice), Great Expectations, 1998, Hush, 1998, A Perfect Murder, 1998, Shakespeare in Love, 1998, The Talented Mr. Ripley, 1999, Duets, 1999, The Intern, 2000, Bounce, 2000, The Anniversary Party, 2001, The Royal Tenenbaums, 2001, Shallow Hal, 2001, Possession, 2002, View From the Top, 2003, Sylvia, 2003; TV films: Cruel Doubt, 1992, Deadly Relations, 1993; Theatre: Picnic, The Adventures of Huck Finn, Sweet Bye and Bye, The Seagull, Proof. Won Golden Satellite Best Actress in a Motion Picture Emma, 1997, Best Actress Oscar, American Academy Awards, Shakespeare in Love, 1999; Golden Globe Awards, Best Actress, Shakespeare in Love, 1999, Best Actress FFCC, 1999. Mem. Screen Actors Guild (Outstanding Performance with others). Office: Creative Artists Agy c/o Rick Kurtzman 9830 Wilshire Blvd Beverly Hills CA 90212-1804 also: Screen Actors Guild 5757 Wilshire Blvd Los Angeles CA 90036-3635*

PALUMBO, LORRAINE REIKO MINATOISHI, architectural historian; b. Honolulu, June 3, 1966; d. Merton Chikayuki and Eleanor Machiko (Suda) M.; m. Charles Haigler Palumbo, Feb. 16, 1995; children: Sara Minatoishi, Hana Machiko. BArch, U. Hawaii, 1989; MArch, U. Oreg., 1993; postgrad., Waseda U., Tokyo, 1994-95, PhD in Archtl. History, 1999. Designer, draftsperson DMJM Architects, Engrs. Planners, Honolulu, 1989-91; rsch. intern Mizusawa Constrn. Co., Tokyo, 1992-93; archtl. historian Mason Archs., Inc., 2000—. Seminar leader Waseda U., 1996-97. Editor Hawaii Buddhism Newsletter, 1999—. Grad. tchg. fellow U. Oreg., 1991, Patricia Roberts Harris fellow U.S. Govt., Oreg., 1991-92; recipient Japanese Mombusho scholarship Japanese Govt. Min. of Edn., 1994-98; grantee Toyota Corp. Fellowship, 1997-98. Mem. Archtl. Inst. Japan, Hist. Hawaii Found., U. Oreg. Alumni Assn. Avocations: travel, ocean activities, visiting architectural sites. Office: Mason Archs Inc 119 Merchant St Ste 501 Honolulu HI 96813 E-mail: imp@masonarch.com.

PALUMBO, LOUISE COREY, fashion and special events administrator; b. Charleston, W.Va., Aug. 19, 1931; d. George N. and Bahia (George) Corey; m. Mario Joseph Palumbo, Apr. 13, 1933; children: Mario Joseph Jr., Corey Lee. BA, Morris Harvey Coll., 1955. Trainee Saks Fifth Ave., N.Y.C., 1956; asst. fashion coord. Ind. Retailers Syndicate, N.Y.C., 1956-59; corp. fashion and spl. events dir. Stone & Thomas, Charleston, W.Va., 1959—2004; ret.; freelance fashion shows. Host TV show Fashion Today. State dir. Friendship Force, W.Va., 1983—; founder, chmn. River Lights, Charleston, 1982—; coord. Uniforms for Spl. Olympics, W.Va., 1992; chmn. Inaugural Balls for Gov. Rockefeller, W.Va., 1983, 87; mem. Preservation of Gov. Mansion, W.Va., 1992—, Women's Arts, W.Va., 1994—, Symphony League for Women, W.Va., 1994—; trustee Sunrise Mus., Charleston, 1983-89; chair Clay Ctr. Art and Sci. Mus. opening. Recipient Mayor's Award for the arts Fund for the Arts, 1992, Creative Achievement award Advt. Club Huntington, 1971, Cert. of Appreciation Nat. Coun. Jewish Women, 1992. Democrat. Ea. Orthodox. Avocations: tennis, skiing. Home: 1838 Louden Heights Rd Charleston WV 25314-1565

PALUMBO, LUCILLE A. microbiologist; d. Dominick J. and Regina R. Palumbo. AAS in Med. Lab. Tech., Bronx C.C., 1972; BS in Med. Lab. Sci., Hunter Coll., 1974; MA in Math., Herbert H. Lehman Coll., 1980. Lab. technologist Montefiore Med. Ctr., Bronx, 1973—88; sys. analyst Jacobi Med. Ctr., Bronx, 1988—89; lab microbiologist Mycobacteriology Lab. N.Y.C. Dept. Health, 1989—95, assoc. lab microbiologist, 1995—; lab supr. Mycobacteriology Lab., 1999—. With anthrax outbreak Bioterrorism Response Lab., 2001—02. Avocations: genealogy, travel.

PALUMBO, RUTH ANN, state legislator; b. Lexington, Ky., July 7, 1949; d. James Keith and Dorothy Calvin (Carrier) Baker; m. John Anthony Palumbo II, June 29, 1974; children: John A. III (dec.), Joseph Edward, James Thomas, Stephen Baker. BA in Secondary Edn., U. Ky., 1972. Sales Chez Lissette Boutique, Leysin, Switzerland, 1966; sales, shoes Purcell's Dept. Store, Lexington, Ky., 1966-70; organist Ctrl. Bapt. Ch., Lexington, Ky., 1968; clk. Good Samaritan Hosp., Lexington, Ky., 1968-73; sec. Dr. Joseph Keith, Lexington, Ky., 1971-73; senate clk. aide Ky. Gen. Assembly, Frankfort, Ky., 1974; pub. rels. Palumbo Properties, Lexington, 1974-92; state rep. Ky. Gen. Assembly, 1991—. Mem. LWV, Lexington, 1990-92, Ky. Women's Polit. Caucus, Louisville, 1991-92, NAt. Order Women Legislators, Washington, 1992; sec. Ctrl. Ky. Caucus, Lexington, 1991-92. Mem. Greater Lexington Dem. Women, fin. v.p., 1982; mem. Nat. Order of Women Legislators, Washington, 1992; legis.liaison ACS Breast Cancer Detection Task Force, Ky., 1992; adv. coun. Bryan Sta. Youth Svcs. Ctr., Lexington, 1992; ball chmn. Lexington Philharmonic Women's Guild, 1990; govt. affairs Am. Symphony Orch. League Vol. Coun., Washington, 1992; bd. dirs. Philharmonic Women's Guild, pres., 1986-88; bd. dirs. Am. Cancer Soc., pres., 1988-89; bd. dirs. Lexington Phulharmonic Soc. Recipient Dorothy Moomaw Miles Svc. award Sayre Sch., 1986, Govs. Vol. Activist award Gov. Wallace G. Wilkinson, 1989, named Lexington's Outstanding Young Woman Bluegrass Jr. Woman's Club, 1982, Leadership Lexington, C. of C., 1988, Leadership Am. Found. for Women's Resources, Washington, 1989. Fellow U. Ky. Devel. Coun.; mem. Jr. League LExington (sec. 1989-90), Prof. Women's Forum, Gamma Phi Veta (pres. 1980-82). Baptist. Avocations: playing piano, singing, collecting stamps, music boxes, family. Home: 10 Deepwood Dr Lexington KY 40505-2106 Office: House of Reps State Capitol Frankfort KY 40601

PALVINO, NANCY MANGIN, retired librarian; b. Rochester, N.Y., Nov. 22, 1937; d. John Bernard and Miriam Lucille (Fox) Mangin; m. Lawrence Robert Palvino, July 2, 1960; children: Mark, Laurie, Lisa, Katharine, Thomas. BS, SUNY, Geneseo, 1959; MLS, U. Buffalo, 1993. Cert. libr., N.Y. Libr. Spencerport (N.Y.) Elem. Sch., 1959-60; tchr. East Greenbush (N.Y.) Elem. Sch., 1960-63; libr. # 41 Sch., Rochester, 1993–2001; ret., 2001. Author: (bibliography) Autism, 1991. Fundraiser Rochester Philharm. Orgn., 1970; mem. women's bd. dirs. St. Mary's Hosp., Rochester, 1980—, giftshop chairperson, 1989-92, exec. coun., 1989-92, chmn. of ball, 1985, Imperial Ball Meml. Art Gallery, 1987, Holiday Open House, 1988; v.p. women's coun. Meml. Art Gallery, Rochester, 1989-91. Grantee DeWitt Wallace Reader's Digest Fund, 1994. Mem. ALA, N.Y. Libr. Assn. (scholarship 1992), Greater Rochester Areas Media Specialists (chmn. scholarship com. 1994-95, scholarship 1992), Phi Delta Kappa. Avocations: golf, reading, walking, knitting. Home: 80 Winding Creek Ln Rochester NY 14625-2175

PAMERLEAU, SUSAN L. career officer; BA in Sociology, U. Wyo., 1968; grad., Squadron Officer Sch., 1975, Air Command and Staff Coll., 1977, Indsl. Coll. Armed Forces, 1985. Commd. 2d lt. USAF, 1968, advanced through grades to maj. gen., 1997; exec. support officer 3d Civil Engring. Squadron, Kunsan Air Base, South Korea, 1973-74; chief cen. base adminstrn. 435th Tactical Airlift Wing, Rhein-Main Air Base, West Germany, 1978-79; chief force programs divsn. Dir. Plans, Programs & Analysis Air Force Mil. Pers. Ctr., Randolph AFB, Tex., 1985-87; comdr. 3700th Pers. Resources Group Air Force Mil. Tng. Ctr., Lackland AFB, Tex., 1988-89; exec. officer plans and policy divsn. Internat. Mil. Staff, NATO Hdqs., Brussels, 1989-92; chief resource allocation divsn. and pers. and support team Hdqs. USAF, Washington, 1992-93; vice comdr. Air Force Mil. Pers. Ctr., Randolph AFB, Tex., 1993-94; commandant Maxwell, Ala. Air Force Res. Officer Tng. Corps, Maxwell AFB, Ala., 1994-96; comdr. Air Force Pers. Ctr., Randolph AFB, Tex., 1996-98; dir. pers. force mgmt., dep. chief of staff pers. Hdqs. USAF, Washington, 1998—. Decorated Def. Superior Svc. medal, Legion of Merit, Meritorious Svc. medal with 2 oak leaf clusters. Office: HQ USAF/DPF 1040 Air Force Pentagon Washington DC 20330-1040

PAMIN, DIANA DOLHANCYK (DIANA DOLHANCYK), poet; b. Cleve., Dec. 13; d. Peter and Diana (Dribes) Dolhancyk; m. Leonard Pamin, Aug. 28; children: Diana Anne, Louis Peter. Grad., Titus Coll. Cosmetology. Author: The Parting in Journey of the Mind, 1994 (Editor's Choice award), The Parting in East of the Sunrise, 1995 (Editor's Choice award), Stormy in Songs on the Wind, 1994 (Editor's Choice award), Stormy in Beyond the Stars, 1995 (Editor's Choice award), Shadow Side in At Water's Edge, 1995 (Editor's Choice award), Eclipse in A Delicate Balance, 1995 (Editor's Choice award), Burnt By Love in Windows of the Soul, 1995 (Editor's Choice award), Web of Guilt in Where Dawn Lingers, 1996 (Editor's Choice award), The View in A Muse to Follow, 1996 (Editor's Choice award), The View in Portraits of Life, 1996 (Editor's Choice award), Photographer in Fields of Gold, 1997 (Editor's Choice award), Photographer in Dappled Sunlight, 1997 (Editor's Choice award), Shadow Side II in Of Moonlight and Wishes, 1997 (Editor's Choice award), Love No More in Best Poems of 1996 (Editor's Choice award), The Happening in Best Poems of the '90s, 1997 (Editor's Choice award), Rain in Journey to Our Dreams, 1996 (Accomplishment of Merit award for Literary Achievement), CAT in Promises to Keep, 1996 (Editor's Preference award of Excellence for Lit. Achievement), CAT in Starburst Jour., Winter Wedding, in Of Sunlight and Shadows, 1997 (Editor's Preference award of Excellence for Lit. Achievement), Unrequited Love, Web of Guilt, Sighs of Love, Autumn Symphony, A Dream, Happiness, Swan Song, Lost Song, in Of Sunlight and Shadows, 1997, Red Satin Box, in The Golden Wings of Time, 1997 (Editor's Preference award of Excellence for Lit. Achievement), Snowscape, Rain, Letters, Love No More, Happiness, in Best New Poems, 1996, 10 Elite award winning poems for Lit. Excellence in The Fourth Dimension, 1998, The Swing, Seasons of Love, The Goodbye, Betrothal, Not Our Own, Association, Gypsy, Healy Lilacs, Our Enchantment, Love No More, Sea of Dreams, A Furtive Tear, The Treasure, When Lips Cared, others; Association (poem), artwork cover Starburst Jour., 1996, Sea of Dreams, Starburst Jour., 1999 (elite award lit. excellence), Winter Wedding, Winds of the Universe, You, Loves Deception, The Soothing, Caress, He in Starburst Jour., 1997, His Name is Peter, "But, Isn't The Flower Lovely?," PaPa, in the Sparrowgrass Family Poetry Album, 2000, others. Inducted Internat. Poetry Hall of Fame Mus. Mem. Internat. Soc. Poets (life), Poet's Guild, Internat. Soc. Authors and Artists, Nat. Authors Registry. Home: 6282 Akins Rd North Royalton OH 44133

PAMMER, LESA GAIL, marketing professional; b. Chgo., Apr. 26, 1957; d. Frank James and Elene M. (Lieberman) Bobele; m. Fred Ross Pammer, May 7, 1978; children: David Ross, Daniel Matthew. AS, Prairie State Coll., 1977. Sportswear sales rep. Roselee, Matteson, Ill., 1975-80; editor market rsch. Bryles Survey, Crestwood, Ill., 1975-85; owner Pammer Rsch. Inc., Mokena, Ill., 1985—. Mem. Market Rsch. Assn. (chmn. arrangements 1994-95, chmn. PIP 1993-94). Jewish. Avocations: travelling, fishing, cooking. Home: 18925 Meadow Creek Dr Mokena IL 60448-9110

PAMPE, PAMELA MARY, textiles executive; consultant; b. Gary, Ind., Mar. 6, 1951; d. John Ambrose and Teresa Rita (Cassidy) Simonetto; m. Robert Allen Pampe, Dec. 29, 1970; children: Ryan Allen, Erin Amelia. BA in English, U. West Fla., 1974; student, San Diego (Calif.) State U., 1975—77, cert., 1977. Cert. quilt appraiser Am. Quilter's Soc., 1994. Employee rels. mgr. Citicorp Savings Fla., Miami, 1983—84, pub. rels. mgr., 1984—86; pres. Pampe Assocs., Miami, 1986—91, Miami (Fla.) Quilt Designs, 1998—. Pres. Am. Quilt Study Group, Lincoln, Nebr., 2000—02, bd. dirs. 1998—2003. Mem. com. Boy Scouts/Girl Scouts, Miami, 1986—; chief staff Pine Acres Cmty. Assn., Miami, 1995—97. Mem.: Am. Quilters Soc., Prof. Assn. Appraisers (pres. 1996—98). Roman Cath. Office: Miami Quilt Textile Designs 8841 SW 132nd St Miami FL 33176

PAMPUSCH, ANITA MARIE, foundation administrator; b. St. Paul, Aug. 28, 1938; d. Robert William and Lucille Elizabeth (Whaley) P. BA, Coll. of St. Catherine, St. Paul, 1962; MA, U. Notre Dame, 1970, PhD, 1972. Tchr. St. Joseph's Acad., St. Paul, 1962-66; instr. philosophy Coll. of St. Catherine, St. Paul, 1970-76, assoc. acad. dean, 1979, acad. dean, 1979-84, pres., 1984-97; Am. Council fellow Goucher Coll., Balt., 1976-77; pres. Bush Found., St. Paul, 1997—. Bd. dirs. St. Paul Cos.; head Women's Coll. Coalition, 1988-91. Author: (book rev.) Philological Quarterly, 1976; contbr. articles to profl. jours. Mem. adv. com. Instl. Leadership project, Columbia U., 1986—; dist. chmn. Rhodes Scholarship Selection com., Mo., Neb., Minn., Kans., N.D., S.D., 1987—; exec. com. Women's Coll. Coalition, Washington, 1985—. Mem. Coun. for Ind. Colls. (bd. dirs. 1987—, chair 1991—), Am. Philos. Assn., St. Paul C. of C. (bd. dirs. 1986—), St. Paul's Athletic Club, Mpls. Club, Phi Beta Kappa. Roman Catholic. Avocations: swimming, camping, reading, music. Home: 161 Stonebridge Rd Saint Paul MN 55118

PAN, ELIZABETH LIM, information systems company executive; b. Manila, Dec. 6, 1941; came to U.S., 1961, naturalized, 1967; d. Lim Hu and Maria (Ramos) Lim; m. Jeff T. S. Pan, Jan. 17, 1962 (dec. 1978); children: Jeffrey, James. Student, U. Philippines, Quezon City, 1959-61; BA, U. Ill., 1963, MS, 1966; PhD, Rutgers U., 1974. Pres. Trulim, Inc., Inst. Info. Studies, Inc.; CEO, chmn. bd. dirs. PSI Internat. Collection Mgmt., 1977-80; editor: Annual Rev. Rehab., 1980-83; contbr. articles to profl. publs. Pres. Nat. Fedn. 8(a) Cos. (pres.) Home: 3220 Lake Edge Way Oakton VA 22124-2028 Office: 10306 Eaton Pl Ste 400 Fairfax VA 22030-2201

PANAGOS, REBECCA JEAN HUFFMAN, university educator, researcher, consultant; b. Shreveport, La., Aug. 19, 1952; d. Richard Herbert and Betty Jean (Lilly) Huffman; m. Dennis Lee Panagos, Dec. 12, 1976; children: Ryan Edward, Anne Rebecca, Alexander. BA, La. Tech. U., 1973, MA in Edn., 1974; PhD, U. Mo., 1996. Cert. vocat. evaluator, tchr., Mo, Tchr. civics, English, journalism Bethel Christian Sch. Ruston, La., 1973-74, counselor Goodwill Industries Denver, 1975-76; guidance counselor Spl. Sch. Dist. St. Louis County, Mo., 1976-95; assoc. prof. tchr. preparation Lindenwood U., St. Charles, Mo., 1995—. Ednl. cons., 1993—. Author: Career Self-Efficacy for Adolescents with Learning Disabilities, 1996; editor Nat. Vocal. Assessment in Edn. Profile, 1993-96; contbr. articles to profl. jours. in spl. edn. Mem. Order of Ea. Star, 1970—, Order of Rainbow for Girls, 1970—, Internat. Families, 1984—. Recipient Outstanding Tchr. of Yr. award Nat. Assn. Vocat. Spl. Needs Edn., 1995, Outstanding Rsch. of Yr. award Am. Vocat. Assn., 1996. Mem. Coun. for Exceptional Children (interdisciplinary com. for vocat. assessment and evaluation 1993-97, faculty advisor student chpt. 1996—, pres. chpt. 212). Democrat. Methodist. Avocations: promoting international adoptions, research, publishing, jogging. Office: Lindenwood Univ 209 S Kingshighway St Saint Charles MO 63301-1693

PANCOAST, BRANDY ELIZABETH, music educator; b. Colville, Wash., Jan. 4, 1976; d. Robert Daniel and Valerie Francis Richartz; m. Tedric Howard Pancoast, July 11, 1999. BM in Piano Performance, BA in Music, Colo. Christian U., Lakewood, 1998. Cert. profl. piano tchr., profl. piano tchr. Wash., lic. Musikgarten instr. Piano tchr., owner Pancoast Sch. of Music, Kettle Falls, Wash. Mem.: Spokane Music Tchrs. (workshop coord. 2001—04, Musiklink coord. 2001—04), Foothills Music Tchrs. (chair Commencement Day 1998—2000, tchr. mentor 1998—2000, v.p. membership 1999—2000), Wash. State Music Tchrs. Assn., Music Tchrs. Nat. Assn. (v.p. student chpt. 1995—96, pres. student chpt. 1996—98), Am. Coll. Musicians (chair guild adjudication 2001—04). Avocations: gardening, reading, travel, music advocacy. Home: PO Box 809 Kettle Falls WA 99141

PANELLI, JEWEL D. elementary school educator; b. Springfield, Oreg., Mar. 7, 1970; d. Doris Jean and Buddy Dean Chafee, Carole Dawn Cameron and Julius Eugene Pool; m. Sal A. Panelli, Feb. 3, 2000; children: Emily Christine Benjamin, Dominic Michael. BA, Mont. State U., Bozeman, 1993. Tchr. Freedom Mid. Sch., Bakersfield, Calif., 1994—. Home: 10013 Polo Trail Ave Bakersfield CA 93312

PANICCIA, PATRICIA LYNN, journalist, writer, lawyer, educator; b. Glendale, Calif., Sept. 19, 1952; d. Valentino and Mary (Napoleon) P.; m. Jeffrey McDowell Mailes, Oct. 5, 1985; children: Alana Christine, Malia Noel. BA in Comm., U. Hawaii, 1977; JD, Pepperdine U., 1981. Bar: Hawaii 1981, Calif. 1982, U.S. Dist. Ct. Hawaii 1981. Extern law clk. hon. Samuel P. King U.S. Dist. Ct., Honolulu, 1980; reporter, anchor woman Sta. KEYT-TV, Santa Barbara, Calif., 1983-84; reporter Sta. KCOP-TV, L.A., 1984-88; reporter CNN, L.A., 1989-93. Adj. prof. comm. law Pepperdine Sch. Law, 1987, gender & the law, 1994—; adj. prof.; profl. surfer, 1977-81. Author: Worksmarts for Women: The Essential Sex Discrimination Survival Guide, 2000. Recipient Clarion award Women in Comm., Inc., 1988. Mem. ABA (chair of law and media com. young lawyers divsn. 1987-88, nat. conf. com. lawyers and reps. of media 1987-91), Calif. State Bar (mem. com. on fair trial and free press 1983-84, pub. affairs com. 1985-87), Hawaii Bar Assn., Phi Delta Phi (historian 1980-81). Office: PO Box 881 La Canada CA 91012-0881

PANICH, DANUTA BEMBENISTA, lawyer; b. East Chicago, Ind., Apr. 9, 1954; d. Fred and Ann Stephanie (Grabowski) B.; m. Nikola Panich, July 30, 1977; children: Jennifer Anne, Michael Alexei. AB, Ind. U., 1975, JD, 1978. Bar: Ill. 1978, U.S. Dist. Ct. (no. dist.) Ill. 1978, U.S. Dist. Ct. (ctrl. dist.) Ill. 1987, U.S. Ct. Appeals (7th cir.) 1987, U.S. Dist. Ct. (no. dist.) Ind. 2001, U.S. Dist. Ct. (ea. dist.) Mich. 2003, U.S. Ct. Appeals (6th cir.) 2003. Assoc. Mayer Brown & Platt, Chgo., 1978-86, ptnr., 1986—2001, Mayer Brown Rowe & Maw, LLP, Chgo., 2002—. Bd. dirs. Munster (Ind.) Med. Rsch. Found. Pub. Interest Law Initiative, 1990—. Mem. ABA, Fed. Bar Assn., Ill. Bar Assn. (mme. pub. interest law initiative, 2003—). Republican. Roman Catholic. Office: Mayer Brown Rowe & Maw LLP 190 S La Salle St Ste 3900 Chicago IL 60603-3441 E-mail: dpanich@mayerbrownrowe.com.

PANIK, SHARON MCCLAIN, primary education educator, writer; b. Detroit, May 29, 1952; d. Robert and Phyllis L. McClain; m. Steven Panik, May 25, 1974; 1 child, Todd. BS, Ctrl. Mich. Univ., 1973; MA, U. No. Colo., 1978. Tchr. primary grades Poudre R-1, Fort Collins, 1974—. Co-author: (with Marilyn Parke) A Quetzalcoatl Tale of Corn, 1992 (Parents' Choice Gold award paperback of yr. 1992), A Quetzalcoatl Tale of the Ball Game, 1992, A Quetzalcoatl Tale of Chocolate, 1994. Mem. Internat. Reading Assn., Soc. Children's Book Writers and Illustrators, Nat. Edn. Soc., Colo. Coun. Internat. Reading Assn. (membership dir.). Office: 1209 Parkwood Dr Fort Collins CO 80525-1930

PANNULLO, DEBORAH PAOLINO, lawyer, training and consulting company executive; b. Providence, Apr. 2, 1953; d. Joseph and Lena (Wilde) Paolino; m. Thomas J. Pannullo, Apr. 23, 1971 (div. 1973); 1 child, Melissa Jean; m. Domonic Joseph Ennamorato, Oct. 11, 1998. BA in Econs., R.I. Coll., 1977; cert. in mfg. mgmt., Bryant Coll., 1982, MBA, 1987; JD, Roger Williams U. Law Sch., 1997. Bar: R.I. 1997. Payroll analyst Bostitch/Textron, East Greenwich, R.I., 1977-79, cost analyst, 1979-80, U.S. mfg. coord., 1980-82, quality circles mgr., 1982-85; productivity mgr. Stanley Fastening Systems, East Greenwich, 1985-87; dir. quality assurance-productivity improvement Stanley-Bostitch, East Greenwich, 1987-91, plant mgr., 1991-95; pvt. mgmt. cons., trainer, 1995—; pres. Pannullo and Assocs.; v.p. ops., in-house counsel Polytop Corp., Slatersville, RI, 1998—. Adj. faculty R.I. Coll.; part-time instr. Bryant Coll.; cons. Small Bus. Devel. Ctr. Bd. dirs. R.I. Anti Drug Coalition. Named outstanding Woman of Yr. WMCA, 1985. Mem. NAFE, Am. Soc. Quality Assurance, Internat. Assn. Quality Circles (pres.1984-85, bd. dirs. R.I. chpt. 1985—), R.I. Bar Assn., R.I. Tech. Coun. (chmn. quality assurance subcom.), R.I. Coll. Alumni Assn. (exec. bd. dirs.), Delta Mu Delta. Roman Catholic. Avocations: walking, tennis, reading. Home: 65 White Pine Dr North Scituate RI 02857-1170 Office: Polytop Corp 100 Graham Dr Slatersville RI 02876 E-mail: dpannullo@polytop.com

PANTELAKOS, LAURA C. state legislator; b. Bath, Maine, Aug. 12, 1935; m. Charles Pantelakos (dec.); 7 children. Attended h.s., Bath. N.H. state rep. Rockingham County Dist. 86; mem. criminal justice and safety com. N.H. Ho. of Reps.; mem. Portsmouth City Coun., 1998—. Chmn. Portsmouth City Del., 1991-92, 1997-98; mem. Portsmouth Fire Commn., 1990-94; mem. exec. bd. Rockingham County Del. Mem. Women of Moose. Office: 528 Dennett St Portsmouth NH 03801-3621 E-mail: lpantelakos@comcast.net.

PANTENBURG, MICHEL, hospital administrator, health educator, holistic health coordinator; b. Denver, Oct. 6, 1926; d. Arthur Robert and Alice (McKenna) P. Diploma, Providence Nursing Sch., Kansas City, Kans., 1951; BS in Nursing Edn., St. Mary Coll., Leavenworth, Kans., 1958; M.in Nursing, Cath. U. Am., 1960. Joined Sisters of Charity, Roman Catholic Ch., 1945; lic. amateur radio operator. Dir. nursing Providence Hosp., Kansas City, Kans., 1958-62; nursing coordinator Sisters of Charity, Leavenworth, 1962-67; hosp. adminstr. St. Mary Hosp., Grand Junction, Colo., 1967-73, St. Vincent Hosp., Billings, Mont., 1973-84; dir. focus on leadership program Gonzaga U., Spokane, Wash., 1985-92; chaplain pastoral care dept. St. Marys Hosp. and Med. Ctr., Grand Junction, Colo.,

1994-99, integrative medicine, 1999—. Dir. Norwest Bank, Billings Co-author, editor: Management of Nursing (CHA award 1969) 1967 Bd. dirs. De Paul Hosp., Cheyenne, Wyo., 1980-85, Ronald McDonald House, Billings, 1982-85, St. Joseph Hosp., Denver, 1994-97. Named Woman of Yr., Bus. and Profl. Women, Billings, 1979 Mem. Cath. Hosp. Assn. (bd dirs. sec.), Am. Hosp. Assn. (regional del. 1975-80), Am. Coll. Hosp. Adminstrn., Mont. Hosp. Assn. (pres.), Billings C. of C. (v.p. 1977-78). Avocations: hiking; skiing. Office: Pastoral Care Dept St Marys Hosp & Med Ctr Grand Junction CO 81502

PANUSH, IRENE E(STHER), social worker; b. Detroit, Jan. 31, 1921; d. Martin and Regina (Eichner) Siegel; m. Irving Panush, Aug. 30, 1942; 1 child, Deborah Aviva. BS, Wayne State U., 1943; postgrad., U. Mich., 1947-48; MS with honors, Columbia U., 1960; MSW, Wayne State U., 1980. Clin. social worker, Mich.; diplomate Nat. Bd. Examiners in Clin. Social Work. Wayne State U. Gen. Libr., Detroit, 1960-62; asst. prof. anatomy and physiology Oakland Community Coll. Highland Lakes, Auburn Hills, Mich., 1971-78; therapist Community Mental Health Ctr., Highland Park, Mich., 1978-79, Cath. Social Svcs. Oakland County, Royal Oak, Southfield, Mich., 1979-88; pvt. practice, Birmingham, Mich., 1988-99; retired. Cons. Ostomy Assn. Oakland County, Mich., 1988—. Editor: (booklet) Facts About Bloomfield Hills Schools, 1970. V.p., community chmn. LWV, Detroit, 1957-58, bd. dirs., community chmn., Birmingham, Bloomfield, Mich., 1968-75. Med. Coll. scholar Student Aid Found., 1942-44, grad. scholar Wayne State U., 1978-80; Libr. Sch. fellow Columbia U., 1959-60. Fellow Am. Orthopsychiat. Assn.; mem. Friends of Mich. Psychoanalytic Assn., Mich. Soc. Clin. Social Workers, Nat. Assn. Social Workers, Alliance Mental Health Svcs., Planned Parenthood, NOW, Women of Religions for Abortion, Beta Phi Mu. Jewish. Deceased.

PANZER, MARY CAROLINE, historian, museum curator; b. Flint, Mich., May 29, 1955; d. Milton and Caroline Alice (Weis) P. BA, Yale U.; MA, Columbia U., 1980; PhD, Boston U., 1990. Asst. prof. U. Kans., Lawrence, 1989-91; curator photographs Spencer Mus. Art, Lawrence, 1989-91; asst. dir. SMART Mus. Art U. Chgo., 1991; curator photographs Nat. Portrait Gallery Smithsonian Instn., Washington, 1992-2000; ind. historian N.Y.C., 2000—. Author: Philadelphia Naturalistic Photography, 1982, Rudolf Eickemeyer, Jr. and the Art of the Camera, 1986, Mathew Brady and the Image of History, 1997, Halsman: A Retrospective, 1998, Brady 55, 2001, Hine 55, 2002; contbg. editor Am. Photo, 2002; editor, Separate, But Equal, 2002. Mem. Am. Studies Assn., Coll. Art Assn., Oracle, Mid-Atlantic Radical Historians Orgn., Orgn. Am. Historians.

PANZER, MARY E. state legislator; b. Waupun, Wis., Sept. 19, 1951; d. Frank E. and Verna L. P.; 1 adopted child, Melissa. BA, U. Wis., 1974; mem., Wis. State Ho. Reps. from 53rd dist. Rep. State of Wis., Madison, 1980-93; mem. Wis. Senate from 20th dist., Madison, 1993—. Home: 635 W Tamarack Dr West Bend WI 53095-3653 Office: Wis State Senate State Capital Madison WI 53702-0001

PAOLILLO, REGINA M. information technology consulting executive; b. 1959; Dir. ops. GartnerGroup, 1993; sr. v.p. contr. GartnerMeasurement, 1995-97, pres., CEO, 1997-99; CEO, exec. v.p. fin., adminstrn. Gartner Inc. (previously Gartner Group Inc.), Stamford, Conn., 1999—. Office: PO Box 10212 55 Top Gallant Rd Stamford CT 06904-2212 Fax: 203-316-1100. E-mail: help@garnter.com.

PAOLONI, VIRGINIA ANN, insurance company executive; b. Scranton, Pa., July 26, 1961; d. Edmund James and Virginia (Borick) P. BS in Mktg., King's Coll., 1983; MBA in Mktg., U. Scranton, 1995. Underwriter Reliance Ins., Phila., 1983-85; account exec. The Walsh Co., Phila., 1984-87; pres. Paoloni Ins. Agy., Olyphant, Pa., 1987—. Adv. bd. Everett Cash Mut. Ins. co.; mem. pres. coun. King's Coll., mentor. Participant Leadership Lackawanna, Scranton, 1991—; bd. dirs. fin. planning Holy Name of Jesus Ch., Scranton, 1990-94; mem. allocation steering com. United Way, 1992-93; bd. dirs., chair corp. sponsorship Am. Heart Assn.; mem. pub. rels. com. Habitat for Humanity, 1993—. Recipient 1st Agent of Yr. award United 1st Ins. Co., 1997. Mem. Greater Scranton Ins. Assn. (bd. dirs., chair edn. com. 1989—, 1st v.p.), Jr. League (chair strategic planning). Republican. Roman Catholic. Avocations: running, gourmet cooking. Office: Paoloni Ins Agy 766 N Valley Ave Olyphant PA 18447-1716 Home: 766 N Valley Ave Olyphant PA 18447-1716 Office Phone: 570-489-7820.

PAOLUCCI, ANNE ATTURA, playwright, poet, English and comparative literature educator, educational consultant; b. Rome; d. Joseph and Lucy (Guidoni) Attura; m. Henry Paolucci(dec.). BA, Barnard Coll.; MA, Columbia U., PhD, 1963; hon. degree, Lehman Coll., CUNY, 1995. Mem. faculty English dept. Brearley Sch., NYC, 1957-59; asst. prof. English and comparative lit. CCNY, 1959-69; univ. rsch. prof. St. John's U., Jamaica, NY, 1969-75, prof. English, 1975-77, acting head dept. English, 1973-74, chmn. dept. English, 1982-91; dir. doctor of arts degree program in English, 1982-97; ednl. cons.; editl. cons. Bagehot Coun. Fulbright lectr. in Am. drama U. Naples, Italy, 1965-67; spl. lectr. U. Urbino, summers 1966-67, U. Bari, 1967, univs. Bologna, Catania, Messina, Palermo, Milan, Pisa, 1965-67; disting. adj. vis. prof. Queens Coll., CUNY; bd. dir. World Centre for Shakespeare Studies, 1972— ; spl. guest Yugoslavia Ministry of Culture, 1972; rep. US at Internat. Poetry Festival, Yugoslavia, 1981; founder, exec. dir. Council on Nat. Lits., 1974— ; mem. exec. com. Conf. Editors Learned Jour.-MLA, 1975—85; del. to Fgn. Lang. Jours., 1977—85; mem. adv. bd. Commn. on Tech. and Cultural Transformation, UNESCO, 1978—80; vis. fellow Humanities Rsch. Centre, Australian Nat. U., 1979; rep. US woman playwright Inter-Am. Women Writers Congress, Ottawa, Ont., Can., 1978; organizer, chmn. profl. symposia, meetings; TV appearances; hostess Mag. in Focus, Channel 31, NYC, 1971-72; mem. N.Am. Adv. Council Shakespeare Globe Theatre Ctr., 1981— ; mem. Nat. Grad. Fellows Program Fellowship Bd., 1985—87; mem. Nat. Garibaldi Centennial Com., 1981; trustee Edn. Scholarship, Grants Com. of NIAF, 1990-94; guest speaker with E. Albee Ohio No. State U., 1990; Appointed by Pres. Reagan to Nat. Council on the Humanities, 1986-1993; One of the 10 top Women in Bus. in Queens, 2003. Author (with H. Paolucci) books, including: Hegel On Tragedy, 1962, new edition, 2001, From Tension to Tonic: The Plays of Edward Albee, 1972, new edit., 2000, Pirandello's Theater: The Recovery of the Modern Stage for Dramatic Art, 1974, 2 edit. 2002, Henry Paolucci: Selected Writings on Literature and the Arts; Sci. and Astronomy; Law, Govt., and Pol. Sci., 1999, Dante's Gallery of Rogues, 2001, Do Me a Favor (and other short stories), 2001 (nominated for the Pulitzer Prize); Poems Written for Sbek's Mummies, Marie Menken, and Other Important Persons, Places, and Things, 1977, Eight Short Stories, 1977, Sepia Tones, 1985, 2nd edit., 1986; plays include: Minions of the Race (Medieval and Renaissance Conf. of Western Mich. U. Drama award 1972), video version, 2002, Cipango!, 1985, pub. as book, 1985, 86, videotape excerpts, 1986, revision, 1990; performed NYC and Washington, 1987-88, Winterthur Mus., U. Del., 1990; The Actor in Search of His Mask, 1987, Italian translation and prodn., Genoa, 1987, The Short Season, Naples, 1967, Tre Cubiculo, NY, 1973, German translation, Vienna, 1996, mini-prodn. of Minions of the Race, The Players, 1999, video prodn. 2002, In the Green Room (play), 1999, Three Short Plays, 1995; poems Riding the Mast Where It Swings, 1980, In the Green Room (orig. play), 1999; Gorbachev in Concert, 1991, Queensboro Bridge (and other Poems), 1995 (Pulitzer prize nominee 1995-96), Terminal Degrees, 1997; contbr. numerous articles, rev. to profl. jour.; editor, author intro. to: Dante's Influence on Am. Writers, 1977; gen. editor tape-cassette series China, 1977, 78; founder Coun. on Nat. Lit.; gen. editor series Rev. Nat. Lit., 1970-2000, CNL/Quar. World Report, 1974-76, semi-ann., 1977-84, ann., 1985-2000; full-length TV tape of play Cipango! for pub. TV and ednl. TV with original music by Henry Paolucci, 1990; featured in PBS psl. Italian-Americans II: A Beautiful Song, 1998; translations of Poems by Leopardi (with Thomas

Bergin), 2004; In Wolf's Clothing, (mystery), 2004. Pres. Reagan appointee Nat. Grad. Fellows Program Fellowship Bd., 1985—86, Nat. Coun. Humanities, 1986—, Ann. award FIERI, 1990; bd. dirs. Am. Soc. Italian Legions of Merit, chmn. cultural com., 1990—; bd. dirs. Italian Heritage and Culture City-wide com., 1986—; pres. Columbus: Countdown 1992 Fedn.; mem. Gov. Cuomo's Heritage Legacy Project for Schs., 1989—; trustee CUNY, 1996—, chairwoman bd. trustees, 1997—99; mem. adv. com. on edn. N.Y. State Senate, 1996—. Decorated cavaliere Italian Republic, commendatore Order of Merit (Italy); named one of 10 Outstanding Italian Ams. in Washington, awarded medal by Amb. Rinaldo Petrignani, 1986; recipient Notable Rating for Mags. in Focus series N.Y. Times, 1972, Woman of Yr. award Dr. Herman Henry Scholarship Found., 1973, Amita award, 1970, award Women's Press Club N.Y., 1974, Gold medal for Quincentenary Can. trustee NIAF, 1990, ann. awards Consortium of Italian-Am. Assns., 1991, Am.-Italian Hist. Assn., 1991, 1st Columbus award Cath. Charities, 1991, Leone di San Marco award Italian Heritage Coun. of Bronx and Westchester Counties, 1992, Children of Columbus award Order of Sons of Italy in Am., 1993, 1st Nat. Elena Cornaro award Order of Sons of Italy, 1993, Golden Lion award, 1997, Can.'s Gold medal Christopher Columbus Can. Commn., 1992, Ann. award Am. Italian Cultural Roundtable, 1997, Am. Italian Tchrs. Lifetime Achievement award, 1997, Italian-Am. Legislator's award, Albany, 1997, N.Y. State Italian-Am. Legis. Lifetime Achievement award, 1997, Columbus Citizens Fedn. Ann. award, 1997, Italian Welfare League award, 1998, Queens Coun. on Arts award, 1998, N.Y. State Conservative Party Bronx com. award, 1998, Woman of Distinction award Kingsborough C.C./CUNY, 1999; named one of "Ten Top Queens Women in Bus., 2003; Columbia U. Woodbridge hon. fellow, 1961-62; Am. Coun. Learned Socs. grantee Internat. Pirandello Congress, Agrigento, Italy, 1978; recipient Woman of Distinction award N.Y. State Senate, 2000. Mem. Internat. Shakespeare Assn., Shakespeare Assn. Am., Renaissance Soc. Am., Internat. Comparative Lit. Assn., Am. Comparative Lit. Assn., MLA, Am. PEN, Hegel Soc. Am., Dante Soc. Am. (v.p. 1976-77), Am. Found. Italian Arts and Letters (founder, pres.), Pirandello Soc. (pres. 1978-85), Am. Soc. Italian Legions of Merit (bd. dir. 1990-93). Achievements include pioneering work in multi-comparative literary studies.

PAONESSA, M. SUZANNE, budget analyst; b. Albany, N.Y., May 1, 1974; d. Thomas and Mary Laura (Maresca) Paonessa. BS in Fin., Siena Coll., 1996. Fin. mgmt. specialist U.S. Dept. Energy, Schenectady (N.Y.) Naval Reactors Office, 1996-99; assoc. dir. fin. aid Siena Coll., 1999-2001; assoc. dir. budget and bus. svcs. U. Maine, Orono, 2001—, instr., Profl. Employees Adv. Coun. (PEAC). Treas. Schenectady Naval Reactors Office Employee Assn., 1997—98. Vol. YMCA; ch. lector, greeter; co-dir. Siena Coll. Friendly's Fanfest, 1997—98; mem. Siena Coll. Career Adv. Network. Mem.: Nat. Youth Sports Coaches Assn., DOE Women's Golf League (treas. 1998—, named Most Improved Player 1998), Fin. Mgmt. Assn., 21st Century Leaders Soc., Kensho Do Karate Club (asst. instr. 1998—2000, brown belt), Sigma Beta Delta, Delta Epsilon Sigma, Alpha Kappa Alpha. Roman Catholic. Avocations: Karate, golf, softball, soccer, volleyball. Home: 398 Old County Rd Apt 9 Hampden ME 04444-1936 E-mail: sqboo@yahoo.com.

PAPA, KATHLEEN NICOLE, music educator; b. Cherry Hill, N.J., Jan. 12, 1971; d. Robert Stephen and Carole Ann Papa. MusB, Immaculate Coll., Pa., 1993; M in Elem. Edn., Rowan U., N.J., 2002. Instrumental music dir. Burlington (N.J.) Twp. Sch. Dist., Voorhees (N.J.) Twp. Sch. Dist.; music specialist Maple Shade (N.J.) Sch. Dist., Woodlynne (N.J.) Sch. Dist. Mem.: Music Educator's Nat. Conf. Democrat. Lutheran. Avocations: reading, dance. Home: 901 A Oswego Ct Mount Laurel NJ 08054 Office: Fountain Woods Elem Sch 601 Fountain Ave Burlington PA 08016

PAPAI, BEVERLY DAFFERN, library director; b. Amarillo, Tex., Aug. 31, 1949; d. Clarence Wilbur and Dora Mae (Henderson) Daffern; m. Joseph Andrew Papai, Apr. 3, 1976. BS in Polit. Sci., West Tex. State U., Canyon, 1972; MSLS, Wayne State U., 1973. Head extension dept. and Oakland County Subregional Libr. The Farmington Cmty. Libr., Farmington Hills, Mich., 1973-79, coord. adult svcs., br. head, 1980-83, asst. dir., 1983-85, dir., 1985—. Cons. U.S. Office of Edn., 1978, Battelle Meml. Inst., Columbis, Ohio, 1980; presenter in field. Contbr. articles to profl. jours. Bd. dirs. Mich. Consortium, 1987-91, Oakland Literacy Coun., 1998—, vice chair, 2000-01, chair, 2001—; trustee Libr. of Mich., 1989-92, vice chair, 1991, 97-98, chair, 1992; del. White House Conf. on Librs. and Info. Svcs., 1991; founder, treas., fiscal agt. METRO NET Libr. Consortium, 1993—; mem. edn. com. Child Abuse and Neglect Coun. of Oakland County, 1998-2000; mem. Commn. on Children, Youth and Families, 1996—, Multiracial Cmty. Coun., 1995—; chair Edn. and Tng. Com., 2000—. Recipient Athena award Farmington/Farmington Hills C. of C. and Gen. Motors, 1994, Chairperson's Rainbow award, 2001; Amarillo Pub. Libr. Friends Group fellow, 1972, Wayne State U. Inst. of Gerontology fellow, 1972. Mem. ALA (officer), Mich. Libr. Assn. (chair specialized libr. svcs. roundtable 1975, chair conf. program 1982, chair pub. policy com. 1988-89, chair devel. com. 1994-95, chair ann. conf. and program coms. 1995-96, pres. 1996-97, Loleta D. Fyan award 1975), LWV of Mich., Farmington Exch. Club, Coun. on Resource Devel. Democrat. Roman Catholic. Home: 6805 Wing Lake Rd Bloomfield Hills MI 48301-2959 Office: The Farmington Cmty Libr 32737 W 12 Mile Rd Farmington Hills MI 48334-3302 E-mail: papaibev@farmlib.org.

PAPALIA, DIANE ELLEN, human development educator; b. Englewood, N.J., Apr. 26, 1947; d. Edward Peter and Madeline (Borrin) P.; m. Jonathan Finlay, June 19, 1976 (div. 1999); 1 child, Anna Victoria Finlay. AB, Vassar Coll., 1968; MS, W.Va. U., 1970, PhD, 1971. Asst. prof. child and family studies U. Wis., Madison, 1971-75, assoc. prof., 1975-78, prof., 1978-87, coord. child and family studies, 1977-79. Adj. prof. psychology in pediatrics U. Pa. Sch. Medicine, 1987-89. Author (with Sally W. Olds and Ruth D. Feldman): A Child's World: Infancy Through Adolescence, 1975; author: (with others) Human Development, 1978, with others: 9th edit., 2004, Psychology, 1985, 2d edit., 1988; author: (with Harvey Sterns, Cameron J. Camp and Ruth D. Feldman) Adult Development and Aging, 1996, 2d edit., 2002; contbr. articles to profl. jours.; author (with Dana Gross and Ruth Feldman): Child Development: A Topical Approach, 2003. NSF fellow, 1971, Am. Coun. on Edn. fellow, 1979-80; U. Wis. grantee. Fellow: Gerontol. Soc.; mem.: APA, Nat. Coun. Family Rels., Soc. Rsch. in Child Devel., Am. Psychol. Soc., Psi Chi. Home: 316 E 18th St New York NY 10003-2803 E-mail: depapalia@aol.com.

PAPANDREOU-SUPPAPPOLA, ANTONIA, electrical engineering educator; b. Famagusta, Cyprus, Oct. 9, 1966; came to U.S., 1985; d. Theodoros and Eleni Papandreou; m. Seth Bowen Suppappola, Aug. 14, 1993; 1 child, Saul. BS, U. R.I., 1989, MS, 1991, PhD, 1995. Rsch. ast. prof. U. R.I., Kingston, 1996-99; asst. prof. elec. engring. Ariz. State U., Tempe, 1999—. Contbr. articles to profl. jours. Grantee Naval Undersea Warfare Ctr., Newport, R.I., 1995, Office of Naval Rsch., Arlington, Va., 1996; Nat. Sci. Found., 2000. Mem. IEEE, IEEE Signal Processing Soc., Comm. Soc., Women in Engring. Soc. Greek Orthodox. Avocations: reading, travel. Office: Ariz State U Tempe AZ 85287

PAPARONE, PAMELA ANN, nurse practitioner; b. Jersey City, N.J., Apr. 16, 1953; d. Thomas Richard and Betty Ann (Richter) Devine; m. Philip William Paparone, Oct 2, 1976; children: Philip, Paige. BSN, Rutgers U., 1974; MSN, Seton Hall U., 1977. RN, N.J.; cert. nurse practitioner; med.-surg. clin. nurse specialist. RN Atlantic City Med. Ctr., 1974-75, surgical inservice nurse, 1975-76, clin. nurse specialist, 1978-80; instr. Russell Sage Coll., Troy, N.Y., 1977-78; nurse practitioner, clin. nurse specialist Philip Paparone, D.O., Absecon, 1978—. Lectr. Stockton State Coll., Pomona, 1978-80. Author: The Lyme Disease Coloring Book, 1989; editl. review bd. Jour. Spirochetal and Tick Borne Diseases, 1994-99; contbr. articles to profl. jours. Recipient Nurse Educator of the Year award Am. Assn. Office Nurses, 1989. Mem. Am. Acad. Nurse Practitioners, Sigma Theta Tau. Home: 800 N Harvard Ave Ventnor City NJ 08406-1124 Office: 72 W Jimmie Leeds Rd Absecon NJ 08205-9406

PAPAS, IRENE KALANDROS, English language educator, poet, writer; b. Balt., Mar. 16, 1931; d. Louis and Kounia (Stamatakis) Kalandros; m. Steve S. Papas, Sept. 10, 1952; children: Fotene Stephenie Tina, Barbara Counia. AA with highest honors, Balt. C.C.; BA magna cum laude, Goucher Coll., 1968; MA in English Lang. and Lit., U. Md., 1974, postgrad., 1980—. Lic. theology profl. Tchr./tutor various schs., Balt., 1965—; tchr. theology U. Md. Free Univ., College Park, 1979—; author/pub. Ledger Publs., Silver Spring, Md., 1982—; TV producer Arts and Humanities Prodns., Silver Spring, 1991—. Lectr. in English, philosophy, Montgomery Coll., Goucher Coll.; instr. English Composition, World Literature, U. Md., College Park, 1968—; adj. faculty various colls.; White House duty, 1997—. Author: Irene's Ledger Songs of Deliverance, 1982, Irene's Ledger Song at Sabbatyon, 1986, Small Meditations, Leaves for Healing, 1996; prodr./dir. tv. progs. Election judge, Montgomery County (Md.) Suprs. Bd. of Elections, 90's; tutor in literacy, 1989, 90. Recipient First Prize Arts and Culture Category Smithsonian Inst., 1991; honored 6th Annual Awards Ceremony Montgomery Community, 1991. Mem. AAUP, Internat. Platform Assn., Nat. Poetry Assn., Phi Beta Kappa. Democrat. Greek Orthodox. Avocations: art/iconography, calligraphy, music, needlepoint. Office: PO Box 10303 Silver Spring MD 20914-0303

PAPATHOMAS, GEORGIA NIKOLAKOPOULOU, communications technbology executive, communications engineer; b. Kato Achaia, Greece, Sept. 11, 1950; d. Andreas and Corina (Fotopoulou) Nikolakopoulos; m. Thomas Vergil Papathomas, Aug. 15, 1976; children: Lia Natassa, Alexander Vergil. BS in Engring. Sci., Columbia U., 1973, MS in Engring. Sci., 1974, PhD in Engring. Sci., 1978; cert. in bus. devel., U. Pa., 1994, cert. in strategic mktg., Harvard U., 1995. Mem. tech. staff Bell Labs., Murray Hill, N.J., 1978-84, supr. Whippany, N.J., 1984-90, program mgr., 1990-93; dir. strategy AT&T, Morristown, N.J., 1993-96, dir. ops. Bedminster, NJ, 1996—2002; v.p. network solutions Lucent Tech., 1998—2002; v.p. info. tech. Pfizer, 2003—. Adj. asst. prof. engring. Rutgers U., New Brunswick, NJ, 1979—82. Sloan Found. rsch. fellow, N.Y.C., 1974. Mem. ASCE, Soc. Women Engrs., Sigma Xi.

PAPE, PATRICIA ANN, social worker, consultant; b. Aurora, Ill., Aug. 2, 1940; d. Robert Frank and Helen Louise (Hanks) Grover; children: Scott Allen, Debra Lynn. BA in Sociology, Northwestern U., 1962; MSW, George Williams Coll., 1979. Cert. addictions counselor, Ill.; lic. clin. social worker, sch. social worker, Ill. Pvt. practice family counseling, 1979—; coord. community resources DuPage Probation Dept., Wheaton, Ill., 1977-80; dir. The Abbey Alcoholism Treatment Ctr., Winfield, Ill., 1980-81; prin. Pape & Assocs., Wheaton, 1982—; dir. alcoholism counselor tng. program Coll. of DuPage, Glen Ellyn, Ill., 1982-87. Chgo. affiliate Employee Assistance Program, 1982—; cons. Luth. Soc. Services Ill., 1979-82. Contbr. articles to profl. jours. Mem. alcohol drug task force Ill. Synod Luth. Ch. Am., Chgo., 1985—. Named Woman of Yr., Entrepreneur Women in Mgmt., Oak Brook, Ill, 1986, Social Worker of Yr. Fox Valley Dist., 1998. Mem. Assn. Labor-Mgmt. Adminstrs. Cons. Alcoholism (women's issues com. 1984—), Acad. Cert. Social Workers, Am. Assn. Marriage Family Therapists, Nat. Assn. Soc. Workers, Women in Mgmt. Home: 1330 Shagbark Ln Wheaton IL 60187 Office: Pape & Assocs 618 S West St Wheaton IL 60187-5038

PAPELL, HELEN GERTRUDE, poet, retired librarian; b. N.Y.C., Apr. 8, 1924; d. Henry and Anna (Gimpel) Sobel; m. Robert Papell, June 1, 1949; 1 child, David H. BA, U. Mo., 1949; MLS, Pratt Inst., 1969; cert. profl. pub. libr., SUNY, 1973. Libr. trainee Bklyn. Pub. Libr., 1967-69, libr., storyteller, puppeteer, sr. libr., supervising libr., 1969-84; libr., cataloger Jewish Women's Resource Ctr. Nat. Coun. Jewish Women, N.Y.C., 1984-98; ret., 1998. Puppeteer in librs., schls., chs., st. fairs, N.Y.C., Bklyn., 1969-84. Author: (poems) Talking with Eve, Leah, Hagar, Miriam, 1996, Caretaker's Mask, 2003; contbg. editor Jewish Women's Lit. Ann. Grantee Poets and Writers, 1991, 93. Mem. Nat. Coun. Jewish Women, Phi Beta Kappa. Avocations: reading judaica, folklore and mysteries, visiting museums, attending plays. Home: 720 W End Ave New York NY 10025-6299

PAPEN, MARY KAY, state senator; Car dealer; Dem. senator dist. 38 N.Mex. State Senate. Mem. pub. affairs com. N.Mex. State Senate, vice chair edn. com. Home: 904 Conway Ave Las Cruces NM 88005 Office: NMex State Senate State Capitol Mail Rm Dept Santa Fe NM 87503 E-mail: senate@state.nm.us.

PAPER, SUSANNE ABBY BABIN, science educator, writer; b. Rochester, N.Y., Feb. 4, 1944; d. Gregory and Lillian Kiener Babin; m. Lawrence Phillip Paper, Aug. 14, 1965; children: Shawn Alan, Kim Sandra. BS, U. Md., 1966. Elem. sch. tchr. Montgomery County Pub. Schs, Rockville, Md., 1981—97; 8th grade sci. tchr. Montgomery County Pub. Schs., Rockville, Md., 1997—. Webmaster Westland Mid. Sch., Bethesda, Md., 1999—2000; mentor to new sci. tchrs. Montgomery County Pub. Schs., Rockville, Md., 2000—03. Editor: (sci. articles) Nat. Sci. Tchrs. Assn., 1998—; author: Math Black Line Masters, 1985 (Broome award, 1983), Airlift For Young Minds. Lobbyist Local/State Tchrs. Union, 1995—2003; dem. pres. and ctrl. com. Dist. 15, Montgomery, Md., 1998—2002; rep. for sci. tchrs. Coun. on Tchg. and Learning, Montgomery County Pub. Schs., 2001—. Grantee numerous grants, Md. State, 1983—2001. Mem.: MCEA Union (sci. rep. 2001—), D15 Dem. Club (v.p. leader). Democrat. Jewish. Avocations: snow skiing, jazz, tap dancing. Home: 12001 Ambleside Dr Potomac MD 20854

PAPERA, ROSEMARIE MARUCCI, speech pathologist; b. Orange, NJ, Feb. 6, 1967; d. Anthony Charles and Jean Marucci; m. Frederick John Papera, Dec. 30, 2000; 1 child, Maria Rose. MA, Montclair State Coll., 1989—91, BA, 1987—89. Certificate of Clinical Competence Am. Speech/Lang./Hearing Assn., 1992, Speech/Language Specialist NJ. Dept. of Edn., 1991, Teacher of the Handicapped NJ. Dept. of Edn., 1995. Speech/lang. pathologist Springfield Pub. Schs., NJ, 1991—2003; clin. supr. Montclair State U., Upper Montclair, NJ, 1992—; speech/lang. pathologist Hanover Twp. Pub. Schs., Whippany, NJ, 2003—. Clinicial fellowship yr. supr. Springfield Pub. Schools, Springfield, NJ, 1993—2002, student tchr. supr., 1993—. Sunday sch. tchr. St. Lawrence Roman Cath. Ch., Chester, NJ, 1981—85; sec. Albernose Women's Social Club, Orange, NJ, 1995—98; vol. Am. Cancer Soc., Parsippany, NJ, 1991—2003. Recipient Governor's Tchr. award, State of NJ, 1995. Mem.: NJ. Speech/Lang. Hearing Assn. (assoc.), Am. Speech/Lang./Hearing Assn. (assoc.). R-Consevative. Roman Catholic. Avocations: traveling, exercise, reading, theater, music. Home: 16 Rockaway Valley Rd Boonton NJ 07005 Office: Hanover Twp Pub Schs Reynolds Ave Whippany NJ 07981 Office Phone: 973-464-5220. Personal E-mail: rpapera@optonline.net. E-mail: rpapera@springfieldschools.com.

PAPICH, MARY JO, secondary school educator, department chairman; Grad., Truman State U., Bradley U. Band dir. Woodruff H.S., Peoria, Ill., 1982—92; dist. fine arts coord. K-12 Peoria Pub. Schs., 1992—2001; fine arts chair Highland Park (Ill.) H.S. Founder, dir. Peoria Jazz AllStars; staff Bands of Am. camp Ill. State U.; mem. Mid-west Band and Orch. Adv. Panel, 2001; adjudicator and presenter in field. Recipient YWCA Leader in the Arts award, Peoria Players Outstanding Music Theatre award, Tri-County Outstanding Educator award. Mem.: NARAS, ASCD, Ill. Arts in Edn. Alliance, Music Educators Nat. Conf., Sisters in Jazz (founder Ill. unit), Internat. Assn. Jazz Educators (treas., planning chair Leadership Inst. 2002), Ill. Music Edn. Assn. (v.p., organizer All State Jazz programs). Home: Apt 101 1601 Oakwood Ave Highland Park IL 60035

PAPPAL, JENNIFER M. musician, educator; m. Scott A. Pappal, July 31, 1999. BS in Music Edn., Duquesne U., 1999, MusM in Music Edn., 2003. Cert. tchr. Pa. Violinist Altoona/Johnstown (Pa.) Symphony, 1997—; music tchr. Riverview Area Sch. Dist., Oakmont, Pa., 1999—2000, Hollidaysburg (Pa.) Area Sch. Dist., 2000—.

PAPPALARDO, FAYE, academic administrator; b. Phila. d. Gregory and Helen (Gregory) P. BS, St. Mary's U., 1968; MS, Johns Hopkins U., 1978; MA, Columbia U., 1991, EdD, 1992. Dept. chair fgn. lang. Cath. Girls High Sch., Balt., 1970-72; dean of coll. Bay Coll. Md., Balt., 1972-76; dir. student life C.C. of Balt., 1978-83, dean student affairs, 1983-88, Carroll C.C., Westminster, Md., 1988-91, exec. v.p., 1991—. Cons. Sci. Rsch. Assn., N.Y.C., 1974-76. Bd. dirs. Multiple Sclerosis Soc., Westminster, 1991-93; mem. Md. Tomorrow, Westminster, 1989-90. Recipient fellowship Franciscian Community, Paris, 1974. Mem. AAUW, Am. Assn. Women in C.C., Am. Assn. Women in Higher Edn. (treas. 1991—, Outstanding Adminstr. award 1994), Md. Assn. Higher Edn. (treas. 1991—), Md. State Deans of Student Affairs (chairperson 1992-93), Johns Hopkins U. Alumni Assn., Columbia U. Alumni Assn. Roman Catholic. Avocation: reading. Office: Carroll CC 1601 Washington Rd Westminster MD 21157-6944

PAPPAS, EFFIE VAMIS, language educator, finance educator, writer, poet, artist; b. Cleve., Dec. 26, 1924; d. James Jacob and Helen Joy (Nicholson) Vamis; m. Leonard G. Pappas, Nov. 3, 1945; children: Karen Pappas Morabito, Leonard J., Ellen Pappas Daniels, David James. BBA, Western Res. U., 1948; MA in Edn., Case Western Res. U., 1964, postgrad., 1964-68; MA in English Lit., Cleve. State U., 1986; postgrad., Ind. U. Pa., 1979-86. Cert. elem. and secondary tchr. Ohio. Tchr. elem. schs., Ohio, 1963-70; office mgr. Cleve. State U., 1970-72, adminstr. pub. rels., 1972-73; med. adminstr. Brecksville (Ohio) VA Hosp., 1974-78; lectr. English, econs./bus. mgmt., math., comm., composition Cuyahoga CC, Cleve., 1978-92. Tchg. asst. Case Western Res. U., 1979—80; lectr. bus. comm. Cleve. State U., 1980; participant in sci. and cultural exch. dels. Am. Inst. Chemists, China, 1984, Russia, 89. Feature writer: The Voice, 1970—78, editor, writer: Cleve. State U. newsletter and mag., 1970—73. Cub scout leader Boy Scouts Am., Brecksville, 1960; mem. local coun. PTA, 1965—70; sec. St. Paul's Coun., 1990—91; mem. membership com. St. Paul Ladies Philoptohos, 1990—2004; active Women's Equity Action League, 1995—2003; mem. Greater Cleve. Learning Project; Sunday sch. tchr., mem. choir Brecksville United Ch. of Christ, 1975—76, mem. bd. missions, 1966—67, mem. membership com., 1993; mem. planning com. edn. Case Western Res. U.; mem. 75th Anniversary steering com. Cleve. Coll. Recipient Editor's Choice award for outstanding achievement in poetry, Nat. Libr. Poetry, 1995, 2000; grantee, Cuyahoga CC, 1982. Mem.: AARP, AAUW (legis. chair, del. Ohio meetings 1993—94, del. Ohio Coalition for Change 1993—94, mem. Ohio and Cleve. br. del. Gt. Lakes regional meeting 1994, co-chair Cleve. br. 1994, 1996—97, legis. chair 1997—98, del. to S.W. regional meeting 1995, del. to Internat. Fedn. Univ. Women triennial meeting Stanford U. 1992), NAFE, NAE, Ohio Edn. Assn. (rep. assembly Columbus 1994, 1999—2001, 2002—03), Nat. Mus. Women in Arts (hon. roll. mem.). Avocations: travel, art, legal studies, theater, correspondence with national and international friends. Home: 8681 Brecksville Rd Brecksville OH 44141-1912

PAPPAS, SANDRA LEE, state senator; b. Saint Paul, Minn., June 15, 1949; m. Neal Gosman, 1976; 3 children. BA, Met. State U., 1986; MPA, Harvard U., 1994. Mem. Minn. Ho. of Reps., St. Paul, 1984-90, Minn. Senate, St. Paul, 1990—. Part-time coll. instr. Mem. Dem. Farmer Labor Party. Home: 182 Prospect Blvd Saint Paul MN 55107-2136 Office: Minn State Senate 120 State Capitol 75 Martin Luther King Jr Blvd Saint Paul MN 55155-1601

PAQUIN, ANNA, actress; b. Winnipeg, MB Canada, July 24, 1982; d. Brian and Mary Paquin. Actor: (films) The Piano, 1993 (Academy Award best supporting actress, 1993, Golden Globe nomination best supporting actress, 1993), Jane Eyre, 1995, Fly Away Home, 1996, Amistad, 1997, A Walk on the Moon, 1988, Hurly-burly, 1998, Begin the Beguine, 1998, Sleepless Beauty, 1998, A Walk on the Moon, 1999, She's All That, 1999, X-Men, 2000, Almost Famous, 2000, Finding Forrester, 2000, Buffalo Soldiers, 2001, Darkness, 2002, 25th Hour, 2002, X2: X-Men United, 2003; (TV films) Member of the Wedding, 1997, Hercules (voice only), 1988, All the Rage, 1999. Office: Double Happy Talent c/o Gail Cowan PO Box 9585 Wellington New Zealand also: William Morris Agy One William Morris Pl Beverly Hills CA 90212

PARADIS, JUDY, state legislator; b. St. Agathe, Maine, Jan. 17, 1944; m. Ross Paradis, 1970. BS, postgrad., U. Maine. Former mem. Dist. 150 Maine Ho. of Reps., mem. appropriations and fin. affairs coms., mem. Dist. 1 Maine Senate; tchr. Frenchville, Maine. Chair Senate Haelth and Human Svcs. Com., ranking mem. Agr., Conservation and Forestry Com. Columnist St. John Valley Times. Co-host Maine Dem. Conv., 1998; mem. John Valley Hist. Assn., Maine Women's Lobby; co-pres. State Franco-Am. Conseil. Recipient Disting. Legislator award, 1990; Toll fellow, 1991. Mem. AAUW, Bus. and Profl. Women's Club, Assn. of French Speaking (Parliamentarian, pres. Maine sect. 1997), Optimists. Home: 40 US Route 1 Frenchville ME 04745-6151 Office: Maine State Senate State Capitol 3 State House Sta Augusta ME 04333-0003 Fax: 728-6374. E-mail: rody@nbnet.nb.ca.

PARASHAK, DEBRA SUE, civil engineer; b. St. Louis, Aug. 28, 1954; d. Paul Michael Parashak and Anita Marie Gettinger. BSCE, So. Ill. U., 1977. Profl. women's basketball player All AM. Redheads, 1975—77; installation and repair technician SBC, St. Louis, 1978—83, mgr. installation and repair, 1984—87, mgr. maint. ctr., 1987—88, mgr. cable repair, 1988—89, mgr. contract adminstrn. Fenton, Mo., 1989—91, mgr. constrn. splicing, 1991—93, mgr. constrn. placing, 1993—99, mgr. constrn. mgmt. ctr., 1999—2003, mgr. constrn. Converse, Tex., 2003—. Vol. basketball coach Gt. NW Recreation, San Antonio, 1998; softball coach Christian Youth Orgn., St. Louis, 1985; vol. San Antonio Sports Found., San Antonio, 2000—. With Corps of Engrs. U.S. Army, 1972—74. Recipient St. Louis Women's Sports Achievement award as mem. of All Am. Redheads, 2001. Mem.: Women's Basketball Hall of Fame as mem. of All Am. Redheads 1999. Eastern Rite Catholic. Avocations: travel, sports.

PARCHMENT, YVONNE, nursing educator; b. Kingston, Jamaica, July 2, 1943; came to U.S., 1979; d. George Augustus Leslie and Evelyn Maude (Brown) Mitchell; m. Neville McDonald Parchment, Feb. 2, 1963; children: Suzanne Marie, April A. Parchment-Knight, Neville Wade, Everton Jerome. AA, AS, Miami (Fla.) Dade Cmty. Coll., 1982; BSN, U. Miami, 1984, MS in Nursing, 1989; postgrad., Fla. Internat. U., 1996—. RN, Fla. Tchr. elem. sch. Alpha Infant Sch., Kingston, 1974-79; nurse South Miami Hosp., 1979-95; clin. nurse specialist Mt. Sinai Med. Ctr., Miami, 1989-95; clin. asst. prof. Fla. Internat. U., Miami, 1995—. Contbr. articles to profl. jours. Bd. dirs. mental health com. Cmty. Health Ctr., Miami, 1996—. Capt. Army Nurse Corps., USAR, 1989—. Rsch. grantee Fla. League Nursing, 1996. Mem. AACN, Fla. Nurses Assn. (bd. dirs. dist. 5), Jamaica Nurses Assn. of Fla. (past v.p., v.p. 1997—, mem. edn. com., cultural diversity com.), Sigma Theta Tau (mem. by-laws com.). Episcopalian. Avocations: dance, reading, sewing. Office: Fla Internat U North Campus Miami FL 33181

PARDUE, KAREN REIKO, elementary school educator; b. Honolulu, June 13, 1947; d. Rex Shinzen and Ruth Fujiko (Arakawa) Ishiara; m. Jerry Thomas Pardue, Oct. 21, 1978 (dec. Sept. 1994); 1 child, Holly; m. Nicholas Lambiase, Mar. 17, 1998 (div. July 1999). BS, Western Ill. U., 1969; MA, U. No. Colo., 1971, 72. Tchr. home econs. Galesburg (Ill.) H.S., 1969-70; tchr. spl. edn. Jefferson County Pub. Schs., Golden, Colo., 1973-85, 87-94; tchr. 2d and 3d grade Englewood (Colo.) Christian Sch., 1985-86; tchr. 2d grade Jefferson County Pub. Schs., 1994—. Adj. instr. Colo. Christian U., Lakewood, 1989—; mem. recommended basic list com. Jefferson County Pub. Schs., 1993-95. Grantee Colo. Dept. Edn., 1976, Jefferson Found. Venture, 1988. Mem. ASCD, Colo. Coun. Learning Disabilities, Jefferson County Ednl. Assn., Jefferson County Internat. Reading Assn., Delta Kappa Gamma (rec. sec. 1988-89, pres. 1990-92, treas. 1994-96, Values award for exemplary performance 2001-2002). Avocations: reading, sewing. Home: 6827 S Webster St Unit D Littleton CO 80128-4469

PARDUE, MARY-LOU, biology educator; b. Lexington, Ky., Sept. 15, 1933; d. Louis Arthur and Mary Allie (Marshall) P. BS, William and Mary Coll., 1955; MS, U. Tenn., 1959; PhD, Yale U., 1970; D.Sc. (hon.), Bard Coll., 1985. Postdoctoral fellow Inst. Animal Genetics, Edinburgh, Scotland, 1970-72; assoc. prof. biology MIT, Cambridge, 1972-80, prof., 1980—, Boris Magasanik prof. biology, 1995—. Summer course organizer Cold Spring Harbor Lab., NY, 1971—80; mem. rev. com. NIH, 1974—78, 1980—84, nat. adv. gen. med. scis. coun., 1984—86; sci. adv. com. Wistar Inst., Phila., 1976—; mem. health and environ. rsch. adv. com. U.S. Dept. Energy, 1987—94; bd. trustees Associated Univs., Inc., 1995—97; mem. Burroughs Wellcome Adv. Com. on Career Awards in Biomed. Scis., 1996—2000, now bd. dirs.; chair Inst. of Medicine Com. on Biol. Basis of Sex and Gender Differences, 1999—2001. Contbr. articles to profl. jours. Mem. rev. com. Am. Cancer Soc., 1990-93, Howard Hughes Med. Inst. Adv. Bd., 1993-2000. Recipient Esther Langer award Langer Cancer Rsch. Found., 1977, Lucius Wilbur Cross medal Yale Grad. Sch., 1989; grantee NIH, NSF, Am. Cancer Soc. Fellow AAAS, NAS (chmn. genetics sect. 1991-94, coun. 1995-98), Am. Acad. Arts and Sci. (coun. mem. 1992-96); mem. NRC (bd. on biology 1989-95), Genetics Soc. Am. (pres. 1982-83), Am. Soc. Cell Biology (coun. 1977-80, pres. 1985-86), Phi Beta Kappa, Phi Kappa Phi, Sigma Xi. Office: MIT Dept Biology 68-670 77 Massachusetts Ave Dept 68-670 Cambridge MA 02139-4307 Office Phone: 617-253-6741. Business E-Mail: mlpardue@mit.edu.

PARELLA, MARY A. state legislator; b. Bristol, R.I., Feb. 10, 1957; BA, Emmanuel Coll., 1979; M in Cmty. Planning, U. R.I., 1982. Program dir. Pawtucket Sch. Dept.; mem. Bristol Town Coun., 1986-92, R.I. Senate, Dist. 45, Providence, 1992—. Mem. judiciary com., health, edn. and welfare com., and joint com. on vets. affairs, R.I. State Senate. Mem. Bristol Rep. Town Com.; bd. dirs. Self Help, Inc.; chief marshall Bristol 4th of July Celebration, 1995. Mem. Am. Planning Assn. (R.I. sect.), Bristol Jaycees. Home: 259 High St Bristol RI 02809-2222

PARENT, LOUISE MARIE, lawyer; b. San Francisco, Aug. 28, 1950; d. Jules D. and Mary Louise (Bartholomew) P.; m. John P. Casaly, Jan. 5, 1980. AB, Smith Coll., 1972; JD, Georgetown U., 1975. Bar: N.Y. 1976, U.S. Dist. Ct. (so. dist.) N.Y. 1976. Assoc. Donovan Leisure, N.Y.C., 1975-77; various positions, then gen. counsel Am. Express Info. Svcs. Corp., N.Y.C., 1977-92; dep. gen. counsel Am. Express Co., N.Y.C., 1992-93, exec. v.p., gen. counsel, 1993—. Bd. dirs. A Better Chance Inc., Cooke Ctr. for Learning and Devel., Nat. Womens Law Ctr; trustee Smith Coll.; mem. adv. bd. Studio in a Sch. Mem. ABA (com. depts. corp. law), N.Y.C. Bar Assn., N.Y. State Bar Assn., Coun. on Fgn. Rels. Home: 1170 5th Ave New York NY 10029-6527 Office: Am Express Co Am Express Tower World Fin Ctr New York NY 10285-0001

PARENT, MARY, film company executive; Past agt. trainee ICM; dir. develop. to v.p. prodn. New Line Cinema, 1994—97; sr. v.p. prodn. Universal Pictures, Universal City, Calif., 1997—2000, exec. v.p. prodn., 2000—01, co-pres. prodn., 2001—03, vice chmn., worldwide prodn., 2003—. Office: 100 Universal City Plaza Universal City CA 91608

PARETSKY, SARA N. writer; b. Ames, Iowa, June 8, 1947; d. David Paretsky and Mary E. Edwards; m. S. Courtenay Wright, June 19, 1976; children: Kimball Courtenay, Timothy Charles, Philip William. BA, U. Kans., 1967; MBA, PhD, U. Chgo., 1977. Mgr. Urban Rsch Ctr., Chgo., 1971-74, CNA Ins. Co., Chgo., 1977-85; writer, 1985—. Author: (novels) Indemnity Only, 1982, Deadlock, 1984 (Friends of Am. Writers award 1985), Killing Orders, 1985, Bitter Medicine, 1987, Blood Shot, 1988 (Silver Dagger award Crime Writers Assn., 1988), Burn Marks, 1990, Guardian Angel, 1992, Tunnel Vision, 1994, Hard Time: A V.I. Warshawski Novel, 1999, also numerous articles and short stories. Pres. Sisters in Crime, Chgo., 1986-88; dir. Nat. Abortion Rights Action League Ill., 1987—; mentor Chgo. inner-city schs. Named Woman of Yr. Ms mag., N.Y.C., 1987; recipient Mark Twain award fot disting. contbns. to midwestern lit., 1996. Mem. Crime Writers Assn. (Silver Dagger award 1988), Mystery Writers Am. (v.p. 1989), Authors Guild, Chgo. Network Achievements include being the founder of two scholarships at U. Kans. Address: Sally McCartin Assoc PO Box 432 Millerton NY 12546-0432

PARHAM, BETTY ELY, credit bureau executive; b. Drumright, Okla., Aug. 14, 1928; d. Wayne Albert and Edith May (Ledgerwood) Bingamon; m. Richard D. Ely, Dec. 22, 1946 (dec. Jan. 1971); children: Richard Wayne, Stephen Wyatt; m. Billy S. Parham, Mar. 10, 1991. BS, East Cen. U., Ada, Okla., 1962, M Teaching, 1965. Office mgr. Louiis M. Long, Loans, Ada, 1946-78; owner Credit Bur. Ada, 1956—, mgr., 1978—. Mem. Soc. Cert. Credit Bur. Execs., Assoc. Credit Burs. Okla. (bd. dirs. 1980—, pres. 1990), AAUW (cert. of achievement 1989), Ada Bus. and Profl. Women (chmn. YC, Pres.'s award 1991), Toastmasters (pres. Ada 1984, Presdl. Excellence award 1984), Kiwanis (bd. dirs. Ada 1990-92). Democrat. Avocations: boating, travel, reading. Home: PO Box 506 Ada OK 74821-0506 Office: Credit Bur Ada 304 E 12th St Ada OK 74820-6510

PARHAM, CAROL SHEFFEY, school system administrator; b. Balt. m. William N. Parham, Jr.; children: William N. III, Julie Desai. BA in Social Studies Edn., U. Md.; M in Edn. Guidance and Counseling, postgrad. studies, Johns Hopkins U.; EdD, U. Md. Social studies tchr. Balt. City Schs., personnel specialist, acting staff specialist, personnel assoc.; supr. office personnel Howard County Pub. Schs., 1985-89; dir. personnel Anne Arundel County Pub. Schs., 1989—. Bd. dirs. Anne Arundel Trade Coun., United Way Ctrl. Md.; mem. task force Md. State Dept. Edn.; mem. edn. adv. com. Johns Hopkins U. Sch. Continuing Studies; mem. adv. bd. Leadership Anne Arundel; trustee Western Md. Coll., Mt. Washington Pediat. Hosp. Recipient Outstanding Achievement in Leadership award Md. State Tchrs. Assn., Good Scout award Baltimore Area Coun. Boy Scouts Am., Martin Luther King Peacemaker award, 1998, Kathleen Kennedy Townsend award; named Woman of Yr., Glen Burnie Chpt. Nat. Fedn. Bus. Profl. Women, Md. Supt. of Yr., 1995, Md.'s Top 100 Women, 1996, 98, 99. Mem. Pub. Sch. Supts. Assn. Md., Assn. Sch. Bus. Officials Md. and DC (past pres.), Md. Pers. Assn. (past pres.), Coalition 100 Black Women, Wash. Area Sch. Study Coun. (pres.), Rotary, Delta Sigma Theta. Office: Office of Supt 2644 Riva Rd Annapolis MD 21401-7305

PARHAM, ELLEN SPEIDEN, nutrition educator; b. Mitchells, Va., July 15, 1938; d. Marion Coote and Rebecca Virginia (McNiel) Speiden; m. Arthur Robert Parham, Jr., Dec. 16, 1961; children: Katharine Alma, Cordelia Alyx. BS in Nutrition, Va. Poly. Inst., 1960; PhD in Nutrition, U. Tenn., 1967; MSEd in Counseling, No. Ill. U., 1994. Registered dietitian; lic. clin. profl. counselor. Asst. prof. to prof. nutrition No. Ill. U., DeKalb, Ill., 1966—, coord. programs in dietetics, 1981-86, 90—, coord. grad. faculty sch. family, consumer, nutrition scis., 1985-87. Cons. on nutrition various hosps., clins. and bus., Ill., 1980—; founder, dir. Horizons Weight Control Program, DeKalb, 1983-91; founder, leader "Escaping the Tyranny of the Scale" Group, 1994—; co-chair Nutrition Coalition for Ill., 1989-90, ptnr., mgr. Design on Fabric, 1986 ; adj. counselor Ctr. for Counsel, Family Svc. Agy. of DeKalb County. Bd. editors Jour. Nutrition Edn., 1985-90, 97—, Jour. Am. Dietetic Assn., 1991-97; contbr. articles to profl. jours. Recipient Fisher award, No. Ill. U. Coll. Health and Human Svcs., 2001, Sullivan award, 2002. Mem. Am. Inst. Nutrition, Soc. Nutrition Edn., Am. Dietetic Assn. (named Ill. Outstanding Dietetics Educator 2001, Excellence in Dietetics Edn. award 2001), Soc. Nutrition Edn. (treas. 1991-94, chair divsn. nutrition and weight realities 1995-96, Weight Realities Cert. of Achievement 1999), N.Am. Assn. Study Obesity. Avocations: painting in watercolor, gardening, reading.

PARHAM-HOPSON, DEBORAH HOPSON, health administrator; BSN, U. Cin.; MS in Pub. Health, PhD in Pub. Health, U. NC. Rear adm. USPHS Commd. Corps.; assoc. adminstr. HAB, 2000—01, 2002—, HRSA HIV/AIDS Bur., HHS. Office: US Dept Health and Human Svcs Health Resources Svcs Adminstrn 5600 Fishers Ln Rm 7-05 Rockville MD 20857

PARIAG, HAIMWATTIE RAMKISTODAS, information management administrator; b. Golden Fleece, Guyana, Aug. 31, 1967; came to U.S., 1977; d. Ramkisto Das and Surujpati Ramkistodas; m. Moolchand Pariag. BS in Med. Records Adminstrn., C.W. Post Coll., 1988. Registered health info. mgmt. adminstr.. Med. records clk. Mary Immaculate Hosp., Jamaica, N.Y., 1986-87; coder Parkway Hosp., Forest Hills, N.Y., 1987, adminstrv. coord., 1987-88, dir. health info. mgmt. svcs., 1988-91; dir. med. records Massapequa Gen. Hosp., Seaford, N.Y., 1991—; dir. health info. svcs./telecom. Brunswick Hosp. Ctr., Amityville, NY, 2000—01; dir. med. records, privacy officer Parker Jewish Inst. Healthcare and Rehab., Hyde Park, NY, 2001—. Mem. Am. Health Info. Mgmt. Assn., N.Y. Health Info. Mgmt. Assn., L.I. Health Info. Mgmt. Assn., Health Info. Mgmt. Assn. N.Y.C. Democrat. Hindu. Avocations: volleyball, raquetball, tennis. Home: 197 E 2nd St Deer Park NY 11729-6005

PARIENTE, BARBARA J. state supreme court justice; b. N.Y.C., Dec. 24, 1948; m. Frederick A. Hazouri; 3 children. Grad. with high honors, Boston U., 1970; JD with highest honors, George Washington U., 1973. Bar: Fla. 1973; cert. civil trial lawyer Fla. Bar; cert. Nat. Bd. Trial Advocacy. Law clk. to hon. Norman C. Roettger, Jr. U.S. Dist. Ct. (so. dist.) Fla., 1973-75; assoc. Cone Wagner Nugent, 1975—77, ptnr., 1977—83, Pariente & Silber, P.A., 1983; pvt. practice, 1983—2001; judge U.S. Ct. of Appeals (4th dist.), 1993-97; justice Fla. Supreme Ct., Tallahassee, 1997—. Participant Twenty-First Century Justice Conf.; mem. Jud. Cir. Grievance Com., 1989-92, chair, 1990-92; mem. nominating com. U.S. Ct. Appeals (15th cir.), 1980-84; past faculty mem. Supreme Ct. Justice Tchg. Inst. Contbr. articles to profl. jours. Bd. dirs. Fla. Bar Found.; mentor Take Stock in Children; active Palm Beach County Youth Ct. program, 1997, Cities in Schs. mentoring program, 1993, Temple Judea, Palm Beach County Sephardi Fedn., Jewish Cmty. Ctr., Ballet Fla., Palm Beach County Commn. on Status of Women; vol. judge Palm Beach County Youth Ct. Program; chair Supreme Ct. Steering Com. on Families and Children in the Courts Fla. Supreme Ct.; liaison Supreme Ct. Task Force on Treatment-Based Drug Courts, 1999—; mem. nat. judges adv. com. Balanced and Restorative Justice Project Dept. Justice. Recipient award for disting. svc. to the arts Palm Beach County Bar Assn., 1987, Civil Litigation Pro Bono award Legal Aid Soc., 1993, Lifetime Achievement award Palm Beach County Jewish Fedn., 1998, Disting. Jud. Svc. award Fla. Coun. on Crime and Delinquency, 2000, Breaking the Glass Ceiling award Jewish Mus. Fla., 2002. Mem. ABA (mem. Coalition for Justice 2000-03, Law Day Speech award 1998), Nat. Assn. Women Judges, Am. Inns. of Ct. (founding mem. Palm Beach County chpt.), Acad. Fla. Trial Lawyers (bd. dirs., chair Spkr.'s Bur. program 1984-87, outreach com. 1991-92, co-chair Workhorse Seminar 1991-92), Assn. Trial Lawyers Am. (vice chair profl. rsch. and devel. dept. 1980-82, chair comml. litig. sect. 1984-85, women's trial lawyer caucus 1986-87; mem. ethics com. 1989-90, conv. planning com. 1992-93), Fla. Assn. Women Lawyers (Lifelong Dedication award 2000), Order of Coif. Office: State Supreme Ct of Florida 500 S Duval St Tallahassee FL 32399-1925 Business E-Mail: supremecourt@flcourts.org.

PARISEAU, PATRICIA, state legislator; b. St. Paul, Aug. 10, 1936; d. James Martin and Mary Margaret (May) Wright; m. Kenneth Edward Pariseau, July 9, 1960; children: Susan M., Douglas C., Penny A., Linda D., Barbara J., Jacqueline. RN, Ravenswood Hosp. Sch. Nursing, Chgo., 1957. Staff nurse Ravenswood Hosp., Chgo., 1957-58, St. Joseph's Hosp., St. Paul, 1958-59, Office of Drs. Roy & Hilker, St. Paul, 1959-60; aide to U.S. Senator Rudy Boschwitz, St. Paul, 1982-88; mem. Minn. Senate from 37th dist., St. Paul, 1989—2002, Minn. Senate from 36th Dist., St. Paul, 2003—. Mem. adv. bd. St. Paul chpt. ARC, 1986-88; vol., officer Minn. Ind. Rep. Com., 1972-83; bd. dirs. Ind. Sch. Dist. 192, Farmington, Minn., 1976-79. Mem. Minn. Waterfowl Assn., Farmington C. of C., Dakota Arts Coun., Ducks Unltd., Eagles Aux., Am. Legion Aux. (sec. Farmington chpt.), VFW Aux., So. Dakota County Sportsmen Club. Avocations: needlework, knitting, drawing, painting, traveling. Office: Minn Senate 117 Stat Office Bldg Saint Paul MN 55155-1232

PARISI, CHERYL LYNN, music educator; b. Tonawanda, N.Y., Aug. 26, 1967; d. John and Bonnie Cirrito; m. Joseph Parisi, July 6, 1991; 1 child, Joey. B in Music Edn., Potsdam Coll., 1989; M in Music Edn., Ithaca Coll., 1991. Music tchr. Decatur County Sch. Sys., Bainbridge, Ga., 1990—96, Grady County Sh. Sys., Cairo, Ga., 1996—2002, St. Thomas More, Kansas City, 2002—. Pvt. instr., 1991—; music dir. So. Ga. Performing Arts Ctr., Cairo, 1996—2002. Mem.: Pilot Club Internat. (advisor 1991—96). Home: 540 E 129th Terr Kansas City MO 64145

PARISI, PAULA ELIZABETH, writer, photographer, editor; b. N.Y.C., Feb. 27, 1960; d. Alfred John and Patricia Ann (Delucas) P. BA, Rutgers U., 1982; photography classes, Phila. Coll. Art, 1978-82. Reporter TVSM Inc./The Cable Guide, Horsham, Pa., 1982-84; assoc. editor Home Viewer Publs., Phila., 1984-85, mng. editor, 1985-87; home video cable TV, technology editor The Hollywood Reporter, Los Angeles, 1987—, editorial dir., 2000—. Contbr. articles to Billboard, Film & Video Prodn., Mix, Hollywood Reporter, Phila. Inquirer; photographs published in Phila. Inquirer, Washington Jour., Miami Herald, Circus, Us, Sixteen, others. Republican. Roman Catholic. Office: The Hollywood Reporter 5055 Wilshire Blvd Ste 600 Los Angeles CA 90036-4396

PARK, ALICE MARY CRANDALL, genealogist; b. Loda, Ill., Oct. 4, 1901; d. Frederick Adam and Sarah Elizabeth (Clemens) Crandall; m. Lee I. Park, Aug. 29, 1925 (dec. Aug. 24, 1978); children: Lee Crandall, Nancy Park Kern. BS, U. Chgo., 1924. Tchr. U. Chgo. Lab. Sch., 1924-25; genealogy rschr. Washington, 1925—. Author: Park/e/s and Bunch on the Trail West, 1974, rev. edit., 1982, Schenck and Related Families in New Netherlands, 1992, One Crandall Family 1651-1996, 1996, supplement, 1999, Our Immigrant Ancestors from Scotland: George Smith and His Wife, Mary Baird and Their Descendants, 2002. Pres. Falls Church (Va.) PTA, 1941-42, LWV, Fairfax County, Va., 1947-48. Mem. DAR, Nat. Soc. Colonial Dames Am., Nat. Soc. Sons and Daughters of Pilgrims, Nat. Soc. Daughters Am. Colonists, Friends Holland Soc., Nat. Hubenot Soc., Nat. Soc. U.S. Daughters 1812, Chevy Chase Club, Met. Club Washington, Farmington Country Club Va. Avocations: gardening, travel, cooking, music. Home: #314 4200 Cathedral Ave NW Washington DC 20016-4931

PARK, BEVERLY GOODMAN, lawyer; b. Boston, Nov. 10, 1937; d. Morris and Mary (Keller) Goodman; divorced; children: Glynis Forcht, Seth, Elyse. BS, Simmons Coll., 1959; MS, Ea. Conn. State U., 1968, JD, Western N.E. Coll. Law, 1998. Bar: Mass. 1998. Asst. dir. cmty. svc. Hartford (Conn.) Courant, 1976-79; mayor Borough of Colchester, Conn., 1979-83; lifestyle editor Chronicle, Willimantic, Conn., 1980-82, suburban editor, 1982-84; officer mktg. & comm. U. Conn. Health Ctr., Farmington, 1984—97; pvt. practice juvenile law BGP, 2000—. Selected team mem. radiation exposure info. study Belorussia, 1993; mem. adv. bd. Hosp. News; mem. women's affairs com. U. Conn. Health Ctr. Women's Networking Task Force; mem. Univ. Adminstrv. Staff Coun.; mem. minority awards com. U. Conn. Health Ctr., mem. John N. Dempsey hosp. disaster plan com. Designer: (libr. studies curriculum) Classroom Instruction on the Use of Books and Libraries, 1972; pub.: (ednl. booklets) Have You Made Plans for the Future?, 1977-78; editor of edn. holiday and bridal supplements The Chronicle, 1980-84; editor: U. Conn. Health Ctr. Anniversary Mag., 1986, U. Conn. Health Ctr. Med. Catalog, 1986, (ann. pub.) Salute, 1988, U. Conn. Health Ctr. 30th Anniversary Supplement, 1991. Bd. dirs. Ea. Conn. Found. for Pub. Giving, Norwich, 1990-96; women's club officer Dem. Town Com., Colchester, Conn., 1963-90; active Hadassah, Northampton/Amherst, 1996—, Women's League for Conservative Judaism. Recipient Lifestyle Page award New England Press Assn., 1980, Media Excellence in Covering Human Svcs. award Conn. chpt. NASW, 1982, Ragan Report Arnold's Admirables award for excellence in graphics and typography, 1985, Gold award Healthcare Mktg. Report, 1987, award for video ACS, 1990. Mem. NOW (membership com. Southea. chpt., mem. legis. task force, Meritorious Svc. award Southea. Conn. chpt. 1985), Am. Soc. for Hosp. Mktg. and Pub. Rels., Am. Mktg. Assn., Assn. Am. Med. Colls. (mem. group on pub. affairs), Conn. Hosp. Assn. (participant hosp. pub. rels. conf.), State of Conn. Pub. Info. Coun. (mem. steering com.), Mass. Bar Assn., Hampshire County and Franklin County Bar Assns., New England Hosp. Pub. Rels. and Mktg. Assn. (bd. dirs. 1987, 88). Avocations: swimming, hiking, spending time with grandchildren. Home and Office: 116 N Main St Florence MA 01062-1220 E-mail: parklegal@aol.com.

PARK, DOROTHY GOODWIN DENT (MRS. ROY HAMPTON PARK), broadcast executive, publishing executive; b. Raleigh, NC; d. Walter Reed and Mildred (Goodwin) Dent; m. Roy Hampton Park, Oct. 3, 1936; children: Roy Hampton, Adelaide Hinton. Student, Peace Jr. Coll., 1925—33; AB, Meredith Coll., 1936. Sec., dir. RHP, Inc., Ithaca, NY, 1945—, Park Comm., Inc., Ithaca, NY, 1983—95. Pres. Park Found. Inc., Ithaca, 1994—; Bd. visitors Peace Coll., Raleigh, 1968—. Mem.: LWV, DAR (1st vice regent 1955—57), Svc. League Ithaca, Colonial Order of Crown, Sovereign Colonial Soc. Ams. Royal Descent, Daus. Am. Colonists, Nat. Soc. Magna Charta Dames, Descs. Knights of Garter, Ithaca Woman's Club, Garden Club (Ithaca). Presbyterian. Home: 205 Devon Rd Ithaca NY 14850-1409

PARK, JANIE C. provost; children: Christopher, Eric. BSN, Baylor U., 1968; MS in Cell and Molecular Biology, Fla. Inst. Tech., 1979, PhD in Cell and Molecular Biology, 1982. Nurse Holmes Regional Med. Ctr., Melbourne, Fla., 1968-69; grad. student tchg. asst. Fla. Inst. Tech., Melbourne, 1977-82, instr. biol. scis., 1982-84, asst. prof. biol. scis., 1984-89, chair preprofl./premed. program, 1986-93, assoc. prof. biol. scis., 1989-93, assoc. dean coll. sci. and liberal arts, 1990-93; dean coll. arts and scis., prof. biol. scis. Mont. State U., Billings, 1993-96, provost, acad. vice chancellor, prof. biol. scis., 1996—. Rsch. dir. Ctr. for Interdisciplinary Rsch. in Aging, 1988-90; rsch. dir. elctron microscopy svcs. Joint Ctr. Advanced Therapy and Biomed. Rsch. Fla. Inst. Tech. and Holmes Regional Med. Ctr., 1991-93; spkr. in field. Contbr. articles to profl. jours. Bd. dirs. St. Vincent's Regional Med. Ctr., Youth Dynamics, Inc.; mem. steering com. Billings Town and Gown; mem. Bldg. a Healthy Cmty. Task Force. Mem. Microscopy Soc. Am., Am. Assn. of State Colls. and Univs., Southeast Electron Microscopy (sessions chair ann. meeting 1991, 92), Soc. for Neurosci., Rocky Mountain Deans' Assn. (ann. meeting organizer 1995), Assn. for Rsch. in Otolaryngology (mem. membership com. 1991-97, chair membership com. 1993-97), Fla. Soc. for Electron Microscopy (v.p. 1983, bd. dirs. 1983-93, session chair ann. meeting 1989-92, pres.-elect 1989, pres. 1990-91, mem. local arrangements com. 1991, meeting registration chair 1990—), Coun. Colls. of Arts and Scis. (session chair ann. meeting 1995), Coun. Arts and Scis. of Urban Univs., Billings Rotary Internat., Leadership Billings Alumni Assn. Office: Mont State U Office Acad Vice Chancellor 1500 N 30th St Billings MT 59101-0245

PARK, KATHLEEN JEONGSOO, portfolio manager, risk management consultant; BA, U. Chgo., 1993. Ptnr., equity options mkt. maker Beemac Traders LP, San Francisco, 1995—99; global client svcs. Moody's KMV Inc., San Francisco, 2000—02; sr. global fixed income portfolio mgr. Samsung Life Ins. Asset Mgmt. Group, Seoul, Republic of Korea, 2003—. Cray Rsch. scholar, 1989—92. Mem.: San Francisco Internat. Film Soc., Wealthy Women Group, U. Chgo. Alumni Assn. Avocations: art, films, writing, music. Office: Samsung Life Ins Co Ltd 3d Fl 150 Taepyeongro 2-Ga Jung-Gu Seoul 100-716 Republic of Korea

PARK, LINDA SUE, writer; b. Ill. BS in English, Stanford U. Pub. rels. writer major oil co., 1981—83; writer, 1997—. Author: Seesaw Girl, 1999, The Kite Fighters, 2000, A Single Shard, 2001 (Newbery Medal, 2002), When My Name Was Keoko, 2002. Avocations: cooking, travel, movies, crossword puzzles. Office: Clarion Books 215 Park Ave S New York NY 10003

PARK, MARY WOODFILL, information consultant; b. Nevada, Mo., Nov. 20, 1944; d. John Prossor and Elizabeth (Devine) Woodfill; m. Salil Kumar Banerjee, Dec. 29, 1967 (div. 1983); children: Stephen Kumar, Scott Kumar; m. Lee Crandall Park, Apr. 27, 1985; stepchildren: Thomas Joseph, Jeffrey Rawson. BA, Marywood Coll., 1966; postgrad., Johns Hopkins U., 1983, Goucher Coll., 1986. Asst. to dir. U. Pa. Librs., Phila., 1968-69; investment libr. Del. Funds, Phila., 1969-71; investment officer Investment Counselors Md., Balt., 1980-84, 1st Nat. Bank Md., Balt., 1984-85; founder Info. Consultancy, Balt., 1985—. Lectr. Loyola Coll., Balt., 1991-92, Cath. U., 1993. Author: InfoThink—Practical Strategies for Using Information in Business, 1998; editor, contbr. to profl. publs. Vol. Internat. Visitors' Ctr., Balt., 1979-80, 91; del. White House Conf. on Librs.; v.p. bd. dirs. Friends of Goucher Libr., 1988-90; mem. industry applications com. Info. Tech. Bd., State of Md., 1993-96; mem. info. tech. com. of the Tech. Coun., Greater Balt. Com., 1993-98. Named One of Md.'s Top 100 Women, Warfield's Bus. Publn., 1996. Mem.: DAR, MD Women's Health Initiative, Huguenot Soc. Md. (1st v.p. 2003—05), Nat. Huguenot Soc., Md. Found. for Psychiatry (bd. mem. 1998—), Assn. Ind. Info. Profls., Info. Futures Inst., Spl. Librs. Assn. (pres. Md. chpt. 1991—92, v.p. network coord. coun. Sailor project 1993—95, govt. rels. chair 1998—2003, pub. rels. chair 2003—), Nat. Inst. Geneal. Rsch. Alumnae Assn., Nat. Soc. of the Sons and Daus. of the Pilgrims, Nat. Soc. Colonial Dames XVII Century (state rec. sec. 2003—05), Nat. Soc. of U.S. Daus. of 1812 (Md. state rec. sec. 2003—05), Soc. of Daughters of Holland Dames, Descendants of Ancient and Honorable Families of New Netherland, Friends of New Netherlands, Nat. Soc. Dames Ct. Honor, Nat. Soc. Daus. Am. Colonists (Md. state 1st vice regent 2003—05, regent Joppa Trail chpt., corr. sec. 2003—), Three Arts Club Homeland, Hamilton St. Club (bd. dirs. 1989—92). Episcopalian. Office: The Information Consultancy 308 Tunbridge Rd Baltimore MD 21212-3803 E-mail: mwpark@informationconsultancy.com.

PARK, SUSAN YOUNG, radar systems engineer; b. Seoul, Aug. 20, 1961; d. Benjamin N. and Ann C. Park; m. Esko A. Jaska, Dec. 21, 1990; children: Arlan Jaska, Ender Jaska. BSEE, Ga. Inst. of Tech., 1984, MSEE, 1987. Aircraft engr. Lockheed-Ga. Co., Marietta, Ga., 1984-85; rsch. engr. Ga. Tech. Rsch. Inst., Atlanta, 1985-90; program mgr. SM&A Corp., Arlington,

Va., 1993-99; dept. mgr. Solers, Inc., Arlington, 1999—. Contbr. articles to profl. jours. With U.S. Peace Corps., Koforidua, West Africa, 1991-92. Office: Solers Inc 3811 N Fairfax Dr Ste 350 Arlington VA 22203 E-mail: spark@solers.com.

PARKE, CAROL REEVES, retired librarian; b. Bridgeport, Conn., Dec. 23, 1935; d. William and Elizabeth Lee (Chappell) Reeves; children: Zoe Elizabeth Parke Andrews, Amy Parke Spencer. BA, Conn. Coll., 1958; MLS, Columbia U., 1966. Asst. children's libr. N.Y. Pub. Libr., N.Y.C., 1966-68; ref. libr. Yale U. Libr., New Haven, 1968-70, documents libr., 1970-76; head ref. dept. Va. Commonwealth U. Libr., Richmond, 1977-82, asst. dir. pub.. svcs., 1982-83, adminstrv. svcs. libr., 1983-84; asst. dir. libr. for pub. svcs. U. Del., Newark, 1984-86; assoc. univ. libr. for pub. svcs. Syracuse (N.Y.) U. Libr., 1987-2001; ret., 2001. Mem. program com. ALA/RASD ann. conf., L.A., 1981-83. Mem. exec. com. Ctr. N.Y. Libr. Resources Coun., 1988-89. Mem.: ALA, Shares Exec. Group, Rsch. Librs. Group, N.Y. Libr. Assn., Assn. Coll. and Rsch. Librs. (heads readers/pub. svcs. discussion group 1985—92, chair 1989—90, com. on instnl. priorities and rewards 1996—97). Democrat. Episcopalian. Home: 4620 Devonshire Rd Richmond VA 23225

PARKE, JANET DIANE, interior designer; b. Winnemucca, Nev., Aug. 20, 1930; d. Willard Virdell and Lois (Carlson) Booth; m. Jack Evan Parke, June 11, 1950; children: Deborah Diane Parke Smith, Cary Evan, James Robert. BA, Brigham Young U., 1950. Interior designer Brunson Homes, Reno, 1972—74, Bakers Interiors, Reno, 1976—81, Tristan Parke Interiors, Reno, 1981—86, Carson Furniture, Reno, 1988—93; designer, mem. sales staff. Thomasville Furniture, 1993—96, Joanies Fashions, 1997—98; sales assoc. Boutique Casablanca, 1998—. Designer showcase homes Designs Ltd., 1987—. Com. mem. Congressman Jim Santini, Reno; bd. dirs. Nev. Jr. Miss Competition, 1969—79; hostess Miss Nev., Reno, 1974—77. Mem.: AIA (assoc.), Nev. Home Builders Assn. (assoc.), Daus. of Nile, Order Ea Star, Sigma Nu (pres. White Rose chpt. 1952—53). Democrat. Mem. Lds Ch.

PARKE, MARILYN NEILS, writer; b. Libby, Mont., June 5, 1928; d. Walter and Alma M. Neils; m. Robert V. Parke, Aug. 25, 1951; children: Robert, Richard, Gayle Crawford, Lynn Parke Castle. BA, U. Mont., 1950; MEd, Colo. State U., 1973. Tchr. Poudre R-1, Fort Collins, 1973—. Co-author: (with Sharon Panik) A Quetzalcoatl Tale of Corn, 1992, A Quetzalcoatl Tale of the Ball Game, 1992 (Parent's Choice Gold award paperback of yr. 1992), A Quetzalcoatl Tale of Chocolate, 1994. Mem. Internat. Reading Assn., Soc. Children's Book Writers and Illustrators, Nat. Edn. Assn., Colo. Coun. Internat. Reading Assn. Avocations: gardening, cooking, sports, reading, travel.

PARKE, PAULA MARIE, nurse; b. Dorchester, Mass., Sept. 21, 1959; d. Robert Daniel and Carol Ann (Young) McEachern; m. Carlton William Parke, Aug. 7, 1982; children: Stefanie J., Caitlin M. Diploma, N.E. Deaconess Hosp., 1980, postgrad., St. Joseph's Coll., 1995-97, Excelsior Coll., 1998—. RN N.H., Mass., Okla., cert. Profl. Utilization Rev., Med. Surg. Nurse. Staff nurse Hampstead (N.H.) Hosp., 1981-85, supr., 1985-87; staff nurse Exeter (N.H.) Hosp., 1987-92; nurse reviewer Alicare Med. Mgmt., Inc., Salem, N.H., 1992-94, team leader, 1994-96, mgr., 1996-98; account mgr., cons. Interqual Products Group, Marlborough, Mass., 1998-2000; case mgr. Parkland Med. Ctr., Derry, N.H., 2000—; dir. utilization and case mgmt. Alicare Med. Mgmt., Inc., Salem, NH, 2000—. Mem. ANA, NAFE, Am. Assn. Managed Care Nurses, N.H. Nurses Assn. Avocations: sewing, community involvement, hiking. Home: 15 Blueberry Cir Hampstead NH 03841-2064

PARKER, ALICE, composer; b. Boston, Dec. 16, 1925; d. Gordon and Mary (Stuart) P.; widowed; children: David, Timothy, Katharine, Mary, Elizabeth. BA, Smith Coll., Northampton, Mass., 1947; MS, Juilliard Sch., N.Y.C., 1949; MusD (hon.), Hamilton U., 1979, Macalester Coll., St. Paul, 1989, Bluffton (Ohio) Coll., 1991, Westminster Choir Coll., Princeton, N.J., 1996. Arranger Robert Shaw Chorale, N.Y.C., 1948-66; artistic dir. Melodious Accord, N.Y.C., 1985—. Tchr., workshop leader Westminster Choir Coll., Princeton, N.J., summers, 1972-98; McDonald chair Emory U., 2003. Composer 4 operas, 35 cantatas, 8 song cycles and numerous anthems and suites. Recipient composer's award ASCAP, 1968—, AGO Disting. Composer of the Yr., 2000, Barlow Endowment, 1992, spl. award Nat. Endowment Arts, 1976, Gottschalk award Pioneer Valley Symphony, 2003. Fellow Hymn Soc., Hymn Soc. Am.; mem. Am. Choral Dirs. Assn., Am. Condrs. Guild, Chorus Am. (Founders award 1994), Am. Music ctr., Sigma Alpha Iota. Office: Melodious Accord Inc Park West Sta PO Box 20801 New York NY 10025-1523

PARKER, ARLENE SANDRA, social worker; b. N.Y.C., June 7, 1948; d. Sam and Sylvia Brotman; m. Franklin Fernandes Parker, Nov. 27, 1983; 1 child, Samantha Joy. BA, SUNY, Albany, 1970; MA, U. Pa., 1971; MSW, Adelphi U., 1977. Diplomate in clin. psychotherapy; ACSW CSW N.Y.; credentialed alcohol and substance abuse counselor N.Y. Asst. social work Cath. Charities, Rockville Centre, NY, 1973—77; sch. social worker Oceanside (N.Y.) Pub. Schs., 1977—. Psychotherapist, Baldwin, NY, 1985—. Scholar Nat. Def. Scholarship, 1969. Mem.: Acad. Cert. Social Workers, NASW, Sisterhood Ctrl. Synagogue. Avocation: travel. Home: 289 Princeton Rd Rockville Centre NY 11570 Office: 865 Merrick Rd Ste 305 Baldwin NY 11510

PARKER, DIANA LYNNE, restaurant manager, special events director; b. Eureka, Calif., June 21, 1957; d. Carol Dean and Lynne Diane (Havemann) P. BA in English, Humboldt U., 1981, postgrad., 1982-84. Lic. real estate agent, Calif. Retail clk. Safeway, Inc., Eureka, 1977-84; caterer, owner TD Catering, Eureka, 1982-84; asst. buyer Macy's Calif., San Francisco, 1984-85; realtor Mason-McDuffie, Alameda, Calif., 1985-87; host, Rotunda Restaurant Neiman Marcus, San Francisco, 1987-89, asst. mgr. Rotunda Restaurant, 1989—96, dir. spl. events, 1989—96, mgr. dining room Rotunda Restaurant, 1996—. Mem.: San Francisco Visitor and Conv. Bur., Women Chefs and Restauranteurs, Mus. Modern Art, Commonwealth Club Calif. Republican. Avocations: gourmet chef, artist, antique collecting. Office: Rotunda at Neiman Marcus 150 Stockton St San Francisco CA 94108-5807

PARKER, H. STEWART, biotechnology company executive; BA, MBA, U. Wash. V.p. corp. devel. Immunex, 1981—91; pres., CEO, dir. Targeted Genetics, 1989—. Chmn. bd. CellExSys, Inc. (subs. Targeted Genetics, Inc.), 2000—. Bd. visitors U. N.C.; Arts & Sciences Coun. U. Wash.; bd. dirs. Pilchuck Glass Sch. Recipient Small Bus. Person of the Year for Western Wash., Small Bus. Admin., 2001. Mem.: Biotechnology Industry Orgn. (exec. com., bd. dirs.). Office: Targeted Genetics Corp 1100 Olive Way Ste 100 Seattle WA 98101

PARKER, JACQUELINE YVONNE, lawyer, educator; b. Urbana, Ill., Jan. 14, 1947; d. Melvin M. and Florence L. (Katz) Pick; m. Bruce Richard Parker, May 30, 1969; children: Kenneth R.L., Michael P., Deborah M. BA, Tufts U., 1969; student law, U. Calif., Berkeley, 1976-77; JD, New Eng. Sch. Law, 1977; LLM, Harvard U., 1981. Bar: Mass. 1978, U.S. Ct. Appeals (1st cir.) 1978, U.S. Supreme Ct. 1990. Asst. prof. law New Eng. Sch. Law, Boston, 1978-81, Albany (N.Y.) Law Sch., 1981-84; assoc. Parker Coulter Daley & White, Boston, 1984-92; atty. Connelly & Norton P.C., Boston, 1992—2000. Author, co-author (4 vol. treatise) Contemporary Family Law: Principles, Policy & Practice, 1988; contbr. articles to law revs. Mem. Children's Adoption & Foster Care Coalition, Boston, 1991—. United Way scholar, 1975, New Eng. Sch. Law Trustee's scholar, 1975-76. Mem. ABA, Nat. Assn. of Counsel for Children (bd. dirs. 1991-2002), Mass. Bar Assn. (family law legis. subcom., com. for pub. counsel svcs., bd. dirs. 1993-2000). Avocations: hiking, jogging, tennis. Office: Law Office of Jacqueline Y Parker Box 554 Newton Center MA 02459 E-mail: jyparker@worldnet.att.net.

PARKER, JANET RUTH, town official; b. Boston, June 8, 1945; d. Nathan Oscar and Ruth Norma (Bishop) Gardner; m. David Storer Parker, Sept. 20, 1969; children: Jonathan, Scott, Rachel. AS, Garland Jr. Coll., Boston, 1965; BS, U. Maine, 1967. Dietitian Stouffer Foods, Boston, 1967-70; town clk. Town of Seekonk, Mass., 1996—. Pres. Save A Pet, Seekonk, 1987-95; docent Roger Williams Park Zoo, Providence, 1997—. Mem. New Eng. Assn. Town Clks., Mass. Town Clks. Assn. Republican. Avocations: reading, animal studies, cooking. Office: Seekonk Town Hall 100 Peck St Seekonk MA 02771-5199

PARKER, JENNIFER WARE, chemical engineer, researcher; b. Berkeley, Calif., Apr. 18, 1959; d. Raymond Paul and Maureen Christina (Trehearne) Ware; m. Henrik Davidson Parker, July 30, 1983; children: Katherine Joyce, Nathaniel Henrikson. BSChemE, Princeton U., 1980; MSChemE, UCLA, 1983, PhDChemE, 1986. Devel. engr. Am. Pharmaseal, Glendale, Calif., 1980-81; rsch. engr. Crump Inst. Med. Engring, UCLA, 1986-87; sr. engr. The BOC Group, Murray Hill, NJ, 1987-90, lead engr., 1990-92; sr. rsch. engr. CFM Techs., Inc., West Chester, Pa., 1993-97; v.p. CFMT Inc., Wilmington, Del., 1997-99, pres., 1999—2001, Mattson Tech. IP, 2001—02; founder Adondo Corp., Wayne, Pa., 2002—. Contbr. articles to profl. jours. Mem. Am. Inst. Chem. Engrs., N.Y. Acad. Scis. Avocations: sports, music, gardening. Home: 201 W Country Club Ln Wallingford PA 19086-6507 E-mail: jhparker@comcast.net.

PARKER, KATHLEEN KAPPEL, state legislator; b. Pitts., Sept. 21, 1943; m. Keith Parker; 2 children. BA, U. Miami, 1968. Tax assessor Northfield Twp., 1979-83; mem. Regional Transp. Authority Bd., 1983-95; del. Ill. and Nat. Rep. Convs., 1988; Northfield Twp. coord. George Bush's Presdl. Campaign, 1988; mem. U.S. Archtl. and Transp. Barriers Compliance Bd., 1991-94; Ill. state sen., 1995—. Mem. Fin. Inst., vice chair Pub. Health and Welfare Coms., Transp. Com., 1995—, chair; co-owner Keith Parker and Assocs., 1985—; pres., bd. dirs. Chgo. divsn. Busch Jewelry Co., 1988-93. Chair Mental Health Task Force. Mem. Northeastern Ill. Planning Coun., Met. Planning Coun. Office: 191 Waukegan Rd Northfield IL 60093-2756

PARKER, LETITIA, secondary school educator; b. Waukegan, Ill., Jan. 12, 1947; d. Robert Edwin and Lettie M. Parker. AA, Gulf Park Coll., Long Beach, Miss., 1970; BS, Fla. State U., 1972, MS, 1975. Tchr. St. John Elem. Sch., Quincy, Fla., 1972—75, LaFayette Art Ctr., Tallahassee, 1975—76, Henry County Sch., Collinsville, Va., 1976—79, Milton (Wis.) HS, 1979—. Regional chair WAEA Visual Art Classic Competition U. Wis., Whitewater, Wis. Mem.: AAUW, Wis. Art Edn. Assn. (bd. mem., Hunziker Endowment bd. mem. 2000—, Pres. award for svc. 1990, 2002), Nat. Art Edn. Assn. Christian Scientist. Avocations: travel, theater. Office: Milton High Sch 114 W High St Milton WI 53563 E-mail: parkerl@mail.milton.k12.wi.us.

PARKER, LINDA BATES, professional development organization administrator; Grad., U. Dayton, U. Cin., Harvard U., 1991. Pres., founder Black Career Women, Cin. Dir. Career Devel. Ctr., mgmt. prof. U. Cin. Author: Career Portfolio; columnist for Nat. Black Collegian Mag.; presenter in field. Office: Black Career Women PO Box 19332 Cincinnati OH 45219-0332

PARKER, LYNDA CHRISTINE RYLANDER, secondary school educator; b. Bremerton, Wash., Apr. 21, 1949; d. Richard Algot and Marian Ethelyn (Peterson) Rylander; m. Joseph Hiram Parker, Feb. 7, 1981; 1 child, Joseph Hiram IV. BA in English, Sociology, Pacific Luth. U., 1971, MA in Ednl. Administrn., 1981, prin.'s credential, 1982, postgrad. Tchr. lang. arts Cen. Kitsap Schs., Silverdale, Wash., 1971-74; tchr. English gifted Okanagan Schs., Kelowna, B.C., Can., 1974-78; tchr. lang. arts gifted Federal Way (Wash.) Schs., 1978-86; tchr. lang. arts, remedial reading, humanities gifted Bethel Sch. Dist., Spanaway, Wash., 1986—. Counselor Okanagan Sch. Dist., Kelowna, 1974-78; advisor Ski Club, Cheerleaders, Svc. Club, Pep Club, Kitsap Schs., Silverdale, 1971-74, Cheerleaders, Pep Club, Svc. Club, Ski Club, annual, newspaper, class advisor, Okanagan Sch. Dist., Kelowna, 1974-78, newspaper, Cheerleaders, Bethel Schs., Spanaway, 1986—; multimedia, at-risk program, gifted program, 1996-; presenter of workshops for parents, tchrs., adminstrs., 1988—. Named Christa McAuliffe Outstanding Tchr. of Yr. State of Wash., 1988. Mem. NEA, ASCD, NAFE, Nat. Assn. Secondary Sch. Prins., Wash. Edn. Assn., Wash. Assn. Secondary Sch. Prins., Bethel Educators Assn. Republican. Lutheran. Avocations: piano, snow skiing, body building. Home: 1721 169th Street Ct S Spanaway WA 98387-9141

PARKER, LYNDA MICHELE, psychiatrist; b. Sept. 28, 1947; d. Albert Francis and Dorothy Thomasina (Herriott) P. BA, C. W. Post Coll., 1968; MA, NYU, 1970; MD, Cornell U., 1974; postgrad., N.Y. Psychoanalytic Inst., 1977-82. Diplomate Am. Coll. Forensic Examiners. Intern N.Y. Hosp., N.Y.C., 1975; resident in psychiatry Payne Whitney Clinic, N.Y.C., 1975-78; psychiatrist-in-charge day program Cabrini Med. Ctr., N.Y.C., 1978-79, attending psychiatrist, supr. psychiatry residents, 1978-96, supr. long-term psychotherapy, 1980-82; attending psychiatrist N.Y. Hosp., Cornell Med. Ctr., 1979-96; practice medicine specializing in psychiatry N.Y.C., 1979-96; from instr. psychiatry to asst. prof. Cornell U. Med. Coll., 1979-96; instr. psychiatry N.Y. Med. Coll., 1978-96; assoc. prof., regional chair dept. psychiatry Tex. Tech. U. Health Scis. Ctr., Amarillo, 1996-99, No. region dir. correctional mental health scis., 1999—2002, clin. dir. PAMIO, 1999—2002; pvt. practice, 2002—. Assoc. prof. pharmacy practice in psychiatry Tex. Tech U. Sch. Pharmacy, 1996-99; psychiat. cons. Bldg. Service 32BJ Health Fund, 1983-89, Inwood House, N.Y.C., 1983-86, Time-Life Inc., 1986-96, Ind. Med. Examiners, 1986-96, Epilepsy Inst., 1986-87, asst. med. dir., 1987-88, med. dir., 1988; ind. med. examiner Rep. Health Care Rev. Sys. Mem. adv. bd. St. Bartholomew Community Presch., N.Y.C., 1990-96. Martin Luther King Jr. scholar NYU, 1968-70. Mem. AAUW, Am. Psychiat. Assn., Am. Womens Med. Assn., Tex. Soc. for Psychiat. Physicians, Tex. Med. Assn. Episcopalian. Office: 1616 S Kentucky Ste C-200 Amarillo TX 79102 Office Phone: 806-457-9200. Personal E-mail: LyParker@aol.com.

PARKER, MARIETTA, prosecutor; Asst. U.S. atty. Dept. Justice, Kansas City, Mo.; U.S. atty. Dept. Justice, Kansas City, Mo., 1993—. Office: US Attys Office 1201 Walnut St Ste 300 Kansas City MO 64106-2136

PARKER, MARY-LOUISE, actress; b. Ft. Jackson, S.C., Aug. 2, 1964; 1 child, William Atticus. Attended, Bard Coll. Actress: (theatre) Hay Fever, 1987, The Miser, 1988, The Art of Success, 1989, The Importance of Being Earnest, 1989, Prelude to a Kiss, Broadway, 1990-91 (Theatre World award, Clarence Derwent Award, Tony nomination, 1990), Babylon Gardens, 1991, How I Learned to Drive, 1997 (Lucille Lortel Award for outstanding actress, OBIE Award, 1997), Proof, Broadway (Tony award for best actress in a play, 2001);(films) Signs of Life, 1989, Longtime Companion, 1990, Grand Canyon, 1991, Fried Green Tomatoes, 1991, Mr. Wonderful, 1993, Naked in New York, 1994, The Client, 1994, Bullets Over Broadway, 1994, Boys on the Side, 1995, A Portrait of a Lady, 1996, Reckless, 1995, Murder in Mind, 1997, The Maker, 1997, Let the Devil Wear Black, 1998, Goodbye, Lover, 1998, Five Senses, 1999, Pipe Dream, 2002, Red Dragan, 2002, The Best Thief in the World, 2004, others; (TV movies) Too Young the Hero, 1988, A Place for Annie, 1994, Sugartime, 1995, Legalese, 1998, Saint Maybe, 1998, The Simple Life of Noah Dearborn, 1999, Cupid & Cate, 2000, Master Spy: The Robert Hanssen Story, 2002; (TV miniseries) Angels in America, 2003 (Golden Globe for best supporting actress 2004); (TV series) Ryan's Hope, 1975, West Wing, 2001- (Emmy nomination, 2002). Office: William Morris Agy care Scott Henderson 151 S El Camino Dr Beverly Hills CA 90212-2775*

PARKER, NANCY WINSLOW, artist, writer; b. Maplewood, N.J., Oct. 18, 1930; d. Winslow Aurelius and Beatrice (Gaunt) P. BA, Mills Coll., 1952; student, Sch. Visual Art, N.Y.C., Art Students League. Pub. rels. exec. N.Y. Soccer Club, N.Y.C., 1961-63; with RCA, N.Y.C., 1964-67; art dir. Appleton-Century-Crofts, N.Y.C., 1968-70; staff designer Holt Reinhart & Winston, N.Y.C., 1970-73; free lance writer, illustrator, 1974—. Author, illustrator: The Man with the Take-Apart Head, 1974, The Party at the Old Farm, 1975, Mrs. Wilson Wanders Off, 1976, Love from Uncle Clyde, 1977, The Crocodile Under Louis Finneberg's Bed, 1978, The President's Cabinet, 1978, rev. edit., 1991, The Ordeal of Byron B. Blackbear, 1979, Puddums, The Cathcarts' Orange Cat, 1980, Poofy Loves Company, 1980 (ALA Notable Book, 1980), The Spotted Dog, 1980, The President's Car, 1981, Cooper, The McNally's Big Black Dog, 1981, Love from Aunt Betty, 1983, The Christmas Camel, 1983, The United Nations from A to Z, 1985, Working Frog, 1992; co-author: Money, Money, Money, 1995, Locks, Crocs and Skeeters, The Story of the Panama Canal, 1996, Land Ho! Fifty Glorious Years in The Age of Exploration with 12 Important Explorers, 2001; illustrator Oh, A Hunting We Will Go!, 1974, Warm as Wool, Cool as Cotton, The Story of Natural Fibers, 1975, The Goat in the Rug, 1976, Willy Bear, 1976 (Christopher award, 1976), Sweetly Sings the Donkey, 1976, The Substitute, 1977, Hot Cross Buns and Other Old Street Cries, 1978, No Bath Tonight, 1978, My Mom Travels a Lot, 1981 (Christopher award, 1981), Paul Revere's Ride, 1985, General Store, 1988, Aren't You Coming Too?, 1988, Peter's Pockets, 1988, The Jacket I Wear in the Snow, 1989, At Grammy's House, 1990, Black Crow, Black Crow, 1991, When The Rooster Crowed, 1991, Barbara Frietchie, 1992, The Dress I'll Wear to the Party, 1992, Sheridan's Ride, 1993, Here Comes Henny, 1994, The Bag I'm Taking to Grandma's, 1995, We're Making Breakfast for Mother, 1996, The House I'll Build for the Wrens, 1997, I'm Taking a Trip on My Train, 1999, I'm Not Feeling Well Today, 2001, Our Class Took a Trip to the Zoo, 2002. Sec. East 74th St. Block Assn., 1974-83. Recipient various awards, 1974—; Jane Tinkham Broughton fellow, Breadloaf, Vt., 1975. Mem. Author's Guild, Mills Coll. Club of N.Y., Mantoloking Yacht Club. Home: Apt 3R 51 E 74th St New York NY 10021-2717 E-mail: nwparker52@aol.com.

PARKER, OLIVIA, photographer; b. Boston, June 10, 1941; d. Harvey Perley and Barbara Ellen (Churchill) Hood; m. John Otis Parker, Apr. 4, 1964; children: John Otis, Helen Elizabeth. BA, Wellesley Coll., 1963. Tchr. photog. workshops, 1975—. Photographer, 1969— ; author: (monographs) Signs of Life, 1978, Under the Looking Glass, 1983, Weighing the Planets, 1987; portfolios of black and white photographs Ephemera, 1977, Lost Objects, 1980; one-woman shows include, Vision Gallery, Boston, 1976, 77, 79, 82, 83, 86, 87, Friends of Photography, Carmel, Calif., 1979, 81, Marcuse Pfeifer, N.Y.C., 1980, 83, George Eastman House, Rochester, N.Y., 1981, Art Inst. Chgo., 1982, Photo Gallery Internat., Tokyo, 1983, 84, 87, Fotografic Forum Gallery, Frankfurt, Germany, 1985, Lieberman and Saul, N.Y.C., 1988, Mus. Photgraphic Arts, San Diego, 1988, Photographers' Gallery, London, 1990, Brent Sikkema, N.Y.C., 1990, 91, Parco, Tokyo, 1991, ICAC/Weston, Tokyo, 1992, Vision, San Francisco, 1993, Robert Klein, Boston, 1993, 96, 99, Wooster Gardens, N.Y.C., 1996, (with Jerry Uelsmann) Isabella Stewart Gardner Mus., Boston, 1997, Huntington (W.Va.) Mus. of Art, 2000, Lancaster (Pa.) Mus. of Art, 2000, Toledo (Ohio) Art Mus., 2002, Visual Arts Ctr. Coll. of Santa Fe, 2003; group shows include, Mus. Fine Arts, Boston, 1978, 92, 93, 96, 99, Chgo. Art Inst., 1978, Internat. Ctr. Photography, N.Y.C., 1985, 87, Fogg Art Mus. Harvard U., 1989; represented in permanent collections, Mus. Modern Art, N.Y.C., Art Inst. Chgo., Boston Mus. Fine Arts, Victoria and Albert Mus., London, (TV documentary) Africans in America, 1998. Bd. dirs. MacDowell Colony, 1988—; trustee Art Inst. Boston, 1992—. Artists Found. fellow, 1978; recipient Wellesley College Alumnae Achievement award, 1996. Mem. Soc. for Photog. Edn. Clubs: Chilton. Office: Robert Klein 4th Fl 38 Newbury St Fl 4 Boston MA 02116-3210

PARKER, PAM, apparel manufacturing company executive; b. San Francisco, 1960; BA, U. Calif., Berkeley; MBA, Stanford U., 1989. Cons. Bain and Co.; co-founder, co-pres. Ariat Internat., Inc., San Carlos, Calif., 1990—. Office: 26 Heritage Dr San Rafael CA 94901-8308

PARKER, PAMELA JEAN, vice principal; b. St. Louis, Mo., Oct. 27, 1947; d. Edward L. and Vaneater K. Peery; m. Henry L. Parker; 1 child, Jennifer J. ; 1 child, Ronald O. Martin Jr. BA, U.Ill., Chgo., 1969; MA in Sch. Guidance and Counseling, Roosevelt U., Chgo., 1974; EdD in Ednl. Psychology, No. Ill. U., De Kalb, 2002. Author: (Book) Resiliency Among African-Am. H.S. Grads., 2002. Bd. dirs. Girl Scouts USA, Chgo., 2001—. Recipient Honor pin, Girl Scouts USA, 2003. Mem.: ASCD, Phi Delta Kappa, Delta Sigma Theta. Avocations: reading, travel, youth work vol.. Office: Paul Revere Sch 1010 E 72nd St Chicago IL 60619 E-mail: pjpparker82@hotmail.com.

PARKER, REBECCA MARY, special education facility administrator, educator; b. Biloxi, Miss., Sept. 1, 1961; d. Peter John and Mary Laura (Whittington) Pitalo; m. David Alan McKee, Oct. 5, 1985 (div. Mar. 1992); 1 child, Daniel Owen McKee; m. Charles L. Parker, Feb. 3, 1994; 1 child, Mary Caroline, 1 child, Jessica Hart. BS in Spl. Edn., U. So. Miss., 1985, M of Behavioral Disorders, 1992; postgrad., Boston U., Berlin. Double A cert. Miss. State Dept. Edn. Tchr. learning disabilities Jackson County Schs., Biloxi, 1985-86; learning impaired specialist Dept. of Def. Dependent Schs., Berlin, 1986-89; tchr. day treatment program Gulf Oaks Psychiat. Facility, Biloxi, 1989-95; behavioral interventionist Jackson County Schs., Vancleave, Miss., 1986-89; exec. dir. recreation integration program O'Keefe Found., New Hope Ctr., Ocean Springs, Miss., 1997—. Adj. faculty U. So. Miss., Gautier, 1993—; spkr. on attention deficit Ctr. for Child Abuse, Gulfport, Miss., 1997; spkr. on applied behavioral analysis Juvenile Shelter Staff, Pascagoula, Miss., 1997; spkr. on recreational integration Gulfport Exch. Club, 1997; cons. on behavior issues Ocean Springs Schs., 1997-98; condr. parenting classes New Hope Ctr., Ocean Springs, 1997; mem. tng. staff on inclusion YMCA, Jackson, and Gulf Coast region, 1997-99; presenter in field. Conductor tng. sems. YMCA's, Jackson and Gulf Coast. Acad. scholar Miss. Gulf Coast Jr. Coll., 1981. Mem. CEC, Assn. for Retarded Citizens (audit bd. 1997—), Assn. for Severe Handicap, Ocean Springs C. of C. Methodist. Avocation: raising three children. Home: 4701 Gibson Rd Ocean Springs MS 39564-6009 Office: New Hope Ctr 1904 Government St Ocean Springs MS 39564-3933

PARKER, SARA ANN, librarian, consultant; b. Cassville, Mo., Feb. 19, 1939; d. Howard Franklin and Vera Irene (Thomas) P. BA, Okla. State U., 1961; M.L.S., Emporia State U., Kans., 1968. Adult svcs. librarian Springfield Pub. Libr., Mo., 1972-75, bookmobile dir., 1975-76; coord. S.W. Mo. Libr. Network, Springfield, 1976-78; libr. developer Colo. State Libr., Denver, 1978-82; state librarian Mont. State Libr., Helena, 1982-88, State Libr. Pa., Harrisburg, 1988-90; Pa. commr. librs., dep. sec. edn. State of Pa., Harrisburg, 1990-95; state libr. State of Mo., Jefferson City, 1995—. Cons. and lectr. in field. Author, editor, compiler in field; contbr. articles to profl. jours. Sec., Western Coun. State Librs., Reno, 1984-88, mem. Mont. State Data Adv. Coun., 1983-88, Mont. Telecommunications Coun., 1985-88, WLN Network Coun., 1984-87, Kellogg ICLIS Project Mgmt. Bd., 1986-88; mem. adv. com. Gates Libr. Initiative, 1998—; mem. OCLC Strategic Directions and Governance Study Adv. Coun., 2000-01. Recipient Pres.'s award, Nature Conservancy, 1989, Friends award, Pa. Assn. Ednl. Comms. and Techs., 1989, Friend of Sch. Librs. award, Mo. Sch. Librs. Assn., 2000, Bohley Libr. Cooperation award, 2001; fellow Inst. Ednl. Leadership, 1982. Mem. ALA, Chief Officers State Libr. Agys. (pres.

1996-98), Mont. Libr. Assn. (bd. dirs. 1982-88), Mountain Plains Libr. Assn. (sec. chmn. 1980, pres. 1987-88). Home: PO Box 554 Jefferson City MO 65102-0554 Office: Mo State Libr PO Box 387 600 W Main St Jefferson City MO 65101-1532

PARKER, SARAH ELIZABETH, state supreme court justice; b. Charlotte, N.C., Aug. 23, 1942; d. Augustus and Zola Elizabeth (Smith) P. AB, U. N.C., 1964, JD, 1969; LHD (hon.), Queens Coll., 1998. Bar: N.C. 1969, U.S. Dist. Ct. (mid., ea. and we. dists.) N.C. Vol. U.S. Peace Corps, Ankara, Turkey, 1964-66; pvt. practice Charlotte, 1969-84; judge N.C. Ct. Appeals, Raleigh, 1985—92; assoc. justice N. C. Supreme Ct., Raleigh, 1993—. Bd. visitors U. N.C., Chapel Hill, 1993—97; pres. Mecklenburg County Dem. Women, Charlotte, 1973; N.C. ct. commr., 1999—; bd. dirs. YWCA, Charlotte, 1982—85. Recipient Disting. Woman of N.C. award, 1997, Woman of Achievement award Nat. Fedn. Women's Clubs, 1997. Mem. ABA, Inst. Jud. Adminstrn., N.C. Bar Assn. (v.p. 1987-88), Mecklenburg County Bar (sec.-treas. 1982-84), Wake County Bar Assn., N.C. Internat. Women's Forum, Women Attys. Assn. (Gwyneth David Pub. Svc. award 1986). Episcopalian. Office: NC Supreme Ct PO Box 1841 Raleigh NC 27602-1841

PARKER, SARAH JESSICA, actress; b. Nelsonville, Ohio, Mar. 25, 1965; m. Matthew Broderick May, 1997; 1 child: James. Actress: (theatre) The Innocents, 1976, The Sound of Music, 1977, Annie, 1978, The War Brides, 1981, The Death of a Miner, 1982, To Gillian on Her 37th Birthday, 1983, 84, Terry Neal's Future, 1986, The Heidi Chronicles, 1989, How to Succeed in Business Without Really Trying, 1996, Once Upon a Mattress, 1996—, (films) Rich Kids, 1979, Somewhere Tomorrow, 1983, Firstborn, 1984, Footloose, 1984, Girls Just Want to Have Fun, 1985, Flight of the Navigator, 1986, L.A. Story, 1991, Honeymoon in Vegas, 1992, Hocus Pocus, 1993, Striking Distance, 1993, Ed Wood, 1994, Miami Rhapsody, 1995, If Lucy Fell, 1996, Mars Attacks!, 1996, The First Wives Club, 1996, Extreme Measures, 1996, 'Til There Was You, 1997, The Substance of Fire, 1996, (voice) A Life Apart: Hasidism in America, 1997, Isn't She Great, 1999, Dudley Do-Right, 1999, State and Main, 2000, Life Without Dick, 2001; (TV movies) My Body, My Child, 1982, Going for the Gold: The Bill Johnson Story, 1985, A Year in the Life, 1986, The Room Upstairs, 1987, Dadah Is Death, 1988, The Ryan White Story, 1989, Twist of Fate, 1989, In the Best Interest of the Children, 1992, (TV series) Square Pegs, 1982-83, A Year in the Life, 1987-88, Equal Justice, 1990-91, Sex and the City, 1998-2004 (Best Supporting Actress Golden Globe award 1999, 2000, 01, 02, 04, Emmy nominee for Outstanding Lead Actress 1999-2002, Outstanding Performance by Female Actor in Comedy Series award 2001), (TV pilots) The Alan King Show, 1986; guest appearances The Ben Stiller Show, 1992, The Larry Sanders Show, 1992; co-exec. prodr. Sex and the City. Nat. amb. U.S. Fund for UNICEF. Recipient, Am. Civil Liberties Union award, 1995. Office: Creative Artists Agy care Jane Berliner 9830 Wilshire Blvd Beverly Hills CA 90212-1804*

PARKER, SHEILA, newscaster; Reporter, Orlando, Fla.; anchor Tallahassee; reporter WSAV-TV, Savannah, Ga., 1999—. Avocations: news, travel, reading, college football. Office: WSAV-TV3 1430 E Victory Dr Savannah GA 31404

PARKER, SUSAN BROOKS, healthcare executive; b. Newport, NH, Nov. 7, 1945; d. Ronald Elliott and Elizabeth Louise (Wiggins) P.; m. Allen D. Avery, 1967 (div. 1978); children: Jeffrey Roberts Avery, Mark Brooks Avery. BS in English and French, U. Vt., 1968; MSW/MSP, Boston Coll., 1978. EMT, Vt., 1973-76. Resort hotel mgr., retail buyer Avery Vt. Inns, 1967-75; aftercare psychiatric worker Orange County Mental Health, Bradford, Vt., 1974-76; exec. dir. Grafton County Planning Coun., Lebanon, N.H., 1978-80, N.H. Developmental Disabilities Planning Coun., Concord, N.H., 1980-87; commr. Dept. of Mental Health, Augusta, Maine, 1987-89; assoc. commr. U.S. Social Security Adminstrn., Balt., 1989-93; sec. gen. Rehab. Internat., NYC, 1993—98; sr. adv., interim dir. disability program Internat. Labor Office, Geneva, 1998—2001; dir. policy and rsch. Office Disability Employment Policy US Dept. Labor, Washington, 2002—. Cons. Nat. Gov.'s Assn., Washington, 1985-86, Office of Health and Devel. Svcs., Washington, 1987; bd. dirs. Nat. Assn. Devel. Disabilities, Washington, 1983-87, Ctrl. NH Mental Health Ctr., Concord, 1985-87, World Com. Disability, Washington, 1997—, Roeher Inst., Toronto, Ont., Can., 1997-2000, Orah.com, Geneva, 2002—, NH Devel. Disabilities Coun., 2002—; bd. dirs. US Coun. for Internat. Disability, Washington; hon. coun. Rehab. Internat. and mem. World Assembly, NY. Author: (poetry) Scheme, 1965, Jamaican Collection, 1973; contbr. articles to newspapers and profl. jours. Pres. Parent Tchr. Orgn., Fairlee, Vt., 1972-73; founder and dir. Ford Sayre Ski Program, Dartmouth Coll. Skiway, Fairlee, 1972-76, United Way, Concord, 1983-86; bd. dirs. PTO Rundlett Jr. H.S., Concord, 1982-85; pres. U.S. Coun. for Internat. Rehab., 1993. Recipient Assn. Retarded Citizens Children's Disability Pub. Policy award, 1992, Kathryn C. Arneson award from People to People, 1992, Commr.'s citation for outstanding efforts in developing policy U.S. Social Security Adminstrn., 1992, Commn.'s citation for outstanding exec. leadership, 1993; named Outstanding Alumnus Boston Coll., 1991. Avocations: skiing, gardening, canoeing, mountain climbing, reading.

PARKER, SUSAN D. state official, auditor; b. Eva, Ala., Sept. 30, 1955; m. Paul Parker. AS magna cum laude, Calhoun C.C., 1975; BS in Edn. magna cum laude, Athens State Coll., 1977; MA in Counseling magna cum laude, U. Ala., Birmingham, 1979; PhD in Adminstrn. Higher Edn., U. Ala., Tuscaloosa, 1984. Admissions clk., office mgr., dir. job placement, asst. dean Calhoun C.C., 1972-88; asst. to pres. for external affairs, chief devel. officer Athens State Coll., 1988-96; pres. Parker Plus Cons., 1996-98; state auditor State of Ala., Montgomery, 1998—. Past mem. numerous bd. dirs. nonprofit, charitable orgns., including Ala. bd. dirs. Am. Heart Assn.; past pres. county chpts. Am. Heart Assn., Am. Cancer Soc., Leukemia Soc., Boys and Girls Club, C. of C. leadership programs, Mental Health Assn., United Way, Cmty. Unity; former Sunday sch. tchr. 1st Bapt. Ch., Hartselle, Ala. Named One of 10 Outstanding Young Ams., U.S. Jaycees, 1987, One of 10 Outstanding Young Alabamians and Outstanding Citizen of Hartselle, Hartselle Jaycees, Ala.'s Most Outstanding Young Career Woman, Ala. Bus. and Profl. Women's Assn., Outstanding United Way Vol. Morgan County; named to Alumni Hall of Honor, Ala. Coll. Sys. Avocations: walking, golf, travel, fishing. Office: State Auditor's Office PO Box 300200 Montgomery AL 36130-0200 Fax: 334-242-7650. E-mail: sparker@auditor.state.al.us.

PARKER, VENUS CRISTELA, music educator, musician; b. San Pedro Sula, Honduras, Sept. 16, 1969; d. Jose David Pineda and Sonia Emilia Melara; m. Jamie Scott Parker, June 17, 1995. MusM, Ga. State U., 1994—96; MusB, U. of So. Miss., 1991—93. Cert. Teacher GA, 1996. Music educator Lilburn Mid. Sch., Lilburn, Ga., 1996—99; sales dir. Mary Kay Cosmetics, Dallas, 1999—2001; music educator Parkview H.S., Lilburn, Ga., 2001—. Pvt. violin instr., Snellville, Ga., 1994—. Musician: musical performances include those with Ray Charles and The Moody Blues, (violin sonata) Vitali Chaconne (Miss. Music Teachers Assn. Sr. Divsn. Winner, 1994). Musician and mem. Atlanta Internat. Ch. of Christ, Lilburn, Ga., 2000—03. Recipient Jr. Divsn. Winner, Miss. Music Teachers Assn., 1992; Full scholarship, Columbus Coll., 1987, U. of So. Miss., 1991, Grad. Assistantship, Ga. State U., 1994. Mem.: Atlanta Fedn. of Musicians, Ga. Music Educators Assn. Avocations: interior decorating, sewing, crafts, cooking, arranging music. Office: Parkview High School 998 Cole Dr Lilburn GA 30039

PARKHURST, CAROLYN, writer; b. 1971; BA, Wesleyan U.; MFA in creative writing, Am. U. Author: The Dogs of Babel, 2003 (Best Fiction Book Fort Worth Star-Telegram, 2003, Notable Book New York Times, 2003), (short stories) (included in) North Am. Review, Minn. Review, Hawaii Review, Crescent Review. Office: c/o Douglas Stewart Curtis Brown Ltd 10 Astor Pl New York NY 10003*

PARKHURST, DENICE DELRAY, music educator; b. Newport, R.I., Feb. 21, 1965; d. Buford Delray and Margaret Louise Baker; m. Douglas Edward Parkhurst; children: Marion Louise, Molly Ruth, Berkley Daniel. MusB in Edn., John Brown U., Siloam Springs, Ark., 1987. Cert. tchr. Maine, 1988. Choral music educator MSAD#49, Fairfield, Maine, 1988—92; dir. choral music MSAD#47, Newport, Maine, 1993—98; ch. choir dir. and organist Getchell St. Bapt. Ch., Waterville, Maine, 1993—99, First Congl. Ch., Durham, Maine, 1999—2003; artistic dir. Greater Freeport Cmty. Chorus, Freeport, Maine, 2002—; ch. choir dir. North Yarmouth Congl. Ch., North Yarmouth, Maine, 2003—; dir. choral music Freeport (Maine) Schs., 1998—. Accompanist Maine Music Educators Assn., 1988—, guest condr., 1990—. Recipient award of distinction, FIESTAVAL, 2003; Bradley fellow, Freeport HS, 2003. Mem.: Music Educators Nat. Conf., Nat. Teachers Assocation, Freeport Edn. Assn., Maine Music Educators Assn. (assoc.), Am. Choral Directors Assn. (assoc.; pres. Maine chpt. 2003—). Republican. Evangelical Free Ch. Avocations: quilting, travel, acting and directing musicals. Home: 824 Royalsborough Rd Durham ME 04222 Office: Freeport Sch System 30 Holbrook St Freeport ME 04032 Personal E-mail: pmstudio@prodigy.net. E-mail: denice_parkhurst@coconetme.org.

PARKHURST, VIOLET KINNEY, artist; b. Derby Line, Vt., Apr. 26, 1926; d. Edson Frank and Rosa (Beauchiene) Kinney; student Sch. Practical Arts, Boston, 1941-42, Baylor U., Waco, Tex., 1943, Calif. State U., Los Angeles, 1950-51; m. Donald Winters Parkhurst, Apr. 10, 1948. Fgn. corr. 5 Brazilian mags., 1946-53; tech. illustrator, 1954-55; owner five galleries including Ports of Call, San Pedro, Calif.; artist, specializing in seascapes; work included in permanent collection of Stockholm Mus., many pvt. collections including Presidents Richard M. Nixon, Ford, Reagan, Bush, Gov. Wilson, Mayor of Kobe, Japan, Mayor Yorty of L.A., Rory Calhoun, Barbara Rush, Jim Arness, David Rose; one-shows shows at prominent galleries; numerous paintings published. Winner 30 blue ribbons for art. Fellow Am. Inst. Fine Arts. Mem. Ch. of Religious Sci. Author: How to Paint Books, 1966; Parkhurst on Seascapes, 1972. Paintings reproduced on covers South West Art, Arizona Living; ltd. edit. prints published, also ltd. edit. plates. The first artist in the world invited to present a painting to Pres. Jiang Zemin, Beisin, China, 2002; the first western artist to have a painting in China Nat. Mus. of Fine Arts and the Hall of the People. Office: Parkhurst Gallery Ports of Call Village San Pedro CA 90731

PARKINSON, DIAN, actress; Student, Lee Strasberg Studio, Los Angeles. Talk show hostess The Women's Side; appeared on TV shows The Price is Right, The Tonight Show Starring Johnny Carson, Vegas, Bob Hope's Desert Classic, The Bob Hope Christmas Show (Emmy Award Citation); model on cover of Bert Stein, Master of Contemporary Photography, Cosmopolitan mag., commls., posters, billboards, other mags. Named Miss U.S.A. Office: Jo-Ann Geffen & Assocs 3151 Cahuenga Blvd W Suite 235 Los Angeles CA 90068

PARKS, BLANCHE CECILE, public administrator; b. Leavenworth, Kans., Feb. 2, 1949; d. Nile Eugene Sr. and Fern (Dickinson) Williams; m. Sherman A. Parks Jr.; children: Michael A., Stacy M. BEd, Washburn U., 1971, MEd, 1976, postgrad., 1983-84. Tchr. Topeka Pub. Schs., 1971-76, reading specialist, 1979-84; ins. regulator Kans. Ins. Dept., Topeka, 1984-88; spl. asst. to sec. Kans. Dept. Human Resources, Topeka, 1988-92; real estate lease adminstr. State of Kans., Topeka, 1992—. Pres. Kans. Children's Svc. League, 1990-94, YWCA, Topeka, 1992-94; chmn. Topeka Human Rels. Commn., 1991-93; mem. Topeka Pub. Schs. Found., 1993-94; participant Leadership Topeka, 1994, Leadership Kans., 1994 Named The Outstanding Young Woman of Kans. Jaycee Women, 1984, 85, one of Outstanding Young Women Am., 1985. Mem. Jr. League of Topeka (Gold Rose award 1993), Jack and Jill Am., Kans. C. of C. (leadership award 1985), Links, Phi Kappa Phi, Phi Delta Kappa, Alpha Delta Kappa, Delta Kappa Gamma, (life) Delta Sigma Theta (v.p. 1980-82). Republican. Mem. A.M.E. Ch. Home: 1727 SE 36th Terrace Topeka KS 66605

PARKS, GRACE SUSAN, bank official; b. N.Y.C., Oct. 14, 1948; d. Marco A. and Gloria (Alvino) Vale; m. Louis Parks, Feb. 14, 1988; 1 child, Adam. BS, Pa. State U., 1970; MA, New Sch. for Social Rsch., 1974; cert. in mgmt., Adelphi U., 1979, MBA, 1980; cert. in entrepreneurship, Hofstra U., 1996. Bus. office rep. N.Y. Tel. Co., Rockville Centre, 1971-74; social worker Children's Aid Soc., N.Y.C., 1974-75; EEO officer Edwin Gould Svcs., N.Y.C., 1976-79; v.p. fin. instns. and global markets Bankers Trust Co., N.Y.C., 1979-92; v.p. compensation human resources Chase Manhattan Bank, 1992-96; pres. Loodie Prodns., Inc., 1996; instr. mgmt. Adelphi U. Grad. Sch. Bus. Adminstrn., 1981—; notary pub. State N.Y., 1978—. Mem. Human Resource Planning Soc., Assn. MBA Execs., Am. Compensation Assn., Wall St. Compensation and Benefits Assn. (chmn. 1994-96, pres. 1993-94), N.Y. Compensation Assn., Adelphi U. Businesswomen's Alumni Assn. (pres. 1980-82).

PARKS, J. ANNE, state representative, funeral director; b. Greenwood, S.C., July 1, 1955; d. James Lloyd and Julia (Arnold) Parks. BS, Johnson C. Smith U., 1976; grad., Gupton-Jones Sch. Mortuary Sci., 1977. Mortician Parks Funeral Home, funeral dir.; real estate agent; state rep. S.C. Legis., 1997, state rep. dist. 12, 1999—, mem. med., mil., pub. and mcpl. com. Mem. Stop the Violence Com.; budget com. Uniter Way, 1996; mem. Orgn. Concerned Citizens, Greenwood City Coun., 1988—96. Mem.: NAACP, Greenwood C. of C., Epsilon Nu Delta, Delta Sigma Theta. Democrat. Baptist. Home: PO Box 181 Greenwood SC 29648 Office: State Capitol 434D BlattBldg Columbia SC 29211 Address: 232 N Hospital St Greenwood SC 29648 E-mail: JAP@scstatehouse.net.

PARKS, JEAN ANNE, retired acute care nurse practitioner; b. Grand Rapids, Mich., Aug. 3, 1940; d. Edwin Charles and Ruth Katherine (Skellenger) Paepke; m. Charles Wilbur Parks, Nov. 24, 1961; children: Charles Edwin, Catherine Ann, Michael Allan. Diploma in Nursing, Blodgett Meml. Hosp., 1961; BS summa cum laude in Health Studies, Western Mich. U., 1987; MA magna cum laude in Health and Humanities, Mich. State U., 1994. RN. Staff nurse Blodgett Meml. Hosp., Grand Rapids, 1961—62; nurse Ctrl. Mich. Cmty. Hosp., Mt. Pleasant, 1962—64; med.-surg. staff Blodgett Meml. Hosp., 1964—70, part-time staff, 1979—2003; part-time Medicaid evaluator for Kent County, Mich. Dept. Pub. Health, Lansing, 1987—88. Mem. Grand Rapids Symphony Chorus, 1987—2003. Baptist. Avocations: travel, music (toured with chorus to numerous countries).

PARKS, KRISTIN M. pediatrics health nurse, educator and practitioner; b. Lynn, Mass., Feb. 24, 1953; d. James B. and Phyllis (Hannaway) Parks; m. Roderick M. Fuqua, Sept. 10, 1977; children: Sarah, Emily, Abigail. BSN, U. Mass., 1974; MS, Boston U., 1977. RN, Mass.; cert. PNP, ANCC. Staff nurse McLean Hosp., Belmont, Mass.; clin. nurse specialist Beth Israel Hosp., Boston; asst. prof. Massaqoit C.C., 1980-91; prof. Quincy (Mass.) Coll., 1991—, chair RN program. Mem. ANA, Mass. Nurses Assn., Mass. Assn. for Advancement ADN. Home: 42 Clinton Rd Weymouth MA 02189-3010 E-mail: kparks@quincycollege.edu.

PARKS, MICHELLE M. academic administrator; b. Jersey Shore, Pa., Dec. 14, 1977; d. James A. and Suanne L. Parks. BA in Sociology summa cum laude, Lycoming Coll., 2000. Customer svc. rep. Sovereign Bank, Williamsport, Pa., 1997—2000; asst. dir. admissions Lycoming Coll., Williamsport, Pa., 2000—. Mem.: Phi Kappa Phi, Pi Gamma Mu. Office: Lycoming Coll 700 College Pl Williamsport PA 17701

PARKS, PATRICIA JEAN, lawyer; b. Portland, Oreg., Apr. 2, 1945; d. Robert and Marion (Crosby) P.; m. David F. Jurca, Oct. 17, 1971 (div. 1976). BA in History, Stanford U., 1963-67; JD, U. Penn., Phila., 1967-70. Bar: N.Y. 1971, Wash. 1974. Assoc. Milbank, Tweed, Hadley & McCoy, N.Y.C., 1970-73, Shidler, McBroom, Gates & Lucas, Seattle, 1974-81, ptnr., 1981-90, Preston, Thorgrimson, Shidler, Gates & Ellis, Seattle, 1990-93; pvt. practice Seattle, 1993-99; spl. counsel Karr Tuttle Campbell, 1999—. Active Vashon Allied Arts, Mountaineers. Mem.: ABA, Wash. Native Plant Soc., Pension Roundtable, Western Pension Conf., Employee Stock Ownership Plan Assn., Seattle-King County Bar Assn., Washington Women in Tax, Wash. State Bar Assn. (past pres. tax sect., past chair gift and estate tax com.), Wash. Native Plant Soc., Vashon Athletic Club, Wash. Athletic Club. Avocations: kayaking, hiking, contra dancing, bird watching, Karate. Office: 1201 3rd Ave Ste 2900 Seattle WA 98101-3284 Office Phone: 206-224-8094. E-mail: pparks@karrtuttle.com.

PARKS, ROSA LOUISE, civil rights activist; b. Tuskegee, Ala., 1913; Stidemt, Ala. State Coll.; hon. degree, Shaw Coll. Former seamstress and housekeeper, Montgomery, Ala., Detroit, from 1957; office mgr. for Congressman John Conyers, Jr., from 1965; co-founder Rosa and Raymond Parks Inst. for Self-Devel., Detroit, 1987—. Author: Quiet Strength, 1994 Formerly active Montgomery Voters League; mem. youth coun. NAACP, sec. Montgomery br., 1943; active SCLC. Recipient Spingarn medal NAACP, 1970, Martin Luther King Jr. award, 1980, Congl. Gold Medal of Honor, 1999, 31st NAACP Image award for outstanding supporting actress in a drama series for Touched by an Angel, 2000. Office: Rosa & Raymond Park Inst Ste 2200 Cadillac Sq Detroit MI 48226-1002

PARKS, SUZAN LORI, playwright; b. Fort Knox, KY, 1964; d. Donald and Francis Parks; m. Paul Oscher, 2001. BA, Mount Holyoke Coll., 1985. Guest lecturer Pratt Institute, N.Y.C., 1988, U. Mich., Ann Arbor, Mich., 1990, Yale U., New Haven, 1990—91, NYU, 1990—91; prof. of playwriting Eugene Lang Coll., N.Y.C., 1990; writer-in-residence New School for Social Research (now New School U.), N.Y.C., 1991—92; dir. Theater Projects Calif. Inst. Arts, Valencia, 2000—. Author: (plays) The Sinner's Place, 1985, Betting on the Dust Commander, 1988, Imperceptible Mutabilities in the Third Kingdom, 1990 (Obie award, 1990), Devotees in the Garden of Love, 1992, The Death of the Last Black Man in the Whole Entire World, 1992, The America Play, 1993, Venus, 1996 (Obie award, 1996), In the Blood, 1999, Topdog/Underdog, 2001 (Pulitzer Prize for drama, 2002), (screenplays) Anemone Me, 1990, Girl 6, 1996, (novels) Getting My Mother's Body, 2003. Recipient Rockefeller Foundation grant, 1990, N.Y. Found. for the Arts grant, 1990, Whiting Found. Writers award, 1992, Ford Found. grant, 1995, CalArts/Alpert award, 1996, PEN-Laura Pels award, 2000; fellow MacArthur Found., 2001, Guggenheim Found., 2000; grantee Mary E. Woolley fellowship, 1989, Naomi Kitay fellowship, 1989, Nat. Endowment for the Arts playwrighting fellowship, 1990—91. Office: Calif Inst Arts 24700 McBean Pkwy Valencia CA 91355*

PARLE, BERTHA IBARRA, writer; b. El Paso, Tex., Nov. 14, 1947; d. Arnulfo and Bertha (Soto) Ibarra; m. Dennis Jerome Parle, Aug. 16, 1969; children: Joseph, Mónica, Angélica. BA in French, Spanish, U. Tex., El Paso, 1968; MA in Spanish, U. Kans., 1970, H.S. tchg. cert., 1971; postgrad. courses in French, U. Houston, 1990-95. Bilingual tchr. Kansas Remedial Edn. Program, Sharon Springs, 1967, 71, 72; Spanish tchr. Ottawa (Kans.) H.S., 1971-74; ESL instr. North Harris Coll., Houston, 1977-83; modern lang. prof. N. Harris Montgomery C.C. Dist., Houston, 1983-97, head lang. inst., 1997—2002. Cultural cons., sponsor Hispanic students North Harris Coll. and Montgomery Coll., 1983-97, organizer Hispanic cultural events, 1983—, sponsor Cath. Newman Club, 1985-95; lectr., slide show The Nahua Mexica Legacy, 1994-96; participant in field seminars; NEH and Fulbright Ecuador field experience. Poetess; Spanish poetry publ. in Tejidos, Grito al Sol, 1972-94. Hispanic leader St. Leo's Cath. Ch., Houston, 1982-92; del. People to People Am. Program to S. Africa, 2000. Recipient Tchg. Excellence award North Harris Coll., 1997, Excellence award Nat. Inst. for Staff and Orgn. Devel., 1998; Am. Coun. Tchrs. Fgn. Langs. summer scholar U. Montreal, 1999. Mem. AAUW, Am. Coun. Tchrs. Fgn. Langs., Computer Assisted Lan. Instruction Consortium, Am. Assn. C.C. Women, Tex. Fgn. Lang. Assn., Inst. Hispanic Culture., North Harris United Faculty Avocations: creative writing, study of indigenous language cultures, hispanic students and hispanic issues in the community. Office: North Harris Coll 2700 W W Thorne Dr Houston TX 77073 E-mail: bertha.parle@nhmccd.edu.

PARLETTE, LINDA EVANS, state senator; m. Bob Parlette; 2 children. BS in Pharmacy, Wash. State U. Pharmacist; orchardist; Rep. rep. dist. 12 Wash. Ho. of Reps., 1997-2000; Rep. senator dist. 12 Wash. State Senate, 2000—. Mem. agr. and internat. trade, health and long-term care, higher edn. and ways and means coms. Wash. State Senate; chair Nat. Coun. State Legislators' Children, Family and Health Com.; bd. dirs. Wash. State Ag-Forestry Edn. Found. Mem. Lake Chelan United Meth. Ch.; former chair Lake Chelan Sch. Bd.; former mem. Lake Chelan Hosp. Guild. Recipient Trail Blazer award Lewis and Clark Elem. Sch., Margaret Chase Smith award Wash. State Rep. Women, 1995, award Friend of Rural Health Care, 1997-98, Rural Legislator of Yr. award Wash. State Hosp., 2000, Outstanding Legislator award Nat. Fedn. Ind. Bus., 2000. Mem. Wash. State Pharm. Assn., Wash. State Hort. Assn., Wenatchee Rotary (founder Lunch Buddy program). Office: PO Box 40412 106A Irv Newhouse Bldg Olympia WA 98504-0412 Fax: 360-786-7819. E-mail: parlette_li@leg.wa.gov.

PARLOW, CYNTHIA MARIA, professional soccer player; b. Memphis, May 8, 1978; BS in Nutrition, U. N.C., 1998. Profl. soccer player Atlanta Beat, 2001—03. Mem. U.S. Women's Nat. Soccer Team, 1996—, U.S. Under-20 Nat. Team, Nordic Cup championships, Denmark, 1997, U-16 Nat. Team pool. Named All-ACC and ACC Rookie of Yr., 1995, Soccer Am. Freshman of Yr., 1995, Most Valuable Player, 1995 Under-17 U.S. Youth Soccer nat. tournament, World Cup Champion, 1999; recipient Gold medal, Centennial Olympic Games, 1996, Herman Trophy, Mo. Athletic Club Player of Yr. award, 1997, Silver medal, Sydney Olympic Games, 2000. Achievements include helped U. N.C. to NCAA Championship 1996, 97; 1st-Team All-ACC selection in 1997; named to 1997 NCAA All-Tournament Team. Office: US Soccer Fedn 1801-1811 S Prairie Ave Chicago IL 60616

PARNELL, JANINE E. conductor, violinist; b. Augusta, Ga., Jan. 23, 1965; d. Howard Carlton Craig and Bernice Lawrence Parnell. MusB, Winthrop Univ., Rock Hill, S.C., 1987, MEd Music, 1988; Mus D, Cath. Univ. Am., 2003. Orch. dir. Mecklenburg Sch., Charlotte, NC, 1989—90, Florence Dist. Sch., SC, D.C. Sch., Washington, 1996—98, Prince William Country Sch., Dumfries, Va., 1998—2001, Atlanta. Pub. Sch., 2001—. Violinist Arlington Symphony, Va., 2001, Prince William Symphony, Manassas, Va., 2001; freelance violinist southeastern U.S., 1985—. Bd. mem. NOVA/Manasas Cmty. Orch., Va., 2001. Recipient H.S. Orch. Dir. of the Yr., Atlanta Pub. Sch., 2002—03. Mem.: Delta Omicron Internat. Music Soc., Music Educators Nat. Conf., Phi Kappa Phi. Office: North Atlanta H S 2875 Northside Dr Atlanta GA 30305 Office Phone: 770-316-7634.

PARODE, ANN, lawyer; b. L.A., Mar. 3, 1947; d. Lowell Carr and Sabine Parode. BA, Pomona Coll., 1968; JD, UCLA, 1971. Bar: Calif. 1972, U.S. Dist. Ct. (so. dist.) Calif. 1972, U.S. Ct. Appeals (9th cir.) 1975, U.S. Supreme Ct. Assoc. Luce, Forward et al, San Diego, 1971-75; gen. counsel, exec. v.p., sec. San Diego Trust & Savs., 1975-94. Judge pro tem San Diego Mcpl. Ct., 1978-84; campus counsel U. Calif., San Diego, 1997—. Bd. dirs. San Diego Cmty. Found., 1989-97, chmn., 1994-96; bd. dirs. The Burnham Inst., 1995-2001, Girard Found., 1990-. Mem. Calif. Bar Assn. (corp. law com. 1980-83, client trust fund commn. 1986-90, chmn. 1989-90), San Diego County Bar Found. (founder, bd. dirs. 1979-86, 98-2001, pres.

1980-83), San Diego Bar Assns. (bd. dirs. 1977-81, v.p. 1977-78, 80-81, treas. 1979-80), Law Libr. Justice Found. (pres. 1994). E-mail: aparode@ucsd.edu.

PARR, CAROLYN MILLER, federal judge; b. Palatka, Fla., Apr. 17, 1937; d. Arthur Charles and Audrey Ellen (Dunklin) Miller; m. Jerry Studstill Parr, Oct. 12, 1959; children: Kimberly Parr Trapasso, Jennifer Parr Turek, Patricia Audrey Smith. BA, Stetson U., 1959; MA, Vanderbilt U., 1960; JD, Georgetown U., 1977; LLD (hon.), Stetson U., 1986. Bar: Md. 1977, U.S. Tax Ct. 1977, D.C. 1979, U.S. Supreme Ct. 1983. Gen. trial atty. IRS, Washington, 1977-81, sr. trial atty. office of chief counsel, 1982; spl. counsel to asst. atty. gen. tax divsn. U.S. Dept. Justice, Washington, 1982-85; judge U.S. Tax Ct., Washington, 1985-2000, sr. judge, 2001—. Nat. Def. fellow Vanderbilt U., 1959-60; fellow Georgetown U., 1975-76; recipient Spl. Achievement award U.S. Treasury, 1979. Mem. ABA, Md. Bar Assn., Nat. Assn. Women Judges, D.C. Bar Assn. Office: US Tax Ct 400 2nd St NW Washington DC 20217-0002

PARR, VIRGINIA HELEN, retired librarian; b. Mansfield, Ohio, May 23, 1937; d. Bernard Franklin and Frances Cole (Downes) P.; m. Marvin E. Lickey, June 14, 1959 (div. 1972); children: Sarah Elizabeth, David Andrew, Rachel Alison; m. Laurence E. Steadman, Nov. 27, 1993. AB, Oberlin Coll., 1959; AM, U. Mich., 1961; MLS, U. Oreg., 1973. English and social studies tchr. Whittier Jr. High Sch., Livonia, Mich., 1961-64; libr. U. Oreg. Libr., Eugene, 1973-79, head edn. and psychology, 1979-80, acting asst. univ. libr. for pub. svcs., 1980-82; head reference, rsch. and instrn. svcs. U. Cin., 1982-89, reference libr., bibliographer, 1989—2002, ret., 2002—. Chair, mem. budget com. Eugene Sch., 1976-79. Founding editor: Behavioral and Social Scis. Libr., 1978; contbr. articles to profl. jours. Bd. dirs. Eugene Jr. Symphony Assn., 1979-82; mem. adv. bd. various mental health groups, Eugene, 1971-79. Mem. Assn. Coll. and Rsch. Librs. of ALA (various offices edn. and behavioral sci. sect. 1977-86, numerous coms. reference and adult svcs. divsn. 1981-92), Beta Phi Mu, Pi Lambda Theta. Democrat. Episcopalian. Avocations: reading, classical music, travel. Home: 5532 S Shore Dr 12F Chicago IL 60637-1990 E-mail: v_parr@sbcglobal.net.

PARRA, ELENA BATRIZ-GUADALUPE, psychologist, educator; b. Nogales, Sonora, Mexico, Feb. 1, 1951; d. Francisco Batriz/Parra and Guadalupe Esther (Hoyos) Batriz; m. Fernando Tapia, Dec. 20, 1984 (div. Mar. 2, 1989); m. Ra,pm Castillon; children: Fernando Luis Parra Tapia, Gabriela Guadalupe Tonanzin P Castillon, Tamara Celic parra Castillon. AA, Pima C.C., Tucson, 1972; BA, U. Ariz., 1974, Master, 1975, PhD, 1983, postdoctoral, 1986. Cert. profl. counselor Bd. Behavioral Health Examiners, 2000; lic. psychologist, Ariz., 2001, cert. sch. psychologist Ariz. State Bd. Edn., diplomate Am. Coll. Cert. Forensic Counselors, cert. domestic violence counselor. Assoc. prof. Pima C.C., Tucson, 1975—85; sch. dir. Proyecto de Colores, Tucson, 1976—77; mental health outpatient supr. Santa Cruz Family Guidance Ctr., Nogales, Ariz., 1979—81; sch. psychologist-bilingual diagnostic team Tucson Unified Sch. Dist., 1982—84; clin. psychologist and children's unit supr. San Antonio Mental Health, Bell Gardens, Calif., 1987—89; asst. prof. Calif. State U., Fullerton, 1989—92; clin. dir. Eloy (Ariz.) Mental Health Ctr., 1992—94; head psychologist Ariz. Dept. of Youth Treatment & Rehab., Tucson, 1992—94; psychologist II Children's Evaluation Ctr., Tucson, 1992—93; clin. dir. Eloy Mental Health Ctr., 1994—95; clin. cons., psychologist La Frontera Clinic, 1995—2000, pres. Multicultural Counseling Ctr., Tucson, 1997—; adj. asst. prof., project coord. U. Ariz., Tucson, 2002—; prof. U. Guadalajara, Mexico. Cons. Chicanos Por La Causa, Tucson, Willcox Eloy, Ariz., 2002—. Author: Daily Life Problems-Recuperation, Adaptation & Adjustment Processes-Spanish, 1993; contbr. articles to profl. jours. Chair Legal Com. for Bilingual Edn., Tucson, 2000—03; dir. Latino Self Help Group, Tucson, 2000—03. Scholar, League Mexican Am. Women and Vocat. Rehab., 1970—74. Mem.: APA, Tucson Assn. for Bilingual Edn., Nat. Assn. Mexican Psychologists and Psychologists in Jalisco (hon.). Roman Catholic. Avocations: poetry, writing, travel, painting, study of Mexican, Mexican-American, Latino-Mexican Indigeneous cultures. Home: 7340 S Camino Bello Tucson AZ 85746 Office: U Ariz Multicultural Counseling Ctr 3901 W Valencia Tucson AZ 85746 Personal E-mail: geparra@u.arizona.edu.

PARRA, NICOLE M. state representative; b. Bakersfield, Calif., Feb. 3, 1970; BA in Econs., U. Calif., Berkeley, 1992; JD, Cath. U. Columbus, 1998. Dist. dir. U.S. Rep. Cal Dooley, legis. asst., 1992—98, campaign mgr., 2000; field dir. Supr. Pete Parra, 1996; GOTV coord. Calif. Assemblyman Dean Florez, 1998; co-chair Gov.'s Econ. Devel. Subcom., 2000—; mem. Calif. Assembly, 2002—. Alumna Hispanas Organized Polit. Equality, 1998—; adv. bd. San Joaquin Valley Hosp., 2001; mem. San Joaquin Valley Empowerment Initiative; bd. dirs. County, 1999—. Mem.: Latina Leaders Kern. Democrat. Roman Catholic. Office: PO Box 942849 Rm 2160 Sacramento CA 94249 Address: 1800 30th St Ste 330 Bakersfield CA 93301

PARRAMORE, BARBARA MITCHELL, education educator; b. Guilford County, N.C., Aug. 29, 1932; d. Samuel Spencer and Nellie Gray (Glosson) Mitchell; m. Lyman Griffis Worthington, Dec. 23, 1956 (div. 1961); m. Thomas Custis Parramore, Jan. 22, 1966 (dec. Jan. 2004); children: Lisa Gray, Lynn Stuart. AB, U. N.C., Greensboro, 1954; MEd, N.C. State U., 1959; EdD, Duke U., 1968. Counselor, tchr. Raleigh City Schs., 1954-59, sch. prin., 1959-65; prof. dept. of curriculum and instrn. N.C. State U., 1970-96, prof. emeritus, 1996—. Acad. specialist Office Internat. Edn., U.S. Info. Svcs., sec. sch. initative program, The Philippines, 1987. Author: The People of North Carolina, 1972, 3rd edit. 1983. Japan Inst. Social and Econ. Affairs fellow, 1980; N.C. AAUW award for juvenile lit., 1973, Holladay medal for excellence N.C. State U., 1994. Mem. ASCD, N.C. ASCD (pres. 1994-96), N.C. Coun. for Social Studies (pres. 1985-87), Assn. Tchr. Educators, Delta Kappa Gamma, Kappa Delta Pi. Home: 5012 Tanglewood Dr Raleigh NC 27612-3135

PARRETTE, ANNE MARIE, music educator, conductor, musician; b. Orlando, Fla., Jan. 29, 1965; d. Robert Olin and Willmarie Wester Parrette. B in Music Edn., Fla. State U., 1987, M in Music Edn., 1994. Cert. tchr. Fla. Orch. condr. Polk Dist. Schs., Lakeland, Fla., 1988—92, DePhillips Sch. Arts, Orlando, 1994—2000; cons. music programs Brevard Dist. Schs., Vierra, Fla., 2000—02; orch. condr. Blake Sch. Arts, Tampa, Fla., 2002—. Condr. orchs. Fla. State U. Summer Camp, Tallahassee, 1996, Fla. So. Coll. Summer Camp, Lakeland, 1999—2003; guest condr. in field. Musician: (recording) Marble Feather, 2000. Active Human Rights Campaign Fund, Tampa, 2000. Mem.: Fla. Orch. Assn. (dist. chair 1998—99, sr. high chair 2000), Crescendo Women's Chorus, Pi Kappa Lambda. Democrat. Episcopalian. Avocations: music, racquetball.

PARRINELLO, KATHLEEN ANN MULHOLLAND, nursing administrator, educator; b. Syracuse, N.Y., June 26, 1953; d. Bernard Joseph and Mary Catherine (Wicke) Mulholland; m. Richard John Parrinello, June 30, 1973; children: Michael, Jeffrey, Stephen. BS, U. Rochester, 1975, MS, 1983, PhD, 1990. RN, N.Y. Staff nurse U. Rochester (N.Y.)-Strong Meml. Hosp., 1975-78, asst. head nurse, 1976-77, head nurse, 1978-83, assoc. clin. chief, 1983-86, coord. ambulatory care, 1986-88, clin. chief, asst. prof. Sch. Nursing, 1990—; practitioner tchr., asst. prof. Rush Presbyn. St. Luke's Med. Ctr., Chgo., 1988-89. Cons. in nursing U. Wis. Hosps. and Clinics, 1990, 91; prin. investigator State of N.Y. Dept. of Health, 1991. Author pamphlet Arterial Bypass Surgery Patient Booklet, 1981; contbr. articles to profl. publs. Workforce Demonstration grantee N.Y. Dept. Health. Mem. Am. Acad. Ambulatory Nursing Adminstrn. (bd. dirs. 1989-92), Am. Orgn. Nurse Execs., Genesee Valley Nurses Assn., Sigma Theta Tau. Office: Strong Meml Hosp 601 Elmwood Ave Rochester NY 14642-0002

PARRINO, CHERYL LYNN, federal agency administrator; b. Wisconsin Rapids, Wis., Jan. 21, 1954; m. Jack J. Parrino, Sept. 1, 1990; 1 child, George. BBA in Acctg., U. Wis., 1976. Auditor Pub. Svc. Commn. Wis., Madison, 1976-82, dir. utility audits, 1982-86, exec. asst. to chmn., 1986-91, commr., 1991-98, chmn., 1992-98; chmn., CEO Universal Svc. Adminstrv. Co., Madison, 1998—. Mem. adv. bd. Bellcore, 1991; vice chmn. bd. dirs. Wis. Ctr. Demand Side Rsch., Madison, 1991-92; chmn. bd. dirs. Wis. Pub. Utility Inst., Madison, 1992-95 Mem. Gov.'s Task Force Gross Receipts Tax, Madison, 1991-92, Gov.'s Task Force Alternative Fuels, Madison, 1992-98, Gov.'s Task Force Clean Air, Madison, 1992-98, Gov.'s Task Force Telecom., Madison, 1993-94. Mem. Nat. Assn. Pub. Utility Commrs. (exec. com. 1991, chmn. comm. com. 1992-98, pres. 1995-96, pres. Gt. Lakes conf. 1996). Republican. Lutheran. Avocations: snow skiing, tennis, traveling. Office: Universal Svc Adminstrv Co 583 Donofrio Dr Ste 201 Madison WI 53719-2096 Fax: (608) 827-8893.

PARRIS, NINA GUMPERT, curator, writer, researcher, photographer; b. Berlin, Sept. 11, 1927; came to U.S., 1937, naturalized, 1944; d. Martin and Charlotte (Blaschko) Gumpert; m. Arthur Parris, Feb. 13, 1949 (div. 1974); children: Carl Joseph, Thomas Martin. BA, Bryn Mawr Coll., 1968; MA, U. Pa., 1969, PhD, 1979. Tchg. fellow U. Mich., Ann Arbor, 1969-70; lectr. Phila. Coll. Art, 1970-71; rsch. asst. Phila. Mus. Art, 1970-71; curator, lectr. U. Vt. Robert Hall Fleming Mus., Burlington, 1971-79; chief curator Columbia (S.C.) Mus., 1979-89; resident faculty visual arts Vt. Coll. Norwich U., 1991—; chair visual arts Burlington Coll., 1996-99. Author: Prints, Paintings and Drawings in Collection of Robert Hall Fleming Mus., 1979 (exhbn. catalog) Through a Master Printer, 1985, The South Carolina Collection of the Columbia Museum, 1987; columnist State newspaper, Columbia, 1984-88; solo shows at Meteor Gallery, Columbia, 1993, Living Learning Ctr., U. Vt., 1994, St. Michael's Coll. McCarthy Arts Ctr., 1995, Colburn Gallery, U. Vt., 1996; group shows at Westbeth Gallery, N.Y.C., 1993, Thomas Waterman Wood Gallery, Vt., 1994, 96, 2001, 02, Firehouse Gallery, Burlington, 1996, Box Car Exhbn., Burlington, 1996, 98, Soho 20 Gallery, N.Y.C., 1996, 97, 98, Flynn Dog Gallery, 2003. Bd. dirs. Photography Coop., Montpelier, Vt., 1977-79, Chittenden Arts Coun., Burlington, 1976-78. Woodrow Wilson fellow, 1968, Univ. fellow Ford Found., 1968-72; grantee NEA, NEH, S.C. Com. Humanities, Vt. Coun. Arts. Mem. Am. Assn. Museums (pres. curator's com. 1985-87, v.p. 1983-85). E-mail: ninag@together.net.

PARRIS, REBECCA (RUTH BLAIR MACCLOSKEY), musician, educator; b. Needham, Mass., Dec. 28, 1951; d. Edmund Myer and Shirley (Robinson) MacCloskey; m. Robert Louis DeGrassie, Sept. 28, 1980 (div. June 1985). Student, Boston Conservatory of Music, 1969-70. Artist-in-residence Monterey (Calif.) Jazz Festival, 1995, Howard U., Washington, 1991; clinician U. N.H., 1991, U. Wash., 1994. Vocalist, prodr., arranger: (mus. rec.) Love Comes and Goes, 1991 (Boston Music award 1991); vocalist: (mus. recs.) A Beautiful Friendship, 1995, Spring, 1993 (Grammy award nomination 1993); vocalist, lyricist: (mus. recs.) It's Another Day, 1994 (Grammy award nomination 1994), A Passionate Fling, 1984, Live at Chans, 1985, Double Rainbow, 1986. The Secret of Christmas, 2002 Performer, fundraiser Poor People's United Fund, Boston, 1984-95,; Germane Lawrence Sch. 2001-2003, AIDS Benefit, 1988, Holiday Project, 1989, Starlight Found., 1991, Living with AIDS, 1991, Stuff for Kids, 1993, Child and Family Svcs., 1993, AIDS Action, boston, 1986-95, ABCD, Boston, 1995, numerous others. Named Outstanding Jazz Vocalist, Boston Music Awards, 1987-95, Outstanding Jazz Album, 1991, recipient Outstanding Svc. to Jazz Edn. award Internat. Assn. Jazz Educators, 1993 Mem. AFTRA, ASCAP. Democrat. Avocations: horseback riding, swimming. Office: Parish and Assoc 19 Elm St Duxbury MA 02332-4955

PARRIS, SALLY NYE, real estate agent; b. Evanston, Ill., Apr. 5, 1946; d. Harry Gale Nye Jr. and Bettye (Herb) Sollitt; m. Thomas Baxter Parris, Mar. 25, 1988 (div. Sept. 1985); 1 child, Samantha Ross. AA, Bradford Jr. Coll., 1966; BS in Secondary Edn., Northwestern U., 1968; cert. real estate, Conn. Real Estate Inst., Norwalk, 1985. Lic. real estate agt., Conn. Dir. girls phys. edfn. Latin Sch. of Chgo., 1967-68; dir. Greenwich (Conn.) YWCA, 1972-79; English tchr. Inlingua Sch. Langs., Stamford, Conn., 1981-84; real estate agt. Curtis Assocs., Realtors, Greenwich, Conn., 1985—. Chair profl. divsn. United Way, Greenwich, 1995-98, chair real estate sect. profl. divsn., 1993-94, co-chair campaign kickoff Septemberfest, 1985-99, co-chair Greenwich Pro-Am. Lit. Vol. Benefit, 1995—; v.p., bd. dirs. YMCA, Greenwich, 1993—, chair spl. events com., 1994—, co-chair annual campaign, 1998; bd. dirs., benefit chair Cmty. Answers, Greenwich, 1994—; co-chair 350th Yr. parade Town of Greenwich, 1990; mem. benefits com. Literacy Vols., 1991-93. Recipient Vol. Recognition award Literacy Vols. Am., 1996, Town of Greenwich, 1991, United Way of Greenwich, 1985-97, Thomas Shepard award, 1995, 96. Mem. Conn. Assn. Profl. Women, Greenwich Bd. Realtors (advisor pub. rels. 1985-87, grievance com. 1999), Riverside Yacht Club (winter mem., social register 1960—), Greenwich Country Club (paddle tennis com. co-chmn. 1984-86, quar. editor 1982-86). Republican. Episcopalian. Avocations: swimming, racquet sports, golf, sporting clays, needlepoint. Office: Colwell Banker/Curtis Assocs 278 Sound Beach Ave Old Greenwich CT 06870-1626

PARRISH, CATHY WALDRON, elementary school educator; b. Harrisonburg, Virginia, July 2, 1944; d. Elmo Preston and Lillian Virginia (Paris) Waldron; m. James Walter Parrish, Aug. 16, 1969; children: James Preston, Cristan Elizabeth. MusB, U. N.C., 1966; MA in Tchg., Winthrop Univ., Rockhill, S.C., 1982; attended 30 hours, Furmar Univ., Greenville, S.C., 1990. Elem. tchr. band and strings Raleigh City Schools, NC, 1967—72; elem. tchr. gen. music Gadsden County Schools, Quincy, Fla., 1972—73, Leon County Schools, Tallahassee, 1973—76, Monroe City Schools, NC, 1977—82; instr. music edn Wingate Univ., NC, 1982—85; elem. tchr. gen music Union County Schs., Monroe, NC, 1985—87, Bethel Elem. Schools, Greenville, SC, 1987—. Dir. Bethel Elem. Chorus, Simpsonville, SC, 1987—; children's music dir. Westminster Presbyn. Ch., Greenville, SC, 1994—97, St. Giles Presbyn. Ch., Greenville, SC, 1997—98. Mem. Greenville County Civic Band, Greenville, SC, 1989—, Westminster Presbyn. Ch. Choir, Greenville, SC, 1989—, Westminster Presbyn. Hand Bell Choir, Greenville, SC, 1992—97. Recipient Tchr. of the Yr., Bethel Elem. Sch., 1996—97, Greenville County Fine Arts Ctr., 1999. Mem.: S. C. Foothills Chap. Am. Orff - Schulwerk Assn., Music Educators Nat. Conf., S. C. Music Educators Assn. (v.p. 2003—, pres. elem. divsn. 2001—03). Republican. Presbyterian. Achievements include Bethel Elem. Chorus performing in the Nat. Children's Choir at Carnegie Hall, 1999 and Walt Disney World, Fla., 1997. Avocations: genealogy, reading, cross stitch, furniture refinishing. Home: 509 Kenilworth Dr Greenville SC 29615-2330 Office: S C Music Educators Assn SC Office Phone: 864-967-1866.

PARRISH, DENISE KAY, regulatory accountant; b. Garden City, Mich., May 20, 1954; d. Lewis William and Carol Ruby (Doederlein) P.; m. Michael Joseph Krause, Oct. 10, 1986 (div. Apr. 1992); m. Joseph Rickie Walsh, Oct. 2000. BA in Acctg., Mich. State U., 1976. Analyst Mich. Pub. Svc. Commn., Lansing, 1977-81; sr. fin. analyst Colo. Pub. Utilities Commn., Denver, 1981-85; chief rate analyst Ariz. Residential Utilities Consuemr Office, Phoenix, 1985-86, Ariz. Corps. Commn., Phoenix, 1986-91; mgr. rates and pricing Wyo. Pub. Svc. Commn., Cheyenne, 1991—2003, dep. adminstr. office of consumer advocate, 2003—. Faculty mem. Inst. Pub. Utilities Mich. State U. Mem. ch. coun. local Luth. Ch., 1999—2001, chmn. long range planning com., 2000. Mem. Nat. Assn. Regulatory Utility Commrs. (chair SEC/FASB Task Force 1992-98, vice chmn. 1997-2000, mem. oversight com. on joint telecomm. audits 1991-92, 96-2001, chmn. acctg. subcom. 2000-03). Lutheran. Avocations: crafting, reading, teaching sunday school, gardening. Office: Wyo Office Consumer Advocate 2515 Warren Ave Ste 304 Cheyenne WY 82001-3113 Office Phone: 307-777-5743. Business E-Mail: dparri@state.wy.us.

PARRISH, JILL N. judge; JD, Yale U., 1985. Clk. Hon. David K. Winder U.S. Dist. Ct., Utah, 1985; atty. Parr, Wadddoups, Brown, Gee & Loveless, Salt Lake City, shareholder, 1990; asst. U.S. atty. Civil Divsn. U.S. Dist. Ct., Utah, 1995—2002; judge Utah Supreme Ct., Salt Lake City, 2003—. Supr. Fin. Litigation Unit U.S. Attys. Office. Mem.: Fed. Bar Assn. (pres.). Office: Utah Supreme Ct PO Box 140210 Salt Lake City UT 84114-0210

PARRISH, LORI NANCE, commissioner; b. Evansville, Ind., July 31, 1948; m. Geoffrey Cohen; children: Gary Brown, Brandi Schmidt. Student, Fla. Atlantic U., 1969, Nova/Davie Cmty. Sch., 1974-75, Broward C.C., Davie, Fla., 1980, Clemson U., 1982, Fla. Atlantic U., 1986; student, Fla. Internat. U., 1988; LHD (hon.), Keiser Coll., 1996; postgrad., U. Ctrl. Fla., 1996—98. Toll operator So. Bell Telephone Co., 1966-68; adminstrv. asst. appraisal and cons. loan dept. Hollywood Fed. Savings and Loan Assn., 1968-72; acct., qualifying agt. Victor Purdo Painting Co., 1972-81; fin. mgr. CRG, Inc., 1982-83; bookkeeper I county and vocational Sch. Bd. Broward County South Plantation H.S., 1983-84; commr. dist. 5 Broward County, Fla., 1988—, chair, 1990-91, 97-98, vice-chair, 1989-90, 96-97, chair, 2001—02. Spl. projects coord. Davie/Cooper City C. of C.; adminstrv. asst. to bldg. ofcl. City of Cooper City, 1972-81; landscape contractor, owner Earthy Interiors; Lake Shore Motel and Swap Shop, Inc., 3290 Sunrise Investments, Inc., 3291 Sunrise Investments, Inc. (dba Swap Shop), Swap Shop Management LLC, 1994—. Adv. bd. Broward County Libr., 1979-85, Mommas and Poppas of Cooper City High, 1982-90, Broward C.C. Women's Programs Adv. Com., 1981-82; chair Cooper City Elem. Sch. Adv. Com., 1980-82, sec., 1979-80; chair South Ctrl. Area Adv. Com., 1982-83, sec., 1981-82; legis. chair Broward County Libr. Adv. Bd., 1982-84; active Broward County Sch. Bd., 1984-88, vice-chair, 1986-87, chair, 1987-88; bd. dirs. Pembroke Pines Human Resource Ctr. Adv. Com., 1984-88, others. Recipient Legislator of Yr. award Broward County Fire Fighters and Paramedics, 1994, Humanitarian of Yr. award Soref Jewish Cmty. Ctr., 1995, award Manatee Survival Found., 1996, Dream Maker award Jr. League Greater Fort Lauderdale, 1996, Jesse Portis Helms award Dolphin Dem. Club, 1996, Par Excellence award Miramar High Cmty. Sch., 1997, Ray Lisanty Meml. award GUARD, 1999, Gracias award Hispanic Unity, 1999, Polit. Leader of Yr. award The Vanguard Chronicle, 1999; named to Broward County Women's Hall of Fame, 1997. Mem. ALA, Southeastern Libr. Assn., Davie/Cooper City Friends of Libr. (founder), Fort Lauderdale Friends of Libr., Broward County Friends of Libr. Office: Office County Commr Govtl Ctr 115 S Andrews Ave Ste 421 Fort Lauderdale FL 33301-1801 also: Dist Office One North University Dr Ste 111-A Plantation FL 33324-2031 E-mail: ldrip01@bellsouth.net., lparrish@broward.org.work.

PARRISH-PORTER, VALLERIE, controller; b. Baxley, Ga., July 12, 1951; d. Robert and Evelyn (Howell) Parrish; m. Julius Devan Porter, May 8, 1987. BS, So. U., Baton Rouge, La., 1971; MBA, U. Miami, Fla., 1973. Auditor Price Waterhouse & Co., Miami, 1973-77; fin. mgr. Post Newsweek div. Washington Post, Miami, 1977-80; acctg. supr. Schlumberger, Houston, 1981-83, controller, 1983-90, Princeton, N.J., 1990—. Mem. Nat. Assn. Accts., NAACP, Urban League. Avocations: tennis, chess, running, writing.

PARRISH-ST. JOHN, FLORENCE TUCKER, writer, educator, retired government official; b. Greenville, Miss., Nov. 12, 1925; d. Victor Amos and Martha Buchannan (Binkley) Denslow; m. Joseph Nathaniel Tucker Jr., Nov. 9, 1946 (dec. Dec. 1955); children: Joseph Nathaniel Tucker III, Frederick Steven Tucker, James Denslow Tucker; m. Noel Francis Parrish, June 25, 1983 (dec. Apr. 1987); m. Adrian St. John, Jan. 29, 1998. Diploma in piano, Ward-Belmont Coll., Nashville, 1945; studied piano with Michael Field, N.Y.C., 1945-46; B of Music Edn., Delta State U., Cleveland, Miss., 1960; MS in Counseling, U. So. Miss., 1971; EdD in Human Resources, George Washington U., 1983. Tchr. music Gulfport (Miss.) Pub. Schs., 1959-63; recreation therapist VA Hosp., Gulfport, 1964-70; edn. counselor USAF, Miss. and Japan, 1971-74, edn. svcs. officer Kunsan, Republic of Korea, 1974-75; asst. dir. sr. tng. CAP nat. hdqrs., 1975-77; EEO officer D.C. Dept. Labor, 1977-80; bur. chief complaints processing and adjudication Office EEO, U.S. Geol. Survey, Reston, Va., 1980-82; mgr. human resources Dept. Interior, 1982-84; internat. forum coord. Inspire 85 Pres.'s Com. on Employment of Handicapped, 1985; commr. Alexandria Commn. on Aging, Va., 1985-88, chmn. edn. and cultural affairs com., 1985-88, sec., 1987-88; lead scholar pilot project Nat. Coun. Aging. Mem. adv. bd. Inst. Conflict Analysis and resolution George Mason U., 1993—, vice chair adv. bd. Inst. Conflict Analysis and resolution, 1995—97, chmn. adv. bd. Inst. Conflict Analysis and resolution, 1998—2000, adv. bd. mem. emeritus, 2003—. Feature writer on aging issues: Alexandria Gazette-Packet, 1986—92; contbr. articles to profl. jours. Pianist/organist Sr. Living Cmty., Fairfax, 2003—. Mem.: Nat. Press Club (events com., chmn. oral history com., sr. rep. NPC trip to China and Hong Kong 1998, presenter 6 panel programs, Vivian award 1998, 1999, 2000, Vivian award, 2002, 2003), Va. Assn. on Aging, World Affairs Count., Women in Comm., Nat. Tuskegee Airmen Inc. Orgn., Smithsonian Assocs., Friends of Kennedy Ctr., Ret. Officers Assn., Miss. Soc. Washington, Am. Inst. Wine and Food, NATO Def. Coll. Anciens Assn., USAF Assn. (v.p. for cmty. programs Gen. Charles Gabriel chpt. 1991—98, Pres.'s award 1998, Woman of Distinction award Thomas Anthony chpt.), Washington Opera Guild. Address: Stonehurst 9302 Arlington Blvd Fairfax VA 22031-2503 Home: 9110 Belvoir Woods Pky Apt 118 Fort Belvoir VA 22060-2717

PARR-JOHNSTON, ELIZABETH, economy and policy consultant; b. N.Y.C., Aug. 15, 1939; d. Ferdinand Van Siclen and Helene Elizabeth Parr; m. David E. Bond, Dec. 28, 1962 (div. July 1975); children: Peter V.S., Kristina Aline; m. Archibald F. Johnston, Mar. 6, 1982; children: James, Heather, Alexandra, Margaret. BA, Wellesley Coll., 1961; MA, Yale U., 1962, PhD, 1973; postgrad., Harvard U., 1986. Various positions Govt. of Can., Ottawa, Ont., 1973-76, INCO Ltd., Toronto, 1976-79; chief of staff, sr. policy advisor Ministry of Employment and Immigration, Govt. of Can., 1979-80; various positions Shell Can. Ltd., Calgary, Alta., 1980-90; pres. Parr-Johnston & Assocs., Calgary, 1990-91; pres., vice-chancellor Mt. St. Vincent U., Halifax, Nova Scotia, N.S., 1991-96, The U. New Brunswick, Fredericton, Canada, 1996—2002; pres. Parr Johnston Econ. and Policy Cons., Chester Basin, Canada, 2002—. Instr. U. We. Ont., London, 1964—67, U. B.C., Vancouver, 1967—71; vis. scholar Wesleyan U., Middletown, Conn., 1971—72; acad. rsch. assoc. Carleton U., Ottawa, 1972—73; bd. dirs. Nova Scotia Power, Emera Ltd., Bank of Nova Scotia, Social Rsch. and Demonstration Corp., Can. Found. Sustainable Devel. Tech., Can. Millennium Scholarships Found.; spkr. and presenter in field. Mem. editl. bd. Can. Econ. Jour., 1980-83; contbr. articles to profl. jours. Planning chmn. John Howard Soc., 1980—84; mem. policy adv. com. C.D. Howe, 1980—85; mem. Ont. Econ. Coun., 1981—84; bd. dirs. Dellcrest Home, 1980—84, Calgary S.W. Fed. Riding Assn., 1985—91, The Learning Ctr., Calgary, 1989—91, Halifax United Way, 1991—92, North/South Inst., 1992—96, Coun. for Can. Unity, 1993—, Vol. Planning N.S., 1992—93, Social Sci. Human Rsch. Coun., 1995—98, FPI Ltd., 1996—2001, Empire Co., 1994—2002, Symphony Nova Scotia, Nat. Theatre Sch. Recipient Canada 125 medal, Queen's Jubilee medal; Hon. Woodrow Wilson fellow, 1962. Mem. Assn. Atlantic Univs. (chair 1994-96), Assn. Univs. and Colls. in Can. (bd. dirs., mem. exec. com. 1994-96), Women in Acad. Adminstrn. (adv. bd. 1991-96), Calgary Coun. Advanced Tech. (exec. 1990-91), Can. Econs. Assn., Inst. Pub. Adminstrn. Can., Sr. Women Acad. Adminstrs. Can., Assn. Commonwealth Univs. (former mem. exec. com.), Phi Beta Kappa. Anglican. Avocations: golf, sailing, travel. Home: PO Box 219 Chester Basin NS Canada B0J 1K0 E-mail: EPJ@chesterbasin.com.

PARRON, DELORES L. federal agency administrator; b. Red Bank, N.J., Jan. 14, 1944; d. James W. and Ruth Pitts Parron. BA, Georgian Ct. Coll., 1966; MSW, Cath. U., 1968, PhD, 1977. Psychiat. social worker Hillcrest

Children's Ctr., Washington, 1969—71; asst. prof. dept. psychiatry Howard U. Coll. Medicine, Washington, 1971—78; social sci. analyst Pres. Commn. on Mental Health, Washington, 1977—78; sr. program officer Inst. Medicine, NAS, Washington, 1978—83; assoc. dir. Nat. Inst. Mental Health, Rockville, Md., 1983—99; dep. asst. sec. for planning and evaluation U.S. Dept. Health and Human Svcs., Washington, 1999—2001; sci. advisor for capacity devel. NIH, Bethesda, Md., 2001—. Trustee Georgian Ct. Coll., Lakewood, NJ, 1996—2001, Ctr. for the Advancement Health, Washington, 1995—2001. Recipient Disting. Alumnae award, Cath. U. Am., 1993. Fellow: Nat. Acad. Pub. Adminstrn.; mem.: APA (Disting. Leader for Women in Psychology award 1998, Disting. Achievements award minority fellowship program adv. com. 1998). Office: NIH 9000 Rockville Pike Bethesda MD 20892 E-mail: parrond@mail.nih.gov.

PARROTT, JANICE MORTON, medical and surgical nurse, nursing researcher; b. Atlanta, Apr. 27, 1954; d. James C. and Dorothy Fowler Morton; m. Danny J. Parrott, Feb. 16, 1980; children: Ashley, Olivia. Diploma, Grady Meml. Hosp. Sch. Nursing, Atlanta, 1978; BTh, Christian Life Sch. Theology, 1999, MTh, 2003. Staff nurse Grady Meml. Hosp., 1978-89; rsch. nurse/cardiology Emory U. Sch. Medicine, Atlanta, 1989-91, rschr. preventive medicine, 1991-93, project coord., 1993—99, clin. dir. women's heart rsch., 1999—2003, supr. rsch. nursing, 2003—. Rschr. in field. Assoc. pastor Christian Life Ctr., Covington, Ga. Home: 195 Trotters Walk Covington GA 30016-8118 Office: Emory U Sch Medicine 69 Butler St SE Atlanta GA 30303-3073

PARROTT, LOIS ANNE, humanities educator; b. Willmar, Minn., Aug. 9, 1948; d. Bernard and Janetta Den (Hartog) Muyskens. BA, Dakota Wesleyan U., 1970; MEd, U. North Tex., 1972; PhD, Tex. A&M U., 1982. Tchr. Dallas Ind. Sch. Dist., 1972—75; prof. Richland Coll., Dallas, 1975—. Dir. pub. rels. EBLC, Dallas, 1987—92; multimedia cons. LeCroy Telecomm.-Dallas County C.C. Dist., Dallas, 1991—93; dir. Dist. -wide Computer Users Group, Dallas, 1992—94; spkr. in field. Contbr. articles to profl. jours. Mem. staff-parish rels. Whiterock United Meth. Ch., youth sponsor, 1999—; vol. Nat. PTA, 1993—94; mem. Dallas County Truancy Task Force; bd. trustees Dallas County Schs., 1994—96; sch. bd. trustee Dallas Ind. Sch. Dist., 1997—. Named Tchr. of Yr., Nat. Inst. Staff and Orgnl. Devel., 1995—96; recipient Cmty. Svc. award, Jane Douglas DAR, 2000; grantee NEH, 1987—89. Avocation: piano.

PARROTTI, LAURA DAVIDIAN, theater educator; b. Cleve., Mar. 25, 1949; d. Bert and Margaret Jean Davidian; children: Talia, Olivia, Jesse, Parrotti. BFA in Acting, Goodman Sch. Drama, 1972; MA in Theater and Voice, SUNY, 1976; student, Binghamton U., 2003—. Cert. voice and speech N.Y., 1976. Lectr. Dalhasie U., Halifax, Canada, 1976—77; asst prof. Ohio U., Athens, Ohio, 1978—94, assoc. prof., 1994—. Chmn. performace programs Ohio U., 2002—; workshop leader in field; dialect coach The Cin. (Ohio) Playhouse. Dir.: (plays) Ohio U., Ohio Valley Summer Theater, The Oldest Story Ever Told, The Cleve. Playhouse, Bloody Poetry, off Broadway, N.Y.C., 1998; actor: ; co-author: Health Inform, 1998; contbr. articles to profl. jours. Mem.: Theatre Comms. Guild, Voice and Speech Theater Assn., Am. Theatre in Higher Edn., West Side Cmty. Orgn. Avocations: cooking, skiing. Home: 11 Maple St Athens OH 45701 Office: Ohio University Kantner Hall College St Athens OH 45701

PARRS, MARIANNE M. paper and lumber company executive; b. N.Y.C. m. Walter Parrs; 3 children. Grad., Brown U. Joined Internat. Paper Co., 1974, sector controller, printing papers, staff v.p., worldwide responsibility tax planning and compliance, CFO, sr. v.p., 1995—99, exec. v.p. adminstrn., info. tech. and human resources, 1999—. Office: Internat Paper Co 2 Manhattanville Rd Purchase NY 10577-2196 Fax: 914-397-1650.

PARRY-ROLAND, ANN, writing educator; b. N.Y. d. Lester and Mary Ann Parry; m. Leonard Roland; m. Michael Grab; children: Susan Grab, Lauren Grab. BA in Secondary Edn. - English, SUNY, New Paltz, 1973; MA in Secondary Edn. with specialization in reading, Hofstra U., 1976. Tchr. Bellmore-Merrick Cen. H.S. Dist., Bellmore, NY, 1973—. Adviser lit. art jour. Illusions Grand Ave. Mid. Sch., Bellmore, NY, 1999—. Recipient Silver medal, Columbia Scholastic Press Assn., 2000, 2001, 2002, Disting. Achievement award, EdPress-J.H./Mid. Sch. Student Pub., 2000, 1st Place, Nat. Scholastic Press Assn., 2001. Mem.: Columbia Scholastic Press Assn., Nat. Scholastic Press Assn.

PARRY-SOLA, CHERYL LEE, critical care nurse; b. Bristol, Pa., Oct. 27, 1960; d. Edmund H. and F. Renee (Platt) P. ADN, Bucks County C.C., 1982. RN, N.J.; CCRN. Formerly asst. head nurse Deborah Heart and Lung Ctr., Browns Mills, N.J.; charge nurse med. ICU Holy Spirit Hosp., Camp Hill, Pa., 1995—2002, tng. ctr. coord., 2001—. Office: Holy Spirit Hosp Edn/Tng/Devel 503 N 21st St Camp Hill PA 17011-2288

PARSHALL, KAREN VIRGINIA HUNGER, mathematics and science historian; b. Virginia Beach, Va., July 7, 1955; d. Maurice Jacques and Jean Kay (Wroton) Hunger; m. Brian J. Parshall, Aug. 6, 1978. BA, U. Va., 1977, MS, 1978; PhD, U. Chgo., 1982. Asst. prof. math. Sweet Briar (Va.) Coll., 1982-87, U. Ill., Urbana, 1987-88; asst. prof. math. and history U. Va., Charlottesville, 1988-93, assoc. prof. math. and history, 1993—99, prof. math. and history, 1999—. Author: (with David Rowe) Emergence of American Mathematics Research Community, 1994; (with others) Experiencing Nature, 1997, James Joseph Sylvester: Life and Work in Letters, 1998, (with others) Mathematics Unbound: The Emergence of an International Mathematical Community, 1800-1945,, 2002; year's ago editor Mathematical Intelligencer, N.Y.C., 1990-93; book rev. editor Historia Mathematica, San Diego, 1990-93, mng. editor, 1994-95, editor, 1996-99; contbr. articles to Archive for History Exact Scis., History Sci., Jour. of the History of Biology, Archives internationales d'histoire des sciences, Annals of Sci., History of Sci., Notices of the Am. Math. Soc., Am. Math. Mo., Revue d'histoire des mathématiques. Scholars award NSF, 1986-87, 90-93, NSF VPW award, 1996-97; John Simon Guggenheim Found. fellow, 1996. Mem. AAAS, Am. Math. Soc., History Sci. Soc., Math. Assn. Am., Académie Internationale d'histoire des sciences (corr.), Phi Beta Kappa. Office: U Va Depts Math and History Dept Mathematics P O Box 400137 Charlottesville VA 22904

PARSKY, BARBARA, utilities executive; BA, Rollins Coll. Various mgmt. positions Gen. Electric Co.; ptnr. Porter Novelli, gen. mgr.; prin., owner; v.p. corp. comms. Edison Internat., Rosemead, Calif., 2002—. Office: Edison International 2244 Walnut Grove Ave Rosemead CA 91770

PARSONS, ANNE, performing company executive; m. Donald Dietz; 1 child. BA, Smith Coll., 1980. Staff Nat. Symphony Orchestra, Wash., DC, 1981—83; orchestra mgr. Boston Symphony Orchestra, 1983—91; gen. mgr. Hollywood Bowl, LA, 1991—98, NY City Ballet, 1998—2004; exec. dir. Detroit Symphony Orchestra, 2004—. Fellow Am. Symphony Orchestra League, 1980—81. Office: Detroit Symphony Orchestra Max M Fisher Music Ctr 3711 Woodward Ave Detroit MI 48201*

PARSONS, CHRISTINA ANNE, writer, photographer; b. Fresno, Calif., Oct. 25, 1979; d. Daniel Charles and Susanne Lee Parsons. Cert. in Mgmt. and Supr., Portland (Oreg.) C.C., 2001. Internet sales office mgr. Lexus of Westminster, Calif., 1999; sales asst. Fancy Publications, LA, 1999—2000; editl. content prodr. I-xposure, Irvine, Calif., 2000; corp. comm. writer Qsent, Portland, 2000—01; travel writer and photographer (freelance) IgoUgo.com, N.Y.C., 2001—; mktg. strategist and writer Modus Design and Devel., Long Beach, Calif., 2001—02, Alling Henning Assocs., Vancouver, Wash., 2001—02; mktg. strategist Drake Certivo, Newport Beach, Calif., 2002. Freelance writer; freelance editor; freelance publicist. Author: The Metrician's Estuous Phraseology published in Praxis, 2000; contbr. photographs Hawaiimagazine.com (Photo of the Day multiple times; entire Hawaii photo collection on Hawaii Mag. web site, 2001), articles and photographs to mags. (Editor's Pick (several were awarded this), 2001). Chmn. mktg. com. Clark County Luth. Schs. Assn., Vancouver, Wash., 2001—02. Recipient Gold Medal award, Academic Decathlon Calif. U.S., 1993, Silver Medal award, Academic Decathlon, 1996, Soroptimist Club, Whittier, Calif., 1996, Century Club award, Fancy Pubs., 1999. Liberal. Avocations: travel, walking, reading, writing, photography. Personal E-mail: christina_a_parsons@hotmail.com.

PARSONS, CYNTHIA, writer, consultant; b. Cleve., Jan. 1, 1926; d. Sanford Sherman Clark and Elenore Mann. BA, Principia Coll., 1948; MA, Putney/Antioch Coll., 1956; EdD, Norwich U., 1985. Tchr. various pvt. and pub. schs., 1948-62; edn. editor Christian Sci. Monitor, Boston, 1962-69, 74-82; sr. program office Nat. Inst. for Edn., Washington, 1970-73; founder, dir., coord. SerVermont, Chester, Vt., 1985—2001. Instr. new math Madison Project, Syracuse, N.Y., 1959-61; edn. editor World Bank, Washington, 1969-70; vis. instr. Dartmouth Coll., Hanover, N.H., 1982, 83, 88, U. Vt., Burlington, 1983-88; edn. cons. Robert Coll., Istanbul, Turkey, 1984. Author: Seeds, 1985, Service Learning From A to Z, 1991, George Bird Grinnell, 1992, The Early History of Christian Science in Vermont, 1996, The Discoverer, Mary Baker Eddy, 2000; co-author: Eleven Awesome Vermont Women, 2003; contbr. newspaper series on edn. Mem. Commn. on Edn. Issues, Boston, 1975-81; bd. mem. Grad. Record Examination, Princeton, N.J., 1978-82, Vt. Coun. on the Humanities, Morristown, 1993-97. Recipient Eleanor Roosevelt medal for pub. svc., Val-kill, N.Y., 1992; grantee Edwin Gould Found. for Children, N.Y. and Vt., 1985-95, MacArthur Found., Chgo. and Vt. Mem. Edn. Writers Assn. (pres. 1970-71). Democrat. Christian Scientist. Avocations: reading, travel, listening to classical music. Home: 4713 N 77th Pl Scottsdale AZ 85251

PARSONS, DEBRA LEA, elementary school educator; b. Redding, Calif., May 13, 1960; d. Gary Leon and Leta Barbara Cox. BA in Music Edn., Columbia Christian Coll., 1983; M Music Edn., U. Portland, 1989. Cert. tchr. Calif. Music tchr. David Douglas Sch. Dist., Portland, Oreg., 1984—85, Harold Oliver Sch., Portland, 1987—97, Shasta County Schs., Redding, Calif., 1997—; pvt. music instr. Parsons Music Sch., Shasta Lake City, Calif., 1997—; pvt. tutor math. and lang. arts,computer skills, spanish, and German Parsons Tutoring Svcs., Shasta Lake City, 1997—. Adj. prof. music Columbia Christian Coll., Portland, 1985—91; adj. music instr. Warner Pacific Coll., Portland, 1990—95; adjudicator music competitions Oreg. Music Educators Assn., Portland, 1989—92; grad. tchr. asst. U. Portland, 1986—87. Contbr. poetry to lit. publs. (Editor's Choice award, 98, 99, 00, 01). Vol. Providence Med. Ctr., Portland, 1984—86; asst. sect. leader, libr. Choral Arts Ensemble; asst. dir. Columbia Christian Band. Recipient award for acad. performance, Bank of Am., John Phillips Sousa Band award. Mem.: Music Educators Nat. Conf./Calif. Music Educator's Assn., Delta Kappa Gamma (music chmn. 1996—). Republican. Mem. Ch. Of Christ. Avocations: collecting sea shells, coins, porcelain dolls, sports cards, needlecrafts. Home and Office: 1988 Cabello St Shasta Lake CA 96019 E-mail: debip@jett.net.

PARSONS, ESTELLE, actress, film director, film producer; b. Lynn, Mass., Nov. 20, 1927; d. Eben and Elinor (Mattson) P.; m. Richard Gehman, Dec. 19, 1953 (div. Aug. 1958); children: Martha and Abbie (twins); m. Peter L. Zimroth, Jan. 2, 1983; 1 child, Abraham. BA in Polit. Sci., Conn. Coll. Women, 1949; student, Boston U. Law Sch., 1949-50. Stage appearances include Happy Hunting, 1957, Whoop Up, 1958, Beg, Borrow or Steal, 1960, Threepenny Opera, 1960, Mrs. Dally Has a Lover, 1962, Ready When You Are C.B, 1964, Malcolm, 1965, Seven Descents of Myrtle, 1968, And Miss Reardon Drinks a Little, 1971, Mert and Phil, 1974, The Norman Conquests, 1975-76, Ladies of the Alamo, 1977, Miss Margarida's Way, 1977-78, The Pirates of Penzance, 1981, The Shadow Box, 1994; adapted, dir., performer Orgasmo Adulto Escapes from the Zoo, 1983, The Unguided Missile, Baba Goya, 1989, Shimada, 1992, Grace & Glorie, 1996, The Last of the Thorntons, 2000-01, Morning's At seven, 2002; film appearances include Bonnie and Clyde, 1966; Rachel, Rachel, 1967, I Never Sang for My Father, 1969, Dick Tracy, 1990, Boys On The Side, 1995, Looking for Richard, 1996, That Darn Cat, 1997; TV appearances include Roseanne, 1990—, NBC Today, 1951-56; artistic dir. N.Y. Shakespeare Festival Players, 1986, Actors' Studio, 1997-2003; dir. (Broadway play) Salome, the Reading, 2003. Recipient Theatre World award, 1962-63, Obie award, 1964; recipient award Motion Picture Acad. Arts and Scis., 1967; Recipient Medal of Honor, Conn. Coll., 1969 Home: 924 West End Ave Apt T5 New York NY 10025-3543

PARSONS, IRENE ADELAIDE, management consultant; b. North Wilkesboro, N.C. d. Everett T. and Martha (Minton) P. BS in Bus. Edn. and Adminstrn., U. N.C., 1941, LLD (hon.), 1967; MS in Pub. Adminstrn., George Washington U., 1965. Tchr. Roanoke Rapids (N.C.) High Sch., 1941-42; rep. U.S. Civil Svc. Commn., 1942-43; with VA, 1946-74, asst. adminstr. vets. affairs, dir. personnel, dir. equal employment opportunity, 1965-74; mgmt. cons., 1974—. Exec. com. Pres.'s Study Group Careers for Women. Served to lt. USCGR, 1943-46. Recipient Fed. Woman's Outstanding Achievement award, 1966, Silver Helmet award Amvets, 1971, Career Svc. award Nat. Civil Svc. League, 1972, Disting. Alumni Achievement award George Washington U., 1973; named to Brevard Coll. Hall of Fame, 1984 Mem. Assn. Fed. Woman's Award Recipients (chmn. 1972-76) Address: PO Box 2046 North Wilkesboro NC 28659-2046

PARSONS, LISA KAY, artist, writer; b. Portland, Oreg., Mar. 23, 1955; d. Norman Elliott and Virginia Ruby Parsons. BA in Art History, Portland State U., 1984; MA in Liberal Studies, NYU, 1989. Cert. in mus. studies N.Y. Dir. Littman Gallery Portland State U., 1981—83, dir. White Gallery, 1982—83; intern Isamu Noguchi Garden Mus., Long Island City, NY, 1988, Mus. of Modern Art, N.Y.C., 1989; acct. exec. Culture Mag., 2003—; instr. art Sellwood Cmty. Ctr., Portland, 2003—; instr. art and writing Portland, Gresham area schs., Oreg., 2003. Writing instr. McCarty Mid. Sch., Gresham, Oreg., 2003; art instr. Robert Gray Mid. Sch., Portland, 2003; program aide YMCA, Portland, 2003—. One-woman shows include Cup and Saucer Cafe, 2004; author: (poetry) included in Into the Teeth of the Wind, 2001; Exhibited in group shows at N.W. Artist's Workshop, Portland, 1983, Internat. House, N.Y.C., 1989, Oreg. Hist. Soc., Portland, 1992, Paparazzi Studio, 2002, exhibitions include The Old Kerr Nursery, 1991, Windows Alive, 2003. Mem.: Willamette Writers.

PARSONS, LORRAINE LEIGHTON, nurse, pre-school administrator; b. Albany, Maine, Feb. 7, 1939; d. Alfred Elmer Leighton and Arlene Rachael Winslow; m. Jack Arnol Greig (div. July 1982); children: Scotty, Kim; m. Robert Davis Parsons, Dec. 20, 1991. Student, U. Maine. RN, Maine. Office nurse Charles Hannigan, MD, Auburn, Maine, 1961-64; with Stephens Meml. Hosp., Norway, Maine, 1964-69; tchr. spl. edn. W. Paris (Maine) Sch., 1969-73; tchr. reading and math. Buckfield (Maine) Sch., 1974-78; nurse Ledgeview Nursing Home, W. Paris, 1979-80, Central Maine Med. Ctr., Lewiston, 1980-96; child care profl. Marwin Cons. Co., Raymond, Maine, 1996—. Author: Families of the Fox and Geese Quilt, 1997, Homesteads of Hartford, 1997, Quilting is Qumforting, 1999, Town of Hartford, 2000, Military Service, 2000, Marston Homestead, 2000, Crazy Quilt, 2000, Winslow Home, 2001, The Alfred E. Leighton Family, 2001, Rokomeko - Native Americans, 2002, Life - 1870, 1879 & 1881, 2003; co-author: Hartford in Pictures, 1984; author: Rokomeko Indians Native Americans, 2002. Pres., founder Hartford (Maine) Heritage Soc., 1976; program chairwoman Hartford Bicentennial, 1997-98. Recipient Cert. of Honor Bicentennial, State of Maine, 1998, Double-Trouble Nature category Internat. Libr. Photography, 2000; grantee Maine Arts, 1998. Avocations: dolls, stamps, town histories. Home: PO Box 493 Canton ME 04221-0493

PARSONS, MARCIA PHILLIPS, judge; Bankruptcy judge U.S. Bankruptcy Ct. (Tenn. ea. dist.), 6th circuit, Greeneville, 1993—. Office: US Courthouse 101 W Summer St Greeneville TN 37743-4944

PARSONS, MINDY (MINDY ENOS), newsletter editor, publisher, non-profit organization executive; b. Cin., May 18, 1962; d. Max Allen and Margery Ann (White) Enos; m. Judd Lewis Parsons, Sept. 4, 1993; children: Cody Robert and Savannah Anne (twins). AA in Liberal Arts, Brevard Community Coll., 1983; BSBA, Fla. Inst. Tech., 1986; MBA, N.Y. Inst., Boca Raton, Fla., 1992. Mem. adminstrv. support staff IBM, Boca Raton, 1980, 81; dir. mktg. Progressive Pub., Melbourne, Fla., 1986; owner, pub. Echelon Pub. Inc., Melbourne, 1986-87; editor Keuthan Communications Inc., Melbourne, 1987-89; staff writer First Mktg. Corp., Pompano Beach, Fla., 1989-90; assoc. editor Billboard Publs. Inc., Coral Springs, Fla., 1990-92, Caribbean Clipper, Inc., Clearwater, Fla., 1992-93; reporter South Fla. News Network, Coral Springs, 1993-94; owner Creative Communications, Delray Beach, Fla., 1993-96; newsletter editor, pub., founder Breast Cancer Survivor Network Corp., 1997—. Author: How to Save for Your Child's Education, 1990; editor: Soccer for Children, 1988, History of Bahamas, 1990; editor, pub. Breast Cancer Survivor newsletter, 1997—; contbr. articles to profl. publs. Vol. Humane Soc. of Broward County, Coral Springs, 1990-91; founder Breast Cancer Survivor Network; mem. Palm Beach County Breast Cancer Coalition. Mem. NAFE, Newsletter Publishers Assn. Republican. Methodist. Avocations: volleyball tournaments, U.S. Masters swim meets, reading. Home: 221 SE 34th Ave Boynton Beach FL 33435-8632

PARTEE, BARBARA HALL, linguist, educator; b. Englewood, N.J., June 23, 1940; d. David B. and Helen M. Hall; m. Morriss Henry Partee, 1966 (div. 1971); children: Morriss M., David M., Joel T.; m. Emmon Bach, 1973 (div. 1996); m. Vladimir B. Borschev, 1997. BA with high honors in Math., Swarthmore Coll., 1961; PhD in Linguistics, MIT, 1965; DSc (hon.), Swarthmore Coll., 1989, Charles U., Prague, Czechoslovakia, 1992, Russian State Humanities U., Moscow, 2001. Asst. prof. UCLA, 1965-69, assoc. prof., 1969-73; assoc. prof. linguistics and philosophy U. Mass., Amherst, 1972-73, prof., 1973-90, Disting. Univ. prof., 1990—2003, Disting. Univ. prof. linguistics and philosophy emerita, 2004—, head dept. linguistics, 1987-93; fellow Ctr. for Advanced Study in Behavior Scis., 1976-77. Mem. bd. mgrs. Swarthmore Coll., 1990-2001. Author: (with Stockwell and Schachter) The Major Syntactic Structures of English, 1972, Fundamentals of Mathematics for Linguists, 1979, (with ter Meulen and Wall) Mathematical Methods in Linguistics, 1990, (with Hajicova and Sgall) Topic-Focus Articulation, Tripartite Structures, and Semantic Content, 1998, Compositionality in Formal Semantics: Selected Papers of Barbara H. Partee, 2004; editor: Montague Grammar, 1976; co-editor: (with Chierchia and Turner) Properties, Types and Meaning, Vol. I: Foundational Issues, Vol. II: Semantic Issues, 1989, (with Bach, Jelinek and Kratzer) Quantification in Natural Languages, 1995, (with P. Portner) Formal Semantics: The Essential Readings, 2002; mem. editl. bd: Language, 1967-73, Linguistic Inquiry, 1972-79, Theoretical Linguistics, 1974—, Linguistics and Philosophy, 1977—. Recipient Chancellor's medal U. Mass., 1977; NEH fellow, 1982-83; Internat. Rsch. and Exchanges Bd. fellow, 1989-90, 95, Fulbright fellow 2000. Fellow AAAS, NAS (chair anthropology sect. 1993-96), Am. Acad. Arts and Scis., Sigma Xi; mem. Linguistic Soc. Am. (pres. 1986), Am. Philos. Assn., Assn. Computational Linguistics, Royal Netherlands Acad. Arts and Scis. (fgn.). Home: 50 Hobart Ln Amherst MA 01002-1321 Office: U Mass Dept Linguistics Amherst MA 01003 E-mail: partee@linguist.umass.edu.

PARTEN, PRISCILLA M. medical and psychiatric social worker, educator; b. Lowell, Mass., Dec. 7, 1944; d. Ralph Bailey and Margaret Lillian (McDonagh) Newton; m. Samuel L. Parten, June 27, 1965; children: Delora Parten Power, Edward Bailey, Ethan Rogers. BA, Northeastern U., 1968; MSW, Adelphi U., Burlington, Vt., 1987. Lic. ind. clin. social worker, Mass., N.H., lic. clin. social worker, Maine; bd. cert. diplomate NASW. Family support coord. Easter Seal Early Intervention, Derry, N.H., 1988-91; med. and psychiat. social worker Salem (N.H.) Vis. Nurses, 1992-96; home sch. coord. Timberlane Regional Sch. Dist., Plaistow, N.H., 1992—; dir. Priscilla M. Parten, MSW, ACSW, BCD, Londonderry, N.H., 1992—. Spkr., author, presenter in field, interviewed on Nat. Pub. TV. Bd. dirs. Norwich U. Parents' Assn., 1st v.p., 1999—2001. Recipient commendation Pres.'s Com. on Mental Retardation, 1968. Mem. NASW, Nutfield Exch. Club (bd. dirs. 1994-96). Democrat. Congregationalist. Avocations: skiing, photography, crocheting, gardening, snorkeling. Office: 50 Nashua Rd Londonderry NH 03053-3444

PARTHEMORE, JACQUELINE GAIL, internist, educator, hospital administrator; b. Harrisburg, Pa., Dec. 21, 1940; d. Philip Mark and Emily (Buvit) Parthemore; m. Alan Morton Blank, Jan. 7, 1967; children: Stephen Eliot, Laura Elise. BA, Wellesley Coll., 1962; MD, Cornell U., 1966. Diplomate Am. Bd. Internal Medicine. Resident in internal medicine N.Y. Hosp./Cornell U., 1966-69; fellow in endocrinology Scripps Clinic and Rsch. Found., La Jolla, Calif., 1969-72; rsch. ednl. assoc. VA Hosp., San Diego, 1974-78; staff physician VA San Diego Health Care Sys., 1978-79, asst. chief, med. svc., 1979-83, acting chief, med. svc., 1980-81, chief of staff, 1984—; asst. prof. medicine U. Calif. Sch. Medicine, San Diego, 1974-80, assoc. prof. medicine, 1980-85, prof. medicine, assoc. dean, 1985—. Mem. nat. rsch. resources coun. NIH, Bethesda, Md., 1990-94. Contbr. chapters to books, articles to profl. jours. Mem. adv. bd. San Diego Opera, 1993—; mem. Roundtable and Channel 10 Focus Group, San Diego Millennium Project, 1999; bd. dirs. San Diego Vets. Med. Rsch. Found., 1989—, Nat. VA Rsch. and Edn. Found., 2001—. Recipient Bullock's 1st Annual Portfolio award, 1985, San Diego Pres.'s Coun. Woman of Yr. award, 1985, YWCA Tribute to Women in Industry award, 1987, San Diego Women Who Mean Bus. award, 1999, Excellence in Leadership award Am. Hosp. Assn., 2002. Fellow ACP (gov.-elect Region III 2004), Am. Assn. Clin. Endocrinologists; mem. Endocrine Soc., Nat. Assn. VA Chiefs Staff (pres. 1989-91), Wellesley Coll. Alumnae Assn. (1st v.p. 1992-95), San Diego Wellesley Club (pres. 1997-99), San Diego Herb Soc. (co-pres. 2003-2004). Avocations: gardening, reading, sailing, cooking, travel. Office: VA San Diego Healthcare Sys 3350 La Jolla Village Dr San Diego CA 92161-0002 Office Phone: 858-552-7419. E-mail: jparthemore@ucsd.edu.

PARTON, DOLLY REBECCA, singer, composer, actress; b. Sevier County, Tenn., Jan. 19, 1946; d. Robert Lee and Avie Lee (Owens) P.; m. Carl Dean, May 30, 1966. Country music singer, rec. artist, composer, actress, radio and TV personality. Entrepreneur, owner entertainment park Dollywood, established 1985. Radio appearances include Grand Ole Opry, WSM Radio, Nashville, Cass Walker program, Knoxville; TV appearances include Porter Wagoner Show, from 1967, Cass Walker program, Bill Anderson Show, Wilburn Bros. Show, Barbara Mandrell Show; rec. artist, Mercury, Monument, RCA, CBS record cos.; star movie Nine to Five, 1980, The Best Little Whorehouse in Texas, 1982, Rhinestone, 1984, Steel Magnolias, 1989, Straight Talk, 1991; albums include Here You Come Again (Grammy award 1978), Real Love, 1985, Just the Way I Am, 1986, Portrait, 1986, Think About Love, 1986, Trio (with Emmylou Harris, Linda Ronstadt) (Grammy award 1988), 1987, Heartbreaker, Great Balls of Fire, Rainbow, 1988, White Limozeen, 1989, Home for Christmas, 1990, Eagle When She Flies, 1991, Slow Dancing with the Moon, 1993 (Grammy nomination, Best Country Vocal Collaboration for Romeo (with Tanya Tucker, Billy Ray Cyrus, Kathy Mattea, Pam Tillis, & Mary-Chapin Carpenter), (with Tammy Wynette and Loretta Lynn) Honky Tonk Angels, 1994, The Essential Dolly Parton, 1995, Just the Way I Am, 1996, Super Hits, 1996, (with others) I Will Always Love You & Other Greatest Hits, 1996, Hungry Again, 1998, Trio II, 1998, Grass is Blue, 1999 (Grammy award for best bluegrass album), Best of the Best-Porter & Doll, 1999, Halos and Horns, 2002, For God and Country, 2003, Makin' Believe, 2003;

appears on song "Creepin' In" with Norah Jones, 2004; composer numerous songs including Nine to Five (Grammy award 1981, Acad. award nominee and Golden Globe award nominee 1981); author: Dolly, 1994. Recipient (with Porter Wagoner) Vocal Group of Yr. award, 1968; Vocal Duo of Yr. award All Country Music Assn., 1970, 71; Nashville Metronome award, 1979; Am. Music award for best duo performance (with Kenny Rogers), 1984; named Female Vocalist of Yr., 1975, 76; Country Star of Yr., Sullivan Prodns., 1977; Entertainer of Yr., Country Music Assn., 1978; People's Choice award, 1980, 88; Female Vocalist of Yr., Acad. Country Music, 1980; Dolly Parton Day proclaimed, Sevier County, Tenn., designated Oct. 7, 1967, Los Angeles, Sept. 20, 1979; recipient Grammy awards for best female country vocalist, 1978, 81, for best country song, 1981, for best country vocal performance with group, 1987; co-recipient (with Emmylou Harris and Linda Ronstadt) Acad. Country Music award for album of the yr., 1987; named to Small Town of Am. Hall of Fame, 1988, East Tenn. Hall of Fame, 1988. Address: RCA 6 W 57th St New York NY 10019-3901 Office: Dollywood Co 1020 Dollywood Ln Pigeon Forge TN 37863-4101*

PARTON, STELLA MAE, entertainer; d. Robert Lee Parton and Avie Lee Ownes; 1 child, Timothy C. Rauhoff. Author: Really Cookin', vol.1, Country Cookin'; actor: (Broadway plays) Seven Brides for Seven Brothers, The Best Little Whorehouse in Texas, Pump boys, Dinettes, Gentlemen Prefer Blonds; (films) Cloud Dancer, The Loner, Country Gold; (TV films) The Dukes of Hazard, The Color of Love; singer: (singles) I Draw From the Well, I Want To Hold You In My Dreams Tonight (ASCAP Songwriter award), Ragged Angel, Ode To Olivia, You've Crossed My Mind, I'm Not That Good at Goodbye, Standard Lie Number One, Undercover Lovers, Steady As The Rain, I'll Miss You, Cross My Heart, Legs, Up In The Holler, Smooth Talker, Try Him You'll Like Him, It's Not Funny Anymore (ASCAP Recording Artist award), the Mood I'm In, Neon Woman, The Danger of a Stranger, Four Little Letters, Stormy Weather (ASCAP Recording Artist award), Room at the Top of the Stairs, Young Love, I Don't Miss You Like I Used To, Picture in a Frame, (albums) In The Garden, I Want to Hold You in my Dreams, Stella Parton, The Best of Stella Parton, Ture to Me, Stella Parton Favorites, vol. 1, A Woman's Touch, Appalachian Blues, Appalachian Gospel, Stella and The Gospel Carrolls, Country Sweet, Love Ya, So Far, So Good, Always Tomorrow, Picture in a Frame, Anthology, Blue Heart; performer: (videos) Cross My Heart, A Woman's Touch, Up in the Holler. Nat. spokewoman Christian Appalachian Project. Nominee Mainstream Country Artist award, CCMA, 2001, Songwriter of the Yr. award, 2002, Video of the Yr. award, 2002; named Mainstream Country Artist, 2002; recipient Hon. Ambassador of Country Music, La., Ky., Pa., New Zealand, Most Promising Internat. Act, GBCM, Stormy Weather/Recording Artist, ASCAP, Tenn. Dem. Chmn.'s award, 2001, Summerfest Country Female Vocalist & Entertainer, 2001. Office: Attic Entertainment PO Box 120871 Nashville TN 37212

PARTRIDGE, CAROLYN, farmer, state representative; b. Hackensack, N.Y., Jan. 21, 1949; m. Alan C. Partridge; 3 children. BA, NYU, 1971. Farmer; rep. Vt. State Ho. Reps., 1999—. Comm. Windham (Vt.) Regional Planning; mem. Windham (Vt.) Cmty. Orgn., Cultural Heritage Tourism Adv. Coun.; deacon Windham (Vt.) Congl. Ch.; chmn. Windham (Vt.) Sch. Bd.; exec. bd. Windham (Vt.) Regional Planning. Democrat. Protestant. Home: 1612 Old Cheney Rd Windham VT 05359

PARULIS, CHERYL, English, drama and speech educator; b. Charlotte, N.C., Apr. 11, 1944; d. Francis August and Evelyn Louise (Scott) Bogacki; m. Albert William Parulis, June 25, 1966 (Apr. 1984); children: Albert William Jr., Christa Suzanne. M in Sports Adminstrn., Mercyhurst Coll., Erie, Pa., 1962-63; student, Indiana U. Pa., 1963-64, U. Que. at Trois Riviers, Can., 1987; BA in English Lit., Clarion U. Pa., 1987, MA in English Lit., 1989; BEd, permanent cert. in English edn., St. Thomas U., Miami, Fla., 1995. Permanet cert. English tchr., Fla. Substitute tchr. Brigantine (N.J.) Pub. Sch. Sys., 1970-72, Dubois (Pa.) Area Sch. Sys., 1982-84, Clarion Intermediate Unit 6, 1984-86; residential aide Pathways, Inc., Clarion, 1987-88; asst. Writing Ctr., Clarion U. Pa., 1987-88, grad. asst., English and computer tutor, 1988-89; tchr. English, St. Jospeh Sch., Miami Beach, Fla., 1991-93, Msgr. Edward Pace H.S., Miami, 1993-98; adj. prof. composition, speech, Am. lit. and drama St. Thomas U., 1994—; adj. prof. English and lit. Internat. Fine Arts Coll., Miami, 1998—. Partitipant Fla. Thespian Festival, 1997, 98; presenter in field; cheerleading coach, Miami, 1995-98. Hospice vol., Miami, 1993-94; vol. Miami Beach Dem. Com., 1994—. Habitat for Humanity, Miami, 1998-99. Recipient Msgr. Edward Pace Golden Apple award of excellence, 1994, 97. Mem. Nat. Coun. Tchrs. English, Dade County Tchrs. Assn., Sigma Tau Delta (life). Roman Catholic. Avocations: theatre, film, decorating, stage directing, dance. Home: 1812 Barber St Sebastian FL 32958-6256

PASAKARNIS, KATHLEEN FALLON, health services consultant; b. Hinsdale, Ill., Nov. 19, 1954; d. William Leo and June Marie Fallon; m. Stephen Edward Pasakarnis, Aug. 7, 1976; children: Timothy Stephen, Christopher William. BS in Elem. Edn., U. Ill., Champaign, 1976; MEd. in Spl. Edn., U. Hartford, 1982. Internat. Bd. Cert. Lactation Cons. Internat. Bd. Lactation Cons. Examiners, 2001. Dir., tchr. Prince of Peace Nursery Sch., Coventry, Conn., 1992—93; tchr. Our Savior Presch. and Childcare, South Windsor, Conn., 2000—02; lactation cons. Nurturing Family Lactation Svs., South Windsor, Conn., 2001—, MCH Services/Aetna, Hartford, Conn., 2003—. Co-chair edn. com. Conn. Breast Feeding Coalition, 2001—02; treas. Assn. Conn. Lactation Cons., South Windsor, 2002—. Vol. breast feeding educator La Leche League Internat., South Windsor, 1989—2003; vol. breastfeeding educator WIC, Rockville, Enfield, Conn., 2000—03; tchr./supt. Sunday sch. Zion Ev. Luth. Ch./Our Savior Luth. Ch., Conn., 1982—2003. Mem.: Internat. Bd. Lactation Cons. (assoc.). Home and Office: Nurturing Family Lactation Svs 98 Woodland Dr South Windsor CT 06074 Personal E-mail: nurturingfamily@aol.com.

PASCAL, AMY, film company executive; b. 1958; BA, U. of Calif., Los Angeles. V.p. of prod. Fox, 1986—87, Columbia, 1987—89, exec. v.p. of prod., 1989—94; pres. of prod. Turner Pictures, 1994—96; pres. Columbia Pictures, Culver City, Calif., 1996-99, chmn., 1999—; vice chmn. Sony Pictures Entertainment, 2002—. Bd. trustees Rand Corp. Office: Columbia Pictures 10202 Washington Blvd Culver City CA 90232-3119*

PASCAL, NAOMI BRENNER, editor-at-large, publishing executive; b. Bklyn., Mar. 13, 1926; d. Mortimer and Sylvia (Freehof) Brenner; m. Paul Pascal, June 27, 1948; children: David Morris, Janet Brenner. BA, Wellesley Coll., 1946. Editor Vanguard Press, Inc., N.Y.C., 1946-48, U. N.C. Press, Chapel Hill, N.C., 1948-50, 52-53, U. Wash. Press, 1953-75, editor-in-chief, 1976—2002, assoc. dir., 1985—2002. Dir. Assn. Am. Univ. Presses, 1976-78; cons. editor Scholarly Pub. jour., Toronto, Ont., Can., 1979— ; del. Wash. State Gov.'s Conf. on Library and Info. Services, Olympia, 1978-79. Co-author: Glossary Typesetting Terms, 1994; contbr. chpts. to books, articles to profl. jours. Durant scholar, 1945; recipient constituency award Assn. Am. Univ. Presses, 1991. Mem. Women in Scholarly Pub., Assn. Asian Am. Studies, Native Am. Art Studies Assn., Phi Beta Kappa (treas. Alpha of Wash. chpt. 1975-78). Office: U Wash Press PO Box 50096 Seattle WA 98145-5096

PASCALE, JANE FAY, pathologist; b. New Haven, Conn., May 20, 1932; d. John Adam and Madeline J. (Pompano) P.; m. Joseph H. Kite Jr., Aug. 6, 1970. BA, Mount Holyoke Coll., 1954; MD, U. Chgo., 1959. Cert. anat. and clin. pathology Am. Bd. Pathology; diplomate Nat. Bd. Med. Examiners. Intern, resident in pathology Yale-New Haven Hosp., 1959-63; NIH-NCI spl. fellow dept. microbiology Yale U. Sch. Medicine, 1963-64; NIH-NCI spl. fellow Inst. de Recherches Scientifiques sur le Cancer, Villejuif, France, 1964-66; asst. in pathology Mass. Gen. Hosp. and Harvard Med. Sch., Boston, 1966-68; asst. prof. clin. pathology Yale U. Sch. Medicine, New Haven, 1968-69; attending pathologist Erie County Med. Ctr., Buffalo, N.Y., 1969-95; clin. asst. prof. pathology SUNY, Buffalo, 1969-90, clin. asst. prof. microbiology, 1991—. Mem. scientific adv. bd. Infectech, Inc., Sharon, Pa., 1995—; scientific del. Citizen Amb. Program People-to-People Internat. Contbr. articles to profl. jours. Recipient Physician's Recognition award AMA, 1981-99. Fellow Am. Soc. Clin. Pathologists, Coll. Am. Pathologists; mem. AMA, N.Y. Acad. Scis., Am. Soc. Cytopathology, Assn. Clin. Scientists. Methodist. Achievements include research in immunopathology of tuberculosis and autoimmune disease.

PASCHAL, RHODA JONES, voice educator; b. Savannah, Ga., Apr. 5, 1956; d. Charles Alexander and Rhoda Johnson Jones; m. Robert Sheldon Paschal, June 16, 1979; children: Rhoda Jane, Ann Sheldon. D of musical arts, U. of SC., 1992—95. Certified Teacher of Music Education SC, 2003, International Baccalaureate Music Educator Internat. Baccalaureate Orgn., 2003. Music staff: alto soloist First Presbyn. Ch., Columbia, SC, 1981—; singer, voice tchr. Paschal Acad. of Music, Columbia, SC, 1990—; founder, dir. Palmetto Girls Ensemble, Columbia, SC, 2000—; internat. baccalaureate music educator A. C. Flora High Sch., Richland Sch. Dist. One, Columbia, SC, 2002—. SC dist. chmn. Met. Opera Nat. Coun. Auditions, Columbia, SC, 1990—; artist in residence SC Arts Commn., Columbia, 1990—, cmty. performing tour, 2001—; art affiliate Columbia Music Festival Assn., SC, 2002—; founder Paschal Academy of Music: a comprehensive music program including piano, voice and choral instrn. Singer: performances include operas, recitals, oratorios and musicals; dir.: (plays) including The Sound of Music, Grease, Anything Goes, Music Man. Bible moderator First Prebyterian: Women of the Ch., Columbia, SC, 1980—85; cmty. rsch. Jr. League, Columbia, SC, 1980—85; chmn., jr. garden club Columbia Garden Club, 1980—85. Grad. Assistantship fellowship, Women's Ensemble; SC. Opera Theater: U. of SC, 1988—90, 1992—95. Mem.: Music Educators Nat. Conf. (assoc.), SC. Music Teachers Assn. (assoc.), Nat. Assn. of Teachers of Singing (assoc.), Greater Columbia Opera Guild (assoc.). R-Consevative. Christian/ Presbyterian. Avocations: travel, tennis, bridge. Home: 1713 Roslyn Dr Columbia SC 29206 Office: Paschal Academy of Music 1713 Roslyn Dr Columbia SC 29206 E-mail: paschaliii@msn.com.

PASCHAL, VERONA, real estate agent, small business owner; b. Jamaica, British West Indies, Oct. 6, 1952; d. John and Hennritta Dennisor; m. Fred L. Paschal, Jan. 26, 1983; children: Kevin, Yolanda, Bryan. Grad., Pitman Inst., London. Owner Paschal & Assocs., Palmetto Bay, Fla., 1986—, Paschal Mortgage Corp., Palmetto Bay, 1999—. Mem.: Coun. Residential Specialists (10 Yr. Svc. award). Avocations: boating, fishing. Office: 15321 S Dixie Hwy Ste 205 Miami FL 33157 E-mail: VeronaPaschal@Realtor.com.

PASCOE, CLARA P. public relations executive, property manager; arrived in U.S., 1981; d. Jairo Buritica and Consuelo Antolinez; m. Armon Vakneen, Feb. 14, 2002. A in Bus. Adminstrn., West L.A., 1987; BBA, U. Phoenix, Los Angeles, 2002, MBA, 2004. Sec., receptionist Indec Fin. Inc., San Jose, Costa Rica, 1975—81; property mgr., acct. Accurate Records, Inc., L.A., 1987—94; property mgmt. agt. Proactive, L.A., 1994—97; asst. dir. pub. rels. Simon Wiesenthal Ctr., L.A., 1997—. Tax cons. H&R Block, L.A., 1991—95. Avocations: art, dance, writing, reading, sports.

PASCOE, PATRICIA HILL, former state legislator; b. Sparta, Wis., June 1, 1935; d. Fred Kirk and Edith (Kilpatrick) Hill; m. D. Monte Pascoe, Aug. 3, 1957; children: Sarah, Edward, William. BA, U. Colo., 1957; MA, U. Denver, 1968, PhD, 1982. Tchr. Sequoia Union H.S. Dist., Redwood City, Calif. and Hayward (Calif.) Union H.S. Dist., 1957-60; instr. Met. State Coll., Denver, 1969-75, Denver U., 1975-77, 81, rsch. asst. bur. ednl. rsch., 1981-82; tchr. Kent Denver Country Day Sch., Englewood, Colo., 1982-84; freelance writer Denver, 1985—; mem. Colo. Senate, Dist. 32, Denver, 1989—93, Colo. Senate, Dist. 34, Denver, 1995—2003; chair minority caucus Colo. Senate, Denver, 1996-2000, chair policy and planning com., 2001, chair edn. com., 2002. Commr. Edn. Commn. of the States, Denver, 1975-82, 2001—. Contbr. articles to numerous publs. and jours. Bd. dirs. Samaritan House, 1990-94, Cystic Fibrosis Found., 1989-93, ACLU of Colo., 2003—; pres. East H.S. Parent Tchr. and Student Assn., Denver, 1984-85; mem. Moore Budget Adv. Com., Denver, 1966-72; legis. chmn. alumni bd. U. Colo., Boulder, 1987-89; del. Dem. Nat. Conv., San Francisco, 1984, N.Y.C., 1992; mem. Denver Woman's Press Club, 1986—, Colo. Arts Coalition, 1988-97, Conflict Ctr. Bd.; bd. dirs. Opera Colo., 1996-2002, ACLU Colo. Mem. Soc. Profl. Journalists, Common Cause (bd. dirs. Denver chpt. 1986-88), Lions Club, Phi Beta Kappa. Democrat. Presbyterian.

PASHGIAN, MARGARET HELEN, artist; b. Pasadena, Calif., Nov. 7, 1934; d. Aram John and Margaret (Howell) P. BA, Pomona Coll., 1956; MA in Fine Arts, Boston Univ., 1958; student, Columbia U., 1957. Art instr. Harvard-Newton Program Occidental Coll., 1977-78; artist in residence Calif. Inst. Tech., 1970-71. Grants panelist Calif. Arts Coun., Sacramento, 1993. Artist: solo shows include Rex Evans Gallery, L.A., 1965, 67, Occidental Coll., 1967, Kornblee Gallery, N.Y.C., 1969-72, U. Calif., Irvine, 1975, U. Calif. Santa Barbara, 1976, Stella Polaries Gallery, L.A., 1981, 82, Kaufman Galleries, Houston, 1982, Modernism Gallery, San Francisco, 1983, Works Gallery, Long Beach, Costa Mesa, Calif., 1986, 87, 88, 89, 90, 91, 92, Malka Gallery, L.A., 1997; group exhibitions include Pasadena Art Mus., 1965, Carson Pirie Scott, Chgo., 1965, Calif. Palace of Legion of Honor, San Francisco, 1967, Esther Bear Gallery, Santa Barbara, 1967, 69, Lytton Ctr. of the Visual Arts, L.A., 1968, Salt Lake Art Inst., Salt Lake City, 1968, Mus. Contemporary Crafts, Internat. Plastics Exhibition, 1969, Second Flint (Mich.) Invitational, 1969, Milw. Art Ctr., 1969, U.S.I.S. Mus., N.Y.C., Mus. Contemporary Art, Chgo., 1970, Studio Merconi, Milan, 1970, Calif. Inst. Tech., Baxter Art Galley, 1971, 1980, Calif. Innovations, Palm Springs Dessert Mus., 1981, Calif. Internat. Arts Found. Mus. of Modern Art, Paris, 1982, L.A. Artists in Seoul, Donsangbang Gallery, 1982, An Artistic Conversation, 1931-82, Poland, USA, Ulster Mus., Belfast, Ireland, 1983, Madison (Wis.) Art Ctr., 1994, Calif. State U., Fullerton, 1995, Oakland (Calif.) Mus., 1995, Molly Barnes Gallery, LA, Calif., 2000, Pasadena (Calif.) Mus. Calif. Art, 2002; represented in pub. collections at River Forest (Ill.) State Bank, Atlantic Richfield Co., Dallas, Frederic Weisman Collection, L.A., Security Pacific Bank, L.A., Singapore, Andrew Dickson White Mus. of Art, Cornell U., Ithaca, N.Y., L.A. County Mus. of Art, Santa Barbara Art Mus., Laguna Beach Mus. of Art, Portland (Oreg.) Art Mus. Trustee, Pomona Coll, Claremont, Calif., 1987—; parade judge Tournament of Roses Centennial Parade, Pasadena, 1987; bd. dirs. L.A. Master Chorale, 1992—. NEA grantee, 1986. Home: 731 S Grand Ave Pasadena CA 91105-2424

PASIEKA, ANNE W. elementary school educator; b. Chgo., July 20, 1943; d. George Hales and Elizabeth Schultz Wilson; m. Ralph Snodgrass, Jan. 1965 (div. 1977); m. Mark Pasieka, Dec. 17, 1977; children: Helena, Brian, Jeff. BS in edn., Drake U., 1964; MS in adminstrn., Nat. Coll., 1976. Tchr. Quincy (Ill.) Pub. Schs., 1964-67, Univ. City (Mo.) Pub. Schs., 1967-68, Harford County (Md.) Pub. Schs., 1968-70, Comm. Consol. Sch. Dist. 59, Arlington Heights, 1970—. Instructional coun. mem. Byrd Sch., Elk Grove Village. Recipient Tchr. of the Year award Jaycees, Elk Grove Village, Ill., 1974. Mem. AAUW (pres. 1999-2000), NEA, Ill. Edn. Assn., ISTE, ICE, NICE, Delta Zeta, Phi Delta Kappa. Avocation: genealogy. Home: 414 W Hawthorne St Arlington Heights IL 60004-5427

PASKAWICZ, JEANNE FRANCES, pain specialist; b. Phila., Mar. 3, 1954; d. Alex and Lillian (Pyluck) P. BSc, Phila. Coll. Pharmacy; MA, Villanova U., 1973; postgrad., St. Joseph U., 1979; PhD, Kensington U., 1984. Mem. anesthesiology staff Einstein Med. Ctr., Phila., 1990-94, Temple U. Hosp., 1994—; mem. detox./rehab. staff Presbyn. Med. Ctr., Phila., 1984—; house officer Tenet Hosps., Elkins Park, Pa., 1990—; mem. psychiatry staff Hahnemann U. Hosp., Phila., 1984-90; hostage negotiator Office of Mental Health, Phila., 1984-90; mem. surgery/anesthesiology staff Mt. Sinai Hosp., Phila., 1989-91. Bd. dirs. Phila. Coll. Pharmacy, St. Joseph U. Mem. NAFE, Am. Pain Soc., Nat. Parks Conservation Assn., North Shore Animal League, Amvets, DAV Comdrs. Club, Lambda Kappa Sigma.

PASKER, DEBBIE ANN, protective services official; b. Homestead AFB, Fla., Nov. 25, 1960; d. Wayne Chandler and Sharon Kaye (Boke) Gainey; m. Michael Harold Pasker, Dec. 31, 1988; children: Matthew Michael, Daniel Chandler. BS in Pub. Adminstrn., Fla. Atlantic U., 1998. Police sgt., grant specialist City of Sunrise, Fla., 1982—. Bd. dirs. Broward chpt. Fla. Informed Parents, Ft. Lauderdale, 1988-89; pres. Broward County D.A.R.E. Officers Assn., 1996. Named officer of yr. Sawgrass Optimists Club, 1996. Mem. Nat. Drug Abuse Resistance Edn. Officer's Assn. (Most Outstanding Student award 1991), Fla. Drug Abuse Resistance Edn. Officer's Assn., Fla. Assn. Sch. Resource Officers (treas. Broward chpt. 1988-89), Fla. Juvenile Officers Assn., Broward Crime Prevention Officers Assn. (sec.-treas. 1988-89). Democrat. Roman Catholic. Avocations: writing children's stories, quilting, reading. Office: 10440 W Oakland Park Blvd Sunrise FL 33351-6822

PASMANICK, FRANCES VIRGINIA COHEN, admissions director; b. Portsmouth, Va., Jan. 24, 1923; d. Meyer and Lillian (Walker) Cohen; m. Kenneth Pasmanick, Dec. 22, 1946; children: Philip, Anne. Student, Am. Univ., 1941-46. Editl. analyst Army-Navy Electronics Prodn. Agy., Washington, 1941-48; adminstrv. asst. CIO Polit. Action Com., Washington, 1948-50, Nat. Farmers Union, Washington, 1950-52; adminstrv. asst. spl. project aging Com. Nat. Health, Washington, 1960-63; dir. admissions Georgetown Day Sch., Washington, 1963—. Writer, editor (newsletter) Georgetown Day Sch., 1971-73. Tchr. Reevaluation Counseling, 1975-85. Recipient Extraordinary Efforts award Black Student Fund, 1978. Mem. AAUW, Women's Action Nuc. Disarmament (founder Washington chpt. 1984). Democrat. Jewish. Avocations: travel, taichi, writing, poetry, grandparenting. Address: 5227 Chevy Chase Pkwy NW Washington DC 20015-1747

PASSTY, JEANETTE NYDA, English language educator, writer; b. LA, Calif., Jan. 19, 1947; d. Walter Isaac and Mollie Sarah Nyda; m. Gregory Bohdan Passty, June 18, 1976; 1 child, Benjamin. AA, L.A. Valley Coll., 1966; BA, UCLA, 1968; MA, U. So. Calif., 1974, PhD, 1982. Cert. tchr. instr., Calif. Tchg. asst., lectr., assoc. dir. freshman English program U. So. Calif., 1971-78; lectr. English dept. U. Tex., Austin, 1983-85; vis. asst. prof., adj. assoc. prof. Tex. Luth. U., Seguin, 1983, 85-87; from instr. to asst. prof. St. Philip's Coll., San Antonio, Calif., 1988-92, assoc. prof., 1992—. Lectr. UCLA, U. Tex., Austin, Western Mich. U., U. Louisville, Salisbury State U., Morehead State U., Tex. Tech. U., U. Wales, Bangor; humanities book reviewer CHOICE (ALA Jour.), 1985—86; manuscript reviewer Fairleigh Dickinson U. Press, 1991—; editl. cons. CONNECTIONS: Online Distance Learning Faculty Forum, 2002—. Author: Eros and Androgyny: The Legacy of Rose Macaulay, 1988, The Lion Tells Her Story: A Biography of the Honorable N.P. Brooks Hinton, 1998, Bringing Denis Home: The Hero from Hope, Kansas, 2001; annotator: Alice Crawford's Paradise Pursued, 1995; contbr. articles to encyclopedia and profl. jours.; guest Sta. KSPL Radio in Touch With, 1989; appearance Sta. KENS-TV, 1992; Channel 12 Morehead, KY, 1998, CNN, 1995, Roadside (entr'acte with G.S. Bailey), 2000. Mem. Nat. Abortion Rights Action League, Tex. Abortion Rights Action League, Greenpeace, Environ. Def. Fund, The Nature Conservancy, NOW, Sierra Club, Handgun Control Inc., Orgn. Internat. Conf. on the Holocaust, San Antonio, 2000. Recipient Elizabeth K. Pleasants Tchg. award, U. So. Calif., 1974, letters of appreciation, Lord Bonham-Carter, 1987, HRH Princess Margaret, 1989—90, Oustanding Acad. Book award, ALA, 1989, Women Honoring Women award, Am. Assn. Women in C.C.s, 1997, Katherine Anne Porter Lit. prize, 1999, NISOD Internat. Conf. on Tchg. and Leadership Excellence Award, 2003, St. Philip's Coll. Tchg. Excellence award, 2003—04; Vierling Kersey scholar, L.A. Valley Coll., 1964—66, NEH grantee, Tex. Luth. U., 1986. Mem. AAUW, MLA, Nat. Coun. Tchrs. English, South Ctrl. Soc. 18th Century Studies, Virginia Woolf Soc. Avocations: academic decathlon, taekwondo, arctic travel. Office: St Philip's Coll English Dept 1801 Martin Luther King Dr San Antonio TX 78203-2098 Office Phone: 210-531-3373.

PASSWATER, BARBARA GAYHART, real estate broker; b. Phila., July 10, 1945; d. Clarence Leonard and Margaret Jamison; m. Richard Albert Passwater, June 2, 1964; children: Richard Alan, Michael Eric. AA, Goldey-Beacom Coll., 1963; BA, Salisbury State U., 1981. Notary pub., Md. Sec. DuPont, Wilmington, Del., 1963-65, Nuclear-Chgo., Silver Spring, Md., 1965-67; office mgr. Montgomery County Sch. System, Wheaton, Md., 1977-79; adminstrv. asst. Solgar Nutritional Rsch. Ctr., Berlin, Md., 1979-94, asst. to v.p. R&D, 1995—2001; assoc. broker Prudential-Groff Realty, Berlin, Md., 1983-87, ReMax, Inc., Berlin, Md., 1987-88; broker, mgr., developers rep. River Run Sales Ctr., Berlin, Md., 1988-96; broker Solger Realty LLC, Berlin, Md., 1997-98, CAMBR Realty LLC, Berlin, 1998—. Treas. Ocean Pines (Md.) Vol. Fire Dept. Aux., 1981—84, emergency med. tech., 1983—95, life mem., 1996—; sec. Ocean Pines Fire Dept., 1990—95; mem. Citizens Rev. Bd., Snow Hill, Md., 1984—; state bd. del. Child Protection Sys.; bd. dirs. Worcester Gold, 2002—; mem. Worcester County Panel on Child Abuse and Neglect, 2002—; Worcester County organizer Rainbows, 2003—; Sunday sch. tchr. Cmty. Ch. of Ocean Pines, 1999—2004, co-chair nature and edn. com., 2000—04. Mem. Coastal Assn. of Realtors of Md., Inc., Beta Sigma Phi, Phi Kappa Phi. Avocations: photography, golf, grandchildren. Office: CAMBR Realty LLC 11017 Manklin Meadows Ln Berlin MD 21811-9340 Office Phone: 410-208-9006. E-mail: cambr@dmv.com.

PASTAN, LINDA OLENIK, poet; b. N.Y.C., May 27, 1932; d. Jacob L. and Bess (Schwartz) Olenik; m. Ira Pastan, 1953; children: Stephen, Peter, Rachel. BA, Radcliffe Coll., 1954; MLS, Simmons Coll., 1955; MA, Brandeis U., 1957. Author: (poetry) A Perfect Circle of Sun, 1971, On the Way to the Zoo, 1975, Aspects of Eve, 1975, The Five Stages of Grief, 1978 (Alice Fay di Castagnola award Poetry Soc. Am. 1978), Setting the Table, 1980, Waiting for My Life, 1981, PM/AM: New and Selected Poems, 1982 (Am. Book award nomination 1982), A Fraction of Darkness: Poems, 1985, The Imperfect Paradise, 1988, Heroes in Disguise, 1991, An Early Afterlife, 1995, Carnival Evening: New and Selected Poems, 1968-98 (nat. Book award nomination 1998), The Last Uncle, 2002. Recipient Dylan Thomas Poetry award Mademoiselle, 1958, Virginia Faulkner award Prarie Schooner, 1992, Charity Randall citation Internat. Poetry Forum, 1996, Ruth Lilly Poetry prize, 2003; NEA fellow; grantee Md. Arts Coun.; poet laureate of Md., 1991-95. Jewish. Office: 11710 Beall Mountain Rd Potomac MD 20854-1105 E-mail: lpastan@att.net.

PASTEN, LAURA JEAN, veterinarian; b. Tacoma, May 25, 1952; d. Frank Larry and Jean Mary (Slavich) Brajkovich. BA in Physiology with distinction, Stanford U., Davis, 1970; BA in Physiology, U. Calif., Davis, 1970, DVM, 1974; postgrad., Cornell U., 1975. Veterinarian Nevada County Vet. Hosp., Grass Valley, Calif., 1975-80; pvt. practice vet. medicine, owner Mother Lode Vet. Hosp., Grass Valley, 1980-96; veterinarian for Morris the 9-Lives cat (of TV comml. fame), 1985-94. Lectr. in field; spokesperson Nat. Cat Health Month; guest Today Show on wildlife. Author: Malignant, Tarantula Whisperer, Rocky Point Murders; contbg. author: Rocky Point Murders; pub. video How Smart is Your Puppy? Bd. dirs. Aguajito Property Owners Assn., Serrano Ranch Property Owners Assn., Sierra Svcs. for the Blind. Mem.: AOPA, AVMA, ASPCA, Bay Area Vet. Assn., Monterey Bay Vet Assn. (Carmel wildlife ednl. com., vet. coord. Monterey County Animal Disasters), Carmel Wildlife Edn. Com., Citizens Against Raccoon Extermination, Monterey SPCA, Denver Area Med. Soc.,

Am. Animal Hosp. Assn. (Mother Lode Hosp. cited for excellence), Mother Lode Vet. Assn., Calif. Vet. Med. Assn., Fund Animals Defenders Wildlife, Def. Animals, Inst. Protection Animals, In Def. of Animals, Humane Soc. U.S., Nature Conservancy, Am. Intenrat. Fund Animal Welfare, Internat. Vet. Med. Assn., Sierra Club, Big Sur Land Trust, Nat. Assn. Underwater Instrs., Rep. Womens Found. (bd. dirs.), Ninety-Nines Pilots Assn., Menoa. Republican. Lutheran. [illegible] Office: [illegible] Schulte Rd Carmel CA 93923-9477 E-mail: LPasten@aol.com.

PASTER, JANICE DUBINSKY, lawyer, former state legislator; b. St. Louis, Aug. 4, 1942; BA, Northwestern U., 1964; MA, Tufts U., 1967; JD, U. N.Mex., 1984. Bar: N.Mex. 1984. Atty. in pvt. practice, 1984—; mem. N.Mex. State Senate from 10th dist., 1988-96. Democrat. Home and Office: 5553 Eakes Rd NW Albuquerque NM 87107-5529

PASTERNAK, JOANNA MURRAY, humanities educator; b. Houston, Feb. 9, 1953; d. Lee Roy and Evelyn Mary (Kirmss) Murray; children: Sheila Ann Tanner, Lawrence Ross Tanner IV; m. Allen Pasternak, Jan. 9, 1993. BA in Liberal Arts with honors, Our Lady of the Lake, San Antonio, 1990; MA in Liberal Arts, U. St. Thomas, Houston, 1998. Acctg. clk. Houston Post, 1981-85; owner, art cons. Tanner Fine Art, Houston, 1985-92; spl. edn. tchr. Houston Ind. Sch. Dist., 1991-94, dept. chmn., 1994—, secondary social studies tchr., 2000—02; prof. and dept. chair humanities U. Phoenix, Houston, 2001—03. Art cons. Plz. Gallery, Houston, 1985; mem. benefits com. Houston Ind. Sch. Dist., 1992-2001; presenter Am. Fedn. Tchrs. Nat. Edn. Conf., 1994; staff rep. Houston Fed. Tchrs., 2003-. Contrb. articles to profl. jours. Vol. legis com. nat. health care campaign AFL-CIO; bd. dirs. PTA, SDMC; Dem. campaign worker, 1993—; precinct and state del. Dem. Senate, 1994-96, 98; sec. Dist. 13 Dem. Com., 1998; v.p. Houston Ind. Sch. Dist. Elem. Chess League, 1996-99; mem. edn. com. Harris County Dem. Com., mem. exec. com.; sec.-treas. Coalition of Cmty. and Commerce, 1997-2000; commr. Houston Bldg. and Stds. Commn., 1999-2002; precinct judge, chmn. precinct 139, Houston. Recipient Vick Driscoll award Tex. Commerce Bank, 1996. Mem. Am. Assn. Children with Learning Disabilities, Tex. Fedn. Tchrs. (bd. dirs. quality ednl. stds. in tchg. 1993, legis. com., chmn. 1993-99), Houston Fedn. Tchrs. (chmn. legis. liaison com. 1993-99, v.p. 1992-99, staff rep. 2003—), River Oaks Roadwomen, Delta Mu Delta. Democrat. Avocation: civic and political activities. Home: 2141 Colquitt St Houston TX 77098-3310

PASTOR, JENNIFER, sculptor; b. Hartford, 1966; BFA, Sch. Visual Arts, 1988; MFA in Sculpture, UCLA, 1992. One-woman shows include Richard Telles Fine Art, 1994, Studio Guenzani, Milan, Italy, 1995, Mus. Contemporary Art, Chgo., 1996, exhibited in group shows at Regen Projects, L.A., 1993, Richard Telles Fine Art, 1994, Studio Guenzani, Milan, 1996, La. Mus. Modern Art, Humleback, Denmark, 1997, Whitney Mus. Am. Art, N.Y.C., 1997, Mus. Modern Art, San Francisco, 1997, others. Louis Comfort Tiffany grantee, 1995. Office: c/o Richard Telles Fine Art 7380 Beverly Blvd Los Angeles CA 90036-2501

PASTORE, DONNA LEE, physical education educator; BA in Phys. Edn., U. Fla., 1981, MA in Phys. Edn., 1983; PhD, U. So. Calif., 1988. Instr. Pa. State U., Beaver, Pa.; asst. prof. Sch. Health Ohio State U., assoc. prof. Advisor Sports Mgmt. Club. Editl. bd. Jour. Sport Mgmt.; rev. Strategies. State coord. Nat. Girls and Women in Sport Day, 1992. Recipient NAGWS Linds to to Leadership award, 1982, NAGWS Rsch. award, 1983, Mabel Lee award, 1995. Mem. Ohio AHPERD (chair rsch. sect. higher edn., v.p.-elect sports sci. divsn., eastern dist. bylaws & oper. code com.), N. Am. Soc. Sports Mgmt. Office: Ohio State U Sch Phys Activity and Ednl Svcs 455 Larkins Hall 337 W 17th Ave Columbus OH 43210 E-mail: pastore.3@osu.edu.

PASTULA, LEAH LYNN, mental health services professional; d. Wendy Jo Haworth and Richard Joseph Pastula. BS, U. Tenn., 1994; MA, Mid. Tenn. State U., 1998; DD (hon.), Universal Life Ch., 1999. Psychol. intern Cmty. Devel. Svcs., Martin, 1994, Tenn. Prison Women, Nashville, 1996—97; crisis response specialist, triage supr., hosp. liaison Centerstone Cmty. Mental Health Centers, Inc., Nashville, 1999—2001; crisis response specialist Vol. Behavioral Health Care Sys., Gallatin, Tenn., 2002—. Recipient 1st Pl. 7th Ann. U.S. Open, Tae Kwon Do Championship, 1993, Gold and Silver medal, Tae Kwon Do Championship, U.S., 1994. Mem.: APA, Pinnacle (life), Psi Chi (life; sec. U. Tenn. Martin chpt. 1993—94), Phi Kappa Phi (life). Achievements include research in determining decision making power and relationship satisfaction among heterosexual married, heterosexual cohabiting, and lesbian cohabiting couples. Avocations: guitar, sports, computers, video games.

PASULA, ANGELA MARIE, lawyer; b. Michigan City, Ind., Oct. 2, 1956; d. Edward Joseph Pasula and Theresa Jeanette (Stella) Hack; m. David Mark Prusa, June 19, 1982. BA in Polit. Sci. cum laude, Western Mich. U., 1977; JD, Valparaiso U., 1980. Bar: Mich. 1980. Asst. pros. atty. Kalamazoo (Mich.) Prosecutors Office, 1980-82, Berrien County Prosecutors Office, Niles, Mich., 1982—. Office: Berrien County Prosecutors Office 1205 Front St Niles MI 49120-1627

PATAN, SYBILL PETRA, research scientist; b. Wetzlar, Germany, Feb. 8, 1955; arrived in U.S., 1994; d. Walter Wilhelm and Ingeborg Ursula Schmidt; m. Ulrich Helmut Patan, Sept. 2, 1983; 1 child, Maximilian Patan. MD, Justus-Liebig U., Giessen, Germany, 1980, Dr.med., 1988. Postdoctoral fellow Inst. Anatomy U. Bern, Switzerland, 1989—94; postdoctoral fellow dept radiation oncology Mass. Gen. Hosp., Boston, 1994—99; postdoctoral fellow dept. medicine Albert Einstein Coll. Medicine, Bronx, NY, 1999—2001, instr. dept. medicine, 2001—02. Asst. prof. anatomy and cell biology SUNY, 2002—. Contbr. articles to sci. publs. Recipient Gian Töndury award, Swiss Soc. Anatomy, 1990; grantee, Swiss and German Rsch. Founds., 1994—95, 1996—98. Mem.: Am. Heart Assn. (Scientist Devel. grantee 2001—04), Am. Assn. for Cancer Rsch., Union of Swiss Socs. for Exptl. Biology. Achievements include research in analysis of cellular mechanisms of intussusceptive microvascular growth in development and different states of disease; analysis of function of Tie-1 and Tie-2 Angiopoietin growth factor/receptor system. Office: SUNY Downstate Med Ctr 450 Clarkson Ave Brooklyn NY 11203-2098 Office Phone: 718-270-1016.

PATCHETT, ANN, writer; b. Los Angeles, Calif., 1963; BA, Sarah Lawrence College. Writer-in-residence Allegheny Coll., 1989—90; vis. asst. prof. Murray State U., 1992. Author: (novels) The Patron Saint of Liars, 1992 (James A. Michener/ Copernicus award for a book in progress, 1990, TV movie, 1997), Taft (also screenplay), 1994 (Janet Heidinger Kafka prize for the best work of fiction, 1994), The Magician's Assistant, 1997 (Nashville Banner Tennessee Writer of the Year Award), Bel Canto, 2001 (PEN/Faulkner prize, 2002), (non-fiction) Truth & Beauty, 2004; contbr. articles The New York Times Magazine, Chicago Tribune, Boston Globe, Vogue, GQ, Elle, Gourmet. Fellow Bunting Fellowship, Mary Ingrahm Bunting Institute at Radcliffe College, 1993, Guggenheim, 1994; grantee Residential fellowship, Fine Arts Work Ctr., Provincetown, Mass., 1990. Mailing: c/o HarperCollins Publishers 10 East 53rd Street New York NY 10022*

PATCHIN, REBECCA J. anesthesiologist, educator, administrator; b. Detroit, Dec. 8, 1949; d. Robert Ira and Doris J. (Hubert) P.; m. Carl W. Anderson, 1988. ASN, Pacific Union Coll., 1969; BSN, Walla Walla Coll., 1971; MD, Loma Linda U., 1989. Diplomate in anesthesiology and pain mgmt. Am. Bd. Anesthesiology. Resident in internalmedicine Loma Linda (Calif.) U. Med. Ctr., 1989-90, resident in anesthesiology, 1990-93, fellow in pain mgmt. dept. anesthesiology, 1993-94; asst. prof. anesthesiology Loma Linda U., 1994—; assoc. med. dir. Ctr. for Pain Mgmt., Loma Linda, 1995—. Presenter in field. Contbr. abstracts to profl. jours. Mem. AMA (mem. credentials com. 1986—, mem. awards com. bd. trustees 1988-89, del. ho. of dels. 1990—, mem. reference com. 1994—, chair coun. on med. [illegible] trustee 2002—), Internat. Anesthesiology Rsch. Soc., Internat. Assn. for Study of Pain, Am. Soc. Anesthesiology, Am. Pain Soc., Am. Soc. Regional Anesthesia, Am. Acad. Pain Medicine, Calif. Soc. Anesthesiology (del. resident component 1991-93, mem. com. on young physicians 1994—96, chair com. on young physicians 1996—), Calif. Med. Assn. (mem. reference com. 1988, trustee 1991-93, mem. com. on health professions and licensure 1992—, chair com. on health professions and licensure 1993-96, mem. coun. on legislation 1995-96, chair coun. on legislation 2000—), So. Calif. Cancer Pain Initiative, Riverside County Med. Assn. (sec.-treas 2002, pres. 2004), San Bernardino County Med. Soc. Office Phone: 951-413-0200.

PATE, JACQUELINE HAIL, retired data processing company executive; b. Amarillo, Tex., Apr. 7, 1930; d. Ewen and Virginia Smith (Crosland) Hail; children: Charles (dec.), John Durst, Virginia Pate Edgecomb, Christopher. Student, Southwestern U., Georgetown, Tex., 1947-48; grad., Real Estate Inst., 1998. Exec. sec. Western Gear Corp., Houston, 1974-76; adminstr., treas., dir. Aberrant Behavior Ctr., Personality Profiles, Inc., Corp. Procedures, Inc., Dallas, 1976-790; mgr. regional site svcs. programs Digital Equipment Corp., Dallas, 1979-92; ret., 1992. Realtor Keller Williams Realty, Austin, Tex., 1996—. Active Austin Bd. Realtors, PTA, Dallas, 1958-73. Mem. Daus. Republic Tex. (treas. French Legation state com. 1996). Methodist. Home: 6501 Brush Country #118 Austin TX 78749

PATÉ-CORNELL, MARIE-ELISABETH LUCIENNE, management and engineering educator; b. Dakar, Senegal, Aug. 17, 1948; arrived in U.S., 1971; d. Edouard Pierre Lucien and Madeleine (Tournissa) Paté; m. C. Allin Cornell, Jan. 3, 1981; children: Phillip Cornell, Ariane Cornell. Eng. Degree, Inst. Polytechnique de Grenoble, France, 1971; MS in Ops. Rsch., Stanford U., 1972, PhD in Engring.-Econ. Systems, 1978. Asst. prof. in civil engring. MIT, 1978-81; asst. prof. indsl. engring. Stanford (Calif.) U., 1981-84, assoc. prof. indsl. engring., 1984-91, prof. indsl. engring., 1991—, chmn. dept. indsl. engring., 1997-99, chmn. dept. mgmt. sci. and engring., 2000—. Cons. Electric Power Rsch. Inst., 1995, SRI Internat., 1993, Atty. Gen. of N.Mex., 1995, Halliburton, 2000, Swiss Re, 2002; mem. adv. coun. NASA, 1995—98; mem. Marine Bd. NRC, 1995—97; mem. Army Sci. Bd., 1995—97, Air Force Sci. Bd., 1998—2002, Calif. Coun. on Sci. and Tech., 2000—, Pres.'s Adv. Bd. on Fgn. Intelligence. Contbr. numerous articles to profl. jours. Numerous rsch. grants. Mem.: Nat. Acad. Engring. (councilor 2001—), Inst. for Mgmt. Scis., Ops. Rsch. Soc. Am., Soc. for Risk Analysis (councilor 1985—86, pres. 1995). Avocations: tennis, swimming, chess, music. Home: 110 Coquito Way Menlo Park CA 94028-7404 Office: Stanford U Dept Mgmt Sci and Engring Stanford CA 94305 E-mail: mep@leland.stanford.edu.

PATEL, MARILYN HALL, judge; b. Amsterdam, N.Y., Sept. 2, 1938; d. Lloyd Manning and Nina J. (Thorpe) Hall; m. Magan C. Patel, Sept. 2, 1966; children: Brian, Gian. BA, Wheaton Coll., 1959; JD, Fordham U., 1963. Bar: N.Y. 1963, Calif. 1970. Mng. atty. Benson & Morris, Esq., N.Y.C., 1962-64; sole practice N.Y.C., 1964-67; atty. U.S. Immigration and Naturalization Svc., San Francisco, 1967-71; sole practive San Francisco, 1971-76; judge Alameda County Mcpl. Ct., Oakland, Calif., 1976-80, U.S. Dist. Ct. (no. dist.) Calif., San Francisco, 1980—; now chief judge U.S. Dist. Ct. for No. Dist. Calif., San Francisco, 1998—. Adj. prof. law Hastings Coll. of Law, San Francisco, 1974-76 Author: Immigration and Nationality Law, 1974; also numerous articles Mem. bd. visitors Fordham U. Sch. Law. Mem. ABA (litigation sect., jud. adminstrn. sect.), ACLU (former bd. dirs.), NOW (former bd. dirs.), Am. law Inst., Am. Judicature Soc. (bd. dirs.), Calif Conf. Judges, Nat. Assn. Women Judges (founding mem.), Internat. Inst. (bd. dirs.), Advs. for Women (co-founder), Assn. Bus. Trial Lawyers (bd. dirs.). Democrat. Avocations: piano playing; travel. Office: US Dist Ct PO Box 36060 450 Golden Gate Ave Ste 36052 San Francisco CA 94102-3482

PATERIK, FRANCES SUE, secondary school educator, actress; b. Bloomington, Ill., Feb. 10, 1953; d. Francis LaVerne and Magaline Wilken. Student, Am. Cons. Music, Chgo., 1976—78, N.W. Ind. Opera Co., 1980, Hinsdale Opera Co., Ill., 1981; BA, MA, Western Ill. U., 1984. Tchg. asst. Western Ill. U., Macomb, 1982—84; music tchr. Cardinal Cmty. Schs., Eldon, Iowa, 1985—89, Johnston (Iowa) Cmty. Schs., 1990—94; music/performing arts tchr. Colfax (Iowa)-Mingo Cmty. Sch., 1995—2002, Merrill Middle Sch., Des Moines, 2002—. Dir. handbell choir First Christian Ch., Des Moines, 1996—2000; soprano soloist Des Moines Concert Singers, 1989—, Des Moines Choral Soc., 2002—. Actress : (various comedic roles) Ingersoll Dinner Theatre; Playhouse; Drama Workshop; Stage West. Mem.: Iowa Choral Dirs. Assn., Am. Choral Dirs. Assn., Music Educators Nat. Conf., Nat. Wildlife Fedn., Sierra Club. Democrat. Avocations: gardening, animal welfare, dance. Office: Des Moines Pub Schs Des Moines IA 50312

PATERSON, KATHERINE WOMELDORF, writer; b. Huaiyin, China, Oct. 31, 1932; came to U.S., 1940; d. George Raymond and Mary Elizabeth (Goetchius) Womeldorf; m. John Barstow Paterson, July 14, 1962; children: Elizabeth Polin, John Barstow, David Lord, Mary Katherine Nah-he-sah-pe-che-a. AB, King Coll., Bristol, Tenn., 1954; post grad., Kobe Sch. Japanese Lang., 1957-60; MA, Presbyn. Sch. Christian Edn., 1957; MRE, Union Theol. Sem., 1962; LittD. (hon.), King Coll., Bristol, Tenn., 1978; LHD (hon.), Otterbein Coll., 1979; LittD (hon.), St. Mary's of the Woods, 1981, Washington and Lee U., 1982, U. Md., 1982, Shenandoah Coll., 1982; LHD, Washington and Lee U, 1982, Norwich U., 1990, Mount St. Vincent U., Halifax, N.S., Can., 1994; LittD, Hope Coll., 1997; DLitt (hon.), Prebyn. Coll., 2002. Tchr. Lovettsville Elem. Sch., Va., 1954-55; missionary Presbyn. Ch., Japan, 1957-61; master sacred studies and English Pennington Sch. for Boys, NJ, 1963-65. Author: The Sign of the Chrysanthemum, 1973, Of Nightingales That Weep, 1974, The Master Puppeteer, 1976, Bridge to Terabithia, 1977, The Great Gilly Hopkins, 1978, Angels and Other Strangers, 1979, Jacob Have I Loved, 1980, Rebels of the Heavenly Kingdom, 1983, Come Sing, Jimmy Jo, 1985, (with John Paterson) Consider the Lilies, 1986, Park's Quest, 1988, The Tale of the Mandarin Ducks, 1990, The Smallest Cow in the World, 1991, Lyddie, 1991, The King's Equal, 1992, Who Am I?, 1992, Flip-Flop Girl, 1994, A Midnight Clear: Stories for the Christmas Season, 1995, A Sense of Wonder, 1995, The Angel and the Donkey, 1996, Jip: His Story, 1996, Marvin's Best Christmas Present Ever, 1997, (with John Paterson) Images of God, 1998, Parzival, 1998, Celia and the Sweet, Sweet Water, 1998, Preacher's Boy, 1999, The Wide-Awake Princess, 2000, The Field of the Dogs, 2001, Marvin One Too Many, 2001, The Invisible Child, 2002, The Same Stuff as Stars, 2002; translator: The Crane Wife, 1981, The Tongue-Cut Sparrow, 1987. US nominee for Hans Christian Andersen award, 1979, 89, 97; recipient Nat. Book award, 1977, 79, Newbery medal, 1978, 91, Newbery honor, 1979, New Eng. Book award New Eng. Booksellers Assn., 1982, Union medal Union Theol. Sem., 1992, Scott O'Dell award for hist. fiction, 1997, May Hill Arbuthnot Lectr. award, 1997, Hans Christian Andersen award, 1998, Lion award NY Pub. Libr., 1998, Literary Light award Boston Pub. Libr., 2000, Living Legend award Libr. of Congress, 2000, Jefferson cup Va. Libr. Assn., 2000, Vt. Gov.'s award for excellence in arts, 2001. Mem. Authors Guild, Children's Book Guild Washington. Democrat. Office: Clarion Books 215 Park Ave S New York NY 10003-1603*

PATMORE, KIMBERLY S. financial services executive; BBA, U. Toledo. CPA, Colo. With Ernst & Young; joined First Data Corp., Inglewood, Colo., 1992, exec. v.p., CFO, 2000—. Mem. Gov.'s Commn. on Sci. and Tech., Colo. Bd. dirs. Coors Tek, Girls Scouts, Family Tree Found. Office: First Data Corp 6200 S Quebec St Inglewood CA 90301

PATON WALSH, JILL, writer; b. London, Apr. 29, 1937; d. John Llewelyn and Patricia (Dubern) Buss; m. Antony Edmund Paton Walsh, Aug. 5, 1961; Children: Edmund, Margaret, Clare. Author: Hengest's Tale, 1966, The Dolphin Crossing, 1967, Fireweed, 1969, (World Book Festival award 1970), Wordhoard, 1969, Goldengrove 1972, Farewell Great King, 1972, Toolmaker, 1973, The Dawnstone, 1973, The Emporer's Winding Sheet, 1974 (Whitbread prize 1974), The Huffler, 1975, The Island Sunrise: Preshistoric Culture in the British Isles, 1975, Unleaving, 1976 (Boston Globe, Horn Book award 1976), Children of the Fox: Crossing to Salamis, 1977, The Walls of Athens, 1978, Persian Gold, 1978, A Chance Child, 1978, The Green Book, 1981, Babylon, 1982, Parcell of Patterns, 1983 (Universe prize 1984), Lost and Found, 1984, Gaffer Samson's Luck, 1984 (Smarties Grand prix 1984), Lapsing, 1985, A School for Lovers, 1989, Birdy and the Ghosties, 1990, "Grace", 1991, Matthew and the Sea Singers, 1992, When Grandma Came, 1992, The Wydham Case, 1993, Knowledge of Angels, 1994, A Piece of Justice, 1995, Connie Came to Play, 1995, Thomas and the Tinners, 1995, The Serpentine Cave, 1997, When I Was Little Like You, 1997, (with Dorothy L. Sayers) Thrones, Dominations, 1998, A Desert in Bohemia, 2000, (with Dorothy L. Sayers) A Presumption of Death, 2002. Fellow Royal Soc. of Lit. (CBE award 1996). Address: care David Higham Assocs 5-8 Lower John St Golden Sq London W1R 3PE England

PATRICK, BETH PELLETIER, art educator; b. San Francisco, Calif., Oct. 1, 1947; d. Betty Mary Pelletier; m. Richard Lynn Patrick; 1 child, Ellen. BA in Comprehensive Music Edn., West Liberty State Coll., 1969; MMus, Kent State U., 2000; postgrad., Ashland U., 2002. Cert. in supervision and adminstrn., Pathwise Level II, Orff Schulwerk - Level I, Level II. Educator Indian Creek Sch. Dist., Wintersville, Ohio, 1969—75, Canton City Sch. Dist., Canton, Ohio, 1989—95, specialist fine arts curriculum, 1995—2001; coord. dept. human resources Canton City Schs., 2002—; adj. prof. Ashland U. - Stark Campus, Ashland, Ohio, 1995—, Malone Coll., Canton. Adv. com. mem. Arts Stds. Ohio Dept. Edn., Columbus, 1998—, Praxis III state assessor, trainer Pathwise Level I, Ohio First Trainer of Trainers, entry yr. adv. coun. mem., mem. adv. com. State Arts Edn.; Education Adv. Bd. mem. Malone Coll., Canton, 1997—; com. mem. Kent State U./CCS, Kent, 2001—; mem. adv./steering com. Stark County Arts Stark County Ednl. Svc. Ctr., Canton, 1995—. Contbr. articles to profl. jours. Mem.: ASCD, NEA, Ohio Art Edn. Assn. (conf. presenter 1998—2002), Ohio Music Edn. Assn. (sec.-treas. East Ctrl. chpt.), Ohio Music Edn. Assn., Ohio Mid. Sch. Assn., Nat. Mid. Sch. Assn., Music Edn. Nat. Conf. (conf. presenter), Ohio Edn. Assn., Canton Profl. Edn. Assn., Ohio Alliance for Arts Edn. (pres. 2000—), Ohio Citizens for Arts. Avocations: knitting, embroidery, travel. Home: 1916 Hillocke St Louisville OH 44641 Office: Canton City School District 617 McKinley Ave SW Canton OH 44707 Home Fax: 330-875-9095; Office Fax: 330-875-9095. Personal E-mail: bpatrick@neo.rr.com. Business E-Mail: patrick_b@ccsdistrict.org.

PATRICK, ERLINE M. federal agency administrator; BA in Biology, Talladega Coll., 1960; MEd in Urban Edn., U. Hartford, 1971, 6th yr. cert. adminstrn. and supervision, 1974; PhD, U. Conn., 1992. Secondary sch. math. and sci. tchr., Pa., N.C. and Conn., 1960-71; vice prin. Hartford (Conn.) Bd. Edn., 1971-78, prin., 1978-84; exec. asst. program devel. Sys. Mgmt. Am. Corp., Arlington, Va., 1984-85; profl. staff mem. U.S. Senate Small Bus. Com., Washington, 1985-89; assoc. adminstr. minority small bus. devel. program U.S. Small Bus. Adminstrn., Washington, 1989-91, dir. office program rev., 1991-94, asy. liaison to Dept. HUD for Pres.' Empowerment Initiative, 1994, dep. assoc. adminstr. small bus. devel. ctrs., 1994-95, asst. adminstr. OEO Civil Rights, 1995—. Contbr. articles to profl. jours. Corporator Hartford Sem. Found., 1978—; active various civic and charitable orgns. NSF grantee Columbia U., 1963, Franklin and Marshall Coll., 1965; Nat. Edn. Policy fellow George Washington, 1978-79; apptd. Adm. Great Navy of State of Nebr., 1989-91; recipient Svc. award Nat. Urban League, 1981, citations for Outstanding Ednl. Leadership, City of Hartford and State of Conn., 1982-84, Disting. Alumni award U. Hartford, 1978-84, Charlotte Jazz Club award, 1962, various trade assn. awards for leadership and svc., 1989—. Mem. NAACP, Exec. Women in Govt., Greater Washington Talladega Alumni Assn. (pres. 1993—). Address: 417 S 96th St Omaha NE 68114-4968

PATRICK, LAURA DAPHENE LAYMAN, retired physicist; b. Pensacola, Fla., Mar. 29, 1968; d. Richard and Faye Layman; m. Brian C. Patrick, Apr. 3, 1993. BS in Physics, U. Ala., Huntsville, 1993. Analyst Delta Rsch., Inc, Huntsville, Ala., 1993—2001; ret. Home: 112 Blackberry Lane Gurley AL 35748

PATRICK, MARY KATHLEEN, freelance/self-employed writer, food service executive; b. Daytona Beach, Fla., Aug. 19, 1976; d. William Minor and Mary Kathleen Hawk; m. Mark Andrew Patrick, June 20, 1998. BA in Pub. Adminstrn., BA in Sociology, U. Ctrl. Fla., 2001. Freelance writer. Poet: www.poetry.com, 2001. Mem.: ASPA, Internat. Soc. of Poets, Nat. Writer's Union. R-Consevative. Avocations: swimming, hiking, reading, writing, cooking. Personal E-mail: kathleenpatrickm@yahoo.com.

PATRICK, MICHELE MARY, government official; b. Phila., Apr. 18, 1963; d. George Robert and Mary Elizabeth (Pristic) P. BA with honors in Econs., La Salle U., 1985; M in Govt. Adminstrn., U. Pa., 1990. Intern Phila. Water Dept., 1987; intern, asst. to exec. dir. Global Interdependence Ctr., Phila., 1988-89; intern, asst. to dep. dir. Phila. Fin. Dept., 1989, asst. to fin. dir., 1990; asst. mng. dir. City of Phila., 1990-91, 93-96; speechwriter to U.S. Senator Frank R. Lautenberg, 1996-97; speechwriter to Hon. Donna Shalala U.S. Sec. Health and Human Svcs., 1997—. Speaker in field. Author: Haunted Prague; co-author: sect. of Municipal Dept. Handbook; trivia writer Merit Inds., Bensalem, Pa., 1993-95; monthly columnist Global Stamp News, 1994-96. Recipient Fulbright fellowship, U.K., Bd. Fgn. Scholarships, Washington, 1985, Nat. Resource fellowship, Pacific-Asian Mgmt. Inst., U. Hawaii, 1984, Lindback award, La Salle U., Phila., 1985, Pa. Forensic Assn., State Championships, 1982, 83, 85, Nat. Forensic Assn. Nat. championship, 1985, Meyerson fellowship, U. Pa., Phila., 1987, Pres. Classroom scholarship, Pres. Classroom for Young Ams., Washington, 1982, James and Helen Hovorka scholarship, Coun. Higher Edn., Brookfield, Ill., 1982, 83, 84. Mem. Amnesty Internat., Am. Friends of Czech Republic, Fulbright Alumni Assn., Omicron Delta Epsilon. Avocations: historical travel, classical music, british and russian studies.

PATRICK, RUTH (MRS. RUTH HODGE VAN DUSEN), limnologist, diatom taxonomist, educator; b. Topeka, Kans. d. Frank and Myrtle (Jetmore) Patrick; m. Charles (IV) Hodge, July 10, 1931; 1 child, Charles (V). BS, Coker Coll., 1929; MS, U. Va., 1931, PhD, 1934; LLD (hon.), Coker Coll., 1971; LHD (hon.), Chestnut Hill Coll, 1974; DSc (hon.), Beaver Coll., 1970, PMC Colls., 1971, Phila. Coll. Pharmacy and Sci., 1973, Wilkes Coll., 1974, Cedar Crest Coll., 1974, U. New Haven, 1975, Hood Coll., 1975, Med. Coll. Pa., 1975, Drexel U., 1975, Swarthmore Coll., 1975, Bucknell U., 1976, Rensselaer Poly. Inst., 1976, St. Lawrence U., 1978, U. Mass., 1980, Princeton U., 1980, Lehigh U., 1983, U. Pa., 1984, Temple U., 1985, Emory U., 1986, Wake Forest U., 1986, U. S.C., 1989, Clemson, 1989, Glassboro State Coll., 1992. Assoc. curator microscopy dept. Acad. Natural Scis., Phila., 1939-47; curator Leidy Micros. Soc., 1937-47, curator limnology dept., 1947—, chmn. limnology dept., 1947-73; occupant Francis Boyer Research Chair Acad. Natural Scis., Phila., 1973—, chmn. bd. trustees, 1973-76, hon. chmn. bd. trustees, 1976—; lectr. U. Pa., 1950-70, adj. prof., 1970—; guest Fellow of Saybrook Yale, 1975. Participant Am. Philos Soc. limnology expdn. to Mexico, 1947; leader Catherwood Found. expdn. to Peru and Brazil, 1955; del. gen. assembly Internat. Union Biol. Scis., Bergen, Norway, 1947; bd. dirs. E.I. Du Pont, Pa. Power and Light Co.; chmn. algae com. Smithsonian Oceanographic Sorting Ctr., 1963—68; mem. panel on water blooms Pres. Sci. Adv. Com., 1966; mem. panel on water resources and water pollution Gov.'s Sci. Adv. Com., 1966; mem. nat. tech. adv. com. on water quality requirements for fish and other aquatic life and wildlife Dept. Interior, 1967—68; mem. citizen's adv. coun. Pa. Dept. Environ. Resources, 1971—73; mem. hazardous materials adv. com. EPA, 1971—74, exec. adv. com., 1974—79; chmn. com.'s panel on ecology, 1974—76; mem. Pa. Gov.'s Sci. Adv. Coun., 1972; mem. exec. adv. com. nat. power survey FPC, 1972—75; mem. coun. Smithsonian Instn., 1973—; mem. Phila. Adv. Coun., 1973—76; mem. energy R&D adv. coun. Pres.s Emergy Policy Office, 1973—74; mem. adv. coun. Renewable Nat. Resources Found., 1973—76, Electric Power Rsch. Found., 1973—77; mem. adv. com. for rsch. NSF, 1973—74; mem. gen. adv. com. ERDA, 1975—77; mem. adv. bd. Sec. Energy, 1975—89; mem. com. on human resources NRC, 1975—76; trustee Biological Abstracts, 1974—76; mem. adv. coun. dept. biology Princeton U., 1975—80; mem. com. on sci. and arts Franklin Inst., 1978—; mem. univ. coun. com. Yale Sch. Forestry and Environ. Studies, 1978—80; mem. sci. adv. coun. World Wildlife Fund-US, 1978—80; trustee Aquarium Soc., Phila., 1951—58, Henry Found.; bd. dirs. Wissahickon Valley Watershed Assn.; bd. govs. Nature Conservancy; bd. mgrs. Wistar Inst. Anatomy and Biology. Author: (series of volumes) Rivers of the United States Vol. 1, 1994, Rivers of the United States Vol. 2, 1997, Chemical and Physical Characteristics Vol. 3, 1995, Rivers of Atlantic and Eastern Gulf Drainage Vol. 4, The Mississipi River and Major Tributaries; co-author (with C.W. Reimer): Diatoms of the United States Vol. 1, 1966, Vol. II, Part 1, 1975; co-author: (with others) (books) Ground Water Contamination in the United States, 1983, 2nd edit.; co-author: (with others) (book) Surface Water Quality: Have the Laws Been Successful?, 1992; mem. editorial bd.with C. W. Reimer: sci. jours. Science, 1974—76, mem. editorial bd.: sci. jours. American Naturalist; contbr. articles over 150 to profl. jours. Recipient Disting. Dau. of Pa. award, 1952, Richard Hopper Day Meml. medal, Acad. Nat. Scis., 1969, Gimbel Phila. award, 1969, Gold medal, YWCA, 1970, Lewis L. Dollinger Pure Environment award, Franklin inst., 1970, Pa. award for excellence in sci. and tech., 1970, Eminent Ecologist award, Ecol Soc. Am., 1972, Phila. award, 1973, Gold medal, Pa. State Fish and Game Protective Assn., 1974, Internat. John and Alice Tyler Ecology award, 1975, Gold meda;, Phila. Soc. for Promoting Agr., 1975, Pub. Svc. award, U.S. Dept. Interior, 1975, Iben award, Am. Water Resources Assn., 1976, Outstanding Alumna award, Coker Coll., 1977, Francis K. Hutchinson medal, Garden Club of Am., 1977, Golden medal, Royal Zool. Soc., Antwerp, 1978, Green World award, N.Y. Bot. Garden, 1979, Hugo Black award, U. Ala., 1979, Sci award, Gov. Pa., 1988, Founders award, Soc. Environ. Toxicology and Chemistry, 1982, Environ. Regeneration award, Rene DuBois Ctr., 1985, Disting. Citizen award, Pa., 1989, Excellence award, N. Am. Benthological Soc., 1993, Benjamin Frankln medal, Am. Philosophical Soc., 1993, U.S. medal of svc., Pres. Bill Clinton, 1996, Nat. medal for sci., 1997, Nat. Wetlands award, 2000, Sci. Edn. Ctr. named in her honor, U. S.C., 1989. Fellow: AAAS (com. environ. alternatives 1973—74); mem.: Internat. Phycol. Soc., Am. Inst. Biol. Scis., Ecol. Soc. Am., Am. Soc. Naturalists (pres. 1975—76), Am. Soc. Limnology and Oceanography (Lifetime Achievement award 1996), Am. Soc. Plant Taxonomy, Internat. Soc. Plant Taxonomists, Internat. Limnological Soc., Phycol Soc. Am. (pres. 1954), Bot. Soc. Am.. (mem. Darbarker prize com. 1956, Merit award 1971), Am. Acad. Arts and Scis., Assn. Metro. Sewage Agys. (Environ. award 1995), Am. Philos. Soc. (Benjamin Franklin Outstanding Sci. Achievement award 1993), Nat. Acad. Engring. (com.environ. engr. study explicit criteria for power plant siting 1973), Nat. Acad. Scis. (chmn. panel com. on pollution 1966, mem.environ. measures panel com. remote sensing earth resources survey 1973—74, mem. nominating com. 1973—75, mem. com. sci. and public policy 1973—77), Water Pollution Control Fedn. (hon.), Soc. Study Evolution, Sigma Xi. Presbyterian. Office: Acad Natural Scis 19th at Benjamin Franklin Pkwy Philadelphia PA 19103

PATRICK, SUSAN D. government agency administrator; B in English, Colo. Coll.; M in Comm. Mgmt., U. So. Calif. Dir. distance learning campus Old Dominion U.; coord. Digital State Survey 2002 State of Ariz.; dep. dir. Office Edn. Tech. U.S. Dept. Edn., Washington. Office: US Dept Edn Rm FB6-7E208 400 Maryland Ave SW Washington DC 20202

PATRIE, CHERYL CHRISTINE, elementary school educator; b. Dobbs Ferry, N.Y., June 8, 1947; d. Edward F. and Antoinette C. (Patrie) P. BA in Edn., U. Fla., 1969; MS in Edn., U. Miami, 1979. Cert. assoc. master tchr., Fla. Tchr. Marion County Sch. Bd., Ocala, Fla., 1970, Dade County Sch. Bd., Miami, 1973—. Mem. faculty coun. Lorah Park lem. Sch., Miami, 1979-89, 1991—, career lab. cons., 1983-85, human growth and devel. cons., 1983—, phys. fitness co-chmn., 1984-90, chair dept., 1993—; coord. quality instrn. incentives program, 1984-89; mem. Dade County Elem. Sch. Day Task Force, 1987-88. Mem. United Tchrs. Dade (bldg. union steward 1979-89, mem. crisis in inner city task force 1984-85, Disting. Svc. award 1984). Home: 1127 Robin Ave Miami FL 33166-3129 Office: Lorah Park Elem 5160 NW 31st Ave Miami FL 33142-3439

PATRON, JUNE EILEEN, former government official; b. N.Y.C., May 15; d. Irving B. and Mollie Patron. BA in Govt. with honors, Clark U., Worcester, Mass., 1965; MA, Am. U., 1967. With U.S. Dept. Labor, 1966-95, dir. Black Lung benefits program, 1976-79, asst. adminstr. pension and welfare benefit programs, 1979-84, assoc. dir. pension and welfare benefit programs, 1984-88, dir. program svcs., 1988-95; ret., 1995. Mem. Sr. Exec. Svc.; ind. contractor, mgmt. cons., 1997—. Vol. alumni admissions program Clark U., 1998—. Van Ness Neighborhood Network, 2003—. Recipient various awards Dept. Labor. Mem. Nat. Assn. Ret. Fed. Employees, Sr. Execs. Assn. Home: 3001 Veazey Ter NW Washington DC 20008-5454 E-mail: jpdcny@aol.com.

PATSTONE, CHERYL, public relations executive; b. Boston, May 4, 1955; d. Harold E. and Anna M. Brown; m. Walter Patstone, Nov. 10, 1979. BA in Econs. and French, Tufts U., 1977. Sr. economist, editor electronic bus. forecast Cahners Pub. Co., San Jose, Calif., 1977-87; mgr. pub. rels. Nat. Semiconductor Corp., Santa Clara, Calif., 1987-91, Marcom team leader comm. and computing group, 1991-96, dir. product pub. rels., 1996-99, dir. strategic Marcom programs, 1999—; v.p. comm. Autoweb-.com, Inc., Santa Clara, 2000—; dir. corp. comm. Atheros Comms., Inc., Sunnyvale, Calif., 2001—. Mem. Internat. Assn. Bus. Communicators, No. Calif. Bus. Mktg. Assn. (bd. dirs., v.p. programs 1999-2000). Office: Atheros Comms 529 Almanor Ave Sunnyvale CA 94085 E-mail: cheryl@atheros.com.

PATTEN, BETSEY LELAND, state legislator; b. Newton, Mass., Apr. 26, 1945; m. Richard C. Patten; 1 child. Student, Kings Coll. State rep. N.H. Ho. Reps., chmn. mcpl. and county govt. com. Chmn. Joint Legis. Com. on Adminstrv. Rules, Assessing Standards Bd., Carroll County Rep. Com., 1996—; mem. state exec. com. N.H. State Rep. Party, 1996—. Home: HC62 Box 415 46 Patten Hill Rd Center Harbor NH 03226 E-mail: rcpatten@worldpath.net.

PATTEN, CHRISTINE TAYLOR, artist; b. L.A., Oct. 17, 1940; d. Malcolm Clark and Virginia (Strong) Patten; children: Robert Roy Powell Jr., Jonathan Taylor Powell, Matthew Clark Powell, Michael Neal Powell; m. Gendron Jensen, Aug. 15, 1987. Student, Pasadena City Coll., 1958-59, 70-72, U. Oreg., 1959-60; BFA, Otis Art Inst., L.A. County, 1974. Tchr. drawing and painting Pacificulture-Asia Mus., Pasadena Art Mus., 1973-74. Author: O'Keeffe at Abiquiu, 1995, Miss O'Keeffe, 1992; exhibitions include SITE Santa Fe, Calif. Mus. Sci. and Industry, L.A., Armory for the Arts, Santa Fe, Mus. N.Mex., Mus. Fine Arts, Santa Fe, Santa Barbara (Calif.) City Coll., Pepperdine U., Malibu, Calif., Ctr. for Contemporary Arts, Santa Fe, exhibited in group shows at Addison-Ripley Gallery, Washington, Albuquerque Mus., Horwitch LewAllen Gallery, Santa Fe, exhibitions include Coll. Santa Fe, Knoedler Gallery, N.Y.C., Exit Art, others, Represented in permanent collections L.A. County Mus. Art, Albright-Knox Art Gallery (Mus.), Buffalo, Albuquerque Mus., U. N.Mex., Mus. N.Mex., Mus. Fine Arts, Harwood Mus., The Old Jail Mus., James Kelly Contemporary, Santa Fe, pvt. collections. Santa Fe Arts Coun. grantee, 1985. Home: PO Box 194 Vadito NM 87579-0194 E-mail: murasaki@laplaza.com.

PATTERSON, BEVERLY ANN GROSS, not-for-profit fundraiser, consultant, social services administrator; b. Pauls Valley, Okla., Aug. 5, 1938; d. Wilburn G. Jack and Mildred E. (Steward) Gross; m. Kenneth Dean Patterson, June 18, 1960 (div. 1976); children: Tracy Dean Patterson, Nancy Ann Patterson-McArthur, Beverly Jeanne Patterson-Wertman. AA, Modesto (Calif.) Jr. Coll., 1958; BA in Social Sci., Fresno (Calif.) State U., 1960; M in Community Counseling, Coll. Idaho; postgrad., Stanislaus State Coll., Turlock, Calif., U. Idaho, Boise (Idaho) State U. Cert. secondary tchr., Calif., Idaho, lic. real estate agt., Idaho. Secondary tchr., Ceres and Modesto Calif., Payette and Weiser Idaho, Ontario Oreg., 1960-67; dir. vol. svcs. mental retardation and child devel. State of Idaho, 1967-70, cons. dir. vol. svcs. health and welfare, 1970-72; dir. Ret. Sr. Vol. Program, Boise, 1972-74; exec. dir. Idaho Nurses Assn., Boise, 1974-76; community svcs. adminstr. City of Davis, Calif., 1976-78; dir. devel. and fundraising Mercy Med. Ctr., Nampa, Idaho, 1978-85; exec. dir. St. Alphonsus Med. Ctr. Found., Boise, 1985-87; dir. devel. and gift planning Idaho Youth Ranch, Boise, 1989-94; fund devel. cons. Mercy Housing, Nampa, Idaho, 1994-96, Pratt Ranch Boys Home, Emmett, Idaho, 1994-96, Northwest Childrens Home, Lewiston, Idaho, 1994-96, Idaho Spl. Olympics, Boise, 1994-95, Idaho Found. for Parks and Lands, Boise, 1994-95, St. Vincent de Paul, Inc., Boise, 1995-96, Nampa Shelter Found., Inc., 1994-95, Turning Point Inc., Nampa, 1994-95, Port of Hope Treatment Ctr. Inc., Boise, 1994-97, Idaho Theater for Youth, Inc., Boise, 1995-96, Boise Tennis Coalition, Inc., 1995-2000, El Ada Cmty. Action Ctr., Boise, 1995, Hemophilia Found. Idaho, 1995-96, Boise YWCA, 1996, Marsing (Idaho) Sch. Dist., 1996-98. Founder Fellowship Christian Adult Singles, Boise, 1974; cons., exec. dir. Boise Hotline, 1988-90; co-dir. ACOA workshop leader Child Within Concepts, Inc., Boise, 1987—; cons. coord. Rural Hosp. Edn. Consortium, 1988; cons. hosp. fund devel. and cmty. resources Gritman Meml. Hosp., Moscow, Idaho, 1987-88; cons., conf. coord. State of Idaho, 1987-88; counsel Adult Children of Alcoholics, 1991; pres. Nonprofit Solutions, Inc., Boise, 1995—; co-dir. Child Within Concepts, Inc., Meridian, 1996—; cmty. resource devel. specialist Idaho Dept. Health and Welfare, 1997-2000, United Way Portland, 2000; chmn., pres. Creative Solutions P.A., 2000—; grant writing cons. sch. dist. # 3JT, Oreg., Tillamook Sch. Dist., Oreg., Banks Sch. dist., Oreg., North West Regional Edul. Svcs. Dist., Oreg. Contbr. articles to profl. jours. Coord. Idaho Golf Angels Open Pro-Am Tournament, Boise, 1989-91; founding exec. v.p. Coll. Fund for Students Surviving Cancer, 1993-96; bd. dirs. Arthritis Found., Idaho, 1984-86, Idaho Mental Health Assn., 1978-97; founder Ctrl. Vol. Bur., Boise, 1971. Named Idaho Statesman Disting. Citizen, 1985. Mem. Nat. Assn. for Hosp. Devel. (accredited, treas. 1980, accreditation chmn. 1984-86, conf. chmn. 1982, 85), Assn. Healthcare in Philanthrophy (accredited), Nat. Soc. Fund Raising Execs., Idaho Devel. Network, Choices in Giving, Inc. Avocations: golf, family activities. Address: 9451 N Polk Ave Portland OR 97203-1630

PATTERSON, CAROLYN F. retired English educator; b. Winnsboro, S.C., Nov. 7, 1935; d. William Lyle and Alma (Wilson) Ferguson; m. Marion Symmes Patterson, Dec. 16, 1956; 1 child, Marion. AB, Lander U., 1957; MEd, Clemson U., 1973. English tchr. Greenwood (S.C.) Sch. Dist. #50, 1958-89; asst. prin. Greenwood H.S., 1989-94, Emerald H.S., 1994-97. Mem. Ch. of Jesus Christ of Latter-Day Saints. Home: 1814 N Echo Ave Fresno CA 93704-6046 Address: Calif Fresno Mission 1814 N Echo Ave Fresno CA 93704-6046

PATTERSON, CHAN, food service executive; Dir., prin. instr. Everyday Gourmet, Jackson, Miss. Featured on Miss. Morning (WJTV), recipes appeared in nat. mags. Mem.: Internat. Assn. Culinary Profls., Am. Inst. Wine and Food. Office: Everyday Gourmet 1625 E County Line Rd Jackson MS 39216

PATTERSON, CLAIRE ANN, career techincal educator; b. Cin., Dec. 28, 1950; d. Lloyd E. and Ruth T. (Flaherty) Lachtrupp; m. Calvin Stanley Patterson, Jr., July 14, 1973; children: Christopher, Alicia. BS, U. Cin., 1973, MEd, 1980. Cert. elem. tchr., elem. supr., secondary math, secondary prin., asst. supt., Ohio., Va., P.R. Third grade tchr. Academia de Aguidilla, P.R., 1973-74; fifth grade tchr. Our Lady of the Rosary, Norfolk, Va., 1974-76; jr. high math and sci. tchr. Yavneh Hebrew Day Sch., Cin., 1976-79; math tchr. Winton Woods City Schs., Cin., 1979-80; math. coord. Great Oaks Inst. of Tech. and Career Devel., Cin., 1980-86, benefits coord./personnel profl., 1986-88, career devel. mgr., 1987-93, asst. dir., 1993-97, dean of instrn., 1998-99, mgr. testing and assessment, 1999—2001, mgr. profl. devel., 2001—03, dir. human resources, 2003—. Ednl. cons. schs. in Ohio, 1988—. Author: Let's Celebrate Math, 1991; contbr. articles to profl. jours. Mem. Ohio Career Devel. Task Frce, 1991-93. Recipient Career Coord. award State of Ohio, 1993. Mem. Ohio Vocat. Assn. (com. chmn. 1990-93, pres. 1997-2000, Pacesetter award 1991, 92, 93, Trendsetter award 1998, 99), Career Edn. Assn. (pres. 1992-93), Nat. Coun. Local Adminstrs., S.W. Career Coun. (pres. 1991-92), Ohio Vocat. Edn. Leadership Inst. (grad. 1993). Republican. Roman Catholic. Avocations: writing murder-mystery plays, travel, reading. Office: Great Oaks Inst Tech and Career Devel 3254 E Kemper Rd Ste 3 Cincinnati OH 45241-1581 Home: 279 Beechridge Dr Cincinnati OH 45216 E-mail: pattersc@greatoaks.com.

PATTERSON, DEB, university women's head basketball coach; Grad., Rockford Coll., 1979. Asst. coach, recruiting coord. No. Ill. U., 1986-91; asst. coach So. Ill. U., 1991-92; top asst. coach, recruiting coord. Vanderbilt U., 1992-96; head coach Kans. State U., 1996—. Asst. coach 1997 World U. Games; women's sr. nat. team asst. coach USA Invitational Tournament of Champions, 1997. Named Women's Coll. Basketball Coach of the Yr. Kans. Basketball Coaches Assn., 1997, Coach of Yr. Ill. H.S. Assn., 1985, Conf. Coach of Yr., 1985, 86. Office: Kansas State U 1800 College Ave Manhattan KS 66502-3308 Fax: 785-532-6093.*

PATTERSON, DENISE QUITINA, principal; b. Shelby, N.C., June 21, 1972; d. Dennis Conroy Giles and DiAnne Patterson. BS, U. N.C., Greensboro, 1994; MEd, U. N.C., Charlotte, 2000; MSA, Gardner-Webb U., 2002; EdD, U. N.C., 2002—. Tchr. Battleground Elem. Sch., Lincolnton, NC, 1994—98; gifted tchr. Lincoln (N.C.) County Schs., 1998—2000; asst. prin. North Brook Elem. Sch., Vale, NC, 2000—03, prin., 2003—. Mem. edn. com. Lincoln (N.C.) County, 2003—; spkr. in field; presenter in field. Sec. young adult missionary soc. Oak Grove A.M.E. Zion Ch., lay coun. sec., mem. usher bd. Scholar, Gardner-Webb U., 2000—02. Mem.: State and Nat. Congress Parents and Tchrs. Assn., N.C. Coun. Tchrs. Math., N.C. Assn. Gifted and Talented, N.C. Assn. Sch. Adminstrs., Assn. Supr. and Curriculum Devel. Avocations: walking, collecting crystal.

PATTERSON, ELIZABETH JOHNSTON, retired congresswoman; b. Columbia, SC, Nov. 18, 1939; d. Olin DeWitt and Gladys (Atkinson) Johnston; m. Dwight Fleming Patterson, Jr., Apr. 15, 1967; children: Dwight Fleming, Olin DeWitt, Catherine Leigh. BA, Columbia Coll., 1961; postgrad. in polit. sci., U. S.C., 1961, 62, 64; LLD (hon.), Columbia Coll., 1987; D Pub. Svc. (hon.), Converse Coll., 1989, M in Liberal Arts, 1999; LLD (hon.), Wofford Coll., 1999. Pub. affairs officer Peace Corps, Washington, 1962-64, VISTA, OEO, Washington, 1965-66; D Pub. Svc. Head Start and VISTA, OEO, Columbia, 1966-67; tri-county dir. Head Start, Piedmont Community Actions, Spartanburg, S.C., 1967-68; mem. Spartanburg County Coun., 1975-76, S.C. State Senate, 1979-86, 100th-102nd Congresess from 4th S.C. dist., 1987-93; dir. continuing edn., converse II program Converse Coll., 1993—2003; ret. Adj. prof. Spartanburg Meth. Coll., 1993-2001. Trustee Wofford Coll., 1978-90; bd. dirs. Charles Lea Ctr., 1978, Spartanburg Coun. on Aging; pres. Spartanburg Dem. Women, 1968; v.p. Spartanburg County Dem. party, 1968-70, sec., 1970-75, pres. 2004-; trustee Columbia Coll., 1991-2003; chmn., bd. dirs. Bethlehem Cmty. Ctr., 1998—; bd. dirs. S.C. Ind. Colls. and Univs., 1995-99. Mem. Bus. and Profl. Women's Club, Alpha Kappa Gamma. Democrat. Methodist. E-mail: lizjpatterson@charter.net.

PATTERSON, FRIEDA MORGAN, retired medical secretary, computer professional; b. Charlotte, N.C., Sept. 2, 1922; d. Creed Worth and Esta Lee (Mitchell) M.; widowed; 1 child, Kristine Morgan Patterson Udall. Student, Columbia U.; BA, Pitzer Coll., 1983. Elem. sch. sec. Pomona (Calif.) Unified Sch. Dist., 1960-75; bookkeeper, officer mgr. Wessels Cons., Diamond Bar, Calif., 1976-84; pathology sec., computer mgr. Pomona (Calif.) Valley Med. Ctr., 1984-99. Systems advisor Met. Systems La. County Librs., Pasadena, 1975-82. Trustee City of Pomona Libr., 1976-88. Democrat. Secular Humanist. Avocations: swimming, reading, gardening, folklore research. Home: 3768 Live Oak Dr Pomona CA 91767-1071

PATTERSON, GINA LYNN, psychologist; b. Zanesville, Ohio, Feb. 8, 1971; d. Gregory Alan Patterson and Virginia Leigh Labaki; m. Joseph Michael Smith, Oct. 3, 1998; 1 child, Isabel Patterson Smith. BA, Ohio Dominican Coll., 1993; D in Psychology, Wright State U., Dayton, Ohio, 1997. Lic. psychologist Ohio. Intern Mich. State U., East Lansing, Mich., 1996—97, NE Ohio Health Svcs., Beachwood, 1997—98, psychologist, 1998—99, The Counseling Ctr., Wooster, Ohio, 1999—2002, Every Woman's House, Wooster, Ohio, 2002—. Adj. faculty Baldwin Wallace Coll., Berea, Ohio, 1997—99. Mem.: Ohio Psychol. Assn., APA, Amputee Coalition of Am. Democrat. Roman Catholic. Avocations: swimming, reading, travel. Office: Every Woman's House 104 Spink St Wooster OH 44691

PATTERSON, JULIA, state legislator; m. Pat Patterson; children: Alex, Erin, Caitlin. BS in Soc. and Justice, Wash. State U.; BA in English cum laude, U. Wash. Mem. Wash. Legislature, Olympia, 1997—, chair mem. state and local govt. com., mem. human svcs. and corrections com., mem. transp. com., mem. Gov.'s com. on alcohol, tobacco and drug prevention, mem. substance abuse adv. com., mem. Gov.'s Coun. on Substance Abuse, mem. substance abuse prevention adv. com. Mem. Wash. Coun. for the Prevention of Child Abuse and Neglect; bd. dirs. Judson Park Ret. Cmty.; past mem. King County Human Svcs. Roundtable; vol. Highline Sch. Dist.; mem. Valley View PTA. Mem. LVW, Wash. Coun. on Aging, Audubon Soc. Democrat. Office: 422 John Cherberg Bldg Olympia WA 98504-0001

PATTERSON, MARIA JEVITZ, microbiology-pediatric infectious disease educator; b. Berwyn, Ill., Oct. 23, 1944; d. Frank Jacob and Edna Frances (Costabile) Jevitz; m. Ronald James Patterson, Aug. 22, 1970; children: Kristin Lara, Kier Nicole. BS in Med. Tech. summa cum laude, Coll. St. Francis, Joliet, Ill., 1966; PhD in Microbiology, Northwestern U., Chgo., 1970; MD, Mich. State U., 1984. Diplomate Am. Bd. Med. Examiners, Am. Bd. Pediatrics Gen. Pediatrics, Am. Bd. Pediatrics Infectious Diseases. Lab. asst., instr. med. microbiology for student nurses Med. Sch. Northwestern U., Chgo., 1966-70; postdoctoral fellow in clin. microbiology affiliated hosps. U. Wash., Seattle, 1971-72, asst. prof. microbiology and pub. health Mich. State U., East Lansing, 1972-77, assoc. prof., 1977-82, assoc. prof. pathology, 1979-82, lectr. dept. microbiology and pub. health, 1982-87, resident in pediatrics affiliated hosps., 1984-85, 86-87, clin. instr. dept. pediatrics and human devel., 1984-87, assoc. prof. microbiology-pub. health-pediatrics-human devel., 1987-90, prof., 1990—. Staff microbiologist dept. pathology Lansing Gen. Hosp., 1972-75; dir. clin. microbiology grad. program. Mich. State U., 1974-81, staff microbiologist, 1978-81; postdoctoral fellow in infectious diseases U. Mass. Med. Ctr., Worcester, 1985-86; asst. dir. pediatrics residency Grad. Med. Edn. Inc., Lansing, 1987-90; med. dir. Pediatrics Health Ctr. St. Lawrence Hosp., Lansing, Mich., 1987-90, Ingham Med. Ctr., 1990-94; cons. clin. microbiology Lansing Gen. Hosp., 1972-75, Mich. State U., 1976-82, Mich. Dept. Pub. Health, 1976—, Ingham County Health Dept., 1988—, Am. Health Cons., 1993, State of Mich. Atty. Gen. Office, 1994-98, Lansing Sch. Dist., 1998—, Mich. Antibiotic Resistence Reduction, 1998—; cons. to editl. bd. Infection and Immunity, 1977; cons. Mich. State U. AIDS Edn. Tng. Ctr, 2001—; presenter seminars. Contbg. author: Microbiology: Principles and Concepts, 1982, 4th edit., 1995, Pediatric Emergency Medicine, 1992, Principles and Practice of Emergency Medicine, 1997, Rudolph's Pediatrics, 2002; item writer certifying bd. examination Bd. Am. Acad. Pediats., 1990—, Am. Bd. Osteopathy, 1997—; contbr. articles to profl. jours. and publs. Mem. hon. com. Lansing AIDS Meml. Quilt, 1993. Recipient award for tchg. excellence Mich. State U. Coll. Osteo. Medicine, 1977, 78, 79, 80, 83, Disting. Faculty award Mich. State U., 1980, Woman Achiever award, 1985, excellence in pediatric residency tchg. award, 1988, 2001, 03, Alumni Profl. Achievement award Coll. of St. Francis, 1991, excellence in diversity award Mich. State U., 2000, Weil Endowed Disting. Pediat. Faculty award, 2001; grantee renal disease divsn. Mich. Dept. Pub. Health 1976-82. Fellow Pediatric Infectious Diseases Soc., Infectious Diseases Soc. Am., Am. Acad. Pediatrics; mem. Am. Coll. Physician Execs., Am. Soc. Microbiology, Am. Soc. Clin. Pathologists (affiliate, bd. registrant), South Ctrl. Assn. Clin. Microbiology, Mich. Infectious Diseases Soc., N.Y. Acad. Scis., Kappa Gamma Pi, Lambda Iota Tau. Roman Catholic. Home: 1520 River Ter East Lansing MI 48823-5314 Office: Mich State Univ Microbiology/Molecular Genetics/Pediat East Lansing MI 48824-4320

PATTERSON, MARTHA ELLEN, artist, art educator; b. Anderson, Ind., Mar. 12, 1914; d. Clarence and Corrine Ringwald; m. John Downey, Nov. 27, 1935 (div. 1946); 1 child, Linda Carol; m. Raymond George Patterson, May 6, 1947. Student, Dayton Art Inst., Bendell Art Sch., Bradenton, Fla. Beauty operator WRENS, Springfield, Ohio, 1932-40; co-owner Park Ave. Gallery, Dayton; window decorator; art tchr. Tchr. art; judge art shows. One-woman shows Springfield (Ohio) Mus. Art, 1998, as well as N.C.R. Country Club, Bill Turner Interiors, U. Dayton, High Street Gallery, Trails End Club, The Designerie, Riverbend Park, Statesman Club, State Fidelity Bank, Wegerzyn Hort. Ctr., Pebble Springs, Backstreet, First City Fed. Bank, Bradenton, Fla., Alley Gallery, Merrill Lynch, Miami U., Gem. City Bank, Dayton, Ohio, Winters Bank, Dayton, Sherwin Williams, Howard Johnsons, Dayton Woman's Club, Bergamo, Dayton Meml. Hall, Bob and Arts, Del Park Med. Soc., The Dayton Country Club, Christ Methodist Ch., Unitarian Ch., The Metropolitan, Rikes, Dr. Pavey's, Dr. Chaney's, Dayton Convention Ctr., The Yum Yum, Jan Strunk Interiors, Park Avenue Gallery, Ohio Mus. of Art, Springfield, 1997, New Carlisle Chiropractic Ctr., 2003, Springfield Art Mus. Yearly Show, 2003; artist: (water colors, oils, acylics, inks and pastels); group exhbns. include: Dayton Art Inst., Meml. Hall of Dayton, Dayton Country Club, Bergamo, Women's Club of Dayton, Am. Watercolor Soc., Sarasota Art Ctr., Art League of Manatee County, Butler Inst., Riverbend Park, First City Fed., NCR Country Club, Springfield (Ohio) Mus., Springfield Art Mus., Longboat Key Art Ctr., others; represented in permanent collections of Mr. and Mrs. Richard Nixon, Virginia Graham, Les Brown, Paul Lynde, Air Force Mus. at Wright Patterson, U. Dayton-Ohio, Dr. Stephen House, Doug Yeager and others. Vol. Christian Woman's Soc. of Am., Twig Children's Hosp., Dayton, The Utopians; mem. Tri Art Dayton, Long Boat Key Art Ctr., Fla. Recipient first prize Dayton

Soc. Painters and Sculptors Show Rikes, First Prize, 1976, 77, First Prize, Best in Show, 1978, Beavercreek Art Assn. First Place, Best in Show, Artist and Sculpture Yearly Show, 1966, 68 2d place, Dayton Art Inst. 2d prize, Tri County Hon. Mention, Walker Motor Sales 2d place, Bendell Art Gallery 2d and 3d, Montgomery County Fair Best in Show, Springfield Art Mus. Big Show, 2003. Mem. Art League of Manatee County (Fla.), Nat. Mus. Women In Art, Nat. Soc. Altrusa, Am. Watercolor Soc., Springfield Mus. Art, Dayton Soc. Painters, Long Boat Key Art League, Tri Art. Republican. Methodist. Avocations: art mus., books, music, travel, gourmet cooking. Home: 3853 Lawrenceville Dr Springfield OH 45504-4459

PATTERSON, MARY JANE, religious organization administrator; b. Marietta, Ohio; BA in Philosophy and Acctg., MSW, Ohio State U. Ordained elder Presbyn. Ch. U.S.A., 1960. Acct. IRS; fin. dir. Columbus (Ohio) YWCA, asst. dir. for teenage programs, 1964-66; career missionary, cmty. developer, social work cons. Commn. Ecumenical Mission-Rels. Presbyn. Ch. East Africa, Nairobi, Kenya, 1966-68; cmty. organizing specialist and ombudsman Protestant Cmty. Svcs. of L.A. Coun. Chs., 1969-71; assoc. dir. Washington Office United Presbyn. Ch. U.S.A., 1971-76, dir., 1976—89; past pres. World Conf. on Religion and Peace, U.S.A., N.Y.C. Participant crisis im the nation program Nat. Coun. Chs., Chgo., L.A., 1968; participant local, regional, nat. and internat. Presbyn. Ch. and interdenominational and ecumenical couns. Mem. nat. bd. UN Assn., PAX World Svc., Washington Office on Africa, Ams. United for Separation Ch. and State, Internat. Human Rights Internship Program.; former mem. bd. dirs. U.S. sect. Amnesty Internat.; past mem. Pres. Carter's Presdl. Adv. Bd. for Ambassadorial Appointments. Recipient numerous awards for civil and human rights, peace and justice issues. Women of Faith Award, Presbyn. Church U.S.A., 1998. Mem. NASW, Nat. Assn. Black Social Workers. Office: World Conf Religion and Peace USA 777 United Nations Plz New York NY 10017-3521

PATTERSON, MILDRED LUCAS, retired teaching specialist; b. Winston-Salem, N.C., Jan. 24, 1937; d. James Arthur and Lula Mae (Smith) Lucas; m. James Harrison Patterson Jr., Mar. 31, 1961; children: James Harrison III, Roger Lindsay. BA, Talladega Coll., 1958; MEd, St. Louis U., 1969; postgrad., Webster U., 1970. Classroom tchr. Winston-Salem (N.C.) Pub. Schs., 1959-61, St. Louis Bd. Edn., 1961-72, reading specialist, 1972-88, co-host radio reading show, 1988-91; tchr. specialist Reading to Achieve Motivational Program, St. Louis, 1991-99; ret., 1999—. Bd. dirs. Supt.'s Adv. Com., University City, Mo., 1994—; presenter Chpt. I Regional Conf. Co-author: Wearing Purple, 1996. Bd. dirs. Gateway Homes, St. Louis, 1989-93; mem. com. University City Sch. Bond Issue, 1994; mem. Univ. City Arts and Letters Commn., 1998-99. Recipient Letter of Commendation, Chpt. I. Regional Conf., 1991, Founders' award Gamma Omega chpt. Alpha Kappa Alpha, 1985. Mem. Internat. Reading Assn. (Broadcast Media award for radio 1990, Bldg. Rep. award St. Louis chpt. 1990). Avocations: reading, arts and crafts, storytelling, motivational speaking. E-mail: mildred9@bellsouth.net.

PATTERSON, PEYTON R. bank executive; b. Weisbaden, Germany; m. Thomas Patterson; 1 child. Degree in Polit. Sci., European Inst. Study, 1977; AB in Polit. Sci., Kenyon Coll., 1978; MBA in Mktg., George Washington U., 1983. From asst. v.p. group product mgr. retail deposit products to v.p. Corestates Fin. Corp., Phila., 1983—85, v.p., 1985—89; from v.p. group product mgr. to sr. v.p. Chemical Banking Corp., N.Y.C., 1989—90, sr. v.p., 1990—95; sr. v.p., dir. nat. fin. svcs. group Chase Manhattan Bank, N.Y.C., 1995—96; exec. v.p., gen. mgr. consumer fin. svcs. Dime Bank Corp., N.Y.C., 1996—2001; chmn., pres., CEO New Haven (Conn.) Savings Bank, 2002—. Co-chmn. Greater N.Y. March of Dimes; mem. Regional Leadership Coun., Arts Coun. Greater New Haven; bd. dirs. United Way. Named One of 25 Most Powerful Women in Banking, U.S. Banker Mag., 2003; Rockefeller fellow, 2000—01, Henry Crown fellow, Aspen Inst. Office: New Haven Savings Bank 195 Church St New Haven CT 06510*

PATTERSON, SALLY JANE, government affairs consultant; b. Ontario, Calif., May 28, 1948; d. James Lowell and Barbara Verle (Griffin) Swain; 1 child, Robert Elias Sandoval. BA, Calif. State U., Fullerton, 1970, MA, 1974. Adminstrv. asst. Congressman Jerry Patterson, U.S. House of Reps., Washington, 1978-81; v.p. Pub. Response Assocs., Washington, 1981-87, Hamilton & Staff, Washington, 1987-90; v.p. pub. affairs Planned Parenthood Fedn. of Am., N.Y.C., 1990-93; internat. cons. Mgmt. Systems Internat., Washington, 1993—; v.p. Wagner & Assocs. Pub. Affairs Cons., Inc., N.Y.C., Washington, 1994-99; pres. Radiant Comms. Inc., 2000—. Cons. Nat. Dem. Inst., Washington, 1994—. Author: Supporting Democracy in The Newly Independent States of The Former Soviet Union, 1994, Women in Government Relations: 20 Years of Vision, Leadership, Education and Networking, 1995, Pursuing a Paradox: Public Attitudes vs. Public Action on Campaign Finance Reform, How does Congress Approach Population and Family Planning Issues?, 1999. Trainer Nat. Women's Campaign Fund. Recipient Gold Key award PR Soc. Am., 1992; named one of 74 Women Shaping Am. Politics, Campaigns and Elections, 1993. Mem. Women in Govt. Rels., Inc. (disting. mem., chair leader found. 1985-87, v.p. 1987-88, pres. 1988-89), Coun. Excellence in Govt. (prin.), NARAL (chair, bd. dirs.). Democrat. Episcopalian. Office: Radiant Comms Inc 2121 K St NW Ste 800 Washington DC 20037-1829

PATTERSON, SHIRLEY DRURY, genealogist, editor-in-chief; b. Sterling, Colo., Dec. 30, 1933; d. Carl Walter Drury and Muriel Avis Sheaffer; m. James Riley Patterson, Mar. 28, 1981; m. Donald Eugene Loomiller, May 24, 1953 (div. Jan. 3, 1963); children: Craig Douglas Loomiller, Cynthia Anne Loomiller. BA, U. No. Colo., 1968, N.C. State U., 1984. Editor in chief Towne Family Assn., Inc., Auburn, Calif., 1988—; profl. genealogist Pvt. Practice, Loveland, Colo., 1980—. V.p. Towne Family Assn., Inc., Auburn, 1996—, genealogist, 1994—97, assoc. genealogist, 1997—. Editor: (journal) About Towne (Cert. of Distinquished Svc., 2001, 1995, Cert. of Disting. Svc., 2002), Atlantic Waves, (newsletter) Columbine Brewgle (Lit. Achievement award, 1998). Mem. of caucus Dem. Party, Ft. Collins, Colo., 1996—2000. Mem.: Boulder County Geneal. Soc. (assoc.), Hardin County Geneal. Soc. (assoc.), South Bend Area Geneal. Soc. (assoc.), The Essex Soc. of Genealogists (assoc.), New Eng. Hist. Geneal. Soc. (assoc.), DAR (life). Democrat-Npl. Bapt. Avocations: travel, collector of history books, golf. Home: 4020 Boxelder Dr Loveland CO 80538-2178 Office: Towne Family Assn Inc 24093 Eucalyptus Ct Auburn CA 95602-8226

PATTERSON DEHN, CATHLEEN, pediatrics administrator; b. Akron, Feb. 25, 1958; d. James Edward and Doris Elizabeth (Boyd) P.; m. James Keith Dehn, June 27, 1981. BSN, U. Akron, 1980; MSN, Case Western Res. U., 1988; MA Applied Psychology, NYU, 1995, postgrad., 1995—. RN, N.Y.; cert. PNP, ANCC. Nurse technician Children's Med. Ctr. Akron, 1979-80, staff nurse, 1980-81; pediatric and advanced clin. nurse, asst. head nurse, clin. nurse specialist Rainbow Babies and Children's Hosp., Cleve., 1981-91, edn. coord., 1991-93; PNP, project coord. divsn. nursing, NYU The Child Health Ctr., Brooklyn, 1994-96; PNP dept. pediat. Inst. for Neurology and Neurosurgery Beth Israel Med. Ctr., N.Y.C., 1996-2000; case mgr. dept. pediats. St. Vincent's Hosp. and Med. Ctr., N.Y.C., 2001—. Lectr., clin. instr. Frances Payne Bolton Sch. Nursing, Case Western Res. U., Cleve., 1990-93; mem. adj. faculty divsn. nursing NYU, 1994-96; project coord. Dance Cleve., 1990-91; regional instr. Neonatal Resuscitation Program, Am. Heart Assn., Am. Acad. Pediatrics. Exec. prodr. videos: Getting to Know the Unique Behavioral Capabilities of the Newborn, 1987, One Step at a Time: A Family's Guide to the Neonatal Intensive Care Unit, 1991. Co-founder Sick Kids Need Involved People, Cleve., 1987; team-walk capt. March of Dimes, Cleve., 1989-92 (Edn. grantee 1991); mem. Nat. Mus. Women in Arts. Recipient Samuel E. and Rebecca Elliott award for Cmty. Svc. Case Western Res. U., 1988; named One of Outstanding Young Women of Am., 1988; Fed. Profl. Nurse Trainee scholar, 1986-87. Mem. APA, Am. Ednl. Rsch. Assn., Kappa Delta Pi, Sigma Theta Tau, Pi Lambda Theta. Avocations: health outcomes research, teaching, educational evaluation. Home: 1 University Pl Apt 10L New York NY 10003 1518

PATTON, NICKI, former political organization executive; BA, MA, U. Ky. Childcare cons.; campaign worker Ky. Dem. Party, 1996-98, exec. dir., 1998-99, chmn., 2000—02. Chair Early Childhood Task Force, Govt. of Ky., 1999—. Office: Early Childhood Task Force 700 Capital Ave Ste 100 Frankfort KY 40601

PATTON, SHARON F. museum director; BA, Roosevelt U., 1966; MA, U. Ill., 1969; PhD in Art History, Northwestern U., 1980. Mem. faculty U. Houston, 1976—79, U. Md., 1979—85; dir. art galleries Montclair State Coll., NJ, 1986—87; chief curator Studio Mus., N.Y.C., 1988—91; assoc. prof. art history U. Mich., Ann Arbor, 1991—98, dir. Ctr. for Afroamerican and African Studies, 1996—98; prof. art Oberlin Coll., 1998—2000; mem. adv. bd. Nat. Mus. African Art, Washington, 2000—, dir., 2003—. Author: Memory and the Metaphor, the Art of Romare Bearden, 1991, African-American Art, 1998 (Choice Outstanding Book of Yr. award); contbr. articles to publs. in field. Mem. Rapid Transit Pub. Art Commn., Cleve., ArtTable, Cleve.; mem. visual arts jury Cleve. Arts Prize, 2000—02; mem. African Am. adv. coun. and Acquisition adv. com. Cleve. Art Mus. Mem.: Assn. Art Mus. Dirs., Am. Assn. Museums. Office: Nat Mus African Art Smithsonian Instn MRC 708 PO Box 37012 Washington DC 20013-7012*

PAUGH, NANCY ADELE, secondary school educator, school system administrator; BS, N.Y. U., 1975, MA, 1978. Tchr. H.S. math. Woodbridge (N.J.) Schs., 1975-87, supr. math. and music, 1987—. Contbr. articles to mags. Mem. Ocean Grove (N.J.) Auditorium Choir, 1984—; organist, choir dir. St. Paul's United Meth. Ch., Tottenville, NY, 1967—71, 1975—. Grantee, NSF, 1995—2001. Mem.: ASCD, Am. Guild Organists, Music Educators Nat. Conf., Am. Math. Soc., Mat. Assn. Am., Nat. Assn. Elem. Sch. Prins., Nat. Assn. Secondary Sch. Prins., Am. Assn. Sch. Adminstrs., Pi Lambda Theta. Office: Woodbridge Schs PO Box 428 Woodbridge NJ 07095-0428 Office Phone: 732-602-8564. E-mail: nancy.paugh@woodbridge.k12.nj.us.

PAUGH, PATRICIA LOU, business consultant; b. Pitts., Oct. 30, 1948; d. Marshall Franklin and Helen Jeanne (Graham) P. BA in English, Columbia U., 1982. Adminstrv. asst. Katz, Robinson, Brog & Seymour, N.Y.C., 1972-75; office mgr. Michael D. Martocci, N.Y.C., 1975-80; adminstrv. mgr. O'Melveny & Myers, N.Y.C., 1982-85, Latham & Watkins, N.Y.C., 1985-88; mgr. Nationwide Legal Svcs., N.Y.C., 1988-89; mgr. legal adminstrn. Aluminum Co. of Am., Pitts., 1990-93; ptnr. Domestic & Overseas Countertrade and Consulting Svcs., Ltd., 1986—; pres. Domestic & Overseas Trading Corp., Pitts., 1993—; mng. dir. Gen. Comml. Svcs., Ltd., 1994—. Mem. Am. Mgmt. Assn., Pitts. C. of C. Republican. Episcopalian. Office: Apt 20F 320 Fort Duquesne Blvd Pittsburgh PA 15222-1133 Home: 2104 Charlemagne Cir Pittsburgh PA 15237-2919

PAUL, AMY, lawyer; b. Santa Monica, Calif. d. Philip and Elaine P.; m. Mark A. Czepiel. Student, UCLA, 1990; JD cum laude, U. San Diego Law Sch., 1993. Bar: Calif.; U.S. Ct. Appeals (9th cir.). Assoc. bus. and tech. group Brobeck Phleger & Harrison LLP, 1993-95; dir. contracts and legal affairs Advanced Fibre Comm., Inc., Petaluma, Calif., 1995-99, v.p., gen. counsel, corp. sec., 1999—. Office: Advanced Fibre Comm Inc 1 Willowbrook Ct Petaluma CA 94954-6507

PAUL, CAROL ANN, retired academic administrator, biology educator; b. Brockton, Mass., Dec. 17, 1936; d. Joseph W. and Mary M. (DeMeulenaer) Bjork; m. Robert D. Paul, Dec. 21, 1957; children: Christine, Dana, Stephanie, Robert. BS, U. Mass., 1958; MAT, R.I. Coll., 1968, Brown U., 1970; EdD, Boston U., 1978. Tchr. biology Attleboro (Mass.) High Sch., 1965-68; asst. dean., mem. faculty biology North Shore Community Coll., Beverly, Mass., 1969-78; master planner N.J. Dept. for Higher Edn., Trenton, 1978-80; assoc. v.p. Fairleigh Dickinson U., Rutherford, N.J., 1980-86; v.p. acad. affairs Suffolk Community Coll., Selden, N.Y., 1986-94, prof. biology, 1994-98; ret. Faculty devel. cons. various colls., 1979-98, title III evaluator, 1985-98. Author: (lab. manual and workbook) Minicourses and Labs for Biological Science, 1972 (rev. edit., 1975); (with others) Strategies and Attitudes, 1986; book reviewer, 1973-77, 94-98. V.p. LWV, Beverly, 1970—74, Cranford, NJ, 1982—83; alumni rep. Brown U., 1972—92; mem. Cape Cod Area LWV, 2001—03; bd. dirs. YMCA of Cape Cod, clk. of bd., 1998—2003. Commonwealth Mass. scholar, 1954-58; recipient Acad. Yr. award NSF, 1968-69, Proclamation for Leadership award Suffolk County Exec., 1989. Mem.: AAUW, AAWCC, AAHE, Nat. Coun. for Staff (nat. exec. bd. 1979—80), Profls. and Orgn. Developers (planning com. 1977—79), Brown Alumni Club of Cape Cod (bd. dirs. 2001—, sec. 2001—), Pi Lambda Theta, Phi Theta Kappa. Roman Catholic. Avocation: swimming. Address: 26 Martin Circle Winslowe's View at Pine Hills Plymouth MA 02360

PAUL, CHARLOTTE PATRICIA PEGGRAM, nursing educator; b. Clarendon, Texas, Jan. 13, 1941; d. William Clyde Peggram and Sibyl (Rattan) Jones; m. Robert M. Paul, Apr. 4, 1964; children: Peter, Lauraine. Attended, Amarillo Coll., Tex., 1958-65; diploma, St. Anthony's Hosp. Sch. Nursing, Amarillo, Tex., 1961; BS, Syracuse Univ., N.Y., 1972, MS, 1973; post grad., Wright State U., 1977-79; PhD in Edn. adminstrn., Syracuse Univ., N.Y., 1979; post grad., U. Tex., El Paso, 1983-86. Nurse St. Anthony's Hosp., Amarillo, Tex., 1961-65; evening charge nurse VA Hosp. Gen. Hosp., Syracuse, NY, 1965-66, Upstate Med. Ctr. State Univ. N.Y., Syracuse, NY, 1966-68; asst. to head nurse Meml. Hosp., Syracuse, NY, 1966-68; nurse IV therapy Cmty. Gen. Hosp., Syracuse, NY, 1968-72; instr. Syracuse Ctr. Sch. Sys., NY, 1972; asst. dir. in svc. edn. House of Good Samaritan Hosp., Watertown, NY, 1973-74; instr. State Univ. N.Y. Sch. Nursing, Syracuse, NY, 1974-75, Syracuse U. Sch. Nursing, NY, 1975-76; asst. dean Wright State Univ., Dayton, Ohio, 1977-79; assoc. prof. Edinboro Univ., Pa., 1979-86, prof., 1986—2001, chairperson, dept. grad. studies, 1980-82, chairperson dept. nursing, 1987-89. Spl. project officer William Beaumont Army Med. Ctr., Ft. Bliss, Tex., 1982—85; adj. assoc. prof. U. Tex., El Paso, 1982—85; cons. in field. Contbr. articles and papers to profl. jour. Bd. dir. ARC, Syracuse, NY, 1970—77; bd. dis. Erie County Emergency Mgmt. Agy., cons., 1987—89; mem. Coun. on Aging Com. on Long Term Care, Dayton, Ohio, 1977—78. Lt. col., ret. USAR, 1977—2001. Named to Hall of Fame, Internat. Bus. and Profl. Women, 1994; recipient Unit Citation Award, CAP, 1968, Excellence in Nursing Edn. Award, 1992, Leadership and Svc. Award, Lake Area Health Edn. Ctr., 1994, Comdr. Commendation Award, 1995; fellow Nightingale Soc. fellow, 1988; grantee Gladys Post scholar, 1958—61, Nellie Hurly scholar, 1971—72, Rodney Horle scholar, 1971—72, HEW, 1977, Wright State Univ., 1977—78, Edinboro Univ., 1979—80, William Beaumont Army Med. Ctr., 1986. Mem.: U.S. Nightingale Soc., Syracuse Univ. Alumni Assn., St. Anthony's Hosp. Sch. Nursing Alumni Assn., Res. Officers Assn. (life), Assn. Mil. Surgeons (life), Nat. Ski Patrol (life), Kiwanis (bd. dirs. Edinboro chpt. 1987—95, pres. 1988—89, v.p. 1987—88), Sigma Theta Tau (advisor 1987—94), Pi Lambda Theta (life; pres. local chpt. 1973—75). Republican. Office: Edinboro Univ Pa 139 Centennial Hall Edinboro PA 16412 E-mail: peggram_01@yahoo.com.

PAUL, CONNIE SUE, educational media specialist, school librarian; b. St. Louis, Feb. 9, 1944; d. Frederick Edward and Lillian Ozelle (West) Niewald; m. Charles R. Jameson, May 25, 1963 (div. 1979); children: Joel Charles, Mark Edward; m. Henry Neill Paul III, Sept. 25, 1982. BS in Edn., Cen. Mo. State U., 1964, MA, 1965; MLS, Rutgers U., 1973, postgrad., 1979-85. Cert. secondary English tchr., ednl. media specialist. English tchr. Hamilton Jr. High Sch., Elizabeth, NJ, 1965-67; instr. speech Cen. Mo. State U., Warrensburg, 1968-69; English tchr. Freehold (NJ) Regional High Sch. Dist., 1969-71, ednl. media specialist, 1973—, exec. dir. Mem. exec. bd. h.s. task force NJ Libr. Network Region V, 1989—95, v.p. Ctrl. Jersey Regional Libr. Coop., 1993; cons. Daily Racing Form, Hightstown, NJ, 1985, 91; exec. dir. Ctrl. Jersey Regional Libr. Coop., 1997—. Worship chair Hope Luth., Freehold, 1989—95, mem. ch. coun., 1980-82, 89—2002; tutor Open Door, Freehold, 1990-91. Recipient Pres. award, EMA NJ, 2001, NJ Libr. of Yr., 2002. Mem. AAUW (cultural com. 1990—93), NJ Edn. Assn., Monmouth Ednl. Media Assn., Ednl. Media Assn. NJ (exec. bd., exhibits com., 1993-94). Avocations: writing liturgy, reading, traveling. Home: 58 Lancaster Rd Freehold NJ 07728-2719 Office: Central Jersey Reg Library Coop 4400 Rt 9S Freehold NJ 07728

PAUL, EVE W. retired lawyer; b. N.Y.C., June 16, 1930; d. Leo I. and Tamara (Sogolow) Weinschenker; m. Robert D. Paul, Apr. 9, 1952; children: Jeremy Ralph, Sarah Elizabeth. BA, Cornell U., 1950; JD, Columbia U., 1952. Bar: N.Y. 1952, Conn. 1960, U.S. Ct. Appeals (2nd cir.) 1975, U.S. Supreme Ct. 1977. Assoc. Botein, Hays, Sklar & Herzberg, N.Y.C., 1952-54; pvt. practice Stamford, Conn., 1960-70; staff atty. Legal Aid Soc., N.Y.C., 1970-71; assoc. Greenbaum, Wolff & Ernst, N.Y.C., 1972-78; v.p. legal affairs Planned Parenthood Fedn. Am., N.Y.C., 1979—91, v.p., gen. counsel, 1991—2003; ret., 2003. Bd. dirs. Ctr. Advancement of Women, Inc. Contbr. articles to profl. jours. Trustee Cornell U., Ithaca, N.Y., 1979-84; mem. Stamford Planning Bd., Conn., 1967-70; bd. dirs. Stamford LWV, 1960-62. Harlan Fiske Stone scholar Columbia Law Sch., 1952. Mem.: ABA, Stamford/Norwalk Regional Bar Assn., Assn. Bar of City of N.Y., Conn. Bar Assn., Phi Kappa Phi, Phi Beta Kappa. E-mail: evewpaul@aol.com.

PAUL, JULIA, ancient history researcher; b. Kharkhov, Ukraine, Russia, Dec. 5, 1927; came to U.S., 1937; d. Malham H. and Marazie D. David; m. Joash E. Paul, Feb. 15, 1947; children: Joyce, Joan, Dean, Timothy (dec.), Therese, Bernadette, David. BA, Calif. State U. Stanislaus, Turlock, 1990. Owner Paul's Motel, 15 yrs.; rschr. ancient history and Assyrian history. Host KBSY-TV, Modesto, Calif., 1997—; edn. chair Assyrian Am. Nat. Fedn., 1992-94; entertainment chair Calif. State U. Stanislaus Oratorio Soc. Composer music; handbell player, mem. choir Sacred Heart Ch., Turlock. Founder, organizer Dem. Women's Club of Turlock, 1979, United for Life of Stanislaus County, 1973. Mem. UN Assn. Stanislaus (v.p.). Avocations: golf, bowling, cooking assyrian dishes.

PAUL, KAREN S. diversified financial services company executive; b. Burlington, Vt., Jan. 15, 1960; d. R. Allan and Elsie E. Paul; m. Mark W. Saba; children: Andrew, Adam, Caroline. AB in Polit Sci. and Econ., Mt. Holyoke Coll., 1982; degree in finance, Coll. Fin. Planning, 1990. CFP. Paralegal Casey, Haythe and Krugman, N.Y.C., 1982—83; reg. rep. Merrill Lynch, Burlington, 1983—84; v.p. Thomson McKinnon Securities, Inc., Burlington, 1984—86, Progressive Investing, Inc., Burlington, 1986—88; CEO, Paul Fin. Svcs., Inc., Burlington, 1988—. Bd. dirs. Burlington Electric Light Commn.; chmn. Formula Ford, Inc., South Barre, Vt., 1999—2002; bd. dirs. Vt. World Trade Office. Contbg. editor: Burlington Free Press, 1989—, Rutland Herald, 1998—, Barre-Montpelier Times Argus, 1998—. Mem. capital campaign com. Trinity Coll., 1993—94; bd. dirs. Child Protection Network, 1999—, Ohavi Zedek Synagogue, 1997—2000, Vt. World Trade Office, 1999—, Greater Burlington YMCA, 2003—, Burlington Police Commn., 2002—. Mem.: Assn. Internat. Mgmt. and Rsch., Vt. C. of C. (bd. dirs. 1997—2003). Office: PO Box 1272 Burlington VT 05402 Office Phone: 802-862-1545. Business E-Mail: karen@paulfinancial.com.

PAUL, LOIS, public relations company executive; BA in Journalism summa cum laude, Temple U.; MS in Computer Info. Systems, Bentley Coll. Former sr. editor/software Computerworld; former exec. editor/features, founding mem. PC Week; founder, pres. Lois Paul & Ptnrs., Burlington, Mass., 1986—. Chmn. Bentley Coll. Grad. Sch. Mktg. Adv. Coun; bd. on Fleishman-Hillard, 2000. Recipient Disting. Sch. of Comm. and Theater Alumnus award Temple U. Office: Lois Paul and Ptnrs 150 Presidential Way Woburn MA 01801-1179

PAUL, MARY, automotive executive; b. Tipton, Ind., Apr. 29, 1952; d. John A. and Inez Marie (Clark) Meyer; 1 child, Regina. BS, U. Evansville, 1974; MBA, So. Ill. U., 1987. Mgr. The Children's Shops, St. Louis, 1980-86; cons., trainer Edison Bros. Stores, St. Louis, 1987; program mgr. Anheuser-Busch Cos., 1988-94; human resources devel. mgr. Campbell Taggart, Inc. (divsn. Anheuser-Busch Cos. Inc.), St. Louis, 1994-96; from orgnl. devel. and tng. mgr. powertrain ops. to corp. sr. mgr. Harley Davidson, Inc., Milw., 1996—2002, sr. mgr. corp. orgnl. devel., 2002—. Active Coro Found. Mem. ASTD, Profl. Woman Network, Profl. Dimensions, Women in Leadership Alumnae. Home: 5801 S Oak Rd West Bend WI 53095 Office: Harley Davidson Motor Co 3700 W Juneau Ave Milwaukee WI 53208-2865 E-mail: mary.paul@harley-davidson.com.

PAUL, NORA MARIE, media studies educator; b. White Plains, N.Y., Mar. 1, 1953; d. Keith and Nancy Miller Doig; m. Robert Lavon Medley, June 1973 (div. Nov. 1974); m. Robert Nathan Paul, Dec. 24, 1982; children: Nathan Augustus, Spencer Bernard. BA, Tex. Women's U., 1975, MLS, 1976. Reference libr. Houston Pub. Libr., 1976-77; cons., co-founder Freelance Rsch. Svc., Houston, 1977-79; editor info. svcs. Miami (Fla.) Herald, 1979-91; faculty Poynter Inst. for Media Studies, St. Petersburg, Fla., 1991—; dir. Inst. for New Media Studies U. Minn. Cons. AP, N.Y.C., 1993-95; vis. faculty European Journalism Ctr., Maastricht, The Netherlands, 1996—. Author: (book) Computer-Assisted Research: A Guide to Tapping Online Information, 4th edit., 1999; co-author: (book) Great Scouts!: Cyber-Guides to Subject Searching on the Web, 1999; contbr. articles to mags. Mem. Spl. Librs. Assn. (Hennebry award news divsn. 1995), Investigative Reporters and Editors. Avocations: writing, tile work. Office: U Minn Inst New Media Studies 111 Murphy Hall 206 Church St SE Minneapolis MN 55455-0488 E-mail: npaul@tc.umn.edu.

PAUL, OUIDA FAY, music educator; b. Deatsville, Ala., Jan. 18, 1911; d. Elza Bland and Martha Eleanor (Hinton) P. AB in Math. and English, Huntingdon Coll., 1930, BS in Music Edn., 1933; MA in Music and Music Edn., Columbia U., 1943, EdD in Music and Music Edn., 1957; postgrad., U. Ill., 1968; studied oil painting, Gloria Foss Sch. of Art, 1978—83. Tchr. math., English and music pub. schs., Ala., 1930—42; tchr. math. Sacred Heart Convent Sch., N.Y.C., 1942-43; tchr. h.s. choral music Kingsport, Tenn., 1943-45; instr., asst. prof. music edn. Greensboro (N.C.) Coll., 1945-49; asst. prof. U. Fla., Gainesville, 1949-61, U. Hawaii, Honolulu, 1961-68; tchr. musicology and voice Leeward C.C., Pearl City, Hawaii, 1968-77; pvt. tchr. voice, Honolulu, 1977-95, Gainesville, 1996—. Choir dir. 1st Presbyn. Ch., Gainesville, 1950-61, Protestant Chapel, USN, Honolulu, 1962-68, Cmty. Ch., Honolulu, 1969-78, Wesley United Meth. Ch., Honolulu, 1978-94; contralto soloist various chs., 1950-94; adjudicator solo and choral auditions and festivals, 1945-94. One-woman shows include Honolulu Cmty. Theatre, 1980, 84, First United Meth. Ch., 1980; group shows with Honolulu Artists, others; permanent collections René Malmezac, Tahiti; contbr. articles to profl. jours. Cons. to com. on edn. Hawaii Gov.'s Commn. on Status of Women, 1965; English lang. tutor Hawaii Literacy, Inc., Honolulu, 1978-95. Recipient Alumni Achievement award, Huntingdon Coll. Alumnae Assn., 1998. Mem. Music Educators Nat. Conf. (1st v.p. Hawaii 1969-70), Am. Choral Dirs. Assn. (Hawaii chmn. 1963-66), Nat. Assn. Tchrs. Singing, Altrusa (pres. Gainesville 1960-61, past pres. Honolulu), Delta Kappa Gamma (pres. Hawaii Theta chpt. 1963-64, past state music chmn., named one of Makers of Destiny Hawaiian Style 2002.). Methodist. Avocation: oil painting. Home: 8015 NW 28th Pl Apt B210 Gainesville FL 32606-8607 E-mail: weefae@webtv.net.

PAUL, ROCHELLE CAROLE, special education educator; b. East Liverpool, Ohio, July 8, 1951; d. Homer Neil and Dolores Elizabeth (Seiler) P. BS, Clarion State Coll., 1973; MS, Clarion U., 1987; MDiv, Trinity Luth. Sem., Columbus, Ohio, 1992. Cert. tchr., Pa., Ohio. Spl. edn. tchr. Dorchester County Bd. Edn., Cambridge, Md., 1973-78, Forest Area Sch. Dist., Tionesta, Pa., 1979-88; edn. coord. juvenile-probate divsn. Common Pleas Ct. of Licking County, Newark, Ohio, 1993-95; instr. Ctrl. Ohio Tech. Coll., Newark, 1994—; prevention specialist Ctr. Alternative Resources, Newark, 1996-98; program dir. early childhood devel. Ctrl. Ohio Tech. Coll., Newark, 1999-2000; exec. dir. Literacy Network Ctrl. Ohio, 2000—; intervention specialist Treca Digital Acad., 2002—. Rep. Pres.'s adv. bd. Trinity Luth. Sem., 1991-92; active St. Paul's Evang. Luth. Ch., Newark, Ohio; mem. head start cmty. assessment com., LEADS, 1999—, trustee, 2000—, policy coun. chair head start, 2000—. Mem. ASCD, AAUW, Coun. Exceptional Children (chpt. pres. 1972-73, 98—), Nat. Assn. Edn. of Young Children, Alcohol and Drug Abuse Prevention Assn. Ohio, Ohio Coalition of Assoc. Degree Early Childhood Programs. Avocations: tai chi, reading, writing, vocal and instrumental music, travel. Home: 164 Newton Ave Newark OH 43055-4758 Office: Literacy Network Ctrl Ohio COTC Baker House 1179 University Dr Newark OH 43055-1707 E-mail: rcpaulteacher@netscape.net.

PAUL, YVONNE C. retired elementary school educator; b. Chgo., July 9, 1934; d. Reuben Douglas Adams and Gladys Winters Bacot; m. William Ralph Paul, Nov. 13, 1962; adopted children: Vanessa, Jonathan. BA, U. Ill., Chgo., 1956; MA in Counseling, San Francisco State U., 1976, MA in Adminstrn., 1983. Classroom tchr. Chgo. Pub. Schs., 1956-59; sch. tchr. Dep. Schs. Europe, Eritrea, East Africa, 1959-60, Stuttgart/Ludwigsburg, Germany, 1960-62; dir. pre-sch. AFB, Killeen, Tex., 1962-63; classroom tchr. Jericho (N.Y.) Sch. Dist., 1964-65; sch. tchr. middle grades Balt. County Schs., Towson, Md., 1965-69; vice prin., tchr. Pittsburg (Calif.) Unified Sch. Dist., 1969-99; ret., 1999. Resource mgr., reading and sci. leadership; classroom tchr., lead math., leader Pittsburg Unified Sch. Dist., 1969-99. Cadet leader Girl Scouts Am., Killeen, 1962; hosp. vol. Killeen Gen. Hosp., 1963; Parent's Booster Club. Technol. Edn. Contra Costa Sch. grantee Alameda/Contra Costa Office Edn., Hayward, Calif., 1985; grant writer awards Technol. Edn. Contra Costa. Mem. No. Calif. Math. Assn., Assn. Calif. Sch. Adminstrs., Artist Guild, Phi Delta Kappa. Roman Catholic. Avocations: writing for publication, reading, gardening, interior design, children's science theater. Home: 488 Lakeview Dr Brentwood CA 94513-5070

PAULEY, JANE, television journalist; b. Indpls., Oct. 31, 1950; m. Gary Trudeau; 3 children. BA in Polit. Sci, Ind. U., 1971; D of Journalism (hon.), DePauw U., 1978. Reporter Sta. WISH-TV, Indpls., 1972—75; co-anchor WMAQ-TV News, Chgo., 1975—76, The Today Show, NBC, N.Y.C., 1976—90; from co-anchor to corr. NBC News, N.Y.C., 1976—; prin. writer, reporter NBC Nightly News, 1980—82, substitute anchor, 1990—2003; co-anchor Early Today, NBC, 1982—83; prin. corr. Real Life With Jane Pauley, NBC, 1991; co-anchor Dateline NBC, N.Y.C., 1992—99, prin. anchor, 1999—2003; anchor Time & Again MSNBC, 1999—2003. Mem. adv. bd. Childrens Health Fund, Internat. Coun. Freedom From Hunger; bd. dirs. Pub. Edn. Needs Civic Involvement in Learning. Named Broadcaster of Yr., Internat. Radio and TV Soc., 1986, Best in Bus., Washington Journalism Rev., 1990; named to Broadcasting and Cable Hall of Fame; recipient Emmy award, Edward R. Murrow award, Gabriel award, Nancy Susan Reynolds award, Maggie award, Humanitas award, Commendation award, Am. Women in Radio and TV, Gracie Allen award, Clarion award, Assn. for Women in Comm., Wilbur award, Religious Pub. Rels. Coun., Salute to Excellence award, Nat. Assn. Black Journalists, Leonard Zeidenberg First Amendment award, Radio TV News Dirs. Found., Paul White award, NTNDA. Fellow: Soc. for Profl. Journalists (hon. chair Jane Pauley task force on mass comm. edn.).*

PAULEY, SHIRLEY STEWART, religious organization executive; b. Boston, Sept. 13, 1938; d. Charles Norris and Nellie Consuelo (Yorke) Stewart; m. Edward Haven Pauley, May 29, 1964; children: David Stewart, Deborah Jeanne. BA, Gordon Coll., 1960; postgrad., Ariz. State U., 1961, Boston U., 1963. Sec./receptionist Atwell Co., Boston, summer 1956; sec., typist Kelley Girl, Boston, 1956-60; asst. office mgr. Radiator Chem. Corp., Scottsdale, Ariz., 1960-62; sec., clerical worker GM, Westwood, Mass., 1962-64; v.p. Truth Alive Ministries, Dallas, 1995—. Spkr. At Large, Boston, 1956-60; Sunday sch. tchr. Blaney Meml. Bapt. Ch., Boston, 1956-60; choir dir. Sherwood Bapt. Ch., Phoenix, 1961-62, co-youth dir., 1961; co-youth dir. Blaney Meml. Ch., Boston, 1964-66; mem. book store com. Prestonwood Bapt. Ch., Dallas, 1994—; messenger Bapt. Gen. Conv. Tex., Ft. Worth, 1996. Republican. Avocations: photography, reading, music. Office: Truth Alive Ministries PO Box 794945 Dallas TX 75379-4945

PAULIK, MARY THERESA, retired municipal official, researcher; b. Flushing, N.Y., Sept. 17, 1939; d. Joseph Percival and Gertrude Veronica (Mahony) Melanson; m. William Paul Paulik, Jan. 21, 1961 AA in Social Scis., Suffolk Community Coll., Brentwood, N.Y., 1979; BA in Human Rels. in Mgmt., St. Joseph's Coll., Patchoque, N.Y., 1980; MPA, L.I. U., 1986. Teller, clk. Chase Manhattan Bank, Flushing, 1957-58; adminstrv. corp. sec. Ginn & Co./Ednl. Textbooks, N.Y.C., 1960-61, regional supervisory mgr., 1961-66; various per diem positions Writing/Rsch. Cos.-Bus. Firms, L.I., N.Y., 1967-70; adminstrv. sec. Town of Islip, Brentwood Water Dist., 1972-88, water dist. coord., 1988—93; ret., 1993. Officer bus. and polit. orgns.; mem. environ. groups. Contbr. articles to profl. jours. Fundraiser United Way, Suffolk, N.Y., 1987-88, team coord., 1989—, assn. for retarded, 1987-88, unit coord., 1989—; fundraiser March of Dimes; mem. Bayshore Rep. Club, N.Y., 1989—, pres., 1992; mem. Islip Rep. Women, 1989—. Mem. AAUW, Bus. and Profl. Women (mem. exec. bd. Bay Shore chpt. 1989—, pres. 1994, Woman of Yr. 1994), Cousteau Soc. (environmentalist), Nat. Audubon Soc., Nat. Geog. Soc. (environmentalist), Nat. Wildlife Soc. (environmentalist), Wilderness Soc., Sigma Iota Chi. Roman Catholic. Avocations: writing, sports, environmental and political research.

PAULIN, AMY RUTH, civic activist, consultant; b. Bklyn., Nov. 29, 1955; d. Ben and Alice Lois (Roth) P.; m. Ira Schuman, May 25, 1980; children: Beth, Sarah, Joseph. BA, SUNY, Albany, 1977, MA, 1978, postgrad., 1979—. Instr. SUNY, Albany, 1978, Queens (N.Y.) House of Detention, 1979; fundraiser United Jewish Appeal Fedn., N.Y.C., 1979-83; dir. devel. Altro Health & Rehab., Bronx, N.Y., 1983-86; fundraising cons. N.Y.C., 1986-88; pres. LWV, Scarsdale, N.Y., 1990-92, Westchester, N.Y., 1992-95; trustee Scarsdale (N.Y.) Village, 1995-99; exec. dir. My Sisters' Place, 1999—. Mem. adv. coun. Family Ct.; co-chair woman Westchester Womens Agenda, Westchester Dept. Social Svcs.; mem. adv. com. Fund for Women & Girls; bd. dirs. Mid. Sch. PTA,, 1995-97, Westchester Coalition for Legal Abortion, Scarsdale Open Soc. Assn., 1992-95, United Jewish Appeal Fedn. Scarsdale Women's Campaign; v.p. Westchester Children's Assn.; troop leader Girl Scouts U.S., 1992-96; mem. Town Club Edn. Com., 1983-89; mem. Scarsdale Bowl com., 1992-95, chair, 1994-95; mem. Scarsdale Japanese Festival, 1992-93; mem. Westchester Women's Equality Day, 1987-92; mem. nominating com. Heathcote Neighborhood Assn., 1991-92; bd. advisors Westchester County Found., 1994—; mem. Scarsdale Village Youth Bd., 1992-95; mem. U.S. legislators task force on families at risk Westchester County Bd., 1994—; mem. Updating Voting Equipment Com., 1994; mem. Tobacco Free Westchester, 1993-95, chair 1995—; co-chair Parent Tchr. Coun. Sch. Budget Study, 1991-94; planning chair Kids Base Bd., 1992-95, dir. 1992-94chair parking and traffic subcom. Village Downtown Devel. Com., 1994-95; mem. Westchester Commn. Campaign Fin. Reform, Westchester Commn. Child Abuse, 1996-87; exec. com. Westchester Mcpl. Offcls. Assn., 1996-97; adv. com. Jr. League, 1996-99. Named Westchester County Woman of Yr., 1995, Bridge Fund award, 1998, Women's Health NNetwork Ann. award, 1999. Mem. LWV (bd. dirs. women and children's issues Westchester chpt., dir. social policy N.Y. state), State Communities Aid Assn. (econ. securities com.), N.Y. State Pub. Health Assn. (bd. dirs. Lower Hudson Valley chpt.), N.Y. State Coalition Choice, New Yorkers Against Gun Violence (bd. dirs.). Avocations: swimming, dance. Home: 12 Burgess Rd Scarsdale NY 10583-4410

PAULL, ELSIE BEHREND, editorial stylist, interpreter; b. Washington, Feb. 18, 1912; d. Edwin and Frances (Sanders) Behrend; m. Francis Swann, June 6, 1936 (div. July 1943); m. Joseph Paull, July 11, 1947; children: Kathryn P. Brown, Elizabeth Jane O'Connell, Paris Mase. Diplomate, U. Nancy, France, 1930, U. Paris, 1931-32; BA, Barnard Coll., 1933. Intelligence analyst Fgn. Econs. Adminstrn., Washington, 1942-43; vol. tchr. of French lang. Washington, 1955; editl. stylist, interpreter E.J. Lieberman, Washington, 1990—. Democrat. Avocations: theater, symphony. Home: 4827 Nebraska Ave NW Washington DC 20016-1833

PAULOS, CHRISTINE ANN, academic administrator; b. St. Paul, Sept. 17, 1956; d. Peter and Linda Joy (Kastner) P. BS in Phys. Edn. and Sociology, U. Minn., 1981; MA in Psychology and Counseling, Liberty U., Lynchburg, Va., 1990. Coach U. St. Thomas, St. Paul, 1980-81; coach, instr. Macalaster Coll., St. Paul, 1981-85; with admissions Century Coll., St. Paul, 1985—2001. Cons. Facility Mgmt., Minn., 1984-86. Author (jour.) The Balancing Act-Athletics and Academics, 1992 (award of excellence for innovations in acad. support Athletic Mgmt. Mag. 1994). Named to Softball Hall of Fame, U. Minn., 1989; named Softball All-Am. Am. Softball Assn., 1980, Outstanding All-Time Athlete-Field Hockey, U. Minn., 1995. Mem.: Am. Assn. Collegiate Registrars and Admissions Officers. Home: 9409 Grand Ave S Bloomington MN 55420-4218 Office: Century College 3300 Century Ave No Saint Paul MN 55110

PAULS, JANICE LONG, state legislator; m. Ron Pauls. BS, Sterling (Kans.) Coll., 1973; JD, U. Kans., 1976. Rep. dist. 102 Kans. Ho. of Reps., mem. Judiciary, rules and regulations, transp., corrections and juvenile justice coms. Democrat. Home: 1634 N Baker St Hutchinson KS 67501-5621 Office: Kans Ho of Reps State Capitol Topeka KS 66612

PAULSEN, ANNE M. state legislator; B.S., Framingham State Coll.; M.A., Boston State Coll. Mem. Belmont School Committee, 1976—85, Belmont Board of Selectmen, 1986—92, Mass. Ho. of Reps., 1993—. Address: State House Rm 22 Boston MA 02133

PAULSEN, VIVIAN, magazine editor; b. Salt Lake City, May 10, 1942; d. Paul Herman and Martha Oline (Blattmann) P. BA, Brigham Young U., 1964, postgrad., 1965, U. Grenoble, France, 1966. Cert. tchr., Utah. Tchr. French Granite Sch. Dist., Salt Lake City, 1966-67; assoc. editor New Era mag., Salt Lake City, 1970-82; mng. editor Friend mag., Salt Lake City, 1982—. Am. Field Service scholar, 1959; grad. fellow Brigham Young U., 1964-66 Republican. Mem. Ch. of Jesus Christ of Latter-day Saints Office: The Friend 50 E North Temple # F23 Salt Lake City UT 84150-0002

PAULSON, GWEN O. GAMPEL, government relations consultant; b. Detroit, Mar. 16, 1945; d. Maurice V. and Lilyan Victor; divorced; children: Jill Susan, Mindy Beth; m. Jerome A. Paulson, July 2, 1989. BA, Mich. State U., 1966; MA, Wayne State U., 1974; postgrad., U. Mich., 1981. Lectr. Oakland (Mich.) U., 1979—80, U. Mich., Ann Arbor, 1981; legis. asst. U.S. Rep. Pete Stark, Washington, 1982—85; mem. profl. staff, ways and means health subcom. U.S. Ho. of Reps., Washington, 1985—89; v.p. for health Capitol Assocs., Washington, 1989—90; pres. Congl. Cons., Washington, 1990—. Author: Women and the Structure of Society, 1984. Edward S. Beck fellow U. Mich., Ann Arbor, 1978-79; Rackham Dissertation grant U. Mich., Ann Arbor, 1980. Mem. Women in Govt. Rels., Bus. and Profl. Women, Fedn. Am. (co-chair 1999—2001), Am. League Lobbyists, Greater Washington Soc. Assn. Execs., Phi Alpha Theta, Tau Sigma. Avocations: collecting contemporary glass, travel, history, politics, reading. Office: Congl Cons LLC 1113 N Howard St Alexandria VA 22304-1627 E-mail: gwencc@comcast.net.

PAULSON, LORETTA NANCY, psychoanalyst; b. L.A., Nov. 5, 1943; d. Frank Morris and Rose (Kaufman) Fargo; m. Maurice Krasnow; 1 child, Kira. BA, U. So. Calif., 1966; MS in Social Work, Columbia U., 1969; cert. psychoanalyst, C.G. Jung Inst., N.Y.C. Cert. clin. social worker, N.Y., Conn., N.J. Pvt. practice psychoanalysis, N.Y.C., 1976—. Vice.- chmn. CGJ Inst. Tng. Bd. Mem. NASW (diplomate in clin. social work), Internat. Assn. for Analytical Psychology (past del., bd. dirs.), N.Y. Assn. for Analytic Psychology (past pres., past chair program com.), Conn. Soc. Clin. Social Work (com. on psychoanalysis), C.G. Jung Inst. Address: 334 W 86th St Apt 1A New York NY 10024-3130

PAULSON-CRAWFORD, CAROL, conservator, educator; b. Ashland, Ohio, Jan. 15, 1961; d. Donald Howard Paulson and Mary Katherine (Dafoe) Paulson Harris; m. Craig Alan Crawford, May 6, 1995; 1 child, Cole Monroe. BFA, Ohio State U., 1984; MA, U. Wis., 1987, MFA, 1989. Book and paper conservator Wis. Hist. Soc., Madison, 1987-91; conservator Libr. of Congress, Washington, 1992-99; book and paper conservator S.C. Dept. Archives and History, Columbia, 1999-2000; lab. dir., sr. conservator U. S.C., State Park, 2000—02; book and paper conservator Crawford Construction Inc., 2002—. Author, editor: Boxes for the Protection of Books, 1994; also articles; exhibited at Rockville (Md.) Manson, 1996. Mem. S.C. Archivists Assn., S.E. Regional Conservation Assn., Am. Inst. for Conservation (profl. assoc.), Guild Book Workers, Washington Conservation Guild. Avocations: biking, gardening. Home and Office: 2305 Cardington Dr Columbia SC 29209-3209 E-mail: craigcarolc@aol.com.

PAULUS, ELEANOR BOCK, professional speaker, author; b. N.Y.C., Mar. 12, 1933; d. Charles William Bock and Borghild (Nelson) Garrick; m. Chester William Paulus Jr., Sept. 6, 1952; children: Chester W. III, Karl Derrick, Diane Paulus Henricks. Student, Smith Coll., 1952-53. Owner, founder Khan-Du Chinese Shar-Pei, Somerset, N.J., 1980—; dir. Pet Net, Santa Fe, N.Mex., 1992—; co-owner, CFO Am. Dream TV Prodns., Washington, 1993—; co-owner, exec. prodr. Capitol Ideas, 1995-2001, Pierre Salinger's Round Table, 1997; pets and animals columnist www-.goodnewsbroadcast.com, 2000—. Lectr., cons. on Chinese Shar-Pei and canine health, 1980—; internat. con., lectr. on pet care and health. Author: Health Care Handbook for Cats, Dogs and Birds, The Proper Care of Chinese Shar-Pei; contbr. articles to mags. and jours. including Dog Fancy, chpts. to books, including The World of the Chinese Shar-Pei; creator, prodr. World of Dogs, 1996—. Dir. bd. trustees Rutgers Prep. Sch., Somerset, 1970-76, v.p. bd. trustees, 1976-81, pres. PTA, 1966-76; chmn. Raritan River Festival, New Brunswick, N.J., 1980-91. Named Woman of Yr., City of New Brunswick, 1982. Mem. Dog Writers Am. Assn., Dog Fanciers N.Y.C., Bonzai Clubs Internat., Koi Internat. N.Y., Raritan Valley Country Club, Chinese Shar-Pei Club of Am. (v.p. 1982-86, bd. dirs. east sect. 1980-82, Humanitarian award 1986). Avocations: travel, dog related activities, gardening. Home: 321 Skillman Ln Somerset NJ 08873-5325 Office: E B Paulus 20 Sutton Pl S # 5A New York NY 10022-4165

PAULUS, NORMA JEAN PETERSEN, lawyer; b. Belgrade, Nebr., Mar. 13, 1933; d. Paul Emil and Ella Marie (Hellbusch) Petersen; m. William G. Paulus, Aug. 16, 1958; children: Elizabeth, William Frederick. LL.B., Willamette Law Sch., 1962; LL.D. (hon.), Linfield Coll., 1985; LittD (hon.), Whitman Coll., 1990; LHD (hon.), Lewis & Clark Coll., 1996. Bar: Oreg. 1962. Sec. to Harney County Dist. Atty., 1950-53; legal sec., 1953-55; sec. to chief justice Oreg. Supreme Ct., 1955-61; of counsel Paulus and Callaghan, Salem; mem. Oreg. Ho. of Reps., 1971-77; sec. of state State of Oreg., Salem, 1977-85; supt. pub. instrn., 1990-99; of counsel Paulus, Rhoten & Lien, 1985-86. Mem. Oreg. exec. bd. U.S. West, 1985-97; adj. prof. Willamette U. Grad. Sch., 1985; mem. N.W. Power Planning Com., 1986-89. Mem. adv. com. Def. Adv. Com. for Women in the Svc., 1986, Nat. Trust for Hist. Preservation, 1988-90; trustee Willamette U., 1978—; bd. dirs. Oreg. Grade Instn. Sci. and Tech., 1985-2001, Edn. Commn. States, 1991-99, Coun. Chief State Sch. Officers, 1995-98, Nat. Assessment Governing Bd., 1996-99, Oreg. Garden Found., 1997—, Oreg. Coast Aquarium, 1999—; bd. dirs., adv. bd. World Affairs Coun. Oreg., 1997—; overseer Whitman Coll., 1985—; bd. cons. Marion-Polk Boundary Commn., 1970-71; mem. Presdl. Commn. to Monitor Philippines Election, 1986; dir. Oreg. Hist. Soc., 2001—. Recipient Disting. Svc. award City of Salem, 1971, LWV, 1995, Path Breaker award Oreg. Women's Polit. Caucus, 1976; named One of 10 Women of Future, Ladies Home Jour., 1979, Woman of Yr. Oreg. Inst. Managerial and Profl. Women, 1982, Oreg. Women Lawyers, 1982, Woman Who Made a Difference award Nat. Women's Forum, 1985; Eagleton Inst. Politics fellow Rutgers U. Mem. Oreg. State Bar, Nat. Order Women Legislators, Women Execs. in State Govt., Women's Polit. Caucus Bus. and Profl. Women's Club (Golden Torch award 1971), Delta Kappa Gamma.

PAULY, JENNIFER L. director, graphics designer; d. Ronald R. and Clarice M. Pauly. BS in Mass Comm., Advt., St. Cloud State U., 1992. Chair dept.-comml. art Fla. Met. U., Tampa, 1996—2002; coord. programs-design studies S.W. Fla. Coll., Tampa, 2002—. Graphic designer, owner JP Creations, Brandon, Fla., 1996—. Adj. faculty quarter Fla. Met. U., 1997; catalog designer Lowry Pk. Zoo Ednl. Dept., Tampa, 2002—03; vol. designer Am. Heart Assn., St. Petersburg, Fla., 2003. Scholar, Gen. Mills, 1987-1990. Mem.: Nat. Assn. Photoshop Profls. (assoc.), Am. Advt. Fedn. (assoc.), Tampa Bay Advt. Fedn. (assoc.), Creative Club Tampa Bay (assoc., membership chair 1996—2000). Office: SW Fla Coll 10210 Highland Manor Drive Ste 200 Tampa FL 33610

PAUXTIS, MARY JO, academic administrator; b. Phila., Sept. 16, 1949; d. Francis Xavier and Mary Ella Daley; m. Richard J. Pauxtis, Mar. 2, 1985; m. James Michael Huver, Nov. 22, 1969 (div.); 1 child, Jessica Michele Huver. AS, Gwynedd Mercy Coll., Gwynedd Valley, Pa., 1969; BBA cum laude, U. Pa., 1987, MGA, 2001. Med. sec. ULMI, Inc., Hahnemann Med. Sch., Phila., 1969—71; lupus coord. Hahnemann U., Phila., 1978—90; office mgr. MPB Archs., Phila., 1990—93; fin. coord. dept. dermatology U. Pa., Phila., 1993—96; mgr. of adminstrn. and fin. Ctr. for Rsch. on Reproduction and Women's Health, U. Pa., Phila., 1996—. Pres. borough coun. Narberth Borough, 2001—03, borough councillor, 1991—2003; com. person Lower Merion/Narberth Dem. Com., 1989—2003; mem. Narberth (Pa.) Cmty. Libr., 1991—96. Mem.: Lower Merion Hist. Soc. (corr.; corr. sec. 2000). Democrat. Avocations: reading, knitting, gardening. Home: 1294 Montgomery Ave Narberth PA 19072 Personal E-mail: mj.pauxtis@verizon.net.

PAVEK, BRYN CARPENTER, director arts administration; b. Phoenix, Mar. 7, 1955; d. John Leon and Lenore Maxine (Stapp) Carpenter; m. Charles Christopher Pavek, Dec. 18, 1977. BFA in Theatre magna cum laude, Ariz. State U., 1977; student, U. Ariz., 1973. Freelance designer, Phoenix, 1973—77; box office mgr. Ariz. State U. Theatre, Tempe, 1976; creative drama specialist City of Phoenix, summer 1976; box office ticketing asst. U. So. Calif., L.A., 1977; co. and stage mgr. Hartford (Conn.) Stage Co. Youth Theatre, 1978, adminstrv. mgr., 1979—80; budget analyst U.S. Naval Mil. Command, Arlington, Va., 1981; prodn. supr. Arlington County Visual & Performing Arts, 1981—84; dep. dir. McLean (Va.) Cmty. Ctr., 1984—87; exec. dir. Reston (Va.) Cmty. Ctr., 1987—97; dir. adult and cmty. edn. Fax Ct. Pub. Schs., 1998—2003; prin., owner Home Instead Sr. Care, Reston, Va., 2003—. Prodn. chair Southeastern Theatre Conf., Arlington, 1984; mem. Drug Free Recreation for Youth Task Force, Fairfax, Va., 1988—, Dogwood Edn. Task Force, Reston, 1989—. Mem. com. Fairfax County Coun. of the Arts, 1987—, Purple Sage Cluster Assn. Social Commn., Reston, 1988; mem. organizing com. Fairfax County Summit Youth Issues, 1989. Recipient Human Rights award Fairfax County, Va., 1991, Leadership Fairfax Grad., 1996. Democrat. Unitarian Universalist. Avocations: travel, swimming. Home: 2515 Fowlers Ln Reston VA 20191-2101

PAVEL, PATRICIA L. elementary school educator; b. Dearborn, Mich., May 10, 1951; d. Louis Charles and Phyllis Jean Pavel. BA, Hope Coll., 1973. Substitute tchr. Holland (Mich.) Pub. Schs., 1973—74; tchr. White Pigeon (Mich.) Cmty. Schs., 1975—. Sec. computer com. White Pidgeon (Mich.) Cmty. Schs., 1980—83, sec. gifted and talented com., 1979—80, sec. math and sci. com., 1980—92, sec. profl. coun., 1990—2003. Jehova's Witness. Avocations: sewing, crafts. Office: White Pigeon Comm Schs PO Box 488 White Pigeon MI 49099

PAVELKA, ELAINE BLANCHE, mathematics educator; b. Chgo. d. Frank Joseph and Mildred Bohumila (Seidl) P. BA, MS, Northwestern U.; PhD, U. Ill. With Northwestern U. Aerial Measurements lab., Evanston, Ill.; tchr. Leyden Cmty. H.S., Franklin Park, Ill.; prof. math. Morton Coll., Cicero, Ill. Invited prof. Internat. Congress on Math. Edn., Karlsruhe, Germany, 1976. RecipientSci. Talent award Westinghouse Electric Co. Mem. Am. Edn. Rsch. Assn., Am. Math. Assn. 2-Yr. Colls., Am. Math. Soc., Assn. Women in Math., Can. Soc. History and Philosophy of Math., Ill. Coun. Tchrs. Math., Ill. Math. Assn. C.C., Math. Assn. Am. Math. Action Group, Ga. Ctr. Study and Tchg. and Learning Math., Nat. Coun. Tchrs. Math., Sch. Sci. and Math. Assn., Northwestern U. Alumni Assn., U. Ill. Alumni Assn., Am. Mensa Ltd., Intertel, Sigma Delta Epsilon, Pi Mu Epsilon. Home: PO Box 7312 Westchester IL 60154-7312

PAVIET-HARTMANN, PATRICIA, chemist, researcher; b. Cormeilles, France, June 8, 1964; came to U.S., 1997; d. Roland Jean and Josette Juliette (Camus) Paviet; m. Thomas Hartmann, Apr. 27, 1996; 1 child, Josephine Caroline. BS, U. Nice, France, 1986, MS, 1988; PhD in Chemistry, U. Paris XI, 1992. Rsch. scientist Commissariat a l'Energie Atomique, Cadarache, France, 1990-92; postdoctoral fellow Lawrence Livermore Nat. Lab., Livermore, Calif., 1992-93; mem. staff Forschungszentrum, Karlsruhe, Germany, 1993-97, Los Alamos Nat. Lab., 1997—. Project leader in actinide chemistry, 2000—. Contbr. articles to profl. jours.; patentee in field. Mem. Am. Chem. Soc., Am. Nuclear Soc. Roman Catholic. Avocations: painting, piano, languages (french, english, german, italian, spanish). Office: Los Alamos Nat Lab Environ Sci MS A141 Carlsbad NM 88220 Home: 4770 Quemazon Los Alamos NM 87544-1672 E-mail: ppaviet-hartmann@lanl.gov.

PAVLAKOS, ELLEN TSATIRI, sculptor; b. Athens, May 25, 1936; d. Andrew and Katherine (Fliskanopoulou) Tsatiri; m. Andrew George Pavlakos, Nov. 2, 1952; children: James, John Andrew. Student, Arsakeion, Athens, 1952, Norton Sch. Art, West Palm Beach, Fla., 1975-79, Nat. Acad. Design, N.Y.C., 1980-81. Solo shows include Brevard Art Mus., 1981, Hess Galleries, Allentown, Pa., 1983, Cultural Ctr. Athens, 1990, 5th Ave. Art Gallery, Melbourne, Fla., 1994, 98; group shows include Le Salon des Nations, Paris, 1984, Nat. Exhbn. of Contemporary Realism in Art, Springfield, Mass., 1984, Springville Mus. Art, Utah, 1985, Capitol Gallery, Fla. Dept. Cultural Affairs, Tallahassee, 1988, Outstanding Am. Women Artists Invitational, Sarasota, 1993, Chamber of fine Arts and Min. of Edn. and Civilization Symposium, Nicosia, Cyprus, 1994, Mus. of Art and Sci., Melbourne, 1996, Appleton Mus. Art, Ocala, Fla., 1997, Sculpture '97,

Thessaloniki, Greece, 1997, Dunedin (Fla.) Fine Arts Ctr., 1998, Orlando City Hall Gallery, 1998, 621 Gallary, Tallahassee, Fla., 1999, Lee County Alliance of the Arts, Fort Myers, Fla., 1999, La. State U., Shreveport, 2000, Mt. Dora (Fla.) Art Ctr., 2000, U. Fla. Arts Ctr., Gainesville, 2001, DeLand (Fla.) Mus. Art, 2001, Oceola Art Ctr., Kissimmee, 2002, Visual Arts Ctr. of NW Fla., Panama City, Fla., 2002, Brevard Mus. of Arts and Sci., Melbourne, Fla., 2003, [illegible] Arts Ctr., Lake Wales, Fla., 2004, Atlantic Ctr. for the Arts at Harris, 2004; bronze sculpture commd. The Harry T. Moore Monument, Titusville Social Svcs. Ctr., 1985, wall relief Knowledge, Brevard Libr., 1993, bronze sculpture Mother Earth, Penakotheke, Athens, 1990, painting Interlude, Penakotheke, Hydrostone sculpture The Flame Keeper, Kennedy Space Ctr., Fla., 1992, Stephen Girard relief Girard Coll., Phila., 1999, Welcoming Jesus, bronze sculputre, Holy Name of Jesus CH., Fla., 2004. Recipient best of Show award Brevard Art Mus., 1980; grantee Brevard County Art in Pub. Places, 1990, 93. Mem. Acad. Artists Assn., Medalic Sculpture Assn., Chamber of Visual Arts in Greece, Ten Women in Art. Greek Orthodox. Avocations: art collecting, gardening. Studio: 331 Coral Way W Indialantic FL 32903-4401

PAVLEY, FRAN J. state representative; b. LA, Nov. 11, 1948; m. Andy Pavley; children: Jennifer, David. BA, Calif. State U., Fresno, 1970; MA, Calif. State U., 1985. Cert. tchr. Calif. Mem. Calif. Assembly, 2000—. Founder Agoura Hills Disaster Response Team, 1987—; adv. com., bd. Santa Monic Mountains Conservancy, 1990—; coastal commn. State of Calif., 1995—2000; councilmember, mayor Agoura Hills, Calif., 1981—97. Democrat. Office: PO Box 942849 Rm 3126 Sacramento CA 95814 Address: 6355 Topanga Canyon Blvd Ste 205 Woodland Hills CA 91367-2108

PAVLICK, PAMELA KAY, nurse, consultant; b. Topeka, Aug. 16, 1944; d. Cy Pavlick and June Lucille Dull. Diploma nursing, St. Luke's Hosp., Kansas City, Mo., 1966; BA in Psychology magna cum laude, U. North Fla., 1982, MS in Health Adminstrn. summa cum laude, 1987. RN, Mo., Ill., Fla.; cert. ins. rehab. specialist; lic. rehab. providor, Fla., Ga. Clin. instr. St. Luke's Hosp., Kansas City, 1966—70; instr. lic. practical nursing Springfield (Ill.) Sch. Bd., 1970—72; nursing supr. Jacksonville Beach (Fla.) Hosp., 1972—74; pub. health nurse State of Fla., Ocala, 1974—76; dir. nursing Upjohn Health Care, Jacksonville, Fla., 1976—77, mem. adv. com.; med. rep. Travelers Ins. Co., Jacksonville, 1977—84; rehab. cons. Aetna Life & Casualty, Jacksonville, 1985—, rep. nurse cons. adv. coun., 1988—90. Mem. ANA., Am. Assn. Rehab. Nurses, Nat. Assn. Rehab. Providers, Phi Kappa Phi. Republican. Episcopalian. Avocation: boating. Home: 14023 Tontine Rd Jacksonville FL 32225-2025 Office: Aetna Life & Casualty PO Box 2200 Jacksonville FL 32203-2200 Office Phone: 904-221-7811.

PAVONE, JILL RUSSELL, special education educator; b. Jan. 25, 1954; BSEd, SUNY, Geneseo, 1976, MSEd, 1985. Dir. Autism Family Support, Rochester, 1986-91; cons. in pvt. practice, Rochester, 1988—; pvt. instr. Early Intervention, Rochester, 1995—; spl. edn. tchr. Rochester Area Schs., 1977—. Involved in parent and staff tng., 1980—; instr. SUNY Coll. Edn., Geneseo, 1989—. Author: A Sister Named Lily; contbr. articles to profl. jours. Mem. Coun. Exceptional Children, Autism Soc. Am. (pres., v.p.), Rochester Tchrs. Assn. Office: 54 Corwin Rd Rochester NY 14610-1308

PAVONE, MARIANNE, medical/surgical nurse; b. Passaic, N.J., June 20, 1957; d. Roger Arthur and Mary Elizabeth Knight; m. James Michael Pavone, Sept. 8, 1979; children: Victoria Elizabeth, Ainslie Rose. Assoc. Degree, Passaic C.C., Paterson, N.J., 1979; student, Felician Coll., 1975—77. RN N.J.; cert. CPA, reach for recovery. RN ICN St. Josephs Med. Ctr., Paterson, 1979; RN rehab. Kessler Inst., West Orange, 1980; RN Dr. Kane-IMCC, Newton, 1996—98; RN rehab. Newton Meml. Hosp., 1998—2000; RN supr. Andover (N.J.) Care Ctr., 2000—. Author: (poetry book) Memories and Tantiles, 1993. Vol. Stillwater Vol. Fire Dept., 1989—; active Stillwater (N.J.) Sch. PTA, 1985—; mem. planning bd. Stillwater Twp., mem. welfare bd. Mem.: Am. Cancer Soc. (counselor). Republican. Presbyterian. Avocations: sailing, travel, poetry, gardening. Home: 916 Dove Island Rd Newton NJ 07860 Office: Andover Care Ctr Mulford Rd Andover NJ 07821

PAWELKO, KATHARINE ANN, recreation educator; b. N.Y.C., Mar. 26, 1952; d. Martin Anthony and Muriel Henrietta P. BSE, SUNY, College at Cortland, N.Y., 1974, MSE, 1978; PhD, U. Md., 1994. Cert. tchr. recreation edn. and phys. edn. K-12, N.Y. Instr. U. Maine, Presque Isle, 1979-84, U. Md., College Park, 1982-88; adj. assoc. prof. Prince George's C.C., Largo, Md., 1986-94; asst. prof. Western Ill. U., Macomb, 1994—. Rsch. asst. Nat. Park Svc., Washington, 1983, U. Md., College Park, 1984-86, 87-88, U.S. Forest Svc., 1985, 86; fitness instr., mgr. Healthpro, Inc., U.S. Dept. of Agriculture, Beltsville, Md., 1989-94. Author: Exploring the Nature of River Recreation Visitors and Their Recreational Experiences on The Delaware River, 1994, (with others) Issues in Therapeutic Recreation: A Profession in Transition, 2nd edit., 1996. Lifeguard ARC, 1977-94, water safety instr., 1977—; mem. Presque Isle Cmty. Adult Edn. Tri-Coun., 1981-82, Presque Isle YMCA Adv. Bd., 1981-83. Mem. AAHPERD (life), Nat. Recreation and Park Assn., Nat. Wildlife Assn. (life), N.Y. State Outdoor Edn. Assn. (life), Quebec-Labrador Found./Atlantic Ctr. for the Environment, Phi Kappa Phi, Kappa Delta Pi, Phi Alpha Epsilon, Omicron Delta Kappa. Republican. Episcopalian. Avocations: canoeing, hiking and camping, gardening, photography, fitness activities. Office: Western Ill U 1 University Circle 400 Currens Hall Macomb IL 61455

PAWLUK, ANNETTE MARIE, secondary school educator; b. Sharon, Pa., Nov. 12, 1960; d. Joseph Louis and Helen Katherine (Janosko) A.; m. Paul Pawluk, June 22, 2002. Student, Pa. State U., 1983-85; BE, Edinboro (Pa.) U., 1989; MS in Edn., Youngstown (Ohio) U., 1996. Math. tchr. Farrell (Pa.) Area Sch. Dist., 1990—. Head math. dept., 1992—. Mem. NEA, Pa. State Edn. Assn. Avocations: walking, weightlifting, aerobics, reading, sunbathing. Office: Farrell Area Sch Dist 1660 Roemer Blvd Farrell PA 16121-1754 Home: 744 N Darby Rd Hermitage PA 16148-9303

PAXTON, KATHLEEN MARIE, special education educator; b. Chicago, Ill., Mar. 11, 1960; d. Kenneth Alan and Patricia Nell Brown; m. Kevin Michael Paxton, July 14, 1984; children: Kaitlyn Mae, Kelly Meagan, Keegan Michael. BS, Ill. State U., Normal, 1982. Cert. learning disabilities Ill. State U., 1984. Spl. edn. tchr. Forman HS, Manito, Ill., 1982—85, Pleviak Elem. Sch., Lake Villa, Ill., 1985—86, Wenona (Ill.) Jr. HS, 1987—91, Bloomington (Ill.) HS, 1991—92, Fieldcrest Mid. Sch., Wenona, Ill., 1992—94, Salem Children's Home, Flanagan, Ill., 1994—98, Esmen Sch., Pontiac, Ill., 1998—2002; guidance counselor Morton (Ill.) HS, 2002—. Chairperson Gridleyfest, Gridley, Ill., 1992—99. Home: 18175 E 3100 North Rd Gridley IL 61744 Office: Morton High Sch 350 N Illinois Ave Morton IL 61550 Personal E-mail: lablover42@hotmail.com. E-mail: paxtkam@mortonpotters.org.

PAXTON, MARY JEAN WALLACE, science educator; b. Gary, Ind., Nov. 10, 1930; d. John James Wallace and Ruth Isobel Johnson; m. Robert Gerard Haagens, Dec. 27, 1971 (dec. Feb. 14, 1976); 1 child, Jan Gerard Haagens ; m. David Grant Paxton, Dec. 27, 1978. BS, St. Mary's Coll., 1957; PhD, U. Notre Dame, 1964. Asst. then assoc. prof. St. Mary's Coll., Notre Dame, Ind., 1964—69; rsch. fellow Harvard Sch. Pub. Health, Boston, 1969—71, Mass. Gen. Hosp., Boston, 1971—73; asst. prof. biology R.I. Coll., Providence, 1973—78; asst. to full prof. biology Jacksonville (Ala.) State U., 1978—93, dir., in service edn., 1990—93, acting dir. continuing edn., 1990—93; adj. instr. life scis. Palomar Coll., San Marcos, Calif., 1994—. Co-author: Biological and Medical Aspects of Contraception, 1965; author: The Female Body in Control, 1981, Endocrinology: Biological and Medical Perspective, 1986. Fellow coop. grad. fellow, NSF, 1962. Mem.: AAUW. Avocations: gardening, reading, crossword puzzles, fitness. Home: 3050 Skyline Dr Oceanside CA 92056 E-mail: mjw-paxton@cox.net.

PAYNE, ANITA HART, reproductive endocrinologist, researcher; b. Karlsruhe, Baden, Germany, Nov. 24, 1926; came to U.S., 1938; d. Frederick Michael and Erna Rose (Hirsch) Hart; widowed; children: Gregory Steven, Teresa Payne-Lyons. BA, U. Calif., Berkeley, 1949, PhD, 1952. From rsch. assoc. to prof. U. Mich., Ann Arbor, 1961-96, prof. emeritus, 1996—; assoc. dir. U. Mich. Ctr. for Study Reproduction, Ann Arbor, 1989-94; sr. rsch. scientist Stanford (Calif.) U. Med. Ctr., 1995—. Vis. scholar Stanford U., 1987-88; mem. reproductive biology study sect. NIH, Bethesda, Md., 1978-79, biochem. endocrinology study sect., 1979-83, population rsch. com. Nat. Inst. Child Health and Human Devel., 1989-93. Assoc. editor Steroids, 1987-93; contbr. book chpts., articles to profl. jours. Recipient award for cancer rsch. Calif. Inst. for Cancer Rsch., 1953, Acad. Women's Caucus award U. Mich., 1986, Mentor award Women in Endocrinology, 1999. Mem. Endocrine Soc. (chmn. awards com. 1983-84, mem. nominating com. 1985-87, coun. 1988-91), Am. Soc. Andrology (exec. coun. 1980-83), Soc. for Study of Reproduction (bd. dirs. 1982-85, sec. 1986-89, pres. 1990-91, Carl G. Hartman award 1998, Disting. Svc. award 2004). Office: Stanford U Med Ctr Dept OB GYN Divsn Reproductive Biology Stanford CA 94305-5317

PAYNE, DEBORAH ANNE, medical company officer; b. Norristown, Pa., Sept. 22, 1952; d. Kenneth Nathan Moser and Joan (Reese) Dewhurst; m. Randall Barry Payne, Mar. 8, 1975 (div.). AA, Northeastern Christian Jr. Coll., 1972; B in Music Edn., Va. Commonwealth U., 1979. Driver, social asst. Children's Aid Soc., Norristown, Pa., 1972—73; mgr. Boddie-Noell Enterprises, Richmond, Va., 1974—79; retail food saleswoman Hardee's Food Systems, Inc., Phila., 1979—81; supr., with tech. tng. and testing depts. Cardiac Datacorp., Phila., 1981—95; tng. supr. Raytel Cardiac Svcs., Forest Hills, NY, 1995—98, supr. tech. support Haddonfield, NJ, 1998—2000; ret., 2000. Mem. bd. advisers Am. Biog. Inst., 1989—. Mem. NAFE, Delta Omicron (pres. Alpha Xi chpt. 1978-79, pres. Epsilon province 1980-85, chmn. Eastern Pa. alumni 1986-88, Star award 1979), Am. Soc. Profl. and Exec. Women. Democrat. Avocations: music, sports. Home: 7400 Roosevelt Blvd Apt A10 Philadelphia PA 19152-4324 E-mail: Deborah.A.Payne@att.net.

PAYNE, FRANCES ANNE, literature educator, researcher; b. Harrisonburg, Va., Aug. 28, 1932; d. Charles Franklin and Willie (Tarvin) P. BA, B.Mus., Shorter Coll, 1953; MA, Yale U., 1954, PhD, 1960. adj. fellow St. Anne's Coll., Oxford Eng. Instr. Conn. Coll., New London, 1955-56, U. Buffalo, 1958-60, lectr., 1960, asst. prof., 1960-67; assoc. prof. SUNY, Buffalo, 1967-75, prof. English and medieval lit., 1975—. Adj. fellow St. Anne's Coll., Oxford, Eng., 1966—. Author: King Alfred and Boethius, 1968; Chaucer and Menippean Satire, 1981. Contbr. articles to scholarly publs. AAUW fellow, Oxford, 1966-67; Research Found. grantee SUNY Central, Oxford, 1967, 68, 71, 72; recipient Julian Park award SUNY-Buffalo, 1979. Mem. Medieval Acad. Am., New Chaucer Soc., Internat. Soc. Anglo-Saxonists, Pi Kappa Lambda Office: SUNY-Buffalo 306 Clemens Hall Buffalo NY 14260-4600 Office Phone: 716-645-2575 2557. E-mail: fapayne@buffalo.edu.

PAYNE, GLORIA MARQUETTE, business educator; b. Elkins, W.Va., Dec. 21, 1923; d. Anthony and Roselyn Marquette; m. Carl Wesley Payne, Mar. 6, 1950; 1 child, Mary Debra Payne Moore. BA, MHL (hon.), Davis and Elkins Coll.; MA, W.Va. U.; PhD, U. Pitts., 1975; postgrad., NYU Fashion Inst. Tech. Cert. designed appearance cons. Sec. Equitable Ins. Co., Elkins, 1943-44; tchr., dept. head Spencer (W.Va.) H.S., 1944-45; prof. bus. Davis & Elkins Coll., Elkins, 1945-93; image cons. Elkins, 1988-93; bus. cons., 1970-93; mgr. Elkins Wallpaper Shop, 1945-65; owner Merle Norman Cosmetic Studio, Elkins, 1950-56. Dir. tchr. workshops W.Va. U., Marshall U., State Dept. Edn., Charleston, W.Va., summers; dir. machine shorthand workshops for tchrs. throughout the U.S.; dir. designer appearance World Modeling Assn., N.Y.C., 1989—; instr. modeling Davis & Elkins Coll., 1980-93. Author: A Methods Class is Interesting and Challenging, 1970, The Oak or the Pumpkin; mem. editl. bd. Nat. Assn. of Business Teachers Edn. Pub., 1993, 94; contbr. articles to profl. jours. Chair Bi-Centennial, City of Elkins; dir. Elkins Fair, City of Elkins; pres. St. Brendans Parish; judge Mountain State Forest Festival Parades, 1988-94; rep. Region I at Dallas Nat. Cov., 1994 (one of five nat. finalists); div. chair bus., econs., and tourism. Recipient Outstanding Prof. award Sears-Roebuck Co., Lois Latham award for Excelence in Tchg., Cmty. Svc. award Elkins C. of C., 1992, Outstanding Educator award BPW, 1997, WVBEA, W.Va. Vocat. Assn., 1994, 97, Region I award for Outstanding Vocational Educator, Outstanding Collegiate Tchr. Bus. award, 1997, 1st recipient James S. McDonnell Found. Fully Endowed Acad. Chair in Bus. and Econs.; named Educator of Yr., W.Va. Women's Club, Outstanding Educator AAUW, Randolph County C. of C. Citizen of Yr., 1998. Mem. Am. Bus. Writers Assn., W.Va. Edn. Assn. (past pres., Outstanding Prof., Outstanding Svc. award, Outstanding Bus. Educator award), Tri-State Bus. Edn. Assn. (historian, outstanding svc. award, Tchr.-Educator of the South award 1991), World Modeling Assn. (v.p. 1988-95, modeling award 1989), Designed Appearance U.S. (dir. 1990-98), W.Va. Bus. Edn. Assn. (award 1977, 85, 94, 97), Bus. & Profl. Women's Orgn., W.Va. C. of C., The Fashion Club (advisor), Beta Sigma Phi (advisor), Beta Alpha Beta (advisor), Pi Beta Phi, Phi Beta Lambda (advisor). Democrat. Roman Catholic. Avocations: flower arranging, modeling. Home: 301 Davis St Elkins WV 26241-4030 Office: Davis & Elkins Coll 100 Sycamore St Elkins WV 26241-3996

PAYNE, JOANNE LESLEY, broadcast executive; b. Leeds, Eng., Jan. 21, 1958; arrived in US, 1995; d. Rowland Kenneth and Marjorie (Meekley) Cockill; m. Michael Dermot Kavanagh, June 14, 1986 (div. Mar. 1989); m. Gregory Banks Payne, Oct. 28, 1995. Attended, North of England Bus. Sch., England, 1975. Sales admin. Trident TV, Leeds, England, 1976—81; sales mgr. Television South (Telso), London, 1982—90; cons. Yorkshire TV, London, 1990—91; sr. v.p. Link Entertainment, London, 1991—95, L.A., 1995—2000; pres. Foothill Entertainment, Santa Barbara, Calif., 2000—. Exec. prodr.: (TV series) Pirate School, 2004. Exec. com. mem. Muscular Dystophy Assn., Santa Barbara, 2003. Mem.: Acad. of TV, Arts and Sci., British Acad. of Film and TV. Avocations: golf, tennis, music, art, travel. Office: Foothill Entertainment Inc 1231 State St 208 Santa Barbara CA 93101

PAYNE, MARY LIBBY, retired judge; b. Gulfport, Miss., Mar. 27, 1932; d. Reece O. and Emily Augusta (Cook) Bickerstaff; m. Bobby R. Payne; children: Reece Allen, Glenn Russell. Student, Miss. U. for Women, 1950-52; BA in Polit. Sci. with distinction, U. Miss., 1954, LLB, 1955. Bar: Miss. 1955. Ptnr. Bickerstaff & Bickerstaff, Gulfport, 1955-56; sec. Guaranty Title Co., Jackson, Miss., 1957; assoc. Henley, Jones, & Henley, Jackson, Miss., 1958-61; freelance rschr. Pearl, Miss., 1961-63; solo practitioner Brandon, Miss., 1963-68; exec. dir. Miss. Judiciary Commn., Jackson, 1968-70; chief drafting & rsch. Miss. Ho. Reps., Jackson, 1970-72; asst. atty. gen. State Atty. Gen. Office, Jackson, 1972-75; founding dean, assoc. prof. Sch. Law Miss. Coll., Jackson, 1975-78, prof., 1978-94; judge Miss. Ct. Appeals, Jackson, 1995—2001; ret., 2001. Mem. bd. disting. alumnae Miss. U. Women, 1988—2000. Contbr. articles to profl. jours. Founder, bd. dirs. Christian Conciliation Svc., Jackson, 1983-93; bd. dirs. Exchange Club's Child Abuse Prevention Ctr. of Jackson, 1999-2001; counsel Christian Action Com. Rankin Bapt. Assn., Pearl, 1968-92; advisor Covenant Ministerial Fellowship, 1995-2002. Named Miss. Coll. Lawyer of Yr., Miss. Coll. Sch. Law Alumni Assn., 1998, Outstanding Woman Lawyer, Miss. Women Lawyers Assn., 1999, Susie Blue Buchanan award, Women in Profession Com. of Miss. Bar, 2000; recipient Book of Golden Deeds award, Pearl Exch. Club, 1989, Excellence medallion, Miss. U. Women, 1990, Woman of Yr. award, Miss. Assn. Women Higher Edn., 1989, Power of One award, Miss. Govs. Conf., 1996. Fellow Am. Bar Found.; mem. Miss. Bar Found., Christian Legal Soc. (nat. bd. dirs. 1992-2001, Skeeter Ellis Svc. to Law Students award 1999, Lifetime Achievement award 2002). Baptist. Avocations: public speaking, travel, needlepoint, sewing, reading.

PAYNE, MEREDITH JORSTAD, physician; b. St. Louis, Feb. 7, 1927; d. Louis Helmar and Cleone Gladys (Branian) Jorstad; m. Spencer Payne, 1948 (div. 1959); m. James McGarity, 1965 (div. 1977); children: Maureen Meredith, James Louis. AB, Washington U., St. Louis, 1947, MD, 1950; MBA, Lindenwood U., 1999. Diplomate Am. Bd. Surgery, Am. Bd. Plastic Surgery. Intern gen. surgery St. Louis City Hosp., 1950-51, asst. resident surgery, 1951-54; chief surg. resident Roswell Park Meml. Hosp., Buffalo, 1954-55; chief plastic surgery resident Allentown (Pa.) Gen. Hosp., 1955-57; clin. instr. surgery Washington U. Med. Sch., 1957-70; vis. surgeon Homer G. Phillips Hosp., St. Louis, 1957-70; staff St. Luke's, St. Louis and Bethesda, 1957—, St. Mary's, 1988—; chief plastic surgery Vets. Hosp., 1986-98; assoc. prof. plastic surgery (clin.) St. Louis U. Sch. Medicine, St. Louis, 1986—. Med. dir. Unity Clft Palate Clinic; asst. dir. Bethesda Delworth Nursing Home, 1997—2001; attending physician Concentra Med. Ctrs., 1994—. Contbr. articles to profl. jours. Fellow ACS; mem. AMA, Am. Soc. Plastic and Reconstructive Surgery, Mo. Med. Assn. (del., councillor 1988X), St. Louis Met. Med. Soc. (councillor 1983-86, sec. 1998-99, v.p. 1999-00), Am. Cleft Palate Assn., Roswell Park Surgery Assn., So. Med. Assn., Washington U. Med. Alumni Assn., Am. Geriatrics Soc., Midwestern Assn. Plastic Surgeons, Pan Am. Med. Assn., City Hosp. Alumni Assn., Soc. Head and Neck Surgeons, St. Louis Area Soc. Plastic Surgeons (pres. 1990-93), City Hosp. Alumni Assn. (v.p. 1995-97, pres. 1997-99), Mo. Assn. Plastic and Reconstructive Surgery (treas. 1995X, v.p. 1997, pres. 1998), St. Louis Surg. Soc. (v.p. 1998), AMWA (treas. St. Louis chpt. 1995), Order Eastern Star, Zonta (St. Louis pres. 1968-69), College Club (bd. dirs. St. Louis 1983-85). Avocations: skiing, tennis, sewing, knitting, gardening. Home: 7314 Westmoreland Dr Saint Louis MO 63130-4240

PAYNE, PAULA MARIE, minister; b. Waukegan, Ill., Jan. 13, 1952; d. Percy Howard and Annie Maude (Canady) P. BA, U. Ill., 1980; MA, U. San Francisco, 1986; MDiv, Wesley Theol. Sem., 1991, postgrad., 1995—. Ordained to ministry United Meth. Ch., 1990. Chaplain for minority affairs Am. U., Washington, 1988-89; chaplain, intern NIH, Bethesda, Md., 1989-90; pastor Asbury United Meth. Ch., Charles Town, W.Va., 1990—. Supt. ch. sch. United Meth. Ch., Oxon Hill, Md., 1989-90; mem. AIDS task force Wesley Theol. Sem., Washington, 1988-89; mem. retreat. com. Balt. Conf., 1990—; chair scholarship com. Asbury United Meth. Ch., 1990—. Bd. dirs. AIDS Task Force Jefferson County, Charles Town, 1991—, Cmty. Ministries, Charles Town, 1991—; formerly N.H. state v.p. Ch. Women United, now pres.; mem. ethics com. Concord Hosp. Tech. sgt. USAF, 1984-88; chaplain Army N.G., Md., 1994-96, Mass. 2001; chaplain USAFR, 1997. Maj. Air N.G. Recipient Cert. of Recognition, Ill. Ho. of Reps., 1988, 20th Century award of Achievement Internat. Biog. Ctr., Cambridge, Eng., 1993, 1st Five Hundred, Cambridge, 1994, Citizen's citation, City of Balt., 1994, others; Ethnic Minority scholar United Meth. Ch., 1988-89, Brandenburg scholar, 1988-89, Tadlock scholar, 1989-90, Calvary Fellow scholar Calvary United Meth. ch., 1989-90. Mem. AAUW, U. Ill. Alumni Assn. (bd. dirs. 1987-88), Alpha Kappa Alpha (pres. local chpt. 1974-76, v.p. 1973). Republican. Home: PMB 286 39 Nathan Ellis Hwy Mashpee MA 02649-3267 E-mail: revpmpumc@msn.com., revpmpumc@hotmail.com.

PAYNE, SARA MARLENE, school librarian; d. Wayne and Marlene Genske; m. Ronnie C. Payne, Mar. 20, 1993. BA in Journalism, U. of Wis., 1990; MLS, Tex. Woman's U., 1997. Cert. tchr. Tex., 1998. Tchr. Chisholm Trail Mid. Sch., Rhome, Tex., 1998—99, libr., 1999—. Mem. com. N.W. Ind. Sch. Dist., Fort Worth, Tex., 2001—02; mem. site based com. Chisholm Trail Mid. Sch., Rhome, Tex., 2002—03. Recipient Bright Idea award, N.W. Edn. Found., Highsmith award, Tex. Libr. Assn.; grantee Devel. Grant, N.W. Edn. Found., 2000, 2002, 2003. Mem.: Tex. Libr. Assn., U. of Wis. Alumni, Soc. of Children's Book Writers and Illustrators. Office: Chisholm Trail Middle School 583 Fm 3433 Rhome TX 76078

PAYNE, SUSAN FRANTZ, fundraiser, artist; b. N.Y.C., Feb. 17, 1941; d. Frederick P. and Caroline (Campbell) Frantz; m. John H. Payne III, Aug. 24, 1963; children: John H. IV, Sarah S. BS, Simmons Coll., 1963. Dir. edn. Am. Indian Archaeol. Inst. (now Inst. Am. Indian Studies), Washington, Conn., 1976-83, exec. dir., 1983-85; devel. assoc. New Milford (Conn.) Hosp. Found., 1991—2001; devel. dir. Roxbury (Conn.) Land Trust, 2001—. Mem. adv. coun. Women's Ctr. Greater Danbury, Conn., 1993—; trustee Steep Rock Assn., Washington, 1991—, chair of Land Preservation Com. Vol. Re-election Campaign Nanncy Johnson, 1996, Conservation Plan, Washington, 1995-2000; devel. cons. Am. Montessori Soc., N.Y.C., 1997-2000; chair Greenways Com., Town of Wash. Conservation Commn., 2001—. Mem. Oriental Brush Artists Guild (pres. 1993-94). Avocations: horticulture, japanese gardening, hiking, travel, chinese brush painting.

PAYSON, HERTA RUTH, psychotherapist, theater educator; b. Oak Park, Ill., Jan. 31, 1933; d. Joseph Hale and Lily Brush (Bagley) P.; m. Elliott Proctor Joslin, Oct. 12, 1961 (div. Oct., 1984); children: Allen Payson, Rachel Elizabeth, David Elliott. BA, Goddard Coll., 1979; MA, Vt. Coll., 1982; PhD, The Union Inst., 1996. Tchr., dir. Queens (N.Y.) Cmty. Dance Sch., 1954-63; theatrical costumer N.Y.C., 1955-69; costumer Nat. Theatre of the Deaf, Waterford, Conn., 1970-84; asst. prof., theater dept. Conn. Coll., New London, 1970—; pvt. practice psychotherapy Groton, Conn., 1980—; with Conn. Ctr. Massage Therapy, 2003—. Co-owner SYZYGY for little b., N.Y.C., 1964-69; coord. small groups Friends Conf. Religion and Psychology, Haverford, Pa., 1975-79, co-clk., 1978-83. Author: The Dragon's Eye: Envisioning Women's Wisdom, 1998; choreographer for As You Like It, Two Gentlemen of Verona and Romeo & Juliet for N.Y. Shakespeare Festival, Alice in Wonderland for The Little Orch. Soc., others. Mem. Am. Counseling Assn., Conn. Assn. Jungian Psychology, Nat. Guild Hypnotists, Soc. of Layerists in Multi-Media, Fiber Artists on the Cutting Edge. Avocations: gardening, weaving, quilting, home improvement. Office: 73 Laurelwood Rd Groton CT 06360-5654 Office Phone: 860-445-8083.

PAYTON-WRIGHT, PAMELA, actress; b. Pitts., Nov. 1, 1941; d. Gordon Edgar and Eleanor Ruth (McKinley) Payton Wright; m. David Arthur Butler, May 8, 1978 (div. 1989); 1 child, Oliver Dickon Hedley. Grad., St. Mary's Jr. Coll., 1961; BA, Birmingham So. Coll., 1963; postgrad., Royal Acad. Dramatic Arts, London, 1963-65. Theatre debut Diary of a Scoundrel, 1965, Broadway debut The Show-Off, 1968, Broadway appearances Exit The King, The Cherry Orchard, 1968, Jimmy Shine, 1969, The Crucible, 1972, Mourning Becomes Electra, 1972, All Over town, 1975, Glass Menagerie, 1976, Romeo and Juliet, 1977, A Streetcar Named Desire, 1988, Night of the Iguana, 1988, M. Butterfly, 1988-90, Something Unspoken, 1995, Long Day's Journey Into Night, 2003, Off-Broadway appearances The Effect of Gamma Rays on Man-In-The Moon Marigolds, 1970-71, Jesse and the Bandit Queen, 1975, The Seagull, 1980, Don Juan, 1982, Hamlet, 1982, Mrs. Warren's Profession, 1992, The Replacement, 1995, Richard III, 'Til the Rapture Comes, 1998, What You Get and What You Expect, 2000, Fifth of July, 2003, regional theater appearances Skin of Our Teeth, 1972, Aimee, 1973, Othello, Troilus and Cressida, As You Like It, 1976, Lunch Girls, 1977, Summerfolk, 1978, The Greeks, 1982, The Misanthrope, 1982, Tobacco Road, 1984, Passion, 1984-85, Cat on a Hot Tin Roof, 1985, Little Eyolf, 1985, On the Verge, 1986, Our Town, 1987,

The Road to Mecca, 1990, Picnic, 1991, The Way of the World, 1991, Quartermaine's Terms, 1993, Misalliance, 1993, Six Degrees of Separation, 1993, Ghosts, 1994, Sea Gull, 1994, The Show-Off, 1995, The Rivals, 1996, Touch of the Poet, 1996, Glass Menagerie, 1997, Voir Dire, 1997, She Stoops to Conquer, 1997, Blithe Spirits, 1998, Transit of Venus, 1998, Seagull, 1999, Long Day's Journey Into Night, 1999, Sweet Bird of Youth, 1999, A Fair Country, 2000, Philadelphia Story, 2001, Long Days Journey Into Night, 2002, Seascape, 2002, Outward Bound, 2002, others, film appearances At the Dark End of the Street, 1980, Going in Style, 1981, Starlight, 1985, My Little Girl, 1985, Ironweed, 1987, The Freshman, 1989, In Dreams, 1999, TV appearances Look Homeward Angel, 1972, The Haunting of Rosalind, 1973, The Prodigal, Brother to Dragons, 1973, The Adams Chronicles, 1976. Nominee Lucille Lortel, 2003; recipient Fulbright award, 1963, Spl. medal, Edmund Gray prize for high comedy, Herbert Beerbohm Tree citation, Royal Acad. Dramatic Art, 1963—65, Obie award, 1970, 1975, Clarence Derwent award, Variety Critics' Poll citation, 1970, Drama Desk award, 1972, Best Actress citation, Dallas Theater Critics' Forum, 1994, Balt., 1997, Dean Goodman award, 1999; Fox Grant fellow, 1999. Mem. Actors Equity Assn., AFTRA, Screen Actors Guild. Episcopalian. Office: Bauman & Assocs 250 W 57th St New York NY 10019-3741

PAZDON, DENISE JOAN, speech pathology/audiology services professional; b. Bklyn., Aug. 28, 1953; d. Robert Edward and Mildred Ella (Volinsky) Strauss; m. John Joseph, Jr. Pazdon, Nov. 3, 1973 (dec.); children: Melissa Joann, John Robert. AS, Coll. Lifelong Learning, Portsmouth, N.H., 1995; BS in Comm. Disorders summa cum laude, Coll. Lifelong Learning, 1997; MS in Comm. Disorders, U. N.H., 2000. Cert. tchr. N.H., lic. speech-lang. pathologist N.H. Speech lang. asst. Garrison Pub. Sch., Dover, NH, 1988—95; speech lang. specialist Kingston-Bakie Sch., Kingston, NH, 1995—98; speech lang. pathologist Pollard Sch., Plaiston, NH, 1998—2001; lang. pathologist, ednl. specialist North Hampton Sch., NH, 2001—03; spl. edn. cons. U. N.H., Durham, 2003—, coop. tchr., supr., 2001—; program designer/instr. Coll. for Lifelong Learning, Portsmouth, 2003—. Contbr. articles to profl. jours. Staff-adult advisor Youth to Youth, Ohio, 1985—87; sch. vol. City of Diver, 1987; bd. dirs. Concerned Citizens for Drug and Alcohol Prevention, Dover, 1980—87. Mem.: Am. Speech Lang. Hearing Assn., N.H. Speech Lang. Hearing Assn., Alpha Sigma Lambda. Avocations: kayaking, travel, skiing, vocalist in band. Home: 41 Ayers Ln Dover NH 03820 Office: North Hampton Sch 201 Atlantic Ave North Hampton NH 03862

PAZICKY, DIANA LOERCHER, literature educator; d. Gustav Arthur Loercher and Ellen Hazel Sederlund; m. Edward P. Pazicky; 1 child, Luke. BA in English, Wellesley Coll., 1963; MA in Comparative Lit., U. Chgo., 1964; PhD in English, Temple U., 1995. Proofreader, copy editor Atlantic Monthly, Boston, 1967—69; feature writer, art critic Christian Sci. Monitor, Boston, 1970—80, N.Y.C., 1970—80; freelance writer, 1980—85; grants writer, mgr. NJN Pub. TV, Trenton, NJ, 1997—2000; asst. prof. Temple U., Phila., 2000—. Author: Cultural Orphans in America, 1990; contbr. articles to mags. and newspapers. Avocation: playwrighting. Office: Temple Univ 580 Meeting House Rd Ambler PA 19002

PEABODY, ARLENE L. HOWLAND BAYAR, retired, nurse; b. Deposit, NY, June 26, 1931; d. Burt and Olive (Oralls) Howland; m. Atilla C. Bayar, Dec. 8, 1956 (div.); m. Norman R. Peabody, Feb. 1, 1975 (dec.); children: Tildy Anne Bayar Sparrow, Carol A. Digilio; m. Robert A. Ehlers, Feb. 15, 2003. Diploma, Harrisburg Hosp. Sch. Enterostomal Therapy, 1971; AAS, Empire State Coll., 1985; BS in Edn., SUNY, Oneonta, 1990. RN, N.Y.; cert. therapeutic touch practitioner, natural force healing practitioner, enterostomal nurse. Sec. pres.'s office Cornell U., Ithaca, NY, 1949—55; exec. sec. Rudolph Lang, Office Execs. Assn. N.Y. and Prestige Expositions Inc., N.Y.C., 1955—69; enterostomal therapy nurse M.I. Bassett Hosp., Cooperstown, NY, 1972—89; pvt. practice enterostomal therapy nurse Oneonta, NY, 1989—2002. Spkr. in field. Vol. Am. Cancer Soc., 1972-2002, Catskill Area Hospice, 1990-02, Glimmerglass Opera, 1975-2002; bd. dirs. Del. Heritage Inc., 1996-2002; trustee Unitarian Universalist Soc.; active Storytelling Ctr. of Oneonta, Oneonta Concert Assn., Oneonta Contradance. Mem. AARP (bd. dirs. 1986-2002), N.Y. State Hist. Assn., Delaware County Hist. Assn., Wound Ostomy and Continence Nurses Soc., United Ostomy Assn. (N.Y. state field svcs. rep.), Order Ea. Star. Avocations: heirloom quilting, traditional folk music, coutourier clothing, costuming, dance. Home: 13511 Pebblebrook Dr Houston TX 77079-6023

PEACOCK, FLORENCE F. professional musician, soprano, voice teacher; b. Covington, Ga., June 13, 1937; d. Robert Raphael and Louly (Turner) Fowler; m. James Lowe Peacock, Aug. 4, 1962; children: Louly Peacock-Konz, Sara Claire, Natalie F. BA, Hollins Coll., 1959; MMusic, Yale U., 1962. Instrumentalist, singer, dancer Javanese Gamelon, Indonesia, 1963, 64, 96; paticipant, soprano soloist Oberlin Coll.: Baroque Performance Inst., 1978-2001; soprano soloist Franz Schubert Inst., Baden-bei-Wien, Austria, 1995. Presented in recital and concert in Japan, Russia, Indonesia, Eng., Austria, Can. and U.S.; appeared on Nat. Pub. Radio in Performance Today. Bd. dirs. Triangle Opera, Research Triangle Park, N.C.; mem. adv. bd. Chapel Hill-Carrboro Cmty. Chorus; soprano soloist United Meth. Ch. Choir, pres., 1987-88; bd. dirs. nat. devel. coun. U. N.C., Chapel Hill; pres. Preservation Soc., Chapel Hill, 2001; bd. dirs. Chapel Hill Mus., 1999-2001. Recipient citation Chapel Hill Preservation Soc., 1995. Mem. PEO, Nat. Assn. Music Tchrs., Chapel Hill Music Tchrs. Assn. (program chair 1997-98), U. N.C. Woman's Club (pres. 1998-99). Democrat. Methodist. Avocations: swimming, tennis, walking. Home and Office: 306 N Boundary St Chapel Hill NC 27514-7800

PEACOCK, JUDITH ANN See ERWIN, JUDITH

PEACOCK, MARILYN CLAIRE, primary education educator; b. Harvey, Ill., Aug. 2, 1952; d. Carmen Anthony and Helen Elaine (Welch) R. AA with high honors, Thornton C.C., 1972; BS in Edn. with high honors, Ill. State U., 1974; MEd, Nat.-Louis U., 1990. Cert. K-9, Ill. Tchr. kindergarten Primary Acad. Ctr., Markham, Ill., 1976-91, tchr. K-3, 1991—. Ill. State scholar, 1969. Mem. Ill. Edn. Assn. (assn. rep. 1976-88), Kappa Delta Pi, Phi Theta Kappa. Republican. Avocations: music, travel. Home: 2447 Clyde St Homewood IL 60430-3103 Office: Acad Ctr 3055 W 163rd St Markham IL 60426-5626 Personal E-mail: mcrpeacock@hotmail.com.

PEACOCK, MARY WILLA, magazine editor; b. Evanston, Ill., Oct. 23, 1942; d. William Gilbert and Mary Willa (Young) P. BA, Vassar Coll., 1964. Assoc. lit. editor Harper's Bazaar mag., N.Y.C., 1964-69; staff editor Innovation mag., N.Y.C., 1969-70; editor in chief, co-founder Rags mag., N.Y.C., San Francisco, 1970-71; co-founder, features editor Ms. mag., N.Y.C., 1971-77; pub., pres. Rags mag., N.Y.C., 1977-80; sr. editor Village Voice, N.Y.C., 1980-85, style editor, 1985-89; editor-in-chief Model mag., N.Y.C., 1989—, editorial cons., 1991—; fashion dir. Lear's Mag., N.Y.C., 1992-93; dep. editor In Style Mag., 1993-94, Mirabella mag., 1994-95; cons., 1995—. Internat. editor InStyle; writer and cons. in field.

PEACOCK, MOLLY, poet, educator; b. June 30, 1947; d. Edward Frank and Pauline Ruth (Wright) P. BA magna cum laude, Harpur Coll., Binghamton, N.Y., 1969; MA with hons., Johns Hopkins U., 1977. Adminstr., lectr. in english SUNY, Binghamton, 1970-76; instr. english Friends Sem., N.Y.C., 1981-92; poet-in-residence Bucknell U., 1993-94, Cathedral St. John the Divine, 2000. Author: And Live Apart, 1980, Raw Heaven, 1984, Take Heart, 1989, Original Love, 1995, Paradise, Piece by Piece, 1998, How To Read A Poem and Start A Poetry Circle, 1999, The Private I: Privacy in A Public World, 2001, Cornucopia: New and Selected Poems, 2002, The Shimmering Verge: A One-Woman Show in Poems, 2003; contbg. writer House and Garden mag., 1996-2001; contbr. poems to The New Yorker, The New Republic, The Nation. Danforth Found. fellow, 1970, Yaddo fellow, 1980, 82, 89, Ingram Merrill Found. fellow 1981, 86, Lila Wallace/Woodrow Wilson fellow 1994, 95, 96, 2001; grantee Creative Artists Pub. Svc. Program, 1977, N.Y. Found. for Arts, 1985, NEA, 1991; Regents scholar U. Calif., Riverside, 1998. Mem. PEN, Poetry Soc. Am. (governing bd. 1988—, pres. emeritus). Home: 109 Front St E #1041 Toronto M51 4P7 Canada also: 109 Front St Apt 1041 Toronto ON Canada M5A 4P7 E-mail: peacockmol@aol.com.

PEACOCK, PENNE KORTH, ambassador; b. Hattiesburg, Miss., Nov. 3, 1942; m. Fritz-Alan Korth, Dec. 15, 1965 (div. 1997); children: Fritz-Alan Jr., Maria Korth Chieffalo, James Frederick; m. Andrew Peacock, Sept. 21, 2002. Student, U. Tex., 1960—64. Sr. Washington assoc., client liaison and rep. trust and estate div. Sotheby's, 1986-89; amb. to Mauritius, Port Louis, 1989-92; pres. Firestone and Korth Ltd., Washington, 1993-97; commr. US Adv. Commn. Pub. Diplomacy, 1997—. Bd. dir. Chevy Chase Bank, 1993—; rep. Sotheby's Internat., 1997—. Co-chmn. Am. Bicentennial Presdl. Inauguration, Washington, 1988—99; mem. adv. bd. Washington Ballet, 2002—; bd. dirs. Hillwood Mus. and Gardens; counselor Meridian Internat. Ctr.; bd. dirs. Coun. of Am. Ambs., 1994—. Mem.: Assn. for Diplomatic Studies and Tng. (bd. dir. 1996—). Office: 11 Gladswood Gardens Apt #5 Double Bay 2028 NSW Australia

PEACOCK, VIRGINIA C. artist; b. Harrisburg, Pa., June 25, 1958; d. M. Edwin Jr. and Karon Cliffe Green; m. Foulis Munro Peacock, Apr. 20, 1996. BA, Mount Holyoke Coll., 1980. Sec. Mus. Modern Art, N.Y.C., 1982; pub. info. assoc. Nat. Acad. Design, N.Y.C., 1983-87; graphics specialist Fortune Mag., N.Y.C., 1987-95; creative mgr. Bus. Week Mag., N.Y.C., 1995-99. One-woman shows include Ridge Street Gallery, N.Y.C., 1992, 92, 94, Artra Gallery, N.Y.C., 1992, Mercedes-Benz Manhattan, Inc., N.Y.C., 1995, 97, Mercer St. Gallery, N.Y.C., 1999; group exhbns. include The Weisner Gallery, Bklyn., 1987, The New Waterfront Mus., Bklyn., 1987, The Studio Gallery, Bklyn., 1989, B4 ART Gallery, N.Y.c., 1991, The Kentler Internat. Drawing Ctr., Bklyn., 1991, Montserrat Gallery, N.Y.C., 1992, Brookwood Child Care Ctr., Bklyn., 1992, Bklyn. Waterfront Artists Coalition, 1993-96, Time-Warner, N.Y.C., 1993, Krasdale Corp., Bronx, N.Y., 1994, Ridge St. Gallery, N.Y.C., 1994, Fort Hunter Mus., Harrisburg, Pa., 1995, Harbor Cove Cafe, Sag Harbor, N.Y., 1995, St. John's Episcopal Ch., Southampton, N.Y., 1996. Republican. Methodist. Avocations: horse riding, running, gardening, cooking, tennis.

PEAKE, CANDICE K. LOPER, data processing professional; b. Sublette, Kans., Oct. 29, 1953; d. Robert Franklin and Marion Joyce Loper; m. Eugene E. Peake, Aug. 12, 1993. Student, McPherson (Kans.) Coll., 1971—72; lic. in cosmetology, Crums Beauty Sch., Manhattan, Kans., 1974; student, Garden City (Kans.) Community Coll., 1975—76, Diablo Valley Coll., 1988—89, U. Phoenix, 2002—. ICCP cert. data processor. Owner, operator Candi's For Beautiful Hair, Garden City, 1974-78; systems project librarian Bank of Am., San Francisco, 1980, analyst, 1981, systems analyst, 1981-82, sr. systems analyst, 1982-83, cons., 1983-84, systems cons., team leader, 1984; project mgr. Wells Fargo Bank, Concord, Calif., 1984-86; systems analyst 1st Nationwide Bank, San Francisco, 1986-88; adv. systems engr. Bank Am., Concord, Calif., 1988-89; owner Candi's Visions, Independence, Mo., 1988—; sr. mgr. Computer Scis. Corp., Independence, 1989—. Home: 3419 S Home Ave Independence MO 64052-1239 Office: Computer Scis Corp 3419 S Home Ave Independence MO 64052-1239 Office Phone: 816-358-7475. Personal E-mail: cpeake@csc.com. Business E-Mail: candice@go4thevision.com.

PEALE, RUTH STAFFORD (MRS. NORMAN VINCENT PEALE), religious leader; b. Fonda, Iowa, Sept. 10, 1906; d. Frank Burton and Anna Loretta (Crosby) Stafford; m. Norman Vincent Peale, June 20, 1930; children: Margaret Ann (Mrs. Paul F. Everett), John Stafford, Elizabeth Ruth (Mrs. John M. Allen). AB, Syracuse U., 1928, LLD, 1953; LittD, Hope Coll., 1962; LHD (hon.), Judson Coll., 1988. Tchr. math. Cen. High Sch., Syracuse, NY, 1928—30; nat. pres. women's bd. domestic missions Ref. Ch. Am., 1936-46; sec. Protestant Film Commn., 1946-51; chmn. Am. Mother's Com., 1948-49; pres., editor-in-chief, gen. sec., CEO, chmn. bd. dirs., chmn. emeritus Guideposts Peale Ctr. for Christian Living, 1940—; nat. pres. bd. domestic missions Ref. Ch. in Am., 1955-56; mem. bd. N. Am. Missions, 1963-69, pres., 1967-69; mem. gen. program council Ref. Ch. in Am., 1968—; mem. com. of 24 for merger Ref. Ch. in Am. and Presbyn. Ch. U.S., 1966-69; v.p. Protestant Council N.Y.C., 1964-66; co-founder, pub. Guideposts, N.Y.C., 1945—, pres., 1985-92, chmn. bd., 1999—2003, chmn. emeritus, 2003—; pres. Fleming H. Revell, Tarrytown, N.Y., 1985-92. Appeared on : (nat. TV program) What's Your Trouble, 1952—68; author: I Married a Minister, 1942, The Adventure of Being a Wife, 1971, Secrets of Staying in Love, 1984, A Lifetime of Positive Thinking, 2001; founder, pub. (with Dr. Peale) Guidepost mag., 1945—, co-subject with husband (film) One Man's Way, 1963. Named N.Y. State Mother of Yr., 1963, Disting. Woman of Yr., Nat. Art Assn., Religious Heritage Am. Ch. Woman of Yr., 1969, Woman of Yr., AAUW, 2000; recipient Cum Laude award Syracuse U. Alumni Assn. N.Y., 1965, Honor Iowans award Buena Vista Coll., 1966, Am. Mother's com. award for religion, 1970, Disting. Svc. award Coun. Chs., N.Y.C., 1973, Disting. Citizen award Champlain Coll., 1976, Disting. Svc. to Cmty. and Nation award Gen. Fedn. Women's Clubs, 1977, Horatio Alger award, 1977, Religious Heritage award, 1979, joint medallion with husband Soc. for Family of Man, 1981, Soc. Family of Man award, 1981, Alderson-Broaddus award, 1982, Marriage Achievement award Bride's mag., 1984, Gold Angel award Religion in Media, 1987, Adela Rogers St. John Roundtable award, 1987, Disting. Achievement award Am. Aging, 1987, Paul Harris award N.Y. Rotary, 1989, Leader's award Arthritis Found. Dutchess County, 1992, Dave Thomas Well Done! award, 1994, Norman Vincent Peale award for positive thinking, 1994, Master of Influence award, 1995, The Leadership award Worldwide Leadership Coun., 1998, Cert. for Disting. Svc., N.Y. State Fedn. Women's Clubs, 1999, Light award CANDL Found., 2000, Woman of Distinction awd RCA Women, 2001. Mem. Blanton-Peale Inst. (bd. exec. com.), Am. Bible Soc. (trustee 1948-93, hon. trustee 1993—, bd. dirs.), Nat. Bible Assn. (bd. dirs.), United Bible Soc., Interch. Ctr. (bd. dirs. 1957-92, chmn. 1982-90), Nat. Coun. Chs. (v.p. 1952-54, gen. bd.; treas. gen. dept. United Ch. Women, vice chmn. broadcasting and film commn. 1951-55, program chmn. gen. assembly 1966), N.Y. Fedn. Women's Clubs (chmn. religion 1951-53, 57-58), Home Missions Coun. N.A. (nat. pres. 1942-44, nat. chmn. migrant com. 1948-51), Internat. Platform Orgn. (bd. govs. 1994-2000), Cmty. Action Network (adv. bd. 1998—), Wainwright House (hon. trustee, advisor 2001), PEO, Sorosis (pres. 1953-56, hon. pres.), Alpha Phi (Frances W. Willard award 1976). Republican. Office: Peale Ctr Christian Living 66 E Main St Pawling NY 12564-1409

PEARCE, BETTY MCMURRAY, manufacturing company executive; b. Hastings, Nebr., Oct. 11, 1926; d. Frank Madry and Scereta (Mudd) McMurray; BS in Aerospace, U. Tex., Austin, 1949; 1 child, Karen A. Harsley. Draftsman, Koch & Fowler, Civil Engrs., Dallas, 1945-47; with Ling Temco Vought-Aircraft Products Group-Aircraft Maintenance and Support Group, Dallas, 1949—, project engr., 1955-77, engring. project mgr., 1977-83, dir. engring., 1983-89, engring. mgr. advanced sys. concepts, 1989-90; program mgr. PAMPA 2000, 1990-92; ret., 1992; dir. LTV Fed. Credit Union, v.p. LTV Mgmt. Club; cons. Active Aux. St. Joseph's Hosp.; pres. St. Andrews Catholic Ch. Coun., Fort Worth, 1977-78; mem. Bishop's Adv. Coun. Fort Worth Diocese, 1980-87, chmn. svc. com., 1980-81, pres., 1981-82, 84-85; mem. Allied Cmtys. of Tarrant, 1982— . Mem. AIAA, Tech. Mktg. Soc. Am. Home: 3613 W Biddison St Fort Worth TX 76109-2704

PEARCE, CHRISTIE PATRICIA, professional soccer player; b. Broward County, Fla., June 24, 1975; m. Chris Rampone, Nov. 9, 2001. BS in spl. edn., Monmouth U., N.J., 1997. Mem. N.Y. Power, WUSA, 2001—; soccer player, defender U.S. Women's Nat. Team, 1997, mem. World Cup championship team, 1999. Founding player N.Y. Power, WUSA, 2001. Named First Team All-Mid-Atlantic Region, 1995, 1996, Player of Yr., N.E. Conf., 1995, 1996. Office: US Soccer Fedn 1801 S Prairie Ave Chicago IL 60616*

PEARCE, DRUE, government official, former state legislator; b. Fairfield, Ill., Apr. 2, 1951; d. H. Phil and Julia Detroy (Bannister) P.; m. Michael F.G. Williams; 1 child, Tate Hanna Pearce-Williams. BA in Biol. Scis., Ind. U., 1973; MPA, Harvard U., 1984; cert. exec. program Darden Sch. Bus., U. Va., 1989. Sch. tchr., Clark County, Ind., 1973-74; curator of edn. Louisville Zoo, 1974-77; dir. Summerscene, Louisville, 1974-77; asst. v.p., br. mgr. Alaska Nat. Bank of the North, 1977-82; legis. aide to Rep. John Ringstad Alaska Ho. of Reps., Juneau, 1983, mem., 1984-88, minority whip, 1986; mem. Alaska Senate; chmn. com. oil and gas, mem. exec. com. energy coun., 1989-90; chmn. com. labor and commerce, mem. exec. coms. western state conf., coun. state govts., energy coun., 1991-92; co-chmn. senate fin., chmn. energy coun., vice chmn. com. energy, nat. coun. state govts., 1993-94; mem. select com. legis. ethics and legis. coun., 1993—; pres. senate, mem. exec. com. energy coun., vice chmn. senate coms. resources and rules, 1995-96; co-chmn. com. senate fin., mem. exec. com. energy coun., vice chmn. com. senate judiciary, 1997—98. Senate pres., 1999-2000, 1995-96, senate rules chmn., 2001; ptnr. 4150 Co., Anchorage and Kotzebue, Alaska, 1983-2002, Cloverland N., Anchorage, 1993—; resources cons. Arctic Slope Regional Corp., Anchorage, 1987-91, 95-96; sr. adv. Sec. Interior for Alaska Affairs, 2001-. Former bd. dirs. Alaska Women's Aid in Crisis, Anchorage Econ. Devel. Coun., Alaska Aerospace Devel. Corp., Alaska Spl. Olympics, Gov.'s Bd. Mem. DAR, Commonwealth North, Resource Devel. Counc., Alaska Miners Assn., Alaska Fedn. of Republican Women, Aircraft owners & Pilots Assn., United States Trotting Assn. Republican. Home: 221 E Seventh Ave #313 Anchorage AK 99501 Office: Office of the Secretary Dept of the Interior 1849 C St NW MS 6020 Washington DC 20240-

PEARCE, PATSY BEASLEY, elementary education educator; b. Dunn, N.C., Apr. 13, 1945; d. Marvin Franklin and Christine (Bryant) Beasley; m. Robert Michael Cole, Aug. 15, 1970 (div.); 1 child, Matthew Bryant Cole; m. Elwood Glenn Pearce, Mar. 1, 1980. BSEd, E. Carolina U., 1966. Cert. collegiate profl., Va. Primary tchr., 1st and 2d grade Va. Beach (Va.) City Schs., 1966-75; primary tchr., 1st. and 3rd grade Jasper County Schs., Hardeeville, S.C., 1976-78; tchr., 4th grade Campbell County Schs., Lynchburg, Va., 1979; kindergarten tchr. Aesop Acad., Portsmouth, Va., 1981-84; primary tchr., 1st grade Chesapeake (Va.) City Schs., 1984—2001; ret., 2001. Mem. social studies adoption com. Chesapeake City Schs., 1996-98, colleague mentor, 1997-98, Pizza Hut Book-It chairperson, 1997-2001; United Way chair, 1995-97; sch. rep. Chesapeake Reading Coun., 1986-95, colleague mentor, 1988-90; equity tutor Camelot Elem. Sch., Chesapeake, 1994, grade level chmn., 1990-95, coop. tchr., 1990-91; mem. tech. tng. Va. Stds. Learning Tng., 1999-2001, 2001. Sunday sch. tchr. Cradock United Meth. Ch., Portsmouth, Va., 1982, worship com. chmn. 1990-91, Acolyte chmn., 1984-89; vacation Bible sch. tchr. Thail United Meth. Ch., Virginia Beach, 1969; com. chmn., treas. Cub Scout Pack 251, Portsmouth, Va., 1980-91; roundtable commr. Merrimac Dist. Boy Scouts Am., Portsmouth, 1989-90, dist. chmn. Scouts Ann. Mall Show and Pinewood Derby Race, 1987-89; children's choir dir. Kempsville Ch. of Christ, Virginia Beach, 1979-80. Named Camelot's Tchr. of Yr., 1995-96. Mem. NEA, Va. Edn. Assn., Chesapeake Edn. Assn., Chesapeake Reading Coun., Internat. Reading Coun., PTA (corr. sec. 1997-98). Avocations: gardening, needlework crafts, travel, granddaughter. Home: 2233 Ferndale Rd Chesapeake VA 23323-5016

PEARCE, SERENA RAY, performing arts educator, music director; b. Charlotte, Nc, Dec. 21, 1950; d. Archie Sereno and Blanche Horton Ray; m. Clyde Thomas Pearce, May 19, 1973; 1 child, Christa Pearce Honeycutt. MusB, U. of NC - Greensboro, Greensboro, NC, 1973; MusM, Meredith Coll., Raleigh, NC, 1987. Lic. tchr. of Music K-12 NC. Chorus and drama dir. Zebulon GT Magnet Mid. Sch., Zebulon, NC, 1973— ; adult choir, drama and handbell dir. Bethany Bapt. Ch., Wendell, NC, 1973—. Cultural arts chmn. Zebulon GT Magnet Mid. PTA, Zebulon, NC, 1989—. Mem.: Am. Choral Directors Assn., Music Educators Nat. Conf. Baptist. Avocation: music director for over five groups at a local baptist church.

PEARCEY, LYNNE G. university dean, nursing educator; ADN, Paducah Jr. Coll., 1967; BSN with distinction, Eastern Ky. U., 1974; MSN, U. Ky., 1975, PhD in Ednl. and Counseling Psychology, 1982. Instr. Midway (Ky.) Coll., 1975-77, U. Ky., Lexington, 1977-79; asst. prof. dept. nurisng U. West Fla., Pensacola, 1981-82; assoc. prof., chmn. cmty.-mental health dept. U. South Ala. Coll. Nursing, Mobile, 1982-89; assoc. dean, prof. U. N.C., Greensboro, 1989-90, acting dean, prof., 1990-91, dean Sch. Nursing, prof., 1991—. Adj. prof. anesthesia Bowman Gray Sch. Medicine of Wake Forest U., Winston-Salem, N.C., 1990— Contbr. articles to profl. jours. Mem. ANA, Nat. League for Nursing, So. coun. on Collegiate Edn. for Nursing (bd. dirs. 1993-95, mem. nominating com. 1995-96, membership com. 1995-97), Am. Assn. for Higher Edn., Am. Assn. Colls. of Nursing, Ala. State Nurses Assn. (outstanding nurse educator 1984), Mobile County Nurses' Socj. (excellence in profl. nursing 1985), Sigma Theta Tau. Office: U NC Sch Nursing Office of Dean PO Box 26172 Greensboro NC 27402-6172

PEARL, ALISON B. music educator; d. Barbara M. and Louis R. Sparano; m. Daniel M. Pearl, July 4, 1995; children: Timothy children: Nicholas. BA, CUNY, Flushing, 1994, MS in Edn., 1997. Cert. permanent music edn. K-12 N.Y., 1999. Tchr., elem. orch. dir. Uniondale (N.Y.) Union Free Pub. Schs., 1994—96, Massapequa (N.Y.) Union Free Pub. Schs., 1996—. Curriculum com. mem. Massapequa Union Free Pub. Schools, Massapequa, NY, 2003—. Composer: (music book) Elementary Sight Reading Exercises (not yet pub.); composer: (author) (string method book) String Achievements (work in progress). Violist Nassau Pops Symphony Orch.; violist, violinist local coll. orchs.; mem. Massapequa Park (N.Y.) Rep. Club, 1988—2003. Mem.: L.I. String Festival Assn. (elem. festival chair 1999—2000, elem. v.p. 2000—03, adjudication chair 2003—), Nassau Music Educators Assn. (Divsn. I West chair 1996—97, Divsn. I East chair 1997—98), N.Y. State Sch. Music Assn. (cert. adjudicator 1999—), Music Educators Nat. Conf. Republican. Avocations: bowling, bicycling. Office: Massapequa Pub Schs 350 Unqua Rd Massapequa NY 11758

PEARL, HELEN ZALKAN, lawyer; b. Washington, Sept. 12, 1938; d. George and Harriet (Libman) Zalkan; m. Jason E. Pearl, June 27, 1959; children: Gary M., Esther H., Lawrence J. BA with honors, Vassar Coll., 1959; JD, U. Conn., 1978. Bar: Conn. 1978, U.S. Dist. Ct. Conn. 1978. Mkt. rsch. analyst Landers, Frary & Clark, New Britain, Conn., 1960-61, managerial statistician, 1961-62; real estate salesperson Denuzze Co., New Britain, 1966-70; property mgr. self-employed New Britain, 1970-75; legal asst. Atty. Gen. Office, State of Conn., Hartford, 1978; assoc. Weber & Marshall, New Britain, 1978-83, ptnr., 1983-99, Weber & Carrier, New Britain, 1999—. Hearing officer Commn. on Human Rights and Opportunities, State of Conn., 1980—98; spl. master Conn. Jud. Dept., 1986—. New Britain rep. to Ctrl. Conn. Regional Planning Agy., 1973-75, 84—, chmn., 1990-92; mem. New Britain Bd. Fin. and Taxation, 1973-77; founder, mem. Conn. Permanent Commn. on Status of Women, 1975-82, bd. dirs. Human Resources Agy., 2001—, others. Recipient Women in Leadership award, YWCA of New Britain, 1988, Book award for torts, Am. Jurisprudence, 1976. Mem. AAUW (pres. 1970-72), Conn. Bar Assn., New Britain Bar Assn., LWV (Conn. specialist 1987—, local pres. 1995-97, co-pres. 2003-), Hartford Vassar Club, Phi Beta Kappa. Democrat. Jewish. Avocations: travel, theater, reading, cooking. Home: 206 Hickory Hill Rd New Britain CT 06052-1010 Office: Weber & Carrier 24 Cedar St New Britain CT 06052-1302 Office Phone: 860-225-9463. Personal E-mail: hzpearl@msn.com. Business E-Mail: hpearl@webercarrier.com.

PEARL, NANCY LINN, librarian; b. Detroit, Mich., Jan. 12, 1945; d. Sidney and Anne Linn; m. Joseph Harold Pearl; children: Eily Raman, Katie. MLS, U. Mich., 1967. Exec. dir. Washington Ctr. Book Seattle Pub. Lib., 1993—; head collection devel. Tulsa City County Libr., Okla. Author: Now Read This: A Guide to Mainstream Fiction, 1978-1998, 1999, Now Read This II: A Guide to Mainstream Fiction, 1990-2001, 2002, (book) Book Lust: Recommended Reading for Every Mood, Moment and Reason, 2003. Named Fiction Reviewer of Yr., Libr. Jour. Magazine, 1998; recipient Allie Beth Martin award, Pub. Libr. Assn., 2001, Open Book award, Pacific Northwest Writer's Conf., 1997, Humanities Washington award, 2003. Office: Seattle Pub Libr 800 Pike St Seattle WA 98101 Office Fax: 206 386 4672. Business E-Mail: nancy.pearl@spl.org.

PEARLMAN, AMALIA CECILE, artist, educator; b. Zborov, Czechoslovakia, Oct. 10, 1918; d. Charles David and F. Rachel (Weissman) Rappaport; m. Lester S. Pearlman, June 18, 1939 (dec. 1992); children: Leslie Ellen, Austin Cecil, Lise Ann, Jared Salom, Justin Dana. BA, Bklyn. Coll., 1939; MFA, NYU, 1965, PhD, 1970. Sr. rsch. scientist curriculum devel. for creative arts NYU Sch. Edn.; adj. prof. art De Anza Coll., Calif.; prof. art So. Conn. Coll.; docent in great literature Bridgeport (Conn.) Engring. Inst.; prof. art and art history Western Conn. Coll. Panelist, spkr. in field. One-person shows at Creative Gallery, N.Y., Silvermine Guild Artists, Mystic Art Assn. Gallery, Western Conn. Coll., Mali's Gallery, Rocky Neck Gloucester, San Francisco Open Studios; exhibited in group shows at Collectore of Am. Art, Bloomfield Hills, Ill. (Purchase prize), Hartford (Conn.) Atheneum (Berthe Dion Tucker award), Alameda (Calif.) Fairgrounds (1st Hon. Mention award), Norton Gallery, Palm Beach, Fla. (1st Hon. Mention), Courtyard Mexico City (1st Hon. Mention), Ligoa Duncan Galleries, Paris (Prix de Paris), Silvermine Guild of Artists (Best New Eng. Landscape award), Riverside Mus., N.Y.C., Norwich (Conn.) Art Assn.; represented in archives Nat. Mus. for Women in the Arts, Washington; prodr. audiovisual documentary: Jerusalem, The Living Past, The Emerging Future. Dir. urban evaluation and planning program at Harlem Sch., AIA. Grantee Kress Found., 1975-77, Vinmount Found., 1972, 73. Mem. Rocky Neck Art Assn. (annual demonstrations), Mechanics Inst. Chess Club, Commonwealth Club, Sierra Club. Avocations: reading, gardening, chess, great-grandchildren, theater. Home: Apt 720 2180 Post St San Francisco CA 94115 E-mail: amaliap@pacbell.net.

PEARLMAN, ELLEN LOIS, writer, photographer, computer consultant; b. Bklyn., May 22, 1952; d. Sol and Norma (Fischel) P. BA, Hofstra U., 1974; postgrad., Naropa Inst., 1977, Sch. of Mus. Fine Arts, Boston. Asst. to Oleg Grabar dept. fine arts Harvard U., Cambridge, Mass., 1980; photo/performance collaborator Internat. Sch. Ballet, Flex Dance Co., Berlin, 1983; teaching asst. Internat. Ctr. Photography, 1984; owner photo studio, Denver, 1985-87; freelance photojournalist Colo. Daily, 1985-87; editor Vajradhatu Sun, 1988; transcription editor Allen Ginsberg, 1990; conservation & restoration painter Presevar, Inc., 1991; writer Tricycle Mag., 1991 (UTNE award 1992, 93); adj. faculty mem. Columbia U., Baruch Coll., CUNY; prof. CTA program Columbia U., 1996; sr. cons. IBM/Catapuit Tng.; prof. New Sch. U., Parsons Sch. Design; residency Vt. Studio Ctr., 1997, 2000; writers residency Banff Ctr., 2004-. Rsch. editor Journey Throuth the Wheel of Time-The Kalachakra Sand Mandala, 1992; contbg. writer Tricycle Mag., 1992-95; writer Shambhala Sun, Halifax, N.S., 1992; editor-at-large Bklyn. Rail, 2001— (UTNE award 2002, 2003); writer Turning Wheel Mag.; pub. Tibetan Sacred Dance Inner Traditions, 2002. Grantee Am. Inst. Indian Studies, Harvard Med. Sch., 1981, Ctr. Holographic Arts, NYC; non-fiction scholar Breadloaf Writers Conf., 1994; fellow Vt. Studio Ctr., 1997, Pres.'s fellow, 2003; Banff Mountain Ctr. grantee, 2003, writers grantee Great River Arts Inst., Patzluaro, Mex., 2001. Mem. Shambhala Lodge. Buddhist. Avocations: pumping iron, travel, meditation, martial arts (black belt). Office: 302 Bedford Ave Ste 345 Brooklyn NY 11211

PEARSON, APRIL VIRGINIA, lawyer; b. Martinsville, Ind., Aug. 11, 1960; d. Clare Grill and Sheila Rosemary (Finch) Rayner; m. Randall Keith Pearson, Dec. 10, 1988; children: Randall Kyle, Austin Finch, Autumn Virginia. BA, Calif. State U., Long Beach, 1982; JD, Pepperdine U., 1987; cert. indsl. fire brigade, Tex. A&M U. Bar: Calif. 1987, Idaho 1993, D.C. 1989. Assoc. counsel Union Oil Co. Calif., LA, 1988-2001; owner Avrilex, Chino Hills, Calif., 2001—. V.p. Pa's Bier, Long Beach, Calif., 1988—98, Ammonia Safety Tng. Inst., sec., 1995—98, gen. counsel, 1997—; mem. pub. works commn. City of Chino Hills, 1999—. Mem.: Chem. Industry Coun. Calif. (chair regulatory affairs com. 1995), Am. Corp. Counsel Assn., Women Lawyers Long Beach (v.p. 1990—93). Avocations: running, Tae Kwon Do. Office: Avrilex 13462 Montserrat Ct Chino Hills CA 91709-1327 Office Phone: 909-517-3838. E-mail: april@avrilex.com.

PEARSON, BARBARA JOY, small business owner; b. St. Louis, Oct. 1, 1942; d. Emerson Maness and Marie (Barlett) Elgin; m. Herby Otto Pearson, Mar. 26, 1963; children: Herby, Christina. Student, Roosevelt U., St. Louis; Diploma, Revlon Sch. Make Up Artistry, 1977; Advanced Facial Tng., Repechage, 1987. Lic. cosmetologist; cert. makeup technician, Am. Bd. Permanent Make Up Tech., Calif. Mgr. safety equipment Reis Equipment, St. Louis, 1958-65; makeup artist Revlon Cosmetics, N.Y.C., 1969-73; facialist, makeup artist Saks Fifth Ave., St. Louis, 1973-85; owner, operator James Pearson Beauty Salon & Day Spa, Frontenac, Mo., 1985—. Mem. Nat. Assn. Women Bus. Owners, Alstisition Profls. St. Louis. Republican. Lutheran. Avocations: investing, watercolor painting, writing poetry, reading, studying makeup artistry. Home: 1949 Lanchester Ct Chesterfield MO 63017-7906 Office: James Pearson Beauty Salon Le Chateau Village 10411 Clayton Rd Saint Louis MO 63131-2928

PEARSON, CAROLYN SUE, primary school educator; b. Almont, Mich., Nov. 16, 1951; d. Ralph and Zola Smith; m. William Pearson, May 11, 1974 (div. Mar. 1980); 1 child, Michelle Costa. BS, Ctrl. Mich. U., 1973; MA, Ea. Mich. U., 1980. Presch. tchr. Wayne Westland Schs., Westland, Mich., 1974—95, kindergarten tchr., 1995—. Mem.: U.S. Tennis Assn., Ann Arbor Ski Club, Am. Sailing Inst. E-mail: pearcar@netscape.net.

PEARSON, CLARA, elementary school educator, music educator; b. Morristown, N.J., Nov. 22, 1956; d. Everett and Lucia Olimpia vander Putten; m. Marshall J. Pearson, July 7, 1995; children: Michaela, Matthew. BA in Music Edn., Kean Coll., 1978. Music tchr. grades K-8 Washington Twp., Robbinsville, NJ, 1978—. Musical dir. Millstone (N.J.) Players, 1979—81; curriculum coord. Washington Twp., Robbinsville, 1999—2003. Children dir. Christmas Show Laurelton Pk. Bapt., Brick, NJ, 1998, 1999. Recipient PTA Lifetime award, 2001. Mem.: Music Educators Nat. Conf. Home: 16 Cherry Ln Howell NJ 07731

PEARSON, DENISE ANNE, music educator; b. Bryn Mawr, Pa., Aug. 16, 1954; d. Albert Hamilton and Helen Pope Anderson; m. James L. Pearson, June 27, 1981; children: James M., Kate E., David A. BS in Music Edn., Indiana U. Pa., 1976. Tchr. Alleghany County Sch. Dist., Covington, Va., 1976—78, Loyalsock Twp. Sch. Dist., Williamsport, Pa., 1978—81, Warren (Pa.) County Sch. Dist., 1996—. Tchr. summer sch. Warren County Summer Music Sch., 1993—. Mem. panel Pa. Ptnrs. in Arts, Erie, 2001—02; chair com. Russell (Pa.) Elem. PTA, 1988—95; dir. choirs First Luth. Ch., Warren, Pa., 1982—; bd. dirs. Warren Concert Assn., 1994—96. Mem.: Philomel (Music Tchr. of Yr. 2001), Delta Kappa Gamma. Republican. Lutheran. Avocations: reading, gardening, cooking, music. Home: 61 S Main St Russell PA 16345 Office: Youngsville Elem Middle Sch 232 Second St Youngsville PA 16371

PEARSON, GAYLE MARLENE, writer; b. Chgo., July 12, 1947; Student, Taylor U., 1965-67; BS in Edn., No. Ill. U., 1970. Asst. news editor Vance Pub., Chgo., 1970-71; child care specialist Ming Quong Children's Ctr., Los Gatos, Calif., 1974-75; area dir. Santa Clara County Info. and Referral, San Jose, Calif., 1977-81; edn. writer, editor free lance San Francisco, 1982-97; author children and young adult lit., 1980—. Author: (books) Fish Friday, 1986 (Best Children's Book 1986 Bay Area), The Coming Home Cafe, 1988, One Potato Tu, 1992, The Fog Doggies and Me, 1993, The Secret Box, 1997, Don't Call it Paradise, 1999. Bd. dirs. Bethany United Meth. Ch., San Francisco, Calif., 1991-92. Mem. Soc. Children's Book Writers and Illustrators. Democrat. Avocations: hiking, painting, gardening. Home and Office: 326 S Maple Ave Apt 3F Oak Park IL 60302 E-mail: G_Pearson@earthlink.net.

PEARSON, LANDON, Canadian senator; b. Toronto, Nov. 16, 1930; 5 children. BA in Philosophy and English, U. Toronto, 1951; MEd in Psychopedagogy, U. Ottawa, 1978, DU, 2002; LLD (hon.), Wilfrid Laurier U., 1995, U. Victoria, 2001, U. Carleton, 2002. Vice-chairperson Can. commn. Internat. Yr. of Child, 1979; pres., chairperson Can. Coun. on Children and Youth, 1984—90; founding mem., chairperson Can. Coalition for Rights of Children, 1990—94; senator The Senate of Can., Ottawa, 1994—. Advisor Children's Rights to the Min. of Fgn. Affairs, 1996; personal rep. Prime Min. to the 2002 UN Spl. Session on Children, 1999. Author: Children of Glasnost, Letters from Moscow; contbr. articles to profl. jours. Liberal. Office: 210 East Block The Senate of Canada Ottawa ON Canada K1A 0A4

PEARSON, MARGIT LINNEA, management advisor; b. Weymouth, Mass., Nov. 6, 1950; d. Eric Gustav and Evelyn (Forest) P. BA, Simmons Coll., 1972; MBA, Harvard U., 1975. With McKinsey & Co., Inc., N.Y.C., 1975-83; pres. Berkey, Inc., Conn., 1987-89, APC Corp., NJ, 1990-91, Sunset Mgmt., NY, 1993-97; prin. CFN, NY, 1998—; CEO Neoptis, Inc., NY, 2000, HipnTasty, Inc., NY, 2001—. Bd. dirs. theguystore.com, 1999—. Bd. dirs. Desert Chorale, N. Mex., 1994—, Tchrs. Network, NY, 1996—, iKindi, NY, 2002-, Isopulse, Calif., 2002-. Avocations: art, skiing, travel. Home: 9 E 96th St New York NY 10128-0778 Office: 14 W 95th St New York NY 10025-6706

PEARSON, SELA, poet, speaker; b. Bklyn., Aug. 10, 1952; d. Thomas Turner and Thelma (Brown) Razor; m. Nassar Anwar Jonathan. BS, St. Joseph's Coll., Bklyn., 1988. LPN. Psychiat., pediat. nurse Syosset (N.Y.) Hosp., 1974-78; sales agent Combined Life Ins. Co. N.Y., Albany, 1978-80; med., surg. nurse Bapt. Med. Ctr., Bklyn., 1980-86; nurse counselor Riker's Island Prison Hosp., Queens, N.Y., 1986-88; clinic nurse St. Christopher Ottilie, Queens, 1988-90; intensive case mgr. AIDS Ctr. Queens County, 1990-92; quality assurance, utilization rev. nurse Vanderbilt U. Med. Ctr., Nashville, Tenn., 1992-94; program dir. Boys and Girls Club, Franklin, Tenn., 1994-95; spkr., writer, nurse Akanke Creations, Brentwood, Tenn., 1996—; ind. health contractor Clayton County Crisis Unit, 1997-98; nurse Phoenix Program FHC of Nashville, 1998-99; nurse Murci Homes, 1999—. Cons. Murphy Alternative Ctr., Nashville, 1996, Serendipity House, Nashville, 1996, Family and Ednl. Adv. Assocs., Inc., Nashville, 1996, Growing In Grace Leadership Sch., Nashville, 1996; storyteller, presenter poetry recitals; ind. contractor Crisis Group Home, Riverdale, Ga. Author: New York Poetry Foundation Anthology, 1986, Beyond the Stars, 1995 (Editors Choice 1995), Sela's Sounds of Silence, 1995, A Soulful Journey, 2000; performer (video) A Soulful Journey, 1995, The Magic of Peace, 1996, Our Voices, 1996; author numerous poems; contbr. articles to profl. jours., mags. Vol. Williamson County Libr., Franklin, 1995—, Boys and Girls Club, Franklin, 1996—, TPAC; bd. dirs. Nashville Peace Action, 1996—; mem. New Gospel Singers Choir, 1995—; storytelling del. to South Africa People to People Amb. Programs, invited Women in Soc. rep., Egypt, 2000—; mem. Coun. for the Written Word. Recipient Vol. Svc. award Berksheire Nursing Ctr., West Babylon, N.Y., 1977. Mayor's award for svc. in cmty. in the arts, 2001; icluson of poem Faith to Wm. Kings Regl. Art Ctr., 1999, Cmty. Svc. award Edith Taylor Langster, Ho. of Reps., 54th Dist., 2003. Mem. Nat. Spkrs. Assn., Brentwood Early Risers Toastmasters (v.p. membership 1996—, various awards), Tenn. Writers Alliance, Harpeth Storytelling Group, Nat. Storytelling Assn., Internat. Soc. Poets (Poets Choice award 1995, Internat. Poet of Merit award 1995), Tenn. Writers Group Franklin, Tenn. Assn. Perpetuation Preservation Storytelling, Ga. Writers Group, Creative Artists Tenn., Tenn. Spkrs. Assn., Women Vision Enhancing Network (cert., dir. pub. rels.), Cherokee Wolf Clan (tribal coun. mem.). Avocations: piano playing, travel, reading. Address: PO Box 111341 Nashville TN 37222-1341 Office Phone: 615-365-3187. E-mail: serenityrises@aol.com.

PEARSON, SUSAN, elementary school educator; b. Port Arthur, Tex., July 10, 1942; d. Alfred McCallum and Alibel (Elkins) Sherwood; m. Thomas David Pearson, Feb. 1, 1964; children: Kyle, Christopher. BS in Elem. Edn., Lamar U., Beaumont, Tex., 1966. Cert. tchr. of gifted/talented. Tchr. Kirbyville (Tex.) Ind. Sch. Dist., 1964, Gonzales (La.) Elem. Sch., 1964-66, Dixie Elem. Sch., Lexington, Ky., 1966-70, Roanoke (Tex.) Elem. Sch., 1984-85; gifted/talented coord. Denton (Tex.) Ind. Sch. Dist., 1992-96; tchr. Southwood Valley, Coll. Sta., Tex., 1997-2000; tchr. civics and world history 7th and 8th grades Acad. Sci. and Fgn. Langs., Huntsville, Alaska, 2003—; tutor Diplomat to Kransnadar Kri., Russia, 2003. Cons. Dixie Elem. Sch., 1968; bd. dirs. City/County Day Sch., Denton, 1994, St. Michael's Acad., Bryan, Tex., 1996-97; long term subsitute, Madison, Ala.; Region 5 North Ala. dir. Project Citizen. Chmn. ball invitations Benefit League, Denton, Tex., 1994—96. Mem. AAUW, PEO, Denton County Women's Club (pres. 1989-91), Delta Zeta, Delta Kappa Gamma (treas.). Episcopalian. Avocations: gourmet cooking, arts and crafts, reading, travel. Home: 1811 Cross Creek Rd Huntsville AL 35802 E-mail: stp0742@knology.net.

PEASE, ELEANOR JEANNE, humanities educator; b. Phila., Apr. 28, 1935; d. Harold Chandler and Elizabeth (Wright) Hill; m. Richard Bruce Pease, May 26, 1956; children: Richard Bruce Jr., Sharon Pease Andrews. BA in English, Gordon Coll., 1970; MEd in English, Westfield State U., 1973. Educator Gateway Regional Schs., Huntington, Mass., 1970-74; missionary in Japan Christian & Missionary Alliance Hdqrs., Colorado Springs, Colo., 1963-68, 74-93; educator Pasadena (Calif.) Unified Schs., 1989-95; prof., head dept. TESOL, Nyack (N.Y.) Coll., 1995—. Guest lectr. Caransebes Bible Sch., 1996; co-chair Support A Mother project com., 2001--. Contbr. articles to profl. publs. Dir. Womens Ministries, Pasadena Alliance Ch., 1991-95, English Tchrs. Seminar, Hiroshima, 1980-82, 85, 86; coord. homework assistance program Pasadena Schs., 1990-95; vice chmn. Hiroshima (Japan) Internat. Sch. Bd., 1980-83; pres. South Pacific Alliance Women, Pasadena, 1991-93. Mem. TESOL. Avocations: reading, travel. Home: 61 Summit Ave Spring Valley NY 10977-5351 Office: Nyack Coll 1 S Boulevard Nyack NY 10960-3604

PEASE-PRETTY ON TOP, JANINE B. community college administrator; b. Nespelam, Wash., Sept. 17, 1949; d. Benjamin and Margery Louise (Jordan) Pease; m. Sam Vernon Windy Boy, July 30, 1975 (div. Jan. 1983); children: Rosella L. Windy Boy, Sam Vernon Windy Boy; m. John Joseph Pretty On Top, Sept. 15, 1991. BA in Sociology, Anthropology, Ctrl. Wash. U., 1970; MEd, Mont. State U., 1987, EdD, 1994; HHD (hon.), Hood Coll., 1990; LLD (hon.), Gonzaga U., 1991; DHL (hon.), Teikyo/Marycrest U., 1992; EdD (hon.), Whitman Coll., 1993; HHD (hon.), Rocky Mountain Coll., 1998. Dep. dir. Wash. State Youth Commn., Olympia, 1971; tutor student svcs. Big Bend C.C., Moses Lake, Wash., 1971-72, upward bound dir., 1972-75; women's counselor Navajo C.C., Many Farms, Ariz., 1972; dir. adult & continuing edn. Crow Ctrl. Edn. Commn., Crow Agy., Mont., 1975-79; ednl. cons. Box Elder, Mont., 1979-81; dir. Indian career svc. Ea. Mont. Coll., Billings, 1981-82; pres. Little Big Horn Coll., Crow Agency, 1982—. Exec. com. Am. Indian Higher Ednl. Consortium, Washington, 1983—; bd. dirs. Am. Indian Coll. Fund, N.Y.C., 1988—; sec. Indian Nations at Risk U.S. Dept. Edn., Washington, 1990-91, collaborator task force, 1990-91; 2d vice chmn. Nat. Adv. Coun. Indian Edn., Washington, 1994—. Chmn. Bighorn County Dem. Ctrl. Com., Hardin, Mont., 1983-88; mem. coun. First Crow Indian Bapt. Ch., 1989—; bd. dirs. Ctr. for Rocky Mountain West, 1998—; chmn. Mont. State Reappt. an dDistructing Commn., 1999—. MacArthur fellow John D. & Catharine MacArthur Found., 1994. Mem. Nat. Indian Edn. Assn. (Indian educator of yr. 1990), Mont. Assn. Chs. (bd. dirs. 1997—), Crow Tribe Nighthawk Dance Soc. Office: Little Big Horn Coll PO Box 370 Crow Agency MT 59022-0370

PEASLEE, JANICE L. state legislator, agricultural products executive; b. Auburn, Maine, Jan. 20, 1935; m. Bert H. Peaslee; five children. Co-owner Peaslee's Vt. Potatoes; mem. Vt. Ho. of Reps., Montpelier, 1989—. Mem. govt. ops. com., clk. transp. com., Vt. Ho. Reps; mem. state bd. trustees, Rep. state exec. com., state legis. com. Former town auditor, former pres., mem. Essex County Sch. Bd.; chmn. Coos-Essex Com. for Agrl. Awareness. Mem. Farm Bur., Eastern Star, 4-H Club (orgn. leader), Conn. Valley Sno-Riders. Home: PO Box 12 Guildhall VT 05905-0012 Office: Vt House of Reps Office of House Mems Montpelier VT 05602

PEASLEE, JAYNE MARIE, computer scientist, educator; b. Corning, N.Y., Mar. 1, 1958; d. Frank and Alice Joyce (Thresher) Walters; m. Kenneth Stewart Peaslee, June 28, 1980; children: Mary Alice, Brent Kenneth. BA, SUNY, Geneseo, 1980; postgrad., SUNY Binghamton, 1984-86; MS, Elmira Coll., 1987. Tchg. asst. Corning-Painted Post (N.Y.) Sch. Dist., 1980-81; instr. computer sci. Corning C.C., 1981—, mid. states chmn. Profl. cert. nat. chair Acad. Leadership Tng., 1996. Leader Seven Lakes Girl Scouts U.S. Council, Corning, 1994-2000. Recipient Honor plaque Data Processing Mgmt. Assn., 1985. Mem. AAUW, Assn. Computer Machinery, Nat. Mus. Women in Arts, Math. Assn., Corning Quilters Guild. Methodist. Avocations: sewing, ice skating, swimming, drawing, painting. Office: Corning CC 1 Academic Dr Corning NY 14830-3297

PEASLEE, MARGARET MAE HERMANEK, zoology educator; b. Chgo., June 15, 1935; d. Emil Frank and Magdalena Bessie (Cechota) Hermanek; m. David Raymond Peaslee, Dec. 6, 1957; 1 dau., Martha Magdelena Peaslee-Levine. AA, Palm Beach Jr. Coll., 1956; BS, Fla. So. Coll., 1959; med. technologist, Northwestern U., 1958, MS, 1964, PhD, 1966. Med. technologist Passavant Hosp., Chgo., 1958-59; med. technologist St. James Hosp., Chicago Heights, Ill., 1960-63; asst. prof. biology Fla. So. Coll., Lakeland, Fla., 1966-68; asst. prof. of biology U. S.D., Vermillion, SD, 1968-71, assoc. prof., 1971-76, prof., 1976, acad. opportunity liaison, 1974-76; prof., head dept. zoology La. Tech. U., Ruston, La., 1976-90, assoc. dean, dir. grad. studies and rsch., prof. biol. scis. Coll. Life Scis., 1990-93; v.p. for acad. affairs U. Pitts. at Titusville, Titusville, Pa., 1993—. Contbr. articles to profl. jours. Fellow AAAS; mem. AAUP, Am. Inst. Biol. Scis., Am. Soc. Zoologists, S.D. Acad. Sci. (sec.-treas. 1972-76), N.Y. Acad. Scis., Pa. Acad. Sci., La. Acad. Sci. (sec. 1979-81, pres. 1983), Sigma Xi, Phi Theta Kappa, Phi Rho Pi, Phi Sigma, Alpha Epsilon Delta. Office Phone: 814-827-4473. Business E-Mail: peaslee@pitt.edu.

PEATTIE, LISA REDFIELD, urban anthropology educator; b. Chgo., Mar. 1, 1924; d. Robert and Margaret (Park) Redfield; m. Roderick Peattie, June 26, 1943 (dec. 1962); children: Christopher, Sara, Miranda, Julia; m. William A. Doebele, 1973 (div.). MA, U. Chgo., 1950, PhD, 1968. Faculty mem. dept. urban studies MIT, Cambridge, 1965—, prof. urban anthropology, 1968-85, now prof. emeritus, sr. lectr. Cons. World Bank, 1975, 76, 81, UN, 1980 Author: The View from the Barrio, 1968, Thinking About Development, 1982, (with W. Ronco) Making Work, 1983, (with Martin Rein) Women's Claims, 1983, Planning: Rethinking Ciudad Guayana, 1987. Recipient Paul Davidoff award Am. Soc. Collegiate Schs. of Planning, 1989. Mem. Am. Anthrop. Assn., Soc. Applied Anthropology

PECK, ANNETTE BIEMOND, retired social worker, writer; b. Amsterdam, Netherlands, Nov. 11, 1928; d. Cornelis Biemond and Maria Johanna Kam; m. Claude J. Peck Jr. (dec. 2001); 4 stepchildren. Advanced MSW, Sch. Social Work, Amsterdam, 1968. Home visiting social worker Royal Sch. for the Blind, Huizen, Netherlands, 1954—63; program dir. Sch. Drop-outs Program, Amsterdam, Netherlands, 1963—68; exec. dir. Coun. Internat. Programs, Chgo., 1976—81. Cons. The Exec. Svc. Corps. Chgo., 1988—. Author: Our Father's House, 2000; contbr. articles to pubs. Mem. vestry, 2002—; bd. dirs. Youth Comm., 2002—. Grantee Travel grant, Fulbright Assn., 1969. Mem.: The Winnetka Fortnightly (pres. 1998—99). Episcopalian. Avocations: writing, genealogy, needlecrafts, cooking, art research. Home: 589 Sunset Rd Winnetka IL 60093

PECK, CAROLE, food service executive; m. Bernard Cabernet. Student, Culinary Inst. Am.; apprentice with Fernand Granger, Le Pavillon. Exec. chef Hilton Head Sea Pines Plantation Resort, Fisher Island, Miami, Fla., Cafe Greco, N.Y.C.; opened Carole Peck's restaurant, Hunt Hill Farms, Conn.; owner, chef Good News Cafe, Woodbury, Conn. Selected chef Julia Child Cookbook Awards. Named one of Nation's Top Young Chefs, Food Arts mag., 1992, 1994; named to honor roll of eight chefs from around the country, Eating Well mag., 1994. Avocation: collecting American folk art. Office: Good News Cafe 694 Main St South Woodbury CT 06798

PECK, CAROLYN, professional basketball coach; b. Jefferson City, Tenn. BA in Comm., Vanderbilt U., 1988. Mktg. cons., Nashville; salesperson; profl. basketball player Nippondenso Corp., Japan, 1991-93; asst. coach U. Tenn., U. Ky., 1995-96, Purdue U., West Lafayette, Ind., 1996-97, coach, 1997-98; head coach, gen. mgr. Orlando (Fla.) Miracle, 1999—. Asst. coach USA Jones Cup team, 1997. Named AP Coach of the Yr., 1999, IKON/WBCA Div. I Nat. Coach of the Yr., 1999. Office: Orlando Miracle Two Magic Pl 8701 Maitland Summit Blvd Orlando FL 32810-5915

PECK, DIANNE KAWECKI, architect; b. Jersey City, June 13, 1945; d. Thaddeus Walter and Harriet Ann (Zlotkowski) Kawecki; m. Gerald Paul Peck, Sept. 1, 1968; children: Samantha Gillian Gildersleeve, Alexis Hilary. BArch, Carnegi-Mellon U., 1968. Architect P.O.D. R&D, 1968, Kohler-Daniels & Assocs., Vienna, Va., 1969-71, Beery-Rio & Assocs., Annandale, Va., 1971-73; ptnr. Peck & Peck Architects, Occoquan, Va., 1973-74, Peck Peck & Williams, Occoquan, Va., 1974-81; corp. officer Peck Peck & Assocs., Inc., Woodbridge, Va., 1981—. CEO interior design group Peck Peck & Assocs., 1988—; mem. archtl. rev. bd. Prince William County, 1998—, chair 2000—. Work pub. in Am. Architecture, 1985. V.p. Vocat. Edn. Found., 1976; chmn. architects and engrs. United Way, Indsl. Devel. Authority of Prince William, 1976, vice chair, 1977, mem. 1975-79; mem. Health Sys. Agy. of No. Va., commendations 1977, Washington Profl. Women's Coop.; developed rsch. project Architecture for Adolescents, 1987-88; mem. inaugural class Leadership Am., 1988, Leadership Greater Washington, D.C. Coun. Metrication, 1992—, D.C. Hist. Preservation League, Rep. Nat. Com. Recipient commendation Prince William Bd. Suprs., 1976, State of Art award for Contel Hdqrs. design, 1985, Best Middle Sch. award Coun. of Ednl. Facilities Planners Internat., 1989, Creativity award Masonry Inst. Md., 1990, First award, 1990, Detailing award, 1990, Govt. Workplace award for renovations of Dept. of Labor Bldg., 1990, Creative Use of Materials award Inst. of Bus. Designers, 1991, 1st award Brick Inst. Md., 1993, award Brick Inst. Va., 1994, Bull Elephant award Prince William County Young Reps., 1995, Detailing & Craftsmanship award Washington Builder's Congress, 1998; winner Archtl. Design Competition Vis. Pavillion Bur. Engraving and Printing, 2002; named Best Instl. Project Nat. Comml. Builders Coun.; subject of PBS spl.: A Success in Howard Co. Mem. Soc. Am. Mil. Engrs., Prince William C. of C. (bd. dirs.), Soroptimist Club. Roman Catholic. Research on inner-city rehab., adolescents and the ednl. environ. Office: 2050 Old Bridge Rd Woodbridge VA 22192-2447 Personal E-mail: dpeck@peckpeck.com.

PECK, ELLIE ENRIQUEZ, retired state administrator; b. Sacramento, Oct. 21, 1934; d. Rafael Enriquez and Eloisa Garcia Rivera; m. Raymond Charles Peck, Sept. 5, 1957; children: Reginaldo, Enrico, Francisca Guerrero, Teresa, Linda, Margaret, Raymond Charles, Christina. Student polit. sci., Sacramento State U., 1974. Tng. svcs. coord. Calif. Divsn. Hwys., Sacramento, 1963-67, tech. and mgmt. cons., 1968-78; expert examiner Calif. Pers. Bd., Sacramento, 1976-78; tng. cons. Calif. Pers. Devel. Ctr., Sacramento, 1978; spl. cons. Calif. Commn. on Fair Employment and Housing, Sacramento, 1978; cmty. svcs. rep. U.S. Bur. of Census, No. Calif. counties, 1978-80; project dir. Golden State Sr. Discount Program, 1980-83; dir. spl. programs Calif. Lt. Gov., 1983-90; ret., 1990; pvt. cons., 1990—. Project dir. SSI/QMB Outreach Project, 1993-94; cons., project dir. nat. sr. health issues summit Congress Calif. Srs. Edn. and Rsch. Fund, 1995; project dir. various post-White House Conf. on Aging seminars and roundtables, 1995-97; coord. Calif. Sr. Legis., 2000-03; exec. dir. SMART Coalition Calif., 1997—2004. Mem. editl. adv. bd. Latino Jour. Mag., 1996—2002. Campaign workshop dir. Chicano/Latino Youth Leadership Conf., 1982—; chmn. ethnic minority task force Am. Diabetes Assn., 1988—90; steering com. Calif. Self-Esteem Minority Task Force, 1990—93; v.p. Comision Femenil Nacional, Inc., 1987—90; del. Dem. Nat. Conv., 1976, White House Conf. Aging, 1995—2004; mem. exec. bd. Calif. Dem. Ctrl. Com., 1977—95, mem., 1997—2001; bd. dirs. Sacramento/Sierra Am. Diabetes Assn., 1989—90; trustee Stanford Settlement Inc., Sacramento, 1975—79; bd. dirs. Sacramento Emergency Housing Ctr., 1974—77, Sacramento Cmty. Svcs. Planning Coun., 1987—90, Calif. Advs. for Nursing Home Reform, 1990—96, Calif. Human Devel. Corp., 1995—2003. Named Outstanding Advocate on Aging Issues, Calif. State Senate, 1998, Dem. Yr., Sacramento County Dem. Com., 1987; recipient Outstanding Cmty. Svc. award, Comunicaciones Unidos de Norte Aztlan, 1975, 1977, Vol. Svc. award, Calif. Human Devel. Corp., 1998, Outstanding Svc. award, Chicano/Hispanic Dem. Caucus, 1979, Vol. Svc. award, Calif. Human Devel. Corp., 1981, Outstanding Advocate award, Calif. Sr. Legis., 1988—89, Meritorious Svc. to Hispanic Cmty. award, Comite Patriotico, 1989, Cert. Recognition, Sacramento County Human Rights Commn., 1991, Tish Sommers award, Older Women's League/Joint Resolution Calif. Legislature, 1993, Latino Eagle award in govt., 1994, Mentor Yr. award, Latina Leadership Network, 2002, Outstanding Vol. Svs. Throughout Yrs. award, Calif. Sr. Legislature, 2003. Mem. Hispanic C. of C., Older Women's League, Nat. Coun. Silver Haired Legislators, Nat. Coun. La Raza, Latina Leadership Network (Mentorship award 2002). Home and Office: 101 Simmons Way Folsom CA 95630

PECK, MARYLY VANLEER, retired academic administrator, chemical engineer; b. Washington, June 29, 1930; d. Blake Ragsdale and Ella Lillian (Wall) VanLeer; m. Jordan B. Peck, Jr., June 15, 1951; children: Jordan B. III, Blake VanLeer, James Tarleton VanLeer, Virginia Ellaine.; m. 2d, Walter G. Ebert, Sept. 3, 1983 (dec. June 1990); m. 3d Edwin L. Carey, Apr. 13, 1991. Student, Ga. Inst. Tech., 1948, 55-58, Duke U., 1947-48; B.Ch.E., Vanderbilt U., 1951; MSE., U. Fla., 1955, PhD, 1963. Chem. engr. Naval Research Lab., Washington, 1951-52; chem. engr. Med. Field Research Lab., Camp LeJeune, N.C., 1952; asso. research and instr. U. Fla., Gainesville, 1953-55; chem. engr., research asso. Ga. Tech. Expt. Sta., Atlanta, 1956-58; lectr. Ga. State Coll., Atlanta, 1957-58; lectr. math. East Carolina Extension, Camp Lejeune, 1959; sr. research engr. Rocketdyne div. N.Am. Aviation Co., 1961-63; self-employed as lectr., 1963; assoc. prof. Campbell Coll., Buie's Creek, N.C., 1963-66, prof., 1966; acad. dir. St. John's Episcopal Sch., Upper Tumon, Guam, 1966-68; chmn., prof. phys. scis. U. Guam, Agana, 1968-73, dean Coll. Bus. and Applied Tech., 1973-74, dean Community Career Coll., 1974-77; pres. Cochise Coll., Douglas, Ariz., 1977-78; systems planning analyst Urban Pathfinders, Inc., Balt., 1978-79; dean undergrad. studies U. Md. Univ. Coll., College Park, 1979-82; pres. Polk Community Coll., Winter Haven, Fla., 1982-97, pres. emeritus, 1997—; headmaster All Saints' Acad., 1997-99. Cons. in field. Founder, pres. Guam Acad. Found., 1972-77; bd. dirs. Cochise Coll. Found., 1977-78; charter bd. dirs. Turnaround Inc., 1987-91, chmn. 1990-93; bd. dirs. United Way Ctrl. Fla., 1986-95, vice-chmn., 1992, chair elect, 1993, chmn. 1994; founding mem. Prince George's Ednl. TV Cable Coalition; mem. Prince George's Cable TV Ednl. Adv. Group, 1980-82, Polk County Coun. Econ. Edn., 1982; sec. Polk C.C. Found., 1982-97; mem. Polk County Coord. Coun. Vocat. Edn., 1982-91, PRIDE Adv. Coun.; vice-chmn. Fla. Job Tng. Coord. Coun., 1983-87, Fla. Edn. Fund Bd., 1988-93; active Girls Inc. Bd., 1992—, pres., 2000-2001; trustee All Sts.'s Acad. 1991-2002; mem. Vanguard Sch. Fdn. Bd., 2001-; bd. dirs. Theater Winter Haven, 2000—, chair, 2002-03. Named Disting. Alumnus U. Fla., 1992, Woman of Distinction, 1997, Woman of Distinction Girls Scouts U.S.A., 1994; fellow NSF, 1961-63; recipient She Knows Where She's Going award Girls Inc. of Winter Haven, 1995, Cmty. Svc. award Jr. League Winter Haven, 2002. Fellow Soc. Women Engrs. (nat. v.p. 1962-63); mem. AAUW, AIChE, Am. Chem. Soc., NSPE, Am. Assn. for Higher Edn., Am. Assn. Cmty. and Jr. Colls., Am. Assn. Univ. Adminstrs., Rotary (pres.-elect 2003-04, centennial pres. 2004—), Sigma Xi, Tau Beta Pi, Chi Omicron Gamma, Phi Kappa Phi, Delta Kappa Gamma. Episcopalian. Home: 1290 Howard Ter NW Winter Haven FL 33881-3158 E-mail: mpeck@tampabay.rr.com.

PECK, NATALIE DEANNE, music educator; b. Macon, Ga., July 12, 1954; d. Jesse Dean Cheek and Susie Pearl Stringer; m. Michael Owen Peck, June 28, 1975; children: Jennifer Michelle, Jameson Michael. BME, Ga. Coll., 1976; MEd, U. Ga., 1986; diploma in edn. leadership, adminstrn. and supr., State U.West Ga., 2001. Nat. registered music educator MENC, 1993. Asst. min. music First United Meth. Ch., Milledgeville, Ga., 1973—74; choral dir., music tchr. Northside HS, Worker Robins, Ga., 1976—79, Boddie Jr. High/Baldwin High, Milledgeville, Ga., 1979—86; music tchr. DD Crawford Primary, Tennille (Ga.) Elem., 1988—90; music specialist The Chilren's Sch., Atlanta, 1992—94; choral dir., music tchr. Nash/Campbell Mid. Sch., Smyrna, Ga., 1994—2000, Herschel Jones Mid. Sch., Dallas, Ga., 2000—. Exploratory team leader Nash/Campbell Mid. Sch., Smyrna, Ga., 1995—96; bldg. rep. PAGE, Smyrna, Ga., 1998—2000. Grantee 2 Grants, Jr. League, 1995—96. Mem.: Prof. Assn. of Ga. Educators, Music Educator's Nat. Conf., Pi Tau Chi, Sigma Alpha Iota. Baptist. Avocations: reading, bowling. Home: 1802 Cabot Ct Marietta GA 30064

PECKHAM, ELLEN, artist, poet; b. Rochester, NY, Sept. 28, 1938; d. Walter Fredrick and Florence Albertina (Schmanke) Stoepel; m. Anson Wheeler Peckham, Sept. 10, 1976. Exhibitions include Atelier A/E Enterprises, N.Y.C., 1994—, Instituto Cultural Peruano Norteamericano, Peru, 1997—, Art Internat., N.Y.C., 1998, Boston Printmakers, 1999—, Katonah (N.Y.) Mus., 1999—, Collage/Assemblage Soc., N.Y.C., 2000—02, Brand Libr. and Art Ctr., Glendale, Calif., 2001—, Springfield (Mo.) Art Mus., 2001, Stocker Ctr., Elyria, Ohio, 2001, U. Richmond, Va., 2002, N.W. Arts Coun./Ill. Arts Coun., Woodstock, Ill., 2002, Sothebeys, NY, 2002, Pacific States Biennial, Hilo, Hawaii, 2002, No. Ariz. U., Flagstaff, 2002, Multi-sensory Hera Gallery, Warwick, RI, 2003, Solarplate Traveling Exhibits, NY and Mass., 2003;, author numerous poems; exhibitions include Zimmerli Mus., Rutgers U., N.J. Avocations: gardening, theatre.

PEDEN, KATHERINE GRAHAM, industrial consultant; b. Hopkinsville, Ky., Jan. 2, 1926; d. William E. and Mary (Gorin) P. Student pub. schs. Vice pres. radio sta. WHOP-CBS, Hopkinsville, 1944-68; owner sta. WNVL, Nicholsville, Ky., 1961-71; commr. commerce Ky., 1963-67; mem. Gov. Ky. Cabinet, Frankfort, 1963-67; pres., cons. Katherine G. Peden & Assos. Inc., Louisville, indsl. and community developers. Bd. dirs. Westvaco Corp.; mem. adv. bd. Norfolk So. Corp. Chmn. Louisville and Jefferson County Riverport Authority, 1975-80; civilian aide to Sec. of Army, 1978-82; mem. com. Pres.'s Commn. on Status of Women, 1961-62; mem. Pres.'s Commn. on Civil Disorders, 1967; pres. Ky. Derby Festival, 1979-80; Dem. nominee U.S. Senate, 1968; mem. adv. coun. U. Ky. Coll. Bus.; trustee Spalding U., 1980-86. Named Woman of Year Hopkinsville, 1952 Mem. Fedn. Bus., Profl. Women's Clubs (pres. state 1955-56, 1st nat. v.p. 1960-61, nat. pres. 1961-62). Mem. Christian Ch. (deaconess 1956-59, 60-63). Home: 3818 Washington Sq Louisville KY 40207-1954 Office: PO Box 6268 Louisville KY 40206-0268

PEDERSEN, DARLENE DELCOURT, publishing executive, psychotherapist; b. Westbrook, Maine; 1 child, Jorgen David. BSN, U. Conn., 1967; postgrad., U. B.C., 1974-75; MSN, U. Pa., 1997. RN Pa., N.J., N.Y., cert. clinical specialist in adult psychiatric and mental health nursing, ANCC. Various nursing positions, psychiat.-cmty health, 1967-79; assoc. editor JB Lippincott Co., Phila., 1979-84; acquisition editor WB Saunders Co., Phila., 1984-88, v.p., editor in chief, 1988-91, sr. v.p., editorial dir. books divsn., liaison to London office, 1991-95; domestic and internat. pub. cons. Phila., 1995—; psychotherapist pvt. practice Secaucus, NJ, 1997—. Team leader Northwestern Human Svcs. Delaware County, 1998—99; dir. PsychOptions, 2000—; v.p. contents ops. MedCases, Phila., 2000—03; exec. editor Thomson Physicians World, 2003—04; mng. editor FA Davis Co., Phila., 2004—. Author (with others): (book) Canadian Nurse, 1976; co-author: Basic Nursing Skills, 1977; acquisition editor: book Saunders Manual of Medical Practice. Mem.: ANA, Internat. Soc. Traumatic Stress Studies, U.S. Dressage Fedn., Inc., Am. Orthopsychiat. Assn., Internat. Platform Assn., Assn. Profl. Comm. Cons., Manuscript Soc., Forum Exec. Women, Internat. Soc. Psychiat. Mental Health Nurses, Med. Mktg. Assn., Assn. Am. Pubs., Med. Mktg. Assn., Am. Med. Writers Assn., Am. Med. Pubs. Assn., Am. Group Psychotherapy Assn., Am. Psychiat. Nurses Assn., Am. Group Psychotherapy Assn., Montgomery County C. of C., Emily's List, Sigma Theta Tau (Xi chpt.). Avocations: autograph and art collection, travel, francophile, french music, reading. Office: FA Davis Co 1915 Arch St Philadelphia PA 19103 E-mail: ddped@aol.com.

PEDERSEN, KAREN SUE, electrical engineer; b. Indianola, Iowa, Apr. 27, 1942; d. Donald Cecil and Dorothy Darlene (Frazier) Kading; m. Wendell Dean Pedersen, May 6, 1961; children: Debra Ann Pedersen Schwickerath, Michael Dean. AA, Grand View Coll., Des Moines, 1975; BSEE, Iowa State U., 1977; MBA, Bentley Coll., Waltham, Mass., 1989. Registered profl. engr., Mass., Iowa, Ill. Engr. Iowa Power & Light Co., Des Moines, 1978-80, rate engr., 1980-84; sr. rsch. engr. Boston Edison Co., Boston, 1984-87, sr. engr., 1987-94, prin. rsch. analyst, 1994-98; sr. engr. MidAmerican Energy Co., Davenport, Iowa, 1998—. Ops. chmn. Old South Ch., Boston, 1989-98. Mem. IEEE (chmn. Iowa ctrl. sect. 1983-84, sec. Iowa-Ill. sect. 2003), NSPE (v.p. 1999-2000, v.p. North Ctrl. region 2001-03), Mass. Soc. Profl. Engrs. (pres. 1992-93), Eta Kappa Nu. Republican. Congregationalist. Office: MidAmerican Energy Co 106 E 2nd St # D Davenport IA 52801-1502 E-mail: kspedersen@mchsi.com.

PEDERSEN, PEDIE, physiology educator; b. Milan, Tenn., Apr. 12, 1948; d. E.E. and Bettye M. Pedersen. BA, Rhodes Coll., 1970; MS, U. Ala., 1972; BS, U. New Orleans, 1977; PhD, Tulane U., 1986. Tchr. biology Holy Name Sch. and Chapelle H.S., New Orleans, 1978-81; vis. instr., postdoctoral fellow Tulane U., New Orleans, 1986-87; asst. prof. physiology Delgado C.C., New Orleans, 1987-91, assoc. prof., 1991—. Author: Human Anatomy and Physiology: Lecture Outlines and Self Tests I and II, 1995. Mem. Human Anatomy and Physiology Soc., Sweet Adelines, Sigma Xi. Office: Delgado Cmty Coll 615 City Park Ave New Orleans LA 70119 Office Phone: 504-483-4426.

PEDERSON, RENA, newspaper editor; b. San Angelo, Tex. children: Gregory Gish, Grant Gish. B in Journalism with honors, U. Tex., 1969; M in Journalism, Columbia U., 1970. With UPI, AP; with Washington Bur. Houston Chronicle; with Dallas Morning News, 1973—, Fed. beat, city hall, features, TV critic, editl. writer, op-ed editor, v.p., editl. page editor, 1986—2002, editor-at-large, 2002—. Mem. Pulitzer Prize Bd., 1989—. Author: What's Missing? Inspirtation for Women Seeking Faith and Joy in Their LIves, 2003; co-author (with Lee Smith): What's Next? Women Redefining Their Dreams in the Prime of Life, 2001. Named one of Most Powerful Women in Tex., Tex. Monthly Mag.; recipient award, Headliners Club, Dallas Press Club, AP Mng. Editors. Mem.: Am. Soc. Newspaper Editors, Coun. on Fgn. Rels., Nat. Conf. Editl. Writers (former pres.). Methodist. Office: The Dallas Morning News PO Box 655237 508 Young St Dallas TX 75265

PEDERSON, SALLY, lieutenant governor; b. Muscatine, Iowa, Jan. 13, 1951; d. Gerald and Wineva Pederson; m. James A. Autry, Feb. 6, 1982; children: Rick, Jim Jr., Ronald. Grad., Iowa State U., 1973. With Meredith Corp., 1973-84; sr. food editor Better Homes & Gardens mag.; lt. gov. State of Iowa, 1999—. Pres. Polk County Health Svcs.; bast bd. trustees Nat. Alliance for Autism Rsch.; pres. bd. trustees Autism Soc. Iowa; founding pres. The Homestead Living and Learning Ctr. for Adults with Autism; past cmty. bd. svcs. includes Des Moines Cmty. Playhouse, Very Spl. Arts Iowa, YWCA Aliber Child Care Ctr., YMCA Ctr. Br.; parent rep. Heartland AEA Autism Steering Com.; mem. Iowa State Spl. Edn. Adv. Bd; bd. dirs. Blank Children's Hosp., Mid-Iowa Health Found.; gov.'s appointee State Spl. Edn. Adv. Panel. Democrat. Office: Office of Lt Governor State Capitol Bldg Des Moines IA 50319-0001*

PEDESCLEAUX-MUCKLE, GAIL, business analyst, writer; b. Cleve., June 20, 1949; d. Alfonso Pedescleaux and Belle Pinkard Pedescleaux; m. Kirk Muckle, Oct. 24, 1997; 1 stepchild, Christopher Corey Muckle. BA in English Lit., Ctrl. Mich. U., 1971. Acct. asst. Travelers Ins. Co., Southfield, Mich., 1972—79, underwriter Garden City, NY, 1979—81, Commerce and Industry, N.Y.C., 1981—83; sr. underwriter Firemans' Fund, N.Y.C., 1983—85; bus. analyst Am. Internat. Group, N.Y.C., 1985—94, sr. quality assurance analyst Livingston, NJ, 1994—2000, sr. bus. analyst Parsippany, NJ, 2000—. Author: (anthology) America at the Millennium, 2000 (Editor's Choice, 2000), Poetry's Elite: The Best Poets of 2000, 2001 (Editor's Choice, 2001), Throwing Stardust, 2003 (Editor's Choice, 2003), Celebrating Poetry, 2003, Theatre of the Mind, 2003. Mem. DAV: Comdr.'s Club, 1993—, Nat. Multiple Sclerosis Soc., 1994—, Nat. Trust, 1993—, Am. Mus. Natural History, 1996, Nat. Civil Rights Mus., 2002, So. Poverty Law Ctr., 2002, Susan G. Komen Breast Cancer Found., 2003. Avocations: jazzercise, photography, writing, theater, writing children's stories and poetry. Home: 54 Rainford Rd Edison NJ 08820-2903 Office: Am Internat Group 9 Entin Rd Parsippany NJ 07054

PEDRICK, JEAN, poet; b. Salem, Mass. d. Laurence Davis and Elfrieda Augusta (Virchow) P.; m. Frank John Kefferstan II, Feb. 8, 1948; children: Laurence Dick, John Pedrick. BA, Wheaton Coll., 1943. Sec. to editor Houghton Mifflin Co., Boston, 1944-47; staff writer Beacon Hill News Cmty. Press, Inc., Boston, 1965-95. Founding mem. Alice James Books, Cambridge, Mass., 1974; pres. Rowan Tree Press, Boston, 1980; instr. poetry Northeastern U., Ext., Boston, 1967-70, Boston Ctr. Continuing Edn., 1972-76. Author: The Fascination, 1947; (poetry) Wolf Moon, 1974, Pride & Splendor, 1976, Greenfellow, 1981, Catgut, 2003. Democrat. Avocations: photography, crafts, travel.

PEEBLES, ALLENE KAY, manufactured housing company executive; b. Waukegan, Ill., Feb. 9, 1938; d. Allan Laverne and Kathryn Bernice (McGill) Sedlmayr; m. William Ross Peebles, July 9, 1960; children: Ross William, Robb Allan, Raymond John, Renda Kay (Mrs. Christopher Sivak). BS with high honors, U. Wis., 1960, MS, 1967; grad., Realtors Inst., 1968. Cert. home economist. Tchr. Horicon (Wis.) High Sch., 1960-61, Oconomowoc (Wis.) High Sch., 1961-67; freelance writer, 1967-70; v.p. Luxury Homes, Inc., Watertown, Wis., 1970-93, Land Devel. Plus Devel. Inc., Watertown, 1970—; co-developer Hidden Meadows Condominium Community, Watertown, 1976-96; gen. ptnr. W and A Elderly Housing Ltd. Partnership, Watertown, 1988—; pres. Housing Am., Inc., 1991—. Gen. ptnr. Sunrise Housing Ltd. Ptnrship., 1990—; builder new and rehab low-income housing, 1983—. Active Wis. Gov.'s Conf. on Family, 1980, long range planning team, 1996—; membership chmn. Boy Scouts Am., 1984—90; chmn. Ams. Abroad Am. Field Svc., Oconomowoc, 1982—87; del. Wis. Rep. Conv., 1997—; chmn. adminstrv. bd. United Meth. Ch., Oconomowoc, 1974—77, 1996—99, lay leader, 2000—03, pres. United Meth. Women, 2002—, chmn. family ministry Wis. Conf., del. to Wis. conf., 2000—03. Recipient Dist. award of Merit Potawatomi Area coun. Boy Scouts Am., 1986. Mem.: AAUW (pres. Oconomowoc br. 1981—83, pres. Oconomowoc 1983—85, officer's bd. 1984—93, fin. advisor 1995—2002), NAFE, Wis. Assn. Family and Consumer Scis. (state bd. 1999—, state housing chmn. 2000—02), Met. Builders Assn. Greater Milw., Internat. Fedn. Home Economists (USA internat. del. 1997—), Wis. Manufactured Housing Assn. (bd. dirs. 1979—90, chmn. bd. 1985—88, Mem. of Yr. award 1986), Wis. Builders Assn., Waukesha Bd. Realtors, Wis. Assn. Realtors, Am. Assn. Family and Consumer Scis., Nat. Assn. Realtors, Wis. Home Economists in Bus. (state chmn. 1987—88, internat. rep. 1998—2000, Home Economist in Bus. of Yr. 1987), Internat. Profl. and Bus. Women, Nat. Assn. Home Builders, Nat. Home Economists in Bus. (internat. com. 1985—87, regional U.S. advisor 1990—92), Wis. Home Econs. Assn. (parliamentarian 1988—90), Am. Home Econs. Assn., Phi Lambda Theta, Kappa Omicron Nu, Phi Upsilon Omicron, Phi Kappa Phi. Republican. Avocation: writing. Home: 37788 Mapleton Rd Oconomowoc WI 53066 Office: Housing Am Inc W1140 Marietta Ave Ixonia WI 53036-9748 E-mail: peebles@execpc.com.

PEEBLES, LUCRETIA NEAL DRANE, policy and administration educator; b. Atlanta, Mar. 16, 1950; d. Dudley Drane and Annie Pearl (Neal) Lewis; divorced; 1 child, Julian Timothy. BA, Pitzer Coll., 1971; MA, Claremont Grad. Sch., 1973, PhD, 1985. Special edn. tchr. Marshall Jr. High Sch., Pomona, Calif., 1971-74; high sch. tchr. Pomona High Sch., 1974-84; adminstr. Lorbeer Jr. High Sch., Diamond Bar, Calif., 1984-91; prin. Chapparal Mid. Sch., Moorpark, Calif., 1991-92, South Valley Jr. High Sch., Gilroy, Calif., 1992—95; asst. prof. dept. edn. Spelman Coll., Atlanta, 1995—97; asst. prof. Coll. Edn. U. Denver, 1997—. Co-dir. pre-freshman program, Claremont (Calif.) Coll., 1974; dir. pre-freshman program, Claremont Coll., 1975; cons., Claremont, 1983—. Author: Negative Attendance Behavior: The Role of the School, 1985, Teaching Children Proactive Responses to Media Violence, 1996, Validating Children: A Collaborative Model, 1996, The Challenge of Leadership in Charter Schools, 2000, Charter School Equity Issues: Focus on Minority and At-Risk Students, 2000, Millennial Challenges for Educational Leadership: Revisiting Issues of Diversity, 2000. Active Funds Distbn. Bd.-Food for All, 1987—, Funds Distbn. Task Force-Food for All, 1986; mem. Adolescent Pregnancy Childwatch Task Force. Named Outstanding Young Career Woman Upland Bus. and Profl. Women's Club, 1978-79; Stanford U. Sch. Edn. MESA fellow, 1983, NSF fellow Stanford U., 1981, Calif. Tchrs. Assn. fellow, 1979, Claremont Grad. Sch. fellow, 1977-79, fellow Calif. Edn. Policy Fellowship Program, 1989-90; recipient Woman of Achievement award YWCA of West Edn., 1991. Mem. Assn. Calif. Sch. Adminstrs. (Minigrant award 1988), Assn. for Supervision and Curriculum Devel., Nat. Assn. Secondary Sch. Principals, Pi Lambda Theta. Democrat. Am. Baptist. Home: 2080 Shoreline Loop #270 San Ramon CA 94583-5502

PEEBLES, MARY LYNN, nursing home administrator; b. Camden, Tn., Feb. 27, 1943; d. Leonard Nathaniel and Luada Gertrude (Cooper) Peebles; div. 1974; children: Jamie Johnson, Rachel Iversen, Jenny Odle-Madden. AA, Brevard C.C., Cocoa, Fla., 1976; B in Gen. Studies, Rollins Coll., 1978; postgrad. in healthcare adminstrn., U. Tex., Austin, 1983. Administrator Spring Valley ARA, Houston, 1983-84, Rosewood Manor, Memphis, 1984-86, Hillhaven Raleigh, Memphis, 1986-87, Carriage Hill VHA Long Term Care, Fredricksburg, Va., 1988-91; regional v.p. VHA, Memphis, 1991-93; administrator Roper Nursing Ctr., Charleston, S.C., 1993-95; v.p. ops. Diversified Health Svcs., Memphis, 1995-97, regional v.p., 1997-98; pres. Age to Age, 1998-99; regional Cara Vita Sr. Svcs., Roswell, Ga., 1999—. Author: (children's book) The Squirrel's Secret, 1975. V.p. Women's Club. St. James Ch., Memphis, 1985; v.p. Tenn. Health Care Assn., Memphis, 1986; trustee Environ. of God, 1996. Mem. Am. Health Care Assn., S.C. Health Care Assn. (mem. pub. rels. com. 1995), Cruseau. Avocations: writing, photography, reading, hiking. Office: Caravita 9755 Dogwood Rd Ste 300 Roswell GA 30075-4663

PEEBLES, SHEILA KAY, music educator; b. Springfield, Mo., Dec. 8, 1957; d. H. Wayne and Shirleen M. Grisham; children: Ashley, Andy, Alex. BS in Music Edn., Southwest Mo. State U., 1978, M in Music Edn., 1900. Music instr., grades 6-8 North Kansas City Pub. Schs., Kansas City, Mo., 1979—80; dir. children's music Blue Ridge Presbyn. Ch., Raytown, Mo., 1979—80; music instr., grades K-6 Lebanon (Mo.) Pub. Schs., 1980—81; music instr., grades 7-12 Springfield (Mo.) Pub. Schs., 1981—87; dir. youth and children's choir 1st and Calvary Presbyn. Ch., Springfield, Mo., 1981—87, dir. music, 1987—. Pres. bd., concept organizer Boys Choir of Springfield, 1999—. V.p. Field Elem. PTA Bd., Springfield, 1998—99, sec., 2000—01, fundraising chair, 2001—02; reflectoins creative arts chair Pershing Mid. Sch. PTSA Bd., Springfield, 1996—; pres. Vocal Music Boosters Glendale H.S., Springfield, 2001—. Named Disting. Woman of Yr., Girl Scouts Am., Dogwood Trails, Springfield, 1997. Mem.: Presbyn. Assn. Musicians, Mo. Music Educators Assn., Am. Choral Dirs. Assn. Home: 3230 S Valleyview Ave Springfield MO 65804 Office: 1st and Calvary Presbyn Ch 820 E Cherry St Springfield MO 65806

PEEK, STEPHANIE, artist; b. N.J., Jan. 17, 1940; d. James Desmond and Adeline (Peek) Shevlin; 1 child, Matthew Chase Peek. BA, Wellesley Coll., 1961; MFA, U. Calif., Berkeley, 1996. Artist, San Francisco, 1990—; graphic designer Stephanie Peek Graphic Design, San Francisco, 1971-92. Vis. artist Am. Acad. Rome, Italy, 1997; vis. lectr. U. Calif., Berkeley, 1997. Books, Giardini del Sogno, 1997, Time Capsule, 1995, one-woman shows include Triangle Gallery, San Francisco, Friesen Gallery, Seattle & Sun Valley, Represented in permanent collections Harvard, Stanford, Univ. Calif., Berkeley, San Cruz. Virginia McPheter Stoltz fellow U. Calif., Berkeley, 1994, J. Ruth Kelsey Travel grantee, 1996, Susan B. Irwin scholarship in visual arts, 1995; recipient Borsa di Studio award Rignano, Italy, 1997. Mem. Am. Inst. Graphic Artists, Art Alumni Group (chair 1997-99), Women's Caucus for Art. Christian Scientist.

PEELE, KATHERINE N. architect; BArch (summa cum laude), NC State U., 1988. With Boney, PLLC, Raleigh, NC, 1988—, dir. Raleigh office, 1992—, COO, 2002—. Sch. constrn. support com. Wake County Pub. Sch. Sys. Fellow: AIA (pres. 2000, chair com. arch. edn. 2001, adv. bd. nat. com. arch. edn.); mem.: NC Ednl. Facility Planners (pres. 1999). Office: 5511 Capital Ctr Dr Ste 105 Raleigh NC 27606 Office Phone: 919-851-9393. E-mail: knp@booneyarchitects.com.

PEELE-BURKHOLDER, TAMMY SUE, nurse; b. Cheverly, Md., July 27, 1971; d. Betty Ann Swartz; m. Paul Francis Burkholder, June 3, 1995; 1 child, Caitlin Rose Peele. Nail technician, Wards Corner Beauty Sch., Norfolk, Va., 1990; nurse aide, Madison Career Ctr., Norfolk, Va., 1991;

med. office asst., Kees Bus. Coll., Norfolk, Va., 1992. Cert. nurse aide. Nail technician, helper Empress Beauty Salon, Norfolk, 1990—92; nurse aide Sentra Nursing Home, Virginia Beach, Va., 1992—93, Winchester, Va., 1995—2002, Continuing Care, Strasburg, Va., 2002—. Kennel helper Carpenter and Pope Vets., Norfolk, 1991—92; cashier Wal-Mart, Winchester, 2001—02; writer Inst. Children's Lit., West Redding, Conn., 2003—. Republican. Adventist. Avocations: art, reading.*

PEET, AMANDA, actress; b. Jan. 11, 1972; d. Charles and Penny Peet. BA in History, Columbia U., 1994. Actor: (TV series) Law & Order, 1995, Central Park West, 1995—96, The Single Guy, 1996, Spin City, 1997, Seinfeld, 1997, Jack & Jill, 1999, Partners, 1999; (TV films) Ellen Foster, 1997, Date Squad, 2001; (films) Animal Room, 1995, She's the One, 1996, One Fine Day, 1996, Virginity, 1996, Grind, 1997, Touch Me, 1997, Sax and Violins, 1997, 1999, 1998, Southie, 1998, Playing by Heart, 1998, Origin of the Species, 1998, Simply Irresistible, 1999, Jump, 1999, Two Ninas, 1999, Body Shots, 1999, Isn't She Great?, 2000, The Whole Nine Yards, 2000, Takedown, 2000, Whipped, 2000, Saving Silverman, 2001, High Crimes, 2002, Changing Lanes, 2002, Igby Goes Down, 2002, Whatever We Do, 2003, Identity, 2003, Something's Gotta Give, 2003, The Whole Ten Yards, 2004. Office: The Gersh Agy Ste 201 232 N Canon Dr Beverly Hills CA 90210*

PEIFER, MILLIE R. computer company executive; b. Phila., Dec. 14, 1954; d. George Brinton Rombold and Elsie Helen Gimbel; m. William F. Peifer, Apr. 7, 1979; children: Allan, Brinton stepchildren: William D., Nysha-Lynn, Eric. Grad. H.S., Albuquerque, 1972. Field asst. Circle K Corp., Albuquerque, 1991—94, asst. mgr., 1994—96; sales assoc. Circuit City, Albuquerque, 1996—98; COO Peifer Computing Solutions, Albuquerque, 1998—. Sec. Allan Peifer Meml. Found., Albuquerque, 1998—2002. Avocations: needlecrafts, designing wedding gowns.

PEIRCE, CAROL MARSHALL, English educator; b. Columbia, Mo., Feb. 1, 1922; d. Charles Hamilton and Helen Emily (Davault) Williams; m. Brooke Peirce, July 12, 1952. AB, Fla. State U., 1942; MA, U. Va., 1943; PhD, Harvard U., 1951. Head English dept. Fairfax Hall, Waynesboro, Va., 1943-44; instr. English Cedar Crest Coll., Allentown, Pa., 1944-46; instr. Harvard U., 1952-53; asst. dean Radcliffe Coll., Cambridge, 1950-53; head English extension home study U. Va., Charlottesville, 1953-54; asst. dir. admissions Goucher Coll., Towson, Md., 1956-62; prof. English and comm. design U. Balt., 1968—2003, chmn. dept., 1968-94, gen. edn. core coord., 1985-87, Disting. teaching prof. Coll. Liberal Arts, 1981-82, chmn. humanities div., 1972-79; gen. edn. dir., 1995-97; chmn. bd. New Poets Series, 1975—. Vis. scholar Lucy Cavendish Coll., U. Cambridge, Eng., 1977-78; co-coord. On Miracle Ground: The Internat. Lawrence Durrell Conf., 1980, 82, 90, 2000; co-coord. conf. Evermore! Celebrating the 150th Anniversary of Edgar Allan Poe's "Raven," 1995. Author: (with Brooke Peirce) A Study of Literary Types and an Introduction to English Literature from Chaucer to the Eighteenth Century, 1954, A Study of Literary Types and an Introduction to English Literature from the Eighteenth Century to the Present, 1954; editor: (with Lawrence Markert) On Miracle Ground: Second Lawrence Durrell Conference Proceedings, 1984; guest editor: (with Ian S. MacNiven) Lawrence Durrell Issue, Parts 1 and II, Twentieth Century Literature, Fall, Winter, 1987; contbr. essays to: Poe and Our Times, 1986, Critical Essays on Lawrence Durrell, 1987, Into the Labyrinth: Essays on the Art of Lawrence Durrell, 1989, On Miracle Ground: Essays on the Fiction of Lawrence Durrell, 1990, Dictionary of Literary Biography Yearbook, 1990, St. James Reference Guide to English Literature, 1991, Poe's Pym: Critical Explorations, 1992, Selected Essays on the Humor of Lawrence Durrell, 1993, Lawrence Durrell: Comprehending The Whole, 1994, D.H. Lawrence: The Cosmic Adventure, 1996, Anais Nin: A Book of Mirrors, 1996, others; assoc editor: Deus Loci: The Lawrence Durrell Jour., 1990-92, co-editor, 1993—. McGregor fellow, DuPont fellow U. Va., 1943; Harvard tutor, Anne Radcliffe traveling fellow Harvard U., 1951. Mem. MLA, Edgar Allan Poe Soc. of Balt. (bd. dirs. 1973-89, pres. 1989—), Lawrence Durrell Soc. (bd. dirs. 1983-93, 99—, nat. pres. 1980-82, internat. pres. 1994-98), Md. Assn. Depts. English, Phi Beta Kappa, Chi Delta Phi, Phi Alpha theta, Phi Kappa Phi. Home: 705 Warren Rd Cockeysville Hunt Valley MD 21030-2824 Office: Univ Balt Divsn English/ Comm Dsgn Baltimore MD 21201 E-mail: cpeirce@ubalt.edu.

PEIRIS, SUHITHI MAHESICA, research chemist; b. Colombo, Sri Lanka, Nov. 23, 1965; d. Suran A. and Marguerite M. Peiris; m. Brett M. Goodman, Apr. 28, 2001. BS with honors, U. Mich., 1991; PhD in Inorganic Chemistry, U. Chgo., 1996. Postdoctoral fellow U. Chgo., 1996-97; staff scientist Nova Rsch. Inc., Alexandria, Va., 1997-98; rsch. chemist Naval Rsch. Lab., Washington, 1998-2000, Naval Surface Warfare Ctr., Indian Head, Md., 2000—. Contbr. articles to profl. jours. Sci. fair judge, Washington, 1999, Indian Head, 2000. Recipient Outstanding Young Scientist award, Gordon Rsch. Conf., 2000. Mem. Am. Chem. Soc. Avocations: swimming, reading. E-mail: peirisSM@ih.navy.mil.

PEISCH, ALICE HANLON, state legislator; BA, Smith Coll.; JD, Suffolk U. Law Sch. Town clerk Wellesley, 2000—03; state rep. Mass. House, 2003—. Bd. dirs. Wellesley Edn. Found., 1999—; bd. overseers Newton-Wellesley Hosp., 1996—; mem. League of Women Voters of Wellesley, 1986—; bd. mem. Senior Living, Inc., 2001—; mem. Wellesley Svc. League, 1988—. Democrat. Office: Rm 26 State House Boston MA 02133

PEJSA, JANE ELIZABETH, writer, retired computer scientist; b. Mpls., Aug. 12, 1929; d. Walter U. and Irene M. (Melgaard) Hauser; m. Franz J.F. Gayl, Dec. 19, 1951 (div. Jan. 1968); children: Ilse E. Gayl, Franz J. Gayl; m. Arthur J. Pejsa, May 26, 1975. BA, Carleton Coll., 1951. Computer engineer, researcher Honeywell, Mpls., 1971-86. Author: The Molineu Affair, 1984, The Molineu Affair, 3d. edit., 1988 (finalist Edgar Allen Poe Fact Crime award Mystery Writers Am., 1985), Matriarch of Conspiracy, Ruth von Kleist 1867-1945, 1991, soft cover edit., 1992, German edit., 1996, Japanese edit., 1998, Polish edit., 2003 (Best Book Overall Midwest Ind. Pubs., 1992, Best Biography Minn. Book award Minn. Office Libr. Devel. and Svcs., 1992, Golden Ex-Libris award Pomorska, Poland, 2003), Gratia Countryman, Her Life, Her Loves and Her Library, 1995 (finalist Best Biography Minn. Book award Minn. Office Libr. Devel. and Svcs., 1995), To Pomerania, in Search of Dietrich Bonhoeffer, a Traveler's Companion, 1995, 2d. edit., 1998, To Pomerania Where Dietrich Bonhoeffer Met the Holocaust, 2000, Emily Peake, One Dedicated OJIBWE, 2003 (written under grant from Minn. Hist. Soc.), Romanoff, Prince of Rogues, The Life and Times of a Hollywood Icon, 1997; contbr. articles to profl. jours. Chair philanthropy The Woman's Club, Mpls., 1993-95. Recipient Disting. Achievement award Carleton Coll., 1988; Artist's Fellowship grantee The Bush Found., St. Paul, 1986. Mem. Phi Beta Kappa. Congregationalist. Achievements include patents for energy submetering sys., 1986. Avocations: piano, software design. Home: 1314 Marquette Ave Apt 906 Minneapolis MN 55403-4105 Office Phone: 612-332-5073.

PEKOL, MARILYN PATRICIA, music educator, musician; b. Rhinelander, Wis., Jan. 16, 1962; d. Joseph Edward and Janet Etta (Kelly) Baer; m. James Brian Pekol, June 16, 1984; children: Brian Joseph, Robert James. MusB edn., U. of Wis., Stevens Point, Stevens Point, Wis., 1980—85. Cert. Instrumental Music Wis. Dept. of Pub. Instrn., 1985. Banjo player/ drummer Jim Pekol Orch., Phillips, Wis., 1983—; music tchr. Butternut Sch. Dist., Butternut, Wis., 1986—88, St. Anthony's Sch., Pk. Falls, Wis., 1987—88; prin. flutist Wausau Symphony and Band, Wausau, Wis., 1989—; music tchr./ band instr. Rhinelander Cath. Ctrl. Sch., Rhinelander, Wis., 1989—. Clarinetist Wausau City Band, Wausau, Wis., 1984—; banjo player Bridge St. Dixieland Rev., Wausau, Wis., 1985—; clarinet/ saxophone player Jerry Goetsch Orch., Wausau, Wis., 1986—92; dir. Rhinelander City Band, Rhinelander, Wis., 1996—97; drummer Greiner Bros. Orch., Wausau, Wis., 1996—99. Musician: (orch.) Annie /Northwoods Players, The King and I/ Northwoods Players, Hello Dolly/ Northwoods Players, My Fair Lady/ Northwoods Players, Hello Dolly/ Wausau Cmty. Theater, The Pajama Game/ Wausau Cmty. Theater. Den leader Cub Scout Troop 540, Phillips, Wis., 1996—99, advancement chmn., 2000—02, vol. Phillips Pub. Libr., Phillips, Wis., 2002—03. Mem.: Wis. Sch. Music Assn., Nat. Cath. [illegible] Band Assn. Catholic. Avocations: reading, travel, blacksmithing, ping pong/table tennis, cross country skiing. Home: N7791 County Road K Phillips WI 54555 Office: Rhinelander Catholic Central School 103 East King Street Rhinelander WI 54501 E-mail: rhicc@newnorth.net.

PELAEZ, OFELIA, addiction and HIV/AIDS counselor; b. Havana, Cuba, Apr. 27, 1944; came to the U.S., 1990; d. Adalberfo and Ofelia del Pilar (Fernánder) P.; m. Francisco Iglesias, May 28, 1960 (div. Sept. 1972); children: Francisco, Mijail. Nursing asst. cert., Internat. Tng. Ctr. Inst., 1995, cert. patient care technician, 1997; degree in counseling for addictions, cert. HIV/AIDS counselor, U. Miami, 1998. Tchr. Little Pumpkin Day Care, Hialeah, Fla., 1991-93; cons. One 2 One Co., Miami, Fla., 1993-97; behavior svcs. profl. A. Jung Mgmt. Svcs. Inc., Miami, 1997—; crisis counselor. Social asst. Total Med. Ctr., Miami, 1994-95; cons. in field. Author: Organizacion de Escuelas Juveniles, 1980. Women's group educator Bapt. Ch., Hialeah, 1991-97; vol. Switchboard of Miami. Democrat. Avocations: arts and crafts, reading and writing articles psicoterapia, sewing, travels. Home: Lot 49 2775 W Okeechobee Rd Lot 49 Hialeah FL 33010-1058

PELAVIN, DIANE CHRISTINE, small business owner; m. Sol H. Pelavin, Aug. 14, 1966. BA, So. Ill. U., 1965; MS, San Jose (Calif.) State U., 1979. Tchr., 1965—68; planning analyst EPRI, Palo Alto, Calif., 1977—78; rsch. analyst NTS Rsch. Corp., Durham, NC, 1978—82; v.p., co-founder Pelavin Assocs., Inc., Washington, 1982—94; pres., co-founder Chesapeake Inst., Washington, 1991—94; sr. v.p. Am. Insts. for Rsch., 1994—. Contbr. articles to profl. jours. U. Chgo. fellow, 1966, NSF fellow, 1968. Mem. Am. Edn. Rsch. Assn. Office: 1000 Thomas Jefferson St NW Washington DC 20007-3835

PELCYGER, ELAINE, school psychologist; b. Jersey City, N.J., Apr. 13, 1939; d. Maurice C. and Bessie (Schneider) Morley; m. Iran Pelcyger, June 4, 1956; children: Stuart Lawrence, Gwynne Ellice, Wayne Farrol. BA magna cum laude, L.I. U., 1983; MS, St. John's U., Flushing, N.Y., 1985. Cert. sch. psychologist N.Y., N.Y.C., nat. cert. sch. psychologist, group psychotherapist, N.Y. Sch. psychologist N.Y.C. Bd. Edn., 1985—; trauma and loss sch. specialist. Mem. Nat. Assn. Sch. Psychologists, Am. Group Psychotherapists, N.Y. Assn. Sch. Psychologists, Psi Chi. Avocations: handicrafts, reading, old time radio. Office: Com Spl Edn Dist 10 5500 Broadway Bronx NY 10453 Office Phone: 718-584-8002 3174.

PELHAM, JUDITH, health system administrator; b. Bristol, Conn., July 23, 1945; d. Marvin Curtis and Muriel (Chodos) Pelham; m. Jon N. Coffee, Dec. 30, 1992; children: Rachel Welch, Molly, Edward. BA, Smith Coll., 1967; MPA, Harvard U., 1975. Various govt. postions, 1968-72; prin. analyst Urban Systems, Cambridge, Mass., 1972-73; dir. devel. and planning Roxbury Dental and Med. Group, Boston, 1975-76; asst. to dir. for gen. medicine and ambulatory care Peter B. Brigham Hosp., Boston, 1976-77, asst. dir. ambulatory care, 1977-79; asst. v.p. Brigham and Women's Hosp., Boston, 1980-81; dir. planning and mktg. Seton Med. Ctr., Austin, Tex., 1980-82, pres., 1982-92, CEO, 1987-92; pres., CEO Daughters of Charity Health Svcs., Austin, 1987-92, Mercy Health Svcs., Farmington Hills, Mich., 1993—2000, Trinity Health (merger of Mercy Health Svcs. and Holy Cross Health Sys.), Novi, Mich., 2000—. Bd. dirs. Amgen, Cath. CEO Healthcare Connection; cons. Robert W. Johnson Found., 1979—80; mem. mgmt. bd. Inst. for Diversity in Health Mgmt., 1994—97; chair Coalition for Non-Profit Healthcare, 1997—2000, exec. com., 1997—2002; mem. Healthcare Rsch. and Devel. Inst., 1998—, bd., 2003—. Contbr. articles to profl. jours. Trustee A. Shivers Radiation Therapy Ctr., Austin, 1982—92, Marywood Maternity and Adoption Agy., 1982—86; bd.dirs. Quality of Life Found., Austin, 1985, Austin Rape Crisis Ctr., adv. bd. mem., 1986—88; bd. dirs., trustee League House, 1992—93, Seton Fund, 1982—93, Greater Detroit Area Health Coun.; mem. Gov.'s Job Tng. Coordinating Coun., 1983—85; mem. adv. coun. U. Tex. Social Work Found., 1983—85; charter mem. Leadership Tex., Austin, 1983—93. Recipient Leadership award, YWCA Austin, 1986. Fellow: Am. Hosp. Assn., Am. Coll. Healthcare Execs. (bd. dirs. 1987—95); mem.: Cath. Health Assn. (sec., treas. 1982—95, com. on govt. rels. 1984—91, chair fin. com. 1992—95, bd. dirs. 1987—95), Tex. Conf. Health Facilities (bd. dirs. 1985—89, pres. 1988), Austin Area Rsch. Orgn., Tex. Hosp. Assn. (various couns. 1982—87). Office: Trinity Health 27870 Cabot Dr Novi MI 48377

PELISH, SUSAN MARION, sculptor, painter; b. Poughkeepsie, N.Y., Mar. 31, 1946; d. John Curtis and Genevieve Francis (Chance) Caulkins; m. James Detmer Pelish, Feb. 2, 1966; children: Jason, Amber. Student, Pratt Inst., 1964-66, SUNY, New Paltz, 1966-68; BFA, Fla. Atlantic U., 1994. One woman shows at Mid Hudson Mus. Arts and Scis., Poughkeepsie, 1981, Esparante, Palm Beach Cultural Coun. Sculpture Ctr., 1995, Steiner Gallery, Bal Harbour, Fla., 1996, Art and Culture Ctr. of Hollywood, Fla., 1996, Pembroke Pines Mcpl. Ctr., 1997; group shows include Boca Raton Mus., 1982 (2d prize), Soc. of Four Arts, Palm Beach, 1983, Broward Art Guild, Ft. Lauderdale, Fla., 1984 (Excellence in Oil award), Fla. Atlantic U. Gallery, 1994 (Hon. Mention), XS Best of Gallery MONA, Ft. Lauderdale, 1995-96, SOFA, Miami, 1995, Weaton Village Internat. Glass Expo, N.J., 1996, Glass Canvas Gallery, St. Petersburg, Fla., 1997, Vespermann Gallery, Atlanta, 1998, Palm Beach Art Expo, 1998; represented in corp. collections at W.R. Grace Hdqrs., Boca Raton, Fla., Norwegian Cruise Ship, Norwegian Sky, King World, Deerfield, Fla., Exxon Corp., West Palm Beach, New Port Bus. Ctr., Gumbo Limbo Nature Ctr., Boca Raton, Boca Raton Elem. Sch., Boca Raton Libr., Capitol Bldg., Tallahassee, 1997, Poughkeepsie H.S., N.Y., 1964, Boca Raton Art Mus., Hollywood Art and Culture Mus. Mem. Boca Raton Beautification Com., Nat. Grand Champion Tree Com. AAUW scholar, 1964; Art Dreams Inc. grantee, 1981; recipient Key to City, Boca Raton, 1997. Mem. Glass Art Soc. Achievements include pioneering cold welded glass sculpture. Home: # 35 850 NE Spanish River Blvd Boca Raton FL 33431-6156 E-mail: susan@pelish.com.

PELLEGRINO, SISTER MARY R. nun; b. Pitts., Sept. 1, 1963; d. Americo R. and Virginia R. Pellegrino. BA in Journalism, Indiana U. of Pa., 1985; MS in Religious Edn., Fordham U., 1994. Campus min. Cath. Campus Ministry Assn., 1997. Campus min. Robert Morris Coll., Moon Township, Pa., 1988—89; dir. of religous edn. Christ the King Parish, Ambridge, Pa., 1989—92; campus min., pastoral assoc. Newman Ctr., St. Thomas More U. Parish, Indiana, Pa., 1992—98; dir. of vocation ministries Sisters of St. Joseph of Baden, Pa., 1998—; program dir. Visitation House, Pitts., 2002—. Young adult leadership team Diocese of Pitts., 2002—; conf. presenter Nat. Religious Vocation Conf., 2001—; conf. facilitator 3d Continental Congress on Vocations, 2003; presenter, facilitator various religious comtys., Pa. and N.Y. Contbr. articles to profl. jours. Mem.: Pitts. Religious Vocation Coun. (chairperson 1999—2001), Nat. Religious Vocation Conf. (region III chairperson 2000—02), Cath. Campus Ministry Assn. (assoc.). Roman Catholic. Avocations: writing, reading. Office: Sisters of St Joseph 1020 State St Baden PA 15005 Personal E-mail: mrpcsj@yahoo.com. E-mail: membrcsj@usaor.net.

PELLER, MARCI TERRY, realtor; b. Upland, Pa., Nov. 5, 1949; d. Max Maclyn and Lucille Eugenia (Zucker) P. AA, Harcum Jr. Coll., Bryn Mawr, Pa., 1971; student, Villanova U., 1971-73. With sales dept. William H. Cartwright Real Estate, North Palm Beach, Fla., 1985-91; realtor-assoc. Fin. Realty Group, Lake Park, Fla., 1991—. Owner Cards By Marci. Republican. Jewish. Avocations: theater, football, golf, attending concerts. Office: Gerald H Grant Inc 2247 Palm Beach Lakes Blvd West Palm Beach FL 33409 E-mail: m.peller@att.net.

PELLETIER, MARSHA LYNN, secondary school educator, poet; b. Mt. Pleasant, Mich., July 20, 1950; d. Eugene Russell and Mary Ellen (Eude) Mingle; m. Arthur Joseph Pelletier, May 19, 1973; 1 child, John Frederick. BS in Home Econs. and Edn., Kans. State U., 1971, MS in Edn. Guidance and Counseling, 1972. Lic. real estate broker N.H. Conf. coord., guidance counselor Kans. State U., Manhattan, 1971-73; tchr. home econs. Franklin (Mass.) HS, 1974, Exeter (N.H.) HS, 1974-75, Barrington (N.H.) Mid. Sch., 1975-81, Pentucket Regional Jr. HS, West Newbury, Mass., 1981-82; realtor assoc. Century 21 Ocean and Norword Realty, Portsmouth, NH, 1983-86; tchr. interior design, cons. U. N.H., Durham, 1986-87; tchr. family and consumer sci. Dover (N.H.) Mid. Sch., 1983—2001; tchr. Dover HS, 2001—; mem. legis. adminstrn. com. N.H. Ho. of Reps., Concord, 1992—94, 1996—2002; ind. real estate broker Dover, 1986-2000. Bd. dirs. N.H. State Profl. Bd. Stds., 1999—; assessor Nat. Bd. Profl. Tchg. Stds., 2001; tchr. assessor Nat. Tchrs. Bd. Cert., 2002—. Author: (poems) Arriving at the Crossroads, 2003; costume dir. & designer : Guys and Dolls, 2004. Bd. dirs. Dover Adult Learning Ctr., 1995—98; mem. Health Task Force, Dover, Concord, 1993—94, Cornerstone Dancers, Dover Friends of Pub. Libr., 1996—, bd. supt. adv. com., 2001—03, poetry judge, 2003—04; trustee St. John's Meth. Ch., 1995—97. Mem.: NEA (local pres., negotiator, v.p., membership chair, mem. leadership exec. com., bldg. rep. 1979—, N.H. del. to nat. conv.), Seacoast Writers Assn., Nat. Coalition Consumer Econ., Alpha Delta Kappa (v.p., historian, altruistic chmn. 1984—89). Democrat. Avocations: gardening, aerobics, poetry, sewing, cooking. Home: 94 Back River Rd Dover NH 03820-4411

PELLETIER, SHO-MEI, musician, educator; b. Tucson, July 25, 1952; d. Harold W. and Mary Pelletier; m. Dwight E. Shambley, Aug. 12, 1979; children: Aaron Joshua Pelletier-Shambley, Alexis Jessica Pelletier-Shambley. Student, No. Ariz. U., 1966, student, 1965, Ariz. State U., 1965, student, 1966; MusB in Violin, Ind. U., 1974. Asst. prin. violinist Dallas Symphony Orch., assoc. prin. violinist, 1975—, solo violinist, 1993, 1995; assoc. prin. violinist Santa Fe Opera, Santa Fe, 1973—98; prin. violinist Dallas Chamber Orch., 1975—92, Dallas Bach Soc., 1975—95. Mem. youth edn. svc. quintet Dallas Symphony Orch., 1978—, charter tchr. Young Strings Minority Scholarship program, 1988; part-time tchr. Booker T. Washington Arts Magnet HS, Dallas, 1982—85. Musician (solo violinist): Walden Ensemble, 1975—, New Arensky Piano Trio, 1975—, Anton A Piano Trio, 1975—, Kodaly Duo, 1975—, Voices Change Ensemble, 1975—; author: (book) The Simple Dictionary for Classical Musicians, 2000. Charter mem. Nat. Mus. Women Art, Washington; mem. Klanwatch So. Poverty Law Ctr. Named concertmaster, Ariz. All-State Orch., 1968, 1969, Outstanding Young Women of Am., 1982; recipient awards, Plano Art Soc., 1980—, Richardson Art Soc., 1980—. Mem.: Nat. Geog. Soc. Avocations: painting, drawing, photography. Home: 9648 Whitehurst Dr Dallas TX 75243 Office: Dallas Symphony Orch 2301 Flora St Dallas TX 75201-2497 Personal E-mail: shambley@mindspring.com.

PELLICCIOTTO, NICOLE ALYSSA, special education services professional, consultant; b. Virginia Beach, Va., Feb. 15, 1970; d. Ted and Wanda Pellicciotto; m. Stephen Carl Karcha, Feb. 12, 1994. MEd, postgrad. in PhD program, George Mason U., 1994—. Cert. Severe and Profound 2-21 Va., 1995, Early Childhood Spl. Edn. Va., 1995. Pvt. cons. early intervention, Fairfax, Va., 1995—; project mgr. RGB Group, Inc., Fairfax, 2000—. Contbr. chapters to books. Recipient Tech. award, Va. Assistive Tech. Systems, 1996. Mem.: Coun. for Exceptional Children (assoc.). Personal E-mail: nicpellicc@yahoo.com.

PELLMAR, TERRY C. neurophysiologist, researcher; b. Bklyn., Nov. 4, 1951; d. Ruben and Frances (Freilich) P.; m. Howard Louis Leikin, Jan. 4, 1981. ScB in biology magna cum laude, Brown U., 1973; PhD, Duke U., 1977. Fellow Marine Biological Lab., Woods Hole, Ma., 1978, Armed Forces Radiobiology Rsch. Inst., Bethesda, Md., 1977-80, Nat. Inst. Alcohol Abuse & Alcoholism, Rockville, Md., 1980-82; rsch. physiologist physiology dept. Armed Forces Radiobiology Rsch. Inst., 1982-84; adj. asst. prof. physiology dept. Georgetown U., Washington, 1983-90; project mgr. neurophysiology physiology dept. Armed Forces Radiobiology Rsch. Inst., Bethesda, Md., 1984-95, chmn. radiation pathophysiology and toxicology dept., 1995—99; dir. neuroscience & behavioral health Inst. of Medicine, Washington, 1999—. Mem. VA Merit Rev. Bd. in Neurobiology, 1991-94; mem. neurology disorders program rev. A com., NIH, 1995—. Contbr. articles to profl. jours. Rsch. Peer Review Com. mem. Am. Heart Assn., 1989-92. Mem. N.Y. Acad. Scis., Soc. Neurosci., Oxygen Soc., Assn. Women in Sci., Oxygen Club Washington (councilor 1988-91, sec. 1991-94, pres. elect 1994, pres. 1995), Sigma Xi. Office: Board on Neuroscience and Behavioral Hlth Inst Med 500 5th St NW Washington DC 20001

PELOSI, NANCY, congresswoman; b. Balt., Mar. 26, 1940; d. Thomas J. D'Alesandro Jr.; m. Paul Pelosi; children: Nancy Corinne, Christine, Jacqueline, Paul, Alexandra. Grad., Trinity Coll., 1962—62. Former chmn. Calif. State Dem. Com., 1981; committeewoman Dem. Nat. Com., 1976, 80, 84; fin. chmn. Dem. Senatorial Campaign Com., 1987; mem. U.S. Congress from 5th Calif. dist., 1987-93, U.S. Congress from 8th Calif. dist., 1993—; mem. appropriations com., intelligence com.; mem. House Dem. Whip, 2002; Ho. Dem. Leader, 2002—. Democrat. Office: 2371 Rayburn House Office Bldg Washington DC 20515*

PELTIER, JANIS JANOSEK, real estate agent, astrologer; b. Cleve. d. John George and Mary Theresa (Elias) Janosek; m. William H. Peltier, Feb. 10, 1968 (div. Mar. 1980); children: William Brian, Janine Mary Janosek. Student, Chgo. Mus. Coll., 1960-63. Media and rsch. asst. Lang, Fisher & Stashower, Cleve., 1963-65; new bus. asst. Griswold Eshelman, Chgo., 1965-67; asst. dir. rsch. Feldman & Norton, Chgo., 1967-68; freelance advt. and mktg. cons., Chgo., 1978-81; astrologer, lectr., 1976—; saleswoman Cyrus Realtors, Evanston, Ill., 1981-91, Baird & Warner, 1991—2001, Coldwell Banker, 2001—. Bd. dirs. YMCA, Evanston, 1973-77, Santa Claus for the Very Poor, Chgo., 1988—; vol. recovery room Evanston Hosp.; vol. publicity dir. YMCA Brillianteen Orgn. Mem. Nat. Assn. Realtors, Nat. Coun. Geocosmic Rsch. (sec. Chgo. 1976-82). Avocations: investments, amateur theatre, physical fitness. Home: 8 Salem Cir Evanston IL 60203-1216

PELTO, GRETEL H. nutritional anthropologist, educator; b. Mpls., May 6, 1940; d. Isaac L. and Deana (Harris) Hoffman; m. Pertti J. Pelto, July 27, 1968 (div. Dec. 1995); children: Jonathan, Dunja, Ari; m. Jean-Pierre Habicht, June 13, 1997. Student, Bennington Coll., 1957-60; BA, U. Minn., 1963, MA, 1967, PhD, 1970; DSc (hon.), U. Helsinki, 1996. Clin. assoc. U. Conn. Sch. Medicine, Farmington, 1970-74; asst. prof. anthropology U. Conn., Storrs, 1974-77, prof. nutritional scis., 1977-92; scientist, child health divsn. WHO, Geneva, 1992-98; prof. nutritional scis. Cornell U., Ithaca, N.Y., 1998—. Mem. adv. bd. divsn. diarrheal disease control WHO, 1987-92; mem. adv. bd. subcom. on maternal and infant nutrition NAS, Washington, 1980-83; cons. UN U., Washington and Tokyo, 1985, Population Coun., N.Y.C., 1980-82. Co-author: Anthropological Research, 1978, Community Assessment of Natural Food rces of Vitamin A; co-editor: Nutritional Anthropology, 2000. Bd. dirs. Parent-Child Rsch. Ctr. for Eastern Conn., 1974-79; mem. task force Hartford (Conn.) Area Health Edn. Ctr., 1980-82; mem. adv. com. Travelers Ctr. on Aging, Hartford, 1988-89. Fulbright grantee, 1984; hon. rsch. fellow U. Birmingham, Eng., 1994-97; U.S. AID rsch. grantee, Mex., 1982-87. Fellow Soc. for Applied Anthropology; mem. Soc. for Internat. Nutritional Rsch. (bd. dirs. 1989-92), Coun. on Nutritional Anthropology (pres. 1982-84, v.p. 1998-00), Am. Soc. Nutritional Scis. (mem. long range planning com.), Soc. for Med.

Anthropology (bd. dirs. 1980-82). Avocations: photography, cooking. Home: 129 Eastlake Rd Ithaca NY 14850-9700 Office: Cornell U Div Nutritional Sci MVR 3M1 Ithaca NY 14853 Office Phone: 607-255-6277. Business E-Mail: gp32@cornell.edu.

PELTZ, CISSIE JEAN, art gallery director, cartoonist; d. Morton Dunbar Liebshutz and Myrtle Jewel Friedman; m. Richard Walter Peltz, Jan. 1, 1953 (dec. Feb. 21, 1975); 1 child, David Lee. BA, U. Chgo., 1947. Freelance cartoonist Milw. Jour., 1975—77, Chgo. Tribune, 1948—68, Today's Health, Chgo., 1959—71, Cosmopolitan mag., N.Y.C., 1950—85, Look Mag., N.Y.C., 1950—85, N.Y. Times, N.Y.C., 1950—85, Saturday Rev., N.Y.C., 1950—85, Chgo. Mag., 1950—85, Great Books Found., Chgo., 1950—85; owner, dir. Peltz Gallery, Milw., 1989—. Illustrator: book Everyday Speech, 1949, Laugh Your Way to Work, 1977, illustrator: booklets, advt. filmstrips. Named Communicator of Yr., Univ. Chgo., 1963. Mem.: Milw. Art Mus. Contemporary Art Soc., Mil. Art Mus. Print Forum (v.p., pres. 1987—89, bd. dirs. 1989—2002), Milw. Art Dealers Assn. Democrat. Avocations: grandchildren, collecting art, theater, movies. Office: Peltz Gallery 1119 E Knapp St Milwaukee WI 53202

PELTZ, PAULETTE BEATRICE, corporate lawyer; b. Bklyn., May 30, 1954; BA, SUNY, Binghamton, 1976; JD, Am. U., 1979. Bar: D.C. 1980, Va. 1982, Md. 1986. Atty. U.S. EPA, Washington, 1979-83; assoc. Mahn, Franklin & Goldenberg, Washington, 1983-85, Deso, Greenberg & Thomas, P.C., Washington, 1985-87; corp. gen. counsel Western Devel. Corp., Washington, 1987-91; v.p. and corp. gen. counsel Mills Corp., 1992-94; sr. v.p., gen. counsel Charter Oak Ptnrs., 1994—. Office: Charter Oak Ptnrs 8000 Towers Crescent Dr Ste 950 Vienna VA 22182-6208

PELZ, CAROLINE DUNCOMBE, retired educational administrator; b. White Plains, N.Y. d. David Sanford and Helena (Ebert) Duncombe; m. Edward Joseph Pelz, July 11, 1942; children: Caroline Pelz Elbow, Margaret L. (dec.), Patricia Pelz Hart, Sanford M. AB, Barnard Coll., 1940. Adjustments supr. R.H. Macy & Co., N.Y.C., 1940-42; admissions interviewer Barnard Coll., 1960-63; alumni sec. Allen-Stevenson Sch., N.Y.C., 1967-70, admissions asst., 1969-70; adminstrv. asst. Ednl. Records Bur., N.Y.C., 1970-72; dir. admissions Grace Ch. Sch., N.Y.C., 1972-87. Trustee Barnard Coll., 1963-67. Recipient Columbia U. Alumni Fedn. medal, 1991. Mem. Barnard Coll. Alumnae Assn. (pres. 1963-66), Woman's Nat. Farm and Garden Assn. (scholarship chmn. N.Y.C. met. br. 1981-99, treas. 1989-99), English-Speaking Union. Republican. Episcopalian. Home: PO Box 395 Berlin NY 12022-0395

PEÑA, ELIZABETH, actress; b. Elizabeth, N.J., Sept. 23, 1961; d. Mario Peña and Margarita Toirac. Grad., Sch. Performing Arts. Actor: (plays) Rome and Juliet, Antigone, Blood Wedding, Night of the Assassins, Italian-American Reconciliation, Cinderella, Act One and Only; (films) El Super, 1979, Times Square, 1980, They All Laughed, 1981, Crossover Dreams, 1984, Down and Out in Beverly Hills, 1985, La Bamba, 1986, Batteries Not Included, 1987, Vibes, 1988, Blue Steel, 1989, Jacob's Ladder, 1990, The Waterdance, 1991, Across the Moon, 1992, Free Willy II, 1994, Dead Funny, 1995, Lone Star, 1996, The Pass, 1997, Strangeland, 1997, Rush Hour, 1998, Seven Girlfriends, 1999, Imposter, 2000, Tortilla Soup, 2001, Ten Tiny Love Stories, 2001, Zig-Zag, 2001, Keep Your Distance, 2003, Sueño, 2003, How the Garcia Girls Spend Their Summer, 2003; dir.: The Brothers Garcia, 2002; actor: Down in the Valley, 2004; (TV films) Fugitive Among Us, 1992, It Came From Outer Space II, Contagious, 1996, Dead Man's Gun, 1997, Aldrich Ames: America Betrayed, 1998, Border Line, 1999, Hollywood Dead Moms Society, 2003; (TV miniseries) Drug Wars: The Camarena Story, The Invaders; (TV series) Saturday Night Live, Hillstreet Blues, Cagney and Lacey, Dellaventura, I Married Dora, 1987—, Shannon's Deal, Tough Cookies, Resurrection Blvd., 2000—02; actor, actor: (TV series) Boston Public, 2003, C.S.I. Miami, 2003; dir.: (plays) Celebrando La Diferencia, 1992; (TV series) Resurrection Blvd., 2002. Mem.: AFTRA, SAG, Dirs. Guild Am., Actors' Equity Assn. Office: Paradigm care Joel Rudnick 10100 Santa Monica Blvd Fl 25 Los Angeles CA 90067-4003

PENA, MARIA GEGES, academic services administrator; b. Torrance, Calif., Nov. 27, 1964; d. Nicholas John and Dina Connie (Vengel) Geges; m. Vicente Gregorio Pena, June 22, 1991. AA, El Camino Coll., 1985; BA, U. Calif., San Diego, 1987; MS, San Diego State U., 1989, postgrad., Claremont Grad. Sch., 1990—, Western State U., 1995—. Peer counselor El Camino Coll., Torrance, Calif., 1982-85; peer advisor U. Calif., San Diego, 1985-87, vice chancellor student affirmative action rsch. intern, 1986-87, outreach asst. disabled student svcs., 1986-89; coord. student svcs. Mira Costa Coll., Oceanside, Calif., 1989—. Contbr. articles to profl. jours. Mem. Calif. Assn. Postsecondary Educators of Disabled. Democrat. Greek Orthodox. Avocations: law, education, cd collecting, collecting beatles memorabilia. Office: Mira Costa Coll 1 Barnard Dr Oceanside CA 92056-3820

PENCE, JEAN VIRGINIA (JEAN PENCE), retired real estate broker; d. William Roscoe and Sophie Cottrell; m. Robert Albert Pence, June 14, 1947; children: Marjorie Tuinstra, Robert. Grad., Realtors Inst., Ill. Assn. Realtors. Cert. residential specialist Ill. Assn. of Realtors. Sales assoc. William Knight Co., Realtors, LaGrange, Ill., 1962—70, sales mgr., 1970—76; pres. Pence & Co., Realtors, LaGrange, Ill., 1976—86; freelance writer Sun City Center, Fla., 1999—. Bd. dir., treas. LaGrange Bd. Realtors, 1972; pres. West Suburban Women's Coun. Realtors, Berwyn, Ill., 1979—81. Author: (genealogy) The Cottrell Adventure With the Wright Connection, (novel) The Apprentice Angel, short stories. Sec. bd. deacons St. Andrew Presbyteriam Ch., Sun City Center, Fla., 2003—. Mem.: DAR (vice regent Clearwater chpt. 1984—86), CNW Fla. Freelance Writers Assn., South Bay Genealogy Club, Pierre Chastain Family Assn. (press chmn. 1998—2001), Red Hat Soc., Sun City Ctr. Computer Club.

PENCEK, CAROLYN CARLSON, treasurer, educator; b. Appleton, Wis., June 13, 1946; d. Arthur Edward and Mary George (Notaras) Carlson; m. Richard David Pencek, July 10, 1971; children: Richard Carlson, Mallory Barbara Rowlinds. BA in Polit. Sci., Western Coll., 1968; Ma in Polit. Sci., Syracuse U., 1975; EdD, Temple U., 1999. Investment analysts asst. Bankers Trust Co., N.Y.C., 1969-71; substitute tchr. Lackawanna Trail Sch. Dist., Factoryville, Pa., 1971-81; instr. polit. sci. Keystone Coll., La Plume, Pa., 1972-73; USGS coding supr. Richard Walsh Assocs., Scranton, Pa., 1975-76; instr. polit. sci. Pa. State U., Dunmore, 1976-77; treas. Creative Planning Ltd., Dunmore, 1988—. Bd. trustees Lourdesmont Sch., Clarks Summit, Pa., 1989—, v.p., 2000—. Bd. dirs. Lackawanna County Child and Youth Svcs., Scranton, 1981—, pres., 1988-90; founding mem., sec. Leadership Lackawanna, 1982-84; bd. dirs. N.E. Pa. Regional Tissue and Transplant Bank, Scranton, 1984-88, Vol. Action Ctr., Scranton, 1986-91; founding mem. Women's Resource Ctr. Assn., Scranton, 1986—, pres., 1986-87; v.p. sch. improvement coun. Lackawanna Trail Sch. Dist., 1995-96, sec., 1996-97; mem. adv. bd. Pa. State U., Worthington Scranton, 1998—. Named Vol. of Yr. nominee, Vol. Action Ctr., 1985; Temple U. fellow, Phila., 1991-92. Mem. AAUW (sec. 1973-75, state sel. com. 1979-81), Assn. Jr. Leagues Internat. (area II coun. mem. 1978-79), Jr. League Scranton (v.p. 1980, pres. 1981-83, Margaret L. Richards award 1984), Philharmonic League (v.p. 1976, pres. 1977). Episcopalian. Home: RR 2 Box 2489 Factoryville PA 18419-9649 Office: Creative Planning Ltd 1100 Dunham Dr Dunmore PA 18512-2653 E-mail: spot717@aol.com.

PENCZARSKI, JENNIFER MARIE, music educator; b. Barberton, Ohio, Sept. 11, 1974; d. Terry Blake and Rita Jeanette Messner; m. Michael Andrew Penczarski, Aug. 22, 1998. MusB in Performance, MusB in Edn., Miami (Fla.) U., 1996; MEd, Ashland (Ohio) U., 2003. Mng. dir. Miami (Fla.) U., 1994—96; band dir. Tuslaw Schs., Massillon, Ohio, 1997—. Named to All Star Stark County Tchg. Team, Mix 94.1, 2003. Avocations: tennis, animals, sewing, crocheting, mentoring. Home: 769 Chris Circle NW Canal Fulton OH 44614 Office: Tuslaw Local Schools 1723 Manchester Ave NW Massillon OH 44647

PENDER, NANCY, newscaster; b. Concord, Calif., 1960; BBus in mktg. with honors, Sacramento State U. Freelance reporter, LA and San Francisco; dep. press sec. Calif. Assembly Spkr. Willie J. Brown, Jr.; with KCRL-TV, Reno, Orange County Newschannel, Calif., KMST-TV, Monterey, KJEO-TV, Fresno, KCOY-TV, Santa Maria; morning news anchor KUSI-TV, San Diego; weekend news anchor and reporter WFLD-TV, Chgo., 1997—. Office: WFLD-TV 205 N Mich Ave Chicago IL 60601

PENDERGRAFT, JANICE GAYLE, volunteer; b. San Antonio, Mar. 9, 1950; d. Janice Gayle and John Joseph Pendergraft(Stepfather); m. Pete E. Kraus, Nov. 3, 1973 (dec. Aug. 3, 1987); 1 child, Heather Kraus ; m. John Joseph Pendergraft, June 18, 1988. Cert. dental asst., L.A. Coll. Med. and Dental Assts., San Bernardino, Calif., 1969. Cert. dental asst. Vol. M.A.D.D., San Bernardino, 1995—, Ronald McDonald House, Loma Linda, Calif., 1998—. Author poetry. Active Yucaipa Edn. Bd., Calif., 1980—98. Recipient several poetry awards, 1998—2002. Office: Ronald Mcdonald House Barton Rd Loma Linda CA 92353

PENDLETON, GAIL RUTH, newspaper editor, writer, educator; b. Franklin, N.J., May 8, 1937; d. Waldo A. and Ruby (Bonnett) Rousset; m. John E. Tyler, Mar. 10, 1956 (div. 1978); children: Gwenneth, Victoria, Christine; m. Jeffrey P. Pendleton, Oct. 1, 1978 (dec. 1992). BA, Montclair (N.J.) State Coll., 1959; M in Div., Princeton (N.J.) Theol. Sem., 1973; MA in English, William Paterson Coll., 1998. Ordained minister Presbyn. Ch., 1974. Tchr. Epiphany Day Sch., Kaimuki, Oahu, Hawaii, 1956-58; editor Women's Sect. Daily Record, Morristown, N.J., 1959-62, reporter, 1963-65; tchr. Hardystown Twp. Sch., Franklin, 1968-69; asst. pastor 1st Presbyn. Ch., Sparta, N.J., 1973-74; reporter N.J. Herald, Newton, 1976-78, editor lifestyle sect., 1978-93, editor Friday entertainment sect., 1993-95, editor spl. sect., 1995-97; pres. Crystal Palace Networking Inc., Newton, 1995—. Adj. prof. Ramapo Coll. of N.J., Mahwah, 1998, County Coll. of Morris, Randolph, N.J., 1998, Sussex County C.C., Newton, N.J., 1998—, Centenary Coll., Hackettstown, N.J., 1999—; tchr. Univ. H.S., Newark, 1999-2000. Recipient Ruth Cheney Streeter award Planned Parenthood N.W. N.J., 1985. Mem. N.J. Press Assn. (family sect. layout award 1985, 87, 88, 89, 91, 2nd feature columns award 1986).

PENDLETON, GLORIA BELL, lay worker; b. Washington, Dec. 30, 1927; d. Alton and Helen P. (Williams) Bell; m. Calvin Pendleton, Dec. 7, 1950; 1 child, Mark Alton. B in Gen. Studies, George Washington U., 1977; MDiv., Howard U., 1991. Vol. positions including elder, supt. ch. sch., tchr., others. various Presbyn. chs.; lay minister Northminster Presbyn. Ch., 1963—, Protestant chaplain intern Commn. of Mental Health, St. Elizabeth campus, Washington; pastoral counselor Pastoral Counseling and cons. Ctrs. Greater Washington, 1992-96; chaplain Washington Hosp. Ctr. Chair com. for women Nat. Capital Presbytery, 1985-88, com. on ministry, ministerial and parish rels., 1979-85. Advocate fair housing Neighbors, Inc., Washington, 1965-69; mgr. fed. women's program Dept. Navy, Washington, 1983-87; vol. chaplain George Washington U. Hosp. Mem. AAAW, Federally Employed Women, Chevy Chase Bus. and Profl. Women. Democrat. Home: 11912 Viewcrest Ter Silver Spring MD 20902-1553 Office: Nat Capital Presbytery 4915 45th St NW Washington DC 20016-4080

PENDLETON, JOAN MARIE, microprocessor designer; b. Cleve., July 7, 1954; d. Alvin Dial and Alta Beatrice (Brown) P. BS in Physics, Elec. Engring., MIT, 1976; MSEE, Stanford U., 1978; PhDEE, U. Calif., Berkeley, 1985. Sr. design engr. Fairchild Semiconductor, Palo Alto, Calif., 1978-82; staff engr. Sun Microsystems, Mountain View, Calif., 1986-87; cons., designer Computer Sci. Dept. U. Calif., Berkeley, 1988-90; dir. engring. Silicon Engring. Inc., Scotts Valley, Calif., 1994-95; CEO Harvest VLSI Design Ctr., Inc., San Jose, Calif., 1988—; dir. ASIC devel. Poseidon Tech., San Jose, 1997-98. Founder Aurora VLSI, Inc., Santa Clara, Calif., 1998—. Contbr. articles to profl. jours.; inventor, patentee serpentine charge transfer device. Recipient 1st, 2d and 3d place awards U.S. Rowing Assn., Fairchild Tech. Achievement award, 1982, 1st place A award Fed. Internat. Soc Aviron, 1991. Mem. IEEE, Assn. for Computing Machinery, Los Gatos Rowing Club, U.S. Rowing Assn. Avocations: rowing, skiing, backpacking.

PENDLETON, MARY CATHERINE, foreign service officer; b. Louisville, June 15, 1940; d. Joseph S. and Katherine R. (Toebbe) Pendleton. BA, Spalding Coll., 1962; MA, Ind. U., 1969; cert., Nat. Def. U., 1990; D (hon.), U. N. Testemitanu, Moldova, 1994. Cert. secondary tchr. Ky. Tchr. Presentation Acad., Louisville, 1962-66; vol. Peace Corps, Tunis, Tunisia, 1966-68; employment counselor Ky. Dept. for Human Resources, Louisville, 1969-75; gen. svcs. Am. Embassy, Khartoum, Sudan, 1975-77, counsular officer Manila, 1978-79, adminstrv. officer Bangui, Central African Republic, 1979-82, Lusaka, Zambia, 1982-84; post mgmt. officer Dept. of State Bur. European and Can. Affairs, Washington, 1984-87; adminstrv. counselor Am. Embassy, Bucharest, Romania, 1987-89; dir. adminstrv. tng. divsn. Fgn. Svc. Inst., Arlington, Va., 1990-92; ambassador Am. Embassy, Chisinau, Moldova, 1992-95, adminstrv. counselor Brussels, 1995-98; consul gen. U.S. Consulate Gen., Montreal, 1998-2001; mgmt. counselor Am. Embassy, Cairo, 2001—. Bd. dirs. Cairo Am. Coll., 2001—, Am. Sch. Bucharest, 1987—89. Named to, Hon. Order Ky. Cols., 1988. Democrat. Roman Catholic. Avocations: family history research, outdoor activities. Home: Unit 64900 Box 3 Apo AE 09839-4900 Office: 8 Kamel El-Din Salah St Garden City Cairo Egypt E-mail: pendletonmc@state.gov.

PENDLETON, YVONNE, astrophysicist; m. Dale Cruikshank; two children. BS in Aerospace Engring., MS in Aeronautics and Astronautics; PhD in Astrophysics, U. Calif., Santa Cruz, 1987. Astrophysicist Ames Rsch. Ctr., Moffett Field, Calif., infrared observational astronomer, Planetary Systems Branch. Avocations: reading, scuba diving, tennis, piano playing. Office: Ames Rsch Ctr Moffett Field CA 94035*

PENGRA, R. RENE, lawyer; b. 1967; BA, U. Wyo., 1988; JD, NYU, 1993. Bar: Ill. 1995, N.Y. 2000. Law clk. to Hon. David B. Sentelle U.S. Ct. Appeals, D.C. Cir., 1993; with Sidley Austin Brown & Wood, Chgo., 1993—, ptnr., 2002—. Office: Sidley Austin Brown and Wood Bank One Plz 10 S Dearborn St Chicago IL 60603*

PENICHEIRO, TICHA NUNES, professional basketball player; b. Portugal, Sept. 18, 1974; d. Joao Penicheiro. Degree comm. and interdisciplinary studies, Old Dominion. Profl. basketball player Sacramento Monarchs, 1998—. Named 3d Rookie of Yr., 1998, All-WNBA 1st Team, 1999, All-WNBA 2nd Team, 2001. Mem.: Portuguese Nat. Team. Avocation: music. Office: Arco Arena 1 Sports Pkwy Sacramento CA 95834 Business E-Mail: monarchs@arcoarena.com.

PENLEY, JULIE ANNE, psychologist, educator; b. Chicago, Ill., July 13, 1967; d. John and Marcheta Isabelle Dietzen; m. Howard Lawson Penley. PhD, U. Tex., 2001. Tchg. asst. U. Tex., El Paso, 1995—96, rsch. asst., 1996—2001; instr. Dona Ana C.C., Sunland Park, N.Mex., 1999; part-time instr. El Paso C.C., 2000—02, full-time instr., 2002—; evaluation coord. U. Tex., El Paso, 2001—02. Mem.: APA, Soc. Behavioral Medicine, Am. Edn. Rsch. Assn., Am. Evaluation Assn. Lutheran. Office: El Paso Community Coll PO Box 20500 El Paso TX 79998-0500

PENN, AUDREY S. retired federal agency administrator; BA, Swarthmore Coll., Pa., 1956; MD, Columbia U., N.Y.C., 1960. Intern, asst. resident Bronx Mcpl. Hosp. Ctr., Albert Einstein Coll. Medicine, 1960—62; asst. resident in neurology, neurol. inst. Columbia Presbyn. Med. Ctr., N.Y.C, 1962—64; asst. and instr. in neurology Coll. Physicians and Sutgeons, Columbia U., N.Y.C., 1964; from instr. to assoc. prof. neurology U. Pa., Phila., 1967—73; prof. neurology Coll. Physicians and Surgeons, Columbia U.; neurologist Columbia Presbyn. Med. Ctr.; dir. Am. Bd. Psychiatry and Neurology; deputy dir. Nat. Inst. Neurol. Disorders and Stroke, dep. and acting dir. Bd, dirs. Am. Bd. Psychiatry and Neurology, 1975—82, exec. com, 1981—82; mem. immunological soc. study sect. NIH, 1982—86; mem. rev. panel for rsch. tng. fellowships Howard Hughes Med. Inst., 1989—91, chair rev. panel, 1992—94; mem. nat. adv. neurol. disorders and stroke coun. NIH, 1992—95. Mem.: AAAS, Assn. Rsch. in Nervous and Mental Disease, Harvey Soc., Am. Acad. Neurology, Am. Neurological Assn. (pres. 1994). Office: Nat Inst Neurol Disorders & Strokes 8a 52 Bldg 81 Center Dr Bethesda MD 20892

PENN, DAWN TAMARA, entrepreneur; b. Knoxville, Tenn., July 22, 1965; d. Morton Hugh and Virginia Audra (Wilson) P. AS, Bauder Fashion Coll., Atlanta, 1984; postgrad., U. Tenn., 1986; grad., Rasnic Sch. Modeling, Knoxville, 1986. Gen. mgr. Merry-Go-Round, Knoxville, 1984-86; mgr., dancer Lady Adonis Inc. Performing Arts Dance Co., Knoxville, 1987-90; owner, pres. Lady Adonis, Inc. Performing Arts Dance Co., Knoxville, 1990—, also chmn.; owner, pres. Penn Mgmt. and Investment Co. Comml. Real Estate, Knoxville, 1989—; deputized bonded rep. Knox County Sheriff's Dept., Knoxville, 1989-90. Fgn. dance tours include Aruba, Curacao, Caracas, Barbados, Ont., Que., Montreal, Nfld., Labrador, N.S., New Brunswick; cons. The John Reinhardt Agy., Winston-Salem, N.C., 1987—, Gen. Talent Agy., Monroeville, Pa., 1990—, Xanadu, Inc., Myrtle Beach, S.C., 1991—. Author, editor: Lady Adonis Performing Arts promotional mag., 1988; TV and motion picture credits include: Innocent Blood, 1992, The Phil Donahue Show, N.Y.C., 1989, 91. Coord. bridal fair Big. Bros./Big Sisters Knox County, Knoxville, 1985, 86; judge Southeastern Entertainer of Yr. Pageant, Knoxville, 1992—, Miss Knoxville U.S.A. Pageant, Knoxville, 1990—; active Knoxville Conv. and Visitors Bur., 1993-94. Recipient 1st Pl. award for swimsuit TV comml. and runway modeling Internat. Model's Hall of Fame, 1986, 1st Pl. award for media presentation Modeling Assn. Am. Internat., 1986; nominee The Pres.'s Commn. on White House Fellowships, U.S. Office Pers. Mgmt., 1994-95. Mem. Internat. Platform Assn., Profl. Assn. Diving Instrs. (cert.). Methodist. Avocations: scuba diving, racquetball, horseback riding, piano, theology. Home: 7320 Old Clinton Pike Apt 9 Knoxville TN 37921-1064 Office: Lady Adonis Inc/Penn Mgmt Ste 9 7320 Old Clinton Hwy Knoxville TN 37921-1064 E-mail: ldyadonis1@aol.com.

PENN, VERNITA LYNN, government agency administrator; d. Welborne L. and Bonita L. Richmond; m. Ray C. Penn, Mar. 21, 1992 (div. Oct. 1994); 1 child, Courtney James. BA, Langston U., 1980; MA, U. Okla., 1992. Lic. tchr. Okla., cert. mediator. Instr. COPE Inc., Oklahoma City, 1998—99; inventory mgmt. specialist Tinker AFB, Midwest City, Ohio, 1999—. Bd. dirs. Credit Advisors Am., Midwest City. Mem. Ambs. Concert Choir, Oklahoma City, 1999—, Oklahoma City Beautiful, 2001—. Mem.: Okla. Assocs. Black Journalist, Tinker Mgmt. Assn., Okla. Acad. Mediators and Arbitrators, Nat. Assn. Female Execs., Okla. Bar Assn. (assoc.), Tinker Officers Club, Alpha Kappa Alpha (Silver Soror award 2002). Democrat. Baptist. Avocations: singing, dance, writing, opera, symphony. Home: PO Box 14871 Oklahoma City OK 73113 Office: Tinker AFB 3001 Staff Dr Tinker Afb OK 73145

PENNEY, BETH, English educator, editor, writer; b. Carmel, Calif., Feb. 7, 1955; d. William Carroll Penney and Raylyn Thyrza (Crabbe) Moore. BA in Journalism and English, Calif. State U., Fresno, 1978, MA in English Lit., 1985. Mng. editor Paul Kagan Assocs., Inc., Carmel, Calif., 1980-89; tech. writer Computer Svcs. Corp., Monterey, Calif., 1989-90; publs. mgr. Data Rsch. Assocs., Inc., Monterey, 1990-98; English faculty Monterey (Calif.) Peninsula Coll., 1990—. Creator tech. writing program Monterey (Calif.) Peninsula Coll.; feature writer, reviewer Carmel Pine Cone, 1994—97. Newsletter editor Monterey Peninsula Dickens Fellowship, Pacific Grove, Calif., 1991—, Unitarian Universalist Ch. of the Monterey Peninsula, 1990-97, The Dickens Project, U. Calif., Santa Cruz, 1995-98; reviewer, editor Gothic Jour. mag., Elko, Nev., 1994—. Pres. Pacific Grove (Calif.) Feast of Lanterns, 1995-2000, Friends of the Dickens Project, 1995—; founder, hon. sec. Monterey Peninsula Dickens Fellowship, 1991—. Mem. Pacific Grove C. of C. (newsletter editor 1995—). Democrat. Avocations: reading, needlework, collecting depression glass. Home: PO Box 604 Pacific Grove CA 93950-0604 Office Phone: 831-646-4159.

PENNEY, DIXIANNE MCCALL, mental health services researcher, administrator; b. N.Y.C., Aug. 30, 1937; d. Marsh and Josephine Wetherell (Suddards) McCall; m. Thomas Penney III; children: Anne, Thomas. BA, Smith Coll., 1958; MPH, Columbia U., 1980, D Pub. Health, 1996. Spl. asst. to dir. Westchester Devel. Disabilities Svcs. Office, Tarrytown, N.Y., 1982-84, dir. pub. info., 1990-96; dir. cmty. edn. and info. Harlem Valley Psychiat. Ctr., Wingdale, N.Y., 1984-88; asst. regional dir. adult svcs. N.Y.C. Regional Office/N.Y. State Office Mental Health, 1988-90; asst. dir. Ctr. for Study of Issues in Pub. Mental Health, Orangeburg, N.Y., 1996-97, adminstrv. dir., 1998—. Mem. legis. adv. com. for mental health N.Y. State Senate, Albany, 1983-88; pres. bd. dirs. Westchester Exceptional Children, North Salem, N.Y., 1972-74; pres. bd. visitors Rockland Children's Psychiat. Ctr., Orangeburg, 1972-74. Contbr. chpt. to book: Quality Assessment in Hospitals, 1982. Pres. bd. dirs. Friends of Karen, North Salem, N.Y., 1979-87; trustee Katonah (N.Y.)-Lewisboro Free Sch. Dist., 1982-88; bd. dirs. AHOME, Chappaqua, N.Y., 1988-94. Mem. APHA, Treatment and Rsch. Advancements Assn. for Personality Disorders (exec. bd. 1994—), Internat. Soc. Personality Disorder. Home: 25 Truesdale Lake Dr South Salem NY 10590-1317 Office: Ctr Studies Issues in Pub Mental Health Nathan Kline Inst 140 Old Orangeburg Rd Orangeburg NY 10962-1157

PENNEY, SHERRY HOOD, university president, educator; b. Marlette, Mich., Sept. 4, 1937; d. Terrance and B. Jean (Stoutenburg) Hood; m. Carl Murray Penney, July 8, 1961 (div. 1978); children: Michael Murray, Jeffrey Hood; m. James Duane Livingston, Mar. 30, 1985. BA, Albion Coll., 1959, LLD (hon.), 1989; MA, U. Mich., 1961; PhD, SUNY, Albany, 1972; hon. degree, Quincy Coll., 1999. Vis. asst. prof. Union Coll., Schenectady, N.Y., 1972-73; assoc. higher edn. N.Y. State Edn. Dept., Albany, 1973-76; assoc. provost Yale U., New Haven, 1976-82; vice chancellor acad. programs, policy and planning SUNY System, Albany, 1982-88; acting pres. SUNY, Plattsburgh, 1986-87; chancellor U. Mass., Boston, 1988-95; pres. U. Mass. Sys., Boston, 1995; chancellor U. Mass. Boston, 1996-2000, endowed prof., 2001—. Chmn., bd. dirs. Nat. Higher Edn. Mgmt. Sys., Boulder, Colo., 1985-87; mem. commn. on higher edn. New Eng. Assn. Schs. and Colls., Boston, 1979-82, Mid. States Assn. Schs. and Colls., Phila., 1986-88; mem. commn. on women Am. Coun. Edn., Washington, 1979-81, commn. on govt. rels., 1990-94; bd. dirs. NSTAR, (Boston Edison Co.), 1990—, Carnegie Found. for Advancement of Teaching, 1994-2002. Author: Patrician in Politics, 1974; editor: Women and Management in Higher Education, 1975; contbr. articles to profl. jours. Nat. adv. com. Nat. Initiative for Women in Higher Edn., 2001—; mem. Internat. Trade Task Force, 1994—96; mem. exec. com. Challenge to Leadership, 1988, chair, 1995—98; mem. Mid-Am. adv. bd. HERS, 1992—, Mary Baker Eddy Libr., Boston, 2001—; trustee Berkeley Div. Sch., Yale U., 1978—82, John F. Kennedy Libr. Found., 1988—2001; bd. dirs. Albany Symphony Orch., 1982—88, U. Mass. Found., 1988—2000, Mcpl. Rsch. Bur., Boston, 1990—2001, New Eng. Coun., 1990—2000, Greater Boston C. of C., 1989—2002, Met. Affairs Coalition, chair, 1999—2001; bd. overseers New Eng. Aquarium, 1990—; bd. dirs. Greater Boston One to One Leadership

Coun., 1990—2000, NASULGC Commn. Urban Affairs, 1990—2000, The Ednl. Resource Inst., chair, 1996—; bd. dirs. The Environ. Bus. Coun., 1991—97; bd. visitors WEIU, 2002—. Recipient Disting. Alumna award Albion Coll., 1978, Disting. Citizen award for racial harmony Black/White Boston, 1994, Am. Coun. on Edn./Nat. Identification Program Mass. Leadership award, 1995, New Eng. Women's Leadership award, 1996, Pinnacle award for Lifetime Achievement Greater Boston C. of C., 1998, Abigail Adams award, Mass. Women's Polit. Caucus, 2003. Mem. Orgn. Am. Historians, St. Botolph Club, Comml. Club (Boston). Unitarian Universalist. Office: U Mass Boston 100 Morrissey Blvd Boston MA 02125-3300 E-mail: sherry.penney@umb.edu.

PENNEYS, REBECCA ANN, musician; b. L.A., Oct. 2, 1946; d. Alexander and Rose (Kaplan) Penneys. Faculty N.C. Sch. of the Arts, 1972-74; artist faculty to chmn. piano dept. Chautauqua Instn., 1976—, 86—; faculty Wis. Conservatory of Music, 1974-81, chmn. piano dept., 1975-80; prof. of piano with tenure Eastman Sch. of Music, 1980—, student advisor, 1987—, acad. affairs com., 1980-83, 90-93. Founder, pianist New Arts Trio, 1974—; vis. prof. piano Ind. U. Sch. Music, 1981, Peabody Conservatory Music, 1992; soloist at numerous colls., univs. and music tchr.'s convs. worldwide, including Skidmore Coll., 1997, Am. Liszt Soc./Vanderbilt U., Nashville, 1997, Grinnell Coll., Iowa, 1997, New Eng. Conservatory of Music, Boston, 1997, Longy Sch. of Music, Boston, 1997, Chgo. Musical Coll., 1997, N.C. Music Tchrs. Assn./Meth. Coll., Fayetteville, N.C., 1996, others; grantee for concert tours.; lectr. in field; profl. mgr. Brigit Schmid-Salm, Artists Internat. Mgmt., Inc., 1996—, Jean Pilcher, 1988-96, others. TV and video presentations include Rebecca Penneys Live Master Class, 1990, 92, 93, 94, New Arts Trio in Concert From Kilbourn Hall, 1983, Piano Video Exch. with Rebecca Penneys, 1992—, Musical Encounters Series: The Piano and Its Moods, 1989— (PBS TV Spl.), Beethoven Triple Concerto, Milw. Symphony Orchestra, 1983, Rebecca Penneys Live in Recital, Tokyo, 1970, Children Are People, L.A., 1958; recordings include The Voice of the Piano Works by Mendelssohn, Schubert, Mozart, Gershwin, 1992, Complete Chopin Etudes, 1993, Arensky Trios, Beethoven's Arrangements for Piano Trio, Brahms Hungarian Dances, Ballades Opus 10, 1998, Fantasies, Opus 166, 1998, Arensky and Beethoven, 1998; co-author: (books) The Fundamentals of Flow in Learning Music, 1993, 2nd edit. 1994; contbr. articles to profl. publs. Recipient numerous awards in field, including Special Critics prize Chopin Internat. Piano Competition, 1965, Naumburg Chamber Music award N.Y., 1980, 82, Disting. Young Woman of Am. award Milw., 1977, Most Outstanding Musician prize 5th Vianna Da Motta Internat. Piano Competition, Lisbon, Portugal, 1971, top prize 2nd Paloma O'Shea Internat. Piano Competition, Santander, Spain, 1975, others. Mem. Coll. Music Soc., Am. Fedn. of Musicians, Music Tchrs. Nat. Assn., AAUP. Avocations: gardening, reading. Office: Eastman Sch of Music 26 Gibbs St Rochester NY 14604-2599

PENNIMAN, LINDA SIMMONS, real estate agent; b. Springfield, Ill., Sept. 26, 1943; d. Robert Leonard Simmons and Frances Jane Day; m. Nicholas Griffith Penniman, IV, Mar. 7, 1938; children: Rebecca, Nicholas G. V. AA, Springfield Jr. Coll. Sales assoc. Edward L. Bakewell, Inc., St. Louis, 1978—2000. Chmn., founder Realtors' Housing Assistance Fund, St. Louis, 1996—2000; chair Housing Resources Fund, St. Louis, 1996—2000. Chair Old Town Assn., Clayton, Mo., 1996—2000, Stop Metrolink Com., Clayton, 1998—99; asst. leader, program chair Greater Naples Leadership, 2003—, bd. dirs., 2003—, vol. com., 2003—; founder Women's Com. Forest Park Forever, St. Louis, Butterfly House, St. Louis. Recipient Charles H. Evermann Disting. Svc. award, St. Louis Assn. Realtors, 1994. Avocations: golf, reading, politics.

PENNINGER, BEVERLY LYNN, television producer, writer; b. Charlotte, N.C., May 5, 1961; d. William Ferris and Nancy (Bailey) Penninger. BA, U. N.C., 1983. Exec. prodr. Sta. WBTV, Charlotte, 1983—89; coordinating prodr. Creative Sports, Charlotte, 1989—93; exec. prodr., owner Naka Prodns., Charlotte, 1993—. Writer, prodr. (documentaries) The SAVE Story, 1995, Wild in Corolla, 1996 (Aurora award, 1996), Moving America's Lighthouse, 2000 (Telly award, 2002). Creator, co-chair Sisters Act!, Charlotte, 1993—97. Named Top 100 Prodrs., A/V Multimedia Prodr., 2001, Citizen Cool, Ben & Jerry's, 2001; recipient Gold Quill award, IABC, 2000. Mem.: IDA, Nat. Acad. TV Arts and Scis. Avocations: hiking, cooking, travel, music, reading. Office: Naka Prodns PMB # 251 Charlotte NC 28278 Business E-Mail: beverlychakatv.com.

PENNINGER, FRIEDA ELAINE, retired English language educator; b. Marion, N.C., Apr. 11, 1927; d. Fred Hoyle and Lena Frances (Young) P. AB, U. N.C., Greensboro, 1948; MA, Duke U., 1950, PhD, 1961. Copywriter Sta. WSJS, Winston-Salem, N.C., 1948-49; asst. prof. English Flora Macdonald Coll., Red Springs, N.C., 1950-51; tchr. English Barnwell, S.C., 1951-52, Brunswick, Ga., 1952-53; instr. English U. Tenn., Knoxville, 1953-56; instr., asst. prof. Woman's Coll., U. N.C., Greensboro, 1956-58, 60-63; asst. prof., assoc. prof. U. Richmond (Va.), 1963-71; chair., dept. English Westhampton Coll., Richmond, 1971-78; prof. English U. Richmond, 1971-91, Bostwick prof. English, 1987-91; ret., 1991. Author: William Caxton, 1979, Chaucer's "Troilus and Criseyde" and "The Knight's Tale": Fictions Used, 1993, (novel) Look at Them, 1990; compiler, editor: English Drama to 1660, 1976; editor: Festschrift for Prof. Marguerite Roberts, 1976. Fellow Southeastern Inst. of Mediaeval and Renaissance Studies, 1965, 67, 69. Democrat. Presbyterian. Home: 2701 Camden Rd Greensboro NC 27403-1438

PENNINGTON, BEVERLY MELCHER, financial services company executive; b. Vermillion, SD, Feb. 8, 1931; d. Cecil Lloyd and Phyllis Cecelia (Walz) M.; m. Glen D., Sept. 1, 1965 (dec. Aug. 1986); 1 child, Terri Lynn. BS, U. S.D., Vermillion, 1952. Enrolled agt. cert. IRS 1989. Sec. budget dept. Bur. of Indian Affairs, Aberdeen, S.D., 1952-53, pvt. sec., 1953-54, U.S. P.H.S. Indian Health, Aberdeen, 1954-55; adminstr. asst. U.S. Pub. Health Svc., Anchorage, 1955-58, U.S. Pub. Health, Dental Pub. Health, Washington, 1958-61; grant adminstr. Dental Pub. Health, Washington, 1961-65; co-owner Penn Mel Marina, Platte, S.D, 1965-74, Pennington Tax Service, Platte, 1974-86, owner, 1986-93; pres., CEO, White Tiger Fin. Svc., Inc., Platte, 1994—. Contbr. articles to profl. jours. Mem. Platte Women's Club, sec., 1965-68, pres., 1968-70, 89-91; mem. Libr. Bd., Sec., 1982-85, treas., 1995—. Fellow Am. Soc. Tax Profls. (sec. 1989-91, 2d v.p. 1995, 1st v.p. 1996, pres. 1997); mem. NAFE, Platte C. of C. (v.p. 1989, pres. 1990), Lyric Theatre Mus. Soc. (pres. 1988-92), U.S.C. of C., Washington Dakota Cen. Com. Republican. Presbyterian. Avocations: collecting jewelry, reading, dress designing, gourmet cooking. Office: White Tiger Fin Svc Inc 420 Main St Platte SD 57369

PENNINGTON, KAREN HARDER, lawyer; b. Amarillo, Tex., June 7, 1956; d. Alvin L. and Rosemary Herskowitz Harder; m. Richard R. Pennington, Oct. 13, 1979. J.D., U. of Tex., Austin, 1986; BS cum laude in biology, W. Tex. State U., 1977. Bar: Calif. 1986, Tex. 1998, US Patent and Trademark Office 1993, Hopi Tribal Ct. 1993. Assoc. atty. Thelen, Marrin, Johnson & Bridges, L.A., 1986—89, Quinn, Emanuel & Urquhart, L.A., 1989—91, Crosby, Heafey, Roach & May, L.A., 1991—92; atty. Law Office of Karen H. Pennington, Long Beach, Calif., 1993—97, Cath. Charities Immigration Counseling Svcs., Dallas, 1998—2000; joint project, immigration atty. Law Office of Karen H. Pennington, Dallas, 2000—. Recipient cover story, Sept. 9 issue, Tex. Lawyer mag., 2002. Mem.: Dallas Bar Assn., LA County Bar Assn., Tex. Bar Assn., Calif. Bar Assn., Am. Immigration Lawyers Assn., North Tex. Coalition Just Peace, United For Peace and Justice, Dallas Peace Ctr. Roman Catholic. Achievements include representation of post-Sept. 11 immigration/national security detainees both before the courts and in FBI interrogations. Avocations: social justice activist, travel, international affairs. Office: Law Office of Karen H Pennington Ste 100 2501 Oak Lawn Ave Dallas TX 75219 E-mail: penningtonlaw@yahoo.com.

PENNY, SUSAN CAROLINE VOELKER, investment manager; b. N.Y.C., July 26, 1949; d. Friedrich and Anna Voelker; m. Ralph E. Penny, Aug. 31, 1974 (div. 1989); m. Radomir Stevanovic, Mar. 14, 1992. BA, Syracuse U., 1970; MBA, Columbia U., 1972. CFA. Securities analyst Shearson, Hammill & Co., Inc., N.Y.C., 1972-73; investment analyst, v.p. The Equitable Life Assurance Soc. of the U.S., N.Y.C., 1973-85; mng. dir. Equitable Capital Mgmt. Corp., N.Y.C., 1985-91, sr. v.p., 1991-93, Alliance Corp. Fin. Group, Inc., N.Y.C., 1993-96; prin. August Ptnrs., LP, N.Y.C., 1996-98, corp. fin. cons., 1998-2000; mng. ptnr. Associated Mezzanine Investors LLC, New Canaan, 2000—. Vice-chair trustees Syracuse U., N.Y., 1997-2002, chair trustees investment and endowment com., 1996-2002, trustee exec. com., 1994-2002, acad. affairs com., 1995-2000, mem. bd. orgn. and nominating com., 2000-02, mem. adv. bd. Maxwell Grad. Sch. of Citizenship and Pub. Affairs, 1991—; bd. dirs. Elderhostel Inc., 2001—. Mem. AIMR. Republican. Lutheran. Avocations: reading, hiking, opera. Office: 436 Frogtown Rd New Canaan CT 06840-4411 E-mail: scpenny@aol.com.

PENQUITE, MARY C. realtor; b. Sapulp, Okla., Nov. 6, 1940; d. John Robert and Nancy Jewel Mobley; m. Jon Arthur Penquite, Nov. 11, 2000; m. H. L. Payne (div. 1965); children: Pamela Sue, Samuel Kevin. Student in Nursing, Tulsa (Okla.) Jr. Coll.; student in Real Estate, 1976. Real estate assoc. Boh-Monr Realtors, Tulsa, 1976, John Hausam Realtors, Tulsa, 1980—2001; real estate broker McGraw Davisson Steart Realtors, Grove, Okla., 2001—. Bd. dir. RPAC, Tulsa, 1990. Mem.: Grand Lake Assn., Grand Lake C. of C. Democrat. Avocations: fishing, boating, RVing, travel, piano. Office: McGraw Davisson Stewart Realtors 414 E 3d PO Box 450998 Grove OK 74344 Home: PO Box 452514 Grove OK 74345-2514

PENROD, HAZEL L. music educator; b. Lonepine, La., Dec. 3, 1915; d. John Izac LaFleur and Sally Elizabeth McDonald; widowed Feb. 1994; 1 child, Paula Jean. MusM, Inst. Music, St. Louis, 1957. Piano tchr. Monfrey Music Studio, San Antonio, 1985; pvt. practice piano tchr. San Antonio, 1959. Tchr. ch., San Antonio, Nat. Guild Piano Tchrs., Austin, 1960. Inductee Hall of Fame Piano Guild USA. Mem. Tex. Music Tchrs. Assn., San Antonio Music Tchrs. Assn. Baptist. Home: 503 Wayside Dr San Antonio TX 78213-2842

PENSACK, SUSAN, elementary school educator; b. Somerville, N.J., Mar. 13, 1956; d. Charles Florence and Eloise Joyce Green; m. Rodney Drew Pensack, June 25, 1977; children: Heather, Ryan. BA in Edn., Rider Coll., 1978; MS in Edn., E. Stroudsburg U., 1991. Cert. elem. tchr. K-8, tchr. handicapped K-12, N.J.; cert. learning disabilities tchr. cons., N.J., 2002. Dir. nursery sch. Surprise House, Belvidere, N.J., 1978-79; head tchr. NORWESCAP, Phillipsburg, N.J., 1979-81; impaired tchr. Washington Nursery, Washington, N.J., 1981-90; tchr. intermediate perceptually Washington Schs., Washington, 1990-91; tutor Masons/Allentown Learning Ctr., Allentown, Pa., 1998—; resource ctr. tchr. Hope Twp. Sch., Hope, NJ, 1991—2001; supr. trainee Masons-Allentown Learning Ctr., Allentown, 1999—; tchr. Lebanon Twp. Valley View Sch., 2001—; resource ctr. tchr. Lebanon Twp. Sch., Califon, NJ, 2001—. Learning disabilities tchr. cons. Lebanon Twp. Sch. Svc. unit dir./leader Girls Scouts Great Valley Coun., Allentown, 1983—; sec. Lower Mt. Bethel Sports. Assn., Martins. Creek., Pa., 1986-94, treas. 1994—. Recipient Outstanding Vol. Leadership award, Girl Scouts, Allentown, 1992, Outstanding Leader, Valley Coun., 1990, Great Valley award, 2000. Mem. NEA, Coun. Exceptional Children, Internat. Dyslexia Assn., N.J. Edn. Assn., Assn. Learning Cons. Democrat. United Meth. United Methodist. Avocations: girl scouts, reading, fitness, walking. Home: 10317 Upper Little Creek Rd Bangor PA 18013-4447 E-mail: pens@epix.net.

PENSKY, CAROL, political organization administrator; Past nat. chair Womens Leadership Forum/Democratic Nat. Com., Washington; past treas. Democratic Nat. Com., Washington. Office: Womens Leadership Forum 430 S Capitol St SE Washington DC 20003-4024

PENSYL, CHRISTINA A. special education educator; d. Rodger L. and Brenda K. Pensyl. BS in Elem. Edn., West Chester U., 1995; M in Spl. Edn., East Stroudsburg U., 2002. Tchg. cert.-instrnl. II Pa., 2001. Spl. edn. tchr. Lincoln Mid. Sch., Catasauqua, Pa., 1996—2003, Unionville-Chadds Ford Sch. Dist., Kennett Square, Pa., 2003—. Avocations: reading, working with children, gardening, scrapbooks, travel. Office: Unionville-Chadds Ford School District 760 Unionville Rd Kennett Square PA 19348

PENTERMAN, CAROL A. opera company executive; b. Lincoln, Nebr., June 18, 1955; BMus, U. Nebr., 1977; MM in Voice and Opera, Coll. Cons. Music, 1981. Performer, 1981-84; prodn. stage mgr. Lyric Opera, Kansas City, Mo., 1985-95, Des Moines Metro Opera, Des Moines, 1985-95, Opera Carolina, 1985-95, New Orleans Opera, 1985-95, Balt. Opera, 1985-95; exec. dir. Nashville Opera, 1995—. Recipient achievement award Frist Found. Mem. Opera Am., Am. Guild of Musical Artists. Home: 5500 Cottonport Dr Brentwood TN 37027-7640 Office: Nashville Opera Ctr 3628 Trousdale Dr Ste D Nashville TN 37204-4523

PEOPLES, CAROLYN Y. federal agency administrator; b. Md. BS in Fin., U. Balt., 1982, MBA, 1984. Mgr. St. Andrews House, Balt., 1977—80; program adminstr. for aging divsn. Cath. Charities, Balt., 1980—85, adminstr. housing aging divsn., 1985—90, property mgr. aging divsn., 1980—90, dir. ops. for the housing divsn., 1990—99; founder, CEO Jeremiah Housing Svcs., Inc., 1999—2001; asst. sec. for fair housing and equal opportunity HUD, Washington, 2002—. Pres. edn. com. Beacon Inst.; trustee Mid-Atlantic Nonprofit Health and Housing Assn.; bd. govs. U. Balt. Mem.: Am. Assn. of Homes and Svcs. for the Aging (mem. hos. of dels.). Office: US Dept HUD 451 7th St SW Washington DC 20410*

PEOPLES, CRYSTAL D. state legislator; 1 child, Rashaun. BS in Elem. Edn., M in Student Adminstrn., Buffalo State Coll. Legislator 7th Dist. Erie Co., 1993—2002; state rep. N.Y. House, 2003—. Chair Erie Co. Legislature Fin. Com. Democrat. Office: 792 E Delavan Ave Buffalo NY 14215

PEPELEA, KIMBERLI RAE, case manager; b. Clinton, Ind., Sept. 14, 1963; d. Charles W. and Sally Luft; m. Rockie Gene Pepelea, Sr., Jan. 19, 1990. AA, Southeastern C.C., West Burlington, Iowa, 1999; BA in Psychology and Criminal Justice, Iowa Wesleyan Coll., 2001. Cert. activity dir. Nurses aide Clinton (Ind.) Nursing Home, 1982-87; asst. activity dir. BMC Klein Unit, Burlington, Iowa, 1992-98; case mgr. Hamilton Ctr., Rockville, Ind., 2002. Avocations: cross-stitch, computers.

PEPPER, DOTTIE, professional golfer; b. Saratoga Springs, N.Y., Aug. 17, 1965; Student, Furman University. Top ranked player LPGA Tour, 1992. 3 time NCAA All-American; recipient Rolex Player of the Year Award, 1992; recipient Vare Trophy, 1992; leading money winner LPGA, 1992. Achievements include winning tournaments including Mazda Classic, 1989, Crestar Classic, 1990, Nabisco Dinah Shore, 1992, Sega Women's Championship, 1992, Welch's Classic, 1992, Sun-Times Challenge, 1992, LPGA Leading Money Winner, 1992, Wendy's Three-Star Challenge, 1992, PING/Welch's Championship, 1995, JC Penney/LPGA Skins Game, McCall's LPGA Classic, wom four tournaments: Rochester Internat., ShopRite LPGA Classic, Friendly's Classic and Safeway LPGA Golf Champ., 1996, 24 tournaments earning $293,652, 1997, tied 2nd at Rochester Internat., tied 3rd at Star Bank LPGA Classic, tied fourth at ShopRite LPGA Classic, 1997, Solheim Cup, 1998, Nabisco Dinah Shore, 1999. Address: care LPGA 100 International Golf Dr Daytona Beach FL 32124-1082

PEPPER, FLOY CHILDERS, educational consultant; b. Broken Arrow, Okla., Mar. 14, 1917; d. James Alexander and Louise Lena (Barber) Childers; m. James Gilbert Pepper, Mar. 23, 1940; children: James G., Suzanne Pepper Henry. BS, Okla. State U., Stillwater, 1938; MS, Okla. State U., 1939; postgrad., Oreg. U. Home econs. tchr. Bur. Indian Affairs, Ft. Sill, Okla., 1939-40, Chemawa, Oreg., 1940-42, Portland (Oreg.) Pub. Schs., 1945-65; instr. Portland State U., 1967-85; supr. spl. edn. Multnomah Ednl. Svc. Dist., Portland, 1965-83; orientation specialist N.W. Regional Ednl. Lab., Portland, 1983-85; curriculum writer Oreg. State Bd. Edn., Salem, 1987-90; evaluator Native Indian Tchr. Edn. Program U. B.C., Vancouver, 1987-89; cons. Indian edn. Portland Pub. Sch., 1989—. Co-author: Maintaining Sanity in the Classroom, 1971, revised edit., 1982; contbr. articles to profl. jours. Recipient Ed Elliot Human Rights award Oreg. Edn. Assn., 1996 Mem. Indian Curriculum Com. (alternative chmn. 1990-99), Oreg. Soc. of Individual Psychology, Multicultural Task Force (co-chmn. 1990-99, Dist. Svc. award 1990-91). Republican. Avocations: writing, reading, dance, presenting workshops. Home: 7799 Sw Scholls Ferry Rd Apt 138 Beaverton OR 97008

PERA, MCCALL, newscaster; B in Broadcast News, U. Ga. Intern WSB-TV, Atlanta; anchor, reporter CNN Affiliate, Athens, Ga.; weekend reporter, spl. projects prodr. WSAV-TV, Savannah, Ga., 1999—2003; weekend reporter, anchor WUPN-TV, Winston-Salem, 2003—. Recipient two Ga. Associated Press Broadcast awards for spot news coverage. Office: WUPN-TV 3500 Myer Lee Dr Winston Salem NC 27101

PERANICH, DIANE C. state legislator; b. Biloxi, Miss., Jan. 11, 1940; m. A. John Peranich. State legislator Miss. Ho. of Reps., Jackson, 1988—. Vice chmn. banks and banking com. Miss. Ho. of Reps., mem. apportionment and elections, appropriations, county affairs and transp. coms. Active State Exec. Commn. Miss. Dem. Party; bd. dirs. Crimestoppers; adv. coun. constitution study com. State Bd. of Econ. Devel. Home: 25176 Le Chene Dr Pass Christian MS 39571 Office: State Capitol Bldg Rm 400 E PO Box 1018 Jackson MS 39215-1018

PERDIGO, LUISA MARINA, foreign language and literature educator; b. Havana, Cuba, Dec. 25, 1947; came to U.S. 1962; d. Mario and Hortensia Dolores (Alvarez) P. AB, CUNY, 1971, MA, 1974, PhD, 1981; MA, Columbia U., 1987. Cert. translator English/Spanish, Am. Translators Assn. Asst. prof. Spanish, asst. dean St. Thomas Aquinas Coll., Sparkill, N.Y., 1982-87; asst. prof. Spanish and French CUNY, La Guardia, 1987-88, asst. prof. Spanish, City Coll., 1988-89; asst. prof. Spanish St. Peter's Coll., Jersey City, N.J., 1989-91; asst. prof. Spanish and French Clarion U., Pa., 1992-94, Rockland Coll. SUNY, 1995-96, Mercy Coll., 1998—. Author: La Estética de Octavio Paz, 1975, The Origins of Vicente Huidobro's Creacionismo (1911-1916) and its Evolution (1917-47), 1994, The Lyrics of the Troubadour Perdigon, 2002, (poetry) Desde el Hudson/From the Hudson, 1993, Huellas/Footprints, 1997, America at the Millenium, 2000, The Best Poems and Poets of 2002, Theatre of the Mind, 2003; author numerous poems; contbr. articles to profl. jours. Participant seminar in poetry, NEH, U. Kans., 1991; Rsch. fellow Orgn. Am. States, Chile, 1981; grantee CUNY, 1975; scholar Columbia U., 1982-84. Mem. MLA, Clarion Hist. Soc., Circulo de Cultura Panamericano, Sigma Delta Pi, Pi Delta Phi.

PERDIKOU, KIM, information technology executive; BSc. Comp. Sci. and Operational Rsch., Paisley U., Scotland; MA Info. Systems, Pace U. Dir. Network Svcs. Knight Ridder; VP, CIO Women.com Networks, Inc., 1999—2000; CIO Juniper Networks, Inc., Calif., 2000—. Office: Juniper Networks Inc 1194 N Mathilda Ave Sunnyvale CA 94089*

PERDUE, BEVERLY E. lieutenant governor, geriatric consultant; b. Grundy, Va., Jan. 14, 1948; d. Alfred P. and Irene E. (Morefield) (dec.) Moore; m. Robert W. Eaves, Jr.; children: Garrett, Emmett. BA, U. Ky., 1969; MEd, U. Fla., 1974, PhD, 1976. Pvt. lectr., writer, cons., 1980-86; pres. The Perdue Co., New Bern, N.C., 1985—; rep. N.C. State Gen. Assembly, Raleigh, 1986-90; senator N.C. Gen. Assembly, Raleigh, 1990-2001; lt. gov. State of N.C., 2001—. Bd. dirs. Nations Bank, New Bern. Bd. dirs. N.C. United Way, Greensboro, 1990-92; exec. mem. N.C. Dem. Party, Raleigh, 1989—; mem. N.C. travel bd. Nat. Conf. State Legislators. Named Outstanding Legislator, N.C. Aging Network, 1989, 92, 100 to Watch, Dem. Leadership Coun. 2003; Toll fellow Nat. Conf. State Legislators, Lexington, Ky., 1992. Mem. Nat. Coun. on Aging, Bus. and Profl. Women, Rotary. Democrat. Episcopalian. Office: Hawkins-Hartness House 310 North Blount Street Raleigh NC 27603 E-mail: bperdue@ncmail.net.*

PERDUE, KAREN, state agency administrator; BA in Biology, Stanford U., 1978. Reporter, photographer Fairbanks (Alaska) Daily News-Miner, 1969-74; editor River Times, Fairbanks, 1974-75; foreman, expeditor Teamsters Union, Alaska Pipeline, 1975-76; health planner Tanana Chiefs Conf., Fairfanks, 1977; instr., counselor Stanford (Calif) Med. Ctr., 1978; rsch. dir. Fairbanks Town and Village Assn., 1978-79; legis. aide/press sec. U.S. Senator Ted Stevens, Washington, 1979-80; spl. asst. to lt. gov. Terry Miller State of Alaska, 1980-82; dir. Divsn. of Cmty. Devel., Dept. of Cmty. and Regional Affairs, Juneau, 1982-85; dep. commr. Dept. of Health and Social Svcs., Juneau, 1985-90; cons., ptrn. Northern Rsch. and Planning, 1991—; commr. Alaska Dept. of Health and Social Svcs., 1995—. Office: Health & Social Svcs Dept Office Commr PO Box 110601 Juneau AK 99811-0601 E-mail: karen_perdue@health.state.ak.us.

PERDUE, KATHY, operations research specialist; Exec. asst. Warner Ctr. Hilton, Woodland Hills, Calif.; lead network ops. ctr. analyst Computer Scis. Corp./JPL, L.A. V.p. Women Of Color Investment Group, Woodland Hills, 1991. Personal E-mail: kateyes.c.you@verizon.net. E-mail: kathy.perdue@jpl.nasa.gov.

PEREIRA, MELANY, elementary school educator; b. Bombay, Oct. 17, 1945; arrived in U.S., 1976; d. Joseph and Mary Pereira. Assoc. in Music, Mt. Aloysius Coll., 1980; degree in elem. edn., St. Francis U., 1983, MEd, 1989. Tchr. elem. edn. St. Ann's Sch., Secunderabad, India, 1969—75, St. Aloysius Sch., Cresson, Pa., 1984—89, All Sts. Cath. Sch., Pa., 1989—. Mission procurator Propagation of Faith, Ebensburg, Pa., 1976—. Named Outstanding Cath., Diocese of Altoona; recipient Educator award, Johnstown, Pa., 1999—2000. Avocations: gardening, sewing, cooking, music, collecting stamps. Office: Mt St Ann Retreat House PO Box 328 Ebensburg PA 15931-0328

PERES, JUDITH MAY, journalist; b. Chgo., June 30, 1946; d. Leonard H. and Eleanor (Seltzer) Zurakov; m. Michael Peres, June 27, 1972; children: Dana, Avital. BA, U. Ill., 1967; M Studies in Law, Yale U., 1997. Acct. exec. Daniel J. Edelman Inc., Chgo., 1967-68; copy editor Jerusalem (Israel) Post, 1968-71, news editor, 1971-75, chief night editor, 1975-80, editor, style book, 1978-80; copy editor Chgo. Tribune, 1980-82, rewriter, 1982-84, assoc. fgn. editor, 1984-90, nat. editor, 1990-95, nat./fgn. editor, 1995-96, specialist writer, 1997—; Yale Law fellow, 1996-97. Recipient Media award, U. Mich., 2000. Office: Chicago Tribune 435 N Michigan Ave Chicago IL 60611-4066 E-mail: jperes@tribune.com.

PERET, KAREN KRZYMINSKI, health services administrator, consultant; b. Springfield, Mass., Mar. 8, 1950; d. Edward S. and Doris L. (Beaudry) Krzyminski; m. Robert J. Peret, June 19, 1971 (div. Sept. 2003); children: Heather, James, Kaitlin, Matthew. BSN, St. Anselm's, 1972; MS in Nursing Adminstrn., Boston U., 1980; EdD in Orgnl. Devel., U. Mass.,

1993. RN, Mass. Staff nurse Boston VA's Hosp., 1972—73; staff nurse pediat. Harrington Meml. Hosp., Southbridge, Mass., 1973—74, instr. edn., 1974—75, relief day asst. dir. nursing, 1975; coord. continuing edn. Ctrl. Maine Med. Ctr., Lewiston, 1975—76; asst. dir. nursing Monson Devel. Ctr., Palmer, Mass., 1977—83, DON, 1983—94; exec. nursing cons. Liberty Healthcare, Waltham, Mass., 1994—98, v.p. ops. Phila., 1998—; ind. mgmt. cons., 1993—. Instr. Quinsigamond Cmty. Coll., Worcester, Mass., 1972-73. Contbr. articles to profl. jours. Mem. ANA, Mass. Nurses' Assn., Am. Assn. on Mental Retardation, Sigma Theta Tau. Home: 79 Sturbridge Rd Holland MA 01521-3123 Office: 401 E City Ave Ste 820 Bala Cynwyd PA 19004-1130 Office Phone: 800-331-7122. E-mail: karenperet@aol.com.

PERETSMAN, NANCY B. investment banker; b. Worcester, Mass., Mar. 27, 1954; d. George Peretsman and Norma (Burofsky) O'Haire. AB with hons., Princeton U., 1976; MPPM, Yale, 1979. V.p. Blyth, Eastman, Dillon & Co., N.Y.C., 1979—83; dir., head of media group Salomon Bros., N.Y.C., 1983—95; exec. v.p., mng. dir. Allen & Co., N.Y.C., 1995—. Bd. mem. Charter Comm., Inc. Charter trustee, Princeton U., 1976—.*

PERETTI, MARILYN GAY WOERNER, human services professional; b. Indpls., July 30, 1935; d. Philip E. and Harriet E. (Meyer) Woerner; children: Thomas A., Christopher P. BS, Purdue U., 1957; postgrad., Coll. DuPage, 1980—2002, U. Wis., 1981—95. Nursery sch. lab. asst. Mary Baldwin Coll., Staunton, Va., 1957-58; tchr. 1st grade, nursery sch. No. Ill. area schs., 1958-61; asst. tchr. of blind Glenbard E. H.S., Lombard, Ill., 1978-80; adminstrv. asst. Elmhurst Coll., 1980-81; dir. vol. svcs. DuPage Convalescent Ctr., Wheaton, 1981-95; dir. cmty. outreach Sr. Home Sharing, Inc., Lombard, Ill., 1996-97; asst. to dir. of Career Vision, graphic designer The Ball Found., 1997-98; adminstrv. asst. Christ Ch. of Oak Brook, 1998-99; asst. for comms. Lombard Mennonite Peace Ctr., 2000—02; owner freelance computer bus., web design Pages by Peretti, 2002—. Prodr. ednl. slide programs on devel. countries, 1988-98; initiator used book collection for libr. project U. Zululand, S. Africa, 1997-98; designer, developer websites for Loretto Ctr., Wheaton, Ill. Maya Ministry, Westchester, St. Luke Luth. Ch., Glen Ellyn. Author, pub. (poetry): Poems of a Woman, 1999, Crack the Rifle in Two, 1999, To Love Cranes, 2000, Let Wings Take You, 2003; editor/designer (newsletters) Our Developing World's Voices, 1994-98, The Leaflet, Nature Artists' Guild of the Morton Arboretum, 1997-2000, Ill. State Poetry Soc., 1997-98, LOVE in Action, 2002—; exhbns. include Danada Nature Art Show, 2002, St. Thomas Celebration of the Arts, 2002, Wheaton Libr., 2003, Glen Ellynb Libr., 2003, Hanging Gardens Gallery, Genoa, Ill., 2004. Bd. dirs. Lombard YMCA, 1977-83, pres., 1980; vol. Chgo. Uptown Ministry, 1979; participant fact finding trips El Salvador, 1988, Honduras, 1989, Nicaragua, 1989, Republic of South Africa, 1991, Guatemala and El Salvador, 1997; mem. Nature Artists Guild of Morton Arboretum, exhibitor, 1992—; vol. homeless shelter, 1994-97; initiated sponsorship of ch. missionaries to Guatemala, 2003. Recipient 1st prize for poetry, Current, Ann Arbor, Mich., 2001, 2d prize for poetry, Nat. Conf. on Aging, 2003. Avocations: swimming, poetry writing, desktop publishing, third world concerns, botanical and animal watercolors.

PEREZ, DIANNE M. medical researcher; b. Cleve., Dec. 13, 1959; BA in Chemistry and Biology with honors, Coll. of Wooster, 1982; PhD in Chemistry, Calif. Inst. Tech., 1988. Grad. rsch. asst. dept. chemistry Calif. Inst. Tech., Pasadena, 1982—87, grad. tchg. asst. introductory chemistry and biochemistry, 1982—87; sr. rsch. scientist Specialty Labs., Inc., Santa Monica, Calif., 1987—88; fellow dept. eye rsch. Doheny Eye Inst., L.A., 1988—89; fellow dept. heart and hypertension rsch. Cleve. Clinic Found., 1989—91, rsch. assoc. dept. cardiovasc. biology, 1992—93, project scientist dept. molecular cardiology, 1993—95, mem. asst. staff dept. molecular cardiology, 1996—. Coord. Molecular Cardiology's Protein Group Seminar Series Cleve. Clinic Found., 1994—95, supr. DNA Synthesis Core Facility Rsch. Inst., fellow's rep. Dept. Heart and Hypertension Rsch. to Divsn. Com.; adj. asst. prof. dept. pharmacology U. Ky., Lexington, 1994—; manuscript referee Molecular Pharmacology, Circulation Rsch., Cardiovasc. Rsch., Jour. Pharmacology and Exptl. Therapeutics, Gene, Biochemistry; lectr. in field. Contbr. articles to profl. jours.; patentee in field. Recipient Nat. Rsch. Svc. award, NIH, 1991; grantee Glaxo, 1994—; scholar Lubrizol, Coll. of Wooster, 1980. Mem.: AAAS, Am. Soc. Biochemistry and Molecular Biology, Am. Chem. Soc. (cert.), Am. Heart Assn. (Established Investigator award 1996), Am. Soc. Pharmacology and Therapeutics, Sigma Xi, Iota Sigma Pi, Phi Beta Kappa.

PEREZ, EDITH R. lawyer; BA, U. Calif., Davis, 1976; JD, U. Calif., Berkeley, 1980. Bar: Calif. 1982. Vis. atty. Sergio Augusto Malta Advogados, Rio de Janeiro, Pablo Martinez Cano y Asociados, Mexico City; with Latham & Watkins, L.A., 1984—. Mem. adv. com. on women in svcs. U.S. Dept. Def.; mem. bd. dirs. Hugh O'Brian Youth Leadership Found., Nat. Conf. Christians and Jews, Cmty. Enhancement Corp., Mex.-Am. Legal Def. and Ednl. Fund, ARC, Latino Mus. History, Art and Culture; bd. regents Loyola Marymount U.; mem. adv. coun. on equal opportunity to CEO of So. Calif. Edison; mem. Calif. Gov.'s Task Force on Diversity and Outreach. V.p. L.A. Bd. Recreation and Pks. Commrs., 1994—95; pres. L.A. Bd. Police Commrs., 1997—99; mem. bd. dirs. Nat. Recreation Found., Ctr. for Study of L.A., Loyola Marymount U., Oakwood Sch. Named one of 25 Up-and-Coming Attys. Who Are Making a Difference in Calif., L.A. Daily Jour., 1994, 100 Most Influential Hispanics in U.S., Hispanic Bus. Mag., 1996; recipient Bringing Up Daughters Differently award, NOW Legal Def. and Edn. Fund, 1996, Redesigning Policing award, Nat. Ctr. for Women and Policing, 1997, Cmty. Commitment award, Calif. Latino Civil Rights Network, 1998, Women of Achievement award, Anti-Defamation League, 1998, Legal Svcs. award, Mex.-Am. Legal Def. and Ednl. Fund., 1998, Twice a Citizen award, L.A. Police Res. Found., 1999. Mem.: ABA, Mex. Am. Bar Assn., L.A. County Bar Assn., Calif. State Bar Assn. Office: Latham and Watkins LLP 633 W Fifth St Ste 4000 Los Angeles CA 90071*

PEREZ, ELENA N. professional society administrator, writer; b. Gainesville, Fla., Dec. 8, 1972; d. Ellen D. Lanahan and Mario Perez; life ptnr. Colin M. Davis, Sept. 1, 2002. BA, Oberlin Coll., 1994. Outreach coord. Animal Protection N.Mex, Albuquerque, 1995—96; program dir. Calif. Nat. Orgn. Women, Sacramento, 1997—. Author (editor): (activist training manual) Action for Justice; editor (co-author): (discussion guide) A Passion for Justice; author: (newspaper column) The Vegetarian Kitchen in La Cocina; contbr. articles to profl. jours. Event organizer N.W.C., Sacramento, 1997—2003; bd. mem. Sacramento Co-Traditional Circles, 1997—2001; artist Chalk It Up, Sacramento, 1999—2003. Grantee, Ben & Jerry's Found., 1996. Mem.: Orangevale Grange. Office: Calif Nat Orgn Women 926 J St Ste 424 Sacramento CA 95814 E-mail: programs@canow.org.

PEREZ, JOSEPHINE, psychiatrist, educator; b. Tijuana, Mex., Feb. 10, 1941; came to the U.S., 1960, U.S. citizenship, 1968. BS in Biology, U. Santiago de Compostela, Spain, 1971, MD, 1975. Nuc. medicine technician, EEG technician, supr. Electrographic Labs., Encino, Calif., 1963—69; clerkships in internal medicine, gen. surgery, otorhinolaryngology, dermatology and venereology Gen. Hosp. of Galicia, Spain, 1972-75; resident in gen. psychiatry U. Miami, Jackson Meml. Hosp. and VA Hosp., Miami, Fla., 1976-78; practice medicine specializing in psychiatry, marital and family therapy, individual psychotherapy Miami, 1979—. Emergency room physician Miami Dade Hosp., 1975; attending psychiatrist Jackson Meml. Hosp., 1979—, asst. dir. adolescent psychiat. unit, 1979-83; mem. clin. faculty U. Miami Sch. Medicine, 1979—, clin. instr. psychiatry, 1979—. Mem. AMA (Physicians' Recognition award 1980, 83, 86, 89, 98, 2000, 01), Am. Assn. for Marital and Family Therapy (cert. clin. mem., treas. 1982-84, pres.-elect 1985-87, pres. 1987-89), Am. Psychiat. Assn., Am. Med. Women's Assn., Assn. Women Psychiatrists, Fla. Psychiat. Soc., South Dade Women Physicians Assn. Office: 420 S Dixie Hwy Ste 4A Coral Gables FL 33146-2228

PEREZ, JULIE ANNA, audio engineer; b. Miami, Fla., Sept. 2, 1961; d. Miguel Angel and Dorothy Elizabeth (Headford) P. Student, U. Miami, 1979-83. Audio engr. NBC, Inc., N.Y.C., 1984—; pres. BDC Prodns. Ltd. Asst. music mixer (TV shows) Saturday Night Live, 1987-93, Late Night with David Letterman 7th Anniversary Spl., 1989; music mixer Late Night with David Letterman, summer 1989, Late Night in L.A. with Conan O'Brien, 1993—; audio engr. Later with Bob Costas, Friday Night Videos, Brokaw Reports; co-founder TECHNET, Nabet Diversity Com.; sem. chair AES Women in Audio, 1991, Saturday Night Live, 1993. Editor: Music Engrng. Tech. newsletter, 1983; audio engr. TV talk-show Donahue, 1985-87 (Emmy nomination); recorded and mixed Live from 6A, CD music performances from Late Night with Conan O'Brien; music mixer (NBC Millennium Spl.) Sting Concert Live from Studio 8H. Contbr. Planned Parenthood Fedn. Am., 1986—, Women in the Arts. Recipient Down Beat award Down Beat mag., 1982, Best Engineered Live Performance award Down Beat mag. Mem. NARAS, NOW, ACLU, NATAS, (Emmy nomination for sound mixing 1986), Acad. TV Arts and Scis. (Emmy nomination for sound mixing 1993), Audio Engrng. Soc., Nat. Assn. Broadcast Employees and Technicians (co-chair local diversity com.), Women in Music. Democrat. Office: NBC Inc 30 Rockefeller Plz Rm 901W2 New York NY 10112-0002 Home: c/o Ellen Nernberg 9776 SW 147th Ct Miami FL 33196-1637

PEREZ, LUCILLE C. NORVILLE, medical association administrator, pediatrician; BA, Manhattanville Coll., Bklyn., N.Y., 1974; MD, N.Y. Med. Coll., 1979. Pres. Nat. Med. Assn., Washington, 2001—; assoc. dir. ctr. for substance abuse, prevention, mental health svcs. adminstrn. Dept. Health & Human Svcs., Washington, 2001—. Asst. prof. Mount Sinai Sch. Medicine; assoc. prof. clin. pediat. SUNY Health Sci. Ctr., Bklyn., St. George's Sch. Medicine, Grenada, West Indies; lectr. in field. Recipient Spl. Achievement award, Congl. Black Caucus, Disting. Svc. award, Sec. Health & Human Svcs. Mem.: AMA, Nat. Med. Assn., Medico-Chirurgical Soc. of D.C., Acad. Pediat. Office: Nat Med Assn 1012 Tenth St NW Washington DC 20001

PEREZ, LUZ LILLIAN, psychologist; b. Ponce, P.R., Aug. 7, 1946; d. Emiliano and Maria D. (Torres) P.; children: Vantroi, Maireni. BA, Herbert H. Lehman Coll., 1974; PhD, NYU, 1989. Lic. bilingual (Spanish and English) psychologist, N.Y. Staff psychologist Soundview Throgs Neck Community Mental Health Ctr., Bronx, 1980-88; coord. early childhood program Crotona Park Cmty. Mental Health Ctr., Bronx, 1988-91; cons. psychologist Highbridge Adv. Coun. Presch. Program, Bronx, N.Y., 1991-93, Coalition for Hispanic Family Svcs., Bklyn., N.Y., 1991-95, Marathon Child Devel. Ctr., Queens, N.Y., 1993-94, Bronx Orgn. for Learning Disabled, 1993—, Village Child Devel. Ctr., N.Y.C., 1994-97, Graham-Windham Svcs. to Families and Children, 1994-95, Jackson Child Devel. Ctr., Jackson Heights, N.Y., 1996-97, Leake & Watts Svcs., Inc., Yonkers, N.Y., 1996—. Grantee NIMH, 1974-77. Mem. Assn. Hispanic Mental Health Profls. Avocation: flamenco dancing.

PEREZ, MARY CHRISTINE, guidance counselor, small business owner; b. Miami, Fla., Dec. 5, 1967; d. Marta Miranda Perez. BA, Fla. Internat. U., 1989, MS, 1995. Cert. K-12 tchr., sch. guidance counselor, Fla. Tchr.'s aide Dade County Pub. Schs., Miami, 1986-87, tchr.'s asst., 1987-89, elem. tchr., 1989-95, guidance counselor, 1995—, chmn. student svcs. dept. Ruben Dario Mid. Sch., 1996—, mem. curriculum coun., 1996—. Sec.-treas., part owner K Lucky Transp. Svc., Miami, 1997—. Active Young Rep. Club, Miami, 1997. Named Role Model, 1st Union Nat. Bank and Hot Wheels Skating Ctr., 1997. Mem. Fla. Counseling Assn., Dade County Counseling Assn. Roman Catholic. Avocations: animals, music, sports, creative writing. Office: Ruben Dario Mid Sch 350 NW 97th Ave Miami FL 33172-4107 Home: 901 Golden Cane Dr Weston FL 33327-2429

PEREZ, ROSE (ROSE A. PEREZ), painter; b. Santiago, Cuba, Sept. 28, 1937;, US1954; d. Mercedes Riera (Gomez) Sanchez; m. Pedro P. Perez, June 27, 1957; children: Peter P., Anthony P. Attended, Fla. Fine Arts Inst.; degree in concert piano, Conservatory of Music, Cuba. Art tchr. Tillamook County Art Assn., 1976—77, Clatsop Cmty. Coll., 1977—81, Portland Cmty. Coll., Oreg., 1981—85. Exhibitions include Coos Bay Art Mus., Oreg., 2000—03 (Peoples Choice award, 2001), Ventura County Maritime Mus., Calif., 2001 (Merit award, 2001), Nestucca Valley Fine Arts Festival, Oreg. (Best of Show award), Salem State Fair Fine Art Exhibit, Fla. Bicentennial Fine Art Exhibit, Fla., Pacific City Gallery, Oreg. Coast, Pacific Marine Gallery, Wash.; pub.: Headlight Herald, 1992, News Guard newspaper, 1995, Visuel mag., 1995—96, Ruralite mag., 1995, Ctrl. Oreg. Coast guide, 1999, Oreg. Coast mag., 2000, News Time newspaper, 2000; contbr. articles to various profl. jours. Oreg. state pres. Nat. League Am. Pen Women, Wash. DC 1977—78, hon. mem., Tampa Fla. Br., 1975—77; mem. Oreg. Coast Coun. for Arts, Newport, 1994—97, Tillamook County Art Assn., Oreg., 1976—89. Mem.: Nestucca Valley Artists (founder 1992—), Nat. Mus. Women in the Arts (charter 1986—), Am. Soc. Marine Artists. Avocations: music, beach walks, study rsch. of ocean.. Home: POB 9 Pacific City OR 97135

PEREZ, ROSIE, actress; b. Bklyn. d. Ismael Serrano and Lydia Perez. Dramatic appearances include: (TV) 21 Jump Street, WIOU, Rosie Perez Presents Society's Ride, 1993, Happily Ever After: Fairy Tales for Every Child, 1995, Subway Stories: Tales From The Underground, 1997, (film) Do the Right Thing, 1989, White Men Can't Jump, 1992, Night on Earth, 1992, Untamed Heart, 1993, Fearless, 1993 (Acad. award nom. Best Supporting Actress 1994), It Could Happen To You, 1994, Somebody to Love, 1995, A Brother's Kiss, 1997, Perdita Durango, 1997, 24-Hour Woman, 1998, Louis and Frank, 1998, The Road to El Dorado, 2000, (TV series) House of Buggin, 1995. Office: Parks Palmer Turner & Yemenidjian c/o Diane Schroeder 1990 S Bundy Dr Ste 600 Los Angeles CA 90025-5291

PEREZ, SYLVIA, newscaster, reporter; married; 2 children. B, U. Okla. Sch. of Journalism. Reporter KRPC-TV, Houston, Denver, Lawton, Okla.; weekend anchor and reporter WLS-TV, Chgo., 1989—, med. reporter, anchor 11am news. TV journalist with prodr. Holly Grisham HealthBeat, WLS-TV (Silver Dome award, 2001), TV journalist with prodr. Christine Tressel Desktop Doctors (Peter Lisagor award, 2002). Office: WLS-TV 190 N State St Chicago IL 60601

PERFETTO, LISA ANN, quality assurance professional; b. Erie, Pa., Aug. 19, 1969; d. Dan Anthony and Judith Ann (Meyer) P. BS in Human Devel., Pa. State U., 1992; MS in Higher Edn., West Chester U., 1996. Dir. of tutoring, Act 101 asst. dir. West Chester U., 1994-96, coord. acad. support svcs., 1997—98; supr. instrnl. svcs. Ind. Blue Cross, Phila., 1999—2002, adminstr. continuous quality, 2002—. Owner Pathfinder Consulting; academic coach for students with learning disabilities, attention deficit disorder coach; presenter in field. Democrat. Roman Catholic. Home: 12 Manor Dr West Chester PA 19380-3932 Office: Independence Blue Cross 1901 Market St Philadelphia PA 19103 E-mail: cheflisa19@comcast.net.

PERGAL, THERESA MARIA, artist; b. Boston; d. Ernest Arthur and Theresa Maria Golia; m. Frank Joseph Pergal; 2 children. BFA, Otis Parsons, L.A., 1979; diplomate, R.H. Ives, Boston, 1998. One-woman shows include Katherine Lorilland Wolfe Art Club, N.Y.C., 1998, 2002, Pastel Soc. Am., 1998, Allied Artists Am., 1998, Am. Artist Profl. League, 1998, 2000, 2001, Acad. Artists Assn., Springfield, Mass., 2000, Allied Artists Am., N.Y.C., 2000, Hudson Valley Art Assn., N.Y., 2001, 2002, Audubon Artists 60th Exhbn., N.Y.C., 2002; subject (feature article) Am. Artist Mag., 1999, Portraiture, The Artists Mag. (Mag. Finalist award, 2003). Recipient Am. Artist Mag. award, Pastel Soc. of Am., 1998, Jurors' Choice Best in Show award, Acad. Artists Assn., Springfield, Mass., 2000. Mem.: North Shore Art Assn., Rockport Art Assn. (juror 2001—02), Am. Artist Profl. League (Best in Show 1998, Finalist award 2003, Helen DeCozen award 2001). Avocations: gardening, jogging. E-mail: tmp@cove.com.

PERHACS, MARYLOUISE HELEN, musician, educator; b. Teaneck, N.J., June 15, 1944; d. John Andrew and Helen Audrey (Hosage) P.; m. Robert Theodore Sirinek, Jan. 27, 1968 (div. Jan. 1975). Student, Ithaca (N.Y.) Coll., 1962-64; BS, Juilliard Sch., 1967, MS, 1968; postgrad., Hunter Coll., 1976, St. Peter's Coll., Jersey City, N.J., 1977. Cert. music tchr., N.Y., N.J. Instr. Carnegie Hall, N.Y.C., 1966-69; program developer, coord., instr. urban edn. program Newburgh (N.Y.) Pub. Sch. System, 1968-69; adj. prof. dept. edn. St. Peter's Coll., Jersey City, 1976-92; tchr. brass instruments Indian Hills High Sch., Oakland, N.J., 1976; tchr. Jersey City Pub. Schs., 1976-77, N.Y.C. Pub. Sch., Bronx, 1980-84; pvt. tchr. Cliffside Park, N.J., 1976—; vocal music tchr. East Rutherford, N.J., 1990; tchr. music Bergen County Spl. Svcs. Sch. Dist., 1990-91; tchr. gen. music Little Ferry (N.J.) Pub. Schs., 1991-92; tchr. mid. sch. instrumental Paramus (N.J.) Pub. Schs., 1993-94; tchr. vocal music West New York (N.J.) Pub Schs., 1995—. Tchr. music summer enrichment program, West New York, NJ, 1999, 2000, summer instrumental music program Park Ridge (N.J.) H.S., 1995, 96, Waldwick Concert Band, 2003-04; tchr., singer, trumpeter Norwegian Caribbean Lines, 1981-82, Jimmy Dorsey Band, Paris and London, 1974; music and edn. lecture cir., 1992—. Singer with Original PDQ Bach Okay Chorale, 1966, Live from Carnegie Hall Recordings, 1970, St. Louis Mcpl. Opera, 1970, Ed Sullivan Show, 1970; singer, dancer, actress (Broadway shows) Promises, Promises, 1969-71, Sugar, 1971-72, Lysistrata, 1972; trumpeter (Broadway shows) Jesus Christ Superstar, 1973, Debbie!, 1976, Sarava!, 1979, Fiddler on the Roof, Lincoln Ctr., 1981, Sophisticated Ladies, 1982, Waldwick Concert Bd., 2003; writer, host series on women in music Columbia Cable/United Artists, 1984; recordings: Carnegie Hall Live, Avery Fisher Hall, Lincoln Ctr. Cons. to cadette troop Girl Scouts U.S., Jersey City, 1967-68, Bergen County N.J. Coun., 1995—. Mem. NEA, AFTRA, Actors Equity Assn., Am. Fedn. Musicians (mem. theatre com. local 802 N.Y.C. 1972—, chmn. 1973), Music Educators Nat. Conf., N.J. Music Educators Assn., N.J. Sch. Music Assn., N.J. Edn. Assn., Internat. Women's Brass Conf. (charter mem.), Internat. Trumpet Guild, Mu Phi Epsilon. Democrat. Episcopalian. Avocations: cats, cake decorating, food sculpting, horticulture, sewing. Home and Office: 23 Crescent Ave Cliffside Park NJ 07010-3003

PERHAM, LEIGH WELLINGTON, art educator, art historian; b. NYC, June 2, 1951; d. C. Burleigh and Jean Willett Wellington; children: Britiany Titania, Cameron Jake. BA in Art History and English, Tufts U., 1973, MA in Edn., 1975; Cert. in Mus. Scis. in Art History, Harvard U., 2000; MFA in Creative Writing, Bennington Coll., 2005. Cert. K-12 tchr. Mass. Tchr. Boston Children Mus.; mid. sch. tchr. Stoneham, Mass.; tchr., dir. Red Sneakers/Wellington Sch., Stoneham; edn. cons. Tufts U., Medford, Mass.; tchr. Gov. Dummer Acad., Byfield, Mass.; lectr. art history Mus. Fine Art, Boston, Harvard U., Cambridge, Mass. Homesch. tchr., Beverly, Mass. Coord. Fresh Air Fund, North Shore Region, Mass., chairperson; vol. Greenpeace, Mass., World Wildlife Fund, Mass. Avocations: writing, painting, archaeology.

PERI, LINDA CAROL, librarian; b. Johnsville, Pa., Sept. 8, 1943; d. Willard and Ethel F. (Furness) Hinkle. BA, Juniata Coll., 1965; MA, Columbia U., 1967; MLS, Emporia State U., 1995. Sr. lectr. Oslo Inst. Bus. Adminstrn., Norway, 1967-72; Fulbright sr. lectr. Tech. U . Wroclaw, Poland, 1972-75; acad. dir. Inlingua Sch. Langs., Singapore, 1975-82; nat. accts. coord. United Van Lines, Denver, 1982-94; libr. Arapahoe Libr. Dist., Littleton, Colo., 1995-99; libr. Bus. Resource Ctr. Aurora (Colo.) Ctrl. Libr., 1999—. Editor: Mystery in Malacca, 1981. Mem. Am. Libr. Assn., Colo. Libr. Assn., Beta Phi Mu. Avocations: yoga, bridge, book discussion, travel. E-mail: lperi@ci.aurora.co.us.

PERICAK-VANCE, MARGARET A. health facility administrator; PhD in Med. Genetics, Ind. U., 1978. Dir., chief sect. med. genetics dept. medicine Duke Ctr. for Human Genetics, Duke U., Durham, NC. Named to Century Club: 100 People to Watch as We Move to the Next Millennium, Newsweek Mag., 1997. Mem.: Am. Coll. Med. Genetics (founding fellow, bd. cert. PhD med. geneticist). Office: Duke U Med Ctr Ctr for Human Genetics Box 3445 Durham NC 27710

PERICH, TONI ANNETTE, sales executive; b. Galveston, Tex., Sept. 22, 1946; d. Daniel John, Jr. and Adelaide Lucia (Lopez) Traverso; m. Thomas Joseph Perich, June 3, 1978 (div.); children: Matthew John, Stephen Christopher. Designated assoc. surety and fidelity bonding Ins. Inst. Am., CPCU. Comml. svc. rep. various ins. agys., Houston, 1965-87; field rep., outside sales Old Republic Surety, Houston, 1987-90; owner Galerie d'Alexandria, Galveston, Tex., 1990-92; ins. cons. various law firms, Houston, 1990-91; comml. svc. rep. The Houston Agys., Inc., 1992-94; field rep., outside sales Universal Surety of Am., Houston, 1994-95; field rep., sales exec. RLI Ins. Co., Dallas, 1995—. Pvt. practice piano tchr., Sugarland, Tex., 1994—. Editor: Surety Newsfacts, 1996—, Reporting Cover, 1999—. Schoolsite liaison Am. Heart Assn., Upper Pinellas County, 1996—98, dir., 1997—98. Recipient Gold medal, Internat. Piano Recording Festival, 1956, 1st pl., 1963, Paderweski Gold medal, Nat. Guild Piano Tchrs., 1964; Music scholar, N. Tex. State U., 1964. Mem.: Houston Surety Assn., Fla. Surety Assn. (v.p. 1998—99), Ins. Women St. Petersburg (treas. 1997—98, v.p. 1998), Nat. Assn. Ins. Women (mem.-at-large 1995—96, mem. tech. panel 1998—99, pres.-elect 2000—, legis. liaison Tex. coun. 2000—, pres. 2001—02, edn. found. amb. Tex. coun. 2002, chair pub. rels. Houston NAIW, Inc., edn. found. website com. chmn., Profl. of the Yr. Tex. Coun. 2001, Profl. of Yr. 2002), Am. Coll. Musicians, Blue Bird Circle. Roman Catholic. Avocations: reading, handwork, golf, crossword puzzles. Office: RLI Surety Ste 1020 3010 Lyndon B Johnson Fwy Dallas TX 75234-7006 E-mail: Tonitp@aol.com.

PERKINS, ESTHER TYE, pastor; b. Eufaula, Ala., Aug. 4, 1921; d. James Hutchin and Florence W. Tye; m. Charles Grant Perkins, Dec. 22, 1937 (div. May 1983); children: Charles G. Jr., Patricia P. Cert. reverend SC, 1983. Min. Home Br. Bapt. Ch., Manning, SC, 1958—63, Bloomingvale Bapt. Ch., Andrews, SC, 1965—67, Corinth Bapt. Ch., New Ellenton, SC, 1967—74, West End Bapt. Ch., Manchester, Ga., 1974—76, Pine Bluff Bapt. Ch., Columbia, SC, 1976—83; pastor Eason Mem. Bapt. Ch., Eastover, SC, 1989—97, Pine Bluff Bapt. Ch., 1999—. Assn. music dir. Santee Assn., Manning, SC, Screven Assn., Holly Hill, SC; co-dir Columbia Christ. Men's Group Svc. Ctr., Columbia. Author: (biography) For Such A Time As This, 1996. So. Bapt. Achievements include first to first woman pastor of a So. Bapt. Ch. in SC. Avocations: fishing, reading. Home: 3970 Caesars Rd West Columbia SC 29170

PERKINS, NANCY ANN, nurse; b. American Fork, Utah, Jan. 31, 1961; d. George Thorvald and Ann Elizabeth (Williamson) Gardner; m. Layne Todd Perkins, Sept. 6, 1986; children: Christian H., Nathaniel B. BSN, Westminster Coll., 1982. RN, BLS, AHA, Utah. LPN med./surg. unit staff nurse Holy Cross Hosp., Salt Lake City, 1980-81; RN staff nurse renal St. Marks Hosp., Salt Lake City, 1982-86, RN charge nurse diabetic unit, 1986-87, RN diabetic educator, 1986-87, RN, community educator, 1991—94, RN, charge nurse med. psych. unit, 1987-93; SIU nurse auditor IHC Health Plans, SLL, 2000—, catastrophic care mgr., 1998—2000; RN resource nurse IHC, Salt Lake City, 1993—. Author/educator: (class design syllabus) Adoptive Parenting, 1991. Active Prenatal Boarding Home, Children's Aid Soc., Ogden, Utah, 1992-94; jr. leader Girl Scouts U.S., Salt Lake City, 1984-86; charge first aid clinic Presbyn. USA Gen. Assembly, Salt Lake City, 1990. Mem. Utah Nurses Assn. (Clin. Nurse Practice award 1988). Democrat. Presbyterian. Avocations: hiking, camping, wind surfing, swimming, counted cross stitch, crochet. Home: 3682 S 2110 E Salt Lake City UT 84109-4320 Office: [illegible] Health Plans Dpl Investigation Unit PO Box 30192 Salt Lake City UT 84130-1472

PERKINS, NANCY JANE, industrial designer; b. Phila., Nov. 5, 1949; d. Gordon Osborne and Martha Elizabeth (Keichline) P. Student, Ohio U., 1967-68; BFA, U. Ill., 1972. Indsl. designer Peterson Bednar Assocs., Evanston, Ill., 1972-74, Deschamps Mills Assos., Bartlett, Ill., 1974-75; dir. graphic design Cameo Container Corp., Chgo., 1975-76; indsl. design cons. Sears Roebuck & Co., Chgo., 1977-88; cons. indsl. design, 1988—. Lectr. CUNY, 1995; founder Perkins Design Ltd., Anna Wagner Keichline Gallery, Bellefonte, Pa.; adj. prof. grad. design seminar U. Ill. Chgo., 1982, 88, 91, 93, adj. instr. undergrad. design, 1984, 88, 91, 93; adj. instr. Ill. Inst. Tech., 1987, 91; vis. assoc. prof. Carnegie-Mellon U., 1991; juror annual design rev. Indsl. Design mag., 1986; mem. tech. rev. com. Ben Franklin Partnerships, 1991—; keynote spkr. several major U.S. design groups; spkr. Design in Am. symposium, Nagoya, Japan, 1989. Contbg. author: Design and Feminism, 1999; featured in Bard Grad. Ctrs.' Exhibit, N.Y.C., 2000; contbr. articles to profl. jours.; patents in field. Co-leader Cadette troop DuPage County coun. Girl Scouts U.S., 1978-79. Recipient Outstanding Alumni award U. Ill. Alumni Jour., 1981, Goldsmith award, 1992; profiled in Indsl. Design mag., 1986, Feminine Ingenuity (by Anne L. Macdonald), 1992, Dun & Bradstreet Reports, 1993; profiled The Phila. Inquirer Mag., 1994; featured in Chgo. Athenaeum "33 plus 20", 1993, Pratt Manhattan Gallery, N.Y.C., 1994. Fellow Indsl. Designers Soc. Am. (treas. Chgo. chpt. 1977-79, vice chmn. 1979-80, chmn. 1981, mem. dist. membership com. 1982, mem. ann. conf. com. 1983, mem. publs. com. 1985-86, dir.-at-large 1987-88, v.p. Midwest dist. 1989-90, nat. sec.-treas. 1991-92, del. Internat. Coun. of the Socs. Indsl. Design 1989, dist. conf. speaker Mideast, 1993, Midwest, 2000, co-founder women's sect. 1992). E-mail: njperkins@earthlink.net.

PERKINS, NANCY LEEDS, lawyer; b. Washington, June 19, 1956; d. Roswell Burchard and Joan (Titcomb) P. AB, Harvard U., 1979, M in Pub. Policy, JD, Harvard U., 1987. Bar: Pa. 1988, D.C. 1989, U.S. Dist. Ct. D.C. 1990. Jud. clk. U.S. Dist. Ct. (ea. dist.) N.Y., Bklyn., 1987-88; spl. counsel Arnold & Porter, Washington, 1988—. Contbr. articles to profl. jours. Recipient Pro Bono svc. award Internat. Human Rights Law Group, 1990. Democrat. Avocation: tennis. Office: Arnold & Porter 555 12th St NW Washington DC 20004-1206

PERKYNS, JANE ELIZABETH, music educator, composer; b. St. John, New Brunswick, Can., Jan. 17, 1960; arrived in U.S., 1990, naturalized, 2000; d. Joseph Archibald Gormley, Carmelita Anne Gormley; m. John Stephen Perkyns, Aug. 20, 1983; children: Stephen, Nicholas. MusB, Dalhousie U., Halifax, N.S., Can., 1982; MusM, Juilliard Sch., 1983; D in Musical Arts, U. B.C., Vancouver, B.C., Can., 1990. Music adminstr., tchr. Jewish Cmty. Ctr., Houston, 1990—94; adj. music faculty Tex. So. U., Houston, 1990—96, asst. prof. music, 1996—2001, assoc. prof. music, 2001—. Founder, dir. Curtyn Calls Theatre and Pub. Co., Houston, 1995—; co-dir. spl. edn. programs Theatre Under the Stars, Houston, 2000—; dir. Charles P. Rhinehart Piano Festival, 2001—03. Composer: (Musical) The Gift, 1994, Pinnojokio, 1996, Love is a Disability, 1998, Medea's Children, 1999, musician Solo/collaborative recitals. Panelist Cultural Arts Coun. Houston/Harris County, 2000—02. Grantee Mayor's Initiative Grant, Cultural Arts Coun. Houston/Harris County, 2001, Gen. Assistance Grant, Cultural Arts Coun., 2003, Office Civil Rights, 2003. Mem.: Am. Musicological Soc., Royal Conservatory Music (coord. of exams Houston area 1994—2003), Houston Music Tchrs. Assn. (bd. mem., chair scholarship event 1995—2002), Tex. Music Tchrs. Assn., Music Tchrs. Nat. Assn. (cert.), Coll. Music Soc., Houston Tuesday Musical Club. Avocations: children's arts and crafts, cooking, yoga. Home: 5634 Benning Dr Houston TX 77096 Office: Tex So Univ 3100 Cleburne Houston TX 77004 Office Fax: 713-313-1869. Personal E-mail: perkyns_je@tsu.edu. Business E-Mail: perkyns-je@tsu.edu.

PERLESS, ELLEN, advertising executive; b. N.Y.C., Sept. 9, 1941; d. Joseph B. and Bertha (Messinger) Kaplan; m. Robert L. Perless, July 2, 1965. Student, Smith Coll., 1958-59; BA, Bard Coll., 1962. Copywriter Doyle, Dane Bernbach, N.Y.C., 1964-70, Young & Rubicam, N.Y.C., 1970-74, creative supr., 1974-76, v.p., creative supr., 1977, v.p., assoc. creative dir., 1978, sr. v.p., assoc. creative dir., 1979-84; v.p., assoc. creative dir. Leber Katz Ptnrs., 1984-85, sr. v.p., creative dir., 1986-87; sr. v.p., sr. creative dir. Foote Cone & Belding, N.Y.C., 1987-93, sr. v.p., group creative dir., 1994—2002; sr. v.p., sr. creative dir. Euro RSCG Life Becker, N.Y.C., 2003—04. Author: (poetry) Riverside 4, Approach, Margie. Recipient Clio awards, Andy awards, awards Art Dirs. Club N.Y., N.Y. Festivals, One Club. Home: 37 Langhorne Ln Greenwich CT 06831-2611 E-mail: ellen@perless.com.

PERLIS, SHARON A. lawyer; b. New Orleans; d. Rogers I. and Dorothy Perlis. BA in French, Principia Coll., 1967; JD, Tulane U., 1970. Officer, dir. Perlis, Inc., New Orleans, 1973—2003; pres. SILREP Internat. Co., Metairie, 1984—; officer, dir. Internat. Adv. Svcs., Inc., New Orleans, 1985-89; prin. Perlis & Assocs., Metairie, 1985—2003; pres. Sharon A. Perlis P.C., 2001—. Legal counsel La. Ins. Rating Commn., 1980-84; adminstrv. law judge State of La., 1980-84, mem. Econ. Devel. Adv. Coun., 1982-84; exec. com. small bus. coun. Bd. of Trade, 1987-89, chmn. small bus. coun., 1988, exec. com. East Jefferson coun., 1989-96; dir. World Trade Ctr., 1985-2003, vice chmn. internat. bus. com.; dir. New Orleans br. Fed. Res. Bank of Atlanta, 1982-88, chmn., 1984, 86, 88; dir. Metairie Bank & Trust, 1997-2003; bd. of commr. Port of New Orleans, 1992-96, vice chmn., 1995, chmn. bd., 1996; del. U.S. Def. Dept.'s Joint Civilian Orientation Conf., 1997; adj. prof. A.B. Freeman Sch. Bus., Tulane U. Mem. human rels commn. City of New Orleans, 1992-93, Commn. To Reorganize Govt., Leadership La., 2001; mem. exec. bd. La. Coun. Econ. Edn., 1986-89, Pvt. Enterprise Edn. Found., 1986-89; state del. White House Conf. on Small Bus., La. rep. internat. trade issues, 1986; dir. Metro YMCA, 1990-97; exec. com. agy. rels. United Way, 1987-90; mem. exec. com. Jr. Achievement Project Bus., 1987; vice chmn. La. Dist. Export Coun.; bd. dirs. Bur. Govtl. Rsch.; bd. dirs. La. Internat. Trade Commn.; mem. adv. bd. Internat. Program for Non-profit Leadership; mem. Econ. Devel. Commn., state of La.; mem. New Orleans Leadership Inst. Recipient Achiever's award Woman Bus. owners Assn., 1994, Jefferson Econ. Devel. Commn. award, 1994, Advocacy of Yr. award Small Bus. Adminstrn., 1988, 89, Iberville award New Orleans Pub. Group, 1996, Women of the Yr. award New Orleans Pub. Group, 2000, Patty Strong award Jefferson-25, 2000; named Young Leadership Coun. Role Model, 2001. Mem. ABA, Bankers Assn., Am. Arbitration Assn. (arbitrator/mediator), Jefferson Bar Assn., Orleans Bar Assn., Federal Bar Assn., Adv. Coun. Federalist Soc., La. Estate Planning Coun., La. Bar Assn., Gov.'s Commn. on Internat. Trade Devel., New Orleans Regional C. of C. (bd. dirs. 1990—), New Orleans Regional Leadership Inst., New Orleans Area Polit. Action Coun. (pres.), Leadership La., Greater New Orleans Found. Avocations: reading, sailing, tennis. Office: Perlis & Assocs 6069 Magazine St New Orleans LA 70118-6006

PERLMAN, JUDITH FAITH, think-tank associate, researcher; d. Ida Lillian Balbert and Charles Bernstein; life ptnr. Roni Lynn Kugler; children: Eric M, Alaine. M, Calif. State U., Northridge, 1981. MFCC Bd. of Behavioral Scis., 1983. Survey coord. UCLA, Westwood, Calif.; survey dir. RAND, Santa Monica, Calif., 1982—. Contbr. articles to profl. jours. (Article of Yr. award, 1996). Pres. Homeowners' Assn., Calabasas, Calif., 2000—03. Office: Rand Corp 1700 Main St Santa Monica CA 90407

PERLMUTTER, DIANE F. marketing executive; b. N.Y.C., Aug. 31, 1945; d. Bert H. and [illegible] ([illegible]) P. Student, NYU Grad. Sch. of Bus., 1969—70; BA in English, Miami U., Oxford, Ohio, 1967. Writer sales promotion Equitable Life Assurance, N.Y.C., 1967-68; bus. adminstr. de Garmo, Inc., N.Y.C., 1968-69, asst. account exec., 1969-70, account exec., 1970-74, v.p., account supr., 1974-76; mgr. corp. advt. Avon Products, Inc., N.Y.C., 1976-79, dir. comm. Latin Am., Spain, Can., 1979-80, dir. brochures, 1980-81, dir. category merchandising, 1981-82, group dir. motivational comm., 1982-83, group dir. sales promotion, 1983-84, v.p. sales promotion, 1984, v.p. internat. bus. devel., 1984-85, area v.p. Latin Am., 1985, v.p. advt. and campaign mktg., 1985-87, v.p. U.S. operational planning, 1987; cons. N.Y.C., 1987-88; sr. v.p. Burson-Marsteller, N.Y.C., 1988-90, exec. v.p., mng. dir. consumer products, 1991-93, bd. dirs., 1992—, chief oper. officer, 1993-94, chief oper. officer, 1994-96, chmn. mktg. practice/U.S., 1996-98. Vice chmn., CEO Cohn & Wolfe, N.Y.C., 1998—2000; CEO Gilda's Club Worldwide, 2001—; chair ann. meeting Direct Selling Assn., Washington, 1982; v.p. Nat. Home Fashions League, N.Y.C., 1975—76; adj. instr. SUNY/ Fashion Inst. Tech., 1992—; vice chmn. Columbia-Greene Hosp. Found., 2000—; vice chmn., bd. dirs. Olana Partnership, 2000—03; bd. dirs. Double L.P. Industries, Inc. Bd. dirs. Hudson Opera House, 2002—. Named to YWCA Acad. Women Achievers, 1996. Mem.: Women in Comm., Advt. Women of N.Y., Pub. Rels. Soc. Am., Women's Econ. Round Table (bd. dirs. 1998—2000), Miami U. Alumni Assn. (pres., chair 1986), The Women's Forum (bd. dirs. 1998—2000, pres. 2002—04), YMCA of Greater N.Y. (bd. dirs. 1996—2003), Publicity Club N.Y. (bd. dirs. 1994—96), Beta Gamma Sigma. Avocation: interior design. Office: Gilda's Club Worldwide 322 8th Ave 14th Flr New York NY 10001 Business E-Mail: dperlmutter@gildasclub.org.

PERLMUTTER, DONNA, music critic, dance critic; b. Phila. d. Myer and Bessie (Krasno) Stein; m. Jona Perlmutter, Mar. 21, 1964; children: AAron, Matthew. BA, Pa. State U., 1958; MS, Yeshiva U., 1959. Music and dance critic L.A. Herald Examiner, 1975-84; contbr. L.A. Times, 1984—, N.Y. Times, 1994—. Dance critic Dance Mag., NYC, 1980—; music critic Opera News, NYC, 1981-98, Ovation Mag., NYC, 1983-89, Hollywood Reporter, 2001—, L.A. City Beat, 2003—, NY Mag., 1995—, L.A. Mag., 1996—, Daily News, L.A., 1996-97, New Times, L.A., 1997-2002, Performing Arts Mag., 1996-2002; panelist, spkr. in field. Author: Shadowplay: The Life of Antony Tudor, 1991. Recipient Deems Taylor award for excellence in writing on music ASCAP, 1991. Mem. Music Critics Assn. Home: 10507 Le Conte Ave Los Angeles CA 90024-3305

PERLOFF, CAREY, performing company executive, theater director, playwright; children: Lexie, Nicholas. B.A. in classics and comparative lit., Stanford U., 1980. Artistic dir. Classic Stage Co., N.Y.C, 1986—92; faculty, Tisch School of the Arts N.Y.U., 1986—92; artistic dir. Am. Conservatory Theater Found., San Francisco, 1992—. Playwright, dir.: The Colossus of Rhodes, 2001. Recipient Obie award for Artistic Excellence, The Village Voice, 1988; Fulbright Fellow, Oxford, 1981. Mem.: Phi Beta Kappa. Office: Am Conservatory Theater Found 30 Grant Ave San Francisco CA 94108-5800

PERLOFF, MARJORIE GABRIELLE, English and comparative literature educator; b. Vienna, Sept. 28, 1931; d. Maximilian and Ilse (Schueller) Mintz; m. Joseph K. Perloff, July 31, 1953; children: Nancy Lynn, Carey Elizabeth. AB, Barnard Coll., 1953; MA, Cath. U., 1956, PhD, 1965. Asst. prof. English and comparative lit. Cath. U., Washington, 1966-68, assoc. prof., 1969-71, U. Md., 1971-73, prof., 1973-76; Florence R. Scott prof. English U. So. Calif., LA, 1976—; prof. English and comparative lit. Stanford (Calif.) U., 1986—, Sadie Dernham prof. humanities, 1990—, prof. emerita, 2000. Vis. prof. U. Utah, 2002; scholar-in-residence U. So. Calif., 2004—. Author: Rhyme and Meaning in the Poetry of Yeats, 1970, The Poetic Art of Robert Lowell, 1973, Frank O'Hara, Poet Among Painters, 1977, 2nd edit., 1998, The Poetics of Indeterminacy: Rimbaud to Cage, 1981, 2d edit., 1999, The Dance of the Intellect: Studies in the Poetry of the Pound Tradition, 1985, 2d edit., 1996, The Futurist Moment: Avant-Garde, Avant-Guerre and the Language of Rupture, 1986, 2d edit., 2003, Poetic License: Essays in Modern and Postmodern Lyric, 1990, Radical Artifice: Writing Poetry in the Age of Media, 1991, Wittgenstein's Ladder: Poetic Language and the Strangeness of the Ordinary, 1996, Frank O'Hara, 2d edit., 1998, Poetry On and Off the Page: Essays for Emergent Occasions, 1998, Twenty-first Century Modernism, 2001, The Vienna Paradox, 2004; editor: Postmodern Genres, 1990; co-editor: John Cage: Composed in America, 1994; contbg. editor: Columbia Literary History of the U.S., 1987; contbr. preface to Contemporary Poets, 1980, A John Cage Reader, 1983. Guggenheim fellow, 1981-82, NEA fellow, 1985; Phi Beta Kappa scholar, 1994-95. Fellow Am. Acad. Arts and Scis.; mem. MLA (exec. coun. 1977-81, Am. lit. sect. 1993—, 2d v.p. 2004-), Comparative Lit. Assn. (pres. 1993-94, mem. adv. bd. Libr. of Am.), Lit. Studies Acad. Home: 1467 Amalfi Dr Pacific Palisades CA 90272-2752 Office: Stanford U Dept English Stanford CA 94305 E-mail: mperloff@earthlink.net.

PERLOV, DADIE, management consultant, consultant; b. N.Y.C., June 8, 1929; d. Aaron and Anna (Leight) Heitman; m. Norman B. Perlov, May 29, 1950; children— Nancy Perlov Rosenbach, Jane, Amy Perlov Schenkein BA, NYU, 1950; postgrad., Adelphi U., 1963, Vanderbilt U., 1973. Cert. assn. exec., N.Y. Exec. dir. ops. Open City, N.Y.C., 1962-64; field svcs. dir. Nat. Coun. Jewish Women, N.Y.C., 1968-74; exec. dir. N.Y. Libr. Assn., N.Y.C., 1974-81, Nat. Coun. Jewish Women, N.Y.C., 1981-90; founder, prin. Consensus Mgmt. Group, N.Y.C. and Washington, 1989—. Cons. HEW 1975-76; pres.-elect Internat. Coun. Libr. Assn. Execs., 1979-80; exec. mem. Conf. of Pres., 1981-90; strategic planner, lectr., merger facilitator; mgmt. cons. ABA, Am. Bankers Assn., ALA, Nat. Assn. Home Builders, Am. Coll. Healthcare Execs., Nat. Assn. Ind. Insurers, and more than 500 other maj. trade and profl. assns. Co-author: The Ultimate Association Diet: How to Stay Fit and Trim in the 21st Century; author monthly column Dear Dadie for Assoc. Trends; contbr. articles to profl. jours. Dem. committeewoman, 1966; mem. N.Y. Zool. Soc., 1959—, adv. bd. Nat. Inst. Against Prejudice and Violence, 1985-89; bd. visitors Pratt Inst., Bklyn., 1980-84; bd. dirs. Pres. Coun. on Handicapped, 1981—; facilitator Nursing Summit, 1994. Recipient Recognition award N.Y. Libr. Assn., 1978, BUDDY award NOW Legal Def. and Edn. Found., 1989, cert. N.Y. State Legislature, 1978; named N.Y. State Exec. of Yr., 1980, One of Am.'s 100 Most Important Women, Ladies' Home Jour., 1988. Fellow Am. Soc. Assn. Execs. (cert. 1978, evaluator 1980-91, bd. dirs. 1987-90, bd. found. 1990-92, Excellence award 1983); mem. LWV (chpt. pres. 1960-62), N.Y. Soc. Assn. Execs, (pres. 1985, Outstanding Assn. Exec. 1989, Outstanding Svc. award 1991), Global Perspectives in Edn. (bd. dirs.), Nat. Orgn. Continuing Edn. (coun.), Audubon Soc., N.Y. Citizens Coun. on Librs. (bd. dirs. 1981-84), Am. Arbitration Assn. (mem. panel). Avocations: writing, mycology, history, music, art. Fax: 212-874-8068.

PERNER, DARLENE E. special education educator, consultant, editor; b. Chgo., Dec. 1, 1948; d. LaVerne Perner; m. Lance C. Nielsen, Aug. 3, 1976; 1 child, Jaron M. Nielsen. BA in Fine Arts, Knox Coll., 1970; MEd. in Curriculum Devel. and Urban Edn., SUNY, Buffalo, 1972, MS in Spl. Edn., 1973; EdD in Spl. Edn., U. B.C., 1986. Permanent sch. prin. cert. N.B., Can., permanent tchr.'s cert. N.B., Can., permanent tchr. cert. N.Y. Art and elem. tchr. Chgo. Pub. Schs., 1970—71; spl. edn. tchr. West Seneca (N.Y.) Devel. Ctr., 1973—78; instr. SUNY, Buffalo, 1978; asst. prof. U. N.B., Fredericton, 1980—81; ednl. cons. N.B. Dept. Edn., Fredericton, 1981—82, cons., 1986—93, rsch. and policy devel. cons., 1993—96, rsch. and policy analyst, 1996—98; supr. Sch. Dist. 20, St. John, 1982—86; assoc. prof. Bloomsburg U. of Pa., 1998—. Author: (curriculum guide) Changing Teaching Practices Using Curriculum Differentiation to Respond to Student's Diversity, (curriculum instruction) Implementing Inclusive Edn. [illegible] How to Use Differentiated Instrn. with Students with Develop. Disabilities in the Gen. Edn. Classroom, 2002; contbr. chapters to books; author: (curriculum guide) UNESCO, 2001—. Grantee, Ednl. Rsch. Inst. of B.C., 1979—80, N.B. Dept. of Advanced Edn. and Labour's Job Experience for Tomorrow, 1995, 1997; Can. Works grantee, 1985. Mem.: TASH (assoc.), Am. Assn. on Mental Retardation (assoc.), Northea. Ednl. Rsch. Assn. (assoc.; co-editor newsletter 1999—2002), Coun. for Exceptional Children (assoc.; program proposal reviewer 2001—, pres. chpt. # 365 1999—, newsletter editor divsn. devel. disabilities 2000—). Avocations: vegetarian cooking, organic gardening, travel, running, reading. Office: Bloomsburg U of Pa 400 E 2nd St Bloomsburg PA 17815 E-mail: dperner@bloomu.edu.

PEROTTI, ROSE NORMA, lawyer; b. St. Louis, Aug. 10, 1930; d. Joseph and Dorothy Mary (Roleski) Perotti. BA, Fontbonne Coll., St. Louis, 1952; JD, St. Louis U., 1957. Bar: Mo. 1958. Trademark atty. Sutherland, Polster & Taylor, St. Louis, 1958-63, Sutherland Law Office, 1964-70, Monsanto Co., St. Louis, 1971-85, sr. trademark atty., 1985-91, assoc. trademark counsel, 1991-94, trademark counsel, 1994-96, Polster, Lieder, Woodruff & Lucchesi, 1996—. Honored with dedication of faculty office in her honor, St. Louis U. Sch. Law, 1980. Mem. ABA, Mo. Bar, Bar Assn. Met. St. Louis, Am. Judicature Soc., Friends St. Louis Art Mus., Mo. Bot. Garden. Office: Polster Lieder Woodruff & Lucchesi 12412 Powers Court Dr Ste 200 Saint Louis MO 63131-3615 Office Phone: 314-238-2400. Business E-Mail: rperotti@patpro.com.

PERRAUD, PAMELA BROOKS, human resources professional; m. Jean-Marc Francois Perraud; children: Marc Alexander, Andrea Elizabeth. BA, Conn. Coll., 1970; MA in Urban Studies, Occidental Coll., 1972; MA in Indsl. Rels., U. Minn., 1977. Cert. sr. profl. in human resources, compensation profl., benefits profl., relocation profl., global renumeration profl. Dir. personnel Mpls. Housing and ReDevel. Authority, Mpls., 1973-75; dir. adminstrn. United Svcs. Orgn., Paris, 1976-78; dir. office svcs. Pechiney Ughine Kuhlmann, Greenwich, Conn., 1979-80; lectr., trainer Monodnock Internat., London, 1981-85; personnel recruiter IBM Europe, Paris, 1989; prof. bus. Am. Bus. Sch., Paris, 1988-92; pres. Women's Inst. for Continuing Edn., Paris, 1992-93; human resource cons. N.Y.C., 1994-97; pres. Global Transitions, 1998—. Chair Women on the Move, Paris, 1990-93; pres. Women's Inst. for Continuing Edn., Paris, 1990-91; Non-govtl. Orgn. rep. at UN for Fedn. Am. Women's Clubs Overseas, 1998—; bd. dirs. METRO Internat., 1998-02, Assn. Am. Residents Overseas, Families in Global Transitions. Co-author: Living in France, 1994. Co-founder Focus Info. and Referral, London, 1982, Women in Mgmt., Mpls., 1973; trustee Conn. Coll., New London, 1970-72. Fellow in Pub. Affairs, Coro Found., L.A., 1970. Mem. Friends of WICE, World at Work Assn., Soc. for Human Resources Mgmt., Soc. for Intercultural Edn., Tng. and Rsch., Fgn. Policy Assn., Mayflower Soc. of Minn. Avocations: tennis, skiing.

PERRIGUEY, GEORGIA DÉSIRÉE, poet, educator; b. Las Cruces, N.Mex., June 26, 1957; d. Billy Joe Carter and Patricia Rae Morgan; m. Michael Gregory Perriguey, May 17, 1985; children: Dustin Travis, Tara Jacqueline. BS in Edn., N.Mex. State U., 1991, MA in Ednl. Adminstrn., 1995; paralegal degree, U. Tex., El Paso, 1999. Adminstrv. asst. Honeywell, Las Cruces, N.Mex., 1983—86; tchr. Las Cruces Pub. Schs., Las Cruces, 1991—99, spl. edn. summer sch. prin., 1993, 1994; tchr. Alamagordo (N.Mex.) Pub. Schs., 1999—2000. Chairperson child story team Las Cruces Pub. Schs.-Tombaugh Elem., 1992, 93, 94. Author poetry. Vol. victim assistance unit Las Cruces Police Dept., 2001—02. Crimson scholar, N.Mex. State U., 1991. Mem.: Phi Delta Kappa, Golden Key. Democrat. Methodist. Avocations: reading, writing.

PERRINI, NANCY BROWN, writer, consultant; b. St. Louis, July 28, 1934; d. Linwood Alvis and Esther Elizabeth Neblett; m. Sidney Alsop McClanahan, Dec. 15, 1956 (div. Dec. 1970); 1 child, William Alvis McClanahan ; m. John Anthony Brown, June 14, 1973 (dec. Feb. 1978); m. Nicholas John Perrini, Aug. 29, 1985. BA, Lindenwood Coll., 1956; MA, Ohio State U., 1980. Dir. alumnae affairs Lindenwood Coll., St. Charles, Mo., 1966—73, acting dean students, 1968—69, dir. admissions, 1971—73; dir. corp./found. rels. Capital U., Columbus, Ohio, 1980—99; freelance writer, cons. Columbus, 1999—. Bd. dirs., v.p. Ctrl. Ohio chpt. Nat. Soc. Fundraising Execs., Columbus, 1990—92; bd. dirs., pres. Stuart Pimsler Dance and Theater, Columbus, 1985—88; bd. dirs. S.E. Ohio Symphony Orch., New Concord, 1976—80. Co-author: Educational Administration in Two Year Colleges, 1980. Mem. YWCA, Columbus, Women's Fund Ctrl. Ohio. Mem.: Coun. for Advance and Support Edn. (life). Roman Catholic. Avocations: traveling, ballroom dancing, golf, gardening. Home: 1524 Tiffany Ct Columbus OH 43209 E-mail: nperrini@columbus.rr.com.

PERRONI, CAROL, artist, painter; b. Boston, July 28, 1952; d. Michael John and Mary Agnes (Collett) P.; m. John Richard Mugford, May 23, 1987; 1 child, Jonathan Perroni. Student, Boston Mus. Sch., 1970-71; BA in Art, Bennington Coll., 1976; student, Skowhegan Sch. Painting and Sculpture, 1978; MFA in Art, Hunter Coll., 1983; MEd, The Coll. Santa Fe, 2003. Studio asst. for artist Isaac Witkin, Bennington, Vt., 1973-74; libr. asst. Simmons Coll. Libr., Boston, 1977-78; studio asst. for artist Mel Bochner, N.Y.C., 1979; bookkeeper Internat. House, N.Y.C., 1979-80; studio asst. for Lee Krasner, East Hampton, N.Y., 1980; rsch. asst. Art News Mag., N.Y.C., 1981; intern Greenespace Gallery, N.Y.C., 1982-83; tech. asst. Avery Architectural and Fine Arts Libr. Columbia U., N.Y.C., 1981-83; libr., rechr. Kennedy Galleries, Inc., N.Y.C., 1984-86; program specialist, art tchr. Swinging Sixties Sr. Citizen Ctr., Bklyn., 1986-87; with Arts in Edn. Program, R.I., 1993-96. One-woman shows include Boston City Hall, 1978, Hunter Coll. Gallery, N.Y.C., 1983, Ten Worlds Gallery, N.Y.C., 1986, Gallery X, New Bedford, Mass., 1993-94, Hera Gallery, Wakefield, R.I., 1995, 98, AS220, Providence, R.I., 1996, C.C. of R.I., Lincoln, 1996, Boyden Libr., Foxboro, Mass., 1997; group shows include Salem State Coll., Mass., 1978, Fuller Mus. Art, Brockton, Mass., 1989-90, Danforth Mus. Art, Framingham, Mass., 1989, Attleboro Mus., Mass., 1989, Gallery One, Providence, 1992, Gallery X, New Bedford, Mass., 1992-98, Grove St. Gallery, Worcester, Mass., 1993, Bell St. Chapel, Providence, 1994-95, AS220, Providence, 1994, 98, Hera Gallery, Wakefield, R.I., 1993-99, 2000, 2001, St. Andrew's Sch., Barrington, R.I., 1994, McKillop Gallery, Salve Regina U., Newport, R.I., 1995, North River Arts Soc., Marshfield Hills Village, Mass., 1995, Providence Art Club, 1995, The Sarah Doyle Gallery, Brown U., Providence, 1995-96, R.I. Watercolor Soc. Slater Meml. Park, Pawtucket, 1995, Fed. Reserve Bank, Boston, 1996, Art Advisory/Boston, Quincy, Mass., 1996, Rotch-Jones-Duff Mus., New Bedford, Mass., 1997, Dryden Galleries, Providence, 1997, Renaissance Gallery, Fall River, Mass., 1997, 98, Island Arts Gallery, Newport, 1997, Harwood Art Ctr., Albuquerque, 1998, Branigan Cultural Ctr., Las Cruces, N.Mex., 1999, 2000, Atrium Gallery, Providence, R.I., 2000, New Haven Pub. Libr., New Haven, 2000, Angelo State U., San Angelo, Tex., 2000, Rockport (Tex.) Ctr. Arts, 2001, Lorain C.C., Elyria, Ohio, 2001, Hiestand Galleries, Miami U., Oxford, Ohio, 2001, South Broadway Cultural Ctr., Albuquerque, 2001, N.Mex. State U. Art Gallery, Las Cruces, 2001, Sedona (Ariz.) Arts Ctr., 2002, Cork Gallery, Avery Fisher Hall, Lincoln Ctr., N.Y., 2002, 2003, Keystone Bldg., Santa Fe, N.Mex., 2003, Tishman Hall, The Coll. Santa Fe, 2004; represented in permanent collection at R.I. Hosp. Art Collection and pvt. collections. Bd. dirs. Hera Ednl. Found., 1994—2001. Grantee Artists Space, 1986, Flintridge Found., 1993, fellow Vt. Studio Ctr., Johnson, 1990,

Dorland Mountain Arts Colony, 1993. Mem.: SOHO 20 Gallery (nat. affiliate mem.), Am. Acad. Women Artists (assoc.). Home: 2089 Plaza Thomas Santa Fe NM 87505-5438 E-mail: carolpi56@msn.com.

PERRY, BARBARA MITCHELL, retired librarian; b. Chgo., Oct. 14, 1933; d. Raymond O. and Ann (Ashcraft) Mitchell; m. Lee R. Perry, July 2, 1955; children: Christopher R., Constance A. Perry Genrich, Geoffrey M. BS, U. Ariz., 1955. Cert. tchr., libr., Ariz. Libr. Washington Sch. Dist., Phoenix, 1983—98, ret., 1998. Recipient Louis Slomaker award, 1965, Alumni Appreciation award U. Ariz., 1965. Mem. AASL, ALA, Ariz. State Libr. Assn., Ariz. Edn. Media Assn. Home: 106 N Country Club Dr Phoenix AZ 85014-5443

PERRY, BETH BENTLEY, writer, artist; b. Oklahoma City, Apr. 4, 1928; d. Warren Edward and Ollie Antoinette (Kerr) Bentley; m. Kenneth Alvin Perry, Dec. 23, 1925; children: Pamela Lynn, Scott Kenneth, Angela Beth. AA, Fla. Jr. Coll., 1976; BA, U. North Fla., 1978, BFA magna cum laude, 1983. Pres. Univ. Art League, Jacksonville, 1980-81; sec. Jacksonville Coalition for Visual Arts, 1986-87. Author: From the Same Cloth, 1994, Eyes of the Osprey, 1991. Vol. Dem. Party, Jacksonville, 1991-94, Taylor Sr. Residences, Jacksonville, 1980-95, Pub. TV, Jacksonville, 1978-85; bd. dirs. Am. United, Jacksonville, 1995-98. Recipient Grumbacher award for best in show, 1984, U.S. Navy Squadron 8 Commemerative medallion. Democrat. Avocations: opinion writing to editors, reading, women's issues, writing organizational newsletters, geneology. Home: 7926 Praver Dr W Jacksonville FL 32217-4156

PERRY, BLANCHE BELLE, physical therapist; b. New Bedford, Mass., Sept. 2, 1929; d. Joseph Rudolph and Beatrice (Farial) Andrews;m. Louis Perry, Nov. 26, 1953 (dec. 1980); children: Marcia, Susan, Tracey, Evelyn (dec.). BS, Ithaca (N.Y.) Coll., 1951; MA, Assumption Coll., Worcester, Mass., 1978. Office and hosp. phys. therapist, Mass. and N.Y., 1961-65; dir. rehab. svc. St. Luke's Hosp., New Bedford, 1967-89, ret., 1989. Profl. adv. com. Vis. Nurse Assn. Wareham, 1980; mem. faculty continuing edn. Newbury Coll., 1986; corporator Compass Bank for Savs. Chmn. Mattapoisett Sch. Com., 1970; vice chmn. Mass. Sch. Commn. Area IV, 1972-75; sec. Old Colony Regional Vocat. Sch. Com., 1973—, asst. treas.; trustee Abner Pease Scholarship Found.; chmn. com. opportunity ctr. CARE, New Bedford, 1987; pres. St. Luke's Hosp. Retirees, 1996. Grantee, Elks Nat. Found., 1965; scholar, Mattapoisett Land Trust, 2003, Mattapoisett Scholarshop Commn., 2003. Mem. Am. Phys. Therapy Assn., Delta Kappa Gamma, Mattapoisett Women's Club (pres. 1996). Home: 41 Aucoot Rd Mattapoisett MA 02739-2401 E-mail: beebee41@comcast.net.

PERRY, CATHERINE D. judge; b. 1952; BA, Univ. of Okla., 1977; JS, Wash. Univ. Sch. of Law, 1980. Sec., law clk. Gillespie, Perry & Gentry, Sentinel, Okla., 1970, 77-78; with Armstrong, Teasdale, Kramer & Vaughn, St. Louis, 1980-90; magistrate judge U.S. Dist. Ct. (Mo. ea. dist.), 8th circuit, St. Louis, 1990-94; dist. judge U.S. Dist. Ct. (ea. dist.), 8th circuit, St. Louis, 1994—. Mem. Fed. Magistrate Judges Assn., Nat. Assn. of Women Judges, Am. Bar Assn., Mo. Bar Assn., Bar Assn. of Metropolitan St. Louis, Women Lawyers Assn. of Greater St. Louis. Office: US Courthouse 1114 Market St Rm 319 Saint Louis MO 63101-2038

PERRY, DAWN ANNA, music educator; b. Biloxi, Miss., Nov. 10, 1972; d. Donald Fulford and Carolyn (Eller) Perry. B in Music Edn., Appalachian State U., 1995, M in Music Edn., 1999. Tchr. Davidson County Schs., Lexington, NC, 1995—98, Alice (Tex.) Ind. Sch. Dist., 1999, Alexander County Schs., Taylorsville, NC, 2000, New Hanover County Schs., Wilmington, NC, 2001—; interim dir. Appalachian State U., Boone, NC, 2000—01. Adminstr., dean women Cannon Music Camp Appalachian State U., Boone, 1993—. Mem.: Music Educators Nat. Conf., Nat. Band Assn., N.C. Bandmasters Assn. (bd. dirs., auditions chair eastern dist. 2003—). Avocations: music, sports, reading. Business E-Mail: daperry@nhcs.k12.nc.us.

PERRY, E. LYNN, lawyer; b. Tucson, Mar. 23, 1949; d. Eldon G. Perry and Doris E. (Wismer) Noonan BA, U. Ariz., 1970; JD, Loyola U., 1976. Bar: Ill. 1977, U.S. Dist. Ct. (no. dist.) Ill. 1977, N.Y. 1980, U.S. Dist. Ct. (no. and ea. dists.) N.Y. 1984, Calif. 1984, U.S. Dist. Ct. (no., ea. and cen. dists.) Calif., U.S. Ct. Appeals (9th cir.). Flight attendant Pan American World Airways, N.Y.C. and L.A., 1971-75; asst. state's atty. Cook County State's Atty., Chgo., 1977-79; assoc. Kass, Goodkind, Wechsler & Labaton, N.Y.C., 1980-81; assoc. counsel MasterCard Internat., Inc., N.Y.C., 1981-84; assoc. Townsend and Townsend and Crew, San Francisco, 1984-89, ptnr., 1989—2002, Thelen Reid & Priest, 2002—. Speaker and author in field. Recipient scholarship U. Ariz., Tucson, 1967, Loyola U., L.A., 1975. Mem. ABA (Governing Com. Forum Franchising 1991—93), Internat. Trademark Assn. (Trademark Reporter 1985—, reviewer 1990—, panel of neutrals 2001), Calif. State Bar (trademarks chair 1990-91, Exec. Com. Intellectual Property Sect. 1991—94), San Francisco Patent and Trademark Assn. (program chair 1987-88), Profl. Writing Competition (competitions com. chair, 2004) Avocations: tennis, yoga, skiing. Office: Thelen Reid & Priest 101 2nd St Ste 1800 San Francisco CA 94105

PERRY, EVELYN REIS, communications company executive; b. N.Y.C., Mar. 09; d. Lou L. and Bertl (Wolf) Reis; m. Charles G. Perry III, Jan. 7, 1968; children: Charles G. IV, David Reis. Student, Am. Acad. Dramatic Arts, 1958-59, U. N.Mex., 1963-64; BA, U. Wis., 1963. Lic. real estate broker, N.C. Vol. ETV project Peace Corps, Colombia, 1963-65; program officer-radio/tv Peace Corps, Washington, 1965-68; dir. Vols. in Svc. to Am. (VISTA), Raleigh, N.C., 1977-80; exec. dir. CETA Program for Displaced Homemakers, Raleigh, 1980-81; cons. exec. dir. to Recycle Raleigh for Food and Fuel, Theater in the Park, 1981-83; pres., CEO Carolina Sound Commn., MUZAK, Charleston, S.C., 1984—; pub. rels. account exec. various cos. Washington, Syracuse, N.Y., 1969-71; cons. pub. rels. and orgn. Olympic Organizing Com., Mexico City, 1968; cons. pub. rels., fundraising, arts mgmt. pub. speaking Ill., Pa., N.C., 1971-77; orgnl. and pub. speaking cons. Perry & Assocs., Raleigh, 1980—. Spkr. Nat. Syss. Contrs. Assn., 1993, 95, 97; founder Nat. Assn. Women Bus. Owners, Charleston, S.C., 1998; bd. dirs. Charleston Area Br. Banking and Trust, 1999—; bd. dirs. Nat. fed. of Indep. Bus, 1986-, mem. adv. bd., 1999-. Contbr. articles to Sound and Comm. mag. Mem. adv. bd. Gov.'s Office Citizen Affairs, Raleigh, 1981-85; mem. Involvement Coun. of Wake County, N.C., Raleigh, 1981-84; mem. Adv. Coun. to Vols. in Svc. to Am., Raleigh, 1980-84; mem. Pres.'s adv. bd. Peace Corps, Washington, 1980-82; v.p., bd. dirs. Voluntary Action Ctr., Raleigh, 1980-84, bd. dirs., Charleston, 1988-94; sec. bd. dirs. Temple Kahil Kadosh Beth Elohim, 1987-89, sec. fin., 1989-90, v.p. programming, 1990-93, v.p. adminstrn. 1993-95, v.p. sisterhood, 2001—; bd. dirs. Chopstik Theater, Charleston, 1989-90; del., chmn. S.C. Delegation to White House Conf. Sml. Bus., 1995; S.C. del. Congl. Sml. Bus. Summit, 1998. Named Bus. Women Adv. of Yr., SBA, 2002. Mem. N.C. Coun. of Women's Orgns. (pres., v.p. 1982-84), Charleston Hotel and Motel Assn., N.C. Assn. Vol. Adminstrs. (bd. dirs. 1980-84), S.C. Restaurant Assn., Nat. Assn. Women Bus. Owners (founder lowcountry chpt. 1998, pres. 1998—2001), Internat. Planned Music Assn. (chmn. conf. 1993), bd. Branch Banking & Trust, 1999—, Nat. Fedn. Ind. Bus. (mem. adv. bd. 1987—, chmn. leadership coun. 1994-2000, del. Congl. Summit, Washington, pres. 2003), Internat. Platform Assn., Theaterworks (bd. dirs. 1994-96), Internat. Planned Music Assn. (bd. dirs. 2000—, v.p. 2001-2003, pres. 2003—). Office: Carolina Sound Comm Inc 1941 Savage Rd Ste 200G Charleston SC 29407-4789 E-mail: evelyn@carolina-sound.com.

PERRY, HELEN, medical/surgical nurse, secondary school educator; b. Birmingham, Ala., Mar. 4, 1927; d. Van Mary Ellenol (Thornton) Curry; m. Charlie Pitts, May 1960 (div.); 1 child, Charlenia Pitts ; m. George Perry (dec. 1989); children: Hattie Mae(dec.), George Jr., Bishop, Jose Sr. Student, LaSalle Extension U., Chgo., 1968, Georgetown U., 1979; Doctorate/Mayanuis Mosaic Soc., Duke Univ., San Antonio, 1979. Cert. paramedic; LPN. Tchr. Wenona HS City Bd. Edn., Birmingham, 1977—. Notary pub., Ala., 1975—; home health nurse U. Ala. Birmingham Hosp., 1988—. Trustee Nat. Crime Watch, 1989; mem. adv. bd. Am. Security Coun., Va., 1969—91; mem. Coalition for Desert Storm; others; vol. ARC, Birmingham, 1970—; mem. crime watch Am. Police, Washington, 1989; mem. Hall of Fame Pres. Task Force, Washington, 1983—91, Image Devel. Adv. Bd.; nominee Nat. Rep. Com., Washington, 1991, 1992; selected VIP guest del. Rep. Nat. Conv., Houston, 1992; life mem. Rep. Presdl. Task Force, Washington, 1992; mem. Jefferson Com., 2001; mem. adv. bd. Nat. Congl. Com., Washington; mem. fin. com. fundraiser Middleton for Congress Campaign, 1994, Dist. # 59 Bd. Reps.; mem. exec. com. Jefferson County Rep., chairperson legis. dist. 52; chair Harriet Tubman Rep. Com.; del. Commonwealth of Ky. So. Rep. Leadership Conf., 2000; min. Greater Emmanuel Temple Holiness Ch., Birmingham, 1957—, ordained elder, vice champion mother bd.; mem. Nat. Law Enforcement Assn., 1989. Nominee Presdl. Election Registry, Rep. Presdl. Task Force, 1992; named Good Samaritan, Law Envforcement Officers; recipient award, Ala. Sheriff Assn., 1989, Navy League, 1989—91, cert. of appreciation, Pres. Congl. Task Force, 1990, Rep. Nat. Com., 1994, Diamond award, U.S.A. Serve Am., 1992, Rep. Presdl. award, Legion of Merit, 1994, Royal Proclamation, Royal Highness Kevin, Prince Regent of Hutt River Province, 1994, Royal Ceremonial jewel, Svc. award, Ala. Bd. Nursing, Outstanding Sr. Citizen's cert. of recognition. Mem.: Ala. Nurses Assn., Nat. Assn. Unknown Players, Nat. Rep. Women Assn., LaSalle Ext. U. Alumni (life). Avocations: singing, writing, speaking, reading, planting flowers. Home: 2021 10th Ave S Apt 513 Birmingham AL 35205-2716

PERRY, HELEN THOMAS, artist; b. Bryan, Tex., Jan. 31, 1925; d. Frank Lincoln and Mable Clare (Randal) Thomas; m. John Vivian Perry Jr., Feb. 5, 1946; children: John V. III, Judith Ann, Joan Thomas. BS in Art, Tex. Womans U., 1945; student, Tex. A&M U., 1973—75. Illustrator Tamu Mus., Coll. Sta., Tex., 1942—43; draftsman U.S. Navy, Wash., DC, 1945—46, Tamu Oceanography-Meteorology, Coll. Sta., 1951—53; tchr. H.S., Coll. Sta., 1970—78. Ct. room artist KBTX TV, 1975. Sunlight & Shadows, Collected & Selected, exhibitions include Salamagudy Gallery, N.Y.C., 1980, one-woman shows include 10. Docent Tamu Arts Collection; mem. cemetary com. Coll. Sta. City, Coll. Sta. Recipient Anderson award, Arts Coun., 1988. Mem.: The Woman's Club (life). Home: 516 Kyle Ave College Station TX 77840

PERRY, JACQUELIN, orthopedic surgeon; b. Denver, May 31, 1918; d. John F. and Tirzah (Kuruptkat) P. B.E., U. Calif., Los Angeles, 1940; MD, U. Calif., San Francisco, 1950; DSc (hon.), U. So. Calif., 1996. Intern Children's Hosp., San Francisco, 1950-57; resident in orthopedic surgery U. Calif., San Francisco, 1951-55; orthopedic surgeon Rancho Los Amigos Hosp., Downey, Calif., 1955 ; chief pathokinesiology Rancho Los Amigos Med. Ctr., 1961—; chief stroke service Rancho Los Amigos Hosp., 1972-75; mem. faculty U. Calif. Med. Sch., San Francisco, 1966—, clin. prof., 1973—; mem. faculty U. So. Calif. Med. Sch., 1969—, prof. orthopedic surgery, 1972—, dir. polio and gait clinic, 1972—. Disting. lectr. for hosp. for spl. surgery and Cornell U. Med. Coll., N.Y.C., 1977-78; Packard Meml. lectr. U. Colo. Med. Sch., 1970; Osgood lectr. Harvard Med. Sch., 1978; Summer lectr., Portland, 1977; Shands lectr.; cons. USAF; guest speaker symposia; cons. Biomechanics Lab. Centinela Hosp., 1979—. Served as phys. therapist U.S. Army, 1941-46. Recipient Disting. Svc. award Calif. Assn. Rehab. Facilities, 1981, Pres.'s award, 1984, Milton Cohen award Nat. Assn. Rehab., 1993, Isabelle and Lenard Goldenson award for tech. United Cerebral Palsy Assn., 1981, Jow Dowling award, 1985, Profl. Achievement award UCLA, 1988, Amistad award Rancho Las Amigos Med. Ctr., Calif. 1990, Shands award Orthop. Rsch. Soc., 1998, Tribute, Ruth Jackson Orthopedic Soc., 2004; named Woman of Yr. for Medicine in So. Calif., L.A. Times, 1959, Alumnus of Yr., U. Calif. Med. Sch., 1980, Physician of Yr. Calif. Employment Devel. Dept., 1994; Jacquelin Perry Neuro Trauma Inst. Rancho Clin. Bldg. named in her honor, 1996. Mem. AMA, Am. Acad. Orthop. Surgeons (Kappa Delta award for rsch. 1977, orthupaedic rsch. svc., 1976), Am. Orthop. Assn. (Shands lectr. 1988), Western Orthop. Assn., Calif. Med. Soc., L.A. County Med. Soc., Am. Phys. Therapy Assn. (hon. Golden Pen award 1965), Am. Acad. Orthotists and Prosthetists (hon.), Scoliosis Rsch. Soc., LeRoy Abbott Soc., Am. Acad. Cerebral Palsy, Gait & Clin. Movement Analysis Soc. (mem. emeritus, Lifetime Achievement award 2000), Orthop. Rsch. Soc. (Shands award 1998, 99). Home: 12319 Brock Ave Downey CA 90242-3503 Office: Rancho Los Amigos Med Ctr 7601 Imperial Hwy Downey CA 90242-3456 E-mail: pks@larei.org.

PERRY, JANE A. service assistant; b. Anderson, IN, Mar. 14, 1960; d. Richard L. Ward, Shirley A. Ward; m. Will C. Perry, Mar. 14, 1992; 1 child, Devin Ward. A in Bus. Mgr., Acctg. Sci., Indiana Bus. Coll., Anderson, IN, 1990—93. Designee Cardinal Svc. Mgmt. Svcs., New Castle, Ind., 1990—97; caterer Plain J&W Catering, Indianapolis, Ind., 1998—2001; svc. asst. Ind. Ins. Agents Ind., Indianapolis, Ind., 1997—. Planner Ind. Ins. Agents Ind., Indianapolis, 1998—2001. Human rights com. Cardinal Svc. Mgmt. Svcs., New Castle, 1997—2001. Apostilic. Avocations: horseback riding, swimming. Home: 10927 Cornell Ave Indianapolis IN 46280-1134 Business E-Mail: perry@bigi.org.

PERRY, JANIS DOLORES, elementary school educator; d. John W. and Florence C. Perry; 1 child, Justin K. Bagley. AA, Seminole Jr. Coll., 1975; BA, Fla. Tech. U., 1977. Tchr. 1st, 2d, 4th grades Idyllwilde Elem. Sch., Sanford, Fla., 1979—99, home sch. liaison, 1999—2002, tchr. 1st grade, 2002—. Chmn. sch. adv. coun., Sanford, 1999—2001; mem. Seminole County Discipline Com., 1999—2003; membership chmn. PTSA, 2001—02. Mem.: Fla. Notary Assn., Assn. Curriculum & Devel., Phono-Graphix Assn. Reading. Democrat. Avocations: stamp collecting, bowling. Home: 2070 Ruff Rd Sanford FL 32771

PERRY, JEAN LOUISE, dean; b. Richland, Wash., May 13, 1950; d. Russell S. and Sue W. Perry. BS, Miami U., Oxford, Ohio, 1972; MS, U. Ill., Urbana, 1973, PhD, 1976. Cons. edn1. placement office U. Ill., 1973-75; adminstrv. intern Coll. Applied Life Studies, 1975-76, asst. dean, 1976-77, assoc. dean, 1978-81, asst. prof. dept. phys. edn., 1976-81; assoc. prof. phys. edn. San Francisco State U., 1981-84, prof., 1984-90, chair, 1981-90; dean Coll. of Human and Community Scis. U. Nev., Reno, 1990—. Named to excellent tchr. list U. Ill., 1973-79. Mem. AAHPERD (fellow research consortium, pres. 1988-89), Am. Assn. Higher Edn., Am. Ednl. Research Assn., Nat. Assn. Phys. Edn. in Higher Edn., Nat. Assn. Girls and Women in Sports (guide coordinator, pres.), Delta Psi Kappa, Phi Delta Kappa. Home: 3713 Ranchview Ct Reno NV 89509-7437 Office: U Nev Coll Human Cmty Scis 136 Reno NV 89557-0001

PERRY, JEANINE, state representative; b. Apr. 3, 1942; married; 2 children. BEd, U. Toledo. State rep. dist. 49 Ohio Ho. of Reps., Columbus, 1998—, ranking minority mem., transp. and pub. safety com., mem. agr. and natural resources, econ. devel. and tech., homeland security engring. and archtl. design, and human svcs. and aging coms., mem. natural resources, parks and recreation subcom. Councilwoman Toledo City Coun., 1993—98. Named Legislator of Yr., Point Place Bus. Assn., 1999; recipient Outstanding Svc. award, Toledo PTA Pub. Schs. Mem.: U. Toledo Alumni Assn., Friends of the Libr., Fraternal Order of Police Aux., Toledo Power Squadron (hon.), Ohio PTA (life). Democrat. Office: 77 S High St 10th fl Columbus OH 43215-6111

PERRY, KATHRYN ABBOTT, telecommunications engineer; b. Mobile, Ala., Mar. 19, 1958; d. Thomas William South and Nancy Jeanne (Abbott) Smith; m. Russell Owen Perry, July 2, 1988. Student, DeVry Tech. Inst., 1997—. Network analyst Trust Co. Bank, Atlanta, 1980-85; network coord. Crawford & Co. Risk Mgmt., Atlanta, 1985-88; telecomm. ops. mgr. First Interstate Bank Tex., Houston, 1988-90; sr. sys. engr. LDDS World Comm. (formerly Wiltel), Atlanta, 1990-98; sr. ops. mgr. Rapid Link USA, Marietta, Ga., 1998—. Co-founder AT&T Sys. 75 User Group. Episcopalian. Avocations: gardening, fishing. Office: Rapid Link USA 1000 Circle 75 Pkwy SE Atlanta GA 30339-3026

PERRY, MARGARET, librarian, writer; b. Cin., Nov. 15, 1933; d. Rufus Patterson and Elizabeth Munford (Anthony) P. AB, Western Mich. U., 1954; Cert. d'etudes Francaises, U. Paris, 1956; MSLS, Cath. U. Am., 1959. Young adult and reference libr. N.Y. Pub. Libr., N.Y.C., 1954-55, 57-58; libr. U.S. Army, France and Germany, 1959-63, 64-67; chief circulation U.S. Mil. Libr., West Point, N.Y., 1967-70; head edn. libr. U. Rochester, N.Y., 1970-75, asst. prof., 1973-75, assoc. prof., 1975-82, asst. dir. librs. for reader svcs., 1975-82, acting dir. librs., 1976-77, 80; univ. libr. Valparaiso U., Ind., 1982-93; ret., 1993. Mem. Task Force on Coop. Edn., Rochester, 1972; freelance writer Mich. Land Use Inst., 1995-01. Author: A Bio-bibliography of Countee P. Cullen, 1903-1946, 1971, Silence to the Drums: A Survey of the Literature of the Harlem Renaissance, 1976, The Harlem Renaissance, 1982, The Short Fiction of Rudolph Fisher, 1987; also numerous short stories; contbr. articles to profl. jours. Bd. dirs. Urban League, 1978-80 Recipient 1st prize short story contest Armed Forces Writers League, 1966; 2d prize Frances Steloff Fiction prze, 1968, 1st prize short story Arts Alive, 1990, 2d prize short story Willow Rev., 1990; seminar scholar Schloss Leopoldskron, Salzburg, Austria, 1956, 3d prize short story West Shore C.C., Scottville, Mich., 1995. Mem. ALA. Democrat. Roman Catholic. Avocations: violin and viola, collecting book marks, gardening, reading, travel. Home: 8 Muriel St Ithaca NY 14850 Office Phone: 607-257-3997. E-mail: mperry515@yahoo.com.

PERRY, NANCY ESTELLE, psychologist; b. Pitts., Oct. 30, 1934; d. Simon Warren and Estelle Cecelia (Zaluski) Reichard; children: Scott, Karen, Elaine. BS, Ohio State U., 1956, MA in Psychology, 1969, PhD in Psychology, 1973. Nurse various locations, 1956-63; psychologist Pub. Schs., Columbus, Ohio, 1970-72; human devel. specialist Madison County (Ohio) Schs., 1972-75; pvt. practice clin. psychology; cons. psychology, 1975-80; tchr. U. Wis. Sch. Nursing, Milw., 1980-88. Milw. Devel. Ctr., 1980-83; pvt. practice Assoc. Mental Health Svcs., 1983-87, Glendale Clinic for Stress Mgmt. and Mental Health Clinics, 1987-98, Cambridge Group, 1999—; pvt. practice life transactions therapy Milw. and Santa Fe, 1999—. Mem. faculty Wis. Profl. Schs.; adj. faculty U. Wis., Milw. Ohio Dept. Edn. grantee, 1973-76. Bd. dirs. Youth Shelters & Family Svcs., Santa Fe. EPDA fellow Ohio State U., 1973; Ohio Dept. Edn. grantee, 1973-76. Fellow Internat. Soc. Study of Dissociation (sec.-treas. 1995-98), Wis. Psychol. Assn.; mem. APA, Am. Soc. Clin. Hypnosis, Am. Assn. Marriage and Family Therapists. Office: 355 E Palace Ave Santa Fe NM 87501 Home: 47 Avenida Frijoles Santa Fe NM 87507-3431

PERRY, NANCY TROTTER, former telecommunications company executive; b. Cleve., Jan. 1, 1935; d. Charles Hanley and Mable Dora (Lowry) Trotter; m. Robert Anthony Perry, Apr. 27, 1957. Student, Dunbarton Coll., 1952-53; BA, W.Va. U., 1999. Svc. rep. C&P Telephone Co., Balt., 1956-60, adminstrv. asst., 1960-67, staff supr., 1967-69; staff mgr., 1969-79; mgr. consumer affairs C&P Telephone Co., Balt., 1979-91. Bd. dirs., founding dir. Balt. Mus. Industry, Md., Info. and Referral Providers Coun., 1990-2003, sec., 1994-98, v.p. 1999-2002; bd. dirs. Learning Ind. Through Computers, Inc., 1991-99, pres., 1994-96; bd. dirs. Md. Gerontol. Assn., 1991, Md. Consumer Coun., 1991-2000, chair, 1994-96; bd. dirs. Fgn.-Born Info. and Referral Network, 1992-96; bd. dirs. Hearing and Speech Agy., 1989-94, exec. v.p. 1991-94; founding dir. Tele-Consumer Hotline, 1986-92; mem. responding to crisis panel United Way, 1995-2003, vice chmn., 1995-99, 2001-03. Mem. Soc. Consumer Affairs Profls. in Bus., Nat. Fedn. of Blind, Alliance for Pub. Tech., Sons of Italy (v.p. 1997-99, 2001—, trustee 1999—, editor Il Giornale). Avocations: travel, reading. Home: 7200 3rd Ave C150 Sykesville MD 21784-5208 E-mail: ntperry@prodigy.net.

PERRY-CAMP, JANE, music educator, pianist; b. Durham, N.C., Oct. 5, 1936; d. Harold Sanford and Margrid (Hagelberg) Perry; m. John Barton Camp, Aug. 20, 1960 (div. Sept. 1970); m. Harold Anthony Schiffman, June 10, 1978. AB magna cum laude, Duke U., 1958; MusM in Piano Performance, Fla. State U., Tallahassee, 1960, PhD in Music Theory, 1968; studied piano with, Edward Kilenyi, Ernst von Dohnanyi. Asst. prof. music Brevard C.C., Cocoa, Fla., 1968-69; faculty St. Petersburg (Fla.) Coll., 1969-73; asst. prof., assoc. prof. Sweet Briar (Va.) Coll., 1974-80; assoc. prof., prof. Sch. Music, Fla. State U., Tallahassee, 1980-96, prof. emeritus, 1996—, Orpheus chair musicology, 1999. Mem. adv. bd. Fla. State U., Music Theory Soc., Tallahassee, 1982-88; bd. dirs. Fla. State U. Friends of Libr., Tallahassee, 1985-87. Pianist: (CDs) Schiffman: Spectrum, My Ladye Jane's Booke: Eighteeen Fugues and Postludes for Piano, 1996, Concerto for Piano and Orchestra, 1999, (LPs) Fantasy for Piano, 1986, Chamber Concertino for Piano and Double Wind Quintet, 1987; contbr. articles to profl. jours. and anthologies. Fellow NEH, Paris, London, 1973-74; faculty fellow Sweet Briar Coll., 1979-80; recipient rsch. grants Fla. State U. Found., 1985-86, Internat. Rsch. and Exch. Bd., Krakow, Poland, 1986. Mem. Am. Soc. 18th Century Studies (pres. 1991-92), SE Am. Soc. 18th Century studies (pres. 1987-88), Mozart Soc. Am. (bd. dirs. 1996-2001), Internat. Soc. Study of Time, Am. Musicol. Soc., Coll. Music Soc. Avocations: gardening, hiking, needlework (knitting, crocheting, sewing). Home: 2304 Don Andres Ave Tallahassee FL 32304-1313 E-mail: jperrycp@mailer.fsu.edu.

PERRY-WIDNEY, MARILYN (MARILYN PERRY), international finance and real estate executive, television producer; b. N.Y.C., Feb. 11, 1939; d. Henry William Patrick and Edna May (Bown) Perry; m. Charles Leonidas Widney (dec. Sept. 1981). BA, Mexico City Coll., 1957. Pres. Marilyn Perry TV Prodns., Inc., N.Y.C., 1970—, C.L. Widney Internat., Inc., N.Y.C., 1977—. Mng. dir. Donerail Corp., N.Y.C., 1980-88, Lancer, N.Y.C., 1980-88, Assawata, N.Y.C., 1980-88. Prodr., host TV program Internat. Byline, series of more than 100 documentaries on the UN; host 80 radio and 200 pages on Internet series regarding environ. and devel. issues; author: (reference book) Leaders of the World, 2003; contbr. pages on environ. and devel. issues to radio and Internet sites; internat. byline-mem. nations UN exec. com. HNCA, 1998, PBS, in S.C., N.C., Ga., Tenn. Bd. dirs. UN After Sch. Program; ambassadorial candidate Pres. Bush., 1989. Recipient U.S. Indsl. Film Festival award, CINE Golden Eagle award, Bronze medal Internat. Film & TV Festival of N.Am., Bronzenen Urkinde, Berlin, award for superior quality Intercom-Chgo. Internat. Film Festival, Knights of Malta Trophy award for superior programming from Min. of Tourism, Internationales Tourismus award Film festival, Vienna, Manhattan Cable Ten Year award for continuous programming, citations from former pres. Ford and Carter, King Hussein Jordan, Pres. Clinton, pres. Maumoon Gayoon, Maldives, pres. Jacques Chirac, France. Mem. UN Corrs. Assn., UN After Sch. Programs, Rep. Presdl. Task Force (charter, journalist). Avocations: music, travel, antiques. Home: 211 E 70th St Apt 3A New York NY 10021-5206

PERSELL, CAROLINE HODGES, sociologist, educator, author, researcher, consultant; b. Ft. Wayne, Ind., Jan. 16, 1941; d. Albert Randolph and Katherine (Rogers) Hodges; m. Charles Bowen Persell III, June 17, 1967; children: Patricia Emily, Stephen David. BA, Swarthmore Coll., 1962; MA, Columbia U., 1967, PhD, 1971. Sr. assoc., then nat. coord. Nat. Scholarship Svc. and Fund for Negro Students, N.Y.C., 1962-66; project dir. Bur. Applied Social Rsch., N.Y.C., 1968-71; asst. prof. NYU, 1971-76, assoc. prof., 1976-86, prof., 1986—, dir. grad. studies dept. sociology, 1984-87, chair dept. sociology, 1987-93, Robin Williams Disting. lectr., 1993-94. Author: Education and Inequality, 1977, Understanding Society, 1984, 3d edit., 1990; author: (with Cookson) Preparing for Power, 1985, Making Sense of Society, 1992; author: (with Maisel) How Sampling Works, 1996; assoc. editor: Tchg. Sociology, 1983—85, Sociology of Edn., 1991—95, Gender & Society, 1992—95; contbr. articles to profl. jours. Carnegie scholar Advancement of Tchg., 2000-01; grantee Fund for Improvement of Postsecondary Edn., 1989-92, NSF Equipment Fund, 1993-96; recipient Faculty Devel. award NSF, 1978-79, Women Educators' Rsch. award, 1978. Mem.: Sociologists for Women in Soc., Ea. Sociol. Soc. (pres. 1995—96), Am. Ednl. Rsch. Assn., Am. Sociol. Assn. (chair sect. 1983—84, chmn. publs. com. 1987—89, chair sect. 1988—89, v.p.-elect 2003—04). Avocations: violin, gardening, opera, sports. Office: NYU Dept Sociology 269 Mercer St New York NY 10003-6633 Office Phone: 212-998-8350. E-mail: chp1@nyu.edu.

PERSONETTE, LOUISE METZGER (SISTER MARY ROGER METZGER), mathematics educator; b. Indpls., Dec. 21, 1925; d. Frank Alexander and Frances Lee Ann (Durham) Metzger; m. Marlen William Personette, Dec. 9, 1967 (div. Dec. 1985); 1 stepson: Lyle Scott. BS in Elem. Edn., Athenaeum of Ohio, 1952; MEd, Xavier U., 1964. Nun St. Francis Convent, Oldenburg, Ind., 1942—67; elem. tchr. Cath. Schs., Cin., 1945-56, secondary math tchr. Middletown, Ohio, 1957-63, Evansville, Ind., 1964-65, Hamilton, Ohio, 1966-67; elem. tchr. Kent (Wash.) Schs., 1968-72, math specialist, 1973-82; math cons. greater Seattle Schs., 1983—; GED instr. Muckleshoot Indian Tribe, Auburn, Wash., 1998—2000. Dir. Heatherhill Edn. Ctr., Kent, 1982—, Homework House, Kent, 1987—90; adj. instr. Seattle Pacific U., 1975—95, City U., Seattle, 1975—95; SAT prep. math tutor, 2002—. Co-author: S.O.S. Story Problems, 1980. Mem. Nat. Coun. Tchrs. Math., Math. Assn. Am., Washington State Math Coun., Puget Sound Coun. Tchrs. Math., New Horizons. Home and Office: Heatherhill Education Ctr 11830 SE 263rd Ct Kent WA 98031-8407 E-mail: louisamath@msn.com.

PERSONS, FERN, actor; b. Chgo., July 27, 1910; d. John William and Alpha Valeska (Solberg) Ball; m. Max I. Persons, Oct. 17, 1935 (dec. Nov. 1971); 1 child, Nancy Janice Persons Rockafellow. BA, Kalamazoo Coll., 1931; BFA, Carnegie-Mellon U., 1933. Faculty mem. speech and drama Ferry Hall, Lake Forest, Ill., 1934-35. V.p. SAG, L.A., 1977-81, nat. bd., 1982-98. Appeared in (films) Prelude to a Kiss, Straight Talk, Curly Sue, Field of Dreams, Hoosiers, Risky Business, Class, Grandview U.S.A., On the Right Track, The Golden Gloves Story, (tv feature films and series) Mario and the Mob, Hard Knox, The Impostor, Under the Biltmore Clock, The Chicago Story, Jack and Mike, Jon Sable, ER, Early Edition, also in regional theatre prodns., 1972-95. Recipient Otto Kahn prize Carnegie-Mellon U., Pitts., 1933; Fern Persons Day in Chgo. named in her honor Mayor Richard M. Daley, Chgo., July 27, 1999. Mem. AFTRA (bd. mem., v.p.), AAUW (scholar 1927), Zeta Phi Eta (v.p. 1971, Disting. Svc. award 1994). Democrat. Methodist. Avocations: travel, reading, walking, gardening, theatre. Home: 2700 Woodland Rd Evanston IL 60201-2034

PERSYN, MARY GERALDINE, law librarian, law educator; b. Elizabeth, N.J., Feb. 25, 1945; d. Henry Anthony and Geraldine (Sumption) P. AB, Creighton U., 1967; MLS, U. Oreg., 1969; JD, Notre Dame U., 1982. Bar: Ind. 1982, U.S. Dist. Ct. (no. and so. dists.) Ind. 1982, U.S. Supreme Ct. 1995. Social scis. libr. Miami U., Oxford, Ohio, 1969-78; staff law libr. Notre Dame (Ind.) Law Sch., 1982-84; dir. law libr. Valparaiso (Ind.) U., 1984-87, law libr., assoc. prof. law, 1987—. Editor Journal of Legislation, 1981-82; mng. editor Third World Legal Studies, 1986—. V.p. Ind. Coop. Libr. Svcs. Auth., 1997-98, pres., 1998-99. Mem. ABA, Ind. State Bar Assn., Am. Assn. Law Librs. Ohio Regional Assn. Law Librs. (pres. 1990-91), Ind. State Quilt Guild (pres. 1996-2000). Roman Catholic. Home: 1308 Tuckahoe Park Dr Valparaiso IN 46383-4032 Office: Valparaiso U Law Libr Sch Law Valparaiso IN 46383 E-mail: mary.persyn@valpo.edu.

PERTHOU, ALISON CHANDLER, interior designer; b. Bremerton, Wash., July 22, 1945; d. Benson and Elizabeth (Holdsworth) Chandler; m. A.V. Perthou III, Sept. 9, 1967 (div. Dec. 1977); children: Peter T.R., Stewart A.C. BFA, Cornish Coll. Arts, 1972. Pres. Alison Perthou Interior Design, Seattle, 1972—, Optima Design, Inc., Seattle, 1986-89; treas. Framejoist Corp., Bellevue, Wash., 1973-90; pres. Classics: Interiors & Antiques, Inc., 1988—. Cons. bldg. and interiors com. Children's Hosp., Seattle, 1976—; guest lectr. U. Wash., Seattle, 1980-81. Mem. bd. trustees Cornish Coll. Arts, Seattle, 1973-80, sec. exec. com., 1975-77; mem. procurement com. Patrons of N.W. Cultural and Charitable Orgn., 1985—, mem. antiques com., 1991—. Mem.: Am. Soc. Interior Design, Sunset Club, Seattle Tennis Club (mem. house and grounds com. 1974—75). Office: 563 Lake Washington Blvd E Seattle WA 98112-4226 Fax: 206-322-2335.

PERVALL, STEPHANIE JOY, management consultant; b. San Antonio, Sept. 10, 1963; d. Jessie Elizabeth and Joseph Henry Frank Pervall. Student, Lehigh U., Bethlehem, Pa., 1981—85. Software engr. RCA Missile and Surface Radar, Moorestown, NJ, 1985—88; systems analyst AT&T Chief Fin. Orgn., Piscataway, NJ, systems devel. and support mgr. Basking Ridge, NJ, 1992—96; campus presence mgr. AT&T Chief Fin. Orgn. - Recruiting, 1994—2000; project mgr. AT&T Chief Fin. Orgn., 1996—97; contract writer AT&T Bus. Svcs., Bridgewater, NJ, 1997—2000; ops. mgr. AT&T Bus. Sales, Phila., 2000—01; sr. tech. staff mem. AT&T Consumer Svcs., Somerset, NJ, 2001—02; bus. analyst - contract specialist Chief Process Officer Orgn., Bridgewater, NJ, 2002—. Elder Willingboro Presbyn. Ch., choir dir. Mem.: Lehigh U. Alumni Assn. (bd. dirs.). Presbyterian.

PESCH, ELLEN P. lawyer; BA, Barat Coll., 1986; JD, John Marshall Law Sch., 1989; LLM, DePaul U., 1991. Bar: Ill. 1989, U.S. Dist. Ct. (no. dist.) Ill. With Sidley Austin Brown & Wood, Chgo., 1989—, ptnr., 2001—. Mem.: ABA, Internat. Swaps and Derivatives Assn., Stable Value Investment Assn. Office: Sidley Austin Brown and Wood Bank One Plz 10 S Dearborn St Chicago IL 60603*

PESCOSOLIDO, PAMELA JANE, arts and craft supply store owner, graphic designer; b. Chgo., Dec. 28, 1960; d. Carl Albert Jr. and Linda Clark (Austin) P.; m. Larry Carl Vangroningen, Mar. 5, 1994 (div.); 1 child, Harley Austin. BA, Scripps Coll., 1983; JD, Vt. Law Sch., 1990. Bar: Maine 1990. Office mgr., asst. chef The Elegant Picnic, Stockbridge, Mass., 1983; receptionist, sec. Sequoia Orange County, Exeter, Calif., 1983-84; A/R clk. Tropicana Energy Co., Euless, Tex., 1984-85; owner, calligrapher Calligraphic Arts, Great Barrington, Mass., 1986-87; legal intern Pine Tree Legal Assistance, Augusta, Maine, 1989, Office of the Juvenile Defender, Montpelier, Vt., 1990; bookkeeper Badger Farming Co., Exeter, 1991—; owner, legal drafter and researcher Legal Rsch. Svc., Visalia, Calif., 1990—; owner, graphic designer Hourglass Prodns., Visalia, 1995—; owner, mgr. The Angel Within, Artists, Supplies and Gallery, Exeter, Calif. Rsch. editor Vt. Law Rev., Vt. Law Sch., South Royalton, 1989-90. Designer, graphic artist polit. propaganda for Libertarian Party of Calif.; contbr. poetry to Nat. Coll. Poetry Rev. Mem. county cen. com., chair Valley Libertarians, Libertarian Party of Calif., Visalia, 1996—; candidate Libertarian Party Dist. 19, Calif. U.S. Congress, 1996; candidate Libertarian Party Calif. State Contr., 1998. Chase scholar Vt. Law Sch., 1989. Mem. ACLU, AAUW (newsletter editor 1994-96), ABA, Nature Conservancy. Avocation: artistic endeavors of all kinds. Office: The Angel Within LLC 137 North E St Exeter CA 93221-1728

PESICKA, HARLENE NEAVE, mental health services professional; b. Aberdeen, SD, July 27, 1937; d. Harlan Michael and Margaret Marie (Hatzenbeller) Loye; m. William John Pesicka, Dec. 23, 1956; children: William Michael, Sandra Sue, Charlene Marie, Dennis John. BS, No. State U., 1992, MS in Edn. (Counselling and Guidance), 1997. Lic. profl. mental health counselor. Clk. J.J. Newberry, Aberdeen, 1955-56, IHS, Aberdeen, 1957-58, staff asst. Office of Environ. Health Indian Health Svc., Aberdeen, 1958-90; exec. dir. battered women shelter Resource Ctr. for Women, Aberdeen, 1990-92; exec. dir. S.D. Coalition Against Domestic Violence and Sexual Assault, Aberdeen, 1992-95; edn. aide May Overby Sch., Aberdeen, 1996; grad. asst. dept. psychology No. State U., Aberdeen, 1997; therapist, case mgr. Northeastern Mental Health Ctr., Aberdeen, 1997—. Bd. dirs. Resource Ctr. for Women; founding mother Aberdeen Area Rape Task Force, 1976, advocate, spkr., 1977—; bd. dirs. S.D. Peace and Justice, v.p., 1996, pres., 1997, 98; mem. S.D. Advocacy Network for Women, 1984—, pres., 1987; mem. various coms. and bd. dirs., Brown County United Way, chmn. bd., 1980; den mother Boy Scouts Am., also instnl. rep.; mem. S.D. NOW, 1974—, state coord., 1980-90; mgr. Fed. Women's Program Com., nat. EEO counselor, 1975-76; vol. mem. 4-person team on sexism and racism Am. Luth. Ch., N.E. S.D. Dist., 1978-80 Named S.D. Vol. of Yr., 1983, Nat. Vol. of the Yr., Dept. Health and Human Svcs., 1983; recipient award U.S. Dept. Justice, 1992, Athena award Aberdeen C. of C., 1997. Mem.: AAUW, Am. Coll. Cert. Forensic Counselors (diplomate clin. forensic counseling), Pi Gamma Mu, Phi Beta Kappa. Democrat. Home: 13529 386th Ave Aberdeen SD 57401-8754 Office: Northeastern Mental Health Ctr PO Box 550 Aberdeen SD 57402-0550

PESIN, ELLA MICHELE, journalist, public relations professional; b. North Bergen, N.J., Aug. 29, 1956; d. Edward and Helene Sylvia (Rattner) P. BA, Sarah Lawrence Coll., 1978. Press rep. CBS-TV News and Entertainment, N.Y.C., 1978-80; publicist Newsweek Mag., N.Y.C., 1980-81; freelance journalist N.Y.C., 1982-85; publicist Universal Studios MCA Inc., L.A., 1982-83; with publicity and mktg. NBC-TV News, N.Y.C., 1985-86; media exec. Burson Marsteller Pub. Rels., N.Y.C., 1986-87; prin. Pesin Pub. Rels., 1987—. Contbg. editor Cable Age mag., TV Radio Age mag., Advt. Forum, Facts Figures & Film, Advt. Compliance Svc.; syndicated newspaper columnist. Active Israel Bonds/United Jewish Appeal, N.Y.C., Rudolph Giuliani for N.Y.C. Mayor campaign. Mem. Pub. Rels. Soc. Am., Women in Comm., Publicity Club N.Y., Healthcare Pub. Rels. and Mktg. Soc. Avocations: photography, sculpture, modern dance, tennis, skiing. Home and Office: 303 E 83rd St Apt 27J New York NY 10028-4323 E-mail: eem75p@aol.com.

PESNER, CAROLE MANISHIN, art gallery owner; b. Boston, Aug. 5, 1937; m. Robert Pesner (dec. 1983); children: Ben, Jonah; m. Martin Cherkasky, 1995 (dec. 1997). BA, Smith Coll., 1959. Asst. dir. Kraushaar Galleries, Inc., N.Y.C., 1959-86, dir., 1986-90, pres., 1991—. Author, editor publs., catalogues in field. Mem. Art Dealers Assn. Am., Internat. Fine Print Dealers Assn. Office: Kraushaar Galleries Inc 724 5th Ave New York NY 10019-4106

PESTERFIELD, LINDA CAROL, retired school administrator, educator; b. Pauls Valley, Okla., May 3, 1939; d. D.J. and Geneva Lewis (Sheegog) Butler; m. W.C. Peterfield, Aug. 30, 1958; children: Ginger Carol, Walt James, Jason Kent. Student, E. Cen. State U., Ada, Okla., 1957, 76, 79; BS, Okla. State U., 1961; postgrad., Ottawa U., Ottawa, Kans., 1970, Okla. U., 1979. Tchr. Sumner Elem. Sch., Perry, Okla., 1961-62; tchr. Whitebead D-16, Pauls Valley, Okla., 1964-65, Cen. Heights Unified, Ottawa, Kans., 1969-71; prin., tchr. Whitebead D-16, Pauls Valley, 1975-91; adminstrv. asst., curriculum dir. Pauls Valley Sch., P.V., 1991—2003; ret., 2003. Mem. profl. standard bd. State Dept. Edn., Okla., 1988—; presenter in field. Bd. dirs. Positively Pauls Valley, 1987-97; county chmn. Nat. and Okla. 4-H Fund Drive, Garvin County, Okla., 1987-88; mem. organizational com. C-CAP-Child Abuse Prevention Orgn., Pauls Valley, 1987—; mem. vision 2000 com. Garvin County Assn. Svcs. Named to Gov.'s Honor Roll Recognition and Appreciation for Community Activities, Pauls Valley, Okla., 1985-86; named Pauls Valley Citizen of Yr., 1996; Paul Harris fellow, 1997. Mem. Cooperative Coun. Okla. Sch. Adminstrn., Whitebead Ednl. Assn., Okla. Orgn. Dependent Sch., Okla. Assn. Elem. Sch. Prins., AAUW, All Sports Club (v.p. 1984-89, pres. 1985, 90), Okla. Heritage Assn., Pauls Valley Hist. Soc., Pauls Valley C. of C. (pres. 1997, pres. exec. bd. dirs. 1998—), State Found. for Acad. Excellence Forum Com., Rotary (bd. dirs. 1993-96, 1999-2001, 2003—), Pauls Valley Gen. Hosp. Bd., Delta Kappa Gamma (past local auditor, parliamentarian, v.p., pres. 1979-96), Phi Delta Kappa. Democrat. Mem. Ch. of Christ. Home: RR 3 Box 306 Pauls Valley OK 73075-9232 E-mail: wlpest@itlnet.net.

PETCHESKY, ROSALIND POLLACK, political scientist, educator, social sciences educator; b. Bay City, Tex., Aug. 16, 1942; BA, Smith Coll., 1964; MA, Columbia U., 1966, PhD, 1974. Prof. Hunter Coll. CUNY. Author: The Individual's Rights and the International Organization, 1966, Abortion and Women's Choice: The State, Sexuality and Reproductive Freedom, 1984 (Joan Kelly Meml. prize Am. Hist. Assn., 1984), Abortion and Women's Choice: The State, Sexualoty and Reproductive Freedom, 2d edit., 1990; co-editor: Negotiating Reproductive Rights: Women's Perspectives Across Countries and Cultures, 1998. Founder Internat. Reproductive Rights Rsch. Action Group. Fellow, MacArthur Found., 1995. Office: CUNY Hunter Coll Dept Polit Sci 695 Park Ave New York NY 10021-5024 E-mail: rpetches@igc.org.

PETERA, ANNE PAPPAS, state official; b. Richmond, Va., Feb. 13, 1950; d. Evangel Thomas and Margaret Theresa (McGuire) Pappas; m. Ronald Petera, Sept. 15, 1968; 1 child, Paul Evangel. BS, Va. Commonwealth U., 1980; grad., Realtors Inst. Br. officer Ctrl. Fidelity Bank, Richmond, 1972-79; asst. v.p. Signet Bank, Richmond, 1979-85; sales assoc. Hermitage Realty, Richmond, 1985-92; assoc. broker Napier Old Colony, Richmond, 1992-95, Bowers, Nelms & Fonville & Jefferson-Jones, Richmond, 1995-96; chair Va. Dept. Alcoholic Beverage Control, 1996-97; sec. Commonwealth of Va., 1998—2002; chief of staff to Atty. Gen. of Va., 2002—. Mem. faculty Richmond Assn. Realtors Sch. Real Estate, 1991-96; bd. visitors Va. Commonwealth U., 2001—, vice rector, 2003—. Vice-chmn. Hanover (Va.) County Rep. Com., 1990-92, chmn., 1992-94; chmn. 1st Congl. Dist., Rep. Party Va., Richmond, 1994-98, budget dir., 1996-98, treas. 1998-2001; mem. Rep. Nat. Com., 2001—. Named Disting. Achiever, Richmond Assn. Realtors, 1986, 87, 89, 90, 91, 92, 93, 94. Mem. Nat. Alcohol Beverage Control Assn. (dir. 1996-98), Nat. Assn. Realtors, Nat. Assn. Bank Women. Republican. Roman Catholic. Avocations: golf, reading, travel. Office: Office of the Atty Gen 900 E Main St Richmond VA 23219-2725 also: Old Finance Bldg PO Box 2454 Richmond VA 23218-2454 E-mail: annepetera@aol.com.*

PETERMAN, DONNA COLE, communications executive; b. St. Louis, Nov. 9, 1947; d. William H. Cole and Helen A. Morris; m. John A. Peterman, Feb. 7, 1970. BA in Journalism, U. Mo., 1969; MBA, U. Chgo., 1984. Mgr. employee comm. Sears Merchandise Group, Chgo., 1975-80; affairs and mktg. comm. Seraco Real Estate, Chgo., 1980-82; dir. corp. comm. Sears, Roebuck and Co., Chgo., 1982-85; sr. v.p., dir. corp. comm. Dean Witter Fin. Svcs. Group, N.Y., 1985-88; sr. v.p., mng. dir. Hill and Knowlton, Inc., Chgo., 1988-94, exec. v.p. N.Y.C., 1994-96; sr. v.p., dir. corp. comm. Paine Webber Group, Inc., N.Y.C., 1996-2000; mng. dir., regional head comms. and mktg. The Americas, UBS Americas Inc., 2000—03; sr. v.p., dir. corp. comm. PNC Fin. Svcs. Group Inc. Pitts., 2003—. Media chair DeKalb County Comm., Ga., 1975; media dir., Mo. Atty. Gen., 1971, Rep. Govs. Conf., 1974; copywriter Govt. of Mo., 1971. Trustee Securities Industry Found. for Econ. Edn. Mem. Internat. Assn. Bus. Communicators, Pub. Rels. Soc. Am., Univ. Club, Women Execs. in Pub. Rels., Arthur Page Soc., Pub. Rels. Seminar, The Wise Men. Republican. Roman Catholic. Avocations: tennis, golf, sailing, skiing, bridge. Office: The PNC Fin Svcs Group Inc 1 PNC Plaza 249 5th Ave Pittsburgh PA 15222-2707

PETERS, AULANA LOUISE, lawyer, former government agency commissioner; b. Shreveport, La., Nov. 30, 1941; d. Clyde A. and Eula Mae (Faulkner) Pharis; m. Bruce F. Peters, Oct. 6, 1967. BA in Philosophy, Coll. New Rochelle, 1963; JD, U. So. Calif., 1973. Bar: Calif., 1974. Sec., English corr. Publimondial, Spa, Milan, Italy, 1963-64, Fibramianto, Spa, Milan, 1964-65, Turkish del. to Office for Econ. Cooperation & Devel., Paris, 1965-66; adminstrv. asst. Office for Econ. Cooperation & Devel., Paris, 1966-67; assoc. Gibson, Dunn & Crutcher, L.A., 1973-80, ptnr., 1980-84, 88—; commr. SEC, Washington, 1984-88. Bd. dirs. 3M Corp., Merrill Lynch & Co., Mobil Corp., Northrop Grumman, Callaway Golf Co. Recipient Disting. Alumnus award Econs. Club So. Calif., 1984, Washington Achiever award Nat. Assn. Bank Women, 1986, Critics Choice award nat. Women's Econ. Alliance, 1994, Women in Bus. award Hollywood C. of C., 1995. Mem. ABA, State Bar of Calif. (civil litigation cons. group 1983-84), Los Angeles County Bar Assn., Black Women Lawyers Assn. L.A., Assn. Bus. Trial Lawyers (panelist L.A. 1982), Women's Forum, Washington. Office: Gibson Dunn & Crutcher 333 S Grand Ave Ste 4400 Los Angeles CA 90071-3197

PETERS, BARB WATERMAN, artist, educator; b. Topeka, Nov. 3, 1944; d. L.E. Clifton Bailey and Gertrude Minnie McFarland; m. John Herman Waterman, Dec. 21, 1965 (div. Dec. 1985); m. Larry Dean Peters, May 30, 1986. BFA, Washburn U., 1973; MFA, Kans. State U., 1998. Adj. instr. Washburn U., Topeka, 1985-88, adj. asst. prof., 1989—96, 1999—2001; grad. tchg. asst. Kans. State U., Manhattan, 1997-98. Mus. specialist ednl. svcs. Mulvane Art Mus., Topeka, 1987; faculty advisor Washburn Art Students Assn., Topeka, 1994-96; guest curator Water Marks exhbn. Mulvane Art Mus., Topeka, 1995-96; exhbn. juror in field; spkr., reviewer in field. One-woman shows include Bedyk Gallery, Kansas City, Mo., 1983, 88, Collective Art Gallery, Topeka, 1988-90, 96-97, 1999-2000, 2002-2004, Yost Gallery-Highland (Kans.) C.C., 1989, 95, Art Craft Gallery, Denver, 1994-95, 97, Fourth St. Gallery, Kansas City, 1997, Michael Cross Gallery, Kansas City, 1999-2000, Wichita Ctr. Arts, 2001, Kanas Artist Gallery, Mulvane Art Mus., 2002; group shows include Holman Art Gallery-Trenton State Coll., 1979, N.Mex. Art League, Albuquerque, 1980, Nat. Soc. Painters, N.Y., 1980 (Michael Engle Meml. award), Ball State U. Art Gallery, Muncie, Ind., 1981, Portsmouth (Va.) Cmty. Ctr., 1982, Nelson-Atkins Mus., Kansas City, 1982, Owensboro (Ky.) Mus. Fine Art, 1982 (award), Joslyn Art Mus., Omaha, 1988, others, Women's Conf., Beijing, 1995, Jan Weiner Gallery, Kansas City, 1995, The Columbian Art Gallery, Wamego, Kans., 1997, 2002, Topeka and Shawnee County Pub. Libr., 1997, 2002, Strecker Gallery, Manhattan, Kans., 1999-2000, Cedar Rapids (Iowa) Mus. Art, 1997, Wichita Ctr. for the Arts, 2000, 02, Birger Sandzen Gallery, Lindsborg, Kans., 2001, U. Kans. Art and Design Gallery, 2002, Strecker-Nelson Gallery, Manhattan, Kans., 2002, Mulvane Art Mus., Topeka, 2003, Emporia Art Ctr., Kans., 2003, Gallery of Framewoods, Topeka, 2004; visual artist Andrew J. and Georgia Neese Gray Theatre, Washburn U., 1999--; contbr. articles to profl. jours. Vol. art gallery Topeka and Shawnee County Pub. Libr., 1986—; panelist Kans. Arts Commn., Kans. Presswomen, 1990—; bd. dirs. Arts Coun. Topeka, 2002-04, Raymer Soc., 2004—; mem. ad hoc com. Kans. Arts Commn., 2002-04, mem. fellowship selection panel, 2004; mem. ad. hoc com. Topeka Cmty. Found., 2002-03. Recipient Outstanding Achievement award, Am. Inst. Banking, Topeka, 1977, assistantship in lithography, Kans. Arts Commn., 1981, Woman of Distinction in the Arts award, Kaw Valley Girl Scouts, Topeka, 1996, Artist's Residency award, The Raymer Soc., 2001—04, Cert. of Recognition Outstanding Contributions, State Kans., 2003. Mem. Nat. Mus. Women in the Arts, Chgo. Artists' Coalition, Kansas City Artists Coalition, St. Louis Artists Guild, Mulvane Art Mus., Lawrence Art Ctr., Libr. Friends of Art Topeka and Shawnee County Pub. Libr., The Collective (charter, treas. 1987-89, v.p. 1990-94, 99-00, pres. 2001-04, newsletter editor 2000—), Friends of Art Bd. Beach Mus. Art (collections com. 1997—), Kans. Citizens for Arts, Kans. Author's Club, Raymer Soc. (bd. dirs.), Assn. Cmty. Arts Agencies of Kansas, Manhattan Arts Ctr. Avocations: reading, writing, travel. Home: 2223 SW Knollwood Dr Topeka KS 66611-1623 E-mail: barbara.r.peters@att.net.

PETERS, BERNADETTE (BERNADETTE LAZZARA), actress; b. Queens, N.Y., Feb. 28, 1948; d. Peter and Marguerite (Maltese) Lazzara. Student, Quintano Sch. for Young Profls., N.Y.C. Ind. actress, entertainer, 1957—. Appeared on TV series All's Fair, 1976-77; frequent guest appearances on TV; (films) The Longest Yard, 1974, Silent Movie, 1976, Vigilant Force, 1976, W.C. Fields and Me, 1976, Silent Movie, 1976, The Jerk, 1979, Heartbeeps, 1981, Tulips, 1981, Pennies from Heaven, 1981 (Golden Globe award best actress), Annie, 1982, Slaves of New York, 1989, Pink Cadillac, 1989, Impromptu, 1991, Alice, 1990, Anastasia (voice), 1997, Cinderella, 1997, Snow Days, 1999, Prince Charming, 2001, Bobbie's Girl, 2002, A Few Good Years, 2002, It Runs in the Family, 2003; (TV movies) Cinderella, ABC-TV, 1997, Holiday in Your Heart, 1997; (stage appearances) This is Google, 1957, The Most Happy Fella, 1959, Gypsy, 1961, Curly McDimple, 1967, Johnny No-Trump, 1967, George M!, 1968 (Theatre World award, 1968), Dames at Sea, 1968 (Drama Desk award, 1968), La Strada, 1969, On the Town, 1971, Tartuffe, 1972, Mack and Mabel, 1974, Sally and Marsha, 1982, Sunday in the Park with George, 1983-85 (Tony nom., 1983), Song and Dance, 1985-86 (Drama League award best actress, 1985, Tony award best actress, 1986, Drama Desk award best actress, 1986), Into the Woods, 1987, The Goodbye Girl, 1992-93, Annie Get Your Gun 1998-1999 (Tony award best actress, 1999, Outer Critics Circle award best actress, 1999, Drama Desk award best actress, 1999), Gypsy, 2003-; TV mini-series The Odyssey, 1997; rec. artist: (MCA Records) Bernadette Peters, 1980, Now Playing, 1981; CD's include I'll Be Your Baby Tonight, Angel Records, 1996 (Grammy nomination), Sondheim Etc: Bernadette Peters Live at Carnegie Hall, Angel Records, 1997 (Grammy nom.), solo concert Radio City Music Hall, 2002. Recipient Hasty Pudding Theatrical award, 1987 Woman of Yr. award, Sara Siddons Actress of Yr. award, 1993-94, Actors Fund medal for artistic achievement, 1999; named Woman of Yr., Police Athletic League, 1999; named to Theatre Hall of Fame. Office: William Morris Agency c/o Jeff Hunter 1325 Ave of the Americas 15th Fl New York NY 10019*

PETERS, BRENDA IRENE, computer specialist, government official; b. Bethesda, Md., Feb. 2, 1952; d. William Elbert and Helen Gertrude (Monroe) P.; m. James Wayne Bradley, Dec. 21, 1972 (div. May 1976). AA in Computer Sci., Bus., Montgomery Coll., 1972. Clk.-typist NIH, Bethesda, Md., 1972, HEW, Rockville, Md., 1972; card punch operator Pope AFB, Fayetteville, N.C., 1973-74, David Taylor R & D Ctr., Bethesda, Md., 1974-75, computer operator, 1975-77; computer programmer, analyst Carderock div. Naval Surface Warfare Ctr., Bethesda, 1977-86, computer specialist, 1986—, acting dep. br. head bus. sys., 1997—98. Cons. Kengla Flag Co., Washington, 1988-95, Mt. Airy (Md.) Vol. Fire Co., 1995. Sunday sch. tchr. Germantown (Md.) Bapt. Ch., 1981-2003, asst. pianist, chmn. mission outreach, rec. sec., 1989-2003; children's choir dir. Germantown (Md.) Bapt. Ch., 2000-03. Bd. trustees grantee Montgomery Coll., Rockville, Md., 1970-72. Avocations: sewing, cross-stitch, piano, quilting. Office: Naval Surface Warfare Ctr 9500 Macarthur Blvd Bethesda MD 20817-5700

PETERS, CAROL ANN DUDYCHA, counselor; b. Ripon, Wis., Dec. 23, 1938; d. George John and Martha (Malek) Dudycha; m. Milton Eugene Peters, Aug. 27, 1960. AB, Wittenberg U., 1960, MEd, 1963; leadership devel. cert., Ctr. for Creative Leadership, Greensboro, N.C., 1986; postgrad., U. Toledo, 1973-97, U. Findlay, 1997-99. Lic. profl. counselor, Ohio;

nat. cert. counselor, nat. cert. career counselor Nat. Bd. Cert. Counselors, Inc.; cert. basic critical incident stress mgmt. Internat. Critical Incident Stress Found., 1999. Tchr. Springfield (Ohio) City Schs., 1960-62, Mad River-Green Local Schs., Springfield, 1962-63; counselor Napoleon (Ohio) Area Schs., 1963-70, Findlay City Sch., Ohio, 1970-2000; field counselor Career Relocation Corp. Am., Armonk, 1992-95, 98-99; sr. lectr. U. Findlay, 1999—2002. Cons., prin. Peters and Peters, Findlay, 1979—; leader Creative Edn. Found., Buffalo, 1980-91, colleague, Hadley, Mass., 1985—; founder ednl. corp. Career Info. Bur. Hancock County, 1974. Pres. Big Bros./Big Sisters Hancock County, 1982-83; bd. dirs. Citizens Opposing Drug Abuse (C.O.D.A.), Findlay, 1982—; advisor, leader Hancock Addictions Prevention for Youth (H.A.P.P.Y.), 1985-91; mem. Hancock County Community Devel. Found. Edn. Com., 1990-93, Findlay/Hancock County Am. 2000 New Sch. Design Team, 1991-92; mem. Hancock County Crisis Response Team, 1991-97, 99—; mem. assets/needs assessment com. United Way, 1997-98; mem. Findlay Juvenile Diversion Task Force, 1997-98 Named One of Outstanding Young Women of Am., 1967; named Outstanding Woman in Edn., Bus. and Profl. Women, 1983; recipient Outstanding Citizenship award The Lincoln Ctr., Findlay, 1989, Meritorious Svc. award Big Bros./Big Sisters Hancock County, 1988. Mem. ACA, AAUW (Findlay br.), NEA (life), Nat. Career Devel. Assn., Ohio Ret. Tchrs. Assn. (life), Ohio Counseling Assn., Findlay-Hancock County C. of C. (sec. edn. com. 1984-90), Ohio Career Devel. Assn. Lutheran. Avocations: sailing, flower arranging, cooking.

PETERS, CAROL BEATTIE TAYLOR (MRS. FRANK ALBERT PETERS), mathematician; b. Washington, May 10, 1932; d. Edwin Lucius and Lois (Beattie) Taylor; B.S., U. Md., 1954, M.A., 1958; m. Frank Albert Peters, Feb. 26, 1955; children— Thomas, June, Erick, Victor. Group mgr. Tech. Operations, Inc., Arlington, Va., 1957-62, sr. staff scientist, 1964-66; supervisory analyst Datatrol Corp., Silver Spring, Md., 1962; project dir. Computer Concept, Inc., Silver Spring, 1963-64; mem. tech. staff, then mem. sr. staff Informatics Inc., Bethesda, Md., 1966-70, mgr. systems projects, 1970-71, tech. dir., 1971-76; sr. tech. dir. Ocean Data Systems, Inc., Rockville, Md., 1976-83; dir. Informatics Gen. Co., 1983-89; pres. Carol Peters Assocs., 1989—. Home and Office: 12311 Glen Mill Rd Potomac MD 20854-1928 E-mail: cbpeters@msn.com.

PETERS, CRYSTAL HARRINGTON, music educator, consultant; b. Cynthiana, Ky., Aug. 29, 1971; d. Gary Lynn and Beverly Mattox Harrington; m. Ryan Michael Peters, June 29, 1996. MusB, U. S.C., 1993. Cert. early & middle childhood music Nat. Bd. for Profl. Tchg. Stds., Va., 2002. Music tchr. Cobb County Schools, Marietta, Ga., 1996—; ind. arts cons. the GRAMMY Found., Santa Monica, Calif., 2001—. Presenter in field. Active Cobb Wind Symphony. Recipient Tchr. of the Yr. award, Harmony Leland Elem. Sch., Mableton, Ga., 2000—01; music scholar, U. S.C., 1989—93. Mem.: Ga. Music Educator's Assn. (assoc.), Music Educator's Nat. Conf. (assoc.), Delta Omicron (life; second v.p. 1991—93), Tau Beta Sigma (life). Home: 5175 Willow Tarn Acworth GA 30102 Office: Harmony Leland Elem Sch 5891 Dodgen Rd Mableton GA 30126 Personal E-mail: crystalpeters@comcast.net.

PETERS, ELEANOR WHITE, retired mental health nurse; b. Highland Park, Mich., Aug. 11, 1920; d. Alfred Mortimer and Jane Ann (Evans) White; m. William J. Peters, 1947 (div. 1953); children: Susannah J., William J. (dec.). BA, Jersey City State Coll., 1968; postgrad., U. Del., 1969-70; MS, SUNY, New Paltz, 1983. RN, N.J., N.Y. Staff various hosps., N.J., 1941-58; indsl. nurse Abex, Mahwah, N.J., 1958-68; nurse Liberty (N.Y.) Ctrl. Sch., 1971-76; coord. practical nurse program Hudson County C.C., Jersey City, 1979-80; cmty. mental health nurse Letchworth Village, Thiells, N.Y., 1981-96; ret., 1996. Historian, Bishop House Found., Saddle River, N.J. Mem. AAUW (pres. Liberty-Monticello br. 1988-92), Am. Sch. Health Assn., Alpha Delta Kappa (sec. Mu chpt. 1973-75), Sigma Theta Tau (Kappa Eta chpt.). Republican. Lutheran. Avocations: antiques, history, traveling, education of children. Home: PO Box 224 Saddle River NJ 07458-0224

PETERS, ELIZABETH, media organization director; Degree in film, U. Tex. Dir. Austin (Tex.) Film Soc., 1995—98; exec. dir. Assn. Ind. Video and Filmmakers, Inc., N.Y.C., 1999—; pub. The Ind. Film & Video Monthly, 1999—. Tchr. prodn. classes. Prodr., dir. Women's Action Coalition, asst. editor (documentary) The Maine Coast, (feature film) Office Space. Office: Assn Ind Video & Filmmakers Inc 304 Hudson St 6th Fl N New York NY 10013 Business E-Mail: elizabeth@aivf.org.*

PETERS, ELIZABETH ANN HAMPTON, retired nursing educator; b. Detroit, Sept. 27, 1934; d. Grinsfield Taylor and Ida Victoria (Jones) Hampton; m. James Marvin Peters, Dec. 1, 1956; children: Douglas Taylor, Sara Elizabeth. Diploma, Berea Coll. Hosp. Sch. Nursing, 1956; BSN, Wright State U., Dayton, Ohio, 1975; MSN, Ohio State U., Columbus, 1978. Therapist, nurse Eastway, Inc., Dayton, Ohio, 1979-81; therapist, family counseling svc. Good Samaritan-Cmty. Mental Health Ctr., Dayton, Ohio, 1981-83; instr. Wright State U. Sch. Nursing, Dayton, 1983-84; clin. nurse specialist, pain mgmt. program UPSA, Inc., Dayton, 1983-86; staff nurse Hospice of Dayton, Inc., 1985-86, dir. vol. svcs., 1986-89, dir. bereavement svcs., 1986-87; asst. prof. Cmty. Hosp. Sch. Nursing, Springfield, Ohio, 1990-93, prof., 1993-97; ret., 1997; parish nurse Honey Creek Presbyn. Ch., 1998—2003. Co-author (with others): Oncologic Pain, 1987. Mem. Clark County Mental Health Bd., Springfield, 1986-95; mem. New Carlisle (Ohio) Bd. Health, 1990-2003. Mem.: Sigma Theta Tau. Home: 402 Flora Ave New Carlisle OH 45344-1329

PETERS, ELLEN ASH, judge, retired Supreme Court chief justice; b. Berlin, Mar. 21, 1930; came to U.S., 1939, naturalized, 1947; d. Ernest Edward and Hildegard (Simon) Ash; m. Phillip I. Blumberg; children: David Bryan Peters, James Douglas Peters, Julie Haden Dreisch. BA with honors, Swarthmore Coll., 1951, LLD (hon.), 1983; LLB cum laude, Yale U., 1954, MA (hon.), 1964, LLD (hon.), 1985, U. Hartford, 1983; LLD (hon.), Georgetown U., 1984; LLD (hon.), Yale U., 1985, Conn. Coll., 1985, N.Y. Law Sch., 1985; HLD (hon.), St. Joseph Coll., 1986; LLD (hon.), Colgate U., 1986, Trinity Coll., 1987, Bates Coll., 1987, Wesleyan U., 1987, DePaul U., 1988; HLD (hon.), Albertus Magnus Coll., 1990; LLD (hon.), U. Conn., 1992; LLD, U. Rochester, 1994, Detroit Mercy Coll. Law, 2001. Bar: Conn. 1957. Law clk. to judge U.S. Circuit Ct., 1954-55; assoc. in law U. Calif., Berkeley, 1955-56; prof. law Yale U., New Haven, 1956-78, adj. prof. law, 1978-84; assoc. justice Conn. Supreme Ct., Hartford, 1978-84, chief justice, 1984-96; judge trial referee Superior Ct., Hartford, 2000—. Author: Commercial Transactions: Cases, Texts, and Problems, 1971, Negotiable Instruments Primer, 1974; contbr. articles to profl. jours. Bd. dirs. Nat. Ctr. State Cts., 1992—96, chmn., 1994; bd. mgrs. Swarthmore Coll., 1970—81; trustee Yale-New Haven Hosp., 1981—86, Yale Corp., 1986—92; mem. conf. Chief Justices, 1984—, pres., 1994; hon. chmn. U.S. Constl. Bicentennial Com., 1986—91; mem. Conn. Permanent Commn. on Status of Women, 1973—74, Conn. Bd. Pardons, 1978—80, Conn. Law Revision Commn., 1978—84; bd. dirs. Hartford Found., 1997—. Recipient Ella Grasso award, 1982, Jud. award Conn. Trial Lawyers Assn., 1982, citation of merit Yale Law Sch., 1983, Pioneer Woman award Hartford Coll. for Women, 1988, Disting. Svc. award U. Conn. Law Sch. Alumni Assn., 1993, Raymond E. Baldwin Pub. Svc. award Quinnipiac Coll. Law Sch., 1995, Disting. Svc. award Conn. Law Tribune, 1996, Nat. Ctr. State Cts., 1996; named Laura A. Johnson Woman of Yr. Hartford Coll., 1996. Mem. ABA, Conn. Bar Assn. (Jud. award 1992, Spl. award 1996), Am. Law Inst. (coun.), Am. Acad. Arts and Scis., Am. Philos. Soc. Office: Superior Ct 95 Washington St Hartford CT 06106-4431 Fax: 860-548-2887. Office Phone: 860-548-2850.

PETERS, EVELYN JOAN, artist; b. Anchorage, Alaska, Mar. 25, 1927; d. Algernon Sidney Jones and R. Lee (Bartholf) Jones-Lange; m. Curtis Gordon Chezem, Sept. 29, 1945 (div. Oct. 1956); children: Joanne Lee Chezem, David Gordon Chezem; m. Frederick William Peters Jr., May 30, 1958. Student, U. Oreg., 1945-50, Oreg. State Coll., 1955-56. Pvt. sec. Pub. Svc. Commn., Las Vegas, Nev., 1957-58; tech. sec. Los Alamos (N.Mex.) Nat. Lab., 1958-70; sr. sec. EG&G, Los Alamos, 1970-71. Chmn. bd. dirs. Buchanan Arts and Crafts, Inc., Buchanan Dam, Tex., 1980, 86. One-woman shows include Frame Corner Gallery, Farmington, 1996, San Juan Coll., 1998, invitational retrospective St. Francis Newman Ctr., Silver City, N.Mex., 1994, exhibited in group shows at Inn of Loretto, Santa Fe, 1982, Capital Rotunda, Austin, Tex., 1983, Golub Gallery, Steamboat Springs, Colo., 1985, Cowtown Invitational, Ft. Worth, 1987, Safari Park Hotel, Nairobi, Kenya, 1990 (Artistic Expressions award, 1990, Gold medal, 1990), St. John's Coll., Cambridge, Eng., 1992 (Bronze medal, 1992), Western N.Mex. U., Silver City, 1993, Sixth Bear River Western Hist. Art Exhbn., Craig, Colo., 1994, Fed. Hall Mus., N.Y.C., 1994, 1997, Ann. COGAP Exhbn., Governor's Island, N.Y., 1994 (George Gray award, 1993), Apples, Aspen and Art, Cedaredge, Colo., 1995 (Most Popular Painting), Western and Wildlife Art Show, Estes Park, Colo., 1995, Sheraton-on-the-Park Hotel, Sydney, Australia, 1995, Colo. Indian Market, Denver, 1995, Art Concepts Gallery, Tacoma, Wash., 1997, Keble Coll., Oxford, Eng., 1997, Sunwest Bank, Farmington, 1997, Rotunda Canon Office Bldg., U.S. Ho. of Reps., Washington, 1997, Alpine Holiday, Ouray, Colo., 1997, 1999, 2000, Durham (Eng.) Art Gallery, Arts for the Parks, 2000, Represented in permanent collections Aviation Heritage Mus., Anchorage, Daystar Found., Oklahoma City, Eleanor Bliss Ctr. Arts, Steamboat Springs, Marble Falls Depot Mus., Mus. N.W. Colo., Craig, Nat. Gallery Rural Art, Bonner Springs, Kans., Pioneer and R.R. Mus., Temple, Tex., San Juan Coll., Farmington, N.Mex., USCG, art, numerous mags., books, calendars and catalogs. Pres. Highland Arts Guild, Marble Falls, Tex., 1977, 90, 2d v.p., 1989; sec. Highland Lakes Arts Coun., Marble Falls, 1986. Recipient Marine Safety award Olin-Matheson, 1968, cert. of appreciation USCG Aux., 1969, 70, 1st and purchase award Kiwanis Art Competition, Granbury, Tex., 1983, 2d Pl. award Tex. Women Western Artists Show, Cresson, Tex., 1983, 2d and 3d pl. awards Llano Rodeo Art Show, 1986, 1st pl. award 9th Nat. Small Painting Western Show, 1987, 1st and purchase award Gt. Am. Art Competition, 1988, Most Popular Painter award 3d Ann. Invitational Art Show, Waco, Tex., 1988, Best of Show award Bear Valley Hist. Art Show, Craig, 1989, Best of Show, 1st Watercolor, 1st Oil, 1st Sculpture, Highland Lakes Arts Competition, Kingsland, Tex., 1991, Internat. Woman of Yr. in art Internat. Biog. Ctr., 1991-92, Most Popular Painting award Western Colo. Ctr. for Arts, 1996, Purchase award NWNMAC, Farmington, 1997, Purchase award Ouray Coll. 39th Ann. Art Exhibit, 1999, choice award 8th Ann. Nat. Christian Art Show, San Juan Coll., Farmington, N.Mex., 2000, Top 200 Arts for the Parks, 2000, 1st pl. Gateway Regional Art Show, Farmington, N.Mex., 2000, Internat. Peace prize United Cultural Conf., 2003, numerous others. Mem. N.W. N.Mex. Arts Coun., signature mem. Nat. Acrylic Painters Assn. (bd. dirs. 2002—, invitation cover award 5th Internat. Open Exhibit 2000), ofcl. Coast Guard Artist, 1987—, Salmagundi Club, 1989-95, World Found. of Successful Women (charter mem.), Nat. Oil and Acrylic Painters Assn., Nat. Soc. Painters in Casein and Acrylic (assoc.), Am. Biog. Inst. Rsch. Assn. (life, dep. gov. 1989, Gold Cup 1993, Medal of Honor 1992, Woman of Yr. 1994, 95), World Inst. of Achievement (life, Excellence as Painter award 1988), N.W. N.Mex. Arts Coun. (acting exec. dir. 1998-2003, Internat. Peace prize United Cultural Conv. 2003). Avocations: gardening, photography, reading, travel. Studio: Evelyns Studio 1646 16th Ave SE Rio Rancho NM 87124 Office Phone: 505-892-2324. E-mail: petersart@sprynet.com.

PETERS, JACQUELINE MARY, secondary school educator; b. Milw., Oct. 6, 1947; d. Arnold Martin and Rosalie Ellen (Mulherin) Fladoos; divorced; children: Casey Martin, Ann Marie. Student, Clarke Coll., Dubuque, Iowa, 1965-67; BA, Calif. State U., Long Beach, 1970; MA in History and Tchg., LaVerne (Calif.) U., 1973. Reading tchr. Chaffey H.S., Ontario, Calif., 1971-78, tchr. phys. edn., 1976-78, English tchr., 1978-90, tchr. history, 1990—. Mentor AAUW, cmty. schs., 1997-99. State rep. Trans Nat. Golf Assn., 1963-75; bd. dirs. Cmty. Challenge Grants, Ontario, 1996-00. Named to Sports Hall of Fame, Dubuque Sr. H.S., 1996; Med-Cal grantee, 1996, Project Yes grantee, 1997-99. Mem. AAUW (bd. dirs., br. pres. 1995-99, Edn. Foun. Gift Honoree 1998), Calif. Tchrs. Assn. Republican. Roman Catholic. Avocations: golf, fly fishing, pysanka, poetry, bridge. Home: 320 W 21st St Upland CA 91784-1413 Office: Chaffey HS 1245 N Euclid Ave Ontario CA 91762-1923

PETERS, JANICE C. cable company executive; b. Harlan, Ky., Apr. 23, 1951; m. Mike Peters; 2 children. BS, Wayne State U., 1972; MBA in Mgmt., Stanford U., 1989. Customer svc. rep. Mich. Bell, 1973-78; with AT&T Corp., Chgo., 1978-85, U.S. West, Denver, Seattle, London, from 1985, MediaOne, Englewood, Colo., CEO, pres., 1997—. Bd. dirs. Primus. Office: c/o MediaOne 188 Inverness Dr W Englewood CO 80112

PETERS, JEAN THERESA, sales executive; b. Boulder, Colo., July 22, 1944; d. Barney Clifford and Frances Kathrine (Tholen) Neff; m. Ford Gordon Peters, Jr., Jan. 29, 1982; 1 child, Christopher Samuel. Student, U. Colo., 1962-63; lic., Brown Radio-TV Sch., 1975. Reception clk. first aide and water safety dept. Denver chpt. ARC, 1960-62; reception clk. Takcom Jewelry, N.Y.C., 1963-64; mem. promotion staff Calla Records, N.Y.C., 1965-67; detail sales rep. Alright Med. Labs., N.Y.C., and R.I., 1971-74; engr., tech. dir. WTNH-TV, New Haven, 1975-76, KWGN-TV, Denver, 1976-79; engr. KBTV (name now KUSA-TV), Denver, 1976; adminstrv. asst., v.p. sales broadcast equipment G.P. Enterprises, Inc., Port Aransas, Tex., 1980—, pres., 2000—. Mem. Bowie HS PTSA, Arlington, 1991—. Mem.: Soc. Motion Pictures and TV Engrs., Wilderness Soc., Humane Soc., World Wildlife Fund, Port Aransas Garden Club (2d v.p. 2001—, pres. 2002—), Arlington Herb and Garden Club. Avocations: gardening, wildlife and animals, reading, theater, travel. Office: G P Enterprises Inc PO Box 626 Port Aransas TX 78373-0626

PETERS, JUDITH GRIESSEL, foreign language educator; b. Albany, N.Y., Sept. 30, 1939; d. Edward Ernest and Miriam Anne Griessel; m. Howard Nevin Peters, Aug. 24, 1963; children: Elisabeth Anne, Nevin Edward. BA, Valparaiso (Ind.) U., 1961; PhD, U. Colo., 1968. Mem. faculty Valparaiso U., 1965—98, internat. svc. program chair, 1993—98, chair dept. fgn. langs., 1995—98, prof. emerita fgn. langs. and lit., 1998—. Faculty fellowship Lilly Endowment, 1989, NDEA Title IV fellowship U.S. Govt., 1961-64. Avocations: canoeing, gardening, travel, volunteering. Home: 860 N 500 E Valparaiso IN 46383-9743

PETERS, MARY ANN, ambassador; m. Tim McMahon; 2 children. BA, Santa Clara U.; M Internat. Studies, Johns Hopkins U. With U.S. Fgn. Svc., 1975—, dep. chief of mission, econ. counselor Moscow, prin. officer, vice consul, dep. dir. Office of Pakistan, Afghanistan and Bangladesh Affairs, U.S. State Dept., 1988—90, dep. chief of mission U.S. Embassy, ambassador to Bangladesh, 2000—; dir. European and Can. affairs Nat. Security Coun. White House, Washington. Office: US Embassy Madani Ave Baridhara Dhaka 1212 Bangladesh*

PETERS, MARY CATHERINE, journalist, researcher, broadcaster; d. Thomas Peters and Agnes Columba Griffin. Journalist La - The Irish Lang. Newspaper, Belfast, Ireland, 1970—2004, Radio na Gaeltachta, Ireland, 1970—2004, Radio Eireann, vaious Irish Lang. shows; dir. Clann na hEireann USA (Reuniting Irish Am. Families), Naples, Fla. Rschr. family surnames Clans of Ireland Office, Tipperary, Ireland; creator, rschr. SBB Show for Telefis Eireann (Irish TV), Dublin. Actor: Letters of a Successful TD; contbr. columns in newspapers. Named Internat. Writer of Merit, Holder, C.P.C. Internat. Transp.; recipient Cert. Coop. Devel. Personal E-mail: mnicp2@cs.com.

PETERS, MARY E. federal agency administrator; m. Terry Peters; 3 children. B, U. Phoenix; attended govt. program for state & local govt., Harvard U. Dir. Ariz. Dept. Transp., 1985—2001; fed. hwy. adminstr. U.S. Dept. Transp., Washington, 2001—. Past bd. dirs. Project Challenge, Nat. Guard; past chair adv. bd. Hwy. Expansion Loan Program; mem. Gt. Ariz. Develop. Authority; past mem. Growing Smarter Commn. Named Women of Yr., Women's Transp. Seminar; named one of Most Influential Person in Ariz. Transp., Ariz. Bus. Jour. Mem.: We. Assn. State Hwy. Transp. Officials, Am. Assn. State Hwy. Officials (past chair standing com. on planning, assest mgmt. task force, reauthorization steering com. 2001). Office: US Dept Transp Fed Hwy Adminstrn 400 7th St SW Washington DC 20590

PETERS, MELODIE M. state legislator; b. Springfield, Mass., July 22, 1947; m. Earl Peters; two children: Troy, Lalisa. Grad. sch. nursing, Winthrop Cmty. Hosp. Mem. Dist. 20 Conn. Senate, Hartford, 1993—; nurse Quaker Hill, Conn. Mem. adv. bd. Conn. Occupational Health Clinic, Conn. Legis. Task Force on Safety in Workplace; chair Waterford Dem. Town Com. Office: Conn State Senate 210 Capitol Ave Hartford CT 06106-1535

PETERS, ROBERTA, soprano; b. N.Y.C., May 4, 1930; d. Sol and Ruth (Hirsch) Peters; m. Bertram Fields, Apr. 10, 1955; children: Paul, Bruce. Ed. privately; Litt.D., Elmira Coll., 1967; Mus. D., Ithaca Coll., 1968, Colby Coll., 1980; L.H.D., Westminster Coll., 1974, Lehigh U., 1977; D.F.A., St. John's U., 1982; LittD, Coll. New Rochelle, 1989; MusD, U. R.I., 1992, Fla. Atlantic U., 1997. Author: Debut at the Met; singer: (Operas) Met. Opera debut as Zerlina in Don Giovanni, 1950, recorded numerous operas, (appeared motion pictures including) Tonight We Sing, 1996, frequent appearances radio and TV, (stage appearances include) The King and I, 1973, Bittersweet, Merry Widow, The Sound of Music, Royal Opera House, Vienna State Opera, Munich Opera, West Berlin Opera, Salzburg Festival, The White House, debuts at festivals in Vienna and Munich, premiered Ani M'amin, Carnegie Hall, 1973, concert tours in U.S., Soviet Union, Scandinavian countries, Israel, China, Japan, Taiwan, South Korea, (debut) Kirov Opera, sang at Bolshoi Opera (1st Am. recipient Bolshoi medal). Trustee, bd. dirs. Carnegie Hall; trustee Ithaca Coll.; dir. Met. Opera Guild; chmn. Nat. Inst. Music Theater, 1991—; apptd. by Pres. Bush to Nat. Coun. Arts, 1991; overseer Colby Coll., Bklyn. Coll. Performing Arts Ctr.; past chair Nat. Cystic Fibrosis Found.; active Israel Bonds, AIDS rsch. Named Woman of Yr., Fedn. Women's Clubs, 1964; recipient honored spl. ceremony on 35th anniversary with Met. Opera Co., 1985, Nat. Medal of Arts, Pres. Clinton, 1998. Avocation: tennis. Office: ICM Artists Ltd 40 W 57th St Fl 16 New York NY 10019-4098

PETERS, SARAH WHITAKER, art historian, writer, lecturer; b. Kenosha, Wis., Aug. 17, 1924; d. Robert Burbank and Margaret Jebb (Allen) Whitaker; m. Arthur King Peters, Oct. 21, 1943; children: Robert Bruce, Margaret Allen, Michael Whitaker. BA, Sarah Lawrence Coll., 1954; MA, Columbia U., 1966; student, L'Ecole du Louvre, Paris, 1967-68; diplome, Ecole des Trois Gourmandes, Paris, 1968; PhD, CUNY, 1987. Freelance critic Art in Am., N.Y.C. Lectr.-in-residence Garrison Forest Sch., Owings Mills, Md.; adj. asst. prof. art history C.W. Post, U. L.I.; lectr. Bronxville (N.Y.) Adult Sch., Internat. Mus. Photography, 1979, Tufts U., 1979, Madison (Wis.) Art Ctr., 1984, Meml. Art Gallery, Rochester, N.Y., 1988, 91, Caramoor Mus., Katonah, N.Y., 1988, Yale U. Art Gallery, New Haven, Conn., 1989, The Cosmopolitan Club, N.Y.C., 1977, 91, Sarah Lawrence Coll., Bronxville, 1992, The Phillips Collection, Washington, 1993, Mpls. Inst. Arts, 1993, Whitney Mus. Am. Art, Champion, 1994, U. Wis., Parkside, 1994, Nat. Mus. Wildlife Art, Jackson Hole, Wyo., 1995, The Georgia O'Keeffe Mus., Santa Fe, 1997, Bronxville Pub. Libr., 1998, Weatherspoon Art Mus., Greensboro, NC, 2003, Amon Carter Mus, Ft. Worth, 2003, Pa. Acad. Fine Arts, Phila., 2004. Author: Becoming O'Keeffe: The Early Years, 1991, 2d edit., 2001, Pattern of the Past: A Kenosha Memoir, 2001; contbr. essays to Portraits of American Women, 1991, The Dictionary of Art, 1996, Frames of Reference; Works from the Whitney Museum of American Art, 1999, American Art Review, 2003; TV appearances include: BBC, London, The Late Show, 1993, A&E Network Biography series on Georgia O'Keeffe, 2004; radio interview: Art Today, Australia Broadcasting Corp., 1999; contbr. articles to profl. jours. Mem. Coll. Art Assn., Bronxville Field Club, The Cosmopolitan Club. Avocations: horseback riding, rock climbing, tennis, cooking. Home: 14 Village Ln Bronxville NY 10708-4806

PETERSEN, ANNE C.(CHERYL), foundation administrator, educator; b. Little Falls, Minn., Sept. 11, 1944; d. Franklin Hanks and Rhoda Pauline (Sandwick) Studley; m. Douglas Lee Petersen, Dec. 27, 1967; children: Christine Anne, Benjamin Bradfield. BA, U. Chgo., 1966, MS, 1972, PhD, 1973. Asst. prof., rsch. assoc. Dept. Psychiatry U. Chgo., 1972-80, assoc. prof., rsch. assoc., 1980-82, prof. human devel., head Dept. Individual and Family Studies Pa. State U., University Park, 1982-87, dean Coll. Health and Human Devel., 1987-92, prof. health and human devel., 1987-92; dean grad. sch., v.p. for rsch. throughout state U. Minn., Mpls., 1992-94, prof. adolescent devel. and pediatrics, 1992-96; dep. dir., COO NSF, Arlington, Va., 1994-96; sr. v.p. programs W.K. Kellogg Found., 1996—. Vis. prof., fellow Coll. Edn., R&D Psychology, Roosevelt U., Chgo., 1973-74; cons. Ctr. for Health Adminstrn. Studies U. Chgo., 1976-78, Ctr. for New Schs., Chgo., 1974-78, Robert Wood Johnson Found. Mathtech, Inc., 1987-89; coord. clin. rsch. tng. program Michael Reese Hosp. and Med. Ctr., Chgo., 1976-80, dir. Lab. for Study of Adolescence, 1975-82; mem. faculty Ill. Sch. for Profl. Psychology, 1978-79; statis. cons. Coll. Nursing U. Ill. Med. Ctr., 1975-83; assoc. dir. health program MacArthur Found., 1980-82, also cons. health program, 1982-88; chair sr. adv. bd. NIMH, 1987-88; mem. nat. adv. mental health coun. NIH, 1997—; trustee Nat. Inst. Statis. Scis., 1998—. Author: Sex Related Differences in Cognition Functioning: Developmental Issues, 1979, Promoting Adolescent Health: A Diolog on Research and Practice, 1982, Firls at Puberty: Biological and psychosocial Perspectives, 1983, Brain Maturation and Cognitive Development: Comparative and Cross Cultural Perspectives, 1991, Narrowing the Margins: Adolescent Unemployment and the lack of a social role, 1991, Grofit: A Fortran Program for the Estimation of Parameters of a Human Growth Curve, 1972, Girls at Puberty: Biological and Psychosocial Perspectives, 1983, Adolescence and Youth: Psychological Development in a Changing World, 1984, Youth Unemployment and Society, 1994, Transitions Through Adolescence: Interpersonal Domains and Context, 1996; reviewer Jour. Youth and Adolescence, 1975-80, Devel. Psychology, 1979—, Sci., 1979—, Jour. Edn. Psychology, 1979—, Child Devel., 1980—, Jour. Edn. Measurement, 1980, Ednl. Rschr., 1980, Am. Ednl. Rsch. Jour., 1981—, Jour. Mental Imagery, 1982-92, Sex Roles, 1984—; cons. editor Psychology of Women Quar., 1978-82, assoc. editor, 1983-86; adv. editor Contemporary Psychology, 1985-86; mem. editl. bd. various profl. jours.; contbr. chpts. to books and articles to profl. jours. Bd. overseers Lewis Coll., Ill. Inst. Tech., 1980-82; mem. adv. bd. longitudinal data archive project Murray Ctr., Radcliffe Coll., 1985-91, mem. sci. adv. bd., 1983-91 Fellow: APA (chmn. task force on reproductive freedom 1979—81, program chmn. 1981—82, chmn. task force on long range planning 1986—89, pres. divsn. 7 1992—93), AAAS; mem.: NAS (nat. forum on future children and their families 1987—91, chmn. panel on child abuse and neglect 1991—93, mem. forum on adolescence Inst. of Medicine 1997—2000, chair bd. on behavioral, cognitive and sensory scis. 1997—), Soc. for Rsch. on Adolescence (pres. 1990—92, past pres. 1992—94, chmn. nominations com. 1992—94), Acad. Europaea, Psychometric Soc., Behavior Genetics Assn.,

Assn. Women in Sci. (bd. dirs. 1996—2000), Am. Ednl. Rsch. Assn. (various offices), Internat. Soc. for the Study of Behavioral Devel. (coun. mem. 1995—2001, pres. elect 2002—04), Inst. for Medicine. Home: 3715 Blackberry Ln Kalamazoo MI 49008-3333

PETERSEN, CATHERINE HOLLAND, lawyer; b. Norman, Okla., Apr. 24, 1951; d. John Hays and Helen Ann (Turner) Holland; m. James Frederick Petersen, June 26, 1973 (div.); children: T. Kyle, Lindsay Diane; m. Lester E.R. Doty, Apr. 17, 2004. BA, Hastings Coll., 1973; JD, Okla. U., 1976. Bar: Okla. 1976, U.S. Dist. Ct. (we. dist.) Okla. 1978. Legal intern, police legal advisor City of Norman, 1974-76; sole practice Norman, 1976-81; ptnr. Williams Petersen & Denny, Norman, 1981-82; pres. Petersen Assocs., Inc., Norman, 1982—. Adj. prof. Oklahoma City U. Coll. Law, 1982, U. Okla. Law Ctr., 1987; instr. continuing legal edn. U. Okla. Law Ctr., Norman, 1977, 79, 81, 83, 84, 86, 89-95; instr. Okla. Bar Assn., ABA, Am. Acad. Matrimonial Lawyers. Bd. dirs. United Way, Norman, 1978-84, pres., 1981; bd. dirs. Women's Resource Ctr., Norman, 1975-77, 82-84; mem. Jr. League, Norman, 1980-83, Norman Hosp. Ayx., 1982-84; trustee 1st Presbyn. Ch., 1986-87. Named among Outstanding Okla. Women of 1980s, Women's Polit. Caucus, 1980, Outstanding Young Women of Am., 1981, 83. Fellow Am. Acad. Matrimonial Lawyers (pres. Okla. chpt. 1990-91, bd. govs. 1991-95); mem. ABA (family law sect., faculty Family Law Inst. 1993—), Cleveland County Bar Assn., Okla. Bar Assn. (chmn. family law sect. 1987-88), Phi Delta Phi. Republican. Home: 4716 Sundance Ct Norman OK 73072-3900 Office: PO Box 1243 314 E Comanche St Norman OK 73069-6009

PETERSEN, JANET, state representative; b. DesMoines, Aug. 1, 1970; BA, U. No. Iowa; MA, Drake U. Constituency coord. 1992 Clinton-Gore Campaign; comm. specialist Am. Heart Assn.; sr. account exec. Strategic Am.; mem. Iowa Ho. Reps., DesMoines, 2001—, mem. commerce and regulation com., mem. econ. devel. com., mem. appropriations com., mem. edn. com., mem. local govt. com. Active Beaverdale Neighborhood Assn., Walnut Hills Meth. Ch.; bd. mem. DesMoines Arts Festival, United Way Ctrl. Iowa, Women in Pub. Policy, Polk County Housing Trust Fund. Democrat. Office: State Capitol East 12th and Grand Des Moines IA 50319 also: 1346 47th St Des Moines IA 50311

PETERSEN, JEAN SNYDER, association executive; b. N.Y.C., Oct. 16, 1931; d. Peter Eugene and Helyn Brownell (Parker) Snyder; m. Elton Reed Petersen, Sept. 16, 1954; children— Bruce Brownell, Craig Reed. Student, N.Y. U., 1949-51; degree fgn. banking, Am. Inst. Banking, 1952. Fgn. credit investigator Chase Nat. Bank Hdqrs., N.Y.C., 1952-56; nat. exec. dir. Assn. Children and Adults with Learning Disabilities (name changed to Learning Disabilities Assn. of Am.), Pitts., 1972—. Mem. exec. com., treas. Jr. League, Pitts.; bd. dirs. Found. for Children with Learning Disabilities, N.Y.C., Children's Hosp., Pitts., Music for Mt. Lebanon, Vocat. Rehab. Ctr., Pitts.; bd. dirs., v.p., mem. exec. com. Assn. Retarded Citizens Pa.; ptnr. UN Internat. Yr. of Disabled; ruling elder Presbyn. Ch.Assn. Retarded Citizens Pa.; mem. exec. com. Pat Buckley Moss Nat. Children's Charity Found; chmn. bd. dirs. Masonic Learning Ctrs. for Children. Recipient Sustainers award Jr. League, 1977, Recognition award, 1975, Pres.'s award, 1978 Mem. AAUW, Meeting Planners Internat. (treas.), Am. Soc. Assn. Execs. Republican. Presbyterian. Home: 343 Shadowlawn Ave Pittsburgh PA 15216-1239 Office: 4156 Library Rd Pittsburgh PA 15234-1349 Fax: (412) 5634537.

PETERSEN, MAUREEN JEANETTE MILLER, management information consultant, former nurse; b. Evanston, Ill., Sept. 4, 1956; d. Maurice James and M. Joyce (Mielke) Miller; m. Gregory Eugene Petersen, July 7, 1984; children: Trevor James, Tatyana Brianne. BS in Nursing cum laude, Vanderbilt U., 1978; MS in Biometry and Health Info. Systems, U. Minn., 1984. Nurse U. Iowa Hosps. and Clinics, Iowa City, 1978—82; research asst. Sch. Nursing, U. Minn., Mpls., 1982—83; mgr. Accenture, Mpls., 1984—2001, PMP; sr. mgr. clin. systems Park Nicollet, Eden Prairie, Minn., 2003—. Mem.: Project Mgmt. Inst., Mensa. Methodist. Avocation: travel. Home: 1050 County Rd C2 W Roseville MN 55113-1945 Office: Park Nicollet 7905 Golden Triangle Dr Eden Prairie MN 55344 E-mail: peters1050@aol.com., petema@parknicollet.com.

PETERSEN, MEG JOANNA, education educator, language educator; b. Peterborough, N.H., Oct. 8, 1956; d. Walter Rutherford Peterson and Dorothy Donovan; m. Carlos E. Gonzalez (div. Aug. 1995); children: Sam, Marc, Max. BA, Franklin Pierce Coll., Rindge, N.H., 1977; PhD, Univ. N.H., Durham, 1991. Therapeutic tchr. Philbrook Ctr., Concord, NH, 1977—81; tchr. Devon Lane Sch., Devonshire, Bermuda, 1981—85; tchg. asst. U. N.H., Durham, 1985—87; prof. English U. Catolica Madrey Maestra, Santiago, Dominican Republic, 1987—88, U. Pedro Henriquez, Santo Domingo, 1988—91; lang. coord. Entrena S.A., Santo Domingo, 1989—91; assoc. prof. Plymouth (N.H.) State Coll., NH, 1991—. Cons. writing various orgns., 1987—; coord. English grad. program in edn. Plymouth State Coll., 1995—; dir. Plymouth Writing Project, 2001—. Editor: (book series) Plymouth Writers Group Anthologies, 1995—, (jour.) PSC Jour. of Writing Across the Curriculum, 1998—, H.S. Voices, 1999—. Recipient New Eng. Poet of Yr., New Eng. Asn. Tchrs. English, 1998. Mem.: N.H. Assn. Tchrs. English, N.H. Writers' Project, Nat. Assn. Tchrs. English. Home: 7 Pleasant St Plymouth NH 03264 Office: Plymouth State Coll English MSC #40 Plymouth NH 03264 E-mail: megp@mail.plymouth.edu.

PETERSEN, RUTH ANNE, performing arts educator; b. Onawa, Iowa, Aug. 23, 1969; d. Charles Louis and Joan Marie Petersen; life ptnr. Sherry Louise Blevins, Nov. 13, 1988; 1 child, Christina Korey. MusM Edn., U. of NC at Greensboro, 1991—92, MusB Edn., 1987—91. National Board Certified Music Teacher: Early Adolescence-Young Adult Nat. Bd. for Profl. Tchg. Standards, 2002. Band dir. J. M. Smith Mid. Sch., Charlotte, NC, 1992—98, Francis Bradley Mid. Sch., Huntersville, NC, 1998—. Music in our schools month coord. Bradley Mid. Sch., Huntersville, NC, 1998—; cert. and program designer Charlotte-Mecklenburg Schools Honors Band Com., Charlotte, NC, 1993—, Charlotte-Mecklenburg Schools Elem. Honors Chorus Com., 2002—; bd. mem. Bradley Mid. Sch. Band Boosters, Huntersville, NC, 1998—; team leader Bradley Mid. Sch. Elective Team, 2002—03; team rep. Bradley Mid. Sch. Leadership Team. Editor: (music theory book series) Fundamentals of Music Theory for the Wind Band Student. Recipient Ben Craig Outstanding Educator Finalist, Wachovia, 2002, Harris Tchr. of the Yr. Semi-finalist, Charlotte Cultural Edn. Collaborative, 1998, Disney's America's Tchr. Award Nominee, Disney Co., 2002, Cable in the Classroom Award Winner, Time Warner Cable, 1992; grantee $10, 000 for Performing Artists-in-Residence, Charlotte Arts & Sci. Coun., 1993, Learning Village Website, IBM, 1999—2003. Mem.: Women Band Directors Internat. Assn. (assoc.), Nat. Band Assn. (assoc.), Internat. Trombone Assn. (assoc.), NEA (assoc.), Music Educators Nat. Conf. (assoc.). D-Liberal. Avocations: music, art, computers, reading, walking. Office: Francis Bradley Middle School 13345 Beatties Ford Road Huntersville NC 28078 Personal E-mail: roothieap@aol.com. E-mail: r.petersen@cms.k12.nc.us.

PETERSEN, STEPHANIE BURTON, bond analyst; b. San Rafael, Calif., Sept. 3, 1958; d. George and Marie Burton; m. Christopher Michael Petersen, May 4, 1991. BS, U. San Francisco, 1980; MBA, Golden Gate U., 1984, JD, 1987. Bar: Calif. 1987. Analyst Fireman's Fund Ins. Co., San Francisco, 1980-85; law clk. Consolidated Capital, Emeryville, Calif., 1985-86; underwriting officer Fireman's Fund Ins. Co., 1986-87; sr. underwriting officer Capital Guaranty, San Francisco, 1987-92; v.p. mcpl. rsch. Charles Schwab & Co., San Francisco, 1992—. Co-author: Mastering Your Professional Image, 1995. Bd. dirs. Bay Area coun. Campfire Boys and Girls, San Francisco, 1995—, pres., 1997—. Mem. ABA, Nat. Fed. Mcpl. Analysts.

PETERSON, ANDREA LENORE, law educator; b. L.A., July 21, 1952; d. Vincent Zetterberg and Elisabeth (Karlsson) P.; m. Michael Rubin, May 29, 1983; children: Peter Rubin, Eric Rubin, Emily Rubin. AB, Stanford U., 1974; JD, U. Calif., Berkeley, 1978. Bar: Calif., 1979, U.S. Dist. Ct. (no. dist.) Calif., 1979. Law clk. to Judge Charles B. Renfrew U.S. Dist. Ct. (no. dist.) Calif., San Francisco, 1978-79; lawyer Cooley, Godward, Castro, Huddleson & Tatum, San Francisco, 1979-80; law clk. to Justice Byron R. White U.S. Supreme Ct., Washington, 1980-81; lawyer Heller, Ehrman, White & McAuliffe, San Francisco, 1981-83; prof. law Boalt Hall U. Calif., Berkeley, 1983—. Contbr. articles to profl. jours. Office: U Calif Sch Law Boalt Hall Berkeley CA 94720

PETERSON, ANN SULLIVAN, physician, health care consultant; b. Rhinebeck, N.Y., Oct. 11, 1928; A.B., Cornell U., 1950, M.D., 1954; M.S. (Alfred P. Sloan fellow 1979-80), M.I.T., 1980. Diplomate Am. Bd. Internal Medicine. Intern, Cornell Med. Div.-Bellevue Hosp., N.Y.C., 1954-55, resident, 1955-57; fellow in medicine and physiology Meml.-Sloan Kettering Cancer Ctr., Cornell Med. Coll., N.Y.C., 1957-60; instr. medicine Georgetown U. Sch. Medicine, Washington, 1962-65, asst. prof., 1965-69, asst. dir. clin. research unit, 1962-69; assoc. prof. medicine U. Ill., Chgo., 1969-72, asst. dean, 1969-71, assoc. dean, 1971-72; assoc. prof. medicine, assoc. dean Coll. Physicians and Surgeons, Columbia U., N.Y.C., 1972-80; assoc. prof. medicine, assoc. dean Cornell U. Med. Coll., N.Y.C., 1980-83; assoc. dir. div. med. edn. AMA, Chgo., 1983-86, dir. div. grad. med. edn., 1986-89; v.p. mgmt. cons. corp., 1989-93; ind. cons., Chgo., 1993—; mem. bd. regents Uniformed Svcs. U. of Health Scis., 1984-90. John and Mary R. Markle scholar, 1965-70. Fellow ACP; mem. Mortar Board, Alpha Omega Alpha, Alpha Epsilon Delta. Contbr. articles to med. jours.

PETERSON, BARBARA ANN BENNETT, history educator, television personality; b. Portland, Oreg., Sept. 6, 1942; d. George and Hope Bennett; m. Frank Lynn Peterson, July 1, 1967. BA, BS, Oreg. State U., 1964; MA, Stanford U., 1965; PhD, U. Hawaii, 1978; PhD (hon.), London Inst. Applied Rsch., 1991, Australian Inst. Coordinated R, 1995. From prof. history to prof. emeritus U. Hawaii, 1967—95, prof. emeritus, 1995—; prof. history Oreg. State U., 2000—03. Prof. Asian history and European colonial history and world problems Chapman Coll. World Campus Afloat Semester At Sea, 1974, European overseas exploration, expansion and colonialism U. Colo., Boulder, 1978, Modern China, Modern East Asia, The West in the World U. Pitts., 1999; assoc. prof. U. Hawaii-Manoa Coll. Continuing Edn., 1981; Fulbright prof. history Wuhan (China) U., 1988-89; Fulbright rsch. prof. Sophia U., Japan, 1967; rsch. assoc. Bishop Mus., 1995-98; lectr. Capital Spkrs., Washington, 1987—; prof. world civilization Hawaii State Ednl. Channel, U. Hawaii Sys., 1993-97; adj. fellow East-West Ctr., Honolulu, 1998-99; prof. history U. Pitts. Semester at Sea, fall 1999; adj. prof. Hawaii Pacific U., East-West Ctr., Hawaii, 1998-99. Co-author: A Woman's Place is in the History Books, Her Story, 1962-1980: A Curriculum Guide for American History Teachers, 1980; author: America in British Eyes, 1988, John Bull's Eye on America, 1995, Sarah Childress Polk, First Lady of Tennessee and Washington, 2002 (nominated for Pulitzer prize 2003, Avery O. Craven award 2003, Merle Curti award 2003, Albert J. Beveridge award 2003), Emalani, 2003; editor: Notable Women of Hawaii, 1984, (with W. Solheim) The Pacific Region, 1990, 91, American History: 17th, 18th and 19th Centuries, 1993, America: 19th and 20th Centuries, 1993, Notable Women of China, 2000 (nominated for Pulitzer prize 2001), Hawaii in the World, 2000; assoc. editor Am. Nat. Biography, 1998 (Dartmouth medal); contbr. articles to profl. publs. Participant People-to-People Program, Eng., 1964, Expt. in Internat. Living Program, Nigeria, 1966; chmn. 1st Nat. Women's History Week, Hawaii, 1982; pres. Bishop Mus. Coun., 1993-94; active mem. Hawaii Commn. on Status of Women; fundraiser local mus. and children's activities. Fulbright scholar, Japan, 1967, sr. tchg. Fulbright scholar, China, 1988-89; NEH-Woodrow Wilson fellow Princeton U., 1980; recipient state proclamations Gov. of Hawaii, 1982, City of Honolulu and Hawaii State Legis., 1982, Outstanding Tchr. of Yr. award Wuhan (China), U., 1988, Woman of Yr. award, 1991; inducted into the Women's Hall of Fame, Seneca Falls, N.Y., 1991; co-champion Hawaii State Husband and Wife Mixed Doubles Tennis Championship, 1985. Fellow: World Lit. Acad. (Eng.); mem.: AAUW, Am. Studies Assn. (Hawaii chpt. pres. 1984—85), Women in Acad. Adminstrn., Hawaii Found. History and Humanities (mem. editl. bd. 1972—73), Am. Coun. on Edn., Fulbright Assn. (founding pres. Hawaii chpt. 1984—88, mem. nat. steering com. chairwomen ann. conf. 1990, pres. 1998—99), Am. Hist. Assn. (mem. numerous coms., nominated Albert J. Beveridge award 2003), Maison Internat. des Intellectuals, Phi Kappa Phi, Pi Beta Phi (mem. mortar bd.). Avocations: writing, cooking, fund raising for charity and children's organizations and museums, gardening, travel. Office: East West Ctr Burns Hall 1601 East West Rd Honolulu HI 96848-1601 also: Oreg State U History Dept 306 Milam Hall Corvallis OR 97331

PETERSON, BARBARA OWECKE, retired real estate agent, artist, nurse; b. Winona, Minn., Nov. 25, 1932; d. Adelbert Paul and Hermanda Gilda Bittner; m. Jerome Francis Owecke, Nov. 28, 1953 (div. 1974); children: Paul Richard Owecke, Michael Jerome Owecke, Margaret Francis Owecke (dec.), Stacy Ann Owecke, Wendy Alane Owecke (dec.), James William Owecke, William Harold Owecke; m. Roy Eugene Peterson, May 28, 1983. RN, St. Francis Sch. Nursing, 1953; B Individualized Study, George Mason U., 1994. RN, Va., Wis., Mich., Ill., Ohio, Fla. Staff nurse Commonwealth Hosp., Fairfax, Va., 1973-74; telemetry nurse Fairfax Hosp., 1974-76; med. sales rep. CB Fleet Pharm., Lynchburg, Va., 1976-78; territory mgr. Bristol-Myers Squibb, Northern Va., Washington, 1978-92; realtor Century 21 United, Fairfax, Va., 1974-91; ret., 1992; artist, 1992—. Bd. dirs. Fauquier Artists' Alliance, Warrenton, Va., 1993-96, pres., 1994-95. Exhibited in group shows at Fauquier Artists' Alliance, Warrenton, 1994—97, Alexandria Art League, 1994—98, Ctr. for Creative Art, Fredericksburg, Va., 1994—98, George Mason U., Fairfax, Va., 1994, Neighborhood Art Show, The Plains, Va., 1994—97, Japanese Embassy, Washington, 1996, The Campagna Ctr., Alexandria, 1996—97, The Torpedo Factory, Alexandria, Va., 1994—98, Petersburg Area Art League, Va., 1998, Brush Strokes Gallery, Ft. Pierce, Fla., 1998—2001, Treasure Coast Art Assn., Ft. Pierce, 1998—2004, Vero Beach Mus., 1999—2004, Waterways Gallery, 2003—, Backus Gallery, 2004. RN Fauquier Free Clinic, Warrenton, 1993-98; mem. Goldvein Vol. Fire Dept., 1989-94. Mem. Internat. Registry Artists and Artwork, Nat. Mus. Women in the Arts (charter mem.), Archives of Nat. Mus. Women in the Arts, Vero Beach Art Club, Vero Beach Mus., Treasure Coast Art Assn., Art Assocs. of Martin County, Jensen Beach Art League. Roman Catholic. Avocation: tennis. Home: 403 Southstar Dr Ocean Village Fort Pierce FL 34949 E-mail: BaMaBi66@aol.com.

PETERSON, CLARA MARGARET, elementary school educator; b. Thorp, Wis., June 25, 1930; d. Matthew and Pearl H. Olejniczak; m. Donald Richard Peterson, Dec. 27, 1954; 1 child, Mark Gregory. BS, Wis. State U., Eau Claire, 1964; MS Elem. Edn., U. Wis., LaCrosse, 1975. Tchr. 2d grade pub. sch., Gilman, Wis., 1950—53, tchr. 1st grade Eau Claire, 1953—54, tchr. 2d & 4th grades Trenton, NJ, 1955—56, tchr. 2d grade St. Paul, 1957—58, substitute tchr. La Crosse, Wis., 1964—67; tchr. math. 3d & 5th grades La Crosse Pub. Schs., 1967—93. Co-treas. Senate Dance Club, La Crosse; treas. PTA. Mem.: NEA, AAUW, Wis. Ret. Educator's Assn., La Crosse Edn. Assn., We. Wis. Edn. Assn., Wis. Edn. Assn., Delta Kappa Gamma, Kappa Delta Pi. Avocations: piano, swimming, golf, bicycling.

PETERSON, DARLENE DENISE, budget officer; b. Augusta, GA., Aug. 8, 1965; d. Rufus Albert and Dorothy Mosley Peterson. BS, Clemson U., 1986, MS, 1988. Assoc. policy analyst Gov.'s Office of Planning and Budget, Atlanta, 1989-91; fin. analyst United Parcel Svc., Atlanta, 1991-93; policy analyst Gov.'s Office of Planning and Budget, Atlanta, 1993-96; budget officer Ga. Dept. Edn., Atlanta, 1996—. Mem. Jr. League Atlanta, 1991-99, chair membership outreach, 1999; mem. Stone Mountain, Ga., 1999. Mem. Assn. Ednl. Fed. Fin. Adminstrs., Ga. Fiscal Mgmt. Coun., Delta Sigma Theta (historian, journalist). Baptist. Avocations: photography, reading, traveling. Office: Ga Dept Edn 205 Butler St SE Ste 1970 Atlanta GA 30334-9049 Fax: (404) 657-6821. E-mail: dpeterso@doe.k12.ga.us.

PETERSON, DONNA RAE, gerontologist; b. Wichita, Kans., Aug. 29, 1948; d. Raymond Houston and Edna Brooks (Waddell) Hobbs; m. William E. Peterson, Nov. 7, 1993; 1 child, Shauna Layne Reed. Student, Wichita State U., 1968-70; BS in Mgmt., N.W. Christian Coll., 1996, MA in Interdisciplinary Studies Gerontology, 2000. Adminstrv. asst. postgrad. edn. Med. Sch. U. Kans., Wichita, 1974-80; activity coord. continuing med. edn. Wesley Med. Ctr., Wichita, 1980-84; mgr. support svcs. 9th dist. Farm Credit Svcs., Wichita, 1984-88; sales and mktg. mgr. Amb. Travel, Eugene, 1988-93; mktg. dir. Peterson Design Devel., Eugene, Oreg., 1993-95; pres. Davinci Designs, Eugene, 1996-2000; owner 2nd Half Dynamics, 2000—; dir. Alzheimer's program Sunwest Mgmt., Inc., 2002—04; owner 2nd Half Dynamics, 2000—. Cons. Jr. League Wichita, 1983, Plancon, Inc., Martinsville, N.J., 1987-88, Changing Creatively, 1997; continuing edn. instr. Lane C.C., 2000—; mem. adv. bd. Lane C.C. Ctr. for Leisure and Learning, 2000—. Mem. Wichita Conv. and Visitors Bur., 1987; mem. events com. Wichita Festivals, Inc., 1987; mem. Eugene Conv. and Visitors Bur., 1988—; mem. Eugene Airport Commn., 1991—, chmn., 1992-93; bd. dirs. Campus Life, chmn., 1993-94; mem. steering com. Eugene Celebration, 1991-94, Oreg. Women Bus. Owners Conf., 1997; bd. pres. Of Coun. for Bus. Edn., 1999-2000. Mem. AAUW, Am. Mktg. Assn. (pres. S.W. chpt. 1991—, pres. 1992-94, bd. dir.), Soc. Travel Agt. in Govt., Adminstrv. Mgmt. Soc., Forum for Exec. Bus. Women, Gt. Plains Bus. Adminstrn. Group, Assn. Travel Exec., Eugene C. of C. (bus. devel. com. 1990-91), The Gerontol. Soc. Am. (student mem. campus rep. 1999), mem., 2000-present, mem., Alzheimers Assn., Oreg. chapt., edn. com., 2002-present, Eugene High Ground Assoc. (chmn.), Delta Gamma Alumni Assn. Republican. Avocations: decorating, writing, snow skiing, water skiing, camping. Home: 1460 Olive St Apt 32 Eugene OR 97401-3991 Office Phone: 541-687-9318. E-mail: gerovision@aol.com.

PETERSON, DOROTHY LULU, artist; b. Venice, Calif., Mar. 10, 1932; d. Marvin Henry and Fay (Brown) Case; m. Leon Albert Peterson, June 21, 1955; 1 child, David. AD, Compton (Calif.) Coll., 1950. Artist Moran Printing Co., Lockport, N.Y., 1955—; caricature artist West Seneca and Kenmore Creative Artist Socs., 1973-86; commd. artist in pvt. practice, 1986—. Comml. artist Boulevard Mall, Kenmore (N.Y.) Arts Soc., 1974—. Works include portraits of Pres. and Mrs. Reagan in Presdl. Libr. Collection, also portraits of Geraldine Ferraro, Presidents Clinton, Bush, Nixon, Ford, also Bette Davis, Lucille Ball, Bing Crosby, Elizabeth Taylor, 1971-94; sculpture of Pres. Bush, Princess Diana, John Kennedy Jr.; caricature sculptures of Joan Rivers, Erma Bombeck, Lucille Ball; author articles, poems. Recipient awards West. Seneca Art Soc., 1975, Kenmore Art Soc., 1982, 86. Recipient Editors award Nat. Poetry Soc., 1997, Editors Choice award Nat. Libr. of Poetry, 1998, Best Poems and Poets of 2001, Internat. Poet of Merit Silver Bowl award, 2002; named to The Best Poems and Poets of the 20th Century, Internat. Libr. of Poets. Democrat. Baptist. Home: 247 Pryor Ave Tonawanda NY 14150-7407

PETERSON, E. ANNE, federal agency administrator; married; 3 children. MD, Mayo Med. Sch.; MPH, Emory U. Cert. bd. cert. gen. preventive medicine and pub. health, lic. Va., Ga., Minn., Zimbabwe. Resident Emory U.; commr. health State of Va., 1998—2001; asst. adminstr. bur. global health USAID, Washington, 2001—. Cmty. devel., pub. health tng. and AIDS prevention, Kenya, Zimbabwe. Office: USAID RRB 1300 Pennsylvania Ave NW Washington DC 20523-3900

PETERSON, EILEEN M. state agency administrator; b. Trenton, N.J., Sept. 22, 1942; d. Leonard James and Mary (Soganic) Olschewski; m. Lars N. Peterson, Jr., 1970 (div. 1983); children: Leslie, Valerie, Erica. Grad., Internat. Guide Acad., 1998. Cert. Tour dir. Globus, Cosmos, Archers, 1999-2000. Adminstrv. sec. State Ins. Fund, Boise, 1983-85; legal asst. Bd. Tax Appeals, Boise, 1985-87, exec. asst., 1987-92, dir., 1992-98; asst. shore excursion mgr. Renaissance Cruises, 2000-01. Ind. distbr. nutritional products USANA Health Scis., Inc.; lic. realtor, 2002—04. Vol. tutor ESL Idaho Refugee Svc., 1997—98; docent Boise Art Mus., 1998—99, 2001—03. Recipient Gov's. Cert. of Recognition for Outstanding Achievement, 1995. Mem. Mensa, Investment Club (pres.), Mountain West Outdoor Club (treas. 1996-98), Idaho Rivers United, Internat. Platform Assn. Avocations: white water rafting, non-fiction reading, teaching esl. Home: 3317 Mountain View Dr Boise ID 83704-4638

PETERSON, JANE WHITE, nursing educator, anthropologist; b. San Juan, P.R., Feb. 15, 1941; d. Jerome Sidney and Vera (Joseph) Peterson; 1 child, Claire Marie. BS, Boston U., 1968; M in Nursing, U. Wash., 1969, PhD, 1981. Staff nurse Visiting Nurse Assn., Boston, 1964-66; prof. Seattle U., 1969—, dir. nursing home project, 1990-92, chair pers. com., 1988-90; chair dept. Community Health and Psychiat. Mental Health Nursing, 1987-89. Sec. Coun. on Nursing and Anthropology, 1984-86; pres. Wash. League Nursing, Seattle, 1988-90; pres. bd. Vis. Nurses Svcs., Seattle, 1988-90; contbg. cons. CSI Prodn., Okla., 1987; cons. in nursing WHO/U. Indonesia, Jakarta, fall 1989, Myanmar (Burma), Yangon, winter 1995, Beijing, 1995. Contbr. articles to profl. jours., chptrs. to books. Co-owner (with Robert Colley) North End Train Ctr., Seattle; mem. Seattle Art Mus., 1986—. Fellow: Soc. for Applied Anthropology; mem. Am. Anthropological Assn., Soc. for Med. Anthropology, Nat. League for Nursing, Am. Ethological Soc. Office: Seattle U Sch Nursing Broadway and Madison Seattle WA 98122

PETERSON, JILL SUSAN, elementary school educator; b. Richland, Wash, July 26, 1946; d. Clarence Edward and Doris Edeline (Ostby) Lange; m. Wallace Peterson Jr., Aug. 10, 1968 (dec. Jan. 1991); 1 child, Dawn Sa Ra. BA, Pacific Luth. U., 1968; MA, U. St. Thomas, 1984; post grad., Augsburg Coll., U. Minn., U. St. Thomas, U. Calif., Irvine. Tchr. Little Can. Elem. Sch., 1968—74; title I tutor Red Oak Elem., St. Paul, 1975—79; lead tchr. Sand Creek Elem., Mpls., 1979—88, Andover Elem., Mpls., 1988—. Adj. instr. multicultural edn. Hamline U., 1995—99; instr. Seeking Ednl. Equity and Diversity, 1995—. Human rights commr. City Arden Hills, Minn., 1987—90; pres. Children of the World, 1995—99; vol. Ctr. for Victims of Torture, Mpls., 2000—; Women in Soc. del. to Brazil People to People Ambassador Program, 2003; mem. coun. Roseville Luth. Ch., Minn., 1986—88, 1994—96. Recipient Award of Excellence, Minn. Elem. Sch. Prin. Assn., 1992. Mem.: NEA, Anoka-Hennepin Edn. Minn., Edn. Minn., Alpha Delta Kappa (pres. Alpha Omicron chpt. 1993—94, Regional Scholar of Merit 1994, Tchr. Outstanding Performance 2000). Avocations: reading, swimming, travel, volunteering. Home: 3061 Highpointe Curve Roseville MN 55113 Office: Andover Elem Sch 14950 Hanson Blvd NW Andover MN 55304

PETERSON, JULIE, public information officer; b. Ft. Dodge, Iowa; m. John P. Wesley; 2 children. BA, St. Olaf Coll., Northfield, Minn.; MA, Sarah Lawrence Coll. Previously in edn.; mem. Vt. Legislature; with Office of Gov. of Vt., 1991—, now chief of staff, 1991—. Office: Office of the Gov 109 State St Montpelier VT 05609-0001

PETERSON, KATHERINE DIANNE, ministry assistant; b. Poplarville, Miss., Dec. 10, 1956; d. Juel Billy and Ruby Lee Smith; m. Kelvin Ray Peterson, Sept. 26, 1975; children: Kelvie Dianne Culpepper, Kalena Rae Wells, Kidron Dishon. AAS, Pearl River C.C., Poplarville, Miss. Student trainee NASA, Stennis Space Ctr., Miss., 1995; adminstrv. office asst. Naval Rsch. Lab., Stennis Space Ctr., 1995—97; cert. ministry asst. Steep Hollow Bapt. Ch., Poplarville, 1997—. Mgr. office Pete's Auto Sales, Poplarville, 1997; sec. Poplarville Family Chiropractic, 2001—. Sun. sch. tchr. Steep Hollow Bapt. Ch., Poplarville, 1996—. Mem.: Phi Beta Lambda. Home: 97 Sandy Smith Rd Poplarville MS 39470 Office: Steep Hollow Bapt Ch 2272 Hwy 53 Poplarville MS 39740*

PETERSON, KATHERINE H. federal agency administrator, former ambassador; b. Pasadena, CA; Student, Nat. War Coll.; BA, U. Calif., Santa Cruz. Mem. staff Foreign Svc., 1976, Bureau of African Affairs, Washington; deputy chief of mission Amer. Embassy, Windhoek, Namibia, 1993—96; U.S. ambassador to Lesotho U.S. Dept. State, Washington, 1998—2001; dir. Fgn. Service Inst., Washington, 2001—. Office: Fgn Service Inst 4000 Arlington Blvd Washington DC 22204-1500*

PETERSON, LAUREN KAY, social worker; b. Hammond, Ind., Nov. 4, 1959; d. John Lee and Darlene Fay Schoon; m. Jeffrey Marvin Peterson, Nov. 25, 1983; children: Daniel John, Calelo Russell; m. Jeffrey Lawrence Federoff, Apr. 20, 1979 (div. June 1982); children: Elisabeth Ann, Jeffrey James. BA, Purdue U., 1992; MSW, Ind. U., 2000. LCSW. Client asst. The Caring Place, Valparaiso, Ind., 1993—95; behavioral health tech. INPACT, 1994—95; client asst. St. Jude House, Crown Point, Ind., 1995—96; family resource specialist Kidspace Nat. Ctrs., Merrillville, Ind., 1996—2000; social worker White's Family Svcs., Hobart, Ind., 1999—2001; clinician II Soutlake Ctr. Mental Health, Merrillville, 2000—. Ct. apptd. spl. adv. Youth Svc. Bur., Portage, Ind., 1996—2003. Mem.: NASW, Phi Alpha. Avocations: reading, skiing, water-skiing. Home: 13829 Huseman Cedar Lake IN 46303 Office: Southlake Ctr Mental Health 8555 Taft St Merrillville IN 46410

PETERSON, LINDA H. English language and literature educator; b. Saginaw, Mich., Oct. 11, 1948; BA in Lit. summa cum laude, Wheaton Coll., 1969; MA in English, U. R.I., 1973; PhD in English, Brown U., 1978. From lectr. to assoc. prof. Yale U., New Haven, 1977-92, prof., 1992—, dir. undergrad. studies English, 1990-94, chair, 1994-2000, acting chair, 2003, Niel Gray Jr. prof. of English, 2002—. Dir. Bass writing program Yale Coll., 1979-89, 90—; mem. various departmental and univ. coms. Yale U., 1977—; presenter in field. Author: Victorian Autobiography: The Tradition of Self-Interpretation, 1986, Traditions of Victorian Women's Autobiography: The Poetics and Politics of Life Writing, 1999; co-author: Writing Prose, 1989, A Struggle for Fame: Victorian Women Artists and Authors, 1994; co-editor: Wuthering Heights: A Case Study in Contemporary Criticism, 1992, The Norton Reader, 10th edit., 2000, Instructor's Guide to the Norton Reader, 2000; mem. editl. bd. Writing Program Adminstrn., 1983-85, Coll. Composition and Comm., 1986-88, Auto/Biography Studies, 1990—;, Victorian Poetry, 2002—; contbr. articles to profl. jours. Resident fellow Branford Coll., 1979-87, Mellon fellow Whitney Humanities Ctr., 1984-85, fellow NEH, 1989-90, fellow Harry Ransom Humanities Rsch. Ctr., U. Tex., 1997; life fellow Clare Hall, Cambridge, Eng., 1998—. Mem. MLA (del. assembly 1984-86, mem. program com. 1986-89, mem. nonfiction divsn. com. 1988-92, mem. nominating com. 1993-94, mem. teaching of writing divsn. 1993-98), Nat. Writing Program Adminstrs. (mem. cons.-evaluator program 1982-95, mem. exec. bd. 1982-84, 89-90, v.p. 1985-86, pres. 1987-88), Nat. Coun. Tchrs. English (mem. CCCC nominating com. 1985, mem. coll. sect. com. 1987-90). Home: 53 Edgehill Rd New Haven CT 06511 1343 Office: Yale U Dept English PO Box 208302 New Haven CT 06520-8302

PETERSON, LINDA S. lawyer; b. Grand Forks, N.D., Mar. 15, 1952; BA summa cum laude, U. N.D., 1973; JD, Yale U., 1977. Bar: N.D. 1977, D.C. 1978, U.S. Dist. Ct. D.C. 1979, U.S. Ct. Appeals (D.C. cir.) 1979, U.S. Ct. Appeals (3d cir.) 1982, Calif. 1986, U.S. Ct. Appeals (fed. cir.) 1986. Law clk. Ct. of Appeals for D.C., Washington, 1977-78; ptnr. Sidley & Austin, L.A., 1978—. Dep. counsel Webster Commn., 1992; mem. bd. trustees Southwestern U. Sch. Law, 1995. Recipient Dean Phillips Memorial Award, Vietnam Veterans of America. Mem. State Bar Calif. (rules of ct. com. 1988-91), L.A. County Bar Assn. (conf. dels. 1987-90), Women Lawyers Assn. L.A. (bd. dirs. 1989-95), Phi Beta Kappa. Office: Sidley & Austin 555 W 5th St Ste 4000 Los Angeles CA 90013-3000

PETERSON, MARJORIE, former mayor; b. Chisholm, Minn., Aug. 16, 1924; d. Martin and Catherine Mihelich Champa; m. Andrew Levchak, July 6, 1946 (dec. Mar. 2, 1975); children: Carol, Andrea, Richard, Lisbeth; m. Walter C. Peterson, Sept. 25, 1976. Bookkeeper Ford Sales & Svc., Chisholm, Minn.; dental asst. Office of Dr. J.E. Hoffman, Chisholm, 1960—65; podiatrist asst. Office of Dr. Larson, Hibbing, Minn., 1967; divsn. sec. Fin. Programs, Hibbing, 1967—74; mem. city coun. City of Chisholm, 1977—85, ofcl., 1989—95, mayor, 1996—98. Mem. Pub. Utilities Bd., Chisholm. Contbr. poetry to anthologies. Pres. Range Assn. Sch. and City, Chisholm; chmn. Chisholm-Hibbing Airport Authority, Hibbing, 1991—2001; v.p. bd. dirs. Mus. Mining, 2002; mem. Friends of Libr.; bd. dirs. League Minn. Cities, St. Paul, 1984. Recipient C.C. Ludwig award, League Minn. Cities, 1984, Silver award, World of Poetry, 1990, Golden Poet award, 1998, Famous Poet, Famous Poet Soc., 2000. Mem.: Moose. Democrat. Roman Catholic. Achievements include being first woman elected to City Council in Chisholm, and first woman elected as mayor. Avocations: reading, volunteer work, travel, cards. Home: 405 7th St NW Chisholm MN 55719

PETERSON, MARY L. state agency official; BA in English, Carleton Coll., 1972; MA in Tchg. in Edn. and English, Duke U., 1974; postgrad., U. Utah, 1977-80. Tchr. English, New Canaan (Conn.) Sch. Dist., from 1973, Brighton Ctrl. Sch. Dist., Rochester, N.Y., Davis County Sch. Dist., Kaysville, Utah, until 1977; rsch. asst. in cultural founds. and ednl. adminstrn. U. Utah, Salt Lake City, 1977-79; prin. St. Nicholas Elem. Sch., Rupert, Idaho, 1979-81; cons. Nev. Dept. Edn., Carson City, 1981-92, dep. supt. instrnl., rsch. and evaluative svcs., 1992-94, supt. pub. instrn., 1994—. Assessor Nev. Assessment Ctr., Nat. Assn. Secondary Sch. Prins.; mem. accreditation team N.W. Assn. Schs. and Colls.; trainer Tchr. Effectiveness for Student Achievement, Correlates Effective Schs.; facilitator Assisting Change in Edn.; mem. state team Nat. Coun. for Accreditation Tchr. Edn. Asst. editor: Work, Family and Careers (C. Brooklyn Derr), 1980; contbr. to profl. publs. Scholar Carleton Coll., Duke U. Mem. Phi Kappa Phi, Delta Kappa Gamma. Office: Nev Dept Edn Capitol Complex 700 E 5th St Carson City NV 89701-5096

PETERSON, MARY N. state representative, lawyer; b. Buffalo, Apr. 3, 1960; m. Barrett Peterson; 4 children. BA summa cum laude in Govt., St. Lawrence U., 1982; JD, Northwestern U., 1985. Atty.; state rep. State of Vt., 2003—. Chair Williston Selectboard, 2001—; mem. Taft Corners Task Force, Future Develop. Com., Williston Sch. Growth Planning Com.; past mem. Williston Planning Commn., Williston Conservation Commn., Colchester Planning Commn.; mem. Williston Fed. Ch. Mem.: Vt. League of Cities and Towns (bd. dirs.). Democrat. Avocations: skiing, canoeing, camping. Office: 2588 N Williston Rd Williston VT 05495 E-mail: marypeterson@adelphia.net.

PETERSON, MILLIE M. state senator; b. Merced, Calif., June 11, 1944; BS, U. Utah, 1979, MSW, 1984. Mem. Utah Senate, Dist. 12, Salt Lake City, 1991—. Susa Young Gates Award, 1998. Mem. NASW. Democrat. Address: 7131 W 3800 S West Valley City UT 84128-3416 Office: Senate House 319 State Capitol Salt Lake City UT 84114 E-mail: mpeter7131@aol.com.

PETERSON, NANCY, special education educator; AS, Webster State Coll., 1963; BS in Elem. Edn. magna cum laude, Brigham Young U., 1964, MS in Ednl. Psychology, 1966, PhD in Ednl. Psychology, 1969. Instr. in tchr. edn. Brigham Young U., Provo, Utah, 1966-69; asst. prof. edn. dept. spl. edn. U. Kans., Lawrence, 1969-74, dir. spl. edn. classes for handicapped children Clin. Tng. Ctr., 1969-89, project dir. head start tng., 1973-74, coord. edn. univ. affiliated facility Clin. Tng. Ctr., 1969-74, coord. pers. tng. programs in mental retardation, 1973-76, assoc. prof. edn., 1974-88, project dir. pers. tng. programs, 1986-93, prof. edn. dept. spl. edn., 1988—, dept. chair, 1994—. Rsch. sci. Bur. Child Rsch., U. Kans., 1969—; prin. investigator for Kans. U. Kans. Early Childhood Rsch. Inst., 1977-82 Recipient J.E. Wallace Wallin award Internat. Coun. Exceptional Children, 1993. Office: U Kans Dept Spl Edn 3001 Dole Bldg Lawrence KS 66045-0001

PETERSON, NANCY L. federal agency administrator, volunteer; b. Des Moines, Sept. 15, 1939; d. Leonard Edward and Arlene Mae (Brubaker) Peterson; 1 child, Ted. BA, DePauw U., 1961; MA in Edn., UCLA, 1965. Tchr. U.S. Bur. Indian Afairs, Crownpoint, N.Mex., 1961—74, L.A. City Sch., 1964—65; mgr. fed. women program U.S. Dept. Health Edn. and Welfare, San Francisco, 1974—85, mgr. equal employment opportunity, 1985—95; ret.; with Planned Parenthood Assn., San Francisco, 1980—. Author: Our Lives for Our Selves Women Who Have Never Married, 1981, The Ever Single Woman Life Without Marriage, 1982. Pres. UN Assn., San Francisco, 1997—; area rep. Am. Women Internat. Understanding, 1995—2000. Named Hon. Alumnus, Pacific Luth. Theol. Sem., 2003. Mem.: Sierra Club. Lutheran. Home: 839 Washington Ave Albany CA 94706 E-mail: nlpeterson@aol.com.

PETERSON, PATTY, radio personality; d. Willie and Jeanne Arland Peterson; m. Stuart Paster; 4 children. Radio show host Sta. WCCO Radio, Mpls., 1997—. Singer: (albums) The More I See You. Recipient 7 time Minn. Music award winner for Best Female Vocalist and Best Group. Office: WCCO 625 2nd Ave S Minneapolis MN 55402 Mailing: P.O. Box 390697 Minneapolis MN 55439-0697

PETERSON, ROBYN GAYLE, museum curator; b. San Francisco, Jan. 17, 1958; BA, UCLA, 1979; MA, U. Wis., 1982, PhD, 1987. Goldsmith, 1974-80; collections acquisition asst. social studies bibliographer Meml. Libr./U. Wis., 1984-86; curator of collections The Rockwell Mus., Corning, N.Y., 1988-99; dir. collections and rsch. Turtle Bay Exploration Park, 1999—. Author: American Frontier Photography, 1993, Edward Borein, 1997, Warp and Weft: Cross-cultural Exchange in Navajo Weavings, 1997, Transforming Trash: Bay Area Fiber Art, 2000; contbg. author: Allgemeines Künstlerlexikon, 1998—; editor/contbr.: Collector's Choice Review: Masterpieces of Glassmaking, Frederick Carder and the Steuben Glass Works, 1993, Brilliance in Glass: The Lost Wax Glass Sculpture of Frederick Carder, 1993, Journey to Justice: The Wintu People and the Salmon, 2002, The Other Side of the Looking Glass: The Glass Body and Its Metaphors, 2003; mng. editor: Frederick Carder and Steuben Glass: American Classics (Thomas P. Dimitroff), 1998; contbr. articles to profl. jours.; peer reviewer IMLS. Mem. Coll. Art Assn., Soc. Advancement of Scandinavian Studies, Glass Art Soc., Am. Assn. Mus. Office: Turtle Bay Exploraton Park PO Box 992360 Redding CA 96099-2360 E-mail: rpeterson@turtlebay.org.

PETERSON, ROSE ANN, artist; b. Salt Lake City, June 15, 1935; d. Phillip Arthur Snell and Vera Langford; m. Bennett Pulley Peterson, Dec. 20, 1957; children: Rose Marie, Alan, Bruce, Jenny. BA with honors, U. Utah, 1957. Tchr. home econs. Davis County Sch. Dist., Bountiful, Utah, 1957—59, Alexandria (Va.) Sch. Dist., 1959—60; instr. art Bountiful Davis Art Ctr., 1989—. Exhibitions include Simon's Art, Laguna Beach, Calif., 1988—94, Repartee, Salt Lake City, 1994—98, Apple Frame Gallery, Bountiful, 1995—; designer ch. gardens at Temple Sq., LDS Ch., Salt Lake City, 1995—, artist watercolors, lithographs; Represented in permanent collections LDS Ch., Brigham Young U., Sundance Inst., Salt Lake Art Ctr., Crown Prince of Norway. Mem. com. Bountiful-U.S. Centennial Celebration, 1976; art cons. Woman's LDS Ch. Relief Soc., Salt Lake City, 1982; coord. Mus. Ch. History and Art, Salt Lake City, 1983—99. Mem.: DAR, Utah Watercolor Soc. (life; Signature mem., founding pres. 1974—78, bd. dirs. 1978—81), Omicron Nu, Phi Kappa Phi. Mem. Lds Ch. Avocations: gardening, travel, family. Home: 1501 E Mueller Park Rd Bountiful UT 84010

PETERSON, SOPHIA, international studies educator; b. Astoria, N.Y., Nov. 24, 1929; d. George Loizos and Caroline (Hofstetter) Yimoyines; m. Virgil Allison Peterson, Dec. 28, 1951; children: Mark Jeffrey, Lynn Marie. BA, Wellesley (Mass.) Coll., 1951; MA, UCLA, 1956, PhD, 1969; DHL (hon.), Wheeling Jesuit U., 1997. Instr. Miami U., Oxford, Ohio, 1961-63; with W.Va. U., Morgantown, 1966—, assoc. prof., 1972-79, prof., 1979-97, prof. emerita, 1997—, dir., internat. studies maj., 1980-92. Dir. W.Va. Consortium for Faculty & Course Devel. in Internat. Studies, Morgantown, 1980-97, founding dir., 1997—. Author: monograph Monograph Series in World Affairs, 1979. Recipient gold medal semi-finalist CASE Prof. of Yr. award Coun. for Advancement and Support of Edn., 1987, Outstanding Tchr. award W.Va. U., W.Va. U. Coll. Arts and Scis., 1988, finalist Prof. of Yr. award W.Va. Faculty Merit Found., 1991, Heebink award for disting. state svc. W.Va. U., 1984. Mem. W.Va. Polit. Sci. Assn. (pres. 1984-85). Democrat. Avocations: sailing, travel. Home: 849 Vandalia Rd Morgantown WV 26501-6247 Office: WVa U Dept Polit Sci Morgantown WV 26506

PETERSON, V. SPIKE, political science educator; d. Charles Russell and Mattie Lois Peterson. BS in Psychology and Philosophy, U. Ill., 1970, MA in Social Scis. and Anthropology, 1975; PhD in Internat. Rels., American U., Washington, DC, 1988. Adj. asst. prof. U. So. Calif., Los Angeles, 1988—89, American U., Washington, 1989—90; asst. prof. U. Ariz., Tucson, 1990—96, assoc. prof., 1996—. Vis. rsch. scholar Australian U., Canberra, 1995, U. Bristol, Eng., 1998, U. Goteborg, Sweden, 2000. Author: Critical Rewriting of Global Political Economy, 2003; co-author: Global Gender Issues, 1999; editor: Gendered States: Feminist (Re)Visions of International Relations Theory, 1992; contbr. articles to profl. jours. Grantee MacArthur Found., 1996; recipient Nat. Mentor award Soc. for Women in Internat. Polit. Economy, 2000, Provost Gen. Edn. Tchg. award, 2001. Office: Dept Polit Sci U of Arizona 315 Social Scis Tucson AZ 85721

PETERSON, VERONICA MARIE (RONNIE PETERSON), clinical nurse manager; b. Washington, Feb. 29, 1956; BA, U. Wis., Eau Claire, 1978; BSN, U. Wis., Madison, 1990, MS, 1993. Oncology staff nurse U. Wis. Hosp. and Clinics, Madison, 1990-93, nursing supr., 1993-97, nurse mgr., 1998—. Author: Just the Facts: A Pocket Guide to Basic Nursing, 1994, 2d edit., 1998; author: (poetry) SunFlowers, 1997, Listen, 1996, Learning to Soar, 1997, Alone, 1997, My Grandmother's Quilt, 1998, Sisters, 1998, others; author/dir. videos: Understanding Changes in Your Health After Cancer Treatment, 1993, Reflections on Nursing, 1994; contbr. articles to profl. jours.; compiled, dir., participant dinner theatre prodn.: Reflections on Nursing. Recipient Nat. Presdl. award for Lit. Excellence Iliad Press, 1997, 98. Mem. Wis. Nurses Assn. (bd. dirs. 1993-97, nurse liaison to Wis. State Med. Soc.994-97, Image of Nursing award 1993, 95), Madison Dist. Nurses Assn. (2d v.p. 19-94, pres. 1995-97), Internat. Soc. Poets, Oncology Nursing Soc., Pi Kappa Delta (nat. oratory champion 1978).

PETITAN, DEBRA ANN BURKE, elementary school educator; b. Chgo., Mar. 12, 1932; d. James Marcellus and Susan Florence (Hines) Burke; m. Kenneth Charles Petitan, Aug. 9, 1952; 1 child, Susan Florence. AA, Wilson Jr. Coll., Chgo., 1951, N.Y. Inst. Photography, 1952; BS in Primary Edn., Chgo. State U., 1956, MS in Indsl. Edn., 1967; DSc in Applied Sci. and Tech., London Inst. Tech., 1971; postgrad., U. Wis., Bradley U., U. Calif., U. Ill.; grad., Inst. Children's Lit., West Redding, Conn., 1991; cert. in Childrens' Portraiture, North Light Art Sch., 1997. Tchr. Chgo. Bd. Edn., 1958-71, guidance counselor, 1976-84, now tchr., cons.; nat. dir. edn. Nation of Islam, 1971-75; design engr. Fed. Sign and Signal Corp., Chgo., 1975-76; CEO, owner Petitan's Creative Projects, Inc. Nat. adv. bd. Nat. Right to Work Orgn., 1976-85; cons. ednl. devel., 1978; computer libr. cons.; owner, CEO, Fayzah's Fin. Svcs., Instrn. Svcs. in Trading and Investing, Fayzah's Creative Projects, Inc.; ednl. cons. tech. analysis and chart reading stock market; participant summer writing festival U. Iowa, 1991. Photographer VISTA News, 1969-70; writer children's lit.; author curriculum introducing computer-aided design techniques in the pub. schs., 1965. Cmty. svc. rec. sec. 9600 Block Club; navigator, pub. rels. officer IL wing Squadron 8, capt. CAP, 1953—56; chmn. Career Women for Johnson/Humphrey, Chgo., 1965; dir. Christian edn. Trinity United Ch. Christ, Chgo., 1978—81, family counselor, 1978—81; organizer, leader family counseling ministry, lic. lay Eucharistic min. Episcopal Ch. St. Edmund, Chgo. Episc. Diocese, 1989. Named Woman of Yr. Iota Phi Lambda, 1978; recipient 250 Hr. medal Ground Observer Corps, 1952, 25 Yr. Service medal Chgo. Bd. Edn., 1987. Mem. Off-Campus Writer's Workshop (editor newsletter), Soc. of Children's Book Writers, Am. Contract Bridge League, Am. Bridge Assn. (life master, rec. sec.), Children's Reading Roundtable, Green River Writers, Epsilon Pi Tau. Achievements include introduction of Computer Aided Design curriculum to field of education. Office: Fayzah's Analytical Guidance Svc Chicago IL 60628 E-mail: drdap1@ameritech.net.

PETITO, MARGARET L. foundation administrator; b. Dallas, Sept. 28, 1950; d. Jacob Charles and Eileen (Shank) Loehr; m. John Haven Petito, 1978 (div. 1984); children: John Christian Robert, David Nelson. BA, So. Meth. U., 1972. Mem. Action/Vista Program U.S. Govt., Middlesex, NY, 1972—74; dir., curator Oliver House Mus., Penn Yan, NY, 1975—77; staff asst. Williams & Jensen, P.C., Washington, 1986—89; dir. fed. rels. Chambers Devel. Co., Inc., 1989—92; dir. fed. affairs DSSI-U.S. Biotech., Washington, 1992—94; cons., dir. pub. affairs Embassy Ecuador, Govt. Ecuador, Washington, 1994—96; prin. Petito & Assocs., Washington, 1994—. Dir. external events Internat. Cancer Alliance, Bethesda, Md., 1996—97, Sch. of Bus., Georgetown U., Washington, 1998—99; pres., exec. dir. Friends of Rule of Law in Ecuador, Inc., 2001—. Spl. legis. advisor Drugwatch Internat., Chgo., 1993—; mem. Women's Coun. Energy and Environ., Washington, 1990—94; bd. dirs. Nyumbani Orphanage for Kenyan Children with AIDS, Washington, 1989—99; dir. Marshall Ho. Mus., Lambertville, NJ, 1980—82; mem. task force Women in Govt. Rels., Washington, 1990—96; founder, co-chair Forum for Environ., Washington, 1989—91; pres. Cultural Partnership of the Ams., Washington, 1999—. Mem.: Tex. State Soc., Tex. Breakfast Club. Roman Catholic. Avocations: squash, needlepoint, fishing. Home and Office: Friends of Rule of Law in Ecuador Inc 6008 34th Pl NW Washington DC 20015-1607 E-mail: mlp3@starpower.net.

PETITTO, BARBARA BUSCHELL, artist; b. Jersey City; d. John Edward and Anna (Barnaba) Buschell; m. Joseph Bruno Petitto; children: Vincent John, Christopher Joseph. Studio art cert., N.J. Ctr. Visual Arts, Summit, 1985; student, Art Students League, N.Y.C., 1980, 89-92, Montclair Art Mus., 1991-93. Artist-in-resident art faculty Acad. St. Elizabeth, Convent Stations, NJ, 1989—91; art faculty Morris County Art Assn., Morristown, NJ, 1989; curator Olcott Studio Gallery Art Show, Bernardsville, NJ, 1985, Color/Divine Madness Ward-Nasse Gallery, N.Y.C., 1996; demonstrator Acad. St. Elizabeth Convent Sta., 1989—90, DuCret Sch. Arts Student Art Exhbn.; organizer for acad. students, 1989; dir. Student's Art Festival WNET/Thirteen, Acad. St. Elizabeth, 1989. One-woman shows include County Coll. Morris, 1989, Allied Corp., N.J., 1989, Corner Gallery, World Trade Ctr., N.Y.C., 1989—90, Ward-Nasse Gallery, 1997—98, Johnson & Johnson World Hdqrs., New Brunswick, N.J., 1998—, Hanover Twp. Mcpl. Bldg., 1999, Dominion County Club, Tex., 1999, Nexus Gallery, N.Y.C., 1999, 2001—02, N.J. Ctr. Visual Arts, Summit, 2001, Morris City Libr., 2003, exhibited in group shows at N.A.W.A., Chelsea, N.Y.C., 2000—01, Atelier 14, Chelsea, N.Y., 2000, Internat. Salon, 2000—02, Nat. Soc. Painters in Casein and Acrylic, Balt. Convention Ctr., 2000, numerous others, Represented in permanent collections Nat. Assn. Women Artists, Inc., exhibited in group shows at Denise Bibro Gallery, Chelsea, N.Y.C., 2001, Salmagundi Club, 2001, Morris County Libr., 2003, Somerset Art Assn., 2003, Nat. Assn. Women Artists, N.Y.C., N.Y., 2003, NAWA "Illuminations" Group, 2003, Word-Nasse, Chelsea, N.Y.C., 2003, Represented in permanent collections Ethicon Corp., New Brunswick, N.J., Allied Corp., N.J., Interior Sensations, Marinac, N.Y., Palisades Amusement Pk. Hist. Soc., Cliffside Park Libr., ACI Art Communication Internat., The Best Contemporary Art, Chgo., Salon. Named Miss Livingston N.J., Livingston C. of C.; recipient Rudolph A. Voelcker Meml. award Art Ctr. N.J., 1982, Excellence award Hunterdon Art Mus., 1988, award for excellence Artists League Ctrl. N.J., 1989, Cornelius Low House, Middlesex County Mus., 1989, Montclair Art Mus., 1990, award for mixed media Millburn-Short Hills Art Assn., 1989, 1st Pl. award N.E. Caldwell Arts Festival, 1989, award Nabisco Brands, Inc., East Hanover, N.J., 1990, Excellence award Ann. Tri-State Artists League Ctrl. N.J., 1991-92, Winsor & Newton plaque, Visual Arts League, Edison, N.J., 1992, Excellence award Manhattan Arts Internat. Cover Art Competition, 1994-2000, Hunterdon Art Mus. award for acrylic/mixed media, 1996, Newark Acad., 1996, Livingston Art Assn., 1996, Midland Gallery, Montclair, N.J., 1998 ADP Corp., 1998, Group Liv. Art Assn., 1998, Mary K. Karasick Meml. award, 2000, award N.J. Ctr. Visual Arts, 2001; juried show Somerset Art Assn., 1997-98. Mem. Nat. Soc. Painters in Casein and Acrylic, Nat. Assn. Women Artists, Inc., N.J. Ctr. Visual Arts, Nat. Mus. Women in Arts, Jersey City Mus., Catherine Lorillaird Wolfe Art Club, World Wildlife Fedn., Somerset Art Assn. Avocations: opera, vocalist, piano, concerts, museums. Office: PO Box 515 Whippany NJ 07981-0515

PETOSA, JANET FRANCES, recruiting executive, publishing executive; b. Hartford, Conn., Sept. 10, 1954; d. Paul and Agnes Casmiras (Kamarauskus) Aiello; m. Frank Joseph Petosa, May 17, 1980; children: Allison Marie, Justin Paul-Charles. BA, Ctrl. Conn. State U., New Britain, 1976, MS in Orgn. and Mgmt., 1995. Mgr. clerical divsn. Hobson Assocs., Southington, Conn., 1978-80; br. mgr. Uniforce Temporary Svcs., Hartford, 1985; exec. dir. Women in World Trade-Conn., Inc., Suffield, 1995-96; pres. Computext, Bristol, Conn., 1996—, Global Recruiters, Bristol, 1996—, Computext, Bristol, 1996—. Editor-in-chief Global Job Bank, 1997. Hon. mem. Permanent Commn. on the Status of Women, Conn., mem. Congl. Dist. 6 adv. coun., 1996-98. Mem. AAUW, NAFE, Am. Entrepreneur's Assn. (charter), Am. Seminar Leaders Assn., Am. Women's Econ. Devel. Corp., Nat. Assn. Women Bus. Owners (congl. adv. coun. 1995-96). Democrat. Roman Catholic. Avocations: piano, statistical research, internet. Address: 200 Blakeslee St Apt 237 Bristol CT 06010-8804

PETRAS, CHERYL ANN, nursing administrator; b. Richmond Heights, Ohio, Mar. 23, 1967; d. Stephen and Barbara Ann Petras. AA in Nursing, Cuyahoga C.C., 1992. RN Ohio, 1992. Lab. tech. asst. Marymount Hosp., Garfield Heights, Ohio, 1989—92; staff nurse, supr. Heather Hill Inc.,

Chardon, 1992—99; nurse supr. Mt. Alverna Home, Parma, 1999—2003, Slovene Home for Aged, Cleve., 2003—. Republican. Roman Catholic. Avocations: animal rescue, gardening, travel, baking, photography. Home: 863 Overlook Ridge Dr Cleveland OH 44109 Office: Slovene Home for Aged 18621 Neff Rd Cleveland OH 44119

PETRAUSKAS, HELEN O., automobile manufacturing company executive; b. 1944; married. BS, Wayne State U., 1966, JD, 1971. Chemist, group supr. Sherwin-Williams Co., 1966-71; various positions Ford Motor Co., Dearborn, Mich., 1971-79, asst. dir. emissions and fuel economy cert., 1980-82, exec. dir. environ. and safety engring and rsch. staff, 1982-83, exec. dir. engring. and tech. staff, 1983, corp. v.p. environ. and safety engring., 1983—. Office: 1 American Rd Dearborn MI 48126-2701

PETREE, BETTY CHAPMAN, anesthetist; b. Emmetsburg, Iowa, Sept. 25, 1950; d. David Jr. and Wilma Ruby (Jones) Chapman; m. Howard Gray Petree, Sept. 21, 1974; children: Zachary Gray, Lynsey Taylor. Diploma, Davis Hosp. Sch. Nursing, 1970; cert., N.C. Bapt. Hosp. Sch. Nursing, 1974. RN, N.C. Clin. mgr. pre admit testing N.C. Bapt. Hosp., Winston-Salem, chief nurse anesthetist outpatient surgery, 1990—, asst. dir. nurse anesthesiology, 1997—. Mem. AANA Nat. Re-certification Coun., 1996—2003, v.p., 1997—99, vice chmn., 1998—2002, chmn., 1999—2003. Author: Anesthesia for Kidney Transplantation, Thoracic Aortic Trauma. Recipient Excellence in Teaching award, 1984, 86, 100 Great N.C. Nurses award, 1992. Mem. AANA (Clin. Practitioner award 1988), NCANA (program chmn. 1984-85), NCBH Anesthesia Alumni (sec. 1975-76, pres. 1993-95).

PETRELIS, STELLA MARSHA, writer; b. Tulare, Calif., May 29; d. George Peter and Mersa Soultana Petrelis; m. R.E. Stiles (dissolved). Student, U. Calif., Berkeley, 1962. Freelance writer Fresno (Calif.) Bee, 1981—93, Visalia (Calif.) Times-Delta, 1983—91. Recipient Poetry award, Writer's Digest, 1983. Avocations: art, photography, music, horticulture.

PETRI, CHRISTINE ANN, music educator; b. Trenton, N.J. d. Swen Albert Gilberg and Elizabeth Catherine Schutte; m. Joseph Carmen Petri, July 21, 1994. MusB in Music Edn., Westminster Choir Coll., 1971; MA in Music Performance, The Coll. N.J., 1974. Cert. tchr. N.J., 1971. Choral music dir. Hunterdon Ctrl. HS, Flemington, NJ, 1971—84, Hightstown (N.J.) HS, 1984—. Musical dir., prodr. Drama Dept. Hightstown (N.J.) HS, 1984—; pvt. voice and guitar tchr., NJ, 1967—90. Performer: worldwide, 1984—. Mem.: NEA, Ctrl. Jersey Music Educators Assn., Music Educators Nat. Conf., N.J. Edn. Assn. Avocations: antiques, classic cars, cats, guitar, costuming. Home: 1617 Miriam Drive North Brunswick NJ 08902 Office: Hightstown High School 25 Leshin Lane Hightstown NJ 08520

PETRIE, AMY ELIZABETH, speech pathology/audiology services professional; b. Madisonville, Ky., July 7, 1975; d. David Harold and Janice Carol Vincent; m. Gregory Thomas Petrie, Feb. 20, 1999; 1 child, Nathan Thomas. BSc, We. Ky. U., 1997, MSc, 1998. Cert. Am. Speech-Lang. Hearing Assn., lic. Ky. Bd. Speech Pathology and Audiology. Speech lang. pathologist Muhlenberg County Bd. Edn., Greenville, Ky., 1999—. Mem. coun. Pennyrile Rural Electric, Hopkinsville, Ky., 2003. Republican. Baptist. Avocations: reading, family, church, pets, travel.

PETRILLO, NANCY, public relations executive; CFO, exec. v.p. Edelman Pub. Rels. Worldwide, Chgo. Office: Edelman Pub Rels Worldwide 200 E Randolph St Fl 63D Chicago IL 60601-6436

PETRUSKI, JENNIFER ANDREA, speech and language pathologist; b. Kingston, NY, Jan. 28, 1968; d. Andrew Francis and Judith (Cruger) Petruski. BS, SUNY, Buffalo, 1990, MSEd, 1992. Cert. tchr. speech-hearing handicapped N.Y., lic. speech-lang. pathology N.Y. Speech-lang. pathologist Kingston (N.Y.) City Schs., 1992—, student rev. team facilitator, 2002—; clin. practicum supr. SUNY, New Paltz, 1996—. Cooperating tchr. SUNY, New Paltz, 1995—2002; ind. contr. speech svcs. Ulster County, 1997; cooperating tchr. Coll. St. Rose, 1997, 2004; summer sch. tchr. New Paltz Sch. Dist., 2002. Mem.: Bd. Regional Assn. Pres., N.Y. State Speech-Lang. and Hearing Assn., Am. Speech and Hearing Assn., Speech and Hearing Assn. Hudson Valley (corr. sec. 1995—98, newsletter editor 1995—2002, membership com. 1995—2002, treas. 1997, pres. 1999—2000, nominating com. 1999—2000, membership chair 2000—02, legis. chair 2000—, past. pres. 2001—, website adminstr. 2001—, historian 2001—, continuing edn. adminstr. 2002, program com. 2003, newsletter com. 2003—), Bd. Regional Presidents (membership chair 2000—02, public info. chair 2003—). Home: PO Box 88 Hurley NY 12443 E-mail: jpetruski@aol.com.

PETTERCHAK, JANICE A. researcher, writer; b. Springfield, Ill., Sept. 15, 1942; d. Emil H. and Vera C. (Einhoff) Stukenberg; m. John J. Petterchak, Oct. 5, 1963; children: John A., Julie Gilmour, James. AA, Springfield Coll., 1962; BS, Sangamon State U., 1972, MA, 1982. Supr. hist. markers Ill. State Hist. Soc., Springfield, 1973-74, asst. exec. dir., 1985-87; curator photographs Ill. State Hist. Libr., Springfield, 1974-79, assoc. editor, 1979-83, rep. local history svcs., 1983-85, libr. dir., 1987-95. Project dir. NEH/Ill. newspaper cataloging project. Author: Mapping a Life's Journey: The Legacy of Andrew McNally III, 1995, Jack Brickhouse: A Voice for All Seasons, 1996, Researching and Writing Local History in Illinois: A Guide to the Sources, 1987, Taming the Upper Mississippi, 2000; To Share: The Heritage, Legend and Legacy of Nathan Cummings, 2000, Out To Sea Again: A Naval Armed Guard in World War II, 2002, Lone Scout: W.D. Boyce and American Boy Scouting, 2003; editor: Illinois History: An Annotated Bibliography, 1995; assoc. editor Illinois Historical Jour.; contbr. articles to profl. jours. Grantee NEH, 1987-95. Mem. Ill. State Hist. Soc., Stephen A. Douglas Assn., Sangamon County Hist. Soc. (bd. dirs. 1991-94, 99-2002, v.p. 1996-97, pres. 1995-96), Soc. of Midland Authors. Home: 11381 Mallard Dr Rochester IL 62563-8011 E-mail: petterchak@biogwriter.com.

PETTI, NANCY A. information technology manager; BS, Pace U., 1986. Market rsch. analyst Nielsen Market Rsch., N.Y.C., 1986—87, account coord., 1987—88; mktg. svcs. coord. Pfizer Inc., N.Y.C., 1988—90, mktg. asst. bus. devel., 1990—92, asst. mgr. bus. devel., 1992—93, asst. mgr. sales planning, 1993—96, mgr. sales planning, 1996—99, mgr. sales ops., 1999—2000, project mgr., 2000—. Mem.: Am. Mktg. Assn. Office: Pfizer Inc 150 East 42nd St - 150/3/65 New York NY 10017 E-mail: nancy.a.petti@pfizer.com.

PETTIGREW, JO ARNOLD, educational association administrator; MA in Speech and Drama, North Tex. State U.; EdD in Ednl. Adminstrn., Okla. State U. Asst. exec. dir. Okla. State Sch. Bds. Assn., 1983—95; exec. dir. United Suburban Schs. Assn., 1996—. Bd. dirs. S.W. Ednl. Lab., Austin, Tex., 2002—, sec. bd. dirs., 2003—. Mem.: Okla. Edn. Coalition. Office: SEDL 211 E 7th St Austin TX 78701-3281

PETTIGREW, L. EUDORA, retired academic administrator; b. Hopkinsville, Ky., Mar. 1, 1928; d. Warren Cicero and Corrye Lee (Newell) Williams; children: Peter W. Woodard, Jonathan R. (dec.). MusB, W.Va. State Coll., 1950; MA, So. Ill. U., 1964, PhD, 1966; PhD honoris causa, U. Pretoria, South Africa, 2002, Holy Family Coll., 2002. Music/English instr. Swift Meml. Jr. Coll., Rogersville, Tenn., 1950-51; music instr., librarian Western Ky. Vocat. Sch., Paducah, 1951-52; music/English instr. Voorhees Coll., Denmark, S.C., 1954-55; dir. music and recreation therapy W.Ky. State Psychiatric Hosp., Hopkinsville, 1956-61; research fellow Rehab. Inst., So. Ill. U., Carbondale, 1961-63, instr., resident counselor, 1963-66, coordinator undergrad. ednl. psychology, 1963-66, acting chmn. ednl. psychology, tchr. corps instr., 1966; asst. prof. to assoc. prof. dept. psychology U. Bridgeport, Conn., 1966-70; prof., chmn. dept. urban and met. studies Coll. Urban Devel. Mich. State U., East Lansing, 1974-80; assoc. provost, prof. U. Del., Newark, 1981-86; pres. SUNY Coll. at Old Westbury, 1986-98. Cons. for rsch. and evaluation Hall Neighborhood House Day Care Tng. Project, Bridgeport, 1966-68, U.S. [illegible] Regional Lab. Edn. Devel. Ctr., Newton, Mass., 1967-69; coordinator for edn. devel., 1968-69; cons. Bridgeport Public Schs. lang. devel. project, 1967-68, 70; Lansing Model Cities Agy., Day Care Program, 1971; U. Pitts., 1973, 74, Leadership Program, U. Mich. and Wayne State U., 1975, Wayne County Pub. Health Nurses Assn., 1976, Ill. State Bd. Edn., 1976-77; assoc. prof. U. Bridgeport, 1970, Ctr. for Urban Affairs and Coll. of Edn., Mich. State U., East Lansing, 1970-73; trustee L.I. Community Found.; program devel. specialist Lansing Public Schs. Tchr. Corps program, 1971-73; coord. workshop Conflict Resolution The Woman's Role in Our World, 4th Internat. UN Conf. on Women, Beijing, China, 1995; lectr. in field; condr. workshops in field; mem. adv. com. Economists Allied for Arms Reduction, 1996; guest spkr. Internat. Conf. on The New Role of Higher Edn. in the Context of an Ind. Palestinian State, An-Najah Nat. U., Nablus, Palestine, 1996. Tv/radio appearances on: Black Women in Edn, Channel 23, WKAR, East Lansing, 1973, Black Women and Equality, Channel 2, Detroit, 1974, Women and Careers, Channel 7, Detroit, 1974, Black Women and Work: Integration in Schools, WITL Radio, Lansing, 1974, others; editor: Universities and Their Role in World Peace, 2003; contbr. articles to profl. jours. Mem. Commn. U. Peace, Costa Rica; bd. dirs. U. Pretoria (South Africa) Found., Nat. Peace Garden Found. Recipient Diana award Lansing YWCA, 1977, Outstanding Profl. Achievement award, 1987, award L.I. Ctr. for Bus. and Profl. Women, 1988, Educator of Yr. 100 Black Men of L.I., 1988, Black Women's Agenda award, 1988, Woman of Yr. Nassau/Suffolk Coun. of Adminstrv. Women in Edn., 1989, Disting. Ednl. Leadership award L.I. Women's Coun. for Equal Edn. Tng. and Employment, 1989, L.I. Disting. Leadership award L.I. Bus. News, 1990, Disting. Black Women in Edn. award Nat. Coun. Negro Women, 1991; named Outstanding Black Educator, NAACP, 1968, Oustanding Woman Educator, Mich. Women's Lawyers Assn. and Mich. Trial Lawyers Assn., 1975, Disting. Alumna, Nat. Assn. for Equal Opportunity in Higher Edn., 1990, Woman of Yr., Nassau County League of Women Voters, 1991, Disting. Alumna So. Ill. U., 1997, N.Y. State Senate resolution of commendation, 1998; Elected to Achievers Hall of Fame: Long Island Bus. and Profl. Women's Orgn., 2001 Mem. AAAS, Nat. Assn. Acad. Affairs Adminstrs., Internat. Assn. Univ. Pres. (exec. com., v.p.), Phi Delta Kappa.

PETTINATO, MAUREEN J. special education educator; b. Scranton, Pa., May 28, 1954; d. Robert Andrew and Ellen Pauline (Delaney) Smith; m. Ronald Joseph Pettinato, July 14, 1984; children: Melanie Ann, Dean Anthony. BS, East Stroudsburg U., 1976; MS, U. Scranton, 1997. Cert. tchr. Pa. Spl. edn. tchr. Northeastern Ednl. Intermediate Unit, Archbald, Pa., 1980—. Transition coord. Lakeland Sch. Dist. Mem.: Coun. for Exceptional Children. Avocations: jogging, skiing, reading.

PETTINE, LINDA FAYE, physical therapist; b. New London, Conn., Nov. 11, 1958; d. Robert Anderson and Pauline Priscilla (Johnson) Erwin; m. H. Louis Pettine, Jr., Mar. 6, 1982. BS, U. Conn., 1980; post grad., Quinnipiac Coll., Hamden, Conn., 1989-91. Registered phys. therapist Conn. Staff phys. therapist Hahneman Hosp., Worcester, Mass., 1980, Newport Hosp., RI, 1980-82, Middlebury Orthop. Group, Waterbury, Conn., 1982, Easter Seal Rehab. Ctr., Ctrl. Conn., Meriden, Conn., 1982-84; hosp. and rehab. ctr. coord. Easter Seal Rehab. Ctr., Ctrl. Conn., Meriden, Conn., 1984-86; co-founder Pettine and McDiarmid Phys. Therapy, Cheshire and Wallingford, Conn., 1986-88; pres. Keystone Phys. Therapy and Sports Medicine P.C., Cheshire and Wallingford, Conn., 1988-99; facility adminstr. Keystone Phys. Therapy and Sports Medicine, Cheshire and Wallingford, Conn., 1999—2001; facility dir. Conn. Phys. Therapy, LLC, Wallingford, 2001—04, dist. dir., 2002—04; dir. outpatient rehab. Hosp. of St. Raphael, Wallingford, Conn., 2004—. Lectr. Diabetes Edn. Program, Meriden, Conn., 1985; cons. Waterbury Nursing Ctr., Conn., 1986—87; guest spkr. Conn. chpt. Am. Diabetes Assn., Meriden, 1986, Arthritis Support Group, Meriden, Conn., 1986, Meriden Indsl. Mgr. Assn., Conn., 1986. Mem. adv. bd. Waterbury Continuing Edn. Program, Conn. Katherine Wyckoff and Margaret Wyckoff Moore Endowed Scholar, 1991. Mem.: MD Health Plan (phys. therapist and chiropractor liaison com. 1997). Avocations: reading, needlecrafts, quilting.

PETTIS-ROBERSON, SHIRLEY MCCUMBER, retired congresswoman; b. Mountain View, Calif. d. Harold Oliver and Dorothy Susan (O'Neil) McCumber; m. John J. McNulty (dec.); m. Jerry L. Pettis (dec. Feb. 1975); m. Ben Roberson, Feb. 6, 1988; children: Peter Dwight Pettis, Deborah Neil Pettis Moyer. Student, Andrews U., U. Calif., Berkeley; PhD (hon.), Loma Linda U., 2002. Mgr. Audio-Digest Found., L.A., Glendale; sec.-treas. Pettis, Inc., Hollywood, 1958-68; mem. 94th-95th Congresses from 37th Calif. Dist., mem. coms. on interior, internat. rels., edn. and labor. Pres. Women's Rsch. and Edn. Inst., 1979-80; bd. dirs. Kemper Nat. Ins. Cos., 1979-97, Lumbermens Mut. Ins. Co.; bd. dir. Kemper Corp. Mem. Pres.'s Commn. on Arms Control and Disarmament, 1980-83, Commn. on Presdl. Scholars, 1990-93; trustee U. Redlands, Calif., 1980-83, Loma Linda (Calif.) U. and Med. Ctr., 1990-95; chair Loma Linda U. Children's Hosp. Found.; mem. Former Mems. Congress, 1988—. Mem.: Morningside Country Club (Rancho Mirage, Calif.).

PETTUS, CANDICE, social sciences educator; b. Inglewood, Calif., June 2, 1967; d. Barbara Ann and Nicolas Van Cina; m. Marvin Thomas Pettus, Sept. 22, 1995; children: Jackson Thomas, Cameron Ann. AA, Orange Coast Coll., 1989—91; BA, Calif. State U., 1992—93, MA, 1998—2000. Human resources, mgmt., adminstrv. Nordstrom, 1984—98; instr. of sociology and anthropology Orange Coast Coll., Costa Mesa, Calif., 2001—. Candidate Santa Ana Unified Sch. Bd., Calif., 2003; cons. Preparing For A Degree, Santa Ana, Calif.; advisor United Student Sociologists, Costa Mesa, Calif., 2002—03. Peg Taylor Forensic Scholarship, Orange Coast Coll., 1991. Mem.: Faculty Assn. of Calif. Cmty. Colleges. Office: Orange Coast Coll 2701 Fairview Rd Costa Mesa CA 92628 E-mail: cpettus@occ.cccd.edu.

PETTY, M. S. MARTY, publisher; b. St. Louis, Mo., Dec. 17, 1952; Publisher Hartford Courant, 1997—. Office: Hartford Courant 285 Broad St Hartford CT 06115-2510

PETTY, MARGE D. state senator; b. Ft. Wayne, Ind., Feb. 26, 1946; m. Tyrus C. Petty, 1968; children: Brandon, Megan. BS, Tex. Christian U., 1968; MEd, Kans. U., 1978; JD, Washburn U. Sch. Law, 1990. Tchr., 1968-69; mgmnt. consultant, 1981-; health educator, 1978-81; mem. City Council of Topeka, 1985-89; dep. mayor Topeka, Kans., 1986; mem. Kans. Senate, 1988-. Mem. Topeka Metro. Ballet, Chamber of Commerce, Mulvane Art Ctr. Episcopalian. Home: 106 SW Woodlawn Ave Topeka KS 66606-1241 Address: Kansas Senate State Capitol Rm 422-S Topeka KS 66612

PETTY, MARTY, publishing executive; m. Mark Petty; 2 children. BJ, U. Mo., 1975; MS in Mgmt., Harvard Grad. Ctr., 1989. Asst. mng. editor Kansas City Star and Times; mng. editor The Hartford Courant, 1983-86, v.p., dep. exec. editor, 1986-89, assoc. pub. for projects and planning, 1989, sr. v.p., gen. mgr., pub., CEO, 1997—2000; exec. v.p. St. Petersburg Times, 2000—. Editor The Electronic Times, 1991-92. Mem. journalism bd. Wm. Randolph Hearst Found., 1987-89; mem. CEO adv. bd. Greater Hartford Arts Coun.; pres. bd. Camp Courant; bd. dirs. Hartford Courant Found., Hartford Hosp. Holding Co.; mem. The MetroHartford Growth Couns. millennium mgmt. com. Mem. Newspaper Assn. of Am. (Ptnrs. 2000 com., Copyright Clearance Ctr. adv. bd.), Soc. Newspaper Design (pres. 1985, active cons.), Am. Soc. Newspaper Editors, Am. Press Inst., AP Mng. Editors, Poynter Inst. Office: St Petersburg Times 490 1st Ave S Saint Petersburg FL 33701-1121

PETTY, PRISCILLA HAYES, writer, columnist, producer; b. Nashville, Aug. 22, 1940; d. Anderson Boyd and Margaret Louise Hayes; m. Gene Paul Petty, Jan. 10, 1961; children: Eric, Damon, Boyd. BA in English, Vanderbilt U., 1962; postgrad., Lang. Inst., Dartmouth Coll., 1965. Cert. tchr. Ohio. Tchr. English Cin. Suburban Pub. Schs., 1962-65, head dept. English, tchr., 1971-79; newspaper columnist Cin. Enquirer, 1978-89; also syndicated newspaper columnist Gannett News Svc., Washington, 1982-89. Cons. Arthur Andersen & Co., 1981-82; writer United Western Corp., 1982; exec. producer, on camera interviewer national TV documentary, 1992; commentator nat. bus. TV show, 1992; pres., owner, Petty Cons. Prodns., producer Total Quality Tng. Tapes. speaker W. Edwards Deming Seminars; cons. in field. Author: History of a Boardsman (oral history), 1979, Under a Lucky Star: The Story of Frederick A. Hauck, 1986, What's in It for You and the Firm: CEOs and Presidents Look at Community Involvement. Mem. Cin. Coun. World Affairs; chmn. Cin. Media-Bus. Exch., 1983; founder, pres., bd. trustees Cin. Oral History Found., 1984—. Named Outstanding Tchr., Project Teach, Ohio Edn. Assn., 1978; recipient WICI Great Lakes Regional Communicators' award; Pulitzer Prize nominee for Harvard U. Bus. Rev. article. Mem. Women in Comms. (Outstanding Communicator of Yr. 1985), Oral History Assn., Soc. Profl. Journalist, Wyo. Woman's Club. Home: 229 Oliver Rd Cincinnati OH 45215-2638

PETTY, RACHEL, academic administrator; BS in Psychology, MS, Howard U.; postgrad., George Washington U.; PhD in Human Devel., U. Md. Former mem. faculty dept. edn. Howard U., Washington; instr. dept. psychology Fed. City Coll. (now U. D.C.); from asst. prof. to prof. dept. psychology U. D.C., from asst. dean to dean Coll. Arts and Scis., v.p. acad. affairs, 2001—. Sch. psychologist D.C. Pub. Schs. Title I program, Prince George's County Pub. Schs.; staff psychologist, cons., clin. program dir. St. Ann's Infant and Maternity Home; consulting psychologist Bd. of Child Care, United Meth. Ch., Balt.-Washington Dist.; cons. child and family svcs. divsn. D.C. Dept. Human Svcs.; cons. Ednl. Testing Svc.; cons., evaluator Everyday Theater Youth Ensemble; cons. D.C. Ednl. Licensure Commn. Contbr. articles to profl. jours. Active Md. State Foster Care Rev. Bd., Conf. on Developing World Class Ednl. Stds. for D.C., Luth. Social Svcs. of Nat. Capital Area, D.C. Child Welfare Consortium. Named one of Outstanding Young Women of the Carolinas; recipient award, Nat. Assn. Equal Opportunity in Higher Edn.; fellow Minority Dissertation, State of Md. Mem.: AAUW, APA, D.C. Psychol. Assn. (bd. dirs.), Am. Psychol. Soc., Psi Chi. Office: U DC 4200 Connecticut Ave NW Washington DC 20008

PETURA, BARBARA BRADLEY, academic administrator; b. Milw., June 24, 1943; d. Donald C. and Elizabeth Conger Bradley; m. Richard C. Petura, Aug. 3, 1968. BA in English magna cum laude, Lawrence U., 1965. English tchr. New Canaan (Conn.) HS, 1965—68; reporter Morris County Citizen, Parsippany, NJ, 1969—70; news bur. staff writer U. Idaho, Moscow, 1970—71, news bur. asst. mgr., 1971—72, news bur. mgr., 1972—79; news bur. dir. U. Oreg., Eugene, 1979—85; news and info. svcs. dir. Wash. State U., Pullman, 1985—91, asst. v.p. univ. rels., 1991—2002, assoc. v.p. univ. rels., 2003—. Author: (book) Cross-Strain Breeding of Racing Siberian Huskies, 1983; editor: The Seppala Siberian, 1987; webmaster (website) WorkingDogWeb.com. Mem., v.p., pres. Pullman Civic Trust, 1985—93; v.p. campaign com. United Way Pullman, 1997—2003. Mem.: Coun. Advancement and Support Edn. (mem. instl. rels. com., nat. case 1978—82, chair elect bd. dirs. dist. VIII 1982—84, chair bd. dirs. dist. VIII, nat. trustee 1984—86, mem. commn. communication and mktg. 1999—2002, nat. trustee, chair commn. communication and mktg. 2002—, Dist. VIII Bronze award 1991, Dist. VIII Silver award 1998), Mortar Bd., Phi Beta Kappa, Kappa Delta. Avocations: gardening, travel, reading about archaeology, community service. Office: Wash State U French Adminstrn Bldg 446 Pullman WA 99164-1040 E-mail: petura@wsu.edu.

PETZEL, FLORENCE ELOISE, textiles educator; b. Crosbyton, Tex., Apr. 1, 1911; d. William D. and Eloise Petzel. PhB, U. Chgo., 1931, AM, 1934; PhD, U. Minn., 1954. Instr. Judson Coll., 1936-38; asst. prof. textiles Ohio State U., 1938-48; assoc. prof. U. Ala., 1950-54; prof. Oreg. State U., Corvallis, 1954-61, 67-75, 77, 77, prof. emeritus, 1975—, dept. head, 1954-61, 67-75; prof., divsn. head U. Tex., 1961-63; prof. Tex. Tech. U., 1963-67. Vis. instr. Tex. State Coll. for Women, 1937; vis. prof. Wash. State U., 1967. Author: Textiles of Ancient Mesopotamia, Persia and Egypt, 1987; contbr. articles to profl. jours. Effie I. Raitt fellow, 1949-50. Mem. Met. Opera Guild, Sigma Xi, Phi Kappa Phi, Omicron Nu, Iota Sigma Pi, Sigma Delta Epsilon. Home: 150 Downs Blvd Apt A206 Clemson SC 29631-2043

PETZOLD, CAROL STOKER, state legislator; b. St. Louis, July 28; d. Harold William and Mabel Lucille (Wilson) Stoker; m. Walter John Petzold, June 27, 1959; children: Ann, Ruth, David. BS, Valparaiso U., 1959. Tchr. Parkwood Elem. Sch., Kensington, Md., 1960-62; legis. aide Md. Gen. Assembly, Annapolis, 1975-79; legis. asst. Montgomery County Bd. Edn., Rockville, Md., 1980; cmty. sch. coord. Parkland Jr. H.S., Rockville, 1981-87; mem. Md. Ho. of Dels., Annapolis, 1987—, mem. constl. and adminstrv. law com., 1987-93, mem. judiciary com., 1994—, chair subcom. on criminal justice, 2003—, vice chair Montgomery County del., 1995—, dep. majority whip, 1999—2002. Mem. transp. planning bd. Nat. Capitol Region, 1989—; vice chmn. assembly on fed. issues Nat. Conf. State Legislatures, 1996-97, chair adv. com. on energy, 1997-99, chair energy and transp. com., 1998-99, vice chair spl. com. drug and alcohol abuse, 1999—. Editor Child Care Sampler, 1974, Stoker Family Cookbook, 1976. Pres. Montgomery Child Care Assn., 1976-78; mem. Md. State Scholarship Bd., 1978-87, chmn. 1985-87; chmn. Legis. Com. Montgomery County Commn. for Children and Youth, 1979-84; mem., v.p. Luth. Social Services Nat. Capitol Area, Washington, 1980-86; mem. exec. com. coun. Montgomery United Way, 1981-2000. Named Mother of Yr., March of Dimes, 2000; named one of Top 100 Md. Women, Daily Record, 2002, 2004; recipient Statewide award, Gov.'s Adv. Bd. on Homelessness, 1994, recognized for outstanding commitment to children, U.S. Dept. HEW, 1980, Award of Excellence, MADD, 2002, Disting. Legislator award, 2003, Impaired Driving Coalition, 2003, Legis. award, Md. Coalition Against Domestic Violence, 2003. Mem.: AAUW (honoree Kensington br. 1971, 2002, honoree Md. divsn. 1981), Women Legislators of Md., Md. Women Legislators Caucus, Women's Polit. Caucus (chmn. Montgomery County 1981—83, exec. com. 2003—04). Democrat. Lutheran. Home: 14113 Chadwick Ln Rockville MD 20853-2103

PEVEAR, ROBERTA CHARLOTTE, retired state legislator; b. Bethel, Maine, July 4, 1930; d. Frank Albert Sr. and Thirza Estella (Hickford) Gibson; m. Edward Gordon Pevear, Aug. 21, 1971. Diploma in Comml. Art, Gould Acad., 1947. Sec. Wilner Wood Products, South Paris, Maine, 1947-50; sec. export dept. Whitaker Cable, North Kansas City, Mo., 1951-56; sec. br. and dist. Anheuser-Busch, Inc., Kansas City, Mo., 1957-59; legal sec. Johnson & Johnson, New Brunswick, N.J., 1960-65, St. John, Ronder & Bell, Kingston, N.Y., 1966; sec., adminstrv. asst. Sears-Roebuck & Co., Overland Park, Kans., 1967-70, Exeter, N.H., 1971-77; salesman Avon Products, Hampton Falls, N.H., 1978-86; mem. ho. reps. State of N.H., 1979-88, ret., 1988. Commr. Rockingham Planning Commn., N.H., 1979-88, N.H. Planning Com., 1985-88; clk. Environment and Agrl. Com. N.H. Ho. Reps., 1983-88; del. mem. Rockingham County, 1979-88, exec. bd., 1984-88; chmn. Rockingham County Home, 1987-88. Civil Def. dir., Hampton Falls, NH, 1980—88. Recipient Community Citizen award

Hampton Falls Grange, 1982, Seacoast Retired Sr. Service award, 1985. Mem. Nat. Order Women Legislators, N.H. Order of Women Legislators, DAR. Avocations: writing, genealogy, travelling.

PFAELZER, MARIANA R. federal judge; b. L.A., Feb. 4, 1926; AB, U. Calif., 1947; LLB, UCLA, 1957. Bar: Calif. 1958. Assoc. Wyman, Bautzer, Rothman & Kuchel, 1957-69, ptnr., 1969-78; judge U.S. Dist. Ct. (ctrl. dist.) Calif., 1978—. Mem. Jud. Conf. Adv. Com. on Fed. Rules of Civil Procedure. Pres., v.p., dir. Bd. Police Commrs. City of L.A., 1974-78. UCLA Alumnus award for Profl. Achievement, 1979, named Alumna of Yr., UCLA Law Sch., 1980, U. Calif. Santa Barbara Disting. Alumnus award, 1983. Mem. ABA, Calif. Bar Assn. (local adminstrv. com., spl. com. study rules procedure 1972, joint subcom. profl. ethics and computers and the law coms. 1972, profl. ethics com. 1972-74, spl. com. juvenile justice, women's rights subcom. human rights sect.), L.A. County Bar Assn. (spl. com. study rules procedure state bar 1974), Ninth Cir. Dist. Judges Assn. (pres.). Office: US Dist Ct 312 N Spring St Ste 152 Los Angeles CA 90012-4703

PFAFF, JUDY, artist; b. London, 1946. Student Wayne State U., 1965-66, So. Ill. U., 1968-69; B.F.A., Washington U.-St. Louis, 1971; postgrad. Yale U., 1970, M.F.A., 1973. One-woman exhbns. include: Webb and Parsons Gallery, New Canaan, Conn., 1974, Artists Space N.Y., 1975, Theatre Gallery, U. So. Fla., Tampa, 1977, Los Angeles Contemporary Exhbn., 1978, Holly Solomon Gallery, N.Y., 1980, Daniel Weinberg Gallery, Los Angeles, 1984, Wacoal, Japan, 1985, Holly Solomon Gallery, 1986, Nat. Mus. Women in the Arts, Washington, 1989, Cleve. Ctr. for Contemporary Art., Cleve., 1990, Fabric Workshop, N.Y., 1991, Rotunda Gallery, N.Y., 1993; group exhbns. include: Whitney Mus. Am. Art, 1975, Hallwalls Gallery, Buffalo, 1976, Art Mus., U. Calif.-Santa Barbara, 1979, Neuberger Mus., SUNY-Purchase, 1979, Contemporary Arts Mus., Houston, 1980, Contemporary Arts Ctr., Cin., 1980, Mus. Modern Art, N.Y.C., 1984, Venice Biennale, 1984, Rotunda Gallery, Bklyn., 1984, Bklyn. Mus., 1985, WHitney Mus. Am. Art., N.Y., 1988, Internat. Art Projects, Asia, 1990, Mis. Modern Art., 1989, Inst. Contemporary Art, Phila., 1991, Cultural Space, N.Y., 1992, Henie-Onstad Art Ctr., Norway, 1992, Whitney Mus. Am. Art at Champion, Stamford, Conn., 1993, Drawing Ctr., N.Y., 1993; commd. work Spokane City Hall, 1981. Nat. Endowment Arts grantee, 1979; Guggenheim fellow, 1983.

PFAFFLIN, SHEILA MURPHY, psychologist; b. Pasadena, Calif., July 31, 1934; d. Leonard Anthony and Honora (Shields) Murphy; m. James Reid Pfafflin, Sept. 7, 1957. BA, Pomona Coll., 1956; MA, Johns Hopkins U., 1958, PhD, 1959. Mem. tech. staff AT&T Bell Labs., Murray Hill, N.J., 1959-75; dist. mgr. AT&T, Morristown, N.J., 1975-98. Chair subcom. on womem Com. on Equal Opportunities in Sci. and Tech., NSF, Washington, 1981-85; mem. adv. coun. Math/Sci. Tchr. Supply and Demand, N.J. Dept. Higher Edn., 1982-83; mem. adv. bd. for Maths., Sci. and Computer Sci. Teaching Improvement Grants, N.J. Dept. Higher Edn., 1984-89. Co-editor: Expanding the Role of Women in the Sciences, 1978, Scientific Technological Change & the Role of Women in Development, 1981, Psychology & Educational Policy, 1987; contbr. articles to profl. jours. Trustee Ramapo Coll. of N.J., Mahwah, N.J., 1984-96; adv. bd. Project "SMART", Girls Clubs of Am., N.Y.C., 1984-94, Consortium for Ednl. Equity, Rutgers U., New Brunswick, N.Y., 1983-90; pres. Assn. for Women in Sci. Ednl. Found., Washington, 1982-98. Fellow AAAS, N.Y. Acad. Scis., Am. Psychol. Assn., Assn. for Women in Sci. (pres. 1980-81, Women Scientist award, Met. Chpt., 1987); mem. Phi Beta Kappa, Sigma Xi. Avocation: sailing. Home: 173 Gates Ave Gillette NJ 07933-1719

PFAHL, FLORADELLE ATWATER, civic worker; b. Miami, Fla., Nov. 30, 1926; d. Jay Charles and Gertrude Luella (Glasby) Atwater; m. John Kerch Pfahl, June 19, 1948 (dec.); children: Jay charles, John Christopher, Susan Kay. BS in Edn., U. Akron, 1948; LHD (hon.), Ohio Dominican Coll., 1994. Office mgr. S.S. Pierce and Co., Boston, 1948-49; asst. to state home demonstration leader Ohio State U., Columbus, 1949-51, asst. to dean of women, 1951-53. Co-chmn. capital campaign Max Fisher Sch. Bus., Ohio State U., 1997—; mem. governing bd. dirs. Columbus Found., 1991—, chmn., 1995-97; trustee Ohio Dominican Coll., 1995—, Greater Columbus Arts Coun., 1997—, Luth. Social Svcs., 1995—; mem. devel. com. Promise for Life Meml., 1997—, Circle of Women, 1996—; bd. dirs. Columbus Mus. of Art, 1975-97, Pro Musica Svc. Bd., 1992—, United Cmty. Coun., 1972-78, Ohio State U. Found.; past pres. Action for Children; bd. dirs., Ctr. of Sci. and Industry, 1982-96, auction chmn., 1982; bd. dirs., Opera Columbus, 1989-95, chmn. ball, 1990; bd. dirs., past chmn. Riverside Meth. Hosp. Found.; bd. dirs. Riverside Meth. Hosp., 1991-92; vice chmn. United Way of Franklin County, 1993-94, campaign cabinet mem., 1982-83; bd. dirs., treas., past chmn. Ohio United Way; mem. Columbus Area Leadership program, 1970-76, Mayor's Com. for Bicentennial, 1975-76; vol. WBNS Call for Action, 1982-84, 6 On Your Side, 1985-90, Planned Parenthood, 1934-37, Cub Scouts and Boy Scouts Am., 1965-67, Girl Scouts U.S., 1967-72; mem. Holy Trinity Evang. Luth. Ch., vol. bookkeeper 1956-71, coun. mem. 1973-81, chmn. 1979-81, ch. choir 1953-78, altar guild 1981-90; bd. Ohio State U. Found., 1998—. Recipient Gov.'s Spl. Recognition, Gov. of Ohio, 1990, Women of Achievement award, Columbus YWCA, 1991, Mayor's medal for vol. svc., Mayor of Columbus, 1984, Mobius Club award Ctr. of Sci. and Industry, 1984; named Woman of Yr., Upper Arlington Rotary, 1975. Mem. Phi Mu (treas. 1945-48, omicron chpt. advisor 1958-60, 70-74, nat. housing com. 1968-70, Leadership award 1968, Outstanding Alumni award 1970), Scioto Country Club, Capital Club. Avocations: collecting, tennis, golf, travel, gourmet cooking. Home: 1427 Roxbury Rd Apt C Columbus OH 43212-3212

PFANSTIEL PARR, DOROTHEA ANN, interior designer; b. San Antonio, Nov. 10, 1931; d. Herbert Andraes and Ethel Missouri (Turner) Pfanstiel; m. Thurmond Charles Parr, Jr., Sept. 15, 1951; children: Thurmond Charles, III, Richard Marshall. AA, Coll. San Antonio, 1951. Asst. dean evening divsn. Alamo C.C., San Antonio, 1951; tchr., cons., dir. Humpty Dumpty Early Childhood Devel. Ctr., San Antonio, 1951-58; exec. sec., cons. Thurmond C. Parr, Jr. & Co., San Antonio, 1960-61; founder, pres. Creative Designs, Ltd., San Antonio, 1962—. Liaison, coord. Internat. Students Lang. Sch., Lackland AFB, San Antonio, 1959-65. Adv., cons. Urban Renewal Inner City San Antonio, 1959-61. Named Notable Woman of Tex., Awards and Hons. Soc. Am., 1984-85. Republican. Presbyterian. Avocations: travel, swimming, reading, studying, walking. Office: Creative Designs Ltd PO Box 6822 San Antonio TX 78209-0822

PFEFFER, CYNTHIA ROBERTA, psychiatrist, educator; b. Newark, May 22, 1943; d. Edward I. and Ann Pfeffer. BA, Douglas Coll., 1964; MD, NYU, 1968. Assoc. dir. child psychiatry inpatient unit Albert Einstein Coll. Medicine, Bronx, N.Y., 1973-79; chief child psychiatry inpatient unit N.Y. Hosp. Cornell Med. Ctr., White Plains, N.Y., 1979-95; assoc. prof. clin. psychiatry Weill Med. Coll. Cornell U., N.Y.C., 1984—. Prof. psychiatry Cornell U. Med. Coll., 1989—; pres. N.Y. Coun. on Child and Adolescent Psychiatry, N.Y.C., 1989—; dir. childhood bereavement program Weill Med. Coll. Cornell U., 1999—. Author: The Suicidal Child, 1986, Difficult Moments in Child Psychotherapy, 1988; editor: Youth Suicide: Perspectives on Risk and Prevention, 1989, Intense Stress and Mental Disturbance in Children, 1996; co-editor: Neurologic Disorders: Developmental and Behavioral Sequelae for Child and Adolescent Psychiatric Clinics of North America, 1999. Recipient Erwin Stengel award Internat. Assn. Suicide Prevention, 1987, Wilford Hulse award N.Y. Coun. on Child & Adolescent Psychiatry, 1989, Sigmund Freud award Am. Soc. Psychoanalytic Physicians, 1994. Fellow Am. Psychiat. Assn., Am. Acad. Child and Adolescent Psychiatry (councillor-at-large 1989—, Norbert Rieger award 1988), Am. Psychopathological Assn.; mem. Am. Assn. Suicidology (pres. 1987, Young Contbrs. award 1981, 82). Office: NY Hosp Westchester Div 21 Bloomingdale Rd White Plains NY 10605-1504 also: 1100 Madison Ave New York NY 10028-0327

PFEIFFER, ANGELA MCGLAUN, psychologist; b. Houston, Tex., Dec. 10, 1967; d. Bill Glenn and Sharon Ann McGlaun; m. John Francis Pfeiffer, July 20, 1968; children: Emily, Braden. BS psychology, Tex. A&M U., Coll. Sta., Tex., 1986—90; MS psychology, Memphis State U., Memphis, Tenn., 1990—94; PhD clin. psychology, U. of Memphis, Memphis, Tenn., 1994—96. Lic. Psychologist Tex. State Bd. of Examiners of Psychology, 1998. Clin. psychologist Tex. Children's Hosp., Learning Support Ctr., Houston, Tex., 2000—, head, teammates program, 1998—2000. Girl scout leader Girl Scouts of Am., Sugar Land, Tex., 2000—03; mem., cmty. based leadership team Lexington Creek Elem., Ft. Bend Ind. Sch. Dist., Mo. City, Tex., 2002—03, mem., emergency preparation team Mo.City, Tex., 2002—03. Mem.: Ft. Bend Psychol. Assn. Avocations: gardening, cooking, camping, reading, travel. Office: Texas Children's Hospital 6621 Fannin Street MC3-2340 Houston TX 77030 Personal E-mail: angelampfeiffer@aol.com. E-mail: ampfeiff@texaschildrenshospital.org.

PFEIFFER, JANE CAHILL, former broadcasting company executive, consultant; b. Sept. 29, 1932; d. John Joseph and Helen (Reilly) Cahill; m. Ralph A. Pfeiffer, Jr., June 3, 1975. BA, U. Md., 1954; postgrad., Cath. U. Am., 1956-57; LHD (hon.), Pace Coll., 1978, U. Md., 1979, Manhattanville Coll., 1979, Amherst U., 1980, Babson Coll., 1981, U. Notre Dame, 1991, Bryant Coll., 1995. With IBM Corp., Armonk, N.Y., 1955-76, sec. mgmt. rev. com., 1970, dir. comm., 1971, v.p. comm. and govt. rels., 1972-76, bus. cons., 1976-78; chmn. NBC, Inc., N.Y.C., 1978-80; bus. cons., 1980—. Dir. Ashland Oil Co., Mony Fin. Svcs., Internat. Paper Co., J.C. Penney Co.; trustee The Conf. Bd., 1991. Mem. pres.'s adv. com. White House Fellows, 1966, Pres.'s Gen. Adv. Commn. on Arms Control and Disarmament, 1977-80, Pres.'s Commn. Mil. Compensation; trustee Rockefeller Found., U. Md., Carnegie Hall, 1981-1986, U. Notre Dame; bd. mem., Catholic Univ. of Am., 1973-1978, Rockefeller Found., 1973-1985, White House Fellows, 1976-1981, Kettering Found., 1975-1979. Recipient Achievement award Kappa Kappa Gamma, 1974-80, Eleanor Roosevelt Humanitarian award N.Y. League for Hard of Hearing, 1980, Disting. Alumna award U. Md., 1975, Humanitarian award NOW, 1980, Centennial Alumna medallion U. Md., 1988; White House fellow, Washington, 1966, Making Waves award, Greatest 50 Women in Radio and Television-AWRT, 2002. Mem. Coun. Fgn. Rels., Overseas Devel. Coun., Econ. of N.Y. Club. Office: C/O Jonathan L Smith Chesapeake Asset Mgmt LLC 1 Rockefeller Plz Rm 1210 New York NY 10020-2002 Home: Johns Island 1050 Beach Rd Apt 1G Vero Beach FL 32963-3413

PFEIFFER, MARGARET KOLODNY, lawyer; b. Elkin, N.C., Oct. 7, 1944; d. Isadore Harold and Mary Elizabeth (Brody) K.; m. Carl Frederick Pfeiffer II, Sept. 2, 1968. BA, Duke U., 1967; JD, Rutgers U., 1974. Bar: N.J. 1974, N.Y. 1976, D.C. 1981, U.S. Supreme Ct. 1979. Law clk. to Hon. F.L. Van Dusen U.S. Ct. Appeals 3d cir., Phila., 1974-75; assoc. Sullivan & Cromwell, N.Y.C. and Washington, 1975-82, ptnr., 1982—. Contbr. articles to profl. jours. Trustee Am. Found. for Blind, Nat. Law Ctr. on Homelessness and Poverty; mem. bd. visitors Trinity Coll. of Duke U. Mem. ABA, Internat. Bar Assn., D.C. Bar Assn., N.Y. State Bar Assn., Assn. of Bar of City of N.Y., Am. Soc. of Intl. Law. Avocations: gardening, reading, music. Office: Sullivan & Cromwell 1701 Pennsylvania Ave NW Washington DC 20006 5866 E-mail: pfeifferm@sullcrom.com.

PFEIFFER, MICHELLE, actress; b. Santa Ana, Calif., Apr. 29, 1957; d. Dick and Donna P.; m. Peter Horton (div.); 1 adopted child, Claudia Rose; m. David Kelley, Nov. 13, 1993. Student, Golden West Coll., Whitley Coll. Actress: (feature films) Falling in Love Again, 1980, Hollywood Knights, 1980, Charlie Chan and the Curse of the Dragon Queen, 1981, Grease II, 1982, Scarface, 1983, Ladyhawke, 1985, Into the Night, 1985, Sweet Liberty, 1986, Amazon Women on the Moon, 1987, Witches of Eastwick, 1987, Married to the Mob, 1988, Tequila Sunrise, 1988, Dangerous Liaisons, 1988 (Acad. award nominee for best supporting actress, 1989, BAFTA award, 1990), The Fabulous Baker Boys, 1989 (L.A. Film Critics Assn. award for best actress, 1989, D.W. Griffith award Nat. Bd. Rev., 1989, N.Y. Film Critics award, 1989, Nat. Soc. Film Critics award for best actress, 1990, Golden Globe award for best actress drama, 1990, Acad. award nominee for best actress, 1990), The Russia House, 1990, Frankie & Johnny, 1991, Love Field, 1992 (Acad. award nominee for best actress, 1993), Batman Returns, 1992, The Age of Innocence, 1993, Wolf, 1994, Dangerous Minds, 1995, Up Close and Personal, 1996, To Gillian on her 37th Birthday, 1996, One Fine Day, 1996, A Thousand Acres, 1997, The Prince of Egypt (voice), 1998, The Story of Us, 1998, A Midsummer Night's Dream, 1999, Deep End of the Ocean, 1999, What Lies Beneath, 2000, I Am Sam, 2001, White Oleander, 2002, Sinbad: Legend of the Seven Seas (voice), 2003; (TV movies) The Solitary Man, 1979, Callie and Son, 1981, The Children Nobody Wanted, 1981, Splendor in the Grass, 1981, One Too Many, 1983, Tales from the Hollywood Hills: Natica Jackson, 1987, Power, Passion and Murder, 1987; (TV series) Delta House, 1979, B.A.D. Cats, 1980; prodr: (films) A Thousand Acres, 1997; exec. prodr.: (films) One Fine Day, 1996. Named Woman of the Yr., Harvard's Hasty Pudding Theater Club, 1995; recipient Crystal award, Women in Film, 1993. Office: care ICM 9830 Wilshire Blvd Beverly Hills CA 90211-1934*

PFEIFFER, PHYLLIS KRAMER, publishing executive; b. N.Y.C., Feb. 11, 1949; d. Jacob N. and Estelle G. Rosenbaum-Pfeiffer; m. Stephen M. Pfeiffer, Dec. 21, 1969; children: Andrew Kramer, Elise Kramer. BS, Cornell U., 1970; postgrad., U. San Diego, 1976-78. Instr. Miss Porter's Sch., Farmington, Conn., 1970; tchr. Dewey Jr. H.S. N.Y.C. Bd. Edn., 1970-73; rschr. Hunter Coll., N.Y.C., 1971-72; account exec. La Jolla (Calif.) Light, 1973-75, advt. dir., 1975-77, gen. mgr., 1977-78, pub., 1978-87; exec. v.p. Harte Hanks So. Calif. Newspapers, 1985-87; gen. mgr. San Diego edit. L.A. Times, 1987-93; pres., pub. Marin Ind. Jour., Novato, Calif., 1993-2000; v.p. advt. and mktg. Contra Costa Times, 2000—. Dir. comm. ctr. San Diego State U., 1980-93. Bd. dirs. La Jolla Cancer Rsch. Found., 1979-82, YMCA, San Diego Ballet, 1980, Dominican Coll., San Rafael, Calif, 1994—, Marin Theater Co., Alvarado Hosp., 1981-88, chmn. fin. com., 1986, sec. bd., 1986; co-chmn. Operation USS La Jolla, USN, 1980—; mem. mktg. com. United Way, 1979-81, chmn., 1983; trustee La Jollan's Inc., 1975-78, Nat. Pk. Trust, 2000-02, Dogs for the Blind, 2001-; mem. Conv. and Visitors Bur. Blue Ribbon Com. on Future, 1983; mem. resource panel Child Abuse Prevention Found., 1983—; bd. overseers U. Calif., San Diego; mem. violent crimes task force San Diego Police Dept.; dir. Guide Dogs for the Blind, Oveland Mus. Grantee N.Y. Bd. Edn., 1971-72; named Pub. of Yr., Gannet Co., Inc., 1995. Mem. Newspaper Assn. Am., Calif. Newspaper Pubs. Assn. (bd. dirs., exec. com.), Chancellor's Assn. U. Calif.-San Diego, Clairemont Club. Office: Contra Costa Times 2640 Shadelands Dr Walnut Creek CA 94598 E-mail: ppfeiffer@cctimes.com.

PFEIFFER, SOPHIA DOUGLASS, state legislator, lawyer; b. N.Y.C., Aug. 10, 1918; d. Franklin Chamberlin and Sophie Douglass (White) Wells; m. Timothy Adams Pfeiffer, June 7, 1941; children: Timothy Franklin, Penelope Mesereau Keenan, Sophie Douglass. AB, Vassar Coll., 1939; JD, Northeastern U., 1975. Bar: R.I. 1975, U.S. Ct. Appeals (1st cir.) 1980, U.S. Supreme Ct. 1979. Editl. rschr. Time, Inc., N.Y.C., 1940-41; writer Officer War Info., Washington, 1941-43, N.Y.C., 1943-45; editl. staff Nat. Geog. Mag., Washington, 1958-59, 68-70; editor Turkish Jour. Pediatrics, Ankara, 1961-63; staff atty. R.I. Supreme Ct., Providence, 1975-76, chief staff atty., 1977-86; mem. Maine Ho. Reps., 1990-94; lectr. U. So. Maine, 1995. Bd. dirs. Death and Dying project. Contbr. in field. Chair bioethics study League Women Voters; pres. Karachi (Pakistan) Am. Sch., 1955-56; chair Brunswick Village Rev. Bd., 1986-89; trustee Brunswick Sewer Dist., 2000—, vice chmn., 2003; bd. dirs. Coll. Guild, 2003—. Home: 15 Franklin St Brunswick ME 04011-2101 E-mail: aminta@gwi.net.

PFEIFFER-KENNEDY, NATALIE PATRICIA ANITA, public relations executive, social sciences educator, consultant; b. Freeport, N.Y., Mar. 26, 1966; d. Richard William Pfeiffer and Nora Natalie Ferrato Bily; m. Brian Edward Kennedy, Jan. 14, 1995; children: Andrew Brian Kennedy, Christina Nora Antoinette Kennedy. Graduate, Barbazon Sch. Modeling, 1983; BA, N.Y. Inst. of Tech., 1988, AA in Social Sciences, BFA magna cum laude in Comm. and Arts, N.Y. Inst. of Tech., 1995, MA with honors in Public Rels. and Advt., 1998. Broadcast journalist Long Island News Tonight, 1986—88; polit. cons., media specialist Long Island, N.Y. Polit. Campaigns, 1988—; pub. rels. cons. Women on the Job Task Force, 1996—98; prin., owner Politcal Image Cons., Kings Park, NY, 1998—. Pub. and polit. liaison COMPASS, Kings Park, NY, 2002—. Dir.: (short film) Nanny Gate; contbr. articles to mags. Treas. Kings Pk. (N.Y.) Coun. Schs., 2003—; family massteam leader, catechist St. Joseph's Roman Cath. Ch., Kings Park, 2001—. Mem.: Pk. View Parent Faculty Assn. (chmn. cultural arts 2002—). Avocations: travel, cooking, history, entertaining, writing.

PFISTER, KARSTIN ANN, human services administrator; b. Phila., Apr. 26, 1955; m. William Howard Pfister, July 10, 1979; children: Caitlin Justine, Rebecca Danielle. BA, Cornell Coll., Mount Vernon, Iowa, 1977; MEd, George Mason U., Fairfax, Va., 1983; postgrad., Va. Poly. and State U., 1986, EdD, 1990; grad., Dept. Defense Exec. Leadership Program,Dick Cheney, Sec. of Defense, 1991. lic. profl. counselor, Va.; nat. cert. counselor, lic. marriage and family therapist, cert. clin. mental health counselor, contracting officer's rep. Instr. Nat. Meteorol. Inst., Kabul, Afghanistan, 1977-78; instr. faculty of medicine, faculty of letters Kabul U., 1978-79; program coord. Pepperdine U., Calif., 1979-81; counselor family svc. ctr. Individual Devel. Assoc., Inc., Arlington, Va., 1981-87; acting dir., program coord. family svc. ctr. Hdqrs. Marine Corps., Henderson Hall, 1987-88; dir. family svc. ctr. Hdqrs. Marine Corps., Arlington, Va., 1988—99, dir., personal svc. divsn., 1999—. Author: Counseling the Military Family: A Conceptual Framework, Virginia Counselors Journal, 1987; Recognition Memory Processes in Bilingual Students, paper presented at the Iowa Acad. of Sci. ann. meeting, 1979. Recipient Cert. Appreciation U.S. Amb. to Afghanistan, 1979., commendation for Superior Civilian Svc., Commendant of the Marine Corps 1995 and 2002, cert. of recognition from the Sec. of Def., 2002. Mem.: Phi Delta Kappa, Kappa Delta Pi. Office: Personal Svc Divsn MCCS HQBN MCNCRC Henderson Ha Arlington VA 22214

PFLAUMER, KATRINA C. lawyer; BA in English Lit. cum laude, Smith Coll.; MA in Tchg. English, Columbia U.; JD, NYU. Tchr. English and Am. Lit. Westtown Sch., Pa., 1970-72; staff atty. Seattle King County Defender Assn., 1975-77, Fed. Pub. Defender's Office, Seattle, 1977-80; pvt. practice, 1980-93; U.S. atty. Dept. Justice (we. dist.) Washington, 1993-01. Pro tem judge King County Superior Ct.; adj. prof. U. Puget Sound Sch. Law; guest lectr. U. Washington, Hastings, Cardozo, Nat. Inst. Trial Advocacy programs; lawyer rep. 9th Cir. Jud. Conf.; named to Atty. Gen. Adv. Com., 1994-95. Mem. Fire Brigade Emergency Response Team. Mem. FBA (pres. we. dist. Washington 1991, chair implementation of gender task force report com.), Nat. Assn. Criminal Def. Lawyers (mem. nominating com.), U.S. Sentencing Commn. (practitioners adv. group), Am. Civil Liberties Union (mem. legal com.), Seattle-King County Bar Assn. (mem. jud. conf. com.), Washington Assn. Criminal Def. Lawyers (pres. 1988-89), State Bench Bar (mem. press com.), Phi Beta Kappa. Office: US Dept Justice 601 Union St Ste 5100 Seattle WA 98101

PFLUM, BARBARA ANN, pediatrician, allergist; b. Cin., Jan. 10, 1943; d. James Frederick and Betty Mae (Doherty) P.; m. Makram I. Gobrail, Oct. 20, 1973; children: Christina, James. BS, Coll. Mt. St. Vincent, 1967; MD, Georgetown U., 1971; MS, Coll. Mt. St. Joseph, 1993. Cons. Children's Med. Ctr., Dayton, Ohio, 1975—, dir. allergy clinic, 1983-89; dir. allergy divsn. Hopeland Splty. Clinic, Dayton, 1998-2000. Fellow Am. Acad. Pediatrics, Am. Acad. Allergy and Immunology, Am. Coll. Allergy and Immunology; mem. Ohio Soc. Allergy and Immunology, Western Ohio Pediatric Soc. (pres. 1985-86). Roman Catholic. Office: 207 E Stroop Rd Dayton OH 45429-2825 Office Phone: 937-293-8263. E-mail: bapflum@hotmail.com.

PHAIR, LIZ, recording artist, pop vocalist; b. Cin., Apr. 17, 1967; d. John and Nancy Phair. Diploma, Oberlin Coll., 1990. Freelance artist, 1990; singer, songwriter, 1992—. Albums include: Exile in Guyville (name Album of Yr. Village Voice), 1993, Whip-Smart, 1994, Whitechocolatespaceegg, 1998. Named Best New Female Vocalist Rolling Stone Critic's Poll. Office: Matador Records 625 Broadway New York NY 10012-2611

PHALP-RATHBUN, STEPHANIE DAWN, music educator; b. Kansas City, Mo., July 30, 1978; d. Stephen Douglas and Gloria Dean Phalp; m. Robert Eric Rathbun, Sept. 6, 2002. BS, William Jewell Coll., Liberty, Mo., 2000. Dir. orch. Independence (Mo.) Sch. Dist., 2000—01, Park Hill Sch. Dist., Kansas City, 2001—. V.p. orchs. Kansas City Metro Dist. No. 3, 2002—. Mem.: Mo. Music Educators Assn., Music Educators Nat. Conf., Am. String Tchrs. Assn. (vol. coord. chpt. 2000—). Office: Park Hill HS 7701 NW Barry Rd Kansas City MO 64153

PHAM, LARA BACH-VIEN, small business owner; b. Ba-Xuyen, Vietnam, Jan. 11, 1962; d. Thi Van and Huong Thi Nguyen; m. Thien Van Pham, Apr. 17, 1982; children: Minh-Thu, Sheena, Lisa, Jimmy. Diploma, Brand's Beauty Coll., Charlotte, NC, 1990. Lic. securities NASD, life and health ins., in property and liability, in real estate sales. Hair stylist, owner Hair Studio, Charlotte, 1990—; beauty cons. Beauti Control, Charlotte, 1990—93, 2001—; flower arranger weddings, Charlotte, 1995—.

PHAN, CHRISTINA, electronic analog design executive; b. Can Tho, Vietnam, Oct. 24, 1961; came to U.S., 1979; d. Thoi Thanh and Loan Kim (Nguyen) Phan; m. Manh Van An, Nvo. 3, 1990; children: Steven An, Jessica An. BSEE, U. Calif., Berkeley, 1983; MSEE, U. Santa Clara, Calif., 1988. Design engr. Nat. Semicondr. Corp., Santa Clara, 1984-97, analog design mgr., 1997—. Patentee in field. Buddhist. Avocation: singing. Home: 5338 Canyon Hills Ln San Jose CA 95138-2438

PHAN, KIM THAN NGUYEN, psychologist, educator; b. Hanoi, Vietnam, June 1, 1949; arrived in U.S., 1966; d. Thuat Nang Nguyen and Thi Thi Pham; m. Sonny Ngoc Phan, Oct. 10, 1974; children: Jay Lawrence, Sarah Kim. AA in Liberal Arts, Cottey Coll., 1971; BA in Sociology, U. Kans., 1973, MA in Sociology, 1977; PhD in Clin. Psychology, U.S. Internat. U., 1998. Lic. psychologist. Social worker Holt Adoption Agy., Saigon, Vietnam, 1973—74; med. social worker Providence Hosp., Sandusky, Ohio, 1980—87; dir. social svcs. Willard (Ohio) Meml. Hosp., 1987—88; sr. social worker Children and Family Svcs., Orange, Calif., 1988—98; clin. psychologist Children and Youth Svcs., Westminster, Calif., 1998—. Lectr. U. Calif., Irvine, 2000; adj. prof. U.S. Internat. U., Irvine, 2000; staff mem. County of Orange Health Care Cultural Competency and Multiethnic Svcs.; mem. County of Orange Social Svcs.-Multicultural Task Force. Co-founder Vietnamese-Am. Human Svcs. Assn., Westminster, Calif., 2003—, Vietnamese Handicapped Support Group, Westminster, 1994—95; mem. adv. bd. MAA Acculturation Svcs. of Vietnamese Social Svcs. Comty. Ctr., Santa Ana, Calif., 1994; comty. liaison Team of Advocates for Spl. Kids. Recipient minority scholarship, U.S. Internat. U., 1993—96, PEO Internat. Women scholarship, Cottey Coll., 1969—71, fgn. exch. student scholarship, Am. Field Svcs., 1966—67, Appreciation award,

Team of Advocates for Spl. Kids, 1999. Mem.: APA, Calif. Psychol. Assn. Roman Catholic. Avocations: gardening, beach walking, Vietnamese music. Office: County of Orange Health Care Agy Behavioral Health Svcs Ste 155 14140 Beach Blvd Westminster CA 92683 E-mail: kphan@hca.co.orange.ca.us.

PHAN, TÂM THANH, medical educator, psychotherapist, consultant, researcher; b. Hue, Vietnam, June 10, 1949; d. Quê'Dinh and Chánh Thi (Tô) P. BA, Adams State Coll., 1979; MA, Western State Coll., 1980; PhD in Nutrition, Am. Coll. Nutrition, 1983; D of Nutrimedicine, John Kennedy Nutrisci., Gary, Ind., 1986; PhD in Counseling, Columbus Pacific U., 1988; DSc, Lafayette U., 1989. Lic. profl. counselor, marriage and family therapist; cert. nutrimedicine specialist. Counselor Lamar U., Beaumont, Tex., 1980-82; cons. Vietnamese Cmty., Golden Triangle, Tex., 1980—, The Wholistic Clinic, Beaumont, 1980—. Mem. adv. bd. Internat. Homeopathic Clearance, Mo., 1993—. Author: How Western Culture..., 1988, Natural Preventive Medicine, The Wholitic Approach, 1992, How to Prevent Mental Illness, 1995, How to Prevent Diabetes, 1996. Fellow Internat. Nutrimedicine Assn., Am. Nutrimedicine Assn.; mem. Interant. Alliance of Nutrimedical Therapists, Internat. Holistic Med. Soc. (bd. dirs. 1996, Cert. of Merit 1996). Avocations: writing, reading, swimming, cooking, knitting. Office: The Wholistic Clinic 1995 Broadway St Beaumont TX 77701-1941

PHARES, LYNN LEVISAY, public relations communications executive; b. Brownwood, Tex., Aug. 6, 1947; m. C. Kirk Phares, Aug. 22, 1971; children: Laura, Margaret, Adele, Jessica. BA, La. State U., 1970; MA, U. Nebr., 1987. Asst. to advt. mgr. La. Nat. Bank, 1970-71; writer, producer, asst. v.p., account exec. Smith, Kaplan, Allen & Reynolds, Inc., Omaha, 1971-80; assoc. dir. pub. affairs U. Nebr. Med. Ctr., 1980-83; dir. pub. rels. ConAgra Inc., Omaha, 1985-87, v.p. pub. rels., 1987-90, v.p. pub. rels. and cmty. affairs, 1990-97, v.p., corp. rels., 1997-2000. Pres. ConAgra Found., Feeding Children Better Found. Office: ConAgra Inc 1 ConAgra Dr Omaha NE 68102-5001

PHARISS, SUSAN WILLIS, dietitian; b. Lawrenceburg, Tenn., Dec. 12, 1948; d. Wylie Richard and Mary (Dishongh) Willis; m. Glen Allen Phariss, Jul. 3, 1971; children: Martha, Paula. BS in food and nutrition, Middle Tenn. State Univ., 1970. Registered dietitian. Clinical dietitian St. Elizabeth's Hosp., Belleville, Ill., 1971-72; chief clinical dietitian Christian Hosp., St. Louis, Mo., 1972-76; assoc. prof. St. Louis Cmty Coll. at Florissant Valley, 1976-78; sub. tchr. Westminster Christian Acad., St. Louis, 1990—. Exec. bd. mothers club Westminster Christian Acad., 1996—, edn. com., 1992-98, bd. dirs., 1994-98, treas., 1996—. Mem. Am. Dietetic Assn., Gateway Dist. Deitetic Assn. (v.p. 1971-73), St.Louis Dietetic Assn., Bible Study Fellowship (leader 1981-89). Avocations: skiing, reading, needlework, chorus. Home: 419 Country Oak Dr Chesterfield MO 63017-2821

PHARR, PAIGE ELIZABETH, interior designer, real estate broker; b. New Iberia, La., Sept. 20, 1965; d. Fitzgerald Parker Pharr and Sheila Ferguson Mankin. Student, U. of La. at Lafayette, 1983—86, Am. Intercontinental U., 2001—03. Paralegal Nat. Ctr. for Paralegal Tng., 1990. Paralegal Webb, Carlock, Copeland, Semler & Stair, Atlanta, 1990—92, Resolution Trust Corp., Atlanta, 1992—94; real estate account exec. Koll Real Estate Co., Atlanta, 1994—96, Cushman & Wakefield, Walnut Creek, Calif., 1996—97; v.p. Ackerman & Co., Atlanta, 1997—99; owner Ecclectique, Atlanta, 1999—2003; assoc. dir. Insignia/ESG, Atlanta, 1999—2002; pres. Aria Enterprises, Inc., Atlanta, 2002—. Counsel cancer patients Egleston Children's Hosp., Atlanta, Ga., 1977—83. Mem.: Comml. Real Estate Women. R-Consevative. Episcopal. Avocations: interior design, travel, cooking, photography. Office: Aria Enterprises Inc 3097 Hudson Way Decatur GA 30033 Personal E-mail: paige@ariaenterprises.com. E-mail: paige@ariaenterprises.com.

PHEFFER, AUDREY IRIS, state legislator; b. Aug. 14, 1941; d. Alex and Ruth Fagin; children: Mitchell, Stacey. Grad. cum laude, Queens Coll./CUNY, 1982. Advisor spl. edn. Occupational Tng. Ctr., 1973-77; mem. Neighborhood Stblzn. program N.Y.C. Commn. Human Rights, 1977, acting dir. Far Rockaway office, organizer Rockaway Interracial Coun.; exec. asst. N.Y. State Senator, 1980; spl. asst. to Pres. of City Coun., N.Y.C., 1986; mem. N.Y. State Assembly, 1987—. Mem. aging com., alcoholism and substance abuse com., govt. employees com., higher edn. com., social svc. com., vet. affairs com. Mem. 1st Police Precinct Cmty. and Youth Coun. Home: 108-14 Cross Bay Blvd Ozone Park NY 11417 Office: NY State Assembly 941 Legislative Ofc Bldg Albany NY 12248

PHELAN, ELLEN, artist; b. Detroit, Nov. 3, 1943; d. Thomas Edward and Katherine Louise (Gojlewicz) P; m. Joel Elias Shapiro, Nov. 22, 1978. BFA, Wayne State U., 1969, MFA, 1971. Instr. Wayne State U., Detroit, 1969-72, Fairleigh Dickinson U., 1974, Mich. State U., East Lansing, 1974-75, Calif. Inst. Arts, 1978-79, Bard Coll., 1980, NYU, 1981, Sch. of Visual Arts, 1981-83, Calif. Inst. Arts, 1983; prof. of practice of studio art Harvard U., Cambridge, Mass., 1995—. Milton Avery vis. lectr. Bard Coll., 1994. One-woman exhbns. include Willis Gallery, Detroit, 1972, 74, Artist's Space, N.Y.C., 1975, Susanne Hilberry Gallery, Birmingham, Mich., 1977, 79, 81, 82, 84, 86, 88, 90, 92, 94, Wadsworth Athenaeum, Hartford, Conn., 1979, Ruth Schaffner Gallery, L.A., 1979, The Clocktower, N.Y.C., 1980, Hansen-Fuller-Goldeen Gallery, San Francisco, 1980, 82, Dart Gallery, Chgo., 1981, Barbara Toll Fine Arts, N.Y.C., 1982, 85, 86, 87-88, 89, 90, 92, 93, Asher/Faure, L.A., 1989, 92, 94, Balt. Mus. Art, 1989, Albright-Knox Art Gallery, Buffalo, 1991, U. Mass. Amherst Fine Arts Ctr., 1992, Saidye Bronfman Ctr., Montreal, Que., 1993, Contemporary Mus., Honolulu, 1993, John Stoller, Inc., Mpls., 1993, Cin. Art Mus., 1994; exhibited in group shows at Detroit Inst. Arts, 1970, 80, Willis Gallery, Detroit, 1971, 79, J.L. Hudson Gallery, Detroit, 1972, Cranbrook Acad. Art, Bloomfield Hills, Mich., 1972, 79, 84, Grand Rapids (Mich.) Art Mus., 1974, Paula Cooper Gallery, N.Y.C., 1975, 76, 77, 78, 79, 90, Fine Arts Bldg., N.Y.C., 1976, Acad. der Kunste, Berlin, 1976, Susanne Hilberry Gallery, Birmingham, 1976-77, 83, 85, 91, Willard Gallery, N.Y.C., 1977, Kansas City (Mo.) Art Inst., 1977, N.A.M.E. Gallery, Chgo., 1977, Hallwalls, Buffalo, 1977, Mus. Modern Art, N.Y.C., 1978, 89, 92, Weatherspoon Art Gallery U. N.C., Greensboro, 1979, 92, Albright-Knox Gallery, Buffalo, 1979, Brown U., Providence, 1980, XIII Olympic Winter Games, Lake Placid, N.Y., 1980, Jeffrey Fuller Fine Art, Phila., 1980, Portland (Oreg.) Ctr. for Visual Arts, 1980, The Drawing Ctr., N.Y.C., 1980, 82, Brooke Alexander Gallery, N.Y.C., 1980, Mus. Contemporary Art, Chgo., 1980, 81, P.S. 1 Mus., N.Y.C., 1981, 92, Art Latitude Gallery, N.Y.C., 1981, Leo Castelli Gallery, N.Y.C., 1981, Sutton Place, Guildford, Eng., 1982, Gallerie d'Arte Moderna di Ca'Pesaro, Venice, Italy, 1982, Inst. Contemporary Art of Virgini Mus., Richmond, Va., 1982, Galerie Biedermann, Munich, 1982, Thomas Segal Gallery, Boston, 1983, Fuller-Goldeen Gallery, San Francisco, 1983, 86, William Paterson Coll., Wayne, N.J., 1983, 89, Artist's Space, N.Y.C., 1983, 84, Harborside Indsl. Ctr., Bklyn., 1983, Orgn. Ind. Artists, N.Y.C., 1984, Bernice Steinbaum Gallery, N.Y.C., 1984, Brentwood Gallery, St. Louis, 1984, U. Calif., Irvine, 1984, U. No. Iowa Gallery Art, Cedar Falls, 1984, Hudson River Mus., N.Y.C., 1984, Barbara Toll Fine Arts, N.Y.C., 1984, 85, 86, 87, Detroit Focus Gallery, 1984, Cable Gallery, N.Y.C., 1984, Wayne State U., Detroit, 1984, Matthews Hamilton Gallery, Phila., 1984, Barbara Krakow Gallery, Boston, 1984, BlumHelman Warehouse, N.Y.C., 1984, Pam Adler Gallery, N.Y.C., 1985, Daniel Weinberg Gallery, L.A., 1985, 89, Knight Gallery, Charlotte, N.C., 1985, Bank of Boston, 1986, Whitney Mus. Am. Art, Stamford, Conn., 1987, 89, Scott Hansen Gallery, N.Y.C., 1987, Saxon-Lee Gallery, L.A., 1987, Parrish Art Mus., East Hampton, N.Y., 1987, Curt Marcus Gallery, N.Y., 1988, Loughelton Gallery, N.Y.C., 1988, 90, Whitney Mus. Am. Art, N.Y.C., 1988, 91, Hillwood Art Gallery C.W. Post Campus, Brookville, N.Y., 1989, USIA traveling exbhn., 1989, Edward Thorp Gallery, N.Y.C., 1989, Pine Street Lobby Gallery, San Francisco, 1989, Fuller Gross Gallery, San Francisco, 1989, Solo Press/Soho Gallery, N.Y.C., 1989, Maxwell Davidson Gallery, N.Y.C., 1989, Blum Helman Gallery, N.Y.C., 1989, R.I.S.D., Providence, 1989, Graham Modern, N.Y.C., 1990, Hood Mus. Art Dartmouth Coll., Hanover, N.H., 1990, 92, New Britain Mus. Am. Art, Hartford, Conn., 1991, Asher-Faure, L.A., 1991, Annina Nosei Gallery, N.Y.C., 1991, Lintas Worldwide, N.Y.C., 1991, Nina Fredenheim Gallery, Buffalo, 1991, Molica Guidarte Gallery, N.Y.C., 1991, Squibb Gallery, Princeton, N.J., 1991, Cleve. State U. Gallery, 1992, Ind. Curators Inc., N.Y.C., 1992, Wexner Ctr. for the Arts, Columbus, Ohio, 1992, Transamerica Corp., San Francisco, 1992, The Gallery Three Zero, N.Y.C., 1992, Haggerty Mus. Art, Milw., Barbara Methes Gallery, N.Y.C., Asher Fauve Gallery, L.A., Hillwood Art Mus., Brookville, N.Y., Pamela Auchincloss Gallery, N.Y.C., Leo Castelli Gallery, N.Y.C.; represented in permanent collections Mus. Modern Art, N.Y.C., Whitney Mus. Am. Art, N.Y.C., Bklyn. Mus., Walker Art Ctr., Mpls., Balt. Mus., Toledo Mus. Art, Hood Mus. Dartmouth Coll., High Mus. Art, Albright-Knox Art Gallery, Moderna Museet, Stockholm, Mus. Contemporary Art, Mexico City, Detroit Inst. Arts, MIT, Whitehead Inst., Philip Morris, Inc., Volvo Corp., Chase Manhattan Bank, Chem. Bank, BankAm., Bank of Am., Prudential Ins. Co., U.S. Trust & Co., Inter Metro Industries, Lannan Found., numerous pvt. collections. Nat. Endowment for Arts grantee, 1978-79; recipient Am. Acad. Arts and Letters award, 1995, Arts Achievement award Wayne State U., 1989.

PHELAN, MARTHA ARMSTRONG, realtor; b. Shelby, Ohio, July 26, 1927; d. George Woodburn and Anna Louise (Wood) A.; m. Vincent Roche Phelan, Aug. 9, 1952 (dec. July 2000); children: Elizabeth Ann Riley, David Woodburn, Anne Louise. BA, Oberlin Coll., 1949. Sec. U.S. Govt., Washington, 1950-52; adminstrv. officer Com. for Free Asia, N.Y.C., 1952-53; legal sec. Atty. V.R. Phelan, Shelby, Ohio, 1975-79; realtor Mattox Realtors, Mansfield, Ohio, 1976-93, Hancock Agy., Shelby, Ohio, 1993—. Precinct committeeman Rep. Orgn., Shelby, 1965—; poll worker Richland County Bd. Elections, Shelby, 1960—; mem. exec. com. Richland County Reps., Mansfield, 1965—; mem. Kingwood Ctr. Gardens; elder Presbyn. Ch., mem. choir, pres. Presbyn. Women, 2002—. Mem. Nat. Assn. Realtors, Mansfield Bd. Realtors, Rotary, Shelby Garden Club (pres. 1997-99), Shelby Women's Club (sec. 1990-01), Presyn. Choir 45 yrs., ch. session 7 yrs., Pres. Presbyn. Women 20 yrs. Republican. Presbyterian. Avocations: gardening, reading, creative arts and crafts, swimming, music. Home: 26 Woodland Rd Shelby OH 44875

PHELAN, MARY MICHENFELDER, public relations executive, writer; b. St. Louis, Oct. 6, 1936; d. Albert A. Michenfelder and Ruth Josephine Donahue; m. Gerald Leo Phelan, Aug. 16, 1958; children: Gerald (Grady) Leo, Jr., Joseph (Joe) Leo. BS, St. Louis U., 1958; M in Liberal Arts, Washington U., St. Louis, 1995. PRSA Accreditation Pub. Rels. Soc. of Am., 1987. Counselor, v.p. Fleishman-Hillard, Inc., St. Louis, 1982—94; dir., corp. comm. BJC HealthCare, St. Louis, 1995—2001; sr. counselor Patrick Davis Comm., Inc., St. Louis, 2001—. Author: (children's books) ABCs of Celebration, ABCs of the City of Man. Chair, pub. rels. com. Confluence St. Louis, 1981—85; mem. Friends of KWMU, Nat. Pub. Radio, St. Louis, 1991—2003, pres., 1997—99. Recipient One of Top 5 PR Teams in U.S. award, PR WEEK Mag., 2000, Wall of Fame for Achievement in Bus., Nerinx Hall HS, 2001. Mem.: Pub. Rels. Soc. of Am. (life; pres. St. Louis chpt. 1992, Coll. of Fellows 2003).

PHELPS, GERRY CHARLOTTE, economist, minister; b. Norman, Okla., Oct. 15, 1931; d. George and Charlotte LeNoir (Yowell) P.; 1 child, Scott. BA, U. Tex., 1963, MA, 1984; MDiv, San Francisco Theol. Seminary, 1981. Cert. tchr., Calif. Lectr. in econs. U. Houston, 1966-69; pastor United Meth. Ch., Kelseyville, Calif., 1980-82; sr. pastor Bethany United Methodist Ch., Bakersfield, Calif., 1982-84; founding exec. dir. Bethany Svc. Ctr., Bakersfield, 1982-84; pres., founding exec. dir. Concern for the Poor, Inc., San Jose, Calif., 1985-92; pastor United Meth. Ch., Flatonia, Tex., 1993-97; founding exec. dir. CRISES, Austin, 1994-98, v.p. devel., 1998-99; pvt. practice cons. poverty issues, 1999—. Cons. in ch. growth, 2001—. Co-author: Nutrition for Better Living, 1999, Budgeting for Better Living, 1999; author: Out of the Iron Furnace, 2000, Up and Out: A Guide to True Compassion for the Poor, 2001. Mem. Task Force on the Homeless, San Jose, 1987, Santa Clara County, 1991. Recipient commendation Mayor of Bakersfield, 1984, Santa Clara County Bd. Suprs., 1992. Avocations: latin american studies, refugee assistance, homeless assistance, study of connections between economic and social problems. E-mail: gphelps@austin.rr.com.

PHELPS, JAYCIE, gymnast, Olympic athlete; b. Indpls., Sept. 26, 1979; Mem. U.S. Women's World Gymnastics Team, 1994-95, U.S. Olympic Team, Atlanta, 1996. Recipient Sagamore of the Wabash award State of Ind., 1995, Gold medal team competition Olympic Games, Atlanta, 1996; placed 3rd in all around U.S. Olympic Festival, St. Louis, 1994, 2d for team Team World Championships, Dortmund, Germany, 1994, 3rd in all around Coca-Cola Nat. Championships, New Orleans, 1995, 3rd for team World Championships, Sabae, Japan, 1995. Avocations: coaching, swimming, shopping. Office: care USA Gymnastics Pan Am Plz 201 S Capitol Ave Ste 300 Indianapolis IN 46225-1058

PHELPS, MARY ANN BAZEMORE, elementary school educator; b. Cofield, N.C., Sept. 17, 1940; d. Hugh Bazemore and Bertha Elmyra Willoughby; m. Russell Vastie Phelps, Aug. 12, 1967; 1 child, Ann Hope. BS, E. Carolina U., 1962. Cert. elem. tchr. Tchr. Weeksville H.S., Elizabeth City, N.C., 1962-65, Sheep-Harney Sch., Elizabeth City, 1965-67, Colerain (N.C.) Elem. Sch., 1967-92, Windsor (N.C.) Elem. Sch., 1992-93, Ahoskie (N.C.) Christian Sch., 1996-99; tutor Ahoskie, 1996-99. Mem. adv. bd. Bertie County Schs., Windsor, 1985. Mem. Ridgecroft Sch. Bd., Ahoskie, 1993-97; mem. visitor's bd. Chowan Coll., Murfreesboro, N.C., 1994-98; mem. U. N.C. Parents Assn., 1995-99. Mem. NEA, N.C. Assn. Educators (sec. 1963-64). Baptist. Avocations: reading, crossword puzzles, golfing, biking. Home and Office: 128 Berkley Rd Ahoskie NC 27910-9575

PHENIS-BOURKE, NANCY SUE, educational administrator; b. Anderson, Ind., Oct. 29, 1943; d. Wilma (Anderson) Baker; m. Richard W. Phenis, June 11, 1966; 1 child, Heidi L. BA, Ind. State U., 1965; MA, Ball State U., 1974, postgrad., 1985. Elem. tchr. Highland Park (N.J.) Schs., 1966-68, Anderson City Schs., 1969-71; elem. tchr., tchr. gifted and talented South Madison Schs., Pendleton, Ind., 1974-85, elem. prin., 1985—. K-12 curriculum dir. South Madison Schs., 1984; mem. CAPE grant com. Eli Lilly Found., 2000. Bd. dirs. South Madison Community Found., Pendleton, 1991, First Am. Bank FirstGrant; devel. bd. St. John's Health Care Systems; mem. Prin.'s Leadership Summit, U.S. Dept. Edn., 2000. Recipient Outstanding Contbn. award Internat. Reading Assn., 1991; grantee Eli Lilly Found., 1993. Mem. NAESP (Ind. state rep. 1998—, membership adv. com. 1999), AAUW (pres. 1985-87), Ind. Assn. Sch. Prins. (bd. dirs. 1994—), First Am. (bd. dirs. 1992-95), Phi Delta Kappa (historian 1987, Leadership award 1994), Delta Kappa Gamma (sec. 1990-92, pres. 1992-94, Leadership/Adminstr. award 1993). Office: East Elem Sch 893 E Us Highway 36 Pendleton IN 46064-9580

PHILBIN, ANN M. art facility director; b. Boston, Mar. 21, 1952; d. Richard Moore and Ann Theresa (Muller) P. BA, BFA, U. N.H.; MA, NYU, 1982. Rschr. Frick Art Reference Libr., N.Y.C., 1977-79; asst. to dir., program coord. Artists Space, N.Y.C., 1979-80; asst. curatorial coord. The New Mus., N.Y.C., 1980-81; curator Ian Woodner Family Collection, N.Y.C., 1981-83; asst. dir. Grace Borgenicht Gallery, N.Y.C., 1983-85; dir. Curt Marcus Gallery, N.Y.C., 1985-88; account dir., dir. Art Against AIDS Livet Reichard Inc., N.Y.C., 1988-90; dir. The Drawing Ctr., N.Y.C., 1990, UCLA Hammer Museum, Los Angeles. Bd. dirs. Elizabeth Streb, Ringside, N.Y., 1990, HIV Law Project, N.Y.C., 1993; founding mem. Women's Action Coalition, N.Y.C., 1991. Address: UCLA Hammer Museum 10899 Wilshire Blvd Los Angeles CA 90024

PHILIPP, ALICIA, community foundation executive; BA, Emory U.; MBA, Ga. State U. Exec. dir. Met. Atlanta Cmty. Found. Inc., Atlanta, 1977-99, pres., 1999—. Bd. dirs. Ctrl. Atlanta Progress, Ind. Sector, Funders Concerned About Aids, Investment Fund for Founds, Policy Bd. of Atlanta Project. Mem. Jr. League, Internat. Women's Forum, Acad. of Women. Recipient Roz Cohen Cmty. Action award YWCA; named as One of Top Women Mgrs. in U.S. Working Woman mag. Office: Met Atlanta Cmty Found The Hurt Bldg Ste 449 Atlanta GA 30303

PHILIPS, SUZANNE MARGUERITE See CASEY, SUE

PHILLIPS, AMY RENEA, assistant principal; b. Evansville, Ind., Nov. 1, 1974; d. William Anthony and Judith Ann Phillips; m. Jeremy Todd Guest, Mar. 14, 1998 (div.). BS in Speech Comm. Edn., So. Ill. U., 1997; MS in Secondary Sch. Adminstrn., S.W. Bapt. U., 2003. Cert. profl. tchg. cert. Mo., Ill. Tchr. Sanford Brown Coll., Granite City, Ill., 1997—; mgmt. in tng. Three Rivers Fed. Credit Union, Ft. Wayne, Ind., 1997; tchr. Ombudsman Ednl. Inst., St. Ann, Mo., 1997—98; program dir. YMCA, St. Louis, 1998—99; tchr. Bayless H.S., St. Louis, 1999—2003, athletic dir., 2002—03; asst. prin. Hillsboro (Mo.) H.S., 2003—. Avocations: singing, writing, football, softball. Office: 123 Leon Hall Pkwy Hillsboro MO 63050

PHILLIPS, ANGELA L. psychotherapist; b. Fridley, Minn., May 21, 1971; d. Ronald L. and Judith L. (Lind) Phillips. BA Sociology of Law, Criminology & Deviance, U. Minn., 1993; MA Marriage, Family, Child Counseling, U. San Diego, 1998. Ntern Children's Outpatient Psychiatry Clinic, San Diego, 1997—. Mediator Victom-Offender Reconciliation Program, San Diego, 1995—. Mem.: Calif. Assn. Marriage & Family Therapists, Chi Sigma Iota. Methodist. Avocations: boating, skiing, travel, reading. Home: Unit E 12517 El Camino Real San Diego CA 92130-4024

PHILLIPS, ANN Y. art advisor; b. Omaha, July 9, 1955; d. Irvin and Annette Swezey Yaffe; m. Lee Stuart Phillips, Aug. 12, 1984; children: S. Perry, Lucy A. BA, Yale U., 1977; grad., Hunter Coll., 1979-81. Adminstr. Pace Gallery, N.Y.C., 1978-79; asst. dir. Rosa Esman Gallery, N.Y.C., 1979-82; dir. Bette Stoler Gallery, N.Y.C., 1982-87; assoc. Hirschl & Adler Galleries, N.Y.C., 1987-93; v.p., art advisor Citibank Art Adv. Svc., N.Y.C., 1993-2000; pvt. art. adv., 2000—. Mem. art com. Montclair (N.J.) Art mus., 1997—. Co-author catalog: Prints of Eugene Delacroix, 1977; co-author, editor catalog: From Architecture to Object--Masterworks from the American Arts and Crafts Movement, 1989; organizer, co-author catalog: Cross Currents: Americans in Paris, 1993. Mem. Am. Assn. Museums, Art Table. Avocations: reading, gardening. Office: Ann Yaffe Phillips Fine Art 329 Park St Montclair NJ 07043-2210

PHILLIPS, BERNICE CECILE GOLDEN, retired vocational education educator; b. Galveston, Tex., June 30, 1920; d. Walter Lee and Minnie (Rothsprack) Golden; m. O. Phillips, Mar. 1950 (dec.); children: Dorian Lee, Loren Francis. BBA cum laude, U. Tex., 1945; MEd, U. Houston, 1968. cert. tchr., tchr. coord., vocat. tchr., Tex. Dir. Delphian Soc., Houston, 1955-60; bus. tchr. various private schs., Houston area, 1960-65; vocat. tchr. coord. office edn. program Pasadena (Tex.) Ind. Sch. Dist., 1965-68, Houston Ind. Sch. Dist., John H. Reagan High Sch., 1968-85, ret., 1985. Bd. dirs. Regency House Condominium Assn., 1991-93. Recipient numerous awards and recognitions for vocat. bus. work at local and state levels. Mem. AAUW (life, 50 yr. mem., Houston Br. v.p. ednl. found. 1987-90, pres. 1992-94, bd. dirs. 1987-96, 50-Yr. mem. cert.), NEA, Nat. Bus. Edn. Assn., Am. Vocat. Assn. (life), Tex. State Tchrs. Assn. (life), Tex. Classroom Tchrs. Assn. (life), Tex. Bus. Edn. Assn. (emeritus, Life Mem. award, numerous other awards), Vocat. Office Edn. Tchrs. Assn. Tex. (past bd. dirs.), Greater Houston Bus. Edn. Assn. (reporter), Houston Assn. Ret. Tchrs., Tex. Assn. Ret. Tchrs., Delta Pi Epsilon (emeritus), Beta Gamma Sigma. Avocations: bridge, reading, arts, crafts, travel. Home: 1123 Royston Pl Apt D Bel Air MD 21015-4614

PHILLIPS, BETTY LOU (ELIZABETH LOUISE PHILLIPS), writer, interior designer; b. Cleve. d. Michael N. and Elizabeth D. (Materna) Suvak; m. John S. Phillips, Jan. 27, 1963 (div. Jan. 1981); children: Bruce, Bryce, Brian; m. John D.C. Roach, Aug. 28, 1982. BS, Syracuse U., 1960; postgrad. in English, Case Western Res. U., 1963-64. Cert. elem. and spl. edn. tchr., N.Y.; cert. interior designer, Calif. Tchr. pub. schs., Shaker Heights, Ohio, 1960-66. Sportswriter Cleve. Press, 1976-77; spl. features editor Pro Quarterback Mag., N.Y.C., 1976-79; bd. dirs. Cast Specialties Inc., Cleve. Author: Chris Evert: First Lady of Tennis, 1977, Picture Story of Dorothy Hamill, 1978 (ALA Booklist selection), American Quarter Horse, 1979, Earl Campbell: Houston Oiler Superstar, 1979, Picture Story of Nancy Lopez, 1980 (ALA Notable book), Go! Fight! Win! The NCA Guide for Cheerleaders, 1981 (ALA Booklist), Something for Nothing, 1981, Brush Up on Your Hair, 1981 (ALA Booklist), Texas..The Lone Star State, 1989, Provençal Interiors-French Country Style in America, 1998, French by Design, 2000, French Influences, 2001, Villa Décor: Decidedly French and Italian Style, 2002 (Foreword Mag. Best Non-Fiction Book, 2003), Unmistakably French, 2003 (Tex. Inst. Letters Best Children's Book, 2003), Emily Goes Wild, 2003 (Tex. Inst. Letters Best Children's Book, 2004), Secrets of the French, 2004; contbr. articles popular mags.; author: Secrets of French Design, 2004. Mem.: Am. Soc. Interior Designers (profl. mem., cert.), Soc. Children's Book Writers, Delta Delta Delta. Republican. Roman Catholic. Home: 4278 Bordeaux Ave Dallas TX 75205-3718

PHILLIPS, CAROLYN KAE, marketing professional; b. Santa Rosa, Calif., May 27, 1958; d. John Harmon and Marlene Kae (Welsh) P. BA, U. Mich., 1980; MBA, Northwestern U., 1982. Asst. acct. exec. Leo Burnett, 1982-85; acct. exec. Foote, Cone & Belding, 1985-87; mktg. mgr. The Nutra Sweet Co., 1987-89, Coca-Cola, Irvine, Calif., 1989-91; dir. mktg. Intellivoice, Atlanta, 1991-92, One-On-One Sports, Chgo., 1993—99, v.p. mktg.; dir. mktg. and pub. rels. World Bus. Chgo., 2001—. Roman Catholic. Avocations: scuba diving, golf, walking, travel, horseback riding. Office: World Business Chgo 177 N State St Ste 500 Chicago IL 60601

PHILLIPS, DOROTHY KAY, lawyer; b. Nov. 2, 1945; d. Benjamin L. and Sadye (Levinsky) Phillips; children: Bethann P., David M. Schaffzin. BS in English Lit. magna cum laude, U. Pa., 1964; MA in Family Life & Marriage Counseling, NYU, 1975; JD, Villanova U., 1978. Bar: Pa. 1978, N.J. 1978, U.S. Dist. Ct. (ea. dist.) Pa. 1978, U.S. Dist. Ct. N.J., 1978, U.S. Ct. Appeals (3d cir.), 1984, U.S. Supreme Ct. 1984. Tchr. Haddon (N.J.) Twp. H.S., Haddon Heights H.S., 1964-70; lectr., counselor Marriage Coun. of Phila., U. Pa., Hahnemann Med. Schs., Phila., 1970-75; atty. Adler, Barish, Daniels, Levin & Creskoff, Phila., 1978-79, Astor, Weiss & Newman, Phila., 1979-80; ptnr. Romisher & Phillips P.C., Phila., 1981-86; prin. Dorothy K. Phillips & Assocs., LLC, 1986—. Faculty Sch., of Law Temple U.; guest spkr. on domestic rels. issues on radio and TV shows; featured in newspaper and mag. articles; bd. mem. Anti-Defamation League of B'nai B'rith, Nat. Mus. Jewish History; mem. friend's circle, Athenaeum, Phila., shareholder. Contbr. articles to profl. jours. Mem. ABA, ATLA (membership com. 1990-91, co-chair 1989-90), Pa. Trial Lawyers Assn. (chair membership com. family sect. 1989-90, presenter ann. update civil litigators-family law, author procedures practice of family law Phila. County Family Law Litigation Sect. County practiced database 1991) Pa. Bar Assn. (continuing legal edn. com. 1990-92, faculty, lectr. Pa. Bar Inst. Continuing Legal Edn. 1990, panel mem. summer meeting 1991), N.J. Bar Assn., Phila. Bar Assn. (chmn. early settlement program 1983-84, mem. custody rules drafting com. for Supreme Ct. Pa., spl. events spkr. on pensions, counsel fees, written fee agreements 1989-91, co-chair and moderator of panel mandatory continuing legal edn. 1994), Nat. Bus. Inst. (lectr. 1997—, Cust. and Visitation in PA, 1998, Planning, Taxation and Divorce, 2002, Custody Modification, 2003), Phila. Trial Lawyers Assn., Montgomery County Bar Assn., Lawyers Club. E-mail: dkp@dkphillipslaw.com.

PHILLIPS, DOROTHY LOWE, nursing educator; b. Jacksonville, Fla., June 3, 1939; d. Clifford E. and Dorothy (MacFeeley) Lowe; m. Dale Bernard Phillips, Feb. 14, 1973; children: Francis D., Sean E., Dorothy F. AA in Nursing, Ventura Coll., 1969; BSN, Calif. State U. Consortium, San Diego, 1984; M. Nursing, UCLA, 1987; EdD, Nova Southeastern U., 1995. Cert. community colls. tchr., Calif.; RN, Calif., pub. health nurse, Calif., clin. nurse specialist maternal/child. Staff nurse Cmty. Meml. Hosp., Ventura, Calif., 1969-70; charge nurse women and children's clinic Ventura County Regional Med. Ctr., Ventura, 1974-76; staff nurse, RN II Pleasant Valley Hosp., Camarillo, Calif., 1978-85; lead instr. cert. nursing asst. program div. adult edn. Oxnard (Calif.) Union H.S. Dist., 1984-89; staff rsch. assoc. UCLA, 1988; clin. instr. Ventura C.C. Sch. Nursing, 1988; college nurse Ventura Community Coll., 1989; lectr. Sch. of Nursing UCLA, 1989, lectr., coord. maternity nursing Sch. of Nursing, 1989-90, 90-91; vocat. nursing dir., health scis. coord. Oxnard Union H.S. Dist., 1990-99; assoc. dean health occupations Allan Hancock Coll., 1999—. Vis. educator health careers unit Calif. Dept. Edn., 1992-94; cons. Oxnard Adult Sch.; mem. adv. com. nursing asst./home health aide program Ventura County Regional Occupational Program; presenter in field. Competitive events judge !st Annual Leadership Conf., Health Occupations Students of Am., Anaheim, Calif.; active St. John's Regional Med. Ctr. Health Fair, 1991, Pleasant Valley Hosp. Health Fair, 1991; seminar leader "Babies and You", March of Dimes, 1988. Grad. Div. Rsch. grantee UCLA, 1986; Calif. State PTA scholar UCLA, 1986, Ventura County Med. Secs. scholar, 1967, Audrienne H. Mosley Grad. scholar, 1987. Mem. Nat. League for Nursing, Calif. Assn. Health Career Educators (pres. 1994), So. Calif. Dirs. Vocat. Nursing Programs (rec. sec. 1996—), So. Calif. Vocat. Nurse Educators (exec. bd.), Assn. Calif. C.C. Adminstrs., Nat. Coun. Instrnl. Adminstrs., Calif. C.C. Assn. Occupl. Edn., No. Calif. ADN Dirs., Santa Maria Valley Leadership Class, Sigma Theta Tau. Republican. Lutheran. Avocations: skiing, reading, exercise, travel, backpacking. Home: 1448 Oakridge Park Rd Santa Maria CA 93455-4560 Office: Allan Hancock Coll 800 S College Dr Santa Maria CA 93454-6399

PHILLIPS, DOROTHY REID, retired medical library technician; b. Hingham, Mass., Apr. 21, 1924; d. James Henry and Emma Louise (Davis) Reid; m. Earl Wendell Phillips, Apr. 22, 1944; children: Earl W., Jr., Betty Herrera, Carol Coe. Cert., Durham Vocat. Sch., 1952; B.S. in Comml. Edn., N.C. Central U., 1959; postgrad. U. Colo., 1969; M.Human Relations, Webster Coll., 1979; postgrad. Grad. Sch. Library Sci., U. Denver, 1983. Vocat. nurse Meml. Hosp., U. N.C., Chapel Hill, 1955-59; vol. work, Cairo, Egypt, 1965-67; library technician Base Library, Lowry AFB, Colo., 1960-65, Fitzsimons Med. Library, Aurora, Colo., 1976-93; ret. 1993; mem. Denver Mus. Natural History, Denver Art Mus., Mariners. Mem. AARP, NARFE, AAUW (chpt. community rep. 1982-83, state chmn. edn. found. 1982-84, pres. Denver br. 1984-86), Altrusa Internat. (corr. sec. Denver 1982-83, bd. dirs. 1984-85, pres. Denver chpt. 1988), Friends of Library, Peace Links, Colo. Coordinating Coun. of Womens Orgn., Inc. (pres. coun.), Colo. Library Assn., Council Library Technicians, Federally Employed Women, Delta Sigma Theta (corr. sec. Denver 1964-66), Women's Assn. of Peoples Presbyn. Ch., League of Women Voters, Denver Urban League. Democrat. Presbyterian. Home: 3085 Fairfax St Denver CO 80207-2714

PHILLIPS, ELIZABETH JOAN, marketing professional; b. Cleve., July 8, 1938; d. Joseph Tinl and Helen Walter; m. Erwin Phillips, June 1956 (div. 1960); 1 child, Michael A. BA, Fordham U., 1980. Acct. exec. David Cogan Mgmt., NYC, 1969—77, N.F.L. Films, NYC, 1977—78; mgr. sports programs Avon Products, NYC, 1978—83; v.p. Needham, Harper & Steers (now D.D.B. Needham), NYC, 1983—86, Ted Bates Event Mktg., NYC, 1986—87; pres. Custom Event Mktg., 1987—. Adj. prof. NYU, NYC, 1987—. Exec. com. Vanderbilt YMCA, NYC, 1976—84; ofcl. Olympic Games, LA, 1984; referee Women's Olympic Marathon, LA, 1984; pres. Met. Athletics Congress, NYC, 1980—83. Mem.: Women's Sports Found. (bd. adv. 1983—94), Road Runners Club Am. (bd. dirs. 1992—98), NY Road Runners Club (v.p., exec. com. 1976—, pres. 1970—98, bd. dirs. 1992—98). Office: Custom Event Mktg Inc 444 E 75th St Apt 10D New York NY 10021-3448

PHILLIPS, GAIL, state legislator; b. Juneau, Alaska; m. Walt Phillips; children: Robin, Kim. BA in Bus. Edn., U. Alaska. Mem. Homer (Alaska) City Coun., 1981-84, Kenai Peninsula Borough Assembly, 1986-87; chmn. legis. com. Alaska Mcpl. League; mem. Alaska Ho. of Reps., 1991-2000, house majority leader, 1993-94, spkr., 1995-98. Former owner, mgr. Quiet Sports; ptnr. Lindphil Mining Co.; pub. rels. cons. Active Homer United Meth. Ch., Rep. Ctrl. Com. Alaska, Kenai Peninsula Coll. Coun.; past mem. com. bd. and race coord. Iditarod Trail Dog Sled Race. Mem. Western States Legis. Coun. (exec. com.), Am. Legis Exch. Coun. (former state chmn.), Resource Devel. Coun. Alaska, Western Legis. Conf. (exec. bd.), Western States Coalition (exec. bd.), The Energy Coun. (exec. bd.). Home: PO Box 3304 Homer AK 99603-3304 also: Alaska Ho Reps State Capitol Juneau AK 99801-1182

PHILLIPS, GAIL SUSAN, elementary school educator; b. Spokane, Wash., Apr. 17, 1962; d. Vern and Jane Phillips. AA, Spokane (Wash.) Falls CC, 1982; MB, BE, Ea. Wash. U., 1985, MA, 1992. Tchr. Port Townsend (Wash.) HS, 1986, Gonzaga Prep. HS, Spokane, Wash., 1987—88, Auburn (Wash.) Sch. Dist., 1988—93, Mead (Wash.) Sch. Dist., 1993—94, Totem Jr. High, Federal Way, Wash., 1994—97, Kalles Jr. High, Puyallup, Wash., 1997—. Sec. MENC Student Chpt., Cheney, Wash., 1983—84; v.p. Ea. Wash. MENC Chpt., Spokane, 1987—88; PTA faculty adv. Totem Jr. High, Wash., 1996—97. Office: Kalles Jr High 515 3rd St SE Puyallup WA 98372 Office Phone: 253-841-8729. Business E-Mail: gphillips@nyallup.k12.wa.us.

PHILLIPS, GENEVA FICKER, academic editor; b. Staunton, Ill., Aug. 1, 1920; d. Arthur Edwin and Lillian Agnes (Woods) Ficker; m. James Emerson Phillips, Jr., June 6, 1955 (dec. 1979). BS in Journalism, U. Ill., 1942; MA in English Lit., UCLA, 1953. Copy desk Chgo. Jour. Commerce, 1942-43; editl. asst. patents Radio Rsch. Lab. Harvard U., Cambridge, Mass., 1943-45; asst. editor adminstrv. publs. U. Ill., Urbana, 1946-47; editl. asst. Quar. of Film, Radio and TV UCLA, 1952-53; mng. editor The Works of John Dryden, Dept. English UCLA, 1964—2002. Bd. dirs. Univ. Religious Conf., L.A., 1979— . UCLA teaching fellow, 1950-53, grad. fellow 1954-55. Mem. Assn. Acad. Women UCLA, Friends of Huntington Libr., Friends of UCLA Libr., Friends of Ctr. for Medieval and Renaissance Studies, Samuel Johnson Soc. So. Calif., Assocs. U. Calif. Press, Conf. Christianity and Lit., Soc. Mayflower Descendants. Lutheran. Home: 213 First Anita Dr Los Angeles CA 90049-3815 Office: UCLA Dept English 2225 Rolfe Hall Los Angeles CA 90024

PHILLIPS, GLYNDA ANN, editor; b. Riverside, Calif. d. Henry Grady and Patricia (Loflin) P. BA in English, Millsaps Coll., 1977; MS in Comms., Miss. Coll., 1996; postgrad., Inst. Children's Lit., 1998—2002. News editor The Magee (Miss.) Courier, 1981-84; editor Miss. Farm Country mag., Jackson, 1984—. Contbr. articles to profl. jours. Recipient first place personal column Nat. Fedn. Press Women, 1984, first place personal column Miss. Press Women's Assn., 1984, first place feature articles Miss. Press Women's Assn., 1984, Best Media Campaign award AFBF Info. Contest, 1996.

PHILLIPS, GRETCHEN, social worker; b. Erie, Pa., July 14, 1941; life ptnr. Beverly Campbell, June 10, 1989. BA, Mercyhurst Coll., 1966; MSW, Yeshiva U., 1972; postgrad., Advanced Ctr. Psychotherapy, 1972-73, Washington Sq. Inst., 1973-77. Diplomate clin. social work, cert. social worker N.Y. Psychiat. social worker, forensic social worker Creedmoor Psychiat. Ctr., Queens Village, NY, 1972-80; med. social worker Bellevue Hosp. Ctr., N.Y.C., 1980-83; intake probation officer N.Y.C. Probation, Family Ct., Bklyn., 1983—. Mem.: NASW, Internat. Soc. Traumatic Stress Studies (N.Y. chpt.). Home: 125 Radford St Apt 3C Yonkers NY 10705-3014 Office: Probation Intake Kings Family Ct 283 Adams St Brooklyn NY 11201-2804

PHILLIPS, JANET COLLEEN, retired educational association executive, editor; b. Pittsfield, Ill., Apr. 29, 1933; d. Roy Lynn and Catherine Amelia (Wills) Barker; m. David Lee Phillips, Feb 7, 1954; children— Clay Cullen, Sean Vincent. BS, U. Ill, 1954. Reporter Quincy (Ill.) Herald Whig, 1951, 52, soc. editor, 1953; editorial asst. Pub. Info. Office U. Ill.-Urbana, 1953-54, asst. editor libr., 1954-61; asst. editor Assn. for Libr. and Info. Sci. Edn., State College, Pa., 1960-61, mng. editor, 1961-89, exec. sec., 1970-89; adminstrv. dir. Interlibr. Delivery Svc. of Pa., 1990-99; ret. Mem. Palmer Mus. Arts, State Coll. Cmty. Theatre, Mt. Nittany Med. Ctr. Mem. Assn. for Libr. and Info. Sci. Edn., Embroiderer's Guild Am., Pa. State Blue Golf Course Club, Faculty Women's Club, C.A.L.L., Delta Zeta. Presbyterian. Avocations: travel, golf, sewing, needlecraft. Address: 471 Park Ln State College PA 16803-3208 E-mail: janph2@aol.com.

PHILLIPS, JEANNE L. ambassador; b. Ark., Sept. 1939; Grad., So. Meth. U. Pres., CEO Jeanne Johnson & Co., Dallas; mng. dir. Pub. Strategies, Inc., Dallas; U.S. rep. to Orgn. for Econ. Cooperation and Devel., 2001—. Mem. M.D. Anderson Bd. Visitors; assoc. bd. mem. Cox Sch. Bus., So. Meth. U.; bd. dirs. John G. Tower Ctr. for Polit. Studies, So. Med. U.; exec. dir. 54th Presdl. Inaugural Com.; dep. chmn. ops. Rep. Nat. Com., Washington; bd. mem. Dallas Jr. League, Inc., Charter 100, Dallas Assembly. Office: DOS Amb Orgn for Econ Cooperation and Devel Washington DC 20521

PHILLIPS, JEANNETTE VERONICA, management consultant, gerontologist; b. Batesburg, S.C., Sept. 29, 1940; d. Katherine Louise (Ramey) Ray; s. William Alfred Phillips, June 23, 1962; children: Veronica Lynn, Marguerite Kathleen. BA in Sociology, Ohio Wesleyan U., 1962; MA in Pub. Adminstrn., William Paterson Coll., 1980. Cert. vocat. rehab. counselor. Asst. teen program dir. YWCA, Toledo, 1962-66; recreation therapist Mo. Inst. Psychiatry, St. Louis, 1967-70, rehab. specialist, 1970-72; counselor, mgr. Vocat. Bur. of Rehab., Toledo, 1972-74; skills ctr. dir. Passaic County Bd. Tech. & Vocat. Edn., Wayne, N.J., 1974-76, personnel dir., 1976-81; asst. personnel dir. City of Stamford, Conn., 1981-87; sec., treas. Phillips Packaging, Inc., Orange, Conn., 1985—; exec. dir. commn. aging City of Stamford, 1987-92; exec. dir. social svcs., 1992-96; dir. eldercare Team, Inc., Derby, Conn., 1996-98; dir. Elder Options Resource Ctr., Shelton, Conn., 1998—2002. Mgmt. cons. pvt. practice, Orange, Conn., 1986—. Sec. Stamford United Way, 1991-96, mem. Cystic Fibrosis Found., 1986-97; commr. Orange Conn. Cmty. Svcs. Commn., 1997—. Named Woman of Yr., Conn. Am. Assn. Univ. Women, 1990. Mem.: AAUW (state v.p. membership 1995—98, Conn. state pres. 1998—2000, nat. membership com., chair 2003—, past pres.), S.W. Conn. Agy. on Aging (pres. 1990—92), Orange Conn. Lions Club (pres.), Lions Club Internat. Avocations: walking, swimming, knitting. Home: 520 Hundred Acre Rd Orange CT 06477-3705 Office: Phillips Packaging PO Box 831 Orange CT 06477-0831

PHILLIPS, JILL META, novelist, critic, astrologer; b. Detroit, Oct. 22, 1952; d. Leyson Kirk and Leona Anna (Rasmussen) P. Student pub. schs., Calif. Lit. counselor Book Builders, Charter Oak, Calif., 1966-77; pres. Moon Dance Astro Graphics, Covina, Calif., 1994—. Author: (with Leona Phillips) A Directory of American Film Scholars, 1975, The Good Morning Cookbook, 1976, G.B. Shaw: A Review of the Literature, 1976, T.E. Lawrence: Portrait of the Artist as Hero, 1977, The Archaeology of the Collective East, 1977, The Occult, 1977, D.H. Lawrence: A Review of the Literature and Biographies, 1978, Film Appreciation: A College Guide Book, 1979, Annus Mirabilis: Europe in the Dark and Middle Centuries, 1979, (with Leona Rasmussen Phillips) The Dark Frame: Occult Cinema, 1979, Misfit: The Films of Montgomery Clift, 1979, Butterflies in the Mind: A Précis of Dreams and Dreamers, 1980; The Rain Maiden: A Novel of History, 1987, Walford's Oak: A Novel, 1990, The Fate Weaver: A Novel in Two Centuries, 1991, Saturn Falls: A Novel of the Apocalypse, 1993, Birthday Secrets, 1998, Your Luck is in the Stars, 2000; columnist Dell Horoscope Mag., Astrology Your Daily Horoscope Mag., 1998—; contbr. book revs. to New Guard mag., 1974-76; contbr. numerous articles to profl. jours. including Dell Horoscope, Midnight Horoscope, Astrology-Your Daily Horoscope, Am. Astrology. Mem. Young Ams. for Freedom, Am. Conservative Union, Elmer Bernstein's Film Music Collection, Ghost Club London, Count Dracula Soc., Dracula Soc. London, Richard III Soc. Republican. E-mail: queenofwands52@aol.com.

PHILLIPS, JOAN ELIZABETH, recreational therapist, educator; b. Norman, Okla., May 18, 1953; d. Raymond and Celia Morris Phillips; children: Carrie Reiser, Amelia Reiser. M in Psychology, Duquesne U., 1977; M in Art Therapy, Emporia (Kans.) State U., 1981. Registered and bd. cert. art therapist Art Therapy Credentials Bd. Art therapist, counselor Art Therapy Ctr., Norman, 1990—; grad. adj. assoc. prof. U. Okla., Norman, 1994—. Bd. dirs., pres. Art Therapy Credentials Bd., Inc., Greensboro, NC, 1999—. Mem. Human Rights Commn., Norman, 1994—98. Mem.: Am. Profl. Soc. on Abuse of Children, Am. Art Therapy Assn. (bd. dirs. 1996—98, Disting. Svc. award 1995). Episcopalian. Avocations: art, poetry, travel. Office: Art Therapy Ctr 123 E Tonhawa Ste 108 Norman OK 73069 Office Phone: 405-364-2008. E-mail: joanphillips@ou.edu.

PHILLIPS, KAREN A. urban planner; b. Ocilla, Ga. BA landscape architecture, Sch. Environ. Design U. Ga.; MA landscape architecture, Harvard U. Grad. Sch. Design, 1982. Urban planner, Atlanta, N.Y.C.; project mgr. econ. devel. dept. N.Y. State Urban Devel. Corp.; co-founder, pres., CEO Abyssinian Devel. Corp., N.Y.C., 1989—2002; mem. N.Y.C. Planning Commn., 2002—. Adj. prof. Sch. Architecture and Environ. Studies, City Coll, N.Y., 1992; cmty. devel. fellow Milano Grad Sch., New Sch. U., 2002—03. Mem. Parks Coun., Urban Design Inst., Preservation League of NY, Hamilton Heights Homeowners Assn., Manhattan Coun. Boy Scouts Am.; apptd. design com. Martin Luther King., Jr. Nat. Monument Project. Fellow: Am. Soc. Landscape Arch.; mem.: Assn. Real Estate Women. Office: NYC Dept City Planning 22 Reade St New York NY 10007-1216*

PHILLIPS, KAREN BORLAUG, economist, railroad industry executive; b. Long Beach, Calif., Oct. 1, 1956; d. Paul Vincent and Wilma (Tish) Borlaug. Student, Cath. U. P.R., 1973-74; BA, BS, U. N.D., 1977; postgrad., George Washington U., 1978-80. Rsch. asst. rsch. and spl. programs adminstrn. U.S. Dept. Transp., Washington, 1977—78, economist, office of sec., 1978—82; profl. staff mem. (majority) Com. Commerce Sci., Transp. U.S. Senate, Washington, 1982—85, tax economist (minority) com. on fin., 1985—87, chief economist (majority) senate com. on fin., 1987—88; commr. Interstate Commerce Commn., Washington, 1988—94; v.p. legis. Assn. Am. Railroads, Washington, 1994—95, sr. v.p. policy, legis. and comm., 1995—98; pres. Policy & Advocacy Assocs., Alexandria, Va., 1998—2000; v.p. U.S. pub. and govt. affairs Can. Nat. Ry. Co., Washington, 2000—. Contbr. articles to profl. jours. Recipient award for Meritorious Achievement, Sec. Transp., 1980, Spl. Achievement awards, 1978, 80, Outstanding Performance awards, 1978, 80, 81. Mem. Am. Econ. Assn., Women's Transp. Seminar (Woman of Yr. award 1994), Transp. Rsch. Forum, Assn. Transp. Law, Logistics and Policy, Tax Coalition, Can.-Am. Bus. Coun. (bd. dirs.), Blue Key, Phi Beta Kappa, Omicron Delta Epsilon. Republican. Lutheran. Office: Can Nat Rlwy Co Ste 500 601 Pennsylvania Ave NW Washington DC 20004 Office Phone: 202-347-7816. E-mail: karen.phillips@cn.ca.

PHILLIPS, KAREN SUZANNE, psychologist; b. Jackson, Miss., Dec. 4, 1959; d. Lawrence and Betty Mae (Riberdy) P. AA, Hinds C.C., 1986; BS, U. So. Miss., 1989; M of Comty. Counseling, Miss. Coll., 1992. Intern Hospice of Cen. Miss., Jackson, 1991-92; psychology technician Miss. State Hosp.-Oak Cir. Ctr. Adolescent Unit, Whitfield, 1992-94; psychologist I Miss. State Hosp.-Jaquith Nursing Home Cons. Svc., Jackson, 1994—. Vol. counselor Hospice of Cen. Miss., Jackson, 1992—. Democrat. Episcopalian. Avocations: travel, swimming, reading, water skiing, horseback riding. Home: 159 S Canton Club Cir Jackson MS 39211-3427

PHILLIPS, LINDA, county official; b. Kansas City, Mo., Mar. 11, 1956; d. Harold Edwin and Louise Anderson; m. Van Keith Phillips, Sept. 27, 1980; children: Andrew Keith, Matthew Harold, Christopher Anderson. AAS, SUNY, N.Y.C., 1977; BS, Purdue U., West Lafayette, Ind., 1978, MSM, 1980. Cons. Jones and Phillips Assocs., Inc., Lafayette, Ind., 1991—99; co-director Tippecanoe County Bd. of Election and Registration, Lafayette, Ind., 2000—02; clk. of the tippecanoe county circuit ct. Tippecanoe County Govt., Lafayette, Ind., 2003—. Mem. Lafayette Redevelopment Commn., Ind., 1996—97; pres., sec. Tippecanoe County Rep. Women's Club, Lafayette, Ind., 1991—2003; mem. Lafayette City Coun., Ind., 1998—99; dir., 4th congl. dist. Ind. Fedn. of Rep. Women, Indpls., 2000—03; bd. mem. Fairfield Twp. Bd., Lafayette, Ind.; bd. mem., treas. Montessori Parents, Inc., West Lafayette, Ind., 1990—99; sec., bd. mem. Wabash Valley Trust for Hist. Preservation, Lafayette, Ind., 1994—2002; treas. Tippecanoe County Hist. Assn., Lafayette, Ind., 2000—03; mem., treas. YWCA, Lafayette, Ind., 2000—; pres. Friends of Downtown, Lafayette, Ind., 2001—01. Mem.: Assn. of Ind. Clks., Internat. Assn. of Assembly Mgrs. Home: 534 S 7th St Lafayette IN 47901 Office: Tippecanoe County Govt 301 Main St Lafayette IN 47901

PHILLIPS, LINDA FOX, social worker, consultant, healthcare educator; b. Boston, Apr. 7, 1947; d. Kenneth Russell and Eleanor Pihl Fox; m. Kenneth Kaas Kugel, Sept. 19, 1970 (div. Dec. 17, 1981); m. Stephen John Phillips, July 3, 1982; children: Ethan, Andrew, Nicholas. BA, Brown U., 1968; MS, Simmons Coll., 1970. LCSW N.H. Social worker, therapist Crownsville (Md.) State Hosp., 1970—71; outpatient Providence Mental Health, 1971—72; outpatient therapist Carroll County Mental Health, North Conway, NH, 1972—75, outpatient coord., 1975—80, area dir., 1980—2000; instr. U. N.H., Conway, NH, 1980—; cons. Shelley Assocs., Albany, NH, 2001—. Co-chair So. Carroll County Wellness Com., NH, 1996—2000. Contbr. articles to profl. jours. Pres., bd. dirs. Carroll County Health Care Svcs., NH, 1973—77; chair environ. project Carroll County, 1978—82; incorporator, No. N.H. Found., 2000—; chmn. membership com. Mt. Washington Valley Econ. Coun.; elected trustee Conway Pub. Libr., 2003; dep. campaign mgr. Epstein for State Senate, NH, 1999—2000. Recipient Maida Solomon award, Simmons Coll., 1976, 1978, Leadership award, Brown U., 1994. Mem.: Acad. Cert. Social Workers. Avocations: reading, horseback riding, coaching boys athletic teams. Home and Office: 597 Passaconaway Rd Conway NH 03818 E-mail: lindafoxphillips@adelphic.net.

PHILLIPS, LINDA GOLUCH, plastic surgeon, educator, researcher; b. Chgo., Nov. 11, 1951; d. Edward Walter and Rosemarie (Tomasek) Goluch; m. William Anthony Phillips, July 12, 1975; children: Cooper William, Nolan Edward, Spencer Geoffrey, Corinna Lee. BA, U. Chgo., 1974, MD, 1978. Diplomate Am. Bd. Surgery, Am. Bd. Plastic Surgery (mem. qualifying examination team 1993—). Intern U. Chgo., 1978-80; resident in gen. surgery Northwestern U., Chgo., 1980-83, instr., surgeon, 1982-83; asst. prof. Wayne State U., Detroit, 1985-88; asst. prof. plastic surgery U. Tex. Med. Br., Galveston, 1988-91, assoc. prof. plastic surgery, 1991-95; prof. plastic surgery, 1995—; Truman G. Blocker Jr., MD, Disting. chairperson U. Tex. Med. Br., Galveston, chief divsn. plastic surgery, 1994—; mem. consulting med. staff Shriners Burns Inst., Galveston, Tex., 1988—. Chmn. basic rsch. grants com. Plastic Surgery Edn. Found., Chgo., 1992-95, bd. dirs., 1995-98, 2000-03, mem. ednl. assessment com., mem. scholarship com., 1987-92, mem. plastic surgery-in-svc. exam. com., 1987-88, 89-93, mem. instrnl. course com., 1991-92, mem. rsch. fellowship com., mem. rsch. fund proposals com., 1993, 94; parliamentarian Plastic Surgery Rsch. Coun., 1991-93, pres., 1996-97; program chmn., 1996, pres., 1997, Morestin lectr. Nat. Med. Assn., 1991; guest spkr. Royal Coll. Surgeons, Eng., 1993; spkr. in field. Co-author book chpts.; contbr. articles, abstracts to profl. jours. Pres. Blue Marlin Swim Team, Houston, 1993; active Clear Creek Ind. Sch. Dist., Houston, 1992. Grantee in field. Fellow ACS; mem. AMA, Am. Assn. Plastic Surgeons, Am. Burn Assn. (orgn. and delivery of burn care com. 1988-91, ednl. com., 1991-94), Am. Soc. Plastic and Reconstructive Surgeons (program com. 1991-92, exhibits com. 1992, 93, chair, 1993-94, sci. program com. 1994), Am. Soc. Maxillofacial Surgeons (news com. 1992, membership com. 1992-93), Am. Assn. Surgery of Trauma (search com. editor of Jour. Trauma 1992), Am. Soc. Aesthetic Plastic Surgery, Fedn. Assn. Women Surgeons (chair, bd. trustees), Am. Assn. Hand Surgery, Am. Geriat. Soc., Am. Diabetes Assn., Surg. Infection Soc., Assn. Women Surgeons (pres. 1992-94, v.p.-pres.-elect 1990-92, chair program com. 1990-92, chair membership com. 1988-89, nominating com. 1989-92), Blocker-Lewis Surgery Soc. (exec. sec. 1988-92), Assn. Acad. Chairmen of Plastic Surgery (prerequisite com. 1990, 91), Wound Healing Soc. (honors and awards com. 1993, chmn. 1996—), Singleton Surg. Soc. (chmn. 1997), Soc. Head and Neck Surgeons, Tex. Soc. Plastic Surgeons, Assn. Acad. Surgery, N.Y. Acad. Scis., Tex. Med. Assn., Galveston Med. Soc., Plastic Surgery Rev. Com. (chmn. 2002-2003, vice-chair 2000-2001), Am. Bd. Plastic Surgery (chmn. written exam. com. 2003-, dir. 2000-, qualifying exam. team 1993-, certifying (oral) exam. team, comprehensive adv. coun. 1999-), Sigma Xi. Roman Catholic. Avocations: salt water tropical fish, gardening, gourmet cooking. Home: 15823 Sylvan Lake Dr Houston TX 77062-4795 Office: U Tex Med Br 6 124 Mccullough Bldg Galveston TX 77555-0001

PHILLIPS, LYNN ALICE, pre-school educator; b. Lima, Ohio, Mar. 15, 1963; d. Lewis Benson and Jeanne Caroline Barger; m. John Coolidge Phillips, Jr., Nov. 24, 1984; children: Sara Jean Ruth, Calvin Lewis. AA in Childhood Devel., St. Thomas U., 1993. Preschool tchr. aide North Miami (Fla.) Early Childhood, 1993; preschool tchr. Friendly Woods, Crestview, Fla., 1994—96, Youthland Acad., Mason, Ohio, 1996—98; preschool dir. Ross Ave. Child Care, Hamilton, Ohio, 1998—99, Precious Resources, Felicity, Ohio, 1999—2001; trainer Missing Children Help Ctr., Blue Ashe, Ohio, 2001; preschool tchr. Mt. Mariah Ark of Learning, Cin., 2001—. Mem.: Ea. Star Claremont (line officer 2002—). United Meth. Avocations: clowning, sewing. Home: 420 W Walnut St PO Box 68 Felicity OH 45120 Office: Mt Moriah Ark of Learning 681 Mt Moriah Drive Cincinnati OH 45245

PHILLIPS, M. CATHERINE, elementary school educator; b. Wells, Austria, Feb. 17, 1954; arrived in US, 1956; d. Jack Berard Phillips and Mary A. Keller. BA in Edn., Mt. St. Joseph, Cin., 1978; MA in Pastoral Ministry, St. Thomas U., 1991; MA in Edn. and Counseling, Xavier U., Cin., 2002. Tchr. St. Veronica Sch., Cin., 1978—90, Immaculate Conception Sch., Hialeah, 1983—85; dir. religious Edn. St. Vivian Parish, Cin., 1990—91; tchr. Mt. Notre Dame H.S., Cin., 1994—96, Corryville Cath. Sch., Cin., 1998—. Test adminstr. for home schooled students, Cin., 1995—. Facilitator St. Ignatius Peace and Justice Com., Cin., Little Rock Bible Study, Cin.; youth min. St. Ignatius Parish, Cin. Mem.: Nat. Cath. Educators Assn. Avocations: quilting, cooking, sewing, gardening.

PHILLIPS, MARGARET A. pharmacology educator; BS in Biochemistry, U. Calif., Davis, 1981; PhD in Pharm. Chemistry, U. Calif., San Francisco, 1988. Prof. dept. pharmacology U. Tex. Southwestern Med. Ctr., Dallas. Office: U Tex Southwestern Med Ctr Dept Pharmacology 5323 Harry Hines Blvd Dallas TX 75390-9041

PHILLIPS, MARGARET RACKLEY, retired elementary school educator; b. Smithfield, N.C., July 20, 1942; d. William Hector Rackley, Sr. and Elizabeth Tyson Rackley; m. R. Douglas Phillips, July 11, 1965; children: Christa Lynn, Scott Hamilton. BA, Meredith Coll., 1964. Cert. art edn. tchr. grades K-12 N.C. Dept. Pub. Instrn. Art tchr. jr. h.s. Winston-Salem/Forsyth County Schs., Winston Salem, NC, 1964—65; social studies and art tchr. Halifax (N.C.) County Schs., 1966—70; asst. site mgr. hist. Halifax N.C. Dept. Cultural Resources, Raleigh, 1974—83, site mgr. hist. Halifax, 1983—95; art tchr. grades K-5 Weldon (N.C.) City Sch., 1995—2001, ret., 2001. Author, editor: History of Halifax Baptist Church, A Continuation, 2001. Pres. Haywood Home Demonstration Club, Halifax, NC, 1976—78; pres., chairperson Coastal Plains Arts and Crafts, Rocky Mount, NC, 1978—79; active, pres., sec., treas. Halifax Fire Dept. Ladies Aux., 1990—2003. Mem.: Hist. Halifax Restoration Assn. (bd. dirs., treas. 1985—98), Halifax County Hist. Assn. (com. mem. 1982—, vice chair 1992—95, home restoration award 1998), Elizabeth Montfort Ashe DAR (sec., vice regent, regent 2001—03). Democrat. Bapt. Avocations: art, drawing faces, reading, genealogy. Address: PO Box 411 Halifax NC 27839-0411

PHILLIPS, MARION GRUMMAN, writer, civic worker; b. N.Y.C., Feb. 11, 1922; d. Leroy Randle and Rose Marion (Werther) Grumman; m. Ellis Laurimore Phillips, Jr., June 13, 1942; children: Valerie Rose (Mrs. Adrian Parsegian), Elise Marion (Mrs. Edward E. Watts III), Ellis Laurimore III, Kathryn Noel Phillips, Cynthia Louise (Mrs. Charles Prosser). Student, Mt. Holyoke Coll., 1940-42; BA, Adelphi U., 1981. Civic vol. Mary C. Wheeler Sch., 1964-68, Historic Ithaca, Inc., 1972-76, Ellis L. Phillips Found., 1960-91. Bd. dirs. North Shore Jr. League, 19660-61, 64-65, 68-69, Family Svc. Assn. Nassau County, 1963-69, Homemaker Svc. Assn. Nassau County, 1959, 61. Author: (light verse) A Foot in the Door, 1965, The Whale-Going, Going, Gone, 1977, Doctors Make Me Sick (So I Cured Myself of Arthritis), 1979; editor: (with Valerie Phillips Parsegian) Richard and Rhoda, Letters from the Civil War, 1982, Wooden Shoes the story of my Grandfather's Grandfather (F.M. Sisson), 1990, Irish Eyes, family hist. of McTarsneys and Sissons, 1990, The Log Chapel, A History of the Congregational Community Church, Rockwood, Maine, 1999; editor Jr. League Shore Lines, 1960-61, The Werthers in America-Four Generations and their Descendants, 1987; A B-Tour of Britain, 1986; contbr. articles on fund raising to mags. Mem. New Eng. Hist. Geneal. Soc., N.Y. Geneal. Biographical Soc., Creek Club, Hannah Adams Womens Club, PEO Sisterhood. Congregationalist. Address: 279 North St Medfield MA 02052-1211

PHILLIPS, MICHELLE GILLIAM, actress, writer; b. Long Beach, Calif., June 4, 1944; d. Gardner Burnett and Joyce Leon (Poole) Gilliam; m. John Phillips, Dec. 31, 1962 (div. 1970); children: Gilliam Chynna Phillips, Austin D. Hines, Aron S. Wilson. Grad. high sch., Ft. Jones, Calif. Model Francis Gill Agy., N.Y.C., 1962-64; singer Mamas and Papas, 1965-69. Guest appearances in TV shows include Vega$, 1980, The Fall Guy, 1983, Santa Barbara, 1984, Murder, She Wrote, 1984, Scene of the Crime, 1985, Alfred Hitchcock Presents, 1985, T.J. Hooker, 1985, Star Trek: The Next Generation, 1988, Herman's Head, 1994, Diagnsos Murder, 1994, 99, Burke's Law, 1994, Lois & Clark: The New Adventures of Superman, 1995, Too Something, 1996, Beverly Hills, 90210, 1997, 98, Pauly, 1997, The Magnificent Seven, 1998, 99, 2000, The Love Boat: The Next Wave, 1998, Rude Awakening, 1999, Providence, 1999, Twice in a Lifetime, 2000; appeared in tv movies The Death Squad, 1974, The California Kid, 1974, The Useres, 1978, Moonlight, 1982, Murder Me, Murder You, 1983, Secrets of a Married Man, 1984, Covenant, 1985, Paint Me a Murder, 1985, Stark: Mirror Image, 1986, Assault and Matrimony, 1987, Mike Hammer: Murder Takes All, 1989, Trenchcoat in Paradise, 1989, Appearances, 1990, Rubdown, 1993, Rock 'n' Roll Revolution: The British Invade America, 1995, 919 Fifth Avenue, 1995, No One Would Tell, 1996, Pretty Poison, 1996, Sweetwater, 1999; appeared in feature films Monterey Pop, 1969, The Last Movie, 1971, Dillinger, 1973, Valentino, 1977, Bloodline, 1979, The Man with Bogart's Face, 1980, Savage Harvest, 1981, American Anthem, 1986, Let It Ride, 1989, Flashing on the Sixties: A Tribal Document, 1990, Scissors, 1991, Army of One, 1993, Anna Petrovic, You Rock!, 1998, Lost in the Pershing Point Hotel, 2000, TV series Aspen, 1977, The French Atlantic Affair, 1979, Hotel, 1983, Knots Landing, 1979, Second Chances, 1993, Malibu Shores, 1996, Knots Landing: Back to the Cul-de-Sac, 1997; author: California Dreamin', 1986, Monday Monday (Grammy award). Recipient medal of Honor for Stop War Toys Campaign Alliance for Survival, 1987, Soap Opera Awards for Best Villainess, 1990.

PHILLIPS, PATRICIA DOMINIS, lawyer; b. Los Angeles, July 21, 1934; d. Anthony P. and Louise Dominis (Brown) Phillips; m. John T. Phillips, Jan. 1, 1964; children: Toni, Lisa, Paul, Samantha, John. BA psychology, U. Calif., Santa Barbara, 1956; JD, Loyola U., Los Angeles, 1967. Bar: Calif. 1968, US Supreme Ct., US Dist. Ct. (cen. dist.)/Calif., US Dist. Ct. (so. dist.)/Calif. Law clk. Los Angeles County Superior Ct., Los Angeles, 1968; assoc. Beardsley, Hufstedler, Los Angeles, 1969—72; ptnr. Hufstedler, Miller, Carlson & Beardsley, Los Angeles, 1972, predecessor firm Beardsley, Hufstedler & Kemble, Los Angeles, 1972; lectr. continuing edn. of the bar Rutter Group. Contbr. articles profl. jour. Mem.: Loyola U. Law Sch. (bd. vistors 1985—), Los Angeles County Bar Assn. (pres. 1984—85, bd. gov. 1986—), State Bar Calif., Am. Acad. Matrimonial Lawyers, ABA, U. So. Calif. (bd. councillors 1983), Chancery. Office: Hufstedler Miller Carlson & Beardsley 700 S Flower St Ste 1600 Los Angeles CA 90017

PHILLIPS, PAULA BRADY, speech pathology/audiology services professional; b. New Bern, N.C., Sept. 26, 1956; d. Paul Carraway and Dora Simpson Brady; m. Michael Craig Phillips, June 27, 1981; children: Michael Craig Jr., Catherine Caroline. BS, E. Carolina U., 1978, MS, 1980. Speech/lang. pathologist Caswell Ctr., Kinston, NC, 1980—84; dir. speech/lang. svcs. Howell's Ctr., New Bern, 1984—89; speech/lang. pathologist Pamlico County Schs., Bayboro, NC, 1989—92, Pitt County Schs., Greenville, NC, 1992—. Mem.: Speech and Hearing Area Resource Exch. (pres.), Am. Speech and Hearing Assn. Avocations: reading, gardening, water-skiing. Home: 625 Heartwood Dr Grimesland NC 27837 E-mail: wer4ecu@earthlink.net.

PHILLIPS, PAULA L. foundation administrator, visual artist; b. Tuskegee, Ala., Oct. 3, 1949; d. Paul Jr. and Thelma Lee (McDaniel) Phillips; m. Lloyd Thomas Pate, Apr. 28, 1978 (div. Dec. 1987); children: Chance Edmund, Lloyd Thomas II, Brandy Bianca. BA cum laude, Tex. Wesleyan U., Ft. Worth, 1994; MFA, Md. Inst. Coll. Art, Balt., 1996. Art therapy facilitator Oakgrave Ctr., Ft. Worth, 1990-94; instr. art Friends Sch., Balt., 1996-97, The Md. Inst., Coll. of Art, Balt., 1996-97; instr. comprehensive art Suitland H.S., District Heights., Md., 1997-99; instr. art Anne Arundel C.C., Arnold, Md., 1995—; asst. dir. Cmty. Arts Partnership, Md. Inst. Coll. ARt, Balt., 1998—; dir. Superkids Camp, The Parks and People Found., Balt., 1997—. Exhibited works (mixed media paitings) Smithsonian Anacostia Exhbn., 1999, Govt. House, 1999, Eubie Blake Jazz and Cultural Theater, 1998. Cmty. activist. Named Tchr. of Yr., Suitland H.S., 1997-99. Mem. Creative Alliance Fells Point. Democrat. Avocations: swimming, camping, horseback riding. Home: 1115 Hunter St Baltimore MD 21202-3821 Office: Cmty Arts Partnerships 1300 W Mount Royal Ave Baltimore MD 21217-4134

PHILLIPS, RAELENE E. writer, educator; b. Lima, Ohio, Aug. 5, 1950; d. Floyd Arley and Vondale Wood; m. Dan L. Phillips, Aug. 9, 1969; children: Sonya Renee' Wilkie, Kyer Toney. Inspirational speaker; ch. pianist; tchr. Sunday Sch.; choir dir. Author: (novels) Freedom in White Mittens, Freedom's Destiny Fulfilled, Freedom's Tremendous Cost, (humorous devotional book) Puppy in the Pulpit, (devotional gift book) Where is Your Pineapple?; contbr. composite book Living by Faith (hon. mention/inclusion in book, 2003), children's devotional books Keys for Kids. Named a Class Communicator, CLASServices, Inc. Avocations: speaking, reading, travel. Home: 9310 Cowpath Road Saint Paris OH 43072 E-mail: danrae@erinet.com.

PHILLIPS, RENEÉ, editor-in-chief, writer, educator; b. Freeport, N.Y. Student, Art Students League, 1979, Am. Art Sch., 1979, Fashion Inst. Tech., 1980, New Sch. for Social Rsch., 1980. Dir., founder Artopia, not-for-profit art orgn., N.Y.C., 1980-84; pub., editor-in-chief Manhattan Arts Internat., N.Y.C., 1983—2000; editor-in-chief www.Manhattan Arts.com. Juror Excellence in Arts Awards, 1988, N.Y. Lung Assn. Ann. Exhbn., 1990, Manhattan Arts Internat. Ann. Internat. Art Competition, 1992—; juror, co-curator Redefining Visionary Art, Doma Gallery, N.Y.C., 1989; curator Synthesis of Painting and Sculpture exhbn., 1st Women's Bank, N.Y.C., 1984, Salute to Liberty internat. art exhbn., N.Y.C., 1986, HerStory exhbns., 1999-2004, Small Works, 2004, The Healing Power of Art, 2002, 03, 04; organizer over 40 art and cultural events; editor-in-chief www.ManhattanArts.com; curator I Love Manhattan, N.Y.C., 2003, The Healing Power of Art, N.Y.C., 2003; bd. dirs., v.p. Women's Studio Ctr., L.I., N.Y., 2003—; spkr. in field; lectr. in field. Author: New York Contemporary Art Galleries Annual Guide, 1995-02, The Complete Guide to New York Art Galleries, 2004, Presentation Power Tools for Fine Artists, 1998, 2d edit., 2000, 3rd edit., 2002, Success Now! for Artists: A Motivational Guide, 1998, 2nd edit., 2003, editor-in-chief Success Now!, 1991—. Recipient award of merit Muscular Dystrophy Assn., 1986, award for outstanding contbns. to arts Mayor of N.Y.C., 1987. Mem. Internat. Assn. Art Critics, N.Y. Artists Equity (former bd. dirs.). Office: Manhattan Arts Internat 200 E 72nd St New York NY 10021-4537 E-mail: info@ManhattanArts.com.

PHILLIPS, SHIRLEY FLOWERS, food service executive; Co-chair Phillips Seafood Restaurants, Ocean City, Md., 1956—. Bd. vis. U. Md.; bd. trustees Balt. Internat. Coll., 1999; aux. bd. Washington Coll. Chestertown Md. Office: Phillips Seafood Restaurants 2004 N Philadelphia Ave Ocean City MD 21842-3560 Fax: 410-289-2053.

PHILLIPS, SUSAN MEREDITH, financial economist, university administrator; b. Richmond, Va., Dec. 23, 1944; d. William G. and Nancy (Meredith) Phillips. BA in Math., Agnes Scott Coll., 1967; MS in Fin. and Ins., La. State U., 1971, PhD in Fin. and Economics, 1973. Asst. prof. La. State U., 1973—74, U. Iowa, 1974—78; econ. fellow Directorate of Econ. and Policy Rsch., SEC, 1976—78; assoc. prof. fin. dept. U. Iowa, 1978—83, assoc. v.p. fin. and univ. svcs., 1979—81; commr. Commodity Futures Trading Comm., 1981—83, chmn., 1983—87; prof. fin. dept., v.p. fin. and univ. svcs. U. Iowa, Iowa City, 1987—91; bd. govs. Fed. Res. Bd., Washington, 1991—98; dean Sch. of Bus., prof. fin. dept. George Washington U., Washington, 1998—. Bd. dirs. Chgo. Bd. Options Exchange, 2000—, Nat. Futures Assn., 2000—, Assn. to Advance Collegiate Schs. Bus., 1999—, Kroger Co.; trustee State St. Mut. Rsch. Funds, 1998—. Co-author (with J. Richard Zecher): The SEC and the Public Interest; contbr. articles to profl. jours. Fellow Brookings Econ. Policy fellow, 1976—77. Office: George Washington U Sch Bus and Pub Mgmt 710 21st St NW Ste 206 Washington DC 20052-0001

PHILLIPS, TARI, professional basketball player; b. Mar. 6, 1969; Student, U. Ga.; grad., Ctrl. Fla. U., 1991. With Orlando Miracle Women's Basketball Team, Fla., 1999, N.Y. Liberty, N.Y.C., NY, 2000—; player USA Basketball Women's Nat. Team, 2002, 2004. Named Most Improved Player, WNBA, 2000; named to All-WNBA Second Team, 2002; recipient Gold Medal, World Championships, 2002. Office: New York Liberty 2 Penn Plz 14th Fl New York NY 10121*

PHILLIPS, VICKI L. school system administrator; b. Marion, Ind., Jan. 15, 1958; d. Denver Phillips and Vivian (Burnette) Fuqua. BS in Edn., Western Ky. U., 1980, MA in Psychology, 1987; doctoral student, U. Ky., 1988—; EdD in instrnl. leadership, U. of Lincoln, Eng., 2002. Dir. devel. tng. dept. Panorama, Bowling Green, Ky., 1978—80; tchr. learning and behavior disorders Simpson County Bd. Edn., 1981—85; exceptional child cons. Ky. Dept. Edn. Office Edn. for Exceptional Children, 1986—90; chief exec. asst. to edn. commr. Ky. Dept. of Edn., 1986—93; dep. dir./chief of staff Nat. Alliance for Restructuring Edn., Wash., DC, 1993—95; dir. Greater Phila. First Partnership for Reform; exec. dir. Children Achieving Challenge; supt. Sch. Dist. of Lancaster, 1998—2003; sec. of edn. Pa. Dept. Edn., Harrisburg, 2003—. Mem. ASCD, Nat. Coun. for Exceptional Children, Coun. for Behavior Disorders, Nat. Assn. for Sch. Psychologists, Ky. Assn. Sch. Adminstrs., Ky. Assn. for Psychology in the Schs., Ky. Assn. for Family-Based Svcs., Ky. Families for Family-Based Svcs., Ky. Families as Allies. Office: 333 Market St Harristown 2 Harrisburg PA 17126-0333

PHILLIPS, VICKY LYNN, elementary school educator; b. Oskaloosa, Iowa, Mar. 21, 1947; d. Irvin and Dena Ott; m. Michael Robert Phillips; children: Jeffrey Michael, Jill Patricia Gardner. BA in Elem. Edn., William Penn Coll., Oskaloosa, Iowa, 1965; MA in Elem. Edn., U. Iowa, 1987; MEd in Ednl. Adminstrn., U. S.C., 1994. Cert. Early Childhood/Generalist Nat. Bd. For Profl. Tchg. Standards, 2002. Elem. educator Sigourney (Iowa) Cmty. Schools, 1969—89, Richland One Sch. Dist., Columbia, SC, 1991—. Mem.: NEA, Richland County Edn. Assn., S.C. Edn. Assn., Delta Kappa Gamma. Home: 124 Stonehill Rd Chapin SC 29036 Office: W S Sandel Elem 2700 Seminole Rd Columbia SC 29210 Personal E-mail: vickyphil@aol.com.

PHILLIPS, VIRGINIA A. judge; BA magna cum laude, U. Calif., Riverside, 1979; JD, Boalt Hall, 1982. Ct. commr. Calif. Superior Ct., Riverside, 1991-95; magistrate judge U.S. Dist. Ct., L.A., 1995-99, dist. judge, 1999—. Office: US Courthouse 3470 Twelfth St Riverside CA 92501

PHILLIPS, WINIFRED PATRICIA, radio producer, composer; b. Mobile, Ala., Apr. 13, 1972; d. Winifred Waldron Phillips. BA summa cum laude in Comms., Kean U., 1994. Composer, prodr., actress, writer Nat. Pub. Radio, Washington, 1996—2002; composer, prodr., actress, writer Radio Tales XM Satellite Radio Dramas, Washington, 2002—; owner music and audio prodn. co. Gens. Prodns. Composer, prodr., actress, writer (National Public Radio dramas) Generations Radio Theater Presents: Radio Tales, 1996—2002, (radio dramas) Radio Tales, XM Satellite Radio, 2002—, composer, prodr., actress (radio drama) The Odyssey Trilogy, 2003, Arabian Nights Trilogy, 2003, The Gift of the Magi, 1996, The Yellow Wallpaper, 1996, The Fall of the House of Usher, 1998, Sleepy Hollow, 1998, The Time Machine, 1999, Gulliver's Travels, 1999, The Mummy, 1999, The Island of Doctor Moreau, 2000, Dr. Jekyll and Mr. Hyde, 2000, Journey to the Center of the Earth, 2000, The Pit and the Pendulum, 2000, The Hunchback of Notre-Dame, 2001, Jason and The Argonauts, 2001, War of the Worlds, 2001, Phantom of the Opera, 2001, Beowulf, 2001, Twenty Thousand Leagues Under the Sea, 2001, The Invisible Man, 2001, The Lost World, 2002, composer, actress, author (radio musicals) Celtic Hero, 2000; composer, actress, author: radio musicals Lord of the Celts, 1998; author: (short stories) Breaking Point, 1991, Celtic Beauty for Sword and Sorceress 20 book anthology, 2003, (radio drama script) Light of Truth, 1985. Recipient GRACIE award for best nat./network drama series, Am. Women in Radio and TV, 2001, 2003, 2004, N.Y. Festivals award, Internat. Radio Festivals, 1997, AUDIE Honors award, Audio Pubs. Assn., 1999, GOLDEN REEL Merit award, Nat. Fedn. Cmty. Broadcasters, 2001, GRACIE award for outstanding achievement by an actress, Am. Women in Radio and TV, 1998, N.Y. Festivals award, Internat. Radio Festivals, 2001; grantee Endowment grantee, Wallace Reader's Digest Funds, 1996—2002, NEA, 1996—2002, Durkin Hayes Publ., 1998. Mem.: SAG, BMI, NARAS. Avocations: reading, Web design, computer art, travel. Business E-Mail: phillips@radiotales.com.

PHILLIPS, ZAIGA ALKSNIS, pediatrician; b. Riga, Latvia, Sept. 13, 1934; came to U.S., 1949; d. Adolfs and Alma (Ozols) Alksnis; (div. 1972); children: Albert L., Lisa K., Sintija. BS, U. Wash., 1956, MD, 1959. Fellow Colo. Med. Ctr., Denver, 1961-62; sch. physician Bellevue and Issaquah (Wash.) Sch. Dists., 1970-77; pvt. practice Bellevue, 1977—; staff pediatrician Overlake Med. Ctr., 1977—, Childrens Hosp. and Med. Ctr., Seattle, 1977—, Evergreen Med. Ctr., 1977—. Attending physician Allergy Clinic, Childrens Hosp., Seattle, 1988—; cons. and contact to pediatricians in Latvia, 1988—; team mem. to Latvia, Healing the Children Contact with Latvia, 1993-97; bd. mem. Bellevue's Stay in Sch. Program, 1994-97. Mem. Am. Latvian Assn., 1972—, Wash. Latvian Assn., Seattle, 1972—; pres. Latvian Sorority Gundega, Seattle, 1990-93; bd. dirs. Sister Cities Assn., Bellevue, 1992-98, Wash. Asthma Allergy Found. Am., 1992-99. Fellow Am. Acad. Pediat.; mem. Am. Latvian Physicians Assn. (bd. dirs. 1998—), Wash. State and Puget Sound Pediatric Assn. Office: Pediatric Assn 2700 Northup Way Bellevue WA 98004-1463 E-mail: zap@u.washington.edu.

PHILLIPS-LESANE, FAY M. mental health professional; b. Petersburg, Va., Feb. 2, 1956; d. Orlando F. Phillips Sr., Mary E. Phillips. BSW cum laude, Va. State U., 1978; MSW summa cum laude, Howard U., 1981; postgrad., Am. Sch. Profl. Psychology, 1995. LCSW Va., LICSW D.C. Psychiat. social worker Ctrl. State Hosp., Petersburg, Va., 1978—79; mental health specialist Alexandria Cmty. Mental Health, Alexandria, Va., 1979—82; social worker supr., program dir. Luth. Social Svcs., Washington, 1982—88; clin. adminstr. Commn. on Mental Health, Washington, 1988—96; prevention specialist U. D.C., Washington, 1996—2000; pres., CEO Agape Mental Health, Woodbridge, Va., 1998—. Bd. dirs. U. D.C. Dept. Social Work, Christian Hope Child Care, Woodbridge; mem. adv. bd. Nat. Consortium for Am. Children; dir. Inst. Human Devel. Nat. Consortium for African Am. Children. Mem.: Alpha Kappa Alpha. Democrat. Avocations: music, sports, travel, art, bowling. Home: 13400 Forest Glen Rd Woodbridge VA 22191 Office: Agape Mental Health 13319 Woodbridge St Woodbridge VA 22191

PHILLIS, MARILYN HUGHEY, artist; b. Kent, Ohio; d. Paul Jones and Helen Margaret (Miller) Hughey; m. Richard Waring Phillis, Mar. 19, 1949; children: Diane E., Hugh R., Randall W. Student, Kent State U., 1945; BS, Ohio State U., 1949. Chemist Battelle Meml. Inst., Columbus, Ohio, 1949-53; illustrator periodical Western Res. Hist. Mag., Garrettsville, Ohio, 1974-78; illustrator book AAUW, Piqua, Ohio, 1976; art instr. Edison State C.C., Piqua, Ohio, 1976; watermedia instr. Springfield (Ohio) Mus. Art, 1976-84. Juror art exhbns. state and nat. art groups, 1980—; painting instr. state and nat. orgns., 1980—; lectr. art healing Wheeling (W.Va.) Jesuit Coll., 1994—96; founder, coord. Nat. Creativity Seminar, Stretching Boundaries for Creative People, 1993, 1995, 1997, 1999, 2002. Author: Watermedia Techniques for Releasing the Creative Spirit, 1992, (chpt.) Bridging Space and Time, 1998; contbr. The Art of Layering: Making Connections, 2004, articles and illustrations to profl. jours.; one-woman shows include Stifel Fine Art Ctr., Wheeling, Va., Springfield Art Mus., Zanesville (Ohio) Art Ctr., Ohio U., Lancaster, Ohio U. East. St. Clairsville, Cleve. Inst. Music, Columbus Mus. Art, Cheekwood Mus. of Art, Bot. Hall, Nashville, Idaho Falls Art Ctr., Monroe (Mich.) C.C., exhibitions include, N.Y.C., Wheeling, W.Va, Butler Mus. Am. Art, Youngstown, Ohio, Taiwan Art Edn. Inst., Taipei, 1994, Represented in permanent collections Ohio U., Lancaster and St. Clairsville, Springfield (Ohio) Mus. Art, Heritage Hall mus., Talladega, Ala., Ohio Watercolor Soc., also corp. collections. Co-chmn. Cmty. Health and Humor Program, Wheeling, 1992. Recipient First awards Watercolor West, Riverside, Calif., 1990, Hudson Soc. award Nat. Collage Soc., 1995, Art Masters award Am. Artist Mag., 1996; elected to Hall of Fame, Kent, Ohio, 2000, Hall of Fame, Wheeling, Va., 2000. Mem. Internat. Soc. Study of Subtle Energies and Energy Medicine (art cons. sci. jour. 1992—, art and healing workshop 1995), Am. Watercolor Soc. (dir. 1991-93, newsletter editor 1992—,chmn. Jury of Awards, 2003, Osborne award 1975), Soc. Layerists in Multi-Media (nat. v.p. 1988-93), Ohio Watercolor Soc. (sec. 1979-82, v.p. 1982-89, pres. 1990-96, dir. biennial creativity seminars 1993-95, 97, 99, 2002, Gold medal, Best of Show 1993), Nat. Watercolor Soc. (chmn. selection jury 2001), Int. Noetic Sci., West Ohio Watercolor Soc. (pres. 1979-80, 2nd award 1982), Allied Artists N.Y., W.Va. Watercolor Soc. (1st award 1993), Ky. Watercolor Soc., Ga. Watercolor Soc., So. Watercolor Soc. (pres. 1997-98, Silver award 1999). Avocations: hiking, reading, genealogy, music, travel. Home and Office: Phillis Studio 72 Stamm Cir Wheeling WV 26003-5549

PHINNEY, JEAN SWIFT, psychology educator; b. Princeton, N.J., Mar. 12, 1933; d. Emerson H. and Anne (Davis) Swift; m. Bernard O. Phinney, Dec. 11, 1965; children: Peter, David. BA, Wellesley Coll., 1955; MA, UCLA, 1969, PhD, 1973. Asst. prof. psychology Calif. State U., L.A., 1977-81, assoc. prof. psychology, 1981-86, prof. psychology, 1986—. Editor: Children's Ethnic Socialization, 1987; asst. editor Jour. Adolescence; mem. editl. bd. Jour. Adolescent Rsch., Identity: An Internat. Jour.; contbr. articles to profl. jours. NIH and NSF grantee. Fellow APA; mem. Soc. for Rsch. in Child Devel., Soc. for Rsch. in Adolescence, Internat. Assn. Cross-Cultural Psychology. Avocations: skiing, hiking, travel. Office: Calif State U Dept Psychology 5151 State University Dr Los Angeles CA 90032-4226

PHIPARD, NANCY MIDWOOD, retired special education educator, prof.; b. Boston, Jan. 31, 1929; d. William Henry and Jean Estelle (Dubbs) McAdams; m. Kenneth E. Brown, June 17, 1949 (div.); children: Christopher M. Brown, Jennifer Progodich, Michael H. Brown, Jeffrey D. Brown; m. Arnold J. Midwood, Jr., July 2, 1980 (dec.); m. Harvey F. Phipard, Jan. 14, 1998. Student, Mt. Holyoke Coll., 1946-48; BA, Wellesley Coll., 1973; MEd, Boston Coll., 1975. Dir. confs. and insvc. tng., chmn. bd. Mass. Assn. for Children with Learning Disabilities, Waltham and Framingham, 1969-75; chmn. cdn. teams, cons. to spl. programs, grant writer Needham (Mass.) Pub. Schs., 1974-79; ret., 1979; pres., feature writer S.D. Assocs., Inc., Wellesley, Mass., 1980-81; dir. pub. rels., women's career conf. Babson Coll., Wellesley, 1982. Mem. program evaluation team Mass. Dept. Edn., Quincy, 1978. Author (as Nancy Brown, with Louis Dickstein): Psychological Reports, 1974; author: (poems) Portraits of a Life, 1996, Fields of Gold, 1996, Ever-Flowing Stream, 1997, Best Poems of 1998, 1998, Colors of the Past, 2000, Echoes of Yesteryear, 2000, America at the Millennium, The Best Poems and Poets of the 20th Century, 2000, Memories of Tomorrow, 2000, Journey to Infinity, 2000, The Best Poems of 2002. Bd. dirs., fundraiser Hospice Palm Beach (Fla.) County S., 1993—97; bd. dirs. La Coqueille Villas, Inc., Manalapan, Fla., 1994—98; bd. dirs., chair cmty. rels. Lincoln Child Ctr., Oakland, Calif., 1983—85; docent Calif. Hist. Soc., San Francisco, 1982—87. Recipient Editor's Choice award, Internat. Libr. Poetry, 1996, 1998, 2000, 2003. Mem.: Internat. Soc. Poets (disting. mem.), Phi Beta Kappa. Avocations: tennis, travel, duplicate bridge. Home: 1630 Lands End Rd Manalapan FL 33462-4762

PHIPPS, JUDITH A. social worker; b. Youngstown, Ohio, Oct. 19, 1945; d. Sidney and Dorothy Loretta (Zola) Greenberger; m. Bruce E. Phipps. BS, Boston U., 1967; MSS, Bryn Mawr Coll., 1978, M Law & Social Policy, 1984. Lic. Pa., 1990, LCSW Pa., 2001. Staff physical therapist St. Christopher's Hosp. Children, Phila., 1968—69, Magee Meml. Hosp.,

1969—72; dir. phys. therapy VNA Abington, 1972—76; staff social worker Doylestown Hosp., 1978—84, VNA No. Chester County, Phoenixville, 1984—89; hospice social worker Wissahickon Hospice, Phila., 1986—89, North Pa. VNA, Lansdale, 1989—90; sr. mgr. The Partnership Group, 1990—93; dir. of. rehab. Manor Care, Pottstown, 1993—99; team supr. Magellan Behavioral Health, King of Prussia, 2000—. Mem.: NASW, Pa. Hospice Network. Avocations: flying, skiing, water-skiing. Home: 1231 Archer Ln Lansdale PA 19446 Office: Magellan Behavioral Health 1100 1st Ave King Of Prussia PA 19406 Office Phone: 610-783-4223. E-mail: j.a.phipps@comcast.net.

PHIPPS, PATSY DUNCAN, retired auditor; b. New Bern, N.C., July 10, 1934; d. Lawrence C. and Pagie P. Duncan; m. Robert A. Phipps, Sept. 27, 1953 (div. Feb. 2, 1992); children: Kathryn Phipps Sublett, Patricia Phipps Bryant. Cert. in Acctg., U. N.C., Greensboro, 1953; postgrad., U. N.C., 1973; BAI in Auditing, U. Wis., 1986. Regional instr. First Citizens Bank, New Bern, 1976—78; br. mgr. First Citizens Bank & Trust Co., New Bern, 1974—76, supr. account svcs. and ops., 1963—74, v.p., regional audit supr., 1978—97; v.p, auditor So. Bank and Trust Co., Mt. Olive, NC, 1997—99. Cons. Millennia Cmty. Bank, Greenville, NC, 2000—04. Active Broad St. Christian Ch. Mem.: Nat. Assn. Bank Women (sec. Ea. N.C. group sec. 1975—76, chmn. 1978—80), Inst. Internal Auditors, New Bern Bus. and Profl. Women's Club (treas. 1973—74, 3d v.p. 1974—75, treas. 1981—82), N.C. Bus. and Profl. Women's Assn. (trustee 1976—82), Nat. Assn. of Bus. and Profl. Women's Club. Disciples Of Christ. Home: 1105 Peach Tree Ln New Bern NC 28562-8327 Office: Vespect Consulting Co 1105 Peach Tree Ln New Bern NC 28562-8327 Office Phone: 252-637-3408. Personal E-mail: patsinfo@newbernnc.com.

PIANO, PHYLLIS J. communications executive; b. Milw., Feb. 1956; BA, U. Wis., 1977. Pub. rels. staff GE Co., 1978—95; v.p. pub. affairs Cooper Industries, Inc., Houston, 1995—99; v.p., v.p. corp. affairs and comm. Raytheon Co., Lexington, Mass., 1999—. Office: Raytheon Co 141 Spring St Lexington MA 02421

PIAZZA, MARGUERITE, opera singer, actress, entertainer; b. New Orleans, May 6, 1926; d. Albert William and Michaela (Piazza) Luft; m. William J. Condon, July 15, 1953 (dec. Mar. 1968); children: Gregory, James (dec.), Shirley, William J., Marguerite P., Anna Becky; m. Francis Harrison Bergtholdt, Nov. 8, 1970. MusB, Loyola U., New Orleans; MusM, La. State U.; MusD (hon.), Christian Bros. Coll., 1973; LHD (hon.), Loyola U., Chgo., 1975. Singer N.Y.C. Ctr. Opera, 1948, Met. Opera Co., 1950; TV artist, regular singing star Your Show of Shows NBC, 1950-54; entertainer various supper clubs Cotillion Room, Hotel Pierre, N.Y.C., 1954, Las Vegas, Los Angeles, New Orleans, San Francisco, 1956—; ptnr. Sound Express Music Pub. Co., Memphis, 1987—. Bd. dirs. Cemrel, Inc. Appeared as guest performer on numerous mus. TV shows. Nat. crusade chmn. Am. Cancer Soc., 1971; founder, bd. dirs. Marguerite Piazza Gala for the Benefit of St. Jude's Hosp., 1976; bd. dirs. Memphis Opera Co., World Literacy Found., NCCJ; v.p., life bd. dirs. Memphis Symphony Orch.; nat. chmn. Soc. for Cure Epilepsy. Decorated Mil. and Hospittaler Order of St. Lazarus of Jerusalem; recipient svc. award Chgo. Heart Assn., 1956, svc. award Fedn. Jewish Philanthropies of N.Y., 1956, Sesquicentennial medal Carnegie Hall, St. Martin De Porres award So. Dominicans, 1994, Lifetime Achievement award Germantown Arts Alliance, 1998; named Queen of Memphis, Memphis Cotton Carnival, 1973, Person of Yr., La. Coun. for Performing Arts, 1975, Woman of Yr., Nat. Am. Legion, Woman of Yr., Italian-Am. Soc. Mem. Nat. Speakers Assn., Woman's Exchange, Memphis Country Club, Memphis Hunt and Polo Club, New Orleans Country Club, Summit Club, Beta Sigma Omicron, Phi Beta. Roman Catholic. Home: 2813 Central Ave Memphis TN 38111-1822

PIAZZA, ROSANNA JOY, paralegal; b. Lincoln, Nebr., Sept. 10, 1950; d. Augustine Joseph Piazza and Mary Lou Pease; m. Pennell Spencer, Sept. 20, 1972 (div. Dec. 1979); children: Madeleine, Adrian, Aurora, Angelica, Marissa, Raquel. BA in Psychology, BA in Sociology, U. Calif., Santa Barbara, 1987, postgrad., 1987-89. Legal asst. Legal Aid, Pacoima, Van Nuys, Calif., 1980-81, Tomas Castelo, Santa Barbara, 1982-84; counselor Battered Women's Network, Santa Barbara, Calif., 1984-89; pres. The Venus Found., Livingston, Mont., 1993; legal asst. Lyman H. Bennett III, Bozeman, 1996—. Poet Mont. Poets, Bozeman, 1989—. Author: (Liberté) (poetry) The Magical Mystical Miracle, 1977, Gods in Exile, Zonderzonde, 1999, The Littlest Buddha, 1999, The Littlest Page of Lancelot de Lac, 1999. Senate candidate dist. 14 Natural Law Party, Bozeman, 1998; mem. disaster emergency team ARC, Fiver Rivers chpt., 1999—; sec. mission for life Pro Life Orgn., 1998. Mem. AAUW (natual law party), Bus. Women's Assn., Mont. Assn. of Paralegals, Mont. Paralegal Assn., Nat. Assn. of Legal Secs., Mont. State Bar Assn. (paralegal sect.). Avocations: writer, poetry, songwriting, folk guitar and mandolin. Home: PO Box 141 Bozeman MT 59771-0141 Office: Lyman H Bennett III PO Box 1168 Bozeman MT 59771-1168

PICKARD, MYRNA RAE, dean; b. Sulphur Springs, Tex., Oct. 10, 1935; d. George Wallace and Ellie (Williams) Swindell; m. Bobby Ray Pickard, May 17, 1957; 1 child, Bobby Dale BS summa cum laude, Tex. Wesleyan Coll., 1957, MEd, 1964; MS, Tex. Women's U., 1974; EdD, Nova U., 1976. Instr. John Peter Smith Hosp., Fort Worth, 1956-58; pub. health nurse Forest County Health Dept., Hattiesburg, Miss., 1958-60; asst. nurse adminstrn. John Peter Smith Hosp. Sch. Nursing, Fort Worth, 1960-70, nurse adminstr., 1970-73; assoc. dean, dean U. Tex. System Sch. Nursing, Fort Worth, 1971-76; dean U. Tex. Sch. Nursing, Arlington, 1976-95; prof. nursing, 1976-98; dir. Rural Health Outreach U. Tex., Arlington, 1998—. Cons. in field; adv. com. Rural Health Rsch. Ctr., U. N.D., 1990. Mem. editorial bd. Jour. Rural Health, 1985-92, 94; contbr. articles to profl. jours., chpt. in book. Pres. Tex. League for Nursing, 1986-89; bd. mgrs. Tarrant County Hosp. Dist., 1995—; trustee Columbia Pla. Med. Bd., 1992—. Fellow Am. Acad. Nursing; mem. ANA, Nat. League Nursing, Nat. Rural Health Assn. (bd. dirs., treas. 1990-92), Sigma Theta Tau, sec. Ctr. Rural Health Initiatives, Austin TX, 1997—. Methodist. Avocations: jogging; gardening. Office: U Tex PO Box 19407 Arlington TX 76019-0001

PICKEL, DIANE DUNN, education educator; d. Donald A. and Janice Dietz Dunn; m. David E. Pickel, May 30, 1987; 1 child, Emily N. BS in mktg., Pa. State U., 1976—80, MBA, 1985—86. Adj. faculty Harrisburg Area C.C., Pa., 1993—2000; prof., bus. adminstrn. Ctrl. Pa. Coll., Summerdale, Pa., 1997—; pub. rels. coord. Huth/PSC Engineers, Lancaster, Pa., 1987—91; mktg. rep. Brinjac, Kambic & Associates, Harrisburg, Pa., 1991—94. Vol. Elizabethtown Boys Club Cheerleading Competition, Elizabethtown, Pa., 1997—2003; parent vol. Elizabethtown area sch., 1994—. Sam M. Walton Free Enterprise fellowship, Students In Free Enterprise (SIFE), 1999—2002. Mem.: Am. Mktg. Assn. Office: Ctrl Pen Col College Hill and Valley Rd Summerdale PA 17093 Office Phone: 800-759-2727. E-mail: dianepickel@centralpenn.edu.

PICKENS, FRANCES JENKINS, artist, educator; b. Dodd's, Tex., Feb. 26, 1927; d. John Morgan and Mary (Burton) Jenkins; m. Alexander Pickens, Aug. 20, 1955. BA, North Tex. U., 1947, MA, 1954; MEd, U. Hawaii, 1976. Tchr. art pub. schs., Dallas, 1948-55, Dearborn, Mich., 1955-58, White Plains, N.Y., 1958-59, Athens, Ga., 1960-62; gallery lectr. Honolulu Acad. Arts, 1962—63; tchr. art Punahou Sch., Honolulu, 1963-65, The Kamehameha Schs., Honolulu, 1965-85; jewelry and metal artist Honolulu, 1963—. Instr. jewelry U. Hawaii, Honolulu, 1967, 75, 77. Exhibited works in shows at Mus. of Contemporary Crafts, N.Y., Schmuckmuseum, Germany, Renwick Gallery, Washington, Wichita Nat., Women in Design Internat., Mich. Influence, 1981, Materials Hard and Soft, United States Metal, Hawaii Craftsmen Ann., Artists of Hawaii, 1965— (Disting. Artist 1991), East-West Ctr. Gallery, 2003, retrospective Honolulu Acad. Arts, 2001; represented in permanent collection at Acad. of Arts, The Contemporary Mus., Honolulu, Hawaii State Art Mus., Renwick Gallery, Washington, Wichita Art Assn., Kans.; photographs of work included in Goldsmith's Jour., Jewelry, Contemporary Design and Technique, Jewelry/Metalwork Survey, The Metalsmith's Book of Boxes and Lockets; contbr. articles to Arts and Activities mag., Sch. Arts, Ornament mag. Chmn. state crafts State Fair Tex., Dallas, 1954; Crafts Symposium planning com. Hawaii State Found. Culture and Arts, Honolulu, 1968-69; workshop for instrs. U.S. Army Arts and Crafts, Ft. Shafter, 1975. Named Distinguished Artist of Hawaii, Honolulu Acad. Arts, 1991. Mem. Soc. N.Am. Goldsmiths, Dallas Craft Guild, Hawai Craftsmen (charter, v.p., pres.), Renwick Alliance. Avocations: travel, jewelry, metalwork. Home: 1471 Kalaepohaku St Honolulu HI 96816-1804

PICKET, LYNN SNOWDEN, magazine editor, writer; b. Norfolk, Va., May 26, 1958; d. Robert and Valerie (Opshinsky) S. BFA, Va. Commonwealth U., 1979. Freelance photographer, Richmond, Va., 1978-79; model Prestige/Elite Modeling Agy., N.Y.C., 1980-84; staff writer Spy Mag., N.Y.C., 1986-87; contbg. editor N.Y. Woman Mag., N.Y.C., 1989-92, Harper's Bazaar Mag., N.Y.C., 1994—99; contbg. editor, editor-at-large Mademoiselle, N.Y.C., 1996—2001; contbg. writer Am. Thunder, 2003—. Online host Live Girl, America Online, 1996-98; guest panelist Politically Incorrect with Bill Mahr TV show, 1994—; on-air corr. Rock Candy on VH-1, 1999. Contbr. articles to Spin, Esquire, Vogue, Glamour, Working Woman, Cosmopolitan, George, Gear, Mirabella, Premiere, Outside, New York Times, Oprah Mag., Budget Living, Prevention, Elle, Vibe, GQ, Self, Rolling Stone, US; author: Nine Lives - From Stripper to Schoolteacher: My Yearlong Odyssey in the Workplace, 1994; Looking for a Fight, A Memoir, 2000.

PICKETT, BETTY HORENSTEIN, psychologist; b. Providence, R.I., Feb. 15, 1926; d. Isadore Samuel and Etta Lillian (Morrison) Horenstein; m. James McPherson Pickett, Mar. 10, 1952. AB magna cum laude, Brown U., 1945, ScM, 1947, PhD, 1949. Asst. prof. psychology U. Minn., Duluth, 1949-51; asst. prof. U. Nebr., 1951; lectr. U. Conn., 1952; profl. assoc. psychol. scis. Bio-Scis. Info. Exch., Smithsonian Instn., Washington, 1953-58; exec. sec. behavioral scis. study sect. exptl. psychology study sect. div, research grants NIH, Bethesda, Md., 1958-61; rsch. cons. to mental health unit HEW, Boston, 1962-63; exec. sec. rsch. career program NIMH, 1963-66, chief cognition and learning sect. div. extramural research program, 1966-68, dep. dir., 1968-74, dir. div. spl. mental health programs, 1974-75, acting dir. div. extramural rsch. program, 1975-77; assoc. dir. extramural and collaborative rsch. program Nat. Inst. Aging, 1977-79; dep. dir. Nat. Inst. Child Health and Human Devel., Bethesda, Md., 1979-81, acting dir., 1981-82, dir. Div. Rsch. Resources, 1982-88. Mem. health scientist adminstr. panel CSC Bd. Examiners, 1970-76, 81-88; mem. coun. on grad. edn. Brown U. Grad. Sch., 1989-91. Contbr. articles to profl. jours. Mem. APA, Am. Psychol Soc., Psychonomic Soc., Assn. Women in Sci., AAAS, Phi Beta Kappa, Sigma Xi. Home: Morgan Bay Rd PO Box 198 Surry ME 04684-0198

PICKETT, CYNTHIA LORELLE, psychologist, educator; b. Enid, Okla., Oct. 13, 1972; BA, Stanford U., 1994; PhD, Ohio State U., 1999. Asst. prof. psychology U. Ill., Champaign, 1999—2002, U. Chgo., 2002—. Mem.: APA, Am. Psychol. Soc. Office: U Chgo 5848 S Univ Ave Chicago IL 60637

PICKETT, SHERRY M. social worker; d. Theo H. and Mable K. McClendon; m. Henry C. Pickett, Mar. 26, 1966; children: Klatra M., Jason A. AS, Oakland C.C., Auburn Hills, Mich., 1992; MSW, U. Mich., 1994. Cert. social worker Mich. Bd. Examiners Social Workers. Social worker State Mich.-Dept. Social Svcs Family Ind. Agy. Children & Family Svcs., Taylor, 1972—97; mgr. Theo & Mable McClendon Found., 1997—. Editor: (newsletter) Bookwomen, 1998—. Pres., founder Theo & Mable McClendon Found., Southfield, Mich., 1994—. Mem.: Bookwomen Reading Club, Lions Club Internat., Detroit Westown Hartford Lions Club (bd. dirs. 2000—, Achievement award 2002, Pres. Appreciation award 2003). Avocations: travel, reading. Office: Theo & Mable McClendon Found PO Box 2623 Southfield MI 48037

PICKETT, TINA L. state representative; b. Kingston, Pa., May 28, 1943; 1 child, Lynne. Pres. Ctrl. Bradford C. of C., 1992—94; commr. Bradford County, 1996—; state rep. Pa., 2001—. Owner Pickett's Dairy, 1964—68, The Fireplace Restaurant, 1968—85, The Williamston Inn, 1977—. Mem. CCAP Tax Reform Com., 2000—; bd. mem. Endless Mts. Vacation Bur., 1975—; v.p. Ptnrs. in Family and Cmty. Devel., 1998—; pres. Wysox Mcpl. Sewer Authority, 1994—. Mem.: Young Men's Christian Assn., Towands Lions Club (pres.). Republican. Office: 155A E Wing Harrisburg PA 17120-2020 E-mail: tpickett@pahousegop.com.

PICKOVER, BETTY ABRAVANEL, retired executive legal secretary, civic volunteer; b. N.Y.C., Apr. 20, 1920; d. Albert and Sultana (Rousso) Abravanel; m. Bernard Builder, Apr. 6, 1941 (div. 1962); children: Ronald, Stuart; m. William Pickover, Aug. 23, 1970 (dec. Nov. 1983). Student, Taft Evening Ctr., 1961-70. Sec. U.S. Treasury Dept., Washington, 1942-43; exec. legal sec. various attys., Bronx, N.Y., 1956-70, Yonkers, N.Y., 1971-83, ret., 1983. Chair Uniongram Sisterhood of Temple Emanu-El, Yonkers, N.Y., 1975—, Honor Roll, 1975—, v.p. 1995-97, 98, 99, 2003; sr. citizen cmty. leader Yonkers Officer for Aging, 1984—, Westchester County Sr. Adv. Bd., White Plains, N.Y., 1989-96; v.p. Mayor's Cmty. Rels. Com. of Yonkers, 1985—, historian, photographer, 1988—; mem. Yonkers Flag Day Observance Com., 1998—; mem. adv. coun. Westchester County Office Aging Srs., 1993—; mem. bd. Legislators Task Force for Sr. Citizens Westchester County, 1995-97, 98, 99; Mayor Silver City Coun. Yonkers, 1989; mem. Mayor's Adv. Coun. on Sr. Citizens, 1990. Named to Sr. Citizen Hall of Fame, 1992; recipient Cert. of Appreciation, Westchester County, 1992, Pres. Coun. City of Yonkers, 1992, Merit cert., 1993, Cmty. Svc., City Mayor Yonkers, 1995, 96, 97, 98, 99, John E. Andrus Meml. Vol., 1995, Cert. of Appreciation, Westchester County Office of County Exec., 1993, 94, Cert. of Disting. Svc., 1997, Merit cert., N.Y. State Senator, 1994, N.Y. State Senator, 1995, 97, 98, 99, 2000, Cert. of Congratulations, N.Y. State Senator, 2001, Merit cert., Proclamation Mayor of Yonkers, 1985, 89, 92, 2 awards, U.S. Ho. of Reps., 1992, Woman of Excellence, Yonkers C. of C., 1993, awards, Mayor of Yonkers, 1985-97, 98, 99, 2000, Cert. of Appreciation, Mayor of City of Yonkers, 2001, awards, N.Y. State Senator and Assemblyman, 1987—97, City of Yonkers, 1993, Cert. of Merit, N.Y. State Assembly, 2001, Cert. of Appreciation, Westchester County Bd. Legislators, 1996, 99, City Coun. Pres., Yonkers, N.Y., 1999, Cert. of Recognition, 2000, Proclamation, Westchester County Bd. Legislators, 2003. Democrat. Jewish. Avocations: writing, photography, entertaining at all nursing homes in yonkers, history, public relations. Home: 200 Valentine Ln Yonkers NY 10705-3607

PICKUS, GLORIA B. retired secondary school educator; b. Bluefield, W.Va., Aug. 14, 1933; d. J.V. "Jack" and Tobie Slifkin Blank; children: Kimberly, A. Scott. AA, Stephens Coll., 1952; BS, Ohio State U., 1954; MS, Radford U., 1976. Tchr. McDowell County Schs., Northfork, W.Va., 1955—56, Mercer County Schs., Bluefield, W.Va., 1959—81, ret., 1956. Vol. Am. Cancer Soc., 1955—, Am. Heart Assn., 1955—; vol. bd. mem. Cancer Rsch. Network, Hollywood, Fla., 1998—; assoc. dir. Preliminary Miss Am. Pagent, Bluefield, 1955—63; bd. dirs. Ohio Valley Sch. Dist., 1966—69; v.p., pres. Sisterhood Temple, Bluefield, 1965—67, pres., 1967—69. Mem.: AAUW (vol. fundraiser 1954—, bd. mem.). Avocations: boating, bridge, waterskiing.

PICULIN, LAURETTE M. mediator; b. N.Y.C., Aug. 26, 1956; d. Carl Piculin and Josephine Hnatt. BA, Pa. State U., 1978. Fed. mediator Nat. Mediation Bd., Washington, 1981—. Mem.: ABA, Assn. for Conflict Resolution, Nat. Trust for Hist. Preservation.

PIECH, MARGARET ANN, mathematics educator; b. Bridgewater, N.S., Can., Apr. 6, 1942; d. Frederick Cecil and Margaret Florence (Laschinger) Garrett; m. Kenneth Robert Piech, June 19, 1965; children: Garrett Andrew, Marjorie Ann. BA, Mt. Allison U., Sackville, N.B., Can., 1962; PhD, Cornell U., 1967. Asst. prof. SUNY, Buffalo, 1967-72, assoc. prof., 1972-78, prof. math., 1978—. Cons. NSF, Washington, 1980-81, Aspen Analytics, Buffalo, 1986—; v.p. Seventy Niagara Svcs., 1990—. Contbr. articles to profl. jours. Woodrow Wilson fellow, 1962-63; grantee NSF, 1976-85, U.S. Army Rsch. Office, 1985-89. Mem. IEEE, Am. Math. Soc., Assn. Computing Machinery, Henry's Fork Found. Avocation: fly fishing. Office: U Buffalo Dept Math 244 Mathematics Bldg Buffalo NY 14260-0001

PIECH, MARY LOU ROHLING, medical psychotherapist, consultant; b. Elgin, Ill., Jan. 20, 1927; d. Louis Bernard and Charlotte (Wylie) Rohling; m. Raymond C. Piech, Feb. 12, 1950 (dec. Feb. 1985); 1 child, Christine Piech. BA, U. Ill., 1948, MA, 1953; postgrad., Ill. Inst. Tech., 1966-68, Union Inst., 1991-98. Cert. clin. psychologist, Ill.; diplomate Am. Bd. Med. Psychotherapy. Instr. psychology Elmhurst (Ill.) Coll., 1955-61; asst. prof. psychology North Cen. Coll., Naperville, Ill., 1961-67, Elmhurst (Ill.) Coll., 1968-81; med. psychotherapist Shealy Pain & Health Rehab. Ctr., La-Crosse, Wis., 1977-82, Shealy Inst. Comprehensive Health Care, Springfield, Mo., 1982—. Author, editor: (video series) Mental Health, 1982, (audio tape series) Holistic Mental Health, 1983. Recipient award Lilly Found., Elmhurst Coll., Shealy Inst., 1977. Fellow Am. Bd. Med. Psychotherapy; mem. APA, N.Am. Soc. Adlerian Psychology, Assn. Psychol. Type (life), Phi Beta Kappa, Phi Kappa Phi, Mortar Bd. Office: Shealy Institute Wellness Ctr 5607 S 222nd Rd Fair Grove MO 65648-8192

PIEKNIK, REBECCA ANNE, technologist, educator; b. Detroit, Sept. 30, 1960; AA in Allied Health, Baker Coll. Flint, 1998, BS in Health Svc. Adminstrn., postgrad., Baker Coll. Flint, 2002—. Cert. surg. technologist. Clin. instr. Baker Coll. Flint, 1999—; cert. surg. technologist Pontiac Osteopathic Hosp., Mich., 2001—02; program dir. surg. tech. Oakland C.C./William Beaumont Hosp., 2002—. Home: 5190 Timber Ridge Trl Clarkston MI 48346 Office Phone: 248-898-7685.

PIELOU, EVELYN C. biologist; b. Eng. m. Patrick Pielou, June 22, 1944; 3 children. B.Sc., U. London, 1950, PhD, 1962, DSc, 1975; LLD (hon.), Dalhousie U., 1993; DSc (hon.), U. B.C., 2001. Research scientist Can. Govt., 1963-67; vis. prof. N.C. State U., 1968, Yale, New Haven, 1969; prof. biology Queen's U., Kingston, Ont., 1969-71, Dalhousie U., Halifax, N.S., 1971-84; vis. prof. U. Sydney, Australia, 1975; oil sands environ. vis. research prof. U. Lethbridge, Alta., 1981-86. Author: Introduction to Mathematical Ecology, 1969, Population and Community Ecology, 1974, Ecological Diversity, 1975, Mathematical Ecology, 1977, Biogeography, 1979, Interpretation of Ecological Data, 1984, World of Northern Evergreens, 1988, After the Ice Age, 1991, Naturalist's Guide to the Arctic, 1994, Fresh Water, 1998, The Energy of Nature, 2001; contbr. articles to profl. jours. Recipient Lawson medal Can. Bot. Assn., 1984, Eminent Ecologist award Ecol. Soc. Am., 1986, Disting. Statis. Ecologist award Internat. Congress Ecology, Commemorative medal for 125th Anniversary of Confedn. of Can., 1992. Mem. Brit. Ecol. Soc. (hon. life), Am. Acad. Arts and Scis. (fgn. hon. mem.), Ecol. Soc. Am. (hon. life).

PIEPER, PATRICIA RITA, artist; b. Paterson, N.J., Jan. 28, 1923; d. Francis William and Barbara Margaret (Ludwig) Farabaugh; m. George F. Pieper, July 1, 1941 (dec. May 3, 1981); 1 child, Patricia Lynn ; m. Russell W. Watson, Dec. 9, 1989. Student, Baron von Palm, 1937-39, Deal (N.J.) Conservatory, 1939, 40, Utah State U., 1950-52; student Baron von Palm, 1937—39, student Deal (N.J.) Conservatory, 1939—40, student Utah State U., 1950—52. One-woman shows include Charles Russell Mus., Great Falls, Mont., 1955, Fisher Gallery, Washington, 1966, Tampa City Libr., 1977-81, 83, 84, Ctr. Pl. Art Ctr., Brandon, Fla., 1985; exhibited in group shows Davidson Art Gallery, Middletown, Conn., 1968, Helena (Mont.) Hist. Mus., 1955, Dept. Commerce Alaska Statehood Show, 1959, Joslyn Mus., Omaha, 1961, Denver Mus. Natural History, 1955, St. Joseph's Hosp. Gallery, 1980, 82, 84-86; represented in pvt. collections. Pres. Bell Lake Assn., 1976-78, 79; mem. Pasco County (Fla.) Water Adv. Coun., 1978—, chmn., 1979-82, 83-84, 86-88, 92—; gov.'s appointee to S.W. Fla. Water Mgmt. Dist., Hillsborough River Basin Bd., 1981-82, 84-87, sec., 1988-91, vice chmn., 1992; active Save Our Rivers program, 1982-84, 85-86, 92—; ad hoc chmn., 1991-92; mem. adv. bd. Fla. Suncoast Expwy., 1988-90; pres. Bell Lake Assn., 1986, 87; mem. adv. bd. Tampa YMCA, 1979-80. Winner photog. competition Gen. Tel. Co. of Fla., 1979; recipient Outstanding Svc. award Bell Lake Assn., 1987, Meml. award Land O'Lake Bd. of Realtors, 1989, Appreciation award Southwest Fla. Water Mgmt. Dist., 1993, finalist, Awds. of Excellence, Photographers winner in top 100 out of 8,000 Nat. Wildlife Fedn. competition, 1986, 1st place photography MacDill AFB, 1991. Mem. VFW (life), Nat. League Am. Pen Women (v.p. Tampa 1976-78, Woman of Yr. award 1977-78), Tampa Art Mus., Ret. Officer's Wives Assn., Land O'Lakes C. of C. (bd. dirs. 1981-82, Outstanding Svc. award 1980), Fla. Geneal. Soc., West State Archaeol. Soc. (distaff mem.), Ret. Officer's Assn., Lutz Club, Land O'Lakes Women's Club, Moose. Home: 3304 E Derry Dr Sebastian FL 32958-8577

PIERCE, CATHERINE MAYNARD, history educator; b. York County, Va., Oct. 11, 1918; d. Edward Walker Jr. and Cassie Cooke (Sheppard) Maynard; m. Frank Marion Pierce Jr., Oct. 4, 1940 (dec. 1974); children: Frank Marion III, Bruce Maynard. BS in Sec. Edn., Longwood Coll., Farmville, Va., 1939; postgrad., Coll. William and Mary, Williamsburg, 1948, 58, 68. Tchr. York County Pub. Schs., Va., 1939-45; instr. Chesapeake (Va.) pub. schs., 1946-49, 57-74; cons. Vol. Svcs., Williamsburg, Va., 1975—. Author audio-visual hist. narratives for use in pub. schs., 1965-86. Organizer The Chapel at Kingsmill on the James, Williamsburg, 1987—, chmn. governing bd., 1987-97. Mem. DAR (regent Williamsburg chpt. 1980-83). Baptist. Avocations: antiques, genealogy, historic research. Address: Kingsmill on the James 4 Bray Wood Rd Williamsburg VA 23185-5504

PIERCE, DEBORAH MARY, educational administrator; b. Charleston, W. Va. d. Edward Ernest and Elizabeth Anne (Trent) P.; m. Henry M. Armetta, Sept. 1, 1967 (div. 1981); children: Rosse Matthew Armetta, Stacey Elizabeth Pierce. Student, U. Tenn., 1956-59, Broward Jr. Coll., 1968-69; BA, San Francisco State U., 1977. Cert. elem. tchr., Calif. Pub. relations assoc. San Francisco Internat. Film Festival, 1965-66; account exec. Stover & Assocs., San Francisco, 1966-67; tchr. San Francisco Archdiocese Office of Cath. Schs., 1980-87; part-time tchr. The Calif. Study, Inc. (formerly Tchr's. Registry), Tiburon, Calif., 1988—; pvt. practice as paralegal San Francisco, 1989—; tchr. Jefferson Sch. Dist., Daly City, Calif., 1989-91. Author: (with Frances Spatz Leighton) I Prayed Myself Slim, 1960. Pres. Mothers Alone Working, San Francisco, 1966, PTA, San Francisco, 1979, Parent Tchr. Student Assn., San Francisco, 1984; apptd. Calif. State Bd. Welfare Cmty. Rels. Com., 1964-66; block organizer SAFE, 1996; active feminist movement. Named Model of the Yr. Modeling Assn. Am., 1962. Mem. People Med. Soc., Assn. for Rsch. and Enlightenment, A Course in Miracles, Commonwealth Club Calif, Angel Club San Francisco, San Diego Chat Club, Deepak Chopra 7 Spiritual Laws Group. Mem. Unity Christ Ch. Avocation: chess. Address: 3346 Taravel St San Francisco CA 94116 E-mail: deborahmpierce@hotmail.com.

PIERCE, DIANE JEAN, artist; b. Evanston, Ill., Apr. 9, 1952; d. Kenneth William and Marjorie J. (Hansen) P.; m. William Carry Reuling, Sept. 8, 1991 (div. July 1992). BFA in Drawing and Painting, U. Utah, 1976. Illustrator Ensign Mag., Salt Lake City, 1977-79, Scott Foresman & Co. Pubs., Glenview, Ill., 1980, Children's Press, Chgo., 1981-82; mansion artist Adnan-Khoshagi's Devereaux Mansion, Salt Lake City, 1984-87; illustrator Friend Mag./Era Mag., Salt Lake City, 1978-88; artist painter Lido Gallery, Park City, Utah, 1990-93, Thomas Charles Gallery, Las Vegas, Nev., 1994, Art Dimensions Gallery, Hollywood, Calif., 1994-96, Meyer Gallery, Park City, Utah, 1996-98; with Don Huntsman Gallery, Aspen, Colo., 1999—2001; artist Winter Olympics, Park City, Utah, 2002. Apprentice photographer Reynel Salgado Mirando, 1980 Elections, Acapulco, Mexico, 1980; juror exhbn. com. Alliance Gallery, Salt Lake Art Ctr., 1984, 85, invitational artist, fundraiser for Town and Country magazine: Women in Need, N.Y., 1998. Exhibited in group shows at New Genre, 1985, 5 Star Auction Invitational, 1985, Springville Nat. Salon, 1985, Utah Women Artists, 1985, Chase Mansion Guthrie Artists Show, 1986, Guthrie Artists, 1986, NAD, 1986, Eccles Art Ctr., 1986, 1987, Women's Show, 1987, 1989, 1991, 1993, Park City Open Painting Competition, 1989—90, 1993, Mus. Art, Alliance Gallery, Chase Mansion, Salt Lake Art Ctr., Tivoli Gallery, Cliff Lodge Gallery, U. Utah Mus. Art, Devereaux Mansion, 1984—87, Utah divsn. Assn. Women Artists traveling show, 1989—90, 100 Yrs.-100 Women traveling show, N.Y.C., 1989—91, Springville Mus. Art, 1992, Nat. Assn. Women ann. nat. competition, 1993, Janet Dumbar Interiors, Sun Valley, Idaho, 1991—93, Lido Gallery, 1990—93, Elouises' Interiors, Park City, Utah, 1993—98, Thomas Charles Gallery, 1994, Art Dimensions Gallery, 1994—96, Springville Mus. Art nat. competition, Art Space, 1995, Gallery Stroll, 1995, Nat. Assn. Women Artists ann., Soho, N.Y., 1995, Nat. Assn. Women Artists, Athens, Greece, 1996, NAWA NY Soho Show, 1999, Springville Mus. Natl. 75th April Salon, 1999—2000, Soho Nat. Assn. Women Artists, 1999, Represented in permanent collections Girl Scouts Hdqs., Salt Lake City, Profl. Figure Skaters Hdqs., Sun Valley, Springville Mus. Art, Moonie & O'Conner, Cin., Van Cott, Bagley, Cornwall & McCarthy, Salt Lake City, also pvt. collections; contbr. color plates Painting and Sculptors by Serdirect, Olphin, 1985, color plates in Visual Selling and Design by Mary Irish, 1990, articles to profl. jours. Recipient Art Dirs. award, Era Mag., 1979, Dirs. award, U. Utah Statewide Competition, Springville Mus. Fine Art, 1987, Best of Show, Eccles Statewide Competition, Ogden Utah, 1987, Best Traditional Painting, Nat. Assn. U. Women, Utah divsn., Ogden, 1989, Best of Show, Open Painting Exhbn., Kimball Art Ctr., Park City, Utah, 1989, 3rd pl. open painting competition, Kimball Art Ctr, 1990, Visual Merchandising & Design Mag. award, Designer Excellence, 1990, Best of Show open painting exhbn, Kimball Art Ctr., Park City, 1993, award of merit, Springville Mus. Fine Art, 1995; grantee, Artists Fellowship, Inc., N.Y.C., 1993. Mem. Nat. Assn. Women Artists (N.Y. chpt., Susan Kahn award 1987), Nat. Mus. Women in Arts.

PIERCE, DIANNE S. city clerk; b. Hertford, N.C., Nov. 4, 1945; d. Delmar and Mae Curlings Spear; m. William Edward Pierce, June 27, 1964; children: William Mark, Charles David. AAS, Coll. of the Albemarle, 1976. Office mgr. Hertford Frame, Inc., 1973-75; adminstrv. asst. Albemarle Law & Order, Elizabeth City, N.C., 1975-80; adminstrv. sec. City of Elizabeth City, 1980-86, city clk., 1986—; owner, operator Black Gold Express, Inc., Elizabeth City, 1993—. Founding mem. Elizabeth City Teen Svcs. Ctr., 1994-99, dir., 1996-99; active N.C. Transp. Pub. Safety, Raleigh, 1995-97, Mayor's Adv. Bd., Elizabeth City, 1995-97. Mem. Internat. Inst. Mcpl. Clks. (cert. mcpl. clk. 1989, advance acad. edn. 1996, first sustaining edn. 1999, master mcpl. clk., 2003), N.C. Assn. Mcpl. Clks. (dir. 1996-99). Democrat. Baptist. Avocations: reading, traveling, tennis, dance. Home: 125 Nancy Dr Elizabeth City NC 27909-9247 Office: City of Elizabeth City 306 E Colonial Ave Elizabeth City NC 27909-4306 also: PO Box 347 Elizabeth City NC 27907-0347

PIERCE, HILDA (HILDA HERTA HARMEL), painter; b. Vienna; arrived in U.S., 1940; m. Herman J. Slutzky; 1 child, Diana Rubin Daly (dec.). Student, Art Inst. Chgo.; studied with Oskar Kokoschka, Salzburg, Austria. Art tchr. Highland Park (Ill.) Art Ctr., Sandburg Village Art Workshop, Chgo., Old Town Art Ctr., Chgo.; owner, operator Hilda Pierce Art Gallery, Laguna Beach, Calif., 1981-85. Guest lectr. maj. art mus. and art tours, Carribean cruises, France, Switzerland, Austria, Italy, Mex., San Diego, China, India, 1998—2002, Russian river cruise and major art mus., St. Petersburg, Moscow, 1994; lectr., Mexico, 2002—04, U. Calif. Geisel Libr., San Diego, 2003; founder, chmn. Art Encounters, San Diego. One-woman shows include Fairweather Hardin Gallery, Chgo., Sherman Art Gallery, Marshall Field Gallery, exhibited in group shows at Old Orchard Art Festival, Skokie, Ill., Union League Club, North Shore Art League, ARS Gallery, Art Inst. Chgo., Represented in permanent collections U. Calif. San Diego Art Libr., La Jolla, numerous pvt. and corp. collections, 1200 large monoprints, oils, 17 murals for Carnival Cruise Lines megaliner M.S. Fantasy, 17 murals consisting of 49 paintings for megaliner M.S. Imagination, U. Calif. San Diego Geisel Libr.; featured (video) Survivors of the Shoa, Stephen Spielberg Found., 1996; contbr. articles to profl. jours. and newspapers. Founder, chair Art Encounters, San Diego. Recipient Outstanding Achievement award, Chgo. Immigrants Svc. League. Office Phone: 858-558-7556.

PIERCE, LISA MARGARET, telecommunications executive, product and market development manager, lecturer; b. Nyack, NY, June 2, 1957; d. William and Elizabeth Pierce. BA with honors, Gordon Coll., Wenham, Mass., 1978; MBA, Atkinson Sch., Salem, Oreg., 1982. Campaign mgr. Carter/Mondale, Manchester, Mass., 1976; investigator Dept. Social Svcs., Nyack, 1977-78; paralegal Beverly, Mass., 1978-79; campaign mgr. Reagan Presdl. Primary, Rockland County, N.Y., 1980; cons. Sidereal, Portland, Oreg., 1981-82; performance analyst Dept. Social Svcs., Pomona, N.Y., 1982; market analyst Momentum Techs., Parsippany, N.J., 1983; cons. Booz Allen & Hamilton, Florham Park, N.J., 1984, Deloitte-Touche, Morristown, N.J., 1985; market researcher, forecaster AT&T, Bedminster, N.J., 1985-87, asst. pvt. line product mgr., 1987-89, Integrated Svcs. Digital Network product mgr., 1989-93; dir. Telecom. Rsch. Assocs., St. Marys, Kans., 1994-98; v.p., rsch. fellow Giga Info. Group/Forrester Rsch., Cambridge, Mass., 1998—. Panelist, contbr. TeleComms. Assn., San Diego, Internat. Comm. Assn., Atlanta, Ea. Comm. Forum, NY, Nat. Engring. Consortium, Chgo., Super Comm., Soc. Telecom. Consultants, MPLS Forum, Mid Atlantic Venture Assn., GSA Fed. Telecom. Svc. Forums, others; contbr. NY State ISDN/Internat User's Group; feature commentator Nat. Pub. Radio (All Things Considered), Pub. Broadcasting Svc. (Nightly Bus. Report), MSNBC, CNN and CNBC, Radio Wall Street, CBS Evening News. Columnist Network World, 2001—02, Bus. Comm. Rev., 2002—. Named one of Top 10 Most Influential IT Analysts, Tech. Mktg. Mag., 2002, 2003; grantee in field. Mem.: IEEE. Business E-Mail: lpierce@forrester.com.

PIERCE, MARIAN MARIE, writer, educator; b. Cleve., Mar. 7, 1959; d. William Moses and Thelma Lee Pierce. BA, U. Iowa, 1981, MFA, 1996. Creative writing instr. Marylhurst (Oreg.) U., 1999—, UCLA Ext. Writer's Program, 2000—. Author short stories. Named Frederick Exley Fiction Competition Winner, GQ mag., 1995; fellow Paul Engle fellow, The Iowa Writers' Workshop, 1996—97, MacDowell Colony fellow, The MacDowell Colony, 1997. Personal E-mail: marian.pierce@juno.com.

PIERCE, MARY E. retired educator, public relations consultant; b. Chgo. d. Henry Harris and Eva Irene (Hanes) P. BE, Chgo. Tchrs. Coll., 1944. One room sch. tchr. Will County, Monee, Ill.; tchr. 5th grade Peotone (Ill.) Sch. Dist.; tchr. elem. and jr. h.s. Steger (Ill.) Sch. Dist., chair lang. arts dept.; ret., 1979; chair sch. improvement plan; pub. rels. cons. Former pres. Steger Edn. Assn.; chmn. bd. dirs. #194 Employee Credit Union, Steger, 1972-95. Village clk. Village of Richton Park, 1992—; pres. Friends of Libr., Richton Park, 1980—, v.p.; bd. dirs. So. Suburban Cancer Soc., Tinley Pk., Ill., 1994—, S.E. Chpt. Ill. Credit Union, Calumet City, Ill., 1994-95. Recipient Cmty. Svc. award Cook County Sheriff's Office, Chgo. Mem. Delta Kappa Gamma (treas. 1979-2003). Avocation: golf. Home: 22147 Karlov Ave Richton Park IL 60471-1721

PIERCE, NAOMI ELLEN, biology educator, researcher; b. Denver, Oct. 19, 1954; d. Arthur Preble and Ruiko (Ishizaka) P; m. Andrew James Berry, Mar. 9, 1996; children: Kate Clark Berry, Megan Elizabeth Berry. BS, Yale U., 1976; PhD, Harvard U., k1983. Fulbright postdoctoral fellow Griffith U., Brisbane, Australia, 1983-84; rsch. lectr. Christ Ch., U. Oxford, Eng., 1984-86; asst. prof. Princeton U., N.J., 1986-91; Sydney A. and John H. Hessel prof. biology, curator lepidoptera Harvard U. and Harvard Mus. Comparative Zoology, Cambridge, Mass., 1991—. Contbr. articles to profl. jours. MacArthur Found. fellow, Chgo., 1988-93. Fellow Harvard Soc. of Fellows (sr.). Office: Harvard U 26 Oxford St Cambridge MA 02138-2902

PIERCE, PATRICIA ANN, university administrator; b. Harriman, Tenn., Feb. 13, 1949; d. Fred Ernest and Lela Nora (Jones) P.; m. Jacky Albert Goss, Sept. 21, 1991; children: Wesley Matthew Goss, James Michael Goss. BS, U. Tenn., 1973; cert., Bryn Mawr Coll., 1991. Cert. secondary edn. tchr., Tenn.; cert. diversity trainer. Field rep. Tenn. Human Rights Commn., Nashville, 1973-76, compliance dir., 1976-78; assoc. dir.Opportunity Devel. Ctr. Vanderbilt U., Nashville, 1978-81, dir., 1981—. Cons. Pierce Consulting, Nashville, 1985—; presenter in field. Contbr. articles to profl. jours. Chairperson Mayor's Adv. Com. for People with Disabilities, Nashville, 1988-89; pres. bd. dirs. League for Hearing Impaired, Nashville, 1994-95, Nashville YWCA, 1996-98; spkr. Nat. Intramural Recreation Sports Assn., Nashville, 1994; del. People to People Internat. Learning Disability Del., Beijing, 1995; nongovtl. rep. NGO Forum, 4th World Conf. on Women, Beijing, 1995; People to People Internat. del. to Cuba, 2003; active Gov. Adv. Com. on Equal Employment Opportunity, 1996-98; mem. Leadership Nashville, 2003. Recipient Jean Harris award Rotary 1998, Mary Jane Werthern award Vanderbilt 1997, Nashville ATHENA award, 2003; named to Leadership America 2000; inducted in Acad. of Women of Achievement, 2002. Mem.: Women in Higher Edn. in Tenn. (historian 1999—, pres.), CABLE Profl. Womens Networking Orgn. (pres. 1991—92, historian 2000—, Promote Women award 1993), Am. Coun. Edn. (state facilitator 1994—95, bd. mem. 1994—, mem. Tenn. planning com., Outstandging Contbns. cert. 1995), Internat. Assn. Higher Edn. and Disability (pres. 1988—89, Ronald Blosser Dedicated Svc. award 1989), Women's Polit. Caucus (v.p. 2001—02), Fundraising for Women Polit. Candidates (bd. mem. 2000—, pres. 2003). Avocations: hiking, tennis, photography. Home: 954 Caney Creek Rd Harriman TN 37748 Office: Vanderbilt U VU Station B 351809 Nashville TN 37235-1809 E-mail: patricia.a.pierce@vanderbilt.edu.

PIERCE, PONCHITTA ANN, TV host, producer, journalist, writer, consultant; b. Chgo., Aug. 5, 1942; d. Alfred Leonard and Nora (Vincent) P. Student, Cambridge (Eng.) U., summer 1962; BA in Journalism cum laude, U. So. Calif., 1964; DHL, Franklin Pierce Coll., 1986. Asst. editor Ebony mag., 1964-65, assoc. editor, 1965-67; editor Ebony mag. (N.Y.C. office), 1967-68; chief N.Y.C. editl. bur. Johnson Pub. Co., 1967-68; corr. news divsn. CBS, N.Y.C., 1968-71; contbg. editor McCall's mag., 1971-77; editl. cons. Philps Stokes Fund, 1971-78; staff writer Reader's Digest, 1976-77, roving editor, 1977-80; co-prodr., host Today in New York, Sta. WNBC-TV, N.Y.C., 1982-87; freelance writer, TV broadcaster, media cons. Co-host Sunday WNBC-TV, 1973—77, The Prime of Your Life, 1977—80; author: Status of American Women Journalists on Magazines, 1968, History of the Phelps Stokes Fund 1911-1972; contbg. editor: Parade mag., 1993, Earth Times Monthly, 2002. Del. to WHO Conf., Geneva, 1973; bd. dirs. Morris-Jumel Mansion, Hirshhorn Mus. and Sculpture Garden, Xavier U. of La., Housing Enterprise for the Less Privileged, Third St. Music Sch. Settlement, Inner-City Scholarship Fund, Josephson Inst. Ethics, Marina del Rey, Sta. WNET-TV; mem. women's bd. Madison Sq. Boys and Girls Club; mem. Columbia Presbyn. Health Scis. Adv. Coun. Recipient Penney-Mo. mag. award excellence women's journalism, 1967; John Russwurm award N.Y.C. Urban League, 1968; AMITA Nat. Achievement award in communications, 1974 Mem. NATAS, Women in Comm. (Woman Behind the News award 1969, Nat. Headliner award 1970), Fgn. Policy Assn. (mem. bd. govs., bd. dirs.), Coun. on Fgn. Rels., Calif. Scholarship Fedn. (life), Econs. Club N.Y., Lotos Club, Nat. Honor Soc., Mortar Bd.

PIERCE, SARAH FAITH, counseling administrator, secondary school educator, elementary school educator; b. Oak Ridge, Tenn., Aug. 26, 1955; BS in Elem. Edn., TTU, 1978, MA in Seed Biology, 1986, ED.S. in Adminstrn & Supr., 1988. Lic. profl. adminstr. Tenn. Dept. Edn., cert. elem. edn. biology, gen. sci., anatomy and physiology, elem. secondary principalship, guidance counselor. With Putnam County Bd. Edn., Cookeville, Tenn., 1978—91, biology tchr., 1991—98, tchr. biology and math, 1998—. Grant writer, guidance adminstr. Adv. bd. mem. Project DARE, Tenn., 1988—93; mem. intake sector Putnam County Readiness/Emergecy Response Team, Cookeville, 2002—. Mem.: Tenn Counselor's Assn., Upper Cumberland Counselor's Assn., Nat. Edn. Assn., Tenn. Edn. Assn. Avocations: gardening, interior decorating, crafts. Office: PCAHS 1060 E Spring St Cookeville TN 38501

PIERCE, SHAHEEDA LAURA, midwife, consultant; b. Jersey City, Apr. 13, 1959; d. Lawrence Everett Pierce and Mary Dean Applegate Swing; m. James Shuffield, May 28, 1994; children: Juniper, Rama, Jasmine, Elijah, Jamila, Tara. AAS, Pima Coll., 1984. Cert. paralegal, cmty. meditation svcs., dance leader Dances Universal Peace; cert. profl. midwife. Pvt. practice mediation and paralegal svcs., Tucson, 1991-95, 96-98, Maui, Hawaii, 1995-96, Silver City, N.Mex., 1998-99, Vashon Island, Wash., 1999—. Nat. coord. group Movement For A New Soc., Phila., 1982-83; bd. dirs. Food Conspiracy Cooperative, Tucson, 1993-95; steering com. S.W. Sufi Cmty., Silver City, 1994-95, bd. dirs., 1995-97; mem. faculty adv. bd. Nat. Coll. Midwifery, 2002—; midwife, holistic health cons. Author: Recipes for the New Children, 1978; contbr. articles to profl. jours.; creator (bd. game) The Healing Game of Life, 1993; composer (musical album on cassette) Full Moon Woman, 1994; co-coord., disc jockey weekly women's radio program KXCI Cmty. Radio, Tucson, 1983. Active Georgians Against Nuc. Energy, Atlanta, 1980-81; organizer Nuc. Free State, Tucson, 1981-82; draft counselor Daring Disarmers, Phila., 1982; vice-chair heavy metals remediation com. Vashon Maury Island Cmty. Coun., 2003. Recipient Ordinary Extraordinary Women's award, 1982. Mem. N.Mex. Midwives Assn., Ariz. Assn. Midwives (co-coord. AHCCCS reimbursement task force 1997-98), Midwives' Alliance Hawaii, Washington Alliance Rural Midwives. Avocations: art, music, dance, nature.

PIERCE, SUE, sales executive; b. Shawano, Wis., Oct. 6, 1953; d. Virginia Anne and William Harry Pierce. Student, U. Wis., Superior, 1976—92; grad., Sgt. Maj. Acad., Ft. Bliss, Tex., 1990. Staff sgt. U.S. Army, Ft. McClellan, Ala., 1971—78; sgt. 1st class Ohio Army N.G., Toledo, 1979—83; sales rep. Steam Economies Co., Toledo, 1983—86, Douglas Steam Splty., Menasha, Wis., 1986—90; sales engr. Hercules, Inc., Appleton, Wis., 1990—92; regional sales mgr. The Johnson Corp., Three Rivers, Mich., 1993—. Budget com. chair U.S. Army Women's Mus. Found., Ft. Lee, Va., 2002—03. Command sgt. maj. USAR, 1971—98. Decorated Legion Of Merit U.S. Army. Mem.: Tech. Assn. of Pulp and Paper Industry (sec. 2002—03). Avocations: travel, water sports, golf. Home: 713 W 1st St Shawano WI 54166 Office: The Johnson Corp 805 Wood St Three Rivers MI 49094 Office Phone: 312-961-8169. Personal E-mail: spierce@joco.com.

PIERCE, SUSAN RESNECK, academic administrator, literature educator; b. Janesville, Wis., Feb. 6, 1943; d. Elliott Jack and Dory (Block) Resneck; m. Kenneth H. Pierce; 1 child, Alexandra Siegel. AB, Wellesley Coll., 1965; MA, U. Chgo., 1966, PhD, U. Wis., 1972. Lectr. U. Wis., Rock County, 1970-71; from asst. prof. to prof. English Ithaca (N.Y.) Coll., 1973-82, chmn. dept., 1976-79; program officer Nat. Endowment for Humanities, 1982-83, asst. dir., 1983-84; dean Henry Kendall Coll. Arts and Scis. U. Tulsa, 1984-90; v.p. acad. affairs, prof. English Lewis and Clark Coll., Portland, Oreg., 1990-92; pres. U. Puget Sound, Tacoma, 1992—2003. Vis. assoc. prof. Princeton (N.J.) U., 1979; bd. dirs. Janet Elson Scholarship Fund, 1984-1990, Tulsa Edn. Fund, Phillips Petroleum Scholarship Fund, 1985-90, Okla. Math. & Sci. High Sch., 1984-90, Hillcrest Med. Ctr., 1988-90, Portland Opera, 1990-92, St. Joseph's Hosp., 1992—, Seattle Symphony, 1993—; cons. U. Oreg., 1985, Drury Coll., Springfield, Mo., 1986; mem. Middle States and N. Cen. Accreditation Bds.; mem. adv. com. Fed. Women's Program, NEH, 1982-83; participant Summit Meeting on Higher Edn., Dept. Edn., Washington, 1985; speaker, participant numerous ednl. meetings, sems., commencements; chair Frederick Ness Book Award Com. Assn. Am. Colls., 1986; mem. award selection com. Dana Found., 1986, 87; mem. Acad. Affairs Council, Univ. Senate, dir. tchr. edn., chmn. adv. group for tchr. preparation, ex-officio mem. all Coll. Arts and Scis. coms. and Faculty Council on Internat. Studies, all U. Tulsa; bd. dirs. Am. Conf. Acad. Deans; bd. trustees Hillcrest Med. Ctr.; participant Aspen Inst. Md. 1999, Annapolis Group Media Roundtable, 1996, Harvard Seminar, 1992; former bd. dirs. Assn. Am. Colls. and Univs., 1989-92, Am. Conf. of Academic Deans, 1988-91, Am. Assn. Colls., 1989-92. Author: The Moral of the Story, 1982, also numerous essays, jour. articles, book sects., book revs.; co-editor: Approaches to Teaching "Invisible Man"; reader profl. jours. Bd. dirs. Arts and Humanities Coun., Tulsa, 1984-90; trustee Hillcrest Hosp., Tulsa, 1986-90; mem. cultural series com., community rels. com. Jewish Fedn., Tulsa, 1986-90; bd. dirs. Tulsa chpt. NCCJ, 1986-90, Kemper Mus. 1996—, Seattle Symphony, 1993-96, St. Joseph Hosp., 1992-93, Portland Opera, 1990-92. Recipient Best Essay award Arix. Quar., 1979, Excellence in Teaching award N.Y. State Edn. Council, 1982, Superior Group Service award NEH, 1984, other teaching awards; Dana scholar, Ithaca Coll., 1980-81; Dana Research fellow, Ithaca Coll., 82-83; grantee Inst. for Ednl. Affairs, 1980, Ford Found., 1987, NEH, 1989. Mem. MLA (adv. com. on job market 1973-74), South Ctrl. MLA, NIH (subcom. on college drinking), Assn. Governing Bds. (coun. of pres.), Nat. Inst. on Alcohol Abuse (presl. advisory group), Soc. for Values in Higher Edn., Assn. Am. Colls. (bd. dirs.), Am. Conf. Acad. Deans (bd. dirs. 1988-91), Coun. of Presidents, Assn. Governing Bds., Phi Beta Kappa, Phi Kappa Phi, Phi Gamma Kappa.

PIERCE, THRESIA KORTE (TISH PIERCE), primary school educator; b. Maize, Kans. d. Herman and Marie Adeline (Lubbers) Korte; children: Judith, John, Mark. BS, Friends U., 1955; MS, U. Nev., Las Vegas, 1978. Cert. tchr., Nev., Nev. Life Ins. lic. Office worker Internat. Trust Co., Denver, Colo., 1951, Motor Equipment Co., Wichita, Kans., 1952-53; tchr. Wichita Pub. Schs., 1960-69, Clark County Sch. Dist., Las Vegas, Nev., 1970-2000. Author numerous short stories; contbr. acticles to profl. jours. Senator Clark County Edn. Assn., Clark County Classroom Tchrs. Mem. NEA, Epsilon Sigma Delta (v.p. 1962). bd. dirs. Kansas Newman U., Wichita, 1966-68. Home: 3105 Cardinal Dr Las Vegas NV 89121-2204

PIERCE, V. RENEE, music educator; d. Oscar Rudolph and Wylodine Glass; m. D. Thomas Pierce, Aug. 18, 1973; children: Adam, Dustin, Alison. MusB in Edn., U. Montevallo, 1975. Cert. tchr. Tex., Ala. Pvt. piano instr., Oneonta, Ala., 1991—95; elem. music tchr. Pky. Christian Acad., Birmingham, Ala., 1995—98; music assoc. First Bapt. Ch., Boaz, Ala., 1998—2002; choral dir. Boaz H.S., Boaz, Ala., 2000—. Dir. Young Musician Choir, Boaz, 1998—; pianist First Bapt. Ch., Boaz. Vol. Oneonta City Sch., 1983—98. Mem.: Music Educators Nat. Conf., Ala. Singing Women. Baptist. Avocations: travel, home projects, gardening. Office: Boaz HS 907 Brown St Boaz AL 35957 Personal E-mail: tpierce809@aol.com.

PIERCY, MARGE, poet, writer; b. Detroit, Mar. 31, 1936; d. Robert Douglas and Bert Bernice (Bunnin) P.; m. Ira Wood, 1982. AB, U. Mich., 1957; MA, Northwestern U., 1958; DHL (hon.), Hebrew Union Coll., 2004, Union Coll., 2004. Instr. Gary extension Ind. U., 1960-62; poet-in-residence U. Kans., 1971; disting. vis. lectr. Thomas Jefferson Coll., Grand Valley State Colls., fall 1975, 76, 78, 80; vis. faculty Women's Writers Conf., Cazenovia (N.Y.) Coll.; Elliston poetry fellow U. Cin., 1986. DeRoy Disting. vis. prof. U. Mich., 1992. Author: Breaking Camp, 1968, Hard Loving, 1969, Going Down Fast, 1969, Dance the Eagle to Sleep, 1970, Small Changes, 1973, To Be of Use, 1973, Living in the Open, 1976, Woman on the Edge of Time, 1976, The High Cost of Living, 1978, Vida, 1980, The Moon is Always Female, 1980, Braided Lives, 1982, Circles on the Water, 1982, Stone, Paper, Knife, 1983, My Mother's Body, 1985, Gone to Soldiers, 1988, Available Light, 1988 (May Sarton award 1991), Summer People, 1989, He, She and It, 1991, Body of Glass, 1991 (Arthur C. Clarke award 1993), Mars and Her Children, 1992, The Longings of Women, 1994, Eight Chambers of the Heart, 1995, City of Darkness, City of Light, 1996, What Are Big Girls Made Of?, 1997 (Notable Book award ALA 1997), Storm Tide, 1998, The Art of Blessing the Day, 1999, Early Grrrl, 1999, Three Women, 1999, (with Ira Wood) So You Want to Write: How to Master the Craft of Writing Fiction and the Personal Narrative, 2001, Sleeping With Cats, A Memoir, 2002, Colors Passing Through Us, 2003, Third Child, 2003; (CD) Louder: We Can't Here You Yet, 2004; editor Leapfrog Press, 1997—; poetry editor Lillith, 1999—; fiction editor Seattle Rev., 2003—; author of poetry. Cons. N.Y. State Coun. on Arts, 1971, Mass. Found. for Humanities and Coun. on Arts, 1974; mem. Writer Bd., 1985-86; bd. dirs. Transition House, Mass. Found. Humanities and Pub. Policy, 1978-85, Am. ha-Yam, 1988-98, v.p., 1995-96; gov.'s appointee to Mass. Cultural Coun., 1990-91, Mass. Coun. on Arts and Humanities, 1986-89; artistic adv. bd. ALEPH Alliance for Jewish Renewal, Am. Poetry Ctr., 1988—; lit. adv. panel poetry NEA, 1989. Recipient Borenstone Mountain Poetry award, 1968, 74, Lit. award Gov. Mass. Commn. on Status of Women, 1974, Nat. Endowment of Arts award, 1978, Carolyn Kizer Poetry prize, 1986, 90, Shaeffer-Eaton-PEN New Eng. award, 1989, Golden Rose Poetry prize, 1990, Brit ha-Dorot award The Shalom Ctr., 1992, Notable Book award, 1997, Paterson poetry prize, 2000. Mem.: NOW, PEN, Am. Poetry Soc., Writers Union, Authors League, Authors Guild, Citizens for the Preservation of Wellfleet, Mass. Audubon Soc., New Eng. Poetry Club. Address: PO Box 1473 Wellfleet MA 02667-1473

PIERIK, MARILYN ANNE, retired librarian, piano teacher; b. Bellingham, Wash., Nov. 12, 1939; d. Estell Leslie and Anna Margarethe (Onigkeit) Bowers; m. Robert Vincent Pierik, July 25, 1964; children: David Vincent, Donald Lesley. AA, Chaffey Jr. Coll., Ontario, Calif., 1959; BA, Upland (Calif.) Coll., 1962; cert. in teaching, Claremont (Calif.) Coll., 1963; MSLS, U. So. Calif., L.A., 1973. Tchr. elem. Christ Episcopal Day Sch., Ontario, 1959-60; tchr. Bonita High Sch., La Verne, Calif., 1962-63; tchr., libr. Kettle Valley Sch. Dist. 14, Greenwood, Can., 1963-64; libr. asst. Monrovia (Calif.) Pub. Libr., 1964-67; with Mt. Hood C.C., Gresham, Oreg., 1972-98, reference libr., 1983-98, chair faculty scholarship com., 1987-98, campus archivist, 1994-98; ret., 1998; pvt. piano tchr., 1998—. Pvt. piano tchr., 1998; mem. site selection com. Multnomah County (Oreg.) Libr., New Gresham br., 1987, adv. com. Multnomah County Libr., Portland, Oreg., 1988-89; bd. dirs. Oreg. Episcopal Conf. of Deaf, 1985-92. Bd. dirs. East County Arts Alliance, Gresham, 1987-91; vestry person, jr. warden St. Luke's Episc. Ch., 1989-92; vestry person St. Aidan's Episcopal. Ch., 2000—; founding pres. Mt. Hood Pops, 1983-88, orch. mgr., 1983-91, 93—, bd. dirs., 1983-88, 91—. Recipient Jeanette Parkhill Meml. award

Chaffey Jr. Coll., 1959, Svc. award St. Luke's Episcopal Ch., 1983, 87, Edn. Svc. award Soroptimists, 1989. Mem. AAUW, NEA, Oreg. Edn. Assn., Oreg. Libr. Assn., ALA, Gresham Hist. Soc. Avocations: music, reading. E-mail: pierikm@teleport.com.

PIERPOINT, KAREN ANN, marriage, family and child therapist; b. Puyallup, Wash., Sept. 1, 1944; d. Peyton Randolph Winn and Jessie Mae (Kenoyer) Kalmen; m. Randall Dean Pierpoint, Mar. 19, 1966; children: Janet, Wendy, Elizabeth, Nathan. BA, U. Oreg., 1966; MS in Counseling, San Diego State U., 1988. Lic. marriage, family and child counseling, Calif. Elem. tchr. Lane County Dist. 4, Eugene, Oreg., 1966-67, Umatilla County Dist. 19-R, Weston, Oreg., 1967-70; internat. student ministry staff mem. Campus Crusade for Christ, Internat., San Bernardino, Calif., 1970-75; dir. Christian edn. Graeagle (Calif.) Community Ch., 1975-83; dir. women's ministries Pine Valley (Calif.) Community Ch., 1983-87; lectr. counselor edn. dept. San Diego State U., 1988-89; mental health cons. San Diego City Schs., 1988-89; staff therapist Heartland Bibl. Counseling, El Cajon, Calif., 1987-90, Shepperson Psychol. Assocs., Fullerton, Calif., 1990-91; pvt. practice family therapist Brea, Calif., 1992—. Ednl. cons. New Life Acad. Home Edn., San Diego, 1984-90; allied profl. Coastal Communities Hosp., Costa Mesa, 1991; allied health profl. Yorba Hills Hosp., Yorba Linda, Calif., 1991, Calif. Psychiat. Ctr., Santa Ana, 1992-95; profl. provider Ocean Hills Med. Group, 1996-97. Columnist Free Indeed Mag., 1976-78. 4-H club leader Mohawk Valley 4-H Club, Plumas County, Calif., 1976-83, Mt. Empire 4-H Club, San Diego County, Calif., 1984-87; 4-H club advisor Mohawk Valley 4-H Club, Plumas County, 1982-83. Named for 4-H Ten Yrs. of Leadership, Mt. Empire 4-H Club, 1986. Mem.: Am. Assn. Christian Counselors, Christian Assn. for Psychol. Studies (clin.), Am. Acad. Experts in Traumatic Stress (clin.), Am. Assn. Marriage and Family Therapy (clin.), Calif. Assn. Marriage and Family Therapists (clin.), Brea C. of C., Phi Kappa Phi. Republican. Avocations: reading, classical and folk music, writing, travel, sewing. Office: 749 S Brea Blvd Ste 43 Brea CA 92821-5388

PIERRARD-MUTTON, MARY V. artist, educator; b. Steubenville, Ohio, Sept. 22, 1921; d. Frank David and Mary E. (Huffman) Nation; m. Charles Joseph Pierrard, Sept. 5, 1942 (dec. May 1979); children: Karen Marie, Charles Joseph; m. James Mutton, May 27, 1994. Grad., Midway (Pa.) H.S., 1940. Tchr. China painting home studio, Midway, 1979—, sr. citizen group, California, Pa., 1993; artist Krauses, Washington, Pa., 1980-85. Demonstrator Pitts. Ctr. of Arts, 1990, Woman's Club, McDonald, Pa., 1992, Garden Club, McDonald, 1992, Fireman's, Midway, 1991, Pitts. Dist. of Chs., Legonier, Pa., 1993. Exhibited in group shows at Washington County Woman's Club, 1981, 90(1st Pl. award), 1990, Pa. Fedn. Woman's Club, 1989, 90 (1st Pl. award), S.W. Dist. Woman's Clubs, 1983 (1st Pl. award); contbr. drawing to book: Years of Duncan, 1980, cover to Internat. Porcelain Artists. Mem. Internat. Porcelain Art Tchrs., Inc., Nat. Mus. Women in Arts, Pitts. Porcelain Artists (treas. 1994 97), Pa. Porcelain Artists (treas. 1985-87), China Painters (pres. Pitts. chpt. 2003-2004), McDonald Woman's Club, Pa. Woman's Club. Home: PO Box 85 Midway PA 15060-0085

PIERRE, MIRELLE, physician, psychotherapist, health facility administrator; b. Port au Prince, Haiti, July 21, 1950; came to U.S., 1970; d. Gustave Pierre and Madeleine Defay; m. Serge Elie, Sept. 30, 1972 (div. Nov. 1981); children: Richard, Lesly Elie. MD, U. Autonoma de Nuevoleon, Monterrey, Mex., 1989; PhD, South Tex. Sch. Nutrition, 1995, postgrad., Clayton Coll. Nat. Health, 1997; CCN, San Antonio Sch. Homeopathy. Physician Guadalpue Psychiat. Ctr., Monterrey, 1990-92; physician, nutritionist Advanced Wellness Clinic, San Antonio, 1993-95; pres., physician, nutritionist Chalumi Health Enterprises, Inc., Bklyn., 1996—. Author: An Ounce of Prevention, 1999, (cassettes) Series of Success Collection, 1999. Mem. Am. Naturopathic Med. Assn., Coalition for Natural Health. Democrat. Pentecostal. Avocations: reading, writing, music. Office: 304 E 35th St Brooklyn NY 11203-3906

PIERRI, MARY KATHRYN MADELINE, cardiologist, educator, emergency physician, educator; b. N.Y.C., Aug. 12, 1948; d. Charles Daniel and Margaret Loyola (Pesce) P. BA, Manhattanville Coll., 1969; MD, Med. Coll. Pa., 1974. Diplomate Am. Bd. Cardiology. Med. resident Med. Coll. Pa., Phila., 1974-77; fellow in cardiology N.Y. Hosp., N.Y.C., 1977-79; asst. physician Meml. Hosp., N.Y.C., 1980-89, assoc. physician, 1989-97, chief cardiology svc., 1991—2002, attending physician, 1997—. Assoc. prof. medicine Cornell Med. Coll., 1989—97, prof. clin. medicine, 1997—. Fellow Am. Coll. Cardiology, N.Y. Cardiological Soc.; mem. ACP, Soc. Critical Care Medicine, Alpha Omega Alpha. Office: Meml Hosp Sloan Kettering Cancer Ctr 1275 York Ave New York NY 10021-6094

PIERSON, ANNE BINGHAM, physician; b. N.Y.C., June 9, 1929; d. Woodbridge and Ursula Wolcott (Griswold) Bingham; m. Richard N. Pierson Jr., July 10, 1954 (div. Aug. 1974); children: Richard N. III, Olivia Tiffany Jacobs, Alexandra deForest Griffin, Cordelia Stewart Comfort Smela; m. Richard Taliaferro Wright, Nov. 25, 1978 (div. Sept. 1997); m. Paul H. Altrocchi, May 9, 1998. Student, Katharine Branson Sch., Ross, Calif., 1943-47; BA, Vassar Coll., 1951; MD, Columbia U., 1955, MPH, 1972. Intern Lenox Hill Hosp., N.Y.C., 1955-56; substitute internship AUH, Beruit, Lebanon, 1955; mem. staff 7th Day Adventist Hosp., Taipei, Taiwan, 1957; clinic physician, med. dir. Planned Parenthood of Bergen County, Hackensack, N.J., 1960-74, also bd. dirs., 1966-69; asst. clin. prof. dept. ob-gyn. Columbia U. Coll. Physicians and Surgeons, Internat. Inst. Study of Human Reproduction, 1972-74; med. dir. Memphis Assn. for Planned Parenthood, Inc., 1974-75; staff physician N.Y. Telephone Co., 1976-87; med. dir. Planned Parenthood Assn. Hudson County, 1976-79; physician Sonalysts, Waterford, Conn., 1988—. Mem. nat. med. adv. com. Planned Parenthood-World Population, 1966-69. Pres. Vassar Class 1951, 1986-91; artist mem. Clinton Art Soc., 1989—, East Lyme Art League, 1991—; active Jr. League, 1964-69, sustainer, 1969—. Mem. AMA (Physicians Recognition award 1973—), Nat. Soc. Colonial Dames (life, asst. sec. 1991-94, 2d v.p. 1994-97), Cosmopolitan Club, Lyme Art Assn. (treas. 1998-99, pres. 1999—), Mystic Art Assn., Essex Art Assn. Office: Sonalysts 215 Parkway N Waterford CT 06385-1209

PIERSON, JUANITA (NITA PIERSON), secondary school educator; b. Shreveport, La., Oct. 28, 1921; d. Henry and Rodessa (Scott) Thomas; m. Floyd Allen Pierson, Sept. 18, 1938; children: Annette Marilyn Pieson Poulard, Frederick Allen. Student, U. Md., 1965-66, Centennary Coll., 1967-68, So. U. Coll., 1967-69, Prairie View A&M U., 1969-70, Santa Clara U., 1974; BA, Wiley Coll., 1954; MS, La. Tech., 1975; postgrad., Northwestern U., 1972-74; D (hon.), Shreveport Bible Coll., 1987. Sec. Mooretown Sch., Shreveport, 1957-67; elem. music splst. Caddo Parish Schs., La., 1967-70; secondary edn. tchr., 1970-79. Ptnr. Pierson's Allendale Plz., Shreveport, 1979—; bookkeeper F & F Food Store, Shreveport, 1978—; artistic dir. Performing Arts Studio, 1983—; dir. music Antioch Baptist Ch., 1997—. Instr. Christian Edn., Shreveport, 1970—; organist Shiloh Bapt. Ch., Shreveport, 1975-78; mem. ways and means com. Greenwood Acres Civic Club, 1975-81, mem. econ. devel. and planning com., 1980-81; mem. Ctr. for Families, Shreveport, 1992-99; mem. music and art cultural awareness project, Jackson Heights Housing Cmty., Shreveport, 1998; mem. Shreveport Symphony Guild, Shreveport Little Theatre, Shreveport Opera Guild; min. music Antioch Bapt. Ch., music dir. Jackson Heights Housing Ctr., Avenue B.C. Shreveport. Grantee La. Divsn. Arts, 1995-99, Shreveport Regional Arts Coun., 1995-99; named Educator of Yr. Caddo Parish Sch. Bd., 1978; hon. state senator, La., 1980-81; recipient Cert. of Recognition of Svc. award, Antioch Bapt. Ch., Shreveport, La., 2000; honorarium during African-Am. History Month Celebration, 2002, Movers and Shakers award, Pan Hellinic Coun. of Greek Orgn., 2002 Mem. NEA, Nat. Coun. Tchrs. English, Shreveport Regional Area Coun., La. Coun. Tchrs. English, Music Tchrs. Nat. Assn., La. State Music Tchrs. Assn., Greater Shreveport Music Tchrs. Assn., Greater Shreveport C. of C. (Woman of the Century award, 2000), Univ. Club, Phi Delta Kappa, Basileus-Sigma Gamma Rho, Sorority Inc., Eta Psi Sigma Chpt. Baptist. Avocations: music, performing arts. Office: Performing Arts Studio 2332 Jewella Ave Shreveport LA 71109-2412

PIERSON, KAREN ARLENE, poet; b. Maquon, Ill., Jan. 25, 1940; d. Charles Frances and Wilma Lois (West) Little; m. Jackie Lee Pierson, Jan. 7, 1962 (dec. July 1982); children: Debra, Tammie. Student, Carl Sandburg Coll., Galesburg, Ill., 1990, 92, cert. tutor literacy coalition, 1997. Author: Poetic Scraps of Literature, 1996; contbr. poetry to Nat. Libr. Poetry (Editor's Choice awards 1993, 95-97), World of Poetry (Silver award 1990, Golden Poet award 1988, 92, hon. mentions), Poetic Voices of America, Famous Poets Soc. (Diamond honor award 1996), Poetry Guild. Vol. VFW, 1996; adult tutor Carl Sandburg Coll. Literacy Coalition, 1997—2002; vol. various hosps., including Iowa City VA Hosp.; mem. com. class reunion Galesburg H.S., 1998; vol. Galesburg Dem. Com., 1994. Mem.: DAV, VFW (chmn. POW-MIA com. 1997—98, Ladies Aux. membership chair 1997—2002, Ladies Aux. POW-MIA chair 1997—2002, jr. v.p. 1998—, Poppu chmn. 1998—, Ladies Aux. pres. 1999—2001), ASPCA, Songwriters Am., Internat. Soc. Poets (life), Parktrust, Arbor Day Soc., Audubon Soc., Nat. Fedn. (cert. backyard wildlife habitat), Am. Legion. Methodist. Avocations: yard and garden, reading, boating, dance. Home: 109 Lincoln St Galesburg IL 61401-3945

PIERSON, MARILYN EHLE, financial planner; b. Cleve., Feb. 27, 1931; d. Ernest John and Helen Irene (Steudel) Ehle; m. Edward G. Pierson, July 17, 1954; children: Melanie K., Edward G. III. BSBA, Miami U., 1953; grad., Coll. Fin. Planning, 1990, Inst. Cert. Divorce Planners, 1997. CFP. Sr. fin. advisor, advanced planner group Am. Express Fin. Advisors, Cleve., 1987—. Corp. presenter, fin. educator East Ohio Gas, AT&T, Cleve., Master Builders, Cleve., Preformed Line Products, Cleve., Parker Hannifin, Cleve.; guest lectr. Chagrin Valley C. of C., Chagrin Falls, Ohio; lectr. adult edn. Shaker Heights (Ohio). Fin. columnist Bainbridge Banter newspaper. Chair stewardship and resources Valley Presbyn. Ch., Bainbridge, Ohio, elder, 1991-93, planned giving chmn., 1991-95, 2000—. Mem. Fin. Planning Assn. (treas. exec. com. NE Ohio chpt. 1994-98), Exec. Women Internat. (advisor, bd. dirs. 1997, pres. 1996), Estate Planning Coun. Cleve. Avocation: travel. Home: 8178 Chagrin Mills Rd Chagrin Falls OH 44022-3807 Office: Am Express Fin Advisors 22901 Mill Creek Blvd #375 Cleveland OH 44122-4556 E-mail: marilyn.e.pierson@aefa.com.

PIGNATELLI, DEBORA BECKER, state legislator; b. Weehawken, N.J., Oct. 25, 1947; d. Edward and Frances (Fishman) Becker; m. Michael Albert Pignatelli, Aug. 22, 1971; children: Adam Becker, Benjamin Becker. AA, Vt. Coll., 1967; BA, U. Denver, 1969. Exec. dir. Girl's Club Greater Nashua, N.H., 1975-77; dir. tenant svcs. Nashua Housing Authority, 1979-80; vocat. counselor Comprehensive Rehab. Assocs., Bedford, N.H., 1982-85; specialist job placement Crawford & Co., Bedford, 1985-87; mem N.H. Ho. of Reps., Concord, 1986—91, mem. appropriations com., 1986-91, asst. minority leader, 1989—91, mem. N.H. Senate, Concord, 1992—2003, dep. Dem. whip, vice chair judiciary com., mem. capital budget com., chair enrolled bills com., long range capital budget overview com.; dir. Sky Meadow Condominium Assn., 2003—. Del. Am. Coun. Young Polit. Leaders, Germany, 1987. Mem. Nashua Peace Ctr., 1980—; asst. coach Little League Baseball, Nashua, 1987-90; steering com. Gephardt for Pres. Campaign, N.H., 1987-88, del. Dem. Nat. Conv. 1988; Gore del. Dem. Nat. Conv., 2000; bd. dirs. Sky Meadow Condominium Assn. Named One of 10 Most Powerful Women in N.H., N.H. Editions mag., 1995; recipient Meritorious Svc. award N.H. Women's Lobby, 1997, John F. Kennedy award Hillsborough County Dems., 2001. Mem. N.H. Children's Lobby, Women's Lobby. Jewish. Avocations: skiing, swimming, boating. Home: 22 Appletree Grn Nashua NH 03062-2252

PIGOTT, IRINA VSEVOLODOVNA, educational administrator; b. Blagoveschensk, Russia, Dec. 4, 1917; came to U.S., 1939, naturalized, 1947; d. Vsevolod V. and Sophia (Reprev) Obolianinoff; m. Nicholas Prischepenko, Feb., 1945 (dec. Nov. 1964); children: George, Helen. Grad., YMCA Jr. Coll., Manchuria, 1937; BA, Mills Coll., 1942; cert. social work, U. Calif.-Berkeley, 1944; MA in Early Childhood Edn., NYU, 1951. Dir.-owner Parsons Nursery Sch., Flushing, N.Y., 1951-59; dir. Montessori Sch., N.Y.C., 1966-67; dir., tchr. Head Start Program, Harlem, 1967-68; founder, dir. East Manhattan Sch. for Bright and Gifted, N.Y.C., 1968—, The House for Bright and Gifted Children, Flushing, N.Y., 1988-93. Organizer, pres., exec. dir. Non-Profl. Children's Performing Arts Guild, Inc., N.Y.C., 1961-65, 87—. Organizer Back Yard Theatre, Bayside, N.Y., 1959-61. Democrat. Greek Orhtodox. Avocations: music, dance, theatre, art, sports. Office: East Manhattan Sch 201 E 17th St 2H New York NY 10003

PIHOS, SANDRA M, state representative; b. Pittsburgh, Pa., June 11, 1946; m. William Pihos; children: Andria, Peter, Deanna, Michael. BA, Mount Union Coll., 1968; MS, Northern Ill. Univ., 1971. State Rep. House of Rep., Dist. 42, Ill., 2002 ; v.p. Pihos Enterprises, 1993—2000; Guidance Counselor Downers Grove N. HS, Dist. 99, 1970—74, 1988—93; tchr. Edison Jr. HS, Dist. 200, 1969—70. Mem.: Glenbard Enrollment Adv. Comm. (mem. 1991—92), Parternership for Ed. Progress Found. (trustee 1993—, sec. 1996—), Parkviewf Elem. Sch. Parent/Tchr. Assoc. (pres. 1985—86), Michael's Pl. Lit. Ctr. (Founder/Ex-Oficio, Dir./Vol. 2000—), Holy Apostles Ch. Women's Org. (sec. 1990—95), Glen Ellyn Lifelong Learning Partnership (Sec. 1992—94), Glen Ellyn Lib. Adv. Bd. (mem. 1990—92), Glen Crest Jr. High Student/Tchr./Parent Coun. (pres. 1989—90, 1992—94), DuPage County Workforce Develop. Bd. (Exec. sec. 2000—01), Citizens Adv. Coun., 1989-1997 (v.p. 1992—93), Local Gov., Glenbard Twp., Dist. 87 (v.p. 1997, pres. 2001—), Consumer Protection, Commerce & Bus. Develop., Appropriations - Human Svc., Appropriations - Elem. & Sec. Republican. Christian (Greek Orthodox). Office: Capitol 214-N Stratton Office Bldg Springfield IL 62706 also: District 799 E Roosevelt Rd Bldg 2 Suite 11 Glen Ellyn IL 60137

PIIRMA, IRJA, chemist, educator; b. Tallinn, Estonia, Feb. 4, 1920; came to U.S., 1949; d. Voldemar Juri and Meta Wilhelmine (Lister) Tiits; m. Aleksander Piirma, Mar. 10, 1943; children: Margit Ene, Silvia Ann. Diploma in Chemistry, Tech. U., Darmstadt, Fed. Republic of Germany, 1949; MS, U. Akron, 1957, PhD, 1960. Rsch. chemist U. Akron, Ohio, 1952-67, asst. prof., 1967-76, assoc. prof., 1976-81, prof., 1981-90, prof. emerita, 1990—, dept. head, 1982-85. Author: Polymeric Surfactants, 1992; editor: Emulsion Polymerization, 1982; contbr. articles to profl. jours. Recipient Extra Mural Rsch. award BP Am., Inc., 1989. Mem. Am. Chem. Soc. Avocations: swimming, skiing. Home: 3528 Adaline Dr Cuyahoga Falls OH 44224-3929 Office: U Akron Inst Polymer Sci Akron OH 44325-3909 Office Phone: 330-972-7504. E-mail: irjapiirma@cs.com.

PIKE, NANCY M. librarian; b. Rockford, Ill., June 23, 1938; d. Hjalmar Magnusson and Violet Lucille Kirby; m. David E. Pike, Aug. 26, 1960; children: Christopher David Pike, Kimberly Ann Pike Greer. BA, Rockford Coll., 1960; MLS, U. Wis., 1984. Tchr. English Keith Country Day Sch., Rockford, 1963-66, 68-70; tchr. Romper Room Sch. Sta. WCEE-TV, WQAD-TV, Moline, 1966-67; libr. asst. L.D. Fargo Pub. Libr., Lake Mills, Wis., 1973-80; libr. technician U. Wis. and Wis. Inter Libr. Svcs., Madison, 1980-84; pub. svcs. libr. Venice (Fla.) Pub. Libr., 1985-87, head libr., 1987-2000; dir. Sarasota County Libr. Sys., 2000—. Bd. dirs. United Way So. Sarasota County, Venice, 1988—, pres., 1994; bd. dirs. Human Svcs. Planning Assn., Sarasota, 1994-2000, chair, 1997-99; bd. dirs. Tampa Bay Libr. Consortium, 2000—, treas. 2001-2003, v.p. 2003-2004. Recipient Gerd Meuhsam award Art Librs. Soc. N. Am., 1983; named Woman of Impact, Sarasota County Commn. on Status of Women, 1995, Woman of Distinction, Women's Support and Enrichment Ctr., 1998. Mem. ALA, Fla. Libr. Assn. (v.p. 2004-, writer column 1992—, Fla. Librs. award 1998), Pub. Libr. Assn., Libr. Adminstrn. and Mgmt. Assn. Home: 420 Baynard Dr Venice FL 34285-3301 Office: Twin Lakes Park Cmty Svcs Bus Ctr 6700 Clark Rd Sarasota FL 34241-2498 E-mail: nmpike@scgov.net.

PIKE, SHIRLEY, school psychologist; b. Ottumwa, Iowa, Aug. 2, 1949; d. Harold Dewey Pike and Marguerite Cleone Berntsen; m. Michael John Hemmingson, Nov. 9, 1984; children: Marguerite Isajoy, Sara Jean. BA in Psychology, Calif. State U., 1971, MA in Psychol. Svcs., 1975. Nat. cert. sch. psychologist, Md. Sch. psychologist L.A. Unified Schs., 1976-79, S.W. Cook County Edn. Assn., Orland Park, Ill., 1979-81, Grant Wood AEA, Cedar Rapids, Iowa, 1981—. Bd. dirs. Children and Adults with Attention Deficit Disorder, Cedar Rapids, 1989-97; profl. devel. chair East Ctrl. UniServ Unit, Cedar Rapids, 1995-97. Co-author: Assessment and Intervention Children with ADHD, 1994. Pres., past v.p. North Ctrl. region Sri Sathya Sai Baba Orgn., 1995—; precinct capt., steering com. Linn County Dems., Cedar Rapids, 1999; v.p. Inter-Religious Coun. of Linn County, 1998—, past sec., treas.; bd. dirs. Faith in Action, 1997-98. Grantee Iowa Dept. of Pub. Instrn., 1985, 86. Mem. Iowa State Edn. Assn. (exec. bd.), Nat. Orgn. of Sch. Psychologists, Samaritan Counseling Ctr. (bd. dirs.), Phi Beta Kappa, Phi Kappa Phi. Office: Grantwood Area Edn Agy 4401 6th St SW Cedar Rapids IA 52404-4432 Home: 3925 Willowbrook Dr Marion IA 52302-6155

PIKEN, MICHELE RENEÉ (PENN), artist, photographer; b. Richmond, Va., Mar. 19, 1946; d. Sam and Dorothy (Klaff) Penn; m. Gerald Piken, Dec. 3, 1967; children: Lara Eden Piken Polner, Charly Brooke Piken. BS, Franklin Sch. Sci. and Arts, 1965; student, Art Inst. Ft. Lauderdale, 1980-81. Photographer, supr. Twin Lakes Travel Park, Ft. Lauderdale, Fla., 1979-81; photographer Miami (Fla.) Jewish fedn., 1988-89; designer Dressed To A Tee Inc., Miami, 1983-85; pres., owner Tickle Pink Inc., Miami, 1985 90; designer, pres. N.V. US Inc., Miami, 1992-95; visual merchantdizer Macy's Inc., Aventura, Fla., 1991-92; bookeeper Piken & Assocs. PA, Miami, 1996—. Freelance photographer The Miami Herald, 1998-99. One-woman shows include Eyes of Israel, U. Miami, 1984, Photo Exhibn. of Israel, Yafta Gallery, 1993, Tommy, Houshang Gallery, 1997, Africa & Beyond, Ft. Lauderdale City Hall, 1999. Staff photographer Diabetes Rsch. Found., Miami, 1981-90; vol. Israeli Army, Negev, 1985, Camillus House, Miami, 1988-91, Aventura Regional Hosp., 1994-97. Mem. Dade County Art in Pub. Places, Palm Beach Photographic Ctr. Avocations: painting, sculpting, gardening, candy making, antique restoration. Home: 2466 Eagle Run Way Weston FL 33327-1431

PILANEN, CAROLYN L. music educator; b. Boston, Jan. 18, 1963; d. Rose-Marie and Patrick F. Doherty; children: Peter John, Joshua Patrick. BA, U. Lowell, 1985. Cert. tchr. Mass. Choral dir./music tchr. Meml. Mid. Sch., Beverly, 1985—93, Beverly (Mass.) H.S., 1993—, musical dir., choreographer, 1993—, color guard dir., 1996—. Named Rotary Club Tchr. of the Yr., Beverly Rotary Club, 2001. Mem.: Mass. Music Educators Assn. Home: 2 Bartlett St Beverly MA 01915 Office: Beverly High School 100 Sohier Rd Beverly MA 01915 Personal E-mail: carolyn.pilanen@verizon.net.

PILCH, MARGARET L. grant consultant; b. Tacoma, Wash., Mar. 6, 1948; d. Bernard Joseph Kern, Jean Katherine Kern; m. Edward Samuel Pilch; 1 child, Christopher Neal Richards. AA, Washburn U., 1979, BA, 1982; MPA, Kans. U., 1987, PhD, Union Inst. and U., 2002. Cert. legal asst. 1979, grant specialist 2003. Paralegal John Wilkinson, Atty., Topeka, 1978—82, Frank Sabatini, Atty., 1982—84; comml. realtor High Plains Realty, 1984—85; comml. leasing agent Pembroke Commercial Realty, Virginia Beach, Va., 1985—91; paralegal Goicoechea & DiGrazia, Attorneys, Elko, Nev., 1992—95, Darlene Reiter, Atty., Sheridan, Wyo., 1995—96, 1997—99; asst. budget dir. Sheridan County Government, 1996—97; loan processor Sheridan State Bank, 1999—2000; grant cons., 1998—2004; grant reviewer Wyo. Dept. Edn., 2002—03. Editor: (Handbook) Legal Rights of Women in Wyoming, 2001; author: (Catalog) Catalog for Individuals Seeking Rural Research Grants, 2001, (Dissertation) Workplace Attitudes of Nonfarm Rural Working Women in Sheridan County, Wyoming, 2001; editor: Where to Find Help People and Places, 2004. Coll. coach Daniels Fund Coll. Prep and Scholarship Program, 2002—03; mem. legal/legis. com. Wyo. Coun. Women's Issues, 2000—; pres. Citco Fed. Credit Union Bd., 2000—; judge H.S. contest FCCLA, 2004; grad. student supr., 2002—; mem. Spring Creek Assn. Architecture com., 1992—93; bd. dirs. Wyo. Substance Abuse Treatment and Recovery Ctr., 2003; dist. chmn. Republican Party, Virginia Beach, 1990—91; legis. aide Senator Ben Vidrickson, Topeka, 1984—85; arbitrator Better Bus. Bur., Topeka, 1984—85; rape counselor Citizen's Crime Com., Topeka, 1983—85. Recipient Certificate of Merit, Am. Cancer Soc., 1994, Outstanding Achievement award, 1994-1995; grantee, Wyo. Women's Found., 2001. Mem.: AAUW, Inst. Women's Policy Rsch., Am. Assn. Grant Profls., Kans. Legal Assistance Soc. (founder 1977—), Assn. Profl. Rschrs. for Advancement, Rural Sociol. Soc., Women in Rural America Task Force. Avocations: writing, travel, weightlifting. Home: 875 Lower Prairie Dog Road Sheridan WY 82801

PILCHARD, MELISSA MEYER, realtor, appraiser; b. NYC, Apr. 3, 1936; d. Halsey and Dorothy May Meyer; m. Charles Edward Pilchard, Sept. 1, 1956; children: Edward, Benjamin. BS, U. Md., 1958. Lic. real estate broker. Tchr. Rockville (Md.) H.S., 1958-61, Plainfield (N.J.) H.S., 1970-73; realtor McCulloch Realtors, Newtown, Conn., 1978-84; v.p. Realtech Realtors, Newtown, 1985-92; broker William Pitt, Newtown, 1993—. Treas. Bd. Realtors, Newtown, 1988-90, v.p., 1994, pres., 1997; dir. Conn. Assn. Realtors, Hartford, 1992, 1995, 1997. Vice chmn. Newtown City Coun., bd. fin., v.p., 1994—. Named Realtor of Yr., Newtown Bd. Realtors, 1991, 97. Mem. Nat. Assn. Realtors, Conn. Assn. Realtors (dir.), Newtown Bd. Realtors (pres. 1997). Democrat. Episcopalian. Home: 6 Poor House Rd Newtown CT 06470-1830 Office: William Pitt 13 Church Hill Rd Newtown CT 06470-1612

PILDES, SARA, artist; b. N.Y.C. d. Isidore and Minnie (Friedlander) Philipson; m. Harry Pildes, Dec. 1930; children: Michael, Jane, Daniel, Robert. BS, CCNY, 1953. Mem. panel C.W. Post Coll., L.I. U.; lectr. Temple U., Phila. Represented in permanent collections Doane Coll. Mus., Crete, Nebr., Bismarck (N.D.) State Coll.; one-woman shows include Gov.'s Mansion, Lincoln, Nebr., Rotunda Gallery, Washington, Raymond Duncan Gallery, Paris, Nat. Arts Club, Gramercy Park, Gallery Internat., N.Y.C. Mem. Nat. Assn. Women Artists, Met. Painters and Sculptors (treas., lectr.), Burr Artists, N.Y. State Soc. Women Artists, Visual Individualists United, Nat. Mus. Women in Arts (charter). Home: 2 Franklin Town Blvd Philadelphia PA 19103-1238

PILETTE, PATRICIA CHEHY, healthcare organizational management consultant; b. Rutland, Vt., June 28, 1945; d. John Edward and Mary T. (McNamara) Chehy; m. Wilfrid Pilette, July 22, 1972; 1 child, Patrick John. Diploma, Jeanne Mance Sch. Nursing, 1966; BSN magna cum laude, St. Anselm Coll., 1971; MS summa cum laude, Boston U., 1974, EdD in Counseling and Human Svcs. Adminstrn. summa cum laude, 1984. RN, Mass. Clin. specialist adult psychiatry counseling practice, Natick, Mass.; employee assistance counselor St. Elizabeth's Med. Ctr., 1984—. Contbr. articles to profl. publs., chpts. to books. Mem.: Am. Mental Health Counselors Assn., N.Am. Soc. Employee Assistance, Assn. for Humanistic Psychologists, Am. Psychotherapy Assn. (diplomate), N.E. Soc. Group Psychotherapists, N.E. Assn. for Specialists in Group Work, Mass. Orgn. Nurse Execs., Sigma Theta Tau, Pi Lambda Theta.

PILGRIM, DIANNE HAUSERMAN, retired museum director; b. Cleve., July 8, 1941; d. John Martin and Norma Hauserman; divorced. BA, Pa. State U., 1963; MA, Inst. Fine Arts, NYU, 1965; postgrad., CUNY, 1971-74; LHD (hon.), Amherst Coll., 1991, Pratt Inst., 1994. Chester Dale fellow Am. wing. Met. Mus. Art, N.Y.C., 1966-68, rsch. cons. Am. paintings and sculpture, 1971-73; asst. to dirs. Pyramid Galleries, Ltd., Washington, 1969-71, Finch Coll. Mus. Art, Washington, 1971; curator dept. decorative arts Bklyn. Mus., 1973-88, chmn. dept., 1988; dir. Cooper-Hewitt Nat. Design Mus., N.Y.C., 1988-2000, dir. emeritus, 2000—. Mem. adv. com. Gracie Mansion, N.Y.C., 1980; mem. design adv. com. Art Inst. Chgo., 1988; mem. Hist. House Trust N.Y.C., Mayor's Office, 1989-94. Co-author, curator: (book and exhbn. catalogue) Mr. and Mrs. Raymond Horowitz Collection of American Impressionist and Realist Paintings, 1973, The American Renaissance 1876-1917, 1979; (book) The Machine Age in America 1918-1941, 1986 (Charles F. Montgomery prize Decorative Arts Soc.). Bd. dirs. Nat. Multiple Sclerosis Soc., 1989. Recipient Disting. Alumni award Pa. State U., 1991. Mem. Decorative Arts Soc. (pres. 1977-79), Art Deco Soc., Victorian Soc., Art Table.

PILL, CYNTHIA JOAN, social worker; b. N.Y.C., Mar. 30, 1939; d. Alfred and Edna (Strauss) Fruchtman; m. Robert Pill, July 29, 1961; children: Laura, Daniel, Karen. BS cum laude, Jackson Coll., Tufts U., 1961; MS in Social Work, Simmons Coll., 1963, PhD in Social Work, 1987. Lic. ind. clin. social worker. Clin. social worker Concord (Mass.) Family Sc., 1965-78; coord. family life edn. Family Counseling Svc., Newton, Mass., 1979-83; pvt. practice clin. social work Newton, 1979—; adj. asst. prof., rsch. advisor Smith Coll. Sch. for Social Work, 1988—99. Adj. asst. prof. Simmons Coll. Sch. Social Work, Boston, 1989-93. Contbr. articles to profl. jours. Vol. coord. Hospice at Home, Sudbury, Mass., 1986-88. Mem. NASW, Mass. Soc. Clin. Social Work, Register Clin. Social Workers (bd. cert. diplomate). Address: 14 Mason Rd Newton Center MA 02459-1506

PILLOTE, BARBARA WIEGAND, volunteer; b. Washington, Jan. 31, 1930; d. Martin Tripp and Elizabeth Beryl (Wagner) Wiegand; m. Robert Lawrence Pillote, July 25, 1953; children: Margaret Lynn, Katherine Elizabeth, Robert Lawrence, Jr. BA, Conn. Coll., New London, 1951. Lab technician Hunter Labs., Washington, 1951-52; sec. Bur. Svc. Mil. Personnel, Luth. Ch. Am., Washington, 1953-54. Pres., bd. trustees Nat. Luth. Home for Aged, 1991-93; active St. Paul's Luth. Ch., Washington, Montgomery County Lung Assn. Recipient Achievement award Montgomery County Lung Assn., 1977-85. Mem. Woman's Club Chevy Chase Md. (pres. 1973-75), Montgomery County Fedn. Women's Clubs (pres. 1990-92), Md. Fedn. Women's Clubs (first v.p. 1996-98, pres. 1998-2000, Md. Clubwoman of Yr. 1980), Md. Assn. Parliamentarians, Conn. Coll. Alumni Assn. Republican. Avocations: knitting, golf, family activities.

PILON, A. BARBARA, language and literature educator; b. Providence; d. Francis L. and Alice F. (Kelly) Cummings; m. Albert J. Pilon Jr., Feb. 6, 1954. AB, Brown U.; MEd, R.I. Coll.; PhD, Ind. U., 1969. Lang. arts cons. Johnston (R.I.) Sch. Dist., 1962-64; instr. Westfield (Mass.) State Coll., 1964-65; asst. prof. Ind. U., Indpls., 1969-71; prof. dept. edn. Worcester (Mass.) State Coll., 1972-87, prof. dept. langs. and lit., 1987-94. Prof. U. Conns. Confratute, summers 1980—. Author: Concrete Is Not Always Hard, Teaching Language Arts Creatively in the Elementary Grades; contbr. articles, tapes, monographs to profl. jours. and chpts. in books. Mem. Nat. Assn. Gifted Children (sec., rec. sec., past bd. dirs., awards), Nat. Coun. Tchrs. English (award), New Eng. Reading Assn. (past bd. dirs.). Home: Concord, Mass. Died Feb. 20, 2000.

PIMBLE, TONI, artistic director, choreographer, educator; b. Eng. Student, Elmhurst Sch. Ballet and Dramatic Arts, Royal Acad. Dancing, London. Resident choreographer Dance Aspen Co. Project; artistic dir., resident choreographer Eugene (Oreg.) Ballet Co., 1978—; artistic dir. Ballet Idaho, Boise. Past mem. faculty Dance Aspen Summer Dance Sch. Choreographer (festival) Carlisle Choreographer's Showcase, Pa. and Colo., (ballets) Two's Company, N.Y.C., Common Ground, Atlanta, 1994, Playing Field, Indlps., Borderline, Alice in Wonderland, Nebr., 1994, Wash., 1996, Quartet in Blue, Oreg., 1994, Petrushka, Nev., 1994, 95, Children of the Raven, India, Bangladesh, Sri Lanka, Syria, Jordan, Tunisia, 1995, 96, A Midsummer Night's Dream, Nev., 1997, numerous tours and sch. performances; choreographer, tchr. U. Iowa, Interlochen Sch. Arts; resident choreographer Dance On Tour Nat. Endowment Arts; artistic dir. Ballet Idaho. Active outreach programs Young Audiences Oreg., Wash. State Cultural Enrichment Program. Oreg. Arts Commn. artist fellow, Nat. Endowment Arts grantee; co-recipient Gov.'s Arts award, Oreg., 1996. Office: Ballet Idaho 501 S 8th St Ste A Boise ID 83702-7108

PIMENTAL, NANCY M. scriptwriter, actress; BS in Chem. Engring., Worcester Poly. Inst., Mass. Author: (major motion picture) The Sweetest Thing, (TV show) South Park (Emmy nomination); actor: (co-host TV show) Win Ben Stein's Money (Emmy nomination).

PINCHIN, JANE, literature educator; BA, SUNY, Binghamton, 1964; MD, Columbia U., 1965, PhD, 1973. Instr. Bklyn. Coll., 1966—67; prof. English Colgate U., Hamilton, NY, 1969—, interim pres., 2001—02, v.p. academic advancement. Author: Alexandria Still: Forster, Durrell and Cavafy, 1977; contbr. articles to profl. jours., chpts. to books. Office: Colgate U 309 James B Colgate Hall 13 Oak Dr Hamilton NY 13346

PINCOMBE, JODI DORIS, health facility administrator; b. Jersey City, Mar. 16, 1954; d. John Joseph and Dorothy Lillian (Wurster) Niemynski; m. JosephAlbert Corvino, Dec. 1, 1973 (div. June 1986); children: Joseph Albert, Jr., Jennifer Lynn, James Michael; m. Raymond Charles Pincombe, July 9, 1988. Student, Saddleback Coll., 1998—. Cert. procedural coder Am. Acad. Procedural Coders, cert. profl. coder hosp. Data adminstr. KeyProcessors, Inc., Cypress, Calif., 1985-88; supr. Ashton-Tate, Torrance, Calif., 1988-90; front office mgr. WillowTree Podiatry, Laguna Hills, Calif., 1990-92; billing mgr. Med. Svcs. Orgn., Laguna Hills, 1990-96; acct. mgr. Argus Med. Mgmt., Long Beach, Calif., 1997—; dir. ops. PFS Tenet Healthcare Sys., Santa Ana, Calif., 1997—. Leader seminar Jodi Pincombe, CPC, CPC-H, Mission Viejo, Calif., 1996—. Mem. Am. Acad. Profl. Coders (mem. adv. bd. 1997-2000, Coder of Yr. 1996), Assn. So. Calif. Procedural Coders (pres. 1994-98, pres. elect. Long Beach chpt. 1997-98), Profl. Assn. Healthcare Office Mgrs., Health Care Compliance Assn., 2000. Republican. Home: 26272 Montarez Cir Mission Viejo CA 92691-5302 Office: Tenet 1500 S Douglas Rd Anaheim CA 92806

PINCUS, ANN TERRY, federal agency administrator, editor, writer; b. Little Rock, Sept. 12, 1937; d. Fred William and Cornelia (Witsell) Terry; m. Walter Haskell Pincus, May 1, 1965; children: Ward, Adam, Cornelia Battle. BA, Vassar Coll., 1959. Editorial asst., writer Glamour Mag., 1963; reporter Ridder Pubs., Washington, 1963-66; freelance writer Washington, 1966-76; dir. info. select com. on U.S. population U.S. Ho. Reps., Washington, 1977-79; nat. publicist Nat. Pub. Radio, Washington, 1979-83; press sec. U.S. Sen. Charles Mathias, Washington, 1983-87; profl. staff mem. Senate Com. on Rules, Washington, 1983-87; v.p. communications Stas. WETA-TV/Radio, Washington, 1987-93; dir. Office of Rsch., USIA, Washington, 1993-99, Office Rsch., Bur. Intelligence & Rsch., Dept. State, 1999-2001. Pres. bd. dirs. Woodley House. Editor: Kennedy Center Cookbook, 1977; contbr. articles to profl. jours. Avocations: politics, reading, walking, tennis. Home: 3202 Klingle Rd NW Washington DC 20008-3403 Office: US Dept of State SA-44 301 4th St SW Rm 352 Washington DC 20547-0009

PINCUS, NANCY, architect, web site designer; d. Samuel and Shirley Pincus; 1 child, Ava Leigh Ichikawa. BArch, The Cooper Union for the Advancement of Sci. and Art, 1986. Project arch. Gensler, N.Y.C., 1994—97; archtl. project cons. HLW Internat., N.Y.C., 1997—2001. Designer, developer, webmaster iHaus.com. Vol. Clinton-Gore Campaign, N.Y.C., 1991—92. Mem.: DNC. Achievements include development of iHaus.com, Babybytes.net. Avocations: painting, internet, design, writing, politics. Personal E-mail: npincus@optonline.net.

PINCUS, STEPHANIE HOYER, dermatologist; b. Lakehurst, NJ, Feb. 28, 1944; d. Ernest Carl and Aviva (Silbert) Hoyer; m. David Frank Pincus, Aug. 22, 1965 (div. Dec. 1984); children: Matthew Jonah, Tamara Hope; m. Allan Roy Oseroff, Mar. 24, 1985; 1 child, Benjamin Henry Oseroff. BA, Reed Coll., 1964; MD cum laude, Harvard U., 1968; MBA, Northwestern U., 1998. Diplomate Am. Bd. Dermatology, Am. Bd. Internal Medicine. Intern Boston City Hosp., 1968-69; rsch. fellow U. Wash., Seattle, 1969-71, resident internal medicine, 1971-72; resident-fellow dermatology U. Washington, Seattle, 1972-74; fellow instr. dept. dermatology Harvard Med. Sch., Boston, 1974-75; asst. prof. medicine U. Wash., Seattle, 1975-77; lectr. Sch. Medicine Boston U., 1977-89; asst. prof. medicine Sch. Medicine Tufts U., Boston, 1977-82, mem. dept. immunology, 1977-89, asst. prof. dermatology, 1979-82, assoc. prof. dermatology and medicine, 1982-89; prof. medicine and dermatology, chairperson dermatology SUNY, Buffalo, 1989-2000; chief acad. affiliations officer Dept. Vets. Affairs, Washington, 2000—. Dermatology Found. fellow, Evanston, Ill., 1974-75, 77-78; Vets. Adminstrn. rsch. assoc., 1975-77; recipient Clin. Investigator award NIH, Bethesda, Md., 1979-81. Mem. Am. Contact Dermatitis Soc. (mem. liaison com. 1993—), Women's Dermatologic Soc. (bd. dirs. 1992—), Soc. Investigative Dermatology (chmn. com. on govt. and pub. rels. 1992-96), Profs. of Dermatology (mem. program com. 1993—), Internat. Soc. for Study of Vulvar Disease (mem. exec. com. 1993-95), Harvard Med. Alumni (pres. 1995-96), Phi Beta Kappa, Alpha Omega Alpha. Office: Dept Vets Affairs Office Acad Affiliations 810 Vermont Ave Washington DC 20420

PINDELL, HOWARDENA DOREEN, artist; b. Phila., Apr. 14, 1943; d. Howard Douglas and Mildred Edith (Lewis) P. BFA, Boston U., 1965; MFA, Yale U., 1967; DFA (hon.), Mass. Coll. Art, 1997, New Sch./Parsons Sch. Design, 1999. Curatorial asst. Mus. Modern Art, N.Y.C., 1969-71, asst. curator, 1971-77, asso. curator dept. prints and illus. books, 1977-79; asso. prof. art SUNY, Stony Brook, 1979-84, prof. art, 1984—. Contbr. articles to profl. jours.; exhbns. include, Mus. Modern Art, Stockholm and 5 European mus., 1973, Fogg Art Mus., Cambridge, Mass., 1973, Indpls. Mus., Taft Mus., Cin., 1974, Gerald Piltzer Gallery, Paris, 1975, 9th Paris Biennale, Mus. Modern Art, Paris, 1975, Vassar Coll. Art Gallery, 1977; represented in permanent collections, Mus. Modern Art, N.Y.C., Fogg Art Mus., Met. Mus., N.Y.C., Whitney Mus. Am. Art; represented in travelling exhbns. Brandeis U., U. Calif. at Riverside, Clev. Inst. Arts, SUNY, Potsdam, New Paltz, Wesleyan U., Davison Art Ctr., others. Recipient Artist award Studio Mus. of Harlem, 1994, Joan Mitchell Painting award Joan Mitchell Found., 1994/95, Women's Caucus for Art award for Disting. Contbns. and Achievement in Arts, 1996, Cmty. Svc. award N.Y. State United Tchrs., 1998, Juneteenth award Heckscher Mus., 1999, IAM Pioneer award, 2000; Japan/U.S. Friendship fellow, 1981-82, Guggenheim fellow, 1987-88; Ariana Found. grantee, 1984-85. Mem. Arts Coun. African Studies Assn., Coll. Art Assn. (Best Exhbn./Performance award 1990), Internat. Assn. Art Critics, Internat. House of Japan (acad.). Office: SUNY/Stonybrook Art Dept Stony Brook NY 11794-0001 Fax: (631) 632-7261. E-mail: Howardena.Pindell@sunysb.edu.

PINE, BESSIE MIRIAM, social worker, editor, columnist; b. Toronto, Jan. 6, 1919; d. Moses and Annie (Rosenberg) Hadler; m. Kurt Pine, Mar 24, 1943 (dec. May 1962); children: Alfred Marc, Annie Laurie Reuveni. BA in Psychology, U. Toronto, 1939; M in Social Work, U. Pitts., 1944. Lic. social worker, N.Y. Br. dir. YM-YWHA, Toronto, 1940-42; case worker Family Svc. of Greater New Haven, Conn., 1944-47, Jewish Family Svc., Phila., 1947-49; divsn. unit supr. Ednl. Alliance, N.Y.C., 1949-51; older adult supr. Kings Bay YM-YWHA, Bklyn., 1955-59; editor pers. reporter Jewish Comty Ctr. Program Aids, dir. part time pers. bur., N.Y.C., 1962-67; assoc. dir. pers. svcs. Jewish Comty. Ctrs. Assn., N.Y.C., 1967-93. Editor: (booklet) Viewpoints on Social and Social Work Issues, 1965; author: (rsch. study) Making Retirement Count: Options and Opportunities, 1989; author: (publ.) Looking Back and Looking Forward: A 75 Year Retrospective on the Assn. of Jewish Center Workers, 1993. Recipient Florence G. Heller award Jewish Comty. Ctrs. Assn., N.Y.C., 1994. Mem. Com. to Strengthen Group Work in Jewish Comty. Ctrs. (co-chair 1992-99), Assn. of Jewish Ctr. Profls. (columnist Ask Bessie 1994—, Profl. of Yr., Phila. 1990, Tikkun Olam award Balt. 1993), Nat. Assn. Social Workers (cert. social worker). Home: 150 Beaumont St Brooklyn NY 11235-4119

PINE, PATRICIA PALMER, aging services administrator; b. Portland, Maine, Mar. 14, 1940; d. Maurice George and Elizabeth Wadsworth (Syphers) Palmer; m. James Erlon Hannaford, Oct. 1, 1960 (div. June 1970); children: Paula L., Brenda J.; m. Vanderlyn Russell Pine, Aug. 9, 1974; stepchildren: Gordon K., Brian T., Daniel R. AB, Vassar Coll., 1972; MA, Columbia U., 1975; PhD, SUNY, Albany, 1993. Dir. Dutchess County Office for the Aging, Poughkeepsie, N.Y., 1976-80; assoc. dir. Hudson Valley Health Systems Agy., Tuxedo, N.Y., 1980-83; exec. dir. Hospice Assn. of Ulster County, Kingston, N.Y., 1983-84; assoc. exec. dir. WellCare N.Y., Kingston and Newburgh, 1984-86; dir. Ulster County Office Aging, Kingston, 1986-95; exec. dep. dir. N.Y. State Office For The Aging, Albany, 1995-2001, dir., 2001—03; prof. pub. svc. SUNY Albany Sch. Social Welfare, 2003—. Adj. prof. SUNY, New Paltz, 1973-95, Marist Coll., Poughkeepsie, 1976-79, 95, Adelphi U., L.I. City, 1983; pres. CEO The Gerontol Inst., 1993—; mem. faculty Brookdale Ctr. of Hunter Coll., 2000-03. Pres. United Way of Ulster County, Kingston, 1989-90; mem. N.Y. State Adv. Commn. on Aging-In Initiative, 1991-2003; trustee The Kingston Hosp., 1993-96; co-chair Panel for Elderly Prescription Ins. Program, 2001-03; chair Gov.'s Osteoporosis Edn. and Prevention Com., 2001—. Gerontol. Soc. Am. fellow, 1987, Paul Harris fellow Rotary Internat., 1989; named Vol. of the Yr., United Way of Ulster County, 1990. Fellow Gerontol. Soc. of Am.; mem. NASW, Nat. Coun. on Aging, N.Y. State Assn. Area Agys. on Aging (rec. sec. 1978-80, chair statewide conf. 1980, chair tng. com. 1986-88, pres. 1995). Avocations: travel, family, reading. Home: 18 Plattekill Ave New Paltz NY 12561-1917

PINENO, MARIAM DAVIS, retired music educator, poet; b. Nelson, Pa., Feb. 13, 1929; d. Frank Leonard and Rhea J. Chilson Davis; m. Francis Louis Pineno, June 24, 1951; children: Jonathan Phillip, Elizabeth Gayl Pineno Barron, Michael Davis, Martha Louise Pineno Hess. BS in Music Edn., Mansfield State U., 1950; M in Music Edn., Pa. State U., 1953; diploma writing for children & teenagers, Inst. Children's Lit., 1995. Music educator grades 6-8 Olean (N.Y.) Pub. Schs., 1950-51; music educator grades 1-12 Otto Twp., Duke Ctr., Pa., 1951-53; music educator pre K-5 Shikellamy Sch. Dist., Sunbury, Pa., 1967-92. Author of poetry and stories. Choir dir., organist United Meth. Ch., Selinsgrove, 1954-67; pvt. piano instr., Selinsgrove, 1954-67; workshop leader Music Edn. Students, Mansfield, Pa.; vol. hostess Nonprofit Cygnet Studios, Elizabethtown, Pa., 1990-99, poetry reader, 1999. Mem. Pa. Music Educators Assn. (mem. GO com., elem. region IV rep., citation of excellence in elem. music tchg. for dist. 8 1992), Acad. Am. Poets (assoc.), Pa. Assn. Sch. Retirees (Snyder County chpt.), Soc. of Children's Book Writers and Illustrators. Avocations: reading, writing, traveling, decorating. Home: 513 N 9th St Selinsgrove PA 17870-1610 E-mail: writemuse@webtv.net.

PINEROS, ELIZABETH, social services administrator, psychotherapist; b. Bogota, Colombia, Mar. 27, 1956; d. Marco Antonio and Ana Lucia (Parra) P.; m. Michael Selvggio, Sept. 18, 1982 (div. July 1988); 1 child, Leonardo. MSW, NYU, N.Y.C., 1982, advaned cert. social work, 1987, PhD, 2000. Diplomate Am. Bd. Clin. Social Work. Case mgr. Mt. Carmel Guild, Union City, N.J., 1982-84; coord. Jersey City Med. Ctr., 1985; clin. supr. La Casa, Newark, 1986-89; clinician II U. Medicine and Dentistry N.J., Newark, 1989-90; clin. dir. Proceed, Inc, Elizabeth, N.J., 1990—. Cons. Dover (N.J.) Bd. Edn., 1990-91, Union County Youth Svc., Linden, N.J., 1993-97; mem. Gov.'s Com. on Children's Planning, State of N.J., 1989-91; mem. Profl. Adv. Com. on Alcohol and Drug Abuse, N.J., 1990—; workshop presenter, 1992, 93. Named Person of Spl. Value, Mental Health Asn., Union County, 1999. Mem. Acad. Cert. Social Workers. Roman Catholic. Home: 112 Belgrade Ave Clifton NJ 07013-1004 Office: Proceed Inc 815 Elizabeth Ave Ste 202 Elizabeth NJ 07201-2788

PINGREE, DIANNE, sociologist, educator, psychotherapist; b. Dallas; BFA magna cum laude, So. Meth. U., 1976, MLA, 1989; PhD in Sociology, Tex. Woman's U., 1994. Diplomate Am. Psychotherapy Assn.; lic. marriage and family therapy assoc., cert. family life educator. Found., editor, pub. Tex. Woman Mag., 1977-80; pres. Tex. Woman Inc., 1980-85; owner, pres. Dianne Pingree & Assoc., 1985-88; pub. cons. Tex. Elite Publications, Dallas, 1988-89; mediator Ctr. for Dispute Resolution Denton County, 1991; grad. tchng. assoc. Tex. Woman's U., 1990-92; postgrad. clin. intern SW Family Inst., Dallas, 1993-94; therapist J&L Human Sys. Devel., Dallas, 1994-95; psychotherapist Child and Family Svc. Inc., Austin, 1995-96; cons. Austin, 1996-98; dir. Liaison Assocs. Profl. Devel. Consultants, 1998—2001; psychotherapist, assoc. clin. staff mem. Austin Acad. for Individual and Relationship Therapy, 2001—03; psychotherapist Capital Area Mental Health Ctr., 2003; pvt. practice, 2004—. Spkr. in field. Vol., vice chmn. Mental Health and Wellness Com. United Way Capital Area, 1998—99; vol., legal adv. Safeplace; mem. Leadership Austin, 2000—01. Recipient Matrix award Women in Comms., Women Helping Women award, Women's Ctr. Dallas, Dallas Press Club award. Mem.: Tex. Coun. Family Rels. (bd. dirs. 2004—), Nat. Coun. Family Rels., Am. Psychotherapy Assn. (diplomate), Tex. Assn. for Marriage and Family Therapy, Am. Assn. for Marriage and Family Therapy, Internat. Sociology Honor Soc., Alpha Kappa Delta (pres. TWU chpt. 1992). Office: PO Box 160277 Austin TX 78716-0277

PINGREE, ROCHELLE M. state legislator; b. Mpls., Apr. 2, 1955; m. Charles F. Pingree, 1975; chidlren: Hannah, Cecily, Asa. BA, Coll. of the Atlantic, 1976. Mem. Dist. 21 Maine Senate, 1993-95, mem. Dist. 12, 1995—, chmn. housing and devel. com., 1992-94, mem. maine resources and agrl. coms., 1992-96, majority leader, 1996—; co-chair Maine Econ. Growth Coun., 1997—. Mem. Eastern Maine Devel. Corp., Midcoast Devel. Corp., Econ. Devel. Incentive Commn. Mem. Inter-Island League, Grange, North Haven Devel. Corp. Office: PO Box 243 North Haven ME 04853-0243

PINK, (ALECIA MOORE), singer; b. Doylestown, Pa., Sept. 8, 1979; With Arista Records, 2001—. Singer: (albums) Can't Take Me Home, 2000, M!ssundaztood, 2001, Try This, 2003 (Grammy for best female rock performance for single Trouble, 2004); singer: (with Mya, Lil' Kim, Christina Aguilera) (songs) Lady Marmalade, 2001 (Grammy award Song Yr., MTV Video Music award, Song Yr.). Office: Box #390 5701 E Circle Dr Cicero NY 13039*

PINKARD, ANNE MERRICK, foundation administrator; b. Baltimore, Feb. 8, 1924; d. Robert Graff M.; m. Walter Devier Pinkard, Sept. 24, 1949 (dec. June, 1994); children: Walter D. Jr., Robert Merrick, Gregory Clyde, Peter McEvoy. BA, Goucher Coll., 1946; student, Cornell U., 1942—43; LLD (hon.), Johns Hopkins U., 1994. Bd. dirs. Citizens Planning and Housing, Balt., 1950-60; bd. dirs., sect. Soc. Md. Antiquities, Balt., 1955-63; pres. women's bd. Johns Hopkins Hosp., Balt., 1968-72, bd. dirs., 1976-92; pres. France Merrick Found., Balt., 1990—. Bd. dirs. Johns Hopkins U., Balt., 1972-94, trustee, 1972-94; trustee St. Mary's Sem. and U., 1974-80. Home: 613 Brightwood Club Dr Lutherville MD 21093-3632 Office: France Merrick Found 1122 Kenilworth Dr Baltimore MD 21204-2139

PINKETT-SMITH, JADA, actress; b. Balt., Sept. 18, 1971; m. Will Smith, 1997; 2 children. Appeared in films Menace II Society, 1993, The Inkwell, 1994, Jason's Lyric, 1994, A Low Down Dirty Shame, 1994, Tales From The Crypt Presents Demon Knight, 1995, The Nutty Professor, 1996, Set It Off, 1996, Scream 2, 1997, Woo, 1998, Return to Paradise, 1998, Bamboozled, 2000, Ali, 2001, The Matrix Reloaded, 2003.

PINKHAM, ELEANOR HUMPHREY, retired university librarian; b. Chgo., May 7, 1926; d. Edward Lemuel and Grace Eleanor (Cushing) Humphrey; m. James Hansen Pinkham, July 10, 1948; children: Laurie Sue, Carol Lynn. AB, Kalamazoo Coll., 1948; MS in Libr. Sci., Western Mich. U., 1967. Pub. svcs. libr. Kalamazoo Coll., 1967-68, asst. libr., 1969-70, libr. dir., 1971-93, ret., 1993. Vis. lectr. Western Mich. U. Sch. Librarianship, 1970-84; mem. adv. bd., 1977-81, also adv. bd. Inst. Cistercian Studies Libr., 1975-80. Alice Louise LeFevre scholar, 1967. Mem. ALA, AAUP, ACRL (chmn. coll. libr. sect. 1988-89), Mich. Libr. Assn. (pres. 1983-84, chmn. acad. divsn. 1977-78), Mich. Libr. Consortium (exec. coun. 1974-82, chmn. 1977-78, Mich. Libr. of Yr. 1986), OCLC Users Coun., Beta Phi Mu. Home: #103 4040 Greenleaf Cir Kalamazoo MI 49008-2582

PINKHAM, ROBIN REMICK, corporate financial executive; b. Bridgeport, Conn., May 5, 1944; d. Irving Grant and Theresa Helena (Busci) Pinkham. BA in English, Conn. Coll. Women, 1965; postgrad., NY Inst. Fin., 1965—66. Registered investment adv. With Paine, Webber, NYC, 1965—68, Scudder, Stevens & Clark, NYC, 1969—72, Wood Walker, NYC, 1972—73; asst. treas. pension fund investment mgr. Nat. Forge Co., NYC, 1973—87; 1st v.p. Smith Barney Shearson, 1987—. Vol. Lighthouse for the Blind, 1966—68. Mem.: Fin. Analysts Fedn., NY Soc. Security Analysts. Republican.

PINKINS, TONYA, actress; b. Chicago, May 30, 1962; 4 children. Attended, Northwestern U., Summer Theater Inst., Chicago, 1978; student, Carnegie Mellon U., 1980—81; BA, Columbia Coll., Chicago, 1996; student, Calif. Western Law Sch., San Diego. Private acting instr. Montclair School of Dance, 1993; visual arts instr., 6th to 8th grades LAUSD, 2000—01; private coach voice, music performance, acting, 2002. Playwriting com. Playwrights' Preview Prodn., 1986—88; instr. cold reading Univ. Calif., San Diego, 2000. Actor: (Broadway plays) Merrily We Roll Along, 1981, Jelly's Last Jam, 1992 (Tony award Best Featured Actress in a Musical, 1992, Drama Desk award Best Featured Actress in a Musical, 1992, Clarence Derwent award, 1992, Outer Critics Circle award Best Featured Actress in a Musical, 1993), Chronicle of a Death Foretold, 1995, Play On!, 1997 (Tony award nomination Best Actress in a Musical, 1997), The Wild Party, 2000, Caroline, Or Change, 2004— (Tony award nomination Best Actress in a Musical, 2004), (Off Broadway plays) Little Shop of Horrors, 1983, A...My Name Alice, 1985, Just Say No, 1988, Believin'/Psychoneurotic Fantasies, 1990, The Caucasian Chalk Circle, 1990, The Merry Wives of Windsor, 1994, The Vagina Monologues, 2000, The House of Flowers, 2003; (plays) Stealin', Joe Turner's Come and Gone, 1989, The Piano Lesson, 1989, Approximating Mother, 1991, No Niggers, No Jews, No Dogs, 2000, Thoroughly Modern Millie, 2000; (TV series) As the World Turns, 1983—86, University Hospital, 1994, All My Children, 1991—95, 2003—; (TV films) American Dream, 1981, Rage of Angels: The Story Continues, 1986, Strapped, 1993, Against Their Will: Women in Prison, 1994, (TV Guest appearances) Crime Story, 1986, The Cosby Show, 1990, Law & Order, 1990, The Guardian, 2002; (films) Beat Street, 1984, See No Evil, Hear No Evil, 1989, Above the Rim, 1994, Love Hurts, 2002; voice (audio books) The Women of Brewster Place, 1992, The Book of

Virtues I and II, 1993, The Moral Compass, 1995, Chocolate for a Woman's Soul, 1997, The Silent Cradle, 1998; singer: (albums) Live @ Joe's Pub. Achievements include co-founder of OPERATION Z: zero tolerance of violence against women and children. Office: Innovative Artist Talent and Lit Agy 1776 Broadway Ste 1810 New York NY 10019-2002*

PINN, VIVIAN W. pathologist, federal agency administrator; b. Halifax, Va., 1941; BA, Wellesley Coll., 1963; MD, U. Va., 1967. Intern in pathology Mass. Gen. Hosp., Boston, 1967-68, rschr. in pathology, 1968-70; asst. pathologist Tufts U. New England Med. Ctr. Hosp., 1970-77, pathologist, 1977-82; from asst. to assoc. prof. pathology Tufts U., 1971-82, asst. dean student affairs, 1974-82; prof., dept. chair pathology Howard U., 1982-91; first dir. Office Rsch. on Women's Health, NIH, Bethesda, Md., 1991—, assoc. dir. rsch. women's health, 1994—, dir. Office Women's Health Rsch. Office: NIH Office Rsch on Women's Health 9000 Rockville Pike Bldg 1 Rm 201 Bethesda MD 20892

PINSKER, PENNY COLLIAS (PANGEOTA PINSKER), television producer; b. Miami, Fla., Aug. 22, 1942; d. Theodore Peter and Agatha Madge (Bridgeman) Collias; m. Raymond Robert Elman, Feb. 19, 1962 (dec. 1967); 1 child, Alan; m. Lewis Harry Pinsker, Oct. 22, 1968. Grad. high sch., Miami, Fla. Operator So. Bell Telephone Co., Miami, 1960-67; asst. dir. pub. affairs Sta. WCKT-TV, Miami, 1968-70; dir. pub. affairs Sta. WOR-AM, N.Y.C., 1971-78; reporter documentary and consumer affairs Sta. WTFM, N.Y.C., 1978-81; dir. editorials and sta. svcs. Sta. WOR-TV, N.Y.C. and Secaucus, N.J., 1981-87; mgr. community affairs and spl. projects Sta. WWOR-TV, N.Y.C., Secaucus, N.J., 1987-91, dir. cmty. affairs and spl. projects Secaucus, 1991-2000, exec. prodr., pub. affairs programming and spl. projects, 1994—, dir. pub. affairs, 2000—02; cons. Penny Pinsker Comms., 2003—. Author, editor: (resource directory) Sta. WOR on Crime, 1982 (recipient George Washington Medal Honor Freedom Found., Emmy award for Outstanding Editorial, 1981), The Changing Family, 1982 (recipient Broadcast Media award San Francisco State U., Emmy nominated), A Child is Missing, 1983 (recipient Broadcast Media award San Francisco State U., Emmy nominated), Taking the High Out of High School, 1984 (recipient Broadcast Media award San Francisco State U, Angel award Religion Media, Bronze medal Internat. TV and Film Soc.); project mgr. A+ For Kids (Emmy award 1989, also Emmy nomination, named 12th nat. Point of Light, 1989), A+ For Kids. Project Director National, (Emmy nominations 1989-91; N.Y. Emmy award 1989, 1991; Nat. Edn. Assn. award 1991; Commr.'s award for child abuse prevention U.S. Dept. HHS 2003). Media advisor N.J. Crime Prevention Officers Assn.; mem. comm. com. N.J. affiliation Am. Heart Assn., Am. Cancer Soc.; bd. dirs. Queensboro Soc. Prevention Cruelty to Children, 1978-83, Hoboken Chamber Orch., 1989-90, N.J. Edn. Found., 1991-92; pub. mem. N.J. Gov.'s Task Force on Child Abuse and Neglect, 1988-97; mem. N.J. Task Force on Cild Abuse and Neglect, 1997—; trustee Assn. for Children of N.J., 1990—; mem. exec. coun. for comm. AARP-N.J., 2002—; mem. N.J. Coun. on Adult Edn. and Literacy, 1992-93; mem. exec. com. Partnership for a Drug Free N.J., 1997—; mem. N.J. Bus.-Edn. Summit, 1997-99, Am. Diabetes Assn. Nat. mktg. and Comm. Com., 2003-. Recipient Disting. Svc. award, N.J. Speech-Lang.-Hearing Assn., 1987, Cmty. Svc. award, Urban League Hudson County, 1986, Media award for achievement in preventing child abuse, N.J. Child Assault Prevention Project, 1993, Cmty. Svc. award, N.J. Gov.'s Conf. in Divesity, 1998, Seton Hall U., 2000, Triangle award for excellence in comms., March of Dimes, 2001, US Dept Health and Human Services Commissioner's award, NJ for Child Abuse Prevention, 2003. Mem.: AARP-N.J. (exec. coun. mem. comm. 2002—), NAFE, N.J. Broadcasters Assn. (bd. dirs. 1992—99, state legis. chair 1999—2001), Advt. Coun. N.J. (trustee 1986—2000), Nat. Broadcast Assn. Cmty. Affairs, Nat. Broadcast Editl. Assn. (bd. dirs. 1986—87), Meadowlands Regional C. of C. (bd. dirs. 1991—92), Leadership N.J. Grad. Orgn. Avocation: breeder thoroughbred horses. Home: Wintercrowd Farm 449 Kingwood-Locktown Rd Flemington NJ 08822 Office: 9 Broadcast Plz Secaucus NJ 07094-2913 Office Phone: 201-330-2148. E-mail: ppinsker@att.net.

PINSKY, JOANNA K. artist, artistic director; b. Bklyn., July 22, 1942; d. Arthur and Miriam (Kapit) Leff; m. Mark Allan Pinsky, Dec. 23, 1963; children: Seth, Jonathan, Lea. BFA, Cornell U., 1964. Co-artistic dir., founder Art Encounter, Evanston, Ill., 1978-94, artistic dir., 1994—. One-woman shows include Nancy Lurie Gallery, Chgo., 1978, 80, 82, Perimeter Gallery, Chgo., 1986, 90, 93, 96, 99, 2003, Air Gallery, N.Y.C., 1991, Shimer Artworks, 2002; group shows include Ill. State Mus., 1981, Charles Wustum Mus., Racine, Wis., 1988, Osaka (Japan) Triennial, 1990, Shidoni Galleries, Santa Fe, N.Mex., 1994, Art St. Louis, Mo., 1999, Koehnline Gallery, Des Plaines, Ill., 2000, N.E. U., Ill., 2001, Noyes Cultural Arts Ctr., Evinston, Ill., 2001, Chgo. (Ill.) Athenaeum, Schaumberg, Ill., 2002, 03, Coll. Lake County, Ill., 2003. Bd. dir. Ill. chpt. Nat. Women's Art Mus., 2002—. Grantee Ill. Arts Coun., 1980. Mem.: Nat. Women in the Arts, Inc., Chgo. (Ill.) Artists Coalition. Home: 1223 Grant St Evanston IL 60201-2614 Office Phone: 847-328-9222.

PINSON, ARTIE FRANCES, retired elementary school educator; b. Rusk, Tex., June 20, 1933; d. Tom and Minerva (McDuff) Neeley; m. Robert H. Pinson, Dec. 14, 1963 (div. Nov. 1967); 1 child, Deidre R. BA magna cum laude, Tex. Coll., 1953; postgrad., U. Tex., 1956, North Tex. U., 1958, 63, New Eng. Conservatory, 1955, 57, 59, 62, Tex. So. U., 1971-72; MEd, U. Houston, 1970. Music tchr. Bullock High Sch., LaRue, Tex., 1953-59; music tchr., 9th grade English tchr. Story High Sch., Palestine, Tex., 1959-64; 6th grade tchr. Turner Elem. Sch., Houston, 1964-66; 3d, 5th and 6th grade tchr. Kay Elem. Sch., Houston, 1966-70; 6th grade tchr. Pilgrim Elem. Sch., Houston, 1970-75; 3d to 6th grade gifted and talented math. tchr. Pleasantville Elem. Sch., Houston, 1975-79; kindergarten to 5th grade computer/math. tchr. Betsy Ross Elem. Sch., Houston, 1979—2003; ret., 2003. Instnl. coord.; lead tchr. math./sci. program Shell/Houston Ind. Sch. Dist., 1986-87, Say "Yes" program, 1988-89; math. tchr. summer potpourri St. Francis Xavier Cath. Ch., 1991; math. tchr. sci. and engring. awareness and coll. prep. program Tex. So. U., 1993-2003; participant Project Sail math. curriculum devel., Prairie View U., 1997-98, 99; presenter confs. in field; condr. tchr. tng. workshops.= Author computer software in field; contbr. articles to mags. Musician New Hope Bapt. Ch., Houston, 1991—, Sunday sch. tchr.; pianist Buckner Bapt. Haven Nursing Home, Houston, 1990-91, inspirational spkr.; mem. N.E. Concerned Citizens Civic League. Recipient Excellence in Math. Teaching award Exxon Corp., 1990. Mem. Assn. African Am. Math. Educators (Salute to Math. Tchrs. award 1991, treas. 1991-93, sec. 1993-95), Nat. Coun. Tchrs. Math., Tex. Coun. Tchrs. Math. (Excellence in Math. Tchg. award 1988), Houston Coun. Tchrs. of Math. (Excellence in Math. Tchg. award 1993), Heoines of Jericho, Palestine Negro Bus. and Profl. Women (charter mem.). Avocations: needlework, number puzzles, piano, photography, gardening. Home: 5524 Makeig St Houston TX 77026-4021 Office: Betsy Ross Elem Sch 2819 Bay St Houston TX 77026-3203 E-mail: artpin@msn.com.

PINTO, MARIE MALANIA, academic administrator, consultant; b. Tulare, Calif., Aug. 30, 1963; d. Joe Martin and Marie Inez Simoes; m. Joe John Pinto, Dec. 30, 1953; children: Jonathon Joseph, Jameson Jesse, Andrew Clayton, Jordan Michael. B in Bus. Mgmt., U. Phoenix, 2000, MBA, 2002; M in Ednl. Adminstrn., Calif. State U., Fresno, 2003. Cert. vocat. instr. Calif., 1996. Dept. mgr. Gottschalks, Visalia, Calif., 1984—91, tng. mgr., 1989—91, asst. buyer Fresno, 1991—94, asst. store mgr. Santa Maria, 1994—95; vocat. instr. Tulare Adult Sch., 1996—2002, work experience coord., 1999—, adminstrv. intern, 2003—. Staff devel. trainer, cons. Marie Pinto & Associates, Visalia, 1998—. Cons., vol. Visalia C. of C. Recipient School-to-Career Partnership award, Tulare County Office Edn., 2001. Mem.: Assn. Calif. Sch. Adminstrs., Calif. Tchrs. Assn. Democrat. Roman Catholic. Avocations: aerobics, travel, reading, entertaining, volunteer work. Home: 5548 W Vine Ct Visalia CA 93291 Office: Tulare Adult Sch 575 W Maple Tulare CA 93274 Personal E-mail: jjpmmp98@aol.com. E-mail: marie.pinto@tulare.k12.ca.us.

PINTO, ROSALIND, retired educator, civic volunteer; b. NYC; d. Barney and Jenny Abrams; m. Jesse E. Pinto (dec.); children: Francine, Jerry, Evelyn. BA in Polit. Sci. cum laude, Hunter Coll.; MA in Polit. Sci., History, Columbia U.; postgrad., Queens Coll., LaGuardia C.C. Lic. social studies tchr. jr. HS, NY, per diem substitute; cert. secondary sch. social studies grades 7-12, NY. Substitute tchr., 1966-69, 90, 91—; tchr. social studies I.S. 126Q, LI, NY, 1969-88, Jr. HS 217 Briarwood, NYC, 1988-89; ret., 1989; part-time cluster tchr. social studies and communication arts Pub. Sch. 140, Bronx, NY, 1990-92; substitute tchr. I.S. 227Q, 1992-93. Participant seminars and workshops. Author curriculum materials; contbr. study guide for regent's competency test, 1990; author numerous poems; contbr. articles to profl. jours. Enrollment asst. Insight Heart Team, 1989; vol. receptionist Whitney Mus., N.Y.C.; mem. com. on pub. transp. Cmty. Bd. 6, Queens, 1990—96, mem. com. on history, 1990—, chmn. beautification com., 1992—, mem. com. on planning and zoning, 1996—, mem. com. on environ. sanitation, 1999—; mem. Forest Hills Action League, 1999; advocate Census 2000 participation; active Gt. Smokies Song Chase Warren-Wilson Coll., NC, 1992; mem. Queens Hist. Soc., Forest Hills Van Ct. Homeowners Assn.; bd. dirs. Ctrl. Queens Hist. Soc.; past mem.. Rego Park Coalition Against Crime; mem. Forest Hills Civic Assn., 1996—97; vol. local polit. campaigns. Recipient Cert. Appreciation for participation, Dept. Probate Cmty. Svc. Project, 1993, award for participation in Make a Difference Day, 1994—95, award for projects, Beautification Com., 1995, Rosemary Gunning award, Queens Borough Pres. for Women's History month, 2000, Editor's Choice award, Best Poems and Poets of 2001, 2002, Poet of Merit award, Poetry Conv., 2002, 2003, Cert. Appreciation for joining graffiti cleanup, 112th Precinct Cmty. Coun., 2002—03, Cert. of Appreciation for help in Night Out Against Crime, 2002—03, 2003, Editor's Choice award, 2003, Fellow Mcpl. Art Soc. (hon. mention design 2000 award); mem. NAFE, Internat. Soc. Poets (life mem. adv. panel, Internat. Poet of Merit award 1993, 2000, Editor's Choice award 2001), NY Insight Alumni Assn., Columbia U. Grad. Sch. Arts and Scis. Alumni Assn., Hunter Coll. Alumni Assn., Robert F. Kennedy Dem. Assn. (bd. dir.), Ctr. for Sci. in the Pub. Interest. Avocations: poetry, reading, long distance walking, art shows, plays.

PINTON, CRISTINA COSTANTINA, artist, educator; b. Hartford, Conn., July 6, 1976; d. Giorgio Alberto and Margaret Bertha Pinton. BFA, Alfred U., N.Y., 2000; MS in Arts Edn., Mass. Coll. Art, Boston, 2003. Cert. tchr. grades 5-12 visual arts Mass. Youth worker, tchr. Bridge Youth Shelter, West Hartford, Conn., 1998—99; pre-GED tchr. Dept. Corrections, Enfield, Conn., 1999—2000; after-sch. art tchr. Conservatory Lab Charter Sch., South Boston, Mass., 2000; art dir. summer program Wediko Children's Svcs., Boston, 2001; intern Boston Arts Acad., 2001—02; art tchr., dept. co-chair Acad. of the Pacific Rim, Hyde Park, Mass., 2002—. Illustrator The Art of Rhetoric, 1996, Universal Right - Giambattista Tico, 2000; exhibitions include Apertures: Scenes Before the Eye, Agora Gallery, N.Y., 2001, Kennedy Gallery, Boston, 2001, Canton Artists Guild Gallery on the Green, Canton, Conn., 1999—2000. Mem.: Nat. Art Edn. Assn. Avocations: African dance, classical singing, piano.

PINTOZZI, CHESTALENE, librarian; b. Macomb, Okla., Apr. 4, 1947; d. Otis William and Edith Marie (Jordan) Bowerman; m. Nicola Francis Xavier Pintozzi, Aug. 2, 1967 (div.) Student, U. Okla., 1965-67; BA in English, No. Ill. U., 1969; MLS, U. Tex., 1981. Geology libr. U. Tex., Austin, 1982-84; environ. libr., Ann Marbut Environ. Libr. Sarasota (Fla.) County Pub. Libr. Sys., 1985-87; temporary reference libr. Sci.-Engring. Libr. U. Ariz., Tucson, 1989-90, reference libr. Sci.-Engring. Libr. Tuscon, 1990—. Mem. ALA (Whitney-Carnegie award 1993), Beta Phi Mu, Phi Kappa Phi. Democrat. Office: U Ariz Bldg 54 Rm 216 Tucson AZ 85720

PIOTROWSKI, NANCY ANN, psychological scientist; b. Jersey City, May 8, 1963; d. Anthony John Piotrowski. BA in Psychology, Rice U., 1985; MA in Clin. Psychology, U. Houston, 1989, PhD in Clin. Psychology, 1992. Rsch. technician, Health Sci. Ctr. U. Tex., Houston, 1986-88; rsch. asst., project dir., psychiatry Baylor Coll. Medicine, Houston, 1988-92; practicum trainee, psychology svc. Houston VA Med. Ctr., 1988-89, predoctoral intern, psychology svc., 1990-91; rsch. asst., psychology U. Houston, 1989-90; postdoctoral fellow U. Calif., San Francisco, 1992-94, Berkeley, 1994-96, assoc. scientist alcohol rsch. group, 1994—; core faculty and interim chair addiction psychology Capella U., Mpls., 1999—; adminstrv. program dir. Japan MA Clin. Psychology Program Alliant Internat. U., CSPP, San Francisco, 2002—. Reviewer Jour. Health Psychology, 1992—, Jour. Cmty. Psychology, 1993—, Cognitive Therapy and Rsch., 1994—, Addiction, 1995—. Vol. counselor, trainer, speaker, Crisis Intervention Hotline, Inc., Houston, 1983-92; vol. telephone counselor, Friendship Line, San Francisco, 1993-94; active Sierra Club, 1983—. NIAAA grantee, 1997—. Mem. APA (mem.-at-large divsn. 28, 1999-2002, divsn.50, 2002-05), ACLU, Assn. for the Advancement of Behavior Therapy. Avocations: hiking, music, travel, collecting incense. Office: 3450 Geary Blvd Ste 107 San Francisco CA 94118

PIPCHICK, MARGARET HOPKINS, advance practice nurse, marriage and family therapist; m. Robert Pipchick; children: Christine, Kevin. BSN, Seton Hall U., 1968; MA, NYU, 1974; grad., Blanton Peale Grad. Inst., N.Y.C., 1981; PhD, The Union Inst., 2001. Various staff positions hosps., N.Y./N.J.; teaching asst. Seton Hall U., South Orange, N.J., 1971-72; staff therapist, faculty Blanton-Peale Counseling Ctr., Cranford, N.J., 1974-90; pvt. practice individual, couple and family therapy Cranford, 1981—. Adj. faculty Fairleigh Dickenson U., Teaneck, N.J., 1989-93, Kean Coll., 1994, 95. Drew U., 2003. Contbr. chpt. to Founds. Psychiat. Mental Health Nursing. Mem. ANA, N.J. State Nurses Assn., Am. Assn. Marriage and Family Therapists, Soc. Advanced Practice Psychiatric Nurses (pres.), Sigma Theta Tau.

PIPER, ADRIAN MARGARET SMITH, philosopher, artist, educator; b. N.Y.C., Sept. 20, 1948; d. Daniel Robert and Olive Xavier (Smith) P.; m. Jeffrey Ernest Evans, June 27, 1982 (div. 1987). AA, Sch. Visual Arts, 1969; BA in Philosophy, CCNY, 1974; MA, Harvard U., 1977, PhD, 1981; student, U. Heidelberg, Germany, 1977-78; LHD (hon.), Calif. Inst. Arts, 1992, Mass. Coll. Art, 1994. Asst. prof. U. Mich., Ann Arbor, 1979-86; Mellon rsch. fellow Stanford (Calif.) U., 1982-84; assoc. prof. Georgetown U., Washington, 1986-88, U. Calif., San Diego, 1988; prof. philosophy Wellesley (Mass.) Coll., 1990—. Disting. scholar Getty Rsch. Inst., 1998—; speaker, lectr. on both philosophy and art. Artist: one-woman exhbns. include N.Y. Cultural Ctr., N.Y.C., 1971, Montclair (N.J.) State Coll., 1976, Wadsworth Atheneum, Hartford, Conn., 1980, Nexus COntemporary Art Ctr., Atlanta, 1987, The Alternative Mus., N.Y.C., 1987, Goldie Paley Gallery, Phila., 1989, Power Plant Gallery, Toronto, 1990, Lowe Art Mus., Coral Gables, Fla., 1990-91, Santa Monica (Calif.) Mus. Contemporary Art, 1991, John Weber Gallery, N.Y.C., 1989, 90, 91, 92, Whitney Mus. Am. Art, N.Y.C., 1990, Hirschorn Mus., Washington, 1991, Ikon Gallery, Birmingham, Eng., 1991, Cornerhouse, Manchester, Eng., 1992, Cartwright Hall, Bradford, Eng., 1992, Kunstverein, Munich, Germany, 1992, Indpls. Ctr. Contemporary Art, 1992, Manasterio de Santa Clara, Moguer, Spain, 1992, Grey Art Gallery, N.Y.C., 1992, Paula Cooper Art Galler, 1992, 94; group exhbns. include Paula Cooper Gallery, 1969, Dwan Gallery, N.Y.C., 1969, 70, Seattle Art Mus., 1969, Stadtisches Mus., Leverkusen, Germany, 1969, Kunsthalle Berne, Berne, Switzerland, 1969, N.Y. Cultural Ctr., 1970, Allen Mus., Oberlin, Ohio, 1970, Mus. Modern Art, N.Y.C., 1970, 88, 91, Musee d'Art Moderne, Paris, 1971, 77, 89, Inhibodress Gallery, New South Wales, Australia, 1972, Calif. Inst. Arts, Valencia, 1973, Samuel S. Fleischer Art Meml., Phila., 1974, Mus. Contemporary Art, Chgo., 1975, Newberger Mus., Purchase, N.Y., 1978, Mass. Coll. Art, Boston, 1979, Artemesia Gallery, Chgo., 1979, A.I.R. Gallery, N.Y.C., 1980, Inst. Contemporary Arts, London, 1980, The New Mus., N.Y.C., 1981, 83, 85, Kenkeleba Gallery, N.Y.C., 1983, The Studio Mus. Harlem, N.Y.C., 1985, 89, Mus. Moderner Kunst, Vienna, Austria, 1985, Intar Gallery, N.Y.C., 1988, Whitney Mus. Downtown, N.Y.C., 1988, Art Gallery Ont., Toronto, 1988, Long Beach (Calif.) Art Mus., 1989, Simon Watson Gallery, N.Y.C., 1990, Feigen Gallery, Chgo., 1990, Barbara Krakow Gallery, Boston, 1990, Milw. Art Mus., 1990, Contemporary Arts Ctr., Houston, 1991, John Weber Gallery, 1991, Anne Plumb Gallery, N.Y.C., 1991, Hirschorn Mus., 1991, The Albuquerque Mus. Art, 1991, The Toledo Mus. Art, 1991, Denver Art Mus., Fukui Fine Arts Mus., Fukyui-ken, Japan, 1992-93, N.J. State Mus., Trenton, 1992-93, Philippe Staib Gallery, N.Y.C., 1992, New Loom House, London, 1992, Espace-Lyonnais D'Art Contemporain, Lyon, France, 1993, Am. Acad. Inst. Arts and Letters, N.Y.C., 1993; permanent collections include Met. Mus. Art, Whitney Mus., L.A. Mus. Contemporary Art, San Francisco Mus. Modern Art, The Bklyn. Mus., Denver Art Mus., Kunstmuseum Berne, Musee d'Art Moderne, The Mus. Contemporary Art, Chgo., The Wadsworth Atheneum, Met. Mus. Art; art performances include RISD, 1973, The Whitney Mus. Am. Art, 1975, Kurfurstendamm, Berlin, 1977, Hauptstrasse, Heidelburg, Germany, 1978, Allen Meml. Mus., Oberlin, Ohio, 1980, Contemporary Art Inst. Detroit, 1980, San Francisco Art Inst., 1985, Calif. Inst. Art, 1984, The Studio Mus. Harlem, 1988; performances on video, 1987—; contbr. articles to profl. jours. Recipient N.Y. State Coun. on Arts award, 1989, Visual Arts award, 1990, Skowhegan medal for sculptural installation, 1995, Dance Theatre Workshop award for New Genres, 2000; NEH Travel fellow, 1979, NEA Visual Artists' fellow, 1979, 82, Andrew Mellon Postdoctoral fellow, 1982-84, Woodrow Wilson Internat. Scholars fellow, 1988-89, Guggenheim Meml. fellow, 1989, nonresident fellow N.Y. Inst. for Humanities, NYU, 1996—; NEA Artists Forums grantee, 1987; rsch. fellowship NEH, 1998, Getty Rsch. Inst. Disting. scholarship, 1998—, Internat. Forschungszentrum Kulturwissenschaften fellow Vienna. Mem. AAUP, Am. Philos. Assn. (mem. ea. divsn.), Am. Soc. Polit. and Legal Philosophy, N.Am. Kant. Soc. Avocations: medieval and renaissance music, fiction, poetry, yoga, German. Office: Wellesley Coll 106 Central St Wellesley MA 02481-8268

PIPER, J. K. See GILES, KATHARINE EMILY

PIPER, KATHLEEN, former political organization administrator; b. Ida County, Iowa; d. Pat and Rita Donahey McGuire; m. James Carl Piper, 1971; 2 children. Student, U. Iowa, Morningside Coll., Mt. Marty Coll. Co-owner Pied Piper Flower Shop, Yankton, S.D., 1986; vice chair Yankton County Dem. Com., 1980-95, state ctrl. committeewoman, 1995—; commr. Yankton County, 1986—, chair, 1996; state ctrl. com. S.D. Dem. Party, 1989-99, exec. bd., 1992-99, chairwoman, 1996-99. Mem. health care adv. com. Senator Tom Daschle, 1991—. Del. Nat. Dem. Conv., N.Y.C., 1992; mem. Gold adv. coun. appointed by Gov., 1993-95; participant Pres. Clinton and Hillary Rodham-Clinton's Health Care Inbitiative Rev., White House, 1993, Gt. Plains Rural Health Summit, 1994, Pres., Clinton and SBA Chief Roundtable Discussion Small Bus. and Health Care Reform, Washington, 1994; appointed del. White House Conf. Small Bus., 1994. Recipient Woman of Yr. award Ed Yankton Daily Press and Dakota, 1986, Emerging Leader for S.D. award Sioux Falls Argus Leader, 1990. Mem. S.D. County Commr. Assn. (exec. bd. 1992-94). Roman Catholic. Home: PO Box 737 Sioux Falls SD 57101-0737 Office: PO Box 43 Yankton SD 57078-0043

PIPER, MARGARITA SHERERTZ, retired school system administrator; b. Petersburg, Va., Dec. 20, 1926; d. Guy Lucas and Olga Doan (Akers) Sherertz; m. Glenn Clair Piper, Feb. 3, 1950; children: Mark Stephen, Susan Leslie Piper Weathersbee. BA in Edn., Mary Washington Coll U. Va., Fredericksburg, 1948; MEd, U. Va., 1973, EdS, 1976. Svc. rep. C&P Telephone, Washington, 1948-55, adminstrv. asst., 1955-56, svc. supr., 1956-62; tchr. Culpeper (Va.) County Pub. Schs., 1970-75, reading lab dir., 1975-80; asst. prin. Rappahannock (Va.) County Pub. Schs., 1980-81, prin., 1981-88, dir. pupil pers., spl. programs, 1988-95; ret., 1995. Chair PD 9 regional transition adv. bd. Culpeper, Fauquier, Madison, Orange and Rappahannock Counties, Va., 1991-94; vice chair Family Assessment and Planning Team, Washington, 1992-95. Recipient Va. Gov. Schs. Commendation cert. Commonwealth of Va., 1989-93. Mem. NEA, Va. Edn. Assn., Va. Coun. Adminstrs. Spl. Edn., Va. Assn. Edn. for Gifted, Rappahannock Edn. Assn. Democrat. Methodist. Avocations: creative writing, music, walking, crosstitch, knitting.

PIPER, ODESSA, chef; m. Terry Theise. Chef L'Etoile Restaurant, Madison, Wis., 1976—. Contbr. Wis. Pub. Radio, NPR; cons. Ctr. for Integrated Agrl. Sys., U. Wis., Madison. Contbr. Fine Cooking, Food & Wine, Bon Appetit, Eating Well, Wine Spectator, Sierra. Recipient award, James Beard Found., 2001. Mem.: Women Chefs and Restauranteurs (mem. scholarship com.), Chefs Collaborative 2000 (bd. dirs.). Office: L'Etoile Restaurant 25 N Pinckney Madison WI 53711

PIPES, SALLY C. think-tank executive; Asst. dir. Fraser Inst., Vancouver, B.C., Can.; pres., CEO Pacific Rsch. Inst. for Pub. Policy, San Francisco. Co-author (with Spencer Star): Income and Taxation in Canada, (with Michael Walker) 7 editions of Tax Facts; has appeared nationally on TV programs such as 20/20 and Politically Incorrect, Dateline, Inside Politics and PBS's Think Tank; regularly asked to comment on timely issues by radio and print journalists; opinion editls. have been published in various newspapers including San Francisco Chronicle, L.A. Times, Investor's Business Daily, L.A. Daily News, The Orange County Register; writes a bi-monthly column in Chief Executive mag. Bd. dirs. Fin. Instns. Commn. (B.C.), 1982— (chmn. 1989—); mem. Vancouver City Planning Commn.; trustee St. Luke's Hosp. Found. in San Francisco; bd. dirs. Ind. Women's Forum; mem. bd. advisors Western Jour. Ctr. and Citizens for Term Limits, San Francisco Lawyers chpt. of the Federalist Soc.; commr. Calif. Commn. on Transp. Investment, 1996; bd. govs. Donner-Can. Found. Mem. Mont Pelerin Soc., Nat. Assn. Bus. Economists, Can. Assn. for Bus. Econs. (pres. 2 terms), Assn. Profl. Economists of B.C. Office: Pacific Rsch Inst Pub Policy 755 Sansome St Ste 450 San Francisco CA 94111-1709

PIPKIN, MARY MARGARET, artist; b. San Angelo, Tex., Mar. 17, 1951; d. Raymond G. and Lillie Marie S. (Billie) Pipkin; m. Robert Boisture; children: Will, John, Jamie. BA U. Tex., MA U. Tex. One-woman shows include Addison Tate Gallery, Washington, Zigler Mus., Jennings, La., 2002, Louisburg (NC) Coll., 2003, Art Sta., Stone Mountain, Ga., 2003, Anderson (Ind.) Art Ctr., Ind., 2003, Mus. S.W., Midland, Tex., 2003, exhibitions include White House, Washington.

PIRKLE, MÄNYA HIGDON, artist, craftsman; b. Norris, Tenn., July 3, 1935; d. Samuel Lyle and Mertie Johnson Higdon; m. John Ward Pirkle, Nov. 26, 1967; 1 child, Jonathan Ward ; m. William Bullard Monroe, June 18, 1956 (div. 1962); children: Mänette Monroe Frank, Lydia Leigh Monroe Krieps. Illustrator Am. Mus. of Atomic Energy, Oak Ridge, Tenn., 1962, Am. Mus. of Sci. Energy, Oak Ridge, Tenn., 1974; owner/operator Mänya Art & Graft Gallery, Gatlinburg, Tenn., 1979—81, Oak Ridge, Tenn., 1981—84; instr. Univ. Tenn., Knoxville, Tenn., 1987—88; owner/operator Mänya Collection Art Gallery, Knoxville, Tenn., 1988—92. Exhibitions include clay sculpture, Am. Crafts Coun., 2001, drawings, Knoxville Mus. of Art, 2002. Bd. dirs. Appalacian Ballet. Mem.: Knoxville Art Mkt., Knoxville Art Coun., Knoxville Mus. of Art, Southern Highland Handcraft Guild, Foothills Craft Guild (charter mem., standard com.). Avocations: sewing, gardening, crafts, painting, photography. Home: 12312 Bluffshore Dr Knoxville TN 37922

PIROZZOLI, HEATHER JO, food company professional; b. Bridgeport, Conn., June 8, 1971; d. Charles Louis and Josephine Ann Pirozzoli. BS, U. Fla., 1992, MS, 1995. Lic. real estate salesperson, Fla. Instr., interim safety specialist U. Fla., Gainesville, 1993-95; safety and tng. supr. Tyson Foods, Jacksonville, Fla., 1995-97, complex safety mgr. Union City, Tenn., 1997-98, area safety mgr. Springdale, Ark., 1998-2000, team leader, 2000— Cons. Nat. Ag Safety Database (Conceptual Arts), Gainesville, 1996. Author article and instructional videos. Bd. dirs. ARC, Union City, 1997-98; vol. Habitat for Humanity, Rogers, Ark., 1998-2000; instr. first aid and CPR, Fla., Tenn., Ark., 1994-2000. Workforce Tng. grantee, 1997. Mem. Am. Soc. Safety Engrs. (editor Ark. chpt. newsletter, profl.), Nat. Inst. for Farm Safety, Alpha Zeta. Avocations: antiques, golf. Office: Tyson Foods PO Box 2020 Springdale AR 72765-2020 E-mail: heather.pirozzoli@tyson.com.

PIRSCH, CAROL MCBRIDE, county official, former state senator, community relations manager; b. Omaha, Dec. 27, 1936; d. Lyle Erwin and Hilfrie Louise (Lebeck) McBride; m. Allen I. Pirsch, Mar. 28, 1954 (dec.); children: Pennie Elizabeth, Pamela Elaine, Patrice Eileen, Phyllis Erika, Peter Allen, Perry Andrew. Student, U. Miami, Oxford, Ohio, U. Nebr., Omaha. Former mem. data processing staff Omaha Pub. Schs.; former mem. wage practices dept. Western Electric Co., Omaha; former legal sec. Omaha; former office mgr. Pirsch Food Brokerage Co., Inc., Omaha; former employment supr., mgr. pub. policy U.S. West Comm., Omaha; mem. Nebr. Senate, 1979-97; commr. Douglas County, 1997—, chair, 1999, 2004, 2004, vice chair, 2001, 2003. Founder, 1st pres., bd. dirs. Nebr. Coalition for Victims of Crime (Lifetime award 2002); bd. dirs. Centris Fed. Credit Union, 1st v.p., 2003—. Mem. Omaha Douglas County Bldg. Commn., 1997-2003, sec., 2000-03; cmty. advisor Omaha Jr. League. Recipient Golden Elephant award, Kuhle award, 1986, Nebr. Coalition for Victims of Crime, Outstanding Legis. Efforts award YWCA, 1989, Breaking the Rule of Thumb award Nebr. Domestic Violence Sexual Assault Coalition, 1989, Cert. of Appreciation award U.S. Dept. Justice, 1988, Partnership award N.E. Credit Union League, 1995, Wings award LWV Greater Omaha, 1995, N.E. VFW Spl. Recognition award for Exceptional Svc., 1995, Victim Rights Week Recognition award, 1995, Victim Adv. Lifetime Achievement award, 2002; Crime Victims Adv. award Nebr. Atty. Gen., 1995. Mem. VASA, Nat. Orgn. Victim Assistance (Outstanding Legis. Leadership award 1981), Freedom Found., Tangier Women's Aux., Footprinters Internat. (bd. dirs., sec.), Douglas County Hist. Soc., Nebr. Taxpayers Assn., Keystone Citizen Patrol (Comm. Network of Citizen Patrols award, 1995), Audubon Soc., N.W. Cmty. Club, Keystone Task Force (Keystoner of the month, 1987, Queen Keystone, 2002), Benson Rep. Women's Club. Office: Legis Chambers 2 Douglas County Civic Ctr Omaha NE 68102 E-mail: cpirsch@aol.com.

PIRTLE, LAURIE LEE, women's university basketball coach; b. Columbus, Ohio, Jan. 1, 1958; BS in Phys. Edn., Ohio State U., 1980. Asst. coach girl's basketball William Fisher H.S., Lancaster, Ohio, 1981-82; coach women's basketball Capital U., Columbus, Ohio, 1982-86, U. Cin., 1986—. Named Coach of Yr. Dist.III Ohio Athletic Commn. and Converse III, 1985-86, Ohio Intercoll. Coaches Assn., 1985, Metro Conf., 1989, Conf. USA, 1999, Leading Woman in Cin., 2000. Mem. Women's Basketball Coaches Assn., Greater Cin. and No. Ky., Women's Sports Assn. (mem. com.). Office: U Cin Athletics Dept PO Box 210021 Cincinnati OH 45221-0021

PISCATELLI, NANCY MARIE, secondary school educator; b. Boston, Feb. 11, 1953; d. Joseph Murphy and Eleanor Elizabeth (Jeffers) Kelley; m. Thomas George Piscatelli, Apr. 17, 1976; 1 child, Thomas Joseph. BS, Bridgewater State Coll., 1975, MEd, 1979, Boston Coll., 1977; EdD, Northeastern U., 1989. Lead tchr. Boston Pub. Schs., 1975—; cons. Boston Plan for Excellence in the Pub. Schs., 1997; dir. Latin Sch. summer test preparation program, 2003—. Cons. Tchrs. Corp. Network, 1979-80. Author/editor: (handbook) The Paraprofessional Handbook, 1979; contbr. articles to profl. jours. Campaign worker Dem. Com., Quincy, Mass., 1975—; active sch. vol. pet project of Mrs. George Bush. Mem. Am. Fedn. Tchrs., Nat. Coun. Tchrs. Math., Internat. Reading Assn., Ea. Educators Rsch. Assn., Boston Tchrs. Union, MassCue. Roman Catholic. Avocations: literature, traveling. Home: Pheasant Hill 10 Chickadee Dr Norfolk MA 02056-1741 Office: Boston Pub Schs 26 Court St Boston MA 02108-2505

PISCIOTTA, VIVIAN VIRGINIA, psychotherapist; b. Chgo., Dec. 7, 1929; d. Vito and Mary Lamia; m. Vincent Diago Pisciotta, Apr. 1, 1951; children: E. Christopher, Vittorio, V. Charles, Mary A. Pisciotta Higley, Thomas Sansone. BA in Clin. Psychology, Antioch U., 1974; MSW, George Williams Coll., 1984; postgrad., Erickson Inst. of No. Ill., 1990. Lic. clin. social worker, Ill.; diplomate in clin. social work. Short-term therapist Woman Line, Dayton, Ohio, 1976-79; psychotherapist Cicero (Ill.) Family Svcs., 1982-83, Maywood (Ill.) - Proviso Family Svcs., 1983-84, Maple Ave. Med. Ctr., Brookfield, Ill., 1985-88, Met. Med. Clinic, Naperville, Ill., 1986-88; allied staff Riveredge Psychiat. Hosp., Forest Park, Ill., 1986-97; psychotherapist, pvt. practice Oakbrook, Ill., 1988-96; psychotherapist, co-founder Archer Austin Counseling Ctr., Chgo., 1988-89; founder Archer Counseling Ctr., Chgo., 1989-97; psychotherapist Columbia Hospitals' Columbia Riveredge Hosp., Forest Park, Ill., 1997; allied staff Linden Oaks Psychiat. Hosp., Naperville, 1990-97; psychotherapist pvt. practice, 1988—; founder Archer Ctr., Ariz., 1997-99. Substitute tchr. Chgo. Pub. High Sch., 1981; instr. Ariz. State U. Livelong Learning Acad., 2002-03. Author treatment prog., workshops in field. Co-founder Co-op Nursery Sch., Rockford, Ill., 1956; leader Great Books of the Western World series, Piqua, Ohio, 1977, Rockford, 1960-65; leader Girl Scouts U.S., St. Bridget Sch., Rockford, 1968-71. Mem. Assn. Labor-Mgmt. and Cons. on Alcoholism, Soc. Clin. Exptl. Hypnosis, Nat. Assn. Social Workers, Acad. Cert. Social Workers, Nat. Social Work Register (cert.), Antioch Univ. Alumnus Assn. Rockford Coll. Alumnae Orgn. (newsletter contbr. 1972-73), Soc. for Clin. and Exptl. Hypnosis (assoc. mem.), Internat. Soc. for Clin. and Exptl. Hypnosis (assoc. mem.). instr., Ariz. State U. West, Life Long Learning Acad., 2002-03. Republican. Roman Catholic. Avocations: reading, travel, study/research, music, religion. Office Phone: 623-810-9517. E-mail: arch3456@aol.com.

PISCITELLI, NANCY L. retired special education educator; children: Gina, Joanne, John. BS, Pacific Oaks Coll., 1965, MA, 1978. Coord. tchr. Head Start Pasadena Cmty. Found., Calif., 1965—66; presch. tchr. Villa Esperanza, Pasadena, 1966—67, dir. infant ctr. devel., 1966—80, program dir., 1980—89. Bd. dirs. Villa Esperanza Svcs., Pasadena, 2003—. Chief fin. officer Bone Cancer Internat., Newbury Park, Calif. Home: 6072 N Shadycreek Dr Agoura Hills CA 91301

PISKOR, CHRYSTAL LEA, service company owner; b. San Diego, Feb. 1, 1963; d. Gilbert E. Chostner and Sheila I. Radley. BA, Lindenwood Coll., 1984. Cert. assoc. contract mgr. Sr. estimator Teledyne Ryan Aero., San Diego, 1985-89; sr. contract pricing adminstr. Sundstrand Power Systems, San Diego, 1989-91, sr. supplier cost analyst, 1991-93; from contracts adminstr. to contracts mgr. Photon Rsch. Assocs., Inc., San Diego, 1993-98, dir. contracts, 1998-99; owner El Cajon Sidekicks Martial Arts Acad., 1997-98; sr. contract closeout adminstr., contract closeout mgr. Ball Sys. Engrng. Ops., San Diego, 1999—2001; sr. contract rep. Sci. Applications Internat. Corp., 2001—03, dep. group contracts dir., 2003—04, contracts mgr., 2004—. Cons. CLC Enterprises, San Diego, 1992—97; ptnr. Ecosense LLC, 1999—2001. Advisor Jr. Achievement, San Diego, 1985. Mem. Soc. Cost Estimating and Analysis (dir. edn. 1987, 88, v.p. 1989, treas. 1990), Nat. Contract Mgmt. Assn., Nat. Mgmt. Assn. (co-chair scholarship fund 1985). Republican. Seventh-day Adventist. Avocations: horseback riding, cycling, skiing, reading, taekwondo instr. (2d degree black belt). Office: Sci Applications Internat Corp 16701 W Bernardo Dr San Diego CA 92127

PISKOTI, CAROL LEE, art educator; b. Stockton, Calif., Jan. 13, 1949; d. Kyman and Clara Lee; m. James Piskoti, June 16, 1984. BA in Fine Art, Calif. State U. Stanislaw, Turlock, 1971. Tchg. credential Calif. Tchr. Sacramento City Sch. Dist., 1973—. Facilitator, staff Calif. Consortium for Arts Edn., Sacramento, 2002—03. Recipient Hon. Svc. award, PTA-John F. Kennedy H.S., 1989. Mem.: Crocker Art Mus. (mem. tchg. adv. bd. 2002—), Nat. Art Edn. Assn., Calif. Art Edn. Assn. (chmn. vols. 2001, chair youth art month 2004, Award of Merit 2001). Avocations: painting, drawing. Office: John F Kennedy HS 6715 Gloria Dr Sacramento CA 95831

PISTERZI, CANDY, special education educator; b. Moline, Ill., Nov. 15, 1945; d. Homer Noel Jackson and Gladys L. Jackson-Meyer; m. Mike Pisterzi, June 1, 1968; children: Maria Ann, John Anthony, Laura Elaine. BA, Ill. State U., 1967; MA, Columbia U., 1971. Spl. edn. tchr. Homer (Ill.) Sch. Sys., 1967—68, Poughkeepsie (N.Y.) City Sch. Sys., 1968—70, Dutchess County Bd. Coop. Ednl. Svcs., Poughkeepsie, 1971—72, 1989—, Cardinal Hayes Sch., Millbrook, NY, 1986—89. Grantee, Dutchess County BOCES, 1994, 2003. Mem.: Coun. for Exceptional Children, Crochet Guild, Pi State Delta Kappa Gamma (state nominations com. 2003—), Delta Kappa Gamma (pres. Alpha Zeta chpt. 2001—). Avocations: sewing, crocheting, reading, travel. Office: Dutchess County BOCES 5 BOCES Rd Poughkeepsie NY 12601

PITCHER, SUSAN INGRID, art dealer; b. Gloucestershire, Eng., Feb. 7, 1967; d. Clive Anthony and Judith (Chandler) P. BA in Art History, Kent (Ohio) State U., 1991. Gallery asst., slide libr. Sch. of Art Kent State U., 1989-91; prodn. artist Line Art Unltd., Chagrin Falls, Ohio, 1992; gallery dir. Michael Thompson Gallery, San Francisco, 1992-95; mktg. assoc. NRG Studio, San Francisco, 1995—; art cons. Mus. West, San Francisco, 1995—96; prin., owner Chandler Gallery, 2003—. Asst. coord. Camp Okizu Art Auction, San Francisco, 1995; mem. Cartoon Art Mus., San Francisco; vol. Sportsbridge. Mem. Sierra Club. Avocations: hiking, camping, dog walking.

PITERNICK, ANNE BREARLEY, librarian, educator; b. Blackburn, Eng., Oct. 13, 1926; emigrated to Can., 1956, naturalized, 1965; d. Walter and Ellen (Harris) Clayton; m. Neil Brearley, 1956 (div. 1971); m. George Piternick, May 6, 1971. BA, U. Manchester (Eng.), 1948, F.L.A., 1983. Mem. library staff U. B.C., Vancouver, Can., 1956-66, head sci. div., 1960-61, head social scis. div., 1965-66, prof. Sch. Library, Archival and Info. Studies, 1966-91, prof. emerita, 1991—, assoc. dean Faculty of Arts, 1985-90. Mem. Nat. Com. Bibliog. Svcs. Can., 1975-80, chmn. com. on bibliography and info. services for social scis. and humanities, 1981-84; mem. adv. acad. panel Social Scis. and Humanities Research Council, 1981-84; mem. adv. bd. Nat. Libr. Can., 1978-84; mem. Nat. Adv. Com. Culture Stats., 1985-90; organizer Confs. on Can. Bibliography, 1974, 81; pres. Can. Assn. Spl. Librs. Info. Svcs., 1969-70, Can. Libr. Assn., 1976-77. Author articles on electronic info. svcs. and scholarly communication. Bd. dirs. Vancouver Friends of Chamber Music, 2001—. Recipient Queen's Silver Jubilee medal, 1977, award for Spl. Librarianship Can. Assn. Spl. Librs. and Info. Svcs., 1987, 75th Anniversary medal U.B.C., 1990, Can. 125 medal, 1993; fellow Coun. on Libr. Resources, 1980. Mem. Assn. Profs. Emeriti U. B.C. (pres. 2003-04). Home: 1849 W 63rd Ave Vancouver BC Canada V6P 2H9 E-mail: annebp@interchange.ubc.ca.

PITILLI, LORETTA ANN, special education educator; b. Bklyn., Oct. 7, 1948; d. Dominick LoBrutto and Nancy Liotta; m. Lawrence Pitilli, Aug. 18, 1974 (div. June 2003); children: James, Brian, Darren, Thomas, Alexander. BA cum laude, L.I. U., 1972; MA, NYU, 1976. Tchr. spl. edn. Crossroads Acad., Bklyn., 1974—75, Buckingham Sch., 1969—74; vocat. counselor pvt. practice, 1990—95, tchr. home sch., 1996—2002; learning specialist ADD learning disabled St. Cecliia Sch., 2002—03, DGK Sch., 2003—. Author children's stories. Mem.: Optimists CLub L.I. U. Avocations: drawing, painting, sculpting, violin. Office Phone: 917-923-8054. E-mail: justbelp33@yahoo.com.

PITMAN, URSULA WALL, curator, educator; d. Thomas Joseph and Emily Hruby Wall; m. Lawrence Clymer Pitman, Aug. 19, 1961 (dec. Jan. 1996). BA in History, Northeastern U., 1968, BS in Art History, 1983; MA in History, Boston Coll., 1971, PhD in History, 1978. Cert. history tchr., IBM sys. svc. rep. Computer demonstrator, lectr. IBM, N.Y.C., 1956—59, data processing instr. Boston, 1959—61; art educator Fitchburg (Mass.) Art Mus., 1978—83, curator 13 ednl. exhbns., 1979—89, dir./instr. docent program, 1982—2000, developer in-mus. and outreach programs for Ctrl. Mass., 1982—2000, grant writer, 1982—2000. Advisor on fundraising activities Fitchburg (Mass.) Art Mus., 1978—2000, dir. funded lectr. series, 1980—90, mem. edn. com., 1983—2000; art lectr. Jr. League Boston Sch. Program, Lincoln, Mass., 1976—77; co-dir. Tchrs. Workshop DeCordova Mus., Lincoln, 1980; grant writer Mass. Cultural Coun., Boston, 1986—89, Inst. Mus./Libr. Svcs., Washington, 1986—; co-grant writer, implementer Nat. Endowment for the Arts, Washington, 1982—2000. Vol. Harvard U. docent Sachler Mus., Fogg Art Mus., Busch Reisinger Mus., Cambridge, Mass., 1983—93; vol. docent DeCordova Mus., Lincoln, 1976—83; vol. libr. asst. Lahey Clinic, Burlington, Mass., 1996; vol. Nat. Heritage Mus., Lexington, Mass., 1997—. Named Vol. of the Yr., Nat. Heritage Mus., 1999. Avocations: travel, reading, visiting museums, theater. Home: 61 Willard Grant Rd Sudbury MA 01776

PITT, JANE, medical educator; b. Frankfurt, Fed. Republic Germany, Aug. 25, 1938; came to U.S., 1939. d. Ludwig Friederich and Vera (Aberle) Ries; m. Martin Irwin Pitt, Aug. 12, 1962 (dec. 1980); children: Jennifer, Eric Jonathan; m. Robert Harry Socolow, May 25, 1986; stepchildren: David, Seth. BA, Radcliffe Coll., 1960; MD, Harvard U., 1964. Diplomate Am. Bd. Pediatrics, Am. Bd. Pediat. Infectious Diseases. Resident Children's Hosp. Med. Ctr., Boston, 1964-66; fellow Tufts U. Med. Sch., Boston, 1966-67, Harvard U. Med. Sch., Boston, 1967-69; asst. prof. SUNY Downstate Sch. Medicine, N.Y.C., 1970-71; asst. prof. Coll. Physicians and Surgeons Columbia U., N.Y.C., 1971-75, assoc. prof. Coll. Physicians and Surgeons, 1975-2000; prof. Coll. Physicians and Surgeons, 2000—. Mem. instl. rev. bd. Columbia Health Scis. Campus, N.Y.C., 1982—; mem. NIH study sect. Reviewer Jour. of Infectious Diseases, New Eng. Jour. Medicine, 1976—; contbr. articles to profl. jours. NIH grantee, 1974—. Fellow Infectious Disease Soc., Pediat. Infectious Disease Soc., Soc. Pediat. Rsch., Am. Pediatric Soc. Democrat. Jewish. Home: 34 Westcott Rd Princeton NJ 08540-3060 Office: Columbia U Coll Physicians Surgeons 630 W 168th St New York NY 10032-3702 E-mail: jp25@columbia.edu.

PITT, RUTH ANNE, school system administrator, music educator; b. Jamestown, N.Y., Feb. 28, 1963; d. Gerald L. Fox and Janet E. McClure; m. Douglas A. Pitt, Aug. 27, 1988; children: Jonathan, Hannah. MusB, Grove City (Pa.) Coll., 1985; MEd, Coll. of William & Mary, 2003. Cert. tchr. Va. Dept. of Edn., 2003. Choral music tchr. Stonewall Jackson Mid. Sch., Mechanicsville, Va., 1993—. Mem.: Va. Music Educators' Assn. (chmn. 2001—03), Kappa Delta Pi. Home: 307 Beechview Ave Jamestown NY 14701-2111 Personal E-mail: jd5mom@msn.com.

PITTARELLI, DIANA, entrepreneur; b. Chgo., Sept. 5, 1951; d. Maurice Seymour Mazel and Harriet Marguerite (Hodgini) Hodges; m. Martin Barry Shapiro, Mar. 4, 1972 (div. June 1989); m. John Pittarelli, Apr. 7, 1990. BA cum laude, Barry U., 1991, MBA, 1993. Lic. real estate sales agt., Fla. Securities broker Herzfeld & Stern, Miami Beach, Fla., 1978-79; NASD broker, dealer IMF Corp., Miami, Fla., 1979-81; outside sales agt. Gold Key Travel, Miami, 1981-84, Maduro Travel/Embassy Travel, Miami, 1981 84; owner, mgr. restaurant/nightclub Biscayne Baby, Coconut Grove, Fla., 1984-89; mgr. Skyline State Bank, Plantation, Fla., 1991-97, pvt. investor. Co-patentee bottle carrying device with pivotable spout; choreographer Miss Fla. USA Pageant, 1988. Mem. Dade County Pub. Rels. Coun., Bob Graham Campaign for Gov., Miami, 1980; capt. cheerleading Miami Dolphins, 1980-85; exec. com. Miami Beach Sr. High Alumni Assn., 1999—, co-chmn. class reunions, 1979, 89, 99. Biscayne Baby named one of Best Night Clubs in U.S. by Playboy mag., 1995. Mem. Am. Bus. Women's Assn., Barry U. Alumni Assn. Avocations: hiking, snow skiing, theater, travel. Home: Apt 201 201 Van Buren St Hollywood FL 33019-1712

PITTMAN, CATHERINE SYLVIA, secondary school educator; b. Brunswick, Ga., Apr. 24, 1962; m. David Pittman; children: Drew, Meghan. BS, Ga. So. Coll., 1984, MEd, 1989, EdS, 1993. Tchr. grade 7,8 Risley Middle Sch., Glynn County, 1985-89; tchr. grades 9-12 Brunswick High Sch., Glynn County, 1989—. Named Ga. Tchr. of Yr., 1995, 1996, Milken Family Found. Nat. Educator, 1995; recipient YMCA Tribute to Women's Leaders, 1999. Mem. Glynn County Assn. of Educators, Ga. Assn. of Educators, Nat. Edn. Assn., Ga. Council of Social Studies, So. Assn. of Student Councils, Nat. Assn. of Student Activity Advisors. Home: 103 Marsh Landing Dr Brunswick GA 31523-9387 Office: Brunswick High Sch 3920 Habersham St Brunswick GA 31520-2799

PITTMAN, CONSTANCE SHEN, endocrinologist, educator; b. Nanking, China, Jan. 2, 1929; came to U.S., 1946; d. Leo F.-Z. and Pao Kong (Yang) Shen; m. James Allen Pittman, Jr., Feb. 19, 1955; children: James Clinton, John Merrill. AB in Chemistry, Wellesley Coll., 1951; MD, Harvard U., 1955. Diplomate Am. Bd. Internal Medicine, sub-bd. Endocrinology. Intern Baltimore City Hosp., 1955-56; resident U. Ala., Birmingham, 1956-57; instr. in medicine U. Ala. Med. Ctr., Birmingham, 1957—59, fellow dept. pharmacology, 1957-59, from asst. prof. to assoc. prof., 1959-70, prof., 1970—. Prof. medicine Georgetown U., Washington, 1972—73; mem. diabetes and metabolism tng. com. NIH, Bethesda, Md., 1972—76, mem. nat. arthritis, metabolism and digestive disease coun., 1975—78, mem. gen. clin. rsch. ctrs. com., 1979—83, 1987—90; bd. dirs. Internat. Coun. for Control of Iodine Deficiency Diseases, 1994—; mem. Iodine Deficiency Disorders Elimination Steering Com. Kiwanis Internat., 2002—. Master ACP; mem. Assn. Am. Physicians, Am. Soc. for Clin. Investigation, Endocrine Soc. (coun., 1978-79, pres. women's caucus 1978-79), Am. Thyroid Assn. (pres. 1990-91), Kiwanis (mem. iodine deficiency disorders steering com.). Achievements include research in activation and metabolism of thyroid hormone; kinetics of thyroxine conversion to triiodothyrine in health and disease states; control of iodine deficiency disorders. Emails. Office: U Ala Div Endocrinology/Metab Lab Med Ctr Birmingham AL 35294-0001 E-mail: cpittman@uab.edu.

PITTMAN, JACQUELYN, retired mental health nurse, nursing educator; b. Pensacola, Fla., Dec. 22, 1932; d. Edward Corry Sr. and Hettie Oean (Wilson) P. BS in Nursing Edn., Fla. State U., 1958; MA, Columbia U., 1959, EdD, 1974. Physician asst. Med. Ctr. Clinic, Pensacola, 1953-55; clin. instr., asst. dir. nursing svc. Sacred Heart Hosp., Pensacola, 1955-56; instr. psychiat. nurse Fla. State Hosp., Chattahoochee, 1958; instr. psychiat. nursing Pensacola Jr. Coll., 1959-60, 62-63; chmn. div. nursing Gulf Coast C.C., Panama City, Fla., 1963-66; asst. prof. U. Tex., Austin, 1970-72, assoc. prof., 1972-80; prof. nursing, coord. curriculum and tchg. grad. program La. State U. Med. Ctr., New Orleans, 1980-99, rep. faculty senate, 1997-99; pres.-elect faculty assembly Sch. Nursing La. State U. Med. Ctr. Sch. Nursing, New Orleans, 1997-98, pres., 1998-99; ret., 1999. Curriculum cons. Nicholls State U., Thibodaux, La., 1982, Our Lady of Lake Sch. Nursing, Baton Rouge, 1983; rsch. liaison So. Bapt. Hosp., New Orleans, 1987-89, Med. Ctr. La., 1992-99; mem. adv. bd. Sister Henrietta Guyot Professorship; mem. planning com. Nichols State U./La. State U. Med. Ctr. Partnership, 1996-99. Mem. ethics com., trustee Hotel Dieu Hosp., New Orleans, 1987—91; judge Internat. Sci. and Engring. Fair Assn., 1990, 1992; del. La. State Nurses' Assn. State Conv., 1992, 1994; assoc. Libr. of Congress, Smithonian Instn.; mem. Dem. Nat. Comm., Presdl. Task Force, 1992, Ctr. for Study of Presidency; tchr. Christian edn. program for mentally retarded St. Ignatius Martyr Ch., 1979—80; tchr. initiation team Rite of Christian Initiation of Adults, Our Lady of the Lake Cath. Ch., Mandeville, La., 1983—86; v.p., bd. dirs. St. Tammany Guidance Ctr., Inc., Mandeville, 1987—91; mem. parish outreach meals-on-wheels program St. Tammany, Covington, La., 2001—02. Mem. ANA, LWV, Am. Assn. Adv. Sci. Directory, N.Y. Acad. Scis., Acad. Polit. Sci., Libr. of Congress Assocs., Nat. Trust for Hist. Preservation, La. Endowment for Humanities, La. Nurses Assn. (archivist 1987-99, state task force com. to preserve hist. documents 1987-99), So. Nursing Rsch. Soc., Nat. League Nursing, Boston U. Nursing Archives, Women's Inner Cir. Achievement N.Am. Cmtys., Internat. Order of Merit, World Found. Successful Women, Wilson Ctr. Assocs., Kappa Delta Pi, Sigma Theta Tau. Democrat. Roman Catholic. Avocations: swimming, golf, travel, reading, louisiana history. Address: 204 Woodridge Blvd Mandeville LA 70471-2604 Office Phone: 985-845-4631.

PITTMAN, LISA, lawyer; b. Limestone, Maine, Jan. 4, 1959; d. William Franklin and Rowena Paradis (Umphrey) P.; 1 child, Graham Edward Paradis. BA, U. Fla., 1980, postgrad., 1981, JD, 1984; LLM, George Washington U., 1988. Bar: Fla. 1984, D.C. 1993, U.S Supreme Ct. 1993. Spl. asst. to gen. counsel Nat. Oceanic and Atmospheric Adminstrn., Washington, 1984-85, atty., advisor, 1985-87; minority counsel Com. on Mcht. Marine & Fisheries, Ho. of Reps., Washington, 1987-95; dep. chief counsel Com. on Resources U.S. Ho. of Reps., Washington, 1995-2001, chief counsel Com. on Resources, 2001—02, 2003—, chief counsel, dep. chief of staff, 2002—03. Home: 7325 Eldorado St Mc Lean VA 22102-2904 Office: US House of Reps 1324 Longworth HOB Washington DC 20515-0001

PITTS, GERTRUDE LOUISE, minister; d. Samuel Norris and Myrtle Lewis; m. Robert David Pitts, Aug. 25, 1956 (dec. Mar. 14). Student, Buffalo Bible Inst.; BTh, Am. Bible Inst.; DD, A. E. W. Inst. of Cathedral of the Living Word, Balt., 1986. Apptd. bishop 1996. Nat. pres. Youth Ch. Mt. Calvary Holy Chs. of Am., Inc., 1941—83, nat. missionary pres., dist. mother Wis.-Ohio-Mich. dist.; pastor Mt. Calvary Ch., Milw., 1957—. Active Neighborhood Action Group, 2001. Recipient Cert. Merit and Honor, U. Wis.-Milw. Dept. Edn., Min. of Yr. award, Inner City Travel Svc., Inc., 1984, Black Excellence award, Milw. Times, Econo Print, and Mils. Jour./Sentinel, 1996, citation, Wis. State Assembly, 2001. Pentecostal. Avocations: collecting pigs, reading, listening to music and singing. Home: 2152 N Halyard St Milwaukee WI 53205 Personal E-mail: jhumphrey1@wi.rr.com.

PITTS, VIRGINIA M. human resources executive; b. Boston, Nov. 22, 1953; d. Harold Francis and Connie (Caico) Cummings; m. Daniel J. Pitts, Mar. 12, 1977. Student, Northeastern U., 1982-85, Harvard U., 1997—. Adminstrv. asst. J. Baker Inc., Hyde Park, Mass., 1980-82, fin. adminstr., 1982-84; dir. human resources Casual Male Corp., Hyde Park, Mass., 1984—; 1st sr. v.p. J. Baker Inc., Hyde Park, Mass., 1991—. Trustee New Eng. Joint Bd. AFL-CIO, Quincy, Mass., 1984-89; guest lectr. Aquinas Jr. Coll.; mem. bd. dirs. Boston Crusaders, Drum & Bugle Corps. Instr. Boston Crusaders Drum and Bugle Corps, 1973-85; regional v.p. 210 Charitable Assn., Watertown, Mass., 1989-90; bd. dirs. Handi-Kids, Boston Crusaders Drum and Bugle Corps. Mem. Am. Mgmt. Assn., Am. Compensation Assn. (cert. profl.), Soc. Human Resource Mgrs. Avocations: dressage, gardening. Office: Casual Male Corp 555 Turnpike St Canton MA 02021-2791 E-mail: gpitts@cmal.com.

PITZER, BETTY BRAUN, social services administrator; b. Springfield, Ohio, Aug. 7, 1912; d. Frank J. and Alnora (Hageman) Braun; m. Elwood Gilbert Pitzer, Oct. 2, 1936; children: Philip Elwood, Richard Alan. BA in Bus. Adminstrn. cum laude, Wittenberg U., 1933, LHD (hon.), 2001. Asst. mgr. Baker's Cafeteria, Springfield, 1933-41; fin. sec. Credit Life Ins. Co., Springfield, 1933-41; pres. Ohio Assn. Alpha Delta Pi, Springfield, 1956-58; nat. treas. Alpha Delta Pi Sorority, Atlanta, 1963-79; assoc. dir. United Way Clark County, Springfield, 1965-69; exec. dir. Elderly United Springfield and Clark County, Springfield, 1969-91. Com. mem. Area Agy. on Aging, Dayton, Ohio, 1979-83, Ohio Gov.'s Conf. on Aging, Columbus, 1979-81, Home Care Adv. Com., Springfield, 1981-84, Ohio Commn. on Aging State Fair, Columbus, 1979-82; Clark County coord. White House Conf. on Aging, 1971. Pres. Adelphean Found., Atlanta, 1964-71; mem. fiscal rev. com. City of Springfield, 1982; mem. alumni coun. Wittenberg U., Springfield. Recipient Disting. Alumna award Wittenberg U., 1975, gov.'s award State of Ohio, 1982, Svc. to Mankind award Sertoma Club, Springfield, 1984, Meritorious Svc. award Community Hosp. Bd. Trustees, Springfield, 1977-86, Clark County Cmty. Action award, 1986, Hall of Fame award United Way Clark County, 1987, Kiwanis Cmty. Svc. award, 1991, Area Agy. Aging Svc. award, 1991, Springfield Urban League Svc. award, 1991, Clark County ADMH Bd. Svc. award, 1993, Ohio Sr. Citizen Hall of Fame, 1995. Mem. Ohio Assn. Sr. Ctrs., Ohio Citizens Coun. (policy bd.), Miami Valley Coun. on Gerontology, Zonta (pres. Springfield 1970-72), Alpha Delta Pi (Alumna of Yr. award 1987). Republican. Lutheran. Avocation: being involved with civic affairs. Home: 111 Englewood Dr Springfield OH 45504

PIVEN, FRANCES FOX, political scientist, educator; b. Calgary, Alta., Can., Oct. 10, 1932; arrived in U.S., 1933, naturalized, 1953; d. Albert and Rachel (Paperny) F.; 1 dau., Sarah. BA, U. Chgo., 1953, MA, 1956, PhD, 1962; L.H.D. (hon.), Adelphi U., 1985. Mem. faculty Columbia, 1966-72; prof. polit. sci. Boston U., 1972-82, Grad. Ctr., CUNY, 1982—. Co-author: Regulating the Poor: The Functions of Public Welfare, 1971, 2d edit., 1993, The Politics of Turmoil: Essays on Poverty, Race and the Urban Crisis, 1974, Poor People's Movements, 1977, New Class War, 1982, The Mean Season, 1987, Why Americans Don't Vote, 1988; editor: Labor Parties in Post Industrial Societies, 1992, The Breaking of the American Social Compact, 1997, Why Americans Still Don't Vote, 2000, Work, Welfare and Politics, 2002, The War at Home, 2004. Recipient C. Wright Mills award Soc. Study Social Problems, 1971, Fulbright Disting. Lectureship award U. Bologna, 1990, President's award APHA, 1993, Annual award Nat. Assn. Sec. of State, 1994, Lifetime Achievement award Pol. Sociology Am. Sociological Assn., 1995, Disting. Career award, 2000, Pub. Understanding of Sociology award, 2003; Guggenheim fellow, 1973-74; Am. Coun. Learned Socs. awardee, 1982. Mem. Am. Polit. Sci. Assn. (v.p. 1981-82), Soc. Study Social Problems (pres. 1980-81, Lee founders award 1992), ACLU (dir.). Home: PO Box N Millerton NY 12546-0651 Office: CUNY Grad Sch 365 5th Ave New York NY 10016-4309

PIVIN, JEANETTE EVA, psychotherapist; b. Fall River, Mass., Feb. 24, 1932; d. Oscar and Ida Antoinette (Gauthier) P. B in Edn., Cath. Tchrs. Coll., 1956; MA in Theology, U. Notre Dame, 1967; cert. clin. pastoral edn., Worcester State Hosp., 1975; cert. interior design, Hall Inst. Tech., 1989; cert. divorce mediator, Roger Williams Univ, 1995. Tchr. St. Matthew Sch., Cranston, R.I., 1956-64; asst. prof. religious studies Salve Regina U., Newport, 1967-74; staff counselor La Salette Counseling Svcs., Attleboro, Mass., 1975-80; pastoral counselor Interfaith Counseling Ctr., Providence, R.I., 1975—; pvt. practice Providence, 1980—. Mem.: Am. Assn. Pastoral Counselors. Achievements include research in the determination of phosphorus together with other 6 elements in chrome steel in one solution by using a nonoxidizing acid first in world; searched out of the direct and quantitative relationship between solubility and charges and radii of ions first in world; promotion of simple natural sieve method to prove infinity of prime twins and derivation of simple and most accurate formula in world to estimate number of prime twins; discovery of relationship between phase graphs and differential thermal analysis curves; co-developer chemical polymerization of polyaniline and polypyrrole on Langmuir-Blodgett trough; discovery of method to monitor polymerizations by Langmuir-Blodgett computerized techniques; created a breakthrough software program used to compute the octane number and other characters for gasoline using GC data. Home and Office: 139 Woodbine St Providence RI 02906-2543

PIZZAMIGLIO, NANCY ALICE, performing company executive; b. Oak Park, Ill., Aug. 22, 1936; d. Howard Joseph and Marian Louise (Henne) Gilman; m. Ernest George Lovas, May 17, 1957 (div. Nov. 1976); children: Lori Dianne, Randall Gilman; m. Albert Theodore Pizzamiglio, Mar. 27, 1978. Student, North Tex. State U., 1955-56. Stewardess North Cen. Airlines, Chgo., 1956-57; receptionist Leo Burnett Advt. Agy., Chgo., 1957-59; office mgr. Judy Stallons Employment Agy., Oak Brook, Ill., 1973-75; mgr. and escort Prestige Vacations, Inc., Oak Brook, Ill., 1975-76; corp. dir. Al Pierson Big Band U.S.A., Inc., Aubrey, Tex., 1976-2000, Al Pierson, Inc., Aubrey, Tex., 1978—, corp. pres., 1997—, Gilman, Inc. Artists Mgmt., Aubrey, 1982-2000; owner Dancing Horse Ranch, Aubrey, Tex., 1983—; bus. mgr. Guy Lombardo's Royal Canadians, Aubrey, Tex., 1989—. Editor: (newsletter) Property Owners Assn., 1972-73; contbr. articles to profl. jours. Recipient expert award NRA, 1952. Mem. U.S. Lipizzan Registry (bd. dirs. 1986-89, 1996-98, treas. 1996, 97, 98), Dallas Dressage Club (bd. dirs. 1988-94), Am. Horse Shows Assn., U.S. Dressage Fedn. (qualified rider 1989, third/all breeds, first level 1989, first/all breeds, fourth level 1991, third Vintage Cup, fourth level 1991, third all-breeds first level 1992, third vintage cup first level 1992), Dallas-Ft. Worth Labrador Retriever Club Inc. (bd. dirs. 2000-03). Republican. Episcopalian. Avocations: showing, breeding, and training labrador retrievers, world travel, chinese history, gem stones. Address: Al Pierson Inc 2469 Spring Hill Rd Aubrey TX 76227-3911 E-mail: dancehorse@aol.com.

PIZZINGRILLI, KIM, state official; BBA Econ., U. Pitts., Johnstown, 1981; M Govtl. adminstrn., U. Pa., 1988. Auditor, acct., and asst. dir. bur. of audits Pa. Treasury Dept., 1981-87; sr. regulatory analyst Pa. Ind. Regulatory Rev. Commn., 1987-95; spl. asst. to sec. Dept. of State, Harrisburg, Pa., 1995-96, dep. sec. regulatory programs, 1996-98, acting sec., 1998-99, sec. of the commonwealth, 1999—2002; commr. Pa. Pub. Utility Comm., 2002—. Mem. Bd. of Property, Bd. of Fin. and Revenue, State of Pa.; mem. Pa. State Athletic Commn., Pa. State Nav. Commn. for the Delaware River and its Navigable Tributaries, mem. Pa. Mcpl. Retirement Bd.; keeper Great Seal of the Commonwealth. Mem. Nat. Assn. Sec. of State, Women Exec. in State Govt. Republican. Office: Pennsylvania Pub Utility Commn P O Box 3265 Harrisburg PA 17105-3265*

PIZZO, PIA, artist, educator; arrived in U.S., 1982, permanent resident, 1985; d. Rosario Pizzo and Rosa Greco; m. Chin Hsiao, Apr. 28, 1962 (div. May 1979); 1 child, Samantha Hsiao (dec.) ; m. Delbert O. Thompson, June 18, 1985. Diploma, Coll. of Art Orsoline, Milano, Italy, 1956; student, Brera Acad. Art, Milano, Italy, 1957—60; BFA, Ministry Pub. Instrn., Roma, Italy, 1957. Founder, propr. Sama Press, Long Beach, Calif., 1995—. Instr. design and color theory Brooks Coll. Design, Long Beach, Calif., 1998—; instr. art and creativity Dept. Parks, Recreation, Marine, Long Beach, Calif., 1987—; lectr. Dept. Art and Tech. Calif. State U., Long Beach, Calif., 1995—96. Exhibitions include 32 solo exhbns., Europe and USA, 1962—2003, 83 group shows, Europe, USA, Brasil, Taiwan, 1957—2002; author: The World is Waiting for the Sunrise, 1985 (hon. mention, 1987); co-author (with blind students): 6'x 8' tactile sculptural book-perm. pub. art, 1988; contbr. articles to profl. publs.; author (designer): adult and children books, 1970, 1981. Named Artist of Yr., Disting. Visual Artist, PCA Pub. Corp. for Arts, 1989; recipient Cert. Recognition award, Accademia Tiberina, Roma, Italy, 1957, cert. of Appreciation in Recognition of Outstanding Svc., City of Long Beach, Calif., 2000, permanent pub. art sign project, City of Gardena, Calif., 2001; fellow, Pollock-Krasner Found., NYC, 1984, Calif. Arts Coun., Sacramento, 1987, Pub. Corp. for the Arts, Long Beach, Calif., 2000. Mem.: Long Beach Mus. Art Artist's Coun. (solo exhbn. 1998), The Smithsonian Inst., Internat. Campaign for Tibet, Children Internat., Amnesty Internat. Avocations: classical piano, reading, concerts, museums, languages. Home and Studio: Artist's Studio 1022 E 1st St # 7 Long Beach CA 90802

PIZZORNO, LARA ELISE, medical writer, editor; b. N.Y.C., Oct. 5, 1948; d. Daniel A. and Elinor M. (Kugel) Udell; m. John James Leary Jr. (div. 1979); m. Joseph E. Pizzorno; children: Galen Udell. BA magna cum laude, Wheaton Coll., 1970; MAR in Philos. Theology, Yale U., 1973; MA in English Lit., U. Wash., 1986. Lic. massage therapist. Instr. philosophy Edmonds (Wash.) C.C., 1974-78; grants writer Seattle U., 1978-79, asst. dir. devel., 1979-81; devel. cons. Bastyr U., Seattle, 1981-83, copyeditor Textbook of Natural Medicine, 1986-89; instr. English North Seattle C.C., 1986-89; dir. publs. Trillium Health Products, Seattle, 1992-93; owner WordWorks, Seattle, 1993—2000; sr. med. editor Salugenecists, Inc., 2000—. Mem. adv. bd. Bastyr U., Seattle, 1989—. Author: The Complete Book of Bread Machine Baking, 1993; co-author: Natural Medicine Instuctions for Patients, 2001, Ency. of Healthy Foods, 2004; editor, contbg. writer: Integrative Medicine: AClinician's Jour., Choices, Natural Lifestyle and Nutrition mag.; editor, contbg. writer: Total Wellness, 1996-2001; contbr. numerous articles to popular mags. Mem. Am. Med. Writers Assn., Ctr. Spiritual Living, Phi Beta Kappa. Avocations: healthy cooking, weight training, gardening, cycling, scuba diving. Home and Office: 4220 NE 135th St Seattle WA 98125-3836

PLACE, JANEY, banking consultant, former bank executive; b. Denver, Jan. 25, 1946; m. Michael Hiles. BA, MA, UCLA, PhD in semiology, 1975, attended Grad. Sch. Mgmt. Info tech. mgr. Hughes Aircraft Co.; corp. mgr. Strategic Tech. Planning Tosco Corp.; sr. v.p. internet strategy, R&D Wells Fargo Bank, 1990—94; exec. v.p. Strategic Tech. Group Bank of Am., 1994—99; pres. Mellon Lab and Online Svcs., N.Y.C., 1999—2003; exec. v.p. Mellon Fin. Corp., N.Y.C., 1999—2003; founder, pres., CEO digitalthinking.com, 1999—. Past lectr. in sys. and comm. theory U. Calif., Santa Cruz, Calif.; bd. dirs. PortBlue; spkr. in field. Contbr. articles to profl. jours.; author: The Western Films of John Ford, 1974, The Non-Western Films of John Ford, 1979. Named One of 25 Women to Watch in Banking, U.S. Banker Mag., 2003.*

PLACHE, KIMBERLY MARIE, state legislator; b. Racine, Wis., Jan. 4, 1961; Student, U. Wis., Whitewater, 1978-81; BS, U. Wis., Parkside-Kenosha, 1984. Legis. asst. to state rep. Jeff Neubauer, 1984-88; mem. Wis. Assembly from 21st dist., madison, 1988-96, Wis. Senate from 21st dist., Madison, 1996—. Mem. NOW, AAUW, Wis. Action Coalition. Address: 2614 17th St Racine WI 53405-3522 Office: Wis State Assembly State Capital Madison WI 53702-0001

PLAGEMANN, SUSAN, publishing executive; Dir. fashion and advt. Madamoiselle, 1992—95; advt. mgr. Esquire, 1995, advt. dir., 1995—96, assoc. pub., 1996—97, Cosmopolitan Mag., 1997—99; publisher Cosmopolitan Magazine, N.Y.C., 1999—2002; v.p., pub. Lifetime Mag., N.Y.C., 2002—. Office: Hearst Magazines 224 W 57th St New York NY 10019-3212

PLAINE, LLOYD LEVA, lawyer; b. Washington, Nov. 3, 1947, d. Marx Leva and Shirley P. Leva, MD; m. James W. Hill. BA, U. Pa., 1969; postgrad., Harvard U.; JD, Georgetown U., 1975. Bar: DC 1975. Legis. asst. to US Rep. Sidney Yates, 1971-72; with Sutherland, Asbill & Brennan, Washington, 1975-82, ptnr., 1982—. Fellow Am. Bar Found., Am. Coll. Trust and Estate Counsel (past regent), Am. Coll. Tax Counsel; mem. ABA (past chmn. real property, probate and trust law sect., coun. sect. of taxation). Office: Sutherland Asbill & Brennan Ste 6 1275 Pennsylvania Ave NW Washington DC 20004-2415

PLAISANCE, MELISSA, retail executive; b. Feb. 12, 1960; BSBA cum laude, Bucknell U., 1982; MBA, UCLA, 1990. Sr. v.p. fin. investor rels. Safeway Inc., Pleasanton, Calif.; v.p. Bankers Trust Co. Corp. Fin., L.A. Office: Safeway Inc PO Box 99 5918 Stoneridge Mall Rd Pleasanton CA 94566-0009

PLAISTED, CAROLE ANNE, elementary school educator; b. Meredith, N.H., Apr. 3, 1939; d. Morris Holman and Christina Martin (Dunn) Plaisted. EdB with honors, Plymouth (N.H.) Tchrs. Coll., 1960; MA, Columbia U., 1966; cert., N.Y. Inst. Photography, 1990. Cert. tchr., N.H. Tchr. Lang St. Sch., Meredith, 1960-61, Mechanic St. Sch., Laconia, N.H., 1961-62, Wheelock Lab. Sch., Keene, N.H., 1963-94; asst. prof. emeritus Keene State Coll. Summer tchr. Cheshire County Headstart, Hinsdale, N.H., 1965; tchr. children's lit. Keene State Coll., 1974, 75; classroom evaluator D.C. Heath Co., Lexington, Mass., 1985-86; dist. trainer for drug edn. supervisory unit, Keene, 1988-94. Author: The Graduates Speak, 1990; co-author curriculum materials; contbr. Kindergarten: A Sourcebook for School and Home, 1984. Trustee Reed Free Libr., Surry, N.H., 1988-2000; program chair Wheelock Sch. PTA, 1964-65. Named Outstanding Elem. Tchr. of Am., 1973. Mem. Cheshire County Ret. Tchrs. Assn., Delta Kappa Gamma (pres. Alpha chpt. 1996-98, 2000-02, corr. sec. Alpha chpt. 1972-76, state scholarship chmn. 1985—, Beta Alpha state scholarship 1989, Founders award, 2001). Avocations: reading, gardening, photography.

PLAISTED, JOAN M. diplomat; b. St. Peter, Minn., Aug. 29, 1945; d. Gerald A. and Lola May (Peters) Plaisted. Student, U. Grenoble, France, 1965—66, U. Calif., Berkeley, 1966; BA in Internat. Rels., Am. U., 1967, MA in Asian Studies, 1969; grad., Nat. War Coll., 1988. Korea desk officer Commerce Dept., Washington, 1969-72, Japan desk officer, 1972-73; comml. officer Am. Embassy, Paris, 1973-78; internat. economist Orgn. Econ. Cooperation & Devel., Paris, 1978-80; econ. officer Am. Consulate Gen., Hong Kong, 1980-83; trade negotiator White House Office of Spl. Trade Rep., Geneva, 1983-85; deputy dir. China desk State Dept., Washington, 1985-87; acting dep. dir., chief econ./comml. sect. Am. Inst. in Taiwan, Taipei, 1988-91; chargé d'affaires, dep. chief of mission Am. Embassy, Rabat, Morocco, 1991-94; dir. Thai and Burma affairs Dept. of State, Washington, 1994-95; sr. advisor U.S. Mission to UN N.Y.C., 1995; amb. to Republic of Marshall Islands and Republic of Kiribati, 1996—2000; amb., sr. advisor U.S. Mission to the UN, N.Y.C., 2000—. Recipient Lodestar award, Am. U., 1993, Disting. Civilian Svc. decoration, Sec. of the Army, 2000, Alumna of Yr. award, Am. U. Sch. Internat. Svc., 2001, Supr. award, State Dept., 2002. Mem.: Am. Fgn. Svc. Assn., Asia Soc., Washington Inst. Fgn. Affairs, Hong Kong Wine Soc. (founding), Phillips Collection. Avocations: wine tasting, gastronomy, history, skiing, scuba diving. Address: 1310 33rd St NW Washington DC 20007-2818

PLANK, BETSY (MRS. SHERMAN V. ROSENFIELD), public relations counsel; b. Tuscaloosa, Ala., Apr. 3, 1924; d. Richard Jeremiah and Bettye (Hood) P.; m. Sherman V. Rosenfield, Apr. 10, 1954. Student, Bethany (W.Va.) Coll., 1940-43; AB, U. Ala., 1944. Continuity dir. radio sta. KQV, Pitts., 1944-47; account exec. Mitchell McKeown Orgn., Chgo., 1947-54; pub. rels. counsel Chgo. chpt. A.R.C., 1954-57; dir. pub. rels. Chgo. Coun. on Fgn. Rels., 1957-58; v.p. Ronald Goodman Pub. Rels. Counsel, Chgo., 1958-61; exec. v.p., treas., dir. Daniel J. Edelman, Inc., Chgo., 1961-73; dir. pub. rels. planning AT&T, N.Y.C., 1973-74; asst. v.p. corp. comm. Ill. Bell, Chgo., 1974-90; prin. Betsy Plank Pub. Rels., Chgo., 1990—. Dep. chmn. VII World Congress on Pub. Rels., 1976; co-chmn. nat. commn. on Pub. Rels. Edn., 1984-87; mem. adv. bd. Ill. Issues, 1975—. Bd. dirs. United Way Chgo., 1986-90; chmn. Citizenship Coun. Met. Chgo., 1990-96, Betsy Plank chpt. Pub. Rels. Student Soc. Am., No. Ill. U.; trustee Found. for Pub. Rels. Rsch. and Edn., 1975-80; nat. bd. dirs. Girl Scouts U.S., 1975-85. Recipient Millennium award Coll. Journalism, U. Fla., 2000, Alexander Hamilton award, Inst. Pub. Rels., 2000; named one of World's 40 Leading Pub. Rels. Profls., Pub. Rels. News, 1984. Fellow Pub. Rels. Soc. Am. (accredited, nat. pres. 1973, Outstanding Profl. award 1977, Outstanding Cmty. Svc. award 1989, Disting. Svc. award 2001); mem. Publicity Club Chgo. (pres. 1963-64, Outstanding Profl. award 1961), Ill. Coun. on Econ. Edn. (past chmn. bd. trustees, Extraordinary Leadership award 2001), Internat. Pub. Rels. Assn., Chgo. Network (chmn. 1980-81), Arthur W. Page Soc. (lifetime achievement award 2000), Union League Club of Chgo., Econ. Club Chgo., Zeta Tau Alpha. Presbyterian. Home and Office: 421 W Melrose St Chicago IL 60657-3848

PLANK, JUDITH ANNE, television production coordinator; b. Sacramento, Feb. 17, 1958; d. Howard Robert Plank and Barbara Jean Wibom. BA in English, U. Calif., Davis, 1980; MA in Counseling Psychology, JFK U., 1994. Alcohol, drug and mental health specialist Yolo County Mental Health, Woodland, Calif., 1998—2002; tutor after-sch. program Calif. State U., Sacramento, 2002—03; prodn. coord. Davis (Calif.) Comty. TV, 2003—. Dir., founder Davis Film Festival, 2003—. Author: (chapbook) Poems, 1992, Anais Dug No Bones, 1996. Vol. Animal Savers, Sacramento, 2002—, Yolo Crisis Nursery, Davis, 2002—; vol. prodr. Davis Comty. TV, Davis, 1998—2003. Recipient award, Davis Comty. TV, 2000—02. Mem.: U. Calif.-Davis English Club (founder, pres. 1978). Avocations: films, classical guitar, screenwriting, hiking, bicycling.

PLANK, TERRY, geochemistry educator; BA in Earth Scis. summa cum laude, Dartmouth Coll., 1985; PhD with distinction, Columbia U., 1993. NSF postdoctoral fellow Cornell U., 1993-94; asst. prof. U. Kans., 1995-99; assoc. prof. Boston U., 1999—. Mem. com. for the study of the earth's deep interior AGU, 1994-95; mem. U.S. Sci. Adv. Com., Ocean Drilling Program, 1995-98; mem. rev. panel NSF GEO-Profl. Opportunities for Women in Rsch. and Edn., 1997, NSF OCE-Marine Geology and Geophysics, 1997-98; mem. steering com. NSF MARGINS Initiative, 1997—, MARGINs Theoretical and Exptl. Inst., Inside the Subduction Factory, 1999-2000; vis. prof. U. Rennes, France, 1998; presenter in field. Mem. editl. bd. Geology, 1997-99; mem. adv. editl. bd. Earth and Planetary Sci. Letters, 1997-2000; contbr. articles to profl. jours. Recipient Houtermans Young Scientist medal European Assn. Geochemistry, 1998, Donath medal Geol. Soc. Am., 1998; summer undergrad. rsch. fellow GSO, U. R.I., 1984, grad. fellow NSF, 1985-88, postdoctoral fellow NSF, 1993-94. Mem. Phi Beta Kappa. Achievements include research on the study of magmas associated with the plate tectonic cycle, at both divergent and convergent plate margins, experimental determination of trace element partition coefficients by laser ablation microprobe, the volatile content of arc magmas melt inclusions, volatile-tracers, effects on magma evoluation, high quality, trace element analysis of volcanic rocks by inductively-coupled plasma mass spectrometry, global relationships. Office: Boston Univ Dept Earth Scis 685 Commonwealth Ave Boston MA 02215 Fax: 617-353-3290. E-mail: tplank@bu.edu.

PLASTERER, TAMARA J. music educator, theater educator; d. Theodore and Erma J Stoica; m. Jared S. Plasterer; 1 child, Kimberly J. MusB. in Edn., Ohio State U., 1984; MFA in Theatre, U. Akron, 1994. Cert. profl. tchr. music K-12 Ohio, 1984. Music and math tchr. Lumen Cordium H.S., Bedford, Ohio, 1984—87; dir. vocal music and theatre Padua Franciscan H.S., Parma, Ohio, 1987—, fine arts dept. chair, 2002—. Stage mgr. Stage Partners, Wooster, Ohio, 1995—. Mem.: Ednl. Theatre Assn., Ohio Music Edn. Assn. (com. chair 2002—03), Music Educators Nat. Conf. Office: Padua Franciscan High Sch 6740 State Rd Parma OH 44134

PLATER-ZYBERK, ELIZABETH MARIA, architectural educator; b. Bryn Mawr, Pa., Dec. 20, 1950; d. Josaphat and Maria (Meysztowicz) P.-Z.; m. Andres M. Duany, June 12, 1976. BA in Architecture, Princeton U., 1972; MArch, Yale U., 1974. Registered architect, Fla. Architect, prin. Andres Duany & Elizabeth Plater-Zyberk, Architects, Miami, Fla., 1979—; prof. U. Miami, 1979—; dean Sch. Architecture U. Miami, 1995—. Contbr. numerous articles to profl. jours. and popular publs. Mem. adv. coun. Princeton (N.J.) U. Sch. Architecture, 1982—, trustee 1987-91, 93-2003; mem. vis. com. MIT Sch. Architecture, 1990—. Mem. AIA, Archtl. Club Miami (pres. 1982-87). Office: Duany Plater-Zyberk & Co 1023 SW 25th Ave Miami FL 33135-4824

PLATIS, MARY LOU, media specialist; b. East Chicago, Ind., Jan. 21, 1946; d. Walter James and Mary Helen (Taus) Campbell; m. James George Platis, Aug. 16, 1974. BS, Ind. State U., 1972, MS, 1974. Tchr. 4th grade Holy Trinity Sch., East Chicago, Ind., 1968-72; tchr. phys. edn. Washington Elem. Sch., East Chicago, Ind., 1972-86; media specialist Ctrl. High Sch. Libr., East Chicago, Ind., 1986—. Recipient 47 Ind. track and field individual state medals, 1983-98, 99, 2000, 2001, 64 Ind. state regional individual medals, 1983-98, 99, 2000, 01, 02, 25 All Am. certs., 12 times Masters track and field All Am., 1989-98, 37 Ill. Grand Prix individual titles, 1989-93, 43 Midwest track and field individual titles, 1989-95, 3 times Nat. Masters track and field champion, 7 times Nat. runner-up; nat. sr. Olympics qualifier, 1997, 99, 2001, 03; winner 6th pl. ribbons (2) Nat. Sr. Olympics, 1999; nat. and world ranked masters track and field, 1989-98; individual championship titles in racquetball; inducted into East Chicago Sports Hall of Fame, 1992. Mem. Nat. Assn. Basketball Coaches. Avocations: racquetball, tennis, working out. Home: 938 Troon Ct Schererville IN 46375 Office: Ctrl High Sch Libr 1100 W Columbus Dr East Chicago IN 46312-2582 E-mail: mlplatis@aol.com.

PLATT, ELLEN L. financial planner; b. Boston, Aug. 8, 1940; d. Jack and Evelyn Miriam Platt. Student, U. Fla., 1958—60. Bookkeeper/cashier Bank of Hollywood, Fla., 1960—63; clk. note dept. Pacific Nat. Bank, San Francisco, 1963—67; ops./office mgr. Walter C. Gorey Co., San Francisco, 1967—73; registered rep. Bache & Co., Hallandale, Fla., 1973—81; fin. advisor UBS Fin. Svcs. (formerly Paine Webber), Hallandale, 1981—89, Plantation, Fla., 1989—95, Ft. Lauderdale, Fla., 1995—. Pres. Jewish Family Svc. Broward County, 1992—95; dir. exec. com. Assn. of Jewish Family and Children Agencies, 2001—; dir., v.p. Literacy Coalition of Broward County, 2001—. Recipient Outstanding Bd. Mem. award, Assn. of Jewish Family and Children Agencies, 2003, Esther Lowenthal award, Jewish Family Svc., 1993, Lifetime Achievement award, 2000. Mem.: C. of C. Hallandale (pres. 1988). Jewish. Avocations: reading, needlepoint. Office: UBS Financial Svcs 1 E Broward Blvd Ste 1810 Fort Lauderdale FL 33301

PLATT, JAN KAMINIS, county official; b. St. Petersburg, Fla., Sept. 27, 1936; d. Peter Clifton and Adele (Diamond) Kaminis; m. William R. Platt, Feb. 8, 1963; 1 child, Kevin Peter. BA, Fla. State U., 1958; postgrad., U. Fla. Law Sch., 1958-59, U. Va., 1962, Vanderbilt U., 1964. Pub. sch. tchr. Hillsborough County, Tampa, Fla., 1959-60; field dir. Girl Scouts Suncoast Coun., Tampa, 1960-62; city councilman Tampa City Coun., 1974-78; county commr. Hillsborough County, 1978-94, 96—; chmn. Hillsborough County Bd. County Commrs., 1980-81, 83-84, 98-99, ret., 1994, re-elected, 1996, chmn., 1998-99. Chmn. Tampa Bay Regional Planning Coun., 1982, West Coast Regional Water Supply Authority, Tampa, 1985, Hillsborough County Coun. Govts., 1976, 79, Agy. Bay Mgmt., Hills Environ. Protection Commn., Sunshine Amendment Drive 7th Congrl. Dist., Tampa, 1976, Cmty. Action Agy., Tampa, 1981, 83-84,chmn. pro tem Tampa Charter Revision Commn., 1975, chmn. Prison Sitting Task Force, Tampa, 1983, Tampa Housing Study Com., 1983, Met. Planning Orgn., Tampa, 1984, Bd. Tax Adjustment, Tampa, 1984, Hartline, 2002-03, Friendship Trailbridge Oversight Com., 2002-03, Tampa Bay Water, 2003-04; appointee Constn. Revision Commn., Fla., 1977, HRS Dist. IV Adv. Coun., Fla.; mem.

Hillsborough County Expy. Authority, Taxicab Commn., Ch. Hills Cmty. Youth Coun.; vice chmn. steering com. Nat. Counties Environ. Task Force; pres. Suncoast Girl Scout Coun., 1973-74, Head Start Cmty. Found., 1996. Bd. dirs. March of Dimes, Tampa, The Fla. Orch., Tampa, Tampa Bay Sierra, Tampa Audubon; trustee Hillsborough County Hosp. Authority, Tampa, 1984-94; pres. Citizens Alert, Tampa, Bay View Garden Club; v.p. Hillsborough County Bar Aux.; mem. adv. bd. Northside Cmty. Mental Health Ctr., Access House, Tampa; active Arts Coun. Tampa-Hillsborough County, 1983-85, 96-2001, Drug Abuse Coordinating Coun. Orgn., Tampa, Bd. Criminal Justice, Tampa, Fla. Coun. on Aging, Inebriate Task Force, Tampa, Tampa Downtown Devel. Authority Task Force, Tampa Sports Authority, Tampa Area Mental Health Bd., Children's Study Commn., Manahill Area Agy. on Aging, Tampa, Athena Soc., Tampa Area Com. Fgn. Affairs, LWV; pres. Hills Children's Coun., Headstart Found.; bd. dirs. Arts Coun.; exec. com. Tampa Performing Arts Ctr.; mem. Com. of 100. Recipient Athena award, Women in Comm., 1976, Spessard Holland Meml. award, Tampa Bay Com. for Good Govt., 1979, First Lady of Yr. award, Beta Sigma Phi, 1980, First Ann. Humanitarian award, Nat. Orgn. of Prevention of Animal Suffering, 1981, Women Helping Women award, Soroptimist Internat. Tampa, 1983, Good Govt. award, Tampa Jaycees, 1983, LWV, 1983, John Books Meml. award, Fla. Audubon Soc., 1989, Girl Scout Woman of Distinction award, 1996, Girl Scout Thanks award, 1996, Libery Bell award, Hillsborough County Bar Assn., 2000, Black Bear award, Suncoast and Tampa Bay Groups of the Sierra Club, 2001, Eliza Wolff award, Tampa United Meth. Ctrs. Mem. Am. Judicature Soc., State Assn. County Commrs. Fla. (at-large dir.), AAUW (bd. dirs.), Mortar Board, Garnet Key, Phi Beta Kappa (pres. local alumni), Phi Kappa Phi. Democrat. Episcopalian. Home: 3531 Village Way Tampa FL 33629-8914 Office: PO Box 1110 Tampa FL 33601-1110 Office Phone: 813-272-5730.

PLATT, KATRINA VONTELLE, music educator; b. Mullins, SC, June 4, 1956; d. Hazel W. Johnson and Mary Grace Foxworth; children: Katrell Antonio, Wrakyia Katrina Platt-Gregg. BS in Music Edn. cum laude, NC A&T State U., 1978. Tchr. band, chorus Sampson County Schs., NC, 1980—82; tchr. band, chorus, music Marion Sch. Dist. #3, SC, 1985—88, Marion Sch. Dist. #2, Mullins, 1990—2000; dir. band, music Corinth-Holders Sch., Zebulon, NC, 2000—. Guest clinician, condr. Williamsburg County Schs., Kingstree, SC, 1992; min. of music New Born Assembly Ch., Mullins, 1993—2000. Mem.: NEA (assoc.), Music Educators Nat. Conf. (assoc.). Office: Corinth-Holders Sch 3976 NC Hwy 231 Zebulon NC 27597-7280 Personal E-mail: vonnie@bbnp.com.

PLATTI, RITA JANE, secondary school educator, draftsman, writer, inventor; b. Stockton, Calif., Aug. 29, 1925; d. Umbert Ferdinand and Concettina Maria (Natoli) Strangio; m. Elvin Carl Platti, July 27, 1955; 1 child, Kimberley Jane. Student, Dominican Coll., 1943-45; AB in Math, U. Pacific, 1947, postgrad., 1947-52, 68. Farmer, almond grower, Escalon, Calif., 1943—; tchr. math St. Mary's High Sch., Stockton, 1947-49, 52, 54; chem. analyst Petri Winery, Escalon, 1949; draftsman Kyle Steel Co., Stockton, 1950-52; pvt. practice as draftsman Stockton, 1952-66; tchr. math Montezuma Sch., Stockton, 1956-57, Davis Elem. Sch., Stockton, 1957-58; with rental bus., 1958-81; tchr. math Amos Alonzo Stagg High Sch., 1961-80, Humphreys Coll., 1981-83, Hamilton Jr. High Sch., 1984-90. Owner, involved in prodn. and mktg. R.J. Creations, 1991—; farm realtor Century 21, Escalon, Calif., 1996-97; spkr. workshops Stanislaus State U., 1992, Calif. Math. Coun., Fresno State U., 1992, Nat. Sci. Found. Conf., 1993; spkr. math./sci. conf. Calif. State U., Bakerfield, 1994-96; evaluator Math. Framework (K-12) Calif. State Dept. Edn. Author: Math Proficiency Plateaus, 1979, Preparing Fundamentals of The Use of Sound in the Teaching of Mathematics, 1994, Book of Poems, 2002; author, pub. series, 1979-86; 3 patents in field. Mem. NEA, Calif. Tchrs. Assn. Democrat. Roman Catholic. Avocations: inventing, mathematics theoretical development, poetry, piano, environmental clean up.

PLAUT, JANE MARGARET, art educator; b. Bklyn., Mar. 31, 1948; d. Charles and Jane Elizabeth (Moore) Rifenberg; m. Harold J. Plaut, Dec. 14, 1968 (div. 1981); 1 child, Harold Jonathan Jr. AAS, N.Y.C. C.C., Bklyn., 1968; BA, Bklyn. Coll., 1978; MA, NYU, 1986. Permanent cert. H.S. art tchg. Staff artist Pastarnack Assn., N.Y.C., 1968, 69; tchr. St. Joseph's Coll., Yokohama, Japan, 1970, St. Maur Internat. Sch., Yokohama, 1970, Good Shepherd Sch., Bklyn., 1978-82, Our Lady Help of Christians, Bklyn., 1978-82, Bishop Kearney H.S., Bklyn., 1982—. Tchr. Saturday humanities enrichment program St. John's U., 2000. One-woman shows include 80 Washington Square East, N.Y.C., 1985, 39 5th Ave., N.Y.C., 1996; works exhibited in group shows at The Paul VI Inst. for Arts, Washington, 1982, 86, Querini Stampali, Venice, Italy, 1983, 84, Bishop Kearney H.S., Bklyn., 1988, 89, Selena Gallery-L.I. U., Bklyn., 1988, St. John's U., Queens, N.Y., 1990, Cathedral Basilica St. James, Bklyn., 2000, others; author, illustrator (children's book): Pierre Le Car, 2001. Recipient commendation for outstanding contbn. to edn. St. Francis Coll., 1991, 92, 94, Gold Photo award Bay Ridge Cmty. Coun., 1999; Fashion Inst. Tech. fellow, 1997; named Internat. Visual Artist of Yr., 2004. Mem. Internat. Ctr. Photography, Nat. Art Edn. Assn., Nat. Mus. Women in the Arts (charter) Met. Mus. Art, Bklyn. Mus. Avocations: painting, photography, reading. Office: Bishop Kearney HS 2202 60th St Brooklyn NY 11204-2599 Office Phone: 718-236-6363 ext. 269.

PLAVINSKAYA, ANNA DMITRIEVNA, artist; b. Moscow, Nov. 26, 1960; came to U.S., 1989, naturalized, 1995; d. Dmitri Petrovich and Nina Nicolaevna; m. Gennady Ioffe, Jan 9, 1988 (div. July 1993). Diploma in Costume Design, Theatrical Art Coll., Moscow, 1976-80. Costume designer Evgeny Vahtangov Theater, Moscow, 1980-82; artist freelance Moscow, 1983-89; art restorer pvt. studio, N.Y.C., 1990-93; artist freelance N.Y.C., 1993—. Exhibited in group shows at art coll., Moscow, Gallery of Moscow Artists, 1983, Ctrl. Exhbn. Hall, Moscow, 1984, 88, Kuznetzky Most Gallery, Moscow, 1985, Tbilisi Acad. of Art, Georgia, 1986, Tallinna Moepaevad '87, Tallinn, Estonia, 1987, Remizovo St. Gallery, Moscow, 1988, Pushkin Sq. Gallery, Moscow, 1988, The Textile Art Ctr., Chgo., 1991, The Russian Nobility Assn., NYC, 1991, 11th Cleve. Internat. Drawing Biennale, Middlesbrough, Eng., 1993 (2d prize), BWA Gallery, Wroclaw, Poland, 1994, BWA Gallery, Lublin, Poland, 1994, Elblag (Poland) Gallery, 1994, Tatraniska Gallery, Poprad, Tatry, Slovakia, 1994, State Gallery, Ostrova, Czech Republic, 1994, Botanica '94, Port Royal Mus. Gallery, Naples, Fla., 1994, Art Addiction Gallery, Stockholm, 1996-98 (cert. merit 1997), Art Addiction Gallery, Venice, Italy, 1998, Internat. Platform Assn., 1998, (1st place, best of show), 1999 (1st place award), Le Salon, Paris, 2000 (Bronze medal), 45th Salon Internat. des Arts Plastiques, Beziers, France, 2001 (Bronze medal), Le Salon, Paris, 2002; 46th Salon Internat. Beziers, 2002 (Prix de La Societe Des Beaux Arts 2002), 47th Salon Internat. des Arts Plastiques, Beziers, France, 2003, Le Salon, Paris, 2003; represented in permanent collections Cleve. Contemporary Art Collection, Middlesbrough, Eng., Zimmerli Art Mus., Norton and Nancy Dodge Collection, NJ. Mem. Nat. Fedn. French Culture. Russian Orthodox. Avocations: fashion design, antique textile restoration, tennis. Home: 815 W 181st St Apt 3E New York NY 10033-4530

PLAWECKI, JUDITH ANN, nursing educator; b. East Chicago, Ind., June 5, 1943; d. Joseph Lawrence and Anne Marilyn (Hamnik) Curosh; m. Henry Martin Plawecki, June 10, 1967; children: Martin H., Lawrence H. BS, St. Xavier Coll., Chgo., 1965; MA, U. Iowa, 1971; PhD, 1974. Asst. prof. Mt. Mercy Coll., Cedar Rapids, Iowa, 1971-73; asst. dept. chmn., assoc. prof., 1974-75; assoc. prof. U. Iowa, 1975-76; asst. dean, assoc. prof. U. Minn., 1976-81; acting dean, assoc. dean and prof. U. N.D., Grand Forks, 1981-82, dean and prof. nursing, 1982-83, Lewis U., Romeoville, Ill., 1983-87; dean U. South Fla., Tampa, 1987-95, prof. nursing, 1987—. Univ. Iowa Fellow, 1973. Mem. AHNA, Nat. League for Nursing, Older Women's League, Sigma Xi, Sigma Phi Omega, Sigma Theta Tau, Phi Lambda Theta. Office: U South Fla Coll Nursing MDC 22 12901 Bruce B Downs Blvd Tampa FL 33612-4742

PLAX, KAREN ANN, lawyer; b. St. Louis, June 20, [illegible]; d. George J. and Evelyn G. Zell; m. Stephen E. Plax, Dec. 19, 1968; 1 child, Jonathan. BA magna cum laude, U. Mo., St. Louis, 1969; JD with distinction, U. Mo., Kansas City, 1976. Bar: Mo. 1976, U.S. Supreme Ct. 1980. Atty. Thayer, Gum & Wickert, Grandview, Mo., 1976-84, Plax & Cochet, Kansas City, Mo., 1984-87; pvt. practice Kansas City, 1987—. Past chair divsn. 3, region IV Mo. Supreme Ct. Com. to review ethical conduct of attys., 1997-98. Author: Missouri Bar Practical Skills, 1998; asst. editor: Racial Integration in the Inner Suburb, 1970; contbr. articles to profl. jours. Recipient Pub. Svc. award U. Mo. Kansas City Law Found., 1998, Woman of Yr. award Assn. Women Lawyers of Greater Kansas City, 1999. Fellow: Am. Acad. Matrimonial Lawyers (pres. Mo. chpt. 1999—2001); mem.: ABA (family law sect. 1976—), Mo. Bar Family Law (legis. chair 1997—98, v.p. 1999—2000, Spl. Commendation for Legis. Role in Family Law 1998), Kansas City Met. Bar Assn. Office: Ste 300 1310 Carondelet Dr Kansas City MO 64114-4803 Personal E-mail: kaplax@swbell.net.

PLAYER, AUDREY NELL, research scientist; b. Houston, July 17, 1955; d. Tom and Justine Player. BA, N. Tex. State U., 1977; PhD, Wright State U., 1986. Staff scientist Bayer/Triton, Emeryville, Calif., 1990-2000, Nat. Inst. Health, Bethesda, 2000—. Former mem. bd. dirs. Brookdale Cmty. Ctr., Oakland, Calif., former mentor. Mem. Am. Assn. Cancer Rsch. Democrat. Avocations: tennis, hiking.

PLAYER, THELMA B. librarian; b. Owosso, Mich. d. Walter B. and Grace (Willoughby) Player. BA, Western Mich. U., 1954. Reference asst. USAF Aero Chart and Info. Ctr., Washington, 1954-57; reference libr. USN Hydrographic Office, Suitland, Md., 1957-58, asst. libr., 1958-59; tech. libr.br. head USN Spl. Project Office, Washington, 1959-68, Strategic Sys. Project Office, Washington, 1969-76. Mem. ALA, AAUW, English Speaking Union, Spl. Librs. Assn., Nat. Geneal. Socl, Internat. Soc. Brit. Genealogy and Family History, Ohio Geneal. Soc. Royal Oak Found., Daus of Union Vets. of Civil War, David Ackerman Descs. Episcopalian. Home: 730 24th St NW Washington DC 20037-2546

PLAZA, EVA M. lawyer; b. Torreon, Coahuila, Mex., Feb. 13, 1958; d. Sergio and Eva (Torres) P. BA cum laude, Harvard U., 1980; JD, U. Calif., Berkeley, 1984. Trial atty. U.S. Dept. Justice, Washington, 1984-86; assoc. Arent, Fox, Kintner, Plotkin, Washington, 1986-88, Seyfarth, Shaw, Fairweather & Geraldson, Washington, 1988-93; dep. asst. atty. gen. U.S. Dept. Jutice, 1993-97; asst. sec. U.S. Dept. Housing and Urban Devel., 1997—. Mem. ABA, Tex. Bar Assn., Pa. Bar Assn., D.C. Bar Assn., Hispanic Bar Assn. (pres. D.C. chpt.). Democrat. Roman Catholic. Home: 201 E Gravers Ln Philadelphia PA 19118-2802*

PLEASANT-JACKSON, TONYA, therapist, consultant; b. Washington, Oct. 27, 1960; d. Oscar and Carolyn Estelle Pleasant; m. Anthony L. Jackson Sr., July 15, 1989; children: Anthony L. Jr., Amara N. V. BS in Family Therapy, U Md., 1984; D in Ministry, Friends Internat. Christian U., 1994; M in Rehab. Counseling, U. Md., 1996. Lic. mariage and family therapist, Va.; cert. rehab. counselor, Md., nat. cert. counselor, rehab. provider, Va., rehab. svc. provider, Md.; ordained to ministry Integrity Ch. Internat., 1993. Dir. counseling ministry Integrity Ch. Internat., 1990—; rehab. coord., vocat. evaluator, rehab. cons. St. Luke's Ho., Bethesda, Md., 1997-98; rehab. coord. CHI Ctrs., Silver Spring, Md., 1998—; pvt. practice therapist Greenbelt, Md., 1998—; therapist, cons. Residential Care Inc., 1999—. Outstanding Svc. award Regional Inst. Children and Adolescents, Md., 1986. Mem. Assn. Mental Health Counselors, Am. Assn. Christian Counelors. Avocations: singing, physical fitness. Office: 9841 Greenbelt Rd Ste 208 Lanham Seabrook MD 20706-6270

PLEDGER, MYRNA JOAN, counselor; d. James Monroe Washington and Johnie Mae Owens-Washington; m. James Pledger, Oct. 18, 1986 (div. Aug. 2003); children: Jennifer, Sara, Margaret. BA, Roosevelt U., 1982; MA, Chgo. State U., 2001. Cert.: Roosevelt U. (paralegal); lic. profl. counselor Ill. Tchr. Chgo. Bd. Edn., 1986—2001, Success Lab., Chgo., 1999—2001; counselor mental health DeltaT, Oak Brook, Ill., 2001—. Author: I Wish So Much to Hold You, 2002, Vegetables, Vitamins and Water, 2002, Liking Me, 2003. Avocation: writing.

PLEIN, KATHRYN ANNE, retired secondary school educator; b. Ashland, Wis., Jan. 28, 1945; d. Donald and Frances (Tankersly) Smith; m. Arvid Arthur Plein, Dec. 19, 1970; children: Marty, Michelle. BS in Broadfield Sci., Northland Coll., 1967; MS in Tchg., U. Wis., Superior, 1973. Cert. secondary science tchr., Wis. 7th grade sci. tchr. Wausau (Wis.) Sch. Dist., 1967-73; tchr. John Muir Mid. Sch., Wausau, 1977; ret., 2000. Mem.: AAUW (pres.-elect 1997—2000). Roman Catholic. Home: R 8800 Hwy J Schofield WI 54476

PLESHETTE, SUZANNE, actress; b. N.Y.C., Jan. 31; d. Eugene and Geraldine; m. Thomas Joseph Gallagher III, Mar. 16, 1968 (dec. Jan. 2000); m. Tom Poston, May 11, 2001. Student, Sch. Performing Arts, Syracuse U., Finch Coll., Neighborhood Playhouse Sch. of Theatre. Founder, prin. The Bedside Manor (later div. of J.P. Stevens). Theatre debut in Truckline Cafe; star in Broadway prodns. Compulsion, The Cold Wind and the Warm, The Golden Fleecing, The Miracle Worker, Special Occasions; star TV series Bob Newhart Show, 1972-78, Suzanne Pleshette is Maggie Briggs, 1984; starred in TV series Bridges to Cross, 1986-87, Nightingales, 1988-89, The Boys Are Back, 1994-95, The Single Guy, 1996-97; host (CBS spl.) Where Are They Now?, 1997, (TV series spl. appearance) Will & Grace, 2001, (TV series) Good Morning Miami, 2002—; star 30 feature films including The Birds, Forty Pounds of Trouble, If It's Tuesday This Must Be Belgium, Nevada Smith, Support Your Local Gunfighter, Hot Stuff, Oh God! Book II, Lion King II Simba's Pride, Spirited Away; TV movies include Flesh and Blood, Starmaker, Fantasies, If Things Were Different, Help-Wanted Male, Dixie Changing Habits, One Cooks, The Other Doesn't, For Love or Money, Kojak, The Belarus file, A Stranger Waits, Alone in the Neon Jungle, Leona Helmsley: The Queen of Mean, 1990, Battling for Baby, 1991-92, A Twist of the Knife, 1993; writer, co-creator, producer two TV series; published author.

PLETSCH, MARIE ELEANOR, plastic surgeon; b. Walkerton, Ont., Can., May 3, 1938; came to U.S. 1962; d. Ernest John and Olive Wilhemina (Hossfeld) P.; m. Ludwig Philip Breiling, Aug. 25, 1967; children: John, Michael, Anne. MD, U. Toronto, 1962. Diplomate Am. Bd. Plastic Surgery. Intern Cook County Hosp., Chgo., 1962-63, resident, gen. surgery, 1963-64, St. Mary's Hosp., San Francisco, 1964-66; resident in plastic surgery St. Francis Hosp., San Francisco, 1966-69; practice med. specializing in plastic surgery Santa Cruz, Calif., 1969—; Monterey, Calif., 1990—; adminstr. Plasticenter, Inc., Santa Cruz, 1976-88, med. dir., 1987-88. Mem. AMA, Am. Soc. Plastic and Reconstructive Surgeons, Calif. Soc. Plastic Surgeons (mem. coun. 1986-89, sec. 1989-93, v.p. 1994-95, pres. elect 1995-96, pres. 1996-97), Am. Soc. Aesthetic Plastic Surgeons, Calif. Med. Assn., Assn. Calif. Surgery Ctrs. (pres. 1988-92), Santa Cruz County Med. Soc. (bd. govs. 1983-88, 1992-94), Santa Cruz Surgery Ctr. (bd. dirs. 1988-93). Roman Catholic. Office: Santa Cruz Can Am Med Group 1669 Dominican Way Santa Cruz CA 95065-1523 : 24571 Silver Cloud Ct Monterey CA 93940 Office Phone: 831-462-1000. E-mail: pletsch@pacbell.net.

PLETTE, SANDRA LEE, retired insurance company executive; b. Cambridge, Mass., June 15, 1950; d. Warren M. and K. Towneley Rohsenow; m. André F. Plette, June 23, 1973; children: Nicole Corris, Kristen Towneley. BBA with high distinction, U. Mich., 1972, MBA with high honors, Boston U., 1980. CFA. Investment rsch. assoc. New Eng. Life Ins. Co., Boston, 1972—76; account mgr. ADP Network Svcs., Boston and L.A., 1976—78; various investment positions UNUM Corp., Portland, Maine, 1980—89, v.p. investor rels., 1989—90, v.p. underwriting, 1990—93, v.p. fin., 1993—98. Pres. Union Mutual Employees Credit Union, Portland, 1984—88. Fin. com. United Way Greater Portland, 1995—; chmn. Tng. Resource Ctr., Portland, 1998—2001; pres. bd. dirs. Girl Scouts Kennebec Coun., 2000—; chaplain Maine Med. Ctr., Portland, 2002—; treas. Foreside Cmty. Ch., Falmouth, Maine, 1999—2003; bd. dirs. Coastal Enterprises, Wiscassett, Maine, 1988—91. Mem. United Ch. Of Christ. Avocations: singing, golf, hiking, reading.

PLETZ, DARCY L. sales executive; b. Harrisburg, Pa., July 23, 1977; d. Dennis Robert and Dorothy Carol Pletz. BS in Ins., Pa. State U., 1999. Agt./intern N.Y. Life, Harrisburg, 1998—99; underwriter Cigna, Phila., 1999—2000; actuary Aegis, Harrisburg, 2000—01; field underwriter IBSi, Lancaster, Pa., 2001, regional agy. mgr., 2003—; account mgr. USI Colburn, Mechanicsburg, 2004. Coach girls' basketball Rutherford Youth Club. Mem.: Pa. State Alumni Assn., Phi Gamma Nu. Avocations: sports, interior design, dog training, painting, gardening. Home: 1022 Wooded Pond Dr Harrisburg PA 17111 Office Phone: 717-691-4721. E-mail: psudarc@hotmail.com.

PLIEGO-STOUT, PATRICIA, travel company executive; b. Mex. City; Founder, pres., CEO Alamo Travel Group, 1982—. Bd. mem. San Antonio Hispanic C. of C., San Antonio Greater C. of C., Sports Found., Libr. Found., 2001—02; pres. San Antonio Chpt. Nat. Assn. Women Bus. Owners; apptd. to San Antonio's Blue Ribbon com. internat. affairs; vice-chair Tex. Assn. Mex.-Am. C. of C. (TAMACC); apptd. by Gov. George W. Bush to State Commr. Tex. Bd. Lic. and Regulation. Named Entrepreneur Yr., San Antonio Hist. C. of C., 1992, Small Bus. Woman Yr., Rep. Women's Leadership Forum, 2000; named to San Antonio Women's Hall Fame, 1997; recipient RNC Hispanic Spirit Enterprise award, Nat. Assn. Women Bus. Owners, San Antonio chpt., 1999, Latina Excellence award, Hispanic mag., 2001, Bus. Entrepreneurship award, 2002. Achievements include led Alamo Travel Group to second place rankings in travel in San Antonio; recognized by Continental Airlines and Delta Airlines as top prodr. in federal and military sales for 1999; award incentive nat. contracts by Dell, Lehman Bros., Lockheed Martin and Am. Inst. Rsch; featured in Latina mag., Reader's Digest, Hispanic Bus. mag., Federal Reserve Bank Report 1995, vanidades mag., Federal Times, Travel Weekly, Bus. Travel mag. Office: Alamo Travel Corp HQ 9000 Wurzbach Rd San Antonio TX 78240 Office Phone: 210-593-0084. Office Fax: 210-614-2448.*

PLIMPTON, PEGGY LUCAS, trustee; b. Nov. 3, 1931; d. David Nicholson and Margaret (MacMillan) Lucas; m. Hollis Winslow Plimpton, June 11, 1955; children: Victoria P. Babcock, Priscilla P. Morphy, Hollis Winslow Plimpton III. AB, Duke U., 1954. Trustee Cape Cod Conservatory of Music, 1989—. Bd. trustees Carleton Williard Retirement Home, Bedford, Mass., 1968—, Cape Cod Conservatory Music, 1990—; bd. dirs. Episcopal Ch. Women, 1968-78, Brigham & Women's Hosp., Boston, 1975—; pres. Boston Lying-In Hosp., 1970-72; chmn. Mass. Nat. Cathedral Assn., Boston, 1978-80, 1985-88; pres. bd. trustees Women's Ednl. and Indsl., Boston, 1980-83. Mem. New Eng. Farm and Garden Club (bd. dirs. 1965—, pres. 1995—), Chestnut Hill Garden Club (bd. dirs. 1970-74), Jr. League Garden Club (pres. 1981-83), Colonial Dames (bd. mgrs. 1983-89, v.p. 1993-98, pres. 1998—), Vincent Club, Chilton Club. Republican. Episcopalian. Avocations: gardening, golf, bridge, grandchildren.

PLISKOW, VITA SARI, anesthesiologist; b. Tel Aviv, Sept. 13, 1942; arrived in Can., 1951; came to U.S., 1967; d. Henry Norman and Renee (Mushkatel) Stahl; m. Raymond Joel Pliskow, June 30, 1968; children: Tia, Kami. MD, U. B.C., Vancouver, 1967. Diplomate Am. Bd. Anesthesiology. Ptnr. Olympic Anesthesia, Bremerton, Wash., 1971-84, pres., anesthesiologist, 1974-84; co-founder Olympic Ambulatory Surgery Ctr., Bremerton, 1977-83; ptnr., anesthesiologist Allenmore Anesthesia Assocs., Tacoma, 1983—. Staff anesthesiologist Harrison Meml. Hosp., Bremerton, 1971-95, Allenmore Hosp., Tacoma, 1983—. Trustee Tacoma Youth Symphony Assn., 1994—; active Nat. Coun. Jewish Women, 1972—. Fellow Am. Coll. Anesthesiologists, Am. Coll. Chest Physicians; mem. Am. Soc. Anesthesiologists (del. Wash. State 1987—), Wash. State Med. Assn. (del. Pierce County 1993-94), Wash. State Soc. Anesthesiologists (pres. 1985-87), Pierce County Med. Soc. (sec.-treas. 1992). Avocations: classical music, opera, singing (mezzo soprano). Office: PO Box 65274 University Place WA 98464-1274

PLOTKIN, JUDY ANN, special education educator; b. L.A., Apr. 9, 1949; d. Donald Olaus and Georgia Maye (Burrus) Nelson; m. Phillip Harold Plotkin, Feb. 11, 1970; children: Amy Louise, Mark Andrew. AA in Religious Studies, Valley Coll., San Bernardino, Calif., 1979; BA in Religious Studies, U. Calif., Riverside, 1982; MEd, Calif. State U., San Bernardino, 1987; EdD, U.S. Internat. U., 1998. Cert. tchr., spl. edn. tchr., Calif. Tchr. spl. edn. Advocate Sch., San Bernardino, 1983-84, Colton (Calif.) Sch. Dist., 1984-85, Carmack Sch., San Bernardino, 1985-91, Harmon Sch., San Bernardino, 1991-92, North Verdemont Sch., San Bernardino, 1992—. Head tchr. Harmon Sch., 1991-92. Rsch. asst. Adoptees Liberty Movement Assn., Redlands-Riverside, Calif., 1982—; active Bike-A-Thon, Epilepsy Soc., San Bernardino, 1982. Mem. Coun. for Exceptional Children (sec. 1983-84), AAUW, San Bernardino Epilepsy Soc., Phi Kappa Phi. Republican. Avocations: bowling, swimming, camping, arts and crafts. Office: N VerdemontSch 3555 W Meyers Rd San Bernardino CA 92407-1911

PLOTTEL, GLORIA SUSANNE STONE, marketing professional; b. N.Y.C., Feb. 16, 1966; d. Leroy Saul and Karen Lila Stone; m. Philip Benjamin Plottel, June 9, 1996. BA cum laude Univ. Profs. Program, Boston U., 1988; MS in Forest Resources Mgmt, SUNY, Syracuse, 1992; MBA, NYU, 2002. Mgr. dept. geography Boston U., 1989-90; tchg. asst. coll. environ. sci. and forestry SUNY, Syracuse, 1990-92; asst. acct. exec. Lowe and Ptnrs./SMS, N.Y.C., 1993-95; asst. mgr. Champion Internat. Corp., Stamford, Conn., 1995-97; mktg. mgr. Bus. New Haven, 1997-98. Cons. Mass. Dept. Environ. Mgmt., Boston, 1993, No. Forest Lands Coun., Concord, N.H., 1993. Screenwriter: Seasoned Trails, 1989. Mem. exec. bd. U. Profs. Program, Boston U., 1997—; coun. mem. YMCA-YWCA Camping Svcs. of Greater N.Y., 1998—. SUNY internat. conf. grantee, 1991. Avocations: hiking, camping, swimming, ballroom dancing.

PLOTTEL, JEANINE PARISIER, foreign language educator; b. Paris, Sept. 21, 1934; came to U.S., 1943; m. Roland Plottel, 1956; children: Claudia S., Michael E., Philip B. Baccalauréat lettres, Lycée Français de N.Y., 1952; BA with honors, Barnard Coll., 1954; MA, Columbia U., 1955, PhD with distinction, 1959. Lectr. dept. French and Romance philology Columbia U., N.Y.C., 1955-59; rsch. assoc. fgn. lang. program MLA of Am., N.Y.C., 1959-60; lectr. dept. romance langs. CUNY, N.Y.C., 1960; asst. prof. div. humanities Julliard Sch. Music, N.Y.C., 1960-65; dir. lang. labs. Hunter Coll. CUNY, N.Y.C., 1965-69; asst. prof. dept. romance langs. Hunter Coll. CUNY, N.Y.C., 1965-69, assoc. prof. dept. romance langs., 1969-81, prof. dept. romance langs., 1981—2000, assoc. prof. French doctoral program grad. sch., univ. ctr., 1980-81, prof. French doctoral program grad. sch., univ. ctr., 1981—2000, prof. emeritus, 2000—. Exec. dir. AAVP NY state conf., 2002-. Extensive adminstrv. experience in CUNY including chair dept. Romance langs. Author: Les Dialogues de Paul Valéry, 1960; pub., editor N.Y. Literary Forum, 1978-88; contbr. articles to profl.

jours., chpts. to books. Pres. Maurice I. Parisier Found., Inc. Named Officer des Palmes Acad., 1999; recipient NEH fellowship, 1979; grantee N.Y. Coun. for the Humanities, 1986, Helena Rubenstein Found., 1986, Florence J. Gould Found., 1986, 88, N.Y. Times Found., 1986. Mem. AAUP (exec. dir. N.Y. State Conf. 2002—), Maison Française (bd. dirs. Columbia U.), Peyre Inst., CUNY, Soc. French Am. Cultural Svcs. & Ednl. Aid, Hunter Coll. Art Galleries. Home: 50 E 77th St Apt 14A New York NY 10021-1836 Office: Hunter Coll-CUNY 695 Park Ave New York NY 10021-5024 Office Phone: 212-535-6668. E-mail: plottel@worldnett.att.net.

PLOUFFE, DIANE MARIE, music educator; b. Woonsocket, R.I., Aug. 29, 1970; d. George Lucien and Carole Anne Pichette; m. Kevin Matthew Plouffe, June 11, 1994; children: Danielle Marie, Marie Adele. BA in Violin Performance, The Boston Conservatory, 1992; MA in Music Edn., U. N.H., 1994. Tchr. music Bridgewater/Raynham Pub. Schs., Raynham, Mass., 1994—95; string tchr. Fall River Pub. Schs., Mass., 1995—97, Franklin Pub. Schs., Franklin, Mass., 1997—. Pvt. music tchr., Woonsocket, 1994—; guest condr. R.I. Music Educators Assn., 1996—97; performer New Bedford Symphony, 1994—, Plymouth Philharmonic, 1994—, Claflin Symphony, 1994—. Mem.: Nat. Sch. Orch. Assn., Am. String Tchrs. Assn. Roman Catholic. Avocations: camping, hiking, racquetball.

PLUMMER, AMANDA, actress; b. N.Y.C., Mar. 23, 1957; d. Christopher and Tammy (Grimes) Plummer. Student, Middlebury Coll. Has appeared in theatre roles: A Taste of Honey, 1981; A Month in the Country, 1980; N.Y.C. debut: Artichoke, 1979; The Glass Menagarie, 1983-84; motion picture debut: Cattle Annie and Little Britches, 1981, The World According to Garp, 1982, Daniel, 1983, Hotel New Hampshire, 1984, Static, 1985, Made in Heaven, 1987, Prisoners of Inertia, 1989, Joe Versus the Volcano, 1990, The Fisher King, 1991, Freejack, 1992, The Lounge People, 1992, So I Married an Axe Murderer, 1993, Needful Things, 1993 (Saturn award, 1994), Pax, 1994, Nostradamus, 1994, Pulp Fiction, 1994, The Final Cut, 1995, The Prophecy, 1995, Search and Destroy, 1995, Butterfly Kiss, 1995, Hysteria, 1996, Freeway, 1996, Dead Girl, 1996, American Perfect, 1997, Drunks, 1997, A Simple Wish, 1997, You Can Thank Me Later, 1998, October 22, 1998, L.A. Without a Map, 1998, Elizabeth Jane, 1998, Great Sex, 1999, Eight and a Half Women, 1999, The Million Dollar Hotel, 2000, Seven Days to Live, 2000, Triggermen, 2002, Ken Park, 2002, TMA, 2002, Pulp Fiction: The Facts, 2002, My Life Without Me, 2002, The Last Angel, 2002; (TV movies) The Dollmaker, 1984, True Blue, 1989, Kojak: None So Blind, 1990, Sidney Sheldon's The Sands of Time, 1992, Last Light, 1993, Whose Child Is This? The War for Baby Jessica, 1993, Under the Piano, 1995, Don't Look Back, 1996, The Right to Remain Silent, 1996, (voice) Hercules, 1997, Shadow Realm, 2002, Get a Clue, 2002, Broadway: The Golden Age, by the Legends Who Were There, 2002; other theatre roles include: Agnes of God (Tony, Drama Desk award, Outer Circle Critics award), 1982; A Lie of the Mind, 1985; TV appearances include Hallmark Hall of Fame: Miss Rose White (Emmy award supporting actress, 1992), TV series L.A. Law, Moonlighting, The Equalizer, The Outer Limits, (Emmy award best guest actress, 1996). Office: Innovative Artists Ste 2850 1999 Avenue Of The Stars Los Angeles CA 90067-4612*

PLUMMER, ORA BEATRICE, nursing educator, trainer; b. Mexia, Tex., May 25, 1940; d. Macie Idella (Echols); childeren: Kimberly, Kevin, Cheryl. BSN, U. N.Mex., 1961; MS in Nursing Edn., UCLA, 1966. Nurse's aide Bataan Meml. Meth. Hosp., Albuquerque, 1058-60, staff nurse, 1961-62, 67-68; staff nurse, charge nurse, relief supr. Hollywood (Calif.) Cmty. Hosp., 1962-64; instr. U. N.Mex. Coll. Nursing, Albuquerque, 1968-69; sr. instr. U. Colo. Sch. Nursing, Denver, 1971-74, asst. prof., 1974-76; staff assoc. III, Western Interstate Commn. for Highr Edn., Boulder, Colo., 1976-78; DON, Garden Manor Nursing Home, Lakewood, Colo., 1978-79, nurse surveyor, cons., 1979-87; ednl. coord. Colo. Dept. Health, Denver, 1987—96. Active in faculty devel. Colo. Cluster of Schs.; bd. dir. Domestic Violence Initiative, 2000—. Contbr. articles to profl. jours. Mem. adv. bd. Affiliated Children's and Family Svcs., 1977; mem. Colo. Instnl. Child Abuse and Neglect Adv. Com., 1984-92; trustee Colo. Acad., 1990-96; mem. planning com. State Wide Conf. on Black Health Concerns, 1977; mem. staff devel. com. Western Interstate Commn. for Higher Edn., 1978, mem. minority affairs com., 1978, mem. coordinating com. for baccalaureate program, 1971-76; active in minority affairs, U. Colo. Med. Ctr., 1971-72; mem. ednl. resources com., pub. rels. com., rev. com. for reappointment, promotion and tenure U. Colo. Sch. Nursing, 1971-76, mem. regulatory tng. com., 1989-93; mem. gerontol. adv. com. Met. State Coll., 1989-94; mem. expert panel long term care tng. manual Health Care Financing Adminstrn., Balt., 1989; mem. employee diversity com. Colo. Dept. Health, 1989-96. Mem. ANA, ASTD, NAFE, Colo. Nurses Assn. (affirmative action com. 1977-79, 93—), Phi Delta Kappa. mem. Nurse Delegation to Cuba, 2000. Nightingale Nominee, Colorado, 2003. Avocations: public speaking, training. Office: 4300 Cherry Creek South Dr Denver CO 80246-1523

PLUMMER, PATRICIA LYNNE MOORE, chemistry and physics educator; b. Tyler, Tex., Feb. 26; d. Robert Lee and Jewell Ovelia (Jones) Moore; m. Otho Raymond Plummer, Apr. 10, 1965; children: Patrick William Otho, Christina Elisa Lynne. BA, Tex. Christian U., Ft. Worth, Tex., 1960; postgrad., U. N.C., 1960-61; PhD, U. Tex., Austin, 1964; grad., Bryn Mawr Summer Inst., 1992. Instr., Welch postdoctoral fellow U. Tex., Austin, 1964-66; postdoctoral fellow Dept. Chemistry, U. Ark., Fayetteville, 1966-68; rsch. assoc. Grad. Ctr., Cloud Phys. Rsch., Rolla, Mo., 1968-73; asst. prof. physics U. Mo., Rolla, 1973-77; assoc. dir. Grad. Ctr. Cloud Phys. Rsch., 1977-79, sr. investigator, 1980-85; assoc. prof. physics U. Mo., 1977-85, prof. dept. chemistry and physics, 1986—. Mem. internat. sci. com. Symposium on Chemistry and Physics of Ice, 1982—, vice chair, 1996—; nat. judge Siemens-Westinghouse Sci. Projects, 1999—. Assoc. editor Jour. of Colloid and Interface Sci., 1980-83; contbr. articles to profl. jours., chpts. to books. Rsch. grantee IBM, 1990-92, Air Force Office Rsch., 1989-91, NSF, 1976-86, NASA, 1973-78; Air Force Office Rsch. summer fellow, 1988, Bryn Mawr Summer Inst., 1992, Faculty fellow Cherry Emerson Ctr. for Sci. Computation, Emory U., 1998-99. Mem. Am. Chem. Soc., Am. Phys. Soc., Am. Geophys. Union, Sigma Xi (past pres., UM-Rolla chptr.). Democrat. Baptist. Avocations: sailing, gardening, tennis, photography. Office: U Mo 201 Physics Bldg Columbia MO 65211-0001 Fax: (573) 882-4195. E-mail: plummerp@missouri.edu.

PLUMSTEAD, KRISTINE LAURA, music educator; b. Willingboro, N.J., Aug. 3, 1976; d. Edward P. and Sandra S. Quairoli; m. Keith James Plumstead, Oct. 14, 2000. MusB in Music Edn., Trenton State Coll., Ewing, N.J., 1999. Band dir. Hillsborough (N.J.) HS, 1999—2000, Hamilton (N.J.) HS West, 2000—03, dir. of bands, 2003—. 2nd lt N.J. NG U.S. Army, 1996—2000, Lawrenceville, N.J. Mem.: Music Educators Nat. Conf. Office: Hamilton High Sch West 2720 South Clinton Ave Hamilton NJ 08610 Office Phone: 609-631-4168 3305. Personal E-mail: klqkjp@yahoo.com. E-mail: kplumstead@hamilton.k12.nj.us.

PLUNKET, DOLORES, art and archaeology educator; b. Chgo., Sept. 2, 1916; d. John Nagoda and Evangeline Kompare; m. John T. Plunket, July 15, 1944; children: Lucy Silver, Robert, John T. Jr., Patricia. BS, U. Ill., 1937; MA in Pre-Colombian Art, Nat. U. Mexico, Mexico City, 1975. V.p. Mexican-N.Am. Cultural Inst., Mexico City, 1985-88; dir. lecture series Selby Libr., Sarasota, Fla., 1992-96; lectr. in field. Co-author: (with A.R. L'huillier) Vision del Mundo Maya, 1978; editor Gardening in the Federal District, 1986; contbr. articles to profl. jours. V.p. Friends Selby Libr., 1992-95; pres. Mexico City Garden Club, 1985; bd. dirs. Am. Soc. Mexico, 1986-88. Home: 1301 N Tamiami Trail apt 406 Sarasota FL 34236-2423 E-mail: jplunket@aol.com.

PLUNKETT, MELBA KATHLEEN, manufacturing company executive; b. Marietta, Ill., Mar. 20, 1929; d. Lester George and Florence Marie (Hutchins) Bonnett; m. James P. Plunkett, Aug. 18, 1951; children: Julie Marie Plunkett Hayden, Gregory James. Educated pub. schs. Co-founder, 1961, since sec.-treas., dir. Coils, Inc., Huntley, Ill. Mem. U.S. C. of C., U.S. Mfg. Assn., Ill. C. of C., Ill. Notary Assn. Roman Catholic. Home: 15n170 Sleepy Hollow Rd West Dundee IL 60118-9113 Office: 11716 Algonquin Rd Huntley IL 60142-7176

PLUNKETT, SARA L. communications company executive; BA in Acctg., U. Ala. CPA, Ala., Ga. Acct. Price Waterhouse, Atlanta, 1978-88; with ITC/DeltaCom, Huntsville, Ala., 1989—, v.p. fin., treas. Office: ITC/DeltaCom 700 Boulevard South SW Huntsville AL 35802-2115

POAD, FLORA VIRGINIA, retired librarian and educator, retired elementary school educator; b. Roanoke, Va., Oct. 8, 1921; d. Thomas Franklin and Ethlind (Wertz) Huff; m. Stanley Theodore Benton, Dec. 24, 1942 (div. Oct. 1983); children: Peggy, Betty, Mary Jo, Lucy; m. James Joseph Poad, June 6, 1986. Student, Radford Coll., 1939-41, Ohio U., 1956-57; BS in Edn., Ohio No. U., 1960; MA in LS, U. Toledo, 1964; postgrad., Kent State U., 1964-66, 71. Reference asst. Roanoke Pub. Libr., 1939-42; catalog asst. Univ. Libr., Emory U., Atlanta, 1942; sec. ARC, Atlanta, 1943; catalog asst. Pickerington (Ohio) Pub. Libr., 1950-51; tchr. Celina (Ohio) Pub. Schs., 1957-62; tchr., libr. Toledo Pub. Schs., 1962-64; libr. supr. Oregon (Ohio) Pub. Schs., 1964-85; instr. U. Toledo, 1970, reference libr., 1971-86; tchr. Sylvan Learning Ctr., Toledo, 1985-92, ret., 1992. Mem. evaluation team Ohio Dept. Edn., Columbus, 1973; rep. Ohio Gov.'s Conf. on Librs., Columbus, 1974; chmn., mem. adv. bd. libr. sci. dept. Cmty.-Tech. Coll., 1965-69. Editor Ohio Assn. Sch. Librs. Bull., 1968-71. Vol. Am. Cancer Soc., Toledo, 1946—48, 1986—87, Mobile Meals, Toledo, 1986—93, Helping Hands, Toledo, 1994—2001. Mem. Am. Assn. Ret. Persons, Delta Kappa Gamma, Pi Lambda Theta, Kappa Delta Pi, Phi Kappa Phi. Avocations: reading, walking, crafts. Home: 3544 Bayberry Pl Oregon OH 43616-2475

POCIERNICKI, JANICE LOUISE, artist; b. Rochester, Pa., June 27, 1941; d. Raymond Joseph and Emma Louise Kercovich; m. William Ignatius Pociernicki, June 30, 1966; children: Jennifer Catherine Bitters, William Chad. Sec., Robert Morris U., 1959—60. Art com. mem. Merrick Art Gallery /Mus., New Brighton, Pa., 2002—; pres. Beaver Valley Artists, New Brighton, Pa., 1996—97, historian, 1995—96. Exhibitions include Beaver Valley Artists Annual, West Hills Art League Ann. Show, Pitts. Watercolor Soc. Ann., North Hills Fall Multi Media Show, Pitts. Progressive Artists Show, 6 internat., 4 nat., and 11 regional shows. Mem.: Pitts. Soc. of Artists, West Hills Art League (pres. 1995—96), Beaver Valley Artists (pres. 1996—97), Pitts. Prog. Artists, Pitts. Watercolor Soc., Pa. Watercolor Soc. (assoc.). Avocations: travel, knitting, sewing, reading. Home: 270 Southward Drive Moon Township, PA 15108-3150

PODD, ANN, newspaper editor; b. Buffalo, Jan. 15, 1954; d. Edward and Florence (Bojan) P.; m. Timothy Murray, 1980; children: Laura, Gregory. AB, Syracuse U., 1976; MBA, SUNY, Buffalo, 1981. Reporter AP, 1977, Buffalo Courier-Express, 1977-80, bus. editor, 1980-82, Bergen (N.J.) Record, 1982-88, New York Daily News, 1988-90, assoc. editor, 1990-92, assoc. editor, dir. human resources, 1992-93; dep. spot news editor Wall St. Jour., N.Y.C., 1994, spot news editor, 1994—2000, nat. TV editor, 2000—03, day editor, 2003—. Office: Wall St Journal 200 Liberty St New York NY 10281-1003

PODELL, JEAN ELIZABETH MESBERG, artist; b. Eveluth, Minn., Feb. 19, 1917; d. George and Clara (Belond) Mesberg; m. William B. Podell, Nov. 30, 1941 (dec. 1973); 1 child, Penny E. Podell Ballantyne. Student, Layton Sch. Art, Milw., 1935-36. Mem. Wis. Designer Craftsman, Milw., 1957-71, pres., 1962-64, dir., 1965-68; profl. enamelist. One-woman shows Charles Dix Gallery, Delafield, Wis., Marian Studios Mt. Mary Coll., Milw., Alverno Coll. Floretti Gallery, Milw., Kenosha (Wis.) Mus., Chgo. Pub. Libr.; exhibited in group shows Smithsonian Inst., Rochester (Minn.) Art Ctr., Madison (Wis.) Art Ctr., others; represented in permanent collections Milw. Art Ctr., St. Mary and Alverno Colls., pvt. collections in no. Calif. and other locations. Mem. Wis. Designer-Craftsman (pres. 1962-64, dir. 1965-68), Am. Craftsman Coun., Lamorinda Arts Alliance. Avocation: watercolor painting.

PODHAJSKI, BLANCHE RITA, language foundation administrator; b. New Britain, Conn., Sept. 4, 1945; d. Charles Anthony and Blanche Margaret (Poplawski) P.; m. Kenneth R. Kreiling, June 22, 1990. BS in Speech and Hearing, Boston U., 1967; MS in Speech Pathology, U. Vt., 1969; PhD in Learning Disabilities, Northwestern U., 1980. Speech/lang. pathologist Ctr. Disorders of Comm. Med. Ctr. Hosp. of Vt., Burlington, 1968-70, acting dir. Ctr. Disorders of Comm., 1970-71, dir. Ctr. Disorders of Comm., 1971-78; asst. prof. learning disabilities Northwestern U., Evanston, Ill., 1980-81; pvt. practice as lang. and learning disabilities specialist Aesculapius Med. Ctr., South Burlington, Vt., 1981-83; founder, pres. Stern Ctr. for Lang. and Learning, Williston, Vt., 1983—; clin. assoc. prof. neurology dept. neurology U. Vt. Med. Sch., Burlington, 1971—. Field faculty Goddard Coll., Plainfield, Vt., 1973-76, summer vis. prof., 1980; adj. faculty Johnson (Vt.) State Coll., 1975-79; adj. faculty dept. comm. sci. and disorders, 1983—; mem. Vt. State Dept. Edn. Task Force, Vt. Spl. Edn. Evaluation Project, 1985; exec. bd. dirs. Vt. New Eng. br. Orton Dyslexia Soc., 1986; presenter in field. Co-author: Sounds Abound; contbr. articles to profl. jours. Commencement speaker Pine Ridge Sch., Williston, 1991, bd. dirs., edn. com. chair, 1989; steering com. Vt. State Colls. Am. Reads, 1997; adult edn. consortium Md. State Dept., 1997; mem. collaborative program com. Vt. Lab. Sch. Collaborative, 1998. Grantee Found. for Children with Learning Disabilities, 1985, Vt. Dept. Spl. Edn., 1986, Vt. Dept. Vocat. Rehab., 1992, Kresge Found., 1994, Freeman Found., 1994-00, Alma Gibbs Donchian Found., 1995-99; Turrell scholar, 1994-98. Mem. Am. Speech Lang. and Hearing Assn. (cert. clin. competence), Coun. for Exceptional Children (divsn. for children with learning disabilities), Vt. Speech and Hearing Assn. (pres.-elect 1977-78, clin. achievement award 1989), Vt. Assn. for Learning Disabilities (lifetime hon., outstanding leadership award for contbns. to learning disabled 1976, lamp of knowledge award 1983), Orton Soc. Office: 135 Allen Brook Ln Williston VT 05495-9209

PODSIADLO, MARIA J. human resources analyst; b. Cleve., July 13, 1977; d. Boguslaw and Theresa Maria Podsiadlo. BS in Psychology, John Carroll U., Cleve., 1999. Human resources analyst ICI Paints, Cleve., 1999—. Vol. work. Mem.: Cleve. Soc. Human Resource Mgmt., Nat. Soc. Human Resource Mgmt. Avocations: dance, reading, fgn. langs., music, travel.

PODUSKA, T. F. artist; b. Cedar Falls, Iowa, Dec. 6, 1925; d. Everett Fleming and Vessie Mitchell; m. Robert D. Poduska, Dec. 27, 1948; children: Ann Poduska McCue, Sue Poduska Niksic. BA, Univ. No. Iowa, 1948. Trustee Denver Art Mus., Denver, 1977—83; bd. mem. Foothills Art Ctr., Golden, Colo. Exhibitions include invitational exhibitions Foothills Art Ctr. 35th Anniversary, 2003, Bus. of Art Ctr., Colo. Springs, Colo., 2003, Gallery of Contemporary Art, U. Colo., 2001, Miriam Perlman Gallery, Chgo., Ill., 1996, Reiss Gallery, Denver, Colo., 1996, exhibitions include Juried Shows Ctr. of The Arts, Tubac, Ariz., 1995, Level to Level, Johnson-Humrikhouse Mus., 1990, Exhibition to India, Bombay, India, 1989, NAWA, 100 Works: 100 Yrs., Nat. Travelling Exhibition, 1989, Nat. Assoc. Women Artists, N.Y.C., 1985, Represented in permanent collections Littleton Hist. Mus., Littleton, Colo., Denver Art Mus., Denver, Colo., Atlantic Richfield Corp., Amoco, Petro-Lewis Corp., Empire Savings, Bill Walters, Exeter, USD West, Mitchell Energy Corp., Piton Found., Ctrl. Bank, Glendale Fed., Laguna Hills, Calif., Marriott Hotels, Syracuse, N.Y., IBM. Recipient Colo. Gov. award, State of Colo., 1977, Cile Bach award, Denver Art Mus., 1991. Mem.: Foothills Art Ctr., Soc. of Layerists in Multimedia, Denver Art Mus. Home: 10233 W Powers Ave Littleton CO 80127

PODWALL, KATHRYN STANLEY, biology educator; b. Chgo., Oct. 14; d. Frank and Marie C. Stanley. BS, U. Ill.; MA, NYU. Prof. biology Nassau C.C., Garden City, NY. Developmental reviewer West Ednl. Pub., Amesbury, Mass. and Highland Park, Ill., 1989, 91-92; reviewer AAAS, Washington, 1970—; exec. bd., advisor Women's Faculty Assn., Nassau C.C., 1990—, pres, 2000-2002; lectr. in field. Author: Tested Studies for Laboratory Teaching, vol. 5, 1993; editor: (books and cassettes) Rhyming Simon Books and Cassettes, 1990, Sight Reading Syncopation, 1998, Today's Way To Play the Standards, 2000, Today's Way To Play the Classics, 2000, (book and CD) Cartoons & Car Tunes, 2001, Cartoons & Kid Tunes, 2002, Cartoons and Christmas Tunes, 2003. Recipient L.I. Alzheimer's Found. Svc. award, 2002, Excellence award, Nat. Inst. for Staff and Orgnl. Devel., 2003. Mem. AAUW, Nat. Assn. Biology Tchrs. (life), Nat. Sci. Tchrs. Assn. (life), Soc. for Coll. Sci. Tchrs., Am. Women in Sci., Met. Assn. Coll. and Univ. Biologists, Nat. Cathedral Assn., N.Y. Acad. of Scis., Friends of Archives (charter), Xerces Soc., Southampton Colonial Soc., LaSalle County Hist. Soc. (life), Garden City Hist. Soc. (life), Soroptimists (bd. dirs. club 1 1994-96, club pres. 1992-94, Nassau County Pres. award 2001), U. Ill. Alumni Assn. (life). Avocations: travel, gardening, zoological pursuits. Office: Nassau Community College One Education Dr Garden City NY 11530 Office Phone: 516-572-7575. Business E-Mail: podwalk@ncc.edu.

POE, CHERYL TONI, music educator; b. Denver, Sept. 23, 1943; d. Anthony Joseph Kotwica and Dorothy Jean Rusch; m. Gerald Dean Poe (div. Aug. 1999); children: Lauren, Russell. BA, Western State Coll., 1965; M in Music Edn., U. Portland, 1974. Music tchr. Minot (N.D.) State Coll., 1969—71, Portland (Oreg.) Pub. Schs., 1975—76, Eugene (Oreg.) 4-J Schs., 1976—80, Howard Bishop Mid. Sch., Gainesville, Fla., 1980—82; clk. Sabine Music Ctr., Gainesville, 1983—85; music tchr. Martha Manson Acad., Gainesville, 1985—88, Sch. Bd. Alachua County, Gainesville, 1988—. Pres, bd. mem. Alachua County Youth Orch., Fla., 1984—; bd. mem. Found. for Promotion Music, Gainesville, 1998—. Children's ch. choir dir. St. Augustine Cath. Ch., Gainesville, 2000—. Mem.: Am. Orff Schuwerk Assn., Fla. Elem. Music Educators (pres. 2000—03), Delta Kappa Gamma, Phi Delta Kappa.

POE, LAURA, nursing educator, administrator; b. Salt Lake City, July 20, 1962; d. William D. and Laree Jardine (Birch) P. Grad., Utah Tech. Coll., 1980; assoc. degree, Brigham Young U., 1984, B., 1986, MS, 1988. Asst. dir. Divsn. Occupl. and Profl. Licensing Utah Bd. Nursing, exec. dir. Author: (with others) Geri-Assistant Care Manual; contbr. articles to profl. jours. Mem. Utah Nurses Assn. (del., chair govt. rels. com.), Nightingale Soc., Phi Kappa Phi, Sigma Theta Tau.

POEN, KATHRYN LOUISE, music educator, performing arts association administrator; b. Decorah, Iowa, Mar. 4, 1927; d. Arthur Nicolai and Emma Margaret Lomen; m. Roger Dean Walker, Nov. 25, 1949 (div. June 5, 1974); children: Bonnie Jo Walker, Marcia Lee Walker, Randall Craig Walker; m. Monte Mac Poen, May 22, 1982. BA, Iowa State Tchrs. Coll., 1949; MusM, U. Ariz., 1968. Music educator pub. schs., Iowa, 1950—55, 1960—61, 1962—76, Flagstaff, Ariz., 1976—90; founder, dir. Flagstaff Light Opera Co., 1995—. Mem. Flagstaff Festival of Arts, 1992—93; dir., mem. Flagstaff chpt.Sweet Adelines, 1990—2000. Composer songs. Mem.: Am. Choral Dirs. Assn., Ariz. Tchrs. of Music Assn., Ariz. Music Educators Assn., Music Educators Nat. Conf. Avocations: travel, collecting. Home: 3703 N Grandview Dr Flagstaff AZ 86004 E-mail: pianomewsik@aol.com.

POETHIG, EUNICE BLANCHARD, clergywoman; b. Hempstead, N.Y., Jan. 16, 1930; d. Werner J. and Juliet (Stroh) Blanchard; m. Richard Paul Poethig, June 7, 1952; children: Richard Scott, Kathryn Aileen, Johanna Klare, Margaret Juliet, Erika Christy. BA, De Pauw U., 1951; MA, Union Theol. Sem., 1952; MDiv, McCormick Theol. Sem., N.Y.C., 1975, STM, 1977; PhD, Union Theol. Sem., 1985. Ordained to ministry Presbyn. Ch., 1979. Missionary United Presbyn. Ch. USA to United Ch. of Christ, The Philippines, 1956-72; mem. faculty Ellinwood Coll. Christian Edn., Manila, 1957-61; mem. faculty, campus ministry Philippine Women's U., Manila, 1962-68. Bd. dirs. Jane Addams Conf., Journey's End Refugee Resettlement Agy., Coun. of Bishops and Execs. of Buffalo Area Met. Ministries; trustee Presbyn. Found., 1991-94, Gen. Bd. Nat. Coun. Chs. Christ, 1995-97; editor New Day Pubs., Manila, 1969-72; curriculum editor Nat. Coun. Chs., Manila, 1962-72; assoc. exec. Presbytery Chgo., 1979-85; exec. Presbytery of Western N.Y., 1986-93; dir. congl. ministries divsn. gen. assembly Gen. Assembly Coun., Presbyn. Ch. (U.S.A.), 1994-98; mem. Coun. Execs., Ill. Coun. Chs., 1980-85. Author: Bible Studies in Concern Response, A.D., 1975, (book) Good News Women, 1987, Sing, Shout and Clap for Joy: Psalms in Worship, 1989, Friendship Press Study on Philippines, 1989, Liturgy 9:1, 1990, Hunger Program Workbook, 1991; editor: (hym book series) Everybody, I Love You, 1971—72, 150 Plus Tomorrow: Churches Plan for the Future, 1982, 1985, Our Living Tradition, 1994, Women of Faith: 1986-1996, 1997, From Slavery to Promised Land, 1999, The Struggle for Equality: Women in Mission, 1999. Mem. Environ. Def. Fund; mem. planning com. Celebrate Adult Curriculum, 1987—93; mem. Erie County (N.Y.) Environ. Mgmt. Coun., 1990—93, NGO Forum UN Fourth World Conf. Women, Beijing, 1995; chmn. governing bd. Stony Point Ctr., 2003—; mem. planning com. Transatlantic Dialogue, 2003; mem. Women's Ordination Conf. Nat. Presbyn. Ch. Com., Presbyn. Gen. Assembly Challenge to the Ch. Fund., 1989; mem. design team Covenant People Curriculum, 1997; mem. futures com. Highland Presbyn. Ch., chair, 1997—99; mem. organizing bd. Asian Ctr. Theology and Strategy, Chgo., 1974; bd. dirs. Ch. Women United, Chgo., 1974—79; trustee McCormick Theol. Sem., Chgo., 1974—75; bd. dirs., mem. exec. com. Presbyn. Cmty. Ctr., Louisville, 1999—2001; bd. dirs. More Light Presbyns., 2000—03. Recipient Walker Cup, DePauw U., 1951; Nettie F. McCormick fellow in Old Testament Hebrew, McCormick Sem., Chgo., 1975; recipient Disting. Alumni award DePauw U., 2003. Mem. Internat. Platform Assn., Soc. Bibl. Lit., Soc. Ethnomusicology, Assn. Exec. Presbyters (bd. dirs., chairperson 1991-93), Am. Schs. Oriental Rsch., Witherspoon Soc., Nat. Assn. Religious Women, Internat. Assn. Women Mins., Nat. Assn. Presbyn. Clergywomen. Home: 1000 E 53rd St #613 Chicago IL 60615

POETTKER, MARY THERESE, music educator; b. Belleville, Ill., Aug. 29, 1950; d. Delmar Julius and Catherine Rita Thouvenot; m. Robert H. Poettker, Aug. 12, 1972; children: Christina, Scott, Jason, Jennifer. B in Music Edn., So. Ill. U., Edwardsville, 1972, M in Music Edn., 1974. Cert. tchr. vocal and instrument music tchr. K-12 Mo. Vocal music tchr. Ferguson (Mo.)-Florissant Sch. Dist., 1972—79, St. Elizabeth-St. Robert Regional Sch., St. Charles, Mo., 1981—. Dir. music St. Elizabeth Ann Seton Ch., St. Charles, 1983—. Nominee Disney Am. Tchr., Disney Co., 2001. Mem.: Mo. Music Educators Assn. (v.p. jr. high vocal and gen. music St. Louis Metro Dist. 8 1988—2000, Merit award St. Louis Metro Dist. 8 2001), Music Educators Nat. Conf., Nat. Pastoral Musicians (chpt. dir. 1998—, Outstanding Sch. Music Edn. 1996). Roman Catholic. Avocations: gardening, camping, crafts. Home: 112 Travelers Trail Saint Peters MO 63376-7149

POGREBIN, LETTY COTTIN, writer, lecturer; b. N.Y.C., June 9, 1939; d. Jacob and Cyral (Halpern) Cottin; m. Bertrand B. Pogrebin, Dec. 8, 1963; children: Abigail and Robin (twins), David. AB cum laude with spl. distinction in English and Am. Lit, Brandeis U., 1959. V.p. Bernard Geis Assocs. (book pubs.), N.Y.C., 1960-70; columnist The Working Woman column Ladies Home Jour., 1971-81; contbg. editor Tikkun mag., 1988—, Family Circle, 1989—; founding editor Ms mag., N.Y.C., 1971-87, columnist, editor at large, 1987-89, contbg. editor, 1990—; columnist The N.Y. Times, Newsday, Washington Post, Moment Mag., Washington, 1990—, Moment Mag., Washington, 1990—. Cons. Free to Be, You and Me projects, 1972—; lectr. women's issues and family politics, changing roles of men and women, friendship in Am., non-sexist child rearing and [illegible], Judaism and feminism, Mid-East politics. Author: How to Make It in a Man's World, 1970, Getting Yours: How to Make the System Work for the Working Woman, 1975, Growing Up Free, 1980, Stories for Free Children, 1982, Family Politics, 1983, Among Friends, 1986, Deborah, Golda, and Me: Being Female and Jewish in America, 1991, Getting Over Getting Older: An Intimate Journey, 1996, Three Daughters: A Novel, 2002; mem. editl. bd. Tikkun Mag., Commonquest mag.; contbr. articles to N.Y. Times, Washington Post, Boston Globe, The Nation, TV Guide, Family Circle, Elle, Travel & Leisure, also other mags., newspapers. Pres. Author's Guild, 1998-2002; bd. dirs. Ms. Found. for Edn. and Comm., New Israel Fund, Jewish Fund for Justice, Commn. on Women's Equality, Am. Jewish Congress, PEN Am.; mem. Task Force on Women Fedn. Jewish Philanthropies, Women's Forum. Pointer fellow Yale U., 1982, MacDowell Colony fellow, 1979, 89, 94, 2000, Cummington Colony Arts fellow 1985, Edna St. Vincent Millay Colony fellow, 1985; recipient Matrix award Women in Comm., 1981, Gloria Steinem Women of Vision award Ms. Found. for Women, 1990, Abram L. Sachar medal Brandeis U., 1994, Woman of Valor award Jewish Fund for Justice, 1997, Woman of Achievement award N. Shore Child and Family Assn., 1997, Hannah G. Solomon award Nat. Coun. Jewish Women, 1997, Woman of Distinction award Kingsborough Coll., 1998, U.S./Israel Women-to-Women award, 1999, N.Y.C. Contr.'s Jewish Heritage award, 1999; named Woman of Yr. Fifty-Plus Expo, 1997, Outstanding Scholars 21st Century, 2000, Vet. Feminists of Am. Hon. Roll, 2002. Address: care Rosenstone/Wender 3 E 48th St New York NY 10017-1027*

POHL, CATHERINE M. principal, educator; b. Ft. Benning, Ga., Mar. 18, 1958; d. Thomas D. Greisch and Mary L. Biever-Greisch; m. Michael A. Pohl, Mar. 31, 1990; children: Andrew, Daniel. BA, Marquette U., 1980, postgrad. Tchr. Christ King Sch., Wauwatosa, Wis., 1980—2001; prin. Our Lady of the Lakes Cath. Grade Sch., Random Lake, Wis., 2001—. Dist. rep. MAEPA, Milw., 2002—. Parade coord. Pt. Washington (Wis.) Fish Day, 1980—; pres. Pt. Washington Fish Day, 1991—93; parade coord. Simplicity Mfg., 1997, The Wall That Heals, 1998. Recipient Key to City, Pt. Washington Fish Day, 1993. Roman Catholic. Avocations: watching sports, knitting, gardening, children, organizing. Home: 1890 Jay Rd Belgium WI 53004 E-mail: ourladyrls@archmil.org.

POHL, ELIZABETH, contracting company executive; b. Dec. 15, 1957; CEO TC Enterprises, Inc., Albuquerque, 1986—. Mem.: Albuquerque Hispano C. of C. Office: TC Enterprises Inc 6000 Indian School Rd NE Albuquerque NM 87110-4178 Fax: 505-883-6275.

POHL, KATHLEEN SHARON, editor; b. Sandusky, Mich., Apr. 7, 1951; d. Gerald Arthur and Elizabeth Louise (Neukamm) P.; m. Bruce Mark Allen Reynolds, June 11, 1982. BA in Spanish, Valparaiso U., 1973; MA in English, No. Mich. U., 1975. Producer, dir. fine arts Sta. WNMU-FM, Marquette, Mich., 1981-82; instr. communications Waukesha County (Wis.) Tech. Inst., 1983; editor Ideals mag., Milw., 1983-85; editor, mng. editor Raintree Pubs., Milw., 1985-87; mng. editor, now exec. editor Country Woman mag., Greendale, Wis., 1987—; exec. editor Country Handcrafts mag., Greendale, 1990-93, Taste of Home Mag., Greendale, Wis., 1993—; editor Talk About Pets, Greendale, 1994-95. Author nature book series, 1985-87; sr. editor: Country Woman Christmas Book, 1996—; mng. editor: Irwin the Sock (Chgo. Book Clinic award 1988); exec. editor Taste of Home's Quick Cooking Mag., 1998—, Down the Aisle Countr Style, 2000, Taste of Home's Light & Tasty Mag., 2000—. Mem. Nat. Mus. of Women in Arts, Alpha Lambda Delta (hon.). Home: N54 W26326 Lisbon Rd Sussex WI 53089-4249 Office: Country Woman Mag 5400 S 60th St Greendale WI 53129-1404

POHLMANN, EVELYN GAWLEY, music educator, consultant; b. Pasadena, Calif., May 3, 1942; m. John Ogden Pohlmann, Aug. 8, 1964; children: Alison Pohlmann Espinosa, Victoria Elizabeth. BA, Occidental Coll., 1964. Life tchg. credential Calif. Studio piano tchr., Seal Beach, Calif., 1971—. Tchr. cons. Internat. Piano Tchg. Found., 1976—. Recipient Ruby Sword of Honor, Delta Province, Sigma Alpha Iota, 1964. Mem.: Music Tchrs.' Assn. Calif. (pres. 1988—90), Long Beach Symphony Guild (pres. 1994—95).

POIANI, EILEEN LOUISE, mathematics educator, college administrator, higher education planner; b. Newark, Dec. 17, 1943; d. Hugo Francis and Eileen Louise (Crecca) P. BA in Math., Douglass Coll., 1965; MS in Math., Rutgers U., 1967, PhD in Math., 1971. Tchg. asst., grad. preceptor Rutgers U., New Brunswick, N.J., 1966-67; asst. counselor Douglass Coll., New Brunswick, 1967, 69-70; instr. math. St. Peter's Coll., Jersey City, 1967-70, asst. prof., 1970-74, dir. of self-study, 1974-76, assoc. prof., 1974-80, prof., 1980—, asst. to pres., 1976-80, asst. to pres. for planning, 1980-96, exec. asst. to pres., 1996-98, v.p. for student affairs, 1999—. Chair U.S. Commn. on Math. Instrn., NRC of NAS, Washington, 1983-90; founding nat. dir. Women and Math. Lectureship Program, Washington, 1975-81, adv. bd., 1981—; project dir. Consortium for Advancement of Pvt. Higher Edn., Washington, 1986-88; mem. N.J. Math. Coalition, 1991—, Nat. Seminar on Jesuit Higher Edn., 1990-94, strategic planning com. N.J. Assn. Ind. Colls. and Univs., 1990-92; charter trustee Rutgers U., 1992-2004; Nutley panelist Centennial Celebration, 2002; advisor NSF Funded Project of Bank St. Coll. and EDC/Ctr. for Children and Tech., 2003—. Author: (with others) Mathematics Tomorrow, 1981, Encyclopedia of Mathematics Education; contbr. articles to profl. jours. Mem. Newark Mus., Nutley (N.J.) Hist. Soc., Friends of Newark Libr.; trustee Nutley Free Pub. Libr., 1974-77, St. Peter's Prep. Sch., Jersey City, 1986-92; active fee arbitration commn. N.J. Supreme Ct., 1983-86, ct. ethics com., 1986-90; U.S. nat. rep. Internat. Congress Math. Edn., Budapest, Hungary, 1988; statewide planning com. NCCJ, 1988-92, youth leadership coun., 1992—; chair evaluation teams Mid. States Assn. Coll. and Schs.; U.S. del. Internat. Congress on Math; trustee The Cath. Advocate, 1993-2003; adv. NSF Funded Project Bank St. Coll. & Ed. Ctr. for Children & Tech., 2003-. Recipient George F. Johnson, S.J. Alumni Faculty award, 1976, Douglass Soc. award Douglass Coll., 1982, Outstanding Cmty. Svc. award Christopher Columbus Found., N.J., 1994, Outstanding Svc. award Middle States Assn. Colls. and Schs., 1994, Cert. of Appreciation for outstanding contbns. as nat. dir. women and math. program, 1993, Varsity Letter plaque for leadership and svc. St. Peter's Prep, 1997; named Danforth Assoc., Danforth Found., 1972-86, SPC Legend, Students of St. Peters Coll., 2002, Humanitarian award NCCJ, 2003, N.J. Women of Achievement award N.J. State Fedn. Women's Clubs, 2003, Alumnae Recognition award Douglass Coll., 2003; named to Nutley Hall of Fame, 2003. Mem. AAUP, Math. Assn. Am. (bd. dirs. lectureship program, gov. NJ chpt. 1972-79, chair human resources coun. 1991-96, Outstanding Coll. Tchg. award 1993), Nat. Coun. Tchrs. Math. (spkr. 1974—), Soc. Coll. and Univ. Planning (program com. 1989—, spkr. nat. conf. 1986, 88-90, judge grad. paper competition), Com. on Math. with Disabilities, Com on Devel. of Man, Pi Mu Epsilon (pres. 1987-90, C.C. MacDuffee award for disting. svc. to math. 1995), Phi Beta Kappa, Alpha Sigma Nu, Tri Beta. Roman Catholic. Avocations: gourmet cooking, travel, golf. Office: St Peter's Coll 2641 Kennedy Blvd Jersey City NJ 07306-5997 Office Phone: 201-915-9018.

POINDEXTER, BARBARA GLENNON, secondary school educator; b. Dallas, Oct. 19, 1937; d. Victor and Ruth (Gaskins) Ward; m. Noble Turner Poindexter, Aug. 2, 1994; 1 child, Victoria Angela Russo. BS, Tex. Woman's U., 1958; postgrad., Kans. State U., 1969-70; grad., U. Northern Iowa, 1986. Cert. tchr. S.C., Kans., N.Mex., Tex. Drama and English tchr. Linn (Kans.) H.S., 1968-69; tchr. Mosquero (N.Mex.) H.S., 1973-74, Sumter (S.C.) Sch. Dist., Maywood Sch., 1974-76, Harleyville (S.C.) H.S., 1976-78, Hampton (S.C.) H.S., 1978-79, Centerville Sch., Cottageville, S.C., 1979-80; tchr. English Scurry-Rosser Sch., Scurry, Tex., [illegible]; tchr. French and Spanish Christ the King, Dallas, 1982-83; tchr. French and English, chmn. fgn. lang. dept. Wilmer-Hutchins H.S., Dallas, 1983-94; tchr. French and English Molina H.S., Dallas, 1997—. Mem.: Theta Alpha Phi. Democrat. Methodist. Home: 5315 Maple Springs Blvd Dallas TX 75235-8326 Office: Molina HS 2355 Duncanville Rd Dallas TX 75211-6532

POIRIER, ELIZABETH A. state representative, state legislator; Degree, Johnson & Wales Univ. State rep. legis., Mass., 1999—. Republican. Office: State Ho Rm 541 Boston MA 02133 also: Dist Office 117 Grove St North Attleboro MA

POKRAS, SHEILA FRANCES, retired judge; b. Newark, Aug. 5, 1935; m. Norman M. Pokras, 1954; children: Allison, Andrea, Larry. Student, Beaver Coll., 1953-54; BS in Edn., Temple U., 1957; JD cum laude, Pepperdine U., 1969. Bar: Calif. 1970, U.S. Dist. Ct. D.C. 1970, U.S. Dist. Ct. Calif. 1970, U.S. Supreme Ct. 1975. Tchr. elem. and secondary schs., Phila. and Newark, 1957-59; pvt. practice law Long Beach, Calif., 1970-78; city councilwoman Lakewood, Calif., 1972-76; judge Long Beach Mcpl. Ct., 1978-80, L.A. Superior Ct., 1980-98; ret., 1998. Supervising judge, 1986; del. Calif. State Dem. Cen. Com., 1975, Calif. State Conv., 1975; mem. Com. on Gender Bias in Calif. Courts, 1986-89 Advisor Jr. League, 1980-85; mem. early childhood adv. bd. Long Beach City Coll.; bd. dirs. Long Beach Alcoholism Coun., 1979-80, Boys and Girls Club Am., 1981-89, Long Beach Symphony, 1985, Jewish Community Fedn., 1982-86, past mem. community rels. com.; active Nat. Women's Polit. Caucus, LWV. Named Woman of Yr. NOW, Long Beach, 1984; recipient Torch of Liberty award B'nai B'rith Anti-Defamation League, 1974; honoree Nat. Conf. Christians and Jews, 1986. Mem. ABA, AAUW, Nat. Assn. Women Judges (dist. supr. 1986), Calif. Bar Assn. (judges div.), Calif. Judges Assn. (mem. ann. seminar com. 1981-89), Mcpl. Cts. Judges Assn. (mem. Marshall com. 1979-80), L.A. County Bar Assn. (judges div., mem. arbitration com.), Women Lawyers Assn., L.A. (judges sect.), Women Lawyers Assn. Long Beach, Long Beach Legal Aid Found. (v.p. 1976-78), Long Beach Bar Assn. (active various coms., bd. govs. 1977-78, Judge of Yr. 1987), Long Beach C. of C. (bd. dirs.). Avocations: swimming, golf, jogging, classical music, movies.

POLAN, ANNETTE LEWIS, artist, educator; b. Huntington, W.Va., Dec. 8, 1944; d. Lake and Dorothy (Lewis) Polan; m. Arthur Lowell Fox, Jr., Aug. 31, 1969 (div. 1994); children: Courtney Van Winkle Fox, Arthur Lowell Fox III. 1st degree, Inst. des Profs. de Francaise, Paris, 1965; BA, Hollins U., 1967; postgrad., Corcoran Coll. Art and Design, 1968-69. Prof. Corcoran Coll. Art and Design, Washington, 1974—, chmn. painting dept., 1991—. Vis. artist Art Therapy Italia, Vignale, Italy, 1986; dir. summer program La Napoule Art Found., Chateau de la Napoule, France, 1987, Chateau de la Napoule, 88, Chateau de la Napoule, 90; guest lectr., China, 89, China, 96, Japan, 89, Japan, 96. Say What I Am, 1989, Relearning the Dark, 1991, Doers of the Word, 1995, portrait commn., Sandra Day O'Connor, Va. Gov. Gaston Caperton, George Calvert, 1st Lord Baltimore, Edward Villela. Bd. dirs. Washington Project Arts/Corcoran Mus., 1994—2000, v.p., 1995—; bd. dirs. Smith Farm. Mem.: Corcoran Faculty Assn. (pres. 1988—89), Washington Women's Forum, Internat. Women's Forum. Avocations: equitation, skiing. Office: Corcoran Coll Art and Design 1801 35th St NW Washington DC 20007-2211 E-mail: apolan@aol.com.

POLAN, MARY LAKE, obstetrics and gynecology educator; b. Las Vegas, N.Mex., July 17, 1943; Student, Smith Coll., Paris, 1963—64; BA cum laude, Conn. Coll., 1965; PhD in Biophysics and Biochemistry, Yale U., 1970, MD, 1975. Diplomate Am. Bd. Ob-Gyn., Am. Bd. Reproductive Endocrinology, Nat. Bd. Med. Examiners. Postdoctoral fellow dept. biology, NIH postdoctoral fellow Yale U., New Haven, 1970—72, resident dept. ob-gyn. Sch. Medicine, 1975—78, fellow in oncology, then fellow in endocrinology-infertility, 1978—80, asst. instr., then lectr. molecular biophysics-biochemistry, 1970—72, instr., then asst. prof. ob-gyn., 1978—79, 1980—85, assoc. prof., 1985—90; clin. clk. in ob-gyn. and pediat. Radcliffe Infirmary, Oxford (Eng.) U. Med. Sch., 1974; instr. Pahlavi U., Shiraz, Iran, 1978; Katharine Dexter McCormick and Stanley McCormick Meml. prof. Stanford (Calif.) Sch. Medicine, 1990—, chmn. dept. gynecology and obstetrics, 1990—. Vis. prof. Hunan Med. Coll., Changsha, China, 1986; mem. med. bd. Yale-China Assn., 1987—90; liaison com. on ethics in modern world Conn. Coll., New London, 1988—90; mem. med. adv. bd. Ova-Med Corp., Palo Alto, Calif., 1992—95, Vivus, Menlo Park, Calif., 1993—; bd. dirs. Metra Biosys., Mountain View, Quidel, San Diego, Am. Home Products, Madison, NJ, 1994—; mem. reproductive endocrinology study sect. NIH, 1989—90, co-chmn. task force on opportunities for rsch. on woman's health, 1991. Author: Second Seed, 1987; guest editor: Seminars in Reproductive Endocrinology, 1984, Infertility and Reproductive Medicine Clinics of North America: GnRH Analogues, Vol. 4, 1993; editor, with DeCherney: Surgery in Reproductive Endocrinology, 1987; ; editor: (with DeCherney, S. Boyers and R. Lee) Decision Making in Infertility; ad hoc reviewer: Jour. Clin. Endocrinology and Metabolism, Fertility and Sterility, Ob-Gyn., others; contbr. chapters to books, articles to med. jours. Fellow, NSRA, 1981—82; grantee, NIRA, 1982—85, HD, 1985—90, NRSA, 1987—88, Johnson & Johnson, 1993—96; scholar, Assn. Acad. Health Ctrs., 1993—96. Fellow: ACOG (PROLOG task force for reproductive endocrinology and infertility 1988—89, rep. to CREOG coun. 1994—97); mem.: Bay Area Reproductive Endocrine Soc., San Francisco Gynecologic Soc., Inst. Medicine (com. on rsch. capabilities of acad. depts. ob-gyn. 1990—91, bd. on health scis. policy 1992—96), Am. Gynecologic and Obstetric Soc., Soc. for Reproductive Endocrinologists, Soc. for Gynecologic Investigation, Am. Fertility Soc., Phi Beta Kappa. Home: 4251 Manuela Ct Palo Alto CA 94306-3731 Office: Stanford U Sch Medicine Dept Gyn OB 300 Pasteur Dr Stanford CA 94305-5317*

POLASCIK, MARY ANN, ophthalmologist; b. Elkhorn, W.Va., Dec. 28, 1940; d. Michael and Elizabeth (Halko) Polascik; m. Joseph Ellie, Oct. 2, 1973; 1 dau., Laura Elizabeth Polascik Jr. BA, Rutgers U., 1967; MD, Pritzker Sch. Medicine, 1971. Jr. pharmacologist Ciba Pharm Co., Summit, N.J., 1961-67; intern Billings Hosp., Chgo., 1971-72; resident in ophthalmology U. Chgo. Hosp., 1972-75; practice medicine specializing in ophthalmology Dixon, Ill., 1975—. Pres. McNichols Clinic, Ltd.; cons. ophthalmology, Jack Mabley Devel. Ctr., 1976-93; mem. staff Katherine Shaw Bethea Hosp. Bd. dirs. Sinnossippi Mental Health Ctr., 1977-82, Dixon Cmty. Trust Mental Health Ctr., 1989—. Mem. Am. Acad. Ophthalmology, Alpha Sigma Lambda, Galena Territory Club. Roman Catholic. Office: 1700 S Galena Ave Dixon IL 61021-9695

POLASKI, ANNE SPENCER, lawyer; b. Pittsfield, Mass., Nov. 13, 1952; d. John Harold and Marjorie Ruth (Hackett) Spencer; m. James Joseph Polaski, Sept. 14, 1985. BA in Psychology, Allegheny Coll., 1974; MSW, U. Pa., 1976; JD, George Washington U., 1979. Bar: D.C. 1979, U.S. Dist. Ct. (D.C. dist.) 1980, U.S. Ct. Appeals (D.C. cir.) 1980, Ill. 1982, U.S. Dist. Ct. (no. dist.) Ill. 1982, U.S. Ct. Appeals (7th cir.) 1982. Law clk. to assoc. judge D.C. Ct., Washington, 1979-80; trial atty. Commodity Futures Trading Commn., Chgo., 1980-84, sr. trial atty., 1984, dep. regional counsel, 1984-88; assoc. Gottlieb and Schwartz, Chgo., 1988-91; staff atty. Chgo. Bd. of Trade, 1991-92, sr. atty., 1992-94, asst. gen. counsel, 1994—. Mem. ABA, Chgo. Bar Assn. Office: Chgo Bd of Trade 141 W Jackson Blvd Chicago IL 60604-2992 E-mail: apolaski@cbot.com.

POLATTY, ROSE JACKSON, civic worker; b. Atlanta, Sept. 17, 1922; d. James Wilmot and Esther Ann (Sweeny) Jackson; m. George Junius Polatty,Nov. 27, 1942; children: George Junius, Robert Wilmot, Rose Crystal, Richard James. AB in Journalism, U. Ga., 1943; postgrad., Oglethorpe U., 1962-63, Ga. State U., 1963. Active U. Ga. Alumni Soc.; pres. Class of 1943 Alumni, 1948-58, bd. mgr., 1966-69; v.p., 1971-73; chmn. seminar, 1971; exec. sec. Atlanta Boy Choir, 1968-69; bd. dirs. Atlanta Arts Coun., 1968-69; adv. com. Kennesaw Coll. on Wheels, 1974-78; bicentennial chmn. City of Roswell (Ga.), 1975-76; sec. hist. preservation commn., 1978-82; chmn., 1983-84. Active Ga. Trust Hist. Preservation, Ga. Conservancy. Mem. adminstrv. bd., chmn. altar guild, Roswell United Meth. Ch., 1977-89. Recipient Recognition award Nat. 4-H Alumni, 1959, Svc. award City of Roswell, 1976, Cmty. Svc. award Roswell Optimist Club, 1977, Roswell Jaycees Leadership award, 1977, Cmty. Svc. award Zion Bapt. Ch., 1977, Vol. award Friends Roswell Libr., 2000. Mem. Roswell Hist. Soc. (charter 1971), Atlanta Symphony Assocs., Colonial Dames XVII Century (charter Nicholas Wallingford chpt. 1979, v.p. 1980-81, pres. 1982-83), U.D.C. (No. Fulton chpt.), Altanta Audubon Soc., High Mus. Art (charter), PEO (chpt. AA, Ga., charter 1977), DAR (Joseph Habersham chpt.), Roswell Women's (charter 1948, pres. 1966-68), Roswell Garden (charter 1951, pres. 1975-77), N. Fulton Coun. Garden Clubs (charter 1975, pres. 1975-77), Kappa Delta,Delta Omicron, Phi Beta Kappa, Phi Kappa Phi, Kappa Delta Pi. Home: 889 Mimosa Blvd Roswell GA 30075-4436 E-mail: rosejp@aol.com.

POLEMITOU, OLGA ANDREA, accountant; b. Nicosia, Cyprus, June 28, 1950; d. Takis and Georgia (Nicolaou) Chrysanthou. BA with honors, U. London, 1971; PhD, Ind. U., Bloomington, 1981. CPA Ind. Asst. productivity officer Internat. Labor Office/Cyprus Productivity Ctr., Nicosia, 1971-74; cons. Arthur Young & Co., N.Y.C., 1981; mgr. Coopers & Lybrand, Newark, 1981-83; dir. Bell Atlantic, Reston, Va., 1983-97; v.p. corp. auditing Columbia Energy Group, Herndon, 1997—2000; pres., CEO Aristion, Inc., Reston, Va., 2000—. Chairperson adv. coun. Extended Day Care Cmty. Edn., West Windsor Plainsboro, NJ, 1987—88. Contbr. articles to profl. jours. Bus. cons. project bus. Jr. Achievement, Indpls., 1984—85. Mem.: AICPAs, NAFE, Princeton Network Profl. Women, Va. Soc. CPAs, N.J. Soc. CPAs (sec. mem. in industry com.), Ind. CPA Soc., Nat. Trust Hist. Preservation. Avocations: water-skiing, tennis. Home: PO Box 2744 Reston VA 20195-0744 Office: 11921 Freedom Dr Ste 550 Reston VA 20190

POLENZ, JOANNA MAGDA, psychiatrist; b. Cracow, Poland, Oct. 20, 1936; came to U.S., 1961; d. Mieczyslaw and Nusia (Goldberger) Uberall; m. Daryl Louis Polenz, July 8, 1962 (div. 1991); children: Teresa Ann, Daryl Philip, Elizabeth Sophia. MD, U. Sydney, Australia, 1960; MPH, Columbia U., 1992. Diplomate Am. Bd. Psychiatry and Neurology. Intern Bklyn. Hosp., 1961-62; resident in psychiatry Mt. Sinai Med. Ctr., N.Y.C., 1962-65, ednl. fellow, 1965-66, rsch. assoc., 1966-67; med. dir. Tappan Zee clin. Phelps Meml. Hosp., Tarrytown, NY, 1968-71, dir. dept. psychiatry, 1972-77; sr. attending psychiatrist Meml. Hosp. Ctr., 1972-93; pvt. practice Briarcliff Manor, NY, 1971-91; physician Joint Commn. Accreditation of Healthcare Orgns., Oakbrook Terrace, Ill., 1993—; pres. Sch. of Health-.com, N.Y.C., 1998—. Lectr. in field. Author: In Defense of Marriage, 1981; (with other) Test Your Marriage IQ, 1984, Test Your Success IQ, 1985, The Last Sick Generation, 2000; contbr. articles to profl. jours.; numerous TV appearances including Phil Donahue, 1988, Oprah Winfrey 1984. Grant Found. grant, 1970. Fellow Am. Psychiat. Assn.; mem. AMA, Am. Coll. Physician Execs., N.Y. Acad. Scis., Pan Am. Med. Assn., Westchester Psychiat. Assn. (sec. 1982-85, chmn. fellowship com. 1989-98). Avocations: travel, international affairs. Home: 123 E 75th St Apt 10B New York NY 10021 Office: SchoolofHealth.com 123 E 75th St Ste 10B New York NY 10021 Fax: 212-828-2507. E-mail: JPolenz@nyc.rr.com.

POLESE, KIM, software company executive; BS, U. Calif., Berkeley, 1984; student, U. Wash. Product mgr. Sun Microsys., 1988—95; co-founder, pres., CEO Marimba, Inc., 1996—2000, chmn., 1996—2003, bd. dirs., 1996—. Bd. dirs. TechNet. Bd. dirs. Do Something, Global Security Inst., U. Calif. President's Bd. Sci. and Innovation, Carnegie Mellon Computer Sci. Advisory Coun. Named one of Time Mags. Most Influential Ams. Mem.: Silicon Valley Mfg. Group. Achievements include a pivotal role in launching Java. Office: Marimba Inc 440 Clyde Ave Mountain View CA 94043-2232

POLESHUK, ALICIA L. alcohol/drug abuse services professional; d. William and Nina Poleshuk. BA with honors, Montclair State U., 1995; MSW, Rutgers U., 1998; MS, postgrad., Seton Hall U., 2002—. Lic. social worker N.J. Recreational therapist vol. Bergen Regional Med. Ctr., Paramus, NJ, 1996—97; social work intern Palisades Learning Ctr., Paramus, NJ, 1996—97; student assistance counselor Council on Alcoholism and Drug Abuse of Bergen, Inc., Hackensack, NJ, 1997—; therapist Pascack Mental Health Ctr., Park Ridge, NJ, 1999—. Scholar Hugh McGee scholar, Hackensack U. Med. Ctr., 1995. Mem.: NASW, Marriage and Family Student Assn. (exec. bd. dirs. 2001—), Am. Assn. Marriage and Family Therapy, Am. Psychol. Assn., End DWI. Roman Catholic. Personal E-mail: apoleshuk@aol.com.

POLETO, MARY MARGARET, orthopedic nurse; b. Troy, N.Y., May 4, 1959; d. Vincent P. and Marianne (DiDomenicantonio) P. BSN, Russell Sage Coll., 1981. Cert. Orthopedic Nurse. Staff nurse Albany (N.Y.) Med. Ctr., 1981-84, asst. nurse mgr., 1984-91, staff nurse, 1991—. Vol. post anesthesia care nurse Albany Plasticare Internat., Dominican Republic. Mem. Nat. Assn. Orthopedic Nurses, Capital Dist. Nurses Assn., Am. Assn. Spinal Cord Injured Nurses, Sigma Theta Tau. Republican. Roman Catholic. Avocations: reading, decorative painting. Home: 11 Cooper Ave Troy NY 12180-2703 Office: Albany Med Ctr Hosp New Scotland Ave Albany NY 12208-3491

POLEVOY, NANCY TALLY, lawyer, social worker, genealogist; b. N.Y.C., May 27, 1944; d. Charles H. and Bernice M. (Gang) Tally; m. Martin D. Polevoy, Mar. 19, 1967; children: Jason Tally, John Gerald. Student, Mt. Holyoke Coll., 1962—64; BA, Barnard Coll., 1966; MSW, Columbia U., 1968, JD, 1986. Bar: N.Y. 1987. Caseworker unmarried mothers' svc. Louise Wise Svcs., N.Y.C., 1967, caseworker adoption dept., 1969-71; caseworker Youth Consultation Svc., N.Y.C., 1968-69; asst. rsch. scientist, psychiat. social worker NYU Med. ctr., N.Y.C., 1973-81; adv. ct. apptd. spl. advs. Manhattan Family Ct., N.Y.C., 1981-82; cons. social work, 1981-86; matrimonial assoc. Ballon, Stoll & Itzler, 1987, Herzfeld & Rubin, P.C., 1987-88; pvt. practice N.Y.C. Contbr. articles to profl. jours. Mem. parents' adv. bd. Riverdale Country Sch., 1988—93; mem. outreach bd. Manhattan divsn. United Jewish Appeal Fedn., 1990—94, exec. bd. Manhattan divsn., 1992—94, mem. met. campaign cabinet, 1994—95, mem. task force aging, 2004—; trustee Am. Jewish Hist. Soc., 1992—, asst. treas., 1995—98, v.p., 1998—2003; trustee Jewish Assn. Svcs. to Aged, 1996—, v.p., 1999—2003; bd. dirs. Ctr. Jewish History, 1996—; mem. archives com. Ctrl. Synagogue, 1991—, chmn., 1994—. Recipient French Govt. prize, 1963, honor for lifetime cmty. svc., United Jewish Appeal Fedn. N.Y., 2003. Mem.: NASW, Acad. Cert. Social Workers, N.Y. State Bar Assn., Assn. Bar City of N.Y., Barnard Coll. Alumni Assn. (v.p. 1966, class pres. 1966 1996—). Home and Office: 1155 Park Ave New York NY 10128-1209

POLIKOWSKY, MARY ELIZABETH, retired English educator; b. St. Louis, June 2, 1938; d. James Franklin and Elizabeth Arminda (Durham) Heaton; m. Lawrence Burdette Cobb, Jr., Dec. 23, 1958 (wid. Aug. 1971); 1 child, Stephen Lawrence; m. John Hughes Polikowsky, June 25, 1993. AB, Okla. Bapt. U., 1959; MA, U. Wash., 1969, PhD, 1984. Tchr., English North Kansas City, Mo. Sch. Dist., 1960; thcr., lang. arts and social studies, jr. high Seattle Sch. Dist., 1961-67, tchr., lang. arts and social studies, h.s.,

1967-87; lectr. in English Western Wash. U., Bellingham, 1987-89, asst. prof. English, 1989-94. Dept. head English, Ingraham H.S., Seattle, 1977-83; co-dir. Puget Sound Writing Project, U. Wash., 1989-90, Fourth Corner Writing Project, Western Wash. U., 1991-94. Bd. dirs. ACLU, Bellingham, 1989-90; tutor Snohomish County Literacy Coalition, Everett, Wash., 1995-2003. Recipient Spl. Commendation, Citizen Com. for Acad. Excellence, Seattle Pub. Schs., 1981; summer rsch. grantee Western Wash. U., 1990; grantee U.S. Dept. Edn., Berkeley, Calif., 1992-94. Democrat. Avocations: reading, snorkeling, kayaking. Home: 9205 Olympic View Dr Edmonds WA 98020-2396 E-mail: marypoli3@hotmail.com.

POLIN, JANE L. foundation official; b. N.Y.C., Sept. 30, 1958; BA, Wesleyan U., Middletown, Conn., 1980; MBA, Columbia U., 1988. Asst. dir. ann. giving Wesleyan U., 1980-82; centennial fund assoc. Met. Opera Assn., N.Y.C., 1982-84; devel. officer Columbia U., N.Y.C., 1984-88; program mgr., comptr. GE Fund, Fairfield, Conn., 1988-99; v.p. cmty. devel. and corp. affairs Sperry & Hutchinson, Inc., 1999—2000, philanthropic advisor, 2001—. Panelist arts-in-edn. Nat. Endowment for Arts, Washington, 1989—90, 1994—95, NEH, 1997; adv. bd. mem. ARC, 1991—99, United Way Am., 1991—99, Inst. for Internat. Econs., 1995—99, Young Audiences, N.Y.C., 1991—2000, advt. coun., 1998—2003; judge Frances Hesselbein Cmty. Innovation Fellows Program, 2001—02, Peter F. Drucker Award for Nonprofit Innovation, 1996—2000. Mem.: Alpha Delta Phi. Home and Office: 67 Riverside Dr Apt 7D New York NY 10024-6136 Fax: 212-873-1568. E-mail: janepolin@aol.com.

POLINGER, IRIS SANDRA, dermatologist; b. N.Y.C., Feb. 10, 1943; m. Harvey I. Hyman, Feb. 6, 1972. AB, Barnard Coll., 1964; PhD, Johns Hopkins U., 1969; MD, SUNY Downstate, Bklyn., 1975. Diplomate Am. Bd. Dermatology. Teaching positions various schs. including NYU Coll. Dentistry and Harvard Med. Sch., 1969-73; med. intern Baylor Coll. Medicine, 1975-76, resident in dermatology, 1976-79; pvt. practice dermatology Houston, 1979—. Bd. dirs. Ft. Bend County Women's Ctr., Richmond, Tex., 1993—. Mem. Am. Bus. Women's Assn. (chair scholarship com. 1992, 96, chair scholarship event com. 1993—). Office: 4915 S Main St Ste 104 Stafford TX 77477-4601

POLINSKY, JANET NABOICHECK, retired state official, former state legislator; b. Hartford, Conn., Dec. 6, 1930; d. Louis H. and Lillian S. Naboicheck; m. Hubert N. Polinsky, Sept. 21, 1958 (div.); children: Gerald, David, Beth. BA, U. Conn., 1953; postgrad., Harvard Bus. Sch., 1954. Mem. Waterford 2d Charter Commn. (Conn.), 1967-68, Waterford Conservation Commn., 1968-69; Waterford rep. Town Meeting, 1969-71, S.E. Conn. Regional Planning Agy., 1971-73; mem. Waterford Planning and Zoning Commn., 1970-76, chmn., 1973-76; mem. Waterford Dem. Town Com., 1976-92. Del. State Dem. Conv., 1976, 78, 80, 82, 84, 86, 90, 92; mem. Conn. Ho. of Reps. from 38th Dist., 1977-82, asst. majority leader, 1981-83, chmn. appropriations com., 1983-85, 87-89, ranking mem., 1985-87, minority whip, 1985-86, dep. spkr., 1989-92; dep. commr. dept. adminstrv. svcs. State of Conn., 1993-94, chmn., 1994-95, asst. sec. of state, 1995, commr. utilities ctrl. auth., 1995-97. Trustee Eugene O'Neill Meml. Theatre Ctr., 1973-76, 81-92; corporator Lawrence and Meml. Hosps., 1987-88; mem. New Eng. Bd. Higher Edn., 1981-83; mem. fiscal affairs com. Eastern Conf. Coun. State Govts., 1983-88; mem. Limoge Village Bd., 2000-02; sec. Cascades, 2000—, sec., 2002—. Named Woman of Yr., Waterford Jr. Women's Club, 1977, Nehantic Women's Bus. and Profl. Club, 1979, Legislator of Yr., Conn. Libr. Assn., 1980. Mem. Order of Women Legislators, Delta Kappa Gamma (hon.). Home: 7141 Haviland Cir Boynton Beach FL 33437-6463 E-mail: naboi1@aol.com.

POLITE, CARLENE HATCHER, writer, educator; b. Detroit; d. John and Lillian Hatcher; m. James S. Patrick, July 21, 2003; children from previous marriage: Glynda Morton, Lila Ashaki. Student, Martha Graham Sch. Dance, N.Y.C., 1952-56; diploma, Acad. Leonardo da Vinci, Rome, 1980. Dancer, student Martha Graham Sch., N.Y.C., 1952-56; dancer Alvin Ailey Dance Co., N.Y.C., 1957-58, Edith Stephen Co., N.Y.C., 1958; dancer, actress Vanguard Playhouse, Detroit, 1960-62; prof. English SUNY, Buffalo, 1971—2000, chair dept. Am. Studies, 1981, prof. emerita, 2000. Tchr. Golden Dragon Kung Fu Acad., 1974-75, Himalayan Inst. Yoga, 1980-82; panelist NEA, Washington, 1981, N.Y. State Coun. Arts, N.Y.C., 1982, N.Y. Found. Arts, 1983, Seattle Arts in Pub. Places, 1989. Author: The Flagellants, 1966, Paris edit., 1967, N.Y. edit., 1968, also other European edits. (Pulitzer prize nominee, 1967, NEA grant, 1967, Rockefeller grant, 1968), Sister X and The Victims of Foul Play, 1975. Coord. Walk to Freedom with Martin Luther King, Detroit, 1963; del., participant UN-Non-Govtl.Orgns. 4th World Conf. on Women, Beijing, 1995. Recipient numerous nat. and internat. awards as artist and educator; invited 1st Ann. Conf. African Presence, Paris, 1991, Internat. Educators and Writers Oxford U., 1997. Avocation: yoga.

POLITE, EVELYN C. retired middle school educator, counselor, evangelist; b. Pineland, S.C., Dec. 25, 1937; d. Martin and Mary Brantley Coger, m. Horace Polite, Jan. 1, 1958 (dec. Jan. 1987); children: Horace Lenton, Tracy Polite Floyd. BS, Allen U., 1960; M in Elem. Edn., Armstrong-Savannah (Ga.) State U., 1976; cert. specialist of arts in theology, Zoe U., Jacksonville, Fla., 2000; PhD in Christian Counseling, Zoe U., 2001. Tchr. math. Beaufort County Bd. Edn., Bluffton, SC, 1960—61, Florence County Bd. Edn., Florence, SC, 1961—63, Jasper County Bd. Edn., Ridgeland, SC, 1963—64, 1991—92, Savannah Pub. Schs., 1964—90; math. tutor Dept. Family and Children, Savannah, 1992—94. Mem. curriculum devel. com. Savannah Pub. Schs., 1983—84, mem. staff devel. coun., 1983—84; test-item writer Ednl. Testing Svc., Princeton, NJ, 1990. Pres. 42d St Civic Club, Savannah, 2000—; exec. v.p. Cuyler-Brownsville Neighborhood Orgn., Savannah, 2001—. Recipient Outstanding Tchr. award, Math.-Sci. Roundtable, Atlanta, 1990. Mem. Ch. Of God. Avocations: world missions, travel, physical fitness, reading Christian literature. Office: Coastal Cathedral Ch of God 2208 E DeRenne Ave Savannah GA 31406 Home: 33 Wild Heron Villas Rd Savannah GA 31419-8981

POLITI, BETH KUKKONEN, publishing services company executive; b. Englewood, N.J., Sept. 18, 1949; d. Andrew and Beatrice G. (Druskin) Kukkonen; m. Joseph Politi, Oct. 21, 1982; children: Andrew, Joseph. BS in Mktg., Miami U., Oxford, Ohio, 1971. Media buyer Schwab, Beatty & Porter, Inc., 1971-72; media planner Adler, Schwartz & Connes, 1972-73; media buyer/planner Schwab Beatty divsn. Marstellar, 1973-74; dir. insert advt. Benjamin Co., Inc., Elmsford, N.Y., 1975-78, prodn. mgr., 1978-80, v.p. client svcs., 1980-83, editor supr., 1979-83; v.p. Bergen County Profl. Svcs., Ft. Lee, N.J., 1983—. Assoc. pub. various books Benjamin Co., Inc., 1981-83; freelance proofreader Montge Media, Montvale, N.J., 1999—. Trustee bd. edn. Pascack Valley Regional H.S. Dist., 1999—; mem. dist. fee com. Office of Atty. Ethics of Supreme Ct. of NJ, 2001—; del. exec. com. Bergen County Sch. Bd. Assn., 2003—. Home: 4 Smoke Rise Ct Montvale NJ 07645-1139

POLK, CONSTANCE CHRISTINE, language educator, education educator; b. Madera, Calif., Dec. 8, 1934; d. Joe Coronado and Belle R. (Gonzalez) Contreras; m. Arthur Clayton Polk, Oct. 16, 1960 (div. Aug. 1965); children: Susan Polk-Hoffses, Lance Arthur. BA, U. Calif., Berkeley, 1972, MA, 1973, postgrad., 1976; EdD, U. San Francisco, 1998. Multiple subject credential, 1991, single subject credential Spanish, 1991, adminstrv. credential, 1995. Prin., dir. New World Univ. H.S., San Francisco, 1978-85; tchr. Oakland (Calif.) Unified Sch. Dist., 1985-90; instr. Sch. of Edn. Wash. U., Pullman, 1996—. Presenter in field. Merit scholar U. San Francisco, 1994-95. Mem. AAUW, NEA, Nat. Assn. Bilingual Edn. (editor of column), Am. Ednl. Rsch. Assn., Am. Assn. Sch. Adminstrs., Calif. Assn. Bilingual Edn., Calif. Assn. Sch. Adminstrs., U. Calif. Berkeley Alumni Assn. Democrat. Avocations: tennis, folk dancing, singing, public speaking, writing. Home: 21 Crescent Ave San Francisco CA 94110-5821

POLK, DORA BEALE, literature educator; b. Pontnewydd, Wales, Jan. 30, 1923; arrived in U.S., 1948; d. Arthur Edward and Margaret Jones Beale. BA in English, U. Wales, Cardiff, 1943; MA in Polit. Sci., U. Colo., 1950; MA in English, U. Calif., Irvine, 1966, MFA, 1967, PhD in English, 1970. From asst. prof. to prof. creative writing and English Lit. Calif. State U., Long Beach, 1969—90, prof. emeritus, 1990—. Author: Vernon Watkins and the Spring of Vision, 1977, A Book Called Hiraeth, 1982, The Island of California, 1991, 1995, Something Must Be Done, 2003 (Arts Coun. of Wales grantee, 2002), numerous other books; contbr. articles to profl. jours. Recipient Profl. Achievement award, U. Calif.-Irvine Alumnus Assn., 1974; Emeritus grantee, Calif. State U., 2003.

POLK, EMILY DESPAIN, conservationist, writer, designer; b. Aberdeen, Wash., July 6, 1910; d. John Dove Isaacs and Constance Ashley (DeSpain) Van Norden; m. Benjamin Kauffman Polk, Aug. 23, 1946. Student, U. Oreg., 1928-29, Oreg. State U., 1929-31, Rudolph Shaefer Sch. of Art, San Francisco, 1931-32. Head display & design V.C. Morris, San Francisco, 1931-37; founder, CEO DeSpain Design, L.A. and N.Y.C., 1937-44, 63-64; ornamental & interior design arch. Benjamin Polk Arch., Calcutta and New Delhi, 1952-63; owner Galeria de San Luis, San Luis Obispo, Calif., 1966-68; founder, CEO Small Wilderness Area Preservation, Los Osos, Calif., 1969-79. Author: Poems and Epigrams, 1959 (All India Book award 1959), Delhi Old and New, 1963, A Wild Part of California, 1991, Rockpool Trilogy, 1995, Shadows: A Giant Tree, Vols. I-II, 1995-96, A Pilgrimage through Time, 1996, A Moment in the Mind, 1997, Invisible Thresholds, 1997, Poems for Drums and Woodwinds, 1999, Praises-Hymns Without Music, 2000, From Stress to Serenity, 2001, The Rustle of Leaves-New Poems, 2001; co-author: (with B. Polk) India Notebook, 1987, (with others) Sri Lanka Buddhist Shrines, 1991; editor (poetry): Calcuttan Magazine, 1961-63; contbr. articles to jours.; designer interior and exhibits Internat. Wool Secretariat, World Trade Fair, New Delhi, 1955; hon. interior designer Pres. of India, New Delhi, 1955, Maharanee of Tripura, Calcutta, India, 1962-63, King of Nepal, Kathmandu, 1962-63, Princess Pema Choki, Gantok, Sikkim, 1963; solo exhbns. paintings and montages India, 1963, U.S., 1963, 75, 89, 91, 98, 99, Eng., 1987, jewelry, U.S., 1948, fashion, India, 1955. Mem. coun. Nat. Mus. Women in the Arts, Washington, 1991-93; del., spkr. Pan Asian Cultural Conf., Calcutta, 1963, India House, N.Y., 1963, The Women's Club, 1964, AAUW, 1998. Recipient Kiwanis Citizenship Plaque Inscription, 1928, Golden Bear Conservation award Calif. Pks. and Recreation, Sacramento, 1972, Nat. Conservation award Am. Motors, 1972. Mem. Soc. Women Geographers (Calif. del., spkr. 50th Anniversary Celebrations 1972, Libr. of Congress Oral History Women of Achievement Program 1995), Small Wilderness Area Preservation, Calif. Hist. Soc., Calif. Oaks Found., Am. Women's Club (pres. 1962), Nat. Indian Assn. Women (pres.), English Speaking Union (bd. dirs.), Gyan Chakra Literary Gp. (founder). Home: 1945 Solano St #202 Los Osos CA 93402-2341

POLLACE, PAMELA L. public relations executive; b. San Jose, Calif., May 1953; BA, U. Santa Clara, 1975. Acct. mgr. mktg. comm. Oxbridge, Inc.; acct. supr. Burson Marsteller; spokesperson, mgr., dir. Intel Corp, Santa Clara, Calif., 1987-96, v.p., dir. worldwide press rels., 1996—2000; v.p. dir. corp. comms. Intel Corp., Santa Clara, Calif., 2000—. Office: Intel Corp Worldwide Press Rels PO Box 58119 Santa Clara CA 95052-8119

POLLACK, FLORENCE K.Z. management consultant; b. Washington, Pa. d. Charles and Ruth (Isaacson) Zaks; divorced; children: Melissa, Stephanie. BA, Flora Stone Mather Coll., Western Res. U., 1961. Chmn., CEO Exec. Arrangements, Inc., Cleve., 1978—. Lobbyist Ohio Citizens Com. for Arts, Columbus, 1975-83; mem. Leadership Cleve., 1978-79; trustee jr. com. Cleve. Orch., mem. pub. rels. adv. com.; trustee Great Lakes Theatre Festival, 1989-90; mem. pub. rels. adv. com., Cleve. Ballet, Dance Cleve., Jr. Com. of No. Ohio Opera Assn., Cleve. Opera, Shakers Lakes Regional Nature Ctr., Cleve. Music Sch. Settlement, Playhouse Sq. Cabinet, Cleve. Ctr. Econ. Edn., ARC, Cleve. Conv. and Visitors Bur., domed stadium adv. com.; bd. dirs. ARC, Great Lakes Theatre Festival, City Club of Cleve., Cleve. Ballet. Named Idea Woman of Yr., Cleve. Plain Dealer, 1975, to Au Courrant list Cleve. Mag., 1979, one of Cleve.'s 100 Most Influential Women, 1985, one of 1988 Trendsetters Cleve. Woman mag. Mem. Cleve. Area Meeting Planning, Skating Club, Univ. Club, Women's City Club, Playhouse Club, Shoreby Club. Avocations: arts, traveling, reading. Office: Exec Arrangements Inc 24800 Chargin Blvd Cleveland OH 44122 E-mail: executivearrange@ameritech.net.

POLLACK, JESSICA GLASS, lawyer; b. Bridgeport, Conn., June 29, 1964; d. MacEllis Kopel and Judith Wilson Glass; m. Russel Leon Pollack, Apr. 19, 1964; children: Nathaniel Bruce, Jason Henry. BA, Barnard Coll., 1986; JD, U. Chgo., 1990. Assoc. Shearman & Sterling, London, N.Y.C., 1990-94, White & Case, Budapest, N.Y.C., 1994-96; corp. counsel securities and fin. Colgate-Palmolive Co., N.Y.C., 1996—. Office: Colgate-Palmolive Co 300 Park Ave Fl 8 New York NY 10022-7499 Home: 2500 Johnson Ave Apt 10G Bronx NY 10463-4932

POLLACK, PHYLLIS ADDISON, ballerina; b. Victoria, B.C., Can., Aug. 31, 1919; d. Horace Nowell and Claire Melanie (Morris) Addison; m. Robert Seymour Pollack, Sept. 6, 1941 (dec. Jan. 2003); children: Robert Addison, Gwenda Joyce, Victoria Jean, Phyllis Anne. Student, SUNY, 1941-42, San Mateo Tech. Coll., 1958-62, U. Calif., San Francisco, 1962. Owner, dir. Phyllis Addison Dance Studio, Victoria, 1936-38; ballerina Taynton Dancers/Marcus Show Ballet Troupe, 1939-41, Ballet Russe, 1941; x-ray therapy tech. Meml. Hosp., N.Y.C., 1943-45; corr. fgn. tellers dept. N.C.B., N.Y.C., 1945-46; owner, designer The Dancing Branch Studio, Sonoma, Calif., 1988—. Floral designer J. Noblett Gallery, Sonoma, 1988-94. Pres. PTA, 1955-56, 62-63; mem. Assistance League San Mateo, Calif., 1960-70. Mem. Metro Club, Bay Area Arrangers Guild, Ikebana Internat., Lifelong Learning Inst. Democrat. Unitarian Universalist. Avocations: dance, choreography, fashion modelling, photography, reading. Home: 384 Avenida Barbera Sonoma CA 95476-8069

POLLACK, SONYA A. artist; b. Phila., Nov. 17, 1932; d. Herman and Helene (Spindor) Glick; m. Alfred Pollack; children: Harry, Kenneth, Helena, Daniel. Grad., Pa. Acad. Fine Arts, 1973; BFA, Phila. Coll. Art, 1975. One-woman shows include 3d Street Gallery, Phila., 1982, 84, Woodmere Art Mus., Phila., 1987, Phila. Art Alliance, 1991, 2003, Samuel S. Fleisher Art Meml., Phila., 1999, The X Gallery, 1995; represented in juried and invited group shows at Internat. House, Phila., 1972, Univ. Art League, Phila., 1973, Eastern Coll., Bryn Mawr, Pa., 1973, Vendo Nubes Gallery, Phila., 1973, Woodmere Gallery, Phila., 1975, 76, 79, 81, Civic Center Mus., Phila., 1975, 78, 81, Peale House, Phila., 1981, 84, 85, Allentown (Pa.) Mus., 1982, 84, 86, 94, Glassboro (N.J.) State Coll., 1982, Phila. Art Alliance, 1975, 82, 83, 91, Montgomery County Ct. House, Norristown, Pa., 1982, 83, 84, 3d Street Gallery, 1983, 84, 85, Lancaster (Pa.) Coummunity Gallery, 1984, West Chester (Pa.) State Coll., 1984, Noyes Mus., N.J., 1984, Lehigh (Pa.) U., 1984, Woodmere Art Mus., Phila., 1984, 86, 89, 94, Marion Locks Gallery, Phila., 1984, Pa. Acad. Fine Art Fellowship, Phila., 1984, Cheltenham (Pa.) Ann. Painting Exhbn., 1973, 85, 89, 92, 94, Hopkins House Gallery, N.J., 1987, Pa. Acad. Fine Arts, 1972, 87, Port of History Mus., Phila., 1988, Del. Art Mus., Wilmington, 1989, Muhlenberg Coll., Allentown, 1989, 90, The X Gallery, Nantucket, Mass., 1991, 92, 93, Long Beach Island Found. Arts and Scis., 1991, Berman Mus. Art Ursinus Coll., Collegeville, Pa., 1992, Morris Gallery, Phila., 1994, The X Gallery, Nantucket, Mass., 1999, The American Coll., Bryn Mawr, Pa., 2000, Main Line Art Ctr., N.Y.C., 2002, Satillite Gallery, Phila., Pa., 2003; group shows include: 80 Washington Square East Galleries, N.Y.C., N.Y., 1998, The X Gallery, Nantucket, Mass., 1999, The Am. Coll., Bryn Mawr, pa., 2000, numerous others; contbr. articles to profl. jours. Recipient Hunt award Artist Equity, Drake Press award Pa. Acad. Fine Arts, 1972, Gimble award Pa. Acad. Fine Arts, 1972, Alexander award Cheltenham Ctr. for Arts, 1989, Curator's Choice award Muhlenberg Coll., 1990, Tobeleah Wechsler award Cheltenham Ctr. for Arts, 1994. Mem. Pa. Acad. Fine Arts Fellowship (v.p. 1981-83, chairperson trust fund 1983-88, bd. dirs.). Home: 609 Fairview Rd Narberth PA 19072-1415

POLLAK, JOANNE E. lawyer; b. Cleve., July 16, 1944; m. Mark Pollak, Dec. 26, 1976; children: Elizabeth, Joshua, Rebecca, Benjamin, Jonathan. BA magna cum laude, Dickinson Coll., 1965; JD with honors, U. Md., 1976. Bar: Md. 1976. V.p., gen. counsel The Johns Hopkins Health System Corp./Johns Hopkins Medicine, Balt.; assoc., ptnr. and head of health care practice group Piper & Marbury Law Offices, 1976-93. Instr. bus. of medicine Sch. Medicine, Johns Hopkins U., Internat. Bus. Sch. Bd. dirs. Charlestown Cmty., Inc., 1992—, Mid-Atlantic affiliate Am. Heart Assn., 1991—, chair bd. dirs., 2002—03, chair rsch. for life campaign, 1999. Named One of Md.'s Top Women, Daily Record, 1996, 98, 2000. Office: Johns Hopkins Health Sys Corp 600 N Wolfe St Baltimore MD 21287-1974

POLLAK, LISA, columnist; Grad., U. Mich., 1990. Columinist Balt. Sun. Recipient Pulitzer prize for feature writing, 1997. Office: Balt Sun 501 N Calvat St Baltimore MD 21278-0001

POLLAN, CAROLYN JOAN, state legislator, job research administrator; b. Houston, July 12, 1937; d. Rex and Faith (Basye) Clark; m. George A. Pollan, Jan. 6, 1962; children: Cee Cee, Todd (dec.), Robert. BS in Radio and TV, John Brown U., 1959; postgrad, NYU, 1959; PhD in Edn., Walden U., 1993. Mem. Ark. House of Reps., 1974-98, asst. to gov., legis. dir., 1999—. Sr. Rep. mem., asst. speaker pro-tempore, 1993; apptd. by Gov. numerous coms., commns.; ex-officio mem. Workplace Literacy Project Adv. Bd. U.S. Dept. Labor & Ednl. Testing Svc., 1990-93, Nat. Adult Literacy Survey, 1990-93; del. Am. Soviet Seminar, Am. Council Young Polit. Leaders, Exeter, N.H., 1976; co-developer Total Touch Test; owner Patent Model Mus.; v. chmn. Ark. Rep. Com., 1972-76; del. Rep. Nat. Conv., 1976; bd. dirs. Ark. Cancer Soc., Ark., Easter Seals Soc.; bd. dirs. Greg Kistler Treatment Ctr. for Physically Handicapped, Ark. Found. Assoc. Colls., 4-H Found. for Sebastian County; trustee John Brown U.; mem. legis. adv. com. So. Regional Edn. Bd., chmn. edn. com. So. Legis. Conf., 1994-96. Recipient Conservation Legislator of Yr. award Ark. Wildlife Fedn., Nat. Wildlife Fedn., Sears Roebuck & Co., 1976, Outstanding State Legislator of Yr. award Ark. Pub. Employees Assn., 1979, Lifetime Mem. award Ark. PTA, 1994, Ark. Kids Count award, 1997, many others; named 1 of 10 Outstanding Legislators, Assembly of Govtl. Employees, 1980, Legislator of Yr., Ark. Human Svc. Providers Assn., 1982, Citizen of Yr. by Ark. Social Workers, 1993, Outstanding Women in Ark. Politics by Ark. Dem., 1990, One of 10 Top Legislators in 1993 Ark. Dem. Gazette, 1993, onf of Top 100 Women in Ark., Ark. Bus. Publ., 1995, 96, 97, Woman of Yr., Fort Smith Bus. and Profl. Women, 1997; voted 1 of Ft. Smith's 10 Most Influential Citizens, S.W. Times Record Readers, 1979. Mem. Ark. Internat. Woman's Forum (founding mem.), Ft. Smith Car Restoration Assn. (bd. dirs.). Baptist. Office: Gov's Office State Capitol Little Rock AR 72201-1088

POLLARD, BETTE MARLENE, computer scientist; b. Knoxville, Iowa, July 24, 1943; BA in History, U. Calif., Berkeley; MS, U. Chgo. Cert. in Data Comm. (Am. Inst.), Client Server Computing (Learning Tree Inst.), Computer Programming (Prince Georges Coll.). Computer scientist NIH, Bethesda, Md., 1983—. Pres. Fox Hills Civic Assn., Potomac, Md., 1979-82; v.p. Area III adv. bd., Bethesda, 1979-82; treas. U. Chgo. Alumni Assn., Washington, 1982. Recipient 4 meritorious svc. awards NIH, 1985, 87, 89, 93. Mem. Internet Soc. Avocation: painting. Office: NIH DHHS 9600 Rockville Pike Bethesda MD 20814-3929

POLLARD, MARGARET LOUISE, association administrator; b. Leominster, Mass., Nov. 15, 1934; d. Edward Francis and AliceMary (Sosvielle) Sasseville; m. Walter Howard Pollard III, Mar. 10, 1957 (dec. Oct. 1974); children: Caroline Pray, Walter Howard IV, Margaret Peirce, Melissa Anne; m. James L. Baird Jr., Jan. 9, 1993. BS, Simmons Coll., 1956; MS, Boston U., 1983. Editor Hist. Soc. Western Pa., Pitts., 1971-75; mgr. advtr. and promotions F.W. Faxon Co., Westwood, Mass., 1976-80; owner, mgr. Peg Pollard Communications, Boston, 1981-84; dir. comms. Mass. Dental Soc., Natick, 1984-93; coord. vols. Lyman Allyn Art Mus., New London, Conn., 1993-96; exec. dir. Norwich (Conn.) Heritage Trrust, 1994-96. Editor LWV, Westwood, 1966, pres., Greensburg, Pa., 1968-71; bd. dirs. First Night, Inc., Boston, 1982-89, Friends Boston Ctr. for Arts, 1985-88; mem. Leu Botanical Gardens, Friends of Orlando Philharm. Mem. Am. Soc. Assn. Execs., Am. Soc. Med. Writers, New Eng. Soc. Assn. Execs., Publicity Club New Eng. (Bellringer award 1984), Morse Mus. of Am. Arts Assoc. (sec.), Friends of the Orlando Philharmonic Bd., Univ. Club Winter Park. Avocations: historical research, reading, walking, theater, golf. Home: Nantucket, Mass. Died July 17, 2003.

POLLARD, SHIRLEY, employment training director, community services administrator, consultant; b. Brunswick City, Va., July 8, 1939; 1 child, Darryl. Degree in bus. adminstrn., Upper Iowa U., 1978. Adminstr. East. Balt. Cmty. Corp.; tng. coord. Balt. County Concentrated Employment Tng. Program; exec. dir. Park Heights Cmty. Corp., Balt.; dir. Linkages, Inc., Balt. Contbr. articles to Afro Am. newspaper. Pres. Park Hts. Cmty. Devel. Corp., United Black Fund, Balt., 1989—, Presdl. Task Force, 1992; active Balt. Urban League, Balt. Welfare Rights Orgn.; founder, pres. Balt. County Polit. Action Coalition, 1982—; founder, dir. Linkages, Inc., 1980; founder, dir. Tng. and Placement Svcs., 1989; active United Svc. Orgn., Md. Minority Contractors Assn., U.S. Civil Rights Mus. and Hall of Fame, Smithsonian Instn.; founder African Am. Culture Ctr.; co-founder Project Lou, Inc.; founder The Afro Fund, Inc.; active Fund for a Free South Africa's Founding Assocs. Leadership Coun., Nat. Women's Hall of Fame, Nat. Abortion Rights Action League, Srs. Coalition, Md. Edn. Coalition, CORE, So. Christian Leadership Conf., Nat. Trust for Hist. Preservation; presdl. appointment Md. Selective Svc. Bd., 1993, Exec. Com. of Am. Friends Svc. Com.; mem. women's adv. coun. Sinai Hosp., 1994—. Recipient Outstanding Achievement award Md. Minority Contractors Assn., Mayor's Citation, Martin Luther King Civil Rights award, 1987, Md. State Dept. Edn. award, 1987, congl. Achievement award, Kool Achiever awards, 1990, Nat. Black Caucus Spl. award, 1990, Congressional Achievement award, 1988, Svc. award The Writers Club, 1991, USO Meritorious Svc. award, 1991, Gov.'s Vol. award, 1992, Acad. of Excellence award, 1992, Signs of Hope award, 1995, Mayor's citation, 1984, Gov.'s citation, 1995, Senatorial award, 1995; recipient Bud Achiever award 1996. Mem. Am. Soc. Pers. Adminstrn., Am. Soc. Health/Manpower/Edn./Tng., Assn. for Providers Employment and Tng., NAACP (founder, pres. Randallstown chpt. 1988-95, Signs of Hope award), Balt. Coun. on Fgn. Affairs, Transafrica, USO, Md. Minority Contractors Assn. (Achievement award 1986, bd. dirs. 1984-89), Smithsonian Assoc., Md. C. of C. (greater Balt. com. 1985). Office: PO Box 32051 Baltimore MD 21282-2051

POLLARD, VERONICA, automotive executive; m. Joel Dreyfuss; 1 child, Justin. Student, U. Wis.; Bachelor's Degree, Boston U.; Master's Degree, Columbia U. First grade tchr., NY; mgr. internat. affairs Cosmo Pub. Rels. Corp., Tokyo; staff writer San Francisco Chronicle; asst. dir. pub. affairs Newsweek Mag.; publicist ABC TV Network, mgr. bus. info.; dir. corp. comm. Capital Cities/ABC, Inc.; v.p. corp. pub. rels. ABC; v.p., external affairs Toyota Motor Corp. Services N.Am., 1998—2002; group v.p. corp. comm. Toyota Motor N.Am., Inc., 2002—. Bd. dirs. Granite Broadcasting Corp.; mem. individual investor adv. com. N.Y. Stock Exch.

Former dir. Nat. YMCA of the U.S.A., YMCA Greater N.Y.; trustee Mus. for African Art, NY; active YMCA; hon. bd. mem. West Side YMCA, NY, 1990—98, bd. chair; dir. The Doe Fund, NY. Mem.: Women's Forum. Office: Toyota Motor NAm Ste 4900 Nine West 57th St New York NY 10019*

POLLARD, WENDY HIGGINS, counselor; b. Ft. Jackson, S.C., July 8, 1955; d. Ruel Ai and Reba Ruth (Beauchamp) Higgins; m. Larry Clay Schalitzky, 1977 (div. 1982); 1 child, Larry Clay Jr.; m. John Wesley Pollard Jr., Apr. 4, 1998. AA, Midlands Tech. Coll., 1976; BA, Newberry (S.C.) Coll.; MEd, U. S.C., 1989, Ed.S., 1991. Lic. profl. counselor, S.C. Owner Exploring Alternatives, Newberry; home-sch. liaison Newberry County Schs.; prevention specialist Newberry Commn. on Alcohol and Drug Abuse. Displaced homemaker liaison S.C. Women's Work, Cola, 1996-98; co-chmn. Newberry Literacy Coun., 1994-96. Recipient Human Rights award Newberry County Sch. Counselors. Fellow S.C. Assn. Adult Educators, S.C. Sch. Counselor Assn., Am. Counseling Assn. Avocations: reading, painting. Office: Exploring Alternatives 1303 Main St Ste 206 Newberry SC 29108-3464

POLLEY-SHELLCROFT, THERESA DIANE, university educator; b. Huntington, W.Va., July 11, 1945; m. John Wesley, II Shellcroft, Jan. 24, 1970; 1 child, Christopher Shellcroft. BS in Art Edn., W.Va. State Coll., Institute, W. Va., 1964—68. Coll. instr. Victor Valley CC, Victorville, Calif., 1980—; h.s. art tchr. Hesperia Unified Sch. Dist., Hesperia, Calif. Painting, quilt art, lecturer, exhibitor, African Inspirations Curator - Exhibit, Road to California, Quilt Show Teacher African American Quilting Trends Agora Gallery, SOHO New York, 2002 (Nat. Endowment for the Humanities, Black Film Studies, 2001; Art Educator of the Yr., 1997; Ca. Visual and Performing Arts Framework Com., 2001). Mem.: Calif. Teachers Assn., NEA, Afro Am. Quilters of LA, San Bernardino Arts Coun., Delta Sigma Theta Sorority. Avocation: travel, reading, swimming,. Office: Studio One Artworks PO Box 2336 Victorville CA 92393 Personal E-mail: tshellcrof@aol.com. E-mail: tshellcrof@aol.com.

POLLINA, KRISTEN MITTL, child and adolescent psychologist; b. Park Ridge, Ill., Nov. 17, 1973; d. Mary Mittl and Ronald Robert Pollina. BA in Psychology, summa cum laude, New Eng. Coll., Henniker, N.H., 1995; MA in Clin. Psychology, Ill. Sch. Profl. Psychology, Rolling Meadows, 1997, D in Clin. Psychology, 1999. Lic. clin. psychologist State of Ill., 2001. Undergrad. intern in psychology Rape and Domestic Violence Crisis Ctr., Concord, NH, 1993—94, Anna Philbrook Psychiat. Hosp. for Children and Adolescents, Concord, NH, 1994—95; pre-doctoral practicum student in clin. psychology St. Therese Med. Ctr. Behavioral Medicine Unit, Waukegan, Ill., 1996—97, The Family Stress Clinic, Libertyville, Ill., 1997—98; pre-doctoral intern in clin. psychology Depke Juvenile Justice Complex / Hulse Detention Ctr., Vernon Hills, Ill., 1998—99; postdoctoral fellow in clin. psychology Connection's Therapeutic Day Sch., Waukegan, Ill., 1999—2000, clin. dir., dir. of clin. tng., 2000—. Instr. Columbia Coll., Park City, Ill., 2000—01. Vol. Connection Crisis Hotline, Libertyville, Ill., 1992—95, A Safe Place, Waukegan, Ill., 1992—95; pres. and mem. Womyn's Network, Henniker, NH, 1991—95; 1st female pres. New Eng. Coll. Greek Coun., Henniker, NH, 1992—95; victim adv. in Jane Doe cases of sexual harassment and assault New Eng. Coll. Jud. Bd., Henniker, NH, 1993—95. Mem.: APA, Assn. for the Advancement of Psychology, Psi Chi, Kappa Phi Sigma (founding pres. 1991—95). Independent. Roman Catholic. Avocations: travel, reading, my pets, yoga. Home: 1253 N Sheridan Rd Lake Forest IL 60045 Office: Connection's Therapeutic Day Sch 31410 Hwy 45 Libertyville IL 60048 Personal E-mail: dr.kmpollina@comcast.net. Business E-Mail: kpollina@connectionsdayschool.net.

POLLNER, JULIA A. financial executive; BBA, Miami U., Oxford, Ohio. CPA, Ohio. With Red Roof Inns Inc., Columbus, Ohio, 1987; v.p., contr., asst. treas. Metatec Internat. Inc., Columbus, v.p. fin., sec., treas., 1997—. Mem. AICPA, Ohio Soc. CPAs, Fin. Execs. Inst. Office: Metatec Internat Inc 7001 Metatec Blvd Dublin OH 43017-3219

POLLOCK, KAREN ANNE, computer analyst; b. Elmhurst, Ill., Sept. 6, 1961; d. Michael Paul and Dorothy Rosella (Foskett) P. BS, Elmhurst Coll., 1984; MS, North Cen. Coll., 1993. Formatter Nat. Data Corp., Lombard, Ill., 1985; computer specialist Dept. VA, Hines, Ill., 1985—. Lutheran. Avocations: cross-stitch, mystery books, bowling, bicycling, softball.

POLLOCK, MARGARET LANDAU PEGGY, elementary school educator; b. Jefferson City, Mo., Oct. 18, 1936; d. William Wold and Grace Elizabeth (Creamer) Anderson; children by previous marriage: Elizabeth, Charles, Christopher, Jeffrey; m. William Whalen Pollock, Jan. 30, 1993. AA, Stephens Coll., 1956; BS in Elem. Edn., U. Mo., Columbia, 1958; MA in Reading Edn., U. Mo., Kansas City, 1987. Cert. elem. tchr., Mo. Kindergarten tchr. Columbia Schs., 1958-59, Moberly (Mo.) Schs., 1960-62; 1st grade tchr. Kansas City Schs., 1962-63; kindergarten tchr. Independence (Mo.) Schs., 1966-75; chpt. I reading specialist Thomas Hart Benton Elem. Sch., Independence, 1975-93; book reviewer Corpus Christi (Tex.) Caller Times, 1994—; children's libr. Corpus Christi Pub. Libr., 1995-97; dir. Johnson City (Tex.) Libr., 1997—. Cons., presenter in field. Bd. dirs. Boys and Girls Club, Independence, 1990-93; coord. Independence Reading Fair, 1989-93; coord. books and tutoring Salvation Army, Kansas City, 1990-92. Mem. AAUW, Internat. Reading Assn. (People to People del. to USSR 1991, local v.p. 1990-91, pres. 1991-92), Internat. Platform Assn., Austin Writer's League, Archeol. Inst. Am., Tex. Libr. Assn., Earthwatch, Nature Conservancy, Sierra Club, Phi Kappa Phi, Pi Lambda Theta (pres. Beta Upsilon chpt. 1992-93). Avocations: native american history, rights and education, archeology, reading, travel, conservation. Home: PO Box 482 Johnson City TX 78636-0482

POLLOCK, MELANY TAWANDA, paralegal, legal assistant; b. Washington, Nov. 12, 1971; d. William Calvin Jr. and Brenda Lee (Bullock) P. BA, Radford U., 1993; MA, Am. U., 1998. Adminstrv. asst. Fed. Dept. Ins. Corp., Washington, 1992, 93, 94; asst. physician recruiter Humana Group Health Plan, Washington, 1995; paralegal specialist Legal Svc. No. Va., Falls Church, Va., 1995-96; legal asst. King & Spalding Law Firm, Washington, 1996—. Mem. Nat. Black Am. Paralegal Assn., Nat. Capital Area Paralegal Assn., Nat. Coun. Negro Women, Nat. Press Club, Women in Video & Film, Women in Comm., Alpha Kappa Alpha. Baptist. Avocations: sewing, writing, reading, pottery, running. Home: 11109 Ascot Cir Fredericksburg VA 22407-5059 Office: Baker-Hostetler 1050 Connecticut Ave NW Ste 11 Washington DC 20036-5351

POLLOCK, RACHEL ELIZABETH, costume designer; b. Minot, N.D., June 9, 1972; d. Mark Alan and Eugenea Carole Pollock. BA, U. Tenn., 1994. Freelance costumer Boston Ballet, 1998, Emerson Stage, Boston, 1998—2000, Boston U. Theatre, 1999, Huntington Theatre, Boston, 1999—2001; pattern drafter, designer Black Labs. Leathersmiths, Boston, 1999—2001; staff craft artisan and dyer Am. Repertory Theatre, Cambridge, Mass., 2000—. Costume designer TrusT Co., Knoxville, Tenn., 1993, Coll. Light Opera Co., Falmouth, Mass., 1995, Scarlet Theatre Co., Evanston, Ill., 1995. 7th Biennial Art to Wear Juried Exhbn. Fundraiser Nat. Multiple Sclerosis Soc., Boston, 2003. Mem.: Golden Key, Phi Beta Kappa, Delta Delta Delta (life; historian 1993—94). Buddhist. Avocations: writing, quilting, deejaying. Office: Am Repertory Theatre 64 Brattle St Cambridge MA 02138

POLLOCK-O'BRIEN, LOUISE MARY, public relations executive; b. Tarentum, Pa., Mar. 14, 1948; d. Louis P. and Amelia M. (Ballay) Pollock; m. Vincent Miles O'Brien. BS, Ind. U. of Pa., 1970. Tchr. Archbishop Wood H.S., Warminster, Pa., 1970-75; spokesperson, publicist Calif. Olive Industry, Fresno, 1976-78; account exec. Ketchum Pub. Rels., N.Y.C., 1979-81, account supr., 1982-83, v.p., 1984, v.p., group mgr., 1985-88, sr. v.p., group mgr., 1988-89, assoc. dir., dir. food mktg., sr. v.p., 1990-91; chmn. Aronow & Pollock Comm., Inc., N.Y.C., 1991—. Mem. pub. rels. adv. com. Mayor's Vol. Action Com., N.Y.C., 1986; mem. food svc. adv. bd. L.I. City Coll., Bklyn., 1987-88. V.p. fundraiser West 76th St. Block Assn., N.Y.C., 1982. Mem. Internat. Foodservice Editl. Coun. (v.p., bd. dirs. 1984-85). Avocations: watercolor painting, skiing. Office: Aronow & Pollock Comm Inc 665 Broadway New York NY 10012-4408 Office Phone: 212-941-1414. E-mail: LPollock@apc-pr.com.

POLO, KRISTINE CAROL, accountant, educator; b. N.Y.C., Nov. 16, 1965; d. Robert Kenneth and Carol Ruth Polo; 1 child, Alexander Charles Bengal. BS in Acctg., U. Fla., 1987; MBA, Palm Beach Atlantic U., 1998. CPA Fla., 1997. Corp. acct. Ocwen Fin. Corp., West Palm Beach, 1990—93; asst contr. Nat. Golf Found., Jupiter, Fla., 1994; ptnr. Douglass & Co., P.A., Boynton Beach, Fla., 1994—2002; owner K C Polo, CPA, P.A., West Palm Beach, 2002—. Assoc. prof. Palm Beach Atlantic U., West Palm Beach, 1999—; chmn. Ficpa -Fed Tax Conf., Tallahassee, 1999—. Mem. event com. Leukemia Lymphoma Soc., West Palm Beach, 2002—; mem. Ficpa-Elder Care Com., Tallahasse, 2003, Women's C. of C., Palm Beach County, West Palm Beach, 2002—; tchr. Sunday ch. St. Marks Episcopal Ch., West Palm Beach, 2001. Recipient Nat. Leadership award, Nat. Republican Congl. Com., 2003. Mem.: Palm Beach Atlantic U. MBA Alumni Assn. (life; bd. mem. 1999—2001). R-Liberal. Episcopalian. Avocations: sailing, skiing, surfing, reading. Office: K C Polo CPA PA 2240 Palm Beach Lakes Blvd 101 West Palm Beach FL 33409

POLOS, IRIS STEPHANIE, artist; b. Oakland, Calif., Feb. 14, 1947; d. Theodore C. and Catherine (Pappas) P.; 1 child Apollo Papafrangou. BFA, Calif. Coll. Arts and Crafts, Oakland, 1968, MFA, 1971. Instr. figure drawing Am. Sch. of Art, Athens, Greece, 1969-71 summers; instr. advanced drawing U. Calif. Extension Open Exchange, San Francisco, 1978-79; artist in residence Chabot Elem. Sch., Oakland, Calif., 1986-92, Mus. of Children's Art, Oakland, 1988—96; art tchr. Arrowsmith Acad., Berkeley, 1991—; instr. Oakland children's hosp. MOCHA, 1995—96. Artist: selected exhibitions include: San Francisco Mus. of Modern Art, 1971, Richmond (Calif.) Art Ctr., 1973, Calif. Coll. of Arts and Crafts, Oakland, 1973, Art for Art Sake Gallery, San Francisco, 1977, Jehu Wong Gallery, San Francisco, 1979, Triangle Gallery, San Francisco, 1981, Bond Gallery, N.Y.C., 1985, 86, Berkeley (Calif.) Art Ctr., 1987, 88, Emanuel Radnitzky, San Francisco, 1990 (2 shows), San Francisco Art Commn. Gallery, 1991, Fine Arts Ctr., Irvine, Calif., 1991, Trojanowska Gallery, San Francisco, 1991, Nelson Morales Gallery, San Francisco, 1992, Morphos Gallery, L.A., 1993, 94, Morphos Gallery, San Francisco, 1994, 95, Hotel Triton Art Fair with Morphos Gallery, San Francisco, 1995, Moreau Galeries, Notre Dame, Ind., 1995, Fort Mason Found., San Francisco, 1995, Magic Theater Lobby, San Francisco, 1995, Chgo.-Artspace, Lima, Ohio, 1997, Catherine Clark Gallery, San Francisco, 1997, 98, 99, Circle Elephant Art Gallery, L.A., 2001, 04, others; permanent collections include the Oakland Mus., Catharine Clark, Gary Noguera, Helen Salz, Daniel Soto, Caroline Zecca, di Rosa Found., Sonoma County, and others; her works also include book illustration and theatre set design; featured artist in Juxtapoz mag., Fall 1998, Chicago Art Fair with C. Clark Gallery, 2001-02, mural projects with Arrowsmith Acad. at Oakland Zoo and at St. Marks Ch., Berkeley. Grantee: Arts in Edn. grant Cultural Arts Divsn., Oakland, 1991-96, Berkeley Repertory Theater, 1995. Democrat. Home: 5801 Broadway Oakland CA 94618-1524 Office: Arrowsmith Acad Art Dept Berkeley CA 94704

POLSBY, GAIL K. psychotherapist; b. Washington, Jan. 13, 1939; d. Thomas Edward and Elise Wildman (Hammer) Kissling; m. Allen I. Polsby, Aug. 30, 1963; children: Daniel, Abigail. BA, U. Md., 1960; MSW, Cath. U., 1963. Mem. faculty Washington Sch. Psychiatry, 1967—2001, chmn. bd. dirs., 2001—; pvt. practice psychotherapy, Chevy Chase, Md., 1969—; cons. doctoral program Clin. Social Work Inst., Washington, 1999—. Sec., bd. dirs. Washington Sch. Psychiatry, 1995—2001, chair faculty coun. Editor quar. newspaper Washington Sch. Psychiatry News, 1997. Mem. Am. Group Psychotherapy Assn., Nat. Fedn. Clin. Social Workers. Avocations: hiking, biking. Home: 5651 Bent Branch Rd Bethesda MD 20816-1049

POLUGA, JUDITH, education educator; b. Budapest, Hungary, Jan. 1, 1952; came to U.S., 1959; d. Laszlo and Irene Takacs; m. Charles Poluga, Dec. 16, 1972; children: Adam Charles, Mia Kyung-Choi, Nathan Lee, Hope Kyung-Choi, David Jonathan, Krystal Kyung-Choi, Danielle Marie (dec.). BS in Edn., Kent State U., 1980, MEd, 1990, postgrad. Cert. tchr., prin. Ohio. Kindergarten tchr. Mother of Sorrows Sch., Ashtabula, Ohio, 1980-85; kindergarten, 4th grade tchr. Ashtabula City Schs., 1985-97; prof. early childhood edn. Kent State U., Ashtabula, 1995—; prin. Kingsville elem. Buckeye Local Schs., Ashtabula, 1997—. Dir. of edn. Intercultural Student Exch., Ashtabula, 1997—. Bd. dirs. Cath. Svc. League, Ashtabula, 1996; mem. Garden Trails Garden Club, Ashtabula, 1987-93. Martha Holden Jennings scholar Martha Holden Jennings Found., 1993. Mem. ASCD, AAUW, Assn. for Childhood Edn. Internat., Comparative and Internat. Edn. Soc., Am. Ednl. Rsch. Assn., Nat. Assn. for the Edn. of Young Children, Phi Delta Kappa. Roman Catholic. Avocations: woodworking, crafts. Home: 4005 W 13th St Ashtabula OH 44004-2109 Office: Buckeye Local Schs Kingsville 5875 Rt 193 Kingsville OH 44048

POMPA, LOUISE ELAINE, secondary school educator; b. Spangler, Pa., Sept. 26, 1958; d. Harry Gregory and Lois Vida Beers; m. David Richard Pompa, Jan. 18, 1985; 1 child, Emilee Louise stepchildren: Angelo, Mary Beth. BS, Pa. State U., 1982; MEd, Ind. U. Pa., 1994. Cert. profl. tchr. Pa. Adult day care provider for mentally handicapped persons Mid-State Intermediate Care Facility for the Mentally Retarded, Altoona, Pa., 1983—84; spl. edn. tchr. Altoona Area Sch. Dist., 1984—86; tchr. Cambria County Children and Youth, Ebensburg, Pa., 1986—87; spl. edn. tchr. Greater Johnstown (Pa.) Vocat.-Tech. Sch., 1987—88, Appalachia Intermediate Unit 8, Ebensburg, 1988—90; spl. edn. tchr., secondary learning support Cambria Heights Sch. Dist., Patton, Pa., 1990—. Author: A Review of the Literature on Motivation and Strategies for Improving Motivation in the Learning Disabled Adolescent: A Comparative Analysis, 1994. Mem.: Kappa Delta Pi, Phi Kappa Phi. Democrat. Roman Catholic. Avocations: health and fitness, gardening, collectibles, quilting. Office: Cambria Heights Sch Dist 426 Glendale Lake Rd Patton PA 16668

PONCELET, PAULETTE, school system administrator; 1 child, Dominique Marie. PhD, Cleve. State U., 1999. Dir. of rsch. and evaluation Cleve. Mcpl. Sch. Dist., Cleve., 1999—. Catechist The Cath. Diocese of Cleve., Cleve. Mem.: Nat. Coun. on Measurement in Edn., Am. Evaluation Assn., Am. Ednl. Rsch. Assn.

POND, PATRICIA BROWN, library science educator, university administrator; b. Mankato, Minn., Jan. 17, 1930; d. Patrick H. and Florence M. (Ruehle) Brown; m. Judson S. Pond, Aug. 24, 1959. BA, Coll. St. Catherine, St. Paul, 1952; MA, U. Minn., 1955; PhD, U. Chgo., 1982. Sch. libr., Minn., N.Y., 1952-62; asst. prof. libr. sci. U. Minn., 1962-63; reference libr. U. Mont., 1963-65; asst. prof. U. Oreg., 1967-72, assoc. prof., 1972-77; prof., dept. chair, assoc. dean Sch. Libr. and Info. Sci. U. Pitts., 1977-85. Mem. ALA (life), Phi Beta Kappa, Beta Phi Mu, Delta Phi Lambda, Kappa Gamma Pi. Home: 15829 SW Village Cir Beaverton OR 97007-3532

POND, PHYLLIS JOAN RUBLE, state legislator, educator; b. Warren, Ind., Oct. 25, 1930; d. Clifford E. and Rosa E. (Hunnicutt) Ruble; m. George W. Pond, June 10, 1951; children: William, Douglas, Jean Ann. BS, Ball State U., Muncie, Ind., 1951; MS, Ind. U., 1963. Tchr. home econs., 1951-54; kindergarten tchr., 1961-98; mem. Ind. Ho. of Reps., Inpdls., 1978—, majority asst. caucus chmn., vice chmn. ways and means com., 1995. Active Rep. Precinct Com., 1976—; del. Ind. Rep. Conv., 1976, 80, 84, 86, 88, 90, 92, 96, 2000; alt. del. Rep. Nat. Conv., 1980, del., 1996; alt. del. to Rep. Nat. conv., 2000. Mem. AAUW, Regional Red Cross Bio Med. Bd., New Haven Am. Legion Aux., New Haven Woman's Club. Lutheran.

PONDER, ANNE, dean; b. Asheville, N.C., Apr. 26, 1950; d. Herschel Doyle and Mary Eleanor (Israel) Ponder; m. John Christopher Brookhouse, Mar. 3, 1973; stepchildren: Stephen Christopher, Nathaniel. AB, U. N.C., 1971, MA, 1973, PhD, 1979. Dir. honors Elon Coll., N.C., 1977-85; assoc. acad. dean Guilford Coll., Greensboro, N.C., 1985-89; acad. dean, prof. Kenyon Coll., Gambier, Ohio, 1989—. Mem. Nat. Collegiate Honors Coun. (pres. 1988-89), N.C. Honors Assn. (pres. 1983), Order of Valkyries. Episcopalian. Office: Kenyon Coll 105 Park St Gambier OH 43022

PONDER, CATHERINE, clergywoman, author; b. Hartsville, S.C., Feb. 14, 1927; d. Roy Charles and Kathleen (Parrish) Cook; 1 child, Richard. Student, Worth Bus. Coll., 1948; BS in Edn., Unity Ministerial Sch., 1956; doctorate (hon.), Unity Sch., 1976. Ordained to ministry Unity Sch. Christianity, 1958. Min. Unity Ch., Birmingham, Ala., 1958-61, founder, min. Austin, Tex., 1961-69, San Antonio, 1969-73, Palm Desert, Calif., 1973—. Author: (books) The Dynamic Laws of Prosperity, 1962, The Prosperity Secret of the Ages, 1964, The Dynamic Laws of Healing, 1966, The Healing Secret of the Ages, 1967, Pray and Grow Rich, 1968, The Millionaires of Genesis, 1976, The Millionaire Moses, 1977, The Millionaire Joshua, 1978, The Millionaire from Nazareth, 1979, The Secret of Unlimited Prosperity, 1981, Open Your Mind To Receive, 1983, Dare To Prosper!: The Prospering Power of Prayer, 1983, The Prospering Power of Love, 1984, Open Your Mind to Prosperity, 1984, The Dynamic Laws of Prayer, 1987, (memoir) Prosperity Love Story, From Rags to Enrichment, 2003. Office: 73-669 US Hwy 111 Palm Desert CA 92260-4033

PONKO, VERA, artist, museum intrepreter; b. Lysander, N.Y., Aug. 1, 1931; d. Amos W. and Myrtle (Brown) Vest; m. Charles W. Ponko, Mar. 1956 (div. June 1979); children: Velton, John, Ronald, Terry, Stephen. Former mus. intrepretor Frederic Remington Art Mus., Ogdensburg, NY; mem. vis. artist program tchg. masonry art. Tchr. St. Lawrence-Lewis Boces Sch. Sys., 2003. Exhibited stained glass in art exhbn., Heuvelton, Gibson Gallery, SUNY, Potsdam, 2002; masonry and glass designer; builder of custom designed windows. Avocations: gardening, stained glass, cooking, masonry designing. Home: PO Box 322 Heuvelton NY 13654-0322 E-mail: vponko@stlawrfcu.net.

PONTON, LYNN E. psychiatrist, educator; b. Stevens Point, Wis., Oct. 3, 1951; d. William and Elizabeth (Loos) Ponton; m. Fred Waldman, May 17, 1981; children: Sarah, Anne. BA, U. Wis., Madison, 1973, MD, 1978. Resident adult psychiatry U. Pa., Phila., 1979—80; resident adult psychiatry Langley Porter Psychiat. Inst. U. Calif., San Francisco, 1980—81; adj. asst. prof., 1983—88, adj. assoc. prof., 1988—94, prof. psychiatry, 1994—. Mem. bd. govs. in child, adolescent psychiatry Am. Bd. Psychiatry, 1990—. Author: The Sex Life of Teenagers, The Romance of Risk (Disting. Publ. award, Handbook of Adolescent Health Risk Behavior, 1996), The Textbook of Adolescent Psychiatry. Recipient Frank Meml. Lecture award, Mount Sinai Hosp., 1999. Fellow: Am. Acad. Child and Adolescent Psychiatry (officer coun.-at-large 1999—2002, mem. adv. bd. Sex etc.), Am. Psychiat. Assn.; mem.: San Francisco Psychiat. Inst. Democrat. Achievements include Contributions to theory of adolescent risk-taking. Avocations: cooking, exercising, reading, swimming. Office: 201 Edgewood Ave San Francisco CA 94117 E-mail: lynnponton@aol.com.

PONZI KAY, MARYLOU, human resources specialist; b. N.Y.C., Oct. 14, 1950; d. Bruno and Constance Louise (DeLuca) P.; m. William J. Kay, Jr., Oct. 24, 1993. BA, SUNY, Geneseo, 1972; MA, U. Iowa, 1974, SUNY, Buffalo, 1979; cert. in advanced study in labor rels., N.Y. Inst. Tech., 1995. Cert. sr. profl. in human resources Soc. for Human Resources Mgmt. Cert. Inst., 2002. Pers. adminstr. Michelin Tire Corp., Lake Success, N.Y., 1978-83; tech. recruiter 1st Data Resources, Lake Success, N.Y., 1983-84; mgr. human resources Chem. Bank, Jericho, N.Y., 1984-87; pers. officer J.P. Morgan Inc., N.Y.C., 1987-89; mgr. employment Am. Express Inc., N.Y.C., 1989-92; dir. human resources RockBottom Stores, Inc., 1992-95; asst. dir. human resources Canon U.S.A., Lake Success, N.Y., 1995-97, dir. human resources, 1997-2000, dir. corp. human resources and devel., 2000; dir. human resources Esselte Ams., Melville, NY, 2000—02; v.p. global compensation benefits and svcs. Esselte Corp., 2002—. Adj. prof. human resources N.Y. Inst. Tech., 2000—; instr. French and Spanish, Amityville H.S. Adult Edn., 1986-96. Editor: New England Guide, 1982, Canada Guide, 1982. Pres. LeBourget Alliance, Amityville, N.Y., 1995-97; pres. bus. adv. coun. Adults and Children with Learning Disabilities, 1994-97, trustee, 1997—. Mem. ASTD, N.Y. Compensation Assn., Soc. Human Resources Mgmt., Human Resources Strategic Issues Coun., World at Work. Roman Catholic. Avocations: languages, travel, cooking, sports. Office: 48 S Service Rd Melville NY 11747 Office Phone: 631-675-3236. Personal E-mail: mwk93@aol.com. E-mail: mponzi@esselte.com.

PONZO, KAREN DIANE, music educator; b. Oswego, N.Y., Oct. 4, 1971; d. Keith Leroy and Diane Marie Fryer. MusB, SUNY Fredonia; MusM, No. Ill. U. Tchr. band Malta Sch. Dist., Ill., Elgin U., Ill. Mem.: Music Educators Nat. Conf.*

POOL, MARY JANE, writer, lecturer; d. Earl Lee and Dorothy (Matthews) P. Grad., St. de Chantal Acad., 1942; BA in Art with honors, Drury Coll., 1946; LHD (hon.), Drury U., 2002. Mem. staff Vogue mag., N.Y.C., 1946-68, assoc. merchandising editor, 1948-57, promotion dir., 1958-66, exec. editor, 1966-68; editor House and Garden mag., 1969, editor-in-chief, 1970-80. Cons. Baker Furniture Co., 1981-94, Aves Advt., Inc., 1981-94, bd. dirs.; mem. bd. govs. Decorative Arts Trust; past mem. bd. govs. Fashion Group, Inc., N.Y.C. Author: The Gardens of Venice, 1989, The Gardens of Florence, 1992, Gardens in the City-New York in Bloom, 1999; co-author: The Angel Tree, 1984, The Angel Tree—A Christmas Celebration, 1993, The Christmas Story, 2001; editor: 20th Century Decorating, Architecture, Gardens, Billy Baldwin Decorates, 26 Easy Little Gardens. Mem. bus. com. N.Y. Zool. Soc., 1979-86; trustee Drury Coll., 1971— ; bd. dirs. Isabel O'Neil Found., 1978— . Recipient award Nat. Soc. Interior Designers, Disting. Alumni award Drury Coll., 1961, Edith Wharton Women of Achievement award, 1999. Address: 1 E 66th St New York NY 10021-5854

POOLE, EVA DURAINE, librarian; b. Farrell, Pa., Dec. 20, 1952; d. Leonard Milton and Polly Mae (Flint) Harris; m. Tommy Lynn Cole, May 15, 1970 (div. Sept. 1984); 1 child, Tommy Lynn Cole; m. Earnest Theodore Poole, Sept. 22, 1990; 1 child, Aleece Remelle Poole. BA in LS, Tex. Woman's U., 1974, MLS, 1976; postgrad., U. Houston, 1989. Libr. asst. Emily Fowler Pub. Libr., Denton, Tex., 1970-74; children's libr. Houston Pub. Libr., 1974-75, 1st asst. libr., 1976-77; children's libr. Ector County Libr., Odessa, Tex., 1977-80; head pub. svcs. Lee Davis Libr. San Jacinto Coll., Pasadena, Tex., 1980-84; libr. dir. San Jacinto Coll. South, Houston, 1984-90; libr. svcs. mgr. Emily Fowler Pub. Libr., Denton, 1990-93, interim dir., 1993; dir. librs. Denton Pub. Librs., 1993—. Mem. Libr. Svcs. Constrn. Act Adv. Coun., 1994-97, Libr. Svcs. Tech. Act Adv. Coun., 1997-2000; mem. TEXSHARE adv. bd. Tex. State Libr. and Archives Commn., 1999—, chmn., 2003—; bd. dirs. Denton Area Tchrs. Credit Union, 2003—; mem. adv. bd. U. North Tex. Sch. Libr. and Info. Sci., 2000—. Bd. dirs. Amigos Libr. Svcs., 2000-03, Girl Scouts Cross Timbers Coun., 2002-04, United Way of Denton County, 2002—, exec. com., Friends of Librs. U.S.A., 2003—, . Named to Outstanding Young Women of Am., 1991. Mem. ALA (chair Loleta Fyan jury com. 1999-2000), Pub. Libr. Assn. (mem. budget and fin. com. 1999-2002, chair budget and fin. com. 2001-2002, nat. conf. com. 2002-04, chair bylaws and orgn. 2002-03), Libr. Adminstrn. and Mgmt. Assn. (program com. 1994-97, mem.-at-large bd. dirs. 2000-02, chair cultural diversity com. 2000-01, com. on orgn. 2002—, rep. to Freedom to Read Found. 2002-03), Tex. Libr. Assn. (pub. libr. divsn. sec. 1995-96, chair 1997-98, leadership devel. com. 1995-97, leadership devel. com. chair 1996-97, alumnae 1st class Tex. Accelerated Libr. Leaders 1994, legis. com. 1997-99, Dist. 7 coun. 1996-99, exec. bd. 1998-2000, 2002-, ad hoc comn. on pub. lib. stds. com. chair 1998-2000, 2002 conf. local arrangements com. 2001-02, chair 2000 conf. program com. 1998-2000, chair awards com. 2001-02, pres.-elect 2002-03, pres. 2003-04), Pub. Libr. Adminstrs. North Tex. (vice chair 1994-95, chair 1995-96), Tex. Mcpl. Libr. Dirs. Assn. (pres. 1995-96, grantee 1993, Libr. of Yr. 1998), Denton Rotary Club, Tex. Mcpl. League (bd. dirs. 1997-2000). Office: Denton Pub Libr 3020 N Locust St Denton TX 76209 Office Phone: 940-349-8750. E-mail: eva.poole@cityofdenton.com.

POOLE, NANCY GEDDES, art gallery curator; b. London, Ont., Can., May 10, 1930; d. John Hardy and Kathleen Edwards (Robinson) G.; m. William Robert Poole, Aug. 15, 1952; 1 child, Andrea Mary. BA, U. Western Ont., 1956, LLD, 1990. Owner, dir. Nancy Poole's Studio, Toronto, Ont., Can., 1969-78; acting dir. London Regional Art Gallery, Ont., Can., 1981—, exec. dir., 1985-89; dir. London Regional Art and Hist. Museums, Ont., Can., 1989-95. Chair governing coun. Ont. Coll. Art, 1972-73; bd. dirs. Robarts Rsch. Inst., 1995. Author: The Art of London 1939-1980, 1984; editor Jack Chambers, 1978, The Collection, 1990. Bd. govs. U. Western Ont., 1974-85; bd. dirs. Western Area Youth Svcs., 1996. Fellow Ont. Coll. Art. Office: 420 Fanshawe Park Rd London ON Canada N5X 2S9

POOLER, ROSEMARY S. federal judge; b. 1938; BA, Brooklyn Coll., 1959; MA, Univ. of Conn., 1961; JD, Univ. of Mich. Law Sch., 1965. With Crystal, Manes & Rifken, Syracuse, 1966—69, Michaels and Michaels, Syracuse, 1969—72; asst. corp. counsel Dir. of Consumer Affairs Unit, Syracuse, 1972—73; common counsel City of Syracuse Pub. Interest Rsch. Group, 1974—75; chmn., exec. dir. Consumer Protection Bd., 1975—80; commr. N.Y. State Pub. Services Commn., 1981—86; staff dir. N.Y. State Assembly, Com. on Corps., Authorities and Commns., 1987—94; judge Supreme Ct., 5th Jud. Dist., 1991—94; dist. judge U.S. Dist. Ct. (no. dist.) N.Y., Syracuse, 1994—98; cir. judge U.S. Ct. Appeals, 2nd cir., 1998—. Vis. prof. Syracuse Univ. Coll. of Law, 1987—88; v.p. legal affairs Atlantic States Legal Found., 1989—90. Mem.: Assn. of Supreme Ct. Justices of the State of N.Y., Women's Bar Assn. of the State of N.Y., N.Y. State Bar Assn., Onondaga County Bar Assn. Office: 40 Foley Square New York NY 10007*

POON, CHRISTINE A. pharmaceutical executive; BS in Biology, Northwestern U.; M in Biology and Biochemistry, St. Louis U.; MBA in Fin., Boston U. Various mgmt. positions Bristol-Myers Squibb, 1985—2000, v.p., sr. v.p. for Can. and L.Am. pharm. ops., pres., gen. mgr. Squibb Diagnostics' Can. operation, 1994, pres. Med. Devices, 1997—98, pres. internat. medicines, 1998—2000; co. group chmn. pharm. group Johnson & Johnson, New Brunswick, NJ, 2000—01, worldwide chmn. pharms. group, 2001—. Bd. dirs. Fox Chase Cancer Ctr., Phila. Named Woman of Yr., Healthcare Businesswomen's Assn., 2004. Office: Johnson & Johnson 1 Johnson and Johnson Plaza New Brunswick NJ 08901*

POOR, JANET MEAKIN, III, landscape designer; b. Cin., Nov. 27, 1929; d. Cyrus Lee and Helen Keats (Meakin) Lee Hofer; m. Edward King Poor III, June 23, 1951; children: Edward King IV, Thomas Meakin. Student, Stephens Coll., 1947-48, U. Cinn., 1949-51, Triton Coll., 1973-76. Pres. Janet Meakin Poor Landscape Design, Winnetka, Ill., 1975—. Chmn. bd. dirs. Cgho. Horticultural Soc., Chgo. Botanic Garden. Author, editor: Plants That Merit Attention Vol. I: Trees, 1984, Vol. II: Shrubs; contbr. articles to profl. jours. Participant in long range planning City of Winnetka, 1978-82, archtl. and environ. bd., 1980-84, beautification commn., 1978-84, garden coun., 1978-82; adv. coun., Sec. of Agr. Nat. Arboretum, Washington; nat. adv. bd. Filoli, San Francisco; trustee Ctr. Plant Conservation at Mo. Bot. Garden, St. Louis, also mem. exec. com.; mem. adv. coun. The Garden Conservancy, 1989—, chmn. Open Days Program Garden Conservancy; trustee Winnetka Congl. Ch., 1978-80; bd. dirs. Lady Bird Johnson Wildflower Ctr., Austin, Tex., McKee Bot. Garden, Vero Beach, Fla. Recipient merit award Hadley Sch. Blind, 1972, Medal of Honor Garden Club Am.; named Vol. of Yr. Hadley Sch. Blind. Mem. Chgo. Hort. Soc. (chmn. bd. dirs. 1987-93, medal 1984, gold medal garden design, exec. com., chmn. rsch. com., women's bd., designer herb garden Farwell Gardens at Chgo. Botanic Garden, Hutchinson medal 1994), Am. Hort. Soc. (bd. dirs., Catherine H. Sweeney award 1985), Garden Club Am. (chmn. nat. plant exchange 1980-81, chmn. hort. com. 1981-83, bd. dirs., 1983-85, corresponding sec. 1985-87, Horticulture award Zone X1 1981, Creative Leadership award 1986), Fortnightly Club, Garden Guild (bd. dirs.), Garden Club Am. (v.p. 1987-89, medal awards chmn. 1991-93, Medal of Honor 1994). Republican. Avocations: gardening, writing, music, lecturing, horticulture research.

POOR, SUZANNE DONALDSON, advertising and public relations executive; b. Somers Point, N.J., Oct. 6, 1933; d. James Watt and Roberta (Radford) Donaldson; m. Richard Sumner Poor, Mar. 19, 1955 (div. Sept. 1983); children: Jonathan Scott, Jeffrey Sumner, Sara Suzanne. AB, Mt. Holyoke Coll., 1955; MA, Montclair State Coll., 1975; postgrad., NYU, 1977-83; MPhil, Drew U., 1994, PhD, 1998; photography student, New Sch. Social Rsch., 1979-82. Reporter, copy writer WFLB, WFLB-TV, Fayetteville, N.C., 1955-56; dir. public relations Montclair YMCA, N.J., 1965-69, Girl Scouts Greater Essex County, Montclair, 1969-74; assoc. pub. relations dept. Nat. League Nursing, N.Y.C., 1974; freelance public relations, photography Montclair, 1974-76; dir. communications Insts. Religion and Health, N.Y.C., 1976-78; ptnr., pres. Miller/Poor Assocs., Verona, N.J., 1978—. Pres. bd. trustee Doubletree Gallery, Montclair, 1977-79; trustee Friends of N.J. Network, 1986-93. Mem. NAFE, Am. Woman's Econ. Devel. Corp., Exec. Women N.J. (bd. dirs. 1980-83), NJ Ad Club (bd. govs. 1983—, pres. 2001-03, editor Ad Talk 1982—, inductee NJ Advt. Hall of Fame, 2001), Am. Soc. Media Photographers (editor Exposure newsletter 1993—), Author's Guild. Democrat. Episcopalian. Avocations: bicycling, swimming, tennis, furniture restoration. Home: 30 Plymouth St Montclair NJ 07042-2625 Office: Miller Poor Assocs 280 Bloomfield Ave Verona NJ 07044-2426

POORMAN, CHRISTINE K. television producer; b. Rochester, N.Y., Oct. 19; d. Paul G. and Barbara L. (LiVecchi) Kozlowski; m. Jack Edward Poorman, Sept. 9, 1995. B in Journalism/Fin., U. Ga., 1990. With CNN, Atlanta, 1990, prodn. asst., 1990-94, assoc. prodr., 1995—, producer, 1995-99. Vol. Junior League, 1993—, United Way. Avocations: acting, tennis, travel, food. Office: CNN One CNN Ctr 7-S Atlanta GA 30303

POPADAK, GERALDINE L. organizational development consultant, educator; b. Warren, Ohio, Sept. 14, 1948; d. John Edward and Leona Margaret (Franko) P. BA, Hiram Coll., 1984; postgrad., The Am. U., 1990; PhD, Union Inst., Cin., 1995. Supr. mfg., gen. supr. mfg., ops. devel. cons. GM Packard Elec. Divsn., Warren, 1966-91; cons. and trainer UAW-GM Human Resource Ctr., Auburn Hills, Mich., 1991-93; cons. GM Vehicle Devel. & Tech. Ops. Group, Warren, Mich., 1993-95, GM Powertrain Group, Pontiac, Mich., 1995—. Vis. lectr. Oakland U. Grad. Sch. Psychology, Rochester, Mich., 1992-93; adj. faculty Hiram (Ohio) Coll., 1995—, U. Phoenix Mich. Campus, Southfield, 1996—; mem. bd. governance Grad. Sch. Mgmt., U. Phoenix, Southfield, 1997. Vol. mediator The Resolution Ctr., Mt. Clemens, Mich., 1995—; mediator U.S. Postal Svc. Mem. APA, AAUW, Assn. Psychol. Type, Nat. Psychology Adv. Bd., Internat. Soc. Gen. Semantics, ODNetwork, Assn. Mgmt. Orgn. Design (bd. dirs. 1995), Inst. Noetic Scis. Democrat. Roman Catholic. Avocations: reading, walking, gardening, spiritual journeys. Home: 303 Baker St Royal Oak MI 48067-2205 Office: General Motors 777 Joslyn Ave Pontiac MI 48340-2925

POPE, ANNE B. agency head, business executive, lawyer; Degree, Vanderbilt U.; degree Cumberland Sch. of Law, Samford U. Bar: Tenn., DC. Commr. State of Tenn. Dept Commerce and Ins., 1999—2003; fed. co-chair Appalachian Regional Commn., 2003—; assoc. atty. Webster, Chamberlain and Bean, Washington, 1988—92; pres., CEO, v.p., CFO, Parks-Belk Co., 1992—95; pres. Proffitts of the Tri-Cities, 1995—97; exec. dir. Tenn. Film Entertainment, and Music Commn., 1997—99; clk. US Dist. Judge James D. Todd, Jackson, Tenn. Mem. Gov. Sundquist's Coun. of Excellence in Higher Edn., 1997, Gov. Sundquist's Commn. on Practical Govt., 1999. Mem.: Johnson City C. of C. Office: 1666 Connecticut Ave NW Washington DC 20009-1068

POPE, ARLETTE FARRAR, insurance company professional; b. Paterson, N.J., Jan. 30, 1958; d. Arthur James Jr. and Mildred Louise (Johnson) Farrar; m. Leonard Pope, Aug. 12, 1990; children: Tyrell D., Trenace D., Leonard II. BSBA, Fairleigh Dickinson U., 1980. Claim svc. rep. State Farm Ins. Co., Paramus, N.J., 1983-88, claim automation and processing specialist Wayne, N.J., 1988—. Notary pub. State of N.J., 1985—. Trustee The New Beginning Is Now, Paterson, N.J., 1989—; adminstrv. asst. New Christian Tabernacle COGIC, Paterson, 1981—; bd. trustees New Christian Tabernacle Faith in Action Mins., v.p., 1999. Avocations: crossword puzzles, reading, travel. Home: 38 Audrey Ct Stroudsburg PA 18360-8981

POPE, INGRID BLOOMQUIST, sculptor, poet; b. Arvika, Sweden; became U.S. citizen. d. Oscar Emanuel and Gerda (Henningson) Brostrom; m. Howard Richard Bloomquist, Feb. 14, 1941 (dec. Nov. 1982); children: Dennis Howard, Diane Cecile Connelly, Laurel Ann Shields; m. Marvin Hoyle Pope, Mar. 9, 1985 (dec. June 1997). BA cum laude, Manhattanville Coll., 1979, MA in Humanities, 1981; MA in Religion, Yale U., 1984. Exhbns. include Manhattanville Coll., Purchase, N.Y., Yale Div. Sch., Ch. of Sweden in N.Y.C., Blessings, 2003, First Ch. of Round Hill; author: (books) Musings, 1994, Hosannah, Help Please, 1999, Blessings, 2003. Past bd. dirs. N.Y.C. Mission Soc., Greenwich YWCA, Greenwich Chaplaincy, Greenwich Acad. Parents' Assn., past pres; past trustee First Ch. Round Hill, Greenwich; pres. Ch. Women United, Greenwich, 1989-91. Mem. AAUW, Nat. Assn. Pen Women, English Speaking Union, Nat. Wildflower Assn., Yale Club N.Y.C., Lakeview Club (Austin, Tex.), Acad. Am. Poets, Nat. Mus. of Women in the Arts, Yale Alumnae Club (Austin and Greenwich, Conn.). Home: 538 Round Hill Rd Greenwich CT 06831-2641

POPE, KATHLEEN MARIE, library director; d. Walter and Cecilia O'Connor; m. Francis Joseph Pope; children: Michelle, Meredith, Jennifer. BS in Edn., Duquesne U., 1972, MLS, 1973. Libr. Red Land H.S., New Cumberland, Pa., 1972—76, Horton Watkins H.S., Ladue, Mo., Waubonsie Valley H.S., Aurora, Ill.; libr. dir., dept. chair Neuqua Valley H.S., Naperville, Ill. Home: 2509 Braddock Dr Naperville IL 60565 Office: Neuqua Valley High Sch 2360 95th St Naperville IL 60564

POPE, LENA ELIZABETH, human resources specialist; b. Brookhaven, Miss., Jan. 25, 1935; d. James S. and Elease (Edwards) Smith; m. Roland Van Pope, Dec. 22, 1955 (dec. 1967); children: Nikki D., Ronald V., Ouida. BS, Alcorn A&M Coll., 1955; student, Northwestern U., 1961, DePaul U., 1975-78; MA, Nat. Coll., 1987. Asst. to registrar Alcorn A&M Coll., Lorman, Miss., 1955-57; tchr. Alexander High Sch., Brookhaven, 1957-60, Magnolia High Sch., Moss Point, Miss., 1960-62; asst. student pers. Jackson (Miss.) State Coll., 1962-64; tchr. Chgo. Pub. schs., 1964-65, 78-80; adminstrv. asst. aide U.S. Senator Charles H. Percy, Chgo., 1965-78; tchr. Citywide Colls., Chgo., 1976-79; v.p. human resources Human Resources Devel. Inst., Chgo., 1982—. Cons. Foundatin I, Harvey, Ill., 1989—, Safer Found., Chgo., 1990—, Foster Park Community Orgn., Chgo., 1991—. Office mgr. Percy for Senator, Chgo., 1966, 70, 74, 78; transp. dir. Rep. Nat. Conv., Kansas City, Kans., 1976; vol. Thompson For Gov., Chgo.; sec. Oakdale Covenant Ch., 1985-89. Mem. Alcorn State Alumni (sec., con. 1990—), Eta Phi Beta (Soror of Yr. 1987; pres. Alpha Lambda chpt. 1999—). Republican. Avocations: desk top publishing, traveling, reading. Office: Human Resources Devel Inst 222 S Jefferson St Chicago IL 60661-5603

POPE, MELISSA LOPEZ, law educator; b. Detroit, May 8, 1969; d. Eugene Joe Lopez and Linda Rose Cunningham, Richard Lee Cunningham (Stepfather); m. Morgan Emmor Pope, July 29, 1995; 1 stepchild, Ian Charles. B in Lit., Sci. and Arts, U. Mich., Ann Arbor, 1992; JD, Thomas M. Cooley Law Sch., Lansing, Mich., 1999. Bar: Mich. 1999. Acad. adminstrv. intern Office of Academic Multicultural Initiatives, U. Mich., Ann Arbor, 1992—93, multicultural program assoc., 1993—95; receptionist to Spkr. of the House, Mich. Ho. of Reps., Lansing, 1996—97, legal asst. to majority counsel, 1997—98; adj. prof., fed. Indian law Thomas M. Cooley Law Sch., Lansing, Mich., 1999—, asst. dir. and diversity coord. for admissions, 1999—2003, adj. prof., intro. to law, 2000—03, dep. dir., JD program Rochester, Mich., 2003—. Vol. Ann Arbor Pow Wow, Mich., 1988—; participant Native Am. Critical Issues Conf., Mich., 1993—; law student rep. Am. Indian Law Sect., Lansing, Mich., 1996—99; intern Mich. Commn. on Indian Affairs, Lansing, 1999—99; advisor Native Am. Law Student Assn., Cooley Law Sch., Lansing, Mich., 1999—2003; founder, mem. Thomas M. Cooley Law Sch. MLK Day Planning Com., 1999—; mem. So. Poverty Law Ctr., Montgomery, Ala., 2000—; sec./treas. Am. Indian Law Sect., State Bar of Mich., Lansing, 2000—01; mem. Holocaust Meml. Mus., Washington, 2000—; participant Nat. Conf. on Race and Ethnicity, 2000—; chair-elect Am. Indian Law sect. State Bar Mich., Lansing, 2001—02, chair Am. Indian Law sect., 2002—03; advisor student bar assn. diversity coalition Cooley Law Sch. Oakland U., 2003—, dep. dir. Thomas M. Cooley Law Sch., 2003—, ex-officio Am. Indian Law sect., 2003—. Mem.: Nat. Women's Law Alliance (founding mem., treas. 2002—). D-Liberal. Achievements include Head of Delegation, Four Directions Council, Native American Student Secretariat. Successfully lobbied for inclusion of Indigenous Peoples in the UN Conference on Population & Development document. Office: Thomas M Cooley Law Sch 472 O'Dowd Rochester/Oakland Univ Rochester MI 48309 E-mail: popem@cooley.edu.

POPE, SUSAN W. state legislator; Grad., Centenary Coll. Mem. Mass. Ho. of Reps., Boston, 1997—, mem. health care com., mem. local affairs, mem. ethics com. Mem. subcoms. Redistricting for 2001, SBAB funding, zoning issues, cardiac task study. Mem. Wayland Rep. Town Com., Wayland Sch. Com., Bd. Selectman. Mem. Mass. Mcpl. Assn. Republican. Office: Mass State Legis Rm 237 State House Boston MA 02133-2305

POPE-ROBERTS, SONDY, state legislator; b. Apr. 27, 1950; Student, Edgewood Coll. Mem. Wis. State Assembly, Madison, 2002—, mem. aging and long-term care com., mem. edn. com., mem. rural affairs com., mem. small bus. com. Democrat. Office: State Capitol Bldg Rm 420 W PO Box 8953 Madison WI 53708 Address: 3426 Valley Woods Dr Verona WI 53593

POPIAN, LUCIA, artist; b. Bacau, Romania, Sept. 1, 1956; arrived in U.S., 1999; d. Vasile and Maria Bocanet; m. Gabriel Popian, Apr. 11, 1981; 1 child, John. Degree, Nicolae Grigorescu, Bucharest, Romania, 1982; postgrad., Internat. Ctr. Study Presevation and Restoration of Cultural Property, Rome, 1996. Pres. G&L Popian, Pty Ltd., Sydney, Australia, 1993—99, G&L Popian, Inc., N.Y.C., 1999—. Exhibited in group shows at Orizont Art Gallery, Romania, 1985, Juan Miro Competition, Spain, 1986, exhibitions include Fgn. Residents in Italy, 1987. Served with inf. Romanian Marines, 1982. Recipient Sydney Cove medallion, Gov. NSW, Sydney, 1998. Mem.: Nat. Trust of Am. Republican. Eastern Orthodox. Avocations: pottery, gardening, pet care, tennis, reading. Home: 14-19 33d Rd Apt 10C Long Island City NY 11106 E-mail: archoan@aol.com.

POPIO, DONNA MARIE, music educator; b. Youngstown, Ohio, Apr. 11, 1969; d. Paul and Theresa Margaret Vukovinsky; m. John Donald Popio, Aug. 20, 1993; children: Anthony John-Paul, Brandon Michael-Donaldo. B of Music Edn., Youngstown StateU., 1991; MA, Nova Southeastern U., 2003. Tchr. vocal music Youngstown City Schs., Ohio, 1992—2000; music dir. Jewish Cmty. Ctr., 1993—94, Youngstown Playhouse, 1995; dept. head Youngstown City Schs., 1996—2000; tchr. vocal music Liberty Local Schs., 2000—. Mem.: NEA, Ohio Music Educators Assn. Roman Catholic. Avocations: music, reading. Office: Liberty Local Schs 4115 Shady Rd Youngstown OH 44505

POPKIN, ALICE BRANDEIS, lawyer; b. N.Y.C. d. Jacob H. and Susan Brandeis Gilbert; m. Jordan J. Popkin; children: Susan Cahn, Anne, Louisa. AB magna cum laude, Radcliffe Coll., 1949; JD, Yale U., 1953. Bar: N.Y. 1953, U.S. Dist. Ct. (so. dist.) N.Y. 1956, U.S. Ct. Appeals (2nd cir.) 1959, U.S. Supreme Ct. 1962, D.C. 1972, Mass. 1987. Assoc. Cahill Gordon & Reindel, 1953—61; dir. internat. programs Peace Corps, 1961—63; project co-dir. Georgetown Inst. Criminal Law and Procedure, 1967—72; spl. counsel Senate Sub-Com. to Investigate Juvenile Delinquincy, 1972—74; atty., prof. Antioch Sch. Law, 1974—77; assoc. adminstr. EPA, 1977—79; pvt. practice cons. on internat. environ. issues, 1979—81; practicing atty., 1981—87; of counsel Toabe and Riley, Chatham, Mass., 1987—. Fellow Brandeis U.; bd. trustees Radcliffe Coll.; mem. Chatham Harbor Mgmt. Com.; trustee Eldredge Pub. Libr., 1994—. Mem. ABA, Mass. Bar Assn., Barnstable County Bar Assn., Estate Planning Coun. Cape Cod, Planned Giving Coun. Cape Cod. Office: Toabe & Riley Box 707 154 Crowell Rd Chatham MA 02633-2800

POPMA, RENA M. psychologist; d. Dan Christian Popma and Jonnie Marie Arons. BS, McMurry U., 1985; MS, Miss. State U., 1988; PsyD, Antioch New Eng., 1998. Lic. psychologist Tex. Clin. mgr. Deer Oaks Mental Health Assn., Austin, Tex., 1998—. Office: Deer Oaks Mental Health Assn 1600 W 38th St # 214 Austin TX 78731 Home: 901 W Belt Line Rd Desoto TX 75115-3741

POPOVA, NINA, dancer, choreographer, director; b. Novorossisk, USSR, 1922; ed. in Paris, studied ballet with Olga Preobrajenska, Lubov Egorova, Anatole Vilzak, Anatole Oboukhov, Igor Schwezoff. Ballet debut with Ballet de la Jeunesse, Paris, London, 1937-39; soloist Original Ballet Russe, 1939-41, Ballet Theatre (now Am. Ballet), 1941-42, Ballet Russe de Monte Carlo, 1943, 47, Ballet Alicia Alonso, Cuba; mem. faculty Sch. Performing Arts, N.Y.C., from 1954; later artistic dir. Houston Ballet, 1975; tchr. Nat. Acad. Arts, Champaign, Ill., also N.Y.C., 1975—, now Eglevsky Ballet Sch., L.I.; tchr. ballet Mexico City, Mex.; asst. choreographer mus. comedy Birmingham So. Coll., Ala., 1960; numerous appearances on Broadway stage, TV; former mem. regular cast Your Show of Shows; currently tchg. N.Y.C. Address: 33 Adams St Sea Cliff NY 11579-1614

POPOVIC, BOZENA (BO POPOVIC), artist; b. Kostajnica, Croatia, Jan. 2, 1957; d. Milorad and Dragica Skvorc; life ptnr. John Richard Tomasello. AA in Mdse., Fashion Inst. of Design & Mdse., San Francisco and L.A., 1977; BFA in Painting, Calif. Coll. Arts & Crafts, 1980; MPA in Pub. Policy Devel., Calif. State U., Hayward, 1997. Adminstr. Claims Tech. Svcs., Oakland, Calif., 1990-93; co-pub., owner Weekender Mag., West Contra Costa Ed., 1993—95; office mgr. Wild Oats Market, San Francisco, 1996-97; cons. fed. funded project Workers to Bus. Owners, Alameda, Calif., 1997; bus. rels. cons. Better Bus. Bur., San Francisco, 1998-99; rschr. Dominican U. of Calif., San Rafael, 1999—2002; devel. assoc. Found. Osteoporosis Rsch. and Edn., Oakland, 2002; devel. coord. Easter Seals No. Calif., Novato, 2002—. Bd. dirs. Women's Refuge, Oakland, 1999; outreach coord. San Pablo Hotel, Oakland, 1995; asst. dir. Voter Registration Project, San Francisco, 1987; active Re-Elect Marge Gibson campaign, Oakland, 1987, Don Perata campaign, Alameda, 1986-87. Mem.: AAUW, San Francisco Bus. Arts Coun., Assn. Fundraising Execs., Calif. Assn. Rschrs. for Advancement, Assn. Profl. Rsch. for Advancement, Soroptimists Internat. (regional del.). Avocations: reading, hiking, sketching. Office: Easter Seals No Calif 20 Pimentel Ct Ste A1 Novato CA 94949 Home: 335 Silvio Ln Novato CA 94947-5121 E-mail: bpopovic@ca-no.easter-seals.org.

POPP, ANN L. elementary school educator, music educator; b. Gloversville, N.Y., Sept. 6, 1972; d. Arthur Leo and Mary Ann Popp. BS in Music Edn., Coll. St. Rose, 1994, MS in Edn., 1999. Tchr. music Notre Dame, Schenectady, NY, 1994—95; tchr. elem. sch. music Glorversville Schs., 1995—. Dir. music The Glove Theatre, Gloversville, 1999—. Avocations: photography, reading, bicycling. Home: PO Box 651 Northville NY 12134 E-mail: countrygirl72@frontiernet.net.

POPP, CHARLOTTE LOUISE, health facility administrator; b. Vineland, N.J., July 26, 1946; d. William Henry and Elfriede Marie (Zickler) P. Diploma in Nursing, Luth. Hosp. of Md., Balt., 1967; BA in Health Edn., Rowan U., 1972; MA in Human Devel., Fairleigh-Dickinson U., 1981. Cert. Sch. Nurse, N.J., Health Educator, N.J. Charge nurse Newcomb Hosp., Vineland, N.J., 1967-71; supr. Vineland Rehab. Ctr., 1971-72; charge nurse Bridgeton (N.J.) Hosp., 1972-73; dir. insvc. edn. Millville (N.J.) Hosp., 1973-76; dir. hosp. insvc. edn. Vineland Devel. Ctr. State of N.J., 1976-78, program asst. Vineland Devel. Ctr., 1978-87; dir. habilitation planning services State of N.J., Vineland Devel. Ctr., 1987—, lead program coord. Vineland Devel. Ctr., 1981—2001. Exam proctor State of N.J. Bd. Nursing, Newark, 1973-91. Editorial rev. bd. (jour.) Nursing Update, 1973-77. Instr. basic life support, Am. Heart Assn., bd. dirs. Tri-county chpt., 1979-83, South Jersey chpt., 1983-90. Mem. ANA, N.J. State Nurses Assn., Am. Assn. Mental Retardation, South Jersey Insvc. Exch. (life), Smithsonian Assn., Luth. Hosp. of Md. Alumni Assn., Glassboro State Coll./Rowan U. Alumni Assn., Fairleigh-Dickinson U. Alumni Assn. Lutheran. Avocations: reading, travel, collectable plates, animals, horseracing. Office: Vineland Devel Ctr 1676 E Landis Ave Vineland NJ 08361-2943

POPP, LILIAN MUSTAKI, writer, educator; b. N.Y.C. d. Peter and Mae Claire (Cary) Mustaki; m. Robert J. Popp. BA, Notre Dame Coll.; postgrad., Columbia U.; MS in Edn., Hunter Coll. Tchr. English McKee Vocat. and Tech. H.S., S.I., N.Y., 1946-63, chmn. acad. studies, 1963-71; prin. William Howard Taft H.S., Bronx, N.Y., 1971-79; adj. prof. Wagner Coll., S.I., 1960-85; instr. Richmond Coll., CUNY, 1968-70; prof. St. John's U., 1991-93. Mem. Cmty. Sch. Bd., 1980—93, chmn., 1989—90, chmn. legis. com., chmn. substance abuse and adolescent issues com., chmn. pupil pers. svcs. com.; chmn. curriculum com.; asst. examiner N.Y.C. Bd. Edn., 1960—85. Author, editor: Journeys in Science Fiction, 1961, Four Complete World Novels, 1961, Gertrude Lawrence as Mrs. A., 1961, Four Complete Modern Novels, 1962, Four Complete Heritage Novels, 1963, Four Complete Novels of Character and Courage, 1964; contbr. articles to profl. jours. Chmn. vols. N.Y.C. Child Abuse Prevention Program, 1984—86; regional dir., mem. exec. bd. March of Dimes; book discussion leader Snug Harbor Cultural Ctr., 1981—; pres. Com. for a Nuclear-Free Island, 1986—91; v.p. Staten Islanders Against Nuclear Weapons, 1991—95; pres. Staten Island chpt. Brandeis U. Nat. Women's Com., 1996—99, leader News and Shmews; founder, pres. Coalition of S.I. Women's Orgns., 1996—; mem. edn. com. Staten Island Cmty. TV; mem. Libr. com. Staten Island Hist. Richmond Town; pres. Staten Island Youth Coun.; mem. libr. com. Coll. Staten Island; cmty. outreach chair Women for Women of Sierra Leone, 2001; bd. dirs. Staten Island Mental Health Soc. Recipient Women Helping Women award Soroptimists, 1985, Thomas

Wilson award for Substance Abuse Prevention, 1990, S.I. Advance Woman of Achievement award, 1994, Cmty. Hero award S.I. Register, 1996, Woman of Distinction award World of Women, 1998, Paul O'Dwyer Humanitarian award Staten Is. Dem. Assn., 1999, Distinction award Bus. and Profl. Women's Club, Staten Island, N.Y., 2004; named Outstanding Woman by N.Y. State Sen. Vincent J. Gentile, 1998, Women's History Month award N.Y. City Coun. Spkr. Peter Vallone and Councilmen Jeremiah O'Donovan, Oddo and Fiala, 2001, Bus. and Profl. Women's CLub S.I. award of distinction, 2004. Mem. AAUW, Belles Lettres Lit. Soc. (pres.), S.I. Hist. soc., N.Y.C. Assn. Tchrs. English (pres. 1967-71), Nat. Coun. Tchrs. English (bd. dirs. 1968-69), Acad. Pub. Edn., McKee Tchrs. Assn. (pres. 1969), H.S. Prins. Assn. (exec. bd.), Arista Hon. Soc. (hon.), Delta Kappa Gamma (pres.), Phi Delta Kappa (v.p. 1990-92). Avocations: travel, reading, photography, jewelry making. Home: 40 Flagg Pl Staten Island NY 10304-1119

POPPLER, DORIS SWORDS, lawyer; b. Billings, Mont., Nov. 10, 1924; d. Lloyd William and Edna (Mowre) Swords; m. Louis E. Poppler, June 11, 1949; children: Louis William, Kristine, Mark J., Blaine, Claire, Arminda. Student, U. Minn., 1942-44; JD, Mont. State U., 1948. Bar: Mont. 1948, U.S. Dist. Ct. Mont. 1948, U.S. Ct. Appeals (9th cir.) 1990. Pvt. practice law, Billings, 1948-49; sec., treas. Wonderpark Corp., Billings, 1959-62; atty. Yellowstone County Attys. Office, Billings, 1972-75; ptnr. Poppler and Barz, Billings, 1972-79, Davidson, Veeder, Baugh, Broeder and Poppler, Billings, 1979-84, Davidson and Poppler, P.C., Billings, 1984-90; U.S. atty. Dist. of Mont., Billings, 1990-93; field rep. Nat. Indian Gaming Commn., Washington, 1993-2000. Pres. Jr. League, 1964-65; bd. dirs., pres. Yellowstone County Metre Bd., 1982; trustee Rocky Mt. Coll., 1984-90, mem. nat. adv. bd., 1993—; mem. Mont. Human Rights Commn., 1988-90; bd. dirs. Miss Mont. Pageant, 1995—; elected to Billings City Coun., Billings, Mont., 2002; elected dep. mayor coun. woman Ward4, 2002—. Recipient Mont. Salute to Women award, Mont. Woman of Achievent award, 1975, Disting. Svc. award Rocky Mt. Coll., 1990, 1st ann. U. Montana Law Sch. Disting. Female Alumna award, 1996. Mem. AAUW, Mont. Bar Assn., Nat. Assn. Former U.S. Attys., Nat. Rep. Lawyers Assn., Internat. Women's Forum, Yellowstone County Bar Assn. (pres. 1990), Alpha Chi Omega. Republican.

PORDON, JUDITH, writer, poet, artist; life ptnr. Ezequiel Rodriguez Gallegos. Dir. Casa Poema Writers' Retreat, Puerto Vallarta, Jalisco, Mexico, 2000—. Author poetry. Socialist. Mystic. Office: CasaPoema Writers' Retreat Jalisco Puerto Vallarta Mexico Personal E-mail: casapoema@hotmail.com.

PORIES, MURIEL H. business executive, loan consultant; b. Milw., Dec. 19, 1925; d. Jacob and Jean Aronson; m. Walter J. Pories, Aug. 1951 (div. Apr. 1977). BS, U. Wis., Milw., 1951; MA, John Carroll U., 1979; JD, Am. Coll. Law, Brea, Calif., 1984. Cert. prin. Tchr. Rochester (N.Y.) Bd. Edn., 1952-56, Irondequoit (N.Y.) Bd. Edn., 1956-59, Shaker Heights (Ohio) Pub. Schs., 1973—77; counselor Lawyers Referral Svc., Santa Ana, Calif., 1983; mng. ptnr. Pories and Klein, Fullerton, Calif., 1984; mktg. analyst Display Techniques Internat., Santa Ana, Calif., 1986; dir. mktg. Peninsula Shipyard, Newport Beach, Calif., 1987-89; pres., owner Mar-Bruc Inc., Laguna Beach, Calif., 2002—. Loan cons. CPM Fin., Ont., 1999; pioneered open edn. Shaker Heights Bd. Edn., 1974; adj. prof. Am. Coll. Law, Anaheim, Calif., 2002—. Author: "That's Because We Love You," 1976, A Program for Dropout Reduction, 1978. Mem.Am. Coll. Law Alumni (pres. 1999). Democrat. Achievements include co-inventor of E-Z cycle light. Avocations: swimming, table tennis. Home: 231 Cozumel Laguna Beach CA 92651-4447

PORITZ, DEBORAH T. state supreme court chief justice, former attorney general; b. Bkln., Oct. 26, 1936; married; 2 children. BA, Brooklyn Coll., City U. NY, 1958; JD, U. Penn., 1977. Dep. atty. gen. NJ Dept. Law and Pub. Safety, 1977—81, asst. chief environ. protection section, 1981—84, dep. atty. gen. in charge of appeals, chief banking, ins. and pub. securities section, 1984—86, asst. atty. gen., dir. divsn. law, 1986—89; chief counsel to Gov. Thomas Kean, 1989—90; ptnr. Jamieson, Moore, Peskin and Spicer law firm, Princeton, 1990—94; atty. gen. State of N.J., 1994—96; chief justice Supreme Ct. N.J., Trenton, 1996—. Office: Supreme Ct NJ Hughes Justice Complex PO Box 23 Trenton NJ 08625-0023*

PORPER, MARY, comptroller; V.p., comptroller Suissa Miller, L.A. Office: Suissa Miller 11601 Wilshire Blvd Fl 16 Los Angeles CA 90025-1770 Fax: 310-392-2625.

PORTA, SIENA GILLANN, sculptor, educator; b. NYC, Nov. 5, 1951; d. Vincent Anthony Porta and Barbara Ann Gill Porta Hutchinson; m. Robert Christopher Dell, May 30, 1986; 1 child, Malcolm Vincent Dell. BS in Studio Arts, Bklyn. Coll., CUNY, 1977; MFA in Sculpture, Pa. State U., 1979. Sci. illustrator Columbia U./Lamont-Doherty Geol. Obs., Palisades, NY, 1980-87; scenic artist Saturday Night Live, NYC, 1986-89, Met. Opera, NYC, 1987-92; master scenic artist numerous Broadway prod., including Frankie and Johnny, Boiler Rm., Sorrows and Rejoicings, 1992—; adj. prof. contemporary arts Ramapo Coll., 2000—; adj. prof. of art St. Thomas Aquinas, Sparkill, NY, 2000—; represented by Noho Gallery, NYC. Adj. prof. Bergen CC, Paramus, NJ, 1984—85; artist-in-residence Brisons Veor, Cornwall, England, 2003. One-woman shows include 14 Sculptors Gallery, NYC, 1984-85, 88, 90, Mid-Hudson Arts and Sci. Ctr., Poughkeepsie, NY, 1992-93, Dominican Coll., Blauvelt, NY, 1980, Noho Gallery, NYC, 2003; group shows at A.B. Condon Gallery, NYC, 1982-83, Terrain Gallery, NYC, 1984, Am. Cultural Ctr., Reykiavik, Iceland, 1988, Notre Dame U., South Bend, Ind., 1990, Lehigh U., Phila., Blue Hill Cult. Ctr., Pearl River, NY, 1995, Eighth Floor Gallery, NYC, 1996, NJ City U., Jersey City, Nassau C.C., Garden City, NY, The Interchurch Ctr., Riverside Dr., NY, 1998, Adelphi U., NY, 2000, St. Thomas Aquinas Coll., Sparkhill, NY, 2000, Galleri Ofeigur, 2001, Noho Gallery, 2001-02, Snaefelsness Regl. Museum, 2002, Hafnarborg Ctr. for Culture, Mus, 2002-03, Regional Mus. of Hornafjordur, 2003, Rutgers U., 2003, others; represented in collections at Fulbright Commn., Reykjavik, Bergen C.C., Paramus, NJ, 1988, St. Philip R.C. Ch., Norwalk, Conn., Jacob Riis Nat. Park US Embassy, Iceland; subject of video Me and The Mirror, 1990; contbr. articles to popular mag. Pa. State Arts Coun./Hershey Med. Coll. grantee, 1978-79; NY State Coun. on the Arts grantee, 1986; USIA-Ptnrs. of Ams. travel grant to St. Lucia, W.I., 1992, NY Fdn. for the Arts grantee, 2002.; artist resident Brisons Veor, Cornwall, Eng., 2003. Mem. Zen Ctr. of San Diego. Home: PO Box 46 Palisades NY 10964-0046

PORTANOVA, CAROLYN AMICK, religious organization administrator; b. Bedford, Pa., July 30, 1945; d. James T. and Elizabeth D. (DiLbert) Amick; m. Andrew J. Portanova, Apr. 17, 1982. BS, Pa. State U., 1967; MEd, U. Rochester, 1974. Supr. Cath. Family Ctr. Substance Abuse Svcs., Rochester, N.Y., 1974-83, dir., 1983-89; pres., CEO Cath. Family Ctr., Rochester, N.Y., 1989—. Chairperson monitoring com. N.Y. State Bd. Regents, Rochester, 1989—; bd. trustees Coun. Accrediation, Rochester, 1996—; adv. bd. Blue Cross/Blue Shield, Rochester, 1996—; com. mem. Family Svcs. Am., Rochester, 1996. Bd. dirs. United Neighborhood Ctrs., Rochester, 1995—, Monroe County Bar, 1996—; mem. corp. body United Way, Rochester, 1992—. Recipient Outstanding Contbn. award N.Y. State Div. Substance Abuse Svc, 1986, Leadership, Faith and Courage award Interfaith Action Cmty., 1997; named Exec. Yr. United Way Greater Rochester, 1992. Mem. Rotary. Avocations: photography, travel. Office: Catholic Family Ctr 25 Franklin St Fl 7 Rochester NY 14604-1002

PORTER, BARBARA, anchorwoman, writer, educator; m. Henry Stroud Elms III; children: Tommy, Dorian. Anchorwoman NBC Radio; dir. pub. affairs George Washington U., Washington. Tchr. in dramatics and journalism; writer cable TV children's programming. Office: George Washington Univ Ste 1200 2121 I St NW Rm 512 Washington DC 20052-0001

PORTER, CHRISTINE ANN, music educator; b. Philadelphia, Pa., Nov. 19, 1971; d. Matthew Adam and Eileen Delores Kicinski. BMus, U. Hartford, 1995. Cert. OCCS presch. tchr. 1997. Presch. tchr. Beacon Hill Nursery Sch., Boston, 1997—99; owner, instr. YoungSong, Randolph, Mass., 1999—. Spkr. New Eng. Kindergarten Conf., Providence, 2001—02, mem. steering com., 2002—03. Dir.(touring theater prodn.): Wiz of the West, 1999, (musical prodn.): Funny Thing Happened on the Way to the Forum, 2002; actor(film): The Romance Department, 1996 (nominated for ACE Cable Award, 1996); prodr.(recording): YoungSong Sings Out!, 2000. Mem.: Music Educators Nat. Conf., Nat. Assn. Edn. Young Children, Children's Music Network, People to People Amb. Programs (founder New Eng. chpt. 2001—02, ednl. delegation to Cuba 2001). Avocations: dog training, theater, singing, camping, hiking. Home: 116 Pond St Randolph MA 02368 Office: YoungSong 10 Mazzeo Dr Suite 201E Randolph MA Personal E-mail: yngsong@aol.com. Business E-Mail: yngsong@aol.com.

PORTER, ELSA ALLGOOD, writer, lecturer; b. Amoy, China, Dec. 19, 1928; d. Roy and Petra (Johnsen) Allgood; m. Raeford B. Liles, Mar. 19, 1949 (div. 1959); children: Barbara, Janet; m. G. Hinckley Porter, Nov. 22, 1962; children: David, Brian, Wendy. BA, Birmingham-So. Coll., 1949; MA, U. Ala., 1959; M in Pub. Adminstrn., Harvard U., 1971; LHD (hon.), U. Ala., 1986. With HEW, Washington, 1960-73; with U.S. CSC, Washington, 1973-77; asst. sec. Dept. Commerce, Washington, 1977-81; disting. practitioner in residence Washington Pub. Affairs Ctr., U. So. Calif., Washington, 1982-84; v.p. R & D The Maccoby Group, Washington, 1990-96; sr. fellow Meridian Internat. Inst., 1990—. Chair comml. adv. subcom. NASA, 1997—2003. Fellow World Acad. Art & Scis., Nat. Acad. Pub. Adminstrs.; mem. Women's Nat. Dem. Club. Home: 2309 SW 1st Ave Apt 742 Portland OR 97201-5008

PORTER, JEANNETTE UPTON, elementary school educator; b. Mpls., Mar. 5, 1938; d. Robert Livingston and Ruby Jeannette (Thomas) Upton; divorced; children: Steven, Fritz, Susan Porter Powell. BS, U. Minn., 1960, Mankato State U., 1968; postgrad., St. Thomas U., 1991. Camp dir. St. Paul's Epsicopal Ch., Mpls., 1956-66; tchr. elem. sch. Bloomington (Minn.) Pub. Schs., 1967—, dir. title I, 1975-82, tchr. spl. assignment of rsch. and devel., 1990-91; ednl. adminstrn. Conf. Ctr. Office, Lac du Flambeau, Wis., 1991—. Cons. in ednl. change and innovations The Inst.; team cons. Hillcrest Cmty. Sch., Bloomington, 1990—95; res. tchr. spl. assignment, 1996—; vol. music therapist The Pines Sr. Care, Pine City, Minn., 2001—; edn. cons., 1996—; vol. Nature Conservancy, Avon Park, Fla., 2001—; exchange tchr. Minn./China Tchr., Hangzhou, China, 2002—03; Minn./China exch. tchr., Zhenjiang, China, 2002—03. Tutor Telephone Hot Line Minn. Fedn. Tchrs., Mpls., 1988-92; crisis counselor Neighborhood Improvement Programs, Mpls., 1988-93; adult literacy counselor Right to Read, Mpls., 1987-89; vol. Abbott Northwestern Hosp.; bd. dirs. The Inst. (profl. ednl. think tank, Lac du Flambeau), 1997—. Recipient 1st Bank award Mpls., Red Apple award, Mpls., 1988; named Minn. Tchr. of Excellence, 1988, 89. Mem. Assn. Early Childhood Edn. (treas. 1990-94), Bloomington Edn. Found., Delta Kappa Gamma (1st v.p. 1992-93), PEO (past pres. A.C. chpt.). Avocations: fishing, photography, back packing, global volunteer, music. Home: 4400 W 44th St Minneapolis MN 55424-1064 E-mail: porterfl@strato.net.

PORTER, JENNIE LEE, health facility administrator, entrepreneur; d. Jay Hamilton and Willie Ovella Gregory; m. Jack MacArthur Porter, Oct. 9, 1993. BS, Fresno State U., 1996; cert. in gerontology, San Francisco State U., 1997; Master Degree (hon.), Jones Internat. U., 2000; cert. in healthcare adminstrn. (hon.), Capella U., 2002, PhD (hon.), 2003. Registered dietitian Calif., 1997; notary public Calif., 1998, lic. real estate salesperson Calif., 1994. Food svc. mgr. Kings/Tulare Area Agy. on Aging, Lemoore, Calif., 1985—96; CEO/owner JP Svcs., Lemoore, 1994—; dietitian cons. HM Composite, Livermore, Calif., 1997—98; area dir. Gambro Healthcare, Lemoore, 1998—2000, regional dir., 2000—02, v.p. alt. modalities, 2002—. Dietitian cons. State of Calif., 1994—. Chairperson Emmanuel Pentecostal Churches, 1989—2003. Named Woman of the Yr., Soroptomist Internat., 1990. Mem.: Calif. Dietitic Assn. (assoc.; pub. rels. 1994—96, scholarship 1996), Am. Dietitic Assn. (assoc.). Personal E-mail: jp40404@aol.com. E-mail: jennie.porter@us.gambro.com.

PORTER, JENNIFER MADELEINE, producer, director; b. Milw., Oct. 3, 1962; d. John Hamlin and Helen Meak (Smith) P. BA in Comm., Bowling Green State U., 1984. Audio visual supr. Liberty Mutual Ins. Group, Berwyn, Pa., 1985-88; sr. prodr. audio visual Prudential Ins. Co., Mpls., 1988-93; proprietor Shoot The Moon Prodns., Mound, Minn., 1993-96, Shoot the Moon Prodns., Mpls., 1996—. Prodr., dir., writer: (audio visual programs) Phantom Lake... A Lifetime of Memories, 1991 (Best of Show 1991, Script award Assn. for Multi-Image Internat. 1991), Vision... The Gamma Phi Beta Foundation, 1992 (First Place award 1993), prodr., prodn. coord. Stadium Theatre Experience-College Football Hall of Fame (Silver award Assn. for Multi-Image Internat. 1996), the Making of Homo Heights, 1997 (Women in Dirs. Chair Walker Art Ctr.). Mentor U. Minn., Mpls., 1989-96; fundraiser Gamma Phi Beta Found. Philanthropy-Spl. Camping for Girls, Minn., Wis., 1991—; chairperson 100th Celebration, Phantom Lake YMCA Camp, Mukwonago, Wis., 1994-96. Mem. Assn. for Multi-Image Internat. (exec. bd. local 1986-88), Gamma Phi Beta (internat. officer, pub. rels. speaker/prodr. 1991—). Avocations: travel, music, sports, camping, canoeing. Home and Office: Shoot The Moon Prodns 5104 26th Ave S Minneapolis MN 55417-1317 E-mail: shootthemoon@usinternet.com.

PORTER, JILL, journalist; b. Phila., Aug. 5, 1946; d. Sidney and Mae (Merion) Chalfin; m. Eric Porter, Mar. 7, 1970 (div. 1975); m. Fred Hamilton, Oct. 28, 1983; 1 child, Zachary. BA, Temple U., 1968. Pub. rels. Manning Smith P.R., Phila., 1968-69; reporter Norristown Times Herald, Norristown, Pa., 1969-72, The Trentonian, Trenton, N.J., 1972-75, The Phila. Daily News, Phila., 1975-79, columnist, 1979—. Instr. Temple U., 1976-80. Contbr. articles to numerous mags. Vol. Phila. Futures, 1994, 95, 96, Phila. Cares, 1997. Recipient numerous journalism awards. Avocations: dance, biking, reading. Home: 134 Rolling Rd Bala Cynwyd PA 19004-2615 Office: Phila Newspapers Inc Phila Daily News 400 N Broad St Philadelphia PA 19130-4015

PORTER, JOYCE KLOWDEN, theatre educator and director; b. Chgo., Dec. 21, 1949; d. LeRoy and Esther (Siegel) Klowden; m. Paul Wayne Porter, June 8, 1980; 1 child, David Benjamin. BA in Speech Edn., U. Ill., 1971; MA in Theatre, Northwestern U., 1972; postgrad., Northeastern U., Chgo., 1980, 89, 98, Ill. State U., 1985-90. Prof. theatre, play dir. Moraine Valley C.C., Palos Hills, Ill., 1972—2002, emeritus, 2002—, acting theatre coord., 1986-87, theatre coord., 2001—02. Adj. faculty Columbia Coll., 1988—92, Triton Coll., 2004; text reviewer Harcourt Brace Pub., 1997, Simon & Schuster, 1998, Mayfield, 1999, Martins, 2000—, Pearsons Ednl., 2001—03; actress, Chgo., 1972—. Author: (textbook) Humanities on the Go, 1992, Experiencing the Arts, 2000. Mem. adv. bd. Oak Park (Ill.) Park Dist., 1983; co-chmn. Moraine chpt. Chgo. Area Faculty for nuclear Freeze, Palos Hills, 1985-87; announcer for blind Chgo. Radio Info. Svc., 1982-83; bd. dirs. Festival Theatre, Oak Park, 1989—, sec. 1996-97, pres., 1997-99, v.p. 2002-2003, pres., 2003—; mem. play selection com. Village Players of Oak Park, 1992; guest dir. Triton C.C., 2000. Mem. Assn. for Theatre in Higher Edn., U.S. Inst. for Theatre Tech., Ill. Theatre Assn., C.C. Humanities Assn (presenter midwest conf. 1993, presenter & planning com. nat. conf. 1999), Ill. Fedn. Tchrs., Nature Conservancy, Zeta Phi Eta. Avocations: acting, singing, foreign travel, antiquities and antiques. Office: Moraine Valley CC 10900 S 88th Ave Palos Hills IL 60465-2175 E-mail: porter@morainc.valley.edu.

PORTER, JUDITH DEBORAH REVITCH, sociologist, educator; b. Phila., Mar. 26, 1940; d. Eugene and Esther (Tulchinsky) Revitch; m. Gerald Joseph Porter, June 26, 1960; children: Daniel, Rebecca, Michael. Student, Vassar Coll., 1958-60; BA, Cornell U., 1962, MA, 1963; PhD, Harvard U., 1967. Lectr. Bryn Mawr (Pa.) Coll., 1966-67, asst. prof., 1967-73, assoc. prof., 1973-79, prof. sociology, 1979—, chair dept. sociology, 1987-93. Author: Black Child, White Child: The Development of Racial Attitudes, 1971; contbr. articles to profl. jours. Committeeperson Haverford Twp. Dem. Party, 1976-96; bd. dirs. Phila. AIDS Fund, 1992-98; Congreso de Latinos Unidos, Inc.; vice-chair Mayor's Commn. on Drugs and Alcohol, City of Phila. Recipient Shannon award NIMH, 1992-94; Ford Found. fellow, 1973-74; NSF fellow, 1967; NIDA grant Co-PI, 1998-2001. Mem. APHA, Am. Sociol. Assn., Phi Beta Kappa, Phi Kappa Phi. Jewish. Address: 161 Whitemarsh Rd Ardmore PA 19003-1634 Office: Bryn Mawr Coll Dept Sociology Bryn Mawr PA 19010 E-mail: jporter@brynmawr.edu.

PORTER, LEAH LEEARLE, biological researcher, industry executive; b. Remington, Va., Sept. 19, 1963; d. James Wallace and Earline Yvonne (Moore) P. BS, U. Md., 1985; MS, Cornell U., 1990, PhD, 1993. Biol. technician U.S. Dept. Agr., Beltsville, Md., 1981-85; agrl. cons. Md. Dept. Agr., College Park, 1985; grad. rsch. asst. Cornell U., Ithaca, N.Y., 1986-94; mgr. internat. project Glahe Cons. Group, Washington, 1994-95; rsch. mgr. Am. Chemistry Coun., Washington, 1995-97; sci. mgr. ILSI, Washington, 1997-98; exec. dir. CropLife Am., Washington, 1999—2003; v.p. sci. affairs Chocolate Mfgs. Assn., 2004—. Cons., mktg. asst. Le Earle Enterprises, Ithaca, 1988—93. Pres. Cmty. Ministry Prince George's County, 1999—, bd. dirs., 1999—. Md. State Senate scholar, 1984-85; faculty grad. fellow Cornell U., 1986-87. Fellow N.Y. Acad. Scis.; mem. Am. Phytopathological Soc., Assn. Women in Sci., Alpha Chi Sigma, Zeta Phi Beta. Democrat. Baptist. Avocations: church volunteer, reading, music, church volunteer, reading, music.

PORTER, LILIANA ALICIA, artist, photographer, painter, print and filmaker; b. Buenos Aires, Oct. 6, 1941; came to U.S., 1964, naturalized, 1982; d. Julio and Margarita (Galetar) P.; m. Luis Camnitzer, 1965 (div. 1978); m. Alan B. Wiener, May 28, 1980 (div. 1991). Grad., Nat. Sch. Fine Arts, Argentina, 1963. Co-dir., instr. Studio Camnitzer-Porter summer workshops, Lucca, Italy, 1974, 75, 76, 77; prof. art Queens Coll., CUNY, N.Y.C., 1991—. Adj. lectr. SUNY Coll., Old Westbury, N.Y., 1974-76, Purchase br., 1987; co-dir. Studio Porter-Wiener, N.Y.C., 1979-87. One-woman shows of prints/paintings/photographs include Galeria Artemultiple, Buenos Aires, Argentina, 1977, 78, Galleria Arte Comunale, Adro, Brescia, Italy, 1977, Hundred Acres Gallery, N.Y.C., 1977, Mus. Modern Art, Cali, Colombia, 1978, Center for Interamerican Relations, N.Y.C., 1980, Galeria Arte Nuevo, Buenos Aires, 1980, Barbara Toll Fine Arts, N.Y.C., 1979, 81, 82, 84, Galerie Jolliet, Montreal, 1983, Museo de Arte Contemporaneo, Panama City, Panama, 1984, Dolan/Maxwell Gallery, Phila., 1985, U. Alta., Edmonton, 1985, Dolan/Maxwell Gallery, Phila., 1985, Galería Luigi Marrozzini, San Juan, P.R., 1986, Galería-Taller, Museo de Arte Moderno, Cali, Colombia, 1987, The Space, Boston, 1988, Syracuse U., N.Y., 1990, Steinbaum-Krauss Gallery, N.Y.C., 1993, Galeria Ruth Benzacar, Buenos Aires, 1994, U. Art Gallery, N.Mex. State U., Las Cruces, 1995, Monique Knowlton Gallery, 1996, Ruth Benzacar Gallery, N.Y., 1997, Mus. de Bellas Artes Juan Manuel Blanes, Montevideo, Uruguay, 1997, Espacio Minimo, Murcia, Espana, 1998, Annina Nosei Gallery, N.Y., 1999, Artcore Gallery, Toronto, Can., 1999, Espacio Minimo, Murcia, Spain, 2000, Ruth Benzacar Gallery, Buenos Aires, 2000, Sicardi Gallery, Houston, 2000, Annina Nosei, N.Y., 2000, Ctr. Photography, Woodstock, N.Y., 2000, Phoenix Mus., 2000, Galeria Espacio/Mimimo, Madrid, 2000, Brito-Cimino, Sao Paulo, Brazil, 2001, Annina Nosei Gallery, N.Y., 2002, Sicardi Gallery, Houston, 2002, Casas Riegmer Gallery, Miami, Fla., 2003, Hosfelt Gallery, San Francisco, 2003, Galeria Espacio Minimo, Madrid, Spain, 2003, Centro Cultural Recolete, Buenos Aires, 2003; retrospective exhibits 1968-90 Fundacion San Telmo, Buenos Aires, 1990, Museo Nacional de Artes Plasticas, Montevideo, Uruguay, 1991, Centro de Recepciones del Gobierno, San Juan, P.R., 1991, Bronx Mus. Art, N.Y.C., 1992, retrospective exhibit Archer Huntington Art Gallery U. Tex. Austin, 1993, Staller Ctr. for the Art SUNY at Stony Brook, N.Y., 1998, Centro Cultural Recoleta, Sla Cronopios, Buenos Aires, Argentina, 2003; exhibited in numerous group shows including most recently El Mus. del Barrio, N.Y.C., 2000,Casa de America, Madrid, 2000, Contemporary Mus., Balt., 2000, N.Y., others, Mass. Coll. Art, Huntington Gallery, Boston, 2001, ARCO, Madrid, 2001, Centro Cultural Borges, Buenos Aires, 2001, Peter Lewis Theater, Guggenheim Mus., N.Y., 2001, Hosfelt Gallery, San Francisco, 2001, Fundacion Telefonica, Madrid, 2001, Fundacion Joan Miro, Barcelona, 2001, Carrie Secrist Gallery, Chgo., 2001, Contemporary Art Ctr., N.Y., 2001, The Mahady Contemporary Gallery at Marywood U., Scranton, Pa., 2002, Kunst Werke, Berlin, 2003; represented in permanent collections Mus.Phila., Mus. Modern Art, N.Y.C., RCA Corp., N.Y.C., N.Y. Public Library, N.Y.C., La Biblioteque Nationale, Paris, France, Museo del Grabado, Buenos Aires, Museo Universitario, Mexico City, Mexico, Museo de Art Moderno, Cali, Colombia, Museo de Bellas Artes, Caracas, Venezuela, Met. Mus. Art, N.Y.C. Recipient 1st prize Argentinian Art 78 Mus. Fine Arts, Buenos Aires, 1978, Grand Prix XI, Internat. Print Biennial, Cracow, Poland, 1986, 1st prize VII Latin Am. Print Biennial, San Juan, Puerto Rico, 1986; fellow Guggenheim Found., 1980-81, N.Y. Found. for the Arts, 1985, grantee, 1999. Address: 720 Greenwich St 10G New York NY 10014 Office Phone: 718-997-4800. E-mail: lilianaporter@frontiernet.net.

PORTER, LOUISA S. federal judge; Apptd. presiding magistrate judge so. dist. U.S. Dist. Ct. Calif., 1991. Office: 1140 US Courthouse 940 Front St San Diego CA 92101-8994 Fax: (619) 702-9925.

PORTER, MARIE ANN, neonatal nurse; b. St. Paul, June 29, 1961; d. Theodore J. Morrison and Betty Ann Verdick; 1 child, Angela. ADN, Columbia Basin Coll., 1988. RN, Wash.; cert. neonatal resuscitation, Neonatal Resuscitation Program instr., ACLS; cert. nurse life care planner Am. Assn. Life Care Planners, 2003. Staff RN Kennewick (Wash.) Gen. Hosp., 1988-95; legal nurse cons. Richland, Wash., 1995—; owner, pres. Porter Med. Cons. Active March of Dimes. Mem. Wash. State Trial Lawyers Assn., Richland C. of C. (amb.).

PORTER, NANCY LEFGREN, reading recovery educator; b. Council Bluffs, Iowa, Apr. 26, 1945; d. Elvin W. and Verna V. (Hansen) Lefgren; m. Eugene D. Porter, Apr. 3, 1965; children: Theresa McFarland-Porter, M.S., Dr. Tracy K.P. Gregg. BS, U. Iowa, 1976, completed devel. activities program, 1983, MS, 1992. Cert. Reading Recovery trained tchr., reading specialist, 1993. Tchr. Iowa City Sch. Dist., 1976-93, reading recovery Title I tchr., 1993—. Mem. After Sch. Tutoring Program, Iowa City; instr. U. Iowa, 1997. Author (curriculum) Lites and Shadows, 1993, reading curriculum, 1997 (Blue Ribbon award 1997); presenter (cmty. collaboration) NSCI At-Risk, 1994. Precinct chair Dem. Party, Johnson City, Iowa, 1990-96; exec. bd. LWV, 1989-90; WELCA chair Gloria Dei Luth. Ch. Women; mem. corp. bd. Alpha Xi Delta. Grantee K-3 At Risk Grant, 1992, State of Iowa, 1992-97; named Educator of Yr. East Ctrl. Uniserve Unit, 1992. Mem. Iowa State Edn. Assn. (exec. bd. 1993—, Friend of Edn. award 1997, student ISEA), Iowa City Edn. Assn. (pres. 1983-84, 97, govtl. affairs chair 1983—, Educator of Yr. 1992), Delta Kappa Gamma (pres. 1995-96), Pi Delta Kappa (program chair 1994-95). Democrat. Lutheran. Avocations: biking, camping, dance, reading, enjoying grandchildren. Home: 2519 Potomac Dr Iowa City IA 52245-4827

PORTER, PRISCILLA MANNING, artist; b. Balt., Feb. 1, 1917; d. William Hamilton and Amy Russell (Manning) P. BA in Sci., Bennington Coll., 1940. Lab. technician Coll. of Physicians and Surgeons, N.Y.C., 1940-43; sci. tchr. The Brearley Sch., N.Y.C., 1943-45, The Chapin Sch., N.Y.C., 1946-52; ceramic tchr. Mus. Modern Art, N.Y.C., 1952-61; owner fused glass studio, Washington, Conn., 1960—. Contbr. articles to profl. publs. Trustee Steep Rock Assn., Washington, 1993—. Mem. Soc. Conn. Craftsmem, Washington Art Assn. Episcopalian. Avocations: choral singing, gardening. Home and Office: 24 Plumb Hill Rd Washington CT 06793-1511

PORTER, ROBERTA ANN, counselor, educator, school system administrator; b. Oregon City, Oreg., May 28, 1949; d. Charles Paul and Verle Maxine (Zimmerman) Zacur; m. Vernon Louis Porter, Dec. 27, 1975 (div. Dec. 1998). B in Bus. Edn., So. Oreg. Univ., 1971, M in Bus. Edn., 1977; cert. in counseling, Western Oreg. U., 1986; postgrad., Lewis and Clark Coll., 1995. Cert. in leadership Nat. Seminars. Tchr. Klamath Union H.S., Klamath Falls, Oreg., 1971-73, Mazama Mid./H.S., Klamath Falls, 1973-83; instr. Oreg. Inst. Tech., Klamath Falls, Oreg., 1975-92; counselor Mazama H.S., Klamath Falls, 1983-93; vice prin. Bonanza (Oreg.) Schs., 1993-95; counselor Klamath County Sch. Dist., Oreg., 1995—; TAG coordinator Lost River Jr./Sr. H.S., 1995—2002, gender equity team, 1997—. Participant Clinton Cuban-USA Edn. Initiative, Oct. 2000; Blue/Gold Officer USN Acad., 2000—; sch. improvement com. Klamath County Sch. Dist., 2000—; presenter Oreg. and Nat. Assn. Student Coun., 1989-92, Oreg. Sch. Bds. Assn., Sch. Counselor Assn., 1995, state mini workshops counselors/adminstrs., Western Region Br. leadership tng. ACA, 1999, Klamath Youth Summit, 1999; task force for ednl. reform in Oreg., 1993-94; trainer asst. Leadership Devel. Am. Sch. Counselor Assn.; trainer ACA. Mem. editl. bd. Eldorado Wellness, 1996—. Trainer U.S. Army and Marines Recruiters, Portland and Medford, Oreg., 1988-89; master trainer Armed Svcs. Vocat. Aptitude Battery/Career Exploration Program, 1992—; candidate Klamath County Sch. Bd., Klamath Falls; interpreter AMTRAK svc. Klamath Dept. Tourism and Nat. Parks, 1998—; mem. Klamath County Crisis Team. Recipient Promising, Innovative Practices award Oreg. Sch. Counselors, 1990. Mem. NEA, ACA (western region parliamentarian 1999-2001), COSA, ASCD, ASCA, Oreg. Sch. Counseling Assn. (presenter, v.p. h.s. 1988-91, mem. com. 1991-93, pres. 1992-95, pres.'s award), Oreg. Edn. Assn., Oreg. Counseling Assn. (pres. award 1995, parliamentarian 1994-95, area 8 rep. 1995-97, pres.-elect 1997-98, pres. 1998-99, past pres. 1999-2000), Oreg. Assn. Student Couns. (bd. dirs. activity advisors 1989-91), Nat. Assn. Student Couns., Klamath Falls Edn. Assn. (bldg. rep. 1990-93, sec. 1991-92, negotiations team 1992-93), Elks, Delta Kappa Gamma (exec. bd. Alpha chpt. 1985-94, pres. 1990-92, state conv. chmn. 1992, state legis. com. 1991-93, chmn. 1993-95, state expansion com., World Fellowship chair Alpha chpt., scholarship chair 2002—), Elks (scholarship chair, 2003). Avocations: boating, travel, reading, fishing. Home: 3131 Derby St Klamath Falls OR 97603-7313 Office: Lost River Jr/Sr High Sch 23330 Highway 50 Merrill OR 97633-9706

PORTER, VERNA LOUISE, lawyer; b. May 31, 1941; BA, Calif. State U., 1963; JD, Southwestern U., 1977. Bar: Calif. 1977, U.S. Dist. Ct. (ctrl. dist.) Calif. 1978, U.S. Ct. Appeals (9th cir.) 1978. Ptnr. Eisler & Porter, L.A., 1978-79, mng. ptnr., 1979-86; pvt. practice, 1986—. Judge protempore L.A. Mcpl. Ct., 1983—, L.A. Superior Ct., 1989—, Beverly HIlls Mcpl. Ct., 1992—; mem. subcom. landlord tenant law, State Calif., panelist conv.; mem. real property law sect. Calif. State Bar, 1983; mem. client rels. panel, vol. L.A. County Bar Dispute Resolution; ct. appointed arbitrator civil cases, fee arbitrator L.A. Superior Ct.; mem. Better Bus. Bur. Arbitrator Automobile Lemon Laws, 2000—. Editl. asst., contbr. Apt. Bus. Outlook, Real Property News, Apt. Age. Mem. adv. coun. Freddie Mac Vendor, 1995—; mem. World Affairs Coun. Mem. ABA, L.A. County Bar Assn. (client-rels. vol. dispute resolution fee arbitration 1981—; arbitrator lemon law claims), L.A. Trial Lawyers Assn., Wilshire Bar Assn. Women Lawyers' Assn., Landlord Trial Lawyers Assn. (founding, pres.), Da Camera Soc. Republican. Office: 2500 Wilshire Blvd Ste 1226 Los Angeles CA 90057-4365

PORTERFIELD, SHERRI LOU, music educator; b. Poplar Bluff, Mo., Feb. 2, 1958; d. Harold Ray and Nancy Lou Porterfield. BS in Music Edn., U. Memphis, 1980; MusM in Choral Conducting, U. Mo., Kansas City, 1991. Choral music dir. Fort Zumwalt Sch. Dist., O'Fallon, Mo., 1980—89, Olathe (Kans.) Unified Sch. Dist. #233-Frontier Trail Jr. High, 1989—2002; dir. choirs Austin (Tex.) Ind. Sch. Dist.-Murchison Mid. Sch., 2002—03, Leander Ind. Sch. Dist.-Cedar Park (Tex.) Mid. Sch., 2003—. Adj. asst. prof. music edn. U. Mo., Kansas City, 1995; presenter, guest clinician in field; guest condr. in field. Composer over 175 compositions. Bd. govs. U. Mo., Kansas City, 1995—97. Mem.: ASCAP, Tex. Choral Dirs. Assn., Am. Choral Dirs. Assn., Tex. Music Educators Assn., Music Educators Nat. Conf. Roman Catholic. Avocations: stained glass design, reading, dogs. Office: Cedar Park Mid Sch 2100 Sun Chase Blvd Cedar Park TX 78613 E-mail: sporterfld@aol.com.

PORTMAN, NATALIE, actress; b. Jerusalem, June 9, 1981; BS in Psychology, Harvard U. Appeared in motion pictures including The Professional, 1994, Developing, 1995, Heat, 1995, Everyone Says I Love You, 1996, Beautiful Girls, 1996, Mars Attacks!, 1996, Star Wars: Episode I-The Phantom Menace, 1999, Anywhere But Here, 1999, Where the Heart Is, 1999, Zoolander, 2001, Star Wars Episode II-Attack of the Clones, 2002, Cold Mountain, 2003, Garden State, 2004, True, 2004; appeared in stage prodns. including Diary of Anne Frank, 1997, The Seagull, 2001. Office: Internat Creative Mgmt 8942 Wilshire Blvd Beverly Hills CA 90211-1934*

PORTNOW, KATHRYN EMILY, psychologist, educator; b. New York, Jan. 17, 1949; BA, Goddard Coll., 1971; MS, Bank Street Coll. Edn., 1984; EdD, Harvard Grad. Sch. Edn., 1996. Instr. in edn. Wheelock Coll., Boston, 1996—2002; rsch. assoc. Harvard Grad. Sch. Edn., Cambridge, Mass., 1997—2001; instr. in human devel. Wheelock Coll., 2003—. Bd. dirs. Parenting Edn. Network of Mass., Boston, 2000—02; presenter in field. Contbr. articles to profl. jours. Achievements include research in Co-author of qualitative rsch. study on adult ABE/ESOL learners' expriences. The level of develpoment, acculturation and parenting history shapes the coherence of ABE/ESOL family literacy students. Office: Wheelock Coll 200 The Riverway Boston MA 02215

PORTNOY, LESLIE SNYDER, art educator, artist; b. Balt., Oct. 5, 1953; d. Irvin and Shirley Snyder; m. David Norman Portnoy, June 24; children: Jessica, Ben. BS, U. Md., Coll. Pk., 1975; MFA in Edn., Md. Inst. Coll. of Art, Balt., 1981. Part-time art instr. Baltimore County Pub. Schs., 1982—2000; adj. faculty art edn. Loyola Coll., Balt., 1984—; instr. art edn. Md. Inst. Coll. of Art, 1988—, instr. continuing studies, 1994—; instr. Goucher Coll. Day Sch., 1998; instr. 2 dimension design Goucher Coll., 2003. Curator Mid-Atlantic Region Art League, 1998; docent lectr. Balt. Mus. of Art, 1995. Exhibitions include Washington Women's Art Ctr., 1975, Md. Inst. Coll. of Art Grad. Show, 1981, Essex C.C., 1985, Balt. Mus. Art Sales and Rental Gallery, 1985, Md. Inst. Coll. of Art Faculty Show, 1986, Md. Fedn. of Artists, 1988, Artscape, 1988, Md. Inst. Coll. of Art, 1994, Artscape '94, 1994, Chesapeake Art Gallery, Harford C.C., 1995, Morris Mechanic Art Gallery, 1995, Resurgam Gallery, 1995, Clay Works Artist Sudios Tours, 1996, Beneath the Surface, 1999, Meet the Masters, Jewish Cmty. Ctr. Faculty Show, 2001, Art Effects Gallery, 2003 . Recipient Outstanding Svc. award, Md. Art Edn. Assn., 1984, Outstanding Svc. of Art Edn. award, 1984, Outstanding Svc. award, Loyola Coll., 1989; grad. assistantship, Md. Inst. Coll. of Art, 1979. Jewish. Avocations: gardening, tennis, reading, travel, hiking. Home: 1308 Pine Ridge Ln Pikesville MD 21208 Studio: Leslie Snyder Portnoy Studios 330 W 23rd St Baltimore MD 21211

PORTNOY, LYNN ANN, fashion retailer; b. Detroit, June 13, 1938; d. Morris and Betty (Diamond) P. Student, U. Wis., 1956-57, Harvard U., 1957; BA, U. Mich., 1960. Buyer trainee Joseph Magnin, San Francisco, 1960-65; buyer, pub. rels. Claire Pearone, Troy, Mich., 1968-80; owner, pres. Lynn Portnoy Women's Clothier Inc., Detroit, 1980-97, Southfield, Mich., 1997—. Author: (book) Going Like Lynn, Paris (A Series of Liberating Travel Primers for Women), 1999, Going Like Lynn, New York, 2000, Going Like Lynn, Florence, 2001. Vol. Internat. Vis. Council, South Oakland Shelter, Alzheimers Assn., Mich. Abortion Rights Action League. Mem. Nat. Assn. Women Bus. Owners, Womens Economic Club, U. Mich. Alumni. Avocations: travel, reading, writing, cooking, walking. Office: 29260 Franklin Rd Southfield MI 48034-1161 E-mail: info@goinglikelynn.com.

PORTNOY, SARA S. lawyer; b. N.Y.C., Jan. 11, 1926; d. Marcus and Gussie (Raphael) Spiro; m. Alexander Portnoy, Dec. 13, 1959 (dec. 1976); children: William, Lawrence. BA, Radcliffe Coll., 1946; LLB, Columbia U., 1949. Bar: N.Y. 1949, U.S. Dist. Ct. (so. dist.) N.Y. 1952, U.S. Dist. Ct. (ea. dist.) N.Y. 1975, U.S. Ct. Appeals (2d cir.) 1975, U.S. Supreme Ct. 1975. Assoc. Seligsberg, Friedman & Berliner, N.Y.C., 1949-51; atty. AT&T, N.Y.C., 1951-61; vol. atty. Legal Aid Soc. of Westchester, NY, 1966-74; assoc. Proskauer Rose Goetz & Mendelsohn, N.Y.C., 1974-78, ptnr., 1978-94; ret., 1994. Mem. Commn. on Human Rights, White Plains, N.Y., 1973-78; mem. bd. visitors Columbia Law Sch., 1996-02; bd. dirs. Legal Aid Soc. of Westchester County, N.Y., 1975-83, Columbia Law Sch. Assn., 1990-94, Mosholu Montifiore Cmty. Ctr., 1998—; mem. Pres.'s Coun. Yaddo; dir. Muscular Dystrophy Assn., 2000-03. Mem. Assn. Bar City of N.Y. (chair com. legal support staff 1994, mem. Com. on Homeless, Sr. Lawyer's Com. and chair Pub. Svc. Network 2003—), South Fork Country Club (dir. 1997—), The Children's Storefront (dir. 1998—).

PORTO, MARISA JOSETTA, editor; b. New Haven, Conn., Apr. 17, 1965; d. Carl and Henrietta Maria (Louese) Porto. BA, U. S.C., 1987. Intern Palm Beach (Fla.) Post (copydesk) Greensboro (NC) News and Record (reporting), 1985—87; city, environ. reporter Lakeland (Fla.) Ledger, 1987—88; cops, county and schs. reporter Florida Today, Melbourne, 1988—92; cops reporter, fill-in ACE, Sun Sentinel, Ft. Lauderdale, Fla., 1992—93; bus. editor Charlotte Sun Herald, Port Charlotte, Fla., 1993—97; editor Venice (Fla.) Gondolier, 1997—98; mng. editor Coshocton (Ohio) Tribune, 1998—99; editor Zanesville Times Recorder, Coshocton Tribune, Ohio, 1999—. Cmty. editing seminar Am. Press Inst., 1997, discussion leader, 2001—02. Bd. dirs. Big Brothers, Big Sisters, Venice, Fla., 1996—97, Girl Scouts Heart of Ohio, Zanesville, 2000—; adv. bd. Big Brothers Big Sisters, Zanesville, Ohio, 2001—02. Recipient First Place features, Fla. Soc. Newspaper Editors, 1995, Third Place In-Depth writing, Fla. Press Club, 1996, 2d Place Bus. writing, 1996, 3d Place 5th Amendment Defense, Fla. Press Assn., 1997, 1st Place Govt. writing, Fla. Press Club, 1997, First Place Feature writing, 1998, First Place 1st Amendment Defense, Fla. Press Assn., 1999, First Place Edtl. writing, Ohio Associated Press, 2000, First Place Column writing, 2001, First Place Edtl. writing, 2001, Presstime 20 under 40 Dec., 2002. Mem.: Associated Press Mng. Editors, Nat. Assn. Hispanic Journalists. Office: Zanesville Times Recorder 34 S 4th St Zanesville OH 43701 E-mail: mporto@nncogannett.com.

PORTOGHESE, CAROLINE LOUISE PARKE, occupational therapist; d. Robert John and Barbara Ann Parke; m. Stephen Philip Portoghese, May 10, 1996; children: Isabella Christine, Annelisa Barbara. BA, Macalester Coll., 1990; BS, U. Minn., 1995. Rsch. asst. U. Minn., Mpls., 1994—95; occupl. therapist, casual, 1996; occupl. therapist St. Paul, 1996—98; seating practitioner Tamarack Clinic - Fairview, 1998—. Clin. instr. U. Minn., Mpls., 1999—99; guest lectr. Coll. St. Catherine, St. Paul, 2000—03, Century Coll., White Bear Lake, 2000—03; item writer cert. exam. Nat. Bd. Certification Occupl. Therapy, Gaithersburg, Md., 2003—; presenter in field. Dewitt-Wallace scholar, Macalester Coll., 1986—89. Mem.: Am. Occupl. Therapy Assn., Minn. Occupl. Therapy Assn. (chair com. 2000—03, newsletter editor, asst. editor 1998—2000, Svc. award 2000, 2002, cert. appreciation 2003). Office: Tamarack 2200 Univ Ave W Ste 110 Saint Paul MN 55114

POSEN, SUSAN ORZACK, lawyer; b. N.Y.C., Nov. 5, 1945; BA, Sarah Lawrence Coll., 1967; JD, Bklyn. Law Sch., 1978. Bar: N.Y. 1979. Assoc. Stroock & Stroock & Lavan, N.Y.C., 1978-83, 84-86; ptnr. Stroock, Stroock & Lavan, LLP, N.Y.C., 1987-2000; asst. gen. counsel Cablevision Systems Corp., Woodbury, N.Y., 1983-84; co-founder, ptnr. DIVA Capital LLC, N.Y.C., 2000—01; CEO Outspoke LLC, 2001—. Office: Outspoke LLC 13-17 Laight St New York NY 10013

POSER, JOAN RAPPS, artists agent; b. Plainfield, N.J., Apr. 10, 1940; d. Mandel Max and Marion Davidson Rapps; m. Jay Sanford Poser, Nov. 15, 1964; children: Lester Philip, Toby Anne. BA, U. Conn., 1962. Self-employed travel cons., Lancaster, Pa., 1976-79; tchr. McDonogh Sch., Balt., 1982-90; artist's agt. Joan E. Poser Assocs. Agts. in the Arts, Balt., 1978—; co-owner, v.p. Poser's Apparel, Inc., Pa., 1990-95; co-owner Poser's Accessories Sales Reps., 1995—. Cons. Charmelle, Inc., San Francisco, 2002—. Pres. Lancaster Town Fair, 1974, Temple Beth El Sisterhood, Lancaster, 1973—77, donor chmn., 2000—03; pres. and devel. chmn. Md. Assocs. for Dyslexic Adults and Youth, Inc., 1989—91; campaign chair Bus. and Profl. Women, Assoc. Jewish Charities, Balt., 1985; spl. events chair Cultural Arts Inst. Chizuk Amuno Congregation, 1986—90, trustee, 1986—90; chmn. Lancaster Jewish Community Ctr. 50th Anniv. Gala, 1994, Temple Beth El 50th Anniv. Gala, 1995; bd. dirs. Temple Beth El, 1991—92, Janus Sch., Lancaster, 1991—94, Lancaster Jewish Community Ctr., 1991—93. Mem. Hadassah. Democrat. Avocations: opera, sports, architecture, travelling, writing. Home: 119 Greenview Dr Lancaster PA 17601-4988 Office Phone: 717-560-7976. Personal E-mail: jerapps@localnet.com.

POSEY, ADA LOUISE, human resources specialist; BA, Carleton Coll. Expense mgmt. and pension operation staff Prudential Ins. Co., 1978—85, internal auditing staff, 1985—89; corp. budgeting staff Minn. Mut., 1989—93; assoc. dir. for gen. svcs. Office Adminstrn., The White House, Washington, 1993-96, dep. dir., 1996-97, dir., 1997-99; spl. advisor Office of Nat. Drug Control Policy, Washington, 1999—; sr. policy advisor Dept. of Energy, Washington, 1999-2001; pres. Posey Cons. Group, 2001—03; dir. diversity and compliance Raytheon Tech. Svcs., Reston, Va., 2003—. Trustee Carleton Coll.; mem. Capital City Links chpt., Washington. Office: Raytheon Tech Svcs 12160 Sunrise Valley Dr Reston VA 21910 E-mail: ada_l_posey@raytheon.com., noah0496@aol.com.

POSEY, FAITH E. artist; b. Deercreek, Minn., Apr. 6, 1944; d. Clark B. Posey and Iva L. Bitner-Posey-Huffman; m. Kenneth S. Vitale, Sept. 19, 1969 (div. July 26, 1981). BFA, Sch. Art Inst., Chgo., 1967. Cert. art tchr. Ill., journeyman glazier Glazier's Union . Art instr. Chgo. Pk. Dist., 1968—72; art tchr. Sears Sch., Kenilworth, Ill., 1973—74, Green Briar Sch., Northbrook, Ill., 1974—76; art glazier apprentice Drehobl Bros. Art Glass, Chgo., 1980—84; owner Glassart Studio, Chgo., 1984—; constrn. glazier various contractors, Chgo., 1985—. Aesthetic cons., Chgo., 1990—. Stained glass, Byer Mus. Arts, 1983, Casa Mexicana, Chiapas, Mex., 1993, series of 56 paintings, Mujeres Trabajando, 1991. Women's rights advocate in constrn. trades, Chgo., 1985—; cmty. adv. Oakwood Blvd. Improvement Assn., Chgo., 1989—2002. Recipient Juror's award, 59th Rockford and Vicinity Show, 1983, Hon. Mention, Artscape '96, Chgo. (represented by Metamorphosis Art Gallery, Patagonia, Ariz., 1996. Mem.: Glaziers Union, Mus. Women in Arts (charter mem.), Chgo. Artists Coalition. Avocations: restoring houses, landscaping, walking. Address: PO Box 895 Sonoita AZ 85637

POSGAY, BETTY MARIE, medical equipment company executive, artist; b. Frankenstein, Mo., Dec. 15, 1933; d. August Peter and Gertrude Johanna (Koenigsfeld) Stiefermann; m. John George Posgay, Jr., June 12, 1954; children: Elaine Marie, Laura Elizabeth, Martin John. Student, U. Mo., 1952-54. Receptionist St. Mary's Hosp., Jefferson City, Mo., 1951; sec. March of Dimes, St. Louis, 1954-57; demonstrator CDI, St. Louis, 1983-86; sec. Archway Med. Supply, Inc., Clayton, Mo., 1988-96; pres. Crown Med. Equipment, Inc. (Southtown), St. Louis, 1996—. Exhibited in group shows at St. Louis Artists Guild/Two Oak Knoll Park, Clayton, Mo., 1998, Am. Art Alliance, St. Louis, 1997. Chmn. Am. Cancer Soc., Affton, Mo., 1984-85; former crusader Heart Fund, and March of Dimes, Affton. Mem. Am. Art Alliance (sec. 1997), Mo. Bot. Garden, Friends of Art Mus. Roman Catholic. Avocations: playing piano, sketching, writing in diary, painting, walking. Office: Crown Med Equipment Inc 5639 S Kingshighway Blvd Saint Louis MO 63109-3508

POSIN, KATHRYN OLIVE, choreographer; b. Butte, Mont, Mar. 23, 1943; d. Daniel Q. and Frances (Schweitzer) P. BA in Dance, Bennington Coll., 1965; MFA in Interdisciplinary and World Dance, NYU, 1994; studies in composition, 1965-78, studies in ballet, 1965-90, studies in modern dance, 1967-80. Mem. dance co. Am. Dance Theater at Lincoln Ctr., 1965; dancer Anna Sokolow Dance Co., 1965-73; artistic dir. Kathryn Posin Dance Co., NYC, 1972-91; choreographer Eliot Feld Ballet, NYC, 1978, Netherlands Dance Theater, Den Hague, Switzerland, 1980, Alvin Ailey Am. Dance Theater, NYC, 1980; mem. dance faculty U. Wis., Milw., 1984-86, choreographer, 1984-88; tchr., choreographer UCLA, 1988-90, Trinity Coll., Hartford, Conn., 1990-91. Mem. dance faculty, choreographer U. Calif., Santa Barbara, 1986; tchr. dance technique and performance Tchr.'s Coll. Columbia U., spring 1990; tchr. composition and technique Nat. Inst. of Arts, Taiwan, 1991; founding chair Joffrey Ballet Sch., New Sch. U. BFA in Dance, 1998. Choreographer (performing cos./orgns.) Cherry Orchard, Lincoln Ctr., NYC, 1978, Alvin Ailey Am. Dance Theater 1981, Netherlands Dans Theater 84182, Extemporary Dance Co. London, Balletmet, Columbus, Ohio, Milw. Ballet, 1991, 93, 95, 96, Cin. Ballet, 1997; (prin. works) Salvation, Off-Broadway, NYC, 1969, Waves, 1975 (Am. Dance Festival commn.), The Cherry Orchard, NY Shakespeare Festival, 1979, Mary Stuart, Acting Co., 1980, Shady Grove (grantee joint program of Ohio Arts and Humanities Couns. 1991), The Tempest, Am. Shakespeare Festival, Strratford, Conn., 1982, Midsummer Night's Dream, Arena Stage, Washington, 1982, Boys From Syracuse, Am. Repertory Theater, Harvard U., 1983, The Paper Gramophone, Hartford Stage, 1989, Of Rage and Remembrance, 1990 (Premiere of Yr. in Music and Dance, Milw. Jour.), Stepping Stones, 1993 (co-recipient Meet the Composer/Choreographer award Milw. Ballet 1993), many others; subject of documentary Kathy's Dance. Grantee Guggenheim Found., 1978, NY State Coun. on Arts, 1977, 79, 80, Jerome Robbins Found., 1972; grantee Nat. Endowment for Arts 1981, 82, 85-87, choreography fellow, 1995-96; Doris Humphrey fellow Am. Dance Festival, New London, Conn., 1968. Office: Kathryn Posin Dance Co 20 Bond St New York NY 10012 2406 E-mail: Pozndance@aol.com.

POSNER, KATHY ROBIN, communications executive; b. Oceanside, N.Y., Nov. 3, 1952; d. Melvyn and Davonne Hope (Hansen) P. BA in Journalism, Econs., Manhattanville Coll., 1974. Fin. planner John Dreyfus Corp., Purchase, N.Y., 1974-80; corp. liaison Gulf States Mortgage, Atlanta, 1980-82; dir. promotion Gammon's of Chgo., 1982-83; coordinator trade show mktg. Destron, Chgo., 1983-84; pres. Postronics, Chgo., 1984-87; v.p. Martin E. Janis & Co., Inc., Chgo., 1987-90; chmn. Comm 2 Inc., Chgo., 1990—. Editor: How to Maximize Your Profits, 1983; contbg. editor Internat. Backgammon Guide, 1974-84, Backgammon Times, 1981-84, Chgo. Advt. and Media; columnist Food Industry News. Bd. dirs. Chgo. Beautification Com., 1987, Concerned Citizens for Action, Chgo., 1987; mem. steering com. Better Boys Found.; campaign mgr. Brown for Alderman, Chgo., 1987; mem. bd. cons. Little City Found.;'mem. benefit bd. C.A.U.S.E.S. Mem. NATAS, NOW, Women in Comm., Am. Soc. Profl. and Exec. Women, Women in Film-Chgo. (bd. dirs.), Mensa, Acad. Arts (v.p.), Ill. Restaurant Assn. (mem. adv. bd.), Chgo. Area Pub. Affairs Group, City Club Chgo. (bd. dirs.), Chgo. Legal Clinic (bd. dirs.). Republican. Jewish. Avocations: politics, reading. Home: 100 E Huron # 3505 Chicago IL 60611 E-mail: kathyposner@aol.com., krp01@aol.com.

POSNER, LINDA IRENE, retired government official, marketing consultant; b. Balt., Feb. 6, 1939; d. Morris and Rosabelle (Hankin) Rosen; m. Allan Bernard Posner, Dec. 29, 1957; children: Larry Gregg, Michael Glenn, Robert Ira. BA summa cum laude, Coll. of Notre Dame, 1989. Dir., lectr. Montgomery Ward's Fashion, Modeling and Charm Sch., Md., 1962-66; fashion and pub. rels. dir. Montgomery Ward, Md., 1966-75; freelance writer Balt., 1975-76; pres., co-owner Designer's Circle Ltd., Balt., 1976-78; TV writer, producer Dept. of Def., Ft. Meade, Md., 1979-87; TV mgr. Dept. Def., Ft. Meade, Md., 1980-87, sr. edn. and tng. mgr., 1987-91, performance technologist, 1991-94, multi-media ops. mgr., 1994-96, sr. corp. mktg. strategist, 1996-98; mktg. and multimedia cons., 1999—. Regional dir. The Fashion Group, Balt., 1972-74. Mem. com. March of Dimes, Balt., 1976-78; chairperson Combined Fed. Campaign Com., 1987, U.S. Savs. Bonds, 1989. Dept. of Def. scholar, 1987-88. Mem. Women in Communications, Human Resources Mgmt. Assn., AFTRA. Jewish. Avocations: travel, writing. Home: 640 Grove Ave SW Cleveland TN 37311 E-mail: travelers_pos@msn.com.

POSNER, SYLVIE PEREZ, lawyer; b. Havana, Cuba, Nov. 17, 1954; d. Carlos Miguel Perez and Emilia Ines Amezaga; m. Michael J Posner, Aug. 23, 1987; 1 child, Christopher Barrett. BS, Fla. State U., Tallahassee, Florida, 1975—80; JD, U. Miami, Coral Gables, Florida, 1984—88. Bar: Fla. 1989, Fla. So. Dist. 1989, US Ct. Appeals, 11th Cir. 1989. Rsch. asst. U. of Miami Sch. of Law, Coral Gables, Fla., 1987—88; cert. legal intern Dade County Pub. Defender, Miami, 1986—87; law clk. Frumkes and Greene, P.A., Miami, Fla., 1987—88, Fourth Dist. Ct. of Appeal, West Palm Beach, Fla., 1990—94; asst. atty. gen. Office of the Atty. Gen., Fort Lauderdale, Fla., 1994—2000; sr. staff atty. Fourth Dist. Ct. of Appeal, West Palm Beach, Fla., 2000—; legislative aide Fla. Senate, Tallahassee, 1981—84. Mem. Phi Alpha Delta Legal Frat., Coral Gables, Fla., 1985—88, Health and Law Soc., Coral Gables, Fla., 1985—88; participant Trial Advocacy Program, Nat. Inst. of Trial Advocacy, Coral Gables, Fla., 1987; mem. Appellate Law Sect., Fla. Bar, Fla., 1994—, Govt. Law Sect., Fla. Bar, Fla., Broward County Hispanic Bar Assn., Fort Lauderdale, Fla., 1998—2000, Fla. Assn. of Police Attorneys, Fla., 1994—2000; mem. appellate law clk. edn. com. Fla. Supreme Ct., 2002—. Vol. lawyers program The Fla. Bar, Miami, Fla., 1989—90; vol. tel. crisis counselor Switchboard of Miami, Inc., Miami, Fla., 1981—83; supporting mem. Norton Art Mus., West Palm Beach, Fla., 2003; mem. Emily's List, Washington, D.C., DC, 2002; apptd. mem. Dade County Dem. Exec. Com., Miami, Fla., 1982—84; exec. v.p. Dade County Young Democrats, Miami, Fla., 1988—89; del., fla. dem. conv. Fla. Dem. Party, Orlando, Fla., 1988, del., state dem. conv. Miami, Fla., 1984. Nominee Outstanding Young Women of Am., Nat. Fedn. of Dem. Women, 1985. Mem.: Wellington Country & Golf. Independent. Avocations: reading, computer research, swimming, listening to music, writing. Office: Fourth District Court of Appeal 1525 Palm Beach Lakes Boulevard West Palm Beach FL 33401 Personal E-mail: sylverbyrd@aol.com. Business E-Mail: posners@flcourts.org.

POSPICHAL, MARCIE W. neuroscientist, psychologist, educator; b. Great Lakes, Ill., Feb. 22, 1959; BS in Psychology, Fla. So. Coll., 1985; MA in Psychology, Neurosci., Vanderbilt U., Nashville, 1990, PhD in Psychology, 1991. Tchg. asst. Vanderbilt U., Nashville, 1988—91, faculty lectr. dept. psychology, 1991—95, rsch. assoc. dept. psychology, 1991—97, editl. asst. Jour. Comparative Neurology, 1992—97, asst. dir. programs Ctr. for

Molecular Neurosci., 1996—2001, coord. grad. studies Vanderbilt Brain Inst., 1997—2001, asst. dir. programs in neurosci. edn. Vanderbilt Brain Inst., 1999—2001; adj. instr. dept. psychology Fla. So. Coll., Lakeland, 2001—. Neurosci. cons. Bd. of Nat. Health Mus., 1999; lectr. in field; condr. seminars in field; mem. neurosci. coun. com. Vanderbilt U., Nashville, 1999—2001; Assoc. Vice-Chancellor's planning com. for the 2001 Consortium on Neurogenetics Vanderbilt Med. Ctr., 1999—2001, Vice-Chancellor's Com. on Cmty. Outreach, 1998—2001; mem. neurosci. PhD curriculum com. Vanderbilt U., 1997—2001; adj. mem. Ctr. for Molecular Neurosci. Faculty Recruitment Com., 1997—2001. Contbr. articles and abstracts to profl. jours. Vol. WDCN, Nashville, 1999; mem. Safe and Drug-Free Nashville Metro Schs. Com., 1997; vol. reader for the blind WPLN Listening Libr., Nashville, 1992—93. Co-recipient NSF grantee, 1999; recipient Rsch. Svc. award, Nat. ., 1995; fellow postdoctoral fellow, Vanderbilt U., 1996, 1993—94, 1991—92, grad. rsch. fellow, 1986—88, 1991; grantee Fight for Sight Postdoctoral Tng. grantee, 1992—93. Mem.: Internat. Brain Rsch. Orgn., Soc. for Neurosci. (com. on neurosci. liberacy 2001—), Assn. of Neurosci. Depts. and Programs. Achievements include research in in neuroanatomy; neurotoxic and electrolytic stereotaxic brain lesioning in rodents; also in pressure injectin and iontophoretic application of tract tracing substances such as HRP and its conjugates in non-human primates; also in tract tracing using live slice tissue preparation in non-human primates; other areas. Office: thern Coll Dept Psychology Lakeland FL

POSPISIL, JOANN, historian, archivist; b. Schulenburg, Tex., Dec. 10, 1947; d. Edwin James and Jossie Annie (Mica) Krametbauer; m. Gerald Joseph Pospisil, Nov. 19, 1966; 1 child, Ryan Joseph. BA summa cum laude, U. Houston, 1992, MA, 1994. Cert. archivist Acad. Cert. Archivists, 2001. Sec. to v.p. Bohler Bros. of Am., Inc., Houston, 1972-75, asst. corp. sec., 1975-77; archival intern Sul Ross State U. Archives of the Big Bend, Alpine, Tex., 1993; rsch. asst. U. Houston Recovering U.S.-Hispanic Literary Heritage, 1993-94; archive technician Houston Acad. Medicine-Tex. Med. Ctr. Jesse H. Jones Libr., 1995-98; asst. archivist Baylor Coll. Medicine Archive, Houston, 1997—. Task force mem., rsch. cons. Houston Urban Coun., 1993; contbg. historian Candelilla Wax Industry, Tex. Archeol. Rsch. Lab., 2004. Contbr. articles to profl. jours. Sec. handbook com. Clay Road Bapt. Parent-Tchr. Orgn., Houston, 1980-81; coord. Houston Police Dept., Houstonians on Watch, 1982-91; sec., membership chair, libr. aide Spring Branch Ind. Sch. Dist. Parent-Tchr. Assn., Houston, 1983-89; presenter geographical and cultural topics to classrooms in Spring Br. Elem. Sch., Northbrook H.S., Houston, 1985-95; interviewer oral history program Alliance Am. Quilts, 1999-; pres., pub. chair Spring Braneh Addition Civic Assn. Inc., sec., 2002-. Recipient Spanish award Houston C.C., 1985, Josephine Del Barto scholarship in history U. Houston, 1989-90, Helen M. Douthitt scholarship in history, 1990-91;named Sadie Iola Daniels scholar Assn. for Study of African Am. Life and History, Washington, 1990. Mem. Ctr. for Big Bend Studies, Soc. Am. Archivists, Tex. Czech Geneal. Soc. (charter), Archvists Houston Area (charter), Soc. Southwest Archivists, Tex. Hist. Assn., West Tex. Hist. Assn., Tex. Oral History Assn., Phi Kappa Phi, Phi Alpha Theta. Avocations: bicycling, hiking, photography, whitewater rafting, reading non-fiction. Home: 9418 Railton St Houston TX 77080-1431 Office: Baylor Coll Medicine Chancellor's Office/Archive One Baylor Plaza Ste 177 A Houston TX 77030

POST, BARBARA JOAN, elementary school educator; b. Passaic, NJ, June 29, 1930; d. John Ward and Florence Barbara (Barnum) Post; m. Edward Wayne Poppele, Apr. 10, 1954 (dec. Mar. 1978); children: E. Scott Poppele, Sara Elizabeth Poppele, Andrew John Poppele. BSE, William Paterson Coll., 1953; cert. in counseling, Rutgers U., 1981; postgrad., Columbia U., 1983, Northeastern U., 1983. Cert. tchr., N.J. Elem. tchr. Cen. Sch., Glen Ridge, N.J., 1953-55, Middletown (N.J.) Village Sch., 1956, Our Lady of Perpetual Help, Highlands, N.J., 1981-85; reading tchr. Monmouth Reading Ctr., Long Branch, N.J., 1985; tchr. gifted/talented Harmony Sch., Middletown, 1987-88; edn. coord. for Monmouth County Nat. Coun. on Alcoholism, Freehold, N.J., 1988-89; coord. math./sci. consortium Brookdale Community Coll., Lincroft, N.J., 1989-90; tchr., owner Learning Post and Creative Garden of Art for Children, Middletown, 1991—; dir. art Hillel Sch., Ocean, N.J., 1991—. Dir.-owner Learning Post, Middletown, 1986—; art tchr. Art Alliance of Monmouth County, Red Bank, N.J., 1986-88; vol. case mgmt. worker St. Matthews House, Naples, Fla., 1997-98. Author: (poem) The Lift, 1988 (short story) Sarah-Grand, 1984, Hooked on the Classics, 1988; artist (program cover) Country Christmas, 1990, 91. Demonstrator Family Reading Fair, Lincroft, 1989; participant Muscular Dystrophy Telethon, Eatontown, N.J., 1986; tchr. Tower Hill Vacation Bible Sch., Presbyn. ch., Red Bank, N.J., 1998. Mem. AAUW (tchr., mentor for teen women 1989-92, Appreciation award 1989-90), Nat. Soc. DAR (chairperson 1961-62), N.J. Shore Rose Soc. (exhibitor, 2d and 3d prize for roses 1986). Republican. Presbyterian. Avocations: art, swimming, choir, roses, golf. Home: 167 Crown Dr Naples FL 34110 E-mail: post@mymailstation.com

POST, DIANA CONSTANCE, retired librarian; b. Anoka, Minn., Oct. 17, 1929; d. Kenneth Fred and Emma Constance (Fredrickson) Davis; husband dec., June 1996; children: Leslie Post, Paul Post, Tom Post. BS, U. Minn., 1970, MLS, 1976. Cert. libr., media specialist, Minn. Libr., media specialist Lake City (Minn.) H.S., 1970-94. Bd. dirs. Zumbrota (Minn.) Pub. Libr.; mem. SELCO governing bd. regional libr. sys., Rochester, Minn., 1980-86; pres. SELCO exec. com., 1984-86; SELS adv. com., 1990-94. Editor Lake City Sch. Dist. News, 1988-89. Scholar LaVerne Noyes Found., 1947-48, Delta Delta Delta, 1949. Mem. Beta Phi Mu. Avocations: golf, swimming, volunteering. Home: 695 Jefferson Dr Zumbrota MN 55992-1103 E-mail: DPost3@aol.com.

POST, JOANN JESSON, librarian; b. Trenton, N.J., July 16, 1949; d. Joseph Ephraim and Irene Jesson; m. Edward Harry Post, Jan. 22, 1983; 1 child, Jennifer Elaine. Cert. elem. tchr., ednl. media specialist. Rsch. asst. N.J. Edn. Assn., Trenton, 1972—81; dir. spl. sci. collection N.J. Dept. Environ. Protection, Trenton, 1981—87; part-time ref./adult svcs. librarian Monroe Twp. Libr., Monroe, NJ, 1990—. Mem. Christian And Missionary Alliance. Avocations: bicycling, sewing, reading. Office: Monroe Twp Pub Libr 4 Municipal Plz Monroe NJ 08831 E-mail: jpost@lmxac.org.

POSTER, ELIZABETH C. dean; BSN, Boston U., 1968, MSN in Child Psychiatric Nursing, 1970; PhD in Ednl. Psychology, Boston Coll., 1981. Asst. prof., asst. dean student affairs Sch. Nursing UCLA, 1981-84, dir. nursing rsch. and edn. Neuropsychiatric Hosp., 1984-95; dean, prof. Sch. Nursing U. Tex., Arlington, 1995—. Bd. dirs. Tex. Bd. Nurse Examiners. Editor Jour. Child, Adolescent Psychiatric Nursing, 1992—. Office: U Tex Arlington Sch Nursing Box 19407 411 S Nedderman Dr Arlington TX 76019-0407 Fax: 817-272-5006. E-mail: poster@uta.edu.

POSTER, MERYL, film company executive; With William Morris Agy.; exec. asst. to co-chmn Harvey Weinstein Miramax Film Corp., 1989—91, dir. devel., 1991—93, v.p. east coast prodn., 1993—94, sr. v.p. prodn., 1994—97, exec. v.p. prodn, 1997—98, co-pres. prodn., 1998—. Exec. prodr.: (films) Smoke, 1995, Marvin's Room, 1996, The Pallbearer, 1996, Cop Land, 1997, Wide Awake, 1998, Shakespeare in Love, 1998 (Acad. Award for Best Picture), Cider House Rules, 1999, Chocolat, 2000, Bounce, 2000, The Shipping News, 2001, Kate and Leopold, 2001, Blow Dry, 2001, Chicago, 2002 (Acad. Award for Best Picture), Duplex, 2003; co-prodr.: Music of the Heart, 1999. Office: Miramax Film Corp 375 Greenwich St Fl 3 New York NY 10013*

POSTON, ANITA OWINGS, lawyer; b. Sylacauga, Ala., Sept. 24, 1949; d. John T. and Margaret Owings; m. Charles E. Poston, June 9, 1973; children: Charles E. Jr., John W., Margaret Elizabeth. BA, U. Md., 1971; JD, Coll. William & Mary, 1974. Bar: Va. 1974. Atty. Vandeventer Black LLP, Norfolk, Va., 1974—. Substitute judge Norfolk (Va.) Gen. Dist. Cts., 1982-90; mem. Bar Examiners Bd.; mem. bd. vistors Coll. William and Mary Mem. State Bd. for Community Colls., Richmond, 1985-90, chmn. 1988-89; mem. Norfolk Sch. Bd., 1990-2002, chmn. 1998-2002; bd. dirs. WHRO Pub. Broadcasting, chair, 2002-03; bd. dirs. Learning Bridge Acad., Govs. Sch. for the Arts Found. Mem. ABA (law fellows), Va. Bar Assn. (pres. 2000), Norfolk-Portsmouth Bar Assn. (pres. 1998-99), Va. Law Fellows, Am. Inn of Ct. Office: Vandeventer Black LLP 500 World Trade Ctr Norfolk VA 23510-1679 Fax: 757-446-8670. E-mail: aposton@vanblk.com.

POSTON, REBEKAH JANE, lawyer; b. Wabash, Ind., Apr. 20, 1948; d. Bob E. and April (Ogle) P. BS, U. Miami, 1970, JD, 1974. Bar: Fla. 1974, Ohio 1977, U.S. Dist. Ct. (so. and mid. dists.) Fla., U.S. Ct. Appeals (11th cir.). Asst. U.S. atty. U.S. Atty.'s Office, Miami, Fla., 1974-76; spl. atty. organized crime and racketeering sect. Strike Force, Cleve., 1976-78; ptnr. Fine, Jacobson, Schwartz, Nash & Block, Miami, 1978-94, Steel Hector & Davis, Miami, 1994—. Adj. prof. U. Miami Law Sch., Coral Gables; mem. U.S. sentencing guidelines com. So. Dist. of Fla., Miami. Named one of Best Lawyers in Am., Fla.'s Elite Lawyers, Fla. Trend Mag. Mem. Fla. Bar Assn., Nat. Assn. Criminal Def. Attys., Nat. Directory Criminal Lawyers, Am. Immigration Lawyers Assn., Dade County Bar Assn. Democrat. Lutheran. Avocations: power boat racing, swimming. Home: 1541 Brickell Ave Apt 3706 Miami FL 33129-1229 Office: 200 SE 2nd St Miami FL 33131 E-mail: rposton@steelhector.com.

POSUNKO, LINDA MARY, retired elementary education educator; b. Newark, Dec. 24, 1942; d. Joseph and Mary (Prystauk) P. BA, Newark State Coll., Union, N.J., 1964; MA, Kean U., Union, 1974. Cert. permanent elem. tchr., supr., prin., N.J. Elem. tchr Roselle (N.J.) Bd. Edn., 1964—65; head tchr. 1st grade Garwood (N.J.) Bd. Edn., 1965—76, 1982—95, head tchr., 1974—76, 1979—82, 1984—86, 1987—88, head tchr. 3d grade, 1976—82, acting prin., 1978, lead tchr. early childhood edn., 1993—95; ret., 1995. Cooperating tchr. to student tchrs.; instr. non-English speaking students and children with learning problems; mem. affirmative action, sch. resource coms.; conductor in-svc. workshops on early childhood devel. practices, 1993. Recipient honor cert. Union County Conf. Tchrs. Assn., 1972-73, The Garwood award N.J. Gov.'s Tchr. Recognition Program, 1983, 88, Outstanding Tchr. award N.J. Gov.'s Tchr. Recognition Program, 1988, Tchr. Recognition award Spanish Nat. Honor Soc., 1999, Most Memorable Tchr. Recognition award Spanish Nat. Honor Soc., 1999; nominee N.J. Gov.'s Tchr. Recognition award, 1993-94. Mem. ASCD, NEA, Internat. Reading Assn. (bd. dirs. suburban coun.), N.J. Edn. Assn., Garwood Tchrs. Assn. (sec., v.p., pres.), High/Scope Ednl. Found. Home: 17 Drake Rd Mendham NJ 07945-1805

POSVAR, MILDRED MILLER, opera singer; b. Cleve. d. William and Elsa (Friedhofer) Mueller; m. Wesley W. Posvar, Apr. 30, 1950; children: Wesley, Margot Marina, Lisa Christina. MusB, Cleve. Inst. Music, 1946; hon. doctorate, Cleve. Ins. Music, 1983; artists' diploma, New England Conservatory Music, 1948, hon. doctorate, 1966; MusD (hon.), Bowling Green State U., 1960; hon. doctorate, Washington and Jefferson U., 1988. Founder Opera Theater of Pitts., 1978—; mem. music faculty Carnegie-Mellon U., 1996—. Operatic debut in Peter Grimes, Tanglewood, 1946; appeared N.E. Opera Theater, Stuttgart State Theater, Germany, 1949-50, Glyndebourne Opera, Edinburgh Festival; debut as Cherubino in Figaro, Met. Opera, 1951; 23 consecutive seasons Met. Opera; radio debut Bell Telephone Hour; TV debut Voice of Firestone, 1952; appeared in films including Merry Wives of Windsor (filmed in Vienna), 1964; Vienna State Opera debut, 1963, appearances with San Francisco, Chgo. Lyric, Cin. Zoo, San Antonio, Berlin, Munich, Frankfurt, Pasadena, Ft. Worth, Kansas City, Pitts., Tulsa and St. Paul operas. Bd. dirs. Gateway to Music. Recipient Frank Huntington Beebe award for study abroad, 1949, 50, Grand Prix du Disque, 1965, Outstanding Achievements in Music award Boston C. of C., 1959, Ohioana Career medal, 1985, Outstanding Achievement in Opera award, Slippery Rock U., 1985, YWCA Ann. Tribute to Women award, 1989, Keystone Salute award Pa. Fedn. Music Clubs, 1994; named one of outstanding women of Pitts., Pitts. Press-Pitts. Post-Gazette, 1968, Person of Yr. in Music, Pitts. Jaycees, 1980. Mem. Nat. Soc. Arts and Letters (pres. 1989-90, Gold medal 1984), Disting. Daus. Pa. (pres. 1991-93), Tuesday Mus. Club, Phi Beta Kappa, Phi Delta Gamma, Sigma Alpha Iota. Office: Opera Theater of Pittsburgh PO Box 110108 Pittsburgh PA 15232-0608

POTASH, JEREMY WARNER, public relations executive; b. Monrovia, Calif., June 30, 1946; d. Fenwick Bryson and Joan Antony (Blair) Warner; m. Stephen Jon Potash; 1 son, Aaron Warner. AA, Citrus Coll., 1965; BA, Pomona Coll., 1967. With Forbes Mag., N.Y.C., 1967-69, Japan External Trade Orgn., San Francisco, 1970-75; v.p., co-founder, pres. Potash & Co. Pub. Rels., Oakland, Calif., 1980—. Founding exec. dir. Calif.-Asia Bus. Coun., Oakland, 1991—; editor Cal-Asia Member Alert, 1991—; exec. dir. Customs Brokers and Forwarders Assn., San Francisco, 1990—; adv. bd. Asia Pacific Econ. Rev., 1996—; mem. No. Calif. Dist. Export Coun., 2000—, Pacific Coun. Internat. Policy, 2000—. Editor: Southeast Asia Environmental Directory, 1994; editor: Southeast Asia Infrastructure Directory, 1995-96. Co-founder J.L. Magnes docent program, 1980; pres. WAORT, Calif., 1985—86; bd. dirs. Temple Sinai, Oakland, 1984—86, Judah L. Magnes Mus., Berkeley, 1981—94. Named Export Citizen of Yr., U.S. Dept. Commerce, 1998. Mem. Oakland Women's Lit. Soc., Book Club Calif. Office: Potash & Co Pub Rels 1919 Clement Ave Bldg 11 Alameda CA 94501-5213

POTASH, VELLA ROSENTHAL, lawyer, educator; b. Balt., Oct. 3, 1937; d. Joseph and Rona (Glasner) Rosenthal; m. Michael Donald Potash, June 20, 1957 (div. Aug., 1982); children: James Bennet, John Lawrence. BA in Edn., Goucher Coll., 1959; JD, U. Balt., 1974. Bar: Md. 1975, Pa. 1975, Family Mediation Fla., 1992. Tchr. Balt. Sch. System, 1959-62; pub. rels. dir. Citizens Planning & Housing Assn., Balt., 1966-69; asst. pub. defender Pub. Defender's Office, Balt., 1975-78; lawyer pvt. practice, Balt., 1978-82, Guardian Ad Litem Program Family Law Sect., Broward County, Fla., 1987—; family mediator pvt. practice, Broward County, 1992—. Pres., lectr. The Changing Am. Family. Rev. bd. Palm Beach County Foster Care, 1999—. Mem. NOW (bd. dirs., chair women's ctr. Boca Raton), Md. Bar, Pa. Bar, Broward County Bar Assn. (assoc.), So. Fla. Goucher Alumnae Assn. (pres.), Broward County Mediation Assn. (bd. dirs.). Avocations: bus. investment, golf, reading. Home: 2900 N Palm Aire Dr Apt 301 Pompano Beach FL 33069-3445

POTEMPA, KATHLEEN, dean; Diploma in nursing, Providence Hosp. Sch. Nursing, Southfield, Mich., 1970; BA in Psychology summa cum laude, U. Detroit, 1974; MS in Nursing, Rush U., 1978, D of Nursing Sci., 1986. Charge nurse coronary ICU Holy Cross Hosp., Ft. Lauderdale, Fla., 1970-71; staff nurse, charge nurse cardiovasc. ICU Henry Ford Hosp., Detroit, 1971-74; nurse practitioner Rush-Presbyn.-St. Luke's Med. Ctr., Chgo., 1974-75; nursing edn. coord. dept. nursing Michael Reese Hosp. and Med. Ctr., Chgo., 1975-77, nursing supr., 1977-78; asst. unit leader dept. gerontol. nursing Rush U. Coll. Nursing, Chgo., 1978-79, asst. chmn., 1979-80, assoc. chmn., asst. prof. gerontol. nursing, 1980-85, asst. prof. gerontol. nursing, 1985-86; asst. prof. nursing, dept. internal medicine, practitioner Rush Med. Coll., Rush U., 1987-88; asst. then assoc. prof. dept. med.-surg. nursing Coll. Nursing, U. Ill., Chgo., 1988—, dir. tng., pre and postdoctoral fellowship instnl. rsch., 1992—, exec. assoc. dean Coll. Nursing, 1994-95, interim dean Coll. Nursing, 1995-96; prof., dean Sch. Nursing Oreg. Health Scis. U., Portland, 1996—. Rsch. assoc. Robert Wood Johnson Tchg. Nursing Home Project, VA Edward Hines Jr. Hosp., Hines, Ill., 1985-86, co-dir. Exercise Rsch. Lab., 1985-86; dir. nursing Johnston R. Bowman Health Ctr. for Elderly, Rush Presbyn. St. Luke's Med. Ctr., Chgo., 1980-85. Contbr. articles to profl. jours. Fellow Am. Acad. Nursing; mem. ANA (coun. nurse rschrs.), Am. Soc. Hypertension, Gerontol. Soc. Am., Midwest Nursing Rsch. Soc., Heart Assn. Met. Chgo., Am. Heart Assn. Oreg., Ill. Coun. Nurse Rschrs., Am. Heart Assn. (coun. cardiovasc. nursing, coun. hypertension, coun. on stroke), Sigma Theta Tau. Office: SN ADM Oreg Health Scis U Sch Nursing 3181 SW Sam Jackson Park Rd Portland OR 97201-3011

POTENZA, DAISY MCKASKLE, newspaper executive; b. Houston, Mar. 5, 1906; d. George Washington and Dora Amy (Crump) McKaskle; m. Julius Orian Potenza, Sept. 26, 1928; 1 child, Marjorie Ann (Mrs. William L. Hale) (dec.). Student, Sinclair Bus. Coll., 1925. With Houston Chronicle, 1926-87, adminstrv. asst. to editor-in-chief, 1930-79, adminstrv. asst. to sr. v.p., cons., 1979-87, apptd. cons., 1994—. Exec. sec. Houston Endowment, Inc., 1968-69, participated in oral history project Jesse H. Jones Archive, Houston Endowment Inc., 1997-98; bd. dirs. Pin Oak Charity Horse Show, 1978, 79, 80, 81, 82, 83, 84. Recipient award United Fund, 1967—; tribute for exec. svc. to Chronicle, 1983; Outstanding ticket sales awardee Pin Oak Charity Horse Show, Tex. Children's Hosp., 1975-83, 84. Mem. Nat., Tex. press women, Women in Comms., Press Club Houston (hon. life), Farm and Ranch Club. Methodist. Home: 2405 San Felipe St Houston TX 77019-3403 Office: 801 Texas St Houston TX 77002-2904

POTOCKY-TRIPODI, MIRIAM, social worker, educator; b. Prague, Czech Republic, Feb. 28, 1962; arrived in U.S., 1969; d. Pavel Potocky and Vlastimila Potocka; m. Tony Tripodi. BA, U. of Colo., 1984; MSW, U. of Kans., 1989, PhD, 1993. Assoc. prof. Fla. Internat. U., Miami, Fla., 1993—. Author: Where Is My Home? A Refugee Journey, 2000, Best Practices for Social Work with Refugees and Immigrants, 2002; contbr. articles 25 to profl. jours. Office: Fla Internat U Sch Social Work University Park ECS 460 Miami FL 33199 Business E-Mail: potockym@fiu.edu.

POTOK, NANCY ANN FAGENSON, federal agency administrator; b. Detroit, May 20, 1955; d. William and Harriet Fagenson; m. Barry Potok, May 16, 1976; children: Benjamin, Leah. BA, Sonoma State U., 1978; MAS, U. Ala., 1980. Cert. govt. fin. mgr. Presdl. mgmt. intern U.S. Dept. Transp., Washington, 1980-82; budget examiner U.S. Office Mgmt. & Budget, Washington, 1982-89; deputy asst. adminstr. fin. and budget Adminstrv. Office U.S. Cts., Washington, 1989-95; controller U.S. Census Bur., Washington, 1995-97, prin. assoc. dir., CFO, 1997—2002; vis. exec. Nat. Opinion Research Ctr., U. Chgo., 2003—. Pres., treas. Women's Transp. Sem., Washington, 1983-84; advisor Presdl. Mgmt. Intern Career Devel. Group, Washington; co-chmn. Census Bur. Labor-Mgmt. Partnership coun., 1997-2002; assoc. mem. exec. orgn./mgmt. panel, Nat. Acad. Pub. Adminstrn., 2000—, bd. dirs. The Public Manager, 2002—. Contbr. articles to profl. jours. Chmn. Citizens Adv. Com., Crofton, Md., 1996-98; mem. exec. bd. PTA, Crofton, 1990-95; judge Odyssey of the Mind Creative Problem Solving Competition, Md., 1995; coach Destination Imagination, Creative Problem Solving 1st Pl. Team, 1999. Recipient Arthur S. Flemming award, 1991, Silver medal Sec. Commerce, 1998. Mem. Am. Asn. Budget & Program Analysts, Am. Soc. Pub. Adminstrn., Assn. Govt. Accts. Avocations: writing, music. Office: US Census Bur Fob 3 Washington DC 20233-0001 E-mail: Nancy.A.Potok@census.gov.

POTSIC, AMIE SHARON, photographer, educator, artist; b. Chgo., Dec. 11, 1971; d. William P. and Roberta K. Potsic. BA, Ind. U., 1993; MFA, San Francisco Art Inst., 1999. Cert. Teaching English as a Foreign Language to Adults U. Cambridge, 1996. Adj. faculty, photography instr. San Francisco Art Inst., 1999—; adj. faculty photography instr. U. Calif. Berkeley, 2001—; adj. faculty, photography instr. Ohlone Coll., Fremont, Calif., 2003—. Art/photography cons. Amie Potsic Photography, San Francisco, 2004—. One-woman shows include Seduce Me, Quotidian Gallery, 2000, Thin Skinned Thick, 2002, Doppelganger, The Painted Bride Art Ctr., 2003, publication, exhbn., Ritual and Resilience (Second Pl. Photoessay award, San Francisco Bay Guardian, 1998), publication, Prayer - Jerusalem, Israel (Jerusalem 3000 First pl. award Jewish Exponent, 1996), Casa do Vaticano, Graficos Burti Brazil, exhibited in group shows at Documenta USA, The Mus. of New Art, 2001, Fotosemana, Meseo de Arte Moderno de Bogota, 2002, Piece Process, Athens Inst. Contemporary Art, 2004. Program coord., instr. Shooting Back, Washington, 1993—94. Recipient Award of Excellence, Manhattan Arts Internat. Mag., 1996, Award of Excellence, Coll. Photography Ann., Photographer's Forum, 1999. Mem.: Coll. Art Assn. Personal E-mail: apotsic@yahoo.com.

POTTEBAUM, SHARON MITCHELL, health educator; b. Champaign, Ill., Jan. 7, 1948; d. Robert D. and Louise M. (Straits) Mitchell; m. Joseph R. Pottebaum; children: Pamela, Nicholas. BS in Secondary Health Edn., Ohio State U., 1969, MA in Health Edn., 1978. Cert. occupl. hearing conservationist 1984, health edn. 7-12 Ohio Dept. Edn., 1969, health edn. K-12 Ohio Dept. Edn., 1978. Health edn. supr. Ctr. Sci. and Industry, Columbus, Ohio, 1970—72; jr. h.s. health tchr., dist. health coord. Scioto-Darby City Bd. Edn., Hilliard, Ohio, 1972—74; Drug, Alcohol, Tobacco & Human Behavior Project coord. Ohio State U., Columbus, 1974—75, instr. health edn., 1975—76; pub. health edn. cons. child health unit Ohio Dept. Health, Columbus, 1978—79; dir. edn. and tng. Family Hosp., Milw., 1980—85; instr. health edn. U. Wis.-Whitewater, 2000—03; mgr. farms, Ill., 2003—. Health edn. cons., tchrs. aide Hillside Elem. Sch., Brookfield, Wis., 1988—97; ind. sales rep. World Book-Childcraft, Brookfield, 1985—88; Head Start tng. tech. assistance project cons. Westinghouse Health Systems, 1979—82; profl. continuing edn. coord. Gtr. Milw. Assn. Hosp. Staff Devel. Dirs. and Wis. Soc. Health Edn. and Tng., 1980—85; adv. mem. geriatric edn. planning com. and indsl. medicine task force coms. Family Hosp., Milw., 1981—84. Co-author (textbook): Teaching Health Science in Middle and Secondary Schools, 1981, Toward A Healthy Lifestyle Through Elementary Health Education, 1980; editor: (monthly newsletter) The Post Graduate, 1990—92 (Wisconsin's "Nellie Bly" First Place Award for Outstanding Branch Newsletter, category of 100+ members, 1992). Recipient cert. of leadership, YWCA Gtr. Milw., 1984. Mem.: AAUW (editor bull. West Suburban Milw. 1990—92, fundraiser 1990—, treas. 1992—94, pres.-elect 1995—96, pres. 1996—97, chair travel group 1997—2000, historian, bd. dirs. Wis. 1998—2000, bd. dirs. Wis. chpt. 1999—2001, historian 1999—2001, chair Women's History Month 1999—2001, scholarship honoree, 5-star br. award 1997), Wis. Assn. Health, Phys. Edn., Recreation and Dance, Upside Investment Club (sec. 2000—01). Avocations: travel, photography, painting, scrapbooks, woodcarving. Home: 2815 Almesbury Ave Brookfield WI 53045

POTTER, ALICE CATHERINE, clinical laboratory scientist; b. Oil City, Pa., June 24, 1928; d. Howard Taylor and Hilda Marian (Lewis) P. BA, U. Findlay, 1949; postgrad., Springfield (Ohio) City Hosp., 1949-50. Registered med. technologist Am. Soc. Clin. Pathologists; cert. clin. lab. scientist. Med. technologist Mercy Hosp., Springfield, 1950-54, Oil City Hosp., 1954-67; staff med. technologist Thomas Jefferson U. Hosp., Phila., 1968-83, sr. med. technologist, 1983—97, retired, 1997. Vol. Acad. Natural Scis., Phila., 1995—. Mem. Am. Soc. Clin. Lab. Scientists, Pa. Soc. Clin. Lab. Scientists (membership chmn. Delaware Valley chpt. 1977-78, chmn. pub. rels. 1982-94, 96-97, bd. dirs. 1989-91, 97-98, 98-99, 99—, pres.-elect 1991-92, pres. 1992-93, Scrimshaw award 1992). Republican. Avocations: travel, needlework. Home: 1701 Wallace St Philadelphia PA 19130-4300

POTTER, BLAIR BURNS, editor; b. Spartanburg, SC, Mar. 11, 1946; d. Leonard Hill and Nancy Milner (Vaughan) Burns; m. Robert Arthur Potter, May 24, 1974; children: Lillian Howard, Gordon Leonard. BA, Hollins Coll., Roanoke, Va., 1968; MA, U. N.C., Chapel Hill, 1971. Manuscript editor Science, Washington, 1970—74; freelance editor, 1974—85; assoc. editor Health Adminstrn. Press/U. Mich., Ann Arbor, 1985—87; freelance editor NAS, Inst. Medicine, Office Tech. Assessment, Washington,

1987—92; assoc. editor Science News, Washington, 1992, mng. editor, 1992—98; dir. Urban Inst. Press, Washington, 1998—2000, dir. acquisitions, 2000—01; freelance editor, 2000—. Editl. cons. Surgeon Gen.'s Report on Youth Violence, Washington, 2000-2001, White House Task Force on Infant Mortality, Washington, 1990, Nat. Commn. on Orphan Diseases, Washington, 1988-89, Nat. Comm. on Children, Washington, 1992-93, White House Commn. on Complementary & Alternative Medicine Policy, Washington, 2002; lay mem. protocol com. Nat. Heart, Lung and Blood Inst., Bethesda, Md., 1973. Whittaker fellow, 1969-70; Hollins Coll. scholar, 1964-68, English-Speaking Union scholar, 1967. Mem.: Am. Soc. Mag. Editors, Nat. Press Club. Avocations: gardening, historic preservation, antique american furniture, sailing. Address: 8607 North Bend Circle Easton MD 21601-7327 Home and Office: 8607 Northbend Cir Easton MD 21601-7327

POTTER, CYNTHIA M. art educator, artist; b. Balt., July 15, 1950; d. Percel Celon and Nancy Jane (Williams) Harris; m. Willis M. Potter, Oct. 11, 1975; 1 child, Shomaree. BA, Norfolk State U., 1973, MA, 1983; postgrad., Old Dominion U., 1979, Hampton U., 1984, Va. Commonwealth U. Cert. designated gifted alternative, inservice tng. program for mainstreaming, leadership skills. Summer enrichment art tchr. African Am. art Norfolk (Va.) Pub. Schs., photojournalist tchr., art tchr. Contbr. articles to profl. newsletters. Chair planning com. Ruth Winstead Diggs Scholarship Fund, Inc., 1988—; dir. minority concerns com., 1990—. Recipient Cert. of Recognition, Superior Art Instrn. of Appreciation, 1989; fellow for travel study in West Africa; named Tidewater Elem. Art Tchr. of Yr., for Outstanding Svc., 1988. Mem. Nat. Art Edn. Assn., Nat. Conf. of Artists (exec. sec. 1991-93). Home: 1433 Flintfield Cres Chesapeake VA 23321-2824

POTTER, DEBORAH ANN, news correspondent, educator; b. Hagerstown, Md., June 10, 1951; d. Peter R. and H. Louise (McDevitt) P.; m. Robert H. Witten; children: Cameron, Evan. BA, U. N.C., 1972; MA, Am. U., 1977. Assignment editor Sta. WMAL-TV, Washington, 1972-73, prodr., 1973-74; reporter Voice of Am., Washington, 1974-77; anchor Sta. KYW, Phila., 1977-78, CBS Radio, N.Y.C., 1978-81; White House corr. CBS News, Washington, 1981-85, state dept. corr., 1985-87, congl. corr., 1987-89, environ. corr., 1989-91; contbg. corr. 48 Hours, 1989-90; host Nightwatch CBS News, Washington, 1991; Washington corr. Cable News Network, Washington, 1991-94; asst. prof. Sch. Comm. Am. U., Washington, 1994-95. Mem. faculty Poynter Inst. Media Studies, St. Petersburg, Fla., 1995-98; exec. dir. NewsLab, Washington, 1998—. Co-author: Poynter Election Handbook; host (video prodns.) Beyond the Spotted Owl, 1993, Health Beat, 1994, Risk Reporting, 1995, Kids at Risk, 1997, (PBS series) In the Prime, 1996-97. Mem. adv. coun. Environ. Journalism Ctr., Radio and TV News Dirs. Found., Washington, 1994—; lay reader St. Alban's Episc. Ch., Washington, 1988-89, vestry, 1998-01. Mem. Radio TV News Dirs. Assn., Investigative Reporters and Editors, Assn. for Edn. in Journalism and Mass Comm., Nat. Press Photographers Assn., U. N.C. Alumni Assn. (bd. dirs. 1990-93, Disting. Young Alumna award 1990). Office: NewsLab 1900 M St NW Ste 210 Washington DC 20036-3530 E-mail: potter@newslab.org.

POTTER, EMMA JOSEPHINE HILL, language educator; b. Hackensack, N.J., July 18, 1921; d. James Silas and Martha Loretta (Pyle) Hill; m. James H. Potter, Mar. 26, 1949. AB cum laude with honors in classics, Alfred U., 1943; AM, Johns Hopkins U., 1946. Tchr. Latin, Balt. County Pub. Schs., 1943-44; instr. French and Spanish, Balt. Poly. Inst., 1950-83, instr. Spanish adult edn. classes, 1946-48; treas. Bruno-Potter, Inc. Trustee James Harry Potter Gold Medal award of ASME. Donor commemorative plaque in honor of Martha Pyle Hill to Chenango County Coun. Arts, 1996. Mem. Internat. Platform Assn., Clan Hay Soc. Scotland (Am. br.), John Hopkins U. Faculty Club. Democrat. Home: 419 3d Ave Avon By The Sea NJ 07717-1244

POTTER, JUNE ANITA, small business owner; b. La Crosse, Wis., Jan. 22, 1938; d. Christian John and Ethel Marie (Stafslien) Stefferud; m. James Oscar Potter, June 18, 1961; children: Jill Potter Rutlin, Todd. BA in Home Econs., St. Olaf Coll., Northfield, Minn., 1960; postgrad., N.Y. Sch. Interior Design, 1964; MS in Edn., U. Wis., Menomonie, 1977. Sr. high home econs. tchr., FHA advisor Tomah (Wis.) H.S., 1960-64, Black River Falls (Wis.) H.S., 1971-83; freelance interior designer Warrens, Wis., 1964-97; ptnr., mgr. James Potter Cranberry Marsh, Inc., Warrens, 1968—; substitute tchr. Tomah Schs., 2001—. Co-pubr.: Warrens Centennial Book, 1968, Wisconsin Cranberry Centennial Book, 1989. Active various charitable and church orgns.; bd. dirs. Warrens Cranberry Festival, 1984—, chair 25th Anniversary Book, 1997; mem. Warrens Area Bus. Assn., 1990-98; sec. Wis. Cranberry Bd., Inc., 1990—; sec. Warren Mills Cemetery Assn., 1993-2000; mem. com. Wis. Alice in Dairyland Finale, 1993 (state Alice award, 2000); mem. Jellystone Campground Ministry, Warrens Wis., 1970-, Millennium Tree Com., Washington, 1999; found. bd. Wis. Exec. Residence, 1994—2003; pres. Gloria Dei Luth. Ch. Women, 1997-2000. Mem.: AAUW (v.p. 1983—2001), Wis. State Cranberry Growers Assn. (mem. centennial com. 1988—, pub. rels. com. 1994—2000, State Pres.'s award 2000, Agri-Communicator of Yr. 2004), Tomah Pkwy. Garden Club (corr. sec. 2002—04), Beta Sigma Phi (com. mem. 1961—, officer, Nat. Order of Rose 1983, Silver Cir. award 1985, Girl of Yr.). Lutheran. Avocations: flowers, photography, travel, collecting foreign country items. Home and Office: 28353 County Hwy EW Warrens WI 54666-7513 Office Phone: 608-378-4749. E-mail: jpotter@tomah.com.

POTTER, LORRAINE K. career military officer; m. Robert Saunders. BS, Keuka Coll.; MDiv, Colgate Rochester Div. Sch. Former pastor, N.Y.; clin. pastoral educator Yale-New Haven Med. Ctr.; commd. 2d lt. USAF, 1971, advanced through ranks to maj., 2001; various assignments to command chaplain Hdqtrs. Air Edn./Tng. Command, Randolph AFB, Tex., 1998-99; dep. chief of Chaplain Svc. Hdqtrs. USAF, Bolling AFB, D.C., 1999—. At-large mem. Am. Bapt. Chs. Gen. Bd.; active Ministers Coun. for Chaplains and Pastoral Counselors. Office: Chief Chaplain HQ USAF/Bolling AFB 112 Luke Ave SW Washington DC 20332-5113

POTTER, MYRTLE S. research and development company executive; B, U. Chgo. Formerly with Merck and Co.; v.p. strategy and econ. Bristol-Myers Squibb, 1996, pres.; exec. v.p. Genetech, Inc., South San Francisco, 2000—01, exec. v.p. comml. ops., COO, 2001—. Bd. dirs. Calif. Healthcare Inst., 2001—. Office: Genetech Inc 1 DNA Way South San Francisco CA 94080

POTTER, ROSEMARY, state legislator; b. Apr. 15, 1952; m. Steve Nichols, 1994. BA, U. Wis., Milw., 1974, MA, 1983. Former dist. dir. Combined Health Appeal Wis. Ho. of Reps.; chairwoman Dem. Caucus; Wis. state assemblywoman Dist. 20, 1989-98; pub. polit. advocate Foley & Lardner, Milw., 1998—. Former tchr. Office: Doley & Lardner 1st Star Center 777 E Wisconsin Ave Ste 3800 Milwaukee WI 53202-5367 Home: W314n8709 Winchester Trl Hartland WI 53029-9525

POTTER, SUSAN K. bank executive; BA, Cornell U., 1988; MBA, U. Pa.; student, Harvard U. Sr. mgr. Sotheby's; bus. analyst McKinsey & Co., Cleve., 1994—98, engagement mgr., 1998—2002; exec. v.p. product mgmt. Consumer Banking Group KeyCorp, Cleve., 2002—. Named One of 25 Women to Watch, U.S. Banker Mag., 2003. Office: KeyCorp 127 Public Square Cleveland OH 44114-1306*

POTTER, SUZANNE PEYTON, elementary school educator; b. Hollandale, Miss., June 20, 1950; d. Harris Bailey and Dorothy Bland Peyton; m. Emmett Thaddeus Jr. Potter, Aug. 23, 1969; children: Thaddeus Shelton, Emmett Peyton. B of Music Edn., Delta State U., 1972, M of Music Edn., 1985. Music tchr. Deer Creek Sch., Arcola, Miss., 1972—75, 1999—; music dir. 1st Bapt Ch., Leland, Miss., 1987—93, 1st Presby. Ch., Greenville, Miss., 1993—. Founder, dir. Delta Children's Choir, Greenville, 1994—; founder Miss. All-State Boy Choir, Jackson, 2001—. Mem.: Presbyn. Assn. of Musicians, Am. Choral Dirs. Assn. (chair state boy choir Miss. div. 1998—), Miss. Music Educator's Assn. Baptist. Avocation: sewing. Home: PO Box 2647 Wayside MS 38780 Office: 1st Presby Ch 1 John Calvin Cir Greenville MS 38701 E-mail: deltacc1@tecinfo.com.

POTTER, SYLVIA, education educator; b. Buchanan County, Va., Feb. 4, 1942; d. Kelly C. and Virgie E. (Osborn) Runyon; m. Hersel E. Potter, Apr. 23, 1961 (div. 1992); children: Barbara L., Timothy H., Jonathan, Amanda. AS summa cum laude, Southwest Va. Cmty. Coll., 1985; BS summa cum laude, Pikeville Coll., 1987; MA with honors, Va. Tech. Inst., 1994. Lic. reading specialist, early edn. educator, mid. edn. educator, spl. edn., Va. LPN Grundy (Va.) Hosp., 1962-72; tchr. Buch County Schs., Grundy, 1972-76, 89-92, Commonwealth of Va. Dept. of Corrections, Hanover, 1993—. Mem. curriculum com. Dept. Correctional Edn., 1997-99, mem. interview panel for hiring com., 1996-2001. Mem. com. Office on Youth, Grundy, 1991-93; scout leader Boy Scouts Am., 1986-93, com. mem. Matlapanai coun. 1996-99, Order of Arow Brotherhood, Sequoyah coun., 1990-94. Mem. Correctional Edn. Assn., Va. Assn. Correctional Edn., Internat. Reading Assn., VA Assn. for Gifted. Democrat. Mem. Ch. of Christ. Avocations: reading, physical work outs, scouting, camping, travel. Home: 8601 S Fork Ct Fredericksburg VA 22407-8723

POTTER, TERESA PEARL, adult education educator; b. Lakeport, Calif., June 11, 1954; d. William Everett and Irene Evelyn (Hennegar) Heath; m. Gideon Steven James Potter, Mar. 18, 1978 (div. Sept. 1987); 1 child, Abraham Jesse. AA, Portland City Coll., 1976; BA, Pacific Oaks Coll., 1989, MA, 1991. Cert. tchr., Calif. Actress, co-prodr. The Wonder Faire Theater., Portland, Oreg., 1978-81; tchr. Temple Beth Meier Sch., Studio City, Calif., 1982-83; dir. Progress Presch., Santa Monica, Calif., 1983-89, Hill An'Dale Family Learning Ctr., Santa Monica, Calif., 1989-92; tchr. Samata Yoga Studio, L.A., 1989-93, L.A. Unified Sch. Dist., 1992-93; lead tchr. Adult Edn., Parent Edn. Programs San Juan Unified Sch. Dist., Sacramento, Calif., 1993—. Co-host (cable show) License to Parent, 1997-2000. Pres. Sacramento Parent Edn. Consortium 1997—; chmn. Santa Monica Child Care Task Force, 1997. Mem. Calif. Coun. for Adult Edn., Nat. Assn. for Edn. in Young Children. Democrat. Avocations: golf, reading, swimming, tennis, yoga. Office: San Juan Unified Sch Dist 900 Morse Ave #C Sacramento CA 95864-7710

POTTER-HUGHES, KAREN ANN, secondary school educator; b. Rome, N.Y., June 17, 1951; d. Robert Francis and Ada Marie (Hoskins) P.; m. Roger Allen Hughes, June 10, 2000. AA in Liberal Arts, Mohawk Valley C.C., Utica, N.Y., 1978; BA in English, Syracuse U., 1980; MEd, Lincoln Meml. U., 1986; postgrad., Union Coll., 1988. Tchr. English, Camden (N.Y.) Cul. Schs., 1980-82; Middlesboro (Ky.) Ind. Schs., 1983—; city reporter Daily News, Middlesboro, 1982-83. Mem. adj. faculty S.E. C.C., 1986-92, Clear Creek Bapt. Bible Coll., 2000 ; writing cons. summer workshops Ea. Ky. U. Consortium, Richmond, 1993, 94, mem. adv. bd. satellite campus, 1992-94; site-based coun. mem. Middlesboro H.S., 1991-95. Ruling elder, clk. of session First Presbyn. Ch., Rome, N.Y., 1972-75; ruling elder First Presbyn. Ch., Middlesboro, 1983-86, 92-95, 95-98, chair worship com., 1994 98; mem. Tri-State Cmty. Choir, Harrogate, Tenn., 1994-98. Recipient Excellence in Tchg. award Campbellsville Coll., 2001. Mem. ASCD, Ky. Edn. Assn. (del. 1991), Nat. Coun. Tchrs. English, Middlesboro Edn. Assn. (sec. 1985—), Delta Kappa Gamma (rec. sec. 1993-95), Alpha Delta Kappa (chaplain 1998-2000, corr. sec. 2000—). Democrat. Avocations: gardening, bicycling, baking, singing, writing. Home: 2930 Cumberland Ave Middlesboro KY 40965-1542 Office: Middlesboro HS 4404 Cumberland Ave Middlesboro KY 40965-2626

POTTERTON, BARBARA ALICE, artist, educator, illustrator; b. San Francisco, Feb. 17, 1930; d. Dale Howard and Marjorie Louise (Wilson) Drullinger; m. Kenneth Eugene Potterton, May 30, 1948; children: Kathleen Dale Millen, Kenneth Leon. Student, San Francisco Jr. Coll., 1947-48. Exclusive Seascape artist for the following galleries: Mendocino (Calif.) Art Ctr., 1965-73, Gallery Mendocino, 1973-90, Jack London Sq. Gallery, Oakland, Calif., 1978-80, Village Artistry, Carmel, Calif., 1979, Winters Gallery, 1980-83, Calico Whale Gallery, Mendocino, 1991-95, Franki Waters Gallery, Bodega Bay, Calif., 1995-96, Color and Light, Mendocino, 1996-97, Gallery One, Mendocino, 1997-2000; tchr. Gallery Mendocino, Plein Air Class, 1975-85, pvt. studio classes, Rancho Cordova, Calif., 1989—; workshop lectr., demonstrator Lincoln City (Oreg.) Art Ctr., 1979, Golden Valley Art Ctr. Yuba City, Calif., 1983-85. Artist specializing in seascape paintings: over 1500 of her paintings are in private collections throughout the world; illustrator: (childrens' books) Song of the Calico Whale, 1995, Watch Out for Tule Petunia, 1997; (interdisciplinary study unit) Journey to Africa, 1996. Recipient Best of Show awards, Roseville, Calif. Art Ctr. 1970, Stanford Ctr., Palo Alto, Calif., 1975, one-woman show Calif. State U., Sacramento, 1978. Mem. Crocker Art Mus., Soc. Marine Painters (Merit award 1970), Nat. Mus. Women in Arts, N.Y. Met. Mus. of Art (assoc.). Avocations: writing, reading, music, gardening, bird watching. Home: 707 Sunrise Ave Apt 131 Roseville CA 95661-4533

POTTORFF, JO ANN, state legislator; b. Wichita, Kans., Mar. 7, 1936; d. John Edward McCluggage and Helen Elizabeth (Alexander) Ryan; m. Gary Nial Pottorff; children: Michael Lee, Gregory Nial. BA, Kansas State U., 1957; MA, St. Louis U., 1969. Elem. tchr. Pub. Sch., Keats and St. George, 1957-59; cons., elem. specialist Mid Continent Regional Edn. Lab., Kansas City, Mo., 1971-73; cons. Poindexter Assocs., Wichita, 1975; campaign mgr. Garner Shriver Congl. Camp, Wichita, 1976; interim dir. Wichita Area Rape Ctr., 1977; conf. coord. Biomedical Synergistics Inst., Wichita, 1977-79; real estate sales asst. Chester Kappelman Group, Wichita, 1979-98, J.P. Weigard & Sons, Wichita, 1998—; state rep. State of Kans., Topeka, 1985—. Mem. exec. com. Nat. Conf. State Legis. Com. Mem. sch. bd. Wichita Pub. Schs., 1977-85; bd. dirs. Edn. Consol. and Improvement Act Adv. com., Kans. Found. for the Handicapped; mem. Children and Youth Adv. com. (bd. dirs.); active Leadership Kans.; chairperson women's network Nat. Conf., State Legislators; mem. Wichita Children's Home Bd.; vice chmn. Nat. Assessment Governing Bd.; chair edn. com. assembly on state issues Nat. Conf. State legislators. Recipient Disting. Svc. award Kans. Assn. Sch. Bds., 1983, Outstanding Svc. to Sch. Children of Nation award Coun. Urban Bds., 1984, awards Gov.'s Conf. for Prevention of Child Abuse and Neglect, Kans. Assn. Reading. Mem. Leadership Am. Alumnae (bd. dirs., sec) Found. for Agr. in Classroom (bd. dirs.), Jr. League, Vet. Aux. (pres.), Bd. Nat. State Art Agys., Rotary, Ky. Assn. Rehab. Facilities (Ann. award), Nat. Order Women in Legislature (past bd. dirs.), Nat. Conf. State Legislatures (chmn. edn. assembly state issues, exec. com.), Rotary, Chi Omega (pres.). Avocations: politics, traveling. Office: Weigard 6530 E 13th St N Wichita KS 67206-1247

POTTS, ALISON JEAN, neuroscience medical liaison; b. NYC, Sept. 3, 1966; d. Douglas Gordon and Ann Frank Potts. BA summa cum laude, Middlebury Coll., 1988; MA, U. Toronto, 1993, PhD, 1998. Addictions counsellor Cmty. Care Ctr. for Substance Abuse, Barrie, Canada, 1990—92; tchg. asst. U. Toronto, 1992—97; clin. rsch. assoc. Eli Lilly Can. Inc., Scarborough, 1998—2000, med. liaison assoc., 2000—01; neurosci. med. liaison Eli Lilly and Co., Indpls., 2001—. Mem. support services com. Amyotrophic Lateral Sclerosis Soc. of Can., Toronto, 1997—99. Grantee, Clarke Inst. of Psychiatry, 1996—97; scholar, Med. Rsch. Coun. of Can., 1992—97. Mem.: APA, Phi Beta Kappa. Avocation: running.

POTTS, BARBARA JOYCE, retired historical society executive; b. L.A., Feb. 18, 1932; d. Theodore Thomas and Helen Mae (Kelley) Elledge; m. Donald A. Potts, Dec. 27, 1953; children: Tedd, Douglas, Dwight, Laura. AA, Graceland Coll., 1951; grad., Radiol. Tech. Sch., 1953; grad. program for sr. execs. in state and local govt., Harvard U., 1989. Radiol. technician Independence (Mo.) Sanitarium and Hosp., 1953, 58-59, Mercy Hosp., Balt., 1954-55; city coun. mem.-at-large City of Independence, 1978-82, mayor, 1982-90; exec. dir. Jackson County Hist. Soc., 1991-97; ret., 1997. Chmn. Mid-Am. Regional Coun., Kansas City, Mo., 1984-85; bd. dirs. Mo. Mcpl. League, Jefferson City, 1982-90, v.p., 1986-87, pres., 1987, 88; chmn. Mo. Commn. on Local Govt. Cooperation, 1985-90; chair ind. adv. bd. Mercantile Bank, 1997-99; bd. dirs. Women's Found. of Greater Kansas City, 1997-2003; mem. chancellor's adv. bd. UMKC Women's Ctr., 1996-; mem. adv. bd. Comprehensive Mental Health Svcs., 1997-. Author: Independence, 1985. Mem. Mo. Gov.'s Conf. Edn., 1976, Independence Charter Rev. Bd., 1977; bd. dirs. Hope House Shelter Abused Women, Independence, 1982—, Vis. Nurses Assn., 1990-93, Mid-Continent coun. U.S. Girl Scouts, 1991-95, adv. bd. Ewing M. Kauffman Fund, 2002—, Greater Kansas City Cmty. Found., 1999-02, Salvation Army, 1999—; pres. Child Placement Svcs., Independence, 1972-89, Greater Kansas City region NCCJ, 1990—; bd. dirs. Harry S. Truman Libr. Inst., 1995—, Truman Med. Ctr., 2001—, Coun. on Philanthropy, 2001-03; bd. vis. UMKC Sch. Medicine, 2002—; trustee Independence Regional Health Ctr., 1982-90, 94-2001; trustee Park Coll., 1989-99, chmn. bd. trustees, 1995-99; mem. Nat. Women's Polit. Caucus, 1978—; mem. adv. bd. Greater Mo. Focus on Leadership, mem. steering com., 1989-; bd. dirs. Truman Heartland Cmty. Found., 1990-2003, bd. chmn., 1997-99; trustee Eye Found. Kansas City, 1997-99; bd. dirs. Leadership 20/20 Vision. Recipient George Lehr Meml. award for cmty. svc., 1989, Woman of Achievement award Mid-Continent coun. Girl Scouts U.S.A., 1983, 75th Anniversary Women of Achievement award Mid-Continent coun. Girl Scouts, 1987, Jane Adams award Hope House, 1984, Cmty. Leadership award Comprehensive Mental Health Svcs., Inc., 1984, 90, Graceland Coll. Alumni Disting. Svc. award 1991, Disting. Citizen award Independence C. of C., 1993, Outstanding Cmty. Svc. award Jackson County Inter-Agy. Coun., 1994, Outstanding Cmty. Svc. award Cmty. Svcs. League, 1996, Jackson County Humanitarian of Yr. award, 1997, Disting. Citizen award, 1997, Paul Harris award Ind. Rotary Club, 1997, Outstanding Svc. award City of Independence Human Rels. Commn., 1999, Greater Kans. City Coun. Philanthropy Vol. of Yr. award, 2000; named Friend of Edn. Indpendence NEA, 1990. Mem. LWV (Cmty. Svc. award 1990), Jackson County Hist. Soc., Nat. Trust for Hist. Preservation. Mem. Reorganized Lds Ch. Home: 18508 E 30th Ter S Independence MO 64057-1904

POTTS, GLENDA RUE, music educator; b. Butler, Ala., Nov. 26; d. Jennings Herschel and Erma Rue (Holdridge) Moseley; m. Billy Wayne Blackwell, June 23, 1963 (div. Aug. 1977); children: William Stephen, Melton Jennings; m. Willis Jones Potts, Jr., July 13, 1985; 1 stepchild, Timothy Brendon. BM in Music, Auburn U., 1963. Organist Beverly Meth. Ch., Birmingham, 1964-65; music tchr. grades 3-8 Birmingham Pub. Schs., 1964-65; music tchr. grades 7-9 Chattanooga Pub. Schs., 1965-66; tchr., owner piano/pipe organ studio Kreative Keyboards, Prattville, Ala., 1967-93, Savannah, 1993-99, Rome, Ga., 1999—. Pipe organist 1st Bapt. Ch., Prattville, 1969-85, 87-93, music asst. dir., 1980-85; pianist, dir. children's choirs, asst. organist Bull St. Bapt. Ch., Savannah, 1995-99; sec., mem. chair Savannah Symphony Women's Guild, 1993-99; soprano Savannah Symphony Chorale, 1993-94; mem. chair Savannah Newcomer's, 1994-95; substitute organist and pianist First Baptist Ch., Rome, Ga., 2000-. Honored as one of Top 400 Women Grads. of Centennial of Admission of Women Students, Auburn U., 1992. Mem. Ga. Music Tchrs. Assn. (pres. Savannah chpt. 1997-99, pres. Rome chpt. 2001-03, treas. 2003—), Music Tchrs. Nat. Assn. (nat. and state cert. tchr. and adjudicator), Nat. Guild of Piano Tchrs. (nat. cert. tchr. and adjudicator, established audition ctrs., chmn. Prattville 1967-93, Rome area fall 2001—, Hall of Fame 1990), Am. Coll. Musicians. Republican. Baptist. Home: 2614 Horseleg Creek Rd SW Rome GA 30165-8583 E-mail: glenda@itxmail.net.

POTTS, MARTHA LOU, elementary school educator; b. Enid, Okla., May 30, 1939; d. Hugh David and Luaddie (Williamson) P. BA, Northwestern Okla. U., 1961; postgrad., U. Hawaii, 1966, Phillips U., 1967, 75, Citadel, 1980. Tchr. music pub. schs., Vici, Okla., 1961-62, Enid, 1962-67, Tulsa, 1987-88, Garden City, Kans., 1967-70, Dept. Def., Iwakuni, Japan, 1970-76, pub. schs., Charleston, S.C., 1976-86, Hudson, N.H., 1986-87, San Antonio, 1988—. Mem. tribal coun. Tex. Cherokee and assoc. bands. Vol. Cancer Soc., 1977-87, Dem. Party, Charleston, Enid, San Antonio, 1977-97, Neighborhood Watch, San Antonio, 1990-97; mem. tribal coun. Tex. Cherokees Associated Bands, 1998—. Mem. Am. Assn. Profl. Educators, Music Educators Nat. Conf., Am. String Tchrs. Assn. (People to People award 1997), Tex. Orch. Dirs. Assn., Japanese Am. Cultural Soc., Irish Am. Cultural Soc., Tex. Rangers Assn., Sons and Daus. of Cherokee Strip, Bexar County Geneal. Soc. Civil War Round Table. Roman Catholic. Avocations: traveling, genealogy, civil war. Home: 12647 Sandtrap St San Antonio TX 78217-1822 Office: Connell Middle Sch 400 Hot Wells Blvd San Antonio TX 78223-2602

POU, LINDA G. interior designer, architectural designer; b. Huntsville, Ala., Oct. 26, 1942; d. Louis and Lillian Maurice (Garvin) Grabensteder; m. Robert LeRoy Pou, Aug. 27, 1965; children: Susan Caroline, Stephanie Lynn. B of Interior Design, Auburn U., 1964; postgrad., Ecoles D'Art Americaines, 1964. Interior designer Martin Interiors, Huntsville, 1963, Blance Reeves Interiors, Atlanta, 1964-65, Militare, Atlanta, 1965, Loveman's Dept. Store, Huntsville, 1966, Southea. Galleries, Charleston, SC, 1967; draftsman Brown Engring., Huntsville, 1967-68, Naval Electronics Systems Command, SC, 1968, Leland Engr., Charleston, 1968-69; owner Drafting Svc., Mobile, Ala., 1977-78, The Design Svc., Prattville, Ala., 1980-92, Savannah, Ga., 1992—. Composer songs including (adult anthems), Sing for Joy, 1983, Sing Hallelujah to the Lord, He's the Rainbow in My Life, 1984, (children's)_Lord of Harvest, 1984, Sing a Song to the Lord of Earth, 1985, (children's musical) Six Myths of Christmas, 1986; compiler and editor book of poetry, Nana's Legacy. Mem. jr. bd. Florence Crittendon Home for Unwed Mothers, Mobile, Ala., 1977-79, Prattville Planning Commn., 1980-92, chmn., 1985-88, vice-chmn., 1988-92; mem. Prattville Hist. Re-devel. Authority, 1988-89; children's choir dir. 1st United MEth. Ch., 1979-83, 87-89, adminstrv. bd., 1987-89, bldg. commn., 1987-89, trustee, 1990-92; mem. Savannah Symphony Women's Guild, 1993-95; mem. exec. bd. Keep Marietta Beautiful, 2003—. Mem. ASCAP, Spinners (treas. 1982-83), Prattville C. of C., Garden Club of Savannah (2nd v.p. 1995-97, pres. 1997-99), Charlton Forge Garden Club (1st v.p. 2000, pres. 2000-2002), Alpha Gamma Delta. Avocations: reading, gardening, playing the piano, singing. Home and Office: 980 Marbury Ct SW Marietta GA 30064-2991

POU, NELLIE, assemblywoman; Degree in mcpl. budget and fin., Rutgers U. Assemblywoman N.J. Gen. Assembly, 1997—; assembly asst. minority leader, 2000—01; dep. spkr., 2002—. Mem. N.J. Dept. Health, Profl. Adv. Com., 1991—92, Passaic County Human Svcs. Adv. Coun., 1991—95, Passaic County-Bergen County HIV Health Svcs. Adv. Coun., 1993—97; chair Mayor's Health Planning Task Force, 1988—97; mem. Passaic County Planning and Policy Partnership Com., 1996—. Commr. Paterson Pub. Libr. Bd. Trustees, 1983—84; mem. N.J. Task Force on Child Abuse and Neglect, 1997—. Democrat. Office: 100 Hamilton Plz Ste 1403-05 Paterson NJ 07505 E-mail: AswPou@njleg.org.

POUILLON, NORA EMANUELA, food service executive; b. Vienna, Oct. 26, 1943; came to U.S., 1965; d. Leopold and Gertraude (Mayr) Aschenbrenner; m. Pierre Pouillon, Dec. 3, 1965 (separated 1978); children: Alexis, Olivier; m. Steven Damato; 1 child, Nina Fiona Emanuela.

Baccalaureat, Neuland Schule, Vienna, 1961; Moderne Rechentechnic, Technische Hochschule, Vienna, 1962-63; Bus. Degree, Handelsakademie, Vienna, 1964; drawing cert., Corcoran Sch. Art, 1967; diploma, Internat. Sch. Interior Design, 1968. Tchr. and owner Guerilla Gourmet, Washington, 1973-76; owner Food for Friends, Washington, 1973-76; chef Tabard Inn Hotel, Washington, 1977-78; co owner, chef Restaurant Nora, Washington, 1979—, City Cafe, Washington, 1986—; Food writer Washington Mag., 1975-76; Sponsor Pub. Voice, Washington, 1991—, Voters for Choice, Washington, 1991—, Share Our Strength, Washington, 1991—; active with food safety advocacy groups. Named Outstanding Chef Am. 2000, 1990, Best Restaurant Dossier Mag., 1987-89, Outstanding Restaurant Pub. Voice, 1990; recipient Excellence in Restaurant Industry award Dinesty, 1990, Achievement in Culinary Arts award Gault Millau, 1990. Avocations: synergy exercise, yoga, hiking, downhill and cross-country skiing. Home: 1910 Biltmore St NW Washington DC 20009-1510 Office: Restaurant Nora 2132 Florida Ave NW Washington DC 20008-1925

POULIN, MARIE, Canadian government official; b. Sudbury, Ont., Can., June 21, 1945; d. Alphonse-Emile and Lucille Charette; m. Bernard A. Poulin, May 21, 1977; children: Elaine, Valérie. BA magna cum laude, Laurentian U., Sudbury, 1966; M of Social Svcs., U. Montréal, Que., Can., 1969; PhD (hon.), Laurentian U., Sudbury, 1995. Lectr. U. Montreal, 1969-70, Coll. of Gen. and Profl. Instrn., Hull, Que., 1972-73; rschr. Ctr. Social Svcs., Hull, 1972-73; interviewer, rschr. French Radio and TV, Ottawa, Ont., 1973-74; prodr. Sta. CBOF-CBC, Ottawa, 1974-78; founder and dir. svcs. in N.E. and N.W. Ont. Sta. CBON (French Network-CBC), Sudbury, 1978-83; exec. dir. regional programming CBC, Ottawa, 1983-84, assoc. v.p. regional broadcasting, 1984-88, v.p., sec. gen., 1988-90, v.p. human resources, 1990-92; dep. sec. for comm. and consultation The Privy Coun. Govt. of Can., Ottawa, 1992-93; founding chmn., CEO Can. Artists and Prodrs. Profl. Rels. Tribunal, Ottawa, 1993-95; senator Can. Govt., Ottawa, 1995—. Mem. Senate Standing com. Internal Economy, Budgets and Adminstrn.; former chair Senate Standing Com. on Transport and Comms., Can.'s Competitive Position in Comms.; first woman to chair Senate Liberal Caucus; first sen. to chair No. Ontario Liberal Caucus; bd. dirs. Cité Collégiale, Ottawa, 1989-91. Commr. for French lang. svcs. Province of Ont., 1986-89; regent U. Sudbury, 1979-83; bd. dirs. Laurentian Hosp., Sudbury, 1980-83, Cambrian Coll.Found., Sudbury, 1983-88; v.p. Art Ctr., Ottawa, 1988-90; pres. Regroupement gens d'affaires, Ottawa, 1991-92, Bell Globemedia, 2001-03. Recipient medal for contbn. to Can. Culture, Coun. of French-Am. Life, 1987, Prix Marcel-Blouin for best morning program in Can., 1983, Profl. Woman of Yr. award Réseau des femmes d'affaires professionnelles, 1990; named Chevalier Ordre de la Pléiade, 1995, Officier de l'Ordre national de la Legion d'Honneur de la France, 2003; named CEO of Yr., ACTRA Fraternal Benefit Soc. Mem. various parliamentary assns. and friendship groups including Canadian-Japan Inter-Parliamentary Group (co-chmn.), Can.-France Fedn. (pres.), Can.-Japan Inter-Parliamentary Group (co-chair). Avocations: running, reading, swimming. Office: Senate Can Ottawa ON Canada K1A 0A4 E-mail: poulim@sen.parl.gc.ca.

POULIOT, ASSUNTA GALLUCCI, retired business school owner and director, consultant; b. West Warwick, R.I., Aug. 14, 1937; d. Michael and Angelina (DeCesare) Gallucci; m. Joseph F. Pouliot Jr., July 4, 1961; children: Brenda, Mark, Jill, Michele. BS, U. R.I., 1959; MS, U. R.I., 1971. Bus. tchr. Cranston High Sch., R.I., 1959-61; bus. dept. chmn. Chariho Regional High Sch., Wood River Junction, R.I., 1961-73; instr. U. R.I., Kingston, 1973-78; founder, dir. Ocean State Bus. Inst., Wakefield, R.I., 1977-95, fin. aid cons., 1995—, ednl. cons., 1996—. Dir. Fleet Nat. Bank, 1985-91; bd. mgrs. Bank of New Eng., 1984-85; commr. Accrediting Coun. Ind. Colls. and Schs., 1995-98, chair accreditation com. team visits, 1998-2001, intermediate rev. com., 2000-01, rev. bd., 2000—; spkr. in field including Glencoe/McGraw-Hill Pub. Co., 1995—. Ednl. author, Glencoe McGraw Hill Pub. Co., 1999-2002. Pres. St. Francis Women's Club, Wakefield, 1975; sec. St. Francis Parish Coun., Wakefield, 1980; mem. Econ. Devel. Commn., Wakefield, 1981-85; mem. South County Hosp. Corp., Wakefield, 1978-97; fin. dir. Bus. and Profl. Women's Club, Wakefield, 1982-84; chmn. Ladies Golf Charity, 1985-91; mem. Computer Info. Systems Com., Chariho Regional Career and Tech. Ctr. Mem. R.I. Bus. Edn. Assn. (newsletter editor 1979-81), New Eng. Bus. Coll. Assn. (sec. 1984-86, pres. 1985-87), R.I. Assn. Career and Tech. Schs. (treas., bd. dirs. 1979-95), Eastern Bus. Edn. Assn. (conf. leader), Nat. Bus. Edn. Assn. (conf. leader), Career Coll. Assn. (conv. speaker, pub. rels. com., govt. rels. com., membership com., key mem., nominating com., evaluator), Assn. Colls. and Schs. (commr. commn. on postsecondary schs. accreditation 1994-98), R.I. Women's Golf Assn., Am. Cancer Soc., U. R.I. Alumni Assn. (Excellence Bus. award 1992), Phi Kappa Phi, Delta Pi Epsilon (pres., newsletter editor). Clubs: Point Judith Country (past ladies golf chmn., R.I. Women's golf rep.). Roman Catholic. Avocations: golfing, gardening. Home and Office: 137 Kenyon Ave Wakefield RI 02879-4242 Office: 15835 Sandy Point Dr Fort Myers FL 33917-5464 E-mail: sjpouliot@aol.com.

POULOS, CLARA JEAN, nutritionist; b. L.A., Jan. 1, 1941; d. James P. and Clara Georgie (Creighton) Hill; m. Themis Poulos, Jan. 31, 1960. PhD in Biol., Fla. State Christian U., 1974; PhD in Nutrition, Lafayette U., 1984; D in Nutritional Medicine, Hearts of Jesus and Mary Coll., 1986. Registered nutritionist, cert. hypnotherapist, clin. densitometry technician, in diabetes edn. Dir. rsch. Leapou Lab., Aptos, Calif., 1973—76, Monterey Bay Rsch. Inst., Santa Cruz, Calif., 1976—2001; nutrition specialist Santa Cruz, 1975—2001; dir. nutritional svcs., health enhancement, lifestyle planning, 1983—97; chief tech. and rsch. Osteoporosis Diagnostic Ctr., Santa Cruz, 2000—. Instr. Stoddard Assocs. Seminars; cons. Biol-Med. Lab., Chgo., Nutra-Med Rsch. Corp., NY, Akorn-Miller Pharmacal, Chgo., Monterey Bay Aquaculture Farms, Threshold Lab., Calif., Resurrection Lab., Calif. Author: Alcoholism-Stress-Hypoglycemia, 1976, The Relationship of Stress to Alcoholism and Hypoglycemia, 1979; assoc. editor: Internat. Jour. Bio-Social Research, Health Promotion Features; editor: Nutrition and Dietary Consultant Jour.; columnist: The Connection Newspaper; contbr. articles to profl. jours. Recipient Najulander Internat. Rsch. award, 1971, Wainwright Found. award, 1979, various state and local awards. Fellow: Internat. Acad. Nutritional Consultants, Am. Nutritionist Assn., Internat. Coll. Applied Nutrition; mem.: AAAS, Internat. Fishery Assn. (health assoc.), Calif. Acad. Sci., Am. Public Health Assn., Am. Heart Assn. (pres. Santa Cruz br. 1990—91), Internat. Platform Soc., Am. Diabetes Assn. (profl., pres. Santa Cruz chpt., editor newsletter The Daily Balance Santa Cruz chpt., sec. No. Calif. chpt.), MUSE-Computer Users Group, Am. Women's Bowling Assn., Quota, Toastmistress. Office: 9029 Soquel Ave Santa Cruz CA 95062 E-mail: cjp1918@netscape.net.

POULOS, PAIGE M. public relations executive; b. Woodland, Calif., Apr. 26, 1958; d. Paul William Jr. and Frances Marie (Gibson) Poulos; m. John Stuart Woolley, Jr., Feb. 3, 1990. Student, U. Calif., Davis, 1977-80. Mgr. pub. rels. Somerset Wine Co., N.Y.C. and San Martin, Calif., 1982-88; dir. comm. The Beverage Source, San Francisco, 1988-89, Rutherford (Calif.) Hill Winery, 1989-90; pres. Paige Poulos Comm., Berkeley, Calif., 1990—. Founder, chmn. WINECOM, 1992—; adj. lectr. Culinary Inst. Am./Greystone, 2002, adj. prof. lime comm., 2003 Pub. rels. editor: Practical Winery & Vineyard, 1994; wine, epicurean travel editor Focus Mag. Mem. Pub. Rels. Soc. Am. (accredited 1993, bd. dirs. 1993-95, editor newsletter food and beverage sect. 1993-95, pres. East Bay chpt. 1994-96, sec. 1994, counselors acad. 1994, chmn. food and beverage sect. 1996-97), Women in Comm., Acad. Wine Comm. (program chair 1994, sec. 1998, pres. 2000), Internat. Assn. Bus. Communicators, Am. Inst. Wine and Food, Internat. Assn. Culinary Profls., San Francisco Profl. Food Soc., Sonoma Culinary Guild (bd. dirs. 1998-99). Republican. Episcopalian. Avocations: horseback riding, diving, skiing, wine collecting. Office: Paige Poulos Comm PO Box 8087 Berkeley CA 94707-8087 E-mail: paige@paigepoulos.com.

POULTON, ROBERTA DORIS, nurse consultant; b. Balt., Oct. 10, 19[illegible]; d. Charles Robert and Mary Doris (Guercio) P. Nursing diploma, Md. Gen. Hosp., 1964. Staff nurse Md. Gen. Hosp., 1964-67, Project Hope, Colombia, 1967, 1969-70, St. Agnes Hosp., Balt., 1968-69, team leader, 1972-83, staff nurse-preceptor, 1983-88, nurse mgr. pediatric emergency rm./ambulatory svcs., 1988-93, pediat. hemophilia coord., 1993—2003. Pediat. ambulatory specialty clin. nurse; hemophilia nurse Johns Hopkins Med. Instn., Balt., 1998-2003; cons. Girl Scouts U.S.A., Balt., 1972—, Bapt. Conv. Md., 1963—. Mem.: ANA, Md. Nurses Assn. Democrat. Baptist.

POUNDSTONE, SALLY HILL, library director; m. Robert Bruce Poundstone; children: Nancy Katrina, Holly Megan, Angus Bruce, Alice Heather. BA, U. Ky., 1954, MA in Libr. Sci., 1955. Asst. head ref. dept. Louisville Free Pub. Libr., 1955-59; libr. Folger Shakespeare Libr., Washington, 1959-60; chief acquisition dept. White Plains (N.Y.) Pub. Libr., 1960-62; libr. Bedford Hills (N.Y.) Pub. Elem. Sch., 1965-66; dir. Mamaroneck (N.Y.) Free Libr. and Emelin Theatre, 1966-87, Westport (Conn.) Pub. Libr., 1987-98; prin. SHP Libr. Consultants, 1998—. Instr. libr. sci. N.Y. U., 1968-69, Coll. of New Rochelle (N.Y.), 1970-71; adv. coun. mem. Pratt Inst. Grad Sch. of Libr. and Info. Sci., 1978-87; adminstrv. svcs. chmn. N.Y. Met. Ref. and Res. Libr. Agy., 1977-79, bd. trustees, 1979-88, 2d v.p. and chair, 1984-85, pres., 1985-88; planning and devel. com. mem. Bibliomation, Inc., 1988-90; chair Conn. State Adv. Coun. for Libr. Planning and Devel., 1988-90. Pres. Garden Club of Mamaroneck, 1969-70, Larchmont-Mamaroneck Film Coun., 1971-72, Mamaroneck Hist. soc., 1976-77, bd. mem., 1976-87; vice chmn. Village of Upper Nyack Planning Bd., 1988-89; leadership com. and task force mem. Westchester 2,000, 1984-87; com. mem. Rotary Club of Westport, 1987—; active Downtown Westport Adv. Com., 1989-90, Rep. Town. Com., Weston, Conn., 1990-93, Westport Bridge & Traffic Com., 1990-97, Honorable Order of Ky. Cols., 1995—, United Way Profl. Adv. Com., 1994-97, Westport Telecomm. Com., 1994-96, and others; v.p., dir. Woodcock Nature Ctr., 1998—, pres., 2001—; mem. Wilton Rep. Town Com., 2000—, Planning & Zoning Bd. Commns., 2000—. Mem. ALA, Conn. Libr. Assn., Fairfield Libr. Adminstrs. Group, Archons of Colophon, Pub. Libr. Dirs. Assn. Westchester County (various offices and chairs), N.Y. Libr. Assn. (sec. treas. adult librs. assn. 1970-72, pres. pub. librs. sect. 1981-82, chair planning com. 1984-85). Home and Office: 48 Sharp Hill Rd Wilton CT 06897-3531

POUR-EL, MARIAN BOYKAN, mathematician, educator; b. NYC; d. Joseph and Mattie (Caspe) Boykan; m. Akiva Pour-El; 1 child. AB, Hunter Coll.; A.M., Harvard U., 1951, PhD, 1958. Prof. math. U. Minn., Mpls., 1968—2000, prof. emeritus, 2000—. Mem. Inst. Advanced Study, Princeton, N.J., 1962-64; mem. coun. Conf. Bd. Math. Scis., 1977-82, lectr. internat. congresses in math. logic and computer sci., Eng., 1971, Hungary, 1967, Czech Republic, 1973, 1998, Germany, 1983, 96-97, Japan, 1985, 88, China, 1987; lectr. Polish Acad. Sci., 1974; lectr. Fed. Republic of Germany, 1980, 1983, 87, 89, 91, 96 Japan, 1985, 87, 90, 93, China, 1987, Sweden, 1983, 94, Finland, 1991, Estonia, 1991, Moscow, 1992, Amsterdam, 1992; mem. Fulbright Com. on Maths., 1986-89; invited spkr. Internat. Congress on Computability and Complexity Theory, Kazan U., Russia, 1997, Workshop on Computability and Complexity in Analysis, held in conjunction with 23rd Internat. Symposium on Math. Founds. of Computer Sci. and Computer Sci. Logic, Brno, Czech Republic, 1998, IEEE Workshop on Real Number Computation, 1998 Author: (with I. Richards) Computability in Analysis and Physics, 1989; contbr. articles to profl. jours. Named to Hunter Coll. Hall of Fame, 1975; NAS grantee, 1966. Fellow AAAS, Japan Soc. for Promotion of Sci.; mem. Am. Math. Soc. (coun. 1980-88, numerous com., spkr., orgn. spl. sessions on math. logic), Assn. Symbolic Logic, Math. Assn. Am. (nat. panel vis. lectr.), Phi Beta Kappa, Sigma Xi, Pi Mu Epsilon (mathematics), Sigma Pi Sigma (physics). Achievements include research in mathematical logic (theoretical computer science) and in computability and noncomputability in physical theory—wave, heat, potential equations, eigenvalues, eigenvectors. Office: U Minn Sch Math Vincent Hall Minneapolis MN 55455-0488 E-mail: pour-el@math.umn.edu.

POURMOTABBED, TAYEBEH, biochemist; b. Kermanshah, Iran, Mar. 25, 1959; d. Ali Akbar Pourmotabbed and Molouk Ghovaalla; m. James Aflaki, Jan. 3, 1998. BA, Coll. of Notre Dame, 1981; PhD, U. Md., 1986. Asst. lectr. gen. chemistry U. Md., Balt., 1985, grad. tchg. asst., 1981-86, supr. undergrad. rsch., 1986-88, postdoctoral rsch. asst. College Park, 1986-88; instr. organic chemistry Howard C.C., Columbia, Md., 1986-87; asst. prof. U. Tenn., Memphis, 1989-92, 1993-98, assoc. prof., 1998—. Vis. prof. Wash. U., Seattle, 1995; invited lectr. in field. Contbr. articles to profl. jours., chpts. to books. Named Disting. Aumnus of Yr., U. Md., 2000. Mem. AAAS, Am. Chem. Soc., Am. Soc. for Biochemistry and Molecular Biology, Am. Coll. Rheumatology, N.Y. Acad. of Scis., Phi Lambda Epsilon. Office: Univ Tenn Molecular Sci Dept 858 Madison Ave Ste G1 Memphis TN 38163-0001 E-mail: tpourmotabbe@utmem.edu.

POUSADA, LIDIA, physician; b. Mt. Kisco, N.Y., July 21, 1957; d. Manuel and Maria Nieves (Mejuto) P.; m. Andrew Kemper Goodman, June 26, 1983 (div. Sept. 1986); 1 child, Sara Pousada Goodman; m. Wayne William Maibaum, Apr. 11, 1987 (div. July 1993); 1 child, Anna Pousada Maibaum; m. James Paul Kreindler, Mar. 2, 1996; 1 child, Victoria Pousada Kreindler. BS, CUNY, N.Y.C., 1978; MD, N.Y. Med. Coll., 1980. Diplomate Am. Bd. Internal Medicine, Am. Bd. Geriatric Medicine. Student geriatric fellowship NYU Med. Sch., N.Y.C., 1978-80; resident in internal medicine Montefiore Med. Ctr., Bronx, N.Y., 1980-83, dir. geriatric unit, 1986-89; with nat. health svc. North Cent. Bronx Hosp., 1983-84, Morris Heights Health Ctr., Bronx, 1985; instr. City Coll. Med. Sch., N.Y.C., 1982-85, Albert Einstein Coll. Medicine, Bronx, 1983-84, 86-89, asst. prof. medicine, 1988-89; assoc. prof. clin. medicine N.Y. Med. Coll., 1993—; pvt. practice geriatric medicine, 2002—. Dir. geriatric cons. svc. Montefiore Med. Ctr., 1987—89, assoc. chief divsn. geriatrics, 1988—92; chief divsn. geriatrics and gerontology Sound Shore Med. Ctr., 1992—2002. Author: Geriatric Diagnostics, 1983, Emergency Medicine for the House Officer, 1986, 2d edit., 1995, Emergency Medicine for Nurses, 1989, Perioperative Medical Care of the Geriatric Patient, 1989, Case Studies in Emergency Medicine for the House Officer, 1993. Physician scholar Nat. Health Svc., 1978-80. Fellow ACP, Gerontol. Soc. Am., Am. Geriatric Soc.; mem. Physicians for Social Responsibility. Office: 141 North State Rd Briarcliff Manor NY 10510

POVICH, LYNN, journalist, magazine editor, internet executive; b. Washington, June 4, 1943; d. Shirley and Ethyl P.; m. Stephen B. Shepard, Sept. 16, 1979; children: Sarah, Ned. AB, Vassar Coll., 1965. Rschr., reporter, writer, editor, sr. editor Newsweek mag., N.Y.C., 1965-91; editor-in-chief Working Woman mag., N.Y.C., 1991-96; mng. editor, sr. exec. prodr. East coast programming MSNBC Interactive, Secaucus, NJ, 2001—. Co-chair Internat. Women's Media Found., 2002—; adv. com. women's rights divsn. Human Rights Watch. Recipient Matrix award N.Y. Women in Comms., 1976; named to Acad. of Women Achievers YWCA, 1993.

POWDRELL-CULBERT, JANE E. state representative; b. Albuquerque; B, postgrad. in MPA program. Liaison between cmty. groups and Albuquerque Police Dept.; exec. dir. N.Mex. Commn. on Status of Women; tchr. rifle safety NRA, Va.; apptd. N.Mex. Parole Bd., 1999—2003; state rep. dist. 44 N.Mex. Ho. of Reps., Santa Fe, 2002—, mem. bus. and industry, transp. and enrolling and engrossing-A coms. Republican. Office: State Capitol Room 203GCN Santa Fe NM 87503

POWELL, ALMA JOHNSON, writer, advocate, foundation administrator; b. Birmingham, Al., Oct. 27, 1937; d. Robert and Mildred Johnson; m. Colin L. Powell, Aug. 1962; children: Michael, Linda, Annemarie. BA, Fisk U., 1957; LHD (hon.), Emerson Coll., 1996. Audiologist Boston Guild Hard of Hearing, 1959—62; co-chair America's Promise Alliance Youth, 1997—. Author: (children's books) America's Promise, 2003, My Little Wagon, 2003. Bd. trustees Kennedy Ctr., 1991—, vice chair, 1993; chair nat. coun. Best Friends Found., 1989—. Named one of 100 Most Powerful Women in Wash., Washingtonian mag., 2001.*

POWELL, ANICE CARPENTER, retired librarian; b. Moorhead, Miss., Dec. 2, 1928; d. Horace Aubrey and Celeste (Brian) Carpenter; m. Robert Wainwright Powell, July 19, 1948 (dec. 1979); children: Penelope Elizabeth, Deborah Alma (dec.). BS, Delta State U., 1961, MLS, 1974. Libr. Sunflower (Miss.) Pub. Libr., 1958—61; tchr. English Isola (Miss.) H.S., 1961—62; dir. Sunflower County Libr., Indianola, Miss., 1962—97, ret., 1997. Mem. adv. bd. libr. svcs. and constrn. act com. Miss. Libr. Commn., 1978-80; mem. state adv. coun. adult edn., 1988-92 mem. steering com. NASA cmty. involvement program Miss. Delta C.C., 1990, mem. adult edn. adv. com., mem. dist. workforce coun., 1994—; commn. mem. Mid Delta Empowerment Zone Alliance, 1995—, exec. com. Sunflower County Alliance for Youth, 1998-99. Mem. AAUW, NOW, ALA (spkr. senate subcom. on illiteracy 1989, honoree ALA 50th Ann. 1996), Miss. Libr. Assn. (exec. dir. Nat. Libr. Week 1975, steering com. 1976, chmn. Right to Read com. 1976, co-chmn. 1987, chmn. legis. com. 1979, chmn. intellectual freedom com. 1975, 80, legis. com. 1973-86, 96, 98, chmn. membership com. 1982, 98, pres. 1984, chmn. nominating com. 1986, chmn. election com. 1989, co-chmn. awards com. 1998, legia. com. 1998, Peggy May award 1981), Sunflower County Hist. Soc. (pres. 1983-87), Sierra Club. Methodist. Home: PO Box 310 Sunflower MS 38778-0310

POWELL, ANNE ELIZABETH, editor; b. Cheverly, Md., Nov. 11, 1951; d. Arthur Gorman and Barbara Anne (MacAran) P.; m. John Alan Ebeling Jr., 1972 (div. 1983). BS, U. Md., 1972. Reporter Fayetteville (N.C.) Times, 1973-75; home editor Columbus (Ga.) Ledger-Enquirer, 1976; assoc. editor Builder mag., Washington, 1977-78; architecture editor House Beautiful's Spl. Publs., N.Y.C., 1979-81; editor Traditional Home mag., Des Moines, 1982-87, Mid-Atlantic Country mag., Alexandria, Va., 1987-89; editor in chief publs. Nat. Trust for Hist. Preservation, Washington, 1989-95; editor-in-chief Landscape Architecture Mag., Washington, 1995-98, Civil Engrng. Mag., Washington, 1998—. Author: The New England Colonial, 1988. Mem. Nat. Press Club, Am. Soc. Mag. Editors. Home: 1105 Park St NE Washington DC 20002-6317 Office: American Society of Civil Engrs Civil Engring Mag 1801 Alexander Bell Dr Reston VA 20191-4344 E-mail: apowell@asce.org.

POWELL, CHRISTA RUTH, educational training executive; b. Dodgeville, Wis., Mar. 3, 1957; d. Robert Franklin and RAchel Jean (Edge) Powell; m. Fred L. Neff, Sept. 10, 1989; 1 child, Rosalena Pauline Neff. BSN, Viterbo Coll., 1979. RN, Minn. Staff nurse Abbott Northwestern Hosp., Mpls., 1979-81, 83-87, asst. head nurse, 1981-83; legal asst. Hyatt Legal Assts., St. Paul, 1981-83, comms. dir. Minn. region, 1983-86; office coord. Neff Law Firm, P.A., Mpls., 1986—; pres., bd. dirs. Profl. Devel. Inst., Bloomington, Minn., 1994—. Cons. A Basic Legal Svc., Bloomington, 1990-94. Editor: Mysterious Persons, 1990, Great Puzzles in History, 1990; co-host TV program Great Puzzles in History, 1989-91. Investigator ethics com. Hennepin County Bar, Mpls., 1989-90; v.p. Endless Fist Soc., Inc. Scholar Gerry Graber Scholarship Com., 1975; State of Wis. honors grantee, 1975. Mem. Edina C. of C. Avocations: reading, sewing, walking, knitting, gardening. Home: 4515 Andover Rd Edina MN 55435-4031 Office: Neff Law Firm PA 7760 France Ave S Bloomington MN 55435-5800

POWELL, DEBORAH ELIZABETH, pathologist, dean; b. Lynn, Mass., Nov. 28, 1939; MD, Tufts U., 1965. Diplomate Am. Bd. Pathology. Intern Georgetown Med. Ctr., Washington, 1965-66; resident in pathology NIH, Bethesda, Md., 1966-69; exec. dean, vice-chancellor clin. affairs U. Kans. Sch. Medicine, Kansas City, 1997—2002; dean, asst. v.p. for clin. affairs U. Minn. Med. Sch., Mpls., 2002—. Past pres. U.S. & Can. Acad. Pathology, Inc.; trustee Am. Bd. Pathology. Mem.: Inst. Medicine, Internat. Assn. Pathologists, Am. Assn. Pathologists. Office: U Minn Med Sch Dean's Office 420 Delaware St SE MMC 293 Minneapolis MN 55455 Business E-Mail: dpowell@umn.edu.

POWELL, ELAINE MARIE, consultant, educator, writer; b. St. Louis, Nov. 25, 1946; d. Edsel Arthur and Jessie Louise (Whitelaw) Hatfield; m. David Eugene Powell; children: Steven, Bryan. Grad. H.S., Florissant, 1964. Sec. U. Mo., Columbia, 1969—71, Francis Howell Sch. Dist., St. Charles County, Mo., 1985—93; scrapbook instr., cons., 1996—. Author: The Family Heritage Album. Coun. tng. staff Boy Scouts Am., 1980-85, dist. tng. chmn., 1982-85; mem. long range planning coun. Francis Howell Sch. Dist., 1989-93, others. Recipient Dist. award of merit Boy Scouts Am., 1983, Howell of Fame award, 1987, Silver Beaver award Boy Scouts Am., 1991. Mem.: First Families St. Louis, Ctrl. Fla. Geneal. Soc. (pres. 2003—). Republican. Presbyterian. Home and Office: 4620 Saddleworth Cir Orlando FL 32826-4126

POWELL, ENID LEVINGER, writer, educator; b. Bklyn., Nov. 24, 1931; d. Herbert Roosevelt and Selma Esther (Sherman) Levinger; m. Bert Powell, Nov. 5, 1950; children: Pip Irene, Jon Lawrence. BA in English, Barat Coll., 1974; MA in English and Creative Writing, U. Ill., Chgo., 1978. Staff writer The Young and the Restless, L.A., 1983-94; tchr. Columbia Coll., Chgo., 1993-95, Newberry Libr., Chgo., 1994—; freelance writer Chgo. Co-author: The Big Steal, 1980, The Divorce Handbook, 1982; contbr. short stories and poetry to popular mags. Nominee for Best Writing award NATAS, 1986, 87, 90-91, 91-92. Mem. ACLU, NOW, Common Cause. Avocations: theater, traveling. Home: 1300 N Lake Shore Dr Apt 21B Chicago IL 60610-5152

POWELL, JEANNE, publishing executive, consultant, writer, advocate; d. Ambrose and Blanche Powell. BA, Wayne State U.; JD, U. San Francisco. Pres. Nob Hill Urban Neighbors, San Francisco, 1991—2001; CEO Meridien PressWorks, San Francisco, 1996—; treasurer Lower Polk Neighbors, San Francisco, 2003—. Founder Celebration of the Word spoken word series. Author: (book) February Voices, 1994, Cadences, 1996, Celebration of the Word, 2003. Mem. bd. suprs. Task Force on neighborhood issues, San Francisco, 1995—96. Named Outstanding spoken word series, North Beach NOW, 1998. Mem.: Alliance Francaise San Francisco, Commonwealth Club. Protestant. Avocation: study of ancient religions and spiritual practices. Office: PO Box 640024 San Francisco CA 94164

POWELL, JEANNE MARIE, accountant; b. N.Y.C., Sept. 5, 1947; d. Vincent and Genevieve (Josephs) Calabretta; children: Lisa M., Roger J. Jr. Student, CUNY, 1968. Cert. tax profl.; registered rep.; accredited tax advisor; accredited tax profl. Owner, pres. Jeanne Powell Assocs., Howard Beach, N.Y., 1972—. Bd. dirs. Putnam Investment Co., Boston, 1987-90, bd. govs., 1990—, mem. adv. bd., 1993—. Fundraiser for Geraldine Ferraro, Queens, N.Y., 1991, for Al Stabile, 1997. Mem. Nat. Soc. Pub. Accts., Nat. Assn. Tax Profls., Nat. Soc. Tax Profls., N.Y. Soc. Ind. Accts. (pres. Queens chpt. 1995-98, state 2d v.p. 1997, state pres. 2002-03). Roman Catholic. Office: 15552 101st St Howard Beach NY 11414-2818

POWELL, KARAN HINMAN, academic administrator; b. Great Lakes, Ill., May 25, 1953; d. David Daniel and Mary Anne (Buretz) Hinman; m. David Leonidas Powell, Feb. 14, 1987; children: Meloni (dec.), Erik. BS, We. Ill. U., 1975; MDiv, B Sacred Theology (hon.), Loyola U., Chgo.,

1981; PhD, George Mason U., 1998. Cert. tchr., Ill., Va.; cert. orgn. devel. profl. Tchr. St. Hugh Cath. Sch., Lyons, Ill., 1975-77, Lay Ministry Tng. Program, Chgo., 1980-81, Jackson, Miss., 1981-83; adminstr. Inst. Creation Centered Spirituality Mundelein Coll., Chgo., 1978-79; exec. dir. North Am. Forum Catechumenate, Washington, 1983-88; dir. Profl. Devel. Program, tchr. theol. studies, tng. cons., exec. devel., direct contact tng. Georgetown U., Washington, 1988-94, dir. organization devel. program, 1991-95, mng. acad. dir., 1995, assoc. dean, 1998—, v.p., chief learning officer. Assoc. pastor Annunciation Cath. Ch., Columbus, Miss., 1981-83; cons. dioceses in U.S., Can., 1983—; cons. to fed. govt., profit and non-profit corps.; pres. Powel and Assocs., 1994—; cons. leadership devel. Am. Mgmt. Systems Inc., 1998—; v.p., dir., exec. dir., chief learning officer AMS U. Author: How to Form a Catechumenate Team, 1985; editor: Breaking Open the Word of God series, 1986-88, The Ninety Days, 1989; contbr. articles Cath. mags.; spkr. in field. Active on Blessed Sacrament RCIA Team, Alexandria, Va., 1984-86; apptd. to Va. State Child Fatality Review Team, 1996-99, 99—. Recipient tchr.'s scholarship State of Ill., 1971-75, cert. recognition KC, Columbus, Miss., 1982; George Mason U. fellow, 1994-97. Mem. ASTD, Orgn. Devel. Inst., Acad. of Mgmt., Assn. Psychol. Type, N.Am. Forum Catechumenate (cons. 1982—), Cath. Edn. Future's Project (mem. com. 1985-88, Va. SIDS Alliance, 1991—, state steering com. 1993-94, bd. dirs., 1993-94, pres. 1994-96), Orgn. Devel. Network (presenter nat. conf. 1996, 97), Internat. Acad. Bus. (reviewer for spirituality and work 1998), Acad. Mgmt. (reviewer mgmt. edn. divsn. 1998). Democrat. Avocations: sailing, music, crafts, travel, foreign exchange student hosting. Office: 4000 Legato Rd Fl 10 Fairfax VA 22033-4055 E-mail: karan_powell@ams.com.

POWELL, KATHLEEN TRESTKA, artist, educator, editor; b. Oceanside, N.Y., July 3, 1953; d. Andrew Anthony and Ann Trestka; m. David Allen Powell, Aug. 4, 1972; children: Pamela Joy, David Andrew. Student, Greenfield (Mass.) C. C., 1988-91, Smith Coll., 1995. Tchr. English Mt. Snow Acad., W. Dover, Mass. Arts editor, arts cons. Nat. Evaln. Sys., Amherst, Mass.; guest lectr. Smith Coll., Northampton, Mass.; art critic Brattleboro (Vt.) Reformer. Author: poems Mem. NOW, Acad. Am. Poets, Nat. Writers Union, Phi Beta Kappa. Home: 62 Hendrick St Easthampton MA 01027 Office: 380 Dwight St Holyoke MA 01040-5842

POWELL, LAURA ELIZABETH, music educator; b. Aurora, Ill., May 4, 1977; d. Gerald John and Anne Marie Engelhardt; m. David Leland Powell, June 30, 2001. BME and BM, Ill. Wesleyan U., 1999. Choral dir. Evang. United Meth. Ch., Bloomington, Ill., 1998—99; music assoc. Calvary Temple, Springfield, Ill., 2000; choral dir. and tchr. gen. music Calvary Acad., Springfield, 2000—. Mem. music adv. bd. IESA, Bloomington, Ill., 2002—03; mem. fine arts focus group ROE, Springfield, 2001. Mem.: Music Educators Nat. Conf. Office: Calvary Acad 1730 W Jefferson St Springfield IL 62702

POWELL, LILLIAN MARIE, retired music educator; b. DeLand, Fla., June 1, 1927; d. Francis Charles and Jessie Agnes (Niven) P.; m. James Armbruster, May 1950 (div. 1957); children: Jeffrey L. Armbruster, Leslie J. Armbruster; m. Dwight M. Liller, Dec. 8, 1957 (div. June 1972). B. Pub. Sch. Music, Capital U., 1950; MA, Ohio State U., 1957. Lic. tchr., N.Y., N.J., Va., Ohio. Vocal and instrumental music tchr. Community Sch., Stoutsville, Ohio, 1949-50, Roosevelt Jr. High Sch., Newark, 1950-51; elem. music tchr. at several schs. Norfolk, Va., 1951-53; music tchr. Naval Base Sch., Guantanomo Bay, Cuba, 1953-55; instr. voice Otterbein Coll., Ohio, 1955-56; music tchr. several elem. and jr. high schs. Lorain, Ohio, 1956-60; music cons. elem. schs. South Orange, N.J., 1960-61; music tchr. elem. schs. Livingston, N.J., 1963-66; music tchr. Roosevelt Jr. high Sch., West Orange, N.J., 1965-72; instr. music lit. County Coll. Morris County, Dover, N.J., 1970-72; elem. sch. tchr. music Pub. Sch. 86, Jamaica Heights, N.Y., 1973-75; tchr. Satellite East Jr. High Sch. for Gifted, Bklyn., 1977-89, Stephen Halsey Jr. High Sch., N.Y.C., 1989-96, ret., 1996. Music theater dir. Children's Theater, Guantanamo Bay, 1953-55; ch. choir dir. Naval Base Chapel, Guantanano Bay, 1953-55; ch. choir dir., soloist Congregational Ch., Lorain, Ohio, 1956-60; ch. soloist, organist Religious Sci. Ch., Morristown, Ohio. CORO associate orgn. activities CORO Leadership Found., Manhattan, N.Y., 1985—; vol. vocal/drama coaching Vocal Students for Profl. Goals and Producing Major Musical Prodn., Bklyn., 1977-85. Named Outstanding Woman of State of N.Y., N.Y. State Senate, 1984. Eckankar. Avocations: equestrian activities, astrology, writing, musical composition. Home: 4551 College Ave Ellicott City MD 21043-6817 E-mail: LeeMPowell@aol.com.

POWELL, LURA J. science association administrator; b. Balt., Aug. 26, 1950; m. Arthur J. King, May 22, 1982; 2 children. BS in Chemistry, U. Md., 1972, PhD (hon.), 1978. Rsch. chemist inorganic analytical rsch. divsn. Nat. Inst. Stds. & Tech., 1987-88, acting deouty dir. nat. measurement lab., 1987-88, dir. program office nat. measurement lab., 1988-89, deputy dir. Ctr. Chem. Tech. nat. measurement lab., 1989-91, chief biotech. divsn. nat. measurement lab., 1991-95, chief biotech. divsn., 1995—. Recipient Disting. Pub. Svc. award Internat. Personnel Mgmt. Assn., 1991, Silver medal Dept. Commerce, 1992. Mem. Am. Chem. Soc., Exec. Women Govt., Sigma Xi. Methodist. Office: Nat Inst Stds & Tech Dept Commerce Rm A333 Adminstrn Bldg Gaithersburg MD 20899-0001

POWELL, MARGARET ANN SIMMONS, computer scientist; b. Gulfport, Miss., May 26, 1952; d. William Robert and Nancy Rita (Schloegel) Simmons; m. Mark Thomas Powell, Sept. 11, 1983. AS in Math., N.W. Miss. Jr. Coll., 1972; BS in Edn., Memphis State U., 1977; BS in Computer Sci., U. Md., 1988; MS in Computer Sci., Johns Hopkins U., 1991. Tchr. Sacred Heart Sch., Walls, Miss., 1973-80; office mgr. Hyman Builders Supply, Memphis, 1980-84; tech. instr. Bendix Field Engring. Corp., Greenbelt, Md., 1985-87; software engr. Assurance Technology Corp., Alexandria, Va., 1987-89, Naval Rsch. Lab., Washington, 1989-93; computer scientist Naval Info. Systems Mgmt. Ctr., Washington, 1993-97; head software product assurance office Naval Rsch. Lab., Washington, 1997—. Bd. dirs. Greenbrook Village Homeowners Assn., 1992-96; sec. Greenbelt East Adv. Com., 1994, chair, 1995-96. Recipient Navy Meritorious Civilian Svc. award, 1997, Standardization award Dept. Def., 2001.; named one of Outstanding Young Women Am., 1977, Tech. Leadership award Govt. Exec. Mag., 1996. Mem. IEEE Computer Soc., Assn. for Computing Machinery, Phi Kappa Phi, Kappa Delta Pi, Phi Theta Kappa, Mu Alpha Theta. Episcopalian. Avocation: needlework. Home: 4652 Kell Ln Alexandria VA 22311-4917 Office: Naval Rsch Lab Code 8101 3 4555 Overlook Ave SW Washington DC 20375-0001

POWELL, MARILYN LINDEBERG, minister; b. Oakland, Calif., Nov. 10, 1924; d. Niels David Lindeberg and Azalia Covington; m. Joseph Harllee Powell, Sept. 14, 1943; children: David, Dorian, Cristina, Mark. Student, U. South, 1982—83, t. Lukes Sch. Theology, 1984—85. Deacon Episcopal Ch., 1985. Program dir. Dubose Conf., Monteagle, Tenn., 1983—84; deadon St. James Epsicopal Ch., Sewanee, 1985—86; co-dir. Mid-Cumberland Mountain Ministry, Monteagle, 1986—91; deacon Ch. Our Saviour, Charleston, SC, 1991—96, St. James Episcopal, 1996—99, St. Stephen's Episcopal Ch., 2000—. Founder Cmty. Action, Sewanee, Family Violence Program, Grundy County; hosp. vol. Cuba. Named Citizen of Yr., Civic Assn., Sewanee, 1984; recipient Good Folks award, Tenn. Mag., 1990. Democrat. Avocations: reading, shelling. Home: 1 Gadsden Way C-7 Charleston SC 29412

POWELL, MARSHA N. federal program analyst; b. Culver City, Calif., Aug. 31, 1960; d. Raymond Edward Powell and Wynonne Raye Keeling. B Music Edn., S.W. Bapt. U., Bolivar, Mo., 1984. Cert. K-12 music (vocal) tchr., Mo. Music tchr. Carroll Christian Acad., Westminster, Md., 1984-85; receptionist, PBX operator Criswell Coll., Dallas, 1985-87; critical care asst. Baylor U. Med. Ctr., Dallas, 1987-90; elem. and music tchr. Star of Bethlehem Christian Acad., Triangle, Va., 1990-91; sec. FAA, Washington, 1991-95, program analyst, 1995—. Composer songs. Music dir. Women's Ministries/Immanuel Bible Ch., Springfield, Va., 1998—, choir mem. and officer, 1991—, dir. Ladies Ensemble, 1999—. Avocations: music, sports, Bible, Dr. Pepper paraphernalia, people. Home: 7908 Inverton Rd Unit 302 Annandale VA 22003-4835 Office: FAA 800 Independence Ave SW Washington DC 20591-0001

POWELL, MICHELE HALL, music educator; b. Norfolk, Va., May 20, 1958; d. Wadsworth and Mable Hall; m. Raymond Powell (div. 1999). BS in pub. sch. music edn., Norfolk State U., 1981, MusM, 1994. Cert. tchr. Va., 1981. Choral, music tchr. Barstow (Calif.) Cogic Christian Sch., 1982—83, Nuernburg, Germany, 1984—87, Amelia County Mid. and HS, Va., 1987—88; tchr. asst. Ruffner Mid. Sch., Norfolk, Va., 1988—89; music specialist Windsor Woods Elem. Sch., Va. Beach, Va., 1989—99; choral, music tchr. Brandon Mid. Sch., Va. Beach, 1999—. Mem. Sch. Planning Coun., Va. Beach, 2002—03, PTA Bd., Va. Beach, 2002—03. Mem.: Music Educator's Nat. Assoc. Home: 1038 Smoke Tree Ln Virginia Beach VA 23452 Office: Brandon Mid Sch 1700 Pope St Virginia Beach VA 23464 E-mail: mipowell@vbcps.k12.va.us.

POWELL, NANCY J. ambassador; b. Cedar Falls, Iowa; Dep. chief of mission, Lome, Togo, 1990—92; polit. counselor New Delhi, 1993—95; consul gen. Calcutta, India; dep. chief of mission US Embassy, Khaka, Bangladesh, 1995—97; U.S. amb. to Uganda U.S. Dept. State, Kampala, 1997—99, prin. dep. asst. sec. African affairs, 1999—2001, acting asst. sec. African affairs, 2001, U.S. amb. to Ghana Accra, 2001—02, U.S. amb. to Pakistan Islamabad, Pakistan, 2002—. Office: Embassy of USA Diplomtic Enclave PO Box 1048 Ramna 5 Islamabad Pakistan Office Fax: +92 51 214222.

POWELL, PATRICIA HRUBY, writer, dancer; b. Chgo., July 6, 1951; d. Norbert Joseph and Dolores Marie Smith Hruby; m. Morgan Edward Powell, Jan. 7, 1938. Diploma of dance, London Sch. Contemporary Dance, 1973; BFA in Dance, U. Ill., 1979; MFA in Dance, Temple U., 1987; MS, U. Ill., 1994. Artistic, exec. dir. One Plus One, 1976—91; free-lance storyteller, dancer, writer Champaign, Ill., 1993—. Author: Blossom Tales: Flower Stories of Many Folk, Zinnia: How the Corn Was Saved, (Operas) A Woodland Tale; performer: (dance music theatre) Indeterminancy Principle, In the Beginning., (choreographed history of dance). Recipient Choreographic award, Ill. Arts Coun., 1983, 1991, Writing and Performance award, Ragdale Found., 1992, 1995—97, 2000—02; fellow, NEA, 1980, Temple U., 1986—87. Mem.: Soc. Children's Book Writers and Illustrators (assoc.). Personal E-mail: phpowell@talesforallages.com.

POWELL, PATRICIA LYNN, education educator, educator, special education educator, educator; b. Columbus, Jan. 4, 1954; d. Roger Lee and Geraldine (Porter) Triemstra; m. Richard Wayne Powell, Apr. 5, 1980; children: Joshua, Aaron, Kaitlyn. AB in Music and Elem. Edn., Calvin Coll., 1975; EdM in Hearing Impairments, U. Airz., 1976; postgrad., U. Ill., Chgo., 2003—. Tchr. hearing impaired Ariz. State Sch. for the Deaf and Blind, Tucson, 1976—81; music tchr. disabled students Elim Christian Sch., Palos Heights, Ill., 1986—2001; asst. prof. edn. and spl. edn. Trinity Christian Coll., Palos Heights, 1999—. Mem. com. on disabilities Reformed Ch. in Am., NJ, 2002—03. Recipient Open Hearts award, Pathways Awareness Found., 2001. Mem.: ASCD, Coun. for Exceptional Children, Am. Ednl. Rsch. Assn. Avocations: flute, quilting, reading, boating, gardening. Home: 12300 Nagle Ave Palos Heights IL 60463 Office: Trinity Christian Coll 6601 W College Dr Palos Heights IL 60463

POWELL, RUTH AREGOOD, music educator; b. Rising City, Nebr. d. August Walter and Gussie Hobson (Bray) Aregood; m. Jack William Powell, June 27, 1953; children: Stephen Mark, Linda Lou, Timothy Vaughn. BA, Nebr. Wesleyan, Lincoln, 1949; MA, Northwestern U., Evanston, Ill., 1952. Dir. edn. Wauwotosa (Wis.) Meth., 1952-54; self-employed piano tchr. Wis., Hawaii, Ohio, 1955—. Mem. Music Tchrs. Nat. Assn. (pres. East Ctrl. Divsn. 1990-92), Nat. Guild Piano Tchrs., Ohio Music Tchrs. Assn. (pres. 1984-88, pres. ctrl. east dist. 1992-96, named Cert. Tchr. of Yr. 2000-01), Westerville Womens Music Club. Methodist. Avocations: reading, sewing.

POWELL, SANDY, costume designer; b. London, Jan. 12, 1959; Costumer designer for films including Caravaggio, 1986; The Last of England, 1987; Stormy Monday, 1988; Venus Peter, 1989; Killing Dad, 1989; For Queen and Country, 1989; Shadow of China, 1991; The Pope Must Die, 1991; Edward II 1991; The Miracle, 1991; Orlando, 1992 (Nominated BAFTA Award, Academy Award; Best Costume Design, 1994); The Crying Game, 1992; Wittgenstein, 1993; Being Human, 1993; Interview with a Vampire, 1994 (Nominated BAFTA Award, Best Costume Design, 1995); Rob Roy, 1995, Michael Collins, 1996; The Wings of a Dove, 1997 (Nominated Golden Satellite Award, BAFTA Award; Best Costume Design, 1998); The Butcher Boy, 1997; Velvet Goldmine, 1998 (Nominated Academy Award, Best Costume Design; Won Best Costume Design, British Academy Awards, 1998); Hilary and Jackie, 1998; Shakespeare in Love, 1998 (Won Academy Award, Best Costume Design; Nominated BAFTA Award, Best Costume Design, 1998). Office: c/o Costume Designers Guild 13949 Ventura Blvd Ste 309 Sherman Oaks CA 91423-3570

POWELL GEBHARD, JOY LEE (BOK SIN LEE), small business owner; b. Jan. 29, 1936; arrived in U.S., 1956, naturalized, 1962; d. Yong Joon and Chun Jal Lee; m. Jimmy Wayne Powell, Sept. 24, 1960; children: Chun Jal Lee, Miran Victoria, D. Gibbhard; m. Karl Ten Eyck Gebhard, Oct. 15, 1995. Student, Internat. Speech Coll., Pusan, Korea, 1952, Nat. U. Pusan, 1953—55, McMurry Coll., Abilene, Tex., 1956—58; BA, Wayland Bapt. U., Plainview, Tex., 1966; postgrad., Cen. State U., Okla., 1967—68. Cert. antique appraiser and cons. Nurse Rok Med. Sch., Pusan, 1950—53; news announcer Pusan Radio Sta., 1953; sec., ret. choir organizer chaplain's office U.N. Army divsn. 8069, Pusan, 1954—56, Meth. Mission, Pusan, 1955—56, U.S. A.S.C. Office, Ploydada, Tex., 1958, Am. U., Washington, 1958—60; with Washington Post, U.S. Acad. Sci., 1960; with spl. study of prejudice among children grades 1 to 12 Pub. Opinion and Propaganda, 1965—66; tchr. Oklahoma City Sch. Sys., 1968—70; head social studies dept. Dunjee H.S., 1968; tchr. Spanish Carl Albert H.S., 1969; owner Internat. Antiques, Upperville, Va., 1973—; founder, dir. Healing Inc., 1997—. Co-founder, charter mem. lit. mag. Mang Hiang. Contbr. articles to profl. jours., poetry New Voices in American Poetry, 1978, poems and essays to Korean periodicals. Mem.: World Affairs Coun. Washington, Nat. History Preservation, Smithsonian Assocs. Avocations: music, writing, swimming, collecting, travel. Home and Office: PO Box 221 Upperville VA 20185-0221

POWER, A. KATHRYN, social services administrator; m. Brian Power; children: Matthew, Brendan. BA, St. Joseph's Coll., Md.; MEd, Western Md. Coll.; postgrad. Harvard U. Tchr. various pub. schs.; computer systems analyst U.S. Dept. Def.; exec. dir. R.I. Coun. Cmty. Mental Health Ctrs., 1985—90; dir. R.I. Office Substance Abuse, Gov.'s Drug Program, R.I. Anti Drug Coalition, R.I. Dept. Mental Health, Retardation and Hosps., Ctr. for Mental Health Svcs., Rockville, Md., 2003—. Capt. USNR. Fellow Toll fellow, Coun.. State Legislators, 1991. Mem.: Nat. Assn. State Mental Health Program Dirs. (pres. 1997). Office: Substance Abuse/Mental Health Svcs Ctr for Mental Health Svc 5600 Fisher Ln Parklawn Bldg #12 Rockville MD 20857*

POWER, BARBARA LOUISE, artist, educator; b. Niskayuna, N.Y., Jan. 14, 1958; d. Thomas Dunbar and Norma Virginia Power; m. Joshua Arthur Muskin, July 5, 1992; 1 child, Saul E. Muskin. BS, Western Mich. U., Kalamazoo, 1980; MA in Art Edn., R.I. Sch. of Design, Providence, 1985; MFA, Vt. Coll. assoc. with Norwich U., Montpelier, 1998. Cert. tchr. Va., 2001. Adj. instr. Bainbridge Coll., 1992—98, Valdosta (Ga) State U., 1997; pt. time instr. FACE, Tallahassee, 1998; adj. instr. Frederick (Md.) Cmty. Coll., 1999; tchr. Langley HS, McLean, Va., 1999—2002. Summer student Penland Sch., NC, 1989, 95, Fla. State U., Tallahassee, 1993, Anderson Ranch, Snowmass, Colo., 1994; instr. summer Corcoran Sch. of Art, Washington, 1999, Md. Coll. of Art and Design, Silver Spring, 1999. One-woman shows include Cole Pratt Gallery, New Orleans, 1999, Roles and Rels., Divsn. of Cultural Arts, Tallahassee, 1995, Holden Gallery, Warren Wilson Coll., 1999. Chmn. United Way, Tallahassee, 1993—94; tutor Laubach Literacy, Tallahassee, 1992—95. Scholar Grassroots Cultural Program, Bainbridge (Ga.) Coll., 1995; Kast Grant, Germantown Acad., Ft. Wash., Pa., 1995. Mem.: Nat. Mus. of Women in the Arts, Washington Sculpture Group, Capitol Hill Art League. Democrat. Avocations: bicycling, reading, walking, yoga. Home: 8004 Piney Br Rd Silver Spring MD 20910 Office: Barbara Power Scuptor and Mixed Media Drawing 8004 Piney Br Rd Silver Spring MD 20910

POWER, MARY SUSAN, political scientist, educator; b. Hazleton, Pa., July 5, 1935; d. Younger L. and Cleo (Brook) Power; 1 child, Catherine Laverne. BA, Wells Coll., 1957; postgrad., Exeter (Eng.) U., 1955-56, Yale U., 1958-59; MA, Stanford U., 1960; PhD, U. Ill., 1961. Asst. prof. Susquehanna (Pa.) U., 1961-64; assoc. prof. U. Ark., Fayetteville, 1965-68; assoc. prof. polit. sci. Ark. State U., State University, 1968-79, prof., 1979—2000, prof. emeritus, 2000—. Author: (book) Before the Convention, Religion and the Founding Fathers, 1984, Jacques Maritaln and the Quest for a New Commonwealth, 1992, Political Philosophy & Cultural Renewal: Collected Essays of Francis Wilson, 2001; contbr.: Jonesboro Sun, 2003—; contbr. articles to profl. jours. Mem. Fed. Edn. Commn. States, 1982—84; N.E. chair Arkansans for Progress, 1990—96; alt. del. Rep. Nat. Conv., 1972, 1976, 1988, del., 1992; mem. State com. Ark. Rep. Com., 1968—96, sec., 1978—80; mem. Craighead County Election Commn., 1986—88; chmn. Craighead County GOP, 1986—88, vice chmn., 1990—96, N.E. regional chmn., 1988—96; chmn. Craighead County Sheffield for Gov., 1990; mem. exec. com. Ark. Rep. Party, 1990—96, N.E. regional chair, 1988—96; treas. women's soc. Blessed Sacrament Ch., Jonesboro, 1996—2000, chmn. jubilee 2000; chair Silver Caths., 2002—. Relm Found. fellow, 1960, NSF-Am. Polit. Sci. Assn. fellow, 1963, Nat. Def. Seminar fellow, Nat. War Coll., 1973, NEH fellow, 1978, Pres.'s fellow, Ark. State U., 1988—89. Mem.: AAUP (state sec. 1978—80, pres. 1983—90), So. Polit. Sci. Assn., Am. Polit. Sci. Assn., Ark. Polit. Sci. Assn. (bd. dirs., v.p. 1992—93, pres. 1993—94), Phi Kappa Phi (pres. 1991), Phi Gamma Mu (sec.-treas. 1990—2000), Phi Sigma Alpha. Republican. Roman Catholic. Personal E-mail: spower@fastdata.net.

POWER, PEGGY ANN, elementary school educator; b. Chgo., Sept. 17, 1973; d. Edward and Lois Power. BA, U. Ill., Chgo., 1994, MEd, 1996. Cert. elem. sch. tchr., Ill. Rsch. asst. U. Ill., Chgo., 1991-96; sales asst. Chgo. Bd. Trade, 1991-96; spl. edn. tchr. Gladstone Elem. Sch. Chgo. Bd. Edn., 1995—. Poet: Outstanding Poets of 1994, Best Poems of the 90's, 1992, Distinguished Poets of America, 1993. Active Wis. Dairy Coun., 1996—, Lawry's Menu for Success, Chgo., 1996—, After-Sch. Acad. Ctr., Chgo., 1996—; rep. Chgo. Tchr.'s Union, 1997—, bd. dirs. Recipient Gwendolyn Brookes Poet Laureat award, 1990; Baer Darfler scholar Morgan Park Women's Assn., 1994-96; Marilyn Mucha fellow U. Ill., Chgo., 1995. Mem. ASCD, Coun. Exceptional Children, Nat. Coun. Tchrs. English, U. Ill. Chgo. Alumni Club, Pi Lambda Theta. Democrat. Roman Catholic. Avocations: triathlons, computer programming, Karate, poetry, pottery. Home: Apt 407 710 Oakton St Evanston IL 60202-2927

POWER, SAMANTHA, academic administrator, writer; b. Ireland, 1970; Grad., Yale U.; Harvard U. Law Sch. Lectr. pub. policy, founding exec. dir. Carr Ctr. for Human Rights, Harvard U.; reporter covering wars in former Yugoslavia US News and World Report and Economist, 1993—96; polit. analyst Internat. Crisis Group. Author: (book) A Problem from Hell: America and the Age of Genocide (Pulitzer prize, 2003); co-editor (with Graham Allison): Realizing Human Rights, 2000. Office: Harvard U John F Kennedy Sch Govt 79 John F Kennedy St Eliot-217 Cambridge MA 02138

POWERS, CLAUDIA MCKENNA, state legislator; b. Key West, Fla., May 28, 1950; d. James Edward and Claudia (Antrim) McKenna; children: Gregory, Theodore, Matthew, Thurston. BA in Edn., U. Hawaii, 1972; MA, Columbia U., 1975. Cert. tchr., N.Y. Mem. Greenwich Rep. Town Meeting, Conn., 1979-93, sec. bldg. com., 1982-84, sec. legis. com., 1986—88, 1990—93; mem. Conn. Ho. of Reps., Hartford, 1993—, ranking mem. govt. adminstrn. and elections com., 1995-96, asst. minority leader, 1997-98, vice chmn. Rep. bill rev. com., 1997—, house minority whip, 1999—2003, dep. minority leader, 2003—, mem. spl. com. of inquiry into impeachment of the gov., 2004. Mem. editl. bd. Greenwich Mag., 1995-98. Conn. commr. Edn. Commn. of the States, 2000—; campaign chmn. Greenwich Rep. Town Com., 1984, 85, chmn., 1986-90; sec. Rep. Round Table, Greenwich, 1988-90; bd. govs. Riverside Assn., Greenwich, 1987-91, sec., 1991-92; class mother Riverside Sch., Greenwich, 1984-90; mem. altar guild Christ Ch., Greenwich, 1990—, lay eucharistic min., 2004—; adminstrv. coord. Greenwich Teen Ctr., 1990-91; alt. del. Rep. Nat. Conv., New Orleans, 1984—, San Diego, 1996; v.p. LWV of Greenwich, 1990-91; bd. trustees Norwalk Maritime Ctr., 2001—; bd. dirs. Gov.'s Prevention Partnership, 2004—. Episcopalian. Home and Office: 15 Hendrie Ave Riverside CT 06878-1808

POWERS, DORIS HURT, retired engineering company executive; b. Indpls., Jan. 17, 1927; d. James Wallace Hurt Sr. and Mildred (Johnson) Devine; m. Patrick W. Powers, Nov. 12, 1950 (dec. 1989); children: Robert W. Powers, Jaye P., Laura S. Powers. Student, So. Meth. U., 1944-45; BS in Engring., Purdue U., 1949; postgrad., U. Tex., W. Tex., 1952-53, Ecole Normale Du Musique, Paris, 1965-68; grad., Harford County Leadership Acad., 1991. Flight instr. Red Leg Flying Club, El Paso, Lawton, Okla., 1951-57; check pilot Civil Air Patrol, El Paso, Lawton, Okla., 1952-57, ground instr. Washington, Tex., Okla, 1957-61; exec. v.p. T&E Internat., Inc., Bel Air, Md., 1979-88, pres., 1989-91; exec. v.p. T.E.I.S., Inc., Bel Air, 1979-88, pres., 1989-91, Shielding Technologies, Inc., Bel Air, 1987-95; retired, 1995. Mem. Purdue U. Engring. Vis. Com., 1999—2002. Mem. Northeastern Md. Tech. Coun., 1991—; bd. dir. Leadership Acad., 1991-94; mem. vis. com. dept. engring. Purdue U., 1998-2002. Recipient Svc. award U.S. Army, 1978, Cert. of Appreciation U.S. Army Test and Evaluation Command, 1988, Woman of Distinction award Soroptimist Club, 1996; selected as Old Master Purdue U., 1995. Mem. CAP (lt. maj. 1951-58), Soc. of Women Engrs. (sr., v.p. 1977, treas. 1979, sec. rep. 1986-88, 98-00, mentor 1986—, spkr. 1978—, selected to Coll. of Fellows 1993), Engring. Soc. Balt. (spkr. 1980—), 99's (pres. 1951-53), Am. Soc. Indsl. Security, Am. Def. Preparedness Assn., Harford County Econ. Devel. Coun., Assn. of U.S. Army, Northeastern Md. Tech. Coun. Avocations: ice dancing, music. Home: 11 Glen Gate Ct Bel Air MD 21014-5682

POWERS, ELIZABETH WHITMEL, lawyer; b. Charleston, S.C., Dec. 16, 1949; d. Francis Persse and Jane Coleman Cotten (Wham) P.; m. John Campbell Henry, June 11, 1994 (dec. Jan. 1997); m. Henry C. B. Lindh, June 16, 2000. AB, Mt. Holyoke Coll., 1971; JD, U. S.C., 1978. Bar: S.C. 1978, N.Y. 1979. Law clk. to justice S.C. Cir. Ct., Columbia; assoc. Reid & Priest, N.Y.C., 1978—86, ptnr., 1986—97; of counsel LeBoeuf, Lamb, Greene & MacRae, N.Y.C., 1997—2004, ptnr., 2004—. Exec. editor S.C. Law Rev., Columbia, 1977-78. Vol. N.Y. Jr. League, N.Y.C., 1983—; bd. dirs. The Seamen's Ch. Inst., 1996—; sec. The Seamen's Ch. Inst., 1999—;

trustee Ch. Club, 1991—94, 1997—2001, v.p., 1992—94. Mem.: Nat. Soc. Colonial Dames in State of N.Y. (pres. 1992—95), Nat. Soc. Colonial Dames of Am. (parliamentarian 1994—2000, regent Gunston Hall 2001—02), S.C. Bar Assn., ABA.

POWERS, GAY HAVENS-MONTEAGLE, artist, educator; b. L.A., Mar. 19, 1946; d. Lionel Standar and Johanne Havens-Monteagle; m. William Pringle, 1969 (div. 1972); m. Joseph Stevens, 1978 (div. 1979). AS in Electronics, Monterey Peninsula Coll., 1972; BA, U. Calif., Davis, 1986; MFA, Mills, 1990. Cert. tchg. multiple subject. Microwave technician Comsat, Carmel Valley, Calif., 1974—79; mgr. univ. art mus. bookstore U. Calif., Berkeley, 1979—80; owner Bonjour Baguette, Davis, Calif., 1981—2000; artist, 2000—; art tchr. Dixon HS, 2003—. One-woman shows include John Natsoulas Gallery, Davis, 1990—2003, exhibitions include Judith Weintraub Gallery, Sacramento, 1989—90, Davis, 1993—, exhibited in group shows at San Francisco Mus. Modern Art Rental Gallery, 1998—2001. Organizer Martin Luther King Freedom Walk, Davis, 1993, Thong Meml. Ann. Awards Dinner, Davis, 1992—93; mem. Human Rels. Commn., Davis, 1993—96. Presdl. grantee, U. Calif. Davis, 1984—86. Mem.: Phi Kappa Phi. Democrat. Home: 1737 E 8th St Davis CA 95616-2408

POWERS, MALA, actress; b. San Francisco, Dec. 20, 1931; d. George Evart and M. Dell (Thelen) P.; 1 child, Toren Michael Vanton. Student, UCLA; studied with Michael Chekhov. V.p. Book Pubs. Enterprises Inc., 1985; internat. lectr. Chekhov Drama Method; entertainer troops USO, Korea, 1951-52; founder, bd. dirs. West Coast Michael Chekhov Drama Group, 1988—; presenter bus. and theater workshops and seminars. Writer, narrator: (sponsored by telephone cos. in various cities) Children's Story, Tele-Story and Dial-A-Story, 1979— (sponsored nationally 1988—); author: Follow the Year, 1985, French edit. 1986; editor: The Secret Seven and the Old Fort Adventure, 1972; rec.: Advent calendar and author book Follow the Star, 1980, Spanish edit., 1981, Italian edit., 1982; films: Cyrano de Bergerac, 1950, Outrage, Edge of Doom, Yellow Mountain, Bengazi, Tammy, Cheyenne, Daddy's Gone A'Hunting, Six Tickets to Hell, 1975;, Hitters, 2003; rec. artist, RCA, records for pre-Christmas, 1977, album Follow the Star; stage prodns. include Absence of a Cello (Broadway), 1964-65; Hogan's Goat, Night of the Iguana, Bus Stop, Far Country, The Rivalry, Mr. Shaw Goes to Hollywood, 2003; also starred in radio and TV prodns. including Medical Story, Ironside, Charlie's Angels; co-star with Anthony Quinn in The Man and the City, 1971-72, Murder She Wrote, 1990. Chmn. So. Calif. Mothers' com. March of Dimes, 1972—; bd. dirs. Layman's Nat. Bible Com., 1981—. Mem. NATAS, Acad. Motion Picture Arts and Scis. (fgn. film com.), ANTA (v.p., exec. com. 1974-75), PEN, Actors Equity Assn.,, Women in Film, Authors Club (London). Mem. Christian Community Ch. Home: 10543 Valley Spring Ln Toluca Lake CA 91602-2852

POWERS, MARIAN, accounting educator; PhD in Acctg., U. Ill. Acctg. faculty Kellogg Grad. Sch. Mgmt. Northwestern U., Evanston, Ill., 1980-88; dept. acctg. U. Ill., Chgo., 1989-92; prof. acctg. Allen Ctr. Exec. Edn., 1987; vis. assoc. prof. acctg. Kellogg Grad. Sch. Mgmt. Northwestern U., 1993—. Rschr. in field. Contbr. articles to profl. jours.; co-author software. Mem. Am. Acctg. Assn., Ill. CPA Assn., European Acctg. Assn., Internat. Assn. Acctg., Edn. and Rsch., Am. Soc. Women Accts. (past pres. Chgo. chpt.), Edn. Found. Women in Acctg. (trustee 1999). Office: The Allen Ctr Northwestern U 633 Clark St Evanston IL 60208-0001

POWERS, PATRICIA KENNETT, retired music educator; b. Detroit, Feb. 25, 1925; d. Frank and Dorothy (Hurley) Kennett; m. Jack Powers, Jr., June 4, 1948; 1 child, Brian K. BA in Music, Kalamazoo Coll., 1946; MA in Music History, U. Mich., 1947. Instr. music U. Ark., Fayetteville, 1947-49; pvt. tchr. music, Corpus Christi, Tex., 1953-62, 68-72, Beeville, Tex., 1972-99; ret., 2002. Adj. instr. group piano, theory, applied piano and organ music Bee County Coll., Beeville, 1974-89. Pres. Beeville Concert Assn., 1992-94. Mem. Music Tchr. Nat. Assn. (cert.), pres. South Ctrl. divsn. 1992-94, bd. dir. 1994-96, South Ctrl. divsn. rep. to ho. of dels. 1996-98), Tex. Music Tchr. Assn. (sec. and pres.-elect, pres. 1986-88, former cert. chmn., and South Ctrl. divsn. rep. on nat. cert. bd.), Am. Guild Organists, Music Educators Nat. Conf., Tex. Music Educators Conf., Midland Music Tchr. Assn. Episcopalian. Avocation: music and computers. Home: 113 Abell Hanger Circle Midland TX 79707 E-mail: ppow@swbell.net.

POWERS, PAULINE SMITH, psychiatrist, educator, researcher; b. Sept. 23, 1941; m. Henry P. Powers; children: Jessica, Samantha. AB in Math., Washington U., 1963; MD, U. Iowa, 1971. Med. intern Emanuel Hosp., Portland, Oreg., 1971-72; psychiatry resident U. Iowa, Iowa City, 1972-74, U. Calif., Santa Barbara, 1974-75; from asst. prof. to assoc. prof. psychiatry Coll. Medicine U. So. Fla., Tampa, 1975-85, prof., 1985—, dir. eating disorder program, 1979—, dir. psychosomatic medicine divsn., 1979—. Author: Obesity: The Regulation of Weight, 1980; editor: The Current Treatment of Anorexia Nervosa and Bulimia, 1984. Fellow: Am. Psychiat. Assn. (Rush Gold Outstanding Exhibit medal 1976, Dorfman Jour. Paper award 1987); mem.: Nat. Eating Disorders Assn. (pres.-elect 2003—), Acad. Eating Disorders ((founding pres.), Women Helping Women award 1995, Profl. Excellence award 1997, Outstanding Clinician award 2000). Office: U So Fla Coll Medicine Dept Psychiatry 3515 E Fletcher Ave Tampa FL 33613-4706 E-mail: ppowers@hsc.usf.edu.

POWERS, REBECCA ANN, psychiatrist, health facility administrator; b. Portland, Oreg., Sept. 28, 1955; m. Gary A. Gusewitch. B in Tech. and Med. Tech., Oreg. Inst. Tech., 1977; M in Pub. Health, Loma Linda U., 1983, MD, 1990. Cert. Am. Bd. Psychiatry and Neurology. Receptionist and vet. asst. Gresham (Oreg.) Vet. Clinic, 1969-77; micobiologist clin. lab. Portland Adventist Med. Ctr., 1977-86; rsch. asst. dept. microbiology Loma Linda (Calif.) U. Med. Ctr., 1987, residency gen. psychiatry, 1990-93; cons. psychiatrist arrowhead home Geriatric Psychiat. Home, San Bernardino, Calif., 1992-93; gen. psychiat. review instr. nat. med. bds. Arc Ventures, Pasadena, Calif., 1992-93; fellowship child and adolescent psychiatry Stanford (Calif.) U. Hosp., 1993-95; psychiat. disability evaluations state Calif. Sunnybrook, Amberstone and Stanford Med. Groups, 1994-95; cons. child and adolescent psychiatry Seneca Ctr. Day Treatment, Fremont, Calif., 1994—; attending staff physician comprehensive pediatric care unit, med. psychiat. unit Stanford U. Hosp., 1995-97, developer and med. dir. clin. faculty co. Terminus Adolescent Alcohol and Drug Treatment Program, 1995-96; pvt. practice physician Child, Adolescent, Adult and Family Psychiatry, Los Gatos, Calif., 1995—; attending for eating disorders clin., clin. faculty co. Terminus Lucile Salter Packard Children's Hosp. at Stanford, 1995—. Founder and pres. Art Soc., 1976-77; planning com. Portland Adventist Med. Ctr., 1982-83, team capt. fund raising program, 1984, cmty svc., 1983-86, instr. clin. lab, 1977-86; cons. pub. health Clackamas County Health Dept., 1983; pub. rels. officer Med. Sch. Class 1990, 1987-90; PULSE rep. Loma Linda U. Sch. Med., 1988-90; rsch. aid, schizophrenia dopamine receptor rsch. Jerry L. Pettis VA Meml. Hosp., Loma Linda, 1991; lecturer Am. Lupus Soc., 1991, Loma Linda U. Med. Ctr., 1992; mem. com. Treatment Improvement Group for anxiety and personality disorders Behavioral Medicine Ctr. Loma Linda U. Med. Ctr., 1991-92;psychiat. evaluations smoking cessation Wellburtin Study Jerry L. Pettis Va Meml. Hosp., Loma Linda, 1992-93; co-founder, pres. elect L.A. Preventive Psychiatry Tak Force So. Calif. Psychiat. Soc., 1992-93; del. Calif. Med. Assn. Calif. House Officer Med. Soc.; developer and coord. Pediatric Psychiatry Lecture Series for pediatricians and other primary care physicians Lucile Salter Packard Children's Hosp. at Stanford, 1994-95; com. Forensic Cmty. Project for Oakland Neighborhood Steering and Oakland Planning Commn., 1994; dir. Pediatric Psychiatry Screening Stanford U., 1994; appointment prevention com. Am. Acad. Child and Adolescent Psychiatry, 1994-97, com. Well Being Physicians Calif. Med. Assn., 1995—, adv. bd. Adult and Adolescent Alcohol and Drug Treatment Program, Stanford U. Hosp, 1995-96; assoc. mem. Consortium Med. Educators in Substance Abuse, 1994; program development adolescent alcohol and drug treatment Stanford U. Med. Ctr., 1995-96; vol. clin. instr. and supervisor Stanford U. Hosp., 1995—. Asst. editor newsletter Lab Lines, 1984-86; planned and presented symposium Everything you always wanted to know about Mediacl Practice, San Bernardino County Med. Soc., 1989; contbr. chpts. to books. Recipient Janssen Clin. Scholar award U.S. Psychiat. and Mental Health Congress, 1994, Presdl. Scholar award Am. Acad. Child and Adolescent Psychiatry, 1995. Mem. AMA, Am. Acad. Child and Adolescent Psychiatry, Am. Assn. Orthopsychiatry, Am. Lupus Soc., Am. Psychiatric Assn., Calif. Acad. Preventive Medicine, Calif. Med. Assn. (com. for Well Being of Physicians), Calif. Soc. Addiction Medicine, Healthy Young 2000, No. Calif. Psychiat. Soc., No. Calif. Region Child and Adolescent Psychiat. Home: 36275 Easterday Way Fremont CA 94536-1671 Office: Stanford U Child Psychiatry 401 Quarry Rd MC 5540 Stanford CA 94305-5540 also: 14651 S Bascom Ave Ste 225 Los Gatos CA 95032-2005

POWERS, RUNA SKÖTTE, artist; b. Anderstorp, Sweden, Oct. 29, 1940; d. Gösta Nils Folke and Kristina Torborg (Andersson) S.; m. David Britton Powers, Mar. 13, 1965; children: Kristina, Davis. Student, Art Inst. So. Calif., 1976-83; BMA, U. So. Calif., 1986. Exhbns. include Newport Festival Arts, Newport Beach, 1980, Costa Mesa Art League, 1980, Orange County Fair, Costa Mesa, 1980, Art Inst. So. Calif., Laguna Beach, 1976-83, Studio Sem Ghelardini, Pietrasanta, Italy, 1983, Design House, Laguna, 1984, Vorpal Gallery, 1983-84, Laguna Beach Mus. Art, 1984, Gallery Sokolov, Laguna Beach, 1985-93, Margareta Sjödin Gallery, Malibu, 1988, Ana Izax Gallery, Beverly Hills, 1988, Envision Art, 1991, Gallery Slottet, Hörle, Sweden, 1990-92, J.F. Kennedy Performing Arts Ctr., Washington, 1991, Internat. Art Expn., L.A., 1985, N.Y., 1986-87, San Bernardino County Mus., 1993. Founder Found. Hörle Manor House, Värnamo, Sweden, 1987—. Avocations: music, reading, cooking, swimming. Home: 1831 Ocean Way Laguna Beach CA 92651-3235

POWERS, THERESA MACK, medical/surgical nurse, psychotherapist; b. Thief River Falls, Minn., June 13, 1928; d. Frank John and Alice Genevieve (Denery) Mack; m. Lester Jean Kile, Nov. 18, 1995; stepchildren: Vickie Nussbaumer, Larry Kile, Jeannie Kendall, Cindy Kile; m. Charles James Powers, Sept. 4, 1948 (div. Sept. 11, 1989); children: Maureen, Pam Toffer, Kevin, Peggy Warren, Laurie, Jeff. RN, O.R. Tech., St. Cloud Sch. of Nursing, St. Cloud, Minn., 1948; RN, Columbia Basin Coll., Pasco, Wash., 1963; BA, Tri City Univ. and Eastern Wash. Univ., Cheney, Wash., 1988; MSW, Eastern Wash. Univ., Cheney, Wash., 1990. Lic. Wash.; LCSW Wash. Oper. rm. tech. Our Lady of Lourdes Hosp., Pasco, Wash., 1948—50; oper. rm. tech. (on call) Kennenick Gen., Kennenick, Wash., 1950—63; oper. nurse, office nurse Ray Rose MD Surgeon, Pasco, Wash., 1965—75, Robert Lukson MD Surgeon, Kennenick, Wash., 1965—75; counselor domestic violence A Woman's Pl., Richland, Wash., 1987—89; psychotherapist Cath. Family Svc., Spokane, Wash., 1990—96; dream therapist/analyst pvt. practice, Spokane, Wash., 1996—. RN Red Cross Blood Dr. Am. Nat. Red Cross, Wash., 1960—76; tchr. music, tap dancing, 1960. Performer comedy. Democrat. Roman Cath. Avocations: piano, reading, sewing, walking, ballroom dancing. Home and Office: 5304 N Wash Spokane WA 99205-5144

POY, VIVIENNE, Canadian senator; b. May 14, 1941; BA, McGill U.; diploma in Fashion Arts, Seneca Coll.; MA in History, postgrad., U. Toronto. Founder Vivienne Poy Mode, 1981—95; pres. Vivienne Poy Enterprises, 1995—, Calyan Pub.; senator The Senate of Can., Ottawa, 1998—. Author: A River Named Lee, Building Bridges: The Life and Times of Richard Charles Lee, Hong Kong, 1905-1983. Chmn. Lee Tak Wai Holdings Ltd.; bd. dirs. Bank of East Asia; gov. McGill U.; hon. patron Chinese Cultural Ctr. Greater Toronto, Chinese Cultural Ctr. Greater Vancouver. Recipient Internat. Women's Day award, 1996, Arbor Award for Outstanding Vol. Svc., U. Toronto, 1997. Liberal. Office: 205 Victoria Bldg The Senate of Canada Ottawa ON Canada K1A 0A4

POYNTER, DEENA ROUSH, elementary school educator, music educator; b. Maryville, Mo., Mar. 13, 1962; d. Charles Amos and Barbara Carmichael Roush; m. Phillip Mark Poynter, July 12, 1997; children: Adam Paul Knorr, Charisse Gabrielle Knorr stepchildren: Jeremy, Jonathan. BS in Elem. and Secondary Music, N.W. Mo. State U., 1984, MS in Edn., 1993. Elem. music tchr. North Andrew Sch. Dist., Bolckow, Mo., 1984—85; mid. sch./H.S. music tchr. N.E. Nodaway Sch. Dist., Ravenwood, Mo., 1985—87; elem. music tchr., gifted coord. North Nodaway Sch. Dist., Pickering, Mo., 1987—2002, elem. music tchr., 2002—. Music dir. First Christian Ch., Maryville, 1991—; piano accompanist N.W. Mo. State U., Maryville, 2002—. Mem. various ch. coms. including worship and fine arts First Christian Ch., Maryville, Mo., 1983—. Mem.: Cmty. Tchrs. Assn., Mo. State Tchrs. Assn., Music Educators Nat. Conf.

POZNIAKOFF, RITA OPPENHEIM, education software consultant; b. Munich, Nov. 19, 1949; (parents Am. citizens); d. Lester and Pearl Tobia (Waldman) Oppenheim; m. Theodore A. Pozniakoff, Dec. 29, 1985. BS, Cen. Mo. State U., 1973. Dept. mgr. Venture Dept. Stores div. May Co., St. Louis, 1973-75; dist. sales mgr. Seven Up Co., St. Louis, 1975-76; account exec. Christmas Club A Corp., Easton, Pa., 1976-83, Bankers Systems Inc., St. Cloud, Minn., 1983-85; edn. svcs. rep. Control Data Corp., Mpls., 1985-86; edn. specialist Radio Shack bus. products Tandy Corp., Ft. Worth, 1986-87, dist. govt. and edn. mktg. mgr., 1987-88, area edn. mktg. mgr., 1988-89, mgr. govt. accounts Grid Systems Corp. div. Parsippany, N.J., 1989; sr. account rep. N.Y.C. schs. Unisys Corp., White Plains, N.Y., 1989-90; mktg. mgr. N.Y. schs. Jostens Learning Corp., Phoenix, 1990-92, TRO Learning, Inc., Edina, Minn., 1993-96; govt. and edn. sales mgr. CompUSA, Inc., N.Y.C., 1996—. Republican. Home and Office: 7004 Boulevard East 3 1-C Guttenberg NJ 07093-5029

POZZO, MARY LOU, retired librarian, writer; b. L.A., Calif., June 18, 1945; d. Clayton Oliver and Violet Elizabeth (Webb) Straub; m. Richard Louis Pozzo, Nov. 10, 1984; stepchildren: Heidi, Peter; m. Richard Lee Horttor, Apr. 15, 1968 (div. 1969). AA, Pasadena C.C., 1965. Asst. legal dept. L.A. City Attys. Office, L.A., 1968—72; sec. fgn. law dept. L.A. County Law Libr., L.A., 1972—78; libr. Musick, Peeler & Garret, L.A., 1979—84, Bronson, Bronson & McKinnon, L.A., 1984—90, Bolton Hall Mus., L.A., 1992—. Pres. Zinnia Press of Tujunga. Author: When Hollywood Came to Sunland-Tujunge-1920-1995, 1997, Founding Sisters: Life Stories of Tujunga's Early Women Pioneers 1886-1926. Trustee Verdogo Hills Cemetary, Tujunga, Calif., 1992—; regional v.p. Calif. Conf. Hist. Socs., L.A.; docent Bolton Hall Mus., Tujunga, 1992—; co-founder Sunland-Tujunga Historic Home & Garden Tour. Mem.: Sunland-Tujunga Little Landers Hist. Soc. (pres. 1995—96), The Westerners L.A. Corral, Sunland-Tujunga Women's Club, Bus. & Profl. Womens Club (Cmty. Woman of Yr. award 1998). Avocations: travel, reading, gardening, cooking, animal rescue. Home and Office: 10966 Hillhaven Ave Tujunga CA 91042

PRACHAR, MICHELE C. elementary school educator; b. Trenton, NJ, Apr. 3, 1978; d. Barbara and John Hanusi; m. Alan M. Prachar, June 11, 2000. B.A. in Early Childhood Edn., Montclair State U., 1996—2000. Elementary School Teacher NJ., 2001. Tchr. fourth grade Lincoln Ave. Sch., Orange, NJ, 2000—01; tchr. seventh grade lang. arts Lakewood (NJ) Mid. Sch., 2001—. Tchr. counselor Camp Victory, South Toms River, NJ, 2002—. Mem.: ASCD (assoc.), Lakewood Edn. Assn. (assoc.; assn. rep. 2002—03), Phi Sigma Sigma - Epsilon Theta Chpt. (life; pres. 1999—2000, Bertha S. Bodian Meml. Scholarship 1999). Office: Lakewood Middle School 755 Somerset Ave Lakewood NJ 08701 Personal E-mail: mprachar@optonline.net.

PRADERE, SONIA, accounting administrator; b. Bklyn., Sept. 22, 1965; d. Miguel Mercado and Candita P.; m. Mario Pradere, July 18, 1986; children: Michael, Stephanie. BS in Human Resource Mgmt., Palm Beach Atlantic Coll., 1995; M Acctg., Nova Southeastern U., 1998. Asst. controller Diversified Comms., Inc., West Palm Beach, Fla., 1990-95; sr. acct. Oxbow Corp., West Palm Beach, 1995-99; acctg. mgr. Sara Lee Branded Apparel, West Palm Beach, 1999—. Office: Prado Medical Park Inc 485 NE 28th Rd Boca Raton FL 33431-6830

PRAEGER, SANDY, state legislator; b. Oct. 21, 1944; m. Mark A. Praeger. Student, U. Kans., 1966. V.p. Douglas County Bank; mem. Kans. Senate from 2nd dist., Topeka, 1992—. Vice chmn. Douglas County Rep. Cent. Com.; chmn. Leadership Kans.; pres. bd. dirs. United Way. Home: 3601 Quail Creek Ct Lawrence KS 66047-2134 Office: Kans State Senate State Capitol Rm 128S Topeka KS 66612

PRAGER, ALICE HEINECKE, music company executive; b. N.Y.C., Aug. 2, 1930; d. Paul and Ruth (Collin) Heinecke; m. George L. Drescher, 1963. BA, Russell Sage Coll., 1951; postgrad., NYU, 1952-55. V.p. SESAC Inc., N.Y.C., 1956-73, pres., 1973-78, pres., chmn. bd., 1978-92. Chmn. bd. Personal Touch, Inc. Mem. Internat. Radio and TV Soc., Am. Inst. of Mgmt., NARAS, Country Music Assn. (bd. dirs., 1986, life), Gospel Music Assn. (life). Office: The Personal Touch Inc 68-34 Fleet St Forest Hills NY 11375-5051 E-mail: apd3700@aol.com.

PRAGER, SUSAN WESTERBERG, law educator, provost; b. Sacramento, Dec. 14, 1942; d. Percy Foster Westerberg and Aileen M. (McKinley) P.; m. James Martin Prager, Dec. 14, 1973; children: McKinley Ann, Case Mahone. AB, Stanford U., 1964, MA, 1967; JD, UCLA, 1971. Bar: N.C. 1971, Calif. 1972. Atty. Powe, Porter & Alphin, Durham, N.C., 1971-72; acting prof. law UCLA, 1972-77, prof. Sch. Law, 1977—, Arjay and Frances Fearing Miller prof. of law, 1992-99, assoc. dean Sch. Law, 1979-82, dean, 1982-98; provost Dartmouth Coll., Hanover, N.H., 1999—. Bd. dirs. Pacific Mut. Life Holding Co., Newport Beach, Calif. Editor-in-chief, UCLA Law Rev., 1970-71. Trustee Stanford U., 1976-80, 87-97. Mem. ABA (council of sect. on legal edn. and admissions to the bar 1983-85), Assn. Am. Law Schs. (pres. 1986), Order of Coif. Address: Dartmouth College Office of the Provost 6004 Parkhurst Hall Rm 204 Hanover NH 03755-3529

PRAGER-KAMEL, NANCY ANN, investment banker, artist, business development firm executive; b. N.Y.C., Mar. 17, 1943; d. Sigmund Godfrey and Eleanor Pauline Prager; BA Cooper Union, MS, Maxwell Sch. Polit. Sci. Syracuse U., BFA, Accademia de Belle Arte, Florence, Italy, 1964-65; m. Barry Lawrence Benett, June 19, 1966 (div.); children: Lara Christina, Andrew Bernard, Ariane Alison; m. Ahmed Abdul Monein Kamel, Aug. 28, 1993. Founder, pres. Boskoff-Präger Group Ltd.; pres., founder ARK Devel. Group, 1992-, mng. dir., gen. ptnr. Wolff Investment Group, 1996-98, mng. dir. investment banking Bottom Line Fin. Group, 1998-99; sr. v.p. bus. devel. Resource Recovery Assocs. Inc., 1998-99; exec. v.p., head investment banking U.S. Securities and Futures, 1999—; pres. Lampert Bros. Internat.; pres. Lempert Bros. Internat. USA, 2003—. Dir. Bus. devel. Merchant Bank-Continental Capital; mng. dir. Selby; past dir. World's Children's Day NGO, U.N., 1984-91. Work exhibited in mus. and univ. one woman and group shows, U.S., Can., Turkey, Italy, France, Eng., also Am. Consulate, Istanbul, Turkey, Resim ve Hey Kel Mus., Dolmabahce Palace, Istanbul, UN; represented pvt. and corp. collections, U.S., Italy, Eng., Turkey, Can., France; tchr. Met. Mus. Art and Black Emergency Cultural Coalition, State of N.Y. Prison System; dir. aux. events Suliman the Magnificent Exhbn.; prodr. Dance exhbn. at Costume Inst. Met. Mus., 1986-87. Chmn. bd. Prep. Sch. Mannes Coll. Music, 1975-76. Author: Turkish Costumes in the Collection of Metropolitan Museum. Bd. dirs. Georgetown U. Sch. Lang. and Linguistic, Amalfi Coast Consortium, TV Acad. Arts and Sci., Acad. Arts and Sci., Am. Ballet Theatre II, Mid. East Ctr. Conservation and Preservation, Human Rights Watch, Fgn. Press Assn., Vital Voices for Women, Global Acad.; dir. for devel. and pub. rels. UN World Children's Day; bd. dirs. UNICEF (vice chmn. exec. bd. N.Y. Metro Area), 1991-2002; adv. Global Acad. Head U.N. Artists Group. Recipient Prix de Paris, 1975, Grand Prix Humanitaire de France, 1976. Bd. dirs. Immigration and Refugee Svc. Am. Mem. Am.-Scandinavian Found., Les Surindependants Societaire, Graphic Art Assn., Am. Italian Found. Cancer Research (bd. dirs., editor Research for Life), Smithsonian Assos., Met. Mus., Archaeology Inst. Am. Presbyterian. Club: Saltaire Yacht (bd.). Work noted in Artist USA Bicentennial, N.Y. Art Yearbook, Nouvelle Littaire, Art News Mag., Arts Mag., Fine Art Mag., 2002. Office: 667 Madison Ave New York NY 10021 E-mail: npk@lempertusa.com.

PRAGUE, EDITH G. state legislator; b. Methuen, Mass., Nov. 23, 1925; m. Franklyn Prague, 1946; 4 children. BS, MA, Ea. Conn. State U.; MSW, U. Conn. Newspaper columnist, Columbia, Conn.; mem. Dist. 19 Conn. Senate, Hartford, 1995—. Mem. Columbia Bd. Edn., 1977-82, Conn. Ho. of Reps.; del. White House Conf. on Aging, 1980—; commr. State Dept. Aging, Mass., 1991-93. Mem. Beta Sigma Phi Internat. (First Lady of Yr. 1986). Democrat. Office: Conn Senate Rm 3800 Legislative Office Bldg Hartford CT 06106

PRAIRIE, CELIA ESTHER FREDA, biochemistry educator; b. Buenos Aires, Sept. 30, 1940; came to U.S., 1963; d. Rafael Emilio A. and Celia Esther (Seijo) Freda; m. James Roland Prairie, Sept. 19, 1970; children: James Roger, Caryn Elizabeth. BS, U. Buenos Aires, 1961, MS, 1963; PhD, U. Pa., 1967. Fellow Nat. Rsch. Inst., Buenos Aires, 1961-63; rsch. assoc. dept. therapeutic rsch. U. Pa., Phila., 1967-70; postdoctoral rsch. assoc. Lab. Molecular Embryology, Arco Felice, Naples, Italy, 1970; lectr. biology and chemistry depts. Holy Family Coll., Phila., 1974-75, asst. prof. biology dept., 1975-80, assoc. prof., 1980-85, prof. biochemistry, 1985—, chmn. dept. natural scis. and math., 1986-88, acting chmn. biology dept., 1982-86. Sr. teaching staff assoc. Marine Biol. Lab., Woods Hole, Mass., 1968-69. Contbr. articles to profl. jours. Bd. dirs. Lower Bucks County Community Ctr., 1970—. Fellow USPHS, 1963-65, U. Pa., 1965-66, Am. Coun. Edn. and Fund for the Improvement of Post Sec. Edn., 1983-84. Mem. AAAS, Nat. Sci. Tchrs. Assn., Am. Inst. Biol. Scis., N.Y. Acad. Scis., Sigma Xi, World Federalist Assn. Democrat. Mem. Religious Soc. of Friends. Avocations: tai chi, yoga, swimming. Home: 31 Full Turn Rd Levittown PA 19056-1924 Office: Holy Family Coll Frankford and Grant Ave Philadelphia PA 19114-2094

PRAIRIE-STEBER, CHERYL LEE, art educator, graphics designer; b. Mannheim, Germany, July 1, 1964; d. Dean Joseph and Ursula Helga Prairie; m. Alan Lee Steber, Feb. 5, 1988; 1 child, Johannes Nikolaus Lee Steber. Degree in German Kindergarten Edn., Alice Schule, Giessen, Germany, 1985; BA, Ill. State U., 1997, BS (hon.), 2002. Kindergarten tchr. Katholic Kirche Buseck, Buseck, Germany, 1985—87, Gemeinde Reiskirchen, Germany, 1988; substitute tchr. Normal (Ill.) Sch. Dist., 1998—2003; art educator El Paso (Ill.) Cmty. Unit Sch. Dist., 2003—. Graphic designer, Hudson, Ill., 2001—; art instr. City of Bloomington, 2003—. Logo, Ill. Art Edn. Assn. Ctrl. Coun., poster, American Beauty (Seymour Better Design award, Best of Show in Design, 2003). Grantee, Sun Found., 2003. Mem.: Ill. Art Edn. Assn., Nat. Art Edn. Assn., Golden Key Honor Soc. (life). Avocations: quilting, watercolor, bookdesign, reading. Home: PO Box 133 Hudson IL 61748 Office: El Paso HS 600 N Elm Street El Paso IL 61738

PRANSKY, JOAN E. lawyer, community organizer; b. N.Y.C., Apr. 26, 1946; d. John and Sharon (Harris) P.; 1 child, Leah. BS, Syracuse U., 1967; JD, Seton Hall U., 1974. Bar: N.J. 1974, U.S. Dist. Ct. N.J. 1974. Social worker Dept. Social Svcs., N.Y.C., 1967; elem. sch. tchr. V.I. Bd. Edn., St. Thomas, 1968; lawyer Essex-Newark Legal Svcs., 1974-83; supervising trial atty. Urban Legal Clinic, prof. Rutgers U. Sch. Law, Newark, 1983-86; atty. in pvt. practice Montclair, N.J., 1986—; atty., N.J. State Bar fellow Seton Hall Law Sch. Ctr. for Social Justice, Newark, 1992-94. Legal counsel N.J. Tenant Orgn., 1984—; legal counsel, advisor City-wide Tenant Orgns., East Orange, Newark, Paterson, Elizabeth, Orange, Jersey City, 1976-90; adv. mem. N.J. State Com. on Rent Control,, N.J. State Com. on Multifamily Dwellings, 1983-85. Editor, co-founder Shelterforce, 1976-85; contbr. articles to N.Y. Times, others. Bd. dirs. N.J. Citizen Action, 1990-94; mem. budget adv. com. Montclair Bd. Edn., 1996; co-founder Support Integrated Pub. Edn., Montclair, 1996; co-founder, mem. steering com. Montclair Civil Rights Coalition, 1997. Recipient Equal Justice medal Legal Svcs. N.J., 1989, Ronald B. Atlas Meml. award N.J. Tenant Assn., 1988, Cmty. Svc. award N.J. Citizen Action, 2002; named one of Women You Should Know, YWCA, 1999. Mem. N.J. State Bar, N.J. Nat. Lawyers Guild. Avocations: singing in chorus, hiking, whitewater rafting, jogging. Home: 11 Stephen St Montclair NJ 07042-5031 Office: 460 Bloomfield Ave Montclair NJ 07042-3552

PRATHER, LENORE LOVING, former state supreme court chief justice; b. West Point, Miss., Sept. 17, 1931; d. Byron Herald and Hattie Hearn (Morris) Loving; m. Robert Brooks Prather, May 30, 1957; children: Pamela, Valerie Jo, Malinda Wayne. BS, Miss. Univ. Women, 1953; JD, U. Miss., 1955; D (hon.), Miss. Univ. Women, 2003. Bar: Miss. 1955. Practice with B. H. Loving, West Point, 1955-60; sole practice, 1960-62, 65-71; assoc. practice, 1962-65; mcpl. judge City of West Point, 1965-71; chancery ct. judge 14th dist. State of Miss., Columbus, 1971-82, supreme ct. justice Jackson, 1982-92, presiding justice, 1993-97, chief justice, 1998-2001; interim pres. Miss. U. for Women, Columbus, Miss., 2001—02. V.p. Conf. Local Bar Assn., 1956-58; sec. Clay County Bar Assn., 1956-71 1st woman in Miss. to become chancery judge, 1971, and supreme ct. justice, 1982, and chief justice, 1998-2000. Mem. Miss. State Bar Assn., DAR, Rotary, Pilot Club, Jr. Aux. Columbus Club. Episcopalian.

PRATHER, SOPHIE S. educational administrator; b. Selmer, Tenn., Jan. 23, 1948; d. Argie D. and Doris Prather; 1 child, Kimberly. BEd, Lane Coll., Jackson, Tenn., 1969; MEd, Trevecca U., Nashville, 1987. Cert. ednl. adminstr. K-12, Tenn. Tchr. Milw. Pub. Schs., 1971-72, Juneau Acad., Milw., 1972-76, McNairy County Schs., Selmer, 1977-93; psychiat. tchr. counselor Timber Springs Adolescent Ctr., Bolivar, Tenn., 1993-95, prin., 1995-96, program dir., 1996-98; supr. spl. edn. McNairy County Schs., Selmer, 1998—. Mem. McNairy County Devel. Bd. 1998, McNairy County Health Coun. Adv. Bd., 2001—; mem. bd. trustees Western Mental Health Inst.; mem. adv. coun. S.W. Headstart, McNairy County Family Resource Ctr.; mem. DCS Child Abuse Rev. Team; mem. S.W. Commn. on Children and Youth. Mem. NEA, NAFE, Tenn. Edn. Assn., Phi Delta Kappa, Delta Kappa Gamma. Methodist. Avocations: crafts, embroidery. Office: Spl Edn Ctr 491 High School Rd Selmer TN 38375-3252 E-mail: prathers@k12tn.net

PRATHER, SUSAN LYNN, public relations executive; b. Melrose Park, Ill. d. Horace Charles and Ruth Anna Paula (Backus) P.; divorced. BS, Ind. U., 1973, MS, 1975. Arts administr. Lyric Opera Chgo., 1975; jr. account exec. Morton H. Kaplan Assocs., Chgo., 1976-78, sr. account exec., 1978-81; account supr. Ketchum Pub. Relations, Chgo., 1981-83, v.p., 1983-87, v.p., group mgr., 1985-87; v.p., dir. pub. relations Cramer-Krasselt, Chgo., 1987-95, sr. v.p., dir. pub. rels., 1996—. Cons. Velamints, Foster Wheeler, Kellogg Co., Battle Creek, Mich., 1985—, Village of Rosemont, Ill., PrincCo Personal Comm., Sr. Friendlys, Anti-Cruelty Soc. Chgo., Ill. State Toll Hwy. Authority. Singer various recitals; founder, dir. Chgo. Sports Hall of Fame, 1976-81. Mem. archives com. Chgo. Symphony Orch., 1986—, mem. long term planning com., 1987-89; mem. press advance team Papal Visit to Chgo., 1978; mem. White House Press Advance Team, Chgo., 1976-80. Mem. Pub. Rels. Soc. Am. (bd. dirs. Chgo. chpt. 1987—), Internat. Pub. Rels. Assn., Publicity Club (bd. dirs. 1986—, Merit award 1982, Golden Trumpet awards, Silver Trumpet awards), Bus. and Profl. Assn. Lutheran. Avocation: figure skating. Home: 155 N Harbor Dr Apt 2212 Chicago IL 60601-7321

PRATT, ALICE S. music educator; b. Rochester, N.Y., Sept. 28, 1952; d. Nunzio and Elisa Pierleoni Sciscioli; m. Ronald J. Pratt, Aug. 23, 1975; children: Rebecca, Kathryn. BS in Music Edn., Nazareth Coll., 1974. Permanent tchrs. cert. N.Y. Page Rochester Pub. Libr., 1970—73; pvt. piano tchr. Rochester, 1973—; vocal music tchr. Rochester City Schs., 1974—. Presenter in field. Composer: America, America, 2003, Seven Days of Kwanzaa, 2003, various childrens songs for chorus and Orff ensemble. Recipient Rochester Philharm. Music Educator's award, Rochester Philharm. Orch., 1994. Mem.: N.Y. State Sch. Music Assn. (elem. classroom chair 1996—98), Am. Orff Schulwerk Assn. (pres. Greater Rochester chpt. 1985—87, 1994—96), Music Educators Nat. Conf. Avocations: cultural events, camping, travel, gardening, reading. Home: 352 Pine Brook Dr Rochester NY 14616 Office: Rochester City Sch 321 Post Ave Rochester NY 14616

PRATT, CARIN, television executive; b. Marshfield, Mass., Aug. 22, 1956; m. John Echeverria; children: Nicholas, Edward. BA, Harvard U., 1978. Staff mem. Nieman Found. Harvard U., Boston, 1977-79; staff mem. Tex. R.R. Commn. Campaign, 1979-80; asst. to Tex. bur. chief Washington Post, Austin, 1981-83, rschr., 1981-83, editor, 1981-83; asst. to assoc. prodr. Face the Nation CBS News, N.Y.C., 1984-87, sr. prodr. Face the Nation, 1987-93, exec. prodr., Face the Nation with Bob Schieffer, 1993—. Office: CBS News 2020 M St NW Washington DC 20036-3369

PRATT, CHRISTINA CARVER, social work and women's studies educator; b. N.Y.C., Dec. 5, 1951; d. Harry S. and Frances Carver (Shaw) P.; 1 child, Cherish Marie. AAS, Rockland U., 1973; BA, Fairleigh Dickinson, 1975; MSW, Columbia U., 1976; D, CUNY. Cons., educator Orange County Cmty. Mental Health, Goshen, NY, 1976-80; prof. social work and gender studies Dominican Coll., Orangeburg, N.Y., 1980—; prof. social work and women's studies NYU, N.Y.C., 1985—98. Exec. dir. Ptnrs. of Ams., Rockland, NY, 1987—97; tng. cons. Govt. of St. Lucia, 1987—93; commr. Coun. on Social Work Edn., Washington, 1990—93; del. NGO Forum-4th World Conf. on Women, 1995; trustee Green Meadow Waldorf Sch., NY, 1996—2000; bd. dirs. Hopf Enterprises, Englewood, NJ. Film maker (video documentaries) India: The Cultural Past, 1985, India: Rural Villages and Urban Villagers, 1986, Tunisia, 1990; editor Jour. Social Devel., 1987—; contbr. articles to profl. jours. Fulbright scholar, India, 1981, Pakistan, 1983; Malone Faculty fellow Nat. Coun. U.S./Arab Rels., Tunisia, 1989, Israel, Syria, Jordan and Palestine, 1991. Mem. NASW, NOW, AAUW, Amnesty Internat., Am. Adoption Congress. Buddhist. Avocations: jazz, opera, hiking, photography, cooking. Office: Dominican Coll 470 Western Hwy Orangeburg NY 10962-1210

PRATT, IRENE AGNES, state legislator; b. Jaffrey, N.H., Mar. 30, 1924; m. Philip E. Pratt (dec.); 4 children. Student, U. N.H., Mass. Gen. Sch. Nursing, 1946. N.H. state rep.; mem. children and family law com. N.H. Ho. of Reps.; ret. pub. health nurse Dept. Health, N.H., 1988. Bd. dirs. Monadnock Family Svc., 1984-89, Big Bros. & Big Sisters of Monadnock Region, 1984-89; active Home Health Care & Cmty. Svc.; Keene Interdisciplinary Child Abuse Team, 1980-88. Mem. C&H Health Sys. Monadnock Region. Office: NH State Senate Legislative Office Bldg Concord NH 03301

PRATT, JOAN M. comptroller; b. Balt., Jan. 15; BS, Hampton Univ., 1976; M, U. Balt., 1978. Comptroller Office of Mayor, Balt., 1995—. Office: Office of Comptroller City Hall 100 N Holliday St Ste 204 Baltimore MD 21202-3417

PRATT, KATHERINE MERRICK, environmental consulting company executive; b. Alexandria, Egypt, July 4, 1951; d. Theodore and Bettie (Curland) R.; m. Harry Kenneth Todd (div.); 1 child, Kirsten Todd Pratt. BBA in Mgmt. Systems, U. Iowa, 1980; postgrad., U. Tex., 1985-87. Program data mgr. Rockwell Internat., Dallas, 1981-85; support coord. GTE Govt. Systems, Taunton, Mass., 1987-89, support engr., 1989-93; pres. Enviro-Logistics Inc., Harwood, Md., 1993—; sole Internat. Soc. Logistics. Recipient Rear Admiral Bernard Eccles award, 1997, Cert. Commendation for Superior Performance as Dist. Dir., 1997. Mem. Soc. Logistics Engrs. (officer, mem. standing com. environ. applications, bd. dirs. New Eng. dist. 1996, dir. New Eng. dist., nat. chpt. newsletter judge), U.S. Pony Club (Ctrl. New Eng. championship chmn., nat. recognition for outstanding contbn. 1997). Avocations: sailing, reading, equitation. Office: Enviro-Logistics Inc PO Box 723 West River MD 20778-0723 E-mail: envirolog@earthlink.net

PRATT, MARY, retired educator; b. Bridgeport, Conn., Nov. 30, 1918; d. William Young Pratt and Daisy Edna Gore. BS, Boston U., 1940; MS, U. Mass. Tchr. Quincy (Mass.) Sch. Dept., 1941-65, 68-86; profl. baseball player All Am. Girls Profl. Baseball League, Chgo., 1943-47; recreation supr. Quincy, 1948-68; assoc. prof. Salem (Mass.) State U., 1965-68; tchr. Braintree (Mass.) Sch. Dept., 1986-88, ret., 1988. Mem., archivist Mass. Assn. Health, Phys. Edn., Recreation and Dance, 1941-88. Named Hon. Aux., Sargent Coll., Boston, 1939, Twiness, 1940. Mem. Mass. Interscholastic Athletic Assn., Boston U. Alumni Assn., Sargent Coll. Alumni Assn., Boston U. Hall of Fame (Moose Washburn award 1990), Weymouth Tennis and Fitness Club, Nat. Fedn. H.S. Assn. Hall of Fame. Avocations: gardening, tennis. Home: 1428 Quincy Shore Dr Quincy MA 02169-2333

PRATT, MARY LOUISE, librarian, writer; b. Iowa City, Iowa, May 31, 1953; d. William Winston and Helen Virginia Pratt. BA in Eng., Pa. State U., 1974; MLS, Clarion U. Pa., 1987. Dir. written comm. The Fine Arts Connection, State College, Pa., 1980—81; mgr. Unimarts, Inc., State College, 1981—84; reference libr. Evansville-Vanderburgh County Pub. Libr., Ind., 1987—88; ref. libr. Cabell County Pub. Libr., Huntington, W.Va., 1989—96, adult svcs. coord., 1996—. Cons. br. libr. Cabell County Pub. Libr., Huntington, 1989—, pub. computer instr., 1998—. Actor: (plays) A Christmas Carol, Deathtrap, The Boys Next Door; editor: (jour.) Rural Libraries; columnist: Who Said it?; author: (poem) Mr. Lonely in the City (1st pl. Ctrl. Pa. Festival of Arts Poetry Competition., 1977, 1st pl. Calamity Cafe Poetry Slam, 1999); contbr. articles to profl. jours. Mem. Cabell-Huntington Coalition for the Homeless, W.Va., 1998—2003. Mem.: W.Va. Libr. Assn., ALA, Guyandotte Poets, Acad. Am. Poets (assoc.). D-Conservative. Presbyterian. Avocations: acting, autograph collecting, hiking, travel. Home: 1368 13th St Huntington WV 25701 Office: Cabell County Pub Libr 455 9th St Plaza Huntington WV 25701 Office Phone: 304-528-5700. Personal E-mail: mlpratt007@aol.com. E-mail: mpratt@cabell.lib.wv.us.

PRATT, RENEE GILL, state legislator; BA, Dillard U.; MEd, U. New Orleans. Teacher; mem. for dist. 91 La. Ho. of Reps., Baton Rouge, 1991—. Named Spl. Educator of Yr. Mem. Nat. Honor Soc., Alpha Kappa Mu. Democrat. Roman Catholic. Office: 1636 Toedano St Ste 304 New Orleans LA 70115 Address: 1636 Toledano St Ste 304 New Orleans LA 70115-4542

PRATT, SUSAN G. architect; b. Kansas City, Mo., Sept. 24, 1951; d. John Bohman and Alice Marguerite (Harris) Grow; m. W. Scott Pratt; children: David, Alice; stepchildren: David, Laura. BArch, Kans. State U., 1973. Registered architect, Mich., Wis. Project arch. Skidmore Owings & Merrill, Chgo., 1973-78, 83-85, Murphy/Jahn, Inc., Chgo., 1978-82, 86—, now v.p.; sr. project arch. Froelich & Marik, L.A., 1982-83, Marshall & Brown, Kansas City, 1985-86. Prin. works include New World Ctr., Hong Kong, Group Repertory Theatre, North Hollywood, Calif., Bi State Indsl. Park, Kansas City, Mo., State of Ill. Ctr., Chgo., John Deere Harvester Works Office Facility, Moline, Ill., Two Liberty Pl., Phila., Livingston Pla., Bklyn., North Loop Block 37, Chgo., 1st and Broadway, L.A., Kudamm 119, Berlin, Cologne/Bonn Airport, Cologne, Jeddah Airport, Saudi Arabia, Sony European Hdqrs., Berlin, Munich Airport Ctr., 21st Century Tower, Shanghai, China, South Pointe Condominiums, Miami Beach, Kaufhof Dept. Store, Chemnitz, Germany, Andersen Cons. Hdqrs., Frankfurt, Germany, Deutsche Post Hdqrs., Bonn, Shen Zhen Conv. Ctr., China, Mannheim (Germany) Ins. Co. Hdqrs., Skyline Towers, Munich, Kempinski Hotel, Tokyo Sta., Tokyo, Am. Airlines Terminal, Chgo., Horizon Serono Headquarters, Geneva, Switzerland. Mem. First Presbyn. Ch., Evanston, Ill. Mem. AIA (corp. mem.). Presbyterian. Office: Murphy/Jahn 35 E Wacker Dr Ste 300 Chicago IL 60601-2157 Office Phone: 312-427-7300. E-mail: sspratt@msn.com.

PRATT, SUZANNE, producer, reporter; BA in History, Tulane U.; MS in Journalism, Columbia U. Reporter Bucks County Courier Times, Pa.; reporter, editor McGraw-Hill News; with. N.Y. bur. Nightly Bus. Report, N.Y.C., 1990—, sr. prodr., reporter, 1997—; contbr. Morning Bus. Report, Miami. Office: NBR 74 Trinity Pl New York NY 10006-2003

PRAZAK, BESSMARIE LILLIAN, science educator; b. Chgo., June 6, 1941; d. William Felix and Bess Blanch (Kostka) Kolar; m. Charles J. Prazak III, June 15, 1963; 1 child, Robin Marie. BS, Rosary U., 1963; MS, Northwestern U., 1965. Rsch. asst. Argonne Nat. Lab., Lemont, Ill., 1965-68; tchr. Morton Coll., Cicero, Ill., 1968-2000, tchr. emeritus, 2000—. Chair curriculum com. Morton Coll., 1984—2000. Author: Laboratory Manual of Anatomy and Physiology, 1997, Laboratory Manual of Microbiology, 1997, Photo Albums of Anatomy and Physiology Histology, 2002, 2d edit., 2003. Mem. AAAS, Nat. Assn. Biology Tchrs., Ill. Assn. C.C. Biologists (sec.-treas. 1978), Human Anatomy and Physiology Soc. Avocations: painting, photography.

PREBLE, SARAH HAMILTON, art librarian, author, writer; b. N.Y.C., Sept. 19, 1939; d. John Leonard and Elizabeth (Collier) Hamilton; m. Duane Preble, Mar. 13, 1961; children: Jeffrey Hamilton, Kristen Malia. BA in Psychology, U. Hawaii, 1962, MLS, 1980. Reference libr. U. Hawaii, Honolulu, 1981-89; libr. Manoa Pub. Libr., Honolulu, 1989-90; art libr. Hawaii State Libr., Honolulu, 1990—2000; ret., 2000. Co-author: (book) Artforms, 2d edit., 1978, 6th edit., 1998. Bd. dirs. Life of the Land, Honolulu, 1972. Mem.: Authors Guild, Honolulu Acad. Arts, Hawaii Libr. Assn., Contemporary Mus. Home: 3347 Anoai Pl Honolulu HI 96822-1419

PREECE, BARBARA G. librarian; b. Fall River, Mass., July 27, 1952; children: Ellen, Molly. MA, U. Minn., 1979. Coord. tech. and automated svcs. Shawnee Libr. Sys., Carterville, Ill., 1981—85; cataloger So. Ill. U.-Morris Libr., Carbondale, 1985—93, asst. access svcs. libr., 1993—98, dir. for sys. svcs., 1998—2000, acting assoc. dean for tech. and automation svcs., 1999—2000; exec. dir. Boston Libr. Consortium, 2000—. Vis. asst. libr. U. Calif., Davis, 1989—90. Contbr. articles to profl. jours. Mem.: ALA. Office: Boston Library Consortium 700 Boylston St Rm 317 Boston MA 02117 Office Fax: 617-262-0163. E-mail: bpreece@blc.org.

PREECE, LYNN SYLVIA, lawyer; b. Birmingham, Eng., June 13, 1955; d. Norman and Sylvia Florence (James) Preece. LLB, Leeds (Eng.) U., 1976; postgrad., Washington U., St. Louis, 1978-79; JD, Loyola U., 1981. Bar: Ill., 1981. Assoc. Barnes Richardson, Chgo., 1980-86; from assoc. to ptnr. Burditt & Radzius, Chgo., 1986-88; ptnr. Katten Muchin & Zavis, Chgo., 1988-96, Baker & McKenzie, Chgo., 1996—. Adj. prof. John Marshall Law Sch., 1998—. Contbr. articles to profl. jours. Chair customs com. Chgo. Bar Assn., 1986-87, Am. Bar Sect. Internat. Law, Washington, 1993-95, practitioners workshop bd., 1995-97; sec., dir. Women in Internat. Trade, Chgo., 1986-89, British Am. C. of C., Chgo., 1990; dir. Chgo. Internat. Sch., 1994-96. Recipient Gold medal Duke of Edinurghs award Scheme, London, 1973. Mem.: ABA (program officer, coun. mem., newsletter editor 1996—98), Internat. Bar Assn., Ct. Internat. Trade Bar Assn. Avocations: gardening, dogs. Office: Baker & McKenzie Ste 3500 130 E Randolph Dr Chicago IL 60601-6342 Office Phone: 312-861-8022. E-mail: Lynn.S.Preece@Bakernet.com.

PREESHL, ARTEMIS SUSAN, choreographer, actor, director; b. St. Paul, Apr. 15, 1962; d. F. Warren Preeshl and Marcelaine Evelyn (Wotschke) Westergren. BA in French-Psychology with high honors, Bates Coll., 1984; MA in Dance, Ohio State U., 1988; MFA in Drama, U. Ariz., 1989; cert. movement analyst, Laban Inst. Movement Studies, N.Y.C., 1992; cert. Labanotation tchr., Dance Notation Bur., N.Y.C., 1994. Lic. series 7 and 63 Nat. Assn. Securities Dealers; cert. personal trainer Am. Coun. Exercise, 1996. Choreographer, pres. Artemis and The Wild Things, N.Y.C., 1987—; dancer Pooh Kaye & Eccentric Motions, N.Y.C., 1992, Avodah Dance Ensemble, N.Y.C., 1992-93, Elizabeth Strebl/Ringside, N.Y.C., 1993-94; asst. prof. theatre arts and movement specialist Utah State, Utah, 1994—; asst. choreographer Caesar's, Atlantic City, 1994; broker The Wellington Group, N.Y.C., 1994; actor, dance capt. Creative Faires, N.Y.C., 1994-96; media asst. Young & Rubicam, N.Y.C., 1995-96; personal trainer Peninsula Spa, N.Y.C., 1996; with Movement Matters, N.Y.C., 1996; stage mgr. Theater Works USA, 1999—2000; asst. Arthur Andersen, 2000—02; practice adminstr. KPMG, 2002—03; tax preparer H&R Block, 2003. Tchg. assoc. Ohio State U., 1985-88; trainer Aline Fitness, N.Y.C., 1995, In High Form, N.Y.C., 1995; mem. Dance Theater Workshop, 1994-96; co. mem. Love Creek Prodns. Theater, 1994-99; asst. dir. Show Me New York, 1996-97; personal trainer; personal asst. to Ronald A. Wilford, Columbia Artists Mgmt., 1997-98. Actor Fall Prodns., N.Y.C., 1996, Eclipse Pictures, 1997, (soap opera) Diary, The Riant Theatre, 1997-97, Our Town, Steel Magnolias, Measure for Measure, Twelfth night, Macbeth, Romeo & Juliet, Hamlet, The Tempest, Antony & Cleopatra, The Jazz, Winter's Tale, Much Ado About Nothing, As You Like It, Taming of the Shrew, Troilus & Cressida, King Lear, Henry VI, Part I, A Midsummer's Night Dream. Dana scholar Bates Coll., 1981-84; fellow U. Ariz., 1988-89; grantee Lehman Bros., Manhattan Cmty. Arts Fund, Field's Emerging Artist Challenge, Freed of London, Ltd., the Puffin Found., The Fund for Creative Cmtys., N.Y. Found. Arts, Non-Profit Recovery, Dept. Cultural Affairs, N.Y.C., Utah Humanities Coun. Mem. Cum Laude Soc., Phi Beta Kappa. Avocations: horseback riding, scuba diving, swimming, weightlifting.

PREIS, MARY LOUISE, commissioner, former state legislator; b. Jacksonville, Ill., Oct. 10, 1941; m. Frederick G. Preis; children: Elizabeth, John, Mary. BA, U. Strasbourg, France, 1963; MS, Georgetown U., 1967; JD, U. Md. Sch. Law, 1983. Bar: Md. 1983, U.S. Dist. Ct. Md. 1984, U.S. Ct. Appeals (4th cir.) 1986. Tchr. Notre Dame Prep., Balt., 1966—67, Rose Tree Sch., Media, Pa., 1967—69; reporter The Record, Havre de Grace, Md., 1975—79; dir. devel. Loyola H.S., 1979—80; dep. dir. cmty. and govt. rels. Md. Dept. Econ. and Employment Devel., 1983—84; counsel Office Atty. Gen., Balt., 1984—86, asst. atty. gen., 1986—90; lawyer Bel Air, Md., 1991; del. Md. Ho. Reps., Balt., 1991—99; commr. Divsn. Fin. Regulations, Balt., 1999—. Adv. bd. Harford County Econ. Devel., 1992—98; bd. mem. Md. Commn. on Future of Cts., 1995—97, Md. Commn. on Alternative Dispute Resolution, 1997—, Coll. Notre Dame Md., Women in Millennium Com., 1999. Adv. bd. Md. Bar Jour., 1990. Bd. mem. State Bank Suprs. Edn. Found., 1999, United Way of Ctrl. Md., 1995, Rockford Found. Bel Air, 1996, Harford C.C. Found., 1990—99. Recipient Disting. Svc. award, Rte. 40 Bus. Assn., 1998. Mem.: U. Md. Law Sch. Alumni Assn. (bd. mem. 1995), Chesapeake Heritage Conservancy (bd. dirs.), Harford County Bar Assn., Md. Bar Assn. (Exceptional Svc. award 1995).

PREISS-HARRIS, PATRICIA, music educator, composer, pianist; b. N.Y.C., May 19, 1950; d. Fredric H. and Madeline (Robbins) P.; m. Eric A. Lerner, Nov. 1970 (div. 1975); m. William H. Harris, Aug. 13, 1995. BA, Harvard U., 1973; MFA, Calif. Inst. Arts, 1987. Performer, bassist Carla Bley Band, Willow, NY, 1977—78; instr. piano, composition The Hall Sch., Pittsfield, Mass., 1983—84; instr. music Santa Monica (Calif.) C.C., 1989; tchr. piano The Hackley Sch., Tarrytown, NY, 1991; tchr. piano and composition Fraioli Sch. of Music, Greenwich, Conn., 1991—2002; accompanist SUNY, Purchase, NY, 1991—95; performer, pianist Gary Wofsey Jazz Orchestra, 1996—, The Jones Factor Big Band, 1999—. Pvt. piano tchr., NY, 1990—, Conn., 1990—, Mass., 1980—84; pianist Greenwich Regency Hyatt Hotel, 1995—; solo and ensemble pianist, 1980—; accompanist Blue Notes vocal ensemble, 2000—; attendee Cummington (Mass.) Cmty. of Arts, 1981. Performer Trust in Love, 1981; composer, pianist Jamaica's Album, 1984; composer Messages (piano & flute), 1980, Invocations (women's choir, medieval instruments), 1981, Complete Enlightenment (woodwinds, spkr.), 1986. Performance grantee Cambridge (Mass.) Arts Coun., 1977, Artists grantee No. Berkshire Coun. on Arts, 1983 Mem.: Schubert Club. Home: 162 Toms Rd Stamford CT 06906-1031 Office Phone: 203-249-1067. E-mail: patti@pattipreiss.com.

PREMACK, ANN J. writer; b. Shanghai, Jan. 5, 1929; interned in Japanese detention ctr., 1943-45; came to the U.S., 1945; d. John Joseph James and Mae Victoria Parker; m. David Premack, Oct. 26, 1951; children: Ben, Lisa, Tim. BS with distinction, U. Minn., 1951. Author: Why Chimps Can Read, 1975; co-author (with D. Premack): The Mind of An Ape, 1983; co-editor: Causal Cognition: A Multidisciplinary Debate, 1995; co-author (with D. Premack): Original Intelligence: Unlocking the Mystery of Who We Are, 2003, French translation, 2003; contbr. chapters to books, articles to profl. jours. Avocation: owning and running an avocado grove. Home: 6163 Heatherton Dr Somis CA 93066-9716 E-mail: dpremack@aol.com.

PRENDERGAST, CAROLE LISAK, musician, educator; b. Chgo., Mar. 15, 1949; d. Chester Matt and Emily Julie (Krupa) Lisak; m. Joseph Thomas Prendergast, Oct. 19, 1974; children: Karin, Colin. MusB, DePaul U., 1971; MA in Ch. Music and Liturgy, St. Joseph's Coll., Rensselaer, Ind., 2002. Tchg. cert. K-14, Ill. Substitute organist St. Adalbert Ch., Chgo., 1965-76; music tchr. Chgo. Pub. Schs., 1971-74; music dir. St. Adalbert Ch., 1976-88; freelance musician, 1988—; choir accompanist St. Luke Ch., River Forest, Ill., 1993—, music dir., 2000—. Piano tchr., Chgo., 1970—. Chairperson welcome com. Queen of Martyrs Ch., Evergreen Park, Ill., 1990—. Ill. state scholar, 1968-71, DePaul scholar, 1968. Mem. Am. Guild Organists, Nat. Assn. Pastoral Musicians, Music Tchrs. Nat. Assn., Chgo. Fedn. Musicians, Chgo. Area Suzuki Tchrs., Suzuki Assn. of the Ams. Roman Catholic. Avocations: gardening, travel, antique collecting, cooking. Home: 10417 S Hamlin Ave Chicago IL 60655-3115 Office: St Luke Ch 528 Lathrop River Forest IL 60305 Office Phone: 708-771-8250.

PRENTICE, ANN ETHELYND, university dean; b. Grafton, Vt., July 19, 1933; d. Homer Orville and Helen (Cooke) Hurlbut; divorced; children: David, Melody, Holly, Wayne. AB, U. Rochester, 1954; MLS, SUNY, Albany, 1964; DLS, Columbia U., 1972; LittD (hon.), Keuka Coll., 1979. Lectr. sch. info. sci. and policy SUNY, Albany, 1971-72, asst. prof., 1972-78; prof., dir. grad. sch. library and info. sci. U. Tenn., Knoxville, 1978-88; assoc. v.p. info. resources U. South Fla., Tampa, 1988-93; dean Coll. Info. Studies, U. Md., College Park, 1993—, acting asst. v.p. for info. resources, 1994-98. Y2K compliance coord. U. Md., 1998—. Author: Strategies for Survival, Library Financial Management Today, 1979, The Library Trustee, 1973, Public Library Finance, 1977, Financial Planning for Libraries, 1983, 2d edit., 1996, Professional Ethics for Librarians, 1985; editor Pub. Libr. Quar., 1978-81; co-editor: Info. Sci. in its Disciplinary Context, 1990; assoc. editor Library and Info. Sci. Ann., 1987-90. Cons.

long-range planning and pers. Knox County Libr. System, 1980, 85-86, Richland County S.C. Libr. System, 1981, Upper Hudson Libr. Fedn., N.Y., State Libr. Ohio, 1986, Am. U., 1996; trustee Hyde Park (N.Y.) Free Libr., treas., 1973-75, pres., 1976; trustee Mid-Hudson Libr. System, Poughkeepsie, N.Y., 1975-78; trustee adv. bd. Hillsborough County Libr., 1991-93. Recipient Disting. Alumni award SUNY, Albany, 1987, Columbia U., 1991. Mem. ALA, CAUSE, Am. Soc. Info. Sci. (exec. bd. 1986-89, conf. chmn. 1989, pres. 1992-93, chmn. info. policy com. 1994-96), Assn. for Libr. and Info. Sci. Edn. (pres. 1986). Office: Univ Md Coll Libr and Info Svcs 4105 Hornbake Bldg College Park MD 20742-0001

PRENTICE, MARGARITA, state legislator, nurse; Student, Phoenix Coll., Youngstown U.; RN, St. Joseph's Hosp. Sch.; student, U. Wash. RN, Wash. Nurse, Wash.; mem. Wash. Senate, Dist. 11, Olympia, 1988—; majority caucus vice chair Wash. Senate, Olympia, 1993-94; mem. agr. and rural econ. devel. com. Wash. Legislature, Olympia, mem. transp. com. Mem. Dem. Nat. Com. Recipient Legislator of Yr. Retail Assn. and Mortgage Bankers Assn., Wash. Health Care Assn., Wash. State Labor Coun., Wash. State Nurses Assn., Home Health Care Assn., King County Nurse of Yr., Champion of Health Care award Valley Med. Ctr., Disting. Svc. award Wash. Assn. Homes for Aging, Legislator of Yr. Wash. State Dental Hygienists Assn. Mem. ACLU, Amnesty Internat., Wash. State Nurses Assn. (1st v.p. 1968-72, labor officer 1974-78), Sierra Club, Renton Hist. Soc., Audubon Soc., Humane Soc. U.S. Democrat. Office: 419 John Cherberg Bldg Olympia WA 98504-0001

PRENTISS, C. J. state legislator; BA in Edn., Cleve. State U., 1969, MEd, 1975; cert., Kent State U., 1976; grad. Weatherhead Sch. Mgmt., Case Western Res. U., 1978. Mem. Ohio Ho. of Reps. from 8th dist., Columbus, 1990-98, Ohio Senate from 21st dist., Columbus, 1999—; mem. econ. devel., tech. and aerospace com., edn. com., fin. and financial instns. com., health, human svcs. and aging com. Chair edn. policy Ohio legislative Black Caucus and Black elected Democrats of Cleve., vice-chair edn. com. Nat. Conf. State Legislatures; past vice-chair HouseEdn. com., ways and means, ins.; mem. State Bd. Edn., 1984-90, chair lit. and youth-at-risk com., legis. stds. com., past chair joint select com. on infant health and family support. Past Vice-chair Black Leadership Cleve. Alumni; past mem. gov.'s com. Socially Disadvantaged Black Males. Office: Senate Bldg Rm 57 Columbus OH 43215

PRESCOTT, BARBARA LODWICH, educational administrator; b. Chgo., Aug. 15, 1951; d. Edward and Eugenia Lodwich; m. Warren Paul Prescott, Dec. 2, 1979; children: Warren Paul Jr., Ashley Elizabeth. BA, U. Ill., Chgo., 1973, MEd, 1981; MA, U. Wis., 1978; postgrad., Stanford U., 1983-87. Cert. tchr., learning handicapped specialist, cmty. coll. instr., Calif. Grad. rschr. U. Ill., Chgo., 1979-81; learning handicapped specialist St. Paulus Luth. Sch., San Francisco, 1981-83; grad. rsch. asst. Sch. Edn. Stanford (Calif.) U., 1983-87, writing cons. for law students, 1985-86; learning handicapped specialist/lead therapist Gilroy Clinic Speech-Hearing-Learning Ctr., Crippled Children's Soc., Santa Clara, Calif., 1988-89; ednl. dir. Adolescent Intensive Resdl. Svc. Calif. Pacific Med. Ctr., San Francisco, 1989-95; exec. dir. Learning Profiles, South Lake Tahoe, Calif., 1995—. Instr. evening San Jose City Coll., 1988-92. Contbr. articles to profl. jours.; author: Proceedings of Internat. Congress of Linguistics, 1987; editor: Proceedings - Forum for Research on Language Issues, 1986; author videotape: Making a Difference in Language and Learning, 1989. Recipient Frederick Bork Teaching Trainee award San Francisco State U., 1983; Ill. State scholar, 1973. Mem. Calif. Assn. Pvt. Specialized Edn. and Svcs., Phi Delta Kappa (v.p. 1984-86), Pi Lambda Theta (sec. 1982-83), Phi Kappa Phi, Alpha Lambda Theta.

PRESKA, LORETTA A. federal judge; b. 1949; BA, Coll. of St. Rose, 1970; JD, Fordham U., 1973; LLM, NYU, 1978; LHD (hon.), Coll. of St. Rose, 1995. Assoc. Cahill, Gordon & Reindel, N.Y.C., 1973-82; ptnr. Hertzog, Calamari & Gleason, N.Y.C., 1982-92; fed. judge U.S. Dist. Ct. (so. dist.) N.Y., N.Y.C., 1992—. Mem. N.Y. State Bar Assn., N.Y. County Lawyers Assn., Fed. Bar Coun., Fordham Law Alumni Assn. (v.p.). Office: US Courthouse 500 Pearl St Rm 1320 New York NY 10007-1316

PRESKA, MARGARET LOUISE ROBINSON, education historian, administrator; b. Parma, N.Y., Jan. 23, 1938; d. Ralph Craven and Ellen Elvira (Niemi) Robinson; m. Daniel C. Preska, Jan. 24, 1959; children: Robert, William, Ellen Preska Steck. BS summa cum laude, SUNY, 1957; MA, Pa. State U., 1961; PhD, Claremont Grad. Sch., 1969. Instr. LaVerne (Calif.) Coll., 1968-75, asst. prof., asso. prof., acad. dean, 1972-75; instr. Starr King Sch. for Ministry, Berkeley, Calif., summer, 1975; v.p. acad. affairs, equal opportunity officer Minn. State U., Mankato, 1975-79, pres., 1979-92; project dir. Kaliningrad (Russia) Mil. Re-Tng., 1992-96; disting. svc. prof. Minn. State U. Sys., 1993—; pres. Inst. for Effective Tchg. Minn. State U., Winona, 1993—98; owner BuildaBikeInc.com, 2000—. Bd. dirs. XCEL Energy Co., Milkweed Edits.; pres. emerita Minn. State U., Mankato, 1992—; provost, CEO AbuDhabi Campus, Zayed U., United Arab Emirates, 1997-99. Pres. Pomona Valley chpt. UN Assn., 1968-69, Unitarian Soc. Pomona Valley, 1968-69, PTA Lincoln Elem. Sch., Pomona, 1973-74; pres., chmn. bd. Nat. Camp Fire Boys and Girls, 1984-88; mem. Pomona City Charter Revision Commn., 1972; chmn. The Fielding Inst., Santa Barbara, 1983-86; bd. dirs. Elderhostel Internat., 1983-87, Minn. Agrl. Interpretive Ctr. (Farmam.), 1983-92, Am. Assn. State Colls. and Univs., Moscow on the Mississippi - Minn. Meets the Soviet Union; nat. pres. Campfire, Inc., 1985-87; chmn. Gov.'s Coun. on Youth, Minn., 1983-86, Minn. Edn. Forum, 1984; mem. Gov.'s Commn. on Econ. Future of Minn., 1985—, NCAA Pres. Commn., 1986-92, NCAA Cost Cutting Commn., Minn. Brainpower Compact, 1985; commr. Great Lakes Govs.' Econ. Devel. Coun., 1986, Minn Gov.'s Commn. on Forestry. Carnegie Found. grantee Am. Coun. Edn. Deans Inst., 1974; recipient Outstanding Alumni award Pa. State, Outstanding Alumni award Claremont Grad. Sch., YWCA Leader award 1982, Exch. Club Book of Golden Deeds award, 1987; named One of top 100 alumni, SUNY, 1895-1985, 1985, Hall of Heritage award, 1988, Wohelo Camp Fire award, 1989. Fellow Fielding Inst.; mem. AAUW (pres. Mankato 1990-92), LWV, Women's Econ. Roundtable, St. Paul/Mpls. Com. on Fgn. Rels., Am. Assn. Univ. Adminstrs., Rotary, Horizon 100. Unitarian Universalist. Home: 10 Sumner Hls Mankato MN 56001-3931 E-mail: mpreska@hickorytech.net.

PRESLEY, EVA LUISE VON SCHRILTZ, counselor, writer; b. Jamestown, Md., Mar. 3, 1955; d. Armin Ernst and Elizabeth Louise (White) Graber; children: Melissa, Jason, Christopher. BA, Ft. Hays State U., 1974; Tchr. Cert., U. Colo., 1976; AS, Pikes Peak C.C., 1979; MA, U. No. Colo., 1995. Cert. addictions counselor III; cert. counselor; lic. profl. counselor. Mgr. Fontasia Heisley Advt., Colorado Springs, Colo., 1982-85; bus. owner Design-Tech, Colorado Springs, Colo., 1985-90; freelance writer, 1990—; residential adolescent counselor Chins Up, Colorado Springs, 1993; counselor/clinician Pikes Peak Mental Health Ctr., Colorado Springs, 1993-94; counselor Parkview Episcopal Med. Ctr., Pueblo, Colo., 1995-96; clin. dir. Rocky Mountain Behavioral Health, Cañon City, Colo., 1996-97; clin. program coord. Centura Health St. Mary-Corwin Recovery Ctr., Pueblo, 1997—99; crisis evaluator Spanish Peaks Mental Health Ctr., 1999—2000; pvt. practice, 1998—. Team clinician So. Colo. CISM Team, Colorado Springs, 1995-96; vol. Child Abuse Prevention Project, El Paso County Health Dept., Colorado Springs, 1992-93., exec. dir. Alpine Family Counseling Svcs., Inc., 2000—. Mem. bd. United We Stand Women's Svcs., Colorado Springs, 1992-92; co-founder Youth Employment Svc., Colorado Springs, 1992; chair parent steering com. Dare to Be You Parenting Program, Colorado Springs, 1993. Recipient scholarship Nat. Coun. Alcoholism and Drug Dependence, 1992, scholarship AAUW, 1993. Mem. ACA, Internat. Assn. Addictions and Offender Counselors (pres.-elect local chpt.) Republican. Roman Catholic. Avocations: reading, writing fiction, crochet, cooking, stained glass. Office: St Mary-Corwin Recovery Ctr Centura Health 1008 Minnequa Ave Pueblo CO 81004-3733

PRESLEY, LISA MARIE, musician; b. Memphis, Tenn., Feb. 1, 1968; d. Elvis and Priscilla Presley; m. Danny Keough, 1988 (div. 1994), children: Danielle Riley Keough, Benjamin Storm Keough; m. Michael Jackson, 1994 (div. 1997); m. Nicholas Cage, 2002 (div. 2002). Mgmt. Elvis Presley Trust; owner, chmn. bd. Elvis Presley Enterprises, Inc.; co-owner with mother Priscilla Elvis Presley's Memphis nightclub, operated by Presley Estate, 1997—2003. Musician: (albums) To Whom It May Concern, 2003 (cert. Gold), (songs) Lights Out, 2003; actor: (music video) You Are Not Alone, Michael Jackson, (car commercial), 1989; appeared on (cover of Vogue mag.), 1996. Internat. spokesperson Citizens Commn. on Human Rights; co-founder (with Isaac Hayes) LEAP (Literacy, Edn., and Ability Program). Office: Elvis Presley Enterprises Inc PO Box 16508 3734 Elvis Presley Blvd Memphis TN 38186-0508*

PRESLEY, PAULA LUMPKIN, retired editor; b. Des Arc, Ark., June 8, 1938; d. Herbert Eugene and Clara Erline (Jones) Lumpkin; m. Clifton Jay Presley, Apr. 19, 1958 (div. Mar. 1988); children: Richard Jay, Steven James, Susan Jean. BA in History, Truman State U., Kirksville, Mo., 1985, MA, 1989; MLS, U. Iowa, 1991. Copy and prodn. editor Sixteenth Century Jour., Kirksville, 1982—; asst. editor Thomas Jefferson U. Press, Kirksville, 1986-91, assoc. editor, 1991-98; dir., editor-in-chief Truman State U. Press (formerly Thomas Jefferson U. Press), Kirksville, 1998—2003, ret., 2004; owner Paula Presley Editl. Svcs. Editor (Keywords newsletter): Am. Soc. Indexers, 1997—98; editor: Editing History newsletter, 1996—97; co-editor: Habent sua libelli or, Books Have Their Own Destiny, 1998; contbr. chpts. to books; contbg. author: What Else Can You Do with a Library Degree: Career Options for the 90s and Beyond, 1997. Mem.: ALA, Conf. Hist. Jours., Calvin Studies Soc., Soc. for Scholarly Pub., Am. Soc. Indexers (newsletter editor 1997—98), Am. Mensa, Kirksville Rotary Club. Democrat. Presbyterian. Avocations: book indexing, copyediting, research in printing, incunabula, religious history/theology. Home: 820 E Meadow Ln Kirksville MO 63501-2568 Office Phone: 660-627-1359. Personal E-mail: bookwoman2003@yahoo.com.

PRESLEY, PRISCILLA, actress; b. Bklyn., May 24, 1945; m. Elvis Presley, 1967 (div. 1973); 1 child, Lisa Marie. Studied with Milton Katselas; student, Steven Peck Theatre Art Sch., Chuck Norris Karate Sch. Co-owner Bis and Beau Boutique; co-executor, pres. Elvis Presley Enterprise, Memphis. Launched internat. fragnance line. Appearances include (films) The Naked Gun, 1988, The Adventures of Ford Fairlaine, 1990, The Naked Gun 2 1/2, 1991, The Naked Gun 33 1/3, 1994, (TV series) Those Amazing Animals, 1980-81, Dallas, 1983-88, (TV movies) Love Is Forever, 1983, Breakfast With Einstein, 1998, Hayley Wagner, Star, 1999, After Dallas, 2002; prodr. (TV movie) Elvis and Me, 1988; exec. prodr. The Road to Graceland, 1998; author: Elvis and Me, 1989. Office: Michelle Bega c/o Rogers & Cowan 1888 Century Park E Los Angeles CA 90067-1702

PRESLEY, VIVIAN MATHEWS, junior college administrator; b. West Point, Miss., Oct. 12, 1952; d. Beatrus and Lula (Butler) Mathews; m. Dwight Presley, Sept. 12, 1971; 1 child, Julian. BA, Miss. State U., 1973, MA, 1975, Cert. Edn. Specialist, 1978, EdD, 1983. Counselor Coahoma Jr. Coll. (named changed to Coahoma Community Coll.), Clarksdale, Miss., 1975-80; title III coordinator Coahoma Jr. Coll., Clarksdale, Miss., 1981-82, asst. to pres., 1982-83, v.p., 1983—. Vice chairperson Miss. State Council on Vocat. Edn., Jackson, Miss., 1984. Named One of Outstanding Young Woman of Am., 1981, 84, 85, 88. Mem. Nat. Assn. Female Execs., Assn. Univ. Women, Nat. Council for Resource Devel., Psi Kappa Psi, Delta Sigma Theta. Democrat. Methodist. Avocations: reading, biking. Home: 3240 Friars Point Rd Clarksdale MS 38614-9359 Office: Coahoma Community Coll RR 1 Box 616 Clarksdale MS 38614-9801

PRESNELL, JENNY LYNN, librarian; b. Cin., Jan. 24, 1961; d. Joseph Hobart and Carmen Jeanne (Thomas) P. BA in History, Miami U., 1983; MLS, Ind. U., 1984; MA in History, Xavier U., 1992. Libr. Xavier U., Cin., 1984-88, Miami U., Oxford, Ohio, 1988—. Contbr. articles to profl. jours., encys. and books. Mem. ALA, Assn. for History and Computing, Greater Cin. Libr. Consortium. Methodist. Avocations: knitting, gardening. Office: Miami U King Libr Oxford OH 45056 Office Phone: 513-529-3937. Business E-Mail: presnejl@muohio.edu.

PRESPARE, DEBORAH SUN, financial analyst; arrived in U.S., 1976; d. William and Sun Prespare. BA summa cum laude, Cornell Coll., 1998; MA in Writing, Johns Hopkins U., 2003—. Office asst. Am. Embassy, Nairobi, Kenya, 1992—92; statis. rschr./intern Cedar Rapids (Iowa) C. of C., 1997—97; intern FDIC, Washington, 1997—97; fin. systems analyst Fed. Res. Bd., Washington, 1998—. Nominee All-American scholar, Cornell Coll., 1997; scholar, Am. Fgn. Svc. Assn., 1994—98; Presdl. scholar, Cornell Coll., 1994—98. Mem.: Motar Bd., Phi Beta Kappa. Avocations: writing, reading.

PRESS, AIDA KABATZNICK, former editor, writer, poet; b. Boston, Nov. 18, 1926; m. Newton Press, June 5, 1947; children: David, Dina Press Weber, Benjamin Presskreischer. BA, Radcliffe Coll., 1948. Reporter Waltham (Mass.) News-Tribune, 1960-63; freelance writer, 1960-63; editl. cons. Mass. Dept. Mental Health, Boston, 1966-72; Waltham/Watertown reporter Boston Herald Traveler, 1963-70; dir. news and publs. Harvard Grad. Sch. Design, Cambridge, Mass., 1972-78; publs. editor Radcliffe Coll., Cambridge, 1978-81, dir., editor of publs., 1981-83, editor Radcliffe Quar., 1971-93, dir. pub. info., 1983-93; cons. editor Regis Coll. Alumnae Mag., Weston, Mass., 1994. Editor emerita Radcliffe Quar., 1993—; contbr. articles to newspapers and mags. Recipient Publs. Distinction award Am. Alumni Coun., 1974, Top 5 coll. Mag., Coun. for Advancement and Support of Edn., 1984, Top 10 Univ Mags., 1991, Gold medal Coll. Mags., 1991, Alumnae Achievement award Radcliffe Coll., 1994, Radcliffe Coll. Presdl. Commendation, 1992. Mem. Phi Beta Kappa. Avocations: hiking, playing recorder.

PRESS, BETH, publishing executive; Sr. account mgr. Conde Nast's GQ, 1998-99; dir. advt. Teen Magazine, 1999-2000, group pub., 2000—. Office: EMAP USA 6420 Wilshire Blvd Los Angeles CA 90048-5502

PRESSEISEN, BARBARA ZEMBOCH, retired educational director, researcher; b. Dayton, Ohio, June 15, 1936; d. William and Ida (Wise) Zemboch; m. Ernst Leopold Presseisen, June 30, 1963; children: Joshua William, Benjamin David. BA, Brandeis U., 1958; MAT, Harvard U., 1959; EdD, Temple U., 1972. Tchr., counselor Sequoia Union High Sch. Dist., East Palo Alto, Calif., 1959-63; lectr. No. Ill. U., De Kalb, 1963-65; teaching assoc. Temple U., Phila., 1967-69; asst. prof. Swarthmore (Pa.) Coll., 1969-71; curriculum coord. Rsch. for Better Schs., Phila., 1971-75, project dir., 1975-80, asst. dir., 1980-85, dir. nat. networking, 1985-99; ret., 1999. V.p. edn. Nobel Learning Communities, Inc., Media, Pa., 1996-99. Author: Unlearned Lessons, 1985; editor and author: At-Risk Students and Thinking, 1988, Teaching for Intelligence, 1999; contbr. editor: (newsletter) Teaching Thinking and Problem Solving, Phila., 1981-96. Bd. trustees Friends Select Sch., Phila., 1987-95. Mem. ASCD (task force 1981—), Am. Ednl. Rsch. Assn., Pi Lambda Theta (editl. bd. 1983—), Nat. Ind. Pvt. Sch. Assn. (bd. dirs. 1998—), Phi Delta Kappa (Ralph D. Owen scholar 1958), Brandeis U. Alumni Assn. (Phila.). Democrat. Office: 1943 Pine St Philadelphia PA 19103-6616

PRESSER, HARRIET BETTY, sociology educator; b. Bklyn., Aug. 29, 1936; d. Phillip Rubinoff and Rose (Gudowitz) Jabish; m. Neil Nathan Presser, Dec. 16, 1956 (div.); 1 child, Sheryl Lynn. BA, George Washington U., 1959; MA, U. N.C., 1962; PhD, U. Calif., Berkeley, 1969. Statistician Bur. Census, Washington, 1959; research assoc. Inst. Life Ins., N.Y.C., 1962-64; lectr. demography U. Sussex, Brighton, England, 1967-68; staff assoc. Population Council, N.Y.C., 1968-69; asst. prof. sociomed. scis. Columbia U., N.Y.C., 1969-73, assoc. prof. sociomed. scis., 1973-76; prof. sociology U. Md., College Park, 1976—99, dir. Ctr. on Population, Gender, and Social Inequality, 1988—2001, disting. faculty rsch. fellow, 1993-94, disting. univ. prof., 1999—; fellow in residence Netherlands Inst. for Advanced Study in Humanities & Social Sci., Wassenaar, The Netherlands, 1994-95. Fellow-in-residence Ctr. for Advanced Study in the Behavioral Scis., Stanford, Calif., 1986-87, 91-92, 2003-04; bd. dirs. Population Reference Bur., 1993-99; scholar-in-residence Russell Sage Found., N.Y.C., 1998-99,2000; resident scholar Bellagio Study and Conf. Ctr., Rockefeller Found., 2000; acad. visitor Gender Inst. London Sch. Econs and Polit. Scis. Editl. bd. Time and Soc., 1991-95, Social Forces, 1984-87, Signs, 1975-85, Applied Population and Policy, 2002—, Rose Monograph Series, 2003—, Jour. of Marriage and the Family, 2003; assoc. editor Jour. Health and Social Behavior, 1975-78; co-editor (with Gita Sen) Women's Empowerment and Demographic Processes: Moving Beyond Cairo, 2000; author: Working in a 24/7 Economy: Challenges for Am. Families, 2003 Nat. Inst. for Child Health and Devel. grantee, 1972-78, 83-88, Population Coun. grantee, 1976-79, NSF grantee, 1982-83, 90-94, 2000-03, Rockefeller Found. grantee, 1983-85, 88-94, William and Flora Hewlett Found. grantee, 1989—, Andrew W. Mellon Found. grantee, 1994-95, W. T. Grant Found., 1996-99, Russel Sage Found., 1976-79, 2003-; recipient Rosabeth Moss Kanter award for excellence in work-family rsch., 2001, Lawrence R. Klein award, 2003. Fellow AAAS (elected 2002); mem. Population Assn. Am. (bd. dirs. 1972-75, 2nd v.p. 1983, 1st v.p. 1985, pres.-elect 1988, pres. 1989), Am. Pub. Health Assn. (council mem. population sect. 1976-79), Am. Sociological Assn. (coun. mem. at large 1990-93, chmn., coun. mem. population sect. 1978-83), Sociological Rsch. Assn. (elected 1987). Office: U Maryland Dept Sociology College Park MD 20742-0001 Office Phone: 301-405-6422.

PRESSER, JANICE, business executive; b. N.Y.C., Feb. 14, 1946; m. Barry S. Perlman; 2 children. BA, CCNY, 1967; BSN, Columbia U., 1978; MA, Hunter Coll., 1981; PhD, Union Inst., 1990. Pres., CEO The Gabriel Inst., Phila. Libertarian candidate for N.J. House, 1995, 97; Libertarian candidate for U.S. House 3rd dist., N.J., 1996, 98; chair N.J. Libertarian Party, 1998-99. Office: The Gabriel Inst 1601 Market St Ste 1500 Philadelphia PA 19103-2301 E-mail: jpresser@thegabrielinstitute.com.

PRESSLEY-ULMER, DARA AYANNA, web site designer; b. N.Y.C., June 15, 1971; d. George and Diana Ursula Pressley; m. Patrick Ulmer, July 6, 1971; 1 child, Ariyanna Simone Ulmer. BA, Scripps Coll., 1993; MA in Tchg. Writing, MFA in Writing, Columbia Coll., 1999. Cert. mulitmedia U. Wash., 2000. Writing instr. Columbia Coll., Chgo., 1997—98; web developer, designer By The Moon, Kirkland, Wash., 2000—. Jr. Fellow, Scripps Coll., 1992, Follett fellow, Columbia Coll., 1995. E-mail: d@bythemoon.com.

PREST, NERISSA, newscaster; married; 1 child. Grad., Calif. State U., Columbia Grad. Sch. Journalism. News asst. CNN Bus. News, N.Y.C.; gen. assignment reporter, fill-in anchor Sarasota (Fla.) News Now; anchor, reporter, prodr. WFMZ-TV, Allentown, Pa.; anchor WFLA-TV, Tampa, Fla., 2000—. Office: WFLA-TV PO Box 1410 Tampa FL 33601

PRESTO, CATHERINE ANN (KAY PRESTO), small business owner, media specialist, consultant; b. Erie, Pa., Apr. 26, 1929; d. Frank Peter and Mary Alice Vogel; m. Leon Anthony Presto, Apr. 14, 1951; children: Deborah Ann, Richard Anthony, Lee Ann, Anthony Frank. Student, Chaffey Coll., Calif. State Poly. U., Calif. State U., San Bernardino. Cert. tchg. jr. coll. adult edn. R.O.P. Comm. Arts. Newcaster, creator, supr. spl. mktg. surveys Sta. KSOM Radio; med. features editor Italics of Health Mag. Riverside Advt. Agy.; pub. info. supr. L.A. County Fair; mgr. pub. rels. dept. Theta Cable TV; media rels. mgr. Ont. Conv. Ctr.; owner Presto Prodns. Talk Show Host WICU-TV; comml. actress; prod. and broadcaster CNN & ESPN Speedweek, Mut. Radio, ABC, NBC, WBBM, KFWB radio networks; spkr. in field. Co-author (non-fiction): Power Basics of Auto Racing, 1986 (2nd place nat., 1987); contbr. articles to books and mags. Promoter House of Ruth Women's Shelter, Claremont, Calif., 1991; condr. drive for supplies Crossroads, Inc., Claremont, Calif., 1998; condr. political campaign Mayor of Ontario, Calif., 1971; bd. dirs. A Spl. Wish Found., Inc. Calif. Divsn., 1998—99; adv. bd. dirs. Inland Valley Daily Bulletin, Ontario, Calif., 1996. Recipient Age of Achievement award, Nordstrom Dept. Stores, 1994, Ava Doner Pioneer award, Women's Referral Svc., Calif., 2001, of 52 nat. and state awards, in TV, radio, pub. rels., journalism photography, Outstanding Alumni award, Villa Maria Acad., 2003. Mem.: AFTRA (newscaster, sportscaster), Press Club Southern Calif. (former bd. dirs., scholarship chmn.), Am. Writers and Broadcasters Assn. (past western v.p.), Toastmasters Internat. (v.p. pub. rels. dist. 12). Avocations: travel, classical music, reading classics, working to prevent intentional child murder by their parents. Office: Presto Prodns 1711 N Leeds Ave Ontario CA 91764-1143 Business E-Mail: prestoprod@juno.com.

PRESTON, COLLEEN ANN, lawyer; b. Monterey, Calif., Oct. 11, 1955; d. Howard Houston and Catherine (Reid) Harrison; m. Raymond C. Preston Jr., June 12, 1982. BA, U. Fla., 1975, JD, 1978; LLM, Georgetown U., 1985. Bar: Fla. 1979, U.S. Ct. Claims 1979, U.S. Ct. Appeals (fed. cir.) 1979. Assoc. Akerman, Senterfitt & Eidson, Orlando, Fla., 1978-79; atty. advisor, office of gen. counsel Sec. USAF, 1979-83; counsel com. on armed svcs. U.S. Ho. Reps., Washington, 1983-89, gen. counsel, 1990-93; spl. asst. to Sec. Def. for legal matters Dept. Def., Washington, 1993, dep. under sec. of def. for acquisition reform, 1993-97. Cons. Preston & Assocs., 1997—. Capt. USAF, 1979-83. Avocations: golf, tennis, cross country and downhill skiing, water skiing.

PRESTON, FRANCES WILLIAMS, performing rights organization executive; children: Kirk, David, Donald. Hon. degree, Lincoln (Ill.) Coll.; degree (hon.), Berklee Sch. Music. With BMI (Broadcast Music Inc.), Nashville, 1958—, v.p., 1964-85; sr. v.p. performing rights BMI, N.Y.C., 1985, exec. v.p., chief exec. officer, 1986, pres., chief exec. officer, 1986—, also bd. dirs. Mem. Film, Entertainment and Music Commn. Adv. Council State of Tenn.; founding mem. bd. dirs. Leadership Nashville; past pres. bd. dirs. John Work Meml. Found.; chmn. bd. dirs. Country Music Found., Inc., 1983-85, trustee, past pres., chmn. bldg. com.; mem. Commn. on White House Record Library, Carter adminstrn., Pres.'s Panama Canal Study Com., Carter adminstrn.; bd. dirs. Rock & Roll Hall of Fame; mem. adminstrv. council Internat. Confedn. of Socs. of Authors and Composers; v.p. Nat. Music Council; past bd. dirs. Peabody Awards; hon. trustee Nat. Acad. Popular Music; pres. bd. dirs. T.J. Martell Fedn. for Leukemia, Cancer and AIDS Rsch.; established Frances Williams Preston Rsch. Labs. for T.J. Martell Fedn., 1993; bd. dirs. R&B Found. Recipient achievement award Women's Equity Action League, spl. citation award NATAS, Golden Baton award Young Musicians Found., Humanitarian award Internat. Achievement in Arts award, 1995, Creative Achievement award Elaine Kaufman Cultural Ctr., 1996, Lester Sill Humanitarian award, 1996, Nat. Trustees award Grammys, 1998; named one of Am.'s 50 Most Powerful Women Ladies' Home Jour.; named to Country Music Hall of Fame. Mem. Country Music Assn. (life mem. bd. dirs., Irving Waugh Award of Excellence), Nashville Symphony Assn. (past sec., bd. dirs.), NARAS Found. (bd. dirs., pres.'s adv. bd.), Nashville Songwriters Assn. (life mem., bd. dirs.), Gospel Music Assn. (life mem. bd., past chmn., past pres.), Am.

Women in Radio and TV (past nat. dir.). Clubs: (Friars Found. Applause award). Lodges: Rotary (1st woman mem. Nashville club), Friars. Presbyterian. Office: BMI 320 W 57th St Fl 3 New York NY 10019-3790

PRESTON, KELLY, actress; b. Oct. 13, 1962; m. John Travolta, 1991; 2 children. Student, U. So. Calif., UCLA. Represented by Internat. Creative Mgmt., Beverly Hills, Calif. Appeared in films, including Mischief, 1985, Space Camp, 1986, 52 Pick-Up, 1986, A Tiger's Tale, 1987, Spellbinder, 1988, Twins, 1988, The Experts, 1989, Run, 1991, Love is a Gun, 1994, Jerry Macguire, 1996, Citizen Ruth, 1997, Addicted to Love, 1997, Nothing to Lose, 1997, The Holy Man, 1998, Jack Frost, 1998, For Love of the Game, 1999, Battlefield Earth, 2000, Daddy and Them, 2001, View from the Top, 2003, What a Girl Wants, 2003, The Cat in the Hat, 2003.*

PRESTON, LETRICIA ELAYNE, financial planner; b. El Paso, Tex., Oct. 19, 1947; d. Leon A. and Doris (Jones) Curry; m. Elisha I. Preston, May 22, 1965 (div.); children: Rhonda E. Eastman, Stacy A. Milburn Student, El Paso C.C. Lic. real estate broker. Sec. S.I.C. Fin. Co., El Paso, 1966-67; sec., credit investigator, asst. cashier First City Nat. Bank, El Paso, 1967-79; real estate agt. Allied Agts., El Paso, 1979-80, Coldwell Hovious, El Paso, 1980-83; asst. v.p. First Fin. Savs., El Paso, 1983-86; sec. Kelly Svcs., El Paso, 1986-87; sales-securities br. mgr. First Investors Corp., El Paso, 1987-93; br. mgr. Linsco Pvt. Ledger Corp., El Paso, 1993—. Avocations: dance, travel, reading, bowling, crossword puzzles. Office: Linsco Pvt Ledger Corp 1790 N Lee Trevino Dr Ste 303 El Paso TX 79936-4525

PRESTON, PATRICIA ANN, language educator, researcher; b. Milw., Mar. 11, 1933; d. Charles Francis Preston, Dorothy Catherine Engman. BA in Spanish magna cum laude, Bryn Mawr Coll., 1955; MA in Spanish, Cath. U. Am., 1961, PhD in Spanish, 1964. Joined Sch. Sisters of Notre Dame. Prof. Spanish and bilingual edn. Mt. Mary Coll., Milw., 1964—, acad. dean, 1971—76, 1984—92, dir. Ctr. for Assessment, 1998—. Founder, dir. Project Head Start Coun. for the Spanish Speaking, Milw., 1965—71, founder, dir. Guadalupe Ctr., 1966—71; cons., in-svc. trainer Milw. Pub. Schs. Bilingual Program & other local and regional schools and districts, Milw., Waukesha, Kenosha, Wis., 1969—; mem. corp. bd. Mt. Mary Coll., Milw., 1971—96; co-founder, bd. dirs. Milw. Spectrum Alternative H.S., 1972—95; cons., examiner North Ctrl. Assn. Colls., Chgo., 1974—77; co-rschr. Cath. Colls. Milw., 1981; vis. prof. English Notre Dame Women's Coll., Kyoto, 1990. Author: (Book) A Study of Significant Variants in the Poetry of Gabriela Mistral, 1964; contbr. Book Wagering on Transcendence, 1997. Active mem. Coun. on Urban Edn., Milw., 1965—68; apptd. mem. Wis. State Day Care Adv. Bd., Madison, 1967—70; chairperson, bd. dirs. Coun. for the Spanish Speaking, Milw., 1970—74; chairperson Project Head Start Coalition Bd., Milw., 1970—74; bd. dirs. Cath. Social Svcs., Milw., 1971—76; mem. edn. commn. Wis. Cath. Conf., Madison, 1975—79; apptd. mem. Wis. State Adv. Com. on Bilingual-Bicultural Edn., Madison, 1978—82. Recipient Edn.: A Family Affair award of excellence, U. Wis.-Milw., Milw. Pub. Schs., Wis. Dept. Pub. Edn., 1999; fellow, Woodrow Wilson Found., 1960—61, 1963—64, Fellow, Summer Seminar in Spain, Fulbright Found., 1966, Summer Seminar Fellow - Bilingualism, NEH, 1977, Summer Seminar Fellow - European Autobiography, 1993. Mem.: TESOL, Am. Nystagmus Network, Nat. Assn. for Bilingual Edn., Wis. Assn. Fgn. Lang. Tchrs., Am. Assn. for Tchrs. of Spanish and Portuguese. Avocation: active advocate for disabled, mentally ill, poor, under-educated persons, immigrants, children and youth. Office: Mount Mary Coll 2900 Menomonee River Pkwy Milwaukee WI 53222-4597 Home Fax: 414-256-0195; Office Fax: 414-256-0195. Personal E-mail: prestonp@mtmary.edu. Business E-Mail: prestonp@mtmary.edu.

PRESTRIDGE, PAMELA ADAIR, lawyer; b. Delhi, La., Dec. 25, 1945; d. Gerald Wallace Prestridge and Louis Baugh and Peggy Adair (Arender) Martin. BA, La. Poly. U., 1967; M in Edn., La. State u., 1968, JD, 1973. Bar: U.S. Dist. Ct. (mid. dist.) La. 1975, U.S. Dist. Ct. (so. dist.) Tex. 1982, U.S. Ct. Appeals (5th cir.) 1982, U.S. Supreme Ct. 1990. Law clk. to presiding justice La. State Dist. Ct., Baton Rouge, 1973-75; ptnr. Breazeale, Sachse & Wilson, Baton Rouge, 1975-82, Hirsch & Westheimer P.C., Houston, 1982-92; pvt. practive, Houston, 1992—. Counselor Big Bros./Big Sisters, Baton Rouge, 1968-70; legal cons., bd. dirs. Lupus Found. Am., Houston, 1984-93; bd. dirs. Quota Club, Baton Rouge, 1979-82, Speech and Hearing Found., Baton Rouge, 1981-82, The Actors Workshop, Houston, 1988-93, Tex. Satsang Soc., 2000—. Recipient Pres.'s award Lupus Found. Am., 1991, cert. of appreciation Assn. Atty. Mediators, 1992, Outstanding Profl. Woman of Houston award Fedn. Profl. Women, 1984. Mem. ABA, La. Bar Assn., Tex. Bar Assn., Houston Bar Assn., Houston Bar Found., Assn. Atty. Mediators (bd. dirs. 1994-96, Citation for Outstanding Mems. 1993), Profl. Atty.-Mediators Coop. (v.p. 1994, bd. dirs. 1994-96, pres. 1995), Phi Alpha Delta. Eckankar. Avocations: acting, ultralite flying. Home: 1701 Hermann Dr Unit 407 Houston TX 77004-7345 Office: 3200 Southwest Freeway Ste 3300 PO Box 130987 Houston TX 77219-0987

PRESZLER, SHARON MARIE, psychiatric home health nurse; b. L.A. d. Rudolph Edward Wirth and Bertha Marie (Thornton) Paddock; m. Alan Preszler, Aug. 31, 1966; children: Brent, Alison. BS in Nursing, Loma Linda (Calif.) U., 1963, MS in Marriage and Family Counseling, 1978. RN, Calif., Idaho; cert. pub. health nurse. Team leader med. fl. Loma Linda U. Hosp., 1963-64; office nurse Dr. Lowell Johnson, Redlands, Calif., 1964-65, Dr. H. Glenn Stevens, Loma Linda, 1965-72; team leader women's oncology Loma Linda U. Hosp., 1974-75; pub. health nurse Riverside County Pub. Health, Hemet, Calif., 1975-78; nurse, staff psychologist Dept. Health and Welfare, Idaho Falls, Idaho, 1989-91, Boise, Idaho, 1991-92; psychiat. nurse Cmty. Home Health, Boise, 1992-94, Mercy Home Health & Hospice, Nampa, Idaho, 1995-99; hospice nurse, home health nurse Mercy Med. Ctr., 1995-99, personal care supr. nurse for medicaid, 1996—; case mgr. Assisted Living of Idaho, 2001, Ada Can, 2001—. Instr. YWCA, Bartlesville, Okla., 1984-88; tchr. Bartlesville Pub. Sch., 1984-88, Heritage Retirement, Boise, 1994. Contbr. to Focus, 1986. Mem. Am. Assn. Marriage and Family Therapy, Sigma Theta Tau. Avocations: reading, tennis.

PREUIT, THERESA, librarian; b. Florence, Ala., Mar. 6, 1960; d. Richard Gordon and Rose Mary Preuit. BA, Judson Coll., 1981; MLS, U. of Ala., 1982. Reference libr. U. of Ala. Librs., Tuscaloosa, Ala., 1982—85; humanities reference libr. U. of West Fla., Pensacola, Fla., 1985—89, interim dir. campus libr. Fort Walton Beach, Fla., 1989, humanities reference libr. Pensacola, 1990—93, head circulation dept., 1993—99; head, access services dept. Old Dominion U., Norfolk, Va., 1999—2001; assoc. dir. for pub. svcs. Mercer U. Libraries, Macon, Ga., 2001—. Treas. Innovative Users Group, 2003—; editor, the southeastern libr. Southeastern Libr. Assn., Atlanta, 1993—97, chair, southeastern libr. editl. bd., 1998—99; editor, fla. chpt. newsletter Assn. of Coll. and Rsch. Libraries, Pensacola, Fla., 1988—95; editor, coll., u., and spl. libraries divsn. page Ala. Libr. Assn., Tuscaloosa, Ala., 1984—85, mem., ala. libr. exec. bd., 1984—85; asst. to libr. dir. U. West Fla., Pensacola, 1988—90; online rsch. coord. U. Ala. Librs., Tuscaloosa, 1984—85. Mem.: ALA, Ala. Libr. Assn. (chmn. pubs. com. 1985—85), Fla. Libr. Assn. (bd. mem. academic librs. caucus 1988—95, chmn. Fla. electronic access com. 1999—99), Va. Libr. Assn. (chmn. pub. svcs. forum 1999—2000), Ga. Libr. Assn., Assn.Coll. and Rsch. Librs., Gulf Coast Online and Automated Librs. (sec., treas. 1986—87, v.p. 1988—89, pres. 1989—99, pres. elect 1988—89), Beta Phi Mu. Office: Mercer University 1300 Edgewood Avenue Macon GA 31207 E-mail: preuit_t@mercer.edu.

PREUSS, LINDA PALMBAUM, music educator; b. Doylestown, Pa., June 11, 1957; d. Harry Milton Palmbaum and Roslyn Spigel; children: Benjamin, Rebecca. BA in Music, SUNY, Stonybrook, 1980. Cert. music tchr. N.Y. Music dir. Studio 101 Sch. of Piano, Sound Beach, NY, 1980—2000, Rolling Hills Day Camp, Coram, NY, 1991—94; choral accompanist elem. and high schs., 1990—99; keyboard instr. Frank & Camille's, Lake Grove, NY, 1994—99; elem. music tchr. William Floyd Sch., Mystic Beach, NY, 2000—01, Rocky Point (NY) Schs., 2001—03, S. St. Elem., Manorville, NY, 2003—. Choral accompanist SWE Cmty. Chorus, Shoreham, NY, 1990—99. Contbr. poetry to lit. publs. Recipient Norman Dello Joio Honor award, Boston U., 1975—77, scholarships, Chautauqua Inst., 1977—79, Nat. Poet of Merit award, winner, Albany Symphony Piano Competition; scholar, Albany League of Arts, 1975. Mem.: L.I. Orff Soc., Music Educators Nat. Conf., Suffolk County Music Educators Assn. Home: 101 Westbury Dr PO Box 588 Sound Beach NY 11789 Office Phone: 516-707-8135. Personal E-mail: LPalmbaum@aol.com.

PREVE, ROBERTA JEAN, librarian, researcher; b. Wilmington, Del., Feb. 27, 1954; d. Burton Hugo Sanders and Betsy (Kan) Klein; m. Thomas Alan Preve, Sept. 23, 1978; children: Stephanie Jean, Melanie Marie. BA, U. N.H., 1975; MLS, Simmons Coll., 1985. Rschr. U. N.H., Durham, 1974-75; rsch. asst. Eikonix Corp., Burlington, Mass., 1976-79; asst. cashier, credit dept. mgr. Dania (Fla.) Bank, 1980-83; rsch. assoc. Ctr. for Strategy Rsch., Cambridge, Mass., 1984-86; info. svcs. Braxton Assocs., Boston, 1986-87; mktg. adminstr. Summit Tech., Waltham, Mass., 1987-91; mgr. market rsch. AT&T Capital Corp., Framingham, Mass., 1991-95; mgr. Bus. Info. Ctr. Raytheon Co., Lexington, Mass., 1995—. Co-owner T&R Pest Mgmt., Attleboro, Mass., 1988-95. Mem. Spl. Librs. Assn., New England Online (dir., logistics chair 1986-90), Beta Phi Mu. Avocations: hiking, reading, needlework, sports. Office: Raytheon Co Bus Info Ctr 870 Winter St Waltham MA 02451

PREW, DIANE SCHMIDT, information systems executive; b. Orange, N.J., Jan. 21, 1945; d. Herman and Elfriede (Witt) Schmidt; m. Jonathan Prew, Jan. 27, 1968; 1 child, Heather Diane. BSBA, U. N.H., 1967. Programmer analyst Eastman Kodak Co., Rochester, N.Y., 1967-70; program and system mgr. Nat. Acad. Scis., Washington, 1970-72; owner Active Info. Systems, Nashua, N.H., 1974-79; dir. info. svcs. City of Manchester, N.H., 1980—. Bd. dirs. Members First Credit Union, vice chair, 1993—. Mem. Data Processing Mgmt. Assn. (sec. 1982-84, exec. v.p., 1984-85, pres. 1985-86, treas. 1986-95, Bronze award 1988, Silver award 1991), Rotary Club. Avocations: gardening, swimming, hiking. Office: City of Manchester Info Systems Dept 100 Merrimack St Manchester NH 03101-2210

PREWITT, DEBRA A. state legislator; b. Livonia, Mich., Apr. 19, 1963; BA in Bus. Adminstrn., Eckerd Coll., 1998. Mem. New Port Richey (Fla.) City Coun., 1989-91; vice-mayor New Port Richey, 1991-92; mayor, 1992-94; mem. Fla. Ho. of Reps., Tallahassee, 1994—. Mem. cmty. colls. and career prep com., tourism com., juvenile justice com.; exec. dir. Deaf Svc. Ctr. of Pasco/Hernando County. Mem. Breast Cancer Awareness Task Force, 1996—; v.p. Deaf Svc. Ctr. Assn., 1992. Democrat. Office: State Capitol Rm 1402 Tallahassee FL 32399-1300

PREWITT, JEAN, not-for-profit organization executive; Degree, Harvard U.; degree in law, Georgetown U. Formerly lawyer Donovan Leisure Newton & Irvine; sr. v.p., gen. counsel United Internat. Pictures, 1982—89; with Nat. Telecomm. and Info. Adminstrn. U.S. Dept. Commerce, 1989—94; prin. Podesta.com, Washington, 1994—99; pres. Am. Film Mktg. Assn., L.A., 2000—. Office: AFMA 10850 Wilshire Blvd 9th Fl Los Angeles CA 90024*

PREY, YVONNE MARY, real estate broker; b. Milw., Mar. 14, 1945; d. Irvin Raymond Reindl and Viola Rose Schneider Maresh; m. John V. Prey, Sept. 2, 1967 (div. Dec. 1984); children: James Carter, Jacquelyn Rue. BS in Sociology, U. Wis., Oshkosh, 1967, postgrad., 1967-69. Lic. real estate broker, Wis.; cert. residential specialist, relocation profl. Social worker Winnebago State Hosp., Oshkosh, 1967-69, Div. Family Svcs., State of Wis., Fond du Lac, 1969-72, Green Bay, 1972-75; real estate broker Action Realty, Inc., Wausau, Wis., 1975-81, Williams Realty, Inc., Wausau, 1982-92, RE/MAX of Wausau, 1992—. Active Habitat for Humanity, Friends of Wausau Hist. Landmarks; sponsor Wis. River Valley Jour. Mem. NAFE, LWV, Wausau Area C. of C. (bd. dirs. Coun. Women Bus. Owners 1990—, Amb. 1975-89, edn. com.), Marathon County Hist. Soc., Wausau Bd. Realtors, Wis. Realtors Assn., Realtors Nat. Mktg. Inst. Roman Catholic. Avocations: reading, gardening, gourmet food preservation. Home: 811 Becher Dr Wausau WI 54401-2177 Office: RE/MAX of Wausau 1314 Grand Ave Wausau WI 54403-6672

PRIBANICH, CHERYL MARIE, music educator; b. Allentown, Pa., Jan. 6, 1955; d. Ronald Earl and Isabel Marie Maurey; m. Mark Michael Pribanich, Aug. 20, 1977; children: Scott Michael, Jenna Marie, Steven Mark. BS Music Edn., Ind. U. of Pa., 1976; M of Music Edn., Temple U., 1982. Music tchr. Parkland Sch. Dist., Orefield, Pa., 1977—78, Allentown (Pa.) Sch. Dist., 1979—. Organist, choir dir. Boulevard E.C. Ch., Allentown, Pa., 1984—92; musician Mcpl., Pioneer, Marine Bands, Allentown, 1970—86. Asst. scout master and troop com. chmn. Boy Scouts of Am., Allentown, 1999—, counselor, 1998—, com. mem., 1997. Mem.: Nat. Edn. Assn., Allentown Edn. Assn., PA State Edn. Assn., Music Educators Nat. Conf., Am. Fed. Musicians. Avocations: singing, needlepoint, reading, performing. Home: 3621 Manchester Rd Allentown PA 18104 Office: Allentown Sch Dist 31 N Penn St Allentown PA 18102 E-mail: pribanichc@allentownsd.org.

PRIBBLE, ELIZABETH J. retired airline administrator; b. Dixon, Ill., Oct. 8, 1929; d. Steve John and Isabel Elizabeth Gall; m. Robert Isom Pribble, Sept. 4, 1954 (dec. Dec. 1970); children: Stephanie Catherine Kerstetter, John Patrick. BS in Edn., No. Ill. U., 1951. Tchr. h.s. Milledgeville (Ill.) Schs., 1951-52; stewardess TACA Internat. Airlines, New Orleans, 1952-54; tool planner Rohr Aircraft Corp., Riverside, Calif., 1954-59; documents libr. U. Calif., Riverside, 1961-66; flight attendant instr. West Coast Airlines, Seattle, 1966-68; flight attendant mgr. Northwest Airlines, Seattle, 1968-94. Campaign mgr. City Coun., Federal Way, Wash., 1995; safety com. advisor Northwest Airlines, Inc., Seattle, 1991-94. Commr., Fire Dept., Federal Way, 1996; mem. Human Svcs. Commn., Federal Way, 1995-98; mem. social justice com. St. Vincent DePaul Ch., 1998—; vol. St. Francis Hosp. Mem. AAUW (bd. dirs. 1995—, v.p. membership), St. Francis Hosp. Vols., Alpha Sigma Alpha (Alumnae Star award 1995). Roman Catholic. Avocations: volunteer work, coin collecting, reading, travel. Home: 4301 40th Ave NE Tacoma WA 98422-2492

PRICE, ALICE LINDSAY, writer; b. Augusta, Ga., Oct. 21, 1927; d. William Lloyd and Orlana Jerome (Gould) P. BA in Art English Lit., Okla. State U., 1949; MA in English, U. Tulsa, 1970. Mus. asst. Philbrook Art Mus., Tulsa, 1949-51; recreation supr. U.S. Army Europe, 1951-54; neighborhood ctr. dir. City of Monterey (Calif.) Parks and Recreation Dept., 1955-59; art gallery dir., co-owner Gallerie Quais de la Roquette, Arles, France, 1960-62; program dir. City of Tulsa (Okla.) Parks and Recreation Dept., 1963-69; instr. English lit. and creative writing Holland Hall Sch., Tulsa, 1970-86; artist-in residence Okla. State Arts Coun., Oklahoma City, 1986-91; scholar in residence Tulsa City-County Libr. of NEH, Tulsa/Washington, 1988, 90, 91; pub. HCE Publs./ Riverrun Press, Tulsa, 1974—. Acquisitions editor Coun. Oak Books, Tulsa, 1986-89; lectr. Gilcrease Inst., Tulsa, 1984, 86, 90, 94, Trumpeter Swan Soc., Mpls., 1997, Kans. State U., Manhattan, 1997. Author: (poetry) Faces of the Waterworld, 1970, Our Dismembered Shadow, 1981 (Pegasus award 1981); author/illustrator Swans of the World: Nature, Hist., Myth, Art, 1994 (Feldman award 1993), Cranes: The Noblest Flyers in Natural History and Cultural Lore, 2001. Bd. edn. chair Swan Lake Waterfowl Soc., Tulsa, 1986—; mem. lit. arts com. Arts and Humanities Coun., 1990—; creative writing workshop dir. Tulsa Ctr. Phys. Ltd., Tulsa, 1990. First pl. Folger scholarship Kans. City Art Inst., 1945; grantee Arts and Humanities Coun., 1990, 92. Mem. Trumpeter Swan Soc., Author's Guild, Pen West, Internat. Wild Waterfowl Assn., Tulsa Artists Coalition (First Pl. 1997), Living Arts (poetry coord. 1978-85), Phi Beta Kappa. Avocations: traveling, listening music, photography. Office: HCE Pubs/Riverrun Press 3113 S Florence Ave Tulsa OK 74105-2407

PRICE, ALICIA HEMMALIN, psychotherapist, researcher; b. New Bedford, Mass., Nov. 24, 1937; d. William Alton Disbury and Hazel Rogers; m. John Paul Hemmalin, Aug. 11, 1957 (div. Nov. 1970); m. John Barrett Price, Nov. 3, 1983 (dec. Aug. 1998); children: Karen, Roxanne, Eric. Attended, Mass. Coll. of Art, 1957; BA in psychology, U. R.I., 1972; MA in counseling, R.I. Coll., 1978; cert. Jungian/Depth Counseling, Interfaith Counseling Ctr., Providence, R.I., 1989—90. Cert. chem. dependency profl. Internat. Cert. Reciprocity Consortium for Alcoholism and Other Drug Dependencies, 1993. Creative artist therapist Health Care Industry, RI, 1976—84; family counselor Family Focus Program, Edgehill Newport, RI, 1987—93; social worker Thundermist Health Assoc., Woonsocket, RI, 1990—91; clinician rsch. team Miriam Hosp., Providence, 1991—. Reader, spkr. various lectures and workshops, RI, 1987—. Mem.: Jean Baker Miller Tng. Inst. Stone Ctr., East Providence Substance Abuse Prevention Task Force, Nat. Assoc. for Alcoholism and Drug Abuse Conselors, Nat. Mus. of Women Artists, Providence Art Club. Independent. Avocations: photography, writing, dance, bicycling. Home: 111 Sheffield Hill Rd Exeter RI 02822 Office: Miriam Hosp The Lifespan Brown U Ctr for Behavioral and Preventive Medic 1 Hoppin St 5-14 Providence RI 02903

PRICE, AMELIA RUTH, not-for-profit foundation president, artist, small business owner; b. Bklyn., Sept. 4, 1942; d. Dr. Alphonse Frederick Pagano and Adele Marie Savarese; 1 child, Ean James. BA, Georgian Ct. Coll., Lakewood, NJ, 1964; MA in Art Hist., Cath. U. of Am., Washington, DC, 1968. Cert. Permanent Certificate, Art State of N.Y. Edn. Dept., 1971. Art tchr. Bd. Coop. Ednl. Svcs., Patchogue, NY, 1967—68; art director Roland Advt. Co., N.Y.C., 1968—69; art dept. chair Bd. Coop. Ednl. Svcs. II, Deer Park, NY, 1969—78; v.p. Delicious Selections Ltd, White Plains, NY, 1991—95; pres., owner Parker Commodities Ltd, Kings Park, NY, 1995—; owner Bubbling Oaks Samoyeds, Commack, NY, 1974—. Co-founder bubbling oaks samoyeds kennels Bubbling Oaks Samoyeds, Commack, NY, 1974—2002. Samoyed Newsletter and other publs.featuring Samoyeds, 1999—; contbr. articles on Samoyeds and their care to various publs. ., 1999. Pres. Samoyed Club of Am. Edn. and Rsch. Found., Inc., Madison, Wis., 2001—, v.p., 1997—2001. Recipient # 1 Samoyed Bitch, Kennel Rev., 1974, 1975, 1976, 1977, 1978, 1983, 1984, # 3 Samoyed, Dogs in Canada, 1976, Top Winning Team, Orgn. for the Working Samoyed Inc., 1986, 1988. Mem.: Habour Lights Painter, Decorative Artists LI, Soc Decorative Painters, Nat. Assn. Woman Bus. Owners (pub. affairs com. 2003—), Suffolk County Kennel Club Inc. (chmn. hospitality 1989—99, bd. dirs. 1996—99), Westbury Kennel Association (chmn. of trophies 1985, chmn. judges' transport. 2000), Samoyed Club of America Inc. (pres. 1997—99, Top Winning Bitch 1975, 1976, 1985, Top Winning Team 1985, Top Winning Bitch 1986, Top Winning Team 1987). Home: 128 Cowie Rd Commack NY 11725 Personal E-mail: arprice@optonline.net.

PRICE, ANITA W. music educator, consultant; b. Langley Field, Va., Oct. 17, 1943; d. Ralph Neil and Clara Frances Wirthin; m. James Robert Price, Sept. 24, 1966; children: James Robert Jr., Jennifer Lynne Price Pollard. BA, Mary Washington Coll., Fredericksburg, Va., 1965, M in Arts and Liberal Studies, 1986. Band dir. grades K-12 Spotsylvania (Va.) Schs., 1965—67; choral and band dir. Stafford County Schs., Stafford, Va., 1974—95, Bonner County Schs. K-12, Clarkfork, Idaho, 1996—98; dir. bands elem. and h.s. Sandpoint (Idaho) Schs., 1998—2003; tchr. band, chorus, drama and humanities Sandpoint Charter Sch., 2003—; owner, dir. Keys to Music, Sandpoint, 2003—. Owner, dir. Yamaha Music Sch., Fredericksburg, Va., 1975—85; dir. Fredricksburg Children's Musical Theatre, Va., 1980—82; cons. to talented and gifted programs, Caroline Couny, Va., 1985; guest dir. and judge State Music Sch. Competitions, 1990—95. Composer: 2 original commd. symphonic compositions. Bd, dirs. Panida Theatre, SandPoint, Idaho, 1998—2000; bd. dirs. Sandpoint Festival, Idaho, 1998—2000; mem. Student Festival scholarship com. Mem.: NEA, Music Educators Nat. Conf., Bonner County Edn. Assn., Idaho Edn. Assn. Avocations: antiques, home decorating, music, skiing. Home: PO Box 1201 Sagle ID 83860

PRICE, ANNA MARIA, university administrator; b. Dallas, Feb. 17, 1943; d. Lumpkin Calier and Lulu Belle (Smith) Benjamin; m. Hollis Freeman Price Jr., June 22, 1963 (div. Jan. 1981); children: Stacey Ellen (dec.), Hollis Freeman III. BA, Ctrl. State U., 1970; MA, Wright State U., 1971; PhD, U. Miami, 1988. Dir. upward bound U. Miami, Coral Gables, Fla., 1973-88, coord. acad. support athletics, 1988-91, asst. athletic dir., 1991-94, asst. provost, asst. athletic dir., 1994-96, asst. provost, asst. prof., 1996—; dean students Fla. Meml. Coll., Miami, 1983-84. Cons. Nat. Coun. Ednl. Opportunity Assn., Washington, 1986, 87, 96, Western Ky. U. Program Evaluation, Nashville, Tenn., 1988, SAEOPP Tng. Authority, Atlanta, 1987. Contbr. articles to profl. jours. Mayor City of South Miami, Dade County, Fla., 1997, commr., 1996; 1st vice chmn., bd. trustees Hist. Mus. of So. Fla., Dade County, 1997; bd. dirs. Recording for Blind and Dyslexic, 1995—; min., dir. of cmty. missions; mem. Dem. Women's Club, Coral Gables, pres. 1979-80; pres. Hemispheric Congress for Women, 1977. Named Woman of Yr. King of Clubs, 1991, Cmty. Headliner Women in Comms., 1990; recipient Black Achievers award Family Chrisitan Assn. of Am., 1988. Mem. Rotary Club of South Miami, Fla. Sports Found., Omicron Delta Kappa. Democrat. Office: City of South Miami 6130 Sunset Dr South Miami FL 33143-5093

PRICE, ARTIS J. retired secondary school educator; b. Hoopeston, Ill., Dec. 10, 1929; d. John William and Marian Elizabeth (Moore) Little; m. Harry Mackey Price, Nov. 28, 1958; 1 child, Kathryn Elizabeth. BS, Purdue U., 1952; postgrad., U. Colo., 1955, Northwestern U., 1958. Cert. tchr. h.s. English, Spanish, speech and phys. edn., Ill. Tchr. English, Spanish and speech Onarga (Ill.) H.S., 1952-53; tchr. English and Spanish Reavis H.S., Oak Lawn, Ill., 1953-58; tchr. phys. edn. Niles Twp. H.S., Skokie, Ill., 1958-59; substitute tchr. Libertyville (Ill.) H.S., 1959-97; tchr. water ski clinics Chgo. Boat Show, 1960-97, Midwest Boat Show, Chgo., 1960-97. Tchr. water ski clinics Boy Scouts, Girl Scouts, Lions Club, Chgo. and suburbs, 1961-98; mem. adv. bd. Lambs Farm Retarded Facility, Libertyville, 1965-68; nutrition cons. Dr. Harry Price, Northbrook, Ill., 1964-98; cons., editor Diamond Video Prodns., Libertyville, 1976-99. Editor: Water Skiing with Champions, 1969. Vol., Adlai Stevenson Presdl. Campaign, Chgo., 1953-54; founder Ann. Lambs Show Tournament, 1965-99. Recipient 51 Nat. 1st Place Championships, U.S.A. Water Ski, 1957-2002, 4 World 1st Place Championships, 1984, award of distinction U.S.A. Water Ski Hall of Fame, 1998. Mem.: Am. Water Ski Ednl. Found. (award of distinction 1998), U.S.A. Water Ski Assn., Lambs Water Ski Club (hon.; pres. 1965—70), Diamond Lake Water Ski Club (hon.; pres. 1959—64). Christian. Home: 1660 Blackwelder Rd De Leon Springs FL 32130-3914

PRICE, BARBARA GILLETTE, college administrator, artist; b. Phila., June 26, 1938; d. Philip and Frances (Bressler) Gillette; 1 child, Michelle Cutler. BFA, U. Ala., Tuscaloosa, 1966, MA, 1968. Acting chair dept. art Judson Coll., Marion, Ala., 1969; faculty Corcoran Sch. of Art, Washington, 1970-78; acad. dean Cranbrook Acad. of Art, Bloomfield Hills, Mich., 1978-82; v.p. acad. affairs Md. Inst. Coll. of Art, Balt., 1982-93; pres. Moore Coll. of Art and Design, Phila., 1994-98; art edn. cons., 1998—. Bd.

dirs. AICAD, Washington, Fleisher Art Meml., Phila. One person shows include Cranbrook Acad. Art Mus., Bloomfield Hills, 1980, Robert Kidd Gallery Assocs., Birmingham, Mich., 1980, Ferris State, Big Rapids, Mich., 1981, Schweyer Galdo Galleries, Birmingham, 1982, Md. Inst. Coll. of Art, Balt., 1982, 94, Coll. of Notre Dame of Md., Balt., 1985, Columbia (Md.) Assn. Ctr. for Arts, 1989, Loyola Coll., Balt., 1991, Artshowcase, Balt., 1993; group exhbns. include Gallery 641, Washington, 1975, Washington Women's Art Ctr., 1975, Foundry Gallery, Washington, 1975, 76, Rutgers U., New Brunswick, N.J., 1975, Olympia Internat. Art Ctr., Kingston, Jamaica, 1975, Robert Kidd Gallery Assocs., Birmingham, 1980, Grimaldis Gallery, Balt., 1983, Artscape, Balt., 1986, Md. Inst. Coll. of Art, Balt., 1983, 85, 91, 92, 93, Art in the Bell Tower, Balt., 1988, Morris Mechanic Theatre Gallery, Balt., 1989, Artshowcase, Balt., 1990, 91, 92, 93, Frostburg State U., 1991. Bd. dirs. Friends of Logan Square, Phila., 1994-95, Phila. Vol. Lawyers Arts, Phila., 1994-95. Mem. Nat. Assn. Schs. of Art and Design (bd. dirs., sec. exec. com.), Nat. Coun. Art Adminstrs., Coll. Art Assn. (assoc.), Am. Assn. Higher Edn., Soc. for Coll. and Univ. Planning.

PRICE, BETTY JEANNE, choirchime soloist, writer; b. Long Beach, Calif., June 12, 1942; d. Grant E. and Miriam A. (Francis) Sickles; m. Harvey H. Price, Aug. 6, 1975; children: Thomas Neil Gering, Timothy Ray (dec.), Pamela Kay (dec.). Degree in Acctg., Northland Pioneer Coll., Show Low, Ariz., 1977. Youth missionary Open Bible Standard Missions, Trinidad, 1958-59; typographer Joel H. Weldon & Assocs., Scottsdale, Ariz., 1980-89; exec. chief acct. Pubs. Devel. Corp., San Diego, 1991-93; coord. music and worship College Ave. Bapt. Ch., San Diego, 1994-95; ChoirChime soloist, 1986—; exec. acct. Advance Reprographics, San Diego, 1996—, 1996—. Author: 101 Ways to Fix Broccoli, 1994, ABC's of Abundant Living, 1995, Breaking Free from Financial Bondage: A Guide to Living Debt Free, 2004; co-author: God's Vitamin C for the Spirit, 1995, Bounce Back, 1997, You Can Bounce Back Too, 1998, Pathway of Love, One Man's Remarkable Journey, 2002, One Man's Remarkable Journey, 2002; dir.(chime choir): La Habra Hills Presbyn. Ch. Dir. handchime choir La Habra Hills Presbyn. Ch. E-mail: pricecan@juno.com.

PRICE, CLARA SUE, state legislator; b. Sept. 10, 1953; m. Gary Price; 1 child. BA in Bus. Adminstrn., Minot State U., 1977. Mem. N.D. Ho. of Reps., 1991—, chmn. Rep. caucus, 1993-94, vice chair human svcs. com., 1995, mem. transp. com., chmn. human svcs., 1997—. Employee benefit specialist BCBS of N.D., 1982-87; stockbroker INVEST, 1988-90; sec. Cal-Dak Cabinets, 1975—; owner, operator Dakota Gardens & Herbs, 1993—. Past mem. Minot Commn. Status of Women; bd. dirs. Trinity Health. Mem. Internat. Peace Garden, C. of C. Republican. Lutheran. Home: 3520 30th St NW Minot ND 58703-0312 Office: ND Ho of Reps State Capitol Bismarck ND 58505 E-mail: cprice@state.nd.us.

PRICE, DONNA J. nurse; b. Edmond, Okla., May 23, 1953; d. Robert Burton and Lois Mae (Cagle) Gaylord; children: Amanda Leigh. Assoc., Okla. State U., Oklahoma City, 1989. Kindergarten tchr. Logos Christian Sch., Oklahoma City, 1980-87; nurse technician St. Anthony Hosp., Oklahoma City, 1988-90, staff nurse, 1990-92; infusion specialist Curaflex Infusion Co., Oklahoma City, 1992-93; managed care nurse Blue Cross/Blue Shield, Oklahoma City, 1993—. Fundraising chmn. Mustang (Okla.) H.S. Band, 1998, sec., 1999; Sunday Sch. tchr. First Bapt. Ch., Mustang, 1998—. Mem. NMA (treas. Oklahoma City chpt. 1996-98, pres. 1999-2000). Republican. Baptist. Avocations: music, reading, cross stitching, car shows, traveling. Office: Blue Cross/Blue Shield Okla 3401 NW 63rd St Oklahoma City OK 73116-3716

PRICE, ELIZABETH ANNE, lawyer; b. Boston, Aug. 23, 1960; BA, George Washington U., 1983, JD with honors, 1986. Bar: Ga. 1986, U.S. Dist. Ct. (no. dist.) Ga. 1986, U.S. Ct. Appeals (11th cir.) 1986, U.S. Supreme Ct. 1995. Ptnr. Alston & Bird, Atlanta, 1986—. Mem. Atlanta Bar Found. Police Scholarship Commn., 1993—, bd trustees continuing legal edn., 1994—. With U.S. Army, 1978-81. Mem. Nat. Assn. Law Placement Found. (nat. adv. bd.), State Bar Ga. (environmental law sect., access to justice com., ct. futures com., programs com.), Atlanta Bar Assn. (bd. dirs. 1996—, chmn. continuing legal edn. com. 1991-92, environmental law sect., exec. com. 1999—). Office: Alston & Bird 1 Atlantic Ctr Atlanta GA 30309-3400

PRICE, GAYL BAADER, residential construction company administrator; b. Gothenburg, Sweden, Mar. 1, 1949; arrived in U.S., 1951; d. Harold Edgar Anderson and Jeanette Helen (Hallberg) Akeson; m. Daniel J. Baader, Nov. 27, 1971 (div. Sept. 1980); m. Leigh C. Price, Feb. 28, 1983 (dec. Aug. 2000); children: Heidi, Heather. BA in Fgn. Lang., U. Ill., 1971. Asst. buyer The Denver, 1971-73, buyer, 1973-75; escrow sec. Transam. Title, Evergreen, Colo., 1975-76, escrow officer, 1976-78, sr. escrow officer, 1978-79, br. mgr., 1979-84, sr. account mgr. Denver, 1984-87, sales mgr., 1987-91, v.p., 1991-94; cmty. mgr. Village Homes of Colo., Littleton, Colo., 1994-2000, mgr. mktg. ops., 2000-01, v.p. mktg. ops., 2001—03, v.p. sales and mktg., 2003—. Vol. Safehouse for Battered Women, Denver, 1986—, Spl. Olympics, 1986—, Adult Learning Source, 1993—, Kids Cure for Cancer, 1994—. Mem. Nat. Assn. Homebuilders (Most Profl. award 1997), Home Builders Assn. Met. Denver (bd. dirs. 1989-93, exec. com. 1991, assoc. mem. coun. 1988-93, co-chair 1990, chair 1991, Arthur Gaeth Assoc. of Yr. 1989), Sales and Mktg. Coun. Met. Denver (bd. 1986-92, 95—, Major Achievement in Merchandising Excellence chair 1989-90, Most Profl. award 1989, 97, Sales Master award 1995, Silver MAME award 1996, Gold MAME award 1997), Zonta (charter Denver II chpt., pres. 1990, Zontian of Yr. award 1988), Colo. Assn. Homebuilders (Assoc. of Yr. award 1992), Million Dollar Cir. (Platinum award 1996-2000). Avocations: cooking, volunteer work, travel. Home: 1975 Linda Ln Evergreen CO 80439 Office: Village Homes 6 W Dry Creek Cir Ste 200 Littleton CO 80120-8031

PRICE, GLENDA DELORES, university dean; b. York, Pa., Oct. 10, 1939; d. William B. Price and Zelma E. Holmes McGeary. BS, Temple U., 1961, MEd, 1969, PhD, 1979. Clin. lab. specialist. Cytotechnologist Temple U. Hosp., Phila., 1961-67; faculty Coll. Allied Health Professions, Temple U., Phila., 1967-79, asst. dean allied health, 1979-86; dean allied health Sch. Allied Health Professions, U. Conn., Storrs, 1986—. Contbr. articles to profl. jours., chpts. to books. Bd. trustees U. New Eng., Biddeford, Maine, 1989—; bd. dirs. Windham Hosp., Willimantic, Conn., 1989—, E. Hartford VNA, 1989—; allied health adv. Pew Health Prof. Commn., Durham, N.C., 1991—. Recipient Leadership Award SUNY-Buffalo, 1982; named Mem. of the Yr., Pa. Soc. for Med. Tech., 1979; decorated Legion of Honor, Chapel of Four Chaplains, 1977. Mem. Am. Soc. Allied Health Professions (sec. 1985-87), Am. Soc. for Med. Tech. (pres. 1979-80), Alpha Kappa Alpha, Alpha Mu Tau, Alpha Eta, Phi Kappa Phi. Democrat. Baptist. Office: U Conn 358 Mansfield Rd Storrs Mansfield CT 06269-9000

PRICE, HELEN (LOIS) BURDON, artist, retired nurse educator; b. St. Louis, Sept. 23, 1926; d. Kenneth Livingston and Estelle Lois (Pemberton) Burdon; m. John Bryan Price, Jr.; children: Diane Price Baker, Jeannette B., John Bryan III. BS, La. State U., 1946; BS, RN, Johns Hopkins U., 1949; postgrad., Boston U., 1951-52. Head nurse in pediatrics Johns Hopkins Hosp., Balt., 1949-51; instr. nursing sch. Boston Children's Hosp., 1951-52; physician's aide, sec. U.S. Army-Osaka (Japan) Hosp., 1952-54; instr. pediat. nursing Holy Name Hosp., Teaneck, N.J., 1965-67; primary nurse Englewood (N.J.) Hosp., 1974-79; dir.- curator Vineyard Theatre Gallery, N.Y.C., 1980-90; bd. mem., coord. pub. lecture series Ward Nasse Gallery, N.Y.C., 1987-92. Program planner, judge, panel participant, curator Salute to Women in the Arts, Bergen County, N.J., 1977-95. Fund raiser Women's Aux., Presbyn. Med. Ctr., N.Y. Hosp. Fund, N.Y.C., 1982-90. Mem. Nat. Assn. Women Artists (past sec., v.p., pres., permanent advisor, Akston Found. award 1987, Blake award 1991, Bronze medal 1995, Kreindler Meml. award 1998, Blum Meml. award 1999). Avocations: bird watching, mycology. Home: 151 Tweed Blvd Nyack NY 10960-4913 Office: Burdon Price Studio 151 Tweed Blvd Nyack NY 10960-4913

PRICE, HELEN HOGGATT, counseling administrator; b. Lafeyette, La., Aug. 1, 1959; d. Buford James and Barbara Boggan Hoggatt; m. Jahncke Earl Price, Mar. 11, 1978; children: Gretchen Ann, Kayla Ann. BS in Social & Rehab. Svc., U. So. Miss., 1987; M in Counseling & Psychology, Miss. Coll., 1994. Lic. Profl. Counselor Miss., 95, cert. Nat. Cert. Sch. Counselor Nat. Bd. Cert. Counselors, 99, lic. Marriage & Family Therapist Miss., 2000, cert. Psychologist Miss., 2000. Sch. counselor North Pike Elem., Summit, Miss., 1991—95; exec. dir. Crisis Pregnancy Ctr., McComb, Miss., 1995—98; regional dir. S.W. Miss. Mental Health, McComb, 1998—99; sch. counselor McComb Jr. H.S., McComb, 1999—. Contbr. Family Counseling in the Schools, 1994, Counselmate, 1994. Scholar Keith Parks scholarship, Miss. Bapt. Conv. Bd., 1993. Mem.: Miss. Marriage & Family Counselors (pres. 1996—98), Miss. Counseling Assn. (pres. 1999—2000, Dr. Charles Scott scholarship 1994, Spl. Recognition award 2001). Republican. So. Baptist. Office: Harrison Ctrl HS 15600 Sch Rd Gulfport MS 39503 E-mail: hprice@harrison.k12.ms.us.

PRICE, ILENE ROSENBERG, lawyer; b. Jersey City, July 2, 1951; d. Irwin Daniel and Mildred (Riesberg) Rosenberg; m. Jeffrey Paul Price, Feb. 18, 1973. AB, U. Mich., 1972; JD, U. Pa., 1977. Bar: Pa. 1977, D.C. 1978, U.S. Dist. Ct. D.C. 1979, U.S. Ct. Appeals (D.C. cir.) 1979. Assoc. Haley, Bader & Potts, Washington, 1977-80; staff atty. Mut. Broadcasting System Inc., Arlington, Va., 1980-82, asst. gen. counsel, 1982-85; gen. counsel MultiComm Telecommunications Corp., Arlington, 1985-88; east coast counsel Westwood One, Inc., Arlington, 1988-91; gen. counsel Resource Dynamics Corp., Vienna, Va., 1991—. Mem. Fed. Communications Bar Assn., Wash. Met. Area Corp. Counsel Assn., Women's Bar Assn. D.C. (bd. dirs. 1984-87). Office: Resource Dynamics Corp 8605 Westwood Center Dr Vienna VA 22182-2240 E-mail: ileneprice@aol.com.

PRICE, JOANNA SAEGUSA, psychotherapist; b. Balt., July 10, 1939; d. Torakichi Thomas and Martha Ellen (Brooks) Saegusa; m. Warren Wayne Price, Aug. 13, 1960; children: Portia Brooks, Jessica Clark Price Vaughan. BA, Carson-Newman Coll., 1961; MA, U. Ky., 1967, PhD, 1974; MEd, Coll. William & Mary, 1986, EdS, 1988. Lic. profl. counselor Va., marriage and family therapist Va., registered play therapist, cert. clin. hypnotherapist, family mediator. Tchr. French Morristown City Schs., Tenn., 1961—62, Henry County Schs., New Castle, Ky., 1962—65; instr. French, psychology Southeastern Christian Coll., Winchester, 1973—79; lang. specialist, dir. Early Childhood Devel. Ctr., 1977—81; physicians asst. Williamsburg Family Practice Ctr., Va., 1982—87; psychotherapist Peninsula Pastoral Counseling Ctr., Newport News, 1986—. Mem. Nat. Bd. for Cert. Clin. Hypnotherapists. Mem.: Am. Psychotherapy Assn., N.Am. Assn. Masters in Psychology, Am. Assn. for Marriage and Family Therapists, Assn. for Conflict Resolution, Am. Assn. Pastoral Counselors, Am. Guild Organists. Avocations: reading, writing, movies, walking, aerobics. Office: Peninsula Pastoral Counseling Ctr 707 Gum Rock Ct Newport News VA 23606 Office Phone: 757-873-2273.

PRICE, JULIA LARKIN, art educator; d. John I. and Margaret (Gardner) Larkin; m. Michael E. Price, Mar. 21, 1987; children: Jessica, Ian. BFA, U. Denver, Colo., 1982; MA, U. Colo., 1990. Art tchr. K-12 Adams City Sch. Dist 50, Colo., 1982—, dept. chmn., 1983—. Elder St. Andrew Presbyn. Ch., Boulder, Colo., 2003. Named Featured Artist, Sterling Art Assn., 1989. Mem.: Colo. Art Edn. Assn., Nat. Art Edn. Assn. Avocations: ceramics, quilting, skiing, travel. Home: 485 Muirfield Ct Louisville CO 80027-9598 E-mail: novelimage@aol.com.

PRICE, KATHLEEN VERMILLION, priest; b. Newport News, Va., Apr. 11, 1946; d. Ervin Davis and Charlotte Smith Farmer; m. Geoffrey M Price, Apr. 22, 1995; children: Meredith, Holly, Anna; m. Hunter S Vermillion, June 29, 1968 (div. Mar. 1986). BSHE, UNC, 1968; MEd, William and Mary Coll., 1991; MDiv, Va. Theological Seminary, 1994; D of ministry, Howard U. Divinity Sch., 1998. Cert. Myers Briggs Type Indicator 1999. Asst. rector Grace Ch., Yorktown, Va., 1994—95, St. John's Norwood, Chevy Chase, Md., 1995—98; rector All Saints Ch., Md., 1998—. Provincial chaplain D. of the King, 2000—. Recipient Clergy Leadership, Project Trinity, NY, NY, 2000. Avocations: antiques, art, reading. Office: All Saints Episcopal Ch Oakley Parish P O Box 307 21659 Oakley Rd Avenue MD 20609 E-mail: kvprice@erols.com.

PRICE, LEONTYNE, concert and opera singer, soprano; b. Laurel, Miss., Feb. 10, 1927; d. James A. and Kate (Baker) Price; m. William Warfield, Aug. 31, 1952 (div. 1973). BA, Central State Coll., Wilberforce, Ohio, 1949, DMus, 1968; student, Juilliard Sch. Music, 1949-52; pupil, Florence Page Kimball; LHD, Dartmouth Coll., 1962, Fordham U., 1969, Yale U., 1979; MusD, Howard U., 1962; Dr. Humanities, Rust Coll., 1968. Singer: (Operas) (debut) in 4 Saints in 3 Acts, 1952, (appeared) Bess in Porgy and Bess, Vienna, Berlin, Paris, London, under auspices U.S. State Dept., N.Y.C. and U.S. tour, 1952—54; recitalist, soloist (symphonies) U.S., Can., Australia, Europe, 1954—, appeared concerts in India, 1956, 1964, soloist Hollywood Bowl, 1955—59, 1966, Berlin Festival, 1960, role as Mme. Lidoine in Dialogues des Carmelites, San Francisco Opera, 1957; singer: (Operas) NBC-TV, 1955—58, 1960, 1962, 1964, San Francisco Opera Co., 1957—59, 1960—61, 1963, 1965, 1967, 1968, 1971, as Aida at La Scala, 1957; : (Operas) Vienna Staatsoper, 1958, 1959—60, 1961, Berlin Opera, 1964, Rome Opera, 1966, 1968, (recital) Brussels Internat. Fair, auspices State Dept., 1958, Verona Opera Arena, 1958—59, Yugoslavia for, State Dept., 1958; rec. artist RCA-Victor, 1958—, appeared Covent Garden, London, 1958-59, 70, Chgo. Lyric Theatre, 1959, 60, 65, Oakland (Calif.) Symphony, 1980, soloist Salzburg Festival, 1959—63, appeared Tetro alla Scala, Milano, 1960-61, 63, 67, Met. Opera, N.Y.C., 1961-62, 64, 66, 75, 76, since resident mem., until 1985, soloist Salzburg Festival, 1950, 60, debut Teatre Dell'Opera, Rome, 1967, Teatro Colon, Buenos Aires, Argentina, 1969, Hamburg Opera, 1970, recordings A Christmas Offering with Karajani, God Bless America with Charles Gerhardt, Arias from Don Giovanni, Turandot, Aida, Emani, Messa di Requiem, Trovatore, Live at Ordway, The Prima Donna Collection, A Program of Song with D. Garvey, Right as the Rain with André Previn. Co-chmn. Rust Coll. Upward Thrust Campaign; trustee Internat. House.; hon. vice-chmn. U.S. com. UNESCO; Hon. bd. dirs. Campfire Girls. Decorated Order at Ment Italy; named Musician of Year, Mus. Am. mag., 1961; recipient Merit award for role of Tosca in NBC-TV Opera, Mademoiselle mag., 1955, 20 Grammy awards for classical vocal recs. Nat. Acad. Rec. Arts and Scis., citation YWCA, 1961, Spirit of Achievement award Albert Einstein Coll. Medicine, 1962, Presdl. medal of freedom, 1964, Springarn medal NAACP, 1965, Schwann Catalog award, 1968, Nat. Medal of Arts, 1985, Essence award, 1991, others. Fellow: Am. Acad. Arts and Sci.; mem.: AFTRA, Actors Equity Assn., Am. Guild Mus. Artists, Delta Sigma Theta, Sigma Alpha Iota. Office: Price Enterprises 1133 Broadway Ste 920 New York NY 10010-7901

PRICE, LINDA K. small business owner; b. Dearborn, Mich., Mar. 7, 1952; d. Leroy G. and Mary Anne (Antos) Hollen; m. Tracy L. Price, Oct. 7, 1989; children from previous marriage: Shannon M. Shepley, Matthew F Gooldy, Krystle E Gooldy. Cert. Ceramic Instr. Mich., 1981. Pres. T.L.C. EnterPrices, Ltd., Canton, Mich., 1991—; co-owner The Handmade Soap Co., Canton, Mich., 2001—. Cath. Achievements include patents pending for Handmade Lamp. Avocation: personal improvement. Office: TLC EnterPrices Ltd PO Box 87356 Canton MI 48187 Office Phone: 734-454-9028. E-mail: getsometlc@aol.com.

PRICE, LINDA RICE, community development administrator; b. Norman, Okla., Sept. 17, 1948; d. Elroy Leon and Esther May (Wilson) Rice; m. Michael Allen Price, May 17, 1970 (div. June 1998); children: Justin R, Mathew Lyon, David F. BA in Am. History, U. Okla., 1970, M. Regional and City Planning, 1975. Dir. U. Okla. Crisis Ctr., Norman, 1969-70; cardio-pulmonary technician Bethany Med. Ctr., Kansas City, Kans., 1970-72; mgr. congressional campaign Barsotti for Congress, Kansas City, 1972; planning intern City of Seminole (Okla.), 1973-74, City of Tecumseh (Okla.), 1974-75; planner I City of Norman, 1975-76, planner II, 1975-80, community devel. coord., 1980-96, revitalization mgr., 1996—. Adj. prof. U. Okla., Norman, 1986-93; cons. in field, Norman, 1980—; mem. Homeless Here Coalition, Social Svcs. Coordinating Coun. Past pres., mem. LWV Norman, 1979—; chmn. Norman Arts & Humanities Coun., 1983—86; v.p. Oakhurst Neighborhood Assn., Norman, 1991—94; bd. dirs. Women's Resource Ctr., Norman, 1991—92; mem., past pres. bd. Thunderbird Clubhouse, 1992—95; bd. dirs. Ind. Living Svcs. for Youth, pres., 2001—03; gov.'s appt. Rural Housing Incentive Study Task Force, 2000. Named to Leadership Norman, Norman C. of C., 1992, for Exemplary Mgmt. Practice, The Urba. Inst., 1989, for Outstanding Performance, HUD, 1988; recipient Citation of Merit, Okla. State Hist. Preservation, 1991, Spl. Recognition, Okla. Hist. Soc., 1991, John J. Gunther Blue Ribbon Practices in Comty. Devel. award, 1997; Best of the Best Practice award HUD, 1999, 2 Best Practice awards, 1999, Okla. Best Practice award, 2000; named to Okla. Mcpl. League Honor Roll of Svc., 2001. Mem. Am. Inst. Cert. Planners (cert.), Am. Planning Assn. (sec. Okla. chpt. 1980-82), Planning and Women (regional coord. 1987-90), Assn. Cen. Okla. Govt. (areawide planning and tech. adv. com. 1979—), Nat. Cmty. Devel. Assn., (bd. dirs. 1998-99, state whip 1988-97, chair nat. membership 1994-96), Rotary. Democrat. Presbyterian. Avocations: softball, travel, music, reading, political activities. E-mail: linda.price.ci.norman.ok.us. Office: City of Norman PO Box 370 Norman OK 73070-0370 Office Phone: 405-366-5439. Business E-Mail: linda.price@ci.norman.ok.us.

PRICE, MARIAN L. state legislator; b. Page, Nebr., Aug. 6, 1938; children: Mark Reed Price, Penni Lou Price Godemann, Randall Joseph Price, Ronald Noble Price. Student, Wesleyan U., 1955-56; grad., Bryan Meml. Hosp. Sch., 1959. RN, Nebr. With Bryan Meml. Hosp., 1959—63; co-owner family restaurants, Lincoln, Nebr., 1971—90; mem. Nebr. Legislature from 26th dist., Lincoln, 1998—. Bd. dirs. Home Health Svcs. for Independent Living, Inc., VITAL Inc. Mem. Lincoln Bd. Edn., 1985-98, pres., 1994-97, chair legis. subcom., 1997-98; chair Lancaster County Reorgn. Com., 1990-98; pres. Ednl. Svc. Unit No. 18, 1991-96; del. Nat. Sch. Bds. Assns. Fed. Rels. Network, 1989-98; mem. Bethany Christian Ch., Lincoln, past pres., mem. Christian women's fellowship, past ch. wedding coord.; past bd. dirs. Lincoln Cmty. Playhouse Guild. Mem. Bryan Meml. Sch. Nursing Alumnae Assn. (past bd. dirs.), Bethany Women's Club, Alpha Gamma Delta Alumnae Assn. (past bd. dirs.), Phi Sigma Alpha (past pres., bd. dirs.). Home: 6735 Lexington Cir Lincoln NE 68505-1338 Office: State Capitol Dist 26 PO Box 94604 Rm 1117 Lincoln NE 68509-4604

PRICE, MARILYN, lawyer; BS in Human Devel., Cornell U.; JD, Hofstra U. With Certilman Balin Adler & Hyman LLP, 1983, of counsel, 1993, ptnr., 1997—. Instr. Acad. Law, Nassau County Bar Assn.; vice chair adv. bd. Hofstra U. Named March of Dimes Woman of Distinction, 2001; named one of Top 50 Long Island Women, 2001. Mem.: Long Island Builders Inst., Cornell Alumni Ambs. Admissions Network (chairperson), Cornell Club Long Island (past pres., treas.). Office: Certilman Balin Adler & Hyman LLP 90 Merrick Ave East Meadow NY 11554

PRICE, MARY SUE SWEENEY, museum director; d. William Robert Sweeney; m. Clement A. Price, 1988. BA in English, Allegheny Coll., 1973; D.H.C. (hon.), Caldwell Coll. With textbook pub. co., N.Y.C.; supr. pub. rels. Newark Mus., 1975, dep. dir., 1990—93, dir., 1993—, with, 1995—. Past pres. ArtTable Inc.; v.p. ArtPrice NJ Inc.; bd. dirs. St. Vincent Acad., Newark Arts Coun. Mem.: Assn. Art Mus. Dirs., Am. Assn. Mus., NJ Assn. Mus. (bd. dirs.). Office: Newark Mus 49 Washington St PO Box 540 Newark NJ 07101-0540*

PRICE, RUTHE GEIER, actress, writer, educator; b. New Brunswick, N.J., Dec. 16, 1922; d. Morris Payenson and Anne (Payenson) Dorfman; m. Arnold Geier, July 1, 1951 (div. Nov. 1976); children: Donald Lloyd, Michael Jay; m. Nathaniel Wolfred Price, Oct. 9, 1988 (dec. Nov. 2003). Student, State Tchrs. Coll., Trenton, N.J., 1941-43; BS in Edn., NYU, 1945, MA in Theater, 1946. Dir. Parker Playhouse, Plainfield, N.J., 1947, Newark Acad. Dramtic Art, 1948; asst. dir., theater chair Essex Conservatory, Newark, 1949-51; soc. editor Edison Jour., Miami, Fla., 1954; comptroller Nat. Ins. Cons., Miami, 1974-76; actress Miami, 1977—; mng.editor Starbooks Inc., 1999—. Drama coach, Fla., 1990—; media cons., Fla., 1983—. Appeared in films including Let It Ride, Making Mr. Right, Italian Taxi Driver, The Bellboy, Hardly Working, Last Plane Out; TV appearances include Miami Sands, Miami Vice, The Sunset Gang; plays include Save Me a Place at Forest Lawn, Pocket Watch, Ladies in Retirement, Hamlet, You Can't Take it With You, The Male Animal, Blithe Spirit, Lady Precious Stream, As You Like It, Guest in the House, Godperson, Forty Carats, Medea, Skin of Our Teeth, Romeo and Juliet, A Choice to Make; hostess TV talk show Ruthe Geier Presents; hostess radio show Spotlight on Stars; Author: (book) Acting in On-Camera Commercials, 2001; contbr. poetry to Harper's mag. Recipient CLIO award, 1982, Emmy award, 1982, Addy award, 1982. Mem. AFTRA (columnist 1985-93, v.p. 1985-93), Screen Actors Guild (bd. dirs. so. dist. 1990-93), Actors Equity Assn. Avocations: stamp collecting/philately, reading, music, theater, travel. E-mail: writegal@bellsouth.net.

PRICE, THEODORA HADZISTELIOU, individual, child and family therapist; b. Athens, Greece, Oct. 1, 1938; arrived in U.S., 1967; d. Ioannis and Evangelia (Emmanuel) Hadzisteliou; m. David C. Long Price, Dec. 26, 1966 (div. 1989); children: Morgan N., Alkes D. L. BA in History/Archaeology, U. Athens, 1961; DPhil, U. Oxford, Eng., 1966; MA in Clin. Social Work, U. Chgo., 1988; diploma in piano tchg., Nat. Conservatory, Athens, 1958. LCSW, bd. cert. diplomate in clin. social work. Mus. asst., resident tutor U. Sydney, Australia, 1966-67; instr. anthropology Adelphi U., N.Y.C., 1967-68; archaeologist Hebrew Union Coll., Gezer, Israel, 1968; asst. prof. classical archaeology/art U. Chgo., 1968-70; jr. rsch. fellow Harvard Ctr. Hellenic Studies, Washington, 1970-71; clin. social worker Harbor Light Ctr., Salvation Army, Chgo., 1988-89; therapist Inst. Motivational Devel., Lombard, Ill., 1989-90; caseworker Jewish Family & Cmty. Svc., Chgo., 1989-90; staff therapist Family Svc. Ctrs. of South Cook County, Chicago Heights, 1990-91; pvt. practice child, adolescent, family therapy Bolingbrook, Ill., 1991—; dir. counseling svcs., clin. supr., psychotherapist Family Link, Inc., Chgo., 1993; staff therapist Cen. Bapt. Family Svcs., Gracell Rehab., Chgo., 1991, 91-92; casework supr., counselor Epilepsy Found. Greater Chgo., Chgo., 1992-93; therapist children, adolescents and families dept. foster care Cath. Charities, Chgo., 1993-94; individual and family therapist South Ctrl. Cmty. Svcs. Individual-Family Counseling Svcs., Chgo., 1994-97. Bd. dirs., counselor Naperville Sch. Gifted and Talented, 1982—84; lectr. in field. Author: (monograph) Kourotrophos, Cults and Representations of the Greek Nursing Deities, 1978; contbr. articles to profl. jours. Eleutherios Venizelos scholar, 1962—65, Meyerstein Traveling grantee, Oxford, Eng., 1963, 1964. Mem.: NASW, Ill. Clin. Social Workers, Nat. Acad. Clin. Social Workers. Avocations: yoga, piano playing, Byzantine chanting, writing. Home and Office: 10 Pebble Ct Bolingbrook IL 60440-1557 Office Phone: 630-378-1187.

PRICE BODAY, MARY KATHRYN, choreographer, small business owner, educator; b. Fort Bragg, N.C., May 20, 1945; d. Max Edward and Katharine (Jordan) P.; m. Les Boday (div. 1982); children: Shawn Leon Boday, Irmali Ferecho Boday; m. Richard A. Weil, May 1, 1986. BFA, U. Okla., 1968, MFA, 1970; studies with David Howard, 1972-74. Soloist dancer Mary Anthony Dance Co., N.Y.C., 1971-74, Larry Richardson Dance Co., N.Y.C., 1971-73; dancer Pearl Lang Dance Co., N.Y.C., 1971-73, Gaku Dance Theater, N.Y.C., 1972-74; ballet mistress and soloist dancer St. Gallen Ballet, Switzerland, 1974-75; dancer, tchr. Zurich Ballet, Switzerland, 1975-76; asst. prof. U. Ill., Champaign-Urbana, 1976-79; artist-in-residence Cornish Inst., Seattle, 1979-80; pres. The Dance Works, Inc., Seattle, 1981-90; dir. Seahurst Ballet, 1982-84; pres. The Dance Works, Inc., Erie, Pa., 1990-94; dir. dance dept., asst. prof. Mercyhurst Coll., Erie, Pa., 1990-94; dir. Peoria Ballet, 1994-99; asst. prof. Bradley U., Peoria, 1994—; dir. Ill. Ballet (formerly Ctrl. Ill. Ballet), 1999—. Tchr. Harkness Ballet N.Y., Mary Anthony Dance Sch., Zurich Ballet, Nat. Acad. Arts Ill., Jefferson High Sch. Performing Arts Portland, also choreographer; tchr. Summer Dance Lab.; choreographer Mary K. Price Dance Co., U. Ill., Nat. Acad. Arts, Cornish Inst., Seahurst Ballet; tchr. Kneeland Workshops, Port Townsend, Wash., 1988; tchr., co-dir. Kneeland Seminars, Las Vegas, Nev., Port Townsend, summers 1989, 90, Oklahoma City U., summer 1990, Am. Coll. Dance Festival, 1991, 92, 93; tchr. Pa. Gov's. Sch. of the Arts, 1991, 92, 94, David Howard summer seminar Mercyhurst Coll., summer 1992, David Howard Summer Workshop with Tulsa Ballet Theatre, 1993, 94, David Howard workshop Seattle tchrs., 1996, David Howard workshop U. Ill., 1997, David Howard-Western Mich. U., 1999; guest artist, asst. prof. Slippery Rock U., 1994; owner The Dance Works, Peoria, Ill., 1994—; guest artist, Southern Ballet Theatre, summer 2000, 2001, David Howard and Mary Price Boday Summer Intensives, Worcester, summer 2000, 2001, 2002, Mt. Hood Ballet Acad., 2002, 03; lectr. Knox Coll., 2000—. Choreographer 3 ballets Ballet Co. St. Gallen, 1988, dance concert Mary & Friends, Seattle, 1990, The Nutcracker for Warner Theatre Erie; co-choreographer The Nutcracker Ballet, 1991-93, Coppelia, 1993, The Little Mermaid of Lake Erie at the Warner Theatre, 1994; choreographer Peoria Ballet, Nutcracker, Civic Ctr., 1995, 30 Yr. Gala, 1995, Alice in Wonderland, 1996, Little Mermaid of Lake Peoria, 1997; staged Swan Lake, 1999; choreographer (with Ill. Ballet) Rudolph the Red Nose Reindeer at the Shrine Mosque, 2000, Evanston Dance Ctr., 2004; choreographer Rock Ballet and The Lion, Witch, and Wardrobe at the Peoria Civic Ctr. Theatre, 2001, Hansel and Gretel, 2002, Power of Dance, 2002; restaged ballet Coppelia, 2002, Sleeping Beauty, Peoria (Ill.) Civic Ctr., 2003, The Nat. Ballet Panama, 2003. Outstanding Dancer award U. Okla., 1968; named one of Outstanding Young Women of Am., 1977, 25 Women in Leadership Week TV, 2003. Address: 719 W Moss Ave Peoria IL 61606-1931

PRICHARD, ANNE W.B. librarian; b. Birmingham, Ala., July 14, 1937; d. Ben F. and Lilie S.G. Johnson; m. Joseph B. Dallett, June 7, 1966 (div. July 31, 1989); 1 child, Timothy B. Dallett ; m. Robert E. Prichard, May 16, 1992 (dec. Mar. 9, 1995). BA, Mills Coll., 1959; MLS, U. Calif., Berkeley, 1965. Asst. to curator Oberlin (Ohio) Coll., 1960—61; asst. art librarian Smith Coll., Northampton, Mass., 1965—66; librarian MacOdrum Libr., Carlton U., Ottawa, Canada, 1974—75; cataloguer Ottawa Pub. Libr., 1977—84; reference librarian Fayetteville (Ark.) Pub. Libr., 1998—2001; spl. collections, reading rm. supr. U. Ark., Fayetteville, 2001—. Contbr. articles to profl. jours. Bd. dirs. Fayetteville Pub. Libr., Washington County Hist. Soc., Fayetteville, Unitarian Universalist Fellowship of Fayetteville. Mem.: ALA, NOW, AAUW. Unitarian Universalist. Avocations: reading, stewardship of family farm, music, walking, birdwatching. Home: 3150 W Pear Ln Fayetteville AR 72701-8873

PRICHARD, BARBARA ANN, English educator; b. Muskogee, Okla., Jan. 11, 1947; d. Carl Howard Fullbright and Iris Oleta (Staffan) Evans; children: Shelia DeLynn, Katherine Elizabeth, David Warren III. BS, Northeastern Okla. State U., 1976; MEd, U. Okla., 1990. Cert. reading specialist, tchr. nat. bd. Tchr. Muldrow (Okla.) Pub. Schs., 1976-77, Stafford (Mo.) Pub. Schs., 1977-79, Oklahoma City C.C., 1991—, Moore (Okla.) Pub. Schs., 1979—. Sponsor, state pres. Moore West Nat. Jr. Honor Soc.; global classroom dir., chair reading dept. Moore West Sch. Bd. dirs. Moore Parks & Recreation, 1988-89. Mem. NEA, Oklahoma Edn. Assn., Okla. Reading Coun., Okla. Romance Writers Am.)v.p.), Romance Writers Am., Moore Assn. Classroom Tchrs. Avocations: travel, writing, reading, painting, golf. Office: Moore Pub Schs 9400 S Pennsylvania Ave Oklahoma City OK 73159-6903

PRICHARD, LONA ANN, retired elementary education educator; b. Mt. Washington, Ky., Jan. 13, 1938; d. Emil Hoke and Ernestine Ray (Hall) Harris; m. Robert Eugene Russell (div.); 1 child, Dora Lynn Russell; m. Richard John Prichard, June 26, 1982; stepchildren: Linda, Rick, Susan, Rita, Pat. Student, Cumberland Coll., Williamsburg, Ky., 1956-58; BS in Elem. Edn., Eastern Ky. State U., Richmond, 1961; MS in Elem. Edn., Berry Coll., Rome, Ga., 1974. Cert. tchr. Tchr. 5th and 6th grade Mt. Washington (Ky.) Elem. Sch., 1958-59; thcr. one-rm. sch., grades 1-8 Pulaski County, Somerset, Ky., 1961-62; tchr. 1st grade Osburn Sch., Chickamauga, Ga., 1963-66; tchr. Rock Spring (Ga.) Elem. Sch., 1966-71, North Rossville Elem. Sch., 1971-93; tchr. 1st grade and spl. edn. Rossville Elem. Sch., 1993-2000, ret., 2000. Mem. social studies and math. curriculum coms. Walker County Bd. Edn. Mem. NEA, Ga. Assn. Educators, Walker County Edn. Assn. Baptist. Avocations: reading, painting, tutoring, tchg. conversational english. Home: 1300 Michael Ln Hixson TN 37343-4334

PRIDDY, JEAN MARIE, music educator, voice educator; b. Andrews AFB, Md., Apr. 12, 1962; d. Sandra J. and George J. Wanner; m. Greg A Priddy, June 7, 1986. AS, BA cum laude, Bluefield Coll., 1986; MA in Music Edn., Case Western Res. U., 1990. Profl. Music Edn. Cert. K-12 State of Ohio, 1990. Music tchr. St. Mary's Sch., Collinwood, Ohio, 1990—92, St. Felicitas Sch., Euclid, Ohio, 1990—91; music dir. Lake Cath. H.S., Mentor, Ohio, 1991—2002; voice tchr. Rabbit Run Cmty. Arts Assn., Madison, Ohio, 2002—, Fairport Exempted Village Schs., 2003—, JM-Priddy Voice Studios, Mentor, Ohio, 2002—. Sec. Lake County Music Educator's Assn., Mentor, Ohio, 1992—95; pres. Ohio Coll. Music Edn. Assn. CWRU Chpt., 1989—90; mem. play selection com. Rabbit Run Cmty. Arts Assn., Madison, Ohio, 2002. Dir.: (musical theater) Once Upon a Mattress, Bye Bye Birdie, Little Shop of Horrors, Starmites, Gold Dust, Anything Goes; singer: Four Spirituals by Needham (World Premier); dir.: Babes In Arms; singer (mother): (opera) Amahl and the Night Visitors; singer: South Pacific at Rabbit Run Theater. Recipient Dennison U. Tchg. Excellence award, Dennison U., 2000, Coll. of Wooster Excellence in Tchg. award, Coll. of Wooster, 2000. Mem.: Lake County Music Educators Assn. (sec. 1992—95, treas. 2003—), Ohio Music Edn. Assn., Music Edn. Nat. Conf., AAUW. Avocations: reading, cooking, jewelry, music, musical theater. Home: 6265 Glenwood Dr Mentor OH 44060 Office: Fairport Schs 329 Vine St Fairport Harbor OH 44077 Personal E-mail: jmpriddy@multiverse.com.

PRIDE, MIRIAM R. college president; b. Canton, China, June 6, 1948; d. Richard E. and Martha W. Pride; divorced. Grad., Berea College Found. Sch., 1966, Coll. of Wooster, 1970; MBA, U. Ky., 1989. Intern in administrn. in higher edn., head resident Coll. of Wooster, Ohio, 1970-72; accounts payable clk., dir. Boone Tavern Hotel, head resident, dir. student activities Berea Coll., 1972-88; eligibility worker dept. human resources State of Ky., 1975-76; asst. in undergrad. advising Coll. Bus., U. Ky., 1987-89; asst. to pres. for campus life, v.p. for administrn., pres. Blackburn Coll., Carlinville, Ill., 1989—. Chmn. United Way Berea, Carlinville, 1989—92; fin. chmn. Carlinville Hosp., 1995—97; mem. Ill. Commn. on Status of Women; bd. dirs. Land of Lincoln Girl Scouts, 1993—2000, fin. chmn., 1995—2000, mem. nominating com., 2000—; bd. dirs. Carlinville Area Hosp., 1993—97, Assn. Presbyn. Colls. and Univs., Fedn. Ill. Colls. and Univs., 1993—, Federated Ch. Bd., 1998—2001. Mem. Carlinville C. of C. (bd. dirs.), Rotary (bd. dirs. 1996—). Mem. Federated Ch. Avocations: reading, walking, knitting. Office: Blackburn Coll Office of the President Carlinville IL 62626

PRIDGEN, HEATHER DAWN, financial analyst; b. Laurinburg, N.C., Oct. 2, 1975; d. Fred Lee and Gloria Jean Pridgen; m. Marty Edward McKinley, June 26, 1999 (div. Apr. 27, 2001). BBA in Finance, U. Ga., Athens, 1997. Loan officer Fed. Credit Union, Charleston, 1997—98, br. mgr., 1998—99; fin. svcs. officer S.C. Fed. Credit Union, Charleston, 1999—2000; from fin. asst. I to fin. asst. II EMA, Charleston, 2000—03; sr. fin. analyst Titan Systems Corp., Charleston, 2003—. Mem.: NAFE. Avocations: bicycling, running, swimming, tennis, walking. Home: 1481 Center St Extension Mount Pleasant SC 29464 Office: Titan Systems Corp Ste 300 2457 W Aviation Ave Charleston SC 29406 E-mail: heather.pridgen@navy.mil.

PRIESAND, SALLY JANE, rabbi; b. Cleve., June 27, 1946; d. Irving Theodore and Rosetta Elizabeth (Welch) P. BA in English, U. Cin., 1968; B.Hebrew Letters, Hebrew Union Coll.-Jewish Inst. Religion, 1971, MA in Hebrew Letters, 1972; D.H.L. (hon.), Fla. Internat. U., 1973; DD (hon.), Hebrew Union Coll., 1997. Ordained rabbi, 1972. Student rabbi Sinai Temple, Champaign, Ill., 1968, Congregation B'nai Israel, Hattiesburg, Miss., 1969-70, Congregation Shalom, Milw., 1970, Temple Beth Israel, Jackson, Mich., 1970-71; rabbinic intern Isaac M. Wise Temple, Cin., 1971-72; asst. rabbi Stephen Wise Free Synagogue, N.Y.C., 1972-77, assoc. rabbi, 1977-79; rabbi Temple Beth El, Elizabeth, N.J., 1979-81, Monmouth Reform Temple, Tinton Falls, N.J., 1981—; chaplain Lenox Hill Hosp., N.Y.C., 1979-81. Author: Judaism and the New Woman, 1975. Mem. commn. on synagogue rels. Fedn. Jewish Philanthropies N.Y., 1972-79, mem. com. on aged commn. synagogue rels., 1972-75; mem. task force on equality of women in Judaism pub. affairs com. N.Y. Fedn. Reform Synagogues, 1972-75; mem. com. on resolutions Ctrl. Conf. Am. Rabbis, 1975-77, com. on cults, 1976-78, admissions com., 1983-89; chmn. Task Force on Women in Rabbinate, 1977-83, chmn. 1977-79, mem. exec. bd., 1977-79, com. on resolutions, 1989-92, chmn. com. conv. program, 1993-96; mem. joint commn. on Jewish edn. Ctrl. Conf. Am. Rabbis-Union Am. Hebrew Congregations, 1974-77; mem. task force on Jewish singles Commn. Synagogue Rels., 1975-77; mem. N.Y. Bd. Rabbis, 1975—, Shore Area Bd. Rabbis, 1981—; mem. interim steering com. Clergy and Laity Concerned, 1979-81; bd. dirs. NCCJ, N.Y.C., 1980-82, Jewish Fedn. Greater Monmouth County, trustee, 1988-2000, strategic planning commn., 1996—, hon. v.p., 2000—; trustee Planned Parenthood of Monmouth County, 1982-90; v.p. Interfaith Neighbors, 1988-96, pres., 1997—; mem. UAHC-CCAR Joint Commn. on Synagogue Affiliation, 1992—2002; bd. govs. Hebrew Union Coll.-Jewish Inst. Religion, 1993—; trustee Union Am. Hebrew Congregations, 1994 98. Cited by B'nai Brith Women, 1971; named Woman of Yr. Temple Israel, Columbus, Ohio, 1972, Woman of Yr. Ladies Aux. N.Y. chpt. Jewish War Vets., 1973, Woman for All Seasons N. L.I. region Women's Am. ORT, 1973, Extraordinary Women of Achievement NCCJ, 1978, Woman of Achievement Monmouth County Adv. Commn. on Status Women, 1988; recipient Quality of Life award Dist. One chpt. B'nai B'rith Women, 1973, Medallion Judaic Heritage Soc., 1978, Eleanor Roosevelt Humanities award Women's div. State of Israel Bonds, 1980, Rabbinical award Coun. Jewish Fedn., 1988, Woman of Leadership award Monmouth Coun. Girl Scouts U.S., 1991, The Woman Who Dares award Nat. Coun. Jewish Women, 1993, Women's Studies Disting. Alumnae award Friends of Women's Studies U. Cin., 1997; named to Alumni Hall of Fame, Fairview Park H.S., 2002. Mem. Hadassah (life), Ctrl. Conf. Am. Rabbis, NOW, Am. Jewish Congress, Am. Jewish Com., Assn. Reform Zionists Am., Jewish Women Internat. (life), Jewish Peace Fellowship, Women's Rabbinic Network, Nat. Breast Cancer Coalition, HUC-JIR Rabbinic Alumni Assn. (sec., treas. 1997-99, v.p. 1999-2001, pres. 2001-03). Home: 10 Wedgewood Cir Eatontown NJ 07724-1203 Office: 332 Hance Ave Eatontown NJ 07724-2730 Office Phone: 732-747-9365. E-mail: spriesand@monmouth.com.

PRIEST, HARTWELL WYSE, artist; b. Brantford, Ont., Can., Jan. 1, 1901; d. John Frank Henry and Rachel Thayer (Gavet) Wyse; m. A.J. Gustin Priest, Aug. 4, 1927; children: Paul Lambert, Marianna Thayer. BA, Smith Coll. Former tchr. graphic art Va. Art Inst., Charlottesville. Former lectr. on prints and lithography; juror art exhbn. Unitarian Ch., 1993. One-woman shows include Argent Gallery, N.Y.C., 1955, 58, 60, 73, 77, 81, Va., 1969, 71, Nantucket, Mass., 1956, Ft. Lauderdale, Fla. Art Ctr., 1956, McGuffey Gallery, Charlotsville, Va., 1998; Pen & Brush, N.Y.C., 1973, 91, 97, invitational retrospective exhbn. McGuffey Art Ctr., Charlottesville, Va., 1984, Va., N.Y., 1984, 88; work represented in permanent collections Library of Congress Washington, Norton Gallery, Palm Beach, Fla., Soc. Am. Graphic Artists, Hunterdon County Art Ctr., Longwood Coll., Smith Coll., Va. Mus., Richmond, Carnegie Mellon U. and numerous others; solo exhbn. of prints McGuffey Art Ctr., Charlottesville, Va., 1988, 90, 93, Woodstock Artist Gallery, 1990, Soc. Am. Graphic Artists, 1988-89, 92, Bombay, 1989, U. Va. Hosp., 1989, Bergen Mus. Art and Sci., 1991; represented in group shows McGuffey Gallery, 1988, 94, Gallery Show, Richmond, Va., 1988, Nat. Assn. Women Artists, Florence, Italy, 1972, N.Y.C., 1989, 96, ann. show Ojibway Hotel Club, Pointe au Baril, Georgian Bay, Ont., Can., 1991, Soc. Am. Graphic Srts, N.Y.C., 1989, 92, Woodstock, N.Y. Art Assoc., 1990, McGuffey Art Ctr., Charlottesville, Va., 1990, 94, 98, Pen and Brush ann. Graphic Show, N.Y.C., 1991 (award for etching Spring, Ada Rosario Cecere Meml. award), Bergen Mus., N.J., 1991, Ojibway Club, Ont., Can., 1991; Pen and Brush Christmas exhbn., 1994-95, Showing of a Video, Harrisonburg, Va.; represented in traveling group shows Nat. Assn. Women Artists, Puerto Rico, 1987, India, 1989, N.Y.C., 1994; pvt. collection U. Va. Hosp., Charlottesville, 1989; subject of TV documentary Hartwell Priest: Printmaker, 1995. Recipient awards for lithograph Field Flowers, Longwood Coll., 1965, Nat. Assn. Women Artists, 1965, lithograph West Wind, A Buell award, 1961, print Streets of Silence, T. Giorgi Meml. award, 1973, lithograph Blue Lichen, Pen & Brush, 1984, award for collage, 1985; 1st award for graphics Blue Ridge Art Show, 1985, Gene A. Walker award for print Glacial Rocks, 1986, award for print Blue Ridge Show, 1987, Philip Isenburg award for graphic PreCambrian Rock Pattern, 1988, Ada R. Cecere Meml. award Pen and Brush, 1991, Art award Piedmont Coun. Arts, 1993. Mem. Nat. Assn. Women Artists (Travelling Printmaking Exhbn. 1987-89), Pen and Brush, Soc. Am. Graphic Artists, Washington Print Club, 2d St. Gallery, Charlottesville, McGuffey Art Ctr. Avocations: walking, singing in choir, gardening, playing Bach and Mozart, playing recorder and piano. Home: 41 Old Farm Rd Charlottesville VA 22903-4725

PRIEST, SHARON DEVLIN, association executive, former state secretary of state; b. Montreal; m. Bill Priest; one son Adam. Tax preparer, instr. H & R Block, Little Rock, 1976-78; owner, founder Devlin Co., Ark., 1983-86; account exec. Greater Little Rock C. of C., 1990-94; vice mayor Little Rock, 1989-90, mayor, 1991-92; Sec. of State State of Ark., 1994—2002; exec. dir. The Downtown Partnership, 2002—. Bd. dir. Invesco Inc., New Futures. Bd. dir., past pres. Metroplan (Environ. Svc. Award 1982), YMCA, Southwest Hosp.; mem. Advt. and Promotion commn., Ark. Internat. Visitors Coun., Pulaski Are Transp. Svc. Policy Com., St. Theresa's Parish Coun., Exec. com. for Ark. Mcpl. League, Nat. League of Cities Trans. and Comm. Steering Com. and Policy Com., adv. bd. M.M. Cohn., Little Rock City Beautiful Commn., 1980-86; former bd. dir. Downtown Partnership, S.W. YMCA, 1984, 86, sec.; former mem. Cmty. Housing Resource Bd., 1984-86, Pub. Facilities Bd. S.W. Hosp., 1985-86, S.W. Merchants' Assn., 1985—, 2d v.p., 1985; chmn. Little Rock Arts and Humanities Promotion Commn.; led petition dr. for appropriation for Fourche Creek Plan 7A. Recipient of the Fighting Back Freedom Fighter Award, 1995; Environ. Svc. Award from the Little Rock Metroplan Comm., 1982. Mem. Leadership Inst. Alumni Assn. (4 Bernard de la Harpe Awards). Achievements include being selected by Ark. Bus. as one of the Top 100 Women in Ark. Office: Downtown Partnership PO Box 1937 Little Rock AR 72203 E-mail: spriest@downtownlr.com.

PRIETO, MONIQUE N. artist; b. L.A., 1962; BFA, UCLA, 1987, Calif. Inst. Arts, 1992, MFA, 1994. One-woman shows include include ACME, Santa Monica, Calif., 1994, 1995, 1996, 1997, Bravin Post Lee, N.Y.C., 1996, one-woman shows include Anderson Gallery, Va. Commonwealth U., Richmond, 1997, Pat Hearn Gallery, N.Y.C., 1998, Robert Prime, London, 1998, exhibited in group shows at Wight Gallery, UCLA, 1987, Bacilla Hernandez Gallery, Long Beach, Calif., 1989; actor: Lockheed Gallery, 1994; Exhibited in group shows at Pat Hearn Gallery, N.Y.C., 1996, 1997, Factory Place Gallery, L.A., 1996, Armand Hammer Sales and Rental Gallery, 1997, ACME, Santa Monica, 1997, Orange County Mus. Art, Newport Beach, Calif., 1997. Herb Alpert scholar, 1992—93, Philip Morris fellow, 1992—94, Skowhegan Sch. Painting and Sculpture fellow, 1994. Office: c/o Pat Hearn Gallery 530 W 22nd St New York NY 10011-1108

PRIMERANO, LAVINA S. volunteer; b. Snow Camp, N.C., June 20, 1918; d. Passmore Harrison Stephens and Manie Mae Culberson-Stephens; widowed; children: Joseph Stephens, Jane Roberta. BS Guilford Coll., 1938, MA U. Ky., 1941. Cert. tchr. N.C., N.J. Tchr. Pine Hall (N.C.) H.S., 1939—40; dean Blackstone (Va.) Jr. Coll., 1940—42; substitute Morris County (N.J.) Schs., 1960—62; 3d grade tchr. Jefferson Twp., NJ, 1962—64, math tchr., 1963—76, dept. chmn., 1969—70; ret., 1976. Vol. tchr. St. Lucie County Schs., Ft. Pierce, Fla., 1985—; svc. officer Nat. Assn. Ret. Fed. Employees, 1993—; pres. River Park Homeowners Assn., Port St. Lucie, Fla., 1994—99, 2002—. Recipient Good Neighbor award, McDonald's, 1995—96, Prime Time award, RSVP, St. Lucie County, 1995—96. Mem.: Pi Mu Epsilon.

PRIMO, JOAN ERWINA, retail and real estate consulting business owner; b. Detroit, Aug. 28, 1959; d. Joseph Carmen and Marie Ann (Nash) P.; m. David James Yared, Sept. 20, 1997; 1 son, Benjamin Primo Yared. BA, Wellesley Coll., 1981; MBA, Harvard U., 1985. Acct. exec. Michigan Bell, Detroit, 1981-82, AT&T Info. Sys., Southfield, Mich., 1983; planning analyst Gen. Motors, Detroit, 1984; v.p. Howard L. Green & Assocs., Troy, Mich., 1985-89; prin., founder The Strategic Edge, Inc., Southfield, 1989—. Contbr. articles to profl. jours. Founders soc. mem. Detroit Inst. Arts, 1989—. Mem.: Internat. Coun. Shopping Ctrs. (faculty, seminar leader 1987—), Ivy Club Detroit (bd. dirs. 1994—, sec. 1995—99), Harvard Bus. Sch. Club Detroit (bd. dirs. 1994—98, v.p. 1995—96, exec. v.p. 1996—97), Wellesley Club Southeastern Mich. (pres. 1994—98). Republican. Avocations: antiques, travel, theatre, gourmet cooking. Home: 224 Woodwind Dr Bloomfield Hills MI 48304-2172 Office: The Strategic Edge 24333 Southfield Rd Ste 211 Southfield MI 48075-2849

PRINCE, GINGER LEE, actress, choreographer, educator; b. Stuart, Fla., June 3, 1945; d. Hugh Frederick and Gladys Inez (Davis) P.; children: Jessica Elizabeth McMaster, Jennifer Lee Hall. Student, Stephens Coll. Performing Arts, 1961. Faculty, bd. dirs. Sande Shurin Acting Studio, N.Y.C., 1981—; adj. prof. Marymount Manhattan Coll., N.Y.C.; guest tchr., dir., chor. Stephens Coll., Columbia, Mo., 1997; lectr. Va. Intermont Coll.; ensemble dir., asst. choreographer Theatre Under the Stars; co-dir., choreographer-in-residence, ballet mistress The Atlanta Ballet; assoc. dir. Southern Ballet of Atlanta; active the Charleston Ballet, Lexington Ballet, Bristol Concert Ballet, Augusta Ballet Co., Louisville Ballet, Tampa Ballet, Southern Ballet Theatre, Orlando, Capital City Ballet, Atlanta, Ruth Mitchell Concert Dance, Atlanta. Choreographer: Tribute to Patti LuPone, Taking My Turn, New Lawrence Welk Show, She Loves Me, Big Band at the Savoy, Company, Lawrence Welk Family Christmas (with the Lennon Sisters), 2000, Carousel, 2001; actress: (Broadway) Gypsy, Ain't Broadway Grand; (off-Broadway) Steel Magnolias (original Broadway cast), After the Dancing in Jericho, The Jericho 7, Tribute to David Merrick; (U.S. nat. tours) La Cage Aux Folles, Pippin, George M!!, Can-Can, Oklahoma, Most Happy Fella; (regional theatre) Pippin, Gilligan's Island, Same Time, Next Year, Vanities, Bus Stop, The Rainmaker, The Odd Couple; (stock) Guys and Dolls, Gypsy, Mame, Peter Pan, Sweet Charity, Pippin, Annie, Something's Afoot, Pal Joey, Goldiggers of 1633, I Do, I Do, Kiss Me Kate, Dames at Sea, Brigadoon, Showboat, Music Man, Oklahoma, Damn Yankees, Driving Miss Daisy, 2000. Appointed mem. by Gov. Jimmy Carter Ga. Coun. for the Arts, 1970-74. Nat. Choreography grantee NEA, 1976, 85. Mem.: SAG, AFTRA, Nat. Assn. Am. Dance Artists, Dance Educators Am., Actor's Equity Assn., Soc. Stage Dirs. Choreographers.

PRINCE, LEAH FANCHON, art educator and research institute administrator; b. Hartford, Conn., Aug. 12, 1939; d. Meyer and Annie (Forman) Berman; m. Herbert N. Prince, Jan. 30, 1955; children: Daniel L., Richard N., Robert G. Student, U. Conn., 1957-59, Rutgers U., Newark, 1962; BFA, Fairleigh Dickinson U., 1970; postgrad., Caldwell Coll. for Women, 1973-75, Parsons Sch. of Design, N.Y.C., 1978. Cert. tchr. art, N.J. Tchr. art Caldwell-West Caldwell (N.J.) Pub. Schs., 1970-75; pres. Britannia Imports Ltd., Fairfield, N.J., 1979-89; tchr. religious studies Bohrer-Kaufman Hebrew Acad., Randolph, N.J., 1981-82; co-founder, corp. sec. Gibraltar Biol. Labs., Inc., Fairfield, 1970—; dir., co-founder Gibraltar Inst. for Rsch. and Tng., Fairfield, 1984—. Cons. Internat. Antiques and Fine Arts Industries, U.K., 1979-89; cons. in art exhibitry Passaic County Coll., Paterson, N.J., 1989-93; art curator Fairleigh Dickinson U., Rutherford, N.J., 1972-74; curator history of design Bloomfield (N.J.) Coll., 1990-91; lectr. Am. Soc. Microbiology, New Orleans, 1989; spkr. in field. Exhibited in group shows at Bloomfield (N.J.) Coll., 1990, Caldwell Women's Club, N.J., 1991, State Fedn. Women's Clubs Ann. Show, 1992 (1st pl. award 1992), Newark Art Mus., 1992, West (N.J.) Essex Art Assn., 1990, Somerset (N.J.) Art Assn., 1994, Mortimer Gallery, Gladstone, N.J., 1994 (1st pl. award 1998), Tewksbury His. Soc. (1st pl. award 1994), Tewksbury Hist. Soc., 2001, 02, Nat. Meeting Am. Pen Women, Calif., 2002, Washington DC, 2004; one-woman shows include Passaic County Coll., N.J., 1990, Caldwell Coll., N.J., 1990; author children's stories. Chair ann. juried art awards Arts Coun. of Essex Bd. Trustees, Montclair, N.J., 1984-90; chair fundraising Arts Coun. Essex County, N.J., 1989. Recipient 1st place award, N.J. Tewksbury Hist. Soc., 1994, 1998, Juried Art award, 2001, 2002. Mem. AAUW, Soc. Childrens Book Writers and Illustrators, Somerset Art Assn., Nat. League Am. Pen Women (pres. N.J. br., Juried Art award 2001), Barnegat Light Yacht Club. Republican. Avocations: boating, tennis, opera, painting, travel. Home: 5 Standish Dr Mendham Twp Morristown NJ 07960-3224

PRINGLE, BARBARA CARROLL, state legislator; b. N.Y.C., Apr. 4, 1939; d. Nicholas Robert and Anna Joan (Woloshinovich) Terlesky; m. Richard D. Pringle, Nov. 28, 1959; children: Christopher, Rhonda. Student, Cuyahoga C.C. With Dunn & Bradstreet, 1957-60; precinct committeewoman City of Cleve., 1976-77; elected mem. Cleve. City Coun., 1977-81; mem. Ohio Ho. of Reps., Columbus, 1982—. 20th dist. state ctrl. committeewoman, 1982-92; asst. minority leader econ. devel. & small bus. com., pub. utilities com.; mem. Children & Family Svcs. com.; mem. Ohio Legis. Svc. Commn.; mem. Ohio Children's Trust Fund, Midwestern Legis. Conf. Coun. State Govts.' Com. Status Children. Vol. Cleve. Lupus Steering Com., various community orgns.; charter mem. Statue of Liberty Ellis Island Found. Recipient cert. of appreciation Cleve. Mcpl. Ct., 1977, Exch. Club Bklyn., 1978, Cmty. Recreation Appreciation award City of Cleve., 1978, Key to City of Cleve., 1979, Cleve. Area Soapbox Derby cert., 1976, 77, 81, cert. of appreciation Ward 9 Youth League, 1979-82, No. Ohio Patrolman's Benevolent Assn. award, 1983, Cuyahoga County Firefighters award, 1983, Outstanding Pub. Servant award for Outstanding Svc. to Hispanic Cmty., 1985, Nat. Sr. Citizen Hall of Fame award, 1987, cert. of appreciation Cleve. Coun. Unemployed Workers, 1987, Ohio Farmers Union award, 1990, award of appreciation United Labor Agy., 1993, Susan B. Anthony award, 1995. Mem. Nat. Order Women Legislators, Fedn. Dem. Women of Ohio, Nat. Alliance Czech Catholics, St. Michael Ch. Altar and Rosary Soc., Ward 15 Dem. Club, Polish Falcons. Democrat. Home: 708 Timothy Ln Cleveland OH 44109-3733

PRINGLE, NORMA JEAN POARCH, translator, educator; b. Kansas City, Mo., May 29, 1934; d. Travis and Frances Gertrude (Millard) Poarch; m. Robert McClelland Pringle, Feb. 17, 1972 (div. May 1983); 1 child, Travis McClelland. BA, Rockford Coll., 1956; MA, U. Mo., Kansas City, 1968; diploma, Agnese Haury Inst. for Ct. Interpreting, U. Ariz., 1985. Accredited translator by exam. Spanish to English Am. Translators Assn. Adj. instr. Spanish Columbia (Mo.) Coll., 1974—. Trainer, ct. interpreters Transimpex, Kansas City, Mo., 1998—; organizer conf. translators, Columbia, Mo., 1982, Columbia, 92. Author: (course outline for study) Judiciary Interpreting, 1998. Grantee Am. Lit., NEH, 1979. Mem.: Mid-Am. Chpt. Am. Translators Assn. (pres., sec., dir.), Nat. Assn. Judiciary Interpreters, Am. Translators Assn. Avocation: flamenco singing and dancing. Office: Columbia Coll 20th and Rogers Columbia MO 65216

PRINGLE, REBECCA, elementary school educator; b. Phila. m. Nathan Pringle; children: Nathan III, Lauren. BS in Elem. Edn., U. Pitts., 1976; EdM, Pa. State U., 1989. Phys. sci. tchr. Susquehanna Twp. Middle Sch., Harrisburg, Pa. Mem. strategic planning com. on diversity Susquehanna Twp. Sch. Dist.; mem. Inst. for Ednl. Leadership Task Force. Named Cmty. Woman of the Yr., Harrisburg Br. AAUW, 2002; recipient award, Pa. Acad. for the Profession of Tchg. Mem.: NEA (mem. exec. com., bd. dirs., mem. women's issues com., dist. learning task force, chair reading task force 1999—2000), Pa. State Edn. Assn. (bd. dirs., chair human and civil rights award com., task force on minority representation, regional chair leadership devel. com.), Nat. Bd. for Profl. Tchg. Stds. (bd. mem.). Office: Susquehanna Twp Middle Sch 801 Wood St Harrisburg PA 17109

PRINS, JOHANNA, literature educator; PhD in Comparative Lit., Princeton U. Assoc. prof. English and comparative lit. U. Mich., Ann Arbor. Recipient Guggenheim fellowship, 2003. Office: U Mich Dept English and Comparative Lit 3184 Angell Hall Ann Arbor MI 48109

PRINS, LAVONNE KAY, programmer analyst; b. Sibley, Iowa, Feb. 28, 1957; d. Henry Simon and Katherine (Schram) Prins. BA, S.W. State U., Marshall, Minn., 1982; postgrad., Mankato (Minn.) State U., 1982-84. Instr. math. Mankato State U., 1982-84; computer operator Sathers, Round Lake, Minn., 1985; law records analyst ITT Consumer Fin. Corp., St. Louis Park, Minn., 1985-86; systems programmer Metaphor, Eden Prairie, Minn., 1987-89; pres. Ablazon Unltd. Inc., Ramsey, Minn., 1990—97; sr. systems programmer Health Risk Mgmt., Edina, Minn., 1989-91; software engr. Dimensional Medicine, Inc., Minnetonka, Minn., 1992-95; programmer analyst DynaMark Inc., Arden Hills, Minn., 1995-98; sr. programmer analyst United Hardware Distbg. Co., Plymouth, Minn., 1998; ind. contractor, 1999—; inspector Boston Sci. Corp., 2000—02; pres. LaVonne's Home Businesses Inc., 2001—; food insp. USDA, 2002—. Sgt. U.S. Army, 1975-79. Republican. Mem. Reformed Ch. in Am. Avocations: sponsoring needy children, studying foreign languages, writing, piano, travel. Home and Office: 8607 N Zinnia Way Maple Grove MN 55369-4626 Address: 8607 N Zinnia Way Maple Grove MN 55369-4626

PRINTZ, JILLIAN KRUEGER, college program administrator; b. Chgo., Sept. 16, 1942; d. Joseph Davis and Shirley Ann (Sondel) K.; children: Warren Davis, Joseph Granville, Allison Heather. BA in Lit., Bennington Coll., 1964. Asst. curator exhbns. Mus. Art, Ft. Lauderdale, Fla., 1985-86; mktg. coord. Broward C.C., Ft. Lauderdale, Fla., 1986-88, dir. coll. rels., 1988—. Former bd. mem., current assoc. Beaux Arts of the Mus. of Art, Ft. Lauderdale, 1980—; past bd. chair Kids in Distress, Ft. Lauderdale, 1982—, hon. lifetime bd. dirs.; former bd. mem. Women's Polit. Caucus, Ft. Lauderdale, 1990—; media ctr. adminstr. and press liaison, Whitbread Round-the-World Race, Ft. Lauderdale, 1994. Leadership Enhancement and Advancement Program grad., Fla. Dept. Edn. Mem. Nat. Coun. Mktg. and Pub. Rels. (conf. presenter 1992, 96, Gold Medallion Achievement 1995, Silver Medallion Achievement 1994), Women in Comm., Inc. (former bd. com. chair), Leadership Fla., Fla. Assn. C.Cs. (commn. chair 1988—, Jim Mulcahey award 1993). Office: Broward CC 225 E Las Olas Blvd Fort Lauderdale FL 33301-2208 Office Phone: 954-201-7550. Business E-Mail: jprintz@broward.edu.

PRINZ, KRISTIE DAWN, lawyer; b. Columbus, Ga., July 26, 1973; d. Stephen Charles and Helen Ann (Dunlap) P. BA in Spanish and Polit. Sci. summa cum laude, Furman U., 1995; JD, Vanderbilt U., 1998. Bar: Ga. 1998, Calif. 2001. Summer assoc. Rose Immigration Law Firm, Nashville, Tenn., 1996; rsch. asst. Vanderbilt U., Nashville, 1996-97; summer assoc. Bruce, Weathers, Corley, Dughman & Lyle, Nashville, 1997; assoc. Mozley, Finlayson & Loggins, LLP, Atlanta, 1998, Schnader Harrison Segal & Lewis LLP, Atlanta, 1999-2000, Pennie & Edmonds LLP, Palo Alto, Calif., 2000—. Mem. adv. bd. Knoxville Jour., 1990-91. Vol. tchr. English Classes for Refugees, Knoxville, Tenn, 1993; mem. Collegiate Ednl. Svc. Corps. Furman U., Greenville, S.C., 1991-95. Mem.: ABA, Computer Law Assn., Licensing Execs. Soc., Calif. Lawyers for the Arts, Forum for Women Entrepreneurs, Calif. Women Lawyers, Nat. Assn. Women Lawyers, San Francisco Bar Assn., Atlanta Bar Assn. (mem. Therell H.S. Com.), Palo Alto Bar Assn., Churchill Club, Phi Sigma Iota, Sigma Delta Pi, Phi Beta Kappa, Sr. Order Furman U., Kappa Alpha Theta (Elizabeth Staley Leadership award 1995), Phi Sigma Alpha. Avocations: running, playing piano, watching Spanish language movies and programs, tennis.

PRIOLEAU, SARA NELLIENE, dentist; b. Hopkins, S.C., Apr. 10, 1940; d. Willie Oree and Wilhelmina Illorah (Neal) P.; m. William F. McKeever, Aug. 31, 1969 (div. Mar. 1982); children: Kara, William P.; m. William R. Montgomery, Dec. 18, 1984; stepchildren: Sharon, Myra, John. BS, S.C. State U., 1960, MS, 1966; DMD, U. Pa., 1970. Rotating gen. dentist intern Phila. Gen. Hosp., 1970-71; staff dentist Comprehensive Group Health Ctr., Phila., 1971-72; dental dir. Hamilton Health Ctr., 1972-97; CEO Cmty. Dental Assocs., P.C., Harrisburg, 1976—; dental dir. Selinsgrove Ctr., 1999—2002. Cons. Region III Head Start, Phila., 1972—; dental dir. Healthmate HMO-Hamilton Health Ctr., Harrisburg, 1988-96, Healthmate HMO/Health Am., Harrisburg, 1996-97; v. p. bd. dirs. Harrisburg Area C.C., 1990-99, v.p., 1997-99; adv. bd. Mellon Bank Commonwealth Region, Harrisburg, 1995-2001, Capital Area Math./Sci. Alliance, Harrisburg, 1995-99. Named one of 50 Best Women in Bus., Dept. of Commerce and Econ. Devel., Harrisburg, 1997; recipient Athena award C. of C., 1995. Fellow Internat. Coll. Dentists; mem. ADA, Am. Assn. Women Dentists, Nat. Dental Assn., Pa. Dental Assn., Harrisburg Area Dental Soc. (v.p. 2000-01, pres. 2001-02), Soroptimist Internat. (past pres. Harrisburg chpt.), The Links Inc (past pres. Herrisburg chpt.). Republican. Baptist. Avocations: travel, golf, shopping. Home: 1094 Cardinal Dr Harrisburg PA 17111-3730 Office: Cmty Dental Assocs PC 2451 N 3rd St Harrisburg PA 17110-1902 Office Phone: 717-238-8163.

PRISSEL, BARBARA ANN, paralegal, law educator; b. Plum City, Wis., July 7, 1946; d. John Henry and Mary Ann Louise (Dankers) Seipel; m. Stephen Joseph Prissel, Dec. 16, 1967; children: Angela, Benjamin. Graduate with honors, Mpls. Bus. Coll., 1966; student, Moraine Park Tech. Coll., Wis., 1983—. Cert. interactive TV, adult edn. instr. Legal sec. Mott, Grose, Von Holtum & Hefferan, Mpls., 1966-67, Whelan, Morey & Morey Attys. at Law, Durand, Wis., 1967-70, Murry Law Office, River Falls, Wis., 1968-70, Potter, Wefel & Nettesheim, Wisconsin Rapids, Wis., 1970-71; sec. to adminstr. Moraine Park Tech. Coll., Fond du Lac, Wis., 1971-72; paralegal Kilgore Law Office, Ripon, Wis., 1985—2004, Grant Law Office, Waupun, Wis., 2004—. Chmn. legal adv. com. Moraine Park Tech. Coll., Fond du Lac, Wis., 1996-98, mem. adminstrv. assts. adv. com., 1984-86; mem. legal adv. commn. Moraine Park Tech. Coll., 1984—. Contbr. poems to newspapers. Ch. rep. Ch. Women United, Ripon, Wis., 1984-87; pianist Christian Women's Orgn., Ripon, 1985-95; pianist, organist Our Lady of [illegible] Ch., [illegible], Wis., 1987— . Mem.: NALS, Legal Profls. Assn. (East Ctrl. Wis. pres. 1994—95, sec. 1995—96, chmn. Day-In-Ct. 1999, NALS Fedn. liaison 2000—02, sec. 2001—02, v.p. 2003—, state legal ed. task force 2003—, chmn. ednl. liaison com., Legal award of Excellence 1995—96), Wis. Assn. Legal Secs. (state legal ednl. liaison com. 1997—, state legal edn. task force 2003—), Nat. Assn. Legal Secs. Roman Catholic. Avocations: teaching and playing piano, creative writing, cooking, swimming, exercising. Home: 129 Wolverton Ave Ripon WI 54971-1144

PRITCHARD, BETTY JEAN, retired art educator; b. Dana, Ind., Nov. 25, 1934; d. Terrence Ellis and Mary Ethel (Wishard) P. BS in Arts and Crafts, Ind. State U., 1957; MA in Art Edn. and Painting, Purdue U., 1972; postgrad., Ball State U., 1958, 66; postgrad. computer graphics works, Ind. U., Bloomington, 1985. Cert. pub. sch. tchr., supt., Ind., Ky., Ill. Art tchr. 1-12 Sheridan (Ind.) H.S., 1957-60; art tchr. 3-12 Danville (Ind.) City Schs., 1961-62; art tchr. 1-12 Brownsburg (Ind.) Comm. Schs., 1962-64; art tchr. 7-12 Blue River Valley S.C., New Castle, Ind., 1964-67; art tchr. 1-8 Twin Lakes Sch. Corp., Monticello, Ind., 1967-69; art tchr. 1-6 Tippecanoe Sch. Corp., Lafayette, Ind., 1972-75; art tchr., children's art Art Ctr. Sch., Albuquerque, 1977-78; tutor supr. Albuquerque Pub. Schs., 1977-78, art lab. asst., 1978-79; art tchr. 7-12 Attica (Ind.) Consolid. Schs., 1979-80; art tchr. 1-8 Southwest Parke C.S., Mecca, Ind., 1983-85; painting instr. Danville Area C.C., Ill., 1987-88; substitute tchr. Albuquerque Pub. Schs., 1989-2000; ret., 2000. One-artist and group shows of paintings at Purdue U., Jonson Gallery, U. N.Mex., Union Bldg., U. N.Mex., 1976, 77, 88. One-woman and group shows include Purdue U., Jonson Gallery, U. N.Mex., Union Bldg., U. N.Mex., 1976-78, Arts and Crafts Benefit. Mem. Neighborhood Watch, Bernalillo, N.Mex., 1995—97; mem. animal legal The Nature Conservancy; docent Albuquerque Mus.; vol. greeter Albuquerque Biol. Park; charter mem. WWII Meml. Women's History Mus.; vol. youth exhibit Arts and Crafts Fair. Grantee Wabash Valley Projects, Tippecanoe Arts Fedn. and Nat. Endowment of the Arts, Lafayette, 1987. Mem.: Animal Protection Inst., Sierra Club, Animal Legal Def., Internat. Fund for Animal Welfare, Nat. Wildlife Fedn., Doris Day Animal League, U.S. Defenders of Wildlife, The Wilderness Soc., Mus. of Albuquerque Found., Nat. Resources Def. Coun. Methodist. Avocations: animal rights and environ. issues, music, art. Home: 324 E Avenida Bernalillo Bernalillo NM 87004-9018

PRITCHARD, SARAH MARGARET, library director; b. Boston, Feb. 8, 1955; d. Wilbur Louis and Kathleen Hunton (Moss) P.; m. Timothy John Brennan, Aug. 20, 1977 (div. 1993). BA, U. Md., 1975; MA in French, U. Wis., 1976, MLS, 1977. Intern Libr. Congress, Washington, 1977-78, reference specialist in women's studies, 1978-88, head microform reading rm., 1988-90; sr. program officer Assn. Rsch. Librs., Washington, 1990-91, assoc. exec. dir., 1991-92; acad. libr. mgmt. intern Coun on Libr. Resources Princeton U., N.J., 1988-89; dir. librs. Smith Coll., Northampton, Mass., 1992-99; univ. libr. U. Calif., Santa Barbara, 1999—. Editl. advisor Women's Rsch. and Edn. Inst., Washington, 1987-92; bd. dirs. Western Mass. Regional Libr. Sys., 1997-98; bd. dirs. U. Calif. So. Regional Libr. Facility, 1999—, Gold Coast Libr. Network, Libr. of Calif., 2003—. Editor: The Women's Annual, 1984; compiler ARL Stats., 1990-92; contbr. articles to profl. jours.; mem. editl. bd. Jour. Acad. Librarianship, 1993-99, Portal: Librs. and the Acad., 2000—; contbg. editor Libr. Issues, 1994-99. Trustee Leroy C. Merritt Humanitarian Fund, 1991-94. Named Wis. Alumni Rsch. Found. fellow, 1975-77, Outstanding Alumna U. Wis. Sch. of Libr. and Info. Studies, 1997. Mem. ALA (chair machine assisted reference sect. 1986-87, chair women's studies sect. 1989-90, coun. 1990-98, 2000—, chair stds. com. 1998-2002, chair ethics com. 2002—, Equality award 1997), Nat. Women's Studies Assn., Cosmos Club. Democrat. Office: U Calif Davidson Libr Santa Barbara CA 93106

PRITCHARD, TIFFANY MAXWELL, writer, educator; b. Fredericksburg, Va., Dec. 2, 1974; d. David John Douglas and Patricia Elaine (Bryant) Maxwell; m. Walter Eric Pritchard, Sept. 12, 1998; 1 child, Kassidy Blayne. AA in Bus. and Mktg., No. Va. U., 1994; degree in Fashion Design and Merchandising, Strafford U.; student in English Lit., Stratford U. Tchr. various schs., Va., 1994—. Author: (poem) Someday, 2001 (Editors Choice award, 01), Blowing Kisses to Heaven, 2002 (Pub. Choice award, 02). Mem. Nat. Campaign for Tolerance; vol. Hope House, Fredericksburg, Va., Mary Washington Hosp., Fredericksburg, Human Soc., Fredericksburg. Mem.: ASPCA, Nat. Mus. Women in Arts, Humane Soc. U.S. Avocation: modelling. Home: 10713 Holly Brooke Dr Spotsylvania VA 22553

PRITCHETT, LORI L. real estate broker, secondary school educator; b. Redding, CA, Dec. 21, 1966; d. Lane L. and Linda L. Pritchett. BA, Univ. of the Pacific, Stockton, Calif., 1985—90. Cert. Real Estate Broker Calif., 1993, Tchg. credential Calif., 1989. HS tchr. Red Bluff HS, Red Bluff, Calif., 1989—90; Jr. HS tchr. Anderson Mid. Sch., Anderson, Calif., 1990—91; Jr. HS substitute Evergreen Mid. Sch., Cottonwood, Calif., 1991—; real estate broker Running L Realty, Cottonwood, Calif., 1993—. Mem. Multiple Listing Com., Shasta Assn. of Realtors, Redding, Calif., 1995—, Edn. Com., Shasta Assn. of Realtors, Redding, Calif., 1995—97, Bus. and Tech. Com., Sahsta Assn. of Realtors, Redding, Calif., 1998—2001, chmn., 1999; chair Multiple Listing Com., Shasta Assn. of Realtors, Redding, Calif., 2003—04. Multiple listing com. chmn. Shasta Assn. of Realtors, Redding, Calif., 2003—03. Mem.: Nat. Assn. of Realtors, Shasta Assn. of Realtors, Calif. Assn. of Realtors. R-Conservative. Avocations: travel, ranching, computer tech., sports. Office: Running L Realty PO Box 616 Cottonwood CA 96022 Home: 15790 Bowman Cottonwood CA 96022 E-mail: lori@runningl.com, lori@runningl.com.

PRIVES, CAROL, biologist, educator; Prof. biology Columbia U., N.Y.C., NY, chmn. Dept. Biol. Scis. Mem. sci. adv. bd. NIH Virology Study Section; mem. Damon Runyon Fellowship Com.; mem. sci. adv. bd. N.J. Cancer Commn., Howard Hughes Med. Inst. Mem. editl. bd.: Cell, Genes & Devel., Jour. Biology, Chemistry and Cancer Rsch.; editor: Jour. Virology, 1991—99. Fellow: Am. Acad. Arts and Scis. Office: Dept Biological Scis Columbia Univ 816 Fairchild Center MC422 1212 Amsterdam Ave New York NY 10027

PRIVETT, CARYL PENNEY, judge; b. Birmingham, Ala., Jan. 7, 1948; d. William Kinnaird Privett and Katherine Speake (Binford) Ennis. BA, Vanderbilt U., 1970; JD, NYU, 1973. Bar: Ala. 1973, U.S. Dist. Ct. (so. dist.) Ala. 1973, U.S. Dist. Ct. (no. dist.) Ala. 1974, U.S. Ct. Appeals (5th cir.) 1974, U.S. Ct. Appeals (11th cir.) 1981. Assoc. Crawford & Blacksher, Mobile, Ala., 1973—74, Adams, Baker & Clemon, Birmingham, Ala., 1974—76; asst. US atty. no. dist. Ala. US Atty.'s Office, US Dept. Justice, Birmingham, Ala., 1976—94, first asst. US atty., 1992—93, US atty., 1995—97, chief asst., 1997—98; pvt. practice Birmingham, Ala., 1998—2003; city prosecutor City of Mountain Brook, 1998—2003; cir. judge 10th Jud. Cir. of Ala., 2003—. Adj. prof. Cumberland Sch. Law Samford U., 1998—. Active Downtown Dem. Club, Birmingham, Ala.; bd. dir. Planned Parenthood Ala., Birmingham, Ala., Legal Aid Soc., Birmingham, Ala., 1986—88, pres., 1988; sec., founder Lawyers for Choice Ala., 1989—92; chair domestic violence com. City of Birmingham, Ala., 1989—91; sustaining mem. Jr. League Birmingham, Ala.; mem. Photography Guild; active Birmingham Mus. Art, Ala. Named, Outstanding Young Women Am., 1977, 1978; recipient Cert. in Color Photography, U. Ala. Birmingham, 1989, Commr.'s Spl. citation, Food and Drug Adminstrn. Mem.: ABA, Ala. Law Inst., Adminstrv. Dir., Ala. Acad. Atty. Mediators (pres. 2002), Birmingham Bar Found. (pres. 2001), Birmingham Bar Assn. (exec. com. 1996-98), Ala. Bar Assn. (chmn. women in the profession com. 1997-99), Fed. Bar Assn. (pres. Birmingham chpt. 1979), Ala. Solution, Leadership Birmingham, Women's Network, Women's Fund, Altamont Alumni Assn., Summit Club. Presbyterian. Avocation: photography. Home: 20 Norman Dr Birmingham AL 35213-4310 Office: 660 [illegible] Courthouse 716 Richard Arrington Blvd Birmingham AL 35203 E-mail: carylprivett@mindspring.com.

PRIVETTE, NANCY ANNETTE, school system administrator; b. Fayetteville, N.C., Sept. 20, 1967; d. Grady Lee and Nancy Carol (Shatley) P.; m. Patrick Donovan Darnell, 2001. BA, U. N.C., 1989, MA in Pub. Adminstrn., 2000. Reporter Statesville (N.C.) Record & Landmark, 1990-94, audio-text coord., 1994-95; mng. editor Mooresville (N.C.) Tribune, 1995-97; pub. info. officer, dir. before and after sch. program Mooresville Sch. Sys., 1997—2000; pub. info. coord. Charlotte-Mecklenburg Schs., 2000—01, City of Concord, 2001—. Chair Woods Tech. Adv. Com., Mooresville, Chamber Edn. Com., Mooresville, Mitchell C.C. Adv. Bd., Mooresville, centennial fundraising com. U. N.C., Greensboro; bd. dirs. United Way. Mem. N.C. Press Assn., Mooresville/South Iredell C. of C., U. N.C. Greensboro Alumni Assn. (bd. dirs.), Mooresville Civitan Club (sec., bd. dirs.). Democrat. Baptist. Avocations: golf, tennis, reading, cross-stitch.

PRIZIO, BETTY J. volunteer, retired property manager; b. LA, Jan. 23, 1928; d. Harry W. and Irene L. (Connell) Campbell; divorced; children: David P., John W., Robert H., James R. AA in Social Sci., L.A. City Coll., 1949. Owner, mgr. indsl. bldgs. and condominiums, mktg. exec., Tustin, Calif., 1976—. Co-chair silent auction Am. Lung Assn., Santa Ana, 1997-2001, co-chair Big Breath Easy charity event; bd. dirs. Founders Chpt. Aux., Providence Speech and Hearing Ctr., 1986-88, aux. pres., 1986-89; vol. Western Med. Ctr. Aux., 1985-89, chmn. gift shop com., 1987-88, 2d v.p., 1992, aux. pres., 1999, jr. vol. adv., bd. dirs. fundraising group, scholarship com., Focus on Women com. 1990—, buyer for gift shop, 1998—, 4th v.p. gift shop, 1993, pres., 1999-2001; adv. coun. Chapman U., Orange, Calif., 1986-87; bd. dirs. Pres. Assocs., 1985-86, Chapman Music Assocs., 1986—, Santa Ana YWCA, 1976-77; adv. coun. Orange County chpt. Freedoms Found. at Valley Forge, 1985—; active United Meth. Ch., Olive Crest Treatment Ctr.; pres. Western Medicine Ctr. Disciplinary, 1999. Named Vol. of Yr., Gift Shop, 1999, Vol. of Nov., hosp. staff and physicians, 2003. Mem.: Tustin Hist. Soc. (bd. dirs. 1988—90), Western Med. Ctr. Aux. (life; pres. 1999, 2000, 2001, Col. of Yr. 1999). Republican. Avocations: gardening, arts and crafts, travel, photography. Home: 2522 N Tustin Ave Unit D Santa Ana CA 92705

PROCTOR, BARBARA GARDNER, advertising agency executive, writer; b. Asheville, N.C. d. William and Bernice (Baxter) Gardner; m. Carl L. Proctor, July 20, 1961 (div. Nov. 1963); 1 son, Morgan Eugene. BA, Talladega Coll., 1954. Music critic, contbg. editor Down Beat Mag., Chgo., 1958—; internat. dir. Vee Jay Records, Chgo., 1961-64; copy supr. Post-Keyes-Gardner Advt., Inc., Chgo., 1965-68, Gene Taylor Assos., Chgo., 1968-69, North Advt. Agt., Chgo., 1969-70; contbr. to gen. periodicals, 1952—; founder Proctor & Gardner Advt., Chgo., 1970—, pres., CEO. Pres., CEO Proctor Comm. Network, Chgo. Mem. Chgo. Urban League, Chgo. Econ. Devel. Corp.; cons. pub. rels. and promotion, record industry. Author: (TV documentary) Blues for a Gardenia, 1963. Bd. dirs. People United to Save Humanity, Better Bus. Bur. Recipient Armstrong Creative Writing award, 1954; awards Chgo. Fedn. Advt., Frederick Douglas Humanitarian award, 1975; named Chgo. Advt. Woman of Yr., 1974. Mem. NARAS, Chgo. Media Women, Women's Advt. Club, N.Y. Art Dirs. Club, Woman's Day Club, Cosmopolitan C. of C. (dir.), Female Execs. Assn., Internat. Platform Assn., Smithsonian Instn. Assos.

PROCTOR, BETTY JANE, English language and literature educator; b. Houston, June 10, 1952; d. H.D. and Opal Jimmie (Givens) P. BA, U. Houston, 1973, MA, 1974; PhD, Tex. A&M U., 1978. Instr. English, Tex. A&M U., College Station, 1977-78, U. Houston, 1978-80, dir. devel. English, 1980-82; instr. English, Houston C.C., 1982—. Editor: Southwestern Studies, 1993—, Tchg. English in C.C., 1993—. Vol. Harris County Rep. Com., Houston, 1988-95; founding mem. The Guild of Baylor Coll. of Medicine. Mem. South Cen. MLA, Coll. English Assn., Phi Kappa Phi. Avocations: decorating, gourmet cooking, sewing, fiction writing, screenwriting.

PROCTOR, BRILEY ELIZABETH, psychologist, educator; b. Tallahassee, Fla., Apr. 5, 1969; d. Ralph E. Proctor, Jr. and Rebecca Proctor; m. Matthew Claps, Apr. 27, 2002. PhD in Sch. Psychology, U. Fla., 1999. Faculty mem. Fla. State U., Tallahassee, 1999—. Grantee, Williams Family Found., 2001—03, Coll. Edn., 2002, U. South Fla., 2003—. Mem.: Fla. Assn. Sch. Psychologists (exec. bd. 1999—). Achievements include research in learning disabilities, attention deficit disorders, academic interventions, and policy issues affecting children and education. Office: Florida State University 307 Stone Building Tallahassee FL 32306

PROCTOR, CHERYL ANN, music educator; b. Ashtabula, Ohio, Aug. 29, 1957; d. Milton Eugene and Verna Maxine Proctor. B in music edn., Mt. Union Coll., 1975—79; M in edn. in sch. counseling, Kent State U., 1988. Permanent Music Tchg. Cert. State of Ohio Dept. of Edn., 1987, Provisional Cert. for Sch. Counseling State of Ohio Dept. of Edn., 2002. Elem. music tchr. Newbury Local Schools, Ohio, 1979—. Handbell choir dir. Newbury Cmty. Ch., Ohio, 2002—03. Grant, Frohring Found., 1983. Mem.: United Methodists in Music and Worship Arts (assoc.; north east ohio sec. 1994—96), Music Educator's Nat. Conf. (assoc.), Newbury Edn. Assn. (assoc.; sec. 2002—), Delta Kappa Gamma (assoc.), Mu Phi Epsilon. Protestant. Avocations: reading, gardening, nature watcher. Home: 13333 Glen Hill Dr Chesterland OH 44026 Office: Newbury Local Schools 14775 Auburn Rd Newbury OH 44065 E-mail: ne_proctor@lgca.org.

PROCTOR, GEORGANNE C. company executive; b. 1957; m. Robert Proctor. BS in Bus. Mgmt., U. S.D.; MBA in Fin., Calif. State U., Hayward. From fin. analyst Bechtel Financing Svcs. (now part of Bechtel Enterprises), 1982-89; mgr. Bechtel Info. Tech. Group., 1989-91, mgr. project cost controls for Disney MGM Studio project, 1991; dir. fin. and acctg. Internat. Home Video divsn. Disney Co., 1991-93; dir. fin. Walt Disney Imagineering, 1993-94; CFO Bechtel Enterprises, 1994-97; sr. v.p., CFO Bechtel Group, Inc., San Francisco, 1997—2002, senior v.p., 1997—. Amb. Calif. State. U., Hayward. Office: Bechtel Group Inc PO Box 193965 San Francisco CA 94119-3965*

PROCTOR, MILLICENT CARLÉ, social worker; b. Chgo., Mar. 9, 1944; d. Harry and Erene (Merriweather) Vinée; m. Donald Proctor (div. 1972); m. James Smith (dec. 1995). BA in Polit. Sci. and History, U. Ill.; MSW, Loyola U.; PhD, 1986. Cert. social worker, Ill.; master addiction counselor. Caseworker, case work supr. Cook County (Ill.) Dept. Pub. Aid; social work supr. dept. children and family svcs. State of Ill.; exec. dir. Adler Adoption Agy., Chgo.; dir. pub. health social svc. Chgo. Dept. Health, coord. mental health info. and edn. Contbr. articles to profl. jours. Active women's bd. Wesley Hosp., materials mgmt. vol. Mem. Am. Pub. Health Assn., Chgo. Child Care Soc., Ill. Child Care Soc., Ill. Psychiat. Assn., Blind Assn. Ill., Acad. Cert. Social Workers, Am. Psychologists Assn., Nat. Assn. Forensic Counselors. Office: Ste 1305 8 S Michigan Ave Chicago IL 60603-3375

PROCYSON, MARY G. WALTON, critical care nurse; b. Coatesville, Pa., May 4, 1948; d. Marvin O. and Florence G. (Johnson) W.; m. Michael Procyson, 1991. Diploma in Nursing, Brandywine Hosp. Sch. Nursing, Coatesville, 1970. RN, Pa.; CCRN. Critical care nurse Brandywine Hosp.,

Coatesville, Pa., 1970-82, Coatesville VA Med. Ctr., 1982-85, 86-87, Wilmington (Del.) VA Med. Ctr., 1985-86, 91—, Chester County Hosp., West Chester, Pa., 1987-91; ind. contractor as critical care nurse, 1994-95. Mem. AACN (cert.). Home: 520 Main St Parkesburg PA 19365-1014

PROENZA, THERESA BUTLER, adult education educator, writer; b. Savannah, Ga., Jan. 18, 1961; d. Lee Bradford Sr. and Theresa Zipperer Butler; m. Luis Mariano Proenza, July 2, 1983. BS in Biology with Spanish minor, U. Ga., 1982; MBA, U. Alaska, 1991. Biology, Spanish and Math. tchr. Jefferson (Ga.) HS, 1982—85; mgr. Gazebo Interiors, Athens, Ga., 1985—86; grant writer, conf. and lectr. corrd. U. Alaska, Fairbanks, 1986—90; rsch. asst. Alaska Dept. Trans. Rsch., Fairbanks, 1990—91; dir. U. Alaska Fairbanks Small Bus. Devel. Ctr., 1991—94; asst. dir. Purdue Ctr. for Internat. Bus. Edn. Rsch., West Lafayette, Ind., 1994—96; adminstrv. dir. Purdue U. Tech. Transfer Initiative, West Lafayette, Ind., 1996—97. Chair elect governance com. Summa Health Sys., Akron, 2003; mem. Ohio Supreme Ct. Task Force on Rules of Profl. Conduct, Columbus, 2003—; chair, pers. budget com., lay mem. Ohio Supreme Ct. Bd. Commrs. for Grievances and Discipline; mem. fin. com. Summa Health Sys. Hosps., mem. ethics com.; chair Stan Hywet Hall and Gardens Found. Bd. Dirs. Guest columnist (newspaper bus. column) Fairbanks Daily News-Miner, 1992—94. Recipient Top 100 Women of Summit County, YWCA, 2001. Lutheran. Avocations: cooking, sailing, bicycling, reading, scuba diving.

PROKOP, SUSAN, disability rights advocate; b. Washington, Aug. 30, 1956; d. Jerome and Lotus (Therkelsen) P.; m. James Shafter Turpin, May 16, 1998. B in Govt., Georgetown U., 1978; MPA, U. Va., 1980. Legis. asst. to Del. James Almand, Richmond, 1980, 81; housing mgmt. specialist Va. Housing Devel. Authority, Richmond, 1981-82; staff asst. Aerospace Industries, Washington, 1982-83; sr. legis. asst. to Congresswoman Marcy Kaptur Washington, 1983-89; dir. health policy Am. Soc. Internal Medicine, Washington, 1989-97; assoc. advocacy dir. Paralyzed Vets. of Am., Washington, 1997—. Mem. Consortium for Citizens with Disabilities, Am. Pub. Health Assoc., Washington, 1997—, Women in Govt. Rels., Washington, 1990—. Bd. dirs. Cmty. Residences, Inc., Arlington, Va., 1995—, Arlington Arts Ctr., 1996-99; del. Dem. Nat. Conv., 1996; mem. Arlington Dem. Comm., 1975—. Democrat. Methodist. Avocations: photography, writing, painting. E-mail: Turkop@worldnet.att.net.

PRONESTI, ROSA C. artist; b. W. Nantmeal Twp., Pa., Aug. 27, 1932; d. Salvatore Maria and Frances (Bavuso-Volpe) P. Student, Hussian Art Sch., Phila., 1954. With Deco Art, Phila., 1950-51; asst. artist Fliesher Art Meml., Phila., 1951-68; mech. artist William F. Bird Studio, Phila., 1952-65, Designers Frank Nofer Inc., Phila., 1968-85. One-woman shows include Cathedral Village Retirement Home, Andora, Pa., 1996, 98, Stone Harbor Miniature 2x3 Art Shows, 1993 2002, Jewish Comm. Ctr., 2001-02; group shows include Atlantic City (N.J.) Art Ctr., 1997-2003, Long Beach Island Miniature Show, 1985-2001 Surf City, N.J., Yellow Springs Art Show, Chester Springs, Pa., 1997-2001, Ocean City Libr., 2003. Mem. Atlantic City Art Ctr. (1st and 2d Pl. awards), Nat. Mus. Women in the Arts, Del. Artist Guild, Woodmere Mus. Art (1st and 2d Pl. awards), Phila. Water Color Soc. Roman Catholic. Home: 28 N Frontenac Ave Margate City NJ 08402-1853

PRONOVOST, VICKI S. special education educator; b. Pasco, Wash., Apr. 10, 1977; d. Renee G. Pronovost. MEd, Portland State U., 2000; BS, We. Oreg. U., 1998. Spl. edn. tchr. Beaverton Sch. Dist., Oreg., 2002—, Multnomah Ednl. Svc. Dist., Portland, Oreg., 2000—02. Ford Family Ednl. Scholarship, Ford Family Found., 1995—2000. Mem.: Coun. for Exceptional Children (assoc.). D-Conservative. Avocations: softball, soccer, camping, volleyball. Home: 19737 SW Deepwell Ct Aloha OR 97007 Personal E-mail: vickipro@juno.com.

PROPST, CATHERINE LAMB, biotechnology company executive; b. Charlotte, N.C., Mar. 10, 1946; d. James Pinckney and Eliza Mayo (Mills) P. BA magna cum laude, Vanderbilt U., 1967; M of Philosophy, Yale U., 1970, PhD, 1973. Head microbiology div. GTE Labs., Waltham, Mass., 1974-77; various mgmt. positions Abbott Labs., North Chgo., Ill., 1977-80; v.p. rsch. and devel. Ayerst (Wyeth) Labs., Plainview, NY, 1980-83; v.p. rsch. and devel. worldwide Flow Gen. Inc., McLean, Va., 1983-85; pres., CEO Affiliated Sci. Inc., Ingleside, Ill., 1985-97; pres., chmn. and CEO Tex. Biotech. Found., Hempstead, Tex., 1997—. Vis. prof. genetics U. Ill., Chgo., 1989—90; founder, exec. dir. Ctr. for Biotech., Northwestern U., 1990—95; pres. Ill. Biotech. Ctr., 1995—97; bd. dirs. several cos.; bd. dirs., mem. sci. adv. bd. Keystone Symposia on Molecular and Cellular Biology, 1997—2002. Author and editor: Computer-Aided Drug Design, 1989, Nucleic Acid Targeted Drug Design, 1992; contbr. articles to profl. jours. Named to Outstanding Working Women in the U.S., 1982; recipient many sci. and bus. awards. Fellow Soc. Indsl. Microbiology (bd. dirs. 1990-93), Nat. Coun. Biotech Ctrs. (bd. dirs. 1995-97); mem. AAAS, Nat. Wildlife Fedn., Consortium for Plant Biotech. Rsch. (bd. dirs. 1994-99), Phi Beta Kappa, Sigma Xi. Episcopalian. Avocations: horseback riding, skiing, raising Black Angus and Black Brangus cattle. Office: Texas Biotech Found PO Box 17 Hempstead TX 77445-0017 Fax: 979-826-9710.

PROST, SHARON, federal judge; b. Newburyport, Mass., May 24, 1951; m. Kenneth F. Greene, June 24, 1984; 1 child, Matthew Prost-Greene. BS, Cornell U., 1973; MBA, George Washington U., 1975, LLM in Taxation, 1984; JD, Am. U., 1979. Bar: D.C. Labor rels. specialist Office of Personnel Mgmt., 1973-76; with Gen. Acctg. Office, 1976-79; trial atty. Fed. Labor Rels. Authority, 1980-83; atty. chief counsel's office Dept. of Treasury, 1983-84; assoc. solicitor Nat. Labor Rels. Bd., 1984-89; chief minority labor counsel Senate Com. on Labor and Human Resources, 1989-93; minority chief counsel Senate Com. on the Judiciary, 1993—2001; judge U.S. Court of Appeal, Federal Cir., 2001—. Office: US Court Appeals Fed Cir 717 Madison Pl NW Washington DC 20439

PROTHO, JESSIE, vocational school educator; d. Duncan and Julia Mae (Edmond) McKenzie; widowed; children: Phyllis Noble, Carl Protho. Diploma, Scientific Beauty Sch., 1947; student, Walker Beauty Coll.; BS in Edn., Indiana U., 1968, MS in Edn., 1971. Lic. vocational dir. Indiana State U., 1979. Cosmetology tchr. Gary (Ind.) Area Career Ctr.; with Johnie's Beauty Shop, 1947-53, Jewelry Tng. Svc., 1948-49, Swartchild and Co., 1949-53; self-employed beauty shop owner, 1953-65; educator Gary (Ind.) Community School Corp., 1965—. Mem. AAUW, NAACP, Ind. U. Alumni Assn., Nat. Cosmetology Assn., Vocat. Indsl. Club, Alpha Phi Omega, Phi Delta Kappa (sec. 1991-92, Tchr. of Yr.). Avocations: bowling, sewing, cooking, creative hair styling. Home: 6710 Adams St Merrillville IN 46410-3407

PROTHROW-STITH, DEBORAH, academic administrator, public health educator; MD, Harvard U., 1979. Resident Boston City Hosp.; state commr. health Pub. Health Commonwealth Mass., 1987; assoc. dean govt. and faculty devel. Sch. Pub. Health Harvard U., Boston, prof. pub. health practice. Author: Peace by Piece: A Guide for Preventing Community Violence, 1995. Mem. Nat. Commn. Crime Control and Prevention, 1995. Recipient Sec. Health and Human Svc. award, 1989, World Health Day award, 1993. Office: Harvard Sch Pub Health Dept Health Policy & Mgmt 718 E Huntington Ave Boston MA 02115 Fax: 617-495-8543. E-mail: dp-s@hsph.harvard.edu.

PROULX, (EDNA) ANNIE, writer; b. Norwich, Conn., Aug. 22, 1935; d. George Napolean and Lois Nellie (Gill) Proulx; m. James Hamilton Lang, June 22, 1969 (div. 1990); children: Sylvia Marion Bullock Clarkson, Jonathan Edward Lang, Gillis Crowell Lang, Morgan Hamilton Lang. BA cum laude, U. Vt., 1969; MA, Sir George Williams U., Montreal, Can., 1973; DHL (hon.), U. Maine, 1994; LLD, Concordia U., Montreal, 2002; DLitt (hon.), U. Toronto, 2000. Author: Heart Songs and Other Stories, 1988, Postcards, 1991 (PEN/Faulkner award 1993), The Shipping News, 1993 (Chgo. Tribune Heartland award 1993, Irish Times Internat. Fiction award 1993, Nat. Book award for fiction 1994, Pulitzer Prize for fiction 1994), Accordion Crimes, 1996 (Dos Passos prize for lit. 1996), Brokeback Mountain, 1998 (Nat. Mag. award 1998), Brokeback Mountain, 1998, Close Range: Wyoming Stories, 1999, That Old Ace in the Hole, 2002; contbr. more than 50 articles to mags. and jours.; editor: Best American Short Stories of 1997. Recipient Dos Passos prize for Lit., Longwood Coll., 1997, Ambassador Book award English Speaking Union, 2000, Best Fiction 1999 Book award The New Yorker, 2000, Willa award, 2000, Evil Companions Lit. award, 2001; Kress fellow Harvard U., 1974, fellow Vt. Coun. Arts, 1989, NEA, 1991, Guggenheim Found., 1992; rsch. grantee Inter.-U. Ctr., 1975; resident Ucross Found., 1990, 92. Mem. PEN Am. Ctr., Phi Beta Kappa, Phi Alpha Theta. Avocations: canoeing, reading, fishing. Office: c/o Simon & Schuster 1230 Ave of Americas New York NY 10020

PROUT, KATHLEEN SOLIOZY, realtor; b. Newport, R.I., Dec. 22, 1947; d. Charles Steven and Sadie (Hidson) Soliozy; m. James Gregory Prout III, Aug. 8, 1971 (dec. May 1995); children: Brendan Charles, Heather Kathleen, James Gregory Prout IV. BA, Salve Regina U., 1971. Cert. tchr. R.I., realtor Calif. Tchr. Norfolk Schs., Va., 1972, Charleston Schs., SC, 1972—73; sales rep. Pyckles Buttons & Bows, 1983—84; tchr. Assets Sch., Honolulu, 1992—94. Realtor Calif. Assn. Realtors, San Diego, 2001—. Chmn. Armed Svcs. YMCA Avangard, San Diego, 1999—; bd. dirs. Coronado Schs. Found., 1996—2001. Mem.: Naval Officers Spouse Club (advisor 1995—96). Republican. Avocations: gardening, theater, history, travel.*

PROVENCHER, JEANNE STANSFIELD, secondary school educator; b. Methuen, Mass., June 30, 1948; d. Ernest Daniel and Rita Marie (Vayo) Stansfield; m. Richard Leonard Provencher, Dec. 15, 1978; children: Matthew, Ryan. BA, Newton Coll., 1970; MA, Rivier Coll., Nashua, N.H., 1990. Cert. tchr., Mass.; cert. experienced educator, N.H. Tchr. St. Francis Acad., Nevada, Mo., 1970-71, Salem (NH) H.S., 1971-72, Pelham (NH) Meml. Sch., 1983-87; tchr. English and women's studies Nashua (N.H.) HS South, 1987— . Critical reader Grammar Workshop, 1994; contbg. reader Adventures in Appreciation, 1994; reader/evaluator A.P. Lang. Exams, 2003, 04; presenter in field. Lector St. Kathryn Ch., Hudson, N.H., 1988—. Mem. NOW, N.H. NOW, Nat. Coun. Tchrs. English (state judge for student lit. mags. 1994—), New Eng. Coun. Tchrs. English, N.H. Coun. Tchrs. English. Avocations: reading, gardening, working for equity, bicycling. Office: Nashua HS South 36 RIverside Dr Nashua NH 03062 Office Phone: 603-589-8244.

PROVENSEN, ALICE ROSE TWITCHELL, artist, author; b. Chgo. d. Jay Horace and Kathryn (Zelanis) Twitchell; m. Martin Provensen, Apr. 17, 1944; 1 child, Karen Anna. Student, Art Inst. of Chgo., 1930-31, U. Calif., L.A., 1939, Art Student League, N.Y., 1940-41; D.H.L. (hon.), Marist Coll., 1986. With Walter Lanz Studios, Los Angeles, 1942-43; OSS, 1944-45. Author, illustrator Karen's Opposites, 1963, Karen's Curiosity, 1963, What is a Color?, 1967, author, illustrator (with Martin Provensen) Who's in the Egg?, 1970, author, illustrator The Provensen Book of Fairy Tales, 1971, Play on Words, 1972, My Little Hen, 1973, Roses are Red, 1973, Our Animal Friends, 1974, The Year at Maple Hill Farm, 1978, A Horse and a Hound, A Goat and a Gander, 1979, The Owl and Three Pussycats, 1981, Town and Country, 1984, Shaker Lane, 1987, The Buck Stops Here, 1990, Punch in New York, 1991 (Best Books N.Y. Times, 1991), My Fellow Americans, 1995, Count on Me, 1998 (Book of Yr. Parenting Mag., 1998), The Master Swordsman, 2001, The Magic Doorway, 2001, A Day in the Life of Murphy, 2003 (named One of the Three Best Childrens Books, 2003), illustrator (with Martin Provensen) Mother Goose Book, 1976, illustrator Old Mother Hubbard, 1977, A Peaceable Kingdom, 1978, The Golden Serpent, 1980, A Visit to William Blake's Inn, 1981 (Caldecott honor book, 1981), Birds, Beasts and the Third Thing, 1982, The Glorious Flight, 1984 (Caldecott medal, 1984), The Voyage of Ludgate Hill, 1987, also textbooks; exhibitions include with Martin Provensen Balt. Mus., 1954, exhibitions include Am. Inst. Graphic Arts, N.Y., 1959, Botolph Group, Boston, 1964, one-woman shows include Henry Feiwel Gallery, N.Y.C., 1991, Children's Mus., Washington, 1991, Moscarelle Mus. Art, Williamsburg, Va., 1991; books represented Fifty Book of Yr. selections Am. Inst. Graphic Arts, 1947, 1948, 1952 (The Charge of the Light Brigade named Best Illustrated Children's Book of Yr. N.Y. Times, 1964, co-recipient medal Soc. Illustrators, 1960). Named to Soc. Illustrators Hall of Fame, 2000.

PROVINE, LORRAINE, retired mathematics educator; b. Altus, Okla., Oct. 6, 1944; d. Claud Edward and Emmie Lorraine (Gasper) Allmon; m. Joe A. Provine, Aug. 14, 1966; children: Sharon Kay, John David. BS, U. Okla., 1966; MS, Okla. State U., 1900. Tchr. math. U.S. Grant High Sch., Oklahoma City Schs., 1966-69; tchr. East Jr. High Sch., Ponca City (Okla.) Schs., 1969-70; tchr. Ponca City High Sch., 1978-79, 81-96; lectr. dept. math. Okla. State U., Stillwater, 1996-99. Mem.: NEA, Ponca City Assn. Classroom Tchrs. (treas. 1983—86, 1991—96), Assn. Women in Math, Okla. Coun. Tchrs. Math, Okla. Edn. Assn., Sch. Sci. and Math Assn., Nat. Coun. Tchrs. Math, Math Assn. Am., Internat. Soc. Tech. in Edn., Coun. for Exceptional Children, Okla. Assn. Mothers Club (life; state bd. dirs. 1977—87, pres. 1984—85), Delta Kappa Gamma (Delta chpt. treas. 1996—98, Gamma state essay com. 1999—2003, Gamma state comm. com. 2003—, Eta chpt. treas. 2000—). Republican. Baptist. Avocations: reading, knitting, sewing, genealogy. Home: 1019 Greenway Cir Norman OK 73072-6125 E-mail: lorraineprovine@cox.net.

PROVIS, DOROTHY L(OUISE), retired artist, sculptor; b. Chgo., Apr. 26, 1926; d. George Kenneth Smith and Ann Hart (Day) Smith Guest; m. William H. Provis Sr., July 28, 1945; children: Timothy A., William H. Jr. Student, Sch. Art Inst., Chgo., 1953-56, U. Wis.-Milw., 1967-68, 69-70. Sculptor, Port Washington, Wis., 1963-97; ret., 1997. Pres. bd. dirs. West Bend Gallery of Fine Arts, Wis., 1984-86, bd. dirs., 1987-89; speaker, presenter in field. Co-curated exhbn. West Bend Gallery of Fine Arts, 1992. Author, lobbyist Wis. Consignment Bill, Madison, 1979; presenter Art of Bead Making Charles Allis Art Mus., Milw., 1991, Fimo, polymer clay jewelry techniques Moraine Valley C.C., Palos Hills, Ill., 1992; panelist Women's Caucus for Art Conf., Phila., 1983, Coalition Women's Art Orgn. at Coll. Art Assn. Conf., Seattle, 1993; mem. adv. bd. Percent for Art Pro., 1985-87; mem. adv. bd. Wis. Arts Bd., salary assistance program, 1991; pres. workshop Milw. Art Mus., 1990; conf. panelist Coll. Art Assn., N.Y.C., 1990. Wis. Arts Bd. Designer-Craftsmen grantee, NEA, 1981. Mem. Coalition of Women's Art Orgns. (del. to continuing com. Nat. Women's Conf. 1979, panelist conf. 1981, v.p. for membership/nominations, 1981-83, pres. 1983-85, nat. pres. 1985-87, 89-91, 91-93, 93-95, 95-97, v.p. communications 1987-89, editor CWAO newsletter 1985-97, rep. CWAO at Am. Coun. for Arts Advocacy Day, Washington, 1993, panelist Southeastern Coll. Art Conf. 1995), Wis. Painters and Sculptors (life mem., pres. 1982-84, editor newsletter 1982-85), Wis. Women in Arts (legis. liaison 1978-80), Nat. Women's Studies Assn. (conf. presenter 1988), Artists for Ednl. Action (corr. 1979-85), Wis. Designer Crafts Coun. (membership chair 1991-93, editor newsletter 1993-95), Women's Caucus for Art (panelist 1981, 83, 86, 87, conf. com. panelist 1987, presenter 1989), Chgo. Artists Coalition. Home: Port Washington, Wis. Died June 5, 2002.

PROVOST, RUTH W. state legislator; Student, U. Mass. Mem. 2d Dist. Mass. Ho. of Reps., Boston, 1997—, mem. election laws com., mem. energy com. Mem. Sandwich Dem. Town Com., Mass. PTA, Citizens for Pub. Schs., Cape and Isla nds Dem. Coun., Plymouth County Dem. League. Mem. Mass. Assn. Schs. Coms. Office: Mass State Legis Rm 26 State House Boston MA 02133

PROVUS, BARBARA LEE, executive search consultant; b. Washington, Nov. 20, 1949; d. Severn and Birdell (Eck) P.; m. Frederick W. Wackerle, Mar. 29, 1985. Student, NYU, 1969-70; BA in Sociology, Russell Sage Coll., 1971; MS in Indsl. Rels., Loyola U., Chgo., 1978; postgrad., Smith Coll., 1971. Sec. Booz, Allen & Hamilton, Chgo., 1973-74, mgr. tng., 1974-77, dir. rsch., 1977-79, cons. search, 1979-80; mgr. mgmt. devel. Federated Dept. Stores, Cin., 1980-82; v.p. Lamalie Assocs., Chgo., 1982-86; prin., founder Sweeney, Shepherd, Bueschel, Provus, Harbert & Mummert, Inc., Chgo., 1986-91; founder Shepherd Bueschel & Provus Inc., Chgo., 1992—. Bd. dirs. Anti-Cruelty Soc., Chgo., 1990—, pres., 1996-97; trustee Sage Colls., Troy, N.Y., 1999-2000. Mem. Assn. Exec. Search Cons. (dir. 1989-92), The Chgo. Network (bd. dirs. 1993—, chair 2002-03), Econ. Club Chgo. Avocations: collecting rubber bands, modern art, baseball. Home: 3750 N Lake Shore Dr Chicago IL 60613-4238 Office: Shepherd Bueschel & Provus Inc 401 N Michigan Ave Ste 3020 Chicago IL 60611-4257 Office Phone: 312-832-3020.

PRUDEN, NANCY PARIS, artist; b. St. Louis, Mar. 14, 1946; BFA, U Ga., 1968. Designer Montag Stationery, Atlanta, 1968—72; illustration and card designer Paris Pruden Inc., 1972—83; designer Nu Art, Inc., Chgo., 1983—85; portrait painter Paris Pruden Portraits, Houston, 1985—; instr. Paris Pruden Sch. Fine Arts, 2002—. Office: Paris Pruden Portraits 710 Tirrell St Houston TX 77019

PRUDEN, TREVA ANN, music educator; b. Newburgh, Ind., Nov. 27, 1959; d. Vernon P. and Evalon Cowan; m. Randy Gene Pruden, Apr. 11, 1981; children: Darrell, Jason. AA in Acctg., Lockyear Coll., 1982, MusB in Edn., U. Evansville, 1995. Music tchr. Warrick County Schs., Boonville, Ind., 1995—. Sec. R&T Constrn., Newburgh, Ind., 1981—; organist Morningside Ch., Evansville, Ind., 1980—85; adjudicator Ind. Fedn. Music, Evansville, 1993—95. Musician: (plays) Castle HS, 1999—. Nominee Am. Tchr. award, Disney Learning, 2001. Mem.: Music Educators Nat. Conf. Avocation: piano.

PRUETT-LAWSON, JO ANN, marketing professional, special events coordinator; b. Jacksonville, Fla., Feb. 27, 1961; d. Billy Earl Pruett and Mildred Ann (Reedy) Jewell. AS in Bus. Adminstrn., Fla. C.C., Jacksonville, 1991; BS in Bus. Adminstrn. and Mktg., U. North Fla., Jacksonville, 1993; nail technician lic., Roffler, Jacksonville, Fla., 1994. Cert. image cons., makeup artist; cert. promotional mgr. Owner, CEO Black and White Prodns., Jacksonville, 1991—, Depeche Mktg. Group, Inc., Jacksonville, 1996—. Color and makeup cons. Carol Jackson-Color Me Beautiful, Fla., 1990, Fernand Aubrey, Fla., 1990; educator Advanced Edn. for Nail Profls., Jacksonville, 1993—; territory supr. Mktg. Force, Jacksonville, 1993-95; specialty events mgr., Jacksonville, 1993—; sales rep. KMart Corp., Jacksonville, 1995-97; specialty events mgr. Greater Jacksonville Agrl. Fair, 1996. Bd. dirs. Sutton Pl. Homeowners Assn., 1997—. Mem.: First Coast Car Coun. (v.p., show chmn. 14th Ann. Car, Truck, and Motorcycle Show 2001), CMOJ, SCCA, SVCCA, JCNA (mem. BMWCCA First Coast chpt. 1998—), Jaguar Car Club North Fla. (pres. 2000 , founder).

PRUETZ, ADRIAN MARY, lawyer; b. Nov. 13, 1948; Student, U Wis., 1966—69; BA, Loyola U., Chgo., 1972, postgrad., 1972—73; JD magna cum laude, Marquette U., 1982. Bar: Wis. 1982, Calif. 1985. With Quinn Emanual et al, L.A.; assoc. Whytz and Hirschboeck, SC, 1982—84, Monison and Foerster, 1984—88, ptnr., 1988—94, Quinn Emanuel, 1994—. Spkr., lectr. Price Waterhouse Intellectual Property Forum, Licensing Execs. Soc., Am. Soc. Indsl. Security. Named one of Most Influential Trial Lawyers in Calif., L.A. Daily Jour., 2002, State's Top 25 Copyright, Trademark and Patent Legal Minds, head STRONG, 2003, Calif.'s Most Successful Lawyers, Calif. Law Bus. Mem.: ABA (past chair com. U.S. lit. affecting internat. patent problems, past chair com. impact 1991 amendments), Women Lawyer's Assn. L.A., Los Angeles County Bar, State Bar Calif., Fed. Bar Assn. (spkr., lectr.). Office: 865 S Figueroa St 10th Fl Los Angeles CA 90017 Business E-Mail: emp@quinnemanuel.com.

PRUGH, PATRICIA ALICE, psychotherapist; b. Phila., July 19, 1951; d. Tommy J. and Lorraine DeRewal Prugh; m. Michael John Furman, June 5, 1980; children: Stephanie Ann Furman, Mary Elizabeth Furman. MA in Art Therapy, George Wash. U., 1982. Registered art therapist Am. Art Therapy Assn., 1988, cert. group psychotherapist Am. Group Psychotherapy Assn., 1999. Project dir. Bethany Women's Ctr., Washington, .DC., 1984—90; art therapist Wash. Urban League, Sr. Ctr. for Homeless Elderly, Washington, 1987—91; ind. contr. Balt. Mental Health Systems, Inc., Balt., 1991—2000; sr. art therapist Sheppard and Enoch Pratt Hosp., Balt., 1993—; program dir. Women's Mural Project, Washington, 1995—. Clin. instr. George Wash. U., Washington, 1986—99; clin. asst. prof. U. of Md., Dept. of Psychiatry, Balt., 1991—93; art therapy coord. D.C. Ofice of Cmty. Residential Programs, Washington, 1988; workshop coord. Internat. Very Spl. Arts Festival, Orlando, Fla., 1981; film festival coord. Internat. Sculpture Conf., Washington, 1980; spkr. Sheppard Pratt Speakers Bur., Balt. Dir.: (cmty. arts) The Magic Theatre, My Sisters' Garden (Baltimore's Best Murals, 1998). Co-founder Womens Murals Project, Washington, 1995—2003. Grantee, Path Project grantee, 1995—97, Md. Arts Coun. grantee, 1995—97, Arts award, Mayor's Adv. Com. on Arts and Culture, 1996, Video grantee, Am. Art Therapy Assn., 1992. Mem.: Potomac Art Therapy Assn. (assoc.; nat. affiliate represnetative 1989), Md. Art Therapy Assn. (assoc.; nat. affiliate rep. 1996). Office: Sheppard & Enoch Pratt Hospital 6501 N Charles St Baltimore MD 21285-6815 E-mail: pprugh@sheppardpratt.org.

PRUITT, ALICE FAY, mathematician, engineer; b. Montgomery, Ala., Dec. 17, 1943; d. Virgil Edwin and Ocie Victoria (Mobley) Maye; m. Mickey Don Pruitt, Nov. 5, 1967; children: Derrell Gene, Christine Marie. BS in Math., U. Ala., Huntsville, 1977; postgrad., Calif. State U., Northridge, 1978-79. Instr. math. Antelope Valley Coll., Quartz Hill, Calif., 1977-78; space shuttle engr. Rockwell Internat., Palmdale, Calif., 1979-81; programmer, analyst sci. support svcs. Combat Devel. and Experimentation Ctr., Ft. Hunter-Liggett, Calif., 1982-85; sr. engring. specialist Loral Vought Sys. Corp., Dallas, 1985-92; dir. concepts and analysis, advanced sys. engring. Nichols Rsch. Corp., Huntsville, Ala., 1992-99; sr. prin. engr. Computer Sci. Corp., Huntsville, Ala., 1999—. Mem. DeSoto (Tex.) Coun. Cultural Arts, 1987-89. Mem. AAUW (sch. bd. rep. 1982, legal advocacy fund chairperson 1989-91), Toastmasters, Phi Kappa Phi. Republican. Methodist. Avocations: dance, gourmet cooking. Office: PO Box 400002 4090 S Memorial Pky Ste A Huntsville AL 35815-1502 Personal E-mail: afpruitt@comcast.net. Business E-Mail: apruitt@csc.com.

PRUITT, ANNE LORING, academic administrator, education educator; b. Bainbridge, Ga., Sept. 19, 1929; d. Loring Alphonzo and Anne Lee (Ward) Smith; m. Harold G. Logan; 1 child, Leslie; stepchildren: Dianne, Pamela, Sharon, Ralph Pruitt, Jr., Harold, Minda, Andrew Logan. BS, Howard U., Washington, 1949; MA, Columbia U., N.Y.C., 1950, EdD, 1964; HumD hon., Ctrl. State U., Wilberforce, Ohio, 1982. Counsel for women Howard U., 1950-52; tchr., dir. guidance Hutto H.S., Bainbridge, 1952-55; dean students Albany State Coll., Ga., 1955-59, Fisk U., Nashville, 1959-61; prof. edn. Case Western Res. U., Cleve., 1963-79; prof. ednl. policy and leadership Ohio State U., Columbus, 1979-95, prof. emeritus, 1995—; assoc. dean Ohio State U. Grad. Sch., Columbus, 1979-84; assoc.

provost Ohio State U., Columbus, 1984-86, dir. Ctr. for Tchg. Excellence, 1986-94; dean in residence Coun. Grad. Schs., Washington, 1994-96, scholar in residence, 1996—2002. Cons. So. Regional Edn. Bd., Atlanta, 1967-78, So. Edn. Found., Atlanta, 1978-87; co-dir. Preparing Future Faculty program, 1994-2002. Author: New Students and Coordinated Counseling, 1973, Black Employees in Traditionally White Institutions in the Adams States, 1973-77, 1981, In Pursuit of Equality in Higher Education, 1987; co-author: (with Paul Isaac) Student Services for the Changing Graduate Student Population, 1995, (with Jerry Gaff and Richard Weibl) Building the Faculty We Need: Colleges and Universities Working Together, 2000, (with Jerry Gaff and Joyce Jentoft) Preparing Future Faculty in the Sciences and Mathematics, 2002, (with Jerry Gaff, Leslie Sims and Daniel Denecke) Preparing Future Faculty in the Humanities and Social Sciences: A Guide for Change, 2003. Trustee Urban League, Cleve., 1965-71, Ctrl. State U., 1973-82, Case Western Res. U., 1987-02, Columbus Area Leadership Program, 1988-91; bd. dirs. ARC, Cleve., 1978-79, Am. West Airlines Found., 1992-95; mem. adv. com. USCG Acad., New London, Conn., 1980-83; Ohio State U. rep. to AAUW, 1989-94; univ. co-chairperson United Way, 1990-91; trustee Marburn Acad., 1991-95; mem. Columbus 1992 Edn. Com., 1988-92; mem. edn. subcom. Columbus Found., 1991-94; mem. exec. com. Renaissance League, 1992-94; mem. vis. panel on rsch., Ednl. Testing Svc., 1996-02; mem. Commn. on Future Clemson U., 1997-98; bd. dirs. Black Women's Agenda, Inc., 1997-, pres. 1998-2002; deacon Peoples Congregational United Ch. of Christ, 1998—; mem. B.E.S.T. Expert Panel, 2002-04; evaluation external expert NSF Grad. Tchg. Fellows in K-12 Edn. Program, 2002-04. Recipient Outstanding Alumnus award Howard U. Alumni Assn., 1975; Am. Council on Edn. fellow, 1977; named one of Am.'s Top 100 Black Bus. and Profl. Women Dollars & Sense Mag., 1986; recipient Disting. Affirmative Action award Ohio State U., 1988; named Sr. Scholar Am. Coll. Personnel Assn., 1989, Woman of Achievement award YMCA, 1993. Mem. NSF (mem. com. on equal opportunities in sci. and engring. 1989-95), Am. Coll. Pers. Assn. (pres. 1976-77), Coun. Grad. Schs. in U.S. (chairperson com. on minority grad. edn. 1980-84), Am. Ednl. Rsch. Assn., Ohio Assn. Counselor Edn. (pres. 1966-67), Links Inc., Cosmos Club, Alpha Kappa Alpha.

PRUITT, LINDA KAY, special education educator; b. Sayre, Okla., Jan. 6, 1952; d. Clinton Forrest Forgay and Wilma Laverne Anderson; m. Bobby Gene Pruitt, May 19, 1991; m. Gary Wayne Brooks, June 20, 1969 (div.); children: Charles Clayton Brooks, Lindsay Renae Brooks. Assoc. cum laude, Southwestern Okla. State U., Sayre, Oklahoma; BA magna cum laude, Southwestern Okla. State U., Weatherford, Oklahoma. Cert. Spl. Edn. Tchr. K-12th Okla. Spl. edn. tchr. Olive Jr. H.S., Drumright, Okla., 2002—. Non-Denominational. Achievements include National Board Teacher Certification Candidate. Avocations: fishing, hunting, travel. Home: 9448 S 437 W Place Drumright OK 74030

PRUITT, MARY ANN, chiropractor; b. Glen Rose, Tex., Mar. 2, 1930; d. Sterling Holder Sr. and Oveda Jean (Wade) P.; widowed. DC, Palmer Coll. Chiropractic, 1949; postgrad., Tex. Christian U., 1951, Tex. Wesleyan U., 1952-53. Chiropractor, owner Pruitt Chiropractic Clinic, Ft. Worth, Tex., 1949—. Appointee state peer rev. bd. Tex. Bd. Chiropractic Examiners; appointee Tex. Indsl. Accident Bd., Chiropractic Adv. Com. Precinct chair Dem. Party, Tarrant County, county del. state conv., county del.; mem., base operator Citizens on Patrol, Ft. Worth, 1994-95. Recipient Mabel Palmer award World of Congress of Women Chiropractors, 1993; fellow Palmer Coll. Acad. Fellow Internat. Chiropractors Assn. (mem. legis. com. 1993-94), Palmer Acad. Chiropractic; mem. Chiropractic Soc. Tex. (treas., Sterling Pruitt Humanitarian award 1994), Tex. Coalition for Concerned Chiropractors (treas. 1993), Congress of Ind. Chiropractors, Palmer Alumni Assn. Tex. (regional officer, past bd. dirs.), Assn. for Chiropractic Ednl. Stds. (treas. and sec. 1994-97), Sigma Phi Chi (Hon. Supreme Kiatrus). Methodist. Office: Pruitt Chiropractic Clinic 2214 Hemphill St Fort Worth TX 76110-2014

PRUITT, MARY H. social worker; b. Marianna, Ark., Dec. 12, 1944; d. Florzell and Bonnetta Thelma (Harris) Hawkins; children: Woodie III, Rita Marie. AB, U. Ark., 1967; MSW, Washington U., St. Louis, 1971. Lic. clin. social worker. Case worker Grace Hill Settlement House, St. Louis, 1967-69; social worker Dept. Mental Health, St. Louis, 1972-94; pvt. practice St. Louis, 1990-2000; case mgr. Magellan Behavior Health, St. Louis, 2000—; group leader Liberty Program, St. Louis, 1995—. Bd. dirs. Women in Cmty. Svcs., St. Louis, 1982; mem. Betterment Commn. City of Berkeley, Northside Aides Coun., St. Bartholomew Ch.; supporter numerous charities. Mem. Nat. Assn. Social Workers, Am. Bd. Social Workers, Am. Coun. Social Workers, Assn. Black Social Workers. Home: Po Box 845 Marianna AR 72360-0845

PRUITT-STREETMAN, SHIRLEY IRENE, small business owner; b. Atlanta, May 22, 1936; d. Len Harris Strickland, Ellen Jay chadwick-Strickland; m. Charles Carter Pruitt, June 5, 1954 (dec. Sept. 1993); children: Gary C. Pruitt, Patricia L. Pruitt, Dianne S. Pruitt; m. James Dorsey Streetman, Aug. 19, 1999. Student, U. Notre Dame, Ind., 1976, U. Notre Dame, 1978, Degree in Bus. Mgmt., 1980; student in profl. interior design, Sheffield Sch. Interior Design, N.Y.C., 1990. Sec. spl. ins. Hurt & Quin Ins. Co., Atlanta, 1954—56; with Globe Ticket Co., Atlanta, 1956—57, Emmett C. Bennett, CPA, Atlanta, 1958—59; acctg., ptnr. Pruitt's Furniture, TV and Appliances, Alpharetta and Cumming, Ga., 1958—93, owner, pres. Cumming, Ga., 1993—. Contbr. poetry to local papers; co-author: (ch. history) 150 Years of Church History, 1986. Adv. bd. Key Distbrs. of Ga., Clarksville, Ga., 1993—. Recipient Pride award, Dealerscope Mag., 1979, Retailer of the Mo. award, Ga. Retailing Mag., 1976. Mem.: C. of C. Baptist. Avocations: reading, crocheting, embroidery, sketching, genealogy. Office: Pruitts Furniture TV and Appliances 606 Veterans Memorial Blvd Cumming GA 30040

PRUSSING, LAUREL LUNT, public interest lobbyist, economist, auditor; b. N.Y.C., Feb. 21, 1941; d. Richard Valentine and Maria (Rinaldi) Lunt; m. John Edward Prussing, May 29, 1965; children: Heidi Elizabeth, Erica Stephanie, Victoria Nicole Johanna. AB, Wellesley Coll., l962; MA, Boston U., l964; postgrad., U. Calif., San Diego, l968-69, U. Ill., l970-76. Economist Arthur D. Little, Cambridge, Mass., l963-67, U. Ill., Urbana, l971-72; mem. county bd. Champaign County, Urbana, 1972-76, county auditor, 1976-92; legis. dir. ERA Ill., 2002—03; founder ERA Yes!, 2003. Mem. local audit adv. bd. Office Ill. Compt., Chgo., 1984-92. Contbr. to Illinois Local Government: A Handbook, 1990. Founding mem. Citizens Forum on Gambling and Campaign Fin. Reform, 1999; downstate program dir. Citizen Action/Ill., 1999; lobbyist AAUW, Ill., Inc., 2001, 2004; mem. Champaign-Urbana Mass Transit Dist. Bd., 2004—; state rep. 103d dist. Ill. Gen. Assembly, 1993—95; Dem. nominee Ill. 15th dist. U.S. Congress, 1996—98. Named Best Freshman Legislator Ind. Voters Ill., 1994; recipient Friend of Agriculture award Ill. Farm Bur., 1994; named to Legis. Honor Roll Ill. Environ. Coun., 1994. Mem. AAUW, NAACP, LWV, Govt. Fin. Officers Assn., U.S. and Can. (com. on acctg., auditing and fin. reporting 1980-88, Fin. Reporting award 1981-91, Disting. Budget award 1986), Nat. Assn. Local Govt. Auditors (charter), Ill. Assn. County Auditors (pres. 1984-85). Democrat. Home: 2106 Grange Dr Urbana IL 61801-6609 Office Phone: 217-328-2071.

PRUTER, MARGARET FRANSON, editor; b. Oak Park, Ill., Jan. 16; d. Frederick G. and Margaret K. (Svoboda) Franson; m. Robert D. Pruter, July 22, 1972; 1 child, Robin. AB, Dominican U., 1961; MA, Northwestern U., 1965. Asst. editor Am. People's Ency., Chgo., 1961-62; rsch. assoc. AMA, Chgo., 1962-63; asst. editor New Standard Ency., Chgo., 1964-66, assoc. editor, 1966-75, sr. editor, 1975-96; editl. dir. Elmhurst (Ill.) Editl. Svcs., 1996—; editor McDougal Littell, Evanston, Ill., 1997—. Exec. dir. Militaria Archives, Elmhurst, Ill., 1972—. Co-author: DuPage Roots, 1985 (Ill. State Hist. Publ. award 1986). Mem. Elmhurst Hist. Commn., 1981—, v.p., 1995—2000, pres., 2000—01; mem. Friends of Elmhurst Pub. Libr., Elmhurst Art Mus. Found.; exec. bd. North Ctrl. Coll. Parents Assn., 1995—98; bd. dirs. DuPage County Hist. Soc., Wheaton, Ill., 1982—, DuPage County Sesquicentennial Com., 1988—89. Mem.: AAUW (bd. dirs. Elmhurst br. 1993—99), Nature Conservancy, Arch. Conservancy, Am. Studies Assn., Nat. Women's History Mus., Nat. Trust Historic Preservation, Orgn. Am. Historians, Nat. Parks and Conservation Assn., Elmhurst Hist. Soc., Ill. Hist. Soc., Chgo. Hist. Soc., World Wildlife Fed., Sisters in Crime, Byrd's Nest Chapel Questers (pres. 1992—94, 2003—), Chgo. Architecture Found., Chgo. Women in Pub., Sierra Club. Office: Elmhurst Editorial Svcs PO Box 768 Elmhurst IL 60126-0768

PRUTZMAN, PENELOPE ELIZABETH, elementary school educator; b. Vancouver, Wash., Apr. 25, 1944; d. Delbert Daniel and Jessie May (Lowry) P. BA in Sociology, CUNY, 1975; diploma, Grand Diplôme Cooking Sch. Tchr. Mt. Carmel-Holy Rosary Sch., N.Y.C., 1968—. Active Vol. Svcs. for Children, N.Y.C., 1980—83; vol. St. Mary's Ch., Manhattanville, 2001—. Recipient 10 Yr. Service to Cath. Schs. of Harlem award Office of Supt. Sch. Archdiocese of N.Y., 1979, 20 Yrs. to Cath. Sch. award Archdiocese of N.Y., 1986; named one of Outstanding Elem. Tchrs. of Am., 1974. Mem.: Nat. Cath. Edn. Assn., Fedn. Cath. Tchrs. (sch. del. 1974—94, exec. coun. 1974—95, negotiating com., Cert. of Honor 1982). Democrat. Episcopalian. Avocations: gourmet cooking, traveling, collecting cookbooks. Home: 35-25 34th St Apt C44 Astoria NY 11106-1953 Office: Mt Carmel-Holy Rosary Sch 371 Pleasant Ave New York NY 10035-3745

PRYCE, DEBORAH D. congresswoman; b. Warren, Ohio, July 29, 1951; BA cum laude, Ohio State U., 1973; JD with honors, Capital U., 1976. Bar: Ohio 1976. Former asst. city prosecutor, asst. city atty., first asst. city prosecutor, Columbus, Ohio; former judge Franklin County Mcpl. Ct., Columbus; mem. U.S. Congress from 15th Ohio dist., Washington, 1993—; mem. rules com.; mem. select com. on homeland security. Republican. Presbyterian. Avocation: skiing. Office: US Ho Reps 221 Cannon Ho Office Bldg Washington DC 20515-0001

PRYCE, MONICA ELIZABETH, music educator; b. Washington, Apr. 7, 1968; d. Frederick Thaddeus Hezikiah and Linett Joyce P. BM, Carleton U., 1995. Cert. tchr. Ch. organist Luth. Ch., Ottawa, Ont., 1985-93, SDA Ch., Ottawa, Ont., 1985-95; piano tchr. Ottawa, 1985-95; ch. pianist United Meth. Ch., Atlanta, 1996—; piano tchr. Atlanta, 1996—; music tchr. DeKalb County Sch. Sys., Atlanta, 1998—. Mem. Music Tchrs.' Nat. Assn. (registered). Avocations: music, sports, reading. Home: 4893 Hairston Pl Stone Mountain GA 30088-1941 Office: Dekalb County Sch Sys 3770 N Decatur Rd Decatur GA 30032-1005

PRYGA, SUZANNE MARIE, gender equity consultant, sociology educator, academic administrator; b. Chgo., Apr. 19, 1969; d. John Michael and Rosemarie Jean (Weldin) Pryga. BA in Sociology, MA in Sociology, DePaul U., 1992. Gender equity cons. Ill. State Bd. of Edn., Springfield, 1993-97; adj. faculty Joliet (Ill.) Jr. Coll., 1995—2001, co-dir. Women's Coll., 1997—2001; prof. sociology Prairie State Coll., Chgo. Heights, Ill., 2001—. Author: Fairness: A Guide To Gender Equity In Illinois Schools, 1999. Vol. advocate Northwest Action Against Rape, Schaumburg, Ill., 1993; mem. gender equality commn., Ill., 1997—. Mem. AAUW (co-chair of initiative for ednl. equity, 1995—), Am. Sociol. Assn. Democrat. Roman Catholic. Avocation: exercise. Office: Prairie State College 202 South Halsted St Chicago Heights IL 60411

PRYOR, CAROL GRAHAM, obstetrician, gynecologist; b. Savannah, Ga. m. Louis O.J. Manganiello, June 11, 1950; children: Carol Helen, Victoria Manganiello Mudano. AB, Ga. Coll., 1943; MD, Med. Coll. Ga., 1947. Rotating intern City Hosps., Balt., 1947-48; asst. resident pathology Baroness Erlanger Hosp., Chattanooga, 1948; intern. obstetrics City Colls., Balt., 1949; coll. physician Ga. State Coll. for Women, Milledgeville, Ga., 1949-50; resident obstetrics City Hosps., Balt., 1950-51; asst. resident gynecology Univ. Hosp., Balt., 1951-52, sr. resident ob-gyn. Augusta, Ga., 1952; pvt. practice ob-gyn. Augusta, 1952—; chmn. ob-gyn. St. Joseph Hosp., Augusta, 1997—. Chair ob-gyn. dept. St. Joseph Hosp., Augusta. Mem., former pres. Iris Garden Club, Augusta; mem. coun. on maternal and infant health State of Ga., Atlanta, 1981-90; mem. edn. found. AAUW, 1961-63, state v.p., state pres., 1963-65. Recipient Cert. of Achievement-Community Leadersip, Ga. div. AAUW, 1982; named Med. Woman of Yr., Ga. br. 51 Am. Med. Women's Assn., 1961; Heritage award Ga. Coll. and State U., 2001, Achievement award, Ga. Coll. U., 1982. Fellow ACS (1st woman mem. Ga. chpt. 1956), ACOG; mem. AMA, Richmond County Med. Soc., So. Med. Assn., So. Surg. Congress, Delta Kappa Gamma. Democrat. Methodist. Office: 2316 Wrightsboro Rd Augusta GA 30904-6220 E-mail: cpryor@bellsouth.net.

PRYOR, VANITA MOON, music educator; b. Lula, Ga., Sept. 4, 1961; d. Howard Joe and Allonia Bostick Moon; m. Marvin Antinio Pryor, Mar. 31, 1990; 1 child, Kierra Janae. MusB in Edn., Brenau Coll., 1983; MusM in Edn., Fla. State U., 1987; EdD in Adminstrn., Lincoln Meml. U., 2000. Music tchr. Lanier Mid. Sch., Suwanee, Ga., 1984—86, J.E. Richards Mid. Sch., Lawrenceville, Ga., 1987—96, Meadowcreek HS, Norcross, Ga., 1994—96, Shiloh Mid. Sch., Snellville, Ga., 1996—. Musician Salem Bapt. Ch., Lilburn, Ga., 2000—03. Condr.: Mid. Sch. Summer Camp, 2000, Dist. Hon. Chorus, 2002. Study leader Women On The Move, Inc., 2000—03. Mem.: Nat. Educators Assn., Music Educators Nat. Conf. (choral music adjudicator 1990—2003), Am. Assn. Christian Counselors, Alpha Kappa Alpha. Avocations: piano, horseback riding. Home: 415 Spring Gate Rd Stone Mountain GA 30087

PRZYBYLSKI, MERCEDES, retired medical and surgical nurse, health facility administrator; Diploma, Hotel Dieu Sch. Nursing, El Paso; BSN, Madonna Coll., Livonia, Mich.; MS in Adminstrn., Cen. Mich. U. Cert. operating room nurse. Dir. operating room svcs. Pontiac (Mich.) Osteo. Hosp.; dir. operative svcs. Mercy Hosp., Toledo; mgr. ambulatory surgical svcs. St. Vincents Mercy Med. Ctr., Toledo; ret., 1998. Mem. Assn. Oper. Rm. Nurses (pres. Mich. Southeastern chpt. 1991), Mich. Assn. Oper. Rm. Suprs., Am. Acad. Med. Adminstrs.

PRZYSTAWSKI, KAREN ANN, registered nurse; b. N.Y.C., N.Y., Jan. 8, 1970; d. Stanley J. and Magdalen K. Przystawski. BS in Psychology, Coll. Mt. St. Vincent, 1992, BSN, 1999. Social worker Vis. Nurse Svc. of N.Y., N.Y.C., 1993—99; staff nurse Cabrini Med. Ctr., N.Y.C., 2000—. Mem.: N.Y. State Nurses Assn. Republican. Roman Catholic. Avocations: aerobics, weightlifting, dance, reading, family. Home: 8228 Ankener Ave Elmhurst NY 11373

PSALTIS, HELEN, medical and surgical nurse; b. Rockford, Ill., Nov. 27, 1931; d. Harry and Martha (Triantafelakis) P. Diploma, St. Margaret Hosp., Hammond, Ind., 1953; BSN, DePaul U., 1961; MS in Health Edn., Purdue U., 1971; MSN, Purdue U., Calumet, Ind., 1988. RN, Ind., cert. sch. nurse, Ind. Staff nurse U. Ill. Hosp., Chgo., 1959—61, U. Chgo. Hosp., Billings, Ill., 1962; sch. nurse Pub. Sch. City of East Chicago, Ind.; asst. supr., staff nurse, instr. St. Catherine Hosp., East Chicago, Ind., 1962—63; instr., head nurse, staff nurse St Margaret Hosp., Hammond, 1953—58, 1989—, 1963; staff nurse U. Ill. Rsch. Hosp./Chgo. Hosp., 1959—61; asst. supr., staff nurse, inst. St. Catherine Hosp., East Chicago, 1981—91. Mem. ANA, AACCN, Soc. of Critical Care Nursing, Nat. League for Nursing, Sigma Theta Tau. Home: 4303 Ivy St East Chicago IN 46312-3026

PUCCIATTI, SANDRA MILSTEIN, opera company director; b. Phila., June 14, 1952; d. Harvey Jack Milstein and Beverly Goldberg; m. Joseph Robert Pucciatti, Oct. 2, 1977; 1 child, Rachel Shabana. MusB summa cum laude, Temple U., 1974, MA, Coll. N.J., 1980. Co-founder, adminstr. The Boheme Club, Inc., Trenton, N.J., 1981-89; co-founder, music dir. Boheme Opera Co. N.J., Trenton, 1989-95, mng. dir., 1995—. Piano and ensemble coach N.J. Gov.'s Sch. of Arts, Ewing, N.J., summers 1993-2000; program coord. Inside Opera program Boheme Opera N.J., Mercer County, 1999—. Co-dir. Congregation Beth Chaim Choir, Princeton Junction, N.J., 1980—. Mem. Opera Am., N.J. Art Pride, Trenton Torch Club. Avocations: chamber music, gardening, lecturing about opera medium. Home: 108 Fetter Ave Trenton NJ 08610-3510 Office: Boheme Opera NJ 1 Municipal Dr Hamilton NJ 08619-3809 E-mail: jrspuce@aol.com.

PUCCI GILES, MICHELLE, legislative staff member, writer; d. Richard and Kathleen Pucci; m. Kevin Giles, Nov. 29, 1997. BA in Journalism, Trenton (N.J.) State Coll., 1990. Staff writer The Home News and Tribune, East Brunswick, NJ, 1989—90, The Observer, Toms River, NJ, 1990—93; dep. dir. comms. N.J. Assembly, Trenton, 1993—2001; legis. liaison N.J. Ratepayer Advocate, Newark, 2001—. Manuscript reader Dorchester Pub., N.Y., 2000—01; polit. campaign writer N.J. Elections, 1993—. Author: (short stories) 75 published in mags. Recipient Fiction award, Women in the Arts, 2000. Roman Cath. Avocation: photography.

PUCK, JENNIFER M. physician, scientist; b. Denver, Aug. 9, 1949; m. Robert L. Nussbaum. BA, Harvard U., 1971, MD, 1975; MA, U. Pa., 1991. Diplomate Am. Bd. Pediatrics. Assoc. prof. U. Pa. Med. Sch., Phila., 1991-93; chief immunologic genetics Nat. Human Genome Rsch. Inst./NIH, Bethesda, Md., 1993—; asst. prof. pediatrics U. Pa. Med. Sch., Phila., 1984-91. Fellow Am. Acad. Pediatrics. Office: Nat Human Genome Rsch Inst/NIH Bldg 49 Rm 49 Convent Dr Msc 4442 Bethesda MD 20892-0001

PUCKETT, ELIZABETH ANN, law librarian, law educator; b. Evansville, Ind., Nov. 10, 1943; d. Buell Charles and Lula Ruth (Gray) P.; m. Joel E. Hendricks, June 1, 1964 (div. June 1973); 1 child, Andrew Charles; m. Thomas A. Wilson, July 19, 1985. BS in Edn., Eastern Ill. U., 1964; JD, MS in L.S., U. Ill., 1977. Bar: Kans. 1978, Ill. 1979. Acquisitions/reader services librarian U. Kans. Law Library, Lawrence, 1978-79; asst. reader services librarian So. Ill. U. Law Library, Carbondale, 1979-81, reader services librarian, 1981-83; assoc. dir. Northwestern U. Law Library, Chgo., 1983-86, co-acting dir., 1986-87; dir./assoc. prof. South Tex. Coll. Law Library, Houston, 1987-89; dir./prof. South Tex. Coll. Law Libr., Houston, 1990-94, U. Ga. Law Libr., Athens, 1994—. Co-author: Evaluation of System-Provided Library Services to State Correctional Centers in Illinois, 1983; co-editor Uniform Commercial Code: Confidential Drafts, 1993. Mem. ABA, Am. Assn. Law Librs. (mem. exec. bd. 1993-96). Avocations: reading, antiques. Office: U Georgia Law Libr Athens GA 30602-6018 Office Phone: 706-542-5078. E-mail: apuckett@uga.edu.

PUCKETT, HELEN LOUISE, retired tax consulting company executive; b. Ripley, Ohio, Oct. 29, 1934; d. Joseph and Gladys Muriel (Madden) Haney; m. Marvin R. Puckett, May 26, 1953 (dec.); children: Steven W., Thomas J. Grad., Columbus Bus. U., 1971. Office mgr., sec.-treas. Al-Win Tng., Inc., West Jefferson, Ohio, 1971—, agt., 1977—99; ret., 1999. Notary pub., 1975-88. Sunday sch. tchr. London (Ohio) Ch. of Christ, pres. Women's Fellowship, 1979-81. Mem. London Bus. and Profl. Women (pres.), Coover Soc., Cornerstone Club at Madison County Hosp. Office: 485 Glade Run Rd West Jefferson OH 43162-9581

PUCKETT, RUBY PARKER, nutritionist, hospital food service administrator, consultant, author; b. Dora, Ala., Nov. 26, 1932; d. John Franklin Parker and Ethel V. (Short) Tuggle; m. Larry Willard Puckett, July 2, 1955; children: Laurel Lynn Puckett Brown, Hollie Kristina Puckett Walker. BS in Food and Nutrition, Auburn (Ala.) U., 1954; postgrad. in vocat. edn., U. Fla., 1970, 80; MA in Health Sci. Edn., Cen. Mich. U., 1976. Registered dietitian, foodservice adminstr. Dietetic intern Henry Ford Hosp., Detroit, 1955; staff dietitian VA Hosp., Houston, 1955-56; dietitian Matty Hersee Hosp., Meridian, Miss., 1957-58; asst. dir. U. Miss. Med. Ctr., Jackson, 1960-61; dir. dietetics Ft. Sanders Presbyn. Hosp., Knoxville, Tenn., 1961-63, Waterman Meml. Hosp., Eustis, Fla., 1963-68; dir. food and nutrition U. Fla. Shands Hosp., Gainesville, 1968-95; pres. Square One Cons. Service, Gainesville, 1979-85; pres., owner Food Svc. Mgmt. Cons., 1995—. Adv. com. on jr. coll. dietetic programs Fla. Dept. Edn., 1967-69; nominating com. Southeastern Hosp. Conf. for Dietitians, 1969, sec., 1974-75; pres. Field Agy. Nutrition, 1970; instr. U. Fla., 1972-73, 82-85, clin. and cmty. coordinated undergrad. dietetic program adv. bd., 1974-89; instr. Santa Fe Jr. Coll., Gainesville, 1977-81; adv. com. Marquis Libr. Soc., Inc., 1974; health project rev. com. North Ctrl. Fla. Planning Coun., 1974-76; named to White House Conf. on Food and Nutrition, 1976, Senate Select Com. on Food and Nutrition, 1976; com. on animal products NRC Adv. Bd. on Mil. Pers. Supplies, 1978-81; site evaluator dietetic programs in colls and univs., 1998—; mem. Commn. on Accrediation Dietetic Edn., 1999—, program reviewer for dietary mgr. tng., 2003—; adv. bd. various corps.; reviewer abstracts, articles Jour. Am. Dietetic Assn.; apptd. faculty mem. Dept. Family Youth and Cmty. Svcs. Internat. Food Svc. Adminstrs. Author: Food Service in Health Care Facilities, 1988, 2d edit., 2004, Basic Nutrition and Diet Modification Shands Hospital, 1992, revised edit., 2002, Managing Foodservice Operations, 1992, HACCP The Future Challenge, 4th edit., Nutrition Diet Modification Meal Patterns, 4th edit., Disaster and Emergency Preparedness for Food Service Operations, 2003, Dietary Managers Course by Correspondence, 9 edits., Nutrition for the Elderly, Safety, Sanitation and Security for Food Service Operations, Topics in Practice: Productivity Measures for Food Service Operations, 2004, Food Service Manual for Health Care Organizations, 2004; mem. editl. adv. com.: Stokes Report, 1980—84, editl. advisor: Food Management: Topics in Clinical Nutrition, 1988—, Aspen's Focus, 1984—91, Aspen's Hosp. Nutrition and Foodservice Forms; contbr. numerous articles to profl. jours.; spkr., seminar leader, developer nutrition and older adult distance edn-.course. Bd. dirs. Campus USA Credit Union, 1978—, v.p., 1980—81, pres.-elect, 1981—82, chmn. bd., 1982—83, 1998; chmn. Shands Hosp. chpt. United Way, 1978, mem. budget and allocations com., 1983—, mem. speakers bur., 1985—86; mem. adv. bd. Harvest Gainesville, 1991—93, Children's Miracle Telethon, 1992—95; adv. bd. Sta. WRUF Pub. Radio, 1988; profl. adv. bd. Shands Home Care; vol. Mothers Supporting Daus. with Breast Cancer, 2000—; bd. dirs. Fla. 4-H Found., 2000—04; mem. Sexual Phys. Abuse Bd.; courtesy faculty appt. Divsn Youth, Family and Ext.; election clk., inspector/dep. Alachua County (Fla.) Elections, 2000—; bd. dirs. North Fla. Regional Vocat. Sch. Named Alumni of Yr., Auburn U. Sch. Home Econs., 1985, Disting. Ind. Study Course award, 1986, 1990, Disting. Woman, Alachua County, Fla., 1992; named to Woodlawn H.S. Hall of Fame, 1982, Fla. Women's Hall of Fame, 1986; recipient Community Leader award, Sta. WRUF-FM, 1972, Ivy award, Restaurateurs of Distinction, 1980, Disting. Pace Setter award, Roundtable for Women in Foodservice, 1984, Award of Distinction, Sch. Human Svc., Auburn U., 1991. Mem.: IFAS (mem. family youth and cmty. svc. sect.), FCSI (mem. task force needs assessment 2003), Fla. Coun. on Aging (sec. nutrition sect. 1974—76, adv. bd. 1974—76, chmn. 1974—76), Nat. U. Continuing Edn. Assn. (disting. ind. study course 1986), Nutrition Edn. Soc. (liaison with industry com. 1974, legis. com. 1974, charter), Dietary Mgr. Assn. Found. (steering com.), Am. Soc. Hosp. Food Service Adminstrs. (edn. com. 1968—71, nomination com. 1978, chmn. publ. com. 1981—82, chmn. legis. com. 1984, bd. dirs., task force HACCP cert.), Gainesville Dietetic Assn. (v.p. 1969, pres. 1970, 1976), Fla. Dietetic Assn. (sec. 1968—70, pres. 1973—74, chmn. by-laws com. 1985, del. 1985—87, numerous other offices), Am. Dietetic Assn. (pres. practice group 41 1982—84, area III coord. 1985—88, 1989—, chair practice group mgmt. in food and nutrition svc. 2001, numerous other offices, Excellence in Mgmt. Practice award 1994, medal 1996, Medallion for Profl. Cmty. and Career Achievement, Marjorie Hulsizer Copher award 2003), Internat. Gold and Silver Plate Soc. (sec. bd. trustees 1983—85), Ivy Soc., Altrusa, Pi Lambda Beta, Kappa Sigma Phi. Democrat. Mem. Lds Ch. Avocations: whitewater rafting, hiking, gardening. Office: 5200 NW 43d St Ste 102-302 Gainesville FL 32606 Office Phone: 352-371-6160. E-mail: puckerp@juno.com.

PUCKO, DIANE BOWLES, public relations executive; b. Wyndotte, Mich., Aug. 15, 1940; d. Mervin Arthur and Bernice Letitia (Shelly) Bowles; m. Raymond J. Pucko, May 22, 1965; children: Todd Anthony, Gregory Bowles. BA in Sociology, Bucknell U., Lewisburg, Pa., 1962. Accredited in pub. rels. Asst. to pub. rels. dir. Edward C. Michener Assocs., Inc., Harrisburg, Pa., 1962-65; advt./pub. rels. coord. Superior Switchboard & Devices, Canton, Ohio, 1965-66; editorial dir. women's svc. Hutchins Advt. Co., Inc., Rochester, N.Y., 1966-71; pres. Editorial Communications, Rochester and Elyria, Ohio, 1971-77; mgr. advt. and sales promotion Tappan Air Conditioning, Elyria, 1977-80; mgr. pub. affairs Kaiser Permanente Med. Care Program, Cleve., 1980-85; corp. dir. pub. affairs Keystone Health Plans, Inc., Camp Hill, Pa., 1985-86; v.p., dir. client planning Young-Liggett-Stashower, Cleve., 1986; v.p., dir. pub. rels. Marcus Pub. Rels., Cleve., 1987-91; sr. v.p. Proconsul, Cleve., 1991-95, also bd. dirs.; sr. ptnr. pub. rels. Poppe Tyson, Cleve., 1995-96; managing dir. Bozell Pub. Rels., Cleve., 1996-97; sr. counsel Pub. Rels. Ptnrs., Inc., Cleve., 1997—2002. Mgr., role model Women in Mgmt. Field Placement program, Cleve. State U., 1983-92; pub. rels. adv. bd. profl. adviser, Pub. Rels. Student Soc. Am., Kent State U., 1988—. Bd. trustees, mem. exec. com., chmn. pub. rels. adv. com. Ronald MacDonald House of Cleve., 1993—2000; bd. dirs., chmn. pub. rels. com. Assn. Retarded Citizens, Cleve., 1987-91; mem. pub. rels.-mktg. com. Beech Brook, 1996—2000; mem. journalism comm. adv. bd. Elon Coll., 1998—2001. Recipient Woman Profl. Excellence award YMCA, 1984, MacEachern award Acad. Hosp. Pub. Rels., 1985, Bell Ringer award Cmty. Rels. Report, 1985, Bronze Quill Excellence award Internat. Assn. Bus. Communicators, 1992, 93, Cleve. Comms. award Women in Comms. Internat., 1993, 95, Tower award Bus./Profl. Advt. Assn., 1993, 95, Creativity in Pub. Rels. award, 1994, Silver Screen award U.S. Internat. Film & Video Festival, 1995, Silver Quill Excellence award Internat. Assn. Bus. Communicators, 1995, 2001, Internat. Assn. Bus. Communicators. Fellow Pub. Rels. Soc. Am. (bd. dirs. 1983-85, 86-94, officer 1991-95, mem. counselors acad. 1986—, Silver Anvil award 1985, Mktg./Consumer Rels. award East Ctrl. dist. 1992, 95, Lighthouse award 1995); mem. Press Club Cleve. (bd. dirs. 1989-96, v.p. 1990-96), Cleve. Advt. Club, Women's City Club Cleve., Nat. Agri-Mktg. Assn. (Nat. Merit award 2000). Republican. Methodist. Avocation: soccer. Home: 656 University Ave Elyria OH 44035-7278 Office: 6100 Rockside Woods Blvd Cleveland OH 44131-2366

PUDICK, DONNA EASTMAN, writer, educator; b. Milford, Mass., Sept. 7, 1939; d. Walter Smith and Theodora Elsa (DeAmicis) Eastman; m. Sheldon Pudick, Jan. 26, 1964; children: Jill Teddie, Glenn Allen. BS, Simmons Coll., 1961. Writer Allyn & Bacon, Inc., Boston, 1961-62; editor Allergy Found., Boston, 1962, Little/Brown, Inc., Boston, 1963-64; writer, editor McGraw-Hill Book Co., N.Y.C., 1964-65; instr., model, pub. rels. coord. Barbizon Schs., Highland Park, NJ, 1972-75; writer, agy. dir. Barbizon Agy., Montclair, N.J., 1975-85; editor Howmark Pub., Elizabeth, N.J., 1985-92; instr. adult edn. Writing for Money, 1993—2000; book editor, line editor, 1992—. Columnist (newspapers) Looking Glass, 1968-72, Mirror-Mirror, 1972-78; contbr.: Inkslingers, 1995; editor, contbr.: Scribblings, 1993, The Brass Ring, 1996. Mem. AAUW (program chair 1995-97), DAR (publicity chair 1994-96, vice regent 2001-03), Am. Pen Women, Ormond Writers League, Poets and Writers Soc. (sec.-treas. 2002-03), Mayflower Soc., Scribblers (sec.-treas.). Avocations: gardening, cooking, pets.

PUERTA, CHRISTY L. construction executive; b. Santa Ana, Calif., May 28, 1966; d. Larry E. and Eileen G. Methvin.; m. Julio E. Puerta, Aug. 28, 1987; children: Nichole, Brittany. BA in Child Devel., Calif. State U., Northridge, 1989. Child care counselor Children's Inst. Internat., L.A., 1985-89; v.p. Larry Methvin Installation Inc., Lodi, Calif., 1984—. Coun. mem. Leadership Prayer Breakfast Coun., 2001—; camp counselor Sch. Bethel Open Bible, Lodi, Calif., 1999—, tchr. Sunday Sch., 2000. Mem. HBANC (assoc.), BIA Superior Calif. (assoc.), Pacific Coast Builders Conf. Republican. Avocations: travel, soccer, family. Office: Larry Methvin Installation Inc 128 N Cluff Ave Lodi CA 95240 Office Fax: 209-367-4938. E-mail: cpuerta@puertafamily.com., lmilodi@aol.com.

PUETZ, PAMELA ANN, human resources executive; b. Lawrence, Mass., Aug. 17, 1949; d. Gregory and Eleanor Christine Bedrosian; m. Tracy Barnum Braun, Jan. 26, 1974 (div. 1985); 1 child, Susannah ; m. Dan Lee Puetz, May 31, 1986. AS, Fisher Jr. Coll., Boston, 1969; BS in Mgmt. with high distinction, Babson Coll., Wellesley, Mass., 1973. Br. mgr. First Security Bank of Utah, N.A., Salt Lake City, 1974-76; bus. mgr. U.S. Ski Team, Inc., Park City, Utah, 1976-77; banking specialist Tracy Collins Bank, Salt Lake City, 1980-83, instr. Fitness Inst., LDS Hosp., Salt Lake City, 1983-85; owner/operator Grapevine Svcs., Redondo Beach, Calif., 1987-88; human resources adminstr. PacifiCare Health Systems, Inc., Cypress, Calif., 1988-89, human resources analyst, 1989-91, human resources project mgr., 1991-93, human resources mgr., 1993—94; sr. mgr. human resources systems Mattel, Inc., El Segundo, Calif., 1994-95; sr. cons., HRIS mgr. PacifiCare Health Systems, Inc., Cypress, Calif., 1995-96, dir. Employee Svc. Ctr., 1996—. Mem., bd. dir. Human Options, 2004—. Mem. Internat. Human Resources Info. Mgmt. Assn., Soc. for Human Resources Mgmt., World At Work. Avocations: scuba, snow skiing.

PUGH, ANNE D. state legislator; b. Rye, N.Y., May 21, 1952; BS, Union Coll., 1974; MSW, Washington U., St. Louis, 1975; CAS, U. Vt., 1990; student, Case Western Res. U. Planning commr. City of South Burlington (Vt.), 1986-92; justice of peace, mem. South Burlington Bd. Civil Authority, 1988—; mem. Vt. Ho. of Reps., 1993—; social worker, educator, cons. City of South Burlington. Mem. gov.'s commn. on women Vt. Ho. of Reps.; chmn. South Burlington Dem. Com.; bd. dirs. Vt. Women's Health Ctr. Trustee Ctr. Human Svc.; chmn. South Burlington Dem. Com. Mem. NASW (past pres.), Nat. Assn. Family Based Svc. (bd. dirs.). Address: 67 Bayberry Ln South Burlington VT 05403

PUGH, DOROTHY GUNTHER, artistic director; b. Memphis, May 8, 1951; Grad. magna cum laude, Vanderbilt U., 1973; studied with Raymond Clay, studied with Donna Carver, studied with David Howard; student, Royal Acad. Dancing, London. Founder, artistic dir. Ballet Memphis, 1985—. Named one of city's influential citizens, Memphis Mag.; recipient Woman of Achievement award for Initiative, 1987, Gordon Holl Artistic Adminstr. of Yr. award, State of Tenn., 1999. Office: Ballet Memphis PO Box 3675 Cordova TN 38088-3675*

PUGH, JOYE JEFFRIES, educational administrator; b. Ocilla, Ga., Jan. 23, 1957; d. Claude Bert and Stella Elizabeth (Paulk) Jeffries; m. Melville Eugene Pugh, Sept. 21, 1985. AS in Pre-law, S. Ga. Coll., 1978; BS in Edn., Valdosta State Coll., 1980, MEd in Psychology, Guidance and Counseling, 1981; EdD in Adminstrn., Nova U., Ft. Lauderdale, Fla., 1992. Cert. tchr., adminstr., supr., Ga. Pers. adminstr. TRW, Inc., Douglas, Ga., 1981-83; recreation dir. Ocilla (Ga.), Irwin Recreation Dept., 1983-84; exec. dir. Sunny Dale Tng. Ctr., Inc., Ocilla, 1984-96; employment cons. TPS Staffing and Recruiting, Douglas, Ga., 1997-98; mgr. Global Employment Solutions, Inc., 1999—2002; freelance writer, 2002—. Pres. and registered agt. Irwin County Resources, Inc., Ocilla, 1988-97, Camelot Ct., Inc., 1994-97. Author: Antichrist-The Cloned Image of Jesus Christ, 1999; contbr. articles on handicapped achievements to newspapers, mags. (Ga. Spl. Olympics News Media award, 1987, Assn. for Retarded Citizens News Media award, 1988). Mem. adv. bd. Area 12 Spl. Olympics, Douglas, Ga., 1984-88, bd. dirs., 1995-2000; pres. Irwin County Spl. Olympics, 1984-97, mem. adv. task force Spl. Olympics Internat. for 6-7 yr. olds, 1995—97; bd. dirs. Ga. Spl. Olympics, 1995-98, 98-99, mem. comm. and mktg. com., 1995-96, mem. nominations com., 1997-98, outreach and edn. com., 1999-2000; exec. dir., fund raising chmn. Irwin Assn. for Retarded Citizens, Ocilla, 1984-97; arts and crafts chmn. Ga. Sweet Tater Trot 5k/1 Mile Rd. Races, 1993-97; founder, chmn. Joseph Mascolo Celebrity Events, 1985—; vol. Am. Heart Assn., 2000-02. Recipient Spirit of Spl. Olympics award Ga. Spl. Olymics, Atlanta, 1986, Award of Excellence Ga. Spl. Olympic Bd. Dirs., 2000, Cmty. Svc. award Ga. Assn. for Retarded Citizens, Atlanta, 1987, Govs.' Vol. award Ga. Vol. Awards, Atlanta, 1988, Presdl. Sports award AAU, Indpls., 1988, Humanitarian award Sunny Dale Tng. Ctr., Inc., Ocilla, 1988, Golden Poet award New Am. Poetry Anthology, 1988, Outstanding Coach-Athlete Choice award Sunny Dale Spl. Olympics, Ocilla, 1992, Dist. Coach award, 1993, Outstanding Unified Sports Ptnr. of Yr. award, 1995, Coach of Yr. award, 1996; carried Olympic Torch, Ocilla, Ga., 1996; Ga. Spl. Olympics State Gold medalist Golf Unified Team, 1996, State Silver medalist Unified Table Tennis Team, 1996, State Bronze medalist Master's Unified Softball Team, 1995. Mem. DAR (Author-Educator-Humanitarian award Nathaniel Abney chpt. 2000), Nat. Soc. Daughters Am. Revolution (mem. Nathaniel Abney chpt.), Mut. Unidentified Flying Object Network (Ga. state sect. dir., asst. state dir., cons. 1994—), Ga. State Assn. for Retarded Citizens, Ctrs. Dirs. Ga., Ocilla Rotary Club (program dir. 1995-97, bd. dirs. 1995-97, sec. 1996-97), Sunny Dale Unified Track Club (founder 1991), Sunny Dale Ensemble (founder), Ocilla/Irwin County C. of C., Irwin Assn. Retarded Citizens Inc. Baptist. Avocations: playing musical instruments, jet skiing, weight lifting, dance, singing. Home and Office: 201 Lakeside Cir Douglas GA 31535-6629 E-mail: drjoye@charter.net.

PUGLIESE, KAREN OLSEN, freelance public relations counsel; b. S.I., N.Y., Aug. 20, 1963; d. Harold Birger and Janet Mildred (Cronk) Olsen; m. John Michael Pugliese Jr., Oct. 21, 1989; children: Emily Olsen, John Michael Pugliese III. BA in Polit. Sci., Union Coll., 1985. Asst. editor Food Mgmt. mag., N.Y.C., 1985-86; account exec. Edelman Pub. Rels., N.Y.C., 1986-87; account exec., sr. v.p., group dir. Creamer Dickson Basford, N.Y.C., 1987-96; freelance pub. rels. counsel, Redding, Conn., 1996—. Recipient Gold Quill, Internat. Assn. Bus. Communicators, 1991, award Internat. Pub. Rels. Soc., 1993, Creativity in Pub. Rels., Inside PR, 1993. Republican. Avocations: tennis, reading, walking.

PUGLIESE, MARIA ALESSANDRA, psychiatrist; b. Phila., Sept. 16, 1948; d. Peter Francis and Ida Agnes (Rosa) Pugliese; m. J. Paul Hieble, Sept. 14, 1985. BS, Chestnut Hill Coll., 1970; MD, U. Pa., 1974. Diplomate Am. Bd. Psychiatry and Neurology; with added qualifications in addiction psychiatry. Intern in pediatrics Children's Hosp. of Phila., 1974-75; resident in psychiatry Inst. Pa. Hosp., Phila., 1975-78, attending psychiatrist, 1978-97, Malvern (Pa.) Inst., 1982—, Pa. Hosp., 1997—. Office: 111 N 49th St Philadelphia PA 19139-2718 E-mail: mariadoc2@cs.com.

PUGLIESE LOCKE, RANADA MARIE, nurse; b. Cleve., Sept. 22, 1950; d. Joan Lee Green; m. Thomas L. Locke; 1 child, Kathryn Marie. AA, Los Angeles Valley Coll., 1974; student, Pepperdine U., 1981-82, U. San Francisco, 1985; BA, St. Mary's Coll., 1998; postgrad., Samuel Merrit Coll., 1998-00. Nurse emergency and ICU St. Joseph Hosp., Burbank, Calif., 1968-76; asst. dir. emergency services Brotman Hosp., L.A., 1976-78; clin. instr. Stanford (Calif.) U., 1978-80; dir. emergency services White Meml. Hosp., L.A., 1980-84; coordinator base sta., flight nurse UCLA, 1982-84; flight nurse, dir. med. ops. CALSTAR, 1984-87; coord. base sta. Tahoe Forest Hosp., 1987-98, base sta. coord., staff nurse, house supr. emergency dept.; staff nurse Santa Monica Hosp., 1980-84; firecaptain, EMS coord. North Tahoe Fire Protection Dist., 1990-98. Mem. Emergency Nurses Assn. (pres. local chpt. 1987-78), Flight Nurse Assn., Critical Care Nurses Assn., Calif. State Firefighters Assn. Avocations: backpacking, snow, waterskiing. Home and Office: 68-151 AU St Ph 8 Waialua HI 96791-9456

PUGLISI, MARY JOANNA, psychologist; b. Towson, Md., June 1, 1966; d. Joseph Anthony Butterhoff, Mary Barbara Butterhoff; m. Terrence Anthony Puglisi; children: Meg, Anthony, Cate, Joanna. BA in Psychology, Loyola Coll., 1988, MS in Counseling Psycholgy, 1993. Lic. clin. profl. counselor Md., 2001. Psychologist St. Elizabeth Sch., Balt., 1994—97; PRIDE program coord. St. Anthony of Padua Sch., Balt., 1997—. Cons. (book) Special Needs Resource Directory, 2001. Local coord./team mem. Cath. Engaged Encounter, Balt., 1991. Mem.: Am. Counseling Assn. Home: 8146 Bell Tower Crossing Pasadena MD 21122 Office: St Anthony of Padua Sch 4410 Frankford Ave Baltimore MD 21206

PULANCO, TONYA BETH, special education educator; b. Portland, Oreg., Apr. 17, 1933; d. Anthony Lorenzo and Adelfa Elizabeth (Dewey) P. BA, San Jose State U., 1955; MA, Columbia U., 1966. Occupl. therapist Langley Porter Hosp., San Francisco, 1958-60, writer ednl. sub contracts Columbia U., N.Y.C., 1961-64; from tchr. to dir. edn. Gateway Sch. N.Y., N.Y.C., 1965—. Mem. Assn. for Children with Learning Disabilities, Am. Occupl. Therapy Assn., Japanese Am. Citizens League. Avocations: tap dancing, walkathons, silversmithing, jazz, opera. Office: Gateway Sch NY 236 2d Ave New York NY 10003

PULITZER, LILLY (LILLIAN MCKIM ROUSSEAU), apparel designer, writer; b. Nov. 1931; m. Peter Pulitzer, 1952 (div. 1969); 3 children ; m. Enrique Rousseau (dec. 1993). Owner Fla. juice stand; dress designer, 1960—84, 1993—. Co-author (with Jay Mulvaney): Essentially Lilly: A Guide to Colorful Entertaining, 2004.*

PULITZER, ROSLYN KITTY, social worker, psychotherapist; b. Bronx, N.Y., Apr. 25, 1930; d. George and Laura Eleanor (Holtz) P. BS in Human Devel. and Life Cycle, SUNY, N.Y.C., 1983; MSW, Fordham U., 1987; postgrad., Masterson Inst., N.Y.C., 1991. cert. in psychoanalytic psychotherapy of the personality disorders, Masterson Inst., N.Y.C.; lic. clin. social worker, N.Y. Clinic dir. Resources Counseling and Psychotherapy Ctr., N.Y.C., 1985-89; social worker, clin. supr. methadone maintenance treatment program Beth Israel Med. Ctr., N.Y.C., 1989-97; psychotherapist pvt. practice, 1989—. Cons. therapist, clin. supr. Identity House, N.Y.C., 1980-97, exec. dir., 1985, clin. dir., 1993-94. Mem. regional adv. coun. N.Y. State Div. Human Rights, N.Y.C., 1975-76; mem. Community Bd. 6, N.Y.C., 1978-81; founder, legis. chmn. N.Y. State Women's Polit. Caucus, 1978-80. Mem. NASW, Acad. Cert. Social Workers, Soc. Masterson Inst., N.Y. Milton Erickson Soc. for Psychotherapy and Hypnosis (cert.). Avocations: photography, snorkeling. Home: 2742 La Silla Dorada Santa Fe NM 87505-6703 Fax: 505-438-2884. E-mail: imagesrkp@aol.com.

PULLEN, PENNY LYNNE, non-profit organization administrator, former state legislator; b. Buffalo, N.Y., Mar. 2, 1947; d. John William and Alice Nettie (McConkey) P. BA in Speech, U. Ill., 1969. Tv technician Office Instnl. Resources, U. Ill., 1966-68; cmty. newspaper reporter Des Plaines (Ill.) Pub. Co., 1967-72; legis. asst. to Ill. legislators, 1968-77; mem. Ill. Ho. of Reps., 1977-93, chmn. ho. exec. com., 1981-82, minority whip, 1983-87, asst. minority leader, 1987-93; pres., founder Life Advocacy Resource Project, Arlington Heights, Ill., 1992—. Exec. dir. Ill. Family Inst., 1993-94; dir. Legal Svcs. Corp., 1989-93; mem. Pres.'s Commn. on AIDS Epidemic, 1987-88; mem. Ill. Goodwill Del. to Republic of China, 1987. Summit conf. observer as mem. adhoc Women for SDI, Geneva, 1985; mem. Nat. Coun. Ednl. Rsch., 1983—88; dir. Eagle Forum of Ill., 1999—2003, pres., 2003—; Del. Rep. Nat. Conv., 1984; mem. Rep. Nat. Com., 1984—88; Del. Atlantic Alliance Young Polit. Leaders, Brussels, 1977; pres. Maine Twp. Rep. Women's Club, 1997—99, Rep. Women of Park Ridge, 2001—03. Recipient George Washington Honor medal Freedoms Found., 1978, Dwight Eisenhower Freedom medal Chgo. Captive Nations Com., 1977, Outstanding Legislator awards Ill. Press Assn., Ill. Podiatry Soc., Ill. Coroners Assn., Ill. County Clks. Assn., Ill. Hosp. Assn., Ill. Health Care Assn.; named Ill. Young Republican, 1968, Outstanding Young Person, Park Ridge Jaycees, 1981, One of 10 Outstanding Young Persons, Ill. Jaycees, 1981. Mem. DAR, Am. Legis. Exch. Coun. (dir. 1977-91, exec. com. 1978-83, 2d vice chmn. 1980-83), Com. on the Status of Women (sec. 1997—).

PULLER, LINDA TODD, state legislator; b. Cedar Rapids, Iowa, Jan. 19, 1945; d. Robert Grant and Margaret Jean (Threlkeld) Todd; m. Lewis Burwell Puller, Apr. 26, 1968; children: Lewis B. III, Margaret Todd. BA in Art History, Mary Washington Coll., 1967. With campaign Moore for Chmn., Fairfax, Va., 1987; adminstrv. aide Chair Bd. Suprs., Fairfax, 1988; polit. cons. Wilder for Gov., 1989; mem. Va. Senate, 1992—. Democrat. Episcopalian. Office: VA Senate State Capitol Richmond VA 23219

PULLIN, TANYA, state representative; b. South Shore, Ky, Sept. 15, 1957; d. Norman Keith and Mildred Pauline (Williams) P. JD, Univ. of Ky., 1986; MA, Duke Univ., 1985; BS, Univ. of Ky., 1980. Bar: Ky., 1986, U.S. Ct. Appeals Fed. Cir. 1987. State Rep. House of Rep., Dist. 98, Ky, 2000—; employed Baker & McKenzie, Hong Kong, China, 1995—97, Deacons, Hong Kong, China, 1990—95, Morgan & Finnegan, 1986—90. Bd. dirs., State YMCA of Ky., Frankfort, 1987—. Mem. N.Y. Soc. of Ky. Women (treas. 1988—), Kentuckians of N.Y. (dinner chmn. 1989—), Rainbow Girls (majority member). Democrat. Christian. Office: Capitol Capitol Annex Rm 432C Frankfort KY 40601 also: Dist Rural Rt 1 PO Box 486 South Shore KY 41175

PULOS, VIRGINIA KATE, communications consultant; b. Dayton, Ohio, Oct. 12, 1947; d. James C. and Mary M. (Maroglou) P.; m. George S. Georgiou; 1 child, Kate. BFA in Music summa cum laude, U. Cin., 1970. Singer, actor Broadway, Off Broadway, Stock, Film, Regional Theatre, more, 1970-89; founder, pres. Ginny Pulos Comm., 1989—. Speech, media and tng. cons.; asst. prof comm. NYU Sch. Continuing and Prolf. Studies; speaker confs. in field. Actress: Portrait of Jenny (Eugene O'Neil award, Richard Rodgers award), regular appearances on TV shows: All My Children, As the World Turns, The Doctors, 1982-88; numerous major opera and musical theatre roles, including: (Broadway) A Little Night Music, (Regional) My Fair Lady, others, 1970—; numerous radio and TV commls., 1970-80; guest soloist: Bklyn. Kingsboro Symphony in the Parks, 1984, 85, others. Program chair The Matrix Awards, 1993, 95, 96, others. Named Corbett Found. Internat. Opera fellow, Hamburg, Germany, 1969, N.Y.C., 1970-77. Mem. Screen Actors Guild, Actors Equity Assn., Am. Fedn. TV and Radio Actors, Greek-Am. Women's Network, N.Y. Women in Comm. (bd. dirs., 1992-99), Internat. Assn. Bus. Communicators, N.Y. Coalition Women in Arts & Media Avocations: theatre, film, food, travel, friends. Office: Ginny Pulos Comms 4th Fl 1120 Ave of the Americas New York NY 10036-6700*

PUMARIEGA, JOANNE BUTTACAVOLI, mathematics educator; b. Coral Gables, Fla., May 27, 1952; d. Ciro Charles and Rosaria Frances (Calabrese) Buttacavoli; m. Andres Julio Pumariega, Dec. 26, 1975; children: Christina Marie, Nicole Marie. BA in Math. and Edn. magna cum laude, U. Miami, 1973, MA in Math., 1974; postgrad., U. Houston, 1991-92. Cert. secondary math. tchr., Tex., Fla., Tenn., N.C. Grad. tchg. asst. U. Miami, Coral Gables, 1973-74; substitute tchr. Dade County Pub. Schs., Miami, 1975; math. instr. Miami Dade C.C., 1975-76; math. and G.E.D. instr. Durham (N.C.) Tech. Inst., 1976-77; math. instr. Durham H.S., 1977-78, Durham Acad., 1978-80, Univ. Sch. of Nashville, 1980-83; pvt. practice math. instr. Houston, 1984-86; tutor Clear Lake Tutoring Svc., Houston, 1987-90; pvt. practice, S.A.T, lang. instr. League City, Tex., 1990-92; pvt. practice math. and S.A.T. instr. Johnson City, Tenn., 1996—; lang. instr. Nelson Elem. Sch., Columbia, 1993-96. Instr. fgn. langs. and math. Lonnie B. Nelson Elem. Sch., Columbia, S.C.; adj. faculty math. East Tenn. State U., 1999—. Author (with F. Rodriguez and A. Pumariega): HIV/AIDS in Children and Adolescents, 1999; co-author (with A. Pumariega): Risk Factors of Mental Illness and Addiction Amongst Hispanic Immigrant Youth, 2002; contbr. articles to profl. jours. Chair bd. edn. St. Mary Parish, League City, 1988-90, lector, 1992, v.p. coun. Cath. Women, Johnson City, 1997-99; C.C.E. tchr. St. John Neumann Cath. Ch., Columbia, S.C. & Johnson City, Tenn., 1993-95, lector, 1992-96; lector St. Mary's Ch., Johnson City, 1996—; treas. St. Thomas More Women's Club, Houston, 1985-86; v.p., then pres. housestaff med. wives Duke U., Durham, N.C., 1978-80; mem. Wash./Unicoi/Johnson County Med. Alliance, 1999-2002, 2003-04, asst. treas., 2002-03, membership chmn., 2003-04, co-chmn. caring com., 2004—. Recipient Above and Beyond award, East Tenn. State U., 2002. Mem. Newcomers of Greater Columbia (chmn. pub. rels. chpt. 1993,95), Newcomers of Greater Colo. (com. chair coord. 1994-95), Welcome Neighbors of Bay Area (v.p., program chmn. 1991-92), Washington/Unicoi/Johnson Co. Med. Aux. (chair pub. rels. com. 1999-2002), Tex. Med. Aux., Bay Area Med. Wives, East Tenn. State U. Women's Club (v.p. 1997-98, pres. 1998-99, parliamentarian 1999-2000), U. S.C. Faculty Women's Club (v.p. 1993-94, pres. 1994-95, parliamentarian, advisor 1995-96), Phi Kappa Phi, Kappa Delta Pi, Delta Kappa Gamma (corr. sec. Gamma chpt. 2004), Alpha Lamba Delta (Woman of Yr. 1972). Roman Catholic. Avocations: reading, public speaking, traveling. Home: 2 Roundtree Court Johnson City TN 37604-1492 Office: East Tenn State U Dept Math PO Box 70663 Johnson City TN 37614-1701 Office Phone: 423-439-4349. Personal E-mail: pumarieg@aol.com.

PUMPHREY, JANET KAY, editor, publisher; b. Balt., June 18, 1946; d. John Henry and Elsie May (Keefer) P. AA in Secondary Edn., Anne Arundel C.C., Arnold, Md., 1967, AA in Bus. and Pub. Adminstrn., 1976. Office mgr. Anne Arundel C.C., 1964—2002; mng. editor Am. Polygraph Assn., Severna Park, Md., 1973—98; owner JKP Publ. Svcs., 1990—; dir. Am. Polygraph Assn. Reference Svc., 1995—98; owner Brooke Keefer Ltd.Editions, 1999—. Editor: (with Albert D. Snyder) Ten Years of Polygraph, 1984, (with Norman Ansley) Justice and the Polygraph, 1985, 2d edit., 1998, A House Full of Love, 1990, Mama, There's A Mouse in My House, 1996; pub. Vergennes, Vermont and The War of 1812, 1999; co-pub.: An Investigator's Guide to Non-Verbal Communication, 3d edit., 2004. Mem. Rep. Nat. Sustaining Com. Mem. NAFE, Am. Polygraph Assn. (hon.), Md. Polygraph Assn. (affiliate), Anne Arundel County Hist. Soc., Alumni Assn. Anne Arundel Community Coll. Republican. Methodist. Avocations: travel, poetry, gardening, mystery writer. Home: 3 Kimberly Ct Severna Park MD 21146-3703 Office: JKP Pub Svcs Brooke Keefer Ltd Edits PO Box 1535 Severna Park MD 21146-8535 E-mail: brookekle@worldnet.att.net.

PUNCH, SHAWNA LYNNETTE, special education educator; b. Houston, July 14, 1973; d. Michael Reynard and Sheryl Lee Herbert; m. Lawrence David Punch, Mar. 14, 1998; children: Caleb Daniel, Jacob Lacy. BS in Interdisciplinary Studies, U. Houston, 1996. Tchr. Cage Elem., Houston, 1996—2002; reading intervention tchr. Roberts Elem., Houston, 2002—. Mem.: Phono-Graphix Assn. Reading Therapists, Houston Fedn. Tchrs., Nature Conservancy, Delta Sigma Theta (sec. 1994—95, pres. 1995—96). Avocations: writing, reading.

PURCELL, ANN KATHRYN, artist, educator, painter; b. Wash., DC, Nov. 18, 1941; d. John Kevin and Mary Rita (Parker) Purcell. BA in painting, George Wash. U., Corcoran Coll. of Art, 1973; MA in liberal studies, NYU, Draper Sch. of Interdisciplinary Studies, 1995. Tchr. The Corcoran Coll. of Art and Design, Wash., 1971—79, Parsons Sch. of Design, Wash., 1983—85; freelance painter. Guest lectr. Ind. State U., Terre

Haute, Ind., 1983; vis. artist Ill. State U., Bloomington, 1987; guest lectr. Nat. Mus. of Am. Art, Wash., DC, 1988, Long Island U., NY, 1989. One-woman shows include Villa Roma Gallery, Mexico, 1971, Corcoran Gallery of Art, Wash., DC, 1976, Tibor de Nagy Gallery, N.Y.C., 1978, 1980, Osuna Gallery, Wash., DC, 1981, 1983, 1987, Reynold C. Kerr Gallery, N.Y.C., 1985, Philip Dash Gallery, 1985, 1987, exhibited in group shows at Corcoran Gallery of Art, Wash., DC, 1974, 1976, Mint Mus. of Art, NC, 1978, Franz Bader Gallery, Wash., DC, 1990, The Studio Mus. in Harlem, N.Y.C., 1990, The Nat. Mus. of Women in the Arts, Wash., DC, 1992, 1994, The Rotunda Gallery, NY, 1998, numberous others, Represented in permanent collections The Nat. Gallery of Art, Wash., DC, The Phillips Collection, The Corcoran Gallery of Art, The Balt. Mus. of Art, Md., Santa Barbara Mus., Calif., The Nat. Mus. of Women in the Arts, Wash., DC, New Orleans Mus. of Art, La., Va. Mus. of Fine Arts, Va., Albright-Knox Members' Gallery, NY, represented in numerous pub. and pvt. collections. Leg. asst. Office of Senator William Proxmire, Wash., DC, 1967—71, Office of Senator George McGovern, Wash., DC, 1971—72. Invitational fellowship, MacDowell Art Colony, 1975, Lester Hereward Cooke Found. grant, 1988, Pollock-Krasner Found. grant, Nat. Gallery of Art, 1989. Home: 155 Henry St 8F Brooklyn NY 11201-2547 E-mail: apurcell2001@aol.com.

PURCELL, ANN RUSHING, state legislator, office manager; b. Reidsville, Ga., May 12, 1945; d. William Robert and Katie (Dasher) Rushing; m. Dent Wiley Purcell, May 26, 1966; children: Edwin Wiley, Mieke Ann, Mikki Marie. BS in Edn., Ga. So. Coll., 1966; hon. degree, Ga. Future Farmers Am., 1999. Cert. secondary tchr. Tchr. math. Evans (Ga.) High Sch., 1966-68; tchr. math., earth and sci. Beaumont Jr. High Sch., Lexington, Ky., 1969-70; substitute tchr. Tallahassee, Fla., 1970's; agt. Noblin Realty, Tallahassee, 1970's; office mgr. Radiation Therapy Assocs., PC, Savannah, Ga., 1979—; state legislator Ho. of Reps. Ga. Gen. Assembly, Atlanta, 1991—. Author: Purcells of South Georgia and Other Related Families, 1976. Bd. dirs. Med. Assn. Ga. Polit. Action Com., Atlanta, 1988-89, Girl Scout Coun. Savannah, 1991-93, Ga. So. U. Found., 1992—. Armstrong Atlantic U. Found., 2004—; mem. adv. com. Effingham County Extension Svc., 1992—; Effingham County fin. chmn. State YMCA, 1991—, vice chmn. steering com., 1999, bd. dirs., 1999; mem. adv. com. Treutlin Home, 1999-; bd. adv. Claxton Youth Detention Ctr.; bd. dirs. Effingham YMCA, 1999—. Hon. comdr. 165th Ga. Air Guard Airlift, 2000—; hon. mem. Civil Air Patrol, 2001—, Ga. State Patrol, 2001. Decorated WA-PO-HE award Ga. Nat. Air Guard, Minuteman award; named Georgia's Legislator of Yr., Ga. Sch. Counselors Assn., 1996, Ga. Legislator of Yr., Coastal Conservation Assn. Ga., 1998; named to Hon. Ga. State Patrol, 2001; recipient Friend of Medicine award, Med. Assn. Ga., 1991, 1993, 1994, 1996, Guardian of Small Bus. award, Nat. Fedn. Ind. Bus., 1992, 1994, 1996, Commendation cert., Ga. Emergency Mgmt. Agy., 1995, Vol. of Yr. award, Effingham 4-H, 1998, Nat. Am. hon. degree, Future Farmers Am., 1999, Friend of State 4-H award, 1999, svc. award, Effingham Recreation Dept., 2000, cmty. svc. award, Guyton Masonic Lodge, 2000, Hon. Family Consumer Cmty. Leaders of Ga. award, 2001, Ga. Pub. Health award, 2003, Ga. Vet. award, Med. Assn. Ga., 2003, Effingham Jr. Adv. Family Connection award, 2003, Environ. Leadership award, Ga. Conservation Voters, 2003, Pub. Rels. award, Ga. Ext. Assn. of Family and Consumer Scis., 2003, Leadership award, Ga. Water Coalition, 2003, Charles Dick award, U.S. Nat. Guard, 2003, Air Nat. Guardsmen award, Savannah Assn. Flying, 2003. Mem. Aux. to the Med. Assn. Ga. (pres. 1985), Aux. to the Ga. Med. Soc. (pres. 1981-82), Ga. Salzburger Soc., Effingham County Pub. Ofcls. Assn., Rotary Internat. (Paul Harris fellow 2003), Ga. Peace Officers Assn. (hon.), Rincon Noon Lions Club, Exch. Club. Republican. Methodist. Avocations: painting, genealogy, fishing. Home: 410 Willowpeg Way Rincon GA 31326-9157 Office: LOB 508 Atlanta GA 30334-1600

PURCELL, CHERYL LINN, music educator; d. Lloyd Howard and Rosaline Elizabeth Goebel; m. Francis Joseph Purcell, Nov. 11, 1977 (dec. May 28, 1980); 1 child, Stephanie Rachel. BS in Edn., U. Mo., 1972, MusM in Edn., 1997. Cert. lifetime tchr. music K-12 Mo., 1972, ch. musician United Meth. Ch. Gen. Bd. Ordained Ministries, 2002. Educator music Gasconade County Schs., Owensville, Mo., 1972—73, Riverview Gardens Sch. Dist., St. Louis, 1973—75, Ft. Zumwalt Sch. Dist., O'Fallon, 1975—78, 1980—; dir. worship arts Faith United Meth. Ch., St. Charles, 1997—. Coord. curriculum performing arts Ft. Zumwalt Sch. Dist., 1999—. Dir.: (performance) Schubert: Mass in G (selected to perform at Carnegie Hall, 2002). Mem.: NEA, Fellowship United Meths. Music and Worship Arts, Ft. Zumwalt Ednl. Assn. (first v.p. 1977—78), Am. Choral Directors Assn., Music Educators Nat. Conf., U. Mo. Alumni Assn. (life), Sigma Alpha Iota (life; v.p. 1971—72). Methodist. Avocations: sewing, gardening, travel. Office: Lewis and Clark Elem Sch 460 McMenamy Rd Saint Peters MO 63376

PURCELL, KAREN BARLAR, physician, nutritionist, vocalist, writer; b. Miami, Fla., Dec. 31, 1947; d. Raymond and Elita (Kitzmiller) Barlar; m. John A. Purcell, June 11, 1977 (div. Dec. 1986); 1 child, Carl; m. Roy Gene Autry, Dec. 31, 1987 (dec. Mar. 2003). MusB, U. Cin., 1969; MusM, New England Conservatory Music, Boston, 1971; post grad tng., Bastyr U., Seattle, WA, 1997-98; D in Naturopathy, Natural Health Acad. Healing Arts, Tenafly, NJ, 1992. Diplomate Am. Bd. Naturopathic Physicians, 1997, cert. master herbalist, Dallas; ordained to mininstry Progressive Universal Life Ch., 1998. Assoc. prof. U. Miami, 1974-77, Dade County Jr. Coll., Miami, 1974-77; pvt. practice, N.Y.C., 1990—. Assoc. prof. NYU, 1988-92, Strasberg Theater Inst., N.Y.C., 1988-92, UN Internat. Sch., N.Y.C., 1992-96; star mgr. Nature's Sunshine Products; profl. spkr. in field, 1990—. Author: Simplified Nutritional Handbook, 1996, How to Survive a Nuclear Disaster, 2002; opera singer, 1970—. Founder WINS Found. for Moderate to Severe Brain Disorders, 1999—, PriceMentors.Com, affordable web sites, 2002. Mem. Am. Naturopathic Med. Assn., Internat. and Am. Assn. Clin. Nutritionists, Internat. and Am. Assn. Counselors and Therapists, Nat. Spkrs. Assn. Avocations: botany, cooking, travel. Office: 666 West End Ave Ste 15S New York NY 10025-7357 E-mail: kbpurcell@aol.com.

PURCELL, LEE, actress, film producer; b. N.C., June 15, 1957; divorced; 1 child, Dylan D. Purcell. Studies with Margot Lister, London; studies with Milton Katselas, Jeff Corey, U.S. Pres., owner Silver Strand Entertainment, L.A., 1995—. Appeared in (films) Adam at 6 A.M., 1970, The Toy Factory, 1971, Dirty Little Billy, 1972, Kid Blue, 1973, Mr. Majestyk, 1974, Almost Summer, Big Wednesday, 1978, Stir Crazy, 1980, Valley Girl, Eddie Macon's Run, 1983, Laura's Dream, 1986, Airplane II, 1989, Trackers, 1990, Money & Murder, 1993, The Joke, 1994, Malaika, 1997, Dizzyland, 1998, The Unknown, 2003, (TV) Hijack, 1973, Stranger in Our House, 1978, Howard, The Amazing Mr. Hughes, 1979, Kenny Rogers as the Gambler, 1980, Killing At Hell's Gate, 1981, My Wicked Wicked Ways: The Legend of Errol Flynn, 1986, Betrayed by Innocence, 1989, Long Road Home (Emmy nominee Lead Actress-Special), 1991, To Heal a Nation, 1992, Dazzle, 1994, Secret Sins of the Father (Emmy nominee Supporting Actress-Special), 1994, Due South (recurring role), 1995-96, Promised Land, 1999, (stage) One Flew Over the Cuckoo's Nest, Richard III, A Streetcar Named Desire, The Taming of the Shrew, A Midsummer's Night Dream. Recipient Bronze Star Halo Career Achievement award So. Calif. Motion Picture Council, 1985, Golden Star Halo award, 1986, Silver Medal award N.Y. Film and TV Festival, 1987. Mem. Actors' Equity Assn., Screen Actors Guild, AFTRA, Acad. Motion Picture Arts and Scis., Acad. TV Arts And Scis. Avocations: writing, collecting antiques and art. Office: PO Box 12581 La Crescenta CA 91224-5581

PURCELL, MARY HAMILTON, speech educator; b. Ft. Worth; d. Josseph Hants and Letha (Gibson) Hamilton; m. William Paxson Purcell, Jr., Dec. 28, 1950; children: William Paxson III, David Hamilton. BA, Mary Hardin-Baylor Coll., 1947; MA, La. State U., 1948; HHD (hon.), Mary Hardin-Baylor Coll., 1986, U. New England, 2000. Instr. dept speech and dramatic arts Temple U., Phila., 1948-53, 60-61; part-time instr. speech Cushing Jr. Coll., Bryn Mawr, Pa., 1966-78. Pres. Pa. Program for Women and Girl Offend, 1968—73, Nether Providence Parent Tchr. Orgn., 1975—76; treas. Virginia Gildersleeve Internat. Fund U. Women, 1975—81, bd. dirs., 1987—93; mem. U.S. del. UN Commn. on Status of Women, 1996; co-chmn. NGO Com. for UNICEF, 1994—2000, mem. global forum, 2001—; mem. Wallingford-Swarthmore Dist. Sch. Bd., 1977—83; bd. dirs. Ministers and Missionaries Fund Am. Bapt. Conv., 1985—94, pres., 1995—, Internat. Devel. Conf., 1986—; bd. dirs. Nat. Peace Inst. Found., 1983—86; Big Bros./Big Sisters of Am., 1985—90; bd. dirs. Citizens Crime Commn. of Phila., 1976—, Pa. Women's Campaign Fund, 1985—88, 1993—. Named Outstanding Alumna, Mary Hardin-Baylor Coll., 1972, Disting. Dau. Pa., 1982, v.p., 1994—95, pres., 1995—97, Woman of Yr., DECO Women's Conf., 1998; recipient Zeta Phi Eta award excellence in comms., 1983, Eleanor Schnurr award, UNA/USA, 2000. Mem. AAUW (Pa. divsn. pres. 1968-70, v.p. mid. Atlantic region, 1973-77, program v.p. 1979-81, pres. 1981-85, rep. to UN 1985-89), Internat. Fedn. Univ. Women (1st v.p. 1986-89, pres. 1989-92, rep. to UN 1992—; pres. UN Dept. Pub. Info. Non Govt. Orgn. ann. conf. 1993), Speech Assn. Am., Pi Kappa Delta, Pi Gamma Mu, Delta Sigma Rho, Alpha Psi Omega, Alpha Chi. Democrat. Baptist. Home: 9 Oak Knoll Dr Wallingford PA 19086-6315

PURCELL, MARY LOUISE GERLINGER, retired adult education educator; b. Thief River Falls, Minn., July 17, 1923; d. Charles and Lajla (Dale) Gerlinger; m. Walter A. Kuyawski, June 9, 1950 (dec. July 1954); children: Amelia Allerton, John Allerton; m. Dale Purcell, Aug. 26, 1962. Student, Yankton Coll., 1941-45, Yale Div. Sch., 1949-50, NYU, 1949; MA, Columbia U., 1959, EdD, 1963. Teenage program dir. YWCA, New Haven, 1945-52; dir. program in family rels. Earlham Coll., Richmond, Ind., 1959-62, asst. prof. sociology and psychology, 1959-62, conf. coord. undergrad. edn. for women, 1962; chmn. divsn. home and cmty. Stephens Coll., Columbia, Mo., 1962-73, chmn. family and cmty. studies, 1962-78; dir. continuing edn. women Learning Unltd., 1974-78; prof. Auburn (Ala.) U., 1978-88, head dept. family and child devel., 1978-84, chmn. search com. for v.p. acad. affairs, 1984, spl. asst. to v.p. acad. affairs, 1985-86, prof. emerita, 1988—. Developer course, cons. Contemporary Am. Woman, 1962; vis. prof. Ind. U. Summer Sch., 1970; cons. student pers. svcs. Trenton (N.J.) State Coll., 1958—59, 1961. Contbr. articles to coll. bulls., jours. V.p. Falls Villate-Canaan Hist. Soc., 1998—2001, pres., 2002—. Recipient Alumni Achievement award, Yankton Coll., 1975; Alumni fellow, Tchrs. Coll. Columbia U., 1959. Mem.: AAUW, Nat. Coun. Family Rels., Groves Conf. Family (nat. program chmn. 1977, dir., chmn.-elect affiliated couns. 1981—82, chmn. 1982—84, chmn. film awards com., chmn. spl. emphases sect., bd. dirs.), Am. Home Econs. Assn. (bd. dirs. 1967—69, chair 1st subject matter unit 1969, family rels. and child devel. sect. 1986—89), Falls Village Can. Hist. Soc. (v.p. 1998—2001, pres. 2002—), Litchfield County Univ. Club (mem. scholarship com. 2001—, bd. dirs. 2001—), Housatonic Camera Club (co-pres. 1996—2000), Delta Kappa Gamma. Congregationalist. Home: 120 Belden St Falls Village CT 06031-1124 E-mail: mlgp@sbcglobal.net.

PURCHASE-OWENS, FRANCENA, human resources specialist, educator; b. Milw., Nov. 14, 1960; d. Johnny and Arlene (Roberts) Purchase. Cert., Mich. Profl. Sch. Modeling, 1980; AA cum laude, Milw. Stratton Coll., 1982; BS in Applied Liberal Studies, Western Mich. U., 1997, M in Ednl. Leadership, 2002. Investment mgmt. sec. M&I Bank, Milw., 1984-85; cons. United Devel. Corp., Milw., 1986-88; paraprofessional Grand Rapids (Mich.) Pub. Schs., 1990-92; temp. helper Dayton Hudson Fortune 500, Grand Rapids, Mich., 1990; customer svc. rep. Kent County Conv. and Visitors Bur., Grand Rapids, 1995; mktg. rschr. Wirthlin Worldwide, Grand Rapids, 1996-98; pres. Creative Works, Grand Rapids, 1988—, Francena Purchase Internat. Honor Soc., Kentwood, Mich., 1999—, Francena Purchase Internat. Applied Studies, Kentwood, 1999—, Purchase Bus. Inst., Kentwood, 1999—, Francena Purchase Internat. Applied Profl. Studies Soc., Kentwood, Mich., 2000—; prof. U. Wis. (Big 10 U. Sys.); adminstrv. asst. to Elizabeth Kubler-Ross Ga. State U., 1980. Sec. Mich. Nat. Bank, Grand Rapids, 1980-81, Internat. Mktg. dept. Am. Seating, Grand Rapids, 1980-81, Volt Tech. Svcs. engrng. firm, Milw., 1980, sec. to various tep. cos. and positions; asst. exec. sec. Manpower Internat. Inc., Milw., 1982-84; cons. NASW; rschr., sec. United Devel. Corp.; human resource asst., computer programmer, sec. Patricia Stevens Coll., Milw., 1985-86; clerk-typist med. recors Spectrum Health (formerly Blodgett Meml. Med. Ctr.), Grand Rapids, 1979, telemarketer Weathermaster Indsutries, Inc., Milw., 1980; computer programming cons. Nat. Assn. Social Workers, Milw., 1980; office asst. to various cos. Access, Milw., 1980; asst.to pres. Alissia Cosmetics, Miss Black Pageant, 1980; legal sec. to attorney David Clowers, Milw., 1980, student asst. Ga. State U. Gerontology dept., Atlanta, 1980; student asst. Maln office, attendance office Ottawa Hills H.S., Grand Rapids, 1976-77, Fed. Govt. contract divsn., Grand Rapids, 19777-78; cashier Helen Smith's Market, Milw., 1972-73; clerk draft typist Ind. Libr. Life Ins. Co. claims dept., Grand Rapids, 1978-79; grad. asst. candidate Dale Carnegie course in Human Rels and Pub. Speaking; grad. student adv. bd. Western Mich. U., Kalamazoo, 2000; mem. Nat. Honor Soc. Iroquois Mid. Sch., 1974-75, Grand Rapids, Ottawa Hills H.S., 1976-79. Co-editor: Smoke Signal, 1975. Vol. United Way, Grand Rapids, 1990, TV (GVSD-TV) fundraiser Grand Valley State U.; reading condr. S.E. Neighborhood Assn., Grand Rapids, 1990; mem. literacy coun. Kent County Literacy Coun., Grand Rapids, 1991—, task force Dwelling Pl., Grand Rapids, 1999, First Call Help United Way, Grand Rapids, 1992; model Miss J. Fashion bd. Jacobson's Dept. store, East Grand Rapids Mich., 1979; finalist Miss Black Wis. pageant, Milw., 1981; bd. dirs. Program and Quality Com., Pers. Com., Fin. Com., Consumer Adv. bd., Touchstone innovaré mental health, Grand Rapids, 2000—, Kent County Cmty. Mental Health, 1999—; mem. Task Force Herkimer Apartment Projects, Weston Apartments Dwelling place of Grand Rapids, 1999; reading program asst. S.E. End Neigborhood Assn., Grand Rapids, 1993; rehab. asst. Kent Comty. Hosp. Complex, Grand Rapids, 1991; intake asst. Baxter Comty. Ctr., Grand Rapids, 1989; tutor Kent County Literacy Coun., Grand Rapids, 1988; facilitator trainer Employers Coalition for Healing Racism, Grand Rapids, 1997, Citizens Cirs. Resource Ctr., Grand Rapids, 1998, Ptnrs. in Pub. Edn., Grand Rapids, 1999, United Way Champions Diversity, Grand Rapids, 1999; project help tutor Iroquois Mid. Sch., Grand Rapids, 1975; student tutor Washington Elem., Kalamazoo, 1974; student rep. Bus. Office Edn. Club, 1978-79 (2nd place Extemporaneous Verbal Coms. 1978, 1st place second divsn. 1979, other leadership awards 1978-79); fundraiser Spl. Olympics Office Edn. Assn. Ottawa Hills H.S., 1978. Recipient shorthand awards taking dictation of 140 words per minute Milw. Stratton Coll., 1981-82, Century award typing 100 words per minute Milw. Stratton Coll., 1982, Machine Transcription award secretarial skills contest seventh place Milw. Area Tech. Coll., 1981, shorthand award Ottawa Hills H.S., 1979; Phillip Morris scholar Alverno Coll., 1981; Nontraditional Student grantee Western Mich. U., 1994, 2000, Thurgood Marshall Profl. Tuition grantee; Thurgood Marshall Assistanship scholar Western Mich. U.1989, 1998; 1st place speaker, 3rd place typist and secretarial job application Office Edn. Assn. Extemporaneous Speaking; 6th place with Letter of Recognition from Senator Berger of Wis. Milw. Area Tech. Coll., 1981; Internat. finalist theatre arts, Milw., 1986; noted as jr. achievement Ottawa Hills H.S., 1978, other different honors, awards, recognitions, accomplishments, etc. Mem. ASCD, ASTD, Am. Mgmt., Am. Cancer Soc., Program Soc. Human Resource Mgmt. (Superior Merit award), Internat. Econ. Assn., Phi Beta Lambda (sec. 1982), Mich. Jaycee, U.S. C. of C., Jr. Chamber Internat., Jaycess Networking and Leads, Alzheimers Assn., Am. Cancer Soc. Program, Profl. Bus. Leaders (sec.-elect), Profl. Secs. Internat., Office Edn. Assn., Grand Rapids Econ. Club, Phi Beta Lambda, others. Avocations: modern dancing, reading, tennis. Address: PO Box 7421 Grand Rapids MI 49510

PURDEE, ALICE MARIE, retired adult education educator; b. St. Louis, Jan. 8, 1931; d. Joseph Louis and Angeline Cecilia (Mozier) P. AA, Belleville Area Coll., 1951; BS, Ill. State U., Normal, 1953, MS, 1954; cert., Sorbonne U., Paris, 1964; PhD, Fla. State U., Tallahassee, 1976. Cert. in music edn., elem. edn., secondary edn., adult edn. Tchg. and grad. asst. Ill. State U., 1953-54; music supr. Princeton (Ill.) Pub. Schs., 1954-55; music dir. Venice (Ill.) Pub. Schs., 1955-72, secondary vocal music dir., 1955-72; coord. literacy program Venice-Lincoln Tech. Ctr., 1983-86, chmn. lang. arts dept., 1983-96; ret., 1996. Tchr. in space candidate, 1985. Mem. St. Louis chpt. World Affairs Coun., UN Assn., Nat. Mus. of Women in the Arts, Humane Soc. of Am.; charter mem. St. Louis Sci. Ctr., Harry S. Truman Inst.; contbr. Old Six Mile Mus., 1981, Midland Repertory Players, Alton, Ill., 1991; chair Cystic Fibrosis Spring Bike-A-Thon, Madison, Ill., 1981, Granite City, Ill., 1985. Named to Ill. Sr. Hall of Fame, 2001, Gov's Sr. Hall of Fame, 2001; recipient Gold medal, Nat. Senior Olympics, 1989, Gold medal, more than 400 others, Sr. World Games, 1992, Generations of Success Alumni award, Belleville Area Coll., 1998, several scholarships. Mem.: AAUW, Am. Fedn. Tchrs. (pres. 1957—58), Ill. Adult and Continuing Educators Assn., Am. Choral Dirs. Assn., Ill. Music Educators Assn. (Svc. award 2002), Music Educators Nat. Conf., Ill. State U. Alumni Assn., Slavic and East European Friends (life), Fla. State Alumni Assn., Lovejoy Libr. Friends, Nat. Space Soc., Western Cath. Union, Croation Fraternal Union, St. Louis Numis. Assn., Friends St. Louis Art Mus., Archaeol. Inst. Am., Travelers Abroad (pres. 1966—68, 1989—), Madison Rotary Club (internat. amb., Humanitarian award 1975). Roman Catholic. Avocations: bowling, travel. Home: PO Box 274 Madison IL 62060-0274

PURDY, LESLIE, community college president; b. Downey, Calif., Aug. 18, 1943; d. Hubert C. and Janice M. (Harker) Noble; m. Ralph Purdy, Aug. 23, 1969; children: Christopher Hugh, George Colin. BA cum laude, Occidental Coll., L.A., 1965; MAT, Oberlin (Ohio) Coll., 1966; EdD, UCLA, 1973. Tchr. Parma (Ohio) Sr. H.S., 1966; ombudsman/instr. social sci. Raymond Coll., U. of Pacific, Stockton, Calif., 1967-69; coord. spl. svcs. ERIC Clearinghouse for C.C.'s, L.A., 1970-74; sr. instrnl. designer Coastline C.C., Fountain Valley, Calif., 1974-84, adminstrv. dean, 1984-94, pres., 1994—. Bd. dirs. Intelecom, Pasadena, Calif.; bd. dirs., pres. Instrnl. Telecom. Coun., Washington, 1987-94; adv. bd. PBS "Going the Distance" program, Washington, 1993-96; cons. Commn. on Innovation, Calif. Colls. Chancellor's Office, 1993-94. Editor: Reaching New Students Through New Technologies, 1983; instrnl. designer Psychology: The Study of Human Behavior, 1989 (Emmy 1990); exec. prodr. (telecourses): Universe: The Infinite Frontier, 1994 (Emmy 1994), Time to Grow, 1992 (Emmy 1992); contbr. articles to profl. jours. Mem. Orange County Forum, 1994—, Ctr. for Studies of Media and Values, L.A., 1990-95, Bread for the World, Washington, 1980—; bd. mem. West County Family YMCA, 1993-2000; bd. mem. Garden Grove Renaissance Found., 1998—; bd. mem. Orange County Nat. Conf. of Cmty. and Justice, 1997—, Orange County Workforce Investment Bd., 2000—; mem. adv. bd. Calif. C.C. Satellite Network, 2001-02. Recipient Emmy awards Am. Acad. TV Arts and Scis., 1987, 90, 92,. 95, Western Region award Instrn. Telecom. Coun., 1995; named one of Women of Distinction City of Garden Grove, 2001. Mem. Assn. of Calif. C.C. Adminstrs., Assn. Ednl. Comms. and Tech., Am. Assn. of Women in C.C.'s, UCLA Alumni Assn. (Doctoral Award in Edn. 1973). Presbyterian. Avocations: backpacking, gardening, conservation, choral singing. Office: Coastline Cmty Coll Office of Pres 11460 Warner Ave Fountain Valley CA 92708 E-mail: lpurdy@cccd.edu.

PURE, PAMELA, information technology executive; Various mgmt., product devel. and mktg. positions Shared Med. Sys. (now divsn. Siemens); COO Channel Health Subs. IDX Sys.; group pres. product devel. and support McKesson Corp., San Francisco, 2001—02, COO, McKesson Info. Solutions, 2002—. Office: 1 Post St San Francisco CA 94104*

PURITZ, HOLLY SUZANNE, obstetrician-gynecologist; b. N.Y.C., Feb. 10, 1957; d. Sheldon and Rubie (Meyers) P.; m. Stephen D. Wohlgemuth, June 26, 1982; children: Zachary, Leah. BS, Tufts U., 1979, MD, 1983. Diplomate Am. Bd. Ob-Gyn. Chief resident Eastern Va. Sch. of Medicine, Norfolk, Va., 1986-87; ptnr. The Group for Women, Norfolk, 1987—, mng. ptnr., 1995—. Chief Dept. Ob-Gyn., Sentara Hosps., Norfolk, 1993-96; chmn. Mid Atlantic Women's Care, PLLC, 1996—. Mem. bd. dirs. Jewish Family Svcs., Norfolk, 1992—, exec. com., sec. 1996, pres.-elect 1998; spkrs. bur. March of Dimes Campaign for Health Babies, 1992-93; active Senara Physician Leadership Coun., 1999—, Hampton Roads Physician Orgn. Exec. Com., 1999—. Mem. Phi Beta Kappa, Alpha Omega Alpha. Jewish. Office: The Group for Women 880 Kempsville Rd Ste 2200 Norfolk VA 23502-3989

PURKERSON, MABEL LOUISE, physician, physiologist, educator; b. Goldville, S.C., Apr. 3, 1931; d. James Clifton and Louise (Smith) P. AB, Erskine Coll., 1951; MD, U. S.C., Charleston, 1956. Diplomate Am. Bd. Pediat. Instr. pediat. Washington U. Sch. Medicine, St. Louis, 1961-67, instr. medicine, 1966-67, asst. prof. pediat., 1967-98, asst. prof. medicine, 1967-76, assoc. prof. medicine, 1976-89, prof., 1989-98, prof. emerita, 1998—, assoc. dean curriculum, 1976-94, assoc. dean acad. projects, 1994-98. Cons. in field. Editl. bd. Am. Jour. Kidney Diseases, 1981-87; contbr. articles to profl. jours. Mem. bd. counselors Erskine Coll., 1971-87; trustee St. Louis Symphony Orch., Erskine Coll., 2000—. USPHS spl. fellow, 1971-72. Mem. Am. Heart Assn. Coun. on the Kidney (exec. com. 1973-81), Am. Physiol. Soc., Am. Soc. Nephrology, Internat. Soc. Nephrology, Ctrl. Soc. Clin. Rsch., Am. Soc. Renal Biochemistry and Metabolism, Am. Osler Soc., Explorer's Club, Sigma Xi (chpt. sec. 1974-76). Home: 20 Haven View Dr Saint Louis MO 63141-7902 Office: Bernard Becker Med Libr Renal Div Dept PO Box 8132 Saint Louis MO 63110-1093 Office Phone: 314-362-4234. E-mail: purkerm@msnotes.wustl.edu.

PURPURA, GRACE, artist, retired art educator; b. N.Y.C., Nov. 3, 1929; d. Michael and Carmela Maligno Purpura; m. Salvatore Andriola; children: Marina, Diana, Valerie. Student, Cooper Union Sch. Art & Arch., 1946-49, CUNY, 1952, San Jose State U., 1969. Cert. elem., secondary, art tchr., Calif. Art tchr. L.A. City Schs., 1957-62; design instr. L.A. City College, 1960; bilingual tchr. Alum Rock Sch. Dist., San Jose, 1969-91; arts commr. City of San Jose, Calif., 1994-98. Mentor tchr. State of Calif. Dept. Edn., Sacramento, 1984-87; mem. Fulbright Scholar L.Am. project Stanford U., China and Korea/Calif. Dept. Edn., 1987, Calif. Internat. Studies mem., 1985. Exhibited paintings, sculptures and drawings at numerous shows regionally, nat. and internat. including Synopsys, Inc., Mountain View, Calif., Lifescan, Milpitas, Calif., Network Gen. Corp., Menlo Park, Calif., Ohlone Coll., Fremont, Calif., Works Gallery, San Jose, Inst. for Contemporary Art, San Jose, Triton Mus., Santa Clara, Calif., de Saisset Mus., Santa Clara, Denver Art Mus., Raychem Corp., Menlo Park, Forum Art Gallery, N.Y.C.; one-woman shows include San Jose Art League, Casa de la Cultura, Livorno, Italy. Bd. dirs. San Jose Art League, 1985-88; arts commr. City of San Jose, 1994-98. Mem. Calif. Art Edn. Assn. Avocations: arts, photography, children's picture books. Home: 2364 Stokes St San Jose CA 95128-4262

PURVES, KAREN E. freelance/self-employed small business owner; d. Purves and Boehmer. MA, Claremont (Calif.) U., Claremont, California, 1995. Cert. coach trainer Coaches Tng. Inst., 2000. Prin., owner Innovative Impact, Hoffman Estates, Ill., 2000—. Adj. faculty Harper Coll., Palatine, Ill., 2001—; mem. U.S. Appropriations Subcommittee, 1997, 2000. Author:

(non-profit curriculum) Compassion Curriculum. Mem.: Meeting Profls. Internat. Avocations: improv, music, cats, travel. Office: Innovative Impact 2549 W Golf Rd 114 Hoffman Estates IL 60194 E-mail: samneph@earthlink.net.

PUSEY, ELLEN PRATT, home economist; b. Milford, Del., Aug. 27, 1928; d. Algeo Newell and Ruby Newton (Boorman) Pratt; m. William W. Pusey, June 12, 1950; children: William W., Patricia A., Cynthia L., Daniel N. BS, U. Md., 1950; MS, 1951; PhD in Home Econs. Edn., U. Md., 1990. Camp dietitian N.Y. Herald Tribune Frsh Air Fund Camps, 1947; supr. cafetaria Roosevelt Hosp., N.Y.C., 1948; supt. sch. cafetaria Seaford, Del., 1964; field faculty home economist Md. Coop. Ext. Svc., Wicomico County, Md., 1967-92, Worcester County, Md., 1992-94; merchandising mgr. Pusey's Country Store, 1994—. Chmn. lower shore coun. Am. Lung Assn., Md., 1978-79; pres. U. Md. Coll. Human Ecology Alumni Bd., 1988-89. Named One of Outstanding Women Wicomico County, Commn. ofro Women, 1989. Mem. Internat. Fedn. Home Econs., Am. Home Econs. Assn., Asian Regional Assn. Home Econs., Md. Econs. Assn., Nat. Assn. Extension Home Economists, Tri-County Home Econs. Assn. (chmn. 1973), Nutrition Jour. Club Eastern Shore, Phi Kappa Phi, Alpha Xi Delta, Soroptimists Club (pres. 1978, 2nd v.p. 1989, South Atlantic region Women Helping Women award 1989. Presbyterian. Home: 301 W Federal St Snow Hill MD 21863-1116 Office: Pusey's Country Store PO Box 265 Snow Hill MD 21863-0265

PUTNAM, RUTH ANNA, philosopher, educator; b. Berlin, Sept. 20, 1927; d. Martin and Marie (Kohn) Hall; m. Hilary W. Putnam, Aug. 11, 1962; children: Samuel, Joshua, Maxima. BS in Chemistry, UCLA, 1954, PhD in Philosophy, 1962. Instr. philosophy UCLA, 1957-59; acting asst. prof. U. Oreg., 1959-62; from lectr. to prof. philosophy Wellesley (Mass.) Coll., 1963-98, chmn. dept., 1979-82, 91-93; ret., 1998. Dir. summer seminar NEH, 1986, 89; mem. extramural grad. fellowships Wellesley Coll., faculty benefits com., com. budget, academic review bd., taskforce on affirmative action, bd. of admissions; presenter in field. Editor: Cambridge Companion to William James, 1997; contbr. chpts. to books, articles to profl. jours., and encys. Mem. Am. Philos. Assn. (program com. ea. divsn. 1977). Jewish. Office: Wellesley Coll 106 Central St Wellesley MA 02481-8268 E-mail: rputnam@wellesley.edu.

PUTNEY, MARY LYNN, bank administrator, educator; b. N.Y.C., Feb. 26, 1948; d. Joseph John Berry and Evelyn Marie (Geoghegan) Schneir; m. Paul Michael McCaffery, May 18, 1968 (div. June 1976); children: Melissa Berry McCaffery, Paul David McCaffery; m. Frederick Bates Putney, May 30, 1992. MBA in Fin., Columbia U., 1982. Various positions Citibank, N.Y.C., 1974-85, v.p. fgn. exch., 1985-88, v.p. leveraged capital, 1988-92, mng. dir. pvt. banking, 1992-95, mng. dir. global equity, 1995—; adj. prof. Columbia Bus. Sch., N.Y.C., 1986—. Dir. Sinter Metal Corp., Cleve.; mem. adv. bd. AIG Millenium Fund, Russia, CVC/Opportunity Ptnrs., Brazil. Contbr. articles to profl. jours. Dir. Project Renewal, N.Y.C., 1995—, Mary Knoll Sch. Theology, Ossining, N.Y., 1994-95. Mem. Emily's List, Women's Campaign Fund, Sleepy Hollow Country Club, Sea Pines Country Club, Beta Gamma Sigma. Avocations: golf, bridge. Office: Citibank NA 153 E 53rd St New York NY 10022-4611

PUTO, ANNE-MARIE, reading specialist; b. Windber, Pa., July 20, 1956; d. John Michael and Ann Theresa (Biel) Puto. BS Elem. Edn., U. Pitts., Johnstown, 1978; EdM in Lang. Comms., U. Pitts., 1981; EdM in Ednl. Psychology, Indiana U. Pa., 1989. Reading specialist Conemaugh Valley Sch. Dist., Johnstown, 1978—79, Upward Bound Program, St. Francis U., Loretto, Pa., 1994—2000, Appalachian Youth Svc., Ebensburg, Pa., 1991—, Children's Aid Home, Somerset, Pa., 1999—, Appalachia Intermediate Unit 08, Ebensburg, 1979—. Mem. Cambria Area Reading Coun. Mem.: Keystone State Reading Assn., Pa. Assn. Fed. Program Coords. Avocations: reading, travel, cross country skiing, needlecrafts, theater. Home: 1093 Tener St Johnstown PA 15904

PUTTERMAN, FLORENCE GRACE, artist, printmaker; b. N.Y.C., Apr. 14, 1927; d. Nathan and Jean (Feldman) Hirsch; m. Saul Putterman, Dec. 19, 1947. BS, NYU, 1947; MFA, Pa. State U., 1973. Founder, pres. Arts Unlimited, Selinsgrove, Pa., 1969—; curator Milton Shoe Collection, 1970—; artist in residence Title III Program Cultural Enrichment in Schs. Program, 1969-70; instr. Lycoming Coll., Williamsport, Pa., 1972-74, Susquehanna U., Selinsgrove, PA, 1984—. One-woman shows include Everson Mus., Syracuse, N.Y., 1976, Hagerstown, Md., 1978, Stuhr Mus., Grand Island, N.B., 1979, Muhlenburg Ctr. for the Arts, Pa., 1985, Harmon Gallery, Fla., 1985, The State Mus. of Pa., 1985-86, Segal Gallery, N.Y., 1986, Canton Inst. Fine Arts, Ohio, 1986, Fla. Biennial Polk Mus., Lakeland, Fla., 1987, 89, Artists Choose Artists, Tampa Mus., 1987, Auburn Works on Paper, 1987, Ala., Ruth Volid Gallery, Chgo., 1989, Polk Mus. Art, Lakeland, Fla., 1989, Lowe Gallery, Atlanta, 1990, Mickelson Gallery, Washington, 1990, Palmer Mus., Pa. State U., 1990, Payne Gallery, Moravian Coll., 1991, Everhart Mus., Scranton, Pa., 1991, Lowe Gallery, L.A., 1992, Center Gallery, Bucknell U., Pa., 1993, Lore Degenstein Gallery, Susquehanna U., Selinsgrove, Pa., 1993, Lowe Gallery, Atlanta, 1993, Down Roll Gallery, Sarasota, Fla., Gallery 10, Washington, Donn Roll Contemporary, Sarasota, Fla., 1996, Grand Central Gallery, Tampa Fla., 1997, Walter Wickiser Gallery, N.Y., Hodges-Taylor Gallery, Charlotte N.C., Ziegenfuss Gallery, Sarasota, Burroughs-Chapin Mus., Myrtle Bend, S.C., Lighthouse Gallery, Tequesta, Fla., 1998, Galerie Lumiere, Savannah, Ga., 1999, Walter Wickiser Gallery, N.Y., 1999, Ellen Noel Art Mus., Odessa, Tex., 1999, Spartansburg County Mus. Art, Spartansburg, S.C., 2000, Saginaw (Mich.) Art Mus., 2000, Art Mus., No. Mich. U., Marquette, Lancaster Mus. Art, 2001, Albany (Ga.) Art Mus., 2002, Walter Wickiser Gallery, N.Y.C., 2003, Mira Mar Gallery, Sarasota, Fla., 2003, Waterworks Visual Art Ctr., Salisbury, N.C., 2003, Robeson Gallery, Pa. State U., 2003; 10-yr. retrospective Susquehanna U., 2003; exhibited in numerous group shows including: Libr. Congress, Smithsonian Traveling Exhbn., Sarasota (Fla.) Biennial Ringling Mus., 2000, Tampa Mus. Art, 2001, Springfield (Mo.) Art Mus., 2002, Chattahoochee Valley Art Mus., 2002, Butler Inst. Am. Art, 2002, Appalachian Corridors, Charleston, W.Va., 2003, La. State U., Baton Rouge, 2004others. Recipient award Silvermine Guild Conn. Appalachian Corridors, Arena, 1976, Gold medal of honor Audubon Artists ann. competition, Whitehead award Boston Printmakers, 1985, Shellenberg award Artists Equity, 1985, award N.C. Print & Drawing, 1985, award Chautauqua Nat., 1985, Johnson & Johnson award 3rd Ann. Nat. Printmaking Coun. of N.J., 1985, Purchase award N.J. State Mus., 1987, Disting. Alumni award Pa. State U. Sch. Arts & Architecture, 1988, Ethel Klassen Meml. award Fla. Artists Group, 1992, Earl Horter award Phila. Watercolor Club, 1992, award of excellence, 1995, Stella Drabkin Meml. award Colorprint Soc., Award for Excellence Phila. Watercolor Club, 1996, Elizabeth Morse Meml. award Fla. Artists Group, 1996, Daniel Serra Y Navas Meml. award Audubon Artists, N.Y., 1996, Purchase award drawing annual Del Mar (Tex.) Coll., 1997, Purchase award Stockton (Calif.) Arts Commn., 1998, LaGrange Nat. Biennial, 2002; Va. Ctr. for the Creative Arts fellow, 1983-84; Nat. Endowment Arts grantee. Mem. Soc. Am. Graphic Artists (v.p.), Nat. Assn. of Women Artists (Nat. Medal of Honor, Elizabeth Blake award). E-mail: Flo2@gte.net.

PUTZEL, CONSTANCE KELLNER, lawyer; b. Balt., Sept. 5, 1922; d. William Stummer and Corinne (Strauss) Kellner; m. William L. Putzel, Aug. 28, 1945; 1 son, Arthur William. AB, Goucher Coll., 1942; LLB, U. Md., 1945, JD, 1969. Bar: Md. 1945. Social worker Balt. Dept. Pub. Welfare, 1945-46; atty. New Amsterdam Casualty Co., Balt., 1947; staff atty. Legal Aid Bur., Balt., 1947-49; mem. Putzel & Putzel, P.A., Balt., 1950-89; pvt. practice Balt., 1989—; instr. U. Balt. Sch. Law, 1975-77, Goucher Coll., 1976-77. Chair character com. Ct. Appeals for 3d Cir., 1976-97. Author: A Practice Guide to Divorce, 1999, Representing the Older Client in Divorce, 1992. Commr. Md. Com. on Status of Women, 1972-76, Com. to Implement ERA, 1973-76; Pres. U. Md. Law Alumni Assn., 1978; bd. dirs. Legal Aid Bur., 1951-52, 71-73. Fellow Am. Acad. Matrimonial Lawyers (chair elder issues com. 1996); mem. ABA (co-chair elder issues com., mem. coun. sr. lawyers divsn. 1996-2000, editl. bd. 1996-99), Md. Bar Assn. (bd. govs. 1972-73, chmn. family law sect. 1978-79, chair sr. lawyers divsn. 2001-03). Home: 7121 Park Heights Ave Unit 401 Baltimore MD 21215-1610 Office: 401 Washington Ave Ste 803 Towson MD 21204 E-mail: lawtowson@aol.com.

PYDYNKOWSKY, JOAN ANNE, journalist; b. Ft. Riley, Kans., Oct. 2, 1951; d. Fredrick Albert and Mary Elizabeth (O'Connor) Gadwell; m. Michael Stanley Pydynkowsky, Mar. 14, 1981; children: Tricia Lynn Glotfelty, Deborah Findley, Alexandra, Royce. BA in Journalism, U. Ctrl. Okla., 1991, MEd in Journalism, 1993. Trust clk. Ill. Nat. Bank, Rockford, 1974-75; engring. aide Barber Colman, Rockford, 1976-77; draftsperson Gen. Web, Rockford, 1979-80, Keeson, Ltd., Rockford, 1981; editor Oklahoma City Marriage Encounter, 1988-89, 94-95; humor columnist UCO Vista, Edmond, Okla., 1990-91; city editor Guthrie (Okla.) Daily Leader, 1991-92; substitute tchr. Edmond (Okla.) Pub. Schs., 1993-94; with N.W. News, Piedmont, Okla., 1994-95, South Oklahoma City Leader, 1995-96; staff writer, columnist, reporter, photographer N.W. News, Piedmont-Surrey Gazette, Okarche Chieftain, Piedmont, 1996—98; city editor Okarche Chieftain, Piedmont, 1996-98, asst. editor, 1998; staff writer, columnist, photographer El Reno (Okla.) Tribune, 1997; horsemanship/hunter/jumper trainer Red Tail Ranch, Piedmont, Okla., 1999-2000. Copywriter, cons., Edmond, 1991—, photographer, 1990—, cartoonist, 1984—, humorist, 1990—; columnist, contbg. writer N.W. News, Piedmont, Okla., 1994-95; reporter and assoc. editor: All About Kids/South Oklahoma City Leader, 1995-96. Artworks include: Turtle (cover), UCO Bus. Rev., winter 2000. Asst. leader Boy Scouts Am., Edmond, 1993-95; league coach Young Am. Bowling Alliance, Edmond, 1993-99; counselor Oklahoma City YWCA Rape Crisis, 1986-88; mem. Tiaras Jr. Women's Honor Soc., 1990-91; mem. selection com. Okla. Journalism Hall of Fame, 1990. Recipient awards State Fair of Okla., 1983-96, 99-2003, Feature Writing award Okla. chpt. Soc. Profl. Journalists, 1992-93, six awards including first place Entertainment, Sports feature, sports column, 1994-95, six awards including first place feature writing, 1995-96, five awards including first place feature writing, 1996-97, eight awards, 1997-98, first place Feature Writing award, State Fair of Okla. Better Newspaper Contest, 1995. Mem. Soc. Profl. Journalists (pres. U. Ctrl. Okla. chpt. 1990, treas. 1989, 91), Kappa Tau Alpha. Roman Catholic. Avocations: writing, photography, horsemanship, art. Home: 301 Reynolds Rd Edmond OK 73013-5121

PYE, JANNA LYNN, music educator; b. Dalton, Ga., Mar. 10, 1975; d. Larry Keith and Janice Karen Masters; m. Lionel Ford Pye III, July 26, 1997; 1 child, Sean Ford. MusB, U. Ga., 1997; MA, So. Oregon U., 2000. Tchg. cert. Ga. Band dir. Gladden Mid. Sch., Chatsworth, Ga., 1997—99; asst. band dir. Rome (Ga.) City Schs., 1999—2002; band dir. Christen Heritage Sch., Dalton, 2002—. Clarinet clinician Renaissance Music Camp, Rome, 1999; guest conductor Encore Music Camp, Milledgeville, Ga., 2000, Bartow County Honor Band, Cartesville, Ga., 2001, N.W. Ga. Music Camp, Rome, 2002—03, Dist. 7 Clinic Band, Rome, 2003. Contbr. articles to profl. jours. Mem.: Internat. Clarinet Assn., Music Educators Nat. Convention, Ga. Music Educators Assn. (guest performing group com. 2000). Presbyterian. Avocations: reading, golf. Home: 1609 Ryman Ridge Rd Dalton GA 30720 Office: Christian Heritage Sch 1600 MLK Blvd Dalton GA 30721

PYLE, CAROL LYNN HORSLEY, small business owner; b. Dallas, Mar. 29, 1946; d. John Otis and Flora Eileen Horsley; m. Michael R. Pyle (dec. 1995). B Music Edn., East Tex. State U., 1970, MusM, 1972. Cert. music and English tchr., Tex. Choral dir. Dumas (Tex.) Jr. H.S., 1970-72, Haltom H.S., Birdville, Tex., 1981-84, Glen Rose (Tex.) Jr. and Sr. H.S., 1986-88, Springtown (Tex.) H.S., 1988-91, Azle (Tex.) H.S., 1991—; choral dir., vocal coord. Weatherford (Tex.) H.S. and Mid. Schs., 1972-81; English reading tchr. Aledo (Tex.) H.S., 1984-86; prin., owner Trebleshooter Edn. Svcs., Weatherford, Tex., 2003—. Mem. adv. bd. Tex. Girls' Choir, Ft. Worth; founder, mus. dir. Parker County Choral Soc., Weatherford, 1984-86. Contbr. articles to profl. jours. Founder, bd. dirs., 1st pres. Weatherford Assn. Performing Arts, 1974-77; pres. Weatherford Classroom Tchrs. Assn., Weatherford, 1979-80; soloist, guest condr. various civic, ch. and cmty. choirs, Tex., 1970—; tchr. Azle Ch. of Christ, 1980—; vol. Tarrant County Fine Arts Coun., Parker County Cancer Soc. Named Tchr. of Yr. Weatherford Ind. Sch. Dist./VFW Aux., 1980, Nat. Finalist Tchr. of Yr., Nat. VFW Aux., 1980. Mem. Tex. Music Educators Assn. (chair region VII 1987-88, region V 1991-92), Tex. Choral Dirs. Assn. (state sec. 1980-81), Assn. Tex. Pub. Educators, Renaissance Consort of Ft. Worth, Schola Cantorum of Tex., Inc. (bd. dirs. 1974-75, Mem. of Yr. 1992), Mu Phi Epsilon, Alpha Chi, Alpha Lambda Delta. Office: Trebleshooter Music Svcs PO Box 443 Weatherford TX 76086

PYLE, CASSANDRA A. service organization executive; Chmn. Acad. Edn. Devel., Washington. Exec. dir. Coun. Internat. Exchange Scholars, 1981-84; v.p. Internat. Edn. at Am. Coun. Edn., v.p. Inst. Internat. Edn.; past pres. NAFSA: Assn. Internat. Educators; bd. dirs. Latin Am. Scholarship Program Am. U., U.S.-Can. Fulbright Commn., Hariri Found., Social Sci. Found. U. Denver, U. Colo. Found. Deans Adv. Coun. Recipient Disting. Svc. award Coun. Internat. Edn. Exchange, U. Colo. Bd. Regents, Fulbright prize, Japanese Fulbright Alumni. Mem. Coun. Foreign Relations. Office: Acad Edn Devel 1825 Connecticut Ave NW Washington DC 20009-5708 Fax: 202-884-8400. E-mail: admindc@aed.org.

PYLE, WILMA J. retired education educator; b. Red Key, Ind., Feb. 7, 1926; d. William Finley and Mae Ellen Pyle. BS, Ball State U., 1946; MA, Ohio State U., 1950; EdD, Wayne State U., 1964. Cert. tchr. Ind. Tchr. Ft. Wayne (Ind.) Pub. Schs., Battle Creek (Mich.) Pub. Schs.; tchr., prin. Pontiac (Mich.) Pub. Schs.; instr. Wayne State U., Detroit; assoc. prof. Mercy Coll., Detroit; prof., asst. dean SUNY, Fredonia; assoc. dean, prof. Fla. Atlantic U., Boca Raton; ret., 1988. Pres. Internat. Reading Assn., Chautauqua County, NY, 1972—74. Author reading series, 1966-1972. Bd. dir. Fla. Bipartisans Civic Affairs Group, Polk County, Fla., 1999—. Named one of Outstanding Women in Fla.; recipient Outstanding Alumni award, Coll. of Edn., Ohio State U., 1979, Outstanding Alumni Achievement award, Ball State U., 1974. Mem.: AAUW (pres. 1996—98, co-pres. 2003—04), Lake Wales Arts Coun. Avocations: painting, reading, walking, gardening.

QUACKENBUSH, MARGERY CLOUSER, psychoanalyst, administrator; b. Reading, Pa., Apr. 30, 1938; d. Carl Brumbach and Katherine Elvina (Althouse) Clouser; m. Robert Mead Quackenbush, July 3, 1971; 1 child, Piet Robert. BA, Pratt Inst., 1960; MA, Calif. Grad. Inst., 1982; PhD in Psychoanalysis, Internat. U. Grad. Studies, N.Y.C., 2001. Cert. in psychoanalysis Ctr. for Modern Psychoanalytic Studies, 1992. Instr. Pratt Inst., Bklyn., 1978-79, Fashion Inst. of Tech., N.Y.C., 1980-81; counselor Wiltwyck, Bronx Ctr., 1981-82; exec. dir. Nat. Assn. for Advancement of Psychoanalysis, N.Y.C., 1982—; instr. Mid-Manhattan Inst. for Psychoanalysis, N.Y.C., 2004—; pvt. practice in psychoanalysis N.Y.C., 1980—. Instr. Mid-Manhattan Inst. Psychoanalysis, 2004—. Mem. Lenox Hill Dem. Club, N.Y.C., 1993-95; spkr. various cmty. groups, 1991—. Recipient Maison Blanche award, 1959, Miriam Berkman Spotnitz award, 1992. Mem. Nat. Assn. for Advancement of Psychoanalysis, Nat. Soc. DAR, Alumni Assn. of the Ctr. for Modern Psych. Studies (sec. 1992-94, Alumni Assn. program dir., v.p. 1995-98). Democrat. Avocations: reading, writing, golf, horseback riding. Home: 460 E 79th St Apt 14E New York NY 10021-1447 Office: Nat Assn Advancement Psychoanalysis 80 8th Ave # 1501 New York NY 10011-5126 Office Phone: 212-741-0515. Personal E-mail: naap72@aol.com.

QUADAY-GRAY, AILENE DIANN, retired speech pathology/audiology services professional; b. Blue Earth, Minn., Aug. 26, 1937; d. Carl Frederick Quaday and Arlene Alice Bunting; m. Maurice Clayton Maine, Aug. 18, 1956 (div. May 1975); children: Keith Mauricé, Kevin Richard; m. Francis Moulton Gray Jr., May 7, 1989 (dec. Dec. 1994). BA, St. Cloud (Minn.) State U., 1971; postgrad., San Diego State U., 1979-81, various colls., 1971-85, West Hills and Fresno Pacific, 1987-94. Lic. speech pathologist, Calif.; cert. presch. tchr., Calif. Speech pathologist Comprehensive Health Ctrs., Inc., San Diego, 1981-82; speech pathologist pilot project Kings Rehab. Ctr., Inc., Hanford, Calif., 1983 summer; tchr., dir. First Luth Ch. Presch., Hanford, 1983-85; speech specialist Fresno (Calif.) County Office of Edn., 1985-87, Kings County Office of Edn., Hanford, 1987-91, Reef-Sunset Unified Sch. Dist., Avenal, Kettleman City, Calif., 1991-94, Kingsburg (Calif.) Joint Union Charter Elem. Schs., 1994-2001; part-time presch. speech therapist Sanger (Calif.) Unified Sch. Dist., 2001—02. Cons. Headstart: Tech. Assistance Mgmt., 1971-72; part-time speech therapist Selma (Calif.) Unified Sch. Dist., 2001—. Vice chmn. bd. edn. St. James Luth., San Diego, 1979-80; del. Consortium on County Health Needs, Wright County, Minn., 1972-75; advisor Wright County Minn. Commrs. on Handicapped, 1973-75; vol. children's waiting rm. Navy Hosp., Bremerton, Wash., 1976-77. Mem. Calif. Speech, Lang. and Hearing Assn. Democrat. Methodist. Avocations: playing flute, teaching language, reading, writing poetry. Home: 2132 14th Ave Kingsburg CA 93631-1731

QUADE, VICKI, editor, writer, playwright, producer; b. Chgo., Aug. 15, 1953; d. Victor and Virginia (Uryasz) Q.; m. Charles J. White III, Feb. 15, 1986 (div. Aug. 1996); children: Michael, David, Catherine. BS in Journalism, No. Ill. U., 1974. Staff reporter news divsn. The News-Tribune, LaSalle, Ill., 1975-77; staff writer news divsn. The News-Sun, Waukegan, Ill., 1977-81; staff writer ABA Jour., Chgo., 1981-85; mng. editor ABA Press, Chgo., 1985-90, editor, 1990-2000, sr. editor, 1994-2000. Author: (poetry) Rain and Other Poems, 1976, Laughing Eyes, 1979, Two Under the Covers, 1981, (biography) I Remember Bob Collins, 2000; playwright Late Nite Catechism, 1993, Room for Advancement, 1994, Mr. Nanny, 1997, (musical) Lost in Wonderland, 1998, (musical) Here Come the Famous Brothers, 2001; prodr. Late Nite Catechism, Mr. Nanny, Here Come the Famous Brothers, Christopher Carter Messes With Your Mind, Forever Plaid, Cast on a Hot Tin Roof; contbr. to numerous anthologies and publs.; contbd. to: 20th Century Chicago: 100 Years, 100 Voices (contbd. the year 1953), owner/operator Crossroads Theater, Naperville, Ill. Recipient numerous awards from Soc. Nat. Assn. Publs., AP, UPI. Mem. Am. Soc. Bus. Press Editors (award), Chgo. Newspaper Guild (award), Am. Soc. Assn. Execs. (Gold Circle award 1989, 90). Avocations: travel, photography.

QUAIFE, MARJORIE CLIFT, retired nursing educator; b. Syracuse, N.Y., Aug. 21; Diploma in Nursing with honors, Auburn Meml. Hosp; BS, Columbia U., 1962, MA, 1978. Cert. orthopaedic nurse; cert. in nursing continuing edn. and staff devel.; BLS instr. Staff instr. Columbia Presbyn. Hosp., N.Y.C., 1968-97, ret., 1997. Content expert for computer assisted instrn. program-ctrl. venous catheters. Contbr. articles to numerous profl. publs. Mem. ANA, N.Y. State Nurses Assn., Nat. Assn. Orthopaedic Nurses, Nat. Assn. Nursing Staff Devel., Nat. Assn. Vascular Access Networks, Intravenous Nurses Soc., Sigma Theta Tau.

QUALLS, ROXANNE, mayor; D (hon.), Cin. State Tech. and C.C., 1996. Former exec. dir. Women Helping Women; former dir. No. Ky. Rape Crisis Ctr.; former dir. Cin. office Ohio Citizen Action; councilwoman City of Cin., 1991-93, mayor, 1993-98, founder youth summer jobs program Artworks, Cin. Homeownership Partnership. Former chairperson Cin. City Council's Intergovtl. Affairs and Environment Com.; former vice chairperson Community Devel., Housing and Zoning Com.; mem. Gov.'s Commn. on Storage and Use of Toxic and Hazardous Materials, Solid Waste Adv. Com. of State of Ohio, Gov.'s Waste Minimization Task Force; former chair bd. commrs. Cin. Met. Housing Authority; bd. dirs. Shuttlesworth Housing Found. Hon. chair Friends of Women's Studies; mem. Jr. League Adv. Coun.; bd. dirs. Nat. Underground Railroad Freedom Ctr., Ctr. Voting and Democracy; past bd. didrs. No. Ky. Cath. Commn. Soc. Justice. Recipient Woman of Distinction award Girl Scouts U.S., 1992, Woman of Distinction award Soroptimists, 1993, Outstanding Achievement award Cin. Woman's Polit. Caucus, 1993, Women of Achievement award YWCA, 1994, Outstanding Svc. award Ohio Pub. Employees Lawyers Assn., 1996, Pub. Offcl. of Yr. award State of Cinn., 1996, Nat. Assn. Soc. Workers, 1996, Nat. Homebuilders Assn., 1997. Mem. Nat. Assn. Regional Couns. (former pres., 1st v.p., 2d v.p.), Ohio Ky. Ind. Regional Coun. Govts. (1st v.p., 2d v.p.). Office: 119 Fayerweather St #1 Cambridge MA 02138-6812 Fax: 513-352-5201.

QUAM, LOIS, healthcare company executive; MA in Philosophy, Politics, Econs., U. Oxford, 1985. Dir. rsch. and eval. United HealthCare, 1989-93, v.p. public sector svcs., 1993; sr. advisor White House Task Force Nat. Health Care Reform, 1993-96; CEO AARP/United divsn. United HealthCare, 1996-98; CEO Ovations (formerly Retiree and Sr. Svcs. Co. United HealthCare), Minnetonka, MN, 1998—. Office: Ovations United Health Group 500 Opus Ctr 9900 Bren Rd E Minnetonka MN 55343-9664

QUAMINA, JOYCE, management consultant; b. Jan. 4, 1937; d. Da Costa and Beryl Jones; m. Ulric Quamina (dec. May 1985); 1 child, Michelle Quamina Reid. From recording sec. to bus. mgr. WIADCA Inc., Bklyn., 1983—2001. Dir. Caribbean Music Festival, Nassau, Bahamas, 1987—2001; cons. Western Union, NJ, 1994—99; v.p. Westchester Carnival Assn., White Plains, NY, 1989—96. Home: 1150 President St B2 Brooklyn NY 11225

QUANN, MEGAN, Olympic athlete; b. Tacoma, Wash., Jan. 15, 1984; Recipient Gold medal 100-meter breaststroke, 4 x 100-meter medley (team) Sydney Olympics, 2000, Silver medal 100-meter breaststroke Pan Pacific Championships, 1999; set Am. record for 100-meter breaststroke U.S. Open Swimming Championships, San Antonio, 1999; winner 100-meter breaststroke title U.S. Spring Nats., 1998, 99, 1st pl. 100m breast stroke, Nat. Championships, 2003. Office: USA Swimming 1 Olympic Plz Colorado Springs CO 80909-5746

QUARLES, BETH, civil rights administrator; Commr. Civil Rights Commn., Indpls. With presdl. task force, Mits task force, Muncie task force ADA; with Pecso CEO Learning Ctr.; active in youth leadership, employment opportunities and law enforcement ADA; hearing impaired cons.; condr. sign lang. classes. Bd. dirs. Open Door Comty., Muncie (Ind.) Pub. Libr., United Way, County Commty. Partnership on Disability, Muncie Civic Theater; vol. interpreter for deaf; mentor numerous minority bus. Recipient Frieda Dawkins award, Presdl. Points of Light award, also state, nat., and internat. awards for theatrical prodns. Office: Civil Rights Commn 100 N Senate Ave Rm W103 Indianapolis IN 46204-2273

QUARTERMAN, CYNTHIA LOUISE, lawyer; b. Savannah, Ga., Apr. 6, 1961; d. Rudolph V. and Bernice Q.; m. Pantelis Michalopoulos, Nov. 2, 1993. BS, Northwestern U., 1983; JD, Columbia U., 1987. Atty. Benson & McKay, Kansas City, 1987-88, Steptoe & Johnson, Washington, 1988—93; dep. dir. Minerals Mgmt. Svc., Dept. Interior, Washington, 1993-95, dir., 1995-99; ptnr. Steptoe & Johnson, Washington, 1999—. Mem. adv. bd. Inst. for Energy Law, co-chair ann. inst. Mem. ABA (vice chair sect. on environment, energy, resources, oil and natural gas exploration and prodn. com. 2002—03), Energy Bar Assn. (chair environment and pub. lands com. 2002—03), Women's Coun. Energy and Environment. Home: 1337 21st St NW Washington DC 20036-1503 E-mail: cquarter@steptoe.com.

QUARTUCCIO, MARYANN, insurance agent, home economist; b. San Jose, Calif., Aug. 26, 1957; d. Anthony Angelo and Catherine Elizabeth (Sunseri) Q. AA, San Jose City Coll., 1979; BS in Home Econs., Calif. Poly. State U., San Luis Obispo, 1984. Lic. ins. agt., Calif. Dept. head Marshall's Dept. Store, San Jose, Calif., 1977-80; food server Servomation Corp., Santa Clara, Calif., 1980-85; sr. customer svc. coord. Prudential Ins., Los Altos, Calif., 1985-90; personal lines account mgr. Alburger Basso Degrosz Ins. Svcs., Belmont, Calif., 1990-95; personal lines mgr. Bandar Covall Ins., San Mateo, Calif., 1995-96, Micheletti & Assocs., San Jose, Calif., 1997-99; personal lines mgr., claims mgr. Dorsey Hazeltine Wynne Ins., Palo Alto, Calif., 1999—2001; ins. agt. Allwest Ins. Brokers, Campbell, Calif., 2001—. Tchg. asst. for the disabled San Jose City Coll., 1978-79. Vol., Second Harvest Food Bank, San Jose, 1999. Mem. Peninsula Ins. Women's Assn. (2d v.p. 1996-97, various coms., Ins. Woman of Yr. 1995), Nat. Assn. Ins. Women. Republican. Roman Catholic. Avocations: cooking/baking, culinary arts, catering, sports, interior decorating. Home: Apt 71 4951 Cherry Ave San Jose CA 95118-2737 Office: Thoits Insurance Svcs 444 Castro St Ste 200 Mountain View CA 94040

QUAST, PEARL ELIZABETH KOLB, retired elementary school educator; b. Omro, Wis., Nov. 21, 1934; d. Frank Kolb and Lavon Opal Buchanan; m. Arthur Roman Quast; children: Arthur R. Jr., Robert F.; 1 child, John M. BS in Edn., Edgewood Coll., Madison, Wisconsin, 1956; MA in Edn., Cardinal Stritch Coll., Milw., 1971. Cert. tchr. unlimited 0743, K-3 Wis., remedial reading 42 and 27 (K-12), reading specialist 42 and 27 (K-12). Tchr. grade 2 Deerfield (Ill.) Pub. Schs., 1956—58; tchr. grade 3 Whitefish Bay (Wis.) Pub. Schs., 1958—60; tchr. reading Milw. Pub. Schs., 1969—75; reading specialist Germantown (Wis.) Pub. Schs., 1975—91. Seminar presenter Reading Assn., Milw., 1982—86; vol. coord. The Cath. Ctr., Sun City West, 1998—99; coord. lectors Our Lady of Lourdes Ch., Sun City West, 1996—2003, lector, cantor, choir mem., Sun City West and Phoenix, 1995—2003. Bd. trustees Found. for Sr. Living, Phoenix, 1998—2001; group leader founding com. Cath. Ctr. for Srs.' Needs, Sun City and Sun City West, 1995—2001; coord. lectors Our Lady of Lourdes Ch., 1996—2003, mem.; del. Phoenix Diocesan Synod, 2002—03; Bd. trustees Symphony of the West Valley, Sun City West, 1996—2002. Mem.: AAUW (v.p. membership 1994—96), West Valley Art Mus. (sec. Woman's League 1994—96), Cath. Ctr. (founding officer, v.p. adv. com. 1996—2000, Cert. Appreciation), Found. for Sr. Living, Weavers West Handweaving Guild, Our Lady of Lourdes Church. Roman Catholic. Avocations: handweaving, travel, singing, reading, cultural arts.

QUATRANO, ANNE, chef, restaurant owner; Grad., Calif. Culinary Acad., San Francisco. Chef, co-owner Bacchanalia, Atlanta, Floataway Cafe, Atlanta, Star Provisions, Atlanta; chef Grolier Club, NY, Bimini Twist, La Petit Ferme. Elected mem. James Beard Found. Office: 1198 Howell Mill Rd Atlanta GA 30301

QUATTRONE-CARROLL, DIANE ROSE, clinical social worker; b. N.Y.C., July 18, 1949; d. Mario Anthony and Filomena (Serpico) Quattrone; m. Rene Eugene Carroll Jr., June 7, 1980; children: Jenna Cristine, Jonathan Rene. BA cum laude, Bklyn. Coll., 1971; MSW, Rutgers U., 1974. Lic. marriage and family counselor, lic. clin. social worker, N.J.; bd. cert. diplomate in clin. social work. Clin. social worker, field instr. Essex County Guidance Ctr., East Orange, N.J., 1974-82; exec. dir. Psychotherapy Info. and Referral Svc., Madison, N.J., 1982-87; pvt. practice Sparta, N.J., 1982—. Nat. Assn. Social Workers. Avocation: travel.

QUAY, JACQUELYN SUE, art educator, consultant; d. Harold Ira and Helen Mary Martin; m. Stanley John Quay, June 12, 1976; children: Patrick William, Kathleen Martin. AB, Wilmington Coll., 1970—73; MEd, Xavier U., 1973—76; EdD, U. of Cin., 1978—87. Music tchr. West Clermont Local Sch. Dist., Batavia, Ohio, 1973—79; adj. prof. U. of Cin., 1988—93; dir., spectra riverside acad. Fitton Ctr. for Creative Arts, Hamilton, Ohio, 1995—. Pres. Ohio Alliance for Arts Edn., 2000—03; co-chair Ohio Arts Edn. Adv. Bd., 2000—02. Co-author: (handbook) Ohio Arts Education Assessment Project Handbook; developed internet graduate courses; contbr. articles. Pres. Sycamore HS Athletic Boosters, Cin., 1995—2000. Nominee Governor's Award for Arts Edn., 2000, 2001, 2002, 2003; recipient Art Adminstr. of the Yr., Ohio Art Edn. Assn., 2003, Arts partnership, Governor's Award, Ohio, 2002, Ohio BEST award, Model Arts Edn. Program, 2002, Model Arts Programming, Ohio Arts Edn. Adv. Com., 2002; Model Arts Demonstration and Dissemination grant, Dept. of Edn., 2000—, 21st Century Learning Cmty. grant, Ohio Dept. of Edn., 2003—, Profl. Devel. Arts Edn. grant, Ohio Arts Coun., Grad. Student scholarship, U. of Cin., 1979—86. Mem.: Ohio Art Edn. Assn. (assoc.), Nat. Assn. of Mid. Schools (assoc.), Americans for the Arts (assoc.), MENC- Ohio Music Edn. Assn. (assoc.), Nat. Art Edn. Assn. (assoc.), ASCD (assoc.), Ohio Alliance for Arts Edn. (assoc.), Phi Delta Kappa (assoc.). Avocations: sewing, golf, softball. Home: 9184 Hopewell Rd Cincinnati OH 45242 Office: Fitton Ctr for Creative Arts 101 South Monument St Hamilton OH 04501-2833 Personal E-mail: jsquay@aol.com. E-mail: jackie@fittoncenter.org.

QUAY, JOYCE CROSBY, writer; b. Dayton, Ohio, Aug. 8, 1928; d. Wilson Hill and Marianne (Mitchell) Crosby; m. John Grier Quay, Nov. 12, 1952; children: Peter Crosby, John Paul, Leslie Quay McMillan. Student, Simmons Coll., 1951, NYU, 1959-60. Ptnr. Quay Assocs., 1961-84. Author: Sam Walton, Founder of Wal-Mart (People to Know), 1994, Early Promise, Late Reward, 1995, (play) Double Destinies, 2000; contbr. articles to popular publs. Mem. Rep. Nat. Com., 1990, 94-95. Presbyterian. E-mail: jcquay@msn.com.

QUAYLE, MARILYN TUCKER, lawyer, wife of former vice president of United States; b. 1949; d. Warren and Mary Alice Tucker; m. J. Danforth Quayle, Nov. 18, 1972; children: Tucker, Benjamin, Corinne. BA in Polit. Sci., Purdue U., 1971; JD, Ind. U., 1974. Pvt. practice atty., Huntington, Ind., 1974—77; ptnr. Krieg, DeVault, Alexander & Capehart, Indpls., 1993—2001; pres. BTC Inc., Phoenix, 2001—. Author (with Nancy T. Northcott): Embrace the Serpent, 1992; author: The Campaign, 1996.

QUEEN, DOROTHY, distribution company executive; b. Carlsbad, N.Mex., Jan. 23, 1946; m. Bill Queen (dec.); 1 child. BS in Biology, N.Mex. State U.; med. tech., Tex. Tech. Co-founder Queen Oil & Gas Co., Inc., Carlsbad, 1972—, pres. Vol. 4H, Future Farmers of Am. Avocations: being outdoors, snow skiing, nature, raising horses, bird watcher. Office: Queen Oil & Gas 3202 S Canal St Carlsbad NM 88220 Fax: 505-887-6485.

QUEEN, EVELYN E. CRAWFORD, judge, law educator; b. Albany, N.Y., Apr. 6, 1945; d. Iris (Jackson) Crawford; m. Charles A. Queen, Mar. 6, 1971; children: Angelia, George. BS, Howard U., 1968, JD, 1975. Bar: N.Y. 1976, D.C. 1977, U.S. Ct. Appeals (D.C. cir.) 1977, U.S. Dist. Ct. (D.C. dist.) 1978, U.S. Supreme Ct. 1980. Park ranger Nat. Park Svc., Washington, 1968-69; pers. specialist NIH, Bethesda, Md., 1969-75; staff atty. Met. Life Ins. Co., N.Y.C., 1975-76; atty. advisor Maritime Adminstrn.-U.S., Washington, 1976-78; asst. U.S. atty.-D.C. Justice Dept., Washington, 1978-81; hearing commr. D.C. Superior Ct., Washington, 1981-86, judge, 1986—2001. Adj. law prof. Howard U., 1988, D.C. Sch. Law, 1993, 94. Contbr. chpt. to book. Recipient spl. achievement awards HEW, 1975, Trefoil award Hudson Valley coun. Girl Scouts U.S.A., 1988, Spl. Achievement award Dept. Justice, 1981, Sigma Delta Tau Jud. Svc. award, 2001. Mem. Nat. Bar Assn., Washington Bar Assn. Office: DC Superior Ct 500 Indiana Ave NW Ste Jm Washington DC 20001-2191

QUEEN, JOYCE ELLEN, elementary school educator; b. Cleve., Mar. 17, 1945; d. Wilbur Raynor and Mae (Reid) Closterhouse; m. Robert Graham Queen, Mar. 17, 1973. BA in Biology, Macalester Coll., 1966; MS in Conservation and Natural Resource Mgmt., U. Mich., 1968. Cert. tchr. biol. and earth scis., Ohio. Exhibitor, docent, coord. Grand Rapids (Mich.) Pub. Mus., 1967-68; tchr., naturalist Rose Tree-Media (Pa.) Outdoor Edn., 1967, Willoughby-Eastlake (Ohio) Schs., 1969-70, Independence (Ohio) Schs., 1970-78; sci. tchr. grades 1-7, coord. sci. field trip Hathaway Brown Sch., Cleve., 1970—, primary sci. educator, 1970—, primary sci. dept. chair, 1998—2002, prime sci. dept. head, 2003. Designer Courtland Woods nature trail, 1986, designer sci. greenhouse, 1990-92; designer sci. classroom Van Dyke Architects/Hathaway Brown Sch., 1990-92; designer, coord. Dampeer Primary sci. courtyard, 1993, Oliva Herb Garden, 1998, Colini Landscape Design/Hathaway Brown Sch., Shaker Hts., Ohio; mem. ednl. adv. com. William G. Mather Vessel Mus., Cleve., 1992, Holden Arboretum, Kirtland, Ohio, 1992-97; workshop leader Lake Erie Islands Hist. Mus., South Bass Island, Ohio, 1992, H.B. Winter Sci. Symposium Workshop, 1994—, Sagamore Adirondacks Great Camps Wksh, 2003; presenter Nat. Assn. Ind. Schs., Columbus, Ohio, 1993; workshop leader for schs. on garden design, sci. labs., and sci. discovery programs; youth divsn. judge Cleve. Botanic Garden Show, 1999, 2000, 2002, NOAA (with Betsy Youngman and Art Traverse) Live From Antarctica, 2003. Contbr. articles to profl. jours. Design cons. Cleve. Bot. Garden and Floral Scape, 1998; active Belize (Ctrl. Am.) Tchrs. Workshop, 1994; Sagamore Adirondack Great Camps Workshop, 2003. Catalyst grantee Hathaway Brown Sch. Gt. Lks. Curriculum, 1991; recipient Environ. Edn. award Ohio Alliance for Environment, 1986, Presdl. Excellence in Elem. Sci. Tchg. award NSF, 1992, Sheldon Exemplary Equipment and Facilities award, 1992; Great Lakes Lighthouse Keepers Assn. scholar; Marine Ecology scholar Marine Resources, Inc., 1989; Internat. Space Sta. Conf. scholar, 2000; Maine Salt Marsh Ecology Curriculum scholar, 2001; Calif. Coastal Wetlands and Desert Study scholar, 2002. Mem. NSTA (recipient Exemplary Environ. and Facilities award with Sheldon Mfg. Co. 1992), Cleve. Regional Coun. Sci. Tchrs., Cleve. Coun. Ind. Schs., Cleve. Natural Hist. Mus., Cleve. Zool. Park, Ind. Sch. Assn. Ctrl. Sts., Internat. Pen Pal Exchange Progam. Presbyterian. Avocations: orchardist, naturalist, horticulturist. Office: Hathaway Brown Sch 19600 N Park Blvd Cleveland OH 44122-1899 E-mail: jqueen@hb.edu.

QUEEN, SALLY ANN CRANNELL, entrepreneur; b. Dallas, Feb. 25, 1949; d. Kenlen Bates Jr. and Eleanor Crannell; m. Bruce Fielding Queen, Apr. 20, 1968; children: Heather Leigh Queen Dennis, Christopher Dyer Queen. BS in Home Econs., U Ariz., 1983. Mgr. Wicker Rocker, Panama City, Fla., 1973-75, House of Fabrics, Alamogordo, N.Mex., 1984-86, Colonial Williamsburg (Va.) Found., 1987-95; owner Calico Queen, Fla., Ariz., Germany, 1975-83, Sally Queen & Assocs., Arlington, Va., 1995—. Creator: (video) Costuming at Colonial Williamsburg, 1995, (costume calendar) Reflections in Time, 1998. Fund raiser various wive's clubs, 1972—; dist. commr. Girl Scouts U.S., Germany, 1978-80. Named Outstanding new member Panama City C. of C., 1975. Mem. Peninsula Women's Network, Costume Soc. Am. (regional bd. dirs. 1992-96, nat. bd. dirs. 1993—, long range planning coord. 1994-96, regional v.p. 1996—), Kappa Omicron Nu, Phi Upsilon Omicron, Omicron Nu. Republican. Mem. Christian Ch. (Disciples Of Christ). Avocation: clothing and textile industry. Office: 2801 S Joyce St Arlington VA 22202-2248

QUEEN, SANDY (SANDRA JANE QUEEN), psychologist, trainer; b. Washington, Jan. 25, 1946; d. Ralph Edward and Nettie Mae (Peeler) Bort; m. Roy Queen (div. 1973); children: David Brice, Lara Renee, Wendy Joy. BS in Psychology summa cum laude, Towson State U., 1975. Staff social svc. dept. St. Joseph Hosp., Towson, Md., 1973-76, outreach dir., 1980-82; legal rsch. aide, office mgr. Ellin and Assocs., Balt., 1976-77; mkt. mgr. east coast Nat. Med. Cons., Kansas City, Mo., 1977-80; owner, dir. Lifeworks Columbia, Md., 1982—, Lifeline Publs., 1995—. Wellness coord. St. Anthony Sch., Balt., 1975—, Goucher Coll., 1981-87, Nat. Wellness Conf., Stevens Point, Wis., 1982—, Nat. Humor Conf., 1996—; adv. coun. Gov.'s Coun. on Phys. Fitness, Balt. 1990-95, Willow Tree Teen Inst., 1996—; cons. Ministry of Sport and Recreation, Australia, 1991-96, Singpore Kidney Found.; nat. peer leadership trainer, 1995-97; mem. Early Childhood Edn. Conf. Wis., 1994—, trainer substance abuse Ky. Drug and Alcohol Sch.; founder Md. Peer Helper Assocs., 1995, Adolescent Leadership Tng. Inst., 1998. Author: Wellness for Children, 1982, Wellness for Youth, 1992, vol. II, 1993; (curriculi) Well and Wonderful, 1982, Child Abuse Resistance, 1985, Teen Empower, 1997. Chmn. edn. com. Nat. Cancer Soc., Towson, 1981-83, pub. info. com. Am. Heart Assn., Balt., 1982-83; race dir. Am. Heart Assn., Balt., 1982-84; commr. Gov's Coun. on Physical Fitness, Balt., 1984-90; active Md. Wellness Com., Balt., 1991—, Md. St. Peer Helper Assn., 1995—. Recipient Spl. Svc. award, Jaycees of Md., 1982, Am. Heart Assn., 1983. Mem. Md. Peer Helpers Assn. (bd. dirs. 1996—). Democrat. Baptist. Avocation: marathon running (6). Office: Lifeworks PO Box 2668 Columbia MD 21045-1668

QUEEN LATIFAH, (DANA OWENS), recording artist, actress; b. N.J., Mar. 18, 1970; d. Lance and Rita O. Student, Borough of Manhattan C.C. CEO Flavor Unit Entertainment. TV appearances include: Living Single, Fresh Prince of Bel Air, In Living Color, Ellen, Hangin' with Mr. Cooper, Mad TV, The Arsenio Hall Show, Mama Flora's Family, 1998, The Queen Latifah Show, 1999-2001, Spin City, 2001, (miniseries) Living with the Dead, 2002; film appearances include: House Party 2, 1991, Jungle Fever, 1991, Juice, 1992, Who's the Man, 1993, My Life, 1993, Set It Off, 1996, Hoodlum, 1997, The Wizard of Oz, 1998, Living Out Loud, 1998, Sphere, 1998, The Bone Collector, 1999, (voice) Bringing Out the Dead, 1999, The Country Bears, 2002, Brown Sugar, 2002, (voice) Pinocchio, 2002, Chicago, 2002 (Acad. award best sup. actress nom., 2003), Bringing Down the House, 2003, Scary Movie 3, Barbershop 2: Back in Business, 2004; albums include All Hail the Queen, 1990, The Nature of Sista, 1991, X-tra Naked, 1992, Black Reign, 1994, Order In The Court, 1998, She's a Queen: A Collection of Hits, 2002. Named Best New Artist, New Music Seminar, 1990, Best Female Rapper, Rolling Stone Readers' Poll, 1990; recipient Grammy award nomination, 1990, Soul Train Music award, 1995, Sammy Davis Jr. award, 1995, Entertainer of Yr. award, 1995, Grammy award for best rap solo performance, 1995. Office: Flavor Unit Entertainment 155 Morgan St Jersey City NJ 07302-2932*

QUELER, EVE, conductor; b. N.Y.C. Student, Mannes Coll. Music, CCNY. Music staff N.Y.C. Opera, 1958-70; assoc. condr. Ft. Wayne (Ind.) Philharm., 1970-71; founder, music dir. Opera Orch., N.Y., 1968; condr. Lake George Opera Festival, Glen Falls, N.Y., 1971-72, Oberlin (Ohio) Music Festival, 1972, Romantic Festival, Indpls., 1972, Mostly Mozart Festival, Lincoln Center, 1972, New Philharmonia, London, 1974, Teatro Liceu, Barcelona, 1974, 77, San Antonio Symphony, 1975; guest condr. Paris Radio Orch., 1972, P.R. Symphony Orch., 1975, 77, Mich. Chamber Orch., 1975, Phila. Orch., 1976, Montreal Symphony, 1977, Cleve. Orch., 1977 (Recipient Martha Baird Rockefeller Fund for Music award 1968, named Musician of Month Mus. Am. Mag. 1972), N.Y.C. Opera, 1978, Opera Las Palmas, 1978, Opera de Nice, 1979, Nat. Theatre of Prague, 1980, Opera Caracas, Venezuela, 1981, San Diego Opera, 1984, Australian Opera, Sydney, 1985, Kirov Opera, St. Petersburg, Russia, 1993, Hamburg Opera, Germany, 1994, Pretoria, South Africa, 1995, Hamilton, Ont., 1995, Hawaii Philharmonic, 1997, Hong Kong Sinfonietta, 1998, Hong Kong Philharmonic, 1999, Orch. dello Stato de Mexico, 1999-2002, Macau Festival, 2000, Festival Euro Mediterraneo, Italy, 2002; Opei Bonn, 1994-96; recording CBS Masterworks, 1974, 76, Hungaroton Records, 1982-85. Decorated Chevalier de l'ordre des Arts et des Lettres; named Woman in Music, N.Y.C., 2002; recipient Butterfly award, Licia Albanese-Puccini Foundation, 1995. Office: Opera Orch 239 W 72nd St Ste 2R New York NY 10023-2734*

QUELL, MARGARET ANNE, special education educator; b. Akron, Ohio, Oct. 21, 1942; d. John A and Donna Geraldine (Castello) Quell. BS with hons., Kent (Ohio) State U., 1966; student Inst. des Etrangers, University de Besancon, France, 1962—63; MS in Edn., U. Akron, Ohio, 1976; Grad. studies, U. Aix-Marseille, Aix-en-Provence France, 1968—69; EdD U. Akron, 1982. Cert. Supt. Ariz., Prin. Ariz. Asst. prin., truant officer Wooster (Ohio) City Schs., 1976—80; prin., dir. edn. Apple Creek (Ohio) Devel. Ctr., 1980—81; asst. prin., athletic dir. Mt. Vernon (Ohio) City Schools, 1981—86; cons. child study Columbiana Bd. Edn., Lisbon, Ohio, 1986—87; dir. spl. edn., coord. instrn. Kenston Bd. Edn., Chagrin Falls, Ohio, 1987—90; dir. children's programs Lake County Bd. Mental Retardation/Developmental Disabilities, Mentor, Ohio, 1990—98; dir. spl. edn. Chinle (Ariz.) Unified Sch. Dist., Navajo Nation, 1998—. Mem. adv. bd. Knox County Children's Svcs/, Mt. Vernon, Ohio, 1981—86; exec. dir. Kenston Found., Chagrin Falls, Ohio, 1988—90; mem. exec. coun. Ariz. Sch. for Deaf and Blind, Tucson, 1998—. Author: (Book) Sex Equity in Educational Leadership, 1982; editor: (Book (Hershberger) Amish Life Through a Child's Eyes, 1985. Co-chair silent auction Deepwood Industries, Mentor, Ohio, 1998—98; Lifetime Fellow New Directions Shelter, Mt. Vernon, Ohio, 1984; mem. Proposition 203 Com., Chinle, Ariz., 2000—01. Recipient Innovative Counseling award, John G. Odgers Assn., 1978; fellow Kellogg Fellowship, Kellogg Found. Leadership Program, 1984; grantee Crossage Mentoring, Navajo Workforce Devel., 2000. Mem.: Coun. for Exceptional Children, Nat. Assn. Suprs. Spl. Edn. Programs. Avocations: equine dentistry, music, reading, running, travel. Office: Chinle Unified Sch Dist P O Box 587 Chinle AZ 86503 Business E-Mail: mquell@netscape.net.

QUENNEVILLE, KATHLEEN, lawyer; b. Mt. Clemens, Mich., July 31, 1953; d. Marcel J. and Patricia (Armstrong) Q. BA, Mich. State U., 1975; JD, Golden Gate U., 1979. Bar: Calif. 1980. Atty. Wells Fargo Bank, San Francisco, 1980-81; staff counsel Calif. State Banking Dept., San Francisco, 1981-83; assoc. Manatt, Phelps, Rothenburg & Tunney, Los Angeles, 1983-84; v.p., assoc. gen. counsel Bank of Calif., San Francisco, 1984-96; sr. v.p., gen. counsel The Mechanics Bank, Richmond, Calif., 1996—. Asst treas. AIDS Legal Referral Panel of the San Francisco Bay Area, 1986-92. Mem. Calif. State Bar Assn. (bus. law sect. corp. law depts. com. 1988-90), Calif. Bankers Assn. (chair regulatory compliance com. 1994-96, legal affairs com. 1996—). Office: The Mechanics Bank 3170 Hilltop Mall Rd Richmond CA 94806-5231

QUESADA, FRANCINE BARBARA, social services administrator, therapist, educator; b. N.Y.C., Nov. 21, 1942; d. Samuel David and Rose (Feiner) Weiss; m. Joseph R. Quesada, Nov. 25, 1979 (dec. Aug. 1988); children: Sherifa, Samora. BS in Human Svcs., Empire State Coll., N.Y.C., 1991; MS in Rehab. Counseling, U. Scranton, 1994. Cert. rehab. counselor, Pa.; nat. cert. counselor; masters addiction counselor; lic. prof. counselor; master practitioner neuro-linguistic programming. Office mgr. Dr. David Richter, N.Y.C., 1973-91; exec. dir. Vision House, Inc., Scranton, Pa., 1992-96; intensive outpatient counselor, couples therapist A Better Today, Inc., Scranton, 1996; inpatient drug and alcohol counselor, lectr., therapist MARWORTH, Waverly, Pa., 1996—. Adj. prof. Marywood Coll., Scranton, 1994—; part-time pvt. practice. Dist. leader Ind. Dem. Club, N.Y.C., 1987-87; sec. exec. bd. Village East Towers, Inc., N.Y.C., 1986-88; mem. Housing Coalition for Scranton Families, 1995—. Avocations: opera, classical music, theater, cooking gourmet vegetarian meals for friends. Office: MARWORTH Lilylake Rd Waverly PA 18471

QUESADA-EMBID, MARY REGINA CHAMBERLAIN, library media specialist; b. Nov. 25, 1947; BA in English Lit., Cath. U. Am., 1969, MSLS, 1972. Libr. media specialist Charles County Pub. Schs., LaPlata, Md., 1972—, Dr. Thomas L. Higdon Elem. Sch., Newburg, Md., 1972—. Vol. St. Ignatius Cath. Ch., Chapel Point, Port Tobacco, Md., 1996—; mem. Dr. Thomas L. Higdon Elem. Sch. PTA, Newburg, Md., 1988—. Mem. So. Md. Reading Coun., Internat. Reading Assn., El Circulo Cultural Hispánico. Home: PO Box 1 Bel Alton MD 20611-0001

QUEST, KRISTINA KAY, art educator, small business owner; b. Fort Atkinson, Wis., Sept. 22, 1952; d. Duane and Kiwa (Kikuchi) Tessman; m. Michael Charles Quest, July 28, 1973; children: Jennifer, Eric, Sarah. BS in Art Edn., U. Wis., 1992; student, U. Wis., Whitewater, 2002—. Lic. tchr., Wis. Substitute tchr., various cities, 1993-97, 99—; summer sch. tchr. Ft. Atkinson Sch. Dist., 1993-97; art tchr. 7th and 8th grade St. Peter's Luth. Sch., Helenville, Wis., 1997; tchr., kindergarten day care tchr. 1st Class Presch., before/after sch. day care at Prospect Elem., Lake Mills, Wis., 1997—99; owner The Oriental Quest, Oshkosh, Wis., 2000—01, Back Acres Mobile Home Park, Oshkosh, Wis., 2000—; art tchr. Wis. Career Acad., Milwaukee, 2002—03; substitute tchr. Lake Mills (Wis.) Sch. Dist., 2003—. Past mem. Jefferson Arts Coun., bd. dirs., 1976-90; workshop fine arts fair judge Lakeside Luth. H.S., Lake Mills, Wis., 1991-92; art fair judge for Fort Fest, Fort Atkinson, Crafters, 1993; owner mobile home park, substitute tchr. Johnson Creek (Wis.) Sch. Dist., Wis. Career Acad., Milw., 2002-03, 6-10th grade art tchr. Author/illustrator: (book) Tiannamen Square, China's Dark Hours, 1987 (Juried Art Show 1993). Participant art donator AIDS Wellness Auction, The Globe, Oshkosh, 1999. Recipient art award Wis. Regional Arts Program/Waukesha Creative Arts League, Madison, 1993. Mem. Wis. Edn. Assn., Nat. Art Edn. Assn., Women in the Arts Nat. Mus., Japanese Am. Pub. Mus., U. of Wis.-Whitewater Alumni Assn., Student Tchr.'s Assn. Lutheran. Avocations: watercolor, sketching, painting, Japanese sumi brushstroke painting, block printing. Office: 105 Aztalan St Johnson Creek WI 53038-9666 E-mail: mkquest@tds.net.

QUICK, JOAN B. state legislator; b. Rochester, N.Y., Mar. 21, 1946; m. Terry Quick; children: Christopher, Scott, Erin, Brooke, Tom, Tim, Elizabeth. Student, Ashland Coll. Mem. dist. 94 R.I. Ho. of Reps., 1990—, dep. minority leader, 1997—; mem. spl. legis. com.; mem. rules com. and joint com. on accounts and claims; health care adminstr. Mem. Am. Legis. Exchange Coun., Rep. State Ctrl. Com., Nat. Fedn. Rep. Women, R.I. Fedn. Rep. Women. Home: 16 Mullin Hill Rd # G Little Compton RI 02837-1957 Mailing: RI Ho of Reps PO Box 433 Adamsville RI 02801-0433

QUICK, JULIA MAY, music educator, musician; b. Plattsburg, N.Y., May 1, 1942; d. Henry James Ehlers and Retta Elberta Wooden; m. David Marvin Quick, July 23, 1966 (div. July 12, 1974); 1 child, Sarah Louise. BS in Music, U. Minn., Duluth, 1964; MA in Violin Performance, San Francisco State Coll., 1966; MFA in Violin Performance and Pedagogy, U. Iowa, 1971, DMA in Violin Performance and Pedagogy, 1977; tng. as nat. Suzuki violin tchr., various workshops and locations, 1983—91. Tchr. strings, pub. sch. orch. A.P. Giannini, San Francisco, 1965—66, West, Iowa City, 1969—70; asst. prof. music U. Nfld., St. Johns, Canada, 1977—79; assoc. prof. music Western State Coll., Gunnison, Colo., 1979—81, Weber State Coll./So. Utah State, Ogden and Cedar City, Utah, 1981—85, 1985—86; artist-in-residence, Suzuki tchr. Fine Arts Ctr. Kershaw County, Camden, SC, 1986—91; prof. music S.C. State U., Orangeburg, 1991—. Violinist regional symphony orchs. throughout U.S.; violinist Classical Music Seminar, Elsenstadt, Austria, 1978, Aspen (Colo.) Music Festival, 1980—81, Grand Teton (Wyo.) Music Festival, 1984, Chapel Hill Music Festival, 1994—97; rschr. violin music by women and African Am. composers and lesser-known composers, 1991—; scholar, performer Taiwan Women's Coll. Arts and Tech., 2001. Reviewer: books and music, violinist, dir.: recitals, violinist: Lake Superior Chamber Orch., 1998—2001, Mojo and Piccolo Spoleto, 1st Night Charleston, 1987,

1989—91, 2000—03, Biltmore Estate, Asheville, NC, 1994—, So. Conf. African-Am. Studies, Inc., 2003—, solo violinist: CD's Grace Notes, 1998, SCARAB, Spiritual Colors, Airs, Rags, And Blues, 2002, Biltmore Estate Christmas Vol. II, 2003. Recipient Fulbright-Hayes fellowship, S.C. State U., 1992. Mem.: Am. Assn. U. Profs. (acad. mem., performer mem.), Music Educators Nat. Confs. (performer mem.), Suzuki Assn. Am. (performer mem.), Am. String Tchrs. Assn. (reviewer books and music 1977—), Nat. Assn. African-Am. Studies (area chair 2000—, performer mem.), Sigma Alpha Iota (reviewer books and music), Pi Kappa Lambda (pres. Eta Omega chpt. 1998—). Avocations: environmental activities, travel, photography, hiking, yoga. Home: 130 Rutledge St NW Orangeburg SC 29115 Office: SC State U PO Box 7193 300 College St NE Orangeburg SC 29117

QUICK, VALERIE ANNE, sonographer; b. Alta., Can., Feb. 14, 1952; came to U.S., 1953; d. Kenneth Conrad and Kathryn (Maller) Bjorge. Grad. high sch., Salinas, Calif. Registered adult and pediatric echocardiographer, abdomen, small parts and ob-gyn sonographer; registered cardiovasc. technician, registered diagnostic cardiac sonographer. Chief EKG technician Natividad Med. Ctr., Salinas, 1978-81, chief ultrasound dept., 1981-94, chief cardiac echo lab., 1995—. Mem. Am. Inst. Ultrasound in Medicine, Am. Soc. Echocardiography, Nat. Soc. for Cardiopulmonary Technicians, Soc. Pediat. ECHO, Soc. Diagnostic Med. Sonographers, Am. Heart Assn., Am. Registry Diagnostic Med. Sonographers. Avocations: reading, photography, travel. Office: PO Box 6694 Salinas CA 93912-6694 Home: PO Box 6694 Salinas CA 93912-6694

QUIGLEY, DEBORAH HEWITT, adult education educator; d. Merritt Lambert and Gertrude Bush Hewitt; m. Edward James Quigley, III; children: Margaret Sarah, Edward James IV. AA, Coll. Marin, 1972; BA in History with honors, U. Calif., Davis, 1974; multiple subject credential, Dominican Coll., 1975. Tchr. Ladybug Presch., Kentfield, Calif., 1975—77; head tchr. Buttons & Bows Nursery Sch., San Rafael, Calif., 1977—78; parent edn. tchr. Nat. City (Calif.) Adult Sch., 1987—, child devel. tchr., 1996—2002, older adult tchr., 2002—. Mem. parent edn. Western Assn. Sch. and Colls. com. Sweetwater Union H.S. Dist., Chula Vista, Calif., 1997—98. Counselor, asst. leader, scout leader Boy Scouts and Girl Scouts, San Diego, 1986—2002; parent assn. mem., newsletter editor Marian Cath. H.S., San Diego, 1998—2002. Lt. j.g. USN, 1978—81. Named Parent Educator of Yr., San Diego Assn. Parenting Educators, 1995, Marian Cath. H.S., 2000, 2002. Mem.: NEA, Calif. Coun. for Adult Edn., Nat. Assn. for the Edn. Young Children. Avocations: reading, sewing, ice skating. Office: Nat City Adult Edn Ctr 517 Miles of Cars Way National City CA 91950

QUIGLEY, JOAN MARIE, state legislator; b. Jersey City, N.J. d. Edward James and Julia M. Duane; m. John J. Quigley Jr.; children: John J. III, Suzanne Rogacki, Robert Duane. BA, St. Peters Coll., 1977; MPA, Rutgers U., 1979. State assemblywoman dist. 32, N.J., 1994—. Exec. asst. Hudson County Dept. Health, 1974-79; v.p. St. Francis Hosp., 1979-85; v.p. external affairs Franciscan Health System of N.J., 1985—; active United Way, Hudson County Red Cross, Hudson County Boys and Girls Club, N.J. Area Coun. Boys and Girls Club (chair 1992-94). Named Woman of Achievement Jersey Jour., 1965, Outstanding Dir. Jr. Clubs Gen. Fedn. Women Clubs,, 1972; recipient Mary T. Norton Congrl. award United Way Hudson County, 1994. Mem. Rotary. Home: 242 10th St Ste 101 Jersey City NJ 07302

QUIGNEY, THERESA ANN, special education educator; b. East Cleveland, Ohio, June 19, 1952; d. James and Lenora Mary (McDonald) Q.; m. Joseph Carl Lang, July 23, 1983. BA, Notre Dame Coll., 1974; MEd, Cleve. State U., 1980; PhD, Kent State U., 1992. Cert. tchr. handicapped K-12; cert. ednl. adminstrv. specialist edn. of exceptional pupils; cert. ednl. supr.; cert. elem. prin.; cert. h.s. prin. cert. tchr. French K-12, Ohio. Spl. edn. tchr. Newbury (Ohio) Local Schs., 1974—80; county supr., specific learning disabilities and behavior handicaps Geauga County Bd. Edn., Chardon, Ohio, 1980—86, 1987—88; asst. prof. spl. edn. West Chester (Pa.) U., 1992—93; asst. prof. edn. Heidelberg Coll., Tiffin, Ohio, 1993—94; assoc. prof. spl. edn. Cleve. State U., 1994—, coord. spl. edn. program Coll. Edn., 2000—02. Ednl. rschr.; presenter in field. Contbr. articles to profl. jours. Vol. cons. Tchrs. for Action Rsch. South Euclid/Lyndhurst (Ohio) Sch. Dist., 1996—; past participant issues task force Ohio Coun. for Exceptional Children; presenter, participant Oxford Round Table, Oxford U., England; past bd. mem. Camp Sue Osborne, Lake County, Ohio; mem. steering com. State Improvement Grant (Edn.), 2000—. Grantee Ohio State Supt.'s Task Force on Spl. Edn., 1997, Cleve. State U. Coll. Edn., 1997, Am. Sch. Counselor's Assn.; recipient achievement recognition Assn. for Children and Adults with Learning Disabilities, Ohio, 1980. Mem. CEC, ASCD, Am. Ednl. Rsch. Assn., Learning Disabilities Assn., Mid-We. Ednl. Rsch. Assn., Coun. for Learning Disabilities, Kappa Delta Pi, Phi Delta Kappa, Pi Lambda Theta (vol. cons. Gamma Epsilon chpt. 1996—). Avocations: travel, writing, reading, sketching. Office: Cleveland State Univ Euclid Ave at E 24th St Cleveland OH 44115

QUILTER, DEBORAH, writer, consultant, educator; b. San Diego, June 24, 1950; d. Edward Sinon and Mary Ann (Murray) Q. BA, San Francisco State U., 1973; postgrad., MIT, 1994. Cert. personal trainer Am. Coun. on Exercise. Consumer reporter, columnist San Francisco Bay Guardian, 1981-82; legal corr. Andrews Litigation Reporter, Westtown, Pa., 1982-85; travel and entertainment editor Better Health and Living, N.Y.C., 1985-87; columnist UDT News, N.Y.C., 1995, Computer Currents mag., N.Y.C., 1997—; contbg. editor Am. Cheerleader, N.Y.C., 1995-96; sr. editor Dance Spirit mag., N.Y.C., 1997—. Cons. and speaker, N.Y.C., 1994—; instr. Marymount Manhattan Coll., N.Y.C., 1996, fitness instr., personal trainer, 1997. Co-author: Repetitive Strain Injury: A Computer User's Guide, 1994; contbg. writer: Total Health for Women, 1995; author: The Repetitive Strain Injury Recovery Book, 1998. Recipient Honorable Mention award for best non-daily newspaper story San Francisco Press Club, 1983. Mem. Authors Guild. Avocations: ballet, theatre, opera. Home: 140 Riverside Blvd # 1106 New York NY 10069

QUINCE, PEGGY A. state supreme court justice; b. Norfolk, Va., Jan. 3, 1948; m. Fred L. Buckine; children: Peggy LaVerne, Laura LaVerne. BS in Zoology, Howard U., 1970; JD, Cath. U. of Am., 1975. Hearing officer Rental Accomodations Office, Washington; pvt. practice Norfolk, 1977-78, Bradenton, Fla., 1978-80; asst. atty. gen. criminal divsn. Atty. Gen.'s Office, 1980; apptd. 2d Dist. Ct. of Appeals, 1994-98; state supreme ct. justice Fla. Supreme Ct., 1998—. Lectr. in field. Former asst. Sunday sch. tchr., former mem. #3 usher bd. New Hope Missionary Bapt. Ch.; active Jack and Jill of Am., Inc., Urban League, NAACP, Tampa Orgn. for Black Affairs. Recipient award Cath.'s Neighborhood Legal Svcs. Clinic. Mem. Nat. Bar Assn., Fla. Bar, Va. State Bar, George Edgecomb Bar Assn., Fla. Assn. Women Lawyers, Tallahassee Women Lawyers, Alpha Kappa Alpha. Office: 500 S Duval St Tallahassee FL 32399-6556 E-mail: supremecourt@flcourts.org.

QUINDLEN, ANNA, journalist, author; b. Phila., July 8, 1953; d. Robert V. and Prudence Quindlen; m. Gerald Krovatin; children: Quin, Christopher, Maria. BA, Barnard Coll., 1974. Reporter New York Post, N.Y.C., 1974-77; gen. assignment, city hall reporter New York Times, N.Y.C., 1977-81, columnist About New York, 1981-83, dep. met. editor, 1983-85, columnist Life in the 30's syndicated, 1986-89, columnist Public and Private, 1990-94. Author: Living Out Loud, 1988, Object Lessons, 1991, The Tree That Came to Stay, 1992, Thinking Out Loud, 1993, One True Thing, 1994, Happily Ever After, 1997, Black and Blue: A Novel, 1998, A Short Guide to a Happy Life, 2000, Blessings, 2002, Loud and Clear, 2004. Recipient Mike Berger award for Disting. Reporting, 1983, Pulitzer Prize for commentary, 1992; named Woman of Yr., Glamour mag., 1991. Office: c/o ICM 40 W 57th St New York NY 10019-4001

QUINLAN, KATHLEEN, actress; b. Pasadena, Calif., Nov. 19, 1954; Actress: (theatre) Taken in Marriage, 1979 (Theatre World award 1979), Accent on Youth, 1983, Les Liaisons Dangereuses, 1988, (feature films) One is a Lonely Number, 1972, American Graffiti, 1973, Lifeguard, 1976, Airport '77, 1977, I Never Promised You a Rose Garden, 1977, The Promise, 1979, The Runner Stumbles, 1979, Sunday Lovers, 1981, Hanky Panky, 1982, Independence Day, 1982, Twilight Zone: The Movie, 1983, The Last Winter, 1983, Warning Sign, 1985, Wild Thing, 1987, Sunset, 1988, Clara's Heart, 1988, The Doors, 1991, Trial by Jury, 1994, Apollo 13, 1995 (Acad. award nominee for best actress 1996), Zeus and Roxanne, 1997, Event Horizon, 1997, Lawn Dogs, 1997, A Civil Action, 1998, My Giant, 1998; (TV movies) Can Ellen Be Saved?, 1974, Lucas Tanner, 1974, Where Have All the People Gone?, 1974, The Missing Are Deadly, 1975, The Turning Point of Jim Malloy, 1975, The Abduction of Saint Anne, 1975, Little Ladies of the Night, 1977, She's in the Army Now, 1981, When She Says No, 1984, Blackout, 1985, Children of the Night, 1985, Dreams Lost, Dreams Found, 1987, Trapped, 1989, The Operation, 1990, Strays, 1991, An American Story, 1992, Stolen Babies, 1993, Last Light, 1993, Perfect Alibi, 1994, Breakdown, 1996, In the Lake of the Woods, 1996, The Doris Duke Story, 1998. Mem. Actors' Equity Assn., Screen Actors Guild.

QUINLAN, MARY LOU, advertising executive; BA, St. Joseph's U., 1975; MBA, Fordham U., 1982; doctorate (hon.), Alvernia Coll., 1996. Dir. comm. St. Joseph's U., 1975-78; dir. advtg. Avon Products, 1978-89; sr. v.p. Ally & Gargan, 1989-91; exec. v.p., mng. ptnr. DDB Needham N.Y., 1991-94; pres N.W. Ayer & Ptnrs., N.Y.C., 1994-99, CEO, 1995—99; vice chairperson The MacManus Group, N.Y.C., 1999; founder, CEO Just Ask a Woman, N.Y.C., 1999—. Bd. dirs. 1800flowers.com, 2002—; lectr. St. John's U., 2004—. Author: Just Ask a Woman: Cracking the Code of What Woman Want and How They Buy, 2003. Bd. dirs. St. Joseph's U., Phila. Named Advt. Woman of Yr., Advt. Women of N.Y., 1995. Mem.: N.Y. Women in Comm. (Matrix Award for Advt. 1997). Office: Just Ask a Woman 670 Broadway Ste 301 New York NY 10012

QUINN, ALICE FREEMAN, literature educator; BA, Manhattanville Coll., 1970; graduate student in English Lit., NYU, 1971. Editor Alfred A. Knopf Pub. Firm, 1976—87; fiction editor The New Yorker, 1987—2001, poetry editor, 1987—. Adj. prof. poetry Columbia U., 1994—; lectr. in field. Contbr. articles to Artforum, The New Yorker, The Forward, and Poetry Ireland. Jury mem. Kingsley & Tate Tufts Poetry Awards, 1994—. Mem.: Poetry Soc. Am. (exec. dir. 2001—). Office: Sch of Arts Columbia U Mail Code 1808 305 Dodge Hall 2960 Broadway New York NY 10027

QUINN, BARBARA ANN, writer; b. Bronx, N.Y., June 10, 1950; d. Anthony Joseph and Alice Rita (Sacchetti) Ferrara; m. Thomas Gerard Quinn, June 30, 1973; 1 child, Bret Thomas. BA, SUNY, Stony Brook, 1972; JD, Pace U., 1979. Bar: N.Y. 1979, U.S. Dist. Ct. (ea. dist.) N.Y. 1979, U.S. Supreme Ct. 1984. Mgr. contracts Matrix Leasing, San Francisco, 1973-76; asst. West. Co. Atty., White Plains, N.Y., 1979-85, town atty. North Salem, N.Y., 1986-87; writer The Scarsdale (N.Y.) Inquirer, 1992; features editor Strictly Scarsdale (N.Y.)/Garrido Assn., 1993-96; mgr. PROSE bd. and contest judge Sixty-Second Novelist Area America OnLine, 1995-98, coord. Amazing Instant Novelist writing area, 1996-97. Legal adviser Lake Katonah Club, Lewisboro, N.Y., 1982-85. Author: Hardhead, 2000; columnist Travels With Duct Tape, 2000—; contbr. short stories; mng. editor, pub. The Rose & Thorn, 2003—. Bd. mem. Friends of the Scarsdale (N.Y.) Libr., 1993-95. Mem. The Fiction Co. (founder, spokeswoman).

QUINN, BRENDA WHALEN, writer, poet; d. Thomas Leo Whalen and Pearl Zalesny Flynn, Richard Patrick Flynn (Stepfather) and Marie Whalen- (Stepmother); m. Paul Arthur Barnes (div. Mar. 25, 1993); 1 child, Dylan Barnes ; m. Paul Gregory Quinn, July 24, 1982 (div. Feb. 1985). BA, U. Wis., Milw., 1995, MA, 1999. Edn. and outreach coord. Endometriosis Assn., 2000—02; devel. resources dir. Blood Ctr. of S.E. Wis., Milw., 2002—. Author: (book) Caring for Milwaukee: The Daughters of Charity at St. Mary's, 1998 (Leslie Cross Non-fiction Book award Coun. for Wis. Writers, 1999, Gurda History award, 1999), poems. Recipient First Pl. Country Lyric Competition, Music City Song Festival, 1986. Roman Catholic.

QUINN, ELIZABETH MARIE, performing arts educator; b. Waukegan, Ill., Nov. 9, 1962; d. John Joseph Quinn Jr. and Marilyn Francis Quinn. MFA in Child Drama, Ariz. State U., 1987; BA in Comm. and Theatre, St. Mary's Coll., 1984; MA in Ednl. Adminstrn., Northeastern Ill. U., 1999. Cert. Drama Tchr. Ill. State Bd. of Edn., 1987, Ednl. Adminstrn. Ill. State Bd. of Edn., 1999. Drama tchr., arts dept. chair Haven Mid. Sch., Evanston, Ill., 1987—; vis. prof. Northwestern U., Evanston, 2003—; assoc. dir. summer theatre lab U. Chgo. Lab. Schs., 1987—2002. Youth group moderator St. Nicholas Ch., Evanston, 2000—03; v.p., sec. Chgo. Children's Theatre, Evanston, 1990—95. Fellow: Ill. Theatre Assn. (v.p. 1993—95); mem.: Am. Alliance for Theatre and Edn. (2d v.p. 2002—, Creative Drama award 1997). Office: Haven Middle School 2417 Prairie Ave Evanston IL 60202 E-mail: irishbq@yahoo.com.

QUINN, ELYSIA D. finance company executive; d. John P. and Regina A. Slivak; m. J. D. Quinn, Aug. 16, 2003; m. Raymond E. Torrance, Oct. 18, 1996 (dec. June 6, 2000); children: Sean, Daniel. Adminstr. Vanguard Group, Valley Forge, Pa., 1993—. Vol. Red Cross, Valley Forge, 1994—2003. Republican. Roman Catholic. Avocations: reading, home decor, gardening, child psychology. Home: PO Box 731 Morgantown PA 19543

QUINN, HELEN RHODA, physicist; b. Melbourne, Victoria, Australia, May 19, 1943; came to U.S. 1961; d. Ted Adamson and Helen Ruth (Down) Arnold; m. Daniel James Quinn, Oct. 8, 1966; children: Elizabeth Helen, James Arnold. BS, Stanford U., 1963, MS, 1964, PhD in Physics, 1967. Vis. scientist Duetsches Elektronen Synchrotron, Hamburg, Germany, 1968-70; postdoctoral researcher Harvard U., Cambridge, Mass., 1971-72, assoc. prof., 1972-76, 1976-77; rsch. scientist Stanford Linear Accelerator Ctr., Palo Alto, Calif., 1978—, edn. officer, 1988-93, asst. to dir. for edn. and pub. outreach, 1993—. Contbr. articles to profl. jours. Pres. Contemporary Physics Edn. Project, Portola Valley, Calif., 1989—; vol., chair Town of Portola Valley Trails Com., 1988—. Alfred Sloan Found. fellow, 1975-79. Fellow Am. Phys. Soc. Avocations: hiking, native plants. Office: Stanford Linear Accelerator PO Box 4349 Palo Alto CA 94309-0450*

QUINN, HOLLI JO BARDO, social worker, educator; b. Muncy, Pa., Jan. 7, 1961; d. Emerson David and Beverly Bair Bardo; m. Joel Paul Quinn, Oct. 15, 1983; children: Tara Jo, Austin Paul. BA in Comm., Shippensburg U., 1982; MS in Bible, Phila. Bibl. U., 1997; MA in Religion, Temple U., 1999, postgrad. in Feminist Studies, 2000—01. Mktg. asst. Lower Bucks Cablevision, Levittown, Pa., 1984—87; English composition instr. Temple U., Phila., 1998, Bible instr., 1999; case worker Bucks County Head Start, Bensalem, Pa., 2001—04; prof. humanities Strayer U., Trevose, Pa., 2003—. Impact study rep. Bucks County Head Start, Morrisville, Pa., 2002—04. Author: Sacrifical Offerings, 1989, Fishing, 1995. Vol. A Woman's Place, Doylestown, Pa., 2002; spkr. Women's Ink, Phila., 1989; campaign chair United Way Bucks County Head Start, Bensalem, Pa., 2002, mem. family partnership planning Morrisville, Pa., 2003; active Safety Corn., Bensalem, 2003—04; founding mem. Nat. Campaign for Tolerance, Montgomery, Ala., 2004. Recipient Discovery award in fiction, Bucks County C.C., 1989, Senatorial citation, Pa. Senate, 1992. Republican. Avocations: gardening, landscaping, writing, reading, swimming. Home: 2224 Bent Rd Langhorne PA 19053 Office: Strayer Univ Lower Bucks County Campus 3600 Horizon Blvd Ste 100 Trevose PA 19053 Office Phone: 215-953-5999.

QUINN, JANE BRYANT, journalist, writer; b. Niagara Falls, N.Y., Feb. 5, 1939; d. Frank Leonard and Ada (Laurie) Bryant; m. David Conrad Quinn, June 10, 1967; children— Matthew Alexander, Justin Bryant. BA magna cum laude, Middlebury Coll., 1960. Assoc. editor Insiders Newsletter, N.Y.C., 1962-65, co-editor, 1966-67; sr. editor Cowles Book Co., N.Y.C., 1968; editor-in-chief Bus. Week Letter, N.Y.C., 1969-73, gen. mgr., 1973-74; syndicated financial columnist Washington Post Writers Group, 1974—2001; contbr. fin. column to Women's Day mag., 1974-95; contbr. fin. column Good Housekeeping, 1995—; contbr. NBC News and Info. Service, 1976-77; bus. corr. WCBS-TV, N.Y.C., 1979, CBS-TV News, 1980-87, ABC-TV Home Show, 1991-93; contbg. editor Newsweek mag., 1978—. Host PBS personal fin. series Take Charge!, 1988; dir. bd. dirs. Bloomberg LP. Author: Everyone's Money Book, 1979, 2d edit., 1980, Making the Most of Your Money, 1991, 2d edit., 1997, A Hole in the Market, 1994; contbr. Quicken Financial Planner, 1995. Mem. bd. advisors Jerome Levy Econs. Inst. Bard Coll. Recipient Emmy award for outstanding coverage fin. on TV, Gerald Loeb award for lifetime achievement and disting. bus. and fin. journalism. Mem. Phi Beta Kappa. Office: Newsweek Inc 251 W 57th St New York NY 10019-1802

QUINN, MAUREEN E. ambassador; b. Spring Lake, N.J. Vice consul, gen. svcs. officer U.S. Consulate Gen., Karachi, Pakistan, 1982—84; econ. officer, comml. attaché Am. Embassy Conakry, Guinea, 1984—86; with Western Hemisphere's Bur. Regional Econ. Affairs, 1986—88, Econ. Bur. Office Internat. Devel. Fin., 1988—90; Pearson fellow U.S. Ho. Reps., Washington, 1990—91; econ. counselor Am. Embassy Dept. of State, Panama, 1991—94, exec. asst., spl. asst. to undersec. for econ., bus. and agrl. affairs, 1994—97, dep. exec. sec., 1997—98, dep. chief of mission Am. Embassy, 1998—2001, U.S. amb. to Qatar, 2001—. Office: DOS Amb 6130 Doha Pl Washington DC 20521

QUINN, PATRICIA K. literary agent; b. Chico, Calif. d. Donald Joseph and Kathleen (Alexander) Q. BA, Bennington Coll., 1971; MFA in Drama, Yale U., 1976. Producer, devel. exec. various Off-Broadway and regional theatres, 1976-84, devel. cons. Sundance Film Inst., Utah, 1983—85; theatrical agt. I.C.M., L.A., 1985-90; v.p. comedy devel. Warner Bros. TV, Burbank, Calif., 1990-92; lit. and packaging agt. Met. Talent Agy., L.A., 1995—2000. Instr. UCLA Ext., 1995—; spkr., lectr. Nat. Assn. of TV Programming Execs., Fla. Bar, NATAS, Media Xchange (Internat.); mem. TV com. Brit. Acad. Film and TV Arts, 2002—; prof. reps. peer group com. NATAS, 2002-. Founding mem. N.Y. Theatre Workshop, N.Y.C., 1980—86. Mem.: Women in Film (v.p. bd. dirs. 1995—2001). Office: Paradigm Talent and Lit Agy 10100 Santa Monica Blvd Los Angeles CA 90067

QUINN, YVONNE SUSAN, lawyer; b. Spring Valley, Ill., May 13, 1951; d. Robert Leslie and Shirley Eilene (Morse) Quinn. BA, U. Ill., 1973; JD, U. Mich., 1976, MA in Econs., 1977. Bar: N.Y. 1978, U.S. Dist. Ct. (ea. and so. dists.) N.Y. 1978, U.S. Ct. Appeals (3d, 5th, 9th, 10th and D.C. cirs.) 1982, U.S. Ct. Appeals (2d cir.) 1992, U.S. Ct. Appeals (4th cir.) 1994, U.S. Supreme Ct. 1982. Assoc. Cravath, Swaine & Moore, N.Y.C., 1977-80, Sullivan & Cromwell, N.Y.C., 1980-84, ptnr., 1984—. Mem. ABA, Assn. of Bar of City of N.Y., India House Club. Office: Sullivan & Cromwell 125 Broad St New York NY 10004-2489 Office Phone: 212-558-3736. Business E-Mail: quinny@sullcrom.com.

QUIÑONES KEBER, ELOISE, art historian, educator; b. LA; d. Rudy Jr. and Margaret (Romero) Q. BA, Immaculate Heart Coll., 1966; MA, UCLA, 1967, Columbia U., 1979, PhD, 1984. Lectr. Columbia U., N.Y.C., 1984-86; prof. art history Baruch Coll., The Grad. Ctr., CUNY, 1986—. Author: Codex Telleriano Remensis: Ritual, Divination, and History in a Pictorial Aztec Manuscript, 1995 (Getty Grant Program Publ. Subvention award, 1992); co-author: Art of Aztec Mexico: Treasures of Tenochtitlan, 1983; editor: Chipping Away on Earth: Studies in Prehispanic and Colonial Mexico in Honor of Arthur J.O. Anderson and Charles E. Dibble, 1995, In Chalchihuitl in Quetzalli: Mesoamerican Studies in Honor of Doris Heyden, 2000, Representing Aztec Ritual: Performance, Text, and Image in the Work of Sahaqún, 2002; co-editor: The Work of Bernardino de Sahagun: Pioneed Ethnographer of 16th-Century Aztec Mexico, 1988, Mixteca-Puebla: Discoveries and Research in Mesoamerican Archaeology and Art, 1994; contbr. articles to profl. jours. Mellon postdoctoral fellow Columbia U., 1984-86, fellow Ford Found./NRC, 1986-87, Am. Coun. of Learned Socs. fellow, 1987-88, 93-94, grantee, 1985, 95, NEH fellow, 1993-94, grantee, 1986, 91; grantee Am. Philos. Soc., 1986; fellow Guggenheim Found., 1998; recipient Ralph Waldo Emerson award Phi Beta Kappa Soc., 1996. Mem. Coll. Art Assn., Assn. Latin Am. Art, Am. Soc. for Ethnohistory. Office: CUNY Grad Ctr Art History Program 365 Fifth Ave New York NY 10016 also: CUNY Baruch Coll Dept Fine and Performing Arts 1 Bernard Baruch Way New York NY 10010-1703 E-mail: Eloise_Quinones-Keber@baruch.cuny.edu., equinones@mindspring.com.

QUINTANA, ANA M. media specialist; b. Chicago, Ill., Oct. 16, 1967; d. Sergio Antonio (Tony) Quintana and Ana Ilia Gonzalez. BA in Comm. cum laude, Loyola U. Chgo., 1989. Cert. Media Rels. Cmty. Media Workshop, 2001, U. of S.C., 2001. Claims rep. Social Security Adminstrn., Chgo., 1993—99, mgmt. support specialist, 2000—01, pub. affairs specialist, 2001—02, acting asst. dist. mgr., 2003, exec. staff asst., 2003—. President-Hispanic task force Gift of Hope Organ and Tissue Donation Network, Elmhurst, Ill., 2002—03. Mem.: Nat. Assn. Hispanic Journalists (mem. Chgo. region Hispanic action com. 1995—, Ill. vice chair 2003). D-Liberal. Avocations: photography, reading, drawing, art shows.

QUIRK, KATHLEEN L. mining executive; BS in Acctg., La. State U. With Mobil Oil Corp., Dallas; from mem. staff to treas. Freeport-McMoRan Copper & Gold Inc., New Orleans, 1989—2000, treas., 2000—, sr. v.p., 2003—, CFO, 2003—. Office: Freeport McMoRan Copper & Gold Inc 1615 PoydrasSt New Orleans LA 70112

QUIROGA, NINOSKA, university official; b. La Paz, Bolivia, Nov. 29, 1968; came to U.S., 1995; d. Marcelo Quiroga and Sara Loza. B Econs., Cath. U. La Paz, 1991; MBA, S.W. Mo. State U., 1997. Jr. rschr. in projects, cons. Coop. Urban dnr Rural Women, La Paz, 1988-90; tchg. asst. Cath. U. La Paz, 1990-92; freelance writer Hoy, newspaper, La Paz, 1992; hostess, co-prodr. Net Bolivian Network, Red Uno de Bolivia, La Paz, 1992-95; news reporter Sta. KMSU, nat. pub. radio, Springfield, Mo., 1995-96; with distbn. ctr. The News Leader, Springfield, 1996—; grad. asst. to dean Sch. Bus., S.W. Mo. State U., Springfield, 1995—. Tchr. Am.-Bolivian Ctr., La Paz, 1991. Recipient award for exceptional help and effort shown throughout yr. Am.-Bolivian Ctr., 1991; named Miss Bolivia, 1993, Miss La Paz, 1993, Best Friend in Miss Bolivia, 1993, Miss Intelligence and Personality of World and Miss Friendship of Am. in Miss World of Ams. and Caribbean, 1994. Mem. UN of USA, Hispanic Assn. Leaders, Delta Sigma Pi. Avocations: making friends, reading. Office: SW Mo State U Coll Bus Glass Hall 400 901 S National Ave Springfield MO 65804-0027 Home: #1st Floor 7396 Kingsbury Blvd Saint Louis MO 63130-4145

QUISENBERRY, NANCY LOU, university administrator, educator; b. Washington, Ind., Jan. 29, 1938; d. Joseph Franklin and Maud Helen (Fitch) Forbes; m. James D. Quisenberry, Feb. 6, 1960; 1 child, James Paul. BS in Home Econs., Ind. State Tchrs. Coll., 1960, MS in Home Econs., 1962; EdD, Ind. U., 1971. Cert. tchr. Ind. Home economics tchr. Honey Creek High Sch., Terre Haute, Ind., 1961-62; third grade tchr. Indpls. Pub. Sch.,

1962-64; sustitute tchr. Dep. of Def., Baumholder, Fed. Republic Germany, 1964-65; first grade tchr. Wayne Twp. Schs., Indpls., 1966-67; assoc. faculty lang. arts Ind. U.-Purdue U., Indpls., spring 1970; prof. curriculum and instruction So. Ill. U., Carbondale, 1971—98, assoc. dean Coll. of Edn., 1976-96, interim dean, 1996-98. Cons. U. N.C., Durham, 1977, Ministry Edn., Bangkok, 1980, Bangkok, 84, DePaul U., 1990, Ill. State U., 2002, U. Miss., 2001, Loyola U., 2002, Gov's State U., 2000; dir. tech. and trg. assistance grant Head Stard-OCD, Carbondale, 1972—74, Cameroon project USAID, Carbondale, 1984—86; mem. Ill. State Tchr. Cert. Bd., 1981—84, 1984—87. Co-author: Early Childhood Education Programs: Developmental Objectives and Their Use, 1975, Play as Development, 1978, Educators Healing Racism, 1999, Racism in the Classroom: Case Studies, 2002. Bd. dirs. Jackson County YMCA, 1988; chair candidacy com. Ctrl. So. Ill. Synod Evang. Luth. Ch. Am., Springfield, 1987—90, sec. multisynodical com. Chgo., 1987—90, synod coun., 1992—95; pres. Epiphany Luth. Ch. Coun., Carbondale, 1984—85, 1989—92, 1994—96. Recipient Dare To Be Great award, Ill. Women Adminstrs. and So. Ill. Region, 1989, Woman of Distinction award, So. Ill. U., 1992; grantee, Bur. Educationally Handicapped, 1979—82, 1990—95. Mem.: World Orgn. for Pre-sch. Edn. (U.S. nat. com., treas. 1997—99, chmn. strategic planning commn. 1999—2002, webmaster 2000—), Assn. Tchr. Educators (chair com. racism from a healing perspective 1995—98), Ill. Assn. Colls. for Tchr. Edn. (pres. 1984—86), Am. Assn. Colls. for Tchr. Edn. (chair adv. coun. state reps. 1987—88, bd. dirs. 1986—88, 1991—94), Nat. Coun. for Accreditation Tchr. Edn. (bd. examiners 1987—98, new profl. tchr. project elem. edn. stds. drafting com. 1996—98, transition team elem. stds. 1998—2000, chair Rubics devel. com. 2001, chair elect Coun. Profl. Preparation of Educators 2002—03, exec. bd. 2002—03), Assn. Childhood Edn. Internat. (chair tchr. edn. com. 1989—93, folio rev. coord. elem. edn. 1989—2001, sec.-treas. 1996—, pres.-elect 1998—2000, pres. 2001—03), Internat. Coun. on Edn. for Tchg. (bd. dirs., N.Am. v.p. 1992—94, pres.-elect 1997—2000, pres. 2000—02). Avocations: gardening, flute, sewing, walking, organ. Home: 1713 E Mumford Dr Urbana IL 61802-8605 Office: So Ill U Coll Edn Carbondale IL 62901-4624 E-mail: nancyq@siu.edu.

QUIST, JEANETTE FITZGERALD, television production educator, choreographer; b. Provo, Utah, July 4, 1948; d. Sherman Kirkham and Bula Janet (Anderson) Fitzgerald; m. G. Steven Quist; children: Ryan, Amy, Michelle, Jeremy. Student, U. Redlands, Calif., 1970; BA, Brigham Young U., 1971; postgrad., Calif. State U., Riverside, 1972, Calif. State U., San Bernardino, 1973. Host, co-producer children's show PBS Sta. KBYU-TV, Provo, 1968-69; buyer ready to wear J.C. Penney & Co., Redlands, 1969-71; tchr. spl. reading program Fontana (Calif.) Elem. Sch. Dist., 1971-73; owner, choreographer Jeanette Quist Creative Dance, Tri Cities, Wash., 1975-79; owner, tchr. Dance Studio, Gridley, Calif., 1979-81; producer, instr. Butte Coll., Oroville, Calif., 1986—. Asst. producer Kate Knight Prodn. Co., Chico, Calif., 1987; video producer Gridley Sch. Dist., 1987-88; cmty. svcs. cons. Biggs-Gridley Meml. Hosp., 1999—; presenter in field. Prodr., editor promotional video Police Acad., 1986, commls. for Butte Coll., 1987—; prodr., dir. telecourse Interior Designer, 1988—; prodr., hostess TV talk shows Crossroads, 1988—, NVCA Today, BCTV Forum, 1991—; prodr. (video) Butte Coll., 1989-90, Intro to Telecommunications, 1994-98, Butte Environ. Coun., 1995, Early Alert for Butte Coll., 1995, City of Chico, 1995, Sports Events for Butte Coll., 1995—, Small Bus. Devel. Ctr., 1996, Work Tng. Ctr., 1996, Project Maestros, 1996, video for bilingual tchrs. recruitment Butte Coll. 1997, American Dream: Unity in Diversity, Butte Coll., 1997, Sentencing Video for the Fed. Defs. Office, Ea. Dist. of Calif., 1998, Butte Coll. Child Devel. Program, 1999, Multimedia Program, 2001, Radio TV Film Program, 2002, Environ. Hort. Program, 2002, EMT/Paramedics Program, 2002, Butte Coll. Tech. Prep. program, 2003; choreographer Kaleidoscope, 1988, South Pacific, 1989, Fantasticks, 1990, Amahl and the Night Visitors, 1990, An Evening of Song and Dance, Butte Coll., 1991, Kiss Me Kate, Butte Coll., 1992, Hello Dolly, Chico Stake, 1992, Tumbleweeds, Butte Theatre, 1994, Joseph and the Amazing Technicolor Dreamcoat, Gridley HS, 1999. State judge Miss. Am. Contest, Provo, 1968; 1st v.p. Friends of Libr., Gridley, 1988; chmn. Regional Fine Arts Festival Tri Cities, 1978; v.p. Gridley High Sch. Parent Club, 1990; chmn. 3D Expo Fine Arts Festival for Oroville, Gridley, and Butte Coll., 1991; cmty. svcs. cons. Biggs-Gridley Meml. Hosp., 1999—, organizer 50th anniversary celebration, 2000. Recipient Acad. Excellence award Butte Coll., 1993-94, What Would We Do Without You award, Butte Coll., 1998; Mask club scholar Brigham Young U., 1967; Project Maestro grantee, 1994, Svc. Learning grantee Butte Coll., 2002. Mem. AAUW (membership v.p. 1989-91, pres. 1997-99, com. for gender equity for Gridley br., Tech Trek chmn. Gridley br. 2001—), Butte County Arts Coun. (spl. com. 1986), Kaleidoscope Arts Coun., Am. Assn. Women in Cmty. Jr. Colls. Republican, Ch. of Jesus Christ Latter-day Saints. Avocations: family, theatre, music, camping, reading.

QUIVERS, ROBIN, radio personality; b. 1953; d. Charles and Louise Quivers. Student, U. Md., 1974. Morning anchor W100, Carlisle, Pa., 1980; joined WWDC, Wash., DC, 1981; radio personality WNBC, N.Y.C., 1982—85, WXRK-FM, N.Y.C., 1985—. Co-author: Quivers: A Life, 1995; actor: (TV films) Deadly Web, 1996; (films) Private Parts, 1997; guest appearance : (TV series) The Fresh Prince of Bel-Air; The Larry Sanders Show. With USAF. Address: WXRK-RADIO 40 W 57th St Fl 14 New York NY 10019-4001

QUNELL, KERRI WYNN, marketing professional; b. Bastrop, Tex., Mar. 16, 1971; d. James Richard Wynn and Lu Ella Johnson; m. Jason Christopher Qunell, Sept. 25, 1999. BA, Tex. State U., 1993. Econ. devel. assoc. Greater Austin (Tex.) C. of C., 1994—97; account exec. Sicola Martin Advt., Austin, 1997—98; mktg. comm. mgr. Dell Computer Corp., Round Rock, Tex., 1998—2001; corp. devel. dir. KEYE - TV, CBS, Austin, 2001—02, cmty. rels. dir., 2002—. Mktg. task force ARC Ctrl. Tex., Austin, 2002—; adv. coun. mem. Girl Scouts Lone Star Coun., Austin, 2002—. Bd. mem. Greater Austin Hispanic C. of C., 2002—03. Recipient Vol. of Distinction award, The Dell Found., 2001, Profiles in Power finalist, Austin Bus. Jour. & FOX TV, 2002. Mem.: Women in Comm. Inc., Am. Women in Radio and TV, Am. Mktg. Assn. (bd. mem. 2001—03), Young Women's Alliance Austin (life; pres. 2001—01), Austin Ballet BARRE. Methodist. Avocations: photography, camping, travel, music, interior decorating. Office: KEYE-TV 10700 Metric Blvd Austin TX 78758

QUTUB, EILEEN, state legislator, real estate appraiser; b. York, Nebr., Mar. 2, 1948; m. Abe Qutub. BS in Mgmt. Human Resources, George Fox Coll. Mem. Oreg. Legislature, Salem, 1996—, mem. jud. com., mem. pub. affairs ocm., dep. co-chair ways and means com., mem. subcom. on transp. and econ. devel. com., asst. majority leader. Precinct Com., alt. del. Oreg. Rep. Orgn.; facilitator engring. dept.-real estate divsn. City of Charlotte, N.C. Republican. Home: 11135 Sw Patridge Loop Beaverton OR 97007 Office: S 210 State Capitol Salem OR 97310 E-mail: qutub.sen@state.or.us.

RAABERG, GLORIA GWEN, literature educator; b. Atlanta, Dec. 31, 1932; d. Lawrence Leslie and Gwendolyn Neff (Ewing) Hill; m. Charles B. Raaberg, Jan. 29, 1955 (div. 1983); children: Charlyn L., Ross W., Valerie R. BA, Col. William & Mary, 1954; MA, Calif. State U., 1971; PhD, U. Calif., Irvine, 1978. Instr. lit. UCLA, 1977-78; Mellon fellow lit. Case Western Res. U., Cleve., 1978-79; asst. prof. U. Tex., Dallas, 1979-85, 87-89; vis. prof. U. Calif., Irvine, 1985-86; Fulbright sr. prof. U. Debrecen, Hungary, 1986-87; prof. English, dir. women's studies Western Mich. U., Kalamazoo, 1989—. Fellow Ctr. Humanities U. Calif., 1985-86, U. Va., Charlottesville, 1996; mem. exec. bd. Ctr. Ethics in Soc., Kalamazoo, Mich., 1991—. Author: Toward a Theory of Literary Collage, 1978; co-editor: Surrealism and Women, 1991; contbr. articles to profl. jours. Mem. Women Civic Leaders Network, Kalamazoo, 1989-92. Lilly Found. grantee, 1991-93, NEH grantee, 1983-85. Mem. MLA, Nat. Women's Studies Assn., Am. Studies Assn. Avocations: hiking, art, archaeology. Office: Western Mich U Kalamazoo MI 49008

RAAD, VIRGINIA, pianist, lecturer; b. Salem, W.Va., Aug. 13, 1925; d. Joseph M. and Martha (Joseph) R. BA in Art History, Wellesley Coll., 1947; spl. student, New Eng. Conservatory Music, 1947-48; diplôme, Ecole Normale de Musique, Paris, 1950; Doctorate with honors (French Govt. grantee 1950-52, 54-55), U. Paris, 1955; student, Alfred Cortot, Jeanne Blancard, Berthe Bert, Jacques Chailley. Artist in residence Salem (W.Va.) Coll., 1957-70; ind. concert pianist, 1960—; musician in residence N.C. Arts Council, at community colls., 1971-72. Adjudicator Nat. Guild Piano Tchrs., Nat. Fedn. Music Clubs; panelist, grant reviewer NEH, 1978-84, 92—; mem. com. Nat. Endowment Arts, 1978; Am. rep. Debussy Centennial Colloque, Paris, 1962. Perfomances, concerts, lectrs. master classes at West Ga. Coll., Carrollton, La Grange (Ga.) Coll., Columbus (Ga.) Coll., Young Harris (Ga.) Coll., U. Fla., Gainesville, Norton Gallery, Palm Beach, Fla., Alliance Française de Rollins Coll., Winter Park, Fla., Dixon Gallery and Gardens, Memphis, St. Jude Children's Rsch. Hosp., Memphis, Cleveland (Tenn.) State C.C., Sampson Tech. Inst., Clinton, N.C., Wayne C.C., Goldsboro, N.C., Brevard (N.C.) Coll., Ctrl. (S.C.) Wesleyan Coll., Ky. Wesleyan Coll., Owensboro, Berea (Ky.), Coll., Alice Lloyd Coll., Pippa Passes, Ky., Coll. of William and Mary, Williamsburg, Va., Eastern Mennonite Coll., Harrisonburg, Va., The Phillips Gallery, Washington, Trinity Coll., Washington, Manhattanville Coll., Purchase, N.Y., Elmira (N.Y.) Coll., Fordham U., N.Y.C., The Piano Tchrs. Congress of N.Y., Middlebury (Vt.) Coll., St. Anselm's Coll., Manchester, N.H., Mount St. Mary's Coll., Hooksett, N.H., Wellesley (Mass.) Coll., Curry Coll., Milton, Mass., So. Conn. State U., New Haven, Slippery Rock (Pa.) U., Seton Hill Coll., Greensboro, Pa., Alliance Française de Pitts. and U. Pitts., Channel 13 WQED (PBS) Pitts., Lincoln U., Oxford, Pa., The Grier Sch., Tyrone, Pa., Mount de Chantal Acad., Wheeling W.Va., Wheeling Jesuit U., among other colls. and univs.; contbg. author: Debussy et l'Evolution de la Musique au XX Siècle, 1965; author: The Piano Sonority of Claude Debussy, 1994; recording artist: EDUCO, 1995—; contbr. articles to profl. jours. Active Amnesty Internat. Urgent Action Network; alumna regional representative Wellesley Coll. Named Outstanding W.Va. Woman Educator Delta Kappa Gamma, 1965; presented biography to Schlesinger Library on History of Women in Am. Radcliffe Coll., 1967; grantee Govt. France, Am. Coun. Learned Socs. Mem. Soc. Française de Musicologie, Am. Musicol. Soc. (regional officer 1960-65), Am. Coll. Musicians, Internat. Musicol. Soc., Music Tchrs. Nat. Assn. (adjudicator, musicology program chair 1983-87), W.Va. Music Tchrs. Assn., Coll. Music Soc., Audubon Activist, Alpha Delta Kappa (hon.). Republican. Roman Catholic. Avocations: hiking, gardening, birding. Address: 60 Terrace Ave Salem WV 26426-1116 E-mail: virginiaraad@aol.com.

RAASH, KATHLEEN FORECKI, artist; b. Milw., Sept. 12, 1950; d. Harry and Marion Matilda (Schwabe) Forecki; m. Gary John Raash, June 13, 1987. BS, U. Wis., Eau Claire, 1972; MFA, U. Wis., Milw., 1978. One-woman and group shows include Sight 225 Gallery, Milw., 1979, 81, Nicolet Coll., Rhinelander, Wis., 1981, Messing Gallery, St. Louis, 1982, Arts Consortium, Cin., 1982, Ctr. Gallery, Madison, Wis., 1982, Otteson Theatre Gallery, Waukesha, Wis., 1982, Foster Gallery, Eau Claire, 1984, Duluth (Minn.) Art Inst., 1984, West Bend (Wis.) Gallery of Fine Arts, 1987, U. Wis., Waukesha Fine Arts Gallery, 1988, Mount Mary Coll., Milw., 1990, Cardinel Stritch Coll., Milw., 1991, West Bend Art Mus., 1995, 2003, Gwenda Jay Gallery, Chgo., 1995, Wis. Acad., Madison, 1996, Nicolet Coll., Rhinelander, Wis., 1997, Wausau (Wis.) Ctr. for Arts, 1998, Riveredge Galleries, Mishicot, Wis., 2000, Union Theater Gallery, Madison, 2000, Gallery 110, Plymouth, Wis., 2001, Bloomington (Minn.) Art Ctr., 2001, Mt. Seanrio Coll., Ladysmith, Wis., 2001, Regional Art Ctr., Eau Claire, 2002, Ctrl. Wis. Cultural Ctr., Wis. Rapids, 2003; exhibited in group shows at River Edge Galleries, Wis., 1990-91, 94-95, 2000, Peltz Gallery, Milw., 1990-94, 96-98, 2000-03, Minnetonka Ctr. Arts, Wayzata, Minn., 1996, Paine Art Ctr., Oshkosh, Wis., 1998, 2002, Woodward Gallery, N.Y.C., 2000-01; represented in permanent collections United Bank and Trust of Madison, Fine Arts Gallery U. Wis., Miller Brewing Co., Independence Bank Waukesha, Fed. Res. Bank, Mpls., Rhinelander Med. Ctr., Univ. Hosp., Madison, Wis. Recipient Purchase award, Madison Art Ctr., 1978, Hon. Mention, Paine Art Ctr., 2002, Percent for Art Direct Purchase award, Wis. Arts Bd., 2001.

RABACA, JOSEFINA RAGSAG, writer; b. Pinili, Philippines, June 17, 1939; d. Benigno Pagdilao Ragsag and Segundina Rapanut Reg; m. Eddie Rabo Rabaca, Mar. 20, 1966 (dec. Oct. 1976); 2 children. BS in Pharmacy, Centro Escolar U., 1964. Registered pharmacist Philippines, 1966. Editor Cader Pub., Sterling Heights, Mich., 2002—03. Author: The Universe: The Hidden Secret of God for the Year 2000, 2002. Vol. Cath. Women's League, 1974—76; election watcher Manila, 1982. Avocations: cooking, sewing, interior decorating, movies. Address: PO Box 6233 Woodland Hills CA 91365-6233

RABADEAU, MARY FRANCES, protective services official; b. Elizabeth, N.J., July 13, 1948; d. Russell John and Frances (Hanley) R. Student, Union Coll., 1967-69; MEd, Kean Coll., 1976. Officer City of Elizabeth Police Dept., N.J., 1978-82, detective, 1982-83, sgt., 1983-87, lt., 1987-91, capt., 1991-92, dir., 1993-95, dep. chief, 1994; chief N.J. Transit Police Dept., Maplewood, 1995—. Instr. Union County Police Acad. Trustee Blessed Sacrament Ch., Elizabeth, N.J., 1989-99; bd. acad. advisors N.J. state police grad. studies program Seton Hall U.; bd. trustees Benedictine Acad., Elizabeth, N.J. Named one of Outstanding Young Women in Am., 1983, Woman Leader N.J. Assn. Women Bus. Owners, 1997; recipient John H. Stamler Police Acad. Svc. award, 1992, Cert. of Recognition award YWCA, 1992, Disting. Grad. award Nat. Cath. Ednl. Assn., 1995; honoree Union County Commn. on the Status of Women, 1993, Hispanic Law Enforcement Assn. of Union County, 1995, Women Helping Women Recognition award Soroptimist Internat. Ams., 2001. Mem. NAACP, Internat. Assn. Chiefs of Police, N.J. State Chiefs of Police, Essex County Chiefs Assn., N.E. Assn. Women Police (cert., Merit award), Elizabeth Police Patrolman's Benevolent Assn., Elizabeth Police Superior Officers Assn. (treas. 1983-91, v.p. 1991), Am. Soc. Law Enforcement Trainers, Emerald Soc., Union County Urban League, Italian Law Enforcement Officers Assn., Fellas Inc. (hon.), Union County Men's Svc. Orgn., Nat. Assn. of Women Law Enforcement Execs. Democrat. Roman Catholic. Office: NJ Transit Police Dept 180 Boyden Ave Maplewood NJ 07040-2494 Home: 184 Riveredge Dr Chatham NJ 07928-3112

RABB, GAEL CAUTION, mental health consultant; b. Nüernberg, Germany, Oct. 24, 1953; U.S. mil. dependent, came to U.S., 1965; d. Gustave Hamilton Jr. and Anne Grace (Richardson) Caution; m. Larry Lebby, Oct. 2, 1970 (div.); children: Lanir, Amanda; m. Moses Rabb Jr., Oct. 16, 1995; children: Mary Anne Grace. BA in Psychology, U. S.C., 1975, PhD in Clin. Psychology, 1984. Lic. ind. social worker. Fellow White House, Washington, 1980-81; dir. psychology Morris Village Alcohol and Drug Tx Ctr., Columbia, S.C., 1985; dir. health and human svcs. Office of the Gov., S.C., 1986; pres. Cautions Consults, Columbia, 1988—. Home: 2324 Washington St Columbia SC 29204-1862

RABB, HARRIET SCHAFFER, academic administrator, educator, lawyer, government official; b. Houston, Sept. 12, 1941; d. Samuel S. and Helen G. Schaffer; m. Bruce Rabb, Jan. 4, 1970; children: Alexander, Katherine. BA in Govt., Barnard Coll., 1963; JD, Columbia U., 1966. Bar: N.Y. 1966, U.S. Supreme Ct. 1969, D.C. 1970. Instr. seminar on constl. litigation Rutgers Law Sch., 1966-67; staff atty. Center for Constl. Rights, 1966-69; spl. counsel to commr. consumer affairs N.Y.C. Dept. Consumer Affairs, 1969-70; sr. staff atty. Stern Community Law Firm, Washington, 1970-71; asst. dean urban affairs Law Sch., Columbia U., N.Y.C., 1971-84, prof. law, dir. clin. edn., 1984-99, George M. Jaffen prof. law and social responsibility, 1991-99, vice dean, 1992-93; gen. counsel Dept. Health and Human Svcs., Washington, 1993—2001; v.p., gen. counsel Rockefeller U., 2001—. Mem. faculty employment and tng. policy Harvard Summer Inst., Cambridge, Mass., 1975-79 Author: (with Agid, Cooper and Rubin) Fair Employment Litigation Manual, 1975, (with Cooper and Rubin) Fair Employment Litigation, 1975. Bd. dirs. Ford Found., 1977-89, N.Y. Civil Liberties Union, 1972-83, Lawyers Com. for Civil Rights Under Law, 1978-86, Legal Def. Fund NAACP, 1978-93, Mex. Am. Legal Def. and Edn. Fund, 1986-90, Legal Aid Soc., 1990-93, The Hastings Ctr., 2004—; mem. exec. com. Human Rights Watch, 1991-93; trustee Trinity Episcopal Sch. Corp., 1991-93; mem. external adv. bd. Columbia U. Ctr. for Bioethics, 2002—. Office: Rockefeller U 1230 York Ave New York NY 10021 Office Phone: 212-327-8070. Business E-Mail: hrabb@rockefeller.edu.

RABBIT, LINDA, construction executive; BA, U. Mich., Ann Arbor; MA, George Wash. U. With KPMG (formerly Peat Marwick), 1981—85, dir. mktg., 1982—85; co-founder, co-owner, exec. v.p. Hart Construction Co., Inc.; founder, pres. Rand Contruction, 1989—. Dir. Watson Wyatt & Co., 2002—. Bd. trustees George Wash. U., Federal City Coun. Named Person of Vision, Arlington C. of C., 1995, Bus. Woman Yr., United Cerebral Palsy, 1996, Wash. Woman of Genius, Trinity Coll., 2002, Washingtonian Yr., Washingtonian mag., 2004; named one of 100 Most Powerful Women, 2001; recipient Working Woman 500, 2001. Mem.: Wash. Bd. Trade (past chair), Comml. Real Estate Women (past pres., Annual Achievement award 2003). Office: Rand Construction Corp 2100 Wash Blvd Ste 175 Arlington VA 22204 Office Phone: 703-553-5511. Office Fax: 703-486-3092.

RABE, ELIZABETH ROZINA, hair stylist, horse breeder; b. Granby, Quebec, Canada, Sept. 28, 1953; d. John I. and Christina Maria (De Vaal) Gluck; m. Oct. 21, 1972 (div. 1981); children: Diana Marie Claire, Michelle Diane. Diploma in hairstyling, Art Inst. Film hairstylist Internat. Alliance Theatrical, Stage Employees and Moving Pictures Machine Operators Local 706, L.A., 1977—2004. Recipient Design Patent hock support horse brace U.S. Design Patent Office, Washington, 1994. Home: 622 Ventura St Altadena CA 91001-4939 Office Phone: 818-385-8269.

RABIDEAU, MARGARET CATHERINE, retired media center director; b. Chgo., Nov. 24, 1930; d. Nicholas and Mary Agnes (Burke) Oberle; m. Gerald Thomas Rabideau, Nov. 27, 1954; children: Mary, Margaret, Michelle, Gregory, Marsha, Grant. BA cum laude, U. Toledo, 1952, MA in Ednl. Media Tech., 1978. Cert. tchr. K-12 media tech., supr. ednl. media, tchr. English and journalism, specialist in edn. Asst. dir. pub. rels. U. Toledo, 1952-55; publicity writer United Way, Toledo, 1974-75; tchr. Toledo Pub. Schs., 1975-80, libr., media specialist, 1980-90; dir. media svcs. Sylvania (Ohio) Schs., 1990—2002, ret., 2002. Task force to evaluate coll. programs Ohio Dept. Edn., 1987; on-site evaluation team, Hiram Coll., Ohio, 1991; north ctrl. evaluation team Northwestern Ohio, 1985—. Citizen task force Toledo/Lucas County Libr., Ohio, 1991, mem. friends of the libr., 1990—; task force Sta. WGTE-TV PBS Sta., Toledo, 1993; mem. tech. com. strategic plan Sylvania Schs., 1997; instr. U. Toledo, 1990— Recipient Disting. Educator for Art Edn. award N.W. Ohio Art Edn. Assn., 1997; nmamed Educator of Yr., Sylvania Schs., 2001. Mem. ALA, U. Toledo Alumni Assn., Ohio Ednl. Libr. Media Assn. (N.W. dir. 1993—, vocat. dir. 1985-89, Libr. Media Specialist of Yr. 1993, disting. educator art edn. 1999), Am. Ednl. Comm. and Tech., Ednl. Leadership Assn. (bd. dirs.), Maumee Valley Computer Assn. (task force), Phi Delta Kappa (Outstanding Newsletter Nat. award 1990, pres. Toledo chpt., svc. key award, 1998). Avocations: running, travelling, cross stitching. Home: 1038 Olson St Toledo OH 43612-2828

RABII, PATRICIA BERG, church administrator; b. Lynn, Mass., Nov. 7, 1942; d. Clarence Oscar and Naomi Ruth (MacHugh) B.; m. S. Rabii, Oct. 26, 1966 (div. 1988); children: Susan M., Elizabeth L. AA, Green Mtn. Coll., Poultney, Vt., 1962; BA cum laude, U. Pa., 1978. Cons. City of Phila., 1981; fin. svcs. officer U. Pa., Phila., 1981-90; asst. to exec. dir. Psi Upsilon Found., Paoli, Pa., 1990-92; parish adminstr. St. David's (Radnor) Episcopal Ch., Wayne, Pa., 1992-98; clergy and parish sec. St. David's Ch., 1998—. Co-dir. career planning/pub. rels. Resources for Women, Phila., 1978-81. Counselor direct patient and care ARC, St. Louis, 1967-69; bd. dirs. Upper Merion PTA, 1976-78, Dental Clinic, King of Prussia, 1976-78; leader Girl Scouts U.S.A., King of Prussia, 1976-77, 80-81. Recipient ACT 101 Svc. award, Penn Cap, 1989. Mem. AAUW, U. Pa. Women's Club (bd. dirs. 1975-80, v.p. 1979-80). Avocations: golf, bridge, travel. Home: 5 Drummers Ln Wayne PA 19087-1503 Office: St Davids Radnor Episcopal 763 Valley Forge Rd Wayne PA 19087-4724 Office Phone: 610-688-7947. E-mail: prabii@stdavidschurch.org.

RABINOF, SYLVIA, pianist, composer, author, educator; b. N.Y.C., Oct. 10, 1913; d. Morris and Fanny (Edelstein) Smith; m. Benno Rabinof, Sept. 16, 1943 (dec. Apr. 1976); m. Charles Rothenberg, Dec. 22, 1978 (dec. April 1992). Student, 3rd St Music Sch. Settlement, N.Y.C., NYU, Juilliard Sch. Music; MusD (hon.), Lincoln Meml. U., 1947; studied with Marguerite Valentine, Mary Emerson, Rudolph Serkin, Ignace Jan Paderewski, Simon Barere, Georges Enesco, Oscar Ziegler, James Bleeker, Charles Haubiel, Albert Stoessel, Philip James. Tchr. piano, improvisation, ensemble theory Juilliard Sch. Music; mem. faculty Brevard Music. Ctr. N.C. Converse Coll., Spartanburg, S.C., Round Top Music Festival, Tex., SUNY, Fredonia; lectr. in field. Author: (textbooks) Musicianship Through Improvisation, 1966, The Improviser, 1967, The Improvisers Key Guidebook, 1969; contbr. composers' biographies to NFMC Jr. Keynotes mag., 1971-98; composer: cantata The Deluge, Three Profiles for Piano, Suite for String Orchestra, children's operetta Hamlet the Flea; published piano arrangements for Warner Bros.; piano solo and duo recordings with Benno Rabinof include Beethoven violin and piano sonatas, violin gypsy classics, Vivaldi concerti, others; performances in Vienna, Zurich, London, Phila., Carnegie Hall, N.Y.C., Boston, Chgo., Toronto, Paris, Moscow, Athens, Rome, Milan, others. Mem. ASCAP, Nat. Fedn. Music Clubs (chair improvisation), Musicians Club N.Y. (pres. 1976-79) Home: 8220 Jog Rd Boynton Beach FL 33437-2938

RABINOVICH, RAQUEL, painter, sculptor; b. Buenos Aires, Mar. 30, 1929; arrived in U.S., 1967, naturalized, 1973; d. Enrique Rabinovich and Julia Dinitz; m. Jose Luis Reissig, Feb. 14, 1956 (div. 1981); children: Celia Karen Reissig, Pedro Dario Reissig, Nora Vivian Reissig. Student, U. Córdoba, Argentina, 1950-53, Sorbonne, Paris, 1957, U. Edinburgh, Scotland, 1958-59. Lectr. Whitney Mus., 1983—86, Marymount Manhattan Coll., 1984—90. Exhibitions include Hecksher Mus., Huntington, N.Y., 1974, Susan Caldwell Gallery, N.Y.C., 1975, CUNY Grad. Ctr., 1978, Jewish Mus. Sculpture Ct., N.Y.C., 1979, Ctr. Inter-Am. Rels., 1983, Bronx Mus. Arts, N.Y.C., 1986, Fordham U. Lincoln Ctr., 1985, Ams. Soc., 1990, Erik Stark Gallery, 1991, Montgomery Ctr., 1992, Trans Hudson Gallery, N.Y.C., 1993, 1998, 2000, Noyes Mus., 1994, Nelson Atkins Mus. Art, 1995, Intar Gallery, N.Y.C., 1996, U. Tex. Mus. Art, 1998, Emergences (Hudson River Project), 2001—, Collaborative Concepts, Beacon, N.Y., 2003, Hudson River Mus., Yonkers, N.Y., 2003, others, —, Represented in permanent collections World Bank Fine Art Collection, Washington, Univ. Art Mus., Austin, Cin. Art Mus., Walker Art Ctr., others. Fellow, NEA, 1991—92; grantee, N.Y. State Coun. Arts, 1995—96, Pollock-Krasner Found., 2001. Avocations: travel, music. Home: 141 Lamoree Rd Rhinebeck NY 12572-3013 E-mail: raquelrabinovich@aol.com.

RABINOWITZ, ANNA, poet; b. Bklyn., May 28, 1933; d. Sam and Ruth (Chernoff) Goldban; m. Martin Jay Rabinowitz, Sept. 12, 1954; children: Steven Michael, Susan Alice, Nancy Jean. BA magna cum laude, Bklyn. Coll., 1953; MFA, Columbia U., 1990. Instr. New Sch. for Social Rsch.,

N.Y.C., 1994-98; fellow NEA, 2000. Author: At the Site of Inside Out, 1997 (Juniper prize U. Mass. Press 1997); editor Am. Letters and Commentary jour., 1992—. Bd. dirs. Jewish Comm. Rels. Coun., Women for Women, N.Y.C., 1993—. Recipient Black Warrior Poetry prize Black Warrior Poetry Rev., U. Ala., 1993. Mem. St. Mark's Poetry Project, Poets and Writers, Poets House, Acad. of Am. Poets, Poetry Soc. Am. (bd. govs. 1990—, v.p. 1993—), Phi Beta Kappa. Home: 850 Park Ave New York NY 10021-1845

RABINOWITZ, DOROTHY, television critic; b. N.Y.C. BA, Queens Coll., N.Y.C.; postgrad., NYU, Pratt Inst. Freelance writer, syndicated columnist, commentator Sta. WWOR-TV News, N.Y.C.; editl. page writer and television critic Wall St. Jour., mem. editl. bd. Author: Home Life, 1970, New Lives, 1976, No Crueler Tyrannies: Accusation, False Witness, and Other Terrors of Our Times, 2003; columnist Dorothy Rabinowitz's Media Log. Recipient Pulitzer prize for Disting. Commentary, 2001. Office: Wall St Jour 1155 Ave of the Americas 5th fl New York NY 10036*

RABKIN, PEGGY ANN, retired lawyer; b. Buffalo, Apr. 13, 1945; d. Anthony J. and Margaret G. (Catuzzi) Marano; m. Samuel S. Rabkin, June 29, 1969. BA, SUNY, Buffalo, 1967, MEd, 1970, MA, 1972, JD, PhD, 1975. Tchr. Buffalo Pub. Schs., 1967-69; grad. teaching asst. SUNY, Buffalo, 1969-72; case analyst U.S. Equal Employment Opportunity Com., 1974; dir. affirmative action U. Louisville, 1975-78, adj. prof. of law, 1976-77; atty. office for civil rights HEW, N.Y.C., 1978; sr. atty. for labor and employment Am. Home Products Corp., N.Y.C., 1978-86, sr. atty., 1986—. Author: Fathers to Daughters, 1980; editor: Buffalo Law Rev., 1974-75; contbr. articles to profl. jours. Commr. Louisville & Jefferson Co. Human Relations Com., Louisville, 1977-78. Recipient Christopher Baldy fellow, SUNY at Buffalo Law Sch., 1974-75, Regents Coll. Scholarship N.Y. State Bd. of Regents, 1963-67. Mem. ABA, Assn. of Bar of City of N.Y., Am. Corp. Counsel Assn., Soc. of Human Resources Mgmt., U.S. C. of C. (labor com. 1991—). Avocations: skiing, reading, cooking, and nutrition.

RABUCK, DONNA FONTANAROSE, English writing educator; b. Edison, N.J., Aug. 2, 1954; d. Arthur Thomas and Shirley Gertrude (Golub) Fontanarose; m. John Frederick Rabuck, July, 28, 1973; 1 child, Miranda Rose. BA in Eng., Rutgers U., 1976, MA in Eng. Lit., 1980, PhD in Eng. Lit., 1990. Prof. writing Pima C. C., Tucson, 1981-86; asst. dir. writing skills program U. Ariz., Tucson, 1983—. Asst. dir. summer inst. writing U. Ariz., Tucson, 1985—, asst. dir. grad. writing inst., 1996—; adj. faculty Pima C. C., Tucson, 1992-95. Author: The Other Side of Silence: Performing Heroinism in the Victorian Novel, 1990, Writing Ctr. Perspectives, 1995; editor: Writing is Thinking: Collected Writings of the Summer Inst., 1985—. Founder, pres. Miles East-West Neighborhood Assn., Tucson, 1983—; dir. Ctr. for Sacred Feminine, Tucson, 1995—; program coord. U. Ariz. Arts and Scis. Minority Retention Program, 1988-93. Rutgers Alumni scholar, 1972-76; Bevier fellow Rutgers U., 1976-78. Mem. Intercollegiate Writing Com. (task force), Commn. Cultural Thinking (task force), Nat. Coun. Tchrs. Eng. Avocations: feminist scholarship, women's rituals, yoga, hiking, meditation. Home: 1115 N Camino Miraflores Tucson AZ 85745-1612 Office: Univ Ariz Writing Skills Program 1201 E Helen St Tucson AZ 85719-4407 E-mail: drabuck@u.arizona.edu.

RACCAH, DOMINIQUE MARCELLE, publisher; b. Paris, Aug. 24, 1956; arrived in U.S., 1964; d. Paul Mordechai and Colette Bracha (Madar) R.; m. Raymond W. Bennett, Aug. 20, 1980; children: Marie, Lyron, Doran. BA, U. Ill., Chgo., 1978; MS, U. Ill., Champaign-Urbana, 1981. Rsch. analyst Leo Burnett Advt., Chgo., 1980-81, rsch. supr., 1981-84, assoc. rsch. dir., 1984-87; pres., pub., owner Sourcebooks, Inc., Naperville, Ill., 1987—; co-CEO Login Pubs. Consortium, Chgo., 1990-99. Author Financial Sourcebooks' Sources, 1987. Recipient Blue Chip Enterprise award, 2000, Ernst & Young Entrepreneur of Yr. Ill. and N.W. Ind., 2000; named to Inc. 500 list; inducted into Univ. Ill. Entrepreneurship Hall of Fame, 2001. Mem. Pubs. Mktg. Assn., Am. Booksellers Assn., Am. Assn. Pubs. Avocations: photography, writing, history. Home: 26 N Webster St Naperville IL 60540-4527 Office: Sourcebooks Inc 1935 Brookdale Rd # 139 Naperville IL 60563-9245 E-mail: dominique@sourcebooks.com.

RACHOW, SHARON DIANNE, realtor; b. St. Joseph, Mo., Apr. 12, 1939; d. Norman DeLos Zancker and Sylvia Lavina (Hawkins) Trouel; m. Thomas Eugene Rachow, Oct. 22, 1968; children: Todd A., Tiffany K. Student, So. Ill. U., 1969-72. Quality svc. cert. Sec. Westab, Inc. (now Mead), St. Joseph, 1957-60, Seitz Packing Co. (now Sara Lee), St. Joseph, 1960-66; exec. asst. to v.p., gen. mgr. Kansas City (Mo.) Chiefs, 1972; co-owner, mgr. Pool 'N Patio Plus, St. Joseph, 1973-84; realtor Coldwell Banker Gen. Realtors, St. Joseph, 1984-93, RE/MAX, 1993—. Trustee Nat. Multiple Sclerosis Soc., Mid Am. chpt., Midland M.S. Express Br., 1993-98. Mem.: Real Estate Buyer's Agt. Coun. (accredited buyers rep. 1996—), St. Joseph Regional Bd. Realtors (cert. residential specialist 1987, Multi-List com. 1993—2002, dir. 1994, forms com. 1994—2002, Top 10, Top Residential Sales award 1986—), Multi Million Dollar Club (life). Republican. Lutheran. Home: 4211 Country Ln Saint Joseph MO 64506-2454 Office: RE/MAX of St Joseph Inc 1119 N Woodbine Rd Saint Joseph MO 64506-2434 E-mail: sharonr@stjoelive.com.

RACITI, CHERIE, artist; b. Chgo., June 17, 1942; d. Russell J. and Jacque (Crimmins) R. Student, Memphis Coll. Art, 1963-65; BA in Art, San Francisco State U., 1968; M.F.A., Mills Coll., 1979. Assoc. prof. art San Francisco State U., 1984-89, prof., 1989—. Lectr. Calif. State U., Hayward, 1974, San Francisco Art Inst., 1978; mem. artist com. San Francisco Art Inst., 1974-85, sec., 1980-81. One woman shows include U. Calif., Berkeley, 1972, Nicholas Wilder Gallery, L.A., 1975, San Francisco Art Inst., 1977, Marianne Deson Gallery, Chgo., 1980, Site 375, San Francisco, 1989, Reese Bullen Gallery, Humboldt State U., Arcata, Calif., 1990, Mills Coll. Art Mus., Oakland, Calif., 1998; group shows include Whitney Mus. Art, 1975, San Francisco Sci. Fiction, The Clocktower, N.Y.C., Otis-Parsons Gallery, Los Angeles, 1984-85, San Francisco Art Inst., 1985, Artists Space, N.Y.C., 1988, Angles Gallery, Santa Monica, 1987, Terrain Gallery, San Francisco, 1992, Ctr. for the Arts, San Francisco, 1993, Santa Monica Coll., 1998, 25/25 25th Anniversary Exhbn., So. Exposure Gallery, San Francisco, 1999, Santa Cruz Mus., 2003. Bd. dirs. New Langton Arts, 1988-92. Eureka fellow Fleishhacker Found., San Francisco; recipient Adaline Kent award San Francisco Art Inst., 1976, Djerassi resident, 1994, Tyrone Guthrie Ctr. resident, Ireland, 1995, Millay Colony for Arts resident 1999, Juror's award Art Coun. Inc. San Francisco. Office: San Francisco State U Art Dept 1600 Holloway Ave San Francisco CA 94132-1722 E-mail: craciti@sfsu.edu.

RACKE, ANNE MOLLER, winery executive; b. Oberwesel, Germany, Dec. 10, 1961; came to U.S., 1981; d. Werner Jacob and Gerda Johanna Brager; m. Marcus Moller Racke, Aug. 27, 1983 (div. 1993); 1 child, dorothé; m. Saul I. Gropman, May 26, 1995. Grad., Fach Hochschule, Boppard, Germany, 1979. Asst. vineyard mgr. Buena Vista Winery, Sonoma, Calif., 1981-83, vineyard mgr., 1983-90, dir. vineyard ops., 1990-98, v.p., 1998—. Bd. dirs. Carneros Quality Alliance, Napa/Sonoma, Calif. Mem. adv. bd. Sonoma Valley Mus. Art, 1999. Roman Catholic. Office: Buena Vista Winery 27000 Ramal Rd Sonoma CA 95476-9791

RACKLIN, BARBARA COHEN, fundraising consultant; b. N.Y.C., Dec. 3, 1950; d. Harry Cohen and Sheri Lillian (Greene) Cohen; m. Arthur Michael Racklin, Aug. 19, 1979; 1 child, Nicholas Michael. BA in Math., U. Tex., 1972; postgrad., U. LaVerne, 1981-82. Cert. histocompatibility technologist, Am. Bd. Histocompatibility and Immunogenetics. Asst. dir. transplant lab. Med. br. U. Tex., Galveston, 1974-76; transplant immunology specialist Montefiore Hosp., Bronx, N.Y., 1976-77; dir. pediat. immunology lab. Cedar Sinai Hosp., L.A., 1977-79; supr. pathology lab. City of Hope Nat. Med. Ctr., Duarte, Calif., 1979-82, rsch. specialist transplant lab., 1982-85; staff coord. vol. devel. City of Hope Deve. Ctr., L.A., 1986-88; coord. fin. devel. events ARC, Pasadena, Calif., 1995-99; co-owner benefit specialists Fundraising Cons., La Cañada, Calif., 1995-99; dir. devel. San Gabriel chpt. ARC, 1999—. Tour chmn. City of Hope Ann. Conv., Duarte, 1987, 89, 91. Contbr. or co-contbr. articles to profl. pubis. Bd. dirs. City of Hope Med. Ctr., 1986-89, mem. bd. govs., 1991-93; mem. steering com. local parcel tax election, La Cañada, 1992, local sch. bd. election, 1995; mem. sch. bd. La Cañada Unified Sch. Dist., 1997—, clk. governing bd., 1999-2000; pres. La Cañada Coun. PTA, 1995-97, City of Hope Aux., 1988-90; bd. dirs. LCF Ednl. Found., past pres., v.p., 1991-97; sec. Children's Hosp. Aux., 1994-97; auditor 1st Dist. PTA, 1997; chairperson youth com. Pasadena Temple, 1996-97; v.p. governing bd. La Canada Unified Sch. Dist., 1998-99; bd. dirs. southwest reg. B'nai B'rith Youth Orgn.; participant Leadership Pasadena, 1999-2000. Recipient Hon. Svc. award La Cañada Coun. PTA, 1996, Svc. award LCF Ednl. Found., 1995, Golden Apple award La Canada Unified Sch. Dist., 1996. Mem. NSFRE. Avocations: skiing, bowling, reading. Office: ARC PO Box 91087 Pasadena CA 91109-1087 Home: 362 Grace Dr South Pasadena CA 91030-1823

RACKOW, SYLVIA, business consultant, educator; b. N.Y.C., May 21, 1931; d. Isaac and Gina Frieder; m. Paul Rackow, Sept. 12, 1962; 1 child, Julianna S. Richter. BA, CUNY, 1955; MA, Columbia U., 1958; cert., U. Straniere, Florence, Italy, 1959. Pub. rels. dir. Pharm. Soc. N.Y. State, N.Y.C., 1960—62; media rels. dir. N.Y. State Med. Soc., N.Y.C., 1963—65; lectr. speech and theater The City Coll., CUNY, N.Y.C., 1965—69; adj. lectr. speech and theater John Jay Coll., CUNY, N.Y.C., 1973—78; cons. Rackow Assocs., N.Y.C., 1980—; adj. lectr. English dept. Baruch Coll., CUNY, N.Y.C., 1985—. Mem., del. profl. staff congress CUNY, 1994—. Contbr. articles to mags. and newspapers. Mem., spokesperson Women-Heart Orgn., Washington, 2002—; vol. recreation dept. Mt. Sinai Hosp., N.Y.C., 1993—2004. Recipient theater fellowship, U. Conn., 1959. Mem.: AAUP, HFCA Ladies Tennis Assn. (chairperson 1983—). Democrat. Jewish. Avocations: tennis, snorkeling, visiting grandchildren, travel, volunteer work. Home: 505 LaGuardia Pl New York NY 10012 Office: Baruch Coll English Dept 10 Lexington Ave New York NY 10010 Personal E-mail: rackow@juno.com. E-mail: sylvia_rackow@baruch.cuny.edu.

RADELL, CAROL K. elementary school educator; b. Rochester, NY, Feb. 22, 1939; d. Harold LaVerne and Ruth Elinor Kruger; m. Eugene Arthur Radell, Apr. 30, 1971 (dec. Jan. 18, 1998); children: Terry Jean(dec.), Steven Paul, Marcie Ann. Elem. edn., Long Beach (Calif.) City Coll., 1959; chemistry, Rochester Inst. Tech., 1961; BA, Long Beach (Calif.) City Coll., 1961. Lab. technician Eastman Kodak, Rochester, NY, 1959—63; assoc. tchr. Henrietta Sch. Dist., NY, 1969—71, Fairport Bd. Coop. Edn., NY, 1986—99, Fairport Sch. Dist., 1999—, East Rochester Sch. Dist., NY, 1999—2001, Hemet Unified Sch. Dist., Calif., 1999—2002, Riverside County, Calif., 2000—02. Mem. Safe Celebration Com., Fairport, 1989—90. Mem.: MADD. Avocations: rock climbing, fast walking, reading, volunteer work. Home: 87 Eaglesfield Way Fairport NY 14450

RADER, ANGELA NICHOLE, music educator; b. Buckhannon, W.Va., Dec. 28, 1974; d. Paul Douglass and Leda Linette Koon; m. Brent David Rader, July 5, 1997; 1 child, Jordan McKenzie. B in Music Edn., W.Va. Wesleyan Coll., 1997. Tchr. Waynesboro (Va.) City Schs., 1997—98; tchr., band dir. Lexington (Va.) City Schs., 1998—; girls' basketball coach. Mem.: Music Educators Nat. Conf., Va. Music Edn. Assn. Republican. Methodist. Avocations: flute, candle making, handbells. Office: Waddell Elem Sch 100 Pendleton Pl Lexington VA 24450

RADER, ELLA JANE See ASHLEY, ELLA JANE

RADFORD, VIRGINIA RODRIGUEZ, retired secondary education educator, librarian; b. Willcox, Ariz., Nov. 17, 1917; d. Domingo Acosta and Maria Ceveriana (Lopez) Rodriguez; m. John Houston Radford, June 5, 1942; children: Mary Jane, Ann Christine, Patricia Mae. BA, BS, univ. tchrs. diploma, U. Kans., 1940; Librarianship, Benedictine Coll., Atchinson, Kans., 1972-76. Cert. life. tchr. K-12, Kans., master tchr., 1970. Tchr. Spanish, French, English Horton (Kans.) High Schs., 1957-60; 4th and 5th grade tchr. St. Leo's Parochial Sch., Horton, 1961-62; tchr. Spanish, French/librarian Horton High Sch., 1962-82. Translator U.S. War Dept., San Antonio, 1942; past pres. Brown County Ret. Tchrs. Assn., People-to-People (Horton chpt.); commd. lay min. St. Leo's Ch., 1990; pres. bd. dirs. Horton Libr., 1975; bd. dirs. Tri-County Manor, Horton, 2001. Named Outstanding Secondary Educator of Am., 1975; inducted Kans. Tchrs. Hall of Fame, 1984. Mem.: AAUW, Bus. and Profl. Women, Friends of Libr., Horton Hosp. Aux. (life), Horton Sr. Citizens Club, Inc. (trustee), VFW Aux. Post 3021 (life; v.p.), Delta Kappa Gamma (pres. Alpha Kappa chpt.). Roman Catholic. Avocations: reading, music, traveling, photography, collecting letter openers. Home: 439 W 8th St Horton KS 66439-1515

RADICE, ANNE-IMELDA, museum director; b. Buffalo, Feb. 29, 1948; d. Lawrence and Anne (Marino) R. AB, Wheaton Coll., 1969; MA, Villa SchiFanoia, Florence, Italy, 1971; PhD, U. N.C., 1976; MBA, Am. U., 1984. Asst. curator Nat. Gallery of Art, Washington, 1972-76; archtl. historian U.S. Capitol, Washington, 1976-80, curator Office of Architect, 1980-85; dir. Nat. Mus. Women in the Arts, 1985-89; chief div. of creative arts USIA, 1989-91; sr. dep. chmn. Nat. Endowment for Arts, Washington, 1991-92; acting chmn., 1992-93; exec. v.p. Gray & Co. II, Miami, Fla., 1993; prodr. World Affairs TV Prodn., 1994; assoc. producer Think Tank, 1994; chief spl. projects, confidential adviser Courtney Sale Ross, 1994-96; v.p., COO ICL Internat., 1996—; exec. dir. Friends of Dresden, 1998—2001; exec. dir. appeal Consci. Found., 2001—03; chief staff U.S. Dept. Edn., 2003—. Cons. in pub. rels. and TV, 1994—. Contbr. articles to profl. jours.

RADKE, ANNE MARIE, assistant principal, writer; b. Mineral Wells, Tex., Oct. 29, 1967; d. Robert Woodward and Joanne Kristol Hornaday; m. David Erik Radke, Aug. 12, 1995; 1 child, Erika Jane. M in Sch. Adminstrn., U. N.C. Charlotte, 1998, M in English, 1995, BA, 1990. Cert. School Adminstr. N.C., 1998, Tchr. Cert. N.C., 1990. Asst. prin. Piedmont Mid. Sch., Monroe, NC, 2000—, Charlotte Mecklenburg Schools, NC, 1998—2000, tchr. grades 9-12, 1990—96. Spl. needs adminstr. Piedmont Mid. Sch., Monroe, 2000—; environ. educator N.C. Dept. Pub. Instrn., Raleigh, 2003—. Author (grant developer): (educational grants for student funding) Wild About School (NC Learn and Serve Grant ($26, 000), 2001). Environ. educator Edfundamentals, Charlotte, 2002—03. Recipient award, Kappa Delta Pi, 1997; fellow, N.C. Prin. Fellows Program, 1996—98; scholar Summer Seminar: Dartmouth Coll., NEH, 1994; Fellow: Grant Writing, N.C. Prin. Exec. Program, 2001. Mem.: ASCD, Union County Prin. and Asst. Prin. Assn. (na). R-Consevative. Lutheran. Avocations: writing, showing and breeding collies, hiking, travel, photography. Office: Union County Schools Piedmont Mid Sch 2816 Sikes Mill Rd Monroe NC 28110-9780 Personal E-mail: aradke@carolina.rr.com. E-mail: anne.radke@ucps.k12.nc.us.

RADKOWSKY, KAREN, advertising research specialist; b. Washington, Nov. 8, 1957; d. Lawrence and Florence (Kramer) R. BA, Columbia U., 1979. Rsch. analyst Cosmair, Inc., N.Y.C., 1979-82, sr. rsch. analyst, 1982-84; asst. rsch. mgr. Am. Express Co., N.Y.C., 1984-85; account rsch. mgr. BBDO, Inc., N.Y.C., 1985-88, v.p., assoc. rsch. dir., 1988-94, sr. v.p., assoc. rsch. dir., 1994-95; sr. v.p., rsch. dir. BBDO N.Y., N.Y.C., 1995-99; sr. ptnr., dir. consumer rsch. Ogilvy & Mather, N.Y.C., 2000—. Bd. dirs. Advt. Rsch. Found., 2001—. E-mail: karen.radkowsky@ogilvy.com.

RADLOFF, MARIE ULREY, music educator; d. Charles Franklin and Patricia Dort Ulrey; m. D. Scott Radloff, July 9, 1996. MusB in Edn., Fla. State U., 1978; MEd, U. of Ctrl. Fla., 1991. Cert. tchr. Fla., 2003. Music specialist Lilburn Elem. Sch., Ga., 1978—87, Bonneville Elem. Sch., Orlando, Fla., 1987—2001, Three Points Elem. Sch., Orlando, 2001—; adj. instr. U. Ctrl. Fla., 2004. Clinician Ctrl. Fla. Orff Chpt., Orlando, Fla., 2002—03; adv. bd. mem., young composers' program Orlando Philharm. Orch., Orlando, Fla., 2003—; chmn. of music assessment writing team Orange County Pub. Schs., Orlando, 2002, clinician on various topics in music edn., 1995—; clinician Fla. Music Educator's Assn., Tampa, Fla., 2002, Arts for a Complete Edn./Fla. Assn. of Arts Educators, Orlando, 2002, U. of Ctrl. Fla., Orlando, 2000, Orange County Pub. Schs. Tchr. Acad., Orlando, 1999; prin. oboist Hollywood Festival Orch., Asian Tour, 2002—03. Author: (book) Making Music Florida Planner. Coun. of ministries mem. First United Meth. Ch., Orlando, 1994—96. Named Tchr. of the Yr., Three Points Elem. Sch., 2002—03; recipient Teacherrific Award for Innovative Tchg. Practices, The Walt Disney Co., 1993, 1994, 2000, Innovative Program/Project award, Fla. Music Educators Assn., 1999; scholar, Orange County Pub. Schs. scholar, 2002. Mem.: Am. Orff Schulwerk Assn., Music Educators Nat. Conf., Fla. Music Educators Assn., Fla. Elem. Music Educators Assn. (dist. chmn. 2003—), Orange County Elem. Music Educators Assn. (dist. chmn. 2000—03), Phi Delta Kappa (chpt. historian 1990—92). Avocations: playing oboe, flute, and handbells, reading, movies. Office: Three Points Elem Sch 4001 S Goldenrod Rd Orlando FL 32822 Personal E-mail: radloffm@earthlink.net. E-mail: radlofm@ocps.net.

RADOGNO, CHRISTINE, state legislator; b. Oak Park, Ill., Dec. 21, 1952; BA, MSW, Loyola U. Mem. Ill. Senate, Springfield, 1997—, mem. appropriations, commerce & industry & pub. health coms. Republican. Office: State Capitol Capitol Bldg M-121 Springfield IL 62706-0001 also: 521 S LaGrance Rd Ste 104 La Grange IL 60525

RADOJCSICS, ANNE PARSONS, librarian; b. Mansfield, Ohio, Mar. 23, 1929; d. Richard Walbridge Parsons and Iva Pearl (Ruth) Kemp; m. Joseph Michael Radojcsics, July 8, 1950; children: Kurt Joseph, Jo Anne Radojcsics Kent. Diploma, Bethel Woman's Coll., Hopkinsville, Ky., 1949; BS, Miss. State U., 1972, MEd, 1974. Cert. secondary tchr., Miss. Chemist Humphries Borg-Warner Co., Mansfield, 1950-53; asst. reference libr. Mansfield Pub. Libr., 1953-59; libr. media specialist Verona (Miss.) Sch., 1970-92, supr. Verona computer lab., 1985-92; libr. media specialist Pierce St. Elem. Sch., Miss., 1992-95; ret., 1995; libr. Saints Libr., Tupelo, Miss., 1995—. Supr. libr. Guntown (Miss.) Scho., 1988-92; chmn. assessment project Miss. Libr. Miss. Dept. Edn., Jacson, 1986-92; coord. region I Miss. Conf. on Libr. and Info. Svc., 1990; mem. Miss. Edn. TV Adv. Coun., 1985-89; cons. content instrnl. prodn. libr. rsch. skills Miss. Ednl. TV., 1995; Equity Adv. Coun. Itawamta Comm. Coll., Tupelo, 1995-99. Author: Clay Tablets to Media Centers: Library Development from Ancient to Modern Times, 1975; (tchr. guide) Media Mania, 1996 Mississippi Educational TV. Bd. dirs., past pres. SAFE, Inc., Tupelo, Miss., 1978-92, bd. dirs. emeritus, 1992—; mem. Lee County Adult Lit. Task Force, Tupelo, 1987-90; v.p. Friends Miss. Libr., Inc., 2002—; N. Ea. regional rep. Friends Lee County Libr., 2002—, sec., 2003—. Recipient Ed Ransdell Instructional TV award, 1991, Woman of Achievement Equity Program award, 1996. Mem. AAUW (pres. Tupelo chpt. 1977-81, 1993-97, Miss. divsn. 1984-86)), Miss. Profl. Educators, Mississippians for Ednl. Broadcasting, Miss. Ednl. Computer Assn., Miss. Libr. Assn. (project chmn. com. on sch. librs. 1989, awards chmn. 1987-88, ednl. comml. and tech. roundtable chair 1993), Miss. Profl. Educators Tupelo/Lee County (treas. 1993-95, pres. 1995-97), Friends Miss. Libr. (N.E. regional rep. 2001—, v.p. 2002—), Friends Lee County (sec. 2003—). Democrat. Episcopalian. Avocations: reading, church music and liturgy, quilt making. Home: Carr Vista 105 Michael St Tupelo MS 38801-8608

RADULOVIC, LJILJANA, psychiatrist, researcher; d. Dimitrije and Bozidarka Radulovic. MD with honors, U. Zagreb Med. Sch., Croatia, 1986—93. Resident in psychiatry SUNY HSC, Bklyn., 1998—2002; addiction fellow Mt. Sinai Sch. of Medicine, N.Y.C., 2002—03, rsch. fellow in devel. disabilities and compulsive, impulsive and anxiety disorder program, 2003—. Rschr. on marijuana and psychotic disorders Ctr. for Addiction and Mental Health, Toronto, 1997—98. Mem.: AMA, APA, Am. Acad. Addiction Psychiatry. Achievements include research in Schizophrenia. Office: Mt Sinai Sch Medicine One Gustave L Levy Pl Box 1230 New York NY 10029 Personal E-mail: ljiljar@att.net.

RADZIKOWSKI, ANTONINA ANGELINA, retired elementary education educator; b. N.Y.C., Oct. 9, 1946; d. Salvatore Joseph and Rose (LaPiana) Bonaccorso; m. Phillip Joseph Radzikowski, July 22, 1972; children: Katherine, Phillip III. BA in Math., Hunter Coll., 1967, MS in Edn., 1970. Cert. elem. tchr., math., ednl. tech., computer edn. lab. Tchr., elem. Manhatten Schs., N.Y.C., 1967-69; tchr., math. Queens Schs., N.Y.C., 1970-83; substitute tchr. Montgomery County Pub. Schs., Rockville, Md., 1984-86; tchr., math. resource, computer lab. coord., young astronauts chpt. leader. Washington Pub. Schs., 1986-91; tchr., math. resource Van Ness Elem. Schs. Washington, 1989-91, Parkview Elem. Sch., Washington, 1991-92; intervention program tchr. Lafayette Elem. Sch., 1992-93; tchr. math., computer sci. Backus Middle Sch., Washington, 1993-97. Adj. prof., math., Montgomery Coll., Rockville, 1985-86; vol. tchr. Treatment and Learning Ctr. Troop leader, Girl Scouts Am., 1981-85. Cafritz Found. fellow, 1987, Inst. Ednl. Leadership fellow, 1988. Mem. Nat. Coun. Tchrs. Math., Nat. Sci. Tchrs. Assn., Washington Coun. Tchrs. Math. Democrat. Roman Catholic. Avocations: ice skating, dance, boating, skiing, swimming.

RADZINOWICZ, MARY ANN, language educator; b. Champaign, Ill., Apr. 18, 1925; d. Arthur Seymour and Ann (Stacy) Nevins; m. Leon Radzinowicz, June 16, 1958 (div. 1978); children: Ann Stacy Radzinowicz Prior, William Francis Henry. BA, Radcliffe Coll., 1945; MA, Columbia U., 1947, PhD, 1953; MA (hon.), U. Cambridge, Eng., 1960. Prof. Vassar Coll., Poughkeepsie, N.Y., 1947-50, 52-59, Girton Coll., Cambridge, Eng., 1960-80, U. Cambridge, 1973-80, Cornell U., Ithaca, N.Y., 1980-90, Jacob Gould Schurman prof. English emeritus, 1990—. Mem. adv. bd. 2d, 3d, 4th Internat. Milton Symposia, 1985—. Author: Toward Samson Agonistes, 1978 (Hanford prize 1979), Milton's Epics and Psalms, 1989, Milton and the Tragic Women of Genesis, 1995 (Hanford prize); editor American Colonial Prose, 1984, Paradise Lost, Book VIII, 1974; mem. editorial bd. Milton Quarterly, 1981—, Christianity and Literature, 1989—. Mem. MLA, Renaissance Soc. Am., Milton Soc. Am. (honored scholar 1987), John Donne Soc. Home: Ballyconry House Ballyvaughan County Clare Ireland Office: Cornell U Dept English Lit Ithaca NY 14850 E-mail: manr@eircom.net.

RAE, BARBARA JOYCE, former employee placement company executive; b. Prince George, B.C., Can., May 17, 1930; d. Alfred and Lottie Kathleen (Davis) Holmwood; m. George Suart, Feb. 14, 1984; children: James, Glenn, John. MBA, Simon Fraser U., Burnaby, B.C., 1975, LLD (hon.), 1998. Chmn., CEO Adia Can., Ltd., Vancouver, B.C., 1953-95; also bd. dirs. Bd. dirs. emeritus Can. Imperial Bank Commerce, Grosvenor Internat. Ltd., Noranda, Inc., Telus, Xerox Can.; dir. VLINX.Com., Can. Inst. Adv. Rsch., 1995-2001, KTCS Pub. Broadcasting; bd. govs. Multiple Sclerosis Soc., 1995—; mem. Fed. Task Force on Future of Can. Fin. Svcs. Sector, 1997-98; past chmn. B.C. Women's Hosp. Found., 1994-97. Chancellor Simon Fraser U., 1987—93; mem. Jud. Appts. .Com., 1988—90; commr. Triennial Commn. Judges Salaries and Benefits; mem. Premier's Econ. Adv. Coun., 1987—91, Prime Minister's Com. on Sci. and Tech., 1989—94; gen. chmn. United Way Lower Mainland, 1987; chair Salvation Army Red Shield Vancouver Campaign, 1986; bd. dirs. Vancouver Bd. Trade, 1972—76; dir. Royal B.C. Mus.; patron Can. Coun. Christians and Jews; mem. adv. bd. Salvation Army, 1985—. Decorated Order of Can., Order of B.C.; recipient Outstanding Alumnae award Simon Fraser U., 1985, Disting. Alumni Svc. award, 1995, Bus. Women of Yr. award Vancouver YWCA, 1986, West Vancouver Achievers award, 1987, B.C. Entrepreneur of Yr. award, 1987, Nat. Vol. award, 1990, Can. Woman Entrepreneur B.C. award, 1992, Queen's Jubilee medal, 2003, Clan Leader award Simon Fraser U., 2004. Home: 2206 Folkestone Way #3 West Vancouver BC Canada V7S 2X7 E-mail: brae@sfu.ca.

RAEDER, MYRNA SHARON, lawyer, educator; b. N.Y.C., Feb. 4, 1947; d. Samuel and Estelle (Auslander) R.; m. Terry Oliver Kelly, July 13, 1975; children: Thomas Oliver, Michael Lawrence. BA, Hunter Coll., 1968; JD, NYU, 1971; LLM, Georgetown U., 1975. Bar: N.Y. 1972, D.C. 1972, Calif. 1972. Spl. asst. U.S. atty. U.S. Atty's Office, Washington, 1972-73; asst. prof. U. San Fransisco Sch. Law, 1973-75; assoc. O'Melveny & Myers, L.A., 1975-79; assoc. prof. Southwestern U. Sch. Law., L.A., 1979-82, prof., 1983—, Irwin R. Buchalter prof. law, 1990, Paul E. Treusch prof. law, 2002; mem. faculty Nat. Judicial Coll., 1993—. Prettyman fellow Georgetown Law Ctr., Washington, 1971-73. Author: Federal Pretrial Practice, 3d edit., 2000; co-author: Evidence, State and Federal Rules in a Nutshell, 4th edit., 2003, Evidence, Cases, Materials and Problems, 2d edit., 1998. Recipient Ernestine Stahlhut award, Women Lawyers L.A., 2003. Fellow Am. Bar Found.; mem. ABA (trial evidence com. litigation sect. 1980—, criminal justice sect. 1994-97, vice-chair planning 1997-98, chair elect 1997-98, chair 1998-99, mem. mag. bd., 2000—, adv. to nat. conf. commrs. uniform state laws drafting com. uniform rules of evidence 1996-1999, Commn. Women in the Profession, Margaret Brent Women Lawyers of Achievement award 2002), Am. Law Inst., Assn. Am. Law Schs. (chair women in legal edn. sect. 1982, com. on sects. 1984-87, chair elect evidence sect. 1996, chair 1997), Nat. Assn. Women Lawyers (bd. dirs. 1991-98, pres.-elect 1993, pres. 1994-96), Women Lawyers Assn. L.A. (bd. dirs., coord. mothers support group 1987-96), Order of Coif, Phi Beta Kappa. Office: Southwestern U Sch Law 675 S Westmoreland Ave Los Angeles CA 90005-3905 E-mail: mraeder@swlaw.edu.

RAFFA, JEAN BENEDICT, author, educator; b. Lansing, Mich., Apr. 23, 1943; d. Ernest Raymond and Verna Lois (Borst) Benedict; m. Frederick Anthony Raffa, June 15, 1964; children: Juliette Louise, Matthew Benedict. BS, Fla. State U., 1964, MS, 1968; EdD, U. Fla., 1982. Tchr. Leon County Sch. Sys., Tallahassee, Fla., 1964-69; coord. children's programming WFTV, Orlando, Fla., 1978-80; cons. edn. Tchr. Edn. Ctr. U. Ctrl. Fla., Orlando, 1980-89; writer Orlando, Fla., 1989—; instr. Disney Inst., Orlando, Fla., 1996. Adj. instr. U. Cen. Fla., 1977-85; vis. asst. prof. Stetson U., DeLand, Fla., 1988-89; cons. Lang. Arts Curriculum Com. Orange County Sch. Sys., 1983; inst. The Jung Center, Winter Park, FL, 1997—. Author: Introduction to Television Literacy, 1989, The Bridge to Wholeness: A Feminine Alternative to the Hero Myth, 1992, Dream Theatres of the Soul: Empowering the Feminine Through Jungian Dreamwork, 1994; contbr. articles to profl. jours., articles and meditations to religious jours. Mistress of ceremonies Young Authors' Conf., Orange and Volusia County Sch. Sys., 1984-85; cons. Young Authors' Conf. Orange and Seminole County Sch. Sys., 1985-89; judge Volusia County Pub. Schs. Poetry Contest, 1983, 84, Seminole County Pub. Schs. Lit. Mag., 1985-89; pres. Maitland (Fla.) Jr. H.S. PTA, 1986-87; pres., bd. dirs. Canterbury Retreat and Conf. Ctr. Episcopal Diocese Ctrl. Fla., 1988-90; chair edn. commn. Episcopal Ch. of the Good Shepherd, 1986-89; sr. warden Vestry of Episcopal Ch. of the Good Shepherd, 1988. Mem. Kappa Delta Pi, Phi Delta Kappa. Democrat. Avocations: antiques, horseback riding, travel, reading. Office: 17 S Osceola Ave Ste 200 Orlando FL 32801-2828

RAFFINI, RENEE KATHLEEN, foreign language professional, educator; b. Racine, Wis., Mar. 10, 1955; d. John Peter and Clara Cecelia (Urli) R.; m. Anthony M. Yezer, Sept. 19, 1984 (div. 1997); children: Claire Eva, Benjamin Anton; m. Mark L. Whipple, June 26, 1999. BA in Econs. and French, U. Wis., 1976; MA in Econs., George Washington U., 1984, MEd, 1996. Cert. secondary edn. tchr. French and social studies, Md. Legis. aide to spkr. Wis. State Assembly, Madison, 1974-78; credit union advisor/auditor U.S. Peace Corps, Bafoussam, Cameroon, 1978-80; exec. aide George Washington U. Med. Faculty Assn., Washington, 1980-84; fin. economist U.S. Securities and Exch. Com., Washington, 1984-89; tchr. of French Bethesda (Md.) - Chevy Chase H.S., 1992-94; history tchr. French Internat. Sch., Bethesda, 1997; tchr. of French Walter Johnson H.S., Bethesda, 1994—. Sponsor Bethesda Comm. Action Team, 1995—; student mentor Walter Johnson H.S., 1994—; advisor U.S. Peace Corps Tchg. Forum, Washington, 1997. Judge of strokes and turns Montgomery County Swim League, Bethesda, 1997; vestry mem. Grace Episcopal Ch., Silver Spring, Md., 1996-97; active mem. Returned Peace Corps Assns., Washington, 1980—. Grantee Youth Rise, State of Md., Annapolis, 1996-97, Neighborhood Empowerment, Rockville, Md., 1996-97. Mem. Am. Coun. Tchrs. of Fgn. Langs., Am. Econs. Assn., Am. Assn. Tchrs. of French, Les Francomeres (founder 1992—), Les Compagnons de la Parole Française, Friends of Cameroon. Democrat. Avocations: sailing, tennis, photography, camping. Office: Walter Johnson HS 6400 Rock Spring Dr Bethesda MD 20814-1913

RAFFLES, LINDA N. secondary school educator; b. New Britain, Conn., June 14, 1948; d. Peter Anthony and Jacqueline Ann Negrini; m. David Anthony Raffles, Sept. 15, 1978 (div. Oct. 1992); children: Anthony, Sara. BA in Math., Ctrl. Conn. State U., 1970, MS in Math., 1972. Math. tchr. Gideon Welles Middle Sch., Glastonbury, Conn., 1970—90, Glastonbury H.S., 1990—. Prof. U. Conn., West Hartford, 1999—; cons. State Dept. Edn., Hartford, 1988—; summer sch. tchr., W. Hartford, Conn., 2000—; cons. Gulf States Project, 2003; pvt. tutor. Author: (textbook) Stepping Stone Math, 1988, Math Connections, 1993. Recipient Presdl. Award in Math., 1987. Fellow: Acad. Nat. Coun. Tchrs. Math. (publicity chair 1995); mem.: Assn. Tchrs. Math. in Conn. (publicity chair 1988). Avocations: crafts, travel, reading. Office: Glastonbury High Sch 330 Hubbard St Glastonbury CT 06033

RAFTER, TRACY, publishing executive; m. Michael Rafter; 1 child, Haley. With advt. sales mgr., Idaho; gen. mgr.; pub.; group pub. Taunton Daily Gazette and The Herald News, Fall River, Mass.; co-owner Valley Times, Milton-Freewater, Oreg., 1999—2002; sr. v.p. advt. and mktg. L.A. Newspaper Group, 2001—04; pub., CEO L.A. Daily News, 2004—. Office: LA Daily News 21221 Oxnard St POBox 4200 Woodland Hills CA 91365

RAGAN, AMANDA, state senator; b. Sept. 1954; m. James Ragan; children: Edith, Charles. Mem. Iowa State Senate, DesMoines, 2002—, asst. minority leader, ranking mem. human resources com., mem. agr. com., mem. econ. growth com., mem. rules and adminstrn. com., mem. state govt. com. Diplomat Mason City C. of C.; active Mason City Sesquicentennial Com.; mem. Birth Defects Adv. Bd., HAWK-I Bd.; bd. dirs. Buena Vista U. Alumni Assn.; active North Iowa Girl Scout Coun.; exec. dir. Meals on Wheels, Mason City, Cmty. Kitchen North Iowa, Inc., Mason City; active Iowa Dem. Party State Ctrl. Com.; bd. dirs. Kinney Pioneer Mus. Named Diplomat of Yr., Mason City C. of C., 1998, 2001. Mem.: Mason City Sunrise Rotary (bd. dirs.). Office: State Capitol Bldg East 12th and Grand Des Moines IA 50319 Home: 20 Granite Ct Mason City IA 50401

RAGAN, LISA CAROL, editor; b. Muncie, Ind., Oct. 30, 1967; d. Jack Ray and Elizabeth (McDowell) R. BS cum laude, Ball State U., 1990; MS in Social Work, U. Tenn., 2000. Editorial intern Good Housekeeping Mag., N.Y.C., 1989; editor Ideals mag., Nashville, 1993—98. Mem. ACLU. Democrat. Avocations: reading, writing, playing piano. Office: Ideals 535 Metroplex Dr Ste 250 Nashville TN 37211-3140

RAGANS, ROSALIND DOROTHY, textbook author, retired art educator; b. Bklyn., Feb. 28, 1933; d. Sidney Guy Gordon and Beatrice (Zuckerman) Safier; m. John Franklin Ragans, July 31, 1965; 1 child, John Lee. BFA, CUNY-Hunter Coll., 1955; MEd, Ga. So. Coll., 1967; EdD, U. Ga., 1971. Cert. tchr. art, Ga. Tchr. art Union City (N.J.) Bd. Edn., 1956-62, tchr. 1st grade Chatham Bd. Edn., Savannah, Ga., 1962-64; instr. art Ga. So. U., Statesboro, 1964-69, asst. prof., 1969-76, assoc. prof., 1976-89, prof. emeritus, 1989—. Keynote speaker art edn. confs., Ind., 1987, 88, Ark., Wis., 1989, Md., 1990, others; presenter GA Art Edn. Conf., 1998, 2000, NAEA, 1999. Author: (textbooks) ArtTalk, 1988, 2d edit., 1994, 3d edit., 1999, Introducing Art, 1997, Exploring Art, 1990, 2d edit., 1997, Understanding Art, 1990, 2d edit., 1997, (sr. author) Art Connections K-5, 1997, 2d edit., 2000. Mem. Nat. Assn. Educators (life), Ga. Assn. Educators (life), Nat. Art Edn. Assn. (Southeastern Art Educator of Yr. 1991, Nat. Art Educator of Yr. 1992), Ga. Art Edn. Assn. (Ga. Art Educator of Yr. 1990), Pilot Club Internat. (Ga. dist., Ga. Profl. Handicapped Woman of Yr. 1988). Jewish. Avocation: painting.

RAGAVAN, ANPALAKI JEYABALASINKHAM, software developer, researcher; arrived in U.S., 1992; d. George Nagularajah and Thangaranee Veluppillai Jeyabalasingham; m. Ragavan Vinasithamby, July 1, 1993. BS(hon.), U. Sri Lanka, 1985, MPhil (hon.), 1989; MS (hon.), U. Nev., 1996, MS in Environ. Engrng., student, U. Nev., 2003—. Cert. BASIC computer programmer, geographic info. sys., Visual Basic programmer, GIS and web design, well drilling with LS 100. Asst. prof. U. Sri Lanka, Kilinochchi, 1989—92; rsch. asst. Ind. State U., Tere Haute, 1992—93; software developer Bur. Labor Stats., Washington, 1996—99; rsch. asst. U. of Nev., Reno, 1999—. Grad. fellow U. Nev., Reno, 1993—96; presenter in field. Contbr. articles to profl. jours. (Excellence in Abstract Submission award Am. Jour. Pub. Health, 2001); author: (book) Introductory Statistics, Lab-Guide - SAS, 1st edition., 1993, (Nev. health divsn. quar. report) Impact Of Discharge Planning On Adherence to Treatment for Inmates with HIV/AIDS in Nevada, 2001, Surveillance Update: Discharge Planning For Inmates with HIV/AIDS in Nevada, 2002. Recipient Excellence in Abstract Submission, APHA, HIV/AIDS Sect., 2001, Cert. Of Appreciation, Nev. State Mental Health and Devel. Services, 2000, Overseas Devel. Adminstrn. scholarship, Govt. Of UK, 1986—89; grantee, State of Nev., 2002; scholar, Asian Inst. Of Tech. in Thailand, 1991, Ind. State U., 1992—93, U. of Nev., Reno, 1993—, Soroptimist Internat. of Reno, Sierra Nev. Region, 2000. Mem.: Am. Statis. Assn., Geol. Soc. Am., Alumni Assn. U. Nev. Mem. Lds Ch. Avocations: dance, music, guitar, swimming, sports. Office: U Nev Dept Internal Med Reno NV 89512 Personal E-mail: ragavan@unr.edu. Business E-Mail: ragavan@unr.edu.

RAGGI, REENA, circuit judge; b. Jersey City, May 11, 1951; BA, Wellesley Coll., 1973; JD, Harvard U., 1976. Bar: N.Y. 1977. U.S. atty. Dept. Justice, Bklyn., 1986; ptnr. Windels, Marx, Davies & Ives, N.Y.C., 1987; judge U.S. Dist. Ct. (Ea. dist.) N.Y., 2002, U.S. Ct. Appeals (2nd Cir.), N.Y.C., 2002—. Office: US Courthouse 225 Cadman Plz E Brooklyn NY 11201

RAGGIO, LOUISE BALLERSTEDT, lawyer; b. Austin, Tex., June 15, 1919; d. Louis F. and Hilma (Lindgren) Ballerstedt; m. Grier H. Raggio, Apr. 19, 1941; children: Grier, Thomas, Kenneth. BA, U. Tex., 1939; student, Am. U. Washington, 1939-40; JD, So. Methodist U., 1952. Bar: Tex. 1952, U.S. Dist. Ct. (no. dist.) Tex. 1958. Intern Nat. Inst. Pub. Affairs, Washington, 1939-40; asst. dist. atty. Dallas County, Tex., 1954-56; shareholder Raggio and Raggio, 1956—. Sec. Gov.'s Commn. on Status of Women, 1970-71; trustee Tex. Bar Found., 1982-86, chmn., 1984-85, chmn. fellows, 1993—, Dallas Women's Found., 1993—, Nat. Conf. Bar Founds., 1986-92. Recipient Zonta award, Bus. and Profl. Women's Club award, So. Meth. U. Alumni award, Woman of Yr. award Tex. Fedn. Bus. and Profl. Women's Clubs, 1985, award Internat. Women's Forum, 1990, Disting. Law Alumni award So. Meth. U., 1992, Disting. Trial Lawyer award, 1993, Outstanding Trial Lawyer award Dallas Bar Assn., 1993, Pacemaker award Nat. Bus. Women Owners Assn., 1994, Thomas Jefferson award ACLU, 1994, Courage award Women Journalists North Tex., 1995, Tex. Lawyer award 1999, Entrepreneur award Fortune Sm. Bus. Mag., 2000, Gillian award 2000, Professionalism award Dallas (Tex.) Bar, 2003; named to Tex. Women's Hall of Fame, 1985; named one of Heroes of Sm. Bus., Fortune Sm. Bus. Mag., 2000. Fellow Am. Bar Found.; mem. ABA (chmn. family sect. 1975-76, Best Woman Lawyer award 1995, Lifetime Achievement award 2002), LWV (pres. Austin 1945-46), State Bar Tex. (chmn. family law sect. 1965-67, dir. 1979-82, citation for law reform 1967, Pres.'s award 1987, Sarah T. Hughes award 1993, named one of 100 Tex. Lawyers of Century, 1999, 50 Yr. Lawyer award 2003), Dallas Bar Found. (pres. fellow com. 1991), Am. Acad. Matrimonial Lawyers (gov. 1973-81, trustee found. 1992—), Bus. and Profl. Women's Club (pres. Town North 1958-59), Phi Beta Kappa (pres. Dallas chpt. 1970-71, 90-92). Unitarian Universalist. Home: 3561 Colgate Ave Dallas TX 75225-5010 Office: Raggio and Raggio 3316 Oak Grove Ave Ste 100 Dallas TX 75204-2338

RAGINSKY, NINA, artist; b. Montreal, Apr. 14, 1941; d. Bernard Boris and Helen Theresa R.; 1 child, Sofya Katrina. BA, Rutgers U., 1962; studied painting with, Roy Lichtenstein; studied sculpture with, George Segal; studied Art History with Allan Kaprow, Rutgers U. Freelance photographer Nat. Film Bd., Ottawa, Ont., Can., 1963-81; instr. metaphysics Emily Car Coll. Art, Vancouver, B.C., Can., 1973-81; painter Salt Spring Island, B.C., 1989—. Sr. artist, jury Can. Coun.; selected Can. rep. in Sweden for Sweden Now Mag., 1979; tchr., lectr. in field, 1973—. One woman shows include Vancouver Art Gallery, Victoria Art Gallery, Edmonton Art Gallery, Art Gallery Ont., San Francisco Mus. Art, Acadia U., Nancy Hoffman Gallery, N.Y.C., Meml. U. Newfoundland Art Gallery; exhibited in group shows at Rutgers U., 1962, Montreal Mus. Fine Arts, 1963, Nat. Film Bd., Ottawa, 1964, 65, 67, 70, 71, 76, 77, Internat. Salon Photography, Bordeaux, France, 1968, Nat. Gallery Ottawa, 1968, Eastman House, Rochester, N.Y., 1969, Vancouver Art Gallery, 1973, 80, Mural for Conf. Ctr. Ottawa, 1973, Field Mus., Chgo., 1976, Edmonton Art Gallery, 1978, 79, Walter Philips Gallery, 1979, Glenbow Mus. Gallery, 1979, Harbour Front Community Gallery, 1980, Hamilton Art Gallery, 1980, Musée Maisil de St. Lambert, 1981, Mendel Art Gallery, 1981, Dunlop Art Gallery, Regina, Can., 1981, Vancouver Art Gallery, 2001; represented in permanent collections Nat. Film Bd. Stills divsn., Ottawa, Ont., Banff (Alta.) Sch. Fine Arts, Nat Gallery Ottawa, Can., George Eastman House, Rochester, NY, Wadsworth Atheneum, Conn., Edmonton Art Gallery, U. Victoria, B.C., various pvt. collections. Bd. dirs. Island Watch, Salt Spring Island, B.C., 1993; founder, coord. Salt Spring Island Ecosys. Stewardship Project, 1993; founder, coord. Salt Spring Island Waterbird Watch Collective, 1994—. Decorated officer Order of Can., 1984; recipient Kees Vermeer award for edn. and conservation Simon Fraser U., 1997. Mem.: Royal Can. Acad. Arts. Avocations: gardening, birding, subject of numerous publs. Home and Office: 272 Beddis Rd Salt Spring Island BC Canada V8K 2J1

RAGLAND, INES COLOM, principal; b. Washington, Mar. 12, 1947; d. Jose Luis Sr. and Frances Yerby (Pannill) Colom; m. Banjamin Michael Ragland, Dec. 17, 1977 (div. May 1991); children: Michelle Elizabeth, Rachael Christine. BA in Secondary Edn., Longwood Coll., 1969, MS in Secondary Adminstrn., 1992. Clk. Va. State Water Control Bd., Richmond, 1969; tchr. Spanish Richmond City Pub. Schs., 1969-74; planning supr. Va. State Water Control Bd., 1974-78; asst. prin., tchr., prin. Grove Ave. Bapt. Christian Sch., Richmond, 1978-83; guidance tchr., asst. prin. Victory Christian Acad., Richmond, 1990—. Cons. in field. Mission participant, El Salvador, 1992. Mem. ASCD. Avocations: civil war research, church. Office: Victory Christian Acad 8491 Chamberlayne Rd Richmond VA 23227-1550

RAGLAND, MARY RUTH, music educator; b. Charleston, SC, Mar. 23, 1947; d. Robert Davidson Harper and Ruth Jeanette Baker; m. Willis Leon Ragland; children: Montgomery Lee, Elizabeth Blair. BA in Music Edn., Columbia Coll., 1968; MA in Integrated Studies, Cambridge Coll., Boston, 2000. Music tchr. Georgetown County Bd. Edn., Andrews, SC, 1968—70, 1974—; cons., tchr. trainer continuing progress for Williamsburg County U. SC, 1970—74. Music dir. Trinity United Meth. Ch., Andrews, 1968—73; dir. music ministries, music tchr. Duncan Meml. United Meth. Ch., Georgetown, SC, 1993—; music tchr. Andrews Elem. Sch.; instr. Coastal Carolina Coll., Georgetown, 2001—; dir. cmty. handball choir, Andrews, 1982—88; music dir. SC Laity Convention, Lakd Junaluska, 1997, SC Meth. Ann. Conf., Spartanburg, 1998; organizer, dir. Bible sch. for Spanish speaking children, Costa Rica, 2003; co-dir arts festival Andrews Pub. Schs., 1986—89. Bd. dirs. Georgetown County Arts Coun., Georgetown, 1988—95; mem. fundraising com. for children's wing Georgetown Hosp., Georgetown County, 1986—87; entertainment organizer hospice ann. Christmas festival, Georgetown County, 1997—99. Mem.: Nat. Music Educators. Methodist. Avocations: gardening, needlework, music. Home: 300 Atlantic Ave Pawleys Island SC 29585 Office: Duncan Meml United Meth Ch 901 Highmarket Georgetown SC 29440

RAGO, ANN D'AMICO, university official, public relations professional; b. Pitts., Aug. 24, 1957; d. Jack and Florence D'Amico; m. John Rago; children: Annie J., Emily J., John Henry. BA, Duquesne U., Pitts., 1979, MA, 1987. From comm. assoc. to dir. pub. rels. Duquesne U., 1979—89, coord. univ. rels., 1989—93, adj. prof. comm., 1990—2000, exec. dir. pub. affairs, 1993—2002; v.p. instnl. rels. Carlow Coll., Pitts., 2002—. Editor University Record, 1989 (silver medal). Bd. dirs. Support, Pitts., 1989-91; sch. dir. Carylnton Sch. Bd., Pitts., 1989-93, pres. sch. bd., 1990. Recipient Gold award for publs./external prospectus 9th Ann. Admissions Advt. Awards, 1994, Gold award for Total Pub. Rels. Campaign, 10th Ann. Admissions Advt. Awards, 1995, Gold award for Total Pub. Rels. Campaign, 11th Ann. Admissions Awards, 1996, 1st Place award in Category 35, Internal Pub. Rels. Campaign, Pitts. chpt. Women in Comm., Inc., 1996, Bronze Cert. for logo and letterhead for Duquesne U.'s Capital Campaign and cert. merit for Duquesne U.'s internal publ. 14th Ann. Admissions Advt. Awards, 1998, Clarion award Assn. for Women in Communications, 2003. Mem. Pub. Rels. Soc. Am. (1st place award 1993), Internat. Assn. Bus. Communicators (award of excellence 1991, award of honor 1993, award of merit 1994), Am. Mgmt. Assn., Assn. for Women in Comm. (Clarion award 2003), Press Club Western Pa., Sigma Delta Chi. Office: Carlow Coll Institutional Relations 3333 Fifth Ave Pittsburgh PA 15213 E-mail: arago@carlow.edu.

RAGO-MCNAMARA, JULIET MAGGIO, artist; b. Chgo., Mar. 21, 1927; d. Henry Clifford and Grace (Canadeo) Maggio; m. Henry A. Rago, Oct. 7, 1950 (dec. 1969); m. Robert J. McNamara, Aug. 14, 1973 (dec. 1995); children: Christina, Carmela, Anthony, Martha. BFA, Sch. of Art Inst., Chgo., 1950; MFA, Sch. of Art Inst., 1973; postgrad., Accademia di Belli Arti, Florence, Italy, 1960-61, Vt. Studio Sch., 1988, Putney Painting Intensive, Vt., 1990. Prof. fine arts Loyola U. Chgo., 1969—; art instr. Barat Coll. of Sacred Heart, Lake Forest, Ill., 1970-71. Solo sculpture shows include U. Ill. Med. Ctr., 1978, Loyola U., Chgo., 1979; group sculpture shows include Evanston Art Ctr., 1987, Nina Owen Gallery, Chgo., 1987; solo painting exhbns. include Kerrigan-Hendricks Gallery, Chgo., 1954, Devorah-Sherman Gallery, Chgo., 1963, 65, Rosary Coll., River Forest, Ill., 1970, Wabash Transit Gallery, Sch. Art Inst., Chgo., 1973, Evanston Art Ctr., 1977, Cloud Hands Gallery, Chgo., 1978, Northwestern U., Chgo., 1983, 84, Sykes Gallery, Lancaster, Pa., 1987, Lawrence Perrin Gallery, Chgo., 1989, Space 900, Chgo., 1992, Chgo. Cultural Ctr., 1993, Gallery 1933, 1994, Lincoln Pub. Libr., 1995, many others; group painting shows include Renaissance Soc. Christmas Shows, 1953-69, Old Orchard Art Fair, Skokie, Ill., 1979, Chgo. Bot. Gardens, Glencoe, Ill., 1985, Ill. Arts Coun. Gallery, Chgo., 1986, Assisi, Italy, 1989, Gallery 1933, 1990, 90, Lincoln Pub. Libr., 1994, Fine Arts Gallery, Chgo., Ill., 2002, Lincoln (Mass.) Pub. Libr., 2003, Emerson Umbrella, Concord, Mass., 2003, others; and pvt. collections. Fellow Yaddo Found., 1971, Skowhegan Sch. Painting, 1972, Va. Ctr. Creative Arts, 1986, Vt. Studio Found., 1987, Ragdale Found., 1987, The Ucross Found., 1988, Byrdcliffe Art Colony, 1991, 92; grantee Ill. Arts Coun., 1979. Mem. Coll. Art Assn. (mem. women's caucus). Avocations: piano, guitar, singing, choirs. Home: 1555 Sherman Ave # 231 Evanston IL 60201-4421

RAGSDALE, ANN F. state representative; b. Wilkes-Barre, Pa., June 4, 1936; married; children: JoAnn, Fran, Bridget. Attended, Front Range C.C. State rep. dist. 35 Colo. Ho. of Reps., Denver, mem. local govt. and transp. and energy coms. Chmn., 2 terms Adams County (Colo.) Dem. Party; mem. Jud. Dist. 17 Victims Compensation Bd.; adv. bd. Adams County Libr. Mem.: Women in Govt., Downtown Dem. Forum, Ad-Dems Club, Dem Fems. Democrat. Roman Catholic. Avocations: sewing, crafts, cross country skiing, reading, furniture refinishing. Office: State Capitol # 357 200 E Colfax Ave Denver CO 80203

RAGSTER, LAVERNE E. academic administrator; b. St. Thomas, Virgin Islands; BS in Biology and Chemistry, U. Miami, 1973; MS in Biology, San Diego State U., 1975; PhD in Biology, U. Calif., San Diego, 1980. Pres. U. Virgin Islands, St. Thomas, asst. prof. then prof., 1980—90, chair divsn. sci. math., sr. v.p., provost. Trustee U. Virgin Islands, St. Thomas, acting v.p. rsch. land grant affairs, v.p. rsch. pub. svc.; sub-sec. gen. Assn. Caribbean Univs. Rsch. Insts.; coord. Consortium Caribbean Univs. Natural Resource Mgmt. Contbr. articles to profl. jours. Mem.: Caribbean Coun. Sci. Tech. (rep. U.S. Virgin Islands), Nature Conservancy (bd. dirs.), Island Resources Found. (bd. dirs.), Caribbean Conservation Assn. (past v.p.), Caribbean Natural Resources Inst. (bd. dirs., past chair bd. dirs.), Caribbean Studies Assn. (past pres.). Office: Office of Pres U Virgin Islands 2 Hohn Brewers Bay St Thomas VI 00802-9990

RAGUSA, ELYSIA, real estate company executive; V.p. Lincoln Property Co.; pres. S.W. corp. svcs. The Staubach Co., Addison, Tex., pres., COO. Grad. Leadership Dallas; assoc. mem. Dallas Citizens Coun.; bd. dirs. Dallas County C.C. Found., Vis. Nurse Assn.; bd. mem. United Way Met. Dallas, former chmn. ctrl. budget com., former mem. exec. com. Mem.: Internat. Women's Forum, Dallas Breakfast Group. Office: The Staubach Co Ste 400 15601 Dallas Pkwy Addison TX 75001

RAGUSA, KAREN ANN, music educator; b. Buffalo, Mar. 27, 1961; d. Edward Anthony and Antoinette (Parisi) Russo; m. John Ragusa, July 7, 1995; children: Brian Sebastian Weinzler, Allison Leigh, Angela Marie. MusB, SUNY Fredonia, 1979—83; EdM, U. Buffalo, 1990—92. Cert. tchr. NY, 1983, Fla., 1983. Music tchr. Greenglade Elem. Sch., Miami, Fla., 1983—86, Dr. John Hugh Gillis Sch., Antigonish, Canada, 1987—88, St. Amelia's Sch., Tonawanda, NY, 1989—90, Starpoint Ctrl. Sch., Lockport, 1991—. Guest conductor Niagara All County Elem. Band. Dir.: (guest conductor) Niagara All County Elem. Band. Mem.: NCMEA (assoc.). Office: Starpoint Central School Dist 4363 Mapleton Road Lockport NY 14094

RAGUSA, OLGA MARIA, retired Italian language educator; b. Catania, Italy, Feb. 11, 1922; came to U.S., 1932; d. Andrea and Anna (von Weiskopf) R. BA summa cum laude, Hunter Coll., 1943; MA, Columbia U., 1947, PhD, 1954. Instr. French and German Rutgers U., Newark, 1946-47; instr. Italian Vassar Coll., Poughkeepsie, N.Y., 1949-52; asst. prof. Columbia U., N.Y.C., 1955-61, assoc. prof., 1961-65, prof., 1965-79, Da Ponte prof. Italian, 1979—2002, chmn. dept., 1973-92; ret., 2002. Co-owner, editor S.F. Vanni (book dealers), 1974—; mem. exec. coun. MLA, 1972-75; mem. selection com. Am. Coun. Learned Socs., 1976-80; mem. area adv. com. for Western Europe, Coun. Internat. Exchange Scholars, 1983-86.

Author: Mallarmé in Italy: Literary Influence and Critical Response, 1957, Verga's Milanese Tales, 1964, Narrative and Drama: Essays in Modern Italian Literature from Verga to Pasolini, 1976, Pirandello: An Approach to His Theatre, 1980; editor: Romance Section: Italian, Columbia Dictionary of Modern European Literature, 1980; editor Italica jour., 1968-84; mem. editorial bd. European Womens Writers Series, U. Nebr. Press, 1984—; contbr. numerous articles, revs. to Am. and European publs. Recipient Disting. Svc. award Am. Assn. Tchrs. of Italian, 1990; Fulbright fellow U. Milan, Italy, 1958-59, Am. Coun. Learned Socs. fellow, 1971-72; decorated knight Order of Merit (Italy), 1982 Mem. Phi Beta Kappa. Roman Catholic. Home: 30 W 12th St New York NY 10011-8635

RAHBAR, ZITA INA, insurance company executive; b. Kaunas, Lithuania, Mar. 15, 1937; arrived in U.S., 1949; d. Stasys and Ona (Eitkeviciute) Carneckas; m. Vytautas Dudenas, June 20, 1960 (div. 1965); m. Darius Rahbar, Mar. 26, 1970. BA, St. Xavier U., Chgo., 1957; postgrad., U. Chgo., 1957-59, MBA, 1978. Mng. editor Lyons & Carnahan divsn. Meredith Corp., Chgo., 1960-68; exec. cons. George S. May Co., Chgo., 1973-75; mgr. program planning Blue Shield Assn., Chgo., 1975-76; dir. corp. planning Blue Shield/Blue Cross Assn., 1976-78, sr. dir. program devel. & implementation, 1978-81; v.p. mktg. Blue Cross Calif., L.A., Oakland, 1981-87; pres. Creative Mktg. Solutions, 1987—, CMS Automotive Inc., 1992—99. Bd. dirs. Bethune Ballet, L.A., 1982—, Wellnes Cmty. Valley, Ventura, Calif., 1999—. Fellow U. Chgo., 1957—58. Mem.: NOW, AAAS, World Affairs Coun. L.A., Chgo. Coun. Fgn. Rels., Town Hall Calif., Women in Pub. (co-foudner 1965), Orgn. Women Execs. (com. mem. 1982—), Am. Mktg. Assn., Am. Mgmt. Assn. Republican. Roman Catholic. E-mail: zic@gte.net.

RAHE, PEGGY ANN, realtor; b. Cin., Oct. 5, 1951; d. William Thomas and Shirley Lee (Court) Sheff; m. Charles Albert Rahe, Sept. 11, 1970; children: Julie Ann, Jennifer Lynn. Office mgr. Creative Promotions, Cin., 1970-80; photographer proprietorship Cin., 1977-85, realtor Keyes Gateway, Inc., Dayton, Ohio, 1985—2002. Mem. T.W.I.G.-Terrific Women in Giving Children's Med. Ctr., Dayton, Ohio, 1984-2000. Recipient Ohio Assn. of Realtors award for 1985-2000, Dayton Area Sales Leader award, 1985-2002. Mem. Dayton Area (Ohio) Bd. Realtors, Cir. Excellence Club, Keyes Gateway Pres. Club, Women's Coun. of Realtors (pres.-elect Dayton chpt. 2000-01). Avocations: roller skating, photography, camping, hiking, traveling. Home: 767 Valleyview Pt Springboro OH 45066 Office: Real Living Realtors 7575 McEwen Rd Centerville OH 45459

RAHEJA, KRISHNA KUMARI, retired medical/surgical nurse; b. Muzzaffargarh, India; d. R.R. and Sharda (Devi) Relan; m. B.D. Raheja, Apr. 29, 1956; children: Dalip, Nishtha. Diploma, Lady Hardinge Hosp., New Delhi, India, 1952; BA, Punjab U., 1954; MS in Nursing, Syracuse U., 1967; EdS, No. Ill. U., 1986; EdD, Northern Ill. U., 1988; PhD, Columbia Pacific U., 1987. Cert. transcultural nurse. Staff nurse, head nurse Lady Hardinge Med. Coll. Hosp. New Delhi, New Delhi, India, 1952-54, 54-56, clin. specialist, lectr., 1956-66; assoc. head. dept. All India Inst. Med. Scis., New Delhi, India, 1967-70; asst. prof. Alfred (N.Y.) U., 1970-71; asst. prof. Coll. of Nursing U. Ill., Chgo., 1971-80; asst. prof. Ctr. for Nursing Northwestern U., Chgo., 1980-90; assoc. prof. St. Xavier U., Chgo., 1989-2000; ret., 2000. Clin. nursing cons. U. Ill. Hosp. Ambulatory Svcs., Chgo., summer 1971; adj. faculty Northpark U., 1992—. Contbr. articles to profl. jours. Recipient Best Tchr. of the Yr. award, 1984, Internat. Transcultural Excellence award Transcultural Nursing Soc., 1999; named to Sigma Theta Tau Omicron Chpt. Mem. ANA, Ill. Nurses Assn., Transcultural Nursing Soc. (treas.), Transcultural Nursing Assn. Internat. Home: 758 Lilac Way Lombard IL 60148-3641 Office: Saint Xavier Univ 3700 W 103rd St Chicago IL 60655-3105

RAHM, MARY ELLEN, statistical clerk; b. Middletown, Ohio, Apr. 15, 1940; d. John Russel and Evelyn Brockamp McDermott; m. Herbert William Rahm Jr., Dec. 28, 1963; children: Evala Rahm Bailey, Herbert William III, John Anthony, Edward Joseph. BA, Ursuline Coll., 1962; MEd, U. Louisville, 1969. Primary tchr. Jefferson County Bd. Edn., 1962-66, substitute tchr., 1966-79; owner, operator J. H. Brockamp Advt. Specialties, 1966-70; with Stevens Rsch., 1979-88; office mgr. Janet McIntyre DMD, 1988-89; statistical clk. U.S. Census Bur., 1989—; part time owner, outside sales rep. Travel Profl. Internat. Mem. Meadow Heights Womens Club, Ascension Cath. Ch. in Louisville, Ascension Womens Club, Ascension PTA, tchr. Confraternity of Christian Doctrine, 1969-72; brownie and jr. leader Girl Scouts Kentuckiana Coun., 1972-76; active Boy Scouts, Old Ky. Home Coun.; coach Upper Highlands Swim Club; dem. judge, 1992; leader parent group 12 step program, 1988-90; aerobic tchr. Walking Program for Sr. Citizens, 1987-97; vol. usher Ky. Ctr. for the Arts, 1989—; fund raiser for Booklawn A Substance Treatment Ctr. for Teens, 1985. pres. Neuropathy Support Group of Louisville, 2003-. Recipient cert. appreciation Ky., Ind. Girl Scout coun., Jefferson County Bd. Elections; Mary Ellen Rahm grantee; cert. achievement Cencus Quality Mgmt., named in Outstanding Women Am., 1971. Mem. AAUW (pres. 1977-81, many other offices state and br. divsn.), Young Execs. Specialty Advt. Assn., Meadow Heights Women Club, Kentuckiana Swim Offls. Avocations: bridge, bunco, gourmet cooking. Home: 2404 Sir Johns Ct Louisville KY 40220-1055

RAHM, SUSAN BERKMAN, lawyer; b. Pitts., June 25, 1943; d. Allen Hugh and Selma (Wiener) Berkman; m. David Alan Rahm, Nov. 23, 1972; children: Katherine, William. BA with honors, Wellesley Coll., 1965; postgrad., Harvard U., 1966-68; JD, NYU, 1973. Bar: N.Y. 1974, D.C. 1988. Assoc. Marshall, Bratter, Greene, Allison & Tucker, N.Y.C., 1973-81, ptnr., 1981-82, Kaye Scholer, LLP, N.Y.C., 1982—, ptnr. chair real estate dept., 1993-98; chair internat. practice group Kaye Scholer, LLP, N.Y.C., 1999—. N.Y. adv. bd., Chgo. Title Ins. Co., 1995. Editor: New York Real Property Service, 1987. Bd. dirs. Girls Inc., 1989-93; mem. aux. bd. Mt. Sinai Hosp., N.Y.C., 1976-78. Recipient cert. of outstanding svc. D.C. Redevel. Land Agy., 1969, She Knows Where She's Going award Girls' Clubs of Am., 1987, Woman of Yr. award CREW.NY, 1999. Mem. ABA, Assn. Bar City N.Y., N.Y. Bar Assn. (real property law com., co-chmn. real-estate devel. . 1987-91), Am. Coll. Real Estate Lawyers, WX formerly known as Comml. Real Estate Women N.Y. (bd. dirs. 1988-94, v.p. 1988-91, pres. 1991-93), Assn. Fgn. Investors in Real Estate, Assn. Real Estate Women (Outstanding Achievement award 2003). Office: Kaye Scholer LLP 425 Park Ave New York NY 10022-3506

RAHMAN, YUEH-ERH, biologist; b. Kwangtung, China, June 10, 1928; came to U.S., 1960; d. Khon and Kwei-Phan (Chan) Li; m. Aneesur Rahman, Nov. 3, 1956; 1 dau., Aneesa. BS, U. Paris, 1950; MD magna cum laude, U. Louvain, Belgium, 1956. Clin. and postdoctoral research fellow Louvain U., 1956-60; mem. staff Argonne (Ill.) Nat. Lab., 1960-72, biologist, 1972-81, sr. biologist, 1981-85; prof. pharmaceutics Coll. Pharmacy, U. Minn., Mpls., 1985—, dir. grad. studies, pharmaceutics, 1989-92, head dept. pharmaceutics, 1991-96, 97-98. Vis. scientist State U. Utrecht, Netherlands, 1968-69; adj. prof. No. Ill. U., DeKalb, 1971-85; cons. NIH.; Mem. com. of rev. group, div. research grants NIH, 1979-83 Author; patentee in field. Recipient IR-100 award, 1976; grantee Nat. Cancer Inst., Nat. Inst. Arthritis, Metabolic and Digestive Diseases. Fellow Am. Assn. Pharm. Scientists; mem. AAAS, Am. Soc. Cell Biology, N.Y. Acad. Scis., Radiation Rsch. Soc., Assn. for Women in Sci. (1st pres. Chgo. area chpt. 1978-79). Unitarian Universalist. Home: 939 Coast Blvd Unit 6G La Jolla CA 92037-4115 Office: Coll Pharmacy U Minn Minneapolis MN 55455

RAHMANI, LORETTA HARDIE, university administrator; b. Burbank, Calif., Dec. 9, 1955; d. Alexander Simpson and Marie Virginia (Kaczmaryn) Hardie; m. Ali Mossaver Rahmani, Oct. 28, 1989. BA, San Diego State U., 1979, MS, 1982; EdD, U. LaVerne, 1994. Coord. residential life Calif. State U., Northridge, 1983-87, asst. dir. housing, 1987-88; asst. mgr. housing UCLA, 1988-89; asst. dean of students U. LaVerne, Calif., 1989-94, assoc. dean of students, 1994-95, dean of student affairs, 1995—. Co-founder Kaleidoscope Leadership Cons., LaVerne, 1995; small coll. network chair NASPA, 1994-95, chair exec. com. Southern Calif. NASPA, 1998—; sec. Cacuho, 1987-88, v.p. 1988-89. Office: U LaVerne 1950 3rd St La Verne CA 91750-4401

RAHMS, BEATRIX ANNA, accountant, artist; b. Oldenburg, Germany, June 17, 1963; came to U.S., 1969; d. Brigitta Maria (Rahms) Terry; m. Eric Scott Castaline, Aug. 15, 1992 (div. Dec. 1996); 1 child, Britta Anne. BA in Mktg., U. South Fla., 1986, BA in Acctg., 1993. Credit mgr. Hyatt Regency Tampa, Fla., 1982-87; computer operator, promotional advisor Carl T. Watkins, CPA, Tampa, 1984-87; reservation sales agt., counselor WORLDSPAN Travel Agy. Info. Svcs./N.W. Airlines, Inc., Kansas City, Mo., 1987-90; sr. staff acct. Associated Marine Inst., Inc., Tampa, 1992-94; sr. acct. Carl T. Watkins, CPA, Tampa, 1990—. Republican. Roman Catholic. Avocations: art, travel, weight lifting/physical exercise.

RAHN, SAUNDRA L. councilwoman; b. Elgin, Ill., Jan. 10, 1936; d. Leonard Herman and Alvina Elizabeth Leetzow; m. Eugene Maurice Rahn, June 25, 1955; children: Connie, Gregory, Pamela. Grad. H.S., Elgin. Councilwoman, Bradenton, Fla., 1970-74, 79-89, 1990-91, 96—. City rep. Nat. Assn. Regional Planning Coun., 1982-84, mem. housing and met. com., 1985-90; city rep. Manatee County Transit Adv. Bd., 1986-90; rep. Ward 5, Bradenton City Coun., 1995-99, met. planning orgn., 1995-97, fire dept. liaison, 1995-97, fin. dept. chmn., 1997-98, pub. works liaison, 1998-99. Pres., lifetime mem. Jr. Woman's Club, Bradenton, 1964; chmn. Tampa Bay Regional Planning Coun., 1973-74, 84, apptd. city rep., 1995-99, legis. chmn., 1999; vice mayor City of Bradenton, 1973, 84; v.p. Sr. Woman's Club, Bradenton, 1989; bd. mem., legis. lobbyist Fla. Regional Planning Coun., 1996-99; rep. City Art League, 1999. Mem. Nat. League Cities (fin., adminstrv. intergovtl. rels. policy com. 1998-99), Fla. League Cities (city rep. intergovtl. rels. com. 1984-90, city rep. fin. and taxation com. 1987-90, intergovtl. rels. com. 1995-97, fin. and taxation com. 1998-99), Woman's Club. Avocations: dance, bowling, gardening, family activities. also: PO Box 25015 Bradenton FL 34206-5015

RAIKHEL, NATASHA V. plant cell biology educator; b. Jan. 11, 1947; MS, Leningrad State U., 1970; PhD, Inst. Cytology, Acad. Scis., Leningrad, 1975. Rschr. Acad. Scis., Inst. Cytology, Leningrad, 1970—75, asst. rsch. scientist lab. cytology of unicellular organisma, 1975—78; postdoctoral assoc. dept. botany U. Ga., Athens, 1979—84, asst. rsch. scientist dept. botany, 1984—86; from asst. prof. to assoc. prof. to prof. Mich. State U., MSU-DOE Plant Rsch. Lab. and Dept. Botany, East Lansing, 1986—94, univ. disting. prof., 1997—2000; Ernst and Helen Leibacher chair prof. plant molecular, cell biology and genetics dept. botany and plant scis. U. Calif., Riverside, Calif., 2001—, dir. Ctr. for Plant Cell Biology dept. botany and plant scis., 2001—, Disting. prof. plant cell biology dept. botany and plant scis., 2001. Sabbatical leave U. Melbourne, Australia, 1996, Nagoya (Japan) U., 1996; mem. adv. panel on Alzheimer's DiseaseUSDA, 92; mem. adv. panel NSF, 1994—97; co-organizer NATO-ASI Course, Maratea, Italy, 1997, 22d Symposium in Plant Biology, 2003. Mem. editl. bd.: Plant Physiology, 1988—92, Jour. Cell Biology, 1995—2000, editor-in-chief: Plant Physiology, 1997—, mem. editl. bd.: Current Opinion in Plant Cell Biology, 1998—. Recipient Guggenheim fellowship, 1996, Fellowship for Rsch. in Japan, 1996. Mem.: Internat. Soc. for Plant Molecular Biology (bd. dirs. 2001), Am. Soc. for Plant Physiologists (mem. publ. com. 1992—93, mem. exec. com. 1996—99), Am. Soc. for Cell Biology (program com. mem. 1998—2000). Office: U Calif Riverside Dept Botany and Plant Scis 2109 Batchelor Hall Riverside CA 92521-

RAIL, KATHY LYNN PARISH, accountant; b. Chewelah, Wash., May 21, 1951; d. John Edward and Margaret Irene (Seefeldt) Rail. BBA, Gonzaga U., 1984. CPA, Wash. Legal sec. Redbook Pub. Co., N.Y.C., 1974-75, Howard Michaelson, Esquire, Spokane, Wash., 1975-76; sec. Burns Internat. Security Svcs., Spokane, 1977-79; sec. to contr. Gonzaga U., Spokane, 1979-81, acctg. asst., 1981-82; staff acct. Martin, Holland & Petersen, CPA's, Yakima, Wash., 1984-87; acct., supr. Strader Hallet & Co., P.S., Bellevue, Wash., 1988-91; acct. Miller & Co., P.S., Woodinville, Wash., 1991-93; pres. Parish Rail, CPA, P.S., Redmond, Wash., 1993—. Treas. White Pass Ski Patrol, Nat. Ski Patrol Systems, Wash., 1987-90; editor, chmn. audit com. Mt. Spokane Ski Patrol, 1983-84. Mem. AICPA, Am. Soc. Women Accts. (charter, editor 1987), Wash. Soc. CPA (sec. Sammamish Valley chpt. 1990-92, pres. 1992-93, 93-94), Washington Soc. of Cert. Pub. Accts. (chair adv. coun. 1995-96, tax com., govt. affairs com., dir. 1996-98), Bus. and Profl. Women of Woodinville (treas. 1994-95), Carnation C. of C. Lutheran. Avocations: snow skiing, piano, golfing.

RAINBOW, DEE DEE, retired art educator, sculptor; b. Seattle, Sept. 3, 1932; d. Cedric Marshall and Edna Beatrice (Lowe) Wardall; m. Peter Opilman Raible (div.); children: Steve Marshall, Robin Starr, Robert Ray, Deborah René. Student, San Francisco (Calif.) State U., 1952, R.I. Sch. Design, 1953; BA in Edn., U. Nebr., 1960. Cert. tchr. Wash. Reservations agent United Airlines, San Francisco, 1951; head art dept. Seattle (Wash.) Pub. Schs., 1964—93, tchr. art, 1964—93. Head childrens sculpture program Seattle (Wash.) Pks. Dept., 1962—70; founder U. Unitarian Fine Arts Gallery Seattle (Wash.) Unitarian Ch., 1963. Editor: Nebr. Newsletter, 1954; dir.: (tile work) Madrona Pk. Water Garden, 1972, (stained glass windows) U. Unitarian Ch., 1968; exhibitions include R.I. Sch. Design Gallery, Henry Gallery, Seattle, Wash., Tacoma (Wash.) Art Mus., Kunstlerhaus Place, Berlin, Germany, Giverney Gallery at Ashleys, Gresham, Oreg., Reid Galleries, Carmel, Calif., one-woman shows include Wing Luke Asian Mus., Seattle, Wash., Represented in permanent collections Ella Fitzgerald's pvt. collection. Recipient Nora award, Madrona Cmty. Coun., 1996, Tribute award, Wash. Art Edn. Assn., 2003. Democrat. Unitarian. Avocations: jazz, dance, theater. Home: 1704 36th Ave Seattle WA 98122

RAINE, MELINDA L. library manager; b. Boston, Feb. 4, 1951; d. James Agee and Marjorie Elizabeth (Gilstrap) Raine; m. Stephen Richard Brogden, Jan. 1, 1983; 1 child, Nathan Raine Brogden. BA, U. Iowa, 1973, MA, 1974. Info. specialist Pub. Libr. Des Moines, 1974-82, libr. mgr., 1982-90; task force coord. Visio 2020 Project, Conejo Future Found., Thousand Oaks, Calif., 1991-92; mgr. engring. libr. Metters Industries, Camarillo, Calif., 1992-94; govt. publs. libr. Pepperdine U., Malibu, Calif., 1994-98, coord. info. resources, 1998—. Author: Options for Our Endangered Environment, 1992, Water: Liquid Gold, 1992, The Housing Crisis, 1992, Solid Ideas for Solid Waste, 1992; co-author (with Elizabeth parang and Trisha Stevenson): Redesigning Freshman Seminar Library Instruction Based on Information Competencies in Research Strategies, 2001. Mem. ALA, AAUW (pub. policy chair 1993-96, v.p. programming 1992-93), Calif. Libr. Assn., Calif. Acad. and Rsch. Librs. Office: Pepperdine U 24255 Pacific Coast Hwy Malibu CA 90263-4786

RAINER, LUISE, actor; b. Vienna, Jan. 12, 1910; Appeared in films Ja, der Himmel uber Wien, 1930, Sehnsucht 202, 1932, Heut kommt's drauf an, 1933, Wenn die Musik nicht war, 1935, Escapade, 1935, The Great Ziegfeld, 1936 (Oscar award for Best Actress 1936), The Good Earth, 1937 (Oscar award for Best Actress 1937), The Emperor's Candlesticks, 1937, Big City, 1937, The Toy Wife, 1938, The Great Waltz, 1938, Dramatic School, 1938, Hostages, 1943, La Dolce vita, 1960, The Gambler, 1997; appeared in TV series Schlitz Playhouse of Stars, 1952, Lux Video Theatre, 1953, Suspense, 1954, Combat!, 1965, The Love Boat, 1983, (TV film) A Dancer, 1988.*

RAINER, RENATA URBACH, artist, photographer, educator; b. Vienna, May 20, 1928; came to the U.S., 1940; d. Robert and Lola (Finkelstein) Urbach; m. George F. Rainer, Feb. 6, 1949; childen: Nina H. Price, Andrew A. Rainer. BA cum laude, CUNY, 1949; MA cum laude, Columbia U., 1967. Cert. art specialist grades K-12, N.Y. Graphic designer Newsweek mag., 1949-52; freelance graphic designer N.Y.C., 1952-65; art specialist Irvington Pub. Schs., N.Y., 1968; art specialist grades K-8 Pocantico Hills Pub. Sch., Sleepy Hollow, N.Y., 1968-71; adj. asst. prof. Marymount Coll., Tarrytown, N.Y., 1980-90; adj. assoc. prof. studio art and photography Manhattanville Coll., Purchase, NY, 1990—2001. Advisor Pelham (N.Y.) Art Ctr. Gallery, 1980-90, Rye (N.Y.) Arts Ctr. Gallery, 1994—; lectr. art history SUNY, Purchase, 1982-85; spkr. N.Y. Coun. for the Humanities, 1988-90, 2003—; artist-in-residence Westchester Pub. Schs., 1990-94. Solo exhbns. include Bridge Gallery, White Plains, N.Y., 1981, Butler Gallery-Marymount Coll., Tarrytown, 1984, Hewlett Packard, Palo Alto, Calif., 1986, Hudson River Mus., Yonkers, N.Y., 1988, Benham Gallery, Seattle, 1997, Wainwright House, Rye, N.Y., 1997, Luchsinger Gallery, 1999, Greenwich Acad., Conn., 1999, Brownson Gallery, Manhattanville Coll., Purchase, N.Y., 2004; curator 150 Years of American History by American Photographers, Pelham Art Ctr., N.Y., 1989, The Feminine Focus: Photographs of Women and Women Who Photograph, Greenburgh Town Hall, Elmsford, N.Y., 1991, Photography Now: Facts and Fantasies, Rye (N.Y.) Arts Ctr., 1994, 95, Of Time and the River, Hastings (N.Y.) Gallery, 1995, Pelham Arts Ctr., 1995, Faces, Through the Lens: Time, Space and Matter, Rye Arts Ctr., 1998, Photography: Intimate Encounters, the Mentoring Relationship, Rye Art Ctr., 2002; exhibited in group shows at Hopkins Ctr., Hanover, N.H., 1976, Hudson River Mus., Yonkers, 1977, Bridge Gallery, White Plains, 1978, Focal Point Gallery, City Island, N.Y., 1980, Fig Tree Gallery, Fresno, Calif., 1980, River Gallery, Irvington, N.Y., 1981, Pace U. Gallery, Briarcliff, N.Y., 1982, Photographics Gallery, New Canaan, Conn., 1984, Mus. Gallery, White Plains, 1985, Sarah Lawrence Coll., Bronxville, N .Y., 1988, Katonah (N.Y.) Gallery, 1988, Candace Perich Gallery, Katonah, 1997, Brownson Gallery, Purchase, N.Y., 1990-2000, Gallery on the Hudson, Irvington, 1998, Paramount Ctr. for the Arts, Peekskill, N.Y., 1999, Westchester Biennial 2000, Castle Gallery, Coll. New Rochelle, N.Y., 2000, Bridgewater/Lustberg & Blumenfeld, N.Y.C., 2000, Westchester Arts Coun. Gallery, 2001, Westchester C.C., Valhalla, N.Y., 2002; included in Imaging the River (The Hudson River Mus., 2003-04) Black & White Photography Manifest Visions, 2000, In the Mind's Eye, 2004; pub. collections include Libr. Rsch. Ctr. Nat. Mus. Women in Arts, Washington, 1990, Boca Raton Mus. Art, Fla., 1992, Lyndhurst Nat. Trust Hist. Preservation, Tarrytown, N.Y., 1996, Neuberger Mus. Art, Purchase, N.Y., 2000, Pfizer Art Coll., Purchase, 2000, Metromedia Fiber Network Hdqrs., White Plains, 2001, The Hudson River Mus., Yonkers, N.Y., 2002, Harry Ransom Humanities Rsch. Ctr., U. Tex., Austin. Recipient Hist. Svcs. award for excellence Lower Hudson Conf. Hist. Agys. and Mus., 1988, No. Westchester Ctr. for the Arts award Mt. Kisco, 2000, All-Star award Assn. for Women in Comms., 2003; grantee N.Y. Coun. for the Humanities, 1988, 2003. Mem. The Ground Glass (founder, past pres.), Photog. Adminstrs., Inc. Avocations: hiking, gardening, cross country skiing. Home: 11 Cottontail Ln Irvington NY 10533-1011 E-mail: grainer153@aol.com.

RAINES, CHARLOTTE AUSTINE BUTLER, artist; b. Sullivan, Ill., July 1, 1922; d. Donald Malone and Charlotte (Wimp) Butler; m. Irving Isaack Raines, Sept. 26, 1941; children: Robin Raines Collison, Kerry Raines Lydon. BA in Studio Arts magna cum laude, U. Md., 1966. One-woman show at Castle Theatre, 1988, C.T.V. Awards Hall, Md., 1993; exhbd. in numerous group shows including Corcoran Gallery, 1980, Md.'s Best Exhbn., 1986, Md. State House, 1990, four-artist video documentary, 1992, U. Md. Univ.-Coll. Gallery, 1996; artist publ. cover Writers' Ctr., 1997, Md. State House Print Exhbn., 1999, Washington Women Artists Millenium Show, 2001, Md. State Ho. Complex, 2003; represented in various pvt. collections and permanent collection at U. Md. Univ.-Coll.; selected works in U.S. Dept. State Arts in Embassies Program; contbr. poems to lit. publs. Mem. Artists Equity Assn., Writers' Ctr., Phi Kappa Phi. Avocations: piano, jogging, gardening. Office: 4103 Longfellow St Hyattsville MD 20781-1748

RAINES, JUDI BELLE, language educator, historian; b. N.Y.C., July 16, 1955; d. Alfonso Don Raines and Belle Margarite Samuels. BA in Elem. Edn., Adelphi U., 1977, MA in Secondary Edn., 1981; MS in Guidance, St. Johns U., 2000. ESL tchr. Lincoln Farm Camp, Roscoe, NY; project leader Operation Crossroads, Anguilla, B.W.I., 1981; English tchr., sr. activities advisor Andrew Jackson H.S., Jamaica, NY, 1981—83; history and art tchr., step team advisor Magnatech Jr. H.S. 231, Jamaica, NY, 1985—97; English tchr., dorm supr. project Double Discovery Upward Bound, Queens Coll., Columbia Univ. and Queens Coll., 1989—93; English tchr., dean, step team advisor August Martin H.S., Jamaica, NY, 1997—; adj. instr. SAT prep. CUNY, Jamaica, 1999—; guidance counselor Flushing H.S. Step advisor N.Y.C. Bd. End.; adj. instr. Coll. Now, York Coll., 2000—02. Dir. chorus Ctrl. Bklyn. Model Cities, 1976—77. Recipient Marva Collins Award, cmty. award, 2000, Editors Choice award, 2000—03, Project Prize Educator, Flushing HS, 2002, Gear Up (counselor), 2003. Mem.: ACA, Guilder Lehrman Tchrs. Inst. Avocations: poetry, chess, swimming, quilt making, computers. Office: Flushing High Sch 35-01 Union St Flushing NY 11354

RAINES, KAREN CORNELL, secondary school educator; b. Columbus, Ohio, Dec. 12, 1956; d. Stanley Buel and Ruth Ellen Cornell; m. Roger Dale Raines, July 5, 1980; children: Mary Katherine, Sandra Beth. MusB, W.Va. U., 1979, MMus, 1983; tchg. cert., William Carey Coll., Gulfport, Miss., 1996. Cert. tchr., Miss. Choral dir. Grace Luth. Ch., Long Beach, Miss., 1992-94, Christ United Meth. Ch., Long Beach, 1994-98; tchr. music Waveland (Miss.) Elem. Sch., 1996-98, North Bay Elem. Sch., Bay St. Louis, Miss., 1996-99; tchr. choral music Robert Smalls Mid. Sch., Beaufort, S.C., 1999—. Mem. dist. curriculum com. Bay/Waveland Schs., Bay St. Louis, 1997-99. Mem. choirs performing at Carnegie Hall, N.Y.C., 1997, internat. choral competition, Verona, Italy, 1999. Mem. Music Educators' Nat. Conf. Democrat. Methodist. Avocations: reading, community choral groups. Home: 109 Lakewood Dr Guyton GA 31312-6562 Office: Robert Smalls Mid Sch 43 W K Alston Dr Beaufort SC 29906-9432

RAINES, SHIRLEY CAROL, academic administrator; b. Jackson, Tenn., Apr. 15, 1945; m. Robert J. Canady; 1 stepchild, Brian Scott Smith. BS, U. Tenn., Martin; MS, EdD, U. Tenn., Knoxville; grad. mgmt. program, Harvard Grad. Sch. of Edn. Dept. head Northeastern State U, 1983—87; assoc. prof. edn. George Mason U., Fairfax, Va., 1987—92; prof. and chmn. dept. of childhood/ lang. arts/ reading U. South Fla., 1992—95; prof. U. Ky. Coll. of Edn., 1995—2001, vice chancellor academic svcs. and dean of coll., 1998—2001; pres. U. Memphis, 2001—. Author books; contbr. articles to profl. jours. Recipient Dist. Svc. to Edn., Phi Delta Kappa, Dist. Paper awards, Ednl. Rsch. Assn. Office: U Memphis 341 Adminstrn Bldg Memphis TN 38152*

RAINES, TAMI JO, principal; b. West Union, Ohio, Mar. 10, 1974; d. Michael David and Carolyn Sue Scott; m. Gregory Alan Raines, July 27, 1996. BS in Social Sci., Shawnee State U., 1995; MA in Ednl. Leadership, U. Dayton, 1998. Tchr. elem. sch. Peebles Elem. Sch., Ohio, 1996—2000; prin. Mt. Orab Elem. Sch., 2000—. Mem.: Reading Recovery, Ohio Assn. Elem. Adminstrs. Home: 80 Rothwell Rd Seaman OH 45679 Office: Western Brown Schs 474 W Main Mount Orab OH 45154 E-mail: tamiraines@yahoo.com.

RAINEY, JEAN OSGOOD, public relations executive; b. Lansing, Mich., Apr. 5, 1925; d. Earle Victor and Blanche Mae (Eberly) Osgood; m. John Larimer Rainey, Nov. 29, 1957 (dec. Oct. 1991); children: Cynthia, John Larimer, Ruth. Grad., Lansing Bus. U., 1942. Pub. rels. dir. Nat. Assn. Food Chains, Washington, 1954-59; v.p. pub. rels. Manchester Orgns., Washington, 1959-61; ptnr. Rainey, McEnroe & Manning, Washington, 1962-73; v.p. Manning, Selvage & Lee, Washington, 1973-79, pres. Washington div., 1979-84, sr. counsellor, 1985; owner Jean Rainey Assocs., Washington, 1986-87; sr. v.p. Daniel J. Edelman Inc., 1987-96; owner Jean Rainey Assocs., Washington, 1996—. Chmn. bd. Windward Mortgage, 1997—2001. Author: How to Shop for Food, 1972. Pres. Hyde Home and Sch. Assn., Washington, 1969-71; co-chmn. Nat. Adv. Com. for Reelection of the Pres., 1972; chmn. bd. trustees St. John's Presch., 1996-99, vice chair, 2003-; pres. Sherwood Forest Endowment Fund, 1995-97; adminstr. A Few Good Women-Advancing the Cause of Women in Govt., 1969-74, 97—; bd. dirs. Westchester Corp., 2001-04. Mem. Internat. Women's Forum, Pub. Rels. Soc. Am. (accredited, Hall of Fame 1999), Am. Women in Radio and TV (pres. Washington chpt. 1962-63, mem. nat. bd. 1963-65), Am. News Women's Club (pres. 1973-75) Clubs: City Tavern. Republican. Episcopalian. Home: 4000 Cathedral Ave NW Apt 250B Washington DC 20016-5279 Office: PO Box 251 Main Lobby W 4000 Cathedral Ave NW Washington DC 20016-5249 E-mail: jorainey@aol.com.

RAINEY, SUSAN J. school system administrator; m. Jack Rainey; 1 child, Jordan. BA, MA, U. Redlands; PhD, U. So. Calif. Tchr. Moore Jr. H.S., Redlands Unified Sch. Dist.; tchr. Palo Alto, Calif., Yucaipa H.S., 1972—76, dir. activities, 1976—78; asst. prin. Monrovia H.S.; h.s. prin. Brea, Calif.; asst. supt. for adminstrv. svcs. Helmet Unified Sch. Dist., asst. supt. for personnel svcs., assoc. supt.; supt. Charter Oak Unified Sch. Dist., Covina, Calif., 1991—98; sutp. Riverside Unified Sch. Dist., 1998—. Office: Riverside Unified Sch Dist 3380 14th St Riverside CA 92501*

RAINVILLE, ANNA MARY, elementary school educator; b. San Jose, Calif., Apr. 3, 1954; d. Willys Irvine and Betty Ruth (Wesson) Peck; m. Donald Rainville, Apr. 21, 1985 (div. Dec. 1996); children: Sarah, Merina. BA, U. Calif., Santa Cruz, 1976; MA, Adelphi U., 1979. Cert. tchr. Mills Coll., Calif., 1978. Tchr. Saratoga (Calif.) Cmty. Garden, 1974—76; summer sch. tchr. Rudolf Steiner Sch., N.Y.C., 1979; Waldorf class tchr. Waldorf Sch., Lexington, Mass., 1979—86; enrichment tchr./aid Saratoga Union Sch. Dist., 1986—87; kindergarten tchr. Lakeside Sch., Los Gatos, Calif., 1987—2000; Waldorf class tchr. Waldorf Sch. of the Peninsula, Los Altos, Calif., 2000—. Instr. Summer Inst. Rudolf Steiner Coll., Fair Oaks, Calif., 1987—; co-founder, dir. Kindergarten Forum, Saratoga, 1989—; dist. art coord. Lakeside Joint Sch. Dist., 1999—2000. Musician: wind and wood musical ensemble. Bd. dirs. Raise the Children in Villages and Faith, 2000—. Mem.: Calif. Kindergarten Assn. (Audrey Sanchez Tchr. Enhancement award 2002), Waldorf Kindergarten Assn. N.Am., Nat. Kindergarten Alliance (bd. mem. 2000—), Elle Lisant Book Club. Office: Waldorf Sch of the Peninsula 11311 Mora Dr Los Altos CA 94024

RAINWATER, JOAN LUCILLE MORSE, investment company executive; b. Chattanooga, Mar. 5, 1943; d. Robert Ora and Alma Lucille (Miller) M.; m. Percy Raymond Rainwater (div. 1987); children: Karen Sue, Steven Jay, Robin Rae, Linda Sue. Student, John Robert Powan Sch. Design, 1977-78, Corcoran Sch. Art, 1985-86, Nova U., 1980, 85, 87. Co-owner Rainwater Concrete, Lorton, Va., 1962-87, Undertaking Gallery, Occoquan, 1977-80; cons. in art edn. Occoquan Elem. Sch., Woodbridge, Va., 1969-73; owner Riverside Gallery, Occoquan, 1980-84, Joamen Investments, Occoquan, 1985—. Author: (poems) At Waters Edge, 1995. Founding mem. Hist. Occoquan, 1970, Women's Mus., Washington; pres., v.p. Woodbridge Art Guild, 1980-82. Recipient numerous awards for paintings, various juried shows Washington area, 1977-87. Mem. Unity Ch. Avocations: hiking, reading, esoteric studies. Office: Rainwater Investments 611 Queen St Alexandria VA 22314-2514

RAIZEN, SENTA AMON, educational administrator, researcher; b. Vienna, Oct. 28, 1924; came to U.S., 1940; d. John and Helen (Krys) Amon; m. Abraham A. Raizen, Apr. 18, 1948; children: Helen S., Michael B., Daniel J. BS, Guilford Coll., 1944; MA, Bryn Mawr, 1945; Tchr. Cert., U. Va., 1960. Rsch. chemist Sun Oil Co., Norwood, Pa., 1945-48; rsch. asst. NAS, Washington, 1960-62; assoc. program dir. NSF, Washington, 1962-69, spl. asst., 1969-72; sr. researcher The Rand Corp., Washington, 1972-74; assoc. dir. Nat. Inst. Edn., Washington, 1974-78; ind. cons. Washington, 1978-80; study dir. NAS, Washington, 1980-88; dir. Nat. Ctr. for Improving Sci. Edn., Washington, 1988—. Cons. Nat. Ctr. for Edn. Stats., Washington, 1987—, Ednl. Testing Svc., Princeton, N.J., 1988—, Nat. Goals Panel, Washington, 1990-2000, Third Internat. Math. and Sci. Study, Internat. Assn. Evaluation Ednl. Achievement, The Netherlands, 1990—, SRI Internat., 1998—, Orgns. for Econ. Cooperation and Devel., Paris, 1998—. Contbr. articles to profl. jours., encys., books, reports in field. Pres. Cooperative Nursery Sch., Arlington, Va., 1953-57; leader Brownies, Girl Scouts, U.S. and Cub Scouts, Boy Scouts, Am., Arlington, 1958-64. Recipient Disting. Lifetime award WestEd, 2000; grantee NSF, U.S. Dept. Edn., U.S Dept. Energy, pvt. founds., 1988-2000, fellowship for grad. study NSF, 1944-45, Meritorious Svc. award, 1968, The Network Pres.' award, 1991. Fellow AAAS; mem. Am. Chem. Soc., Am. Ednl. Rsch. Assn. Avocations: dance, swimming, reading, knitting, stitchery, grandchildren. Home: 5513 31st St N Arlington VA 22207-1532 Office: Nat Ctr Improving Sci Edn 1726 M St NW Ste 704 Washington DC 20036-4524

RAJKUMAR, ROSHINI ANNE, reporter; b. Colombo, Sri Lanka, Nov. 6, 1970; arrived in U.S., 1972; d. Rajadurai and Concy Rajkumar. BA, Boston Coll., 1993; JD, U. Minn., 1997. Reporter KVLY-TV, Fargo, ND, 1998—99, KCCI-TV, Des Moines, 1999—2000, WTVF-TV, Nashville, 2000—02, KMSP/WFTC-TV, Mpls., 2002—. Mem.: NATAS, Minn. State Bar Assn., Investigative Reporters and Editors, Minn. Women Lawyers, Asian Am. Journalists Assn. Avocations: travel, photography, movies. Office: KMSP/WFTC 11358 Viking Dr Minneapolis MN 55344

RAKER, IRMA, judge; b. Bklyn. m. Samuel K. Raker. BA, Syracuse U., 1959; cert. of attendance (hon.), Hague (The Netherlands) Acad. Internat. Law, 1959; JD, Am. U., 1972. Bar: Md. 1973, D.C. 1974, U.S. Dist. Ct. Md. 1977, U.S. Ct. Appeals (4th cir.) 1977. Asst. state's atty. State's Atty.'s Office of Montgomery County, Md., 1973-79; ptnr. Sachs, Greenebaum & Tayler, Washington, 1979-80; judge Dist. Ct. Md., Rockville, 1980-82, Cir. Ct. for Montgomery County, Md., 1982-94, Ct. of Appeals of Md., 1994—. Adj. prof. Washington Coll. Law, Am. U., 1980—; mem. faculty Md. Jud. Inst., Nat. Criminal Def. Inst., 1980, 81, 82; instr. litigation program Georgetown Law Ctr.-Nat. Inst. Trial Advocacy; mem. legis. com. Md. Jud. Conf., mem. exec. com., 1985-89, mem. commn. to study bail bond and surety industry in Md.; mem. spl. com. to revise article 27 on crimes and punishment State of Md., 1991—; mem. inquiry com. atty. Grievance Commn. Md., 1978-81; chairperson jud. compensation com. Md. Jud. Conf., 1997—. Past editor Am. U. Law Rev. Treas., v.p. West Bradley Citizens Assn., 1964-68; mem. adv. com. to county exec. on child abuse Montgomery County, 1976-77, mem. adv. com. to county exec. on battered spouses, 1977-78, mem. adv. com. on environ. protection, 1980; mem. citizens adv. bd. Montgomery County Crisis Ctr., 1980. Recipient Robert C. Heeney award Md. State Bar Assn., 1993, Dorothy Beatty Meml. award Women's Law Ctr., 1994, Rita Davidson award Women's Bar Md., 1995, Margaret Brent Trailblazers award ABA Commn. on Women in the Profession/Women's Bar Assn. Md., 1995, Elizabeth Dole Woman of Achievement award ARC, 1998, Leadership in Law award The Daily Record, 2001, Nat. Assn. Social Workers' Pub. Citizen of Yr. award, 2001, others; named of Md.'s Top 100 Women Warfield's Bus. Record, 1997, 99, 2001. Fellow Md. Bar Found.; mem. ABA (chair criminal justice stds. com. 1995-96, mem. coun. criminal law sect. 1997—, del. nat. conf. state trial judges, active various coms.), Md. State Bar Assn. (chair coun. criminal law and practice sect., mem. bd. govs. 1981, 82, 85, 86, 90, mem. coun. litigation sect., active coms., chair com. to draft pattern jury instrns. in civil and criminal cases 1980—), Nat. Assn. Women Judges, Internat. Acad. Trial Judges, Am. Law Inst., Montgomery County Bar Assn. (chair criminal law sect. 1978-79, mem. exec. com. 1979-80, active other coms., Outstanding Jurist award 2000), Montgomery County Bar Leaders, Women's Bar Assn. Md., Women's Bar Assn. D.C., Hadassah Women's Orgn. (life), Pioneer Women Na'amat (Celebration of Women award 1985), Pi Sigma Alpha. Office: Ct of Appeals of Md 50 Maryland Ave Rockville MD 20850-2320

RAKO, SUSAN, psychiatrist, author; b. Springfield, Mass., Sept. 4, 1939; d. Robert and Ann (Melnikoff) Mandell; 1 child, Jennifer Sarah. Student, Wellesley Coll., 1957-60; BS, U. Cin., 1961; MS in Film, Boston U., 1988; MD, Albert Einstein Coll. Medicine, 1966. Med. rsch. asst. neuroendocrinology Worcester Found. Exptl. Biology, Shrewsbury, Mass., 1959; med. rsch. asst. May Inst., Cin., 1961-62; intern in medicine, surgery Mt. Auburn Hosp., Cambridge, Mass., 1966-67; resident in adult psychiatry Mass. Mental Health Ctr., Boston, 1967-69; tchg. fellow in psychiatry Harvard Med. Sch., Boston, 1967-69, clin. fellow in psychiatry, 1969-70; pvt. practice Newton, Mass., 1970—; clin. instr. psychiatry Harvard Med. Sch., Boston, 1970-75; resident in child and adult psychiatry Beth Israel Hosp., Boston, 1969-70; psychiatrist Mass. Mental Health Ctr., Boston, 1970-77, Newton-Wellesley Hosp., 1982. Cons. Cutler Counseling Ctr., Norwood, Mass., 1983, VA Hosp., San Juan, P.R., 1990-94; spkr. in field. Author: No More Periods? The Risks of Menstrual Suppression, 2003; The Hormone of Desire: The Truth About Testosterone, Sexuality, and Menopause, 1996, 2d edit., 1999, No More Periods? The Risks of Menstrual Suppression, 2003; co-editor: Semrad: The Heart of a Therapist, 1980, (paperback) 2004; film maker Susan and Jenni, 1987. E-mail: susanrako@aol.com.

RAKOV, BARBARA STREEM, marketing executive; b. Bklyn., Jan. 4, 1946; d. Harold B. and Claire (Colbert) Streem; m. Harris J. Rakov, Nov. 20, 1970 (div. Mar. 1972). BS, Boston U., 1967; postgrad. NYU, 1972-74. Market rsch. analyst, product mgr., mktg. mgr. J.B. Williams, N.Y.C., 1967-77; mktg. dir. Del Labs., Farmingdale, N.Y., 1977-78; product mgr., sr. product mgr., asst. to office of pres., dir. mktg. and sales Benelux countries, v.p. group mktg., dir., dir. new products, v.p. bus. devel. Joseph E. Seagram & Sons, 1978-90; pres. BSR Assocs., N.Y.C., 1990-92; v.p. mktg. Del Labs., 1992-94; v.p. mktg. Tsumura Internat., Secaucus, N.J., 1994-96; v.p. mktg. Franco Mfg. Co., Inc., Metuchen, N.J., 1996—. Mem. L'Ordre des Coteaux de Champagne, Les Gastronomes de la Mer, Am. Mgmt. Assn. Avocations: tennis, skiing, squash, reading, water skiing. Home: 415 E 52d St New York NY 10022-6424 Office: Franco Mfg Co Inc 555 Prospect St Metuchen NJ 08840-2271

RAKOW, LANA F. communications educator, humanities educator; b. Valley City, N.D., Apr. 17, 1952; d. William Frederick Rakow and Vera Miranda Angeline Alinder; m. Tony John Stukel, July 1, 1978; children: Caitlin Stukel Rakow, Jack William Rakow Stukel. BA, U. N.D., 1974, MA, 1977; PhD, U. Ill., 1987. News coord. U. N.D., Grand Forks, 1974—75, prof. comm. and women's studies, 1994—, dir. Sch. Comm., assoc. dean Coll. Fine Arts and Comm., 1994—96, coord. Experiential Learning Project, 2000—; dir. pub. info. Minn. Ins. Info. Ctr., Mpls., 1977—78; consumer and cmty. rels. coord. Wausau (Wis.) Ins. Cos., 1978—81; asst. prof. Franklin Coll., 1981—83; asst. and assoc. prof. U. Wis.-Parkside, Kenosha, 1986—94, chair comm. dept., 1990—92, assoc. vice chancellor for undergrad. studies, 1992—94. Mem. Accrediting Coun. on Edn. in Journalism and Mass Comm. Author: Gender on the Line: Women, the Telephone, and Community Life (Book of Yr., Orgn. for Study of Comm., Lang. and Gender, 1993); editor: The Revolution in Words: Righting Women 1868-1871, Women Making Meaning: New Feminist Directions in Communication. Chair comm. com. Grand Forks C. of C., 2000—02. Fellow Spkrs.' grantee to South Korea, USIA, 1997; grantee Women of Color in the Curriculum Project, Ford Found. and U. Wis. Sys., 1989; Spotlight scholar Feminist and Women's Studies Divsn., Nat. Comm. Assn., 1997, Wis. Tchg. fellow, U. Wis. Sys., 1989—90. Mem.: N.D. Profl. Communicators (pres. 2002—04), Internat. Comm. Assn. (co-founder, co-chair Feminist Scholarship Interest Group 1985—87), Assn. Edn. in Journalism and Mass Comm. (chair Com. on Status of Women 1987—89, pres., v.p., sec. tchg. stds. com. 1997—2003), Rotary (chair pub. rels. com. 1997—2001), Phi Beta Kappa. Democrat. Avocation: justice for women and human rights work. Home: 539 Terrace Dr Grand Forks ND 58201 Office: U ND Box 7169 Grand Forks ND 58202 E-mail: lana.rakow@mail.und.nodak.edu.

RALEIGH, JEAN W, museum staff member; b. Newport News, Va., Aug. 24, 1944; d. John B White and Verice Mae; m. Edward Raleigh, Apr. 15, 1968; children: Lloyd, Carolyn. BS, Longwood U., Farmville, VA, 1962—66. Tchr. Alfred I. du Pont Spl. Sch. Dist., Wilmington, Del., 1966—71, Internat. Sch., Geneva, Switzerland, 1979—80; owner Petals, Wilmington, Del., 1984—86; mus. guide Winterthur Mus., Winterthur, Del., 1986—. Bd. mem. People to People, Del. Chpt., Wilmington, Del., 1999—. Registrar Nat. Soc. Col. Dames, Del., 2001—04.

RALPH, LEANN RAE, writer, editor; b. Eau Claire, Wis., Aug. 5, 1958; d. Roy Arthur and Norma Irene Halvorson Ralph; m. Randall Carl Simpson, June 28, 1992. Student, U. Wis., Whitewater, 1985—87, MA in Tchg., 1992. Cert. tchr. Wis., 1992. Reporter The Janesville (Wis.) Gazette, 1987—90; grad. asst. U. Wis., Whitewater, 1990—91; substitute tchr. Whitewater, Jefferson, Ft. Atkinsin Sch. Dists., Wis., 1992—94; English tchr. Whitewater Sch. Dist., 1995—95, Northwestern Mil. and Naval Acad., Lake Geneva, Wis., 1994—95; reporter The Dunn County News, Menomonie, Wis., 1998—98; staff writer The Colfax (Wis.) Messenger and The Glenwood City (Wis.) Tribune Press Reporter, 1998—2003; freelance writer, 2003—. Author: (nonfiction book) Christmas In Dairyland, essays. Choir mem. Norton Luth. Ch., Colfax, Wis., 1997—2003. Mem.: Wis. Regional Writers' Assn. (editor 2001—), Phi Kappa Phi. Home and Office: E6689 970th Ave Colfax WI 54730-4711 Personal E-mail: bigpines@ruralroute2.com.

RALPH, NANCYJO, music educator; d. Alfred M. and Phyllis L. Niles; m. Dwight G. Ralph, Mar. 28, 1970; children: Victoria L. Fortna, Erik C. MusB in Edn., Grove City Coll., 1969; M in Elem. Edn., Edinboro U. Pa., 1974; postgrad. in Music Edn., Kent State U., 1989. Registered music educator. Elem. music tchr. Lakeview Sch. Dist., Sandy Lake, Pa., 1969; h.s. music tchr. Cambridge Springs (Pa.) H.S., Penncrest Sch. Dist., 1970—2000, elem. music tchr., 2000—. Choir mem., pianist, various com. Saegertown (Pa.) United Meth. Ch., 1970—2003; dir. Justified By Faith, Saegertown, 2002—. Mem.: Pa. Music Educators Assn. (curriculum and instrn. chair dist. 2 1993—2003), Pa. State Edn. Assn. (alt. profl. rights and responsibilities commn. 2001—04), Penncrest Area Edn. Assn. (assoc.; v.p. 1982—84, negotiator 1982—86, pres. 1984—86, negotiator 2000—01, v.p. 2001—02, pres. 2001—03). Methodist. Avocations: music, reading, painting. Home: 17768 Grange Center Rd Saegertown PA 16433-4506 Office: Cambridge Springs Elem Sch 130 Steele St Cambridge Springs PA 16403 E-mail: nralph@penncrest.iu5.org.

RALSTIN, BETTY LOU, religious organization administrator; b. Stanford, Ky., Dec. 29, 1935; d. Eugel Harris Anderson and Elizabeth Ella Campbell; m. John Edward Wasson, Aug. 24, 1954 (div.); 3 children ; m. Paul Edward Ralstin, June 23, 1984. Grad. h.s., Manilla, Ind., 1953. Cert. notary Ind., Tenn., Fla. Tax preparation Rafferty & Wood Law Office, Shelbyville, Ind., 1955—61; tax auditing Milligan & Burke Assoc., Orlando, Fla.; sec. GE, Shelbyville, 1955—64; acct. William S. Lee CPA, Orlando, 1965—66; office mgr. Milligan & Burke CPAs, Orlando, 1965—66; controller Hallmark Constrn. Co., Orlando, 1966—72; bookkeeper and tax cons. Laurel, Ind., 1972—86; antique and gift shop owner B's Enterprise, Laurel, 1985—89; supr. Book Market, Knoxville, Tenn., 1992—94; portrait cons. United Photographic Industry, Galion, Ohio, 1994—95; 3rd key Foozles, Crossville, Tenn., 1996—97; adminstr. and sec. Lantana Rd. Bapt. Ch., Crossville, 1997—. Named Mrs. Eagle of Yr., FOE 2036, 1985—86. Baptist. Avocations: gardening, travel, going to flea markets, church activities, making baskets. Home: 33 Will Cir Crossville TN 38555 Office: Lantana Rd Baptist Church 3332 Lantana Rd Crossville TN 38572

RALSTON, BARBARA JO, bank executive; b. Youngstown, Ohio, Apr. 11, 1940; d. Fred Kenneth and Juanita Ruth (Welch) Roof; m. Donald Gene Ralston, Jan. 9, 1960; children: Mark David, Lori Sue. Cert., Pacific Coast Banking Sch. U. Wash., Seattle, 1981; AA in fin., Maricopa County CC. Sec. Bank of Scottsdale, Ariz., 1962-66; adminstrv. asst. Talley Industries, Mesa, Ariz., 1966-73; asst. mgr. Continental Bank, Phoenix, 1973-77; exec. v.p. Continental Bank Service Corp., Phoenix, 1977-85, pres., dir., 1985—86; chmn., pres. to sr. v.p. electronic and convenience banking to exec. v.p. personal banking group Chase Bank of Ariz., exec. v.p., COO; exec. v.p., mgr. northeast Ariz. retail area First Interstate Bank, 1994—95, Phoenix area pres., 1995—96; sr. v.p., mgr. in-store banking Wells Fargo Bank, Ariz., 1996—97; founder, pres., CEO Camelback Cmty. Bank, Phoenix, 1998—. Pres. Ariz. Bus. Leadership. Bd. dirs. Valley Big Bros.-Big Sisters, Phoenix, 1986; mem. Ariz. Acad., Phoenix, 1984; treas. Phoenix Together Town Hall, 1986; chair Am. West Airlines Edn. Found.; immediate past chair, Fresh State Women's Found.; past chair Ariz. Town Hall; past internat. pres. Financial Women Internat. Recipient You Too Can Make A Difference award Valley Christian Ctrs., Phoenix, 1985. Mem. Nat. Assn. Bank Women (state pres. 1981-82), Am. Inst. Banking (state edn. chmn. Ariz. chpt. 1984), Tumbleweed (pres. 1983); Am. Bankers Assn. (state membership chair for Ariz., chair ABA Edn. Found, 2003-), Ariz Bankers Assn. (bd. dirs., 2001-03, pres., 2001-02. Lodges: Soroptimists (pres. 1982, Women Helping Women award 1984). Republican. Methodist. Avocations: reading, travel, sewing. Office: Camelback Cmty Bank 2777 E Camelback Rd Ste 100 Phoenix AZ 85016*

RALSTON, JOANNE SMOOT, public relations executive; b. Phoenix, May 13, 1939; d. A. Glen and Viriginia (Lee) Smoot; m. W. Hamilton Weigelt, Aug. 15, 1991 (dec.). BA in Journalism, Ariz. State U., 1960. Reporter The Ariz. Rep., Phoenix, 1960-62; co-owner, pub. rels. dir. The Patton Agy., Phoenix, 1962-71; founder, pres., owner Joanne Ralston & Assocs., Inc., Phoenix, 1971-87, 92—. Pres. Nelson Ralston Robb Comm., Phoenix, 1987—91, Joanne Ralston & Assocs., Inc., Scottsdale, 1991—, Kapaau, Hawaii, 2000—. Contbr. articles to profl. jours. Bd. dirs. Ariz. Parklands Found,. 1984-86, Gov.'s Coun. on Health, Phys. Fitness and Sports, 1984-86; mem. task force Water and Natural Resources Coun., Phoenix, 1984-86; mem. Hawaii Gov.'s Adv. Bd., 2003—, others. Recipient Lulu awards (36) L.A. Advt. Women, 1964—, Gold Quill (2) Internat. Assn. Bus. Communicators, Excellence awards Fin. World mag., 1982-93, others; named to Walter Cronkite Sch. Journalism Hall of Fame, Coll. Pub. Programs Ariz. State U., 1987; named one of 25 Most Influential Arizonians, Phoenix Mag., 1991. Mem. Pub. Rels. Soc. Am. (counselor sect.), Internat. Assn. Bus. Communicators, Phoenix Press Club (pres. bd.), Investor Rels. Inst., Phoenix Met. C. of C. (bd. dirs. 1977-84, 85-91), Rotary Internat. Republican. Avocations: horses, dog training. Address: PO Box 808 Kapaau HI 96755-0808

RALSTON, SARAH LUCILLE, veterinarian, educator; b. Elyria, Ohio, Apr. 11, 1951; BA, U. Pa., Phila., 1973, VMD, 1980, PhD, 1983; MS, Colo. State U., 1976. Diplomate Am. Coll. Vet. Nutrition. Asst. prof. Colo. State U., Ft. Collins, 1983-89, Rutgers U., New Brunswick, N.J., 1989-95, assoc. prof., 1995—. Chmn. NRC-136 Equine Rsch. Com., 1993-94. Co-editor, author: Large Animal Clnical Nutrition, 1991; sect. editor, author: Current Therapy in Equine Medicine, 1991; editl. bd. Jour. Equine Vet. Sci., 1992—, Jour. Vet. Clin. Nutrition, 1994—; ad hoc reviewer 8 jours., 1991—. Bd. dirs. Spl. People United to Ride, Red Bank, N.J., 1994-95. Recipient Rsch. awards Purina Mills, Inc., 1990-93, Church & Dwight Inc., Princeton, N.J., 1992-94, Chr. Hansen Labs., Am. Cyanamid, 1995-96, Zinpro, 1997-98. Mem. Am. Coll. Vet. Nutrition (v.p. 1995-96, pres. 1997-98), Am. Vet. Med. Assn. (Samuel F. Scheidy award 1991), Am. Assn. Equine Practitioners, N.J. Assn. Equine Practitioners, Equine Nutrition and Physiology Soc. (bd. dirs. 2003), Am. Soc. Animal Sci. Avocations: horseback riding, gardening. Office: Rutgers U Dept Animal Sci Bartlett Hall Lipman Dr New Brunswick NJ 08901

RAMACHANDRAN, PATRICIA PATES, retired social worker; b. Portsmouth, Va., May 25, 1943; d. Carl Stansbury and Louise Barger Pates; m. Thomas Gilmer Booher, Apr. 27, 1968 (div. Mar. 1983); children: Jennifer Lynn Booher, Karin Alicia Booher; m. Seshadri Ramachandran, Sept. 15, 1990. BA, Mary Washington Coll., 1964; MSW, Va. Commonwealth U., 1967. LCSW Va., ACSW, bd. cert. diplomate. Field worker pub. assistance Richmond (Va.) Pub. Welfare Dept., 1964—65, social worker group unit, 1967—69; psychiat. social worker Lorberg Family Guidance Clinic, Richmond, 1969—70, Commonwealth Psychiat. Ctr., Richmond, 1971—74; adj. faculty, field supr. Va. Commonwealth U., Richmond, 1975—76, adj. faculty, supr., 1977—79; clin. social worker adolescent Westbrook Hosp., Richmond, 1977—79; pvt. practice social work Richmond, 1980—97; ret. Adj. faculty womens resource U. Richmond, 1983—89. Chpt. founder Compassionate Friends, Richmond, 1979—82; lobbyist Gen. Assembly Va., Richmond, 1990; ch. group leader Unitarian-Universalist Congregation Marietta, Acworth, Ga.; bd. mem. YWCA, Richmond, 1995—99. Scholar, NIMH, 1966. Avocations: music, reading, refinishing furniture, interior decorating, pastels. Home: 1209 Benbrooke Ct Acworth GA 30101

RAMALEY, JUDITH AITKEN, former university president, endocrinologist; b. Vincennes, Ind., Jan. 11, 1941; d. Robert Henry and Mary Krebs (McCullough) Aitken; m. Robert Folk Ramaley, Mar. 1966 (div. 1976); children: Alan Aitken, Andrew Folk. BA, Swarthmore Coll., 1963; PhD, UCLA, 1966; postgrad., Ind. U., 1967-69. Rsch. assoc., lectr. Ind. U., Bloomington, 1967-68, asst. prof. dept. anatomy and physiology, 1969-72; asst. prof. dept. physiology and biophysics U. Nebr. Med. Ctr., Omaha, 1972-74, assoc. prof., 1974-78, prof., 1978-82, assoc. dean for rsch. and devel., 1979-81; asst. v.p. for acad. affairs U. Nebr., Lincoln, 1980-82; prof. biol. scis. SUNY, Albany, N.Y., 1982-87, v.p. for acad. affairs, 1982-85, acting pres., 1984, exec. v.p. for acad. affairs, 1985-87; exec. vice chancellor U. Kans., Lawrence, 1987-90; pres. Portland (Oreg.) State U., 1990-97, U. Vt., Burlington, 1997—2001; asst. dir. edn. and human resources NSF, 2001—. Mem. endocrinology study sect. NIH, 1981-84; cons.-evaluator North Cen. Accreditation, 1978-82, 89-90; regulatory panel NSF, 1979-82, bioadv. com., 1994-98; mem. Ill. Commn. Scholars, 1980-90; Vt. tech. coun. Gov.'s Bus. Adv. Coun., Vt. Bus. Roundtable, Com. on Econ. Devel., 1997-2001; presdl. prof. biomed. scis. U. Maine, Orono, 2001—; subcom. on coll. drinking Nat. Inst. Alcohol Abuse & Alcoholism, 1998-01. Co-author: Progesterone Function: Molecular and Biochemical Aspects, 1972; Essentials of Histology, 8th edit., 1979; editor: Covert Discrimination, Women in the Sciences, 1978; contbr. articles to profl. jours. Bd. dirs. Family Svc. of Omaha, 1979-82, Albany Symphony Orch., 1984-87, mem. exec. com., 1986-87, 2d v.p., exec. com., 1986-87, Capital Repertory Co., 1986-89, Assn. Portland Progress, 1990-97, City Club of Portland, 1991-92, Metro Family Svcs., 1993-97, Campbell Inst. for Children, Portland Met. Sports Authority, 1994; vice-chair Ore. Campus Compact, exec. com. 1996-97, nat. adv. coun. Sch.-Work Opportunities, 1996—; bd. dirs. NCAA Pres. Commn., 1991, chair divsn. II subcom., 1994, joint policy bd., 1994; chmn. bd. dirs. Albany Water Fin. Authority, 1987; exec. com. United Way Douglas County, 1989-90; adv. bd. Emily Taylor Women's Resource Ctr., U. Kans., 1988-90; mem. Portland Opera Bd., 1991-92, Portland Leaders Roundtable, 1991-97; bd. devel. com. United Way of Columbia-Willamette, 1991-95; active Ore. Women's Forum, 1991-97, Portland Met. Sports Authority, Greater Burlington Industry Corp., 1998—; progress bd. Portland-Multnomah County, 1993-97; trustee Wilmington Coll. Ohio, 1998—. NSF grantee, 1969-83; fellow Margaret Chase Smith Ctr. for Pub. Policy. Fellow AAAS; mem. Nat. Assn. State Univs. and Land Grant Colls. (exec. com., mem. senate 1986-88, vice-chair commn. urban agenda 1992-94, chair 1995-97), Am. Assn. for Higher Edn. (bd. dirs. 2003—), Assn. Am. Colls. and Univs. (bd. dirs. 1995-98, chair nat. panel on greater expectations 2000-02), ACE (commn. on govt. rels. 1996-2000), Kellogg Commn. on Future of State and Land-Grant Univs., Assn. Governing Bds. Coll. & U. (pres.'s coun. 1998-2000), Endocrine Soc. (chmn. edn. com. 1980-85), Soc. Study Reprodn. (treas. 1983-85), Soc. for Neuroscis., Am. Physiol. Soc., Am. Assn. Schs. and Colls., Am. Coun. on Edn. (chmn. commn. on women in higher edn. 1987-88, commn. on govt. rels., bd. dirs. 1999-2001), Assn. Portland Progress (bd. dirs.), Portland C. of C. (bd. dirs. 1995), Western Assn. of Schs. and Colls. (commr. 1994-97). Office: Edn and Human Resources Directorate Nat Sci Found 4201 Wilson Blvd Arlington VA 22230

RAMAZZINI, JUDITH WILLIAMS, curator; b. Milw., Nov. 13, 1945; d. Bruno Bernard and Verna Marie (Williams) R.; m. Jack Allen Porter, Mar. 15, 1975 (div. Oct. 1981); m. Lawrence Anthony Baldassaro, Feb. 26, 1995 (div. Feb. 2001). BA, U. Wis., Milw., 1978. Gallery mgr. Milw. Art Mus., 1968-78, spkr., 1988—; freelance artist, 1980-92; curator Quad Graphics, Pewaukee, Wis., 1992—. Instr. U. Wis., Milw., 1980-85. One-woman show includes Charles Allis Art Mus., 1989; exhibited in group show Bradley Gallery, 1991, Peltz Gallery, 1992-98; creator Sacajawea award design, 1986; author: The Guild: A Sourcebook of American Craft Artists, 1986. Active Jr. League, Milw., 1976-78; bd. dirs. Wis. Arts Alliance, Madison, 1995—, co-chair creative ticket for student success, 1996; bd. dirs. Milw. Mus. Art, 1995, Print Forum Milw. Art Mus., 1995—, v.p., 1996-97, pres. 1997-98; mem. adv. bd. Jazz Series at the Pabst, Milw., 1994—. Recipient 1st place award Wis. Women in the Arts, 1982, award Art and the Law, 1982, award Wis. Designer Crafts Coun., 1976; grantee Amoco Prodn. Co., 1987. Mem. Print Forum (bd. dirs.), Contemporary Art Soc. Avocations: cooking, piano, gardening, cats. Office: Quad Graphics Inc West Allis WI 53214 E-mail: jramazzini@qg.com

RAMBERG, LAURA LOUISE, sculptor; b. Hannibal, Mo., Jan. 22, 1956; d. David Freeman and Joanne R.; m. Charles Alan Seibel, Aug. 28, 1977 (div. 1996); children: Jonah Seibel, Ella Seibel, Julia Seibel, Katy Seibel, Copper. BFA, U. Kans., 1981. Vis. artist Kansas City area, 1989—; art tchr. Douglas County Youth Svcs., 1998—. Prin. works include lifesized carved wooden crucifix, St. Johns The Evangelist, 1995, carved limestone relief falcon Riley County H.S., 1994, original tilework Wheatfields Bakery, 1995, Paradise Cafe, 1992, carved wooden meml. figure St. Alban's Ch., Wichita, Kans., 1998; work featured in Natural Home Mag. Recipient Amsden Book award Kress Found., 1988, Burgess award N.Am. Sculpture Exhbn., 1985; Fine Arts grantee Alpha Delta Kappa, 1981; Fine Arts scholar U. Kans., 1980. Mem. Internat. Sculpture Ctr., Nat. Mus. Women in the Arts. Avocation: gardening. Home: 18641 Stairstep Rd Lawrence KS 66044-8280

RAMBO, DOMINGO H. elementary school educator; b. Marietta, Tex., Apr. 20, 1924; d. Joseph E. and Elvira (Henderson) Johnson; m. Buford Rambo, Oct. 15, 1951; children: Jennifer Joan, George Alford. BA, Huston Tillotson Coll., Austin, Tex., 1951; postgrad., Calif. State U., L.A., Calif. State U., UCLA, Pepperdine U. Cert. elem. tchr., Calif. Tchr. Greenville (Tex.) Ind. Sch. Dist., L.A. Unified Sch. Dist., profl. expert. Co-founder L.A. Bridge Conservatory Performing and Visual Arts, pres., 1992—. Recipient outstanding and merit award for 35-yrs. svc. L.A. Unified Sch. Dist. Mem. NEA, Calif. Tchrs. Assn., UTLA, Phi Delta Kappa.

RAMBO, SYLVIA H. federal judge; b. Royersford, Pa., Apr. 17, 1936; d. Granville A. and Hilda E. (Leonhardt) R.; m. George F. Douglas, Jr., Aug. 1, 1970. BA, Dickinson Coll., 1958; JD, Dickinson Sch Law, 1962; LLD (hon.), Wilson Coll., 1980, Dickinson Sch. Law, 1993, Dickinson Coll., 1994, Shippensburg U., 1996, Widener U., 1999. Bar: Pa. 1962. Atty. trust dept. Bank of Del., Wilmington, 1962-63; pvt. practice Carlisle, 1963-76; from public defender to chief public defender Cumberland County, Pa., 1974-76; judge Ct. Common Pleas, Cumberland County, 1976-78, U.S. Dist. Ct. (mid. dist.) Pa., Harrisburg, 1979-92, chief judge, 1992-99; federal judge U.S. Dist. Ct., Harrisburg, 2000—. Asst. prof., adj. prof. Dickinson Sch. Law, 1974—76; mem. Jud. Conf. Com. of Adminstrn. of Magistrate Judges Sys., 1996—2002, Pa. Bar Assn. Task Force on Legal Svcs. to the Needy, 2000—03. Bd. govs. Dickinson Sch. Law., Pa. State U., 2000—. Mem. Phi Alpha Delta. Democrat. Presbyterian. Office: US Dist Ct Federal Bldg PO Box 868 Harrisburg PA 17108-0868

RAMEY, EUDORA MALOIS, minister; b. Maywood, Ill., Oct. 23, 1926; d. Clenus and Ora Helen Garner; m. Edward F Ramey, July 27, 1947; children: Jonathon, RoseMary, Paul. Edn. counselor Dist. 9 Bd. Edn., McKinley Sch., Chgo., 1966—75; counselor aid Bd. Edn./Whitney Young Sch., Chgo., 1975—80; implementor Job Club/Pres.'s Office/Employment Tng., Chgo., 1980—92. Advisor Garfield Pk. Conservatory, Chgo., 1991—, bd. dirs., 1996—. Mem. Chgo. Urban League, Ill., 1943—2003, PUSH (People United to Serve Humanity), Chgo., 1951—2003; ordained local elder/min. St. Stephen AME Ch., Chgo., 2003—; mem. NAACP, Chgo., 1943—2003. Recipient Trailblazer for Women in Ministry award, 4th Dist. of the AME Ch., 2001, Cert. of Honor, Way of Life /A.M.E.Ch., 1999, Chgo. Sr. Citizen's Hall of Fame, 1997. African Methodist Episcopal (A.M.E.). Avocations: Scrabble, Bingo, reading. Home: 746 S Kilbourn Ave /Ste 1 Chicago IL 60624

RAMEY, LINDA DEE, literature educator, poet; b. Portsmouth, N.H., Dec. 3, 1949; d. Alvin William Miles and Mae Garlonsky; m. Kelly Raymond Ramey, Dec. 26, 1971; children: Brian William, Aaron Jason. BA in Edn., U. Conn., 1972; MFA in English and Creative Writing, U. Md., 1996. Cert. tchr. Conn., R.I. Substitute tchr. Portsmouth Sch. Dist., RI, 1996—99, Middletown Sch. Dist., RI, 1996—99, Newport Sch. Dist., RI, 1996—2001; poetry cons. Goucher C.C., Balt., 1996; English tutoring cons. St. Andrew's Sch., Barrington, RI, 1997; adj. prof. Johnson and Wales U., Providence, 2001—, C.C. of R.I., Warwick, 2003—. Hist. interpreter Newport Restoration Found., 2003—; hist. interpreter for Guilded Age Properties Preservation Soc. of Newport County, 1999—2003. Contbr. poetry to profl. jours. Vol. James L. Maher Ctr., 1990—. Recipient 1st, 2d and 3d prizes, Aspen Writers' Conference, 1997, award, Galway Kinnell Poetry Contest, Pawtucket Art Assn., 1996; fellow R.I. fellow in lit., R.I. State Coun. for the Arts, 1997—98. Mem.: Roger Williams Pk. Zoo, Soc. Am. Poetry. Home: 163 Third St Newport RI 02840-1328

RAMI, JANET SIMMONS, university dean, nursing educator; b. Washington, La. BSN, Dillard U., 1970; MS in Cross-Cultural Nursing, U. So. Miss., 1979; PhD in Edn. Rsch. Methodology, La. State U., 1992. Dir. nursing staff edn. Earl K. Long Hosp., Baton Rouge, 1977-83; coord. nurse staff edn. State La., Office of Hosps., Baton Rouge, 1983-84; asst. prof. So. U. and Agrl. and Med. Coll., Baton Rouge, 1984-85, acting dean, asst. prof., 1985-86, dean, assoc. prof., 1986—. Contbr. articles to profl. jours. Coun. mem. (hon.) city of Baton Rouge, 1984; rep. (hon.) to State of La., 1984. Mem. ANA, Baton Rouge Dist. Nurses Assn., Coun. Acad. Nurse Educators, La. State Nurses Assn., Nat. League for Nursing, Sigma Theta Tau, Alpha Kappa Alpha, Lambda Phi Alpha. Office: S U Sch Nursing Office Dean PO Box 11794 Baton Rouge LA 70813-1794

RAMIREZ, LINDA MANNING, counselor; b. San Antonio, July 13, 1951; d. Elmer Eugene Manning and Celeste E. (Campbell) Siner; m. Javier Ramirez, Oct. 22, 1977; children: Andrea, Xavier, Eric. BSN, U. Tex. Health Sci. Ctr., Houston, 1974; MEd in counseling, U. Tex. Pan-Am., Edinburg, 1993. RN Tex.; lic. profl. counselor supr. Bd. Profl. Counseling, registered play therapist supr. Assn. for Play Therapists. Vol. tchr. Our Lady of Sorrows Sch., McAllen, Tex., 1988-98, counseling intern, 1992—95; pvt. practice counseling children McAllen, 1996—. Presenter profl. continuing edn. workshops, parenting tng.; co-author children's books in English and Spanish. Bd. dirs. Diocese of Brownsville Sch. Coun., 1997-2000. Mem.: Assn. Play Therapists, Tex. Assn. Play Therapy (bd. dir. 1997—99, treas 2002—), Rio Grande Valley Assn. Play Therapy (pres. 1997—99, 2000—01), Border Equestrian Sports Assn. (sec. 1992), Phi Kappa Phi. Republican. Roman Catholic. Avocations: weightlifting, equestrian sports, reading. Home: 12 Villas Jardin Mcallen TX 78503-3138

RAMIREZ, MARIA C(ONCEPCION), retired educational administrator; d. Ines and Carlota (Cruz) R. BA, U. Incarnate Word, San Antonio, 1966; MEd, U. Tex., Austin, 1979; postgrad., S.W. Tex. State U., San Marcos, 1980. Cert. elem. tchr., bilingual tchr., supr. Elem. tchr. regular and bilingual Edgewood Ind. Sch. Dist., San Antonio, 1966-69; elem tchr. regular and bilingual Austin (Tex.) Ind. Sch. Dist., 1969-74, bilingual program coord., 1974-89; instrnl. coord. Austin Ind. Sch. Dist., 1989-91, asst. prin., 1991—96, bilingual instrnl. coord., 1996-97; ret., 1997.

RAMIREZ, MARY CATHERINE, retired secondary school educator; b. McLeansboro, Ill., Feb. 16, 1921; d. George Washington and Mary Margaret (Lane) Tousley; m. John Ramirez, Oct. 30, 1948 (dec. 1975). BS, Ctrl. U., Edmond, Okla., 1942; MA, U. Okla., 1945. Tchr. Bradley (Okla.) High Sch., 1942-43, McLeansboro (Ill.) High Sch., 1943-46, No. Okla. Jr. Coll., Tonkawa, Okla., 1946-47, Draughon Bus. Coll., Springfield, Mo., 1947-48, VA Hosp., Springfield, Mo., 1948-52, Madison, Wis., 1952-63, Madison pub. sch., 1963-85. Mem. AAUW (publicity chmn. Madison br. 1954-60)., NEA, Madison Civics Club. Avocations: travel, photography, coin and stamp collecting, needlework. Home: 971 Wellington Ct Nekoosa WI 54457-9040

RAMIREZ, TINA, artistic director; b. Caracas, Venezuela; d. Gloria Maria Cestero and Jose Ramirez Gaonita. Studied dance with Lola Bravo, Alexandra Danilova, Anna Sokolow. Toured with Federico Rey Dance Co.; founder, artistic dir. Ballet Hispanico, N.Y.C., 1970—. Panelist NEA N.Y. Sate Coun. on Arts; mem. advisory panel N.Y.C. Dept. Cultural Affairs; bd. dirs Dance Theater Workshop. Appearances (Broadway plays) Kismet, Lute Song, (TV series) Man of La Mancha. Recipient Arts and Culture Honor award, Mayor of N.Y.C., 1983, Ethnic New Yorker award, N.Y.C., 1986, Gov.'s Arts award, N.Y. State Gov. Mario Cuomo, 1987, honoree Nat. Puerto Rican Forum, Hispanic Inst. for Performing Arts. Office: Ballet Hispanico 167 W 89th St New York NY 10024-1901

RAMIREZ-CAMPBELL, CHRISTINE M. art council administrator; b. Springfield, Ill., July 1, 1951; d. Philip Joseph Ramirez and Mary Barbara (Dinora); m. R. Michael Patsche, Oct. 1971 (div. 1986); children: Gina Maria Patsche, R. Michael Patsche; m. G. Dennis Campbell, Oct. 1, 1993. AA, Springfield Coll. Ill., 1971; BA, Sangamon State U., 1989. Edn. asst. Ill. State Mus., Springfield, 1989—92; sci. edn. coord. Springfield Children's Mus., 1992—94; dir. cmty. edn. Lincoln Land C.C., Springfield, 1994—2000; exec. dir. Springfield Area Arts Coun., 2000—. Arts trainer, mentor program Ill. Arts Alliance, 2001; v.p. bldg. bd. Springfield Ctr. for the Arts, 2001. Arts chair Springfield Jr. League, 1984; pres. Care Ctr., Springfield, 1984; bd. mem. Brinkenhoff Home Aux., Springfield, 1987. Recipient Paragon award, Assn. Pub. Rels. C.C., 1999, Spl. Recognition Svc. award, Trustees Lincoln Land Cmty. Coll., 2000. Mem.: Downtown Springfield Inc., Springfield C. of C. Office: Springfield Area Arts Coun 526 E Capitol Springfield IL 62701

RAMO, ROBERTA COOPER, lawyer; b. Denver, Aug. 8, 1942; d. David D. and Martha L. (Rosenblum) Cooper; m. Barry W. Ramo, June 17, 1964. BA magna cum laude, U. Colo., 1964; JD, U. Chgo., 1967; LLD (hon.), U. Mo., 1995, U. Denver, 1995; LHD (hon.), U. Colo., 1995; JD (hon.), Golden Gate U., 1996; LLD (hon.), U. S.C., 2001. Bar: N.Mex. 1967, Tex. 1971. With NC. Fund, Durham, 1967-68; nat. tchg. fellow Shaw U., Raleigh, N.C., 1968-70; mem. Sawtelle, Goode, Davidson & Troilo, San Antonio, 1970-72, Rodey, Dickason, Sloan, Akin & Robb, Albuquerque, 1972-74; sole practice law Albuquerque, 1974-77; dir., shareholder Poole, Kelly & Ramo, Albuquerque, 1977-93; shareholder Modrall, Sperling, Roehl, Harris & Sisk, Albuquerque, 1993—. Lectr. in field., bd. dirs. Merrill Lynch Asset Mgmt., Ednl. Credit Mgmt. Corp. Co-author: New Mexico Estate Administration System, 1980; editor: How to Create a System for the Law Office, 1975; contbg. editor: Tex. Probate Sys., 1974; contbr. articles to profl. jours., chpts. to books. Mem. steering com. World Conf. Domestic Violence, 1996—99; mem. Am. Law Inst. Coun., 1997—, exec. com., 2000—; mem. Martindale-Hubbell Legal Adv. Bd., 1996—2000; bd. dirs., past pres. N.Mex. Symphony Orch., 1977—86; bd. dirs. Albuquerque Cmty. Found., N.Mex. First, 1987—90, Santa Fe Opera, Santa Fe, 2001—; bd. regents U. N.Mex., 1989—94, pres., 1991—93; founding bd. mem. Think N.Mex., 1998—; mem. Civitas Initiative, 1997—; chmn. bd. Cooper's Inc., 1999—. Recipient Disting. Pub. Svc. award Gov. of N.Mex., 1993. Fellow: Am. Bar Found.; mem.: ABA (pres. 1995, bd. govs. 1994—97, chmn. London 2000 com., Asia Law Initiatives Coun. 1999—, others), Am. Arbitration Assn (bd. dirs, 1997—, bd. trustees Global Ctr. Dispute Resolution Rsch. 1999—), Law Inst. Coun., Am. Judicature Soc. (bd. dirs. 1988—91), Am. Bar Retirement Assn. (bd. dirs. 1990—94), N.Mex. Bar Assn. (Outstanding Contbn. award 1981, 1984), Albuquerque Bar Assn. (bd. dirs., pres. 1980—81), Greater Albuquerque C. of C. (bd. dirs., exec. com. 1987—91). Address: Modrall Sperling Roehl Harris & Sisk PO Box 2168 Albuquerque NM 87103-2168

RAMO, VIRGINIA M. SMITH, civic worker; b. Yonkers, N.Y. d. Abraham Harold and Freda (Kasnetz) Smith; m. Simon Ramo; children: James Brian, Alan Martin. BS in Edn., U. So. Calif., DHL (hon.), 1978. Nat. co-chmn., ann. giving U. So. Calif., 1968-70, vice chmn., trustee, 1971—, co-chmn. bd. councilors Sch. Performing Arts, 1975-76, co-chmn. bd. councillors Schs. Med. and Engring. Vice-chmn. bd. overseers Hebrew Union Coll., 1972-75; bd. dirs. The Muses of Calif. Mus. Sci. and Industry, UCLA Affiliates, Estelle Doheny Eye Found., U. So. Calif. Sch. Medicine; mem. adv. coun. L.A. County Heart Assn., chmn. com. to endow Chair in cardiology at U. So. Calif.; vice chmn., bd. dirs. Friends of Libr. U. So. Calif.; bd. dirs., nat. pres. Achievement Rewards for Coll. Scientists Found., 1975-77; bd. dirs. Les Dames L.A., Cmty. TV So. Calif.; bd. dirs., v.p. Founders L.A. Music Ctr.; v.p. L.A. Music Ctr. Opera Assn.; v.p. corp. bd. United Way; v.p. Blue Ribbon-400 Performing Arts Coun.; chmn. com. to endow chair in gerontology U. So. Calif.; vice chmn. campaign Doheny Eye Inst,. 1986; co-chair, bd. overseers Keck Sch. Medicine U. So. Calif., 1999—. Recipient Svc. award Friends of Librs., 1974, Nat. Cmty. Svc. award Alpha Epsilon Phi, 1975, Disting. Svc. award Am. Heart Assn., 1978, Svc. award U. So. Calif., Spl. award U. So. Calif. Music Alumni Assn., 1979, Life Achievement award Mannequins of L.A. Assistance League, 1979, Woman of Yr. award Pan Hellenic Assn., 1981, Disting. Svc. award U. So. Calif. Sch. Medicine, 1981, U. So. Calif. Town and Gown Recognition award, 1986, Asa V. Call Achievement award U. So. Calif., 1986, Phi Kappa Phi scholarship award U. So. Calif., 1986, Vision award Luminaires of Doheny Eye Inst., 1994, Presdl. medallion U. So. Calif., 2002, USC Thornton Sch. of Music Founder's award, 2003. Mem. UCLA Med. Aux., U. So. Calif. Pres.'s Cir., Commerce Assocs. U. So. Calif., Cedars of Lebanon Hosp. Women's Guild (dir. 1967-68), Blue Key, Skull and Dagger.

RAMOS, MILDRED, administrative assistant; b. Patterson, N.J., Mar. 12, 1962; d. Rosa Marie Ramos; children: David Orlando Rodriguez, Raymond Michael Rodriguez. Grad. high sch., Camden, N.J. Sec. Camden H.S., NJ, 1989—91; adminstrn. asst. Camden County Tech. Schs., Pennsauken, 1991—. Office: Camden County Tech Schs 6008 Browning Rd Pennsauken NJ 08109

RAMOS, ODETTE TERESA, political organization worker, director; b. Albuquerque, N.Mex., Jan. 25, 1973; d. Juan Ricardo and Mary Jo Ramos. B in Social Justice, Goucher Coll., 1995; MS in Policy Analysis, Rutgers U., 1996. Legislative aide State Del. James W. Campbell, Balt., 1996—97; regional fundraising dir. Mikulski for Senate, Balt., 1997—97; neighborhood programs dir. Greater Homewood Cmty. Corp., Balt., 1997—2000; exec. dir. Balt. Neighborhood Indicators Alliance, Balt., 2000—. Lead organizer Neighborhood Congress of Balt., 1998—2000. Student govt. pres. Goucher Coll., Balt., 1992—95; campaign com. Citizens for Maggie MacIntosh, Balt., 2002; vol. coord. Friends of Mary Pat Clark, Balt., 1995; founder, bd. mem. The Village Learning Pl., Balt., 1997—2001. Harold Martin fellow, Eagleton Inst. of Politics, 1995—96. Mem.: Md. NonProfits (assoc.), Goucher Coll. Alumni Assn. (life), Rutgers U. Alumni Assn. (life). Office: Baltimore Neighborhood Indicators Allian 100 E 23rd St 1st floor Baltimore MD 21218 E-mail: odette@bnia.org.

RAMOS-CANO, HAZEL BALATERO, caterer, chef, innkeeper, restaurateur, entrepreneur; b. Davao City, Mindanao, Philippines, Sept. 2, 1936; came to U. S., 1960. d. Mauricio C. and Felicidad (Balatero) Ramos; m. William Harold Snyder, Feb. 17, 1964 (div. 1981); children: John Byron, Snyder, Jennifer Ruth; m. Nelson Allen Blue, May 30, 1986 (div. 1990); m. A. Richard Cano, June 25, 1994. BA in Social Work, U. Philippines, Quezon City, 1958; MA in Sociology, Pa. State U., 1963, postgrad., 1966-67. Cert. exec. chef, Am. Culinary Fedn. Faculty, tng. staff Peace Corps Philippine Project, University Park, Pa., 1961-63; sociology instr. Albright Coll., Reading, Pa., 1963-64; rsch. asst. Meth. Ch. U.S.A., State College, Pa., 1965-66; rsch. asst. dept. child devel. & family rels. Pa. State U., University Park, Pa., 1966-67; exec. dir. Presbyn. Urban Coun. Raleigh Halifax Ct. Child Care and Family Svc. Ctr., 1973-79; early childhood educator Learning Together, Inc., Raleigh, 1982-83; loan mortgage specialist Raleigh Savs. & Loan, 1983-84; restaurant owner, mgr. Hazel's on Hargett, Raleigh, 1985-86; admissions coord., social worker Brian Corp. Nursing Home, Raleigh, 1986-88, food svc. dir., 1989-90; regional dir. La Petite Acad., Raleigh, 1989-90; asst. food svc. mgr. Granville Towers, Chapel Hill, N.C., 1990-92; mgr. trainee Child Nutrition Svcs. Wake County Pub. Sch. System, Raleigh, N.C., 1993-94; food svc. dir. S.W. Va. 4-H Ednl. Conf. Ctr., Abingdon, 1994-95; caterer, owner The Eclectic Chef's Catering, 1995—; innkeeper, owner Love House Bed and Breakfast, 1996—; pres. Ramos-Cano Inc., 1996—; owner Withers Hardware Restaurant, Abingdon, Va., 2002—; pres. Ramos-Cano Mgmt. Svcs., LLC, 2002—. Cooking instr. Wake Cmty. Tech. Coll., Raleigh, 1986-92; freelance caterer, 1964-95; chair Internat. Cooking Demonstrations Raleigh Internat. Festival, 1990-93. Pres. Wake County Day Care United Coun., 1974-75, N.C. Assn. Edn. Young Children (Raleigh Chpt.), 1975-76; bd. mem. Project Enlightenment Wake County Pub. Schs., 1976-77; various positions Pines of Carolina Girl Scout Council, 1976-85; chmn. Philippine Health and Medical Aid Com., Phil-Am Assn. Raleigh 1985-88 (publicity chmn.); elder Trinity Presbyn. Ch., Raleigh, 1979-81, bd. deacons, 1993-94; elder, session mem. Sinking Spring Presbyn. Ch., 1997—; treas. Abingdon Newcomers Club, 1997—, Presbyn. Women, Sinking Spring Presbyn. Ch., Abingdon, 1999—; master gardener Va. Tech. Master Gardeners Program, 1998—. Recipient Juliette Low Girl Scout Internat. award, 1953, Rockefeller grant Rockefeller Found., 1958-59, Ramon Magsaysay Presidential award, Philippine Leadership Youth Movement, 1957; Gov.'s Cert. Appreciation State N.C., 1990, Raleigh Mayor's award Quality Childcare Svcs., 1990, Recipient award for keeping hist. Abington beautiful Abington Kiwanis Club, 1997. Mem. Am. Culinary Fedn., Presby. Women, Raleigh, (historian 1975-76), Penn State Dames (pres. 1968-69). Democrat. Office: Victoria & Albert INN 224 Oak Hill St Abingdon VA 24210 also: The Love House Bed and Breakfast 210 E Valley St Abingdon VA 24210 Address: Withers Hardware Restaurant 260 W Main St Abingdon VA 24210 Office Phone: 276-628-1111. E-mail: v&ainn@naxs.com., lovehouse@naxs.com.

RAMPERSAD, PEGGY A. SNELLINGS, sociologist, consultant; b. Fredericksburg, Va., Jan. 12, 1933; d. George Daniel and Virginia Riley (Bowler) Snellings; m. Oliver Ronald Rampersad, Mar. 19, 1955; 1 child, Gita. BA, Mary Washington Coll., Fredericksburg, 1953; student, Sch. Art Inst. Chgo., 1953—55; MA, U. Chgo., 1965, PhD, 1978. Grad. admissions counselor U. Chgo., 1954-57, adviser to fgn. students, 1958, dir. admissions Grad. Sch. Bus., 1959-63, rsch. project specialist, 1970 78, pers. mgr., 1979-80, mgr. organizational devel., 1980-82, adminstr. dept. econs., 1983-95; cons. PSR Consulting, Chgo., 1995—. Cons. North Ctrl. Assn. Colls. and Secondary Schs., Chgo., 1964—70, Orchestral Assn. Chgo. Symphony Orch., 1982, Chgo. Ctr. Decision Rsch., 1982, Harvard U., 1993—97. Exhibitions include Va. Mus. Fine Arts, Art Inst. Chgo., others; editor: North Ctrl. Assn. Quar., 1972; contbr. articles to profl. jours. Grad. fellow, U. Chgo., 1963—67. Mem.: AAUW, Am. Acad. Polit. and Social Sci., Am. Econ. Assn., Art Inst. Chgo. (assoc.), Pi Lambda Theta (past pres.). Episcopalian. Avocations: painting and drawing, opera, reading, walking. Home and Office: 28 Seneca Ter Fredericksburg VA 22401-1115

RAMPHELE, MAMPHELA A. medical educator; MD, U. Natal, 1972; PhD in Social Anthropology, U. Cape Town; B in Adminstrn., U. South Africa; diploma in tropical health and hygiene and pub. health, U. Witwatersrand. Sr. rsch. officer U. Cape Town, South Africa, 1986—91, dep. vice chancellor, 1991—95, vice chancellor, 1996—2000; mng. dir. human devel. World Bank, Washington, 2000—. Immediate past chmn. bd. trustees Ind. Devel. Trust; adv. bd. World Bank Econ. Devel. Inst. Author: Across Boundaries; contbr. articles to profl. jours. Student activist Black Consciousness Movement. Recipient of numerous nat. and internat. awards including 17 hon. doctorates, awards for svc. to cmty. Mem.: Inst. of Medicine of NAS. Office: The World Bank 1818 H St NW Washington DC 20433

RAMSAY, KARIN KINSEY, publisher, educator; b. Brownwood, Tex., Aug. 10, 1930; d. Kirby Luther and Ina Rebecca (Wood) Kinsey; m. Jack Cummins Ramsay Jr., Aug. 31, 1951; children: Annetta Jean, Robin Andrew. BA, Trinity U., 1951. Cert. assoc. ch. edn., 1980. Youth coord. Covenant Presbyn. Ch., Carrollton, Tex., 1961-76; dir. ch. edn. Northminster Presbyn. Ch., Dallas, 1976-80, Univ. Presbyn. Ch., Chapel Hill, N.C., 1987-90, Oak Grove Presbyn. Ch., Bloomington, Minn., 1990-93; coord. ecum. ministry Flood Relief for Iowa, Des Moines, 1993; program coord. 1st Presbyn. Ch., Green Bay, Wis., 1994-95; owner, sole proprietor Hist. Resources Press, Corinth and Denton, Tex., 1994—. Dir. Godspell tour Covenant Presbyn. Ch., 1972-75; mem. Presbytery Candidates Com., Dallas, 1977-82, Presbytery Exams. Com. Dallas, 1979-81; clk. coun. New Hope Presbytery, Rocky Mount, N.C., 1989-90; creator, dir. Thee Holy Fools mime/musical group and This Is Me retreats. Author: Ramsay's Resources, 1983—; pub., editor: Patton's Ill-Fated Raid, 2002; contbr. articles to jours. in field. Design cons. Brookhaven Hosp. Chapel, Dallas, 1977-78; elder Presbyn. Ch. U.S.A., 1982—; coord. Lifeline Emergency Response, Dallas, 1982-84. Mem. Internat. Platform Assn., Small Publisher's Assn. of N. Am.,Pub. Marketing Assoc., Writer's League of Tex.

RAMSAY, LINDA, architect; Grad., Clemson U., Ga. Inst. Tech. Prin. Ramsay Sherrill Arch., Savannah, Ga., 1985—. Chair Hist. Dist. Bd. Rev., Savannah, Ga. Fellow: AIA (pres.). Office: Ramsay Sherrill Arch 221 E York St Savannah GA 31401

RAMSDEN, MARY CATHERINE, substance abuse specialist; Diploma, St. Joseph Mercy Hosp., 1966; postgrad., Mason City Jr. Coll., Kirkwood Community Coll. Cert. alcohol and drug counselor; RN Iowa, cert. chem. dependency nurse. Nursing supr. children's unit State Mental Health Inst., Cherokee, Iowa, 1966-69, Iowa Security Med. Facility, Oakdale, 1969; staff nurse psychiatry St. Luke's Meth. Hosp., Cedar Rapids, Iowa, 1969-74, asst. psychiat. nursing instr., 1970-74; mem. staff Sedlacek Treatment Ctr. Mercy Hosp., Cedar Rapids, 1974-85; cons. drug and alcohol CareUnit,

Jacksonville Beach, Fla., 1985-86; nursing mgr. adolescent chem. dependency unit Broadlawns Med. Ctr., Des Moines, 1987-88; tng. mgr. Div. Substance Abuse and Heath Promotion Iowa Dept. Pub. Health, 1988-91; clin. program dir. Forest City (Iowa) Treatment Ctr., 1991-92; facilitator Employee & Family Resources Enhancement Women Pr Iowa Correctional Instn. for Women, Mitchellville, 1992-97; cast mgmt. tng. coord. Employee & Family Resources, Des Moines, 1998-99; substance abuse cons., trainer Des Moines, 1999—; sr. counselor Powell Chem. Dependency Ctr. Iowa Luth Hosp., Des Moines, 1999—2003; case mgr., substance abuse counselor drug ct. 5th Jud. Dist., Employee & Family Resources, 2003—. Mem. licensing rev. com. Iowa Bd. of Nursing. Author: (with others) Nurses Quick Reference, 1989. Lt. Cmdr. Nurse Corps USNR. Named Nurse Expert Coll. Nursing U. Iowa., 1985. Mem.: Iowa Assn. Addiction Profls. (v.p.), Iowa Corrections Assn., Nat. Consortium Chem. Dependence Nurses, Nat. Assn. Alcoholism and Drug Abuse Counselors, Res. Officers Assn. Home: 1519 Idaho St Des Moines IA 50316-2425 Office Phone: 515-242-6582. E-mail: mrrncd@yahoo.com.

RAMSDEN, SALLY ANN, pianist; b. Port Clinton, Ohio, Feb. 23, 1963; d. Donald Burlinson and Vera Edna (Smith) Ramsden. BMusic in Piano, MusB in piano, U. Wash., Seattle, 1986. Student accompanist U. Wash., Seattle, 1981-86, U. Tex., Austin, 1986-87; staff accompanist Cornish, Seattle, 1988—; studio accompanist Stephanie Dudash, Algona, Wash., 1990-96; staff accompanist Highline C.C., Des Moines, 1995—. Author: Igor Denshik Classical Piano, 1996; pianist: (solo performances) TCI Cable TV, 1996. Pianist for benefit dinner Northend Emergency Fund, Seattle; pianist for fundraisers Nature Conservancy, Seattle, Seattle Symphony. Recipient scholarship Kent Music Study Club, 1981, Nat. Sch. Choral award Kent Meridian H.S., 1981. Mem. Washington State Music Tchrs. Assn. Democrat. Avocations: study of classic english literature, classic films, early broadway musicals.

RAMSDEN, WILLA OLDHAM, retired organization executive, columnist, historian, consultant; b. San Diego, Nov. 27, 1911; d. William Henry Stillwell and Martha Ellen Estell; m. Clifton John Oldham (dec. Feb. 1984); m. Percy Herbert Ramsden (dec. Oct. 1993). Field dir. Girl Scout Coun., San Diego, 1934—39, asst. exec., 1945—49, exec. dir. Fresno, Calif., 1939—41, San Jose, Calif., 1942—44, Riverside, Calif., 1949—56; ret., 1956; self-employed feature writer, columnist, 1957—59; feature writer, columnist Boulder City, Nev., 1960—69, Carson City, Nev., 1970—; staff substitute City of Carson City, 1974—92, cons. pers., adminstrn., orgn., 1974—. Spkr. various civic and svc. clubs, schs., Nev., 1960—2001, Hannah Clapp Lecture Series, Carson City, 1999—2000; mem. panel Landmark Soc. series, Carson City, 2001; pres. Region XII Girl Scout Profls.; nat. bd. dirs. Girl Scout Profls. Contbr. over 500 articles to profl. jours., mags. and newspapers; contbr. (anthology) Light From a Thousand Campfires, 1953; weekly columnist: Mayor of Boulder City, Nev., 1963—64; author: pers. manuals and publicity articles, 1974—83, (publicity articles) Coop. Ext. Svc., U. Nev., Reno, 1974—83, Carson-Tahoe Hospital: The Story of a Caring Community, 1987, Carson City - Nevada's Capital City, 1991. Active Nev. State Mus., Carson City, 1972—; organizer Appaloosa Club Clark County, Las Vegas, 1960; docent Nev. State Mus., Carson City, 1972—75; mem. bicentennial commn. Carson City Centennial, 1974—78; mem. organizing com. Friends in Svc. Helping, Carson City, 1977; chmn. All Carson City Ch. Women Leadership Conf., 1978, Western Nev. Sr. Conf., Carson City, 1985; promotion staff for bd. suprs. Marriage Bur., 1991; mem. planning com. Nev. Women's Project, 1997—98; sustaining mem. Rep. Nat. Com., Washington, 1970—2002; mem. Rep. Presdl. Task Force; mem. election bd. Riverside, 1956—59, Carson City, 1971—72; chmn. election bd., 1973—81; dep. election bd., 1982—92; active local Rep. campaigns; bd. deacons 1st Presbyn. Ch., Carson City, 1978—80, chair, 1979—80, 1986—88, organizer sr. Serving Others Loving Others program, deacon, 1978, founder sr. assistance program, 1982, chair social action com., 1982. Nominee Nev. Woman of Yr., 1970; named Hon. Life mem., Nat. Presbyn. Ch. USA, 1976; recipient Thanks badge, Nat. Bd. Girl Scouts U.S., 1957, cert. of appreciation, Nat. Appaloosa Horse Club, 1960, commendation cert., Carson City Centennial/U.S. Bicentennial Commn., City of Carson City, 1979, Ad hoc Recreational Vehicle Com, City of Carson City, 1987. Mem.: Rep. Presdl. Task Force, Heritage Found. Presbyterian. Achievements include a special collection at the Getchell Library of University of Nevada-Reno of her correspondence, manuscripts and writing samples. Avocations: gourmet food study, classical music, travel, reading, computer contacts.

RAMSER, WANDA TENE, library and information scientist, educator; b. Atlanta, June 4, 1951; d. Galen Eugene Ramser and Christine Elizabeth Owen; children: Catherine Nicole Hannabach, David Richmond Hannabach. BA in History with honors, U. Calif., Santa Barbara, 1973; MLIS with honors, UCLA, 1976, MA in Latin Am. Studies, 1977. With UCLA Latin Am. Ctr., 1973—78; literacy coord. County of Los Angeles Libr., 1978—83; assoc. faculty South Orange County C.C. Dist., Mission Viejo, Calif., 1986; libr. youth svcs. County Orange, Calif., 1986—87; libr. City of San Diego Libr., 1993—2001, City of Oceanside, Calif., 2001—. Pres. San Diego chpt. Svcs. to Latinos/REFORMA; bd. dirs. UCLA Club San Diego, Palomar Coll. Libr. Tech. Bd. Active Chicano Fedn. San Diego County, 1993—, Chicano Pk./Barrio Sta. San Diego, 1993—; mem. spkr.'s bur. City of Hope Nat. Cancer Ctr., 2000—. Mem.: AAUW, ALA, Calif. Libr. Assn., City San Diego Latino Employees Assn. (bd. dirs.). Address: PO Box 1484 Beverly Hills CA 90213-1484

RAMSEY, CYNTHIA (CINDY) HORRELL, publishing executive, writer, editor; b. Burgaw, NC, May 20, 1953; d. Roy Barefoot and Eusely Malpass Horrell; m. Steven Pope Ramsey, Oct. 30, 1970; children: Joy Ramsey Stutts, Kimberly Ramsey McCrea, Bradley Steven. BA in English, U. of NC, 1998—99, MFA in creative writing, 2000. Self-employed wallpaper hanger Wonderful Walls, Kelly, NC, 1983—98; tchr. Southport Christian Sch., Southport, NC, 2000; writer Streetmail, NYC, 2000—01; ins. salesman Bankers Life, Wilmington, NC, 2001—02; writer, editor The Pender Post, Burgaw, NC, 2002—02; pub. Pender Pub. Co., Inc. - The Pender Post, 2002—. Author: (short story) Gossip. Youth leader Pender Youth for Christ, Burgaw, NC, 1990—93; coach Burgaw Dixie Youth, Burgaw, NC, 1982—90. Recipient Chancellor's award, U. of NC at Wilmington, 1998—99. Mem.: Topsail Area C. of C. and Tourism, Hampstead C. of C., Burgaw C. of C., NC Press Assn., Phi Kappa Phi. So. Bapt. Avocations: horseback riding, walking, travel, writing, reading. Office: The Pender Post 201-A West Fremont St Burgaw NC 28425 Personal E-mail: chramsey@intrstar.net. E-mail: postnews@intrstar.net.

RAMSEY, ELEANORE EDWARDS, design bookbinder; d. Arthur Decatur Jr. and Eleanore Virginia (Edwards) R.; m. Andrew Thomas Nadell, July 24, 1993. BA, Coe Coll. Bookbindings exhibited in N.Am., Eng., Scotland, France, Belgium and Germany; permanent collections include Libs. of Stanford U., Book Club of Calif., U. Tex., U. Chgo. and Manchester U., Eng. Recipient Wollenberg Internat. Prize for Art Bookbinding Stanford U., 1992, Design prize DeGolyer Triennial Competition Am. Booking So. Methodist U., 2003, Oscar Lewis award for contributions to the Book Arts, Book Club Ca., 2004. Mem. Hand Bookbinders of Calif. (v.p. 1994—99, pres., 1999—2001), Designer Bookbinders (London), Roxburghe Club of San Francisco, Colophon Club (San Francisco), Metropolitan Club San Francisco. Episcopalian. Office: 502 Turney St Sausalito CA 94965-1840

RAMSEY, KIM N. information technology manager; b. N.Y.C., May 7, 1968; d. Thelma Moorer; children: Stephen Donnell Frederick, Christopher Dimetrius Breland, Quentin LaMonte Lee. MEd, S.C. State U., 2002. Cert. tchr. S.C. Bus. edn. instr. Felton Lab. Sch., Orangeburg, SC, 1995—2002; tech. coord. S.C. State U., Orangeburg, 2003—. Cons. Felton Lab. Sch., 1995—2003. Mem.: Delta Sigma Theta (life; rec. sec. 1998—2002). Home: PO Box 1931 Orangeburg SC 29116 Office: SC State U 300 College St Orangeburg SC 29117

RAMSEY, LUCIE AVRA, small business owner, consultant; b. N.Y., Mar. 3, 1942; d. Albert and Mazie (Gordon) Miller; m. Charles Allen Ramsey, Feb. 3, 1968; children: Aaron Ramsey (dec.), Jacqueline Hartigan. BS, U. San Francisco, 1986. Cert. mediator, cert. ct. mediator County Riverside Dispute Resolution Ctr. Office mgr. Quicksilver Products Inc., San Francisco, 1962-66; exec. sec. Far West Lab. for Educ. Rsch. and Devel., San Francisco and Berkeley, Calif., 1966-68; office mgr. The Ark Pub. Co., Tiburon, Calif., 1973-75; adminstrv. asst. Nat. Coun. Jewish Women, San Francisco, 1979-80; asst. to the chief Tiburon Fire Protection Dist., 1980; exec. dir. Zionist Orgn. Am., San Francisco, 1980-87; asst. dir. Bay Area Coun. for Soviet Jews, San Francisco, 1987-89; exec. dir. Jewish Community Rels. Coun., Oakland, Calif., 1989-91; pres. Ramsey Cons., Mill Valley, Calif., 1991—. Leader first ever interreligious task force to the USSR. Author: Concerns of the Jewish Community 1930's/1970's. Civic organizer, planner, chairperson Marin County Clergy Group, San Rafael, Calif., 1975-79; asst. area dir. Am. Jewish Com., San Francisco Bay Area chpt., 1994-96. Democratic. Jewish. Avocations: reading, camping, traveling.

RAMSEY, LYNN ALLISON, trade association, public relations professional; b. Phila., July 31, 1944; d. Charles Edward and Edna Berry (Whetstone) R. Student, Inst. European Studies, Vienna, Austria, 1964-65; BA, Boston U., 1967. Copy editor Am. Heritage Pub. Co., N.Y.C., 1969-71; prodr., writer Rick Carrier Film Prodns., N.Y.C., 1971-72; mng. editor New Ingenue mag., N.Y.C., 1973-75; freelance writer N.Y.C., 1975-80; mgr. pub. rels. Cunningham and Walsh (acquired by Ayer Pub. Rels. 1987), N.Y.C., 1981—; v.p., mgr. Ayer Pub. Rels., N.Y.C., 1988-95; pres., CEO Jewelry Info. Ctr., N.Y.C., 1995—. Author: Gigolos; The World's Best-Kept Men, 1978; photographer: FLY: The Complete Book of Sky Sailing, 1974; contbr. articles to profl. jours. Mem. Fgn. Policy Assn. 1982-87; mem. Chelsea Cmty. Ch. Bd., 1996—, chair, 1999—; sec. U.S.A. Bald Eagle Command, 1975—. Mem. Pub. Rels. Soc. Am. (accredited, bd. dirs. N.Y. chpt. 1993-95), Fashion Group Internat., Women's Jewelry Assn. (bd. dirs. 1993—, treas. 2000—, Award for Excellence 1993), Soc. Jewelry Historians. Avocations: cross-country skiing, traveling, cooking, reading.

RAMSEY, MARGIE, librarian; b. Bay City, Tex., Aug. 29, 1921; d. Cyrus Otis Lansford and Myra Lenore Ferrell; m. Joe Bryan Ramsey, July 29, 1945; children: Ronald Lansford, Kevin Bryan. BA in Libr. Sci., Tex. State U., 1942. Cert. tchr., Tex. Libr. Talco (Tex.) Ind. Sch. Dist., 1942-44; sec. Consolidated Aircraft, San Diego, summer 1943; bookkeeper Lockheed Aircraft, Dallas, 1944; libr. Dallas Pub. Libr., 1944-45; sec. Steck Co., Austin, Tex., 1946-48; libr. U. Tex., Austin, 1948-51. Author, poet:. Vol. libr. Hyde Park United Meth., Austin, 1963-2002, Leander (Tex.) Ind. Sch. Dist., 1982-92; mem. The Internat. Libr. of Poetry. Named Outstanding Vol., Nat. Assn. Ptnrs. in Edn., Kraft-Disney, 1989. Fellow AAUW. Democrat. Avocations: teaching, camping, computers, reading, collecting rare books. Home: 1105 Church St Georgetown TX 78626 E-mail: mramsey@verizon.net.

RAMSEY, MARY CATHERINE, mechanical engineer, consultant; b. dumas, Tex., Sept. 16, 1955; d. E. Edward and Mary V. Roberts; m. Jimmy Paul Ramsey, Aug. 18, 1984. BSME, Tex. Tech U., 1979. Registered profl. engr., Tex. Fatigue and fracture engr. Gen. Dynamics, 1979—80; design engr. Barnard & Burke, Baton Rouge, 1980-81; project engr. Ruston Gas Turbines, Houston, 1981-88, Hawker Siddeley, Houston, 1988-90; project mgr. Northern Engrng., Houston, 1990-95; project devel. mgr. Air Liquide Am., Houston, 1995-97; ind. cons. Cat Spring, Tex., 1997—. NSF rsch. scholar, 1974; Welch Rsch. Found. grantee, 1974; named Nat. Merit finalist, 1974. Avocations: llama breeding, wildlife rehabilitation, needlework, cooking, piano. Office: 17425 Tranquil Ln Cat Spring TX 78933 E-mail: cramsey@industryinet.com.

RAMSEY-GOLDMAN, ROSALIND, physician; b. N.Y.C., Mar. 22, 1954; d. Abraham L. and Miriam (Colen) Goldman; m. Glenn Ramsey, June 29,1 975; children: Ethan Ramsey, Caitlin Ramsey. BA, Case Western Res. U., 1975, MD, 1978; MPH, U. Pitts., 1988, DPH, 1992. Med. resident U. Rochester (N.Y.), 1978-81; chief resident Rochester Gen. Hosp., 1981-82; staff physician Univ. Health Svc., Rochester, 1982-83; rheumatology fellow U. Pitts., 1983-86, instr. medicine, 1986-87, asst. prof., 1987-91, co-dir. Lupus Treatment and Diagnostic Ctr., 1987-91; asst. prof. medicine Northwestern U., Chgo., 1991-96, assoc. prof. medicine, 1996—2001, prof. medicine, 2001—. Dir. Chgo. Lupus Registry, Northwestern U., Chgo., 1991—, chairperson Systemic Lupus Internat. Collaborating Clinics Group, 2003—. Contbr. rsch. articles to profl. jours. Recipient Finkelstein award Hershey (Pa.) Med. Ctr., 1986. Fellow ACP, Am. Coll. Rheumatology; mem. Soc. for Epidemiologic Rsch., Ctrl. Soc. Clin. Rsch. Office: Northwestern U Ward 3-315 303 E Chicago Ave Chicago IL 60611-3093 E-mail: rgramsey@northwestern.edu.

RAN, SHULAMIT, composer; b. Tel Aviv, Oct. 21, 1949;, U.S. m. Abraham Lotan, 1986. Studied composition with, Paul Ben-Haim, Norman Dello, Joio, Ralph Shapey; student, Mannes Coll. Music, N.Y.C., 1963—67. With dept. music U. Chgo., 1973—, William H. Colvin prof. music; composer-in-residence Chgo. Symphony Orch., 1990—97, Lyric Opera of Chgo., 1994—97. Compositions include 10 Children's Scenes, 1967, Structures, 1968, 7 Japanese Love Poems, 1968, Hatzvi Israel Eulogy, 1969, O the Chimneys, 1969, Concert Piece for piano and orch., 1970, 3 Fantasy Pieces for Cello and Piano, 1972, Ensembles for 17, 1975, Double Vision, 1976, Hyperbolae for Piano, 1976, For an Actor: Monologue for Clarinet, 1978, Apprehensions, 1979, Private Game, 1979, Fantasy-Variations for Cello, 1980, A Prayer, 1982, Verticals for piano, 1982, String Quartet No. 1, 1984, (for woodwind quintet) Concerto da Camera I, 1985, Amichai Songs, 1985, Concerto for Orchestra, 1986, (for clarinet, string quartet and piano) Concerto da Camera II, 1987, East Wind, 1987, String Quartet No. 2, 1988—89, Symphony, 1989—90, Mirage, 1990, Inscriptions for solo violin, 1991, Chicago Skyline for brass and percussion, 1991, Legends for orch., 1992—93, Invocation, 1994, Yearning for violin and string orch., 1995, (opera) Between Two Worlds (The Dybbuk), 1995—97, Soliloquy, 1997, Vessels of Courage and Hope for orch., 1998, (flute concerto) Voices, 2000, Three Scenes for solo clarinet, 2000, Supplications for chorus and orch., 2002, Violin Concerto, 2003, commd. pieces include for Am. Composers Orch., Phila. Orch., Chgo. Symphony, Balt. Symphony, Chamber Soc. of Lincoln Ctr., Mendelssohn String quartet, Da Capo Chamber Players, Sta. WFMT, Lyric Opera Chgo., composer and soloist for 1st performances Capariccio, 1963, Symphonic Poem, 1967, Concert Piece, 1971. Named Guggenheim fellow, 1977, 1990; recipient Acad. Inst. Arts and Letters award, 1989, Pulitzer prize for music, 1991, Friedheim award for orchestral music, Kennedy Ctr., 1992. Office: U Chgo Dept Music 1010 E 59th St Chicago IL 60637-1512

RANADA, ROSE MARIE, retired elementary school educator; b. McClure, Ill., Sept. 21, 1936; d. James F. and Agnes T. (Sullivan) Glaab; m. Anthony Ranada, Oct. 25, 1958; children: James, Thomas. BA, San Jose (Calif.) State U., 1958; MA, U. San Francisco, 1975. Elem. tchr. Alum Rock Sch. Dist., San Jose, Calif., Jefferson Union Sch. Dist., Santa Clara, Calif., Sunnyvale Sch. Dist., Calif. Mentor to student tchrs. Sunnyvale Sch. Dist., Calif., 1963—96. Author: (with J. Rust) Child Care Guidebook for Santa Clara County. Grantee Hewlett Packard Co.

RANALD, MARGARET LOFTUS, English literature educator, author; b. Auckland, N.Z., Sept. 5, 1927; came to U.S., 1952; d. Leonard R. and Geraldine (McGrath) Loftus; m. Ralph Arthur Ranald, Feb. 26, 1955; 1 child, Caroline Margaret. AB, U. N.Z., Wellington, 1949, MA honors, 1951; MA, UCLA, 1954, PhD, 1958. Jr. asst. Dept. Prime Min. Govt. N.Z., Wellington, 1944-52; asst. to sec. Princeton (N.J.) U., 1956-57; from instr. to asst. prof. Temple U., Phila., 1957-61; from asst. prof. to prof. CUNY, N.Y.C., 1961—. Assoc. bibliographer MLA, N.Y.C., 1958—; mem. assoc. faculty, mem. adv. com. Columbia U., N.Y.C., 1976—; vis. prof. UCLA, 1970-85, 98, tchg. asst., 1953-55. Author: The Eugene O'Neill Companion, 1984, Shakespeare and his Social Context, 1987, John Webster, 1989; assoc. editor (book series): International Bibliography of Theatre, 1985—. Fulbright fellow, 1952-54; sr. fellow Folger Shakespeare Libr., 1970-72. Mem. MLA, Am. Soc. Theatre Rsch. (exec. sec., v.p. 1976-83), Eugene O'Neill Soc. (coun., pres. 1996-2000), Shakespeare Soc. Am. (former rsch. asst.), Princeton Club N.Y. Avocations: music, drama, theatrical history, travel. Office: CUNY Dept of Eng 65-30 Kissena Blvd Flushing NY 11367

RANCE, SHARON LEE, speech pathology/audiology services professional; d. Harold Rance and Dorothy Diamond; m. Peter Freedman, July 18, 1968 (div. Jan. 1984); children: Barbara Freedman Hammer, Stephanie Freedman. BA, Queens Coll., 1968; MS, U. Wis., 1971. Lic. speech-lang. pathology Tex. Speech pathologist Madison (Wis.) and Bangor Sch. Dists., 1968—73, Albuquerque Pub. Schs., 1973—74, Head Start, San Diego, 1974—75, Wisconsin Rapids (Wis.) Sch. Dist., 1978—79, MHMRA, Johnstown, Pa., 1980—82, Alief Ind. Sch. Dist., Houston, 1983—. Team leader Mata Intermediate, Houston, 1999—2001, shared decision making coun., 2001—03. Vol. Seven Acres Home for the Aged, Houston, 1992. Recipient Summer traineeship, State Dept. Pub. Instrn., Madison, 1970. Mem.: Am. Speech-Lang.-Hearing Assn. (cert. clin. competence), Sigma Alpha Eta. Achievements include produced a carrying case for the Wolf Communication device which was sold throughout the world. Avocations: stained glass, dance, golf, sailing. Office: Mata Intermediate Sch 9225 S Dairy Ashford Houston TX 77099

RAND, JOELLA MAE, retired nursing educator, counselor; b. Akron, Ohio, July 9, 1932; d. Harry S. and Elizabeth May (Miller) Halberg; m. Martin Rand (dec.); children: Craig, Debbi Stark. BSN, U. Akron, 1961, MEd in Guidance, 1968; PhD in Higher Edn. Adminstrn., Syracuse U., 1981. Staff nurse Akron Gen. Hosp., 1953-54; staff-head nurse-instr. Summit County Receiving, Cuyahoga Falls, Ohio, 1954-56; head nurse psychiat. unit Akron Gen. Hosp., 1956-57; instr. psychiatric nursing Summit County Receiving, Cuyahoga Falls, 1957-61; head nurse, inservice instr. Willard (N.Y.) State Hosp., 1961-62; asst. prof. Alfred (N.Y.) U., 1962-76, assoc. prof., assoc. dean, 1976-78, acting dean, 1978-79, dean, 1979-90, dean coll. profl. studies, 1990-91, prof. counseling, 1991-2000; ret., 2000. Cons. N.Y. State Regents Program for Non-Collegiate Sponsored Instrn., 1984; cons. collegiate programs N.Y. State Dept. Edn., 1985, Elmira Coll., 1991, U. Rochester, 1992-93; accreditation visitor Nat. League for Nursing, 1984-92; ednl. cons. Willard Psychiat. Hosp., 1992-93; mem. profl. practice exam. subcom. Regents Coll., 1990-95. Vol. Williard Drug Treatment Ctr., 1997—, bd. dirs., Romulus Zoning Bd., 2002—; vol. Red Cross, 2003—; bd. dirs. Five Point Correctional Facility. Recipient Tchg. Excellence award Alfred U., 1977, Mary E. Gladwin Outstanding Alumni award Akron U. Coll. Nursing, 1983, Alfred Alumni Friends award, 1989, Grand Marshall commencement Alfred U., 1993, Vol. of Yr. award Willard Drug Treatment Ctr., 1999. Mem.: ACA (NAR rep. 2000—), Genesee Valley Edn. Com. (chair 1984—86), Western N.Y. League Nursing (bd. dirs. 1991—93), Genesee Regional Consortium (v.p.), N.Y. State Coun. of Deans (treas. 1984—88), N.Y. State Counseling Assn. (v.p.-elect profl. svcs. 1995—96, 1998—99, v.p. profl. svcs. 1996—98, 1999—2000), Sigma Theta Tau (treas. Alfred chpt. 1984—85). Avocations: boating, fishing, public speaking in areas of family and child abuse. E-mail: drand@rochester.rr.com.

RAND, KATHY SUE, public relations executive; b. Miami Beach, Fla., Feb. 24, 1945; d. William R. and Rose (Lasser) R.; m. Peter C. Ritsos, Feb. 19, 1982. BA, Mich. State U., 1965; MBA, Northwestern U., 1980. Asst. editor Lyons & Carnahan, Chgo., 1967-68; mng. editor Cahners Pub. Co., Chgo., 1968-71; pub. rels. writer Super Market Inst., Chgo., 1972-73; account supr. Pub. Communications Inc., Chgo., 1973-77; divisional mgr. pub. rels. Quaker Oats Co., Chgo., 1977-82; exec. v.p., dep. gen. mgr. Golin/Harris Communications, Chgo., 1982-90; exec. v.p. Lesnik Pub. Rels., Northbrook, Ill., 1990-91; mng. dir. Manning, Selvage & Lee, Chgo., 1991—2002. Dir. midwest region NOW, 1972-74; mem. Kellogg Alumni Adv. Bd.; bd. dirs. Jr. Achievement of Chgo. Mem. Pub. Rels. Soc. Am. (Silver Anvil award 1986, 87), Pub. Club Chgo. (Golden Trumpet awards 1982-87, 90, 94, 95, 97, 98, 99, 2000), Vet. Feminists of Am. (bd. dirs.), Northwestern Club Chgo., Kellogg Alumni Club, Beta Gamma Sigma. Home: 400 Riverwoods Rd Lake Forest IL 60045-2547 E-mail: ksrand@aol.com.

RANDALL, BEVERLY MARILYN, theater director; b. Orlando, Fla., Nov. 17, 1966; d. Jerry D. and Marilyn L. Randall. BA, Baylor U., 1989; MA, U. Tex., 1991, PhD, 1997. Asst. editor Holt, Rinehart & Winston, Austin, Tex., 1997—98; program officer Tex. Coun. for Humanities, Austin, 1998—2000; devel. dir. Alley Theatre, Houston, 2000—. Bd. dirs. Bobbindoctorin Puppet Theatre, Houston; mem. peer panel rev. bd. Cultural Arts Coun., Houston, 2001, Houston, 02. Vol. Planned Parenthood Young Leaders, Houston, 2002, 2003, Found. for the Retarded, Houston, 2001, 2002, 2003. Mem.: Assn. Profession Rschrs. for Advancement, Assn. Fundraising Profls. Democrat. Unitarian Universalist. Office: Alley Theatre 615 Texas Ave Houston TX 77009-1420 also: 205 Fairbanks St Houston TX 77009-1807 E-mail: randall@io.com.

RANDALL, CARLA ELIZABETH, nursing educator; b. Calif., Dec. 28, 1958; d. Lester Lee and Carrie Allen (Helm) R.; m. Dara Reimers, Oct. 4, 1995. Diploma, Luth. Hosp. Sch. Nursing, Ft. Wayne, Ind., 1979; BSN, Coe Coll., 1981; MSN, U. Dubuque, 1987; postgrad., U. B.C., Vancouver, Can., 1996—99; student, U. Victoria, Victoria, B.C., 2000—. RN, Mont. Staff nurse CCU U. Iowa, Iowa City, 1982-84, faculty, 1985-90, Kirkwood C.C., Cedar Rapids, Iowa, 1983-85, Salish Kootenai Coll., Pablo, Mont., 1990-93; nurse supr. West Mont., Polson, Mont., 1991-96; sessional faculty U. Victoria, Canada, 1997—2001; sr. instr. U. So. Maine at LAC, Lewiston, 2003—. Dir., counselor Earth Unbound, 1987-96. Contbr. articles to profl. jours. Bd. dirs. Montana Pride, Helena, 1995-96, Mont. Human Rights Network, Helena, 1994-96, Flathead Reservation Human Rights Coalition, Ronan, Mont., 1990-96, Mont. PFLAG, St. Regis, Mont., 1994-96. Rsch. grantee Sigma Theta Tau, U. Iowa, 1988. Mem. ANA. Avocation: feminist. Office: U So Maine at LAC 51 Westminster St 162-H Lewiston ME 04240

RANDALL, CLAIRE, church executive; b. Dallas, Oct. 15, 1919; d. Arthur Godfrey and Annie Laura (Fulton) R. AA, Schreiner Coll., 1948; BA, Scarritt Coll., 1950; DD (hon.), Berkeley Sem., Yale U., 1974; LHD (hon.), Austin Coll., 1982; LLD (hon.), Notre Dame U., 1984. Assoc. missionary edn. Bd. World Missions Presbyn. Ch., U.S., Nashville, 1949-57, dir. art Gen. Coun. Atlanta, 1957-61; dir. Christian World Mission, program dir., assoc. dir. Ch. Women United, N.Y.C., 1962-73; gen. sec. Nat. Coun. Ch. of Christ in U.S.A., N.Y.C., 1974-84, ret., 1985; nat. pres. Ch. Women United, N.Y.C., 1988-92. Mem. Nat. Commn. on Internat. Women's Yr., 1975-77, Martin Luther King Jr. Fed. Holiday Commn., 1985. Recipient Woman of Yr. in Religion award Heritage Soc., 1977; Empire State Woman of Yr. in Religion award State of N.Y., 1984; medal Order of St. Vladimir, Russian Orthodox Ch., 1984. Democrat. Episcopalian. Avocations: golf, swimming, painting, reading, music. Home: 9965 W Royal Oak Rd # 1214 Sun City AZ 85351

RANDALL, FRANCES, technical writer; b. Frederick, Md., Oct. 6, 1924; d. George Birely and Ruth Carty Delaplaine; m. Myron William Randall, Apr. 10, 1949; children: George Elliott, Myron William Jr., Ruth Ann Randall, Eleanor Jane Randall Luttrell. BA, Hood Coll., 1945; MS, The Johns Hopkins U., 1947. Chemist U.S. Army lab., Frederick, Md., 1947-49; writer-historian The Frederick News-Post, 1965—. Chmn. bd. dirs. The Randall Family LLC, 2001—. Author: (book) Mirror on Frederick, 1998. Bd. dirs. Cmty. Found. of Frederick Co., 1988-96. Recipient vol. yr., Cmty. Found., Frederick Co., 1993, Cmty. Svc. award, Ch. Transfiguration, Braddock Heights, Md., 1999, Thanks Badge, Penn Laurel Girl Scout Coun., 1988, Alumnae Achievement award Hood Coll., 1998, Woman of Distinction award Girl Scouts Am., 2000. Mem. Hood Coll. Alumnae Assn. (pres., sec.), Frederick Woman's Civic Club (publicity chair, pres.); bd. dirs. Penn Laurel Girl Scout Coun., Braddock Heights Cmty. Assn. Avocations: swimming, biking, photography, travel, grand children. Home: 6301 Jefferson Blvd Frederick MD 21703-5809

RANDALL, HERMINE MARIA, retired power plant engineer; b. Vienna, July 22, 1927; came to U.S., 1948; d. Heinrich Georg Adametz and Maria Antonia (Paul) Safranek; m. May 25, 1948 (div. 1975); children: George Eugene, Dorothy Maria. Lic. 1st class stationary engr., Mass. Shift supr. Stony Brook Generating Sta. Mass. Mcpl. Wholesale Electric Co., Ludlow, 1980-82; chief engr. power plant U. Mass., Amherst, 1982-87, mgr. utility generation and distbn., 1987-90, acting dir. engring., 1990-91; dir. engring., 1991-95; ret., 1995. Recipient spl. achievement award Region I, U.S. Dept. Labor, 1980, Chancellor's Citation U. Mass., 1990, Citation for Outstanding Performance, Commonwealth of Mass., 1990. Mem. Nat. Assn. Power Engrs. (pres. Springfield chpt. 1989-90). Republican. Home: 22 Worthington Dr South Hadley MA 01075-3319

RANDALL, KAREN, film company executive; BA cum laude, Vassar Coll., 1973; JD, UCLA, 1976. Ptnr. Wyman Bautzer Kuchel & Silbert, 1976; mng. ptnr. Katten Muchin & Zavi, LA, sr. v.p., gen. counsel Universal Studios, 1996—2000; exec. v.p., gen. counsel Vivendi Universal Entertainment, Universal City, Calif., 2000—. Bd. mem. United Internat. Pictures, Hollywood Sign Trust, Hollywood Canteen Found. Named to, YWCA Acad. Women Achievers, The Am. Lawyer's 1995 edit. of "Forty-Five Under 45"; recipient Women of Distinction award, Hollywood C. of C., Pursuit of Justice award, Calif. Women's Law Ctr., Corp. Leadership award, Big Sisters L.A. Mem.: Motion Picture Assn. Am. (Universal's liaison, bd. dirs., mem. spl. policy group), Am. Corp. Counsel Assn. (nat. bd. dirs.). Office: Vivendi Universal Entertainment 100 Universal City Plaza Universal City CA 91608-1002*

RANDALL, KAY TEMPLE, accountant, retired real estate agent; b. Chattanooga, Sept. 23, 1952; d. James H. Temple and Hortense N. (Dailey) Goodner; m. Gary F. Goodner, Feb. 9, 1968 (div. July 1972); 1 child, Jeffrey F. Goodner; m. Rodney B. Randall, Oct. 3, 1987. Student, Chattanooga State Coll., 1970-77, 82-83, Am. Inst. Banking, 1977-79. Lic. real estate agt., Tenn., ret.; notary public, Tenn. Ins. rep. Colonial Life Accident and Health, Columbia, S.C., 1980-82; real estate appraiser, agt. Chattanooga, 1983-88; acct. Mr. Transmission of Chattanooga, Inc., 1987—; real estate agt. Chattanooga, 1989—. Adminstrv. asst. to legal profession, Chattanooga, 1972-75. Adv. bd. United Meth. Ch., Chattanooga, 1979-82, tchr., 1979-83; fellow cen. br. YMCA, Chattanooga, 1977-97. Fellow Walden's Club. Republican. Episcopalian. Avocation: collecting art. Home: 1858 Rivergate Ter Soddy Daisy TN 37379-5947 Office: Mr Transmission of Chattanooga Inc PO Box 1395 Soddy Daisy TN 37384-1395 E-mail: rodkayj@aol.com.

RANDALL, LILIAN MARIA CHARLOTTE, museum curator; b. Berlin, Feb. 1, 1931; came to U.S., 1938; d. Frederick Henry and Elizabeth Agnes (Ziegler) Cramer; m. Richard Harding Randall, Apr. 11, 1953; children: Christopher, Julia, Katharine. BA cum laude, Mount Holyoke Coll., 1950; MA, Radcliffe Coll., 1951, PhD, 1955; LHD (hon.), Towson State U., 1993; D of Arts (hon.), Mt. Holyoke Coll., 1998. Asst. dir. Md. State Arts Coun., 1972-73; curator manuscripts and rare books Walters Art Gallery, Balt., 1974-85, rsch. curator manuscripts, 1985-95; rsch. cons., 1995-97. Vis. lectr. dept. art history Johns Hopkins U., 1964-68; hon. vis. lectr. U. Mich., Ann Arbor; lectr. in field; bd. dirs. Digital Scriptorium: Electronic Access to Medieval Manuscripts; advisor Union Manuscript Computer Catalogue, 1996—. Author: Images in the Margins of Gothic Manuscripts, 1966; co-editor: Gatherings in Honor of Dorothy Miner, 1974, The Diary of George A. Lucas: An American Art Agent in Paris, 1909-1957, 1979, Illuminated Manuscripts: Masterpieces in Miniature, 1984, Medieval and Renaissance Manuscripts in the Walters Art Gallery, Vol. I, France, 875-1420, 1989, Vol. II, France, 1420-1540, 1992, Vol. III, Belgium, 1250-1530, 1997; contbr. articles to profl. jours. Mem. Williston Libr. com., 1988-89; reviewer, panelist NEH, 1980—; mem. vis. com. Art of Europe dept. Mus. Fine Arts, Boston, 2002—. Grantee AAUW, 1953-54, ACLS, 1960, 65, Bunting Inst., 1961-63, Ford Found., 1967-69, Am. Philos. Soc., 1971, NEA, 1975, Samuel H. Kress Found., 1979, 81-84, NEH, 1977-84, 89-95; grantee publ. subsidy Md. State Arts Coun., 1972, Mcpl. Art Soc. Balt., 1972, Andrew W. Mellon Found., 1988, Getty Grant program, 1990-92, NEA Mus. program, 1992-93; recipient Festschrift, Walters Art Gallery, ed. Elizabeth Burin, 1996, Sesquicentennial award Mount Holyoke Coll., 1987. Fellow Medieval Acad. Am. (libr. preservation com., various coms. 1985-87, 90-93); mem. Internat. Ctr. Medieval Art (bd. dirs. 1978-82, 96-99), Coll. Art Assn. (Arthur Kingsley Porter prize 1957), Balt. Bibliophiles (bd. dirs. 1966-80, pres. 1980-83), Pyramid Atlantic (bd. dirs. 1985-88), Mus. Fine Arts Boston (vis. com. Art of Europe dept. 2002—), Grolier Club, Phi Beta Kappa. Home: 370 Adams St Milton MA 02186-4233

RANDALL, LINDA LEA, biochemist, educator; b. Montclair, N.J., Aug. 7, 1946; d. Lowell Neal and Helen (Watts) R.; m. Gerald Lee Hazelbauer, Aug. 29, 1970. BS, Colo. State U., 1968; PhD, U. Wis., 1971. Postdoctoral fellow Inst. Pasteur, Paris, 1971—73; asst. prof. Uppsala (Sweden) U., 1975—81; assoc. prof. Wash. State U., Pullman, 1981—83, prof. biochemistry, 1983—2000; Wurdock prof. biochemistry U. Mo., Columbia, 2000—. Guest scientist Wallenberg Lab., Uppsala U., 1973-75; study section NIH, 1984-88. Mem. edit. bd. Jour. of Bacteriology, 1982-96; co-editor: Virus Receptors Part I, 1980; contbr. articles to profl. jours. Recipient Eli Lilly Award in Microbiology and Immunology, Am. Soc. Microbiology, Am. Assn. Immunologists, Am. Soc. Exptl. Pathology, 1984, Faculty Excellence Award in Rsch., Washington State U., 1988, Disting. Faculty Address, 1990, Parke-Davis award, 1995. Fellow AAAS, Am. Acad. Microbiology; mem. NAS, Am. Microbiol. Soc., Am. Soc. Biol. Chemists, Protein Soc. Avocation: dance. Office: Univ Mo Dept Biochemistry 117 Schweitzer Hall Columbia MO 65211 Office Phone: 573-884-4160.

RANDALL, LYNN ELLEN, librarian; b. Chgo., Oct. 10, 1951; d. Ward W. and Hazel A. (Nettles) R. BA, King's Coll., 1970; MA, Seton Hall U., 1973; MLS, Rutgers U., 1978. Libr. asst. Newark Coll. Engring, Newark, 1970-75; libr. dir. N.E. Bible Coll., Essex Fells, N.J., 1975-81; reference libr. Seton Hall U., South Orange, N.J., 1983-85; dir. libr. svc. Berkeley Coll., NJ, 1985-89; with Caldwell Coll., NJ, 1989—, exec. dir. libr. svcs. Reference libr., instr. Morris (N.J.) County Coll., 1981-83; panelist/facilitator Middle States Self-Study Inst., 1996, 97, Evaluator, Middle States, 1994-. Mem. N.J. Libr. Assn. (pres. 1996-97), Am. Libr. Assn. Office: Jennings Libr Caldwell Coll 9 Ryerson Ave Caldwell NJ 07006-6109 Office Phone: 973-618-3314. E-mail: lrandall@caldwell.edu.

RANDALL, PRISCILLA RICHMOND, retired travel company executive; b. Arlington, Mass., Mar. 19, 1926; d. Harold Bours and Florence (Hoefler) Richmond; m. Raymond Victor Randall, Mar. 2, 1946; children: Raymond Richmond, Priscilla Randall Middleton, Susan Randall Geery. Student, Wellesley Coll., 1943-44; Assoc., Garland Coll., 1946; student, Winona State U., 1977-81. Pub. relations dir. Rochester Meth. Hosp., Rochester, Minn., 1960-69; dir. pub relations Sheraton Rochester, 1969-71; pres. Med. Charters, Rochester, 1970-75, Ideas Unltd., Rochester, 1969-77; chief exec. officer Randall Travel, Rochester, 1977-89; pres. Randall Travel Delray, Delray Beach, Fla., 1989—2002; ret., 2002. Pres. Bar Harbour Apts. Inc., Delray Beach, 1989, sec., bd. dirs., 2002; social com. chmn., 1999—, sec., 1993-99. Editor, Inside Story, 1960-69, Rochester Meth. Hosp. News, 1960-69; producer Priscilla's World, 1972-75. Pres. Rochester Meth. Hosp. Aux., 1957-59, Downtown Bus. Assn., Rochester, 1985; treas. Class of 1947 Wellesley (Mass.) Coll., 1997-2002. Recipient Woman of Achievement Bus. YWCA, Rochester, 1983, Golden Door Knob, Bus. and Prfl. Women, Rochester, 1979. Mem. Inst. Cert. Travel Agts. (life), Assn. Retail Travel Agts. (life, nat. bd. 1988-90, sec. to bd. 1988-90, sec.-treas. Arlington, Va. nat. bd. 1990), Am. Soc. Travel Agts., Pacific Area Travel Agts., Minn. Exec. Women in Travel, Cruise Line Internat. Assn. (master cruise counselor), Little Club (sec. 2002, v.p. 2003- Gulfstream, Fla.) (sec. women's golf com. 1993-99, sec. bd. govs. 2002, treas. 2002), Hibiscus Garden Club (Delray Beach, Fla.) (pres., corr. sec.), Travelors Century Club (bd. govs.), Circumnavigator Club, Little Club (v.p. 2003—). Avocation: travel writing. Home: 86 Macfarlane Dr Apt 2C Delray Beach FL 33483-6901

RANDALL, RHONDA MICHAELE, music educator; b. Madison, Wis., Jan. 27, 1952; d. Benjamin J. and Phyllis Elaine Talledge, Evelyn Mae Nimmo; m. Karl Arthur Randall, June 9, 1990 (div. May 21, 2003); 1 child, Melissa Mae Bell. BS. in Vocal Music Edn., Mt. Senario Coll., 1974. Music/choral tchr. Lake Holcombe Sch., Wis., 1974—. Dir., soloist Ladysmith (Wis.) Cmty. Singers, 1972—2003; organist, choir dir. Lake Holcombe United Meth. Ch., 1992—2003. Recipient Outstanding Alumnus, Mt. Senario Coll., 1984, 1989. Mem.: Wis. Sch. Music Assn. (cert. adjudicator 1991, music selection com. 1980—, mem. adjudication com. 2002—), Music Educator's Nat. Conf., Lakeland Music Conf. (life). Home: E10768 E Salem Ridge Rd LaFarge WI 54639 Office: Lake Holcombe Sch 27331 262nd Holcombe WI 54745

RANDALL, SHEILA R. real estate company executive; b. Shelby, N.C., Oct. 14, 1955; d. Bobby Randall and Jo Ann (Baldwin) Peeler; m. David Tiller, Aug. 18, 1973 (div. July 1986); children: Matt, Carrie, Katie. Student, Trevecca Nazarene U., 1997. Affiliate broker Folk-Jordan Realtors, Brentwood, Tenn., 1985-90; residential sales rep. Liberty Mus. Ins., Franklin, Tenn., 1990-94; broker ERA-Adams Realtors, Brentwood, Tenn., 1994-98; pres. HomeTrust Real Estate Investments, Brentwood, Tenn., 1996-98; prin. broker First Home Builder's Realty, Gastonia, N.C., 1998—. Recipient numerous real estate sales awards. Mem. Charlotte Regional Realtors Assn., Gastonia C. of C., William County C. of C., Greater Nashville Assn. Realtors, Williamson County Assn. Realtors (edn. com. 1985-96). Baptist. Avocations: dance, boating, reading. Office: First Home Builder's Realty Gastonia NC 28056

RANDER, JOANN CORPACI, musician, music educator; b. Waterbury, Conn., June 24, 1954; d. Anthony and Victoria Corpaci; m. David Rander, July 22, 1983. MusB Piano magna cum laude, Hartt Coll. Music, 1976, MusM Piano magna cum laude, 1980; studied classical piano with Paul Rutnam, Juilliard Sch., N.Y.C.; studied percussion, with Joe (Skinny) Purcaro, Hollywood, Calif. Musician various org., 1964—; music tchr. Fox Mid. Sch., Hartford, Conn., 1976—77, McDonough Sch., Hartford, 1976—77, Kennelly Sch., Hartford, 1976—77, S. Cath. H.S., Conn., 1977—78, St. Brigid Sch., Elmood, Conn., 1978—80, Wolcott Pub. Sch., Conn., 1980—85; pvt. instr. Zinno Music Studio, Waterbury, Conn., 1985—89. Judge Miss Mattauck Pageant, Conn., 1986, Miss Prospect Pageant, Conn., 1986, Miss Watertown Pageant, Conn., 1986, Miss Cheshire Pageant, Conn., 1987, Music Adjudication Festivals, Hartford, others. Performer: with Buddy Rich Big Band, 1973; performances throughout Fla. including Mar-a-Lago, Gov.'s Club, Four Seasons Hotel, others, conductor, accompanist New Brit. Reperatory Theatre, Miss Conn. and Universe Pageants, 1976—87. Recipient Joseph Summa award; scholar Conn. State scholar, Conn. State Union Barbers Assn. Roman Catholic. Achievements include youngest mem. in musicians union, 1968. Avocations: music performance, piano, percussion, singing, dance. Home: 2750 Tecumseh Drive West Palm Beach FL 33409-7446

RANDINELLI, TRACEY ANNE, magazine editor; b. Morristown, N.J., Apr. 6, 1963; d. Andrew R. and Patricia Ann (Brenner) R. BA in Comm., U. Del., 1985. Copywriter Macy's N.J., Newark, 1985-86; editl. asst. Globe Comms. Corp., N.Y.C., 1986-87; from asst. editor to assoc. editor Scholastic Math and DynaMath Mags. Scholastic, Inc., N.Y.C., 1987-89, editor Scholastic Math Mag., 1989-95; mng. editor Zig Zag Mag. Games Pub. Group, N.Y.C., 1995; sr. editor Contact Kids Mag./ Sesame Workshop, N.Y.C., 1996-2001; freelance writer, 2001—02; sr. editor Pearson Learning Group, 2002—. Mem. Soc. Children's Book Writers, Ednl. Press Assn. Am. (Disting. Achievement award feature articles divsn. 1991, 95, coverdesign 1996, how-to feature divsn. 1998, 99). E-mail: pen4kidz@aol.com.

RANDISI, ELAINE MARIE, accountant, educator, writer; b. Racine, Wis., Dec. 19, 1926; d. John Dewey and Alveta Irene (Raffety) Fehd; m. John Paul Randisi, Oct. 12, 1946 (div. July 1972); children: Jeanine Randisi Manson, Martha Randisi Chaney (dec.), Joseph, Paula, Catherine Randisi Carvalho, George, Anthony (dec.); m. John R. Woodfin, June 18, 1994. AA, Pasadena Jr. Coll., 1946; BS cum laude (Giannini scholar), Golden Gate U., 1978. With Raymond Kaiser Engrs., Inc., Oakland, Calif., 1969-75, 77-86, corp. acct., 1978-79, sr. corp. acct., 1979-82, sr. payroll acct., 1983-86; acctg. mgr. Lilli Ann Corp., San Francisco, 1986-89; acting mgr. Crosby, Heafey, Roach & May, Oakland, 1990-98; accounts payable coord. Crosby, Heafy, Roach & May, Oakland, 2003—. Initiated Minority Vendor Purchasing Program for Kaiser Engrs., Inc., 1975-76; corp. buyer Kaiser Industries Corp., Oakland, 1975-77; lectr. on astrology Theosophical Soc., San Francisco, 1979-99; mem. faculty Am. Fedn. Astrologers Internat. Conv., Chgo., 1982, 84. Mem. Speakers Bur., Calif. Assn. for Neurologically Handicapped Children, 1964-70, v.p., 1969; bd. dirs. Ravenwood Homeowners Assn., 1979-82, v.p., 1979-80, sec., 1980-81, mem. organizing com. Minority Bus. Fair, San Francisco, 1976; pres., bd. dirs. Lakewood Condominium Assn., 1984-87; mem. trustee Ch. of Religious Sci., 1992-95; treas. First Ch. Religious Sci., 1994-98, lic. practitioner, pres., 1990-91, sec., 1989-90. Mem. Am. Fedn. Astrologers, Calif. Scholarship Fedn. (life), Alpha Gamma Sigma (life). Home: 742 Wesley Way Apt 1C Oakland CA 94610-2339

RANDLETT, MARY WILLIS, photographer; b. Seattle, May 5, 1924; d. Cecil Durand and Elizabeth (Bayley) Willis; m. Herbert B. Randlett, Oct. 19, 1950 (div.); children: Robert, Mary Ann, Peter, Susan. BA, Whitman Coll., Walla Walla, Wash., 1947. Freelance photographer, 1949—. One-woman shows include Seattle Sci. Ctr., 1971, Western Wash. State U., 1971, Seattle Art Mus., 1971, Art Gallery Greater Victoria, 1972, Alaska State Mus., 1972, State Capitol Mus., 1983, Whatcom Mus. History and Art, Bellingham, Wash., 1986, Janet Huston Gallery, LaConner, Wash., 1990, Gov.'s Gallery, Office of Gov., Olympia, Wash., 1991, Stonington Gallery, Seattle, 1992, Valley Mus. Art, LaConner, 1992, Grad. Sch. Design Dept. Landscape Arch. Harvard U., Cambridge, Mass., 1996, Mus. N.W. Art, LaConner, 1998, others, exhibited in group shows at Am. Soc. Mag. Photographers, 1970, Whatcom Mus., Bellingham, Henry Gallery, Seattle, 1971, 1974, Royal Photg. Soc., 1979, Heard Mus., Phoenix, 1979, State Capital Mus., Olympia, Wash., 1983, 1984, 1988, 1989, 1993, Santa Fe Ctr. for Photography, 1987, Tacoma Art Mus., 1989, Helen Day Art Ctr., Stowe, Vt., 1989, Valley Mus. N.W. Art, LaConner, 1991, 1994, 1996—98, Allen Libr. U. Wash., Seattle, 1991, Wing Luke Asian Mus., 1991, Cheney Cowles Mus., Spokane, 1991, 1998, Security Pacific Gallery, Seattle, 1992, Benham Gallery, 1993, Stonington Gallery, 1993, 1998, Rainier Club, Seattle, 1994, Port Angeles (Wash.) Fine Arts Ctr., 1994, Mus. History and Industry, Seattle, 1994, Whatcom Mus., Bellingham, 1994, Pacific N.W. Annual Bellevue Art Mus., Wash., 1995, Skagit Valley Hist. Mus., LaConner, 1995, Seattle Art Mus., 1996—98, Kirkland (Wash.) Arts Ctr., 1997, Bainbridge Arts and Crafts, Bainbridge Island, Wash., 1997, Lucia Douglas Gallery, Bellingham, 1997, Anchorage Mus. History & Art, 1997, Burke Mus. Natural History and Culture, Seattle, 1998, Henderson House, Turnwater, Wash., 1998, Whatcom Arco Exhibit Gallery, Bellingham, 1998, Sea First Gallery, Seattle, 1998, 1999, Citizens Cultural Ctr., Fujinomita, Japan, 1999, Mus. Am. Indian, N.Y.C., 1999, Cheney Cowels Mus., Spokane, 1999, J. Paul Horiuchi Seattle Asian Art Mus., 2000, Mus. NW Art, 2000, Seattle Art Mus., 2002, Whitney Mus. Am. Art, N.Y.C., 2002, High Mus., Atlanta, 2002, and numerous others, Represented in permanent collections Met. Mus., Nat. Collection of Fine Arts, Nat. Portrait Gallery, Washington State Libr., Manuscript divsn. U. Wash., Pacific Northwest Bell, Seattle, Swedish Med. Ctr., Whatcom Mus., Bellingham, Henry Gallery, Seattle, Wash. State Capitol Mus., Olympia, Phillips Collection, Wash.; works appeared in books The Master and His Fish (Roderick Haig-Brown), 1982, Theodore Roethke: The Journey to I and Otherwide (Neal Bowers), 1982, Mountain in the Clouds (Bruce Brown), 1982, Masonry in Architecture (Louis Redstone), 1982, Writings and Reflections from the World of Roderick Haig-Brown), 1982, Pike Place Market (Alice Shorett and Murray Morgan), 1982, The Dancing Blanket, (Cheryl Samuel), 1982, Collected Poems of Theodore Roethke, 1982, Spires of Form (Victor Scheffer), 1983, Assault on Mount Helicon (Mary Barnard), 1983, New as a Wave (Eve Triem), 1983, Sketchbook: A Memoir of the '30's and the Northwest School (William Cumming), 1983, Good Intentions (Jane Adams), 1985, Blackbirds of the Americas (Gordon Orians and Tony Angell), 1985, Historic Preservation in Seattle (Larry Kreisman), 1985, Down Town Seattle Walking Tours (Mary Randlett and Carol Tobin), 1986, Seattle, the Seattle Book, 1986, When Orchids Were Flowers (Kate Knap Johnson), 1986, Jacob Lawrence, American Painter, (Ellen Wheat), 1986, Manic Power: Robert Lowell and His Circle (Jeffrey Meyers), 1987, The Isamu Noguchi Garden Museum (Isamu Noguchi), 1987, Washington's Audacious State Capitol an its Builders (Norman Johnston), 1988, The Bloedel Reserve: Gardens in the Forest (Lawrence Kreisman), 1988, Washingtonians: A Biographical Portrait of the State on the Occasion of its Centennial, 1988, Directory of Literary Biography: Canadian Writers 1920-59, 2d series, 1989, Crafts of America, 1989, The Lone Tree Tragedy (Bruce Brown), 1989, Northwest Coast Handbook of North American Indians, 1990, Dancing on the Rim of the World, 1990, Openings, Original Essays by Contemporary Soviet and American Writers (eds. Robert Atwan, Valeri Vinokurov), 1990, George Tsutakawa (Martha Kingsbury), 1990, Contemporary American Poetry (ed. Al Polin Jr.), 1991, Natural History of Puget Sound Country (Arthur Kruckberg), 1991, Bones (Joyce Thompson), 1991, Cebu (Peter Basho), 1991, Catalogue of Historic Preservation Publications, 1992, Art in Seattle's Public Places (James Rupp), 1992, The Olympic Rainforest (Ruth Kirk with Jerry Franklin), 1992, Steelhead Fly Fishing (Trey Combs), 1992, Illustrated Guidelines for Rehabilitation Historic Buildings, 1993, A History of African American Artists (Bearden and Henderson), 1994, Childrens Literature Review Vol. 1, 1994, Invisible Gardens: The Search for Modernism the American Landscape (Walker and Simo), 1994, Seeing Seattle (Roger Sale), 1994, Reaching Home (Jay and Matson), 1994, Redesigning the American Lawn: A Search for Environmental Harmony (Gordone Geballe, Diana Balmari and F. Herbert Bormann), 1995, Reaching Home: Pacific Salmon, Pacific People (Foves, Jay and Matson), 1995, Carl F. Gould: A Life in Architecture and the Arts (T. William Booth and William H. Wuksib), 1995, Destination Zero (Sam Hamill), 1996, Market Sketchbook, 25th Anniversary Edition, 1996, Sprir its of the Ordinary, 1997, Instrument of Change: Jim Schoppert 1947-1992, 1997, Looking for Edulabee Dix (Joann Ridley), 1997, Jack Lenor Larsen: A Memoir, 1998, Museo Nacional Centro de Arte Reina (Mark Tobey), 1998, Fountains Splash, and Spectacle: Water and Design from the Renaissance to Present (ed. Marilyn Symmes), 1998, Ghost Dancing (Anna Linzer), 1998, The Flower in the Skull (Kathleen Alcala), 1998, This Great Unknowing: Last Poems (Denise Levertov), 1999, Building Washington (Paul Dorpat, Genevier McCoy), 1999, The Wright Collection, Seattle Art Museum, 1999, Made to Last: Historic Preservation in Seattle and King County (Larry Kreisman), 1999, Isamu Noguchi: A Study of Space (Ana Maria Torres), 2000, The Tiger Iris (Joan Swift), 2000, The Eighth Lively Art (Wesley Wehr), 2000, All Powers Necessary and Convenient (Mark F. Jenkins), 2000, Ice Breakers: Alaska's Most Innovative Artists (Julie Decker), 2000, Over the Line: The Life and Art of Jacob Lawrence (Peter Nesbett and Michelle Dubois), 2000, Iridescent Light: The Emergence of Northwest Art (Delores Tarzan Ament), 2001, Messages from Frank's Landing, 2000, Leo Kenney: A Retrospective, 2000, Building for Learning: Seattle Public Schools History 1860-2000, 2001, Geology and Plant Life, 2001, and numerous others; works also appeared in newspapers and mags., one-woman shows include Iridescent Light: The Emergence of Northwest Art, Mary Randlett Portraits in the Arts Cmty., Wright Exhbn. Space, Seattle, 2002—03, book, Maritime Seattle, 2002, Picture Bainbridge Island: A Pictorial History, Distant Corner, 2003, Child of the Oemulgee. Recipient Wash. State Gov.'s award for spl. commendation for contbns. in field of photography, 1983, Individual Artist award, King County Arts Commn., 1989, Lifetime Achievement award, Artist Trust, 2001, Matrix Table, Seattle Women of Achievement, 1999, Nancy Blankenship Pryor award, 2001, Alumnus of Merit award, Whitman Coll, 2003; grantee, Nat. Endowment for Arts, 1976, Allied Arts Found., 2000. Mem. AIA (hon.), Am. Soc. Mag. Photographers. Home: PO Box 11238 Olympia WA 98508-1238 Office Phone: 360-352-1716.

RANDOLPH, BEVERLEY, production stage manager; b. Norristown, Pa., Aug. 26, 1951; d. Robert Lyman Kratz and Sarah Randolph (McDonnell) DaCosta. BFA magna cum laude, Ithaca Coll., 1973. Prodn. supr. Time and Again Old Globe, San Diego, 1996. Prodn. supr. Follies in Concert, Lincoln Ctr., N.Y.C., 1985, Uptown It's Hot, Phila., 1985, Queenie Pie, Duke Ellington Mus., Phila. and Washington, 1987, Jerome Robbins Broadway, Nat. Tour, Japan, L.A., 1990-91, Tony Awards, 1992, Sansho the Bailiff, Bklyn. Acad. Music, 1993, The Sound of Music, N.Y.C., 1998, The Sound of Music, N.Y.C., 1997, The Hunchback of Notre Dame, Berlin, 1999, Waiting in the Wings, Boston, N.Y.C., 2000, Tom Sawyer, 2001, Into the Woods, N.Y.C., 2002; prodn. stage mgr. Merrily We Roll Along, N.Y.C., 1981, A Doll's Life, L.A., N.Y.C., 1982, Gala Opening of Ky. Ctr. of Performing Arts, Louisville, 1983, End of the World, Washington and N.Y.C., 1984, Grind, 1985, Cabaret, N.Y.C., 1988, Jerome Robbin's Broadway, 1989-90, Kiss of the Spider Woman, Purchase, 1990, N.Y., 1993, Metro, N.Y.C., 1992, Falsettos, N.Y.C., 1992, Kiss of the Spider Woman, 1993, Passion, 1994, Steel Pier, N.Y.C., 1997; stage mgr. Chapter Two, 1979. Stage mgr. Nat. Inst. of Music Theatre, N.Y.C., 1986-87; participant Broadway Cares. Mem. Actors Fund (life), Actor's Equity Assn.

RANDOLPH, LYNN MOORE, artist; b. N.Y.C., Dec. 19, 1938; d. Cecil Howard and Dorothy (Didenhover) M.; m. Robert Raymond Randolph, June 5, 1959 (div. June, 1975); children: Robert Cean, Grayson Moore; m. William Simon, July 22, 1986. BFA, U. Tex., 1961. Pres. Houston chpt. Nat. Women's Caucus for Art, 1979-80. regional v.p., 1982-85, nat. adv. bd. 1986-88, co-chair ann. 1988 ann. conf.; lectr. and conf. participant to art and women's groups, 1980—; set designer, Space, Dance Theater, Houston, 1977, Main St. Theater, 1982; coord. Art Under Duress, El Salvador, Lawndale Art and Performance Ctr., Houston. Artist: solo exhibitions include Graham Gallery, Houston, 1984, 86, 91, Mary Ingraham Bunting Inst., Cambridge, Mass., 1990, Lynn Goode Gallery, Houston, 1995, U. Tex. Health Sci. Ctr., 1997, Ariz. State U. Mus., 1998, Joan Wich Gallery, Houston, 2003; group shows: Contemporary Arts Mus., Houston, 1978, 79, 90, 500 Exposition Gallery, Dallas, 1980, Ga. State U. Gallery, 1982, Mus. Fine Arts, Houston, 1986, Aspen (Colo.) Art Mus., 1987, Nat. Mus. of

Women in Art, Washington, 1988, San Antonio Mus. of Art, 1989, Sewell Gallery, Rice U., 1993, Diverse Works, Houston, 1994; works in pub. collections at Ariz. State U., Tempe, The Menil Collection, Houston, San Antonio Mus. of Art, Mary Ingraham Bunting Inst., Cambridge, Houston Mus. Fine Arts, numerous others. Organizer Houston Area Artist's Call Against U.S. Intervention in Ctrl. Am., 1984. Recipient summer fellowship Yaddo, Saratoga Springs, N.Y., 1987, fellowship Mary Ingraham Bunting Inst., Radcliffe Coll., 1989-90. Mem. The Ilusas (women's drum corps), Artists Bd. Lawndale Art and Performance Ctr., Houston. Home: 1803 Banks St Houston TX 77098-5403 Office Phone: 713-528-0909.

RANEY, CAROLYN E. educational consultant; b. L.A., Aug. 14, 1918; d. Charles Porter Raney and Carrie Elizabeth Schafer; m. Saul Schechtman, July 31, 1952; children: Carol Ruth Kimmel, Julia Schechtman Pabst. MusB, Eastman Sch. Music, 1938; MusM, Case Western U., 1943; PhD in Hist. Music, NYU, 1971; cert. in Bus., Harvard U., 1980. Faculty mem. NYU, N.Y.C., 1968—73, CUNY, S.I., 1968—73, Am. Music and Drama Sch., N.Y.C., 1968—73; dir. grad. dept. Peabody Coll., Johns Hopkins U., Balt., 1973—76; dean arts, v.p. East Stroudsburg (Pa.) State U., 1976—80; faculty Am. creative writing U. Dusseldorf, Germany, 1982—85; dean grad. sch. Schiller Internat. U., Heidelberg, Germany, 1985—90, London, 1985—90, Paris, 1985—90; cons. Mgmt. Inst., Strasbourg, France, 1990—94. Lectr. in field. Author: Francesca Caccini, 1971, (poetry volume) Realities and Unrealities, 1993; contbr. articles to publs. Fulbright fellow, NEA, 1963—64. Mem.: Authors Guild, Internat. Musicol. Soc., Acad. Am. Poets (assoc.), Coll. Music Soc. (life; editor 1975—79). Christian Scientist. Avocations: singing, church organist, voice teacher, career advisor. Home: 134 Cathedral Ave Hempstead NY 11550

RANEY, JEAN PUCKETT, art gallery director, artist; b. San Juan, P.R., May 11, 1954; d. Ralph Puckett and Jean Martha Martin; m. Dixon Flanary Raney, Sept. 11, 1982; children: Lauren Flanary, Dixon Flanary, Jr. BA in Polit. Sci. cum laude, U. Ga., 1976. Cert.: Nat. Ctr. for Paralegal Tng. (legal asst.). Legal asst. Webb, Carlock, Atlanta, 1978—86; owner Wedding Wand, Atlanta, 1984—94, Jean Raney Studios, Atlanta, 1992—. Art instr. Jean Raney Studio, Atlanta, 1995—; tchr. art appreciation Austin Elem., Dunwoody, Ga., 1997—99; judge DeKalb County State of Ga. Reflections Contests, Atlanta, 1998, Atlanta, 99, Outstanding Young Artists Competition, Alpharetta, 2002—03. Author: Paralegal Training Manual, 1980, Training and Procedures Manual for DFAA Gallery, 1995; co-author: Art Appreciation for Elementary Schools, 1996. Fundraiser United Way Atlanta, 1981; spl. events chair, fundraiser Ga. Trust for Hist. Preservation, 1979—81; mem., chair coms. Jr. League Atlanta, 1982—; PTA pres., bd. dirs. Austin Elem. Sch., Dunwoody, 1991—99; Vol., creator and chmn. Downtown Night "Mingle, Jingle & Jazz" Egleston Hosp. Festival Trees, 1979—86; mem. young careers and membership dr. High Mus. Art, Atlanta, 1978—81; co-chmn, mem. Dunwoody Twigs, 1989—2001; mem. social com. Wyntercreek Neighborhood1989, 1989—90; Sunday Sch tchr. 5th and 6th grades St. Luke's Presbyn. Ch., Dunwoody, 1991—93; bd. dirs. Neighbors of Wyntercreek, 1999—2001. Named Selected Artist, So. Living Idea House, 2000, Featured Artist, Wesleyan Sch., 2001. Mem.: Ga. Assn. Legal Assts. (newsletter chmn., bd. dirs.), PACESETTERS (bd. dirs., sec., spl. events chmn.), Dunwoody Fine Arts Assn. (gallery dir. 1995—98, bd. dirs., vol.), Wesleyan Arts Alliance (artist market chair 1999—, pres. 2003), Colonial Dames. Methodist. Avocations: painting in Italy, skiing, reading, studying languages, camping. Office: Jean Raney Studios 5247 Wyntercreek Ct Atlanta GA 30338

RANGE, SHIRLEY QUALLS, academic administrator; b. Montgomery, Ala., Oct. 5, 1954; d. J. E. Qualls, Sr and Ruth Thomas Qualls; m. A. J. Range, Aug. 8, 1987; 1 child, Thomas A. BA, U. of Ala., 1972—76, MA, 1976—78. Resource Development Specialist Coun. for Resource Devel., 1998. Resident dir. U. Housing, U. of Ala., 1976—78; voice instr. Huntingdon Coll., Montgomery, Ala., 1979—81; artist-in-residence Ala. State Coun. on the Arts and Humanities, 1979—81; rsch. assoc. & instr. U. of Ala., 1981—83; cultural resources coord. Ala. Hist. Commn., 1983—88; dir. Bessie Smith Hall, Inc., Chattanooga, 1988—91; staff assoc., office of the vice chancellor for student affairs U. of Tenn. at Chattanooga, 1993—94; devel. writer U. of Ctrl. Fla. Found., Orlando, 1995—96; dir., office of resource devel. Seminole C.C., Sanford, Fla., 1996—. Adv. bd. The SE Inst. for Edn. in Music, U. of Tenn. at Chattanooga, 1989—92; adv. coun. Career Edn. Programs, Chattanooga Pub. Schools, 1992—94. Singer: (feature performer) Heritage Jubilee; author: (black and white slide documentary) Preserving Historic Black Resources in Alabama, (historical photo-text calendar) Keepers of the Faith: Alabama's Historic Black Churches; contbr. interdisciplinary curriculum guide The Culture of Southern Black Women: Approaches and Materials. Steering com., co-chair comm. com. ReVision 2000, Chattanooga, 1992—93; steering com., Chattanooga Insight Chattanooga C. of C., 1992; ch. coun. and lead deaconess Grace Cmty. of Faith, Orlando, Fla., 2001—; mem. Chattanooga Area Conv. and Visitors Bur., 1989—91, Ctr. City Corp., Chattanooga, 1990—92. Mem.: CRD Fed. Funding Task Force (team leader 1996—2002), Assn. of Profl. Researchers for Advancement, Coun. for the Advancement and Support of Edn., Assn. of Fundraising Professionals, Ctrl. Fla. Chpt., Coun. for Resource Devel., Fla. Coun. for Resource Devel. (pres. 2000—02), Delta Sigma Theta Lambda Zeta Chpt., U. of Ala. (charter line 1973—74). Office: Seminole Community College 100 Weldon Blvd Sanford FL 32773-6199

RANKAITIS, SUSAN, artist; b. Cambridge, Mass., Sept. 10, 1949; d. Alfred Edward and Isabel (Shimkus) Rankaitis; m. Robbert Flick, June 5, 1976. BFA in Painting, U. Ill., 1971; MFA in Visual Arts, U. So. Calif., 1977. Rsch. asst., art dir. Plato Lab., U. Ill., Urbana, 1971-75; art instr. Orange Coast Coll., Costa Mesa, Calif., 1977-83; chair dept. art Chapman Coll., Orange, Calif., 1983-90; Fletcher Jones chair art Scripps Coll., Claremont, Calif., 1990—. Represented by Robert Mann Gallery, NYC; overview panelist visual arts Nat. Endowment for Arts, 1983, 84; selector Bingham Ednl. Trust, 1997-2002; scholar-in-residence Borchard Found., Misallac, France, 2004. One-woman shows include Los Angeles County Mus. Art, 1983, Internat. Mus. Photography, George Eastman House, 1983, Gallery Min. Tokyo, 1988, Ruth Bloom Gallery, Santa Monica, 1989, 90, 92, Schneider Mus., Portland, Ore., 1990; Ctr. for Creative Photography, 1991, Robert Mann Gallery, NYC, 1994, 97, Mus. Contemporary Photography, Chgo., 1994, Mus. of Photographic Arts, 2000; represented in permanent collections MOCA, LA, U. N.Mex. Art, Ctr. for Creative Photography, Mus. Contemporary Photography, Chgo., Santa Barbara Mus. Art, Los Angeles County Mus. Art, Mpls. Inst. Arts, St. Louis Art Mus., San Francisco Mus. Modern Art, Art Inst. Chgo., Mus. Modern Art, Lodz, Poland, Princeton U. Art Mus., Stanford U. Art Mus., Contemporary Art Mus., Honolulu, Mus. Contemporary Photography, Art Inst. Chgo., St. Louis Art Mus., others. Active art auction Venice Family Clinic, 1980—. Recipient Graves award in Humanities, 1985; Nat. Endowment for Arts fellow, 1980, 88, US, France fellow, 1989, Agnes Bourne fellow in painting and photography Djerassi Found., 1989; Durfee Chinese/Am. grantee, 2000-2001; City of LA Cultural Affairs grantee, 2001; Borchand scholar-in-residence fellow, France, 2004. Mem. Coll. Art Assn., Los Angeles County Mus. Art, Santa Monica Mus. Art. Home: 3117 N Lansbury Ave Claremont CA 91711-4146 Office Phone: 909-607-4439., 213-683-9679. E-mail: srankait@scrippscollege.edu.

RANKIN, JACQUELINE ANNETTE, communications expert, educator; b. Omaha, Nebr., May 19, 1925; d. Arthur C. and Virdie (Gillispie) R. BA, Calif. State U., L.A., 1964, MA, 1966; MS in Mgmt., Calif. State U., Fullerton, 1977; EdD, U. LaVerne, Calif., 1981. Tchr. Rowland H.S., La Habra, Calif., 1964-66, Lowell H.S., La Habra, Calif., 1966-69, Pomona (Calif.) H.S., 1969-75; program asst. Pomona Adult Sch., 1975-82; dir. Child Abuse Prevention Program, 1985-86; exec. dir. child abuse prevention Calif. Dept. Pub. Svc., 1985-87; instr. Ind. U., Purdue U., 1993; assoc. prof. speech Ball State U., Muncie, Ind., 1993-94; instr. No. Va. U., 1994—, trainer Loudoun campus, 1996. Faculty evening divsn. Mt. San Antonio C.C., 1966-72; asst. prof. speech Ball State U., Muncie, Ind., 1993; instr. No. Va. U., Alexandria, Annandale, Manassas, Woodbridge, 1995—; assoc. faculty dept. comm. and theatre, Ind. U., Purdue U., Indpls., 1993; trainer internat. convs., sales groups, staffs of hosps., others; spkr., writer, trainer, lectr., cons. in field. Columnist: Jackie's World, Topics Newspapers; author: Body Language: First Impressions, Body Language in Negotiations and Sales, Body Language in Love and Romance, Body Language of the Abused Child, 1999, Using body Language That Kids Trust, Ten Tips for Evaluating Body Language of the Abused Child; contbr. articles to Child Law Practice, ABA and other profl. jours. Mem. Fairfax County Dem. Com.; mem. adv. coun., mem. nat. capital chpt. bd. dirs. ARC. Mem. Internat. Platform Assn., Pi Lambda Theta, Phi Delta Kappa. Home and Office: 7006 Elkton Dr Springfield VA 22152-3330 E-mail: jackie.rankin@cox.net.

RANKIN, MARY ANNE, director; b. Hackettstown, N.J., Feb. 2, 1944; d. Joseph Edward and Barbara Jean (Cornish) Sekerke; m. John M. Rankin, June 10, 1966; children: Andrew M., Christopher J. BA, Albion Coll., 1966; MAT, George Washington U., 1968. Tchr. Redlands (Calif.) Ind. Sch. Dist., 1980-86, Colton (Calif.) Ind. Sch. Dist., 1986-88, Concord (Calif.) Ind. Sch. Dist., 1989-90; dir. RSVP, Shreveport, La., 1992—2000; exec. dir. Bossier Coun. Aging, Bossier City, La., 2000—. Mem. Krewe of Elders; capt. Mayor's Women's Commn. Svc. Connection; pres. bd. Am. Heart Assn. Mem.: AAUW, Altrusa Club. Methodist. Avocations: stitchery, floral arrangements, ceramics, sewing. Home: 410 Dunmoreland Cir Shreveport LA 71106-6102 Office: Bossier Council on Aging 706 Bearkat Drive Bossier City LA 71111

RANKS, ANNE ELIZABETH, retired elementary and secondary education educator; b. Omaha, June 10, 1916; d. Salvatore and Concetta (Turco) Scolla; m. Harold Eugene Ranks, Aug. 20, 1955 (dec.). B in Philosophy, Duchesne Coll., Omaha, 1937; MA, Creighton U., 1947. Tchr. Good Shepherd Parochial H.S., Omaha, 1937-38, St. Benedicts H.S., Omaha, 1938-39, Omaha Pub. Schs., 1939-81. Pres. women's divsn. Dem. Cen. Com., Nebr.; chmn. Gov.'s Profl. Practices Commn. Nebr., 1938-39; vol. Bergan-Mercy Hosp., Omaha, 1980-86, 99—, hosp. mem. aux. bd. dirs., 1985-86; vol. Saddleback Hosp., Laguna Hills, Calif., 1989-91; bd. dirs. Sylvia Tischhauser CRTA divsn. Scholarship Found., 1989-94; mem. bd. dirs. Saddleback Valley Ednl. Found., 1990-92; bd. dirs. Orange County Diocesan Coun. Cath. Women, 1989-90, 2d v.p., 1990-94; vol. Bergan Mercy Hosp., 1998-2001. Mem. AAUW (v.p. Laguna Hills br. 1988-91), Nebr. Edn. Assn. (bd. dirs. 1957-60, pres. dist. II 1960-62), Omaha Edn. Assn. (bd. dirs. 1950-55), Womens Club, Cath. Daus. Regent Omaha Ct. (rec. sec. Lake Forest, Calif. Ct. 1988-90), Coll. Club of Leisure World (v.p. 1990-95), Nat. Ret. Tchrs. Assn., Nebr. Ret. Tchrs. Assn., Local Ret. Tchrs. Assn., Cath. Daus. Home: Apt 242 9804 Nicholas St Omaha NE 68114-2180

RANNEY, HELEN MARGARET, internist, hematologist, educator; b. Summer Hill, N.Y., Apr. 12, 1920; d. Arthur C. and Alesia (Toolan) Ranney. AB, Barnard Coll., 1941; MD, Columbia U., 1947; ScD, U. S.C., 1979, SUNY, Buffalo, 1996. Diplomate Am. Bd. Internal Medicine. Intern Presbyn. Hosp., N.Y.C., 1947—48, resident, 1948—50, asst. physician, 1954—60; practice medicine specializing in internal medicine, hematology N.Y.C., 1954—70; instr. Coll. Phys. and Surg. Columbia, N.Y.C., 1954—60; from assoc. prof. to prof. medicine Albert Einstein Coll. Medicine, N.Y.C., 1960—70; prof. medicine SUNY, Buffalo, 1970—73, U. Calif., San Diego, 1973—90, chmn. dept. medicine, 1973—86, Disting. physician vet. adminstr., 1986—91; cons. Alliance Pharm. Corp., San Diego, 1991—. Master: ACP; fellow: AAAS; mem.: NAS, Am. Acad. Arts and Scis., Am. Assn. Physicians, Harvey Soc., Am. Soc. Hematology, Am. Soc. for Clin. Investigation, Inst. Medicine, Alpha Omega Alpha, Sigma Xi, Phi Beta Kappa.

RANNEY, MARY ELIZABETH, business executive; b. Louisville, Nov. 10, 1928; d. James William and Erna Marie Katerina (Hansen) Connell; m. Glen Royal Ranney, July 26, 1947; children: Darleen Diane Ranney Bowie, Nancy Elizabeth Ranney Pieratt. Student, Monmouth Coll., 1946-47. Cert. profl. sec., nursing asst. Nursing asst. Monmouth (Ill.) Hosp., 1957-63; asst. in fin. Bd. Pub. Instrn. Collier County, Naples, Fla., 1964-68; sec. 1st Nat. Bank, Bonita Springs, Fla., 1969-71; founder, dir. Planned Parenthood, Naples, 1972-76; writer Am. Hibiscus Soc., 1977-82; owner Tree Gallery, Naples and Ft. Myers, 1983—. Tchr., seedling judge Am. Hibiscus Soc., 1977-79. Author: (brochure) Abortion, 1976; solo performance Fiddler on the Roof, 1976. Chair Fla. Assn. for Repeal Abortion Laws, Lee and Collier County, 1972; founder Abortion Referral Svc. S.W. Fla., 1972-75; founder, dir. Accordion Band, Naples, 1974-79, Floridian Accordion Band, Ft. Myers, 1989-91; founding officer Naples Concert Band, 1972-79; sponsor Am. hibiscus shows, Naples, 1973-81; founder, codr. City of Ft. Myers String Band, 1998—. Recipient Prominent Woman of Cmty. award Naples Star, 1977, 78, 79, Mover of 70's award Naples NOW Mag., 1980, Shaker, Mover and Star award Naples NOW Mag., 1983, Life Work Feature award Naples Star, 1981, Great Achiever award Naples Star, 1982. Mem. NOW (charter nat. pres. 1975-77), Am. Hibiscus Soc. (life, founder Ranney chpt. 1973—, editor Show Chair Manual 1979, Judges Manual 1980, Pres. Svc. award 1979, Hibiscus of Yr. 1980, 82), Meml. Soc. S.W. Fla. (pres. 1975-77). Democrat. Avocations: musician, seamstress, biker, walker, dancer. Home: 3164 Palm Beach Blvd Fort Myers FL 33916-1579

RANNEY-MARINELLI, ALESIA, lawyer; b. Ithaca, N.Y., 1952; BA, Mich. State U., 1973; JD cum laude, Harvard U., 1977. Bar: Del. 1977, N.Y. 1986. Ptnr. Skadden Arps Slate Flom & Meagher, N.Y.C. Office: Skadden Arps Slate Meagher & Flom 4 Times Sq Fl 24 New York NY 10036-6595

RANSOM, EVELYN NAILL, language educator, linguist; b. Memphis, Apr. 20, 1938; d. Charles Rhea and Evelyn (Goodlander) Naill Ransom; m. Gunter Heinz Hiller, June 7, 1960 (div. Mar. 1964). AA, Mt. Vernon Jr. Coll., 1958; BA, Newcomb Coll., 1960; MA, N.Mex. Highlands U., 1965; PhD, U. Ill., 1974. Cert. secondary tchr., N.Mex. Instr. Berlitz Sch. Langs., New Orleans, 1961; tchr. MillerWall Elem. Sch., Harvey, L.A., 1961-62; teaching asst. N.Mex. Highlands U., Las Vegas, 1963-64; instr. U. Wyo., Laramie, 1965-66; teaching asst. U. Ill., Urbana, 1966-70; prof. English lang. Ea. Ill. U., Charleston, 1970-93; vis. prof. in linguistics No. Ariz. U., Flagstaff, 1990-91, adj. faculty, 1993-94, Ariz. State U., Tempe, 1995-98; retired. Referee Pretext: Jour. of Lang. and Lit., Ill., 1981, S.W. Jour. Linguistics, 1999; co-chair roundtable Internat. Congress of Linguistics, 1987; linguistics del. People to People, Moscow, St. Petersburg, Prague, 1993, China, 1998; dissertation reader SUNY, Buffalo, 1982; vis. scholar UCLA, 1977; conductor workshop LSA summer inst. Author: Complementation: Its Meanings and Forms, 1986; contbr. articles to profl. publs. Organizer Prairie Women's Cir., Champaign, 1981-83. Nat. Def. Fgn. Lang. fellow, 1969; grantee Ea. Ill. U., 1982, 87, 88, NSF, 1988. Mem. Linguistic Soc. Am., Linguistic Assn. S.W. (jour. referee 1999). Avocations: computer applications for the humanities, chess, motorhoming. Home: 201 E Southern Ave # 135 Apache Junction AZ 85219-3740

RANSOM, JUDY LYNN, music educator; b. Plainfield, N.J., Feb. 2, 1959; d. Henry Shade Ransom, Sr. and Eloise Werner (Imrie) Ransom; m. Henry Alfred Faivre, July 27, 1991 (div. June 2001). MusB in Performance, Greensboro (N.C.)Coll., 1981; BS in Music Edn., Old Dominion U., Norfolk, Va., 1989, MS in Music Edn., 1995; DMA, Shenandoah U., Winchester, Va., 2001. Elem. music tchr. Norfolk Pub. Sch., 1989—94, choral dir., 1994—2002; asst. prof. music Mo. Valley Coll., 2002—. Mem. bd. dirs. Va. Children's Chorus, Norfolk, 1999—2001; dir. youth choir Christ-St. Lukes Episcopal Ch., 1996—2002; pianist Catalpa Restaurant, Arrow Rock, Mo., 2002. Mem. Christ-St. Lukes Cantata Chorus, Norfolk, 1996—2001. Recipient Performance Presentation plaque, Va. Music Educators Assn., 1992. Mem.: Mo. Music Educators Assn., Am. Choral Dirs. Assn., Music Educators Nat. Conf., Phi Kappa Lambda. Avocations: running, dance, aerobics, choral and instrumental arrangement. Home: PO Box 441 Marshall MO 65340 Business E-Mail: ransomj@moval.edu.

RANSOM, NANCY ALDERMAN, sociology and women's studies educator, university administrator; b. New Haven, Feb. 25, 1929; d. Samuel Bennett and Florence (Opper) Alderman; m. Harry Howe Ransom, July 6, 1951; children: Jenny Alderman, Katherine Marie, William Henry Howe. BA, Vassar Coll., 1950; postgrad., Columbia U., 1951, U. Leeds, Eng., 1977-78; MA, Vanderbilt U., 1971, EdD, 1988. Lectr. sociology U. Tenn., Nashville, 1971-76; grant writer Vanderbilt U., Nashville, 1976-77, dir. Women's Ctr., 1978-97, instr. sociology, 1972, 74, lectr. sociology and women's studies, 1983, 90-97. Vol. counselor family planning Planned Parent Assn. of Nashville, 1973—77, bd. dirs., 1978—89, mem. adv. coun., 1989—98, v.p., 1981—, pres., 1987—89; bd. dirs. Sr. Citizens, Inc., 1996—, pres., 2001—02, chmn. ann. fund campaign, 2002—03; mem. planning com. ACE/ACE nat. identification program Women in Higher Edn., 1984—92; spkr. at profl. meetings. Recipient Women of Achievement award Middle Tenn. State U., 1996, Mary Jane Werthan award Vanderbilt U., 1998; named to Acad. for Women of Achievement, YWCA, 2000, Molly Todd Cup, 2003; Columbia U. residential fellow, 1951; Vanderbilt U. fellow, 1971. Mem.: LWV, NOW, AAUW, Nat. Women's Polit. Caucus, Cable Club, Phi Beta Kappa (v.p. Alpha of Tenn. 1994—95, pres. 1995—97).

RANSON, DIANA L. language educator; b. Louisville, Sept. 6, 1956; d. Guy Harvey Ranson and Rose Ellen Clark; m. Rachid Seklaoui, May 1, 1979 (div. Feb. 1989); 1 child, Catherine ; m. Ronald Baxter Miller, Sept. 3, 2000. BA, Yale U., 1977; MA, U. Mich., 1981, PhD, 1986. Asst. prof. U. Ga., Athens, 1986—92, assoc. prof., 1992—. Author: Change and Compensation: Parallel Weakening (in Italian, French and Spanish), 1989; co-editor: Essays in Hispanic Linguistics Dedicated to Paul M. Lloyd, 1999; contbr. articles to profl. jours. Mem.: Assn. de Hist. de la Lengua Española, Am. Assn. Tchrs. of Spanish and Portuguese, Am. Assn. Tchrs. of French, Modern Lang. Assn. Avocations: jogging, travel. Home: 279 Imperial Way Bogart GA 30622-1794 Office: U Ga Dept Romance Langs Athens GA 30602-1815 Personal E-mail: dranson@charter.net. Business E-Mail: dranson@uga.edu.

RANTS, CAROLYN JEAN, college official; b. Hastings, Nebr., Oct. 3, 1936; d. John Leon and Christine (Helzer) Halloran; m. Marvin L. Rants, June 1, 1957 (div. July 1984); children: Christopher Charles, Douglas John. Student, Hastings Coll., 1954—56; BS, U. Omaha, 1960; EdM, U. Nebr., 1968; EdD, U. S.D., 1982. Elem. sch. tchr. Ogallala (Nebr.) Cmty. Sch., 1956-58, Omaha Pub. Schs., 1958-60, Hastings Pub. Schs., 1960-64, Grosse Pointe (Mich.) Cmty. Schs., 1964-67; asst. prof., instr. Morningside Coll., Sioux City, Iowa, 1974-82, dean for student devel., 1982-84, v.p. for student affairs, 1984-94, interim v.p. for acad. affairs, 1992-94, v.p. enrollment and student svcs., 1994-96, v.p. adminstrn., 1996-99; exec. dir. enrollment svcs. Western Iowa Tech C.C., 1999—, dean of students, 2000—. Mem. new agy. com., chmn. fund distbn. and resource deployment com. United Way, Sioux City, 1987-94, co-chair, United Way Day of Caring, 1996; mem. Iowa Civil Rights Commn., 1989-97; bd. dirs. Leadership Sioux City, 1988-93, pres., 1992-93; bd. dirs. Siouxland Y, Sioux City, 1985-90, pres., 1988; bd. dirs. Girls, Inc., 1995-2000, Red Cross, 2002—; bd. dirs. New Perspectives, Inc., 1996-2000, pres. 1999, 2000; mem. Vision 2020 Cmty. Planning Task Force, 1990-92; pres. bd. dirs. Siouxland Youth Chorus, 2001—; bd. dirs. Sioux City Symphony, 2001—, treas., 2002—. Mem. Iowa Women in Ednl. Leadership (pres. Sioux City chpt. 1986), Nat. Assn. Student Pers. Adminstrs.(region IV-E adv. bd.), Nat. Assn. for Women Deans, Adminstrs. and Counselors, Iowa Student Pers. Adminstr. (chmn. profl. devel. Iowa chpt. 1988-89, pres. 1991-92, Disting. Svc. award 1992), AAUW (corp. rep., coll./univ. rep. 1994-96), P.E.O. (pres. Sioux City chpt., Tri-State Women's Bus. Conf. (treas., planning com. Sioux City chpt. 1987-89), Quota Club (com. chmn. Sioux City 1987-89, v.p. 1992-94, pres. 1994-95, Siouxland Woman of Yr. award 1988), Sertoma (officer, bd. govs., regional dir.), Omicron Delta Kappa (faculty dir. province X 1996-99), Delta Kappa Gamma (state 1st v.p. 1993-95, state pres. 1995-97, internat. com. 1998-2000, 2002-04), Phi Delta Kappa (pres. 1988-89, Excellence in Leadership award 1998, Spl. Commendation Bessie Gabbard award 2001). Republican. Methodist. Avocations: handbells, cross-stitching. Home: 2904 S Cedar St # 4 Sioux City IA 51106-4246 Office: Western Iowa Tech Comm Coll PO Box 5199 4647 Stone Ave Sioux City IA 51102-5199 E-mail: rantsc@witcc.com.

RANUM, JANE BARNHARDT, state senator, lawyer; b. Charlotte, N.C., Aug. 21, 1947; d. John Robert and Gladys Rose (Swift) B.; m. James Harry Ranum, Mar. 29, 1972; 1 child, Elizabeth McBride. BS, East Carolina U., 1969; JD, Hamline U., 1979. Bar: Minn. 1979, U.S. Dist. Ct. Minn. 1979. Tchr. elem. sch. Durham County, Durham, N.C., 1960-70; tchr. Dept. Def., Baumholder, Germany, 1970-72, Dist. 196, Rosemount, Minn., 1972-76; law cclk. Hennepin County Dist. Ct., Mpls., 1982; asst. county atty. Hennepin County, Mpls., 1982—; mem. Minn. Senate, St. Paul, 1991—. Chmn. legislature commn. on children, youth and their families, 1993—, mem. rep. chem. abuse and prevention resource coun., 1993. Mem. exec. com., lobbying coord. Dem. Farmer Labor Feminist Caucus, St. Paul, 1980-84; bd. dirs. Project 13 for Reproductive Rights, Mpls., 1981-82; state del. Minn. Dem. Farmer Labor Party Conv., 1982, 84, precinct del., 1974—. Named Feminist of Yr., Minn. NOW, 1994, Legislator of Yr., Minn. Assn. for Retarded Citizens, 1994. Mem. Minn. Bar Assn., Minn. Women Lawyers, Minn. Family Support and Recovery Coun., Hennepin County Bar assn. Democrat. Home: 5045 Aldrich Ave S Minneapolis MN 55419-1207 Office: Minn Senate State Capitol Saint Paul MN 55155-0001

RAPHAEL, BONNIE NANETTE, voice, speech, text and dialect coach, educator; b. Bklyn., Mar. 27, 1944; d. David A. and Helen (Rutstein) Newmark; m. Jay E. Raphael, June 21, 1966 (div. Mar. 1988). BA in Speech Edn., Bklyn. Coll., 1964; MA in Theatre, U. Mich., 1965; PhD in Theatre, Mich. State U., 1973. Lectr. theater So. Ill. U., Carbondale, 1971-73; asst. prof. theater Northwestern U., Evanston, Ill., 1973-76; asst. prof. drama U. Va., Charlottesville, 1976-81; assoc. prof. theater U. Mo., Kansas City, 1981-82; voice and speech coach Colo. Shakespeare Festival, Boulder, 1979-83; voice and speech coach, tchr. Denver Ctr. Theater Co., 1982-86; rschr. Rec. and Rsch. Ctr. Denver Ctr. for Performing Arts, 1982-86; voice and speech coach, tchr. Am. Repertory Theatre, Cambridge, Mass., 1986-97; prof. dept. dramatic art U. N.C., Chapel Hill, 1997—. Contbg. author: Professional Voice: The Science and Art of Clinical Care, 1991; mem. editl. bd. Jour. of Voice, 1987—; contbr. articles to profl. jours. Smoking cessation facilitator Am. Cancer Soc., Denver. Recipient Disting. Woman award Am. Theatre Assn., 1977; named one of Outstanding Young Women of Am., 1980. Mem. Voice and Speech Trainers Assn. (life, founding, bd. dirs. 1985), Actors Equity Assn., Assn. for Theatre in Higher Edn. (charter mem.), Voice Found. (Sackler Awards com. 1992-94.). Avocations: travel, hiking, gardening, animals. Office: U NC Dept Dramatic Art CB # 3230 Ctr for Dramatic Art Chapel Hill NC 27599-3230

RAPHAEL, LOUISE ARAKELIAN, mathematician, educator; b. N.Y.C., Oct. 24, 1937; d. Aristakes and Antionette (Sudbeaz) Arakelian; m. Robert Barnett Raphael, June 12, 1966 (div. 1985); children: Therese Denise, Marc Philippe. BS in Math., St. John's U., 1959; MS in Math., Cath. U., Washington, 1962; PhD in Math, Cath. U., 1967. Asst. prof. math. Howard U., Washington, 1966-70, vis. prof., 1981-82, assoc. prof., 1982-86, prof., 1986—; assoc. prof. Clark Coll., Atlanta, 1971-79, prof., 1979-82. Vis.

assoc. prof. MIT, Cambridge, 1977-78, vis. prof., 1989-90; vis. mem. Courant Inst. Math. Scis., NYU, 1996-97; vis. scholar Cornell U., 2004. Contbr. over 40 rsch. articles to profl. jours. Program dir. NSF, Washington, 1986-88; acting adminstrv. officer Conf. Bd. Math. Scis., 1985-86. Grantee NSF, 1975-76, 79-81, 89-91, Army Rsch. Office, 1981-89, Air Force Sci. Rsch., 1981-82, 91-95, Nat. Security Agy., 1994-96. Mem.: Soc. Indsl. and Applied Math., Math. Assn. Am. (1st v.p. 1996—98, chmn. minorities in math. task force 1988), Am. Math. Soc. (coun. 2001—04, com. mem.), Sigma Xi. Democrat. Roman Catholic. Office: Howard U Dept Math Washington DC 20059-0001

RAPHAEL, SALLY JESSY, talk-show host; b. Easton, Pa., Feb. 25, 1942; children: Allison (dec.), Andrea; m. Karl Soderlund; 2 step-daughters, 1 adopted son, also foster children. BFA, Columbia U. Anchored radio program Jr. High Sch. News Sta. WFAS-AM, White Plains, N.Y., 1955; host of cooking program WAPA-TV, San Juan, P.R., 1965-67; radio and television broadcaster Miami and Ft. Lauderdale, Fla., 1969-74; host Sta. WMCA-Radio, N.Y.C., 1976-81; talk show host NBC Talk-net, N.Y.C., 1982-88, ABC Talkradio, N.Y.C., 1988-91; syndicated TV talk-show host N.Y.C., 1983—. Part-time owner of a perfume factory, 1964-68; owner of an art gallery, 1964-69; owner, The Wine Press, N.Y.C., 1979-83; ind. producer TV films, 1991 Author: (with M.J. Boyer) Finding Love, 1984, (with Pam Proctor) Sally: Unconventional Success, 1980; film appearances include: She-Devil, 1989, Resident Alien, 1990, The Addams Family, 1991, The Associate, 1996, Meet Wally Sparks, 1996, (TV movie) No One Would Tell, 1996; TV appearances include: Murphy Brown, Dave's World, The Nanny, The Tonight Show, Nightline, Diagnosis Murder, Conspiracy of Silence, Touched By An Angel, Sabrina the Teenage Witch, John LaRoquette Show; co-exec. producer (mini-series) The 3rd Twin, 1997 (film cameo) Double Whammy, 2000. Recipient Bronze medal, Internat. Film & Television Festival of NY, 1985; Emmy award as outstanding talk-show host, daytime, 1988, Emmy award for outstanding talk show, 1989. Office: USA Studios The Sally Show Fl OF2 15 Penn Plz New York NY 10001-2010

RAPHEL, ROBIN, ambassador; b. Vancouver, Wash., Sept. 16, 1947; 2 children. BA, U. Wash.; Diploma in Hist. Studies, Cambridge U., Eng.; MA, U. Md. Lectr. history Damavand Coll., Tehran, Iran, 1970-72; analyst CIA, 1974-75, USAID, Islamabad, Pakistan, 1975-78; with office investment affairs bur. econs. Dept. of State, 1978-80, staff asst. to asst. sec. Near East and South Asian affairs, 1980-81, econ. officer Israel desk, 1981-82, spl. asst. to under sec. polit. affairs, 1982-84; 1st sec. polit. affairs London, 1984-88; polit. counselor Pretoria, South Africa, 1988-91, New Delhi, 1991-93; asst. sec. South Asian affairs Dept. of State, Washington, 1993-97; U.S. amb. to Tunisia Tunis, 1997-2000; sr. v.p. Nat. Def. U., 2000—. Mem. Am. Econ. Assn., Am. Fgn. Svc. Assn., Phi Beta Kappa. Office: Nat Def U Marshall Hall Fort McNair Washington DC 20319

RAPIN, ISABELLE, physician; b. Lausanne, Switzerland, Dec. 4, 1927; d. Rene and Mary Coe (Reeves) R.; m. Harold Oaklander, Apr. 5, 1959; children: Anne Louise, Christine, Stephen, Peter. Physician's Diploma. Faculte de Medicine, U. Lausanne, 1952, Doctorate in Medicine, 1955. Diplomate Am. Bd. Psychiatry and Neurology. Intern in pediatrics N.Y. U. Bellevue Med. Center, 1953-54; resident in neurology Neurol. Inst. of N.Y., Columbia-Presbyn. Med. Center, 1954-57, fellow in child neurology, 1957-58; mem. faculty Albert Einstein Coll. Medicine, Bronx, N.Y., 1958—, prof. neurology and pediatrics, 1972—; attending neurologist and child neurologist Einstein Affiliated Hosps., Bronx. Mem. Nat. Adv. Neurol. and Communicative Disorders and Stroke Coun., NIH, 1984-88. Contbr. chpts. to books, articles to med. jours. Recipient award Conf. Ednl. Adminstrs. Serving the Deaf, 1988. Fellow: Am. Acad. Neurology (exec. bd. 1995—99); mem.: AAAS, Assn. for Rsch. in Nervous and Mental Diseases (v.p. 1986), Internat. Neuropsychology Soc., Child Neurology Soc. (Hower award 1987), Am. Neurol. Assn. (v.p. 1982—83), Internat. Child Neurology Assn. (sec.-gen. 1979—82, v.p. 1982—86, Frank R. Ford lectr. 1990). Office: Albert Einstein Coll Medicine 1410 Pelham Pky S Bronx NY 10461-1101 E-mail: rapin@aecom.yu.edu.

RAPOPORT, JUDITH, psychiatrist; b. N.Y.C., July 12, 1933; d. Louis and Minna (Enteen) Livant; m. Stanley Rapoport, June 25, 1961; children: Stuart, Erik. BA, Swarthmore Coll., 1955; MD, Harvard U., 1959. Lic. psychiatrist. Cons., child psychiatrist NIMH/St. Elizabeth's Hosp., Washington, 1969—72; clin. asst. prof. Georgetown U. Med. Sch., Washington, 1972—82, clin. assoc. prof., 1982—85, clin. prof. psychiat., 1985—; med. officer biol. psychiatry br. NIMH, Bethesda, Md., 1976—78, chief, child mental illness unit, biol. psychiat. br., 1979—82, chief, child psychiatry lab. of clin. scis., 1982—84, chief, child psychiatry div. intramural rsch. programs, 1984—; prof. psychiatry George Washington U. Sch. Med., Washington, 1979—; prof. pediat. Georgetown U., Washington, 1985—. Cons. in field. Author: (non-fiction) The Boy Who Couldn't Stop Washing, 1989 (best seller literary guild selection, 1989), Childhood Obsessive Compulsive Disorder, 1989. Fellow: Am. Acad. Child Psychiatry, Am. Psychiat. Assn.; mem.: Inst. Medicine, D.C. Psychiat. Assn. Home: 3010 11th Pl NW Washington DC 20016-3557 Office: NIMH Rm 3N202 10 Center Dr Bldg 10 Bethesda MD 20892-0001 E-mail: rapoport@helix.nih.gov.

RAPOPORT, NANCY B. dean, law educator; b. Bryan, Tex., June 29, 1960; m. Jeffrey D. Van Niel, Oct. 13, 1996. BA in legal studies, honors psychology summa cum laude, Rice U., 1982; JD, Stanford Law Sch., 1985. Bar: Calif. 1987, U.S. Dist. Cts. (no., ea., ctrl., and so. dists.) Calif. 1987, U.S. Ct. Appeals (9th cir.) 1987, Ohio 1993, Nebr. 1999, U.S. Dist. Ct. (no. dist.) Tex. Jud. clerk Hon. Joseph T. Sneed, United States Ct. Appeals for Ninth Cir., San Francisco, 1985—86; assoc. bus.dept. of bankruptcy and workouts group Morrison & Foerster, San Francisco, 1986—91; asst. prof. Ohio State U. Coll. Law, Columbus, Ohio, 1991—95, tenured assoc. prof., 1995—98, assoc. dean student affairs, 1996—98, prof., 1998; dean, prof. law U. Nebr. Coll. Law, Lincoln, 1998—2000, U. Houston Law Ctr., 2000—. Invited spkr., panelist, and presenter in field. Co-editor (with Bala G. Dharan): Enron: Corporate Fiascos adn Their Implications, 2004. Bd. trustees Law Sch. Admissions Coun., 2001—04; bd. dirs. Friends of Girl Scouting Adv. Bd., 2001—, Pro Bono Rsch. Group, 2000—, St. Elizabeth Found., 1999—2000, ADL Southwest Regional Bd., 2001—, Houston Area Women's Ctr. Named Legal Pioneer for Women in Law (first woman to serve as dean of Nebr. Law Sch.), Nebr. State Bar Assn., 2000, Outstanding Prof. of Yr., Ohio State U. Coll. Law., 1997; named to Louis Nemzer meml. lectr., 1998; fellow 1998 Fellowship, Am. Bankruptcy Law Jour. Fellow: Am. Bar Found.; mem.: ABA (task force on law student debt 2001—03), Assn. Am. Law Sch.'s Profl. Develop. Com., Ohio State Bar Assn. (legal edn. com. 1997—98), Am. Bankruptcy Inst. (law sch. com. 1994—), Bar Assn. San Francisco, Nebr. Continuing Legal Edn. (long-range planning com. 1998—2000), Nat. Assn. Coll. and U. Attys., Nebr. State Bar Assn. (bankruptcy sect. 1998—2000, exec.com., bankruptcy sect. 1999—2000, access to profession com. 1999—2001), Houston Bar Found. (selection com. Best Article award 2000—), Houston Bar Assn., Am. Law Inst. Avocations: tae kwon do, ballroom dancing, Latin dancing, black and white photography, music. Office: U Houston Law Ctr 100 Law Ctr Houston TX 77204-6060 Business E-Mail: nrapoport@uh.edu.

RAPOPORT, SONYA, artist; b. Boston; d. Louis Aaron and Ida Tina (Axelrod) Goldberg; m. Henry Rapoport; children: Hava Rapoport de Fereres, David, Robert. Student, Mass. Coll. Art, 1941-42; BA, NYU, 1945; MA, U. Calif., Berkeley, 1949. Bd. dirs. LEONARDO, Jour. Internat. Soc. Arts, Scis. and Tech.; mem. adv. com. Berkeley Art Mus. U. Calif. One-woman shows include Peabody Mus., Harvard U., 1978, Calif. Palace Legion of Honor, 1963, N.Y.C. Pub. Libr., 1979, New Sch. Social Rsch., N.Y.C., 1981, NYU Grad. Sch. Bus. Adminstrn., 1982, Sarah Lawrence Coll., Bronxville, N.Y., 1984, Kuopio Mus., Finland, 1992, exhibited in group shows at Union Gallery San Jose (Calif.) State U., 1979, Ctr. Visual Arts, Oakland, Calif., 1979, Walker Art Ctr., Mpls., 1981, Nat. Libr., Madrid, 1982, SUNY Libr., Purchase, 1983, Otis Art Inst. Parsons Sch. Design, L.A., 1984, Cleve. Inst. Art, 1984, SIGGRAPH, 1998, N.Y. Digital Salon, 1995, 1996, 1997, 1998, Copenhagen Film Festival, 1996, Scotland Photo Biennial, 1997, Mill Valley Film Festival, 1997, Internat. Symposium Electronic Art, Mpls., 1993, 1995, 1996, 1999, others, Buenos Aires Biennial, 2002, Represented in permanent collections Mus. Modern Art, N.Y.C., Stedelijk Mus., Amsterdam, Inpls. Mus. Art, Grey Art Gallery, NYU, San Francisco Mus. Modern Art, San Jose State U. Found.-Union Gallery, Crocker Art Mus., Sacramento, Hall of Justice, Hayward, Calif.; book artist: book Shoe-Field, Chinese Connections, About Me, Objects on My Dresser, interactive book Gateway to Your Ka, Your Fate is in Your Feet, Digital Mudra2; prodr.: A Shoe-In, Biorhythm, Coping with Sexual Jealousy, (computer assisted interactive installations) The Animated Soul, Digital Mudra, 1998, Transgenic Bagel, 1994—95, Redeeming the Gene, Molding the Golem, Folding the Protein, 2001, Make Me a Jewish Man: An Alternative Masculinity, 1999, Arbor Erecta, 1998, Make Me a Man, 1997, Objective Connections, 1996, Brutal Myths, 1996, Smell Your Destiny, 1995; Web books, Redeeming the Gene, Molding the Golem, Folding the Protein, 2001. Home: 6 Hillcrest Ct Berkeley CA 94705-2805 E-mail: sonyarap@lmi.net.

RAPOSO, DEBORAH F. nursing administrator; b. Mattapoisett, Mass., July 23, 1962; d. Bradley S. and Susan B. Drake; m. Joseph A. Raposo, June 9, 1984; children: Michael, Kelly Ann. BSN, Salve Regina Coll., 1984; student, St. Joseph's Coll. RN, Mass.; cert. in infant devel. Staff army nurse corps. U.S. Army, El Paso, Tex., 1984-91; dir. women's and children's health St. Luke's Hosp., New Bedford, Mass., 1991—. Recipient Meritorious Svc. medal U.S. Army, 1991, Commendation medal, 1991. Mem. AWONN, Nat. Assn. Neonatal Nurses, Am. Orgn. Nurse Execs. Home: 3 Greenhough Dr Mattapoisett MA 02739-1630 Office: St Lukes Hosp 101 Page St New Bedford MA 02740-3400

RAPP, MELANIE L. state legislator, primary school educator; b. Lake Worth, Fla., Sept. 5, 1964; BA in Internat. Culture and Commerce, Christopher Newport U., 1990. Substitute tchr.; state del. dist. 96 Va. House Dels., 2001. Elected mem. York County Bd. Suprs., 2000; mem. Watermen's Mus., Concerned Women for Am.; ea. vice chmn. Rep. Party Va. Mem.: York Ruritan, York Rep. Women's Club, Va. Soc. Human Life. Republican. Baptist. Office: Gen Assembly Bldg Rm 520 PO Box 406 Richmond VA 23218 Address: Dist Office PO Box 1529 Yorktown VA 23692 E-mail: Del_Rapp@house.state.va.us.

RAPPAPORT, LINDA ELLEN, lawyer; b. Freeport, N.Y., Jan. 12, 1952; d. William Jay and Marcia Ann (Wiland) Rappaport; m. Leonard Chazen, June 1, 1980; 1 child, Matthew Ross Chazen. BA, Wesleyan U., Middletown, Conn., 1974; JD, NYU, 1977. Bar: N.Y. 1977. Law clk. Chief Judge James S. Holden U.S. Dist. Ct. Vt., Rutland, 1978; assoc. Shearman & Sterling, N.Y.C., 1979-85, ptnr., 1986—, elected mem. policy com., 1995—. Bd. dirs. N.Y. Women's Found., N.Y.C., 1995—2001, AIESEC Internat., N.Y.C., 1994—2000. Fellow: Am. Coll. Employee Benefits Coun.; mem.: Bar Assn. City of N.Y. (employee benefits com. 1986—, employment law com. 1986—). Office: Shearman & Sterling 599 Lexington Ave Fl 13 New York NY 10022-6069 E-mail: lrappaport@shearman.com.

RAPPAPORT, MARGARET M.W.E. psychologist, physician, writer, pilot, consultant; b. Nov. 16, 1947; d. Leo J. and Marie L. (Rischle) Williams; m. Herbert Rappaport (div.); children: Amanda, Alexander. BA, U. Buffalo; MA, SUNY; PhD, MD, U. Colo. Zone Perfect cert. instr. Prof., rschr. U. Dar es Salaam, Tanzania; with Rappaport Assocs., Phila., 1974-94; exec. dir. Inst. for Parent/Child Svcs., Phila., 1978-94; pres., CEO, Diabetes Edn. Ctr. of Cape Cod, Inc. Mem. adj. faculty Temple U., Phila., 1974-94; aviation safety counselor FAA; aviation cons.; chair devel. com. Vis. Nurse Assn. Cape Cod; trustee Cape Cod Healthcare Found.; nat./internat. spkr. Pres. Reach New Heights, Inc.; founder Fit to Fly. Mem. adv. coun. VNA Am. Mem. AAUP, Nat. Profl. Spkrs. Assn., Cosmopolitan Club, Orleans Yacht Club. Home: PO Box 1845 Orleans MA 02653-1845 E-mail: rappaportmm@prodigy.net.

RAPPÉ, TERI WAHL, piano educator; b. Missoula, Mont., Apr. 4, 1945; d. Charley Franklin and Mary Evelyn (Beaver) Wheeler; m. Bruce Dennis Wahl, June 20, 1964 (div. 1982); 1 child, Maradee; m. Gerald Alan Rappé, Sept. 19, 1987; stepchildren: Rick, Susan. BMus with honors, U. Mont., 1971. Cert. secondary tchr. Wash.; nat. cert. music tchr. Piano instr., Missoula, Mont., 1962-72, Wenatchee, Wash., 1972—, Wenatchee Valley Coll., 1976—; ch. organist Ctrl. Christian Ch., Wenatchee, 1982-90; ch. pianist First Ch. of God, Wenatchee, 1990—. Accompanist Columbia Chorale, Wenatchee, 1984—98, Appleaires, Wenatchee, 1998—, Apollo Club, 2001—; percussionist Wenatchee Valley Symphony. Performer with Wenatchee Valley Symphony, 1992—, Am. Guild of Organists, 1992-99. Mem. Wash. State Music Tchrs. (pres. 1998-2000), Pi Kappa Lambda, Mu Phi Epsilon. Avocations: reading, backpacking, snowshoeing. Home: 227 Grover Ct Wenatchee WA 98801-1811

RAQUET, MAUREEN GRAHAM, protective services official, educator; b. Seaford, Del., Jan. 28, 1955; d. Robert James and Helen Mary Graham; m. William Jameson Raquet; 1 child, Patrick. BA in Psychology, Lafayette Coll., 1976; MS in Juvenile Justice Adminstrn. and Criminal Justice, Shippensburg U., 1989. Cert. police officer Pa. Police officer Lower Merion Twp. Police Dept., Ardmore, Pa., 1978—80; foster care cons. The Impact Project, Allentown, Pa., 1993—94; juvenile probation officer Montgomery County Juvenile Probation Dept., Norristown, Pa., 1980—92; secure detention coord. Montgomery County Youth Ctr., Norristown, 1992—2000, exec. dir., 2000. Adj. prof. criminal justice West Chester (Pa.) U., 1994—, Montgomery County C.C., Blue Bell, Pa., 1997; mem. adv. bd. Foster Grandparent Program, Norristown, 1998—; bd. dirs. Plays For Living, Norristown, 1995—2000. Recipient Outstanding Scholarship in Juvenile Justice, Pa. Juvenile Ct. Judges' Commn., Ctr. Juvenile Justice Tng. and Rsch., 1989; scholar, Charles A. Dana Found., Lafayette Coll., 1973—76. Mem.: Pa. Assn. Probation, Parole and Corrections, Nat. Coun. Juvenile and Family Ct. Judges, Am. Corrections Assn., Nat. Juvenile Detention Assn., Montgomery County Juvenile Adv. Assn. (v.p. 1991—92), Juvenile Detention Ctrs. Assn. Pa. (mental health adv. bd. 1999—, bd. dirs. tng. commn. 2001—), Alpha Phi Sigma. Office: Montgomery County Youth Ctr 540 Port Indian Rd Norristown PA 19403

RASBERRY, DAWN YVETTE, counselor; b. Aug. 1, 1963; BMusic, U. South Ala., Mobile, 1985; MEd, U. Ga., 1990. Acad. advisor U. Ga., Athens, 1987-90; counselor, therapist County Mental Health, Fairhope, Ala., 1991-93, Columbia, S.C., 1993-94; asst. band dir. Mobile County Schs., Mobile, 1994-95, counselor, choral dir., 1995—. Author: Vashti's Star, 1999. Min. of music Highpoint Bapt. Ch., Mobile, 1992-93, 94-97; musician Lily Bapt. Ch., Mobile, 1997—. Mem. Am. Counseling Assn., Nat. Music Tchrs. Assn., Romance Writers Am., Mobile Educators' Union, Omicron Kappa Delta, Sigma Alpha Iota, Abe Neefoo Kuo Honor Soc. (charter). E-mail: rasberry@hotmail.com.

RASCH, ELLEN MYRBERG, cell biology educator; b. Chicago Heights, Ill., Jan. 31, 1927; d. Arthur August and Helen Catherine (Stelle) Myrberg; m. Robert W. E. Rasch, June 17, 1950; 1 son, Martin Karl. PhB with honors, U. Chgo., 1945, BS in Biol. Sci., 1947, MS in Botany, 1948, PhD, 1950. Asst. histologist Am. Meat Inst. Found., Chgo., 1950-51; USPHS postdoctoral fellow U. Chgo., 1951-53, rsch. assoc. dept. zoology, 1954-59; rsch. assoc. Marquette U., Milw., 1962-65, assoc. prof. biology, 1965-68, prof. biology, 1968-75, Wehr disting. prof. biophysics, 1975-78; rsch. prof. biophysics East Tenn. State U., James H. Quillen Coll. Medicine, Johnson City, 1978-94, interim chmn. dept. cellular biophysics, 1986-94, prof. anatomy and cell biology, 1994—. Mem. Wis. Bd. Basic Sci. Examiners, 1971-75, sec. bd., 1973-75. Contbr. articles to various publs. Recipient Rsch. Career Devel. award, 1967-72, Tchg. Excellence and Disting. award Marquette U., 1975, Kreeger-Wolf vis. disting. prof. in biol. sci. Northwestern U., 1979. Mem. Royal Microscopic Soc., Am. Soc. Cell Biology, Am. Soc. Zoologists, Am. Soc. Ichthyologists and Herpetologists, The Histochem. Soc. (Outstanding Svc. award), Phi Beta Kappa, Sigma Xi. Home: 1504 Chickees St Johnson City TN 37604-7103 Office: East Tenn State Univ Dept Anatomy & Cell Biology PO Box 70582 Johnson City TN 37614-0582 Office Phone: 423-439-2015.

RASHAD, PHYLICIA, actress, singer, dancer; b. Houston; m. Ahmad Rashad; children: William Bowles, Condola Phylea. Grad. magna cum laude, Howard U., N.Y. Mem. Negro Ensemble Co., founder Phylicia Rashad and Co., 1990. Actor: (plays) The Cherry Orchard, 1973, Zora, 1981, A Raisin in the Sun, 1984, (Off-Broadway) The Duplex, 1972, Zooman and the Sign, 1980—81, Weep Not for Me, 1981, In an Upstate Motel, 1981, Puppetplay, 1983, Sons and Fathers of Sons, 1983; (Broadway plays) Ain't Supposed to Die a Natural Death, 1971, The Wiz, 1975, Dreamgirls, 1981, Into the Woods, 1988, Jelly's Last Jam, 1992—93, A Raisin in the Sun, 2004 (Tony nom. best actress in a play, 2004); (films) The Broad Coalition, 1972, The Wiz, 1978, Once Upon a Time When We Were Colored, 1995, Free of Eden, 1999, Loving Jezebel, 1999, The Visit, 2000; (TV films) We're Fighting Back, 1981, Uncle Tom's Cabin, 1987 (Cable ACE award nom. best sup. actress, 1987), False Witness, 1989, Polly, 1989, Polly: Comin Home, 1990, Jailbirds, 1991, Hallelujah, 1993, David's Mother, 1994, The Possession of Michael D., 1995, The Babysitters Seduction, 1996, Free of Eden, 1999, The Old Settler, 2001, Murder, She Wrote: The Last Free Man, 2001; (TV series) One Life to Live, 1983—84, The Cosby Show, 1984—92 (NAACP Image award best actress, 1987, Emmy award nom. best actress, 1985, 1986), Santa Barbara, 1985, Cosby, 1996—2000, (voice) Little Bill, 1999—, : (TV guest appearances) The Love Boat, 1985, A Different World, 1988—90, Blossom, 1991, Touched by an Angel, 1994, 2002, The Cosby Mysteries, 1994, In the House, 1995, Bull, 2001. Office: Care Jim Cota Artisits Agency 10000 Santa Monica Blvd Los Angeles CA 90067-7007*

RASKIN, ROSE ESTHER, veterinary educator; b. Albany, N.Y., Mar. 4, 1950; d. Morris and Helen (Fishman) R.; m. Shengheng Lin, June 23, 1989 (div. Oct., 1994); 1 child, Hannah. BA, Rutgers U., Newark, 1971; DVM, Purdue U., 1976; PhD, Mich. State U., 1987. Diplomate Am. Coll. Vet. Pathologists. Associate vet. Cameron Animal Hosp., Montclair, N.J., 1976-82; resident, instr. vet. medicine Mich. State U., Lansing, 1982-85, sr. resident, instr., 1985-87; asst. prof. U. Fla., Gainesville, 1987-93, assoc. prof. and svc. chief of clin. pathology, 1993—2003; prof. Purdue U., West Lafayette, Ind., 2003—. Co-advisor Pre-veterinary Medicine Club, U. Fla., Gainesville, 1995—2003. Author: Saunders Manual of Small Animal Practice, 1994, Textbook of Small Animal Surgery, 2003, Schalm's Veterinary Hematology, 2000, Clinical Medicine of the Dog and Cat, 2003; editor: Atlas of Canine and Feline Cytology, 2001; contbr. articles to profl. jours. Named Tchr. of Yr., Class of 97 U. Fla., Gainesville, 1995, SCAVMA Tchr. of Yr. (clin. scis.), 1995. Mem. Am. Animal Hosp. Assn., Am. Vet. Med. Assn., Assn. for Women Veterinarians, Vet. Cancer Soc., Am. Coll. Vet. Pathologists, Am. Soc. for Vet. Clin. Pathology. Jewish. Avocations: photography, swimming, cultural events. Home: 2216 Robinhood Ln West Lafayette IN 47906 Office: Purdue U Dept VPB 725 Harrison St West Lafayette IN 47907

RASMUSSEN, KATHLEEN MAHER, nutritional sciences educator; b. Dayton, Ohio, Mar. 1, 1948; AB, Brown U., 1970; MSc, Harvard U., 1975, ScD, 1978. Registered dietitian. Tchr. sci. Cape Hatteras Elem. Sch., Buxton, NC, 1971-72; analytical chemist Berkley Machine Works, Foundry Co., Norfolk, Va., 1972-73; rsch. assoc. dept. nutrition Harvard U., Boston, 1978; instr. div. nutritional scis. Cornell U., Ithaca, N.Y., 1981-83, asst. prof., 1983-88, assoc. prof., 1988-96, assoc. dir. grad. affairs, 1992-95, prof., 1996—, assoc. dean, sec. Univ. Faculty, 1997-2000. Com. mem. NAS, Washington, 1988-96; Pew faculty scholar in nutrition Nat. Ctr. Sci. Rsch., Meudon-Bellevue, France, 1989-90. NIH trainee, 1974-80; NIH grantee, 1984-90, 87—, 93—, 2001—, various other grants and awards, 1982-85, 88-89, 89-92, 92-94, 93-96, 97-99, 2001—. Mem.: Internat. Soc. Rsch. in Human Milk and Lactation (pres. 2002—03), Brit. Nutrition Soc., Am. Soc. Clin. Nutrition, Am. Soc. Nutrition Scis. (sec. 1999—2002, pres. 2004—). Office: Cornell U Div Nutritional Sci 111 Savage Hall Ithaca NY 14853-6301 E-mail: kmr5@cornell.edu.

RASMUSSEN, MARILYN, state legislator; b. Seattle; m. Don Rasmussen; 7 children. Livestock and timber farmer; mem. Wash. Senate, Dist. 2, Olympia, 1992—; chair agr. and rural econ. devel. com. Wash. Senate, mem. commerce, trade, housing and fin. instns. com.; mem. edn. com. Wash. Legislature, Olympia, mem. ways and means capital subcom., mem. vets. and mil. affairs com., mem. Agy. Coun. on Coord. Transp., mem. Nat. Conf. State Legislatures. Mem. Eatonville Sch. Bd., 1980-87; bd. dirs. Marymount Assn. for Sr. Housing, Nisqually River Interpretive Ctr. Found., mem. Rocky Mountain Elk Found.; mem. adv. com. Women of Vision; mem. Gov.'s Prayer Breakfast Com.; mem. adv. com. Harborview Vis.; past bd. dirs. Good Samaritan Mental Health Bd.; eucharistic min. Our Lady of Good Counsel. Mem. Wash. State Dairy Fedn., Kiwanis (Spanaway-Parkland), Am. Agri-Women, Wash. Women for the Survival Agr., Wash. Cattlemen's Assn., Wash. Cattlewomen's Assn., South Pierce County C. of C., Vladivostok Sister City Assn., Am. Tree Farm Sys., Tacoma Sportsmen's Club, Delta Kappa Gamma. Democrat. Office: 409 Legislative Bldg Olympia WA 98504-0001

RASMUSSEN, TINA MARIE, organizational development consultant, writer; b. LaGrange, Ill., Oct. 17, 1963; d. William and Barbara (Meyer) R. BA, No. Ill. U., 1985; MA, The Fielding Inst., 1995, PhD, 1997. Cert. Neurolinguistic Programming Practitioner. Tng. developer Gandalf Tech., Wheeling, Ill., 1981-87; advt. rep. MicroTimes, Hollywood, Calif., 1987-88; trainer Citizen Wristwatch, L.A., 1988-90; asst. v.p. Santa Barbara (Calif.) Bank & Trust, 1990-93; tng., orgn. devel. mgr. Nestle', San Francisco, 1993-94; founder Enteleky Assoc., San Francisco, 1994—. Bd. dirs. Am. Red Cross, Santa Barbara, 1992-93. Author: Leadership in a New Era, 1994, Reflections on Leadership, 1995, In Action: Conducting Needs Assessments, 1995, The ASTD Trainer's Source Book: Diversity, 1995, Leading Organizational Change, 1997. Vol. Holiday Project, Santa Barbara, 1990-93, San Francisco Rescue Mission, 1995, pub. rels. Am. Red Cross, Santa Barbara, 1991-92, Mem. Inst. of Noetic Scis., Bus. For Soc. Responsibilty, OD Network. Avocations: backpacking, running, scuba diving, traveling. Office: PO Box 2447 Mill Valley CA 94942-2447

RASNICK, MELISSA HOPE, music educator, musician; b. Monticello, N.Y., May 21, 1976; d. Bart Alan and Kathleen Ann Rasnick. MusB, Wilkes U., 1998; MusM, E. Carolina U., 2001. Music educator Onslow County Schs., Jacksonville, NC, 1998—2000, Pitt County Schs., Greenville, NC, 2000—. Pvt. clarinet instr., Fallsburg, 1994—98; clarinet player Tar River Cmty. Band, Greenville, NY, 2001—. Mem.: N.C. Assn. Educators, Music Educators Nat. Conf. Avocations: soccer coach/player, cheerleading, reading.

RASOR, DINA LYNN, investigator, journalist; b. Downey, Calif., Mar. 21, 1956; d. Ned Shaurer and Genevieve Mercia (Eads) R.; m. Thomas Taylor Lawson, Oct. 4, 1980. BA in Polit. Sci., U. Calif., Berkeley, 1978. Editorial asst. ABC News, Washington, 1978-79; researcher Pres.'s Commn. on Coal, Washington, 1979; legis. asst. Nat. Taxpayers Union, Washington, 1979-81;

founder, dir. Project on Mil. Procurement, Washington, 1981-89; investigative reporter Lawson-Rasor Assocs., El Cerrito, Calif., 1990-92; pres., CEO, investigator Bauman & Rasor Group, El Cerrito, Calif., 1993—. Author: The Pentagon Underground, 1985; editor: More Bucks, Less Bang, 1983; contbr. articles to profl. jours. Recipient Sigma Delta Chi Outstanding Leadership award Soc. Profl. Journalists, 1986; named to register Esquire Mag., 1986, Nat. Jour., 1986. Mem. United Ch. Christ.

RASOR, DORIS LEE, secondary school educator, educator; b. Gonzales, Tex., June 25, 1929; d. Leroy and Ora (Power) DuBose; m. Jimmie E. Rasor, Dec. 27, 1947; children: Jimmy Lewis, Roy Lynn. BS summa cum laude, Abilene (Tex.) Christian U., 1949. Part-time sec. Abilene Christian U., 1946-50; sec. Radford Wholesale Grocery, Abilene, 1950-52; tchr. Odessa (Tex.) High Sch., 1967-98. Author play: The Lost Pearl, 1946. Recipient Am. Legion award, 1946. Mem. AAUW, Classroom Tchrs. Assn., Tex. Tchrs. Assn., NEA, Tex. Bus. Educators Assn., "W" Club for Women, Alpha Delta Kappa (pres. 1976-78), Alpha Chi. Ch. of Christ. Avocations: reading, cooking, camping, fishing. Home: 3882 Kenwood Dr Odessa TX 79762-7018 E-mail: drjrasor@apex2000.net.

RASSAI, RASSA, electrical engineering educator; b. Tehran, Oct. 15, 1951; d. Farjollah and Farideh (Mofakhami) R. BSEE with high honors, U. Md., 1973, MSEE, 1975, PhD, 1985. Sr. engr. Traycor Electronics Co., Arlington, Va., 1975; project engr. Iran Electronics Industry, Tehran, 1977-79; lectr. U. Md., 1980, 81-91, George Washington U., Washington, 1980-82, George Mason U., Fairfax, Va., 1982; rschr. elec. engring. dept. U. md., 1986-92; prof. No. Va. C.C., Annandale, 1986—, program head engring./elec. engring. tranfer program, 1991. Contbr. articles to profl. jours.; patentee remote telephone links. Mem. NOW Democrat. Avocations: reading, philosophy. Home: 6628 Medinah Ln Alexandria VA 22312-3117

RATCLIFF, DOLORES JEAN, special education educator; d. James Harold and Lottie Irene Jenkins; m. Bruce Laverne Ratcliff, Jan. 23, 1965; children: James Arne, Paige Ada Surguine. BS, Okla. Northwestern U., Alva, Okla., 1966—68; EdM, U. of No. Iowa, Cedar Falls, Iowa, 1977—79. Cert. Permanent Profl. State of Iowa, 1979, Consultant for learning disabilities State of Iowa, 1979, Consultant for behavior disabilities State of Iowa, 1979, Consultant for Mental Disabilities State of Iowa, 1979. Tchr. South Tama Schools, Tama, Iowa, 1968—76; tchr./cons. Area Edn. Agy. 7, Cedar Falls, Iowa, 1977—2000; cons. State of Iowa, Des Moines, 2003—. Pres. Learning Disabilities Assn. of Iowa, Des Moines, 1993—96; mem. bd. of directors Learning Disabilities Assn. of Am., Pitts., 2000—03, chmn. of the advocacy com., 2001—. Recipient Helping Hands, Learning Disabilities Assn., 2002. Mem.: Assn. for Supervision and Curriculum Develop. (ASCD) (assoc.), Learning Disabilities Assn. of Am. (life; see previous). Democrat-Npl. Protestant. Pioneer in Iowa with starting the electronic IEP and trained hundreds of teachers. Created an advocacy (spl. edn.) training kit for parents used across the country and a CD of accommodation ideas for the gen. educator used across Iowa. Office: Iowa Department of Education Grimes State Office Building Des Moines IA 50319

RATCLIFF, MARY CURTIS, artist, educator; b. Chgo., Dec. 3, 1942; d. Francis Kenneth and Marian Elizabeth (Carter) R. AA, Pine Manor Jr. Coll., Wellesley, Mass., 1963; BFA, RISD, 1967; postgrad., U. Calif., Berkeley, 1976-79. Cert. art tchr., Calif. Founding mem. and camera operator Videofreex, Inc., N.Y.C., 1969-71; video prodr. Everson Mus., Syracuse, N.Y., 1972; designer and fabricator, prop dept. Am. Conservatory Theater, San Francisco, 1974; artist in schs. Calif. Arts Coun., various cities, 1976-79; asst. model maker Lucasfilm, Ltd., San Rafael, Calif., 1985-86; visual arts instr. East Bay French Am. Sch., Berkeley, 1986-91; artist and sculptor pvt. studio, 1987—. Instr. Women's Daytime Drop-in Ctr., Berkeley, 1996; mem. adv. bd. No. Calif. Women's Caucus for Art, San Francisco, 1992-93. One-woman shows include Meridian Gallery, San Francisco, 1994, exhibited in group shows at Waitakare Arts Ctr., Titirangi, New Zealand, 1995, Katonah Mus. of Art, N.Y., 2003, Copia-The Am. Ctr. for Wine, Food and the Arts, Napa, Calif., 2003, Galerie Dukon, Marseille, France, 2002, World Trade Ctr., Osaka, Japan, 1999, many others. Fellow Va. Ctr. Creative Arts, 1997, 99. Mem. NOW, Nat. Abortion and Reproductive Rights Action League, Pacific Rim Sculptor's Group (exhbns. com. 1994-97). Avocations: photography, walking, travel. Home: 630 Neilson St Berkeley CA 94707-1505

RATCLIFFE, WALTERENE HARRIS, social worker, educator; b. New Brunswick, N.J., Jan. 27, 1949; d. Walter John Harris and Ann Kovack; m. Barry Lynn Ratcliffe, Oct. 14, 1972; children: Kimberly Lynn, Daniel Joseph. BA in German and Secondary Edn., Cedar Crest Coll., 1971; MEd in Ednl. Psychology, Wayne State U., 1976; postgrad., U. West Fla., 1990—. German tchr. S.G. Smith Middle Sch., Franklin Twp., NJ, 1971—72; edn. counselor Rhein-Main (Germany) Edn. Office, 1974—76; German tchr. Rhein-Main Jr. High, 1976—78; substitute tchr. Edwards AFB (Calif.) Schs., 1980—81; edn. counselor Hurlburt (Fla.) Edn. Office, 1986—94; social svcs. counselor Okaloosa County Health Dept., Ft. Walton Beach, Fla., 1994—. Art smart program dir. Combs-New Heights Elem. Sch., Ft. Walton Beach, Fla., 1989—92, mem. sch. adv. counsel, 1993. Mem.: ACA, APA, Fla. Pub. Health Assn. Avocations: choir, reading, travel, gardening.

RATH, LINDA JOANN, professional organization executive; b. Sioux City, Iowa, June 16, 1950; d. Raymond John and Maxine Joan (Holcomb) Curtin; m. Roger Joseph Rath, June 12, 1976 (div. June 1988). BA in Social Work, Mt. Marty Coll., Yankton, S.D., 1972; MA in Sociology, U. S.D., 1974. Regional program adminstr. Office Resource Mgmt., Sioux Falls, S.D., 1974-79; exec. dir. Minn-Ia-Kota Girl Scout Coun., Sioux Falls, 1974-79; exec. v.p. Harlingen (Tex.) Area C. of C., 1983-95; exec. dir., CEO Moccasin Bend Girl Scout Coun., Chattanooga, 1995—. Founder Leadership Harlingen, 1984; mem. adv. bd. Youth Leadership, Chattanooga; bd. dirs. Family Leadership, State of Tex., 1994-95; mem. adv. com. United Way Am. Humanics, Chattanooga, 1997; sec., bd. dirs. Literacy Ctr., Harlingen, 1993-95; v.p., bd. dirs. Tip o' Tex. Girl Scout Coun., Weslaco, 1990; participant Leadership Texas, 1989, Leadership Chattanooga, 1997. Linda Rath Day proclaimed by City of Harlingen, 1995. Mem. Invest in Children, Southeast Tenn. Coun. on Children and Youth. Democrat. Roman Catholic. Avocations: crossword puzzles, reading, gardening. Office: Moccasin Bend Girl Scouts 1936 Dayton Blvd Chattanooga TN 37415-6410

RATH, MARY LOU, state legislator; b. Buffalo, June 17; d. George Lewis and Margaret M. Whetzle; m. Edward A. Rath, Jan. 10, 1959; children: Allison, Melinda, Edward A., III. BS, Buffalo State U., 1956; Ins. Broker's lic., U. Buffalo, 1965. Home service rep. Nat. Feul Gas, Buffalo, 1958-61; communications affiliate Cummunications Affiliates of N.Y.C., 1961-67; legislator Erie County, N.Y., 1978-93; senator N.Y. State Senate, Albany, 1993—. Mem. N.Y. State Senate, chmn. Senate Local Govt. com., 1982, Buffalo Better Bus. Bur., 1983—, Adminstrv. Regulations Rev. Commn., mem. Alcohol & Drug Abuse, Children & Families, Civil Svc. & Pensions, Edn., Higher Edn. & Taxation, Investigations & Govt. Ops. Coms., various other legis. coms. 1979—. Vice pres. Research and Planning Council, Buffalo and Erie County, 1973-74; pres. Jr. League, 1973-74, mem. admissions com., 1974-78; chmn. Theodore Roosevelt Inaugural Site Restoration com., 1974-78; vol. WBEN "Call for Action", 1974-78; moderator candidates night Coalition for Better Edn., community adv. council SUNY-Buffalo, 1974—, arts adviser, 1981—; mem. Regan Dinner com., 1975; appointed Republican com. woman 8th Dist., Town of Amherst, N.Y., 1979—; trustee Buffalo Sem., 1975-79; bd. dirs. United Way of Buffalo and Erie County, 1977-78; pres. Landmark Soc. of Niagara Frontier, 1977-78; trustee, mem. vestry Calvary Episcopal Ch., Williamsville, N.Y., 1975-78; founding mem. Amherst "Lunch and Issues" program, 1980; bd. dirs. Daemen Coll. Assocs., 1980-81, Buffalo Better Bus. Bur., 1981—, Buffalo Soc. Natural Scis., 1984—; mem. commn. adv. com. State U. of N.Y. at Buffalo, 1985. Recipient Disting. Community Service award Crisis Services, 1984; named Pub. SServant of Yr., Erie County Fedn. Sportsmen's Clubs, 1981, Outstanding Women in Western N.Y., SUNY, 1984; Participant Am. Gas Assn. Lab. Tour, Cleve., 1982 (one of 8 persons invited-nationwide). Mem. Buffalo Philharm. Orchestra Soc., Buffalo Zool. Soc., Erie County Hist. Soc., Landmark Soc. Niagara Frontier, Williamsville Hist. Soc., Amherst C. of C., Buffalo C. of C., Alpha Hon. Soc. Office: 5500 Main St Ste 260 Williamsville NY 14221-6737

RATHBONE, ELIZA E. curator; b. St. Louis; d. Perry Townsend Rathbone and Euretta Cecilia; m. John Andrew Hamilton, Sept. 8, 1979; children: Claudia, Emma, James. Student, Smith Coll., 1967—68; BA, NYU, 1972; MA, U. London, Eng., 1974. Asst. curator Nat. Gallery of Art, Washington, 1977—85; assoc. curator Phillips Collection, Washington, 1985—89, chief curator, 1989—. Decorated chevalier Order Arts and Letters. Office: The Phillips Collection 1600 21st St NW Washington DC 20009-1090

RATHER, LUCIA PORCHER JOHNSON, library administrator; b. Durham, N.C., Sept. 12, 1934; d. Cecil Slayton and Lucia Lockwood (Porcher) Johnson; m. John Carson Rather, July 11, 1964; children: Susan Wright, Bruce Carson. Student, Westhampton Coll., 1951-53; AB in History, U. N.C., 1955, MS in Library Sci., 1957; PhD in History, George Washington U., 1994. Cataloger Library of Congress, Washington, 1957-64, bibliographer, 1964-66, systems analyst, 1966-70; group head MARC Devel. Office, 1970-73, asst. chief, 1973-76, acting chief, 1976-77, dir. for cataloging, 1976-91. Chmn. standing com. on cataloguing Internat. Fedn. Library Assns., 1976-81; sec. Working Group on Content Designators, 1972-77; chmn. Working Group on Corp. Headings, 1978-79, Internat. ISBD Rev. Com., 1981-87. Co-author: the MARC II Format, 1968. Recipient Libr. Congress Disting. Svc. award, 1991, Disting. Alumnus award U. N.C. Sch. Libr. and Info. Sci., 1992. Mem. ALA (Margaret Mann award 1985, Melvil Dewey award 1991), Phi Beta Kappa. Democrat. Presbyterian. Home: 438 Heron Point Chestertown MD 21620-1680

RATHFON, JEANNE LORRAINE, artist; b. Ann Arbor, Mich., June 9, 1929; d. Howard Edward and Betty P. (Laurie) Riggs; m. Sidney Osborn Rathfon, Oct. 21, 1948 (dec. Mar. 2001); children: Paul, Betsy, George, Mary. Art tchr., artist Rathfon Art Studio, Chesaning, Mich., 1990—. Oil painter floral still-life works. Mem.: Arts and Humanities Assn., Charlotte County Arts Assn., Shiawassee County Arts Assn., Chesaning Area Arts Assn. (co-founder, bd. dirs.), Nat. Mus. Women in the Arts.

RATHKE, SHEILA WELLS, strategic and marketing consultant; b. Columbia, S.C., Aug. 9, 1943; d. Walter John and Betty Marie (McLaughlin) Wells; m. David Bray Rathke, Sept. 1966 (dec. 1997); 1 child, Erinn Michele. BA summa cum laude, U. Pitts., 1976, postgrad., 1976-77. Loan coord. Equibank, Pitts., 1961-65; office mgr. U.S. Steel Corp., Pitts., 1966-70; various account and mgmt. positions Burson-Marsteller, Pitts., 1977-87, exec. v.p., gen. mgr., 1987-94, CEO Can. ops. Toronto, Montreal, Ottawa, Vancouver, 1994-95; sr. v.p., dir. corp. devel. Young and Rubicam, Inc., N.Y.C., 1995-99, COO, 1999-2000; asst. provost strategic and program devel. U. Pitts., 2001—. Instr. Slippery Rock Coll., Pitts., 1984-85; adviser Exec. Report Mag., Pitts., 1986-88, A Better Chance, N.Y.C., 1996-2000, N.Y. Philharm., 1997-99. Trustee U. Pitts., 1976-80, mem. alumni bd. dirs., 1990-94; trustee Robert Morris Coll., 1992-95; bd. dirs. Vocat. Rehab. Ctr., 1987-93, Freewheelers, 1989-92, Pitts. Hist. Soc., River City Brass Band, Quantam Theatre, 2003-. Named Disting. Alumnus, U. Pitts., 1992, Legacy Laureate, 2000. Mem. Female Execs. Am., Am. Assn. Advt. Agys. (chair ea. region 1994-95), Pitts. Advt. Club (bd. dirs. 1988-91, pres. 1990), Alpha Sigma Lambda (charter). Avocations: skiing, reading, gardening, traveling, photography. Home: 1819 Sarah St Apt 2 Pittsburgh PA 15203 Office: U Pitts Cathedral of Learning Pittsburgh PA 15260- E-mail: sheilarathke@msn.com.

RATHMANN, PEGGY, writer, illustrator; b. St. Paul; BA in Psychology, U. Minn.; student, Am. Acad. Chgo., Atelier Lack, Mpls., Otis Parsons Sch. Design, L.A. Author: Ruby the Copycat (Most Promising New Author Cuffie award Pubs. Weekly 1991), Good Night, Gorilla (ALA Notable Children's Book 1994), Officer Buckle and Gloria (Caldecott medal 1996), Ten Minutes Till Bedtime, 1998 (ALA Notable Children's Book 1998), The Day The Babies Crawled Away, 2003; illustrator: Bootsie Barker Bites, 1992. Office: Penguin Putnam Inc 345 Hudson St Fl 15 New York NY 10014-4502*

RATHORE, UMA PANDEY, utilities executive; b. Mar. 5, 1950; d. O Nath and R Devi Pandey; m. Ram N.S. Rathore, Dec. 18, 1978; children: Dinesh, Rana. BS, Kanpur U., 1967, MS, 1969. Adviser Consul Gen. of Iceland to India, 1976-85; v.p. Nevaid Cons., 1974-82; with North Jersey Utilities, Mount Freedom, N.J., 1983—, pres. Sr. ptnr. Translantic Cons.; founder Maxim Imports, 1994—; ind. mgmt. cons.; bd. dirs. Revel Inc., N.Y. Mem. ethics bd. Randolph Twp., N.J., 1986-91, county and state rep. Shongum Sch. PTA, 1989—, mem. multicultural com., 1993-94; membership chmn. LWV, 1979-81, com. person Dem. dist. 3 Randolph Twp., 1992, 94, mem. ethics com., 1994, mem. com., 1995; mem. drug action com. Randolph Twp., 1994, 95, 96—; mem. Dem. task force N.J. Women's Polit. Caucus, 1994; county and state rep. Randolph Intermediate Sch. PTA, 1993-94, bd. edn. rep., 1996—; mem. PTA coun. Randolph Twp. Schs.; legis. chair Morris County Coun. PTA, 1997—, counselor Region I; mem. Morris Mus., Macculloch Hall, Frelinghuysen Arboretum; mem. Ctr. for Study of Presidency, 1997; mem. DBE, 1999. Mem. Internat. Platform Assn., Dau. Brit. Empire, Acad. Polit. Sci., Kiwanis Club Smithsonian, Libr. of Congress, Fgn. Policy Assn., N.Y. Acad. Scis., Nat. Trust Hist. Preservation, Nat. Wildlife Fedn. Democrat. Avocations: reading, jogging, hiking, mountaineering. Home and Office: 3 Hickory Pl Randolph NJ 07869-4528

RATHS, BARBARA, political organization worker; b. Maine; BA in Rhetoric with highest honors, Bates Coll., 1996. Various positions in polit. campaigns, Maine; legis. aide, senate caucus dir.; exec. dir., then coordinated campaign dir. Maine Dem. Party, 2000; dep. Sec. of State, Maine; campaign dir. Baldacci for Gov., Michaud for Congress, Dem. State Senate Campaign Com., Dem. State House Campaign Com., Maine AFL-CIO, AFL-CIO, Dem. Nat. Com.; chairwoman Maine Dem. Party, 2002—. Active Valley St. Organic Cmty. Garden, Portland, Maine, Alumni Coun., Bates Coll., Wayside Soup Kitchen, Portland. Office: Maine Dem Party Main Office PO Box 5258 Augusta ME 04332

RATICK, RANDIE H. music educator, elementary school educator; b. Ellenville, N.Y., Apr. 14, 1956; d. Saul and Rose Finkelstein; m. Lawrence Richard Ratick, Oct. 1, 1983; 1 child, Benjamin. BFA, SUNY, Buffalo, 1978, MFA, 1979. Cert. tchr. Music tchr. Circleville (N.Y.) Mid. Sch., 1979—85, Hagan Elem. Sch., Poughkeepsie, NY, 1985—. Grantee, Cmty. Found. Dutchess County, 1992—93, Mid-Hudson Tchrs. Ctr., 2001, 2002, Dutchess County Arts Coun., 2001, 2002. Mem.: Dutchess County Music Educators Assn., Music Educators Nat. Conf., N.Y. State Sch. Music Assn. Avocations: reading, crafts. Home: 454 N Elting Corners Rd Highland NY 12528

RATLEDGE, ELIZABETH ANN GENTRY, social worker; b. Maryville, Tenn., June 14, 1970; d. Bobby Ray Gentry and Doris Jean Brewer-Gentry; m. Charles William Ratledge Jr., Dec. 24, 1990; 1 child, Charles Alexander. BSW, U. Tenn., 1992, MSW, 1997. LCSW. Coord. Blount County br. Big Bros./Big Sisters, Maryville, Tenn., 1992—94; case mgr., group leader Knox Area Rescue Ministries, Knoxville, 1994—96; therapist The Parent Refuge, 1997—99; program mgr. Vols. Am., 1998—2000; owner God's Children, Inc., Maryville, 2000—02; assoc. exec. dir. Harmony Adoptions Tenn., 2000—02; owner, social worker A Blessed Choice Adoptions, Inc., 2002—; clin., med. social worker Covenant Health, Knoxville, 2002—. Temp. psychotherapist Helen Ross McNabb Ctr., Knxoville, 1999; exam writer Assn. Social Work Bds., Culpeper, Va., 2003 . Author of poems. Scholar, Am. Bus. Women's Assn., 1996. Mem.: NASW, Student Social Work Orgn. (pres.-elect 1990—91, pres. 1991—92), Gamma Beta Phi, Phi Kappa Phi. Baptist. Home: 424 N Houston St Maryville TN 37801 Office: 294 Gamble Ave Maryville TN 37801 E-mail: bratledge@charter.net.

RATLIFF, JUDY LYNN, chemist, educator; d. J. E. and O. L. Ratliff; m. Mitchell Douglas Owens, Feb. 5, 2003. BA, Berea Coll., 1985; MEd, Ea. Ky. U., 1988; PhD, U. Ky., 1995. Rank 1, Tchg. Lic. Ky. Dept. of Edn., 1985. Physics tchr. Mason County H.S., Maysville, Ky., 1985—89; tchg., rsch. asst. U. Ky., Lexington, 1989—92; chemistry physics tchr. Clarksville H.S., Ind., 1992—93; asst. prof. chemistry Murray State U., Ky., 1993—99, assoc. prof. chemistry, 1999—, interim chmn. chemistry, 2002—. Cons. USAF Environics Directorate, Panama City, Fla., 1992—93; post doctoral asst. U. Tenn. Knoxville, 1994. Contbr. articles to profl. jours. Grantee Multidisciplinary Sci. Course Devel., Ky. Sci. and Tech. Coun., 1999—2000, Ky. Inst. for Mid. Sch. Sci. Tchrs., Ky. Dept. of Edn., 2002, New Traditions in Chemistry at Murray State U., NSF, 2001—03. Mem.: NSTA, Am. Chem. Soc., Phi Delta Kappa, Sigma Xi, Iota Sigma Pi. Conservative. Baptist. Avocations: quilting, stained glass, flying, French bulldogs. Office: Murray State Univ Chemistry Dept 456 Blackburn Science Building Murray KY 42071-3346 E-mail: judy.ratliff@murraystate.edu.

RATLIFF, KARI LYNNE, music educator; b. Great Falls, Mont., May 1, 1957; d. Harold Perry and Inez Borghild Gaarder; m. Jay Doyl Ratliff, July 28, 1984; children: Jordan, Spencer, Taylor. BS, Mont. State U., 1979. Kindergarten tchr., Philipsburg, Mont., 1979—82; 1st grade tchr. Canyon Creek Sch., Billings, Mont., 1982—89; music tchr. Greenfield Sch., Fairfield, Mont., 1995—. Active Cmty. Choir. Mem.: Jr. Womens Club. Home: 130 4th Ln NE Fairfield MT 59436-9229

RATLIFF, LINDA SUSAN, special education educator, consultant; b. Kenosha, Wis., Aug. 13, 1952; d. Donald Charles and Audrey Catherine (Vick) Martell; m. Roger Neal Ratliff, Nov. 24, 1978. BS, Ea. Mich. U., Ypsilanti, Mich., 1974, MA, 1982. Substitute tchr. Ann Arbor (Mich.) Pub. Schs., 1975—77, U. Mich. Treatment Ctr., Ann Arbor, 1975—77; spl. edn. tchr. EI class Flint Cmty. Schs., 1977—79; spl. edn. tchr. LD class Lapeer Cmty. Schs., 1979—90; spl. edn. cons. East China Schs., St. Clair, Mich., 1990—. Spl. edn. curriculum chair East China Schs., East China, 2002—. Contbr. Paralyzed Vets., 1990—; coach Spl. Olympics Mich., 1998—; fundraiser March of Dimes, 1996—. Mem.: Mich. Assn. Learning Disabled Educators, Mich. Transition Svcs. Assn., Coun. for Exceptional Children (Golden Nugget 1998), Phi Kappa Phi. Avocations: organic gardening, bicycling, scrapbooks, aerobics, guitar. Home: PO Box 542 Saint Clair MI 48079 Office: E China Sch/ St Clair HS 2200 Clinton Rd Saint Clair MI 48079

RATLIFF, MARY JEAN DOUGHERTY, fine arts educator; b. Wichita Falls, Tex., July 25, 1933; d. Robert Byron and Thelma Irene (Dickson) Dougherty; m. Charles Richard Ratliff, Aug. 28, 1953; children: David Charles, Richard Byron, Melany Elaine, James Brett. Student, Tex. Tech. U., 1952-53; AAS, Richland U., 1975; BFA, U. North Tex., 1978. Art instr. Brookhaven Coll., Dallas, 1982-97. Exhibited in Watercolor U.S.A. Show, 1998, 2002. Com. mem. Tex. Bicentennial Com., Farmers Branch, Tex., 1975-76, Imagination Celebration, 1990-91. Named to Notable Women of Tex., 1984-85. Mem.: Internat. Soc. Exptl. Artists (signature mem. status), Nat. Mus. Women in the Arts (charter mem.), Southwestern Watercolor Soc., Tex. Visual Arts Assn. (signature mem. status), Farmers Br. Carrollton Art Assn. (life; founder, twice past pres., v.p., sec., treas.). Republican. Baptist. Avocations: boating, traveling, photography, sewing, ping pong/table tennis. Home: 1202 Mackie Dr Carrollton TX 75007-4835

RATLIFF-SMITH, DEE ANN, bookkeeper; b. Wichita, Kans., Feb. 14, 1943; d. Casey Emil Eichenauer and Dorotha Mary Cox; m. Eugene Leroy Ratliff, Oct. 31, 1987 (dec. Apr. 1997); m. Paul Vernon Smith, Aug. 18, 2001; 1 child, Darin Alan Eichenauer. AS in Edn., Garden City (Kans.) Jr. Coll., 1963; BS in Elem. Edn., Newman U., 2000. Emergency tchr. Unified Sch. Dist. #466, Scott City, Kans., 1997—2000; cashier, stocker Gibsons Discount, Scott City, 1998—99, Caspar Foods, Scott City, 1999—2000; cert. substitute tchr. Unified Sch. Dist. #274, Oakley, Kans., 2000—; bookkeeper Paul's Pharmacy, Oakley, 2001—. Contbr. articles to newspapers. Cub Scout leader, Scott City; student advisor Newman Adv. Coun.; vbs dir., tchr., chior, worship leader Holy Cross Luth. Ch., First Bapt. Ch., United Meth. Ch., Kans. Grantee Kans. Tuition grantee, Newman U., 1998—2000, Wichita C.C., 1998—2000; scholar, Alpha Omega, Scott City, 1961—63, BPW, Dodge City, Kans., 1999—2000. Mem.: Student Tchr. Nat. Edn. Assoc. (sec. 1961—63). Baptist. Avocations: walking, swimming, sewing, home remodeling, travel. Home: 401 Willow Ave Oakley KS 67748-1239

RATNER, ELLEN FAITH, radio talk show host, writer; b. Cleve., Aug. 28, 1951; d. Harry Ratner and Anne Spott. BA, Goddard Coll., 1974; EdM, Harvard U., 1978. Coord. women's svcs. Homophile Comty. Health Svc., Boston, 1971-73; co-dir., co-founder Boundaries Therapy Ctr., Acton, Mass., 1973-86; dir. psychiat. day treatment program South Shore Mental Health Ctr., Quincy, Mass., 1974-81; v.p. rsch., devel. and svc., dir. ARC Rsch. Found. Addiction Recovery Corp., Rockville, Mass., 1986-90; health care cons., dir. found. for Addiction Rsch., 1990-94; pres. Talk Radio News Svc., White House corr. Good Day USA "The Washington Reality Check", Washington, 1991—; pres. Talk Radio News Svc. White House corr. Good Day USA "Washington Day", 1995; polit. analyst Fox News Channel, 1997—; Washington bur. chief Talkers Mag., 1996—; CEO Coll. Media News Co. Tchr. Curry Coll., Milton, Mass., 1979-80; cons. program devel. Addiction Recovery Corp., 1984-86; developer, planner The Art's in Mileau Treatment of Phychiatric Outpatients, Quincy, 1980, New Eng.'s first conf. on Chem. Dependency and AIDS, 1988. Author: The Other Side of the Family: A Book for Recovery from Abuse, Incest and Neglect, 1990, 101 Ways to Get Your Progressive Issues on Talk Radio, 1997; appeared on nat. TV and radio shows including C-SPAN, The Oprah Winfrey Show, CNN, Nat. Empowerment TV, others; mem. adv. bd. The Counselor Mag., 1987-90. Bd. trustees, mem. exec. com., vis. com. presdl. search com. Goddard Col., Plainfield, Vt. 1977-81; bd. trustees Samaritan Coll., L.A., 1988-90; bd. dirs. Nat. Lesbian and Gay Health Found., Washington, 1985-92, pres., exec. com., program com., program chair; v.p. Harry Ratner Human Svcs. Fund, Cleve., 1991—; mem. adv. bd. Women of Washington, Inc., 1992—; bd. dirs. Theater Chamber Players, Kennedy Ctr., Washington, 1988-91, An Uncommon Legacy Found., N.Y.C., 1993—, The Ctr. for Spiritual Enlightment, Falls Church, Va., 1994—. Recipient Comty. Svc. award Lesbian and Gay Counseling Svc., Boston, 1985, The Addams-Brown award Nat. Lesbian and Gay Health Found., 1993. Mem. Nat. Assn. Radio Talk Show Hosts, Mass. Assn. Day treatment Adminstrs. (chair regulations and standards com. 1979-81), Lily Dale Assembly. Democrat. Jewish. Avocation: writing works on spiritualism. Office: Talk Radio News Svc 2514 Mill Rd NW Washington DC 20007-2950

RATNER, GAYLE, special education educator; b. Bronx, N.Y. BS, SUNY, Plattsburgh, 1991, MS in Edn., 1993. Cert. spl. edn. grades K-12 and elem. edn. grades N-6. Spl. edn. tchr. Chazy (N.Y.) Ctrl. Rural Sch., 1991—. Asst. chief reader N.Y. State Tchr. Cert. Examinations, mem. students with disabilities content adv. com.; instr. N.Y. State United Tchrs. Effective Tchg. Program, 1999—; mem. edn. bias and sensitivity com. for 4th and 8th grade state assessments CTB/McGraw Hill and N.Y. State, 2001—. Mem.: N.Y.

State United Tchrs., Chazy Tchrs. Assn. (pres. 1995—), Nat. Bd. for Profl. Tchg. Stds. (bd. mem., spl. edn. and elem. edn. com. 2000—), Phi Delta Kappa. Office: Chazy Ctrl Rural Sch 609 Route 191 Chazy NY 12921

RATNER, MARCIA, research scientist; b. Hartford, Conn., June 24, 1960; d. William and Gertrude Chorches Ratner. BA in Psychology, Boston U., 1995, postgrad., 1996—. Rsch. asst. neurology Boston U. Sch. Medicine, 1994-96, editl. asst., 1996-98, rsch. assoc., 1998—; project mgr. Boston U., 1998—; instr. toxicology and forensic toxicology Boston U. Sch. Medicine, 2000—. CEO, v.p. Chem. Safety Net, Inc., 2002—; counselor Specialized Housing, Brookline, Mass., 1995—. Mem.: N.Y. Acad. Sci., Am. Conf. Govt. Indsl. Hygiene, Soc. Occupl. Environ. Health, Soc. Occupl. Health, Soc. for Neurosci., Mass. Neuropsychol. Soc., Am. Acad. Clin. Toxicology, Internat. Neurotoxicol. Assn., Combined Jewish Philanthropies, Psi Chi, Alpha Phi Omega. Jewish. Avocations: horseback riding, guitar, running, skiing. Office: Boston U Sch Medicine C-329 715 Albany St Boston MA 02118-2526 E-mail: marcia@bu.edu.

RATNER, MARINA, mathematician, educator, researcher; b. Moscow, Oct. 30; MA, PhD, Moscow State U. Asst. High Tech. Engring. Sch., Moscow, 1969-71; lectr. Hebrew U., Jerusalem, 1971-74, sr. tchr. pre-acad. sch., 1974-75; from acting asst. prof. to assoc. prof. U. Calif., Berkeley, 1975-82, prof., 1982—. Alfred P. Sloan rsch. fellow, 1977-79, Miller rsch. prof., 1985-86, John Simon Guggenheim fellow, 1987-88; recipient John J. Carty medal for the Advancement of Science Nat. Acad. of Sciences, 1994. Mem. NAS (John J. Carty Medal for the Advancement of Science, 1994), AAAS. Office: Univ Calif Berkeley Dept Math 970 Evans Hall Berkeley CA 94720-3841

RATZER, MARY BOYD, secondary education educator, librarian; b. Troy, N.Y., Sept. 6, 1945; d. John Leo and Katherine M. (Van Derpool) Boyd; m. Philip J. Ratzer, July 30, 1972; children: Joseph, David. BA cum laude, Coll. of St. Rose, Albany, N.Y., 1967; MA, SUNY, Albany, 1968, MLS, 1981. Cert. secondary tchr., sch. libr. media specialist, N.Y. Secondary tchr. English, Shenendehowa Cen. Sch., Clifton Park, N.Y., 1968-85; sch. libr. media specialist Shendehowa Cen. Sch., Clifton Park, 1985—2003. Coord., mentor tchr. intern program; lectr. SUNY Grad. Sch. Info. Sci. and Policy, Albany; frequent speaker at state-level confs., 1986—; mem. adv. bd. U. Albany Grad. Sch. Info. Sci. and Policy; advocacy cons. Sch. Libr. Sys. Assn. Contbr.: N.Y. State Teacher Resource Guides for Learning Standards; contbr. articles to profl. jours. Recipient grants. Mem. ALA, AASL, N.Y. Libr. Assn., Nat. Coun. Tchrs. English, N.Y. Assn. for Supervision and Curriculum Devel., N.Y. State Acad. for Tchg. and Learning, BIRT, LUERT (past pres.). Home: 433 County Route 68 Saratoga Springs NY 12866-6636

RAU, LOUISE BILLIE, interior designer; b. Saginaw, Mich., June 19, 1946; d. Carl and Belinda (Janni) Dolfi, m. Raymond J. Rau, May 2, 1970; children: Allegra L., Katherine M. BS in Edn., Concordia Tchrs. Coll., 1968; MA in Edn., U. Mich., 1970; postgrad., Baker Coll., 1989-91. Cert tchr. Tchr. grade 2 Birch Run (Mich.) Area Schs., 1968-69, Wayne Westland (Mich.) Schs., 1970-72, Clio (Mich.) Area Schs., 1972-74; floor display mgr. Oscar Rau's, Inc., Flint, Mich., 1985-86, direct mktg. coord. Frankenmuth, Mich., 1986-87, interior designer, 1989—; reading tchr. Reese (Mich.) Middle Sch., 1987-89. Docent Art Goes to Sch., Saginaw (Mich.) Art Mus., 1981-84, pres. Mich. Chapt. of Interior Design Soc., 1998—; adj. fac. interior designer, Baker Coll. Flint, 1998. Contbg. designer feature article on Am. style Saginaw News, 1991; designer "Dream Home" Saginaw Parade of Homes, 1991, contbr. articles to profl. jours. Charter pres. AAUW, Frankenmuth, 1976; bd. dirs. Wickson Meml. Libr., Frankenmuth, 1978; ops. com. Frankenmuth (Mich.) Hist. Mus., 1978; mem. sr. mixed choir St. Lorenz Luth. Ch., Frankenmuth, 1980—, mem. liturical arts com., 1991-93. Mem. Interior Design Soc. (profl.), Founders Soc. Detroit Inst. Arts., Eischer Haus Historical Preservation Com., Frankenmuth, MI, 1999—. Avocations: reading, writing, classical music, traveling, scuba diving. Home: 725 W Tuscola St Frankenmuth MI 48734-1435 Office: Oscar Rau Furniture Inc 360 S Main St Frankenmuth MI 48734-1635 E-mail: rjrau@concentric.net.

RAU, MARGARET E. writer; b. Shantou, Guangdong, China;, (parents Am. citizens); d. George Wright and Mary Victoria (Wolfe) Lewis; m. Neil L. Rau, Jan. 6, 1935 (dec. Nov. 6, 1971); children: Robert, Peter, Mary Margaret Frank, Thomas. Student, U. Chgo., Columbia U.; BA, U. Redlands; student, Riverside Coll. L.S., 1932. Freelance writer. Author: (novels) Band of the Red Hand, 1939; author: (with Neil Rau) (book) My Father Charlie Chaplin, 1960, Act Your Way to Successful Living, 1966, My Dear Ones, Story of the Founding of Recovery, Inc., 1971; author: Dawn from the West, 1964, The Penguin Book, 1965, The Yellow River, The Yangtze River, 1970, Jimmy of Cherry Valley, 1973, Our World: The People's Republic of China, 1974 (notable Children's Trade Book), The People of New China, 1975, Musk Oxen, Bearded Ones of the North, 1976 (Outstanding Sci. Book for Children), The Giant Panda at Home, 1977 (Outstanding Sci. Book for Children), The Gray Kangaroo at Home, 1978, The Snow Monkey at Home, 1979 (Best Non-Fiction Book of the Yr. So. Calif. Coun. Lit. Children), Red Earth Blue Sky, 1981, Minority Peoples of China, 1983, Holding Up the Sky (China's Youth), 1983 (notable Children's Trade Book), Young Women in China, 1989 (Outstanding Book N.Y. Pub. Libr.), The World's Scariest "True" Ghost Stories, 1994, The Ordeal of Olive Oatman, 1997, Wells Fargo's Book of the Gold Rush, 2001, Belle of the West. Fellow: So. Calif. Coun. Lit. Children; mem.: Soc. Children's Book Writers and Illustrators, Authors Guild. Avocation: travel. Home: 5700 Via Real # 97 Carpinteria CA 93013

RAUCH, KATHLEEN, computer executive; b. Franklin Square, N.Y., Oct. 30, 1951; d. William C. and Marian (Shull) R.; B.A., U. Rochester, 1973; M.A. in L.S., U. Mich., 1974; postgrad. N.Y. U., 1981-82. Media specialist Sutton (Mass.) Sch., 1974-76; program cons. Advanced Mgmt. Rsch. Internat., N.Y.C., 1976-79; pub. rels. cons., N.Y.C., 1979; pres. N.Y. chpt. NOW, N.Y.C., 1979-80; computer programmer Blue Cross/Blue Shield of Greater N.Y., N.Y.C., 1981-82; computer programmer analyst Fed. Res. Bank of N.Y., 1983-84; systems officer Citibank, N.A., 1984-85; systems analyst Fed. Res. Bank of N.Y., 1986-89; computer and children's libr. East Meadow (N.Y.) Pub. Libr., 1989-91; pres. Panorama Children's Videos, Inc., 1988-93; microcomputer specialist N.C. State U., 1992-93; prin., v.p. The Computer Lab., Inc., 1993—; prin., v.p., The Computer Lab of Atlanta, Inc., 1994-98. Adv. bd. SafeSkills, Durham, N.C., 1997-98; mem. Coun. on Entrepreneurial Devel., Research Triangle Park, N.C., 1996—. Mem. ALA, NOW (dir. pub. rels. N.Y.C. chpt. 1978, v.p. programs 1978, pres. 1979-80, chmn. bd. 1981, founding mem., sec. Svc. Fund NOW, N.Y.C. chpt. 1981, Raleigh, N.C. chpt.), Assn. for Women in Computing (v.p. membership 1984, exec. v.p. 1985, treas. 1986, mem.-at-large 1987, pres. 1988), Triangle Bus. and Profl. Guild, Friends of the JC Raulston Arboretum. Office: The Computer Lab Inc 2700 Gateway Centre Blvd Morrisville NC 27560-9137

RAULERSON, PHOEBE HODGES, school superintendent; b. Cin., Mar. 16, 1939; d. LeRoy Allen and Thelma A. (Stewart) Hodges; m. David Earl Raulerson, Dec. 26, 1959; children: Julie, Lynn, David Earl, Jr., Roy Allen. BA in Edn., U. Fla., 1963, MEd, 1964. Tchr. several schs., Okeechobee, Fla., 1964-79; asst. prin. Okeechobee Jr. H.S., 1979-81, prin., 1983-84; asst. prin. South Elem. Sch., Okeechobee, 1981-82, Okeechobee H.S., 1982-83, prin., 1984-96, asst. supt. for curriculum and instrn., 1996-98, supt., 1998—. Mem. Dept. Edn. Commr.'s Task Force on H.S. Preparation, 1993-94, chair Task Force Tchr. Preparation and Certification, 1995-96, Edn. Practices Commn., 1998-99, Commr.'s Blue Ribbon Com. on Edn., 1999-2000; mem. shared svcs. network Okeechobee County Exec. Roundtable, 1998-; bd. dirs. Small Sch. Dists. Coun. Consortium, 2001-, Fla. Assn. Dist. Sch. Supts., 1999-; mem. Treasure Coast adv. bd. Fla. Atlantic U., 2001—. Mem. literacy transition team Gov. Jeb Bush, 2002—03; mem. Pres. Frank Brogan's transitional team Fla. Atlantic U., 2003; bd. dirs. Okeechobee County Farm Bur., 1996—. Recipient Outstanding Citizen award Okeechobee Rotary Club, 1986; week named in her honor, Okeechobee County Commrs., 1990. Mem. Am. Bus. Women's Assn., Fla. Assn. Secondary Sch. Prins. (pres. 1993-94, Fla. Prin. of Yr. award 1990), Fla. Assn. Sch. Adminstrs. (bd. dirs. 1992-95), Fla. Assn. Dist. Sch. Supts. (bd. dirs. 2000—), Small Sch. Dist. Consortium Com. (exec. com. 2000—), Okeechobee Cattlewomen's Assn., Okeechobee C. of C. (bd. dirs. 1995-97), Okeechobee Rotary Club, Okeechobee Exch. Club. Republican. Episcopalian. Home: 3898 NW 144th Dr Okeechobee FL 34972-0930 Office: Okeechobee County Sch Dist 700 SW 2nd Ave Okeechobee FL 34974-5117

RAUSCHENBUSCH, STEPHANIE, artist, educator, poet; b. Washington, July 27, 1942; d. Stephen and Josephine Burns Raushenbush; m. Joseph Marchant Hayman, Dec. 29, 1984; m. Louis R. Rowan, June 20, 1964 (div. June 20, 1979); 1 child, Quentin Rowan. BA magna cum laude, Radcliffe Coll., Cambridge, Mass., 1964; MA summa cum laude, Columbia U., NYC, 1966. Treas. Noho Gallery, NYC, 1999—. One-woman shows include Noho Gallery, NYC, 1983, 1987, 1989, 1991, 1993, 1995, 1997, 1999, 2002, exhibited in group shows at Woodstock (NY) Guild, 1986, Art and the Law traveling exhibit, 1988—1889, Biennale d'Arte Contemporanea, Florence, 2001, in pvt. collections; author: (book of poetry) The Heart's Ice Thaws, 1999; contbr. poetry to lit. jours.; exhibitions include, 1986—90, 2003. Trustee Friends Sem., NYC, 1998—2001. Fellow, Woodrow Wilson Found., 1964—65; grantee Kent fellowship grad. studies, Danforth Found., 1966—70. Mem.: NY Soc. of Women in the Arts, Women's Caucus for Art, Catherine Lorillard Wolfe Art Club. Democrat. Mem. Soc. Of Friends. Avocation: gardening. Home: 46 Sherman St Brooklyn NY 11215

RAVECHÉ, ELIZABETH SCOTT, immunologist, educator; b. Stuttgart, Federal Republic of Germany, Nov. 21, 1950; (parents Am. citizens); d. Williard Warren and Justine (Dorney) Scott; m. Harold Joseph Raveché, Jan. 26, 1974; children: John, Justin, Bernice, Beth. BS, Seton Hill Coll., 1972; PhD, George Washington U., 1977. Rsch. scientist NIH, Bethesda, Md., 1972-79, sr. investigator, 1980-85; assoc. prof. immunology Albany (N.Y.) Med. Coll., 1985-89; prof. immunology U. of Medicine and Dentistry, Newark, N.J., 1989-96, prof., 1996—. Contbr. 14 chpts. to books, 75 sci. articles to profl. publs.; mem. editl. bd. Oncology Reports, Procs. Soc. Exptl. Biol. Medicine. Sec. PTA, Hoboken, N.J., 1991. Recipient Disting. Alumna Leadership award, Seton Hall Coll., 2002. Fellow Washington Acad. of Sci. (Outstanding Researcher award, 1983); mem. Am. Assn. Immunologists, Am. Assn. Pathologists, Am. Assn. Cancer Rsch. Office: Dept of Pathology U Medicine-Dentistry NJ 185 S Orange Ave Newark NJ 07103-2757

RAVEN, ABBE, broadcast executive; b. New York, 1953; 1 child. BA in Theater, U. Buffalo, 1974; MA in Cinema and Theater, Hunter Coll. Prodn. mgr., stage mgr. Manhattan Theater Club, Bklyn. Acad. Music, N.Y.C.; mgr. prodn. Hearst/ABC Video Svcs.; dir. prodn. svcs. A&E TV Networks, 1984-88, sr. v.p. prodn., 1988—; sr. v.p. programming and prodn. The History Channel and HTV Prodns., 1995-97; sr. v.p. programming The History Channel, 1997—2000, gen. mgr., exec. v.p., 2000—. Instr. various edn. instns. Active Competition Com. CableACE Awards, chair 12 Ann. Ceremonies; active coms. focusing on violence in TV. Named to, Hunter Coll. Hall of Fame; recipient U. Buffalo Alumni award, National History Day Org. Corp. Leadership Award, 2000. Mem. NATAS, Women in Cable, Am. Women in Radio and TV, PROMAX, Nat. Acad. Cable Programming. Office: A&E TV Networks The Hearst Corp 235 E 45th St 9th Fl New York NY 10017-3305*

RAVEN, LINDA F. mechanical engineer; b. Mishawaka, Ind., Oct. 31, 1972; d. Francis Harvey and Therese Strobel Raven. BSME, U. Notre Dame, 1995. Tech. staff Hughes Space & Comm., El Segundo, Calif., 1995—98; cons. engr. Dynatech Engring., Citrus Heights, 1998—99; environ. edn. intern Nat. Parks Svc., Bar Harbor, Maine, 1999; edn. vol. U.S. Peace Corps, Namibia, 1999—2001, HIV-AIDS coord., 2002; sales support engr. Beacon Power Corp., Wilmington, Mass., 2003—. Asst. scout leader Girl Scouts USA, Roseville, Calif., 1998—99. Avocations: hiking, camping, biking, snowboarding, running. Office: 234 Ballardvale St Wilmington MA 01887

RAVENAL, CAROL BIRD MYERS, artist; b. Bklyn. d. Harry Walter and May (Chalmers) Myers; m. Earl Cedric Ravenal, May 1956; children: Cornelia Jane, John Brodhead, Rebecca Eliza. PhD, Harvard U., 1963. Assoc. prof. R.I. Sch. Design, Providence, 1958—62; asst. prof. R.I. Coll., Providence, 1964-68; assoc. prof. Am. U., Washington, 1969-98; ret., 1998. V.p., pres. Phi Kappa Phi, Washington, 1981-84; chairperson Friends of Art Dept., Washington, 1986-88; v.p. Internat. Psychohistorical Assn., N.Y., 1991-1992; chair Washington Chpt. Internat. Psychohistorical Assn., 1988-90. Contbr. articles to profl. jours.; one-woman exhibits paintings, Harvard, Bkyln. Mus., Providence, Washington, Easton, Md., Germany, Italy. Pres., v.p. Radcliffe Club, 1972-76; bd. mem., chair edn., Acad. of Arts, Easton, Md., 1982-87; bd. mem. Com. Nat. Security, 1984-86; chair Conf. Com. for Nat. Security, 1985; bd. mem. chair, exhbn. com., Art Barn, Washington, 1989-91. Fellow Paul J. Sachs Travelling Harvard U., Sears-Gilbert, Radcliffe Coll.; grantee Am. U., 1979. Mem. Coll. Art Assn., Women's Art Caucus, Internat. Psychohist. Soc., Phi Kappa Phi, Friends of Art Dept. of Am. U., Phi Beta Kappa. Avocations: painting, reading psychobiography, museums, travel, gardening, remodelling historic houses, volunteer teaching. Home: 4439 Cathedral Ave NW Washington DC 20016-3562

RAVID, KATYA, medical educator; m. Shmuel Ravid; children: Yinon Arie, Noga Leah, Jonathan David. BSc, Technion-Israel Inst. Tech., Haifa, Israel, 1979, PhD, 1985. Postdoctoral fellow dept. biochemistry Brandeis Univ., Waltham, Mass., 1986-88; postdoctoral assoc. dept. biology Mass. Inst. Tech., Cambridge, 1988-91; instr. molecular medicine Harvard Medical Sch., Boston, 1992; asst. prof. biochemistry Boston Univ. Sch. Medicine, Boston, 1993-95, assoc. prof. biochemistry rsch. assoc. prof. medicine, 1993—, investigator Whitaker Cardiovascular Inst., 1993—, scientific dir. Core Transgenic facility, 1993—. Peer reviewer Am. Heart Assn. 1995—. Contbr. articles to profl. jours. With Israeli Def. Forces, 1977-79. Recipient numerous rsch. grants. Mem. The Am. Soc. Hematology, Am. Soc. Cell Biology, Am. Soc. Biochemistry and Molecular Biology, Am. Assn. Advancement of Sci. Office: Boston U Sch Medicine Dept Biochemistry 715 Albany St # K724 Boston MA 02118-2526

RAVIN, LINDA, actress; b. N.J., Oct. 21, 1956; d. Frank and Sophie Genevieve (Adams) Ravinsky. BA, Jersey City State Coll.; studies with Ann Countryman, Gene Frankel, Phil Black, Bob Audy. Dancer various prodns. including Salute to Armed Forces, Dance Festival in Park; actress numerous plays including West Side Story, 1977, Sugar Babies, 1979-82, When the Kids Are Away, One Flew Over the Cuckoo's Nest, Detective Story, House of Blue Leaves, My Fair Lady, Pippin, (films) Don Juan, 1975, The Cellar, Dino's Case, Four Friends, 1981, (TV shows) Let's Talk to the Stars, Ryan's Hope, Eddie Capra Mystery, A Little Sex, 1982, The Hamptons. Mem. Actors' Equity Assn., AFTRA, Screen Actors Guild.

RAVITCH, DIANE SILVERS, historian, educator, author, government official; b. Houston, July 1, 1938; d. Walter Cracker and Ann Celia (Katz) Silvers; m. Richard Ravitch, June 26, 1960 (div. 1986); children: Joseph, Steven (dec.), Michael. BA, Wellesley Coll., 1960; PhD, Columbia U., 1975; LHD (hon.), Williams Coll., 1984, Reed Coll., 1985, Amherst Coll., 1986, SUNY, 1988, Ramapo Coll., 1990, St. Joseph's Coll., N.Y., 1991, Middlebury Coll., 1997, Union Coll., 1998. Adj. asst. prof. Tchrs. Coll., Columbia U., N.Y.C., 1975-78, assoc. prof., 1978-83, adj. prof., 1983-91; asst. sec. office ednl. rsch. and improvement U.S. Dept. Edn., Washington, 1991-93, counselor to the sec. edn., 1991-93. Vis. fellow Brookings Instn., Washington, 1993-94, non-resident sr. fellow, 1994-, editor papers on edn. policy, 1997-, Brown chair in edn. policy, 1997-; rsch. prof. NYU, 1994-; mem. Nat. Assessment Governing Bd., 1997-; mem. com. on edn. policy Nat. Acad. Scis., 2003-. Author: The Great School Wars, 1974, The Revisionists Revised, 1977, The Troubled Crusade, 1983, The Schools We Deserve, 1985, National Standards in American Education, A Citizens Guide, 1995, Left Back, 2000, The Language Police, 2003; author: (with others) Educating an Urban People, 1981; author: The School and the City, 1983, Against Mediocrity, 1984, Challenges to the Humanities, 1985, What Do Our 17 Year Olds Know?, 1987; editor: The American Reader, 1990; co-editor: New Schools for a New Century, 1997, City Schools, 2000, The Democracy Reader, 1992, Making Good Citizens, 2001; editor: Learning from the Past, 1995, Debating the Future of American Education, 1995; co-editor: Kid Stuff, 2003. Chair Ednl. Excellence Network, 1988—91, 1994—96; trustee Nat. Humanities Ctr., 1999—2000, N.Y. Pub. Libr., N.Y.C., 1981—87, hon. life trustee, 1988—; trustee N.Y. Coun. on Humanities, 1996—; mem. Landmarks Preservation Commn., Southold, NY, 2000—02; bd. dirs. Woodrow Wilson Nat. Fellowship Found., 1987—91, Coun. Basic Edn., 1989—91, Thomas B. Fordham Found., 1998—, New Am. Found., 2000—, Albert Shanker Inst., 2002—, Core Knowledge Found., 2003—, Hunt Inst. Ednl. Policy and Leadership, 2002—. Recipient Award for Disting. Svc., N.Y. Acad. Pub. Edn., 1994, Wellesley Coll. Alumnae Achievement award, 1989; Guggenheim fellow, 1977-78; Phi Beta Kappa vis. scholar. Mem. Nat. Acad. Edn., Am. Acad. Arts and Scis., Soc. Am. Historians, N.Y. Hist. Soc. (trustee 1995-98), PEN Internat. Office: NYU 26 Washington Sqare E New York NY 10003-6644

RAVNIKAR, VERONIKA A. reproductive endocrinologist, educator; b. Bklyn., Jan. 13, 1950; m. Dr. Leonard Sicilian; 3 children. AB in premedicine magna cum laude, Immaculata (Pa.) Coll., 1971; MD, SUNY Upstate, 1975. Diplomate Am. Bd. Ob-gyn. Resident in ob-gyn Prentice Women's Hosp. of Northwestern Med. Ctr., Chgo., 1975-79; fellow in reproductive endocrinology and infertility Brigham and Women's Hosp.-Harvard Med. Sch., Boston, 1979-81, obstetrician-gynecologist, 1981-89; asst. prof. ob-gyn, and reproductive biology Harvard Med. Sch., 1987-92, part-time lectr., 1992—; prof. U. Mass. Med. Ctr., 1992—, obstetrician-gynecologist, 1993—, dir. divsn. reproductive endocrine and infertility and menopause, 1992—. Cons. in field. Mem. editl. bd. Women's Health Digest Med., 1994. Recipient rsch. paper award Dist. VI meeting, Milw., 1979, rsch. paper award Boston Obstetrical Soc., 1981; Bristol Myers grantee, NIH grantee; Grace La Gendre fellow Com. of Nat. Bus. and Profl. Women's Club in N.Y., 1973. Fellow Am. Coll. Obstetricians and Gynecologists; mem. Am. Fertility Soc., Soc. Reproductive Endocrinologists, The Endocrine Soc., Assn. Gynecologic Laparoscopists, Am. Heart Assn., North Am. Menopause Soc. (founding mem.), others. Home: 423 Commonwealth Ave Newton MA 02459-1301 Office: U Mass Med Ctr S4-717 55 Lake Ave N Worcester MA 01655-0002

RAWLINSON, HELEN ANN, librarian; b. Columbia, S.C., Mar. 30, 1948; d. Alfred Harris and Mary Taylor (Moon) R. BA, U. S.C., 1970; MLS, Emory U., 1972. Asst. children's librarian Greenville (S.C.) County Library, 1972-74, br. supr., 1974-76, asst. head extension div., 1976-78; children's room librarian Richland County Pub. Library, Columbia, 1978-81, sr. adult services librarian, 1981-82, chief adult services, 1982-85, dep. dir., 1985—. Mem. adv. com. S.C. Pre-White House Conf. on Libr. and Info. Svcs., chmn. program com. Recipient Outstanding S.C. Librarian award by S.C. Library Assn., 1998. Mem. ALA, S.E. Libr. Assn., S.C. Libr. Assn. (2d v.p. 1987-89, editl. com. 1993, chmn. pub. libr. sect. 1995), U. S.C. Thomas Cooper Soc. (bd. dirs., v.p., pres.-elect, pres.). Baptist. Home: 1316 Guignard Ave West Columbia SC 29169-6137 Office: Richland County Pub Libr 1431 Assembly St Columbia SC 29201-3101 E-mail: harawlin@richland.lib.sc.us.

RAWLINSON, JOHNNIE BLAKENEY, federal judge; b. Concord, N.C., Dec. 16, 1952; BS in Psychology summa cum laude, NC A&T State U., 1974; JD, U. of Pacific, 1979. Private practice, Las Vegas, 1979—80; staff atty. Nevada Legal Services, 1980; from dep. dist. atty. to asst. dist. atty. Clark County Dist. Atty.'s Office, 1980—98; judge U.S. Dist. Ct. Nev., 1998—2000, U.S. Ct. Appeals (9th cir.), 2000—. Office: 333 Las Vegas Blvd S Rm 7072 Las Vegas NV 89101

RAWLS OLTMANNS, SANDRA KAY, interior designer, educator; b. Ft. Myers, Fla., Feb. 15, 1956; d. Clarence Wilmer and Clara Mae (Arnold) Rawls. BS, Fla. State U., 1976, MS, 1981; PhD, Va. Tech., 1988. Cert. interior designer Nat. Coun. Interior Design Qualification, 1990, lic. Fla., 1998. Asst. prof. U. S.W. La., Lafayette, La., 1981—84, U. Mo., Columbia, Mo., 1988—92, U. N.C., Greensboro, 1992—98; interior designer Tropic Interiors, Naples, Fla., 1998—99, Design Purchasing Network, Naples, 1999—2003. Bd. vis. Found. Interior Design Edn. Rsch., 1992—98, mem. accreditation com., 1998—. Mem.: Interior Design Educators Coun., Internat. Interior Design Assn., Am. Soc. Interior Designers (Joel Polsky Acad. Achievement award 1989). Democrat. Episcopalian. Avocations: designing, writing, reading, study classic films & theatre.

RAWSKI, EVELYN SAKAKIDA, history educator; b. Honolulu, Feb. 2, 1939; d. Evan T. and Teruko (Watase) Sakakida; m. Thomas G. Rawski, Dec. 16, 1967. BA, Cornell U., 1961; MA, Radcliffe Coll., 1962; PhD, Harvard U., 1968. Asst. prof. history U. Pitts., 1967-72, assoc. prof., 1973-79, prof. history, 1980—; univ. prof., 1996—. Author: Agricultural Change and the Peasant Economy of South China, 1972, Education and Popular Literacy in Ch'ing China, 1979, The Last Emperors: A Social History of Qing Imperial Institutions, 1998; co-author: Chinese Society in the Eighteenth Century, 1987, Worshiping the Ancestors: Chinese Commemorative Portraits, 2001; co-editor: Popular Culture in Late Imperial and Modern China, 1985, Death Ritual in Lake Imperial and Modern China, 1988, Harmony and Counterpoint: Chinese Music in Ritual Context, 1996. Grantee Am. Coun. Learned Socs., 1973-74; NEH fellow, 1979-80, Chinese Studies fellow Am. Coun. Learned Socs./Social Sci. Rsch. Coun., 1989, Guggenheim fellow, 1990, Woodrow Wilson Internat. Ctr. fellow 1992-93. Mem. Assn. Asian Studies (China-Inner Asia coun., bd. dirs. 1976-79, v.p. 1994-95, pres. 1995-96). Home: 5317 Westminster Pl Pittsburgh PA 15232-2120 Office: U Pitts Dept History Pittsburgh PA 15260 Business E-Mail: esrx@pitt.edu.

RAWSON, ELEANOR S. publishing company executive; m. Kennett Longley Rawson (dec.); children: Kennett Longley, Linda. V.p., exec. editor David McKay Co.; pres., editor-in-chief Rawson, Wade Publishers, Inc.; v.p. Scribner Book Cos.; pub. Rawson Assocs. (divsn. Macmillan Pub. Co.); v.p., chmn., pub. Rawson Assocs./Scribner/divsn. Simon & Schuster Consumer Grp; teaching staff Columbia U. Lectr. NYU, New Sch., N.Y.; organizer, panelist various writers' confs.; mem. exec. coun., nominating chair Am. Assn. Pubs., 1970-74. Former editorial staff writer Am. mag.; free-lance writer radio and mags., newspaper syndicates; fiction editor Collier's mag., Today's Woman. Trustee, past v.p. Museums at Stony Brook. Mem. Women's Nat. Book Assn., P.E.N., Am. Assn. Museums, Yale Club, Cosmopolitan Club, Old Field Club, Women's Forum, Women In Media, Women in Comms. Office: Rawson Associates 150 E 69th St New York NY 10021-5704

RAWSON, MARJORIE JEAN, lawyer; b. Okolona, Miss., Dec. 5, 1939; d. E.P. and Marjorie J. R. BS, U. Miss., 1961; MS, Ind. U., 1969; JD, John Marshall Law Sch., 1977. Bar: Ind. 1977, U.S. Dist. Ct. (no. dist.) Ind. 1977, U.S. Ct. Appeals (7th cir.) 1983, U.S. Supreme Ct. 1983, Fla. 1988,

U.S. Dist. Ct. (mid. dist.) Fla. 1991, U.S. Ct. Mil. Appeals, 1995. Tchr. Munster (Ind.) High Sch., 1966-77; atty. pvt. practice, Munster, 1977-90; deputy prosecutor Lake County Juvenile Ct., Gary, Ind., 1978-90; pvt. practice Naples, Fla., 1991—. Adj. prof. Ind. U., Gary, 1984-87, Purdue U., Hammond, Ind., 1988-90, John Marhsall Law Sch., Chgo., 1984-87, U. South Fla., Ft. Myers, 1992-97; compliance specialist Collier County Pub. Schs., Naples, 1997-99. Author: A Manual of Special Education Law for Educators and Parents, 2000; editor: Handbook for Legal Assistants, 1987. Past pres. Women's Polit. Caucus, Naples, 1995-97, Women's Rep. Club, Naples, 1992-94; mem. adv. bd. Naples Alliance Children, 1997—. Mem. AAUW, LWV, Collier County Bar Assn. (bd. dirs. 1996-99), Naples C. of C. (bd. dirs. 1997—), Zonta Club. Republican. Avocations: jogging, swimming, music. Office: 400 5th Ave S Ste 300 Naples FL 34102-6556

RAWSON, RACHEL L. lawyer; BA magna cum laude, Kenyon Coll., 1987; JD, Columbia U., 1990. Bar: N.Y. 1991, Ohio 1995. With Jones Day, Cleve., 1992—, ptnr., 2003—. Mem.: ABA (bus. law sect.), Cleve. Bar Assn. (banking and bus. law sect.). Office: Jones Day North Point 901 Lakeside Ave Cleveland OH 44114-1190*

RAY, ANNETTE D. executive secretary; b. Decatur, Ind., Mar. 24, 1950; d. Gilbert O. and Florence L. Hoffman; m. Richard M. Ray, Nov. 28, 1975 (dec. June 1999); children: Michelle Ann, Ellen Marie, Laura Leigh, David Richard, Ruth Anne. AA, Concordia Jr. Coll., Ann Arbor, Mich., 1970; BS, Concordia Tchrs. Coll., Seward, Nebr., 1972; attended, Ctrl. Fla. C.C., Ocala, 1974. Lic. real estate, Ind.; lic. tchr., Ind., Fla. Elem. tchr. St. John's Luth., Ocala, 1972-74; mgr. apt. complex Victoria Sq. Apts., Ft. Wayne, Ind., 1974-75; substitute tchr. East Allen County Schs., Allen County, Ind., 1976-79, Circut A Luth. Schs., Adams and Allen County, Ind., 1977-81; corp. sec., treas., office mgr. Heritage Wire Die, Monroeville, Ind., 1987—. Co-author, co-editor: 1928-1988 A Rememberance, 1988, Coming to America--32 Families 1597-1997. Vol. Monroeville C. of C., 1987—, Concerned Area Residents Quality Edn., Allen County, 1990—, Am. Cancer Soc., Allen County, 1991—, chairperson Celebrity Bagger Day, 1995, 96; bd. dirs. Hoagland (Ind.) Hist. Soc., 1985—, sec. 2002; bd. dirs. Hoagland Area Advancement Assn., 1999—, sec. 2003; contbr. 2005 Allen County (Ind.) History. Lutheran. Avocations: remodeling old homes, reading, genealogy, gardening, floral arranging. Home: 16901 Berning Rd Hoagland IN 46745-9753 Office: Heritage Wire Die Inc 19819 Monroeville Rd Monroeville IN 46773-9113 E-mail: heritagewiredie@yahoo.com.

RAY, DEBRA ANN, music educator; b. Cleve., Ohio, Nov. 6, 1967; d. Roy Preston and Cleata Ann Ray. AA, Tidewater C.C., Porthsmouth, Va., 1988; BSSE, Old Dominion Univ., Norfolk, Va., 1992, MSEd, 2000. Piano tchr. self employed, Chesapeake, Va., 1986—, Greenbrier Christian Acad., Chesapeake, Va., 1994—98, Currituck County Sch., Currituck, NC, 1998—99; music tchr. Little Creek Elem., Norfolk, Va., 1999—. Mem.: Va. Music Nat. Assn., Music Educator Nat. Conf. (presentor, How Music in the Minor Modes affects Children 2000). Republican. Bapt. Avocations: scrapbooks, reading, bicycling, swimming, gardening.

RAY, DIANE MARIE AYERS, music educator; b. Glens Falls, N.Y., Apr. 28, 1965; d. Robert Edson and Margaret LeClaire Ayers; m. Malcolm Earl Ray, Dec. 24, 1988; children: Zachary Edson, Amanda Doris. BS, Castleton State Coll., 1987. Cert. tchr. music, math. Vt., 1987. Co bus. owner Ray's TV, Poultney, Vt., 1989—99; substitute tchr. Rutland SW Supervisory Union, 1999—2002; tchr. music Poultney Elem. Sch., 2002—. Dir. music United Bapt. Ch., Poultney, 1990—. Mem.: Music Educators Nat. Conf. Baptist. Avocations: drama, photography, travel.

RAY, ELISE, gymnast; b. Tallahassee, Feb. 6, 1982; d. Bill and Ellen Ray. Mem. U.S. Gymnastics Team, 1996-2001, U.S. Olympic Team, 2000. Recipient 1st team Internat. Team Championships, 1997; 1st pl. uneven bars, John Hancock U.S. Gymnastics Championships, 1998; 1st pl. fixed bars, John Hancock U.S. Gymnastics Championships, 1999; 1st pl. All Around uneven bars, John Hancock U.S. Gymastics Championships, 2000; 1st pl. All Around vault, uneven bars, fixed bars, Aussie Haircare Gymnastics Invitational, 2000; 1st team All-Around Champion, Sr. Pacific Alliance Championship, New Zealand, 2000, All-Around Champion, NCAA Championships, 2001, 1st pl. balance beam, NCAA Championships, 2002. Mem. Hill's Angels Club. Avocations: shopping, arts and crafts, movies, family. Address: Womens Gymnastics 1000 S State St Ann Arbor MI 48109

RAY, EVELYN LUCILLE, arts facilitator, small meetings planner; b. Phila., Oct. 15, 1949; d. William and Erma Lucille (Chadrick) Ray. Sec. City of Phila., 1967, Free Libr. of Phila., 1972-77, Office of City Solicitor, Phila., 1977-81, Water Dept., Phila., 1981-87; program devel. creative cons. Accoutrements for the Arts, Phila., 1989, creative dir., 1993—, meeting planner for small meetings specializing in theme and site selection, 1995—. Comms. support Pa. Acad. of Fine Arts, Phila., 1987-88; creative cons. West Phila. Cultural Alliance, Phila., 1988-89; mem. adv. bd. Internat. Biog. Ctr., Cambridge, Eng., 1995—, Am. Biog. Inst., Raleigh, N.C., 1995—. Republican. Baptist. Avocations: travel, real estate: interior design and preservation, entertaining, classical music. Office: Accoutrements for the Arts 341 N Robinson St Philadelphia PA 19139-1125

RAY, JANIE MACHELLE (J. R. SHEPARD), software development executive; b. Montebello, Calif., Feb. 23, 1954; d. George Allen and Ada Janette Ray; 1 child, April Lynn. Grad. h.s., Albany, Ga., 1972. Adminstrv. asst. to pres. FRC Office Products, Jacksonville, Fla., 1979-82; adminstrv. asst. to v.p. comml. lending Stockton Savs., Dallas, 1983-84; exec. sec. to v.p. ops. Metromedia Long Distance, Ft. Lauderdale, Fla., 1985-87; owner, pres. RaceCom, Inc., Ormond Beach, Fla., 1986—, ALAdvt., Ormond Beach, 1986-96. Developer computer text file editing system and computer artificial intelligence, optical character recognition neural network software. Vol., co-chair Jazz Matazz, 1992—94, adv. coord., 1995—96; chair Home for the Holidays Parade, 1995—97; vol. Bowling in Daytona, 1995—2000; active Girl Scouts U.S.A., 1960—69, 1981—96; bookfriend Volusia County Libr., 1998—; vol. Halifax Habitat for Humanity, 2001—. Democrat. Methodist. Avocations: photography, skating, country dancing, writing. Home: 10 Cypress View Trail Ormond Beach FL 32174-8295 Office: RaceCom Inc PO Box 730955 Ormond Beach FL 32173-0955

RAY, JESSICA B. artist, poet, educator; b. Houston, Feb. 10, 1937; d. Raymond Merle Brock and Jessie Lee Evans-Brock; m. Louis A. Williams, Dec. 21, 1969 (div. Dec. 1991); 1 child, Elizabeth Lee Williams. BS, Abilene Christian U., 1959, EdM, 1968. Cert. tchr. Tex. Tchr. English and journalism Ft. Worth/Dallas Ind. Schs., 1959—70; freelance artist/poet Tex., 1970—. Singer Ft. Worth Symphony League, 1995—2001; resident artist Tex. Commn. on the Arts, Austin, 2001—03. Author: Mother Earth...Father Sky, 2002; one-woman shows include SoHo Gallery, Ft. Worth Tex., 2002—03, exhibitions include Cook Children's Hosp., Dallas, Tex., 2003, One Main Pl., 1985, First united Meth. Ch., 2000, 2003, N. Tex. Health Sci. Ctr. Atrium Gallery, 2001, 2002, 2003, Quanah Mus., 2003. Recipient Best of Show, Artists, Writers, Composers Am., 2002. Mem.: Ft. Worth Poetry Soc., Tex. Poetry Soc., Nat. League Am. Pen Women, Ft. Worth Astron. Soc. Methodist. Avocations: gardening, singing. Home: 4407 Bellaire Dr South Fort Worth TX 76109

RAY, NELDA HOWTON, financial consultant; Grad., U. Montevallo, Ala., 1962. Fin. cons. Merrill Lynch, Tuscaloosa, Ala. Mem. Rotary Internat. (local and dist. officer). Home: 4704 Oneida Ave Northport AL 35473-1431 Office: Merrill Lynch 302 Merchants Walk Ste 100 Tuscaloosa AL 35406-2214

RAY, RACHAEL, chef; Mgr. fresh foods dept. Macy's Marketplace, NY; store mgr., buyer Agata & Valentina, NY; mgr., pub and rest. Sagamore Resort, Lake George, NY; food buyer Cowan & Lobel, Albany; host 30 Minute Meals, Albany, 30 Minute Meals, Food Network, $40 a Day, Food Network. Author: 30-Minute Meals, 1999, Veggie Meals, 2001, Comfort Foods, 2001, 30-Minute Meals 2, 2003, Get Togethers: Rachael Ray's 30-Minute Meals, 2003. Office: Food Network Studios 604 W 52nd St New York NY 10019*

RAY, SUSAN DAVIS, accountant; b. Savannah, Ga., Sept. 28, 1967; d. Shelley Arthur and Ann Swain D.; m. Kevin Christopher Ray, Feb. 7, 1994. BBA in Acctg., U. Ga., 1990, M Acctg. in Taxation, 1991. CPA, 1994. Acct. Robert A. Shuman, CPA, Savannah, Ga., 1991-96; tax mgr. Boswell Davis and Assocs. PC, Savannah, 1996—. Mem. Am. Inst. CPA's, Ga. Soc. CPA's, Savannah Estate Planning Coun., Inst. Mgmt. Accts. Avocations: cooking, reading, needlepoint. Office: Boswell Davis and Assocs PC 7 E Congress St Ste 600 Savannah GA 31401-3337 E-mail: bdacpa@g-net.net.

RAY, VIRGINIA H. S. columnist, writer; b. Chgo., Aug. 4, 1931; d. Russell Horton and Cora Virginia Stafford; m. Wilson K. Ray, Nov. 8, 1952 (dec. Oct. 14, 2000); 1 child, Virginia Ray Bouchillon. Writer, reporter South Bend (Ind.) Tribune, 1953—58; freelance writer Lausanne, Switzerland, 1963—68, Tokyo, 1973—79; freelance writer, corr. York County Coast Star, Kennebank, Maine, 1989—2002, Biddeford (Maine) Jour. Tribune, 1990—. Newsletter editor Jr. League Pitts., 1969—70, Tokyo Am. Club, 1974—78; founder libr., Fox Chapel, 1st Internat. Fair, Japan, 1974. Active Pitts. Jr. League, 1958—73; chmn. Three Rivers Art Festival, Pitts., 1962; active Kennebankport Hist. Soc., 1990. Mem.: Portland Jr. League, Brick Store Mus. Republican. Avocations: reading, history, travel, tennis. Home: #15 Pt Arundel PO 1144 Kennebunkport ME 04046-1144 Personal E-mail: vsr@gwi.net.

RAYA, MADHAVI, controller; arrived in US, 1987; d. Madhava Gurjal and Suguna Gurjal Reddy; m. Sai Raya, Aug. 4, 1992; children: Shaan, Neil. M, U. Mo., 1991; attended, Baylor U., 1992. Rsch. assoc. City of Hope, Duarte, Calif., 1992—93; mgr. acctg. and adminstrn. ScImage Inc., Los Altos, Calif., 1995—2001; contr. ScImage, Inc., 2001—. Avocations: reading, travel, gardening, interior decoration.

RAYBURN, CAROLE ANN (MARY AIDA RAYBURN), psychologist, researcher, writer, consultant; b. Washington, Feb. 14, 1938; d. Carl Frederick and Mary Helen (Milkie) Miller; m. Ronald Allen Rayburn (dec. Apr. 1970). BA in Psychology, Am. U., 1961; MA in Clin. Psychology, George Washington U., 1965; PhD in Ednl. Psychology, Cath. U. Am., 1969; MDiv in Ministry, Andrews U., 1980. Lic. psychologist, Md. Psychometrician Columbian Prep. Sch., Washington, 1963; clin. psychologist Spring Grove State Hosp., Catonsville, Md., 1966-68; pvt. practice, 1969, 71—; staff clin. psychologist Instl. Care Svcs. Div. D.C. Children's Ctr., Laurel, Md., 1970-78; psychologist Md. Dept. Vocat. Rehab., 1973-74; psychometrician Montgomery County Pub. Schs., 1981-85. Lectr. Strayer Coll., Washington, 1969-70; forensic psychology expert witness, 1973—; guest lectr. Andrews U., Berrien Springs, Mich., 1979, Hood Coll., Frederick, Md., 1986-88; instr. Johns Hopkins U., 1986, 88-89; adj. faculty Profl. Sch. Psychology Studies, San Diego, 1987; adj. asst. prof. Loyola Coll., Columbia, Md., 1987; cons. Julia Brown Montessori Schs., 1972, 78, 82—, VA Ctr., 1978, 91-93. Editor: (with M.J. Meadow) A Time to Weep and a Time to Sing, 1985; contbg. author: Montessori: Her Method and the Movement (What You Need to Know), 1973, Drugs, Alcohol and Women: A National Forum Source Book, 1975, The Other Side of the Couch: Faith of the Psychotherapist, 1981, Clinical Handbook of Pastoral Counseling, 1985, An Encyclopedic Dictionary of Pastoral Care and Counseling, 1990, Religion Personality and Mental Health, 1993; co-editor (with Violet Franks) Springer Focus on Women series; author copyrighted inventories Religious Occupational and Stress Questionnaire, 1986, Religion and Stress Questionnaire, 1986, Organizational Relationships Survey, 1987, Attitudes Toward Children Inventory, 1987, State-Trait Morality Inventory, 1987, Body Awareness and Sexual Intimacy Comfort Scale (BASICS), 1993, Inventory in Religiousness, 1996, Inventory on Spirituality, 1997, Sports, Exercise, Leadership and Friendship Questionnaire, 1997, Peace Inventory, Life Choices Inventory, 1998, Inventory on the Supreme and Work, 1999; cons. editor Profl. Psychology, 1980-83; assoc. editor Jour. Pastoral Counseling, 1985-90, guest editor, 1988; co-proposer (with Lee Richmond) of Theobiology: interfacing of theology and the sciences, 1998; contbr. numerous articles to profl. jours. Bd. dirs. Psychologists Ethical Treatment of Animals, 1998-2000. Recipient Svc. award Coun. for Advancement Psychol. Professions and Scis., 1975, cert. D.C. Dept. Human Resources, 1975, 76, cert. recognition D.C. Psychol. Assn., 1976, 1985; AAUW rsch. grantee, 1983. Fellow: APA (mem. editl. bd. Jour. Child Clin. Psychology 1978—82, divsn. psychology women chair task force on women and religion 1980—81, chair equal opportunity affirmative action divsn. clin. psychology 1980—82, clin. psychology women's sect. 1984—86, divsn. psychology issues in grad. edn. and clin. tng. 1988—, program chair 1991—94, pres. divsn. psychology of religion 1995—96, fellow, divsn. on internat. psychology, divsn. psychology of religion, psychology of women, clin. psychology, cons. psychology, gen. psychology, psychotherapy, state assn. affairs, divsn. media psychology, dir. family psychology, rsch., Mentoring award divsn. clin. psychology, sect. of clin. psychology of women 1997, divsn. psychology of religion 1997, William C. Bier rsch. award divsn. psychology of religion 2000), Md. Psychol. Assn. (editor newsletter 1975—76, chair ins. com. 1981—83, pres. 1984—85, exec. adv. com. 1985—, chpt. recognition 1978), Am. Assn. Applied & Preventive Psychology (sec. 1992—93, chair fellows com. 1992—93), Am. Orthopsychiat. Assn.; mem.: Balt. Assn. Cons. Psychologists (pres. Md. chpt. 1991—92), Assn. Practicing Psychologists Montgomery-Prince George's Counties (pres. 1986—88, editor newsletter 1990—, treas. 1996—98), Internat. Soc. Polit. Psychology, Psi Chi (hon.). Achievements include research on stress in religious professionals, women and stress, women and religion, pastoral counseling, state-trait morality inventory, leadership, clergy stress, psychotherapy, children, body image, intimacy, peacefulness, spirituality, life choices, religiousness, work. Address: 1200 Morningside Dr Silver Spring MD 20904-3149

RAYMAN, PAULA M. economics educator; b. N.Y.C., Feb. 27, 1947; d. Abraham Samuel and Rita (Relkin) R.; m. Robert Russell Read, Apr. 1, 1973; children: Alyssa, Lily. BA, Hunter Coll., 1970; PhD, Boston Coll., 1977. Postdoctoral fellow NIMH, Bethesda, 1982-84; assoc. prof. econs. Wellesley (Mass.) Coll., 1986-94, assoc. prof. sociology, 1990-94, dir. women's sci. program, 1991-94; exec. dir. Radcliff Pub. Policy Inst., Cambridge, Mass., 1994—. Vis. prof. Harvard Med. Sch., Cambridge, 1983-85; mem. faculty Harvard Grad. Sch. Edn., 1995—; disting. vis. scholar Cambridge (Eng.) U., 1992. Editor Temple U. Press, 1983—. Mem. Mass. Jobs Coun., Boston, 1989-98; dir. work-family project Fleet Bank, Boston, 1996-98; bd. dirws. Baumann Found., Washington, 1996—, New England Bd. Higher Edn., 1997—; mem. adv. bd. Working Today, N.Y.C., 1996—. Bunting fellow Radcliffe Coll., 1985-86; grantee NSF, 1985-86; recipient Swedish Bicentennial award, 1990. Mem. Assn. Women Sci. (adv. bd. 1991—), Am. Sociol. Assn. (chair labor sect., Svc. award 1985), Boston Club. Jewish. Avocations: hiking, collage-making. Office: Radcliffe Public Policy Institute 10 Garden Street Cambridge MA 02138

RAYMO, MAUREEN ELIZABETH, geologist, researcher; b. L.A., Dec. 27, 1959; d. Chester Theodore and Maureen Dorothy (Sterett) R.; m. Chris James Marone, May 24, 1986; children: Victoria Ray, Daniel Chester. ScB, Brown U., 1982; MA, Columbia U., 1985, MPhil, 1988, PhD, 1989. Rsch. asst. Lamont-Doherty Geol. Obs., Palisades, N.Y., 1982-83, adj. assoc. rsch. scientist, 1989—; assoc. scientist dept. geology U. Melbourne, Australia, 1989-90; asst. prof. dept. geology and geophysics U. Calif., Berkeley, 1991-92; asst. prof. dept. earth, atmospheric and planetary scis. MIT, Cambridge, 1992—. Prin. investigator rsch. grants NSF, 1991—; mem. ocean history panel Joint Oceanographic Instns. for Deep Earth Sampling, 1992—. Co-author (with C. Raymo): Written In Stone, 1989; contbr. articles to profl. jours. Named Nat. Young Investigator, NSF, 1992. Mem. AAAS, Am. Geophys. Union, Sigma Xi. Democrat. Office: MIT Earth Atmospheric & Planetary Scis E34-254 Cambridge MA 02139

RAYMOND, DOROTHY GILL, lawyer; b. Greeley, Colo., June 2, 1954; d. Robert Marshall and Roberta (McClure) Gill; m. Peter J. Raymond, June 8, 1974. BA summa cum laude, U. Denver, 1975; JD, U. Colo., 1978. Bar: Conn. 1978, Colo. 1981. Assoc. Dworkin, Minogue & Bucci, Bridgeport, Conn., 1978-80; counsel Tele-Communications, Inc., Englewood, Colo., 1981-88; v.p., gen. counsel WestMarc Communications, Inc., Denver, 1988-91, Cable Television Labs., Inc., Boulder, Colo., 1991-96, sr. v.p., gen. counsel, 1996—. Mem. Am. Corp. Counsel Assn. (pres. 1990-91, Colo. chpt. dir. 1988-94), Colo. Assn. Corp. Counsel (pres. 1987), Sports Car Club Am. (nat. champion ladies stock competition 1981, 85, 86, 88). Avocations: sewing, reading, outdoor activities. Office: Cable Television Labs Inc 400 Centennial Pkwy Louisville CO 80027-1266

RAYMOND, DOROTHY SARNOFF, communications consultant, former actress and singer; b. N.Y.C. d. Jacob and Belle (Roossin) S.; m. Milton Harold Raymond, Mar. 15, 1957. BA, Cornell U., 1935. Cons. 5 adminstrns., over 12 years; cons. 5 adminstrns. U.S. Dept. State; founder, chmn. Dorothy Sarnoff Speech Dynamics and Communications Svcs. Inc. subs. Oglivy & Mather, N.Y.C., 1975—2000. Lectr., cons. nat. and internat. orgns., 1975—. Appeared in Broadway plays: Rosalinda, 1942, Magdalena, 1948, The King and I, 1951, My Darling Aida, 1953; debut in opera as Marquerite in Faust, Phila. Opera, 1942; leading roles with N.Y.C., Phila., L.A. and San Francisco Civic Light, New Orleans, St. Louis Mcpl., Salt Lake City operas include La Boheme, Tosca, Tales of Hoffmann, Carmen, Merry Widow, Fleidermaus, Pagliacci, New Moon, Chocolate Soldier, Great Waltz, Vagabond King; soprano soloist with various symphony orchs., soloist and guest on numerous TV programs incl. Ed Sullivan Shows, 1951—; author: Speech Can Change Your Life, 1970, Make the Most of Your Best, 1981, Never Be Nervous Again, 1988, contbr. articles to profl. jours. and mags. Mem. spl. med. adv. bd. N.Y. Cornell Hosp. Recipient Gold Medal of Honor award for disting. svc. to humanity Nat. Inst. Social Scis.; named Woman of Achievement Albert Einstein Med. Coll. Mem. Women's Forum, Women in Communication, Mortar Bd., Tower Club (Cornell U. chpt.), Lotos Club, N.Y. Hosp. Med. Adv. Bd. Home: 150 E 69th St New York NY 10021-5704

RAYMOND, ELIZABETH SOLLARS, vault and monument company executive; b. Washington, Aug. 4, 1927; d. Walter T. and Loucille (Hyde) Sollars; m. Daniel Robert Raymond; children: Michael, Stephen, David. Tchg. cert., Towson State Tchrs. Coll., 1948. Pres. So. Md. Vault & Monument Co., La Plata. Councilwoman Town of La Plata, 1985—, bus. dist. commr. ward III, 1992—, Charles County woman's commn., 1996—, Charles County econ. commr., 1994-96; pres. So. Md. chpt. Md. Mcpl. League. Mem. DAR, Nat. Soc. Colonial Dames. Democrat. Roman Catholic. Avocation: genealogy. Home: PO Box 1307 La Plata MD 20646-1307

RAYMOND, LISA, professional tennis player; b. Norristown, Pa., Aug. 10, 1973; d. Ted and Nancy Raymond. Student, U. Fla. Profl. tennis player WTA Tour, 1993—. Mem. U.S. Fed Cup Team, 1997—98, 2000, 2002—03. Recipient 1 Career singles title, 42 Career Doubles Titles, WTA Tour; winner U.S. Open, 1996, 2002, Wimbledon, 1999, Australian Open Grand Slam doubles, 2000, Wimbledon, 2001, U.S. Open Grand Slam doubles, 2001, WTA Doubles Championship, 2001, Mixed Doubles Roland Garros, 2003; named NCAA Singles Champion, 1992, 93. Avocations: shopping, hanging out with friends, watching television, football, volleyball. Office: US Tennis Assn 70 W Red Oak Ln White Plains NY 10604-3602

RAYNOLDS, VIRGINIA CRANE, nurse; b. Salinas, Calif., June 3, 1959; d. John Fiske Raynolds III and Sinclair Winton. BSN, Coll. St. Catherine, St. Paul, Minn., 1987. RN Minn. Nursing Bd., Minn., 1987. RN- staff AbbottNorthwestern Hosp., Mpls., 1987—2003; patient placement nurse AbbotNorthwestern Hosp., Mpls., 2003—; admission/discharge nurse AbbottNorthwestern Hosp., Mpls., 2003—. Chair profl. practice com. Abbott-Northwestern Hosp., Minneapolis, Minn., 1989—91, new staff preceptor, 1988—2002. Nat. Merit Scholarship, 1976. Mem.: Sigma Theta Tau (assoc.). Independent. Congl. Avocations: gardening, travel, reading. Home: 5529 James Ave So Minneapolis MN 55419-1608 Office: AbbottNorthwestern Hosp 800 East 28th St Minneapolis MN 55407 Personal E-mail: graynolds@mn.rr.com.

RAZ, HILDA, editor-in-chief periodical, English educator; b. Rochester, N.Y., May 4, 1938; d. Franklyn Emmanuel and Dolly (Horwich) R.; m. Frederick M. Link, June 9, 1957 (div. 1969); children: John Franklin Link, Aaron Link; m. Dale Nordyke, Oct. 4, 1980. BA, Boston U., 1960. Asst. dir. Planned Parenthood League of Mass., Boston, 1960-62; edit. asst. Prairie Schooner, Lincoln, Nebr., 1970-74, contbg. editor, 1974-77, assoc. editor, 1977-87, acting editor, 1981-83, 85, poetry editor, 1980-87, editor-in-chief, 1987—; prof. dept English U. Nebr., Lincoln, 1990—, Luschei editor-in-chief. Lectr., reader, panelist in field; participant many workshops, symposia, confs.; panelist creativity arts com. NEA, 2000; judge Kenyon Rev., 1990, Ill. Art Coun./NEA fellowships, 1987; bd. govs. Ctr. for Great Plains Studies, U. Nebr., 1989-95. Author: The Bone Dish, What Is Good, Divine Honors, 1998, Trans, 2001; editor: Best of Prairie Schooner: Fiction and Poetry, 2001, Best of Prairie Schooner: Essays, 2000, Living on the Margins, 1999, other books; editor Nebr. Humanist, 1990. Pres. Assoc. Writing Programs, bd. dirs., 1988-89, ex-officio pres., 1989-90, v.p., 1987-88; bd. dirs. Nebr. Libr. Heritage Assn., 1988-91; mem. Mayor's Blue Ribbon Com. on Arts, 1985-88; bd. dirs. Planned Parenthood League Nebr., 1978-83, sec. bd. dirs., 1979-80, chairperson long-term planning com., 1980-81, 81-82. Recipient Literary Heritage award, Mayor's Art award, Lincoln, 1988, 2002; Bread Loaf scholar editors, 1974, poetry, 1985; Robert Frost fellow, 1988, 89, Mag. Panel fellow, 1993, 94. Avocation: gardening. Home: 960 S Cotner Blvd Lincoln NE 68510-4926 Office: Univ of Nebraska Lincoln Prairie Schooner 201 Andrews Hall Lincoln NE 68588-0334 E-mail: HRaz1@unl.edu.

RAZOHARINORO, archivist, historian, researcher; b. Antsirabe, Madagasikara, Republic of Madagascar, Nov. 19, 1936; d. Rakotonjanahary and Razanamanana; m. Eugene Randriamboavonjy; children: Vonimbolanoro, Soalandy, Tianjanahary. Degree in Archives, Ecole Nat. des Chartes, Paris, 1964. Cert. archivist. Archivist Republic of Madagasikar Nat. Archives, Antananarivo, Madagasikara, 1964-69, chief, dir., 1969-2001; instr. history U. Antananarivo, 1973-2001. Editor Tantara, 1973-95; author articles and revs. Decorated Grand Croix de 2d classe order. Mem. Malagasy Acad. Lutheran.

RAZOR, MARY C. writer; b. Clinton, Iowa, Aug. 12, 1926; d. William Francis and Lillian Anne (Alvis) Curran; m. Al Razor, Jan. 8, 1973. BA magna cum laude, Drake U., 1985. Author: All Our Yesterdays, 1945, Hominy Ridge, 1981, Hello From Hominy Ridge, 1994. Founding mem. Seed Savers Exch.; mem. Iowa Woodland Owners Assn., Iowa Nut Growers Assn., Friends of Walnut Creek, Sea Shepherd, Earth First, Iowa Prairie Network, Beta Beta Beta, Sigma Tau Delta. Avocation: conservationist activities. Home: 10834 Highway 330 N Collins IA 50055-8554

REA, ANN HADLEY KUEHN, retired social organization marketing administrator; b. Arlington, Va, Oct. 14, 1962; d. Alvin Henry Kuehn and Barbara Ann Schanzenbach; m. Burt Richard Rea, June 30, 1990; 3

children. BA in Communications, Va. Poly. Inst. & State U., Blacksburg, 1984; MA in Liberal Studies, Georgetown U., Washington, 1993. Desk asst., prodn. asst. ABC News, Washington, 1986—88; media/info. officer Embassy of Australia, 1988—90; mktg. dir. The Connection for Women & Families, Summit, NJ, 1992—2002, ret., 2002. Mem. LWV. Episcopalian.

REA, ANN W. librarian; b. Jefferson City, Mo., Aug. 3, 1944; d. William H. and Ruby (Fogleman) Webb; m. Glen N. Rea, Sept. 28, 1974; children: Sarah, Rebecca. BA, U. Mo., 1966; MLS, U. So. Calif., 1968. Libr. St. Charles (Mo.) County Libr., 1967-71; libr. adult svcs. Paterson (N.J.) Free Pub. Libr., 1971-74; libr. Beal Coll. Libr., Bangor, Maine, 1983—. Pres. Bairnet. Mem ALA, Maine Libr. Assn.(scholarship and loan com.). Office: Beal Coll Libr 99 Farm Rd Bangor ME 04401 Office Phone: 207-947-4591.

REA, ANNE E. lawyer; b. 1959; AB, Brown U., 1981; JD, U. Cghо., 1984. Bar: Ill. 1984. With Sidley Austin Brown & Wood, Chgo., 1984—, ptnr., 1992—. Selected as one of 15 Rising Stars You Won't Want to Oppose in Ct., Ill. Legal Times. Mem.: ABA, Leadership Greater Chgo., Chgo. Bar Assn., Ill. State Bar Assn. Office: Sidley Austin Brown and Wood Bank One Plz 10 S Dearborn St Chicago IL 60603*

READ, SISTER JOEL, academic administrator; BS in Edn., Alverno Coll., 1948; MA in History, Fordham U., 1951; hon. degree, Lakeland Coll., 1972, Wittenburg U., 1976, Marymount Manhattan Coll., 1978, DePaul U., 1985, Northland Coll., 1986, SUNY, 1986, Lawrence U., 1997, Marquette U., 2003. Former prof., dept. chmn. history dept. Alverno Coll., Milw., pres., 1968—2003. Past pres. Am. Assn. for Higher Edn., 1976-77; mem. coun. NEH, 1977-84; bd. dirs. Ednl. Testing Svc., 1987-93, Neylan Commn., 1985-90; past pres. Wis. Assn. Ind. Colls. and Univs.; mem. Commn. on Status of Edn. for Women, 1971-76, Am. Assn. Colls., 1971-77. Bd. dirs. Jr. Achievement, 1991-2003, State of Wis. Coll. Savs. Bd., 2000-03, Greater Milw. Com., Wis. Found. Ind. Colls., 1990-99, Women's Philanthropy Inst., 1997-2000, Wis. Women Higher Edn. Leadership, 1997-2000; bd. dirs. YMCA, 1989-2003, trustee, 2003—; mem. Profl. Dimensions. First recipient Anne Roe award Harvard U. Grad. Sch. Edn., 1980; recipient Morris T. Keaton award, Coun. for Adult and Experiential Learning, 1992; recipient Jean B. Harris award, Rotary; Paul Harris fellow, Rotary. Fellow Am. Acad. Arts and Scis., Wis. Acad. Arts and Scis. Office: Alverno Coll Office of Pres PO Box 343922 Milwaukee WI 53234-3922 E-mail: joel.read@alverno.edu.

READ, PATRICIA ELLEN, administrator non-profit organization, editor; b. Indpls., Apr. 29, 1952; d. Horace Manson and Patricia (Downtain) R.; m. William A. Shunk, Jr., Dec. 29, 1995. BA in English cum laude, Rockford Coll., 1974; MS in Libr. Sci. with hons., Columbia U., 1978. Mng. editor Neal Schuman Publishers, N.Y.C., 1977-80; dir. publs. The Foundation Ctr., N.Y.C., 1980-84, v.p., sec., 1984-87; cons. N.Y.C., 1987-93; exec. dir. Am. Reading Coun., N.Y.C., 1988-91; cons., mktg. dir. The Feminist Press, N.Y.C., 1991-93; exec. dir. Colo. Assn. Nonprofit Orgns., Denver, 1993—. Contbr. articles in field. Mem. Comm. Network in Philantrophy, Washington, 1981-87, rsch. adv. group Independent Sector, Washington, 1982-87. membership com., 1983-85, adv. com. Giving USA, N.Y.C., 1984-87, adv. com. Nat. Ctr. for Charitable Stats., Washington, 1986-87, task force in classification of non-profit sector, 1984-86; bd. dirs. Support Ctr. of N.Y., 1990-93, Blue Hill Troupe (Gilbert and Sullivan Repertory Co.), N.Y.C., 1989-91, v.p. 1990-91; mem. Colo. Symphony Orch. Chorus, 1993-94; bd. dirs. Denver/Boulder Better Bus. Bur., 1998—; mem. philanthropic adv. stds. rev. panel Coun. Better Bus. Burs., 1999—. Finalist 1994 Women of Achievement, YWCA of Denver, 1994; named one of 50 most influential in the nonprofit sector Nonprofit Times', 1999. Mem. Nat. Coun. Non-profit Orgns. (bd. dirs., chair 1998—), Metro Vols., Denver (bd. dirs. 1993—, mem. transition team for merger with vol. ctr. 1993, co-chair nominating com. 1994, sec. 1998). Office: Colo Assn Nonprofit Orgns 22 E 16th Ave Ste 1060 Denver CO 80202-5109 Home: 1611 Tamarack St NW Washington DC 20012-1034

READ, SARAH J. lawyer; BA cum laude, Yale U., 1978; JD, U. Wis., 1981; postgrad., Ctr. for Conflict Resolution, Chgo., MIT-Harvard U. Bar: Wis. 1981, Ill. 1981, U.S. Dist. (we. dist.) Wis. 1981, U.S. Dist. Ct. (no. dist.) Ill. 1981. Ptnr. Sidley & Austin, Chgo., also mem. telecom., energy and petrochems. practice group, mem. alternative dispute resolution resource group. Mem. Ohio Telecom. Adv. Bd., 1984. Mem. ABA, Wis. Bar Assn., Chgo. Bar Assn., Order of Coif. Office: Sidley & Austin 1 S First National Plz Chicago IL 60603-2000 Fax: 312-853-7036.

READ, SUSAN PHILLIPS, state appeals court judge; b. Gallipolis, Ohio, June 27, 1947; d. Gomer Wesley and Elizabeth Molineaux Phillips; m. Howard John Read. BA summa cum laude, Ohio Wesleyan U., 1969; JD Floyd R. Mechem Prize Scholar, U. Chgo., 1972. Asst. counsel SUNY, 1974—77; in-house counsel GE Co., 1977—88; ptnr. Bond, Schoeneck & King, Albany, NY, 1988—94; dep. counsel to Gov. Pataki, 1995—97; judge Ct. of Claims, 1998—; assoc. judge N.Y. State Ct. Appeals, Schenectady, 2003—. Mem.: Phi Beta Kappa. Office: NY State Ct Appeals 20 Eagle St Albany NY 12207-1095

READE, CLAIRE ELIZABETH, lawyer; b. Waltham, Mass., June 2, 1952; d. Kemp Brownell and Suzanne Helen (Dorntge) R.; m. Earl Phillip Steinberg, Nov. 22, 1980; children: Evan Samuel, Emma Miriam. BA, Conn. Wesleyan U., 1973; JD, Harvard U., 1979; MA in Law and Diplomacy, Tufts U., 1979. Bar: Mass. 1980, D.C. 1983. Sheldon fellow Harvard U., Cambridge, Mass. and, Republic of China, 1979-80; assoc. Ropes & Gray, Boston, 1980-82, Arnold & Porter, Washington, 1982-86, ptnr., 1987—. Exec. editor: International Trade Policy: The Lawyer's Perspective, 1985; contbr. articles to profl. jours. Mem. ABA (co-chair internat. trade com.), D.C. Bar Assn., Council on Foreign Relations, Washington Coun. Lawyers, Women in Internat. Trade. Office: Arnold & Porter 555 12th St NW Washington DC 20004-1206 E-mail: readecl@aporter.com.

READE, KATHLEEN MARGARET, paralegal, author, educator; b. Ft. Worth, Tex., Sept. 6, 1947; d. Ralph S. and Margaret Catherine (Stark) R.; 1 child, Kathryn Michelle Carter. BA in English and Polit. Sci., Tex. Christian U., 1978; student, El Centro Coll.; postgrad., Tex. Christian U., Tex. Tech. Asst. land and legal dept. Am. Quasar Petroleum, Ft. Worth, 1971-74; paralegal and office mgr. Law Offices of George Sims, Ft. Worth, 1974-81; asst. Criminal Cts. #2 and #3 Tarrant County Dist. Atty., Ft. Worth, 1981; ind. paralegal Ft. Worth, 1982-84; paralegal Law Offices of Brent Burford, Ft. Worth, 1982-85; sr. paralegal/litigation Law Offices of Windle Turley, Dallas, 1985-90; major case supr. The Dent Law Firm, Ft. Worth, 1990-96, Whitaker, Chalk, Swindle & Sawyer, LLP, Ft. Worth, 1996—. Cons./instr. paralegal program, U. Tex., Arlington, 1996—; active Tex. Christian U. Writer's Continuous Workshop. Author: Plaintiff's Personal Injury Handbook, 1995; contbg. author: Legal Assistant's Letter Book, 1995; editl. com. Tex. Paralegal Jour.; contbr. articles to profl. jours. Recipient scholarship Tex. Christian U., Ft. Worth. Mem. AAUW, Am. Assn. Paralegal Edn., Assn. Trial Lawyers, State Bar of Tex. (Legal Asst. Divsn.), Nat. Assn. Legal Assts., Nat. Paralegal Assn., Ft. Worth Paralegal Assn., Freelance Writers' Network, Austin Writer's League, Okla. Writers' Fedn., Text and Acad. Authors. Home: PO box 101641 Fort Worth TX 76185-1641 E-mail: kmrparal@aol.com.

READING, PHYLLIS ANN, social welfare administrator; b. Seattle, Apr. 21, 1954; ADN, Shoreline C.C., Seattle, 1975; BSN, Seattle U., 1979; M Nursing in Adminstrn., U. Wash., 1988. RN, Wash., Calif. Relief charge nurse CCU Group Health Hosp., Redmond, Wash., 1979-81; relief supr. pheresis unit Puget Sound Blood Ctr., Seattle, 1981-83; coord. critical care Snoqualmie (Wash.) Valley Hosp., 1983-85, asst. adminstr., 1985-89; staff devel. specialist U. Wash. Med. Ctr., Seattle, 1989-93; edn. specialist AACN, Aliso Viejo, Calif., 1993-94, program devel. and meeting svcs. dir., 1994-96, dir. profl. devel., 1996-97, exec. dir., 1997-2000, program dir. Ctr. for Leadership Excellence, 1994-96, exec. prodr. satellite video confs., 1994-96; exec. dir. Nat. Assistance League, L.A., 2000—02; dir., patient and family services ALS Assn., San Francisco, 2002—. Mem. nat. faculty tchg. improvement project sys. Kellogg Found., 1992. Mem. adv. bd. N.W. Emergency Physicians, Seattle, 1985-89; bd. dirs. Am. Cancer Soc., Kirkland, Wash., 1988-89. Mem. AACN, Am. Soc. Assn. Execs., Sigma Theta Tau. Avocation: tennis. Office: 140 Geary St 4th Fl San Francisco CA 94108

READY, ELIZABETH M. state legislator; b. Burlington, Vt., Oct. 7, 1953; m. John H. McLain; 3 children. BA, U. Vt. Selectman Town of Lincoln, Vt.; mem. Vt. Senate, Montpelier, 1989—. Regional planning commr.; educator. Home: Box 2018 RR 1 Box 5146 Bristol VT 05443 Office: State House 115 State St Montpelier VT 05633-0001

REAGAN, BETTYE JEAN, artist; b. Oviedo, Fla., Jan. 27, 1934; d. Andrew and Mary Alice (Powell) Aulin; m. Joel Edwin McGill, Sept. 16, 1952 (dec. July 15, 1956); children: Daniel Lee, Kathleen Ann; m. Donald Thomas Reagan, Mar. 30, 1957; children: Debbie Lynn, Julie Karin, Andrew Scott, Patrick Kelley. Grad., Oviedo (Fla.) High Sch., 1951; student, Arrowmont Arts and Crafts Sch., 1993—96. Co-chmn. 1st St. Gallery, Sanford, Fla., 1986. One-woman shows include G. Sander Fine Art Gallery, Daytona Beach, Fla., 1986, 1987, Artist Hand Gallery, Oviedo, 1983, two-person shows, Ormond Beach (Fla.) Meml. Mus., 1987, 1998, 1st St. Gallery, Sanford, Fla., 1992, exhibited in group shows at Maitland (Fla.) Rotary Art Festival, 1991, St. Johns River Art Festival, 1994, Heathrow Festival of the Arts, 2001, Winter Park Sidewalk Art Festival, 2000, one-woman shows include Ormond Meml. Art Mus., Ormond Beach, 1998, Hope Barton Fine Arts, Clermont, 2001, Steinway Piano Gallery, 2003. Recipient 2nd Place, Maitland Art Festival, 1995, Award of Distinction, Deland (Fla.) Fall Festival of Art, 1995, 1st Place, Beaux Arts 45th Annual Festival Art, 1996, Cert. of Recognition for leadership and role model, Fla. Ho. of Reps., 2001, Poster Artist, Five Fla. Art Festivals, 1991—2002. Mem.: Sanford Seminole C. of C. (chmn. cultural arts com.), Portrait Soc. Am., Pastel Soc. Am. Republican. Baptist. Avocations: tennis, swimming, beach. Home: 2636 Reagan Tr Lake Mary FL 32746 Office: Reagan Studios 2636 Reagan Tr Lake Mary FL 32746 Office Phone: 407-322-8177. E-mail: donbetreagan@aol.com.

REAGAN, MELODIE A. communications executive; d. Wyman Reagan and Elaine Edwards; m. Frank Slavick, Aug. 7, 1993; children: Aaron Slavick, Bryce Slavick. BSBA Magna Cum Luade, U. Mo., 1986. Acting dir. Sprint, Kansas City, Mo., 1989—93; sr. mgr. Wiltel, Tulsa, Okla., 1993—94; prin. Telechoice, Montclair, NJ, 1994—97; sr. dir. US West Long Distance, Denver, 1997—99; sr. v.p. Level 3 Comm., Denver, 1999—2001; ceo Auromira Exec. Advantage, Superior, Colo., 2001—. Pres., founder Women Bus. Execs., Superior, Colo., 2001—; founder Colo. Bus. Assn. Coun., Denver, 2002—. Contbr. articles to prof. jours.; presenter in field. Chmn. Women Bus. Executives, Superior, Colo., 2001—03; bd. mem. Wellness for Women, Denver, 2002—03; mktg. chair Denver Shares, Denver, 2003—03; advisor Coryhant Iveena, Boulder, Colo., 2002—03. Recipient Nat. Mktg. Hon., Alpha Mu Alpha, 1986, Nat. Bus. Hon., Beta Gamma Sigma, 1986, Women Excellence award, NAFE, 2003. Mem.: Network Denver, Colo. Software Internet Assn., Rocky Women In Tech., Exec. Coun. Avocations: mother, mentor. Office: Auromira Exec Advantage 1825 South Pitkin Ave Superior CO 80027 E-mail: melodie.reagan@auromiraexecutive.com.

REAGAN, NANCY DAVIS (ANNE FRANCIS ROBBINS), former First Lady of the United States, volunteer; b. N.Y.C., July 6, 1921; d. Kenneth and Edith (Luckett) Robbins; step dau. Loyal Davis; m. Ronald Reagan, Mar. 4, 1952; children: Patricia Ann, Ronald Prescott; stepchildren: Maureen, Michael. BA, Smith Coll., 1943; LLD (hon.), Pepperdine U., 1983; LHD (hon.), Georgetown U., 1987. First Lady of the U.S., Washington, 1981—89. Contract actress, MGM, 1949-56; films include Portrait of Jennie, 1948, East Side, West Side, 1949, Doctor and the Girl, 1949, Shadow on the Wall, 1950, The Next Voice You Hear, 1950, Night into Morning, 1951, It's a Big Country, 1951, Shadow in the Sky, 1952, Talk About a Stranger, 1952, Donovan's Brain, 1953, Hellcats of the Navy, 1957, Crash Landing, 1958, You Can't Hurry Love, 1988, Lunar: Silver Star Story, 1992; TV credits include Schlitz Playhouse of Stars, 1951, Climax, 1954, General Electric Theater, 1953, Zane Grey Theater, 1956, The Tall Man, 1960, 87th Precint, 1961, Wagon Train, 1957, Different Strokes, 1978, Dynasty, 1981; Author: Nancy, 1980; formerly author syndicated column on prisoner-of-war and missing-in-action soldiers and their families; author: (with Jane Wilkie) To Love a Child, 1982, (with William Novak) My Turn: The Memoirs of Nancy Reagan, 1989. Civic worker, visited wounded Viet Nam vets., sr. citizens, hosps. and schs. for physically and emotionally handicapped children, active in furthering foster grandparents for handicapped children program; hon. nat. chmn. Aid to Adoption of Spl. Kids, 1977; spl. interest in fighting alcohol and drug abuse among youth: hosted first ladies from around the world for 2d Internat. Drug Conf., 1985; hon. chmn. Just Say No Found., Nat. Fedn. of Parents for Drug-Free Youth, Nat. Child Watch Campaign, President's Com. on the Arts and Humanities, Wolf Trap Found. bd. of trustees, Nat. Trust for Historic Preservation, Cystic Fibrosis Found., Nat. Republican Women's Club; hon. pres. Girl Scouts of Am. Named one of Ten Most Admired Am. Women, Good Housekeeping mag., ranking #1 in poll, 1984, 85, 86; Woman of Yr. Los Angeles Times, 1977; permanent mem. Hall of Fame of Ten Best Dressed Women in U.S.; recipient humanitarian awards from Am. Camping Assn., Nat. Council on Alcoholism, United Cerebral Palsy Assn., Internat. Ctr. for Disabled; Boys Town Father Flanagan award; 1986 Kiwanis World Service medal; Variety Clubs Internat. Lifeline award; numerous awards for her role in fight against drug abuse. Republican. Address: 2121 Avenue Of The Stars Fl 34 Los Angeles CA 90067-5062*

REAGAN, PATRICIA L. secondary school counselor; b. Pitts., Pa., Jan. 11, 1968; d. Russell Joseph and Joan Lorraine (McPeak) Cherry; m. James Stevenson Reagan, Nov. 1, 1996; children: James S. Jr., Russell; 1 child, Jamie L. Svoboda. BA, LaRoche Coll., Pitts., Pa., 1995; EdM, Sippery Rock U., Slippery Rock, Pa., 2003. Cert. Secondary Guidance, (NCC, NCSC bd. eligible). Clk. Mitchell's Deli, Etna, Pa., 1984—89; office mgr. Jim's Auto Reconditioning, Hampton, Pa., 1989—94; intern The Bradley Ctr., Indiana, Pa., 1994; rsch. dir. Internat. Inventors Club, Greentree, Pa., 1995—96; caseworker II AC Children Youth & Families, Southside, Pa., 1996—98; tchr. aide Montessori Ctr. Acad., Glenshaw, Pa., 1999—2000; intern Shaler Area Sch. Dist., Glenshaw, Pa., 2003; guidance counselor Mt. Alvernia H.S., Millvale, Pa. Vol. tutor Wyland Mid. Sch., Hampton, Pa., 1999; facilitator Slippery Rock Univ., Slippery Rock, Pa., 2000—02; vol. facilitator Shaler Area Intermediate, Glenshaw, Pa., 2003. Mem.: Am. Sch. Counseling Assn., Pa. Sch. Counseling Assn., Am. Counseling Assn. Avocations: gardening, swimming, horseback riding, boating, writing. Home: 3009 Woodview Drive Allison Park PA 15101

REAGON, BERNICE JOHNSON, cultural historian, educator, curator, singer, composer; b. Oct. 4, 1942; Student, Albany State Coll., 1959-61; BA in History, Spelman Coll., 1970; PhD, Howard U., 1975. With African Diaspora Program, Festival of Am. Folklife Smithsonian Instn., Washington, 1974-76, dir. Program in Black Am. Culture, Nat. Mus. Am. History, 1976-88, mus. curator, 1988—; disting. prof. history dept. Am. U., Washington, 2000—. Founder, artistic dir. Sweet Honey in the Rock, Washington, 1973—; vocal dir. Black Repertory Theatre, Washington, 1972-77; mem. Freedom Singers, 1962-63; founder, dir. Harambee Singers, Atlanta, 1968-70. Author: Black People and Their Culture: Selected Writings from the African Diaspora, 1976, Compositions One: The Original Compositions of Bernice Johnson Reagon, 1986; author, programmer Voices of Civil Rights Movement, Black American Freedom Songs, 1960-65, three-record album and book Smithsonian Coll. Recs., 1980; recs. include Songs of the South, 1964, Sound of Thunder, 1967, Give Your Hands to Struggle, 1975, River of Life, 1987; (with the Freedom Singers) We Shall Overcome, 1963, (with Sweet Honey in the Rock) B'Lieve I'll Run On, See What the End's Gonna Be, 1978, Good News, 1981, We All...Everyone of Us, 1983, The Other Side, 1985, Feel Something Drawing Me On, 1985, Live at Carnegie Hall, 1988, All for Freedom, 1989, others; mus. cons., composer for films including Eyes on the Prize-I, 1987, We Shall Overcome, 1988, Roots of Resistance, 1990. Program chair Albany (Ga.) Movement, 1961-62; field sec. Student Non-Violent Coord. Com., 1962-64. MacArthur Found. fellow; recipient Charles Frankel prize NEH, 1995. Achievements include pioneering in the development of a focus on African American culture in exhibition and programming at Smithsonian Instn. Office: Smithsonian Instn Nat Mus Am History Div Community Life Washington DC 20560-0001 Address: Am U Dept History 4400 Massachusetts Ave NW Washington DC 20016

REALE, SARA JANE, museum education director; b. Jamestown, N.Y., Jan. 25, 1961; d. Irving Reuben and Frances Goldinger Wolinsky; m. David Anthony Reale, July 28, 1985; children: Michael Joseph, Lauren Rebecca. AS, Jamestown (N.Y.) C.C., 1983; BA, Fredonia (N.Y.) State U., 1985. Mus. tchr. Fenton History Ctr., Jamestown, NY, 1990-95, dir. edn. and pub. programming, 1995—, interim mus. exec. dir., 2003—04. Mem. adv. bd. Roger Tory Peterson Inst., Jamestown, 1997-2001; mem. Chautauqua County Visitors Bur. Motorcoach Com., 1998-; mem. curriculum devel. com. Robert H. Jackson Ctr., Jamestown, 2001—. Mem. AAUW. Avocations: travel, exercise, children's school activities, historical research. Office: 67 Washington St Jamestown NY 14701-6631 Office Phone: 716-664-6256. E-mail: sarawreale@yahoo.com.

REALS ELLIG, JANICE, marketing professional, human resources specialist; b. NYC, May 14, 1946; d. Otto Peter and Anne (Briganti) Astolfi; m. Paul T. Reals, 1971 (div.); m. Bruce Robert Ellig, July 16, 1994; 1 child, Meredith Evans. BBA, U. Iowa, 1968; MA, Rider Coll., Princeton, N.J., 1978. Dir. Shareholders Mgmt., L.A., 1968-71; v.p. human resources Cooper Med. Ctr., NJ, 1971-80; dir. human resources Pfizer, N.Y.C., 1980-86; v.p. human resources Citibank, 1986-91; sr. v.p. mktg., human resources, adminstrn. Ambac Fin. Group, 1991-2000; prin. Heidrick & Struggles, 2000; ptnr. Gould, McCoy, Chadick, Ellig, 2000—. Chmn. bd. Women's Econ. Roundtable, N.Y.C., 1997—98. Author: What Every Successful Woman Knows, 2001. Bd. dirs. Fountain House, N.Y.C., Nat. Exec. Svc. Corp., N.Y.C., WMCA of N.Y., U. Iowa Found., 2003—, pres. club, 2000—; dir. adv. coun. Bus. Sch., U. Iowa, Iowa City, 1998—; bd. dirs. Women in the State and House, Washington, 1998—; mem. bus. com. Met. Mus. Art, N.Y.C., 1994—; mem. Women's Forum, N.Y.C., 1998-2000; mem. adv. coun. Children's Aid Soc., N.Y.C., 1995-97; mem. leadership cir. Women's Campaign Fund, N.Y.C., 1990—. Named Woman of Yr., Rhinelander's Children Ctr./Children's Aid Soc., 1999, Woman of Excellence award TV Channel 21, 2002. Mem. Fin. Women's Assn., Econ. Club N.Y.C. Republican. Avocations: writing, gourmet cooking, reading, travel, tennis. Home: Apt 12G 10 Gracie Sq New York NY 10028-7052 Office: Gould McCoy Chadick Ellig 300 Park Ave New York NY 10022 Business E-Mail: jrellig@gmcsearch.com.

REAME, NANCY, nursing educator; BSN, Mich. State U., 1969; MSN, Wayne State U., Detroit, 1974, PhD, 1977. RN. Postdoctoral fellow U. Mich., Ann Arbor, prof. dept. nursing. Mem.: Inst. of Medicine of NAS. Achievements include research in in brain aging and menopause; long-term satisfaction and outcomes after surrogate pregnancy; bioethics of assisted reproduction; gender and health. Office: Univ Mich Sch Nursing 400 N Ingalls Bldg Rm 2238 Ann Arbor MI 48109-0482

REAMY, MICHAELIN, marriage and family therapist, educator, consultant; b. N.Y.C., Feb. 20, 1938; d. Judson Reamy and Eleanor Stevens (McMichael) R.; m. James Donald Cowie, Aug. 29, 1959; children: Jennifer D., James J., David K., Laura S.; m. Richard Ward Stephenson, Aug. 31, 1979. B.S. with Distinction in Human Ecology, Cornell U., 1960; M.S.W., U. Ga., 1979; student of Carolyn Myss and Norm Shealy, cert. program in intuition and energy medicine. Cert. primordial sound meditation instr. with Deepak Chopra, 1996. Tchr. swimming, Conn., E. Africa, Lebanon, 1968-75; social work intern, grad. asst., Atlanta, 1978-79; dir. social services, assoc. dir. and coordinator family therapy adult treatment program Brawner Psychiat. Inst., Atlanta, 1980-82; dir. extramural tng., marriage and family therapist Atlanta Inst. Family Studies, 1982-87; Perspective Ctr. for Psychotherapy, 1988-98; Natural Color & Design, 1988—. Mem. Atlanta Com. Children, 1983-85; instr. Water Safety ARC, 1957—. Recipient DAR Citizen award, 1956; YMCA Service Award, White Plains, N.Y., 1958. Diplomate NASW; mem. Nat. Assn. Social Workers, Am. Assn. Marriage and Family Therapy (com. on supervision), Cornell U. Human Ecology Alumni Assn., Mortar Bd., Omicron Nu, Phi Kappa Phi. Contbr. articles to profl. jours. Kappa Phi. Contbr. articles to profl. jours. Office: Natural Color & Design PO Box Q Menlo Park CA 94026-6218 Home: 1115 Santa Cruz Ave Menlo Park CA 94025-5002

REAP, SISTER MARY MARGARET, college administrator; b. Carbondale, Pa., Sept. 8, 1941; d. Charles Vincent and Anna Rose (Ahern) R. BA, Marywood Coll., Scranton, Pa., 1965; MA, Assumption Coll., Worcester, Mass., 1972; PhD, Pa. State U., 1979; Doctorate (hon.), U. of Scranton, 1997, Allentown Coll., 1999. Elem. tchr. St. Ephrem's, Bklyn., 1966-67; secondary tchr. South Catholic High, Scranton, Pa., 1967-69, Maria Regina High Sch., Uniondale, N.Y., 1969-72; mem. faculty Marywood U., Scranton, Pa., 1972-86, dean, 1986-88, pres., 1988—. Tchr. Mainland China, Wuhan, 1982, Marygrove Coll., Detroit, 1979; bd. dirs. Moses Taylor Hosp., Scranton Prep. Sch., Mid-Valley Hosp.; mem. Middle States Commn. for Higher Edn., 1998—; bd. dirs. Coun. Ind. Colls., Assn. Ind. Colls. and Univs. of Pa. Contbr. articles to profl. jours. Recipient Local Chpt. Svc. award UN, 1984, Woman of Yr. award Boy Scouts Am., 1993, Humanitarian award Easter Seals, 1998, Country Club Woman of Yr., 1999; named Outstanding Alumna, Pa. State Coll. Edn., 1989. Mem. Am. Assn. Cath. Colls., Phi Delta Kappa (Northeast Woman 1986, 96, Educator of Yr. award 1990). Office: Marywood U Office of the President Scranton PA 18509-1598

REARDEN, CAROLE ANN, clinical pathologist, educator; b. Belleville, Ont., Can., June 11, 1946; d. Joseph Brady and Honora Patricia (O'Halloran) R. BSc, McGill U., 1969, MSc, MDCM, 1971. Diplomate Am. Bd. Pathology, Am. Bd. Immunohematology and Blood Banking, Am. Bd. HIstocompatibility and Immunogenetics. Resident and fellow Children's Meml. Hosp., Chgo., 1971-73; resident in pediatrics U. Calif., San Diego, 1974, resident then fellow, 1975-79, asst. prof. pathology, 1979-86, dir. histocompatibility and immunogenetics lab., 1979-94, assoc. prof., 1986-92, prof., 1992—, head divsn. lab. medicine, 1989-94; dir. med. ctr. U. Calif. Thornton Hosp. Clin. Labs., San Diego, 1993—. Prin. investigator devel. monoclonal antibodies to erythroid antigens, recombinant autoantigens; dir. lab. exam. com. Am. Bd. Histocompatibility and Immunogenetics. Contbr. articles to profl. jours.; patentee autoantigen pinch. Mem. Mayor's Task Force on AIDS, San Diego, 1983. Recipient Young Investigator Rsch. award NIH, 1979; grantee U. Calif. Cancer Rsch. Coordinating Com., 1982, NIH, 1983; scholar Nat. Blood Found. Mem. Am. Soc. Investigative Pathology, Am. Soc. Hematology, Am. Assn. Blood Banks (com. organ transplantation and tissue typing 1982-87, tech. com. 13 and 14 edit. tech. manual 1996-2002). Office: U Calif San Diego Dept Pathology 0612 9500 Gilman Dr La Jolla CA 92093-0612 E-mail: arearden@ucsd.edu.

REARDON, CINDY LU, gifted and talented educator; b. Glendive, Mont., Jan. 19, 1959; d. Betty L. Oxley and Carl L. Maddux; m. D.G. Reardon, Aug. 19, 1978; 1 child, Nathan Jacob. BA, U. Wyo., 1977—87; M in Psychology, U. Conn., 1994—97. Tchr. remedial reading Sweetwater County Sch. Dist. #1, Green River, Wyo., 1987—89; tchr. of the gifted Campbell County Sch. Dist., Gillette, Wyo., 1989—. Cons. Self Employed, Gillette, Wyo., 1995—2003. Fund raising Challenger Learning Ctr./Sci. Complex of NE Wyo., Gillette, Wyo., 2000—03. Independent-Republican. Catholic. Office: Sage Valley Jr HS 1000 Lakeway Road Gillette WY 82718 E-mail: creardon@ccsd.k12.wy.us.

REARDON, NANCY ANNE, human resource executive; b. Little Falls, N.Y., Sept. 19, 1952; d. Warren Joseph and Elizabeth Owen (Tiel) Reardon; m. Steven Jonathan Sayer, Aug. 28, 1976; children: Scott Jason, Kathryn Anne. BS in Psychology, Union Coll., Schenectady, N.Y., 1974; MS in Social Psychology, Syracuse U., 1978. With GE Co., N.Y.C., 1979-85, Avon Products Inc., N.Y.C., 1985-89, Am. Express, N.Y.C., 1989-91; sr. v.p. human resources Duracell Internat., Inc., Bethel, Conn., 1991-97; sr. v.p. corp. affairs & human resources Borden Inc., Columbus, OH, 1997—. Adv. bd. mem. Catalyst, 1995. Mem. Human Resource Planning Soc. (bd. dirs. 1991-94, treas. 1992-93), N.Y. Human Resource Planners (bd. dirs., pres. 1989-91), Sr. Pers. Execs. Forum, Nat. Fgn. Trade Coun. (bd. dirs. 1995). Office: Borden Inc 180 E Broad St Columbus OH 43215-3799

REARDON, TARA G. state legislator; b. Concord, N.H., Jan. 12, 1956; 2 children. AAS, Westbrook Coll., 1976; JD, 1989. Mem. N.H. Ho. of Reps. (dist. 23), Concord, 1996—; pvt. practice Concord. Mem. N.H. Bar Assn., Maine Bar Assn., Concord Area Home Builders. Roman Catholic. Office: NH State Legis State House Concord NH 03301

REARICK, ANNE, photographer, educator; BA in English with honors, U. Mass., 1982; MFA in Photography with honors, Mass. Coll. Art, 1990. Photographer, instr. photography Cambridge Sch. Weston, 1994—. One-woman shows include Dean's Gallery, MIT, Cambridge, 1997, Salle Buscaillet, Bordeaux, France, 2000, exhibited in group shows at Erector Sq. Gallery, New Haven, 1997, Conant Gallery, Groton, Mass., 1997, 1999, Photographic Resource Ctr., Boston, 1997, Tufts U., Aidekman Arts Ctr., Medford, Mass., 1997, Whistler Mus., Lowell, Mass., 1999, Galerie Vu, Paris, 1999, Boise (Idaho) Art Mus., 1999, S.E. Mus. Photography, Daytona, Fla., 2001, Soc. Contemporary Photography, Kansas City, Mo., 2001, FNAC, Paris, 2002, Photographic Ctr., Skopelos, Greece, 2002, exhibited in group shows, Represented in permanent collections St. Botolph's Club Found. Collection, Boston, S.E. Mus. Photography, Daytona, Rose Art Mus., Brandeis U., Waltham, Mass., Internat. Polaroid Collection, Cambridge, Boise Art Mus., Bibliotheque Nationale, Paris. Recipient Blanche E. Colman award, 1992, Golden Lights award, 1996; fellow, New Eng. Found. for the Arts/Mass. Cultural Coun., 1995, John Simon Guggenheim Meml. Found., 2003; grantee, Polaroid Film, 1990, Somerville Arts Coun., 1990, 1993, 1997, 2003, Janet Wu, 1993, St. Botolph's Club Found., 1995; Fulbright fellow, 1990—91. Office: Cambridge Sch Weston 45 Georgian Rd Weston MA 02493

REAST, DEBORAH STANEK, small business owner; b. Phila., Feb. 25, 1955; d. Chester Joseph and Thelma Sylvia (Hop) S. AS, Gwynedd Mercy Coll., 1975; Cert. Mgmt., Villanova U., 1987. Cert. med. mgr.; notary pub., 1985—. Billing clk. Ophthalmic Assocs., Lansdale, Pa., 1971-75, exec. sec., 1975-80, ops. mgr., 1980-99; exec. asst. 24th Sen. Dist., State of Pa., Lansdale, 1999—2002; prin., owner Yours, Mine and Hours-Personal Asst. and Concierge Svcs., Hatfield, Pa., 2003—. Corp. sec., The Wellness Place for the Cancer Cmty. Ch. organist Corpus Christi Parish, Gwynedd, 1970-86, Saint Maria Goretti Parish, Hatfield, 1986—, ch. organist, 1986-96. Mem. Internat. Concierge and Errand Assn., Pa. Assn. Notaries, The Wine Connection, Publicity-St. Maria Goretti Social Com., North Penn C. of C., Hatfield C. of C. Republican. Roman Catholic. Avocations: writing, traveling, collecting. Office Fax: 215-412-7689. Business E-Mail: deb@yoursmineandhours.com.

REATEGUI, LISA J. lawyer; b. 1966; BA magna cum laude, Princeton U., 1988; MA in Latin Am. Studies, Stanford U., 1990; JD magna cum laude, Northwestern U., 1995. Atty. Sidley Austin Brown & Wood, Chgo., 1995—2003, ptnr., 2003—. Chmn. major gifts fund raising Princeton U.; mem. women's bd. The Field Mus., mem. young profl.'s bd. Mem.: ABA, Chgo. (Ill.) Bar Assn. Office: Sidley Austin Brown & Wood Bank One Plz 10 South Dearborn St Chicago IL 60603

REAVES, LORI JO, social worker, educator; b. Chgo., July 25, 1967; d. Larry Jo Goss and Martha Nell Gipson; m. Eric Leon Reaves, Dec. 19, 1987; children: Christopher, Cody, Colton, Courtney, Casey. BSW, Ball State U., 1988; MSW, Ind. U.-Purdue U., Indpls., 1990. LCSW, ACSW, CCSW. Clin. social worker Family Svc. Soc., Marion, Ind., 1990—; outpatient social worker Cornerstone, Marion, Ind., 1990—96; prof. Ind. Wesleyan U., Marion, Ind., 2002—. Spkr. at workshops and meetings Headstart, Marion, 1995—. Vol. Sweetser (Ind.) Elem. Sch., 1996—, Converse (Ind.) Ch. of Christ, 1985—. Mem.: NASW. Avocations: sporting events, reading, walking. Home: 4832 N Brooke Dr Maion IN 46952 Office: Family Svc Soc 101 S Washington St Ste 200 Marion IN 46952

REBELLO, MARLENE MUNSON, speech pathologist; b. San Jose, Calif., Oct. 15, 1948; d. Alfred Vernon and Rose Zita (Pereira) Nunes; m. Steven Del Munson, Mar. 21, 1970 (div. 1982); m. William Wayne Rebello, Dec. 5, 1992. BA, San Jose State U., 1970, MA, 1971; MS in Counseling, U. LaVerne, 1990. Speech pathologist Newark (Calif.) Unified Sch. Dist., 1971—; pvt. practice Fremont and Pleasanton, Calif., 1980—; speech pathologist Washington Hosp., Fremont, Calif., 1980-89. Ednl. cons. Fremont and Pleasanton, 1980—. Recipient Bank of Am. award, 1966, Cabrillo scholarship, Nat. Merit scholarship, 1966, Maria Leonard award Outstanding Sr. Grade Point Average, 1970; fellow VA, 1970. Mem. Calif. Speech and Hearing Assn., Pleasanton Sister City Assn. (v.p. 1996-2002, pres. 2003—), Newark Tchrs. Assn. (treas. 1971—), Save Our Sunol Found., Calif. Tchrs. Assn., Arthur & Elena Court Conservation Soc. Avocations: antique collecting, decorating, gourmet cooking. Home: 10579 Foothill Rd Sunol CA 94586-9464 E-mail: marspot@aol.com.

REBER, CHERYL ANN, consultant, social worker, trainer; b. Cin., Feb. 7, 1956; d. Randland John and Marcella Catherine (Hollstegge) Reber; m. Michael Zaletel. AA, Xavier U., 1976, BA, 1980. Lic. social worker. Social worker Altercrest, Cin., 1977-79, Hamilton County Dept. Human Svcs., Cin., 1979-85, adoption specialist, social worker, 1985-92, trainer, program developer, 1988-92; social worker, AIDS specialist Hospice of the Miami Valley, 1992-95; ind. trainer Inst. for Human Svcs., Cin., 1996—. Trainer Hamilton County Dept. Human Svcs., Cin., 1988-92; permanency planning cons. Ohio Dept. Human Svcs., 1995-2000, Mem. Cmty. Task Force on Adoption, Cin., 1989-91, 95—. Mem. S.W. Ohio Adoption Resource Exch., Beechmont Players. Democrat. Roman Catholic. Avocations: whitewater rafting, community theatre, primitive camping and exploration. Personal E-mail: creber4129@aol.com.

RECANATI, DINA, artist; b. Cairo, Jan. 15, 1928; Student with Jose de Creft, Art Students League, N.Y.C., 1959—62. Represented by Julie M. Gallery, Tel Aviv. Exhibitions include Julie M Gallery, Tel Aviv, Israel, 1981—84, Jewish Mus. Sculpture Garden, NY, 1981—84, Am-Israel Cultural Found., 1984, Hebrew Coll., Boston, 1985, Julie M. Basel Art Fair, 1986, Bklyn. Mus., 1988, Mus. Contemporary Art, Ramat Gan, Israel, 1989, Barbican Art Gallery, London, 1990, Berlin Shafir Gallery, NY, 1990, Tel Aviv Mus. Art, 2001; artist (prin. works) Israel Mus. Jerusalem, Tel Aviv Mus., Ben Gurion Airport, Tel Aviv, Tel Aviv U., Israel, Jewish Mus., N.Y., Herzliya Mus., Continental Grain Collection, N.Y., Israel Embassy, Wash.; prin. works include Hudson Valley, N.Y., NYU, Artomi Fields Sculpture Pk., Hudson Valley, N.Y., Represented in permanent collections Gate (bronze), Ministry of Transportation, Israel, Gates (spl. bronze edit.), Am.-Israel Cultural Found., N.Y., Israel Chancellery, Wash., President's Garden Collection, Jerusalem, Beit Ariella Public Library, Tel Aviv, Weizmann Inst. Sci., Rehovot, Israel; (bibliography) Recent Works by Dina Recanati, 2001, Dina Recanati, From the Artists' Notebook, 2001; contbr. pubs. to Artist's Notebook, Gordon Galleries, Israel, 1975, Tel Aviv Mus. Art, 2001. Recipient Knickerbocker award, Nat. Arts Club, 1961, King Solomon award, Am.-Israel Found., 1977, Louise Waterman Wise award, Am. Jewish Congress, 1976. Address: 136 Grand St #6E New York NY 10013-3127

RECH, SUSAN ANITA, obstetrician, gynecologist; b. Summit, N.J., Nov. 5, 1957; d. William F. and Mary Jane (Crooks) R.; m. Marc R. Sarnow; 1 son, Kyle. BA in Biology, Swarthmore Coll., 1979; MD, U. Medicine Dentistry N.J., Newark, 1984. Diplomate Am. Bd. Ob-Gyn. Resident in ob-gyn. Temple U. Hosp., Phila., 1984-88; pvt. practice, Plattsburgh, N.Y., 1988—; chief dept. ob-gyn CVPH Med. Ctr., Plattsburgh, 1997-2000. Asst. clin. prof. dept. ob-gyn. U. Vt. Sch. Medicine, 1991—; dir. ob-gyn. tchg. program CVPH Med. Ctr., 1998—; bd. dirs. CVPH Med. Ctr., 1999—; mem. med. adv. bd. Planned Parenthood No. N.Y., Plattsburgh, 1989-98, Clinton County Health Dept., Plattsburgh, 1989-96; bd. dirs. Cmty. Providers, Inc., Plattsburgh, 1994-97. Active Newman Ctr., St. Mary's of the Lake Ch., Plattsburgh; mem. alumni coun. Swarthmore (Pa.) Coll., 1994-96; mem. Seton Cath. H.S. Sch. Bd., Plattsburgh, 1995-98. Rsch. grantee U. Medicine and Dentistry N.J., summer 1980. Fellow ACOG; mem. AMA, Am. Med. Women's Assn. (founding pres. Champlain Valley chpt. 1991), Assn. Women Surgeons, No. N.Y. Ind. Practice Assn. (bd. dirs. 1994-98), Champlain Valley Oratorio Soc. (soloist 1989—), Nat. Honor Soc. Avocations: choral singing, skiing, running, gardening, reading. Home: 15 Point Farm West Grand Isle VT 05458-7021 Office: Assocs in Ob-Gyn PC 210 Cornelia St Ste 201 Plattsburgh NY 12901-2318

RECINIELLO, KAREN MARY, language educator; b. Newark, June 20, 1950; d. Michael Nahirny and Helen Petishnok; m. Robert N. Reciniello, Apr. 29, 1972. BA, Montclair State Coll., N.J., 1972, MA, 1982. Tchr. of French Mountain Lakes (N.J.) H.S., 1973; tchr. of Russian Boonton (N.J.) H.S., 1973; tchr. of French Hopatcong (N.J.) H.S., 1974—. Owner Ivy Rock Acres, Hackettstown, NJ, 1995—. Mem.: Am. Tchrs. French, N.J. Lang. Tchrs. Assn., U.S. Dressage Fed. Avocations: dressage riding, travelling in France.

RECUPERO-FAIELLA, ANNA ANTONIETTA, poet; b. Boston, Nov. 22, 1966; d. Vittorio and Anna Maria Recupero; m. Mark Stephan James Faiella, May 30, 1998. Cert. early edn., Wheelock Coll. Tchr. N. Bennet St. Sch., Boston, 1981-87; clk. Post Office, Boston, 1988—. Art coord. N. Bennett Sch., Boston, 1985-87; acting extra films and commls. Author: (poems) A View From the Edge, 1992, Dusting Off Dreams, 1994, Echoes From the Silence, 1995, Treasure the Moment, 1996, Whispers, 1996, Sensations, 1997; co-author: (poems) Distinguished Poets of Amercia, 1993, Outstanding Poets of 1994, 1994, Treasured Poems of America, 1995, Treasured Poems of America, 1996, Best Poems of the 90's, 1996, Best Poems of '97, 1997, Ten Years of Excellence, 1998. Co-chair Wall of Tolerance, 2003. Recipient Editors Choice award, Nat. Libr. Poetry, 1993—97, semifinalist Discover G'Vanni's 500th Art Awd., 1992, semifinalist Internat. Soc. Photography award, 2003, semifinalist Shadows of Tomorrow award, Internat. Soc. Photography, 2003, Internat. Writer Yr. award, Noble House, 2003; scholar Mass. State Gen. Scholarship, 1985. Mem. Internat. Soc. Poets (disting. mem. adv. com. 1994), Nat. Mus. Women Arts, Point of Pines Assn. Democrat. Roman Catholic. Avocations: painting, writing poems, traveling, nascar racing, comedy. Home: 40 Bickford Ave Revere MA 02151-1723

REDD, J. DIANE, professional fundraiser and grants management executive; b. Apr. 10, 1945; d. Robert Fountain and Lillian (Fitts) Redd. BS, W.Va. State Coll., 1967. Instr. bus. subjects Paterson (N.J.) Bus. Edn., 1967—68; with U. Medicine and Dentistry, Newark, 1968—69; adminstrv. asst. rsch. and sponsored programs, 1968—73; asst. dir. health edn., 1973—76; sr. devel. officer, 1976—79; asst. dir. devel., 1979—83; chief devel. and alumni affairs, 1983—89; dir. devel. founds., corps. and major gifts Planned Parenthood Fedn. Am., Inc., N.Y.C., 1989—2002; dir. devel. NAACP-LDF, Inc., N.Y.C., 2002—. Mem. priorities com., devel. com. United Way of Essex and West Hudson, Newark, 1983-85; chmn. human resources com. Cmty. Adv. Bd., U. Medicine and Dentistry N.J., Newark, 1978-82; mem. rsch. bd. advisors Am. Biographical Inst., 1992—. Recipient Recognition of Achievement award Young Women of Am., Inc., Montgomery, Ala., 1979, Black Achiever award YMWCA, 1986. Mem. Coun. Advancement and Support of Edn., Nat. Soc. Fund Raising Execs., Ind. (cert., trustee, v.p., parliamentarian, sec.), Assn. Am. Med. Colls., Exec. Women N.J. (trustee, chmn. scholarship com.), Women in Fin. Devel., Consortium of Devel. and Alumni Profls. of Greater N.Y. Democrat. Office: NAACP Legal Def Fund Inc 99 Hudson St Ste 1600 New York NY 10013

REDD, MARIE E. state legislator, criminal justice educator; b. Huntington, W.Va., Aug. 5, 1954; m. William Redd; 2 children. RBA in Criminal Justice, Marshall U., 1989, MS in Criminal Justice, 1995. Various positions IBM, 1973-92; instr. criminal justice Marshall U., Huntington, W.Va., 1996-97, mem. adj. faculty, 1997—; mem. W.Va. Senate, Charleston, 1999—. Mem. edn. com., govt. orgn. com., health and human resources com., interstate cooperation com., judiciary com., transp. com. Mem. W.Va. Women's Commn.; pres. Women's Orgn., 1st Bapt. Ch., Huntington. Mem. Am. Criminal Justice Assn., Links, Lambda Alpha Epsilon, Alpha Kappa Alpha. Democrat. Office: WVa Senate 1900 Kanawha Blvd E Rm 209W Charleston WV 25305-0009

REDD, VIVIAN CORTEZZA, government agency administrator; b. Harrisonburg, Va., Sept. 18, 1934; d. Manie Minerva Adelia Redd. LLB, LaSalle Ext. U., 1974. Clk. U.S. Patent & Trademark Office, Washington, 1965—66, patent reclassification clk., 1966—67, clk., 1967—72, office copier control clk., 1972, patent classification aid/tech., 1972—77, file integrity tech., 1977—84, sr. documentation projects asst., 1984—86, patent applications asst., 1986—. Avocations: reading, puzzles, crossword puzzles. Home: 320 23d St S Apt 1316 Arlington VA 22202-3791 Office: IS Patent & Trademark Office 2900 Crystal Dr Arlington VA 22202-3513

REDDICK, CATHERINE ANNE (CAT REDDICK), professional soccer player; b. Richmond, Va., Feb. 10, 1982; Majoring in comm., U. N.C., 2000—. Mem. Under-16 Nat. Team, 1998, Under-18 Nat. Team, 1998—99, capt., 2000; mem. Under-21 Nat. Team, 2003; soccer player, defender U.S. Women's Nat. Team, 2000. Co-recipient U-18 Soccer Gold medal, Pan Am. Games, 1999, Nordic Cup, Denmark, 2000, 2001, 2002, 2003; named Defensive MVP, NCAA Final Four, 2000, Freshman All-Am. Team, NSCAA, 2000, Second Team All-Am., 2001, First Team All-Am., 2002; named to First Team All-ACC, 2002. Office: US Soccer Fedn 1801 S Prairie Ave Chicago IL 60616*

REDDING, EVELYN A. dean; b. Gulfport, Miss., Mar. 13, 1945; d. Arthur Edward and Rebecca (Morris) R. BSN, U. Ala., 1967; MS, Fla. State U., 1971; EdD, Okla. State U., 1974; cert. PNP, Tex. Women's U., 1974; MSN, Wichita State U., 1980. Psychiat. nurse Camp Ponderosa, Mentone, Ala., 1967; dir. health svcs. Community Action Agy., Head Start, Dadeville, Ala., 1967-68; pediatric nurse All Children's Hosp., St. Petersburg, Fla., 1968-69; instr. A&M U. Sch. Nursing, Tallahassee, 1969-71; coord. mater and child health Western Ky. U., Bowling Green, 1971-72; dir. grad. program U. Tex. Health Sci. Ctr., Houston, 1974-78; prof., assoc. dean Coll. Nursing U. Tulsa, 1978-81; dean, prof. Coll. Nursing U. Southwestern La., Lafayette, 1981-97, prof., 1997—. Presenter in field. Contbr. articles to profl. jours. Policy adv. bd. Northwest Fla. Family Planning Project, 1969-71, Nurses Coalition for Action in Politics; mem. exec. com. Hospice of Acadiana, 1982-85, pres., bd. dirs., 1984; cons. big Bend Comprehensive Svcs. Clinic, Tallahassee, 1970-71; cons. family planning nurse practitioner program Planned Parenthood Ctr., Houston, 1975-78; cons. grad. edn., nurse clinician program Madigan Army Med. Ctr., Washington, 1975; pres. Dirs. Nursing Edn. and Nursing Svc. Acadiana, 1982-83; docent intern Gilcrease Mus.; chair Tulsa Area Dirs. Nursing Svc. and Nursing Edn. Mem. AAUW (cultural affairs and community com.), ANA, Nat. League for Nursing, ANA Coun. Nurse Researchers, Soc. for Rsch. Nursing Edn., La. State Nurses Assn. (program com. dist. IV 1986), Okla. Nurses Assn. (nurse edn. com. dist. 2 1978-79, by-laws com. 1978-80), Tex. Nurses Assn. (chairperson task force for profl. self-determination 1976-78), Coun. Adminstrs. Nursing Edn. La. (presenter 1987-88), Sigma Theta Tau, Omicron Nu. Avocations: bike riding, reading, fishing, yard work. Office: U Southwestern La Coll Nursing PO Box 42490 Lafayette LA 70504-0001 Home: 14336 Dalton Rd Kaplan LA 70548-6729

REDDINGTON, MARY JANE, retired secondary school educator; b. New Rochelle, N.Y., July 21, 1923; d. Gordon William and Katharine Regina (Coleman) Kann; m. John Martin Reddington, Oct. 11, 1947; children: Terence, Martha, Robert. BA cum laude, Coll. New Rochelle, 1945; postgrad., Columbia U., 1947—49; MA, Hunter Coll., 1954; PhD (hon.), Iona Coll., 1996. Tchr. St. Gabriel's H.S., New Rochelle, NY, 1945—51, Albert Leonard Jr. H.S., New Rochelle, NY, 1960—81; dir. devel. The Ursuline Sch., New Rochelle, NY, 1981—88; ret., 1988. Active Bd. Edn., New Rochelle, 1983—, v.p., 1985—87, pres., 1987—89, Colburn Meml. Home; active New Rochelle Pub. Libr. Found. Bd., New Rochelle Cmty. Svcs. Bd.; vol. Sound Shore Med. Ctr.; bd. dirs. United Way New Rochelle, 1972—, pres., 1979—82, campaign chair, 1976—82; trustee Coll. New Rochelle, 1967—73; lector Holy Family Ch.; active Holy Family Ch. Ladies Guild. Recipient Gold Key award, Columbia Scholastic Press Assn., 1976, Ursula Laurus citation, Coll. New Rochelle, 1962, St. Angela Merici medal, 1970, citation, United Way New Rochelle, 1970—82, Spl. Recognition award, 1986, 2001, St. Angela award, The Ursuline Sch., 1977, Nat. Cmty. Svc. award, AARP, 1994, Loyal Svc. and Dedication award, Colburn Home, 1992, Cmty. Salute honoree, New Rochelle Pub. Libr. Found., 1999, Cmty. Svc. award, New Rochelle YMCA, 2001, honoree, Sr. Pers. Placement Bur., 2002, Interreligious Coun. of New Rochelle, 2002, Meals-On-Wheels of New Rochelle, 2003. Mem.: Bus. and Profl. Women's Club New Rochelle (past pres., Woman of Yr. 1979), So. Westchester Ret. Tchrs. Assn. (co-pres.), Coll. New Rochelle Alumnae Assn. (past pres.), Ladies of Charity (past pres.), Cath. Women's Club Westchester (founder, past pres.), Woman's Club New Rochelle (pres.), LWV, Alpha Delta Kappa (past pres.). Roman Catholic. Avocations: travel, reading, antiques, writing, cross country skiing. Home: 56 Wykagyl Terr New Rochelle NY 10804

REDFEARN, CHARLOTTE MARIE, nursing administrator; b. Tulsa, Nov. 24, 1949; d. John Edward and Mary Loretta Kirkbride; 1 child, John Patrick. Diploma in nursing, Tulsa Jr. Coll., 1986. Admission nurse Tulsa County Jail, 1992—94; skilled unit mgr. So. Hills Nursing Ctr., Tulsa, 1994—96; asst. dir. nursing Pk. Ter. Nursing Ctr., Tulsa, 1996, Georgian Ct., Tulsa, 1996—97, Manor Care Health Svc., Tulsa, 1997—99; dir. nursing Georgian Cts. Rehab., Tulsa, 1999, Maplewood Care Ctr., Tulsa, 2000—. Roman Catholic. Home: 4803 S Lawton Tulsa OK 74107 Office: Maplewood Care Ctr 6202 E 61 Tulsa OK 74136

REDFIELD, JEAN M. electric power company executive; With McKinsey & Co., Inc.; mgr. corp. strategy Detroit Edison Co., 1994-97; pres. Detroit Edison Co. Am., 1997—. Office: Detroit Edison Co 2002 2d Ave Detroit MI 48226

REDFIELD, PAMELA A. state legislator; b. Chicago, Ill., Aug. 11, 1948; m. Jerry Redfield; 6 children. B in edn., U. Nebr., Omaha, 1969. Exec. dir. Omaha-Millard Rotary; libr. spcl.; election cons.; banker; mem. Nebr. Legislature from 12th dist., Lincoln, 1998—. Mem. Ralson Bd. Edn. 1992-1998. Coun. State Govt.; Nat. Conf. State Legislatures; Am. Legis. Exch. Conf.; Nat. Coun. Ins. Legislators.; chmn. Rotary Internat. Office: State Capitol (Dist 12) Rm 1404 PO Box 94604 Lincoln NE 68509-4604

REDFIELD, RITA TAMS, art gallery owner; b. Trenton, NJ, Aug. 30, 1939; d. George Stokes and Henrietta Elizabeth (Tams) Zimmerman; m. George Edward Redfield, Sept. 30, 1961 (dec. July 1992); children: Edward Scott, Elizabeth Tams; m. Witt Kennon Cochrane, May 22, 1993. Owner Redfield Artisans Gallery, Northeast Harbor, Maine, 1977—; asst. libr. Mt. Desert Island H.S., Bar Harbor, Maine, 1983—88; ceramist, 1977—90. Pres. Mt. Desert C. of C., 1983—85; mem. exec. coun. Episcopal Ch. in U.S., 1997—; bd. dirs. Episcopal Relief and Devel., 1997—, Domestic and Fgn. Missionary Soc., 1997—, Great Harbor Collection Mus., Northeast Harbor, 1985—90, Mt. Desert Hist. Soc., 1979—82, Mt. Desert C. of C., 1983—95. Recipient Fred C. Schribner medal, Episcopal Diocese of Maine, 2001. Episcopalian. Avocations: poetry, piano, hiking, travel. Home: PO Box 153 Mount Desert ME 04660

REDLICH, ALLISON DYAN, research psychologist; b. Abington, Pa., Aug. 14, 1970; d. George and Phyllis Redlich; m. John Henry Hornberger, Jr., Jan. 10, 2001; 1 child, Isaac Ethan Hornberger. PhD, U. Calif., Davis, 1999. Rsch. asst. Nat. Inst. of Child Health and Human Devel., NIH, Bethesda, Md., 1992—94; postdoctoral fellow Stanford U., 1999—2001, rsch. scientist, 2001—02; sr. rsch. assoc. Policy Rsch. Assocs., Delmar, NY, 2002—. Author: (book chpt.) Interrogations, Entrapment, and Confessions; contbr. articles to profl. jours. Recipient Violence Prevention Initiative Acad. fellowship, Calif. Wellness Found., 1999, Grant-in-Aid, Soc. for the Psychol. Study of Social Issues, 1998. Mem.: APA, Am. Psychology Law Soc. (Student award 1996). Avocation: crossword puzzles. Office: Policy Rsch Assocs 345 Delaware Ave Delmar NY 12054 E-mail: aredlich@prainc.com.

REDMAN, BARBARA KLUG, nursing educator; b. Mitchell, S.D. d. Harlan Lyle and Darlien Grace (Bock) Klug; m. Robert S. Redman, Sept. 14, 1958; 1 child, Melissa Darlien. BS, S.D. State U., 1958; MEd, U. Minn., 1959, PhD, 1964; LHD (hon.), Georgetown U., 1988; DSc (hon.), U. Colo., 1991. RN. Asst. prof. U. Wash., Seattle, 1964-69; assoc. dean U. Minn., Mpls., 1969-75; dean Sch. Nursing U. Colo., Denver, 1975-78; VA scholar VA Cen. Office, Washington, 1978-81; postdoctoral fellow Johns Hopkins U., Balt., 1982-83; exec. dir. Am. Assn. Colls. Nursing, Washington, 1983-89, ANA, Washington, 1989-93; prof. nursing Johns Hopkins U., Balt., 1993-95; dean, prof. Sch. Nursing U. Conn., Storrs, 1995-98; dean Coll. Nursing Wayne State U., Detroit. Vis. fellow Kennedy Inst. Ethics, Georgetown U., 1993-94; fellow in med. ethics Harvard Med. Sch., 1994-95. Author: Practice of Patient Education, 1968—; contbr. articles to profl. jours. Bd. dirs. Friends of Nat. Libr. of Medicine, Washington, 1987—. Recipient Disting. Alumnus award S.D. State U., 1975, Outstanding Achievement award U. Minn., 1989. Fellow Am. Acad. Nursing. Home: 12425 Bobbink Ct Potomac MD 20854-3005 Office: Wayne State U 5557 Cass Ave Detroit MI 48202-3615

REDMON, CYNTHIA BOUDREAUX, art educator; b. Lafayette, La., July 11, 1953; d. Leslie Bernard and Rita (Thompson) Boudreaux; m. David Eric Redmon, June 22, 1979 (div. Sept. 11, 1998); children: Bret Andrew, Carrie Elizabeth. BA in Interior Design, La. State U., 1975. Interior designer, buyer Ethan Allen, New Orleans, 1975—79; interior designer Clyde W. Smith Co., New Orleans, 1979—81; retail buyer, mgr. Shenandoah Valley Discovery Mus., Winchester, Va., 1996—2001; fine art tchr. Shenandoah Com. Arts Acad., Winchester, 1999—2003, Warren County Pub. Schs., Front Royal, Va., 2001—. Freelance interior designer, Winchester, 1984—. Exhibitions include Burwell Mill Art Show, Millwood, Va. V.p. Old Towne Bus. Assn., Winchester, 1999—2001. Mem.: Mus. Store Assn., Nat. Mus. Women Arts, Little Garden Club Winchester (sec. 1998—2003), Gamma Phi Beta (pres. 1971—). Roman Catholic. Avocations: painting, sculpting, gardening, antiques.

REDMOND-STEWART, AUDREY A. small business owner; b. Mt. Sterling, Ky., July 16, 1938; d. William and Jessette (Rhoades) Redmond; m. William Stewart, July 16, 1988. Office adminstr. St. Paul United Meth. Ch., Fresno, Calif., 1983-86; owner D.A. Cons., Fresno, 1986—. Instr. Fresno Adult Program, 1983-88; instr. Leadership/Legis. 1997-99. Mem. Area Agy. on Aging, Fresno and Madera Counties, Calif. Mem. Am. Bus. Women (pres. Ponderosa chpt. 1994-95), Calif. Press League Assn. (pres. 1997-98), Am. Legion Aux. (v.p. 1997-98, dist. pres. 1998-99, nat. legis. com. 1999—). Republican. Avocations: traveling, music, writing. Office: DA Cons PO Box 11545 Fresno CA 93774-1545

REECE, BETH ELAINE, music educator; d. Robert Wilson and Mary Reece. MusB, Capital U., 1974; EdM, Ohio State U., 1987. Cert. music edn. tchr. grades K-12 Ohio, classroom tchr. grades 1-8 Ohio. Playground leader I and II Columbus Recreation and Pks., 1972—80; unified arts tchr. grades K-5 Prairie Lincoln-Southwestern City Schs., Grove City, Ohio, 1974—77; music tchr. grades K-5, elem. choir tchr. Prairie Norton/Kingston Elem.-Southwestern City Schs., Grove City, 1979—80; music tchr. grades K-4 Prairie Norton Elem.-Southwestern City Schs., Grove City, 1980—2002, Prairie Norton/Darbydale Elems.-Southwestern City Schs., Grove City, 2002—. Mem. curriculum com. Southwestern City Schs., Grove City, tchr. leadership pal mem., 2000—, tchr. leadership PAL, EYT-PAL cadre, 2004, mem. sch. governing com., 2001—02, Grove City, 2002—; mem. OMEA govt. rels. com. Vol. alto Columbus Symphony Chorus, 1985—; vol. Columbus Symphony Pops Concerts Columbus Symphony Orch., 2000, 2003; first alto Columbus Symphony Chamber Choir, 2002—03; vol. Columbus Symphony Pops Concerts Columbus Symphony Orch., 2004. Mem.: NEA, Nat. Am. Orff Schulwerk Assn., Ohio Music Edn. Assn. (govt. rels. com.), Music Educators Nat. Conf. Avocations: painting, designing jewelry, singing. Office: Southwestern City Schs Prairie Norton Elem 117 Norton Rd Columbus OH 43228

REECE, BETH PAULEY, commodities broker; b. Warsaw, Ind., June 4, 1945; d. Lester Elden and Genevene (Walter) Pifer; m. Gyle Barry Reece, June 20, 1987. BA, Grace Coll., 1967; interior design degree, Harrington Inst. Design, Chgo., 1995; summer student, Oxford and Cambridge, Eng., 1987, 95, 97; Trinity Coll., Dublin, 1999, U Edinburgh, 2001; grad., Inst. Spiritual Companionship, 2000—02. Cert. Inst., Companionship Cert., 2002. Grain trader, hedger Ctrl. Soya Inc., Ft. Wayne, Ind., 1973-82; account exec. ACLI Internat. Inc., Chgo., 1982-83, account exec., hedger Ctrl. States Enterprises, Ft. Wayne, 1983-84, account exec. Stotler & Co., Chgo., 1984-89, LaSalle Brokerage Inc., Chgo., 1989—. Mem. Nat. Futures Assn., Spiritual Dirs. Internat., Art Inst. of Chgo., Met. Club. Republican. Presbyterian. Avocations: reading, sailing, traveling. Home: 227 E Delaware Pl Apt 5C Chicago IL 60611-7758 E-mail: bethreece@aol.com.

REECE, GERALDINE MAXINE, elementary school educator; b. L.A., May 13, 1917; d. Charles Kenneth and Bertha (Austin) Ballou; m. Thomas Charles Bauman, Aug. 16, 1942 (div. Oct. 1971); children: Thomas Charles Bauman, Jr., Kathleen Marie Bauman Messenger, Stephen Kenneth Bauman; m. Wilbert Wallingford Reece, Nov. 3, 1973 (dec. 1988). AA, L.A. City Coll., 1942; BA, U. So. Calif., L.A., 1966. Specialist tchr. in reading, elem. edn. Tchr. Archdiocese of L.A., Altadena, Calif., 1962-66; master tchr. Alhambra (Calif.) City and H.S., 1966-79, writer multicultural component early childhood edn. program. Author poetry. Mem. San Gabriel Child Care Task Force, 1984-86; mem. steering com. West San Gabriel Valley Cmty. Awareness Forum, 1985-87; past pres. women's divsn., bd. dirs. San Gabriel C. of C., 1989-90, 98—, publicity chair, 1994-98, incoming pres. women's divsn., 1998—; mem. sch. site and facilities com. Sch. Dist. Unification, San Gabriel, 1992-93; mem. task force Episcopal Parish/Healing Our Cities, San Gabriel, 1992-93; docent San Gabriel Mus., 1989, 92-93; mem. Hearing Our Voice anti-violence com. Episcopal Parish. Recipient Exceptional Svc. awards Am. Heart Assn., West San Gabriel Valley, 1990, 91, 93, 94, 95, Dedicated Svc. award San Gabriel C. of C., 1989, Outstanding and Dedicated Cmty. Svc. award Fedn. Cmty. Coord. Couns., San Gabriel, 1986, 87, 97-98, others, Woman of Yr. award City of San Gabriel, 1994, Diamond Homer trophy Famous Poet Soc., 1995, 96; named Outstanding Older Am., City of San Gabriel, 1999; scholarship named in her honor Divsn. 1 Calif. Ret. Tchrs. Assn. Mem. AAUW (Money Talks sect. chairperson 1981-82, corr. sec.-treas. Alhambra-San Gabriel 1982-85), Calif. Ret. Tchrs. Assn. (pres. 1989-91, Outstanding Svc. plaque 1994, divsn. 1 scholarship named in her honor 1998, bd. dirs. 1999—), DAR (3rd vice regent 1994—, 1st Pl. Poetry award 1996, 3d Pl. Poetry award 1998), Pasadena Women's City Club, St. Francis Guild, San Gabriel Ret. Tchrs. (pres. 1985-89, cmty. rep. 1990-97), San Gabriel Hist. Assn., San Gabriel Cmty. Coord. Coun. (pres. 1986, 1st v.p. 1997-98). Democrat. Episcopalian. Avocations: reading, bridge, writing poetry, stitchery.

REECE, MONIQUE ELIZABETH, marketing, advertising and sales consultant; b. Eldora, Iowa, Jan. 12, 1960; d. Barry Lynne and Vera Marie (Powell) R.; m. Gordon Duane Myron, Mar. 14, 1992 (div. Apr. 2000); children: Morgan Reece, Isabella Monique. BSBA, Regis U., 1991. Mgr. regional advt. Silo, Inc., Denver, 1979-86; dir. mktg. LaserLand Corp., U.S.A., Denver, 1986-87; advt. mgr. King Soopers, Denver, 1987-90; supr. brand devel. Garrison-Lontine Advt., Denver, 1991; pres. Monique Myron and Assocs., Denver and La Jolla, Calif., 1991-94, MarketSmarter, Denver and San Diego, 1994—; v.p. corp. devel. Tactical Mktg. Ventures, LLC, Denver, 1999—2001. Chmn. bus. partnership com. Colo. Mktg. Tech. Advt. Com., Denver, 1987-91; spkr. in field. Co-author: Market Smarter Not Harder, 1996. Mem. publ. rels. com. Make-A-Wish Found., Denver, 1989. Recipient 1st Place Advt. award Nat. Frozen Food Assn., 1988, 89, 90, award Retail Advt. Coun., 1990. Mem. NAFE, ASTD, Nat. Assn. Women Bus. Owners (bd. dirs.), Colo. Women's C. of C., La Jolla C. of C. (bus. profl. com. 1992-93), Denver Met. C. of C., U. Denver Marketing Advisory Bd. Avocations: skiing, running, triathlons, diving, reading. Home and Office: 401 Monaco Pkwy Denver CO 80220-6015 E-mail: moniquer@tmventures.com.

REECE-PORTER, SHARON ANN, international human rights educator; b. Cin., Nov. 28, 1953; d. Edward and Claudia (Ownes) Reece; divorced, 1981; children: Erika Lynn, Melanie Joyce. BS in Textiles and Clothing, Edgecliff Coll., 1975; cert. clerical computer, So. Ohio Coll., 1984; MEd in Gen. Edn., SUNY, Buffalo, 1994; PhD in Internat. Human Rights Devel., Brentwick U., London, 2000; EdD in Global Edn. (hon.), Australian Inst. Coordinated Rsch., Victoria, 1995; postgrad. in photojournalism/profl. photography, NY Inst. Photography, 2002—. Cert. tchr., Ohio. Dept. supr., asst. buyer Mabley & Carew, Cin., 1975-76; claims adjuster Allstate Ins. Co., Cin., 1976-78; sales merchandiser Ekco Houseware, Cin., 1979-80; sales rep. Met. Life Inc., Cin., 1981-83; info. processing specialist GPA/Robert Half/Word Source, Cin., Dallas, 1985-87; tchr. adult edn. Princeton City Schs., Cin., 1984-90; with Rainbow Internat. Non-Profit Adult Ednl. Rsch. Ctr., Honolulu, 1990-98, Norfolk, Va., 1998—; edn. specialist rsch. found. SUNY, Buffalo, 1993. Prof. computer sci. So. Ohio Tech. and Bus. Coll., Cin., 1986-90; computer software tng. cons., 1987-89; part-time tchr. adult GED classes Adult Learning Ctr. Buffalo Bd. Edn., 1994-95; participant Am. Forum for Global Edn., Honolulu; lectr. photography N.Y. Inst. Photography, N.Y.C., N.Y., 2002—. Tutor U.S. div. Internat. Laubach Literacy, Clermont County, Ohio, 1984. Fellow Australian Inst. for Coordinated Rsch. (life); mem. NAFE, ASTD, Internat. DOS Users Group, Am. Ednl. Rsch. Assn., Nat. Assn. Women Bus. Owners, UN Assn., World Assn. Women Entrepreneurs, Assn. Baha'i Studies in Australia, Boston Computer Soc., Cin. Orgn. Data Processing Educators and Trainers, Internat. Platform Assn., Cin. C. of C. (cert. minority supplier devel. coun.). Baha'I. Home: 2941 Chilton Pl Virginia Beach VA 23456 Office: Rainbow Cinema Global Human Rights Inst 4221-125 Pleasant Valley Rd @ 172 Virginia Beach VA 23464 E-mail: Sharaocean@aol.com., SharonAnHumanRts@aol.com.

REED, ANGELICA DENISE, sculptor, writer, illustrator; b. Murfreesboro, Tenn., Dec. 16, 1955; d. Keith Kenyon and Lester Faye (Todd) Reed; m. David Earl Myers, Apr. 19, 1975 (dec. Mar. 1978); m. John Gregory Bettis, May 11, 1979. Student, Mid. Tenn. State U., 1973-75, 77-78, UCLA, 1981-82, Venice Sculpture Studio, 1983-85, Brucchion Sch. of Art, Culver City, Calif., 1987-90. Artist-in-residence Reed Studio and Gallery, Venice, Calif., 1990-95, The Jerry Solomon Gallery, L.A., 1997, Belle Art Galleries, Inc. at Bel Age Hotel, West Hollywood, Calif., 2000—. Cons. Sweet Harmony Music, Sunset Beach, Calif., 1978-83, Bettis Paradise Music, Sunset Beach, 1978-85, John Bettis Music, L.A., 1983—, John Bettis Property Mgmt., L.A., 1986—. Sculptures, illustrations, home landscapings and pencil drawings exhibited in Calif., 1985—. Fundraiser Children's Hosp./Santa Monica Bay Aux., 1991, Nat. Acad. Songwriters, 1985, SEA Environ. Assn., Bonaventure Hotel, L.A., 1990, 91; mem. L.A. com. P.E.T.A. People for the Ethical Treatment of Animals, 1992; vol. St. John Hosp., 1998. Avocations: gymnastics, scuba diving, travel, animals, ballet. Home and Office: 1153 E Main St Murfreesboro TN 37130-3950 E-mail: adreed.reed@verizon.net.

REED, ANNE F. THOMSON, government official; BA, Goucher Coll., 1973; MPA, Harvard U., 1981. Devel. rschr. Office of Alumni Devel. Vanderbilt U., Nashville, 1973-74; jr. cmty. planner Nashville City Planning Commn., 1974-76; staff asst. to asst. dean for adminstrn. Kennedy Sch. Harvard U., Cambridge, Mass., 1976-77, registrar, admissions officer John F. Kennedy Sch. Govt., 1977-80; presdl. mgmt. intern Dept. Navy, Washington, 1981-83, budget analyst for Naval Sea Sys. Command, 1983-86, numerous mgmt. positions Office Comptroller, 1986-93; dep. asst. sec. agr. for adminstrn. USDA, Washington, 1993-96, chief info. officer, 1997—. Office: USDA 14th & Independence Ave SW Washington DC 20250-0001

REED, BERENICE ANNE, art historian, artist, government official; b. Memphis; d. Glenn Andrew and Berenice Marie (Kallaher) R. BFA, St. Mary-of-the-Woods Coll., Ind., 1955; MFA in Painting and Art History, Istituto Pio XII, Villa Schifanoia, Florence, Italy, 1964; ind. art history rsch., Ctr. for Advanced Study in the, Visual Arts, Nat. Gallery of Art, Washington, 1998—. Cert. art tchr., Tenn. Comml. artist Memphis Pub. Co., 1955-56, arts adminstr., educator pub. and pvt. instns., Washington, Memphis, 1957-70; arts adminstr. Nat. Park Svc., 1970-73; mem. staff U.S. Dept. of Energy, Washington, 1973-81, U.S. Dept. Commerce, Washington, 1983-84, Exec. Office of the Pres., Office of Mgmt. and Budget, Washington, 1985; with fin. mgmt. svc. U.S. Treasury Dept., Washington, 1985—. Ind. art history rschr. Nat. Gallery of Art, Ctr. Advanced Study in Visual Arts, Washington, 1998—; cons. on art and architecture in recreation AIA, 1972-73; artist-in-residence St. Mary-of-the-Woods Coll., Ind., 1965; guest lectr. instr. Nat. Sch. Fine Arts, Tegucigalpa, Honduras, 1968; exec. com. Parks, Arts and Leisure Project, Washington, 1972-73; rschr. art projects, Washington, 1981-83. Developer (video) In Your Interest, 1992; TV interviewer Am. Fin. Skylink satellite programs, 1996-98. Bd. dirs. Am. Irish Bicentennial Com., 1974-76; advisor Royal Oak Found. Recipient various awards for painting; installed as Dama of Merit, Sacred Mil. Constantinian Order of St. George, Naples, 1997, awarded Star, 2001, installed as Dama, Order of St. Maurice and St. Lazarus, 2000; named one of 150 Women Who Made A Difference in 150 years of St. Agnes Acad., 2001. Mem. Soc. Woman Geographers, Nat. Soc. Arts and Letters, Ctr. for Advanced Study in Visual Arts, Art Barn Assn. (bd. dirs. 1973-83), Patrons of the Arts in the Vatican Mus., Irish Georgian Soc. Roman Catholic. Avocations: photography, performing arts. Home: PO Box 34253 Bethesda MD 20827-0253 Office: Dept Treasury Fin Mgmt Svc 401 14th St SW Washington DC 20024-2106

REED, CAROL L. secondary school educator, writer; b. N.J., July 8, 1961; m. Thomas M. Callahan, Apr. 1, 1991; 1 child, Katherine E. C. BA, Goucher Coll., Balt., 1983; MLA, Johns Hopkins U., Balt., 1993. Cert. advanced tchr. Md. Educator Balt. County Pub. Schs., 1983—89, Talbot County Pub. Schs., Easton, Md., 1990—, advanced placement tchr., 1997—. Program coord. U. Md., 1988—89; summer writer in residence For the Love of Children Camp, W.Va., 1990; theatre dir., grant writer Talbot County Pub. Schs., Easton, 1992—, literary mag. editor, 1993—, equity advocate coord., 1997—2002. Contbr. articles newspapers, mags., 1984, poetry to mags., 1991; co-prodr.: (video) An End to Violence, 1999—; writer, dir. (video) A Fine Line. Named Tchr. of Yr., Talbot County Pub. Schs., 1999—2000; recipient Team Harmony award, AT&T, 1999, Gov. citation, 1999, 2000. Mem.: ASCD, AAUW (state keynote spker. 2000, Myra Sadker advocate 1995, leader Girls Summit 1993—2001, Eleanor Roosevelt award 1996), Nat. Coalition for Sex Equity Educators, Md. State Tchrs. Assn. (Dorothy Lloyd Women's Right Recipient 2000). Avocations: watercolor painting, photography, writing. Office: Talbot County Pub Schs 723 Mecklenberg Ave Easton MD 21601 E-mail: creed@tcps.k12.md.us.

REED, CAROL LOUISE, designer; b. Pontiac, Ill., Apr. 16, 1938; d. Rollin Kenneth and Lucille Hortence (Myer) Snethen; m. Richard Willis Reed, Feb. 13, 1960 (dec.); children: Rena Louise Davis, Ronda Lee Howle. BBA in Mktg. and Advt., Tex. Tech. U., 1959. Office mgr. Sappington Devel., Inc., Rociada, N.Mex., 1990-91; owner Designs by Carol, Rociada, 1988—. Elected state officer Tierra y Montes Soil and Water Conservation Dist., Las Vegas, 1990—; mem. Mora-San Miguel Water Planning Bd., 1991-94; treas. 1st Meth. Ch., Las Vegas, 1989-90; sec. Calvary Bapt. Ch., Las Vegas, 1991-92; treas. 1st Bapt. Ch., 1996. Recipient award of merit Goodyear Tire and Rubber Co., 1991; named Outstanding Supr. of Tierra y Montes Soil and Conservation Dist., 1992, 94, 95, 97, 98. Mem. Nat. Assn. Conservation Dists., N.Mex. Assn. Soil and Water Conservation Dists. (chair region IV 1994-96, nat. coun., 1995-98, 1st v.p. state 1996-98), Phi Kappa Phi. Republican. Avocations: art, sewing, remodeling, interior design. Home and Office: PO Box 853 Rociada NM 87742-0853

REED, CONSTANCE LOUISE, materials management and purchasing consultant; b. Point Pleasant, W.Va. d. John Melvin Supple and Garnet L. Tooley; m. James Wesley Reed Jr., Sept. 20, 1985; children: Andrew James, Tatiana. Student, Ohio State U., 1974—76, Capital U., 1984—85. Buyer Abex Corp., Columbus, Ohio, 1971-79; maj. component buyer Grumman Corp., Delaware, Ohio, 1979-81; purchasing mgr. Atlantic Richfield (ANATEC), Dublin, Ohio, 1981-85; purchasing agt. Columbus Lodging, Inc., 1986-87, Monitronix Corp., Westerville, Ohio, 1988-89; contracts adminstr. Cellular Communications Inc., Worthington, Ohio, 1989-90; dir. materials mgmt. Fibrebond Corp., Minden, La., 1991-92; v.p. C&P Mgmt. Cons., Powell, Ohio, 1985—. Mem. NAFE, Am. Mgmt. Assn., Nat. Assn. Purchasing Mgmt., Bus. and Profl. Women's Club. Republican. Roman Catholic. Avocations: writing, photography, bear collection. Home: 1245 Windham Rd Columbus OH 43220-4940

REED, CYNTHIA S. manufacturing executive; b. Springfield, Mass., Oct. 29, 1955; Student, Dartmouth Coll., 1976; BA, Wellesley Coll., 1977; JD, Northeastern U., 1980. Bar: R.I., Mass. Assoc. Edwards & Angell, Providence, 1980-86; sr. atty. Hasbro, Inc., Pawtucket, RI, 1986-88, asst. v.p., sr. atty., 1988-92, v.p., 1992-95, sr. v.p., gen. counsel, 1995—2002; pres., CEO LTR Holdings, Providence. Sec., trustee In-Sight R.I.; trustee New Eng. Legal Found./R.I. Adv. Bd.; mem. Wellesley Bus. Leadership Coun.; past pres. Wessley Club R.I., Ocean State Adoption Resource Exch. Wellesley scholar, 1977. Mem. ABA (bus. law sect.), Am. Corp. Counsel Assn., Mass. Bar Assn., R.I. Bar Assn. Office: LTR Holdings 275 Promenade St Providence RI 02908*

REED, DIANE MARIE, psychologist; b. Joplin, Mo., Jan. 11, 1934; d. William Marion and Olive Francis (Smith) Kinney; m. William J. Shotton; children: Wendy Robison, Douglas Funkhouser. Student, Art Ctr. Coll., L.A., 1951-54; BS, U. Oreg., 1976, MS, 1977, PhD, 1981. Lic. psychologist. Illustrator J.L. Hudson Co., Detroit, 1954-56; designer, stylist N.Y.C., 1960-70; designer, owner Decor To You, Inc., Stamford, Conn., 1970-76; founder, exec. dir. Alcohol Counseling and Edn. Svcs., Inc., Eugene, Oreg., 1981-86, clin. supr., 1986, Christian Family Svcs., Eugene, 1986-87; pvt. practice Eugene, 1985-94; co-founder Reed Consulting, Bend, Oreg., 1995—2000; pvt. practice Bend, Oreg., 2000—. Evaluator Vocat. Rehab. Div., Eugene, 1982—; alcohol and drug evaluator and commitment examiner Oreg. Mental Health Div., 1981—86. Named Disting. Alumnus, Ctrl. Oreg. region U. Oreg. Coll. Edn., 2003. Mem.: APA, Sunriver Area C. of. C. (bd. dirs. 1997—98), Bend C. of C., Lane County Psychol. Assn. (pres. 1989—90), Oreg. Psychol. Assn., Ctrl. Oreg. Llama Assn. (pres. 1999—2000), Sunriver Women's Club (comm. chair), Toastmasters Internat., Rotary (pres. 1997—98, Rotarian Yr. 1996—97, 1997—98), U. Oreg. Nat. Alumni (bd. dirs., outstanding alumnus for ctrl. Oreg. 2003). Avocations: photography, skiing, running, hiking, backpacking.

REED, DONNA MARIE, editor, newspaper; b. Dayton, Ohio, Mar. 29, 1950; d. Andrew Levi and Golda Mabel (Branham) Tatman; m. Donald Ray Newsome, May 12, 1973 (div. Sept. 1985); 1 child, Amanda Marie; m. James A. Reed, Sept. 26, 1987. BA, Morehead State U., 1973, MA, 1974. From reporter to state editor Tampa (Fla.) Tribune, 1974-90; dir. comm. Hillsborough County Schs., Tampa, 1990-96; dep. mng. editor Tampa Tribune, 1996—. Bd. dirs. Tampa Edn. Channel; com. mem. Hillsborough Edn. Found., Tampa, 1990—. Recipient Sunshine Medallion award Sunshine State Sch. PR Assn., 1991-96, Prin.'s award Armwood H.S., 1994-95. Mem. Fla. Press Assn., Fla. Soc. Newspaper Editors, Hillsborough Assn. Sch. Adminstrs. (Pub. Rels. award 1991, 95), Plant City Little League, Delta Gamma Alumni Assn. Baptist. Avocations: reading, needlework, sports, bike riding. Office: Tampa Tribune 202 S Parker St Tampa FL 33606-2395

REED, FAITH PATRICIA, health services administrator; b. Phila., June 14, 1946; d. Dorr Leonard and Ruth Alice (Simmons) Van E.; m. Richard Thomas Reed, May 2, 1970; children: Colleen Elizabeth, Todd Richard. BSN, Fla. State U., 1967; MS, Wright State U., 1995. RN, Calif. Supr., staff nurse Castle Nursing Homes, Millersburg, Ohio, 1971-73; staff nurse VA Med. Ctr., San Antonio, 1975-81, nursing supr. Chillicothe, Ohio, 1981-95, coord. women and minority vets., 1995-99, exec. asst. to dir. for quality improvement, women vets., utilization mgmt. and patient safety improvement, 1999—. Collateral women vets coord. VA Med. Ctr., Chillicothe, 1990-95, nursing computer coord., 1993-95, chmn. nursing home screening, 1990-95, chmn. nurse profl. stds. bd., 1999—. Chmn. bd. Ross County Coalition Against Domestic Violence, 1995-99; mem. Ohio gov.'s Adv. Com. for Women Vets., 1996—. Capt. Nurse Corps., U.S. Army, 1965-71. Recipient Spl. Contbn. award Ross Care Partnership, 1996. Mem. ANA, AAUW, Ross County Nurses Assn., Fed. Employees Assn. South Central Ohio (Profl. of the Year 1998), Gamma Sigma Sigma, Sigma Theta Tau. Methodist. Avocations: computers, reading, travel. Home: PO Box 242 Kingston OH 45644-0242 Office: VA Med Ctr 17273 State Route 104 Chillicothe OH 45601-8608

REED, FRANCES BOOGHER, writer, actress; b. Marion, Ky., May 29, 1938; d. Charles Boogher and Evelyn Shelby (Roberts) R.; m. José Joaquín Solís, June 1, 1957 (div. Sept. 1964); children: Julie, Michael Charles; m. Arnold Haslund, Jan. 30, 1965 (div. May 1967); 1 child, Elizabeth Evelyn Marie; 1 adopted child, Leni Ellis. BA in English and Spanish, U. Houston, 1960; MPH, U. P.R., 1970. Tchr. English as 2d lang. Author: A Dream With Storms, 1979, Thoughts, Feelings and Dreams, 1985, Black Mexican Necklace, 1990, TOEIC Test Guide, 1997, Miguel's Aztec Calendar, 1997, (with Koji Shimada) From Chocolate Bars to CEO, A MacArthur's Kid, 2000, (with Francisco Diaz Infante M.) Pockets and Jingles: Something for His Pockets, 2000; actress (television shows) General Hospital, Rescue-911, others, also movies. Mem. Am. Pub. Health Assn., Screen Actors' Guild, Mensa, Phi Kappa Phi. Democrat. Methodist. Avocations: teaching, dance, reading. Home: 239 Beach City Rd Apt 2113 Hilton Head Island SC 29926-4713 also: PO Box 23481 Hilton Head Island SC 29925-3481 E-mail: ML888888@aol.com.

REED, HELEN G. poet; b. South Bend, Ind., Nov. 21, 1923; d. Herman F. and Hulda A. (Kinas) Glaser; m. Arthur L. Reed; children: Michael, James. BS magna cum laude, Kalamazoo Coll., 1946; pre-med., U. Chgo., 1944—45. Exec. dir., clinic adminstr. Saint Joseph County Mental Health Assn., South Bend, Ind., 1957—67; program dir. Chgo. Mental Health Assn., 1967—70; exec. dir. Evanston (Ill.) Mental Health Assn., 1970—80. 1st chairwoman United Way Cmty. Coun., South Bend, 1965—66; bd. dirs. National Mental Health Staff Coun., N.Y.C., 1962—67; mem. faculty Nat. Mental Health Staff Coun. In-svc. Tng. Insts., 1967—69; 1st chairwoman Mental Health Consortium, Evanston, 1969—70, Staff Coun. Tng. Inst., Chgo., 1970; cons., supr. Chgo. Vis. Nurses Assn., Chgo. Jr. League, U. Wis. Mgmt. Seminar, U. Chgo. Social Svcs. Students, etc., Evanston and Chgo., 1970—80. Author (poetry): Pulling Up the Dawn, 1992 (Goodman Prize, 1992); contbr. poems to mags. (Edwin Davin Wickers prize, 1993); author (poetry): Riding the Bubbles Down, 1994 (Am. Chapbook prize, 1994, nom. for Pulitzer prize for lit., 1994, Whetstone Poetry prize, 1994, Atlanta Rev. Internat. Merit award, 1996, Willow Rev. Poetry prize, 2002). Mem. vol. Jr. League, South Bend, 1953—67, Chicago, 1967—70, jr. league, Chicago-North Shore, 1970—80; parent rep. Kalamazoo Coll. freshmen, 1964—65. Recipient "Best of the Best" award, Chicago Poets and Patrons, 1990. Mem.: Poetry Ctr. Chgo., Nat. League Am. PEN Women (Librarian, Poetry Contest Chair 2003), Acad. Am. Poets (assoc.). Avocations: birdwatching, gardening, reading, travel, antiques. Home: 345 Cumberland Ln Crystal Lake IL 60014

REED, JULIA CONSTANCE, financial services executive; b. Dunmore, Pa., Nov. 16, 1954; d. James M. and Dorothy C. Reed. BS in Liberal Sci., SUNY, 1994. Enlisted USN, 1973, advanced through grades to chief petty officer, 1989, command master chief Joint Interoperability Test Ctr., 1991-94, command master chief Naval Med. Ctr. Oakland, Calif., 1994-97, ret., 1997; registered rep. Bayside Fin., Walnut Creek, Calif., 1996-99, registered prin. Middletown, R.I., 1999—; pres. Advantage Tax Svcs., Middletown, R.I., 1997—. Tax cons. R.I. Small Bus. Devel. Ctr., Middletown, 1999—. Bd. dirs. Armed Forces YMCA, Newport, R.I., 1999—, Navy Relief Soc., Newport, 1997—. Recipient Inspirational Leadership award Navy League, 1982. Mem. Fleet Res. Assn., Disabled Am. Vets. Democrat. Roman Catholic. Avocations: reading, golf, chess. Office: Advantage Tax Svcs 1272 W Main Rd Middletown RI 02842-6335 Home: 57 Shoreline Ter Portsmouth RI 02871-2018

REED, KATHLYN LOUISE, occupational therapist, educator; b. Detroit, June 2, 1940; d. Herbert C. and Jessie R. (Krehbiel) R. BS in Occupl. Therapy, U. Kans., 1964; MA, Western Mich. U., 1966; PhD, U. Wash., 1973; MLIS, U. Okla., 1987. Occupl. therapist in psychiatry Kans. U. Med. Ctr., Kansas City, 1964-65; instr. occupl. therapy U. Wash., Seattle, 1967-70; assoc. prof. dept. occupl. therapy U. Okla. Health Scis. Ctr., Oklahoma City, 1973-77, prof., 1978-85, chmn. dept. occupl. therapy, 1973-85; libr. edn. info. svcs. Houston Acad. Medicine Tex. Med. Ctr. Libr., 1988-97. Cons. to Okla. State Dept. Health, 1976-77, Children's Convalescent Ctr., Oklahoma City, 1977-80, Oklahoma City Pub. Schs., 1980-81; vis. scholars program Tex. Woman's U., 1991-94, adj. prof. Sch. Occupl. Therapy, 1992-97, vis. prof., 1997—; prof. Houston Ctr. Author: (with Sharon Sanderson) Concepts of Occupational Therapy, 1980, 2d edit., 1983, 3rd edit., 1992, 4th edit., 1999, Models of Practice in Occupational Therapy, 1983, Quick Reference to Occupational Therapy, 1991, 2d edit., 2000, (with Julie Pauls) Quick Reference to Physical Therapy, 1996, 2d edit., 2004, (with J. Cunningham) Internet Guide for Rehabilitation Professionals, 1997, (with Sally Pore) Quick Reference to Speech-Language Pathology, 1999. Vol. crisis counselor Open Door Clinic, Seattle, 1968-72; mem. exec. bd. Seattle Mental Health Inst., 1971-72; Mem. Citizen Participation Liaison Coun., Seattle, 1970-72. Recipient Award of Merit, Can. Assn. Occupl. Therapists, 1988. Fellow Am. Occupl. Therapy Assn. (Merit award 1983, Slagle lecture award 1985, Svc. award 1985, 2001); mem. N.Am. Riding for Handicapped Assn., World Fedn. Occupl. Therapists, Coun. Exceptional Children, Okla. Occupl. Therapy Assn. (pres. 1974-76), Tex. Occupl. Therapy Assn. (Roster of Merit award 2002), Med. Libr. Assn. (Rittenhouse award 1987, Acad. Health Info. Professions), Am. Occupl. Therapy Found., Assn. Advancement Rehab. Tech., Neuro-Devel. Treatment Assn., Tex. Occupl. Therapy Found. (pres. 1998—), Pi Theta Epsilan, Sigma Kappa (Colby award 1994). Democrat. Home: 6699 De Moss Dr Houston TX 77074-5003 E-mail: klreed3@juno.com.

REED, MARSEEDA, photographer; b. Cambridge, Md., Dec. 16, 1965; d. Jesse Gregory Webb and Dolliejean Reed; children: Jerome Jesse Gregory Harris, Kevin Marquette Harris. Dept. lead tech. District Photo Inc., Beltsville, Md., 1984—; adminstrv. asst. Nat. Bureau Collecting, Laurel, Md., 1990—97. Participant Cure for Breast Cancer, Wash., 2002, 2003. Recipient Foster Parenting award, Mayor Wash. D.C., 2000, 2001, 2002, 2003. Democrat. Ch. God (Holiness). Avocations: swimming, tennis, walking, needlepoint, sewing. Home: 7705 Bender Rd Landover MD 20785 Office: District Photo Inc 10501 Rhode Island Ave Beltsville MD 20705 Office Phone: 240-687-3920. E-mail: MarSeeDa@aol.com.

REED, MARY CAROLYN CAMBLIN, retired music educator, retired county official; b. North Platte, Nebr., June 22, 1938; d. Brick and Evelyn Camblin; m. Paul E. Reed, Dec. 20, 1960. BA, U. No. Colo., 1960; MA, Calif. State U., 1964; PhD in Ednl. Adminstrn., U. So. Calif., 1976. Cert. adminstr. Calif., 1970. Music educator Rowland Unified Sch. Dist, Rowland Heights, Calif., 1960—67; tchr and writer instrnl. TV LA (Calif.) County Office Edn.; asst. to supt. and chief dep. supt. LA (Calif.) County Office of Edn., 1976—79; adminstr. Regional Ednl. TV Adv. Coun., LA, 1979—82; ednl. tech. unit adminstr. Calif. State Dept. Edn., Sacramento, 1982—83; dir. media svcs. Sacramento (Calif.) County Office Edn., 1983—84. Cons. music series PBS Sta. WETA, Washington, 1974—76; bd. dirs. LA (Calif.) Music Ctr., AMAN Folk Dance group, LA, 1975—77, PBS Sta. KQED, San Francisco, 1989—95. Musician: Am. Flute Orch., 2000, 2002, Internat. Flute Orch., 2004, Sacramento (Calif.) Symphonic Bankd, 1996, 2003. Recipient Outstanding Alumnus, U. of No. Colo., 1983. Mem.: Cosumnes Cmty. Orch, West Sacramento Orch. (prin. flutist 1990—2003). Office Phone: 916-684-3929.

REED, MIRIAM BELL, legislative staff member; b. N.Y.C., May 31, 1930; d. Samuel Dennis and Miriam Wilkes Bell; m. John Grady Reed, May 1, 1954; children: Roberta, Christine, Karen, Laura, Margaret, Abigail, Elisabeth. BA, Mount Holyoke Coll., 1952. Asst. to adminstrv. asst. Rep. Harlan Hagan, Washington, 1953-54; asst. to econ. prof. Littauer Sch. Pub. Adminstrn., Cambridge, Mass., 1954; producer, treas. Video Ed Prodns., Inc., Hyattsville, Md., 1974-90; Singapore testing coord. Malaysian Am. Commn. on Ednl. Exch., Singapore, 1991-92; legis. aide Del. Constance A. Morella, Annapolis, Md., 1978-86; legis. asst. Hon. Constance A. Morella, Washington, 1987-90, 92, 94-97; staff Friends of Connie Morella for Congress, 1999-2000. Cons. Arcad. Arrangements Abroad, N.Y.C., 1974-99. Rsch. and writing of ednl. hist. videotapes, 1974-90 (Pratt Libr. award 1986). V.p., pres. bd. LWV, Bronxville, N.Y., 1957-74; mem. Montgomery County Commn. on the Humanities, 1985-88; mem. Montgomery County Com. to Celebrate Md.'s 350th Birthday. Mem. Montgomery County Hist. Soc. (dir. 1998—), C&O Canal Assn. (dir. 2000—). Avocations: swimming, hiking, backpacking. Home: 8221 Burning Tree Rd Bethesda MD 20817-2908 E-mail: mreed8221@aol.com.

REED, NANCY ELLEN, computer science educator; b. Mpls., Aug. 11, 1955; d. Jacob Alen and Mary Emeline (Howser) Lundgren; m. Todd Randall Reed, June 18, 1977. BS in Biology, U. Minn., 1977, MS in Computer Sci., 1988, PhD in Computer Sci., 1995. Rsch. lab. technician gastroenterology rsch. unit Mayo Clinic, Rochester, Minn., 1978-81; phys. sci. technician U.S. Environ. Hygiene Agy., Fitzsimmons Army Med. Ctr., Aurora, Colo., 1982-83; profl. rsch. asst. molecular, cellular, devel. biology dept. U. Colo., Boulder, 1983-84; tchg. asst. U. Minn., 1985-86, rsch. asst., 1985-88; computer programmer Control Data Corp., Arden Hills, Minn., 1986; asst. Artificial Intelligence Lab. Swiss Fed. Inst. Tech., Lausanne, 1989-91; lectr. computer and info. sci. dept. Sonoma State U., Rohnert Park, Calif., 1993-94; lectr. U. Calif., Davis, 1994-95, 96, rschr., 1995, asst. adj. prof. computer sci. dept., 1996—2002; asst. prof. dept. computer and info. sci. Linköping (Sweden) U., 1998—2002; asst. prof. dept. elec. engrs., U. Hawaii, 2002—. Contbr. articles to profl. jours.; presenter in field; spkr. in field; reviewer for Artificial Intelligence in Medicine, Internat. Jour. of Man-Machine Studies, Integrated Computer-Aided Engring. Microelectronic and Info. Scis. Fellowship, 1984-85, Am. Electronics Assn. Fellowship, 1985-89. Mem. IEEE, AAUP, Am. Assn. for Artificial Intelligence (scholarship for travel nat. conf. on artificial intelligence 1992, 94, session chair for spring syposium 1994), Assn. for Computing Machinery, Am. Med. Informatics Assoc., Am. Heart Assoc. Office: Univ Hawaii Dept Elec Engring 2540 Dole St 483 Holmes Hall Honolulu HI 96822

REED, PATSY BOSTICK, former academic administrator; b. Holland, Tex., Dec. 1, 1936; d. William T. and Evelyn R. (Smith) Bostick; m. F. DeWitt Reed, Sept. 6, 1958. BS, U. Tex., 1959, MS, 1967, PhD, 1969. Tchr. pub. schs., Austin and Port Arthur, Tex., 1959-65; fellow U. Va., Charlottesville, 1969-70; rsch. chemist U. Heidelberg, W.Ger., 1970-72; assoc. prof. nutrition Idaho State U., Pocatello, 1973-79; prof. nutrition, adminstr. No. Ariz. U., Flagstaff, 1979-94; dean Coll. Design and Tech., 1981-85; asst. v.p. acad. affairs U. N.C., Asheville, 1985-87, v.p. acad. affairs, 1987-93, interim pres., 1994, chancellor, 1994-99; ret., 1999. Author: Nutrition: An Applied Science, 1980. Mem. AAAS, Am. Chem. Soc., Am. Dietetic Assn., Phi Kappa Phi, Sigma Xi. Office: U NC 1 University Hts Asheville NC 28804-3299

REED, SALLY GARDNER, cultural organization administrator; BA in English, Colo. State U., 1979; MLS, No. Ill. U., 1981. Dir. North Hampton (H.H.) Pub. Libr., 1981-85, Ilsley Pub. Libr., Middlebury, Vt., 1985-93, Ames (Iowa) Pub. Libr., 1993-95; dir. librs. Norfolk (Va.) Pub. Libr., 1995—2001; exec. dir. Friends of Librs. USA, Phila., 2001—. Adv. com. product devel. Rsch. Pub., Inc., 1993-94; bd. trustees Bibliographic Ctr. Rsch., Aurora, Colo., 1994-95. Author: Small Libraries: A Handbook for Successful Management, 1991, 2d edit., 2002, Saving Your Library: A Guide to Getting, Using and Keeping the Power You Need, 1992, Library Volunteers: Worth the Effort!, 1994; editor: Creating the Future: Essays on the Future of Librarianship in an Age of Great Change, 1996, Speaking Out: Voices in Celebration of Intellectual Freedom, 1999, Making the Case for Your Library, 2001, 101+ Great Ideas for Libraries and Friends, 2004; contbr. articles to profl. jours. Bd. dirs. Sheldon Art History Mus., Middlebury, 1988-93, United Way Story County, Ames, 1994-95; mem. cabinet United Way Norfolk, 1996-97, chair city campaign, 1997. Recipient Recognition award Tidewater Area Minority Libr. Network, 1997, Am. Libr. Assoc. Herb & Virginia White award for Promoting Librarianship, 2000. Mem. ALA (exec. bd., intellectual freedom roundtable 1991—, chpt. coun. 1989-93, promotion task force 1989-91, planning budget assembly 1991, adv. com. office libr. outreach svcs. 1993-94, nat. libr. week com. 1993-95, presdl. com. pub. awareness 1994-96, councilor at large 1995-99, chair membership com. 1996, resolutions com. 1997, exec. bd. 1997-2001). Office: Friends Libraries USA 1420 Walnut Ste 450 Philadelphia PA 19102-

REED, SANDY, former magazine editor; m. Bob Ingle. B Journalism, Kans. State U. Reporting and sr. editing positions San Jose (Calif.) Mercury News, Miami (Fla.) Herald, Billings (Mont.) Gazette, Oakland (Calif.) Tribune; exec. editor news ops. InfoWorld, San Francisco, 1984-90, exec. editor Pers. Computing mag., 1985-90, editor-in-chief, 1990-00, exec. editor PC/Computing, 1991-00. Founding editor Macintosh Bus. Rev.; founding editl. dir. New Media Age mag. (now NewMedia mag). Named one of most influential journalists covering computer industry Mktd. Computers mag. Avocations: surfing the web, reading, travel. Office: Infoworld 155 Bovet Rd Ste 800 San Mateo CA 94402-3150

REED, SUELLEN KINDER, school system administrator; BA in History, Polit. Sci. and Secondary Edn., Hanover Coll., 1967; MA in Elem. Edn. and History, Ball State U., 1970, EdD in Adminstrn. and Supervision, LLD (hon.), 1997; EdD (hon.), Vincennes U., 1996; LittD (hon.), U. Indpls., 1997; LHD (hon.), St. Joseph Coll., 1999, Hanover Coll., 2003; postgrad., Fla. Atlantic U., U. Scranton, Purdue U., Earlham Coll., Ind. U., Ind. State U., U. So. Ind., Butler U., U. Alaska, U. Va. at Edinburgh (Scotland) U., Oxford (Eng.) U. Lic. supt., life lic. in elem. edn., U.S. history, world history, govt., adminstrn. and supervision and endorsement in edn. for gifted and talented K-12, Ind.; lic. adminstr., U.S. history, world history, govt., middle sch. lang. arts, social studies, elem. edn., gifted edn., Fla. Tchr. 5th and 6th grades Rushville (Ind.) Consol. Sch. Corp., 1967-70; tchr. Shelbyville (Ind.) High Sch., 1970-71; tchr. 6th, 7th and 8th grade social studies, curriculum Broward County (Fla.) Sch. Corp., 1971-76; tchr. Rushville Jr. High Sch., 1976-77; asst. prin. Rushville Elem. Sch., 1977-79; prin. Frazee Elem. Sch., Connersville, Ind., 1979-87; asst. supt. Rushville Consolidated Schs., 1987-90, supt., 1991-93; supt. pub. instrn., chairperson bd. edn., CEO dept. edn. State of Indiana, Indpls., 1993—. Pres. N. Ctrl. Regional Edn. Lab., Oak Brook, Ill., 1993—97, Oak Brook, 2002; mem. The Ctr. on Congress Outstanding Tchr. Award Selection Com. Contbr. articles to profl. jours. Bd. trustees Hanover Coll., Commn. Drug-Free Ind., Ind. Commn. Cmty. Svc., Ind. Higher Edn. Telecom. Sys., Ctr. Agrl. Sci. Heritage; hon. bd. mem. Rush County Cmty. Found.; alumni bd. Ball State U. Tchrs. Coll., 1999-; bd. dirs. Nat. Children's Film Festival; trustee, mem. New Salem United Meth. Ch.; bd. dirs. Ind. Historic Landmarks Found., Agy. for Instrnl. Tech., Project Lead the Way, Virtual H.S., 2003—; bd. visitors Ind. U.; hon. bd. mem. Indpls. Zool. Soc. Named Outstanding Sch. Edn. Alumnus, Ball State U., 1994, Govt. Leader Yr., Ind. C. of C., 2001; recipient Pres. award, Ind. Assn. Sch. Prins., 1996, Achievement award, Ind. Network Women Adminstrs., 1996, Alumni award, Hanover Coll., 1997, Legis. award, Ind. Assn. for the Edn. Young Children, 1998, Pres. award, Ind. Middle Level Edn. Assn., 2001, Elizabeth Heywood Wyman award for alumnae, Alpha Omicron Pi, 2001, Friend Youth award, Ind. Sch. Counselors, 2001, Hoosier Heritage Civic Leadership award, 2002, Turn Off the Violence award, Ind. Crime Prevention Coalition, 2002, Ind. Sch. Safety Leadership award, 2002, Citizen's award, Ind. Libr. Fedn., Counselor's award, Assn. for Ind. Media Educators. Mem. ASCD (nat. and Ind. chpts.), Internat. Reading Assn., Nat. Coun. for Accreditation Tchr. Edn. (mem. exec. bd.), Nat. Assn. Elem. and Mid. Sch. Prins. (assoc.), Nat. Assn. Gifted Children (nat. adv. bd.), Internat. Tech. Edn. Assn. (mem. adv. com.), Ind. Assn. Pub. Sch. Supts., Ind. Assn. Elem. and Mid. Sch. Prins. (assoc.), Women's Coun. on Literacy for the Ind. Literacy Found., Rose Hulman Inst. Tech., Network Woman Adminstrs., Indpls. Zoo, Indpls. Art Mus., Indpls. Bd. Assocs., Bus. and Profl. Women of Rushville, Connersville Area Reading Coun., Smithsonian, Rushville Rotary Club, Monday Cir., K-12 Compact Learning and Citizenship (chairwoman), Edn. Commn. States (commr., mem. exec. com. 1994-98, 2002—), Council Chief State Sch. Officers (pres.-elect., 2000-01, pres., 2001-02, v.p., 2002-03), Ind. Hist. Soc., Ind. State Mus., Conner Prairie Farm, Order of Ea. Star (Andersonville chpt.), Delta Kappa Gamma (past pres.), Phi Lambda Theta, Phi Delta Kappa (Conner Prairie). Office: Superintendent Edn Dept 229 State House Indianapolis IN 46204-2798*

REED, SUSAN D. prosecutor; m. Robert D. Reed; 1 child. B in Econs., U. Tex., JD, 1974. Bar: Tex., U.S. Dist. Ct. (we. dist.) Tex., Fed. Ct., U.S. Supreme Ct., bd. cert. criminal law: Tex. Bd. Legal Specialization. Judge 144th Dist. Ct.; pvt. practice Souls and Reed; chief pros. 144th and 187th Dist. Cts.; adminstrv. judge Dist. Cts. Bexar County, 1996—97; asst. dist. atty. Bexar County, San Antonio, 1974—82, criminal dist. atty., 1998—. Mem. Criminal Justice Policy Coun., Govs. Juvenile Justice Adv. Bd., Bush-Cheney Transition Team for Dept. Justice, Nat. Adv. Coun. on Violence Against Women. Mem. Regional Anti-Terrorism Task Force; co-chair Anti-Crime Commn., 2002. Recipient Judge of Yr. award, Tex. Gang Investigators Assn. Mem.: Nat. Dist. Attys. Assn., Tex. Dist. and County Attys. Assn. Office: Bexar County Criminal Dist Atty 5th Fl 300 Dolorosa San Antonio TX 78205-3630

REED, VALERIE V. school librarian; b. Wilmington, Ohio, May 5, 1954; d. James Todd and Janice Ann VanDervort; m. David Carl Reed, May 8, 1976; children: Timothy David, Amy Lyn, Ann Michal. BA in Edn., Cinn. Bible Coll., 1976; MEd in Elem. Edn., Xavier U., 1980. Cert. elem. edn. Ohio Dept. Edn., 1979, K-12 libr./media specialist) Ohio Dept. Edn., 2001. 3rd/4th grade tchr. Christian Schs. Greater Cinn., 1976—77; writing lab instr. Mason (Ohio) City Schs., 1993—2000; libr. media specialist Hopewell Jr. Sch., West Chester, Ohio, 2000—. Mem. bd. edn. Lebanon City Schs., 1991—99, Warren County Careet Ctr., Lebanon, 1995—99; bd. trustees Cin. Bible Coll. and Seminary, 2004—; sec. Jewell Edn. Found., Lebanon, 2000. Mem.: Readers Young Adult Lit., Cin. Area Sch. Libr. Assn. (assoc.), Delta Kappa Gamma. Avocations: reading, volleyball. Office: Hopewell Jr Sch 8200 Cox Rd West Chester OH 45069

REED, VASTINA KATHRYN (TINA REED), child and adolescent psychotherapist, family development specialist; b. Chgo., Mar. 5, 1960; d. Alvin Hillard and Ruth Gwendolyn (Thomas) R.; 1 child, Alvin J. BA in Human Svcs. magna cum laude, Nat.-Louis U., Chgo., 1988; MA, Ill. Sch. Profl. Psychology, 1991; tng. cert., Appelbaum Inst. Child Devel.; cert. family devel. specialist, U. Iowa, 2002; theology student of Evangelist Audrey Donson, Good Shepherd Grace Min., 2002—. First aid/CPR cert., ARC. Tchr. early childhood edn. Kendall Coll. Lab. Sch., Evanston, Ill., 1983-85, Rogers Park Children's Learning Ctr., Chgo., 1983-85; child life therapist Mt. Sinai Hosp., Chgo., 1988; child psychotherapist Nicholas Barnes Therapeutic Day Sch., Chgo., 1989-90; presch. instr. YMCA, 1999-2000; crisis line counselor Washington Security Corp., 2000—02; family support specialist Maywood (Ill.) Head Start, 2000—03; health care rep. Care Entrée, 2002—. Den leader Boy Scouts Am., Chgo., 1989-92, scoutmaster, 1992-2000, merit badge counselor, 1999—, troop advisor for Order of the Arrow; vision ptnr., co-labourers Christ Ministry; editor, mem. praise and worship team Christ Outreach Deliverance Ctr. Ministry, 2001—. Recipient Cub Scouter award Boy Scouts Am., 1990, Scoutmaster award of merit, 1993, 94, Scouters Vet. award, 1994, Scouters Tng. award, 1995, Scoutmasters Key award, 1996, Okpik Cold Weather Camping cert., 1994-95, Outstanding Women of 20th Century medal, 2000, Boy Scout Woodbadge Tng. award, 2001; Internat. Who's Who of Profl. & Business Women, 2002-. Mem. APA, Nat. Orgn. for Human Svc. Edn., Order of the Arrow, Ea. Stars (Hon. Lady status 1999—), Charles F. Menninger Soc. (patron), Phi Theta Kappa, Kappa Delta Pi. Democrat. Roman Catholic. Avocations: camping, cruising, classic movies, performing in ministry's ensemble, gospel music. Home: 1872 S Millard Ave Chicago IL 60623-2542

REED, WARLENE PATRICIA, retired librarian; b. Denmark, Tenn., Aug. 3, 1940; d. Wallace Edward and Louise Greer; m. Jerome Batchelor (div. Dec. 10, 1960); children: Angela Batchelor, Edwin Batchelor, Lajuana Batchelor-Counts; m. Billy Matt Reed, Oct. 18, 1964; 1 child, Byron. BA, Lane Coll., 1962; M in Librarianship, Emporia State U., 1972. Cert. English tchr., libr. Tchr. Crockett County Schs., Alamo, Tenn., 1962—63, Madison County Schs., Jackson, Tenn., 1963—66; tchr., libr. Wichita (Kans.) Pub. Schs., 1966—70; libr. Barnes Hosp. Sch. Nursing, St. Louis, 1971, Francis Howell Sch. Dist., St. Charles, Mo., 1971—2001. Pres. St. Louis Area Libr. Suprs., 1993—95; mem. St. Louis Suburban Libr. Assn., 1983—97. Mem. chancellor's adv. com. U. Mo., St. Louis, 1994—; mem. Charter Rev. Com., St. Charles, 1991—92, Citizens Participation and Adv. Com., St. Charles, 1988—89; bd. dirs. MOsaics Arts Festival Assn., St. Charles, 1996—98; trustee St. Charles City-County Libr. Dist., 1998—. Recipient Alumni award, Lane Coll., 1978, Svc. award, 5th Dist. Lay Orgn.-AME Ch., 1983, Howell of Fame award, Francis Howell Sch. Dist., 1990, Lifetime Disting. Svc. award, St. Charles C. of C., 2002. Mem.: AAUW (pres. 1995—97, gift honoree St. Charles br. 1990), Mo. Assn. Sch. Librs., Howell Found. Bd., St. Charles County Hist. Soc. (black history honoree 2001), Vision-St. Charles County, Sigma Gamma Rho. Episcopalian. Avocations: reading, travel, youth volunteer. Home: 1135 Olde Saybrook Dr Saint Charles MO 63301

REEDER, KAREN EMERALD, artist, educator; d. Joe Franklin Reeder and Elizabeth Avyce Bennett; m. Vincent Phillip DiMarco, June 13, 1998. BS in Edn., Tex. Tech U., Lubbock, 1975; MS in Edn., Parsons Sch. Art, 1991. Adobe cert. expert Adobe Systems Inc. Tchr. Lubbock Ind. Sch. Dist., 1977—83, Ruidoso (N.Mex.) Mcpl. Sch. Dist., 1983—2002; instr. Ea. N.Mex U., Ruidoso, 1991—, head art dept., 1995—. Instr. western dancing, ballroom dancing, 1983—87; owner Kaleidoscope, Ruidoso, 1984—89; dept. head fine arts Ruidoso HS, 1991—2001, chair site based com., 1996—2001, chair dept. heads, 1996—2001; assessment coord. Ea. N.Mex U., Ruidoso, 1995—. Exhibited in group shows at Mus. of Horse, Ruidoso, 1996 (Best of Show, 1996), Nat. Mus. Women Arts, 1999, Rio Grande Art Show, 2001 (Hon. Mention, 2001), 2003 (Hon. Mention, 2003), Colored Pencil Am. Nat. Show, 2002, 2003 (Best of Show, 2003). Mem. Ruidoso Madrigal Singers, 1983—86; actress, dir. Ruidoso Little Theatre, 1984—90. Mem.: Colored Pencil Soc. Am., Phi Kappa Phi (life). Home: 113 Rim Rd Ruidoso NM 88345 Office: Ea NMex U Mechem Ruidoso NM 88345 Office Phone: 505-257-2120. Personal E-mail: karen.reeder@zianet.com., flame25@charter.net.

REED-FORD, LILLIE MAE, geriatrics services professional; b. Near Blackville, S.C., Oct. 9, 1939; d. William Henry and Joanne Reed; m. Phinnize Ford; children: Monica D. Ford, Marie C. Ford, William H. Ford, Maude L. Ford, Phinnize E. Ford, Lee A. Ford, Merlinda Ford, Christopher E. Ford. A in Paralegal, Orangeburg (S.C.) Calhoun Tech. Coll., 2000. Pres. usher bd. Thankful Bapt. Missionary, Bamberg, SC; program chairperson Bapt. Usher Bd. Union, Bamberg; therapeutic asst. Northhampton Assocs., Orangeburg, SC, S.C. Mentor Network, Columbia, SC; quality control insp. Allied Signal Aerospace Electronics, Orangeburg; vol. Helpline, Aiken, SC; pvt. caregiver Aiken, SC. Named to Wall of Tolerance So. Poverty Law Ctr., Mont.; recipient Honor award for Internship, Senator Strom Thurmon, 1984, Spl. Recognition award, Continental Challenge II Team, 2003, cert. of Appreciation, Girl Scouts U.S. Mem.: NAACP, Christian Burial Aid Assn. (pres. lodge #46), Smith-Hazel Sr. Citizens Art and Crafts Club. Avocations: quilting, crafts, reading, sewing, dance.

REEDY, CATHERINE IRENE, elementary school educator; b. Suffolk County, N.Y., Dec. 27, 1953; f. Edward and Catherine (Spindler) Grafenstein. AA, Suffolk C.C., Selden, N.Y., 1980; BA in Social Sci. summa cum laude, Dowling Coll., 1983, MS in Edn., 1986. Tchr. coord. sci. & health, tech. regence earth sci. St. Ignatius Sch., Hicksville, NY, 1983—2002, tchr. tech. grades 6-8, 1983—2002. Contbr. poetry to Beyong the Stars, 1996, Walk Through Paradise, 1995, Best Poems of 1996. Recipient Editor's Choice award Nat. Soc. Poetry, 1996, Nat. Libr. Poetry, 1995. Mem. ASCD, AAUW, N.Y. Acad. Scis., N.Y. Sci. Tchrs. Assn., Nat. Assn. Univ. Women, Nat. Poet Soc., Internat. Poets Soc., Alpha Zeta Nu (1st sec.), Phi Theta Kappa, Phi Alpha Sigma, Jappa DeltaPi (pres. Xi chpt. 1985-87). Home: 15 Nikia Dr Islip NY 11751-2630 Office: St Ignatius Sch 30 E Cherry St Hicksville NY 11801-4396

REEDY, SUSAN, painter; BFA, Daemen Coll., 1978; MFA, SUNY, Buffalo, 1981. Gallery dir. Niagara County Cmty. Coll., Sanborn, N.Y., 1984-88, instr., 1983-87; asst. prof. Daemen Coll., Amherst, 1992—. One woman show at Goldman Greenfield Gallery, Amherst, 1985, Castellani Art Mus., Niagara Falls, 1993, Amherst (N.Y.) Mus., 1997; exhibited in group exhibitions at Meml. Art Gallery, Rochester, N.Y., 1995, 96, Goldman-Greenfield Gallery, Amherst, N.Y., 1995, Albright-Knox Art Gallery, Buffalo, N.Y., 1993, 94, 97, Butler Inst. of Am. Art, Youngstown, Ohio, 1990, 92, O.K. Harris Gallery, N.Y.C., 1988, Gallery 84, N.Y.C., 1996, 97, (2 person exhbn.) Marymount Manhattan Coll. Art Gallery, N.Y., N.Y., 2002; permanent collections include Meml. Art Gallery, Castellani Art Mus., Std. Fed. Bank Hdqrs., Rich Products Corp., Hospice Found. of Western N.Y., Mobil Oil Corp. Recipient Dr. J. Warren Penny award Art Dialogue Gallery, 1995, Dirs. Choice award Meml. Art Gallery, 1995, Mfrs. and Traders Trust Co. award Albright Knox Art Gallery, 1980, Dorothy Cripps Salo Meml. award Meml. Art Gallery, 1996, award for outstanding non-representational painting Meml. Art Gallery, 1996. Avocation: figure skating.

REEDY-DEWEY, MADELINE ANNE, retired occupational therapist; b. Milw., Jan. 25, 1954; d. Samuel Smith and Louise Rita (Thomas) Reedy; m. Craig D. Dewey, Sept. 28, 1989. BS in Occupl. Therapy, U. Wis., Milw., 1978. Registered occupl. therapist Wis. Dir. occupl. therapy Hillhaven, Shorewood, Wis., 1978-83, Colonial Manor, Glendale, Wis., 1983-85; Saturday/on-call occupl. therapist Northwest Gen. Hosp., Milw., 1981-84; chief occupl. therapist Silver Spring Convalescent Ctr., Glendale, 1985-86; dir. occupl. therapy Colonia Manor, Glendale, 1986-91; rehab. clin. cons. Therapy Mgmt. Inc. Facilities, various locations, 1991-92; cons./instr. in edn. program W.H. Carter, Inc., Milw., 1994-95; instr. med. terminology and anatomy/physiology Concordia U., Mequon, Wis., 1996; ret., 1996. Clin. practicum supr. occupl. therapy program U. Wis.-Milw., Milw. Area Tech. Coll., 1978—83; bd. dirs. Toner Tech Cartridge Services Inc., Panama City, Fla., 1996—. Vol. Gulf Coast Cmty. Hosp., Panama City, 1985, St. Michael's Hosp., Milw., 1994, St. Francis Children's Ctr., Milw., 1996, Humane Soc. Bay County, Fla., 2000—01, Vocat. Rehab., Panama City, 2001. Mem.: Wis. Occupl. Therapy Assn., Am. Occupl. Therapy Assn. Roman Catholic. Avocations: volunteer work, gardening, cooking, animal husbandry. Home: 314 Massalina Dr Panama City FL 32401 E-mail: cdeweybc@att.net.

REEF, GRACE, government official; b. Portland, Maine; m. Don Green, Nov. 9, 1991; children: Megan, Jamie, Ryan. BA, Colby Coll., 1984. Legis. asst. Sen. George Mitchell U.S. Senate, Washington, 1984-94, legis. asst. Sen. Tom Daschle, 1995-97; dir. intergovt. affairs Children's Def. Fund, Washington, 1997-2001; subcom. staff dir. children and families Office of Senator Chris Dodd, Washington, 2001—. Office: Office of Senator Chris Dodd 448 Russell Bldg Washington DC 20510 E-mail: grace_Reef@labor.senate.gov.

REES, NINA SHOKRAII, federal official, writer; b. Iran; BS in Psychology, Va. Polytech and State U., 1989; MS in Internat. Transactions, George Mason U., 1991. Mem. staff Rep. Porter Gross, Washington, 1990—92; dir. outreach programs Inst. for Justice, Washington, 1992—94; policy analyst Ams. for Tax Reform, Washington, 1994—96; chief edn. analyst The Heritage Found., Washington, 1997—2001; aide to v.p. U.S. Govt., Washington, 2001—02. Contbr. commentaries in newspapers, TV, radio on ednl. issues, 1995. Education adviser to Bush Campaign, Phila., 2000; contbr. to Rep. platform in edn. area Rep. Paty, 2000. Recipient Rita Ricardo Campbell award, Heritage Found., 1999. Office: US Dept Edn 400 Maryland Ave SW Washington DC 20202

REES, NORMA S. academic administrator; b. N.Y.C., Dec. 27, 1929; d. Benjamin and Lottie (Schwartz) D.; m. Raymond R. Rees, Mar. 19, 1960; children— Evan Lloyd, Raymond Arthur BA, Queens Coll., 1952; Ma, Bklyn. Coll., 1954; PhD, NYU, 1959; D of Arts and Letters honoris causa, John F. Kennedy U., 2001. Cert. speech-language pathology, audiology. Prof. communicative disorders Hunter Coll., N.Y.C., 1967-72; exec. officer, speech and hearing scis. grad. sch. CUNY, N.Y.C., 1972-74, assoc. dean for grad. studies, 1974-76, dean grad. studies, 1976-82; vice chancellor for acad. affairs U. Wis., Milw., 1982-85, from 1986, acting chancellor, 1985-86; vice chancellor for acad. policy and planning Mass. Bd. Regents for Higher Edn., Boston, 1987-90; pres. Calif. State U., Hayward, 1990—. Chmn. Commn. Recognition of Postsecondary Accreditation, 1994-96; mem. adv. com. quality and integrity U.S. Dept. Edn., commn. on internat. edn. Coun. on Higher Edn. Accreditation, 2003—. Contbr. articles to profl. jours. Trustee Citizens Govtl. Rsch. Bur., Milw., 1985-87; active Task Force on Wis. World Trade Ctr., 1985-87; bd. dirs. Am. Assn. State Colls. and Univs., 1995-97, Coun. of Postsecondary Accreditation, Washington, 1985-94, Greater Boston YWCA, 1987-90; mem. Calif. Sch. to Career Coun.; bd. dir. Econ. Devel. Alliance for Bus., Alameda County, 1995—; sec. edn. Nat. Adv. Com. Institutional Quality and Integrity, 1998-2002; bd. dirs. Bay Area World Trade Ctr., 2001—, Alameda County Health Care Found., 2002-. Fellow Am. Speech-Lang-Hearing Assn. (honors); mem. Am. Coun. Edn. (com. internat. edn. 1991-93), Am. Assn. Colls. and Univs. (chair task force on quality assessment 1991-92), Nat. Assn. State Univs. and Land Grant Colls. (exec. com. divsn. urban affairs 1985-87, com. accreditation 1987-90), Hayward C. of C. (bd. dirs. 1995-98), Oakland C. of C. (bd. dirs. 1997—). Office: Calif State Univ Hayward 25800 Carlos Bee Blvd Hayward CA 94542-3001 E-mail: nrees@csuhayward.edu.

REESE, DELLA (DELOREESE PATRICIA EARLY), singer, actress; b. Detroit, July 6, 1931; d. Richard and Nellie Early; m. Vermont Adolphus Bon Taliaferro (div.); m. Leroy Basil Gray (div.); m. Franklin Thomas Lett, Jr. Student, Wayne U. Ordained to ministry Ch. Understanding Principles for Better Living Inc., April, 1987. Choir singer, 1938—, with Mahalia Jackson troupe, 1945-49, Erskine Hawkins, N.Y.C.; solo artist, 1957—; organized gospel group at Wayne U.; appearances include: (radio shows) with Robert Q. Lewis; (TV series) Della, 1969, The Voyage of the Yes, 1972, Twice in a Lifetime, 1974, Cop on the Beat, 1975, Chico and the Man, 1974, 76-78, Nightmare in Badham County, 1976 (Emmy nomination), Roots: The Next Generation, 1979, It Takes Two, 1982, Charlie & Co., 1985, 86, The Kid Who Loved Christmas, 1990, The Royal Family, 1991, You Must Remember This, 1992, Touched By an Angel, 1994-2003, A Match Made in Heaven, 1997, Miracle in the Woods, 1997, Emma's Wish, 1998, The Secret Path, 1999, Having Our Say: The Delany Sisters' First 100 Years, 1999; spl. appearances with Jackie Gleason, Ed Sullivan, McCloud, 1971, Sanford and Son, 1972, Welcome Back, Kotter, 1975, The A-Team, 1983, Night Court, 1984, MacGyver, 1985, Designing Women, 1986, L.A. Law, 1986, Married People, 1990, Dream On, 1990, Picket Fences, 1992, Promised Land, 1996, Anya's Bell, 1999, The Moving of Sophia Myles, 2000; guest host The Tonight Show; actress (films) Let's Rock, 1958, Psychic Killer, 1975, Harlem Nights, 1989, A Thin Line Between Love and Hate, 1996, (plays) Same Time Next Year, Ain't Misbehavin, Blues in the Night, The Last Minstrel Show; recs. for Jubilee, RCA Victor Records, ABC Paramount Records, Jazz Ala Carte, AIR Co. (Grammy nomination 1987); author: Angels Along the Way, 1997, (voice) Dinosaur, 2000. Voted Most Promising Singer of Yr. 1957; recipient Image awards, 1996, 98-2000, Star on Walk of Fame, 1994. Office: William Morris Agy c/o Jeff Kolodny 151 S El Camino Dr Beverly Hills CA 90212-2775*

REESE, JANET KAY, purchasing agent; b. Xenia, Ohio, July 27, 1954; AS, N.Mex. State U., 1996. Sec. fgn. tech. divs. Wright Patterson AFB, Dayton, Ohio, 1975-77, sec. dept. of air force Air Force Logistics Command, 1977-83, staff asst. dept. of the air force, 1983-84; procurement asst. nat. aeronautics and space admistrn. White Sands Test Facility, Las Cruces, N.Mex., 1984-97, purchasing agt. nat. aeronautics and space adminstrn., 1997—. Mem. NAFE, Nat. Mgmt. Assn. (White Sands chpt.). Democrat. Avocations: travel, reading, writing. Office: NASA JSC White Sands Test Facility PO Box 20 Las Cruces NM 88004-0020

REESE, KATHERINE ROSE, music educator; b. Mannington, W.Va., July 27, 1937; m. Wallace Reese, July 29, 1955; children: Kyla O'Dell, Ann Landers. BA, W.Va. U., 1986. Cert. profl. music tchr. Artist tchr. of piano Fairmont (W.Va.) State Coll., 1986—. Address: RR 1 Box 122 Mannington WV 26582-9801

REESE, NORMA CAROL, clinical psychologist; b. Biloxi, Miss., Oct. 26, 1946; d. Virgil Stephen and Lila Mae (Shelton) Tatom; m. John Jay Reese, June 5, 1965 (div. Mar. 1983); children: Cher LeAnne, James Steven. AA in Psychology, Dade County Jr. Coll., Kendall, Fla., 1971; BS in Psychology, U. Miami, 1973; MS and PhD in Psychology, U. So. Miss., 1976. Lic. psychologist, Wis., Tex. Rsch. asst. NASA Lang. Rsch. Lab., Coral Gables, Fla., 1971-73; psychology instr. U. So. Miss., Hattiesburg, 1975-76, Grambling (La.) State U., 1976-78; clin. psychologist II Lake Charles (La.) Mental Health Ctr., 1979-83; tng. cons. Human Rels. Cons., Lake Charles, 1983-86; clin. dir. Grafton (N.D.) State Sch., 1986-89; dir. psychol. svcs. State Devel. Ctr., Grafton, 1989-95; ind. contractor, cons. psychol. svcs. Harley Residential Svcs. (name changed to Applied Behavioral Cons., Inc. 1990), Roseville, Minn., 1990-91; pvt. practice MYNDAK Moblie Cons., Minn. and N.D., 1990-95; program dir. for spl. needs Saint Coletta Sch., Jefferson, Wis., 1995-98, human rights and sexual health curriculum coms., 1995—2001; psychol. cons. Tex. Deer Oaks Geriatric Svcs., 1999-2000, Deer Oaks Mental Health Assocs., Harlingen, Tex., 2000-01, ret., 2001. Dir. sexual health project for devel. disabled and mentally retarded N.D. Dept. Human Svcs., Grafton, 1989-95, dir. sex offender and treatment program devel. disabled offenders, 1986-87; mem. adj. faculty grad. clin. psychology dept. U. N.D., Grand Forks, 1994—; presenter in field. Author: The Bulletin of the Psychonomic Soc., 1975-76; author/cartoonist The Worm Runner's Digest, 1975-80. Freedom writer Amnesty Internat., Midwest, 1989; founding mem. Sexual Health Coalition Steel of N.D., 1990; nat. disaster mental health technician, chpt. family svc. worker Red River Valley chpt. ARC, 1993—; mentor Am. Assn. Mental Retardation, 1992—; vol. Red Cross Nat. Disaster Mental Health Team, 1993, Emilys List, 1993. Named Silver Knight candidate, art, Miami (Fla.) Herald News, 1965; nominated Profl. of the Yr., La. Assn. Retarded Citizens, Lake Charles, 1983. Mem. N.D. Psychol. Assn. (legis. action com. 1990-91, mem. disaster action com. 1993-94, mem. women in psychology 1995), Am. Assn. Mental Retardation (sec.-treas. N.D. chpt. 1991), Ft. Worth Psychol. Assn. Republican. Methodist. Avocations: boating, dance, art, travel. Office: RR 8 Box 4396-12 Donna TX 78537-8836

REEVE, PAMELA, communications executive; MBA with distinction, Harvard Bus. Sch.; BA with honors, U. Ga. Pres., CEO Lightbridge, Burlington, Mass., 1989—. Bd. trustees Mass. Software Coun. Office: Lightbridge Inc 67 S Bedford St Burlington MA 01803-5152 Fax: 781-359-4500.

REEVER, WILMA MARIE, educational consultant; b. Denver, Aug. 27, 1943; d. James Albert and Dorothy Josephine Totton; m. Mark Ja'n Reever, June 4, 1966; children: Anna Elizabeth, Sarah Katherine. BA in Elem. and Christian Edn., Hastings Coll., 1965; MS in Home Econs. and Child and Family Studies, U. Wyo., Laramie, 1990. Tchr. pub. schs. Natrona City Sch. Dist. # 1, Casper, Wyo., 1965—68, 1970—71; dir. Christian edn. Shepherd of the Hills Presbyn. Ch., Casper, 1975—83, dir. CDC, 1976—85; dir. presch./child care Our Saviour's Luth. Ch., Casper, 1985—90; dir. Family Resource Ctr. Casper Coll., 1990—96; cons. Early Childhood Svcs., Delta, Colo., 1996—; tng. and curriculum specialist U.S. Army Child and Youth Svcs., Baumholder, Germany, 1999—2001. Mem. child and adult care food program Children's Nutrition, Inc., Casper, 1985—90; dir. resource and referral agy. Care Connections, Inc., Casper, 1989—94; grant writer; presenter in field. Chair gen. coun., mem. various coms. Presbytery Wyo., Casper, 1984—91; bd. dirs., mem. Ret. Sr. Vols., Casper, 1989—91; bd. dirs., mem. family selection com. Habitat for Humanity, Casper, Wyo. and Delta, Colo., 1993—97. Recipient Woman of the Yr. award, Bus. and Profl. Women, 1979. Mem.: Child Care Adv. Coun., Nat. Assn. Edn. Young Children, Wyo. Early Childhood Assn. (pres. 1988—92, bd. dirs., Lifetime achievement award 1995), Surface Creek Valley Hist. Soc. (bd. dirs. 2002—03), Soroptimists Internat. (bd. dirs. 1990—96). Presbyterian. Avocations: reading, puzzles, knitting. Office: Early Childhood Svcs PO Box 61 Delta CO 81416

REEVES, BARBARA, writer, educator; b. Wellington, Tex., Aug. 29, 1931; d. Edward Decatur Reeves and Ruth Caroline Rich; m. Stanley Kolaski, Jan. 15, 1956 (dec. Feb. 1987); children: Anne Marie, Linda Caroline, John Edward. Writing tchr. San Jacinto Coll. Sys., Houston, 1990—. Curriculum cons. San Jacinto Coll. South, Houston, 1998-2000; cons. and mentor in field. Authro: Georgina's Campaign, 1991, The Dangerous Marquis, 1993, The Much Maligned Lord, 1995, My Buffalo Soldier, 2000, Thunder Moon, 2003. Mem. Romance Writers Am. (founder chpt. 30, chairperson, fundraiser for literacy), Bay Area Writer's League (founder, chairperson). Democrat. Roman Catholic. Avocations: social historian, interior design, family history. E-mail: bkwriter@swbell.net.

REEVES, BARBARA ANN, lawyer; b. Buffalo, Mar. 29, 1949; d. Prentice W. and Doris Reeves; m. Richard C. Neal; children: Timothy R. Neal, Stephen S. Neal (dec.), Robert S. Neal, Richard R. Neal. Student, Wellesley Coll., 1967-68; BA (NSF fellow, Lehman fellow), New Coll., Sarasota, Fla., 1970; JD cum laude, Harvard U., 1973. Bar: Calif. 1973, D.C. 1977. Law clk. U.S. Ct. Appeals, 9th Circuit, Portland, Oreg., 1973-74; assoc. firm Munger, Tolles and Rickershauser, L.A., 1977-78; trial atty. spl. trial sect. Dept. Justice (Antitrust div.), 1974-75; spl. asst. to asst. atty. gen. Antitrust div. Dept. Justice, Washington, 1976-77; chief antitrust div. L.A. field office, 1978-81; ptnr. Morrison & Foerster, L.A., 1981-94, Fried, Frank, Harris, Shriver & Jacobson, L.A., 1995-97, Paul, Hastings, Janofsky & Walker, L.A., 1997—. Mem. exec. com. state bar conf. of dels. L.A. Delegation, 1982-91; del. 9th Cir. Jud. Conf., 1984-88; mem. Fed. Ct. Magistrate Selection Com., 1989; bd. dirs. Pub. Counsel, 1988-92, Western Ctr. Law and Poverty, 1992-98; lectr. in field. Editor: Federal Criminal Litigation, 1994; contbg. author: World Antitrust Law, 1995; contbr. articles to profl. jours. Mem. ABA (litigation sect., antitrust sect.), Fed. Bar Assn. (officer 1998—), Assn. Bus. Trial Lawyers (officer 1997—), Am. Arbitration Assn. (arbitrator, mediator, mem. adv. panel large complex case program), L.A. County Bar Assn. (antitrust sect. officer 1980-81, litigation sect. officer 1988-93 trustee 1990-92, chair alternative dispute resolution sec. 1992-95, L.A. County Ct ADR com.). Home: 1410 Hillcrest Ave Pasadena CA 91106-4503 Office: Paul Hastings Janofsky & Walker 555 S Flower St Fl 23D Los Angeles CA 90071-2300

REEVES, DIANA CRIMHILDA ASLAN, chemist, researcher; b. Bucharest, Romania, July 15, 1968; d. Vintila Nerva-Traian and Romanita Stela Aslan. MSChE, Politechnica U., Bucharest, Romania, 1993; PhD in Organic Chemistry, U. Fla., 1998. Postdoctoral assoc. U. Pitts., 1998—2000; rsch. chemist Dow AgroSciences, Indpls., 2000—. Rsch. asst. U. Fla., Gainesville, 1994—98. Contbr. articles to profl. jours. Mem.: Am. Chem. Soc.

REEVES, KATHLEEN WALKER, English and French language educator; b. Mt. Pleasant, Mich., Dec. 7, 1950; d. John J. and Gladys M. W.; m. Daniel H. Reeves, Mar. 10, 1972; children: Sheila, Michael. BA, Ctrl. Mich. U., 1973, MA, 1984. Cert. early adolescent English language arts tchr. English and French tchr. Shepherd (Mich.) High Sch., 1973-76, Chippewa Hills High Sch., Remus, Mich., 1978-79, Onekama (Mich.) Pub. Sch., 1983-86; English tchr. Seaholm High Sch., Birmingham, Mich., 1986—. Field test participant Nat. Bd. Profl. Tchg. Stds., Detroit, 1993—; adv. liaison Instrn. and Devel. of Mich. Ednl. Assn., Lansing, 1994—; bd. dirs. Mich. Assn. Tchr. Edn., Lansing, 1996-97. Troop leader Girl Scouts U.S., Dearborn, Mich., 1988-90; asst. gen. Boy Scouts Am., Dearborn, 1990—. Mem. Nat. Coun. Tchrs. of English (pres. 1973), Assn. for Supervision & Curriculum Devel., Mich. Assn. Tchrs. of French, Birmingham Ednl. Assn. (v.p. 1994—, disting. svc. award 1989, 91, 93). Democrat. Roman Catholic. Avocations: gardening, camping, reading, cooking. Home: 1020 N York St Dearborn MI 48128-1754 Office: Seaholm High Sch 2436 W Lincoln St Birmingham MI 48009-1898

REEVES, LUCY MARY, retired secondary school educator; b. Pewamo, Mich., July 2, 1932; d. Lavaldin Edgar and Marian S. (Lee) Hull; m. Walter Emery Reeves, Jan. 21, 1922. BS, Western Mich. U., Kalamazoo, 1965; postgrad., Western Mich. U., 1965-75. Tchr. Country Sch. One Room, Matherton, Mich., 1956-57, Ionia, Mich., 1957-58, Belding, Mich., 1958-62, Saranac, Mich., Belding, Mich., 1965, Belding (Mich.) Area Schs., 1965-89; ret., 1989. Vol. Frederick Meijers Garden, Grand Rapids, Point Man Internat. Ministries, Shiloh Cmty. Ch., United Meml. Health Ctr., Shiloh Cmty. Ch.; vol. United Meml. Health Ctr., Greenville. Mem. NEA, Mich. Edn. Assn., Belding Area Edn., Profl. Businesswomen's Assn. Avocations: computers, reading, travelling, sewing.

REEVES, MARY JANE W. interior designer; b. Madison, Wis., Oct. 26, 1949; d. Spencer Hunt and Caroline (Griffith) Watkins; m. Michael Leo Reeves, Nov. 26, 1971 (div.); 1 child, Kristin Ann. BS in Biology, Duke U., 1971; MS in Interior Design, U. N.C., Greensboro, 1975. Interior designer Burdines, Miami, Fla., 1975-78, 81-84; mgr., designer Contract Mktg. Group, Miami, 1981-83; interior designer Burdines, Miami, 1983-84; pres., owner MJR Interiors, Inc., Coral Gables, Fla., 1990—. Mem. bd. govs. Design Ctr. of the Americas, Dania, Fla., 1992-93; bd. dirs. Design Access Adv. Bd., South Fla., 1991-92. Vol. Miami City Ballet, 1991-92. Recipient ASIP Design Excellence Awd. (2), IBD Designer of the Yr., most creative awd., Architectural Digest. Mem. Am. Soc. Interior Designers (profl., bd. dirs. 1989-90, 92—, v.p. 1990-91, pres. 1991-92, pres. IDAF, 1997-99, presdl. citation 1991), Capitol Ctr. Planning Commn. appointment, state of Fla., 1999—, Interior Design Assn. Fla., Nat. Trust Hist. Preservation, Miami Design Preservation League. Office: MJR Interiors Inc 855 S Federal Hwy Ste 105 Boca Raton FL 33432-6130

REEVES, PAMELA, lawyer; b. Marion, Va., July 21, 1954; BA, U. Tenn., 9176, JD, 1979. Bar: Tenn. 1979, U.S. Dist. Ct. (ea. and mid. dists.) Tenn. 1979, U.S. Ct. Appeals (6th cir.), U.S. Supreme Ct. Ptnr. Watson Hollow & Reeves, PLC, Knoxville. Lectr. employment related issues, ethics, and professionalism and civil procedure Knoxville Bar Assn., Tenn. Bar Assn., 1991—. Mem. U. Tenn. Law Rev., 1976; contbr. articles to profl. jours. Mem. ABA, Tenn. Bar Found., Tenn. Bar Assn. (pres. 1998, pres. young lawyers cons. 1989-90, ho. dels. 1987-92), Knoxville Bar Assn. (pres. Knoxville barristers 1983, sec. 1994-96), Am. Inns of Ct. (master of the bench, adminstr. 1994), Phi Beta Kappa. Office: Watson Hollow & Reeves PC 1700 First Tennessee Plz PO Box 131 Knoxville TN 37901-0131 E-mail: swaneeves@mindpsring.com.

REEVES, PEGGY, state legislator; b. Macon, Feb. 20, 1941; m. F. Brent Reeves. BS, Dominican Coll., 1963. Neurophysiology rsch. technician, 1963-64; sci. tchr., 1964-65; sales and broker-assoc. Bartran Homes, 1978-80; broker-assoc. Wheeler Realty, 1983—; mem. Colo. Ho. of Reps., Denver, 1982-84, 87-96, Colo. Senate, Dist. 14, Denver, 1996—; mem. appropriations com., mem. legis. audit com.; mem. health, environment, welfare and instns. com.; mem. local govt. com. Mem. Ft. Collins City Coun., 1973-77, 79-82, Ft. Collins Water Bd., 1977-79; mem. Women's Econ. Devel. Coun., 1988X; mem. One West Art Ctr., Ft. Collins Cmty. Found., Alliance for Children with Disabilities; mem. adv. bd. Colo. Mcpl. Bond Supervision, Vet. Medicine. Mem. AAUW, Colo. State U. Women's Assn., Nat. Assn. Realtors, Colo. Assn. Realtors, Ft. Collins Bd. Realtors. Office: State Capitol 200 E Colfax Ave Ste 274 Denver CO 80203-1716

REEVES, SAMANTHA, professional tennis player; b. Redwood City, Calif., Jan. 17, 1979; d. Jack and Jill. Profl. tennis player, 1995—. Recipient Ranked #1 in U.S. 18-and-under divsn., 1996, WTA Tours Doubles Titles, Quebec City, 2001, 2002, Ranked #76, WTA, Ranked #12 Among U.S. Players, Highest Season Ending Singles Ranking #101, 2002, 2 Women's Circuit Singles Titles, ITF, Rookie of the Yr., 2002, World Team Tennis MVP, 2003. Office: WTA Tour Corporate Headquarters One Progress Plz Ste 1500 Saint Petersburg FL 33701*

REEVY-MANNING, GRETCHEN MARIA, psychology educator; b. Cortland, N.Y., Oct. 17, 1964; d. William Robert and Carole May Reevy; m. Todd Royal Manning. AB in Psychology, U. N.C., 1986; PhD in Psychology, U. Calif., Berkeley, 1994. Lectr. psychology dept. Dominican Coll., San Rafael, Calif., 1993—98; lectr. U. Calif., Davis, 1994, Profl. Sch. Psychology, San Francisco, 1995; lectr. psychology dept. Calif. State U., Hayward, 1994—. Grantee, Rand Corp., 1993. Mem.: APA, Soc. Psychol. Study of Social Issues, Western Psychol. Assn., Phi Beta Kappa, Psi Chi. Avocations: swimming, reading. Office: Calif State U Psychology Dept Hayward CA 94542 Business E-Mail: greevy@csuhayward.edu.

REFO, PATRICIA LEE, lawyer; b. Alexandria, Va., Dec. 31, 1958; BA with high honors and high distinction, U. Mich., 1980, JD cum laude, 1983. Bar: Ill. 1983, Ariz. 1996, U.S. Dist. Ct. (no. dist.) Ill. 1988, U.S. Ct. Appeals (7th cir.) 1989, U.S. Ct. Appeals (11th cir.) 1990, U.S. Ct. Appeals (5th cir.) 1992, U.S. Ct. Appeals (9th cir.) 1998, Fed. Trial Bar (no. dist.) Ill. 1993, U.S. Dist. Ct. Ariz. 1996, Ptnr. Jenner & Block, Chgo., 1991-96, Snell & Wilmer L.L.P., Phoenix, 1996—. Mem. evidence rules adv. com., U.S. Jud. Conf. 2000—; mem. faculty Nat. Inst. Trial Advocacy, 1989—; bd. advisors Comml. Lending Liability News; lectr. ALI/ABA and Practicing Law Inst. on various subjects including trial advocacy and lender liaibility. Co-author: Class Action Controversies, 1989, Notice to Members of the Class, IICLE Class Actions Handbook, 1986, Closing Argument: A String of Pearls, Litigation, 1998. Dir. Ariz. Found. for Women, 1999—, Legal Clinic for the Disabled, 1994-96, Chgo. Lawyers' Com. Civil Rights Under Law, 1987-91, Cabrini Green Legal Aid Clinic, 1987-91; mem. adv. bd. Ariz. Acad. Decathlon Assn., 1998—, Mem. ABA (chair sect. litigation 1990 annual meeting, co-chair sect. litigation Pro Bono com. 1990-93, dir. divsns. sect. litigation 1993-94, sec. sect. litigation 1994-98, mem. Ho. of Dels. 1998-2001, chmn. sect. litigation 2003-). Office: Snell & Wilmer LLP One Arizona Ctr Phoenix AZ 85004-2202

REGALA, DEBBIE, state senator; b. Tacoma, Apr. 27, 1945; m. Leo Regala; children: Alisa, Tim, Jonathan. BA in Fgn. Lang., Edn., U. Puget Sound. Dem. rep. dist. 27 Wash. Ho. of Reps., 1994-2000; Dem. senator dist. 27 Wash. State Senate, 2000—. Mem. edn., labor, commerce and fin. instns. and ways and means coms. Wash. State Senate, vice chair environ., energy and water com.; mem. Joint Legis. Audit and Review Com. Mem. bd. dirs. Nature Conservancy, Point Defiance Zool. Soc.; mem. exec. com. Wash. Cmty. Forestry Coun., Puyallup River Watershed Coun.; parent vol. McCarver Elem.; mem. activities coun. Tacoma Art Mus., docent; lector St. Patrick's Cath. Ch., mem. Parish Coun. Marriage Preparation Team; work site supr. 4 environ. restoration projects; commr. Met. Pk. Sits. Tacoma, 1986-92, pres., 1989, 91. Office: PO Box 40427 405 John A Cherberg Bldg Olympia WA 98504-0427 Fax: 360 786-1999. E-mail: regala_de@leg.wa.gov.

REGALMUTO, NANCY MARIE, small business owner, psychic consultant, therapist; b. Bay Shore, N.Y., Aug. 24, 1956; d. Antonio J. Jr. and Agnes C. (Dietz) R. Student, SUNY, Stony Brook. Sales mgr. Fire, Inc., Hempstead, N.Y., 1976-78; sports handicapper Red Hot Sport, J. Dime Sports, Diamond Sports, Hicksville, N.Y., 1978—; small bus. owner, pres. Synergy (vitamin/nutritional product mfr. and distributor), Bellport, N.Y., 1981—. Cons. on medicine, fin., past life, bus. readings, hypnosis, substance abuse, archeology, law enforcement investigations, family, counseling, inter-species comm., animal therapy, psychic surgery, healing, 1989—; lectr. in field, specializing in holistic remedies and therapies, 1989-91. Columnist Daily Racing Form, 1989-91; appeared on numerous TV programs, worldwide radio, mags., newspapers. Lectr., seminar leader, written about in numerous books. Min. Universal Life Ch., 1996, 97, Ch. of Inner Wisdom, 1996, 97. Mem. NAFE, Internat. Platform Assn., Horse Protection Assn., Therapuetic Riding for the Handicapped, World Wildlife Fedn. Office: 18 Woodland Park Rd Bellport NY 11713-2315

REGAN, CHARLOTTE CAME, real estate company executive; b. Salina, Kans., Apr. 10, 1941; d. Charles W. Marie A. (Gunzelman) Came; m. James V. Regan Jr., Feb. 24, 1962; children: Annette Regan Loyd, James V. III, John C., Joseph P. BBA, Marymount Coll. Kans., 1963. Cert. residential specialist. Savs. counselor Gibraltar Savs., Ft. Worth, 1977-78; broker/assoc., property mgr. Award Realtors, Inc., Ft. Worth, 1978-90; broker/assoc. Wm. Rigg Inc., Ft. Worth, 1990-93, Coldwell Banker, Salina, Kans., 1993-99; co-owner John Utsey Properties Inc., Ft. Worth, 1999—2002; owner, broker Sunflower Realty, Inc., 2002—. Membership chair Salina Bd. Realtors, 1996, 97, ednl. chair, 1996, 97, profl. stds. mem., 1996-97. 2d v.p. Kiwanis Internat., Salina, 1996, pres.-elect, 1997. Mem. AAUW (mem.-at-large), Women's Coun. Realtors (party chair, meetings chair 1991-92), Nat. Assn. Realtors Property Mgrs., Cert. Residential Specialist (Kans. chpt.), Salina Kiwanis Club (pres. 1997-98). Republican. Roman Catholic. Avocations: piano, bridge, decorating and refurbishing old homes. Home: 4351 Delarosa Ct Fort Worth TX 76126-2305 Office: Ste 5A 1020 Macon St Fort Worth TX 76102-4562

REGAN, ELLEN FRANCES (MRS. WALSTON SHEPARD BROWN), ophthalmologist, educator; b. Boston, Feb. 1, 1919; d. Edward Francis and Margaret (Moynihan) R.; m. Walston Shepard Brown, Aug. 13, 1955. AB, Wellesley Coll., 1940; MD, Yale U., 1943. Intern Boston City Hosp., 1944; asst. resident, resident Inst. Ophthalmology, Presbyn. Hosp., N.Y.C., 1944-47, asst. ophthalmologist, 1947-56, asst. attending ophthalmologist, 1956-84; instr. ophthalmology Columbia Coll. Physicians and Surgeons, 1947-55, assoc. ophthalmology, 1955-67, asst. clin. prof., 1967-84. Mem. AMA, Am. Ophthal. Soc., Am. Acad. Ophthalmology, N.Y. Acad. Medicine, N.Y. State Med. Soc., Mass. Med. Soc., River Club, Tuxedo Club. Office: PO Box 632 Tuxedo Park NY 10987-0632

REGAN, HELEN BROOKS, education educator, educational consultant; b. Wilmington, Del., Jan. 13, 1945; d. Richard Ensign and Helen Townsend (Lewis) Brooks; m. Richard James Regan, Nov. 22, 1980; 1 child, Katherine Helen. BA magna cum laude, Randolph-Macon Woman's Coll., 1966; MA in Teaching, Yale U., 1967; PhD, U. Conn., 1981. Cert. chemistry tchr., intermediate supr., supt., Conn. Tchr. chemistry Glastonbury (Conn.) High Sch., 1967-75; asst. prin. Daniel Hand High Sch., Madison, Conn., 1975-78, 81-83, acting prin., 1979-80; prin. Amity Sr. High Sch., Woodbridge, Conn., 1983-85; assoc. prof. Conn. Coll., New London, 1985—. Cons. Conn. Dept.

of Edn., Hartford, 1985—. Co-author: The Staff Development Manager, 1991; contbr. articles to profl. jours. Mem. ASCD, AAUP, Am. Ednl. Rsch. Assn., New Eng. Coalition Ednl. Leaders (pres. 1983-85). Avocations: hiking, stitchery, biking.

REGAN, JUDITH TERRANCE, publishing executive; b. Leominster, Mass., Aug. 17, 1953; d. Leo James and Rita Ann (Imprescia) Regan; children: Patrick, Lara. BA, Vassar Coll., 1975. Reporter Nat. Enquirer; sr. editor, v.p. Simon & Schuster, N.Y.C., 1989—94; pres., pub. Regan Books imprint of HarperCollins, N.Y.C., 1994—. TV prodr. Entertainment Tonight, N.Y.C., Geraldo, N.Y.C.; prodr. 20th Century Fox Films, Fox TV; anchor Full Disclosure, Fox TV; host Judith Regan Tonight, Fox News Channel. Editor, pub. (books) The Way Things Ought to Be (Rush Limbaugh), 1992, Rogue Warrior (Richard Marcinko), 1992, She's Come Undone (Wally Lamb), 1992, Shampoo Planet and Life After God (Douglas Coupland), 1992, Private Parts, Miss America (Howard Stern), 1993, Judge Robert Bork, Slouching Towards Gomorrah, 1993, I Can't Believe I Said That (Kathie Lee Gifford), 1994, Microserfs, 1996, Shabby Chic (Rachel Ashwell), 1996, The Zone (Dr. Barry Sears), 1996, Brain Lock (Dr. Jeffrey Schwartz), 1997, Wicked, 1997, Confessions of an Ugly Stepsister (Gregory Maguire), 1997—2000, Girlfriend in A Coma, 1998, I Know This Much is True, 1998, Marilu Henner's Total health Makeover, 1998, Story (Robert McKee), 1998, Have a Nice Day, Mick Foley (Mankind), 1999, The Rock Says, 2000, and others, —; exec. prodr.: (TV series) Growing Up Gotti, 2004—. Office: Regan Books 10 E 53rd St New York NY 10022-5244

REGAN, LAURA ANDERSON, aviation maintenance technician; b. Mpls., Sept. 23, 1962; d. Roger Wayne and Susan Eleanor (Swanson) A. Grad. in Field Artillery Digital Sys. Repair, U.S. Army Field Artillery Sch., Ft. Sill, Okla., 1987; grad. in Electronics Tech., Northwestern Electronics Inst., Columbia Heights, Minn., 1992; grad. in Aviation Maintenance, Red Wing Winona Tech. Coll., Winona, Minn., 1994. Cashier/cook Zantigo Restaurants, Mpls., 1980-85; electronic assembly Lee Data, Eden Prairie, Minn., 1988-89; house painter J&M Painting, Big Lake, Minn., 1985-93; electronic technician Electrosonic, Minnetonka, Minn., 1989-93; delivery driver Air Vantage, Mpls., 1993-94; fund raiser Hudson Bay, Lincoln, Nebr., 1994-95; aviation maintenance technician Duncan Aviation, Lincoln, 1994-97, Northwest Airlines, Duluth, Minn., 1997—. Spkr. Career Day, Winona Tech. Coll., 1994, Women in Aviation Conf., Mpls., 1996. Mem. unit Morale Support Fund Coun., USAR, Faribault, Minn., 1990, retention NCO, 1992; mentor for mentor Big Bros./Big Sister, 1998. With USAR, 1986—99, Air Nat. Guard, 1999—. Recipient David Stumpf Aviation scholarship Winona Tech. Coll., 1993, Equity Program scholarship Winona Tech. Coll., 1994. Mem. Ass. Women in Aviation Maintenance, Women in Aviation, Profl. Aviation Maintenance Assn., Toastmasters (treas. 1995), Vo-Tec Honor Soc. Avocations: weight lifting, aerobics, skiing, reading, promoting non-traditional careers for women. Home: 5413 N Cloquet Rd Duluth MN 55810-2151 Office: Northwest Airlines 4600 Stebner Rd Duluth MN 55803-8201

REGAN, MARIE CARBONE, retired language educator; b. Massena, N.Y., July 18, 1936; d. Dominick Carbone, Josephine Trimboli; m. Robert John Regan; children: Shawn, Denise, Gavin, Bridget, Stephanie. BA, SUNY, Albany, 1957; MA, SUNY, Potsdam, 1977. Tchr. English Massena H.S., 1957—60; prof. English SUNY, Canton, 1970—97; ret., 1997. Exec. com. faculty senate SUNY, Albany, 1987—93; evaluator curriculum for two-yr. coll. liberal arts offerings N.Y. State Edn. Dept., Albany, 1990—95. Mem. econ. devel. com. Town of Potsdam, 1994—, dep. town supr., 1994—; com. mem. St. Lawrence County Dem.s, 1994—; edn. alumni bd. SUNY, Potsdam, 2000—; dir. St. Lawrence Valley Tchrs. Ctr., Canton, NY, 1989—90; trustee St. Mary's Ch., Potsdam, 1993—95; vol. Alliance for Mcpl. Power, St. Lawrence County, NY, 1996—. Named Disting. Faculty, SUNY-Canton, 1989; recipient Disting. Svc. Prof., SUNY, 1990. Mem.: AAUW (bd. dirs. St. Lawrence County br., chmn. 1999—2001), Inst. for Learning in Retirement (founding mem., v.p. 2000—01). Democrat. Roman Catholic. Avocations: reading, dance, cooking. Home: 6869 State Hwy 56 Potsdam NY 13676

REGAN GOSSAGE, MURIEL, librarian; b. N.Y.C., July 15, 1930; d. William and Matilda (Riebel) Blome; m. Robert Regan, 1966 (div. 1976); 1 child, Jeanne Booth; m. Wayne Gossage, 2003. BA, Hunter Coll., N.Y.C., 1950; MLS, Columbia U., 1952; MBA, Pace U., N.Y.C., 1982. Post libr. US Army, Okinawa, 1952-53; researcher P.F. Collier, N.Y.C., 1953-57; asst. libr. to libr. Rockefeller Found., N.Y.C., 1957-67; dep. chief libr. Manhattan Community Coll., N.Y.C., 1967-68; libr. Booz Allen & Hamilton, N.Y.C., 1968-69, Rockefeller Found., N.Y.C., 1969-82; prin. Gossage Regan Assocs., Inc., N.Y.C., 1980-95; pub. svcs. libr. Carlsbad (N.Mex.) Pub. Libr., 1995-2000. Dir. N.Y. Met. Reference and Rsch. Libr. Agy., 1988-95, Coun. Nat. Libr. and Info. Assns., 1991-95; cons. Librs. Info. Ctrs., Gossage Sager Assocs., 2001—. Elder First Presbyn. Ch. of Carlsbad, 1997-99, Stephan min., 2000—, deacon, 2002-03. Mem. Spl. Librs. Assn. pres. 1989-90), Archons of Colophon. Avocations: cats, reading, playing piano, traveling. Home: 604 N Lake St Carlsbad NM 88220-5014 E-mail: murielregan@hotmail.com.

REGAN-STANTON, CHRISTA MARIA, artist; b. Stuttgart, Germany, Dec. 30, 1930; arrived in U.S., 1952; d. Friedrich Wilhelm and Anna Katharina (Schiller) Hohnhausen; m. James Allen Stanton (dec.); m. James Dale Regan, Apr. 27, 1955 (div. 1983); children: Jessica Ute, Jeffrey William. M Interpretive Dance, Tanzmeister Sch. Vock, Stuttgart, Germany, 1950. Tchr. Christa Studio Dance, Stuttgart, Germany, Athens, Ohio, 1952—54, Miami U., 1955—56; mgr. Treehouse Gallery, Oak Ridge, Tenn., 1983—95; studio potter Oak Ridge, Tenn. Bd. dirs. Upstairs Gallery, Oak Ridge, Tenn.; show dir. Foothills Craft Guild, Oak Ridge, Tenn., 1985. Recipient Honorable Mention award, Oak Ridge Mus. Fine Arts, 1982, First Place award, 1983, Second Place award, 1985. Mem.: Nat Mus. Women in Arts, Southern Highland Crafts Guild, Tenn. Arts and Crafts Assn., Am. Craft Coun., Foothills Craft Guild. Home: 119 Cooper Cir Oak Ridge TN 37830-7156

REGES, MARIANNA ALICE, marketing executive; b. Budapest, Hungary, Mar. 23, 1947; arrived in U.S., 1956, naturalized, 1963; d. Otto H. and Alice M. Reges; children: Rebecca, Charles III. AAS with honors, Fashion Inst. Tech., N.Y.C., 1967; BBA magna cum laude, Baruch Coll., 1971, MBA in Stats., 1978. Media rsch. analyst Doyle, Dane, Bernbach Advt., N.Y.C., 1967—70; rsch. supr. Sta. WCBS-TV, N.Y.C., 1970—71; rsch. mgr. Woman's Day mag., N.Y.C., 1971—72; asst. media dir. Benton & Bowles Advt., N.Y.C., 1972—75; mgr. rsch. and sales devel. NBC Radio, N.Y.C., 1975—77; sr. rsch. mgr. Ziff-Davis Pub. Co., N.Y.C., 1977—84; media mgr. Bristol-Myers Squibb Co., 1984—2001, Procter & Gamble Co., 2001—. Mem. Spanish Radio Adv. Coun., N.Y.C., 1986—88, Pan-European TV Audience Rsch. Mgmt. Com., 1988—. Mem. advisor Baruch Coll. Advt. Soc., 1975—; active First Presbyn. Ch., N.Y.C. Mem.: Advt. Rsch. Found., Radio and TV Rsch. Coun., Media Rsch. Dirs. Assn., Am. Advt. Fedn., Am. Mktg. Assn., Anthroposophical Soc., Nature Conservancy, Baruch Alumni Assn., Gilda's Club, Beta Gamma Sigma. Home: 626 E 20th St New York NY 10009-1509

REGIER, ELAINE ROXANNE, elementary school educator, school librarian; b. Oklahoma City, May 12, 1957; d. Dale Gene and Phyllis (Harms) R. BS in Edn., Southwestern Okla. State U., 1980; M in Libr. and Info. Studies, U. Okla., 1999. Cert. libr. media specialist Okla., lic. pvt. pilot lic. 1988. Tchr. kindergarten Anadarko (Okla.) Pub. Schs., 1980—84, tchr. pre-1st grade, 1984—98, tchr. 1st grade, 1998—99; libr. media specialist Wiley Post Elem. Sch., Oklahoma City, 1999—. Vol. U.S. Olympic Festival, Yukon, Okla., 1989, Anadarko Community Libr., 1990; jmem. ch. choir, Celebration Ringers, 2001—. Recipient Excellence in Aviation Edn. award Gen. Aviation Mfr. Assn., 1992; named Okla. Aerospace Educator of Yr., Okla. Aerospace Edn. Assn., 1994-95. Mem. Assn. Profl. Okla. Educators, Ninety-Nines, Delta Kappa Gamma (sec. 1987-90, 2d v.p. 1990-92), Okla. Pilots Assn. Methodist. Avocations: flying, snow skiing, sewing, reading, computers. Office: Wiley Post Elem Sch 6920 W Britton Rd Oklahoma City OK 73132

REGIS, SUSAN, food service executive; b. N.H. Grad., Skidmore Coll. Worked with Lydia Shire Seasons restaurant, 1983; opened Four Seasons Hotel, Beverly Hills, Calif.; exec. chef Biba, Boston, Pignoli, Boston. Named Best Chef in Boston, Improper Bostonian, Am.'s Best Chef N.E., James Beard Found., 1998. Office: Biba 272 Boylston St Boston MA 02116

REGISTER, ANNETTE ROWAN, reading educator; b. Doctors Inlet, Fla., Apr. 5, 1931; d. Ernest Ambors and Frances Perlena (Monroe) R.; Henry Ira Register, Oc. 31, 1954; 1 child, Andrew Henry. RN, Grnville Gen.Hosp.Sch.of Nursi, Greenville, 1948-51; BS, Tex. Woman's U., Denton, 1954; MEd, U. Fla., Gainesville, 1959; SEd, Fla. State U., 1983; student, U. West Fla., Okaloosa Walton C.C. Instrn. dir. nursing edn. Alachua Gen. Hosp., Gainesville, Fla., 1955-57; pub. sch. tchr. Okaloosa County, Ft. Walton Beach, Fla., 1966-93. V.p., Internation Training in Communication Ft. Walton Beach, Fla.; active Inst. Sr. Profls. Okaloosa Walton C.C. Pres. Okaloosa Reading Coun., 1976—80; mem. Okaloosa Walton C.C. Symphony Guild, 1998—; pres. United Meth. Women, Ft. Walton Beach, Fla., 1985—87; dist. v.p. Mem. Fla. C. of C. (amb. 1996—), Phi Delta Kappa (1st v.p.). Methodist. Avocations: crafts, painting, sketching, grandmothering, traveling. Office: Okaloosa County Sch Bd 10 Lowery Pl SE Fort Walton Beach FL 32548 E-mail: registerannette@yahoo.com.

REGN FRAHER, BONNIE, special education educator; BA, U. Calif., Santa Cruz, 1978; EdS, Rutgers U., 1982, MA, 1983. Cert. tchr. of the handicapped, cert. elem. tchr. Tchr. Search Day Program, Wanamassa, NJ, 1978-87; v.p. Fin-Addict Charters, Wall, NJ, 1987-93; v.p., dir. fin. William Cook Custom Homes, Wall, 1987-95; v.p. Archtl. Woodworking, 1993-95; tchr. Elmcrest Hosp., 1996—2003; daycare owner Fraher Acad., West Hartford, Conn., 1996—2003; tchr. West Hartford (Conn.) Sch. Dist., 2003—. Mem. Autism Soc. Am., Am. Sailing Assn., Long Branch Ski Club. Avocation: writing.

REGUEIRO-REN, ALICIA, biomedical researcher; b. Madrid, Oct. 31, 1967; came to U.S., Jan. 1995. d. Joaquin Regueiro and Alicia Miguelez; m. Rex. X.-F. Ren, Dec. 27, 1995. BSc, U. La Laguna, Santa Cruz de Tenerife, Spain, 1990, PhD, 1994. Fulbright postdoctoral fellow Columbia U., N.Y.C., 1995-98; rsch. investigator I Bristol Myers Squibb, NJ, 1998—99, rsch. investigator II, 1999—2001, sr. rsch. investigator I, biomed. investigator, 2001—. Contbr. articles to profl. jours.; patentee in field. Mem. AAAS, Am. Chem. Soc., Sigma Xi. Roman Catholic. Avocations: traveling, reading. Home: 69 Greenview Ter Middletown CT 06457-8738 Office: Bristol Myers Squibb 5 Research Pkwy Wallingford CT 06492-1951 Fax: 203-677-7202. E-mail: alicia.regueiroren@bms.com.

REHA, ROSE KRIVISKY, retired finance educator; b. N.Y.C., Dec. 17, 1920; d. Boris and Freda (Gerstein) Krivisky; m. Rudolph John Reha, Apr. 11, 1941; children; Irene Gale, Phyllis. BS in Bus. and Music Edn., Ind. State U., 1965; MA in Bus. and Psychology, U. Minn., 1967, PhD in Ednl. Psychology and Counseling, 1971. With U.S. and State Civil Svc., 1941-63; tchr. pub. schs., Minn., 1965-66; teaching assoc., instr. U. Minn., Mpls., 1966-68, 68-85; prof. coll. bus. St. Cloud (Minn.) State U., 1968-85, prof. emeritus, 1985—, chmn. bus. edn. & office adminstrn. dept., 1982-83. Advisor Small Bus. Inst., 1972-85, SBA, 1972-85; ct. advocate for women in distress St. Cloud Women's Shelter, 1986-89; adj. prof. profl. and bus. comm. Fla. Atlantic U., Boca Raton, Fla., 1989-90; substitute tchr. Broward County, 1990—; tutor (reading) Lauderdale, Fla., 1990-92; moderator, counselor Posnack Jewish Cmty. Ctr., Davie, Fla.; lectr. in com. Soref Jewish Cmty. Ctr. Continuing Edn. for sr. groups, Sunrise, Fla., 1994—; cons., lectr. in field; small bus. cons. Small Bus. Inst. Coll. Bus. St. Cloud St. U. Minn. Reviewer of bus. comm. and consumer edn. textbooks. Contbr. articles to profl. jours. Camp dir. Girl Scouts U.S., 1960-62; active various cmty. fund drives; sec., mem. relicensure rev. Com. Minn. Bd. Teaching Continuing Edn., 1984-85. Recipient Achievement award St. Cloud State U., 1985, St. Cloud State U. Rsch. and Faculty Improvement grantee, 1973, 78, 83. Mem. Am. Vocat. Assn. (cert.), Am. Counseling Assn. (cert.), Am. Mental Health Counselors Assn. (cert.), Minn. Econ. Assn., Minn. Women of Higher Edn., NEA, Minn. Edn. Assn. (pres. women's caucus 1981-83, award 1983), St. Cloud U. Faculty Assembly (pres. 1975-76), St. Cloud State U. Grad. Coun. (chmn. 1983-85), Fifty-five-plus Sr. Group (moderator North Broward, Ft. Lauderdale moderation counselor for PWP Chptr., 1994-97), Pi Omega Pi (sponsor St. Cloud State U. chpt. 1982-85), Phi Chi Theta, Delta Pi Epsilon, Delta Kappa Gamma. Jewish. Home: Apt 465 3671 Environ Blvd Fort Lauderdale FL 33319-4221 Office: Coll Bus St Cloud State U Saint Cloud MN 56301

REHBERG, KITTY, state legislator; b. Cedar Rapids, Iowa, Oct. 16, 1938; m. Franklin Rehberg; 3 children. Student, Rowly C.C. Mem. Iowa Senate from 14th dist., Des Moines, 1996—; mem. appropriations com., mem. rules and adminstrn. com.; vice chair edn. com.; mem. natural resources and environment com. Republican. Office: State Capitol 9th And Grand Ave Des Moines IA 50319-0001 E-mail: kitty_rehberg@legis.state.ia.us.

REHM, SUSAN, physician; b. 1954; BS, U. Nebr., 1975; MD, U. Nebr., Omaha, 1978. Diplomate Am. Bd. Internal Medicine with subspecialty in infectious disease. Resident in internal medicine The Cleve. Clinic Found., 1978—81, fellow in infectious diseases, 1981—83, assoc. chief of staff, 1997—. Clin. asst. prof. Case Western Res. U., Cleve.; clin. assoc. prof. Ohio State U., Columbus. Mem.: AMA, ACP, Am. Coll. Physician Execs., Infectious Diseases Soc. Am., Am. Soc. Microbiology, Nat. Found. for Infectious Diseases (pres.). Office: The Cleveland Clinic 9500 Euclid Ave Cleveland OH 44195

REHNKE, MARY ANN, academic administrator; b. Faribault, Minn., Jan. 23, 1945; d. Wesley Arthur and Sarah Frances (Smith) Rehnke; m. Charles Orin Willis, Apr. 18, 1924. BA in English, Cornell Coll., 1967; MA in English, U. Chgo., 1968, PhD in Lit., 1974; MS in Ednl Adminstrn., U. Wis., 1975. Head resident Elizabeth Waters Hall, U. Wis., Madison, 1970-73; asst. prof. English No. Ky. U., Highland Heights, 1973-82, acad. adminstr., 1976-77, dir. summer sessions, 1977-80; dir. conf. planning Am. Assn. Higher Edn., Washington, 1980-82; assoc. dean for faculty relations and acad. programs Coll. St. Catherine, St. Paul, 1982-83; assoc. dean of coll. Daemen Coll., Buffalo, N.Y., 1983-85; v.p. ann. programs Council of Ind. Colls., Washington, 1986—. Mem. planning com. nat. identification program Am. Council Edn., Washington, 1978-85; mem. program com. Nat. Conf. Women Student Leaders and Women of Distinction, Washington, 1985-88. Author: Women in Higher Education Administration: A Brief Guide for Conference Planners, 1982, Guide to Spiritual Retreats in the Washington, D.C. Area, 1997; editor: Creating Career Programs in a Liberal Arts Context, 1987; editor newsletter N. Ctrl. Regional Women's Studies, 1978-80; columnist Teaching and Learning, The Independent. Vestry mem Ch. of St. Clement, Alexandria, Va., 1982, vice chair search com., 1986-87. Named one of Outstanding Young Women Am., 1976. Mem. Am. Assn. Higher Edn. (coordinator nat. conf. roundtable 1982-86), Nat. Assn. Women Deans, Adminstrs. and Counselors, N.Am. Assn. Summer Sessions (rsch. chair 1979-80), Soc. for Values in Higher Edn., Jane Austen Soc. N.Am., Phi Beta Kappa, Phi Delta Kappa. Democrat. Episcopalian.

REHNQUIST, JANET, federal agency administrator; Grad., U. Va.; JD, U. Va. Law School. Assoc. counsel to the pres., 1990—93; asst. U.S. atty. Ea. Dist. Va.; inspector gen. Dept. HHS, Washington, 2001—03. Counsel U.S. Senate Permanent Subcom. on Investigations.

REHORN, LOIS M(ARIE) (LOIS MARIE SMITH), nursing administrator; b. Larned, Kans., Apr. 15, 1919; d. Charles and Ethel L. (Canaday) Williamson; m. C. Howard Smith, Feb. 15, 1946 (dec. Aug. 1980); 1 child, Cynthia A. Huddleston; m. Harlan W. Rehorn, Aug. 25, 1981. RN, Bethany Hosp. Sch. Nursing, Kansas City, Kans., 1943; BS, Ft. Hays Kans. State U., Hays, 1968, MS, 1970. RN, N.Mex.; lic. pvt. pilot. Office nurse, surg. asst. Dr. John H. Luke, Kansas City, Kans., 1943-47; supr. nursing unit Larned (Kans.) State Hosp., 1949-68, dir. nursing edn., 1968-71, dir. nursing, 1972-81, ret., 1981. Recipient Order of the Blue Key, 1942-43; named Nurse of Yr. DNA-4, 1986. Mem. Am. Nurses Assn., Kans. Nurses Assn. (dist. treas.), N.Mex. Nurses Assn. (dist. pres. 1982-86, dist. bd. dirs. 1986-88). Avocation: flying (pilot). Home: 1436 Brentwood Dr Clovis NM 88101-4602

REHR, HELEN, social worker; b. NYC, Dec. 16, 1919; d. Philip and Rose (Stern) R. BA, Hunter Coll., 1940; DSc (hon.), CUNY, 1995; MS, Columbia U., 1943, DSW, 1970. Social worker, asst. dir. Sydenham Hosp., N.Y.C., 1943-45; supr. Grasslands Hosp., Valhalla, N.Y., 1945-47; asst. prof. medicine NYU Bellevue Med. Ctr., N.Y.C., 1947-51; med. soc. cons. Dept. Health, Maternal & Child Health, N.Y.C., 1951-52; assoc. dir. Mt. Sinai Med. Ctr., N.Y.C., 1954—70, dir., 1971—89, Edith J. Baerwald prof. cmty. medicine, 1971—89, prof. cmty. med. emerita, 1998—. Dir. Israel/Australia Leadership Project, 1986—; vis. prof. U. Flinders, U. Melbourne, Australia, 1990, Ben Gurion U., Israel, 1991; Kenneth Pray vis. prof. U. Pa., Phila., 1979-80; cons. Mt. Sinai, 1986—. Author, editor books, jour. and articles in field; mem. editl. bd. Social Work in Health Care, Health and Social Work. Bd. dirs. N.Y. Found., Ctr. for Study of Social Work Practice/Columbia U., Joint Commn. on Accreditation of Hosps.; mem. adv. bd. scholarship and welfare fund Hunter Coll., Jewish Bd. Family Chns Svc. Named Disting. Practitioner, Nat. Acad. Practice; named to hall of fame Hunter Coll., 1978, Columbia U. Sch. Social Work, 1998; recipient Ida M. Cannon award Soc. SW Dir., 1975, Knee-Wittman Lifetime Achievement award NASW, 1990. Fellow: Brookdale Ctr. Aging, NY Acad. Medicine, Gerontol. Soc. Avocation: gardening. Home: 27 W 96th St # 6C New York NY 10025-6515 Office: Mt Sinai Med Ctr 1 Gustave L Levy Pl New York NY 10029-6500

REIBMAN, JEANETTE FICHMAN, retired state senator; b. Ft. Wayne, Ind., Aug. 18, 1915; d. Meir and Pearl (Schwartz) Fichman; m. Nathan L. Reibman, June 20, 1943; children: Joseph M. Edward D., James E. AB, Hunter Coll., 1937; LLB, U. Ind., 1940; LLD, Lafayette Coll., 1969; hon. degree, Lehigh U., 1986, Wilson Coll., 1974, Cedar Crest Coll., 1977, Moravian Coll., 1990. Bar: Ind., 1940, U.S. Supreme Ct. 1944. Pvt. practice law, Ft. Wayne, 1940; atty. U.S. War Dept., Washington, 1940-42, U.S. War Prodn. Bd., Washington, 1942-44; mem. Pa. Ho. of Reps., 1956-66, Pa. State Senate, Harrisburg, 1966-94, chmn. com. on edn., 1971-81, minority chmn., 1981-90, majority caucus adminstr., 1992-94. Mem. Edn. Commn. of the States. Trustee emeritus Lafayette Coll.; bd. mem. Pa. Higher Edn. Assistance Agy., Pa. Coun. on Arts, Camphill Schs. Recipient Disting. Dau. of Pa. award and medal Gov. Pa., 1968, citation on naming of Jeanette F. Reibman Adminstrn. Bldg., East Stroudsburg State Coll., 1972, Early Childhood Learning Ctr. Northampton Community Coll., 1992, Pub. Svc. award Pa. Psychol. Assn., 1977, Jerusalem City of Peace award Govt. Israel, 1977; named to Hunter Coll. Alumni Hall of Fame, 1974; U. Ind. Law Alumni fellow, 1993. Mem. Hadassah (Myrtle Wreath award 1976), Sigma Delta Tau, Delta Kappa Gamma, Phi Delta Kappa, Order Ea. Star. Democrat. Jewish. Office: 711 Lehigh St Easton PA 18042-4325 Home: 1332 Kirkland Village Cir Bethlehem PA 18017-4759

REICH, DENISE ELIZABETH, writer, researcher; b. Pozzuoli, Italy, Nov. 7, 1976; BA, Marymount Manhattan Coll., 1999. Freelance writer, artist, rschr., 1992—; editor, rschr., interviewer, writer Children's Express, N.Y.C., 1994—96; editor, translator, spokeswoman Bur. of Young GRAPEs, N.Y.C., 1995—96; choreographer, dance capt. Ujammaa Theater, N.Y.C., 1997—99; disc jockey UCT Radio, Cape Town, South Africa, 2000. Mem. exec. adv. bd. Young Media Partners, N.Y.C. Co-author, illustrator We're In Print! The Whole Story by Kids for Kids; contbr. articles to mags. Recipient hon. mention, City Coll. Poetry Festival, 1993, cert. of merit for excellence in writing, N.Y.C. Assn. Tchrs. of English, 1994; Peggy Deane Meml. scholar, Mensa Edn. and Rsch. Found., 1996. Mem.: Nat. Writers' Union. Zen Anglican. Avocations: ballet, gymnastics, music, swimming, travel. Personal E-mail: dreich@webmail.co.za.

REICH, JILL, dean; B.A., Regis College; Ph. D. in Psychology, Dartmouth Coll. Fmr. dept. chair, assoc. dean Grad. school Loyola; fmr. dean of faculty Trinity College; fmr. exec. dir. of education American Psychology Assoc.; prof., dept. of psychology Bates Coll., v.p. of academic affairs, dean of faculty, 2000—. Office: Bates Coll Lane Hall Rm 120A 2 Andrews Rd Lewiston ME 04240

REICH, VICTORIA J. consumer products company executive; b. Southborough, Mass., 1958; BS in Applied Math. and Econs., Brown U. With GE Co.; v.p., contr. Brunswick Corp., Lake Forest, Ill., 1996-2000, sr. v.p., CFO, 2000—. Office: Brunswick Corp 1 N Field Ct Lake Forest IL 60045-4811

REICHBLUM, AUDREY ROSENTHAL, public relations executive, publishing executive; b. Pitts., June 28, 1935; d. Emanuel Nathan and Willa (Handmacher) Rosenthal; m. M. Charles Reichblum, Jan. 25, 1956; children: Robert Nathan, William Mark. Student, Bennington Coll., 1952-53; BS, Carnegie Mellon U., 1956. Founder, creator, chmn. Pitts. Children's Mus., 1970-73; mag. writer Pitts. Mag., 1978; dir. pub. rels. Pitts. Pub. Theater, 1978-79; pres. arPR audrey reichblum PUB. RELS. inc., Pitts., 1980—, arpr, inc., 1996—; pub. "Knowledge in a Nutshell" Series, 1996—99, "The Edible Game A Smart Cookie", 1996—, "Sweet Smarts The Candy With A Brain", 2004. Pub. rels. cons., bd. mem. Pitts. Planned Parenthood, 1980-84, United Jewish Fedn., Bus. and Profl. Women, Pitts., 1980-85, Pitts. City Theater, 1985-94, Pa. Coun. on Aging, 1996—; chmn. Villa de Marillac Nursing, 1999, Vincencian Collaborative Svcs. Bd. Recipient Gold Cindy award Info. Film Producers Am., 1982, award of excellence Internat. Assn. Bus. Communicators, Pitts., 1986, Matrix award for Three Rivers Arts Festival, Lifetime Achievement award NAWBO-YWCA, Y-Tribute to Women in Comms. award, 1998. Mem. Pub. Rels. Soc. Am. (accredited; award of merit 1983, G. Victor Barkman award for excellence 1984, 1st place award Race For The Cure), Women in Comm. (Matrix-sales promotion award 1987), Nat. Assn. Women Bus. Owners (Life Time Achievement award 1995). Office: 1420 Centre Ave Ste 2213 Pittsburgh PA 15219-3536

REICHELT, SUSAN ANN, career and techical educator; b. Wisconsin Rapids, Wis., May 16, 1958; d. Robert Edgar Hamm, Marjorie Theresa Hamm; m. Blane Thomas Reichelt; 1 child, Kellee. BS, U. Wis., Stevens Point, 1980; MS, Fla. Tech., 1994; PhD, Iowa State U., 2001. Asst. prof. Ea. Ky. U., Richmond, 1997—99; supr. Zayed U., Dubai, United Arab Emirates, 1999—2000; asst. prof. Tex. Tech. U., Lubbock, 2000—. Recipient Outstanding Faculty award, Mortar Bd. Soc., 2001, Outstanding Dissertation Award, Am. Assn. of Family and Consumer Sci., 2002. Mem.: Assn. Career and Tech. Educators, Am. Assn. Family and Consumer Scis., Phi Upsilon Omicron. Avocations: travel, reading. Office: East Carolina U 261 Rivers Greenville NC 27858 Office Fax: 806-742-3042. Business E-Mail: sue.reichelt@ttu.edu.

REICHENBACH, LAURA JEAN, art educator; b. Marshfield, Wis. d. Albert and Mildred Perner. BA, MEd, U. Wis. Art educator Sparta (Wis.) Sch. Dist., 1992—97, Black River Falls (Wi.) Sch. Dist., 1997—. Chmn. Dept. Art Black River Falls (Wis.) Sch. Dist., 1999—. Mem. task force Wis. Dept. Planning Curriculum In Art And Design. Mem.: Onsin Art Edn. Assn. (rep. Wis. West Ctrl. 2000—), Nat. Wis. Art Edn. Assn. (assoc.; rep. West Ctrl. Region 2000—03), Golden Key Honor Soc. (life). Office: Black River Falls High School 1200 Pierce Street Black River Falls WI 54615

REICHGOTT JUNGE, EMBER D. former state senator, lawyer, writer, broadcast analyst, radio personality; b. Detroit, Aug. 22, 1953; d. Norbert Arnold and Diane (Pincich) Reichgott; m. Michael Junge. BA summa cum laude, St. Olaf Coll., Minn., 1974; JD, Duke U., 1977; MBA, U. St. Thomas, 1991. Bar: Minn. 1977, D.C. 1978. Assoc. Larkin, Hoffman, Daly & Lindgren, Bloomington, Minn., 1977-84; counsel Control Data Corp., Bloomington, Minn., 1984-86; ptnr. The Gen. Counsel, Ltd., 1987—; mem. Minn. State Senate, 1983-2000, chmn. legis. com. on econ. status of women, 1984-86, vice chmn. senate edn. com., 1987-88, senate majority whip, 1990-94, chmn. property tax divsn. senate tax com., 1991-92, chmn. senate judiciary com., 1993-94, senate asst. majority leader, 1995-2000, chmn. spl. subcom. on ethical conduct. Dem. endorsed candidate Minn. Atty. Gen., 1998; instr. polit. sci. St. Olaf Coll., Northfield, Minn., 1993; bd. dirs. Citizens Ind. Bank, St. Louis Park, Minn. Host cable TV monthly series Legis. Report, 1985-92. State co-chair Clinton/Gore Presdl. Campaign, Minn. Dem. Farmer-Labor Party, 1992, 1996; del. Nat. Dem. Conv., 1984, 1992, 1996; pres. Minn. Women's Polit. Caucus, 2002—04; trustee, bd. dirs. N.W. YMCA, New Hope, Minn., 1983—88, United Way Mpls., 1989—, Greater Mpls. ARC, 1988—, chair, 2001—03. Recipient Woman of Yr. award North Hennepin Bus. and Profl. Women, 1983, award for contbn. to human svcs. Minn. Social Svcs. Assn., 1983, Clean Air award Minn. Lung Assn., 1988, Disting. Svc. award Mpls. Jaycees, 1984, Minn. Dept. Human Rights award, 1989, Myra Bradwell award Minn. Women Lawyers, 1993, Disting. Alumnae award Lake Conf. Schs., 1993, Disting. Alumnae award St. Olaf Coll., 1998, awards for leadership Am. Lung Assn., 1999, Am. Heart Assn., 1997, Everyday Hero award Up with People, 1995, Unsung Hero award United Way of Mpls., 1999, 1st recipient of award named in her honor for prevention of sexual assault, 2000; charter inductee Robbinsdale H.S. Hall of Fame, 2000; author of Minn. charter sch. law, winner of "2000 Innovations in Am. Govt. award" Harvard U. and Ford Found., others; named One of ten Outstanding Young Minnesotans, Minn. Jaycees, 1984, Policy Adv. of Yr., NAWBO, 1988, Woman of Achievement, Twin West C. of C., 1989, Marvelous Minn. Woman, 1993; youngest woman ever elected to Minn. Senate, 1983. Mem. Minn. Bar Assn. (bd. govs. 1992-96, Pro Bono Publico Atty. award 1990), Hennepin County Bar Assn., Corp. Counsel Assn. (v.p. 1989-96). Home: 7701 48th Ave N Minneapolis MN 55428-4515 Fax: 763-536-1447. E-mail: emberrj@msn.com.

REICHHELD, DEBORAH ANN, secondary school educator; b. Cleve., Feb. 23, 1947; d. John James Pechman Jr. and Ethel M. Pechman; m. Charles A. Reichheld III, Aug. 23, 1969; children: Jennifer Lindsey, Elizabeth Ashley, Deborah Whitney, Chase. BA, Moskingum Coll., 1969; MA Spanish, Kent State U., 1974. Tchr. high sch. Parma City Schs., Ohio, 1969—, dept. chair, 1972—82, 1998—. Scholar, Muskingum Coll., New Concord, Ohio, 1965—69. Mem.: NEA, Parma Edn. Assn., Ohio Edn. Assn., Phi Sigma Iota, United Ch. Of Christ. Avocations: tennis, aerobics, crafts, baseball. Home: 3313 Hamilton Rd Medina OH 44256 Office: Normandy High Sch 2500 W Pleasant Valley Rd Parma OH 44256

REICHL, RUTH MOLLY, editor; b. N.Y.C., Jan. 16, 1948; d. Ernst and Miriam and (Brudno) R.; m. Douglas Wilder Hollis, Sept. 5, 1970 (div. 1985); m. Michael Singer, 1985; 1 child, Nicholas Singer. BA, U. Mich., 1968, MA in History of Art, 1970. Chef, owner The Swallow Restaurant, Berkeley, Calif., 1973-77; food writer, editor New West mag., San Francisco, 1978-84; editor restaurant column L.A. Times, 1984-93, food editor, 1990-93; restaurant critic N.Y. Times, 1993-99; editor-in-chief Gourmet Mag., 1999—. Author: Mmmm: A Feastiary, 1972, The Contest Book, 1977, Tender at the Bone: Growing Up at the Table, 1998, Comfort Me with Apples: More Adventures at the Table, 2001; editor: Modern Library Food Series, 2000—, Endless Feasts: Sixty Years of Writing from Gourmet, 2002, Remembrance of Things Past, 2004, The Gourmet Cookbook, 2004. Office: 4 Times Sq New York NY 10036-6518 E-mail: ruth.reichl@gourmet.com.

REICHMANIS, ELSA, chemist; b. Melbourne, Victoria, Australia, Dec. 9, 1953; arrived in U.S., 1962; d. Peteris and Nina (Meiers) R.; m. Francis Joseph Purcell, June 2, 1979; children: Patrick William, Elizabeth Anne, Edward Andrew, Thomas Alexander. BS in Chemistry, Syracuse U., 1972, PhD in Chemistry, 1975. Postdoctoral intern Syracuse (N.Y.) U., 1975-76, Chaim Weizmann rsch. fellow, 1976-78; mem. tech. staff AT&T Bell Labs., Murray Hill, N.J., 1978-84, supr. radiation sensitive materials and applications, 1984-94, head organic and polymer materials, 1994-95; head polymer and organic materials Lucent Techs., Bell Labs., New Providence, NJ, 1996—2000, dir. materials rsch., 2001—. Panel on advanced materials. Japanese Tech. Evaluation Prog., NSF, Washington, 1986, com. to survey materials. rsch. opportunities and needs for electronic industry Nat. Rsch. Coun., 1986, Nat. Materials Adv. Bd., 1993-98, U.S. Nat. Com. for Internat. Union for Pure and Applied Chemistry, 1996-2001. Editor: The Effects of Radiation on High Tech Polymers, 1989, Polymers in Microlithography, 1989, Irradiation of Polymer Materials, 1993, Microelectronics Technology: Polymers for Advanced Imaging and Packaging, 1995, Micro and Nano Patterning Polymers, 1998; patentee in field; assoc. editor Chemistry of Materials, 1996—; contbr. numerous articles to profl. jours. Recipient Soc. of Women Engrs. Achievement award, 1993, Engring. Materials award ASM, 1996, Arents Pioneer medal Syracuse U., 2001. Fellow: AAAS; mem.: IEEE, Soc. Women Engrs., Am. Phys. Soc., Soc. for Photo-optical Engrs., Soc. Chem. Industry (Perkin medal 2001), Am. Chem. Soc. (mem.-at-large 1986—90, sec. 1991—92, polymer materials sci. and engring. divsn. 1991—, vice chair 1993, chair-elect 1994, chmn. 1995, pres.-elect 2002, pres. 2003, award in applied polymer sci. 1999), Nat. Acad. Engring. (elected mem.). Avocations: music, reading, needlepoint.

REID, DEBORAH E. director; d. Geraldine O. Reid. BS, John Jay Coll. Criminal Justice, 1987; MA, John Jay Coll. of Criminal Justice, 1991. Account exec. Pvt. Industry Coun., N.Y.C., 1985—91; sr. account exec. Consortium for Worker Edn., N.Y.C., 1991—93; mgr. regional tng. ctr. Covenant Ho. N.Y., N.Y.C., 1993—97; asst. dir. Bklyn (N.Y.) Coll. CUNY, Bklyn., 1997—2000; dir. employment svcs. The Salvation Army, N.Y.C., 2001—02; dir. Ctr. Profl. Devel. Fedn. of Protestant Welfare Agys., N.Y.C., 2002—. Educator Sunset Pk. Adult and Family Edn. Ctr., Bklyn., 2000—; tchr. United Cmty. Ctrs., Bklyn., 1998—2001. Author: (manual) Job Preparation Techniques, 1992, (curriculum) Teaching Tolerance: Activities, Lessons, Projects for Life, 2003. Chmn. alumni and friends assn. Coun. for Unity, Inc., Bklyn., 1999; mem. scholarship com. Weil Gotshal and Manges Found., N.Y.C., 1996; founding mem. Village Helpers Group, Bklyn., 1997. Scholar, United Fedn. Tchrs., 1983—87. Office: Federation of Protestant Welfare Agys 281 Park Avenue South New York NY 10010 E-mail: dreid@fpwa.org.

REID, DESIRÉE ANDRÉA, forensic scientist; b. Jersey City, Feb. 4, 1965; d. John Robert and Virginia Claire (Donnarumma) R. BS in Forensic Sci., John Jay Coll. Criminal Justice, 1988. Asst. chemist Union County Prosecutor's Office, Westfield, N.J., 1988-89; forensic scientist N.J. State Police North Lab., Little Falls, 1989—. Pub. spkr. N.J. State Polic., 1989—. Author of profl. papers in field. Fellow Am. Bd. Criminalistics (diplomate); mem. Am. Acad. Forensic Scientists, So. Assn. Forensic Scientists, North Ea. Assn. Forensic Scientists (chair drug analysis sect. 1998, 99). Roman Catholic. Avocations: softball, volleyball, reading, kickboxing. Office: NJ State Police North Lab 1755 Rt 46 E Little Falls NJ 07424

REID, DONNA JOYCE, small business owner; b. Springfield, Tenn., June 25, 1954; d. Leonard Earl Reid and Joyce (Robertson) Kirby; m. Kenneth Bruce Sadler, June 26, 1976 (div. Apr. 1980); m. John Christopher Moulton, Oct. 18, 1987 (div. Dec. 1992); m. Peter Leatherland, Apr. 3, 1993. Student, Austin Peay State U., Clarksville, Tenn., 1972-75. Show writer, producer WTVF-TV (CBS affiliate), Nashville, 1977-83, promotion producer, 1983-85, on-air promotion mgr., 1985-86; gen. mgr. Steadi-Film Corp., Nashville, 1986-90; co-owner Options Internat., Nashville, 1990—2003, Shanti's, Inc., Hermitage, 2003—. Big sister Buddies of Nashville, 1981-87. Named to Honorable Order of Ky. Cols. John Y. Brown, Gov., 1980; recipient Significant Svc. award ARC, 1982, Clara Barton Communications award, 1983. Mem. NAFE, Nat. Assn. TV Arts and Scis., Nat. Film Inst., Nat. Assn. Broadcasters, Internat. Platform Assn., Am. Soc. Prevention of Cruelty to Animals, Humane Soc. U.S. Methodist. Avocations: reading, outdoor sports, travel. Office: Shantis Inc 4715 Andrew Jackson Pkwy Hermitage TN 37076

REID, FRANCES EVELYN KROLL, cinematographer, director, film company executive; b. Oakland, Calif., Mar. 25, 1944; d. William Farnham and Marion Storm (Teller) Kroll. BA, U. Oreg., 1966. Tchr. secondary sch., Los Angeles, 1968-69; sound recordist Churchill Films, Los Angeles, 1971; freelance sound recordist Los Angeles, 1972-75; freelance producer, dir., 1975-78; freelance cinematographer Berkeley, Calif., 1978—; pres. Iris Films, Berkeley, 1977—. Vol. Peace Corps, Malawi, Africa, 1969-70. Producer/dir. Long Night's Journey Into Day, 2000 (Grand Jury award Sundance 2000); dir. (film) In The Best Interests of the Children, 1977 (Blue Ribbon Am. Film Festival 1978), The Changer: A Record of the Times, 1991, Skin Deep, 1995, Talking About Race, 1994, Straight from the Heart, 1994 (Acad. award nominee 1995); cinematographer: (film) The Times of Harvey Milk, 1984 (Oscar 1985), Living with AIDS, 1986 (Student Acad. award 1987), Common Threads: Stories from the Quilt, 1989 (Oscar award 1990), Complaints of a Dutiful Daughter, 1994 (Acad. award nominee 1995). Mem. Film Arts Found., Assn. Ind. Video and Filmmakers, Acad. Motion Picture Arts and Scis. Office: Iris Films 2600 10th St # 413 Berkeley CA 94710-2522

REID, HELEN VERONICA, dean; b. Reading, Eng., Sept. 25, 1956; d. Alan A. and Teresa H. (Thatcher) Ware; m. Gary B. Reid, May 29, 1976; children: Robert, Jennifer, Kristen. BA in Biology, U. Tex., 1976; BSN, U. Tex., Arlington, 1978; MSN, Tex. Women's U., 1983; EdD, U. North Tex., 2000. CCRN, 1980; cert. CPR instr. Asst. nurse coord., staff nurse, float pool nurse Parkland Meml. Hosp., Dallas, 1979-83, float pool nurse, 1987-93; instr. Trinity Valley Community Coll., Kaufman, Tex., 1983-86, freshman team leader, 1986-90; dean health occupations Trinity Valley C.C., Kaufman, Tex., 1990—. Mem.: Tex. C.C. Tchrs. Assn., Nat. Orgn. ADN (pub. rels. dir. 1998—2002), Tex. Orgn. for ADN (sec. 1988—92, nominating com. chair 1995—96, pres.-elect 2002—03, pres. 2003—), Tex. Assn. Vocat. Nurse Educators, Phi Kappa Phi, Sigma Theta Tau. Home: 4332 Crestover Dr Mesquite TX 75150-4452 Office Phone: 972-932-4309. E-mail: reid@tvcc.edu.

REID, INEZ SMITH, lawyer, educator; b. New Orleans, Apr. 7, 1937; d. Sidney Randall Dickerson and Beatrice Virginia (Bundy) Smith. BA, Tufts U., 1959; LLB, Yale U., 1962; MA, UCLA, 1963; PhD, Columbia U., 1968. Bar. Calif. 1963, N.Y. 1972, D.C. 1980. Assoc. prof. Barnard Coll. Columbia U., N.Y.C., 1972-76; gen. counsel youth divsn. State of N.Y., 1976-77; dep. gen. counsel HEW, Washington, 1977-79; inspector gen. EPA, Washington, 1979-81; chief legis. and opinions, dep. corp. counsel Office of Corp. Counsel, Washington, 1981-83; corp. counsel D.C., 1983-85; counsel Laxalt, Washington, Perito & Dubuc, Washington, 1986-90, ptnr., 1990-91; counsel Graham & James, 1991-93, Lewis, White & Clay, P.C., 1994-95; assoc. judge D.C. Ct. Appeals, 1995—. William J. Maier, Jr. vis. prof. law W.Va. U. Coll. Law, Morgantown, 1985-86. Contbr. articles to profl. jours. and publs. Trustee emeritus Lancaster Sem., Pa., 2002—; bd. dirs. Homeland Ministries bd. United Ch. of Christ, N.Y.C., 1978—83, vice chmn., 1981—83; chmn. bd. govs. Antioch Law Sch., Washington, 1979—81; chmn. bd. trustees Antioch U., Yellow Springs, Ohio, 1981—82; trustee Tufts U., Medford, Mass., 1988—98, trustee emeritus, 1999—; trustee Lancaster (Pa.) Sem., 1988—2001; bd. govs. D.C. Sch. Law, 1990—96, chmn., 1991—95. Recipient Emily Gregory award Barnard Coll., 1976, Arthur Morgan award Antioch U., 1982, Service award United Ch. of Christ, 1983, Disting. Service (Profl. Life) award Tufts U. Alumni Assn., 1988. Office: DC Ct Appeals 500 Indiana Ave NW Fl 6 Washington DC 20001-2138

REID, JOAN EVANGELINE, lawyer, stockbroker; b. Mich., Apr. 22, 1932; d. August W. and Evangeline R. (Brozeau) Rogers; m. Belmont M. Reid. AA in Bus., San Jose State U., 1951; JD, McGeorge Sch. Law, 1989. Bar: Nev.; lic. realtor, life, disability and annuity ins. Officer, dir. Lifetime Fin. Planning Corp., San Jose, Calif., 1967-77, Lifetime Realty Corp., San Jose, 1967-77; co-founder, officer, dir. Belmont Reid & Co., Inc., San Jose, 1960-77; officer, corp. counsel, dir. JOBEL Fin. Inc., Carson City, Nev., 1980—. Past sec., treas. Nev. Fedn. Rep. Women; charter pres. Santa Clara Valley Rep. Women Federated. Paul Harris fellow Rotary. Mem. First Jud. Dist. Bar Assn., State Bar Nev., No. Nev. Women Lawyers Assn., Carson City C. of C., Soroptomist Carson City (past pres., sec.), Carson City Rep. Women's Club (past v.p.).

REID, KATHARINE LEE, museum director; d. Sherman E. and Ruth Lee; m. Bryan S. Reid. BA magna cum laude, Vassar Coll.; postgrad., Sorbonne, Paris, 1963, Instiut d'Art et Archaeologie, 1963; MFA, Harvard U., 1966. Mem. curatorial staff Toledo Mus. Art, David and Alfred Smart Mus., U. Chgo., Ackland Art Mus., U. NC, Chapel Hill; asst. dir. Art Inst. Chgo., 1982—86, dep. dir., 1986—91; dir. Va. Mus. Fine Arts., 1991—2000, Cleve. Mus. Art, 2000—. Bd. dirs. Van Gogh Mus., Amsterdam, Netherlands, Nat. Conf. Cmty. and Justice, Am. Fedn. Arts; chmn. vis. com. Frances Lehman Loeb Art Ctr., Vassar Coll., Poughkeepsie, NY. Fulbright scholar, 1963. Mem.: Am. Assn. Mus. (bd. dirs., former mem. accreditation commn.), Am. Assn. Mus. Dirs. (pres. 2000—01, trustee). Office: Cleve Mus Art 11150 East Blvd Cleveland OH 44106*

REID, KATHERINE LOUISE, artist, educator, author; b. Port Arthur, Tex., Mar. 25, 1941; d. Clifton Commodore and Helen Ross (Moore) Reid. BA, Baylor U., 1963; postgrad. in design and illustration, Kans. City Art Inst., 1964; MEd, U. Houston, 1973; cert. supervision, U. Houston-Clear Lake City, 1980; postgrad., San Jacinto Coll., 1982. Litho reprodn. artist Hallmark Cards, Kansas City, Mo., 1963-64; tchr. art high sch. Pasadena (Tex.) Ind. Sch. Dist., 1964-77, supr. art, gifted and talented and photography, 1977-85, supr. art and photography InterAct, 1985-90, instrnl. specialist, 1990-2000, photography and art, 1990-93, instrnl. specialist in art and spl. programs, 1993-96, rsch. planning, data disaggregation, 1996-2000; internet tchr. recruiter, 2001—02; mural artist Old Car Barn, Edna, Tex., 2000—. 4 MAT learning styles trainer DuPont Leadership Devel. Process Trainer, Selective Rsch., Inst., tchr. perceiver specialist, performance quality sys. trainer, coop. learning trainer, outcome based edn. trainer, integrated unit devel. and authentic assessment trainer The Greater Gulf Coast Adminstr. Assessment Project, Assessor, 1990-2000; head crafts, asst. dir., dir. summer, winter discovery program-ski camp Cheley Colo. Camps, Denver, Estes Park, 1967-75; mem. awards com. John Austin Cheley Found., 1990-92; staff artist, media workshop Tex. Edn. Agy., Austin, summer, 1961; art enrichment tchr. Port Arthur Ind. Sch. Dist. (Tex.), summer, 1961; head crafts Camp Waluta, Silsbee, Tex., summer, 1960; mem. Tex. Edn. Agy., Art Leadership Inst., 1989, 90, Tracking Rsch. Com., 1991, Core Strategic Planning Team, 1992-2000, Outcome Based Edn. Dist. Planning Com., 1991-92, Quality Sys. Improvement Team, 1991-92, Outcome Based Edn. Com. Exit Outcomes, 1991; Region IV data disk trainer, 1998-2000, target teach coord., 1993-2000, multiple intelligence trainer, 1997-2000, data disaggregation trainer, 1997-2000, supt.'s rsch. com., 1999. Author: Through Their Eyes, 1989; inventor, patentee Pet Car Seat, U.S.A. and Can. Mem. Friends of Fine Arts-Baylor U., Waco, Tex., 1981—; mem. Scholastic Art awards Regional Bd., Houston, 1978-84, Tex. Edn. Agy.; bd. dirs. Houston Coun. Student Art Awards, Inc., 1984-90. Named Outstanding Secondary Educator of Am., 1975, Tex. Art Educator of Yr., 1985. Mem. ASCD, Tex. ASCD, Tex. Art Edn. Assn. (rep. editor newsletter 1982-85, chmn. supervision divsn. 1982-83, v.p. membership 1978-80, chmn. pub. info. com., regional chmn. youth art month 1980-82; regional chmn. membership com. 1976-78, pres. elect 1986, sec. 1991-93), Tex. Alliance for Arts Edn. (bd. vice chmn. 1984-86, treas. 1988-90), Nat. Art Edn. Assn. (conv. com. 1977, 85), Tex. Assn. Sch. Adminstrs., Houston Art Edn. Assn. (sec. 1969), Tex. Ret. Tchrs. Assn. (Dist. IV historian 2001-03), Pasadena Area Ret. Sch. Employees (parliamentarian 2002—), Delta Kappa Gamma (2d v.p. 1984-86, pres. 2002-2004, state leadership devel. for chpt. pres. com., 2003-2005, state banner com., 2004). Baptist. Home: 106 Ravenhead Dr Houston TX 77034-1520 E-mail: artist@oldcarbarn.com., klreid@mail.esc4.com.

REID, LYNNE MCARTHUR, pathologist; b. Melbourne, Australia, Nov. 12, 1923; d. Robert Muir and Violet Annie (McArthur) R. MD, U. Melbourne, 1946; MA (hon.), Harvard U., 1976. Reader in exptl. pathology London U., 1964-67, prof. exptl. pathology, 1967-76; dean Cardiothoracic Inst., 1973-76; pathologist-in-chief Children's Hosp., Boston, 1976-89, pathologist-in-chief emeritus, 1990—; S. Burt Wolbach Disting. prof. pathology Harvard Med. Sch., Boston, 2001—. Fellow Royal Coll. Physicians (U.K.), Royal Australian Coll. Physicians, Royal Coll. Pathologists, Royal Coll. Radiologists (hon.), Royal Soc. Medicine, Royal Inst. Gt. Britain, Pathol. Soc. Gt. Britain and Ireland, Thoracic Soc., Assn. Clin. Pathologists, Brit. Thoracic Soc., Fleischner Soc., Can. Thoracic Soc., Neonatal Soc., Am. Thoracic Soc., Am. Soc. Pathologists, Fedn. Am. Socs. Exptl. Biology. Office: 300 Longwood Ave Boston MA 02115-5724

REID, MARILYN JOANNE, state legislator, lawyer; b. Chgo., Aug. 14, 1941; d. Kermit and Newell Azile (Hahn) N.; m. M. David Reid, Nov. 26, 1966 (div. Mar. 1983); children: David, Nelson. Student, Miami U., Oxford, Ohio, 1959-61; BA, U. Ill, 1963; JD, Ohio No. U., 1966. Bar: Ohio 1966, Ark. 1967, U.S. Dist. Ct. 1967. Trust adminstr. First Nat. Bank, Dayton, Ohio, 1966-67; assoc. Sloan & Ragsdale, Little Rock, 1967-69; ptnr. Reid and Reid, Dayton, 1969-76, Reid & Assocs., Dayton, 1975—; mem. Ohio Ho. of Reps., 1993-98. Mem. health ins. and HMO's com., chmn. ins. com., vets. com., pub. utilities com. Mem. Ohio adv. bd. U.S. Commn. Civil Rights; trustee Friends Libr. Beavercreek, Ohio; bd. dirs. Beavercreek YMCA, 1985—88; Greene County commr., 2003—; chmn., treas. various polit. campaigns, 1975—; chmn. Greene County Rep. Party; active Mt. Zion United Ch. of Christ. Mem. ABA, Ohio Bar Assn., Greene County Bar Assn., Beavercreek C. of C. (pres. 1986-87), Dayton Panhellenic Assn. (pres. 1982), Altrusa (v.p. Greene County 1978-79, pres. 1979-80), Lions (pres. Beavercreek 1975), Greene County Rep. Party (chmn.), Rotary, Kappa Beta Pi, Gamma Phi Beta (v.p. 1974-75). Mem. Ch. Christ. Avocations: tennis, skiing, boating, bridge. Office: Reid & Buckwalter 3866 Indian Ripple Rd Dayton OH 45440-3448

REID, MARY WALLACE, retired secondary school educator; b. Charlotte, N.C., Oct. 21, 1922; d. Isaac and Mamie Maude (Torrence) Wallace; m. James Samuel Reid, Feb. 13, 1946; 1 child, Virginia Anne. BA, Johnson C. Smith U., 1945; MEd, Temple U., 1970, Secondary Adminstrn. cert., 1982, EdD, 1983. Cert. English, secondary adminstr., French, reading, lang. arts tchr., Pa. Tchr. English, lang, arts, reading Sch. Dist. Phila.; ret., 1988. Title I reading coord., 1976-82; mem. pupil progress com.; past assn. student govt., mem. PFT Bldg. com. Mem. Internat. Reading Assn., Nat. Coun. Tchrs. of English. Home: 1704 Stenton Ave Philadelphia PA 19141-1433

REID, SHARON LEA, educational facilitator; b. Wheeler, Tex., Apr. 24, 1949; d. George S. and Arvazine (Deering) Robinson; m. Thomas Michael Reid, July 9, 1989. BS, McMurry Coll., 1970; MEd, Tarleton State U., 1979. Cert. tchr., edn. adminstr., supr., Tex. Tchr. Fleming Elem. Sch., San Antonio, 1971-72, Peebles Elem. Sch., Killeen, Tex., 1972-84, Sugar Loaf Elem. Sch., Killeen, 1984-85, facilitator, 1985-98, campus instructional specialist, 1998-99, Duncan Elem. Sch., Fort Hood, Tex., 1999—; emotional intelligence trainer Killeen ISD, 1999—. Trainer/dist. Marilyn Burns Problem Solving, Killeen, 1982-85, trainer/campus 4 MAT Lesson Design/Excel, Inc., Killeen, 1994-2000. Mem. Heights Concert Band, Harker Heights, Tex. Recipient music scholarship McMurry Coll., Abilene, Tex., 1968. Mem. ASCD, Nat. Read Across Am. Com., Tex. Elem. Prins. and Suprs. Assn., Tex. State Tchrs. Assn., Internat. Reading Assn., Tex. State Reading Assn., Bell County Reading Assn., Phi Delta Kappa. Avocations: instrumental music, bowling, sewing, cross-stitch. Office: Duncan Elem Sch 52400 Muskogee Dr Fort Hood TX 76544-1099

REID, SUE TITUS, law educator; b. Bryan, Tex., Nov. 13, 1939; d. Andrew Jackson Jr. and Lorraine (Wylie) Titus. BS with honors, Tex. Woman's U., 1960; MA, U. Mo., 1962, PhD, 1965; JD, U. Iowa, 1972. Bar: Iowa 1972, U.S. Ct. Appeals (D.C. Cir.) 1978, U.S. Supreme Ct. 1978. From instr. to assoc. prof. sociology Cornell Coll., Mt. Vernon, Iowa, 1963-72; assoc. prof., chmn. dept. sociology Coe Coll., Cedar Rapids, Iowa, 1972-74; assoc. prof. law. U. Wash., Seattle, 1974-76; exec. assoc. Am. Sociol. Assn., Washington, 1976-77; prof. law U. Tulsa, 1978-88; dean, prof. Sch. Criminology, Fla. State U., Tallahassee, 1988-90; prof. pub. adminstrn. and policy Fla. State U., 1990—. Acting chmn. dept. sociology Cornell Coll., 1965-66; vis. assoc. prof. sociology U. Nebr., Lincoln, 1970; vis. disting. prof. law and sociology U. Tulsa, 1977-78, assoc. dean 1979-81; vis. prof. law U. San Diego, 1981-82; mem. People-to-People Crime Prevention Del. to People's Republic of China, 1982; George Beto Vis. Disting. Prof. criminal justice Sam Houston U., Huntsville, Tex., 1984-85; lecture/study tour of Criminal Justice systems of 10 European countries, 1985; cons. Evaluation Policy Rsch. Assocs., Inc., Milw., 1976-77, Nat. Inst. Corrections, Idaho Dept. Corrections, 1984, Am. Correctional Inst., Price-Waterhouse. Author (with others): Bibliographies on Role Methodology and Propositions Volume D - Studies in the Role of the Public School Teacher, 1962, The Correctional System: An Introduction, 1981, Crime and Criminology, 10th edit., 2003, Criminal Justice, 6th edit., 2002; author: Criminal Law, 6th edit., 2004; editor (with David Lyon): Population Crisis: An Interdisciplinary Perspective, 1972; contbr. articles to profl. jours. Recipient Disting. Alumni award Tex. Woman's U., 1979; named One of Okla. Young Leaders of 80's Oklahoma Monthly, 1980. Mem. ABA, Am. Soc. Criminology, Acad. Criminal Justice Scis., Soc. Criminal Jus. Assn. Avocations: walking, reading, cooking, skiing. Office: Fla State Univ Dept Pub Adminstrn Tallahassee FL 32306 E-mail: suetreid@adelphia.net.

REID, SUSAN L. conductor; b. Charlottesville, Va., Apr. 4, 1958; d. L. Leon and Jane S. Reid, Roseann B. Reid. BM, Westminster Choir Coll., 1980; MS, Okla. State U., 1987; MMus, U. Surrey, Guildford, Eng., 1990; DMA, Ariz. State U., 1995; Cert., Royal Coll. of Church Music, Croydon, Eng., 1980. Tchg. asst. U. Surrey, Guildford, England, 1989—90, Ariz. State U., Tempe, 1990—94; dir. of music First United Meth. Ch., Edwardsville, Ill., 1980—83, First Christian Ch., Stillwater, Okla., 1983—89; faculty assoc. in music Ariz. State U., Tempe, 1994—95; dir. of choral activities S.D. Sch. of Mines and Tech., Rapid City, SD, 1995—2000, James

Madison U., Harrisonburg, Va., 2000—. Prin., owner Integrated Conducting Inc. Bd. dirs., U.S. corr. Internat. Fedn. Choral Music. Office: James Madison U MSC 7301 Harrisonburg VA 22807

REID, TRACY, professional basketball player; b. Nov. 1, 1976; B.Comm., U. N.C., 1998. Forward Charlotte Sting, 1998—. Named Atlantic Coast Conf. Player of the Yr., Player of the Week, 1998; named to 1997 and 1998 Kodak All-Am. First Team, 1998 AP All-Am. First Team; recipient First team All-Am. selection, U.S. Basketball Writers Assn., Women's Nat. Basketball Assn. Rookie of Yr. award, 1998. Office: Charlotte Sting 3308 Oak Lake Blvd Ste B Charlotte NC 28208-7707

REID-BILLS, MAE, magazine editor, historian; b. Shreveport, La. d. Dayton Taylor and Bessie Oline (Boles) Reid; m. Frederick Gurdon Bills (div.); children: Marjorie Reid, Nancy Hawkins, Frederick Taylor, Virginia Thomas, Elizabeth Sharples. AB, Stanford U., 1942, MA, 1965; PhD, U Denver, 1977. Mng. editor Am. West mag., Tucson, 1979-89, cons. editor, 1989—. Gen. Electric fellow, 1963; William Robertson Coe fellow, 1964. Mem. Orgn. Am. Historians, Am. Hist. Assn., Phi Beta Kappa, Pi Alpha Delta. Home and Office: 10 Town Plz #159 Durango CO 81301-5104

REIDELBACH, LINDA, state representative; b. Cin., Apr. 1, 1949; BS, Miami U. Ohio. Exec. v.p. MJR Enterprises, Inc.; state rep. dist. 21 Ohio Ho. of Reps., Columbus, vice chair, banking pensions and securities com., chair, children's healthcare and family svcs. subcom., mem. edn., health, human svcs. and aging, and juvenile and family law coms., and fed. grant rev. and edn. oversight subcom. Mem. Columbus team Abstinence Educators Network; mem. Franklin County Rep. Ctrl. Com., Ohio; bd. dirs. Destiny Training Camp. Mem.: Worthington Christian Ch., Worthington League for Decency. Office: 77 S High St 12th fl Columbus OH 44321-6111

REIDENBACH, FAITH E. medical editor, writer; b. Columbus, Ohio, May 10, 1960; d. William J. and Joann Raudebaugh Reidenbach; life ptnr. Beverly A. Caley, 1986. BA, Ohio State U., 1983. Cert. Bd. of Editors in the Life Scis., 2003. Writer & editor Anadem Pub., Columbus, Ohio, 1984—92; freelance medical editor and writer Medical Pub. Solutions, Cleve., 1992—97; editor ASM Internat., Cleve., 1993—96; from med. journalist to exec. med. editor Reuters Health News, N.Y.C., 1997—99, exec. med. editor, 1999—2001; pvt. practice Caley-Reidenbach Cons. LLP, Ashland, Ohio, 2001—. Contbr. articles to books, newsletters and mags. (Publ. Excellence award, 1996); pub.: newsletter Women's Recovery Network, 1990—93 (Ruth Ellis Meml. award, 2000). Reading tutor Columbus Literacy Coun., Columbus, 1984—86; trustee, sec. of bd. Women's Outreach for Women, Columbus, 1987—90, Women's Cmty. Found., Cleve., 1994—97; mem. adv. bd. Lesbian Health News, Columbus; adult basic and literacy edn. tutor Ashland, 2002—. Recipient Eric Martin Meml. award, 2003, Tex. Media award, Am. Cancer Soc., 2003. Mem.: Nat. Assn. of Sci. Writers, Am. Med. Writers Assn. (Martin award 2003), Phi Beta Kappa. Office: Caley-Reidenbach Consulting LLP PO Box 946 Ashland OH 44805 E-mail: faithreidenbach@aol.com.

REIDY, CAROLYN KROLL, publisher; b. Washington, May 2, 1949; d. Henry August and Mildred Josephine (Mencke) Kroll; m. Stephen Kroll Reidy, Dec. 28, 1974. BA, Middlebury Coll., 1971; MA, Ind. U., 1974, PhD, 1982. Various positions to mgr. subs. rights Random House, Inc., N.Y.C., 1975-83, assoc. pub., 1987-88; dir. subs. rights William Morrow & Co., N.Y.C., 1983-85; v.p., assoc. pub. Vintage Books, N.Y.C., 1985-87, pub., 1987-88, Anchor Books, Doubleday & Co., N.Y.C., 1988; pres., pub. Avon Books, N.Y.C., 1988-92; pres., pub. trade divsn. Simon & Schuster, N.Y.C., 1992—2001, pres. adult publ. divsn., 2001—. Bd. dirs. NAMES Project, 1994—98, Literacy Partners, Inc., 2000—, Nat. Book Found., 2001—. Mem.: NY Women in Comm., Pubs. Lunch Club (recipient Matrix award 2003), Women's Media Group. Office: Simon & Schuster 1230 Avenue Of The Americas Fl Concl New York NY 10020-1586 E-mail: carolyn.reidy@simonandschuster.com.

REIDY, FRANCES RYAN, English language educator, editor, writer; b. St. Louis, Aug. 5, 1955; d. Edward Joseph and Judith H. Bick. BA in English Lit., Washington U., St. Louis, 1978; cert. in book pub., NYU, 1980; MA in English, U. Mo., 1993, MFA, 2001. Mag. prodn. Antiques World, Art News, N.Y.C., 1980-82; mag. promotion Ziff-Davis Pub., N.Y.C., 1982-83; mag. editor Dun & Bradstreet, N.Y.C., 1983-84; prodn. and proofing Valve Line Survey, 1985—86; prodn., freelance editor Behavior Therapist Mag., N.Y.C., 1985-89; writer, editor Davis Design Co., N.Y.C., 1985-90; freelance editor, writer St. Louis, 1990—; prof. English St. Louis C.C., 1994—. Mem. N.Y. Bus. Press Editors, N.Y.C., 1983-86; bd. dirs. St. Louis Poetry Ctr., 1996—; com. mem. adj. staff devel. St. Louis C.C., 1995-97; adj. prof. Washington U., 2000—. Contbr. poetry to lit. jours., anthologies. Mem. Women Athletes of N.Y., N.Y.C., 1983-88, Prep-Privacy Rights Edn., St. Louis, 1990-93. Recipient winner ann. contests for poetry, St. Louis Poetry Ctr., 1992—98; grantee writer's partial work grantee, Vt. Studio Ctr., 1999—2000; scholar Mo. Women's scholar athlete, State of Mo., 1977—78. Mem. Women in Prodn. (mem. publicity com. 1980-83). Avocations: music, history, philosophy, art, dance, athletics. Home: 6820 Delmar Blvd Apt 301 Saint Louis MO 63130-3155 E-mail: ReidyFranR@aol.com.

REIFF, PATRICIA HOFER, space physicist, educator; b. Oklahoma City, Mar. 14, 1950; d. William Henry and Maxine Ruth (Hoffer) R.; m. Thomas Westfall Hill, July 4, 1976; children: Andrea Hofer Hill, Adam Reiff Hill, Amelia Reiff Hill. Student, Wellesley Coll., 1967-68; BS, Okla. State U., 1971; MS, Rice U., 1974, PhD, 1975. Cert. secondary tchr., Okla., Tex. Resident rsch. assoc. Marshall Space Flight Ctr., Huntsville, Ala., 1975-76; rsch. assoc. space physics and astronomy dept. Rice U., Houston, 1975, asst. prof. space physics and astronomy dept., 1978-81, asst. chmn. space physics and astronomy dept., 1979-85, assoc. rsch. sci., 1981-87, sr. rsch. scientist, 1987-90. Adj. asst. prof. Rice U., 1976-78, disting. faculty fellow, 1990-92, prof. 1992—, chmn. dept. space physics and astronomy, 1996-99, dir. Rice Space Inst., 1999—; mem. sci. team Atmosphere Explorer Mission, Dynamics Explorer Mission; co-investigator Global Geospace Sci. Mission, ESA/Cluster Mission, IMAGE Mission; prin. investigator The Public Connection NASA, Mus. Tchg. Planet Earth; cons. Houston Mus. Natural Sci., 1986—; adv. com. on atmospheric scis. NSF, Washington, 1988-92; mem. stategic implementation study panel NASA, Washington, 1989-91; mem. space sci. adv. com. NASA, 1993-98, mem. space sta. utilization subcom., 1995-98; mem. adv. com. Los Alamos Non-Proliferation Divsn., 1998-2001; univ. rep. U. Space Rsch. Assn., Washington, 1993—, chair Coun. of Instns., 2001—; exec. com. George Observatory, Houston, 1989-92, others. Designer Cockrell Sundial/Solar Telescope, 1989; editor EOS (sci. newspaper), 1986-89; contbr. articles to profl. jours. Trustee, Citizens' Environ. Coalition, Houston, 1978-98, pres. 1980-85, adv. com. 1998-2000; mem. air quality com. Houston/Galveston Area Coun., 1980-83, Green Ribbon Com., City of Houston, 1981-83; active coms. Macedonia United Meth. Ch., 1988—. Named rsch. fellow NAS/NRC., 1975, an Outstanding Young Woman Am., 1977, '80, to Houston's Women on the Move, 1990; named Outstanding Aerospace Educator, Women in Aerospace, 1999; NASA grantee 1993, 94, 95, 98, 99; recipient NASA Group Achievement award. Fellow Am. Geophys. Union (fin. com. 1980-82, editor search com. 1992, pub. edn. com.); mem. Cosmos Club, Wellesley Club, Internat. Union of Geodesy and Geophysics (del. 1975, 81, 83, 89, 91, 93, 95, chair working group 2F, 1991-95). Avocations: organic gardening, beef ranching, scouting. Office: Rice U Dept Physics and Astronomy 6100 S Main St Houston TX 77251 E-mail: reiff@rice.edu.

REIFLER, NELLY, writer; b. Poughkeepsie, N.Y., Dec. 17, 1967; d. Samuel Reifler and Ellen Marshall; m. Josh Dorman, Aug. 25, 2001. Student, Harvard Coll., 1985—86; BA, Hampshire Coll., 1991; MFA, Sarah Lawrence Coll., 1996. Grad. asst. Sarah Lawrence Coll., Bronxville, NY, 1994—95; series co-curator Readings at Serena, N.Y.C., 2001, series curator Bklyn. Info. and Culture, 2001—02. Guest curator The Rotunda Gallery, Bklyn., 2001—; guest prof. Sarah Lawrence Coll., Bronxville, 2002—. Author: See Through, 2003; co-editor: (lit. jour.) Aceldama, 1997—2001; asst. editor: anthology I Thought My Father was God and Other True Tales from NPR's National Story Project, 2001; contbr. (anthologies) World Poets, 2000, 110 Stories: NY Writes after September 11, 2002, Lost Tribe: Jewish Fiction from the Edge, 2003; playwright: Satisfaction, 1985; contbr. articles to jours. and mags. Recipient Henfield prize, Henfield Found., 1995. Mem.: Authors' Guild.

REIFSTECK, DOROTHY L. retired health facility executive; b. Fulton, Mo., Mar. 6, 1931; d. William Encil and Mary Elizabeth (Rose) Butterfield; m. William Glenn Reifsteck, Sept. 2, 1949 (dec.); children: Linda Leigh Reifsteck Brooks, Glenna Rose Reifsteck Burre, William E. Student, William Woods U. Bookkeeper Ferrugias' Wholesale, Fulton, 1959-61; legal sec. Baker, Holt & Krumm, Fulton, 1961-68; adminstrv. sec., purchasing audit officer Fulton State Hosp., 1968-86, dir. purchasing, 1986-94, dir. materials mgmt., 1994-95, ret., 1995. Mem. State of Mo. Purchasing Com., 1975-95. Author manual: Purchasing for Fulton State Hospital/Mo. Department of Mental Health. Mem. coun. City of Fulton, 1993—, dep. mayor, 1997—, county commn. liaison 1996—; sec. bd. dirs. United Way of Callaway County, 1978-93; chmn. Callaway Affordable Housing Com., Fulton, 1994—; sec., v.p. Mo. Assn. Legal Secs., 1960's; sec. adminstrv. coun., lay leader, lay spkr. Court Ct. United Meth. Ch., 1995—. Recipient Gov.'s award for quality and productivity State of Mo., 1995, Resolution, Mo. State Ho. of Reps., 1989, 95. Mem. Mo. Assn. Pub. Purchasing (life), Am. Bus. Women's Assn. (local pres., v.p., sec. 1980-97, Woman of Yr. 1989). Avocations: travel, reading, family, swimming, walking. Home: 825 Evergreen Dr Fulton MO 65251-2274

REIG, JUNE WILSON, scriptwriter, television director, television producer; b. Schenectady, N.Y., June 1, 1933; d. Wallace John and Lillian Lucy (Gay) Wilson; m. Robert Maxwell, Nov. 26, 1969. BA summa cum laude, N.Y. State U., 1954; MA in Dramatic Arts, NYU, 1962. Instr. NYU, N.Y.C., 1962-67; prodr., dir. NYU Theater, N.Y.C., 1963-67; dir.-prodr., writer news and pub. affairs NBC TV Network, N.Y.C., 1963-67; dir., writer, prodr. divsn. entertainment NBC-TV Network, N.Y.C., 1967-73; pres. Bunny/Chord Prodns., N.Y.C., 1972-97. Author: (book) Dairy of the Boy King Tut-Ankh-Amen, Charles Scribner's Sons, 1978; writer : (music spl.) The Heart of Christmas, 1965; An Afternoon at Tanglewood (Peabody award); writer, dir. (TV spl.) Stuart Little, 1966 (Peabody award, Prix Jeunesse); writer The Reluctant Dragon, 1968 (Brotherhood award); writer, dir., prodr. Rabbit Hill, 1966 (ALA award); Bill Cosby As I See It, 1970 (Ohio State award); A Day with Bill Cosby, 1971; Jennifer & Me, 1972; prodr., writer Little Women, the ballet, 1976; Tut, the Boy King, 1978 (Peabody award); writer, dir., prodr. : (TV series) Watch Your Child - The Me Too Show, 1973 (Action for Children's TV Achievement award); films in permanent collections Mus. Broadcasting, N.Y.C. Nominee Emmy award, 1966, 1976; recipient Christopher award. Mem.: NATAS, Dirs. Guild Am., Writers Guild Am., Audubon Soc., NYU Alumni Assn., Internat. Soc. Animal Rights, Friends of Animals, Alan Devoe Bird Club (Old Chatham, N.Y.). Avocations: photography, music, animals. Office: care Howard Comart 450 7th Ave Ste 1701 New York NY 10123-1701 Office Phone: 212-582-1551.

REIGSTAD, RUTH ELAINE, lay worker, retired physical therapy consultant; b. Mpls., Apr. 26, 1923; d. Olin Spencer and Amanda Sophia (Fjelstad) R. BA, St. Olaf Coll., Northfield, Minn., 1945; cert., U. Minn., 1947. Lic. phys. therapist, Wash. Phys. therapist Crippled Childrens's Sch., Jamestown, N.D., 1948-52; phys. therapist, clin. instr. Shriners Hosp., U. Minn., Mpls., 1955-58; phys. therapist Rehab. Center, Albuquerque, N.M., 1958-60, Brit. Nat. Health Svc., London; phys. therapy cons. Wash. State Health Dept., Olympia, 1961-73, cons., 1961-74; lay worker Good Shepherd Luth. Ch., Olympia, 1972-75; mem. various coms. Christ Luth. Ch., Tacoma, 1980—. Vol. Children Health Svcs. and Pub. Health of Wash. 1974—; bd. dirs. Morningside Rehab. Orgn., Olympia, Wash., PAVE rehab. orgn. Bd. dirs. Wash. State Phys. Therapy Assn., 1965-68; mem. community planning com. Pierce County Assoc. Ministries. With USCG, 1943-45. Recipient Fellowship award Nat. Easter Seal Soc. Chgo. 1949; Scholarship award US Pub. Health Service Wash. 1962-64. Mem. Am. Phys. Therapy Assn. (life), Am. Pub. Health Assn., Am. Acad. Religion, Luth. Brotherhood Fraternity and Benevolent Orgn. (bd. dirs. Pierce County), Air Force Assn. (exec. coun. Pierce County, 1985—). Mem. Evang. Luth. Ch. Am. Avocations: volunteer work, travel, gardening, public speaking, creative writing. Home: 10420 Gravelly Lake Dr Tacoma WA 98499

REIL, BEVERLY JEAN, director, educator; d. Richard Earle Osgood and Jean Elizabeth Wright; m. Bryan Michael Reil, Mar. 23, 1974; children: Jessica Corinne Cabales, Kelly Elizabeth. BS in Phys. Edn., Wheaton Coll., 1971; MEd in Ednl. Leadership, U. Wash., 2000. Admissions counselor, office mgr. Seattle (Wash.) Pacific U., 1971—74; tennis instr. City of Mercer Island, Wash., 1974; recreation specialist City of Kirkland, Wash., 1988—89; program mgr. evaluations, credentials evaluator Bellevue (Wash.) C.C., 1990—2003. Health and safety chair Spiritridge PTA and Bennett PTA, Bellevue, 1989—91; leader Women's Coun. at Westminster Chapel, Bellevue, 1985—88; treas. Westminster Chapel Missions commn., Bellevue, 1994—98. Recipient Golden Acorn award, Wash. State PTA, 1989, scholarship for classified employees, Assn. of Coll. Adminstrs., 1998—99. Mem.: AAUW, Am. Assn. Women in C.C. (co-pres., treas. 1994—99), N.W. Gifted Child Assn. (bd. dirs. 1985—89), Wheaton Club Western Wash. (dir. 2003), Samena Club. Avocations: motorcycling, swimming, tennis, quilting, writing.

REILEY, MAME CARRIGAN, political consultant; b. Newport News, Va., Dec. 24, 1952; d. Bernard Campbell and Joan (Carrigan) R. BA in Liberal Arts, Sacred Heart Coll., 1974; cert., Cornell U., 1977. Asst. mgr. Watergate Hotel, Washington, 1975-83; real estate agt. Watergate Mgmt., Washington, 1980-84; dir. mktg., producer spl. events Courtesy Assocs., Washington, 1983-90; campaign mgr. Jim Moran for Congress, Alexandria, Va., 1990—; chief of staff Congressman James Moran, 1991—. Guest lectr. Am. U., Washington, 1987; bd. dirs. Rte One Corridor Housing. Mem. fin. com. Dem. Nat. Com., Washington, 1983, Va. State Cen. Com., 1989—; pres. Washington chpt. Internat. Spl. Events Soc. Mem. Washington Performing Arts Soc. (chmn. pub. relations com. 1985-89). Clubs: Nat. Dem. Avocations: swimming, tennis. Office: 501 Slaters Ln Apt 17 Alexandria VA 22314-1114 Home: 7923 Jackson Rd Alexandria VA 22308-1430

REILING, LOIS MAE, librarian; b. St. Paul, May 10, 1938; d. James and Louise (Jamtoos) Kenney; m. Paul Reiling, Sept. 9, 1961; children: Mary Jo, Amy, Molli. BS, U. Ariz., 1980, Master's, 1984. Flight attendant Delta Airlines, L.A., 1958-61. Composer, prodr. (CD) Jazz Mass Traditional, 1997. Mem. ALA, AAUW, Tucson Jazz Soc., Music Therapy Assn., Jazz Educators Internat. Assn. Jazz Educators. Avocations: skiing, music. Office: 492 N Alvernon Way Tucson AZ 85711-1922

REILLY, CATHERINE HERBERT, librarian, educator; b. Milw., May 23, 1950; d. Kevin Barry and Margaret Frances (Lambin) Herbert; m. John Gerard Reilly, Oct. 1, 1977; children: Jane Elizabeth, David Patrick. Cert. profl. photography program, Germaine Sch. Photography, 1971; BA in History, U. Mo., St. Louis, 1975; MLS, U. Mo., Columbia, 1976; postgrad., Washington U., St. Louis, 2000—. Asst. libr. St. Louis Police Libr., 1977—79, libr., 1979—85; reference libr., asst. prof. St. Louis C.C., Ferguson, Mo., 1985—. Part-time reference libr. John M. Olin Libr. Washington U., St. Louis, 1993—94, part-time reference libr. physics libr., 1998; mem. exec. coun. St. Louis Regional Libr. Network, 1984—85; chmn. III OPAC Com., St. Louis, 1999—2000; chmn. fund drive St. Louis (Mo.) C.C., chmn. reference svcs.; designer libr. web pages. Co-author: Handbook of Death and Dying, 2003. Troop leader Girl Scouts Greater St. Louis, 1993—2003; vol. Univ. Sch. Dist., St. Louis, 1990—; co-chmn. seminars Ctr. for Tchg. and Learning; bd. dirs. SLA, St. Louis, 1984—85. Recipient Innovator of the Yr. award, St. Louis C.C. at Florrissant Valley, 2003. Mem.: NEA, ALA, Am. Assn. Women in C.C., Mo. C.C. Assn., Jane Austen Soc. St. Louis (founding mem.). Home: 7117 Waterman Ave Saint Louis MO 63130 Office: St Lous CC at Florissant Valley 3400 Pershall Rd Saint Louis MO 63135 E-mail: creilly@stlcc.edu.

REILLY, CATHERINE REGINA, law administrator; b. Cooperstown, N.Y.; d. John Patrick and Catherine Regina (Dempsey) R.; BA, Coll. of Mt. St. Vincent; MS magna cum laude, Pratt Inst. Libr. Chase Manhattan Bank, N.Y.C., 1972-77, rsch. supr., 1975, asst. treas., mgr. rsch. libr., 1977-81, 2d v.p., systems mgr. info. ctr., 1981-84, bus. systems officer legal dept., 1984-85, v.p., dir. adminstrn. legal dept., 1985—97; exec. dir. Martin, Clearwater & Bell, LLP, 1997-. Trustee Massapequa Pub. Libr., 1986—. Mem. ABA, Assn. Legal Adminstrs. (bd. dirs. 1992-93), Lawnet, Inc. (mem. conf. com. 1988, chair Spl. Interest Group databases 1988-91, bd. dir. 1991—, pres. 1993-95), Phi Beta Mu. Editor, Biz-dex, 1977-81, Bus. and Fin. Newsletter, 1978-81, Info Mation, 1992-94. Office: Martin Clearwater & Bell LLP 220 E 42nd St New York NY 10017

REILLY, JILL MARLENE, school system administrator; b. Chgo., Jan. 27, 1951; d. Jack Louis and Leah M. Cappels; m. Patrick Duane Reilly, May 29, 1971; children: Elizabeth M. Brama, Joseph D., Heather von Mering. BA in English, U. Cin., 1974; MA in Curriculum, U. Minn., 1985; D in Edn. Leadership, U. St. Thomas, St. Paul, 1992. Co-ptnr. Featherstone-Reilly Ednl. Cons., Apple Valley, Minn., 1984-95; mentor program coord. Intermediate Sch. Dist. # 917, Apple Valley, 1985-93; sr. cons. Honeywell, Inc., Mpls., 1993-95; adj. asst. prof. St. Mary's U., Mpls., 1994—; pres. Acad. Holy Angels, Richfield, Minn., 1995—. Author: Mentorship: The Essential Guide for Schools and Business, 1992; co-author: College Comes Sooner Than You Think, 1987. Bd. dirs. guidance div. Nat. Assn. Gifted Children, Mpls., 1988-93; bd. dirs., chair elect Minn. Coun. Gifted and Talented, Mpls., 1991-94. Office: Acad Holy Angels 6600 Nicollet Ave Richfield MN 55423-2498 Office Phone: 612-798-2611. E-mail: jreilly@ahastars.org.

REILLY, NANCY (ANNE CAULFIELD REILLY), painter; b. Bryn Mawr, Pa., Mar. 29, 1927; d. Ralph Caulfield and Claire Helena (Roesch) Goodman; m. Donald Elliot Reilly, May 14, 1949; children: Kevin Caulfield, William Stockbridge, Peter Elliott. Studied with Samuel E. Brown, Westport, Conn., 1955-63; studied with Mimi Jennewein, Larchmont, N.Y., 1964-65. Lectr. portrait painting Bridgeport (Conn.) Art League, Milford (Conn.) Art League, Pen and Brush Club, New Haven, Conn. Classic Arts Assn., Allied Artists Am., Kent (Conn.) Art Assn., SCAN, Newtown, Conn. Exhibited in group shows at Nat. Acad. Design, N.Y.C., 1964, 1965, 1969, 1970, Stamford (Conn.) Mus., 1965, Wadsworth Antheum, Hartford, Conn., 1966, 1972, Nat. Acad. Arts and Letters, N.Y.C., 1971, Mus. Sci. and Industry, Bridgeport, 1972, Salmagundi Club, N.Y.C., Nat. Arts Club, Butler Inst. Am. Art, Youngstown, Ohio, 2001, New Britain (Conn.) Mus. Am. Art, 2001, exhibitions include invitational travelling exhbn. Allied Artists Am., 2003—; included in slide collection Smithsonian Instn., Washington, U. Conn. Health Ctr., Farmington. Vol. artist rehab. unit Norwalk Hosp., 1984—95. Recipient Gold medal for oil painting, Catherine Lorillard Wolfe Art Club, 1965, Silver medal for oil painting, Nat. Arts Club, 1969, George Height award for portrait, 1969, Blanche Farr award, 1991. Fellow: Am. Artists Profl. League; mem.: Conn. Pastel Soc. (signature, J.D. Altobello Meml. award), Artists' Fellowship N.Y., Acad. Artists Assn. Springfield, Kent Art Assn. (Gordon C. Aymar award for oil 1993, Mabel Rowe Aiken award for oil 1995, Frances B. Townley award for portrait 1998, 1999, Best in Show 1991), Hudson Valley Art Assn. (Thora M. Jensen award 1989, Bronze medal for oil painting 1981), Pastel Soc. Am., Nat. Arts Club (Bruce Stevenson award for portrait 1971, 1988, 1991, Silver medal for oil painting 1969), Allied Artists Am. (bd. dirs. 1991—99, participant in travelling exhbn. 2003—), New Haven Paint and Clay Club (Merit award 1992, 1997). Home: 9 Marilane Westport CT 06880-1008

REIMANN, ARLINE LYNN, artist; b. St. Louis, Nov. 25, 1937; d. Albert Robbins and Bess (Kagan) Miller; m. Hans Reimann, Feb. 24, 1957; 1 child, Robert. BA, Rutgers U., 1974; MA, Montclair State U., 1980. Exhibited in group shows at Hunterdon Nat. Print Exhbn., Hunterdon Art Ctr., Clinton, N.J., 1982, Celebration of Women's Week, Galeria San Jeronimo, San Juan, P.R., 1987, Audubon Artists Ann. Exhbn., Nat. Arts Club, N.Y.C., 1988, 90—, Celebration 89, Interch. Ctr., N.Y.C., Nat. Assn. Women Artists Traveling Printmaking Exhbn., Butler Inst. Am. Art, Youngstown, Ohio, 1989, 395 West Broadway Gallery, N.Y.C., 1994, 420 West Broadway Gallery, Soho, N.Y., 1995, Audubon Artists Invitational, Lever House Gallery, N.Y.C., 1995, Selected N.J. Mems. Nat. Assn. Women Artists, Hunterdon Art Ctr., Clinton, N.J., 1996, Art Ctr. Municipality of Athens, Greece, 1996, West Beth Gallery, Montclair in Manhattan, N.Y.C., 1996, ISE Art Found. N.Y.C., 1996, Soc. Am. Graphic Artists, New Rochelle, N.Y., 1997, Gallery Art 54, N.Y.C., 1997, Jane Voorhees Zimmerli Art Mus., New Brunswick, N.J., 1998, 99, Soc. Am. Graphic Artists, N.Y.C., 1999, 2004, Worldwide Feminist Expo, Balt., 2000; represented in permanent collections at Jane Voorhees Zimmerli Art Mus., New Brunswick, N.J., Newark Pub. Libr. Fine Print Collection, Newark, Montclair State U., Bailey Matthews Mus., Sanibel, Fla. Recipient Best in Show award Salute to Women in Arts, Lincoln Ctr., 1981, Hon. mention award Nat. Juried Exhbn. Small Works Montclair State U., N.J., 1995. Aida Whedon Meml. award Nat. Assn. Women Artists, 1996. Mem. Nat. Assn. Women Artists (bd. dirs., chair traveling print exhbn. 1984-89, printmaking jury 1987-89, 95-97), Audubon Artists (bd. dirs., rec. sec. 1991-97), Soc. Am. Graphic Artists, Phi Beta Kappa. Home: 546 Hillrise Pl Walnut Creek CA 94598-4064

REIMER, JUDY MILLS, pastor, religious executive; m. George G. Reimer, 1964; children: Todd, Troy. BA, Emory and Henry Coll., 1962; MDiv, Bethany Theol. Sem., 1994. Ordained into Set Apart Ministry, Ch. of the Brethren, 1994. Vol. Brethren Vol. Svc. NIH, Bethesda, Md., 1962-64, Hessish Lichtenau, Germany, 1964-65; elem. sch. tchr. Pub. and Private Schs., various cities, 1965-76; deacon Ch. of the Brethren, 1966—; mem Virlina Dist. Bd., 1978-90; chair of nurture com. Ch. of the Brethren Virlina Dist., 1979-82, chair of outdoor ministry, 1983-84, conf. speaker, 1992; founding pastor Ch. of the Brethren, Smith Mountain Lake, Va., 1996-98, gen. bd. exec. dir., 1998—; owner, sr. v.p. Harris Office Furniture Co., Roanoke, Va., 1976—. Co-chair and vice-chair of two Virlina Fin. Campaigns, Ch. of the Brethren, 1980s, mem. Gen. Bd., Ch. of Brethren, 1977-90; mem. PTA, United Way Allocation Com., Roanoke Valley Women Owners Assn. (charter mem.); adult advisor Nat. Youth Cabinet. 1991, 92; worship coord. Nat. Youth Conf. 1994 numerous other coms. for Ch. of Brethren; official observer for Nat. Coun. of Chs. at Nicaraguan Election, Feb., 1990; rep. of Ch. of the Brethren, 1989, Atlanta, The Torch of Conscience Campaign to sensitize congregation to the campaign to abolish death penalty; workshop leader across the denomination on leadership devel., pastor/spouse retreats, women's rallies, etc.; ann. conf. moderator elect, 1993-94. Mem. Inst. Indsl. Comml. Chaplains (chmn. bd. dirs. local unit, asst. treas. nat. bd.). Office: Church of the Brethren General Offices 1451 Dundee Ave Elgin IL 60120-1694

REIN, CATHERINE AMELIA, retired insurance company executive, lawyer; b. Lebanon, Pa., Feb. 7, 1943; d. John and Esther (Scott) Shultz. BA summa cum laude, Pa. State U., 1965; JD magna cum laude, NYU ., 1968. Bar: N.Y. 1968, U.S. Supreme Ct. 1971. Assoc. Dewey, Ballantine, Bushby, Palmer & Wood, N.Y.C., 1968-74; with Continental Group, Stamford, Conn., 1974-85, sec., sr. atty., 1976-77, v.p., gen. counsel, 1980-85; sec., asst. gen. counsel Continental Diversified Ops., 1978-80; v.p. human resources Met. Life Ins. Co., N.Y.C., 1985-88, sr. v.p. human resources, 1988-89, exec. v.p. corp. and profl. svcs. dept., from 1989, sr. exec., v.p. bus. svcs. group and corp. svcs., 1998-99; pres, CEO Met. Life Auto and Home, Warwick, R.I., 1999—. Bd. dirs. Bank of N.Y., First Energy Corp. Bd. trustee NYU Sch. Law Found. Mem. ABA, Assn. of Bar of City of N.Y. Episcopalian. Avocations: decorating, restoration, cooking. Home: 21 E 22nd St Apt 8B New York NY 10010-5335 Office: Met Life Ins Co 1 Madison Ave New York NY 10010-3603

REINGLASS, MICHELLE ANNETTE, lawyer; b. L.A., Dec. 9, 1954; d. Darwin and Shirley (Steiner) R. Student, U. Calif., Irvine, 1972-75; BSL, Western State U., 1977; JD, Western State U., Coll. Law, 1978. Bar: Calif. 1979, U.S. Dist. Ct. (ctrl. dist.) Calif. 1979, U.S. Ct. Appeals (9th cir.) 1981, U.S. Dist. Ct. (so. dist.) Calif. 1990. Pvt. practice employee litig., Laguna Hills, Calif., 1979—. Instr. Calif. Continuing Edn. of Bar, 1990—, Western State Coll., 1991, Rutter Group, 1994—; chmn. magistrate selection com. U.S. Dist. Ct. (ctrl. dist.) Calif., L.A., 1991, 93, 94, 95, mem. com., 1997; lectr. in field. Contbr. articles to profl. jours. Pres., bd. dirs. Child or Parental Emergency Svcs., Santa Ana, Calif., 1982-92; bd. dirs. Pub. Law Ctr., Santa Ana, Coalition for Justice, Working Wardrobes; mem. exec. com. and cast CHOC Follies. Recipient Jurisprudence award Anti-Defamation League, 1997; named to Hall of Fame, Western State U., 1993; named one of Best Lawyers, Bestlawyers.com, 2001, 02, 03, one of Top 100 Most Influential Lawyers in Calif., L.A. Daily Jour., 2001, one of Top 30 Female Litigators in Calif., L.A. Daily Jour., 2002. Mem. State Bar Calif., Orange County Bar Assn. (del. to state conv. 1980-94, bd. dirs. 1983-94, chmn. bus. litigation sect. 1989, sec. 1990, treas. 1991, pres.-elect 1992, pres. 1993), Orange County Trial Lawyers Assn. (bd. dirs. 1987-89, Bus. Trial Lawyer of Yr. award 1995), Orange County Women Lawyers (Lawyer of Yr. award 1996), Vols. in Parole (chmn. adv. com. 1990-91), Peter Elliot Inns Ct. (master), Am. Bd. of Trial Advocates. Avocations: distance running, skiing. Office: 23161 Mill Creek Dr Ste 170 Laguna Hills CA 92653-1650 E-mail: michelle@reinglasslaw.com.

REINHARD, DIANE L. university president; Bachelor's elem. edn., master's ednl. psychology, U. Wis.-Milw.; PhD ednl. evaluation, Ohio State U. Faculty mem., assoc. dean, acting dean U. of Oreg.; prof., dept. of ednl. psychology W.Va. U., dean, coll. of human resources and edn., acting pres.; pres. Clarion U., 1990—2003; interim pres. Ind. U. of Pa., 2004—. Office: Clarion U Office of the President Clarion PA 16214*

REINHARD, SISTER MARY MARTHE, educational organization administrator; b. McKeesport, Pa., Aug. 29, 1929; d. Regis C. and Leona (Reese) R. AB, Notre Dame Coll.; MA, U. Notre Dame. Asst. prin. Regina H.S., Cleve., 1960-62, prin., 1963—65, Notre Dame Acad., Chardon, Ohio, 1965-72; pres. Notre Dame Coll. of Ohio, Cleve., 1973-88; dir. devel. Sisters of Notre Dame Ednl. Ctr., Chardon, 1989—2003. Trustee, mem. exec. com. NCCJ, Cleve., 1987; mem. coun. Geagua United Way Svcs., 1990—97, vice chair fund raising, 1991—94, 1995—97; mem. adv. bd. Kent State U., Geauga campus, 1991—94; trustee Leadership Geauga, 1995—96; sec. Notre Dame Edn. Assn., 1990—98, pres., 1998—2001; mem. adv. bd. Regina H.S.; mem. distbn. com. McGinty Family Found., from 1989. Recipient Humanitarian award Cleve. chpt. NCCJ, 1990; named one of 100 most influential women in Cleve., Women's City Club, 1982, one of 79 most interesting people in Cleve., The Cleve. Mag., 1979; named Cleve. United Way Vol. of Yr., 1997, Woman of Yr., Notre Dame Coll. Ohio, 1989; elected to Hall of Excellence, Ohio Found. of Ind. Colls., 1996. Roman Catholic. Died Apr. 19, 2003.

REINHARDT, LINDA KAY, minister; b. Glen Ridge, N.J., Apr. 4, 1950; d. Irving Raymond and Margaret Louise (Mills) Vanderberg; m. Robert Richard Reinhardt, Feb. 16, 1969. B of Liberal Studies summa cum laude, St. Edward's U., 1991; MDiv, Austin Presbyn. Theol. Sem., 1996. Cert. spiritual counselor; ordained to Presbyn. Ch. 1996; commd. Stephen's min. Payroll tax specialist Great So. Life, Houston, 1980-82; comptr. Cayman Constrn., Houston, 1981-83; owner, acct. Reinhardt Acctg. Firm, 1984-93; pastor, dir. The Jeremiah Project, Canyon Lake, Tex., 1994—; restoring creation enabler Mission Presbytery, PC (USA), 1998—. Resource cons. Mission Presbytery, Tex., 1994—; workshop facilitator environtl. theology, 1996—. Author: (booklet) We Can't Have It Both Ways - A Reasoned Approach to Understanding MCS, 2003; editor (newsletter) I Am Jeremiah, 1994—; contbr. articles to profl. publs. Bd. dirs. Tri-Living Cmty. Austin, 1989-91, The Dispossessed Project, 1998—; vol. in parks Fort Davis Nat. Hist. Site, 1986-87; vol. Children's Ctr. for Austin, 1989-91; spokesperson, advocate rights of disabled people, 1969—; worship leader RBJ Retirement Ctr., Austin, 1992-93; worship organizer Brown Schs., Austin, 1991-93. Recipient The Spragens award in Christian Edn., 1996. Mem. Assn. of Civil Litigants (advisor-com. on status of women 1996—), Presbyn. Clergywomen, Friends of the Fort (life), Presbyn. Health, Edn. and Welfare Assn., Christian Environ. Assn., Evangel. Environ. Network, Soc. of the Green Cross. Avocations: environmental concerns, writing, reading, cross stiching. Home and Office: The Jeremiah Project 222 Soft Wind Canyon Lake TX 78133-2414

REINHARDT, SUSAN ELAINE GANTT, family resource center administrator, counselor; b. Newton, N.C., July 17, 1961; d. Charles Lenwood and Brenda Gail (McKee) Gantt; m. Albert Franklin Reinhardt, Dec. 18, 1983; children: Andrew Franklin, Adam Michael. BA in Psychology, U. N.C., 1983; MEd in Counseling, East Tenn. State U., 1985. Elem. sch. counselor Newton-Conover City Schs., Newton, NC, 1985-86; counselor, educator Women's Health Edn. Ctr. Catawba Meml. Hosp., Hickory, NC, 1992-95; instr. human resources Catawba Valley C.C., Hickory, 1995; dir. Footprints Family Learning & Creative Play Ctr., Hickory, 1995—97; sch. counselor Engelmann Sch., Hickory, 1998—99; parent educator Catawba County Schs., Newton, 1999—. Postpartum depression support vol.; Sunday sch. tchr. United Meth. Ch. Mem. Postpartum Support Internat., Newton-Conover Edn. Found. (bd. dirs.). Avocations: school volunteer, computer research, reading. Home: 1792 Cordia Cir Newton NC 28658-7815

REINHARDT, VICTORIA ANN, county official, environmentalist; b. Hastings, Minn., June 30, 1953; d. LeRoy August and Florence Rose (Nogle) R.; m. James Patrick Barone, Oct. 25, 1991; children: Michael Shane Barone, Erich LeRoy Reinhardt. BA, Met. State U., St. Paul, 1996, MBA, 1999. Account clk. Hastings State Hosp., 1972-73; asst. cost analyst Sperry Univac, Roseville, Minn., 1973-77; office mgr. Erhart Law Office, Anoka, Minn., 1980-84; energy auditor No. States Power, White Bear Lake, Minn., 1980-84; prin. asst. Ramsey County Comm. Orth., St. Paul, 1984-86; lobbyist, cons., White Bear Lake, 1986-87; solid waste abatement specialist Anoka County, Anoka, 1987-88; abatement grants adminstr. Met. Coun., St. Paul, 1988-94; problem materials coord. Minn. Office of Environ. Assistance, St. Paul, 1994—; commr. Ramsey County, St. Paul, 1996—. Chmn. White Bear Lake Recycling Adv. Com., 1988-96; mem. Ramsey County Capital Improvements Com., 1994-96, Ramsey County Strategic Planning Com., 1994-96. Contbr. articles to profl. jours. Bd. dirs., charter mem. White Bear Lake Counseling Ctr., 1984-96; vol., spkr. on domestic abuse Law Explorers White Bear Lake Counseling Wilder Found., St. Paul, 1985—; bd. dirs. Recycling Assn. Minn., 1988-95, chmn., 1990-93; pres., steward, co-chair PAC Am. Fedn. State County & Mcpl. Employees, 1990-94; senate dist. affirmative action state ctrl. com. Dem.-Farm-Labor Party; pres. PTO Excellence in Edn. com. Sch. Dist. 624. Recipient Recognition of Svc. award Recycling Assn. Minn., 1993, Recognition of Svc. award Democrat Farmer Labor Party, 1995. Mem. Nat. Recycling Coalition (state recycling orgn. liaison, spkr. 1987—, recycling edn. excellence award 1994), Solid Waste Assn. N.Am., Minn. Assn. Profl. Employees (bd. dirs. polit. action com. 1994-96), Assn. Recycling Mgrs., Minn. Earth Day Network. Democrat. Lutheran. Avocation: cake baking and decorating. Home: 4995 Wood Ave White Bear Lake MN 55110-6645 Office: Ramsey County Commrs Office 220 Courthouse 15 Kellogg Blvd W Saint Paul MN 55102-1635 Office Phone: 651-266-8363.

REINHART, ANNE CHRISTINE, special education educator, consultant; b. Detroit, Mar. 9, 1950; m. Charles Reinhart; children: Kim Meredith, Ted Justin. BS, Ea. Mich. U., 1972; MA, U. Detroit, 1977. Cert. spl. edn., Mich. Spl. edn. tchr. for emotionally impaired State of Mich. Hosp., Pontiac, Berkley (Mich.) Sch. Dist, 1976—. Co-chair ASSET (support group for gifted and talented students), Birmingham, Mich., 1996-98; com. mem. Mich. Dept. of Edn., Office of Spl. Edn.; particpant Mich Pilot Study grant Quality Assurance Rev., 2000-03. Grantee, Dept. Spl. Edn., Mich., 2000—03. Mem. Kappa Delta Pi. Avocations: writing, tutoring, visiting other sch. sites in country. Home: 25925 Romany Way Franklin MI 48025-1909

REINHART, KELLEE CONNELY, journalist; b. Kearney, Nebr., Dec. 15, 1951; d. Vaughn Eugene and Mary Jo (Mullen) Connely; m. Stephen Wayne Reinhart, June 15, 1974; children: Keegan Connely, Channing Mullen. BA, U. Ala., 1972, MS, 1974. Advt. copywriter Stas. WTBC-AM, WUOA-FM, 1970-72; asst. mgr. Ala. Press Assn., 1972-74; asst. to the editor Antique Monthly mag., 1974-75, mng. editor, 1975-77; editorial dir. Antique Monthly and Horizons mags., 1977-89; dir. univ. rels. U. Ala. System, Tuscaloosa, 1989—. Editor: Wild Birds of America: The Art of Basil Ede, 1991, Centennial Memories, Millennial Hopes, 2000, The People's City, 2003. Bd. dirs. Ala. Humanities Found.; bd. dirs. Ala. Writers Forum, pres., 1999—2001. Recipient Druids Arts award, 1995. Mem. Soc. Profl. Journalists, Am. Soc. Mag. Editors, Newcomen Soc. U.S., Art Table, Ala. Writers Forum (pres. 1999-2001), XXXI/U. Ala. Women's Hon. Soc. Office: 401 Queen City Ave Tuscaloosa AL 35401-1551 Office Phone: 205-348-5938. Business E-Mail: kreinhar@uasystem.ua.edu.

REINHERZ, HELEN ZARSKY, researcher, social services educator; b. Boston, Aug. 4, 1923; d. Zachary and Anna (Cohen) Zarsky; m. Samuel E. Reinherz, Aug. 29, 1943; 1 son, Ellis. AB magna cum laude, Wheaton Coll., 1944; MS, Simmons Coll., 1946; S.M., Harvard U., 1962, Sc.D., 1965. Social worker Newton Family Service, Mass., 1946-49, Mass. Gen. Hosp., Boston, 1949-51; supr. psychiat. social work State Hosp., Waltham, Mass., 1958-61; faculty mem. Simmons Coll., Boston, 1965—, prof. methods rsch., 1972—, dir. research Sch. Social Work, 1968-93, dir. PhD program, 1993-96. Prin. investigator Identifying Children at Risk, 1976—84, Adaption in Adolescence, 1987—93, Adult Rsch. Project, 1998—2001, Early Adulthood Rsch. Project, 1993—97, Simms Longitudinal Study, 2001—, Study Adolescent Drug Abuse, 1971—73; rsch. cons. Dept. Mental Health, 1970—80; chmn. Gov.'s Adv. Coun. on Mental Health and Retardation, 1972; mem. adv. com. Mental Health Manpower fo Fed. Govt., 1980—82. Author (with H. Wechler, D. Dobbins): Social Work Research in the Human Services, 1976; author: (with M. Heywood, J. Camp) A Community Response to Drug Abuse, 1976; cons., assoc. editor: Jour. Prevention, 1980—91, mem. fed. adv. com.: Rsch. in Prevention Rev., 1984—87, editl. bd.: Jour. Early Adolescence, cons. editor: NASW Jour.; contbr. articles to profl. jours. Recipient Maida H. Solomon award Simmons Coll. Alumni, 1961; NIH tng. fellow, 1961 65; Grant Found. grantee, 1963; Med. Found. grantee, 1967-69; NIMH grantee, 1975-84, 87—. Fellow Am. Orthopyschiat. Assn.; mem. Acad. Cert. Social Workers, Am. Pub. Health Assn., Council Social Work Edn., Harvard Sch. Pub. Health Alumni Assn. (sec.-treas. 1965-68), Phi Beta Kappa, Delta Omega. Home: 17 Corey Rd Malden MA 02148-1116 Office: Simmons Sch Social Work 300 The Fenway Boston MA 02115 Office Phone: 617-521-3934. E-mail: helen.reinherz@simmons.edu.

REINICHE, DOMINIQUE, food products executive; With Procter & Gamble, Kraft Jacobs Suchard, Coca-Cola Enterprises, 1992—, pres. French divsn., 1998—2003, sr. v.p., pres. European group, 2003—. Office: Coca-Cola Enterprises 2500 Windy Ridge Pkwy Atlanta GA 30339*

REINIKE, IRMA, writer, fine artist, poet, lyricist; b. White Harbor, Long Beach, Miss., Oct. 20, 1927; d. Chester Henry and Edna Claire (Latille) R.; children: Harvey Franklin Linn Shows Jr., George David Shows, Thelma Jewell Shows Hoffman. Student, St. Mary's Dominican Coll.; grad., North Light Art Sch., Cin., 1996, 97, 99. Freelance writer, student Famous Writers Sch., Westport, Conn., 1965—69; freelance writer New Orleans, Long Beach, Miss. Author: Mystery, 1940—41, Long Beach Movie Personality, 1949, My Beach, 1990, Thelma, 1991, (poetry) My Lady of Medjugorje, 1987—88, Irma Reinike Poetry-Book 1, 2000—01, I Love My Flag, 2000, other poems; columnist Round the Town, Long Beach, Miss., 1963—66, (radio-TV paper) The Illustrated Press, Irma Reinike's Personality Parade, New Orleans, 1952; composer: (songs) See You Tomorrow, 1995—96, Days of Love, 1997, The Blue of Your Eyes, 1997, others, (stage play) Ethel Chichester, Peg O' My Heart, Kaye Hamilton, Stage Door, 1949, Song, Dance Dixieland Minstrel and Variety Artists, 1950—51, 1952, Charity Performer, Le Petit Theatre de Vieux Carre' Sunday Salon, 1996, Destruction by Hurricane Camille, Times Picayune, 1970; artist Introduction Camille Book-Hurricane, 1969, exhibited artworks books, St. Thomas, 1992, 2 oil/acrylic paintings, St. Thomas Ch., 1970, artist, fine arts and mixed media (including paintings:) Louisiana Live Oak Tree, Louisiana Noon Sunshine, others. Mem. Nat. Rep. Senatorial Com., 1994-97; mem. Nat. Rep. Congl. Com., 2000; mem. La. Libr. Found., New Orleans Friends of Pub. Libr., 1994-96; charter mem. World War II Monument Meml., Washington. Honored Author, La. Libr. Assn., 1994, 96, La. State Librarian, 1995, Friends Fest New Orleans Pub. Libr., 1994-96, Patron Le Petit Theatre de Vieux Carre, 1996. Mem.: Long Beach Hist. Soc. Republican. Roman Catholic. Avocations: fine arts, songwriting, poetry, lyricist. Home: Apt 3 1568 Carollton Ave Metairie LA 70005

REININGHAUS, RUTH, retired artist; b. NYC, Oct. 4, 1922; d. Emil William and Pauline Rosa (Lazarik) R.; m. George H. Morales, Feb. 20, 1944; children: George James, Robert Charles; m. Allan Joseph Smith, May 28, 1960. Student, Hunter Coll., NYU, Nat. Acad. Sch. of Design, 1960-61, Frank Reilly Sch. of Art, 1963, Art Students League, 1964, 68; studied oil painting, with Robert Beverly Hale and Robert Philips, with Morton Roberts and Frank Reilly, Robert Maione, with Rudy Colao. Instr. art Banker's Trust, N.Y.C., 1971-77, 79-99, Kittredge Club for Women, N.Y.C., 1967-77. Exhibited in group shows at Berkshire Art Mus., 1970s, Hammer Galleries, Inc., N.Y.C., 1974, Far Gallery, N.Y.C., 1974, Mufalli Gallery, N.Y. and Fla., 1983-90, Pen and Brush Club, 1985—, Petrucci Gallery, Saugerties, N.Y., 1988-94, Pastel Soc. Am., 1988—, John Lane Gallery, Rhinebeck, N.Y., 1992-97, Regianni Gallery, N.Y.C., 1994, Catherine Lorillard Wolfe Club, Salmagundi Club, Allied Artists Am., Heidi Newhoff Gallery, N.Y.C., Hudson Valley Art Assn., Knickerbocker Artists, N.Y.C., Pen & Brush Club Inc., Pastel Soc. Am., Heritage Mus.; represented in permanent collections at US Navy Art, US Coast Guard Art Program, Hon. Murtogh D. Guinness; contbr. to popular mags. Recipient 3d prize in Oils, Murray Hill Art Show, 1966, 68; Washington Sq. Outdoor Art Exhibit scholar Nat. Acad., 1960, Frank Reilly Sch. Art, 1963, NYU, 1968, Talens award, 1963, Robert Lehman award, 1968, Richtone Artists award, 1968, Baker Brush award, 1969, Salmagund scholar, 1969; subject NBC TV show You Are an Artist, 1950s. Fellow: Hudson Valley Art Assn. (Claude Parson's Meml. award 1970), Am. Artists Profl. League (Claude Parsons Meml. award 1974, 2d prize oils 1992, 3d prize pastel 1993, Pres. award 1994); mem.: Knickerbocker Artists (Flora B. Giffuni PSA Pres.' award 1990), Oil Pastel Assn. (Pen and Brush award 1987, Strathmore award 1989, Pen and Brush award 1990, Salmagundi Club award 1991), Washington Sq. Outdoor Art Assn. (bd. dirs. 1983—90), Allied Artists Am. (assoc.), Nat. Arts Club (Reciprocal) Artists Fellowship, Soc. Illustrators (hon. 1983—87), Pastel Soc. Am. (bd. dirs. 1988—90, J. Giffuni purchase award 1988, Pastel Soc. of West Coast award 1997), Salmagundi Club N.Y (pres. 1983—87, curator 1989—97, Philip Isenberg award 1974, Salmagundi Club prize 1985, Franklin B. Williams Fund prize 1987, Tom Picard award 1987, Mortimer E. Freehof award 1988, John N. Lewis award 1988—89, Philip Isenberg award 1989—90, Medal of Honor 1989, Helen S. Coes award 1990, Flora B. Giffuni Pres. award 1990, Thomas Moran award 1990, Samuel T. Shaw award 1990, Alice B. McReynolds award 1991, Alphaeus Cole Meml. award 1991, Salmagundi award 1991, Alice B. McReynolds Meml. award 1991, Philip Isenberg award 1992, 1995, Harry Ballinger Meml. award 2000—01, Philip Isenberg award 2001, Jane Impastato award 2003), Pen and Brush Club (Helen Slotman award 1986, OPA Internat. award 1987, Gene Alden Walker award 1988, Pen and Brush Solo award 1992, Margaret Sussman award 1996, 1998, Merit award 2000), Catharine Lorillard Wolfe Art Club (bd. dirs. 1987—, Anna Hyatt Huntington award 1978, Coun. Am. Artists award 1985, Pastel award 1992, Still Life award 1993, 1st prize 2001), Alpha Delta Pi. Lutheran. Avocations: travel, technical illustration, oil, pastel and watercolor painting, collecting antique music boxes and watches. Home: 222 E 93rd St Apt 26A New York NY 10128-3758

REINISCH, JUNE MACHOVER, psychologist, educator; b. N.Y.C., Feb. 2, 1943; d. Mann Barnett and Lillian (Machover) R. BS cum laude, NYU, 1966; MA, Columbia U., 1970, PhD with distinction, 1976. Asst. prof. psychology Rutgers U., New Brunswick, N.J., 1975-80, assoc. prof. psychology New Brunswick, N.J., 1980-82, adj. assoc. prof. psychiatry, 1981-82; prof. psychology Ind. U., Bloomington, 1982-93, dir. Kinsey Inst. Rsch. in Sex, Gender, and Reprodn., 1982-93; prof. clin. psychology Sch. Medicine, Indpls., 1983-93; dir. emeritus Kinsey Inst., 1993—. Dir., prin. investigator Prenatal Devel. Projects, Copenhagen, 1976—, sr. rsch. fellow, trustee The Kinsey Inst., 1993—; pres. R2 Sci. Comms., Inc., Ind., N.Y., 1985—; vis. sr. rschr. Inst. of Preventive Medicine, Copenhagen Health Svcs., Kommunehospitalet, Copenhagen, 1994—; cons. SUNY; sr. cons. Mus. of Sex, N.Y.C., 1998, dir. acquisitions and new exhbns., 2003—, v.p. sci. affairs, 2003. Author: The Kinsey Institute New Report on Sex, 1990, 94, pub. 8 fgn. edits.; editor, contbr. books Kinsey Inst. series; syndicated newspaper columnist: The Kinsey Report; contbr. rsch. reports, revs., articles to profl. jours.; appeared on TV shows including PBS, BBC, ABC and NBC sci. spls., Discovery, ABC Science Specials, 20/20, Oprah Winfrey, Geraldo Rivera, Charles Grodin, Montel Williams, Sally Jessy Rafael, Good Morning Am., Today Show, CBS This Morning; guest host TV shows including CNBC Real Personal, TalkLive, also fgn. appearances. Founders day scholar NYU, 1966; NIMH trainee, 1971-74; NIMH grantee, 1978-80, Ford Found. grantee, 1973-75, Nat. Inst. Edn. grantee, 1973-74, Erikson Ednl. Found. grantee, 1973-74, grantee Nat. Inst. Child Health and Human Devel., 1981-88, Nat. Inst. on Drug Abuse, 1989-95; recipient Morton Prince award Am. Psychopath. Assn., 1976, medal for 9th Dr. S.T. Huang-Chan Meml. Lectr. in anatomy Hong Kong U., 1988, Dr. Richard J. Cross award Robert Wood Johnson Med. Sch., 1991, Award First Internat. Conf. on Orgasm, New Delhi, 1991, Disting. Alumnae award Tchrs. Coll. Columbia U., 1992, award for su contbn. Profl. al Conocimiento dela Sexualidad Humana, Assn. Mexicana de Sexologia, Mexico City, 1996; named Regents lectr. UCLA, 1999. Fellow AAAS, APA, Am. Psychol. Soc., Soc. for Sci. Study Sex; mem. Internat. Acad. Sex Rsch. (charter), Internat. Women's Forum, Women's Forum. Inc., Internat. Soc. Psychoneuroendocrinology, Internat. Soc. Rsch. Aggression, Internat. Soc. Devel. Psychobiology, Am. Assn. Sex. Educators, Counselors and Therapists, Sigma Xi. Office: SUNY HSCB PBL Box 120 450 Clarkson Ave Brooklyn NY 11203-2056 also: The Kinsey Inst Prenatal Devel Project Ind U Bloomington IN 47405 E-mail: DrReinisch@aol.com.

REINIUS, MICHELE REED, executive recruiter; b. San Diego, Jan. 17, 1948; d. Wallace Alvin Reed and Dorothy Louise Austin; m. Robin Patric Reinius, Aug. 4, 1990; 1 child, Joselyn Ann Andrews. Supr. Asosa Personnel, Tucson, 1981-83; recruiter TAD Tech., Tucson, 1983-85; cocowner Migar Personnel, Tucson, 1985-90; mgr. Temps by Encore, Tucson, 1990-2000; pres. Ariz. Recruiting Source, Tucson, 2000—. Democrat. Jewish. Avocations: reading, swimming. Office: Ariz Recruiting Source 7483 E Broadway Tucson AZ 85710

REINKE, DORIS MARIE, retired elementary school educator; b. Racine, Wis., Jan. 12, 1922; d. Otto William Reinke and Louise Amelia Goehring. BS, U. Wis., Milw., 1943; MS, U. Wis., Whitewater, 1967. Tchr. kindergarten Elkhorn (Wis.) Area Sch. Sys., 1943-69, bldg. prin., 1968-70, summer sch. dir., 1974-75, grade 2 tchr., 1970-84, primary dept. chmn., 1971-84, administrv. asst., supervising tchr., 1957-83, student tchr., 1984, ret., 1984; oriented experience tchr. Program Area Sch. Sys., Elkhorn, 1966. Pres. Elkhorn Edn. Assn., 1949-50; rep. dist. State Kindergarten Conf., Oshkosh, Wis., 1966; participant early edn. conf. State Early Edn. Conf., Eagle River, Wis., 1968; tchr. Covenant Harbor Elderhostel, 1997, 98; established Doris M. Reinke Resource Ctr., 2002. Author: Doris' Corner newsletter Walworth County Geneal. Soc., 1992—; author: (with Charlotte and William Gates) Guide to Beckwith's History of Walworth County, 2000; contbr. weekly newspaper column Webster Notes, 1989, monthly column in The Week, 1991. Chmn. Sch. Centennial, Elkhorn, 1987; mem. Elkhorn Hist. Preservation Com., 1991—; chmn. Sesquicentennial com., 1997—; dir. Webster House Mus., 1991—; mem. Walworth County Sesquicentennial Com., 1997—98; mem. sesquicentennial com. Walworth County Fair, 1998—; archivist Sugar Creek Luth. Ch., 1992—, mem. ch. coun., 2003; choir mem. Luth. Ch., 1995—2001; del. dist. constn. conv. Evang. Luth. Ch. Am., Beloit, Wis., 1987; com. mem. Luth. Ch., Elkhorn, 1987; RSVP Vol. Food Pantry, Elkhorn, 1985—2002, bd. dirs., 1985—88, 1995—. Recipient Wis. Edn. Rsch., West Bend, Wis., 1966, Outstanding Elem. Tchrs., Wash., 1973, Wis. Dept. Edn., Madison, 1980, Local History award State Hist. Soc. Wis., 1993, Outstanding Sr. Citizen award Walworth County Fair, 1999, Cmty. Svc. award, Masons, 2000. Mem.: Walworth County Ret. Tchrs. Assn. (v.p. 1988, pres. 1991), Nat. Ret. Tchrs. Assn., Walworth County Geneal. Soc. (bd. dirs. 1991—92), Walworth County Hist. Soc. (treas. 1985—89, v.p. 1990—91, pres. 1991—96, v.p. 1999—2000, pres. 2000—03), Elkhorn Women's Club (sec. 1999—2000, v.p. 2003), Alpha Delta Kappa (state pres. 1968—70, 1976—78, chpt. pres. 2002—03). Avocations: reading, baseball, bird watching, travel. Home: 516 N Wisconsin St Elkhorn WI 53121-1119

REINKE, LINDA JEANETTE, retired social worker; b. Harrisburg, Pa., July 18, 1941; d. William M. and Gladys A. Grabill; m. Marvin E. Reinke, June 1963. BS, George Williams Coll., 1963; MSW, Va. Commonwealth U., 1975. Lic. social worker Ill., cert. Acad. Cert. Social Workers, 1977. Social worker, parole agt. Wis. State Parole, Milw., 1965—67; caseworker Calhoun Co. Dept. Pensions and Securities, Anniston, Ala., 1967—68; supr. counseling and evaluation Goodwill Industries, Sioux City, Iowa, 1969—71; social worker Alexandria Social Svcs., Va., 1971—73, 1975—78; social work supr. Fairfax Social Svcs., Va., 1978—88; clin. coord. splty. svcs. Strong Meml. Hosp., Rochester, NY, 1989—90; coord. vol. svcs. Rochester Rehab., 1990—92; adminstr. homemaker program Salvation Army Family Svcs., Chgo., 1993—98. Guest lectr. Va. Commonwealth U., 1978—88, George Mason U., 1978—88; field instr. social work Cath. U., Va. Commonwealth U., George Mason U., James Madison U.; chair adv. com. social work program George Mason U. Trainer stroke visitor program Vis. Nurse Svc., Rochester; developer stroke support group Strong Meml. Hosp., Rochester; rsch. project, cmty. edn. James City Coun. Social Svcs., Va.; coord. home visitor program Williamsburg Social Svcs., Va.; mem. bd., program devel. Williamsburg Area Faith-in-Action, 2001—;

adv. bd. Lakeview Mental Health Ctr., Chgo., 1992—94. Mem.: Va. NASW (chair polit. action fundraiser 1985, 1987, coord. continuing edn. and lic. classes Ill. chpt. 1998—99, nomination and leadership identification com. 1980—84, mem. Va. chpt.), Va. Coun. Social Welfare (conf. co-chair 1979, conf. chair 1980, conf. track coord., mem. no. chpt. bd.). Avocations: reading, travel, history.

REINKER, NANCY COOKE, artist; b. Owensboro, Ky., July 6, 1936; d. Billie Clayton and Barbara Jane (Mitchell) Cooke; m. Dale Bruce Reinker, Sept. 29, 1956; children: Shahn Elizabeth, Laura Beth, Karen Christian. Student, Kent State U., 1954-55, Cleve. Art Inst., 1956-57; studied sculpture with, Stanley Bleifeld, 1979-80; student, Silvermine Sch. of Art, 1988-89. Owner Nettle Creek Shops of Westport and Cos Cob, Conn., 1974-86, Cross River Design Studio, 1986-89. One-woman shows include Hayes Gallery, 1992, Silvermine Guild Arts Ctr., Art Place, 1993, 1995, 1998, 2000, Silvermine Guild Arts Ctr., Art Pl., 2003, Westport Art Ctr., 1994, Farrell II Gallery, 1998, Ulla Surland Gallery II, 2003; works in traveling exhbn. Internat. Faber Birren Color Show, Stamford Mus., 1990, Conn. Art, Stamford Mus., 1990, Conn. Women Artists, New Britain Mus. of Art, 1991, 1993, 1996, Versions of Childhood, Artspace Gallery, New Haven, Conn., 1994, N.Y./New Haven Artspace Gallery, 1994, Women in Visual Arts, Erector Sq. Gallery, New Haven, Conn., 1994, Nat. Assn. Women Artists, Inc., 1996—98, B.J. Spoke Gallery, Long Island, N.Y., 1997, numerous nat. and internat. exhbns.; sculpture UN, N.Y.C., Rebuilding Torn Societies, 1999; juried and invited shows, Katonah Mus. Art, 2001, Conn. Graphic Arts Ctr., 2001, 42d Art of the Northeast, 44th Art of the Northeast, 45th Art of the Northeast, 52d Art of the Northeast, 2001, 53d Art of the Northeast, Reflections, Norwalk C.C., 2002; Represented in permanent collections, Housatonic C.C. Chmn. Commn. for The Arts, Weston, Conn., 1993-94, Art Bridge-U.S.-Japan, 2000, Gallery Irohani, Sakai City, Japan; pres. Inst. for Visual Artists, New Canaan, Conn., 1992-93; v.p., pres. Art Place Gallery, Southport, Conn., 1991-92, treas., 1998—. Named to 1992 Cir. of Excellence, Soc. Nat. Art Patrons, 1992; recipient 1st prize Spectrum, 1992, 93, 94. Mem. ASID (assoc.), Silvermine Guild of Artists (trustee 1994-99), New Haven Paint and Clay (Merit award 1993, purchase award for permanent collection 1997), Nat. Assn. Women Artists, Conn. Women Artists (Painting award 1991), Greenwich Art Soc. (Randolph Chitwood award 1994), Women's Caucus for Art, Chi Omega. Home: 87 Valley Forge Rd Weston CT 06883-1913 E-mail: ncrtist@aol.com.

REINKING, ANN H. dancer, actress; b. Seattle, Nov. 10, 1949; d. Walter Floyd and Francis Holmes (Harrison) R.; m. Larry Small, 1970; m. Herbert A. Allen; Aug. 25, 1982; (stepchildren): Leslie, Christie, Herbert, Charlie. Student public schs. Guest tchr. NYU, Duke U., Durham, N.C., Rutgers, N.J., Harvard, Cambridge, Mass.; choreographer Pal Joey, Goodman Theater, Chgo., 1988. Broadway appearances include Coco, 1970, Wild and Wonderful, 1972, Pippin, 1973, Over Here, 1974, Goodtime Charlie, 1975, Chicago, 1977, A Chorus Line, 1976, Dancin', 1978, Sweet Charity, 1986-87; TV appearances include Ellery Queen, Doug Henning: Magic on Broadway, 1982, Parade of Stars, 1983, American Treasury, 1985, Salute to Jules Styne, Broadway Salutes Washington, An Introduction to the Dance Gala of the Stars; film appearances include Movie, Movie, 1978, All That Jazz, 1979-80, Annie, 1982, Micki and Maude, 1984; play Ann Reinking ... Music Moves Me, 1984; actor, choreographer Broadway shows: Chicago, 1996 (Tony award 1997), Annie Get Your Gun, 1999 (Tony award 1999), Fosse, 2001; choreographer Broadway shows: Annie Get Your Gun, 1999, Look of Love, 2003 Recipient Clarence Derwent award, 1974, Outer Critics Circle award, 1974, Theatre World award, 1974, Dance Educators Am. award, 1979, Harkness Dance award, 1979, two Tony award nominations, Tony award for Choregraphy, 1997; Ford Found. scholar, 1964-66; Robert Joffery scholar, 1967; Harkness scholar; Nat. Dance Educators award. Mem. Actors Equity, AFTRA, Stage Actors Guild. Avocations: horseback riding, skiing, swimming, hiking. also: Steps Contemporary & Classical Dance 2121 Broadway Fl 3 New York NY 10023-1786*

REINOLD, CHRISTY DIANE, school counselor, consultant; b. Neodasha, Kans., July 21, 1942; d. Ernest Sherman and Faye Etta (Herbert) Wild; m. Willaim Owen Reinold, Dec. 20, 1964; children: Elizabeth, Rebecca. BA Edn., MA in Edn. and Psychology, Calif. State U., Fresno, 1964. Cert. counselor, Family Wellness instr.; lic. mental health counselor, Fla. Tchr. Clovis (Calif.) Unified Sch. Dist., 1965-66, Santa Clara (Calif.) Unified Sch. Dist., 1966-67, Inst. Internat. Chateaubriand, Cannes, France, 1968-69; tchr., vice prin. Internat. Sch., Sliema, Malta, 1969-70; elem. sch. counselor Duval City Schs., Jacksonville, Fla., 1977-82, Lodi (Calif.) Unified Sch. Dist., 1982—. Cons. Calif. Dept. Edn.; mem. Calif. Commn. on Tchr. Credentialing, Sacramento, 1986—. Co-author: The Best for Our Kids; Counseling in the 21st Century; contbr. articles. Chmn. bd. dirs. Oak Crest Child Care Ctr., Jacksonville, 1979-81. Mem.: AAUW (3rd v.p. 1974, 1st v.p. 1980, by-laws chmn. 1990, chmn. pub. policy 1991—93, pres. 1993), Lodi Pupil Pers. Assn. (pres. 1986—87), Calif. Alliance Pupil Svcs. Orgns. (bd. dirs. 1988—95), Fla. Sch. Counselors Assn., Calif. Assn. Counseling and Devel., Calif. Sch. Counselor Assn. (legis. chmn. 1985—90, pres. 1991), Am. Sch. Counselor Assn. (govt. rels. specialist 1993—94). Republican. Avocations: history, travel, politics. Home: 1180 Northwood Dr Lodi CA 95240-0443

REINSHAGEN, YOLANDA P. elementary school educator; b. Recife, Brazil, Mar. 18, 1953; came to U.S., 1977; d. Manoel and Irene Ferreira Pessôa; m. Jerald Alfred Reinshagen Sr., Dec. 22, 1977; children: Jerald Jr., Jerlanda, Janice, Joseph, Judith, Jerson. BA in Theology and Edn., Monte Morelos (Mex.) U., 1979; MA in Health Edn., U. West Fla., 1994. Asst. tchr. Educandarion Advents, Belem de Maria, Brazil, 1972-74; chaplain Hosp. La Carlota, Monte Morelos, 1975-77; tchr. Academia Adventista del Oeste, Mayaguez, P.R., 1979, SDA Elem. Sch., Queens, 1980. Office mgr., treas. Family Practice Clinic, Rockport, Ind., 1985-88; ministry dir. Univ. S.D.A.C., Pensacola, Fla., 1992-94 Counselor Pathfinders, 1999; Spanish transl. SDA, 1990. Mem. SMMA (coord. health project 1997, sec. 1997). SDA. Home: 19 North Pt Hattiesburg MS 39402-7708

REINSTEIN, KATHI-ANNE, state representative, state legislator; BS, Suffolk Univ.; MA, Emerson Coll. State rep. legis., Mass., 1999—. Com. Revere Dem. City, Ins., Pub. Safety. Mem.: Saugus River Watewrshed Coun., Revere C. of C., WILL/WAND, Santa Fund, Revere 1st, Revere Beach Partnership, Moose. Democrat. Office: State Ho Rm 236 Boston MA 02133

REIS, JEAN STEVENSON, administrative secretary; b. Wilburton, Okla., Nov. 30, 1914; d. Robert Emory and Ada (Ross) Stevenson; m. George William Reis, June 24, 1939 (dec. 1980). BA, U. Tex., El Paso, 1934; MA, So. Meth. U., 1935; postgrad., U. Chgo., 1937-38, U. Wash., 1948-49. Tchr. El Paso H.S., 1935-39; safety engr., trainer Safety and Security Divsn., Office of Chief Ordnance, Chgo., 1942-45; tchr. Lovenberg Jr. H.S., Galveston, Tex., 1946; parish sec. Trinity Parish Episcopal Ch., Seattle, 1950-65; adminstrv. sec., asst. Office Resident Bishop, United Meth. Ch., Seattle, 1965-94. Observer Africa U. installation, Mutare, Zimbabwe, 1994; com. on legislation for 1996 gen. conf. Hist. Soc. of United Meth. Ch. Recipient Bishop's award, 1980. Mem. AAUW, Beta Beta Beta. Home: 9310 42nd Ave NE Seattle WA 98115-3814

REISING, JULIET M. information systems executive; m. Lance Reising; children: Nicholas, Michelle. B in Bus. summa cum laude, U. Ga. cert. CPA. Mgmt., CPA Ernst & Young; CFO AvData, Inc, Composit Comms., Inc., InterServ Svcs. Corp.; exec. v.p., CFP MindSpring Enterprises, Inc.; exec. v.p. Cereus Tech. Ptnrs.; exec. v.p., CFP Verso Tech., Inc., 2000—. Office: Verso Technologies Inc 400 Galleria Pkwy Atlanta GA 30339

REISINGER, SANDRA SUE, columnist; b. Washington Court House, Ohio, Feb. 27, 1946; d. Dale E. and Elinor Jean (McMurry) R. BS, Ohio State U., 1968, MA, 1969; JD, U. Dayton, Ohio, 1980. Bar: Ohio 1980. Tchg. asst. Ohio State U., 1968-69; with Dayton Daily News, 1969-81, asst. mng. editor, 1976-81; mng. editor The Miami (Fla.) News, 1981-89, Broward Miami (Fla.) Herald, 1989-93, mng. editor, asst. mng. editor, [illegible], [illegible] editor, 1998-99; columnist The Herald, Ft. Lauderdale, 1999—. Adj. prof. Sinclair (Ohio) C.C., 1971-74, U. Dayton, Ohio, 1980-81. Mem. ABA, AP Mng. Editors Assn. (bd. dirs. 1982-87, exec. com. 1987-94, pres. 1992). Office: The Herald 1520 E Sunrise Blvd Fort Lauderdale FL 33304-2327

REISMAN, JOAN ANN, executive secretary; b. Brooklyn, NY, Sept. 15, 1936; d. David and Betty Rose Sobel; m. Zane Saul Reisman; children: Mitchell, Eve, Lawrence, Beth. Owner Sno White Cleaners, Bklyn., 1967—70; mgr., owner Hill Park Cleaners, Bklyn., 1970—73; with Handher Murray Law Firm, N.Y.C., 1974—76; mgr., owner Joe Taylor Cleaners, S.I., NY, 1977—78; adminstrv. office mgr. Cobble Hill Health Ctr., Bklyn., 1979—2003. Democrat. Jewish. Home: 21 Gemini Ln Manalapan NJ 07726

REISMAN, JUDITH ANN GELERNTER, media communications executive, educator; b. Hillside, N.J., Apr. 11, 1935; MA in Speech Comm., Case Western Res. U., 1976, PhD in Speech Comm., 1980. Faculty dept. anthropology and sociology Haifa U., Israel, 1981—83; rsch. prof. sch. edn. Am. U., Washington, 1983—85; founder, pres. Inst. Media Edn., 1985—. Cons., reviewer grant proposals audio-visual drug programs for youth Dept. Edn., 1987; rsch. design cons. Alcohol and Tobacco Media Analysis in Mainstream Mags., Dept. HHS, 1987—90; cons., field reviewer Drug Free Youth Sch. Candidates Dept. Edn., 1988; lectr., adj. prof. George Mason U., Va., 1990; expert witness Pres.'s Commn. on Assignment of Women in Armed Forces, 1992, U.S. Atty. Gen. Commn. on Pornography, 1985—86, U.S. Atty. Gen. Task Force on Domestic Violence, Washington, 1985, Mapplethorpe Trial, Cin., 1990, Australian Parliament, 1992, Ga. State Senate, 1992; nominated to panel on sex harassment in the Air Force U.S. Inspector Gen., 2003. Author: Images of Children, Crime and Violence in Playboy, Penthouse and Hustler, 1989, Kinsey, Sex and Fraud, 1990, Softport Plays Hardball, 1991, Kinsey, Crimes and Consequences, 1998, 2003; contbr. preme Ct. cases to profl. jours. Co-recipient Scholastic Mag. awards; recipient Dukane award, 1982, Gold Camera award, 1982, Silver Screen award, 1982, Filmstrip of Yr. award, 1981—82, Silver Plaque award, 1982, Family Svc. Assn. Am. 1st pl. award local TV series, 1974, Best of 1965 award, 1965, Scientist of Yr. for Children award, 1993. Mem.: AAAS, Nat. Black Child Devel. Inst., Soc. Sci. Study Sex, N.Y. Acad. Scis., Internat. Comm. Assn., Am. Statis. Assn., Am. Assn. Composers, Authors and Pubs., Nat. Assn. Scholars. Office: 7623 Stonewood Ct Granite Bay CA 95746-9562

REISMAN, ROSEMARY MOODY CANFIELD, writer, humanities educator; b. Des Moines, Iowa, Nov. 18, 1927; d. V. Alton and Lois Gloria (Slee) Moody; m. Michael Ellison Canfield, Sept. 6, 1952 (div. May 1961); children: Michael, John Charles, Celia Catherine, Christopher James; m. Maurice Reisman, May 10, 1986 (dec. 1990). BA in English, U. Minn., 1949, MA in English, 1952; PhD in English, La. State U., 1971. Reporter Ames Tribune, summer 1944; writer, actor Sta. WOI Pub. Radio, Ames, Iowa, 1944-48; dir., writer children's plays Sta. KASI, Ames, 1949; tchg. asst. U. Minn., 1949-52; writer Sta. WOI-TV, Ames, summer 1952; writer, show host Sta. WDGY, Mpls., 1952-54; instr. La. State U., 1961-69, NDEA fellow, 1969-71; asst. prof. English Troy (Ala.) State U., 1971-80, assoc. prof., 1980-90, chairperson dept. English, 1985-90, prof., 1990-94. Mem. honors coun. Troy State U., 1985-94, mem. honors faculty, 1986-94, mem. acad. coun., 1989-92, mem. faculty adv. coun., 1990-92, Rhodes scholar instnl. rep., 1987-91; adj. prof. Charleston So. U., 1996-99, vis. prof., 1999—; coord. sr. honors seminar Coll. of Charleston, 1996-98; writer, cons. Baton Rouge State Times—Morning Adv., 1963-70; prodr., writer Perspectives project films Ala. ETV, 1977-80; chairperson conf. sessions South Ctrl. Soc. for 18th-Century Studies, 1988, Southeastern Am. Soc. for 18th Century Studies, 1991, 93; chairperson workshop Ala. Coun. Tchrs. of English, fall 1987; grant writer, project dir. Ala. Humanities Found., 1980, 89, asst. project dir. summer grad. course, 1990, presenter various instns., 1985-94; grant writer, project dir. Ala. Pub. Libr. Sys., 1977-80; lectr., presenter various pub. librs. for Auburn Ctr. for Arts and Humanities, 1989-97; presenter numerous lectures and lectr. series, various instns., 1970—, resident Richland Co., S.C., 2002—. Author: Perspectives: The Alabama Heritage, 1978; co-author: Contemporary Southern Women Fiction Writers, 1994, Southern Men Fiction Writers, 1998; chairperson editl. adv. bd. Ala. Lit. Rev., 1986-94; mem. editl. bd. Biog. Guide to Ala. Lit., 1985—; guest editor spl. issue Ala. English 7, spring 1995; contbr. essays, articles and revs. to lit. publs. Baldwin County Humanities scholar Ala. Humanities Found., 1983, 84; finalist Ingalls award for Outstanding Tchg., 1991. Mem.: AAUW (past br. pres., mem. steering com.), NEA, Thomas Cooper Soc. (bd. dirs. 2001—), English Spkg. Union (bd. dirs. Charleston 1997—98, pres. 1998—2002, Sourcelist spkr. 1999—2000), Troy State U. Edn. Assn. (pres. 1990—93), Ala. Edn. Assn., Assn. Coll. English Tchrs. of Ala., Assn. Depts. of English (state pres. 1986—88), South Atlantic MLA, Gamma Beta Phi (nat. pres. 1978—79, cert. of merit 1979), Phi Beta Kappa (del. to nat. triennial coun. 1991, alt. 1994, pres. Low Country Assn. 1996—98, del. 1997, bd. dirs. 1998—2001, alt. del. 2000, bd. dirs. 2003—, past pres. S.E. Ala. assn.). Anglican. Home and Office: 121 Innisbrook Bnd Summerville SC 29483-5084

REISS, DALE ANNE, accounting executive, investment company executive; b. Sept. 3, 1947; d. Max and Nan (Hart) R.; m. Jerome L. King, Mar. 5, 1978; children: Matthew Reiss, Mitchell, Stacey. BS, Ill. Inst. Tech., 1967; MBA, U. Chgo., 1970. CPA, Fla., Ill., Mich., Mo. Cost acct. First Nat. Bank, Chgo., 1967; asst. contr. City Colls. of Chgo., 1967-71; dir. fin. Chgo. Dept. Pub. Works, 1971-73; prin. Arthur Young & Co., Chgo., 1973-80; sr. v.p., contr. Urban Investment & Devel. Co., Chgo., 1980-85; mng. ptnr. Ernst & Young LLP, Chgo., 1985-98, Ernst & Young, N.Y.C., 1998-99; global dir. real estate, hospitality and constrn. Ernst & Young LLP, N.Y.C., 1999—. Bd. dirs. Ill. Inst. Tech., Urban Land Inst.; adv. bd. Kellogg Real Estate, Northwestern U., U. Chgo. Grad. Sch. of Bus. Mem. AICPA, Fin. Execs. Inst., Chgo. Network (bd. dirs.), Econ. of Chgo. Club, Met. Club, Chgo. Yacht Club, N.Y. Athletic Club. Office: Ernst & Young 5 Times Sq 16th Fl New York NY 10036-6530 E-mail: dale.reiss@ey.com.

REISS, LENORE ANN, language educator, retired secondary school educator; b. Bklyn., Apr. 17, 1936; d. Morris and Alice Shestack; m. Edward Lawrence Reiss, Sept. 13, 1959 (dec. June 5, 2000); children: Stephanie Lynne, Jonathan David. BA cum laude, Boston U., 1957; student, Middlebury Coll., 1956, NYU, 1958—59, U. Miami, 1979. Tchr. Spanish and French Martin Van Buren HS, Queen Village, NY, 1957—59; pvt. tutor N.Y.C., 1960—77; pvt. sch. tchr. Studio on Eleventh St., N.Y.C., 1960—77; tchr. The Livingston Sch., N.Y.C., 1977—78, Chiaraville Montessori Sch., Evanton, Ill., 1986—87; pvt. tutor Evanton, 1990—95; ret., 1995. Author: White-Robed Recluse: A Study of Emily Dickinson, 1993, Genius of Darkness: A Study of Edgar Allan Poe, 1994, The Good Lady of Nohant: A Study of George Sand, 1995; contbr. poems to jours., articles to profl. jours. Avocations: reading, music, dance, antiques, theater. Home: 2025 Sherman Ave Evanston IL 60201

REISS, SUSAN MARIE, editor, writer; b. Washington, Sept. 14, 1963; m. Paul L. Roney Jr., May 25, 1991. BA in English Lit., U. Va., 1985; MA in English, George Mason U., 1989. Editl. asst. Water Pollution Control Fedn., Alexandria, Va., 1985-87; freelance writer, editor Arlington, Va., 1987-90; staff writer George Mason U., Fairfax, Va., 1988-90, Optical Soc. Am., Washington, 1990-91, news editor, 1991-93, mng. editor, 1993-96; editor On Campus With Women Assn. Am. Colls. and Univs., 1996—2000; freelance writer, editor Arlington, 1996—. Newsletter editor: Arlington County Tennis Assn., 1990-91, On Campus with Women, 1996-2000; contbr. articles to profl. jours. and mags. Mem. Nat. Press Club, Washington Ind. Writers, D.C. Sci. Writers Assn., N.Y. Acad. Scis., Sigma Tau Delta (founding mem. U. Va. chpt.). Avocations: tennis, piano, cross-country skiing. Home and Office: 6814 30th Rd N Arlington VA 22213-1602

REITER, EUNICE HARRIS, accountant; b. Dallas, Jan. 16, 1938; d. Thoedore and Pearl Ann (Baier) Harris; m. Karl H. Reiter, Dec. 29, 1957; children: Joseph, Sheila, Elaine. Student, U. Tex., 1955-56. Acct. White Petrov McHone CPAs, Houston, 1962-80; corp. treas. Perlite of Houston, Inc., 1980-84; owner EH Reiter Acctg. Svcs., Houston, 1984—. Moderator Channel 13 TV Tax Show, Houston, 1986-87. Pres. Fondren Pk. Cmty. Inprovement Assn., Missouri City, Tex., 1972, 73, 87, 88, 89, 91, 92; commr. Planning and Zoning Commn., Missouri City, 1989-94; councilwoman Missouri City Coun., 1994—; bd. dirs. Houston-Galveston Area Coun., 1999—, vice chair audit com., 2002—, trauma care policy com., 2003—; bd. dirs. Tex. Mcpl. League, 2003—. Mem. Am. Soc. Women Accts. (pres. 1983, pres. meml. fund 1993—), Fedn. Houston Profl. Women (v.p. 1989), Hadassah (life, pres. 1979-81). Jewish. Avocations: community service, reading, playing bridge. Home: 11723 N Perry Ave Houston TX 77071-3421 Office: 5005 Woodway Dr Ste 200 Houston TX 77056-1789

REJENT, MARIAN MAGDALEN, retired pediatrician; b. Toledo, Aug. 12, 1920; d. Casimir Stanley and Magdalen (Szymanowski) R. BS, Mary Manse Coll., 1943; MD, Marquette U., 1946; MPH, U. Mich., 1960. Diplomate Am. Bd. Pediatrics. Intern St. Vincent Med. Ctr., Toledo, 1946-47; resident communicable diseases City Hosp., Cleve., 1947-48; resident pediatrics Childrens Hosp., Akron, Ohio, 1948-50; pvt. practice Toledo, 1950-54; chief div. maternal child health Toledo Bd. Health, 1953-64; dir. pediatrics Maumee Valley Hosp., Toledo, 1964-69; assoc. prof. pediatrics Med. Coll. Ohio, Toledo, 1969-76; med. dir. State Crippled Childrens Program, Columbus, Ohio, 1976-78; attendant pediatrician St. Vincent Med. Ctr., Toledo, 1978-80, 87-99; chief pediatric svcs. Wake County Health Dept., Raleigh, N.C., 1980-87; ret. clin. prof. pediatrics Med. Coll. Ohio, 1998; ret., 1999. Exec. com. March of Dimes, 1988-92. Mem. AMA, APHA, Am. Acad. Pediatrics, Am. Med. Women's Assn., Ohio PHA, Ohio State Med. Assn., NW Ohio Pediatric Assn., Acad. Medicine Toledo, Alpha Omega Alpha. Republican. Roman Catholic. Avocations: travel, photography, painting. Home: The Woodlands Apt #401 4030 Indian Rd Toledo OH 43606

REJUNE-ADAMS, GLORIA JEAN, museum director; d. Frank George Rejune and Jean Gloria Salvatore-Rejune; m. Ronald Peter Adams, Oct. 3, 1964; children: Debra Jean Adams-Acquilano, Peter Ronald Adams, Shannon Lynne Adams. Student, Bklyn Coll., 1961—63, Art Students League, N.Y.C., 1960—63. Mus. dir. Cornell Mus. of Art and History, Delray Beach, Fla., 1990—. Liaison Spady Mus. and Historic District; artist-in-residence. Represented in permanent collections Cornell Mus. Art and Hist., Sandoway House Mus., exhibitions include Boca Raton Profl. Artist Guild, 1980, Fla. ATL U. Schmidt Ctr., 1985, Cunningham Gallery, DB, Gallery One, DB, 1980—82, Delray Affair, 1979—88, Photography published in Internat. Libr. Photography, 2004. Sec. Delray Beach (Fla.) Cultural Alliance, 2000—03; mem. Fla. Trust for Hist. Preservation, Tallahassee, 1990—2003. Mem.: Fla. Assn. Museums (art sect. chair 1993—94, 2001—02), Cornell Mus. Art Guild (Mus. Director's Award 2002), Nat. League of Am. Pen Women (sec.), Palm Beach Watercolor Soc., Delray Beach Art League (life; pres. 1981—85). Avocations: art, poetry, photography. Office: Cornell Museum Art and History 51 N Swinton Ave Delray Beach FL 33444 Office Phone: 561-243-7922. E-mail: museum@oldschool.org.

RELJAC, MARY CATHERINE, principal; d. John Franklin and Catherine Pearce Rankin; m. Jason Matthew Reljac, Oct. 31, 1998. BS in Music Edn., Ind. U. of Pa, Indiana, 1995; MEd in Ednl. Leadership, Carlow Coll., Pitts., 2001. Cert. tchr. K-12 music Pa., 1995, elem. and secondary prin. Pa., 2001. Music tchr. Hempfield Area Sch. Dist., Greensburg, Pa., 1996—97, Gateway Sch. Dist., Monroeville, Pa., 1997—2001, acting asst. prin., 2001—02, asst. prin., 2002—03, elem. prin., 2003—. Bd. dirs. Edgewood Symphony Orch., Pa., 2001—; com. chair Pitts. Symphony Orch. Ea. Area Outreach Com., Monroeville, Pa., 2000—. Mem.: Tri-State Reading Assn., Pa. Assn. of Elem. and Secondary Sch. Prins., Nat. Assn. of Elem. and Secondary Sch. Prins., ASCD, Phi Kappa Phi. Avocations: playing piano and organ, reading, travel.

RELKIN, MICHELE WESTON, artist; b. LA, Jan. 17, 1946; d. Ruben and Vivian (Demerer) Weston; m. Stephen Relkin, July 18, 1982; 1 child, Gregory Aaron. Student, Santa Monica Coll. Curator, co-founder Gallery 9, Thousand Oaks, Calif., 1994—. Art instr. for children and adults; artist in residence Walnut Canyon Elem. Sch., Moorpark, Calif. Represented in permanent collections Nat. Archives, Washington, William J. Clinton Presdl. Libr., Ark., Spotty & Barney (Pres. George W. Bush). Recipient Printmaking award Moorpark Coll., 1992. Mem. Nat. Assn. Women Artists, Thousand Oaks Art Assn. (program dir. 1990—, Art awards), Santa Barbara Printmakers Soc. Avocations: walking, pets, nature, teaching children's art. Home: 1944 Woodside Dr Thousand Oaks CA 91362-1265

RELL, M. JODI, lieutenant governor; b. Norfolk, Va., June 16, 1946; m. Lou Rell; children: Meredith, Michael. Student, Old Dominion U., Western Conn. State U.; LLD (hon.), Univ. of Hartford, 2001. Mem., dep. minority leader Conn. Ho. Reps., 1984-94; lt. gov. State of Conn., 1995—. Past vice chmn. Brookfield Rep. Town Com., appt. chair of the Hartford Econ. Devel. Adv. Group, (HEDAG), 1998 ; trustee YMCA Western Conn; played a key role in raising funds for the Conn. Firefighters Meml.; estab. the Lt. Gov.'s Commn. on State Mandate Reform, Lt. Gov.'s Conn. Treasures award. Named Melvin Jones Fellow, Lions Club Internat. Found., 2003; recipient Leadership award, Nat. Order of Women Legislators (NOWL), Impact award, Conn. Tech. Coun., 2001, First Kids 2001 Policy Leadership award, Conn. Voices for Children, Arnold Markle Public Service award. Mem. Nat. Order Women Legislators (past nat. pres., former v.p., treas., corr. sec.), Women Execs. in State Govt., Brookfield Rep. Women's Club (past pres.), Brookfield Bus. and Profl. Women's Club, Prison and Jail Overcrowding comm., Governor's Law Enforcement Coun., Yale Corp., State Finance Advisory Com. Republican. Office: Office Lt Governor State Capitol Rm 304 Hartford CT 06106 E-mail: ltgovernor.rell@po.state.ct.us.*

REMBE, TONI, lawyer, director; b. Seattle, Apr. 23, 1936; d. Armin and Doris (McVay) R.; m. Arthur Rock, July 19, 1975. Cert. in French Studies, U. Geneva, 1956; LL.B., U. Wash., 1960; LLM in Taxation, NYU, 1961. Bar: N.Y., Wash., Calif. Assoc. Chadbourne, Parke, Whiteside & Wolff, N.Y.C., 1961-63, Pillsbury, Madison & Sutro, San Francisco, 1964-71, ptnr., 1971—. Bd dirs. Aegon N.V., The Netherlands, Potlatch Corp., Spokane, Wash., SBC Comms., Inc., San Antonio. Pres. VanLobenSels/RembeRock Charitable Found., San Francisco; trustee Am. Conservatory Theatre, San Francisco. Fellow Am. Bar Found.; mem. ABA, Am. Judicature Soc., State Bar Calif., Bar Assn. San Francisco, Commonwealth Club of Calif. Office: Pillsbury Winthrop LLP 50 Fremont St San Francisco CA 94105-2230

REMER, DEBORAH JANE, secondary school educator; b. Detroit, Dec. 10, 1953; d. Maynard William and Marie Josephine (Wells) R. BS, Mich. State U., 1976, MA in Tchg., 1977. Mich. secondary provisional tchg. cert., 1976, Mich. secondary continuing tchg. cert., 1981. Sci. tchr. grade 8 Walled Lake (Mich.) Middle Sch., 1977-81; substitute tchr. Utica (Mich) Cmty. Schs., 1981-85; sci. tchr. Kingsbury Sch., Oxford, Mich., 1985-86;

sci. tchr. grades 7, 8, sci. dept. chair Walled Lake (Mich.) Consol. Schs., 1986—. Chair 8th grade sci. fair Walled Lake (Mich.) Middle Sch., 1987, 89—, coach sci. competition, 1987-94; mem. K-12 sci. com. Walled Lake (Mich.) Consol. Schs., 1990—. Author: The Joachim Ernest Theodore Remer Family in Michigan, 1980, revised, 1995; contbr. Environmental Conservation Program Design, 1976; author of various booklets and pamphlets. Archaeology program presenter, pianist Rochester Mills (Mich.) Mus. at Van Hoosen Farm, 1988—, co-dir. archaeology programs, 1989—; tallykeeper Rochester Grapers Vintage Base Ball Team. 4-H state winner in conservation Mich. 4-H Clubs, East Lansing, 1971; recipient 4-H Key Club award Mich. 4-H Clubs, Macomb County, Mich., 1972, Earl Borden Historic Preservation award City of Rochester Hills, Mich. Historic Dist. Commn., 1995. Mem. NEA, Nat. Sci. Tchrs. Assn., Nat. Earth Sci. Tchrs. Assn., Mich. Edn. Assn., Walled Lake Edn. Assn., Mich. Earth Sci. Tchrs. Assn., Mich. Sci. Tchrs. Assn. (middle sch. program com. 1977-81, dir.-at-large 1981, conf. presenter 1993-95, finalist Middle Sch. Sci. Tchr. of Yr. 1995), Met. Detroit Sci. Tchrs. Assn. (conf. presenter 1993-94), Nat. Audubon Soc., Macomb Audubon Soc., Cranbrook Inst. Sci., Smithsonian Assocs., Earthwatch, Hist. Soc. Mich., Rochester Avon (Mich.) Hist. Soc. (rec. sec. 1990), Suffolk County (N.Y.) Hist. and Geneal. Soc., New Eng. Historic Geneal. Soc., N. Am. Butterfly Assn., Founders Soc.-Detroit Inst. Arts, Bat Conservation Internat., Archaeol. Inst. Am., Mich. State U. Alumni Assn., Nat. Wildflower Rsch. Ctr., Colonial Williamsburg Found., Mich. Archaeol. Soc. (Clinton Valley chpt.), Detroit Zool. Soc., Oakland County Pioneer and Hist. Soc., Nat. Trust for Historic Preservation, Soc. for the Preservation of Old Mills (Great Lakes chpt.), Mich. Karst Conservancy, Archaeol. Conservancy, Am. Minor Breeds Conservancy, MADD, Alpha Zeta. Republican. Congregationalist. Avocations: archaeology, gardening, reading, music, needlework. Office: Walled Lake Middle Sch 46720 W Pontiac Trl Walled Lake MI 48390-4048

REMER, JANE TOBA, author, arts education consultant; b. Bklyn., Sept. 22, 1932; d. David Louis and Duds Rose (Schwarzbart) Weissman; m. Michael D. Remer, June 18, 1955 (div. Aug. 1967); children: Abby, Harry. BA, Oberlin Coll., 1954; MA, Yale U., 1957. Asst. dir. Young Audiences, N.Y.C., 1965-67, Lincoln Ctr. for Performing Arts/Edn., N.Y.C., 1967-72; program dir. N.Y.C. Bd. Edn.'s Learning Coop., N.Y.C., 1972-73; assoc. dir. John D. Rockefeller 3d Fund, N.Y.C., 1973-79; dir. Capezio-Ballet Makers Dance Found., Totowa, N.J., 1985—; author, cons. N.Y.C., 1980—. Dir. 440 West End Ave. Corp., N.Y.C., 1990—, New Danoe Group, N.Y.C., 1970-85; adj. prof. N.Y. U., N.Y.C., 1992-2003, Tchrs. Coll. Columbia U., N.Y.C., 2003—; advisor City Ctr. for Music/Dance, N.Y.C., 1993—, Manhattan Theater Club, N.Y.C., 1993—, GE Fund, Fairfield, Conn., 1992-97, MacArthur Found., Chgo., 1996, Columbia U. Tchrs. Coll., 1996-98. Author: Changing Schools Through the Arts, 1982, rev. and expanded edit., 1990, Beyond Enrichment: Building Effective Arts Partnerships With Schools and Your Community, 1996.

REMEZ, SHEREEN G. government executive; M. Lee R. Johnson; 1 child: Erik. BA in Psychology and Communications, MA in Edn., Am. U; PhD, U. Md., 1981. Various positions U.S. Govt.; asst. chief info. officer GSA, 1996-97, chief info. officer. Office: GSA 1800 F St NW Rm 6122 Washington DC 20405-0001

REMINGTON, DEBORAH WILLIAMS, artist; b. Haddonfield, N.J., June 25, 1935; d. Malcolm Van Dyke and Hazel Irwin (Stewart) R. BFA, San Francisco Art Inst., 1957. Adj. prof. art Cooper Union, N.Y.C., 1973—97, NYU, 1994—98; tchr. Nat. Acad. Design, N.Y.C., 2003—. One-woman shows include Dilexi Gallery, San Francisco, 1962, 63, 65, San Francisco Mus. Art, 1964, Bykert Gallery, N.Y.C., 1967, 69, 72, 74, Galerie Darthea Speyer, Paris, 1968, 71, 73, 92, Pyramid Gallery, Washington DC, 1973, 76, zola-Leiberman Gallery, Chgo., 1976, Hamilton Gallery, N.Y.C., 1977, Portland (Oreg.) Ctr. for Visual Arts, 1977, Michael Berger Gallery, Pitts., 1979, Mary Ryan Gallery, N.Y.C., 1982, Ramon Osuna Gallery, Washington D.C., 1983, Newport Harbor Art Mus., 1983, Oakland (Calif.) Mus., 1984, Jack Shainman Gallery, N.Y.C., 1987, Shoshana Wayne Gallery, L.A., 1988, Mitchell Algus Gallery, N.Y.C., 2001; group shows include Whitney Mus. Am. Art, N.Y.C., 1965, 67, 72, San Francisco Mus. Art, 1956, 60, 61, 63, 64, 65, Lausanne Mus., Switz., 1966, Fondation Maeght, St. Paul de Vence, France, 1968, Smithsonian Inst., Washington, D.C., 1968, Art. Inst., Chgo., 1974, Inst. Contemporary Art, Boston, 1975, Nat. Gallery Modern Art, Lisbon, Portugal, 1981, Toledo Mus. Art, 1975, The 6 Gallery, 1954-57, Natsoulas Gallery, Davis, Calif., 1990, 1st Trienalle des Ameriques Maubeuge, France, 1993, Tamarind Inst. Retrospective, 2000, Worcester (Mass.) Art Mus., 2001, San Jose (Calif.) Mus. Art, 2002, numerous others; represented in permanent collections Whitney Mus. Am. Art, Nat. Mus. Am. Art, Washington, Art Inst., Chgo., Centre d'Art et de Culture Georges Pompidou, Paris, Carnegie Mus., Pitts. Recipient Hassam and Speicher Purchase award Am. Acad. and Inst. Arts and Letters, 1988; NEA fellow, 1979-80; Tamarind Inst. fellow, 1973; Guggenheim fellow, 1984; Pollock-Krasner Found. grantee, 1999. Mem. NAD (Benjamin Altman prize for painting 178th Ann. Exhbn. 2003). Home: 309 W Broadway New York NY 10013-5325 Office Phone: 212-925-3037.

REMINGTON, MARY, artist, author; b. Kansas City, Mo., Jan. 15, 1930; d. Edwin Jennings and Mary Pauline (Remington) Anderson; m. Robert Alan Smith, Dec. 14, 1957 (div. 1978); 1 child, Susanah Mara Smith. BA, Ottawa (Kans.) U., 1951; postgrad., U. Kans., 1951, Kansas City Art Inst. Artist animation dept. Walt Disney Prodns., Burbank, Calif., 1954-58; pvt. cartoonist Calif., 1977-92; humor and cartooning tchr. Mira Costa Coll. Extension course, Calif., 1992; tchr. So. Oreg. U., 1993. Freelance cartoonist, caricaturist, Calif., Oreg. Author: Long Ago Elf, 1968, Crocodiles Have Big Teeth All Day, 1970; one-woman show at Josephine County Main Libr., Grants Pass, Oreg., Adobe Gallery, San Diego County, Rogue Gallery, Medford, Oreg., Grants Pass Art Mus.; group exhibitions include Yosemite Mus. Gallery, Okla. Art Workshops 15th Nat. Exhbn., Tulsa, Wiseman Gallery, Grants Pass, others; artist for animated films Lady and the Tramp, Sleeping Beauty. Mem. Grants Pass Art Museum. Avocations: history, reading. Studio: 1002 NW Lawnridge Ave Grants Pass OR 97526-1106

REMINI, LEAH, actress; b. Bklyn., June 15, 1970; m. Angelo Pagan, July 19, 2003. Appearances include (TV series) Living Dolls, 1989, Saved By The Bell, 1989, The Man in the Family, 1991, Getting Up and Going Home, 1992, King of Queens, 1999—, (voice) Gabriel Knight: Sins of the Fathers, 1994, (voice) Phantom 2040: The Ghost Who Walks, 1994, The First Time Out, 1995, Glory Daze, 1996, Fired Up, 1997, Follow Your Heart, 1998, also numerous guest appearances, including Cheers, 1982, Who's the Boss?, 1984, Evening Shade, 1990, Blossom, 1992, Diagnosis Murder, 1993, NYPD Blue, 1993, Friends, 1994; TV Movies: Legend of the Lost Tribe, 2002 (voice), Hooves of Fire, 1999 (voice); Films: Old School, 2003, Follow Your Heart, 1998. Office: Gold Marchak & Liedtke 3500 W Olive Ave Ste 1400 Burbank CA 91505-5512*

RENARD, MEREDITH ANNE, marketing and advertising professional; b. Newark, Apr. 12, 1952; d. W. Edward and Lois E. (Velthoven) Young; m. Robert W. Renard, Nov. 11, 1995. BA, Caldwell Coll., 1974. Advt., pub. rels. asst. Congoleum Corp., Lawrenceville, NJ, 1974—77; account mgr. Saatchi & Saatchi Compton, N.Y.C., 1977—82; dir. advt., sales promotion Singer Sewing Co., Edison, NJ, 1982—86, dir. product mktg., 1986—88, dir. nat. accounts, 1988—90; sr. mktg. rep. Walt Disney World Co., Lake Buena Vista, Fla., 1990—91; divsn. mktg. rep. Vista Advt., Walt Disney World Co., Lake Buena Vista, Fla., 1991—92; mgr. advt. Walt Disney World Co., Lake Buena Vista, Fla., 1992—94, mgr. Fla. tourist mktg., 1994—97; mgr. spl. events Disney Cruise Vacations, Celebration, Fla., 1997—; mgr. ops. integration Disney Cruise Line, Celebration, Fla., 2000—02, dir. programming, and ops. integration, 2002—. Contbr. articles to profl. jours. Vol. North Brunswick Dem. Orgn., 1985—87; pub. rels. mgr. Cultural Arts Com., North Brunswick, 1986—87; props chair Adult Drama Group, North Brunswick, 1986—87; mem. mktg. com. Vol. Ctr. Ctrl. Fla., 1993—94. Mem.: Ctrl. Fla. Direct Mktg. Assn. (bd. dirs. 1990—92), Fla. Direct Mktg. Assn. Episcopalian. Avocations: cross stitch, reading. Office: Disney Cruise Line 210 Celebration Pl Ste 400 Celebration FL 34747-4978

RENAUD, BERNADETTE MARIE ELISE, author; b. Ascot Corner, Que., Can., Apr. 18, 1945; d. Albert and Aline (Audet) R. Diploma, Présentation de Marie, Granby, Que., 1962-64. Librarian asst. Schs. of Waterloo, Que., 1964-67, tchr. primary schs., 1967-70; adminstrv. sec. Assn. Medi-Tech-Sci., Montreal, Que., 1972-76. Author: Emilie La Baignoire A Pattes, 1976 (Can. Coun. Children's Lit. prize, 1976, Assn. Advancement of Scis. and Technics of Documentation award, 1976), 2d edit., 2002, Le Chat de l'Oratoire, 1978, Emilie la baignoire á pattes album, 1978, La maison tête de pioche, 1979, La révolte de la courte pointe, 1979, La dépression de l'ordinateur, 1981, Une boîte Magique Très Embêtante, 1981, La grande question de Tomatelle, 1982, Comment on fait un livre?, 1983, The Cat in the Cathedral, 1983, The Computer Revolts, 1984, (book and movie) Bach et Bottine, 1986 (awards for movie, 19 awards across the world, transl. ino 8 langs., subtitled into 18 langs.), Bach and Broccoli, 1986, (short movie) Quand l'accent devient grave, 1989, (novels) Un Homme Comme Tant d'Autres, tome 1, 1992, tome, II, 1993, tome, III, 1994, Prix Germaine Guévremont, 1995, Gala des Arts du Bas-Richelieu (QC); dir., coord.: Ecrire pour la jeunesse, 1990; author: short stories, adaptations of 8 children's classics, 1977—79; dir., coord.: La quête de Kurweena, 1997, Le petit violon muet, 1997, Héritiers de l'éternité, 1998, Les Funambules D'un Temps Nouveau, 2001, Les Chemins d'Eve Tome I, 2002, Les Chemins d'Eve Tome II, 2002, Grand Prix du Livre de la Monteregie, 2001, 2002.

RENAUD, PAULA MARIE, researcher; b. Annapolis, Md., Dec. 16, 1963; d. Frederick Albert and Sarah Marie (Chrobak) Renaud; children: Sarah Irene, Forest Gabriel. AS, Northwest Coll., Powell, Wyo., 1987; BS, U. Wyo., 2001. Receptionist Buffalo Bill Hist. Ctr., Cody, Wyo., 1983—85; gallery owner Raven's Nest Gallery, Greybull, Wyo., 1987—89; art salesperson Harry Jackson Studio, Cody, 1990—92; tutor coord. Learning Skills Ctr., Powell, Wyo., 1992—99, adminstrv. asst., 1992—99; archival maintenance State Hist. Preservation Office, Laramie, Wyo., 2001; rsch. asst. dept. anthropology U. Wyo., Laramie, 2001—. Presenter in field; presenter Ann. Symposium Am. Heritage Ctr., 2002; coord. Shoshone Nat. Forest Ethnohistory Overview, 2003. Contbr. articles and poems to publs., articles to profl. publs. Mem. Rocky Mountain Activists, Laramie, 2000—01. Recipient Outstanding Student Paper award, Plains Anthropologist, 2000, Local Soroptomist award, Park County, Wyo., 1997; grantee Arts and Sci. Rsch. grantee, U. Wyo., 2000, McNair Scholars Rsch. grantee, 2000; scholar Paul Crissman scholar, 2001—02, Ronnie Bathrick Meml. scholar, 2001—02, George Frison scholar, 2001—02, Seibold Meml. scholar, 1999—2001, John Christopher Meml. scholar, 1999—2000, forensic scholar, Northwest Coll., 1989, theater scholar, 1988, 1989; Epscor rsch. scholar, 2001. Mem.: Nat. Assn. Student Anthropologists, Am. Anthropol. Assn., Am. Soc. for Ethnohistory, Smithsonian Instn. (assoc.), Golden Key, Phi Kappa Phi. Avocations: organic gardening, primitive skills, figure drawing, pottery, theater. Home: 610 S 5th Laramie WY 82070 Office: U Wyo Dept Anthropology PO Box 3431 Ivinson St Laramie WY 82070 E-mail: prenaud@uwyo.edu.

RENAUER, MARITA, educational consultant; b. Washington, DC, Jan. 30, 1969; d. Edward John and Rita Renauer. BA in Psychology, U. N.C., Wilmington, 1991; MA in Early Childhood Edn. and Behavior Analysis, U. Kans., 1993, PhD in Developmental and Child Psychology, 2001. Cert. early childhood spl. edn. Asst. dir., program coord. Common Ground Childcare Ctr., Reston, Va., 1993—94; dir. St. Peter's Childcare Ctr., Kanas City, Kans., 1994—95; grad. rsch. asst. Juniper Gardens Children's Project, Kansas City, Kans., 1995—2000; edn. program cons. Kans. State Dept. Edn., Topeka, 2000—. Vol. Neonatal Intensive Care Unit U. Kans. Med. Ctr., Kansas City, 1997—97; vol. Rose Brooks Ctr., 1997; grad. tchg. asst. Children's Mercy Hosp., Kansas City, 1996—97; gov. student state chpt. CEC; vol. Therapeutic Learning Ctr., Kansas City, 1998—. Author: (rev. books) Professional Book Review, Journal of the Association for Childhood Education International, 2001; contbr. tng. manual Project SLIDE:Skills for Learning Independence in Developmentally Appropriate Environments, 2001. Mem.: Assn. for Childhood Edn. Internat., Greater Kansas City Assn. for Edn. of Young Children, Midwest Assn. for Edn. of Young Children, Nat. Assn. for Edn. of Young Children, Clinical Child Psychology divsn. APA, Soc. Pediat. Psychology, Divsn.Early Childhood, CEC. Avocations: running, aerobics, swimming, dance, art. Office: Kans State Dept Edn 120 SE 10th Avenue Topeka KS 66612 E-mail: mrenauer@hotmail.com.

RENDA, LAREE M. retail executive; Exec. v.p. retail ops., human resources, pub. affairs, labor and govtl. rels. Safeway, Inc., Pleasanton, Calif., 1999—, joined, 1974. Office: Safeway Inc 5918 Stoneridge Mall Rd Pleasanton CA 94588

RENDELL, MARJORIE O. federal judge; m. Edward G. Rendell. BA, U. Pa., 1969; postgrad., Georgetown U., 1970—71; JD, Villanova U., 1973; LLD (hon.), Phila. Coll. Textile and Sci., 1992. Ptnr. Duane, Morris & Heckscher, Phila., 1972—93; judge U.S. Dist. Ct. (ea. dist.) Pa., 1994—97, U.S. Ct. Appeals (3d cir.), Phila., 1997—. Asst. to dir. ann. giving Dept. Devel. U. Pa., 1973—78; mem. adv. bd. Chestnut Hill Nat. Bank/East Falls Adv. Bd.; mem. alternative dispute resolution com. mediation divsn. Ea. Dist. Pa. Bankruptcy Conf.; active Acad. Vocal Arts, Market St. East Improvement Assn., Pa.'s Campaign for Choice, Phila. Friends Outward Bound; vice chair Ave. of Arts, Inc.; vice chair bd. trustees Vis. Nurse Assn. Greater Phila. Mem.: ABA, Phila. Bar Found. (bd. dirs.), Phila. Bar Assn. (bd. dirs. young lawyers sect. 1973—78), Pa. Bar Assn., Am. Bankruptcy Inst., Internat. Women's Forum, Forum Exec. Women, Phi Beta Kappa. Office: US Courthouse 601 Market St Rm 21613 Philadelphia PA 19106-1715*

RENDER, ARLENE, ambassador; 2 adopted children. Joined Fgn. Svc., Dept. State, 1970, consular officer, 1971-73, Tehran, Iran, 1973-76, Genoa, Italy, 1976-78, polit. officer, 1978-79, internat. rels. officer AF/C, 1979-81, dep. chief of mission, 1981-84, consul-gen. Kingston, Jamaica, 1984-86, dep. chief of mission Accra, Ghana, 1986-89, mem. sr. seminar, 1989-90, amb. to The Gambia, 1990-93, dir. Office of Ctrl. African Affairs, 1993—96, amb. to Republic of Zambia, 1996-99, dir. So. African Affairs, 1996—99, U.S. amb. Achievements include speaks French and Italian. Office: Dept of State Dir So African Affairs Washington DC 20521-0001 also: US Embassy Rue Jesse Owens 01 BP 1712 Abidjan 01 Cote d'Ivoire

RENDL-MARCUS, MILDRED, artist, economist; b. May 30, 1928; d. Julius and Agnes (Hokr) Rendl; m. Edward Marcus, Aug. 10, 1956. BS, NYU, 1948, MBA, 1950; PhD, Radcliffe Coll., 1954. Economist GE, 1953-56, Bigelow-Sanford Carpet Co., Inc., 1956-58; instr. econs. Hunter Coll. CUNY, 1959-60, Columbia U., 1960-61, rschr., 1961-63; sr. economist Nat. Indsl. Conf. Bd., 1963-66; asst. prof. Pace Coll., 1964-66; assoc. prof. Borough of Manhattan C. of C. CUNY, 1966-71, prof., 1972-85. Lectr. econs. CCNY, 1953-58; vis. prof. Fla. Internat. U., 1986; bd. dirs. N.Y.C. Coun. on Econ. Edn.; cons. in field. Exhibited group shows at in New Canaan Art Show, 1982-85, Am. Soc. Bus. and Behavioral Scis., 1990-96, New Cannan Soc. for Arts Ann., 1983, 85, New Canaan Arts, 1985, Silvermine Galleries, 1986, Stamford Art Assn., 1987, Phoenix Gallery, 1988, N.Y.C., Parkview Point Gallery, 1982-89, Miami Beach, Fla., 1982-89, Art Complex, New Canaan, Miami Beach, 1985—, Lever House, N.Y.C., 1990, Cork Gallery, Lincoln Ctr., N.Y.C., 1990, Women's Caucus for Art, San Antonio, 1990, Artist's Equity, Broome St. Gallery, N.Y.C., 1991, Greater Hartford Architecture Conservancy, 1991, N.H. Arts Ctr., 1997, Just Originals Art Web, Albuquerque, 1999, Ward-Nasse Gallery, N.Y.C., 2000—, Liliana Fine Art Gallery, Lenox, Mass., 2003—, Artists Gallery, Chelsea, N.Y.C., 2003, Nat. Assn. Women Artists, 2003, 115-Yr. Anniversary Show, World Trade Ctr., N.Y.C., 2004; author (with E. Marcus) Investment and Development of Tropical Africa, 1959, International Trade and Finance, 1965, Monetary and Banking Theory, 1965, Economics, 1969, Economic Progress and the Developing World, 1970, Economics, 1978, Fine Art with Many Equilibrium Prices, 1995; editor Women in the Arts Found. Newsletter, 1986-92; contbr. articles to profl. jours. Founder Rendl Fund for Slavic Art, Mus. of Modern Art, N.Y.C., 1999—, Harvard U. Art Mus. Fund for Slavic Art, Cambridge, 2000—, Harvard Mus. Natural History, Peabody Mus. Archeology and Ethnology, Rendl Fund for the Conservation of Slavic Artifacts, 2000—, Rendl Fund for the Conservation of the Ware Collection of Blaschka Glass Models of Plants, 2001—; mem. mus. coun. Harvard Mus. Natural History, 2001—. Recipient Merit award Manhattan Arts Internat., 1998, Excellence award 1998, Artist Showcase award Manhattan Arts Internat., 1999; Dean Bernice Brown Cronkhite fellow Radcliffe Coll., 1950-51, Anne Radcliffe Econ. Rsch. Sub-Sahara Africa fellow, 1958-59; fellow Gerontol. Assn. Mem. AAUW, Internat. Schumpeter Econs. Soc. (founding), Met. Econ. Assns. (sec. 1954-56), Indsl. Rels. Rsch. Assn., Women's Econ. Roundtable (program planning com.), N.Y.C. Women in Arts, Allied Social Sci. Assn. (artist 1994), NYU Grad. Sch. Bus. Adminstrn. Alumni (sec. 1956-58), Radcliffe Club, Women's City Club (art and landmarks com.).

RENEAU, BRENDA, trade association executive; b. Ft. Hood, Tex. d. Norman L. and Marjorie L. (Shaffer) Fallen; 1 child from previous marriage, Jennifer G. Houghton. Student, U. Okla. Dir. edn. Associated Builders and Contractors Western Okla., Oklahoma City, exec. dir.; commr. of labor OK, Okla. City, 1995—. Contbr. articles to trade publs. Mem. Okla. Soc. Execs., Okla. State C. of C., Oklahoma City C. of C. Achievements include 1st female exec. dir. of Assoc. Builders and Contractors Western Okla. Address: 200 W Wilshire Blvd Ste A-12 Oklahoma City OK 73116-7756 Office: Dept of Labor 4001 N Lincoln Blvd Oklahoma City OK 73105-5298

RENEKER, MAXINE HOHMAN, librarian; b. Chgo., Dec. 2, 1942; d. Roy Max and Helen Anna Christina (Anacker) Hohman; m. David Lee Reneker, June 20, 1964 (dec. Dec. 1979); children: Sarah Roeder, Amy Johannah, Benjamin Congdon. BA, Carleton Coll., 1964; MA, U. Chgo., 1970; DLS, Columbia U., 1992. Asst. reference libr. U. Chgo. Libraries, 1965-66; classics libr. U. Chgo. Libr., 1967-70, asst. head acquisitions, 1970-71, personnel libr., 1971-73; personnel/bus. libr. U. Colo. Libr., Boulder, 1978-80; asst. dir. sci. and engring. div. Columbia U., N.Y.C., 1981-85; assoc. dean of univ. librs. for pub. svcs. Ariz. State U. Libr., Tempe, 1985-89; dir. instrnl. and rsch. svcs. Stanford (Calif.) Univ. Librs., 1989-90; assoc. provost for libr. and info. resources Naval Postgrad. Sch., Monterey, Calif., 1993—. Acad. libr. mgmt. intern Coun. on Libr. Resources, 1980-81; chmn. univ. librs. sect. Assn. Coll. and Rsch. Librs., 1989-90. Contbr. articles to profl. jours. Rsch. grantee Coun. on Library Resources, Columbia U., 1970-71, fellow, 1990-92. Mem. ALA, Am. Soc. Info. Sci., Sherlockian Scion Soc., Phi Beta Kappa, Beta Phi Mu. Home: 740 Dry Creek Rd Monterey CA 93940-4208 Office: Naval Postgrad Sch Dudley Knox Libr 411 Dyer Rd Monterey CA 93943-5198 Office Phone: 831-656-2343. Business E-Mail: mreneker@nps.edu.

RENFRO, LINDA GROSSETTA, elementary school educator, librarian; b. Honolulu, Mar. 6, 1947; d. Warren Arthur and Margaret Rose (Nunn) Grossetta; m. Gary Lee Renfro, Jan. 25, 1969; children: Marla, David Lance. BS, U. of Ariz., Tucson, Ariz., 1965—68, EdM, 1970—75. Home economics tchr. Alchesay HS, Whiteriver, Ariz., 1969—70; 1st grade tchr. Blue Ridge Elem. Sch., Lakeside, Ariz., 1976—84, 3rd grade tchr., 1984—87; tchr., libr. Blue Ridge Elem. and Mid Schools, 1987—97, Blue Ridge HS, 1997—; dist. tchr., libr. Blue Ridge Unified Sch. Dist., 1997—. Mem. adv. bd. Larson Meml. Pub. Libr., Lakeside, Ariz., 1997—. Leader 4-H and Guide Dogs for the Blind, Lakeside, Ariz., 1987—99; active, past pres. Pinetop (Ariz.) Fire Dept. Aux., 1996. Recipient Blue Ridge HS Tchr. of the Yr., Rotary Internat., 2000. Mem.: Ariz. Libr. Assn., Nat. Soc. Colonial Dames Am. Avocations: travel, quilting, camping.

RENFROW, PATRICIA ANNE, secondary school educator; b. Oakland, Calif., Dec. 29, 1951; d. Joseph Montez and Suzanne Leona (Anglada) Galindo; m. Victor E. Renfrow, May 10, 1975; children: Mary Suzanne, Alicia Mariane. BA in Polit. Sci., Calif. State U., Chico, 1973. Spl. edn. instrnl. asst. Vintage H.S., Napa, Calif., 1987-91; instr. ESL Napa Valley Adult Sch., 1992, instr. H.S. diploma program for teen parents, 1992-98, sch. to career liaison, 1994-96, coord. cmty. mentor program, 1996; Cal Works student advisor Napa Valley Coll., 1998—. Teen parent task force Napa Valley Adult Sch., 1992-98, Apple Pie subcom. for pregnancy prevention, 1996—; mem. Calif. Alliance Concerned with Sch. Age Parents, Sacramento, 1992-97. Active Vintage Music Boosters, Vintage H.S., Napa, 1993-97; youth counselor First Unith Meth. Ch., Napa, 1994-96. Named Most Caring Woman, Napa Valley Commn. on the Status of Women, 1993. Mem. AAUW (v.p. membership 1996—). Democrat. Avocations: fitness, reading, collecting disneyania. Office: Napa Valley Coll 2277 Napa Vallejo Hwy Napa CA 94558-6236

RENGER, MARILYN HANSON, elementary school educator; b. Shelly, Idaho, July 17, 1949; d. Merril H. and Betty Jean (Hendricksen) Hanson; m. Robert Carl Renger, Sept. 11, 1971; children: Katherine, James. BA in History, U. Calif., Santa Barbara, 1971; postgrad., Calif. Luth. U., 1973-74. Tchr. Ventura (Calif.) Unified Schs., 1974-79, 85-98, asst. prin., 1998—. Cons. State of Calif., 1989-93. Recipient Disting. Tchr. K-12 award Nat. Coun. for Geog. Edn., 1992. Mem. Nat. Coun. Geographic Edn. (Nat. Disting. Teaching award 1992), Calif. Geographic Soc. (steering com. 1989-93, co-dir. summer inst. 1992), Nat. Coun. Social Studies. Office: Balboa Mid Sch 247 S Hill Rd Ventura CA 93003-4401

RENK, KIMBERLY DAWN, social sciences educator; m. Robert William Renk, June 29, 1991; 1 child, Kyle Matthew. BS, U. Ill., 1992; MA, Ill. State U., 1994; PhD, U. South Fla., 2000. Asst. prof. U. Ctrl. Fla., Orlando, 2000—. Svc. provider Nemours Children's Clin., Orlando, 2000—. Contbr. articles to profl. jours. Grantee, U. Ctrl. Fla., 2002; Gala endowment, Fla. Hosp., 2002—03. Mem.: APA, Southeastern Psychol. Assn. Office: U Ctrl Fla Dept Psychology 4000 Central Florida Blvd Orlando FL 32816

RENK, PAMELA JEAN, counselor, psychotherapist; b. Pitts., Feb. 23, 1956; d. James Voris and Nancy Marie (Vessels) McClain; m. Randy Allen Renk, June 20, 1976. BA in Social & Behav. Scis. summa cum, Ind. State U., 1982; M in Clin. and Counseling Psychology, Calif. State U., San Bernardino, 1986. Cert. marriage, family and child counselor Bd. Behavioral Sci. Examiners. Intern counselor U. Calif., Riverside, 1984-85, Fontana (Calif.) Med. Group, 1986-87, Harmonium Inc., Mira Mesa, Calif., 1988-89; owner, marriage family child counselor South Bay Counseling, San Clemente, Calif., 1989—. Spkr. in field. Mem. Calif. Assn. Family Therapists. Avocations: skiing, horseback riding, in-line skating, reading, theatre. Office: South Bay Counseling 302 N El Camino Real # 210 San Clemente CA 92672-4778 Office Phone: 949-361-7880.

RENNA, CATHY, communications executive, activist; Grad., Adelphi U. Vol. Gay and Lesbian Alliance Against Defamation (GLADD), NY, 1990, dir. regional media and cmty. rels., 1996—2001, news media dir., 2001—04; media rels. dir. Fenton Comm., NY, 2004—. Office: Fenton Comm 260 Fifth Ave Ninth Fl New York NY 10001 Office Phone: 212-584-5000. Office Fax: 212-584-5045.*

RENNER, JACQUELINE MARIE, research and development company executive; b. N.Y.C., Feb. 15, 1958; d. Ernest John and Patricia Aurora (Romano) R. BA in Chemistry, U. Pa., 1979; MBA, NYU, 1984. Research chemist Olin Corp., New Haven, 1979-81, comml. devel. mgr. Stamford, Conn., 1981-85, product mgr., 1985-87; comml. dir. Johnson Matthey, West Deptford, N.J., 1987-89; mktg. mgr. FMC Corp., Phila., 1989-91; planning mgr. chemical products group, 1991-92; bus. dir. process additives divsn., 1992-94; acquisition devel. dir. Chgo., 1993—98; comml. dir. Monsanto Co., St. Louis, 1998—2000, v.p. e-business, 2000—02; v.p. and gen. mgr. Fisher Sci. Edn. Fisher Sci. Internat., Chgo., 2003—. Patentee novel functional fluids, 1981. Robert Bosch fellow, 1984-85. Mem. Comml. Devel. Assn. Office: Fisher Sci Edn 4500 Turnberry Dr Hanover Park IL 60133-5491

RENNIE, MILBREY TOWER, television news producer; b. Milw., Aug. 19, 1946; d. William Roxburgh and Jean (Tower) R.; m. David Hendrickson Taylor, Jr., Sept. 15, 1973; children: Rennie, Milbrey. BA, Vassar Coll., 1968. Caseworker Sen. Charles Percy, Washington, 1968-69; campaign asst. to Re-elect Mayor John Lindsay, N.Y.C., 1969; rschr. ABC News, Washington, 1970-71; reporter, prodr. NPACT (PBS), Washington, 1971-75; exec. prodr. CBS News, N.Y.C., 1976—. Trustee Vassar Coll., Poughkeepsie, N.Y., 1989—, Miss Porter's Sch., Farmington, Conn., 1976-81, 93—, Nightingale Bamford Sch., 1994—; dir. OTR Lecture Series, FPA, N.Y.C., 1990—; mem. Counkilon Fgn. Rels. Luce scholar Henry Luce Found., Manila, 1975-76. Avocation: tennis. Office: CBS News Weekend News/Sunday News 524 W 57th St New York NY 10019-2924

RENNINGER, MARY KAREN, librarian; b. Pitts., Apr. 30, 1945; d. Jack Burnell and Jane (Hammerly) Gunderman; m. Norman Christian Renninger, Sept. 3, 1965 (div. 1980); 1 child, David Christian. BA, U. Md., 1969, MA, 1972, M.L.S., 1975. Tchr. English West Carteret High Sch., Morehead City, N.C., 1969-70; instr. in English U. Md., College Park, 1970-72; head network services Nat. Libr. Svc., Libr. of Congress, Washington, 1974-78, asst. for network support, 1978-80; mem. fed. women's program com. Libr. of Congress, Washington, 1978-80; chief libr. divsn. Dept. Vets. Affairs, Washington, 1980-90; chief serial and govt. publs. divsn. Libr. of Congress, Washington, 1991—, mem. fed. libr. com., 1980-90, mem. exec. adv. bd., 1985-90. Mem. USBE pers. subcom., 1982-84; bd. regents Nat. Libr. of Medicine, 1986-90, mem. outreach panel, 1988-89; fed. libr. task force for 1990 White House Conf. on Librs., 1986-90; liaison to The White House Conf. Med. Libr. Assn., 1989-90. Recipient Meritorious Svc. award Libr. of Congress, 1974, Spl. Achievement award, 1976, Performance award VA, ann. 1982-89, Adminstr.'s Commendation, 1985, Spl. Contbn. award, 1986. Mem. ALA (Govt. Documents Roundtable), Libr. Tech. Assn., Med. Libr. Assn. (govt. rels. com. 1985—), D.C. Libr. Assn., Soc. Applied Learning Tech., Med. Interactive Videodisc Consortium, Govt. Documents Roundtable, Knowledge Utilization Soc., Nat. Multimedia Assn. Am., U.S. Tennis Assn., Phi Beta Kappa, Alpha Lambda Delta, Beta Phi Mu. Home: 840 College Pky Rockville MD 20850-1931 Office: Libr of Congress Ser and Govt Pub Divsn Lm 133 Washington DC 20540-0001 Business E-Mail: Kren@loc.gov.

RENO, JANET, former attorney general; b. Miami, Fla., July 21, 1938; d. Henry and Jane (Wood) R. AB in Chemistry, Cornell U., 1960; LL.B., Harvard U., 1963. Bar: Fla. 1963. Assoc. Brigham & Brigham, 1963-67; ptnr. Lewis & Reno, 1967-71; staff dir. judiciary com. Fla. Ho. of Reps., Tallahassee, 1971-72; cons. Fla. Senate Criminal Justice Com. for Revision Fla.'s Criminal Code, spring 1973; adminstrv. asst. state atty. 11th Jud. Circuit Fla., Miami, 1973-76, state atty., 1978-93; ptnr. Steel Hector and Davis, Miami, 1976-78; U.S. atty. gen. Dept. Justice, Washington, 1993-2001. Mem. jud. nominating commn. 11th Jud. Circuit Fla., 1976-78; chmn. Fla. Gov.'s Council for Prosecution Organized Crime, 1979-80. Recipient Women First award YWCA, 1993. National Women's Hall of Fame, 2000. Mem. ABA (Inst. Jud. Adminstrn. Juvenile Justice Standards Commn. 1973-76), Am. Law Inst., Am. Judicature Soc. (Herbert Harley award 1981), Dade County Bar Assn., Fla. Pros. Atty.'s Assn. (pres. 1984-86). Democrat. Address: 11200 N Kendall Dr Miami FL 33176-1108*

RENO, ROSEMARY, marketing professional, real estate agent; b. Chillicothe, Ohio, Jan. 15, 1934; d. James Cullen Varney and Mary Melba (Harlow) Tanner; m. Chester M. Reno, May 18, 1956 (div. 1961); children: Denyce Dianne; m. John S. Wilson, Sept. 6, 1963 (div. 1968); children: Todd Blake Wilson; m. Donald D. Williamson, Mar. 10, 1989. Student, Marin Coll., 1952-53, Santa Rosa Jr. Coll., 1957-58, Glendale Coll., 1975-77, L.A. City Coll., 1977-78. Personal sec. Adj. Gen., Oklahoma City, 1966-70; project coord. Am./West, Glendale, Calif., 1970-76; asst. to pres. United Recording, Hollywood, Calif., 1976-82; dir. mktg. Desarralladora Los Gatos, Rosarito Beach, Mex., 1982-92, Century 21 Coastal, Rosarito Beach, Mexico, 1993—95; office mgr. Globelwide, 1995—99. Mem. Red Cross, Rosarito Beach, 1991; guardian counsel Jobs Daus., Glendale, 1973-76; troop leader Campfire Girls, Oklahoma City, 1968-69; pres. Castillos del Mar Homeowners Assn., 2000-04. Avocations: cooking, fishing, golf, theatre, music. Office: PO Box 439030 PMB L-8 San Diego CA 92143-9030

RENSE, PAIGE, editor, publishing company executive; b. Iowa, May 04; m. Kenneth Noland, Apr. 10, 1924. Editor-in-chief Architectural Digest, L.A., 1970—. Appeared on (television) Good Morning Am., The Today Show, Entertainment Tonight. Named Woman of Yr., LA Times, 1976, to Interior Design Hall of Fame; recipient Pacifica award, So. Calif. Resources Coun., 1978, Editl. award, Dallas Market Ctr., 1978, Golden award, Chgo. Design Resources Coun., 1978, Agora award, 1982, Outstanding Profl. Incomms. award, 1982, Nat. Headliner award, Women in Comms., 1983, Muses, 1986, Woman of Internat. Accomplishment, 1991, Spirit of Achievement award, 1995, Pratt Inst. Founders award, 1997. Office: Archtl Digest The Conde Nast Publ Inc 6300 Wilshire Blvd Fl 11 Los Angeles CA 90048-5204

RENSHAW, JEAN REHKOP, management educator, consultant; b. Canoga Park, Calif., Oct. 15, 1936; d. Al H. and Ada E. (Heins) Rehkop; m. William B. Renshaw (div. 1985); children: Blair, Jeannine, Alan. BS, UCLA, 1959, MS, 1972, PhD, 1974. Economist The RAND Corp., Santa Monica, Calif.; prof. U. So. Pacific, Suva, Fiji, U. Hawaii, Honolulu; prof., chair bus. dept. Ea. Oreg. State Coll., La Grande; prof. mgmt. Pepperdine U., L.A. Cons. AJR Internat. Assocs., San Diego, 1979—; monitor New Zealand Qualification Auth., Wellington, 1989—. Author: Japanese Women Manager, 1996, Kimono in the Boardroom, 1999; contbr. chpt. to book, articles to profl. jours. Cons. Hawaii State, Honolulu, 1990-94. Fulbright sr. rsch. scholar Tokyo, 1990-93. Mem. Womencare, Assn. Asian Studies, Soc. Ind. Scholars. Avocations: sailing, painting.

RENT, CLYDA STOKES, academic administrator; b. Jacksonville, Fla., Mar. 1, 1942; d. Clyde Parker Stokes Sr. and Edna Mae (Edwards) Shuemake; m. George Seymour Rent, Aug. 12, 1966; 1 child, Cason Rent Lynley. BA, Fla. State U., 1964, MA, 1966, PhD, 1968; LHD (hon.), Judson Coll., 1993. Asst. prof. Western Carolina U., Cullowhee, N.C., 1968-70, Queens Coll., Charlotte, N.C., 1972-74, dept. chair, 1974-78, dean Grad. Sch. and New Coll., 1979-84, v.p. for Grad. Sch. and New Coll., 1984-85, v.p. acad. affairs, 1985-87, v.p. cmty. affairs, 1987-89; pres. Miss. U. for Women, Columbus, 1989—. Mem. adv. bd. Nat. Women's Hall of Fame; cons. Coll. Eb. N.Y.C., 1983-89; sci. cons. N.C. Alcohol Rsch. Authority, Chapel Hill, 1976-89; bd. mem. So. Growth Policies Bd., 1992-94; adv. bd. Nat. Women's Hall of Fame, Trustmark Nat. Bank, 1991-97; rotating chair Miss. Instns. Higher Learning Pres. Coun., 1990-91; commn. govtl. rels. Am. Coun. Edn., 1990-93; mem. adv. bd. Entergy/Miss., 1994-97, Freedom Forum 1st Amendment Ctr., 1996-2001; mem. Miss. adv. bd. Trustmark Nat. Bank, 1991-97; mem. Mary Baker Eddy Adv. Group, 2000—; mem. Rhodes Scholar selection com. of Miss., 1996-98; mem. Free Sprit Awards selection com., 1996—; mem. ACE Commn. on Women in Higher Edn., 1999—. Mem. editl. bd. Planning for Higher Education, 1995; contbr. articles to profl. jours.; speeches pub. in Vital Speeches, mem. editl. bds. acad. jours. Trustee N.C. Performing Arts Ctr., Charlotte, 1988-89, Charlotte County Day Sch., 1987-89, bd. visitors Johnson C. Smith U., Charlotte, 1985-89; exec. com. bd. dirs. United Way Allocations and Rev., Charlotte, 1982-88; bd. advisors Charlotte Mecklenburg Hosp. Authority, 1985-89; bd. dirs. Jr. Achievement, Charlotte, 1983-89, Miss. Humanities Coun., Miss. Inst. Arts and Letters, Miss. Symphony, Miss. Econ. Coun.; chair Leadership Miss. and Collegiate Miss.; chmn. bd. dirs. Charlotte/Mecklenburg Arts and Sci. Coun., 1987-88; Danforth assoc. Danforth Found., St. Louis, 1976-88, Leadership Am., 1989; mem. golden triangle adv. bd. Bapt. Meml. Hosp., 1999—; pres. So. Univs. Conf., 1994-95; mem. commn. govt. rels. Am. Coun. Edn., 1990-93; mem. alumni bd. First United Meth. Ch., 1996—. Recipient Grad. Made Good award Fla. State U., 1990, medal of excellence Miss. U. for Women, 1995, Women Who Make a Difference award IWF, 2000; named Prof. of Yr., Queens Coll., 1979, One of 10 Most Admired Women Mgrs. in Am., Working Women mag., 1993, One of 1000 Women of the 90's, Mirabella mag., 1994; Ford Found. grantee, 1981; Paul Harris fellow, 1992; OWHE fellow, 1999—. Mem. Am. Assn. State Colls. and Univs. (bd. dirs. 1994-96, 99), Sociol. Soc., So. Assn. Colls. and Schs. (mem. commn. on colls. 1996-98), N.C. Assn. Colls. and Univs. (exec. com. 1988-89), N.C. Assn. Acad. Officers (sec.-treas. 1987-88), Soc. Internat. Bus. Fellows, Miss. Assn. Colls. (pres. 1992), Newcomen Soc. U.S., Internat. Women's Forum, Univ. Club, Rotary. Achievements include 1st female pres. of Miss. U. for Women (1st pub. coll. for women in Am.). Office: Miss State U Social Scis Rsch Ctr PO Box 5287 Mississippi State MS 39762

RENTELN, ALISON DUNDES, political science educator; b. Bloomington, Ind., Jan. 9, 1960; d. Alan and Carolyn (Browne) Dundes; m. Paul Alexander Renteln, June 9, 1985; children: David Alexander, Michael Alan. BA in History and Lit. cum laude, Harvard U., 1981; postgrad., London Sch. Econs., 1981-82; M of Jurisprudence, U. Calif., Berkeley, 1985, PhD in Jurisprudence and Social Policy, 1987; JD, U. So. Calif., 1991. Acting dir., vis. lectr. law and soc. U. Calif., Santa Barbara, 1986-87; asst. prof. polit. sci. U. So. Calif., L.A., 1987-93, assoc. prof. polit. sci., 1993—2003, prof., 2003—, acting dir. Unruh Inst. Pol., 1995-96, vice-chair dept. polit. sci., 1995—2002. Vis. prof. Sch. Law, U. Calif., Berkeley, 1996-97; vis. prof. dept. polit. sci. Stanford U., 1997; lectr. Calif. State Judges Assn., Nat. Assn. Women Judges, UN Assn., Nat. Assn. Fgn. Student Affairs, L.A. Refugee Forum, Calif. Assn. of Adminstrn. of Justice Educators Delinquency Control Inst.; others; coord. Contemporary Issues in Law and Pub. Policy lectr. series Pasadena Sr. Citizens Ctr.; participant Hearing of U.S. Adv. Bd. on Child Abuse and Neglect. Author: International Human Rights: Universalism Versus Relativism, 1990; co-editor: (with Alan Dundes) Folk Law: Essays on the Theory and Practice of Lex Non Scripta, 1994, The Cultural Defense, 2004; reviewer: Am. Anthropologist, Am. Jour. Comparative Law, Am. Jour. Polit. Sci., Human Rights Quar., Jour. of Peace Rsch., others; contbr. numerous articles to profl. publs. Named Mentor of Distinction, Women's Caucus for Polit. Sci., 1993; Soroptimist Internat. Founder fellow, 1986; grantee Mark De Wolfe Howe Fund for rsch. in civil rights, civil liberties, and legal history Harvard U., 1985, Faculty Rsch. and Innovation Fund, 1988, Irvine Found. for diversity course devel., 1991, Faculty Fund for innovative tchg., 1993, Zumberge Faculty Rsch. and Innovation Fund, 1994. Mem. Am. Polit. Sci. Assn., Law and Soc. Assn., Commn. on Folk Law and Legal Pluralism, Am. Soc. Internat. Law, Internat. Law Assn. Office: U So Calif Dept Polit Sci VKC 327 Los Angeles CA 90089-0044 Office Phone: 213-740-3248. E-mail: arenteln@usc.edu.

RENTOUMIS, ANN MASTROIANNI, psychotherapist; b. New Haven, Apr. 27, 1928; d. Luigi Mastroianni and Marion Dallas; m. George Rentoumis, June 27, 1959; children: Michael, Mary, Anne. BA in Psychology, Vassar Coll., 1949; postgrad., Boston U. Med. Sch., 1949-50; MS in Social Work, Columbia U., 1952. Diplomate Am. Bd. Social Work, Am. Psychotherapy Assn.; lic. cert. social worker; lic. marriage and family therapist. Child and adolescent therapist Bklyn. Psychiat., 1952-55; family therapist Community Svc. Soc., N.Y.C., 1955-58; psychotherapist Bleuler Psychotherapy Ctr., L.I., N.Y., 1958-60, Adolescent Psychiat. Clinic, Tex. Children's Hosp., Houston, 1975-76; pvt. practice Houston, 1976-77, Lauderdale Psychiat. Group, Ft. Lauderdale, Fla., 1978-90, Pompano Beach, Fla., 1990-93, Ft. Lauderdale, 1993—. Bd. dirs. Envirodyne, Inc. Pres. Pine Crest Sch. Mothers Club, 1985-86; v.p. Opera Soc., 1987-88, bd. mem., 1998—, parliamentarian 2000—; bd. govs., v.p. exec. bd. Fla. Philharm Orch., 1988-91, bd. dirs., 1990—; pres. Ft. Lauderdale Philharm. Soc., 1988-90. Recipient Golden Rule award J.C. Penney Co., 1990; named Woman of Yr., Am. Cancer Soc., 1989, Woman of Style and Substance, Ft. Lauderdale Philharm. Soc., 1998. Fellow Am. Psychotherapy Assn., Am. Orthopsychiat. Assn.; mem. Am. Assn. Marriage and Family Therapists, Am. Group Therapy Assn., Harbor Beach Surf Club (v.p. 1986-90). Avocations: piano, tennis, swimming. Home: 2200 S Ocean Ln Ph 6 Fort Lauderdale FL 33316-3836 Office: 1326 SE 3d Ave Fort Lauderdale FL 33316-1260

RENTZ, BESSIE ELIZABETH, adult education educator; b. Wellborn, Fla., Sept. 04; d. Westly Davis and Annie Zow Ingram; m. Eddie James Rentz, June 9, 1958; children: Robyn, Deborah, Darlene, Donna, Lorraine, Eddie Jr.(dec.). EdM, Cambridge Coll., Boston, 1999. Vocat. cert. Fla. Tchr. Blanche Ely High, Pompano Beach, Fla., 1972—81; tchr. vocat. tech. Broward Correctional Instn., Pembroke Pines, Fla., 1981—89; GED instr. AVOC, Pompano Beach, 1989—91; tchr. Hallandale (Fla.) Adult Cmty. Ctr., 1991—. Cons. David's Bridal, Ft. Lauderdale, Fla., 1979—93; liaison, dept. chair Broward Sch. Dist., 1998—. Founding pres. Gemini Women's Club, Ft. Lauderdale, 1970—73; Dem. precinct comitteeperson Broward County, 1970—75; pres. nurses guild Mt. Nebo Bapt. Ch., 2002—. Avocations: designing, catering. Home: 1460 NW 32d Ter Fort Lauderdale FL 33311 Office: Hallandale Adult Cmty Ctr 1000 SW 3d St Hallandale FL 33009

RENZAGLIA, KAREN A. biologist, educator; PhD, So. Ill. U. Vis. prof. dept. plant biology So. Ill. U., Carbondale. Recipient Edgar T. Wherry award Bot. Soc. Am., 1993, Michael Cichan award Bot. Soc. Am., 1999. Office: So Ill U Dept Plant Biology Mail Code 6509 Carbondale IL 62901-6509

RENZETTI, PHYLLIS JEAN, retired technical editor; b. Kingman, Ind., Feb. 3, 1925; d. Claude and Helen (Duchene) A.; divorced; 1 child, Jeanne. BA, Wheaton (Ill.) Coll., 1947; MA, Columbia U., 1950; PhD, Ind. U., 1961. Tchr. Wheaton Coll., 1948-49; tech. editor U.S. Geol. Survey, Reston, Va., Menlo Park, Calif., 1963-94, ret., 1994. Mem. AAAS, Paleontological Soc. Home: 3266 Hanover Dr Lafayette IN 47909-3852

REORDAN, BEVERLY JEAN, artist; d. Albert Wayne Matlaf and Jean Katherine Lang; m. John Robert Suckling, 1951 (div. 1963); children: Leslie Jean Suckling, James Cameron Suckling; m. Robert Geoghegan Reordan, Feb. 1, 1964. Student in Bus., U. So. Calif., 1948—51. Artist, So. Calif., 1965—. Mem. Art A Fair Festival, Laguna Beach, Calif., 1982—, bd. dirs., 1982—87; charter mem. Nat. Mus. Women in Arts, Washington, 1987—; mem. Charter 100 Profl. Women in Orange County, Calif., 1987—89. Original art works pub. by Princess Cruises Fine Arts. Mem. La Quinta (Calif.) Arts Found., 2001—, Palm Springs (Calif.) Desert Mus., 1989—, Artists Coun., Palm Springs, 1990—. Mem.: U. So. Calif. Alumni Assn., Kappa Kappa Gamma. Republican. Avocations: photography, European travel. Home: 35898 Calloway Ln Palm Desert CA 92211

REPKO, LISA, medical/surgical nurse; b. Boston, Oct. 7, 1954; ADN, Regents Coll., Albany, N.Y., 1980, BSN, 1984; MPH, U. Albany, 1995. RN, N.Y. Staff nurse Albany Med. Ctr. Hosp., 1980—.

REPLANSKY, NAOMI, poet; b. Bronx, N.Y., May 23, 1918; d. Sol and Fannie (Ginsberg) R. BA, UCLA, 1956. Author: (book of poems) Ring Song, 1952, Twenty-One Poems, Old and New, 1988, The Dangerous World: New and Selected Poems 1934-1994, 1994. Mem. PEN Am. Ctr., Poetry Soc. Am., Poets House. Avocation: watercolor painting. Home: 711 Amsterdam Ave Apt 8E New York NY 10025-6916

REPLOGLE, JEANNE LONNQUIST, artist; b. Evanston, Ill., Apr. 8, 1932; d. William John Lonnquist and Dorothy Muriel Gittere; m. David Robert Replogle, Nov. 6, 1954; children: William, Bruce, Stewart, James, John. Student, Kathyrn Lord's Studio, Evanston, Ill., Studio of Pepino Mangreviti, Wellesley, Mass., Chgo. Art Inst.; BS, Northwestern U. One-woman shows include South Shore Art Ctr., Cohasset, Mass., 1982 (pres. choice, 1982), Artica Gallery, Duxbury, Mass., 2002, exhibitions include Festival Shows, South Shore Art Ctr., Cohasset, 1983—2002 (blue ribbon show, 1994, 2000, 2001, 2002), Annenburg Gallery, Pine Manor Coll., Chestnut Hill, Mass., 1989, Sailor's Valentine Gallery, Nantucket, Mass., 1988, Harvard Univ., Cambridge, Mass., 1993, Mystic (Conn.) Maritime Gallery, 1994, 1995, 1997, 1998, 1999, Small Works Show/Mystic Maritime Gallery, 1995, 1997, The Art of Giving/Mystic Maritime Gallery, 1996, Art of the Sea/Mystic Maritime Gallery, 1997, Fantasy Folk Art, South Shore Art Ctr, Cohasset, Mass., 1999, Folk Art, 1991, Arts Around Boston, 2000, prin. works include numerous to corp. Mem. Nassau Hosp. Aux., Mineola, NY, 1960—76, Mercy League, Rockville Centre, NY, 1960—76, League of Women Voters, Cohasset, Mass., 1976—80. Mem.: Am Soc. of Marine Artists, Stamford Art Assn., Cape Cod Art Assn., Catherine Lorillard Wolfe Art Club, South Shore Art Ctr. Gallery Artists (curator 1991, 1999). Episc. Avocations: golf, tennis. Home and Studio: 84 Gammons Rd Cohasset MA 02025

REPPERT, NANCY LUE, retired municipal official, legal consultant; b. Kansas City, Mo., June 17, 1933; d. James Everett and Iris R. (Moomey) Moore; m. James E. Cassidy, 1952 (div.); children: James E., II, Tracy C. Student, Ctrl. Mo. State U., 1951-52, U. Mo., Kansas City, 1971-75; cert. legal asst., Rockhurst Coll., Kansas City, 1980, cert. risk mgr., 1979. With Kansas City chpt. ARC, 1952-54, N. Ctrl. Region Boy Scouts Am., 1963-66, Clay County Health Dept., Liberty, Mo., 1966-71, city of Liberty, 1971-80; risk mgr. City of Dallas, 1982-83; dir. Dept. Risk Mgmr., Pinellas County, Fla., 1984-94; ind. legal cons. Cedar Rapids, Iowa, 1994—. Mem. faculty William Jewell Coll., Liberty, 1975-80; vis. prof., U. Kans., 1981; adj. prof. dept. polit. sci. masters program, U. South Fla., 1990; seminar leader, cons. in field. Author: Kids are People, Too, 1975, Pearls of Potentiality, 1980; also contbr. articles to publs. Lay min., United Meth. Ch., 1965—; dir. youth devel., Hillside United Meth. Ch., Liberty; co-chmn. youth dir. Collegiate United Meth. Ch. scouting coord. Palm Lake Christian Ch., Exec. Fellow U. South Fla., mem. Coun. Ministries; advancement chmn. Mid-Iowa Coun. Boy Scouts Am., membership chmn. White Rock Dist. Coun., health and safety chmn. West Ctrl. Fla. Coun., 1985—; scouting coord., chmn. youth dept., bd. dirs., pastor's cabinet, diaconate Palm Lake Christian Ch., 1987—; skipper Sea Explorer ship, 1986—; bd. dirs. Neighborly Sr. Svcs., Inc.; vol. sailing master, instr., Boys & Girls Clubs and Hawkeye Coun. Boy Scouts Am., Cedar Rapids. Recipient Order of Merit, Boy Scouts Am., 1979, Living Sculpture award, 1978, 79; Svc. award Rotary Internat., 1979; Internat. awrd of Merit/Leadership Excellence, IBA, 1992; Exec. fellow, U. South Fla., 1988. Mem. NAFE, Am. Mgmt. Assns., Internat. Platform Assn., Risk Mgrs. Soc., Pub. Risk & Ins. Mgmt. Assn., Am. Soc. Profl. & Exec. Women, Am. Film Inst., U.s. Naval Inst., Nat. Inst. Mcpl. Law Officers. Home: 257 38th Street Dr SE Apt 8 Cedar Rapids IA 52403-1116 E-mail: windsongsailor@netzero.com.

REQUA, VIRGINIA LEE, literature educator, writer; b. San Gabriel, Calif., Dec. 2, 1956; d. Joan Carolyn and Joseph Allen Osborn(Stepfather). BA in English and polit. sci., Calif. State U., Northridge, 1974—79, MA in English, 1979—89. Editl. asst./sec. Javanan Mag., Reseda, Calif., 1990—93; editl. cons. Alegator Books and Cards, Mission Hills, Calif., 1991—; part-time/substitute esl tchr. LA Unified Sch. Dist., Los Angeles, 1995—, emergency permit tchr., 1999—2001; english adj. instr. LA Mission Coll., Sylmar, Calif., 2000—01, LA Valley Coll., Valley Glen, Calif., 2001—, Coll. of the Canyons, Santa Clarita, Calif., 2002—; substitute tchr. LA Unified Sch. Dist., Los Angeles, 2002—, Castaic Union Sch. Dist., Valencia, Calif., 2002—; tutor Profl. Tutors, La Brea, Calif., 2003—. Author: (poetry) The Rival (Hon. Mention and President's award, 1997). Brownie troop leader Girl Scouts of Am., Chatsworth, Calif., 1981. Recipient Hon. Mention and President's award, Iliad Press, 1997; Ednl. Opportunity, State of Calif., 1974. Mem.: Am. Hypnotherapist Assoc., Part Time Instructors Union, WE (Women Educators), CATESOL, CCAE, Humane Soc., Alpha Xi Delta. D-Liberal. Avocations: writing, running, swimming, reading, needlepoint. Home: 18404 Vincennes St Apt 25 Northridge CA 91325 Office: College of the Canyons 26455 Rockwell Canyon Rd Canyon Country CA 91355 E-mail: sashalquay@aol.com.

RESCH, CHARLOTTE SUSANNA, plastic surgeon; b. Charlottesville, Va., Sept. 24, 1957; d. Johann Heinrich and Eleonore Susanne (Stenzel) R.; m. John Arthur Niero, Jan. 31, 1990. Student, Dalhousie U., Halifax, Nova Scotia, Can., 1974-76; MD with distinction, Dalhousie U. Med. Sch., Halifax, Nova Scotia, Can., 1980. Diplomate Dalhousie U., Am. Bd. Plastic Surgery; licentiate Med. Coun. Can.; cert. Bd. Med. Quality Assurance Calif. Intern Ottawa Gen. Hosp., Ont., Can., 1980-81; gen. surgery resident Dalhousie U., Halifax, Nova Scotia, Can., 1981-85; plastic surgery resident Wayne State U., Detroit, 1985-87; pvt. practice San Francisco, 1988-89; pre-ptnr. Southern Calif. Permanente Physicians Group, Fontana, 1989-92, ptnr., 1992—. Contbr. articles to profl. jours. Fellow ACS; mem. Am. Soc. Plastic and Reconstructive Surgeons, Calif. Med. Soc., San Bernardino Med. Soc., Alpha Omega Alpha. Avocations: travel, skiing, bicycling, gardening, gourmet cooking. Office: Kaiser Found Hosp Dept Plastic Surgery 9985 Sierra Ave Fontana CA 92335-6720

RESCH, RITA MARIE, music educator; b. Minot, N.D., Dec. 26, 1936; d. Clement Charles and Magdalena Marie (Zeltinger) Resch. BS in Edn., Minot State U., 1957; MM in Music Lit., Eastman Sch. Music, Rochester, N.Y., 1960; MA in English Lit., U. N.D., 1967; MFA in Voice, U. Iowa, 1973, DMA in Piano Chamber Music/Accompanying, 1974. Music tchr. (vocal) Biwabik (Minn.) Sch. Dist., 1957—58, S. Redford Twp., Detroit, 1958—59; instr. music Fontbonne Coll., St. Louis, 1960—63; asst. prof. music Wis. State U., Stevens Point, 1965—68, Ctrl. Mo. State U., Warrensburg, 1974—, assoc. prof., 1979, full prof., 1989—. Adjudicator for vocal music Mo. State High Sch. Activities Assn., Columbia, Kans. State High Sch. Activities Assn., Topeka, other orgns., 1976—. Author (with Judith E. Carman, William K. Gaeddert, Gordon Myers): Art Song in the United States: An Annotated Bibliography, 1976, 3rd edit., 2001. Assoc. organist Sacred Heart Cath. Ch., Warrensburg, 1980—. Mem.: Mo. Music Tchrs. Assn. (v.p. auditions 1995—98), Music Tchrs. Nat. Assn., Nat. Assn. Tchrs. Singing. Office: Ctrl Mo State U Dept Music Warrensburg MO 64093 E-mail: resch@cmsul.cmsu.edu.

RESING, MARYLORETTO RACHEL, guidance counseling administrator, elementary school educator, pastoral counselor; b. Covington, Ky., Jan. 27, 1949; d. Raymond Anthony and Carole Mary (Glover) Seifert; m. John Joseph Resing, Sept. 6, 1969; children: Jayne Carole, Matthew Raymond-Albert, Markus John, Joseph Thomas. BA, Thomas More Coll., Crestview Hills, Ky., 1984; MEd, Xavier U., Cin., 1989; M of Religious Studies, Athenaeum, Cin., 1994. Cert. elem. tchr. Ky., elem. and secondary guidance counselor Ky., Nat. Cert. Counselor 2002. Tchr. St. Joseph Sch. Diocese of Covington, Crescent Springs, Ky., 1969-70, tchr. St. Cecelia Sch. Independence, Ky., 1984-85, tchr. Covington Cath. H.S. Park Hills, Ky., 1985-90, dir. religious edn. St. Therese Parish Southgate, Ky., 1990-95; guidance counselor Kenton County Sch., Erlanger, Ky., 1995-96; dir. religious edn. St. Agnes Parish Diocese of Covington, Park Hills, 1995-96; tchr., dir. alternative coop. edn. program Covington Ind. Sch., 1997-99; counselor Holmes Jr. H.S., 2000—. Mem. Covington Diocesan Family Life Bd., Erlanger, Ky., 1994-96; initiator, chair Religious Edn. Group, Erlanger, 1991-96. Contbr. to mag. and diocesan newspaper. Active Boy Scouts Am., Independence, Ky., 1983—; bd. dirs. YMCA, Independence, 1986-92; mem. Greater Cin. NCCJ, 1985-90; chair St. Cecilia Sch. Bd., Independence, 1985-89; mem. La Leche League No. Ky., 1970-80, leader, 1976-80; bd. dirs. Nat. Assn. Parish Coords. and Dirs. of Religious Edn., 1997. Mem.: Ky. Sch. Counselor Assn., Corington Edn. Assn., No. Ky. Counseling Assn. (v.p. 2002—03, pres. 2003—, pres.-elect 2004—, 2002—03), Am. Counseling Assn., Ky. Edn. Assn. (rep.), Dirs. of Religious Edn. Support Group, Phi Delta Kappa. Roman Catholic. Avocations: antiques, gardening, reading.

RESNICK, ALICE ROBIE, judge; b. Erie, Pa., Aug. 21, 1939; d. Adam Joseph and Alice Suzanne (Spizarny) Robie; m. Melvin L. Resnick, Mar. 20, 1970 PhB, Siena Heights Coll., 1961; JD, U. Detroit, 1964. Bar: Ohio 1964, Mich. 1965, U.S. Supreme Ct. 1970. Asst. county prosecutor Lucas County Prosecutor's Office, Toledo, 1964-75, trial atty., 1965-75; judge Toledo Mcpl. Ct., 1976-83, 6th Dist. Ct. Appeals, State of Ohio, Toledo, 1983-88; instr. U. Toledo, 1968-69; justice Ohio Supreme Ct., 1988—. Co-chairperson Ohio State Gender Fairness Task Force. Trustee Siena Heights Coll., Adrian, Mich., 1982— ; organizer Crime Stopper Inc., Toledo, 1981— ; mem. Mayor's Drug Coun.; bd. dirs. Guest House Inc. Mem. ABA, Toledo Bar Assn., Lucas County Bar Assn., Nat. Assn. Women Judges, Am. Judicature Soc., Toledo Women's Bar Assn., Ohio State Women's Bar Assn. (organizer), Toledo Mus. Art, Internat. Inst. Toledo. Roman Catholic. Home: 2407 Edgehill Rd Toledo OH 43615-2321 Office: Supreme Ct Office 30 E Broad St Fl 3 Columbus OH 43215*

RESNICK, LYNDA, business executive; Co-owner, vice chmn. Franklin Mint; co-owner Roll Internat. Chmn. Teleflora. Chmn. mktg. com. Conservation Internat.; bd. dirs. Assn. for Cure of Cancer of the Prostate, Cal' CURE, Milken Family Found.; mem. exec. com., trustee, chmn. acquisitions com. L.A. County Mus. Art; mem. com. on sculpture and decorative arts Met. Mus. Art; trustee Phila. Mus. Art. Recipient Gold Effie award, 1983; named one of Top 50 U.S. Women Bus. Owners, Working Women, #1 L.A.-based woman Bus. Owner, L.A. bus. Jour., one of top 100 U.S. art collectors Art & Antiques mag. Office: Roll Internat Corp 11444 W Olympic Blvd Los Angeles CA 90064-1549

RESNICK, LYNDA RAE, consumer products company executive; married; 5 children. Founder, CEO L.A. advt. agy.; with Teleflora, pres., chmn.; co-owner, vice chmn. The Franklin Mint, Franklin Ctr., Pa. Trustee, mem. exec. com. L.A. County Mus. Art, chmn. Acquisitions and Exhbn. Com.; mem. Sculpture and Decorative Arts Com. Met. Mus. Art, N.Y.C.; trustee Phila. Mus. Art; mem. bd. overseers U. Pa.; mem. Acquisition Com. Nat. Gallery Art, Washington; bd. dirs. CaP Cure, Milken Family Found. Named one of top 100 collectors in Am., Art & Antiques, Outstanding Businesswoman of Year, L.A. Advt. Women; recipient outstanding retail concept gold Effie award, 1983. Mem. Conservation Internat. (bd. dirs., chmn. mktg. com.). Achievements include developing concept of Flowers-in-a-Gift pairing fresh flowers with a high-quality keepsake container; expanding Franklin Mint's extensive heirloom product line to include high-fashion jewelry, elegant tableware, porcelain collector dolls and precision crafted diecast cars. Office: The Franklin Mint US Rt 1 Franklin Center PA 19091

RESNICK, RHODA BRODOWSKY, psychotherapist; b. Mar. 22, 1930; d. Isador and Rose (Wasserman) Brodowsky; m. Jack H. Resnick, May 21, 1950; children: Steven E., Caryn B. BS, CCNY, 1951; MS, Queens Coll., 1973; postgrad., Hunter Coll. Tchr. N.Y.C. Bd. Edn., 1960—80, guidance counselor, 1980—; psychotherapist L.I. Cons. Ctr., 1973—77; pvt. practice psychotherapy, 1975—. Fellow, L.I. Inst. Mental Health, 1975. Mem.: PGA, United Fedn. Tchrs., Am. Pers. and Guidance Assn. Home: 340 E 64th St New York NY 10021-7503 E-mail: xrojac@hotmail.com.

RESNICK, ROSALIND, multimedia executive; b. N.Y. BA, MA in Italian Renaissance History, Johns Hopkins U., 1981. Bus. reporter The Miami Herald, 1984-89; freelance writer various computer trade mags., 1990-95; pres., CEO NetCreations, Bklyn., 1995—. Co-author: The Internet Business Guide, 1995. Office: NetCreations 379 W Broadway Rm 202 New York NY 10012-5125

RESNICK, STEPHANIE, lawyer; b. NYC, Nov. 12, 1959; d. Diane Gross. AB, Kenyon Coll., 1981; JD, Villanova U., 1984. Bar: Pa. 1984, N.J. 1984, U.S. Dist Ct. (ea. dist.) Pa. 1984, U.S. Dist Ct. N.J. 1984, N.Y. 1990, U.S. Ct. Appeals (3d cir.) 1993, U.S. Dist. Ct. (so. dist.) N.Y. 1996, U.S. Dist. Ct. (ea. dist.) N.Y. 2001, U.S. Supreme Ct. 1998. Assoc. Cozen and O'Connor, Phila., 1984-87, Fox, Rothschild LLP, Phila., 1987-92, ptnr., 1992—, mem. exec. com., 2003. Mem.: ABA, Womens Way (vice-chair 2002, chair 2003—04), N.Y. Bar Assn., N.J. Bar Assn., Phila. Bar Assn. (investigative divsn. Commn. on Jud. Selection and Retention 1988—94, profl. guidance com. 1992—96, profl. responsibility com. 1992—2000, women's rights com., women in the profession com. 1993—, Comm. on Jud. Selection and Retention 1995—2001, vice-chair 1996, chair 1997, fed. cts. com. 2000—, vice-chair 2001—02, chair 2002—03), Pa. Bar Assn. (disciplinary bd. and study com. 1989—91, prof. liability com. 1991—92, commr. on Women in the Profession 1997—99). Home: 233 S 6th St Apt 2306 Philadelphia PA 19106-3756 Office: Fox Rothschild O'Brien & Frankel 2000 Market St Ste 10 Philadelphia PA 19103-3231

RESOR, PAMELA P. state legislator; b. Lincoln, Nebr., Feb. 26, 1942; d. Roland B. and Margaret L. (Flynn) Phillips; m. Griffith L. Resor III, July 6, 1963; children: Karen E. Resor Savage, Philip G., Kristen M. BA, Smith Coll., 1964. Exec. dir. Mass. Assn. Conservation Com., Belmont, 1986-88; mem. Mass. Ho. Reps., Boston, 1990-99, Mass. Senate, Boston, 1999—. Selectman Town of Acton, Mass., 1981-87. Mem. LWV (pres. 1978-80). Avocations: hiking, skiing. Office: Mass State Senate State House Rm 413-F Boston MA 02133

RESSEL, TERESA MULLETT, federal agency administrator; BS in Engring., MS in Engring., U. Del.; MBA, Rensselaer Poly. Inst., 1990. V.p., chief compliance officer Kaiser Found. Health Plan, Inc., Kaiser Found. Hosps., Inc.; prin. dep. asst. sec. for mgmt. and budget U.S. Dept. Treasury, Washington, 2001—02, asst. sec. for mgmt. and CFO, 2003—. Recipient Presdl. Citation for Outstanding Alumni Achievement, U. Del., 1996, Disting. Svc. award, Dept. Treasury, 2003. Office: US Dept of the Treasury 1500 Pennsylvania Ave NW Washington DC 20220*

RESSETAR, NANCY, foreign language educator; b. Paterson, N.J., Dec. 19, 1947; d. Marino Angelo and Florence Mae (Patterson) DeMattia; m. Michael Ressetar, Jr., Aug. 15, 1981; 1 child, Tatyana Marina. BA, Montclair State U., 1970. Cert. tchr., N.J. Model various agencies, 1953-84; tchr. Spanish Clifton (N.J.) Sch. Sys., 1970—. Sponsor Spanish Club, Clifton, 1981—, Student Leadership, Clifton, 1988—, Travel to Spain, Clifton, 1982-96; campaign worker Dem. Party, Clifton, 1968-72. Recipient Gov.'s award for excellence in tchg. State of N.J., 1996. Mem. NEA, N.J. Edn. Assn., Passaic County Edn. Assn., Clifton Tchrs. Assn. (sec. 1973-75), Fgn. Lang. Tchrs. N.J., Am. Assn. Tchrs. Spanish and Portuguese. Democrat. Lutheran. Avocations: travel, theatre, doll collecting, classic hollywood, tutoring. Home: 20 Robin Hood Rd Clifton NJ 07013-3112

REST, ANN H. state legislator; b. Apr. 24, 1942; 1 child. BA, Northwestern U.; MA, U. Chgo.; MAT, MPA, Harvard U.; MBT, U. Minn. Mem. Minn. Ho. of Reps. dist. 46A, St. Paul, 1985-2000, Minn. Senate from 46th dist., St. Paul, 2001—. Chmn. taxes com., rules and legis. adminstrv. com., mem. ways and means com.; CPA. Recipient Women of Achievment award North Hennepin Bus. and Profl. Women, 1988; named Legislator of Yr., Politics in Minn., 1990. Mem. Resources for Adoptive Parents, Libr. Found. of Hennepin County, YMCA. Democrat. Home: 7611 36th Ave N Apt 322 Minneapolis MN 55427-2085 Office: Minn State Senate 439 State Office Bldg Saint Paul MN 55155-0001

RESTANI, JANE A. federal judge; b. San Francisco, Feb. 27, 1948; d. Roy J. and Emilia C. Restani. BA, U. Calif., Berkeley, 1969; JD, U. Calif., Davis, 1973. Bar: Calif., 1973. Trial atty. U.S. Dept. Justice, Washington, 1973-76, asst. chief comml. litigation sect., 1976-80, dir. comml. litigation sect., 1980-83; judge U.S. Ct. Internat. Trade, N.Y.C., 1983—. Mem. Order of Coif. Office: US Ct Internat Trade 1 Federal Plz New York NY 10278-0001*

RESTOUT, DENISE, musician; b. Paris, Nov. 24, 1915; arrived in US, 1941; d. Fernand Emile Jules and Juliette Louise François Restout. Grad., Nat. Conservatoire de Musique, Paris, 1930. Asst., sec. to Wanda Landowska Ecole de Musique Ancienne, St. Leu-La Foret, France, 1935-41, Lakeville, Conn., 1941-59; dir. Landowska Ctr., Lakeville, 1959—. Mem jury, hon patron Int Bach Competitions, 1969—81; lectr in field. Author: (book) Landowska on Music, 1965; contbr. articles, concert revs to mags; musician (soloist): Chamber Orchestra, 1939; musician: (accompanying harpsicordist) Landowska concert, 1943; musician: (solo harpsicordist) Bach Suites, others; musician: (recorded) Bach Suites (REBI); musician: (solo recorded accompanying harpsicord) Bach ETE with Landowska CCD; musician: recitals; appeared various radio and TV programs: Voice of America, 1950, Radio-Geneve, 1952, CBS Radio, 1960, 1985, Conn Pub Radio, 1985, Radio France, 1990, Video TV, 1999; appeared in documentary film : Visionary; co-prodr.: (several CDs for Pearl and others). Organist St Mary's Ch, Lakeville, 1971—97. Recipient Amicus Poloniae, Poland Mag, 1973, St. Joseph medal, Archdiocese of Hartford, 2002, Pietrzak's prize, Civitas Christiana U., Warsaw, 2003, Cardinal Glemp Gold medal, Polish Ch. Mem.: French and Am Musicological Assn., Am. Guild Organists, French Guild Organists, Am. Fedn. Musicians (Woman of the Yr 1996). Republican. Roman Catholic. Avocations: reading, photography. Home and Office: PO Box 313 63 Millerton Rd Lakeville CT 06039-0313

REUSCHÉ, BARBARA T. writer; b. Louisville, Sept. 15, 1946; d. Charles Allen and Marjorie Ozie (Meador) T.; m.; Richard C. Taylor (wid.), children: Geoff, Christopher, Rachael; m. John McCafferty, nov, 15, 1982 (div. July 1993); m. Robert Reusché, Dec. 12, 2003. BA, U. Louisville, 1980. Author: (pen name Taylor McCafferty/fiction books) Pet Peeves, 1990, Ruffled Feathers, 1992, Bed Bugs, 1993, Thin Skins, 1994, Hanky Panky, 1995, (pen name Tierney McClellan) Heir Condition, 1995, Closing Statement, 1995, A Killing in Real Estate, 1996; co-author: (with Beverly Taylor Herald) Double Murder, 1996, Double Date, 2002. Mem. Mystery Writers of Am., Sisters in Crime. Office: care Richard Parks Agy 138 E 16th St Apt 5B New York NY 10003-3561

RETTELLE, KATHRYNE W. music educator; b. Shreveport, La., July 16, 1947; m. Keith E. Rettelle. BA, Northeast La. State U., 1968; MusM, Northwestern State U., 1970; postgrad., 1985, La. State U., 1993—95. Cert. tchr. La. Tchr. strings St. Mary's Cath. Sch., Natchitoches, La., 1972—73, Rapides Parish Schs., Alexandria, La., 1973—78; tchr. sci. and speech Friendship Acad., Shreveport, 1978—79; tchr. strings Caddo Parish Schs., Shreveport, 1979—. Musician Shreveport Symphony Orch., Four Seasons String Quartet, Marshall Symphony Orch. Bd. dirs. Ark-La-Tex Youth Symphony, 1997; pres., bd. dirs. Amb. for Arts, Shreveport; mem. La. State Mental Health Bd., Shreveport, 1978—87. Named Educator of Week, Shreveport Times, 2001. Mem.: La. Music Educators Assn. (rev. editor 1984—, chair pub. rels. 1983—89), Delta Omicron, Alpha Omicron Pi, Phi Delta Kappa. Baptist. Avocations: travel, sewing. Office: Huntington HS 6801 Rasberry Ln Shreveport LA 71129*

RETZER, MARY ELIZABETH HELM, retired librarian; b. Balt. d. Francis Leslie C. and Edna (Smith) Helm; m. William Raymond Retzer, June 28, 1945; children: Lesley Elizabeth, April Christine. BA, Western Md. Coll., 1940; MA, Columbia U., 1946; postgrad., George Washington U., 1941, Ind. U., 1952, U. Ill., 1958-59, Ill. State U., 1964-66, Bradley U.; PhD, Western Colo. U., 1972. Faculty Rockville (Md.) Bd. Edn., 1940-47, elem. supr., 1945-47; staff Peoria Pub. Libr., 1957-63, homebound libr., 1961-63; cons., organizer libr. Bergan High Sch., 1964-67; condr. libr. sci. course in reference Bradley U., 1966-83. Libr. Hines Elem. Sch., 1963-66, Roosevelt Jr. H.S., 1966-69; head media ctr. Manual H.S., Peoria, Ill., 1969-83. Instr. water safety courses ARC, 1938-93; pres. Entre Nous, 1949-51; pres. women's bd. Salvation Army, 1952-54; pres. Peoria Nursery Sch. Assn., 1953-54; mem. legis. action com. Ill. Congress PTA, 1955-56; mem. Crippled Children's Adv. Com., Peoria, 1957-60; active various community drives; women's adv. bd. Peoria Jr. Star, 1970-73; vol. Sarasota Internat. Airport, 1990-98. Mem. AAUW (life), NEA, ALA (life), Ill. Edn. Assn. (life), Peoria Edn. Assn. (life), Ill. Libr. Assn., Ill. Valley Librs. Assn. (pres. 1971-72), Ill. Assn. Media in Edn. (cert. com. 1973-80), Ill. Audiovisual Assn., Internat. Platform Assn., Order Ea. Star (life), Ill. State U. Adminstrs. Club, Willowknolls Country Club, Sarasota Yacht Club, Ladies Oriental Shrine. Republican. Presbyterian. Home: Unit 308 435 S Gulfstream Ave Sarasota FL 34236-6705

REUBEN, GLORIA, actress; b. Toronto, Ont., June 9, 1964; T.V. and movie actress; backup singer and dancer Tina Turner's World Tour, 2000. T.V. films include The Day They Came to Arrest the Book, 1986, Shadowhunter, 1993, Dead Air, 1994, Indiscreet, 1998, Sara, 1999, Deep in My Heart, 1999, Little John, 2002, Salem Witch Trials, 2002; film appearances include Immediate Family, 1989, Johnny's Girl, 1993, Timecop, 1994, Nick of Time, 1995, Macbeth in Manhattan, 1999, Bad Faith, 1999, Happy Here and Now, 2001; T.V. series include ER, 1995-99 (Emmy Best Supporting Actress nominee 1997, 98), The Agency, 2001-02; T.V. guest appearances in The Flash, 1990, Silk Stalkings, 1991, Homicide: Life on the Street, 1993, others. Recipient SAG Awards, 1998, 99, Q Award, 1997, 98. Office: Gerson Saines Mgmt Ste 2303 250 W 57th St New York NY 10107-2399

REUL, BETTY A. construction executive; b. Bremer County, Iowa, Apr. 3, 1940; d. Hardwig H. Richmann, Emelda B. Richmann; m. David G. Reul, Aug. 16, 1959; children: Julia Weede, Jennifer Marr, Renata Bowers. Student, U. No. Iowa, 1956—57. Payroll acct. Shield Bantam, Waverly, Iowa, 1958—59; bookkeeper Bank of Oconomowoc, Wis., 1959—61; gen. mgr. Oconomowoc Sewing Ctr., 1970—73; self-employed Temporary Office Svc., Oconomowoc, 1973—75; mgr. adminstrn. MSI Gen. Corp., Oconomowoc, 1975—97. Bd. dirs. Luth. Homes Oconomowoc, 1998—. Pres., bd. mem. Oconomowoc Festival of the Arts, 1994—. Mem.: Waukesha Symphony Orch. (bd. mem. 1996—). Lutheran. Avocations: music, travel, tennis, sewing, decorating, cooking. Home: N8530 Ski Slide Rd Ixonia WI 53036

REUTER, HELEN HYDE, psychologist; b. McGehee, Ark. d. John Lloyd and Sallie Elizabeth (Holcomb) Hyde; m. George S. Reuter Jr.; children: Don N., M. Allan, K.L. BA, Westmar U., 1968; AM, U. S.D., 1969; PhD, Westgate U., 1976; LHD (hon.), Sioux Empire Coll.; LLD (hon.), St. John U., New Orleans; DD (hon.), Temple Bapt. Coll. Ordained So. Bapt. minister. Postmaster U.S. Post Office, College Heights, Ark.; sch. counselor various pub. sch. systems, Mo., Iowa; sch. psychologist Oak Park (Ill.) and River Forest High Sch.; v.p., sec. Internat. Assocs. for Christians, Holden, Mo. Cons. in field. Co-author: One Blood, 1964, 2d edit., 1988, Democracy and Quality Education, 1965, 2d edit., 1986. Named Mother of Yr., City of Monticello, 1960; cited as Psychologist of Yr., Internat. U., Lagos, Nigeria, 1992. Mem. P.E.O. (v.p.), Shakespeare Club (v.p.), Garden Club (v.p.). Democrat. Baptist. Avocations: travel, classical music. Home: 3100 Club Dr Apt 320 Lawrenceville GA 30044

REUTER, JOAN COPSON, retired program director; b. London, July 7, 1919; came to US, 1921; d. Denis and Florence (Copson) Soucy; widowed; children: David, Robert N., Joan Ellen Swanson, Alan, Ronald (dec.). AA, Asnuntuck C.C., 1975; BS, N.H. Coll., 1982. Dir. women's ctr. Asnuntuck C.C., Enfield, Conn., 1975—98, ret., 1998. Adj. faculty Asnuntuck C.C., 1984-95, dir. childcare ctr., 1974—; bd. dir. Mentor Program, Town Enfield, After Sch. Program. Bd. dir. Enfield Bd. Edn., 1979-91; justice of peace Town of Enfield, 1980—; sec. Enfield Loan Rev. Com., 1957—. Mem. Women's Club Enfield (sec., bd. dir. 1957—), Asnuntuck Alumni Assn. (v.p., pres.). Republican. Episcopalian. Avocations: reading, walking, gardening. Home: 9 Homestead Dr Enfield CT 06082-4639

REUTHINGER, GEORGEANNE, special education educator; b. Laredo, Tex., Mar. 10, 1952; d. George and Maria Josefina (Elizondo) Ramon; m. David Lawrence Reuthinger, Apr. 5, 1952; 1 child, David L. Jr. AA in Music and Drama, Laredo Jr. Coll., 1972; BS in Speech and Drama Edn., Tex. A&I U., 1974, MS in Edn., 1978; postgrad., Tes. A&M Internat. U. Lic. speech therapist, Tex.; cert. speech therapist, ednl. diagnostician, profl. supervision. Speech and drama tchr. Laredo ISD Martin High Sch., 1974; supr., diagnostician spl. edn. program Laredo ISD Martin H.S., 1992-96, Cigarra H.S., Nixon H.S., 1998—; speech therapist Laredo ISD, 1974-78, ednl. diagnostician, 1978-92, sales assoc. Country Wide Real Estate, Laredo, 1997—; cons. in spl. edn. United Ind. and Laredo Ind. Sch. Dists., 1997-98. Founding mem., lead actress in bilingual theatrical touring co. Tex. A&I U., 1974. Active in fundraising for charities Women's City Club, Boy Scouts Am.; judge UIL Acad. & Fine Arts events, Spl. Olympics. Scholar Art League, 1970, Tex. A&I Alumni, 1972-74; recipient awards U.S. Army, 1973, USO Shows, 1973-74. Mem. Tex. Speech and Hearing Assn. (legis. network 1992-97), Coun. for Exceptional Children (lobbyist 1995, sec. Laredo chpt. 1975), Valley Coun. Adminstrs. and Suprs. in Spl. Edn., ASCD, Tex. Coun. Adminstrs. and Suprs. in Spl. Edn., Delta Kappa Gamma (sec. Alpha Nu chpt. 1977-78). Avocations: directing and acting in theatrical productions, singing in community choirs, special olympics volunteering and judging. Home: 206 Granada Dr Laredo TX 78041-2615 Office: Country Wide Real Estate 1303 Calle Del Norte Ste 6 Laredo TX 78041-6041 also: Laredo Ind Sch Dist 1702 Houston St Laredo TX 78040-4906

REVEAL, ARLENE HADFIELD, retired librarian, consultant; b. Riverside, Utah, May 21, 1916; d. Job Oliver and Mabel Olive (Smith) Hadfield; children: James L., Jon A. BS with honors, Utah State U.; grad. in Librarianship, San Diego State U., 1968; M in Libr. and Info. Sci., Brigham Young U., 1976. Social case worker Boxelder County Welfare, Brigham City, Utah, 1938-40; office mgr. Dodge Ridge Ski Corp., Long Barn, Calif., 1948-65, Strawberry (Calif.) Inn, 1950-65, Pinecrest Permittees Assn., 1955-65; adminstrv. asst. Mono County Office of Edn., Bridgeport, Calif., 1961-67; catalog libr. La Mesa (Calif.)-Spring VAlley Sch. Dist., 1968-71; libr. Mono County Libr., Bridgeport, 1971-96; cmty. grandmother Riverside, Utah, 1996—. Chair Mountain Valley Libr. Sys., 1987-89. Author: Mono Country Courthouse, 1980. Mem. Devel. Disabilities Area Bd. 12, 1974-96, chair, 1990-92. Recipient John Cotton Dana award H.W. Wilson Co., 1974; named Bridgeport Citizen of Yr., 1993, Wild Iris Woman of Yr., Mono County, 1996. Mem. Rebekah (treas. 1973-90), Delta Kappa Gamma (pres. chpt. 1984-88), Beta Sigma Phi (treas. chpt. 1981, 83-85, 91-96, pres. 1982, 85, 89), Beta Phi Mu. Home: 15425 N 5250 W PO Box 156 Riverside UT 84334

REVEIZ, MARIA CRISTINA, osteopath; b. Fort Dodge, Iowa, Oct. 11, 1971; d. Eduardo Roldán and Paulette (Mefferd) Reveiz; m. Robert Vincent Filippone Jr., Aug. 9, 1997; children: Gloria Deia, Eleanor Aida. BS in Psychology, U. Iowa, 1995; DOM, UHS-COM, 1999. Intern Des Moines Gen. Hosp., Iowa, 1999—2000; resident Met. Health Hosp. Case Western Reserve U., Cleve., 2000—01. Locum tenens gen. practice, Webster City, Iowa, 2001—. Speaker, counselor Rape Victim Advocacy Program, Iowa City, 1993—95. Mem.: NOW. Green Party. Unitarian. Avocation: breeding, training St. Bernard dogs. Home and Office: 3863 W 157th St Cleveland OH 44111-5825 E-mail: mreveiz@yahoo.com.

REVERE, VIRGINIA LEHR, clinical psychologist; b. Long Branch, N.J. d. Joseph and Essie Lehr; m. Robert B. Revere; children: Elspeth, Andrew, Lisa, Robert Jr. PhB, U. Chgo., 1949, MA, 1959, PhD, 1971. Lic. cons. clin. psychologist, Va. Intern, staff psychologist Ea. Mental Health Reception Ctr., Phila., 1959-61; instr. Trenton (N.J.) State Coll., 1962-63; psychologist Trenton State Hosp., 1964-65, Bucks County Psychiat. Ctr., Phila., 1965-67; assoc. prof. Mansfield (Pa.) State U., 1967-77; clin. rsch. psychologist St. Elizabeth Hosp., Washington, 1977-81, tng. psychology coord., 1981-83, psychologist, 1985-91; child psychologist Cmty. Mental Health Ctr., Washington, 1983-85; pvt. practice Alexandria, Va., 1980—. Cons., lectr. in field. Author: Applied Psychology for Criminal Justice Professionals, 1982; contbr. articles to profl. jours. Recipient Group Merit award St. Elizabeth's Hosp., 1983, Community Svc. award D.C. Psychol. Assn., 1978, Outstanding Educator award, 1972; traineeship NIH, USPHS, Chgo., 1963-65; fellow Family Svcs. Assn., 1958-59. Mem. APA, No. Va. Soc. Clin. Psychologists, Va. Acad. Clin. Psychologists. Office Phone: 703-780-4872. E-mail: rrevere923@aol.com.

REVESZ, KINGA, chemist, isotope geochemist, researcher; b. Debrecen, Hungary, Apr. 29, 1943; came to U.S., 1975; d. Bela and Katalin (Harsanyi) Lutter; m. Akos Revesz, Jan. 10, 1975; 1 child, Paul. MS, Eotvos Lorant U., Budapest, Hungary, 1966; PhD, Jozset Attila U., Szeged, Hungary, 1977. Head surface chemistry group Tungsram Rsch. Lab., Budapest, 1971-75; chemist Nat. Bur. Stds., Washington, 1977-78, U.S. Geol. Survey, Water Resources Divsn., Reston, Va., 1983-89, chemist nat. rsch. program, 1989—. Contbr. articles to profl. jours.; patentee in field. Mem. Am. Chem. Soc., Am. Geophys. Union, Geol. Soc. Am., Geol. Soc. Washington. Home: 7910 Park Overlook Dr Bethesda MD 20817-2719 Office: US Geol Survey MS 431 Sunrise Valley Dr Reston VA 20192-0001 E-mail: krevesz@usgs.gov.

REVOAL, DEBORAH ANNE LEYDE, primary school educator; b. Sharon, Pa., July 26, 1953; d. Frank Edwin Leyde and Ruth Jane Garhart; m. Walter D. Revoal, June 9, 1978; children: Alexander Boston, Rebecca Jane. BS in Art Edn., Pa. State U.; MA in Edn., U. No. Colo. Kindergarten tchr. Wooden Shoe, Broomfield, Colo.; art tchr. Adams County #14, Commerce City, Colo. Vol. Denver Mus. Nature Sci., 2003. Mem.: NEA, Nat. Art Edn. Assn., Pi Lambda Theta.

REXROAT, VICKI LYNN, occupational child development educator; b. Oklahoma City, Okla., June 12, 1957; d. Troy Bill and Opal Pauline (Flinn) Miller; m. David Edward Rexroat, Sept. 6, 1980; children: Jamie Lynn, Amber Donn, Emily Sue. BS, U. of Sci. and Arts, 1991; MS, U. Ctrl. Okla., 1997. Presch. tchr. Caddo-Kiowa Vocat. Sch., Fort Cobb, Okla., 1981-84, child devel. dir., 1984-89, child devel. instr., 1989—. Rep., advisor Child Devel. Assoc., Washington, 1989—; mem. curriculum team Okla. Dept. of

Vocat. Edn., Stillwater, Okla., 1991—; adv. bd. Child Care Careers, Oklahoma City, 1992—. Contbr. articles to profl. jours. Co-chair Reach Out, Inc. Homeless Shelter, Anadarko, Okla., 1995—; founder, vol. Caddo County Welfare Vols., 1989—; friends for life mem. Fort Cobb Sr. Citizens, 1990—; mem. Fort Cobb Booster Club, 1989—. Named Friend of Children Okla. Inst. of Child Advocacy, 1993, New Tchr. of Yr. Okla. Vocat. Assn., 1993. Mem. Friends in the Okla. Early Childhood Assn. (pres. 1989—), So. Early Childhood Assn., Okla. Assn. for the Edn. of Young Children, Nat. Assn. for the Edn. of Young Children, Am. Vocat. Assn. (dist. v.p. 1989—, New Tchr. of Yr. 1994). Democrat. Bapt. Avocations: basketball games, fishing, boating, student organizations. Office: Caddo-Kiowa Vocat Sch North 7th Fort Cobb OK 73038

REXROTH, NANCY LOUISE, photographer; b. Washington, June 27, 1946; d. John Augustus and Florence Bertha (Young) R. B.F.A., Am. U., 1969; M.F.A. in Photography, Ohio U., Athens, 1971. Asst. prof. photography Antioch Coll., Yellow Springs, Ohio, 1977-79, Wright State U., Dayton, Ohio, 1979-82. Author: Iowa, 1976, The Platinotype, 1977, 1976; exhibited photography at Weinstein Gallery, Mpls. Nat. Endowment Arts grantee, 1973; Ohio Arts Coun., 1981. Mem. Am. Massage Therapy Assn. Democrat. Home and Office: 2631 Cleinview Ave Cincinnati OH 45206-1810 E-mail: rexnex@cinci.rr.com.

REYES, ANNA MARIA, broadcast executive; b. Phoenix, Aug. 21, 1957; d. Perfecto C. and Esperanza (Del Castillo) R. BA in Fin., Ariz. State U., 1983. Radio-Tel. operators permit FCC; notary public, Ariz. Traffic/continuity dir. First Media Corp./KOPA AM and FM, Scottsdale, Ariz., 1978-81, music dir., air talent, 1981-83; bus. mgr., asst. sta. mgr. Cook Inlet Radio Ptnr. KSLX-FM and KOPA-AM, 1983-92; sta. contr., asst. gen. mgr. Jacor/Citicasters KSLX AM/FM, Phoenix, 1992-96; gen. mgr. Jacor Comm. KSLX AM/FM, Phoenix, 1997—. Interviewer KSLX FM/KOPA AM, Scottsdale, 1990. Co-author: INXS Newsletter, 1994. Spokeswoman campaign against radio for men format KSLX FM/KOPA AM, Scottsdale, 1988. Recipient Cert. for Announcing, City of Phoenix-Hello Phoenix, 1985, Bus. Mgr. award Corp. Chain Contest, Phoenix, 1990-92. Mem. AAUW, Am. Women in Radio and TV, Broadcast Cable Fin. Mgmt., Univ. Women London. Democrat. Roman Catholic. Avocations: european travel, ballet, reading, music. Home: 12340 W Elwood St Avondale AZ 85323-9618 Office: KSLX Radio FM/AM 4343 E Camelback Rd Ste 200 Phoenix AZ 85018-8306

REYES, IRMA V. adult education educator; b. Coamo, P.R., Dec. 10, 1951; d. Nazario Reyes and Gloria E. Miranda; 1 child, Catherine M. Hamade. BA in Edn., U. P.R., Rio Piedras, 1974. Cert. secondary tchr. Spanish and sociology P.R., 1974. Tchr. Ergos Sch., Ponce, PR, 1977—79, intermediate sch. tchr., 1979—84, H.S. tchr., 1984—86, asst. dir. academics and register, 1980—86; part-time H.S. tchr. Cristo Rey Acad., Ponce, 1987—89; intermediate sch. tchr. Pedro Albizu Campos Sch., Ponce, 1986—93; GED Spanish tchr. Perth Amboy (N.J.) Adult Sch., 1994—. Moderator of the student counsel and nat. honor soc. Ergos Sch., Ponce, 1980—86. Mem. Nat. Fedn. Bus. and Profl. Women's Club, Ponce, 1975—77. Mem.: N.J. Assn. Lifelong Learning, Profl. Lit. Am. Tchr., Am. Fedn. Tchrs. Roman Catholic. Avocations: reading, poetry. Home: 541 Hazel Ave Perth Amboy NJ 08861 Office: Perth Amboy Adult Sch 178 Barracks St Perth Amboy NJ 08861 Office Phone: 732-376-6240. E-mail: irmareyes@paps.net.

REYES, LORY G. entrepreneur; b. Cuba, Oct. 28, 1952; d. Domingo G. Reyes and Lorena R. Leyva; children: Omar Gonzalez, Gabriella Gonzalez. BA in Mktg., U. Miami, Fla., 1975, BBA in Polit. Sci., 1976. Gen. mgr. Heraldstore Miami Herald, Miami, Fla., 1994—2001; pres. Cultural Colors Corp, Miami, Fla., 2001—. Various mgmt. positions FPL, Miami, Fla., 1982—93; editor Spring Fashion sect., 1980 Fashion Forecasting for Men, Hoy en T.V. (newspaper column); freelance writer various newspapers, including Hay Un Nuevo Estilo Para Ella y El, others. Fundraiser Leukemia and Lymphoma Found., Miami, Fla., 2003; mem. Art and Culture Ctr. of Hollywood, Hollywood, Fla., 1999—2001; bd. mem. Family Counseling Svcs. Greater Miami, Miami, Fla., 1989; mem. Miami Youth Mus., South Miami, Fla., 1987—89. Recipient Addy awards, Fla. Advt. Fedn., 1976—80, First Pl. - Display Category, Internat. Assn. Bus. Communicators, 1985, Internat. Award - Ad Campaign, Editor & Pub., 1980. Mem.: Latin Bus. & Profl. Woman's Club, Product Devel. Mgmt. Assn., Am. Mktg. Assn. Roman Catholic. Avocations: travel, reading, exploring, walking. Home: 16430 SW 103 Lane Miami FL 33196 Office: Cultural Colors Corp 16275 SW 88 St # 218 Miami FL 33196 Personal E-mail: lorygreyes@aol.com. E-mail: lorygreyes@culturalcolors.com.

REYES, MARCIA STYGLES, medical technologist; b. Winchester, Mass., July 15, 1950; d. Bernard Francis and Eleanore Cecilia (Nicgorska) Stygles; m. Carlos Reyes, Aug. 5, 1978. BS in Med. Tech., Merrimack Coll., North Andover, Mass., 1972; MS in Health Scis., SUNY, Buffalo, 1977. Sr. med. technologist Symmes Hosp., Arlington, Mass., 1970-73; sr. microbiologist and serologist Mt. Auburn Hosp., Cambridge, Mass., 1973-75; asst. prof., clin. coord. Quinnipiac Coll., Hamden, Conn., 1976-81; lab. supr. Canberra Clin. Labs., Meriden, Conn., 1981-86, Hill Health Ctr., New Haven, 1984—, clin. lab. mgr., dir., 1995—. Cons. in med. tech. mgmt., allied health edn.; cons. F.Q.H.C. Lab. Devel./Implementation. Mem. adv. bd. to bd. dirs. Sawyer Schs.; mem. adv. bd. New Haven Adult Edn. Programs. Mem. Am. Soc. Clin. Pathologists, Am. Soc. Med. Tech., Conn. Soc. Med. Tech. (Spkr. awards, bd. dirs. 1996—), Am. Soc. Microbiology, Am. Soc. Allied Health Profls. Home: 199 Dover St New Haven CT 06513-4818 E-mail: mreyes@hillhealthcenter.net.

REYES, SARAH, state representative; b. Fresno, Calif. Grad., Fresno City Coll., Calif. State U. Field reporter, news anchor KSEE TV-24, Fresno; field reporter KCRA TV-3, Sacramento; asst. to chancellor State Ctr. C.C. Dist.; mem. Calif. Assembly, 1998—. Bd. dirs. KVPT Channel 18, Radio Bilingue. Elector U.S. Electoral Coll., 1996; bd. dirs. Barrios Unidos Gang Prevention Program; Fresno/Madera Area Agy. Aging; bd. dirs. Rape Counseling Svcs. Fresno. Mem.: Hispanic C. of C. (past pres., founding chair Latina conf.). Democrat. Office: PO Box 942849 Rm 5136 Sacramento CA 94249-0001 Address: 2550 Mariposa Mall STe 5031 Fresno CA 93721

REYES, SUSANA MARIE, utility executive, environmentalist; b. Manila, Philippines, Dec. 18, 1954; d. Virgilio T. and Herminia (Fajatin) Reyes; divorced; children: Freya Suzanne Estreller, Sharon Erin Estreller, Jaimee Lauren Estreller, Carissa Mia Estreller. Cert., Fashion Inst. Design and Mdse., L.A., 1983; BA in Comms., St. Paul Coll., Manila, 1976; MA in Comms., U. Philippines, Manila, 1979. V.p. pub. rels. Apparel Resources Corp., Manila, 1979-81; mdse. specialist Macy's, L.A., 1983-86; mgr. chem. info. ctr. Dept. Water and Power, L.A., 1986-89; mgmt. analyst Dept. Gen. Svcs., L.A., 1990-91; program mgr. city facilities recycling City of L.A., 1991-99; exec. asst. corp. adminstrv. svcs. Dept. Water and Power, L.A., 1999—. Mem. adv. affirmative action com. City of L.A., 1998-99; mem. tech. adv. com. Calif. Resource Recovery Assn., 1992-99. Mem. parent bd. Mayfield Sr. Sch., Pasadena, Calif., 1996; v.p. PTO, Holy Trinity Sch., L.A., 1997. Recipient Good Earthkeeping award City of L.A., 1997. Mem. Sierra Club (mem. polit. com. 1999), All City Employees Benefits Assn. Avocations: reading, writing, event planning, traveling. Office: Dept Water and Power 111 N Hope St Rm 1545 Los Angeles CA 90012-2607

REYES-HERNANDEZ, MIGDALIA, counselor; b. San Juan, P.R., Oct. 27, 1952; d. José Ramón Reyes and Catalina Hernández; m. Carlos Iván Aponte, Dec. 28, 1974 (div. Feb. 1980); m. Wilfred Román, June 30, 1983; children: Ricardo, Natalia. BA in Edn., U. P.R., Río Piedras, 1973; MA in Counseling, U. Phoenix, Guaynabo, P.R., 1999. Cert. tchr. P.R., guidance counselor. Tchr. Dept. of Edn., PR, 1973—75, Colegio María Auxiliadora, Carolina, PR, 1976—99; counselor Univ. del Este, Carolina, 1999—2000, Colegio María Auxiliadora, Carolina, 1999—2003. Spkr. at conf. Sixth P.R. Congress Investigations in Edn., 2001. Author: (hymns) Himno a María Auxiliadora, 1985, Te cantamos Carolina, 2001. Mem.: Am. Counseling Assn., PR Assn. Profl. Counselors (temp. treas. 2000, conf. spkr. 2001). Protestant. Avocations: reading, writing, singing. Home: 1 Fontana Tower Apt 609 Carolina PR 00982 E-mail: migdalia_reyes@hotmail.com.

REYNOLDS, ANNETTE, secondary school educator; Master degree, Ind. U., 1973. 7th and 8th grade physical edn. health tchr. Grissom Mid. Sch., Mishawaka, Ind.; 10th-12th grades physical edn. tchr. Penn HS, Mishawaka, Ind., Tipton HS, Ind.; 9th-12th grades physical edn. tchr. Northridge HS, Middlebury, Ind.; 10th-12th grades dance tchr., gymnastics coach, cheerleader sponsor Richardson HS, Tex. Vol. Iron Kids Triathalon, Am. Heart Assn. Mem. Nat. Assn. Student Activity Advisors, Richardson Edn. Assn., Delta Kappa Gamma (chmn., dir. Flip For Sight fundraiser). Home: 9554 Atherton Dr Dallas TX 75243-6134

REYNOLDS, BILLIE ILES, insurance agent; b. Oakland, Calif., Mar. 26, 1929; d. Walter F. and Frances Olive (Blakesley) Iles; m. William V. Reynolds, June 23, 1950; children: Gilbert, Wendy Lee Bryant, Cynthia Lea Waple, Christy Dirren. Registered fin. rep., fin. counselor, pension and retirement specialist, investment advisor. Ptnr. Reynolds Advt. Agy., 1963-70; asst. exec. dir. Nat. Sch. Transp. Assn., Springfield, Va., 1964-76, exec. dir., 1976-83, Ariz. Landscape Contractors Assn., 1984-86. Registered life and health ins. agt. Freelance writer scripts for radio, TV, newspapers, nat. mags., 1953-70; author: Planning is the Key: Basics of Financial Understanding for Beginners, 1984. Methodist. E-mail: azreynolds@juno.com.

REYNOLDS, DEBBIE (MARY FRANCES REYNOLDS), actress; b. El Paso, Tex., Apr. 1, 1932; m. Eddie Fisher, Sept. 26, 1955 (div. 1959); children— Carrie, Todd; m. Harry Karl, Nov., 1960 (div. 1973); m. Richard Hamlett (div. May 1996). Active high sch. plays; screen debut Daughter of Rosie O'Grady; motion pictures include: June Bride, 1948, The Daughter of Rosie O'Grady, 1950, Three Little Words, 1950, Two Weeks With Love, 1950, Mr. Imperium, 1951, Singin' in the Rain, 1952, Skirts Ahoy!, 1952, I Love Melvin, 1953, The Affairs of Dobie Gillis, 1953, Give a Girl a Break, 1953, Susan Slept Here, 1954, Athena, 1954, Hit the Deck, 1955, The Tender Trap, 1955, The Catered Affair, 1956, Bundle of Joy, 1956, Tammy and the Bachelor, 1957, This Happy Feeling, 1958, The Mating Game, 1959, Say One for Me, 1959, It Started With a Kiss, 1959, The Gazebo, 1959, The Rat Race, 1960, Pepe, 1960, The Pleasure of His Company, 1961, The Second Time Around, 1961, How the West Was Won, 1962, My Six Loves, 1963, Mary, Mary, 1963, The Unsinkable Molly Brown, 1964, Goodbye Charlie, 1964, The Singing Nun, 1966, Divorce American Style, 1967, How Sweet It Is!, 1968, What's the Matter with Helen?, 1971, Charlotte's Web, (voice only) 1973, That's Entertainment!, 1974, The Bodyguard, 1992, Heaven and Earth, 1993, (with Albert Brooks) Mother, 1996, That's Entertainment III, 1994, In & Out, 1996, In and Out, 1997, Zack and Reba, 1998; star TV program The Debbie Reynolds Show, 1969; star Broadway show Irene, 1973-74, Annie Get Your Gun, Los Angeles, San Francisco, 1977, Woman of the Year, 1984, The Unsinkable Molly Brown, 1989-90 (nat. tour); author: If I Knew Then, 1963, Debbie-My Life, 1988; creator exercise video Do It Debbie's Way, 1984; recurring role (TV series) Will and Grace; actress (TV movies) Perry Mason, 1989, Battling for Babies, 1991, Halloweentown, 1998, The Christmas Wish, 1998, A Gift of Love, 1999 (Emmy nominee), Virtual Mom, 1999, These Old Broads, 2001, Return to Halloweentown, 2001, Connie and Carla, 2003. Named Miss Burbank, 1948 Office: Debbie Reynolds Studios care Margie Duncan 6514 Lankershim Blvd North Hollywood CA 91606-2409

REYNOLDS, GAIL SMITH, accountant, bank officer; b. Detroit, May 11, 1945; d. Woodrow and Trannie (McCool) Smith; m. Robert Kenneth Reynolds, Mar. 21, 1975; children: Robert Kenneth Jr., Jonathan Colin. BS in Acctg., Miss. U. for Women, 1985. Acctg. operator First Nat. Bank, Waco, Tex., 1966-67; acctg. clk. Miss. U. for Women, Columbus, 1970-80, accounts payable specialist, 1980-85, head cashier office of comptroller, 1985-86, acctg. supr., 1986—2000; mgr. Miss. U. for Women Fed. Credit Union, Columbus, 2000—. Bd. dirs., mem. Columbus Lowndes Assn. for Handicapped Citizens, 1993-96. Mem. Am. Soc. Women Accts. (pres. 1989-90, bd. dirs. 1985—, Outstanding Woman Acct. of the Yr. Miss. Golden Triangle chpt. 1990), Inst. Mgmt. Accts. Avocation: classic cinema memorabilia collecting. Office: Mississippi Univ for Women Box W41 Columbus MS 39701

REYNOLDS, HELEN ELIZABETH, management services consultant; b. Minerva, NY, Aug. 30, 1925; d. Henry James and Margurite Catherine (Gallagher) McNally; m. Theodore Laurence Reynolds, Feb. 27, 1948; children: Laurence McBride, David Scott, William Herbert. BA, SUNY, Albany, 1967; MA, Union Coll., Schenectady, N.Y., 1971. Grad. Realtors Inst., NY. Owner, mgr. Schafer Studio, Schenectady, 1970-73; co-owner, v.p. Reynolds Chalmers Inc., Schenectady, 1971-97; program coord. Schenectady County, 1980-81; adminstr. Wellspring House of Albany, 1981-94; pres. HR Mgmt. Cons., Port Charlotte, Fla., 1994—2002. Cons., examiner NY State Civil Service, Albany, 1971-81; adv. council SBA, Washington, 1978-80. Planning bd. Town of Niskayuna, NY, 1977-81, town councilwoman, 1986-94; co-chair Great N.E. Festival on the Mohawk River, 1989-90; bd. dirs. HAVEN, Schenectady YWCA; mem. NY State Commn. on The Capital Region, 1994-98, Acad. of Women of Achievement, Schenectady, 1994; pres. Photo Arts Group of Charlotte County, 1998-2003, Buena Vista Property Owners Assn., Port Charlotte, Fla., 1998-2003. Named Woman Vision, 1986-87, Today's Woman, 1987, Schenectady YWCA. Mem. Antique and Classic Boat Soc. (bd. dir. 1974-89, Disting. Svc. award 1979, Founders award 1989), Assn. Adminstrs. Ind. Housing (pres. 1986-88, 92-94), Zonta (pres. 1981-82), Adirondack Mus., Antique Boat Mus., Lake George Antique Boat & Auto Mus. (bd. dir.), Charlotte Symphony League (v.p.), Union Coll. Alumni Assn., Charlotte Harbor Yacht Club, Charlotte County Art Guild. Avocations: photography, reading, golf, skiing, canoeing. Home and Office: 104 Leland St SW Port Charlotte FL 33952-9131

REYNOLDS, JEAN EDWARDS, publishing executive; b. Saginaw, Mich., Dec. 11, 1941; d. F. Perry and Kathrine (Edwards) R.; m. Cary Wellington, Sept. 10, 1975 (div. 1982); children, Bradley, Abigail, Benjamin; m. Jon Haddon, Nov. 8, 1997. BA, Wells Coll., 1963; postgrad., CCNY, 1965-67. Asst. editor, sr. editor trade book div. Prentice-Hall, Englewood Cliffs, N.J., 1963-66, dir. children's books, 1966-69, McCall Pub. Co., N.Y.C., 1969-71; sr. v.p., editorial dir. Franklin Watts Inc., N.Y.C., 1971-75; pres. Pet Projects Inc., Ridgefield, Conn., 1975-81; editor in chief young people's publs. Grolier Inc., Danbury, Conn., 1981-89; founder, pub., exec. v.p. The Millbrook Press, Brookfield, Conn., 1989—. Bd. dirs. Wellington Leisure Products, Atlanta, Kiper Enterprises, Oswego, N.Y., Graduate Inst., New Haven, Conn., Jewish Fedn. Greater Danbury; chairperson Conn. Ctr. for the Book, 1991-94. Mem. Bd. of Govs. for Higher Edn., State of Conn., 2004—; pres. Jewish Fedn. Greater Danbury, 1991—93, 2003—; bd. dirs. Jewish Home for the Elderly, Fairfield, Conn., 1989—90, 1999, Book Industry Study Group, 1991—98, The Wooster Sch., Danbury, Conn., 1992—, chair headmaster search, 2002—; bd. dirs. Temple Shearith Israel, Ridgefield, Conn., 1994—97, chair Kehila campaign, 2002; bd. dirs. The Children's Book Coun., 1996—2000, vice chair, 1997—98, chair, 1998—99; bd. dirs. The Learning Collaborative, 2000—. Mem. ALA, Children's Book Coun., Mensa. Jewish. Avocations: skiing, sailing, needlework. Home: 33 Corntassle Rd Danbury CT 06811-3208 Office: The Millbrook Press Inc 2 Old New Milford Rd Brookfield CT 06804-2426

REYNOLDS, KATHLEEN DIANE FOY (KDF REYNOLDS), transportation executive; b. Chgo., Dec. 9, 1946; d. David Chancy Foy and Vivian Anne (Schwartz) R. Student, San Francisco State U., 1964-68. Taxicab medallion permit holder, City and County of San Francisco, 1995— Studio coord. KTVU-TV, Oakland, Calif., 1968-70; assoc. prodr. KPIX-TV, San Francisco, 1970-72; music publicist Oakland, 1966-70; [illegible], West Coast Women's Press, Oakland, 1974-82, gen. mgr., 1984-86; screen writer Oakland, 1970—; gen. ptnr. Designated Driver Group, Oakland, 1990-97; assoc. owner DeSoto Cab, San Francisco, 1995-98, ptnr., 1998—; mng. ptnr. Foy Scribes, divsn. The Tallahassee Group, Oakland, Calif., 1997—. Coun. mem. West Coast Women's Press, Oakland, 1975-86; founding assoc. Women's Inst. for Freedom of the Press, Washington, 1977—. Author of periodical news, reviews, features, 1974-82; author of six documentaries for comml. and PBS-TV, 1968-73. Mem. Soc. Mayflower Descendants, Casper, Wyo., 1967—, Chabot Space and Sci. Ctr., Oakland, Calif., Fine Arts Museums San Francisco. Mem. LWV, San Francisco Film Soc. Avocations: archery, reading, film festival attendance. Home: PO Box 2742 Oakland CA 94602-0042 Office Phone: 510-261-8807.

REYNOLDS, LOUISE MAXINE KRUSE, retired school nurse; b. Waynesboro, Va., May 28, 1935; d. Emil Herman and Cora Lee (Hammer) Kruse; m. Elbert B. Reynolds Jr., June 13, 1964; children: David Emil, Jane Marie. Diploma, Rockingham Meml. Hosp., 1956; student, Madison Coll., Tex. Tech U. RN, Tex., Va, cert. sch. nurse. Head nurse orthopedic, opthalmology dept. surgery Duke U., Durham, N.C., 1961-62; head nurse surg. fl. Waynesboro (Va.) Hosp., 1962-64; sch. nurse Lubbock (Tex.) Ind. Sch. Dist., 1974-94, ret., 1994. Pres. Vol. Network Luth. Home, Lubbock, Tex., 1996-2000; sec. Luth. Student Coun., Tex. Tech., Lubbock, 1999-2000. Recipient recognition for contbn. to ch. and cmty., Aid Assn. for Luths. Mem. DAR (sec. Nancy Anderson chpt. 2000-02, chpt. chaplain 2002—), Va. Nurses Assn. (dist. sec., chair), Tex. Assn. Sch. Nurses (sec., treas. dist. 17, program chair 1989 state conv.).

REYNOLDS, LOUISE WEBB, retired volunteer, director; b. Demopolis, Ala., Feb. 22, 1946; d. John Cox Webb, III and Marie Suttle Webb; m. Peter Michael Reynolds; children: Peter Michael Jr., Angie Marie, John Webb. BS, U Ala., 1968. Exec. dir. The Demopolis City Schos. Found., Inc., Demopolis, Ala., 1994—99; tchr. English Demopolis City Schs., Demopolis, Ala., 1968—69; clerk Demopolis Stock Yards, Demopolis, Ala., 1969—72; coord. media West Ala. Mental Health Ctr., Demopolis, Ala., 1974—78; clerk Reynolds Cattle Co., Forkland, Ala., 1986—90. Chmn. BOE, 1988—90, 1992—93; chmn. bd. Demopolis City Schs. Bd. Edn., 1988—90; mem. bd. dirs. Bd. Edn., Demopolis City Schs., Demopolis, 1985—95; vol. counselor "Save-a Life" Crisis Pregnancy Ctr., Demopolis, 1990—94; pres. Demopolis Kappa Delta Alumnae, Demopolis, 1990—93; orgnl. pres., first integrated PTA Demopolis Elem. PTA, Demopolis, 1980—81; reorganizational pres. Marengo County chpt. U. Ala. Alumni Assn., Demopolis, 1977—78; orgnl. pres. Marengo County Assn. Brain Damaged Children, Demopolis, 1971—74; vol. coord. The Achievement Ctr. Spl. Children, Demopolis, 1972—74; orgnl. pres. Marengo County chpt. Nat. Assn. Retarded Children, Demopolis, 1972—74; pres. Demopolis Kappa Delta Alumnae, Demopolis, 1976—77; leader Brownie Scout Tombigee Girl Scout Coun., Demopolis, 1979—83; Cub Scout Den Mother Boy Scouts of Am., Prairie Dist., Black Warrior Coun., Demopolis, 1976—79; orgnl. pres. Pastoral Coun., St. Leo's Cath. Ch., Demopolis, 1993—97; orgnl. coord. "RENEW" St. Leo's Cath. Ch., Demopolis, 1983—88; tchr. Confraternity Christian Doctrine, St. Leo's Cath. Ch., Demopolis, 1973—93; Eucharistic min., lector St. Leo's Cath. Ch., Demopolis, chmn. bd., 1992—93. Recipient Disting. Svc. award, Demopolis Jaycees, 1972, Outstanding Chpt. Devel. award, U. Ala., Nat. Alumni Assn., 1979, Paul Harris fellow, Rotary, 2003. Mem.: The Reading Club (pres. Demopolis chpt. 1982—83, 2003—04). Roman Catholic. Avocations: painting, travel. Home: 303 West Lyon Demopolis AL 36732

REYNOLDS, NANCY REMICK, writer, researcher, editor; b. San Antonio, July 15, 1938; d. Donald Worthington and Edith (Remick) R.; m. Brian Rushton, June 25, 1983; 1 child, Ehren T. Park. Student, Sch. Am. Ballet, 1951, 53-61, Juilliard Sch. Music, 1957, Martha Graham Sch. Contemporary Dance, N.Y.C., 1959, U. Sorbonne, Paris, 1962; BA in Art History, Columbia U., 1965; postgrad., Goethe Inst., Prien, 1972, U. Chgo. and Sarah Lawrence Coll., 1974-77. Dancer N.Y.C. Ballet, 1956-61; editor Praeger Pubs., N.Y.C., 1965-71; dir. rsch. book Choreography by George Balanchine: A Catalogue of Works, N.Y., 1979-82 (pub. 1983); dir. rsch. pub. TV spl. Balanchine, N.Y., 1983-84; assoc. editor Internat. Ency. of Dance, (pub. 1998); dir. rsch. The George Balanchine Found., N.Y.C., 1994—. Co-pub. Twentieth-Century Dance in Slides, 1978-93. Author: Repertory in Review: Forty Years of the New York City Ballet, 1977 (De la Torre Bueno prize 1977), The Dance Catalog: A Complete Guide to Today's World of Dance, 1979, co-author: In Performance,1980, Dance Classics, 1991 (rec. for teen age N.Y. Pub Libr.), No Fixed Points: Dance in the Twentieth Century, 2003; editor: Movement and Metaphor: Four Centuries of Ballet (Lincoln Kirstein), 1970, Dance as a Theatre Art: Source Readings in Dance History from 1581 to the Present (Selma Jeanne Cohen), 1974, School of Classical Dance (V. Kostrovitskaya and A. Pisarev), 1978; contbr. (book) Ballet: Bias and Belief, "Three Pamphlets Collected" and Other Dance Writings of Lincoln Kirstein, 1983, also numerous articles and revs. to Dancing Times, Ballet News, Playbill, ArtsLine, Dancemag., Town & Country, Connoisseur, N.Y. Times, Ency. Britannica., Ency. of N.Y.C., others. Ford Found. Travel and Study grantee, 1974; Mary Duke Biddle Found. grantee, 1990. Mem. Dance Critics Assn. (pres. 1986-87), Soc. Dance History Scholars, Soc. for Dance Rsch., Am. Soc. for Theatre Rsch., European Assn. Dance Historians, Internat. Fedn. for Theatre Rsch. in affiliation with Societe Internat. des Bibliotheques et Musees des Arts du Spectacle, Phi Beta Kappa. Home: 9 Prospect Park W Brooklyn NY 11215-1758

REYNOLDS, PAULINE PHYLLIS, retired early education educator, accountant; b. Detroit, Aug. 21, 1924; d. Paul Wesley and Hazel B. (Rolixman) Baughan; m. Douglas Wilcox Reynolds, June 25, 1950; 1 child: Rene Baughan Reynolds. BS, Ea. Mich. U., 1948; MA, Mich. State U., 1950. 2d grade tchr., Perry, Mich., 1944-46; 1st grade tchr. Ovid, Mich., 1946-47; 2d grade tchr. Owosso, Mich., 1948-93; ret., 1993. Sec. Cemetery Assn., 1952—. Mem. AAUW (hon., life), Delta Kappa Gamma (charter). Home: 600 E Bennington Rd Owosso MI 48867-9794

REYNOLDS, ROCHELLE ANNETTA, flight attendant; b. St. Louis, Aug. 1, 1953; d. Joseph Lee Moore, Sr. and Clara Bernice Moore; m. Robert Lee Reynolds, Aug. 26, 1989; children: Joshua Michael, Stacey Karnesha. Student, St. Charles C.C., 2002. Flight attendant U.S. Airways Airline, Charlotte, NC, 1972—2003, St. Louis, 2003—. Dir. Salem Ctr. Summer Camp, St. Louis, 2003—. Sunday sch. tchr. New Salem Missionary Bapt. Ch., St. Louis, 1980—2003; chairperson The Eccles. Ladies, St. Louis, 1983—2002; edn. youth dir. New Salem Youth Dept., St. Louis, 1990—2003; pres. Believers Fellowship Ministers Wives and Widows, St. Louis, 2001—03; dir. Salem Ctr. Summer Camp, St. Louis, 2003—03. Mem.: The Eccles. Ladies (treas. 2002—03, chairperson emeritus 2002). Democrat. Baptist. Avocations: reading, walking, writing, travel. Office: US Airways Airline 2345 Crystal Dr Arlington VA 22227

REYNOLDS, SALLIE BLACKBURN, artist, civic volunteer; b. Kansas City, Mo., Feb. 9, 1940; d. Anton and Sallie Churchill (Blackburn) Zajic; m. Jeffrey Calhoun Loker, Mar. 25, 1959 (div. May 1965); children: Toni Lynne Loker, Michael David Loker, Kathryn Lee Loker Simpson; m. Everett Lee Reynolds, Mar. 29, 1969 (dec. Sept. 1992). Student, William Jewell Coll., 1959, BA magna cum laude, 1977; student, U. Mo., Kansas City, 1966-67, Kansas City Art Inst., 1966-70; Cert., Famous Artists Sch., 1965. Cert. tchr., Mo. From clk. to sec. Hdqrs. Strategic Air Command,

Offutt AFB, Omaha, 1960-62; sec., wage and hr. law enforcement asst., wage-hr. divsn. U.S. Dept. of Labor, Kansas City, 1963-68, exec. sec. to regional manpower adminstr., 1968-71, spl. asst. to regional exec. com., 1971-72, mgmt. asst. Office of Regional Dir., 1972-73; co-owner Claycomo Skelly Svc. Sta. & Garage, 1970—78; from. clk. to sec. air carrier dist. office FAA, Kansas City, 1978-81; from clk. typist contracts divsn. to sec. regional pers. officer Bur. of Reclamation, U.S. Dept. of Interior, Boulder City, Nev., 1982—84; editl. asst. divsn. of planning Bur. of Reclamation, Boulder City, 1984-86; owner, operator B-Bar-L Wandering Star Ranch (registered angus and horses, beefalo, various real estate), Stover, Kansas City, Versailles, Mo., 1989—. Editor newsletter Laurie Fine Art, 1989-90; designer historic landmark plaque Clay County, Mo.; designer hist. painting for annual Dogwood Festival pageants Camden County, Mo., 1994. Ofcl. commr., sec., corr. Clay County (Mo.) Bicentennial Commn., 1974-76; mem. Ozark Brush and Palette, Inc., Camdenton, Mo., 1987—, editor newsletter, 1988-89; v.p., sec., life mem. Clay County Hist. Soc., 1972—, active Nat. Wildlife Fedn. Recipient 1st Pl. award Nat. Soc. DAR Am. Heritage Contest in oil/acrylic painting, 1990, 3d pl., 1991, 1st pl. gold award 1992, 1st pl. award profl. photography Laurie Fine Art Show, 1991; named one of Top 50 Profl. Artists, Mo. State Fair, 1992. Mem. Nat. Soc. DAR (pub. rels. chmn., archives chmn., corr. sec., Niangua chpt. Camdenton 1987—, Eldon Mo. chpt. 1999), Nat. Oil and Acrylic Painters Soc., Phi Epsilon of Phi Beta Kappa, Versailles Saddle Club, Mo. Paint Horse Club (sec. 1998). Presbyterian. Avocations: horses, art, history, cats, needlework, music, photography. Home and Office: B-Bar-L Wandering Star Ranch 23688 S 135 Hwy Stover MO 65078

REYNOLDS, SHERI, writer; b. Conway, SC, 1967; BA in English, Davidson Coll., 1989; MFA in creative writing, Va. Commonwealth U., 1992. Adj. instr. English Va. Commonwealth U., Richmond, 1992—. Author: Bitterroot Landing, 1994, The Rapture of Canaan, 1996, A Gracious Plenty, 1997. Office: VCU Dept English 900 Park Ave Hibbs Bldg 306 PO Box 842005 Richmond VA 23284-2005*

REYNOLDS, VALRAE, museum curator; b. San Francisco, Dec. 18, 1944; d. Ralph Stanley and Valberta May (Eversole) R.; m. Richard Lee Huffman, Sept. 14, 1974; children: Elizabeth Anne, Margaret Lee. BA in Fine Arts with honors, U. Calif., Davis, 1966; MA, NYU, 1969. Asst. curator Asian collections Newark Mus., 1969-70, curator Asian collections, 1970—2002, sr. curator Asian collections, 2003—. Cons. SITES Exhbn., 1988; adj. prof. art history Columbia U., 1996; lectr., presenter in field. Author: From the Sacred Realm, Treasures of Tibetan Art from the Newark Museum, 1999; editor: Newark Mus. Quar., 1976, Tibetan Jour., 1976, Asia Soc., 1977, Arts of Asia, 1989, Explore Tibet, 1992; contbr. over 36 articles and revs. to profl. jours.; prodr. multimedia prodns. in field. Grantee NEA, NEH, 1972-74, 82-83, 85-86, 88-91, 89-92, 99, 2003, J. Paul Getty grantee, 1986, 89-91, Travel grantee Asian Cultural Coun., 1989, NEA grantee, 2003-04, Wallace Found. grantee, 2003-04, Freeman Found. grantee, 2003-04. Office: Newark Mus 49 Washington St Newark NJ 07102

REYNOLDS, VIRGINIA EDITH, sociologist, anthropologist, educator, artist; b. Lafayette, Ind., July 3, 1941; d. Ira Hubert and Harriet G. (Robertson) Reynolds; m. Antonio G. Arroyo, 1961 (div. 1974); children: Mary-Jane R. Arroyo Young, Joanne R. Arroyo Shirley. BS with hons. in Sociology, Columbia U., 1965, MA in Sociology, 1967; postgrad., Pa. State U., 1974—84. Rsch. asst. demographic divsn. Population Coun., N.Y.C., 1968; tchr. CUNY Borough Manhattan C.C., N.Y.C., 1969; asst. prof. sociology and anthropology Lycoming Coll., Williamsport, Pa., 1970—75, Indiana U. Pa., 1975—2001; ret., 2001. Mem. exec. com. Assn. for Asian Studies Mid-Atlantic Region, 1997—99. Exhibited in group shows at Old Courthouse Office Gallery, 2002 (Hon. Mention award, 2002), 2003 (2d Pl. award, 2003). Singer Indiana County Singers and Ch. Choir; Dem. com. woman Indiana County, Pa., 2001—03. Mem.: AAUW. Episcopalian. Avocations: tai chi, community theatre musicals, international folk dancing. Home and Studio: 1699 Church St Indiana PA 15701

REYNOLDS, W(YNETKA) ANN, academic administrator, educator; b. Coffeyville, Kans., Nov. 3, 1937; d. John Ethelbert and Glennie (Beanland) King; m. Thomas H. Kirschbaum; children— Rachel Rebecca, Rex King. BS in Biology-Chemistry, Kans. State Tchrs. Coll., Emporia, 1958; MS in Zoology, U. Iowa, Iowa City, 1960, PhD, 1962; DSc (hon.), Ind. State U., Evansville, 1980; LHD (hon.), McKendree Coll., 1984, U. N.C., Charlotte, 1988, U. Judaism, L.A., 1989, U. Nebr., Kearney, 1992; DSc (hon.), Ball State U., Muncie, Ind., 1985, Emporia (Kans.) State U., 1987; PhD (hon.), Fu Jen Cath. U., Republic of China, 1987; LHD (hon.), U. Nebr., Kearney, 1992, Colgate U., 1993; LHD, No. Mich. U., 1995. Asst. prof. biology Ball State U., Muncie, Ind., 1962-65; asst. prof. anatomy U. Ill. Coll. Medicine, Chgo., 1965-68, assoc. prof. anatomy, 1968-73, rsch. prof. ob-gyn, 1973—, prof. anatomy, 1973—, acting assoc. dean acad. affairs Coll. Medicine, 1977, assoc. vice chancellor, dean grad. coll., 1977-79; provost, v.p. for acad. affairs, prof. ob-gyn. and anatomy Ohio State U., Columbus, 1979-82; chancellor Calif. State Univ. system, Long Beach, 1982-90, prof. biology, 1982-90; chancellor CUNY, 1990-97; pres. U. Ala., Birmingham, 1997—2002. Bd. dirs. Abbott Labs., Maytag, Owens-Corning, Humana, Inc., News-Gasette, Champaign, Ill.; clin. prof. ob-gyn. UCLA, 1985-90; mem. Nat. Rsch. Coun. Com. Undergrad Si. Edn., 1993-97; co-chair Fed. Task Force on Women, Minorities and Handicapped in Sci. and Tech., 1987-90, Pacesetter Program Reform for Secondary Sch. Coll. Bd., 1992-96. Contbr. chpts. to books, articles to profl. jours; assoc. editor Am. Biology Tchr., 1964-67. Active activities involving edn. and the arts; nat. adv. bd. Inst. Am. Indian Arts, 1992-97; bd. dirs. Lincoln Ctr. Inst., 1993—; trustee Internat. Life Scis. Inst.-Nutrition Found., 1987-2001, Southwest Mus. Recipient Disting. Alumni award Kans. State Tchrs. Coll., 1972, Calif. Gov.'s Award for the Arts for an Outstanding Individual in Arts in Edn., 1989, Prize award Cen. Assn. Obstetricians and Gynecologists, 1968; NSF Predoctoral fellow, 1958-62, Woodrow Wilson Hon. fellow, 1958. Fellow ACOG; mem. AAAS, Perinatal Rsch. Soc., Soc. Gynecol. Investigation (sec./treas. 1980-83, pres. 1992-93), Nat. Assn. Systems Heads (pres. 1987-88), Sigma Xi. Office: Ctr for Cmty Outreach Devel Univ Ala 933 19th St S Birmingham AL 35294-2041

REZAC, ROSELYN ANN, graphic designer, business owner; m. Martin R. Skoro, Mar. 4, 1984. BA, U. Minn., 1976, MA, 1978. Counselor, tchr. various orgns., 1971-78; art dir., graphic designer and supr. various cos., 1978-84; prin., owner, graphic designer MartinRoss Design, Mpls., 1984—. Recipient awards for 3M poster design Am. Graphic Design Awards, 1994, logo design, New Am. Logos, 1994, brochure design Best of Brochure Design, 1992, poster and packaging designs Computer Graphics II, 1995, Package Design award Am. Graphic Design Awards, 1997, Package Design award Rockport Pubs., 1997. Avocations: travel, walking, reading. Office Phone: 612-377-5138.

REZENDES, TARA MELISSA, music educator; b. New Bedford, Mass., Apr. 10, 1975; d. Anthony Michael and Leonora Elizabeth Thomas; m. Gilbert Joseph Rezendes III, Aug. 3, 2002; children: Christian Anthony, Dylan Joseph. MusB, Mercyhurst Coll., 1997. Cert. tchr. Mass., Pa. Music dir. Ford Mid. Sch., Acushnet, Mass., 1997—. Piano tchr. Symphony Music Shop, Dartmouth, Mass., 1998—; organist St. Thomas More Ch., Somerset, Mass., 2002—. Singer: Sine Nomine, 1998—, St. Julie Billiart Ch., 1998—; musician: Plymouth (Mass.) Philharm., 2001. Mem.: Kappa Gamma Phi. Democrat. Roman Cath.

RHAU-BERNHARD, ANNA FRIEDA, women's health nurse practitioner; b. Niedernwöhren, Germany, Nov. 5, 1956; d. Wolfgang and Stanislawa Omielska Rhau; m. Douglas Neil Bernhard, June 21, 1980; 1 child, Kristin Bernhard. BSN, Georgetown U., 1978; Nurse Practitioner Cert., U. Colo., Denver, 1984. RN Wash., 1980, Ga., 1998, cert. WHCNP, Wash., 1984, Ga., 1998. Office nurse, then women's healthcare nurse practitioner Evergreen Women's Specialty, Kirkland, Wash., 1980—91, 1991; women's health care nurse practitioner, rsch. coord. Dr. James Kustin, Bellevue, Wash., 1991—93; women's health care nurse practitioner Group Health, Redmond, Wash., 1993—95, Planned Parenthood, Kirkland, 1995—98; women's health care nurse practitioner, physician exam nurse practitioner North Fulton Treatment Ctr., Roswell, Ga., 1998—; women's health care nurse practitioner, nurse rschr. SpectRx, Norcross, Ga., 2000—01. Continuing edn. officer Eastside NPs, Kirkland, 1996—98; nurse practitioner preceptor U. Wash., Kirkland, 1993—98. Vol. Rep. Party of Wash., Bellevue, 1992, 1996. Mem.: AAUW (life), United Advanced Practice RNs of Ga. (founding mem.), Ga. Nurses Assn. Roman Catholic. Avocations: crafts, outdoor activities, gardening, sewing, studying other cultures. Office: North Fulton Treatment Ctr 601 Bombay Ln Roswell GA 30076

RHEA, MARCIA CHANDLER, accountant; b. Columbia, SC, Apr. 27, 1956; d. Foster Frazier and Virginia Elizabeth (Goude) Chandler; m. Randall W. Rhea, Aug. 23, 1980. AA, Bauder Coll., Atlanta, 1975; BA magna cum laude, Coll. of Charleston, S.C., 1981; postgrad., CPA studies. Cert. tax practice ptnr., notary pub., S.C., CPA, S.C. Writer, prodr. U.S. Army C.E., Charleston, 1984; mng. ptnr. Care/Share Prodns., Charleston, 1981—; ptnr. Chandler Rhea, CPA, Johns Island, S.C., 1987—, Homes and Rhea, CPAs, LLC. Ins. agt., registered rep. H.D. Vest Investment Securities; screenwriter; media cons., roving reporter Worldfest-Charleston Internat. Film Festival, 1994. Author: Does It Have to Happen Again?, From Hell's Angel to Heaven's Saint; author (screenplays) The Carolina Storyteller (semifinalist Austin Film Festival, 1999, Fade-in Awards winner 2000, S.C. Film Festival Finalist Winner 2002, Semi Finalist 2002-, AOL Finalist Winner 2004), The Life Shift, The Geriatric Tour, Stargazer; contbr. articles to mags. and profl. jours.; prodr. various films. Adult tchr. Ashley Rivers Bapt. Ch.; mem. Tri-County Advocates for Women on Bds. and Commns. for S.C. Recipient Outstanding Acad. Achievement award Coll. of Charleston, H.D. Vest Svc. award, 2001. Mem. AICPA, Am. Soc. Notaries, S.C. Assn. CPAs, S.C. Motion Picture TV Assn., Charleston Film Soc. (bd. dirs.), Screenwriters Guild of Charleston (charter), Acctg. Assn., Coll. of Charleston Alumni, Film Soc. Coll. Charleston (bd. dirs.), Charleston Film Soc. (bd. dirs.), Phi Kappa Phi, Phi Mu. Republican. Baptist. Avocation: helping to develop an indigenous film industry in south carolina. Office: 102 Wappoo Creek Dr Ste 11 Charleston SC 29412 E-mail: mrhea@homesandrhea.com.

RHEAMS, ANNIE ELIZABETH, education educator; b. Lake Providence, La. d. Curtis Kleinpeter Sr. and Annie Augusta (Webb) Kleinpeter; 1 child, Darryl Jemall Rheams. BA, Grambling (La.) U., 1971; MS, Ala. A&M U., 1975; PhD, U. Wis., Milw., 1989. Cert. tchr. in exceptional edn., adminstrn. Tchr. Ala. A&M U., Normal, 1971-79, adminstr., 1977-79; acad. specialist U. Wis., Milw., 1979-82, Parkside, 1982-84; tchr. diagnostician, adminstr. Milw. Schs., 1984-89; asst. prof. dept. edn. Marquette U., Milw., 1989-96; asst. prin. North Divsn. H.S., Milw., 1996—, Marshall H.S., Milw., 1997—99, tchr. exceptional edn. cognitively disabled, consumer math., 1999—, adminstr., asst. prin., 1999. Career counselor Madison County Career Counseling Svcs., Huntsville, 1975; adj. prof. Oakwood (Ala.) SDA Coll., 1975-78; tchr. Gateway to Engring. Program, Milw., 1984-88; cons. pub. schs./Wee Care Day Care, Milw., 1992-96; condr. workshops in field. Author: P.A.C.E.: A Thematic Approach to Developing Essential Experiences, 1996. Voter registrar/poll watcher NAACP, Lake Providence, 1966; v.p. Work for Wis., Inc., Milw., 1993-94, Messmer H.S. Bd., Milw., 1990-94; com. chmn. Citizen's Rev. Bd., Milw., 1980-82, Met. Milw. Alliance Black Sch. Educators, 1994-95. Assoc. fellow Ctr. for Great Plains Studies, U. Nebr.-Lincoln, 1995; named Outstanding Tchr. Educator, Am. Assn. for Coll. Tchr. Educators Directory, 1995. Mem. Zonta Internat., Alpha Kappa Alpha, Phi Delta Kappa. Avocations: tennis, sewing, ceramics, horseback riding, biking. Home: PO Box 90681 Milwaukee WI 53209-0611 Fax: 414-902-8315. E-mail: rheams@mailandnews.com.

RHEINTGEN, LAURA DALE, research center official; b. Takoma Park, Md., July 13, 1962; d. Robert William and Ethel Frances (Snyder) Schiedel. BA in Internat. Studies and German, W.Va. U., 1984; MA in Internat. Affairs, Am. U., 1988. Rsch. asst. Brookings Instn., Washington, 1986; staff cons. Birch & Davis Assocs., Inc., Silver Spring, Md., 1988-89; devel. analyst Ctr. for Strategic and Internat. Studies, Washington, 1989-92, mgr. devel. rsch. and records, 1992-93, asst. dir. devel., 1994-95, dir. found. rels., 1995-97; assoc. dir. devel. Aspen Inst., Washington, 1997-98; devel. assoc. Nat. Acad. Scis., Washington, 1998-99, devel. officer, 1999; devel. dir. Am. Inst. Contemporary German Studies, Johns Hopkins U., Washington, 1999—. Mem. Women in Internat. Security Studies, German Lang. Soc. Office: Am Inst Contemporary German Studies Johns Hopkins U 1400 16th St NW Ste 420 Washington DC 20036-2216

RHINES, MARIE LOUISE, composer, violinist; b. Boston; BA in History and Polit. Sci., Northeastern U.; postgrad., Yale U.; MusM, New Eng. Conservatory, Boston. Dir. chamber music Groton (Mass.) Sch. for Boys; prof. of violin King's Coll. Choir Sch., Cambridge, Eng.; concertmaster, asst. conductor Cape Cod Symphony, Hyannis, Mass.; producer, announcer, founder The Folk Heritage program Nat. Pub. Radio, Sta. WGBH-FM, Boston; guest faculty U. Colo., Boulder; conductor, Mozart Orch. Harvard U., Cambridge, Mass., 1985-86; panelist Mass. Coun. on Art and Humanities, Boston, 1986; pub., pres., founder Sedona (Ariz.) Music Pub. Co., 1988—; composer, guest soloist USAF Concert Band, Southwestern States, 1990—; guest soloist, composer in residence U.S. Command Band of Air Force Res., Warner Robins AFB, Ga., 1991; artist Ariz. Commn. on Arts and Humanities, Phoenix, 1990—; guest solo violin artist Holland Am. Cruise Lines, 1996. Artist-in-residence U. Calif., LaJolla; composer-artist-in-residence State of Tenn., Nashville; guest poet, musician Ariz. Cowboy Poets Gathering, Prescott, 1990-91, 2002; mem. violin faculty No. Ariz. U. 1993, 2001. Composer, publisher numerous works for solo violin, voice, chamber orchestra, full symphony orch. and opera chorus; solo violin concert appearances at major concert halls and as soloist with symphony orchs. throughout U.S., Can., Europe; numerous radio and TV interviews and documentaries; recording artist, N.Y., Nashville, 1996, RCA Studios. Cmty. Speakers Bureau Lect. Ariz. Humanities Council, 2000-03. Recipient Music Composition award, Artist Found.; Rockefeller grantee Am. Music Ctr. Mem. ASCAP (22 composing and performing awards), Nashville Assn. of Musicians, Meet the Composer. Avocations: mountain climbing, gourmet cooking, gardening, philosophy. Home and Office: PO Box 3075 Sedona AZ 86340-3075

RHOADES, EVA YVONNE, retired elementary school educator; b. Henderson, Tex., Sept. 27, 1935; d. Cecil Milton Andrus and Olga Mae Maddox; m. Samuel Jeffery Rhoades (dec. Jan. 1994). BS in Elem. Edn., U. Tex., 1958; ME in Spl. Edn., U. Tex., Tyler, 1982. Tchr. I.W. Popham Elem. Sch., Austin, 1958—62, Kelso Elem. Sch., Houston, 1962—72; tchr. spl. edn. jr. high West Rusk Ind. Sch. Dist., New London, Tex., 1980—94. Mem.: ATPT, Coun. for Exceptional Children, Anna B. Kelso Elem. PTA (life), Rusk County Poetry Soc., Ex-Students U. Tex. (life). Home: 1900 Castlegate Henderson TX 75654

RHOADES, KITTY, state legislator; b. Hudson, Wis., Apr. 7, 1951; m. Frank Rhoades; 3 children. BA, U. Wis., River Falls, 1973; MA, Ill. State U., 1978. Exec. dir. Hudson C. of C., 1991—96; pres. Suburban C. of C., 1996—; sml. bus. owner; classroom tchr.; mem. Wis. State Assembly, Madison, 1998—, chair aging and long-term care com., mem. colls. and univs. com., mem. edn. com., mem. fin. instns. com., mem. joint legis. coun. Mem. U. Wis. River Falls Alumni Found.; mem. pres.'s adv. coun. Century Coll.; mem. pastoral coun. St. Patrick's Ch.; bd. dirs. Minn. C. of C. Exec. Assn., United Way. Mem.: Rotary. Republican. Roman Catholic. Office: State Capitol Bldg Rm 321 E PO Box 8953 Madison WI 53708-8953 Address: 708 4th St Hudson WI 54016

RHOADES, MARCIA DIANE, career counselor; b. L.A., Sept. 18, 1937; d. Edward Owen Northbrook and Gladys Evelyn (Trano) Pigeon; m. Richard Allison Rhoades, Jan. 29, 1960 (div. 1993); children: Julie, Donald, James; m. James Ferguson, July 20, 2002. BS in Bus. Edn., UCLA, 1960; MS in Counseling with distinction, Calif. State U., Northridge, 1989. Cert. marriage, family and child counselor, Calif.; nat. cert. career counselor; registered counselor, Wash. Counselor Woman at Work, Pasadena, Calif., 1988-91, U. Wash. Extension Career Devel. Svcs., Seattle, 1991-95; tchr. U. Wash. Ext., Seattle, 1995—2000; career cons., Bellevue, 1991-95; v.p. Right Mgmt. Cons., 1995—. Adv. bd. Wash. Cert. in Career Devel. Program, Seattle, 1995-2000; bd. dirs. Puget South Career Devel. Assn., Seattle, 1993-94. Mem. ACA, Nat. Career Devel. Assn. Avocation: photography.

RHOADES, MARGARET, health care association executive; MA, Wellesley Coll.; PhD, Georgetown U. Rsch. analyst U.S. Dept. State Bur. Intelligence and Rsch., 1962-67; assoc. prodr. documentaries NBC News, 1971-77; asst. commr. pub. affairs U.S. Office Edn.; assoc. commr. pub. affairs Social Security Adminstrn.; pub. affairs dir. Brookings Instn., 1981-86; exec. dir. Nat. Leadership Commn., 1986-90, Nat. Coalition on Health Care, 1990—. Office: Nat Coalition on Health Care 1200 G St NW Ste 760 Washington DC 20005-3814 E-mail: info@nchc.org.

RHOADES, NANCY LYBARGER, retired librarian; b. Coshocton, Ohio, Sept. 17, 1915; d. Harry Swayne and Ethel (Finney) Lybarger; m. Rendell Rhoades, Feb. 7, 1953 (dec. Sept. 1976). BA, Westminster Coll., 1939; BS in Libr. Sci., Case-Western Res. U., 1943. Head reference dept., sch. libr. Warder Pub. Libr., Springfield, Ohio, 1939-45; reference asst. history divsn. Cleve. Pub. Libr., 1945-54; reference asst. Columbus (Ohio) Pub. Libr., 1954-56; libr. Starling Jr. High Columbus (Ohio) Pub. Schs., 1956-58; reference asst., serials cataloger Ohio State U. Librs., Columbus, 1958-62; libr. Ashland (Ohio) Theol. Sem., 1963-70; dir. cataloging Coll. of Wooster, Ohio, 1971-74, assoc. editor Atlanta Univ. Black Culture Collection, 1971-74, head tech. svcs., 1974-76; libr. Ashland County Law Libr., 1977-90. Libr. cons. Ohio Agrl. Rsch. and Devel. Ctr., Wooster, 1976; libr., cons. First Presbyn. Ch., Ashland, 1977-83. Author: Croquet: An Annotated Bibliography from the Rendell Rhoades Croquet Collection, 1992. Pres. Ashland Br., AAUW, 1972-73, Ohio State Divsn. Bd. Internat. Rels., 1973-75; Ashland County chmn. Martha Kinney Cooper Ohioana Libr., Columbus, 1974-90. Mem. Ch. and Syngague Libr. Assn. Republican. Presbyterian. Avocations: reading, writing, swimming, sewing, painting. Home: 6000 Riverside Dr Apt C 306 Dublin OH 43017-2060

RHOADS, GERALDINE EMELINE, editor, consultant; b. Phila., Jan. 29, 1914; d. Lawrence Dry and Alice Fegley (Rice) R. AB, Bryn Mawr Coll., 1935. Publicity asst. Bryn Mawr (Pa.) Coll., 1935-37; asst. Internat. Students House, Phila., 1937-39; mng. editor The Woman mag., N.Y.C., 1939-42; editor Life Story mag., 1942-45, Today's Woman mag., N.Y.C., 1945-52, Today's Family Mag., N.Y.C., 1952-53; lectr. Columbia U., 1954-56; assoc. editor Readers Digest, 1954-55; producer NBC, 1955-56; assoc. editor Ladies Home Jour., 1956-62, mng. editor, 1962-63; exec. editor McCall's mag., 1963-66; editor Woman's Day mag., 1966-82, editorial dir., 1982-84, Woman's Day Resource Center, 1984-89; v.p. Woman's Day mag., 1972-77, 78-84, CBS Consumer Publs., 1977-84; cons. Woman's Day, N.Y.C., 1989-91. Editorial cons., dir. Nat. Mag. Awards, 1991-94. Author: (with others) Woman's Day Help Book, 1988. Mem. journalism awards com. James Beard Found., 1993-2001. Recipient award for profl. achievement Diet Workshop Internat., 1977; Elizabeth Cutter Morrow award YWCA Salute to Women in Bus., 1977; Recipient Econ. Equity award Women's Equity Action League, 1982; March of Dimes Women Editor's citation, 1982 Mem.: Women's Forum (bd. dirs. 1985—87), Advt. Women in N.Y. (bd. govs. 1983—85, 2d v.p. 1985—87, 1st v.p. 1987—89, bd. dirs. 1989—90, Pres.'s award 1987), N.Y. Women in Comm. (Matrix award 1975), Am. Soc. Mag. Editors (chmn. exec. com. 1971—73), Fashion Group (bd. govs. 1977—79, 1987—88, chmn. bd. govs. 1978—80, treas. bd. govs. 1983—85, bd. dirs. Found. 1980—81), Nat. Press Club (dir.), Bryn Mawr Coll. Alumni Assn. (bd. dirs. 1989—94), Turtle Bay Assn. (bd. dirs. 1989—92), Literacy Vols. of N.Y.C. (bd. dirs. 1986—93), YWCA Acad. Women Achievers, Bryn Mawr Club of N.Y.C. (bd. dirs. 1994—2000), Women's City Club of N.Y. (bd. dirs. 1996—, chair comm. 2001—). Home: 185 W End Ave Apt 21A New York NY 10023-5548 E-mail: rhoadsge@aol.com.

RHOADS, REBECCA R. electronics executive; BS, MS, Calif. Poly. U.; MA in Bus. Mgmt., UCLA. With Gen. Dynamics, 1979—96; v.p. IT, electronics systems Raytheon Co, Lexington, Mass., 1997—2001, v.p., chief info. officer, 2001—. Office: Raytheon Co 141 Spring St Lexington MA 02421

RHODA, JANICE TUCKER, writer, educator, musician; b. Lynn, Mass., Mar. 24, 1955; d. Robert Samuel and Cecilia Mary Ann (DiTroia) Tucker; m. David Michael Cleary, Jan. 21, 2001. BMus, New Eng. Conservatory of Music, Boston, 1989; Suzuki Tchr. Tng., Ithaca (N.Y.) Coll., 1980—81. Pvt. violin tchr., 1975—; violin tchr. Wakefield Pub. Schs., 1979—80, Newton Pub. Schs., 1979—81, All-Newton Music Sch., 1980—84, McGill U., 1982, 1983, Boston Ctr. for Adult Edn., 1992—95, 1997—98, New Eng. Conservatory of Music, Boston, 2000, Cambridge Ctr. for Adult Edn., Mass., 2003—; dir., tchr. Suzuki program Longy Sch. Music, Cambridge, Mass., 1980—87, Brookline Music Sch., Mass., 1992—94; clinician The ABCs of Strings, 1998—; violin tchr. Royal Conservatory Music, Toronto, 2004. Author: (book series) The ABCs of Strings; concertmistress North-Eastern Dist. Orch., 1972—73, Mass. All-State Orch., 1972. Mem.: Nat. Assn. for Music Edn., Am. String Tchrs. Assn., Suzuki Assn. of Ams., Mu Phi Epsilon. Office: The ABCs of Strings PO Box 400428 Cambridge MA 02140 E-mail: abcsofstrings@comcast.net.

RHODE, DEBORAH LYNN, law educator; b. Jan. 29, 1952; BA, Yale U., 1974, JD, 1977. Bar: D.C. 1977, Calif. 1981. Law clk. to judge U.S. Ct. Appeals (2d cir.), N.Y.C., 1977-78; law clk. to Hon. Justice Thurgood Marshall U.S. Supreme Ct., D.C., 1978-79; asst. prof. law Stanford (Calif.) U., 1979-82, assoc. prof., 1982-85, prof., 1985—; dir. Inst. for Rsch. on Women and Gender, 1986-90, Keck Ctr. of Legal Ethics and The Legal Profession, 1994—; sr. counsel jud. com. Ho. of Reps., Washington, 1998. Trustee Yale U., 1983-89; pres. Assn. Am. Law Schs., 1998; Ernest W. McFarland prof. Stanford Law Sch., 1997—; sr. counsel com. on the jud. U.S. Ho. of Reps., 1998; dir. Stanford Ctr. on Ethics. Author: Justice and Gender, 1989, (with Geoffrey Hazard) the Legal Profession: Responsibility and Regulation, 3d edit., 1993, (with Annette Lawson) The Politics of Pregnancy: Adolescent Sexuality and Public Policy, 1993, (with David Luban) Legal Ethics, 2001, (with Barbara Allen Babcock, Ann E. Freedman, Susan Deller Ross, Wendy Webster Williams, Rhonda Copelon, and Nadine H. Taub) Sex Discrimination and the Law, 1997, Speaking of Sex, 1997, Professional Responsibility: Ethics by the Pervasive Method, 1998, In the Interests of Justice, 2000 (with Geoffrey Hazard, Jr.) Professional Responsibility and Regulation, 2002; editor: Theoretical Perspectives on Sexual Difference, 1990, Ethics in Practice, 2000, The Difference Difference Makes: Women and Leadership, 2002 ; contbr. articles to profl. jours. Mem.: ABA (chmn. commn. on women 2000—02). Office: Stanford U Law Sch Crown Quadrangle Stanford CA 94305

RHODE, KIM, Olympic athlete; b. El Monte, CA, July 16; Recipient Bronze medal in women's skeet 1994 USASNC, bronze medal women's double trap 1995 Seoul World Cup, team Gold medal skeet, team Bronze medal double trap 1995 World Shotgun Championships, Gold medal women's double trap 1995 U.S. Olympic Festival, Gold medal women's double trap Olympic Games, Atlanta, 1996; winner Doubletrap Champion USA Shooting Nat. Championships, 1997.Spokewoman for WPRO 7 Guncleaner & Snake Oil. Mem. Safari Club Internat., Women's Sports Shooting Found. Avocations: skiing, hunting.

RHODES, ALICE GRAHAM, lawyer; b. Phila., June 15, 1941; d. Peter Graham III and Fannie Isadora (Bennett) Graham; m. Charles Milton Rhodes, Oct. 14, 1971 (div. Apr. 21, 1997); children: Helen, Carla, Shauna. BS, East Stroudsburg U. Pa., 1962; MS, U. Pa., 1966, LLB, 1969, JD, 1970, cert. program exec. adminstrn. Bar: N.Y. 1970, U.S. Dist. Ct. (so. and ea. dists.) N.Y. 1971, U.S. Ct. Appeals (2d cir.) 1971, Ky. 1983, U.S. Dist. Ct. (ea. dist.) Ky. 1985. Staff atty. Harlem Assertion Rights, Mobilization for Youth Office Econ. Opportunity, N.Y.C., 1969-70, coord. Cmty. Action Legal Svcs., 1970-72; assoc. dir. in charge of civil representation HUD Model Cities Cmty. Law Offices, N.Y.C., 1972-73; resource assoc. Commn. on Edn. & Employment of Women, N.C. Dept. Adminstrn., Raleigh, 1975; mgr. policies and procedures Div. for Youth, N.C. Dept. Human Resources, Raleigh, 1976; in-house counsel, petroleum transactional atty. Ashland, Inc. (formerly Ashland Oil, Inc.), 1980-82; corp. atty. core group Ashland, Inc., 1985-87, 88-91; mem. Ashland City Commn. Human Rights, 1993-99; mem. bd. regents Ea. Ky. U., 1994-2001; exec. bd., chmn. internal affairs com., academic affairs, 1997-98; asst. county atty. Jefferson County, 1999—2000. Mem. Property Valuation Appeals Commn., 1994; cons. pub. mem. selection and performance stds. review bd. Fgn. Svc., U.S. Dept. State, 1995, Fgn. Agrl. Svc. USDA, 1997; prison program planner, cons. N.Y. City Dept. Corrections, 1971; lectr. N.Y.C. Corrections Acad., Riker's, 1971; lectr. juvenile justice N.C. Law Enforcement Acad., Salemburg, 1976. Mem. usher bd. New Hope Bapt. Ch., Ashland, 1980-94; bd. dirs. YWCA Ashland, 1983-84, Ashland Heritage Pk. Commn., 1983-85; bd. dirs., budget com. United Way, Greenup County, Ky., Ashland, 1988-92; driver Meals on Wheels, 1983-91; vol. Am. Heart Assn., 1982-91; bd. dirs. Our Lady of Bellefonte Hosp. Found. Franciscan Sisters of the Poor, Ky. Health System, 1996-99; mem. adv. com. task force post secondary edn. Gov. of Ky.; bd. dirs. exec. com. Boyd County Dem. Women, 1996-2000; mem. presdl. search com. Ea. Ky. U., 1997-98, Ky. Gov.'s Conf. on Postsecondady Edn., 1999. Recipient Cmty. Svc. award Queens Community Corp., N.Y.C., 1972, Ashland C.C., 1986, Cmty. Svc. award NAACP, Ky.; NSF fellow, 1964, 65, ; faculty friends of Penn scholar U. Pa., 1966-69, Reginald Heber Smith postgrad. fellow cmty. law, 1969-71; named to Hon. Order of Ky. Cols., 1989. Fellow Ky. Bar Found.; mem. AAUW (bd. dirs. Phila. chpt. 1963-65), Nat. Bar Assn., N.Y. Bar, Ky. Bar Assn. (mem. edn. law, corp. house counsel, law sects.), Pilot Club (exec. bd. Ashland 1983), Links, Inc., Penn Club, Assn. Gov. Bds. Colls. and Univs., Pyramid Club of Phila. Democrat. Avocations: interior decorating, sports, dance, gourmet cooking, gardening. Home: PO Box 12408 Philadelphia PA 19151 Address: 658 N 65th St Philadelphia PA 19151

RHODES, ANN FRANCES BLOODWORTH, artist, art history lecturer; b. Gadsden, Ala., Jan. 30, 1940; d. Frederick Allen and Mildred (Chunn) Bloodworth; m. Thomas Willard Rhodes, May 31, 1975; children: Mildred Ruth, Andrew James Howard. BA, Queens Coll., Charlotte, N.C., 1962; MA, Ga. State U., 1972. Computer programmer 1st Nat. Bank, Atlanta, 1962-63; child welfare aide Fulton County Dept. Family and Children Svcs., Atlanta, 1963; tchr. Brandon Hall, Atlanta, 1964-66; lectr. art history Atlanta Coll. Art, 1973-77, mem. adj. faculty, 1987-90; lectr. art history DeKalb C.C., Atlanta, 1975. Vis. prof. Ga. State U., Atlanta, 1985; lectr. DAR, Atlanta, 1997. One-woman show Vines Bot. Garden, Loganville, Ga., 1998; exhibited in group shows Art South, Avondale Estates, Ga., 1995, Level II Gallery, Atlanta, 1996, Creative Arts Guild, Dalton, Ga., 1996, 97, Atelier, Atlanta, 1996 (award of merit), Atlanta Bot. Garden, 1996, Art Sta., Stone Mountain, Ga., 1996, 98, Chateau Elan, Ga., 1997, Quinlan Art Ctr., Gainesville, Ga., 1997, Opus One Gallery, Atlantz, 1997, Madison (Ga.)-Morgan Cultural Ctr., 1998 (award of merit), Roswell (Ga.) Visual Arts Ctr., 1998; represented in collections: Frameworks Gallery, Lynne Farris Gallery, Vermilion Gallery, Atlanta, Gallery One, St. Simon's Island, Ga. Chmn. St. Helena chpt. of women All Saints Ch., Atlanta, 1980, 81, 83, 98, lectr. art history, 1991—, participant numerous on-going outreach programs; chmn. Twigs svc. club Egleston Children's Hosp., Atlanta, 1985; chmn. Party with Purpose, Am. Cancer Soc., Atlanta, 1987. Recipient numerous awards for paintings. Mem. Fine Art Folio, Ansley Park Garden Club (sec. 1993-95, parliamentarian 1995-97). Democrat. Episcopalian. Avocations: reading, swimming, photography, walking, gardening. Studio: Tula K-1 75 Bennett St NW Atlanta GA 30309-5206

RHODES, ANNE GREGORY (PANNY RHODES), state legislator; b. Durham, N.C., July 30, 1942; m. James Thomas Rhodes; children: James Thomas Jr., Anne Gregory. AB in Math., Duke U., 1963. Mem. Va. State Legis., 1992—, mem. appropriations com., mem. health welfare & insts. com., mem. sci. & tech. com. Angler B. Duke scholar. Republican. Episcopalian. Office: Gen Assembly Bldg PO Box 406 Richmond VA 23218-0406

RHODES, DAISY CHUN, writer, researcher, oral historian; b. Kahuku, Hawaii, Nov. 16, 1933; d. Pyung Chan Chun and Shin Ai Park; children: Joseph, Carmella, Thomas Francese. BA in Creative Writing, Eckerd Coll., 1995. Info. specialist Reconstrn. Devel. Corp., Washington, 1970; specialist indigent funding George Washington U. Hosp., Washington, 1971-74; mgr. hosp. assistance Alexandria (Va.) Hosp., 1975-79; asst. editor Employee Futures Rsch., Luray, Va., 1980-84; editor Inside Negotiations, Rochester, N.Y., 1985-87, Educators Negotiating Svc., New Port Richey, Fla., 1987-89; novelist, writer New Port Richey, 1989-95; rschr., oral historian Honolulu, 1994; writer Colorado Springs, 1995—; rschr., cons. Donna Ladd, Writer, Colorado Springs, 1996. Rschr., cons. Donna Ladd, Writer, Colorado Springs, 1996; presenter Asian Studies Conf., Honolulu; presenter scholarly and abstract Korean Picture Brides We. Asian Studies Conf., Boulder, Colo., 1997; lectr. Ctr. for Korean Studies U. Hawaii, 1998. Author: Forever Long-Never End, 1990, Wahaiawa Red Dirt, 1991, At Crossroads of Inspiration, 1993, Shirley Temple Feet, 1993, Remembering the Fallen, 1994, Passages to Paradise: Early Korean Immigrant Narratives from Hawaii, 1998; author: (play) I Know About Olympus, 1993; author: Eye of the Dragon, 1994 (finalist Hemingway 1st Novel Competition, 1994); author: (scholarly and abstract) How Oral History of the First Koreans in America Advances Archival Research, 1996; author: My Father's Voice, Echoes Upon Echoes, 2002, A Place of Noise, 2003. Pres. Colorado Springs Friends of Aquatics, 1997—; bd. dirs. All Souls Unitarian Ch. Recipient Work Study award for profls., Rotary Internat. Found., South Korea, 1998—99. Mem.: Korean Am. Women's Soc. Greater Washington (pres. 1983—84, bd. dirs., Commendation), Korea Soc., Assn. for Asian Studies, West Pasco Kiwanis (pres. 1990—92). Home: 1912 Eastlake Blvd # 502 Colorado Springs CO 80910 E-mail: dyschun@msn.com.

RHODES, KARREN, public information officer; b. Calif., 1947; married; 2 children. Diploma in Journalism, U. Utah, 1984. Journalist, Salt Lake City, 1983—85, UPI, Cheyenne, Wyo., 1985—86, Green River (Wyo.) Star, 1986—88; pub. info. officer Nev. Dept. Employment Security, Carson City, 1989—94, Nev. Dept. Employment, Tng. and Rehab., Carson City, 1994—. Entrepreneur iFreedom Comm., 2000—. Trustee Carson Access Found., Carson City, 1996—2001. Recipient Vol. of Yr. award, State of Utah Gov.'s Office, Salt Lake City, 1984, Best of Nat. Collegiate Photography award, 1984. Mem.: Soc. Profl. Journalists. Avocations: photography, graphic design, writing, travel, mentoring.

RHODES, LINDA JANE, psychiatrist; b. San Antonio, May 23, 1950; d. George Vernon and Lucy Agnes (O'Dowd) R. BA, Trinity U., 1972; MD, U. Tex. Med. Br., 1975. Diplomate Am. Bd. Pediat.; bd. certified, Am. Bd. Psychiatry and Neurology. Resident in pediat. U. Tex. Med. Br., Galveston, 1975-78; fellow in ambulatory pediat. U. Tex. Health Sci. Ctr., Houston, 1978-80, asst. prof. psychiatry San Antonio, 1995—, resident in psychiatry, 1990-92, child and adolescent psychiatrist, fellow in biol. psychiatry, 1992-95; pediatrician Kelsey Seybold Clinic, P.A., Houston, 1980-95. Pediat. rep. Tex. Lay Midwifery Bd. Tex. Dept. Health, Austin, 1994-95. Active San Antonio Conservation Soc., San Antonio Herb Soc., Nat. Trust for Hist. Preservation, San Antonio Mus. Assn., Trinity U. Assocs., 1992-95, Witte Mus. Assn.; patron McNay Art Inst.; bd. dirs. Tex. Found. for Psychiatric Edn. & Rsch., 1997—, sec., 1998-99, treas., 1999-2004. Fellow Am. Acad. Pediat.; mem. Am. Psychiat. Assn., Am. Acad. Child and Adolescent Psychiatry (gifts and endowments com.), Ambulatory Pediat. Assn., Tex. Pediat. Soc., Tex. Soc. Psychiat. Physicians, Tex. Acad. Child and Adolescent Psychiatry, Am. Med. Women's Assn., Am. Soc. Clin. Psychopharmacology, Tex. Med. Assn. (com. on child and adolescent health), AMA, Bexar County Psychait. Soc. (sec. 2000-2001, pres. 2002-2003, past pres. 2003-2004). Office: U Tex Health Sci Ctr-SA Dept Psych/Mail Code 7792 7703 Floyd Curl Dr San Antonio TX 78229-3900

RHODES, LISA DIANE, minister; b. Bklyn., June 7, 1956; d. Henry Anthony and Rebecca Jane Rhodes. BA, Wheeling Coll., 1978; MSW, U. Md., Balt., 1980; MDiv, Candler Sch. Theology, 1991. Hospice chaplain Grady Hosp. Pastoral Care, Atlanta, 1991—93; coord. for minority health Ctrs. for Disease Control, Atlanta, 1993—96; dir. outreach Interdenominational Theol. Ctr., Atlanta, 1996—98; dir. planning and programs Payne Theol. Seminary, Wilberforce, Ohio, 1998—2001; asst. pastor Ebenezer Bapt. Ch., Atlanta, 1995—2000; dean of the chapel Spelman Coll., Atlanta, 2001—. Mem. Mental Health Assn., Jacksonville, Fla., 1985—87; strategic planning cons. Friendship Bapt. Ch., Gastonia, NC, 1997—99; workshop, retreat facilitator Ptnrs. in Faith, Stone Mountain, Ga., 1998—2001. Editor: Transformative Imperatives, 1998; author: Mediation, 2001. Supporter Children's Def. Fund, Washington, 2001—03. Recipient Theol. Exploration of Vocation award, Lilly Endowment, 2002. Mem.: Am. Assn. Colls. and Univs. Avocations: tennis, reading, swimming. Home: 822 Southland Pass Stone Mountain GA 30087 Office: Spelman Coll 350 Spelman Ln SW Atlanta GA 30314

RHODES, LISA FRANCES, elementary school educator; b. Florence, Ala., Apr. 17, 1963; d. Claud Allen Caddell Jr. and Sarah Frances Caddell; m. Wendell Cannon Rhodes, Mar. 5, 1988; 1 child, Karah Frances. BS, U. North Ala., 1984; MA, Auburn U., 1986. Tchr. pre-sch., kindergarten Little Angel Day Sch., Florence, Ala., 1986—88; tchr. 1st grade Harlan Elem. Sch., 1988—. Co-dir. Harlan's Sch.-Wide Reading Program Connections, Florence, 1998—; co-sponsor Author Conf., 1999—2000, Read Across Am., 2000. Vol. Children's Mus. of Shoals, Florence, 2001—. Named Henry Grady Richards Elem. Tchr. of Yr., Rotary, Florence, 1992—93. Mem.: NEA, Harlan Parent Tchr. Orgn., Florence Edn. Assn., Ala. Edn. Assn. Avocation: family. Office: 2233 McBurney Dr Florence AL 35630-1251

RHODES, PAMELA, state representative; m. David; 1 child, Ryan. BSEE. State rep. State of Colo., 2002—, mem. bus. affairs and labor com., mem. info. and tech. com., mem. joint com. on legis. audit. Mem.: MOPS, North Suburban Rep. Forum. Republican. Avocations: reading, travel. Address: 13271 Clermont Cir Denver CO 80241 Office: State Capitol #205 200 E Colfax Ave Denver CO 80203 E-mail: pam.rhodes.house@state.co.us.

RHODY, SUSAN M. director; b. Pitts., Feb. 26, 1976; d. Thomas P. and Marjorie J. Rhody. BS in Psychology, U. Pitts., Johnstown, Pa., 1998; postgrad., Ind. U. Pa., 2002—. Therapeutic staff support/autism program Pressley Ridge Schs., Pitts., 1998—99; child care specialist Southwood Psychiat. Hosp., Pitts., 1999—2000; counselor/tchr. II Eckerd Youth Alternative, Boomer, NC, 2000—01; ltsr specialist Chartier Mental Health/Mental Retardation, Bridgeville, Pa., 2002—02; residence dir. Westminster Coll., New Wilmington, Pa., 2002—. Active Big Brother's and Big Sisters, New Castle, Pa., 2002; adv. Ct. Apptd. Spl. Adv., Hermitage, Pa., 2003; vol. Pitts. AIDS Task Force. Mem.: Am. Coll. and Pers. Assn., Alpha Sigma Alpha (life). Democrat. Roman Catholic. Avocations: camping, travel, the arts. Personal E-mail: rhodysm@westminster.edu.

RHOE, WILHELMINA ROBINSON, retired science educator; b. Columbia, S.C., Nov. 21, 1936; d. William Howard Taft Robinson, Jessie M. Robinson Howard; m. Reginald Mussolini Rhoe, Nov. 28, 1959; children: Chantaine Rhoe-Bulluck, Reginald M., Jandrette, William O. BS in Biology, Benedict Coll., 1958; MS in Sci. Edn., Clemson U., 1980. Tchr. sci. Ruffin H.S., Ruffin, SC, 1958—59; tchr. biology Sterling H.S., Greenville, SC, 1959—60; tchr. sci. Westside H.S., Anderson, SC, 1961—62; tchr. biology, chemistry, physics, math. New Deal H.S., Starr, SC, 1964—68; chemist, statistician Dow-Badische Co., Anderson, 1968—70; tchr. biology, chemistry, physics, math. McDuffie H.S., Anderson, 1971—92; ret., 1992. Bd. dirs. Anderson Civic Ctr., Anderson, SC, 1992—98; del. Dem. Nat. Conv., Chgo., 1996, L.A., 2000; rules committeeperson S.C. Dem., Columbia, 1994—. Mem.: Anderson County Ret. Tchrs., Order Ea. Star (sec. Thomasena chpt. #206 1984—86). Avocations: reading, sewing, travel. Home: 105 Rhoe Cir Anderson SC 29621

RHONE, DIANE CARUSO, music educator; b. Mount Holly, NJ, Apr. 9, 1951; d. Richard Caruso, Evelyn Katharine Caruso; m. Daniel Loy Rhone; children: Bryan, Lisa Rhone-Barnett. BA, Trenton State Coll., 1974. Cert. tchr. N.J., instrnl. II Pa. Instr. music Acad. Musical Arts, Palmyra, NJ, 1977—98; instrumental music tchr. Pennsbury Sch. Dist., Fallsington, Pa., 1992—. Founder First Bapt. Ch. Instrumental Ensemble, Burlington, NJ, 1988—2001. Mem.: Bucks County Music Edn. Assn., Pa. Music Edn. Assn., Nat. Sch. Orch. Assn., Am. String Tchrs. Assn. Baptist. Avocations: astronomy, hiking.

RHONE, SYLVIA MARIE MILLER, recording industry executive; b. Phila., Mar. 11, 1952; BS in Econs.(hon.), U. Pa., 1974; Degree (hon.), Adelphi U., LHD (hon.), 1996. Comml. lending trainee Bankers Trust Co., N.Y.C.; sec. Buddha Records, 1974, nat. promotion coord., Bareback Records; regional promotions mgr. ABC Records, 1976—78, Ariola Records, 1978—79; N.E. regional promotions mgr./special markets Elektra Records, 1980—83, dir. mktg./special markets, 1983—85; dir. nat. black music promotion Atlantic Records, N.Y.C., 1985—88, v.p., gen. mgr. black music ops., 1988—88, sr. v.p., gen. mgr. black music ops., 1988—90; CEO, co-pres. EastWest Records America, N.Y.C., 1990—91; chmn., CEO EastWest/Atco Records, 1991—94; chair/CEO Elektra Entertainment, N.Y.C., 1994—2004. Mem., bd. dirs. Alvin Ailey Am. Dance Theatre, The RIAA, Rock n' Roll Hall of Fame, Jazz at Lincoln Ctr., R&B Found., Studio Mus. of Harlem; bd. dirs. NARAS. Alumni trustee U. Pa., 2001—. Recipient Whitney M. Young Svc. Award, Boy Scouts of Am., 1992, New Music Seminar Joel Webber Prize for Excellence in Music and Bus. award, 1993, Sony Soul of Am. Music Excellence Award, 1993, Legacy Life Mem. award, Nat. Coun. of Negro Women, 1995, Urban Network Exec. Yr. Award, 1995, Herbert H. Wright award, Nat. Assn. Market Developers, 1995, Studio Mus. Corp. award, 1996, Creative Spirit Award, Black Alumni of Pratt Inst., Echo Awards, Trumpet Awards, Turner Broadcasting, 2004. Achievements include became 1st African American and first woman chairman and CEO of a major record company, 1994.*

RHOTEN, JULIANA THERESA, retired school principal; b. N.Y.C., June 28; d. Julius Joseph and Gladys Maude (Grant) Bastian; B.A., Hunter Coll., 1954; M.S., 1956; Ed.S., U. Wis., Milw., 1977; m. Marion Rhoten, Aug. 7, 1956 (dec.); 1 son, Don Carlos. Tchr. elem. schs., Milw., 1957-65, reading specialist, 1965-71, adminstr., 1971-80; prin. Ninth St. Sch., Milw., 1980-83, Parkview Sch., Milw., 1983-90. Bd. dirs. Eisenhower Ctr., 1994—. Mem. ASCD, Internat. Reading Assn., Nat. Assn. Elem. Sch. Prins., Nat. Coun. Tchrs. English, Adminstrs. and Suprs. Council, Phi Delta Kappa, Alpha Kappa Alpha. Home: 7222 N 99th St Milwaukee WI 53224-3802

RIAL, MARTHA, photographer; Grad., Art Inst. Pitts.; postgrad., Ohio U. Staff photographer Jour. Newspapers, Alexandria, Va., Ft. Pierce (Fla.) Tribune, Pitts. Post-Gazette, 1994—. Recipient Recognition award, Pitts. chpt. Women in Comm., Press Club Western Pa., Pitts. Slack Media Fedn., Pulitzer prize. Office: C/O Pitts Post-Gazette Blade Comms 34 Blvd Of The Allies Pittsburgh PA 15222-1204

RIBACK, ESTELLE POSNER, art historian; b. Bklyn., June 8, 1934; d. Max Jacob and Rose (Rosen) Posner; m. Arnold O. Riback, June 17, 1956; children: Phillip Scott, Stephen Craig, Debra Lyn. BS in Psychology, Tufts U., 1956; MS in Elem. Edn., Hofstra U., 1964; MA in Art History, Inst. Fine Art, NYU, 1981; cert. art appraiser, NYU, 1993. Cert. elem. tchr. N.Y. Tchr. reading improvement Glen Cove (N.Y.) Pub. Schs., from 1964; ptnr., v.p. Artlego, N.Y.C., 1980-83; devel. officer East Harlem Tutorial Program, N.Y.C., 1985-86; asst. dir. devel. Ams. Soc., N.Y.C., 1986-89; pres., ptnr. Manley-Riback, Inc., N.Y.C., 1989-96; pres. Estelle Riback Fine Arts Inc., N.Y.C., 1996-98. Curator Am. Barbizon Art. Author: (monograph) Henry Ward Ranger, 2000 (Best Book in art history Bay Area Ind. Book Pub. Assn., 2001). Pres., bd. dirs., chmn. fundraising Azzizz Theatre, Inc., Bklyn., 1993—95, chmn. benefit com., 1993—94; past mem. Hebrew Sch. of Congregation Tifereth Israel Bd. Edn., Glen Cove; past chmn. major gifts Suffolk region Hadassah Med. Orgn., past v.p. fundraising Huntington chpt.; adult edn. com. West End Synagogue, 2000—. Mem.: Nat. Coalition Ind. Scholars, Assn. Historians Am. Art, Assn. Historians of 19th Century Art, Coll. Art Assn., Candlewood Yacht Club, Alpha Xi Delta, Psi Chi. Democrat. Avocations: tennis, sailing, bridge, travel, collecting art and artifacts. Home and Office: 201 E 79th St Apt 19D New York NY 10021-0844

RIBBLE, ANNE HOERNER, communications executive; b. Balt., Oct. 30, 1932; m. John C. Ribble, July 26, 1974. BA, Smith Coll., 1954; MA, Harvard U., 1955. Tech. asst. IBM, N.Y.C., 1958-63, editor Armonk, White Plains, N.Y., 1969-75, mgr. editl. svcs. data processing divsn. White Plains, 1976-77, program adminstr. sys. comm. divsn. N.Y.C., 1977-78, staff tech. edn., fed. sys. divsn. Houston, 1978-80, info. rep., 1980-87; staff info. IBM Fed. Sys. Co., 1988-93; prin. Creative Commn., Houston, 1993—. Mem. allocations com. United Way, Houston, 1989—94; bd. dirs. Stanley Isaacs Cmty. Ctr, N.Y.C., 1968—72, Bayou Bend Docent Orgn., 1999—2001. Mem. Pub. Rels. Soc. Am. (accredited), Internat. Assn. Bus. Communicators (pres. Houston chpt. 1982, cmty. rels. dir. 1989-92, accredited). Home: 6200 Willers Way Houston TX 77057-2808 Office: Creative Commn 6355 Westheimer Rd # 171 Houston TX 77057-5103 E-mail: aribble@houston.rr.com.

RIBBLE, JUDITH GLENN, medical educator; b. Norristown, Pa., Feb. 3, 1938; d. Victor Lewis and Thelma Louise (Coffman) Glenn; m. Darrah Ellsworth Ribble III, June 13, 1959 (dissolved June 1984); children: Darrah, Glenn, Anna; m. Clark Ely Bussey, Aug. 13, 1994; children: Gregory, Will. BA with honors, U. Pa., Phil., 1959; PhD in Social Scis., Med. Coll. Pa., Phil., 1979. Dir. continuing mental health edn. Med. Coll. Pa., Phil., 1979—83, asst. prof. psychiatry, 1979—83; dir. continuing med. edn. Jefferson Med. Coll., Phil., Pa., 1983—84, asst. prof. psychiatry, 1993—95; v.p. profl. edn. Arthritis Found., Atlanta, 1984—87; dir. med. edn. ACP, Phil., 1987—91; dir. continuing med. edn. Lifetime Med. TV, Astoria, NY, 1991—95; v.p. edn. Safeware, Inc., Bellevue, Wash., 1995—96; dir. continuing med. edn. Nat. Ctr. Genome Resources, Sante Fe, 1996—99, Medscape/WebMD, N.Y.C., 2000—. : 1611 Don Gaspar Ave Santa Fe NM 87505-4714

RICARDO-CAMPBELL, RITA, economist, educator; b. Boston, Mar. 16, 1920; d. David and Elizabeth (Jones) Ricardo; m. Wesley Glenn Campbell, Sept. 15, 1946; children: Barbara Lee, Diane Rita, Nancy Elizabeth. BS, Simmons Coll., 1941; MA, Harvard U., 1945, PhD, 1946. Instr. Harvard U., Cambridge, Mass., 1946—48; asst. prof. Tufts U., Medford, Mass., 1948—51; labor economist U.S. Wage Stabilization Bd., 1951—53; economist Ways and Means Com. U.S. Ho. of Reps., 1954; economist, 1957—60; prof. San Jose State U., 1960—61; sr. fellow Hoover Instn. on War, Revolution, and Peace, Stanford, Calif., 1968—95, sr. fellow emerita, 1995—. Lectr. health Stanford U. Med. Sch., 1973—78; bd. dirs. Watkins-Johnson Co., Palo Alto, Calif., Gillette Co., Boston; mgmt. bd. Samaritan Med. Ctr., San Jose. Author: Voluntary Health Insurance in the U.S., 1960, Economics of Health and Public Policy, 1971, Food Safety Regulation: Use and Limitations of Cost-Benefit Analysis, 1974, Drug Lag: Federal Government Decision Making, 1976, Social Security: Promise and Reality, 1977, The Economics and Politics of Health, 1982, 1985, Resisting Hostile Takerovers: The Gillette Company, 1997; co-editor: Below-Replacement Fertility in Industrial Societies, 1987, Issues in Contemporary Retirement, 1988; contbr. articles to profl. jours. Commr. Western Interstate Commn. for Higher Edn. Calif., 1967-75, chmn., 1970-71; mem. Pres. Nixon's Adv. Coun. on Status Women, 1969-76; mem. task force on taxation Pres.'s Coun. on Environ. Quality, 1970-72; mem. Pres.'s Com. Health Services Industry, 1971-73, FDA Nat. Adv. Drug Com., 1972-75; mem. Pres. Reagan's Econ. Policy Adv. Bd., 1981-90, Pres. Reagan's Nat. Coun. on Humanities, 1982-89, Pres. Reagan's Nat. Medal of Sci. com., 1988-91, Pres. Bush's Nat. Medal of Sci. com., 1991-94; bd. dirs. Ind. Colls. No. Calif., 1971-87; mem. com. assessment of safety, benefits, risks Citizens Commn. Sci., Law and Food, Rockefeller U., 1973-75; mem. adv. com. Ctr. Health Policy Rsch., Am. Enterprise Inst. Pub. Policy Rsch., Washington, 1974-80; mem. adv. coun. on social security Quadrennial Health and Human Svcs., 1974-75; bd. dirs. Simmons Coll. Corp., Boston, 1975-80; mem. adv. coun. bd. assocs. Stanford Librs., 1975-78; mem. coun. SRI Internat., Menlo Park, Calif., 1977-90. Mem. Am. Econ. Assn., Mont Pelerin Soc. (bd. dirs. 1988-92, v.p. 1992-94), Harvard Grad. Soc. (coun. 1991-94), Phi Beta Kappa. Home: 26915 Alejandro Dr Los Altos Hills CA 94022-1932 Office: Stanford U Hoover Instn Stanford CA 94305-6010

RICCARDELLI, ROSANNE SHARON, primary school educator; b. Bklyn., Mar. 15, 1950; d. Joseph John Marino and Michelina Victoria Levanti; m. Michael Frank Varone, Aug. 15, 1970 (div. June 1975); 1 child, Michele Lynn Varone Kirvin ; m. Anthony John Riccardelli, Dec. 15, 1979; 1 child, Theresa Rose. BA, Bklyn. Coll., 1971, MS, 1975. Tchr. St. John Evangelist Sch., Bklyn., 1972—89; kindergarten tchr. Our Lady of Grace, Bklyn., 1989—91, St. Agnes Sem., Bklyn., 1991—. Tchr. trainer Diocese of Bklyn./Queens, 1999—. Mem.: Nat. Cath. Edn. Assn. Roman Catholic. Avocations: reading, reiki. Home: 53 Garland Ct Brooklyn NY 11229

RICCI, CHRISTINA, actress; b. Santa Monica, Calif., Feb. 12, 1980; Appeared in films Mermaids, 1990, The Hard Way, 1991, The Addams Family, 1991, The Cemetery Club, 1993, Addams Family Values, 1993, Casper, 1995, Now and Then, 1995, Gold Diggers: The Secret of Bear Mountain, 1995, Bastard Out of Carolina, 1996, The Last of the High Kings, 1996, That Darn Cat, 1996, Ice Storm, 1997, Little Red Riding Hood, 1997, Souvenir (voice) 1998, Pecker, 1999, I Woke Up Early When I Died, 1998, Fear and Loathing in Las Vegas, 1998, Desert Blue, 1998, Buffalo 66, 1998, The Opposite of Sex, 1998, Small Soldiers (voice only), 1998, Souvenir (voice only), 1998, 200 Cigarettes, 1999, No Vacancy, 1999, Sleepy Hollow, 1999, Bless the Child, 2000, The Man Who Cried, 2000, All Over the Guy, 2001, Prozac Nation (also co-prod.), 2001, The Laramie Project, 2002, Pumpkin (also prod.), 2002, Miranda, 2002, The Gathering,

2002, Anything Else, 2003, I Love Your Work, 2003, Monster, 2003; TV appearances include H.E.L.P., 1990, The Simpsons (voice only), 1996, Ally McBeal, 2002, Malcolm in the Middle, 2002. Office: ICM 8942 Wilshire Blvd Beverly Hills CA 90211-1934

RICE, ANNE, writer; b. New Orleans, Oct. 14, 1941; d. Howard and Katherine (Allen) O'Brien; m. Stan Rice, Oct. 14, 1961 (dec.); children: Michele (dec.), Christopher. Student, Tex. Woman's U., 1959-60; BA, San Francisco State Coll., 1964, MA, 1971. Author: Interview with the Vampire, 1976, The Feast of all Saints, 1980, Cry to Heaven, 1982, The Vampire Lestat, 1985, The Queen of the Damned, 1988, The Mummy or Ramses the Damned, 1989, The Witching Hour, 1990 (TV series, 2002), Tale of the Body Thief, 1992, Lasher, 1993, Taltos, 1994, Memnoch the Devil, 1995, Servant of the Bones, 1996, Violin, 1998, The Vampire Armand, 1998, Pandora: New Tales of the Vampires, 1998, Vittorio the Vampire, 1999, Merrick, 2000, Blood and Gold, 2001, The Master of Rampling Gate, 2002, Blackwood Farm, 2002, Blood Canticle, 2003; (as A.N. Roquelaure) The Claiming of Sleeping Beauty, 1983, Beauty's Punishment, 1984, Beauty's Release: The Continued Erotic Adventures of Sleeping Beauty, 1985 (as Anne Rampling) Exit to Eden, 1985, Belinda, 1986 ; screenwriter: Interview with a Vampire, 1994. Office: care Alfred A Knopf Inc 201 E 50th St New York NY 10022-7703*

RICE, ASHLEY LYNN, writer, illustrator; b. Houston, Sept. 8, 1973; d. Darrel Alan and Jeffrey Lynn Rice. BA in English cum laude, Princeton U., N.J., 1996. Web writer and illustrator americangreetings.com; writer and illustrator Blue Mountain Arts. Greeting card lines, Backyard Poetry by Ashley, the Ashley Rice Collection; author - illustrator: childrens books Girls Rule, Friends Rule, Love is Me and You, You Go, Girl: Keep Dreaming!; author: Still Life with Hogs (Grad. Departmental award for Nonfiction, First Pl., 2001). Author BookExpoAmerica, N.Y.C., 2002—02; writing tutor 3d grade Dallas Pub. Schs., Dallas, 2003—03; appeared in Errol Morris' short subject Boston, 2002. Scholar Grad. Assistantship, Emerson Coll., 1999-2001. Mem.: Kappa Kappa Gamma (life; rec. sec. 1992—93). Office: Blue Mountain Arts americangreetingsco Personal E-mail: ashleylynn73@aol.com.

RICE, BARBARA LYNN, stage manager; b. Hartford, Conn., Nov. 9, 1955; d. Joe Roger and Betty Barbara (Baxter) R. BA in Theatre and French, Ind. U., 1978; MFA in Directing, U. Cin., 1982. Freelance stage mgr., N.Y.C.; dir. The Open Eye: New Stagings, N.Y.C., 1989; prodn. stage mgr. Belmont Italian-Am. Playhouse, N.Y.C., 1994, 95; prodn. assn. Silence, Cunning, Exile, N.Y.C., 1995; asst. stage mgr. The Merry Wives of Windsor, N.Y.C., 1995. Dir. The Open Eye: New Stagings, N.Y.C., 1989; stage mgr. 20 Years Ago Today, Cin., 1989, Fourscore & 7 Years Ago, Paramus, N.J., 1989-90, Hanging the President, N.Y.C., 1990; prodn. asst. Kiss of the Spiderwoman, Purchase, N.Y., 1990, (off-Broadway) Beau Jest, N.Y.C., 1992, Belmont Italian-Am. Playhouse, N.Y.C., 1994, 95, Transformations, 1997; listings editor Back Stage, 1998. Mem. Actors' Equity Assn., Stage Mgrs. Assn. Presbyterian. Avocations: music, history, art, reading, foreign languages. Home: 412 W 56th St Apt 10 New York NY 10019-3647 E-mail: cincydame@aol.com.

RICE, CARRIE SOTTILE, public relation director, retired principal; b. Phila., Nov. 2, 1927; d. Gaetano and Lucia Francesca (Domanico) Sottile; children: William Thomas, Steven Malin. BA in Edn., Chestnut Hill. Coll., Phila., 1948; postgrad., U. Pa., Phila., 1948—50; Prin. Cert., Temple U., Phila., 1974; MEd, Beaver Coll., Glenside, Pa., 1974. Fashion model, Phila., 1957—64; tchr. Sch. Dist. Phila., 1948—54, human rels. coord., 1957—72, 1972—76; tchr. Antilles Consolidated Sch. USN, San Juan, PR, 1954—56; prin. Kennedy Crossan Sch., Phila., 1976—91; ednl. cons., fundraiser Phila. Children's Network, Phila., 1992—94; dir. pub. rels. and alumae affairs Nazareth Acad. High Sch., Phila., 1995—. Adj. prof. Chestnut Hill Coll., Phila., 1982—85, Beaver Coll. (now Arcadia U.), Glenside, Pa., 1993—98; supr. teenage br. Frankford br. Free Lib. Phila., Phila., 1947—48; tv model Channels 3, 6, 10, Phila., 1949—54; guest lectr. Spkr.'s Showcase Assocs., Phila., 1968—79; lectr. Holy Family Coll., Phila., 1978—79; tchr. Phila. Modeling and Charm Sch., Phila., 1957—62; apptd. commr. by Gov. Tom Ridge to Jud. Adv. Commn. Phila. County, Commonwealth of Phila., 1995—; pres. Phila. Coun. Adminstrv. Women in Edn., 1983—89; alternate rep. Phila. Orgn. Sch. Adminstrs., 1976—91. Served on merit selection panels Fed. Ct., 2001; vol. Overbrook Sch. Blind, 1972—74, March of Dimes, Am. Red Cross; edn. chmn. N.E. divsn. Am. Cancer Soc., 1981—88, vol.; mem. N.E. divsn. Human Rels.Coun., 1972—78; mem. choir Presentation Cath. Ch., 1980—83; bd. dirs. The Bridge Drug Rehab. Ctr. Phila., 1972—78; sec. women's bd. Arcadia U., 1994—; chairperson 80th Ann. Frankford High Sch., Phila., 1990, 85th Ann. Frankford High Sch., Phila., 1995; state chairperson Cooley's Anemia, 1986—89; mem. pres.'s coun. Manor Jr. Coll., 1989—. Named Woman of the Yr., Columbus Ednl. Forum, 1985; recipient award, Vocat. Indsl. Clubs. Am., 1980, Achievement award for volunteerism, YWCA N.E. divsn., 1981, award, Chapel fo the Four Chaplains, 1982, Adminstrv. Ednl. award, City Coun. Phila., 1985, Disting. Svc. award, N.E. High Sch., 1985, Award of Excellence in Cmty. Svc., Lawncrest, 1985, Pioneer award for achievement, Frankford H.S., 1989, Paul Harris Fellow award, 2003. Mem.: AAUW (v.p. 1990), Women for Gtr. Phila., Sons of Italy (v.p. commn. social justice 1983—89, nat. sec. commn. social justice 1986—91, pres. commn. social justice 1989—90, Judge F.J. Montemuro Lodge), Phi Delta Kappa. Avocations: modeling, reading, singing, public speaking. Home: 802 Knorr St Philadelphia PA 19112 Office: Nazareth Acad 4001 Grant Ave Philadelphia PA 19114

RICE, CHARLENE RUSSELL, human resources professional, consultant; b. Knoxville, Tenn., May 25, 1952; d. Julian Frank and Elizabeth J. (Johnson) Russell; m. Barry L. Rice, Oct. 10, 1980 (div. Oct. 1990); 1 child, Brian C. BS in Bus. Adminstrn., U. Tenn., 1975, MS in Ednl. Psychology, 1985. From staff asst. to employment mgr. U. Tenn. Office Human Resources, Knoxville, Tenn., 1977—2000, employment mgr., 2000—. Cons. Univ. Cons., Knoxville, Tenn., 1989-94. Bd. pres. Planned Parenthood of East Tenn., 1990-93; vice-chmn., mem. Affiliate Pres.'s Coun. Planned Parenthood Fedn. Am., 1992-95; vice-chmn. Southern Region Coun. Planned Parenthood Fedn. Am., 1995—; loaned exec. United Way of Greater Knoxville, Tenn., 1995, co-chair allocation panel, 1997-98, chmn., 1999-2000. Recipient Vol. of Yr. award Planned Parenthood of East Tenn., Inc., 1989. Mem. Am. Compensation Assn. (cert. compensation profl.), East Tenn. Compensation Assn. (pres. 1994-95), Kappa Delta Alumni Assn. (pres. elect 2004). Baptist. Avocations: antiques, needlework, travel, reading. Home: 2319 Gorby Way Knoxville TN 37923-7301 Office Phone: 865-974-7635.

RICE, CONDOLEEZZA, national security advisor; b. Birmingham, Ala., Nov. 14, 1954; BA cum laude, U. Denver, 1974, PhD, 1981; MA, U. Notre Dame, 1975; PhD (hon.), Morehouse Coll., 1991, U. Ala., 1994, U. Notre Dame, 1995, Miss. Coll. Sch. of Law, 2003, U. Louisville, 2004. Asst. prof. dept. polit. sci. to assoc. prof. Stanford (Calif.) U., 1981-93, prof., 1993—99, provost, 1993-99; spl. asst. to dir. of the Joint Chiefs of Staff U.S. Dept. Def., Washington, 1986; spl. asst. to U.S. President Nat. Security Affairs, 1989-91; dir. to sr. dir. Soviet and East European Affairs, 1989—91; sr. fellow Hoover Inst., Stanford, Calif., 1991—93; asst. to the Pres. for Nat. Security Affairs Nat. Security Council, Washington, 2001—. Cons. ABC News, Washington; mem. spl. advisory panel to comdr. and chief strategic air commd.; mem. gov. ind. advisory redistricting the state of Calif.; mem. U.S. Delegation to 2+4 Talks on German Unification. Author: Uncertain Allegiance; The Soviet Union and the Czechoslovak Army, 1984; co-author (with Alexander Dallin): The Gorbachev Era, 1986; co-author: (with Philip Zelikow) Germany Unified and Europe Transformed, 1995. Recipient Sch. of Humanities and Sciences Dean's award for disting. teaching, Stanford U., 1993, Walter J. Gores award for excellence in teaching, Stanford U., 1984. Mem. Coun. Fgn. Rels. Republican. Office: The White House National Security Council 1600 Pennsylvania Ave Washington DC 20500*

RICE, DONNA S. educational administrator; b. Tulsa; d. Grady and Mildred Steed; m. Donald Rice, Aug. 3, 1956 (dec. Jan. 1990); children: Michael, Donna E., Nadine. BA in Linguistics, SUNY, Buffalo, 1971, MA in Linguistics, 1973, PhD in Comms., 1985. LPN, N.Y. Asst. dir. English Lang. Inst. SUNY at Buffalo, 1980-85, assoc. dir. edn. opportunity ctr., 1985-86, staff assoc. office of the pres., 1986-87, dir. ednl. opportunity ctr., 1987-90, assoc. vice provost spl. programs, 1990-91, assoc. v.p. spl. programs, 1991-93, assoc. v.p. student affairs, 1993—. Bd. dirs. N.Y.-Pa. region ARC, 1996—; dir.-in-residence English Lang. Inst. SUNY, Beijing, 1981, chair SUNY Com. Promotion of Tolerance and Diversity, Buffalo, 1993—. Contbr. articles to profl. jours. Bd. dirs. King Urban Ctr., 1998—; scholarship com. Humboldt Pkwy. Bapt. Ch., 1985—; mem. policy adv. bd. Bethel Head Start, 1994-98; bd. dirs. Neighborhood Info. Ctr., 1984-97, Leadership Buffalo, 1989—. Recipient Cmty. Svc. award Neighborhood Info. Ctr., 1997, Outstanding Cmty. Svc. award County of Erie, 1990, Leadership award Great Lakes Bapt. Assn., 1989. Mem. Ptnrs. of Am. (life), Am. Assn. Univ. Adminstrs. (bd. dirs. 1987—), Am. Assn. Higher Edn., Nat. Assn. Student Pers. Adminstrs., Delta Sigma Theta. Democrat. Baptist. Avocations: reading, choir, cooking. E-mail: dsrice168@aol.com.

RICE, DOROTHY PECHMAN (MRS. JOHN DONALD RICE), medical economist; b. Bklyn., June 11, 1922; d. Gershon and Lena (Schiff) Pechman; m. John Donald Rice, Apr. 3, 1943; children: Kenneth D., Donald B., Thomas H. Student, Bklyn. Coll., 1938—39; BA, U. Wis., 1941; DSc (hon.), Coll. Medicine and Dentistry N.J., 1979. With hosp., and med. facilities USPHS, Washington, 1960—61; med. econs. studies Social Security Adminstrn., 1962—63; health econs. br. Community Health Svc., USPHS, 1964—65; chief health ins. rsch. br. Social Security Adminstrn., 1966—72, dep. asst. commr. for rsch. and statistics, 1972—75; dir. Nat. Ctr. for Health Stats., Rockville, Md., 1976—82; prof. Inst. Health & Aging U. Calif., San Francisco, 1982—94, prof. emeritus, 1994—. Developer, mgr. nationwide health info. svcs.; expert on aging, health care costs, disability, and cost-of-illness. Contbr. articles to profl. jours. Recipient Social Security Adminstrn. citation, 1968, Disting. Svc. medal, HEW, 1974, Jack C. Massey Found. award, 1978, UCSF medal, 2002. Fellow: Am. Statis. Assn.; mem.: LWV, APHA (domestic award for excellence 1978, Sedgwick Meml. medal 1988), Assn. Health Svc. Rsch. (President's award 1988), Inst. Medicine. Home: 13895 Campus Dr Oakland CA 94605-3831 Office: U Calif Sch Nursing Calif San Francisco CA 94143-0646 Office Phone: 415-476-2771.

RICE, ELIZABETH OSBURN, music educator, conductor; b. Ferndale, Mich., Aug. 30, 1933; d. Obert Owen Osburn and Mary Elizabeth Kannon; m. William Eli Rice, June 19, 1955 (dec.); children: David Allen, Philip Owen. B in Music, Stetson U., 1955; M in Music, Ga. State U., 1977; postgrad., Columbia Theol. Sem., 1962—63. Contralto soloist Presbyn. Chs., Ohio and Fla., 1955—62; missionary tchr. choir condr. Presbyn. Bd. World Missions, Taiwan, 1963—74; condr. adult choir First Presbyn. Ch., Atlanta, 1976—88, Ctrl. Congl. United Ch. Christ, Atlanta, 1989—. Recitalist1985, 1955; adj. prof. voice Kennesaw Coll., Marietta, Ga., 1981—90, Ga. State U., Atlanta, 1977—2002; cons. voice Columbia Theol. Sem., Decatur, Ga., 1991—98. Editor: (in Chinese) Music for Church Choirs, 1972—73; musician (soloist): Atlanta Symphony Orch. and Chamber Chorus, 1976, 1978. Mem.: Presbyn. Assn. Musicians, Nat. Assn. Tchrs. Singing, Am. Choral Dirs. Assn. Avocations: reading, tennis, walking, gardening. Office: Ctrl ongl United Ch of Christ 2676 Clairmont Rd NE Atlanta GA 30329

RICE, FERILL JEANE, writer, civic worker; b. Hemingford, Nebr., July 4, 1926; d. Derrick and Helen Agnes (Moffatt) Dalton; m. Otis LaVerne Rice, Mar. 7, 1946; children: LaVeria June McMichael, Larry L. Student, U. Omaha, 1961. Dir. jr. and sr. choir Congl. Ch., Tabor, Iowa, 1952-66; tchr. Fox Valley Tech. Inst., Appleton, Wis., 1970-77; activity dir. Family Heritage Nursing Home, Appleton, Wis., 1972-75; dir. activity Peabody Manor, Appleton, Wis., 1975-76. Editor: Moffatt and Related Families, 1981; asst. editor (mag.) Yester-Year, 1975-76; contbr. articles to profl jours. Chmn. edn. Am. Cancer Soc., Fremont County, 1962, 63, 64; founder, 1st pres. Mothers Club Nishna Valley chpt. Demolay for Boys. Mem. DAR, Internat. Carnival Glass Assn., Heart Am. Carnival Glass Assn., Nat. Cambridge Collectors, Heisey Collectors Am., Iowa Fedn. Women's Clubs (Fremont county chmn. 1964, 65, 66, 67, 7th dist. chmn. libr. svcs. 1966-67), Tabor Women's Club (pres. 1962, 63, 64), Jr. Legion Aux. (founder, 1st dir. 1951-52), Fenton Art Glass Collectors Am. (co-founder 1977, sec., editor newsletter 1976-86, editor/sec. 1988-93, pres./editor 1993-95, treas. 1995-96, pres. 2000-01), Mayflower Soc., John Howland Soc., Ross County Ohio Geneal. Soc., Iowa Geneal. Soc., Dallas County Mo. Geneal. Soc., Imperial Collectors Am., Clay County (Ind.) Geneal. Soc., Owen County (Ind.) Geneal. Soc., Fenton Finders of Wis. (chpt. #1 pres. 1988-90). Republican. Methodist: Lodges: Order Ea. Star (worthy matron 1956, 64), Rainbow for Girls (bd. dirs. 1964), Internat. Order Job's Daus. (honored queen 1945). Home: 302 Pheasant Run Kaukauna WI 54130-1802 Office: Rice Enterprises & Rice Mgmt 1050 S Grider St Appleton WI 54914-4858 Office Phone: 920-991-9072.

RICE, FRANCES MAE, physician; b. Oakland, Calif., Apr. 19, 1931; d. George Henry and Clara Evelyn (Youngman) Rice. AB in Psychology cum laude, U. Calif., Berkeley, 1953, MPH in Epidemiology, 1964; MD, U. Calif., San Francisco, 1957. Intern U. Calif. Hosp., San Francisco, 1957-58; pediatric resident U. Calif., San Francisco, 1959-61; pediatric and family physician HMO, Hanford, Calif., 1974-75; clin. pediatrician Kern County Health Dept., Bakersfield, Calif., 1975-76, physician, 1989, Kern Med. Group, Inc., Bakersfield, 1976-83; pvt. practice Shafter, Calif., 1983-89; physician Mercy Medicenter, Bakersfield, 1990-91, K.C.E.O.C. Family Health Clinic, Bakersfield, 1993-98, Berkeley Women's Health Ctr., 1999—. USPHS fellow, 1963—64. Fellow: Royal Soc. Medicine; mem.: N.Y. Acad. Sci. Avocations: music, hiking. Home: 6103 Majestic Ave Oakland CA 94605

RICE, JOY KATHARINE, psychologist, educational policy studies and women's studies educator; b. Oak Park, Ill., Mar. 26, 1939; d. Joseph Theodore and Margaret Sophia (Bednarik) Straka; m. David Gordon Rice, Sept. 1, 1962; children: Scott Alan, Andrew David. BFA with high honors, U. Ill., 1960; MS, U. Wis., 1962, MS, 1964, PhD, 1967. Lic. clin. psychologist. USPHS predoctoral fellow dept. psychiatry Med. Sch. U. Wis., Madison, 1964-65, asst. dir. Counseling Ctr., 1966-74, dir. Office Continuing Edn. Svcs., 1972-78, prof. ednl. policy studies and women's studies, 1974-95, clin. prof. psychiatry, 1995—; pvt. practice psychology Psychiat. Svcs., S.C., Madison, 1967—. Mem. State Wis. Ednl. Approval Bd., Madison, 1972-73; mem. Adult Edn. Commn., U.S. Office Career Edn., Washington, 1978. Author: Living Through Divorce, A Developmental Approach to Divorce Therapy, 1985, 2d edit., 1989; edit. bd. Lifelong Learning, 1979-86; cons. editor Psychology of Women Quar., 1986-88, assoc. editor, 1989-94; cons. editor Handbook of Adult and Continuing Education, 1989, Encyclopedia of Women and Gender, 2001; contbr. articles to profl. jours. Knapp fellow U. Wis.-Madison, 1960-62, tchg. fellow, 1962-63; recipient Disting. Achievement award Ednl. Press Assn. Am., 1992. Fellow APA (exec. bd. psychology of women divsn. 1994—, internat. psychology divsn. 1998—, chair internat. com. for women 2000-02, exec. bd. 1998—, Disting. Leadership award 2000-02); mem. Nat. Assn. Women in Edn. (editl. bd. jour. 1984-88, cons. editor Initiatives 1988-91), Internat. Coun. Psychologists (sec. 2000—, bd. dirs. 2003—), Am. Assn. Continuing and Adult Edn. (meritorious svc. award 1978-80, 82), TEMPO Internat. (bd. dirs., sec. 2000-2003), Big Bros. Big Sisters of Dane County (pres. 2002, bd. dirs. 1995—), Rotary Internat., Phi Delta Kappa. Avocations: interior design, collecting art, gardening, travel. Home: 4230 Waban Hl Madison WI 53711-3711 Office: 2727 Marshall Ct Madison WI 53705-2255

RICE, LEVINA RUTH (SALLY), city council person, former government official; b. Deepwater, Mo., June 8, 1932; d. Earl Jackson and Ruth (Hieronymus) Martin; m. William Samuel Rice, Sept. 20, 1949; children: Sandra Ruth, Sheila Marie (dec.), Sonja Leigh, Shelly Jayne, Sherry Lou, Stacy Alyce. Student, Kansas City C.C., 1973-77. Contract specialist, adminstrv. sec. USDA, Kansas City, Mo., 1961-80; co-owner restaurant Sam & Sally's Nu-Way, 1975-85. Chmn. book com., author: The Hieronymus Story, 1997 (Anne Ford Book award 1999). V.p. Hieronymus Family in Am., 1986-94, pres., 1994-96, treas., 1998—; mayor pro-tem Silver Haired City Coun., Kansas City, 1994-96, 2000—, chmn. fin. com., 1998, city ops. com., 1997-98. Mem. Libr. of Congress. Republican. Baptist. Avocations: genealogy, antiques. Home: 200 E 132d St Kansas City MO 64145-1404 E-mail: sallyrrice@msn.com.

RICE, LINDA ANGEL, music educator; b. New Philadelphia, Ohio, July 23, 1939; d. Leonard Leroy and Anna Mary (Fackler) Angel; m. James Kinsey Rice, June 9, 1963; children: Deborah Lynn, Diane Rice Sequra. BS in Music Edn., Muskingum Coll., 1961. Organist, choir dir., Ohio, 1957-63; organist, 1963-70; tchr. music Jr. High and Elem. Schs., Ohio, 1962-63, Elem. Sch., Calif., 1963-67; organist Albuquerque, 1970—; pvt. practice pvt. practice, Albuquerque, 1970—; founder Albuquerque Girl Choir, 1991—. Pres. N.Mex. Symphony Chorus, Albuquerque, 1991-92, bd. dirs., 1991-95, pres., 1988-89. Mem. Am. Choral Condrs. Guild, Am. Guild Organists (exec. bd. 1967), Sigma Alpha Iota. Avocations: knitting, travel, gardening. Home: 12428 Chelwood Trl NE Albuquerque NM 87112-4628 Office: Albuquerque Girl Choir PO Box 23037 Albuquerque NM 87192-1037

RICE, LINDA JOHNSON, publishing executive; b. Chicgo, Mar. 22, 1958; d. John J. and Eunice Johnson; m. Andre Rice, 1984. BA Journalism, Univ. Southern Calif., L.A., 1980; MBA, Northwestern Univ., Evanston, Ill., 1988. With Johnson Pub. Co., 1980—, past v.p. and asst. to pub., chief operating officer, 1987—2002; pres. Fashion Fair Cosmetics, Ill.; pres., CEO Johnson Pub. Co., Inc., Chgo., 2002—. Office: Johnson Pub Co Inc 820 S Michigan Ave Chicago IL 60605-2191*

RICE, LOIS, mayor; b. Duncan, Okla., May 06; d. William Daniel Wilbourn and Naomi Ruth Lee; m. Karl Gordon Rice, July 18, 1969; 1 child, Phyllis Ann Shepard. Student, Chgo. Inst. Learning. Mgr. Bud's Furniture and Appliance, Plainview, Tex., 1951-69; owner, mgr. Furniture Galleries Canyon, Tex., 1971-96; mayor City of Canyon, 1990—. Governing bd. mem. Better Bus. Bur., Amarillo, Tex., 1996-99; pres. region II, Assn. Mayors, Commn. and Coun., Amarillo, 1996, pres., 1997-99; adv. bd. mem. Atty. Gens. Office, Austin, Tex., 1998. Treas. First United Meth. Ch., 1984—; chmn. bd. Tex. Panhandle Heritage Found., 1988-99; exec. bd. mem. Pvt. Industry Coun., Amarillo, 1988-94; pres. C. of C., Canyon, 1989-90; governing bd. mem. WTAMU Found., 1995—, United Way, 1996—; bd. mem. Tex. Affordable Housing Task Force, Austin, 1998; originator, mentor Boys & Girls Club Canyon, 1999. Recipient Tex. Vocat. Adminstr. and Supr. award Assn. Vocat. Edn., Austin, 1982, Disting. Svc. award Women's Forum, Amarillo, 1991, Regional Svc. award Panhandle Regional Planning Commn., Amarillo, 1997, Career Achievement award Amarillo Womens Network, 1997, Small Town Leadership award Nat. Ctr. for Small Bus., Bentonville, Ark., Washington, 1999; named Citizen of Yr., Canyon C. of C., 1989. Mem. Canyon Rotary Club (past sec. 1997-98, plaque 1998). Republican. Avocations: reading, bridge, traveling, card games. Office: 301 16th St Canyon TX 79015-2828

RICE, LOIS DICKSON, former computer company executive; b. Portland, Maine, Feb. 28, 1933; d. David A. and Mary D. Dickson; m. Alfred B. Fitt, Jan. 7, 1978 (dec. 1992); children: Susan, John Rice. AB magna cum laude, Radcliffe Coll., 1954; postgrad. (Woodrow Wilson fellow), Columbia U., 1954-55; LLD (hon.), Brown U., 1981, Bowdoin Coll., 1984. Dir. counseling services Nat. Scholarship Service and Fund for Negro Students, N.Y.C., 1955-59; with The Coll. Bd., N.Y.C. and Washington, 1959-81, v.p. Washington, 1973-81; sr. v.p. govt. affairs Control Data Corp., 1981-91. Guest scholar The Brookings Inst., Washington, 1991—; bd. dirs. McGraw Hill, Inc., 1987—2003, Internat. Multifoods, 1991—2003, UNUM/Provident Corp., 1992—2003; overseer Tuck Sch. Mgmt. Dartmouth Coll., 1990—94; mem. Pres.'s Fgn. Intelligence Adv. Bd., 1993—2001; trustee George Washington U., 1992—98, co-chair Mgmt. Leadership for Tomorrow, 1994—; trustee CNA Corp. Pub. Agenda Found., Harry Frank Guggenheim Found. Contbr. articles on edn. to profl. publs.; editor: Student Loans: Problems and Policy Alternatives, 1977. Mem. adv. bd. to dir. NSF, 1981—89, chair, 1986—89; mem. Gov.'s Commn. on Future of Postssecondary Edn. in N.Y. State, 1976—77, Carnegie Coun. on Higher Edn., 1975—80; trustee Radcliffe Coll., 1969—75, Stephens Coll., Mo., 1976—78, Beauvoir Sch., Washington, 1970—76, Children's TV Workshop, 1970—73; bd. dirs. Potomac Inst., 1977—92, German Marshall Fund, 1984—94, Joint Ctr. Polit. and Econ. Studies, 1991—94, Reading is Fundamental, 1991—. Recipient Disting. Service award HEW, 1977 Mem. Cosmos Club, Phi Beta Kappa. Episcopalian. Home: 2332 Massachusetts Ave NW Washington DC 20008 Office: The Brookings Instn 1775 Massachusetts Ave NW Washington DC 20036-2103

RICE, LUANNE, writer; b. 1955; Author: Blue Moon, 1994, Home Fires, 1996, Cloud Nine, 2000, Follow The Stars Home, 2001, Firefly Beach, 2001, Dream Country, 2002, Summer Light, 2002, True Blue, 2002, Safe Harbor, 2003, The Secret Hour, 2003, The Perfect Summer, 2003, Dance With Me, 2004. Office: c/o Jane Rotrosen Agency 318 E 51st St New York NY 10022

RICE, MARY ESTHER, biologist; b. Washington, Aug. 3, 1926; d. Daniel Gibbons and Florence Catharine (Pyles) R. AB, Drew U., 1947; MA, Oberlin Coll., 1949; PhD, U. Wash., 1966. Instr. biology Drew U., Madison, N.J., 1949-50; rsch. assoc. Columbia U., N.Y.C., 1950-53; rsch. asst. NIH, Bethesda, Md., 1953-61; curator invertebrate zoology and dir. Smithsonian Marine Sta., Smithsonian Instn., Washington, 1966—2002, sr. rsch. scientist emeritus, 2002—. Mem. adv. panel on systematic biology NSF, Washington, 1977-78; mem. com. on marine invertebrates Nat. Acad. Sci., 1976-81; mem. overseers com. on biology Harvard U., Cambridge, Mass., 1982-88. Assoc. editor Jour. Morphology, Ann Arbor, Mich., 1985-91, Invertebrate Biology, 1995—; editor: (with M. Todorovic) Biology of Sipuncula and Echiura, 1975, 2nd vol., 1976, (with F.S. Chia) Settlement and Metamorphosis of Marine Invertebrate Larvae, 1978, (with F.W. Harrison) Microscopic Anatomy of Invertebrates, Vol. 12, 1993; contbr. articles to profl. jours. Recipient Drew U. Alumni Achievement award in sci., 1980. Fellow AAAS; mem. Am. Soc. Zoologists (pres. 1979), Am. Microscopical Soc. (pres. 1999), Phi Beta Kappa. Office: Smithsonian Marine Sta 701 Seaway Dr Fort Pierce FL 34949-3140

RICE, NANCY E. judge; b. Denver, June 2, 1950; 1 child. BA cum laude, Tufts U., 1972; JD, U. Utah, 1975. Law clerk U.S. Dist. Ct. of Colo., 1975-76, dep. state pub. defender, appellate divn., 1976-77; asst. U.S. atty. Dist. of Colo., 1977-87; dep. chief civil divn. U.S. Attorney's Office, 1985-88; judge Denver Dist. Ct., 1988-98; apptd. judge Colo. Supreme Ct., 1998—. Contbr. articles to profl. jours. Mem. Denver Bar Assn., Colo. Bar Assn. (bd. govs. 1990-92, exec. coun., 1991-92), Women's Bar Assn., Rhone-Brackett Inn of Ct. (master 1993-97), Women Judges Assn. (co-chair nat. conf. 1990). Office: Colo Supreme Ct Colo State Jud Bldg 2 E 14th Ave Fl 4 Denver CO 80203-2115

RICE, PATRICIA OPPENHEIM LEVIN, special education educator, consultant; b. Detroit, Apr. 5, 1932; d. Royal A. and Elsa (Freeman) Oppenheim; m. Charles L. Levin, Feb. 21, 1956 (div. Dec. 1981); children: Arthur David, Amy Ragen, Fredrick Stuart; m. Howard T. Rice, Dec. 16, 1990 (div. Apr. 1994). AB in History, U. Mich., 1954, PhD, 1981; MEd, Marygrove Coll., 1973. Cert. elem. tchr., Mich. Tchr. reading and learning disabled, cons., Detroit Pub. Schs., 1967-76; assoc. prof., coord. spl. edn., Marygrove Coll., 1976-86, adj. prof. Oakland U., 1987-90, U. Miami, 1989-95; edn. curriculum cons. Lady Elizabeth Sch., Jávea (Alicante) Spain, 1988-91; v.p. Machpelah Cemetary Bd., Ferndale, Mich., 1978-87, co-pres., 1987—; adv. bd. Eton Acad., Birmingham, Mich., 1991-93; workshop presenter Dade City Schs., 1992-97; presenter in field. Mem. Mich. regional bd. ORT, 1965-68; mil. affairs and youth svcs. S.E. Mich. chpt. ARC Bd., 1973-79; v.p. exec. bd. Women's Aux. Children's Hosp. Mich., 1968-73; bd. dirs. women's com. United Cmty. Svcs., 1968-73; judge Dade County Schs. for Tchr. Grants, 1996—; bd. dirs. Detroit Grand Opera Assn., 1970-75; com. chair morning of music benefits Detroit Symphony Orch.; torch drive area chmn. United Found., 1967-70; benefactor Fla. Grand Opera, 1990-2001, grand benefactor, 2002—, guild exec. bd., 1992-, v.p., 1998-99, co-pres. 2000-02, chair, found. bd. dirs., 2000-01; guild exec. bd. Miami City Ballet, 1996-2000, Choreographers Cir., 1990-; chair Lincoln Rd. Walk, 1996, co-chair All Star Luncheon, 1996, Ball Com., 1992; active Diabetes Rsch. Inst. & Found. Love & Hope Com., Fla. Concert Assn. Cresendo Soc., 1993-97, Villa Maria Angel, 1996—, v.p. angel bd. 1998—, found. bd. dirs. 2000—; panel judge Dada County Cultural Affairs Coun., 2002—. Mem. NAACP (life), Navy League, Greater Miami Social Register, Citizens Interested in the Arts (charter, grant chair, exec. bd. 1997—), Williams Island Club, Turnberry Isle Golf Club (signature), Miami Shores Country Club, Surf Club, Phi Delta Kappa, Pi Lambda Theta. E-mail: oceania32@msn.com.

RICE, PATRICIA JANE, journalist; b. St. Louis, Oct. 20, 1942; d. Canice T. and Jane Elizabeth Tobin) R. BA, Maryville Coll., 1964; postgrad., St. Louis U., 1965, 66. Copywriter Wohl Co., St. Louis, 1964-67; free-lance journalist Paris, 1967; copywriter D'Arcy Adut. Co., St. Louis, 1968; feature writer, columnist St. Louis Post, 1969-94, religion writer, 1994—. Moderator Rutgers U./Eagleton Ctr. Women in Politics Conf., 1980, 82, 84; lectr. in field. Author: City House, 1968, The Eclectic Shopper, 1973; co-author: In the Running: The New Political Woman, 1981. V.p. The St. Louis Forum, 1997—; bd. dirs. Leadership St. Louis, 1985-90. Recipient Quest award Mo. Press Women's, 1998; Knight Ctr. fellow, U. Md., College Park, 1996. Mem. Journalism Found. Met. St. Louis (pres. 1984-91), St. Louis Newspaper Guild (treas. 1977-87), Soc. Profl. Journalists. Avocations: gardening, skiing. Office: St Louis Post 900 N Tucker Blvd Saint Louis MO 63101-1069

RICE, REBECCA DALE, film producer, writer; b. Albuquerque, May 17, 1953; d. Charles Roy and Marilyn Dale Rice. BS, Tex. Christian U., 1975; MFA, So. Meth. U., 1980. Founding mem., writer, prodr., performer Kids & Co., Dallas, 1979—91; prodr. Tex. Instruments, Dallas, 1989—91; bus. mgr. S.W. Film-Video Archives, Dallas, 1992—95; prodr., writer D-Studios, Dallas, 1994—. Co-dir. Long on Shorts Film Festival, Dallas, 2001—03. Prodr.: (films) FLMKR, 1999 (Cannes Forum selection, 1999), Stealin' Home, 1995 (Best Film Directed by a Black Filmmaker, 1995). Mem.: Women in Film Dallas. Democrat. Unity. Avocations: bicycling, working out, theater patron. Office: D-Studios 8575 Stillwater Cir Dallas TX 75243

RICE, REBECCA KYNOCH, writer, consultant, educator; b. Pittsfield, Mass., June 13, 1954; d. John Hamilton and Nancy Anne (Kynoch) R.; m. Leonard Charles Feldstein, Oct. 17, 1981 (dec. Dec. 1984); m. Bradford Martin Smith, Aug. 14, 1993; 1 child, Oliver Van Santvoord Smith. BA, Sarah Lawrence Coll., 1977; MA, Fairleigh Dickinson U., 1980; MFA, George Mason U., 1996. English tchr. Newark Acad., Livingston, N.J., 1977-79; staff writer, editor Am. Internat. Group, N.Y.C., 1983-85; instr. English George Mason U., Fairfax, Va., 1990-92; mng. editor Green Mtns. Review, Johnson, Vt., 1993-94; freelance writer Johnson, 1994—. Instr. Lone Ridge Writers Group, Redding, Conn., 1998—. Author: A Time to Mourn: One Woman's Journey Through Widowhood, 1990; contbr. articles to pop. publs. Woodrow Wilson fellow, 1977. Mem. Authors Guild. Avocation: tennis. Home: PO Box 157 Ober Hill Rd Johnson VT 05656 Office Phone: 802-635-2727.

RICE, REGINA KELLY, marketing executive; b. Yonkers, N.Y., July 11, 1955; d. Howard Adrian and Lucy Virginia (Butler) Kelly; m. Mark Christopher Rice, Sept. 11, 1981; children: Amanda Kelly, Jaime Brannen. BS in Community Nutrition, Cornell U., 1978. Account exec. J. Walter Thompson Co., N.Y.C., 1978-79; sr. account exec. Ketchum, MacLeod & Grove, N.Y.C., 1979-80; supr. Burson Marstellar, Hong Kong, 1981-83; v.p., dep. dir. food and beverage unit, creative dir. N.Y. office Hill and Knowlton, N.Y.C., 1983-91; mktg. cons. Rice & Rohr, N.Y.C., 1991-93; sr. v.p., dir. consumer mktg. practice Manning, Selvage & Lee, N.Y.C., 1993-97, sr. v.p. global tng. dir., 1999—; chief inspiration officer, dir. corp. devel. Internat. Pub. Rels. Assn., 1999-2001. Writer Fast and Healthy Mag., 1991-2000. Mem. Pub. Rels. Soc. Am. Roman Catholic. Avocation: provence pottery. Office: Pondel Wilkinson/MS&L 12100 Wilshire Blvd Ste 400 Los Angeles CA 90025

RICE, RUTH ELAINE, music educator; d. Lester Ira and Martha Elizabeth Long; m. Frank Lambert Rice, June 21, 1969; children: Suzanne, Kevin, Lauren. BS in Music Edn., Lebanon Valley Coll., 1968; MS in Edn., Johns Hopkins U., 1980. Tchr. music Lower Dauphin Jr. H.S., Hummelstown, Pa., 1968—69; tchr. music K-6 Northwood Elem. Sch., Balt., 1969—73; tchr. Commonwealth Am. Sch. K-8, Lausanne, Switzerland, 1974—76, Yates Elem. Sch., Schenectnady, NY, 1990—97; tchr. elem. music Elsmere Elem., Bethlehem, Md., 1992—95; tchr. Farnsworth Mid. Sch., Guilderland, NY, 1995—96; tchr. mid. sch. gen. choral Van Antwerp Mid. Sch., Niskayuna, NY, 1996—2003. Co-author: (music jour.) Teaching Music, 2002. Music dir. Bethlehem Luth. Ch., Delmar, NY, 1982—; accompanist NYSSMA Zone #7, Albany, NY, 1985—. Lutheran. Avocations: travel, reading, movies. Home: 5 Darroch Rd Delmar NY 12054 E-mail: singasong123@hotmail.com.

RICE, SHARON JEAN, secondary school educator; b. L'Anse, Mich., Feb. 6, 1947; d. Albert George and Beatrice Jeanette Roy; m. Thomas E. Rice, Aug. 23, 1969; 1 child, Scott Thomas. BA in Secondary Edn., We. Mich. U., 1969; mid. sch. endorsement, Ctrl. Mich. U., 1976. Cert. reproductive health Mich. Dept. Edn., 1996, crisis prevention Mich. Dept. Edn., 1999. Substitute tchr. pub. schs., Greenville and Stanton, Mich., 1969—76; adult edn. tchr. Ctrl. Montcalm Pub. Sch., Stanton, 1976—83, alternative edn. tchr., 1983—96, H.O. Steele H.S., Fenwick, Mich., 1996—2001, Montcalm Area Intermediate Sch. Dist. Career Acad., Sidney, Mich., 2001—. Tchr. sch. improvement team, Stanton, 1994—96; graduation spkr. H.O. Steele H.S. and Career Acad., 1997—2004, Teenage Parenting Program (TAPP), 2004—. Mem.: Mich. Ednl. Assn., Greenville Women's Bowling Assn. (league officer, dir. 1989—), Sheridan Women's Bowling Assn. (sec.-treas. 1976—99, pres. 1990—, Hall of Fame). Roman Catholic. Office: TAPP MACC 1550 Sidney Rd Sidney MI 48885 Office Phone: 989-328-6621 329.

RICE, SUE ANN, dean, industrial and organizational psychologist; b. Ponca City, Okla., Sept. 17, 1934; d. Alfred and Helen (Revard) R. BS in Edn., U. Okla., 1956; MA, Cath. U., 1979, PhD, 1988. Ensign USN, 1956, advanced through grades to comdr., 1973; ednl. svcs. officer 9th Naval Dist., Great Lakes, Ill., 1956-58; adminstr., asst. staff, comdr. in-chief Pacific Fleet, Honolulu, 1958-61; head edn. div. Naval Air Sta., Lemoore, Calif., 1961-63; instr., acad. dir. Women Officers' Sch., Newport, R.I., 1963-66; head. tng. div. Naval Command Systems Support Activity, Washington, 1966-70; head, ops. support sec. staff, comdr.-in-chief Lant, Norfolk, Va., 1970-74; sr. U.S. rep. NATO, subgroup 5 orgn. JCS, Washington, 1974-77; ret. USN, 1977; head vocation office Archdiocese of Washington, 1977-78; cons. Notre Dame Inst., Arlington, Va., 1989-97, dean of students, 1990-95. Lectr. Cath. U. Am., Washington, 1983-84; bd. dirs. Villa Cortona Apostolic Ctr., Bethesda, 1984-94. Tech. reviewer Personnel Administration, 1964; editor (newsletter) Vocation News, 1978. Conoco scholarship Continental Oil Co., 1952-56; recipient Meritorious Svc. medal Pres. of U.S., 1977, rsch. grant Cath. U., Sigma Xi, 1986. Mem.: Lay Women's Assn. (internat. v.p., internat. mem. fin. com., nat. v.p.), Cath. War Vets. (nat. membership task force com., nat. youth act com., vets. affairs com.), Gamma Phi Beta, Kappa Delta Pi. Roman Catholic. Avocations: travel, music, gardening, woodworking. Home: PO Box 2742 Ponca City OK 74602-2742

RICE, SUSAN F. fundraising consultant; b. Chgo., Dec. 10, 1939; BA, St. Mary's Coll., 1961; MPA, UCLA, 1976; EdD, Pepperdine U., 1986. Pres. YWCA, Santa Monica, Calif., 1978, League of Women Voters Calif., San Francisco, 1979-81; sr. fundraising profl. adminstr., instr. Santa Monica (Calif.) Coll., 1978-81; dir. govtl. rels. UCLA Alumni Assn., 1981-82; dir. devel. UCLA Grad. Sch. Mgmt., 1982-89; dep. dir. mktg. and devel., dir. major gifts Spl. Olympics Internat., Washington, 1989-90; v.p. devel. Bus. Exec. Nat. Security, Washington, 1991-92; pres., CEO Greater L.A. Zoo Assn., 1992-96; prin. SFR Consulting, L.A., 1996—. Co-author: Women, Money and Political Clout in Women as Donors, Woman as Philanthropists, 1994, Fund Raising in Crisis Mode in Advancing Philanthropy, 1997. Bd. dirs. St. Mary's Coll. Alumnae Assn., Notre Dame, Ind., 1982-84, Santa Monica Coll. Assocs., 1984-94, Internat. Human Rights Law Group, 1990-92; trustee, chair pers. compensation com. L.A. Mus. Nat. History Found., 1982-89; treas. Women's Commn. Refugee Women, 1990-96; vice chmn. pers. commn. Santa Monica Coll. Dist., 1985-89. Recipient Disting. Alumna award St. Mary's Coll., 1986, Humanitarian award, NCCJ-L.A., 1995. Mem. Nat. Soc. Fundraising Execs. (bd. dirs. 1995-97, v.p. Greater L.A. chpt.).

RICE, SUSAN K. school librarian, educator; d. Murl R. and Vivian LaVerne Rice. BA in Edn., Northeastern State U., Tahlequah, OK, 1990; M of Libr. and Info. Studies, U. Okla., Norman, 1994. Cert. tchr. Okla., 1990. Libr. Pryor H.S. Libr., Okla., 1990—. Youth worker Ch. of God, Salina, Okla., 1985—2003. Scholar Edn. Leadership, Okla. Commn. for Tchr. Preparation, 2003. Mem.: ALA, Am. Assn. of Sch. Librs., Delta Kappa Gamma, Kappa Kappa Iota. Office: Pryor HS Libr 1100 SE 9th St Pryor OK 74361

RICE, SUSAN S. social worker; b. Beaufort, S.C., Apr. 20, 1958; d. David and Dorothy Rice; m. David R. Calkins, Sept. 22, 1989; 1 child, Christopher R. Calkins. BS, Wheelock Coll., 1979; MSW, Simmons Coll., 1986. Lic. ind. clin. social worker Mass., 1988. Clin. social worker Children's Hosp., Boston, 1986—88, Beth Israel Hosp., Boston, 1986—93; pvt. practice Brookline, Mass., 1988—96, Concord, Mass., 1999—. Mem.: NASW, Mass. Acad. Clin. Social Workers. Office: 1150 Main St Ste 10 Concord MA 01742

RICE-GOULD, NORMA JANE, home school administrator; b. North Jay, Maine, Jan. 9, 1936; d. Norman Arlin and Beryle Irene (Jones) Plaisted; m. Clifton Holt Rice, Oct. 18, 1957; children: Michael J. Rice, Timothy J. Rice, Peter J. Rice, Rebecca J. Rice; m. Michael Terry Gould, Oct. 9, 1981. Diploma, Maine Med. Ctr. Sch. Nursing, 1957. RN Ctrl. Maine Gen. Hosp., Lewiston, 1957—65; Title I home sch. coord. Auburn (Maine) Sch. Dept., 1966—. Mem. policy coun. Head Start, Androscoggin County, Maine, 1969—. Coord. Christmas Giving Tree United Meth. Ch., Auburn, 1985—. Republican. Methodist. Avocations: music, English handbell ringer, piano.

RICH, ADRIENNE, writer; b. Balt., May 16, 1929; d. Arnold Rice and Helen Elizabeth (Jones) R.; m. Alfred H. Conrad (dec. 1970); children: David, Paul, Jacob. AB, Radcliffe Coll., 1951; LittD (hon.), Wheaton Coll., 1967, Smith Coll., 1979, Brandeis U., 1987, Coll. Wooster, Ohio, 1988, CCNY, Harvard U., 1990, Swarthmore Coll., 1992. Tchr. workshop YM-WHA Poetry Ctr., N.Y.C., 1966-67; vis. lectr. Swarthmore Coll., 1967-69; adj. prof. writing divsn. Columbia U., 1967-69; lectr. CCNY, 1968-70, instr., 1970-71, asst. prof. English, 1971-72, 74-75; Fannie Hurst vis. prof. creative lit. Brandeis U., 1972-73; prof. English Douglass Coll., Rutgers U., 1976-79; Clark lectr., disting. vis. prof. Scripps Coll., 1983-84; A.D. White prof.-at-large Cornell U., 1981-87; disting. vis. prof. San Jose State U., 1984-85; prof. English and feminist studies Stanford U., 1986-93. Marjorie Kovler vis. lectr. U. Chgo., 1989. Author: Collected Early Poems, 1950-1970, 1993, Diving into the Wreck, 1973, The Dream of a Common Language, 1978, A Wild Patience Has Taken Me This Far, 1981, Your Native Land, Your Life, 1986, Time's Power, 1989, An Atlas of the Difficult World, 1991, Dark Fields of the Republic, 1995, Midnight Salvage, 1999, Fox, 2001, The Fact of a Doorframe: Selected Poems 1950-2001, 2002; (prose) Of Woman Born: Motherhood as Experience and Institution, 1976, 10th anniversary edit., 1986, On Lies, Secrets and Silence, 1979, Blood, Bread and Poetry, 1986, What Is Found There: Notebooks on Poetry and Politics, 1993, 2d edit., 2003, Arts of the Possible: Essays and Conversations, 2001. Mem. nat. adv. bd. Nat. Writers Union, Rosenberg Fund for Children. Recipient Yale Series of Younger Poets award, 1951, Nat. Inst. Arts and letters award in poetry, 1961, Eunice Tietjens Meml. prize, 1968, Shelley Meml. award, 1971, Nat. Book award, 1974, Fund for Human Dignity award Nat. Gay Task Force, 1981, Ruth Lilly Poetry prize, 1986, Brandeis U. Creative Arts medal for Poetry, 1987, Nat. Poetry Assn. award, 1989, Elmer Holmes Bobst award arts and letters NYU, 1989, MacArthur fellowship, 1994-99, Dorothea Tanning award Acad. Am. Poets, 1996, others; chancellor Acad. Am. Poets, 1999-2001, Lannan Found. Lifetime Achievement award, 1999, Bollingen prize, 2003, Nat. Found. Jewish Culture award, 2003, others. Mem. PEN, Nat. Writers Union. Office: care W W Norton Co 500 5th Ave New York NY 10110-0002

RICH, ANDREA LOUISE, museum administrator; BA, UCLA, 1965, MA, 1966, PhD, 1968. Asst. prof. comms. studies UCLA, L.A., 1976, asst. dir. office learning resources, 1976, acting dir. Media Ctr., 1977, dir. office of instructional devel., 1978-80, asst. vice chancellor office of instructional devel., 1980-86, asst. exec. vice chancellor, 1986-87, vice chancellor acad. adminstrn., 1987-91, exec. vice chancellor, 1991-95; pres., CEO L.A. County Mus. of Art, L.A., 1995—, pres., Wallis Annenberg dir., 2003—. Office: L A County Mus Art 5905 Wilshire Blvd Los Angeles CA 90036-4597*

RICH, DOROTHY KOVITZ, writer, educational administrator; BA in Journalism and Psychology, Wayne U.; MA, Columbia U.; EdD, Catholic U. Founder, pres. The Home and Sch. Inst., Inc., Washington, 1964—. Adv. coun. Nat. Health Edn. Consortium; adv. com. Ctr. for Workplace Prep. and Quality Edn., U.S. C. of C.; mem. readiness to learn task force U.S. Dept. Edn., urban edn. team Coun. Gt. City Schs.; legislative nat. initiatives including work on Family/Sch. Partnership Act, 1989, Improving America's Edn. Act, 1994; formulator New Partnerships for Student Achievement program, 1987; creator MegaSkills Edn. Ctr. The Home and Sch. Inst. Inc., 1990; designer MegaSkills Leader Tng. for Parent Workshops, 1988, MegaSkills Essentials for the Classroom, 1991, Learning and Working program for sch.-to-work initiatives, 1996, Career Megaskills, 1999, New MegaSkills Bond Tchr./Parent Partnership, 1994, Career MegaSkills materials and tng., 1998, Adult MegaSkills for Profl. Growth, 1999, MegaSkills Behavior Mgmt. Kit, 2002; developer NEA/MegaSkills nat. mentor tng. initiative, 2000—, MegaSkills for the Job, 2002, Adult MegaSkills and MegaSkills for Teachers, 2002., MegaSkills for Teachers Video Programs, 2003. Author: MegaSkills in School in Life: The Best Gift You Can Give Your Child, 1988, rev. edit., 1992, What Do We Say? What Do We Do? Vital Solutions for Children's Educationsl Success, 1997, MegaSkills, 3d edit., 1997, 18 tng. books, MegaSkills: Building Children's Achievement for the Information Age, new and expanced edit., 1998, Improving Student Teaching through MegaSkills; TV appearances include The Learning Channel, NBC Today Show, Good Morning Am.; subject of videos nat. ednl. programs in Thailand, Singapore and China: Families and Schools: Teaming for Success, Survival Guide for Today's Parents. Recipient Am. Woman Leader award, Citation U.S. Dept. Edn., Nat. Gov.'s Assn., Alumni Achievement award in edn. Cath. U., 1992, Golden Apple award for MegaSkills Tchrs. Coll., Columbia U., 1996; grantee John D. and Catherine T. MacArthur Found.; named Washingtonian of Yr. Mem. Nat. Press Club. Office: MegaSkills Edn Ctr Home and Sch Inst Inc 1500 Massachusetts Ave NW Washington DC 20005-1821 Business E-Mail: edstaff@megaskillshsi.org.

RICH, LAURIE M. federal official, educator; b. Dallas, Tex. Grad., U. N. Tex., Denton. Tchr. Dallas Pub. H.S.; spl. asst. and sr. legis. asst. Sen. Phil Gramm, Washington, 1985—93; acting adminstrv. asst. Sen, Kay Bailey Hutcison, Washington, 1993—95; exec. dir. Tex. Office of State-Fed. Rels., Dallas, 1995—2001; asst. sec. for intergovt. and interagy. affairs U.S. Dept. Edn., Washington, 2001—. Dir. of coalitions Bush/Quayle Campaign, Washington, 1992. Office: US Dept Edn 400 Maryland Ave SW Washington DC 20202

RICH, MARY RUTH, music educator; b. Houston, June 20, 1953; d. George Minor and Dolores Tidwell; m. Jerry E. Rich, Jan. 3, 1976; children: Michael Jaye, Jennifer Jane. B.Mus., Baylor U., Waco, Tex., 1975; M.Mus., Baylor U., 1978. Instr. Ind.-Purdue U., Ft. Wayne, Ind., 1987—93; assoc. prof. dept. music Lon Morris Coll., Jacksonville, Tex., 1993—; faculty Baylor U. - Summer Piano Inst., Waco, Tex., 2000—. Adjudicator, Tex., 1993—; presenter Piano Wellness Seminar, NC, 2001—03; pianist, recitals, 1995—. Mem.: Tex. Music Tchrs. Assn. Office: Lon Morris College 800 College Ave Jacksonville TX 75766

RICH, S. JUDITH, public relations executive; b. Chgo., Apr. 14; d. Irwin M. and Sarah I. (Sandock) R. BA, U. Ill., 1960. Staff writer, reporter Economist Newspapers, Chgo., 1960—61; asst. dir. pub. rels. and communications Coun. Profit Sharing Industries, Chgo., 1961—62; dir. advt. and pub. rels. Chgo. Indsl. Dist., 1962—63; account exec., account supr., v.p., sr. v.p., exec. v.p. and nat. creative dir. Edelman Pub. Rels. Worldwide, Chgo., 1963—85; exec. v.p., dir. Ketchum Pub. Rels. Worldwide, Chgo., 1985—89, exec. v.p., exec. creative dir. USA, 1990—97, exec. v.p., chief creative officer worldwide, 1998—2001; pres. Rich Rels. A Creativity Consultancy, Chgo., 2002—. Frequent spkr. on creativity and brainstorming; workshop facilitator. Contbr. articles to popular mags. Mem. pub. rels. adv. bd. U. Chgo. Grad Sch. Bus., Roosevelt U., Chgo., DePaul U., Chgo., Gov.'s State U. Recipient Pub. Rels. All-Star award for Creativity, Inside PR mag., 1999. Mem. Pub. Rels. Soc. Am. (Silver Anvil award, judge Silver Anvil awards), Counselors Acad. of Pub. Rels. Soc. Am. (exec. bd.), Chgo. Publicity Club (8 Golden Trumpet awards). Avocations: theatre, swimming, cycling, racquetball. Office: Rich Rels A Creative Consultancy Ste 2603 2500 N Lakeview Ave Chicago IL 60614

RICHARD, CANDACE L. music educator; d. James S. and Nelda M. (Northrup) Terrill; m. Loren D. Richard, July 20, 1974; children: Christopher L., Colby A. MusB in Edn., Emporia State U., 1970; MusM, Kans. State U., 1993. Cert. tchr. Kans. Vocal music tchr. Unified Sch. Dist. 322, Onaga, Kans., 1970—73, Unified Sch. Dist. 457, Garden City, Kans., 1973—76; vocal and instrumental music tchr. Trinity Cath. HS, Hutchinson, Kans., 1982—84; applied vocal music instr. Cloud County CC, Concordia, Kans., 1985—2000; vocal music tchr. Unified Sch. Dist. 333, Concordia, 1990—2000, Unified Sch. Dist. 480, Liberal, Kans., 2000—. Choral clinician, adjudicator, Kans. Bd. dirs. Cmty. Concert Assn., Concordia, 1987—2000, Liberal, 2000—03. Mem.: NEA, Music Edn. Nat. Conf., P.E.O., Delta Kappa Gamma. Lutheran. Avocation: genealogy.

RICHARD, DIANA MARIE, army officer; b. Dallas, Mar. 24, 1958; d. Dee Will and Dorothy Mae (Scott) R. B.S. with honors, Tex. Coll., 1980; student Dallas Bapt. Coll., 1975-76; M.S., Boston U., 1985. Commd. 2d lt., U.S. Army, 1980, advanced through grades to maj., 1983, bn. chem. officer, Stuttgart, Germany, 1983, corps officer, Nellingen, Ger., 1984-86; asst. prof. mil. sci. Prairie View Agrl. and Mech. U., 1987—, bde chem. officer, Hanau, Germany, 1991-95, sr. divsn. chief engr., Ft. Hood, Tex., 1997-99, hr analyst, City of Dallas, 1999—. Mem. Soc. Chem. Officers, NAACP, Delta Sigma Theta. Democrat. Baptist. Lodge: Mem. Order Eastern Star. Home: 6032 Golden Gate Cir Dallas TX 75241-5258

RICHARD, ELEANOR, minister; b. Hartford, Conn., Aug. 8, 1935; d. Walter Albert, Jr. and Elizabeth Blanche Durham; m. Paul David Juette, Feb. 10, 1957 (div. 1968); children: Christine Alice Reid, Marlene Gail Juette, Michael Paul Juette; m. James Richard Mullen, Mar. 22, 1991. BA, Mills Coll., 1957; MS, Calif. State U., Sacramento, 1982. Lic. Calif. State Bd. Behavioral Health. Tchr. pub. schs., Calif., 1961—69; owner, operator keys & engraving Sacramento, 1969—83; pvt. practice counselor Sacramento, Tahoe City, 1983—97; founding pastor Religious Sci. Ch., Yreka, Calif., 1998—. Co-founder Attitudinal Healing Sacramento, 1973—78. Mem.: Assn. Global New Thought, Religious Scis. Internat. Home: 7515 Sugar Pine Rd Weed CA 96094

RICHARD, ELLEN, theater executive; b. Bridgeport, Conn., Dec. 12, 1957; d. Laurent and Anne (Markham) R. Bus. mgr. Atlas Scenic Studio, Bridgeport, 1977-82; theater mgr. Stamford (Conn.) Ctr. for Arts, 1980-83; bus. mgr. Westport (Conn.) Country Playhouse, 1982-84; gen. mgr. Roundabout Theatre Co. Inc., N.Y.C., 1983—. Mng. dir. Broadway plays including A View From the Bridge, 1997-98 (Tony award Revival of a Play 1998), Cabaret, 1998-2004 (Tony award Revival of a Musical 1998), The Deep Blue Sea, 1998, Side Man, 1998-99 (Tony award Best Play 1999), Little Me, 1998-1999, Death of a Salesman, 1999, The Lion in Winter, 1999, The Rainmaker, 1999-2000, Uncle Vanya, 2000, The Man Who Came to Dinner, 2000, Betrayal, 2000-01, Design for Living, 2001, Major Barbara, 2001, The Women, 2001-02, An Almost Holy Picture, 2002, The Crucible, 2002, The Man Who Had All the Luck, 2002, An Evening with Mario Cantone, 2002, The Boys from Syracuse, 2002, Tartuffe, 2003, A Day in the Death of Joe Egg, 2003, As Long As We Both Shall Laugh, 2003, Nine, 2003 (Tony award Best Revival of a Musical, 2003), The Look of Love, 2003, "MASTER HAROLD"...and the boys, 2003, Big River, 2003, The Caretaker, 2003-04, Twentieth Century, 2004, Assassins, 2004. Mem. N.Y. Cycling Club. Republican. Avocations: cycling, skiing, sailing. Office: Roundabout Theatre Co 231 W 39th St Ste 1200 New York NY 10018-3109

RICHARD, SUSAN MATHIS, communications executive, screenwriter; b. Detroit, June 21, 1949; d. Robert Louis and Maybelle Ann (Kromm) Engel; m. Paul Carl Mathis, May 12, 1973 (div. 1982); m. Robert Stephen Richard, Oct. 26, 1985. BA, U. Mich., 1971. Cert. tchr., Mich. Tchr Carl Brablec High Sch., Roseville, Mich., 1971-73; anchorperson, producer Sta. WNCC-Cable TV, East Lansing, Mich., 1973-76; press asst. Ford-Dole Presdl. Campaign, Washington, 1976; TV and radio reporter Cox Communications, Washington, 1977-81; dep. dir. media rels. White House, Washington, 1981-84, spl. asst. to Pres., dir. media rels., 1985-87; mgr. pub. rels. Walt Disney World, Lake Buena Vista, Fla., 1987-88; v.p. industry communications Nat. Cable TV Assn., Washington, 1989; dep. assoc. adminstr. for pub. affairs NASA, Washington, 1990-93; v.p. Dittus Comm., Washington, 1998-2000; mgr. press rels. INTEL, Washington, 2000—. Mem. exec. com. Radio-TV Corrs. Galleries, Washington, 1978-81. Dir. promotions Action for Children's TV, East Lansing, 1975; mem. Strategic

Planning Adv. Coun. of the Orange County (Fla.) Pub. Schs., 1988; communications dir. Bush-Quayle Fla. Campaign, 1988. Named Outstanding Young Working Woman, Lansing C. of C., 1975, Outstanding Working Woman, Washington Woman mag., 1985. Mem. AAUW (bd. dirs. Lansing chpt. 1974), Am. Soc. Assn. Execs. (Pub. Rels. trophy 1994), Radio-TV News Dirs. Assn., Fla. Youth and Family Svcs. Network (bd. dirs. 1988), Acad. TV Arts and Scis. (pub. rels. com. 1989), Women in Aerospace, Women in Wireless, Women in Film and Video, Washington Women in Pub. Rels., U. Mich. Alumni Assn. (bd. dirs. 1983-85), Gamma Phi Beta Alumnae Assn. Episcopalian.

RICHARDS, ANN, actress, educator, poet; b. Sydney; came to U.S., 1942; d. Mortimer Delaforce and Marion Bradshaw (Dive) Richards; m. Edmond J. Angelo, Feb. 4, 1949 (dec. Mar. 1983); children: Christopher E., Mark R., Juliet M.; m. Paul M. Kramer, Feb. 14, 1987 (dec. Aug. 1996). Student, Stotts Coll., 1936-37, Studio Sch. of Drama, 1936-38. Actress Cinesound Studio, Australia, 1936-42, Metro-Goldwyn Mayer, 1942-45, Hall Wallis-Paramount, 1945-47, R.K.O., 1947, Eagle-Lion Studios, 1947-48, Edmond Angelo Prodns., 1953, Anthony Buckley Prodns., Australia, 1995. Poetry reader with Robert Pinsky's nat. program Lib. of Congress Bicentennial Project, 1999. Author: The Grieving Senses, 1971, Odyssey for Edmond, 1996, New Poems-Old Themes, 1997; contbr. poetry to anthology Poetry From the Art, 1999; actress films including An American Romance, Love Letters, The Searching Wind, Badman's Territory, Sorry, Wrong Number, Lost Honeymoon, Breakdown, Don't Call Me Girlie, Celluloid Heroes, 1994-95; appearances TV program, film, and tape maker Australia, Time Life Assocs., 1977. Vice pres. Tchr. Rememberance Day Found., 1952—; internat. chmn. Apple of Gold Edn. awards, 1953—. Recipient meritorious svc. citation Govs. of Great Britain, U.S., New Zealand, Australia, 1939-46, Star Pattern award Inst. Profl. Direction, 1951, Cert. of Appreciation award Literacy is Reading Program, 1997, Edward Dean Mus., 1996. Mem. AAUW, Nat. Mus. Women in Arts, San Gorgonio Poets Soc., San Gorgonio Artists Soc., Zeta Phi Eta (v.p. nat. coun. 1970-73).

RICHARDS, ANN WILLIS, former governor; b. Lakeview, Tex., Sept. 1, 1933; d. Cecil and Ona Willis; children: Cecile, Daniel, Clark, Ellen. BA, Baylor U., 1954; postgrad., U. Tex., 1954-55. Cert. tchr. Tex. Tchr. Austin Ind. Sch. Dist., Tex.; mgr. Sarah Weddington Campaign, Austin, Tex., 1972, adminstrv. asst., 1973-74; county commr. Travis County, Austin, 1976-82; treas. State of Tex., Austin, 1983-91, gov., 1991-95; sr. advisor Verner, Liipfert, Bernhard, McPherson & Hand, Austin, 1995—; with Pub. Strategies Inc., Austin, 2001—. Chair Dem. Nat. Conv. 1992; Austin Transp. Study, Tex., 1977-82, Capital Indsl. Devel. Corp., Austin, Tex., 1980-81, Spl. Commn. Delivery Human Services in Tex., 1979-81; Dem. com. Southern Governor's Assn. Travis County Dem. com. Author (with Peter Knobler): Straight From the Heart, 1989. Com. mem. strategic planning Dem. Nat. Com., 1983; keynote speaker Dem. Nat. Conv., 1988. Named Woman of Yr. Tex. Women's Polit. Caucus, 1981, 83. Mem. Nat. Govs. Assn. Democrat. Office: Public Strategies Inc 98 San Jacinto Ste 900 Austin TX 78701

RICHARDS, CARMELEETE A. computer training executive, network administrator, consultant; b. Springport, Ind., Feb. 8, 1948; d. Gordon K. and Virginia Christine (New) Brown; 1 child, Annasheril. AA in Elem. Edn., No. Okla. Coll., 1969; BS in Edn., Southwestern State Coll., Weatherford, Okla., 1971; postgrad., Ashland (Ohio) Coll., 1981—; postgrad. in Edn., U. Phoenix, 1994—; postgrad., MEd, AIU. Cert. tchr., Ohio. 6th grade tchr., Scott City, Kans., 1971; salesperson, customer svc. Jafra Cosmetics, 1979-81; br. asst. mgr. Barclays Am. Fin., Columbus, 1981-84; tng. mgr., ednl. dir. Computer Depot, Columbus, Ohio, 1984-85; corp. trainer, exec. sales Litel Telecommunications, Worthington, Ohio, 1985-87; communications cons. Telemarketing Communications of Columbus, Ohio, 1988-89; corp. computer tng. O/E Learning, Troy, Mich., 1989-98; corp. computer trainer ETOP Cols., Ohio, 1989—; dist. asst. network administr. Bexley Sch. Dist., 1998-99; dir. tech., computer instr. MCS, 2001—02; info. tech. specialist, trainer Franklin County Common Pleas Ct., 2002—. Pres. PTA, 1981-82. Recipient Outstanding Participation award Dorothy Carnegie Pub. Speaking; winner Ms. Ohio Beauties of Am. Pageant, 1991. Mem. IEEE, NAFE, Am. Soc. for Tng. and Devel., Columbus Computer Soc., Kappa Delta Pi. Baptist. Avocations: western square dancing, bowling, boating, reading, hiking.

RICHARDS, CAROL ANN RUBRIGHT, editor, columnist; b. Buffalo, Sept. 24, 1944; d. Jesse Bailey and Emma Amanda (Fisher) Rubright; m. Clay F. Richards, Aug. 12, 1967; children: Elizabeth Amanda, Rebecca Diana. BA, Syracuse U., 1966. Reporter Rochester (N.Y.) Times-Union, 1966; legis. corr. Gannett News Svc., Albany, N.Y., 1967-73, White House corr. Washington, 1974-76, regional/nat. editor, 1979-84; founding editor USA Today, Arlington, Va., 1982, mem. editl. bd., 1985-87; dep. editor editl. page Newsday, Melville, N.Y., 1987—. Pres. Washington Press Club, 1981-82; trustee Northport Hist. Soc. Mem.: Women's Press Club N.Y. (named to Hall of Honor 2003), Nat. Press Club. Home: 352 Scudder Ave Northport NY 11768-3021 Office: Newsday 235 Pinelawn Rd Melville NY 11747-4250

RICHARDS, DENISE, actress; b. Downers Grove, Ill., Feb. 17, 1971; m. Charlie Sheen; 1 child. Former model. Actor: (films) Loaded Weapon 1, 1993, Nowhere, 1997, Starship Troopers, 1997, Wild Things, 1998, Lookin' Italian, 1998, Drop Dead Gorgeous, 1999, The World is Not Enough, 1999, Tail Lights Fade Away, 1999, Valentine, 2001, Good Advice, 2001, Empire, 2002, Undercover Brother, 2002, The Third Wheel, 2002, You Stupid Man, 2002, Love Actually, 2003, Scary Movie 3, 2003; (TV films) 919 5th Avenue, 1995, In the Blink of an Eye, 1996, Pier 66, 1996, (guest appearances): (TV series) Spin City, Melrose Place. Office: 722 Elvira Ave #A Redondo Beach CA 90277*

RICHARDS, JACQUELINE, artist, curator; b. Chgo., July 25, 1930; d. Harris Nathan Turner and Henrietta Singer; m. Seymour Richards, Dec. 22, 1949 (div. Dec. 1973); children: Robin, Philip. BS in Cmty. Health, Ga. State U., 1978; postgrad. in art history, U. Chgo., 1949—50; postgrad. in art theory and design, The New Bauhaus, Chgo., 1947—49. Registered dietitian Am. Dietetic Assn., lic. State of Ga. Clin. dietitian Griffin-Spalding Hosp., Griffin, Ga., 1980—86, R.T. Jones Hosp., Canton, Ga., 1986—88; artist, painter Atlanta, 1988—; curator, 2000—, Fulton County Libr., Buckhead Branch, 2004, Northside Atlanta Libr., 2004. Illustrator Raymond Lowey Designs an Automobile for Studebaker, 1950; Fanciful Paintings of Porché Motor Car for Automobile Atlanta, 1993, 100 black ink drawings of The Rubaiyat of Omar Khayyam, 1965, one-woman shows include Art Inst. Chgo., 1952—, Fulton County Libr., Atlanta, 2002—03, exhibited in group shows at Am. Fedn. Arts, 1952—59, House of Color, 2001—; artist, curator Atlanta Bur. Cultural Affairs, 2002. Achievements include development of hypoallergenic skin cream for cancer patients. Home: 479 E Paces Ferry Rd NE Apt 210 Atlanta GA 30305-3308 Office Phone: 404-310-9978.

RICHARDS, JANE C. music educator; b. Phoenixville, Pa., Aug. 31, 1958; d. Henry Hayes Clarke and Doris Virginia Hallman; m. John Theodore Richards, Jr., June 27, 1981; children: Hannah Ruth, Olivia Lynne. BS in Music Edn., West Chester U., 1980; elem. edn. cert., Immaculata Coll., 1996; Master's equivalency, U. of the Arts, 1997. Dir. children's choir and bell choir Sanctuary United Meth. Ch., North Wales, Pa., 1983—; instr. vocal music Abington (Pa.) Sch. Dist., 1985—. Coop. tchr. Temple U., Phila., 1995—, U. of the Arts, Phila., 1995—; prin. flute/piccolo North Pa. Symphony Orch., rehearsal pianist; guest soloist North Pa. Symphony, 1996, 2000, 02. Recipient A.C. Roberts scholarship, Phoenixville H.S., 1976, Charles Swope scholarship, West Chester U., 1979, ednl. grant, Abington Sch. Dist., 1998. Mem.: Am. Guild English Handbell Ringers, North Pa. Choristers Guild (treas. 1999—2003), Sigma Alpha Iota (life; chaplain 1978, scholarship 1979). United Methodist. Avocations: playing flute, reading, jogging. Home: 101 Drayton Cir Lansdale PA 19446

RICHARDS, LACLAIRE LISSETTA JONES (MRS. GEORGE A. RICHARDS), social worker; b. Pine Bluff, Ark. d. Artie William and Geraldine (Adams) Jones; m. George Alvarez Richards, July 26, 1958; children: Leslie Rosario, Lia Mercedes. BA, Nat. Coll. Christian Workers, 1953; MSW, U. Kans., 1956; postgrad, Columbia U., 1960. Diplomate Clin. Social Work, Am. Bd. of Examiners in Clin. Social Work, Nat. Assn. Social Workers; cert. gerontologist. Psychiat., supr., tchg., cmty. orgn., adminstrv., cons. Hastings Regional Ctr., Ingleside, Nebr., 1956-60; supr., cons., adminstrv. VA Hosp., Knoxville, Iowa, 1960-74; field instr. for grad. students U. Mo., 1969-74, 78-90, com. chmn., 1969-70; sr. social worker Mental Health Inst., Cherokee, Iowa, 1974-77; adj. asst. prof. dept. social behavior U. S.D., Cherokee, Iowa, 1974-77, instr. dept. psychiat., 1988-96, Augustina Coll., 1981-86; outpatient social worker VA Med. and Regional Office Ctr., Sioux Falls, S.D., 1978-96, med., surg. and intensive care social worker, 1992-96, 1990-92, sur. and intermediate care social worker, 1992-96, EEO counselor. EEO counselor. Mem. Knoxville Juvenile adv. com., 1963-65, 68-70, sec., 1965-66, chmn., 1966-68; sec. Urban Renewal Citizens' adv. com., Knoxville, 1966-68; mem. United Meth. Ch. task force Expt. Styles Ministry and Leadership, 1973-74, adult choir, ch. and society com.; counselor Knoxville Youth Line program; sec. exec. com. Vis. Nurse Assn., 1979-80; canvasser cmty. fund drs., Knoxville; active Cherokee Civil Rights Commn.; bd. dirs., pub. rels., devel. and program devel. cons. YWCA, 1983-85; bd. dirs. Family Svc. Agy., 1989-90, Food Svcs. Ctr., Inc., 1992-96; active SD Symphonic Choir, 1991—, Youth-At-Risk Task Force and Multicultural Ctr. Advocate; deaconess 1st Evang. Free Ch., 1999-2004. Named S.D. Social Worker of Yr., 1983. Mem. NAACP (chmn. edn. com. 1983-85), AAUW (sec. Hastings chpt. 1958-60), Nat. Assn. Social Workers (co-chmn. Nebr. chpt. profl. standards com. 1958-59), Acad. Cert. Social Workers, S.D. Assn. Social Workers (chmn. minority affairs com., v.p. S.E. region 1980, pres. 1980-82, exec. com. 1985-84, mem. social policy and action com.), Nebr. Assn. Social Workers (chmn. 1958-59), Seventh Dist. S.D. Med. Soc. Aux., Coalition on Aging., Nat. Assn. Social Workers (qualified clin. social worker 1991—), Methodist (Sunday Sch. tchr. adult divsn.; mem. commn. on edn.; mem. Core com. for adult edn.; mem. Adult Choir, mem. Social Concerns Work Area). Home: 1701 E Ponderosa Dr Sioux Falls SD 57103-5019

RICHARDS, LYNN, company training executive, consultant; b. Kansas City, Mo., Sept. 2, 1949; d. Robert A. and Betty (Arnold) Nelson. BS in Edn., U. Kans., 1971; MA in Edn., San Diego State U., 1979. Prin. staff ORI, Inc., Silver Spring, Md., 1980-81; sr. corp. trainer Amerada Hess Corp., Woodbridge, N.J., 1981-83; tng. and devel. mgr. Kimberly-Clark Corp., Beech Island, S.C., 1983-85; orgn. devel. mgr. M&M Mars, Hackettstown, N.J., 1985-89; corp. tng. and devel. mgr. Rohr, Inc., Chula Vista, Calif., 1989-93; customer edn. mgr. ComputerVision, Corp., San Diego, 1993-95; leadership devel. cons. Children's Hosp., San Diego, 1995-97; learning tech. cons. Hewlett-Packard Co., San Diego, 1997-98, site learning ctr. mgr., 1998-99; dir. edn. svcs. N.Am. Peregrine Sys., San Diego, 1999—2001. Cons. in field. Contbr. articles to profl. mags. Mem.: Internat. Soc. Productivity Improvement (chmn. awards com. 1988, presdl. citations, achievement awards).

RICHARDS, PRISCILLA ANN, medical/surgical nurse; b. Providence, R.I., Nov. 10, 1949; d. Frank L. Thornton and Dorothy A. Maker; children: Tanya Rene, Jason Edward. Assoc. Degree Nursing, Lincoln Land C.C., Springfield, Ill., 1980. RN Ill., 1980, R.I., 1997. Cert. nursing asst. Meml. Med. Ctr., Springfield, 1971—73, lic. practical nurse, 1973—80, RN, 1980—97, South County Nursing and Subacute Ctr., North Kingstown, RI, 1997—2000, Elmhurst Extended Care, Providence, 2000—. Sgt. USAF, 1968—71. Baptist. Avocations: reading, swimming, yard work. Home: 71 Wells Ave Warwick RI 02889 Office: Elmhurst Extended Care 50 Maude Street Providence RI 02908 Personal E-mail: paramanri@aol.com.

RICHARDS, RHONDA SUE, accountant; b. Shawano, Wisc., May 27, 1963; d. Thomas Lee and Betty Lou Richards. A in acctg., Northeast Wisc. Tech. Coll., Green Bay, 1988; BA, Lakeland Coll., Sheboygan, 1992. CPA, Wis.; CFM, CBM, Wis. Sr. acct. Oneida Tribe of Indians, Green Bay, Wis., 1995—98; contr. Maple Lane Health Care Ctr., 1998—99; instr. N.E. Wis. Tech. Coll., Green Bay, 1994—; acct. Paper Converting Machine Co., Green Bay, 1985-95; v.p. fin. Claim Mgmt. Svcs., Inc., 1999—. Mem. Inst. Mgmt. Accts. Home: 7526 Lower Rd Sobieski WI 54171-9792

RICHARDS, SUSAN LYNNE, library director; b. Franklin, Pa., Dec. 4, 1956; d. L. Burton and Phyllis D. (Ditzenberger) R.; m. Rex C. Myers, Jan. 10, 1987; stepchildren: Gary Myers, Laura Myers Wight. AB, Grove City Coll., 1978; MA in History, Clarion U., 1980; MLS, Kent State U., 1982; PhD, U. N.H., 2002. Profl. libr. Tech. svcs. libr. Morningside Coll., Sioux City, Iowa, 1983-85; head serials dept. Briggs Libr. S.D. State U., Brookings, 1986-88, head acquisitions dept. Briggs Libr., 1988-91; asst. dir. librs. U. Vt., Burlington, 1992-95; dir. libr. svcs. Western State Coll., Gunnison, Colo., 1995-99; univ. libr. Lawrence U., Appleton, Wis., 1999—. Editor VLA News, Vt. Libr. Assn., 1992-94, Book Marks, S.D. Libr. Assn., 1989-91; gov. bd. dirs. Pathfinder Libr. Sys., Colo.; mem. Vt. Newspaper Project Adv. Bd., 1994-95. Contbr. articles to profl. jours. and mags. Mem. Cmty. Band Bd., Brookings, 1991, City Planning Commn., Brookings, 1989-91, City Historic Preservation Com., Gunnison, 1998-99; judge Nat. History Day, S.D. a nd Iowa, 1984, 85, 88. Grantee NEH, 1984, 2003. Mem.: ALA (com. mem. 1987—), AAUW (local and state officer 1990), Wis. Libr. Assn., Mountain Plains Libr. Assn. (com. chair 1990, 1991), Kiwanis Internat., Beta Phi Mu, Phi Alpha Theta. Avocations: cross country skiing, hiking, gardening. Office: Lawrence U Seeley G Mudd Library 113 S Lawe St Appleton WI 54911-5683

RICHARDS, SUSAN R. management consultant; b. Madison, Ind., Aug. 30, 1948; d. Chester Burns and Martha (Mefford) Goins; m. Kim E. Richards, Sept. 6, 1967 (div. 1969); 1 child, Natalie S. Richards. Student, Ind. U.-Purdue U., Indpls., 1970-72. Co-owner, pres. Baker Bros. Sales & Rentals, Indpls., 1976-87; owner, chmn. Party Concepts, Indpls., 1982-87; asst. dir., adminstr. L.A. Land Co., 1989-90; mgmt. cons. to small bus. cos., Malibu, Woodland Hills, Calif., 1990—. Inner city boys basketball coach, Indpls., 1977; tchr. Profl. Women Entrepreneurs, Indpls., 1980-81, Indpls. chpt. Exec. Women's Network, 1983; mem. Tri Valley Spl. Olympics, 1992—. Mem. Actors and Others for Animals. Republican. Roman Catholic. Avocations: tennis, polo.

RICHARDS, SUZANNE V. lawyer; b. Columbia, S.C., Sept. 7, 1927; d. Raymond E. and Elise C. (Gray) R. AB, George Washington U., 1948, JD with distinction, 1957, LLM, 1959. Bar: D.C. 1958. Sole practice, Washington, 1974—. Lectr. in family and probate law; mem. D.C. Jud. Conf., 1975—2004. Bd. dirs. Coun. for Ct. Excellence. Recipient John Bell Larner award George Washington U., 1958; named Woman Lawyer of Yr., Women's Bar Assn. D.C., 1977. Mem. ABA (ho. of dels. 1988-90), Bar Assn. D.C. (pres. 1989-90, named Lawyer of Yr. 2002), Women's Bar Assn. (pres. 1977-78), Trial Lawyers Assn. of D.C. (bd. govs. 1978-82, 85-2001, treas. 1982-85), D.C. Bar, Fed. Bar Assn. Home: 530 N St SW Washington DC 20024-4546 Office: PO Box 65466 Washington DC 20035-5466

RICHARDS, VIRGINIA M. psychologist; Asst. prof. psychology U. Pa., Phila., grad. group mem. psychology, biomed. engring. and neurosci. Contbr. chpts. to books and articles to profl. jours. Recipient Troland Rsch. award NAS, 1998. Office: Univ Pa Dept Psychology 3815 Walnut St Philadelphia PA 19104 E-mail: richards@cattell.psych.upenn.edu.

RICHARDS-KORTUM, REBECCA RAE, biomedical engineering educator; b. Grand Island, Nebr., Apr. 14, 1964; d. Larry Alan and Linda Mae (Hohnstein) Richards; m. Philip Ted Kortum, May 12, 1985; children: Alexander Scott, Maxwell James, Zachary Alan. BS, U. Nebr., 1985; MS, MIT, 1987, PhD, 1990. Assoc. U. Tex., Austin, 1990—. Named Presdl. Young Investigator NSF, Washington, 1991; NSF presdl. faculty fellow, Washington, 1992; recipient Career Achievement award Assn. Advancement Med. Instrumentation, 1992, Dow Outstanding Young Faculty awd., Am. Soc. for Engineering Education, 1992. Mem. AAAS, Am. Soc. Engrng. Edn. (Outstanding Young Faculty award 1992), Optical Soc. Am., Am. Soc. Photobiology. Achievements include research in photochemistry, photobiology, applied optics and bioengring. Office: U Tex Dept Elec & Computer Engrng Austin TX 78712

RICHARDSON, ALLISON, financial services company official; Grad. in acctg., Fordham U.; MBA in Fin., NYU, 1999. Mgr. assurance and adv. bus. svcs. Ernst & Young, Cleve. Former mentor Adlain Stevenson H.S., N.Y.C.; coord. co. vols. Coun. Fashion Designers Am.-Vogue Initiative/NYC AIDS Fund; counselor to young profls. Recipient Black Achiever in Industry award Harlem YMCA. Mem. Beta Alpha Psi. Office: Ernst & Young LLP 925 Euclid Ave Ste 1300 Cleveland OH 44115-1476

RICHARDSON, ANN BISHOP, foundation executive, lawyer; b. New Rochelle, N.Y., Dec. 15, 1940; d. Erwin Julius and Mary Frances (Stuart) Heilemann; children: Timothy William, Lynn Patricia, Melanie Elizabeth. BA summa cum laude, Georgetown U., 1977; JD, George Washington U., 1984; cert., Oxford (Eng.) U., 1986. Bar: Md. 1988, D.C. 1989. Student counselor Amideast, Beirut, 1967-68, program specialist, 1970-73; adminstrv. asst. UN Devel. Program, Yaounde, Cameroon, 1968-70; adminstrv. mgr. Antioch Sch. Law, Washington, 1977-79; chief adminstrv. officer for internat. ops. Peace Corps, Washington, 1980-84; dir. adminstrn. and fin. African Devel. Found., Washington, 1984-87; atty. Karr and McLain, Washington, 1987-92; v.p., gen. counsel Time Dollar, Inc., Washington, 1992-98; adj. prof. law D.C. Sch. Law, Washington, 1994-98, prof., acad. dean, 1998—. Bd. dirs. Bur. Rehab., Inc. Active Neighbors, Inc., Washington, 1976—, Time Dollar, Inc. Recipient Spl. Achievement award Peace Corps, 1981, 82, African Devel. Found., 1986. Mem. ABA, ACLU, D.C. Bar Assn., Am. Women Univ. Grads., Soc. for Internat. Devel., Phi Beta Kappa. Office: DC Sch Law 4200 Connecticut Ave NW Washington DC 20008-1122

RICHARDSON, BARBARA HULL, state legislator, social worker; b. Danville, Pa., Sept. 30, 1922; d. Robert Alonzo and Clara Lucille (Woodruff) H.; widowed; children: Barbara Follansbee, Lawrence, Christine, Lovel Pratt. BA, Bryn Mawr Coll., 1944; MSW, Smith Coll. School for Social Work, 1973. Social worker child and family svcs. divsn. children and youth svcs. HHS, Keene, N.H., 1969-71, administr. child and family svcs. Concord, N.H., 1975-88, supr. policy writers, 1988-91; mem. N.H. Ho. Reps., Concord, 1992—. Trustee Meeting Sch., 1980—; bd. dirs. Cheshire Housing Trust, 1986-93; adv. bd. Casey Family Svcs. N.H., 1990—; vol. Hospice Monadnock Region, 1991—; mem. community coun. Luth. Social Svcs. New England, 1993—; bd. dirs. Keene Day Care Ctr. Democrat. Home: 101 Morgan Rd Richmond NH 03470-4909 Office: NH Ho of Reps State Capitol Concord NH 03301

RICHARDSON, BECKY D. state representative; b. Chester, SC, Mar. 1, 1943; d. Hiram Ross Davis and Sara Grant McDill; m. J. R. Richardson, July 10, 1999; children: William Layman, James Brennan. BA, Limestone Coll., 1965. Mem. SC Ho. of Reps., 1991—, chmn. ho. ethics com. Pres. United Way, Fort Mill, 1990, campaign chmn., 1989; recycling chmn. Fort Mill, 1988—; women's adv. bd. Piedmont Med. Ctr., 1989—92; solid wste task force York County, 1990—92; chmn. Red Ribbon Week for Drug-Free Am., 1990—2001; adv. bd. Leap Ahead, 1991—99; hon. adv. bd. Teen Challenge, toast of yr., 1993; mem. City Coun., Fort Mill., 1988; pres. women of ch. Unity Presbyn., 1988—90; bd. dirs. Downtown Revitalization Commn., 1988—, Police Athletic League, 1990—92, Fort Mill Mus., 1990—94, Fort Mill Rescue Squad, Tri-County Sisterhelp, 1992—96, Teen Connection, 1996—98. Named Legis. of Yr., SC Wildlife Fedn., 1997, Sierra Club, 1998, SC Optometrist Assn., 1997; recipient Legis. award, Victims' Adv., 1996. Mem.: Fort Mill Area C. of C. (bd. dirs. 1988—91). Republican. Office: State Capitol 519 B Blatt Bldg Columbia SC 29211

RICHARDSON, BETTY H. lawyer, former prosecutor; b. Oct. 3, 1953; BA, U. Idaho, 1976; JD, Hastings Coll. Law, 1982. Staff aid U.S. Senator Frank Church, 1976-77; tchg. asst. Hastings Coll. Law, 1980-82, 1980-82; legal rsch. asst. criminal divsn. San Francisco Superior Ct., 1982-84; jud. law clk. Chamber of Idaho Supreme Ct. Justice Robert C. Huntley Jr., 1984-86; atty. U.S. Dept. Justice, Boise, Idaho, 1993-2001, Richardson & O'Leary, Eagle, Idaho, 2001—. Instr. Boise State U., 1987, 89; mem. U.S. Atty. Gen.'s Adv. Com. subcoms. on environ., civil rights and native Am. issues, others, 1993-2001; mem. hon. adv. bd. for Crime Victims Amendment in Idaho, 1994; mem. Dist. of Idaho Judges and Lawyer Reps. com., gender fairness com., Civil Justice Reform Act com. and criminal adv. com., 1993-2001; Dem. nominee Dist 1 Idaho, U.S. Ho. of Reps., 2003. Mem. Idaho Indsl. Commn., 1991-93, chmn., 1993; mem. adv. bd. Family and Workplace Consortium, 1995-2001; mem. Assistance League of Boise, 2001—; bd. dirs. Tony Patino Fellowship. Recipient Harold E. Hughes Exceptional Svc. award Nat. Rural Inst. on Alcohol and Drug Abuse, 1999; Tony Patino fellow Hastings Coll. Law, 1982. Mem. Idaho Bar Assn. (governing coun. govt. and pub. sectors lawyers sect. 1999-2001, Pro Bono Svc. award 1988), Idaho Women Lawyers, Idaho Dem. Women's Caucus, City Club Boise. Office: Richardson & O'Leary 99 E State St Eagle ID 83616 also: 5796 N Dalspring Boise ID 83713

RICHARDSON, BROWNIE F. accountant; b. Thomaston, Ala., Nov. 29, 1945; d. Cecil G. and Mary G. Foote; divorced; 1 child, Matthew B. BS, U. South Ala., 1997; postgrad., Samford U., Birmingham, Ala., 1998-99. CPA, Ala. Acct. Dudley, Ruland & Chateau, Mobile, Ala., 1990-98, Boohaker, Schillaci & Co., Birmingham, 1998—. Mem. AICPAs, Ala. Soc. CPAs, Ga. Soc. CPAs, Beta Alpha Psi (v.p. 1996). E-mail: brownier@bsccpa.com.

RICHARDSON, DENNISE MARIE, physician assistant; b. Patuxent River, Md., July 16, 1944; d. Hershel Elroy and Suzanne Marie (Ahern) R.; m. Richard Harold Browne, Aug. 10, 1970. BS, Lamar U., 1966, U. Tex., 1995; MS, Okla. State U., 1970, PhD, 1973. Cert. physician asst. Rsch. technician MD Anderson Hosp., Houston, 1967-68; fellow U. Tex., Dallas, 1974-75, rsch. assoc., 1978-93; rsch. immunologist Wadley Insts., Dallas, 1975-76; physician asst. Lakewood Med. Ctr., Dallas, 1996-97, Lewis Group, Dallas, 1997-98; pediat. physician asst. George Monroe, MD, Dallas, 1998—. Fellow Am. Assn. Physician Assts.; mem. People to People Internat., Tex. Acad. Physician Assts., Alzheimer Assn. (group leader), Dallas Com. Fgn. Visitors, Dallas Camera Club (sec.), Beta Beta Beta, Phi Sigma. Republican. Avocations: photography, canoeing, writing. Home: 12045 Inwood Rd Dallas TX 75244-8016

RICHARDSON, DOT (DOROTHY GAY), softball player, physician; b. Orlando, Fla., Sept. 22, 1961; married. Student, Western Ill. U.; BS Kinesiology, UCLA; M in Exercise, Adelphi U.; MD, U. Louisville; PhD (hon.), Western Ill. U., 2003. Mem., captain US Olympic Softball Team; resident in orthopedic surg. U. Calif. Med. Ctr.; med. dir. USA Triathlon Nat. Tng. Ctr., Clermont, Fla., 2001—. Recipient Gold medal Pan. Am. Games, 1979, 87, 95, ISF Women's World Championship, 1986, 94, South Pacific Classic, 1994, Superball Classic, 1995, Atlanta Olympics, 1996, Sydney Olympics, 2000; Rev Linda award, Flo Hyman award, 2002; named All-Am. Am. Softball Assn., MVP Am. Softball Assn. Major Fast Pitch Nat.

Championship, Player of 1980s NCAA. Office: Amateur Softball Assn 2801 NE 50th St Oklahoma City OK 73111-7203 also: Exec Dir USAT Nat Tng Ctr 1099 Citrus Tower Blvd Clermont FL 34711*

RICHARDSON, ELAINA, foundation administrator, former magazine editor; MA, U. Edinburgh, Scotland, 1982; MLitt, Oxford (Eng.) U., 1984 Writer, editor Stills mag., 1984-86, freelance writer, 1986-88; mng. editor In Fashion, 1988, reporter, writer N.Y. Post, 1989; features editor Mirabella mag., 1990-93; mng. editor Elle mag., N.Y.C., 1993-96, dep. editor, editor-in-chief, 1996-00; pres. Yaddo, Saratoga Springs, New York, 2000—. Contbr. to BBC radio program Kaleidoscope, and to various newspapers and mags., including Washington Post, Seventeen, New Women, N.Y., View, Travel and Leisure, and Nat. Pub. Radio. Office: Corp of Yaddo PO Box 395 Saratoga Springs NY 12866-0395

RICHARDSON, ELAINE, state legislator; Student, Bryant Coll., Pima Coll.; U. Ariz.; D (hon.), Tucson U. Comml. real estate broker, Ariz.; small bus. owner; mem. Ariz. Senate, Dist. 11, Phoenix, 1996—. Mem. West Univ. Neighborhood Assn., real estate rev. com. on Edn. Initiatives; precinct com. person legis. dist. #11, Ariz.; mem. adv. bd. Emergency Med. Svcs. for Children, U. Ariz. Health Scis. Ctr.; bd. dirs., community substance abuse adv. coun. Altar Valley Sch. Dist.; del. Jt. Protocol Session, Ariz.-Mex. Commn.; bd. mem. La Frontera Ctr., Inc.; regional dir. Nat. Order of Women Legislators. Recipient Women on the Move award, 1997. Mem. Dems. of Greater Tucson, Ariz. Women's Polit. Caucus, Nat. Conf. of State Legislatures (vice chair energy and transp. com.), Toastmasters, Plateau Club, Sierra Club. Office: PO Box 962 Tucson AZ 85702-0962

RICHARDSON, ELLEN MORRIS, music educator; d. Frank and Kathleen Morris; m. Charles Michael Richardson, Apr. 2, 1977; children: Robert James, Patrick Michael. BA, Queens Coll., 1977, MS, 1984. Cert. N.Y. state solo festival adjudicator. Tchr. Levittown H.S., NY, 1979—81, N.Y.C. Pub. Schs., 1981—94, Elwood Mid. Sch., NY, 1996—97, Kings Pk. Schs., NY, 1997—99, Commack Mid. Sch., NY, 1999—. Mem.: L.I. String Tchrs. Assn. (v.p. 2000—02), Suffolk County Music Educators' Assn. (co-chair 2002—03). Democrat. Office: Commack Middle School Vanderbilt Pky Commack NY 11725 Office Phone: 631-912-2099 x4731. Personal E-mail: batonmama@aol.com. Business E-Mail: erichardson@commack.k12.ny.us.

RICHARDSON, ERIKA, special education educator; b. Meriden, Conn., Sept. 18, 1978; d. Patricia Bailey Cooper; m. Arron Scott Richardson, Mar. 30, 2001. Speech Pathology and Audiology, NC A&T State U., 1996—2000, Spl. Edn. Spl. edn. tchr. SE Mid. Sch., Greensboro, NC, 2000—. Project PISCES scholar, Dr. Cathy Kea, NC A&T State U., 2002. Mem.: Coun. of Exceptional Children. Home: 5253F Fox Hunt Dr Greensboro NC 27407 Personal E-mail: arronsgal@aol.com.

RICHARDSON, GRACE ELIZABETH, consumer products company executive; b. Salem, Mass., Nov. 22, 1938; d. George and Julia (Sheridan) R.; m. Ralph B. Henderson, Mar. 3, 1979. BS, Simmons Coll., 1960; MS, Cornell U., 1962; MBA, NYU, 1981. Textile technologist Harris Rsch. Lab., Washington, 1962-65; instr. Simmons Coll., Boston, 1965-66; dir. consumer edn. materials J.C. Penney, N.Y.C., 1966-73; dir. residential conservation Con Edison, N.Y.C., 1974-81; dir. consumer affairs Chesebrough-Ponds, Greenwich, Conn., 1981-85; v.p. global consumer affairs Colgate Palmolive, N.Y.C., 1985—. Chair Simmons Coll. Leadership Coun., 1993—97; mem. com. Juilliard Sch., 1996—; bd. dirs. SOCAP, 1996—99, Nat. Coalition Consumer Edn., 1983—93; mem. Cornell U. Coun., chair pub. rels. com., 1988—97; bd. mem. UNIFEM, 2002—. Named Nat. Bus. Home Economist of Yr., Home Economists in Bus., 1979. Mem. Women's Forum, Cornell Club N.Y.C. (bd. dirs. 1989—). Home: 180 E 79th St New York NY 10021-0437 Office: Colgate Palmolive Co 300 Park Ave Fl 8 New York NY 10022-7499

RICHARDSON, JUDY MCEWEN, education administrator, consultant, cartoonist; b. Appleton, Wis., June 3, 1947; d. John Mitchell and Isabel Annette (Ruble) McEwen; m. Larry Leroy Richardson, Mar. 19, 1972 (div. Oct. 1983). BA in English, Stanford U., 1968, MA in Edn., 1969; PhD in Higher Edn., U. Wash., 1975. Dir. ednl. rsch. St. Olaf Coll., Northfield, Minn., 1975-79; evaluation specialist Northwest Regional Ednl. Laboratory, Portland, 1980-82; legis. rsch. analyst Ariz. State Sen., Phoenix, 1982-87; dir. sch. fin. Ariz. Dept. Edn., Phoenix, 1987-92, assoc. superintendent, 1992-94; ednl. cons. Scottsdale, Ariz., 1994-96; exec. dir. Ariz. State Bd. for Sch. Capital Facilities, Phoenix, 1996-98; sch. fin. cons. Peacock, Hislop, Staley & Given, Phoenix, 1998—2002, Stone & Youngberg, Phoenix, 2002—. Cartoonist for the Ariz. Capitol Times, 1995-96. Office: Stone & Youngberg LLC 2555 E Camelback Rd Ste 280 Phoenix AZ 85016 E-mail: jrichardson@syllc.com.

RICHARDSON, JULIE G. investment company executive; BA, Univ. Wis. at Madison, 1985; PhD, Stanford Univ. Graduate Sch. of Bus. Mng. dir. Merrill Lynch, 1986—98; vice chmn., co-chair JP Morgan Chase & Co., NYSE, 1998—2003; mng. dir. Providence Equity Prtnrs., Providence, 2003—. Office: Providence Equity Ptnrs 50 Kennedy Plaza, 18th Flr Providence RI 02903

RICHARDSON, KATHY KREAG, state legislator; Ed., Purdue U. Clk. Hamilton County Circuit Ct., 1984-91; mem. from 29th dist. Ind. State Ho. of Reps., 1992—. Mem. cts. and criminal code com., judiciary com., local govt., cityies and towns, county and twp. com., election and apportionment com., family and children com. Mem. Hamilton County Bd. Election Surps. Mem. Assn. Clks. Circuit Cts., Assn. Ind. Counties, Noblesville C. of C. (bd. dirs.), Noblesville H.S. Alumni Assn. (sec.), Kiwanis, Soroptimist, Republican Woman, Hamilton County Hist. Soc. Home: 1363 Grant St Noblesville IN 46060-1925 Office: Ind Ho of Reps State Capitol Indianapolis IN 46204

RICHARDSON, LAURA, psychologist, educator; b. Anoka, Minn., 1970; d. Bruce Carlton Richardson and Julia Louise Gelbart; life ptnr. J.R. Lovell. BA in Psychology(hon.), Pitzer Coll., Claremont, Calif., 1992; MA in Psychology Rsch. (hon.), New Sch. Social Rsch., N.Y.C., 1997; PhD in Clin. Psychology, New Sch. Social Rsch., 2000. Lic. psychologist N.Y., Colo. Instr. dept. of personal counseling and career svcs. Bklyn Coll., CUNY, 1998—99; asst. prof. dept. of counseling and student devel. John Jay Coll. of Criminal Justice, CUNY, N.Y.C., 1999—2001; asst. prof. psychology U. of Guam, Mangilao, 2001—03; staff psychologist, counseling ctr. U. of No. Colo., Greeley, 2003—. Faculty mentor Ronald E. McNair Post-Baccalaureate Achievement Program, N.Y.C., 2000—01. Contbr. articles to profl. jours. Fellow Irene Diamond fellow, New Sch. U., 1995—98; grantee U. Scholars' Summer Rsch. grantee, 1995—96; scholar Univ. scholar, 1992—94. Mem.: APA, Soc. for Personality and Social Psychology, Psi Chi, Phi Beta Sigma (hon.). Home: PO Box 734 Denver CO 80201 Office: Univ of Northern Colorado Cassidy Hall Campus Box 17 Greeley CO 80639 Personal E-mail: richardson_laura@yahoo.com.

RICHARDSON, LAUREL WALUM, sociology educator; b. Chgo., July 15, 1938; d. Tyrrell Alexander and Rose (Foreman) R.; m. Herb Walum, Dec. 27, 1959 (div. 1972); children: Benjamin, Joshua; m. Ernest Lockridge, Dec. 12, 1981. AB, U. Chgo., 1955, BA, 1956; PhD, U. Colo., 1963. Asst. prof. Calif. State U., Los Angeles, 1962-64; postdoctoral fellow Sch. Medicine Ohio State U., Columbus, 1964-65, asst. prof. sociology, 1970-75, assoc. prof., 1975-79; prof. sociology Sch. Medicine Ohio State U., Columbus, 1979—, prof. cultural studies, edn. policy and leadership; asst. prof. sociology Denison U., Granville, Ohio, 1965-69. Mem. editorial bd. Jour. Contemporary Ethnography, Symbolic Interaction, Gender & Soc., Qualitative Sociology, The Sociol. Quar. Author: Dynamics of Sex and Gender, 1977, 3d edit. 1988, The New Other Woman, 1985, Die Neve Andere, 1987, A Nova Outra Mulher, 1987, Writing Strategies: Reaching Diverse Audiences, 1990, Gender and University Teaching: A Negotiated Difference, 1995; editor: Feminist Frontiers, 1983, 5th edit., 2000, Fields of Play Constructing an Academic Life, 1997 (Charles H. Cooley award for best sociology book 1998), (with Ernest Lockridge) Travels with Ernest: Crossing the Literary/Sociological Divide, 2004; assoc. editor Symbolic Interaction; author more than 100 rsch. articles and papers. Ford Found. fellow, 1954-56; NSF dissertation fellow, 1960-62; post doctoral fellow Vocat. Rehab., Columbus, 1964; grantee Ohio Dept. Health, 1986-87, Nat. Inst. Edn., 1981-82, NIMH, 1972-74, NSF, 1963-64, NEH, 1992; recipient Disting. Affirmative Action award Ohio State U., 1983, Feminist Mentor award, 1998. Mem. Am. Sociol. Assn. (com. on coms. 1980-81, com. on pub. info. 1987—), North Ctrl. Sociol. Assn. (pres. 1986-87), Sociologists for Women in Soc. (coun. mem. 1978-80), Ctrl. Ohio Sociologists for Women in Soc. (past pres.), Women's Poetry Workshop, Soc. for Study of Symbolic Interaction (publs. com.). Avocations: hiking, poetry. Office: Ohio State U Dept Sociology 190 N Oval Mall Columbus OH 43210-1328 E-mail: Richardson.9@osu.edu.

RICHARDSON, LILY PENDARVIS, retired occupational health nurse; b. Columbia, N.C., Feb. 23, 1939; d. Theophilus Pendarvis and Comeller (Bowser) Johnson; m. Napoleon Richardson, Apr. 4, 1959; children: Donald Felton, Napoleon Jr. BS cum laude, N.C. A&T U., 1961. RN, D.C. Charge nurse L. Richardson Hosp., Greensboro, N.C., 1961-63; charge nurse medicine Georgetown U. Med. Ctr., Washington, 1963-64; charge nurse of nursery D.C. Gen. Hosp., Washington, 1964-67; occupational health nurse, occupational health adminstr. FBI, Washington, 1967-94, adminstr. nursing program, 1994. Part time instr. practical nurses Dudley High Sch., Greensboro, 1962; cons. Establishing Health Units, 1990-94, Med. Standard Task Force, Washington, 1993, Bloodborne Pathogen Task Force, 1993. Active cmty. svc. Rosemary Hills Sch., Silver Spring, Md., 1992-94, sch. bd., 1993; blood pressure screener, counselor at several cmty. chs. and cmty. health ctrs.; mail worker Health Reform Com., Washington, 1993-94. Mem. NAACP, Nat. Black Nurses Assn., Black Nurses Greater Washington D.C. ARea (rec. sec. 1985—), Met. Washington Assn. Occupational Health Nurses, Teloca Nursing Alumni (parliamentarian 1970—), A&T Alumni, Sigma Theta Tau (Mutau chpt. internat. charter, Gamma Beta chpt. 1 of 100 Extraordinary Nurses 1994). Home: 142 Presidents Dr Durham NC 27704-2168

RICHARDSON, MARGARET MILNER, former accounting firm executive, lawyer; b. Waco, Tex., May 14, 1943; d. James W. and Margaret Wiebusch Milner; m. John L. Richardson, July 22, 1967; 1 child, Margaret Lawrence. AB in Polit. Sci., Vassar Coll., 1965; JD with honors, George Washington U., 1968. Bar: Va. 1968, D.C. 1968, U.S. Dist. Ct. D.C. 1968, U.S. Ct. Appeals (4th, 5th, D.C. and Fed. cirs.) 1968, U.S. Claims Ct. 1969, U.S. Tax Ct. 1970, U.S. Supreme Ct. 1971. Clk. U.S. Ct. Claims, Washington; with Office Chief Counsel IRS, Washington, 1969-77; with Sutherland, Asbill and Brennan, Washington, 1977-80, ptnr., 1980-93; commr. IRS, Washington, 1993-97; ptnr. Ernst & Young, Washington, 1997—2003. Mem. commr.'s adv. group IRS, 1988-90, chair, 1990; bd. advisors George Washington Law Sch.; mem. D.C. Bar Commn. on Multidisciplinary Practice, Presdl. Commn. on Holocaust Assets; bd. dirs. Legg Mason, Inc. Contbr. articles to profl. jours. Assisted Clinton 1992 primary and gen. election campaign; served as team leader Justice Dept./Civil Rights Cluster during Presdl. Transition; mem. bd. Nat. Mus. Women in Arts, Mayor's Transition Team, 1998, Women's Campaign Fund, Nat. Cathedral Sch., Hosp. for Sick Children; bd. trustees Eurasia Found. Mem. ABA, D.C. Bar Assn. (tax sect.), Va. State Bar, Fed. Bar Assn. (com. taxation), Fin. Women's Assn. N.Y., Washington Women's Forum, Internat. Alliance, U.S. Russia Bus. Coun., Woodrow Wilson Ctr. Avocations: travel, antiques, needlepoint, gardening. Personal E-mail: margaretrichardson@yahoo.com.

RICHARDSON, NATASHA JANE, actress; b. May 11, 1963; d. Tony Richardson and Vanessa Redgrave; m. Liam Neeson, July 3, 1994; children: Micheal Richard Antonio, Daniel Jack. Trained, Ctrl. Sch. Speech and Drama. Acting debut on stage at Leeds (Eng.) Playhouse, 1983; appearances include (plays) A Midsummer's Night Dream, Hamlet, 1985, The Seagull, 1985, High Society, 1987, Anna Christie, 1993, (Tony award nominee 1993, Drama Desk award), Cabaret, 1998 (Tony award, Drama Desk award, Outer Critics award), Closer (Broadway, 1999); (TV) In the Secret State, 1984, Sherlock Holmes, The Copper Beaches, 1984, Ghosts, 1986, Suddenly Last Summer, 1992, Hostages, 1993, Zelda, 1993, (Cable Ace nomination), Haven, 2001; (films) Gothic, 1987, A Month in the Country, 1987, Patty Hearst, 1988, Fat Man and Little Boy, 1989, The Handmaid's Tale, 1990, The Comfort of Strangers, 1991, The Favor, The Watch and the Very Big Fish, 1992, Past Midnight, Widow's Peak, 1994, (Best Actress Karlovy Vary), Nell, 1995, The Parent Trap, 1998, Blowdry, 2001, Wakin Up in Reno, 2001, Maid in Manhattan, 2002. Recipient Most Promising Newcomer award Plays & Players, 1986; named Best Actress by London Theatre Critics, Plays & Players, 1990, Evening Standard Best Actress, 1990; Tony Award, actress in a musical, Cabaret, 1999.

RICHARDSON, OPAL MAE, music educator, director; b. Lewistown, Mo., Aug. 10, 1950; d. Harold Leroy and Alice Marie Hinkle; m. Roy John Richardson, Jan. 24, 1971; children: Jonelle, Kristin. BS, U. of Mo., Columbia, MO, 1968—72. Vocal music tchr. Richmond H.S., Richmond, Mo., 1972—75; vocal and instrumental music tchr. Hardin Ctrl. Sch., Hardin, Mo., 1977—84; vocal music tchr. Richmond Mid. Sch., Richmond, Mo., 1984—92, 1996—. Chancel choir dir. Richmond United Meth. Ch., Richmond, Mo., 1985—95, RIchmond, Mo., 1998—, handbell choir dir., Richmond, Mo., 1993—96, Richmond, 1999—. Bd. mem. Ray County Cmty. Arts Assn., RIchmond, Mo., 1992—2002. Mem.: Mo. Music Educators Conf., Music Educators Nat. Conf. Avocations: reading, gardening, family. Home: 9333 Highway T Richmond MO 64085 Office: Richmond Middle School 715 S Wellington Richmond MO 64085

RICHARDSON, PAMELA AUSTIN, music educator; b. Chgo., Jan. 21, 1971; d. William Erwin and Rosemary Austin; m. Darryl Bernard Richardson, Dec. 31, 1995; children: Darielle Breighann, Danyelle Belicia. BA, Bethune-Cookman Coll., Daytona Beach, Fla., 1989—94. Grad. asst. Fla. State U., Tallahassee, 1994—96; instrnl. asst. Bond Elem. Sch., Tallahassee, 1995—96; music tchr. Pinellas County Schs., Palm Harbor, Fla., 1997—. Presenter, music beach camp Pinellas County Music Dept, Largo, Fla., 2003; coun. mem. Sch. Adv. Coun., Palm Harbor, Fla., 1998—99. Founder and elder Agape Covenant Fellowship Ch., Tallahassee, Fla., 1995—97. Grantee, Arts Coun. grantee, 2002—03, Jr. League grantee, 2002—03. Mem.: Fla. Music Educators Assn., Arts For a Complete Edn. Pinellas (arts adv. 2001), Music Educators Nat. Conf., Kappa Delta Pi. Independent. Christian. Avocations: playing musical instruments, reading, scrapbooking, computers, travel. Office: Palm Harbor Elem Sch 415 15th St Palm Harbor FL 34683 Personal E-mail: pam7rich@aol.com.

RICHARDSON, PATRICIA, actress; b. Bethesda, Md., Feb. 23, 1951; d. Laurence Baxter and Elizabeth (Howard) R.; m. Raymond Baker, June 20, 1982; children: Henry, Roxanne, Joseph. BFA, So. Meth. U., 1972. Appearences include (Broadway) Gypsy, Loose Ends, The Wake of Jamie Foster; (off-Broadway) The Collected Works of Billy the Kid, The Frequency, Vanities, The Coroner's Plot, Hooters, Company, Fables for Friends, The Miss Firecracker Contest, Cruise Control; (regional theatre) King Lear, The Killing of Sister George, Relatively Speaking, The Importance of Being Earnest, Of Mice and Men, The Philadelphia Story, Room Service, Fifth of July, About Face; (nat. tours) Gypsy, Vanities; (films) Gas, 1972, You Better Watch Out, Lost Angels, 1988, In Country, 1988, Ulee's Gold, 1997; (TV) Double Trouble, 1984, Eisenhower & Lutz, 1988, FM, 1989-90, Home Improvement, 1991-99 (Lead Actress in a Comedy Series Emmy award nominee, 1994, Golden Globe award nominee, 1993, 94), Sophie and the Moonhanger, 1995, Undue Influence, 1996, Viva Las Nowhere, 2000. Office: William Morris Agy care Jonathon Howard 151 S El Camino Dr Beverly Hills CA 90212-2775

RICHARDSON, PATRICIA JEAN, librarian; b. Walla Walla, Wash., Jan. 31, 1943; d. Francis and Melba Lorraine (Bryant) Hagel; m. Henry Vokes-MacKey Richardson, May 7, 1965 (div. July 1992); children: Shasha L., Kathrine E., Frances du Bruyeres, John E. du Bruyeres; m. Michael E. Ovens, Nov. 1, 1999. AA, Yakima Valley Coll., Yakima, Wash., 1963; BA in English, U. Wash., 1966, MLS, 1994. Cert. libr., Wash. Libr.'s asst. Yakima Valley Regional Libr., Yakima, 1956-63, Microsoft, Redmond, Wash., 1993-94; libr. asst. children's dept. Walla Walla Pub. Libr., 1984-92; libr. for children's svcs. King County Libr. Sys., Seattle, 1993—. Mem. ALA, AAUW (membership chmn. 1971, scholar Walla Walla chpt. 1992), Pacific N.W. Libr. Assn., Wash. Libr. Assn., bd. mem. CAYAS, 1998-2000. Episcopalian. Avocations: gardening, reading, hiking, collecting.

RICHARDSON, POLLIE, principal; b. Stump City, Ark., Nov. 19, 1949; d. L. C. and Daisy Mae Newman; m. John Wesley Richardson, July 7, 1969 (div.); children: Octavia Ethel, Demetrius Donte', Veritie Potere', Bonita Biaute', Carina Danette. BS in Edn., Harris Stowe State Coll., 1981; EdM, U. Mo., St. Louis, 1995. Cert. adminstrn. II/secondary prin. Dept. Elem. and Secondary Edn., 1995, elem. edn. Dept. Elem. and Secondary Edn., 1981, learning disabled Dept. Elem. and Secondary Edn., 1981, mentally handicapped Dept. Elem. and Secondary Edn., 1981, behavioral disorder Dept. Elem. and Secondary Edn., 1981, spl. reading Dept. Elem. and Secondary Edn., 1981, math. Dept. Elem. and Secondary Edn., 1995. Asst. prin. Epworth Campus Sch., St. Louis, 1981—96; prin. Mehlville Sch. Dist., St. Louis, 1996—. Instr. Fontbonne U., St. Louis, 1997—98; dir., pioneer alt. sch. Parent to Parent Tng.; spkr. in field. Contbr. articles to profl. jours. Mem.: Leadership Acad., Nat. Assn. Secondary Prins., Coun. Exceptional Children. Baptist. Avocations: sewing, reading, writing, gardening, travel. Home: 6518 Whitney Ave Saint Louis MO 63133-1426 Office: Mehlville School District 76 Grasso Plaza Saint Louis MO 63123-3108 Office Phone: 314-631-1047. Personal E-mail: pollier@swbell.net. E-mail: richp@mehlville.k12.mo.us.

RICHARDSON, SALLY KEADLE, health care administrator; b. Mar. 2, 1933; d. Okey P. and Viola Miriam (Graybeal) Keadle; m. Don Rule Richardson, Dec. 15, 1961; children: Miriam Paige, Ruth Evan. AB, Vassar Coll., 1954. Regional pub. info. rep. Columbia Gas Sys., Charleston, W.Va., 1958-62; dir. Children's Mus., Charleston, 1963; coord. space-related sci. project Kanawha County Schs., Charleston, 1967-68; vol. dir. Rockefeller for Gov. Campaign, Charleston, 1972, program dir., 1976, 80; dir. admissions W.Va. Wesleyan Coll., Buckhannon, 1974-75; spl. asst. Office of Gov. State of W.Va., 1977, dep. commr. dept. welfare, 1978-79, dep. dir. dept. health, 1979-83; chmn. W.Va. Health Care Cost Rev. Authority, Charleston, 1983-85. Health care cons., Charleston, 1985-89; dir. W.Va. Pub. Employees Ins. Agy., Charleston, 1989-93; vice-chmn. W.Va. Health Care Planning Task Force, 1992-93; mem. White House Health Care Reform Task Force, Washington, 1993; dir. Medicaid Bur., Health Care Financing Adminstrn., U.S. DHHS, Balt., 1993-96; acting dep. adminstr. HCFA, U.S. DHHS, Washington, 1996-97; dir. Ctr. for Medicaid and State Ops., 1997-99; mem. U.S. DHHS Governing Coun. on Children and Youth, 1993-97, co-chmn. U.S. DHHS Children's Health Initiative, 1997-99; co-chmn. U.S. DHHS Home and Cmty. Based Svcs. Task Force, 1996-99; mem. U.S. DHHS Pub. Health Coun.'s D.C. Task Force, 1994-99; mem. Nat. Adv. Com. on Rural Health, DHHS, 2000-04. W.Va. rep. Task Force on So. Children, So. Growth Policies Bd., 1978-79; co-chmn. exec. com. W.Va. Internat. Yr. of Child, 1979; staff mem. Com. on Human Resources Nat. Gov. Assn., 1983-85; bd. trustees U. Charleston, 1994-; bd. dirs. Children's Home Soc., Charleston, 1999—. Mem. Acad. Health, Nat. Rural Health Assn. Democrat. Office: WVa U Inst Health Policy Rsch 3110 Maccorkle Ave SE Rm 3015 Charleston WV 25304-1210

RICHARDSON, SHIRLEY MAXINE, editor; b. Rising Sun, Ind., May 3, 1931; d. William Fenton and Mary (Phillips) Keith; m. Arthur Lee Richardson, Feb. 11, 1950; children: Mary Jane Hunt, JoDee Mayfield, Steven Lee Richardson. Pers. mgr. Mayhill Pubs., Knightstown, Ind., 1967-87, prodn. mgr., 1975-87, editor, 1967-87; info. staff, assoc. editor Ind. Farm Bur., Inc., 1987-89, dir. info. and pub. rels., 1989-94; genealogy editor AntiqueWeek, 1996-2001; exec. editor Knightstown Banner, 2001—. Avocations: travel, reading, boating, quilting. Home: 366 E Carey St Knightstown IN 46148-1208 Office: 24 N Washington St Knightstown IN 46148-1242 Office Phone: 765-345-2292.

RICHARDSON, SHIRLEY R. librarian; b. Brownwood, Tex., Apr. 20, 1943; d. Raymond C. and Leta Z. Richardson. BS in Secondary Edn., Howard Payne U., 1963; MLS, Tex. Woman's U., 1970. Tchr. English Gorman (Tex.) H.S., 1964—65; tchr. art Kirby Jr. High, Converse, Tex., 1965—69; catalog libr. Pittsburg (Kans.) State U., 1971—75, U. Tex., El Paso, 1975—80; serials project libr. U. Houston, 1980—82; catalog libr. Angelo State U., San Angelo, Tex., 1982—. Contbr. short stories and poetry to anthologies. Avocations: writing, reading, animal welfare, classical music. Home: PO Box 3060 San Angelo TX 76902 Office: Angelo State Univ Libr 2601 W Ave N San Angelo TX 76909

RICHARDSON, SUSAN, health facility administrator, writer; b. Denver, May 11, 1956; d. Robert Eugene and Frances Louise Richardson; m. George Wesley Lundy III, Jan. 26, 1985; 1 child, Chandra Alexis Lundy. BA, Colo. State U., 1981. Legal transcriptionist various law firms, Calif., 1982—86; med. clk. USN, San Diego, 1989—90, 1993—94; group sec. IRS Criminal Investigation, San Diego, 1990—92; office automation clk. IRS, Cheyenne, Wyo., 1994—97; med. transcriptionist MedQuist, Englewood, Colo., 1999—. Editl. asst.: Colo. Rev., 1984; mem. prodn. crew Cut Bank Mag. and Hellgate Writers, 1986—87; editl. asst. and poetry editor: Greyrock Rev., 1980—81; author: Rapunzel's Short Hair, 1994; editor: Calypso Mag., Dreaming in Chinese, First Light, author articles, stories and poems. Reading tutor for adults El Cajon Pub. Libr., Calif., 1992; child care provider San Diego Family Ct., 1992; mem. Log Cabin Literary Ctr., Live Poets Workshop. With U.S. Army, 1975—78. Mem.: Phi Kappa Phi. Democrat. Avocations: environmental conservation, miniatures, reading, walking, travel.

RICHARDSON, SUZANNE MAYS, communication consultant; b. Dayton, Apr. 16, 1944; d. Lewell Newton and Virginia Mays; m. Randolph Wade Richardson, Mar. 20, 1993; children: Rebecca (Nash), William (Nash). BA, Brown U., 1966; MA, Columbia U., 1967, U. Mich., 1970. Special asst. commanding gen. U.S. Army Materiel Command, Alexandria, Va., 1986-91; stategic initiatives analyst Office Sec. Defense, Pentagon, Washington, D.C., 1991-93; cons. in field. Chair Colo. Womens Leadership Coalition, 1998-99, sec., 1997; sec. Recording for the Blind and Dyslexic, Denver, 1996-98; bd. dirs. Colo. Women's Hall of Fame, 2000—, co-chair, 2002—04; bd. dirs. Day of Caring for Breast Cancer Awareness, 2002—, v.p., 2004. Recipient Woman Leader of Excellence award Colo. Women's Leadership Coalition, 1997. Mem. Assn. Women in Comms. (pres. Denver chpt. 1996-97), Zonta Club of Douglas County. Unitarian Universalist. Office: 3864 Castle Butte Dr Castle Rock CO 80109-9638

RICHARDSON, VANESSA, education educator; b. Camp Lejeune, N.C., Aug. 31, 1960; d. Matthew and Margaret Ethel (Cox) R. Cert. in traffic mgmt., U.S. Army Transp. Sch., Ft. Eustis, Va., 1985; BS in Urban and Regional Planning, East Carolina U., 1988; MS in Safety and Driver Edn., N.C. Agrl. and Tech. State U., 1990, MS in Reading Edn., 1992; PhD, U.

N.C., Greensboro, 1998. Cert. G grad. level tchr., N.C. Planning intern Pitt County Econ. Devel. Commn., Greenville, N.C., summer 1987; grad. intern in transp. planning City of Greensboro, 1989; transp. adminstrn. mgmt. clk. USMCR, Greensboro, 1985-90; planning/grants coord. City of Fayetteville, N.C., 1990-91; rsch. asst. Sch. Bus. and Econs. N.C. Agrl. and Tech. State U., Greensboro, 1988, grad. asst. Sch. Tech., 1989-90, tutor coord., 1991-92, instr. Upward Bound program, 1992-93, instr., tech. assoc., 1992-94; grad. tchg. asst. U. N.C., Greensboro, 1993-97; cmty. rels. coord. Sch. Tech., N.C. A&T State U, Greensboro, 1997—. Co-author: New Teacher Handbook for Trade and Industrial Educators, 1993, Research on Teaming: Insights from Selected Studies; also author articles. Vol. Greater Greensboro Cities in Schs., 1991-92; coord. Fayetteville Area Sys. Transit campaign United Way. With USMCR. Mem. NEA, ASCD, N.C. Assn. Educators, Internat. Reading Assn., Soc. Tech. Comm., Assn. Grad. Students (v.p.), Am. Planning Assn., N.C. Pub. Transp. Assn., N.C. Driver and Traffic Safety Edn. Assn., Gamma Theta Upsilon, Epsilon Pi Tau, Delta Nu Alpha. Avocations: physical fitness, health, travel. Home: 1504 Cedar Ln Kinston NC 28501-5844

RICHARDSON-MELECH, JOYCE SUZANNE, music educator, singer; b. Perth Amboy, N.J., Nov. 15, 1957; d. Herbert Nathaniel and Fannie Elaine (Franklin) Richardson; m. Gerald Melech, July 28, 1990. MusB, Westminster Choir Coll., 1979, MusM, 1981; postgrad., Rutgers U., 1999—. Cert. music tchr. N.J., supr. N.J. Musical play dir. Perth Amboy H.S., 1989-92, asst. band dir., 1984-94; music tchr. Perth Amboy Bd. Edn., 1981—, gifted and talented music tchr., 1992-96; vocal soloist N.Y.C. Vocal soloist N.Y. Philharm. and Westminster Symphonic Choir, 1977, United Moravian Ch., N.Y.C., 1980-81, Ctrl. Jersey Concert Orch., Perth Amboy, 1994-96; mezzo-soprano soloist in The Messiah, John Hus Moravian Ch., Bklyn., 1998; master tchrs. collaborative with N.J. Symphony Orch., 2000-01, 03. Contbg. author: Teacher's Resource Book, 2000, 2001, 2003; actor. Perth Amboy Adult Cmty. Theatre; illustrator: The Peacock of Half-Way Tree: A Caribbean Fable, 2004. Participant Perth Amboy Adult Cmty. Theatre, 1983. Recipient award for excellence in tchg., NJ Symphony Orch., 2000, 2001, 2003. Mem. NAACP, Am. Fedn. Tchrs., Am. Fedn. Musicians (local 204-373), Music Educators Nat. Conf., Internat. Platform Assn., Am. Mus. Natural History (assoc.), Alliance for Arts Edn. N.J., Ctrl. Jersey Music Educators, N.J. Music Educators Assn., Alpha Phi Omega. Democrat. Mem. African Meth. Episcopal Zion Ch. Avocations: needle-point, cross-stitch, knitting, sewing, crocheting. Home: 148 Carson Ct Somerset NJ 08873-4790 Office: Samuel Shull Sch 380 Hall Ave Perth Amboy NJ 08861-3205 Business E-Mail: joycrichardson@paps.net.

RICHARDS-VITAL, CLAUDIA, small business owner, recreational facility executive; b. Banes, Oriente, Cuba, May 18, 1935; arrived in U.S., 1951; d. Vasper Zacharia Richards and Ana Louisa Coombs - Vital; m. Eugene Blackman, July 22, 1956 (div. Apr. 20, 1965); children: Emery, John, Veronica. AA in Bus. Adminstrn./English, Havana Bus Acad., 1951; diploma in Early Childhood Devel., Miami Dade C.C., 1972. Pvt. practice nanny, Miami Beach, Fla., 1951—56; seamstress Playboy Club, Miami, Fla., 1961—65; prodn. supr. So. Bakery, 1965—69; care mother James E. Scott Cmty. Agy., 1970—75; nurse asst. North Shore Hosp., 1970—75; home health aide Total Care Home Health Agy., 1975—85; site dir. YMCA, 1985—95; sole propr. Veronica's Boutique, 1982—89, Claudia's Formal Wear, 1989—. Pres. Local #249 Am. Bakery and Confectionery Workers Internat. AFL-CIO, Fla., 1966—69. Named Parent of Yr., Metro Dade County, 1993; recipient Diamond Pendant, Queen Elizabeth II, 1965, cert. of Appreciation, YMCA of Miami, Fla., 1990. Mem.: NAFE, NAACP. Democrat. Roman Catholic. Avocations: sewing, decorating, gardening, babysitting, animals. Home: 1915 NW 49 St Miami FL 33142 Office Phone: 305-637-2090.

RICHE, WENDY, television producer; b. N.Y.C., Jan. 8, 1945; d. Elliot and Janice (Fantel) Fields; m. Alan Riche, Dec. 4, 1966; children: Tim, Peter. Student, Syracuse U. Sec. ABC, 1973, program coord. Late Night Programs, 1974, assoc. prodr. In Concert series and specials, 1974; developer, prodr. Levenback/Riche and Wittman/Riche Prodn. Co., 1975-78; prodr. Universal TV, 1978-86; exec. prodr. ABC Entertainment, 1986-89; sr. v.p. prodr. Fox Broadcast Co., 1989-91; exec. prodr. Gen. Hosp. ABC-TV, 1992-99, exec. prodr. Port Charles, 1997-00; exec. prodr. WR Prodns., 2000—. Prodr. (movies of the week) Who Will Love My Children? (8 Emmy award nominations), Madame X, I Saw What You Did, Friendships, Secrets, and Lies, Deadly Care; exec. prodr. (ABC pilot) Never Again, (movies for TV, dir. programming ABC Entertainment) God Bless the Child, David (Emmy award nomination), My Name is Bill W (Emmy award winner), Women of Brewster Place, Unspeakable Acts, Our Sons, Fight for Life, (exec. producer daytime drama) General Hosp. (Emmy award for outstanding drama series 1994/95, 95/96, 96/97, 97/98, 98/99, 99/2000), (after school spl.) Positive: A Journey Into Aids (3 Emmy award nominations). Recipient Soap Opera Update Editors award, 1993, Pub. Svc. award Nat. Kidney Found., 1994, Soap Opera Hall of Fame, 1994, 96, Nancy Susan Reynolds award, 1994, 95, 96, Chair's award Am. Cancer Soc., 1994/95, 15th Media Access award, 1995, Imagen award, 1996, Komen award, 1996, Ryan White Youth Svc. award, 1996, Daytime TV Mag. Readers Poll award for best show, 1996/97, Soap Opera Digest award for Gen. Hosp. favorite show, 1997, 98, 99, 2000, Media Access Michael Landon award, 1997. Mem. Writes Guild Am., Producers Guild Am.

RICHETTI, CINDY L. mental health services professional; b. Jamestown, N.Y., Nov. 2, 1953; d. Marion Larry and Ermina D'Angelo Rizzo; m. Donald Nicholas Richetti, June 7, 1975; children: Ryan Donald, Logan Thomas, Vanessa Louise. BA in Psychology, St. Bonaventure U., Allegany, N.Y., 1975; MS in Edn., Counseling, St. Bonaventure U., 1977. Lic. clin. mental health counselor Fla.; cert. sch. counselor Fla. Parent edn. coord. Midland Intermediate Sch. Dist., Mich., 1990—94; counselor Ocean Palms Elem. Sch., Ponte Vedra Beach, Fla., 1995—2001; counselor in pvt. practice Ponte Vedra Med. Ctr., 1997—2001; pvt. practice counseling Jacksonville Beach, Fla., 2001—. Scholar Undergrad. assistantship, St. Bonaventure U., 1971—75, Grad. assistantship, 1975—77, N.Y. State Regents scholar, 1971—75. Mem.: Am. Counseling Assn. Avocation: tennis. Office: 334 2d Ave N Jacksonville Beach FL 32250

RICHEY, ELLEN, credit card company executive; BA summa cum laude, Harvard U.; JD, Stanford U. Law clk. Hon. Lewis F. Powell, Jr. U.S. Supreme Ct.; law clk. Hon. Charles B. Renfrew U.S. Dist. Ct. (no. dist.); ptnr. Farella, Braun & Martel, San Francisco, 1980—94; from gen. counsel, sec. Providian Fin. Corp., San Francisco, 1995—, exec. v.p., 1997—99, vice chmn. Enterprise Risk Mgmt., 1999—. Office: Providian Financial Corp 201 Mission Street Lobby San Francisco CA 94105

RICHEY, KIMBERLY KAY, singer, actress, composer; b. Zanesville, Ohio, Dec. 1, 1956; Student, Western Ky. U., Bowling Green, 1975-79; BS in Environ. Edn., Ohio U., 1980-82. With Mercury Nashville, 1994—; composer Nobody Wins, Those Words We Said, Believe Me Baby I Lied; rec. artist Kim Richey, 1995, Bitter Sweet, 1997, Glimmer, 1999; opener, headliner various shows. Recipient Grammy nomination, 1996. Office: Mercury Records Ste 300 54 Music Sq E Nashville TN 37203-4386

RICHIE, MICHELLE TRACEY, special education educator; b. Nurenberg, Germany, May 9, 1970; arrived in U.S., 1971; d. Thomas Allen and Mary Jean Brown; married, Nov. 11, 1995; 1 child, Alaina. BA, Rowan State U., 1993. Spl. edn. tchr. Washington Twp. Pub. Schs., Turnersville, NJ, 1993—. Mem.: Reading Coun. So. Jersey, Coun. Exceptional Children, Internat. Reading Assn. Home: 103 Willis Rd Bridgeton NJ 08302 Office: Washington Twp Pub Schs 227 Greentree Rd Turnersville NJ 08012 Business E-Mail: mrichie@wtps.org.

RICHLAND, LISA, library director; b. N.Y.C., July 28, 1945; d. W. Bernard and Pauline Richland; m. Daniel Philip Maciejak, May 28, 1965 (div. Dec. 1992); 1 child, Rafael Luke Maciejak; m. Bruce Edward Saul. BS in Mgmt., Syracuse U., 1985; MLS, U. Ky., 1989. Alumni dir. Bklyn. Friends Sch., 1971-81; libr. dir. Floyd Meml. Libr., Greenport, N.Y., 1989—. Mem. shared decision making com. Shelter Island Sch., 1994-97, budget rev. com., 1992-93; exec. bd. Cmty. Action of Southold Town, Inc., Greenport, N.Y., 1994-2000; mem. standing com. on arts and culture Village of Greenport, 1996—. Dewey fellow N.Y. Libr. Assn., 1994. Mem. ALA, Pub. Libr. Dirs. Assn. Suffolk County (exec. bd. 1990-92, treas. 1992-95, long range plan com., 2003—), Pub. Libr. Assn. Office: Floyd Meml Libr 539 1st St Greenport NY 11944-1399 E-mail: lrichlan@suffolk.lib.ny.us.

RICHMAN, ARLEEN, professional society administrator; b. N.Y.C., Jan. 1, 1941; d. Abraham Friedel and Judith Anne Hecht; m. Sheldon B. Richman, May 26, 1970. AAS, Hofstra Coll., 1960; BBA in Acctg. summa cum laude, Adelphi U., 1969, postgrad., 1969-71. Women's page editor AP, N.Y.C., 1960-69; adminstrv. positions various assns., Washington, 1976-80; mng. editor Trips Travels, Washington, 1980-83; comm. mgr. Appropriate Tech. Internat., Washington, 1984-90; grants adminstr. Coun. for Internat. Devel., Washington, 1990-93; dir. comm. and spl. projects U.S. Parachute Assn., Alexandria, Va., 1993-97; mgr. spl. projects Nat. Soc. Accts., Alexandria, 1997—2001, comm. mgr., 2001—; editor Nat. Pub. Acct., 2001—. Cons. various UN Devel. Program and AID projects, 1986-93; cons., editor, writer Com. on Internat. Liaison for Agr., Puebla, Mexico, 1988-90. Author: Opening the Marketplace to Small Enterprise, 1990; editor: High Impact Case Studies, 1989, (jour.) The Profl., 1995-97; contbr. numerous articles to newspapers and jours. Com. mem. local homeowners assn., Alexandria, 1984—; vol. friend Mental Health Assn., Alexandria, 1992—; vol. mentor Alexandria Jail, 1998—. Recipient Keep Am. Beautiful award Keep Am. Beautiful Fedn., Washington, 1966, Point of Light award Compeer, Alexandria, 1998, 2000. Mem. Am. Soc. Assn. Execs. Jewish. Avocations: tennis, birdwatching. Home: 2741 Carter Farm Ct Alexandria VA 22306-3242 Office: Nat Soc Accts 1010 N Fairfax St Alexandria VA 22314-1504 E-mail: arichman@nsacct.org.

RICHMAN, JOAN M. lawyer; b. Chgo., Dec. 15, 1965; Diploma in Internat. Bus., The Netherlands Sch. Bus., 1989; B of Commerce with distinction, McGill U., 1988; JD, Georgetown U., 1992. Bar: Ill. 1992. Summer assoc. Baker & McKenzie, Chgo., 1991, assoc., 1992—99, ptnr., 1999—. Office: Baker and McKenzie One Prudential Plz 130 E Randolph Dr Chicago IL 60601*

RICHMAN, PHYLLIS CHASANOW, newspaper critic; b. Washington, Mar. 21, 1939; d. Abraham and Helen (Lieberman) C.; m. Alvin Richman, June 5, 1960 (div. 1984); children— Joseph, Matthew, Libby BA, Brandeis U., 1961; postgrad., U. Pa., 1961-63, Purdue U., 1966-70. Exec. food editor Washington Post, 1980-88, food critic, 1976—. Author: Barter, 1976, Best Restaurants, 1980, 82, 85, 89, The Washington Post Dining Guide, 1996, 98, The Butter Did It, 1997, Murder on the Gravey Train, 1999. Mem. Washington Ind. Writers (adv. bd.), James Beard Restaurant Awards (exec. com.). Home: 2118 O St NW Washington DC 20037-1007 Office: Washington Post 1150 15th St NW Washington DC 20071-0002

RICHMOND, ALICE ELENOR, lawyer; b. N.Y.C. d. Louis A. and Estelle (Muraskin) R.; m. David L. Rosenbloom, July 26, 1981; 1 child, Elizabeth Lara. BA magna cum laude, Cornell U., 1968; JD, Harvard U., 1972, grad. Owners and Pres.'s Mgmt. Program, 2001; DLH (hon.), North Adams State U., 1987. Bar: Mass. 1973, U.S. Dist. Ct. Mass. 1975, U.S. Ct. Appeals (1st cir.) 1982, U.S. Supreme Ct. 1985. Law clk. to justices Superior Ct., Boston, 1972-73; asst. dist. atty. Office of Dist. Atty., Boston, 1973-76; spl. asst. atty. gen. Office of Atty. Gen., Boston, 1975-77; asst. prof. New Eng. Sch. of Law, Boston, 1976-78; assoc. Lappin, Rosen, Boston, 1978-81; ptnr. Hemenway & Barnes, Boston, 1982-92, Deutsch, Williams, Boston, 1993-95, Richmond, Pauly & Ault, Boston, 1996—2002; prin. Richmond & Assocs., Boston, 2002—. Asst. team leader, faculty Trial Advocacy Course, 1978—82; examiner Mass. Bd. Bar Examiners, Boston, 1983—; trustee Mass. Continuing Legal Edn., Inc., Boston, 1985—96, Boston, 1998—; treas. Nat. Conf. Bar Examiners, 1995—, chmn. elect., 2002—03; v.p., bd. dirs. Am. Bar Ins., Inc., 1996—. Author (2 chpts.) Rape Crisis Intervention Handbook, 1976; contbr. articles to profl. jours. Mem. Pres. Adv. Com on the Arts, 1995—99; bd. overseers Handel & Haydn Soc., 1985—94, bd. govs., 1994—2002, v.p., 1996—2002; mem. Boston 2000 Millennium Commn., 1997—98; sec., dir. Boston 2000, Inc., 1998—2001; mem., pres. Coun. of Cornell Women, Cornell U. Coun.; trustee Red Auerbach Youth Found., Fund for Justice and Edn.; mem. adv. bd. Ctrl. and Ea. European Law Initiative; mem. Angell Meml. Hosp. Coun. of Fellows, 2001—. Named one of Outstanding Young Leaders Boston Jaycees, 1982; Sloan Found. Urban fellow, N.Y.C., 1969 Fellow: Am. Coll. Trial Lawyers; mem.: NOW, Legal Def. and Edn. Fund (trustee 1995—2002, sec. 1998—2002), ABA (ho. of dels. 1980—, vice chmn. com. on rules and calendar 1986—88, bd. govs. 2002—), Internat. Jud. Acad., Latin Am. Legal Initiatives Coun., Mass. Bar Found. (pres. 1988—91), Mass. Bar Assn. (pres. 1986—87), Am. Law Inst., Boston Club, Harvard Club. Office: Richmond & Assocs 39 Brimmer St Boston MA 02108 E-mail: arichmond@rpalaw.com.

RICHMOND, DEBORAH VANCE, civil engineer; b. Kansas City, Sept. 8, 1947; d. Gerald Griffith and Elizabeth Gosney (Moss) Riegel; m. Thomas Wayne Richmond, Apr. 4, 1987; children: Ray Gerald, Elizabeth Vance. BS in Civil Engring., U. Mo., 1970. Profl. engr. Mo. Engr. Maran-Ingram-Cooke, St. Charles, Mo., 1970-72, Crane & Fleming, Hannibal, Mo., 1972-75; from hwy. designer to project devel. engr. Mo. Dept. Transp., Hannibal, 1978—. Geometric design com. Transp. Rsch. Bd., Washington, 1994-97, friend of low volume roads, 1992—. Mem. Chi Epsilon, Tau Beta Pi. Republican. Episcopal. Avocations: reading, quilting, cross stitching. Office: Mo Dept Transp PO Box 1067 Hannibal MO 63401-1067

RICHMOND, DONNA, speech-language pathologist; b. Huntington, W.Va., Aug. 19, 1961; d. Joseph Roy and Marie (Cunningham) Wright; m. David Lawrence Richmond, Nov. 3,1990; children: Jonathan Andrew, Lydia Brooke. BA in Speech-Lang. Pathology, Marshall U., 1983, MA in Comm. Disorders, 1992; postgrad., U. Ky., 1996-98. Lic. in speech pathology, N.C., Ky.; cert. clin. competence, 1994. Speech therapist, itinerant Greenup County Bd. Edn., Greenup, Ky., 1983-84; speech pathologist Lawrence County Bd. Edn., Louisa, Ky., 1984-94; speech pathologist, floater NOVA, Gallipolis, Ohio, 1993-94; speech pathologist Boyd County Bd. Edn., Ashland, Ky., 1994-98; co-lead speech pathologist Orange County Bd. Edn., Hillsborough, N.C., 1998—. Univ. practicum supr. U. N.C., Chapel Hill. Mem. N.C. Speech-Lang. Assn., Ky. Speech-Lang. Assn., Am. Speech-Lang.-Hearing Assn., Coun. for Exceptional Children (profl.). Avocations: reading, crafts. Home: 7 Chartwell Ct Durham NC 27703-3739 Office: Grady Brown Elem Sch 1100 New Grady Brown School Rd Hillsborough NC 27278

RICHMOND, GAIL LEVIN, law educator; b. Gary, Ind., Jan. 9, 1946; d. Herbert Irving and Sylvia Esther (Given) Levin; children: Henry, Amy. AB, U. Mich., 1966, MBA, 1967; JD, Duke U., 1971. Bar: Ohio 1971, U.S. Claims Ct. 1986, U.S. Ct. Mil. Appeals, 1994; CPA, Ill. Acct. Arthur Andersen & Co., Chgo., 1967-68; assoc. Jones, Day, Cleve., 1971-72; asst. prof. Capital U. Law Sch., Columbus, Ohio, 1972-73, U. N.C. Law Sch., Chapel Hill, 1973-78; vis. asst. prof. U. Tex. Law Sch., Austin, 1977-78, Nova U. Law Ctr., Ft. Lauderdale, Fla., 1979-80, assoc. prof., 1980-81, assoc. prof., assoc. dean, 1981-85, prof., assoc. dean., 1985-93, 95—, prof., acting dean, 1993-95. Author: Federal Tax Research, 6th edit., 2002; co-author: Tax Planning for Lifetime and Testamentary Dispositions, 1997; contbr. articles to profl. jours. Pres. Greater Ft. Lauderdale Tax Coun., 1987-88; trustee Law Sch. Admission Coun., 1994-99, chair audit com., 1991-93, chair svcs. and programs com., 1997-99. Mem. ABA (chair commn. on individual income, tax sect. 2001-03, chair AMT Task Force, tax sect. 2003-2004, chair adj. com., legal edn. sect. 2002-), Am. Assn. Atty.-CPAs (dir. Fla. chpt. 1992-98), Assn. Am. Law Schs. (mem. audit com. 1992, chair sect. adminstrn. of law schs. 1996, pres. S.E. chpt. 1993-94, sec. S.E. chpt. 1995-2002), Broward County Women Lawyers Assn., S.E. Assn. Law Schs. (pres. 2002-03). Democrat. Jewish. Avocation: reading. Office: Nova Southeastern U Shepard Broad Law Ctr 3305 College Ave Fort Lauderdale FL 33314-7721

RICHMOND, MARILYN SUSAN, lawyer; b. Bethesda, Md., Oct. 19, 1949; d. Carl Hutchins Jr. and Elizabeth Adeline (Saeger) R. BA with honors, U. Fla., 1971; JD, Georgetown U., 1974. Bar: Md. 1974, D.C. 1975. Atty. Office of Gen. Counsel, FTC, Washington, 1974-77, antitrust atty. Bur. of Competition, 1977-81; counsel, consumer subcom. of com. on commerce, sci. and transp. U.S. Senate, Washington, 1981-85; assoc. Heron, Burchette, Ruckert & Rothwell, Washington, 1985-87, ptnr., 1987-90; dep. asst. sec. for govtl. affairs U.S. Dept. Transp., Washington, 1990-91, acting asst. sec. for govtl. affairs, 1991-92; cons. Raffaelli, Spees, Springer & Smith, Washington, 1993-94; asst. exec. dir. govt. rels. APA Practice Orgn., 1995—. Lectr. Brookings Instn. Ctr. for Pub. Policy Edn., Washington, 1985-88. Active Lawyers for Bush-Quayle, Washington, 1988. Mem. ABA (antitrust, adminstrv. law sect., vice chair transp. industry com. antitrust sect. 1992-99). Republican. Methodist. Avocations: horseback riding, tennis. Home: Apt 601 2725 Connecticut Ave NW Washington DC 20008-5305

RICHMOND, ROCSAN, television and video producer, director, publicist, actress, dancer, inventor, teacher; b. Chgo., Jan. 30; d. Alphonso and Annie Lou (Combest) R.; divorced; 1 child, Tina S. Student, Wilson Jr. Coll., 1963, 2d City Theatre, Chgo., 1969, Alice Liddel Theatre, 1970; cert. fingerprint classifier, L.A. City Coll., 1996. Lic. 3d class radio/tel. operator FCC. Vegetarian editor Aware mag., Chgo., 1977—78; investigative reporter, film critic Chgo. Metro News, 1975—81; prodr., talk show host Sta. WSSD, Chgo., 1980—81; dir. pub. rels. IRMCO Corp., Chgo., 1981—82; pub. rels. agt., newsletter editor Hollywood (Calif.) Reporter newspaper, 1985—86; exec. prodr. Donald Descendent's Prodns., Hollywood, 1983—, Future News, TV show, 1983—86; pres. Richmond Estates; tchr. TV prodn. Profl. Bus. Acad., Hollywood, 1998—2000, founder & prof. Richmond Acad. Fine Manners, 2000—. Jehovah'S Witness. Achievements include invention of invisible drapery tieback. Office: PO Box 665 Los Angeles CA 90078-0665 E-mail: AAAAAToner@aol.com.

RICHMOND-FRANK, SHERRY RAE, marriage and family therapist; b. Beckley, W.Va., Apr. 7, 1953; d. Percy Eugene and Edna Earl Richmond; m. Donald Frederick Frank; 1 child, Jesse Gabrielle Frank. BS, Concord Coll., Athens, W.Va., 1975; MS, Va. Tech., Blacksburg, Va., 1980; postgrad., Harding Grad. Sch., Memphis, 1983—84, U. New Orleans, 1993—94. Lic. profl. counselor, marriage and family therapist, profl. counselor appraisal privileges, nat. cert. counselor. Practicum student, marriage and family therapy intern Meth. Health Sys., Memphis, 1983—85; family therapist St. Vincent's Family Ctr., New Orleans, 1986—87, Richmond-Frank Family, New Orleans, 1987—; counseling intern The McFarland Inst., New Orleans, 1996—97, contract counselor, 1997—2003; sch. counselor Atonement Luth. Sch., Metairie, La., 1998—2002; pres. Creative Growth Counseling and Coaching Inc., Destrehan, La., 2001—. Home econs. educator Elkhorn Jr. H.S., McDowell County, 1975—77; grad. rsch. asst. Va. Tech., Blacksburg, 1977—78; home econs. ext. agt. W.Va. U., Boone County, 1979—81. Mem. parent adv. com. La. State U. Human Devel. Ctr., New Orleans, 1989—90; sch. team chair safe and drug free schs. Atonement Luth. Sch., Metairie, La., 1998—2001. Mem.: ACA, Am. Rehab. Counseling Assn., La. Assn. for Marriage and Family Therapy, La. Assn. Marriage and Family Counselors, La. Counseling Assn., Internat. Assn. Marriage and Family Counselors, Internat. Coach Fedn., Christian Coaches Network, Am. Assn. Christian Counselors, Am. Assn. for Marriage and Family Therapy. Avocations: photography, poetry, cooking. Office: Creative Growth Counseling and Coaching Inc PO Box 1033 Destrehan LA 70047-1033 Office Phone: 504-473-7871. Business E-Mail: creative-growth@cox.net.

RICHSTONE, BEVERLY JUNE, psychologist, writer; b. N.Y.C., June 8, 1952; d. Max and Rosalyn Richstone. BA summa cum laude, Queens Coll., 1975; MEd, U. Miami, 1978; PsyD, Nova U., 1982. Lic. clin. psychologist. Clin. fellow Harvard Med. Sch., 1982-83; staff psychologist Met. State Hosp., Waltham, Mass., 1983-85; asst. attending psychologist McLean Hosp., Belmont, Mass., 1983-84; asst. psychologist Cambridge Hosp./N. Charles Mental Health Rsch./Tng. Found., Cambridge, Mass., 1984-85; assoc. dir. Coastal Geriatric Svcs., Hingham, Mass., 1985-86, Alpha Geriatric Svcs., Hingham, 1986-87; freelance writer Colorado Springs, Colo. Instr. psychology Harvard Med. Sch., Boston, 1983-84; consulting psychologist Coastal Geriatric Svcs., Hingham, 1985. Author: From Harvard to Humility, 2000; contbg. author: The New Our Bodies, Ourselves, 1992, Our Bodies, Ourselves For The New Century, 1998. Mem. APA, Phi Beta Kappa.

RICHTER, HARVENA, retired english literature and creative writing teacher, writer; b. Reading, Pa., Mar. 13, 1919; d. Conrad Michael and Harvena Maria (Achenbach) R. BA, U. N.Mex., 1938; MA, NYU, 1955, PhD, 1967. Advt. copyrighter Saks 5th Ave., N.Y.C., 1942-43, R.H. Macy, N.Y.C., 1944-46; copy chief Elizabeth Arden, N.Y.C., 1946-47; advt. dir. I. Miller, N.Y.C., 1947-48; European corr. various newspapers, 1948-49; lectr. NYU, N.Y.C., 1952-66, U. N.Mex., 1969-89. Author: The Human Shore, 1959, Virginia Woolf: The Inward Voyage, 1970, Writing to Survive: The Private Notebooks of Conrad Richter, 1988, The Yaddo Elegies and Other Poems, 1995, Green Girls, Poems Early and Late, 1996, The Innocent Island, 1999, Frozen Light, the Crystal Poems, 2002, The Golden Fountains, Sources of Energy and Life, 2002, Passage to Teheran, 2004; contbr. poetry to The New Yorker, Chelsea, New Letters, others; short stories to Sat. Eve. Post, New Am., Blue Mesa Rev.; essays to Atlantic, Modern Fiction Studies, C.S. Monitor, others. AAUW fellow, 1964-65; grantee Yaddo, 1963-64, MacDowell Colony, 1965-66, Wurlitzer Found., Taos, N.Mex., 1968, 73-75, Va. Ctr. for Creative Arts, 1983, 85, Ragdale Found., 1990.. Mem. Author's Guild, Virginia Woolf Soc., Kappa Kappa Gamma. Avocation: gardening. Home and Office: 1932 Candelaria Rd NW Albuquerque NM 87107

RICHTER, JANELL JOHNSTON, principal, minister; b. West Point, Miss., Mar. 20, 1945; d. Alvin Lee Johnston and Lola Marie Wheeler; m. James Franklin Richter, Sr., July 14, 1965; children: James Richter, Jr., Janna Faith, Joanna Felicia. AA, Columbus Coll., Ga., 1965; BS, Columbus U., Ga., 1980. Ordained to ministry Pentecostal Ch. of God. Co-owner, bookkeeper Ye Olde Bible Shoppe/Royal Books, Newnan, Ga., 1972—82; state sec.-treas. corp. Pentecostal Ch. of God, Ga., 1974—75, state dir. christian edn., 1983—90, state dir. women's ministries, 1990—2000; asst. pastor Evangel Temple, Morrow, 1995—97; prin. Evangel Temple Christian Acad., Morrow, 1997—2003. Mem. adv. bd. christian edn. Pentecostal Ch. of God, Joplin, Mo., 1985—95, mem. publicity com., 1985—89, mem. ctrl. com. women's ministries, 1990—2000. Editor (mag.): Spirit, 2002—03; contbr. articles to profl. jours. Curriculum com. Clayton Sch. Bd., Clayton County, Ga., 1994; campaign asst. Rep. Party, Clayton County, Ga., 1990. Recipient plaque for svc., Women's Ministry, Ga., 2000. Mem.: Ga. Music Educators Assn. Republican. Pentecostal Ch. Of God. Avocations: reading, writing, music, vocal/keyboard performance. Office: Evangel Temple Christian Acad 2230 Rex Rd Morrow GA 30260

RICHTER, JUDITH ANNE, pharmacology educator; b. Wilmington, Del., Mar. 4, 1942; d. Henry John and Dorothy Madelyn (Schroeder) R. BA, U. Colo., 1964; PhD, Stanford U., 1969. Postdoctoral fellow Cambridge (Eng.) U., 1969-70, U. London, 1970-71; asst. prof. pharmacology Sch. Medicine Ind. U., Indpls., 1971-78, assoc. prof. pharmacology and neurobiology, 1978-84, prof., 1984—. Vis. assoc. prof. U. Ariz. Health Sci. Ctr., Tucson, 1983; mem. biomed. rsch. rev. com. Nat. Inst. on Drug Abuse, 1983-87; Mem. edit. bd. Jour. Neurochemistry, 1982-87; contbr. numerous articles to sci. jours. Scholar Boettcher Found., 1960-64; fellow Wellcome Trust, 1969-71. Mem. AAAS, Am. Soc. for Pharmacology and Exptl. Therapeutics (exec. com. neuropharmacology div. 1989-91), Am. Soc. for Neurochemistry, Internat. Soc. for Neurochemistry, Soc. for Neurosci., Women in Neurosci., Assn. Women in Sci., Phi Beta Kappa, Sigma Xi. Achievements include research in neuropharmacology, especially barbiturates, neurobiology of mutant mice and dopaminergic systems, and regulation of sensory neuron glutamate release. Office: Ind U Sch Medicine 635 Barnhill Dr Indianapolis IN 46202-5126 Office Phone: 317-274-7593. E-mail: jrichter@iupui.edu.

RICHWINE, HEATHER, technology support manager; d. David and Gayle Richwine. BA, U. N.C., 1991. Legis. asst. Office of Congressman Ike Skelton, Washington, 1991-96; spl. asst. Lightspan Partnership, Washington, 1996-97; tech. support mgr. Deloitte Cons. LLC, Washington, 1997—. Vol. Folger Shakespeare Libr., 1997-99. Mem. Jr. League of Washington. Avocations: hiking, reading, languages. Home: 6705B Washington Blvd Arlington VA 22213-1038 Office: Deloitte Cons 555 12th St NW Ste 450 Washington DC 20004-1200

RICKABAUGH, VICKI, horse farm owner, mayor; b. Phila., June 22, 1951; d. William C. and Marilyn Kirschner; m. Charles David Rickabaugh Jr., Sept. 15, 1973; children: Gloria, George, Peggy, Marc. AA, Brookdale C.C., 1981; BS in Edn., Monmouth U., 1972. RN, N.J., state cert. EMT, N.J.; cert. elem. tchr., N.J. Owner, instr. Blue Spruce Horse Farm Dressage Ctr., Jackson, N.J., 1972—; dep. mayor Jackson Twp. (N.J.) Com., 1996, 99, mayor, 1997-98; owner, instr. Blue Spruce Farm Dressage Ctr. Founder, dressage advisor East Coast Regional Dressage Assn., Medford, N.J., 1993—; lectr. in field. Author: (book) Horse Riding for Beginners, 1985; author: (lecture series) Trace and Equine Circle of Needs, 1982—; contbr. articles on dressage and horses to East Coast Regional Dressage Assn. newsletter, 1994—. Bd. dirs. Jackson Twp. Bd. of Edn., 1991-94, v.p., 1992; Rep. committeewoman Ocean County (N.J.) Rep. Orgn., 1995—; committeewoman Jackson Twp. Com., 1996; founder, mem. Jackson Coun. for Arts, 1998—, Tourism and Bus. Coun., Jackson, 1997-99; EMT Jackson Twp. 1st Aid Squad, 1989-95; mem. Jackson Twp. Mcpl. Alliance for Prevention of Alcohol and Drug Abuse, 1995-99. Recipient Proclamation to Mayor Rickabaugh, N.J. Gov. Christine Todd Whitman, N.J. Exec. Dept., Trenton, 1997, Senate and Gen. Assembly Joint Legis. Resolution for disting. svc. State of N.J., 1997, Svc. award Jackson Coun. for Arts, 1998. Mem. Am. Horse Show Assn. (life), U.S. Dressage Fedn. ("L" judge), Ea. States Dressage and Combined Tng. Assn. (life), Pathfinders (founder). Republican. Avocations: horses, tennis, sailing. Home: 5 Stanley Pl Jackson NJ 08527-4454 Fax: 732-833-0255. E-mail: v.rickabaugh@usa.net.

RICKARD, ANNE COLTON, art educator, artist; b. Cleve., Aug. 28, 1960; d. Theodore Joseph and Nancy Braun Colton; m. John David Rickard, June 27, 1987; 1 child, Georgianna. BA, Ohio No. U., 1982; MA in Liberal Studies, SUNY, Plattsburgh, 1988. Cert. art tchr. grades K-12 N.Y. State Edn. Dept., 1982, elem. edn. grades N-6 N.Y. State Edn. Dept., 1982. Hosp. pharmacy technician Albany (N.Y.) Med. Ctr. Hosp., 1982—84; art tchr., dept. chairperson Lake Placid (N.Y.) Mid./H.S., 1984—. Yearbook advisor Lake Placid Mid./H.S., 1988—91, coord. Winter Carnival, 1995—2000. Authored art exposure project for H.S. students Adirondack Pk. Vis. Interpretive Ctr.; vol., fundraiser Skating Club of Lake Placid, 2000—03. Recipient Tchr. Inst. of Contemporary Art, Sch. Art Inst. Chgo., Nat. Endowment of the Arts, 2001; Art Educator's fellow, Maine Coll. Art, 2003. Mem.: Nat. Art Edn. Assn. (assoc.), N.Y. State Art Tchrs. Assn. (assoc.). Home: 21 Holly Hill Rd Lake Placid NY 12946 Office: Lake Placid Middle/High School 250 Main St Lake Placid NY 12946 Personal E-mail: jrickard@adelphia.net.

RICKARD, LISA ANN, lawyer; b. Englewood, N.J., Oct. 22, 1955; d. Joseph Mitchell and Ann Marie (Samen) Moore; m. J. Scott Rickard, June 18, 1977; children: Jack Taylor, Justin Moore. BA in Govt. and French, Lafayette Coll., 1977; JD, Am. U., 1982. Legis. asst. Bank of Am., Washington, 1977-78; spl. asst. and press asst. to Sen. Richard Stone, Washington, 1978-80; legis. asst. to Sen. Frank Murkowski, Washington, 1981; assoc. and ptnr. Akin, Gump, Strauss, Haver & Feld, Washington, 1982-93; v.p. federal affairs Ryder System, Inc., Washington, 1993-97, sr. v.p. govt. affairs, 1997—. Mem., corp. adv. coun. Women's Rsch. and Edn. Inst., Washington, 1991—. Polit. fundraiser various fed. dem. candidates. Diplome D'Etudes Francaises Cours Moyen, Deuxieme Degres, U. Strasbourg, France, 1976. Mem. D.C. Bar Assn. Episcopalian. Avocation: travel. Home: 10112 Darmuid Green Dr Potomac MD 20854-4852 Office: Ryder System Inc 3600 NW 82nd Ave Miami FL 33166-6623

RICKARD, MARGARET LYNN, retired library director; b. Detroit, July 31, 1944; d. Frank Mathias and Betty Louise (Lee) Sieger; m. Cyriac Thannikary, Nov. 13, 1965 (div. Feb. 1973); 1 child, Luke Anthony Thannikary ; m. Marcos T. Perez, Mar. 1973 (dec. Oct. 1973); m. Lui Gotti, Dec. 23, 1984 (dec. Aug. 1997); m. William A. Rickard, Aug. 22, 1998. AB, U. Detroit, 1968; MLS, Pratt Inst., 1969; postgrad., NYU, 1976-77. Cert. libr. N.Y. Sr. libr. Queens Pub. Libr., Jamaica, NY, 1969-77; libr. dir. El Centro (Calif.) Pub. Libr., 1977-99; ret., 1999. Vice chmn., chmn. Serra Coop. Libr. Sys., San Diego, 1980—82, libr. cons., 1998—; county libr./cons. Imperial County Free Libr., 1993—99. Pres. Hist. Site Found., El Centro, 1988—99, 1992, sec., 1989, trustee, 1989—99, v.p., 1991—92; mem. Downton El Centro Assn., mem. arches bus. improvement dist.; mem. comm. and arts task force Imperial County Arts Coun.; coord. arts and culture com. City of El Centro Strategic Plan; fin. sec. St. Elizabeth Luth. Ch., El Centro, 1988. Recipient Disting. Svc. award, El Dorado County ACSA, 2004, El Dorado County Disting. Employee Svc. award, ACSA, 2004; Title IIB fellow, Pratt Inst., 1968—69. Mem.: AAUW (v.p. El Centro 1988), ALA, Calif. County Librs. Assn., Calif. Libr. Assn., Toastmasters, El Centro C. of C., Women of Moose (sr. regent El Centro 1988—89, ednl. advancment chmn. 1999—2000), Soroptomists (life; v.p. El Centro 1978, corr. sec. 1990—91, 1st v.p. 1991—92, pres. 1992—93, 2d v.p. 1995—96, 1998—99, rec. sec. 1997—98). Democrat. Lutheran. Home and Office: 6169 Terrace Dr PO Box 232 Pollock Pines CA 95726

RICKARD, RUTH DAVID, retired history and political science educator; b. Fed. Republic Germany, Feb. 20, 1926; came to U.S., 1940; d. Carl and Alice (Koch) David; m. Robert M. Yaffe, Oct. 1949 (dec. 1959); children: David, Steven; m. Norman G. Rickard, June 1968 (dec. 1988); 1 stepson, Douglas. BS cum laude, Northwestern U., 1947, MA, 1948. Law editor Commerce Clearing House, Chgo., 1948; instr. history U. Ill., Chgo., 1949-51, instr. extension program Waukegan, 1960-67; instr. history Waukegan Schs., 1960-69; original faculty, prof. western civilization, polit. sci. Coll. of Lake County, Grayslake, Ill., 1969-92. Mem. Inter-Univ. Seminar on Armed Forces and Soc.; mem. Hospitality Info. Svc. for Diplomatic Residents and Families affiliate Meridian Internat. Ctr.; spkr. in field. Author: History of College of Lake County, 1987 (honored by city of Waukegan 1987), (poem) I Lost My Wings, 1989, Au Revoir from Emeritusdom, 1993, Where are the Safety Zones, 1994; contbg. author: History of National Press Club: Reliable Sources, 1997; contbr. articles to profl. jours. Mem. Econ. Devel. Com., Waukegan, 1992-93; working with homeless through Samaritans of Greater Washington area, 2000—. Scholar Freedoms Found. Am. Legion, Valley Forge, Pa., 1967. Mem. AAUW (pres. Waukegan chpt. 1955-57, scholarship named for her 1985, program co-chair McLean chpt. 1997-2000), LWV (charter, v.p. Waukegan chpt.), Nat. Press Club D.C., Northwestern U. Alumni Washington (bd. dirs.). Avocations: writing, travel, lecturing, reading, theater.

RICKEL, ANNETTE URSO, psychology and psychiatry researcher, educator; b. Phila.; d. Ralph Francis and Marguerite (Calcaterra) Urso; 1 child, John Ralph Rickel. BA, Mich. State U., 1963; MA, U. Mich., 1965, PhD, 1972, MD, 1972. Lic. psychologist, Mich. Faculty early childhood edn. Merrill-Palmer Inst., Detroit, 1967-69; adj. faculty U. Mich., Ann Arbor, 1969-75; asst. dir. N.E. Guidance Ctr., Detroit, 1972-75; asst. prof. psychology Wayne State U., Detroit, 1975-81; vis. assoc. prof. Columbia U., N.Y.C., 1982-83; assoc. prof. psychology Wayne State U., 1981-87, asst. provost, 1989-91, prof. psychology, 1987-95; Am. Coun. on Edn. fellow Princeton and Rutgers Univs., 1990-91. AAAS and APA Congl. Sci. fellow on Senate Fin. Subcom. on Health and Pres.'s Nat. Health Care Reform Task Force, 1992—93; clin. prof. dept. psychiatry Georgetown U., Washington, 1995—2000; program officer The Rockefeller Found., 2000—03; pres. The Annette Urso Rickel Found., 2003—. Cons. editor Jour. of Cmty. Psychology, Jour. Primary Prevention; co-author: Social and Psychological Problems of Women, 1984, Preventing Maladjustment..., 1987; author: Teenage Pregnancy and Parenting, 1989, Keeping Children From Harm's Way, 1997, Understanding Managed Care, 2000; contbr. articles to profl. jours Mem. Pres.'s Task Force on Nat. Health Care Reform, 1993; bd. dirs. Children's Ctr. of Wayne County, Mich., The Epilepsy Ctr. of Mich., Reading is Fundamental, Nat. Symphony Orch., Chamber Music Soc. of Lincoln Ctr., Soc. Meml. Sloan Kettering Cancer Ctr., The Kellogg Found., 1996-97, The John D. and Catherine T. MacArthur Found., 1998-99. Grantee NIMH, 1976-86, Eloise and Richard Webber Found., 1977-80, McGregor Fund, 1977-78, 82, David M. Whitney Fund, 1982, Katherine Tuck Fund, 1985-90, NIH, 2000; recipient Career Devel. Chair award, 1985-86. Fellow APA (div. pres. 1984-85); mem. Internat. Women's Forum, Soc. for Rsch. in Child Devel., Soc. for Rsch. in Child and Adolescent Psychopathology, Internat. Assn. of Applied Psychologists, Sigma Xi, Psi Chi. Roman Catholic. E-mail: rickelau@aol.com.

RICKERT, JEANNE MARTIN M. lawyer; b. Cambridge, Mass., May 13, 1953; d. Robert Torrence and Margaret (Mutchler) Martin; m. Scott Edwin Rickert, Aug. 19, 1978. BA, Cornell U., 1975; JD, Case Western U., 1978. Bar: Ohio 1980, U.S. Dist. Ct. (no. dist.) Ohio 1980. Law clk. to presiding justice U.S. Dist. Ct. Ohio, Akron, 1978-80; assoc. Jones, Day, Reavis & Pogue, Cleve., 1980-86; ptnr. Jones & Day, Cleve., 1987—. Author: The Limited Liability Company in Ohio: 1994 Senate Bill 74, with Commentary and Practice Pointers, 1994. Mem. Ohio State Bar Assn. (corp. law com. 1985—). Office: Jones Day Reavis & Pogue N Point 901 Lakeside Ave E Cleveland OH 44114-1190

RICKETTS, MARIJANE GNEGY, poet; b. Mountain Lake Park, Md., July 16, 1925; d. Clyde Columbus Gnegy and Zelda Adeline Stemple; m. Aubrey Eugene Ricketts, Apr. 9, 1950; children: Kenneth, Jennifer Riffer. BA, W.Va. Wesleyan Coll., 1947. Sec. to the adminstrv. asst. Landon Sch. for Boys, Bethesda, Md., 1961—62; sec. to the prin. Montgomery County Pub. Schs., Bethesda/Rockville, Md., 1962—87. Pres. and editor The Writers' League of Wash., Washington, 1989—92; nat. contest poetry judge Nat. League of Am. Pen Women, Washington, 2000—00; poetry programs chairwoman Women's Cmty. Club of Kensington, Kensington, Md., 1997—2000; poet for 50th yr. class reunion Alumni, W.Va. Wesleyan Coll., Buchannon, W.Va., 1997—97; leader, Md. poet laureate program Md. Humanities Coun., Annapolis, Md., 2000—00. Author: (book of poetry) Is it the Onions Making Life Pungent?, 1985; editor: (poetry anthology) The Poets of Ellicott Street, 1989; editor: (and publisher) (writer's league 75th year anthology) A Diamond Anthology of Prose and Poetry, 1992. Prodr. poetry programs Montgomery County Pub. Libr., Kensington, Md., 1997—98; prodr., Christmas readings Women's Cmty. Club, Kensington, 1997—2000. Recipient Grand Prize First Ann. Lit. award, Byline Mag., 1986, First Prize for Poetry, D.C. Commn. on the Arts, 1992, First Prize Poetry, Md. Fedn. Women's Clubs, 1997, Grand Prize, Gen. Fedn. Women's Clubs, 1997, First Prize for Poetry, Writer's League of Wash., 1999, 2000, 2003. Mem.: Live Poets Soc., The Poets of Ellicott St. (pres. 1990—91), The Writers' Ctr., Writer's League of Wash. (archivist 1992—2001). Methodist. Avocations: choir, concerts, museums, gardening, collecting art prints. Home: 10203 Clearbrook Pl Kensington MD 20895-4121 Personal E-mail: marijane@ioip.com.

RICKETTS, SONDRA LOU, librarian; b. McFall, Mo., Aug. 4, 1941; d. Jewell E. and Daisie Glenn (Weller) Rainey; m. Rex Errol Ricketts, June 14, 1964; children: Chad Errol, Trina Rae, Neysa Carrie. BS, U. Mo., 1963—. Cert. tchr., Mo. Libr. East Ladue Jr. High Sch., Ladue, Mo., 1963-65; adminstrv. asst. Jacksonville (Ill.) Pub. Libr., 1965; reference libr. Ill. Coll., Jacksonville, 1965-66; cataloger Stephens Coll., Columbia, Mo., 1966-69; libr. Clark (Mo.) Elem. Sch., 1981-95, Middle Grove Elem. Sch., 1996—2003. Sun. sch. tchr. Presbyn. Ch., Columbia, 1977-84; mem. Hallsville (Mo.) Sch. bond com., 1980; cmty. leader Hallsville 4-H, 1980-82, mem. state com., Columbia, 1985, project leader Hallsville 4-H, 1980-85, 94-2000; bd. dirs. 4-H Found., Columbia, 1991—, sec., 1997-2000; mem. Boone County 4-H Auction com., 1994-2000; mem. ways and means com., hallsville PTA, 1980, publicity com., 1981; co-chmn. Hallsville H.S. All Night Sr. party, 1985, 90. Conf. honoree AIJCA, 1991. Mem. Am. Internat. Charolais Assn., Mo. Assn. of Sch. Librs., Mid.-Mo. Regional Assn. Sch. Librs., Mo. Univ. Alumnae Assn., Boone County Alumnae Assn., Alpha Chi Omega Alumni Assn., U. Mo. Jefferson Club, Pi Lambda Theta. Avocations: crafts, swimming, reading. E-mail: rex.ricketts@gte.net.

RICKETTS, VIRGINIA LEE, historian, researcher; b. Jamestown, Kans., Jan. 12, 1925; d. Roy Earl Eastman and Alma Anna Hunter; m. Clair Keith Ricketts, June 3, 1944; children: Keith Alan, Dennis Lee, Donald Gene. Grad. H.S., Filer, Idaho. Clk. dist. ct., auditor, recorder Jerome County, Idaho, 1972-79; pvt. practice historian, rschr. Jerome, 1979—. Mem. Idaho State Hist. Records Adv. Bd., Boise, 1976-2002; pres. Idaho Assn. Recorders and Clks., 1977-78; cons. Idaho State Supreme Ct., Boise, 1979-81; tour dir., instr. Coll. So. Idaho, Twin Falls, 1984-97; mem. Bur. Land Mgmt. Adv. Bd., Shoshone, Idaho, 1989-95, Upper Snake River Ecosystem Adv. Bd., Idaho, 1995-98; Internat. Toastmistress communicator, 1988; lectr. in field. Author: The History of the North Side-The First 75 Years, 1982, Greater Twin Falls Historical Guide, 1988, A History of the Middle Snake River, 1996, Then and Now in Southern Idaho, 1998. Organizer Friends St. Stricker Ranch, Inc., Twin Falls, 1984. Recipient Cert. of Commendation, Am. Assn. for State and Local History, 1984, Cert. of Resolution of Appreciation, Idaho State Bd. Edn., 1998; named Idaho Disting. Citizen, Idaho Statesmen, 1988, Centennial Citizen, Citizens of Jerome County Idaho, 1990. Mem. Idaho State Hist. Soc. (trustee 1987-99, chairperson bd. trustees 1991-98), Oreg. Calif. Trails Assn. (organizer Idaho chpt. 1984, treas. Idaho chpt. 1985-99), Jerome County Hist. Soc., Inc. (co-organizer 1984, former pres., curator 1985-2004), Idaho Assn. of Mus. (Outstanding Svc. award 1998), Soroptomist Internat. of Am. (Woman of Distinction 1999), PEO (chpt. E Idaho, historian 1987-98). Republican. Presbyterian. Avocations: needlework, gardening, sports, family activities. Home: 516 E 300 S Jerome ID 83338-6747

RICKLEFS, DALE LYNNE, library director; b. Chgo., July 29, 1953; d. Glenn Harley and Eleanor Clara Rogers; 1 child, Reyhan. BA, Ill. Wesleyan U., 1974; MLS, U. Tex., 1977. Libr. Radian Corp., Austin, Tex., 1975—80; libr. dir. City of Round Rock, Round Rock, Tex., 1980—. Mem. ex officio Friends Round Rock Pub. Libr., Round Rock, 1983—, Round Rock Pub. Libr. Found., Round Rock, 1991—. Pres. Round Rock Rotary Club, Round Rock, 2000—01, Bus. and Profl. Women's Club, Round Rock, 1983—84; pres United Way Greater Williamson Co., Round Rock, 2003—; mem. bd. dirs. Round Rock Cmty. Choir, 1998—2003; pres. Main St. Quilt Guild, 2002—03; boy scout dist. cub trainer Boy Scouts of Am. Tomahawk Dist., Austin-Georgetown, Tex., 1991—92. Recipient Dist. Cubscouter of Yr., Boy Scouts Am. Tomahawk Dist., Texas, 1992. Mem.: ALA, Texas Mun. League Libr. Dir.'s Divsn. (pres. 1988—89), Tex. Libr. Assn. (chmn. dist. 3 1984—85). Avocations: quilting, machine embroidery, old house renovations, painting. Office: City Round Rock Pub Libr 216 E Main St Round Rock TX 78664 Business E-Mail: dale@round-rock.tx.us.

RICKS, DALLIS DERRICK BIEHL, pianist; b. Columbia, S.C., June 8, 1938; d. Bennie Carlisle and Pearl (Bradshaw) Derrick; m. Robert W. Burgess, Feb. 15, 1958 (div. 1978); children: Donna Ann Burgess Hegeman, Robert Russell; m. Albert George Biehl Jr., Aug. 19, 1978 (dec. 1989); m. Griffith M. Ricks, Oct. 30, 1991 (dec. 1999); 1 stepchild, Stephen M. Pvt. studies with, Dr. Parker, 1955-56; student, Am. Savs. and Loan Inst., 1970-71; Cert. in Piano, Major Conservator of Music, 1955. With S.C. Nat. Bank, Columbia, 1956-59, First Nat. Bank, Columbia, 1959—65, Standard Savs. & Loan, Columbia, 1970-72, State of S.C., Columbia, 1978-82, State of Fla., Palm Beach, 1988—. Boca Raton (Fla.) Welcome Wagon Club, 1984—. Mem. Nottingham Garden Club, Beta Sigma Phi (v.p. Columbia chpt. 1962-69). Republican. Lutheran. Home: 74 Vista Del Rio Boynton Beach FL 33426-8829

RICKS, JOYCIA CAMILLA, retired lawyer; b. Atlanta, Feb. 17, 1949; d. George Palmer and Johnnie Mae (Ricks) Redd. BBA, Albany State Coll., 1971; MS, Ga. State U., 1977; JD, Woodrow Wilson Coll. Law, Atlanta, 1979, LLM, 1987. Bar: Ga. 1979, US Dist. Ct. (no. dist.) Ga. 1979, US Ct. Appeals (5th cir.) 1979. Acctg. clk. Gulf Oil Corp., Atlanta, 1971; clk. EEOC, Atlanta, 1971-73, paralegal specialist, 1973-79, investigator, 1979-91, supervisory investigator, 1992-2000; complaints mgr. CDC, Atlanta, 2000—03; gen. counsel Albany State Coll. Alumni Assn., 1986-90. Mem. NAACP, Atlanta, 1983—. Recipient Presdl. citation award Equal Opportunity in Higher Edn., Washington, 1981, Spl. Achievement award EEOC, Atlanta, 1982-84, 86-89, Employee of Yr., Atlanta Dist. Office, 1997; Woman of the Yr.: Tara chpt. 1985, 1991, Atlanta Peach Chpt., 2003. Mem. ABA, Atlanta Bar Assn., Ga. Assn. Black Women Attys., Albany State Coll. Alumni Assn. (pres. Atlanta chpt. 1983-85, gen. counsel 1986-90), ATLA, Ga. State U. Alumni Assn., Woodrow Wilson Coll. Law Alumni Assn., Women of the Ch. Presbyn. (hon. life), Am. Bus. Women's Assn. (Woman of Yr., Tara chpt. 1985, 91), Spreading Oak Cmty. Club. Democrat. Presbyterian.

RICO, STEPHANIE ALLCOCK, art educator; b. Washington, Oct. 25, 1955; d. Harry M. and Ann Orlosky Allcock; m. Vincent F. Rico, Sept. 17, 1983; children: Cara Ann, Gianna Ann. BA, U. Md., 1979. Freelance muralist Stephanie Rico Fine Art, Silver Spring, Md., 1978—; visual art educator Studio in the Glen, Montgomery County, Md., 1979—, Montgomery County (Md.) Schs., 1994—. Pres., founder Art Horizons, Brookeville, Md., 1993—; art cons. Miles and Stockbridge, Wash., DC, 1994—2000; advisor, cons. Montgomery County (Md.) Schs., 2000—; bd. dirs. Huntingridge, Brookeville, Md., 2001. Author: (book) Art Horizons American Art, 1997. Mem. Worth Ea. Montgomery County (Md.) Polit. Action Com., 2000—. Mem.: Nat. Assn. Cath. Tchrs., Nat. Mus. for Women in the Arts, Phi Kappa Phi. Avocations: painting, sculpting, photography, gardening. Office: Art Horizons Studio in the Glen 21309 Ridgecroft Dr Brookeville MD 20833 E-mail: arthorizons@comcast.net.

RICO, SUZANNE, newscaster; BA in mass comm., UCLA; MA in broadcast comm., San Francisco State U. Reporter WLS-TV, Chicago, KABC, Los Angeles; anchor, reporter NBC, San Diego, 2000—02; co-anchor, CBS 2 News at 5, 6 and 11pm KCBS, Los Angeles, 2002—. Reporter Olympic Winter Games, Salt Lake City. Contbr. & mem. Muscular Dystrophy Assn.; mem. Los Angeles Mentoring Connection. Office: CBS 2 News 6121 Sunset Blvd Los Angeles CA 90028*

RICORD, KATHY, diversified financial services company executive; Grad., Denison U.; degree in City and Regional Planning and Bus. Adminstrn., Ohio State U. With Nationwide Mutual Ins. Co., 1986—, asst. to CEO, 1997—99, sr. v.p. mktg. and strategy, 2002—03, exec. v.p., chief mktg. officer, 2003—. Office: Nationwide Mutual Ins Co One Nationwide Plaza Columbus OH 43215-2220*

RIDDERHEIM, MARY MARGARET, psychotherapist; b. Chillicothe, Ohio, Mar. 13, 1946; d. Marion Othello and Esther Marie (Justice) Park; m. Denson Coy Pate, Jr., Dec. 19, 1965 (dec. Mar., 1990); children: Elizabeth Jewel, Mary Kathryn, Melissa Fay; m. David Sigfreid Ridderheim, Jr., Oct 19, 1991; stepchildren: Cheryl, Carla, Katie, Kris, David, Joe. BS in Psychology, W. Tex. A&M, Canyon, 1988; MS in Psychology, St. Francis Coll., Fort Wayne, Ind., 1991; postgrad studies in Psychology, Adler Sch. Profl. Psychology, Chgo., 1992-96. Lic. mental health counselor, Fort Wayne, Ind., 1996—; therapist Barry and Barry, Fort Wayne, 1996-98; ind. contractor therapist Luth. Social Svcs., Fort Wayne, 1998—2002. Program dir. After Sch. Activities Forest Hills Sch. Dist., Cin., 1972-74, New Richmond Exempted Sch. Dist., 1973-75; initiator Young Authors Program, New Richmond Sch. Dist., 1976; outpatient svcs. counselor Charter Beacon Hosp., Fort Wayne, 1994-95. Mem. APA, Am. Counseling Assn., Am. Assn. Christian Counselors, Stepfamily Assn. Am. (pres. Ind. chpt.), Ind. Counselors Assn., Alcohol and Drug Abuse, No. Am. Soc. Adlerian Psychology. Home and Office: 12117 Chesterbrook Ct Fort Wayne IN 46845-1965

RIDDIFORD, LYNN MOORHEAD, zoologist, educator; b. Knoxville, Tenn., Oct. 18, 1936; d. James Eli and Virginia Amalia (Berry) Moorhead; m. Alan William Riddiford, June 20, 1959 (div. Jan. 1966); m. James William Truman, July 28, 1970. AB magna cum laude, Radcliffe Coll., 1958; PhD, Cornell U., 1961. Rsch. fellow in biology Harvard U., Cambridge, Mass., 1961-63, 65-66, asst. prof. biology, 1966-71, assoc. prof., 1971-73; instr. biology Wellesley (Mass.) Coll., 1963-65; assoc. prof. zoology U. Wash., Seattle, 1973—75, prof. biology, 1975—2003. Mem. study sect. tropical medicine and parasitology NIH, Bethesda, Md., 1974—78, 1997; mem. Competitive Grants panel USDA, Arlington, Va., 1979, 89, 95; mem. regulatory biology panel NSF, Washington, 1984—88, Washington, 2001; mem. governing coun. Internat. Ctr. for Insect Physiology and Ecology, 1985—91, chmn. program com., 1989—91; chmn. adv. com. SeriBiotech, Bangalore, India, 1989; mem. biol. adv. com. NSF, 1992—95. Contbr. articles to profl. jours. Bd. dirs. Entomol. Found., 1998—2001, Whitney Lab., 2000—04. Recipient Gregor J. Mendel award, Czech Republic Acad. Scis., 1998; fellow, NSF, 1958—63, John S. Guggenheim Found., 1979—80, NIH, 1986—87; grantee, NSF, 1964—, NIH, 1975—, Rockefeller Found., 1970—79, USDA, 1978—82, 1989—. Fellow: AAAS, Entomol. Soc. Am. (Recognition award in insect physiology, biochemistry and toxicology), Royal Entomol. Soc., Am. Acad. Arts and Sci.; mem.: Soc. Devel. Biology, Am. Soc. Cell Biology, Am. Soc. Biochem. and Molecular Biology, Soc. Integrative and Comparative Biology (pres. 1991). Methodist. Home: 16324 51st Ave SE Bothell WA 98012-6138 Office: U Wash Dept Biology PO Box 351800 Seattle WA 98195-1800 E-mail: lmr@u.washington.edu.

RIDDLE, ANNA LEE, retired elementary school educator, retired music educator; b. Washington, Pa., Jan. 19, 1933; d. Don Elliott and Carrie Mae Porter; m. Richard Dean Riddle, Dec. 28, 1954; children: Richard Dean Riddle II, Robert Eliott, Lee Ann Riddle-Fink. MusB, W.Va. U., 1954. Cert. advanced profl. music Md. Dept. Edn. Music tchr. Monongalia County Schs., Morgantown, W.Va., 1954—55; choir dir. First Presbyn. Ch., Elyria, Ohio, 1958—67, Presbyn. Ch. Atonement, Silver Springs, Md., 1968—82; music tchr. Montgomery County Pub. Schs., Rockville, Md., 1970—95; choir dir. First Presbyn. Ch., Weston, W.Va., 1998—. Chmn., founder

Montgomery County Elem. Honors Chorus, Rockville, 1984—95. Sec. Garden Club, Weston, 1998—2001; pres. AAUW, Weston, 1999—2001, Federated Club, Weston, 2000—01; vol. Hosp. Aux., 1998—. Named Md. Music Tchr. of Yr., Md. Music Educators Nat. Conf., 1992. Mem.: DAR, Order Ea. Star. Republican. Presbyterian. Avocations: sewing, ceramics, swimming. Home: 324 E 7th St Weston WV 26452

RIDDLE, AUDREY MAXWELL, healthcare administrator; b. Wilmington, Del., Sept. 2, 1957; d. Richard Lee and Dorothy Jean (Bass) M.; m. Jeffrey W. Riddle; children: Curtis Maxwell Frey, Emily Rose Frey. BS in Edn. with honors, U. Del., 1979; postgrad., Del. Tech. and Community Coll., 1984-85; MBA, Widener U., 1991. Cert. tchr., Del., 1980. Tchr. New Castle County Sch. Dist., Wilmington, Del., 1979-81; pvt. practice as editor New Castle, Del., 1981-83; asst. office mgr. VVM, Inc., Claymont, Del., 1983-86; mktg. coord. Enterprise Pub., Inc., Wilmington, 1986-88; supr. of edn. Alfred I. duPont Hosp. for Children, Wilmington, 1988-90, asst. to rsch. dir., 1990-91, asst. dir. rsch., 1991-96, adminstrv. coord. external programs, 1996-98, area mgr., 1998-99, adminstrv. dir. rsch., 1999-00, asst. adminstr. rsch., 2000—. Cons. Enterprise Pub., Inc., Wilmington, 1988—89. Editor: The Golden Mailbox, 1988; asst. editor: First State Woman, 1988—91; prodn. editor Capitalism for Kids, 1987 (Phila. Book Show award, 1987); tech. reviewer: Pediatric References, 1990—95; mem. editl. bd. Frontiers of Health Svcs. Mgmt., 2001—; contbr. articles to profl. jours. Vol. Girl Scouts Am., Claymont, Del., 1990-95; tchr. St. Paul's United Meth. Ch., Wilmington, Del., 1981-92. Mem. NAFE, Nat. Fedn. Bus. and Profl. Women (pres. 1991-92, sec. 1987-89, Young Careerist award 1989), Am. Coll. Healthcare Execs. (cert. 1998), Kappa Delta Pi. Republican. Baptist. Avocations: antique collecting, reading, decorative arts, outdoor activities. Office: Alfred I DuPont Hosp for Children PO Box 269 Wilmington DE 19899-0269 E-mail: amriddle@nemours.org.

RIDDLE, CLAUDINE, real estate company executive; b. Gatesville, Tex., Apr. 22, 1920; d. James Franklen and Jessie Lavada (Dossay) Maxwell; children: Dicky Joe, Linda Lue Dorran. Grad., Greeley Sch. Bus., 1962, N.Mex. Real Estate Inst., 1970; PhD in Bus. (hon.), Bapt. Christian Coll., 1986. Lic. real estate broker N.Mex. Real Estate Commn. Sec. Sch. Supt., Plains, Tex., 1944—46; libr., purchasing agt. Plains Sch. Dist., 1947—48; operator Riverton (Wyo.) Hosp., 1956; sec. Sch. and County Adminstrn., Farmington, N.Mex., 1960—68; attendance officer Farmington H.S., 1969; broker, owner Claudine's Real Estate, Farmington, 1970—. Founder Redcoats Farmington C. of C., 1974; founding bd. mem. Casa Amego's Halfway House, Farmington, 1982; founder, designer Totah Festival, 1988; mem. new campus com. Diné Coll., Shiprock, N.Mex., 1995—2002; bd. dirs. San Juan County Econ. Devel., Farmington, 1997—2003, Farmington Intertribal Indian Orgn., 2003—. Named Outstanding Assoc. Builder of Yr., State N.Mex., 1979, Women of Yr., 4 Corners Conf. for Women, 1985, Gov. N.Mex., 1986. Mem.: Elks Club, Order Ea. Star. Democrat. Baptist. Avocations: reading, current affairs, gardening, walking. Home: 510 E Comanche Farmington NM 87401 Office: Claudines Real Estate 216 N Auburn Farmington NM 87401

RIDDLE, ELSIE KATHLEEN, elementary school educator, school librarian; b. Phila., Apr. 11, 1939; d. Pervie Olivet and Marian Grasso Riddle. AA, San Jose City Coll., 1961; BA in Edn., San Jose State U., 1966, MLS, 1974; postgrad., Santa Clara U., 1970—97. Cert. elem. tchr. Calif., secondary tchr. Calif., libr. Libr. grades K-6 Sunnyvale Elem. Sch. Dist., Calif., 1966—72, elem. tchr., 1972—98. Tchr. remedial reading Cherry Chase Elem. Sch., Sunnyvale, 1999—2002. Active Triton Mus. Art, Cupertino Sr. Ctr., Santa Clara Sr. Ctr., Nat. Mus. Women in the Arts, Sunnyvale Hist. Assn., Orchard Gardens; mem. vocal music choir Golden Tones, Santa Clara County Reading Coun., Saratoga Hist. Mus. Mem.: AAUW, PTA, NEA, Assn. of Am. Ret. Persons, Sunnyvale Edn. Assn., Calif. Tchr. Assn., Calif. Libr. Assn., Calif. Ret. Tchrs. Assn. (life mem.), San Jose State U. Alumni Assn., Lions Club, Elks, Alpha Delta Kappa. Democrat. Avocations: gardening, reading, travel, hiking, art.

RIDDLE, SUE DORSEY, primary school educator; b. Opp, Ala., June 6, 1951; d. Robert C. and Dorothy S. Dorsey; m. Chase Y. Riddle, July 8, 1972; children: Katie Riddle Hallman, Chad, Rob, Mark. BS in Elem., M in Elem., M in Early Childhood, Troy State U.; adminstrv. cert., Ala. State U. Tchr. Autaugg County, Prattville, Ala.; curriculum specialist Prattville Kindergarten, intervention tchr. Ala. Reading Initiative trainer Ala. Dept. Edn., Ala. math., sci. and tech. trainer; cons. Inservice Regional Ctrs., Ala. Dir. Autauga County Jr. Miss Program, Ala.; chmn. Cotton Cotillion Social Orgn., Ala.; curriculum coord. children's programs First United Meth. Grantee Bright Idea grant, Ala. Electric Cooperative, Autauga County. Mem.: ASCD, Autauga County Reading Coun. (leadership team), Nat. Coun. Tchrs. Math., Internat. Reading Assn., Kappa Kappa Iota (pres. Eta chpt. 1994—95). Office: Prattville Kindergarten 338 First St Prattville AL 36067

RIDDOCH, HILDA JOHNSON, accountant; b. Salt Lake City, July 25, 1923; d. John and Ivy Amia (Wallis) Johnson; m. Leland Asa Riddoch, Nov. 22, 1942 (dec.); children: Ivy Lee (dec.), Leland Mark. Vocal student, Ben Henry Smith, Seattle; student, Art Instrn. Schs. Sales clk., marking room and sec. dist. office Sears, Seattle, 1940-42; with billing dept., receptionist C.M. Lovsted & Co., Inc., Seattle, 1942-51; acct., exec. sec. Viking Equipment Co., Inc., Seattle, 1951-54; acct., office mgr. Charles Waynor Collection Agy., Seattle, 1955-57, Argus Mag., Seattle, 1962-67; acct. Law Offices Krutch, Lindell, Donnelly, Dempsey & Lageschulte, Seattle, 1967-72, Law Offices Sindell, Haley, Estep, et al, Seattle, 1972-77; co-founder, acct. Bus. Svc., Inc. and Diversified Design & Mktg., Fed. Way, Auburn & Orting, Wash., 1975-96; co-founder L & H Advt. and Distbg. Co., Wash., 1992-96. Sec.-treas., dir. Jim Evans Realty Inc., Seattle, 1973-87; agt. Wise Island Water Co., P.U.D., Wise Island, B.C., 1973-88, Estate Executrix, Seattle, 1987-96; exec. sec., acct. Cougar Mountain Assn. Ltd. Partnership, 1964-78. Author: Ticking Time on a Metronome, 1989-90, Beloved Miss Ivy, 1996-97, Siegfield, Earth Angel; writer, dir. hist. video Presidents of Relief Society Thru Ages; writer epic poetry; writer, dir. teenager activation video, 1984; pub., editor Extended Family Newsletter, 1983-96. Dir. speech and drama LDS Ch., 1983-88; ward pres. young women's orgn.; mem. ward and stake choirs, 1963-85; stake genealogy libr., Fed. Way, 1983-85; ward and stake newsletter editor various areas, West Seattle, Seattle, Renton, Auburn, Wash., 1950-90; 1st counselor in presidency, tchr. various courses Ladies' Relief Soc. Orgn., 1965-96; co-dir., organizer 1st Silver Saints Group, 1990-92; interviewer LDS Ch. Employment Svcs., 1992-93; co-resident mgr. Mountain View Estates, Orting, Wash., 1994-96. Recipient Letter of Recognition Howard W. Hunter, Pres. LDS Ch. Mem. NAFE. Avocations: needlework, oil painting, writing, singing, speech and drama. Home: 464 Lariat Cir Idaho Falls ID 83404-7173

RIDE, SALLY KRISTEN, physics educator, scientist, former astronaut; b. L.A., May 26, 1951; d. Dale Burdell and Carol Joyce (Anderson) R.; m. Steven Alan Hawley, July 26, 1982 (div.). BA in English, BS in Physics, Stanford U., 1973, PhD in Physics, 1978. Teaching asst. Stanford U., Palo Alto, Calif., researcher dept. physics; astronaut candidate, trainee NASA, 1978-79, astronaut, 1979-87, on-orbit capsule communicator STS-2 mission Johnson Space Ctr., on-orbit capsule communicator STS-3 mission, mission specialist STS-7, 1983, mission specialist STS-41G, 1984; sci. fellow Stanford (Calif.) U., 1987-89; dir. Calif. Space Inst. of U. Calif. San Diego, La Jolla, 1989-96, pres. space com., 1999-2000; prof. Physics U. Calif. San Diego, La Jolla, 1989—; pres., CEO Imaginary Lines, Inc., 2001—. Mem. Presdl. Commn. on Space Shuttle, 1986, Presdl. Com. of Advisors on Sci. and Tech., 1994—. Author: (with Susan Okie) To Space and Back, 1986, (with T.O'Shaughnessy) Voyager: An Adventure to the Edge of the Solar System, 1992, The Third Planet: Exploring the Earth From Space, 1994, The Mystery of Mars, 1999, Exploring our Solar System, 2003. Office: U Calif San Diego Calif Space Inst 0426 La Jolla CA 92093-0426

RIDELL, CAROL ANNE, reporter; married. BA, Tufts U.; MS in Joournalism, Northwestern U., Evanston, Ill. Reporter WMAQ-TV, Chgo., 1989—92; reporter, host, anchor New York 1 News, N.Y.C., 1992—96; reporter education and children specialist NewsChannel4 NBC, N.Y. C., 1996—. Named N.Y. Cub Reporter of Yr., N.Y. Press Club, 1993, runner -up for Gold Typewrier award; recipient Outstanding Hard News story award, N.Y. State Broadcasters, 2001, Nat. award, Edn. Writers Assn. . Office: NBC 30 Rockefeller Plz New York NY 10112

RIDENHOUR, MARILYN HOUSEL, accountant, consultant; b. Madison, Nebr., July 12, 1931; d. Kenneth Virgil Housel and Edna Christina Reese Housel; m. Henry Clifton Ridenhour, Apr. 25, 1954 (dec.); children: Keith James, Susan Marie Ridenhour Redelfs, Jill Housel Ridenhour Cortese. Student, Nebr. Wesleyan U., 1949—50; BS in Bus. Adminstrn. with distinction, U. Nebr., 1953. CPA Mo., 1957. CPA Price Waterhouse & Co., St. Louis, 1953—54, Adolph Kahn, St. Louis, 1954—57; ptnr., CPA Adolph Kahn & Co., St. Louis, 1957—61, Kahn, Ridenhour & Co., St. Louis, 1961—65, Ridenhour Hylton & Co., St. Louis, 1965—91; cons. Baird Kurtz & Dobson, St. Louis, 1991—92. Mem.: Am. Women's Soc. CPA, Am. Soc. Women Accts. (charter pres.), Dawn Hope Soc., Century Soc., Nat. Law Enforcement (founding mem.), Soaring Eagle, St. Labre Indian Sch. Ednl. Assn., U. Nebr. Alumni Assn., Chancellors Club U. Nebr., Beta Gamma Sigma, Phi Chi Theta, Alpha Lambda Delta, Delta Delta Delta. Methodist. Home: 2043 Kehrs Mill Rd Chesterfield MO 63005

RIDENOUR, JOEY, medical association administrator, operations research specialist; BSc in Nursing, Ariz. State U.; MN, U. Phoenix. RN Ariz. COO Maricopa Health Sys., Phoenix, 1975—95; exec. dir. Ariz. State Bd. Nursing, 1995—98; pres. Nat. Coun. State Bds. of Nursing, Chgo., 1998; exec dir Ariz State bd of nursing. Pres. Ariz. State Bd. Nursing, Phoenix, 1986—89, 1994—95; adj. faculty Ariz. State U. Recipient Disting. Achievement award, Am. Soc. Pub. Adminstrn., Ariz. State U. Coll. Nursing, U. Phoenix; fellow, Wharton. Office: Ariz State Bd of Nursing 1651 E Morten Ste 210 Phoenix AZ 85020-4613

RIDEOUT, PATRICIA IRENE, operatic, oratorio and concert singer; b. St. John, N.B., Can., Mar. 16, 1931; d. Eric Aubrey and Florence May (Chase) R.; m. Rolf Edmund Dissmann, Sept. 3, 1955 (dec. 1975); m. Leonard R. Rosenberg, May 25, 1987. Ed., U. Toronto Opera Sch., Royal Conservatory Music, 1952-55. Tchr. voice Queen's U., Kingston, Ont., 1980-86, Royal Conservatory Music, Toronto, 1980-91. Singer Can. Opera Co., Toronto, 1954-85, leading roles in operas, Stratford, Ont., Vancouver, B.C., Guelph, Ont., 1956-85, CBC, 1958-90. Mem. Actors Equity Assn., Assn. Radio and TV Artists, Toronto Heliconian Club. Unitarian Universalist.

RIDER, FAE B. freelance writer; b. Summit Point, Utah, Mar. 1, 1932; d. Lee Collingwood and Jessie (Hammond) Blackett; m. David N. Rider, Jan. 26, 1952; children: David Lee, Lawrence Eugene. BS, No. Ariz. U., 1971, MA, 1974; postgrad., U. Nev., Las Vegas, 1985-88. Lic. tchr. in elem., reading, spl. edn. Learning specialist, Las Vegas, summers 1974-76; tchr. kindergarten Indian Springs (Nev.) Pub. Schs., 1971-76; reading tchr. Las Vegas Pub. Schs., 1976 80; curriculum coord. Indian Springs Pub. Schs., 1980-91; tchr. 1st grade Las Vegas Pub. Schs., 1991-92, reading specialist, 1992-93; pvt. edn./reading cons. Las Vegas, 1993—. Author booklet: Door to Learning - A Non-Graded Approach, 1978. Bd. dirs. Jade Park, Las Vegas, 1988. Recipient Excellence in Edn. award, 1988, Outstanding Sch.and Cmty. Svc. award, 1990. Mem. Internat. Reading Assn., Ret. Tchrs. Assn., Am. Legion Aux., A.R.E study group, Delta Kappa Gamma (pres., Rose of Recognition), Kappa Delta Phi. Avocations: reading, writing, travel.

RIDER, KATHLEEN MARY, dietician; b. Bronx, N.Y., Mar. 21, 1953; d. William Anthony and Elizabeth Catherine (Gavin) Browne; m. David York Rider, Oct. 15, 1983; children: Kathleen M., Colleen M., David Y., Elizabeth A., Erin M. AAS, Maria Coll., 1976; BS, Empire State Coll., 1978; M of Profl. Studies, SUNY, New Paltz, 1982; cert. alternative & complimentary health, Marist Coll., 1999. Cert. dietitian/nutritionist, N.Y. Food svc. dir./dietitian Lovely Hill Nursing Home, Pawling, N.Y., 1979-81; adminstrv. dietitian Hudson River Psychiat. Ctr., Poughkeepsie, N.Y., 1981-82; cmty. svc. dietitian Wassaic (N.Y.) Developmental Ctr., 1982-83; ind. cons. dietitian, 1981—. Cons. Hudson Haven Health Care Ctr., Bapt. Home, Hospice Inc., Greystone Inc., Mountainview Cafe Nursing Ctr., Assn. for Retarded Citizens, Dutchess Ulster and Orange Counties, Home Care, Alcohol Rehab. Ctr., various other orgns.; advisor Mid Hudson Food Svc. Mgrs. Assn., Poughkeepsie. Vol. nutrition educator area parochial schs., Dutchess County, 1996; instr. religious edn. St. Peter's Ch., Poughkeepsie, 1981-84; team mem. engaged encounter Cath. Engaged Encounter, Dutchess County, 1986-89. Soroptomist scholar, Schenectady, N.Y., 1976. Fellow Am. Dietetic Assn., del. 1999, Flora Wishart Davies Meml. award for Outstanding Caregiver 1994, Outstanding Svc. award); mem. Am. Assn. Diabetes Educators, N.Y. State Dietetic Assn. (state profl. recruitment coord. 1976—, scholar 1976), Mid Hudson Dietetic Assn. (pres. 1992-94). Democrat. Home and Office: 13 Edna Dr Hyde Park NY 12538-2939

RIDGEWAY, JOHANNA BOHACEK, language educator; d. Karel and Luise G. Bohacek; m. Don Ridgeway; children: Eva A. May, Paul C. BA in Russian, Vassar Coll., 1955; MA in History, N.C. State U., 1972. Cert. grad. tchr., supervisory cert. Part-time instr. U. Richmond, 1965—67; adminstr., tchr. ESL Wake County Pub. Schs., Raleigh, 1980—. Mem. Raleigh Planning Commn., 1980—88. Mem.: UNA, League Women Voters, Phi Kappa Phi (award 1972), Phi Beta Kappa (award 1954). Democrat. Office: Wake Co Pub Schs Daniels MS 2816 Oberlin Rd Raleigh NC 27608

RIDGEWAY, LUANN, state legislator; m. Richard Ridgeway. Student, Am. U., 1977; BA in History and Polit. Sci., Westminster Coll., 1978; student, Oxford (Eng.) U., 1978; JD, U. Mo., 1981. Mem. Mo. State Ho. of Reps. Dist. 35, 1992—. Mem. criminal law com., judiciary com., urban affairs com., chldn., youth and families com., civil and administrv. law com., joint com. on administrv. rules. Mem. Mo. Bar Assn. Home: 19405 Platte County Line Rd Smithville MO 64089-8798 Office: Mo Ho of Reps State Capitol Building Jefferson City MO 65101-1556

RIDGWAY, DELISSA ANNE, lawyer; b. Kirksville, Mo., June 28, 1955; d. Kenneth Driggs and Margaret Anne (Warner) R. BA, U. Mo., 1975, postgrad., 1976; JD, Northeastern U., 1979. Bar: D.C. Ct. Appeals 1979, U.S Dist. Ct. D.C. 1980, U.S. Ct. Appeals (D.C. cir.) 1980, U.S. Supreme Ct. 1983, U.S. Ct. Appeals (1st cir.) 1988. Law clk. to presiding justice U.S. Dist. Ct. D.C., Washington, 1979; assoc. Shaw, Pittman, Potts & Trowbridge, Washington, 1979-88, counsel, 1988—. Lectr. nuclear and environ. law to various orgns. Mem. Women's Legal Def. Fund. Hardin-Craig fellow U. Mo., Columbia, 1974. Mem. ABA, Women's Bar Assn. (sec. 1989-90), Fed. Bar Assn. (chair adminstrv. law sect. com. agy. adjudication 1985-89, chair adminstrv. law sect. com. regulatory reform 1984-85). Roman Catholic. Office: Shaw Pittman Potts & Trowbridge 2300 N St NW Fl 5 Washington DC 20037-1172

RIDGWAY, ROZANNE LEJEANNE, retired diplomat; b. St. Paul, Aug. 22, 1935; d. H. Clay and Ethel Rozanne (Cote) R.; m. Theodore E. Deming. BA, Hamline U., 1957, LLD (hon.), 1978, George Washington U., 1986, Elizabethtown Coll., 1990, U. Helsinki, 1992; LLD in Pub. Svc. (hon.), Coll. of William and Mary, 1994; DHL (hon.), Hood Coll., 1994; LLD (hon.), Albright Coll.; DHL in Pub. Adminstrn. (hon.), The Citadel, 2003; DHL (hon.), Ill. Coll., 2003. Career diplomat U.S. Fgn. Svc., 1957-89, amb. at large for oceans and fisheries, 1975-77; amb. to Finland, 1977-80; counselor of Dept. State, 1980-81, spl. asst. to sec. state, 1981, amb. to German Dem. Republic, 1982-85, asst. sec. state Europe and Can., 1985-89; pres. Atlantic Coun. U.S., 1989-92, co-chmn., 1993-96; chmn. Baltic-Am. Enterprise Fund, Washington, 1994—. Bd. dirs. 3M Corp., Emerson Electric Co., The Boeing Corp., Sara Lee Corp., Manpower, Inc., Nat. Geog. Soc., New Perspective Fund. Trustee Hamline U.; bd. dirs. Ctr. for Naval Analyses. Decorated Grand Cross Order of the Lion (Finland); recipient Profl. awards Dept. State, Presdl. Disting. Performance awards, Joseph C. Wilson Internat. Rels. Achievement award, 1982, Sharansky award Union Couns. Soviet Jewry, 1989, U.S. Presdl. Citizens medal, 1989; named Person of Yr. Nat. Fisheries Inst., 1977, Knight Comdr., Order of Merit, Germany; inducted into Nat. Women's Hall of Fame, 1998. Fellow Nat. Acad. Pub. Adminstrn.; mem. Am. Acad. Diplomacy, Met. Club, Army-Navy Country Club. Fax: 703-527-3862.

RIDLEY, ANDREW JEAN, small business owner; b. Tifton, Ga., Apr. 27, 1943; d. Andrew Ridley and Idella (James) Rivers; m. John Columbus Neeley, July 7, 1958 (dec. Jan. 1969); children: Brenda Denise, Sonja Lucille, Cassandra, Jeffery. AA, Wayne County C.C., Detroit, 1976; cert., Madonna Coll., Livonia, Mich., 1976; BA, Wayne State U., 1984; student, Meharry Allied Health Ctr., Detroit, 1988. Cert. real estate broker. Spl. svc. worker State of Mich. Social Svc., Detroit, 1976-78; med. surg. asst. Allied Med. Ctr., Detroit, 1980-84; supr. U.S. Maintenance, Oak Park, Mich., 1985-86; dept. head med. records Detroit Med. Group, 1988-90; office mgr., receptionist Family Med. Clinic, Detroit, 1990-93; CEO Andrea's & Vernell Inc., Detroit, 1996—. Mem. adv. bd., pers. dir. Jefferson & Chalmars, Detroit, 1978-80; mem. adv. bd. cmty. rels. Detroit Pub. Schs., 1980-84; sec. adv. bd. Detroit Bd. Edn. Truency, 1980-84; dir. parents and cmty. coun. Detroit Bd. Edn., 1977-85. Contbr. articles to profl. jours. Asst. sec., resolution vice chair 13th Congl. Dem. Dist., Detroit, 1977-82, co-founder, chairperson cmty. grievence com. Jefferson & Chalmers, Detroit, 1982-84; sec. precinct coun. 13th Congl. Dem. Dist., Detroit, 1984-86; coord. mother's enrichment program City of Detroit, 1982-86; hon. mem. Am. Biog. Rsch. Bd. Advisors, 1996—. Recipient Outstanding Achievement award Jefferson & Chalmers Citizen Dist. Coun. Detroit, 1977, Outstanding Cmty. Svc. award N.E. Guidance Ctr. Mental Health, Detoirt, 1978, Outstanding Svc. award 13th Congl. Dm. Dist., Detroit, 1987-88; named Detroit Afro-Am. Leader Detroit Pub. Sch./Outstanding Volumteerism, 1981-84. Avocations: golf, dance, cooking, travel, recreation. Office: Andrea's & Vernell Inc 3929 Field St Detroit MI 48214-1065

RIDLEY, BETTY ANN, religous educator, lay worker; b. St. Louis, Oct. 19, 1926; d. Rupert Alexis and Virginia Regina (Weikel) Steber; m. Fred A. Ridley, Jr., Sept. 8, 1948; children: Linda Drue, Clay Kent. BA, Scripps Coll., Claremont, Calif., 1948. Christian Sci. practitioner, Oklahoma City, 1973—. Tchr. Christian Sci., 1983—; mem. Christian Sci. Bd. Lectureship, 1980-85. Trustee Daystar Found.; mem. The First Ch. of Christ Scientist, Boston, Fifth Ch. of Christ Scientist, Oklahoma City. Mem. Jr. League Am. Home: 2933 Lansdowne Ln Oklahoma City OK 73120-4343 Office: Suite 100-G 3000 United Founders Blvd Oklahoma City OK 73112 E-mail: BARidley@aol.com.

RIDLEY, ELEANOR HORSEY, retired lawyer; b. Atlanta, Feb. 10, 1947; d. Richard Henry Horsey and Augusta Morgan Collins; m. Clarence Haverty Ridley, Aug. 22, 1969; children: Augusta Morgan, Clare Haverty. BA, Wellesley, 1969; JD, Emory U., 1974. Dep. asst. atty. gen. Ga. State Law Dept., Atlanta, 1974—75; bar exam grader Ga. Supreme Ct., Atlanta, 1986—96, ret., 1996. Bd. dir. Carlos Mus. Emory U., Atlanta, 1999—2003. Mem.: Garden Club Am., Cherokee Garden Club. Independent. Episc. Avocations: gardening, bicycling, travel, cooking, reading. Home: 2982 Habersham Rd NW Atlanta GA 30305

RIDLEY, JOANN D. writer, public relations executive; b. Seattle, Mar. 26, 1925; d. Raymond C. and Hazel Davis; m. John T. Ridley, 1984; m. Frederick J. Patterson (div. 1969); 1 child, Philip S. Student, Whitman Coll.; BA, U. Wash. Pub. rels. dir. Seattle (Wash.) Symphony Orch., 1957—60, Cornish Sch. Allied Arts, Seattle, 1961—65; founding editor The Ark, Tiburon, Calif., 1975; editor Bay and Delta Yachtsman, Alameda, Calif., 1981—82; pub. rels. dir. Gualala (Calif.) Arts Ctr., 1997. Author: High Times - Keeping 'Em Flying, 1993, Looking For Eulabee Dix, 1997, The Barn Book Sea Ranch Foundation, 1997, First & Drream - Belvedere Tiburon Library, 1999; contbr. columns in newspapers.

RIDNER, MELANIE MARIE, writer, composer; b. Dayton, Apr. 18, 1957; d. George Glenn and Lou Gray (Shifflett) Ridner; m. Johnny Edward Clark, Jan. 8, 1977 (div. Apr. 20, 1986); children: Ginay Marion Gray Clark, Dawn Renee Clark; m. Raymond Marion Sissom, Oct. 2, 1976 (div.); 1 child, Gennifer Marie Sissom ; m. Thomas Jefferson Plummer (div. 1988); m. Stephen Michael Sexton (div. 1990); m. David Wayne Cupp (div. 1993). paralegal, civil litigation, computer, Profl. Career Devel. Inst., 1996. Author: (poetry) Romantic Feelings, 1999 (Internat. Libr. Poetry, 1995), (poetry book) Tears On My Shoulder, 2001 (award, 1996), (poetry) Romantic Feelings 2, 1999 (award, 1996); composer: Love Like This, 2001, PennyHeartbreaker, 2001, Country Heartache #1, Country Music Creation, Shattered Hearts and Tears, Holidays Year Round; contbr. poetry to anthologies (awards, 2002);, composer 87 songs, author 4 books of poetry, (short stories) Where Roses Fell, 2002, Where Roses Fall, 2004. Recipient Short Story award Ray Bradbury Contest, New Century Writers, 2002. Mem.: ASCAP, Internat. Libr. Poetry (poet 1995—2002, Poet Laureate 1995—2003), Modern Poetry Assn. (assoc.). Methodist. Home: Lot 71 2318 Hamilton Eaton Rd Hamilton OH 45011 E-mail: melanieridner@netzero.com.

RIDOLFI, DOROTHY PORTER BOULDEN, real estate broker, nurse; b. Staten Island, N.Y., Jan. 24, 1937; d. David Porter and Helen Marie (McCloskey) Boulden; m. Edward Benjamin Ridolfi, Aug. 16, 1958; children: Edward Brian, Judyann Nixon, Jacqueline Ryan. RN, St. Francis Hosp., 1957; student Seton Hall U., 1958, Mercer Community Coll., 1974, 1984, Thomas Edison Coll., 1979-84; real estate cert. S. Jersey Sch. Profl. Bus., 1976. Cert. coronary and critical care nurse; lic. real estate instr., N.J., broker, N.J., sales person, N.J. Owner Stay 'N Play Day Camp, 1963-65; nurse Princeton Med. Ctr. (N.J.), 1972-73; pres., broker Ridolfi Realty Inc., Trenton, 1977-91; nurse Hamilton Hosp. (N.J.), 1982-85; instr. real estate Mercer County C.C. and Career Devel. Sch. Committeewoman Burlington County Democratic Com., Willingboro, N.J., 1966-67, Mercer County Dem. Com. East Windsor, N.J., 1969-72; corr. sec. Hist. Soc., Hightstown, N.J., 1971-72; bd. dirs. Campfire Girls and Boys, 1984. Mem. Soroptimist, Mercer County Bd. Realtors (bd. dirs. 1981-83, treas., v.p., pres. 1988—), N.J. Assn. Realtors (bd. dirs., v.p. 5th dist. 1989, Make Am. Better award 1982), Nat. Fedn. Ind. Bus. (PAC chmn 1989), Nat. Assn. Realtors, Mercer County Multiple Listing, Mercer County C. of C. Democrat. Roman Catholic. Office: Gloria Nilson Realtors GMAC Real Estate 1970 Rt 33 Hamilton Square NJ 08690 Office Phone: 609-890-0007 115.

RIEDEL, BUNNIE, not-for-profit organization executive; m. Daniel M. Gartland; 2 children. Formerly founder, exec. dir. Religious Coalition for Reproductive Choice of So. Calif.; formerly nat. field dir. Ams. United for Separation of Ch. and State; exec. dir. Alliance for Cmty. Media, Washington, 1998—. Spkr. in field. Author: (booklets) Faith and Freedom: Church/State Separation in Our Time, Reflections on Religious Liberty, A Matter of Conscience; contbr. articles to jour., mags., textbooks; appearances on numerous TV and radio programs. Recipient award, V.p. Al Gore, 1999, Recognition for Leadership award, Calif. State Senate. Mem.: Phi Kappa Phi. Office: Alliance for Cmty Media 666 11th St NW Washington DC 20001-4542*

RIEDER, MARY CATHERINE (AHERN), language educator; b. Chgo., Nov. 16, 1942; d. William Bernard Ahern II and [illegible] (O Donnell) Ahern; children: Kristen Rieder Costello, Stephanie Rieder Sullivan, Michael. Student, Sorbonne U., 1962—63; BA, Clarke Coll., 1964; student, U. Que., 1993; MS, U. Wis., 2003. With Oscar Mayer & Co., Madison, Wis., 1958—65; tchr. French and History Edgewood High Sch., Madison, 1965—67; coord. grants & contracts U. Wis. Med. Sch., 1967; v.p., sec., bookkeeper M.J. Rieder, Appleton, 1982—98; tchr. French Appleton Area Sch. Dist., 1994—97. Designer mini-course St. Margaret Mary Sch., Neenah, 1987—88; bd. dirs. Valley Figure Skating Club, Menasha, 1982—87, coord. ice skating show, 1987; docent, lectr. art Bergstrom/Mahler Mus., 1974—84. Bd. dirs. Outagamie County Med. Alliance, Appleton, 1974—98, steering com. Fox. Cities Career Expn., 1984—86; mem.com. on Menasha Cath. Schs.' Centralization Menasha Bd. Edn., 1980—85; mem. ann. food fair com. Xavier H.S., Appleton, 1989—93, mem. ann. fund drive com., 1993; landmarks commr. City of Neenah, 1992—97; mem. future devel. com. Future Neenah, Inc., 2003; dir. ann. fund drive St. Mary's Ctrl. HS, 1989—92. Avocations: piano, golf, reading, travel, art, antiques. Home: 421 Kittiver Ct Neenah WI 54956 Personal E-mail: maryrieder@msn.com.

RIEDLING, ANN MARLOW, education educator; b. New Albany, Ind., July 26, 1952; d. Floyd Guy and Martha Riddle; m. Russell Edward Riedling, Sept. 4, 1982; 1 child, Marlow. BS, Ind. U., 1973; MEd, U. Ga., 1975; EdD, U. Louisville, 1996. Cert. sch. libr. media specialist P-12, elem. edn. Libr. media specialist New Albany/Floyd County Schs., 1984—94, Jefferson County Pub. Schs., Louisville, 1994—96; assoc. prof., chair sch. libr. media dept. Spalding U., Louisville, 1996—2003; assoc. prof. St. Leo U., St. Petersburg, Fla., 2003—, dir. St. Petersburg campus, 2003—. Author: (book) Reference Skills for the School Library Media Specialist, 2000 (Fulbright scholar, 1999), Catalog It! A Guide to Cataloging School Library Materials, 2002 (Metroversity award Tchg., 2000), Learning to Learn, 2002, Helping Teachers Teach, 2002, How We Became Camels, 2003; contbr. numerous articles to profl. jours. Mem.: Fulbright Fellows. Roman Catholic. Avocations: reading, swimming, travel. Home: 1 Key Capri (Treasure Island) Saint Petersburg FL 33706 Office: St Leo University St Petersburg Campus Seminole FL Personal E-mail: ariedling@iglou.com. E-mail: ann.riedling@saintleo.edu.

RIEGLE, ROSALIE GENEVIEVE, English educator, writer; b. Flint, Mich., Feb. 19, 1937; d. John Louis and Eleanor Agnes (Hines) R.; m. Sept. 15, 1962 (div.); children: Kathryn Marie Troester, Maura Clare Troester, Ann Troester Lennon, Margaret Troester Murphy. BA, St. Mary's Coll., 1959; MA, Wayne State U., 1971; D of Arts, U. Mich., 1983. Prof. English Saginaw Valley State U., Univ. Ctr., Mich., 1990—2003. Chair of hons. program Saginaw Valley State U., Univ. Ctr., 1986-93; oral historian Cath. Worker Movement; mem. Jeannine Coallier Cath. Worker Cmty., Saginaw, Mich. Editor: (books) Historic Women of Mich., 1987, Voices from the Catholic Worker, 1993; author: Dorothy Day: Portraits by Those Who Knew Her, 2000. Office: Saginaw Valley State U Dept English University Center MI 48710-0001

RIEGLE KINCH, MARIE EILEEN, art educator; b. Lebanon, Pa., Nov. 9, 1951; d. Delos Norman and Mildred Edna Riegle; m. Michael Ray Kinch, Nov. 8, 1974; children: Eileen Riegle Kinch, Joanne Riegle Kinch. BA, Gettysburg Coll., 1973; MFA, Pa. State U., 1979. Coml. artist Lebanon Valley Offset, Annville, Pa., 1973—77; paste-up artist Strine Printing Co., York, Pa., 1980—81; adj. instr. art Harrisburg (Pa.) Area C.C., 1980, York Coll. Pa., 1981—89; adj. asst. prof. Lebanon Valley Coll., Annville, 1980—2003. Freelance comml. artist Habitat for Humanity, Lancaster, Pa., 1992—93, New Danville Mennonite Sch., Lancaster, 1990, Lancaster, 1992—98, Pa. Chautauqua, Mt. Gretna, Pa., 1995, Mt. Gretna, 2003. Author: Warped Mirror, 1988. Vol. collector Am. Heart Assn., Pa., 1981—2003, Am. Cancer Assn., Pa., 1981—2003; sec. Buck (Pa.) Crime Watch, 1999—2003. Recipient 2d prize for children's fiction story, Inst. Children's Lit., 1995; grantee, Lebanon Valley Coll., 1998, 2001, 2002, 2003. Mem.: Friends of the Suzanne H. Arnold Gallery, Phi Beta Kappa. Avocations: gardening, reading. Office: Lebanon Valley Coll 101 N College Ave Annville PA 17003

RIEHECKY, JANET ELLEN, writer; b. Waukegan, Ill., Mar. 5, 1953; d. Roland Wayne and Patricia Helen (Anderson) Polsgrove; m. John Jay Riehecky, Aug. 2, 1975; 1 child, Patrick William. BA summa cum laude, Ill. Wesleyan U., 1975; MA in Comm., Ill. State U., 1978; MA in English, Northwestern U., 1983. Tchr. English Blue Mound (Ill.) H.S., 1977-80, West Chicago (Ill.) H.S., 1984-86; editor Child's World Pub. Co., Elgin, Ill., 1987-90; freelance writer Elgin, 1990—. Author: Dinosaur series, 24 vols., 1988, UFOs, 1989, Saving the Forests, 1990, Irish Americans, 1995, The Mystery of the Missing Money, 1996, The Mystery of the UFO, 1996, Stegosaurus, 1998, Triceratops, 1998, Tyrannosaurus, 1998, Velociroptor, 1998, A Ticket to China, 1999, Greece, Sweden, 2000, George Lucas, 2001, The Emancipation Proclamation, 2002, The Osage Nation, 2002, The Cree Nation, 2002, Indonesia, 2002, The Plymouth Colony, 2002, The Settling of Jamestown, 2002, The Settling of St. Augustine, 2002, The Siege of the Alamo, 2002, Benjamin Franklin, 2003, Daniel Boone, 2003, The Wampanoag, 2003. Nat. dir. Kids Love a Mystery, 1999-2004. Recipient Summit award for best children's nonfiction Soc. Midland Authors, 1988. Mem. Soc. Am. Magicians, Soc. Children's Book Writers and Illustrators, Mystery Writers of Am. (midwest bd. dirs. 2000-04), Sisters in Crime, Phi Kappa Phi. Democrat. Baptist. Avocations: reading, hiking, dinosaur hunting. E-mail: jr@janetriehecky.com.

RIEHL, JANE ELLEN, education educator; b. New Albany, Ind., Oct. 17, 1942; d. Henry Gabbart Jr. and Mary Elizabeth Willham; m. Richard Emil Riehl, June 15, 1968; 1 child, Mary Ellen. BA in Elem. Edn., U. Evansville, 1964; MS, Ind. U., Bloomington, 1966; postgrad., Spalding U., 1979, Ind. U. S.E., New Albany, 1991—2002. Cert. 1-8 and kindergarten tchr., Ind.; lic. profl. elem adminstrn., reading minor kindergarten tchr., Ind. Elem. tchr. Clarksville (Ind.) Cmty. Sch., 1964-68, 70-75, 81-82, tchr. kindergarten, 1975-81; elem. tchr. Chapelwood Sch. Wayne Twp., Indpls., 1968-70; lectr. edn. Ind. U. S.E., 1988-97, dir. tchg. and rsch. project, 1990-91, 92-93, dir. field and career placement, cert./lic. grad advisor, 1998, coord. elem./spl. edn. field and career placement, license and grad. advisor, 1998—. Cons. Riehl Assocs., Jeffersonville, Ind., 1995—. Co-author: An Integrated Language Arts Teacher Education Program, 1990, The Reading Professor, 1992, Multimedia: HyperStudio and Language Education, 1996, Technology: Hypermedia and Communications, 1997, others; author procs. Parent vol. Girl Scouts U.S.A., Jeffersonville, 1988-95; mem. adminstrtv. bd. Wall Street United Meth. Ch., Jeffersonville, 1993-95; mem. women's health adv. coun. Clark Meml. Hosp., Jeffersonville, 1995—; bd. dirs. Clark Meml. Hosp. Found., vice chair, 1999, chair 2000, sec. 2002-03; team mem. People to People Citizen Amb. Program, 1993, 95, 96; chair internat. bylaws Altrusa Internat., Inc., 2001—. Named Young Career Woman of Yr. Bus. and Profl. Women New Albany and Dist. 13 Ind., 1966; tchg. and rsch. grantee Ind. U. S.E., 1990, 94, 95, 96, 97, 2000; recipient Disting. Tchg. award Ind. U. S.E., 1997, Tchg. Excellence Recognition award, 1997. Mem. Nat. Coun. Tchrs. English, Profs. Reading Tchr. Edn., Ind. State Med. Assn. Alliance (v.p. so. area 1999-2000), Clark County Med. Soc. Alliance (pres.-elect 1997-98, pres. 1998-99), Altrusa Internat. Inc. (internat. bd. 1993-95, dist. gov. 1993-95, svc. award 1995), Phi Delta Kappa (v.p. 1991-92, pres. 1997—, svc. award 1991), Kappa Kappa Kappa (pres. Jeffersonville 1975-76, 90-91, Outstanding Mem. award 1987). Avocations: travel, reading, crafts, decorating. Home: 1610 Fox Run Trl Jeffersonville IN 47130-8204 Office: Ind U SE 4201 Grant Line Rd New Albany IN 47150-2158

RIEHLE, HELEN S, state senator; b. [illegible], May 3, 1950; m. Theodore M. Riehle III; children: Augusta, Emily, Sarah. BS, U. Vt., 1972. Tchr. social studies, South Burlington, Vt.; mem. Vt. Ho. of Reps., 1983-92; mem. dist. 6 Vt. State Senate, 1993—. Bd. dirs. Elizabeth Lund Home; co-chmn. Ward County Rep. Com. Trustee U. Vt., Montpelier, 1985-91; bd. govs. Med. Ctr. Vt. Named Outstanding Conservative Woman Legislator Renaissance mag., 1987. Republican. Congregationalist. Office: Vt House of Reps Office of House Mems Montpelier VT 05602

RIEL, PAULINE, association executive; married; 1 child. BSc in Edn., Ohio U.; MA, Ohio State U. adv. com. Special Standards for Minimum Wages U.S. Dept. Labor; delegate Nat. Rep. Conventions. Second v.p. Nat. Fedn. Rep. Women, Alexandria, Va. GOP chmn.; founding mem. MORCO Water Co., Inc. Named Ohio's first Outstanding Bus. and Profl. Women Mem. of Yr., 1982, Morrow County Outstanding Cmty. Leader Bicentennial Com.; inducted into Ohio Women's Hall of Fame, 1993. Office: Nat Fedn Republican Women 124 N Alfred St Alexandria VA 22314-3011 Fax: 703-548-9836. E-mail: nfrw@worldweb.net.

RIELY, CAROLINE ARMISTEAD, physician, medical educator; b. Washington, Feb. 1, 1944; d. John William and Jean Roy (Jones) Riely. AB, Mt. Holyoke Coll., 1966; MD, Columbia U., 1970. Diplomate Am. Bd. Internal Medicine. Med. intern Presbyn. Hosp., N.Y.C., 1970-71, resident in medicine, 1971-73; fellow in liver disease Yale U., New Haven, 1973-75, asst. prof., 1975-80, assoc. prof., 1980-88; prof. medicine U. Tenn., Memphis, 1988—. Fellow ACP, Am. Coll. Gastroenterology; mem. Am. Assn. Study Liver Disease, Internat. Assn. Study Liver, N.Am. Soc. for Pediatric Gastroenterology and Nutrition. Home: 1756 Central Ave Memphis TN 38104-5116 Office: U Tenn 951 Court Ave Rm 555D Memphis TN 38103-2813

RIENNER, LYNNE CAROL, publishing executive; b. Pitts., Aug. 3, 1945; d. David and Molly (Rice) R. BA, U. Pa., 1967. Exec. v.p., assoc. publisher, editorial dir. Westview Press Inc., Boulder, Colo., 1975-84; pub., owner Lynne Rienner Pub. Inc., Boulder, Colo., 1984—. Pub. cons. various orgns.; lectr. U. Denver Pub. Inst., 1981-84, 93—; panelist nat. meetings Bd. dirs. Boulder Breast Cancer Coalition, 1993-95. Mem. Assn. Am. Pubs. (bd. dirs. 1992-96, 99—, exec. coun. of profl. and scholarly pub. divsn. 1996—). Office: Lynne Rienner Pub Inc 1800 30th St Ste 314 Boulder CO 80301-1026

RIESGRAF, KIM MARIE WOGENSEN, director; b. Mpls., July 30, 1956; d. Lawrence Edward and Caryl Jean (Youngberg) Wogensen; m. Gary (Buck) Raymond Riesgraf, Feb. 7, 1981; children: Christina Marie, Benjamin Robert, Robert Erwin, Jeremy Lawrence, Jason Raymond. BA, U. Minn., 1979, EdD, 2002; MS, U. Wis., Eau Claire, 1984. Cert. dist. supt. Minn., 2000, dir. spl. edn. Minn., 1997, elem. prin. Minn., 1997, tchr. Minn., 1979. Ednl. asst. St. Paul Pub. Schs., 1978—79; early childhood spl. edn. tchr. Minn. River Valley Spl. Edn. Coop., New Prague, Minn., 1979—82; early childhood/exceptional ednl. needs tchr. Eau Claire (Wis.) Area Schs., 1982—88; human devel. ctr. rsch. asst. U. Wis., Eau Claire, 1982—83; early childhood/exceptional ednl. needs tchr. Gilmanton (Wis.) Pub. Schs., 1983—84; grad. asst. U. Wis., Eau Claire, 1983—84; early childhood spl. edn. tchr. Osseo Ind. Sch. Dist. 279, Maple Grove, Minn., 1988—95, lead tchr. early childhood spl. edn., 1995—97, supr./site adminstr., 1997—99, dir. spl. edn., 1999—2003, dir. spl. svcs., 2003—. Sec. exec. com. Coun. for Exceptional Children: Minn. Divsn. for Early Childhood, Mpls., 1995—2000. Recipient Kaye E. Jacobs Meml. award, Minn. Assn. Sch. Adminstrs., 2001. Mem.: ARC, Am. Ednl. Rsch. Assn., Phi Delta Kappa (sec. 1997—2000). Achievements include research in effects of school-based management practices on decision-making for special education; the role of auditory memory in the acquisition of language productions skills. Avocations: gardening, genealogy, skiing, canoeing, hunting. Home: 7451 Dallas Ct Maple Grove MN 55311 Office: Osseo Independent School District 279 11200 93rd Ave N Maple Grove MN 55369 E-mail: riesgrafk@osseo.k12.mn.us.

RIFE, ELIZABETH, musician, music educator; b. Zebulon, Ga., Feb. 23, 1938; d. Jack and Ouida Dorothy (Walker) Bridges; m. Robert M. Hill, June 25, 1959 (div.); 1 child, Dorothy Hill Bremer; m. C. David Rife, Feb. 15, 1986. BS in Music Edn., Ga. State Coll. and U., 1959; postgrad., Ga. State U., 1976-81, Vanderbilt U., 1977-79. Music tchr., Marietta, Ga., 1959—; choir master, organist Holy Trinity Luth. Ch., Marietta, 1966-79. Pres., chmn. bd. Assist, Inc., Marietta, 1982-84. Guest columnist Marietta Daily Jour., 1980-84, Horizons mag., 1997. Dir. WSB-TV Call for Action, Atlanta, 1980—82; spkr. Foster Children Program, Marietta, 1980—83, United Way, 1982—83; sec. bd. dirs. Help for Hispanics, 2002; conducted seminars, workshops on hunger ch. and civic groups, Atlanta, 1981—; concert coord. Musica Sacra Atlanta, 2003; mem. steering com. Presbyn. Answer to Hunger, 1991—. Mem. Music Tchrs. Nat. Assn., Music Educators Nat. Assn., Ga. Music Educators Conf. (adjudicator piano competition 1967—), Cobb County Music Tchrs. Assn., Sigma Alpha Iota. Presbyterian. Avocations: running, reading, travel, fashion consulting, tutoring. Home: 1296 Poplar Pointe SE Smyrna GA 30082-2213

RIFFLE, RHONDA LORENE, construction executive; b. Columbus, Ohio, May 27, 1962; d. Byron Clarence and Madelyn Jane (Powell) R.; m. Manley Clarkson Brown, Feb. 14, 1986 (div. 1994). Trainer Brown Stables, Lexington, 1986-92; mgr. Ballantrae Farms, Lexington, 1992-94, Den Am. Corp., Lexington, 1994-98; owner HH Constrn., Lexington, 1989—, Olajuwon Holdings, 1998—; gen. mgr. Denny's Restaurant, 1994—. With U.S. Army, 1981-83. Mem. NAFE. Republican. Methodist.

RIFKIND, ARLEEN B. pharmacologist, researcher, educator; b. N.Y.C., June 29, 1938; d. Michael C. and Regina (Gottlieb) Brenner; m. Robert S. Rifkind, Dec. 24, 1961; children: Amy, Nina. BA, Bryn Mawr Coll., 1960; MD, NYU, 1964. Intern Bellevue Hosp., N.Y.C., 1964-65, resident, 1965; clin. assoc. Endocrine br. Nat. Cancer Inst., 1965-68; rsch. assoc., asst. resident physician Rockefeller U., 1968-71; asst. prof. medicine Cornell U. Med. Coll., N.Y.C., 1971-82, assoc. prof. medicine, 1983—, asst. prof. pharmacology, 1973-78, assoc. prof., 1978-82, prof., 1983—, chmn. Gen. Faculty Coun., 1984-86. Mem. Nat. Inst. Environ. Health Scis. Rev. Com., 1981-85, chmn., 1985-86; mem. toxicology study sect. NIH, 1989-91, chmn., 1991-93; bd. sci. counselors USPHS Agy. for Toxic Substances and Disease Registry, 1991-95; adv. com. FDA, Spl. Studies Relating to the Possible Long-Term Health Effects of Phenoxy Herbicides and Contaminents, 1995-99; external adv. bd. Environ. Health Scis. Ctr., Wayne State U., 1999—. Assoc. editor Drug Metabolism and Disposition, 1997—; mem. editl. bd. Toxicology and Applied Pharmacology, 1996-2002, Biochem. Pharmacology, 1996—2004; contbr. articles to profl. jours. Chair Friends of the Libr., Jewish Theol. Sem. Am., 1984-86; trustee Dalton Sch., 1986-92; mem. Environ. Health and Safety Coun., Am. Health Found., 1990—; bd. govs. Am. Jewish Com., 1999—; bd. dirs. N.Y. chpt. Am. Jewish Com., 2001-. Recipient Andrew W. Mellon Tchr.-Scientist award, 1976-78; USPHS spl. fellow, 1968-72. Mem. AAAS, Internat. Soc. Study Xenobiotics, Am. Soc. Clin. Investigation, Am. Soc. Pharmacology and Exptl. Therapeutics, Endocrine Soc., Soc. Toxicology. Office: Cornell U Med Coll Dept Pharmacology 1300 York Ave New York NY 10021-4805 E-mail: arifkind@med.cornell.edu.

RIFKIND, IRENE GLASSMAN, legal secretary; b. Houston, June 27, 1921; d. Benjamin Wolf and Celia Pesses Glassman; m. Sydney E. Rifkind, Feb. 8, 1942 (div.); children: Jeffrey Allen, Stephen Paul. Sec. Mo. Dept. Edn., St. Louis, 1967—69, Metal Goods Corp., St. Louis, 1969—71; legal sec. LaBarge Inc., St. Louis, 1971—75; sr. legal sec. [illegible], St. Louis, [illegible]—91, ret., 1991. Recipient Hon. Svc. cert., Office Civil Def., St. Louis, 1945, Meritorious Svc. cert., ARC, St. Louis, 1946. Mem.: Exec. Women Internat. (pres. 1985—86), The Miriam Found. (vol. 1948—, pres. 1958—59). Jewish. Avocations: tennis, sewing, reading, needlework. Home: 10381 Oxford Hill Dr #19 Saint Louis MO 63146

RIFMAN, EILEEN, music educator; b. Bklyn., June 10, 1944; m. Samuel Sholom Rifman, Aug. 12, 1972; children: Edward, Aimee. MusB, Manhattan Sch. Music, 1966, M Music Edn., 1967; MusM, Ind. U., 1970; cert., Fontainebleau, France, 1967. Music specialist N.Y.C. Pub. Sch. System, 1966-67; instr. Long Beach (Calif.) City Coll., 1970-72, Immaculate Heart Coll., Hollywood, Calif., 1971-74, U. Judaism, Hollywood, 1973-74; co-coord. Community Sch. Performing Arts, L.A., 1974-82, instr., 1973-83; pvt. piano tchr. Manhattan Beach, Calif., 1963—; tchr. gifted and talented edn. program GATE, Manhattan Beach, Calif., 1990-91. Tchr. Etz Jacob Hebrew Acad., L.A., 1991-95, Ohr Eliyahu Acad., Culver City, 1995-96; peer counselor Beach Cities Health Dist., 1997—. Performer Pratt Inst., Clinton Hill Symphony, N.Y.C., 1962, Sta. WNYC-FM, 1964. Chair Cultural Arts Com., Manhattan Beach, 1985-86; bd. dirs. Hermosa Beach (Calif.) Community Ctr., 1990-91. Mem. Nat. Fedn. Music Clubs (adjudicator 1970). E-mail: eileenrifman@hotmail.com.

RIGBY, AMANDA YOUNG, paralegal firm executive; b. Yokosuka, Japan, Nov. 15, 1961; d. James Linton Young, Philip T. (stepfather) and Serena Margaret (Murray) Poisson; m. D'Arcy A. Rigby, Apr. 6, 1991; children: Ian A., Helen E. Cert. paralegal, U. San Diego, 1989; AA in Social Sci., Miramar Coll., 1990. Cert. domestic violence counselor, Calif. Sec. Martin & Branfman, Solana Beach, Calif., 1988-89; sr. paralegal Di-Gennaro & Davis, San Diego, 1989-91; owner, pres. paralegal firm AR & Co., San Diego, 1989—. Author poetry in Taking Chances mag., 1992. Vol. clinic coord. San Diego Vol. Lawyer Program, 1989-96; vol. asst. to abuse victims San Diego Police Dept., 1992—; parliamentarian Mira Mesa Town Coun., San Diego, 1992-95; founding mem. Scripps Ranch High Found., San Diego, 1992-95; sec., nat. and state rep. Pomerado Hosp. Mothers of Twins, Poway, Calif., 1994—; mem. Vista (Calif.) Unified Sch. Dist. Common Ground Task Force, 1995-97; staff paralegal San Diego Vol. Lawyer Program, 1994-95; bd. dirs. So. Calif. Mothers of Twins, Inc., 1996—; legal clinic trainer, speaker Community Resource Ctr., 1996—. Mem. ABA. Republican. Methodist. Avocations: reading, writing, sailing, exercising, working on the house. Office: AR & Co 615 Cabezon Pl Fl 2 Vista CA 92083-6309

RIGBY, MARIA DEAN, interpreter, advocate; b. Ogden, Utah, Apr. 15, 1976; d. Donald Ephraim and Orlene Larkins Higgs; m. Alma Brent Rigby, Jan. 15, 2003. AA in Am. Sign Lang., Salt Lake C.C., Utah, 2003. Cert. sign lang. interpreter. Asst. head teller Indsl. Fed. Credit Union, Lafayette, Ind., 1999—2000; customer assoc. Cmty. First Nat. Bank, Salt Lake City, 2000; patient svc. rep. Intermountain Health Care, Salt Lake City, 2000—01; sign lang. interpreter Weber State U., Ogden, Utah, 2002—. Citizen adv. Women for Decency, North Salt lake, Utah, 2002. Mem.: Registered Interpreters Deaf, UT Registered Interpreters Deaf (student liaison 2002—03). Independent. Mem. Lds Ch. Avocations: soccer, camping, nutrition, hiking, volunteering. Home: 693 East 900 North Layton UT 84041 E-mail: buttonhuggs@hotmail.com.

RIGELWOOD, DIANE COLLEEN, insurance adjuster, administrator; b. Savannah, Ga., Apr. 24, 1950; d. William Howell III and Ruth Colleen (Treanor) Bridges; 1 child, Stephanie Michelle Rigelwood Eichstead. Student, Savannah Tech., 1968-69. Ins. adjuster GAB Bus. Svcs., Inc., Savannah, 1974-86, Cramer Johnson White & Assocs., Savannah, 1986-89, Gay & Taylor, Savannah, 1989-94; service location supr. GAB Robins N.A., Inc., Savannah, 1994—. Pres. Isle of Hope PTA, Savannah, 1978; mem. Rep. Nat. Com., Ga. Rep. Party, Savannah Area Rep. Women. Mem. NAFE, Nat. Assn. Ins. Women Internat. (mem. nat. conv. adv. panel 2001), Savannah Claims Assn. (past pres.), Atlanta Claims Assn., Ga. Coun. Nat. Assn. Ins. Women (internat., state dir., immediate past state dir., nat. conv. adv. panel 2001), Ins. Profls. of Savannah (past pres.). Republican. Avocations: walking reading, fishing. Office: GAB Robins N Am Inc PO Box 16955 Savannah GA 31416 E-mail: d.rigelwood@worldnet.att.net.

RIGG, DAME DIANA, actress; b. Doncaster, Yorkshire, Eng., July 20, 1938; d. Louis and Beryl (Helliwell) R.; m. Menahem Gueffen, July 6, 1973 (div. Sept. 1976); m. Archibald Hugh Stirling, Mar. 25, 1981 (div. Apr. 1993); 1 child, Rachael Atlanta. Grad., Fulneck Girls' Sch., Pudsey, Yorkshire; student, Royal Acad. Dramatic Art, London; D (hon.), Stirling U., Eng., 1988, Leeds U., 1992, Southbank U., 1996. Prof. of theater studies Oxford U., 1998—. Stage debut as Natella Abashwilli in The Caucasian Chalk Circle, Theatre Royal, York, Eng., 1957; joined Royal Shakespeare Co., Stratford-on-Avon, 1959, debut as Andromache in Troilus and Cressida, 1960; London debut as Philippe Trincant in The Devils, London, 1961; numerous repertory appearances; joined Nat. Theatre, 1972; appeared in Jumpers, Macbeth, 1972, The Misanthrope, 1973, Pygmalion, 1974, Phaedra Britannica, 1975, Night and Day, 1978, Colette, 1982, Heartbreak House, 1983, Little Eyolf, 1985, Antony and Cleopatra, 1985, Wildlife, 1986, Follies, 1987, Love Letters, 1990, All for Love, 1991, Putting It Together, 1992, Berlin Bertie, 1992, Medea, 1992 (Tony award, Broadway prod., 1994, Eve. Standard award, Variety Club award), Mother Courage and Her Children, 1995, Who's Afraid of Virginia Wolf, 1996, Humble Boy, 2001; film appearances include A Midsummer Night's Dream, The Assassination Bureau, On Her Majesty's Secret Service, Julius Caesar, The Hospital, Theatre of Blood, A Little Night Music, The Great Muppet Caper, Evil Under the Sun, A Good Man in Africa, Parting Shots, 1998; co-starred as Emma Peel in Brit. TV miniseries: Charles II: The Power and the Passion, 2003. TV series The Avengers, 1965-67; star TV series Diana, 1973-74; numerous TV movies including This House of Brede, 1975, Hedda Gabler, 1981, Little Eyolf, 1982, Witness for the Prosecution, 1982, King Lear, 1983, Bleak House, 1984, A Hazard of Hearts, 1987, Worst Witch, 1987, Unexplained Laughter, 1989, Mother Love (Broadcasting Guild Award, BAFTA), 1989, Genghis Cohn, 1994, Zoya, 1995, The Haunting of Helen Walker, 1995, Moll Flanders, 1996, Samson and Delilah, 1996, Rebecca, 1997 (Emmy award, 1997); host PBS series Mystery, 1989—, Mrs. Bradley Mysteries, 1999—. In the Beginning, 2000, The American, 2000, Victoria & Albert, 2001; author: No Turn Unstoned, 1982, U.S. edit., 1983, So To The Land, 1994. Decorated comdr. Brit. Empire; created dame, 1994; recipient Tony award nomination as best actress in Abelard and Heloise and The Misanthrope; Plays and Players award for Phaedra Britannica and Night and Day; Variety Club Gt. Britain award for best actress for Evil Under the Sun; Brit. Acad. Film and TV Arts award for best TV actress in Mother Love, 1989, Award for Women in TV & Film, 2001. Mem. United Brit. Artists (co-founder, dir. 1982—). Address: c/o Lionel Larner Ltd 119 W 57th St New York NY 10019-2303*

RIGGINS, CAROLYN FRANCES, music educator; d. Edward M. and Dorothy G. Riggins. BS in Music Edn., Austin Peary State Univ., Clarksville, Tenn., 1971, MusM, 1977. Choral dir. N.W. HS, Clarksville, Tenn., 1970—; dir. of Music New Providence United Meth., Clarksville, 1982—; adj. music instr. Hopkinsville (Ky.) Cmty. Coll., 2003—. Live entertainment adv. Clarksville (Tenn.) Riverfest, 1989—99; charter mem. Clarksville (Tenn.) Cmty. Choir, 2001—. Recipient Sword of Honor, Sigma Alpha Iota, 1978. Mem.: Middle Tenn. Vocal Assn., Tenn. Music Educators Assn., Music Educators Nat. Conference. Avocations: golf, reading, cross stitch. Office: Northwest HS 800 Lafayette Rd Clarksville TN 37042

RIGGS, CLAUDESTA LAVERN, professional storyteller; b. Wilmington, N.C., May 7, 1957; d. Sylvester Stephen and Frances Claudia Riggs. BS in Telecomms., Mid. Tenn. State U., 1980. Profl. storyteller/sml. bus. entrepreneur. Vol. TC Thompson Children's Hosp., Sunday sch. Avocations: writing, reading, singing. Home and Office: 115 Woodlawn Dr Chattanooga TN 37411 Office Phone: 423-698-6801. Business E-Mail: Lavernscreations@aol.com.

RIGGS, JANE L. performing arts association administrator, consultant; d. Marion Allen and Dorothy Louise Riggs. BA in Music, Capital U. Conservatory, Columbus, Ohio, 1980; MA in Arts Adminstrn., U. Akron, 1986. Cert. lay reader and chalice bearer Episc. Ch., 1999. Sales and mktg. campaign mgr. various arts orgns., various cities, Ohio, 1986—89; gen. mgr. Canton (Ohio) Ballet, 1986—88; performance hall mgr. Veterans Meml. Civic and Conv. Ctr., Lima, Ohio, 1989—2000, ops. mgr., 2000—. Dir. Encore Theatre, Lima, Ohio, 1991—96, prodr. children's theatre, 1997—2000; light designer Stan Tipton & Co., Columbus, Ohio, 1977—80. Dir.: (plays) Boys Next Door (Excellence in Directing from Ohio Cmty. Theatre Assn., 1992), (and lighting designer) Rumors, Cotton Patch Gospel, Gifts of the Magi; singer: (choral) Chapel Choir European Tour. Vol. Our Daily Bread Soup Kitchen, Lima, Ohio, 1993—2002; mem. of bd. Kenyon Conf., Gambier, Ohio, 1996—2001, registrar, Diocese of Ohio and So. Ohio, 1991—2001; vestry mem. & clk. Christ Ch. Vestry, Lima, Ohio, 1996—2003; vol. choir dir. Christ Episcopal Ch., Lima, Ohio, 1996—2003; trustee Encore Theatre, Lima, Ohio, 1994—2000. Recipient Recognition for Svc. to the Pres., White Ho. Presdl. Comm. Agy., 2003, Pres.'s award, Encore Theatre, 1993, New Mem. award, 1991. Episcopalian. Avocations: music, travel, swimming, tinkering with my computer. Office: Veterans' Meml Civic Ctr 7 Town Sq Lima OH 45801 E-mail: jriggs@wcoil.com.

RIGGS, RORY B. pharmaceutical executive; b. Orange, N.J., May 5, 1953; d. Thomas Jeffries and Virginia (Griggs) R. BA, Middlebury Coll.; MBA, Columbia U. Mng. dir. PaineWebber, Inc., CEO RF&P Corp.; mng dir. Pharma Ptnrs. LLC; pres. Biomatrix Inc., Ridgefield, N.J., 1995—. Bd. dirs. Biomatrix, Inc. 1990—; bd. mem. Fibrogen Corp., Spartan Corp., Pharma Ptnrs, LLC. Mem. Young Pres. Orgn. Office: Biomatrix Inc 65 Railroad Ave Ste 3 Ridgefield NJ 07657-2176

RIGGSBY, DUTCHIE SELLERS, education educator; b. Montgomery, Ala., Oct. 26, 1940; d. Malcolm Sellers and Marcelia Sellers Dickman; m. Ernest Duward Riggsby, Aug. 25, 1962; 1 child, Lyn. BS, Troy (Ala.) State Coll., 1962, MS, 1965; postgrad., George Peabody Coll., 1963; EdD, Auburn U., 1972. Cert. tchr., Ala., Ga.; cert. libr., Ga. Tchr. Montgomery Pub. Schs., 1962-63, Troy City Schs., 1963-67; instr. Auburn (Ala.) U., 1968-69; asst. prof. Columbus (Ga.) Coll., 1972-77, assoc. prof., 1978-83, prof., 1983—; coord. Instrnl. Tech. Sch. Edn., 1996-97; program coord. Ednl. Founds., 2001—. Vis. prof. U. P.R., Rio Piedras, 1972—73; leader various workshops, 1989, 1993—; sorfware reviewer NSTA; chmn. publicity Ga. Ednl. Tech. Conf., 1997—, bd. dirs., 1998—; bridal cons. Hist. Moments, Inc., 1998—2001, v.p., 1998—2001; chair scholarship com. Ga. Ednl. Consortium, 1999—. Contbr. more than 90 articles on state, regional, nat., and internat. programs to profl. jours., 1968—. Active Internal Aerospace Edn. CAP, Maxwell AFB, 1980-90; dir. Air and Space Camp for Kids, 1990-98. Recipient STAR Tchr. award NSTA, 1968; named to Lee H.S. Hall of Fame, Montgomery, 1997. Mem. Assn. for Ednl. Comms. and Tech. (non-periodical publs. com. 1994-99, awards com. 1994-96, chair meml. awards com. 1996-99), Nat. Congress on Aviation and Space Edn. (dir. spl. promotions 1986-90), World Aerospace Edn. Orgn. (v.p. for the Ams. 1996-98, pres. for the Ams. 1998—, pres. 1999—), Ga. Assn. Instrnl. Tech. (bd. dirs. 1982-84), Phi Delta Kappa (pres. Chattahochee Valley chpt. 1986-87, Svc. award 1989, Svc. Key award 1993). Baptist. Avocations: photography, mining for gemstones. Office: Columbus State U Coll Edn 4225 University Ave Columbus GA 31907-5679 Office Phone: 706-565-7802.

RIGOLOSI, ELAINE LA MONICA, lawyer, educator, consultant; b. Astoria, N.Y., Oct. 12, 1944; d. Richard Anthony La Monica and Caroline La Monica; m. Robert Salvatore Rigolosi, June 15, 1997. BS, Columbia Union Coll., Takoma Park, Md., 1964; MN, U. Fla., 1967; EdD, U. Mass., 1975; JD, Benjamin N. Cardozo Sch. Law, N.Y.C., 1993. Bar: N.J. 1994, N.Y. 1994, D.C. 1995; RN, N.Y. Chair dept. nursing edn. Tchrs. Coll., Columbia U., N.Y.C., 1988-91, prof. nursing edn., 1982-96, acting chair dept. nursing edn., 1994-96, prof. dept. orgn. and leadership, 1996—, dir. Inst. Rsch. in Nursing, 1981—; health care mgmt. cons. in pvt. practice, N.Y.C., 1974—. Bd. dirs. Hooper Holmes, Inc., Basking Ridge, N.J., 1989—; cons. Delaware Valley Transplant Program, Phila., 1998, U. Tenn. Coll. Pharmacy, Memphis, 1995-98. Author: The Nursing Process: A Humanistic Approach, 1979 (Am. Jour. Nursing Book of Yr. 1979), Management in Health Care, 1994. Dept. HHS grantee, 1977-80, 80-83. Fellow Am. Acad. Nursing; mem. ABA, Assn. Bar City N.Y. (com. on health law 1994-97), Am. Health Lawyers Assn., Am. Assn. Nurse Attys., Am. Coll. Legal Medicine, Sigma Theta Tau. Avocations: tennis, skiing, needlepoint, interior design. Home: 158 Summit Dr Paramus NJ 07652-1312 Office: Tchrs Coll Columbia U 525 W 120th St New York NY 10027-6625

RIGSBY, LINDA FLORY, lawyer; b. Topeka, Kans., Dec. 16, 1946; d. Alden E. and Lolita M. Flory; m. Michael L. Rigsby, Aug. 14, 1963; children: Michael L. Jr., Elisabeth A. MusB, Va. Commonwealth U., 1969; JD, U. Richmond, 1981. Bar: Va. 1981, D.C. 1988. Assoc. McGuire, Woods, Battle & Boothe, Richmond, Va., 1981-85; dep. gen. counsel and corp. sec. Crestar Fin. Corp., Richmond, 1985-99, gen. counsel, 1999-2000; mng. atty. Sun Trust Banks Inc., 2000—. Recipient Disting. Svc. award U. Richmond, 1987; named Vol. of Yr. U. Richmond, 1986, Woman of Achievement, Met. Richmond Women's Bar, 1995. Mem. Va. Bar Assn. (exec. com. 1996-99), Richmond Bar Assn. (bd. dirs. 1992-96), Va. Bankers Assn. (chair legal affairs 1992-95), U. Richmond Estate Planning Coun. (chmn. 1990-92). Roman Catholic. Avocations: music, gardening. Home: 163 W Square Pl Richmond VA 23233-6157 Office: SunTrust Bank 919 E Main St Richmond VA 23219-4625

RIGSBY, SHEILA GOREE, accounting firm executive; b. Macon, Ga., June 13, 1955; d. David Wendell and Carolyn (Canington) Goree; children: Jason, Ryan. Student, Macon Coll., 1979. cert. tax preparer. Tax preparer Better Income Tax Svc., Macon; acct. Bass Tool and Indsl. Supply, Macon, Padgett Bus. Svc., Macon; owner Ind. Acctg. Svcs., Macon. Mem. NAFE, Nat. Fedn. Ind. Businessmen, Nat. Soc. Tax Profls., Nat. Assn. Tax Preparers, Nat. Assn. Tax Practitioners, Ga. Assn. Pub. Accts. Office: 4000 Mercer University Dr Macon GA 31204-5702

RIIKONEN, CHARLENE BOOTHE, international health administrator; b. Washington, June 10, 1942; d. John Edward and Frances Elizabeth (Jett) Boothe; m. Esko Riikonen, 1989; children: Cynthia Lee, Anthony John, Jennifer Elizabeth. AA with high honors, Howard C.C., 1977; BA magna cum laude, U. Md., 1979. Asst. dir. univ. rels., alumni dir. U. Md., Catonsville, 1977-81, assoc. dir. univ. rels. and devel. College Park, 1982-83; sr. devel. officer Internat. Ctr. Diarrhoeal Disease Rsch., Dhaka, Bangladesh, 1984-86; exec. v.p. Child Health Found. (formerly Internat. Child Health Found.), Columbia, Md., 1985-97; pres. Cera Products, LL., Jessup, Md., 1997—, mng. dir., CEO. Cons. to organize symposium oral rehydration therapy Nat. Coun. Internat. Health, Washington, 1987; organizer internat. symposium on food-based oral rehydration therapy Aga Khan U., Pakistan, 1989; organizer consensus conf. cereal-based oral rehydration therapy, Columbia, Md., 1993. Author: (tng. manual) Prevention and Treatment of Childhood Diarrhea with Oral Rehydration Therapy, Nutrition and Breastfeeding, 1992; editor procs. Oral Rehydration Therapy Symposia, 1987, 89, 93, 94; editor Child Health News, 1993—; contbr. articles to profl. jours. Pub. affairs chmn. United Way, Washington Capital Area, Prince Georges County, 1981-83; v.p. Waterfowl Assn.; pres. Windstream Assn., 1988-89; v.p. Waterfowl Terrace Assn., 1994—; mem. pub. rels. com. Md., Del. Cable TV Assn., Balt., 1981-83. Mem. APHA (internat. maternal-child health com.), AAUW, Nat. Coun. Internat. Health Assn., U. Md. Balt. County Alumni Assn. (bd. dirs. 1979-83), Women's Internat. Pub. Health Network. Clubs: Columbia Assn. Athletic (Md.) (capt. women's traveling racquetball team 1979-83). Democrat. Avocations: racquetball, windsurfing, skiing, oil painting. Fax: 410-792-8671. E-mail: criikonen@ceralyte.com.

RIKE, SUSAN, public relations executive; b. N.Y.C., Aug. 29, 1952; d. George Carson and Mildred Eleanor (Geehr) R. BA cum laude, Bklyn. Coll., 1975. Editl. asst. Artforum Mag., N.Y.C., 1975-77; co-owner Say Cheese, Bklyn., 1977-80; editl. asst. The Star, N.Y.C., 1980-82; acct. sec. Robert Marston and Assocs., N.Y.C., 1983-84; asst. acct. exec. Marketshare, N.Y.C., 1984; acct. exec. Doremus Pub. Rels. BBDO Internat., N.Y.C., 1984-86; pres. Susan Rike Pub. Rels., Bklyn., 1986—. Democrat. Avocations: travel, music festivals and concerts, literature. Office: Susan Rike Pub Rels 335 State St Ste 3C Brooklyn NY 11217-1719

RILEY, BARBARA POLK, retired librarian; b. Roselle, N.J., Nov. 21, 1928; d. Charles Carrington and Olive Bond P.; AB, Howard U., 1950; BS, N.J. Coll. Women, 1951; MS, Columbia U., 1955; m. George Emerson Riley, Feb. 23, 1957 (dec.); children: George E., Glenn C., Karen O.; m. William I. Scott, Oct. 6, 1990 (div. 1998). Asst. librarian, Fla. A&M U., 1951-53; with Morgan State Coll., 1955; with Dept. Def., 1955-57, S.C. State Coll., 1957-59, U.Wis., 1958-59; asst. librarian Atlanta U., 1960-68; asst. dir. Union County Anti Poverty Council, 1968; librarian Union County Tech. Inst., Scotch Plains, N.J., 1968-82, Plainfield campus Union County Coll., 1982-95; ret., 1995. Mem. Roselle Bd. Edn., 1976-78; bd. dirs. Union County Anti Poverty Council, 1969-72; mem. Roselle Human Relations Commn., 1971-73, Plainfield Sci. Center, 1974-76, Union County Psychiat. Clinic, 1980-83, Pinewood Sr. Citizens Council, 1981-85; bd. dirs. Project, Women of N.J, 1985-93, Pinewood Sr. Citizen Housing, 1981-85, Black Women's History Conf., 1985-92, pres., 1989-91. Mem. N.J. Library Assn., Council Library Tech., ALA (Black caucas), N.J. Coalition of 100 Black Women, African Am. Women's Polit. Caucus, N.J. Black Librarians Network (bd. dirs.), Links, Inc. (North Jersey chpt.), Black Women's History Conf., Alpha Kappa Alpha. Mem. A.M.E. Ch. Club: Just-A-Mere Lit. Home: 114 E 7th Ave Roselle NJ 07203-2028

RILEY, DOROTHY JOAN, clinical social worker, writer; b. San Francisco, Jan. 19, 1951; d. Harry G. and Sofie Johanna (Schneider) Riley; m. Walter C. Moxley, IV, Nov. 1970 (div. Jan. 1975); children: Michael Joseph Moxley, Theodore John Moxley; m. John F. Keys, Nov. 25, 1981 (div. Jan. 1997). BA in Social Psychology, Park Coll., 1980; Cert. in Graphic Arts, Phila. Sch. Printing and Advt., 1985; MSW, U. South Fla., 1990. Lic. clin. social worker, Fla. Ins. adjuster Crawford and Co., Phila., 1978-80, Continental Ins., Phila., 1980-83, Hanover Ins., Phila., 1983-85; graphic artist Tampa (Fla.) Tribune, 1987-90; program dir., therapist Child Abuse Coun., Inc., Tampa, 1990-96, 98—; family therapist Seminole Tribe Fla., Hollywood, 1996 98. Author: The Purging of Monica Campbell, 1995, (pamphlet) Housekeeping Made Simple, 1992; artist civic mural "Keep Christ in Christmas", 1983. Mem. DAV, Phila., 1980-97; mem., adj. Cath. War Vets., Darby, Pa., 1981-86; chair, asst. scout master Boy Scouts Am., Troop # 123, Darby, 1983-86; mem. Tampa Redevel. Urban Planning Com., 1993-95. With U.S. Army, 1974-77. Mem. Am. Psychotherapy Assn. (diplomate). Democrat. Roman Catholic. Avocations: writing, art, classical music. Home: 1630 Wakefield Dr Brandon FL 33511-2325 Office: Child Abuse Coun Inc 3108 W Azeele St Tampa FL 33609-3059

RILEY, FRANCENA, nurse, retired non-commissioned officer; b. New Smyrna Beach, Fla., May 5, 1957; d. Willard Harrell and Jacqueline Delores (Griffen) R. 1 child, Daniel Albert Cross (dec.). AA, U. Md., Heidelberg, Fed. Republic Germany, 1987; BS, Upper Iowa U., 1994; MA in Edn., Ctrl. Mich. U., 2001. Enlisted U.S. Army, 1980, advanced through grades to sgt. 1st class, 1991, expert field med. badge, parachutist; practical nurse emergency room Keller Army Hosp., West Point, N.Y., 1981; bn. tng. noncommd. officer 34th Med. Bn., Ft. Benning, Ga., 1988-89, practical nurse 2d Mobile Army Surg. Hosp., 1989-91; wardmaster intensive care unit #1 2d MASH, 1990-91; practical nurse pediatric ward Walter Reed Army Med. Ctr., Washington, 1982-84; practical nurse, then nursing supr. 913th Med. Detachment, Kaiserslautern, Fed. Republic Germany, 1984-86; wardmaster surgery clinic Army Regional Med. Ctr., Landstuhl, Fed. Republic Germany, 1987; with 2D MASH 44th med. brigade operation desert shield U.S. Army, Saudi Arabia, 1990-91; ops. non-commd. officer 2d MASH, 1991-92; wardmaster newborn nursery USA MEDDAC, Ft. Polk, La., 1992-94; wardmaster med. surg. unit USAMEDDAC, Ft. Polk, 1994-95; ret., 1995; distbn. clk. USPS, Atlanta, 1995-2000; anesthesia nurse Northside Hosp., Atlanta, 2002—. Maintenance support clk. USPS, Atlanta; adj. instr. Ga. Perimeter Coll., Clarkston, Ga., 2001—. Mem. handbell choir, sr. usher bd. hist. com. Ebenezer Bapt. Ch., Atlanta. Recipient med. badge U.S. Army, 1991. Baptist. Avocations: bicycling, plate collecting, visiting zoos and nature parks. Home: 8773 Valley Lakes Ct Union City GA 30291-6011 E-mail: honedoo2000@yahoo.com.

RILEY, JOCELYN CAROL, writer, television producer; b. Mpls., Mar. 6, 1949; d. G.D. Riley and D.J. (Berg) Riley-Jacobson; m. Jeffrey Allen Steele, Sept. 4, 1971; children: Doran Riley, Brendan Riley. BA in English, Carleton Coll., 1971. Mng. editor Carleton Miscellany, Northfield, Minn., 1971; mkgt. asst. Beacon Press, Boston, 1971-73; freelance writer, editor, prodr., 1973—. Author: Only My Mouth is Smiling, 1982, Crazy Quilt, 1984; prodr.: (TV series) Her Own Words, 1986, Belle: The Life and Writings of Belle Case La Follette, 1987, Gold Medal Internat. Film and TV Festival, 1988, Zona Gale, 1874-1938, 1988, Patchwork, 1989, Prairie Cabin, 1991, Winnebago Women Songs & Stories, 1992, Ethel Kvalheim, Rosemaler, 1992, Her Mother Before Her, 1992, Women in Construction, 1993, America Fever, 1994, Women in Policing, 1994, Sisters & Friends, 1994, Big Sister, Little Sister, 1995, Audrey Handler, Glass Artist, 1995, Women in Dentistry, 1996, Sewing Together, 1996, Women in Nontraditional Careers, 1996, Women in Firefighting, 1996, Women in Machining, 1997, Women in Welding, 1997, Prairie Child, 1997, Math at Work, 1998, Writing on the Lakes, 1998, Women in Engineering, 2000, Work Talk, 2000, Women in Highway Construction, 2001; Women in Building Construction, 2002, The Art of Ethel Kvalheim, 2002, Writing at Work, 2003, Shifting Gears: Changing Careers, 2004; columnist: Wis. State Jour., 1986—91; contbr. articles to profl. jours. Active United Way of Dane County, 1984-90, On-Site Rev. Com., Madison Area Tech. Coll., 1993, Boy Scouts Am., 1996—. Hon. fellow Women's Studies Rsch. Ctr., U. Wis., Madison, 1986-91; Film in the Cities Regional Film/Video grantee; Dane County Cultural Affairs Comm. grantee, 1986-94, 96-97, 2002; Wis. Arts Bd. grantee, 1986, 88-93; Wis. Humanities Coun. grantee, 1997; Wis. Sesquicentennial grantee, 1997, Madison CitiArts grantee, 1986-87, 89-90, 92-93, 96-97, 2002; Bronze Apple award Nat. Ednl. Film & Video Festival, 1988; cert. of commendation Am. Assn. State and Local History, 1988, Gold medal Internat. Film & TV Festival, 1988, cert. of recognition Wis. Dept. Pub. Instrn. Am. Indian History & Culture Program, 1991, Write Women Back into History award Nat. Women's History Project, 1995, ALA award, 1996. Mem. Women in Comms. (pres. Madison chpt. 1984-85, nat. del. 1983, Writer's Cup 1985), Coun. for Wis. Writers (1st pl. for nonfiction article 1986), Authors Guild, Madison Assn. for Multi-Image (pres. 1986-87, nat. del. 1986), Downtown Madison Rotary Club. Address: PO Box 5264 Madison WI 53705-0264

RILEY, JOHNNA WALLER, principal; b. Richmond, Va., May 9, 1962; d. John Garrett and Ellen Nash Waller; m. Martin Lee Riley; children: Jessica Nash, Garrett Ann. BS in Elem. Edn., Va. Commonwealth U., 1984, EdM in Adminstrn. and Supervision, 2003. Cert. prin. grades K-12 Va. Tchr. Henrico County Pub. Schs., Richmond, 1984—2002, prin., 2002—. Strokes and turns judge Tuckahoe Village Recreation Assn., Richmond, 1994—; PTA mem. Varina Elem., Carver Elem., Byrd Mid. Sch., Richmond, 1984—; master ringers mem. Derbyshire Bapt. Ch., Richmond, 1994—, deacon, 1995—, children's and youth handbell dir., 1997—. Mem.: ASCD, Greater Richmond Coun. Tchrs. Math., Richmond Area Reading Coun., Va. Assn. for the Gifted, Am. Assn. Sch. Adminstrs., Nat. Assn. Elem. Sch. Prins., Delta Kappa Gamma. Avocations: swimming, piano, reading, gardening.

RILEY, MATILDA WHITE (MRS. JOHN W. RILEY JR.), sociologist; b. Boston, Apr. 19, 1911; d. Percival and Mary (Cliff) White; m. John Winchell Riley, Jr., June 19, 1931; children: John Winchell III, Lucy Ellen Riley Sallick. BA, Radcliffe Coll., 1931, MA, 1937, DSc (hon.), 1994; DSc, Bowdoin Coll., 1972; LHD (hon.), Rutgers U., 1983, SUNY, Albany, 1997. Rsch. asst. Harvard U., Cambridge, Mass., 1932; v.p. Market Rsch. Co. Am., 1938-49; chief cons. economist WPB, 1941; rsch. specialist Rutgers U., 1950, prof., 1951-73, dir. sociology lab., chmn. dept. sociology and anthropology, 1959-73, emeritus prof., 1973—; Daniel B. Fayerweather prof. polit. econ. and sociology Bowdoin Coll., Brunswick, Maine, 1974-78, prof. emeritus, 1978—, hon. rsch. prof. Assoc. dir. Nat. Inst. on Aging, 1979-91, sr. social scientist, 1991-98, scientist emeritus, Nat. Inst. of Health, 1998—; mem. faculty Harvard U., summer 1955; staff assoc., dir. aging and society Russell Sage Found., 1964-73, staff sociologist, 1974-77; chmn. com. on life course Social Sci. Rsch. Coun., 1977-80; sr. rsch. assoc. Ctr. for Social Scis., Columbia U., 1978-80; adv. bd. Carnegie Aging Soc. Project, 1985-87; mem. Commn. on Coll. Retirement, 1982-86; vis. prof. NYU, 1954-61; cons. Nat. Coun. on Aging, Acad. Ednl. Devel.; mem. study group NIH, 1971-79, Social Sci. Rsch. Coun. Com. on Middle Years, 1973-77; chmn. NIH Task Force on Health and Behavior, 1986-91; cons. WHO, 1987—; Winkelman lectr. U. Mich., 1984, Selo lectr. U. No. Calif., 1987, Boettner lectr. Am. Coll., 1990, Claude Pepper lectr. Fla. State U., 1993, Disting. lectr. Southwestern Social Scis. Assn., 1990, U. N.C., 1997; Standing lectr. SUNY, 1992, Inaugural lectr. Cornell U., 1992; lectr. Internat. Inst. of Sociology, Plenary, 1993, Inter-Univ. Consortium Pol. and Social Rsch., U. Mich., 1993, Duke U., 1993; adv. bd. Internat. Encyclopedia of the Social and Behavioral Sciences, 2000. Author: (with P. White) Gliding and Soaring, (with Riley and Toby) Sociological Studies in Scale Analysis, 1954, Sociological Research, vols. I, II, 1964, (with others) Aging and Society, vol. I, 1968, vol. II, 1969, vol. III, 1972, (with Nelson) Sociological Observation, 1974, Aging from Birth to Death: Interdisciplinary Perspectives, 1979, (with Merton) Sociological Traditions from Generation to Generation, 1980, (with Abeles and Teitelbaum) Aging from Birth to Death: Sociotemporal Perspectives, 1982, (with Hess and Bond) Aging in Society, 1983; editor. (with M. Ory and D. Zablotsky) AIDS in an Aging Society: What We Need to Know, 1989; co-editor: Perspectives in Behavioral Medicine: The Aging Dimension, 1987, (with J. W. Riley) The Quality of Aging, 1989, The Annuals, 1989; mem. editl. com. Ann. Rev. Sociology, 1978-81, Social Change and the Life Course, vol. 1, Social Structures and Human Lives, (with B. Huber and B. Hess) Sociological Lives, vol. II, 1988, (with R. Kahn and Anne Foner) Structural Lag, 1994; contbr. chpts. to books, articles to profl. jours. Former trustee The Big Sisters Assn. Recipient Lindback Rsch. award Rutgers U., 1970, Social Sci. award Andrus Gerontology Ctr., U. So. Calif., 1972, Radcliffe Alumnae award, 1982, Commonwealth award 1984, Kesten Lecture award U. So. Calif., 1987, Sci. Achievement award Washington Acad. Scis., 1989, Disting. Sci. award, 1989, Disting. Creative award Gerontol. Soc. Am., 1990, Presdl. Meritorious award, 1990, Stuart Rice award D.C. Columbia Sociol. Soc., 1992, Kent award Gerontol. Soc. Am., 1992; fellow Advanced Study in Behavioral Scis., 1978-79; Matilda White Riley award in rsch. and methodology established in her honor Rutgers U., 1977; Matilda White Riley prize established Bowdoin Coll., 1987; Matilda White Riley House dedicated Bowdoin Coll., 1996. Fellow AAAS (chmn. sect. on social and econ. scis. 1977-78); mem. NAS, Inst. Medicine of NAS (sr.), Acad. Behavioral Medicine Rsch., Am. Sociol. Assn. (exec. officer 1949-60, v.p. 1973-74, pres. 1986, 91, chmn. sect. on sociology of aging 1989, Disting. Scholar in Aging 1988, Career award 1992), Am. Assn. Public Opinion Rsch. (sec.-treas. 1949-51, Disting. Svc. award 1983), Eastern Sociol. Soc. (v.p. 1968-69, pres. 1977-78, Disting. Career award 1986), Soc. for Study Social Biology (bd. dirs. 1986-92), Am. Acad. Arts and Scis., D.C. Sociol. Soc. (co-pres. 1983-84), Sociol. Rsch. Assn., Internat. Orgn. Study Human Devel., Am. Philos. Soc. (membership lectr. 1987), Phi Beta Kappa, Phi Beta Kappa Assocs. Home: 22 Monument Ln Brunswick ME 04011-8106 Office: Bowdoin Coll Brunswick ME 04011 E-mail: rileym@suscom-maine.net.*

RILEY, NANCY C. state legislator; b. Tulsa, Okla., June 20, 1958; m. Jerry A. Riley; children: Dan, Robin, Patrick stepchildren: Steve, Phil. Student, Okla. Christian U., 1976-79; BSE, UCT Langston, 1985. Tchr. Tulsa Pub. Schs., 1986—; mem. Okla. Senate from 37th dist., Oklahoma City 2001—, Active PTA, Berryhill Hoover, S.W. Tulsa Chamber, Sand Springs Chamber, Bixby Chamber, Green County Campfire Adv. Coun., Interagency Coun. Early Childhood Intervention, Okla. Fedn. Rep. Women, Okla. First Ladies, Tulsa Rep. Men's Club, After Five Rep. Women's Club, Tchr. Recruitment Com. for Minorities. Mem. Tulsa Classroom Tchrs. Assn. (del. 1986-2000), Rolling Oaks Homeowners Assn. (past pres. 1999-2000), Delta Kappa Gamma (sec. 1994-97). Republican. Mailing: State Capitol Bldg Rm 528A 2300 N Lincoln Blvd Oklahoma City OK 73105 E-mail: Rileyn@lsb.state.ok.us.

RILEY, NANCY J. real estate broker; b. Pitts., Pa., Sept. 25, 1947; d. Albert William and Frances Louise (Abaray) Torchia; m. J Thomas Riley, Dec. 31, 1976; children: Jennifer Torchia Davis-Wells, Alison Kathleen Davis-Bearnarth. Cert. Residential Specialist Nat. Assn. Realtors, 1992, Internat.Property Specialist Nat. Assn. Realtors, 2002, Leadership Tng. Grad. Women's Coun. of Realtors. Developer sales Pinellas & Dade County, Fla., 1973—83; broker, owner Country Club Properties, Inc., Clearwater, Fla., 1983—91; broker, assoc. Century 21 Gateway Properties, Inc., St. Petersburg, Fla., 1992—95; residential real estate broker Coldwell Banker Residential Real Estate Co., St. Petersburg, Fla., 1995—. State committee woman Fla. Rep. Party, Pinellas County, 2000—; bd. dirs.. Rep. Party Of Fla., 2001—. Recipient Realtor Of The Yr., Clearwater Assn. Of Realtors, 2000. Mem.: Nat. Assn. Realtors (bd. dirs. 1995—2006), Fla. Assn. Realtors (dist. v.p. 2000—01, treas. 2004—05, sec. 2003—04), Clearwater Assn Realtors (pres. 1999—2000, Realtor of Yr. 2000). Republican. Office: Coldwell Banker Residential Real Estate Co 3401 Fourth St No St. Petersburg FL 33704

RILEY, PAMELA JANERICO, artist; b. Winchester, Mass., Aug. 27, 1970; children: Samuel Adrian Jenkins, James Mark Jenkins. Student, So. Maine Tech. Coll. Ordained to ministry Universal Life Ch., Calif. Data entry clk. Orlando Pub. Libr., 1999. Vol. Caring Unltd., Sanford, Biddeford, Maine, 1999; parent St. Louis Childcare Devel. Svcs., 1999; crime watcher Forest Green Apt. Complex, York County, 1999. Home: PO Box 1984 Biddeford ME 04005-1984

RILEY, SUSAN JEAN, retail executive; b. N.Y.C., Apr. 6, 1958; d. Donald E. and Regina A. (Alt) R.; m. Clive D. Conley, June 22, 1985 (dec. 1994); 1 child, Emily Claire. BS, Rochester Inst. Tech., 1981; MBA, Pace U., 1987. CPA, N.Y. Acct. Goldstein & Viele, Rochester, N.Y., 1979-81; auditor Arthur Andersen & Co., Rochester, 1981-82; internal auditor Bristol Myers Squibb, N.Y.C., 1982-83, sr. fin. analyst, 1983-84, mgr. finance, 1984-85, mgr. treas. ops., 1985-87; internat. fin. mgr. Tambrands Inc., Lake

Success, N.Y., 1987-90, dir. fin. White Plains, N.Y., 1990-92, v.p. fin. Ams. divsn., 1992-94, v.p. corp. fin., 1994-95, CFO, 1995—97; sr. v.p., CFO Dial Corp., 1997—2000; CFO Mt. Sinai Med. Ctr., NY, 2002—04, Abercrombie & Fitch Co., 2004—. Named Fin. Exec. of Yr. Inst. Mgmt. Accts., 1995, one of Acad. of Women Achievers YWCA of N.Y., 1994. Mem. Fin. Execs. Inst. Avocations: youth soccer coach, needlepoint, collecting doll house furniture. Office: Abercrombie & Fitch 6301 Fitch Path New Albany OH 43054*

RILEY-DAVIS, SHIRLEY MERLE, advertising agency executive, marketing consultant, writer; b. Feb. 4, 1935; d. William Riley and Beatrice Estelle (Whittaker) Byrd; m. Louis Davis; 1 child, Terri Judith. Student, U. Pitts., 1952. Copywriter Pitts. Mercantile Co., 1954-60; exec. sec. U. Mich., Ann Arbor, 1962-67; copy supr. N.W. Ayer, N.Y.C., 1968-76, assoc. creative dir. Chgo., 1977-81; copy supr. Leo Burnett, Chgo., 1981-86; freelance advt. and mktg. cons., 1986—. Advt. and mktg. dir. Child and Family Svc., Ypsilanti, Mich., 1992-96; advt. mktg. dir. Jude Entertainment, 1998; vis. prof. Urban League Black Exec. Exch. Program; print, radio, and TV commls. Mem. adv. Cmty. Diabetes, past bd. dirs. People's Hope for Housing, Ypsilanti; mem. adv. bd., founding mem. African Am. Alzheimer's Support Group, Ypsilanti, 1995—; bd. dirs. Housing Bur. for Srs. of the U. Mich. Med. Ctr., 1995-96. Recipient Grand and 1st prize N.Y. Film Festival, 1973, Gold and Silver medal Atlanta Film Festival, 1973, Gold medal V.I. Film Festival, 1974, 50 Best Creatives award Am. Inst. Graphic Arts, 1972, Clio award, 1973, 74, 75, Andy award of Merit, 1981, Silver medal Internat. Film Festival, 1982, Corp. Mgmt. Assistance Program award, 1986, Good Sam award, 1981, Svc. Advt. Creativity of Distinction cert., 1981; Senatorial scholar. Mem. Women in Film, Facets Multimedia Film Theatre Orgn. (past bd. dirs.), Greater Chgo. Coun. for Prevention of Child Abuse, Internat. Platform Assn., Epilepsy Found. Chgo. (past bd. dirs.), Silver Club (mem. adv. bd.), Washtenaw County Sr. Leaders. Democrat. Roman Catholic. Avocations: dance, poetry, design, writing, volunteering. E-mail: beaschild@yahoo.com.

RIMA, INGRID HAHNE, economics educator; b. Fed. Republic of Germany; d. Max F. and Hertha G. (Grunsfeld) Hahne; m. Philip W. Rima; children: David, Eric. BA with honors, CUNY, 1945; MA, U. Pa., 1946, PhD, 1951. Prof. econs. Temple U., Phila., 1967—. Author: Development of Economic Analysis, 1967, 6th edit., 2000, Labor Markets Wages and Employment, 1981, The Joan Robinson Legacy, 1991, The Political Economy of Global Restructuring, Vol. I, Production and Organization, Vol. II, Trade and Finance, 1993, Measurement, Quantification and Economic Analysis, 1994, Labor Markets in a Global Economy, 1996. Fulbright Disting. Lectr. Lingnan U., China, 2000. Fellow Ea. Econ. Assn.; mem. Am. Econ. Assn., History of Econs. Soc. (pres. 1993-4), Phi Beta Kappa. Office: Temple U Broad & Montgomery Ave Philadelphia PA 19122

RIMBACH, EVANGELINE LOIS, retired music educator; b. Portland, Oreg., June 28, 1932; d. Raymond Walter and Viola Clara (Gaebler) Rimbach. BA, Valparaiso (Ind.) U., 1954; MMus, Eastman Sch. Music, Rochester, N.Y., 1956; PhD, Eastman Sch. Music, 1967; student, Pacific Luth. U., Parkland, Wash., 1950-52. Vocal music instr. Goodwin Jr. High Sch., Redwood City, Calif., 1956-57; music instr. Calif. Concordia Coll., Oakland, Calif., 1957-62; prof. music Concordia U., River Forest, Ill., 1964-97, chmn. dept., 1989-97; ret., 1997. Contbg. editor: Church Music, 1965—80; editor: (book) Johann Kuhnau: Magnificat, 1980, (cantata) Johann Kuhnau: Lobe den Herrn, 1993; contbr. (essays) Hymnal Supplement '98 Handbook, Keywords in Church Music, 2004; contbr. articles to profl. jours. Bd. dirs. Civic Symphony of Oak Park-River Forest, 1974-80, concert com. chmn., 1976-78, prog. annotator, 1976-80; mem. choir Grace Luth. Ch., River Forest, 1964-97. AAUW postdoctoral fellow, 1969-70; DAAD grantee, Munich, 1980; recipient Rose of Honor award, Sigma Alpha Iota, 1987. Mem. Am. Musicol. Soc., Assn. Luth. Ch. Musicians (editor newsletter 1998—), Sigma Alpha Iota (Rose of Dedication award 1997). Republican. Lutheran. Avocations: travel, cooking, needlework. Home: Apt L-206 12121 Admiralty Way Everett WA 98204-7507 Fax: 425-265-0837.

RIMEL, REBECCA WEBSTER, foundation administrator; BS, U. Va., 1973; MBA, James Madison U., 1983. Head nurse, emergency dept. U. Va. Hosp., Charlottesville, 1973-74, coord. med. out-patient dept., 1974-75, nurse practitioner dept. neurosurgery, 1975-77, instr. in neurosurgery, 1975-80, asst. prof., 1981-83; program mgr. health Pew Charitable Trusts, Phila., 1983-84; asst. v.p. Glenmede Trust Co., Pew Charitable Trusts, Phila., 1984-85; v.p. for programs Pew Charitable Trusts, Phila., 1985-88, exec. dir., 1988-94, pres., 1994—. Mem. Coun. on Founds., Washington; prin. investigator dept. neurosurgery U. Va., 1981—83; adv. com. Boxing U.S. Olympics, 1983—86; adv. coun. Nat. Inst. of Neurol. Disorders and Strokes, 1988—91, bd. dirs., Thomas Jefferson Meml. Found., Deutsche Banc Flag Investors Fund. Contbr. chpts. in books, articles and abstracts to profl. jours. Recipient Disting. Nursing Alumni award, U. Va., 1988; fellow Kellogg Nat. fellow, 1992. Mem.: APHA, ANA, Va. State Nurses Assn. (membership and credentials com. 1982—86), Emergency Dept. Nurses Assn., Am. Assn. Neurosurg. Nurses, Am. Acad. Nursing.

RIMER, BARBARA K. health facility administrator, educator; b. Wilkes Barre, Pa., Jan. 14, 1949; married. BA in English, U. Mich., 1970, MPH in Med. Care Adminstrn. and Health Edn., 1973; PhD in Health Edn., Johns Hopkins Sch. of Hygiene and Public Health, 1981. Instr. Wayne State U. Sch. Medicine, Detroit, 1973-75; program dir. Nat. Cancer Inst., Bethesda, Md., 1975-77; intervention coord. Johns Hopkins Oncology Ctr., Balt., 1977-79; rsch. assoc. Johns Hopkins Sch. Hygiene and Public Health, Balt., 1977-79; sr. health educator Fox Chase Cancer Ctr., Phila., 1981-87, dir. health comms. rsch., 1981-87, dir. behavioral rsch., 1987-91, dir. population sci. for behavioral rsch., 1990-91; dir. cancer prevention, detection and ctrl. rsch. Duke Comprehensive Cancer Ctr., Durham, NC, 1991-97; sr. fellow Aging Ctr. Duke U. Med. Ctr., Durham, NC, 1991-97, assoc. prof. in cmty. and family medicine, 1991-93, prof. cmty. and family medicine, 1993-97; acting dep. dir. Duke Comprehensive Cancer Ctr., Durham, NC, 1995-96; dir. cancer ctrl. and population scis. Nat. Cancer Inst., Rockville, Md., 1997—. Adj. assoc. prof. dept. health behavior and health edn. U. N.C. Sch. of Public Health, Chapel Hill, NC, 1992-97; adj. mem. Fox Chase Cancer Ctr., Phila., 1992-97; preceptor, lectr. Temple U., 1983-91; guest lectr. Duke U. Med. Ctr., 1991-97, U. N.C. Sch. Public Health, 1991-93; Judith P. Schlager vis. prof. Dana-Farber Cancer Inst., 1995; disting. vis. lectr. Harvard U., 1998; mem. institutional review bd. Fox Chase Cancer Ctr., 1983-88, vice chair, 1988-91; proposal review, site visitor Nat. Cancer Inst., 1985-95; chairperson tech. advisory com. Am. Lung Assn., 1987; external advisory com. Vermont Regional Cancer Ctr., 1988-89; advisory com. Brown U., U. R.I. Cancer Prevention Rsch. unit, 1988-95; mem. Am. Assn. Retired Persons task force on smoking, 1989-91, Health Promotion adv. bd. Wesley Found., 1990-91, program com. annual mtg. Am. Soc. Preventive Oncology, 1990-93, chair, 1993 mtg., expert adv. com. AMC Cancer Rsch. Ctr./Ctrs. for Disease Ctrl. Coop. Agreement, 1991, adult edn. subcom. and tobacco materials review group Am. Cancer Soc., 1991; mem. Nat. Task Force on Breast Cancer Ctrl. Am. Cancer Soc., 1992, chair Nat. and State (NC) Task Force on Breast Cancer Ctrl., 1992; mem. Pub. Edn. subcom. on Adult Edn. Am. Cancer Soc., 1992; mem. adv. bd. Office of Cancer Comms., NCI, 1992; mem. Clin. Cancer com. Duke U. Med. Ctr., 1992-95; mem. Cancer Ctrs.' Support com. NCI, 1993-94, Recruitment and Adherence com. Office of Women's Health NIH, 1993, Report com. Internat. Workshop on Screening for breast cancer NCI, 1993, Detection and Treatment subcom. on Breast Cancer Am. Cancer Soc., 1993, 94, Nominating com. Soc. Behavioral Medicine, 1993-96, adv. com. on cancer coordination and ctrl. State of NC, 1993-97; invited participant and com. chair Frontiers of Behavioral Medicine mtg., Chantilly, Va., 1993; invited co-chair Sec. Shalala's Mtg. to develop nat. strategic plan for breast cancer, Bethesda, Md., 1993; chair, mem. Nat. Cancer Adv. Bd. (presdl. appointment), 1994-97; bd. dirs. Am. Family Life Assurance Corp., 1995—; fellowship selection com. Am. Assn. Cancer Rsch., 1996; mem. exec. com. Acad. Behavioral Medicine Rsch., 1998, Charles S. Mott Selection com. of Gen. Motors Cancer Rsch. Found., 1999, Inst. Medicine com. effective health comm. and behavior change strategies for diverse populations, 2000. Editor: special cancer issue Health Education Research, 1998-89; editl. bd. Health Education Quarterly, 1985-87, guest editl. bd. 1983; editl. bd. Jour. of Compliance in Health Care, 1989-90, Health Edn. Rsch., 1990-98, Cancer Prevention, Epidemiology and Biomarkers, 1990—, Patient Edn. and Counseling, 1994—, Breast Diseases, 1998—, Cancer Causes and Control, 1998—, Effective Clin. Practice, 2000—; assoc. editor: Preventive Medicine, 1990—; reviewer Am. Jour. Preventive Medicine, Am. Jour. Public Health, Annals of Internal Medicine, Health Edn. Quarterly, Health Services Research, Jour. of Am. Med. Assn., Jour. Nat. Cancer Inst., Milbank Quarterly, Women's Health, 1986—; contbr. numerous articles, papers to profl. pubs. Fellow Johns Hopkins Sch. of Hygiene and Public Health, 1979-81, Soc. of Behavioral Medicine, 1997; recipient Mayhew Derryberry award Am. Public Health Assn., 1992, Best Visual Presentation of Session award Soc. of Behavioral Medicine, San Diego, 1995, Citation award Soc. Behavioral Medicine, 1996, Disting. Achievement award Am. Soc. Preventive Oncology, 1997, Herbert J. Block Leadership award Ohio State U., 1997, John P. McGovern award in Health Promotion U. Tex. Sch. Public Health, 1999. Office: Nat Cancer Inst DCCPS Rm 6134 6130 Executive Blvd Exec Plz N Rockville MD 20852 Home: 412 Johns Woods Rd Chapel Hill NC 27516-9236 E-mail: barbara.rimer@nih.gov.

RIMES, LEANN, country music singer; b. Jackson, Miss., Aug. 28, 1982; Singer: (albums) Blue, 1996, Unchained Melody: The Early Years, 1997, You Light Up My Life: Inspirational Songs, 1997, Sittin' on Top of the World, 1998, LeAnn Rimes, 1999, I Need You, 2001, Twisted Angel, 2002; writer : (TV films) Holiday in Your Heart, 1997; guest appearance : (TV series) American Dreams, 2003; (films) Coyote Ugly, 2000. Nominated Best Country Singer award Country Music Assn., 1996; recipient Grammy award (2), 1997, Best New Artist, 1997, Acad. of Country Music award (3), 1997; named Billboard Artist of Yr., 1997. Office: care Curb Records 3907 W Alameda Ave 2d Fl Burbank CA 91505-4332*

RIMLER, ANITA A. secretary of state; Campaign aide, legis. asst. former Del. Rob James, 1975; asst. Atty. Gen. Mary Sue Terry, 1985—91; dir. fin. ops. Terry for Gov. campaign, 1993, Robb for Senate campaign, 1994, Warner's U.S. Senate campaign, 1996; sr. advisor, dir. fin. ops. Warner for Gov. campaign; Sec. of State State of Va., 2002—. Democrat. Office: Office Sec Commonwealth 830 E Main St 14th Fl Richmond VA 23219 Business E-Mail: socmail@gov.state.va.us.*

RINALDO, GINGER LEE, music educator; b. Oneida, N.Y., June 24, 1971; d. Jerry N. and Kathryn A. DuBrey; m. Frederick A. Rinaldo, Aug. 24, 1996; children: Benjamin K, Anna M. A in Music, Onondaga C.C., Syracuse, N.Y.; B in Music Edn., SUNY, Potsdam; M in Reading, SUNY, Cortland. Cert. permanent reading edn., permanent music edn. N.Y. Music educator Sherburne (N.Y.) Earlville Ctrl. Sch., 1993—. V.p. Sherburne Earlville Tchrs. Assn. Mem.: Madison County Music Educators Assn. (sec. 2001—03), N.Y. State Sch. Music Assn. (adjudicator). Home: 7672 Tackabury Rd Earlville NY 13332 Office: Sherburne Earlville Ctrl Sch 15 School St Sherburne NY 13460 Personal E-mail: rinaldog@usadatanet.net. E-mail: rinaldog@secsd.stier.org.

RINALDO, SHARON ANN, special education educator; b. Hartford, Conn., May 13, 1952; d. Jerry and Mary (Sullivan R.). BS, So. Conn. State U., New Haven, 1974, M in Counseling, 1979, postgrad., 1983. Co-dir. summer youth work experiencc program T.E.A.M., Derby, Conn., 1977-82; asst. dir. group home Derby, 1978-79; therapist Cath. Family Svcs., Ansonia, Conn., 1980-81; pvt. therapist, 1980-85; spl. edn. tchr. Derby Bd. Edn., 1974—. Chair bd. dirs. Ansonia Battered Women's Project, 1982-84; cons. Irving After Sch. Program, Derby, 1997-98; counselor DART Program Derby H.S., 1992-95; co-pres. Derby Edn. Assn. Tchrs. Union, 1982-83. Mem. NEA, Coun. Exceptional Children, Conn. Edn. Assn., Derby Edn. Assn. Avocations: travel, reading, woodworking, arts and crafts, exercise. Office: Derby HS 8 Nutmeg Ave Derby CT 06418-1126

RINDO, LINDA SUE, music educator; b. Rifle, Colo., Oct. 23, 1948; d. Raymond Stanley and Marvel Vivian Swanson; m. John Joseph Rindo, Dec. 26, 1966; children: Seth, Jessica Rindo Smith, Micah, Anna. MusB, U. Wis., 1971; MA in Music, U. Minn., 1990. Tchr. Kewaskum (Wis.) H.S., 1971—73; pvt. practice Solon Springs, Wis., 1973—87; tchr. South Shore Sch. Dist., Port Wing, Wis., 1987—88, Maple (Wis.) Sch. Dist., Maple, 1988—94, Randall Sch. Dist., Bassett, Wis., 1994—96, Waterford (Wis.) Sch. Dist., 1995—. Coord. Wis. Coun. Devel. Disabilities, Madison, Wis., 1987—88. Organist, pianist Northwoods Cmty. Ch., Solon Springs, 1974—94. Recipient award, DAR, 1966, Ednl. Excellence award, Assn. Univ. Women, 1997; Wis. Sch. Music Assn. grantee, 1987. Mem.: Music Educators Nat. Conf. Republican. Avocations: boating, walking, reading, piano, travel. Office: Waterford Graded Sch Sys 921 W Main St Waterford WI 53185

RINER, DEBORAH LILLIAN, mental health services professional; b. Brunswick, Ga., Mar. 20, 1960; d. Lee Calvin and Lillian Rosebell Jacobs; m. Thomas Joseph Quinn, Mar. 11, 1978 (div. Dec. 1989); m. Thomas Wallace Riner, Jr., Jan. 1, 1990. Student, Calif. Coll. Health Sci. Cert. hypnotherapist, notary pub. Ga. Exec. sec. Greater Jax Christian Sch., Jacksonville, 1984—87; med. transcription coord. St. Vincent's Med. Ctr., Jacksonville, 1987—89; claims processor Allen Med. Claims Adminstrs., Ft. Valley, Ga., 1990—91; registration technician Houston Health Care Complex, Perry, Ga., 1991—92; med. asst. Peace Sun Med. Clinic, Khamis Mushayt, Saudi Arabia, 1993—95; owner and hypnotherapist Coastal Hypnosis Ctr., Brunswick, 2002—. Mem. Chronic Disease Coalition, Brunswick. Mem.: Nat. Guild Hypnotists, Brunswick Golden Isle's C. of C. Mem. Ch. Of Christ. Avocations: genealogy, travel, antiques, Reiki. Office: Coastal Hypnosis Ctr 40 Carteret Ct Brunswick GA 31525

RING, ALICE RUTH BISHOP, retired preventive medicine physician; b. Ft. Collins, Oct. 11, 1931; d. Ernest Otto and Mary Frances Bishop; m. Wallace Harold Ring, July 26, 1956 (div. 1969); children: Rebecca, Eric, Mark; m. Robert Charles Diefenbach, Sept. 10, 1977. BS, Colo. State U., 1953; MD, U. Colo., 1956; MPH, U. Calif., Berkeley, 1971. Diplomate Am. Bd. Preventive Medicine. Physician cons. Utah State Divsn. Health, Salt Lake City, 1960—65; med. dir., project head start Salt Lake City Cmty. Action Program, 1965—70; resident Utah State Divsn. Health, 1969—71; asst. assoc. regional health dir. USPHS, San Francisco, 1971—75, med. cons. Atlanta, 1975—77, dir. primary care, 1977—84; dir. divsn. diabetes control Ctrs. Disease Control, Atlanta, 1984—88; dir. WHO Collabor Ctr., Atlanta, 1986—91; dir. preventive medicine residency Ctrs. Disease Control, Atlanta, 1988—93; exec. dir. Am. Bd. Preventive Medicine, 1993—98. Trustee Am. Bd. Preventive Medicine, 1990—92; lectr. Emory U. Sch. Pub. Health, 1988—94; bd. dirs. Redwood Coast Med. Svcs., v.p., 1994—; mem. adv. com. Shamli Hospice, Gualala, Calif.; mem. adv. coun. Sonoma County Area Agy. on Aging, Santa Rosa, Calif., 2001—; bd. dirs. Alliance for Rural Cmty Health, Calif. Co-author: Clinical Diabetes, 1991; author: History of the American Board of Preventive Medicine, 2002. Bd. dirs. Diabetes Assn. Atlanta, 1985—90. Recipient Disting. Svc. award, Am. Bd. Med. Splties, 2004. Fellow: Am. Coll. Preventive Medicine (bd. dirs. 1990—94, Spl. Recognition award 1998); mem.: AMA (grad. med. edn. adv. com. 1993—97), Am. Bd. Med. Specialists (Disting. Svc. award 2004), Am. Acad. Pediat., Assn. Tchrs. Preventive Medicine. Office: PO Box 364 Gualala CA 95445-0364 E-mail: ard@mcn.org.

RING, LUCILE WILEY, lawyer; b. Kearney, Nebr., Jan. 2, 1920; d. Myrtie Mercer and Alice (Cowell) W.; m. John Robert Ring, Mar. 28, 1948; children: John Raymond, James Wiley, Thomas Eric. AB, U. Nebr., Kearney, 1944; JD, Washington U., 1946. Bar: Mo. 1946, U.S. Dist. Ct. (ea. dist.) Mo. 1947, U.S. Ct. Appeals (8th cir.) 1972. Atty.-adviser, chief legal group adjudications br. Army Fin. Ctr., St. Louis, 1946-52; exec. dir. lawyer referral svcs. St. Louis Bar, 1960-70; pvt. practice St. Louis, 1960-2000; staff law clk. U.S. Ct. Appeals (8th cir.), St. Louis, 1970-72; exec. dir. St. Louis Com. on Cts., 1972-85. Legal advisor Mo. State Anat. Bd., 1965-95; adj. prof. adminstrv. law Webster Coll., Webster Groves, Mo., 1977-78; mem. Mo. Profl. Liability Rev. Bd., State of Mo., 1977-79. Author, editor: Guide to Community Services - Who Do I Talk To, 1974, 75, 76-79, St. Louis Court Directories, 1972, 73, 74, 75, Felony Procedures in St. Louis Courts, 1975; author: Breaking Barriers: The St. Louis Legacy of Women in Law 1869-1969, 1996; author (series): Women Lawyers in St. Louis History, 1996, Women Breaking Barriers, 1998; contbr. articles to profl. jours. Mem. Mo. Mental Health Authority, 1964-65; bd. dirs., v.p. Drug and Substance Abuse Coun., met. St. Louis, 1976-83; mem. adv. coun. St. Louis Agy. on Tng. and Employment, 1976-83; mem. Mayor's Jud. Reform Subcom., St. Louis, 1974-76. Recipient letter of commendation Office of Chief of Fin., U.S. Army, 1952, Outstanding Alumni award, U. Nebr., Kearney, 1994; Washington U. Sch. Law scholar, 1944—46, 1st Mo. woman nominated for Mo. Ct. Appeals, St. Louis Dist., Mo. Appellate Commn., 1972, 1st woman nominated judgeship Mo. Non-Partisan Ct. Plan, 1972. Mem. Bar Assn. Met. St. Louis (v.p. 1975-76), Legal Svcs. Ea. Mo., Inc. (v.p. 1978-79, dir.), Legal Aid Soc. St. Louis City and County (bd. dirs. 1977-78), HUD Women and Housing Commn. (commr. 1975), Women's Bar Assn. (treas. St. Louis chpt. 1949-50), Mo. Assn. Women Lawyers (treas. 1959-60, pres. 1960-61), Washington U. Dental Faculty Wives (pres. 1972-74), Mortar Board, Pi Kappa Delta, Sigma Tau Delta. Methodist. Home and Office: 2041 Reservoir Loop Rd Selah WA 98942-9616

RING, MIRANDA, psychologist, photographer; d. Martin Robert and Helene Stern Ring; m. Roger Phelps, Aug. 23, 1992; 1 child, Chay Ring Phelps. BA in Dance, Mills Coll., 1971; MA in Counseling Psychology, Lindenwood Coll., 1979; MFA in Dramatic Writing, Brandeis U., 1989; MA in Theatre, Smith Coll., 1990; PsyD in Clin. Psychology, Mass. Sch. Profl. Psychology, 1996; studied photography with Freeman Patterson and Andre Gallant, New Brunswick, Can., 2000, studied photography with Freeman Patterson and Andre Gallant, 2002; student, Maine Photog. Workshops, 1999; studied with Harold Feinstein and Joan Albert, Boston Photo Coop., Boston, 1996—98. Lic. psychologist Maine. Asst. dir. career devel. Smith Coll., Northampton, Mass., 1985—88; counselor and workshop leader Steppingstones, Medford, Mass., 1989—94; sch.-based child therapist Geiger-Gibson Cmty. Health Ctr., Dorchester, Mass., 1995—96; core clinician and interim program dir. intensive outpatient program Boston Med. Ctr., 1997—98; child and family therapist Boston Children's Svcs., 1996—98; clin. psychologist Kennebec Valley Mental Health Ctr., Waterville, Maine, 1998—99, MaineGen. Med. Ctr., Waterville, 1999—, Edmund Cerin Pediat. Ctr., 1999—. Instr. Colby Coll., Waterville, 2002—03. One-woman shows include photography S. Boston Pub. Libr., S. Boston, 2000, one-woman shows include Railroad Sq. Cinema, Waterville, 1999, 2002, Elements Gallery, Rockland, Maine, 2002, exhibited in group shows at Boston Photo Coop., 1998, 1999, 2000, Chocolate Ch. Art Gallery, Bath, Maine, 2000, 2003, Art Carne Coop Gallery, Waterville, 2000—01, Harlow Gallery, Hallowell, Maine, 2001, Elements Gallery, Rockland, 2001, Ctr. Maine Contemporary Art, Rockport, Maine, 2002. Mem. core group/tng. com. Colby Cares About Kids Colby Coll., Waterville, 2001—, 2003. Mem.: APA, Capitol Area Camera Club. Buddhist. Avocations: bicycling, hiking, films, travel. Office: Edmund Ervin Pediatric Ctr Maine Gen Med Ctr 30 Chase Ave Waterville ME 04901 Office Phone: 207-872-4669.

RING, NANCY GAIL, writer; b. Irvington, N.J., Dec. 24, 1956; d. Frank and Dorothy (Kasoff) R.; m. Eric Mark Kaplan, Aug. 1, 1993. Student, Sch. of Mus. of Fine Arts, Boston, 1975-76; BFA, Syracuse U., 1978. Food history columnist, feature food article contbr. N.J. Star Ledger, Newark, 1998—2004. Author, illustrator: Walking on Walnuts, 1996; art exhibited Women Figure, 1990; muralist with pvt. commns., 2000—. Recipient Drawing award Barbara Chase Burke, 1978; fellow Mid-Atlantic Arts Found., 1988, N.Y. Found. for Arts, 1987, Montalvo Ctr. for Arts, 1987. Avocations: baking, cooking, exercise, traveling, reading.

RING, RENEE ETHELINE, lawyer; b. Frankfurt, Germany, May 29, 1950; arrived in U.S., 1950; d. Vincent Martin and Etheline Bergetta (Schoolmeesters) R.; m. Paul J. Zofnass, June 24, 1982; Jessica Renee, Rebecca Anne. BA, Catholic U. Am., 1972; JD, U. Va., 1976. Bar: N.Y. 1977. Assoc. Whitman & Ransom, N.Y.C., 1976-83, Carro, Spanbock, Fass, Geller, Kaster & Cuiffo, N.Y.C., 1983-86, ptnr., 1986, Finley Kumble Wagner et. al., N.Y.C., 1987; of counsel Kaye, Scholer, Fierman, Hays & Handler, N.Y.C., 1988; ptnr. Kaye, Scholer, Fierman, Hays & Handler, LLP, N.Y.C., 1989-97, Hunton & Williams, N.Y.C., 1997—2002. Trustee The Spence Sch., 2001—02; advisor WestWind Found., 2001—; mem. exec. com. Lawyers for Clinton, Washington, 1991—92; team capt. Clinton Transition Team, Washington, 1992—93; mem. Nat. Lawyers Coun. Dem. Nat. Com., 1993—98; trustee The Clinton Legal Expense Trust, 1998—2002, Pound Ridge Land Conservancy, 2003—, Queens Bot. Garden Soc., 2003—; mem. Alumni Coun. U. Va. Sch. of Law, 1997—, 2d v.p., 2000—01, 1st v.p., 2001—03, pres., 2003—. Mem. ABA, N.Y. Women's Bar Assn. Democrat. Roman Catholic.

RING, TRUDY M. writer, editor; b. Galesburg, Ill., Nov. 9, 1955; d. John Robert Ring and Norma Bernice Klinth. BS, No. Ill. U., 1976. Reporter The Register-Mail, Galesburg, 1977—79, The Daily Dispatch, Moline, Ill., 1980—84, Pensions & Investments, Chgo., 1984—91; devel. asst. Chgo. Ho. and Social Svc. Agy., Chgo., 1993—93; commissioning editor Fitzroy Dearborn Pubs., Chgo., 1994—95; reporter Lambda Publs., Chgo., 1995—96; copy editor LPI Media, L.A., 1997—2000, copy chief, 2000—. Editor: (reference book) The International Dictionary of Historic Places, Vols. 1-3; author: (nonfiction book) Careers in Finance; contbr. reference book series Contemporary Authors and Contemporary Authors, New Revision Series, reference book series The International Directory of Company Histories. Vol. Chgo. Ho. and Social Svc. Agy., 1988—92; bd. dirs. NOW, Chgo. Chpt., 1988—93. Recipient Outstanding Vol., Chgo. Ho. and Social Svc. Agy., 1990. Democrat. Avocations: travel, reading, films, theater, music. Home: 1123 N Myers Burbank CA 91506 Office: LPI Media 6922 Hollywood Blvd Los Angeles CA 90028 Personal E-mail: trudyr_1999@yahoo.com. E-mail: tring@lpimedia.net.

RING, TWYLA L. state legislator, newspaper editor; b. Sept. 15, 1937; m. Ardell Ring; 4 children. Student, Cambridge C.C. Mem. Minn. Senate from 18th dist., St. Paul, 1999—. Home: 8500 285th Ave NE North Branch MN 55056-6406 Office: Capitol 75 Constitution Ave Saint Paul MN 55155-1601

RING, YVONNE ANN, special education educator; b. Miami, Fla., Dec. 2, 1960; d. Thomas Charles and Diane Esther Fisher(Stepmother); m. John Michael Ring, Oct. 19, 1991; children: James William Jobbitt, II, Stephanie Ann Jobbitt. BS in Spl. Edn., Piedmont Coll., Demorest, Ga., 1996; MS in Interrelated Spl. Edn., North Ga. Coll. and State U., Dahlonega, 2001; Ednl. Specialist, Piedmont Coll., 2002—03. Cert. tchr. interrelated spl. edn. Ga., 2001, tchr. mental retardation spl. edn. Ga., 1996. Interrelated spl. edn. tchr. Rabun County Mid. Sch., Tiger, Ga., 2000—, North Habersham Mid. Sch., Clarkesville, Ga., 1996—2000. Practicum Clayton Elem., Clayton, Ga., 1994—94. Recipient Spl. Recognition, Coun. For Exceptional Children, 2000—, Recognition of Participation, Hand-in-Hand Mentor Program, 2001—; Tony Molinaro Scholarship, Ga. Coun. of Aminstrs. of Spl. Edn., 2003. Mem.: Profl. Assn. of Ga. Educators (assoc.), Coun. for Exceptional

Children (Phillip Wright br. Ga. chpt.) (assoc.; treas. 2003—), Coun. for Exceptional Children (assoc.), Internat. Dyslexia Found. (assoc.). Lutheran. Avocations: tutoring, travel, continuing education, professional conferences, museums. Home: PO Box 242 Clayton GA 30525-0242 Office: Rabun County Mid Sch 108 Wildcat Hill Drive Tiger GA 30576 E-mail: yring@rabun.k12.ga.us.

RINGER, JENNIFER, dancer; b. New Bern, N.C. m. James Fayette, July 2000. Student, Wash. Sch. Ballet, Sch. Am. Ballet; BA in English, Fordham U., 1997. Apprentice N.Y.C. Ballet, 1989—90, mem. corps de ballet, 1990—95, soloist, 1995—2000, prin., 2000—. Dancer (ballets) Brahms-Schoenberg Quartet, Divertimento No. 15, A Midsummer Nights Dream, The Nutcracker, Gershwin Concerto, Mozart Serenade, The Sleeping Beauty, Swan Lake, Tributary, I Have My Own Room, Correlazione, 1994, Prism, 2000, Appalachia Waltz, 2000, Morgen, Huoah, The Beethoven Seventh. Office: NYC Ballet NY State Theatre 20 Lincoln Ctr Plz New York NY 10023-6913

RINGGOLD, FAITH, artist; b. N.Y.C., Oct. 8, 1930; BS, CCNY, 1955, MA, 1959; DFA (hon.), Moore Coll. Art, Phila., 1986, Coll. Wooster, Ohio, 1987, Mass. Coll. Art, Boston, 1991, CCNY of CUNY, 1991, Russell Sage Coll., Troy, N.Y., 1996, Parsons Sch. Design, 1996; DSc (hon.), Brockport (N.Y.) State U., 1992, Calif. Coll. Arts and Crafts, Oakland, 1993; DHL (hon.), Malloy Coll., 1997; DHL (hon.), U. Chicago Art Inst., 2001; DFA (hon.), Mary Grove Coll., 2000, William Patterson U., 2001, Chgo. Art Inst., 2001, Marymount Coll., 1999. Art tchr. N.Y. Pub. Schs., 1955-73; lectr. Bank St. Coll. Grad. Sch., N.Y.C., 1970-80; prof. art U. Calif., San Diego, 1984—2002, prof. emeritus, 2002—, ret., 2002. Solo exhbns. include Bernice Steinbaum Gallery, 1991, ACA, 2000, Spectrum Gallery, N.Y.C., 1967, 70 10 year retrospective, Studio Mus. in Harlem, N.Y.C., 1984, Bernice Steinbaum Gallerym N.Y.C., 1987-88, Balt. Mus., Deland (Fla.) Mus., Faith Ringgold 25 Yr. Survey Fine Arts Mus. L.I., Hempstead, 1990-93, Textile Mus., Washington, 1993, Children's Mus. of Manhattan, N.Y.C., 1993-95, Hewlett-Woodmere Pub. Libr., Hewlett, N.Y., 1993-94, St. Louis Art Mus., 1994, Athenaeum, La Jolla, Calif., 1995, A.C.A. Gallery, N.Y.C., 1995, 98, Ind. U. of Pa., 1995, Bowling Green State U., Ind., 1996, New Mus. Contemporary Art, N.Y.C., 1998; exhibited in group shows at Harlem Cultural Coun., N.Y.C., 1966, Meml. Exhibit for MLK, Mus. Modern Art N.Y.C., 1968, Chase Manhattan Bank Collection, Martha Jackson Gallery, N.Y.C., 1970, Am. Women Artists, Gedok, Kunstalle, Hamburg, Ger., 1972, Jubliee, Boston Mus. Fine Arts, 1975, Major Contemporary Women Artists, Suzanne Gross Gallery, Phila., 1984, Committed to Print Mus. Modern Art, N.Y.C., 1988, The Art of Black Am. in Japan, Terada Warehouse, Tokyo, Made in the USA, Art in the 50s and 60s U. Calif. Berkeley Art Mus., Craft Today Poetry of the Physical, Am. Craft Mus., N.Y.C., Portraits and Homage to Mothers Hecksher Mus. Huntington, 1987, N.J. State Mus., Trenton, 1992-94, Fukui Fine Art Mus., Fuki, Japan, 1992, Takushima Modern Art Mus., Japan, 1993, Otani Meml. Art Mus., Japan, 1993, Salina Art Atr., Kans., 1993, Bruce Watkins Ctr. Kansas City, Mo., 1993, Barton County C.C., Great Bend, Kans., 1993, Del. State Coll. Arts Ctr. Gallery, Dover, 1993-94, Roswell Mus. and Art Ctr., N.Mex., 1994, Aknaton Gallery, Cairo, Alexandria, Egypt, Exit Art, N.Y.C., 1994, New Mus. Contemporary Art, N.Y.C., 1996, Spellman Coll. Mus., Atlanta, 1996, Whitney Mus., N.Y.C., 1996, Centre Georges Pompidou, Paris, 1997, Mus. Art, Ft. Lauderdale, Fla., 1997, N.J. Ctr. Arts, Summit, N.J., 1997, Trout Gallery Dickenson Coll., Carlisle, Pa., numerous others; represented in collections at Chase Manhattan Bank, N.Y.C., Philip Morris Collection, N.Y.C., Children's Mus., Bklyn., Newark Mus., The Women's House of Detention, Rikers Island, N.Y., The Studio Mus., N.Y.C., High Mus., Atlanta, Guggenheim Mus., Met. Mus. Art, Boston Mus. Fine Arts, MOMA, AARP, Washington, Am. Craft Mus., N.Y.C., Clark Mus., Williamstown, Mass., ARCO Chem., Phila., Coca-Cola, Atlanta, Ft. Wayne Mus. Fine Art, Ind., Harold Washington Libr. Ctr., Chgo., Lang Comm. Corp., Coll., Phila. Mus. Art, Pub. Art Pub. Schs., P.S. 22, Bklyn., Spenser Mus. Lawr., Kans., St. Louis Mus. Art, Balt. Mus., Nat. Mus., Washington, Woman's Mus., Washington, Eugenio Maria de Hostos C.C., N.Y.C., MTA 125th St. IRT subway sta. installation, N.Y.C., numerous others; author: Tar Beach, 1991, Aunt Harriet's Underground Railroad in the Sky, 1992 (Picture Book award 1993, Best Children's Book of Yr. 1993), Dinner at Aunt Connie's House, 1993 (Reading Magic award 1993), We Flew Over the Bridge: Memoirs of Faith Ringgold, 1995, Talking to Faith Ringgold, 1995, Bonjour Lonnie, 1996, My Dream of Martin Luther King, Jr., 1996, The Invisible Princess, 1999, If a Bus Could Talk: The Story of Rosa Parks, 1999, Counting to Tar Beach, 1999, Cassie's Colorful Day with Daddy, 1999, Cassie's Word Quilt, 2000; author: (video prodn.) Goodnight Moon: and Other Sleepy Time Tales, Tar Beach, 2000; contbr. articles to profl. jours. Recipient AAUW travel award to Africa, 1976; John Simon Guggenheim Meml. Found. Fellowship (painting), 1987, N.Y. Found. for Arts award (painting), 1988, Nat. Endowment Arts award (sculpture), 1978, (painting) 1989, La Napoule Found. award (painting in So. of France), 1990, Video and Software award Calif. children's book, 1991, Parent's Choice Gold award, 1991, Artist award Studio Mus., Harlem, 1991, Artist of Yr. award Sch. Art League N.Y., 1991, Coretta Scott King award for illustration, 1992, Dist. Artist award Nat. Coun. Art Adminstrn, 1992, award, 1993, Arts Internat. award (travel to Morocco), 1992, Honors award for outstanding achievement in the visual arts Woman's Caucus Arts, N.Y., 1994, Towsend Harris medal City Coll. Alumni Assn., 1995, N.J. Artist of Yr. award N.J. Ctr. Visual Arts, 1997, 31st NAACP Image award, 1999. Home: PO Box 429 Englewood NJ 07631-0429 Office: ACA Gallery 529 W 20th St Fl 5 New York NY 10011-2800 E-mail: any1canfly@aol.com.

RINGLER, LENORE, educational psychologist, educator; d. Albert Haendel and Ida (Brafstein) Haendel; 1 son., Adam. BA, Bklyn. Coll.; MA, Queens Coll., 1954; PhD, NYU, 1965. Tchr., then reading specialist N.Y.C. Bd. Edn.; prof. NYU, N.Y.C., 1965-98, prof. emerita, 1998—, chmn. dept. ednl. psychology, 1974-79. Ednl. cons. Psychol. Corp., Council on Interracial Books for Children, N.Y.C. Bd. Edn. Author: Skills Monitoring System-Reading, 1977, A Language-Thinking Approach to Reading, 1984, Born to Learn, 2004; author reading series for Holt Rhinehart & Winston, 1989; contbr. articles to profl. jours. Mem. Citizens Com. for Children; mem. Commn. on Reading Nat. Acad. Edn., 1983-85 Grantee U.S. Office Edn., 1968-69, Newspapers in Edn., 1990. Mem. APA, Am. Ednl. Rsch. Assn., Internat. Reading Assn. (past pres. Manhattan coun.), Nat. Reading Conf. (v.p. 1982-84, pres. 1984-85), Pi Lambda Theta (rsch. fellow 1963-64), Kappa Delta Pi. E-mail: lenore.ringler@nyu.edu.

RINGO, SHIRLEY G. state representative; b. Ft. Collins, Colo., Oct. 29, 1940; m. John Ringo; children: Shawn, Stacy, Shelley. BA, Wash. State U., 1962, MAT, 1965. Math. instr. Edmunds C.C., 1969, Madison Jr. H.S., 1962—68, 1969—71, Wash. State U., 1974—76, Moscow Sch. Dist., 1976—2000; state rep. dist. 6B Idaho Ho. of Reps, Boise, 2002—, mem. commerce and human resources, edn., and transp. and def. coms. Chair Latah County Dems., 1992—96, 2000—02; candidate Idaho Ho. of Reps. Dist 5B, 1999—2000. Mem.: NEA, Nat. Coun. Tchrs. Math., Moscow Edn. Assn. (pres. 1976—2000), Idaho Edn. Assn. (pres. region II 1984—86), Am. Assn. Ret. Persons (bd. dirs. 2001—). Democrat. Methodist. Office: State Capitol PO Box 83720 Boise ID 83720-0081

RINGPFEIL, FRAZISKA, dermatologist; b. Sept. 13, 1967; MD, 1992. Diplomate Am. Bd. Dermatology. Pvt. practice dermatology, Phila. Mem.: Am. Acad. Dermatology (Young Investigators award 2001). Home: 1215 Sandringham Rd Bala Cynwyd PA 19004-2024

RINGWALD, MOLLY, actress; b. Sacramento, Feb. 18, 1968; d. Bob and Adele Ringwald. Grad. high sch., Los Angeles. Actress: (stage prodns.) The Glass Harp, 1973, Annie, 1977, Cabaret, 2001, Enchanted April, 2004 (feature films) Tempest, 1982, Spacehunter: Adventures in the Forbidden Zone, 1983, Sixteen Candles, 1984, The Breakfast Club, 1985, Pretty in Pink, 1986, The Pick-Up Artist, 1987, For Keeps, 1988, Betsy's Wedding, 1990, Seven Sunday, 1994, Office Killer, 1996, Kimberly, 1999, Requiem For Murder, 1999, Teaching Mrs. Tingle, 1999, Cut, 2000, In the Weeds, 2000, Ring of Fire, 2000, Not Another Teen Movie, 2001, The Tulse Luper Suitcases: The Moab Story, 2003; (TV movies) Packin' It In, 1983, P.K. and the Kid, Something to Live For: The Alison Gertz Story, 1992, Twice Upon a Time, 1998, Since You've Been Gone, 1998, The Big Time, 2002; (TV mini-series) The Stand, 1994; regular (TV series) The Facts of Life, 1979-80, Townies, 1996; guest-star: (TV shows) Diff'rent Strokes, The Merv Griffin Show; (Album) Molly Sings, 1974. Office: William Morris Agy 151 S El Camino Dr Beverly Hills CA 90212-2775

RINKER, MARIANNE MARIE, rehabilitation nurse; b. Milford, Del., Aug. 5, 1960; d. James Warren and Ann Marie (Vissman) Graham. LPN, Parkview Hosp., Nashville, 1982; BSN, Vanderbilt U., Nashville, 1988. CRRN. Staff nurse West Side Hosp., Nashville, 1982-85; primary nurse Vanderbilt Med. Ctr., Nashville, 1986-89; head trauma coord. Georgetown Pinnacle Rehab., Louisville, 1989-91; clin. mgr. rehab. svcs. Alliant Health Svcs., Louisville, 1991-92; dir. rehab. nursing Healthsouth Med. Ctr., Richmond, Va., 1992-94; program cons. Rehabcare Group, Inc., St. Louis, 1994-98, dir. clin. edn., 1998—. Facilitator Ky. Head Injury Assn., Louisville, 1989-91; surveyor Commn. on Accreditation of Rehab. Facilities, 1997—. Counselor cmty. educator Vanderbilt AIDS Project, Nashville, 1987-88. Mem. Assn. Rehab. Nurses (adminstrv. mgmt. group 1994—). Avocations: music, literature, swimming, running. Home: 21546 Flanders St Farmington Hills MI 48335-5338

RINNAN, BARBARA GUY, retired non-profit organization executive; b. Oak Park, Ill., Dec. 18, 1929; d. Harry Lee and Anna Sophia (Gard) Guy; m. Carl Hagen Bergersen, Sept. 6, 1952 (div. May 1970); children: Laura Marie Bergersen, Paul Andrew Bergersen; m. Robert Malcolm Rinnan, June 3, 1972 (dec. Apr. 1998). BS magna cum laude, U. Ill., 1952. Med. technologist Westlake Cmty. Hosp., Melrose Park, Ill., 1952-54, Dr. Howard M. Sheaff, Oak Park, 1954-56; underwriter Prudential, L.A., 1956-59; comms. dir. Chgo. Sunday Evening Club, 1979-88; midwest rep. Ctr. U.S.-U.S.S.R. Initiatives, San Francisco, 1984-88; founder, pres. Midwest Ctr. Citizen Initiatives, Oak Park, 1988-96. Adv. bd. Caretakers of the Environ. Internat., Wilmette, Ill., 1992-96; sch. bd. mem. Oak Park Pub. Sch. Dist. 97, 1970-81. Democrat. Lutheran. Avocations: reading, writing, community volunteering, collecting russian artifacts, chicago symphony orchestra. Home: 221 N Kenilworth Ave Apt 510 Oak Park IL 60302-2053

RINSCH, MARYANN ELIZABETH, occupational therapist; b. L.A., Aug. 8, 1939; d. Harry William and Thora Analine (Langlie) Hitchcock; m. Charles Emil Rinsch, June 18, 1964; children: Christopher, Daniel, Carl. BS, U. Minn., 1961. Registered occupational therapist Calif., lic. Calif., 2003. Staff occupational therapist Hastings (Minn.) State Hosp., 1961-62, Neuropsychiat. Inst., L.A., 1962-64; staff and sr. occupational therapist Calif. Children's Svcs., L.A., 1964-66, head occupational therapist, 1966-68; researcher A. Jean Ayres, U. So. Calif., L.A., 1968-69; pvt. practice neurodevel. and sensory integraton Tarzana, Calif., 1969-74; pediat. occupational therapist neurodevel. & sensory integration St. Johns Hosp., Santa Monica, Calif., 1991-95; pvt. practice, cons. Santa Monica-Malibu Unified Sch. Dist., 1994-2001; pvt. practice, 2001—. Mem. alliance bd. Natural History Mus., L.A. County, 1983—, pres., 1998-99; cub scouts den mother Boy Scouts Am., Sherman Oaks, Calif., 1986-88, advancement chair Boy Scout Troop 474, 1989-92; mem. Vol. League San Fernando Valley, Van Nuys, Calif., 1985-93; trustee Viewpoint Sch., Calabasas, Calif., 1987-90; bd. dirs. Valley Women's Ctr., 1990-91. Mem. Am. Occupational Therapy Assn., Calif. Occupational Therapy Assn. Home: 19849 Greenbriar Dr Tarzana CA 91356-5428

RINTA, CHRISTINE EVELYN, nurse, air force officer; b. Geneva, Ohio, Oct. 4, 1952; d. Arvi Alexander and Catharina Maria (Steenbergen) R. BSN, Kent State U., 1974; MSN, Case Western Res. U., 1979. CNOR. Staff nurse oper. room Euclid (Ohio) Gen. Hosp., 1974-76, oper. room charge nurse, 1977-79; commd. 1st lt. USAF, 1979, advanced through grades to lt. col.; staff nurse oper. room Air Force Regional Hosp., Sheppard AFB, Tex., 1979-82; staff nurse oper. room, asst. oper. room supr. Regional Med. Ctr. Clark, Clark Air Base, Philippines, 1982-83; chief, nurse recruiting br. 3513th Air Force Recruiting Squadron, North Syracuse, N.Y., 1983-87; nurse supr. surg. svcs. 432d Med. Group, Misawa Air Base, Japan, 1987-89; course supr., instr. oper. room nursing courses 3793d Nursing Tng. Squadron, Keesler Med. Ctr., Keesler AFB, Miss., 1989-92; asst. dir., then dir. oper. room and ctrl. sterile supply Keesler Med. Ctr., Keesler AFB, Miss., 1992-93; comdr., enlisted clin. courses flight 383d Tng. Squadron, Sheppard AFB, Tex., 1993-94; comdr., officer clin. courses flight 383rd Tng. Squadron, Sheppard AFB, Tex., 1994-95; comdr. enlisted courses flight 383rd Tng. Squadron, Sheppard AFB, Tex., 1995-96; ops. officer, oper. room svcs. 74th Med. Ops. Squdron, Wright-Patterson AFB, Ohio, 1996-2000; ret., 2000. Decorated Air Force Commendation medal, Air Force Achievement medal, Meritorious Svc. medal. Mem. ANA, Ohio Nurses Assn., Assn. Operating Rm. Nurses, Air Force Assn., Sigma Theta Tau. Home: 3110 Cymar Dr Beavercreek OH 45434-6355 E-mail: Maxine1988@aol.com.

RIORDAN, JENNIFER L. media relations manager; b. Burlington, Vt., Nov. 11, 1974; d. Peter E. Guerin and Joy L. Lovejoy, K. Gregory Lovejoy (Stepfather) and Darcie Guerin(Stepmother); m. Michael J. Riordan. A, Champlain Coll., Burlington, 1994; BA, U. N.Mex, 1999. Account exec. Cooney, Watsons & Assocs., Albuquerque, 2000—02; sr. pub. affairs rep. U. N.Mex. Health Scis. Ctr., Albuquerque, 2002—. Campaign sect. chair United Way of Ctrl. N.Mex., Albuquerque, 2003—; mem. youth leadership curriculum com. Greater Albuquerque C. of C., 1999—2003; bd. dirs. U. N.Mex. Alumni Rels., 2003—. Named one of N.Mex. Bus. Weekly's 40 Under 40. Mem.: N.Mex. Pub. Rels. Soc. (bd.-elect 2002—), Chi Omega (pres. alumnae assn. 2002—03). Office: U NMex Health Scis Ctr MSC09 5120-1 U NMex Albuquerque NM 87131-0001 E-mail: jriordan@salud.unm.edu.

RIORDAN, ROSEMARY ANN, art educator, consultant; d. Raymond Anthony and Joanne F. Craft; m. Kevin P. Riordan, Nov. 24, 1979; children: Jason, Amber. BFA, Kans. State U., 1978; MS in Edn., Avila U., 1982. Art supr. Shawnee Mission, Overland Pk., Kans., 2000—, art educator, 1990—. Cons. Binney Smith, 1998—, Crayola, 2003—. Poster coord. Nat. Labor Bd., Kans., 2002—03; poster contest coord. Freedom Found., Kans., 2002. Mem.: NEA (named Master Tchr. Emporia State chpt. 2000), Nat. Art. Edn. Assn. (we.region elem. divsn. dir. 2003—), Am. Inst. Arch. (named Art Educator of Yr. 1994, named Preservation Educator of Yr. 1993), Nat. Sci. Tchr. Assn., Kans. Art Edn. Assn. (pres. elect 2003—, elem. divsn. chair, comml. liason, mem. chair., named Elem. Art Educator of Yr. 1995, named Art Educator of Yr. 2000), Nat. Audobon Soc. (Educator award 2003), Nat. Wildlife Soc. (vol. educator 2002—03). Avocations: spinning and weaving, gardening. Office: Shawnee Mission Visual Art Dept 4401 W 103rd Overland Park KS 66207

RIOS, EVELYN DEERWESTER, columnist, musician, artist, writer; b. Payne, Ohio, June 25, 1916; d. Jay Russell and Flossie Edith (Fell) Deerwester; m. Edwin Tietjen Rios, Sept. 19, 1942 (dec. Feb. 1987); children: Jane Evelyn, Linda Sue Rios Stahlman. BA with honors, San Jose State U., 1964, MA, 1968. Cert. elem., secondary tchr. Calif. Lectr. in music San Jose (Calif.) State U., 1969-75; from bilingual cons. to assoc. editor Ednl. Factors, Inc., San Jose, 1969-76, mgr. field rsch., 1977-78; writer, editor Calif. MediCorps Program, 1978-85; contbg. editor, illustrator Cmty. Family Mag., Wimberly, Tex., 1983-85; columnist The Springer, Dripping Springs, Tex., 1985-90. Author, illustrator, health instr. textbooks elem. schs., 1980—82. Author: (book) The Best of It Seems To Me, 2002. Chmn. Dripping Springs Planning and Zoning Commn., 1991—93; music dir. Cambrian Park (Calif.) Meth. Ch., 1961—64; choir dir. Bethel Luth. Ch., Cupertino, Calif., 1965—66, 1968—83; dir. music St. Aban's Ch., Bogota, Colombia; organist Holy Spirit Episcopal Ch., Dripping Springs, 1987—94. Mem.: Am. Guild Organists (dean 1963—64), Phi Kappa Phi (pres. San Jose chpt. 1973—74). Avocations: weaving, stitching, painting. Home and Office: 5700 Maya Ln Atascadero CA 93422-2552

RIPA, KELLY MARIA, television personality; b. Stratford, N.J., Oct. 2, 1970; d. Joseph and Esther Ripa; m. Mark Consuelos, 1996; children: Michael Joseph, Lola Grace, Joaquin Antonio. Student, Camden (N.J.) C.C. Co-host Live with Regis and Kelly, N.Y., 2001—. Dancer (TV series) Dance Party USA, 1986; actor: (TV series) All My Children, 1990—2002 (Soap Opera Digest award, 1996, 1998, 2000, 3 Daytime Emmy nominations); (films) Marvin's Room, 1996, The Stand-In, 1999 (Best Actress award N.Y. Internat. Ind. Film and Video Festival, 1999), It's a Very Merry Muppet Christmas Movie, 2002, Cheaper by the Dozen, 2003; (TV films) Someone to Love, 2001; voice : (films) Kim Possible: A Stitch in Time, 2003; Batman: Mystery of the Batwoman, 2003; actor: (TV series) Hope & Faith, 2003—. Nominee Outstanding Talkshow Host award, Daytime Emmy; named one of 25 Most Intriguing People, People Mag., 2001, Top 20 Entertainers of Yr., E! Entertainment. Office: Live with Regis and Kelly 7 Lincoln Sq New York NY 10023*

RIPPLE, ROCHELLE POYOUROW, educational administrator, educator; b. N.Y.C., Apr. 23, 1936; d. Gerald G. and Hortense (Philips) Bernheimer; m. Julian D. Ripple, Mar. 15, 1985; children: Mitchell, Jill, David. AAS, Fashion Inst. Tech., 1955, Pace U., BPS, 1974; MEd, Temple U., 1977, EdD, 1990. Cert. tchr. handicapped, Pa.; cert. prin., sch. supt., Wyo. Fashion designer Skampalon, Inc., N.Y.C., 1955-60; tchr. fashion design Pleasantville (N.Y.) Cottage Sch., 1969-74; spl. edn. tchr. Horsham Clinic, Ambler and Phila., Pa., 1974-78; fed. project dir. Montgomery County Intermediate Unit, Norristown, Pa., 1978-80; exec. dir. N.E. Wyo. Bd. Coop. Ednl. Svcs., Gillette, Wyo., 1980-86, tchg. assoc. Temple U., Phila., 1986-88; dir. vocat.-tech. edn. Ulster County BOCES, New Paltz, 1988-90; prof. ednl. adminstrn. Columbus (Ga.) State U., 1990—. Contbr. articles to profl. jours. Pres. Yorktown (N.Y.) Cmty. Rels. Coun., 1967-70; mem. adv. bd. Sheridan (Wyo.) Coll. Pace U. Trustee scholar, 1973; named Woman of Yr., Beta Sigma Phi, 1982. Mem. LWV, ASCD, Coun. for Exceptional Children, Am. Assn. Sch. Adminstrs., Assn. Retarded Citizens, Assn. Severely Handicapped, Phi Delta Kappa. Home: 612 Rudgate Rd Columbus GA 31904-2927 Office: Columbus State Univ Dept Edn Columbus GA 31907-5645

RIPPO, OLGA ALICIA, art director; b. Brighton, Mass., Jan. 25, 1923; Student, Boston Trade Sch./Art, 1937—39. Fashion sketch artist, Detroit, 1939—40; boilermaker U.S. Naval Shipyard, Boston, 1941—44; comms. prof. Nat. Weather Bur., San Bruno, Calif., 1946—51; art prodn. supr. Seal Beach Jour., Seal Beach, Calif., 1963—74; graphic artist News Enterprise, Los Alamitos, Calif., 1974—85; catalog prodn. profl. Clifford Rsch. and Devel., Huntington Beach, Calif., 1974—88. Entrepreneur OAR Enteprises, Los Alamitos, Calif., 2001—; "Legal Odyssey" resulted in the establishment of a precedent in Fla. legal system, 1983—92. Author: (novels) (children's story) My Life as a Dime, 1995, Dreams (As I See Them), 2001. Achievements include patent for the Baseball Fan, 2000. Home: 11456 Harrisburg Rd Los Alamitos CA 90720

RIPSTEIN, JACQUELINE, artist; b. Mexico City, Apr. 18, 1952; came to U.S., 1996; d. Maximiliano and Josephine Ripstein; widow; children: Stephanie, Arlette. Grad. high sch., Mexico City. Participant more than 160 expositions and tours, U.S., Mex., Europe. Developer, patentee Invisible Art & Light Technique; group shows include: Libr. Mus. Show, Cuernavaca, Morelos, Mex., 1978, C.V.M. Art. Co., N.Y., 1979, MGM Grand Gallery, Las Vegas, 1980, Govt./Inst. del Petroleo, Mex., 1982, Lanai Gallery, Mex., 1982, Praxis Gallery, 1988, Dyansen Gallery, Beverley Hills, Calif., 1988, CFE Tech. Mus., Mex., 1991, San Carmen Mus., Mex., 1991, Jewish Cmty. Ctr., Houston, 1992, Sefarad, Posada de la Hermandad Art and Cultural Ctr., 1992, 94, Art Expo Phillips-Samuels Gallery, Miami, 1993, Salon d'Automne, Grand Prix de Sud Ouest, 1995, Biennale d'Aquitain (prize 1994): Mus. d'Art Moderne d'Unet, France, 1995 (recognition prize Fort Lauderdale Philarmonic Soc. 1994), Grand Prix de Paris d'Art Plastique: Found. Napoleon, Unet, 1995, Biennale Diploma Honneur/D'EncouragementPub. Paris, Wirtz Gallery, South Beach, Fla., 1996, Kolel Art Show, Caracas, Venezuela, 1996, The World Spritiual U., JR's Art, Heart Sanctuaries, 1998, Art Frenzie, 1998, Vibrations through Music and Art, Steven Halpern and JR's Art, 1999, Vibrations through Music, UN Philarmonica, JR's Art, 1999; spl. events include: Day of Awakenings, Miami Arena, U. Wisdom Found., 1998; commd. Our Lady of the Universe: God's Gift to the World, Thy Will Be Done, Holy Family Inst., Calif., Boston, N.C., Phila., Chgo., New Orleans, Palm Beach, Fla., Naples, Fla., 1997; appeared in publs. Hola Mag., 1994, Fine Art Index N.Am., 1994, Voces Esteticas de Ignacio Flores Antunez, Quinientos Anos Editores, Artistas Plasticos, 1981, Directorio Artistico, 1986, Art Expressions Mag., Sedona Mag., others. Recipient Proclamation, City of Toledo, 1994, Nat. Competition award, Mex., 1994, Laureat prize '95, 1994, Certificate of appreciation, Aspira of Fla., United Way Edn. Program, South Beach Alternative Sch., 1995. Mem. Aventura Mktg. Coun.

RISEN-WHITE, ANGELA LORRI, systems analyst; b. Bloomington, Ind., Nov. 2, 1970; d. Thomas Gary and Margie Bea (Gilbert) Risen; m. Jerry Leslie White, Oct. 19, 1996. BS in Acctg., Ind. U., 1994. CPA, CMA. Bookkeeper Hoosier Hills Food Bank, Bloomington, Ind., 1993-94; fin. devel. program assoc. Baxter Healthcare, Deerfield, Ill., 1995, Baxter Healthcare Can., Mississauga, Ont., 1995-96; with inventory acctg. Allegiance Healthcare, Waukegan, Ill., 1996-97, sr. fin. analyst V. Mueller divsn., 1997-98, sr. fin. ops. analyst V. Mueller divsn., 1998-99, bus. sys. analyst V. Mueller divsn., 1999—. Foster home coord. Guardian Angel Basset Rescue, Ill. Mem. Ill. CPA Soc., Inst. Mgmt. Accts., Jr. Achievement (vol. tutor). Office: Allegiance Healthcare 1430 Waukegan Rd # Kb-b2 Mc Gaw Park IL 60085-6787

RISER, KATHLEEN WALSH, secondary school educator; b. Oak Pk., Ill., Apr. 11, 1960; d. James Edward and Jude Walsh; m. Jody B. Riser, Sept. 1, 2001. MusB, U. Tenn., 1978—83; Peer Assistance Tchr. Tng., U. Memphis, 2001; Classroom Orgn. & Mgmt. Program, Vanderbilt U., Nashville Tenn., 2001. Lic. Profl. Tchr. Dept. of Edn., Tenn., 1984. Travel reservations Holiday Corp., Memphis, 1983—91; tchr. Skyview Acad., Memphis, 1991—94, Memphis Cath. Sch. - Cath. HS, Memphis, 1994—95, Memphis City Schools - Oakhaven HS, Memphis, 1995—98; tchr. & tchr. mentor Memphis City Schools - Georgian Hills Jr., Memphis, 1998—. Tchr. mentor Georgian Hills Jr. HS, Memphis, 2001—. Concert tours, Memphis, Tenn., 1993—2003. Named to Honor Band Counseling Staff, John Phillip Sousa Found., 1991; recipient Outstanding Svc. award, Georgian Hills Jr. HS, 2002, Tchr. of the Month award, 2003. Mem.: West Tenn. Band and Orch. Assn. (assoc.), Music Educators Nat. Conf. (assoc.), Sigma Alpha Iota (life; pres. 1980—82, Sword of Honor 1982). Bapt. Avocations: reading, gardening. Home: 284 Melita Rd Memphis TN 38120

RISHER, MARY LOU BISHOP, artist; b. Tulsa, Jan. 6, 1929; d. George W. and Frances Pearl (Hendrix) Nesmith; m. Thomas Ray Bishop, Sept. 1, 1951 (div. 1996); children: Thomas R. Bishop II, Frances Joann Bishop Faber; m. Jack Risher, May 26, 1998. Student, Columbia U., 1948; BA, U. Houston, 1949, MEd, 1951; student, U. Wash., 1954; postgrad., U. Houston, 1983-84; pvt. studies with, James Jennings, Opal Walls, Ruth Pershing Uhler, Lowell Collins. Cert. tchr., Tex., Wash. Fine artist, painter specializing in portraits, 1951—; freelance artist, 1975—; pvt. tchr. pastels and oils. Condr. portrait seminars Tidwell Art Ctr., Houston. Exhibited in one-woman shows in Washington, Ala., Tex.; group shows at Bellevue Arts Fair, Washington; represented in permanent collections at 1st Bapt. Ch., Houston, Unitarian Ch., Huntsville, Ala., also corp. and pvt. collections in U.S. and Europe; executed murals for Unitarian Ch., Huntsville; portraits represented at Mary Doerr's images of Austin and the Southwest, Austin. Recipient scholarship Houston Mus. Fine Art, 1939-50, numerous awards for art. Mem. AAUW, Houston Soc. Illustrators, Profl. Picture Framer's Assn., Phi Kappa Phi, Phi Theta Kappa, Kappa Delta Pi. Unitarian Universalist. Avocations: portrait work, piano, gardening, landscape painting, travel. Home: 16 Cypress Meadow Loop Slidell LA 70460-5214

RISKIN, VICTORIA, former trade association administrator; d. Robert Riskin and Fay Wray; m. David Rintels. Pres. Writers Guild Am., West, 2001—04. Author: (TV films) My Antonia, 1995; prodr.: (TV films) The Last Best Year, 1990, A Town Torn Apart, 1992, World War II: When Lions Roared, 1994, The Member of the Wedding, 1997.

RISKO, VICTORIA J. language educator; BS, U. Pitts., 1966; MS, W.Va. U., 1969, EdD, 1971; postgrad., U. London, 1975. Fellow Learning Disabilities Inst. W.Va. U., 1969—70; tchr. Johnstown (Pa.) Pub. Sch. Sys., 1967—68; tchr. remedial reading Johnstown (Pa.) Pub. Sch. Dist., 1967; instr. home econs. W.Va. U., 1968—69, instr., supr. reading clinic, 1969; rschr.-tchr. Robert F. Kennedy Youth Ctr., Morgantown, W.Va., 1969—70; tchr.-cons. inservice edn. of tchrs. Belair-Manchester Schs. of Mandeville, Jamaica, 1974—75; instr., asst. prof., assoc. prof., dir. reading clinic programs, mem. grad. faculty SUNY, Fredonia, 1970—75; rsch. scientist Learning Tech. Ctr., mem. faculty interdisciplinary team Child Study Ctr., Kennedy Ctr. Peabody Coll., Vanderbilt U., Nashville, 1978—89, assoc. prof., 1975—94, prof. lang. and learning, 1994—. Vis. prof. reading W.Va. U., 1971. Recipient Disting. Svc. and Leadership award, Coll. Reading Assn., 1995, Disting. Rsch. in Tchr.'s Edn. award, Assn. Tchr. Educators Conf., 1992. Office: Vanderbilt U Peabody Coll Box 330 Nashville TN 37203

RISNER, ANITA JANE, vocational school educator; b. Durant, Okla., Nov. 10, 1946; d. Forrest W. and Jane J. (Nelms) Carter; m. Curt Risner, Jan. 21, 1968; children: Patrick, Brandon. AS, Eastern Okla. Jr. Coll., 1967; BS, Okla. State U., 1971; MEd, Northeastern State U., 1981. Hospitality careers tchr. Pryor (Okla.) Pub. Schs., 1971-73, N.E. Area Vo-Tech, Pryor, 1973-75; child devel. tchr. Tulsa Tech. Ctr., 1976-81, counselor, 1981-89; staff devel. specialist Okla. Dept. of Vo-Tech Edn., Stillwater, Okla., 1989-94; instrnl. coord. Indian Capital Area Vo-Tech Sch., Muskogee, Okla., 1994—; regional career devel. specialist Okla. Dept. Vocat. Tech. Edn., 1994-97; asst. supt. Tri-County Tech. Ctr., Bartlesville, Okla., 1997-99, dep. supt., 1999—. Advisor Vocat. Student Orgns., Tulsa, 1976-89; career adv. com. mem. Bixby (Okla.) Pub. Schs., 1992—; participant Craftmanship 2000 program, Tulsa; presenter in local, state, nat. confs. Editor: (curriculum guide) Integrating Career Days, 1992, Integrating OK Career Search, 1993; editor (newsletter) Classworks, 1995. Mem. ASCD, Am. Vocat. Assn. (Region IV Outstanding Vocat. Educator of Yr. 1994, Outstanding Vocat. Educator of Yr. award 1995), Okla. Vocat. Assn. (Educator of Yr.-Guidance 1993), Okla. Assn. for Supervision and Curriculum Devel., Phi Delta Kappa. Democrat. Avocations: reading, flower gardening. Address: 1729 Melrose Dr Bartlesville OK 74006-7025 Office: Tri-County Tech Ctr 6101 Nowata Rd Bartlesville OK 74006-6029

RISSONE, DONNA, language educator; b. Stamford, Conn., July 13, 1943; d. Thomas and Carmela (Sabato) Galasso; m. Robert Rissone, Aug. 21, 1965; children: Robert, Jeannine. AB in Classics, Rosemont (Pa.) Coll., 1965; MSEd, Nazareth Coll., 1975. Cert. elem. secondary fgn. lang. tchr., N.Y. Tour escort various, Europe; fgn. lang. tchr. W. Irondequoit H.S., Rochester, N.Y., 1973—; treas. Door and Hardware Systems, Rochester, 1972—. Named Activity Advisor of Yr. N.Y. State Advisors/Student Assn., 1996. Avocation: travel. Home: 305 Harbor Hill Dr Rochester NY 14617-1469 Office: W Irondequoit High Sch 260 Cooper Rd Rochester NY 14617-3095

RISTICH, KATHARINE ALEXANDRA, journalist; d. Miodrag and Yvonne Ristich. BA in History, Mt. Holyoke Coll., 1991. Rschr., writer SPIN Mag., N.Y.C., 1991—94; publs. asst. Milbank Meml. Fund, N.Y.C., 1994—96; journalist TheHeart.Org, N.Y.C., NY, 2000—02. Contbg. author: book City Secrets: New York, 2002.

RISTOW, GAIL ROSS, art educator, paralegal, children's rights advocate; b. Carmel, Calif., Oct. 18, 1949; d. Kenneth E. and Lula Mae (Craft) Ross; m. Steven Craig Ristow, Sept. 15, 1971. BS in Biochemistry, Calif. Polytech State U., San Luis Obispo, 1972; MEd, Ariz. State U., 1980. Cert. tchr., Calif. Asst. instr. Calif. State Polytech U., Pomona, 1972; grad. asst. Calif. Polytech State U., Pomona, 1973-74; tchr. Mt. Carmel High Sch., L.A., 1974-76, Cartwright Sch. Dist., Phoenix, 1976-80; pres., owner Handmade With Love, Bay City, Tex., 1984-88; tchr. art Aiken, S.C., 1989-96. Tchr. Community Edn., Bay City, 1986-88, Palacios, Tex., 1987. Sec. Chukker Creek Homeowners, Aiken, S.C., 1989-96; mem. S.C. Foster Care Rev. Bd., 1991-96; vol. tchr. elem. schs., Korea. Mem. AAUW, Am. Chem. Soc., Nat. Soc. Tole and Decorative Painters, Aiken Newcomer's Club (sec. 1989-91), Aiken Lioness Club (pres. 1991-94), Aiken Lions Club, Alpha Delta Kappa (v.p. 1986-87). Avocations: painting, woodworking, sewing, reading, children's rights advocacy. Home: 396 Lombardy Ln Richland WA 99352

RISTOW, THELMA FRANCES, elementary school educator; b. Plymouth, Wis., Sept. 9, 1938; d. Ambrose J. and Marie A. (Lauby) Enders; m. William A. Ristow, Nov. 7, 1964; children: James, Lora, Kim Marie, Robert, Donald. BS, U. Wis., Oshkosh, 1960, MS in Edn., 1995. Cert. elem. tchr. Tchr. Webster Stanley Elem., Wis., 1995—2003; peer coach Oshkosh Area Sch. Dist.; ret., 2003. Contbr. chapters to books; co-author (with Dr. Ava McCall): Teaching State History: A Guide to Developing a Multicultural Curriculum. Mem. ASCD, Internat. Reading Assn. (state coord.), Wis. State Reading Assn., Ctrl. Wis. Reading Coun., Mid-East Reading Coun., Wolf River Reading Coun., Fox Valley Reading Coun., Delta Kappa Gamma, Phi Delta Gamma, Kappa Delta Pi. Home: 1600 Northpoint St Oshkosh WI 54901-3119 Office: Webster Stanley Elem 915 Hazel St Oshkosh WI 54901-4057

RISTUCCIA, LAVERN K. COLE, psychologist, consultant; b. Balt., Mar. 14, 1952; d. Vernon Geyer and Viola Cecilia (Riley) Cole; m. Bruce Michael Ristuccia, Oct. 26, 1990; 2 children. BA, U. Md., Balt., 1974; MA in Clin. Psychology, Antioch Coll., 1982; PhD in Psychology, Nova Southeastern, Ft. Lauderdale, Fla., 1993. Lic. psychologist, N.Y. Practica Nova Southeastern Mental Health Clinic, Ft. Lauderdale, 1987-89; intern psychologist U. Rochester (N.Y.) Med. Ctr., 1989-90; psychologist Monroe Devel. Ctr., Rochester, 1990-92, Lifetime Assistance, Rochester, 1992-94, Park Ridge Hosp., Rochester, 1994-97; psychologist in pvt. practice Rochester, 1997—. Cons. Arbor Hill Living Ctr., Rochester, 1996-97, Indsl. Medicine, Inc., Rochester, 1996-97; adivsor to bd. dirs. Canandaigua (N.Y.) Montessori Sch., 1998-2000. Mem. APA, N.Y. State Psychologists Assn., Genesee Valley Psychol. Assn. Democrat. Methodist. Avocations: travel, antiques. Office: 3180 West St Canandaigua NY 14424-1722

RITCH, KATHLEEN, diversified company executive; b. Harbor Beach, Mich., Jan. 23, 1943; d. Eunice (Spry) R. BA, Mich. State U., 1965; student, Katharine Gibbs Sch., 1965-66. Exec. sec., adminstrv. asst. to pres. Katy Industries, Inc., N.Y.C., 1969-70; exec. sec., adminstrv. asst. to chmn. Kobrand Corp., N.Y.C., 1970-72; adminstrv. to chmn. and pres. Ogden Corp., N.Y.C., 1972-74, asst. sec., adminstr. office svcs., asst. to chmn., 1974-81, corp. sec., adminsr. office svcs., 1981-84, v.p., corp. sec., adminstr. office svcs., 1984-92, v.p. corp. sec., 1992-2000; freelance executive NYC, 2000—. Co-owner Unell Mfg. Co., Port Hope, Mich., 1966-87. Bd. dir. Young Concert Artists, Inc. Mem. Am. Soc. Corp. Secs. Home: 500 E 77th St New York NY 10162-0025

RITCHEY, YVONNE KAY, assistant principal; b. Anderson, Ind., July 10, 1957; d. Kenneth Everett and Constance Florence Wise; m. Randy Dee Jones, Aug. 2, 1980 (div. Apr. 24, 1988); 1 child, Monica Ashley Jones ; m. Stephen Edward Ritchey, June 2, 1990; children: Stephen G., Robert P. BS, Ball State U., Muncie, Ind., 1979, MS Endorsement, 1986, MEd, 1987, postraduate, 2002. 1st grade tchr. Gordon County Schs., Calhoun, Ga., 1979—81; tchr. math. and sci. St. Mary's Sch., Anderson, 1986—89; tchr. sci. Indpls. Pub. Schs., 1989—94; tchr. math. and sci. Anderson Cmty. Schs., 1994—2001, lead tchr., 2001—02, asst. prin., 2002—. Mem.: Am. Assn. Sch. Adminstrs., Phi Delta Kappa. Home: 1516 E 500 N Anderson IN 46012 Office: South Side Middle Sch 101 W 29th St Anderson IN 46016

RITCHIE, BETH BRADLEY, elementary school educator; b. Lynchburg, Va., Feb. 23, 1970; d. Parmer Harding Bradley and Lois Dull (Bradley) Ocheltree; m. Robert John Ritchie, Oct. 9, 1993; children: Elsie Alexander, Caroline Wallace, Virginia Grace. BS in Early Childhood Edn., Longwood Coll., 1992. Learning disabled resource tchr. Thomas Dixon Elem., Staunton, Va., 1992—93, long-term substitute tchr. 6th grade, 1993—94; tchr. sci./health reading 6th grade Bessie Weller Elem., Staunton, 1994—95; tchr. K-4 Sea Island Presbyn. Ch., Beaufort, SC, 1999—2002. Bn. key vol. coord. 3d Bn. / 11th Marines, 29 Palms, Calif., 1996—98; soccer coord. Advent Episcopal Day Sch., 2002—. Recipient Molly Pitcher award, 3d Bn. / 11th Marines, 1998. Mem.: Officer's Wives Club (club officer 1997—98). Republican. Episcopalian. Avocations: running, being with children, gardening. Home: 5016 8th Ter S Birmingham AL 35212

RITCHIE, ELISAVIETTA, poet, writer, educator, editor, translator; b. Kansas City, Mo., June 29; d. George Leonidovich and Jessie Downing Artamonoff; m. Lyell Hale Ritchie (div.); children: Lyell Kirk, Elspeth Cameron, Alexander George; m. Clyde Henri Farnsworth. Student, Cornell U., 1951—53; diploma Mention Tres Bien, Sorbonne, U. Paris, 1951; BA in French, Russian and English, U. Calif., Berkeley, 1954; postgrad., Georgetown U.; MA in French Lit., Am. U., 1976. Instr. The Writers Ctr.; writer, poet, editor, transl., small press pub., pub. rels. profl., tchr. creative writing; poet-in-the-schs., 1967—; pres., now v.p. for fiction Washington Writers' Pub. House. Part-time lectr., then grad. tchg. fellow Am. U., 1968—76. Author: (fiction) In Haste I Write You This Note: Stories and Half-Stories, 2000 (winner Washington Writers' Pub. House premiere fiction competition, 2000), (poetry) The Arc of the Storm, 1998, Elegy for the Other Woman: New and Selected Poems, 1996, (novella in verse) Wild Garlic: The Journal of Maria X., 1995, (poetry) A Wound-Up Cat and Other Bedtime Stories, 1993, (fiction) Flying Time: Stories and Half-Stories, 1982, 1986 (includes 4 PEN Syndicated Fiction winners), (poetry) The Problem with Eden, 1985 (Poetry Soc. of Ga. competition winner, 1985), Raking the Snow, 1982 (Washington Writer's Pub. House competition winner, 1981), Moving to Larger Quarters, 1977, A Sheath of Dreams and Other Games, 1976, Tightening the Circle Over Eel Country, 1974 (Gt. Lakes Colls. Assn.'s New Writer's Prize for Best First Book of Poetry, 1975), (novella in verse) Timbot, 1970; creator, editor: anthologies The Dolphin's Arc: Endangered Creatures of the Sea, 1986, Finding the Name, 1983; contbr. stories, poems, creative non-fiction, photographs to numerous publs. Vol. various pro bono activities. Recipient ann. Poetry Soc. of Am. awards, 1973, 1975, Anamnesis Poetry award, 2001; fellow several fellowships, Va. Ctr. for Creative Arts, 1980; grantee 4 grants, D.C. Commn. for Arts, 1970. Mem.: Writer's Ctr. (instr.). Avocations: tennis, sailing, wildlife conservation. Home: 3207 Macomb St NW Washington DC 20008-3327

RITTEL, KATHLEEN ANN, former assistant principal and school system administrator, middle school educator; d. William Michael and Ann Marilyn; m. Donald Russell Rittel; 1 child, Sophia Anndrina Maria. BA in English and Edn., Queens Coll., 1972, MS in Edn., 1977; postgrad., SUNY, Albany, 1978, Brigham Young U., 1978, McPherson Coll., 1978; PD in Adminstrn. and Supervision, St. John's U., Jamaica, NY, 1982; postgrad., Adelphi U., 1983, U. Mont., 1986, U. N.Mex., 1999, L.I. U., 2000, Coll. St. Rose, 2000, Ind. Wesleyan U., 2003, Endicott Coll., 2003. Cert. tchr., adminstr., supr., N.Y. Tchr. Elijah Clark Jr. H.S., South Bronx, NY, 1972-75, Intermediate Sch. 291, Bklyn., 1975; tchr., dean, asst. prin. Jean Nuzzi Jr. H.S., Queens Village, 1975-83; asst. prin. William Cowper Intermediate Sch., Maspeth, 1983-93; adminstr.-in-charge I.S. 73 Annex, Elmhurst, 1994—97, 51st Ave. Annex for P.S. 7 and P.S. 71, 1997-99; adminstr.-in charge 51st Ave. Annex for P.S. 7 and I.S. 5, 1999; tchr. Jericho Mid. Sch., 2003—. Doctoral fellow Hofstra U., 1990. Mem. Nat. Coun. Tchrs. English, Internat. Reading Assn. Roman Catholic. Avocations: playing piano, roller skating, ice skating, dance, traveling. E-mail: superprofessor1@yahoo.com.

RITTENHOUSE, NANCY CAROL, elementary school educator; b. Humeston, Iowa, May 26, 1941; d. Myrl Matthews and Opal L. (McCartney) Hixson; m. J. Kent Rittenhouse, Dec. 18, 1960 (div. Mar. 1984); children: Brenda L. Carroll, J. Aaron, Timothy K. Grad., Kirksville State Tchrs. Coll., 1960; student, St. Mary of the Plains Coll., 1984-87; degree in elem. edn., Ft. Hays State Coll., 1989. Cert. tchr., Kans. Reading instr. Sacred Heart Sch., Dodge City, Kans., 1984; elem. tchr. Miller Sch., Dodge City, Kans., 1985-86, Washington Sch., Hays, 1987; city-county recreation dir. Sherman County, Goodland, 1988; elem. tchr. Northside Sch., Larned, 1989-90; with Great Bend (Kans.) Tribune. Artist numerous paintings; author poetry. Mem. Menninger Found., Topeka, 1984—; hon. mem. Boy Scouts Am., 1978; camp instr. Spl. Olympics Blind Found., Junction City, Kans., 1985-90, Dodge City, 1984; leader Girl Scouts USA, 1975-77. Recipient Hon. award Spl. Olympics, 1984, 1st pl. poetry award, 1990, watercolor award, 1990, oils award, 1988, pen and ink award, 1984. Mem. AAAS, Nat. Trust for Hist. Preservation, Nat. Geog. Soc., Planetary Soc., Smithsonian Assn., MIT. Republican. Avocations: painting, drawing, walking, swimming, writing prose. Home: PO Box 1872 Great Bend KS 67530-1872 Office: Great Bend Tribune 2012 Forest Ave Great Bend KS 67530-4014

RITTER, ANN L. lawyer; b. N.Y.C., May 20, 1933; d. Joseph and Grace (Goodman) R. BA, Hunter Coll., 1954; JD, N.Y. Law Sch., 1970; postgrad. Law Sch., NYU, 1971-72. Bar: N.Y. 1971, U.S. Ct. Appeals (2d cir.) 1975, U.S. Supreme Ct. 1975. Writer, 1954-70; editor, 1955-66; tchr., 1966-70; atty. Am. Soc. Composers, Authors and Pubs., N.Y.C., 1971-72, Greater N.Y. Ins. Co., N.Y.C., 1973-74; sr. ptnr. Brenhouse & Ritter, N.Y.C., 1974-78; sole practice N.Y.C., 1978—. Editor N.Y. Immigration News, 1975-76. Mem. ABA, Am. Immigration Lawyers Assn. (treas. 1983-84, sec. 1984-85, vice-chair 1985-86, chair 1986-87, chair program com. 1989-90, chair spkrs. bur. 1989-90, chair media liaison 1989-90), N.Y. State Bar Assn., N.Y. County Lawyers Assn., Assn. Trial Lawyers Am., N.Y. State Trial Lawyers Assn., N.Y.C. Bar Assn., Watergate East Assn. (v.p., asst. treas. 1990—). Democrat. Jewish. Home: 47 E 87th St New York NY 10128-1005 Office: 420 Madison Ave Rm 1200 New York NY 10017-1171

RITTER, DEBORAH ELIZABETH, anesthesiologist, educator; b. Phila., May 16, 1947; d. Charles William and Elizabeth Angeline (Coffman) R. BA, Susquehanna U., 1968; MS, U. Pa., 1969; MD, Med. Coll. Pa., 1973. Diplomate Am. Bd. Anesthesiology (assoc. examiner oral bds. 1990, 92). Intern Thomas Jefferson Univ. Hosp., Phila., 1973-74, resident in anesthesia, 1974-76, clin. fellow in anesthesiology, 1976-77; affiliate resident in anesthesia Children's Hosp. Pa., Phila., 1975; assoc. in anesthesiology Frankford Hosp., Phila., 1977-78; clin. instr. anesthesiology Med. Coll. Pa., Phila., 1977-78, Thomas Jefferson U., 1978-80, clin. asst. prof., 1980-86, clin. assoc. prof., 1986—, vice chmn. dept. anesthesiology, 1985—. Contbr. articles to profl. jours. Named Top Doc, Phila. Mag., 1994, 96. Mem. AMA, Am. Women's Med. Assn., Am. Soc. Anesthesiologists, Internat. Anesthesia Rsch. Soc., Soc. Edn. Anesthesia, Assn. Anesthesia Clin. Dirs. Lutheran. Avocations: gardening, music, history, wilderness preservation, american indian culture. Office: Thomas Jefferson U Dept Anesthesiology 111 S 11th St Ste 8490G Philadelphia PA 19107-5084

RITTER, ELISE DAWN, therapist, clinical social worker, writer, artist; b. Balt., Aug. 14, 1952; d. Nelson Fred and Marjorie Jean (Corke) Ritter; m. Philip Anthony Gibson, Apr. 7, 1979 (div. Feb. 1990); 1 child, Christopher Ritter Gibson; m. Victor Wayne Clough, Jr., Mar. 3, 1990; stepchildren: Wesley T., Lindsay, Sharon. Student, Austro-Am. Inst., Vienna, Austria, 1973; BS, U. Kans., 1974; M Psychiatric Social Work, Va. Commonwealth U., 1998. LCSW. Rschr. impeachment inquiry staff U.S. Ho. of Reps., Washington, 1974; rschr. APA, Washington, 1975; editor prodn. The New Republic Mag., Washington, 1976-77; copy editor Time-Life Books, Alexandria, Va., 1977-79, assoc. editor, 1979-83, adminstrv. editor, 1983-87, asst. dir. editl. resources, 1988-90; dir. editl. resources Time Warner, Time-Life Books, Alexandria, 1990-94; pvt. practice therapist, 2000—. With Arlingtonians Ministering to Emergency Needs-AMEN, 1995; vol. Mental Health Program, Visiting Nurse Assn., 1996, Women's Ctr., Vienna, Va., 1997-99, PsychologyNetwork.com, 2000—, DiscoveryHealth.com, 2002-03. Mem.: Rappahannock Art League Studio Gallery.

RITTER, JENNIFER LEIGH, music minister, educator; b. Tacoma, Wash., May 14, 1971; d. Carl Brent Ritter and Shirley Ann Ranus. B in Music Edn., B in Vocal Music Performance, Colo. State U., Fort Collins, 1994. Cert. tchr. Colo., substitute tchr. Colo., lic. Kindermusik educator 2000. Middle sch. & H.S. choir tchr. Lamar (Colo.) Sch. Dist. RE-1, 1994—95; K-12 music specialist Agate (Colo.) Sch. Dist. 300, 1995—96; substitute tchr. Pueblo (Colo.) Sch. Dist. 60, 1996—2000; music minister SunRise Ch., Pueblo, 1997—. Kindermusik educator Rhythm St., Pueblo, 2000—; pvt. piano & vocal tchr., Pueblo, 2000—. Actor: (plays) Damon Runyon Repertory Theater, 1999— (Best Supporting Actress, 2000, Outstanding Sound Design, 2001, Best Female Vocalist, 2002, Most Valuable Person, 2002). Mem.: Colo. Music Educators Assn., Pueblo Choral Soc. Protestant. Avocations: architecture, art, writing, composing, interior design. Office: Jennifer Ritter Studio 1829 S Pueblo Blvd #114 Pueblo CO 81005 E-mail: gracenotes71@yahoo.com.

RITTER, MADELIENE, practical nurse, surgical technologist; b. Camden, N.J., Feb. 11, 1954; m. James W. Ritter. Degree in practical nursing, Ocean County Vocat. Tech. Sch., 1975. Cert. surgical technologist; lic. practical nurse. Staff nurse Cmty. Meml. Hosp., Toms River, NJ, 1975—77, staff nurse/pacu, 1979—85; office nurse Stafford Orthopedics, Manahawkin, NJ, 1985—98; oper. rm. nurse Cmty. Med. Ctr., Toms River, NJ, 1998—2000, So. Ocean County Hosp., Manahawkin, NJ, 1999—, 1999—. Mem. Am. Cancer Soc. Relay for Life, Manahawkin, NJ, 2001, co-captain. Leader Ocean County Girl Scouts, Toms River, NJ, 1982—98; lifetime mem. Girl Scouts of Am.; mem. Barnegat First Aid Squad, Barnegat, NJ; co-leader internat. travel Switzerland/Mex. troops Ocean County Girl Scout Coun., Toms River, NJ. Mem.: Assn. Surg. Technologists, Nat. Assn. Practical Nurse Edn. and Svc.

RITTER, STACY JOY, state legislator, lawyer; b. Washington, June 8, 1960; BA, Rollins Coll., 1982; JD, Nova U., 1985. Bar: Fla. 1985. Mem. Fla. Ho. of Reps., 1996—; mem. regulated svcs. com., 1996-97; mem. civil justice and claims com., 1996-97. Editor Shalom mag. Vice chmn. Coral Springs Civic, Cultural and Ednl. Found., State Pub. Affairs, 1995-96, pres. 1993-95; mem. Cmty. Info. Coun.; mem. leadership Coral Springs Inaugural Class, 1993. Mem. Nat. Coun. Jewish Women (life), Kappa Alpha Theta, Phi Alpha Delta. Democrat. Jewish. Avocations: reading, travel, pilates. Office: Ste 200 3200 N University Dr Coral Springs FL 33065-4100 E-mail: ritter.stacy@myfloridahouse.com.

RITTERHOUSE, KATHY LEE, librarian; b. Hutchinson, Kans., May 24, 1952; d. Fayne Lee and Elizabeth Rose (Tener) R.; m. Michael Raymond Demmitt, July 8, 1972 (div. Apr. 1990). BA in English, Kans. State U., 1974; MLS, U. Okla., 1979. Circulation libr. Grand Prairie (Tex.) Meml. Libr., 1979-80, libr. dir., 1980—. Bd. dirs. Grand Prairie Arts Coun., 1980-2000, pres., 1989. Recipient Women in History award, 1999; named Pub. Svc. Employee of Yr. Grand Prairie C. of C., 1989. Mem.: ALA (intellectual freedom com. 1998—2001), Tex. Libr. Assn. (Tex./SIRS Intellectual Freedom award 1993), Metro Rotary Club (bd. dirs. 1992—99, pres. 2003—04, dist. new generations chair 2001—04), Beta Phi MU. Office: Grand Prairie Meml Libr 901 Conover Dr Grand Prairie TX 75051-1521 E-mail: kritterh@gptx.org.

RITTI, ALYCE RAE, artist; b. Moline, Ill., Jan. 18, 1934; d. Raymond Russell and Alice Linnea Matilda (Arvidson) Keagle; m. Raymond Richard Ritti, Jan. 26, 1957; children: Lesley, Jocelyn, Matthew, Susanna. BA with departmental honors, Grinnell Coll., 1956; MS, Purdue U., 1957; PhD, Columbia U., 1973; postrad., Pa. State U., 1985-90. Advanced cert. Am. Speech, Lang., and Hearing Assn. Speech therapist Rockford (Ill.) Coll. Summer Speech Ctr., summer 1956; instr. speech Cornell U., Ithaca, N.Y., 1957-59; exec. sec. Art Alliance of Cen. Pa., Lemont, 1978-80; test manual coord. NEA, Washington, 1980-82; rsch. assoc. E.P. Sys. Group, State College, Pa., 1980-82; visual artist Pt. Matilda, Pa., 1984—. Com. mem., ad hoc projects Cen. Pa. Festival of Arts, State College, 1988—, artist in action, 1989-91, 93-94, instr. accessible arts collages, 1994-95; artist World's Women Online, 1995-2002; instr. art Cmty. Acad. Lifelong Learning Ctr., State College, 1997-2002, writer Active Life, 1998-2001; artist-in-residence Pa. Coun. on Arts, 2001-03; panelist Art Alliance SCORE Workshops, 1999, 2001; judge Gen. Fedn. Women's Clubs Pa. Arts Festival, 2001. Artist collages and paintings in numerous solo shows including Studio Z Gallery, Pitts., 2002, The Stage Gallery, Merrick, NY, 2002, Woskob Gallery, Pa. State Downtown Theatre, Ctr., State Coll., Pa., 2003; exhibited in internat., nat. and regional shows and galleries, 1990—, including So. Alleghenies Mus. Art Triennial VI, Salon d'Automne, Paris, 2002, 03, Assoc. Artists Pitts. Warhol Mus., 2002, Triennial VII (Mus. Purchase award), Biennial I, Art of the State, State Mus. Pa., Harrisburg, 2003, Great Plains Nat., Hays, Kans., 2004, Alliance Women Artists, City Hall, Oslo, Norway, 2004; contbr. articles to numerous publs. Bd. dirs., officer sch. dist. PTAs, PTOs, couns., Stamford, Conn., 1963-70, State College, 1971-87. Office of Edn. fellow Columbia U. Tchrs. Coll., 1969, 70; Unified Art Event grantee (2) Cen. Pa. Arts Coun., 1984, 86. Mem. Nat. Mus. Women in the Arts, Art Alliance of Ctrl. Pa. (life, bd. dirs. 1981-86, v.p. 1982), Associated Artists Pitts., Alliance of Women Artists, Friends of Palmer Mus. Art, Phi Beta Kappa. Avocations: acting in community theater, attending performing arts and concerts, walking, reading, romping with dog. Home: 170 Cherrywood Way Port Matilda PA 16870-8904

RIVELLI, SUSAN VERONICA, nurse; b. Des Moines, Aug. 28, 1954; d. Thomas James Dobberthein and Naomi M. (Edwards) Dutch; 1 child, Carly Vanessa; m. Prospero Rivelli, Jr., Aug. 20, 1989. Diploma practical nursing, Des Moines Area C.C., 1976; ASN, St. Petersburg Jr. Coll., 1983, AA, 2001; student, U. South Fla., 2000—03. RN, Fla.; cert. risk mgr., Fla.; cert. hospice and palliative nurse. Dir. quality assurance and med. records Horizon Hosp., Clearwater, Fla., 1980-89; DON Palm Gardens of Clearwater, 1989-90; quality assurance/risk mgr. liaison, cons. The Manors, Tarpon Springs, Fla., 1990-94; instr. Ultimate Learning Ctr., Clearwater, Fla., 1994—; shift adminstr. The Manors, Tarpon Springs, Fla., 1994-97; staff nurse Hospice of Fla. Suncoast, Largo, Fla., 1997—2001; sr. staff nurse Hospice of the Fla. Suncast, Largo, 2002—03; admissions nurse Hospice of the Fla. Suncoast, Largo, 2003—. Cons. in field. Pres. Knollwood Civic Assn., Largo, Fla., 1985, editor, pub. newsletter, 1984. Scholar Tampa Bay Orgn. Nurse Exec., 2001. Mem. Am. Health Info. Mgmt. Assn., Nat. Assn. of Quality Assurance Profls., Bay Area Healthcare Risk Mgrs, Nat.

Hospice/Pallrative Care Orgn., Phi Theta Kappa. Roman Catholic. Avocations: writing, reading, alpine skiing. Home: 3149 Harvest Moon Dr Palm Harbor FL 34683-2124

RIVERA, CHERYL A. state representative, lawyer; BA, Northeastern Univ.; JD, Western New Eng. Sch. of Law. State rep., Mass., 1999—; atty. Chairperson Sprinfield Pk. Commn., 1988—2000; com. Springfield Planning Bd., 1999—2000, Mass. Dem. State, 1999—, Energy, Govt. Regulations, House Long Term Debt and Capital Expenditures; mem. Mass. Womens Causus; co-founder, mem. Latino Caucus. Mem.: Mass. Assn. of Hispanic Atty., Hampden County Bar Assn. Democrat. Office: State Ho Rm 540 Boston MA 02133

RIVERA, CHITA (CONCHITA DEL RIVERO), actress, singer, dancer; b. Washington, Jan. 23, 1933; d. Pedro Julio Figuerva del Rivero; m. Anthony Mordente. Student, Am. Sch. Ballet, N.Y.C. Broadway debut: Call Me Madam, 1952; appeared on stage in: Guys and Dolls, Can-Can, Seventh Heaven, Mister Wonderful, West Side Story, Father's Day, Bye Bye Birdie, Three Penny Opera, Flower Drum Song, Zorba, Sweet Charity, Born Yesterday, Jacques Brel is Alive and Well and Living in Paris, Sondheim-A Musical Tribute, Kiss Me Kate, Ivanhoe, Chicago, Bring Back Birdie, Merlin, Jerry's Girls, 1985, The Rink, 1984 (Tony award 1984), Can-Can, 1988, Kiss of the Spider Woman (Tony award, Best Actress in a musical), 1993; performs in cabarets and nightclubs around world; starred in: film Sweet Charity, 1969; numerous TV appearances include Kojak and the Marcus Nelson Murders, 1973, The New Dick Van Dyke Show, 1973-74, Kennedy Ctr. Tonight-Broadway to Washington!, Pippin, 1982, The Mayflower Madam, 1987, Sammy Davis Jr.'s 60th Birthday Celebration, 1990, Ira Gershwin at 100: A Celebration at Carnegie Hall, 1997, Venecia, 2001, Anything Goes, 2000, The Visit, 2001. Recipient Best Actress, Outer Critics Circle award, 1993, Drama League award, Spider Woman, 1993, Ellis Island Medal of Honor, 2000, Best Leading Actress in a Musical, Tony award. Mem. AFTRA, SAG, Actors Equity Assn. Office: William Morris Agy c/o Samuel Liff 1325 Ave of the Ams New York NY 10019

RIVERA, SOPHIE, photographer; Student, New Sch. for Social Rsch., N.Y.C. Lectr. in field; photography resident, Syracuse, N.Y., 1987, SUNY, Buffalo, N.Y., 1987. Solo exhbns. include: Internat. Photo Optical Exhibit, N.Y.C., 1979, El Museo del Barrio, N.Y.C., 1987, En Foco Arts for Transit, N.Y.C., 1989, Windows on White, N.Y.C., 1990, Wilmer Jennings Gallery, N.Y.C., 1995, U. Conn., West Hartford, 1996, Studio Mus. Harlem, N.Y.C., 1997; dual exhbns. include Cork Gallery, N.Y.C., 1980, Casa Aboy, P.R., 1981; group shows include: El Museo del Barrio, 1984, 87, El Museo Nat. del Bellas Artes, Havana, Cuba, 1984, Bronx Mus. Arts, N.Y.C., 1986, Salmagundi Club, N.Y.C., 1987, Camera Club N.Y., 1987, Goddard-Riverside Cmty. Ctr., N.Y.C., 1987, John Jay Coll. Criminal Justice, 1988, Intar Gallery, N.Y.C., 1988, Blum-Helman Warehouse Gallery, N.Y.C., 1989, Mus. Sci. and Industry, Chgo., 1989, Dia Art Found., N.Y.C., 1989, Flossie Martin Gallery, Radford, Va., 1990, Purdue Univ. Galleries, Lafayette, Ind., 1990, En Foco Gallery, 1990, Galleria El Bohio, N.Y.C., 1990, Kince Gallery, N.Y.C., 1990, Ctr. for Book Arts, N.Y.C., 1990, 80 Washington Sq. East Galleries, N.Y.C., 1991, 93, CCNY, 1991, Ctr. for Photography at Woodstock, N.Y., 1991, Scott Alan Gallery, N.Y.C., 1991, Rutgers U., N.J., 1991, Internat. Ctr. for Photography, 1992, Monasterio de Santa Clara, Spain, 1992, Tweed Gallery, N.Y.C., 1993, Mus. at Stony Brook, N.Y., 1993, Kenkeleba Gallery, N.Y.C., 1994, Foto Fest '94, Houston, Hostos Art Gallery, 1995, Marymont Coll., 1997, Smithsonian Inst., 1997, Internat. Ctr. Photography, N.Y.C., 1997. Recipient awards Pub. Art Fund, 1989, N.Y. Found. for the Arts (Photography), 1989. Home: 31 Tiemann Pl New York NY 10027-3302

RIVERA-SINCLAIR, ELSA, psychologist, consultant, researcher; b. Lima, Peru, Dec. 2, 1927; came to U.S. 1954; d. Jorge Maximo Rivera Bodero and Hortencia Resurreccion Vega Alvarado; m. Walter Ward Sinclair, Oct. 30, 1957; children: Harold Anthony, Thomas Edgar (dec.), Ian Paul. AA in Gen. Edn., Montgomery Coll., Takoma Park, Md., 1976; BA in Psychology, U. Md.-College Park, 1979; MA in Clin. Psychoolgy, U. Md.-Balti. County, 1982; PhD in Counseling Psychology, U. Md.-College Park, 1988. Diplomate Am. Bd. Psychological Specialties, 1998. Psychology intern Spring Grove Hosp., Catonsville, Md., 1980-81, Veterans Administrn. Med. Ctr., Washington, 1985-86; clin. psychologist PHS evaluation facility/inpatient care St. Elizabeths Hosp. Immigration/Naturalization, Washington, 1989; clin. psychologist acute care St. Elizabeths Hosp., Washington, 1989; clin. psychologist DC Dept. Mental Health, Washington, 1996—2003. Bd. mem. Mayor of Dist. Ct. Columbia Multicultural Task Force, 1992-94,CMHS, Dept. Human Svcs. Contbr. article to profl. jour. Recipient APA fellowship Am. Psychological Assn., 1982; Vol. award Andromeda Transcultural Hispano Mental Health Ctr., 1998. Mem. APA, Am. Coll. Forensic Examiners, Md. Psychol. Assn., Nat. Hispanic Psychol. Assn., D.C. Psychol. Assn., Phi Kappa Phi. Avocations: traveling, oil painting, reading, poetry, classic music. Home: 116 Fleetwood Ter Silver Spring MD 20910 E-mail: universe@erols.com.

RIVERA-URRUTIA, BEATRIZ DALILA, psychology and rehabilitation counseling educator; b. Bayamón, P.R., Jan. 16, 1951; d. José and Carmen B. (Urrutia) Rivera; m. Julio C. Ribera, July 1, 1978; 1 child, Alejandra B. Ribera. BA, U. P.R., 1972, MA, 1975; PhD, Temple U., 1982. Cert. rehab. counselor Commn. Rehab. Counselor Cert., lic. psychologist P.R. Staff psychologist Learning Plus, Inc., Phila., 1979-80; cons. Hispanic Mental Health Inst., Phila., 1981-82; staff psychologist J.F. Kennedy Cmty. Mental Health Ctr., Phila., 1982-83; prof. U. PR, Rio Piedras, 1983—. Cons. Jewish Employment & Vocat. Svcs., Phila., 1980; staff psychologist San Juan VA Hosp., Rio Piedras, 1990—; coord. grad. program com. Rehab. Counseling Grad. Sch., 2000—, prof., 1995. Contbr. articles to profl. jours. Vol. Parroquia San Juan Apóstol y Evangelista, Caguas, PR, 1988—90, ARC, San Juan, 1990. Grantee Faculty Instnl. Rsch., U. P.R., 1986—87. Mem.: P.R. Lic. Bd. Psychologists (pres. ethics com. 1991—92), P.R. Psychol. Assn. (bd. editors jour. 1984—89, bd. dirs. 1989—91). Avocations: walking, theater. Home and Office: PO Box 22724 San Juan PR 00931-2724 E-mail: ribera@prtc.net.

RIVERA-VELAZQUEZ, MARIA JESUS, marketing professional; d. Juan Prebistero Rivera and Ramona Matias; m. Victor M. Velazquez, Jr., June 27, 1997; 1 child, Mariana Carolina. BA in Econs. cum laude, U. P.R., San Juan, 1993; MA in Econs., U. Wis., Milw., 1995. Statistician Blue Shield P.R., San Juan, 1996—97; rsch. analyst Info. Resources, Inc., Chgo., 1998—2001; sr. rsch. analyst Northwestern Mut., Milw., 2001—. Spkr. Wis. SAS Users Group Conf., Milw., 2003. Active Vecinos Unidos Pro Macun, Toa Baja, PR, 1996—97; vol. United Way campaign Northwestern Mut. Friends, Milw., 2001—; pres. Young Dems. Macun, Toa Baja, PR, 1990—94. Scholar, NEA-P.R. chpt., 1994—95. Mem.: Am. Mktg. Assn. Roman Catholic. Office: Northwestern Mutual 720 E Wisconsin Ave Milwaukee WI 53202

RIVERO, ANDRIA, education educator; b. Alacranes, Matanzas, Cuba, Feb. 04; came to the U.S., 1956; d. Javier and Juana Maria Rivero; m. Hermann E. Diehl (div. Dec. 1983); children: Hermann J., Karina J. BS, Fla. Internat. U., 1974; MS, Nova U., 1981. Elem. tchr. St. Patrick Cath. Sch., Miami Beach, Fla., 1979-81; instr., dean instrn. Ft. Lauderdale Coll., Miami, Fla., 1981-84; prof., disability svcs. advisor St. Thomas U., Miami, 1984-99. Edn. specialist Accrediting Commn. for Colls. and Tech. Career Schs., 1993—; adv. bd. Tech. Career Inst., Miami, 1997-2000; adj. prof. MDC, 2000—, Fla. Internat. U., 2000—. Mem. safety com. City of Miami Beach, 1995-97. Roman Catholic. E-mail: arivero@bellsouth.net.

RIVERO, MARILYN ELAINE KEITH, state legislator; b. Burlington, Vt., Aug. 22, 1942; d. Kenneth Charles and Irene (Haskell) Keith; m. Victor Paul Rivero, Sr., 1966; children: Lina, Mita, Victor Jr., Amy, Nicholas. BS, U. Vt., 1964, MS, 1988; postgrad., Middlebury Coll., 1973, St. Michaels Coll., 1986. Vol. Peace Corps., 1964-66; mem. Vt. Ho. of Reps., 1991—; mem. health and welfare com., 1991—. Recipient Beyond War award. Mem. ANA, Vt. Nurses Assn., Returned Peace Corps. Vol., Am. Assn. Retired People. Roman Catholic. Home: 10 Village Dr Milton VT 05468-3650

RIVERS, ALMA FAYE, secondary school educator; b. Marion, N.C., Oct. 13, 1949; d. Arthur Henry and Lena (Deyton) Letterman; m. Charles Edwin Rivers, June 29, 1980. BA, Mars Hill Coll., 1971; MEd, W. Ga. Coll., 1978. Tchr., choral dir. W. Fannin H.S., Blue Ridge, Ga., 1971-76, W. Fannin Jr. H.S., Blue Ridge, 1976-80; tchr. Truett-McConnell Coll., Young Harris, Ga., 1975-76, 78-80, Sprayberry H.S., Marietta, Ga., 1980—. Student tchr. supr. State of Ga., 1988—, tchr. mentoring program, 1990—; tchr., cons. Kennesaw (Ga.) State U., 1995—; presenter workshops, confs., and confs. on 19th century women's lit. and multiculture lit. Mem. Standing Peachtree NA, Atlanta, 1994—; vol. PGA Tournament. NEH fellow, 1995. Mem. Nat. Coun. Tchrs. English, Ga. Coun. Tchrs. English, Thomas Wolfe Soc., Cooking Club of Am., Alpha Delta Kappa. Methodist. Avocations: golfing, piano, literature, traveling, book collecting. Office: Sprayberry High Sch 2525 Sandy Plains Rd Marietta GA 30066-5799

RIVERS, BEVERLY D. former secretary of the district; b. 1965; JD U. Ala. Sch. Law; BS in bus. mgmt., Oakwood Coll., Huntsville, Ala. Sec. D.C.; spl. asst. CFO; chief legis. asst. State Senator Henry L. Marsh, Richmond, Va.; atty. Hill Tucker Firm, Marsh Firm; acting sec. of dist. Washington, D.C., 1999, sec. of the dist., 1999—2003. Mem.: Nat. Forum Black Pub. Adminstr., Wash. Bar Assn., Ala. Bar Assn., D.C. Bar Assn.*

RIVERS, CHERYL P. state legislator; b. Rutland, Vt. m. Richard H. Rivers; 1 child. Student, U. Vt., Burlington; BS, Castleton State Coll., 1978. Mem., Windsor County Vt. Senate, Montpelier, 1991—; owner River Echo Morgans. Office: Vt State House State Capitol Montpelier VT 05602

RIVERS, JOAN, entertainer; b. N.Y.C., June 8, 1937; d. Meyer C. Molinsky; m. Edgar Rosenberg, July 15, 1965 (dec.); 1 child, Melissa. BA, Barnard Coll., 1958. Formerly fashion coordinator Bond Clothing Stores. Debut entertaining, 1960; mem. From Second City, 1961-62; TV debut Tonight Show, 1965; Las Vegas debut, 1969; nat. syndicated columnist Chgo. Tribune, 1973-76; creator: CBS TV series Husbands and Wives, 1976-77; host: Emmy Awards, 1983; guest hostess: Tonight Show, 1983-86; hostess The Late Show Starring Joan Rivers, 1986-87, Hollywood Squares, 1987, (morning talk show) Joan Rivers (Daytime Emmy award 1990), 1989-93, Can We Shop? Home Shopping Network, 1994, (radio) The Joan Rivers Show, 1997—, E! Pre-awards Show, 1995—; originator, screenwriter TV movie The Girl Most Likely To, ABC, 1973; other TV movies include: How to Murder A Millionaire, 1990, Jackie Collins' Lady Boss, 1992, Tears and Laughter: The Joan and Melissa Rivers Story, 1994; cable TV spl. Joan Rivers and Friends Salute Heidi Abromowitz, 1985; film appearances include The Swimmer, 1968, Uncle Sam, The Muppets Take Manhattan, 1984; co-author, dir.: (films) Rabbit Test, 1978 (also acted), Spaceballs, 1987, Serial Mom, 1994; actress: theatre prodn. Broadway Bound, 1988, Sally Marr...and her escorts, 1994; recs. include: comedy album What Becomes a Semi-Legend Most, 1983; author: Having a Baby Can be a Scream, 1974, The Life and Hard Times of Heidi Abromowitz, 1984, (autobiography with Richard Meryman) Enter Talking, 1986, (with Richard Meryman), Still Talking, 1991, From Mother to Daughter: Thoughts and Advice on Life, Love and Marriage, 1998, Don't Count the Candle, Just Keep the Fire Lit, 1999; debuted on Broadway (play) Broadway Bound, 1988, creator Seminar You Deserve To Be happy, 1995. Nat. chmn. Cystic Fibrosis, 1982—, benefit performer for AIDS, 1984. Recipient Cleo awards for commls., 1976, 82, Jimmy award for best comedian, 1981; named Hadassah Woman of Yr., 1983, Harvard Hasty Pudding Soc. Woman of Yr., 1984. Mem. Phi Beta Kappa. Office: William Morris Agy 151 S El Camino Dr Beverly Hills CA 90212-2775 also: JR Worldwide 150 E 58th St New York NY 10155-0002

RIVERS, JOAN NADIA, graphics designer; b. Santa Ana, Calif., Nov. 1, 1944; d. Hubert Murray and Alix (Bredé) Brown; m. David Allen Rivers, Sept. 3, 1965; 1 child, Kristan David. BFA, U. Tex., 1978. Staff artist Sta. KLRN/KLRU TV, Austin, Tex., 1975-78; art dir. J. Walter Thompson Co., N.Y.C., 1979-81; designer Steck-Vaughn Pub. Co., Austin, 1982-83, Tex. Instruments, Austin, 1984-85; designer, owner Rivers Graphic Design, Austin, 1985—. Author, illustrator cartoon: Word Processing and Info. Systems mag., 1980-83. Recipient Cert. Recognition Nat. Assn. Ednl. Broadcasters, 1977-78, Best of Show award Internat. Assn. Bus. Communicators, 1986, Cert. Merit Printing Industries Am., 1986. Mem. Am. Inst. Graphic Arts, Austin Graphic Arts Soc. (award of Excellence 1986), Soc. Tech. Communication (Achievement award 1986). Democrat. Avocations: fresh water aquarist, gardening.

RIVERS, LORETTA J. film producer, film director, consultant; b. Stafford Springs, Conn., Sept. 7, 1955; d. Everett Joseph and Jean Petrone Rivers. BA Anthropology and Archaeology, U. Conn., 1978, postgrad., 1988—94; postgrad. in history and archive mgmt., postgrad. in film/video prodn., Ctrl. Conn. State U., 1995—96. Mus. tchr., interpreter Old Sturbridge Village, Sturbridge, Mass., 1979—82, 1988; curator edn., asst. dir. Jefferson County Hist. Soc., Watertown, NY, 1983—85; curator edn. Lutz Children's Mus., Manchester, Conn., 1987—88; archives cons. CIGNA Corp., Hartford, Conn., 1988—91; archives asst. dept. Hist. Manuscripts Archives U. Conn., Storrs, 1992—94; exec. dir., founder Lojeri Prodns., Inc., East Hartford, Conn., 1996—. Archaeological rschr. Marc Banks, Archaeologist, Simsbury, Conn., 1999—2000; pub. access vol. Cox Comms., Manchester, Conn., 1995—2001; programming internship CPTV/Channel 24, Hartford, 1996, WGBY/Channel 57, Springfield, Mass., 1995; field crew Mich. State U., East Lansing, Mich., 1979; rsch., lab and field asst. Pub. Archaeology Survey Team, Storrs, Conn., 1977—86. Prodr., dir. : (documentaries) Wadsworth Atheneum Mus. Art, 1995 (1st place, Conn. Higher Edn. Telecom. Assn., 1996); prodr., dir. (documentaries) Mus. Insider, 1995—97 (finalist, Women in Cable and Telecom, New Eng. chpt., 1998); prodr., dir. : (documentaries) Lutz Children's Mus., 1997 (3rd place, Conn. Higher Edn. Telecom. Assn., 1997); prodr., dir. (documentaries) Huntington House, 1997 (Honorable mention, Conn. Higher Edn. Telecom. Assn., 1997, Alliance for Cmty. Media, 1997); prodr., dir.: documentaries Huntington House, 1998; prodr.(, dir.): (comml.) The Learning Ctr. Magnet Sch., 1996 (1st place, Conn. Higher Edn. Telecom. Assn., 1996); mem. editl. bd., contbg. editor (newsletter) Archaeology and Education, 1989—92; contbr. articles to profl. jours.; creator, prodr. (video series) The Mus. Insider, 1995. Conn. History Day judge Conn. Hist. Soc., Hartford, 2001—02, Conn. History Day tchr. workshop, 2001; design com. mem. Rockville (Conn.) Downtown Assn., 2001—03. Recipient award, Connecticare, 1998, Gaylord Hosp., 2000, Am. Savings Bank Found., 2001, George and Grace Long Found., 2001. Mem.: Internat. Documentary Assn., Assn. Ind. Video and Filmmakers, Conn. League History Orgns., Bay State Hist. League, New England Mus. Assn. Avocations: music, cultural events, travel, interior design. Home and Office: Lojeri Prodns Inc PO Box 280304 50 Chapman Pl Studio 209 East Hartford CT 06128 Business E-Mail: info@lojeriproductions.org.

RIVERS, LYNN N. former congresswoman; b. Augres, Mich., Dec. 19, 1956; 2 children. BA, U. Mich., 1987; JD, Wayne State U., 1992. Mem. sch. bd. City of Ann Arbor, Mich., 1984-92; mem. Mich. House of Reps., 1992-94, U.S. Congress from 13th Mich. dist., 1994—2002; mem. edn. and workforce com., sci. com., 1994. Mem.: Nat. Adv. Bd., Univ. Mich. Depression Center, 2003-. Democrat.*

RIVERS, NETTIE TAYLOR, hearing impaired educator; b. Memphis, Dec. 6, 1954; d. Sherman Allen and Elizabeth Lamar Taylor; m. Joel Louis Rivers, Aug. 13, 1977; children: Brett, Joel, Taylor. BS, Miss. U. Women, 1976; Masters, U. Miss., 1977. Tchr. hearing impaired/deaf S. Panola Sch. Dist., Batesville, Miss., 1977—. Head tchr. child devel. ctr. S. Panola Sch. Dist., Batesville, 1995—98; chair dept. spl. edn. S. Panola H.S., Batesville, 1998—, chair local screening com., 1998—. Treas. S. Panola Tiger Booster Assn., Batesville, 1999—2002, Panola Playhouse, Sardis, Miss., 1980—81; pres. Batesville Jr. Aux., 1984—85, 1st v.p., 1983—84, treas., 1982—83; mem. chancel choir 1st United Meth. Ch., Batesville, 1997—, dir. children's choir, 1984—95; mem. exec. bd. S. Panola Found. for Pub. Edn., Batesville, 1992—95, pres., 1995—96. Named Outstanding Educator of Yr., Batesville Civitan Club, 1990—91. Mem.: Coun. Exceptional Children. Methodist. Avocations: singing, scrapbooks, gardening. Home: 108 Hickory Ln Batesville MS 38606 Office: S Panola HS 601 Tiger Dr Batesville MS 38606 Personal E-mail: ntrivers@hotmail.com.

RIVERS, STEPHANIE DENISE WALL, elementary school educator; b. Ft. Bragg, N.C., Oct. 11, 1975; d. Lowell Yates and Brenda Sue (Creech) Wall; m. Jeffery David Rivers, Sept. 16, 2000. BS, U. N.C., Pembroke, 1997. Tchr. South Hoke Elem. Sch., Raeford, NC, 1997—99, Gray's Creek Elem. Sch., Fayetteville, NC, 1999—, co-chair sch. improvement, 2003—, grad level chairperson, 2001—03, coord. Project Excell, 2000—. Named Tchr. of the Yr., Gray's Creek Elem. Sch., 2002—03. Mem.: ASCD. Avocations: dance, reading, swimming. Home: 3505 Shipstone Pl Apt 203 Hope Mills NC 28348 Office: Gray's Creek Elem Sch 2860 Alderman Rd Fayetteville NC 28306

RIVERS, WILGA MARIE, foreign language educator; b. Melbourne, Australia, Apr. 13, 1919; arrived in U.S., 1970; d. Harry and Nina Diamond (Burston) R. BA, U. Melbourne, 1939, diploma in Edn., 1940, MA, 1948; Licence es L., U. Montpellier, France, 1952; PhD, U. Ill., 1962; MA (hon.), Harvard U., 1974; PhD of Langs. (hon.), Middlebury Coll., 1989. H.S. tchr., Victoria, Australia, 1940-48; asst. in English lang., 1949-52; tchr. prep. schs., 1953-58; asst. prof. French No. Ill. U., DeKalb, 1963-64; assoc. prof. Monash U., Australia, 1964-69; vis. prof. Columbia U., 1970-71; prof. French U. Ill., Urbana Champaign, 1971-74; prof. Romance langs. and lit., coord. lang. instrn. Harvard U., 1974-89, prof. emerita, 1989—. Cons. NEH, Ford Found., Rockefeller Found., others; lectr 44 countries and throughout U.S.; mem. adv. bd. Modern Lang. Ctr., Ont. Inst. for Studies in Edn., Nat. Fgn. Lang. Ctr., Lang. Acquire Rsch. Ctr., San Diego. Author: The Psychologist and the Foreign-Language Teacher, 1964, Teaching Foreign-Language Skills, 1968, 2d edit., 1981, Speaking in Many Tongues, 1972, 3d edit., 1983, A Practical Guide to the Teaching of French, 1975, 2d edit., 1988,3rd edit., 2001 (on Web), Opportunities for Careers in Foreign Languages, 1993; co-author: A Practical Guide to the Teaching of German, 1975, 2d edit., 1988, A Practical Guide to the Teaching of Spanish, 1976, 2d edit., 1988, 3rd edit., 2003 (on Web), A Practical Guide to the Teaching of English as a Second or Foreign Language, 1978, Communicating Naturally in a Second Language, 1983, Teaching Hebrew: A Practical Guide, 1989, others; editor, contbr. Interactive Language Teaching, 1978, Teaching Languages in College: Curriculum and Content, 1992, Down Under/Up Top: Creating a Life, 2004; writing translated into 11 langs.; editl. bd. Studies in Second Language Acquisition, Applied Linguistics, Language Learning, Mosaic, System; adv. com. Can. Modern Lang. Rev.; contbr. articles to profl. jours. Decorated Chevalier des Palmes Académiques, 1995; recipient Disting. Fgn. Lang. Leadership award N.Y. State Assn. Fgn. Lang. Tchrs., 1974, Disting. Alumni award U. Ill., 1999. Mem. MLA, Am. Assn. Applied Linguistics (charter pres.), Am. Coun. on Tchg. Fgn. Langs. (Florence Steiner award 1977, Anthony Papalia award 1988), Mass. Fgn. Lang. Assn. (Disting. Svc. award 1983), Tchrs. of English to Spkrs. of other Langs., Am. Assn. Tchrs. French, Linguistic Soc. Am., Am. Assn. Univ. Suprs. and Coords. Fgn. Lang. Programs Northeast Conf. (Nelson Brooks award 1983), Internat. Assn. Applied Psycholinguistics (v.p. 1983-89), Japan Assn. Coll. English Tchrs. (hon.), Am. Assn. Tchrs. German (hon.), Internat. Assn. Lang. Labs. (hon.). Episcopalian. Home and Office: 84 Garfield St Watertown MA 02472-4916

RIVET, JEANNINE M. health plan administrator; BS in Nursing, Boston Coll.; MPH, Boston U. Sch. Public Health. From v.p. health svc. ops. to CEO United HealthCare, Minnetonka, Minn., 1990-98, CEO health plans, 1998—. Office: United HealthCare Group 300 United HealthCare Group Ctr 9900 Bren Rd E Minnetonka MN 55343-9664

RIVLIN, ALICE MITCHELL, federal agency administrator, economist; b. Phila., Mar. 4, 1931; d. Allan C. G. and Georgianna (Fales) Mitchell; m. Lewis Allen Rivlin, 1955 (div. 1977); children: Catherine Amy, Allan Mitchell, Douglas Gray; m. Sidney Graham Winter, 1989. BA, Bryn Mawr Coll., 1952; MA, Radcliffe Coll., 1955, PhD, 1958; LLD (hon.), U. Mich., 1975, U. Md., 1975; DSc (hon.), U. Ind., 1976; LLD (hon.), Yale U., 1984; DSc (hon.), N.J. Inst. Tech., 1998; LLD (hon.), U. Dist. of Columbia, 1999, Harvard U., 2001. Mem. staff Brookings Instn., Washington, 1957-66, 69-75, 83-93; dir. econ. studies Brookings Inst., 1983-87; dir. Congl. Budget Office, 1975-83; prof. pub. policy George Mason U., 1992—93; dep. dir. U.S. Office Mgmt. and Budget, 1993-94, dir., 1994-96; vice chmn., bd. governors Fed. Res. Sys., Washington, 1996-99; chair Fin. Assistance and Mgmt. Authority, 1998—2001; sr. fellow, econ. studies program Brookings Instn., Washington, 1999—; Henry J. Cohen prof. New Sch. U., 2001—; co-dir. Greater Wash. Rsch. Program, Brookings Instn., 2001—. Dep. asst. sec. program coordination HEW, Washington, 1966-68, asst. sec. planning and evaluation, 1968-69; mem. Staff Adv. Commn. on Intergovtl. Rels., 1961-62. Author: The Role of the Federal Governemnt in Financing Higher Education, 1961, (with others) Microanalysis of Socioeconomic Systems, 1961, Systematic Thinking for Social Action, 1971, (with others) Economic Choices 1987, 1986, (with others The Swedish Economy, 1987, (with others) Caring for the Disabled Elderly: Who Will Pay?, 1988, Reviving the American Dream, 1992, The Economic Payoff from the Internet Revolution (co-edited with Robert E. Litan), 2001, Beyond the Dot.Coms: The Economic Promise of the Internet (with Robert E. Litan), 2001. MacArthur fellow, 1983-87, Elliot J. Richardson prize for excellence in pub. svc., 2002, Barnard medal of distinction, Barnard Coll., 2002. Mem. Am. Econ. Assn. (nat. pres. 1986), Nat. Acad. Pub. Administrn., Nat. Acad. of Social Insurance, Coun. on Fgn. Rels., Office: Brookings Instn 1755 Massachusetts Ave Washington DC 20036

RIVLIN, RACHEL, lawyer; b. Bangor, Maine, Sept. 1, 1945; d. Lawrence and A. Sara (Rich) Lait. BA, U. Maine, 1965; MA, U. Louisville, 1968; JD, Boston Coll., 1977. Bar: Mass. 1977, U.S. Dist. Ct. Mass. 1978, U.S. Ct. Appeals (1st cir.) 1983, U.S. Supreme Ct. 1985. Audiologist Boston City Hosp., 1969-72; dir. audiology Beth Israel Hosp., Boston, 1972-74; atty. Legal Sys. Devel., Boston, 1977-78, Liberty Mut. Ins., Boston, 1978-82; counsel, sec. Lexington Ins. Co., Boston, 1982-85, v.p., assoc. gen. counsel, sec., 1985—. Mem. civil rights com. Anti-Defamation League, Boston, 1982—; bd. dirs. DanceArt, Inc., Boston, 1985—92. Mem.: ABA (vice chmn. com. pub. regulation of ins. 1980—81, vice chmn. pub. rels. 1981—84, excess surplus lines and reins com. 1983—, internat. ins. law com. 1983—, chmn. elect 1984—85, chmn. 1985—86, nat. inst. insurer insolvency 1986, vice chmn. 1986—87, chair-elect 1987—88, ann. meeting arrangements chmn. TIPS 1988, nat. inst. reins collections and insolvency 1988, chmn. 1988—89, nat. inst. insurer insolvency 1989, sr. vice chmn. 1989—90, vice chmn. 1997—, task force ins. and corp. counsel interests and involvement 1999—, vice chmn. com. pub. regeulation ins. 1997—), Boston Bar Assn. (chmn. corp. counsel com. 1987, steering com. corp. bus.

law and fin. sect. 1987—89, edn. com. 1987—89, chmn. ins. law com. 1987—90, nominating com. 1988, dinner dance com. 1989, edn. com. 1990—91, chmn. ins. com. 1990—, ethics com. 1993—, dinner dance com. 1994, multi-disciplinary practice task force 2000—02, comprehensive revision Mass. corp. law 2000—, coun., 1983-86 2002—, coun. 1983—86, 2002—), Boston Coll. Law Sch. Alumni Assn. (ann. fund com. 1981—89, coun. 1983—87, chmn. telethon com. 1989 94, nominating com. 1990, search com. for dean 1993, search com. for law sch. fund dir. 1993, leadership gifts exec. com. 1994—98, search com. for dir. instl. advancement 1995, vice chmn. 1997—, reunion com. 2002, Father James Malley award 1996). Home: 122 Lincoln St Newton MA 02461-1528 Office: Lexington Ins Co 200 State St Ste 12 Boston MA 02109-2605

RIVO, SHIRLEY WINTHROPE, artist; arrived in U.S., 1953, naturalized, 1960; m. Julian David Rivo, Mar. 22, 1953; children: Morissa, Sandra, Philip. BA, Kean U., 1977, MA, 1980. Cert. arts tchr. K-12. Window display designer Belgium Stores, Toronto, 1945-53; needlepoint design Creative Kits, Inc., N.J., N.Y., 1965-72. Chair person exhbn. We Love New York, Lever House, 390 Park Ave., N.Y., Sept., 1996. One-woman shows include New Hampshire House, Summit, N.J., 1970, Chemical Bank, N.Y.C., 1977, St. Barnabas Med. Ctr., Livingston, N.J., 1978, N.J. Ctr. for Visual Arts, Summit, 1979, 85, Ciba-Geigy, Summit, 1979, AT&T, Basking Ridge, N.J., 1982, Exxon, Warren, N.J., 1985, Chubb Corp. World HQ, Warren, N.J., 1985, B'nai Jeshurun, Short Hills, N.J., 1987, John Trapp Gallery, Summit, 1988, Johnson & Johnson, New Brunswick, N.J., 1994, 2004, Schering-Plough, Kenilworth, N.J., 1994, photography, Johnson & Johnson Health Care Systems, Piscataway, N.J., 2004; two-person exhbn. Overlook HOsp., Summit, N.J., 2003; group shows include N.J. Ctr. for Visual Arts, N.Y.C., 1970, 72, 76, 81, Kean Coll., Union, N.J., 1972, 80, 87, 88, 89., Visual Arts, Merck & Co., 1990, Papermill Playhouse, N.J., 1972-2000, Somerset Art Assn., 1973, 74, 77, Drew U., Madison, N.J., 1978, Allied Arts of Am., Nat. Arts Club, 1982, Morris County Cultural Ctr., 1983, Morris Mus., Morristown, N.J., 1984, Hunterdon Art Ctr., 1987, Visual Spectrum, Schering-Plough, 1993, 2000, numerous others; permanent collections include Morris Mus., Morristown, Johnson & Johnson, New Brunswick, Nabisco Hdqs., Hanover, N.J., Deloitte and Touche LLP, Parsippany N.J., Nat. Baseball Hall of Fame, Cooperstown, N.Y., Yankee Stadium, Bronx, N.Y., Bklyn. Bot. Garden, Statue of Liberty, N.J. Recipient Best in Show, Millburn Short Hills Art Ctr. 1985, other awards, 1972, 74, 86, 88, 89, 90, 91, 1st prize Papermill Playhouse and in 1995, award of excellence, Pauline Wick award Am. Artists Profl. League Mems. Show, 1990, award for photography Pepermill Playhouse, 2003, numerous others. Mem. N.J. Ctr. Visual Arts (program chair 1979-84, chair spl. events, 1982-84, chair classes 1990-98), Millburn Shorthills Arts Ctr. (trustee, 1990-98, 1st vp. 2003, chair pub. rels. 1986-92, chair corp. exhibits, 1992-96). Avocation: writing. Home: 32 Summit Rd New Providence NJ 07974-2750

RIZER, JANET MARLENE, city tax administrator; b. Warren, Ohio, July 25, 1956; d. Philip F. Zorn and Jessie M. (Salyer) Scott; m. Mitchell L. Betras, Mar. 23, 1978 (div. Mar. 1983); children: Jason P. Betras, Krista L. Betras; m. William F. Rizer, June 8, 1991 (div. Aug. 2000). Grad. high sch., Niles, Ohio. Clk. City of Niles, Office of Treas., 1975-80, chief clk., 1980-90, tax dir., 1990—. Sec. cemetery bd. City of Niles, 1990—, treas. investment bd., 1990—; mem. adv. bd. records commn., City of Niles, 1990—. Mem.: Tricota Tax Assn. (pres. 2002, 2003), Nat. Employee Svcs. and Recreation Assn. (adminstrv. mem. 1999). Home: 36 Lincoln Ave Niles OH 44446-2430 Office: City of Niles Tax Divsn 34 W State St Niles OH 44446-5036 Office Phone: 330-544-9000.

RIZER, MAGGIE, model; b. Watertown, NY, Jan. 9, 1978; Model Elite Modeling Agy.; appeared in ads for Calvin Klein, Versace, the Gap. Actor(guest appearances): (TV series) Sex and the City, The Victoria's Secret Fashion Show, 2001, America's Top Model, 2003. Office: Elite Premier 111 E 22nd St New York NY 10010*

RIZOR, NANCY LUCILE, retired bookkeeper, retired librarian, genealogist; b. Chapel Hill, Tenn., Jan. 2, 1904; d. Samuel Pitts and Gotha Pearl (Rone) Patterson; m. Webb Charles Rizor, Sept. 6, 1927; children: Webb, Hume, Lester, David. Bookkeeper ins. co., Nashville, 1922-30; office mgr. printing firm, Nashville, 1944-45, ice cream plant, Nashville, 1946-53; asst. libr. Disciple of Christ Hist. Soc., Nashville, 1976-93; ret., 1994. Registration staff Little Creek Cmty. House, 1947-50; pres. Civitan Aux., Nashville, 1954-56; tchr. Sunday sch., 1927-1954, Vacation Bible Sch., 10 yrs., Cumberland Presbyn.; deacons, elder Vine St. Christian Ch. Recipient Svc. pin Meth. Women's Misionary Soc., 1960. Mem. Woman's Club Nashville (life, leader dept. 1976). Avocations: reading, traveling, quilting. Home: 1900 Acklen Ave Apt 601 Nashville TN 37212-3729

RIZZI, ALICIA, protective services official; b. Brooklyn, Ny, June 3, 1969; d. John R. and Sue Ann Rizzi; life ptnr. Janice Masters, Sept. 22, 1995; 1 child, William Merick Masters-Rizzi. BS, Weber State U., Ogden, Utah, 1997. Corrections officer Weber County Sheriff's Dept., Ogden, Utah, 1999—. Staff sgt. USAF, 1988—92. Decorated Kuwait Liberation Medal Kingdom of Saudi Arabia USAF, Air Res. Forces Meritorious Svc. medal, Nat. Def. Svc. Medal.

RIZZI, MARGUERITE CLAIRE, music educator; b. New York, NY, Aug. 4, 1955; d. Joan Henderson, Norman Henderson (Stepfather), John N. Rizzi; life ptnr. Brenda June Mottram. BA, Clark U., 1976; MusM, New Eng. Conservatory, 1991; EdD, Boston U., 2000. Cert. std. tchr. cert. music, spl. edn. tchr. Coord. guitar program Boston U., Boston, 1993—99; tchr. Beacon H.S., Brookline, Mass., 1993—2001. Musician (recording): Sympatico, 1999 (listed for grammy nomination, 1999). Capt. sailing vessels. Mem.: Boston Women's Jazz Coalition, Am. Profl. Capt.'s Assn., Internat. Assn. Jazz Edn., Music Educators Nat. Conf. Democrat. Avocations: sailing, bicycling, reading. Office: 74 Green St Brookline MA 02446-3305 Personal E-mail: mottriz@attbi.com.

RIZZO, JOYCE A. environmental services executive; CEO Leak-X Environ Corp, 1990—. Office: Leak-X Environ Corp 790 E Market St West Chester PA 19382-4806

ROACH, KATHLEEN LYNN, lawyer; b. Santa Monica, Calif., Nov. 6, 1962; d. William Russell and Margaret Rose (Balogh) R. AB, U. Calif., Berkeley, 1982; JD, U. Chgo., 1985. Bar: Ill. 1985, Calif. 1988, U.S. Dist. Ct. (no. dist.) Ill. 1985, U.S. Dist Ct. (ea. dist.) Calif. 1988, U.S. Ct. Appeals (7th cir.) 1985. Assoc. Sidley & Austin, Chgo., 1985-93, ptnr., 1993—. Bd. dirs. AIDS Legal Coun., Chgo., 1990—; bd. govs. Chgo. Coun. of Lawyers, 1992—. Office: Sidley & Austin 1 S First National Plz Chicago IL 60603-2000

ROACH, MARGARET, editor-in-chief; Editor., mgr. N.Y. Times; garden columnist Newsday Newspapers; creative developer Martha Stewart Living Omnimedia, 1995; gardening editor Martha Stewart Living; mgr. devel. and execution marthastewart.com; editor-in-chief Martha Stewart Living, N.Y.C., 2001—. Author: A Way to Garden, 1998 (Garden Writers Assn. Am. Best Book, 1998). Office: Martha Stewart Living Omni Advt New York NY 10036

ROACH, MARGOT RUTH, retired biophysicist, educator; b. Moncton, N.B., Can., Dec. 24, 1934; d. Robert Dickson and Katherine (McMillan) R.; m. Franklyn St. Aubyn House, Dec. 20, 1994 (wid. Feb. 2000). B.Sc. in Math. and Physics with honors, U. N.B., Fredericton, Can., 1955; MD, C.M. cum laude, McGill U., Montreal, Can., 1959; PhD in Biophysics, U. Western Ont., Can., 1963; D.Sc. (hon.), U. N.B., St. John, Can., 1981. Jr. intern Victoria Hosp., London, Ont., Can., 1959-60, fellow in cardiology, 1962-63, asst. resident in medicine, 1963-64, Toronto Gen. Hosp., 1964-65; mem. faculty, dept. biophysics U. Western Ont., London, Ont., Can., 1965—, head dept. biophysics, 1970-78, prof., 1971-98, asst. prof. medicine, 1965-72, assoc. prof., 1972-78, prof., 1978-98, prof. emeritus Biophysics & Med., 1998. Mem. staff dept. medicine Victoria Hosp., 1967-72, U. Hosp., London, 1972-98; Commonwealth vis. sci., dept. applied math. theoretical physics Cambridge U., 1975; vis. sci. Bioengring. Inst., Chonqing U., People's Republic of China, 1991; mem. bioengring. grants com. Med. Rsch. Coun. Can., 1993-96; cons. and lectr. in field. Mem. editl. bd.: Imprints. Active civic orgns. and coms. including Univ. Rsch. Coun., 1976-79; mem. interview bd. London Conf. of United Ch., 1967-90; steward United Ch. of Can., 1967-73, elder, 1973-82, chair unified bd. Tatamagouche Pastoral Charge, 2001—; chmn. stewardship devel. com. Colborne St. United Ch., 1990-93. Recipient A. Wilmer Duff prize in physics U. N.B., 1955, Cushing prize in pediatrics, 1959, Ciba Found. award for research in aging, 1959, Teaching award Faculty of Medicine U. Western Ont., 1990, Dean's award, 1997, Women of Distinction award YWCA, 1997; Med. Research Council fellow U. Western Ont., 1960-62, Arthur Guyton award Internat. Soc. Cardiovascular Medicine and Sci., 1997; numerous other fellowships and grants in medicine. Fellow Royal Coll. Physicians (Can.), Am. Coll. Cardiology (Young Investigator's award 1963); mem. Can. Physiol. Soc., Can. Cardiovascular Soc. (off council), Can. Clin. Investigation Soc. (council 1980-84), Can. Biophys. Soc., Can. Soc. Internal Medicine. Address: RR #1 104 Sea Shore Dr Tatamagouche NS Canada B0K 1V0 E-mail: mroach@pchg.net.

ROACH, MAUREEN S. primary school educator; Bachelors Degree, Boston U.; Masters Degree, U. Mass. Primary sch. educator Lyndon Pilot Sch., West Roxbury, Mass. Presenter Nat. Bd. Insts. Mem.: Nat. Bd. for Profl. Tchg. Stds. (bd. mem.). Avocations: cross country skiing, reading. Office: Lyndon Pilot Sch 140 Russett Rd West Roxbury MA 02132*

ROACH, PAM, state legislator; m. Jim Roach; 5 children. BA in History, Brigham Young U., 1970. Mem. Wash. Legislature, Olympia, 1990—, mem. econ. devel. fin. authority com., mem. energy, tech., and telecom. com., mem. jud. com., mem. waysn and means com., mem. sentencing guidelines commn., mem. joint com. on pension policy, mem. statute law com. Guardian mem. Boy Scouts Am.; bd. dirs. Auburn Food Bank; past mem. Gov.'s Juvenile Issues Task Force; mem. local coun. Boy Scouts Am.; past mem. adv. com. Soos Creek Cmty. Plan Tech., Maple Valley Cmty. Summit. Mem. Am. Legis. Exch. Coun., Nat. Conf. State Legislatures, Auburn C. of C. Republican. Office: 202 Irving Newhouse Ofc Olympia WA 98504-0001

ROACHÉ, SYLVIA, social worker; b. Sept. 21, 1923; d. James E. and Iris E. Lawrence; m. Leonard E. Roaché, Oct. 12, 1950; children: Patrick, Grace Roaché Greenidge, Daniel. Diploma, Jamaica Sch. Theology, Wis.; LPN, Practical Nursing Sch., Toledo; BA in Social Work, MSW, U. Pitts. Assoc. pastor 1st Ch. of God, Toledo, Sav-la-mar, Jamaica; nurse Toledo Hosp., Shadyside Hosp., Pitts.; social worker Vintage, Pitts.; co-pastor Lincoln Ave. Ch. of God, Pitts. Contbr. articles to mags. Mem.: Nat. Assn. Ch. of God (founder min.'s wives assn.), Am. Assn. Christian Counselors (charter mem.). Avocations: sewing, writing. Home: 3268 Winter Wood Ct Marietta GA 30062-7001

ROAF, ANDREE LAYTON, judge; b. Mar. 31, 1941; m. Clifton G. Roaf; 4 children. BS in Zoology, Mich. State U., 1962; JD with high honors, U. Ark., 1978; LLD (hon.), Mich. State U., 1996. Bar: Ark. 1978. Bacteriologist Mich. Dept. Health, Lansing, 1963—65; rsch. biologist FDA, Washington, 1965—69; staff asst. Pine Bluff (Ark.) Urban Renewal Agy., 1971—75; biologist Nat. Ctr. for Toxicological Rsch., Jefferson, Ark., 1978—79; assoc. Walker, Roaf, Campbell, Ivory & Dunklin, Little Rock, 1979—86, ptnr., 1986—95; assoc. justice Ark. Supreme Ct., Little Rock, 1995—96; appellate judge Ark. Ct. Appeals, 1997—. Editor: Ark. Law Rev. Mem. PTA bd. Forest Park Elem. Sch., 1972—74, 34th Ave. Sch., 1974—76, 1980—83, Southeast Jr. High, 1976—77; mem. ad hoc com. for voter registration Jefferson County, 1972—73; bd. trustees Southeast Ark. Arts and Scis. Ctr., 1972—75, sec., 1974—75, Pine Bluff OIC Bd., 1972—78, Pine Bluff Police-Cmty. Rels Task Force, 1973; mem. Jefferson County Com. on Black Adoptions, 1973—75, chmn., 1974—75; mem. Ark. Code of Ethics Commn., 1987, Friends of Sta. KRLE-FM, 1982—88, 1990—94, pres., 1985—86; trustee Winthrop Rockefeller Found., 1990—94; mem. Jefferson County Dem. Com., 1980—82; mem. vestry Grace Episcopal Ch., 1995—; bd. dirs. Ark. Coun. on Human Rels., 1972—73, Ark. for Arts, 1983, Ark. Student Loan Authority, 1977—81, Vocals, 1989—. Named Gayle Pettus Pontz outstanding Ark. woman lawyer, 1996; named to Ark. Black Hall of Fame, 1996; recipient disting. alumni award, Mich. State U., 1996. Mem.: ABA, W. Harold Flowers Law Soc., Jefferson County Bar Assn., Pulaski County Bar Assn. (chmn. hist. com. 1986—87), Ark. Bar Assn. (chmn. youth edn. com. 1979—80). Office: Justice Bldg 625 Marshall St Ste 1230 Little Rock AR 72201-1052

ROANE, LELIA DENISE, music educator; d. Arkell R. Roane Sr. and Agnes R. Roane. Bachelor of Music, Va. State U., 1985, Master of Edn., 1991. Cert. music tchr. grades pre-K through 12. Elem. vocal music tchr. Arlington County Pub. Schs., Va., 1987—. Piano accompanist Mt. Olive Bapt. Ch., Arlington, 1997—. Mem.: Delta Kappa Gamma. Avocations: reading, cooking, crocheting, sewing, travel. Office: Barcroft Elem Sch 625 S Wakefield St Arlington VA 22204 E-mail: lroane@arlington.k12.va.us.

ROARK, BARBARA ANN, librarian; b. Evanston, Ill., July 24, 1958; d. Edward B. and Ann H. Rowe; m. Paul E. Roark, Sept. 18, 1982; children: Sarah, John. BA in History, U. Ky., 1981, MLS, 1982. Dir. Hopkins County Madisonville (Ky.) Pub. Libr., 1983-85; ops. mgr. Wurzburg Inc., Nashville, 1985-91; dir. Spies Pub. Libr., Menominee, Mich., 1991-98, Franklin (Wis.) Pub. Libr., 1998—. V.p. adv. coun. Mid-Peninsula Libr. Coop., Mich., 1993-95, sec. adv. coun., 1991-93; chair tech. adv. com. Milwaukee County Federated Libr. Sys., 2001—. Grant writer Title II, 1994, Title I, 1995. Treas. Franklin Area Jr. Woman's Club. Recipient Cert. of Excellence Libr. of Mich., 1995, Cert. of Appreciation Menominee Area C. of C., 1998. Mem. ALA, Wis. Libr. Assn. (pres. and profl. concerns com. 1999—, Muriel Fuller award 2002), Spies Pub. Libr. Found., PEO, Order Ea. Star, U. Ky. Alumni Assn., Franklin Area Jr. Women's Club (treas. 1999—), Kiwanis (pres. Milw. suburban S.W. chpt. 2002—), Zeta Tau Alpha. Methodist. Avocations: golf, reading, cross stitching, travel. Office: Franklin Public Library 9151 W Loomis Rd Franklin WI 53132-9630 E-mail: barbara.roark@mcfls.org.

ROARK, CANDICE RENAU, lawyer; b. Lawton, Okla., Dec. 21, 1970; d. Thomas T. Renau and Michele D. Binkowski; children: Andrew, Elizabeth, Rory. BSc in Psychology and Sociology, U. State N.Y., Albany, 1993; MBA, Cardinal Stritch U., 1997; JD cum laude, Hamline U., 2000. Ordained minister. A.G.E. mechanic USAF, Germany, 1988—92, 1988—92; orgnl. cons. Minn., 1996—99; atty. Pub. Defenders Office, Minn., 1999—2000; arbitrator BBB, 2001—; mediator internat. law, contract lawyer, bd. dirs., min. DEA, 2002—; contract atty. TRANE, 2003—. Arbitrator; nat. spkr. in field. Author: Adolescent God, 1999. Fin. dir. Cmty. Caring for Life, Minn., 1998—99; coord. for jr./sr. h.s. Cmty. Youth, Minn., 1989—98; native am. publicity dir. Native Am. Coun., Incircik, Turkey, 1991—92; mem. parish coun. Minn., 1998—99. Recipient Women's Mil. Meml. award, USAF, Nat. Defense Svc. medal, Humanitarian Svc. medal, MJF award Pub Svc. Mem.: Minn. Women Lawyers, Minn. State Bar Assn., ABA, Mensa. Roman Catholic. Avocations: rollerblading, skiing, writing, fencing.

ROARTY, LOUISE R. writer, realtor; d. Gerald F. St. Louis; life ptnr. Donald C. Wiltse. BS cum laude, So. Ill. U., 1997. Cert. EMT S.C., 1992, nursing asst. II N.C., 1997; assoc. real estate broker Colo., 2001. Author (illustrator): (childrens book) Tales From Grandfather And Bacus The Swamp Troll; book, World of Bern, Bern Porter Collection, Henry Miller enclosures, donation portrait, Christ in Reflection. Donator and supporter of ednl. material St. Bonaventure Indian Mission And Sch., Thoreau, N.Mex., 2002—03. Decorated Good Conduct medal USN, Nat. Def. Svc. medal, Meritorious Unit commendation, Navy and Marine Corps Overseas Svc. medal First award, Navy and Marine Corps Overseas Svc. medal Second award; recipient Letter of commendation. Mem.: South Metro Assn. Realtors, Nat. Realtor Assn., Am. Legion, So. Ill. U. (corr.). R-Consevative. Catholic. Achievements include Framed illustrated Design. Avocations: travel, reading, writing, illustrating.

ROBAK, JENNIE, state legislator; b. Surprise, Nebr., May 4, 1932; m. Cleo F. Robak; children: Karen, Kim, Frank, Kurt, Tony, Andrea. With Fed. Emergency Mgmt. Agy., Kansas City, Mo.; owner, operator RKR Foods, Inc.; mem. Nebr. Senate from 22d dist., Lincoln, 1988—. Trustee Jr. Achievement Columbus; bd. dirs. Platte County Red Cross; den mother Boy Scouts Am. Col. Nebr. Army N.G. Recipient Breaking Rule of Thumb award Nebr. Domestic Violence and Sexual Assault Coalition, 1989, Communicaiton and Leadership award Toastmasters Internat., 1992; named Woman of Distinction Soroptimist Internat. Colubmus, 1990. Mem. VFW Aux., Nat. Orgn. Vol. Leaders, Cath. Daus., Mrs. Jaycees, Kiwanis, Eagles Aux. Office: Rm 1118 State Capitol Lincoln NE 68509

ROBAK, KIM M. academic administrator, lawyer; b. Columbus, Nebr., Oct. 4, 1955; m. William J. Mueller; children: Katherine, Claire. BA with distinction, U. Nebr., 1977, JD with highest distinction, 1985. Tchr. Lincoln Pub. Schs., Nebr., 1978—82; clerk Cline Williams Wright Johnson & Oldfather, 1983; summer assoc. Cooley Godward Castro Huddleson & Tatum, San Francisco, 1984, Steptoe & Johnson, Washington, 1985; ptnr. Rembolt Ludtke Parker & Berger, Lincoln, 1985—91; legal counsel Gov. E. Benjamin Nelson/State of Nebr., 1991—92, chief of staff, 1992—93; lt. gov. State of Nebr., 1993—98; v.p. external affairs, corp. sec. U. Nebr., 1999—. Chair Prairie Fire Internat. Symposium on Edn., 1986. Program com. Leadership Lincoln, 1987—90; chair program com. Leadership Lincoln Alumni Assn., 1987, selection com., 1990; mem. Toll Fellowship Program, 1995; chair Nat. Conf. Lt. Govs., 1996; hon. chair Daffodil Day Campaign An, Cancer Soc.; hon chair Walktoberfest Am. Diabetes Assn.; hon. chair Prevent Blindness Campaign, Nebr.; hon. mem. Red Ribbon Campaign Mothers Against Drunk Driving, 1994—95; active Groundwater Found., 1997, Medicaid Managed Care Commn., 1993—; bd. dirs. Nebr. Health Sys., 1997—, Nat. Found. Women Legislators Found., 1997—98; chair Nebr. Info. Tech. Commn., 1997—98; hon. Christmas chair Salvation Army, 1997; cert. program chair Nat. Order Women Legislators, 1997; bd. dirs. Doane Coll., 1997—, Lincoln Pub. Sch. Found., 1998—, Martin Luther Home Bd., 1999—; mem. Lincoln Partnership for Econ. Devel. Bd., 2000—, Martin Luther Home Soc., 1999—2001, Dem. Gen. Counsel, Nebr., 1985—92; bd. dirs. women's ministries First Congl. Ch., 1988—91, trustee, 1991—99, asst. moderator, 1999—; trustee Plymouth Congl. Ch., 1998—. Named Notable Woman, First Plymouth Congl. Ch.'s Bd. Women's Ministries, 1996; fellow, Leadership Lincoln, 1986—87. Mem.: ABA (steering com. 1997—), Lincoln Bar Assn., Nebr. State Bar Assn. (ethics com. 1987—92, vice chair com. pub. rels. 1988—92, chari com. yellow pages advt. 1988, ho. of dels. 1988—95), Nat. Inst. Trial Advocacy, Alzheimers Assn. (hon. chair Lincoln-Greater Nebr. chpt. 1996—98), Updowntowners, Order of Coif, U. Nebr. Coll. Alumni Assn. (bd. dirs. 1986—89). Office: 3835 Holdrege St PO Box 830745 Lincoln NE 68583-0745 E-mail: Krobak@uneb.edu.

ROBB, BABETTE, retired elementary school educator; b. St. Paul, Minn., Jan. 25, 1923; d. Roy F and Eda Johnson; m. David L Robb, July 23, 1945; children: Deborah G. Jankura, Pamela W. BA, So. Meth. U., Dallas, 1945; Elem. Educator, U. Wis., River Falls, 1948. Asst. to county auditor Washington County, Stillwater, Minn., 1945—46, county sch. tchr. Stillwater, 1947—53; elem. sch. tchr. Stillwater (Minn.) Dist. 834, 1953—81. Author: (elem.sch. text) St. Croix Valley Story, 1970; contbr. articles Childrens Mags., 1979. Chmn. Washington County Young Reps., Stillwater, 1946—50; mem. bd. dirs. Family Svc., Stillwater, Minn.; Grand Marshall of 4th of July Parade Afton (Minn.) Hist. Soc., 1973. Recipient Drama award, Minn. Regional Speech Contest, 1940; chosen to christen army troup transport ship as President's plane dipped it's wings, U.S. Maritime Commn. Mem.: AAUW (life; Founder local chpt. 1946), Minn. Ednl. Assn. (sec. local br. 1953—), Delta Kappa Gamma (Sec. 1972—). Methodist. Achievements include first to introduce Spanish to Elementary Students in 1958. Avocations: modeling, photography, swimming, writing, water biking. Home (Winter): Apt 407 3500 S Ocean Blvd Palm Beach FL 33480 Home (Summer): 2803 S St Croix Tr Afton MN 55001

ROBB, LYNDA JOHNSON, writer; b. Washington, Mar. 19, 1944; d. Lyndon Baines and Claudia Alta (Taylor) Johnson; m. Charles Spittal Robb, Dec. 9, 1967; children: Lucinda Desha, Catherine Lewis, Jennifer Wickliffe. BA with honors, U. Tex., 1966. Writer McCall's Mag., 1966-68; contbg. editor Ladies Home Jour., 1968-80; lectr., bd. dirs. Reading Is Fundamental, 1968—, Lyndon B. Johnson Family Found., 1969-95. Past mem. Va. State Coun. on Infant Mortality, Va. Maternal & Child Health Coun.; mem. Nat. Commn. to Prevent Infant Mortality, 1987-93; chmn. Pres.'s Adv. Com. for Women, 1979-81; pres. bd. dirs. Nat. Home Libr. Found., Ford Theatre; chmn. Va. Women's Cultural History Project, 1982-85; chmn. Reading is Fundamental, 1996-2001. Mem. Zeta Tau Alpha. Office: Reading is Fundamental Ste 400 1825 Connecticut Ave NW Washington DC 20009-5708

ROBBEN, TRICIA ELIZABETH, protective services official; d. Joseph William and Margaret Kelly Robben. BS, John Carroll U., 1993—97; MPA, Fla. Atlantic U., 2002—. Cert. Victim Advocate Office of the Atty. Gen./FL. Rsch. coord. U. Hospitals of Cleve. and Case Western Res. U., 1997—99; sales assoc. First Union Securities, Boca Raton, 1999—2000; elder crime specialist Boca Raton Police Services Dept., Fla. Hospice ethics com. mem. Hospice by the Sea, Boca Raton, Fla. Recipient Civilian of the Month, Dec. 2002 and June 2003, Cmty. Policing award, Internat. Assoc. of Chiefs of Police, 2003, Civilian of Yr. 2003, Chiefs Achievement award, Boca Raton Police Dept., 2003; Stanley scholar, Stanley Found., 1997. Avocation: swimming. Office: Boca Raton Police Services Department 100 NW Boca Raton Blvd Boca Raton FL 33432 Office Phone: 561-338-1239. Business E-Mail: trobben@ci.boca-raton.fl.us.

ROBBINS, ALEXANDRA, journalist, writer; BA summa cum laude, Yale U., 1998. Journalist, writer, spkr. www.alexandrarobbins.com, Washington, 1996—. Spkr., lectr. Author: (book) Secrets of the Tomb: Skull and Bones, the Ivy League, and the Hidden Paths of Power, 2002; co-author: Quarterlife Crisis: The Unique Challenges of Life In Your Twenties, 2001 (Finalist, Books For a Better Life Award, 2002). Judge Books for a Better Life, 2003—. Mem.: Phi Beta Kappa.

ROBBINS, ANNE FRANCIS See REAGAN, NANCY DAVIS

ROBBINS, AUDREY, county official; b. Chgo., Mar. 1, 1932; d. Philip I. and Manya Lehr; children: Dana Merfeld, Cindy Buss. BA, DePaul U., 1993. Mfrs. rep. Museum Reprodns. - Marwall Industries, N.Y.C., 1969—79; asst. to chief counsel Arthur Andersen & Co., Chgo., 1979—98; mem. staff Office of Chief Judge, Cook County Cir. Ct., Chgo., 1999—. Author: Goldblatt's Galloping Gourmets, 1974 (Tribune award, 74). Vol. intensive care infants Northwestern Meml. Hosp., Chgo., 1979—80; vol.

Art Inst. Chgo., 1984—86; touring docent Terra Mus. Am. Art, 1999—; bd. dirs., sec., pres. Nathan & Francis Goldblatt Soc. for Cancer Rsch., 1955—83. Mem.: Golden Key (life). Avocations: art history, watercolors, cooking. Home: 910 N Lake Shore Dr # 718 Chicago IL 60611 Office: Cir Ct Cook County 50 W Washington Chicago IL 60602 Office Phone: 312-603-3900. Business E-Mail: arobbin@cookcountygov.com.

ROBBINS, CARRIE F(ISHBEIN), costume designer, educator; b. Balt., Feb. 7, 1943; d. Sidney W. and Bettye A. (Berman) Fishbein; m. Richard D. Robbins, Feb. 15, 1969. BS, BA, Pa. State U., 1964; MFA, Yale Drama Sch., 1967. Over 30 Broadway shows, NYC, 1968-2001, A Class Act at the Ambassador Theatre, 2001—, Grease (Tony nomination best costumes), Over Here (Tony nomination best costumes), Secret Affairs of Mildred Wilde, Yentl, Cyrano, Iceman Cometh, Octette Bridge Club, Look to the Lillies, Sweet Bird of Youth, Agnes of God, Boys of Winter, The First, Frankenstein, Shadow Box, Samson et Dalila, San Francisco Opera, 1980, LA Opera, 1999, Houston Grand Opera, 2002, Rigoletto, Ixsaison et Ludmilla, Taverner, Bernstein's Mass, Opera Co. Boston, 1975-76, 86, 89, Hamburg State Opera (W.Ger.), 1979, Washington Opera Soc., 1975, designed for NY Shakespeare Festival, Jules Irving's Lincoln Ctr. Repertory Theatre, Tyrone Guthrie Theatre, Mpls. (including Hamlet, Julius Ceasar and Three Penny Opera), Mark Taper Forum, LA (including The Tempest with Anthony Hopkins, Fashion Inst. Tech. Surface Design award, Flea in Her Ear (Dramalogue Critics award), The Wedding Banquet, 2003, Williamstown, Chelsea Theatre Ctr., Bklyn., John Houseman's City Ctr. Acting Co., Juilliard Sch., NYC, WNET and cable TV, off-broadway theatres, NYC including Belle, High Infidelity, Promenade Theatre, It's Only a Play, Big Potato, Women's Project's Exact Center of the Universe, Two-Headed, Westport Country Playhouse Bench's in the Sun, Arclite Theatre Tennessee Williams Remembered, Paper Mill Playhouse Rags; designer sets and costumes Tallulah Hallelujah; tchr. Henry Le Tang Profl. Sch. Tap Dance, 1989-91; vis. guest lectr. costume design U. Ill., UCLA, Oberlin Coll., Pa. State U., others; master tchr. costume design NYU; costume designer: (TV) Saturday Night Live-NBC, 1985-86, The Rita Show; (film) In the Spirit, 1987; designer apparel Rainbow Room, Rockefeller Ctr., 1987-97, Aurora Grill, 1988, Empress Ct., Caesar's Palace, Las Vegas, 1988, Windows on the World Restaurant Complex, 1996 (Image of Yr. award Nat. Assn. Uniform Mfrs. and Distbrs. 1997); regional theatres including Berkshire Theatre, Mass., The Wedding Banquet, Toys in the Attic, Fla. Stage It's Only a Play, Arena Stage, Washington. One-woman show Cen. Falls Gallery, N.Y.C., 1980; exhibited in group shows at Cooper Hewitt Mus., Pa. State U., Wright-Hepburn Gallery, N.Y.C., Scottsdale, Ariz., Cen. Falls Gallery, 1983, Salmagundi Club, 1983-84; illustrations and calligraphy pub. ann. calendar Soc. of Scribes competition, Ms. mag.; original costume work photographed in books; Costume Design, 1983, Fabric Painting and Dying for the Theatre, 1982; original drawing reproduced Time-Life Series: The Ency. of Collectibles; profiled in Costume Design-Techniques of Modern Masters, 1996, Contemporary Designers, 1990, 97; designer loft conversions, comml. lobby space, studios, others; contbr. articles to Theatre Crafts International, Theatre Design & Tech., Theatre Designers & Computers; illustrator: Who Was Wolfgang Amadeus Mozart?, 2003; contbr. to profl. jours. Named Disting. Alumna, Pa. State U., 1979; recipient Antoinette Perry nominations for Best Costumes for a Broadway Show, 1971-72, 73-74, Drama Desk award, Am. Theatre Wing, N.Y.C., 1971, 72, Maharam award for design, Joseph Maharam Found., N.Y.C., 1975, nomination, 1984, Juror's Choice award for surface design, Fashion Inst. of Tech., 1980, Dramalogue Critics' award for Outstanding Achievement in Theatre Costume Design, L.A., 1982, Silver Medal, 6th Triennial of Theatre Design, Novisad, Yugoslavia, 1981, Diplome L'Honneur, 1990, Audelco nomination, 1990, Henry Hewes nomination, 1999, League N.Y. Theatres, N.Y.C., 1971-72, 73-74. Mem. League Profl. Theatre Tng. Programs (steering com.), League Profl. Theatre Women (bd. dirs. 2001—), Graphic Artists Guild, Soc. Scribes, Am. Soc. Interior Designers, United Scenic Artists Local 829; adv. com. The Costume Collection of Theatre Devel. Fund. Home and Office: 11 W 30th St 15th Fl New York NY 10001 E-mail: crobb10001@aol.com.

ROBBINS, DOROTHY ANN, librarian; b. Altha, Fla., Dec. 2, 1939; d. Robert C. and Pauline Johnson; m. Richard N. Robbins, Jan. 16, 1960; children: Cynthia R. Peacock, Pamela T., LeAnne M. Lusk. AA, Gulf Coast C.C., Panama City, 1959. With Bay County Pub. Libr., Panama City, Fla., 1959—, libr. clk., bookmobile clk., br. mgr., circulation supr., literacy dir., pub. svcs. supr. Adv. bd. Literacy Vols. of Bay County, Panama City, 1982-2003; troop leader Girl Scouts of the Apalachee Bend, Panama City, 1972-75. Mem. Greater Panama City Dog Fanciers (sec. 1988-2003), S.E. Bullmastiff Assn. (b. dirs., pres. 1991-2003), Am. Bullmastiff Assn., United Daus. of the Confederacy. Democrat. Baptist. Avocations: showing bullmastiffs, reading, antiques, crafts, gardening. Home: 435 S Palo Alto Ave Panama City FL 32401-3954 Office: Bay County Pub Libr 25 W Government St Panama City FL 32401-2743

ROBBINS, ELLEN SUE, lawyer, educator; b. Chgo., Mar. 15, 1967; d. Sheldon Neal and Barbara Lynn (Corenman) R. BS in Bus. Adminstrn. summa cum laude, U. Ill., 1988; JD magna cum laude, Harvard U., 1991. Bar: Ill. 1991. Jud. clk. to Judge Charles Kocoras U.S. Dist. Ct., Chgo., 1991-92; ptnr. Sidley & Austin, Chgo., 1992—. Adj. prof. law DePaul Coll. Law, Chgo., 1997—. Mem. ABA, Chgo. Bar Assn. Avocations: jogging, golf, sports. Office: Sidley & Austin One First Nat Plz Chicago IL 60603-2003 E-mail: erobbins@sidley.com.

ROBBINS, HULDA DORNBLATT, artist, printmaker; b. Atlanta, Oct. 19, 1910; d. Adolph Benno and Lina (Rosenthal) Dornblatt. Student, Phila. Mus's. Sch. Indsl. Art, 1928-29, Prussian Acad., Berlin, 1929-31, Barnes Found., Merion, Pa., 1939. Poster designer and maker ITE Circuit Breaker Co. Inc., Phila., 1944; instr. serigraphy Nat. Serigraph Soc. Sch., N.Y.C., 1953-60; instr. creative painting Atlantic County Jewish Community Centers, Margate and Atlantic City, N.J., 1960-67. Represented by WIlliam P. Carl, Fine Prints, Boston, The Picture Store, Boston. One-man shows, Lehigh U. Art Galleries, 1933, ACA Galleries, Phila., 1939, 8th St. Gallery, N.Y.C., 1941, Serigraph Gallery, N.Y.C., 1947, Atlantic City Art Center, 1961, 71, numerous group shows, 2d Nat. Print ann. Bklyn. Mus., Carnegie Inst., Library of Congress, LaNapoule Art Found., Am. Graphic Contemporary Art; represented in permanent collections, including, Met. Mus. Art, N.Y.C., Mus. Modern Art, N.Y.C., Bibliotheque Nationale, Smithsonian Instn., Art Mus. Ont., Can., Victoria and Albert Mus., London, U.S. embassies abroad, Lehigh U., Princeton (N.J.) Print Club. Recipient Purchase prize Prints for Children, Mus. Modern Art, N.Y.C., 1941; prize 2d Portrait of Am. Competition, 1945; 2d prize Paintings by Printmakers, 1948 Mem. Am. Color Print Soc., Print Club, Graphics Soc., Serigraph Soc. (mem. founding group, charter sec., Ninth Ann. prize 1948, 49) Home and Office: 16 S Buffalo Ave Ventnor City NJ 08406-2635

ROBBINS, JANE BORSCH, library science educator, information science educator; b. Chgo., Sept. 13, 1939; d. Reuben August and Pearl Irene (Houk) Borsch; married; 1 child, Molly Warren. BA, Wells Coll., 1961; MLS, Western Mich. U., 1966; PhD, U. Md., 1972. Asst. prof. library and info. sci. U. Pitts., 1972-73; assoc. prof. Emory U., Atlanta, 1973-74; cons. to bd. Wyo. State Libr., 1974-77; assoc. prof. La. State U., Baton Rouge, 1977-79; dean La. State U. Sch. Library and Info. Sci., 1979-81; prof., dir. Sch. Library and Info. Studies U. Wis., Madison, 1981-94; dean, prof. Fla. State U. Sch. Info. Studies, Tallahassee, 1994—. Author: Public Library Policy and Citizen Participation, 1975, Public Librarianship: A Reader, 1982, Are We There Yet?, 1988, Libraries: Partners in Adult Literacy, 1990, Keeping the Books: Public Library Financial Practices, 1992, Balancing the Books: Financing American Public Library Services, 1993, Evaluating Library Programs and Services: A Manual and Sourcebook, 1994, Tell It! The Complete Manual of Library Evaluation, 1996; editor Libr. and Info. Sci. Rsch., 1982-92; contbr. articles to profl. jours. Bd. dirs. Freedom to Read Found., 1997-99. Mem.: ALA (councilor 1976—80, 1991—95), Fla. Libr. Assn. (bd. dirs. 1997—99), Wis. Libr. Assn. (pres. 1986), Assn. for Libr. and Info. Sci. Edn. (dir. 1979—81, pres. 1984), Am. Soc. Info. Sci., Beta Phi Mu (exec. dir. 2000—). Democrat. Episcopalian. Office: Fla State U Sch Info Studies Louis Shores Bldg Tallahassee FL 32306-2100 Business E-Mail: robbins@lis.fsu.edu.

ROBBINS, JANE LEWIS, elementary school educator; b. New Iberia, La., Dec. 14, 1942; d. William Lewis and Maurine (James) R. BS, U. Okla., 1965; ME, So. Meth. U., 1972; postgrad., Tex. Women's U., 1981, 83, 85; cert. in edn. adminstrn., Tex A&M U. Commerce, 1991. Tchr. Lone Grove Ind. Sch. Dist., Okla., 1964-65, Concord-Carlisle (Mass.) Regional Sch. Dist., 1966-67, Newton (Mass.) Pub. Schs., 1967-68, Highland Park Ind. Sch. Dist., Dallas, 1968—, instrnl. specialist, dist. appraiser, coord. dist. gifted and talented, coord. student tchrs., mentor new tchrs., coord. instrnl. leadership program, interim elem. prin., 1990-93; asst. prin. McCulloch Intermediate Sch., Dallas. Instr. reading clinic So. Meth. U., 1972-75, Sch. Edn., summer 1978, adj. prof. Div. Ednl. Studies; chmn. English dept. McCulloch Middle Sch.; regional coordinator Tex. Acad. Pentathlon, 1985-89. Mem. ASCD, Tex. Assn. Improvement Reading, Tex. Assn. Gifted and Talented, Assn. Children with Learning Disabilities, Internat. Reading Assn. (North Tex. Coun.), Tex. Elem. Prins. and Suprs. Assn. (Acad. III), Nat. Coun. Tchrs. of English, Tex. Mid. Sch. Assn., Mid. Sch. Consortium, Tex. Assn. Secondary Sch. Prins., Pi Beta Phi, Delta Kappa Gamma. Republican. Episcopalian. Office: McCulloch Intermediate 3555 Granada Ave Dallas TX 75205-2235

ROBBINS, JEANETTE LEE, sales and manufacturing executive; b. Portland, Oreg., July 21, 1956; d. Robert Lee and Norma Yvonne (Smith) Rassi; m. Michael Keith Robbins, May 22, 1981. A in Gen. Sci., Portland C.C., 1982. Cert. engring. aide, Oreg. With prodn. thrift Salvation Army, Portland, 1979, Goodwill Industries, Denver, 1983-87, St. Vincent De Paul, Portland, 1987-88; owner Job Devel. Rsch. Ctr., Portland, 1985 , Eye-Dea Devel. Sales & Mfg., Portland, 1988—. Detective scientist, 1980—; reviewer publs. and forms IRS, 1997—, U.S. Govt., Washington, 1997—, local bus map rev., 1998. Author: (textbook) Prime Factor Pattern, 1991, Prime Pattern of (Square) Root Ends, 1994; contbr. articles and book revs. to profl. publs. and books; artist, author: (visual aid) Artrithmetic, 1982, Patricia Mao, U.S. White House, 1996, Artrithmetic-Reference, 1997, Combination, 1998, Large Combination Deluxe, 1999. Corr., adviser, World Gov., Nat. Gov., State Gov., Local Gov., Private Citizen, Bus. Owners, 1978—, Dem. Nat. Com., Washington D.C., 1993—. With USAF, 1977. Mem. Pub. Libr. Sys. (rschr. 1978—), Nat. Geographic Soc. (corr. 1993—). Avocations: alpinist, photography, languages. Office: Eye Dea Devel Sales & Mfg PO Box 66221 Portland OR 97290-6221

ROBBINS, JENNIFER KATHERINE, music educator; b. New Port Richey, Fla., Dec. 13, 1974; d. Jon Stephen and Christina Rose Robbins. MusB, Fla. State U., 1992—97. Cert. Music K-12th grades, Media Specialist Pre K-12th grades Fla. Dept. of Edn., 1997. Band & chorus dir. Coachman Fundamental Mid. Sch., Clearwater, Fla., 1997—98; music specialist San Antonio Elem. Sch., San Antonio, Fla., 1998—98, KEC Canal Point Elem. Sch., Canal Point, Fla., 1998—2001, Richey & Marlowe Elem. Schools, New Port Richey, Fla., 2001—. Actor: (plays) The Sound of Music. Sec. prin. clarinetist Richey Comty. Orch. Mem.: NEA, Am. Fedn. of Teachers, Fla. Music Educators Assn., Music Educators Nat. Conf., Tau Beta Sigma (membership chair 1996—96). D-Liberal. Roman Catholic. Avocations: reading, travel. Home: 6630 Shelby St # 2 New Port Richey FL 34653 Office: Richey/Marlowe Elementary Schools 6807 Madison St New Port Richey FL 34652 Personal E-mail: fsuass@aol.com. E-mail: jrobbins@pasco.k12.fl.us.

ROBBINS, KELLY, professional golfer; b. Mt. Pleasant, Mich., Sept. 29, 1969; d. Steve and Margie R. BA, U. Tulsa. Mem. Ladies Pro Golf Assn., 1991—. Mem. U.S. Solheim Cup, 1994, 96, 98, 2000, 02, 03. Achievements include 9 Career LPGA victories. Avocations: fishing, tennis, swimming, basketball. Office: c/o Ladies Pro Golf Assn 100 International Golf Dr Daytona Beach FL 32124-1082

ROBBINS, MARY, concert pianist; b. Shelby, N.C., Feb. 14, 1950; d. Clyde Hugh and Hazel Marguerite (Lovett) Robbins; m. Carl Brockman, Jan. 16, 1983. Student, Converse Coll., Spartanburg, S.C., 1968-71; BMusic, U. Tex., 1973, MMusic, 1975, D Musical Arts, 1992. Concert coord. Austin (Tex.) Virtuosi, 1980-82; piano clinician Alfred Music Pub., Van Nuys, Cailf., 1991-94; pianist various chamber org., Austin, 1976-91; pvt. piano instr. for adults and children Austin, 1971—; tchg. asst., instr. piano U. Tex., Austin, 1971-75; founder, prin. pianist A. Mozart Fest, Austin, 1991—, artistic dir., 1991—. Accompanist U. Tex., Austin, 1971-84; invited lectr. Mozart Internat. Bicentennial Congress, Salzburg, Austria, 1991. Composer music and cadenzas following Mozart's style for his piano concertos, 1989—; composer, performer CD, A. Mozart Fest, 1998, CD with Austrian pianist Paul Badura-Skoda, 2002. Presenter, Music Tchr. Nat. Assoc. Conf., 2003 (Presenter of session on stylistic issues of interpretation in Mozart). Vol. music class tchr. First English Luth. Ch., Austin, 1992; founder combined groups Classical Music Consortium, Austin, 1997. Grantee Tex. Commn. on Arts, 1991, 93, City of Austin, 1992—. Mem. Austin Dist. Music Tchrs. Assn. (v.p. 1997-98, chair adult programs 1997—, chair festivals 1997-98, Pre-Coll. Tchr. of Yr. 1998), Mu Phi Epsilon. Lutheran. Avocations: cooking, entertaining, dance, outdoor sports, visual arts. Home: 2600 La Ronde St Austin TX 78731-5924

ROBBINS, NANCY SLINKER, volunteer; b. New Kensington, Pa., Jan. 28, 1923; d. Charles Morris and Nancy Grace (Moore) Slinker; m. James Bingham Murray, Aug. 1, 1946 (div. 1959); m. Daniel Harvey Robbins, Nov. 21, 1964; children: Nancy Caroline, Christina Chapman. BA, Westminster Coll., 1945; grad., U. Pitts., 1946. Cert. tchr. Pa. Tchr. Lower Burrell Sch., New Kensington, 1945-48; asst. buyer Gimbel's, Pitts., 1951-53, buyer, 1953-57, La Salle's, Toledo, 1957-61, Sibley's, Rochester, N.Y., 1961-66. Editor: Fan Fare, 1980-81. Pres. bd. Woman's Edn. and Indsl. Union, Rochester, 1973-76, Women's Coalition for Downtown, Rochester, 1982-84; pres. bd. Ronald McDonald House, Rochester, 1986-90, adminstr. grants program, 1996—; chmn. Pub. TV Auction, Rochester, 1980. Recipient Jefferson award Am. Inst. Pub. Svc., 1988, Forman Flair award for outstanding volunteerism, 1990, DeWitt Clinton awrd for pub. svc. Masons, 1989. Avocations: antique collecting, travel, cooking. Home: 35 Schoolhouse Ln Rochester NY 14618-3231 E-mail: nandan0035@aol.com.

ROBBINS, SUSAN PAULA, social work educator; b. Bklyn., Aug. 15, 1948; d. Harold Jess and Rose (Bernstein) R. AA, Manhattan C.C., 1972; BA summa cum laude, Hamline U., 1974; MSW, U. Minn., 1976; PhD, Tulane U., 1979. Adj. instr. dept. sociology and social work Augsburg Coll., Mpls., 1975-76; part-time instr. women's studies program U. Minn., Mpls., 1976; rsch. and grant cons. Seminole Tribe of Fla., Hollywood, 1978-79, child and adolescent caseworker, program planning cons., 1979-80; coord. criminal justice/corrections program St. Mary's Dominican Coll., New Orleans, 1979-80; asst. prof. social work New Orleans Consortium, 1978-80, U. Houston, 1980-86, assoc. prof., 1986—, assoc. dean acad. affairs, 1998-2000. Cons. ABA Multi Door Program, Houston, Cmty. Svc. Option Program, Houston; mediator Dispute Resolution Ctrs., Houston, 1982—; trainer Tex. Dept. Protective Svcs. Tng. Inst., 1995—. Author (with others): Encyclopedia of Social Work, Social Workers' Desk Reference; contbr. articles and book chpts. to profl. jours. Women's Club of Mpls. fellow, 1975, Nat. Inst. of Mental Health fellow, 1976-78; recipient Nat. Faculty Excellence award Univ. Continuing Edn. Assn., 1998. Mem. NASW, Coun. on Social Work Edn., Social Welfare Action Alliance, Assn. for Cmty. Orgn. and Social Adminstrn., So. Sociol. Soc., Phi Kappa Phi (sec. Houston chpt. 1984—). Democrat. Jewish. Office: Univ Houston 4800 Calhoun Rd Houston TX 77204-4013 E-mail: srobbins@uh.edu.

ROBBINS-WILF, MARCIA, educational consultant; b. Newark, Mar. 22, 1949; d. Saul and Ruth (Fern) Robbins; 1 child, Orin. Student, Emerson Coll., 1967-69, Seton Hall U., 1969, Fairleigh Dickinson U., 1970; BA, George Washington U., 1971; MA, NYU, 1975; postgrad., St. Peter's Coll., Jersey City, 1979, Fordham U., 1980; MS, Yeshiva U., 1981, EdD, 1986; postgrad., Monmouth Coll., 1986. Cert. elem. tchr., N.Y., N.J., reading specialist, N.J., prin., supr., N.J., adminstr., supr., N.Y. Tchr. Sleepy Hollow Elem. Sch., Falls Church, Va., 1971-72, Yeshiva Konvitz, N.Y.C., 1972-73; intern Wee Folk Nursery Sch., Short Hills, N.J., 1978-81, dir. day camp, 1980-81, tchr., dir., owner, 1980-81; adj. prof. reading Seton Hall U., South Orange, N.J., 1987, Middlesex County Coll., Edison, N.J., 1987-88; asst. adj. prof. L.I. U., Bklyn., 1988, Pace U., N.Y.C., 1988—. Ednl. cons. Cranford High Sch., 1988; presenter numerous workshops; founding bd. dirs. Stern Coll. Women Yeshiva U., N.Y.C., 1987; adj. vis. lectr. Rutgers U., New Brunswick, N.J., 1988. Chairperson Jewish Book Festival, YM-YWHA, West Orange, N.J., 1986-87, mem. early childhood com., 1986—, bd. dirs., 1986—; vice chairperson dinner com. Nat. Leadership Conf. Christians and Jews, 1986; mem. Hadassah, Valerie Children's Fund, Women's League Conservative Judaism, City of Hope; assoc. bd. bus. and women's profl. divsn. United Jewish Appeal, 1979; vol. reader Goddard Riverside Day Care Ctr., N.Y.C., 1973; friend N.Y.C. Pub. Libr., 1980—; life friend Millburn (N.J.) Pub. Libr.; pres. Seton-Essex Reading Coun., 1991-94. Co-recipient Am. Heritage award, Essex County, 1985; recipient Award Appreciation City of Hope, 1984, Profl. Improvement awards Seton-Essex Reading Council, 1984-86, Cert. Attendance award Seton-Essex Reading Council, 1987. Mem. N.Y. Acad. Scis. (life), N.J. Council Tchrs. English, Nat. Council Tchrs. English, Am. Ednl. Research Assn., Coll. Reading Assn. (life), Assn. Supervision and Curriculun Devel., N.Y. State Reading Assn. (council Manhattan), N.J. Reading Assn. (council Seton-Essex), Internat. Reading Assn., Nat. Assn. for Edn. of Young Children (life N.J. chpt., Kenyon group), Nat. Council Jewish Women (vice chairperson membership com. evening br. N.Y. sect. 1974-75), George Washington U. Alumni Club, Emerson Coll. Alumni Club, NYU Alumni Club, Phi Delta Kappa (life), Kappa Gamma Chi (historian). Clubs: Greenbrook Country (Caldwell, N.J.); George Washington Univ. Avocations: reading, theatre. Home: 242 Hartshorn Dr Short Hills NJ 07078-1914 E-mail: dr.mrw349@aol.com.

ROBECK, MILDRED COEN, education educator, writer; b. Walum, N.D., July 29, 1915; d. Archie Blain and Mary Henrietta (Hoffman) Coen; m. Martin Julius Robeck, Jr., June 2, 1936; children: Martin Jay Robeck, Donna Jayne Robeck Thompson, Bruce Wayne Robeck. BS, U. Wash., 1950, MEd, 1954, PhD, 1958. Ordnance foreman Sherman Williams, U.S. Navy, Bremerton, Wash., 1942-45; demonstration tchr. Seattle Pub. Schs., 1946-57; reading clinic dir. U. Calif., Santa Barbara, 1957-64; rsch. cons. State Dept. Edn., Sacramento, Calif., 1964-67; prof., head early childhood edn. U. Oreg., Eugene, Oreg., 1967-86; vis. scholar West Australia Inst. Tech., Perth, 1985; v.p. acad. affairs U. Santa Barbara, Calif., 1987-95. Vis. prof. Victoria Coll., B.C. Can., summer 1958, Dalhousie U., Halifax, summer 1964; trainer evaluator U.S. Office of Edn. Head Start, Follow Thru, 1967-72; cons., evaluator Native Am. Edn. Programs, Sioux, Navajo, 1967-81; cons. on gifted Oreg. Task Force on Talented and Gifted, Salem, 1974-76; evaluator Early Childhood Edn., Bi-Ling. program, Petroleum and Minerology, Dhahran, Saudi Arabia, 1985. Author: Materials KELP: Kgn. Evaluation Learning Pot, 1967, Infants and Children, 1978, Psychology of Reading, 1990, Oscar: His Story, 1997, 2nd edit., 2000; contbr. articles to profl. jours. Evaluation cons. Rosenburg Found. Project, Santa Barbara, 1966-67; faculty advisor Pi Lambda Theta, Eugene, Oreg, 1969-74; guest columnist Oreg. Assn. Gifted and Talented, Salem, Oreg., 1979-81; editorial review bd. ERQ, U.S. Calif., L.A., 1981-91. Recipient Nat. Dairy award 4-H Clubs, Wis., 1934, scholarships NYA and U. Wis., Madison, 1934-35, faculty rsch. grants U. Calif., Santa barbara, 1958-64, NDEA Fellowship Retraining U.S. Office Edn., U. Oreg., 1967-70. Mem. APA, Am. Ednl. Rsch. Assn., Internat. Reading Assn., Phi Beta Kappa, Pi Lambda Theta. Democrat. Avocations: dyslexia research, historical research, duplicate bridge, writing. Home: 95999 Highway 101 S Yachats OR 97498-9714 Office Phone: 541-547-3967. E-mail: mrobeck@casco.net.

ROBEK, MARY FRANCES, business education educator; b. Superior, Wis., Jan. 30, 1927; d. Stephen and Mary (Hervert) R. BE, U. Wis., 1948; MA, Northwestern U., 1951; MBA, U. Mich., 1962, PhD, 1967. Tchr. Bergland (Mich.) High Sch., 1948, Tony (Wis.) High Sch., 1948-50, Sch. Vocat. and Adult Edn., Superior, 1950-58; prof. bus. edn. and office tech. Ea. Mich. U., Ypsilanti, 1958-93; instr. Jazyckova Gymnasium, Banská, Slovakia, 1994. Author: Information and Records Management, 1995. Assn. of Records Mgrs. and Adminstrs. fellow, 1992. Mem. Assn. Records Mgrs. and Adminstrs. (life), Inst. Cert. Mgrs. (pres. 1980-81, Emmett Leahy award 2000), Cath. Daus. Am., Delta Pi Epsilon, Delta Kappa Gamma, Pi Lambda Theta. Republican. Roman Catholic. Home: 515 Clough Ave Superior WI 54880 E-mail: RobekMary@aol.com.

ROBEL, LAUREN, law educator; b. Dec. 1953; BA, Auburn U., 1978; JD, Ind. U., 1983. Bar: US Supreme Ct., Ind., Ill. Law clk. to Hon. Jesse Eschbach, U.S. Ct. Appeals (7th cir.), 1983—85; dean, Val Nolan prof. law Ind. U. Sch. Law, Bloomington. Vis. faculty U. Panthenon-Assas, Paris; reporter rules com. U.S. Dist. Ct. (so. dist.) Ind.; mem. rules com. Ind. Supreme Ct. Contbr. articles to profl. jours.; author: Les États des Noirs: Federalisme et question raciale aux États-unis, 2000. Mem.: Ind. State Bar Women (Law Recognition award), Ind. Bar Found. (Pro Bono Publico award), Order of Coif. Office: Ind Univ Sch Law 211 S Indiana Ave Bloomington IN 47405

ROBELOT, JANE, anchor; b. Greenville, S.C., Oct. 9, 1960; married; 1 child. BA in Econs., Clemson U. News and sports dir., reporter WCCP-AM Radio, Clemson, SC; anchor, reporter WSPA-TV, CBS affiliate, Spartanburg, SC, 1983—90; gen. assignment reporter WCAU-TV, Phila., 1990—92, co-anchor 6:00 PM news, 1991—92, co-anchor 11:00 PM news, 1992—95; co-anchor CBS Morning News, N.Y.C., 1995; news reader This Morning CBS News, N.Y.C., 1995—96, co-anchor This Morning, 1996—99, co-anchor CBS Atlanta News, 1999—. Office: Sta WGNX-TV Meredith Corp 1810 Briarcliff Rd NE Atlanta GA 30329-4008

ROBERGE, M. SHEILA, state legislator; b. Manchester, N.H. 2 children. Ed., St. Anselm's Coll. Mem. Dist. 19 N.H. Senate, Concord, 1985—. Chmn. Manchester, N.H., Rep. com., 1979-80; del., Rep. Nat. Conv., 1980, 84; Rep. nat. committeewoman from N.H.; vice-chmn., Rep. Nat. Com., 1980-88. Roman Catholic. Address: Senate House 107 N Main St Rm 312 Concord NH 03301-4951 E-mail: eosman@carltonfields.com.

ROBERSON, DORIS JEAN HEROLD, retired social worker; b. N.Y.C., Oct. 15, 1924; d. Albert and Rosalind (Lowenstein) Herold; m. Lloyd Willis Roberson, Aug. 31, 1949; children: Lynn, Patricia, Katherine, Irene. BA cum laude, Mount Holyoke Coll., 1945; MSW, Fordham U., 1947. Cert. social worker, N.Y. Social worker Children's Aid Soc., N.Y.C., 1947-52, Yonkers (N.Y.) Pub. Schs., 1966-89; ret., 1989. Mem. NASW, Acad. Cert. Social Workers, N.Y. State Sch. Social Workers Assn., Phi Beta Kappa. Home: 145 Hoover Rd Yonkers NY 10710-3408

ROBERSON, JANET L. aircraft manufacturing company official; b. Rochester, N.Y., Oct. 4, 1955; d. Joseph Rollin and Patricia Jean Nightingale; m. Joe Frank Briseno, June 24, 1977 (div. Dec. 1979); 1 child, Bradley Christian; m. Kenneth Mark Roberson, Aug. 9, 1997; stepchildren: Brandon, Ashley. BS in Bus., LeTourneau U., Longview, Tex., 1993. Tech. writer Gen. Dynamics, Ft. Worth, 1979-82, tech. editor, 1982-84, sr. tech. editor, 1984-86; chief tech. data Lockheed Martin, Ft. Worth, 1986—. With USAF, 1976-78. Mem. Inst. Cert. Profl. Mgrs. (cert.), Nat. Mgmt. Assn. Republican. Roman Catholic. Avocations: oil painting, working out, reading. Home: 504 Elderwood Trl Fort Worth TX 76120-1345 E-mail: jan.l.roberson@lmco.com.

ROBERSON, JESSIE HILL, federal agency administrator; Grad., U. Tenn. Nuc. reactor ops. mgr. DuPont, 1982—87; sys. engr. Ga. Power Co., 1987—89; project engring. dir., asst. mgr. environ. restoration Savannah River Site, U.S. Dept. Energy, 1989—96; mgr. Rocky Flats Field Office Dept. Energy, Colo., 1996—99, asst. sec. environ. mgmt., 2001—. Mem. Def. Nuc. Facilities Safety Bd., 2000—01. Named Nat. Black Engr. of Yr. for profl. achievement in govt. Office: Dept Energy Environ Mgmt 1000 Independence Ave SW Washington DC 20585-0001

ROBERSON, LINDA, lawyer; b. Omaha, July 15, 1947; d. Harlan Oliver and Elizabeth Aileen (Good) R.; m. Gary M. Young, Aug. 20, 1970; children: Elizabeth, Katherine, Christopher. BA, Oberlin Coll., 1969; MS, U. Wis., 1970, JD, 1974. Bar: Wis. 1974, U.S. Dist. Ct. (we. dist.) Wis. 1974. Legis. atty. Wis. Legis. Reference Bur., Madison, 1974-76, sr. legis. atty., 1976-78; assoc. Rikkers, Koritzinsky & Rikkers, Madison, 1978-79; ptnr. Koritzinsky, Neider, Langer & Roberson, Madison, 1979-85, Stolper, Koritzinsky, Brewster & Neider, Madison, 1985-93, Balisle & Roberson, Madison, 1993—. Adj. faculty U. Wis. Law Sch., Madison, 1977-2004. Co-author: Real Women, Real Lives, 1981, Wisconsin's Marital Property Reform Act, 1984, Understanding Wisconsin's Marital Property Law, 1985, A Guide to Property Classification Under Wisconsin's Marital Property Act, 1986, Workbook for Wisconsin Estate Planners, 2d edit., 1993, 5th edit., 2003, Look Before You Leap, 1996, Family Estate Planning in Wis., 1992, rev. edit. 2003, The Marital Property Classification Handbook, 1999. Fellow: Family Law Coun. of Cmty. Property States (del. 1996—), Am. Bar Found., Am. Acad. Matrimonial Lawyers (pres. Wis. chpt. 2001); mem.: ABA, Internat. Soc. Family Law, Nat. Assn. Elder Law Attys., Legal Assn. Women, Dane County Bar Assn., Wis. Bar Assn., Divorce Cooperation Inst. (bd. dirs.). Office: Balisle and Roberson PO Box 870 Madison WI 53701-0870 E-mail: lr@b-rlaw.com.

ROBERT, ELISABETH B. toy company executive; b. N.Y.C. children: Catie, Ruthie. Grad., Phillips Acad., 1973; BA in French, Middlebury Coll., 1978; M in Bus., u. Vt., 1984. Asst. to pres. Vt. Gas Systems, 1984-88, exec., 1988-89; campaign mgr. Vt. Gubernatorial Campaign, 1989-90; with computer tech. firm, 1990-95; CRO The Vt. Teddy Bear Co., Shelburne, 1995-97, pres., CEO, 1997—. Bd. dirs. Com. on Temporary Shelter, Vt. Gov.'s Commn. on Women; basketball coach Mater Christi Sch., Burlington, Vt., 1996—. Office: Vt Teddy Bear Co Inc 6655 Shelburne Rd Shelburne VT 05482-6500

ROBERT, ELLEN, university administrator; b. Jackson, Mich., May 24, 1944; d. Paul Jules and Beryl Ruth R.; m. Michael F. Winter, Sept. 6, 1970; children: Christopher Robert-Winter, Laurel Robert-Winter. BA, Western Mich. U., 1966, PhD, 1973. Faculty in sociology Kalamazoo (Mich.) Coll., 1969-70, U. Minn., Morris, 1973-80, faculty in women's studies Mpls., 1980-84; dir. advising San Francisco State U., 1984-91; dir. student learning ctr. U. Calif., Berkeley, 1991-94, dir. McNair scholars program, lectr. sociology Davis, 1995—. Bd. dirs. Davis Cmty. Meals, 1996-98. Mem. Sigma Zi. Democrat. Episcopal. Office: U Calif Davis Grad Studies One Shields Ave Davis CA 95616 E-mail: errobert@ucdavis.edu.

ROBERTS, ANNE MARGARET, secondary school educator; b. Auburn, Ind., Sept. 5, 1972; d. James Alfred and Rachel Sherwood Roberts. BA, Hanover Coll., 1995; MA in French, Purdue U., 2004—. Cert. tchr. Ind., 1995, lic. real estate agt. Ind., 1998. U.S. history and French tchr. Sci. Acad., Mercedes, Tex., 1995—97; real estate agt., realtor Coldwell Banker Roth Wherly Graber, Auburn, Ind., 1998—99; French tchr. Eastside Jr./Sr. H.S., Butler, Ind., 2000—02. Grantee Hanover Coll., 1994. Mem.: Am. Assn. Tchrs. French, Phi Mu (life; Alumnae Chair 1994—95). Avocations: travel, tennis, piano. Home: 1160 Anthrop Dr West Lafayette IN 47906-3844 Personal E-mail: anmrob@hotmail.com.

ROBERTS, BETTY JO, retired librarian, speech therapist; b. Ft. Worth, Tex., Nov. 11, 1927; d. Harry Pulliam and Mamie Josephine (Parker) Easton; m. Robert Lester Roberts, Jr.; children: Jo Lu, Lee Ann. Student, Tex. State Coll. Women, Denton, 1945-47, Tex. Wesleyan Coll.; BS, SW Tex. State U., 1952. Tchr. Milton H. Barry Sch. for Physical Rehab., Houston, United Cerebral Palsy Ctr., Ft. Worth, Tex., San Marcos Pub. Schs., Tex., 1952-53; supr. practice tchrs. S.W. Tex. State, 1952-53; tchr. Waco (Tex.) Ind. Schs., 1953-54; speech therapist Providence Crippled Children's Hosp., Waco; tchr. phonics, creative art Latin Am. Ctr., Waco, 1961-69; ch. librarian Trinity United Methodist Ch., Waco, 1979-88; ch. lib. Cen. United Methodist Ch., Waco, Tex., 1988-91. Compilor, Editor: Swedishes and More 1984. Democrat. Methodist. Address: 3248 Village Park Dr Waco TX 76708-1582

ROBERTS, BETTY WINKLER, retired health agency administrator; b. Ronceverte, W.Va., Aug. 29, 1926; d. James Louis Winkler and Adele L'Artigue Pinckney Pettyjohn; m. Charles Lewis Roberts, Dec. 4, 1954 (div. Nov. 1961); children: Holly Adele, Dean Scott. Diploma, St. Luke's Hosp., 1947; BA, U. Pitts., 1962; MA, Marshall U., 1971. RN. Staff nurse Monongalia Gen. Hosp., Morgantown, W.Va., 1948-50; rehab. nurse Ohio State U. Hosp., Columbus, 1952-53; pub. health nurse Columbus Pub. Health, 1953-54; tchr. English Caroline County Sch. Bd., Bowling Green, Va., 1963-64; rehab. counselor W.Va. Dept. Rehab. Inst., 1964-67; tng. dir. W.Va. Dept. Mental Health, Charleston, 1967-69; editor Jour. Rehab. Nat. Rehab. Assn., Washington, 1970-77; resident health mgr. Westminster Canterbury House, Richmond, Va., 1977-84, dir. assisted living unit, 1984-92; ret., 1992. Mem. Nat. Press Club, Am. Newswomen's Club, Nat. Soc. DAR, Colonial Dames of 17th Century. Avocation: genealogy. Home: 8806 Three Chopt Rd Apt 305 Richmond VA 23229-4736

ROBERTS, CAROLYN JUNE, real estate broker; b. Reading, Mass., June 10, 1938; d. Frank Hiram and Blanche Laura (Robertson) Gifford; m. Roy Dale Roberts, Apr. 4, 1956; children: Kathleen, Charles, Cindy. BS in Microbiology, San Diego State U., 1973, MBA, 1982. Lic. med. tech.; real estate broker, Calif. Microbiologist Kaiser Permanente, San Diego, 1973-74; mgr. anesthesiology U. Calif., San Diego, 1975-81; dir. ambulatory care Merced (Calif.) Community Med. Ctr., 1983-84; mgr. medicine U. Calif., San Francisco, 1984-89, mgr. surgery San Diego, 1989-94. Pres. Acad. Bus. Officers San Francisco (Calif.) Gen. Hosp., 1986-87; chief adminstrv. Dept. Med. Univ. Utah, Salt Lake City. Co-author: (novels) The Forgotten Middle. Mem. Am. Assn. Med. Colls. on Bus. Affairs (program com. 1991-92), Soc. Rsch. Adminstrn. (western sect. pres. elect 1993-94), Sigma Iota Epsilon. Avocations: scuba diving, sailing, traveling. Home: 3174 Central Ave Spring Valley CA 91977-2512

ROBERTS, CELIA ANN, librarian; b. Bangor, Maine, Feb. 6, 1935; d. William Lewis and Ruey Pearl (Logan) Roberts. AA, U. Hartford, 1957, BA, 1961; postgrad., So. Conn. State Coll., 1963—. With catalog, acquisition and circulation depts. U. Hartford Libr., 1956-65; libr. Simsbury Free Libr., Simsbury, Conn., 1965-69; reference libr. Simsbury Pub. Libr., 1969—. Tchr. ballet, 1965—66; tchr. genealogy, 1977—; ballet mistress Ballet Soc. Conn., Inc., 1968—70; with corps de ballet Conn. Opera Assn., 1963—64; active in prodns. Simsbury Light Opera Assn., 1964—69. Contbr. articles to profl. jours. Vol. Family History Ctr., 1970—. Mem.: DAR (Abigail Phelps chpt.), AAUW (past pres. Greater Hartford br.), ALA, Simsbury Hist. Soc., Conn. Libr. Assn., Denison Soc., Inc., Daus. of Scotia, Simsbury Geneal. and Hist. Rsch. Libr., Chateauguay Valley Hist. Soc., New Brunswick Geneal. Soc., Conn. Hist. Soc., Dance Masters Am. (Conn. Dance Tchrs. Club chpt.), Soc. Mayflower Descs. Conn., Conn. Soc. Genealogists (registrar Hartford 1983), Pro Dance, New Eng. Historic and Geneal. Soc., Ont. Geneal. Soc. Unitarian Universalist. Office: Simsbury Public Libr 725 Hopmeadow St Simsbury CT 06070-2243 E-mail: croberts@simsbury.lib.ct.us.

ROBERTS, CORINNE BOGGS (COKIE ROBERTS), correspondent, news analyst; b. New Orleans, Dec. 27, 1943; d. Thomas Hale and Corinne Morrison (Claiborne) Boggs; m. Steven V. Roberts, Sept. 10, 1966; children: Lee Harriss, Rebecca Boggs. BA in Polit. Sci., Wellesley Coll., 1964; hon. degrees, Amherst Coll., Columbia Coll., Loyola U. of the South, Manhattanville Coll., Gonzaga U., Boston Coll., Hood Coll., Chestnut Hill Coll., Miss. Women's U., Notre Dame U. Md., Xavier U., St. Louis U., Duke U. Assoc. prodr., host Altman Prodns., Washington, 1964—66, prodr. L.A., 1969—72; reporter, editor Cowles Comm., N.Y.C., 1967; prodr. Sta. WNEW-TV, N.Y.C., 1968, Sta. KNBC-TV, L.A., 1972—74; reporter CBS News, Athens, Greece, 1974—77; corr. Nat. Pub. Radio, Washington, 1977—, MacNeil/Lehrer Newshour, Washington, 1984—88; spl. Washington corr. ABC News, Washington, 1988—92; interviewer, commentator This Week With David Brinkley, Washington, 1992—96; co-anchor This Week, 1996—2002; chief congrl. analyst ABC News, 1998—. Lectr. in field. Co-host weekly pub. TV program on Congress The Lawmakers, 1981—84, prodr., host pub. affairs program Sta. WRC-TV, Washington; prodr.: Sta. KNBC-TV Serendipity (award for excellence in local programming, Emmy nomination for children's programming); author: We Are Our Mother's Daughters, 1998, Founding Mothers: The Women Who Raised Our Nation, 2004; contbr. articles to newspapers, mags. Bd. dis. Dirksen Ctr., Pekin, Ill., 1988—95; bd. dirs. Fgn. Students Svc. Ctr., Washington, 1990—, Manhattanville Coll., Purchase, NY, 1991—99, Children's Inn at NIH, Bethesda, Md., 1992—. Recipient Broadcast award, Nat. Orgn. Working Women, 1984, Everett McKinley Dirksen disting. reporting of Congress, 1987, Weintal award, Georgetown U., 1988, Corp. Pub. Broadcasting award, 1988, Edward R. Murrow award, Corp. Pub. Broadcasting, 1990, Broadcast award, Nat. Women's Polit. Caucus, 1990, David Brinkley Comm. award, 1991, Mother of Yr. award, Nat. Mother's Day Com., 1992, Emmy award news and documentary, 1992. Mem.: Radio-TV Corrs. Assn. (pres. 1981—82, bd. dirs. 1980—94), U.S. Capitol Hist. Soc. Roman Catholic.*

ROBERTS, DEBRA S. secondary school educator; b. Biddeford, Maine, Nov. 7, 1975; d. Joan L. and William B. Roberts. B in Music Edn., U. Maine, 1998. Tchr. Lake Region H.S., Naples, Maine, 1998—2001, Biddeford (Maine) H.S., 2001—. Named Tchr. from Maine Who Makes a Difference, Sch. Band & Orch. Mag., 2002, 2003. Mem.: Maine Music Educators Assn., Maine Band Dirs. Assn. (sec. 2002—03).

ROBERTS, DENISE (DENISE ROBERTS HURLIN), dancer; Studied dance with Ilene Danek; BFA in dance, SUNY, Purchase. Dancer Paul Taylor Dance Co., N.Y.C., 1989—95. Dancer with Hannah Kahn, Kevin Wynn, Douglas Wright; founding mem., toured with David Parsons Co.; faculty mem. SUNY, The Juilliard Sch., 1989-90; co-founder (with Hernando Cortez), Dancers Responding to AIDS, 1991-; panelist, Arts Alive Grants Com. of Westchester, NY, Broadyway Cares/Equity Fights AIDS Nat. Grants prog. Named Outstanding performer by Joan Acocella, 1994. Office: Dancers Responding to AIDS 165 W 46th St 1300 New York NY 10036*

ROBERTS, DORIS, actress; b. St. Louis, Nov. 4, 1930; d. Larry and Ann (Meltzer) R.; m. Michael E. Cannata, June 21, 1950; 1 child, Michael R.; m. William Goyen, Nov. 10, 1963 (dec.) Student, NYU, 1950-51; studies with, Sanford Meisner, Neighborhood Playhouse, N.Y.C., 1952-53, Lee Strasberg, Actors' Studio, 1956. Ind. stage, screen and TV actress, 1953—. Profl. stage debut, Ann Arbor, Mich., 1953; appeared in summer stock Chatham, Mass., 1955; Broadway debut in The Time of Your Life, 1955; other Broadway and off-Broadway appearances include The Desk Set, 1955, The American Dream, 1961, The Death of Bessie Smith, 1961, The Office, 1965, The Color of Darkness, 1963, Marathon 33, 1963, Secret Affair of Mildred Wilde, 1972, Last of the Red Hot Lovers, 1969-71, Bad Habits, 1973 (Outer Circle Critics award 1974), Cheaters, 1976, Fairie Tale Theatre, 1985, The Fig Tree, 1987, It's Only a Play, 1992; movie debut Something Wild, 1961, film appearances include: Barefoot in the Park, 1968, No Way to Treat a Lady, 1973, A Lovely Way to Die, 1969, Honeymoon Killers, 1969, A New Leaf, 1970, Such Good Friends, 1971, Little Murders, 1971, Heartbreak Kid, 1972, Hester Street, 1975, The Taking of Pelham, One, Two, Three, 1974, The Rose, 1979, Good Luck, Miss Wyckoff, 1979, Rabbit Test, 1979, Ordinary Hero, 1986, #1 with a Bullet, 1987, For Better or for Worse-Street Law, 1988, National Lampoon's Xmas Vacation, 1989, Used People, 1992, The Night We Never Met, Momma Mia, 1994, Walking to Waldheim, 1995, The Grass Harp, 1995, A Fish in the Bathtub, 1997, My Giant, 1998, All Over the Guy, 2001, Dickie Roberts-Child Star, 2003; TV debut on Studio One, 1958, Mary Hartman, Mary Hartman, 1975, Mary Tyler Moore Hour, 1976, Soap, 1978-79, Angie, 1979-80, Remington Steele, 1984-88, Lily Tomlin Comedy Hour, Barney Miller, Alice, Full House, Perfect Strangers, Sunday Dinner, A Family Man, The Fig Tree (PBS), 1987, (TV films) The Story Teller, 1979, Ruby and Oswald, 1978, It Happened One Christmas, 1978, Jennifer: A Woman's Story, 1979, The Diary of Anne Frank, 1982, A Letter to Three Wives, Blind Faith, 1989, A Mom For Christmas, 1990, The Sunset Gang, 1990, Crossroads, 1993, Dream On, 1993, The Boys, 1993, A Time To Heal, 1994, A Thousand Men and a Baby, 1997, One True Love, 2000, Sons of Miseltoe, 2001, A Time to Remember (Hallmark channel) 2003, Raising Waylon, (CBS) 2003. TV series appearances include St. Elsewhere, 1982 (Emmy award best sup. actress drama) Murder She Wrote, 1990, Step By Step, 1994, Burk's Law, 1994, Walker Texas Ranger, 1995, High Society, 1996, Everybody Loves Raymond, 1996- (Amer. Comedy award, 1999, Emmy award best sup. actress comedy, 2001, 02, 03). Mem. SAG (Ensemble award 2002), AFTRA, Actors Equity Assn., Dirs. Guild Am.

ROBERTS, DORIS EMMA, epidemiologist, consultant, public health nurse; b. Toledo, Dec. 28, 1915; d. Frederic Constable and Emma Selina (Reader) Roberts. Diploma, Peter Bent Brigham Sch. Nursing, Boston, 1938; BS, Geneva Coll., Beaver Falls, Pa., 1944; MPH, U. Minn., 1958; PhD, U. N.C., 1967. RN Mass. Staff nurse Vis. Nurse Assn., New Haven, 1938—40; sr. nurse Neighborhood House, Millburn, NJ, 1942—45; supr. Tb Baltimore County Dept. Health, Towson, Md., 1945—46; Tb cons. Md. State Dept. Health, Balt., 1946—50; cons., chief nurse Tb program USPHS, Washington, 1950—57, cons. divsn. nursing, 1958—63; chief nursing practice br. Health Resources Adminstrn., HEW, Bethesda, Md., 1966—75; adj. prof. U. N.C. Sch. Pub. Health, 1975—92. Cons. WHO, 1961—82. Contbr. articles to profl. jours. Capt. commn. corps USPHS, 1945—75. Recipient Disting. Alumna award, Geneva Coll., 1971, Disting. Svc. award, USPHS, 1971, Outstanding Achievement award, U. Minn., 1983. Fellow: APHA (v.p. 1978—79, Disting. Svc. award Pub. Health Nursing sect. 1975, Sedgwick Meml. medal 1979), Am. Acad. Nursing (hon.); mem.: Am. Nursing Assn., Inst. Medicine of NAS, Sigma Theta Tau, Delta Omega. Democrat. Episcopalian. Avocations: needlepoint, gardening, reading, ch. vol. work.. Home: 9707 Old Georgetown Rd Apt 1112 Bethesda MD 20814-1746

ROBERTS, DOROTHY HYMAN, accessory company executive; b. N.Y.C., Dec. 6, 1928; d. Edgar C. and Theresa M. (Marks) Hyman; m. Paul M. Roberts, June 18, 1950 (dec.); children: Lynn, Steven; m. Paul M. Cohen. BA, Conn. Coll., 1950. With Echo Design Group Inc. (formerly Echo Scarfs Inc.), N.Y.C., 1950—, pres., 1978—, chmn., CEO. Mem. The Fashion Group. Office: The Echo Design Grp 10 E 40th St New York NY 10016-0200

ROBERTS, ELIZABETH ANNE STEPHENS, educational consultant; b. Bklyn., N.Y., Oct. 23, 1942; d. Edward Joseph and Mary Agnes (Donlon) Stephens; m. James Patrick Roberts, July 31, 1976; children: Sean Michael, Kerri Elizabeth Stephens. BA in Latin, Seat of Wisdom Coll., Litchfield, Conn., 1967; MA in English, CUNY, 1972; PhD in Adminstrn. and Supervision, L.I. U., 1976. Cert. tchr. Latin N.Y., tchr. English N.Y., sch. adminstrn. and supervision N.Y., sch. dist. adminstrn. N.Y. Tchr. Christ the King HS, Middle Village, NY, 1964—73, asst. prin., 1973—74; asst. prin., tchr. English Elwood (N.Y.) Sch. Dist., 1974—78; ednl. cons. Huntington, NY, 1978—87, 2002—; instr. English, adminstr. Touro Coll, Huntington, 1987—91; tchr. Latin South Huntington (N.Y.) Sch. Dist., 1990—2002, chairperson world langs. dept. grades 6-12, 1997—2002. Coord. student internat. travels South Huntington Schs., 1990—2002. Coord. parish-wide renew program Our Lady Queen Martyrs Ch., Centerport, 1987—90. Mem.: Fgn. Lang. Assn. Chairpersons and Suprs. (pres. 1997—2002), Classical Assn. N.Y. State, N.Y. State Assn. Fgn. Lang. Tchrs., Am. Classical League, Phi Delta Kappa (treas. 1990—). Avocations: travel, reading, crossword puzzles. Home: 24 Platt Pl Huntington NY 11743-3528 Personal E-mail: JSEKR@aol.com.

ROBERTS, ELIZABETH H. state legislator; b. Washington, Apr. 17, 1957; m. Thomas H. Roberts; children: Kathleen, Nora. BA, Brown U., 1978; MBA, Boston U., 1984. Mem. R.I. Senate, Dist. 11, Providence, 1996—. Mem. fin. com. R.I. State Senate, health, edn. and welfare com. Mem. bd. dirs. Childrens Mus. R.I., Southside Cmty. Land Trust. Democrat. Office: RI State Senate State House Providence RI 02903 E-mail: senroberts@rilin.state.ri.us.

ROBERTS, ESTHER LOIS, patent attorney, piano educator, composer, writer; b. Rockwood, Tenn. d. Reva Gretchen (Crowder) H. BA in Biology, BA in Botany, BM in Piano Lit./Pedagogy, MM in Piano Lit./Pedagogy, U. Tenn., Knoxville; JD, U. Tenn, Knoxville, 2001. Pvt. piano instr., Knoxville; law clk. Baker, McReynolds, Byrne, O'Kane & Shea; patent atty. Dept. of Energy, Oak Ridge, Tenn., 2001—. Composer (youth choir cantata) Children of Love, (soprano solo) Corn Husk Moon; author: (children's book series) Sam the Horse, Sam Gets Ready for School, others, 1996; contbr. to Tenn. Law Review. Mem. ABA (student mem.), Okla. Bar Assn., Tenn. Bar Assn., Am. Musicians Coll., Am. Indian Horse Registry, Great Smoky Mountain Indian Horse Club (pres.), Crossroads Dressage Soc., Nat. Soc. DAR, Scottish Clan Donnachaidh. Christian Scientist. Home and Office: Starlight Farm PO Box 32663 Knoxville TN 37930-2663 E-mail: starlight.farm@worldnet.alt.net.

ROBERTS, JANET MOATS, retired secondary school educator; b. Spargusville, Ohio, Sept. 14, 1935; d. John Allen and Irma Pollard Moats; m. David E. Roberts, June 22, 1958; children: Lisa Ellen Roberts-Hahn, Lynne Allene Roberts-Kempton. BS in Elem. Edn., Art Edn., Ohio U., 1967; MA in Art Edn., Ohio State U., 1970. Jr. high tchr. Waverly City Sch., Waverly, Ohio, 1961—66, tchr. h.s., 1966—2000, yearbook advisor, 1969—2000, newspaper advisor, 1974—2000. Contbg. author Lostnes Publ. Financial Advisor, 1974. Fellow: Ohio Art Edn. Assn. (sec., parliamentarian, Ohio Art Educator of the Yr. 1999, Ret. Art Educator of the Yr. 2002); mem.: Prime Tyme Garden Club.

ROBERTS, JANICE, marketing professional; Honors degree in Econs. Dir. mktg. and bus. devel. BICC Techs. Group BICC PLC, 1989, pres. BICC Comm., mng. dir. Data Networking, 1989; v.p., gen. mgr. 3Com Corp., Santa Clara, Calif., Eng., 1992, sr. v.p. bus. devel., pres. 3Com Vemtures. Mem. Chartered Inst. Mktg. Office: 3Com 5400 Bayfront Plz PO Box 58145 Santa Clara CA 95052-8145

ROBERTS, JEANNE ADDISON, retired literature educator; b. Washington; d. John West and Sue Fisher (Nichols) Addison; m. Markley Roberts, Feb. 19, 1966; children: Addison Cary Steed Masengill, Ellen Carraway Masengill Coster. AB, Agnes Scott Coll., 1946; MA, U. Pa., 1947; PhD, U. Va., 1964. Instr. Mary Washington Coll., 1947-48; instr., chmn. English Fairfax Hall Jr. Coll., 1950-51; tchr. Am. U. Assn. Lang. Center, Bangkok, Thailand, 1952-56; instr. Beirut (Lebanon) Coll. for Women, 1956-57, asst. prof., 1957-60, chmn. English dept., 1957-60; instr. lit. Am. U., Washington, 1960-62, asst. prof., 1962-65, asso. prof., 1965-68, prof., 1968-93. Dean faculties Am. U., 1974; lectr. Howard U., 1971-72; seminar prof. Folger Shakespeare Libr. Inst. for Renaissance and 18th Century Studies, 1974; dir. NEH Summer Inst. for HS Tchrs. on Teaching Shakespeare, Folger Shakespeare Libr., 1984-86; dir. NEH summer inst. Va. Commonwealth U. 1995-96 Writings By and About Women in The English Renaissance; group leader inst. Learning in Retirement, Am. U., 1999-2003. Author: Shakespeare's English Comedy: The Merry Wives of Windsor in Context, 1979, The Shakespearean Wild: Geography, Genus and Gender, 1991; editor: (with James G. McManaway) A Selective Bibliography of Shakespeare: Editions, Textual Studies, Commentary, 1975; (with Peggy O'Brien) Shakespeare Set Free, vol. 1, 1993, vol. 2, 1994, vol. 3, 1995, (with Georgianna Ziegler) Shakespeare's Unruly Women, 1997; contbr. articles to profl. jours. Danforth Tchr. grantee, 1962-63; Folger Sr. fellow, 1969-70, 88. Mem. MLA (chmn. Shakespeare div. 1981-82), Renaissance Soc. Am., Milton Soc., Shakespeare Assn. Am. (trustee 1978-81, 87-89, pres. 1986-87), AAUP (pres. Am. U. chpt. 1966-67), Southeastern Renaissance Conf. (pres. 1981-82), Phi Beta Kappa, Mortar Board, Phi Kappa Phi. Episcopalian. Home: 4931 Albemarle St NW Washington DC 20016-4359

ROBERTS, JO ANN WOODEN, school system administrator; b. Chgo., June 24, 1948; d. Tilmon and Annie Mae (Wardlaw) Wooden; m. Edward Allen Roberts Sr. (div.); children: Edward Allen Jr., Hillary Ann. BS, Wayne State U., 1970, MS, 1971; PhD, Northwestern U., 1977. Speech, lang. pathologist Chgo. Bd. Edn., 1971—78, adminstr., 1987—88; project dir. Ednl. Testing Svc., Evanston, Ill., 1976—77; instr. Chgo City C.C., 1976—77; exec. dir. Nat. Speech Lang. and Hearing Assn., Chgo., 1984—86; dir. spl. svcs. Rock Island (Ill.) Pub. Schs., 1988—90; supt. Muskegon Hts. (Mich.) Pub. Schs., 1990—93; dep. supr. Chgo. Pub. Schs., 1993—96; supt. of schs. Hazel Crest (Ill.) Sch. Dist. #152 1/2, 1996—98; cons. Chgo. Pub. Schs., 1998—2000, dep. accountability svcs., 1999—, InterVention officer, 2000—01, chief troubleshooter, 2001—. Hon. guest lectr. Gov.'s State U., U. Pk., Ill., 1983—86; cons. in field. Author: Learning to Talk, 1974. Trustee Muskegon County Libr. Bd., 1990, Mercy Hosp. Bd., Muskegon, 1990, St. Mark's Sch. Bd. Dirs., Southborough, Mass., 1989, United Way Bd., Muskegon, 1990; mem. Mich. State Bd. Edn. Systematic Initiative in Math and Sci., 1991, Gov. John Engler Mich. 2000 Task Force, 1991, Chpt. II Adv. Commn., 1991. Recipient Leadership award Boy Scouts Am., 1990; named finalist Outstanding Young Working Women, Glamour Mag., 1984, Outstanding Educator, Blacks in Govt., 1990. Mem. Am. Assn. Sch. Adminstrs., Nat. Alliance Black Sch. Educators, Mich. Assn. Sch. Adminstrs., Assn. Supervision & Curriculum Devel., Phi Delta Kappa. Avocations: creative writing, poetry, modern dance, theater, drawing. Address: Chgo Pub Schs 125 S Clark St Chicago IL 60603-5200

ROBERTS, JUDITH MARIE, librarian, educator; b. Bluefield, W.Va., Aug. 5, 1939; d. Charles Bowen Lowder and Frances Marie (Bourne) Lowder Alberts; m. Craig Currence Johnson, July 1, 1957 (div. 1962); 1 child, Craig Jr.; m. Milton Rinehart Roberts, Aug. 13, 1966 (div. 1987). BS, Concord State Tchrs. Coll., 1965. Libr. Cape Henlopen Sch. Dist., Lewes, Del., 1965—91; with Lily's Gift Shop, St. Petersburg, Fla., 1991—. Pres. Friends of Lewes Pub. Libr., 1986—90; chmn. exhibits Govs. Conf. Librs.

and Info. Svcs., Dover, Del., 1978; mem. Gov.'s State Libr. Adv. Coun., 1987—91. Mem.: NEA, ALA, Del. Learning Resources Assn. (pres. 1976—77), Del. Library Assn. (pres. 1982—83), Sussex Help Orgn. for Resources Exch. (pres. 1984—85), Del. State Edn. Assn. Methodist. Office Phone: 727-867-7974. Business E-Mail: judyoffice2003@yahoo.com. E-mail: roberts-jud@aol.com.

ROBERTS, JULIA FIONA, actress; b. Smyrna, Ga., Oct. 28, 1967; d. Betty and Walter Roberts; m. Lyle Lovett, Jun. 27, 1993 (div. 1995); m. Daniel Moder, July 4, 2002. Film appearances include Blood Red, 1986, Satisfaction, 1987, Mystic Pizza, 1988, Steel Magnolias, 1989 (Acad. Award nominee, Golden Globe award), Pretty Woman, 1990 (Acad. Award nominee, Golden Globe Award), Flatliners, 1990, Sleeping With the Enemy, 1991, Hook, 1991, Dying Young, 1991, The Player, 1992, The Pelican Brief, 1993, I Love Trouble, 1994, Ready to Wear (Prêt-à-Porter), 1994, Something To Talk About, 1995, Mary Reilly, 1996, Everybody Says I Love You, 1996, Michael Collins, 1996, My Best Friend's Wedding, 1997, Conspiracy Theory, 1997, Stepmom, 1998, Notting Hill, 1999, Runaway Bride, 1999, Erin Brokovich, 2000 (Acad. award for Best Actress), The Mexican, 2001, America's Sweethearts, 2001, Ocean's Eleven, 2001, Full Frontal, 2002, Confessions of a Dangerous Mind, 2002, Mona Lisa Smile, 2003; TV appearances include: AFI's 100 Years...100 Movies, 1998, In the Wild, 1998; TV movies include Baja Oklahoma, 1988 Named Female Star of the Yr., Nat. Assn. Theatre Owners, 1991; recipient People's Choice awards Favorite Motion Picture Actress, 1991, 98, Favorite Comedy/Dramatic Motion Picture Actress, 1992, Favorite Dramatic Motion Picture Actres, 1994; recipient Woman of Yr. award Hasty Pudding Theatricals, 1997, Spl. award Internat. Star of Yr., ShoWest Conv., 1998. Office: c/o Kevin Huvane Creative Artists Agency 9830 Wilshire Blvd Beverly Hills CA 90212-1825*

ROBERTS, KATHARINE ADAIR, retired bookkeeper; b. Columbus, Ga., June 4, 1930; d. William Lynn and Ella Miller (Adair) R. BA, U. Redlands, 1955; postgrad., San Bernardino Valley Coll., 1971-74, Calif. State U., San Bernardino, 1975-78. Bookkeeper Rettig Machine Shop, Inc., Redlands, Calif., 1970-97, ret., 1997. Pres. Dem. Study Club, San Bernardino, 1967-68, Redlands Dem. Club, 1976, Wilsonian Club, San Bernardino, 1986, World Federalist Assn., Redlands/San Bernardino chpt., 1987—; mem. San Bernardino County Dem. Ctrl. Com., treas. 1977-80; San Bernardino leader World Federalist Assn. Program-Ptnrs. for Global Change. Recipient Citizen Achievement award, LWV, 1989. Mem. Dem. Luncheon Club (George E. Brown Amb. of Peace award 2000), Humane Soc. of San Bernardino Valley, Redlands Humane Soc., Redlands Dem. Club (treas.), LWV, Inland Empire Debating Soc. (treas.). Democrat. Home: 798 W 18th St San Bernardino CA 92405-4235

ROBERTS, KATHLEEN JOY DOTY, secondary school educator; b. Jamaica, N.Y., Apr. 19, 1951; d. Alfred Arthur and Helen Caroline (Sohl) Doty; m. Robert Louis Roberts, Nov. 24, 1974; children: Robert Louis, Michael Sean, Kathleen Meagan. BA in Edn., CUNY, 1972, MS in Spl. Edn., 1974; cert. advanced study in ednl. adminstrn., Hofstra U., 1982; Ednl. Specialist, Nova Southeastern U., 2003, PhD Computing Tech. in Edn., PhD, Nova Southeastern U., 2004. Cert. sch. adminstrn., tchr. math., N.Y.; cert. N.Y. Dept. Mental Hygiene; lic. spl. edn. supr., ednl. dminstr., N.Y. Tchr. health conservation Woodside (N.Y.) Jr. H.S., 1973-77; coord. spl. edn. dept. Ridgewood (N.Y.) Jr. H.S., 1977-81; adminstrv. asst., health, compliance and mainstream coord. Grover Cleveland H.S., Ridgewood, 1981—, also coord. transition linkage, resource tchr. mentor, 1981—. Grant writer. Author: Closed Circuit Television and Other Devices for the Partially Sighted, 1971, National Society Colonial Daughters of the Seventeenth Century Lineage Book (Centennial Remembrance edit.), 1999; contbr. to jour. including AACE Jour. Legis. chmn. Fairfield Jr. and Sr. H.S. PTA and Massapequa coun., 1987-92. Mem.: ACM, DAR, NEA, Internat. Soc. Tech. in Edn., N.Y. State Tchrs. Assn., Colonial Dames of the XVII Century, Colonial Daus. of the XVII Century (pres. 1985—91, nat. chmn. hist. activities com. 1988—91, registrar, historian Founders chpt. 1991—94, nat. councillor, publicity chmn. 1991—94, centennial com. 1994—96, registrar gen. nat. soc. 1997—2000, pres. 2000—), Pilgrim Edward Doty Soc. Republican. Home: 52 Hicksville Rd Massapequa NY 11758-5843 Office: Grover Cleveland HS 2127 Himrod St Flushing NY 11385-1299

ROBERTS, KATHLEEN MARY, school system administrator, retired; b. Syracuse, N.Y., Apr. 15, 1947; d. Casimer and Lorrayne Arletta (Molloy) Piegdon; m. James C. Roberts, June 29, 1968 (div. Sept. 1988). BA, Cen. State U., Edmond, Okla., 1968, MEd, 1971; PhD, U. Okla., 1977. Cert. tchr., prin., supt., Okla.; cert. supt., N.Y. Tchr. Putnam City Schs., Oklahoma City, 1960-72; reading specialist Moore (Okla.) Pub. Schs., 1973-74, Crooked Oak Pub. Schs., Oklahoma City, 1974-77, 1990-95; rsch. assoc. Oklahoma City Pub. Schs., 1977-80; supt. Okla. Dept. Corrections, Oklahoma City, 1980-86, Healdton (Okla.) Pub. Schs., 1986-90; supr. Crooked Oak Schs., Oklahoma City, 1990—95; supt. Piedmont (Okla.) Pub. Schs., 1995-98, ret., 1998; registered investment advisor McDonald & Assocs., 1998—. Contbr. articles to profl. publs. Bd. dirs. United Meth. Prism Ministry, Oklahoma City, 1986—, Children's Shelter, Ardmore, Okla., 1989-90; mem. State Vocat. Edn. Coun., Oklahoma City, 1980-85. Recipient citation Okla. State Senate, 1986. Mem. ASCD, Internat. Reading Assn., Am. Assn. Sch. Adminstrs., Okla. Assn. Sch. Adminstrs., Piedmont C. of C. (v.p. 1997—), Phi Delta Kappa, Alpha Chi, Kappa Delta Phi. Democrat. Roman Catholic. Avocations: furniture refinishing, reading, gardening.

ROBERTS, KATHY DESMOND, executive director educational facility; b. Washington, Mar. 24, 1953; d. James Michael and Jean Langrish Desmond; m. John D. Roberts, Aug. 5, 1989; children: John, Kyle, Jenny; stepchildren: Jason, Jesse, Tatum. BA, Coll. New Rochelle, 1981; student, Tchrs. Coll. Columbia. Rsch. asst., 1982-83; founder, pres. Am. Inst. Neuro-Integrative Devel., Fairfield, Conn., 1982—; founder, exec. dir. Giant Steps Sch., Fairfield, Conn., 1992—. Bd. dirs. Autism Soc. Conn.; tissue resource com. Autism Rsch. Found., Boston, 1996—; adv. bd. Autism Soc. Am. Found., 1997—; founder Fairfield County Autism Soc., Conn., 1989. E-mail: SASCO54@aol.com.

ROBERTS, LIA, investor, political organization worker; b. Bucharest, Romania, 1949; arrived in U.S., 1979, naturalized, 1982; married; 1 child. Degree in Geology and Geotechnical Engring., U. Bucharest. Prin., owner, Las Vegas, 1979—93; pvt. investor, 1993—; chmn. Nev. Rep. Party, Las Vegas, 2003—. Mailing: Nevada Republicatn Party Chmn 8625 W Sahara Ave Las Vegas NV 89117

ROBERTS, LINDA, truck transportation services company executive; With Profit Freight Sys.; co-founder Profl. Sales Group Ltd., sales and mtkg. co., 1990, Profl. Transp. Group, Ltd., 1990; with Truck, Net, Inc., 1991, Timely Transp., Inc., 1992, Rapid Transit, Inc., 1995; pres. Profl. Transp. Group, Ltd., Inc., Newport Beach, Calif., 1997—.

ROBERTS, LOUISE NISBET, philosopher, educator; b. Lexington, Ky., Apr. 21, 1919; d. Benjamin and Helen L. Nisbet; m. Warren Roberts, June 14, 1952 (dec.); children: Helen Ward Roberts Hill, Valeria Lamar Roberts Emmett. AB, U. Ky., 1942, MA, 1944; PhD, Columbia U., 1952. Instr. philosophy Fairfax Hall, Waynesboro, Va., 1943—44, Fairmount Casements, Ormond Beach, Fla., 1944—45; mem. faculty Newcomb Coll., Tulane U., 1948—, prof. philosophy, 1969—85, dept. head, prof. emeritus, 1985—. Contbr. articles to profl. jours. Univ. scholar, 1945-46. Mem. AAUW (fellow 1947-48, pres. New Orleans chpt. 1986-88), DAR (vice regent New Orleans chpt. 1987-90, 2002-03), So. Soc. Philosophy and Psychology, Phi Beta Kappa (chpt. pres. 1956-57), Delta Delta Delta (fellow 1946-47). Democrat. Episcopalian. Office: Tulane U Dept Philosophy New Orleans LA 70118

ROBERTS, LYNNE JEANINE, physician; b. St. Louis, Apr. 19, 1952; d. H. Clarke and Dorothy June (Cockrum) R.; m. Richard Allen Beadle Jr., July 18, 1981; children: Richard Andrew, Erica Roberts. BA with distinction, Ind. U., 1974, MD, 1978. Diplomate Am. Bd. Dermatology, Am. Bd. Pediatrics, Am. Bd. Laser Surgery. Intern in pediats. Children's Med. Ctr., Dallas, 1978-79, resident in pediats., 1979-80; resident in dermatology U. Tex. Southwestern Med. Ctr., Dallas, 1980-83, chief resident in dermatology, 1982-83, asst. instr. dermatology and pediatrics, 1983-84, asst. prof., 1984-90, assoc. prof., 1990-99; prof., 1999—; physician Cons. Dermatol. Specialists, Dallas, 1990-93; pres. Lynne J. Roberts, MD, PA, Dallas, 1993—. Dir. dermatology Children's Med. Ctr., Dallas, 1986-2000; dermatology sect. chief Med. City Dallas Hosp., 1994-95, 95-97. Contbr. articles to profl. jours., chpts. to books. Recipient Scholastic Achievement Citation Am. Med. Women's Assn., 1978. Fellow Am. Acad. Dermatology, Am. Soc. Laser Medicine and Surgery (bd. dirs. 1994-97); mem. Soc. Pediatric Dermatology, Am. Soc. Dermatologic Surgery, Tex. Med. Assn., Dallas Zool. Soc., Dallas Arboretum, Kappa Alpha Theta, Alpha Omega Alpha. Avocations: horseback riding, reading, fishing, swimming, camping. Office: Ste 330 7502 Greenville Ave Dallas TX 75231 Office Phone: 469-232-9300.

ROBERTS, MADELYN ALPERT, publishing executive; V.p., assoc. pub. McCall's Magazine, 1993—99; pub. McCall's Gruner & Jahr USA Pub., N.Y.C., 1999—2001; pub. Mode Magazine, 2001; v.p., pub. 360 Youth, N.Y.C., NY, 2003—. Office: Alloy Inc 151 W 26th St New York NY 10001

ROBERTS, MARGARET HAROLD, editor, publisher; b. Aug. 18, 1928; AB, U. Chattanooga, 1950. Editor, pub. series Award Winning Art, 1960-70, New Woman mag., Palm Beach, Fla., 1971-84; editor, pub. BONKERS mag., 1992—2001. Author: juvenile book series Daddy is a Doctor, 1965.

ROBERTS, MARGOT MARKELS, business executive; b. Springfield, Mass., Jan. 20, 1945; d. Reuben and Marion (Markels) R.; children: Lauren B. Phillips, Debrah C. Herman. BA, Boston U. Interior designer Louis Legum Furniture Co., Norfolk, Va., 1965-70; buyer, mgr. Danker Furniture, Rockville, Md., 1970-72; buyer W & J Sloane, Washington, 1972-74, pres. Bus. & Fin. Cons., Palm Beach, Fla., 1976-80, Margot M. Roberts & Assocs., Inc., Palm Beach, 1976—. Dealer 20th century Am. art and wholesale antiques Margot M. Roberts, Inc., Palm Beach, 1989—; v.p., dir. So. Textile Svcs. Inc., Palm Beach. Pres. Brittany Condominium Assn., Palm. Beach, 1983-87; v.p. South Palm Beach Civic Assn., 1983-88; South Palm Beach Pres.'s Assn., 1984-88; vice chmn. South Palm Beach Planning Bd., 1983-88, 90 91; chair Palm Beach County Beach and Shores Coun., 1998—; elected town commr. Town South Palm Beach, Fla., 1991-92, elected vice mayor, 1992-93, elected mayor, 1993—, elected chair Palm Beach Countywide Beaches and Shores Bd., 1998—; apptd. Commn. on Status of Women of Palm Beach County, 1992-95; voting mem. Palm Beach Country Mcp. League, 1991—; apptd. Palm Beach County Intergovtl. Planning and Rev. exec. com., 1999; vice chair Commn. Status of Women of Palm Beach Country, 1994-95; bd. dirs. Palm Beach County Juvenile Justice Bd., 1998-99. Mem. Nat. Assn. Women in Bus., Palm Beach C. of C. Republican. Office: Town Hall South Palm Beach 3577 S Ocean Blvd Palm Beach FL 33480-6450

ROBERTS, MARIE DYER, retired computer systems specialist; b. Statesboro, Ga., Feb. 19, 1943; d. Byron and Martha (Evans) Dyer; m. Hugh V. Roberts, Jr., Oct. 6, 1973 (dec. 2001). BS, U. Ga., 1966; student, Am. U., 1972. Cert. sys. profl.; cert. in data processing. Mathematician, computer specialist U.S. Naval Oceanographic Office, Washington, 1966-73; sys. analyst, programmer Sperry Microwave Electronics, Clearwater, Fla., 1973-75; data processing mgr., asst. bus. mgr. Trenam, Simmons, Kemker et al, Tampa, Fla., 1975-77; mathematician, computer specialist U.S. Army C.E., Savannah, Ga., 1977-81, 83-85, Frankfurt, West Germany, 1981-83; ops. rsch. analyst U.S. Army Constrn. Rsch. Lab., Champaign, Ill., 1985-87; data base adminstr., computer sys. programmer South Pacific divsn. U.S. Army C.E., San Francisco, 1987-93; computer specialist, IDEF repository coord. Functional Process Improvement Expertise/Def. Info. Sys. Agy, Arlington, Va., 1993-95; computer specialist Ctrl. Integration Def. Info. Sys. Agy., MacDill AFB, Fla., 1995—, ret., 2001. Instr. computer scis. City Coll. of Chgo. in Frankfurt, 1982-83. Author: Harris Computer Users Manual, 1983. Recipient Sustained Superior Performance award Dept. Army, 1983, 2 Nat. Peformance Rev. Hammer awards V.P. Al Gore, 1996, DISA Dirs.'s award for Project of Yr., 1999. Mem. Assn. Info. Tech. Profls., U. Ga. Alumni Assn., Sigma Kappa. E-mail: hurob@juno.com.

ROBERTS, NANCY, computer educator; b. Boston, Jan. 25, 1938; d. Harold and Annette (Zion) Rosenthal; m. Edward B. Roberts, June 14, 1959; children: Valerie Friedman, Mitchell, Andrea. AB, Boston U., 1959, MEd, 1961, EdD, 1975. Elem. tchr. Sharon (Mass.) Pub. Schs., 1959-63; asst. prof. Lesley U., Cambridge, Mass., 1975-79, assoc. prof., 1980-83, prof., 1983—99, dir. grad. programs in tech. in edn., 1980—99, dir. Project Bridge, 1987-92, dir. divsn. tchg., learning and leadership, 2001—; dir. Ctr. for Math., Sci. and Tech. in Edn., Cambridge, Mass., 1990-91. Rsch. assoc. MIT, Cambridge, 1976-79;mem. nat. steering com. Nat. Edn. Computing Conf., Eugene, Oreg., 1979-96, co-chmn. nat. conf., 1989, vice chmn. steering com., 1991-95. Author: Dynamics of Human Service Delivery, 1976, Practical Guide to Computers in Education, 1982, Computers in Teaching Mathematics, 1983, Introduction to Computer Simulation, 1983 (J.W. Forrester award 1983), Integrating Computers into the Elementary and Middle School, 1987, Computers and the Social Studies, 1988, Integrating Telecommunications into Education, 1990, Computer Modeling and Simulation in Science and Mathematics Education, 1999; mem. edit. bd. Jour. Ednl. Computing, 1983—, Jour. Rsch. in Sci. Teaching; editor Computers in Edn. book series, 1984-89. Mem. Computer Policy Com., Boston, 1982-84, mem. adv. bd. Electronic Learning, 1989-91; bd. dirs. Computers for Kids, Cambridge, 1983-85; mem. State Ednl. Tech. Adv. Coun., 1990-93, bd. mem. Boston Ctr. Adult Education, 2000-, Citizens for Charter Schs., 1997-. Grantee NSF, 1985-96, DOE, 1994—. Mem. System Dynamics Soc. (bd. dirs. policy com. 1987-89). Republican. Jewish. Home: 300 Boylston St Apt 1102 Boston MA 02116-3940 Office: Lesley Coll 29 Everett St Cambridge MA 02138-2702 Office Phone: 617-349-8419.

ROBERTS, NANCY COHEN, art dealer, marketing professional; b. Washington, Oct. 12; d. Norman G. and Roberta B. Cohen; m. Marc R. Roberts, Aug. 22, 1985; 2 children. BA, U. Pa., Phila., 1976; MBA, NYU, 1982. Actress, 1976—80; exec. tng. program Bloomingdales, 1980—82; advt. salesperson Hearst Corp., N.Y.C., 1982—84; dir. pub. rels./mktg. Karastan, N.Y.C., 1984—86; CEO Nancy C. Roberts Inc., Loveed Corp., N.Y.C., 1987—. Bd. dirs. Manhattan Theatre Club, N.Y.C., Children's Mus. Manhattan, N.Y.C., Auction Live, Washington. Active ann. fundraiser Chapin Sch., N.Y.C.; active capital campaign Riverdale Country Sch., N.Y.C., 1995—2001; grade rep. Edward R. and Rosalind Roberts Found., N.Y.C. Mem.: Breakers Country Club, Club Colette, Army Navy Club, Vassar Club. Office: Nancy C Roberts Inc Loveed Corp 575 Madison Ave New York NY 10022

ROBERTS, NORA, writer; b. Silver Spring, Md., 1950; m. Bruce Wilder, 1985. Author: Promise Me Tomorrow, 1984, Hot Ice, 1987, Sacred Sins, 1987, Brazen Virtue, 1988, Sweet Revenge, 1989, Public Secrets, 1990, Genuine Lies, 1991, Carnal Innocence, 1992, Divine Evil, 1992, Honest Illusions, 1992, reprint, 1993, Private Scandals, 1993, Hidden Riches, 1994, Born in Fire, 1994, Born in Ice, 1995, True Betrayals, 1995, reprint, 1996, Born in Shame, 1996, Daring to Dream, 1996, Montana Sky, 1996, reprint, 1997, Holding the Dream, 1997, Finding the Dream, 1997, Sanctuary, 1997, Rising Tides, 1998, Once Upon a Castle, 1998, Homeport, 1998, Sea Swept, 1998, The Reef, 1998, Inner Harbor, 1999, Jewels of the Sun, 1999, River's End, 1999, Heart of the Sea, 2000, Tears of the Moon, 2000, Carolina Moon, 2001, Heaven and Earth, 2001, The Villa, 2002, Three Fates, 2002, Chesapeake Blue, 2002, Key of Knowledge, 2003, Key of Light, 2003, Once Upon a Midnight, 2003, Birthright, 2003, Blue Dahlia, 2004, Once Upon a Moon, 2004, Northern Lights, 2004, A Little Fate, 2004, Key of Valor, 2004; (under pseudonym J.D. Robb) Naked in Death, 1995, Glory in Death, 1995, Immortal in Death, 1996, Rapture in Death, 1996, Ceremony in Death, 1997, Vengeance in Death, 1997, Holiday in Death, 1998, Loyalty in Death, 1999, Conspiracy in Death, 1999, Judgment in Death, 2000, Witness in Death, 2000, Betrayal in Death, 2001, Seduction in Death, 2001, Interlude in Death, 2001, Purity in Death, 2002, Reunion in Death, 2002, Imitation in Death, 2003, Portrait in Death, 2003, Visions in Death, 2004; author numerous category romances for Silhouette. Recipient Lifetime Achievement award Waldenbooks. Mem. Romance Writers Am. (charter, mem. Washington chpt., inductee Hall of Fame, Centennial award, Lifetime Achievement award 1997), Mystery Writers Am., Sisters in Crime, The Crime League of Am., Novelists, Inc. Office: GP Putnams Sons 375 Hudson St New York NY 10014-3658*

ROBERTS, PAMELA J. lawyer; BA in Econs., U. Calif., Berkeley, 1977; JD, Southwestern U., 1980. Cert.: Supreme Ct. S.C. (mediator) 1997, bar: S.C., Ga., Calif., U.S. Dist. Ct. S.C., U.S. Dist. Ct. (no. and mid. dists.) Ga., U.S. Dist. Ct. (no. dist.) Calif., U.S. Ct. Appeals (4th, 9th and 11th cirs.), U.S. Supreme Ct. Ptnr. Nelson, Mullins, Riley & Scarborough LLP, Colubmia, SC. Instr. Harvard Law Sch., 1999; mediation instr. U.S. Dept. Justice Advocacy Ctr.; presenter in field. Chairwoman bd. trustees EdVenture Children's Mus.; mem. adv. bd. Trinity Housing Corp.; bd. dirs. YWCA of the Midlands. Fellow: S.C. Bar Found., Am. Bar Found.; mem.: ABA (bd. govs. 2002—, former mem. Commn. on Women in the Profession, former mem. Commn. on Opportunities for Minorities in the Profession, chairwoman young lawyers divsn., mem. nominating com., mem. spl. com. on governance), U.S. Fourth Cir. Jud. Conf., Richland County Bar Assn., S.C. Women Lawyers Assn. (bd. dirs., pres. 1999—2001), S.C. Bar (bd. govs., ho. dels.), Nat. Bar Assn., Am. Judicature Soc., Phi Alpha Delta. Office: 3rd Fl 1330 Lady St PO Box 11070 Columbia SC 29211

ROBERTS, PAMELA RANGER, secondary school educator; b. Royal Oak, Mich., May 19, 1960; d. Richard Lee and Carol Bruce (Roland) Ranger; m. John Jack Roberts, Sept. 23, 1989. BA Anthropology, U. Colo., 1983. Retail sales book buyer Neptune Mountaineering, Boulder, Colo., 1985—92; tchr., coach, advisor Phillips Acad., Andover, Mass., 1989; tchr. Spanish Broomfield (Colo.) H.S., 1992—97; retail sales, floor mgr. Neptune Mountaineering, 1997—99; tchr. Spanish Broomfield H.S., 1999—. Dept. chair world lang. Broomfield High Sch., 2001—, mem. emergency first response team, 1999—. Mem.: Am. Assn. Tchrs. Spanish and Portguese, Sigma Delta Pi. Avocations: rock climbing, skiing, surfing, swimming, travel. Home. 130 S 33d St Boulder CO 80305

ROBERTS, PRISCILLA WARREN, artist; b. Montclair, N.J., June 13, 1916; d. Charles Asaph and Florence (Berry) R. Student, Art Students League, 1937-39, Nat. Acad., 1939-43. Represented in permanent collections Met. Mus., Cin. Art Mus., Canton (Ohio) Art Inst., Westmorcland County Mus. Art, Pa., IBM, Dallas Mus., Walker Art Ctr., Mpls., Butler Inst., Youngstown, Ohio, Nat. Mus. Am. Art, Washington, Nat. Mus. Women in the Arts, Washington. Recipient Proctor prize, 1947, popular prize Corcoran Biennial, 1947, prize Westmoreland County Mus., 3d prize Carnegie Internat., Pitts., 1950, Nat. Mus. Women in Arts, Washington, Snite Mus., U. Notre Dame, Ind. Mem. Nat. Acad. Design (Hallgarten prize 1945), Allied Artists Am. (Zabriskie prize 1944, 46), Catherine Lorillard Wolfe Assn. (hon.). Address: PO Box 716 Georgetown CT 06829-0716

ROBERTS, REBA GILL, literature educator; b. McCall Creek, Miss., Jan. 1, 1942; d. Ed and Bessie Johnston Gill; m. Raymond Roberts, Apr. 24, 1999. AA, Copiah-Lincoln C.C., Wesson, Miss., 1960—62; BS, U. So. Miss., Hattiesburg, 1964; MA, U. Southwestern La., Lafayette, 1973. English instr. and dept. chmn. Gloster (Miss.) HS, 1964—66; English instr. Moss Point (Miss.) HS, 1966—67, Pascagoula (Miss.) HS, 1967—68, Brookhaven (Miss.) HS, 1968—73; English instr., dept. chairperson, dist. coord. English Holmes C.C., Goodman and Ridgeland, Miss., 1973—95; adj. English instr. Copiah-Lincoln, Wesson, Miss., 1995—98. Competition coord. Miss. C.C. Creative Writing Assn., Miss., 1983—84, pres., Miss., 1983—84, Miss., 1990—91, state lit. jour. editor, Miss., 1995; sec. So. Lit. Festival, Natchez, Miss., 1996. Author: Leaves Bound in Blue; contbr. poems to lit. jours. Pres. Brookhaven Evening Lions Club, Brookhaven, Miss., 2003—; v.p. United Meth. Women, Brookhaven, Miss., 2002—. Recipient Life Pin, United Meth. Women, 2002, Lion of the Yr. award, Brookhaven Evening Lions Club, 2002. Methodist. Avocations: writing poetry and essays, travel, reading.

ROBERTS, ROBIN, sportscaster; b. Nov. 23, 1960; BA in Comms. cum laude, Southeastern La. U., 1983. Sports dir. WHMD/WFPR Radio, Hammond, La., 1980-83; spl. assignment sports reporter KSLU-FM, 1982; sports anchor, reporter WDAM-TV, Hattiesburg, Miss., 1983-84, WLOX-TV, Biloxi, Miss., 1984-86, WSMV-TV, Nashville, 1986-88, WAGA-TV, Atlanta, 1988-89; with WVEE-FM, Atlanta; host. Sunday SportsDay, contbr. NFL Prime Time, reporter, interviewer ESPN, Bristol, Conn., 1990-95, host, anchor SportsCenter, host In the SportsLight, 1995—; host Wide World of Sports ABC, 1995—. Apptd. adv. bd. Women's Sports Found., 1991; spkr. charity, civic functions. Recipient DAR T.V. Award of Merit, 1990, Women at Work Broadcast Journalism award, 1992, Excellence in Sports Journalism award Broadcast Media Northeastern U. Ctr. Study of Sport in Society and Sch. Journalism, 1993; inducted to Hall of Fame Women's Inst. Sport and Edn. Found., 1994. Office: ESPN Inc Comms Dept ESPN Plz 935 Middle St Bristol CT 06010-1099

ROBERTS, RUTH W. retired elementary school educator; b. Reading, Pa., Jan. 24, 1936; d. Jason W. and Margaret J. (Smith) White; m. James B. Steffy, Dec. 23, 1956 (div. Aug. 1974) ; m. George R. Roberts, Sept. 8, 1995; children: James M., John W., Susan E. BS in Elem. Edn., West Chester (Pa.) U., 1956; MA, Commonwealth of Pa., 1985. Tchr. Selinsgrove (Pa.) Area Schs., 1965-66, Lewisburg (Pa.) Area Sch. Dist., 1966—99. Curriculum cluster leader Lewisburg Area Sch. Dist., 1984—. Mem. NEA, Pa. Edn. Assn., MENSA, PASR (Union County chpt. v.p.). Avocations: cross stitch, reading, traveling. Home: 156 Redtail Ln Lewisburg PA 17837-9615

ROBERTS, SANDRA, editor; b. Humboldt, Tenn., July 22, 1951; d. Harold and Margaret (Headrick) R.; m. Parker W. Duncan Jr., Aug. 11, 1990. Student, Tex. Christian U., 1969-70; BS, U. Tenn., 1972; MLS, Peabody Coll. Libr. The Tennessean, Nashville, 1975-82, editorial writer, 1982-87, editorial editor, 1987—. Pres. Women's Polit. Caucus, Nashville, 1982. Recipient John Hancock award John Hancock Co., 1983, Freedom award Tenn. Trial Laywers Assn., 1988. Mem. Am. Soc. Newspaper Editors, Nat. Conf. Editorial Writers, Sigma Delta Chi (Nat. Headliner award 1982). Mem. Christian Ch. Office: The Tennessean 1100 Broadway Nashville TN 37203-3134

ROBERTS, SUSAN DIANNE GREEN, library media specialist; b. Natchez, Miss., Jan. 23, 1951; d. Vernie Newton and Susie Carolyn (Black) Green; m. Joel David Roberts, Dec. 15, 1990. BS, Miss. State Coll. Women, 1973; MA in Secondary Edn./History, U. Ala., Birmingham, 1976, MA in Sch. Libr. Media, 1982. Cert. secondary history tchr., sch. libr. media specialist. Tchr., libr. Bessemer (Ala.) Acad., 1973-80; libr. media specialist Abrams Elem. Sch., Bessemer, 1980-83, Davis Mid. Sch., Bessemer, 1984-87; head libr. media specialist Jess Lanier H.S., Bessemer, 1983-84, 87-94; libr. media specialist Mountain Brook H.S., Birmingham, 1994—. Chmn. Bessemer City Schs. Librs., 1987-94; mem. Libr. Media Leadership Group ALa. Dept. Edn., 1993—98; chmn. Mountain Brook City Sch. Libr Media Specialists, 1990—98. Mem. NEA, Ala. Edn. Assn., Ala. Instnl. Media Assn., Ala. Libr. Assn., Ala. Cheerleader Coaches & Advisors Assn. (bd. dirs. 1988-2001). Methodist. Avocations: camping, reading, traveling. Office: Mountain Brook HS 3650 Bethune Dr Birmingham AL 35223-1420

ROBERTS, SUSAN STURGEON, art educator, writer; b. Aurora, Colo., Aug. 15, 1953; d. Thomas James Sturgeon, Lela Selby Nagle; m. Eugene Arden Roberts. BS, Calif. State Poly. U., 1978. Tchr. Redlands Unified Sch. Dist., Calif., 1978—80; needle arts tchr. Grants Pass, Oreg., 1974—. Double knits designer Western Textile MIll., Ontario, Calif., 1978. Author: (book) The Complete Needlepoint Guide 400+ Needlepoint Stitches, 2000; sculpture, Stitchin Suzi and Three Ply, 1998. Mem.: Embroiderer's Guild Am. Inc. (asst. editor 1973—76, program dir. 2001—03), Am. Needlepoint Guild Inc. Office: 450 Genverna Glen Grants Pass OR 97527-9570 Home Fax: 541-471-0917; Office Fax: 541-471-0917. Personal E-mail: susanroberts15@hotmail.com. Business E-Mail: susanroberts15@hotmail.com.

ROBERTS, SUZANNE CATHERINE, artist; b. San Antonio, Oct. 27, 1953; d. Thomas Simons and Marceline Margaret (Conrady) Garrett; m. Ted Blake Roberts, May 22, 1976; 1 child, Elizabeth. BS in Radio-TV-Film, U. Tex., 1975, B of Journalism, 1977; MA in Interdisciplinary Studies, Corpus Christi (Tex.) State U., 1982, MS in Gen. Counseling, 1989; MA in Polit. Sci., S.W. Tex. State U., 1995. News announcer Sta. KIXL Radio, Austin, Tex., 1976, Sta. KSIX Radio, Corpus Christi, 1977-78; news anchor Sta. KZTV-TV, Corpus Christi, 1979, news reporter, 1977-80; news announcer, reporter Sta. KRYS-AM-FM, Corpus Christi, 1983-87; freelance reporter United Press Internat., Austin, 1989-94, Tex. State Network, Austin, 1995-97, Des Moines, 1997-2000; artist, 1998—.

ROBERTS, TIFFANY MARIE, former soccer player; b. Petaluma, Calif., May 5, 1977; BA in Comm. Studies, U. N.C., 1998. Mem. U.S. Women's Nat. Soccer Team, 1994—; including CONCAFAF Qualifying Championship Montreal, 1994; 3d place FIFA Women's World Cup, 1995; gold medal U.S. Olympic Team, 1996; mem. Under-20 Nat. Team 1997 Nordic Cup, Denmark; mem. Tri Valley Team, San Ramon, Calif.; profl. soccer player Carolina Courage, 2001—03. Named 1994 Calif. H.S. Player of Yr., Most Valuable Player, Far Western Regional, 1993, World Cup Champion, 1999. Achievements include member U. N.C. NCAA national championship teams, 1996, 97. Office: US Soccer Fedn 1801-1811 S Prairie Ave Chicago IL 60616

ROBERTS, VICTORIA LYNN P. antique expert; b. N.Y.C., Sept. 15, 1953; d. Edgar Alan Parmer and Nina Joyce (Ash) Gross; m. George E. Roberts, Dec. 1, 1978 (div. 1985); 1 child, Joshua Henry. BA in Polit. Sci., Am. govt., const. law, Yale U., 1998; MBA, Fairfield U., 1999. Pres. High Gear Creative Svcs., Savannah, Ga., 1979-81; v.p. Rossignol Modeling Agy., N.Y.C., 1981-82; mgr., dir. Parc Monceau Antiques, Westport, Conn., 1982-85; pres., owner, CEO Victoria & Cie LLC, Custom Furniture Mfg., Norwalk, Conn., 1985—; pres., owner L.L.C. Custon Furniture Mfg. Antiques tchr. Sacred Heart U., Fairfield, Conn., 1988, 89, Norwalk Community Coll., 1989; antique lectr. various hist. socs., Conn., 1989-90; speaker in antiques field; antique expert seminars to interior designers, Norwalk, 1989; creator, sole contbr. spls. on antiques CNBC TV, 1989, 90. Antiques editor Brooks Community Newspaper, Westport, 1989-91; contbr. Antiques Mag., 1991—. Mem. Appraisers Assn. Am. (sr.), Coll. Arts Assn., Yale Club (N.Y.C. admissions com. mem.), Alpha Sigma Lambda. Avocations: scenic photography, bicycling, history, rose gardening. Office: Stamford Industrial Park Canal Street Stamford CT 06902 E-mail: victoria@victoriacie.com.

ROBERTS-BURKE, BERYL D. state legislator, lawyer; b. Columbia, S.C., Aug. 26, 1958; BS, Fla. State U., 1980, JD, 1987; student, Oxford U., Eng., 1981. Bar: Fla. Mem. Fla. Ho. of Reps., 1992—; mem. gen. govt. appropriations com., 1996-97; mem. rules, resolutions and ethics com., 1996-97, 97—. Del. Dem. Nat. Conv., 1988; mem. African-Am. Coun. Christian Clergy; bd. dirs. Concerned African Women, Kids, Miami River of Life. Recipient African-Am. Achievers award 1994, Carter G. Woodson award Postal Employees of United Cmty. Outreach Assn., Up and Comers in Govt. award, 1994; named Citizen of Yr., Miami Chpt. Nat. Black Nurses Assn., 1994. Mem. NAACP, Nat. Bar Assn. (Women Lawyers' divsn.), Dade County Black Lawyer's Assn., Coalition 100 Black Women, Continental Socs., C. of C. (N. Dade and Miami-Dade), Kiwanis, King of Clubs Greater Miami Inc., Omicron Delta Kappa, Alpha Phi Alpha (Beta Lambda chpt.), Delta Sigma Theta, Phi Delta Phi. Democrat. Avocations: reading, playing computer games, studying bible, sewing. Office: Fla Capitol 402 S Monroe St Rm 1402 Tallahassee FL 32399-6526 also: 7900 NE 2nd Ave Ste 705 Miami FL 33138-4424 E-mail: roberts.beryl@leg.state.fl.us.

ROBERTS-DEMPSEY, PATRICIA E. secondary school educator; Tchr. Challenger High Sch., Spanaway, Wash., 1969—. Recipient Wash. State Tchr. of Yr. award, 1991-91. Office: Challenger HS 18020 B St E Spanaway WA 98387-8316

ROBERTS-MAMONE, LISA A. lawyer; BA magna cum laude, Grove City Coll., 1985; JD magna cum laude, Case Wester Res. U., 1988. Bar: Ohio 1988. With Jones Day, Cleve., 1988—, ptnr., 2000—. Trustee The Estate Planning Coun. of Cleve., The Laub Found.; mem. Estate Planning Discussion Group, Cleve.; mem. estate adv. coun. U. Hosps. Cleve. Mem.: Cleve. Bar Assn. (estate planning, probate and trust law sect.), Ohio State Bar Assn. (estate planning, trust and probate sect.). Office: Jones Day North Point 901 Lakeside Ave Cleveland OH 44114-1190

ROBERTSON, ANNE FERRATT, language educator, researcher; b. Dallas, Mar. 19, 1946; d. Thomas Littelle and Elisabeth (Fentress) Ferratt; m. Edwin David Robertson, Sept. 7, 1968; 1 child, Thomas Therit. BA, Hollins Coll., 1968; MA, NYU, 1990, PhD, 1994. Web pub. Ancient Near Eastern Marking, N.Y.C.; profl. cons., 1994—. Author articles. Mem. Am. Oriental Soc., Egyptological Seminar of N.Y. (treas.). Avocation: soprano. Home and Office: 315 E 72nd St Apt 6H New York NY 10021-4627 E-mail: arobe@nyc.rr.com.

ROBERTSON, BRENDA, senator; b. Sussex, NB, Can., May 23, 1929; m. Wilmont W. Robertson (dec.); children: Doug, Leslie, Tracy. BS, Mount Allison U.; DHL (hon.), Mount St. Vincent U., 1973; DSc (hon.), U. Moncton, 1983. Legislator NB Legislature, 1967—83; senator The Senate of Can., Ottawa, 1984—. Progressive. Office: 401 Victoria Bldg The Senate of Canada Ottawa ON Canada K1A 0A4

ROBERTSON, HEATHER ANDERSON, music educator, musician; b. Danville, Va., Apr. 28, 1977; d. S. Wayne and Susan Blair Anderson; m. Jerry Wayne Robertson, July 27, 2002. BA, Averett U., 1999. Music tchr. K-12 Commonwealth of Va., 2001. Info. specialist City of Danville, Va., 2000—01; tchr. music Pittsylvania County Schs., Chatham, 2001—. Ch. musician Chatham Bapt. Ch., 1998—. Author of poems. Mem. The United Friends and Family, Danville, 1999—2001; vol., hon. mem. 4-H, Chatham, 1986—2003; bd. mem. Ext. Leadership Coun., 1993—96. Named 4-H All-Star, Pittsylvania County Coop. Ext., 4-H, 1994. Mem.: Va. Choral Directors' Assn. (assoc.), Am. Criminal Justice Assn. (assoc.), Va. Music Educators Assn. (assoc.), Climax Ruritan Club (hon.). Church Of Christ. Avocations: reading, piano pedagogy, writing, horseback riding, travel.

ROBERTSON, JANE RYDING, marketing executive; b. Dallas, Apr. 11, 1953; d. Ronald and Olive Stacey (Hodgkinson) Pearce; m. James Randall Robertson, May 23, 1974; children: James Andrew, Jessica Ryding. Assoc. degree, Tyler Jr. Coll., 1972; BS, Tex. Tech U., 1974. Store mgr. trainee Montgomery Ward, Dallas, Lubbock, Tex., 1974-75; dist. sales rep. Max Factor & Co., Dallas, 1975-78; sr. asst. buyer cosmetics Sanger Harris, Dallas, 1978-88, also cosmetic mktg.-divisional mktg. account exec., 1978-88; v.p. mktg. Dallas Market Ctr., 1988-90; dir. mktg.-pub. rels. Galleria/Hines Dallas, 1990—2002; sr. v.p. corp. comm. Dallas Market Ctr., 2003. Pub. rels. bd. Easter Seals, 1996—2000; mem. corp. adv. bd. So. Meth. U., 2000—; mem. nat. bd. dir. Susan G. Komen Found. for Breast Cancer, Dallas, 1990—95; bd. dir. Ctr. for Profl. Selling, Baylor U., Waco, Tex., 1989—95. Mem. Internat. Coun. Shopping Ctr. (sr. cert. mktg. dir.), Fashion Group Internat., Univ. Club (bd. dir. profl. women's com. 1990-92). Methodist. Avocations: reading, youth activities, interior decorating. Office: Dallas Market Ctr 2100 Stemmons Freeway MS 25 Dallas TX 75207 E-mail: jrobertson@dmcmail.com.

ROBERTSON, LINDA F. educational adminstrator; b. Powell, Wyo., July 15, 1946; d. Lee and Dorothy W. (Schweighart) Brunk; m. Darrell G. Robertson II, July 2, 1965; 1 child, Michelle. BA in elem. edn., U. Wyo., 1968; MA in edn. adminstrn., U. Akron, 1978; postgrad., Kent State U. Cert. supt., elem. prin., secondary prin., Ohio. Elem. prin. Aurora (Ohio) City Schs., asst. supt., high sch. prin.; dir. Ctr. for Internat. and Intercultural Edn., Kent State U. Named Ohio Prin. of Yr., 1992. Mem.: Kappa Delta Pi, Phi Delta Kappa. Home: 8220 Timber Trl Chagrin Falls OH 44023-5071 E-mail: lfrobert@kent.edu.

ROBERTSON, LISA RAE, music educator; b. Cedar Falls, Iowa, May 2, 1960; d. Robert Dale and Betty Jane Frey; m. Norman Mark Robertson, Feb. 9, 1980. BA in Fine Arts and Humanities, U. Wyo., 1988. Art gallery asst. Sheridan (Wyo.) Inn, 1981—83; music divsn. mgr. Gospel Gardens, Sheridan, 1984; piano tchr. Sheridan, 1980—; art instr. Three Peaks Christian Sch., Sheridan, 1996—; vocal music accompanist Sch. Dist. No. 2, Sheridan, 1984—. Republican. Baptist. Avocations: reading, fitness walking, church involvement. Home: 8 Taxi Dr Sheridan WY 82801 Office: Sch Dist No 2 PO Box 919 Sheridan WY 82801

ROBERTSON, MARIAN ELLA (MARIAN ELLA HALL), small business owner, handwriting analyst; b. Edmonton, Alta., Can., Mar. 3, 1920; d. Orville Arthur and Lucy Hon (Osborn) Hall; m. Howard Chester Robertson, Feb. 7, 1942; children: Elaine, Richard. Student, Willamette U., 1937-39; BS, Western Oreg. State U., 1955. Cert. elem., jr. high. tchr., supt. (life) Oreg.; cert. graphoanalyst. Tchr. pub. schs., Mill City, Albany, Scio and Hillsboro, Oreg., 1940-72; cons. Zaner-Bloser Inc., Columbus, Ohio, 1972-85, assoc. cons., 1985-89; pres. Write-Keys, Scio, 1980-90; owner Lifelines, Jefferson, Oreg., 1991-94. Tchr. Internat. Graphoanalysis Soc., Chgo., 1979; instr. Linn-Benton C.C., 1985-89; del. Oreg. Water Resources Congress at Seaside, 2002; mem. Ptnrs. of the Ams., Costa Rica, 2003. Master gardener vol. Marion County, Oreg. State U. Extension Svc., 1992; floriculture judge Marion County Fair, 1992; master gardener clinic Oreg. State Fair, 1992; sr. intern 5th Congl. Dist. Oreg., Washington1984, mem. sr. adv. coun.; mem. precinct com. Rep. Ctrl. Com., Linn County, 1986, alt. vice chair, 1986, parliamentarian, 1988—; candidate Oreg. State Legislature, Salem, 1986; del. N.W. Friends Yearly Meeting, Newberg, Oreg., 1990—92; clk. Marion Friends Monthly Meeting, 1992—93. Mem.: Ptnrs. of Ams.-Costa Rica., Internat. Platform Assn., Altrusa Internat., Port Orford Heritage Soc. (hon.), Knife and Fork Club. Republican. Mem. Soc. Of Friends. Avocations: piano, organ, violin, gardening, writing. Home: 2757 Pheasant Ave SE Salem OR 97302-3170

ROBERTSON, MARTHA RAPPAPORT, state legislator, consultant; b. Boston, Sept. 14, 1952; d. Jerome Lyle and Nancy (Vahey) Rappaport; divorced; 1 child, Colby. BA, Franklin & Marshall Coll., 1974; MBA, U. Pa., 1976. Mktg. and new bus. devel. exec. Gen. Mills, Inc., Mpls., 1976-91; mem. Minn. Senate from 45th dist., St. Paul, 1993—. Republican. Office: State of Minn 141 State Office Bldg Saint Paul MN 55155-0001

ROBERTSON, MARY LOUISE, archivist, art historian; b. L.A., May 19, 1945; d. Snell and Dorothy (Tregoning) R. BA, UCLA, 1966, MA, 1968, PhD, 1975. Teaching asst. dept. history UCLA, 1967-70; acting instr. UCLA Extension, 1973-74; acting instr. dept. history Pepperdine U., L.A., 1970, Calif. State U., Northridge, 1972-73; asst. curator manuscripts Huntington Libr., San Marino, Calif., 1975, assoc. curator, 1977, chief curator, 1979—. Adj. prof. English Claremont Grad. Sch., 1994. Author: Guide to British Historical Manuscripts in the Huntington Library, 1982; co-author, editor: Guide to American Historical Manuscripts in the Huntington Library, 1979; co-editor: State, Sovereigns & Society in Early Modern England, 1998; contbr. articles on Tudor history to profl. jours. Mabel Wilson Richards dissertation fellow, 1970-72. Mem. Am. Hist. Assn., Soc. Calif. Archivists, N.Am. Conf. on Brit. Studies, Pacific Coast Conf. on Brit. Studies (treas. 1986-88, pres. 1988-90), Phi Beta Kappa. Office: Huntington Libr 1151 Oxford Rd San Marino CA 91108-1299

ROBERTSON, PAULINE DURRETT, publishing executive; b. Amarillo, Tex., Apr. 17, 1922; d. Walter Lucius and Mary Eddie (Jones) Durrett; m. Roy Lewis Robertson, Dec. 18, 1940; children: Kay Linda Robertson Savage, Kent Lewis, Robyn M. Robertson Koock, Paula Jo Robertson Pierce, Roy Durrett, Laurel Annette Robertson Gibson, Virginia Lee Robertson-Baker, Ellen Robertson Neal, Neil Thomas, Carrie Beth. AA, Amarillo Coll., 1969; BA in English Writing, St. Edward's U., Austin, Tex., 1992. Editor project history U.S. Reclamation Bur., Amarillo, 1942-43; editor post newsletter U.S. Army Air Force, Amarillo, 1943-44; freelance writer, 1944-73; writer books of history Staked Plains Press, Canyon, Tex., 1973-77; writer books of history and poetry Paramount Pub. Co., Amarillo, 1977—, pub. house pres., editor, 1977—; tchr. poetry writing and history Amarillo Coll., 1971—2002. Tchr. poetry writing Elderhostel, U. Tex., Austin, 1988-89; writer book revs. Amarillo Globe News, 1968—; spkr. in field. Author: (with R.L. Robertson) Panhandle Pilgrimage: Illustrated Tales Tracing History in the Texas Panhandle, 1976, 77, 81, 85, 90, Tascosa: Historic Site in the Texas Panhandle, 1978, 2d edit., 1995, Mystery Woman of Old Tascosa: The Legend of Frenchy McCormick, 1979, 2d edit., 1995, Cowman's Country: Fifty Frontier Ranches in the Texas Panhandle 1876-1887, 1981, 2d edit., 95, (poetry books) Fringe Benefits: Light Verse From Living, 1985, Borrowed Moccasins: Poems From Other Viewpoints, 1986, Field Notes: Poems on Late Light, 1987; editor and designer: Austin Originals: Chats With Colorful Characters by Robyn Turner, 1982, Long Shadows: Indian Leaders Standing in the Path of Manifest Destiny 1600-1900 (by Jack Jackson), 1985; author, editor: (poetry) Bootsteps: Poems of the West-Then and Now, 1978, 83, Eve's Version: 150 Women of the Bible, 1983; featured in documentary Story Of A Family on NBC-TV, 1960; mem. bd. editors Ch. Women United U.S.A., 2001—. Co-founder, sec. Cerebral Palsy Treatment Ctr., Amarillo, 1948-60, Opportunity House, Amarillo, 1970-87; founder, pres. Children's Cottage, Amarillo, 1964-84, Women's Coalition for Change: Focus on Poverty, Amarillo, 1989-95; founder, dir. for underprivileged children Camp Friendship, Ceta Glen, Tex., 1971-74; chair of elders First Christian Ch., 1979-81; host family Internat. Christian Youth Exch., 1963-64, sending family, 1968, 78; mem. Potter County Hist. Commn., Tex., 1988-96; pres.-elect Ch. Women United of Tex., 1996-98, pres., 1998-2000; chair Amarillo Mayor's Commn. on Early Childhood Nurture/Neglect, 1997—; nat. del. Christian Ch. Named Amarillo's Family of the Yr., Amarillo Globe-News, 1957, Tex. Merit Mother, Am. Mothers Assn., Boston, 1991, 1995 Woman of the Yr. in Amarillo, Beta Sigma Phi, Amarillo, 1995, Yellow Rose Tex., Gov. Anne Richards, 1991, Mayor's Friend of Young Children, 1999, Tex. Mother of Yr., Am. Mothers Assn., Boston, 2003; named to Amarillo HS Hall Fame, 1998; recipient Tex. Panhandle Disting. Svc. award West Tex. A&M U., Canyon, 1977, Lifetime Career Achievement award Amarillo Women's Network, 1996, Woman of Distinction award Girl Scouts Tex. Plains Coun., 2002. Mem. AAUW, LWV (v.p., Amarillo program chair), Western Writers Am., Acad. Am. Poets, Amarillo Photog. Soc. (publicity com., Salon award 1961—), Panhandle Profl. Writers (pres. 1966—, bd. mem.), Poetry Soc. Tex. (founder. area chpt. 1972, pres. area chpt. 1979-81, Tex. state councilor 1973—), Tex. Tchrs. of Creative Writing, Common Cause (area rep. 1971—). Democrat. Avocations: photography, travel, reading, walking, grandchildren. Home: 124 Wayside Dr Amarillo TX 79106-6425 Office: Paramount Pub Co PO Box 3730 Amarillo TX 79116-3730 Office Phone: 806-351-2665.

ROBERTSON, ROSE MARIE, cardiologist, educator; b. Detroit, May 15, 1945; d. Joseph Michael and Rose Marie (Pink) Stevens; m. David Robertson, Oct. 31, 1978; 1 child, Rose Marie. BA, Manhattanville Coll., 1966; MD, Harvard Med. Sch., 1970. Diplomate Nat. Bd. Medicine, 1971, Am. Bd. Internal Medicine, 1974, Cardiovascular Medicine, 1975. Intern in medicine Mass. Gen. Hosp., Boston, 1970-71, resident in medicine, 1970-72; fellow in cardiovasc. medicine Johns Hopkins Med. Sch., Balt., 1973-75, asst. prof. medicine, 1972-78, Vanderbilt U. Med. Ctr., Nashville, 1975-82, assoc. prof. medicine, 1982-89, dir. cardiovasc. tng. program, 1990—2000, assoc. dir. cardiology, 1987—, prof. medicine, 1989—. Mem. adv. bd. Robert Wood Johnson Found., 1990—; chief sci. officer Am. Heart Assn., 2003—; mem. cardiovasc. study sect. NIH, Bethesda, Md., 1993-97; invited spkr., lectr. Contbr. articles to profl. jours., chpts. to books. Fellow Am. Coll. Cardiology, Am. Heart Assn., European Soc. Cardiology; mem. AIAA, Am. Heart Assn. (various offices, pres. 2000-01), Am. Soc. Echocardiography, Am. Fedn. for Clin. Rsch., Am. Soc. Clin. Investigation, Am. Clin. and Climatol. Assn., Assn. Univ. Cardiologists. Home: 4003 Newman Pl Nashville TN 37204-4308 Office: 7272 GreenvilleAve Danville TX E-mail: rmr@heart.org.

ROBERTSON, SANDRA DEE (GRAEN), tax director; b. Denver, Nov. 7, 1953; d. Fredrick Philip Arthur Graen and Dorothea Stone (Bell) Kohler; m. Charles E. Robertson Jr., Aug. 4, 1973 (Jan. 1985); 1 child, Daniel Philip. BS in Bus. cum laude, U. Colo., 1980. CPA, Colo., Ga. Staff acct. Brock, Cordle & Assocs., CPA's, Boulder, Colo., 1980-82; corp. tax acct. Storage Tech. Corp., Louisville, Colo., 1983-87; state tax supr. RJR Nabisco, Inc., Atlanta, 1987-89; mgr. Ernst & Young CPA's, Atlanta, 1989-91; dir. state and local taxes Equifax Inc., Atlanta, 1991-94; dir. state and local tax Ga.-Pacific Corp., Atlanta, 1994—. Bd. dirs. Com. on State Taxation. Served with U.S. Army, 1972-75. Mem. AICPA, Toastmasters, Beta Gamma Sigma. Democrat. Avocations: russian language and history, cajun and zydeco music and dance, reading. Home: 450 Rock Springs Rd NE Atlanta GA 30324-5102

ROBERTSON, SARA STEWART, private investor, entrepreneur; b. N.Y.C., Feb. 4, 1940; d. John Elliott and Mary Terry (Schlamp) Stewart; m. James Young Robertson, Nov. 29, 1975 (dec. Mar. 1988). BA, Conn. Coll., 1961; MBA, Am. U., 1969. From trainee to officer First Nat. Bank/First Chgo. Corp., 1969-75, v.p., 1975-92; prin. Royall Enterprises, Chgo., 1992—; prin., dir. Zeppelin Press, Inc., Miami, Fla., 1995—. Chair individuals fundraising, exec. com. Youth Guidance, Chgo., 1993-95. Bd. dirs. Harbor House Condominium Assn. Chgo., 1990-92; trustee Sherwood Conservatory Music, 1993—, chair bd. devel., 1993-95, 97-99; mem. allocations com. and family priority grants com. United Way-Chgo., 1992-95; co-founder, v.p., sec.-treas. Animal Support Kindness and Kinship, Inc., 1999-2001, v.p., sec., 2001—. Mem.: Club 13 Palm Beach (pres. 1996—98, v.p. 2003—). Home and Office: 339 Westminster Pl West Palm Beach FL 33405-1652 E-mail: saisairob@aol.com.

ROBERTSON, SUSAN JOYCE COE, special education educator; b. Pinedale, Wyo., May 22, 1954; d. Cecil James and Geraldine Ada (Greene) Coe; children: Jamie Michelle, Mark David. BS in Edn., Chadron (Nebr.) State Coll., 1976, MS in Counseling and Guidance, 1977; specialist in emotionally disturbed, U. No. Colo., 1982. Cert. crisis prevention intervention master trainer, peer mediation facilitator. Elem. tchr. pub. schs., Alliance, Nebr., 1976-77; social worker Community Action, Cheyenne, Wyo., 1978-79; Chpt. 1 tchr. Laramie County Sch. Dist. 1, Cheyenne, 1979-81, elem. tchr., 1981-84, tchr. severely emotionally disturbed, 1984-89, cons., specialist for severely emotionally disturbed, 1989-92, behavior intervention team specialist, 1992-95, tchr. learning disabled, 1995-97, tchr. behavior lab., 1997—. Mem. Dist. Placement Com., 1981-92. Mem. Cmty. Commn., Cheyenne, 1981—92; basketball coach YMCA, 1994; competitive soccer asst., 1999—2001; elder Presbyn. Ch., 1996—97. Mem.: PEO, NEA, Cheyenne Tchr. Edn. Assn., Wyo. Edn. Assn., Coun. Exceptional Children (faculty advisor 1991), Am. Guidance and Counseling Assn. Methodist. Avocations: reading, swimming, racquetball, music. Home: 5425 Gateway Dr Cheyenne WY 82009-4035 Office: 6000 Education Dr Cheyenne WY 82009-3991

ROBERTSON, VALERIA BROWER, state legislator, land developer; b. Memphis, Nov. 17, 1932; m. James T. Robertson. Grad. h.s.; student, coll. Mem. Miss. Ho. of Reps., 1996—; mem. constn., county affairs, pub. bldgs. coms.; mem. pub. health com. Commr. DeSoto Election; mem. DeSoto Econ. Coun., Shelby County Equalization; mem. exec. com. Tenn. Rep. Mem. DeSoto and Miss. Fedn. Rep. Women, C. of C. (Olive Branch and Hernando). Republican. Presbyterian. Home: 8570 Jones Rd Olive Branch MS 38654-9001 Office: State Capitol Bldg PO Box 1018 Jackson MS 39215-1018

ROBERTSON, WYNDHAM GAY, university official, journalist; b. Salisbury, N.C., Sept. 25, 1937; d. Julian Hart and Blanche Williamson (Spencer) R. AB in Econs., Hollins Coll., Roanoke, Va., 1958. Rsch. asst. Standard Oil Co., N.Y.C., 1958-61; rschr. Fortune Mag., N.Y.C., 1961-67, assoc. editor, 1968-74, bd. of editors, 1974-81, asst. mng. editor, 1981-86; bus. editor Time Mag., N.Y.C., 1982-83; v.p. comm. U. N.C., Chapel Hill, 1986-96. Bd. dirs. Media Gen. Inc. Contbr. numerous articles to Fortune Mag. Trustee Thomas S. Kenan Inst. for the Arts, U. NC Health Care Sys., Hollins U. Recipient Gerald M. Loeb Achievement award, U. of Conn., 1972. Mem. Phi Beta Kappa. Episcopalian.

ROBERTS-PARAST, ANN TALBOT, English and foreign language educator; b. Roanoke, Va. d. David Charles and Audrey Louise (Cassell) Roberts; m. Rudy M. Parast, Feb. 22, 1980; 1 child, Layla Ann. BA in French, Tulane U.; BA in Fgn. Lang. Edn., U. New Orleans; degree in translating and interpreting, profl. diploma, U. Paris; M English, U. Paris VIII; MA in French, ABD in Comparative Lit., U. Wash. Freelance translator, interpreter, English instr., Paris, 1968-72; French/English instr. pub. and pvt. schs., New Orleans, 1972-78; translator, adminstrv. asst. Ivory Coast Embassy, Washington, 1974-75; tchg. asst. in French U. Wash., Seattle, 1978-83; French tchr. Marine Mil. Acad., Harlingen, Tex., 1983-84, Harlingen H.S., 1984-89; English instr. Tex. State Tech. Coll., 1989—. Freelance translator, interpreter, New Orleans and Seattle, 1975—; French/English interpreter, 1994—; placement of fgn. exch. students, 1990—; mgr., writer Profl. Resume and Writing Svc., Harlingen, 1989—. Contbr. articles to profl. publs. Former bd. dirs. Jr. Peacemaker Club, Harlingen; former bd. dirs. Tex. French Symposium. French Govt. scholar, Vichy, France, 1983. Mem. DAR (chair good citizens com. 1997—), Tex. C.C. Tchrs. Assn., Alliance Française of Lower Rio Grande, Nat. Coun. Tchrs. English. Mem. Baha'i Faith. Home: 2402 E Adams Ave Harlingen TX 78550-2723 Office: Tex State Tech Coll Dept English Harlingen TX 78550 E-mail: eroberts@tstu.edu.

ROBERTS VELIZ, SENORINA, artist, educator; b. McAllen, Tex., Nov. 30, 1959; d. Jose Inez and Beatriz Torres Veliz; m. Jack Franklin Roberts, Nov. 25, 1989. BFA in Fine Arts Studio & Advt. Comml. Art, U. Tex. Pan Am., Edinburg, 1985; MS in Art and Edn. (hon.), Tex. A&I, Kingsville, 1987. Cert. secondary art tchr. Tex., 1985. Artist, muralist, illustrator, sculptor, McAllen, Tex., 1974—; art tchr. Travis Mid. Sch. McAllen Independent Sch. Dist., McAllen, Tex., 1988—99; art educator U. Tex. Pan Am., Edinburg, 1992—98, South Tex. C.C., McAllen, 1998—2000; women's dorm dir. U. Tex. Pan Am., Edinburg, 1983—98; art tchr. McAllen Meml. H.S. McAllen Independent Sch. Dist., Tex., 1999—. Couselor Women's Residence Hall, U. Tex. Pan Am., Edinburg, 1983—98, advisor Internat. Student's Assn., 1982—98; pres. Rio Grande Valley Art Educator's Assn., McAllen, Tex., 1991—93. Painting, Queens of My Heart (Best of Show, 1985), mural, Give and Thou Shall be Blessed, Stop the Violence, Orange Tree Cycle, Gorilla George. Ssunday sch. tchr. Assembly of God -Mission Monte Carmelo, Mission, Tex., 1999—2003. Fellow, U. Tex. Pan Am., 1981 - 1985; grantee A Peek at the Masters, McAllen Edn. Found., 2002 - 2003, 3-D Giants, 2002 - 2003, EDU Rays Piece by Piece - Mosaic Mural, McAllen Chamber of Commerce & the Jr. League of McAllen, 2003, 99 Bottles of Art on the Wall, Jr. League of McAllen, 2003, A Closer Look at the Masters, McAllen Edn. Found., 2001, Ice Sculpting, Jr. League of McAllen, 2001-02, Mylar Sculptures, 2001-02, Beading to the Loom, 2002 -2003, Ice, Ice Breaking, McAllen Edn. Found., 2002 - 2003; scholar Art scholarship, Lemont Wilcox Competitive Scholarship, 1981, 82, 83, 84, & 85. Mem.: Parent Tchr. Student Assn. (assoc.; com. chair to reflections 2002—, Art Educator of Yr. 2002 -2003), Nat. Art Educators Assn. (assoc.), Tex. Art Educator's Assn. (assoc.), Futuro McAllen (assoc.; com. chair to Art in the Pk. 2002—03). Assembly Of God. Home: P O Box 2483 McAllen TX 78502-2483 Office: McAllen Meml HS 101 E Hackberry McAllen TX 78501 Office Phone: 956-632-8855. Personal E-mail: rr1159@sc2000.net.

ROBEY, SHERIE GAY SOUTHALL GORDON, secondary education educator, consultant; b. Washington, July 7, 1954; d. James Edward and Gene Elizabeth Southall; children: m. Robert Jean Claude Robey; children: Michael Aaron Gordon, Robert Eugene Robey, Jamie Lea Robey. BS, U. Md., 1976; MA in Edn. and Human Devel., George Washington U., 1988. Tchr. Esperanza Mid. Sch., Hollywood, Md., 1980-84, Chopticon High Sch., Morganza, Md., 1984—. Coach Odyssey of the Mind, 1985-95; sponsor Future Tchrs. Am., Morganza, 1990-2002, S.H.O.P./S.A.D.D., Morganza, 1990-2002; cons. Ednl. Cosn., Waldorf, 1980—; pres. BNA Swim Team, 1990-2002; driver edn. classroom and lab instr. Greg's Driving Sch., 1996—. Parish com. Good Shepherd United Meth. St. Church, 1999. Mem. Ednl. Rep. Assn. St. Mary's County, Lighthouse Hist. Soc. Methodist. Avocations: swimming, writing, visiting lighthouses, collection miniature lighthouses. Home and Office: 11181 Carroll Dr Waldorf MD 20601-2656 Office Phone: 301-475-0215. E-mail: lightbeacon2@yahoo.com.

ROBFOGEL, SUSAN SALITAN, lawyer; b. Rochester, N.Y., Apr. 4, 1943; d. Victor and Janet (Rosenthal) Salitan; m. Nathan Joshua Robfogel, July 12, 1965; children: Jacob Morris, Samuel Salitan. BA cum laude, Smith Coll., 1964; JD, Cornell U., 1967. Bar: N.Y.1967, U.S. Dist. Ct. (we. dist.) 1968, U.S. Ct. Appeals (2d cir.) 1971, U.S. Supreme Ct. 1971, U.S. Dist. Ct. (no. dist.) 1974, D.C. 1982. From asst. corp. counsel to sr. asst. corp. counsel City of Rochester, N.Y., 1967-70; assoc. Harris, Beach & Wilcox, Rochester, 1970-75; ptnr. Harris, Beach, Wilcox, Rubin & Levey, Rochester, 1975-85, Nixon, Peabody, LLP, Rochester and N.Y.C., 1985—; bd. mem. Office of Compliance, Washington, 1999—. Panel mem., Fed. Svc. Impasses Panel, Washington, 1983-94; mem., past chair Data Protection Rev. Bd., Albany, N.Y., 1984—. Mem. trustees vis. com. U. Rochester Med. Sch., 1990; mem. mgmt. adv. panel SUNY, 1990. Recipient Brockport Coll. Found. Community award, 1989. Fellow Am. Bar Found., N.Y. State Bar Found., Coll. Labor and Employment Lawyers; mem. ABA, N.Y. State Bar Assn., Washington D.C. Bar Assn., Monroe County Bar Assn. (Rodenbeck award 1988). Home: 1090 Park Ave Rochester NY 14610-1728 Office: Nixon Peabody LLP PO Box 1051 Rochester NY 14603-1051 also: 437 Madison Ave New York NY 10022-7001 Business E-Mail: srobfogel@nixonpeabody.com.

ROBIE, JOAN, elementary school principal; Prin. Monteith Elem. Sch., Grosse Pointe, Mich., 1989—. Recipient Elem. Sch. Recognition award U.S. Dept. Edn., 1989-90 Office: Monteith Elem Sch 1275 Cook Rd Grosse Pointe Woods MI 48236-2511

ROBILLARD, LUCIENNE, Canadian government official; b. Montreal, Canada, June 16, 1945; BA, Coll. Basile-Moreau, 1965; MA in Social Work, U. Montreal, 1967; Diploma in Adminstrn., École des hautes études commerciales, Montreal, 1983, MBA, 1986. Social worker, clin. practitioner Maisonneuve-Rosemont Hosp.; appt. min. of labour and fed. campaigns Que., 1995-96; sr. adminstr. Centre de svcs. sociaux Richelieu; youth leader in a kibbutz Israel, 1969-72; apptd. pub. curator City of Quebec, Canada, 1986-89; elected mem. Quebec Nat. Assembly for Chambly, 1989; apptd. min. cultural affairs, 1989-90; apptd. min. higher edn. and science, 1990-92; apptd. min. of edn., 1992-93; min. edn. and science, 1993-94; min. health and social svcs., 1994-95; minister of labor, minister responsible for fed. campaign, 1995; elected mem. parliament Saint-Henri-Westmount, 1995—; min. citizenship and immigration, 1996-99; re-elected to parliament Westmount-Ville-Marie, 1997—; pres. Treas. Bd., 1999—2003; min. infrastructure. Govt. of Canada, 1999—2003, min. industry, 2003—; min. responsible for econ. devel. agy. of Canada for the regions of Quebec, 2003—. Pres. Treasury Bd., Min. responsible for intrastructure; mem. Corp. professionelle des travailleurs sociaux de Québec, 1967—; mem. editl. com. (book) Le travail social et la santé au Québec, 1984-86, departmental study com. psychiatric svcs., Montreal region, 1984-85; pres. Commn. adminstrv. des svcs. de santé mentale of the Conseil régional de la Montérégie, 1983-86, Association des praticiens de service social en milieu de santé du Québec, 1984-86; cons. mental health dossier Rochon Commn., 1986. Mem. editl. com. Le Travail Social et la Santé du Québec, 1985. Mem. Corp Professionelle des Travailleurs Sociaux du Que. Office: 140 O'Connor St East Tower 9th Fl Ottawa ON Canada K1A OR5 also: Industry Canada 11th Fl East Tower CD Howe Bldg 235 Queen St K1A 0H5 Ottawa ON Canada

ROBIN, CLARA NELL (CLAIRE ROBIN), English language educator; b. Harrisonburg, Va., Feb. 19, 1945; d. Robert Franklin and Marguerite Ausherman (Long) Wampler; m. Phil Camden Branner, June 10, 1967 (div. May 1984); m. John Charles Robin, Nov. 22, 1984 (div. Dec. 1990). BA in English, Mary Washington Coll., 1967; MA in English, James Madison U., 1974; postgrad., Jesus Coll., Cambridge, Eng., 1982, Princeton U., 1985-86, Auburn U., 1988, U. No. Tex., 1990-91. Cert. tchr. English, French, master cert., Tex. Tchr. 7th grade John C. Myers Intermediate Sch., Broadway, Va., 1967-68; tchr. 10th grade Waynesville (Mo.) H.S., 1968-70; tchr. 6th, 7th, 8th grades Mary Mount Jr. Sch., Santa Barbara, Calif., 1970-72; tchr. 9th grade Forest Meadow Jr. H.S. Richardson (Tex.) Ind. Sch. Dist., 1972-78, tchr. 10th grade Lake Highlands H.S., 1972-84; tchr. 11th, 12th grades Burleson HS, Burleson (Tex.) Ind. Sch. Dist., 1986—2003; tchr. 9th and 10th grade English Ft. Worth Country Day Sch., 2003—. Instr. composition Hill Coll., 1989-90. Contbg. author: (book revs.) English Journal, 1989-94, (lit. criticism) Eric, 1993. Vol. Dallas Theater Cir., 1990—96; active Kimbell Art Mus., Ft. Worth, 1990—, Modern Art Mus., Ft. Worth, 1992—, KERA Pub. TV, Dallas, 1990—, Amon Carter Mus., Ft. Worth, 2001—. Fellow NEH, 1988, 89, 92, 95, Fulbright-Hays Summer Seminar, 1991; ind. study grantee Coun. Basic Edn., 1990; recipient Chpt. Achievement award Epsilon Nu Delta Kappa Gamma, 1993, Honorable Mention Tex. Outstanding Tchg. of the Humanities award, 1995, Burlesson Independent Sch. Dist., Campus Ednl. Improvement Com., 1997-2000, Dist. Ednl. Improvement Com., 1998-2001. Mem.: United Educators Assn., Nat. Coun. Tchrs. English (spring conf. presenter 2000, 2002), Acad. Am. Poets, Epsilon Nu of Delta Kappa Gamma (1st v.p. 1988—94, v.p. 1992—94, profl. affairs com. 1996—98, comms. chair 1998—). Avocations: bicycling, travel, reading, writing, landscaping. Home: 4009 W 6th St Fort Worth TX 76107-1619 Office: Ft Worth County Day Sch 4200 Country Day Ln Fort Worth TX 76109-4299 E-mail: crobin@fwcds.org.

ROBINER, LINDA GOODMAN, writer, educator; d. Chester Sidney and Marie (Rosenberg) Goodman; children: Steven, Larry. AB, U. Mich., 1958; EdM, John Carroll U., 1978. Adj. prof. Cleve. State U., 1979—84; prodr. WVIZ-Pub. TV, Cleve., 1984—93; adj. prof. John Carroll U., Cleve., 1989—93, Ursuline Coll., Cleve., 1992—93, Cuyahoga C.C., Cleve., 1992—93, Notre Dame Coll., Cleve., 1993—99; writer, educator, cons. The Literary Ctr., Art Studio, Case Western Res. U., Cleve. Author: Reverse Fairy Tale, 1997, poems and short stories; contbr. articles to profl. jours. Office Phone: 216-397-9473.

ROBINOWITZ, CAROLYN BAUER, psychiatrist, educator; b. Bklyn., July 15, 1938; d. Milton Leonard and Marcia (Wexler) Bauer; m. Max Robinowitz, June 10, 1962; children: Mark, David AB, Wellesley Coll., 1959; MD, Washington U., 1964. Diplomate Am. Bd. Psychiatry and Neurology. Chief physician tng. NIMH, Bethesda, Md., 1968-70; dir. pediatric liaison U. Miami Sch. Medicine, Fla, 1970-72, dir. child psychiatry tng., 1971-72; dir. edn. George Washington U. Sch. Medicine, Washington, 1972-74; project dir. Psychiatrist as Tchr., Washington, 1973-75; dep. med. dir. Am. Psychiat. Assn., Washington, 1976-86, dir. Office Edn., 1976-87, sr. dep. med. dir., 1986-94, COO, 1986-94. Assoc. dean Georgetown U. Sch. Medicine, 1995—98, dean, 1998—2000, lectr., 1976—82, professorial lectr., 1982—94, prof., 1995—2000, clin. prof., 2000—; dir. Am. Bd. Psychiatry and Neurology, Evanston, Ill., 1979—86, sec., 1984, v.p., 85, pres., 86; clin. prof. psychiatry and behavioral scis., child health and devel. George Washington U., 1984—98, 2001—; professorial lectr. Uniformed Svcs. U. of Health Scis., 1986—. Editor: Women in Context, 1976; contbr. articles to jours., chpts. to books Admissions com. Wellesley Coll. Club, Washington, 1983-84; active Boy Scouts Am. Served with USPHS, 1966-69 Recipient NIMH Mental Health Career Devel. award, 1966-70, NIMH grantee, 1974-94. Fellow Am. Psychiat. Assn. (Disting. Svc. award 1991, Vestermark award 1995, Adminstrv. Psychiatry award 1999), Am. Coll. Psychiatrists (bd. dirs. 1993-96, 1st v.p. 1996-97, pres. 1999-2000, past pres. 2000—, Bowis award 1994, Disting. Svc. award 2001—); mem. AMA (coun. on sci. affairs 2001—), Assn. for Acad. Psychiatry (pres. 1994-95, dir. 1992-96, 2003—, Lifetime Achievement award 2003), Group for Advancement of Psychiatry (dir. 1982-84, pres. 1989-91), Coun. Med. Splty. Socs. (dir. 1977-82, pres. 1981-82). Office: #514 5225 Connecticut Ave NW Washington DC 20015 E-mail: cbrobinowitzmd@usa.net.

ROBINS, BETTY DASHEW, antiques and arts dealer; b. N.Y.C., Feb. 14, 1923; d. Leon and Esther (Turits) Dashew; m. Arthur Joseph Robins, Sept. 26, 1948; children: Lisa Dale, Michael Lee. BA, NYU, 1952. Field staff Pearl Buck Open Door, N.Y.C., 1944-45; dir. MacArthur House, San Francisco, 1945-47, Georgetown House, Washington, 1948-50; asst. curator S. Asian Collection Mus. of Art and Archaeology, U. Mo., Columbia, 1967-68; owner BDR Assocs. Arts and Antiques, Columbia, 1976—. Founding mem., 1st pres. Columbia Art League, 1959-61; gen. chmn. 1st Tenn. Artist Craftsman Fair, Nashville, 1971-72; bd. mem. Mus. Assocs., Mus. Art and Archaeology, U. Mo., 1975-85, Boone County Hist. Soc., 2001—; mem. S. Asian studies com., 1976-85; coord. Festival of India, 1985-86, Festival of China, 1986-87, Peace Through the Arts, 1987-88, yr.-long programs commemorating 50th anniversary India independence, Columbia, 1997; mem. profl. visual arts adv. com. Mo. Arts Coun., 1980-82; cons. Denver Art Mus., 1991-92; advisor India Arts exhibit U. Mo. Mus. Art and Archaeology, 1997; organizer gallery exhibits, such as carved coconut Scrapers of Malaysia, India, Indonesia, Nat. Inst. of Pub. Adminstrn., Kuala Lumpur, 1989, Traditional Arts of India and U.S.A., U. Mo., 1989, Healing Imagery of Malaysia and U.S.A., U. Mo., 1991, Decorative Arts India, Stephens Coll., 1998, Storytelling through the Everyday Art of Mo. and India, Boone County Hist. Mus., 1998. Co-author: Everyday Art of India, 1968; contbr. articles to profl. jours. Bd. dirs. PAST (hist. preservation of Mo.), 1978-79. Named Woman of the Yr., Women in Comms., 1977-78, Vol. of Yr., Vol. Action Coun., 1983; recipient Quiet Hero award Columbia Pub. Schs., 1998. Home: 2316 Woodridge Rd Columbia MO 65203-1550

ROBINS, LEE NELKEN, medical educator; b. New Orleans, Aug. 29, 1922; d. Abe and Leona (Reiman) Nelken; m. Eli Robins, Feb. 22, 1946 (dec. Dec. 1994); children: Paul, James, Thomas, Nicholas; m. Hugh Chaplin, Aug. 5, 1998. Student, Newcomb Coll., 1938-40; BA, Radcliffe Coll., 1942, MA, 1943; PhD, Harvard U., 1951. Mem. faculty Washington U., St. Louis, 1954—, prof. sociology in psychiatry, 1968-91, prof. sociology, 1969-91, prof. social sci. and social sci. in psychiatry, 1991-2000, prof. emeritus, 2001—. Past mem. Nat. Adv. Coun. on Drug Abuse; past mem. task panels Pres.'s Commn. on Mental Health; mem. expert adv. panel on mental health WHO; Salmon lectr. N.Y. Acad. Medicine, 1983; Cutter lectr. Harvard U., 1997. Author: Deviant Children Grown Up, 1966; editor 11 books; mem. editl. bd. Psychol. Medicine, Jour. Studies on Alcohol, Social Psychiatry and Psychiatric Epidemiology, Epidemiol. e Psichiat. Sociale; contbr. articles to profl. jours. Recipient Rsch. Scientist award USPHS, 1970-90, Pacesetter Rsch. award Nat. Inst. Drug Abuse, 1978, Radcliffe Coll. Grad. Soc. medal, 1979, Sutherland award Am. Soc. Criminology, 1991, Nathan B. Eddy award Com. on Problems of Drug Dependence, 1993, Spl. Presdl. Commendation Am. Psychiat. Assn., 1999, Am. Acad. Arts and Scis., 1999, Commendation and Appreciation award Harvard Inst. Psychiat. Epidemiology and Genetics, 2000, Disting. Sci. Devel. award Soc. Rsch. in Child Devel., 2003; rsch. grantee NIMH, Nat. Inst. on Drug Abuse, Nat. Inst. on Alcohol Abuse and Alcoholism. Fellow Am. Coll. Epidemiology, Royal Coll. Psychiatrists (hon.), Am. Soc. Psychiatrists (hon.), Soc. Study of Addiction (hon.); mem. APHA (Rema Lapouse award 1979, Lifetime Achievement award sect. on alcohol and drug abuse 1994), Internat. Fedn. Psychiat. Epidemiology (com.1992-2002), World Psychiat. Assn. (sect. com. on epidemiology and cmty. psychiatry, 1985-2002, co-chmn. sect. on rsch. instruments in psychiatry), Soc. Life History Rsch. in Psychopathology, Am. Coll. Neuropsychopharmacology, Inst. Medicine, Am. Psychopath. Assn. (pres. 1987-88, Paul Hoch award 1978). Office: Washington U Med Sch Dept Psychiatry Saint Louis MO 63110 E-mail: lro6@aol.com.

ROBINS, MARJORIE MCCARTHY (MRS. GEORGE KENNETH ROBINS), civic worker; b. Oct. 4, 1914; d. Eugene Ross and Louise (Roblee) McCarthy; m. George Kenneth Robins, Nov. 9, 1940; children: Carol Robins Von Arx, G. Stephen, Barbara A. Robins Foorman. Mem. Mo. Libr. Commn., 1937-38; bd. dirs. St. Louis Jr. League, 1945-46, Occupational Therapy Workshop St. Louis, 1941-46, pres., 1945-46; bd. dirs. Ladue Chapel Nursery Sch., 1957-64, pres. bd., 1963-64; past regional chmn. United Fund; past mem. St. Louis Met. Youth Commn., St. Louis Health and Welfare Coun.; bd. dirs. Internat. Inst. St. Louis, 1966-72, 76-92, sec., 1968, v.p., 1981; bd. dirs. Mental Health Assn. St. Louis, 1963-70, Washington U. Child Guidance and Evaluation Clinic, 1968-78, Cen. Inst. for Deaf, 1970—, v.p., 1975-76, pres., 1976-78; bd. dirs. Met. St. Louis YWCA, 1954-74, pres. bd., 1960-63, trustee, 1977—; nat. bd. YWCA, 1967-79, nat. v.p., 1973-76; vol. tchr. remedial reading clinic St. Louis City Schs., 1968-71; trustee John Burroughs Sch., 1960-63, John Burroughs Found., 1965-80, Roblee Found., 1972—, Nat. YWCA Retirement Fund, 1979-88; bd. dirs. Gambrill Gardens United Meth. Retirement Home, 1979-85, Thompson Retreat and Conf. Center, 1981-87, Springboard to Learning Inc., 1980-98, v.p., 1980-90; tutor I Have A Dream Found., 1995-98. Mem. Archaeol. Inst. Am. (bd. dirs. 1993-95, 97-00, treas. St. Louis chpt. 1985-87, 93-95), Vassar Club (sec. and pres. 1939-40), Wednesday Club (dir. 1968-70, 77-81, 93-95), St. Louis. Home: 1 McKnight Pl Apt 265 Saint Louis MO 63124

ROBINSON, ALICE HELENE, English language educator, administrative assistant; b. Cleve., Oct. 16, 1946; d. Alford B. and Willie Helena (Knuckles) R. BA, Cleve. State U., 1968, MA, 1992; postgrad., John Carroll U. Cert. tchr. English, Ohio. English language educator Cleve. Bd. Edn., Ohio. Presenter 1st Celtic Conf. Cleve. State U., 1993. Cleve. Edn. Fund scholar, 1991. Mem.: Cleve. Mus. Art. Episcopalian. Avocations: collecting stamps, plates, and artifacts, word puzzles, logic problems. Home: 3344 E 142nd St Cleveland OH 44120-4009 Office: Cleve Bd Edn 1380 E 6th St Cleveland OH 44114-1606

ROBINSON, ALICE JEAN MCDONNELL, retired drama and speech educator; b. St. Joseph, Mo., Nov. 17, 1922; d. John Francis and Della M. (Mavity) McDonnell; m. James Eugene Robinson, Apr. 21, 1956 (dec. 1983). BA, U. Kans., 1944, MA, 1947; PhD, Stanford U., 1965. Tchr. Garden City (Kans.) High Sch., 1944-46; asst. prof. Emporia (Kans.) State U., 1947-52; dir. live programs Sta. KTVH-TV, Hutchinson-Wichita, Kans., 1953-55; assoc. prof. drama and speech U. Md. Baltimore County, Balt., 1966-99, rsch. theatre history. Author: The American Theatre: A History in Slides, 1992, Betty Comden and Adolph Green: A Bio-Bibliography, 1993; co-editor: Notable Women in the American Theatre, 1989; appeared in plays, including Landscape, 1983, Tartuffe, 1985, Rockaby, 1990. Mem. Am. Soc. Theatre Rsch., Assn. Theatre Higher Edn., Phi Beta Kappa. Republican. Avocations: travel, reading, acting, directing. Home: 111 N Main St Caldwell KS 67022-1535

ROBINSON, ANGELA TOMEI, clinical laboratory technologist, laboratory manager; b. Bklyn., June 5, 1957; d. Leo James and Nina Angela T.; m. John C. Robinson, Sept. 27, 1987. BS, St. John's U., 1979, MS, 1985. Cert. lab. technologist. Exec. sec. Stead-fast Temporaries, Inc., N.Y.C., 1975—79; chief med. technologist Winthrop-U. Hosp., Mineola, NY, 1979—98, adminstrv. lab. coord., edn. coord., lab. info. mgr., 1998—; coord., founder Nat. Med. Lab. Week, Mineola, 1981—; tech. supr., lab. mgr., cons. Hilton Med. Group, Hempstead, NY, 1993—96; lab. technologist Cardiovasc. Group, Garden City, NY, 1996—2000, lab. mgr., 2000—. Lab. cons. Gastroenterology Group, Mineola, NY, 1998—2000; staff contbr. newsletter, in pub. rels. Winthrop-U. Hosp., Mineola, 1981—, com. mem., clin. instr. for rctng. personnel in lab., chmn. com. to petition salary increases, 1987—90, Vision 2000 redesign team, 1997—98; adj. prof. seminar C.W. Post Coll., Westbury, NY, 1992—, edn. coord., 1998—2002; adj. prof. SUNY, Farmingdale, 1999—, advisor, 1999—, com. advisor, Stony Brook, 1995—, Jr. Achievement, 2003; rep. Nassau Suffolk Health Manpower Plan, 1991; team mem. vision 2000 NIH, 1997—98; com. rep. SJU Ann. Clin. Lab Sem., 1998—; jr. vol. cons., 2002; advisor Nassau C.C., 1999—; cons. Mentorship of L.I., 2003—; lectr. in field. Author: (poetry) Our World's Best Loved Poems, 1984 (2d place merit cert. 1983) contbr. articles to profl. jours. Singer Blessed Sacrament Ch. Choir, Bklyn., 1971-73, coord., singer ch. folk group, 1971-79; mem. Mothers Against Drunk Driving, 1985-87, Nat. Rep. Congl. Com., 1984-86, Am. Health Found., 1986-87, DAV, 1984-87, Noise Pollution Clearinghouse, 2003—; fundraiser Statue of Liberty/Ellis Island Found., 1985-86, 95-96, Hands Across Am., 1986, U.S. Olympic Team Spirit, 1992—, U.S. English First, Nat. Mus. Am. Indians; mentoring ptnr. L.I. Mentor, 2003—, jr. vol. mem., 2003—; mem. Noise Pollution Clearinghouse, 2003-. Recipient cert. of merit N.Y. State Senate, 1985, citation Gov. N.Y. State Pres. Soc., 1975; award St. John's U. Med. Tech. Alumni, 1992 Mem. Am. Soc. Clin. Lab. Sci., Profl. Stds. Coalition Clin. Lab. Pers., Am. Soc. Clin. Pathologists (registered), Made in the U.S. Found., N.Y. State Soc. Clin. Lab. Sci. (chmn. govt. liason com., state bd. dirs. 1988—, Outstanding Med. Tech. Student award 1979, Member of Yr. award 1995, founding officer Nassau-Suffolk chpt. 1985-86, bd. dirs., seminar moderator 1985-87, pres. elect 1986-87, 90-91, pres. 1991—, membership com. 1991, state chairperson 1993—), Profl. STDS Coalition (pub. rels. chair 1993—, co-chair 1997—), Theta Phi Alpha (alumni chmn. 1976-77, alumni-collegiate rep. 1986-87). Avocations: piano, guitar, gardening, singing, tennis.

ROBINSON, ANN, state representative; b. Aberdeen, Wash., Oct. 9, 1947; m. Marvin Robinson. AAS, Casper Coll., 1987, AA, 1991. Engring.-regulatory technician Oil and Gas Industry, 1979—86; paralegal Confidential Adoption Intermediary, 1991—; state rep. dist. 58 Wyo. State Legis., Cheyenne, 1997—. Mem. Edn. com. Wyo. State Legis., Cheyenne, mem. Labor, Health and Social Svcs.; editor Wyo. State Dem. Newspaper The Spokesman, 1979—81. Vol. Concerned Citizens for Quality Nursing Home Care. Mem.: DAR, Nat. Fedn. Paralegal Assns., Wyo. Old-Time Fiddlers Assn., Casper Antique and Collectors Club. Democrat. Home: 1923 Grass Creek Rd Casper WY 82601 Office: Capitol Bldg Wyo State Legis Cheyenne WY 82002

ROBINSON, ANNETTE, councilwoman; married; six children. Dist. dir. Office of Congresswoman Majorie Owens; coord., liaison Comptr. Harrison J. Goldin; councilwoman Dist. 36 N.Y.C. Coun., Bklyn., 1992—. Mem. NAACP, Vanguard Ind. Dem. Assn. (exec. com.), Coalition for Cmty. Empowerment (exec. mem.), Knights and Ladies of Peter Claver Ladies Aux., South African Sisters Against Aparteid, African Am. Clergy and Elected Ofcls. Office: Rm 417 1360 Fulton St Ste 417 Brooklyn NY 11216-2600

ROBINSON, ANNETTMARIE, entrepreneur; b. Fayetteville, Ark., Jan. 31, 1940; d. Christopher Jacy and Lorena (Johnson) Simmons; m. Roy Robinson, June 17, 1966; children: Steven, Sammy, Doug, Pamela, Olen. BA, Edison Tech. U., 1958; BA in Bus., Seattle Community Coll., 1959. Dir. perss. Country Kitchen Restaurants, Inc., Anchorage, 1966-71; investor Anchorage, 1971—. Cons. Pioneer Investments, Anchorage, 1983—, M'RAL, Inc. Retail Dry Goods, Anchorage, 1985; owner Cons. Co., Reno, 1998—. Mem. Rep. Presdl. Task Force, Washington, 1984—, Reps. of Alaska, Anchorage, 1987; mem. chmn. round table YMCA, Anchorage, 1986—; active Sta. KWN2, KQLO, Reno, Nev.; active in child abuse issues and prosecution; dir., sec. Hunter Lake Townhouse Assn., Reno, Sta. KSRU and KHOG-Radio, KIHM Cath. Radio, Reno, 1996—, KOZZ Radio, 2000—; ; mem. Cmty. Assn. Inst. Condo/Coop./Townhouse Law, 1999—. Named Woman of Yr. Lions, Anchorage, 1989, marksman first class Nat. Rifle Assn., 1953. Mem. Porsche Club of Am. (racing team 1998—). Avocations: egyptology, theology, archeology, shooting, fishing.

ROBINSON, BARBARA PAUL, lawyer; b. Oct. 19, 1941; d. Leo and Pauline G. Paul; m. Charles Raskob Robinson, June 11, 1965; children: Charles Paul, Torrance Webster. AB magna cum laude, Bryn Mawr Coll., 1962; LLB, Yale U., 1965, Order of the Coif. Bar: N.Y. 1966, U.S. Dist. Ct. (so. and ea. dists.) N.Y. 1975, U.S. Tax Ct. 1972, U.S. Ct. Appeals (2d cir.) 1974. Assoc. Debevoise & Plimpton (formerly Debevoise, Plimpton, Lyons & Gates), N.Y.C., 1966-75, ptnr., 1976—; commr. Mayor's Commn. on Women's Issues, 2003—. Mem. adv. bd. Practicing Law Inst.; bd. dirs. Am. Arbitration Assn., 1987—2003, Sch. Choice Scholarships Found. Mem. bd. editors: Chase Jour., 1997—2001; contbr. articles to profl. jours. Mem. adv. coun., bd. vis. CUNY Law Sch., Queens, 1984—90; active Coun. on Fgn. Rels.; trustee Trinity Sch., 1982—86, pres., 1986—88; bd. dirs. Found. for Child Devel., 1989—2000, 2001—, chmn., 1991—2000; bd. dirs. Catalyst, 1993—, Fund for Modern Cts., 1990—2003, Wave Hill, 1994—, Garden Conservancy, 1996—2002, Lawyers Com. for Civil Rights Under Law, 1997—, William Nelson Cromwell Found., 1993—, Irish Legal Rsch. Found. Inc., 1996—, Citizens Union Found. Inc., 1996—; trustee Bryn Mawr Coll., 2000—. Recipient Laura Parsons Pratt award, 1996. Fellow Am. Coll. Trust and Estate Counsel, Am. Bar Found., N.Y. Bar Found.; mem. ABA (commn. on women in profession 1999-2002), N.Y. State Bar

Assn. (vice chmn. com. on trust adminstrn., trusts and estates law sect. 1977-81, ho. of dels. 1984-87, 90-92, com. ann. award 1993-94), Assn. of Bar of City of N.Y. (chmn. com. on trusts, estates and surrogates cts. 1981-84, judiciary com. 1981-84, coun. on jud. adminstrn. 1982-84, chair nominating com. 1984-85, 99—, exec. com. 1986-91, chair 1989-90, v.p. 1990-91, pres. 1994-96, chair com. on honors 1993-94, com. on long-range planning 1991-94, co-chair coun. on childen 1997-99), Assn. of Bar of City of N.Y. [Fund Inc.] (bd. dirs. 2000-03, pres.1994-96), Women's Forum, Yale Coun., Yale Law Sch. Assn. N.Y. (devel. bd., exec. com. 1981-85, pres. 1988-93), The Century Assn., Yale Club, Washington Club, Order of Coif. Office: Debevoise & Plimpton 919 Third Ave New York NY 10022 E-mail: bprobinson@debevoise.com.

ROBINSON, BERNICE JOYCE, secondary school educator; d. Edwin Samuel and Ruth Selena Mckinley; m. Padmore Agbemabiese, May 2, 2003; children: Marc, Sherri, Sena Agbemabiese, Elikplim Agbemabiese. MA, Hunter Coll., N.Y.C., 1958. Music tchr. N.Y. Bd. Of Edn., N.Y.C., 1958—63, Columbus Bd. of Edn., Ohio, 1965—. Min. of music St. Philip Episc.l Ch., Columbus, 1983—. Dir.(performer): (classical jazz keyboardist). Music condr. Mass Ecumenical Choirs, Columbus, 1975—2003. Recipient Cmty. Svc. award, Omega Psi Phi, 2003. Mem.: Delta Omicron (corr.). Episcopalian. Avocation: drama. Home: 7669 Swindon St Blacklick OH 43004

ROBINSON, BRENDA KAY, editor, public relations professional; b. Flint, Mich., May 15, 1946; d. Albert Coleburn and Kathryn Mary (Salay) Moore; m. Richard F. Robinson, Feb. 6, 1970; 1 child, Kelly Dawn. AS in Fashion, Garland Jr. Coll., 1967. Actress Actor's Workshop and Repertory Co., West Palm Beach, Fla., 1980-82; asst. store mgr. Pavo Real Sculpture Gallery, Boca Raton, Fla., 1987-88; freelance artist, illustrator, coloring book designer Troy, Mich., 1972—; freelance editor, writer Delray Beach, Fla., 1995—; v.p., editor Dick Robinson Co., Delray Beach, 1979—; editor, writer Legacy Scribe LLC, 2003—; pub. rels. dir. Unity of Delray Beach Ch., 1996-99, 2004—; sales office profl. men's dept. and designer salon Saks Fifth Ave., Troy, Mich., 1968-72; actress Actor's Workshop and Repertory Co., West Palm Beach, 2002—03. Cons. Mary Kay Cosmetics, 1983-84. Author, illustrator (coloring book with text) Boca Raton Animal Shelter Coloring Book, 1993. Puppeteer Kids on the Block shows Assn. for Retarded Citizens, West Palm Beach, Fla., 1981-85; bd. treas. Windemere House Condominium Assn., Delray Beach, 1993, bd. sec., 1994, 2003. Republican. Avocations: Web surfing, walking, bichon frise dogs, improvisational comedy acting. Home and Office: 250 S Ocean Blvd Apt 252 Delray Beach FL 33483-6752 E-mail: brenda515@adelphia.net.

ROBINSON, CAROL SUSAN, special education educator; b. Bethesda, Md., Dec. 1, 1958; d. Bryan Wright and Julia Hill Willingham Robinson. BA, Davidson Coll., 1980; MEd, Vanderbilt U., 1983; PhD, Fla. State U., 2002. Tchr. Vanderbilt Child and Adolescent Psychiatry Hosp., Nashville, 1984—87; dir. spl. edn. Christ Presbyn. Acad., Nashville, 1987—97; postdoctoral fellow Fla. Ctr. Reading Rsch., Tallahassee, 2002—03; asst. prof. spl. edun. Ind. State U., Terre Haute, Ind., 2003—. Vol. Reading for Blind, Nashville, 1991—98; vol. food bank Killearn United Meth. Ch., Tallahassee, 1998—2001, tchr. Sunday sch. Thomas Watson fellow, Thomas Watson Found., 1980—81. Mem.: Learning Disabilities Assn., Nat. Coun. Tchrs. Math., Coun. Exceptional Children, Phi Eta Sigma, Phi Kappa Phi, Pi Lambda Theta, Phi Delta Kappa. Democrat. Avocations: photography, piano. Office Phone: 812-237-8455. E-mail: eerobins@isugw.indstate.edu.

ROBINSON, CARRIE, pastor; b. Balt., Jan. 11, 1945; d. Charles Dingle and Anna Lemmon; m. Bill Robinson, Nov. 26, 1977 (dec. June 2, 2003); children: Michael Stukes, Maurice Johnson, Monica Johnson. Doctorate, Interdenominational Coll.; degree in Christian edn., Theol. Sem. and Coll. Notary pub. Pastor Prayer and Faith Ministries Bapt. Ch., Balt., 1987—. Sec. United Bapt. Conf., Balt., 1990—, v.p., 2000—. Mem.: Internat. Women Ministerial Alliance (v.p. 2000—), Order of Ea. Star (Helen Benton House # 34). Avocations: singing, reading, computers, drumming. Home: 1754 Wycliffe Ave Parkville MD 21234-6824 Office: Prayer and Faith Ministries Bapt Ch Inc 1865 N Gay St Baltimore MD 21213 E-mail: crrrbn@aol.com.

ROBINSON, CHALITA BROSSETT, art educator, artist; b. New Orleans, Feb. 3, 1946; d. Ellis Joseph Brossett and Onita Calvey; m. Larry Robinson, Jr., June 24, 1972 (dec. Apr. 22, 1994); children: Lauren Alyce, Dana Estelle. BA, Xavier U., 1967; MFA, Mich. State U., 1969. Prof. art Kern C.C. Dist., Bakersfield, Calif., 1969—. Dir. Bakersfield (Calif.) Coll. Gallery, 1974—79; trustee Bakersfield (Calif.) Mus. Art, 1999—2003; chmn. Art Dept. Bakersfield (Calif.) Coll., 1985—90, 2001—. Prin. works include Passages Suite, 1993, Walls and Windows and Wings, 2000, Eve's Journey, 2003. Named Arts Educator of Yr., Arts Coun. Kern, 1996; recipient, 2002. Home: 2613 Crest Drive Bakersfield CA 93306 Office: Bakersfield College 1801 Panorama Drive Bakersfield CA 93305

ROBINSON, CHERYL JEAN, human services specialist, advocate; b. Bklyn., June 26, 1947; d. George Harry and Maude DeCota Williams; life ptnr. Sybil Virginia Jones, Dec. 1, 1979; children: Zuleika Marie Nathaniel, Karima Melody. AS, San Diego Mesa Coll., 1982. Cert. cmty. econ. devel. San Diego State U., 1997, meeting and event planning San Diego State U., 2002. Asst. storefront dir. Ctr. for Women's Studies and Svcs., San Diego, 1979—84; circulation mgr. The Longest Revolution, San Diego, 1980—84; bookkeeper Potts by Patt, San Diego, 1984—88; human svc. specialist County of San Diego - Health and Human Svc. Agy., 1988—. Treas. U.S.S. Dixion Legal Def. Fund, San Diego, 1980—82, San Diego Gay Ctr., 1981—82; bd. mem. San Diego Lesbians, Gay, Bisexual and Transgender Pride, 1991—2001; student project advisor cmty. econ. devel. cert. program San Diego State U., 1999—; cmty. activist San Diego City Police LGBT Adv. Bd., 2001—; comm. chair Ebony Pride, San Diego, 2002—. Area 1 del. Internat. Assn. of Lesbian, Gay, Bisexual and Transgender Pride Coords., 1993—94; mem. Lesbians of Color, San Diego, 1978—80; facilitator Lesbian Solidarity, San Diego, 1980—83; publicity chair Spectrum, San Diego, 1986—88; promotional chair North Pk. Main St., San Diego, 1996, spring festival chair, 1996—2002; cmty. mem. San Diego Police Lesbian, Gay, Bisexual, Transgender Adv. Bd., San Diego, 2001—03; mem. San Diego Dem. Club, 2002; pers. chair San Diego Lesbian, Gay, Bisexual, Transgender Pride, 1991—2000; mem. San Diego Electric Streetcar, Inc, 2002. Recipient Spl. Commendation, City Coun. San Diego, 1994, City San Diego - Dist. Three, 1997, Cert. of Appreciation, San Diego Lesbian and Gay Pride, 1999, Presidents Award for Com. Mem. of the Yr., North Pk. Main St., 2001. Liberal. Achievements include development of California Main Street Certification. Home: 6372 1/2 Brooklyn Ave San Diego CA 92114-2724 Personal E-mail: cj.robins@cox.net.

ROBINSON, CHERYL JEFFREYS, special education educator, consultant; d. William Charles and Dorothy Crawford Jeffreys; m. Norman Norris Robinson, June 21, 1975; children: Nicole Lorraine, Natalie Lavonne. BS summa cum laude, DC Tchrs. Coll., 1976; MA, George Washington U., 1977; EdD, Nova Southeastern U., 2003. Advanced profl. cert. Md. State Dept. Edn. Diagnostic-prescriptive tchr. Prince George's County Md. Pub. Schs., 1977—83, spl. edn. resource tchr., 1984—90, regional spel. edn. specialist, 1990—, spl. edn. area office mgr., 2001—02. Mem. adv. com. rep. Summer Inst. Nova Southeastern U., Ft. Lauderdale, Fla., 1997; planned and facilitated tchr. ADHD tng., 1998—2001; facilitator sch. staff/parent program ADHD students, 2000—01; mem. sch. CEO's faculty support team, 2003—. Mem.: AAUW (Career Devel. grantee 1997—98), Prince George's County Educators Assn., Nat. Educators Assn., Coun. Exceptional Children, Nat. Coun. Negro Women, Kappa Delta Pi, Alpha Kappa Alpha. Democrat. Baptist. Avocations: art, crafts, antiques, theater. Office: Prince Georges County Pub Schs Oxon Hill Staff Devel Ctr 7711 Livingston Rd Oxon Hill MD 20745 Personal E-mail: robinson@radix.net.

ROBINSON, CLEO PARKER, artistic director; Degree in Dance Edn. Psychology, Denver U., DFA (hon.), 1991. Founder, exec. artistic dir., choreographer Cleo Parker Robinson Dance, Denver. Mem. dance, [expansion] arts and inter-arts panels NEA; bd. dirs. Denver Ctr. Performing Arts; tchr. in workshops. Co-creator (documentary) African-Americans at Festae, Run Sister Run, (film) Black Women in the Arts, (music video) Borderline. Apptd. Nat. Coun. on Arts, 1999. Recipient Thelma Hill Ctr. for the Performing Arts award, 1986; Choreography fellow NEA; named one of Colo. 100, 1992; named to Blacks in Colo. Hall of Fame, 1994. Mem. Internat. Assn. Blacks in Dance (2nd v.p.). Office: Cleo Parker Robinson Dance 119 Parker Ave W Denver CO 80205

ROBINSON, CRYSTAL, professional basketball player; b. Atoka, Okla., Jan. 22, 1974; d. Billy and Nancy Robinson. Grad., S.E. Okla. State, 1996. Forward, WNBA New York Liberty, N.Y.C., 1999—. Named MVP, U.S. Sports Festival, 1993; named to Nat. Assoc. of Intercollegiate Athletics Hall of Fame, 2003; recipient ABL Rookie of the Yr. award, 1996—97.

ROBINSON, DEBORAH J. counselor, educator, educational consultant; b. Buffalo; d. Daniel L. and Barbara A. Robinson. BA, Canisius Coll., Buffalo, 1974; MS in Student Pers. Adminstrn., Buffalo State Coll., 1981. Notary pub., N.Y. Counselor U. Buffalo-Buffalo Ednl. Talent Search, 1982; residential mgr. Women's Residential Resource Ctr., Buffalo, 1986-88; GED coord. aide and tutor JUSENDO, Buffalo, 1988-89; counselor, coord. Trott ACCESS Ctr. Niagara County C.C., Sanborn, N.Y., 1989-91, coord. women in tech. program, 1992, CEOSC counselor, 1992-93, placement counselor, 1993-95, counselor, 1995—. Cons. Cmty. Action Orgn., Edn. Task Force, Buffalo; mem. Ellicott Dist. Concerned Taxpayers, Buffalo; evaluator commn. on higher edn. Middle States Assn. Colls., 1998—. Mentor Buffalo Youth for Golf, Inc., 2002. Recipinet Niagara County Black Achievers, Inc. award, 1998. Mem. AAUW, Career Devel. Orgn., Di GAmma. Avocations: collecting elephants, reading, stock market. Office: Niagara County CC 3111 Saunders Settlement Rd Sanborn NY 14132-9487

ROBINSON, DOROTHY K. lawyer; b. New Haven, Feb. 18, 1951; children: Julia Robinson Bouwsma, Alexandra Toby Bouwsma. BA in Econs. with honors, Swarthmore Coll., 1972; JD, U. Calif., Berkeley, 1975; MA (hon.), Yale U., 1987. Bar: Calif. 1975, N.Y. 1976, Conn. 1981, U.S. Ct. Appeals (2d cir.) 1975, U.S. Dist. Ct. (so. dist.) N.Y. 1981. Assoc. Hughes Hubbard & Reed, N.Y.C., 1975-78; asst. gen. counsel Yale U., New Haven, 1978-79, assoc. gen. counsel, 1979-84, dep. gen. counsel, 1984-86, gen. counsel, 1986-95, dir. fed. rels., 1986-88, acting sec., 1993, v.p., gen. counsel, 1995—. Mem. Calif. Law Rev., 1973-75. Trustee Hopkins Grammar Day Prospect Hill Sch., New Haven, 1983-88, sec., 1986-88; trustee Wenner-Gren Found. Anthrop. Rsch., 1991-2003; bd. dirs. Cold Spring Sch., New Haven, 1990-95; mem. adv. bd. Conn. Mental Health Ctr., New Haven, 1979-89; bd. dirs. Nat. Assn. Ind. Coll. and Univs., 1995-98; mem. alumni coun. Swarthmore Coll., 1999-2002. Fellow Ezra Stiles Coll. Yale U., Am. Bar Found.; mem. ABA, Nat. Assn. Coll. and Univ. Attys. (bd. dirs. 1987-90), Conn. Bar Assn., Calif. Bar Assn., Assn. Bar City N.Y., Phi Beta Kappa. Office: Yale U Office of Gen Counsel PO Box 208255 New Haven CT 06520-8255

ROBINSON, ELLA D. state agency administrator; b. Ky. Bank examiner Dept. Fin. Insts., 1977—84, dir. thrift insts., 1984—93, dir. divsn. supervision, 1993—96, dep. commr., 1996—99, acting commr., 1997—98, 1999, commr., 1999—. Mem. Ky. State Treas. Commn. on Personal Savs. and Investment; chmn. Fin. Insts. Bd.; vice chmn. Dist. II Conf. State Bank Suprs., mem. nom. com., 2002—, mem. planning com.; team mem. PSC Ann. Rev. Mem.: Nat. Assn. Consumer Credit Adminstrs. (past bd. mem.), Nat. Assn. State Credit Union Suprs. (bd. mem. 1985—95, past pres., vice chmn. performance standards com.). Office: 1025 Capital Ctr Dr Frankfort KY 40601

ROBINSON, ELLA GARRETT, editor, writer; b. Decatur, Ala., Apr. 12, 1954; d. Calvis Clemon and Jewell Helms Garrett; m. Daniel Robinson, May 7, 1976. BA, Samford U., Birmingham, AL, 1972—76. Editl. asst. Woman's Missionary Union, Birmingham, Ala., 1976—94; copy editor/writer freelance, Pleasant Grove, Ala., 1994—. Author: (book) A Guide to Literary Sites of the South, 1998. Mem.: Ala. Media Profls. Home: 735 Seventh Pl Pleasant Grove AL 35127 Personal E-mail: ERobnson@aol.com.

ROBINSON, EMILY SUE, music educator; b. Henryetta, Okla., Mar. 1, 1952; d. William Gilbert and Frances (Meyer) Campbell; m. Robert Thomas Robinson, Apr. 16, 1972; children: Juliette Renae Kidd, Tamara Kaye Clemence, Samuel Thomas. MusB, Oklahoma City U., 1974; MusM, U. Okla., 1990. Piano instr., Midwest City, Okla., 1976—; accompanist Rose State Coll., Midwest City, 1986—, adj. prof., 1988—2000, prof., 2000—; accompanist Midwest Choral Soc., Midwest City, 1992—2000. Organist Midwest Blvd. Christian Ch., Midwest City, 1971-74; accompanist Chouteau Acad. Ballet, Oklahoma City, 1972-75, music dir. Eastminster United Presbyn. Ch., Del City, 1975—. Mem. Okla. Music Tchrs. Assn. (adjudicator 1994—), Ctrl. Oklahoma Music Tchrs. Assn. (historian 1996-98). Home: 332 W Campbell Dr Midwest City OK 73110-3318 Office: Rose State Coll 6420 SE 15th St Midwest City OK 73110-2704

ROBINSON, EVELYN EDNA, secondary school educator; b. St. John, Maine, Feb. 23, 1911; d. Registe Jalbert and Olive Michaud; m. Carl Robinson, July 19, 1939; children: Robert, James. BA in Math., U. Maine, 1934; MS, U. N.H., 1963; MEd, Hillyer Coll. U., 1960. Tchr. English and math. Ft. Kent (Maine) H.S., 1934; tchr. English and math., coach girls basketball Madewaska (Maine) H.S., 1935-55; tchr. math. Stamford (Conn.) H.S., 1955-56; tchr. math and English, Bristol (Conn.) H.S., 1956-63; prof. math. Worcester (Mass.) State Coll., 1963-77, chmn. dept., 1970-77. Coord. cmty. bus. Worcester State Coll., 1970-77, class advisor, 1968-72, salary equity bd., 1971-73. Vol. libr. Madawaska Pub. Libr., 1936-55; lector Christ the King, Worcester, 1974-2000. Mem. Delta Kappa Gamma. Republican. Roman Catholic. Avocations: decorating, flower arrangements, ceramics, tailoring. Home: 12 Brookside Ave Worcester MA 01602

ROBINSON, FLORINE SAMANTHA, marketing executive; b. Massies Mill, Va., Feb. 4, 1935; d. John Daniel and Fannie Belle (Smith) Jackson; m. Frederick Robinson (div. 1973); children: Katherine, Theresa, Freda. BS, Morgan State U., 1976; postgrad., U. Balt., 1977-81, Liberty U., 1987. Writer, reporter Phila. Independent News, 1961-63; freelance writer, editor Balt., 1963-71; asst. mng. editor Williams & Wilkins Pubs. Inc., Balt, 1971-76; mktg. rep., then mktg. mgr. NCR Corp., Balt., 1977-93; assoc. minister, trustee Christian Unity Temple, Balt., 1976—; pres. ABCOM, Inc., Balt., 1993—. Bd. dirs. Armstrong & Bratcher, Inc., Balt. Editor: Stedman's Medical Dictionary, 1972; contbr. articles to profl. jours. Active PTA, Balt., 1963-65; bd. dirs. Howard Pk. Civic Assn., Balt., 1967—, pres. 1991—; leader, cons. Girl Scouts USA, 1970-73. Recipient Excellence in Rsch. award Psi Chi, 1976, Citizen citation Mayor of Balt. Mem. NAFE, Mid-Atlantic Food Dealers Assn., Am. Soc. Notaries, Internat. Platform Assn., Edelweiss Club, Order of Eastern Star. Democrat. Avocation: piano. Home: 3126 Howard Park Ave Baltimore MD 21207-6715

ROBINSON, GAIL PATRICIA, retired mental health counselor; b. Medford, Oreg., Dec. 31, 1936; d. Ivan T. and Evelyn H. (Hamilton) Skyrman; m. Douglas L. Smith; children: Shauna J., James D. BS in Edn., Oreg. State U., 1958, PhD in Counseling, 1978; MS in Counseling, Western Oreg. State Coll., 1974. Tchr. Monterey (Calif.) Pub. Schs., 1958-59, Corvallis (Oreg.) Pub. Schs., 1959-62, 69-75, counselor, 1977-81; pvt. practice Corvallis, 1977-95. Vol. therapist Children's Svcs. divsn., Linn and Benton Counties, 1982-83; asst. prof. Western Oreg. State coll., 1977, counselor, 1982-83; mem. grad. faculty Oreg. State U., Corvallis, 1978-95; presenter workshops, lectr. in field. Contbr. articles to profl. jours. Mem. Benton County Mental Health Citizens Adv. Bd., 1979-85, chair, 1982-83; trustee WCTU Children's Farm Home, 1978-84, chair child welfare com., 1982-83, pres., 1984; mem. Old Mill Sch. Adv. Bd., 1979-85, chair, 1979-81; bd. dirs. Cmty. Outreach, 1979-83; mem. Benton Com. for Prevention of Child Abuse, 1979-85, v.p., 1982; mem. Oreg. Bd. Lic. Profl. Counselors and Therapists, 1989-95, chair, 1989-90. Mem. ACA (govt. rels. com. 1988-91, professionalization com. 1988-92, pres. 1996-97), Am. Mental Health Counselors Assn. (chair consumer and pub. rels. com. 1988-91, bd. dirs. Western region 1989-91, chair strategic planning com. 1994-95, pres. 1992-93), Oreg. Counseling Assn. (chair licensure liaison com. 1985-91, exec. bd. 1985-88, steering com. 1986-87, register editorial com. 1985-86, Disting. Svc. award 1985, 87, Leona Tyler award 1989), Oreg. Mental Health Counselors Assn. E-mail: robinsgp@ipns.com.

ROBINSON, GLENDA CAROLE, pharmacist; b. Johnson City, Tenn. d. Harry and Jackie Evelyn Bowers; m. Richard Haynes Robinson, 1967 (div. 1985); children: Rachel Corianne, Fredrick David. BS in Pharmacy, U. Tenn., 1967. Pharmacist supr. Sommers Drug Stores, San Antonio, 1968-69; staff pharmacist Crawford Long Hosp., Atlanta, 1971-72, Rich's Pharmacy, Atlanta, 1973-74; relief staff pharmacist Atchley Drug Ctr., Greeneville, Tenn., 1977-86; staff pharmacist Takoma Hosp. Pharmacy, Greeneville, 1983-86, Greene Valley Developmental Ctr., Greeneville, 1987-91, dir. pharmacy, 1991—. Mem. First Dist. Pharmacy Assn. East Tenn., Greeneville Jr. Women's Club (sec., internat. affairs chair), Greeneville Morning Rotary Club (pres., Polio Plus chair, Outstanding Rotarian 1996-97, Found. Dist. Svc. award 1998-99).

ROBINSON, HELENE M. retired music educator; b. Eugene, Oreg., May 30, 1912; d. Kirkman K. and Emily A. Robinson. BA in Music, U. Oreg., 1935; MusM, Northwestern U., Evanston, Ill., 1945. Piano tchr. No. Ariz. U., Flagstaff, 1952—60, Calif. State U., Fullerton, 1960—61, U. Calif., Santa Barbara, 1961—62, Ariz. State U., Tempe, 1963—77. Author: Basic Piano for Adults, vol. I and II, 1964, Intermediate Piano for Adults, vols. I and II, 1970; author: (with others) Teaching Piano in Classroom and Studio; contbr. articles to profl. jours. Mem.: Music Tchrs. Nat. Assn. (spkr. convs. 1974—76), Phi Beta. Avocation: piano. Home: 1300 NE 16th Ave # 315 Portland OR 97232

ROBINSON, JACQUELINE J. health services administrator, accountant; b. Iola, Kans., Mar. 23, 1947; d. Clarence Leslie and Marie Irene (Pearman) R.; m. Benjamin Thomas Toll, Nov. 27, 1967 (div. Nov. 1987); children: Dacia Ianthe, Thaddeus Nathaniel, Allegra Alexandra. BS in Acctg. and Mgmt. Sci., Avila Coll., 1979, MBA in Acctg., 1981, MBA in Health Care Adminstrn., 1994. Cert. mgmt. acct. Assoc. adminstr. fin. Clinicare Family Health Svcs., Kansas City, Kans., 1979-82; CFO Alexian Bros. Health Mgmt., Kansas City, Mo., 1982-87; internal auditor Hillhaven Corp., Overland Park, Kans., 1987-88; reimbursement specialist Bapt. Med. Ctr., Kansas City, Mo., 1988-90; contr. Parklane Med. Ctr., Kansas City, Mo., 1990-93; decision support mgr. Columbia/HCA, Selma, Ala. and El Paso, 1994-98; decision support specialist Magnolia Regional Health Ctr., Corinth, Miss., 1998-99; decision support coord. Citrus Meml. Hosp., Inverness, Fla., 1999—2001. Mem. Friends of the Zoo, Kansas City, 1986-94. Mem. Nat. Trust for Hist. Preservation, Inst. Mgmt. Accts., Inst. Cert. Mgmt. Accts. Office: 3250 SW 41st Pl Gainesville FL 34608

ROBINSON, JANET L. publishing executive; BA cum laude in English, Salve Regina Coll., 1972; diploma in Exec. Edn., Dartmouth U., 1996; DBA (hon.), Salve Regina U., 1998. Tchr., reading specialist, 1972—83; account exec., Tennis Mag. The N.Y. Times Co., 1983—85, nat. resort and travel mgr., Golf Digest/Tennis, 1985—87, advt. dir., Tennis Mag., 1987—90, v.p. advt. sales and mktg., The Women's Mag. Group, 1990—92, group sr. v.p., advt. sales and mktg., The Women's Mag. Group, 1992—93, v.p., dir. advt., 1994, sr. v.p. advt., 1995, pres., gen. mgr., N.Y. Times newspaper, 1996—, sr. v.p. newspaper ops., 2001—04, exec. v.p., COO, 2004—. Cons. Dept. Edn., Mass., 1977—83. Mem. Literacy Vols. N.Y.; mem. adv. bd. Salve Regina Coll. Named Outstanding Newspaper Exec., Frohlinger's Mktg. Report, 1994. Mem.: Women in Comm., Advt. Women N.Y., Advt. Club N.Y. Office: NY Times 229 W 43rd St New York NY 10036-3959

ROBINSON, JEANNE LOUISE, writer, educator; b. Portland, Oreg., Sept. 12, 1946; d. Louis Darell and Mary Louise (Lane) Gentry; m. Gini Mario Martini, June 13, 1965 (div. 1968); children: Deborah Corinna Martini, Darell James Martini; m. Joseph Ira Robinson, Dec. 5, 1998. Student, Northwestern Coll. Bus., Portland, 1968, Mt. Hood Community Coll., Gresham, Oreg., 1986. Treatment sec. RiverBend Youth Ctr., 1999—2002, ret., 2002. Co-compiler: Lebanon Pioneer Cemetery, 1991, rev. edit. 1995, Visitors' Guide to Oregon Historic Cemeteries, 1999. Apptd. to Oreg. Pioneer Cemetery Commn., 1995-1999 (chair, 1995-99). Mem. Geneal. Coun. Orgn. (sec. 1991-94), Geneal. Forum of Oreg., Oreg. Hist. Cemeteries Assn. (pres. 1992-96, exec. dir. 1997-2002). Avocation: genealogy. Home: 16385 SE 232nd Dr Boring OR 97009-8179 E-mail: ohca@integrity.com.

ROBINSON, JOAN LENORE, retired dietitian; b. Rochester, Minn., May 28, 1931; d. John Silas and Lenore Henrietta (Mittelstadt) Lundy; m. Donald N. Robinson, Sept. 17, 1960; children: Charles Lundy, Jonathan Paul. BS, U. Wash., 1953; MS, U. Minn., 1959. Dietetic intern Mass. Gen. Hosp., Boston, 1954; therapeutic dietitian Faulkner Hosp., Jamaica Plain and Boston, 1954-55; pediatric dietitian St. Mary's Hosp., Rochester, Minn., 1955-56; rsch. dietitian Lankenau Hosp., Phila., 1959-61; chief nutritionist, Children and Youth Project U. Louisville Med. Sch., 1968-69; cons. dietitian Eagleville (Pa.) Hosp. and Rehab. Ctr., 1977-78, North Penn Convalescent Residence, Lansdale, Pa., 1977-80, Ea. Mennonite Home, Souderton, Pa., 1980-81, River Crest, Mont Clare, Pa., 1973, 79-82, Arden Hall, Phila., 1983-84, Presbyn. Home for the Aged, Phila., 1978-95, Manatawny Manor, Pottstown, Pa., 1985-96. Mem. Trinity United Ch. of Christ, Collegeville, Pa., 1974-75, pres. women's guild; mem. Pa. State Extension Family Living Adv. Bd., Skippack, Pa., 1986-98. Mem. AAUW (life; Outstanding Women in Perkiomen Br. 1986), Am. Dietetic Assn., Pa. Dietetic Assn., Phila. Dietetic Assn., Mayo Found. Alumni, U. N.D. Alumni, Cons. Dietiticans in Health Care Facilities (sec.-trea. 1982-83), Collegeville Cmty. Club, Sigma Delta Epsilon. Home: 751 Spring Ln Lansdale PA 19446

ROBINSON, JUDITH RUTTENBERG, educator; d. Milton and Harriette Finestone Ruttenberg; m. Sanford Robinson, Sr., July 10, 1960 (dec. Nov. 1998); children: Sanford Jr., Heather, David. BA, U. Pitts., 1980. Owner, ptnr. RJK Sales, Inc., Pitts., 1987—97; editor Pitts. Ctr. for the Arts, 1987—89; tchr. Acad. Lifetime Learning, Carnegie Mellon U., Pitts., 1998—, C.C. Allegheny County, Pitts., 1999—2001. Lectr., workshop leader Pitts. Pub. Schs., 1997—. Author: (short story collection) The Beautiful Wife, 1996, poetry. Recipient J.D. Johnson award, Poet Mag., 1995, First Pl. Fiction, Taproot Lit. Jour., 1998, 1999. Mem.: Am. Poets and Writers.

ROBINSON, JULIE ANN, judge; b. 1957; BS, U. Kans., 1978, JD, 1981. Bar: Kans. 1981. Asst. U.S. atty. for dist. Kans. U.S. Dept. Justice, Kansas City, Kans., 1983-94, sr. litigation counsel, 1991-94; law clk. to hon. Benjamin E. Franklin, U.S. Bankruptcy Ct. for Dist. Kans., Kansas City, Kans., 1981-83, bankruptcy judge, 1994—2001; judge bankruptcy appellate panel U.S. Ct. Appeals (10th cir.), Kansas City, Kans., 1996—2001. Instr. trial practice U. Kans. Sch. Law, 1989-90. Fellow Am. Bar Found.; mem. ABA, Kans. Bar Assn., Kans. Inn of Ct. Office: US Dist Ct 405 US Courthouse 444 SE Quincy Topeka KS 66683

ROBINSON, JUNE KERSWELL, dermatologist, educator; b. Phila., Jan. 26, 1950; d. George and Helen S. (Kerswell) R.; m. William T. Barker, Jan. 31, 1981. BA cum laude, U. Pa., 1970; MD, U. Md., 1974. Diplomate Am. Bd. Dermatology, Nat. Bd. Med. Examiners, Am. Bd. Mohs Micrographic Surgery and Cutaneous Oncology. Intern Greater Balt. Med. Ctr., Hanover, NH, 1974, resident in medicine, 1974-75; resident in dermatology Dartmouth-Hitchcock Med. Ctr., Hanover, 1975-78, chief resident, clin. instr., 1977-78, instr. in dermatology, 1978; fellow Mohs; chemosurgery and dermatologic surgery NYU Skin and Cancer Clinic, N.Y.C., 1978-79; instr. in dermatology NYU, N.Y.C., 1979; asst. prof. dermatology Northwestern U. Med. Sch., Chgo., 1979, asst. prof. surgery, 1980-85, assoc. prof. dermatology and surgery, 1985-91, prof. dermatology and surgery, 1991-98; prof. medicine and pathology, dir. divsn. dermatology Cardinal Bernardin Cancer Ctr., Loyola U. Med. Ctr., 1998—, program leader skin cancer clin. program, 1998—. Mem. consensus devel. conf. NIH, 1992; mem. panel on use of sunscreens Internat. Agy. for Rsch. on Cancer, WHO, 2000; lectr. in field. Author: Fundamentals of Skin Biopsy, 1985, also audiovisual materials; editor: (textbooks) Atlas of Cutaneous Surgery, 1996, Cutaneous Medicine and Surgery: An Integrated Program in Dermatology, 1996; mem. editl. bd. Archives of Dermatology, 1988-97; sect. editor The Cutting Edge: Challenges in Med. and Surg. Therapeutics, 1989-97, editor, 2004—; contbg. editor Jour. Dermatol. Surgery and Oncology, 1985-88; mem. editl. com. 18th World Congress of Dermatology, 1982; contbr. numerous articles, abstracts to profl. publs., chpts. to books. Bd. dirs. Northwestern Med. Faculty Found., 1982-84, chmn. com. on benefits and leaves, 1984, nominating com. 1988. Grantee Nat. Cancer Inst., 1985-91, Am. Cancer Soc., 1986-89, Skin Cancer Found., 1984-85, Dermatology Found., 1981-83, Northwestern U. Biomed. Rsch., 1981, Syntex, 1984. Fellow: Am. Coll. Chemosurgery (chmn. sci. program ann. meeting 1983, chmn. publs. com. 1986—87, chmn. task force on ednl. needs 1989—90, co-editor bull. 1984—87); mem.: Chgo. Dermatol. Soc., Women's Dermatol. Soc. (pres. 1990—92, Wilma Bergeld, MD Visionary and Leadership award 2002), Soc. Investigative Dermatology, Am. Soc. Dermatol. Surgery (pres. 1994—95), Dermatology Found. (trustee 1995—98), Am. Acad. Dermatology (asst. sec.-treas. 1995—98, sec.-treas. 1998—2001, bd. dirs. 1993—95, Stephen Rothman Lectr. award 1992, Presdl. citation 1992, 2000), Am. Dermatol. Assn., Am. Cancer Soc. (pres. Ill. divsn. 1996—98). Home: 132 E Delaware Pl Apt 5806 Chicago IL 60611-4951

ROBINSON, JUNE P. columnist, retired special education educator; b. Seattle, Wash., June 10, 1925; BA in History, Seattle Coll., 1946; MA in History, Seattle U., 1970. Spl. edn. tchr. Seattle Pub. Schs., 1950—80; adminstrv. asst. office of pub. programs Nat. Archives, Washington, 1982—90; columnist Peninsula Daily News, Port Angeles, Wash., 1995—. Bd. dirs. Arlington Historical Soc., 1982—90; archivist Coun. for Exceptional Children, Arlington, Va., 1980—. Author: (book) Georgetown-That Was A Town, 1979, Pictorial History Clallam County, 2003; co-author: History of Clallam County, 2003. Mem.: Clallam Co. Hist. Soc. Home: 941 E Alder Sequim WA 98382

ROBINSON, LAURIE OVERBY, former assistant attorney general; b. Washington, July 7, 1946; d. Kermit and Ethel Esther (Schlasinger) Overby; m. Craig Baab, Oct. 22, 1977 (div. 1991); 1 child, Teddy Baab ; m. Sheldon Krantz, Dec. 8, 1991. BA in Polit. Sci. magna cum laude, Brown U., 1968. Desk editor Cmty. News Svc., N.Y.C., 1968-71; asst. staff dir. sect. criminal justice ABA, Washington, 1972-74, dir. sect. criminal justice, 1979-93; assoc. dep. atty. gen. U.S. Dept. Justice, Washington, 1993-94, asst. atty. gen. Office Justice Programs, 1994-2000; sr. fellow program on crime policy U. Pa. Jerry Lee Ctr. Criminology, 2000—, exec. dir. Forum Crime & Justice; dir. Master of Sci. in Criminology program U. Pa., 2004—. Mem. ex-officio, bd. regents Nat. Coll. Dist. Attys., Houston, 1979—93; adv. bd. Fed. Sentencing Reporter, N.Y.C., 1990—; chair Nat. Forum Criminal Justice, Washington, 1991—93; bd. dirs. Nat. Ctr. Victims of Crime. Adv. bd. George Mason U. Adminstrn. of Justice Adv. Program.; Clinton transition com. Dept. Justice, 1992; trustee Vera Inst. Justice, 2001—; bd. dirs. Police Found. Mem.: ABA, Phi Beta Kappa. Democrat. Business E-Mail: robinsol@sas.upenn.edu. E-mail: laurieorob@aol.com.

ROBINSON, LINDA GOSDEN, communications executive; b. L.A., Jan. 10, 1953; d. Freeman Fisher and Jane Elizabeth (Stoneham) Gosden; m. Stephen M. Dart (div. June 1977); m. James Dixon Robinson III. Student, UCLA, 1970-72; BA summa cum laude in Psychology, U. So. Calif., 1978. Dep. press sec. Reagan Presdl. Campaign, L.A., 1979; press sec., dir. pub. relations Rep. Nat. Com., Washington, 1979-80; dir. pub. affairs U.S. Dept. Transp., Washington, 1981-83; ptnr. pub. and govt. affairs Heron, Burchette, Ruckert & Rothwell, Washington, 1983; dep. to spl. envoy Office of the Pres., N.Y.C., 1985; sr. v.p. corp. affairs Warner Amex Cable Communications, N.Y.C., 1983-86; chmn., CEO Robinson Lerer & Montgomery, N.Y.C., 1986—. Bd. dirs. Revlon Group, Inc., N.Y.C., VIMRx Pharms., Inc., Stamford Conn.; dir. Group Practice Svcs. Corp. Trustee NYU Med. Ctr., N.Y.C., Hosp. for Joint Diseases; del. Rep. Nat. Conv., 1985. Mem. Nat. Women's Econ. Coun., Phi Beta Kappa. Avocations: horse showing, tennis, golf.

ROBINSON, LINDA SCHULTZ, art educator, artist; b. Oakland, Calif., Mar. 15, 1949; d. James Richie Schultz and Dorothy Louise Koster-Schultz; m. Steven R. Robinson, Aug. 10, 1980; children: Laura Anne, Chelsea Marie, Emily Louise. AA in Art, Mauna Olu Coll., 1970; BA in Criminal Justice, Calif. State U., Sacramento, 1979. Cert.: Calif. (paralegal). Legal typist U.S. Govt., Concord, Calif., 1975—79; paralegal Alternative Legal Choices, Pleasant Hill, Calif., 1985—87; spl. edn. para-profl. Acad. Sch. Dist., Colorado Springs, Colo., 1995—96; pvt. art instr. to spl. needs individuals Colorado Springs, 1999—. Art therapist Meml. Hosp., Colorado Springs, 2001—. Exhibitions include Colorado Springs Art Guild, 2001. Bd. dirs. Interfaith Hospitality Network, Colorado Springs, 1995—99; vol. art tchr. Acad. Dist. 20 Schs., Colorado Springs, 2001—. Avocations: guitar, reading, crafts.

ROBINSON, LYNDA HICKOX, artist; b. Bakersfield, Calif., June 26, 1932; d. George Philip and Naida (Hathaway) Hickox; m. Arthur C. Robinson; children: Jill, Scott. BA, U. Calif., Berkeley, 1953; MA, Mills Coll., 1957. 1st v.p. San Francisco Women Artists, 1985-86, pres., 1986-87; chair gen. meeting East Bay Women Artists, Montclair, Calif., 1994—2004. Invited artist Glasgow Scotland City of Culture Exhbn., 1990. Dancer, tchr. dance, 1957-82; photographer, 1982-89, painter, 1990—; exhbns. include San Francisco Women Artists Gallery, 1992-94, Kaiser Cmty. Gallery, 1992-03, Alta Bates Cmty. Gallery, 1994-02, Valley Art Ctr. Gallery, 1992-02, Royal Ground Gallery, 1994-04, LIndsay Dinkx Brown Gallery, 2003; represented in permanent collections Fuji Vending, Dr. Louise Annand MacFarquar, Prof. and Mrs. Fred Casmir; contbr. artworks to jours. and mags. Recipient Tchg. fellowship Mills Coll., 1954, Francis Coen cash award, 1993. Mem. Phi Beta Kappa.

ROBINSON, MARGUERITE STERN, anthropologist, educator, consultant; b. N.Y.C., Oct. 11, 1935; d. Philip Van Doren and Lillian (Diamond) Stern; m. Allan Richard Robinson, June 12, 1955; children: Sarah Penelope, Perrine, Laura Ondine. BA, Radcliffe Coll., 1956; PhD, Harvard U., 1965. Assoc. scholar Radcliffe Inst. for Advanced Studies, Cambridge, Mass., 1964-65; asst. prof. anthology Brandeis U., 1965-72, assoc. prof., 1972-78, prof., 1978-85, dean Coll. Arts and Scis., 1973-75; assoc. fellow Inst. Internat. Devel. Harvard U., Cambridge, 1978-80, fellow Inst. Internat. Devel., 1980-85, inst. fellow Inst. Internat. Devel., 1985-2000, inst. fellow emeritus Inst. Internat. Devel., 2000—; dir. Cultural Survival Inc., 1981-99, Am. Inst. Indian Studies, Chgo., 1977—, chmn., 1983-84. Cons. Ministry of Fin., Govt. of Indonesia, Jakarta, 1979-92, USAID, 1992-98, Banco Solidario, Bolivia, 1993-95, Bank Rakyat Indonesia, 1994-98, World Bank, 1994-95, Bank Danamon Indonesia, 1995-96, Office of the Comptroller of the Currency, 1996-99, UNESCO, 1997, World Bank, 1997-2003, Bank of Tanzania, 1997, Microfin. Tng. Program Econs. Inst., Boulder, Colo., 1995-2003, Dept. for Internat. Devel., U.K., 2000, Women's World Banking, 2000-02, Govt. of Mex., 2002-03, others. Author: Political Structure in a Changing Sinhalese Village, 1975, Local Politics: The Law of the Fishes, 1988, Pembiayaan Pertanian Pedesaan, 1993, The Microfinance Revolution, Vol. 1: Sustainable Finance for the Poor, 2001, Vol. 2: Lessons from Indonesia, 2002; contbg. author: Cambridge Papers in Social Anthropology 3, 1962, Cambridge Papers in Social Anthropology 5, 1968, Enterprises for the Recycling and Composting of Municipal Solid Waste, 1993, The New World of Microenterprise Finance, 1994, New Perspectives on Financing Small Business in Developing Countries, 1995, Assisting Development in a Changing World, 1997, Agricultural Development in the Third World, 1998, Strategic Issues in Microfinance, 1998, Microfinance: Conversations with the Experts, 1999; contbr. articles to profl. jours. Mem. internat. coun. advisors Calmeadow Found., 1996-2000; pres. The Greatest Gift Corp. Fellow NIH, 1964-65; grantee NSF, 1966-70, Ford Found., 1972-74, 79, Calmeadow Found., 1994; fellow Indo-Am. Fellowship Program-Indo-U.S. Subcommn. on Edn. and Culture, 1976-77, Am. Inst. Indian Studies, 1976-77; grantee Calmeadow Found., 1994. Fellow Am. Anthrop. Assn., Soc. Bunting Inst. Fellows; mem. Assn. Asian Studies, India Internat. Centre.

ROBINSON, MARIETTA S. lawyer; BA, U. Mich., 1973; JD, UCLA, 1978. Bar: Calif. 1978, Mich. 1979, U.S. Dist. Ct. (ea. dist.) Mich. 1979, U.S. Ct. Appeals (6th cir.) 1983, U.S. Supreme Ct. 1989. Data processing mktg. rep. IBM Corp., Flint, Mich., 1973-75; assoc. The Bank of Bermuda Legal Dept., Hamilton, 1978-79; from assoc. to ptnr. Dickinson, Wright, Moon, VanDusen & Freeman, Detroit, 1979-94; ptnr. Sommers, Schwartz, Silver & Schwartz, P.C., Southfield, Mich., 1985-89; owner Law Offices of Marietta S. Robinson, Detroit, 1989—. Dem. nominee for Mich. Supreme Ct., 2000; adj. prof. U. Detroit Sch. of Law, 1982-83, Wayne State U., Detroit, 1983-84; lectr. in field. Contbr. articles to profl. jours. Trustee Dalkon Shield Claimants Trust, 1989-97; appointee Gov. James Blanchard, State of Mich. Bldg. Authority, 1983-89, State Bar Mich./Mich. State Med. Soc. Coalition, 1993—; appointee Transition Team of Wayne County Exec. Robert Ficano, 2002; bd. dirs. Mich. Women's Found., 2003—. Named one of ten Mich. Lawyers of Yr., Lawyers Weekly, 2000. Fellow ABA, Internat. Soc. Barristers (bd. govs.), Am. Bar Found., Mich. State Bar Found.; mem. State Bar Mich., State Bar Calif., ATLA, Mich. Trial Lawyers Assn., Women Lawyers Mich., Am. Bd. of Trial Advocates, Detroit Bar Assn., Oakland Bar Assn., U.S. Ct. Appeals (6th cir.) Jud. Conf. (life). Office: 185 Oakland Ave Ste 260 Birmingham MI 48009 E-mail: mrobin6510@aol.com.

ROBINSON, MARLA HOLBROOK, community care nurse; b. Grass Valley, Calif., Sept. 15, 1934; d. Hilmer Harrison and Mable Lucille (Kline) Holbrook; m. Donald Wilson Robinson Jr., June 25, 1961; children: Jeffrey Brian, Jennifer Lee. BSN, PHN, U. Calif. Chico, 1956. RN; cert. audiometer. Nurse U. Calif. San Francisco Hosp., 1956-59, supr. clinic St. Luke's Hosp., San Francisco, 1959-60; sch. nurse, pub. health nurse San Francisco City and County, 1960-62; sch. nurse All Saints Sch., Carmel, Calif., 1969-79; cmty. care, co-owner Cmty. Care, Monterey, Calif., 1979-94; cmty. care nurse, co-owner Choice Home Healthcare, 1994—. Mem. AAUW, Quata Internat. Monterey Peninsula (pres. 1993), Jacettes (pres. 1967), Long Term Dir. of Nursing Monterey Peninsula, Ea. Star Monterey. Episcopalian. Avocations: growing orchids, crafts, reading, travel. Home: 2841 Acacia Way Placerville CA 95667-4341 Office: Community Care 1900 Garden Rd Monterey CA 93940-5373 E-mail: marlarob@yahoo.com.

ROBINSON, MARY CATHERINE, artist; b. Oshkosh, Wis., Aug. 18, 1934; d. Edward Charles Leupold and Nora Alice O'Laughlin; m. Charles Benjamin Robinson, Sept. 10, 1960; children: Charles Edward, Jeanne Marie, David James. Student, U. Wis., Milw., 1953—54, Ringling Art Sch., Sarasota, Fla., 1954—56, Layton Art Sch., Milw., 1957—58. Owner Tree Top Studio, Nokomis, Fla. Represented by, Karchelles Gallery, Sarasota, Messy Mermaid, Nokomis, Represented in permanent collections Selby Botanical Garden, Sarasota, Fla., exhibitions include Puerto Del Sol/Costa Del Sol, Torremolinos, Spain, 2002. Recipient First prize painting, Fla. State Fair, 1959; scholar, Ringling Art Sch., Sarasota, 1954—56, Layton Art Sch., Milw., 1957—58. Mem.: N.Y. Soc. Portrait Artists, Am. Soc. Portrait Artists, U.S. Tennis Assn. Avocations: painting, sculpting, tennis, photography, fishing. Home: 1609 Hammock Dr Nokomis FL 34275

ROBINSON, MARY ELIZABETH GOFF, retired historian, researcher; b. East Providence, R.I., Jan. 3, 1925; d. Newell Darius and Eva Agnes (Crane) Goff; m. Charles Albert Robinson, July 30, 1954; 1 child, Thomas Goff (dec.). BA, Wheaton Coll., Norton, Mass., 1947. Cataloger, fine arts Chester County Hist. Soc., Pa., 1973-80, trustee, 1974-80. Cataloger artifacts Chadds Ford (Pa.) Hist. Soc., 1992-95. Co-author: (monograph) Ada Clendenin Williamson, 1983, (history) The Ingalls and the Hoyts, The Crane Sawmill, The Ingalls-Crane House, 1995; author: (monograph) The Life of a Young Entrepreneur at the Turn of the Twentieth Century, 1992; editor: A Quiet Man from West Chester, 1974. Mem. Jr. League, Providence, 1957-62, Providence Athenaeum, 1955-63, Providence Preservation Soc., 1959-63, Brandywine Conservancy, Del. Symphony Orch., Winterthur Mus.; donor Newell D. Goff Fund Chester County Cmty. Found.; founder Chester County Artists Register Chester County Art Assn., acting libr., 1994—. Donor T. Morris Longstreth Libr. endowment West Chester U., Greater Lewes (DE) Found., Friends of Lewes Pub. Libr.. Mem. AAUW, R.I. Hist. Soc. (trustee 1994-99, founder Newell D. Goff Inst. for I & E Studies), Danville (Vt.) Hist. Soc., Hershey's Mill Country Club, Hope Club (Providence). Avocations: writing, reading, hiking, travel.

ROBINSON, MARY JO, pathologist; b. Spokane, Wash., May 26, 1954; d. Jerry Lee and Ann (Brodie) R. BS in Biology, Gonzaga U., 1976; DO, Coll. Osteo. Medicine and Surgery, U. Med. Health Scis., 1987. Diplomate Nat. Bd. Osteo. Med. Examiners, Am. Osteo. Bd. Pathology; cert. anatomic pathology, lab. medicine and dermatopathology. Med. technologist Whitman Comty. Hosp., Colfax, Wash., 1977-81, Madigan Army Med. Ctr., Ft. Lewis, Wash., 1981-83; intern Des Moines Gen. Hosp., 1987-88; resident in pathology Kennedy Meml. Hosp., Stratford, N.J., 1988-92; asst. prof. pathology Sch. Medicine U. Medicine and Dentistry of N.J., Stratford, 1995—; staff pathologist Kennedy Meml. Hosp., Cherry Hill, N.J., 1995—; fellow in dermatopathology Jefferson Med. Coll., Phila., 1994. Fellow Coll. Am. Pathologists; mem. AMA, Am. Osteo. Coll. Pathologists (1st prize resident paper 1992), Am. Osteo. Assn., Am. Soc. Clin. Pathologists, N.J. Assn. Osteo. Physicians and Surgeons, Am. Osteo. Coll. Pathologists (pres. 2003-), Am. Osteo. Bd. Pathologists (chmn. 2003-). Avocations: astronomy, antiques, science fiction. Office: Kennedy Health Systems UMDNJ Sch Med Mgmt Svc Ctr 500 Marlboro Rd Cherry Hill NJ 08034- E-mail: m.robinson@kennedyhealth.org.

ROBINSON, MARY LOU, federal judge; b. Dodge City, Kans., Aug. 25, 1926; d. Gerald J. and Frances Strueber; m. A.J. Robinson, Aug. 28, 1949; 3 children. BA, U. Tex., 1948, LL.B., 1950. Bar: Tex. 1949. Ptnr. Robinson & Robinson, Amarillo, 1950-55; judge County Ct. at Law, Potter County, Tex., 1955-59, (108th Dist. Ct.), Amarillo, 1961-73; assoc. justice Ct. of Civil Appeals for 7th Supreme Jud. Dist. of Tex., Amarillo, 1973-77, chief justice, 1977-79; U.S. dist. judge No. Dist. Tex., Amarillo, 1979—. Named Woman of Year Tex. Fedn. Bus. and Profl. Women, 1973. Mem. Nat. Assn. Women Lawyers, ABA, Tex. Bar Assn. (Outstanding 50-Yr. Lawyer award 2002), Amarillo Bar Assn., Delta Kappa Gamma. Presbyterian. Office: US Dist Ct Rm 226 205 E 5th Ave # F13248 Amarillo TX 79101-1559

ROBINSON, MARY LU, retired accountant, artist; b. Bloomington, Ind., Nov. 11, 1919; d. Louis Cleveland and Ruby Olive (King) Welch; m. Robert Newlin Robinson, Sept. 27, 1948; children: Richard Louis, Rebecca Jane. Student, Ind. U., Bloomington, 1937-40, Ind. U., South Bend, 1954-55, Tex. Christian U., Ft. Worth, 1989, 90, 99. Ptnr. Robert N. Robinson, CPA, South Bend, 1950-82. Exhibited in group shows at Composers, Authors, Artists Am., N.Y.C., 1990, Soc. Watercolor Artists, Ft. Worth, 1989—, Internat. Soc. Exptl. Artists, 1992, Womans Club, Ft. Worth, 1989—. Den mother Boy Scouts Am., South Bend, 1956-59; bd. dirs. Neoclassic group Nelson-Atkins Mus. Art, Kansas City, Mo. Mem. DAR, Nat. Assn. Pen Women, Inc. (chpt. pres. 1999—), Colonial Dames XVIIC (chpt. pres. 1995-97), Daus. Colonial Wars (state pres. 1992-95), Magna Charta Soc., Colonial Order of the Crown, Daus. Am. Colonists, Daus. of 1812, Washington Family Descs., Nat. Trust Historic Preservation, Order Eastern star (assoc. matron 1969-70), Johnson County Master Gardner Assn., bd. mem. Neoclassics group, Nelson Atkins Mus. Art, Kansas City, M0. Avocations: geneology, travel, history, bridge, gardening. Home: 3915 W 57th Ter Shawnee Mission KS 66205-3148 E-mail: marylrobinson@sbcglobal.com.

ROBINSON, MELISSA SUE, communications executive, national association administrator; b. Jackson, Mich., July 16, 1950; d. Charles Edward Staelens and Norma Jean Irish; 1 child, Charles Edward Emmons. AA in Humanities; BA in Interdisciplinary Humanities, Mich. State U., 1994. Cert. first aid/CPR ARC, 2000. Adminstr. SBC Comm., Lansing, Mich., 2000—; nat. dir. The NAATP, Lansing, 2000—. Pres. Design Masters Constrn. Co. Inc., Lansing, 1987—98. Author: (poetry and songs) Give Up the Fight and Flying High (Poetry award, 2002). Bush campaign vol. The White Ho.-Rep. Party, Washington, 1992—92; city coun. at large candidate City of Lansing, 1997—97, mayoral candidate, 2003—03; precinct del. Rep. Party, Lansing. Republican. Roman Catholic. Achievements include first to helped in enactment of anti discrimination law; Featured on German TV Network one show; Featured in Janurary 28, 2003 Issue The National Enquirer on Page 10; Featured in Detroit Free Press on Thursday June 12, 2003 Local front page. Avocations: symphony, skydiving, reading, travel, theater. Home: 1121 E Larned St Lansing MI 48912 Office: The NAATP 1121 E Larned St Lansing MI 48912 Personal E-mail: mellorob@ameritech.net. E-mail: melisrob@ameritech.net.

ROBINSON, MYRNA L(ORRAINE), business analyst/program control specialist; b. Fredericksburg, Va., Mar. 31, 1962; d. Charles Edward Sr. and Jeanette Carol R. BS, Morgan State U., 1984; MBA, Averett Coll., 1997. Asst., clk. typist U.S. Army Pentagon, 1984-85; logistics technician E-Sys., Falls Church, Va., 1985-87; cost analyst Applied Rsch., Inc., Arlington, Va., 1987-89; sr. tech. support specialist Cost Based Sys., Inc., Fairfax, Va., 1989-91; program adminstr. EER Sys. Inc., Seabrook, Md., 1992-93; sr. cost analyst, LAN adminstr. Capstone Corp., Alexandria, Va., 1994-95; sr. project control specialist NYMA, Inc., 1995-96; program mgmt. analyst Dynamics Rsch. Corp., Alexandria, Va., 1996-98; bus. analyst Raytheon Sys., Marlboro, Md., 1998; vendor mgr. TRW, McLean, Va., 1998—99; cost mgr. InfoEdge Tech. Inc., 2000—01; cost mgr. cons. Robert Half Mgmt. Resources, 2001—03; cost mgr. Strategic Enterprise Solutions, 2003—. Acct. Quality Catering, Accokeed, Md., 1995—; fin. asst. 2d Baptist Ch. S.W., Washington D.C. Contbg. author: (book) Cost Quality Management Assessment for the Richland Operation Office, 1994, Cost Quality Management Assessment for the Savannah River, 1995, Cost Quality Management Assessment for the Idaho Operations Office, 1995, Cost Quality Management Assessment for the Kansas City Plant, 1995. Nat. dir. mentoring program Reach for Tomorrow. Mem. NAFE, Nat. Coun. of Negro Women, Inc., Am. Assn. Cost Engrs. Internat. Avocations: travelling, sports, computer technology.

ROBINSON, NAN SENIOR, not-for-profit organization consultant; b. Salt Lake City, Jan. 11, 1932; d. Clair Marcil Senior and Lillian (Worlton) Senior Davis; m. David Zav Robinson; Sept. 6, 1954; children: Marc S. Robinson, Eric S. Robinson. BA with hons., Mills Coll., 1952; MA, Harvard U., 1953. Spl. asst. to undersec. Dept. Housing and Urban Devel., Washington, 1966-69; asst. to the pres. U. Mass. Statewide System, Boston, 1970-73, v.p. for planning, 1973-78; dep. commr. Conn. Bd. Higher Edn., Hartford, 1978-81; v.p. adminstrn. The Rockefeller Found., N.Y.C., 1981-90; ret., 1990. Mem. governing coun. Rockefeller Archive Ctr., Pocantico Hills, N.Y., 1986-89; com. mem. Coun. on Founds. N.Y. Regional Assn. Grantmakers, 1985-89; mem. nat. advisory panel on governance Carnegie Found. for the Advancement of Teaching, Princeton, N.J., 1980-82. Trustee, chmn. fin. com. Inst. for Current World Affairs, Hanover, N.H., 1987-90; trustee Calif. Sch. Profl. Psychology, San Francisco, 1985-96; vice chair bd. dirs. Fed. to Preserve the Greenwich Village Waterfront, 1996-99, bd. dirs., 1996—. Recipient Centennial award Am. Assn. U. Women Hartford Br., 1981; named Woman of Yr. Hartford YWCA, 1980; named to Centennial Honor List of 100 Women Barnard Coll., 1989. Mem. Soc. for Coll. and U. Planning (com. chmn. 1985-86, nominating com. 1980-85, regional rep. 1975-77), Phi Beta Kappa. Home: 622 Greenwich St Apt 5B New York NY 10014-3305

ROBINSON, NANCY A. writer; b. Dewey, Okla., June 19, 1939; d. Joseph K. and Velma D. Green; m. McDonald Robinson, June 11, 1961; children: Ehren, Shannon, Adam. BA in Letters and Sci., U. Calif., Berkeley, 1961; MA, Drew U., 1993. Gifted and talented tchr., Lexington, 1962—66; writer AT&T, Morristown, NJ, 1982—85, Santa Barbara (Calif.) Mus. Natural History, 1989—92; founder, pub. Green River Press, Santa Barbara, 1999—. Author: Touched by Adoption, 1999. Founder Bill Downey Writers Scholarship, Santa Barbara, 1996—2003; clk. Santa Barbara Friends Meeting, 2000—03; v.p. Ednl. Found. AAUW, Santa Barbara, 1990—91. Quaker. Office: Green River Press 5880 Hidden Ln Goleta CA 93117

ROBINSON, NANCY ELLEN, artist; b. N.Y.C., Mar. 27, 1949; d. Edwin James Jr. and Marie Josette (Bentivoglio) Robinson. BA in English cum laude, Lawrence U., 1971. Adj. faculty Mpls. Coll. Art and Design, 1999—2001. Vis. artist Mpls. Coll. of Arts and Design, 1983, 97; painting instr. Lakewood C. C., St. Paul, Minn., 1993; mentor Women's Art Registry of Minn., St. Paul, 1991-2002; guest artist spkr. Minn. Mus. Am. Art, St. Paul, 1997; lectr. in field. One woman show Hamline U., St. Paul, 1997, Artemisia Gallery, Chgo., 2000, Flanders Contemporary Art, Mpls., 2001; two person show Flanders Contemporary Art, 1997, U. Minn., St. Paul, 1997, A.I.R. Gallery, N.Y.C., 2001; group shows include Minn. State Arts Bd., St. Paul, 1997, U. Minn., Mpls., 1997, Intermedia Arts, Mpls., 1997, Mpls. Coll. Art and Design, 1997, Mpls. Inst. Arts, 2000, Minn. Hist. Soc., 2002, A.I.R. Galler, 2002; gallery rep.: Flanders Contemporary Art, Mpls. Fellowship Minn. State Arts Bd., 1997, 2001; Jerome Artist grant Blacklock Nature Sanctuary, 1998, travel and study grantee Jerome, Target and Gen. Mills Founds., 2000.

ROBINSON, NANCY NOWAKOWSKI, academic administrator; b. Pitts., Nov. 2, 1945; d. Theodore Joseph Nowakowski and Martha Radick; 1 child, David A. BA cum laude, U. Pitts., 1983, MA, 2000. Founding mem. bd. dirs., treas. Extrasolar Planetary Found., Pitts., 1980—97; mem. adv. com. Nazareth Housing Svcs., 1995—; assoc. Sisters of the Holy Family of Nazareth, Pitts., 1998—; pres. City of God Found., Pitts., 2000—02, bd. dirs. Chaplain and diversity advisor divsn. 7, 8th eastern region U.S. Coast Guard Aux., 2003. Recipient Sister Noel Kernan award, Seton Hill Coll., 1999, Weiner Israel Heritage Nationality Rms. award, U. Pitts., 1999; Dorot Found. grantee for study in Israel, 1999, Pax Christi grantee, Pax Christi,

1999. Mem.: Soc. Bibl. Lit., Am. Acad. Religion, Golden Key. Roman Catholic. Avocations: Jewish/Catholic relations, history, music, travel, outdoors. Business E-Mail: nancy1@pitt.edu.

ROBINSON, OLA MAE, accountant; b. Worsham Ranch, Tex., Nov. 17, 1903; d. Franklin Earle and Jennie Rachael (Gay) R. B of Acctg., Draughons Bus. Coll., 1935. Tchr. rural schs., Tex., 1924-34; bookkeeper Ins. Cos., Wichita Falls, Tex., 1935-40; acct., bookkeeper U.S. War Dept., Washington, 1941-50; acct. Air Force Acctg. & Fin. Ctr., Denver, 1951-65; bookkeeper 1stMeth. Ch., Denver, 1966-70. Author, editor: Robinson Family, 1995. Recipient Pres. award Denver Rose Soc., 1980. Mem. Nat. Assn. Retired Persons, Nat. Genealogical Soc., Am. Rose Soc. (pres.), Clay County Hist. Soc. Republican. Methodist. Avocations: travel, photography, reading, writing, gardening. Home: 400 W 14th Ave #213B Amarillo TX 79101-4140

ROBINSON, PATRICIA ELAINE, women's health nurse practitioner; b. St. Louis, June 30, 1955; d. Harold Winford and Robbie LaVeal (Ferguson) Hammett; m. Kenneth M. Robinson, Nov. 18, 1978 (div.); children: Barry Christopher, Emily Vanessa; m. C. Gilbert, Nov. 20, 1990. ADN, St. Louis Community Coll., 1987; student, Webster U., 1990—; cert. in forensic pathology, St. Louis U., 1975; cert. in pharmacology, St. Louis Coll. Health, 1984; womens health nurse practioner, U. Mo., 1995. Cert. densitometrist. Per diem float nurse St. Louis U. Hosp.; coord. ob-gyn. unit Group Health Plan, St. Louis; staff nurse Barnes Hosp., St. Louis; staff nurse dept. ob-gyn. Washington U. Sch. Medicine, St. Louis, 1990-93; chief exec. study coord. women's health rsch. Obstetric & Gynecologic Diagnosis & Consultation, Florissant, Mo., 1992-96; nurse practitioner and exec. study coord. women's health rsch. Women's HealthPartners, 1996; nurse practitioner James Ottolini, MD, Inc., 1996—. Acting dir. Nurses for Reproductive Health Svcs., St. Louis, 1990-93. Mem. NAFE, Nurse Assn. Am. Coll. Obstetrics and Gynecologists, Med. Group Mgmt. Assn., Nat. Assn. Nurse Practitioners Reproductive Health, Phi Theta Kappa. Office: James L Ottolini MD Inc 222 S Woods Mill Rd Ste 360 Chesterfield MO 63017-3625

ROBINSON, ROBIN, newscaster; b. Chgo. m. Terrence Brantley, 1986 (div. 1989). B, San Diego State U., 1980. Reporter KGTV, San Diego, 1979—81; consumer reporter CBS affiliate, Denver, 1981—84; reporter WBBM-TV, Chgo., 1984—87; co-anchor Fox News at 9 WFLD-TV, Chgo., 1987—. Co-recipient Emmy awards. Office: WFLD-TV 205 N Mich Ave Chicago IL 60601

ROBINSON, ROBIN WICKS, lawyer; b. Roanoke Rapids, NC, June 5, 1961; d. Wallace Wayne and Rozelle Royall Wicks; m. James Hendry Robinson, Jr., Nov. 7, 1992; children: James Hendry Robinson III, Wallace Katherine McLean Robinson. BA in Politics (hon.), Converse Coll., Spartanburg, S.C., 1982; JD, U. N.C., Chapel Hill, 1985. Bar: N.C. 1986; 5th Jud. Dist. 1986, U.S. Dist. Ct. (ea. dist.) 1987; U.S. Dist. Ct. (we. dist.) 1997, 5th Jud. Dist. Arbitrator 1993, Superior Ct. Cert. Mediator, family fin. mediator, specialist in family law, NC. Assoc. atty. Ryals, Jackson & Mills, Wilmington, N.C., 1986-90; ptnr. Pennington & Wicks, Wilmington, N.C., 1990-93; pres, profl. corp. Ryals, Robinson & Saffo P.C., Wilmington, N.C., 1993—. Ethics com. N.C. State Bar, Raleigh, N.C., 1990-93; exec. com. New Hanover County Bar Assn., Wilmington, 1994-97. Bd. mem. Cape Fear Mus. Assocs., Inc., Wilmington, N.C., 1991-2000, v.p. 1994-97, pres. 1997-2000; bd. mem., counsel Wilmington Symphony Orchestra, Inc., Wilmington, N.C., 1991-99; commn. mem. USS N.C. Battleship Commn., Wilmington, N.C., 1989-93; mem. Bd. Deacons First Presbyn. Ch., Wilmington, N.C., 1996-99, Chancel Choir, 1988—. Recipient Women of Achievement New Hanover Commn. for Women, Wilmington, N.C., 1997, Trustee Merit Scholarship Converse Coll., Spartanburg, S.C., 1978-82; named Mortar Bd. Converse Coll., Spartanburg, S.C., 1981—, Crescent Converse Coll., Spartanburg, S.C., 1979-80, Pro bono publico award Legal Svcs. of the Lower Cape Fear, 1997, 2002. Mem. Am. Bar Assn., N.C. Bar Assn., N.C. Acad. Trial Lawyers, New Hanover County Bar Assn., Phi Delta Phi, Phi Sigma Iota, Pi Gamma Mu. Republican. Presbyterian. Avocations: travel, piano, choral, swimming, tennis, sailing. Home: 1940 Hawthorne Rd Wilmington NC 28403-5329 Office: Ryals Robinson & Saffo PC 701 Market St Wilmington NC 28401-4646 E-mail: rrspc@bellsouth.net.

ROBINSON, ROSIE LEE, minister; b. Utica, Miss., Nov. 17, 1946; d. Frank and Mary R.; m. Charles David Robinson, Dec. 5, 1987 (dec. Oct. 31, 2002); children: Eric, Karla, John Marc. D in Div., Internat. U. Grace and Trutch, Indpls., 1995; D in Theology, Aenon Bible Coll., Indpls., 2001. Adminstr. Dept. Navy, San Diego, 1989—95, mgmt. analyst, 1995—2000; chaplain U.S. Chaplaincy Am. Author: Reflections of a Rose, 1997. Exec. sec. Calif. Dist. Coun., 2001—; regional coord. Apostolic Univ. Grace and Ch., 1995—. Mem.: Coaltion of Black Women, Richmond Dem. Club. Democrat. Mem. Apostolic Ch. Avocations: bowling, reading to children, writing, teaching, vacationing. Home: 6863 Caminito Montanoso San Diego CA 92119 Office: Ch Jesus Christ Apostolic 4101 48th St San Diego CA 92105

ROBINSON, RUTH CARLESON, retired secondary school educator; b. Salem, Oreg., Aug. 27, 1937; d. Richard Victor and Opal Charlotte Carleson; m. Kenneth Oliver Robinson, Aug. 2, 1959; children: Grant Kenneth, Victoria Ruth. BS, Oreg. State U., 1959. H.S. tchr. Hillsboro (Oreg.) Sch. Dist., 1959-60, Gresham-Barlow Sch. Dist., Gresham, Oreg., 1976—2002. Site coun. Sam Barlow H.S., Gresham, 1994—2002, chair site coun., 1998—2002. Contbr. Portland Opera Assn., 1982—, Portland Classical Chinese Garden, Portland Art Mus., Met. Mus. Art. Mem. AAII, AAUW, Gresham-Barlow Edn. Assn. (v.p. 1994-95, pres. 1995-96), Multnomah County UniServ (sec. 1989-92, pres. 1993-95). Avocations: opera, travel, collecting. Home: 2934 NE 38th Ave Portland OR 97212-2854

ROBINSON, RUTH HUBBARD, retired elementary school educator; b. Orangeburg, SC, Sept. 18, 1926; d. Charles Harrison and Sarah Hook Hubbard; m. John Samuel Robinson (dec. Aug. 22, 1996); children: Tyrone, Lynn Robinson Miller, Elton. BA in English, Claflin U., Orangeburg SC, 1948; MS in Edn., S.C. State U., 1957. Cert. English S.C. Dept. Edn., elem. edn. S.C. Dept. Edn., reading S.C. Dept. Edn. English tchr. Orangeburg County Tng. Sch., Elloree, SC, 1948—49, Norway (S.C.) H.S., 1951—53; elem. sch. tchr. Allendale (S.C.) Tng. Sch., 1957—59, Bethlehem Elem. Sch., St. Matthews, SC, 1961—63; elem. reading tchr. Orangeburg Sch. Dist. 5, 1963—86; ret. Author: (book of poetry) Images, 1996, poetry. Active Habitat for Humanity, Orangeburg Mission to Families, Family and Cmty. Leaders; co-founder, chair Robinson Scholarship Fund of St. Luke Presbyn. Ch. (USA), Orangeburg, 1994. Recipient Meritorious Svc. award, St. Luke Presbyn. Ch. Bd. Deacons, 1983, Golden Poet award, World of Poetry, 1988, Grand Prize in Quilting, Orangeburg (SC) County Fair, 2000, 2001, Svc. award, Orangeburg Dist. 5, 1986, Outstanding Svc. and Achievement award, Claflin U., 1998. Mem.: VFW Aux. (charter), NAACP (life), Writers Ink, Ch. Women United, Claflin U. Nat. Alumni (life). Democrat. Presbyterian. Avocations: quilting, travel, reading, volunteering. Home: 279 Oakridge Dr NE Orangeburg SC 29115

ROBINSON, SALLY SHOEMAKER, lay associate church social ministries; b. N.Y.C., Dec. 31, 1931; d. Samuel M. and Helen Dominick Smith S.; m. James Courtland Robinson, Dec. 31, 1931; children: Samuel Shoemaker, W. Courtland, A. Alexander, Ellen Whitridge Robinson Mihalski. BA cum laude, Bryn Mawr Coll., 1953; postgrad. studies, Yonsei U. Lang. Inst., Korea, 1960-62, Children's Theatre Assn., 1964; MA, Towson State U., 1974. Ordained elder Brown Meml. Presbyn. Ch., 1985. Commd. missionary to Korea United Presbyn. Ch., 1959-71; dir. Brown Meml. Tutorial Program, 1974-84; exec. dir. Episcopal Social Ministries Diocese of Md., Balt., 1984-97; canon for social ministry Episcopal Diocese of Md., Balt., 1985-96. Met. chmn. 10th Decade Campaign Bryn Mawr Coll.,, 1974-76, nat. chmn. Centennial Campaign. 1980-85, trustee, 1985—; trustee Am. Bible Soc., 1988—, v.p., 1993—, chmn. bd., 1996-2001; chmn. global bd. United Bible Socs., 2001—; trustee United Bd. for Christian Higher Edn. in Asia, 1990-95; trustee emeritus Bryn Mawr Coll., 1997—. Home: 10522 Burnside Farm Rd Stevenson MD 21153-2024 Office: Brown Meml Ch 1316 Park Ave Baltimore MD 21217-4185

ROBINSON, SALLY WINSTON, artist; b. Detroit, Nov. 2, 1924; d. Harry Lewis and Lydia (Kahn) Winston; m. Eliot F. Robinson, June 28, 1949; children: Peter Eliot, Lydia Winston, Sarah Mitchell, Suzanne Finley. BA, Bennington Coll., 1947; postgrad., Cranbrook Acad. Art, 1949; grad., Sch. Social Work, Wayne U., 1948, MA, 1972; MFA, Wayne State U., 1973. Psychol. tester Detroit Bd. Edn., 1944; psychol. counselor and tester YMCA, N.Y.C., 1946; social caseworker Family Svc., Pontiac, Mich., 1947; instr. printmaking Wayne State U., Detroit, 1973—. Tchr. children's art Detroit Inst. Art, 1949-50, now artistic advisor, bd. dirs. drawing and pring orgn. One-woman shows include, U. Mich., 1973, Wayne State U., 1974, Klein-Vogel Gallery, 1974, Rina Gallery, 1976, Park McCullough House, Vt., 1976, Williams Coll., 1976, Arnold Klein Gallery, 1977, exhibited in group shows, Bennington Coll., Cranbrook Mus., Detroit Inst. Art, Detroit Artists Market, Soc. Women Painters, Soc. Arts and Crafts, Bloomfield Art Assn., Flint Left Bank Gallery, Balough Gallery, Detroit Soc. Woman Painters, U. Mich., U. Ind., U. Wis., U. Pitts., Toledo Mus., Krannert Mus., Represented in permanent collections, Detroit, N.Y.C., Birmingham, Bloomfield Hills. Bd. dirs. Planned Parenthood, 1951—, mem. exec. bd., 1963—; bd. dirs. PTA, 1956-60, Roeper City and Country Sch., U. Mich. Mus. Art, 1978; trustee Putnam Hosp. Med. Rsch. Inst., 1978; mem. Gov.'s Commn. Art in State Bldgs., 1978-79; mem. art and devel. coms. So. Vt. Art Ctr., 1987-88; mem. vol. com. Marie Selby Gardens; patron Graphic Art Studio, U. So. Fla., Tampa; patron, benefactor Clark Mus., Williamstown, Mass. Fellow: Williams Coll. Mus. Art (mem. visiting com.); mem.: Bloomfield Art Assn. (program co-chmn. 1956), Birmingham Soc. Women Painters (pres. 1974—76), Detroit Soc. Women Painters, Detroit Artists Market (dir. 1956—, hon. bd. mem.), Founders Soc. Detroit Inst. Art, Bennington Coll. Alumnae Assn. (regional co-chmn. 1954), Cosmopolitan Club (N.Y.C.), Founders Garden Club (Sarasota, Fla.), Garden Club Am. (bd. dirs.), Oaks Club (Fla.), Women's City Club (coord. art shows Detroit 1950), Village Women's Club (Birmingham, Mich.). Unitarian Universalist. Home: 209 Hills Point Rd Charlotte VT 05445-9698 also: 840 N Casey Key Rd Osprey FL 34229-9779

ROBINSON, SHARON BETH, health science association administrator; b. Balt., Sept. 28, 1959; BS, Towson State U., 1981; MS, Johns Hopkins U., 1986. Exec. asst. Congress of Neurol. Surgeons, Balt., 1983-86; office adminstr. Md. Inst. Emergency Med. Svcs., Balt., 1986-87; coord. spl. projects U. Md. Med. Systems, Balt., 1986-88; adminstr. Am. Bd. Med. Genetics, Bethesda, Md., 1988—, Am. Coll. Med. Genetics, Bethesda, 1992-98, Am. Bd. Genetic Counseling, Bethesda, 1993—. Mem. Catonsville Community Coll. Alumni Assn. (bd. dirs. 1984-89, sec. 1986, v.p. 1987, pres. 1988). Office: ABMG/ABGC 9650 Rockville Pike Bethesda MD 20814-3998 E-mail: srobinson@genetics.faseb.org.

ROBINSON, SHARON PORTER, professional society administrator; b. Louisville; B in Edn., English and Psychology, U. Ky., 1966, M in Edn., Curriculum and Instrn., 1976, D in Ednl. Adminstrn. and Supervision, 1979. Tchr., Lexington, Ky., U.S. AFB, Bitburg, Germany; assoc. dir. Jefferson County Edn. Consortium, Ky., late 1970's; dir. instrn. and profl. devel. NEA, 1980-89, dir. R & D arm Nat. Ctr. Innovation, 1989-93; asst. sec. ednl. rsch. and improvement U.S. Dept. Edn., 1993—96; v.p. State and Fed. Regulations EPS, Washington, 1997—98, sr. v.p., COO, 1998—. Cons. Nat. Bd. Profl. Teaching Standards; head tchr. edn. initiative Nat. Ctr. Innovation. Office: EPS 1800 K St NW Washington DC 20006

ROBINSON, SHAWNA, race car driver; b. Des Moines, Nov. 30, 1964; 2 children. Big-rig tractor driver Great Am. Truck Racing Tour, 1980; racecar driver Huffman Racing, 1991. Named winner, Dash Race, 1988, Most Popular Driver, 1988, Rookie of the Yr., 1988, winner, Talladega Pole award, 2000; recipient 3d pl., Goody's Dash Series, 1988, 4th pl., Bondo/Mar-Hyde Series Race, 1999, 2d pl., First Plus Fin. 200, 1999. Office: c/o BAM Racing 11881 Vance Davis Dr Charlotte NC 28269

ROBINSON, SHIRLEY S. coach, educator; b. Miami, Fla., Mar. 10, 1946; d. Henry Early and Catherine Lampley Snell; m. Grover G. Robinson, Mar. 2, 1970 (div. May 1982); 1 child, Wayne Anthony. BA, Bethune Cookman U., 1969; postgrad., U. Miami, 1973-74, Nova U., 1988-89. Staff organizer North Dade Newspaper, Opa Locka, Fla., 1963-64; coach Spl. Olympics, Miami, 1989—, Sports Disabled Program, Miami, 1989—, Shake A Leg, Miami, 1997—. Advisor Miami Edison Sr. H.S., 1989—, Tech. Student Assn., Miami, 1990-92; tchr. ministry Antioch Bapt. Ch., Miami, 1999—; founder Phys. Challenge Club of Miami Edison Sr. High. Mem. 1st delegation Assocs. on Higher Edn. and Disability Profls., Republic of Vietnam, 1993; advocate for people with disabilities; mem. feeding ministry Antioch Bapt. Ch., 1999. Dade County Sch. Bd. grantee for higher edn., 1973-74. Mem. NAACP, Coun. for Exceptional Children (trophy 1982), United Tchrs. of Dade, Bethune Cookman Coll. Alumni Assn. (sec., scholarships com., trophy 1997), Nat. Coun. Negro Women, Sigma Gamma Rho. Home: 15831 NW 37th Ct Opa Locka FL 33054-6333

ROBINSON, SUE L(EWIS), federal judge; b. 1952; BA with highest honors, U. Del., 1974; JD, U. Pa., 1978. Assoc. Potter, Anderson & Corron, Wilmington, Del., 1978-83; asst. U.S. atty. U.S. Attys. Office, 1983-88; U.S. magistrate judge U.S. Dist. Ct. (Del. dist.), 1988-91, dist. judge, 1991—. Mem. Del. State Bar Assn. (sec. 1986-87). Office: US Dist Ct J Caleb Boggs Fed Bldg 844 N King St Lockbox 31 Wilmington DE 19801-3519

ROBINSON, VERNA COTTEN, retired librarian, property management owner; b. Enfield, N.C., Oct. 6, 1927; d. Ernest and Ida (Faulcon) Cotten; m. Elbert Crutcher Robinson, Aug. 14, 1953 (dec. Feb. 1992); children: Angela, Elbert Cotten. BS, N.C. Cen. U., 1948; MS in Libr. Sci., Carnegie Mellon U., 1950. Br. libr. Blyden br. Norfolk (Va.) Pub. Libr., 1950-51; serials libr. Howard U., Washington, 1951-52; sch. libr. Spingarn H.S., Washington, 1952-53, Cardozo H.S., Washington, 1955-60, Roosevelt H.S., Washington, 1960-67, 70-85; ret. D.C. Pub. Schs., 1985. Pres. Robinson Property Mgmt., Inc., Washington, 1993—; bd. dirs. New Birth Corp., Miami, Fla. V.p. D.C. Assn. Sch. Librs., Washington, 1972-74; vice-chair Diaconate Lincoln Congrl. Temple/United Ch. of Christ, 1999—, chair, 2000-02. Recipient Elder Wise Woman award, Ctrl. Atlantic Conf. of United Ch. of Christ, 2002, Pioneer's Achiever's award United Ch. Christ, 1995; Daisy Scarborough scholar N.C. Cen. U., 1946-48, Carnegie Libr. Alumni scholar Carnegie Libr. Sch. Alumni Assn., 1948-50. Mem. African Am. Women's Assn. (internat. com. 1992-95), Delta Sigma Theta (tuition scholar Grand chpt. 1948-50). Avocations: reading, walking.

ROBINSON, WENDY Y. school system administrator; Under grad., DePauw U., Ind. U.-Purdue U., Ball State U. Tchr. Ward Elem., 1973—86; asst. prin. Meml. Pk. Mid. Sch., 1986—87, Weisser Pk. Elem., 1987—89; prin. Price Elem., 1989—91; area admin., asst. supt. Wayne HS, 1991—95; dep. supt. Fort Wayne Comm. Schs., 1995—2003, supt., 2003—. Office: Fort Wayne Comm Sch 1200 S Clinton St Fort Wayne IN 46802

ROBINSON DEROSSI, FLAVIA, photographer, foundation executive; b. Torino, Italy; d. Daniele A. and Anna (Navissano) Derossi; m. Marshall A. Robinson, Oct. 12, 1974. MA, U. Torino, 1949, PhD, 1952. Asst. prof. IPSOA, Torino, 1952-58; dir. CRIS, Torino, 1961-74; fellow OECD Devel. Ctr., Paris, 1967-71; photographer, 1982—. Pres. Daniele Agostino Found., N.Y.C., 1991—. Author: The Mexican Entrepreneur, 1971, The Technocratic Illusion, 1981; one-woman shows include: Soho Photo Gallery, N.Y.C., 1984, 86, 88, 90, Galleria Fotografis, Bologna, 1985, Galleria D'Alessandro, Torino, 1985, Galleria II Canale, Venezia, 1987, Fortezza Pisana, Elba, 1988, Bertha Urdang Gallery, N.Y.C., 1989, 92, Cathedral of St. John the Divine, N.Y.C., 1991, Dutot Mus., Pa., 1995, Piedmont Coll. Art Gallery, Ga., 1994, Vdinotti Gallery, Phoenix, 1997, Caravan House, N.Y.C., 1998, 2000; permanent collections include: Bklyn. Mus., N.Y. Pub. Libr., Bibliotèque Nat. of Paris. Recipient Photography award Ariz. Bot. Soc., N.Y. Audubon Soc., Photographer's Forum. Mem. Cosmopolitan Club. Avocation: travel. Office: Daniele Agostino Found 870 U N Plz Apt 35C New York NY 10017-1820

ROBINSON-HILTON, LORRAINE ANN, music educator; b. Plainfield, N.J., Dec. 11, 1946; d. Kenneth Edward Williams and Ruth Barbara Hatrick; m. Lawrence Raymond Hilton, July 26, 2003; children: Jordan Dean Hilton, Tasha Ann Hilton, Jarvis Drew Hilton; m. Richard Jon Robinson, June 28, 1969 (div.); children: Lindsay Anne Robinson, Kerry Eileen Robinson. BA, Montclair (N.J.) State Coll., 1968; MMusEd, Trenton (N.J.) State Coll., 1972. Cert. tchr. music K-12 N.J., 1968, supr. N.J., 1972. Instrumental music tchr. Franklin Twp. Bd. of Edn., Somerset, NJ, 1968—. Student coun. adv. Hillcrest Sch., Somerset, NJ, 1982—, student activities bursar, 1996—; head tchr. Conerly Rd. Sch., Somerset, NJ, 1980—82; asst. band dir. Franklin HS, Somerset, NJ, 1968—78, band front dir., 1968—77, concert band dir., 1973—77, brass ensemble dir. Treas. Monmouth County Arts Coun., Red Bank, NJ, 1996—2003; pres. The Co. of Dance Arts, Red Bank, NJ, 1992—95, sec., 1997—98, trustee emeritus, 2001—03, trustee, 1990—2001. Named to Master Tchrs. Collaborative, 2004; NEH fellow, 1995. Mem.: NEA, Music Educator's Nat. Conf., Franklin Twp. Edn. Assn., Somerset County Edn. Assn., N.J. Edn. Assn. Independent. Roman Catholic. Avocations: ballet, theater, symphony, visual art, films. Home: 59 Frances St Shrewsbury NJ 07702 Office: Franklin Twp Bd Edn 1755 Amwell Rd Somerset NJ 08873 Personal E-mail: lorraine@monmouth.com.

ROBIRDS, ESTEL, state legislator; Mem. Mo. State Ho. of Reps. Dist. 143, 1993—. Home: Rte 2 Box 2919 Theodosia MO 65761 Office: Mo Ho of Reps State Capitol Building Jefferson City MO 65101-1556

ROBISON, EMILY BURNS, musician; b. Pittsfield, Mass., Aug. 16, 1972; d. Paul and Barbara Burns; m. Charlie Robison, May 1999; 1 child, Charles. Performer Blue Night Express, 1984—89; banjo player, guitarist, vocalist Dixie Chicks, 1989—. Performer: (albums) LIttle Ol' Cowgirl, 1992, Ghank Heavens for Dale Evans, 1992, Shouldn't a Told You That, 1993, Wide Open Spaces, 1998 (Maximum Vision Clip of Yr., Billboard, 1998, Best New Country Artist Clip of Yr., Billboard, 1998, Best Country Album, Grammy Awards, 1998, Album of Yr., Acad. Country Music, 1998, Best Selling Album, Can. Country Music Awards, 1999, Song of Yr., WB Radio Music Award, 1999, Album of Yr., ACM, 1999), Fly, 1999 (Best Country Album, Grammy Awards, 1999, Best Selling Album, Can. Country Musc Awards, 2000, Internat. Album, British Country Music Award, 2000, Country Album of Yr., Billboard Awards, 2000, Album of Yr., ACM, 2000, Album of Yr., CMA, 2000), Home, 2002 (Favorite Country Album, Am. Music Awards, 2002, Best Recording Package, Grammy Awards, 2002, Best Country Album, Grammy Awards, 2002). Named Most Significant New Country Act, Country Monitor, 1998, Top New Country Artist, Billboard, 1998, Top Vocal Group, Acad. Country Music, 1998, Country Artist of Yr., Rolling Stone, 1999, Top Country Artist, Billboard, 1999, Internat. Rising Star, British Country Music Awards, 1999, Artist of Yr. (Country), WB Radio Music Award, 1999, Favorite New Artist (Country), AMA, 1999, Vocal Group of Yr., CMA, 1999, Country Artist of Yr., Billboard, 1999, 2000, Entertainer of Yr., CMA, 2000, ACM, 2000, Vocal Group of Yr., 2001, Entertainer of Yr., 2001, Favorite Musical Group or Band, People's Choice Award, 2002, Vocal Group of Yr., Country Music Assn., 2002, others; recipient Horizon award, CMA, 1998. Office: Monument Sony Nashville 34 Music Sq East Nashville TN 37203*

ROBISON, PAULA JUDITH, flutist; b. Nashville, June 8, 1941; d. David Victor and Naomi Florence R.; m. Scott Nickrenz; Dec. 29, 1971; 1 child, Elizabeth Hadley Amadea Nickrenz. Student, U. So. Calif., 1958-60; BS, Juilliard Sch. Music, 1963. Founding artist, player Chamber Music Soc., N.Y.C., 1970-90, N.Y. ChôroBand, 1994; co-dir. chamber music Spoleto Festival, Charleston, S.C., 1978-88; Filene artist-in-residence Skidmore Coll., Saratoga Springs, N.Y., 1988-89; mem. faculty New Eng. Conservatory Music, 1991—2001; co-dir. Gardner Chamber Orch., Boston, 1995—. Faculty Juilliard Sch., N.Y.C., 1978-82; annual concert series, Met. Mus. Art, N.Y., 1990—, With Art series, P.S. 1 Art Gallery, N.Y., 2000, Mass. Mus. Contemporary Art, 2001; dir.Vivaldi in the Courtyard, Gardner Mus., Boston, 2002—. Soloist with various major orchs., including N.Y. Philharm., London Symphony Orch.; player, presenter Concerti di Mezzogiorno, Spoleto (Italy) Festival, 1970-2003; commd. flute concertos by Leon Kirchner, Toru Takemitsu, Oliver Knussen, Robert Beaser, Kenneth Frazelle; premiered works by Pierre Boulez, Elliott Carter, William Schuman, Thea Musgrave, Carla Bley, John Tavener; premiered Rio Days Rio Nights, Music Theatre Group prodn. in N.Y.C., 1998; participant Marlboro Music Festival, 1999—; author: The Paula Robison Flute Warmups Book, 1989, The Andersen Collection, 1994, Paula Robison Masterclass: Paul Hindemith, 1995, The Sidney Lanier Collection, 1997, Frank Martin: Ballade, 2002, To a Wild Rose, 2003; co-author: Places of the Spirit, 2003; recs. on CBS Masterworks, Music Masters, Vanguard Classics, New World Records, Omega, Arabesque, Sony Classical, King Recs., Mode Recs., Artemis Recs.; featured in PBS documentary and book: Juilliard. Recipient First prize Geneva Internat. Competition, 1966, Adelaide Ristori prize, 1987, Lifetime Achievement award Nat. Flute Assn., 2004; named Musician of Month, Musical Am., 1979, House Musician for Isamu Noguchi Garden Mus., N.Y.C., 1988; Martha Baird Rockefeller grantee, 1966; Nat. Endowment for Arts grantee, 1978, 86; Fromm Found. grantee, 1980; Housewright Eminent scholar Fla. State U., 1990-91. Recipient Disting. Svc. award, Music Tchrs. Nat. Assn., 1989, Laurence Lesser Presdl. award, 1999, Lifetime Achievement award, Usdan Ctr. for Creative and Perfomring Arts, 2000, Hon. Citizen for Life award, City of Charleston, S.C., 2002, Lifetime Achievement award, Nat. Flute Assn., 2004. Mem. Sigma Alpha Iota (hon.). Office: care Matthew Sprizzo 477 Durant Ave Staten Island NY 10308-3006

ROBLE, CAROLE MARCIA, accountant; b. Bklyn., Aug. 22, 1938; d. Carl and Edith (Brown) Dusowitz; m. Richard F. Roble, Nov. 30, 1969. MBA with distinction, N.Y. Inst. Tech., 1984. CPA, Calif., N.Y. Compt. various orgns. various orgns., 1956-66; staff acct. ZTBG CPA'S, L.A., 1966-67; sr. acct. J.H. Cohn & Co., Newark, 1967-71; prin. Carole M. Roble, CPA, South Hempstead, N.Y., 1971-90; ptnr. Roble & Libman, CPAs, Baldwin, N.Y., 1990-93; prin. Carole M. Roble, CPA, Baldwin, N.Y., 1993—. Speaker, moderator Found. for Acctg. Edn., N.Y., 1971—; lectr. acctg. various schs. including New Sch., Queens Coll., Empire State Coll., Touro Coll., N.Y. Inst. Tech., N.Y.C., Parsons Sch., 1971—. Guest various N.Y. radio and TV stas., 2 noted various newspapers. Treas. Builders Devel. Corp. of L.I., Westbury, N.Y., 1985; dir. Women Econ. Devels. of L.I., 1985-87. Recipient Sisterhood citation Nat. Orgn. Women, 1984, 85, cert. of Appreciation Women Life Underwriters, 1988, Women in Sales, 1982, 84; named top Tax Practitioner Money Mag., 1987, one of Top 100 Most Influential People, Acctg. Today, 1999. Mem. AICPA (mem. small firm advocacy com. 1996—), Am. Acct. Assn. (auditing sect.), Am. Soc. Women Accts. (pres. N.Y. chpt. 1980-81), Am. Woman's Soc. CPAs, Nat. Conf. CPA Practitioners (trustee L.I. chpt. 1981-82, sec. 1982-83, treas. 1983-84, v.p. 1984-85, 1st v.p. 1985-86, pres. 1986-87, nat. nominating com. 1983-84, 88-89, nat. continuing profl. edn. chmn. 1988-90, nat. treas. 1991-94, nat. v.p. 1994-96, exec. v.p. 1996-98, first woman nat. pres.

1998-99), Calif. Soc. CPAs, N.Y. State Soc. CPAs (bd. dirs. Nassau chpt. 1981-86, 91-93, bd. dirs. profl. devel., 1982-86, sec., mem. fin. acctg. standards com. 1990-95), Kiwanis (program chmn. County Seat chpt. 1989-90, sec. 1990-91, pres. 1991-92), Baldwin C. of C. (treas. 1990-93). Avocations: golf, gourmet cuisine, water skiing, music. Home: 626 Willis St Hempstead NY 11550-8000

ROBLES, DARLINE P. school system administrator; AA in History, East L.A. Coll., 1968; B in History, Calif. State U., L.A., 1972; MEd, Claremont Grad. Sch., 1976; D in Edn. Policy and Adminstrn., U. So. Calif. Cert. tchr., adminstr. Tchr. Montebello Intermediate Sch., Calif., 1973—79; dir. bilingual program Montebellow Unified Sch. Dist., Calif., 1979—81; prin. Washington Elem., Montebello, Calif., 1981—85, Montebello Intermediate, Montebello, Calif., 1985—88; asst. supt. Montebello Unified Sch. Dist., Montebello, Calif., 1988—91, acting supt., 1991—92, supt., 1992—95, Salt Lake City Sch. Dist., 1995—2002; county supt. schs. L.A. County Office of Edn., 2002—. Office: LA County Office of Edn 9300 Imperial Hwy Rm EC109 Downey CA 90242-2890*

ROBLES-ROMAN, CAROL A. municipal official; b. Bronx, N.Y., 1962; m. Nelson Roman; 1 child, Adriana Roman. BA, Fordham U.; JD, NYU. Bar: N.Y. 1990. Sr. v.p., gen. counsel P.R. Indsl. Devel. Co.; asst. atty. gen. civil rights bur. N.Y. State Dept. of Law; chief staff, counsel to dep. chief adminstrv. judge Hon. Barry Cozier N.Y. State Unified Ct. Sys., spl. insp. gen. bias matters, dir. pub. affairs, spl. counsel to chief adminstrv. judge Hon. Jonathan Lippman; dep. mayor legal affairs, counsel to Mayor Mike Bloomberg City of New York. Counsel to com. promote pub. trust and confidence Unified Ct. Sys. Bd. dirs. N.Y. State Jud. Com. Women and Cts. Named one of N.Y.'s 50 Outstanding Latinas, El Diario/La Prensa. Mem.: NYU Black, Latino, and Asian Pacific Alumni Assn. (pres. 1999—2000). Office: City Hall New York NY 10007

ROBLING, CLAIRE A. state legislator; b. Oct. 22, 1956; m. Tony Robling; 2 children. Student, Coll. St. Catherine. Mem. dist. 35 Minn. Senate, St. Paul, 1996—. Office: 100 Constitution Ave Saint Paul MN 55155-1232 Home: 1169 Butterfly Ln Jordan MN 55352-9476

ROBSON, JUDITH BIROS, state legislator; b. Cleve., Nov. 21, 1939; d. George John and Mary Grace (Millen) Biros; m. Arthur Robson, Sept. 2, 1961; children: Marybeth, Marc, Matthew. BSN, St. John Coll., Cleve., 1961; MS, U. Wis., 1976. RN. Staff nurse Beloit (Wis.) Hosp., 1967-73; nurse practitioner Dr. Ken Gold, Beloit, 1976-78; instr. Blackhawk Tech. Coll., Jonesville, Wis., 1978-87; mem. Wis. Assembly, 1987-98; mem Wis. Senate from 15th dist., Madison, 1998—. Mem. bd. Bedcore, Beloit, 1990, YWCA, Beloit, 1992; sec. Majority Party Caucus, 1990—. Recipient Clean 16 award Environ. Decade. Avocations: biking, skiing, gardening, photography. Office: State Legislature State Capital PO Box 7882 Madison WI 53707-7882

ROBY, ANNIE BETH BRIAN, librarian; b. Lorenzo, Tex., Nov. 20, 1935; d. William Preston and Zona Inez (Cherry) Brian; m. Alexander Eugene Roby, Dec. 23, 1955; children: Rodney, Renee Setser, Rebecca Jordan. BS, Sul Ross State U., Alpine, Tex., 1968; BLS, U. North Tex., Denton, 1986. Cert. tchr., Tex., librarian Am. Libr. Assn., Tex. Tchr. Ector County Ind. Sch. Dist., Odessa, Tex., 1968-73, Bangs Ind. Sch. Dist., Tex., 1973-74, libr., 1990-92; tchr. Brownwood Ind. Sch. Dist., Tex., 1974-82, libr. coord., (retired May 31, 2002), 1992—; libr. Howard Payne U., Brownwood, 1987-89. Cons. Bangs Ind. Sch. Dist., 1990-92, Brownwood Ind. Sch. Dist., 1992—. Mem. Tech. Com., Brownwood, 1995-96; sec. Jr. Twentieth Century Book Club, Brownwood, 1997—. Grantee J.R. Beadel Found., 1995-97. Mem. ALA, AAUW, Tex. Libr. Assn., Rotary, Phi Delta Kappa. Baptist. Avocations: piano, swimming, water skiing, creative writing, sewing. Home: 2505 Southside Dr Brownwood TX 76801-5611 Office: Brownwood Ind Sch Dist 2100 Slayden St Brownwood TX 76801-5456

ROBY, CHERYL J. deputy assistant secretary; b. Fall River, Mass. BS in math. cum laude, Bridgewater State Coll. Various positions Naval Tech. Intelligence Ctr., Suitland, Md., 1975-88, Def. Intelligence Agy., 1988-90; with Office of asst. sec. of def., 1991-92; asst. dep. dir. Intelligence Program Evaluation, 1992-93; dir. programs and evaluations, 1993-96; acting prin. dir. for intelligence Office of Dep. Asst. Sec. of Def., 1996-97, acting dep. asst. sec. of def., 1997-98, dep. asst. sec. of def., 1998—. Office: Dep Asst Sec of Def Programs & Evaluation 6000 Defense Pentagon Washington DC 20301-6000

ROBY, PAMELA ANN, sociology educator; b. Milw., Nov. 17, 1942; d. Clark Dearborn and Marianna (Gilman) R.; m. James Peter Mulherin, July 15, 1977 (div. 1987). BA, U. Denver, 1963; MA, Syracuse U., 1966; PhD, NYU, 1971. Instr. ednl. sociology NYU, 1966; asst. prof. George Washington U., Washington, 1970-71; asst. prof. sociology and social welfare Brandeis U., Waltham, Mass., 1971-73; chair cmty. studies bd. U. Calif., Santa Cruz, 1974-76, 79, assoc. prof., 1973-77, prof. sociology and women's studies, 1977—, dir. sociology doctoral program, 1988-91, chair sociology dept., 1998-2001. Vis. scholar U. Wash., Seattle, 1991-92; mem. anthropology, linguistics and sociology panel NSF, Washington, 1993; mem. sociology program rev. com. Northeastern U., Boston, 1990; assessor Social Scis. and Humanities Rsch. Coun. Can., Toronto, 1993; cons. James Irvine Found., San Francisco, 1986; vice chair Nat. Commn. on Working Women, Washington, 1977-80; mem. social sci. rsch. rev. com. NIMH, Washington, 1976-78; Re-evaluation Counseling (coll. and U. faculty reference person), 1980—. Author: Women in the Workplace, 1981; editor: The Poverty Establishment, 1974, Child Care: Who Cares? Foreign and Domestic Infant and Early Childhood Development Policies, 1973-75; co-author: The Future of Inequality, 1970; adv. editor: Sociol. Quar., 1990-93, Gender and Society, 1986-89. Andrew W. Mellon sr. scholar Wellesley Coll., 1978-79; vis. fellow Indian Coun. Social Sci. Rsch., 1979. Mem. Soc. for Study Social Problems (pres. 1996-97), Sociologists for Women in Soc. (pres. 1978-80), Am. Sociol. Assn. (chair sect. on sex and gender 1974-78, exec. coun. mem.-at-large 1975-78), Internat. Sociol. Assn. (rsch. coun. mem.-at-large 1978-82), Pacific Sociol. Assn. (v.p. 1996-97), Ea. Sociol. Assn. (exec. coun. mem.-at-large 1973-74), Re-evaluation Counseling (internat. ref. person for coll. and univ. faculty), Phi Beta Kappa, Alpha Kappa Delta. Avocations: camping, hiking, painting, swimming, pen and ink drawing. Office: U Calif Dept Sociology C8 Santa Cruz CA 95064

ROCAFORT, JULIA ESTHER, social worker; b. San Juan, P.R., Dec. 9, 1952; d. Julio Rocafort, Esther Campos. BA, U. South Fla., 1975; MSW, Barry U., Miami Shores, Fla., 1978. LCSW, ind. social worker, cert. social worker/counselor Ohio, diplomate in clin. social work, Am. Bd. Examiners in Social Work. Clin. social worker/adj. instr. Jackson Meml. Hosp./U. Miami, 1979—81; svc. chief/minority svcs. coord. County of Orange Mental Health, Santa Ana, Calif., 1981—90; clin. specialist/analyst Preferred Health Care, Irvine, Calif., 1990; mental health asst. adminstr. San Bernardino County Mental Health, Calif., 1990—93; clin. social worker Shasta County Dept. Mental Health, Redding, Calif., 1994; dir. social svcs./support svcs. Redding Specialty Hosp., Redding, 1994—98; clin. supr. North Valley Sch./Family Intervention Cmty. Support, Redding, 1998—. Adj. instr. Calif. State U., Long Beach, 1985—90, U. Miami, 1979—81, Nat. U., Redding, 2002—; cons., social svc. specialist Office of Refugee Resettlement, Washington, 1980; lectr./presenter in field. Mem. Health Improvement Partnership, Redding, Calif., 1996—99; chmn. Shasta Trinity AIDS Consortium, Redding, 1996—98. Named Woman of Achievement, County of Orange, 1989. Mem.: NASW, Internat. Critical Incident Stress Found. Democrat. Roman Catholic. Avocations: kayaking, art appreciation, oil painting. Office: Family Intervention Cmty Support 3300 Churn Creek Ste B Redding CA 96001

ROCCA, CHRISTINA B. federal agency administrator; married; 2 children. BA in History, King's Coll., London, 1980. Intelligence officer CIA, 1982—97; fgn. affairs advisor Senate Sam Brownback; asst. sec. of state South Asian affairs U.S. Dept. of State, Washington, 2001—. Office: US Dept of State South Asian Affairs 2201 C St NW Washington DC 20520-6243

ROCCA, SUE, state legislator; b. May 12, 1949; AS, Ctrl. Mich. Coll. Commr. Macomb County, Mich.; rep. Mich. Dist. 30, 1995-2000. Vice chmn. health policy com. Mich. Ho. Reps., joint com. on adminstrv. rules & regulatory affairs. Office: Office Bd Commrs Macomb County Court Bldg 2nd Fl 40 Clement Ct Mount Clemens MI 48043-5719 Address: Mich State Capitol PO Box 30014 Lansing MI 48909-7514

ROCCO, NIKKI, film company executive; m. Joseph Rocco. Sales dept. Universal Pictures, 1967, asst. to gen. sales mgr., 1981—84, v.p., distbn., 1981—84, 1984—90, sr. v.p., distbn. and mktg., 1990—95, exec. v.p., distbn., 1995—96, pres., distbn., 1996—. Office: Universal Pictures 100 Universal City Plaza Universal City CA 91608*

ROCCO, VANESSA M. art historian, curator, educator; b. Eau Claire, Wis., Aug. 14, 1970; d. Thomas Martin Rocco and Agnes Walsh McKnight; m. Alan Leonard Chin, Apr. 8, 2000. BA, Am. U., Washington, 1992; MPhil, CUNY, N.Y.C., 2002. Mus. asst. Phillips Collection, Washington, 1992—93; dealer's asst. Pace Wildenstein, N.Y.C., 1996—97; curatorial asst. Guggenheim Mus., N.Y.C., 1997—99; curatorial asst., curator Internat. Ctr. Photography, N.Y.C., 2000—02; vis. instr. Pratt Inst., Bklyn., 2003. Curator Kristen Ann Carr Found. Benefit, N.Y.C., 2000; guest curator icon@remotelounge, N.Y.C., 2002. Mem. Film Forum, 2001—, Greenpeace, 2002—. Recipient Presdl. scholarship, Am. U., 1988—92, Peggy Guggenheim studentship, Guggenheim Found., Venice, Italy, 1993; fellow, Grad. Ctr., CUNY, 1996—97, 1999—2000. Mem.: Coll. Art Assn. Democrat. Avocations: political activism, independent films.

ROCHA, CATHERINE TOMASA, municipal official; BA, U. Mo., 1977, MA, 1979. Cert. mcpl. clk. U. Mo., 1991. Student svc. coord., academic advisor U. Mo., Kansas City, 1979-84; dir. records records dept. Jackson County Courthouse, Kansas City, 1984-87; city clk. Office of the City Clk. City of Kansas City, 1988—. Mem. human rels. adv. commn., 1982-84; mem. bd. zoning commn., 1978-79. Author: (oral history) Black Baseball-The Kansas City Monarch Experience, 1978; editor: newsletter CCFOA, 1991-95. Bd. dirs. Trinity Luth. Hosp. Found., 1996, Women's Found. Gtr. Kansas City; chmn. Westside Fountain Com., 1995-97; former trustee, chmn. auction benefit Westport Allen Ctr.; bd. dirs. Trinity Hosp., 1998-99. Harvard U. fellow, 1990; named 25 Most Influential Hispanic Leaders in Kansas City Dos Mundos newspaper, 1994. Mem. Internat. Inst. Mcpl. Clks. (chmn. big cities com. 1991-94, Harvard grant allocation com. 1994-95, profl. status com. 1995-96), Mexican-Am. Women's Nat. Assn., Friends of Art Coun. (mem. exec. bd.), Southwest Blvd. Merchants Assn. (bd. dirs.), Westside Bus. Assn. (pres. 1996-97). Home: 4545 Wornall Rd Kansas City MO 64111-3270 Office: City of Kansas City Mo Office of the City Clk City Hall 25th Fl 414 E 12th St Kansas City MO 64106-2702

ROCHE, BARBARA ANNE, retired minister, editor; b. Long Beach, Calif., Aug. 28, 1934; d. Claire Peter and Agnes Louise (Elford) Roche. BA, Stanford U., 1956; cert., United Theol. Coll., Bangalore, India, 1961; MDiv, Princeton Theol. Sem., 1960; DMin, San Francisco Theol. Sem., 1984. Ordained min. Presbyterian Ch., 74. Clk. typist Smithsonian Instn., Washington, 1956—57; dir. religious edn. Emmanuel Presbyn. Ch., Spokane, 1962—66; area rep. Commn. on Ecumenical Mission and Rels., Chgo., 1966—73; dir. student svcs. Pacific Sch. of Religion, Berkeley, Calif., 1973—76, dean of students, 1976—84; editor Concern Mag. and Newsfold, N.Y.C., 1985—88, Horizons Mag. and Bible Study, Louisville, 1988—97, ret., 1998. Assoc. Consultation on Ch. Union, Princeton, NJ, 1973—80; parish assoc. St. John's Presbyn. Ch., Berkeley, 1981—84; judge H.S. jours. Assoc. Ch. Press, 1998—99. Editor: (jours.) Living the Word, 1999—2000, (mag.) Stewardship Part 2, 1998, (book) Dear House, Mission Becomes You, 2000. Named Woman of Decade, Grad. Theol. Union Women's Ctr., 1975. Mem.: NOW, Assn. Presbyn. Women Clergy, Presbyn. Writers' Guild, Presbyn. Women (life), Amnesty Internat. Democrat. Presbyterian.

ROCHE, GAIL CONNOR, editor; b. Phila., Aug. 14, 1953; d. Donald Russell Connor; m. Richard Roche, Nov. 21, 1981; children: Alex James, Clare Evelyn. AB cum laude, Franklin & Marshall Coll., Lancaster, Pa., 1975; MA with distinction, Rider Coll., 1988. Cert. tchr., Pa. Tchr. Pennsbury Schs., Fallsington, Pa., 1975-76, Cen. Bucks Sch., Doylestown, Pa., 1977-79; reporter Trenton Times, N.J., 1979-82; editor Dow Jones & Co, Princeton, N.J., 1982-95; mem. adv. bd. Dow Jones Women's Network, Princeton, 1990-95; tech. editor Bloomberg News, Princeton, 1995-2000; sr. editor Bloomberg Markets, 2000—. Contbr. articles to mags. Mem. Phi Beta Kappa. Home: 23 Jericho Run Washington Crossing PA 18977-1027 E-mail: groche@bloomberg.net.

ROCHE, PAULINE JENNIFER, artist; b. London, Eng., Sept. 22, 1961; arrived in U.S., 1995; d. Walter Daniel and Doreen Molly Roche; m. Hany Massarany, Feb. 27, 1986; children: Thomas Daniel, Natalie Jane. BS, Monash U., Melbourne, Australia, 1982. Rsch. physiology dept. physiology Monash U., Melbourne, 1983—86; rsch., policy and planning officer Victorian State Govt. Dept. Edn./Pub. Svc. Bd., Melbourne, 1986—92; artist, 1989—. Exhibitions include Sherbrooke Art Award exhbns., 1991—97, Victorian Artists Soc. Ann. Exhbns., 1992—2001, Alice Bale Ann. Nat. Exhbns., 1993—98, Camberwell Rotary Ann. Juried Art Exhbn., 1992—98, 1993, 2000, Kew Gallery Invitational Exhbn., 1994, Victorian Artists Soc. Artist of Yr. Invitational Exhbn., 1997, Salmagundi Club 21st Ann. Open Exhbn., Salmagundi Club, 1997—98, Catherine Lorillard Wolfe Art Club 101st Art Exhbn., 1997, Am. Artists Profl. League 69th Grand Nat. Exhbn., 1997, Newbury Fine Arts Figurative Art Group Exhbn., Boston, 2000, Celebrate! Exhbn., Tucson, 2002, Newbury Fine Arts, Boston, 1998—2004, others, one-woman shows include Cato Gallery, Victorian Artists Soc. Galleries, Melbourne, 1994, Ventana Med. Sys. Nat. Hdqs., Tucson, 2003. Recipient Gold Medal of Honor, Audubon Artists 55th Ann. Exhn., 1997, Hans Heysen award, Sherbrooke Art Soc., 1992, Award for Oil Painting, Alice Bale Nat. Art Awards, 1994, Mavis Hill Acquisitive Award, Sherbrooke Spring Exhbn., 1995, Gordon Moffat award, Victorian Artists Soc., 1997, Highly Commended, Victorian Artists Soc. Dep. Lord Mayor's Exhbn., 1999, N.J. Chpt. award for artistic excellence, Am. Artists Profl. League, 1997, Pres. award, Salmagundi Club, 1997, Artist Showcase award, Manhattan Arts Internat., 1997, 1998, Leonard J. Meiselman Meml. award, Catherine Lorillard Wolfe Art Club, 1997, Sharon and Danielle Ortlip Meml. award, Salmagundi Club, 1998. Mem.: Australian Guild Realist Artists, Portrait Soc. Am., Victorian Artists Soc. (signatory mem., Gordon Moffat award 1997). E-mail: paulinerochepj@aol.com.

ROCHELLE, DOROTHY, educational consultant; b. Danville, Va., Nov. 8, 1922; d. Morton Dean and Eunice Pearl Edwards; m. James Edward Rochelle, Feb. 17, 1946; children: Michael, Deborah, Stephen, Patricia. Diploma in Nursing, St. Phillips Sch. Nursing, Richmond, Va., 1945. RN, Va., Calif. Charge nurse L.A. Gen. Hosp., 1948, Calif. Luth. Hosp., L.A., 1949, White Meml. Hosp., L.A., 1950-52, St. Francis Hosp., Lynwood, Calif., 1952; cmty. liaison L.A. Unified Sch. Dist., 1977—. Title I parent U.S. Congress, Washington, 1973. Mem. Urban League, L.A., 1999—, Black Women's Forum, L.A., 1999—; chairperson 1st Calif. State-wide Parent Conf. on Title I, Marin County, Calif., 1973; mem. L.A. Mayor's Adv. Com. on Edn.; cons. U.S. Dept. Edn. on New Regulations for Title I Funds, 1972-78; founder Advocates for Black Children, L.A., 1999—; life mem. PTA, L.A., 1999—. Recipient Mayor's Human Rels. award, L.A., 1970; hon. by Nat. Assn. Sch. Adminstrs. Mem. NAACP, NOW, Nat. Coalition of ESEA Title I Parents (founding and emeritus). Democrat. Home: 858 E 104th St Los Angeles CA 90002-3253 Office: Los Angeles Unified Sch Dist 450 N Grand Ave Rm G-353 Los Angeles CA 90012-2123

ROCHELLE, LUGENIA, academic administrator; b. Maple Hill, N.C., July 14, 1943; d. John Edward and Ruby Lee (Holmes) R. BA, St. Augustine's Coll., 1965; MS, N.C. A & T State U., 1969; D of Pedagogy, Barbar-Scotia Coll., 1993. Cert. tchr., N.C. Tchr. French, English Butler High Sch., Barnwell, S.C., 1965-67; instr. English N.C. A & T State U., Greensboro, 1970-77, St. Augustine's Coll., Raleigh, N.C., 1977-86, dir. freshman studies program, 1986-91, dean lower coll., 1991-95, asst. to v.p. acad. affairs, 1991-92; dir. gen. studies, asst. prof. English Voorhees Coll., Denmark, S.C., 1996-98, spl. asst. to pres. external affairs, 1999—2002, dir. Hons. Coll., 1999—, dean, Coll. of General Studies, 2002—. Dir. Mellon program St. Augustine's Coll., Raleigh, 1980-83; adv. bd. cooperating Raleigh Colls., 1986—, Off to Coll., Montgomery, Ala., 1993—; mem. profl. practices commn. N.C. Dept. Pub. Instrn., 1994-96; coord. Title III, 1999-00, coord. Bd. Trustees Rels., 1999-02; dir. Ctr. Excellence in Humanities, Vorhees Coll., April 2000-02; Hostess for Radio Talk Show, Views and News from Voorhees Coll., Sept. 2001-03. Author: English Manual of Writing, 1980, (with others) Off to College, 1997, 98, reprinted, 1999, 2000, 01; editor: Can't Nobody Do You Like Jesus, 1998. Judge oratorical contests, Optimist Club, Raleigh, 1985-93; chair pro tem Raleigh Bicentennial Hist. Com., Raleigh, 1991-92; initiated, effected chartering of Phi Eta Sigma St. Augustine's Coll., 1995; bd. dirs. Garner Rd. YMCA, Raleigh, 1994-1996; coord. Honda Campus All-Star Challenge, 1996—; lay min., sec. vestry St. Philip's Episcopal Ch., 1997—; instnl. rep. S.C. Women in Higher Edn., Voorhees Coll., 1998—. Nat. teaching fellow N.C. A & T State U., Greensboro, 1968-70. NCTE Fellow Nat. Coun. Tchrs. English; mem. ASCD (assoc.), Am. Assn. U. Women (pres. Denmark Br.), Cardinal Club. Avocations: reading, collecting antique birds, travel. E-mail: rochelle@voorhees.edu.

ROCHETTE, LAURA CHRISTINE, literature educator; b. Montgomery, Ala., Sept. 6, 1963; d. Kenneth Ferdinand Rochette and Patricia Mary Francoeur. MA, Middlebury Coll., Vt., 1996; BA, U. Calif. L.A., 1985. English tchr. Marlborough Sch., L.A., 1988—. Mem.: UCLA Alumni Assn., Modern Lang. Assn. Avocations: singing, writing, reading, cooking, travel. Office: Marlborough Sch 250 S Rossmore Ave Los Angeles CA 90004 E-mail: laura.rochette@marlboroughschool.org.

ROCK, CARO, publisher; b. Kansas City, Mo., Aug. 4, 1953; d. Paul Jr. and Barbara Uhlmann; m. Robert Henry Rock, Dec. 20, 1975; children: William, Thomas. Student, Wheaton Coll., 1971-72; BA, Tulane U., 1975; postgrad., Temple U. Asst. editor Ames Pub. Co., Phila., 1975-76; lending officer Provident Nat. Bank, Phila., 1976-78; asst. v.p. Fidelity Bank, Phila., 1978-83; spl. sections Montgomery Newspapers, Ft. Washington, Pa., 1987-95; assoc. pub. Main Line Life, Ardmore, Pa., 1995—. Bd. mem. Free Libr. Phila.; chmn. bd. Rock Sch. Ballet; adv. bd. Main Line Art Ctr.; fin. com. Haverford Sch.; assocs. bd. Phila. Art Mus. Named to Pa. Best 50 Women in Bus., 1997. Mem. Main Line C. of C. (bd. mem.).

ROCK, MARY ANN, fine artist, educator, consultant; b. St. Louis, Mar. 2, 1931; d. Clobert Bernard and Mary Henrietta (Jones) Broussard; m. William Ralph Rock, Mar. 18, 1960 (div. Sept. 1967); 1 child, John Henry C. BS, Bennett Coll., 1952; postgrad., Chgo. Art Inst., 1953-54, So. Ill. U., Carbondale, 1955. Instr. arts and crafts Presidio Hill Sch., San Francisco, 1966-71; dir. gallery Cannery House Gallery, Friday Harbor, Wash., 1974-76; co-founder Island Artisans, Friday Harbor, 1980-85; gallery asst. Waterworks Gallery, Friday Harbor, 1986-95; with European study tour, 1996; patron sponsored painting sabbatical, 2001—03; prin., owner Dream Keeper Art Card Co., 2002—. Guest instr. Spring St. Sch., Friday Harbor, 2001, 02. Author, illustrator: DreamKeeper, 1995; illustrator brochures; one-woman and group shows include 13th Salon Internat. del Alpha, Lyon, France, 7th Whatcomb County Museum Bellingham, 1988, Portland C.C., 1990, Chetwynn Stapleton Gallery, Portland, 1989-98, Waterworks Gallery, Friday Harbor, 1986—. Presenter art workshops Friday Harbor Elem. Sch., 1976, 87, Portland C.C., 1989, 90, guest instr. Spring St. Sch., 2001; curator African art exhibit NAACP, San Francisco, 1961. Vt. Studio Ctr. fellow, Johnson, Vt., 1999. Democrat. Avocations: collecting ethnic artifacts, skiing, rock climbing, travel, reading.

ROCKAS, ANASTASIA T. lawyer; b. Rochester, N.Y., 1963; BA, Smith-Coll., 1985; JD with hons., U. Conn., 1990. Bar: Conn. 1990, N.Y. 1993. Atty. Skadden, Arps, Slate, Meagher & Flom LLP, N.Y., 1992, ptnr. Office: Skadden Arps Slate Meagher & Flom LLP Four Times Sq New York NY 10036

ROCKBURNE, DOROTHEA GRACE, artist; b. Montreal, Que., Can;, naturalized; Student, Black Mountain Coll.; PhD, Coll. of Creative Studies, Detroit, 2002. Milton and Sally Avery Disting. prof. Bard Coll., 1986. Trustee Ind. Curators Inc., N.Y., Art in Gen.; artist in residence Am. Acad. in Rome, 1991; vis. artist Skowhegan Sch. Printing and Sculpture, 1984; Rockefeller Found. resident Bellagio (Italy) Conf. and Study Ctr., 1997. Solo exhbns. at Sonnabend Gallery, Paris, 1971, New Gallery, Cleve., 1972, Bykert Gallery, N.Y.C., 1970, 72, 73, Galleria Toselli, Milan, Italy, 1972, 73, 74, Galleria D'Arte, Bari, Italy, 1972, Lisson Gallery, London, 1973, Daniel Weinberg Gallery, San Francisco, 1973, Galerie Charles Kriwin, Brussels, 1975, Galleria Schema, Florence, Italy, 1973, 75, 92, John Weber Gallery, N.Y.C., 1976, 78, Galleria la Polena, Geona, Italy, 1977, Tex. Gallery, Houston, 1979, 80, 81, Xavier Fourcade Gallery, N.Y.C., 1981, 82, 83, 85, 86, David Bellman, Toronto, 1980, 81, Margo Leavin, Calif., 1982, Arts Club of Chgo., 1987, André Emmerich Gallery, N.Y.C., 1988, 89, 91, 92, 94, 95, 10 yr. retrospective Rose Art Mus., 1989, P. Fong & Spratt Galleries, San Jose, Calif., 1991, Sony Music Hdqs., N.Y.C., 1993, Frederick Spratt Gallery, San Jose, 1994, Guild Hall Mus., Easthampton, N.Y., 1995, Portland Mus. of Art, Maine, 1996, Ingrid Raab Gall., Berlin, 1997, Art in Gen., N.Y., 2000, Lawrence Rubin, Greenberg, Van Doren, N.Y., 2000, Dieu Donné Papermill, N.Y.C., 2003, Jan Abrams Fine Art, N.Y., 2003; group exhbns. at Whitney Mus. Am. Art, 1970, 73, 77, 79, 82, Mus. Modern Art, N.Y.C., 71, 73, 84, 86, 91, 93, 94, Buenos Aires, 1971, Kolner Kunst Market, Cologne, Germany, 1971, Stedelijk Mus., Holland, 1971, Spoleto (Italy) Festival, 1972, Palazzo Taverna, Rome, 1973, Nat. Gallery Victoria, Melbourne, Australia, 1973, Art Gallery NSW, Sydney, 1973, Auckland (New Zealand) City Art Gallery, 1973, Inst. Contemporary Art, London, 1974, Mus. d'Arte de la Ville, Paris, 1975, Galerie Aronowitsch, Stockholm, 1975, Stadtiches Mus., Manchengladbach, Germany, 1975, Galleria D'Arte Moderna, Bologna, Italy, 1975, Art Gallery Ont., Toronto, Can., 1975, Mus. Fine Art, Houston, 1975, Contemporary Arts Ctr., Cin., 1973, 75, 81, Mus. Contemporary Art, Chgo., 1971, 77, 86, Corcoran Gallery of Art, Washington, 1975, 87, Städtisches Mus., Leverkusen, Germany, 1975, Cannaviella Studio d'Arte Rome, 1976, Phila. Coll. Art, 1976, 83, Balt. Mus. Art, 1976, New Mus., N.Y.C., 1977, 80, 84, 83, Renaissance Soc. of U. Chgo., 1976, Lowe Art Mus., U. Miami, Fla., 1976, Inst. Contemporary Art, Boston, 1976, Seibu Mus. Art, Tokyo, 1976, N.Y. State Mus., Albany, 1977, Drawing Ctr., 1977, Kansas City (Mo.) Art Inst., 1977, Smithsonian Inst., Washington, 1977, Kassel, Fed. Republic Germany, 1972, 77, Ackland Art Ctr., Chapel Hill, N.C., 1979, 84, Milw. Art Ctr., 1978, 81, Biblioteca Nacional, Madrid, 1980, Gulbenkian Mus., Lisbon, Portugal, 1980, Bklyn. Mus., 1981, 89, Guggenheim Mus., 1982, 88, 89, Albright Knox Art Gallery, Buffalo, 1979, 80, 88, 89, Kuustforeningen Mus., Copenhagen, 1980, Venice Biennale, 1980, Cranbrook (Mich.) Acad. Art, 1981, Mus. Fine Arts, Boston, 1983, Contemporary Arts Mus., Houston, 1983, Norman Mackenzie Art Gallery, U. Regina, Sask., Can., 1983, Galleriet, Sweden, 1983-84, Seattle Art Mus., 1979-84, Nat. Mus. Art., Osaka, Japan, 1984, Fogg Art Mus., Cambridge, Mass., 1984, Am. Acad. and Inst. Arts and Letters, N.Y.C., 1984, 87, L.A. County Mus. Art, 1984, 86, Wadsworth Atheneum, Hartford, Conn., 1981, 84, [illegible] Mus., Fla., 1984, Grey Art Gallery, NYU, 1977, 84, 87, Avery Ctr. Arts, Bard Coll., N.Y., 1985, 87-88, Stamford (Conn.) Mus., 1985, Aldrich Mus., Conn., 1979, 82, 95, Bronx Mus. Arts, N.Y.C., 1985, High Mus., Atlanta, 1975, 81, Phila. Mus. Art, 1986, Nat. Gallery Art, Washington, 1984, 94, 97, Mus. Art, Ft. Lauderdale, Fla., 1986, Nat. Mus. Women in Art, Washington, 1987, Xavier Fourcade Gallery, 1983, 86, 87, L.A. County Mus. Modern Art, 1986-87, The Hague, The Netherlands, 1986, Carnegie-Mellon Art Gallery, Pitts., 1979, 87, Balt. Mus. Art, 1975, 76, 88, Ctr. for Fine Arts, Miami, 1989, Milw. Art Mus., 1989, Cin. Art Mus., 1989, New Orleans Mus., 1989, Denver Art Mus., 1989, Parrish Art Mus., South Hampton, N.Y., 1990, 91, 99, Margo Leavin Gallery, L.A., 1991, Guild Hall Mus., East Hampton, N.Y., 1991, Am. Acad., Rome, 1991, Mus. Contemporary Art, L.A., 1991, 99, Hunter Coll., N.Y., 1991, Centro Cultural/Arte Contemporanea, Mexico City, 1991, Hilton, San Jose, Calif., 1992, Hillwood Art Mus., L.I., N.Y., 1992, Am. Acad. and Inst. Arts and Letters, 1992, Neuberger Mus., 1992, 2000, Kohn-Abrams Galerie, L.A., 1993, The Gallery at Bristol Myers Squibb, N.J., 1993, 94, Friends of Art and Preservation in Embassies, N.Y.C., 1993, Andre Emmerich Gallery, N.Y.C., 1993, Fred Spratt Gallery, San Jose, Calif., 1994, RAAB Galarie, Berlin, 1994, N.Y. Studio Sch., N.Y.C., 1995, Rose Art Mus., Brandeis U., 1996, Addison Gallery Am. Art Philips Acad., Andover, Mass., 1997, Fine Arts Mus. San Francisco, 1997, Wexner Ctr., Columbus, 1997, Dieu Donne Papermill, Inc., N.Y.C., 1998, Pub. Sch. 1, Long Island City, N.Y., 1999, Gemini G.E.L., 1998, Am. Acad. Arts and Letters, 1999, 2001, Parsons Sch. Design, N.Y., 1999, David Dorsky Gallery, N.Y., 2000, Laurence Rubin, Greenberg, Van Doren Fine Art, N.Y.C., 2000, The Ralls Collection, D.C., 2001, Artemis Greenberg Van Doren Fine Art, N.Y.C., 2002, NAD, N.Y.C., 2002, The Armory Show, N.Y.C., 2002, The Nat. Gallery of Art, 2001, Krannert Art Mus., 2002, Selby Gallery, Fla., 2002, Ralls Collection, Washington, 2001, NY Studio Sch., N.Y.C., 2002, The Geffen Contemporary, L.A., 2002, 2004, Marcus Ritter, N.Y.C., 2002, Bowdoin Coll. Mus. Art, 2002, Reina Sophia Mus., Madrid, 2003, Cleve. Mus. Art, 2003, Mus. Fine Arts, Boston, 2003, New Britain (Conn.) Mus. Art, 2003, Mus. New Zealand, 2003, Guggenheim Mus., N.Y.C., 2004, Addison Gallery Am. Art, Mass., 2004, MOCA at Calif. Plz., L.A., 2004, others; print exhbns. at Nat. Gallery, Washington, 1994, 97, 2001, Kate Ganz, Ltd., N.Y.C., 2000, David Adamson Gallery, Washington, 2000, Fine Arts Mus. San Francisco, 1997, Bklyn. Mus., 1989, Mt. Holyoke Coll. Art Mus., 1987, Harcus Gallery, Boston, 1985, Xavier Fourcade Gallery, N.Y.C., 1982, Mus. Modern Art, N.Y.C., 1981, 91, Yale U. Art Gallery, New Haven, 1981, New Gallery Contemporary Art, Cleve., 1978, Art Gallery Ont., Toronto, 1978, Stadtiches Mus., Monchengladbach, Germany, 1971; represented in permanent collections Milw. Art Ctr., Mus. Modern Art N.Y.C., Fogg Mus., Cambridge, Mass., Phila. Mus. Art, High Mus. Art, Atlanta, Houston Mus. Fine Arts, Corcoran Gallery, Washington, Mpls. Art Inst., Mpls. Art Mus., Met. Mus. Art, N.Y.C., Guggenheim Mus., N.Y.C., Ludwig Mus., Aachen, Fed. Republic Germany, Holladay, Washington, Saatchi, London, Bard, Albright-Knox Art Gallery, Buffalo, Whitney Mus. Am. Art, N.Y.C., U. Mich., Ann Arbor, Ohio State U., Columbus, Gilman Paper Co., N.Y., Auckland (New Zealand) City Art Mus., Portland (Oreg.) Art Mus., Aaken Art Mus., Oberlin, Ohio, Highhold Internat., South Africa, U. Ohio Art Gallery, Columbus, HHK Charitable Found., Milw., Art Gallery Ont., Nat. Mus. Women in Art, Washington, Chase Manhattan Bank, N.Y.C.; installations: Hilton Hotel, San Jose, Calif., Sony Music Hdqrs., Aldridge Mus., Conn., Edward T. Gignoux Courthouse, Portland, Maine. Recipient Witowsky prize, 72d Am. Exhbn., Art Inst., Chgo., 1976, Creative Arts award, Brandeis U., 1985, Bard Coll., 1986, Jimmy Ernst Lifetime Achievement award in art, Am. Acad. Arts and Letters, 1999, The Pike award, Nat. Acad. of Art and Design, 177th Ann. Exhbn., 2002, Adolph and Clara Obrig prize, Nat. Acad. Design, 177th Ann. Exhbn., 2002, Omi Internat. Francis J. Greenberger award, 2003, Alliance for Young Artists and Writers Inc. award, 1997, Witowsky Painting award, Art Inst. of Chgo., 1976; fellow, Guggenheim fellow, 1972; grantee, Nat. Endowment Arts, 1974, Am. Acad. Rome, 1991, Pollock Krasner award, 2002. Mem.: AAAL.

ROCKEFELLER, ALLISON HALL W. conservationist; b. Manhattan, N.Y., Nov. 20, 1958; d. George Carroll and JoeAnn (Feeley) Whipple; m. Peter Clark Rockefeller, Dec. 19, 1987; 2 children. BA, Hamilton Coll., Clinton, N.Y., 1980. Asst. dir. pub. rels. Sotheby's Internat. Realty, N.Y.C., 1980-83; dir. pub. rels. and corp. comms. Douglas L. Elliman & Co., N.Y.C., 1983-88; founder residential sales divsn. Elliman East; residential sales assoc. Brown Harris Stevens, N.Y.C., 1988-90; founder Henry Hudson Soc. of Historic Hudson Valley, Inc., 1988—; trustee, devel. com. mem. Mus. of City of N.Y., 1993—; trustee, chmn. devel. com. Student Conservation Assn., Charlestown, N.H., 1987-95, chmn. bd., 1995—. Mem. Pres.'s coun. Mission Soc., N.Y.C., 1994—. Mem. Nat. Soc. Fund Raising Execs., Delta Psi. Presbyterian. Avocations: horticulture, historic houses, american history, writing, landscape architecture. Office: 30 Rockefeller Plz Rm 5600 New York NY 10112-0002

ROCKEFELLER, SHARON PERCY, broadcast executive; b. Oakland, Calif., Dec. 10, 1944; d. Charles H. and Jeanne (Dickerson) Percy; m. John D. Rockefeller IV; children: John, Valerie, Charles, Justin. BA cum laude, Stanford U.; LLD (hon.), U. Charleston, 1977, Beloit Coll., 1978; LHD (hon.), West Liberty State Coll., 1980, Hamilton Coll., 1982, Wheeling Coll., 1984. Founder, chmn. Mountain Artisans, 1968—78; chmn. Corp. Pub. Broadcasting, Washington, 1981—84; bd. dirs. Stas. WETA-TV-FM, Washington, 1987—89, pres., 1989—. Past bd. dirs. Sta. WETA-TV-FM, Washington, pres., 1989—; bd. dirs. Pub. Broadcasting Svc., W.Va. Edn. Broadcasting Authority. Mem.-at-large Dem. Nat. Conv., del., 1976, 1980, 1984; bd. dirs. Rockefeller Bros. Fund. Office: Sta WETA-FM 2775 S Quincy St Arlington VA 22206-2236

ROCKEFELLER, SHIRLEY E. court clerk; b. Sayre, Pa., May 24, 1938; d. Clayton A. and Eva M. Baldwin Wilbur; m. Richard L. Rockefeller, Sept. 27, 1937; 1 child, Randy L. Student, Ridley's Sec. Sch., 1956-57. Legal sec. A.S. Moscrip, Esq., Towanda, Pa., 1961-64; clk. Register and Recorder's Office Bradford County, Towanda, 1965-75; register, recorder and clk. of orphan's ct. Bradford County Courthouse, Towanda, 1976—. Hospitality chmn. Rep. Women, Towanda, 1996-99, scrapbook chmn., 1998—. Mem. DAR (regent), Order of Ea. Star (sec. 1965-99), Tuscarora Hist. Soc., Pa. Register of Wills Assn. (exec. bd. 1998-99). Republican. Mem. United Ch. of Christ. Avocations: crocheting, cooking, traveling, fishing. Home: RR 2 Box 425 Rome PA 18837-9568 Office: Bradford County Courthouse 301 Main St Towanda PA 18848-1824

ROCKLEN, KATHY HELLENBRAND, lawyer; b. N.Y.C., June 30, 1951; BA, Barnard Coll., 1973; JD magna cum laude, New England Sch. Law, 1977. Bar: N.Y. 1978, U.S. Dist. Ct. (so. and ea. dists.) N.Y. 1982, U.S. Dist. Ct. (no. dist.) Calif. 1985. Interpretive counsel N.Y. Stock Exchange, N.Y.C.; 1st v.p. E.F. Hutton & Co. Inc., N.Y.C.; v.p., gen. counsel and sec. S.G Warburg (U.S.A.) Inc., N.Y.C.; mem. Proskauer Rose LLP, N.Y.C. Adj. prof. Fordham Sch. Law. Mem. exec. com. lawyers divsn. Am. Friends Hebrew U.; mem. lawyers' divsn. exec. com. ADL; mem. adv. com. N.Y. Women's Bar Found. Mem. N.Y. State Bar Assn., N.Y. Women's Bar Assn., Assn. Bar City N.Y. (v.p., chmn. exec. com., chmn. drugs and law com., chmn. fed. legis. com., chmn. libr. com., securities law com., sec. 2d century com., sex and law com., young lawyers'com., corp. law com.). Office: Proskauer Rose LLP 1585 Broadway New York NY 10036 E-mail: krocklen@proskauer.com.

ROCKMAN, ILENE FRANCES, librarian, educator, editor; b. Yonkers, NY, Nov. 9, 1950; d. Leon and Margaret (Klein) Rockman; m. Fred Gertler, Mar. 9, 1996. BA, UCLA, 1972; MSLS, U. So. Calif., 1974; MA, Calif. Poly. State U., 1978; PhD, U. Calif., Santa Barbara, 1985. Libr. Wash. State U., Pullman, Wash., 1974—75, Calif. Poly. State U., San Luis Obispo, 1975—98, Calif. State U., Hayward, 1998—2001, office of the [illegible], 2001—; adj. prof. Cuesta Coll., San Luis Obispo, 1982—85; abstracter Women Studies Abstracts, Rush, NY, 1976—91. Contbr. articles to profl. jours.; editor: Reference Svcs. Rev., 1986—; co-author: BLISS-Basic Library Information Sources and Svcs., 1991—95; mem. editl. bd.: Jour. Acad. Librarianship, 2003, Libr. Hi Tech., 1997—, Am. Libr., 1997—99. Del. Dem. Nat. Conv., 1984; bd. dirs. Friends of Hayward Pub. Libr., 2001—. Recipient scholarship, Calif. PTA, L.A., 1973, Literati award, MCB Univ. Press, 2001. Mem.: ALA, Total Libr. Exch. (pres. 1979—80), Am. Ednl. Rsch. Assn., Calif. Assn. Rsch. Librs. (mem. exec. bd. 1998—99), Assn. Coll. and Rsch. Librs. (mem. exec. com. edn. and behavioral sci. sect. 1988—90, mem. exec. com. univ. libr. sect. 1999—2002, Disting. Libr. of Yr. Ednl. and Behavioral Sect. 2003), Calif. Libr. Assn. (mem. coun. 1983—86), Spl. Libr. Assn., Am. Assn. Higher Edn., Calif. Reading Assn. (Exemplary Svc. award 1992), Libr. Assocs. Calif. Poly. State U. (exec. sec. 1981—83).

ROCKWELL, ELIZABETH GOODE, dance company director, consultant, educator; b. Portland, Oreg., Sept. 10, 1920; d. Henry Walton and Elizabeth (Harmon) Goode; m. William Hearne Rockwell, Feb. 3, 1948; children: Enid, Karen, William. BA, Mills Coll., 1941; MA, NYU, 1946. Instr. dance Monticello Jr. Coll., Alton, Ill., 1941-42; dir. masters program in dance Smith Coll., Northampton, Mass., 1946-48; 1st dir. dance dept. High Sch. of Performing Arts, N.Y.C., 1948-51, 53-54; dir. Elizabeth Rockwell Sch. Dance, Bedford, N.Y., 1956-86, Rondo Dance Theater Internat. Dance Touring Co., Bedford, 1971-93; tchr. continuing dance classes CCAE, 1994—; with Martha Graham, 1944-46; with Hanya Holm, 1946-48; with José Limon, 1949-52. Mem. adv. ednl. com. Calif. Ctr. for Arts, Escondido, Calif., 1993-95, dir. dance classes, 1994—; tchr. master class, choreographer Waitukubuli Dance Theater, Dominica, 1999; dir. prime dance performance Artists Coming of Age, U. San Diego, 1999. Choreographer (suite of dances) Jazz Suite, 1966, (50-minute dances) Catch the Wind, 1969, Genesis, 1972, (narrative modern ballet) The Executioner, 1974, Decathalon, 1982; dir. (subscription series) Dance-Art-Poetry-Jazz, 1978-79, (dance/music 1600-1900) Stages in Ages, 1981, (Am. dance revivals) Masterpieces of American Dance, 1982-84, Dances of the Decades, 1985-90, (revival & new choreography) Dances of Our Times, 1991; dir. dance workshops for Calif. Ctr. Arts, 1994, 95, 96; creator, founder performing group of older dancers Golden Connections Dance Ensemble of Women, CCAE, (touring San Diego area), 1996—. Bd. dirs. Coun. for Arts in Westchester, White Plains, N.Y., 1978-79, affiliate, 1978— Recipient Medal for Performance, Israeli Army, 1966, Award for Excellence in Arts Edn. Alumnae of High Sch. of Performing Arts, 1990, Tommy Dance award of distinction San Diego Area Dance Alliance, 1999; various grants N.Y. State Coun. on Arts, 1971-93, Coun. Arts in Westchester, 1973-92, dance touring program grant Nat. Endowment for Arts, 1975-79. Mem. Am. Dance Guild, Westchester Dance Coun. (program dir. 1965-69), Assn. Am. Dance Cos., San Diego Area Dance Alliance (bd. dirs. 1995—). Avocations: writing, swimming, touring, reading. Home: 205 Tampico Gln Escondido CA 92025-7359

ROCKWOOD, MARCIA, magazine editor; Exec. editor Reader's Digest, Pleasantville, N.Y. Office: Reader's Digest Reader's Digest Rd Pleasantville NY 10570-7000*

RODALE, ARDATH HARTER, publishing executive; 5 children. B in art edn., Kutztown U., LLD (hon.), 1995. Chmn. Prevention Mag., Rodale Press, Inc., 1990—; owner, CEO Rodale Press Inc., Emmaus, Pa., 1990—2002. Chmn. emeritus on the bd. Rodale Inst. Author: Climbing Toward the Light, 1989, Gifts of the Spirit, 1997, Reflections: Finding, Love, Hope and Joy in Everyday Life, 2002. Office: Rodale Press Inc 33 E Minor St Emmaus PA 18098-0099

RODAMAKER, MARTI TOMSON, bank executive; m. Bill Rodamaker; children: Mackenzie, Meeghan. BA in Econs., U. No. Iowa; MBA in Fin., U. St. Thomas. Credit analyst Marquette Bank, Mpls., 1984—87; field examiner Norwest Bank, 1987—93; from mem. staff to pres. First Citizens Nat. Bank, Mason City, Iowa, 1993—2000, pres., 2000—. Mem. adv. coun. Fed. Res. Iowa. Chmn. Hosp. Found.; treas. campaign YMCA; bd. regents Luther Coll., 2003—. Named One of 25 Women to Watch, U.S. Banker Mag., 2003. Mem.: Iowa Ind. Bankers Assn. (pres. 2001), Mason City C. of C. (bd. dir.). Office: First Citizens National Bank 2601 Fourth St SW Mason City IA 50401-1708*

RODEKOHR, DIANE E. state official; A in Bus. Mgmt., Nat. Bus. Inst., 1958. Asst. exec. dir. Associated Gen. Contractors of Wyo., 1963-78; field rep. to Sen. Alan Simpson Wyo., 1978-84; state dir. to Sen. Alan Simpson, 1984-96; state dir. to Sen. Michael Enzi, 1997—. Mem. PEO, Cheyenne C. of C., Rotary (sec. 1995-99). Office: Office Sen Michael Enzi 2120 Capitol Ave Ste 2007 Cheyenne WY 82001-3631

RODELLO, DEBBIE A. state representative; b. Espanola, N.Mex., Nov. 28, 1961; m. Thomas Rodella; children: Thomas Rodella Jr., Kara Rodella. AA, No. N.Mex. C.C., 1982, AA, 1983; student, Coll. Santa Fe. Sec. Materials Sci. Technician, San Juan Pueblo, N.Mex., 1998—. Democrat. Roman Catholic. Home: PO Box 1074 San Juan Pueblo NM 87566 Office: New Mexico State Capitol Rm 201A Santa Fe NM 87501

RODEN, CAROL LOONEY, retired language educator; b. Boston, Mass., Jan. 10, 1939; d. William Vincent and Margaret Carey Delaney; m. Vincent James Looney, Feb. 11, 1961 (div. Nov. 1995); children: Vincent J. III Looney, Kara A. Putnam, Douglas B. Looney, John W. Looney; m. Thomas Edward Roden, July 7, 1997. BA, Emmanuel Coll., 1960; postgrad., SUNY, Albany, 1974. Spanish tchr. Hingham (Mass.) H.S., 1960—61, Kennedy H.S., Utica, NY, 1974—80, Waterville (N.Y.) Cen. Sch., 1983—94, Archbishop Carroll H.S., Wayne, Pa., 1995—96; ret., 1996. Author (numerous poems) ; photographer. Pres. PTA, Whitesboro, NY, 1971; v.p. Newcomers Group, Utica, NY, 1970; vol. Puerto Rican Cmty. House, Boston, 1959. Fellow, U. Kans., 1960; scholar Gov. Furcolo scholar, State of Mass., 1956. Mem.: AAUW (v.p. membership 1995—99, Gift honoree 1999, Outstanding Woman of Yr. 2000), Alpha Mu Gamma. Democrat. Roman Catholic. Home: 119 Sawgrass Dr Blue Bell PA 19422

RODENBERG, ANITA JO, academic administrator; b. Dodge City, Kans., Jan. 27, 1956; d. Albert Milton and Anita Marileen (O'Bleness) Kidder; m. Leland Leroy Lambert, Nov. 25, 1972 (div. July 1991); children: Justin, Mason, Vanessa; m. Lindell Vern Rodenberg, Mar. 10, 1994; children: Dawn, Elaina, Lynell. AS in Bus. Adminstrn., Seward County C.C., 1995; BS in Human Resource Mgmt., Friends U., 1996; MS in Edn. Adminstrn., Fort Hays State U., 1999. Cert. devel. edn. specialist Appalachian State U. Co-owner LA Inc., Liberal, Kans., 1980-90; accts. payable clk. Seward County C.C., Liberal, 1990-93, asst. dir. bus. and industry, 1993-95, peer tutor coord., 1995—, coord. devel. edn., 1996—, dir. acad. achievement ctr., 1996—. Mem. adult learning ctr. adv. bd. Seward County C.C., 1996—, mem. continuous quality coun., 1996—. Mem. Liberal Transition Coun., 1996—. Mem. Nat. Assn. for Devel. Edn., Midwest Regional Assn. for Devel. Edn., Coll. Reading and Learning Assn., Seward County C.C. Profl. Employee Assn., Liberal C. of C. (edn. com. 1996—). Home: 2164 N Carlton Ave Liberal KS 67901-2127 Office: Seward County CC 1801 N Kansas Ave PO Box 1137 Liberal KS 67905-1137

RODENBERG, JOY D. sports association executive; Student, Wellesley Coll.; grad., Northwestern U. Mem. Jr. Tennis Coun. U.S. Tennis Assn., 1977-87, mem. nominating com., 1985-87, mem. sanctions and schedules com., 1981-87, mem. jr. ranking com., 1977-80, v.p., 1996—, in charge of Cmty. Tennis Devel. Divsn., in charge of Adminstrn. and [illegible]; chmn. Player Devel. Com., 1988-91, bd. dirs., 1991-97, vol., 1998—. Pres. Missouri Valley Tennis Assn., 1980-84; past umpire U.S. Open. Named to Missouri Valley Hall of Fame, 1994, Nebr. Tennis Hall of Fame, 1989.

RODGER, GINETTE, professional association executive, nurse; b. Amos, Que., Can., Mar. 18, 1943; d. Joseph and Blanche (Gagnon) Lemire; m. William James Rodger; children: Robert, Philippe, Sabrina. Diploma in nursing, U. Ottawa, 1964, BS in nursing, 1966; M.Nursing Adminstrn., U. Montreal, 1971; D.Sci. h.c., U. N.B., 1985. Gen. duty nurse Ottawa Gen. Hosp., Ont., 1964-65; asst. dir. nursing St. Vincent Hosp., Ottawa, summer 1965; gen. duty nurse Queen Mary Hosp. and Jewish Gen. Hosp., Montreal, Que., summer 1966, Hotel-Dieu Hosp., Amos, summer 1967, Queen Mary Hosp., summer 1968; adminstrv. asst. Hosp. Notre-Dame, Montreal, 1968-72, gen. duty nurse, 1972-73, nurse researcher, 1973, asst. dir. nursing, 1973, in-charge nursing research, 1973-74, dir. nursing, 1974-81; exec. dir. Can. Nurses Assn., Ottawa, 1981—, pres., 2000—02. Mem. Can. Council Hosp. Accreditation, 1972-86, chmn., 1981-82; nat. dep. dir. St. John Ambulance for Health Care Program, 1981-86; mem. nat. com. tng. Order of St. John, 1981-86; mem. service adv. com. Victorian Order of Nurses for Can., 1981— ; mem. nat. health com. Can. Red Cross Soc., 1981— ; mem. Que. council Order of St. John, 1975-81, v.p., 1976-79; pres. Assn. St. John, 1976-79; chmn. nursing edn. com. Que. Ministry Edn., 1978-80; mem. Fedn. Que. Health and Social Affairs Adminstrs., 1975-81; mem. com. essential services Que. Ministry Labor, 1978-80; mem. group dirs. nursing Montreal Univ. Hosps., 1980-81. Decorated Serving Sister Can. Order St. John Ambulance, 1979; recipient Vigor prize Que. Fedn. Health Services Adminstr., 1981; officer St. John Ambulance, 1981; Ryerson fellowship award Ryerson Poly. Inst., 1984— . Mem. Can. Coll. Health Service Execs., Can. Hosp. Assn., Ordre des infirmieres et infirmiers du Quebec, Coll. Nurses Ont., Registered Nurses Assn. Ont., Am. Soc. Hosp. Nursing Service Adminstrn., Can. Nurses Found. (sec.-treas. 1981—), Med. Research Council Can., Can. Nurses Protective Soc. (chief exec. officer, treas.). Office: Can Nurses Assn 50 The Driveway Ottawa ON Canada K2P 1E2

RODGER, MARION MCGEE, medical and surgical nurse, nursing administrator; b. Waterville, Maine, Feb. 21, 1949; d. Audrey Renee (Kilgore) McGee. Diploma, Albany Med. Ctr., 1970; student, U. Calif., San Diego, 1994. RN, Calif.; cert. in psychiat.-mental health nursing. Clin. nurse med.-surg. Albany Med. Ctr., 1970-84, mgr. vascular/trauma unit, 1970-78; ICU nurse Sharp Meml. Hosp., San Diego, 1984, divsn. mgr. orth., neuro-pulm., surg., med., 1985-91; br. dir. Nat. Staffing Agy., 1992; health facilities evaluator nurse State of Calif., 1994-99; supr. licensing and cert. div., supr. San Diego dist. office Dept. Health Svcs., State of Calif., 1999—. Home: 731 Avocado Pl Del Mar CA 92014-3943 E-mail: mrodger@ca.gov.

RODGERS, AMBER GAYLE, speech pathology/audiology services professional; b. Houston, Nov. 16, 1971; d. James Cagney and Sandra Gayle Craig; m. Matthew Walker Rodgers, Nov. 20, 1999; children: Dakota Walker, Bailey Gayle. BS in Comm. Disorders, Tex. Tech U., 1994; MA in Comm. Disorders, Our Lady of Lake U., 1997. Speech-lang. pathologist Amistad Nursing Facility, Uvalde, Tex., 1997—2000, Cypress-Fairbanks Ind. Sch. Dist., Houston, 2001—. Speech-lang. pathologist Southwood Nursing Home, Uvalde, 1997—2000, Medina Valley Ind. Sch. Dist., Castroville, Tex., 1998—2000, Spring Ind. Sch. Dist., Tex., 2001, instr. dance, Houston, 2003—. Vol. Big Bros./Big Sisters Orgn., 1991—94, Battered Women's Shelter, 1993. Mem.: Am. Speech and Hearing Assn. (lic.). Baptist. Avocations: dance, sign language. Home: 7055 Hollister #2024 Houston TX 77040*

RODGERS, CYNTHIA, anchor, correspondent; Anchor Sta. WIFR-TV, Rockford, Ill.; Chgo. bur. chief Knight-Ridder Fin. News; corr. CNN Fin. News, Chgo., Washington, anchor, corr. Chgo. Adj. prof. Northwestern U. Sch. Journalism, Evanston, Ill. Office: CNN 435 N Michigan Ave Chicago IL 60611-4066

RODGERS, DENISE V. medical educator; Chief staff Cmty. Health Network, San Francisco, 1997; assoc. dean for cmty. health Robert Wood Johnson Med. Sch., New Brunswick, NJ, 1997—. Office: Robert Wood Johnson Univ Med Group Clinical Acad Bldg 125 Paterson St Ste 1400 New Brunswick NJ 08901-1977

RODGERS, GRACE ANNE, university official; b. South Bend, Ind., Apr. 19, 1936; d. Morris and Barbara Mae (Hamm) Morrow; m. Eugene M. Rodgers, July 7, 1956; children: Craig Eugene, Kimberly Sue. BS, Ind. State U., 1981; pub. mgmt. cert., Ind. U., South Bend, 1991, MPA, 1993. Dir. spl. programs Ivy Tech. State Coll., South Bend, 1990-94, mktg. cons., 1994; mem. assoc. faculty dept. pub. affairs--non-profit marketing and environ. Ind. U., 1994—, dir. internships-student svcs. Sch. Pub.-Environ. Affairs, 1994—, dir. cmty. links, 1997—. Author: (manuals) Resume and Beyond, 1990, Strategic Marketing Plan, 1994. Mem. Youth Svcs. Bur., South Bend Recipient Indiana U. South Bend Student Gov. Lifetime Achievement award. Mem. Ind. U. Sch. Pub. end Environ. Affairs Alumni Assn. (adv. coun. 1993—), Ind. U.-South Bend Alumni Assn., Ind. State U. Alumni Assn., Phi Theta Kappa (hon., award for outstanding svc. 1993), Pi Alpha Alpha (sec. 1996—). Republican. Methodist. Avocations: travel, reading, classical music. Home: 17120 Killarney Ct Granger IN 46530-9771 Office: Ind U 1800 Mishawaka Ave South Bend IN 46615-1621 E-mail: profgrac@aol.com.

RODGERS, JANET AHALT, nursing educator, dean; b. Hershey, Pa. d. Harold A. and Margaret L. (Bittle) Ahalt; m. Terry C. Rodgers. BSN, Wagner Coll., 1957; MA in Psychiat.-Mental Health Nursing, NYU, 1964, PhD Nursing, 1971; cert., N.Y. Med. Coll., 1973. RN, N.Y. Staff N.Y. State Psychiat. Inst., N.Y.C., 1957-59, head nurse, 1959-61; asst. DON Psychiat. Treatment Ctr., N.Y.C., 1961-62; group therapist Creedmoor State Hosp., Queens, N.Y., 1963; instr. Wagner Coll., S.I., N.Y., 1964-66, asst. prof., 1966-68, lectr. psychiat. nursing, 1969-70; asst. prof. psychiat. nursing Lehman Coll. CUNY, 1971-74, coord. psychiat. nursing Lehman Coll., 1971-76, assoc. prof., dep. chmn., 1974-77; prof., chairperson dept. nursing Old Dominion U., Norfolk, Va., 1977-79; cons., 1979-81; prof., chair dept. nursing Lycoming Coll., Williamsport, Pa., 1981-87; dean., prof. Philip Y. Hahn Sch. Nursing U. San Diego, 1987—. Vis. assoc. prof. Sch. Nursing U. Pa., 1981; presenter in field. Contbr. articles to profl. jours. Mem. adv. bd. Lee Hawkins Endowment Fund, Norfolk, Va., 1978-83, N.Y.C. Com. for Children, 1973-77, Bronx Health Manpower Consortium Bd., 1975-76, Ea. Va. Health Edn. Consortium, 1977-79; mem. health adv. bd. Divine Providence Hosp.-Cmty. Mental Health Ctr., 1985-87; bd. dirs. Regional Home Health Svcs., Williamsport, Pa., 1982-87, Divine Providence Hosp., Williamspot, 1986-87, San Diego Hospice, 1989-92, Am. Lung Assn. San Diego and Imperial Counties, 1994-96, Am. Heart Assn., 1996-2000, Assn. Calif. Nurse Leaders, 1996-98; bd. trustees Scripps Health, San Diego, 1998—, The Whittier Inst. for Diabetes, 2001; exec. ptnr. Cmty. Health Improvement Ptnrs., San Diego County, 1999—. Recipient Diane F. Cooper Lifetime Achievement Award, 2002. Fellow Am. Orthopsychiat. Assn., Am. Acad. Nursing; mem. ANA, Am. Assn. Colls. Nursing (bd. dirs. 1987-94, pres.-elect 1990-92, pres. 1992-94, Wagner Coll. Alumni Assn. Achievement award 1977), Wagner Coll. Nat. Alumni Assn. (bd. dirs. 1999—), NYU Alumni Assn. (v.p. 1970-72, Mary Barr Alumni award Sch. Nursing

1993), Pi Lambda Theta, Kappa Delta Pi, Phi Kappa Phi, Sigma Theta Tau (Beta Upsilon and Zeta Mu chpts.). Office: U San Diego Hahn Sch Nurs & Health Svcs 5998 Alcala Park San Diego CA 92110-2492 E-mail: rodgers@acosd.edu.

RODGERS, JOYCE ELLEN, humanities educator; Diploma in fine arts, N.Y.-Phoenix Sch. Design, N.Y.C., 1972; BA, Kean U., 1977; MA, Rutgers U., 1980. Instr. C.C. of Vt., Brattleboro, 1989—; asst. prof. Landmark Coll., Putney, Vt., 1995—. Contbr. Studia Mystica jour. Mem.: Vt. Hist. Soc. Avocation: handweaving. Office: Landmark Coll River Rd S PO Box 820 Putney VT 05346-9446

RODGERS, MARY COLUMBRO, literature educator, writer, academic administrator; b. Aurora, Ohio, Apr. 17, 1925; d. Nicola and Nancy (DeNicola) Columbro; m. Daniel Richard Rodgers, July 24, 1965; children: Robert, Patricia, Kristine. AB, Notre Dame Coll., 1957; MA, Western Res. U., 1962; PhD, Ohio State U., 1964; postgrad., U. Rome, 1964-65; EdD, Calif. Nat. Open U., 1975, DLitt, 1978. Tchr. English Cleve. elem. schs., 1945-52, Cleve. secondary schs., 1952-62; supr. English student tchrs. Ohio State U., 1962-64; asst. prof. English U. Md., 1965-66; assoc. prof. Trinity Coll., 1967-68; prof. English D.C. Tchrs. Coll. U. D.C., 1968—2000; pres. Md. Nat. U., 1972—; chancellor Open U. Am., 1965—; dean Am. Open U. Acad.; ret., 2000; ind. rschr., writer, 2000—. Author: A Short Course in English Composition, 1976, Chapbook of Children's Literature, 1977, Comprehensive Catalogue: The Open University of America System, 1978-80, Open University of America System Source Book, V, VII, VII, 1978, Essays and Poems on Life and Literature, 1979, Modes and Models: Four Lessons for Young Writers, 1981, Open University Structures and Adult Learning, 1982, Papers in Applied English Linguistics, 1982, Twelve Lectures on the American Open University, 1982, English Pedagogy in the American Open University, 1983, Design for Personalized English Graduate Degrees in the Urban University, 1984, Open University English Teaching, 1945-85: Conceptual History and Rationale, 1985, Claims and Counterclaims Regarding Instruction Given in Personalized Degree Residency Programs Completed by Graduates of California National Open University, 1986, The American Open University, 1965 to 1985: History and Sourcebook, 1986, New Design II: English Pedagogy in the American Open University, 1987, The American Open University, 1965 to 1985: A Research Report, 1987, The American Open University and Other Open Universities: A Comparative Study Report, 1988, Poet and Pedagogue in Moscow and Leningrad: A Travel Report, 1989, Foundations of English Scholarship in the American Open University, 1989, Twelve Lectures in Literary Analysis, 1990, Ten Lectures in Literary Production, 1990, Analyzing Fact and Fiction, 1991, Analyzing Poetry and Drama, 1991, Some Successful Literary Research Papers: An Inventory of Titles and Theses, 1991, Catalogue for the Mary Columbro Rodgers Literary Trust, 1992, A Chapbook of Poetry and Drama Analysis, 1992, Convent Poems, 1943-1961, 1992, Catholic Marriage Poems 1962, 1979, 1993, Catholic Widow with Children Poems 1979-1993, 1994, First Access List to the Mary Columbro Rodgers Trust by Year, 1994, Nicola Columbro: A Brief Biography, 3d edit., 1994, Biographical Sourcebook I: Mary Columbro Rodgers 1969-1995, 1995, Catholic Teacher Poems, 1945-1995, 1995, Fables and Farm Stories for Fiction Analysis, 1995, Second Access List to the Mary Columbro Rodgers Literary Trust by Alphabet, 1995, Third Access List to the Mary Columbro Rodgers Literary Trust by Subject, 1996, Fourth Access List to the Mary Columbro Rodgers Literary Trust for K-PhD Open Learning-Open University Methods with Data Batches Delineated, 2002, Journals: Reflections and Resolves 1992-2002, 14 vols., 2002; contbr. articles to profl. jours. Fulbright scholar U. Rome, 1964-65. Fellow Cath. Scholars; mem. U.S. Distance Learning Assn., Poetry Soc. Am., Nat. Coun. Tchrs. English, Am. Ednl. Rsch. Assn., Am. Acad. Poets, Pi Lambda Theta. Home and Office: Coll Heights Estates 3916 Commander Dr Hyattsville MD 20782-1027 E-mail: openuniv@aol.com.

RODGERS, ROBERTA WALKER, music educator; b. Franklin, Tenn., Jan. 24, 1952; d. James Otey Walker Jr. and Nelle Frances (Jackson) Walker; m. John Edward Rodgers Jr., Aug. 25, 1972 (div. July 1990); children: Jennie Rebecca Rodgers Springer, John Edward III. Bachelor of Music Edn., Birmingham-So., 1974; Master of Music Edn., Belmont U., 1990. Tchr. piano, Nashville, 1974—86, Franklin, Tenn., 1974—86; music specialist and choral dir. grades K-8 Harding Acad., Nashville, 1989—98; music specialist grades K-4 Metro Nashville Pub. Sch. Sys., Nashville, 1998—. Choral dir. various music festivals, 1989—, Nashville Children's Choir, 1994—; adj. prof. Belmont U., Nashville, 1999—; presenter in field. Mem. edn. outreach adv. bd. Country Music Hall of Fame, Nashville, 2000—02. Mem.: Music Educators Nat. Conv., Am. Choral Dirs. Assn. Presbyterian. Avocations: sewing, needlecrafts, gardening, cooking. Home: 3000 Hillsboro Pike # 106 Nashville TN 37215

RODGERS, SUZANNE HOOKER, ergonomics consultant, physiologist; b. Rochester, N.Y., Dec. 20, 1939; d. John Ashmead and Priscilla May (Bodman) Rodgers. AB, Vassar Coll., 1961; PhD, U. Rochester Med. Ctr., 1967. Postdoctoral fellow USPHS Middlesex Hosp., London, 1966-68; ergonomist Eastman Kodak Co., Rochester, N.Y., 1968-82; cons. Rochester, N.Y., 1982—. Author: Working With Backache, 1985; tech. editor, prin. author Ergonomic Design for People at Work, 1983, 86, co-editor, contr. Ergonomic Design for People at Work 2d edit., 2003. Bd. dirs., chmn. com., v.p. Rochester Philharm. Orch. Inc., Rochester, 1969-75; bd. dirs. Opera Theatre Rochester, 1969-75; bd. dirs., chmn. com., pres. Monroe County Bd. Health, Rochester, 1979-88. Mem. Soc. Mfg. Engrs., Human Factors and Ergonomics Soc., (pres. Western N.Y. chpt. 1971-72), Am. Coll. Sports Medicine. Avocations: photography, sailing, gardening, reading, enjoying silent films. Home and Office: 169 Huntington Hls Rochester NY 14622-1121 Office Phone: 585-544-3587. Personal E-mail: shrodgers@aol.com.

RODIN, JUDITH SEITZ, academic administrator; b. Phila., Sept. 9, 1944; d. Morris and Sally R. (Winson) Seitz. AB, U. Pa., 1966; PhD, U. Columbia, 1970. Asst. prof. psychology NYU, 1970—72; assoc. prof. Yale U., 1975—79, prof., dir. grad. studies, 1982—89, Philip R. Allen prof. psychology, medicine and psychiatry, 1984—94, chmn. dept. psychology, 1989—91, dean Grad. Sch., 1991—92, provost, 1992—94; pres. U. Pa., Phila., 1994—, prof. psychology, medicine and psychiatry, 1994—. Chmn. John D. and Catherine T. MacArthur Found. Rsch. Network on Determinants and Consequences of Health-Promoting and Health-Damaging Behavior, 1983-93; vice chair coun. press. U. Rsch. Assn., 1994-95, chair, 1995-96; mem. Ind. Panel to Review Safety Procedures at The White House, 1994-95; chair adv. com. Robert Wood Johnson Found., 1994—; mem. Pres. Clinton's Com. Advisors Sci. and Tech., 1994—; mem. Coun. Competitiveness, 1997—; mem. nominating com. N.Y. Stock Exch., 1998—; bd. dirs. Aetna, Electronic Data Sys., AMR. Author: (with S. Schachter) Obese Humans and Rats, 1978, Exploding the Weight Myths, 1982, Body Traps, 1992; chief editor Appetite Jour., 1979-92; contbr. articles to profl. jours. Mem. Pa. Task Force on Higher Edn. Funding, 1994; bd. dirs. Catalyst, N.Y.C., 1994—; trustee Brookings Inst., 1995—; pres. steering com. Am. Reads, 1997—. Fellow Woodrow Wilson Found., 1966-67, John Simon Guggenheim Found., 1986-87; grantee NSF, 1973-82, NIH, 1981—. Fellow AAAS, APA (bd. sci. affairs 1979-82, pres. divsn. 38 health psychology 1982-83, Outstanding Contbn. award 1980, Disting. Sci. award 1977), Am. Acad. Arts and Scis., Soc. Behavioral Medicicine; mem. AAUW (mem. exec. com. 1996—), Am. Philosophical Soc., Inst. Medicine of NAS, Acad. Behavioral Medicine Rsch., Ea. Psychol. Assn. (exec. bd. 1980-82), Phi Beta Kappa, Sigma Xi (pres. Yale chpt. 1986-87). Office: U Pa Office of Pres 100 College Hall Philadelphia PA 19104-6380 also: Univ Pa 3451 Walnut Philadelphia PA 19104

RODIN, RITA A. lawyer; b. N.Y., 1968; BS, Boston (Mass.) Coll., 1990; JD, St. John's U., 1990. Bar: N.J. 1994, N.Y. 1994. Law clk. Hon. Thomas C. Platt U.S. Dist. Ct. (ea. dist.) N.Y., 1993—94; atty. Skadden, Arps, Slate, Meagher & Flom LLP, N.Y., 1994—2001, ptnr., 2001—. Office: Skadden Arps Slate Meagher & Flom LLP Four Times Sq New York NY 10036*

RODKEY, FRANCES THERESA, elementary school educator; b. Germantown, Pa., Sept. 3, 1952; d. Joseph Milton and Elizabeth Jane Parsons; m. Glenn Leroy Rodkey, May 1, 1976; children: Jennifer, Rachel. Student, Immaculata Coll., 1970—72; BS in Elem. Edn., Bloomsburg U., 1975. Cert. emergency edn. Pa., 1986. Substitute tchr. Coatesville Sch. Dist., Pa., 1984—89, tchr. 6th grade, 1989—, head dept. social studies, 2000. Mem.: NEA, Pa. State Edn. Assn. Republican. Roman Catholic. Avocations: reading, camping, hiking. Home: 1111 Oak St Coatesville PA 19320 Office: Coatesville Sch Dist 1515 E Lincoln Hwy Coatesville PA 19320

RODKIN, LOREE, jewelry artist; Studied film making, art history, design, N.Y.C. Hollywood actors mgr., interior designer; jewelry maker Loree Rodkin Gothic Jewelry, Beverly Hills, Calif. Designer of In Memory Ring to honor friend, lover, or family mem. proceeds donated to Elton John AIDS Found. Office: Loree Rodkin Gothic Jewelry 453 Rodeo Dr Beverly Hills CA 90209 Fax: 310-276-8104. E-mail: lrodkin@instanet.com.

RODMAN, SUE A. wholesale company executive, artist, writer; b. Ft. Collins, Colo., Oct. 1, 1951; d. Marvin F. Lawson and Barbara I. (Miller) Lawson Shue; m. Alpine C. Rodman, Dec. 13, 1970; 1 child, Connie, Lynn. Student, Woodbury Bus./Arts Coll., Calif., 1969, Colo. State U., 1970-73. Silversmith Pinel Silver Shop, Loveland, Colo., 1970-71; asst. mgr. Traveling Traders, Phoenix, 1974-75; co-owner, co-mgr. Deer Track Traders, Loveland, 1975-85; v.p. Deer Track Traders, Ltd., Loveland, 1985—. Author: The Book of Contemporary Indian Arts and Crafts, 1985, also numerous children's articles and short stories. Mem. U.S. Senatorial Club, 1982-87, Rep. Presdl. Task Force, 1984-90; mem. CAP, 1969-73, 87-90, pers. officer, 1988-90. Mem. Internat. Platform Assn., Indian Arts and Crafts Assn., Western and English Sales Assn., Crazy Horse Grass Roots Club. Mem. Am. Baptist Ch. Avocations: museums, piano, recreation research, fashion design. Office: Deer Track Traders Ltd PO Box 448 Loveland CO 80539-0448

RODNEY, BONNIE M. music educator; b. Washington, Mar. 15, 1950; d. James Henry Anthony and Mozell Ann Herring; m. Lionel Rodney, July 27, 1990 (div. Sept. 1, 1996). BA, Adelphi U., 1972; MA, Columbia U., 1973, MEd, 1983. Cert. tchr. Mass., N.Y., N.J., Md., DC, early childhood edn., spl. edn. Music tchr., Paterson, NJ, 1986—89, Newark, 1989—90, Cedar Knowles Detention Ctr., Laurel, Md., 1991—92, DC Pub. Schs., 1992—2001, Taft Sch., 2001—. Pvt. piano instr., Washington, 1996—, Md., 1996—; mem. Tchr. Adv. Bd., Washington, 2001—; mem. SCAC com. Washington U., 2001—. Mem. Carter Baron E. Neighborhood Assn., Washington, 1999—2003. Grantee, DC Arts Coun., 2000. Mem.: Music Educators Nat. Conf. (Guitar scholar 2003), Delta Am. Music (hon.), Friday Morning Music Club (mem. chorale ensemble 1999—). Avocations: dance, travel, tennis. Office: 1314 Emerson St NW Washington DC 20011-6906

RODNEY, ROXANNE AUDREY, cardiologist, consultant; BA summa cum laude, Hunter Coll., 1981; MD, Cornell U., 1985. Diplomate Am. Bd. Internal Medicine, Am. Bd. Cardiovasc. Diseases, Am. Bd. Nuc. Cardiology. Resident in internal medicine Montefiore Hosp., Bronx, N.Y., 1985-88; fellow in cardiology N.Y. Med. Coll., Valhalla, 1988-90; fellow in nuc. cardiology Columbia U., N.Y.C., 1990-91; attending physician Columbia-Presbyn. Med. Ctr., N.Y.C., 1991-99; sr. assoc. cons. Mayo Clinic, Jacksonville, Fla., 1999—. Contbr. articles to profl. jours. Mem. Am. Heart Assn. (chair women cardiology com. 1997—, bd. dirs. 1999—), Assn. Black Cardiologists (bd. dirs. 1995-99, chair cardiovasc. diseases women com. 1995—). Office: Mayo Clinic Divsn Cardiology 4500 San Pablo Rd S Jacksonville FL 32224-3899

RODRIGUEZ, ANNABELLE, state attorney general; m. Francisco de Jesus-Schuck; 2 children. BA, JD, U. P.R. From asst. solicitor gen. to solicitor gen. P.R. Dept. Justice; ptnr. Martino, Odell & Calabria, Hato Rey, PR, 1993—96; judge U.S. Dist Ct. (P.R. dist.), 1996; atty. gen. Commonwealth of P.R., 2001—. Democrat. Office: Atty Gen PO Box 9020192 San Juan PR 00902-0192*

RODRIGUEZ, DARLENE, newscaster; married. BA in Broadcast Journalism, U. Miami. Reporter Bronxnet Cable TV, Bronx, NY, 1993—94; gen. assignment reporter WCBS NewsRadio 88, N.Y.C., 1994—98; reporter NewsChannel 4, N.Y.C., 1998—, co-anchor Today in New York, 2003—. Recipient Silurian award, 1998, Latina Excellence award, Hispanic mag., 2000. Office: NBC 30 Rockefeller Plz New York NY 10112*

RODRIGUEZ, DONNA JEANNE ANGLIN, dietician, writer; b. Albuquerque, July 21, 1953; d. Randolph Sterling and Audrey Miriam (Kubach) Anglin; m. Ralph A. Rodriguez, Feb. 19, 1977. BS, N.Mex. State U., 1975; MS, U. N.Mex., 1996. Cert. nutrition support dietitian; registered dietitian. Clin. dietitian U. N.Mex. Hosp., Albuquerque, 1977-91, nutrition support coord., 1991-95, rsch. coord., 1995-96, vis. prof./lectr., 1996-97; profl. healthcare writer Lovelace Healthcare Innovations, Albuquerque, 1997-98; clin. dietitian West Albuquerque Dialysis Ctr., 1999—. Assoc. editor: (jour.) Support Line, 1996—; contbr. articles to profl. jours., chpts. to books. Mem. Am. Soc. Parenteral and Enteral Nutrition, N.Mex. Soc. Parenteral and Enteral Nutrition, Am. Dietetic Assn., N.Mex. Dietetic Assn., Am. Burn Assn. (chmn. nutrition spl. interest group 1994-96). Avocations: camping, needlework.

RODRIGUEZ, ELLEN KAY, special education educator; b. Wagoner, Okla., Feb. 16, 1953; d. John Franklin and Margaret May Seratt; children: Damian Paul, John Ashley. BS in Edn., U. of Okla., 1976. Cert. tchr. Okla., 1976. Learning disabilities tchr. Norman Pub. Schs., Okla., 1979—; upward bound acad. coord. Southwestern Okla. State U., Weatherford, 1985—; learning disabilities tchr. Inola Pub. Schs., Okla. Staff developer Norman Pub. Schs., Okla., 1993—. Recipient, Longfellow Tchr. of the Yr. award, 2003; grantee, Ednl. Leadership of Okla. grantee, 2002. Mem.: Coun. for Exceptional Children (corr.). Democrat-Npl. Roman Catholic. Avocations: travel, gardening.

RODRIGUEZ, GRISELL, librarian, educator; b. Chgo., Apr. 3, 1967; d. Luciano and Margarita (Velazquez) Rodriguez. BA in Philosophy, U. Puerto Rico, Mayaguez, 1993; MLIS, U. Wis., 1996. From cataloger to patents libr. U. Puerto Rico, Mayaguez, 1996—2000, automation dept. head, 2000—02, serial and libr. II, electronic resources collection, 2002—. Grantee Hispanic Serving Instns. grant, U.S. Dept. Edn., 1999—. Mem.: ALA, Soc. Puerto Rico Libr., REFORMA (nat. org. to promote libr. svcs. to spanish speaking), Assn. Coll. & Rsch. Libr. Avocations: reading, music, exercise, travel. Home: Casa G-1 Urb Vista del Rio Anasco PR 00610 Office: Univ Puerto Rico-Mayaguez Gen Libr PO Box 9022 Mayaguez PR 00681-9022 E-mail: g_rodriguez@rumlib.uprm.edu.

RODRIGUEZ, HELEN G. retired social worker; m. Paul H. Rodriguez, Oct. 17, 1998; 1 child, Carina Jon Marie Garcia. Vocat. Nursing degree, St. Phillip's Coll., San Antonio, 1970; BA in Psychology, U. Tex., San Antonio, 1977; MSW (hon.), Our Lady of the Lake U., San Antonio, 1998. Lic. vocat. nurse, Tex., 1970; LMSW Tex., 1998. V.p., cons. Sales Consultants of San Antonio, 1987—90; nurse evaluator, marketer New Medico Head Injury Inc., Boston, 1990—93; adult protective specialist Protective and Regulatory Svcs., San Antonio, 1993—99, guardianship specialist, 1999—2003. Mitigation specialist Tex. Defender Svc., Austin, Tex., 2002—. Adv. and grass roots organizer of civil rights League of United L.Am. Countries, San Antonio, 1967—77; mem. and organizer Am. G. I. Forum, San Antonio. Mem.: NASW, Phi Alpha. Roman Catholic. Avocations: travel, piano, golf, movies, fishing. Home: 9615 Alisa Brooke San Antonio TX 78254 Personal E-mail: rodrighg@aol.com.

RODRIGUEZ, KATHLEEN MOORE, art educator; b. Wynnewood, Pa., Mar. 16, 1971; d. John Francis and Mary Louise (McCahon) N.; married, May 18, 2002. BS, Kutztown U., 1993. Art educator Villa Maria Acad., Malvern, Pa., 1994—, cons. fine arts ctr., 1995-97, dept. chair visual arts, 1996-97; mem. faculty precoll. programs U. of Arts, 2000—. Art tchr. summer enrichment program Archbishop John Carroll H.S., Radnor, Pa., summers 1996, 97; spl. recreation camp counselor, summers 2001--. Bd. dirs. Archdiocesan Curriculum Com. for Fine Arts, Phila., 1996—; vol. tchr. aide GED course Ardmore Libr., 1995. Recipient Connelly Art Connection award Connelly Found., Mus. Am. Art, 1997. Mem. NEA, Nat. Art Edn. Assn., Pa. Art Edn. Assn., Am. Crafts Coun., Phila. Mus. Art, Main Line Art Ctr. Roman Catholic. Avocation: coaching field hockey and basketball. Home: 316 E Athens Ave Ardmore PA 19003-3108

RODRIGUEZ, MERCEDES M. psychiatrist; b. Hato Rey, Puerto Rico, Dec. 31, 1963; d. Amalio Rodriguez and Mercedes Suarez; m. Fernando Castro, Dec. 23, 1988 (div . Apr. 1997); 1 child, Merceditas. Degree, U. Caribe, 1989; degree in psychiatry, U. Puerto Rico, 1993; degree in geropsychiatry, St. Louis U., 1996. Intern U. Puerto Rico Sch. Medicine, Rio Piedras, 1989-90; dir. intermediate care female ward MEPSI Ctr., Bayamon, Puerto Rico, 1993-94; psychiatrist Puerto Rico Mental Health Dept., Bayamon Regional Hosp., 1994-95; staff physician St. Louis VA Med. Ctr., 1996—. Clin. instr. St. Louis U., 1996—; cons. St. Louis Alzheimer's Assn., 1996. Co-contbr. articles to profl. jours. Recipient Silver Apple award St. Louis U., 1995, 96, NIAI Brookdale Found. award Nat. Instn. on Aging, 1997. Mem. AMA, Am. Psychiatry Assn., Am. Geriatric Soc., Eastern Mo. Psychiatry Soc., Am. Assn. for Geriatric Psychiatry, Puerto Rico Coll. Physicians. Roman Catholic. Avocations: tennis, aerobics. Office: Saint Louis U 1221 S Grand Blvd Saint Louis MO 63104-1016 also: Jefferson Barracks VA Psychiatry Svc 1 Jefferson Barracks Rd Saint Louis MO 63125-4181

RODRIGUEZ, NANCY, state legislator; b. San Luis, Colo., Mar. 18, 1953; BBA, MBA. Mem. N.Mex. Senate, Dist. 24, Santa Fe, 1996—; mem. edn. com.; mem. fin. com. Democrat. Office: 1838 Camino La Canada Santa Fe NM 87501

RODRIGUEZ, NORA HILDA, social worker; b. Brownsville, Tex., Dec. 26, 1964; d. Raul and Julia Rodriguez; 1 child, Carlos. AS, Tex. Southmost Coll., 1986; BS, Tex. A&M U., 1987; AA in Social Work, Tex. Southmost Coll., 1997; BA in Sociology, U. Tex., Brownsville, 1997; MSW, U. Tex., 2000. Med. billings Valley Counseling and Wellness, Brownsville; tchr. asst. spl. ed. Garden Pk. Elem. Sch., Brownsville, Tex., 1998; case mgr. Valley AIDS Coun., McAllen, Tex.; case worker Cath. Social Svcs., Brownsville, Tex., 2002—. Scholar, Cath. Daughters Am., 1985; Hispanic scholar, L & F Distributors, Ltd., 1998—99. Fellow: Internat. Fedn. Social Workers (assoc.); mem.: Am. Trauma Soc., Social Work Grad. Alumni Assn. (assoc.), NASW (assoc.), Phi Theta Kappa. D-Conservative. Roman Catholic. Avocations: teaching, travel, hiking, scuba diving, reading. Home: 9401 US Military Hwy 281 Brownsville TX 78520 Office: Catholic Social Svcs 47 W Elizabeth Brownsville TX 78520 Personal E-mail: icbluestars@hotmail.com. E-mail: nrodriguez@cdob.org.

RODRIGUEZ, RAQUEL, lawyer; b. Miami Beach, Fla., 1961; JD, U. Miami, 1985. Assoc. Greenberg Traurig, P.A., Miami, Fla., 1985—97, shareholder, 1993—97, dir. global affiliations, coord internat. practice group, 1999—2002, with lit. dept. Washington, 2002, exec. dir. Multilaw Multinational Assn. Ind. Law Firms, London, 1997—99; gen. counsel to gov. Office Gov. State of Fla., Tallahassee, 2002—. Adj. prof. U. Miami. Office: Office Gov The Capital Tallahassee FL 32399

RODRIGUEZ, RITA MARIA, economist; b. La Havana, Cuba, Sept. 6, 1944; came to U.S., 1960; Tomas and Adela (Mederos) R.; m. E. Eugene Carter, Jan. 7, 1972; 1 child, Adela-Marie R. Carter. BBA, U. PR, 1964; MBA, NYU, 1968, PhD, 1969. Bus. adminstrn. asst. prof., then assoc. prof. Harvard Bus. Sch., Cambridge, Mass., 1969-74, 74-78; fin. prof. U. Ill., Chgo., 1978-82; dir. Export-Import Bank of U.S., Washington, 1982-99. Cons. Polaroid Corp. and Indsl. Devel. Bank in Ecuador (Corporacion Financiera Nacional), 1978-82, U.S. IRS, 1982; bd. dirs. Acad. Ednl. Devel., Washington, 1989-93; bd. advisors Pew Econ. Freedom Fellows, Washington, 1991-94, World Bank, MIGA, Washington, 2000; bd. dirs. Affiliated Mgrs. Group, Boston, 2000-, Pvt. Export Funding Corp., N.Y., 2001—; sr. fellow Woodstock Theol. Ctr., Georgetown U., Washington, 2002—, ENSCO, Dallas, 2003—. Author: (with E. Eugene Carter) International Financial Management, 1976, 2d edit., 1979, 3rd edit., 1984, (with Heinz Riehl) Foreign Exchange Markets: A Guide to Foreign Currency Operations, 1977, Foreign Exchange Management in U.S. Multinationals, 1980 (with Heinz Riehl) Foreign Exchange and Money Markets, 1983, Japanese, Spanish, Portuguese translations, The Export Import Bank at Fifty, 1987; co-editor (with G.C. Hufbauer) Ex-Im Bank: Overview, Challenges, and Policy Options in the Ex-Im Bank in the 21st Century, 2001; editor (with Gary Hufbauer) The Ex-Im Bank in the 21st Century; contbr. numerous fin. articles to profl. publs. Bd. dirs. Am. Friends of Turkey, 2001. Recipient Outstanding Achievement award Nat. Coun. of Hispanic Women, 1986; Outstanding Hispanic Achievement award Hispanic Corp. Achievers, 1988; Nat. Leadership award Government The Nat. Network of Hispanic Women, 1989. Mem.: Coun. Fgn. Rels. Roman Catholic. Avocations: gardening, music. Office: 3075 Ordway St NW Washington DC 20008-3255

RODRIGUEZ, ROCIO, artist; b. Caibarién, Las Villas, Cuba, 1952; BFA, MFA, U. Ga. One-woman shows include Carl Solway Gallery, Cin., 1982, 1985, Young Harris Coll., Ga., 1986, The Arts Exch., Atlanta, 1989, McIntosh Gallery, 1989, Sandler Hudson Gallery, 1991, 1993, 1995, Studio Exhbn., 1992, Brenau Coll., Gainesville,Ga., 1995, Nexus Contemporary Art Ctr., Atlanta, 1996, Fay Gold Gallery, 1998, Hemphill Fine Arts, Washington, 1999, exhibited in group shows at Birmingham (Ala.) Art Mus., 1989, High Mus. Art, Atlanta, 1990, Nexus Contemporary Arts Ctr., 1991, Galerie Simonne Stern, New Orleans, 1992, Montgomery (Ala.) Mus. Fine Arts, 1994, Michael Solway Gallery, Cin., 1996, Spelman Mus., Atlanta, 1997, New Orleans Mus., 1998, numerous others, Represented in permanent collections; contbr. articles to profl. jours. Recipient So. Regional Vis. Artists award, Am. Acad. Rome, 1997; fellow, Ford Found., 1978, Oscar B. Cintas fellow, 1980, Mayor's fellowship in arts, 1990, regional fellow, So. Arts Fedn./NEA, 1990. Office: Fay Gold Gallery 764 Miami Cir Ne Ste 210 Atlanta GA 30324-3026

RODRIGUEZ-WALLING, MATILDE BARCELO, special education educator; b. Santiago, Cuba, Aug. 15, 1950; d. Humberto Jacinto and Matilde Amelia (Cuervo) Barcelo; m. Luis Alfredo Rodriguez-Walling, June 29, 1973; 1 child, Alfredo Luis. BA, U. Miami, Fla., 1972; MS in Diagnostic Tchg., Fla. Internat. U., 1981; EdS, Barry U., 1988. Cert. ednl. specialist computer edn., Fla. Tchr., chair fgn. lang. dept. Notre Dame Acad., Miami, Fla., 1972-80; tchr., coord. English as 2d lang. adult edn. program Dade County Pub. Schs., Miami, elem. sch. tchr., tchr. middle sch. spl. edn. Homestead, Fla., elem. spl. edn. tchr. Miami, 1986—, behavior mgmt. specialist, exceptional edn. dept. chair; tchr. on spl. assignment Fla. Dept. of Edn., 1994—. Mem. spkrs. bur. Nat. Clearinghouse for Professions in Spl. Edn.; sch. adv. chairperson Blueprint 2000; presenter and spkr. at state and nat. profl. confs.; coord. Fla. Spkrs. Bur.; mem. Fla. Edn. Stds.

Commn. Commr. Fla. Edn. Stds. Commn.; mem. State Adv. Com.; mem. Commrs. Blue Ribbon Panel Edn. Governance; co-chair Nat Commn. Improve Spl. Edn. Teaching & Learning. Recipient Gran Orden Martiana, Cuban Lyceum, Miami, 1976. Mem. Coun. Exceptional Children (sec. 1989, v.p. 1990, pres. 1991-92, multicultural chair 1992-93, Mainstreaming Tchr. of Yr. 1983, region finalist Dade County Tchr. of Yr. 1991, Fla. Tchr. of Yr.), Fla. Fedn. Coun. for Exceptional Children (pres. 1997-98, past pres. 1998-99), Coun. Children with Behavior Disorders, Nat. Bd. for Profl. Tchg. Stds. (exceptional needs com.), Internat. Coun. for Exceptional Children (Tchr. of Yr. 1994), Delta Kappa Gamma (Epsilon chpt.). Roman Catholic. Avocations: travel, guitar. Office: Miami-Dade County Pub Schs 1500 Biscayne Blvd Ste 409G Miami FL 33132-1400

RODTS, MARY FAUT, medical/surgical nurse; b. Evanston, Ill., Nov. 4, 1952; d. John Eugene and Mary Margaret (Murphy) F.; m. Thomas Lee Rodts, June 19, 1982; children: Timothy, Sarah, Megan. BSN, Loyola U., 1974; MS, Rush U., 1980; M of Sci. Adminstrn., U. Notre Dame, 1996. Staff nurse pediatrics Rush-Presbyn. St. Luke's Hosp., Chgo., 1974-75, practitioner-tchr., 1975—. Teaching asst. Rush Coll. Nursing, Chgo., 1974-75, asst. prof., 1981—; collaborative practice Orthopaedics & Scoliosis, Ltd., Chgo., 1975—; cons. Ill. Children's Hosp. Sch., Chgo., 1975-89; mem. adv. bd. Scoliosis Assn., N.Y.C., 1977-89. Editor: Nursing Clinics of North America, 1991; mem. editl. bd.: jour. Orthopaedic Nursing Jour., 1990—, editor: jour., 1999—; contbr. chapters to books. Fellow Scoliosis Rsch. Soc.; mem. Nat. Assn. Orthopaedic Nurses (pres. 1982-83, Outstanding Contbn. 1990, 97), ANA, Spine Rsch. Assocs., Sigma Theta Tau. Office: Rush U 1725 W Harrison St Ste 440 Chicago IL 60612-3836

ROE, WANDA JERALDEAN, artist, retired educator, lecturer; b. Batesville, Ark., Nov. 9, 1920; d. William Melvin and Luna Eva (Cockrum) Finley; m. Roy A. Roe, Dec. 25, 1940; children: Ramona Jeraldean, Roy A. II. BS in Edn., U. Cen. Ark., Conway, 1954; MS in Edn., Ark. State U., 1965; diploma Exec. Devel. Ctr., U. Ill., 1984; postgrad., U. Ark., 1981. Cert. educator, Ark.; lic. profl. counselor, Ark. Counselor Fountain Lake H.S., Hot Springs, Ark., 1965-68; instr. art and home econs. Foreman (Ark.) H.S., 1968-72; profl. counselor Pea Ridge (Ark.) H.S., 1972-83; instr. art No. Ark. C.C., Rogers, 1980-90; profl. artist Rogers (Ark.) Art Guild Gallery, 1983-94, Big Spring Gallery, Neosho, Mo., 1989-98, Ark. Artists Registry, Little Rock, 1983—; instr. art Wishing Springs Gallery, Bella Vista, Ark. Dir. workshops State Dept. Edn., Little Rock, 1965-83; supr. for practice tchrs. and counselor interns. Ark. Colls. and Univs., 1968-83; art instr. War Eagle Seminar, 1996; presenter in field. Exhibited in one-person show at Walton Art Ctr., 1996; contbr. poetry to mags.; mem. editorial adv. bd. Cmty. Pubs. Inc., 1994-97; art work pub. Internat. Bu.. Delta Kappa Gamma Soc., 2001. Mem. State Adv. Coun. for Gifted/Talented Edn., Little Rock, 1989-96; mem. Ark. Leadership Acad., 1996, G/T Coalition, 1996-97; juror for art contests; guide for County Constn. Day, Benton County, 1987; pres. United Meth. Women, Pea Ridge, 1973-75; cmty. vol.; sec. Benton County Dem. Ctrl. Com., 1996-2002; White House vol., 1996; mem. rsch. bd. advisors Internat. Directory of Disting. Leadership, 1992—. Travel Study grantee Delta Kappa Gamma, 1987; named Art Educator of Yr., N.W. Art Educators Assn., 1983; recipient numerous art awards. Mem.: AAUW (state pres. 1985—87, state exec. bd.), Rogers Art Guild (pres. 1991—92), Ozark Pastel Soc. (pres. 1990—93, Signature mem.), Internat. Assn. Pastel Socs. (Outstanding Vol. award 1997), Spiva Art Ctr., Ark. Art Educators Assn. (Svc. award for contbn. to art profession 1997), Nat. Art Educators Assn., Dem. Women's Club (v.p. 1996—98), Village Art Club (pres. 1998—2001, bd. dirs. 2002—03, chmn. bd. dirs. 2004—), Delta Kappa Gamma (stete pres. 1983—85, internat. nominations com. 1998—2002, cover artist internat. sem. 2002, state exec. bd.). Democrat. Methodist. Avocations: music, lecturing, directing workshops.

ROEDER, REBECCA EMILY, software engineer; b. Findlay, Ohio, Nov. 2, 1959; d. Brian Eldon and Barbara Lee (Melton) R.; m. Stephen William Bigley, May 28, 1983. BS in Edn. and Computer Sci., Bowling Green State U., 1983, MS in Computer Sci., 1993. Sys. analyst NCR Corp., Dayton, Ohio, 1983-84; sr. sys. analyst Unisys (Burroughs) Corp., Detroit, 1984-88; asst. dir. St. Vincent Med. Ctr., Toledo, 1988-95; sr. cons. Advanced Programming Resources, Inc., Columbus, Ohio, 1996; sr. software engr. Qwest Comm., Dublin, Ohio, 1996—2002; sys. analyst Ohio Bur. of Worker's Compensation, Columbus, 2002—. Active Sta. WGTE/WGLE Pub. Radio, Toledo, 1984—96, Sta. WOSU Pub. Radio, Columbus, 1996—, Sta. WCBE Radio, Columbus, 1996—98, 2001, Toledo Mus. Art, 1988—96, Toledo Zoo, 1993—96, Dawes Arboretum, 1996—, Stratford Festival Friend, 1997—, Columbus Zoo, 1997—, Columbus Symphony Orch. Concerto Club, 1998—; presenter Women in Sci. Career Day, Lourdes Coll., 1992. Marathon scholar Marathon Oil Co., Findlay, 1978, Hancock scholar Findlay Area C. of C., 1978. Mem.: Assn. for Computing Machinery. Unitarian Universalist. Avocations: instrumental and choral music, drum and bugle corps, reading. Home: 4964 Vicksburg Ln Hilliard OH 43026-5740 Office: Ohio BWC 30 W Spring St Columbus OH 43215-2256

ROEDER VAUGHAN, MIMI, small business owner; b. Balt., Nov. 21, 1948; m. Arky Vaughan; children: Gina Pizza, Kelly Vaughan, Ryan Vaughan. BA, U. Tenn., 1970; postgrad., U. Hawaii, 1972. Founder, CEO Roeder Travel, 1973—, Kailua Property, 1973—, Md. Sch. Travel, 1976—, Roland Park Travel, 1984—92, Falls Road Travel, 1990—. Mem. bd. Augusta Bank, 1990—91. Dir., sec. Civic Works, 1998—2000; pres., founder Baskets and Books, 1995—2000; co-founder Kingston Orphanage Group, 2000. Named One of Md.'s Top 100 Women, Daily Record, 1995, 1999, 2001; recipient Sabre Star award, Am. Airlines, 1999, 2000, Gold Spike award, Amtrak, 1998. Mem.: GBC Leadership (bd. dirs. 2000, class rep. 1995 1995—2000), Network 2000 (co-chair mentoring 1999—2000, membership com. 1998—2000). Office: 9805 York Rd Cockeysville Hunt Valley MD 21030

ROEDIGER, JANICE ANNE, artist, educator; b. Trenton, N.J. d. John and Anne Balint; m. Paul Margerum Roediger; children: Pamela Anne, Matthew Paul, Joan Margaret. Student, Beaver Coll., 1975-78; grad. cert., Pa. Acad. Fine Arts, 1988. Instr. multi-media Jane Law Long Beach Island Gallery, Surf City, N.J., 1992-95; instr. drawing Long Beach Island Found., Loveladies, NJ, 1994—2002. Docent Mus. Am. Art, Pa. Acad. Fine Arts, Phila., 1992—. Exhibited in group shows at Rittenhouse Galleries, Phila., 1988-94, Phila. Mus. Art, ASR Gallery, 1992—, Schaff Gallery, Cin., 1995-96, Lambertville (N.J.) Gallery of Fine Arts, 1997—. Mem. vestry, rector's warden St. Anne's Episcopal Ch., Abington, Pa., 1970-73; chair med. staff aux. Abington Meml. Hosp., 1973-7, chair scholarship com., 1974; coord. student com. Pa. Acad. Fine Arts, Phila., 1986-88; active Phila. Mus. Art, 1972—. Recipient Rohm & Haas Outstanding Achievement award Pa. Acad. Fine Arts, 1987, Pearl Van Sciver award Woodmere Mus., 1991, Blumenthal award Cheltenham Ctr. for Arts, 1991, Pres. award, 2001, Lance Lauffler award for visionary painting Pa. Acad. Fine Arts, 1988, Award of Merit Long Beach Island Found., 1994, 96, Woodmere Mus. Memorial Endowment award, 1999, Outstanding Achievement award Long Beach Island Found., 2002. Mem. Nat. Mus. Women in Arts, Phila. Art Alliance, Artists Cultural Exch. (bd. dirs. 1989—). Episcopalian. Avocations: writing, collecting, golf, walking, travel. Home: 1250 Greenwood Ave Jenkintown PA 19046 Studio: 1913 Guernsey Ave Abington PA E-mail: imjanroe@aol.com.

ROEMER, ELIZABETH, astronomer, educator; b. Calif., Sept. 4, 1929; d. Richard Quirin and Elsie Roemer. BA with honors, U. Calif., Berkeley, 1950, PhD (Lick Obs. fellow), 1955. Tchr. adult class Oakland pub. schs., 1950-52; lab technician U. Calif. at Mt. Hamilton, 1954-55; grad. research astronomer U. Calif. at Berkeley, 1955-56; research asso. Yerkes Obs. U. Chgo., 1956; astronomer U.S. Naval Obs., Flagstaff, Ariz., 1957-66; asso. prof. dept. astronomy, also in lunar and planetary lab. U. Ariz., Tucson, 1966-69, prof., 1969-97; prof. emerita, 1997—; astronomer Steward Obs., 1980-97, astronomer emerita, 1997—. Chmn. working group on orbits and ephemerides of comets commn. 20 Internat. Astron. Union, 1964-79, 85-88, v.p. comm. 20, 1979-82, pres., 1982-85, v.p. commn. 6, 1973-76, 85-88, pres., 1976-79, 88-91; mem. adv. panels Office Naval Research, Nat. Acad. Scis., NRC, NASA, researcher and author numerous publs. on astrometry and astrophysics of comets and minor planets including 79 recoveries of returning periodic comets, visual and spectroscopic binary stars, computation of orbits of comets and minor planets. Recipient Dorothea Klumpke Roberts prize U. Calif. at Berkeley, 1950, Mademoiselle Merit award, 1959; asteroid (1657) named Roemera, 1965; Benjamin Apthorp Gould prize Nat. Acad. Scis., 1971; NASA Spl. award, 1986. Fellow AAAS (council 1966-69, 72-73), Royal Astron. Soc. (London); mem. Am. Astron. Soc. (program vis. profs. astronomy 1960-75, council 1967-70, chmn. div. dynamical astronomy 1974), Astron. Soc. Pacific (publs. com. 1962-73, Comet medal com. 1968-74, Donohoe lectr. 1962), Internat. Astron. Union, Am. Geophys. Union, Brit. Astron. Assn., Phi Beta Kappa, Sigma Xi. Office: U Ariz PO Box 210092 Lunar & Planetary Lab Tucson AZ 85721-0092

ROERDEN, CHRIS (CLAIRE ROERDEN), editor, business owner, publishing consultant; b. N.Y.C., Aug. 28, 1935; d. Marion Smolin; m. Harold H. Roerden (div. 1985); children: Ken, Doug. BA in English summa cum laude, U. Maine, 1969, MA in English, 1971. Mem. pub. rels. staff Shell Oil Co., N.Y.C., 1952-55; asst. to pub. rels. dir. Interchem. Corp., N.Y.C., 1956-59; staff editor Newkirk Assocs., Albany, N.Y., 1960-62; instr. in English U. Maine, Portland, 1969-71; mentor Empire State Coll., SUNY, Rochester and Syracuse, 1973-74; mng. editor CPA Digest, Brookfield, Wis., 1983; owner Edit It, Brookfield, 1984—99, Market Savvy BookEditing.com, Greensboro, NC, 1999—. Lectr. U. Wis., Milw., 1991—98, Telesis Inst., Alverno Coll., 1995—97; presenter Pub.'s Mktg. Assn. Pub. U., 1996—, S.E. Mystery Writers of Am., 1998—, Harriette Austin Writers Conf., 2000—, Of Dark and Stormy Nights, 2001. Author: Collections from Cape Elizabeth, 1965, Oops 'n Options Game, 1982, Open Gate: Teaching in a Foreign Country, 1990, What Two Can Do: Sam & Mandy Stellman's Crusade for Social Justice, 2000; editor: Life Skills Parenting Series, 1994-96, Mrs. Wheeler Goes to Washington (Elizabeth Wheeler Colman), 1989, Give This Man a Hand (Earl Harrell), 1990, Genetic Connections: A Guide to Documenting Your Individual and Family Health History, 1995 (Benjamin Franklin award and 6 others), The Safety Minute (R.L. Siciliano), 1995, The Cassidy McCabe Mystery Series (Alex Matthews, Love is Murder Reader's Choice award Best Series Continuing Character 1999): Secret's Shadow, 1995, Satan's Silence, 1997, Vendetta's Victim, 1998, Wanton's Web, 1999, Cat's Claw, 2000, Death's Domain, 2001, Wedding's Widow, 2003, The Body in the Transept (Jeanne Dams), 1995 (Agatha award), Down But Not Out (Jeanne Sexson), 1996, The Battering Syndrome (Michael Groetsch), 1996, Nonviolent Crisis Intervention (Crisis Prevention Inst.) 1996, He Promised He'd Stop (Michael Groetsch), 1997, Failure is Not an Option (Donna Jordan), 1998, New Millennium Guide to Managing Money (John T. McCarthy), 1998, Should I Stay or Go? (Lee Raffel), 1998, The M-Files (Jay Rath), 1998, Walking Tours of Wisconsin, 1998, Citizen Power (Robin Epstein), 1999, Divorcing the Corporation (Rosalyn Reeder), 1999, When the Dead Speak (Sandra Tooley), 1998, The Good Die Twice (Lee Driver), 1999, Nothing Else Matters (S.D. Tooley), 2000, Path to the Soul (Ashok Bedi, M.D.), 2000, Zachronyms (David Zach), 1998, ShapeWalking (Marilyn Bach), 1999, The Herbal Drugstore (Rodale), 2000, Breast Cancer Survivors' Club (Lillie Shockney), 1999, The Susan Chase Mystery Series (Steve Brown), Stripped to Kill, 2000, Dead Kids Tell No Tales, 2000, When Dead is Not Enough, 2001, Radio Secrets, 2000, Fallen Stars, 2001, Hurricane Party, 2002, River of Diamonds, 2002, Rescue, 2002, (Paul Schatzkin) The Boy Who Invented Television, 2002, Sanctuary of Evil, 2003, (Lee Driver) The Unseen, 2004. Pres. Brookfield Civic Chorus, 1986-88; v.p. Brookfield Civic Music Assn., 1989-91. Recipient cert. of honor Korean Nat. Commn. for UNESCO, 1989, Kate Mooney Vol. Svc. award Counseling Ctr. Milw., 1991, Disting. Tech. Commn. awards (2) STC, 1995, award of achievement STC, 1995, Merit award, 1996, 1st pl. tech. editing award MAPA Book awards, 1995, 96, 2d pl. interior design award MAPA Book awards, 1995, 97. Mem.: NOW (Wis. pres. 1978—81, Positive Action award for Leadership 1977), Feminist Bus. and Profl. Women's Forum (coord. 1990—99), Wis. Women's Network (founding), Wis. Bus. Women's Coalition (bd. dirs. 1988), Pubs. Mktg. Assn. (coord. Wis. chpt. 1997—99), Mystery Writers Am. (bd. dirs. S.E. chpt. 2001—), Women in Comm. S.E. Wis. (bd. dirs. 1988), Soc. for Tech. Comm. (Wis. bd. dirs. 1991—95), Mid-Am. Pubs. Assn. (pres. 1995—97), Mensa Internat., Phi Kappa Phi. Address: 3683 Waterwheel Ct Greensboro NC 27409-8103 E-mail: CRoerden@aol.com.

ROESSEL, FAITH, Indian arts and crafts administrator; Bachelor's, Ft. Lewis Coll.; JD, U. N.Mex. Bar: N.Mex., D.C. Legis. asst. to U.S. Senator Jeff Bingaman, Washington; sr. staff atty. Native Am. Rights Fund, Washington; dir. Navajo Nation, Washington Office; dep. asst. sec. Indian Affairs, Washington; staff coord. for White House Domestic Policy Coun.'s Working Group on Am. Indians ans Alaska Natives Dept. of Interior, Washington, spl. asst. to Interior Sec. Bruce Babbitt; chmn. Indian Arts and Crafts Bd., Washington. Bd. dirs. Am. Indians for Opportunity, Child Welfare League Am.; mem. adv. bd. Ariz. U. Law Sch. Mem. ABA, Fed. Bar Assn., Indian Bar Assn. Office: Indian Arts and Crafts Bd 1849 C St NW R4004 Washington DC 20240-0001

ROESSER, JEAN WOLBERG, state official; b. Washington, May 8, 1930; d. Solomon Harry Wolberg and Mary Frances Brown; m. Eugene Francis Roesser, Aug. 3, 1957 (dec.); children: Eugene Francis, Jr., Mary Roesser Calderon, Anne. BA, Trinity Coll., Washington, 1951; postgrad. in econs., Cath. U. of Am., 1951-53. Congl. relations asst. U.S. Info. Agy., Washington, 1954-58; news reporter for Montgomery County Coun., Suburban Record, 1983-86; mem. Md. Ho. of Dels., Annapolis, 1986-94, Md. Senate, Annapolis, 1994—2002; mem. fin. com., ethics com. State Senate, Md. Gen. Assembly, Annapolis, 1994—2002, joint com. welfare reform, 1996, joint com. healthcare delivery & financing, 1996—2002, joint budget & audit com., 1997—2002, chair joint com. on welfare reform, 2002; sec. Md. Dept. Aging, 2003—. Former mem. Md. Gov.'s Task Force on Energy; former pres. Montgomery County Fedn. Rep. Women, Potomac Women's Rep. Club; former 3d v.p. Md. Fedn. Rep. Women; founding mem. Montgomery County Arts Coun.; alt. del. Rep. Nat. Conv., 1992, del., 1996. Named one of Md.'s Top 100 Women, Daily Record, 2002; recipient Cmty. Achievement award, Washington Psychiat. Soc., 1994, 1998, Trinity Coll. Leadership award, 1994, Common Cause Md. award, 1993, Md. Underage Drinking Preventio Coalition award, 1994, Legislator of the Yr. award, Montgomery County Med. Soc., 1996, 2000, Best in Class award, Md. C. of C., 1997, Cmty. Svc. award, Washington Psychiatric Soc., 1998, Legislator of Yr. award, Md. State's Atty.'s Assn., 2000. Mem. Women Legislators Md., also area citizens assns. and chambers commerce. Republican. Roman Catholic. Home: 10830 Fox Hunt Ln Potomac MD 20854-1553

ROESSLER, CAROL ANN, state legislator; b. Madison, Wis., Jan. 16, 1948; d. John J. and Lucile E. (Kraner) Murphy; m. Paul Roessler. BS, U. Wis., Oshkosh, 1972. Dir. nutrition program for older adults County of Winnebago, Wis., 1973-82; mem. Wis. Assembly, Madison, 1983-87, Wis. Senate from 18th dist., Madison, 1987—. Instr. pre-retirement planning Fox Valley Tech. Inst., 1978-81. Home: 1506 Jackson St Oshkosh WI 54901-2942 Office: PO Box 7882 Madison WI 53707-7882 E-mail: Sen.Roessler@legis.state.wi.us.

ROESSNER, BARBARA, journalist; b. Elizabeth, N.J., Sept. 16, 1953; d. Gilbert George and Dorothy Anne (Hector) R.; m. Craig William Baggott, Jan. 20, 1982; children: Craig, Taylor, Liam, Katherine, Elizabeth. BA, Wesleyan U., 1975. Reporter, editor Meriden (Conn.) Record-Jour., 1975-78; reporter The Hartford (Conn.) Courant, 1978-81, chief polit. writer 1981-86, columnist, 1986-90, dep. mng. editor, 1990—. Column distributed worldwide by L.A. Times-Washington Post News Svc. Recipient Best Mag. Column award Soc. Profl. Journalists, 1993, Best Mag. Feature award, 1993. Office: Hartford Courant Co 285 Broad St Hartford CT 06115-3785

ROFFÉ, SARINA, public relations executive; b. Bklyn., Feb. 16, 1955; d. Abe J. and Reneé (Salem) Missry; m. David Roffé, June 4, 1974; children: Simon, Honey, Abraham. BA in Journalism, U. Md., 1992. Reporter Gazette Newspaper, Gaithersburg, Md., 1991—93; news editor Richner Publs., Lawrence, NY, 1993—94; mng. editor Queens Tribune, 1994; interpreter of deaf Montgomery County Pub. Schs., Rockville, Md.; writer, editor freelance Bklyn.; dir. pub. affairs NYC Dept. Juvenile Justice, 1996—2002; founder, exec. dir. NY Speech Ctr., Inc., 1995—; nat. dir. comms. Jewish Nat. Fund, 2002—. Contbg. author: Choices in Deafness-A Parent's Guide, 1987, Cued Speech Resource Guide for Parents, 1993, Jewish Cooking in America, 1994; contbr. articles to profl. jours. Pres. Montgomery County Assn. Hearing Impaired Children, Silver Spring, 1981—83; fundraising v.p., treas. B'nai B'rith Women, Gaithersburg, 1975—93; dir. Magen David Sephradic Congregation Bd., Rockville, 1989—93. Named Best in the Bus., Am. Correctional Assn., 1999; recipient 1st Pl. award, Am. Sephardic Fedn., 1991. Mem.: Am. Sephardi Fedn. (bd. dirs. 2002—), Nat. Cued Speech Assn. (v.p. 1999—2002, pres. 2002—), Sephardic Voters League (v.p. 1999—), Hadassah, Jewish Women Internat., Acad. Women Achievers of the YWCA, Deadline Club. Democrat. Jewish. Avocations: Mid East cooking, Jewish genealogy. E-mail: sarinaroffe@aol.com.

ROGAN, ELEANOR GROENIGER, cancer researcher, educator; b. Nov. 25, 1942; d. Louis Martin and Esther (Levinson) G.; m. William John Robert Rogan, June 12, 1965 (div. 1970); 1 child, Elizabeth Rebecca. AB, Mt. Holyoke Coll., 1963; PhD, Johns Hopkins U., 1968. Lectr. Goucher Coll., Towson, Md., 1968-69; rsch. assoc. U. Tenn., Knoxville, 1969-73, U. Nebr. Med. Ctr., Omaha, 1973-76, asst. prof., 1976-80; assoc. prof. Eppley Inst., dept. pharm. scis. U. Nebr., Omaha, 1980-90, prof. dept. pharm. scis. and dept. biochem. & molecular biol, 1990—. Contbr. articles to profl. jours. Predoctoral fellow USPHS, Johns Hopkins U., 1965-68. Mem. AAAS, Am. Assn. Cancer Rsch., Soc. Toxicology. Democrat. Roman Catholic. Home: 8210 Bowie Dr Omaha NE 68114-1526 Office: U Nebr Med Ctr Eppley Inst 986805 Nebr Med Ctr Omaha NE 68198-6805 Office Phone: 402-559-4095. E-mail: egrogan@unmc.edu.

ROGENESS, MARY SPEER, state legislator; b. Kansas City, Kans., May 18, 1941; d. Frederic A. and Jeannette (Hybskmann) Speer; m. Dean Rogeness, Aug. 31, 1964; children: Emily, James, Paul. BA, Carleton Coll., 1963. Computer analyst Dept. Def., Ft. Meade, Md., 1963-66; freelance writer, editor Longmeadow, Mass., 1982-91; mem. Mass. Ho. of Reps., Boston, 1991—. Editor: Reflections of Longmeadow, 1983. Mem. Longmeadow Rep. Town Com., 1983—; bd. dirs. Goodwill Industries Hartford-Springfield, 1996—; mem. Longmeadow Sch. Com., 1982-88. Mem. Am. Legis. Exch. Coun., World Affairs Coun. of Western Mass. Office: Mass House of Reps State House Rm 124 Boston MA 02133

ROGERS, CAROL ROSENSTEIN, social worker, educator; b. N.Y.C., Apr. 25, 1947; d. Herman R. and Shirley Rosenstein; m. Martin M. Rogers, Aug. 10, 1969; children: Eric J., Beth S. BA cum laude, SUNY, Albany, 1969; EdM, Boston U., 1970, MSW, 1995. LCSW Mass.; permanent cert. tchr. secondary French N.Y., cert. tchr. secondary French and Spanish Mass. Tchr. French and Spanish grades 7-12 Town of Chelmsford (Mass.) Pub. Schs., 1970—81; educator, counselor for infertility and adoption Resolve Inc., Somerville, 1982—86; adoption educator Bedford, 1982—; adoption social worker Concord Family and Adolescent Svcs., Acton, 1997—2000; sch. social worker City of Newton (Mass.) Pub. Schs., 1997—2000; pvt. practice clin. social worker Burlington, 2002—. Mem. Archway interdisciplinary adoption study group; developer, implementor adoption tng. Mass. Gen. Hosp., Boston, Harvard U., Mass. pub. schs.; presenter confs. Com. mem. Bedford Parent-Tchr. Assn., Bedford, Mass., 1987—91; pub. spkr. LWV, Bedford, 1999; bd. dir. Temple Isaiah Sisterhood, Lexington, 1990—92, Open Door Soc./Adoption Cmty. of New Eng., Holliston, Mass., 2000—01. Mem.: NASW, Pi Delta Phi. Avocations: women's causes, travel, cooking, reading, gardening. Home: 47 Glenridge Dr Bedford MA 01730 Office: 1 Garfield Cir Burlington MA 01803 Office Phone: 617-529-4495. Personal E-mail: carol_rogers@comcast.net.

ROGERS, CHERYL ANN, speech pathology services professional; b. Schenectady, N.Y., July 8, 1948; d. George Michael Rogers and Viola Mary Santore. BS Speech and Language Pathology, State Univ. N.Y., Buffalo, N.Y., 1970; MA Speech and Language Pathology, Univ. Buffalo, Buffalo, N.Y., 1972. Lic. CCC/Sp N.Y., cert. tchr. of speech/hearing handicapped. Speech lang. pathologist Aspire, Buffalo, 1971—. Clin. adj. lectr. Univ. Buffalo, 1975—; lectr. Medaille Coll., 1975—; instr. BOCES Region #1, 1980—85. Prof. adv. bd. Hospice, Buffalo, 1980; vol. Luth. Ch. Home; eucharistic min.; pres. union UCPEU Local 3721, Buffalo, 1991—96; co-founder Dignity Buffalo, 1986. Mem.: Amnesty Internat. Human Rights Campaign, Am. Speech Hearing Lang. Assn., Kappa Delta Pi. Democrat. Roman Cath. Avocations: Reiki Level II hypnotherapy, painting, writing. Home: 44 Manchester Pl Buffalo NY 14213 Office: Aspire of NY 4632 Union Rd Cheektowaga NY 14225

ROGERS, DEBORAH S. human biology educator, writer; b. Japan, Oct. 11, 1954; d. Dilwyn J. and Priscilla H. Rogers; children: Even Pay, Maria Miller. BA, Augustana Coll., Sioux Falls, S.D., 1975; MS, U. Wis., 1979. Rschr. Ctr. for Alternative Mining Devel. Policy, Madison, Wis., 1979—80; ecologist The Nature Conservancy, Pierre, SD and Mandan, ND, 1981—82; dir. Tech. Info. Project, Rapid City and Pierre, SD, 1982—94; rschr./writer Rapid City, 1995—; human biology/ecology instr. Oglala Lakota Coll., Kyle, SD, 2001—02; adminstr. NCI rsch. grant Rapid City Regional Hosp., 2003—. Bd. advisors No. Prairies Land Trust, Sioux Falls, 2001—02; apptd. Governor's Mining Task Force, Pierre, 1987; bd. dirs. Dakota Choral Union, Rapid City, 1999. Named West River Notable, Rapid City Jour., 1991, featured South Dakotan, S.D. Pub. TV, 1990; recipient Keller Conservation award, Spearfish Canyon Preservation Trust, 1995. Mem.: Am. Anthropol. Assn. Office: Rapid City Regional Hosp 353 Fairmont Blvd Rapid City SD 57701 Personal E-mail: dsrogers1231@aol.com. E-mail: drogers@rcrh.org.

ROGERS, DESIREE GLAPION, utilities executive; b. New Orleans, June 16, 1959; d. Roy and Joyce Glapion; 1 child, Victoria. B in Polit. Sci., Wellesley Coll., 1981; MBA, Harvard U., 1985. Customer svc. mktg. mgr. AT&T, N.J., 1985-87; dir. devel. Levy Orgn., Chgo., 1987-89; founder, pres. Mus. Ops. Consulting Assocs., Chgo., 1989-91; dir. Ill. State Lottery, Chgo., 1991-97; chief mktg. officer Peoples Energy, Chgo., 1997—. Bd. dirs. Mus. Sci. and Industry, WTTW/Ch. 11, Ravinia; trustee Lincoln Park Zoo. Mem. The Econ. Club, Execs. Club. Office: Peoples Energy 130 E Randolph Dr Fl 18 Chicago IL 60601-6207

ROGERS, EARLINE S. state legislator; b. Gary, Ind., Dec. 20, 1934; d. Earl and Robbie (Hicks) Smith; m. Louis C. Rogers, Dec. 24, 1956; children: Keith, Dana. d. Earl and Robbie (Hicks) Smith; m. Louis C. Rogers, Dec.24, 1956; children: Keith, Dana. BS, Ind. U., 1957, MS, 1971. Mem. Ind. State Ho. Reps, 1982-90, Ind. State Senate from 14th dist., 1990—, asst. minority whip, 1995—96. Mem. appointment and claims com. (ranking minority mem.), edn. com., health and provider svcs. com., rules and legis. procedure com. Mem. NAACP, Nat. Coun. Negro Women, League Women Voters, Urban League, Black Prfl. Women, Am. Fedn. Tchrs., Ind. State Tchrs. Assn. Democrat. Avocations: reading, sewing. Office: Ind State Senate Dist 3 200 W Washington St Indianapolis IN 46204-2728 also: 3636 W 15th Ave Gary IN 46404

ROGERS, ELIZABETH PARKER, chemistry educator; b. Plymouth, Mass., Aug. 27, 1919; d. Edward R. and Helen L. (Barnes) Belcher; m. Warren H. Yudkin, Dec. 23, 1951 (dec. June 1954); children: Michael, David; m. Robert W. Rogers, Nov. 23, 1956; children: Susan, Sarah, John. BA, Mount Holyoke Coll., 1940, MA, 1942; PhD, Northwestern U., 1951. Rsch. chemist Armstrong Cork Co., Lancaster, Pa., 1942-45, Evanston (Ill.) Health Dept., 1951-54; asst. prof. U. Ill., Urbana, 1963-87. Author: (lab book) Beginning Chemistry, 1973, 76, 81, 91, 94, (textbook) Fundamentals of Chemistry, 1987, (with W.H. Brown) General, Organic and Biochemistry, 1980, 83, 87. Staff asst. ARC, France, 1945-46; sec. LWV, Champaign, 1987-89; dir., sec. East Ctrl. Ill. Alzheimer's, Champaign, Ill., 1989-91, pres., 1991-95; dir. Friends of Univ. of Ill. Libr., Champaign, 1989-92. Recipient Achievement award Sid Granet Aging Network, Ill. Area Agys. on Aging, 1992, Cert. of Lifetime Achievement, Ill. Dept. on Aging, 1995. Mem. Am. Chem. Soc. Avocations: golf, reading.

ROGERS, EVA MARIE VANLEUVEN, artist, poet; b. Poughkeepsie, N.Y., May 27, 1958; d. Clyde Benjamin Van Leuven and Gloria Alice (Stanton) Myers and Wilton E. Myers; m. Bruce L. Rogers. Exhbns. include one-woman shows, Adorondack Ctr. for the Arts, Blue Mt. Lake, N.Y., Tinker Street Cafe; group shows include Woodstock Artists Assn., 1994, 95, Springfield Art League 75th Ann. Nat. Exhibit, Small Works '94/Catskill Art Soc., The Tonawanda Ann. Nat. Juried Show/Carnegie Art Ctr., N.Y., Art WYO'94/West Wind Gallery, Casper, Wyo., Baystreet Galleria Nat. Open, Balboa Island, Calif., Nat. Soc. of Artists, '95, Santa Fe, others; prodr. Woodstock pub. access TV. Recipient Fire and Rose award Artspirit Internat., Marlbourgoh, Mass., 1996, Spl. Recognition award Baystreet, Balboa Island, Calif., 1994, awards profl. divsn. Nat. Soc. of Artists, Santa Fe, Tex., numerous others. Mem. Woodstock Artists Assn., Catskill Art Soc. E-mail: vision375@aol.com.

ROGERS, FRANCES EVELYN, author, retired educator and librarian; b. Mobile, Ala., Aug. 30, 1935; d. James Richard Graves and Jessie Reynolds (Butler) Lay; m. Jay Dee Rogers, Mar. 22, 1957; children: Laura, Larry. BA, North Tex. State U., 1957; MSLS, Our Lady of the Lake U., San Antonio, 1975. Cert. tchr., libr., Tex. Tchr. Ector County Ind. Sch. Dist., Odessa, Tex., 1958-59; social dir. svc. club Lackland AFB, San Antonio, 1960-61; tchr. San Antonio Ind. Sch. Dist., San Antonio, 1965-70; tchr., libr. Northside Ind. Sch. Dist., San Antonio, 1970-90, ret., 1990. Author: (hist. novels under name Keller Graves) Brazen Embrace, 1987, Rapture's Gamble, 1987, Desire's Fury, 1988, Velvet Vixen, 1988, Lawman's Lady, 1988, (hist. novels) Tex. Sins, 1989, Midnight Sins, 1989, Wanton Slave, 1990, Surrender to the Night, 1991, A Love So Wild, 1991, Sweet Texas Magic, 1992, Desert Fire, 1992, Desert Heat, 1993, Flame, 1994, Raven, 1995, Angel, 1995, Wicked, 1996, The Forever Bride, 1997, Betrayal, 1997, Hot Temper, 1997, Crown of Glory, 1998, Lone Star, 1999, Longhorn, 2000, Devil in the Dark, 2001, The Loner, 2001, The Grotto, 2002, The Ghost of Carnal Cove, 2002, Dark of the Moon, 2003, (contemporary novels) Second Opinion, 1999, Golden Man, 1999, More Than You Know, 2004. Sec., vol. Opera Guild San Antonio, 1980—; pres. San Antonio Romance Authors, 1997. Recipient Spirit of Romance award Rom Con, 1996, Prism Award Romance Writers Am., 1997, Tex. Gold award East Tex. Romance Writers Am., 1998. Mem. Nat. Soc. Arts and Letters. Home: 2722 Belvoir Dr San Antonio TX 78230-4507

ROGERS, GAIL ELIZABETH, library director; b. Charlotte, N.C., May 6, 1947; d. James Yates and Marian Elizabeth (Church) Rogers. BA, Salem Coll., 1969; MLS, U. N.C., 1971. Cert. libr., Ga. Br. libr. Atlanta Pub. Libr., 1970-77; br. coord. Dekalb Libr. System, Decatur, Ga., 1977-82; asst. dir. West Ga. Regional Libr., Carrollton, 1982-83, Cobb County Pub. Libr., Marietta, Ga., 1983-90, dir., 1991—. Mem. Leadership Cobb, Cobb County, 1985-86. Mem. ALA, Ga. Libr. Assn. (2d v.p. 1987-89), Southeastern Libr. Assn. (v.p.-pres. elect. 1990-92, pres. 1992-94), Urban Librs. Coun., Kiwanis Club Marietta (bd. dirs. 1991-92, sec. 1992-93, sec.-treas. 1993-94, pres. 1995-96). Office: Cobb County Public Lib 266 Roswell St SE Marietta GA 30060-2005

ROGERS, JUDITH W. federal judge; b. 1939; AB cum laude, Radcliffe Coll., 1961; LLB, Harvard U., 1964; LLM, U. Va., 1988; LLD (hon.), D.C. Sch. Law, 1992. Bar: D.C. 1965. Law clk. Juvenile Ct. D.C., 1964-65; asst. U.S. atty. D.C., 1965-68; trial atty. San Francisco Neighborhood Legal Assistance Found., 1968-69; atty. assoc. atty. gen.'s office U.S. Dept. Justice, 1969-71, atty. criminal divsn., 1969-71; gen. counsel Congl. Commn. on Organization of D.C. Govt., 1971-72; coordinator legis. program Office of Dep. Mayor D.C., 1972-74, spl. asst. to mayor for legis., 1974-79, corp. counsel, 1979-83; assoc. judge D.C. Ct. Appeals, 1983-88, chief judge, 1988-94; cir. judge U.S. Ct. Appeals-D.C. Cir., 1994—. Mem. D.C. Law Revision Commn., 1979-83, mem. grievance com. U.S. Dist. Ct. D.C., 1982-83; mem. exec. com. Conf. Chief Justices, 1993-94. Bd. dirs. Wider Opportunities for Women, 1972-74; mem. vis. com. Harvard U. Sch. Law, 1984-90; trustee Radcliffe Coll., 1982-88. Recipient citation for work on D.C. Self-Govt. Act, 1973, Disting. Pub. Svc. award D.C. Govt., 1983, award Nat. Bar Assn., 1989; named Woman Lawyer of Yr., Women's Bar Assn. D.C., 1990. Fellow ABA; mem. D.C. Bar, Nat. Assn. Women Judges, Conf. Chief Justices (bd. dirs. 1988-94), Am. Law Inst., Phi Beta Kappa. Office: US Ct Appeals Fed Cir 717 Madison Pl NW Washington DC 20001-2866*

ROGERS, JULIE, foundation administrator; B, Duke U.; M in tchg., George Wash. U. Staff dir. Coun. DC Com. Human Svcs.; pres. Eugene and Agnes Meyer Found.; joined Meyer Found., 1986—. Founding chair Wash. Regional Assn. Grantmakers, 1992—95; founder Wash. AIDS Partnership, Cmty. Devel. Support Collaborative; dir. Greater Wash. Bd. Trade; bd. mem. Forum Regionals Assn. Grantmakers. Bd. mem. Venture Philanthropy Ptnr., DC Coll. Access Program; adv. com. DC Local Initiatives Support Corp.; bd. Leadership Wash., treas., 1990—91, vice chmn., 1990—91; bd. Found. Ctr., 1991—2000; mem. Federal City Coun., Coun. Found., 2002—. Named one of 100 Most Powerful Women in Wash., Washingtonian mag., 2001; recipient Founder award for leadership and cmty. svc., Leadership Wash., 1997. Mem.: Wash. Women's Forum. Office: Meyer Found 1400 16th St NW Ste 360 Washington DC 20036 Office Phone: 202-483-8294. Office Fax: 202-328-6850.*

ROGERS, KAREN BECKSTEAD, gifted studies educator, researcher, consultant; b. L.A., Nov. 28, 1943; d. Maurice Webster and Helen Dorothy (Nalty) Beckstead; m. William Geoffrey Rogers, Sept. 11, 1965; children: Jeanne Elizabeth Rogers Armstrong, Jennifer Lynn Rogers Hasbrouck, William Carey. BA in Humanities, U. Calif., Berkeley, 1965; MA in Spl. Edn., San Diego State U., 1969; MA in Ednl. Psychology, U. Minn., 1983, PhD in Curriculum and Instrn. Sys., 1991. Cert. elem. tchr., Calif. Pace project coord. West Jr. Paul Schs., 1975-77; Omnibus project dir. Jr. League of Mpls., 1978-83; instr. U. Minn., Mpls., 1985—95; gifted studies instr. U. St. Thomas, Mpls., 1984-87, asst. prof. gifted studies, 1987-93, assoc. prof. gifted studies, 1993-98, prof., 1999—. Cons., Burnsville, Minn., 1978—. Author: Ability Grouping and Gifted Learners, 1991 (Early Scholar award, 1991), Talent Development in Context, 1998, Re-Forming Gifted Education, 2002; contbg. editor Roeper Rev., 1994—, contbg. reviewer Jour. Secondary Gifted Edn., 1994—, Jour. for the Edn. of the Gifted, 1994—, Gifted Edn. Internat., 1998—, Gifted Child Quarterly, 1997—; contbr. 90 articles to profl. jours., 12 chpts. to books. Docent Mpls. Inst. Arts, 1975—. Recipient Lifetime Achievement award Minn. Coun. for Gifted and Talented, 1989. Mem. Coun. for Exceptional Children (pres. The Assn. for the Gifted 1994-96), Nat. Assn. for Gifted Children, Am. Ednl. Rsch. Assn. Democrat. Avocations: art collecting, art history, music appreciation, writing, reading. Home: 14004 Whiterock Rd Burnsville MN 55337-4717 Office: U St Thomas MOH 217 1000 Lasalle Ave Minneapolis MN 55403-2025 Office Phone: 651-962-4386. E-mail: kbrogers@stthomas.edu.

ROGERS, KAREN COOLEDGE, music educator; b. Rochester, N.Y., Jan. 25, 1960; d. Richard Calvin and Barbara Heerich Cooledge; m. Jeffrey Paul Rogers, Dec. 19, 1981; children: Keith Marshall, Renee Michelle, Katie Christine. Bachelor of Music Edn., W.Va. U., 1982. Advanced profl. cert. Md. Tchr. music Antietam Jr. High, Waynesboro, Pa., 1984—86; band dir. N.W. Mid. Sch., Taneytown, Md., 1986—89; band dir. and tchr. music Spring Garden Elem., Hampstead, Md., 1991—. Music dir. St. John's Meth. Ch., Spencer, W.Va., 1982. Elder and deacon 1st United Presbyn. Ch., Westminster, Md., choir dir., 1999—; v.p. and pres. N. Carroll High Choral Booster, Hampstead, Md., 2001—; acting pres. PEO, Westminster, 2003. Mem.: Music Educator's Nat. Conf. Republican. Avocations: water-skiing, tennis, needlecrafts. Office: Spring Garden Elem Sch 700 Boxwood Dr Hampstead MD 21074

ROGERS, KATE ELLEN, interior design educator; b. Nashville, Dec. 13, 1920; d. Raymond Lewis and Louise (Gruver) R.; diploma Ward-Belmont Jr. Coll., 1940; BA in Fine Arts, George Peabody Coll., 1946, MA in Fine Arts, 1947; EdD in Fine Arts and Fine Arts Edn., Columbia U., 1956. Instr., Tex. Tech. Coll., Lubbock, 1947-53; co-owner, v.p. Design Today, Inc., Lubbock, 1951-54; student asst. Am. House, N.Y.C., 1953-54; asst. prof. housing and interior design U. Mo., Columbia, 1954-56, assoc. prof., 1956-66, prof., 1966-85, emeritus, 1985—, chmn. dept. housing and interior design, 1973-85; mem. accreditation com. Found. for Interior Design Edn. Rsch., 1975-76, chmn. stds. com., 1976-82, chmn. rsch., 1982-85. Mem. 1st Bapt. Ch., Columbia, Mo.; bd. dirs. Meals on Wheels, 1989-91. Nat. Endowment for Arts rsch. grantee, 1981-82. Fellow Interior Design Educators Coun. (pres. 1971-73, chmn. bd. 1974-76, chmn. rsch. com. 1977-78); mem. Am. Soc. Interior Designers, (hon., medal of honor 1975), Am. Home Econs. Assn., Columbia Art League (adv. bd. 1988-93), Pi Lambda Theta, Kappa Delta Pi, Phi Kappa Phi (hon.), Gamma Sigma Delta, Delta Delta Delta (Phi Eta chpt.), Phi Upsilon Omicron, Omicron Nu (hon.). Democrat. Author: The Modern House, USA, 1962; editor Jour. Interior Design Edn. and Research, 1975-78.

ROGERS, KATHERINE DIANE, political consultant, commissioner; b. Concord, N.H., Mar. 7, 1955; d. Albert A. and Alta (Whittier) R. BA, Clark U., Worcester, Mass., 1977. Mem. N.H. Ho. of Reps., Concord, 1992-98; county commr. County of Merrimack, 1998—. Bd. dirs. N.H. Bus. Fin. Authority. Mem. City Coun., Concord, 1991—. Democrat. Lutheran. Home: 4 Jay Dr Concord NH 03301-7831

ROGERS, LORENE LANE, university president emeritus; b. Prosper, Tex., Apr. 3, 1914; d. Mort M. and Jessie L. (Luster) Lane; m. Burl Gordon Rogers, Aug. 23, 1935 (dec. June 14, 1941). BA, N. Tex. State Coll., 1934; MA (Parke, Davis fellow), U. Tex., 1946, PhD, 1948; DSc (hon.), Oakland U., 1972; LLD, Austin Coll., 1977. Prof. chemistry Sam Houston State Coll., Huntsville, Tex., 1947-49; research scientist Clayton Found. Biochem. Inst. U. Tex., Austin, 1950-64, asst. dir., 1957-64, prof. nutrition, 1962-80, assoc. dean Grad. Sch., 1964-71, v.p. univ., 1971-74, pres., 1974-79, mem. exec. com. African grad. fellowship program, 1966-71; research cons. Clayton Found. for Research, Houston, 1979-81. Vis. scientist, lectr., cons. NSF, 1959-62; cons. S.W. Research Inst., San Antonio, 1959-62; mem. Grad. Record Exams Bd., 1972-76, chmn., 1974-75; adv. com. ITT Internat. Fellowship, 1973-83; dir. Texaco, Inc., Gulf States Utilities, Republic Bank, Austin. Bd. dirs. Tex. Opera Theatre, Austin Lyric Opera; chmn. bd. trustees Texaco Philanthropic Found.; chmn. council of presidents Nat. Assn. State Univs. and Land-Grant Colls., 1976-77, mem. exec. com., 1976-79; mem. com. on identification of profl. women Am. Council on Edn., 1975-79, mem. com. on govt. relations, 1978-79; mem. target 2000 project com. Tex. A&M U. System; mem. ednl. adv. bd. John E. Gray Inst., Lamar U., Beaumont, Tex. Eli Lilly fellow, 1949-50; Recipient U. Tex. Students Assn. Teaching Excellence award, 1963; Disting. Alumnus award N. Tex. State U., 1972; Outstanding Woman of Austin award, 1950, 60, 71, 80; Disting. Alumnus award U. Tex., 1976; Honor Scroll award Tex. Inst. Chemists, 1980 Fellow Am. Inst. Chemists; mem. AAAS, Am. Chem. Soc. (sec. 1954-56), Am. Inst. Nutrition, Am. Soc. Human Genetics, Nat. Soc. Arts and Letters, Assn. Grad. Schs. (internat. edn. com. 1967-71), Sigma Xi, Phi Kappa Phi, Iota Sigma Pi, Omicron Delta Kappa. Achievements include research in hydantoin synthesis, intermediary metabolism, biochem. nutritional aspects of alcoholism, mental retardation, congenital malformations. Home: 4 Nob Hill Cir Austin TX 78746-3650

ROGERS, MARILYN ROSE, special education educator; d. Bernard George Plaskett and Grace Lucille Landstoffer; m. Jack D. Richardson, July 10, 1954 (div. Nov. 1956); 1 child, Cheryl Lynn Richardson (dec.) ; m. Richard Bernard Doell Rogers, Jan. 11, 1958 (dec. June 2001); children: Sheree Shannon Amber Coe Parten, Michelle Denise Cheeley, Richard Dale. AA, Long Beach City Coll., Calif., 1972; BA in Child Devel., Calif. State U., San Bernardino, 1976, Master's in Spl. Edn., Master's in Sch. Counseling, Calif. State U., San Bernardino, 1980; EdD, Nova Southeastern U., 1994. Cert. child devel. and spl. edn. specialist Calif., lang. devel. specialist Calif., pre-sch. tchr., elem. tchr. Dir. and tchr. Bixby Pk. Parents Coop., Long Beach, 1970—72; tchr. child study ctr. Long Beach City Coll., 1972—76; tchr. and dir. Head Start Moreno Valley Sch. Dist., Calif., 1976—77; tchr. kindergarten and grade 1 Romoland Sch. Dist., Calif., 1977—79, tchr. spl. edn. pre-sch. to grade 8, 1979—88, resource specialist tchr., 1980—2001, coord. spl. edn. and bilingual programs, 1980—90, tchr. home sch. severely disabled, 2001—. Tchr. religious edn. St. Joseph Mission Ch., San Jacinto, Calif., 2001—; tchr., tutor, and counselor The Learning Ctr., Nuevo, Calif., 2001—; child/adult adv. Riverside County Mental Health, Calif., 2002—. Fellow, Calif. Writing Project, 1985. Mem.: Calif. Assn. Resource Specialists (pres. 1986, Resource Specialist of Yr. 1995), Soroptimists, Delta Kappa Gamma (pres., v.p.), Phi Delta Kappa. Roman Catholic. Avocations: doll collecting, gardening, travel. Home: 21925 Garden Dr Nuevo CA 92567-9125 Office: The Learning Ctr 21925 Garden Dr Nuevo CA 92567-9125

ROGERS, NANCY HARDIN, dean, law educator; b. Lansing, Mich., Sept. 18, 1948; d. Clifford Morris and Martha (Wood) Hardin; m. Douglas Langston Rogers, Jan. 30, 1970; children: Lynne, Jill, Kim. BA with highest distinction, U. Kans., 1969; JD, Yale U., 1972. Bar: D.C. 1975, Ohio 1972, U.S. Ct. Appeals (6th cir.) 1973, U.S. Dist. Ct. (no. dist.) Ohio 1974, U.S. Dist. Ct. (so. dist.) Ohio 1975. Law clk. U.S. Dist. Judge Thomas D. Lambros, Cleve., 1972-74; staff atty. Cleve. Legal Aid Soc., 1974-75; vis. asst. prof. Coll. of Law Ohio State U., Columbus, 1975-76, asst. prof., 1976-78, 83-89, assoc. prof., 1989-92, prof., assoc. dean acad. affairs, 1992-97, prof., 1992—, Joseph S. Platt, Porter, Wright, Morris & Arthur prof. law, 1995—2001, vice provost acad. adminstrn., 1999—2001, dean, Michael E. Moritz chair in alternative dispute resolution Michael E. Moritz Coll. Law, 2001—. Adj. prof. Ohio State Coll., 1981-83; vis. prof. law Harvard Law Sch., 2000. Author (with Frank E.A. Sander, Sarah R. Cole, Stephen B. Goldberg): (Book) Dispute Resolution: Negotiation, Mediation and Other Processes), 2003; author: (book with Craig A. McEwen and Sarah R. Cole) Mediation: Law, Policy, Practice, 2nd edit., 1994; mem. (adv. bd.) World Arbitration and Mediation Report, 1991—, Alternatives, 1992—, co-chair (editl. bd. with Frank E.A. Sander) Dispute Resolution mag., 1994—2002; contbr. chapters to books, articles to profl. jours. Bd. dirs. Assn. for Developmentally Disabled, Columbus, 1980-85; Legal Svcs. Corp. 1995-2003. Named Outstanding Prof., Ohio State U. Coll. Law Alumni Assn., 1996; recipient Book prize, Ctr. Pub. Resources for A Student's Guide to Mediation and the Law, 1987, Ctr. Pub. Resources for Mediation: Law, Policy, Practice, 1989, Peacemaker of Yr. award, Cmty. Mediation Svcs. Ctrl. Ohio, 1990, Disting. Svc. Recognition, Soc. Profls. in Dispute Resolution, 1990, Whitney North Seymour sr. medal, Am. Arbitration Assn., 1990, Svc. Recognition award, Legal Aid Soc. Columbus, 1996, Ritter award, Ohio State Bar Found for outstanding contbns. to adminstrn. of justice, 1998; grantee Exxon Edn. Found., 1986, William and Flora Hewlett Found., 1990, Ohio State U. Interdisciplinary Seed, 1990, Ohio State U. Symposium, 1992, William and Flora Hewlett Found., 1992—96, Nat. Sci. Found., 1993—95, State Justice Instn., 1994, Fund for Improvement Post-Secondary Edn., U. Mo., 1996—97, William and Flora Hewlett Found., 1997—2003. Mem. ABA (chair, standing com. dispute resolution 1988-91, D'Alemberte-Raven award sect. on dispute resolution 2002), Phi Beta Kappa. Office: Ohio State U Coll Law 55 W 12th Ave Columbus OH 43210-1306 Business E-Mail: rogers.23@osu.edu.

ROGERS, OLIVIA JOHNSON, elementary school counselor; b. Hays, Kans., Nov. 23, 1947; d. Norman Bruce and La Rene (Miller) Johnson; m. John E. Rogers, Mar. 23, 1991. BS in Edn., Emporia State U., 1971; MS in Edn., Kans. State U., 1976; EdS in Counseling, Wichita State U., 1990. Lic. profl. counselor; nat. cert. counselor. Elem. sch. tchr. Topeka Pub. Schs., 1972-82; spl. edn. tchr. Wichita Pub. Schs., 1982-87, elem. sch. counselor, 1987-91; counselor Diabetes Ctr. at St. Joseph-Via Christi Med. Ctr., Wichita, 1987-91; counselor, clinician CPC Gt. Plains Hosp., Wichita, 1987-91; elem. sch. counselor Salina (Kans.) Pub. Schs., 1991—. Counselor, Child Abuse Prevention Svcs., Salina, 1997—, Rogers Counseling Svcs., Salina, 1997—. Ednl. cons. Topeka Girls Club, 1980-81. Mem. Am. Counseling Assn., Am. Sch. Counselor Assn., Kans. Sch. Counselor Assn., Kans. Mental Health Assn.

ROGERS, PATTIANN, poet, educator, poet, writer; b. Joplin, Mo., Mar. 23, 1940; d. William Tall, Irene Tall; m. John Robert Rogers; children: John, Arthur. BA, U.of Mo., 1961; MA, U.Houston, 1981. Vis. asst. prof. So. Meth. U., Dallas, 1985, U. of Houston, Houston, 1986; field faculty Vt. Coll. Norwich U., Montpelier, Vt., 1986—89; vis. writer U. of Tex., Austin, Tex., 1987; Richard Hugo disting. poet-in-residence U. of Mont., Missoula, Mont., 1988; vis. asst. prof. U. of Tex., 1988—89, U. of Mont., 1993; assoc. prof. U. of Ark., Fayetteville, Ark., 1993—97; vis. prof. Wash. U., St. Louis, 1993. Lectr. in field. Author: The Expectations of Light, 1981 (Best book of Poetry, 1982), The Tattooed Lady in the Garden, 1986, Legendary Performance, 1987, Splitting and Binding, Soerette Diehl Fraser/Natalie Ornish Poetry Award from the Texas Institute of Letters, 1989, Geocentric, 1993, Firekeeper, New and Selected Poems, 1994 (Natalie Ornish award for Poetry, 1995), Eating Bread and Honey, 1997, the Dream of the Marsh Wren, Writing as Reciprocal Creation, 1999, Song of the World Becoming, New and Collected Poems, 1981 - 2001, 2001, numerous poems. Recipient Theodore Roetheke prize, Poetry N.W. U. of Washington, 1981; fellow, Guggenheim Found., 1984—85, Lannan Found., 1991; grantee, Nat. Endowment for the Arts, 1982, 1988, Residency in Bellagio, Italy, Rockefeller Found., 2000. Home: 7412 Berkeley Cir Castle Rock CO 80108

ROGERS, PENNY M. music educator; b. Gastonia, North Carolina, U.S.A., Sept. 7, 1954; d. George Harold and Alberta Helton Miller; m. Steven Mikkelsen Rogers, June 14, 1980; 1 child, Michael Stevensen. B. Music Edn., East Carolina U., Greenville NC., 1972—76. Music tchr. Plainview Mingo Midway EL. Sch., Sampson County, NC, 1976—77; band dir., music tchr. N. Myrtle Beach Primary Elem. & H.S., Loris Elem. Sch., Harris County, SC, 1977—83; band dir. Hartsville Jr. H.S., SC, 1983—99; adj. prof. Coker Coll., Hartsville, SC, 1989—2003; band dir. Chestnut Oaks Mid. Sch., Sumter, SC, 1999—2003. Flag line instr. Hartsville High Sch., Hartsville, SC, 1983—99, Sumter High Sch., Sumter, SC, 1999—2003. Recipient Tchr. Program award, Fulbright Memorial Fund, 2002, Tchr. of the Yr., Chestnut Oaks Mid. Sch., 2003—04. Mem.: Music Educators Nat. Conf., SC. Band Dir. Assn., Am. Sch. Band Dir. Assn. Avocations: reading, needlecrafts. Office: Chestnut Oaks Middle School 1200 Oswego Rd Sumter SC 29153

ROGERS, REBECCA HARRIS, music educator; b. Augusta, Ga., Jan. 14, 1951; d. Waldo Putnam and Hazel McKinnon Harris; m. Richard Sloan Rogers, Dec. 27, 1980; children: George, Mary Alice, Sara Beth. MusB Summa Cum Laude, Shorter Coll., 1972. Pvt. piano tchr., various cities, 1973—. Organist various chs., 1973—2002; children's minister, large music theatre prodns. Arbor Bapt. Ch., Fitzgerald, Ga., 1999—; piano tchr. Abraham Baldwin Coll., Tifton, 1999—; performer grand piano concerts Arts Coun., Fitzgerald. Mem.: Nat. Guild Piano Tchrs. (bd judges), Arts Coun. (bd dirs.). Baptist. Home: 1086 Roanoke Dr Fitzgerald GA 31750

ROGERS, ROSE MARIE, state legislator; b. Wolfeboro, N.H., Sept. 27, 1927; m. Roland N. Rogers (dec.); 2 children. BS, U. N.H., 1949; MSW, U. Conn., 1959. Mem. Ward 1 N.H. Ho. of Reps. (dist. 15), Concord, 1993-94; mem. wildlife and marine resources com. N.H. Ho. of Reps., Concord, 1996—. Active Granite State Sr. Games. Mem. NASW, Am. Assn. Ret. Persons, Acad. Cert. Social Workers. Roman Catholic. Home: 29 Eagle Dr Rochester NH 03868-7038

ROGERS, ROSEMARY, author; b. Panadura, Ceylon, Dec. 7, 1932; came to U.S., 1962; naturalized citizen. d. Cyril Allan and Barbara (Jansze); m. Summa Navaratnam (div.); children: Rosanne, Sharon; m. Leroy Rogers (div.); children: Michael, Adam; m. Christopher Kadison (div.). BA, U. Ceylon. Writer features and pub. affairs info. Associated Newspapers Ceylon, Colombo, 1959-62; sec. billeting office Travis AFB, Calif., 1964-69; sec. Solano County (Calif.) Parks Dept., Fairfield, 1969-74. Part-time reporter Fairfield Daily Republic Author: (novels) Sweet Savage Love, 1974, The Wildest Heart, 1974, Dark Fires, 1975, Wicked Loving Lies, 1976, The Crowd Pleasers, 1978, The Insiders, 1979, Lost Love, Last Love, 1980, Love Play, 1981, Surrender to Love, 1982, The Wanton, 1985, Bound by Desire, 1988, The Tea Planter's Bride, 1995, A Dangerous Man, 1996, Dark Fires: Book 2, 1996, Boomer Babes: A Woman's Guide to the New Middle Ages, 1998, All I Desire, 1998. Mem. Authors Guild of Authors League Am., Writers Guild Am.

ROGERS, ROWENA EMERY, retired land manager; b. Denver, Colo., Dec. 8, 1921; d. Roe and Jeannette (Carpenter) Emery; m. Ranger Rogers, Nov. 1, 1944; children: Susan Livenik, Jeanette Gaffney, Roxana DeSole, Lorna Burgess, Robert Ranger, Sarah Blythe. BA, Vassar College, 1943. Pres., dir. State Bd. Parks, Colo., 1971—77; pres. State Land Bd., 1977—; dir. State Natural Areas Program, 1978—84, State Recreational Trails, 1979—82; chmn. pub. lands com., Interstate Oil Compact Com., Tulsa, Okla., 1982—85, ret. Trustee Vassa College, 1961—63. Mem.: Kent School (bd. dir., Englewood County, Colo. 1962—66), Western States Land Com. Assocs. (pres. 1978—80), Nat. Strategic Materials and Minerals Program Adv. Com., Pony Club (dist. commr., Arapahoe County 1952—), YWCA (bd. dir., Denver 1974—78), Arapahoe (hon.; hon. sec. 1982—). Episc. Home: 7767 N Village Rd Parker CO 80134-6235

ROGERS, SHARON, art educator; b. Detroit, May 6, 1950; d. William Farland and Helen Jane Lowe; m. Bruce M. Rogers, June 6, 1972; 1 child, Katherine Marie. BA, N. Tex. State U., 1972; MA, So. Meth. U., 1982. Art tchr. Slaughter Jr. High, McKinney, Tex., 1975-76, Lakeview Centennial H.S., Garland, Tex., 1977-78, head fine arts dept., 1978—2001; art instr. Naaman Forest H.S., Garland, 2002—. Co-chair dist. fine arts com. Garland Ind. Sch. Dist., 1995—2001; asst. girls' soccer coach Lakeview Centennial H.S., 1999—2001. Adult Sunday Sch. tchr. St. Philip's United Meth. Ch., Garland, 1980—, vol. family ministries, 1990-99 Mem. Assn. Tchrs. Profl.

Edn., Nat. Art Edn. Assn., Garland Tchr.'s Orgn. Avocations: drawing, painting. Home: 1422 Kingsbridge Dr Garland TX 75044-7604 Office: Naaman Forest HS 4834 Naaman Forest Blvd Garland TX 75040

ROGERS, SHARON J. education consultant; b. Grantsburg, Wis., Sept. 24, 1941; d. Clifford M and Dorothy L (Beckman) Dickau; m. Evan D Rogers, June 15, 1962 (div. Dec. 1980); m. Joseph Y. Ruth, Dec. 22, 2003. BA summa cum laude, Bethel Coll., St. Paul, 1963; MA in Libr. Sci., U. Minn., 1967; PhD in Sociology, Wash. State U., Pullman, 1976. Lectr., instr. Alfred (N.Y.) U., 1972-76; assoc. prof. U. Toledo, 1977-80; assoc. dean Bowling Green (Ohio) State U. Librs., 1980-84; univ. libr. George Washington U., Washington, 1984-92, asst. v.p. acad. affairs, 1989-92, assoc. v.p. acad. affairs, 1992-97, co-dir. Univ. Teaching Ctr., 1990-97; cons. in higher edn. and librs., 1997—. Mem Online Computer Library Ctr Users Coun, 1985—92; pres. Online Computer Library Ctr Users Coun., 1989—90, rsch. advt. com., 1990—92; trustee Online Computer Library Ctr., 1992—2002; exec dir Assn Libr. and Info. Sci. Edn., 1997—2000. Contbr. articles to profl jours. Bd dirs CapAccess, 1993—97, treas, 1993—95; bd dirs ACLU, Toledo, 1978—84. Fellow Jackson, Univ Minn, 1964—65; grantee NSF, Wash State Univ, 1969—72. Mem.: ALA (exec coun 1987—91, pub comt 1989—93, chair 1990—93), Universal Serials and Book Exchange (bd dirs, treas 1987), Washington Research Library Consortium (bd dirs 1987—90), Am Sociological Asn, Asn Col and Research Libraries (pres 1984—85). Home: 2922 24th St N Arlington VA 22207 E-mail: sroger7@attglobal.net.

ROGERS, SHERRY ANNE, physician; b. Syracuse, N.Y., Apr. 15, 1943; d. Rodney Wellington and Jayne Hammond; m. Robert Hamilton Rogers, June 30, 1970. BA, Syracuse U., 1969; MD, SUNY, 1969-70. Diplomate Am. Bd. Family Practice, 1973, Am. Bd. Environ. Medicine, 1985. Intern Health Scis. Ctr. Syracuse, 1969-70; pvt. practice pediat., Auburn, N.Y., 1970-71; emergency physician Cmty. Gen. Hosp., Syracuse, N.Y., 1971-72; pvt. practice family medicine, Syracuse, 1972-85; pvt. practice environ. medicine, 1978—. Lectr. in field. Author: (book) Tired or Toxic?, 1990, Wellness Against All Odds, 1994, Chemical Sensitivity, 1995, You Are What You Ate, The E.I. Syndrome, 1997, Depression Cured At Last, 1997, No More Heartburn, 2000, The Cure is in the Kitchen, The Scientific Basis of Environmental Medicine Techniques, 2000, Total Wellness, 2000, 2001, Pain Free in 6 Weeks, 2001, Detoxify or Die, 2003; editor (ed environm med sect): Internal Medical World Report, 1992—93; contbr. articles to profl. jours., book Alternative and Complementary Veterinary Medicine, 1998, chapters to books. Fellow: Am. Coll. Nutrition, Am. Coll. Asthma, Allergy and Immunology. Office: NE Ctr Environ Med 2800 W Genesee St Syracuse NY 13219-1451

ROGERS, STACEY A. mechanical engineer; BSME, MIT, 1989. Sr. project controls engr. Bechtel Corp., various cities, 1993—. Steering com. mem. St. Joseph Basilica Cath. Young Adults Group, Alameda, 1993—95; co-chairperson Bechel Corp.'s San Francisco Office Take Our Daughters to Work Day, 1999; com. mem. Cental Artery / Tunnel Project Diversity Adv. Team, Boston. Lt. USN, 1989—93, lt. col. USNR, 1993—. Recipient Navy Achievement medal, 1993, Navy Commendation medal, 2003. Mem.: VFW (life), Soc. Women Engrs., Naval Res. Assn. Achievements include vet. Operation Desert Storm and Operation Iraqi Freedom. Avocations: travel, reading, gardening.

ROGERS, SUSAN MITCHELL, psychotherapist; b. Atlanta, Apr. 19, 1937; d. George Raymond and Sara Perry Mitchell; children: Eason Jordan, Samuel Worley, III, Dodd Worley Sr. AA, Blue Ridge Coll., 1980; BA, Mercer U., 1987; postgrad., Harvard U., 1988; MSW, U. Ga., Athens, 1989; PhD Internat. U., 2001. Diplomate Am. Psychotherapy Assn.; lic. clin. social worker, Ga. Founder, dir. The Red Door Sch., Atlanta, 1960-65, The Univ. Day Sch., Atlanta, 1964-74; cons. in family therapy Ga. Highlands Mental Health, Dalton, 1989; sr. child therapist Lookout Mountain Mental Health, La Fayette, Ga., 1989-97. Dir. Healing Bridge Counseling Ctr., 1991—; dir. The Appalachian Incest Project, 1991—; cons. in mental health Task Force for the Homeless, Atlanta, Dept. Juvenile Justice. Author, editor: The Women of Healing Bridge, 1997; author: A Survivor's Guide to INcest. Grantee Wardlaw Trust 15-yr grantee, Washington, 1991—. Mem. NASW, ACA, Nat. Assn. Forensic Counselors, Buckhead Girls Club. Home: 4430 Hwy #151 La Fayette GA 30728 Office: 201 West La Fayette Square La Fayette GA 30728

ROGERS, THOMASINA VENESE, federal commissioner; Student, Northwestern U.; JD, Columbia U. Chmn. Adminstrv. Conf. U.S., Washington, 1994-95; presdl. pers. staff The White House, Washington; dep. legal counsel, then legal counsel EEOC, Washington; mem. Occupl. Safety and Health Rev. Commn., Washington, 1998—, chmn., 1999—2002. Bd. dirs. Children's Nat. Med. Ctr. Mem. Am. Arbitration Assn. (bd. dirs.) Office: Occupl Safety and Health Review Commn One Lafayette Ctr 1120 20th St NW Washington DC 20036-3457*

ROGILLIO, KATHY JUNE, musician, piano rebuilder, educator; b. Baton Rouge, La., Nov. 4, 1950; d. David Hunter and Thelma Ruth (Tucker) R. MusB, La. State U., 1972, MusM, 1974. Organist Plains Presbyn. Ch., Zachary, La., 1963-73; teacher's aid Gifted/Talented East Baton Rouge Parish, Baton Rouge, La., 1974-75; staff accompanist La. State U., Baton Rouge, 1975-76; music enrichment tchr. Episcopal H.S., Baton Rouge, 1976-77; organist, choirmaster Grace Episcopal Ch., St. Francisville, La., 1977-82; piano-technician So. U., Baton Rouge, La., 1977-84; apprentice in piano rebuilding and concert tuning, 1978-81; music tchr., organist, choirmaster St. Patrick's Episcopal Day Sch. and Ch., Zachary, La., 1985-86; vis. organist, dir. Numerous Chs., La. and Miss., 1982—; piano rebuilder pvt. practice, Zachary, La., 1986—. Ind. contract work Santi Falcone, Falcone Piano Co., Haverhill, Mass., 1987-88, part time organist/choirmaster St. Patrick's Episcopal Ch., Zachary, La., 1999-2000; pvt. piano tchr. La. Sch. for Visually Impaired, 2000—; recitalist, vis. organist. Arranger: Piano-Trio Arrangement Brahms Intermezzo Opus 118, #2, 1986 (2d pl. Composer's Guild Farmington, Utah, 1986). Treas. Beulah Plains Cemetery Assn., Zachary, La., 1987; mem. Landowners for Equitable Flood Control, Zachary, La., 1994—; Dem. candidate for U.S. Ho. of Reps. from 6th Dist. La., 2000. Mem. Am. Guild Organists, Baton Rouge Musicians' Assn. (exec bd. 1990-92, v.p. 1992-94. pres. 1994-96), La. Endowment for the Humanities, La. Pub. Broadcasting, Pi Kappa Lambda (profl. mus. hons. frat.). Democrat. Episcopalian. Avocations: needlework, cooking, animals. Home and Office: Artist Pianos 18153 Barnett Rd Zachary LA 70791-8114 E-mail: k.rogillio@worldnet.att.net.

ROGIN, RONNE ANN, retired government contract specialist; b. N.Y.C., Oct. 23, 1948; d. Maurice and Marjorie Doris Rogin. BS, George Washington U., 1970, MA, 1972. Head dept. athletics The Potomac Sch., McLean, Va., 1970-80; contract specialist U.S. Geol. Survey, Reston, Va., 1980-90; supervisory contract specialist Dept. Treasury, Washington, 1990-93; contract specialist State Dept., Washington, 1993—99; procurement analyst Office Procurement Treasury, Washington, 1999—2003, dep. dir. Office Procurement, 1999—2003, ret., 2003. Mem. NOW, NAFE, Nat. Contract Mgmt. Assn., Planned Parenthood. Democrat. Home: 13711 Springhaven Dr Chantilly VA 20151-3215

ROGOSKI, PATRICIA DIANA, financial executive; b. Chgo., Dec. 29, 1939; d. Raymond Michael and Bernice Rose (Konkol) R. BS in Acctg. and Econs., Marquette U., 1961, postgrad., 1965-66, NYU, 1966-68, St. John's U., N.Y.C., 1975-76; cert. mgmt. acct., 1979. Sr. fin. analyst Blackhawk Mfg. Co., Milw., 1961-66; mgr., sr. analyst Shell Oil Co., N.Y.C., 1966-71; mgr. data processing Bradford Nat./Penn Bradford, Pitts., 1971-75; asst. mgr. fin. controls ITT, N.Y.C., 1975-79; v.p., comptr. ITT Consumer Fin. Corp., Mpls., 1979-80; sr. v.p. fin. ITT Fin. Corp., St. Louis, 1980-84; v.p., exec. asst., group exec. ITT Coins, Secaucus, N.J., 1984-85; pres. Patron S., Ltd., Wilmington, Del., 1986—; CFO, sr. v.p. Guardsmark, Inc., Memphis, 1989-94; sr. v.p. Peoplemark, Inc., Memphis, 1989-94. Bd. dirs. St. Louis Repertory Theater, 1983-84. Named to Acad. Women Achievers, YWCA, N.Y.C., 1980. Mem. Fin. Execs. Inst., Inst. Mgmt. Acctg., Econ. Club, Memphis Symphony Chorus. Avocation: duplicate bridge. Office: Patron S Ltd 2711 Centerville Rd Ste 400 Wilmington DE 19808-

ROHNER, BONNIE-JEAN, small business owner, computer consultant; b. Waltham, Mass., Aug. 2, 1946; d. Gerrit John and Marjorie Lorraine (Hollis) R.; children: David Harrison Sackett, Amanda Marjorie Sackett. BFA in Fashion, Pratt Inst., Bklyn., 1967; BA in Biology, Adelphi U., Garden City, N.Y., 1983; MS, CIS, U. New Haven, Conn., 1993. Freelance fashion designer, Garden City, 1971-76; owner, mgr. The Printing Workshop, Massapequa, N.Y., 1976-78; personnel mgr. Doron Ltd., Norwich, Conn., 1978-79; computer related trainer Gen. Dynamics, Groton, Conn., 1979-89; acad. computing coord. Three Rivers Com./Tech. Coll., Norwich, 1989-94; owner, mgr. bytestream, Norwichtown, Conn., 1993—. Computer cons. U. New Haven, Groton, 1990-92; tech. advisor Countywide Network Com., 1989-90; sec. Connbug, Rocky Hill, Conn., 1992-93; tech. cons. on Internet Am. Online, 1996—. Mem. NAFE, AAUW, AAUP, ACM, Women's Network of S.E. Conn. Avocations: creative writing, internet.

ROHRABACHER, JANET HAMMOND, geneologist, archivist; b. Williamston, Mich., Apr. 24, 1913; d. Herbert Moore and Anna Eugenia (Lane) Hammond; m. Albert Hazen Rohrabacher (dec.); children: Ardenne Anna Brigham, Jeffrey. Tchg. cert., We. Mich. U., Kalamazoo, 1936; degree in Practical Nursing, McPherson Nursing Sch., Howell, Mich., 1965; student, Mich. State U., East Lansing, 1940. Cert. Geneologist, LPN. Nurse Mich. State Sanatorium, Howell, 1939-41, Ingham County Chest Hosp., Lansing, 1940, Ea. Mich. Sanatorium, Ypsilanty, 1941, McPherson Hosp., Howell, 1942-66; archivist Howell Carnegie Libr., Howell, 1977-2001. Writer Bicentennial History of Howell. Chmn. Livingston County Civil War Obs. Com., 1963; active Bicentennial Com. Howell, 1973-77, Mich. State Sesquicentennial Com., 1985-89; sec. Howell Archives Bd., 1977—. Recipient award, Mich. Geneal. Coun., 1997. Mem. DAR (award 1976), Livingston County Historical Soc. (charter, founder), Livingston County Genealogical Soc. (founder, 1982), Ancient and Honorable Artillery Soc. Mass, Descendents of Early Quakers, Palatines Am., Detroit Soc. Geneol. Rsch., DLKG. Methodist. Avocations: antique collecting, square dancing, genealogical lecturing. Home: 407 W Highland Rd Apt A1 Howell MI 48843

ROHRBACH, HEIDI A. lawyer; b. Buffalo, Jan. 25, 1953; d. William R. and A.T. R.; m. Leonard Lance, Aug. 9, 1996; 1 child, Peter R. Frank. BA, Northwestern U., Evanston, Ill., 1974; JD, Vanderbilt U., Nashville, 1977. Bar: NY, 1978. V.p., asst. gen. counsel J.P. Morgan Chase & Co., NYC, 1985—. Office: J P Morgan Chase & Co 270 Park Ave Fl 40 New York NY 10017-2014 Office Phone: 212-270-5854.

ROHRBOUGH, ELSA CLAIRE HARTMAN, artist; b. Shreveport, La., Sept. 26, 1915; d. Adolph Emil and Camille Claire (Francis) Hartman; m. Leonard M. Rohrbough, June 19, 1937 (dec. Jan. 1977); children: Stephen, Frank, Leonard. Juried exhbns. (painting) Massur Mus. Art, Monroe, La., Mobile (Ala.) Art Gallery, Gulf Coast Juried Exhibit, Mobile, Juried Arts Nat., Tyler, Tex., Greater New Orleans Nat., La. Watercolor Soc. Internat., Ky. Watermedia Nat., So. Watercolor Ann., La. Women Artist, many others. One-woman shows include Le Petit Theatre du Vieux Carre, New Orleans World Trade Ctr.'s Internat. House, Singing River Art Assn., Pascagoula, Miss., La. Font Inn, Pascagoula, Mandeville (La.) City Hall, St. Tammany Art Assn., Covington, La., others; exhibited in groups shows at 1st Guaranty Bank, Hammond, La., St. Tammany Art Assn., Ft. Isabel Gallery, Covington, S.E. La. State U., La. State Archives; represented in permanent collection at St. Tammany Parish Ct. House, Mandeville City Hall, Bellingrath Gardens, Theodore, Ala. Mem.: St. Tammany Art Assn. (bd. dirs. 1985—86, 1987, instr. 1977—78, classes chmn. 1986—88), La. State Assn. (pres. 1998—2000), Nat. League Am. Pen Women (v.p. S.E. La. br. 1986—87, 2002—, pres. 1987—92, 1994—98). Republican. Roman Catholic. Avocations: flower arranging, gardening, ethnic cooking, american antiques. Home: 100 Christwood Blvd Apt 106 Covington LA 70433-4601

ROHREN, BRENDA MARIE ANDERSON, therapist, educator; b. Kansas City, Mo., Apr. 18, 1959; d. Wilbur Dean and Katheryn Elizabeth (Albright) Anderson; m. Lathan Edward Rohren, May 10, 1985; 1 child, Amanda Jessica. BS in Psychology, Colo. State U., 1983; MA in Psychology, Cath. U. Am., 1986. Lic. mental health practitioner, cert. provisional alcohol and drug addiction counselor. Mental health therapist, sr. case mgr. Rappahannock Area Community Svcs. Bd., Fredericksburg, Va., 1986-88, mental health therapist, case mgmt. supr., 1988; rsch. assoc. Inst. Medicine, NAS, Washington, 1988-89; supr. adult psychiat. program Lincoln (Nebr.) Gen. Hosp., 1989, program supr. mental health svcs., 1989-91; adj. instr. S.E. Community Coll., Lincoln, 1990—; assessment & referral specialist Rivendell Psychiat. Ctr., Seward, Nebr., 1993-95; therapist Lincoln Day Treatment Ctr., Lincoln, Nebr., 1993-95. Adj. instr. Coll. of St. Mary, 1994—2001; therapist Rape/Spouse Abuse Crisis Ctr., Lincoln, 1996—2002; substance abuse counselor Independence Ctr., Lincoln, 2002—; computer cons. Syscon Corp., Washington, 1983—84. Author: (report) Bottom Line Benefits: Building Economic Success Through Stronger Families; editor: (newsletter) Alliance for Mentally Ill, Lincoln, 1993-2002. Active Nat. Alliance for the Mentally Ill-Lincoln, Nebr. Domestic Violence/Sexual Assault Coalition. Mem. APA (assoc.), ACA, Nat. Assn. Alcohol and Drug Abuse Counselors, Nebr. Psychol. Assn. (assoc.), Nebr. Counseling Assn Democrat. Roman Catholic. Avocations: interior decorating, reading, landscaping, camping. Home: 3821 S 33rd St Lincoln NE 68506-3806 Office: Independence Ctr 1650 Lake St Lincoln NE 68502 Office Phone: 402-481-5390. Personal E-mail: brenda@neb.rr.com.

ROHRER, SUSAN EARLEY, film producer, writer, director; b. Richmond, Va., Mar. 24; d. Charles Marion Jr. and Gloria Jean (Ripley) Earley; m. Mark Brooks Rohrer. BA in Art cum laude, James Madison U. Prodr., dir., co-story writer (tv shows) Never Say Goodbye, 1988 (Emmy award, Humanitas Prize finalist), Terrible Things My Mother Told Me, 1988 (Emmy nomination, Gold award Nat. Ednl. Film Festival); prodr., dir. (TV movies) For Jenny With Love (TV Movie award), Mother's Day, 1989 (3 Image award nominations), prodr., dir., writer (TV show) The Emancipation of Lizzie Stern, 1991 (Angel award, Bronze award Nat. Ednl. Film Festival, Emmy nomination, Monitor award finalist, TV Movie award), If I Die Before I Wake, 1993 (Emmy nomination, Humanitas Prize finalist, Cine Golden Eagle, TV Movie award); dir. (TV show) Sweet Valley High, 1996; dir. TV pilot Dojo Kids, 1996; prodr., dir., co-writer About Sarah, TV movie, 1998 (award of excellence Film Adv. Bd., Best of Festival award Breckenridge Film Festival, The Christopher award, Angel award, N.Y. Festivals finalist); writer (TV movies) Another Pretty Face, 2002, Book of Days, 2003. Recipient Resolution of Recognition Virginia Beach City Coun., 1988. Mem. ATAS, SAG, Writers Guild Am., Dirs. Guild Am. Office: Josh Schechter IPG 9200 Sunset Blvd Ste 520 Los Angeles CA 90069

ROHSE, ELAINE DAHL, newswriter; b. Portland, Oreg., Apr. 12, 1920; d. Henry Dahl and Irene Lillian Hartman; m. Homer F. Rohse, 1942. BA, U. Oreg., 1942. Columnist News-Register, McMinnville, Oreg., 1969—. Freelance writer to numerous profl. jours. Served McMinnville City Coun., 1971—75. Recipient distinguished svc. award, Dayton FFA Chpt., 2000, svc. plaque, Mid-Valley Rehab., Oregon, 1995. Mem.: Yamhill County Rep. Ctrl. Commn. (v.p.), Yamhill County Hist. Soc. (life; pres.). Avocations: travel, golf, hiking, bridge, reading. E-mail: rohse@onlinemac.com.

ROISMAN, HANNA MASLOVSKI, classics educator; b. Wroclaw, Poland; d. Leon and Eugenia (Shlager-Katz) Maslovski; m. Joseph Roisman, Aug. 5, 1971; children: Elad L., Shalev G. BA in Classics, MA in Classics, Tel Aviv U., Ramat Aviv, Israel, 1977; PhD in Classics, U. Wash., 1981. Lectr. classics Tel Aviv U., 1981-87, sr. lectr. classics, 1987-90; assoc. prof. classics Colby Coll., Waterville, Maine, 1990-94, prof., 1994—. Vis. scholar U. Wash., Seattle, 1983; jr. fellow Ctr. Hellenic Studies, Washington, 1985—86; vis. assoc. prof. (summers) Cornell U., 1986—94; sec. Israel Soc. for Promotion of Classical Studies, 1987—89; vis. scholar Cornell U., Ithaca, NY, 1989, Ithaca, 1995—96, vis. prof. (summers), 1995—97, 2000—03, vis. scholar, 2001—02. Author: Loyalty in Early Greek Epic and Tragedy, 1984, Nothing is as it Seems: The Tragedy of Implicit in Euripides' Hippolytus, 1999; co-author: The Odyssey Re-Formed, 1996, Euripides' Alcestis with notes and commentary, 2003; co-editor: Essays on Homeric Epic, 1993, Studies in Roman Epic, 1994, Essays on the Drama of Euripides, 1997, Essays on Homeric Epic, 2 vols., 2002, Text and Presentation, Jour. Comparative Drama Conf., 1999—2000; contbr. articles to profl. jours. AAUW fellow, 1980-81. Office: Colby Coll Mayflower Hill Waterville ME 04901 Office Phone: 207-872-3480. E-mail: hroisman@colby.edu.

ROISUM FOLEY, AMY KATHRYN, music educator, director; b. St. Louis Pk., Minn., Aug. 7, 1969; d. Donald Andrew and Caroline Markell Roisum; m. David Matthew Foley, Dec. 30, 2001. MusB in Edn., St. Olaf Coll., 1991; MA in Curriculum and Instrn., U. St. Thomas, 1994. Dir. bands McGuire Jr. HS, Lakeville, Minn., 1992—98, U. Prince Edward Island, Minn., 2001, U. Charlottetown, Minn., 2001, Gustavus Adolphus Coll., St. Peter, Minn., 2002, Minn. State U., Mankato, Minn., 2002—. Sec. Lakeville (Minn.) Fedn. Tchrs., 1993—98. Contbr. articles to profl. jours. Mem.: Coll. Band Dirs. Nat. Assn., Music Educators Nat. Conf., Tau Beta Sigma (hon.). Avocations: Tae Kwon Do, dog training. Office: Minnesota State Univ PAC 202 Mankato MN 56001

ROITMAN, JUDITH, mathematician, educator; b. N.Y.C., Nov. 12, 1945; d. Leo and Ethel (Gottesman) R.; m. Stanley Lombardo, Sept. 26, 1978; 1 child, Ben Lombardo. BA in English, Sarah Lawrence Coll., 1966; MA in Math., U. Calif., Berkeley, 1971, PhD in Math., 1974. Asst. prof. math. Wellesley (Mass.) Coll., 1974-77; from asst. prof. to prof. math. U. Kans., Lawrence, 1977—. Author: Introduction to Modern Set Theory, 1990; contbr. articles to profl. jours. Grantee NSF, 1975-87, 92-95. Mem. Assn. Symbolic Logic, Am. Math. Soc., Assn. Women in Math. (pres. 1979-81, Louise Hay award 1996), Kans. Assn. Tchrs. Math., Nat. Assn. Tchrs. Math. Avocation: poetry. E-mail: roitman@math.ukans.edu.

ROIZEN, NANCY J. physician, educator; b. Hartford, Conn. m. Michael F. Roizen; children: Jeffrey, Jennifer. BS, Tufts U., 1968, MD, 1972. Diplomate Am. Bd. Pediats. Staff physician Oakland (Calif.) Children's Hosp., 1976-84; asst. prof. clin. pediats. Johns Hopkins Hosp., Balt., 1984-85; assoc. prof. pediat. and psychiatry U. Chgo., 1985—. Fellow Am. Acad. Pediats.; mem. Soc. for Devel. Pediats. (pres. 1996-98). Office: U Chgo Hosps MC 900 5841 S Maryland Ave Chicago IL 60637-1463

ROJAS, MAZIE, pastor; d. Ceola W. and Willie Mae Woodson; children: Willie Charles, Jr Gilley, Domino Cornelius Gilley, Rodney VanElton Gilley. BA in Human Develop., Eckerd Coll., St. Petersburg, Fla., 1999—2003. Cert. Sr. Pastor Fla., 1984. Sr. pastor Union Hill AME Ch., Monticello, Fla., 1984—, Mt. Sinai AME Ch., Tallahassee, Fla., 1988—89. Sr. pastor St. Paul AME Ch., Safety Harbor, Fla., 1990—92, Wayman Chapel AME Ch., Jacksonville, Fla., 1992—94, St. Paul AME Ch., Safety Harbor, Fla., 1994—97, Leesburg, Fla., 1997—2002, Mt. Olive AME Ch., Tampa, Fla., 2002—. Christian edn. dir. African Meth. Episcopal Ch., Tampa, Fla., 2001—03. Mem.: Order of Ea. Star (chaplain of local and dist. chapters 2003). Democrat-Npl. Methodist. Avocations: reading, writing, singing, volunteer. Home: 1745 W LaSalle Street Tampa FL 33607 Office: African Meth Episc Ch 1747 W LaSalle Street Tampa FL 33607 Personal E-mail: mazierojas@aol.com.

ROKETENETZ, ANNEMARIE, professional society administrator; b. Winchester, Mass., Oct. 14, 1961; d. Joseph Charles and Anne M. (Zevuas) Roketenetz. BA in Career Writing, Roger Williams U., 1983; MA in Journalism and Pub. Affairs, Am. U., 1984. Writer Times Jour. Co., Springfield, Va., 1984—86; assoc. editor Nat. Assn. Realtors, Washington, 1986—90, pub. affairs sr. specialist, mng. dir., 1992—2002, housing opportunity program mgr., 2002—04; pub. dir. Va. Assn. Realtors, Merrifield, 1990—91; pub. affairs specialists U.S. Libr. Congress, Washington, 1992. Pres. Stonewall Farm, Va., 1991—. Contbr. articles to profl. jours. Vol. tchr. Prince William City (Pa.) Sch., 1998—. Mem.: Am. Paint Horse Assn. Democrat. Roman Catholic. Avocations: horseback riding, reading, writing. Home: 12006 Wright Ln Bristow VA 20136 E-mail: aroket@aol.com.

ROLAND, ANNE, registrar Supreme Court of Canada; b. Neuilly-sur-Seine, France, 1947; m. Alphonse Morisette, Dec. 3, 1975; 1 child, Julien. BA Philosophy, Caen, France, 1965; diploma, Inst. Supérieur d'interprétation et de traduction, 1969; lic. in law, Paris, 1969; LLB, U. Ottawa, 1979. Bar: Quebec 1980. Legal trans., revisor, Can., 1971-75; chief trans. svcs. customs and excise Sec. of State, Can., 1975-76; spl. asst. to chief justice Can., 1976-81; chief law editor Supreme Ct. Can., 1981-88, dep. registrar, 1988-90, registrar, 1990. Mem. Can. Bar Assn., Assn. Can. Ct. Adminstrs., Assn. Francophone Jurists, Can. Inst. Adminstrn. Justice, Assn. Reporters Jud. Decisions. Office: Supreme Ct Can Office Reg 301 Wellington St Ottawa ON Canada K1A 0J1

ROLAND, LENORE SUSAN, writer; b. N.Y.C., July 15, 1939; d. David and Frances Richman; m. Howard M. Roland, Dec. 17, 1960; children: Lee Eric, David Andrew, Robert Allen. Student, Alfred U., 1956—58; BA in English Lit., Barnard Coll., 1960; MA in Tchg. English, Columbia U., 1962; MEd in Tchg. Reading, Rollins Coll., 1977. Asst. textbook editor Am. Book Co., N.Y.C., NY, 1963—64; instr./cons. Valencia C.C., Orlando, Fla., 1977—81. Tech. writer Kirchman Corp., Altamonte Springs, Fla., 1981—82; supr. of tech. documentation, sr. tech. writer/editor Travelers/EBS, Maitland, Fla., 1982—86; mgr. of tng. devel., supr. of tng., sr. tng. writer Tupperware Home Parties, Orlando, Fla., 1986—89; writer, Windermere, Fla., 1990—. Contbr. articles and stories to newspapers and lit. jours. and mags. (Fla. Suncoast writing award, 1996, Orlando Sentinel fiction award, 1995). Reading mentor for second-grade student Read2Succeed, Orlando, Fla., 2002—03; writer of auction catalog for fundraiser Orlando Mus. of Art, Orlando, Fla., 1998; planned fundraising trips Atlantic Ctr. for the Arts, New Smyrna Beach, Fla., 1999—2000; harpist Orange County Pub. Schools, Orlando, Fla., vol. tchr. Mem.: Women Writers' Group, The Theater Alliance, Acquisition Trust of the Orlando Mus. of Art, Atlantic Ctr. for the Arts, Women Taking Stock, The Orlando Group. Avocations: travel, reading, folk harp, tennis, art.

ROLAND, MELISSA MONTGOMERY, accountant; b. Houston, Mar. 6, 1961; d. John Edgar and Mariann (Guggino) Montgomery; m. Larry Dean Roland, Sept. 20, 1984. BBA, Tex. A&M U., 1983. CPA, Tex., cert. fraud examiner, Tex. Audit sr. Arthur Andersen & Co., Houston, 1983-87; cons. mgr.-performance improvement group Ernst & Young, San Antonio, 1988-91; COO Roy Smith Shoes, Inc. d/b/a Accenté, Houston, 1991-96; v.p., COO 3d Coast Mgmt., Inc., Jacksonville, Fla., 1996—. Bd. dirs., treas. Grandparents Outreach, San Antonio, 1989—. Mem. AICPA, Tex. Accts.

and Lawyers for the Arts (adv. bd.), Tex. Soc. CPAs, Young Reps., Jr. League Jacksonville, S.W. Found. Forum. Presbyterian. Avocations: running, scuba diving, weight lifting, bicycling. Office: 515 Rutile Dr Ponte Vedra Beach FL 32082-2319

ROLAND, REGINA E. elementary school educator; b. Evanston, Ill., Aug. 1, 1949; d. Melvin J. and Rosemary G. (Malone) Ahrens; m. James I. Roland, Feb. 14, 1970. BA, No. Ill. U., 1971; MEd, Nat. Louis U., 1985. Educator St. John the Bapt. Sch., Winfield, Ill., 1972—74; Spanish/ESL/bilingual tchr. Des Plaines (Ill.) Cmty. Consol. Sch. Dist., 1974—. Presenter workshops in field. Co-author: A Hat for All Seasons, Hats on the Go; contbr. articles to mags. Scholar, Ill. State67. Mem.: NEA, Assisi Animal Found. Roman Catholic. Avocations: reading, walking, jewelry-making, writing, volunteer work. Home: 61 Dundee Ln Barrington IL 60010 E-mail: Regina@avenew.com.

ROLAND, SALLY, secondary resource teacher; b. Omaha, Apr. 22, 1957; d. Chester Henry Sr. and Marie Elaine (Hysom) Dreesen; m. Ronald L. Roland, June 26, 1977 (div.); children: Alexander Jacob, Melissa Christine. BAE, Wayne (Nebr.) State Coll., 1979, MSE, 1998. Cert. in K-12 adminstrn., specific learning disabilities and elem. edn., Nebr.; endorsement in mild/moderate spl. edn. 7-12. K-6 classrm. tchr. Cuming County Dist. 33, Oakland, Nebr., 1979-80; substitute tchr. local sch. dists., 1980-89; itinerant resource tchr. Ednl. Svc. Unit 2, Fremont, Nebr., 1989-93; secondary resource tchr. West Point (Nebr.) H.S., 1993-2000; secondary spl. edn. tchr. Omaha (Nebr.) Pub. Schs., 2000—. Adj. faculty in edn. Wayne State Coll., 1996; pres. Sch. Age Child Care Coalition, West Point, 1990; mem. West Point Cmty. Edn. Bd., 1993-95. Leader, Youth for Christ, West Point, 1992-97; leader 4-H Club, West Point, 1990-96, foods judge at area county fairs, 1997—. Mem. ASCD, NEA, Learning Disabilities Assn., Coun. for Exceptional Children, Nebr. State Edn. Assn., Kappa Delta Pi. Democrat. Lutheran. Avocations: computers, surfing the net, reading, writing, cooking. Home: 5255 S 157th Ct # 165 Omaha NE 68135-6466

ROLINGSON, MARTHA, research archeologist; b. Wichita, Kans., Nov. 6, 1935; BA, U. Denver, 1957; MA, U. Ky., 1963; PhD, U. Mich., 1967. Dir. U. Ky. Mus. Anthropology, Lexington, 1965-68; archeologist Ark. Archeol. Survey, 1968—; dir. rsch. Toltec Mounds Archaeol. State Park, Scott, Ark., 1976—. Mem. Soc. Am. Archaeology, Southeastern Archaeol. Conf. Office: Toltec Mounds Archaeol State Park 490 Toltec Mounds Rd Scott AR 72142

ROLL, MARILYN RITA BROWNLIE, social worker; b. Bay City, Mich., Dec. 7, 1946; d. John P. and Rita (Himpele) Brownlie; m. Charles S. Roll Jr., Dec. 28, 1968; 1 child, Brian. BS, Cornell U., 1969; MSW, Rutgers U., 1986. Lic. clin. social worker, N.J.; cert. practitioner in psychodrama, cert. in EMDR, cert. in Imago relationship therapy for couples and singles, cert. in clin. hypnosis, cert. family life educator, cert. secondary sch. tchr., cert. sch. social worker, N.J., cert. parent effectiveness instr., cert. stepfamily counselor, ACSW; diplomate clin. social work. High sch. home econs. tchr. Scotch Plains Fanwood High Sch., NJ, 1970, 1973—78; dir., co-founder, program developer Family Life Resources, Fanwood, N.J., 1982—; sch. social worker Somerset Elem. Sch., North Plainfield, N.J., 1984-85; psychotherapist, intervention counselor Resolve Community Counseling Ctr., Scotch Plains, 1985-87; pvt. practice psychotherapist Westfield, N.J., 1987—. Evaluative cons. Bank St. Coll. for Internat. Work and Family Life Study, N.Y.C., 1986; program developer, parent educator The Mothers Ctr., Scotch Plains, 1977-83. Researcher: (book-Time, Inc.) The Preschool Years, 1983-85. Mem. Sch. Dist. Substance Abuse com., Scotch Plains, 1987-88. Mem. Nat. Assn. Social Workers, Nat. Coun. on Family Rels., Am. Soc. Group Psychotherapy and Psychodrama, Am. Soc. Clin. Hypnosis, The Stepfamily Found., Family Resource Coalition, Alumni Assn. of Sch. of Social Work Rutgers U., Alumni Assn. Cornell Univ. Sch. Human Ecology, Phi Lambda Theta. Home: 184 Burns Way Fanwood NJ 07023-1604 Office: 128 S Euclid Ave Westfield NJ 07090-5103

ROLLAND, CLARA, pianist, educator; b. Budapest, Hungary, Apr. 20, 1916; arrived in U.S., 1939; d. Alexander and Katalin (Stein) Szekely; m. Paul Rolland, Dec. 24, 1940 (dec. Nov. 9, 1978); children: Peter Thomas, John Paul. M, Royal Franz Liszt Acad. Music, 1939; grad., Cleve. Inst. Music, 1941; diploma (hon.), Franz Liszt Acad. Music, 1990. Founder, instr. prep. dept. piano, theory and ear tng. Simpson Coll., Indianola, Iowa, 1941—45; pvt. studio Urbana, Ill., 1946—73; founder fun with music class Fine Arts Ctr., Clinton, Ill., 1966—70; co-dir. Music Divsn. Nat. Acad. Arts, 1973—79. Lectr. in field; judge Three Rivers Piano Competition, St. Louis, 1978. Performer, WILL-FM, 1950. Mem.: Music Tchr. Nat. Assn. (Baldwin Jr. Achievement award 1972, 1973, 1974, 1975, 1977, Mason & Hamlin Tchr. Achievement award 1974, H.S. Auditions winner 1974), Am. String Tchr. Assn. (life), Mu Phi Epsilon (pres. Mu Alpha chpt. 1961).

ROLLE, MYRA MOSS See **MOSS, MYRA**

ROLLENCE, MICHELE LYNETTE, molecular biologist; b. Takoma Park, Md., Nov. 23, 1955; d. John Francis and Martha Jo (Jackson) R.; m. David H. Specht, June 3, 1978 (div. Sept. 1982). AA, Montgomery Coll., 1976; BS, U. Md., 1978; MS, Johns Hopkins U., 1995. Lab. technician Dairy and Food Labs., San Francisco, 1979-81; rsch. asst. Genex Corp., Gaithersburg, Md., 1981-82, rsch. assoc., 1982-86, sr. rsch. assoc., 1986-88, rsch. scientist, 1989-93; rsch. assoc. Genetic Therapy, Inc., Gaithersburg, Md., 1993—2003; sr. rsch. assoc. Cell Genesys Inc., 2003—. Contbr. articles to profl. publs.; patentee in field. Pres. Explorer Post div. Boy Scouts Am., Gaithersburg, 1973; youth advisor Neelsville Presbyn. Ch., Germantown, Md., 1990. Recipient Nat. Exploration award TRW/Explorers Club, 1973. Mem.: AAAS, Am. Soc. Gene Therapy, Am. Soc. Microbiology, DAR, Pleasant Plains of Damascus. Democrat. Presbyterian. Avocations: bell choir, guitar, dance, hiking. Office: Cell Genesys Inc 500 Forbes Blvd South San Francisco CA 94080 Home: 444 Timberhead Ln Foster City CA 94404-4620

ROLLERI, DENISE MARIE, radiation therapist, business owner; b. Phila., Mar. 16, 1950; d. Albert J. and Marie (Fenerty) R. diploma, diploma, Bryn Mawr Sch. Radiol. Tech., Pa., 1976. Chief technologist dept. radiation therapy Bryn Mawr Hosp., 1970-75; sr. staff therapist Thomas Jefferson U. Hosp., Phila., 1976-85; supr. radiation oncology dept. St. Peter's Med. Ctr., New Brunswick, N.J., 1985-87; pres., CEO, R.T. Temps Inc., Wayne, Pa., 1987—, R.T. Career Edn., Wayne, Pa., 1995—. Pres. Radnor (Pa.) Young Reps., 1976-77. Mem. Am. Hosp. Assn., Soc. Radiation Oncology Adminstrs., Am. Soc. Radiol. Tech. Avocations: boating, walking, pet therapy. Office: RT Temps Inc PO Box 404 Wayne PA 19087-0404

ROLLE-RISSETTO, SILVIA, foreign languages educator, writer, artist; d. Dante and Gladys Rolle. BA in Spanish, BA in French and Italian, Calif. State U., Long Beach, 1987, MA in Spanish, 1990; PhD in Spanish, U. Calif., Riverside, 1996. Assoc. prof. Spanish, grad. coord. and fgn. lang. assessor of Spanish and Italian, dept. world langs. and lit. Calif. State U., San Marcos, 1996—. Participant numerous confs. Author: La Obra de Ana Maria Fagundo: Una Poetica Femenino-Feminista, 1997, Plazas: un lugar de encuentropara la hispanidad (lab manual); contbr. articles to profl. jours.; translator. Recipient Patrons of Italian scholarship U. degli Studi di Siena, 1987. Mem. MLA, Nat. Hispanic Soc., Asociacion de Literatura Femenina Hispanica, Hispanic Assn. of the Humanties, Letra Femeninas, Mairena, Assn. Internat. Hispanistas. Office: Calif State U San Marcos World Langs & Hispanic Lit 333 S Twin Oaks Valley Rd San Marcos CA 92096-0001 Home: 220 Venetia Way Oceanside CA 92057-7655

ROLLIN, BETTY, writer, television journalist, lecturer; b. N.Y.C., Jan. 3, 1936; d. Leon and Ida R.; m. Harold M. Edwards, Jan. 21, 1979. BA, Sarah Lawrence Coll., 1957. Assoc. features editor Vogue mag., 1964; sr. editor Look mag., 1965-71; network corr. NBC News, N.Y.C., 1971-80, contbg. corr., 1985—2003; network corr. ABC News Nightline, 1982-84. Contbr. corr. Religion and Ethics Newsweekly PBS; lectr. in field. Profl. actress : on stage and TV, 1958—64; author: I Thee Wed, 1962, Mothers Are Funnier Than Children, 1964, The Non-Drinkers' Drink Book, 1966, First, You Cry, 1976, reissue, 2000, Am I Getting Paid for This?, 1982, Last Wish, 1985, reissue, 1998; columnist: Hers, N.Y. Times; contbr. articles to popular mags. Bd. mem. Death With Dignity Nat. Ctr., 1997—. Office: care NS Bienstock Inc 1740 Broadway New York NY 10019-4315

ROLLIN, MIRIAM ANN, child advocate; b. Jersey City, Oct. 7, 1960; d. Martin and Shirley (Korasek) Rosenberg; m. Michael David Rollin, May 27, 1990; 1 child, Samantha Elise. BA, Yale U., 1981; JD, Catholic U. Am., 1987. Bar: N.Y. 1988, D.C. 1988, Md. 1989. Nat. dir. Nat. Coalition Ind. Coll. & Univ. Students, Washington, 1981-83; govt. rels. specialist AACD, Washington, 1983-85, Nat. PTA, Washington, 1985-87; asst. dist. atty. King's County Dist. Atty.'s Office, Bklyn., 1987-88; staff atty. child advocacy unit Legal Aid Bur., Riverdale, Md., 1988-90; project atty. ctr. on child & the law ABA, Washington, 1990-92; v.p. policy and program Nat. Assn. Child Advocates, Washington, 1992-96; cons. Children's Law and Policy, Washington, 1996-98; public policy dir. Nat. Network for Youth, Washington, 1998—2001; fed. policy dir. Fight Crime: Invest in Kids, Washington, 2001—. Recipient Unsung Hero award Youth Law Ctr., San Francisco, 1994. Mem. Nat. Assn. Counsel for Children (pres., bd. dirs. 1995-97). Jewish. Avocation: slavic folk singing.

ROLLINGS, JUDITH HARVEY, theater producer, actress, theater director, performing arts educator; d. Roger Donald Harvey and Lillian Maria Theodora Christiansen; m. James Steven Rollings, Sept. 3, 1960 (dec. Dec. 15, 1987); children: Jeffrey Mark, Matthew Charles. BS, Ctrl. Conn. State U., New Britain, Conn., 1960. Artistic dir. Actors Theatre of Phoenix, 1987—96; dir. of performance outreach Herberger Theater Ctr., Phoenix, 1995—. Mem. Ariz. State U. Theater Adv. Bd., Tempe, Ariz., 1993—95; mem., dir. Ariz. Theatre Conf. Panel, Phoenix, 1997; mem., adj. Ariz. Commn. on the Arts Artist Roster Panel, Phoenix, 1987—2000. Dir., author: plays Beginnings and Endings, Coming Full Circle, The Seven Ages of Man; dir.: (plays) Traveller in the Dark (Best Dir. of a Drama, 1988), (producer/creator of program) Brown Bug Theatre (Critics Cir. Award for Innovative Programing, 1991). Recipient Lifetime Award for Outstanding Contbn. to Theatre in Phoenix, ariZoni Awards Orgn., 1995, Actors Theatre of Phoenix, Best Profl. Theatre, New Times Best Of, 1993, Best Drama (dir.), Phoenix Gazette, 1989. Mem.: Actors Equity Assn. Achievements include founder, artistic dir. of actors theatre of Phoenix, the city's first Equity Theatre; founder, innovator, dir. STAGES comprehensive actor tng. program, employed up to 12 instrs. yr; founder, creator, exec. dir. Herberger Theater Ctr. Lunch Time Theater. Avocations: skiing, acrobics, yoga, hiking, bicycling. Office: Herberger Theater Ctr 222 E Monroe Phoenix AZ 85004 Office Phone: 602-254-7399 106. E-mail: jrollings@herbergertheater.org.

ROLLINS, DIANN E. nurse, occupational health nurse; b. Newark, Dec. 13, 1943; d. Lewis Paul and Letitia Lavinia Rollins. RN, Meth. Hosp. Sch. Nursing, Phila., 1964; postgrad., Howard U., 1966, Milton Coll., 1969—72, West Chester State Coll., 1972—79; cert. bldg. maintenance, John F. Kennedy Vocat. Tech., 1992; BSN, Thomas Jefferson U., 2000. RN, Pa., N.J. Nurse Meth. Hosp., Phila., 1964—66, 1967—69, Mercy Hosp., Janesville, Wis., 1969—72, Chester County Hosp., West Chester, Pa., 1972—74, Cheyney U., Pa., 1974—75, Embreville State Hosp., coatesville, 1976—78; agy. nurse Morristown, 1978—86, Medox, Olsten, Kimberly, Phila., 1985-86; RN supr. New Ralston House, Phila., 1986-87, 88-89; agy. nurse Kimberly, Quality Care, Olsten, Medox, others, Phila., 1987-89; info. and referral specialist Nat. Mental Health Consumer Self Help Clearing House, Phila., 1992-93; intern ACT NOW Southeastern Mental Health Program, Phila., 1993-94; nursery sch. tchr. Bambino Gesu Child Devel. Ctr., Phila., 1994-99; primary instr. nursing assts. ARC, 2000—01, Clin. Pathways Educators Ins., 2001—02; supplemental staff nurse Breslin Learning Ctr., 2002—, LPN instr., 2003—; staff nurse Bayada Nurses, 2002—; postal nurse (occupl. health nurse) U.S. Post Office, 2003—. Vol. instr. program Franklin Inst., Phila., 1973-74; vol. multimedia first aide instr. ARC, Wilmington, Del., 1975-83; vol. plan II nurse blood mobiles ARC, S.E. Pa., 1982-85. Mem. Alumnae Meth. Hosp. Sch. Nursing, Four Chaplains Legion of Honor. Avocations: reading, writing, walking. Home: PO Box 34257 Philadelphia PA 19101-4257

ROLLINS, JENNIE ALBIN BROWN, music educator; b. Norfolk, Va., June 3, 1946; d. Theodore Roosevelt and Doris Gwendolyn (Griffin) Brown; m. David Sidwell Rollins, Dec. 10, 1975; 1 child, Brooks Kathlene. AA in Music, Manatee Jr. Coll., 1966; MusB, Hope Coll., 1968; MusM in Edn., Fla. State U., 1976. Elem. music educator Kenowa Hills Pub. Schs., Grand Rapids, Mich., 1968—71, Mt. Pleasant (Mich.) Pub. Schs., 1971—75, Pineview Elem. Sch., Tallahassee, 1976—78; secondary choral music educator Belle Vue Mid. Sch., Tallahassee, 1978—96, Swift Creek Mid. Sch., Tallahassee, 1996—. Coord. all state music Leon County Mid. Sch., Tallahassee, 1985—. Sponsor Red Hills Horse Trials. Named Master Tchr., State of Fla., 1984, 1985. Mem.: Fla. State U. Musical Assocs., Music Educators Nat. Conf. (assoc.), Fla. Music Educators Assn. (assoc.), Fla. Vocal Assn. (assoc.; dist. chmn. 1994—96), United State Pony Club (assoc.; joint dist. commr. 2002—), Delta Kappa Gamma (life). Avocations: travel, vintage cars, sailing. Home: 9110 Oakfair Drive Tallahassee FL 32317 Office: Swift Creek Middle School 2100 Pedrick Road Tallahassee FL 32317 Personal E-mail: rollinsjb@aol.com. E-mail: rollinsj@swiftcreek.leon.k12.fl.us.

ROLLINS, WENDY MILWOOD, media specialist; b. Charleston, S.C., Aug. 26, 1974; d. Jack Ray, Jr. and Linda Carol (Muller) Milwood; m. Robert Bryant Rollins, June 17, 2000. BA in Elem. Edn., U. S.C., Spartanburg, 1997; M in Libr. and Info. Sci., U. S.C., Columbia, 2003. Cert. tchr., sch. libr. media specialist. Phys. edn. asst. Campobello (S.C.)-Gramlin Sch., 1997—98; first grade tchr. Polk-Ctrl. Sch., Mill Spring, NC, 1998—99; libr. media specialist Ford Sch., Lauren, SC, 1999—2001, Beech Springs Intermediate Sch., Duncan, SC, 2001—. Fellow: Delta Zeta Sorority Alum (v.p. 2001—02). Methodist. Office: Beech Springs Intermediate Sch 200 S Danzler Duncan SC 29334

ROLLMAN, CHARLOTTE, artist, educator; b. Harrisburgh, Ill., Oct. 15, 1947; d. Joseph and Beulah (Overton) R.; m. Edward H. Shay, 1971 (div. 1982); m. William B. Holland, 1987; 1 child, Danielle Suzanne Holland. BFA, Murray State U., 1969; MFA, U. Ill., 1971. Instr. art Ball State U., Muncie, Ind., 1971-75; supr. hand-painted silk garments Nicole, Ltd., Chgo., 1980-84; textile designer, stylist Thybony Wallcovering, Chgo., 1983-88; prof. art No. Ill. U., DeKalb, 1987—. Exhibitions include New Harmony (Ind.) Gallery Art, Charlotte Brauer, Munster, Ind., Jan Cicero, Chgo., Roy Boyd, Chgo, Locus, St. Louis, Suzanne Brown, Scottsdale, Ariz, Nestle's Corp., DeKalb, Capitol State Bank, St. Louis, others; illustrator New Internat. Dictionary Music, 1991; AV coord. Women's Caucus Art, Beijing, 1995. Grad. Sch. Rsch. grantee No. Ill. U., 1993, Faculty Enhancement grantee, 1995, Undergrad. Improvement grantee No. Ill. U., 1996. Mem. AAUW, Women's Caucus Art, Nat. Mus. Women Arts, Chgo. Area Women's Studies, DeKalb Area Women's Ctr. Office: No Ill U Sch Art Dekalb IL 60115

ROMAN, MARY, city official; b. Great Barrington, Mass., Sept. 30, 1939; d. Arthur Roger and Beatrice Louise (Cable) Barboza; m. Granville Smith Roman, Apr. 3, 1954; children: Warren David, Kenneth Roger, Michael Stuart, Craig Garfield, Gerald Spencer. Student, Springfield Coll., 1954, Am. Inst. Banking, Stamford, Conn., 1965-69. Teller, loan officer, v.p. Merchants Bank, Norwalk, Conn., 1965-89; br. mgr. Gateway Bank, Norwalk, Conn., 1989-99, Shawmut Bank, Norwalk, Conn., 1989-99, Fleet Bank, Norwalk, Conn., 1989-99; city clk. City of Norwalk, 1999—. Bd. dirs. Soc. to Aid Retarded, Norwalk, Conn., 1992—, Family and Children's Agy., Norwalk, 1997—; mem. Oak Hills Golf Authority, Norwalk, 1998—; mem., past grand marshall Conn. Sr. Olympics; mem. Am. Legion Aux., U.S.A. Track and Field. Recipient awards Celebrate Women, Inc., 1995, Norwalk Old Times, Inc,. 1995. Mem. Oak Hills Women's Golf Assn. (past pres.). Avocations: horseback riding, golf, masters and senior olympics track and field. Home: 1 Birchside Dr Norwalk CT 06850-1513 Office: City of Norwalk 125 East Ave Norwalk CT 06851-5702

ROMAN, NANCY GRACE, astronomer, consultant; b. Nashville, May 16, 1925; d. Irwin and Georgia Frances (Smith) R. BA (Joshua Lippincott Meml. fellow), Swarthmore Coll., 1946; PhD, U. Chgo., 1949; D.Sc., Russell Sage Coll., 1966, Hood Coll., 1969, Bates Coll., 1971, Swarthmore Coll., 1976. Asst. Sproul Obs., Swarthmore Coll., 1943-46; asst. Yerkes Obs., U. Chgo., at Williams Bay, Wis., 1946-48, research asso., 1949-52, instr. stellar astronomy, 1952-55, asst. prof., 1955; research asso. Warner and Swasey Obs., Case Inst. Tech., Cleve., summer 1949; physicist radio astronomy br. U.S. Naval Research Lab., Washington, 1955-56, astronomer, head microwave spectroscopy sect., 1956-58, astronomer cons., 1958-59; head observational astronomy program Office Space Flight Devel., NASA, Washington, 1959-60, chief astronomy and solar physics, geophysics and astronomy programs, 1960-64, chief astronomy and relativity programs, 1964-79, program scientist for space telescope, 1979-80; astronomy cons., 1980-89; prin. scientist Astronomical Data Ctr. (NASA), 1981—. With McDonnell Douglas Space Systems, 1988-94. Contbr. articles to sci. periodicals. Trustee Russell Sage Coll., 1973-78; bd. mgrs. Swarthmore Coll., 1979-83. Recipient Fed. Woman's award., 1962; citation for pub. service Colo. Woman's Coll., 1966; 90th Anniversary award Women's Ednl. and Indsl. Union, 1967; NASA Exceptional Sci. Achievement award, 1969; NASA Outstanding Leadership medal, 1978 Fellow AAAS, Am. Astronautical Soc. (William Randolf Lovelace II award 1980); mem. AAUW, Am. Astron. Soc., Internat. Astron. Union (editor symposia 1956-58), Astron. Soc. Pacific. Acheivements include rsch. on stellar clusters, high velocity stars, radio astronomy; 1st noted correlation of metallic lines in stars with their space velocity; asteroid named Roman, 1989.

ROMAN, TWYLA I. state legislator; m. John Roman; children: Lisa, Sheryl. Student, U. Akron, 1977-78. Trustee Springfield Twp., 1981-94; mem. Ohio State Ho. Reps., Columbus, 1994—. Mem. Summit County Emergency Mgmt. Planning and Exec. Commn. Mem. MADD, S.E. Bd. of Trade, Ohio Twp. Assn., Summit County Twp. Assn., Brimfield Meml. House Assn.

ROMANA, KATHLEEN, writer; b. Boston, Oct. 30, 1957; Student, Mus. Sch. Art, Boston, 1973-75; diploma, Butera Sch. Art, Boston, 1979; AA, Back Bay C.C., Boston, 1981. Freelance illustrator various advt. agys., Boston, 1981-92, freelance copywriter, 1990-92; poet/writer Austin, Tex., 1993—; owner Odyssey Vintage Clothing Store, 2000—. Author, poet, illustrator: Dreamscapes and Other Wanderings, 1998; author, editor, illustrator: Thy Kingdom Come, 1998; author of poetry included in anthologies: Outstanding Poets of 1998, The Isle of View, 1998, Daydreams, 2000, Tides of Memory, 2000, Treasured Poems of America, 2000, Internat. Libr. Poetry, 2000, Ovations, 2001, Best Poems and Poets of 2001 (anthologies) Homecomings, The Silence Within, Acclamations; published Austin Daze Newspaper, Sept. 2003; Austin Poets for Peace, 2003; Illustrator Austin Poets for Peace, 2003; performer, Forest Fest Poetry Festival, 2003; Expressions, Austin 2003 Recipient Editors Choice award and Poet of Merit award Internat. Libr. Poets, Pres.'s award for Lit. Excellence, Iliad Press, 2001, The Pres. award Literary Excellence, 2002; others. Mem. Internat. Soc. Poets (disting.), Nat. Libr. Poetry. Avocations: samurai saber, tai chi, fan form.

ROMANCE, MARY C. library director; b. Rabat, Morocco, June 20, 1957; d. Francis Joseph and Ann (Pickert) Romance. BA in Orgnl. Comms. and Mgmt., U. Mich., Ann Arbor, 1979; MLS, Rutgers U., New Brunswick, N.J., 1992. Libr. coord. Bernardsville (N.J.) Pub. Libr., 1991-93; libr. dir. Rockaway (N.J.) Borough Pub. Libr., 1993-94, Lincoln Park (N.J.) Pub. Libr., 1994-97, Roxbury Twp. Pub. Libr., Succasunna, N.J., 1997—. V.p., 1998, pres., 1999, M.A.I.N. Inc. Planning Coun.. Mem. Roxbury Area C. of C. (bd. dirs.). Office: Roxbury Public Library 103 Main St Succasunna NJ 07876-1417

ROMANO, DARLENE, music educator, composer; b. San Francisco, Sept. 23, 1947; d. Peter Joseph and Pauline Evelyn Silacci; m. James Joseph Sparks, June 25, 1983. D of Mus. Arts, U. So. Calif., L.A.; MA, MusB, San Francisco State U. Prof. music/mus. theatre Coll. of the Desert, Palm Desert, Calif., 1985—, assoc. dean of instrn., 2000—02. Composer (lyricist): (musical) Night of A Thousand Stars. Mem. Civic Arts Com., Arthritis Found., Palm Desert, Calif., Artscope, Nat. Psoriasis Found. Recipient Woman of Distinction in Edn., Soroptimists Internat., Best Musical Dir. Desert Theatre League, Best Dir. of a Musical/Opera, Best Actress in a Musical/Opera, Joan Woodbury Mitchell Acheivement Award, Svc. to the Arts Award, Palm Desert Chamber of Commerce. Mem.: AAUP, Nat. Assn. of U. Women, Calif. Tchrs.' Assn., Actors' Equity Assn., SAG, Pi Kappa Lambda. Catholic. Home: 45-410 Sunbrook Ln La Quinta CA 92253 Office: College of the Desert 43-500 Monterey Ave Palm Desert CA 92260 Personal E-mail: preciousdr@aol.com. E-mail: dromano@collegeofthedesert.edu.

ROMANO, MENA N. artist, educator; b. Bronx, N.Y., Oct. 16, 1943; d. Gerardo and Paulina (Sciurba) DeSanctis; m. Nicholas Romano, Nov. 23, 1963; children: Dina Marie Girola, Nicholas Carmine, Jr.(dec.). AS in Fine Arts, Suffolk County C. C., Selden, N.Y., 1983; BFA summa cum laude, Long Is. U., 1986, MFA, 1988. Mem. faculty, coord. art internships Nassau C.C., Garden City, NY, prof. art, 1996—; adj. asst. prof. art Suffolk County C. C., Selden, NY, 1988—. Vis. artist B.O.C.E.S. Art in Edn. program, 1992-; curator art, exhbns. Chess Collectors Internat., 1990; lectr. in field. Exhbns. include Islip Art Mus., S.W. Tex. State U. Gallery, Fine Art Mus. Long Island, The Pen and Brush Club N.Y.; permanent installations Meditation Garden, Garden City, 13th St. Garden Portals, Chgo. Grantee Artist Space, N.Y., 1990, others. Mem. Nat. Drawing Assn. (chair membership 1990-91), Long Island Craft Guild (pres. 1994-95), Phi Theta, Pi Alpha Sigma. Avocations: travel, gardening.

ROMANO, REBECCA KAY, counselor; b. Zanesville, Ohio, Mar. 26, 1958; Charles Ronald Fulkerson and Margaret Jane (Kiser) Williams; m. Richard Ralph Romano, May 24, 1986; children: Nicholas Robert, Kaitlin Kristine. BA, Walsh U., 1980; MEd, Bowling Green State U., 1981, 82. Lic. profl. counselor; nat. cert. counselor; sex offender treatment provider, Colo. Day program instr. Devel. Opportunities, Cañon City, Colo., 1983-85; clin. behavior specialist Pueblo Regional Ctr. Colo. Divsn. Devel. Disabilities, 1985-86; career devel. tchr. Colo. Dept. Corrections, Cañon City, 1986-87, facility mental health therapist, 1987—2002, devel. disabilities coord., 1991—2002, facility mental health coord., 1995—2002. Therapist sex offender treatment team Colo. Dept. Corrections, 1986—, clin. team leader, 2002--, co-chair state com. to devel. lifetime supervision stds. for devel. disabled sex offenders; presenter in field. Mem. ACA, AAUW, Am. Assn. Mental Retardation (past state bd. dirs. 1987-91), Am. Correctional Assn., Nat. Assn. for Dually Diagnosed, Colo. Assn. Mental Health Counselors, Women of the Evang. Luth. Ch. Am. (exec. bd. mem., newsletter editor 1997, confirmation youth mentor, Sunday Sch. tchr. 1998—). Lutheran.

Avocations: reading, gardening, bicycling, volleyball, walking. Office: Colo Dept Corrections ACC Clin Svcs Box 300 Canon City CO 81215 Home: 332 Crestmoor Rd Canon City CO 81212-2447

ROMANO, SHEILA JUNE, telecommunications industry executive, artist, writer; b. Elko, Nev., June 11, 1951; d. John Lewis and June Florene (Lani) C. BA, U. Nev., 1974. Various svc. positions Citizens Comm. (formerly Alltel-Nevada Inc.), Elko, 1974-78, svc. rep., 1978-84, bus. office supr., 1984-87, bus. supr. Nev. office, 1987-94, bus. supr., state pub. rels. coord., 1994-97, results coord., project mgmt. support person Elk Grove, Calif., 1997, supr. customer ops. escalations and exec. complaints, 1998-2000, specialist state gov. affairs, 2001—02; sr. regulatory analyst Frontier Comm., Elk Grove, 2002—. Active Citizens Amb. program People to People Internat., 1995—98; writer, artist, 1974—. Contbg. author: Fence Post to Fiber, 1998. Officer, organizer Freedom Com., Elko, 1984; mem., treas. Elk Grove Cmty. Action Team, 1997-98. Mem. NOW, AAUW (editor newsletter Elko 1980-82, v.p. programs 1991-93, sec. 1995-96), Soroptimists Internat. (treas. 1992-93, sec. 1993-94, v.p. 1995-96, pres. 1996-97). Office: Frontier PO Box 340 Elk Grove CA 95759-0340

ROMANO-MAGNER, PATRICIA R. English studies educator, researcher; b. N.Y.C., Mar. 22, 1928; d. Al and Nicole (Siriani) Romano; m. Ralpha M. Magner, Dec. 24, 1954. AA, BA, L.A. City Coll.; MA, Calif. State U., L.A.; D (hon.), Stanford U., Cambridge (Eng.) U., Queens Coll. Master tchr. Burbank (Calif.) Unified Sch. Dist., L.A. City Schs., Stanford (Calif.) U. Sch. for the Gifted; prof. Calif. State U., L.A., curriculum lab. asst. LA. Mem. AAUW, AAUP (award 2000), Am. Legion Aux., Sierra Club, Natural Resources Def. Coun., The Friends of the William J. Clinton Presdl. Libr. (founding mem.), Scholarship Soc. of Calif. State U. L.A. Republican. Avocation: horseback riding. Home: 5975 N Odell Ave Chicago IL 60631-2358

ROMANOVICH, PATRICIA M. parochial school educator; b. Akron, Ohio, Dec. 11, 1937; d. Joseph and Mary (Dorosz) Siwik; m. Paul Romanovich, Sept. 13, 1958; children: Paula Marie, Gregory Joseph, Jeffrey John, Martin Paul. BS in Edn., St. John Coll., Cleve., 1971; M.Curriculum and Instrn., Cleve. State U., 1988. Tchr. St. Josaphat Sch., Parma, Ohio, 1964—87, tchr., tech. coord., 1998—; tchr. St. Columbkille Sch., Parma, 1987—90; tchr., computer coord. St. Anthony Sch., Parma, 1990—93, Greenbriar Jr. H.S., Parma Heights, Ohio, 1993—98. Tech. adv. bd. chair St. Josaphat Sch., 1998—2003, curriculum chair, 1998—2003; creator, rschr. flip chart Sch. Crisis Mgmt. Plan, 1999—2003. Named one of Outstanding Elem. Tchrs. of Am., 1974; recipient Excellence in Tchg. award, Diocese of Cleve., 2001; grantee Tech. grantee, Sch. Net, Columbus, 2001. Mem.: Korean War Vets. Assn. Ukrainian Catholic. Avocations: reading, travel, country walks. Home: 5400 Sandy Hook Dr Parma OH 44134 Office Phone: 440-884-1812. Personal E-mail: sandyvalley@msn.com.

ROMBERGER, JEAN LOUISE, retired educator; b. Camp Hill, Pa., Apr. 17, 1935; d. Austin Ira and Elizabeth Ann (Koons) R. BS in Edn., U. Pa., 1957; MS in Edn., Temple U., 1963. Cert. tchr., Pa. Tchr. Camp Hill Sch. Dist., 1957-65, 66-93, Shippensburg (Pa.) U., 1965-66; ret., 1993. Mentor/tutor Harrisburg (Pa.) Sch. Dist., 1994-96. Co-author curriculum in field. Mem. credit com. Susquehanna Valley Fed. Credit Union, Camp Hill, 1993—; vol. Hospice of Ctrl. Pa., Enola, 1994—; mem. Susquehanna Consort, TLC Choir, chmn. Columbarium com., mem. com. on the arts; steering com. The Lion Found. of Camp Hill Scho. Dist.; elections judge Camp Hill Precinct 2, 1997—; pres. Women of Trinity, 1999-2000. Mem. AAUW, NEA (life), Pa. Assn. Sch. Retirees (life), Pa. State Edn. Assn. (life), Capital Area Edn. Assn. (life), Camp Hill Civic Club, Camp Hill Women's Club, Delta Gamma (chpt. pres. 1956-57). Avocations: church activities, volunteer work, music, travel. Home: 300 S 24th St Camp Hill PA 17011-5307

ROMER, CHRISTINA DUCKWORTH, economist, educator; b. Alton, Ill., Dec. 25, 1958; d. Clifford Lee and Carol (Greer) Duckworth; m. David Hibbard Romer, Aug. 20, 1983; children: Katherine, Paul, Matthew. BA, Coll. William & Mary, Williamsburg, Va., 1981; PhD, MIT, Cambridge, Mass., 1985. Asst. prof. Princeton (N.J) U., 1985—88; acting assoc. prof. U. Calif., Berkeley, 1988—90, assoc. prof., 1990—93, prof., 1993—97, Class of 1957 prof., 1997—; co-dir. Monetary Econs. Program Nat. Bur. Econ. Rsch., Cambridge, Mass., 2003—. Rsch. assoc. Nat. Bur. Econ. Rscsh., Cambridge, Mass., 1990—; mem. rsch. adv. bd. Com. for Econ. Devel., Washington, 1994—98; mem. editl. bd. Jour. Econ. History, 1994—97. Editor: (book) Reducing Inflation, 1997; contbr. articles to profl. jours. Recipient Presdl. Young Investigator award, NSF, 1989—94; fellow, John Simon Guggenheim Meml. Found., 1998—99. Mem.: Econ. History Assn. (nominating com. 2001—02), Am. Econs. Assn. (exec. com. 2000—03). Democrat. United Church Of Christ. Achievements include research in new statistical evidence of the effects of monetary policy on output, inflation and interest. Showed that historical macroeconomic indicators overstate the size of business cycles before World War II. Office: Univ Calif Dept Econs Berkeley CA 94720-3880

ROMER, DENISE PATRICE, lawyer; b. Tulsa, Okla., Jan. 11, 1975; d. Franz Karl and Trudy Maria Romer. BS in Sociology, Okla. State U., 1997; M in Alternative Dispute Resolution, JD, Pepperdine U., 2000. Bar: Calif. 2001, Wis. 2002. Clk. Tulsa County Office Dist. Atty., 1998—98, Tulsa Early Settlement - Divsn. Tulsa County Ct. Sys., 1999—99; asst. to counsel Nat. Assn. Securities Dealers, L.A., 1999—99; legal clk. Calif. Lawyers for the Arts, Santa Monica, 2000—00; assoc. atty. Korenberg, Abramowitz & Feldun, Sherman Oaks, Calif., 2001—02; criminal def. atty. Boyle, Boyle & Paulus, S.C., Milw., 2002—03; litig. and employment support GE Med. Systems, Waukesha, Wis., 2003—. Author poetry. Rep. internet team leader Rep. Nat. Com., Milw., 2002—03; supporter/ mem. So. Poverty Law Ctr.-Nat. Campaign for Tolerance, L.A., 2001—03. Mem.: ABA (assoc.), State Bar Calif. (assoc.), State Bar Wis. (assoc.), L.A. County Bar Assn. (assoc.), The Smithsonian Instn. (assoc.), Pepperdine U. Alumni Assn. (life). Conservative. Roman Catholic. Avocations: writing, yoga, travel, dance, reading. Home: 1121 East Pleasant St Milwaukee WI 53202 Personal E-mail: romer33@hotmail.com.

ROMERO, GLORIA, state senator, government agency administrator; 1 child, Soledad. Degree, Barstow Cmty. Coll., 1978, Calif. State U., Long Beach, 1978; PhD in Psychology, U. Calif., Riverside, 1983. Prof. Calif. Coll. Sys., 1980-98; majority whip Calif. State Assembly, Sacramento, 1998—2001; mem. Calif. State Senate, 2001—. Com. mem. 1999-00; v.p. L.A. Cmty. Coll. Bd. Trustees, 1995-97; chair L.A. Elected Charter Reform Commn., 1997; rschr. in field of HIV/AIDS edn. and prevention. Contbr. articles to profl. jours. Chair Hispanic Adv. Coun. to L.A. Police Commn.; co-founder Women's Adv. Coun. L.A. Police Commn.; mem. Domestic Violence Task Force, L.A. Recipient Comision Femenil Cmty. Svc. award, Cmty. Svc. award Mexican-Am. L.A. County Bar Assn., Latin Am. Advancement Edn. and Cmty. award Labor Coun., Cmty. Svc. award San Gabriel Valley League of United Latin-Am. Citizens, Incredible Women Making History award YWCA. Mem. ACLU, Nat. Orgn. Women, Nat. Women's Political Caucus, Nat. Latina Alliance, Calif. Faculty Assn./AFL-CIO, Sierra Club. Office: State Capital Room 4062 Sacramento CA 95814 also: 149 S Mednik Ave Ste 202 East Los Angeles CA 90023 E-mail: gloria.romero@sen.ca.gov.

ROMERO, SYLVIA, social worker; b. Chgo. children: Rebecca, Melissa. AA, Coll. Lake County, Grayslake, Ill., 1985; BA, Barat Coll., 1987; MSW, Jane Addams Coll. Social Work, Chgo., 1990. Sch. social worker Broward County Pub. Schs., Ft. Lauderdale, Fla., 1991—2002; cabin counselor Horizons Bereavement Ctr., Palm Beach, Fla., 2001; instr. (S.T.E.P. program) Project P.A.S.S., Mundelein, Ill., 2002; sch. social worker Cmty. Consolidated Sch. Dist. #46, Grayslake, 2002—. Former write-in candidate for sch. bd. Waukegan Cmty. Unit Sch. Dist. #60, 2003; mem., cmty. leader Bilingual Parent Adv. Coun., Waukegan, Ill., 2003—. Named to Outstanding Minority C.C. Grad. Talent Roster for Disting. Acad. Performance, Ill.; recipient Latino Com. on U. Affairs cert. of achievement, U. Ill. at Chgo.; clin. fellow, Coun. on Social Work Edn., 1999—2002. Mem.: AAUW, ACLU, NASW, Assn. for Advancement of Social Work with Groups, Assn. Latino Social Work Educators (sec. 2003, at-large 2001—03), Soc. Social Work and Rsch., Nat. Coun. of La Raza.

ROMERO-RAINEY, REBECA, bank executive; d. Martin and Cheryl Romero; m. John Rainey. Degree, Wellesley Coll. Pres., CEO Centinal Bank Taos, N.Mex., 1999—, bd. dir., 1999—. Bd. admissions Wellesley Coll. V.p. Taos Chpt. Habitat for Humanity; sec., treas. Bridges Project Edn. Taos; mem. Leadership N.Mex.; treas. N.Mex. Cmty. Found.; bd. dir. Taos (N.Mex.) Feeds Taos; treas. bd. dirs. Rocky Mountain Youth Corps. Named One of 25 Women to Watch, U.S. Banker Mag., 2003. Mem.: Ind. Cmty. Bankers Assn. N.Mex. (bd. dir. 2003—).*

ROMIG, DEBORAH LYNN, secondary school educator; b. Pottstown, Pa., Aug. 27, 1957; d. Norman Linwood and Lucy Ann Romig; m. Richard Alan Mattes, July 12, 1980 (div. Apr. 26, 1997); children: James Alan, Jesse Scot, Gina Marie. BA, Gorden Coll., 1979; MEd, Va. Commonwealth U., 2003. Lic. tchr. Mass., 1979, S.D., 1980, Va., 2003. Tchr. Trinity Sch. Cape Cod, South Yarmouth, Mass., 1979—80; program mgr. Live Ctr., Inc., Lemoh, SD, 1980—87; supr. Bank of Am., Richmond, Va., 1988—98; field force sales rep. Stewart Enterprises, Richmond, Va., 1998—2000; tchr. Manchester HS Chesterfield County Schs., Midlothian, Va., 2000—. Coach track Bailey Bridge Mid. Sch., Midlothian, 2000—03, Manchester HS, 2003; mem. Coun. for Exceptional Children, 2002—. Co-author: Anthology, 1996. Mem. task force Gov., SD. Mem.: Phi Kappa Phi. Avocation: marathon running. Home: 7419 G Newbys Crossing Drive Richmond VA 23235 Office: Manchester HS 12601 Bailey Bridge Rd Midlothian VA 23112

ROMIJN-STAMOS, REBECCA, actress, model; b. Berkeley, Calif., Nov. 6, 1972; m. John Stamos, Sept. 19, 1998; children: Jaap Romihn Stamos, Elizabeth Kuizenga Stamos. Attended, U. Calif., Santa Cruz. Model Sports Illustrated, Christian Dior, Victoria's Secret, Biotherm, Clarins, Dillards, Escada, Furla, Got Milk?, J.Crew, La Senza, Liz Claiborne, Matrix Essentials, Maybelline, Pantene Pro V, Tommy Hilfiger, various others. Actor: (films) Dirty Work, 1998, X-Men, 2000, Rollerball, 2002, Femme Fatale, 2002, X2, 2003, The Punisher, 2004, Godsend, 2004; (TV films) Hefner: Unauthorized, 1999; (TV series) Just Shoot Me, 1999—2000. Mailing: c/o Bragman/Nyman/Cafarelli 9171 Wilshire Blvd Ste 300 Beverly Hills CA 90210*

ROMINE, DONNA MAE, gifted and talented program educator; b. Moreauville, La., Feb. 18, 1949; d. Marvin Peter and Ethel Mae (Young) Bordelon; m. James Rufus Romine, Dec. 4, 1946 (dec. 1999); children: Michael, Shelia, Larry. BA, McNeese State U., 1969; M in Gifted Edn., U. La., 2002. Cert. elem. tchr., La. Tchr. 6th grade Acadia Parish Schs., Rayne, La., 1969-71; tchr. jr. high Basile (La.) High Sch., 1972-77; tchr. 4th and 6th grades Hathaway High Sch., Jennings, La., 1980-82; elgibility worker Acadia Parish Office Family Security, Crowley, La., 1982-87; tchr. Church Point (La.) Mid. Sch., 1987-99; tchr. gifted program Jeff Davis Parish Schs., Jennings, La., 1999—. Leader 4-H, Church Point, 1988—98. Mem.: La. Fedn. Tchrs., Assn. for Gifted and Talented. Democrat. Roman Catholic. Avocations: reading, science fiction films, jeopardy. Home: 223 Violet Ln Iota LA 70543-4320 Office: Jeff Davis Parish Schs 203 E Plaquemine St Jennings LA 70546-5853

ROMNEY-MANOOKIN, ELAINE CLIVE, music educator, composer; b. Salt Lake City, July 11, 1922; d. Joseph Campbell Clive and Katie Winifred Gilroy; m. Eldon Brigham Romney, May 5, 1941 (dec. May 1998); children: Ruth Romney Powell, Frederic Clive Romney, Clive Jay Romney, Stanley Clive Romney, Eldon Clive Romney, Roslyn Kay Romney Reynolds, Rae Lynne Romney Johnson, Vincent Clive Romney; m. Stuart Midgley Manookin. Studied piano, violin and cello, Clive Music Studios, Salt Lake City, 1938; cert., U. Utah, 1941; studied organ, U. S.C., 1954; studied piano with Frederic Dixon, McCune Sch., 1938—42; studied paino with Alton O'Steen, Juilliard, 1936. Musician: Assembly Hall with McCune Symphony, 1941, author organ book for beginning organists; composer: (sch. song) South H.S., 1939, Skyline H.S., 1962, Wasatch Jr. H.S., 1964; organist Grandview Second Ward, 2001—; organist: Columbia (S.C.) Stake Ctr., 1953—54, East Millcreek Stake, 1956—, Monument Pk. Stake, 1955—56. Bd. dirs. Utah Hemophilia Found., Salt Lake City, 1965—99; vol. specialist Welfare Employment; vice chmn. dist. Rep. Party, Salt Lake City, 1970—90. Recipient Dedicated Svc. award, Hemophilia Found., 1991. Mem.: Alpha Dorian Fine Arts Soc. (past pres.), AXO Luncheon Club (pres.), Agalia Mu (past pres.). Avocations: traveling, writing, volunteering. Address: 2987 Hartford St Salt Lake City UT 84106-3468

RONALD, PAULINE CAROL, retired art educator; b. York, Yorkshire, Eng., Feb. 28, 1945; came to U.S., 1966; d. Peter Vincent Leonard and Doris Annie Hume-Shotton; m. James Douglas Ronald, July 16, 1966 (div. 1986); 1 child, Alexia Denise; m. James Donald Wadsworth, Feb. 15, 1991 (div. July 1994). Diploma, Harrogate Sch. Art, Yorkshire, 1965, U. New Castle, Upon Tyne, 1966; MA, Ball State U., 1977. Cert. art tchr., Ind. Art tchr. Knightstown (Ind.) Schs., 1966-67, Dunkirk (Ind.) Schs., 1967-68, Richmond (Ind.) High Sch., 1968-98; ret., 1998. Tchr. Ind. U., Earlham Coll., Richmond 1974-84; set painter Richmond Civic Theatre. Exhibited in numerous group shows; illustrator History of Wayne County, History of Centerville, 1996; represented by Cayam Nat. Gallery. Coach State Acad. Fine Arts State Team Champions, 1988, 96, 2d Pl. for the state, 1989, 95, 97; bd. dirs., mem. permanent collection com. Richmond Art Mus. Recipient Best Set Painting awards, drawing and painting awards Indpls. Art Mus. Mem. NEA, Ind. State Tchrs. Assn., Art Assn. Richmond, Indpls. Mus. Art. Avocations: painting, gardening, cooking, reading, sailing. Home: PO Box 142 Hell West Bay Grand Cayman Island West Indies

RONDEAU, ANN E. career officer; b. San Antonio, Tex. Diploma in History, Eisenhower Coll., 1973; Grad., Officer Candidate Sch., 1974. Commd. 2d lt. USN, 1974, advanced through grades to rear adm.; various assignments to exec. officer Fast Sealift Squad. One, New Orleans, 1987-89; asst. for polit.-mil. analysis Chief of Naval Operation (CNO), 1989-90; various to mil. asst. to Prin. Deputy Under Sec. of Def. for Policy, 1995-96; assigned to Navy's Quadrenniel Def. Rev. Support Office, 1997—; dep. chief of staff Shore Base Mgmt. N46/U.S. Pacific Fleet. Decorated Def. Superior Svc. medal, Legion of Merit, Def. meritorious Svc. medal (2 times), Navy Meritorious Svc. medal (2 times), Navy Commendation medal (3 times); recipient Groben award for Leadership Eisenhower Coll.

RONDEAU, DORIS JEAN, entrepreneur, consultant; b. Winston-Salem, N.C., Nov. 25, 1941; d. John Delbert and Eldora Virginia (Klutz) Robinson; m. Robert Breen Corrente, Sept. 4, 1965 (div. 1970); m. Wilfrid Dolor Rondeau, June 3, 1972. Student Syracuse U., 1959-62, Fullerton Jr. Coll., 1974-75; BA in Philosophy, Calif. State U.-Fullerton, 1976, postgrad., 1976-80. Ordained to ministry The Spirit of Divine Love, 1974. Trust real estate clk. Security First Nat. Bank, Riverside, Calif., 1965-68; entertainer Talent, Inc., Hollywood, Calif., 1969-72; co-founder, dir. Spirit of Divine Love, Huntington Beach, Calif., 1974—; pub., co-founder Passing Through, Inc., Huntington Beach, 1983—; instr. Learning Activity, Anaheim, Calif., 1984—; chmn. bd., prin. D.J. Rondeau, Entrepreneur, Inc., Huntington Beach, 1984—; co-founder, dir. Spiritual Positive Attitude, Inc., Moon In Pisces, Inc., Vibrations By Rondeau, Inc., Divine Consciousness, Expressed, Inc., Huntington Beach, Doris Wilfrid Rondeau, Inc., Huntington Beach, Calif. Author, editor: A Short Introduction To The Spirit of Divine Love, 1984; writer, producer, dir. performer spiritual vignettes for NBS Radio Network, KWVE-FM, 1982-84; author: Spiritual Meditations to Uplift the Soul, 1988. Served with USAF, 1963-65. Recipient Pop Vocalist First Place award USAF Talent Show, 1964, Sigma chpt. Epsilon Delta Chi, 1985, others. Mem. Hamel Bus. Grads., Smithsonian Assocs., Am. Mgmt. Assn., Nat. Assn. Female Execs. Fax: (714) 841-3286. Avocations: long-distance running, body fitness, arts and crafts, snorkeling, musical composition.

RONDOT, SUSAN E. SLADEN, nures, case manager, health facility administrator; b. Washington, Mar. 3, 1949; d. Burt Deale and Lisette B. (Ridgeway) Sladen; m. Peter Rondot, June 2, 2001. AA, Montgomery Coll., Takoma Park, Md., 1978; BA, U. Md., 1971; postgrad., Fla. Internat. U., Miami. RN, Fla.; CRRN; cert. rehab. provider; CCM. Homecare supr., dir. in-svc. edn., dir. health care svcs. Med. Pers. Pool, Miami; rehab. specialist Comprehensive Rehab. Assocs., Inc., Ft. Lauderdale, Fla.; rehab. nurse, case mgr. QRS Managed Care. Ind. case mgr. cons. Mem.: Isaiah Found., Fla. Nursing Assn., Assn. Rehab. Nurses, U. Md. Alumni Assn., Alpha Omicron Pi. Home: PO Box 1114 Floral City FL 34436-1114

RONEN, CAROL, state legislator; b. Chgo., Mar. 28, 1945; BS, Bradley U.; MA, Roosevelt U. Dir. legis. and cmty. affairs Chgo. Dept. Human Svcs., 1985-89; exec. dir. Chgo. Commn. on Women, 1989-90; dir. planning and rsch. Chgo.-Cook County Criminal Justice Commn.; asst. commn. Chgo. Dept. Planning, 1991, Chgo. Dept. Housing; mem. Ill. Ho. of Reps., 1993-99, Ill. Senate from dist. 9, 2001—. Former pres. Ill. Task Force on Child Support; bd. dirs. Cook County Dem. Women, St. Martin De Porres Shelter for Women and Children, Alternatives Youth Orgn., Citizen Action Consumer Rights Orgn.; governing coun. Am. Jewish Congress Midwest Region; mem. Coun. Jewish Women. Democrat. Home: 6033 N Sheridan Rd Chicago IL 60660-3003 Office: Capitol Bldg Rm 413 Springfield IL 62706

RONEY, ALICE LORRAINE MANN, poet; b. Hartford, Mich., Dec. 6, 1926; d. Paul Douglass and Margaret Alice (Widener) Mann; m. Robert Kenneth Roney, Oct. 6, 1951; children: Stephen Paul, Karen Margaret. AA, Santa Monica Coll., 1946; BA, UCLA, 1950. Tech. writer Hughes Aircraft Co., Culver City, Calif., 1949—52; chmn. Ebell Jr. Blind Recording, LA, 1959—63; librarian St. Augustine-by-the-Sea Episcopal Day Sch, Santa Monica, Calif., 1961—68. Author: Those Treasured Moments, 1972, The Seeds of Love, 1975, Psalms for My Lord, 1975; co-author: Singing for Joy, 1989, numerous poems. Sch. bd. Episcopalian Ch., 1964—67, asst. directress altar guild, 1967—69, directress altar guild, 1969—71; treas. Diocese of LA Churchwomen, 1970—73. Recipient Ebell Jr. Svc. award, 1959, 2d pl. for poetry creative writing divsn. marina dist., Calif. Fedn. Women's Clubs Fine Arts Festival, 1979, 3d pl. for inspirational poetry, 1979, 2d and 3d pl., 1981, 1st and 2d pl., 1982, 1st pl., 1985, 2d pl., 1986, 3d pl. for light verse, 1980, 1st pl. for children's stories, 1983, 1985. Fellow: World Lit. Acad.; mem.: PEO (pres. chpt. QB 1969—71, 1976—78, 1986—88), Nat. Fedn. State Poetry Socs., Ky. State Poetry Soc., World Poetry Soc. (life), Calif. State Poetry Soc., Internat. Poetry Soc., Santa Monica Bay Woman's Club (1st v.p. 1980—82, pres. 1982—84, 2d v.p. 1984—86, pres. 1986—). Episcopalian. Home and Office: 1105 Georgina Ave Santa Monica CA 90402-2027

RONEY, JUDITH ROSE, marriage and family therapist; d. Flavius Lee and Nellie Golden Rose; m. Harold Nelson Roney, Feb. 21, 1970 (dec. Dec. 4, 1988). BS, David Lipscomb U., 1963; MA, George Peabody Vanderbilt, 1967. Lic. marital and family therapist Tenn., profl. counselor Tenn. Tchr. elem., h.s. Lake County, Mount Dora, Fla., 1963—65; liason tchr., counselor Tenn. Dept. Mental Health, 1967—70; ednl. cons. Multi County Mental Health Ctr., Tullahoma, 1970—71; supr. AGAPE, Inc., Nashville, 1973—92; therapist pvt. practice, McMinnville, 1992—. Owner Judith R. Roney, M.S., LMFT, LPC-MHSP, McMinnville, Tenn. Mem. McMinnville Warren County C. of C., Tenn.; pres. McMinnville Breakfast Rotary Club, 2001—02, Warren County Ednl. Found. Mem.: Nashville Area Assn. Christian Counselors, Tenn. Assn. Marriage and Family Therapy (pres. 1998—2000, Dedicated Svc. to the Divsn. 2000), Am. Assn. Marriage Family Therapy (mem. and chair ethics com. 2001—03, chmn. 2003). Avocations: theater, reading, music, gardening.

RONEY-O'BRIEN, SUSAN FRANCES, elementary school educator, writer; b. Mass., June 29, 1948; d. Hugh Bernard and Frances Cecilia Roney; m. Philip George O'Brien, Oct. 16, 1971; children: Caitlin Juliet O'Brien, Kevin Hugh O'Brien. BA, U. Mass., Boston, 1970; MA in Edn., Anna Maria Coll., Paxton, Mass., 1990; MFA in Poetry, Warren Wilson Coll., Swannanoah, N.C., 1991. Cert. tchr. 1-6, 5-7 English Mass. Rsch. asst. U. Mass., Boston, 1968—70; genetics technician Boston Hosp. Women, 1970—72; display, sales Westwood (Mass.) Country Store, 1972—73; policy devel. coord. Medicaid Dept. Pub. Welfare, Boston, 1973—80; aide, tutor, reading tchr. Thomas Prince Sch., Princeton, Mass., 1980—90, tchr., 1990—99; tchr. English Wachusett Regional Sch. Dist., Princeton, 1999—. Poetry workshop leader Studio 288, Princeton. Author: (poems) Farmwife, 1999 (William & Kingman Page Book award); editor: (book) Princeton and Wachusett Mountains, 2003, Worcester Rev. Coord. Art is Fundamental Thomas Prince Sch., 1988—; co-founder Princeton Teen Ctr., 2003. Mem.: New Eng. Assn. Tchrs. English (Poet of the Yr. award 2002), Worcester County Poetry Assn. (v.p. 1998—99, Worcester County Poetry award 1988), Ctrl. Mass. Writing Project (tchr., leader 2003—). Avocations: writing, gardening, cooking, drawing. Office: Thomas Prince Sch 170 Sterling Rd Princeton MA 01541

RONSON, BONNIE WHALEY, literature educator; b. Tampa, Fla. d. Terrell Allen and Audie Lou Whaley; 1 child, Tyler Beeby. BA, Mercer U., 1975; MEd, U. Tampa, 1980; DPA, Nova U., 1989. Prof. English, Hillsborough C.C., Tampa, 1988—. Author: (books) Lessons All Around You, 1998, More Lessons All Around You, 1999. Home: 3143 Lakestone Dr Tampa FL 33618 Office: Hillsborough C C Ybor City Campus Tampa FL 33610 Home Fax: 813-908-5791. E-mail: drronson@gte.net.

RONSTADT, LINDA MARIE, singer; b. Tucson, July 15, 1946; d. Gilbert and Ruthmary (Copeman) R. Rec. artist numerous albums including Evergreen 1967, Evergreen Vol. 2, 1967, Linda Ronstadt, The Stone Poneys and Friends, Vol. 3, 1968, Hand Sown, Home Grown, 1969, Silk Purse, 1970, Linda Ronstadt, 1972, Don't Cry Now, 1973, Heart Like a Wheel, 1974, Different Drum, 1974, Prisoner In Disguise, 1975, Hasten Down the Wind, 1976, Greatest Hits, 1976, Simple Dreams, Blue Bayou, 1977, Living in the U.S.A., 1978, Mad Love, Greatest Hits Vol. II, 1980, Get Closer, 1982, What's New, 1983, Lush Life, 1984, For Sentimental Reasons, 1986, Trio (with Dolly Parton, Emmylou Harris), 1986, 'Round Midnight, 1987, Canciones de Mi Padre, 1987, Cry Like a Rainstorm-Howl Like the Wind, 1989, Mas Canciones, 1991, Frenesi, 1992, Winter Light, 1993, Feels Like Home, 1995, Dedicated to the One I Love, 1996, We Ran, 1998, Trio 2, 1999 (with Emmylou Harris & Dolly Parton), Western Wall: The Tucson Sessions (with Emmylou Harris); starred in Broadway prodn. of Pirates of Penzance, 1981, also in film, 1983, off Broadway as Mimi in La Boheme, 1984. Recipient Am. Music awards, 1978, 79, Grammy awards, 1975, 76, 87 (with Emmylou Harris and Dolly Parton), 1988, 89 (with Aaron Neville), 1990 (with Aaron Neville, 1992 (2), 1996, Acad. Country Music award, 1987, 88. Office: Electra Records 75 Rockefeller Plz New York NY 10019-6908

ROOF, SALLY JEAN-MARIE, library and information scientist, educator; b. Cleve., Dec. 29, 1947; d. James William and Marie Monreal Roof; m. Christian John Hoffmann III, Sept. 22, 1973; children: Christian Graham Hoffmann, Joscelyn Nicole Hoffmann, Gavin Leigh Hoffmann. BA in English Lit., Dunbarton Coll. of Holy Cross, Washington, D. C., 1969; MS in Libr. and Info. Sci., Cath. U. of Am., 1972; degree in Profl. Mgmt. (hon.), Miami U., 1976; MA in Elem. Edn., No. Ariz. U., 2001. Cert. tchr. in libr. media ctr. adminstrn. Nat. Bd. of Cert. Tchrs., 2003. Asst. libr. U.S .Postal Svc. Libr., Washington, 1971—72; head of acquisitions George Wash. U. Libr., Washington, 1972—74; libr. adminstr. and mgr. Calgon Corp. Libr. Merck Inc., Pitts., 1974—77; libr. info. specialist U. of Phoenix, 1979—81; reference libr. Grand Canyon U., Phoenix, 1990—91; reference libr. West Campus Libr. Ariz. State U., Phoenix, 1994—95; libr. tchr. info. specialist Madison Meadows Sch., Phoenix, 1998—. Libr. cons. U. of Phoenix, 1981—82; presenter Ariz. Libr. Assn., Scottsdale, 2003; mem., presenter People to People Amb. Program Children's Lit. Del., Spokane, Wash., 2004; cons. in field. Editor: Serial Titles in the Washington, D. C. University Consortium Libraries; designer (school website) Madison Meadows Sch. website; author: (pamphlet) Madison Meadows Library Media Center. Chmn. grade level patroness Nat. Charity League, Phoenix, 1994—99; pres. Phoenix (Ariz.) Mus. of History, 1991—94. Mem.: ALA (assoc.), Ariz. Libr. Assn. (assoc.), Beta Phi Mu, Jr. League of Phoenix. Democrat-Npl. Roman Catholic. Avocations: yoga, fast walking, reading, bicycling. Office: Madison Meadows School 225 W Ocotillo Rd Phoenix AZ 85013 Personal E-mail: sroofhoff@cox.net. E-mail: sroof@msd38.org.

ROOK, JUDITH RAWIE, television producer, writer; d. Wilmer Ernest and Margaret Jane (Towle) Rawie; m. Dr. John Holland, 1964 (div. 1978); children: Daryn Simons, Dawn Reinard; m. Tim Rook, 1993. BA, Loyola-Marymount Univ., 1964; postgrad., U. Calif., San Diego, 1978. Syndicated columnist Environ. Forum, 1971-74; dir. IABC, San Francisco, 1982; dir. programming Westinghouse Cable, 1983-85; dir. devel. Embassy/Nelson Home Entertainment, 1985-87; ptnr. Real Magic, 1987-89; prodr., writer, ptnr. BrantHol Prodns., 1990-93; co-sponsorship Beetle Juice, The Last Emperor, 1987—89; founder, pres. R2 Group, 1990—. Assoc. dir. : (off-broadway play) Arms and the Man, 1967; The Man Who Came to Dinner, 1981; exec. prodr.: Neighborhood Without Bars (Emmy award, 1985, 1986, 1987); prodr., writer : PBS series Focus, 1980; Achieving, 1982 (Emmy award, ACE nominee, PBS nominee); NBC pilot Christmas Comes to Silverton, 1990—93; CNN pilot Clever Encounters, 1991; prodr.: One Creative Moment, Close up: The 60s, 1995—97; assoc. prodr. : Fox Latin Am. Billboard Music Awards, 1998—2000; playwright : Theatre 40 Writer's Workshop Anniversary for Three, 2003. Mem. adv. bd. U. Calif. Irvine Screenwriting/Film Prodn., 1996-2000; mem. adv. bd. Univ. Art Mus., 1996-97, co-pres. contemporary coun., 1996-97; mem. exec. bd. Long Beach Mus. Art, 1995-96; bd. dirs. Counseling 4 Kids, 1998—, bd. sec., 2001—; editor, bd. League Women Voters, Santa Monica. Mem. Am. Film Inst., Women in Film (dir. seminars on women in film), IFP West. Democrat. Episcopalian. E-mail: tirook@earthlink.net.

ROOKS, CHARLES S. foundation administrator; b. Whiteville, N.C., June 29, 1937; BA in English, Wake Forest Coll., 1959; Rockefeller Brothers fellow, Harvard U., 1959-60; MA in Polit. Sci., Duke U., 1964, PhD in Polit. Sci., 1968. Rsch. assoc. Voter Edn. Project, Atlanta, 1969-70, dir. tech. assistance programs, 1970-71, dep. dir., 1971-72; exec. dir. Southeastern Coun. of Founds., Atlanta, 1972-78; dir. mem. svcs. Coun. on Founds., Washington, 1979-80, v.p., 1981-82, acting CEO, 1981-82; exec. dir. Meyer Meml. Trust, Portland, Oreg., 1982—. Instr. polit. sci. Duke U., Durham, N.C., 1963, 65-67; asst. prof. of govt. Lake Forest Coll., Ill., 1967-69; asst. prof. polit. sci. Clark Coll., Atlanta, 1969-71; bd. dirs. Pacific Northwest Grantmakers Forum, Forum of Regional Assns. of Grantmakers; mem. adv. bd. Neighborhood Partnership Fund (Oreg. Cmty. Found.); mem., adv. bd. Giving in Oreg. Coun.; co-chair Northwest Giving Project. Contbr. articles to profl. jours. Home: 2706 SW English Ct Portland OR 97201-1622 Office: Meyer Memorial Trust 425 NW 10th Ave Ste 400 Portland OR 97209-3128

ROOKS, JUDITH PENCE, midwife, public health consultant; b. Spokane, Wash., Aug. 18, 1941; d. Lawrence Cyrus and Christine Atrice (Snow) Pence; m. Peter Geoffrey Bourne, Mar. 1972 (div.); m. Charles Stanley Rooks, Sept. 21, 1975; 1 child, Christopher Robert. BS, U. Wash., 1963; MS, Cath. U. Am., 1967; MPH, Johns Hopkins U., 1974. Cert. edpidemiology, nursing, nurse-midwifery, mediation. Staff nurse King County Harborview Hosp., Seattle, 1963—64, The Clin. Ctr., NIH, Bethesda, Md., 1965; asst. prof. nursing dept. San Jose (Calif.) State Coll., 1967-69; epidemiologist Ctrs. for Disease Control, Atlanta, 1970-78; asst. prof. dept. ob-gyn. Oreg. Health Sci. U., Portland, 1978-79; expert Office of the Surgeon Gen., Dept. HHS, Washington, 1979-80; project officer U.S. AID, Washington, 1980-82; prin. investigator Sch. Pub. Health Columbia U., N.Y.C., 1988-89, assoc. Pacific Inst. for Women's Health, 1993-2001; cons. Portland, 1982—. Mem. tech. adv. com. Family Health Internat., Research Triangle Park, N.C., 1986-97; mem. midwifery adv. com. Frontier Nursing Svc., Hyden, Ky., 1997-2002; mem. com. Inst. of Medicine NAS, Washington, 1983-85; academic faculty cmty.-based nurse midwifery edn. program Frontier Sch. Midwifery and Family Nursing, Hyden, Ky., 1993-95; dir. N.Y. Acad. Medicine/Maternity Ctr. Assn. evidence-based symposium on The Nature and Management of Labor Pain, 1999-01. Author: Midwifery and Childbirth in America, 1997; co-author: Nurse-Midwifery in America, 1986, Reproductive Risk in Maternity Care and Family Planning Services, 1992; mem. editl. bd. Birth, 1996—; editl. cons. Jour. Nurse Midwifery, 1992-2000, Jour. Midwifery and Women's Health, 2002--; contbr. articles to profl. jours. Mem bd. advisors World Affairs Coun. Oreg., Portland, 1987-90; bd. dirs. Planned Parenthood of the Columbia/Willamette, Portland, 1987-90; chm. Ga. Citizens for Hosp. Abortion, Atlanta, 1969-70; assoc. Pacific Coun. on Internat. Policy, 1995-97. Recipient nat. award Nat. Perintal Assn., 1999. Mem. APHA (chair com. on women's rights 1982-83, mem. governing coun. 1976-77, 79-82, Martha May Eliot award for svc. to mothers and children 1993, Hattie Hemschemeyer award for cont. outstanding contbns. to nurse-midwifery and maternal and child health care 1998), Am. Coll. Nurse-Midwives (life, pres. 1983-85). Avocations: gardening, walking, reading, travel, cooking. Home and Office: 2706 SW English Ct Portland OR 97201-1622 E-mail: jprooks1@comcast.net.

ROOKS, LINDA, writer; d. Harold John and Marianna Wieck; m. Marvin Edward Rooks, Dec. 19, 1967; children: Juliana Wolf, Laura Katherine. BA, San Francisco State U., 1965. Tchr. Seminole (Fla.) Jr. H.S., 1970—72; pro-life liaison for Paula Hawkins senatorial campaign Nat. Right to Life, Winter Park, Fla., 1986; asst. editor Ctr. Stage Mag., Maitland, Fla., 1987—89; office coord., newsletter editor Adoption by Shepherd Care, Orlando, Fla., 1994—2000; freelance writer Maitland, 2000—. Scriptwriter: radio and tv Testimony of An Unborn Child (Cammeo Award for Best of Show, 1987); author: (devotional) Tapestry; contbr. articles to profl. jours. Pres. Ctrl. Fla. Right to Life, 1984—85, 1990—96; staff position state coord. for families Bob Dole Presdl. Campaign, Fla., 1995—96; pub. rels. co-chmn. Nat. Right to Life Conv., Orlando, 1983. Mem.: Word Weavers Writers Group (sec. steering com. 2002—). Republican. Protestant. Avocation: travel.

ROOME, KRISTINE ANN, college administrator; b. Pequannock, N.J., Sept. 3, 1967; d. Michael Wesley and Joan Ann (Dooley) Roome. BS, Montclair State U., 1990; postgrad. in anthropology, Columbia U., 1993—. Fin. acct. JP Morgan Co., N.Y.C., 1990-93; sr. acct. Tchr.'s Coll. Columbia U., N.Y.C., 1993, asst. dir. office of instnl. studies, 1993—. Asst. dir. Wright Gallery, N.Y.C., 1994—, curator several exhbns., 1995. Alumni scholar, Student Govt. Assn. scholar Montclair State U., 1989, 90, Columbia U. Tchr.'s Coll. scholar, 1995, travel grantee, 1995, Field Lang./Area Studies fellowship Inst. for African Studies Columbia U., N.Y.C., 1996—. Mem. NAFE, Assn. Inst. Rschrs. Avocations: art, tennis, reading. Office: Tchrs Coll Columbia U 525 W 120th St New York NY 10027-6625

ROONEY, CAROL BRUNS, dietician; b. Milw., Dec. 20, 1940; d. Edward G. and Elizabeth C. (Lemke) Bruns; m. George Eugene Rooney Jr., July 1, 1967; children: Steven, Sean. BS, U. Wis., 1962; MS, U. Iowa, 1965. Registered dietitian; cert. nutrition specialist; disting. health care food svc. adminstr.; cert. dietitian, Wis. Intern VA Med. Ctr., Hines, Ill., 1962-63, resident in nutrition and food svc. Iowa City, 1963-65, dietitian nutrition clinic Hines, 1965-67, 69-70, chief clin. dietetics, 1970-71, chief adminstrv. dietetics, 1971-73, clin. dietitian Memphis, 1967-68; asst. chief nutrition and food svc. Zablocki VA Med. Ctr., Milw., 1974-85, chief nutrition and food svc., 1985-96, divsn. mgr. cons. care, 1996-98, cons. nutrition and food svc. mgmt., 1995—, bus. enterprise mgr., 1998-2000. Adj. lectr. Loyola U. Coll. Dentistry, Maywood, Ill., 1969-72; investigator nutrition VA/Med. Coll. Wis., Milw., 1975-2000, co-dir. ann. clin. nutrition symposium, Milw., 1979-94; chmn. task force on ration allowance VA, Washington, 1977-84, mem. nutrition and food svc. spl. interest users group Washington, 1983-85, chmn. tech. adv. group region IV, 1986; mem. Dept. Vets. Affairs Mktg. Ctr. Subsistence Task Force, 1991-95, dietetic internship adv. bd. St. Luke's Hosp., Milw., 1983-87; mem. Dept. Vets. Affairs Nat. Cost Containment Ctr. Nutrition & Food Svc. Benchmarking Tech. Adv., 1995-96; lectr. in field, 1965—; mem. Dept. Vets. Affairs, Nutrition and Food Svc. Policy Manual Rev. Task Force, 1992-96, Dept. Vets. Chiefs, Food and Nutrition Svc. Mentor Group, 1992-96. Author: (videocassette) VA Ration Allowance as a Management Tool 1976; editor: Nutrition Principles and Dietary Guidelines for Patients Receiving Chemotherapy and Radiation Therapy, 1980; contbr. articles to profl. jours., 1978—. Mem. profl. edn. com. Milw. South unit Am. Cancer Soc., 1976-86, bd. dirs. Milw. South unit, 1984-86, Milw. divsn., 1986-87, Wis. divsn., 1987-91, media spokesperson, 1983-91, del. to Milw. divsn., 1984-85, mem. orgnl. and expansion com. Milw. divsn., 1986-87, profl. edn. com. Milw. divsn., 1986-87, Wis. divsn., 1987-91, mem. taking control Wis. divsn., 1987-91, chmn. nutrition Wis. divsn., 1989-91; mem. med. adv. com. YMCA Met. Milw., 1985—; mem. Marquette U. High Sch. Mothers Guild, 1990-94. Named Dept. Vets. Affairs Dietitian of Yr., 1994; recipient Disting. Svc. award, Am. Cancer Soc. Milw. South unit, 1980, Women of Achievement award, Girl Scouts USA Milw. area, 1987, Leadership award, VA, 1989, Dept. Vets. Affairs Fed. Women's Program cert. merit for outstanding profl. leadership, 1994, commendation, Dept. Vet. Affairs, 2000, rsch. grantee, Paralyzed Vets. Am., 1981—83. Fellow Am. Dietetic Assn. (registered, practice groups in mgmt. responsibilities in health care delivery, gerontology nutrition 1980-2000, dietetics in phys. medicine and rehab. 1983-97, clin. nutrition mgmt. 1987—, amb. nat. media spokesperson 1983-89, Resource Amb. 1991—, Outstanding Svc. award 1983-89), FADA; mem. AAUW, Am. Soc. Health Care Food Svc. Adminstrs. (dir.-at-large Wis. chpt. 1993-95, pres.-elect Wis. chpt. 1995-96, pres. 1996-97, immediate past pres. 1997-98, Disting. Health Care Food Svc. Adminstr. 1995—), Wis. Dietetic Assn. (co-chmn. divsn. mgmt. practice 1976-77, chmn. 1977-78, bd. dirs. 1981-83, coord. cabinet 1984-91, pres. 1988-89, chmn. nominating com. 1989-90, chmn. long-range planning com. 1989-90, legis. com. 1988—, Wis. Medallion award 1986), Milw. Dietetic Assn. (cmty. nutrition and clin. dietetics and rsch. coms. 1975-76, chair ad hoc com. for nutrition and oncology patients 1976-79, clin. dietetics and rsch. study group 1981-90, chair 1983-85, pres. 1982-83, by-laws com. 1983-84, chair policies and procedures com. 1983-87, pub. rels. com. 1983-87, chair nominating com. 1984-85), Fed. Execs. Assn., Coll. Endowment Assn., Leadership Vets. Affairs Alumni Assn. (charter, life), Phi Upsilon Omicron, Kappa Delta, Kappa Delta Alumnae Assn., Milw. Kappa Delta Alumnae Assn. (rep. Milw. Panhellenic coun. 1998-99, treas. 1999-2004). Avocations: tennis, golf. Home: 18230 Le Chateau Dr Brookfield WI 53045-4922

ROONEY, MARIA DEWING, photographer; b. N.Y.C., July 25; d. Madeleine L'Engle Franklin; m. John Bryan Rooney, Jan. 21, 1984; children: Bryson, Alexander. BFA, Phila. Coll. Art. Tchr. photography Bishop Bright Grammar Sch., Leamington Spa, Eng., Mid-Warwickshire Sch. of Further Edn., Leamington Spa, 1976-80; photographer, owner The Studios, Shipston-on-Stour, Eng., 1977-80; photographer Gary Studios & Comini Studios, Dallas, 1980-83; pvt. practice Mystic, Conn., 1990—. Exhibitions include Warwick (Eng.) Gallery, Derby (Eng.) Coll. Art Gallery, Bath (Eng.) Pl. Cmty. Ctr., Midland Group Galley, Nottingham, Eng., Wimbledon Sch. Art, London, Warwich U. Arts Ctr., Birmingham, Eng., Essex Art Assn., 1998, R. J. Julia, Madison, Conn., 1998, State Capitol Hartford, Conn., 1999, Emporium Gallery, 2003, Brick Gallery, Essex, Conn., 2003; contbr. photographs Anytime Prayers, 1994, Mothers and Daughters, 1997, Mothers and Sons, 1999, photographs published in Co-Optic Publs., London, 1976—80; prodr.: series greeting cards with personal photography. Mem. Child and Family Svcs. Mem.: AAUW, Mystic Art Assn., Essex Art Assn. (photography award 1997, 2002, 2003). Avocations: sailing, writing. Home and Office: 77 High St Mystic CT 06355 E-mail: vlad0121@aol.com.

ROOP, KAREN DANSTEDT, elementary and secondary school educator; b. Worcester, Mass., Feb. 20, 1947; d. Robert Spencer and Lucille (Rice) Danstedt; m. William Reed Roop, Sept. 17, 1988; stepchildren; Kim, Matthew. BFA, Boston U., 1969, MFA, 1975; pvt. studies with, Patricia Forrester, 1994-95, George Nick, 1996. Tchr. art Braintree (Mass.) Pub. Schs., 1970—. Mem. state frameworks com. for edn. reform, Braintree, 1995-97, art curriculum revision com. Exhibitor in numerous one-woman and group shows, 1975—; commd. paintings for pub. and pvt. orgns. Reader tapes for the blind Talking Info. Ctr., Marshfield, Mass., 1985-96. Mem. NEA, Nat. Art Edn. Assn., Concord Art Assn., Spenbrook Conservation Assn. (prin. 1995-96). Avocations: local theater set designs, tennis, yoga, boating, travel.

ROOS, PAULA SPARROW, manufacturer's representative; b. Bklyn., Nov. 4, 1932; d. Alexander J. and Tillie A. (Shapiro) Sparrow; m. William J. Roos, Nov. 17, 1951; children: Liza, Sigmund, Joel. Profl. ski instr., Pa., 1962-92; ind. yarn rep., 1983—2002; sec. Maternal & Family Health Svc. N.E. Pa., 2002—. Co-author: Hi Kids - Welcome to the World of Skiing, 1995. Sec., bd. dirs. Scranton (Pa.) Cmty. Concerts, 1960-2003, N.E. Pa. Easter Seal Soc., Scranton, 1971-82; bd. dirs. Pocono coun. Girl Scouts U.S., Scranton, 1955-70, Maternal and Family Health Svc. N.E. Pa., 1974-95, 2003—, Dorflinger-Suydam Wildlife Sanctuary, 1997—, Northeast Regional Cancer Inst., 2003—; mem. com. Dorflinger Glass Mus., Hawley, Pa., 1996, Wayne Hosp. Aux., Honesdale, 1952—. Recipient Brace for an Ace award Easter Seal Soc., 1980, Citizen of Yr. award B'nai B'rith, 1982, Last Bid award PBS-WVIA, 1996. Mem. Ladies Improvement Assn. (pres 1993—), Women's Club of Honesdale (bd. dirs. 1953—, Outstanding Women of Am. award 1965). Avocations: gardening, knitting, travel. Home: 7 Hillcrest Cir Honesdale PA 18431-1442

ROOS, SYBIL FRIEDENTHAL, retired elementary school educator; b. L.A., Jan. 29, 1924; d. Charles G. and Besse (Weixel) Friedenthal; m. Henry Kahn Roos, May 8, 1949 (dec. Dec. 1989); children: Catherine Alane Cook, Elizabeth Anne Garlinger, Virginia Ann Bertrand. BA in Music, Centenary Coll., 1948; MEd, Northwestern State U., 1973. Cert. elem. edn. tchr., spl. edn. tchr. Tchr. Caddo Parish Schs., Shreveport, 1968-75, Spring Branch Ind. Schs., Houston, 1975-85; vol. Houston Grand Opera/Guild, 1979—, Houston Mus. of Fine Arts/Guild, 1990—, Houston Symphony Soc./Guild, 1997—. Author tchrs. guides. Pres. Nat. Coun. Jewish Women, Shreveport, 1958; bd. dirs. Mus. Fine Arts; area coord. Spl. Olympics, Shreveport, 1974-75; bd. dirs. U. Houston Moore Sch. Music. With USN, 1944-46. Mem. AAUW (pres. Spring Valley Houston chpt. 1985-87), Houston Grand Opera Guild (pres. 1989-91), Houston Symphony League, Houston Ballet Guild, Mus. of Fine Arts Guild (bd. dirs.), U. Houston Sch. of Music (bd. dirs.) Am. Needlepoint Guild, Delta Kappa Gamma (bd. dirs., treas. 1987-89), Phi Mu. Republican. Avocations: music, tennis, needlepoint, volunteering. Home: 10220 Memorial Dr Apt 78 Houston TX 77024-3227 E-mail: s.roos@worldnet.att.net.

ROOT, JANET GREENBERG, private school educator; b. Atlantic City, N.J., May 16, 1936; d. Louis and Edith (Shapiro) Greenberg; m. Allen W. Root, June 15, 1958; children: Jonathan, Jennifer, Michael. BS, U. Md., 1958. Tchr. Bd. Edn., Brighton, N.Y., 1958-60; dir. music/art parent program, chmn. dept. arts-humanities Shorecrest Prep. Sch., St. Petersburg, Fla., 1989—. Trustee Shorecrest Prep. Sch., 1980—86, 1990—96, 1998—, dir. cultural enrichment program, 1978—; mem. ednl. bd. Bayfront Ctr., 1993—2000; mem. exhbns. and collections com. Tampa Bay Holocaust Mus., mem. edn. com., 2003—; trustee Salvador Dali Mus., 1998—, chmn. edn. com., mem. long range bldg. com., mem. exec. com.; trustee Order of Salvador, 1999—. Named Honoree, Nat. Philanthropy Day. E-mail: jroot@shorecrest.org.

ROOT, M. BELINDA, chemist; b. Port Arthur, Tex., May 2, 1957; d. Robert A. and Charlene (Whitehead) Lee; m. Miles J. Root, Nov. 8, 1980; children: Jason Matthew, Ashley Erin. BS in Biology, Lamar U., 1979; MBA, U. Houston, 1994. Asst. chemist Merichem Co., Houston, 1979-81, project chemist, 1982-84, instrument chemist, 1984-85, quality assurance coord., 1986-89, product lab. supr., 1989-91; quality control supr. mfg. Welchem Inc. subs. Amoco, 1991—; mgr. Quality Control Petrolite Corp., 1993; mgr. quality control/quality assurance Akzo-Nobel Chems., Pasadena, Tex., 1994—. Mgr. Quality and Environ. Svcs. (Akzo Nobel Catalysts), 1999—. Editor (newsletter) Merichemer, 1989-91. Mem. MADD, 1989—, PTA, 1988—. Recipient Gulf Shore Regional award Cat Fanciers Assn., 1981, Disting. Merit award, 1990. Mem. Am. Soc. Quality Control (cert. quality auditor, quality engr.), Am. Chem. Soc., United Silver Fancier (sec. 1980-82), Lamar U. Alumni Assn., Houston Area Lab Mgrs. Group (chair 2000-01), Beta Beta Beta (sec. 1978-79), Beta Gamma Sigma. Avocations: camping, gardening. Office: Akzo-Nobel Chem Inc 13000 Baypark Rd Pasadena TX 77507-1104

ROOT, NINA J. librarian, writer; b. 1934; d. Jacob J. and Fannie (Slivinsky) R. BA, Hunter Coll.; MSLS, Pratt Inst.; postgrad., USDA Grad. Sch., 1964-65, CUNY, 1970-75. Reference and serials libr. Albert Einstein Coll. Medicine Libr., Bronx, N.Y., 1958-59; asst. chief libr. Am. Cancer Soc., N.Y.C., 1959-62; chief libr. Am. Inst. Aeron. and Astronautics, N.Y.C., 1962-64; head ref. and libr. svcs. sci. and tech. divsn. Libr. Congress, Washington, 1964-66; mgmt. cons. Nelson Assocs., Inc., N.Y.C., 1966-70; dir. libr. svcs. Am. Mus. Natural History, N.Y.C., 1970-97; freelance mgmt. cons. and libr. planning, 1970-99. Trustee Barnard Found., 1984-91; mem. libr. adv. coun. N.Y. State Bd. Regents, 1984-89, trustee Metro, 1987-92; bd. dirs. Hampden/Booth Libr. Players, 1990-97, Sutton Area Cmty., 1997-2001; trustee Mercantile Libr. N.Y., 1993-95; dir. emerita Libr. AMNH, 1998—. Recipient Meritorious Svc. award Libr. of Congress, 1965, Founders medal SHNH, 1997. Mem. ALA (preservation com. 1977-79, chmn. libr./binders com. 1978-80, chmn. preservation sect. 1980-81, mem. coun. 1983-86), Spl. Librs. Assn. (sec. documentation group N.Y. chpt. 1972-73, 2d v.p. N.Y. 1975-76, treas. sci. and tech. group N.Y. 1975-76, mus. arts and humanities divsn. program planning chairperson-conf. 1977), Archons of Colophon (convener 1978-79), Soc. for Hist. of Natural History (N.Am. rep. 1977-85), N.Y. Acad. Scis. (mem. publs. com. 1975-80, 89-91, archives com. 1976-78, search. com. 1976), Explorers Club. Home: 400 E 59th St New York NY 10022-2342

ROOT, PHYLLIS IDALENE, writer; b. Ft. Wayne, Ind., Feb. 14, 1949; d. John Howard and Margaret Esther (Trout) R.; children: Amelia, Ellen. BA, Valparaiso U., 1971. Tchr. complete scholar program U Minn., 1997—; tchr. MFA writing for children Vt. Coll., 1998—. Author: Moon Tiger, 1985, Soup for Supper, 1986, The Listening Silence, 1992, The Old Red Rocking Chair, 1992, Coyote and the Magic Words, 1993, Sam Who Was Swallowed By a Shark, 1994, Rosie's Fiddle, 1997, One Windy Wednesday, 1996, Contrary Bear, 1996, Mrs. Potter's Pig, 1996, Aunt Nancy and Old Man Trouble, 1996, The Hungry Monster, 1996, What Baby Wants, 1998, One Duck Stuck, 1998, Aunt Nancy and Cousin Lazybones, 1998, Turnover Tuesday, 1998, Grandmother Winter, 1999, Here Comes Tabby Cat, 2000, Hey Tabby Cat, 2000, Meow Monday, 2000, Foggy Friday, 2000, Kiss the Cow, 2000, All for the Newborn Baby, 2000, Rattletrap Car, 2001, Soggy Saturday, 2001, Mouse Goes Out, 2002, Mouse All Year Round, 2002, Oliver Finds His Way, 2002, Big Momma Makes the World, 2002, 2003 (Boston Globe Horn Book award for picture books 2003), What's That Noise? (with M. Edwards), 2002. Mem. Authors Guild, Soc. Children's Book Writers and Illustrators. Avocations: gardening, sailing, canoeing.*

ROPER, DENISE MICHELLE, music educator; d. Lewis Wilson and Aleta Leckelt. MusB in Edn., La. State U., 1991, MusM, 1996. Band dir. Oaklawn Jr. HS, Houma, 1992—99, Ellender Meml. HS, Houma, 1999—. Mem.: La. Bandmasters Assn., La. Music Educators Assn., La. Dist. VII Band Dirs. Assn. (2nd v.p. 2002—03). Roman Cath. Home: PO Box 524 Houma LA 70361

ROPER, DONNA C. archaeologist; Rsch. assoc. prof. dept. Sociology & anthrop. Kans. State U., Manhattan. Mem.: Kans. State Hist. Soc., Nebr. Assn. Profl. Archeologists (pres.). Home: 1924 Bluehills Rd Manhattan KS 66502-4503 Office: Kans State U Dept Sociology Anthrop & Social Work 204 Waters Hill Manhattan KS 66506

RORIE, NANCY CATHERINE, retired elementary and secondary school educator; b. Union County, NC, May 31, 1940; d. Carl Evander and Mary Mildred (Pressley) Rorie. BA, Woman's Coll. U. N.C., 1962; MEd, U. N.C., 1967; EdD, Duke U., 1977. Cert. curriculum and instrnl. specialist, social studies tchr. for middle and secondary levels, English tchr., N.C. Social studies and English tchr. Guilford County Schs., Greensboro, NC, 1962—67; social studies instr. Lees-McRae Coll., Banner Elk, NC, 1967—76; social studies and English tchr. Monroe (NC) City Schs., 1977—93, Union County Schs., Monroe, 1993—2002; ret., 2002. Mem.: Monroe Aquatics And Fitness Ctr., Kappa Delta Pi, Phi Alpha Theta. Democrat. Southern Missionary Baptist. Home: 2401 Old Pageland Monroe Rd Monroe NC 28112-8163

RORKE, LUCY BALIAN, neuropathologist; b. St. Paul, June 22, 1929; d. Aram Haji and Karzouhy (Ousdigian) Balian; m. Robert Radcliffe Rorke, June 4, 1960. AB, U. Minn., 1951, MA, 1952, BS, 1955, MD, 1957. Diplomate Am. Bd. Pathology. Intern Phila. Gen. Hosp., 1957-58, resident anat. pathology and neuropathology, 1958-62, asst. neuropathologist, 1963-67, chief pediat. pathologist, 1967-68, chief neuropathologist, 1968-69, chmn. dept. anat. pathology and chief neuropathologist, 1969-73, chmn. dept. pathology, 1973-77, pres. med. staff, 1973-75; practice medicine specializing in neuropathology Phila., 1962—; neuropathologist Children's Hosp., Phila., 1965—, pres. med. staff, 1986-88, acting pathologist-in-chief, 1995-2000. Cons. neuropathologist Wyeth Rsch. Labs., Radnor, Pa., 1961-87, Wistar Inst. Anatomy and Biology, Phila., 1967-93; assoc. prof. pathology U. Pa. Sch. Medicine, Phila., 1970-73, prof., 1973—, clin. prof. neurology, 1979—, clin. prof. pediats., 1997—; forensic neuropathologist Office of Med. Examiner, Phila., 1977—. Author: Myelinization of the Brain in the Newborn, 1969, Pathology of Perinatal Brain Injury, 1982; mem. editl. bd. Jours. Neuropathology Exptl. Neurology, 1980-85, 93—, Pediat. Neurosurgery, 1984-2002, Child's Nervous System, 1984-88, Brain pathology, 1990-95; contbr. articles to profl. jours. NIH fellow in neuropathology, 1961-62; NIH grantee for study of neonatal brain, 1963-68. Fellow Coll. Am. Pathologists; mem. Phila. Gen. Hosp. Med. Staff (pres. 1973-75), Phila. Neurol. Soc. (v.p. 1971-72, editor Transactions 1973, pres. 1975-76),

Am. Assn. Neuropathologists (exec. council 1976-85, v.p. 1979-80, pres. 1981-82, Meritorious Svc. award 1999), Am. Neurol. Assn., AMA, Burlington County Med. Soc., Phila. Coll. Physicians (trustee 2002), Am. Soc. Neuroradiology (hon.). Home: 120 Chestnut St Moorestown NJ 08057-2937 Office: Childrens Hosp Phila 324 S 34th St Philadelphia PA 19104-4304 E-mail: Rorke@email.chop.edu.

ROSA, HELEN, dean, Dean U. Central del Caribe Sch. Medicine, Bayamon, PR, 2002—. Office: Univ Central del Caribe Sch Medicine Office Admissions Call Box 60-327 Bayamon PR 00960-6032

ROSA, MARGARITA, agency chief executive, lawyer; b. Bklyn., Jan. 5, 1953; d. Jose and Julia (Mojica) R.; 1 child, Marisol Kimberly Rosa-Shapiro. BA in History cum laude, Princeton U., 1974; JD, Harvard U., 1977. Bar: N.Y. Assoc. Rosenman & Colin, N.Y.C., 1977-79, Rabinowitz & Boudin, N.Y.C., 1981-84; staff atty. Puerto Rican Legal Def. Edn. Fund, N.Y.C., 1979-81; teaching fellow Urban Legal Studies program CUNY, 1984-85; gen. counsel N.Y. State Div. Human Rights, N.Y.C., 1985-88, exec. dep. commr., 1988-90, commr., 1990-95; exec. dir. Grand St. Settlement, 1995—. Vice chmn. N.Y. State Task force on ADA Implementation, 1991-95; mem. N.Y. Gov.'s Task Force on Sexual Harassment, 1992; mem. Mayor's Commn. on the Judiciary, 2002—, mem. Mayor's commn. on women's issues, 2002—; bd. dirs. Pub. Interest Law Found., NYU Law Sch., 1982-84; adj. prof. law Fordham Law Sch., 1995; adj. prof. pub. policy Wagner Grad. Sch. NYU, 1995—, Baruch Coll. Exec. MPA program, 1998; bd. dirs. Martin Luther King Jr. Commn. N.Y. State, 1990-95, Feminist Press CUNY, 1990-95; mem. adv. bd. N.Y.C. Ind. Budget Office, 1996-2001, vice chair, 2000-01; mem. adv. bd. Women in Mgmt. Inst., Wagner Grad. Sch., NYU, 1995—. Bd. dirs. N.Y. Civil Liberties Union, 1981-86, Lower East Side Family Union, N.Y.C., 1982-84, United Neighborhood Houses, 1995-97, Legal Svcs. for Children, 1999—, Non-Profit Coordinating Com., 2001—. Recipient Hispanic Women Achievers award N.Y. State Gov.'s Office Hispanic Affairs, 1990, Woman of Excellence award CUNY, 1992, Oscar García Rivera award P.R. Bar Assn., 1996, N.Y. State Atty. Gen.'s award for disting. pub. svc. in the legal profession, 2002; Lombard Assn. fellow Office of U.S. Atty., So. Dist. N.Y., 1975; Revson Teaching fellow Charles Revson Found., 1984-85. Mem. N.Y. State Bar Assn. (com. on minorities in the profession 1997—), Assn. Bar City N.Y. (commn. future of CUNY 1999—). Office: Grand St Settlement 80 Pitt St New York NY 10002-3516

ROSA-BRAY, MARILYN, physician; b. Arecibo, PR, Feb. 17, 1970; d. Tomas Rosa and Maria Mercedes Lopez; m. Franklin A. Bray, Mar. 21, 2001; 1 child, Allen M. Bray. BS in Biology, U. P.R., Rio Piedras, 1988—92; MD, U. P.R., San Juan, 1992—97. Cert. MD P.R. Dept. Health, 1997, Mich. State Dept. Health, 1998, Wash. State Dept. Health, 1999, in Internal Medicine ACP, 2003. Instr. KAPLAN, San Juan, PR, 1996—97; intern in neurology San Juan V.A. Hosp., PR, 1997—98; intern McLaren Regional Med. Ctr., Flint, Mich., 1998—99; sr. rsch. fellow U. Wash., Dept. Neurology, Tacoma, 1999—2000; in-patient geriatric physician Western State Hosp., Seattle, 1999—2000; med. and lab. dir. Biomat USA, Seattle, 1999—; anatomy and physiology prof. Shoreline C.C., Wash., 1999—2001, Seattle Pacific U., 2000; physician Va. Mason Med. Ctr., Seattle, 2001—03, Carolyn Downs Family Medicine Ctr., Seattle, 2002—03, Valley Med. Ctr., Newcastle, Wash., 2003—. Mortality and morbidity external reviewer Western State Hosp., Tacoma, 2000—. Spkr., cmty. edn. Golden Care Sr. Group, Renton, Wash., 2003; cmty. educator Va. Mason Med. Ctr., Seattle, 2003. Recipient Outstanding Woman of Hatillo, P.R., Rotary Club, 1992. Mem.: ACP, AMA (assoc.), Med. Assn. P.R. (assoc.), Genesse County Med. Soc. (assoc.), Am. Student Med. Assn. (pres. 1991—92), Biology Honor Soc. (v.p. 1990—92). Avocations: sailing, walking. Office: Valley Med Ctr Int Med 7203 129th Ave SE Ste 200 Newcastle WA 98056-1412 Office Phone: 425-656-5428. Personal E-mail: marilynrosa@hotmail.com. E-mail: marilyn_rosabray@valleymed.org.

ROSADO, ROSSANA, publishing executive, editor-in-chief; b. Bronx, N.Y. married; 2 children. BA in Journalism, Pace U. Reporter El Diario/La Prensa, N.Y.C., editor-in-chief, 1995—, gen. mgr., pub., 1999—; prodr. pub. affairs programming Sta. WPIX-TV, N.Y.C., 1988, pub. svc. dir. Prodr.: (TV series) Best Talk in Town; contbr. articles to mags. V.p. pub. affairs Health and Hosps. Corp., N.Y.C., 1992. Recipient STAR award, N.Y. Women's Agenda, Emmy award, Broadcaster's award, N.Y. State, Folio award. Office: El Diario La Prensa 345 Hudson St 13th Fl New York NY 10014

ROSADO, SHARON L. marketing professional; b. N.Y.C., June 4, 1961; d. Bernice Silverman and Harold Linderman. AA, Kingsborough C.C., Bklyn., 1980. Trade mktg. mgr. Jaret Internat. (CS) Inc., Iselin, NJ, 1996—.

ROSALES, SANDRA JOHNSON, school system administrator; b. Riverside, Calif., June 21, 1944; d. William Emory Johnson and Mildred Alice (Alford) Wimer; m. Wynn Neal Huffman, Feb., 1962 (div. May 1967); 1 child, Kristen Lee; m. Steven Jack Herrera, June, 1985 (div. Dec. 1997); m. Mario Rosales, Sept. 22, 2000. AS in Purchasing Mgmt., Fullerton Coll., 1983; BSBA, U. Redlands, 1985, MA in Mgmt., 1988. Sr. purchasing clk Fullerton (Calif.) Union High Sch. Dist., 1969-77, buyer, 1977-79, coord. budgets and fiscal affairs, 1979-83; asst. dir. fin. svcs. Downey (Calif.) Unified Sch. Dist., 1983-85; dir. acctg. Whittier (Calif.) Union High Sch. Dist., 1985-89; asst. supt. bus. Whittier City Sch. Dist., 1989-91, Oxnard Elem. Sch. Dist., 1991—. Cons. Heritage Dental Lab., El Toro, Calif, 1981-97. Spl. dep. sheriff Santa Barbara (Calif.) County Sheriff's Mounted Posse, 1986-90; spl. dep. marshal U.S. Marshals Posse, LA, 1987-95. Mem. Calif. Assn. Sch. Bus. Ofcls. (treas. S.E. sect. 1985, mem. acct. R & D com. 1983-89, chief bus. ofcls. com. 1989-92), So. Calif. Paraders Assn. (exec. sec. 1976-97), Calif. State Horsemens Assn. (regional v.p. 1986-87, sec. 1988), Alpha Gamma Sigma. Avocations: horseback riding, golf, reading, micro-computers, model trains. Office: Oxnard Elem Sch Dist 1051 S A St Oxnard CA 93036-7442 Home: 1900 Muirfield Dr Oxnard CA 93036-7736

ROSALES, SUZANNE MARIE, hospital coordinator; b. Merced, Calif., July 23, 1946; d. Walter Marshall and Ellen Marie (Earl) Potter; children: Anita Carol, Michelle Suzanne. AA, City Coll., San Francisco, 1966. Diplomate Am. Coll. Utilization Review Physicians. Utilization review coord. San Francisco Gen. Hosp., 1967-74; mgr. utilization review/discharge planning UCLA Hosp. and Clinics, 1974-79; nurse III Hawaii State Hosp., Kaneohe, 1979-80; review coord. Pacific Profl. Std. Review Orgn., Honolulu, 1980-81; coord. admission and utilization reviewq The Rehab. Hosp. of the Pacific, Honolulu, 1981-85; coord. Pacific Med. Referral Project, Honolulu, 1985-87; dir. profl. svcs. The Queen's Healthcare Plan, Honolulu, 1987-88; utilization mgmt. coord. Vista Psychiat. Physician Assocs., San Diego, 1989; admission coord. utilization review San Francisco Gen. Hosp., 1989-91, quality improvement coordinator, 1991—. Cons. Am. Med. Records Assn. Contbr. articles to profl. jours. Mem. Nat. Assn. Utilization Review Profls. Home: 138 Alta Vista Way Daly City CA 94014-1402 Office: San Francisco Gen Hosp 1001 Potrero Ave San Francisco CA 94110-3594

ROSALSKY, BARBARA ELLEN, artist, home health aide; b. N.Y.C., Nov. 16, 1948; d. Ellis M. Rosalsky and Claire (Schwartz) Rosalsky Shapiro; m. Dennis Robinson. BA, SUNY, Plattsburgh, 1970. Sales girl Cambridge (Mass.) Artist mag., 1970-71; artist Pillar of Fire mag., Zarephath, N.J., 1977; home health aide CMR, Bound Brook, N.J., 1978—; designer New Brunswick (N.J.) Tomorrow, 1980-87; art therapist Middlesex Hosp., New Brunswick, 1981-83. One-woman shows include The Bird and Me, 1980, Highland Pk. (N.J.) Libr., 2003, The City, 2003, exhibited in group shows at Other Artists Other Art, 1983. Mem. Cultural Arts Commn., Piscataway, N.J., 1993—. SUNY Plattsburgh scholar, 1970. Mem. Women's Caucus Art, Marriott Swim Club. Democrat. Avocations: piano, swimming, dance, hiking, print making. Home: 114 Woodland Rd Piscataway NJ 08854-4222

ROSATI, ALLISON, newscaster; b. Dover, Del., 1963; married; 4 children. Grad. Speech and Comms. cum laude, Gustavus Adolphus Coll., 1985. Gen. assignment reporter Sta. KTTC-TV, Rochester, Minn., 1985, prodr., co-anchor of 6 pm and 10 pm newscasts, 1986—87; gen. assignment reporter Sta. WGRZ-TV, Buffalo, 1987, anchor 6 pm and 10 pm newscasts; anchor, reporter NBC 5, Chgo., 1990—97, co-anchor 10 pm newscast, 1997—, co-anchor weekday 6 pm newscast. Active Big Brothers/Big Sisters; bd. dirs., organizer Bowl for Kids and Celebrity Golf Outing; active Greater Chgo. Food Depository, March of Dimes, Salvation Army, Ronald McDonald House. Recipient 1st Decade award for Most Accomplished Alumna of the Decade, Gustavus Adolphus Coll., Nat. Emmy award, Excellence in Comms. award, Justinian Soc. Chgo., David award for Achievement in Broadcasting, Joint Civic Com. Italian Ams., Dante award, 2001. Office: NBC 454 N Columbus Dr Chicago IL 60611

ROSCHER, NINA MATHENY, chemistry educator; b. Uniontown, Pa., Dec. 8, 1938; d. Charles Kenneth and Wilma Pauline (Solomon) Matheny; m. David Roscher, Dec. 27, 1964. BS in Chemistry, U. Del., 1960; PhD in Chemistry, Purdue U., 1964. Phys. chemist Nat. Bur. of Standards, 1958-61; rsch. and teaching asst. Purdue U., West Lafayette, Ind., 1960-64, fellow in chemistry, instr. chemistry, 1964-65; instr. U. Tex., Austin, 1965-67; sr. staff chemist Coca-Cola Export Corp., 1967-68; asst. prof. Douglass Coll., Rutgers U., The State U., 1968-74, asst. dean, 1971-74; dir. acad. adminstrn. Am. U., Washington, 1974-76, assoc. prof. chemistry, 1974-79, prof., 1979—, assoc. dean grad. affairs Coll. Arts and Scis., 1976-79, vice-provost acad. svcs., 1979-82, vice provost for acad. affairs, 1982-85, dean faculty affairs, 1981-85, chair chemistry dept., 1991—. Program dir. sci. edn., NSF, 1986-98; lectr. in field. Contbr. articles to profl. jours. Recipient Disting. Alumna award Purdue Univ. Sch. Sci., 1996, Am. Chem. Soc. award for encouraging women into careers in the chem. scis. Camille and Henry Dreyfus Found., 1996, Presdl. Award for Excellence in Sci., Math. and Engring. Mentoring, 1998; Standard Oil fellow, 1961-62, David Ross fellow, 1963-64, Rutgers U. Rsch. Fund, Biomed. Support grantee. Fellow AAAS, Am. Inst. Chemists (profl. opportunities for women com., pres. dist. inst. chemists 1978-79, sec. 1976-77, fin. com. 1983-87, exec. com., bd. dirs. 1986), Assn. Women in Sci., Am. Chem. Soc. (treas. Monmouth County sect. 1970-72, chair 1974, pres. Washington sect. 1995, profl. programs planning and coord. com. 1976-78, admissions com. 1981-89, 91-96, GM scholar 1956-60, Virgil F. Payne award, others); mem. N.Y. Acad. Scis., AAUA, Soc. Applied Spectroscopy, Sci. Manpower Commn. Profls. in Sci. Home: 10400 Hunter Ridge Dr Oakton VA 22124-1616 Office: Am Univ Dept Chemistry Washington DC 20016-8014 E-mail: NRosche@American.edu.

ROSE, ANITA, journalist, minister; b. Marquette, Mich., Apr. 25, 1957; d. Thomas Kyle and Juanita Evelyn Hubbard; m. Robert G. Rose, Oct. 6, 2000; children: Angela, Zachary Hubbard, Thomas, John. AAS, Kaskaskia Coll., 1977; BA, East Tenn. State U., 2000. Ordained min. Ray of Hope World Min., 2002. Sales dir. Mary Kay Cosmetics, Inc., Dallas, 1977—79; broadcast sec. WETS - TV, Johnson City, Tenn., 1995—98; CEO Broken Hearts Ministries, Jonesborough, Tenn., 1996—. V.p. Soc. Profl. Journalists, E. Tenn. State U., 1996. Author: How to Get Mr. Right. Not!, 1994, Comforts in a Time of Storm, 1997, Dear Broken Hearts, 2001. Team mem. Presdl. Prayer Team, Orange, Calif., 2001—04; GOP team leader Rep. Nat. Com., Washington, 2000—04; prayer team mem. Guideposts Mag., N.Y.C., 2002—. Named Famous Poet, Hollywood Famous Poets Soc., 2001, Internat. Libr. of Poetry Bash Winner, 2001; named to Internat. Libr. Poetry, 2001; recipient Famous Poet, Hollywood Famous Poets Soc., 2003, Presdl. award for Literary Excellence, Natl. Authors Registry, 2003, Editor's Choice award, Internat. Libr. Poetry, 2001, 2002, 2003. Mem.: Pi Gamma Mu (life Honors 2000), Psi Chi (life Honors 2000). Avocation: travel. Home: 490 Sand Valley Rd Jonesborough TN 37659 Office: Broken Hearts Ministries PO Box 495 Jonesborough TN 37659 Personal E-mail: therosebuds@cs.com. Business E-Mail: brokenheartsinc@cs.com.

ROSE, ANITA CARROLL, retired educator; b. New Bedford, Mass., Oct. 14, 1922; d. Louis Arthur and Aline (Chicoine) Carroll; m. Anthony E. Rose, Sept. 24, 1955 (dec.); children: Anthony David, Stephen Arthur. BA, U. Mass., Dartmouth, 1971; MAT, R.I. Coll., 1975. Exec. sec. Berkshire-Hathaway, Inc., New Bedford, 1941—55, New Bedford Cancer Soc., 1956-59; tchr. French and English New Bedford Pub. Schs., 1971-88; ret., 1988. Clk. Friends of Coastline Elderly Svcs., Inc., 1991-93; bd. dirs. Our Lady's Haven, 1995—. Pres. New Bedford Jr. Women's Club, 1950-51, Fairhaven Mothers' Club, 1967-69, book chmn., 1989-91, sunshine chmn., 1991-93, nominating com. chmn., 1993—; v.p. Cath. Women's Club, 1957-59, del. Coun. of Women's Orgns., 1989-91; active Fairhaven Town Mtg., Mass., 1965—; trustee Millicent Libr., Fairhaven, 1980—; rec. sec. Fairhaven Improvement Assn., 1982-99; sec. Fairhaven Rep. Town Com., 1980—; bd. dirs. St. Anne Credit Union, New Bedford, 1988—, asst. treas., investment com. 1991-93, pres., chmn. bd., 1993—; adv. coun. Coastline Elderly Svc. Inc., 1988-92; del. Mass. Rep. Conv., 1974, 82, 86, 90, 94, 98; mem Old Dartmouth Hist. Assn., Friends of the Zeiterion Theatre, Friends New Bedford Festival Theatre. Testimonial dinner in her honor for years of cmty. svc. Fairhaven Improvement Assn., 1997. Mem. AAUW (pres. Coll. Club New Bedford 1983-85, 1st v.p. 1989-91, del. nat. conv. 1981, 83, 85, 93, chmn. nominating com. Mass. divsn. 1988-90, chmn. art study group 1992—, honored Mass. chpt. 1986), Tri-County Music Assn. (pres. 1992-95, bd. dirs. 1988—), R.I. Coll. Alumni Assn., U. Mass.-Dartmouth Alumni Assn., Libr. Assocs. U. Mass.-Dartmouth, Ret. Officers Assn., Am. Ex-Prisoners of War, St. Joseph's Couples Club (pres. 1987-88, 2001-02), Fairhaven Colonial Club (2d v.p. 1988-89), MONETA Assocs. Investment Club (chmn. 1998-99), Republican Club Southeastern Mass., Greater New Bedford Garden Club, Friends of Buttonwood Park Zoo. Avocations: travel, music, theater. Home: 49 Laurel St Fairhaven MA 02719-2817 E-mail: fairhavenacr@msn.com.

ROSE, BONNIE LOU, state official; b. Philipsburg, Pa., Feb. 24, 1951; d. Wasil and Ethel Louise (Crain) Harsomchuck; m. James Edward Rose, Aug. 31, 1975 (sept. 1981); m. Geoffrey Alan Clarke, Oct. 23, 1998. Student, Harrisburg Area Community Coll, 1969-70; diploma, Harrisburg Hosp. Sch. Nursing, 1972; postgrad., Pa. State U., 1987. RN, Pa. Charge nurse Plasmapheresis Ctr., Harrisburg, Pa., 1973-75, Longterm Care Facility, Harrisburg, Pa., 1975; nurse Oral Surgery Practice, Harrisburg, Pa., 1975; nurse, utilization review Pa. Dept. Pub. Welfare, Harrisburg, 1975-79; chief planning, implementation Pa. Dept. Pub. Welfare, Office Med. Assistance, Harrisburg, 1979-83, dir. provider inquiry, 1983-87, dir. provider rels., 1987, dir. long term care provider svcs., 1989—. Cons. in field; instr. Pa. Dept. Pub. Welfare, 1985—, stress mgmt., 1985—, burnout, 1986—, facilitator-orgnl. devel., 1987—, team building, 1992—. Mem. Harrisburg Hosp. Alumni Assn. Avocations: golf, reading, cooking, crafts. Home: 1704 Creek Vista Dr New Cumberland PA 17070-2212

ROSE, BRITA MAY, web site designer, writer, peace activist; b. Cuffley, Hertfordshire, Great Britain and Northern Ireland, Aug. 9, 1964; arrived in U.S., 1990; d. John Harold and Irene Evelyn Burden; m. Wesley Anthony Rose, Jan. 19, 1961. BA in History/Philosophy with honors, CUNY, Bklyn., 1997. Dir. Athenaclassicdesigns, Bklyn., 2000—. Web site designer Bklyn Coll., 1997—. Vol. animal rescuer, Bklyn., 1995—2002; bd. of deacons The Village Ch., Greenwich Village, NY, 1997—2002; bd. dirs. So. Exposure Relief Org., N.Y.C., 1999—2000. Scholar Ford Colloquium scholar, Bklyn Coll., 1994—96, Judith Rothenberg scholar, 1996—97. Mem.: ASPCA, Nat. Campaign for Tolerance (cert. of tolerance), Mid. East Web, Defenders of Wildlife, Golden Key. Liberal. Avocations: travel, horseback riding, dance, music. Personal E-mail: britamayrose@hotmail.com.

ROSE, DEBBIE J, music educator; d. Robert P Schliske and Helen Jean Konig; m. Randall K Rose, Aug. 19, 1952; children: Chad M, Brent A, Jeanna K. MusB, U. of Wyo., Laramie, Wyo., 1970—74. Cert. Wyoming Tchg. Wyo. Profl. Tchg. Standards Bd., 1974. K-8 music tchr. Niobrara County Sch. Dist. #1, Lusk, Wyo., 1974—. Editor: (jour.) Windsong/ Wyo. Music Educators Jour. Recipient Wyo. Music Educator of the Yr., Wyo. Music Educators Assn., 1999. Mem.: Nat. Edn. Assn. (NEA), Music Educators Nat. Conf., Delta Kappa Gamma. R-Consevative. Lutheran. Avocations: gardening, golf, reading, needlework.

ROSE, GAIL ELAINE, wholesale trade company manager; b. Chgo., Sept. 14, 1949; d. Edward Vincent and Ollove Lorraine (Ruska) Ruzicka. AAS, Morton Coll., 1969; BA, Nat.-Louis U., Evanston, Ill., 1984. Dental asst. Merrill Shepro, DDS, LaGrange Park, Ill., 1968-71; dental asst. instr. Morton Coll., Cicero, Ill., 1969-71; dental asst. Bernard C. Marker DDS, Niles, Ill., 1971-73; adminstrv. asst. KYB Corp. Am., Oak Brook, Ill., 1973-78, adminstrv. mgr. Lombard, Ill., 1978-87, dir. adminstrv. dept., 1987-90, v.p. adminstrn., 1990-99, KYB Am. LLC, Addison, Ill., 1999—. Mem., assoc. Ill. Sheriffs' Assn., 1982—; mem. Rep. Nat. Com., Washington, 1980—. Mem. Women of Moose. Roman Catholic. Avocations: physical fitness, bicycling, reading. Office: KYB America LLC 140 N Mitchell Ct Addison IL 60101-1490

ROSE, JOANNA SEMEL, cultural activist; b. Orange, NJ, Nov. 22, 1930; d. Philip Ephraim and Lillian (Mindlin) Semel; m. Daniel Rose, Sept. 16, 1956; children: David S., Joseph B., Emily, Gideon G. Cert., Shakespeare Inst., U.K., 1951; BA summa cum laude, Bryn Mawr Coll., 1952; postgrad., St. Hilda's Coll., Oxford U., 1953. Mem. exec. com. Am. Friends of St. Hilda's Coll., former chmn.; former pres. bd. dirs., current bd. dirs. Paper Bag Players, NYC; former bd. dir., current mem. adv. coun. Poets and Writers, Inc., NYC; former chmn. adv. bd. Partisan Rev., NYC; former bd. dir., current mem. adv. coun. Nat. Dance Inst., NYC. Bd. dir. Bay St. Theatre, Sag Harbor, Am. Friends Jewish Mus. Greece; assoc. fellow Berkeley Coll. Yale U.; mem. NY Inst. for the Humanities. Former bd. dirs. Eldridge St. Project, N.Y.C. Mem. Cosmopolitan Club, Bryn Mawr Club of NY, LVIS East Hampton. Home: 895 Park Ave New York NY 10021-0327 also: 1 Lily Pond Ln East Hampton NY 11937

ROSE, JOANNE W. rating service executive; BA in Polit. Sci. and History magna cum laude, U. Rochester; JD, Columbia U. Assoc. White & Case, N.Y.C.; sr. mng. dir., gen. counsel Standard & Poor's Rating Svcs. divsn. McGraw Hill, N.Y.C., 1989—99, chair rating policy bd.; exec. mng. dir., structured fin. ratings Standard & Poor's, N.Y.C., 1999—. Office: Standard & Poors 55 Water St New York NY 10041-0003*

ROSE, JODI, opera company founder and artistic director; b. Phila., Nov. 27, 1952; d. Hubert Michael and Rita Gervase (Schubert) Rosenberger; m. Edward A. Caycedo; children: Gervase-Teresa, Thomas Schubert, Tanya-Katrina, Edward-Michael. Student, Vienna (Austria) Hochshule, 1973; BS in Edn. and Music, Chestnut Hill Coll., Phila., 1974; postgrad. in performing arts, NYU, 1976-77. Leading roles in 35 musicals or operas throughout country, U.S. and Europe, 1974-87; founder, artistic dir. Opera on the Go, Ltd., 1988—. Produced, staged and choreographed many children's and adult operas, including Goldilocks, Little Red Riding Hood, The Tortoise and the Hare, The Pirate Captains, Telephone, Sweet Betsy from Pike, The Medium, and La Pizza Con Funghi. Founder, dir. musical theater workshops for youth, Queens Theater, N.Y., 1993—2002 Recipient numerous cmty. and corp. grants, as well as grants from N.Y. State Coun. on Arts; selected as guest performers at Lincoln Ctr., N.Y.C.; recipient 8-yr. grant N.Y.C. Dept. Youth Svcs. Republican. Roman Catholic. Avocations: ballroom dancing, scuba diving, water skiing, swimming, horseback riding. Office: 603 Delavan Ave Margate City NJ 08402

ROSE, JOY H. playwright, poet; b. Phila., May 24, 1927; d. Abraham Eliazer and Deborah (Feinberg) Hurshman; m. Bernard Rose, June 20, 1948; children: Joan Rose Easley, Linda Rose Hallowell. BA, Temple U., 1950, MFA, 1983. Co-owner, mgr. Roses' Newstand, Media, Pa., 1962-87; mng. dir. Rose and Swan Theater, Media, 1988-93. Author of 5 chap books of poetry; plays include This Is My Land, No Lovers To Scare, Sweet Vibella, Atlantis, In The Shadow of The Liberty Bell, Aunt Bessy and the Ghost of Tomasso, The Dowry. Tchr. Russel Sch. Broomall, Pa., 1992, home-schoolers, Delaware County, 1994; tchr./storyteller, Media Fellowship House, Media, 1995. Recipient prize for short story, Woman's Clubs of Delaware County, 1962, Cmty. Svc. award Media, 1989, Emma Lazarus award Shalom Aleichem Club, Phila., 1954; winner Twin City Sister award Pew Found., 1996; tied 1st place Pa. State Med. Sch., Hershey, 1994. Mem. Theatre Assn. of Pa., Delco Poets Co-op, Phila. Dramatist's Ctr. Jewish. Avocations: designing doll clothes, sketching, gardening, reading, knitting.

ROSE, LEATRICE, artist, educator; b. N.Y.C., June 22, 1924; d. Louis Rose and Edna Ades; m. Sol Greenberg (div.); children: Damon, Ethan; m. Joseph Stefanelli, Oct. 10, 1975. Student, Cooper Union, 1941-45, Arts Students League, 1946, Hans Hoffman Sch., 1947. Solo exhbns. include Hansa Gallery, N.Y.C., 1954, Zabriskie Gallery, N.Y.C., 1965, Landmark Gallery, N.Y.C., 1974, Tibor de Nagy Gallery, N.Y.C., 1975, 78, 81, 82, Elaine Benson Gallery, Bridgehampton, N.Y., 1980, Armstrong Gallery, N.Y.C., 1985, Benton Gallery, Southampton, N.Y., 1987, Cyrus Gallery, N.Y.C., 1989; group exhbns. include Sam Kootz Gallery, N.Y.C., 1950, Peridot Gallery, N.Y.C., 1952, Poindexter Gallery, N.Y.C., 1959, Tanager Gallery, N.Y.C., 1960, 62, Riverside Mus., N.Y.C., 1964, Frumkin Gallery, N.Y.C., 1964, Pa. Acad. Fine Arts, Phila., 1966, N.Y. Cultural Ctr., 1973, The Queens (N.Y.) Mus., 1974, 83, Nat. Acad. Design, N.Y.C., 1974, 75, 76, 92, 93, Weatherspoon Art Gallery, Greensboro, N.C., 78, 81, Whitney Mus. Am. Art, N.Y.C., 1978, Albright-Knox Gallery, Buffalo, 1978, 81, Met. Mus. Art, 1979, Vanderwoude Tananbaum Gallery, N.Y.C., 1982, Benton Gallery, 1986, 87.; public collections include Albrect Gallery, St. Joseph, Mo., Guild Hall Mus., East Hampton, N.Y., Tibor de Nagy, Met. Mus. Art. Grantee N.Y. State Coun. Arts, 1974, The Ingram Merrill Found., 1974, AAUW, 1975, NEA, 1977, Esther and Aldolph Gottlieb Found., 1980, 88; recipient Altman prize NAD, 1974, Phillips prize NAD, 1992, award AAAL, 1992, Am. Inst. Art award. Mem. NAD. Avocations: reading, walking. Office: 463 West St Apt A924 New York NY 10014-2038*

ROSE, MARY ETTA, retired educator; b. Indpls., Oct. 3, 1917; d. Robert and Florence Etta (Brooking) Taylor; divorced, 1972. BS, Ball State U., 1937; MS, Butler u., 1947; DHL, Martin U., Indpls., 1995. Tchr. music Indpls. Pub. Schs., 1943-88. Choir dir., organist Bethel African Methodist Episcopal Ch., Indpls., 1942-64; organist, choir dir. Witherspoon Presbyn. Ch., Indpls., 1978—. Martin Luther King Human Rights award Indpls. Edn. Assn., 1987. Mem. NAACP (life), AAUW, Internat. Soc. Music Educators, Ind. Ret. Tchrs. Assn., Nat. Coun. Negro Women, Ctr. for Black Music Rsch./Columbia Coll., Phi Delta Kappa (sec. 1992-94). Avocations: listening to, performing and teaching about music. Home: 6415 Chapelwood Ct Indianapolis IN 46268-4020 Office: W-PAC 5136 N Michigan Rd Indianapolis IN 46228-2337

ROSE, MERRILL, public relations counselor; b. Beaufort, N.C., Apr. 20, 1955; d. Robert Lloyd Rose and Betty Lou (Merrill) Ellis. Student, U. N.C., 1977. Reporter, editor Consumer News, Washington, 1978-79; v.p. Fraser/Assocs., Washington, 1979-82; sr. assoc. Porter/Novelli, Washington, 1982-85, v.p., 1985-87, sr. v.p., food practice leader N.Y.C., 1989-91, exec. v.p., 1990—, gen. mgr. Chgo., 1991-96; dir. Europe Porter Novelli

Internat., Brussels, 1996-98; exec. v.p. Porter Novelli, N.Y.C., 1998-2000; ind. cons., 2000—. Bd. dirs. CARE, 1991-98; bd. visitors U. N.C. Sch. Journalism, Chapel Hill, 1992—; bd. dirs. Friends of Prentice affiliate Northwestern Meml. Hosp., 1993-2000; mem. accrediting com. Accrediting Coun. for Edn. in Journalism and Comm., 1994-2000. Mem. Am. Inst. of Wine and Food, Pub. Rels. Soc. Am. Office: 43 5th Ave Apt 1N New York NY 10003-4368

ROSE, PEGGY JANE, artist, art educator, gifted education advocate; b. Plainfield, N.J., Oct. 4, 1947; d. Kenneth Earl and Mary Elizabeth (Taylor) R.; m. Byram Soli Daruwala, July 30, 1988; 1 child, Mathew Byram Daruwala. BA magna cum laude, U. Tex., Austin, 1971; BFA with distinction, Acad. of Art Coll., San Francisco, 1980; student of, Burton Silverman. With curriculum devel. com. Calif. Coll. Arts and Crafts, Oakland, 1985-86; with Walnut Creek (Calif.) Civic Arts, 1985-95; with faculty exec. com. Acad. of Art Coll., 1983-97; solo show Dragon Gallery, Mill Valley, Calif., 1987; Brenda Hall Gallery, San Francisco, 1993; featured artist Sausalito (Calif.) Art Festival, 1986; group shows U.S. Art, San Francisco, 1994; Marin open studios Marin Arts Coun., San Rafael, Calif., 1996. Art exhbn. juror, No. Calif., 1994-97; instr. painting, drawing. Editor: Resource Notebook for Teaching Gifted Children; artist (exhibitions) Mercer County Ann. Exhibit, 2003 (Juror's Choice award, West Windsor Arts Coun. award, 2003), Acad. Art Faculty Exhibits, City of Walnut Creek, 1994—97, Carmel Gallery, 1990; prin. works include include portrait and landscape paintings and commns.; author: Whistler's Pastels in Venice. Founder advocacy group Raising Exceptionally Able Children; co-chmn. G&T Resource Com., West Windsor-Plainsboro Regional Sch. Dist.; advocate gifted edn. Recipient Parent of Yr. award, NJ Assn. Gifted Children, 2002, Nat. Assn. Gifted Children. Mem.: Alamo Danville Artists Soc. (Best of Show Gold Medallion 1984), San Francisco Women Artists Gallery (Merit award 1987), N.Y. Soc. Illustrators (Lila Atcheson Wallace award), San Francisco Acad. Art Coll., Marin Soc. Artists (Grumbacher Gold Medallion awards), Arts Coun. Princeton, Audubon Artists, Pastel Soc. West Coast (signature mem., Best of Show 1996, Handell award 1996, Ferrari Color award 1997), Pastel Soc. Am. (Sauter-Margulies award 1998, Bd. Dirs. award 2003), Internat. Assn. Pastel Socs., Allied Artists Am. (signature mem., Gold Medal of Honor 2002), Calif. Art Club, Arts Coun. Princeton (Juror's Choice awards 2001, 2002), Portrait Soc. Am., Catherine Lorillard Wolf Art Club (Gold Medal of Honor 2002). Avocations: music, gifted education advocacy. Studio: 12 Perry Dr Princeton Junction NJ 08550-2803 E-mail: prose47@comcast.net.

ROSE, ROSLYN, artist; b. Irvington, N.J., May 28, 1929; d. Mark and Anne Sarah (Green) R.; m. Franklin Blou, Nov. 26, 1950; 1 child, Mark Gordon Blue (dec.). Student, Rutgers U., 1949-51, Pratt Ctr. for Contemporary, Printmaking, N.Y.C., 1969; BS, Skidmore Coll., 1976. Artist. One-woman shows include Midday Gallery, Caldwell, N.J., 1972, Caldwell Coll., 1972, Kean Coll., Union, N.J., 1973, Art Corner Gallery, Millburn, N.J., 1974, Brandeis U., Mass., 1974, Newark Mus., 1974, George Frederick Gallery, Rochester, N.Y., 1981, Robbins Gallery, Washington, 1981, Arnot Art Mus., Elmira, N.Y., 1982, Douglas Coll. Rutgers U., New Brunswick, 1987, Nathans Gallery, West Paterson, N.J., 1984, 86, 89, 97, 99, The Pen and Brush, N.Y.C., 1998, New Century Artists Gallery, N.Y.C., 2003; exhibited in group shows at Seattle Art Mus., Portland (Oreg.) Mus., NYU U., Montclair Art Mus., N.J., Women in the Arts, Florence and Naples, Italy, Art Ctr. Athens, Greece, Middlesex County Mus., Piscataway, N.J., New Century Artists, N.Y.C., Noyes Mus., Oceanville, N.J., Grounds for Sculpture, Hamilton, N.J., Mountain Art Show, Bernardsville, NJ, 2002 (Best in Show award),Manhattan Arts Internat., N.Y.C. (Artist Howcase award) 2004, J.W. Starks Galleries, Coll. Stat., Tex., 2004, others; represented in permanent collections including N.J. State Mus., Trenton, Citibank of N.Y., Moscow, N.J. State Libr., Trenton, Roddenbery Meml. Libr., Cairo, Ga., Rosenberg Libr., Galveston, Tex., Period Gallery, Omaha, (Dir. award, 2001), Cambridge Art Assn., Cambridge, Mass., Newark Mus., Newark Pub. Libr., AT&T, BASF Wyandotte Corp., First Fed. Bank, Rochester, Gulf & Western Industries, Irving Trust Co., N.Y., McAllen Internat. Mus., Tex., Nabisco Brands Corp., East Hanover, N.J., Verizon, Readers Digest Collection, Voorhees-Zimmerli Mus., Rutgers U., New Brunswick, N.J., The Noyes Mus. (study collection), Oceanville, N.J., others; featured artist New Century Artists Gallery, N.Y.C., 1998-2001, 2003, Internat. Soc. Exptl. Artists, 1999-2000; creator UNCIF cards, 1979-80. Recipient graphic award Westchester (N.Y.) Art Soc., 1973, Best-in-Show award Livingston (N.J.) Art Assn., 1971, Best-in-Show award N.J. Ctr. for Visual Arts, Summit, 1969, Mixed Media Merit award Salmagundi Club, N.Y.C., 1995, Exptl. Art award Western Colo. Art Ctr., 2000; numerous others. Mem.: Nat. Collage Soc. Inc., Collage/Assemblage Soc. NY, Internat. Soc. Exptl. Artists, N.Y. Artists Equity, Nat. Assn. Women Artists (v.p. 1997—2001, exec. bd. 2001—03, Innovative Painting award 1990, Hazel Witte Mem. Computer Art award 2003), Period Gallery (Alternative Photography award 2000, 2001), Pen and Brush Club N.Y.C. (Mixed Media award 1996, 1997, 1998, Photography award 2000, 2001, Best-in-Show award Mountain Art Show 2002). Office: Roslyn Rose Studios 321 Newark St Hoboken NJ 07030-2434 Office Phone: 201-217-9760. Business E-Mail: bluerose@roslynrose.com

ROSE, SARAH ELIZABETH, genealogist, counselor; d. H. S. Agsanian and B. M. Phillips; children: Julie, Tory, Mary, Alesandra, Vinnie, Sasha, Zachary. Grad. with honors, U.S. Army Signal Sch., 1975; grad. with distinction, Non-Commd. Officer's Leadership Acad. U.S. Army, 1977; BA in Social Sci., San Jose State U., 1980; MA in History with honors, Hawking Inst., 2004. Registered profl. geneaologist Oreg. Author: Many Branches, One Tree, 1997, World Wide Roots, 2001, Poetry: A Tribute to Life, 2003, numerous poems. With U.S. Army, 1974—77. Decorated Good Conduct medal, Nat. Def. Svc. medal; recipient Cold War Recognition Cert., U.S. Dept. Def. Mem.: Nat. Fedn. Poetry Socs., Women in Mil. Svc. for Am. (charter mem.), Pioneers of Kans., Ill. Prairie Pioneers, Am. First Families, Nat. Soc. DAR, The Winthrop Soc. (assoc.), Nat. Soc. Daus. of the Am. Colonists, Nat. Soc. Colonial Dames XVII Century, Pioneer Families Nebr., Am. Legion. Avocation: collecting Egyptian, African, Native American objects. Address: PO Box 945 Sutherlin OR 97479 Personal E-mail: genealogical2002@yahoo.com.

ROSE, SUSAN PORTER, consultant; b. Cin., Sept. 20, 1941; d. Elmer Johnson and Dorothy (Wurst) Porter; m. Jonathan Chapman Rose, Jan. 26, 1980; 1 child, Benjamin Chapman. BA, Earlham Coll., 1963; MS, Ind. State U., 1970; HDL (hon.), Rose-Hulman Inst. Tech., 2002. Staff asst. Congressman Richard L. Roudebush, Washington, 1963-64; asst. dean George Sch., Bucks County, Pa., 1964-66; asst. dir. admissions Mt. Holyoke Coll., South Hadley, Mass., 1966-71; asst. dir. correspondence First Lady (Mrs. Nixon) The White House, 1971-72, dir. of scheduling to First Lady Pat Nixon, 1972-74, to First Lady Betty Ford, 1974-77; spl. asst. to asst. atty. gen. Office Improvements in Adminstrn. Justice, Washington, 1977-79; spl. asst. to dep. asst. atty. gen. Justice Mgmt. divsn. U.S. Dept. Justice, Washington, 1978-81; chief of staff to Barbara Bush V.P. of U.S., Washington, 1981-89; dep. asst. to Pres. of U.S., chief of staff to First Lady Barbara Bush, The White House, 1989-93; commr. U.S. Commn. Fine Arts, 1993-98. Bd. dirs. Barbara Bush Found. for Family Lit.; trustee Bush Presdl. Libr.; mem. alumni coun. Earlhem Coll., 1977—78, pres. alumni assn., 1978—81. Recipient Disting. Alumni award, Earlham Coll., 1992, Ind. State U., 1991. Mem.: Ind. Acad. Home: 5955 Ranleigh Manor Dr Mc Lean VA 22101-2428

ROSE, TERESA BETH, psychologist, educator; b. Kansas City, Mo., Aug. 7, 1960; d. Raymond William Rose and Vivian Darlene Sommers. BBA, U. Mo., Kansas City, 1982, MA in Counseling and Guidance, 1995, PhD in Counseling Psychology, 1999; postgrad., Kansas City Inst. for Contemporary Psychoanalysis, 2003—. Lic. psychologist State Com. of Psychologists, Mo., 2000. Adv. mktg. rep. IBM, Kansas City, Mo., 1983—92; psychologist in tng. Kansas City, Mo., 1994—98; cons. Women's Ctr., Kansas City, Mo., 1995—96; adj. prof. U. Mo., Kansas City, 2001—; psychologist Kansas City, Mo., 1998—. Cons. Schuster Kane Alliance, Kansas City, Mo., 1999—2002; sec./treas. exec. adv. bd. Cmty. Counseling Svcs., Kansas City, Mo., 2001—. Author: (book chapter in graduate counseling text) Empathy; columnist Relationship Matters. Grantee, Women's Coun., U. Mo., 1995, 1996. Mem.: APA (psychoanalytic divsn.), Kansas City Assn. for Psychoanalytic Psychology. D-Liberal. Achievements include research in Dissertation entitled Worldview & Empathy: A Study of Police Officers. Avocations: german shepherds, travel, reading, writing. Office: Dr Teresa Rose 7 East Gregory Kansas City MO 64114 Office Phone: 816-363-9500. E-mail: drteresarose@drteresarose.com.

ROSE, VIRGINIA SHOTTENHAMER, secondary school educator; b. San Jose, Calif., Feb. 3, 1924; d. Leo E. and Mae E. (Slavich) Shottenhamer; m. Paul V. Rose, June 21, 1947; children: Paul V. Jr., David P., Alan P. AB, W. Calif., San Jose, 1945, MA, 1972. Tchr. grades 5-6 Evergreen Sch. Dist., San Jose, 1945-47; 6th grade tchr. Washington Sch., San Jose, 1947-57; elem. tchr. San Jose Unified Sch. Dist., 1967-82, reading specialist, tchr. grades 6-8, 1982-92; ret., 1992. Cons. in field; mem. project literacy San Jose Unified Schs., 1987-91; mem. instrnl. materials evaluation panel Calif. State Edpt. Edn., Sacramento, 1988; master tchr. U. Calif., San Jose, 1991. Co-author: Handbook for Teachers' Aides, 1967. Active Alexian Bros. Hosp. League, San Jose, 1965, bd. dirs., chair libr. cart, 1966-76; vol. San Jose Hist. Mus., 1992—. Mem. AAUW (com. chair 1978-81), Internat. Reading Assn., Calif. Reading Assn. (Margaret Lynch award for Outstanding Contbn. to Reading 1999), Santa Clara County Reading Coun. (pres. 1986-87, Asilomar conf. chair 1991, IRA honor coun. pres. club 1987, bd. dirs.), Santa Clara U. Calala Club (bd. dirs. 1994-96), Soroptimist Internat. (sec. 1993-94), Pi Epsilon Tau (pres. 1944-45), Kappa Delta Pi (pres. 1943-45), Pi Lambda Theta (pres. San Jose chpt. 1987-89, auditor 1980, sec. 1985-86, Biennium award 1987). Avocations: reading, hiking, biking, gardening, cooking. Office: Willow Glen Ed Park S 2001 Cottle Ave San Jose CA 95125-3502

ROSE-ACKERMAN, SUSAN, law and political economy educator; b. Mineola, N.Y., Apr. 23, 1942; d. R. William and Rosalie Rose; m. Bruce A. Ackerman, May 29, 1967; children: Sybil, John. BA, Wellesley Coll., 1964; PhD, Yale U., 1970. Asst. prof. U. Pa., Phila, 1970-74; lectr. Yale U., New Haven, Conn., 1974-75, asst. prof., 1975-78, assoc. prof., 1978-82; prof. law and polit. economy Columbia U., N.Y.C., 1982-87; Ely prof. of law and polit. econ. Yale U., New Haven, 1987-92, co-dir. Ctr. Law, Econ. and Pub. Policy, 1988—, Luce prof. jurisprudence law and polit. sci., 1992—. Vis. rsch. fellow World Bank, 1995-96. Author: (with Ackerman, Sawyer and Henderson) Uncertain Search for Environmental Quality, 1974 (Henderson prize 1982); Corruption: A Study in Political Economy, 1978; (with E. James) The Nonprofit Enterprise in Market Economies, 1986; editor: The Economics of Nonprofit Institutions, 1986, (with J. Coffee and L. Lowenstein) Knights, Raiders, and Targets: The Impact of the Hostile Takeover, 1988, Rethinking the Progressive Agenda: The Reform of the American Regulatory State, 1992, Controlling Environmental Policy: The Limits of Public Law in Germany and the United States, 1995, Corruption and Government: Causes, Consequences and Reform, 1999 (Levine Prize 2000), (with Janos Kornai) Building a Trustworthy State in Post-Socialist Transition, 2004, (with Kornai and B. Rothstein) Creating Social Trust in Post-Socialist Transition, 2004; contbr. articles to profl. jours.; bd. editors: Jour. Law, Econs. and Orgn., 1984—, Internat. Rev. Law and Econs., 1986—, Jour. Policy Analysis and Mgmt., 1989—, Polit. Sci. Quar., 1988—. Guggenheim fellow 1991-92, Fulbright fellow, Free U. Berlin, 1991-92; fellow Ctr. for Advanced Study in the Behavioral Scis., Stanford, Calif., 2002, Collegium Budapest, 2002. Mem. Am. Law and Econs. Assn. (bd. dirs. 1993-96, 2002-), Am. Econ. Assn. (mem. exec. com. 1990-93), Am. Polit. Sci. Assn., Assn. Am. Law Schs., Assn. Pub. Policy and Mgmt. (policy coun. 1984-88, treas. 1998-2000). Democrat. Office: Yale U Law Sch PO Box 208215 New Haven CT 06520-8215

ROSEANNE, (ROSEANNE BARR), actress, comedienne, television producer, writer; b. Salt Lake City, Nov. 3, 1952; d. Jerry and Helen Barr; m. Bill Pentland, 1974 (div. 1989); children: Jessica, Jennifer, Brandi, Buck, Jake; m. Tom Arnold, 1990 (div. 1994); m. Ben Thomas, 1994. Former window dresser, cocktail waitress; prin. Full Moon & High Tide Prodns., Inc. As comic, worked in bars, church coffeehouse, Denver; produced showcase for women performers Take Back the Mike, U. Boulder (Colo.); performer The Comedy Store, L.A.; showcased on TV special Funny, 1986, also The Tonight Show; featured in HBO-TV spl. On Location: The Roseanne Barr Show, 1987 (Am. comedy award Funniest Female Performer in TV spl., 1987, Ace award Funniest Female in Comedy, 1987, Ace award Best Comedy Spl. 1987); writer, dir., star of TV series Roseanne ABC, 1988-97 (U.S. Mag. 2nd Ann. Readers Poll Best Actress in Comedy Series, 1989, Golden Globe nomination Outstanding Lead Actress in Comedy Series 1988, Emmy award Outstanding Lead Actress in Comedy Series, 1993), The Real Roseanne Show, 2003; actress: (motion pictures) She-Devil, 1989, Look Who's Talking Too (voice), 1990, Freddy's Dead, 1991, Even Cowgirls Get the Blues, 1994, Blue in the Face, 1995, Unzipped, 1995, Meet Wally Sparks, 1997, Home on the Range (voice), 2004; TV movies: Backfield in Motion, The Woman Who Loved Elvis, 1993; appeared in TV spl. Sinatra: 80 Years My Way, 1995; exec. prodr. Saturday Night Spl., Fox-TV; author: Roseanne: My Life as a Woman, 1989, My Lives, 1994; (host) Roseanne Show, 1998-2000, I am Your Child, 1997 (TV), Get Bruce, 1999. Active various child advocate orgns. Recipient Peabody award, People's Choice award (4), Golden Globe award (2), Am. Comedy award, Humanitas award, Nickelodeon Kids Choice award, 1990, Eleanor Roosevelt award for Outstanding Am. Women, Emmy award, 1993.

ROSEBROUGH, CAROL BELVILLE, cable television company executive; b. Ironton, Ohio, June 5, 1940; d. Lindsey and Bessie (Reed) Belville; m. John R. Rosebrough, Mar. 4, 1960 (dec. Nov. 1974); children: G. Suzanne, John R., Rebecca J. Student, Columbia (Mo.) Coll., 1958-59; BSBA, Franklin U., 1985. Cons. CBR and Assocs., Columbus, 1978-82; dir. adminstrn. United Cerebral Palsy Columbus and Franklin County, 1972-82; bus. mgr. Times Mirror, Newark, Ohio, 1982-83, ops. mgr., 1983-85, gen. mgr. Logan/Waverly/Greenfield, Ohio, 1985-86, Times Mirror doing bus. as Dimension Cable Svcs., Marion, Ohio, 1986-88; v.p., gen. mgr. Cable TV div. Susquehanna Comms. (formerly Times Mirror and Cox Comms.), Williamsport, Pa., 1988—. Fllow Betsy Magness Leadership Inst., 1999—. Bd. dirs United Way, Marion County, 1987-88, Lycoming County, 1989-2000, 2001-, Williamsport/Lycoming C. of C.; personal and bus. coach Coach U., 2002. Named one of Pa.'s Best 50 Women in Bus., 1997, One of Top 100 Bus. Persons in the State of Pa., 1997-99; fellow Betsy Magness Leadership Inst. 1999-2000, Pa. Economy League 2003—. Mem. Ohio Cable TV Assn. (bd. dirs. 1986-88), Pa. Cable TV Assn. (bd. dirs. 1990-96), Pa. Edn. Comms. Sys. (bd. dirs.), Pa. Rural Devel. Coun. (exec. com. telecomms. task force 1992-95), Mid-Ohio Regional Planning Commn. (transp. com. 1980-82), Internat. Women's Writers Guild, Internat. Assn. Counselors and Therapists. Avocations: writing, reading, music, arts/therapies. Office: Susquehanna Comms 330 Basin St Williamsport PA 17701-5216 Personal E-mail: carolcrosebrough@suscom.net. Business E-Mail: crosebro@suscom.com.

ROSELL, SHARON LYNN, physics and chemistry educator, researcher; b. Wichita, Kans., Jan. 6, 1948; d. John E. and Mildred C. (Binder) Rosell. BA, Loretto Heights Coll., 1970; postgrad., Marshall U., 1973; MS in Edn., Ind. U., 1977; MS, U. Wash., 1988. Cert. profl. educator, Wash. Assoc. instr. Ind. U., Bloomington, 1973-74; instr. Pierce Coll. (name formerly Ft. Steilacoom (Wash.) Community Coll.), 1976-79, 82, Olympic Coll., Bremerton, Wash., 1977-78; instr. physics, math. and chemistry Tacoma (Wash.) Community Coll., 1979-89; instr. physics and chemistry Green River Community Coll., Auburn, Wash., 1983-86; researcher Nuclear Physics Lab., U. Wash., Seattle, 1986-88; asst. prof. physics Cen. Wash. U., Ellensburg, 1989—. Faculty senate Ctrl. Washington U., 1992-98. Lector and dir. Rite of Christian Initiation of Adults, St. Andrew's Ch., Ellensburg, Wash., 1993—, mem. parish coun., 1995-2000. Mem. Am. Phys. Soc., Am. Assn. Physics Tchrs. (rep. com. on physics for 2-yr. colls. Wash. chpt. 1986-87, v.p. 1987-88, 94-95, pres. 1988-89, 95-96, past pres. 1996-97), Am. Chem. Soc., Internat. Union Pure and Applied Chemistry (affiliate), Pacific Northwest Assn. Coll. Physics (bd. dirs. 1997-99, 2001—, treas. 2002—), Soc. Physics Students (councilor zone 17 1998—). Democrat. Roman Catholic. Avocations: leading scripture discussion groups, reading, writing poetry, needlework. Home: 1100 N B St Apt 2 Ellensburg WA 98926-2570 Office: Ctrl Wash U Physics Dept Ellensburg WA 98926 E-mail: rosells@cwu.edu.

ROSEMBERG, EUGENIA, physician, educator, medical research administrator; b. Buenos Aires, Apr. 25, 1918; came to U.S., 1948, naturalized, 1956; d. Pedro and Fanny (Hestrin) R. BS, Liceo Nacional de Senoritas, Buenos Aires, 1936; MD, U. Buenos Aires, 1944. Intern Hosp. Pirovano, Buenos Aires, 1940-41; resident Hosp. Nacional de Clinicas, U. Hosp., U. Buenos Aires, 1941-44, assoc. in pediatrics, 1943-48; instr. in anatomy Hosp. Nacional de Clinicas, U. Hosp., U. Buenos Aires (Med. Sch.), 1940-46, instr. pediatrics, 1946-48; practice medicine specializing in pediatrics, 1946-48; research in endocrinology, 1948-51, Worcester, Mass., 1955—; Mead Johnson fellow dept. endocrinology Johns Hopkins Med. Sch., Balt., 1948-49; vis. scientist Med. Sch., U. Montevideo, Uruguay, 1950; research fellow NIH, Bethesda, Md., 1951-53, Nat. Inst. Arthritis and Metabolic Diseases, 1951-53, Med. Research Inst. and Hosp., Oklahoma City, 1953; mem. staff Worcester Found. Exptl. Biology, Shrewsbury, Mass., 1953-62; research dir. Med. Research Inst. of Worcester, Inc., 1962—; cons. Center for Population Research, Nat. Inst. Child Health and Human Devel., NIH, 1969-70, chief contraceptive devel. br., 1970-71; prof. pediatrics U. Md. Hosp., Balt., 1970-73; prof. medicine U. Mass. Med. Sch., Worcester, 1972—; mem. staff Worcester City Hosp., 1955-85, sec. human experimentation com., 1965-83, chmn., 1984-85, dir. clin. research, 1972-85. Sec. subcom. on gonadotropins Nat. Hormone and Pituitary Program, Nat. Inst. Arthritis, Diabetes, Digestive and Kidney Diseases, 1965-69, chmn., 1969-85, mem. med. adv. bd., 1969-72, 73-85, sec. subcom. on standards endocrinology study sect., 1968 Author: Gonadotropins, 1968, (with C.A. Paulsen) The Human Testis, 1970, Gonadotropin Therapy in Female Infertility, 1973, (with C. Gual) Hypothalamic Hypophysiotropic Hormones—Physiological and Clinical Studies, 1973; Mem. editorial bd.: Giner, 1970—, Procs. 1st Ann. Meeting Am. Soc. Andrology, supplement, Vol. 8, 1976, Andrologia, 1978—, Jour. Andrology, 1979-82, Internat. Jour. Andrology, 1978—; assoc. editor: Reproduccion, 1970—, Andrologia jour, 1974-77; Contbr. articles and book chpts. on research in endocrinology to med. texts and jours.; Translator: from Spanish Diagnosis and Treatment of Endocrine Disorders in Childhood and Adolescence (L. Wilkins). Patentee in field, U.S., Can., Europe. Fellow AAAS; mem. Am. Med. Women's Assn., Endocrine Soc. U.S. (mem. com. pub. affairs 1971, v.p. 1975-76), Soc. for Research in Biology of Reproduction, Soc. for Study of Reproduction, Am. Fertility Soc., Peru Fertility Soc. (fgn. corr.), N.Y. Acad. Scis., New Eng. Cardiovascular Soc., Am., Mass. heart assns., Argentine Endocrine Soc., Argentine Pediatric Soc., Sociedad Argentine Para El Estudio de la Esterilidad., Pan Am. Med. Women's Alliance, Am. Soc. Andrology (program chmn. 1975-76, exec. council 1976-78, chmn. publ. com. 1975-80, Disting. Andrologist award 1982), Internat. Com. for Study Andrology (exec. council 1976-79)

ROSEN, ADRIENNE, artist, educator; b. St. Louis, Dec. 18, 1940; d. Charles and Rena Gallop; m. Alex Paul Tucker, June 21, 1961 (dec. June 1965); children: Michele Lori Tucker, Valerie Joy Tucker, Alex Paul II Tucker; m. Martin M. Rosen, Dec. 1967; 1 child, Marissa Angele. BFA, Washington U., St. Louis, 1972. Illustrator, designer Internat. Shoe Co., St. Louis, 1961; owner, illustrator, graphic designer A.R. Art Studio, St. Louis, 1961—; painter portraits of people and pets St. Louis, 1995—. Art tchr. St. Louis Artist Guild; art tchr. Coll. for Kids program Meramec C.C.; pvt. instr. Designer, illustrator (dolls) Bethany Farms Inc., 1990—. Vol. artist Leukemia Soc. Am., St. Louis, 1999, Animal Aid, St. Louis, 1975, Am. Med. Ctr., St. Louis, Cystic Fibrosis Found.; vol. St. Louis Showstoppers for Breast Cancer Rsch. Named Artist of Month, Ballwin, Mo., 2004; recipient 2d pl. award, Jewish Cmty. Ctrs. Assn., St. Louis, 1997, University City Art Assn., St. Louis, 1999, award of mention, South County Art Assn., St. Louis, 1998, Recognition award, Art Happening, 2001—02, 1st pl. award profl. watercolor, Jewish Cmty. Ctrs. Assn., 2002, 2003. Mem.: Greater St. Louis Art Assn. (publicity dir. 1994—99, sec. 1995—98, v.p. 1998—2000, pres. 2000—02, exhibits chair 2002—03, publicity chair 2004—), St. Louis Watercolor Soc., St. Louis Artist Guild (bd. dirs. 1993—94), Art World Art Assn. Avocations: running races, dance, photography, marathon running. Office: A R Art Studio 1717 Seven Pines Dr Saint Louis MO 63146-3713

ROSEN, ANA BEATRIZ, electronics executive; b. Guayaquil, Ecuador, May 16, 1950; came to U.S., 1962; d. Luis A. and Luz Aurora (Rodriguez) Moreira; m. Manuel Jose Farina, Dec. 15, 1979 (dec. Apr. 1990); children: Kevin Farina, Mark Farina; m. Michael G. Rosen, June 6, 1992 (dec. Oct. 2001). AA, Latin-Am. Inst., 1971. Adminstr. asst. M&T Chem. Inc., N.Y.C., 1971-75; mgr. sales Singer Products Co., N.Y.C., 1975-78; v.p. Argil Internat. Ltd., N.Y.C., 1978-83; pres. KMA Enterprises Inc., Bklyn., 1983-94, KMA Industries Inc., Palm Beach Gardens, Fla., 1994—. Mem. U.S Trade Adv. Bd.; v.p. Miro Sales, Inc. Bd. dirs. Palm Beach County chpt. ARC. Mem. ARC, World Trade Coun. (Palm Beach County), Gold Coast Bus. and Profl. Women of the Palm Beaches, County Bus. & Profl. Coun. Roman Catholic. Office Phone: 561-627-5090.

ROSEN, BETH DEE, travel agency executive; b. N.Y.C., June 27, 1945; BA, Queens Coll., 1967, MA, 1970; cert. adminstrn. and supervision, CUNY, 1982. Tchr. N.Y.C. Bd. Edn., 1967-2001; lectr. CUNY, 1971-73; pres. Uniglobe Rainbow Travel Inc., Middletown, NJ, 1982-94; dir. Uniglobe Rainbow Travel Sch., 1983-87; travel counselor Excel Travel, Middletown, NJ, 1994—2001, A-1 Tuscany Travel, 2003—. Mem. reader adv. panel Conde Nast Traveler, 1991, mem. travel agt. adv. panel, 1996—; master cruise counselor, Aussie specialist, Princess cruise expert. Columnist "The Courier" newspaper, Middletown, N.J. Avocations: birdwatching, whale watching, bell collecting.

ROSEN, CAROL MENDES, artist; b. N.Y.C., Jan. 15, 1933; d. Bram de Sola and Mildred (Bertuch) Mendes; m. Elliot A. Rosen, June 30, 1957. BA, Hunter Coll., 1954; MA, CUNY, 1962. Tchr. art West Orange (N.J.) Pub. Schs., 1959-85. Co-curator exhibit Printmaking Coun. N.J., Somerville, 1981; exhibit curator 14 Sculptors Gallery, N.Y.C., 1988; collection: Nat. Collection of Fine Arts, Smithsonian Instn., Newark Mus., N.J. State Mus., Bristol-Myers Squibb, AT&T, Noyes Mus., N.Y. Pub. Libr., Zimmerli Art Mus., Mus. of Modern Art, Whitney Mus., Yale U., Skimore, Libr. Collection Bklyn. Mus., Victoria & Albert Mus., Nat. Art Gallery, London, Mus. of Tolerance, L.A., Tel Aviv U. and The Jewish Nat. & Univ. Libr., Jerusalem, Houghton Libr., Harvard U., Clark Art Inst., Williams Coll. Mus. Art, Nat. Mus. Women in Arts, Oberlin Coll., William Paterson U., Hunterdon Mus. Art. Contbr. articles to arts mags. Recipient Hudson River Mus. award, Yonkers, 1983; fellow, N.J. State Coun. Arts, 1980, 1983. Jewish. Avocations: gardening, reading. Home: 10 Beavers Rd Califon NJ 07830-3433 E-mail: earosen@earthlink.net.

ROSEN, DEBORAH NODLER, poet, writer; b. Phila., Aug. 11, 1935; d. Daniel B. and Anne Kleiman Nodler; m. Lester Rosen; children: Alison Rosen Vogel, Jordan. BA, Wellesley Coll., 1957; JD, U. Pa., 1960. Bar: Ill. 1960. Atty. Brunswick Corp., Chgo., 1961—64; prof. bus. law YMCA C.C., Chgo., 1965—68; freelance writer and poet Chgo., 1970—; editor RHINO Poetry Jour., Chgo., 1998—. Vol. poetry tchr. in schs. Author: Anwar el-Sadat, 1986, poetry; contbr. articles to newspapers and mags. Recipient first prize, Green River Grande Poetry Contest, first pl., Conn. State Poetry Contest, 2nd pl., Ill. State Poetry Contest, 1st pl., Mo. Poetry Soc. Contest; scholar Fulbright Act, 1960; Durant scholar, Wellesley Coll., 1957. Mem.: Soc. Midland Authors, Poetry Ctr. Chgo. (bd. mem. 1988—), Wellesley Club Chgo., Phi Beta Kappa. Avocations: travel, jewelry making. Home: 650 Sycamore Ln Glencoe IL 60022

ROSEN, DIANA, writer; b. Charleroi, Pa., Aug. 4, 1944; d. David and Mae Rosen. BS in Mass. Comm./Journalism, Ariz. State U., 1966. Freelance writer, 1962—. Author: The Coffee Lover's Companion, 1997, The Book of Green Tea, 1998, CHAI: The Spice of Tea in India, 1999, The Ice Cream Lover's Companion, 2000, Taking Time for Tea, 15 Seasonal Parties Tea Parties to Soothe the Soul and Celebrate the Spirit, 2000, Essence of Incense, 2001, American Pride, 2001, Social Security for the Clueless, The Complete Guide to SSA Benefits, 2002, Fifty Jewish Women Who Changed the World, 2003; co-author: Cooking with Tea, Techniques and Recipes for Appetizers, Entrees, Desserts, and More, 2000; editor: Tea Talk, author numerous poems. Pres. Della Robbia Guild Children's Hosp., L.A., 1988. Mem.: Author's Guild. Jewish.

ROSEN, ELLEN FREDA, psychologist, educator; b. Chgo., Jan. 28, 1941; d. Samuel Aaron and Clara Laura (Pauker) R. BA, Carleton Coll., 1962; MA, U. Ill., 1965, PhD, 1968. Instr. psychology U. Ill., Urbana, 1966-67; prof. Coll. William and Mary, Williamsburg, Va., 1967-99; dean grad. studies and dir. Ctr. for Urban Mental Health Rsch. Chgo. State U., 1999—. Cons. Ctr. for Teaching Excellence Hampton (Va.) U., 1988-94; sr. rsch. scientist Behavioral Rsch. Ctr., Hampton U., 1997-99. Author: Ednl. Computer Software, (with E. Rae Harcum) The Gatekeepers of Psychology, 1993; contbr. articles to profl. jours. Mem. Am. Psychol. Soc. Office: Office Grad Studies LIB 338 Chgo State Univ Chicago IL 60628 E-mail: EF-Rosen@csu.edu.

ROSEN, HARRIET R. elementary school educator; m. Neil C. Rosen, Dec. 26, 1959; children: Cindy, Jody, Sherry. BS, Pa. State U.; postgrad., U. Pa., Mercer U., Fau-Fla. Atlantic U. Cert. middle grades 4-8. Tchr. Gwinnett County Schs., Lawrenceville, Ga., Lower Merion Sch. Dist., Ardmore, Pa., Temple Beth Israel, Sunrise, Fla., Beth Tfiloh Sch., Pikesville, Md., Am. Heritage Sch., Delray Beach, Fla. Mem. Nat. Coun. Tchrs. English, Nat. Assn. Preservation Storytellers, Nat. Jr. H.S., Profl. Assn. Gifted Educators, So. Order Storytellers (profl. storyteller). Home: 8597 Chevy Chase Dr Boca Raton FL 33433-1803

ROSEN, RHODA, obstetrician, gynecologist; b. Trenton, N.J., Jan. 17, 1933; d. Max and Gussie (Thierman) R.; m. Seymour Kanter, Aug. 19, 1956; children: Cynthia, Gregg, Larry, Brad. BA, U. Pa., 1954, MD, 1958. Diplomate Am. Bd. Obstetrics and Gynecology. Intern Albert Einstein Phila. Med. Ctr., 1958-59, resident, 1959-62, assoc. staff gynecology exec. com.; clin. prof. ob-gyn. Temple U. Med. Sch., Phila.; attending physician Rolling Hill Hosp., Elkins Park, Pa.; pvt. practice ob-gyn. Phila., 1962—. Chmn. gynpathology com. Albert Einstein Med. Ctr., Phila.; arbitrator N.Y. Stock Exch. Bd. dirs. Joseph J. Peters Inst.; docent Barnes Found., Merion, Pa. Fellow ACOG, ACS; mem. AMA, Nat. Assn. for Arbitrators for N.Y. Stock Exchange, Pa. Med. Soc., Phila. Colposcopy Soc. (past pres.), Ex-Residents Assn. (past pres. Albert Einstein Med. Ctr.), Philadelphia County Med. Soc. (com.), Phila. Bar Assn. (com.). Jewish. Avocations: bicycling, art, swimming, music. Home: 1420 Locust St Apt 35K Philadelphia PA 19102

ROSEN, ROBERTA, philosophy educator; b. Madawaska, Maine, Aug. 9, 1935; d. Bernard and Dolores (Bourgoin) Dionee; m. Frank Rosen, June 8, 1963; children: Ruth, Rachael, David, Sarah. BA, Gov. State U., University Park, Ill., 1975, MA, 1976; PhD, Walden U., 1977; postdoctoral, K.A.M.I.I. Temple. Free-lance writer, Chgo.; dir. religious edn. ASFU, Chgo.; minister All Souls 1st Universalist Soc., Chgo., 1975—95; prof. philosophy Prairie State Coll., Chicago Heights, Ill., 1976—89. Leader seminars on prevention of child abuse, 1976-1999. Author: (novel) Call Her Dolores, (children's) Johnny Linny's Nightmare; contbr. articles to religious jours. Bd. trustees Gov. State U., Unitarian-Universalist Women's Fedn. Recipient Humanitarian award, Humane Soc. award; named Best Tchr. Mem. Unitarian-Universalist Women's Assn. (life). Address: 2444 Madison Rd Apt 1004 Cincinnati OH 45208-1269

ROSEN, RUTH CHIER, retired editor-in-chief; b. Mpls., June 13, 1925; d. Maurice Charles and Esther (Bentson) C.; m. Richard Rosen (dec.); children: Richard A., Roger C. BA, Smith Coll., 1947. V.p., editor-in-chief Rosen Press, N.Y.C., 1950-90, ret., 1990. Author 40 cookbooks. Avocations: reading, travel. Home: 137 E 19th St New York NY 10003-2403

ROSEN, WENDY WORKMAN, arts management and publishing executive; b. Miami, Sept. 17, 1954; d. Robert L. and Mildred E. (Duck) Workman; m. Steven David Rosen, June 22, 1972, children: Rebecca, Jeffrey. AS, Santa Fe Coll., 1974; BS, U. Fla., 1976. Cert. exhbn. mgr. Advt. exec. Balt. News Am., 1978-80, Balt. Mag, 1980-82; pres. The Rosen Group, Inc., Balt., 1982—. Cons. Times Pub. Group, Balt., 1982; gen. ptnr. Mill Ctr. Artists Studios, Balt.; pres. Am. Craft Showroom; founder The Buyers Markets of American Crafts, founder Craft Bus. Inst. Author: Crafting as a Business, Cash For Your Crafts; pub.: Niche mag., Am. Style mag., Market Insider. Bd. mem. Craft Emergency Relief Fund. Mem. Natl. Assn. Exposition Mgrs., Glass Art Soc. Democrat. Jewish. Avocation: gardening. Office: The Rosen Agy 3000 Chestnut Ave Ste 300 Baltimore MD 21211-2769

ROSENBAUM, BELLE SARA, appraiser, interior designer, museum director, educator; b. N.Y.C., Apr. 1, 1922; d. Harry and Hinda (Sits) Heimowitz; m. Jacob H. Rosenbaum, Mar. 12, 1939; children: Linda Zelinger, Simmi Brodie, Martin, Arlene Levene. Cert., N.Y. Sch. Interior Design, 1945; MA in Judaic Art, PhD, U. B.C., 1997. Sr. mem. Am. Soc. Appraisers, Washington, 1979—; tchr. Judaica Yeshiva U., 1984—; dir. Mus. Contemporary Judaica; pres. Jarvis Designs, Inc., Union City, N.J., 1955-75, Design Assocs., BLS, Monsey, N.Y., 1970-78; v.p. Lord & Lady Inc., Union City, 1955-70, Cardio-Bionic Scanning, Inc., Spring Valley, N.Y., 1975-78; v.p., treas. Rapitech Sys., inc., 1985; exec bd. State of Israel Bonds Orgn., 1992—. Author short stories, 1947-48, Chronicle of Jewish Traditions, 1992, Upon Thy Doorposts, 1996; contbr. articles on interior design to profl. jours. Chmn. bd. artifacts Rockland Holocaust Ctr., 1991—; trustee Rockland Ctr. Holocaust Studies, 1994; pres. Ednl. Ctr. Jewish Values Jerusalem Gt. Synagogue, Israel, 1998—; co-chair Nat. Jewish Art Week, 2000; curator arts Holocaust Mus. Rockland County, 2000; Bd. dirs. Midgal Ohr Schs., 1971—, Shaare Zedek Hosp., Jerusalem, 1998—, Jewish Fedn. Rockland County, 1999—, Riverdale (N.Y.) Jewish Mus., 1999—, Am. Guild Judaic Art, 1999—, Judaica Mus. Riverdale, 2001—.

ROSENBAUM, DIANE M. state representative; b. Berkeley, Calif., Nov. 26, 1949; m. Jas Adams. State rep., dist. 42 Oreg. House Rep., Salem, 1999—; pres. Oreg. State Indsl. Union Coun., 1994—; legis. rep. Comm. Workers Am., 1989—. Chair Oreg. Commn. for Women, 1993—. Mem.: ACLU. Democrat. Office: 900 Court St NE H-377 Salem OR 97301 Address: Dist Office 1423 SE Hawthorne Blvd Portland OR 97214

ROSENBAUM, JOAN HANNAH, museum director; b. Hartford, Conn. d. Charles Leon and Lillian (Sharasheff) Grossman; m. Peter S. Rosenbaum, July 1962 (div. 1970). AA, Hartford Coll. for Women, 1962; BA, Boston U., 1964; student, Hunter Coll. Grad Sch., 1970-73; cert., Columbia U. Bus. Sch. Inst. Non Profit Mgmt., 1978; DHL (hon.), Jewish Theol. Sem., 1993. Curatorial asst. Mus. Modern Art, N.Y.C., 1966-72; dir. mus. program N.Y. Council on Arts, N.Y.C., 1972-79; assoc. Michal Washburn & Assocs., N.Y.C., 1979-80; dir. Jewish Mus., N.Y.C., 1980—. Mem. adv. bd. Pub. Ctr., N.Y.C.; bd. dirs. Creative Time. Bd. dirs. Artists Space, 1980-93 ; mem. coun. Am. Jewish Mus., 1981—; mem. policy panel Nat. Endowment Arts, 1982-83. Created knight (Denmark); recipient Disting. Alumni award Boston U. Coll. Libera Arts, 1994, Woman of Distinction award Hadassah, 1997, diploma Chevalier of Order of Arts and Letters (France), 1999; European travel grantee Internat. Coun. Mus., 1972. Mem. Am. Assn. Mus. (cons. 1979—), Assn. Art Mus. Dirs. (com. chair), N.Y. State Assn. Mus. (mem. coun. 1981-90), Art Table. Office: Jewish Mus 1109 5th Ave New York NY 10128-0118

ROSENBAUM, LOIS OMENN, lawyer; b. Newark, Apr. 10, 1950; d. Edward and Ruth (Peretz) Omenn; m. Richard B. Rosenbaum, Apr. 4, 1971; children: Steven, Laura. AB, Wellesley Coll., 1971; JD, Stanford U., 1974. Bar: Calif. 1974, Oreg. 1977, D.C. 1974, U.S. Supreme Ct. 1990, Wash. 2001. Assoc. Fried, Frank, Harris, Shriver & Kampelman, Washington, 1974-75, Orrick, Herrington, Rowley & Sutcliffe, San Francisco, 1975-77, Stoel Rives LLP (formerly Stoel, Rives, Boley, Jones & Grey), Portland, Oreg., 1977-81, ptnr., 1981—. Mem. U.S. Dist. Ct. Mediation Panel. Bd. dirs. Providence Med. Found., 1990-95, Robison Jewish Home, 1994-97, Jewish Family & Child Svc., 1997-2000, Am. Jewish Commn., 2000-04; past mem. Nat. Legal Com. Am. Jewish Com. Wellesley Coll. scholar, 1971. Mem. ABA, Multnomah County Bar Assn. (arbitration panel), Wellesley Club (pres. 1987-88). Office: Stoel Rives LLP 900 SW 5th Ave Ste 2600 Portland OR 97204-1268 Office Phone: 503-294-9293. E-mail: lorosenbaum@stoel.com.

ROSENBAUM, MARY HELÉNE POTTKER, writer, editor; b. Highland Park, Ill., Mar. 13, 1944; d. Ralph Eugene and Olga Norma (Somenzi) Pottker; m. Stanley Ned Rosenbaum, Sept. 2, 1963; children: Sarah Catherine, William David, Ephraim Samuel. Student, Bard Coll., 1962-63; BA magna cum laude, Dickinson Coll., 1975. Writing dir. Black Bear Prodns., Inc., Carlisle, Pa., Boston, Ky., 1989—; co-advisor Dickinson Coll. Hillel, Carlisle, 1991-92; exec. dir. Congregation Beth Tikvah, 1990-92. Coord. Interfaith Family Resources, 1995-97; exec. dir. Dovetail Inst. Interfaith Family Resources, 1997—. Co-author: Celebrating Our Differences: Living Two Faiths in One Marriage, 1994; columnist Interfaith Newsletter, 1995; mem. pubs. com. Cumberland County Hist. Soc.; editl. cons. Writers Cramp Inc., 1989—; assoc. editor Dovetail: A Jour. by and for Jewish/ Christian Families, 1996-98, editor, 1998-2003; contbr. articles to profl. jours. Mem. Cable Commn., Carlisle, 1991-92. Recipient Jean Gray Allen Non-fiction award Harrisburg Manuscript Club, 1978, Founder's Fiction award, 1978. Mem. League Women Voters Carlisle Area (pubs. coord. 1990-92, pres. 1988-90). Democrat. Roman Catholic. Avocations: dramatic reading, walking, cooking, folk singing. Home: 815 Simon Greenwell Rd Boston KY 40107-8524 Office: Dovetail Inst Interfaith Family Resources 775 Simon Greenwell Ln Boston KY 40107

ROSENBERG, ALISON P. public policy official; b. Miami, Fla., Sept. 5, 1945; d. Mortimer I. and Gail (Sklar) Podell; m. Jeffrey Alan Rosenberg, May 4, 1969; 1 child, Robert Aaron. BS in Econs., Smith Coll., 1967. Mng. officer Citibank, N.Y.C., 1967-69; legis. aide Senator Charles Percy, Washington, 1969-80; profl. staff mem. Senate Fgn. Rels. Com., Washington, 1981-85; assoc. asst. adminstr. Agy. for Internat. Devel., Washington, 1985-87; dir. African affairs Nat. Security Coun., Washington, 1987-88; dep. asst. sec. for Africa State Dept., Washington, 1988-92; asst. admnstr. for Africa Agy. for Internat. Devel., Washington, 1992-93; lead partnerships specialist (Africa) The World Bank, Washington, 1993—. E-mail: arosenberg@worldbank.org.

ROSENBERG, AURIA ELEANOR, elementary school educator; b. Detroit, Mar. 27, 1938; d. Paulino and Emelia (Phillip) Aromin; m. Jonah Rosenberg, Jan. 23, 1967 (div. June 1974); children: Pamela Reynée, Jonathan David, Deena Robyn. BA in French, Univ. Wash., 1961; MA in edn., Nat.-Louis Univ., 1992. Cert. tchr. Ill., Wash. Tchr. Tyee Jr H.S., Bellevue, Wash., 1961-62, Bais-Yaakov Parochial Sch., Chgo., 1979-84, Audy Home Cook County Detention Ctr., Chgo., 1984-89, Pleasant Ridge Elem. Sch., Glenview, Ill., 1988-90, Lyon Elem. Sch., Glenview, Ill., 1989-91; chair world lang. dept. Phillips Acad., Chgo., 1991—. Rep. committeewoman of 49th ward, Chgo., 1970-82, mem. Cook County Rep. Committeewomens Orgn. Chgo., 1970-82, sec., 1970-74. Recipient Merit award Excellence for Outstanding Tchr. of Yr., Ill. State Bd. Edn. Mem. Alumni Assn. Univ. Wash., Nat. Coun. of Teaching of Fgn. Languages, Ill. Coun. of Teaching of Fgn. Languages, Internal. Reading Assn., Ill. Reading Assn., Pi Lambda Theta (v.p. 1996-98, sec. 1992), Delta Kappa Gamma (historian 1994—), Phi Delta Kappa. Republican. Avocations: watercoloring, illustration. Home: One Ct of Harborside Northbrook IL 60062

ROSENBERG, CAROLE, art dealer, real estate broker, foundation executive; b. Bklyn., Nov. 16, 1936; d. Hugo and Mildred (Wilinsky) Clemente; m. Melvyn S. Sponder; m. Jerome A. Halsband; children: Michael S. Halsband, Kenneth L. Halsband; m. Alex J. Rosenberg, May 15, 1977. Student, Hunter Coll., 1954-56; BA, Bklyn. Coll., 1958; postgrad., NYU, 1961-62, 64-65. Tchr. N.Y.C. Sch. System, 1958-59, 61-63, Fla. Sch. System, Miami Beach, 1959-61; gallery owner and dir. Original Graphics/Carole Halsband Gallery, N.Y.C., 1971-76; assoc. editor Transworld Art Inc., N.Y.C., 1974-78; exec. dir., curator Alex Rosenberg Gallery/Transworld Art Inc., N.Y.C., 1978-87; exec. dir., v.p. Ardmore Affiliates Ltd., N.Y.C., 1987—; real estate salesperson N.Y.C., 1986-91; real estate broker Carole Rosenberg Properties Internat. Ltd., 1992—. Treas. 3/69 Owners Corp., N.Y.C.1984-87, pres., 1987-91, v.p., 1991-93; chmn. bd. dirs. Friends of the Hofstra U. Arboretum, Hempstead, N.Y., 1991-94. Editor: (art catalogs) Henry Moore, Howard Kanovitz, Mark Tobey, Lila Katzen, 1975; assoc. editor (portfolio) An American Portrait, 1976. Mem. adv. bd. Women Beyond Borders, 1995—, Ludwig Found. Cuba, 1995—; mem. cmty. bd. Water Mill Ctr., 1999—; internat. bd. mem. Tel Aviv Mus. Art, 1999—; bd. dirs. Am. Friends of the Tel Aviv Mus., 2000—; mem. coun. Friends of Upper East Side Hist. Dist., N.Y.C., 1983—96; pres. Am. Friends of the Ludwig Found. of Cuba, 2000—, Lotos Club Found., 2000—. Recipient Lotos medal of merit, 1995, Mgmt. Achievement Award for Innovation, N.Y. Habitat Mag., N.Y.C., 1989. Mem.: Real Estate Bd. N.Y.C., Art Table, N.Y. Hort. Soc. (Longhouse Res. garden com. 1995—, art com. 2001—), Hort. Alliance of the Hamptons, Nat. Arts Club, Mus. Modern Art, Parrish Art Mus. (patron garden com.), Met. Mus. Art, Guggenheim Mus., Women's City Club Am. Hort. Soc., City Gardens Club, Lotos Club (art com. 1989—, chmn. art com. 1992—98, dir. 1993—99). Democrat. Jewish. Avocation: gardening. Business E-Mail: arfineart@aol.com. E-mail: crosenberg@alfc.org.

ROSENBERG, ELLEN Y. religious association administrator; married; 2 children. Student, Goucher Coll.; BS in Edn., Mills Coll.; postgrad., Columbia U. Assoc. dean for acad. affairs Marymount Manhattan Coll., N.Y.C.; exec. dir. Women of Reform Judaism/Fed. Temple Sisterhoods, 1992—. Bd. dirs. Mazon, World Union for Progressive Judaism, Jewish Braille Inst. Am., Union Am. Hebrew Congregations. Jewish. Office: WRJ 633 3rd Ave New York NY 10017-6706

ROSENBERG, JILL, realtor, civic leader; b. Shreveport, La., Feb. 17, 1940; d. Morris H. and Sallye (Abramson) Schuster; m. Lewis Rosenberg, Dec. 23, 1962; children: Craig, Paige. BA in Philosophy, Tulane U., 1961, MSW, 1965; grad., Realtor Inst., 1994. Cert. residential specialist Residential Sales Coun. Social worker La. Dept. Pub. Welfare, 1961-62, 63-64; genetics counselor Sinai Hosp., Balt., 1967-69; ptnr. Parties Extraordinaire, cons., 1973-77; realtor assoc. Robert Weil Assocs., Long Beach, Calif., 1982—. Pres. we. region Pres. we. region, 1972—73, v.p. Jewish Cmty. Fedn. Long Beach and West Orange County, 1983—86, bd. dirs., 1982—86; pres. Long Beach Cancer League, 1987—88, exec. bd. dirs., 1984—96; pres. Long Beach Jewish Cmty. Sr. Housing Corp., 1989—91; v.p. fundraising S.E. unit Long Beach Harbor chpt. Am. Cancer Soc., 1989—90; trustee St. Mary Med. Ctr. Found., 1991—2003; pres. nat. conf. NCCJ, 1994—96, bd. dirs., 1989—, Leadership Long Beach, 1992—2000, pres., 1994—95; hon. bd. govs., 2000—; mem. dean's adv. bd. Sch. Bus. Adminstrn. Calif. State U., Long Beach, 2001—; assoc. coun. Long Beach Edn. Foun., 2003—; bd. dirs. Long Beach Symphony Assn., 1984—85, Westerly Sch. Assoc., 1991—2000, Phoenix Long Beach Mus. Art, 1992—98, Am. Diabetes Assn., Long Beach., Calif., 1997—99, Stramski Children's Devel. Ctr., Long Beach Meml. Med. Ctr., 1998—, Pub. Corp. for Arts, 2002—, Long Beach Day Nursery, 2000—02; leadership devel. chair Pub. Corp. for Arts, 2003—. Recipient Young Leadership award Jewish Cmty. Fedn. Long Beach and West Orange County, 1981, Jerusalem award State of Israel, 1989, Hannah G. Solomon award Nat. Coun. Jewish Women, 1992, Alumnus of Yr. award Leadership Long Beach, 1995, Humanitarian award The Nat. Conf., 1997, Disting. Leadership award Calif. Assn. Leadership Programs, 2000; named Rick Racker Woman of Yr., 1999; scholar La. Dept. Pub. Welfare, 1962, NIMH, 1964. Mem. Rotary Club of Long Beach (bd. dirs. 2000-01). Office: Robert Weil Assocs 5220 E Los Altos Plz Long Beach CA 90815-4251

ROSENBERG, LESLIE KAREN, media buyer; b. Camden, N.J., Mar. 3, 1949; d. Lorimer and Doris Selma (Kohn) R. BS in Radio, TV, Film, U. Tex., 1971. Continuity dir. WEAT-TV/AM/FM, West Palm Beach, Fla., 1971-74; media buyer Wm. F. Haselmire Advt., West Palm Beach, 1974-75, media dir., 1982-85; program and pub. svc. dir. WTBS-TV, Atlanta, 1975-78; nat. traffic coord. WXIA-TV, Atlanta, 1978-80; sr. sales asst. CBS Radio Spot Sales, Atlanta, 1980-82; acct. exec. WRMF-FM, West Palm Beach, 1985; media dir., acct. exec. Merlin Masters & Nomes Advt., West Palm Beach, 1985-88; pres., media dir. Media Magic Plus, West Palm Beach, 1988—; advt. coord. Hearx, Ltd., West Palm Beach, 1996-98; media dir. Fantasma Prodns., Inc., West Palm Beach, 1998—2001; mktg. mgr. Broward Ctr. for Performing Arts, 2001—03. Communications adv. bd. Palm Beach Jr. Coll., Lake Worth, 1972-74; media planner, buyer Hear USA, 2004-. Talent, author various radio commercials (Addy award 1973, 74), talent various TV commercials (Addy award 1974). Bd. dirs. Lake Worth (Fla.) Playhouse, 1989-92, program co-chmn., 1989-91; mem. Internat. Cultural Exch. Program, 1984, 94, 97; producer Lake Worth Playhouse Internat. Cultural Exch. for 1994 trip to Eng., mem. com. for 97 trip to Eng., 1994-97. Mem.: NATAS, NAFE, U.S. Racquetball Assn. (dir. tournament control 1976—80), Advt. Club of the Palm Beaches (bd. dirs. 1983—85). Avocations: singing, tap dancing, theatre, reading, shopping. Office: Media Magic Plus PO Box 19962 West Palm Beach FL 33416-4962 Office Phone: 561-683-7532 X 129. E-mail: LKRose761@aol.com., lrosenberg@hearusa.com.

ROSENBERG, MARILYN ROSENTHAL, artist, visual poet; b. Phila., Oct. 11, 1934; m. Robert Rosenberg, June 12, 1955; 2 children. B in Profl. Studies in Studio Arts, SUNY, Empire State Coll., 1978; MA in Liberal Studies, NYU, 1993. Represented in permanent collections Avant Writing Collection, The Ohio State U. Librs., Whtiney Mus. Am. Art, Frances Mulhull Ancilles Libr., N.Y.C., numerous one-woman shows including most recently, one-woman shows include Marymount Coll., Tarrytown, N.Y., 1993, McHenry County Coll., Crystal Lake, Ill., 1997, John Jay Coll., N.Y.C., 1999, Westchester CC, Valhalla, N.Y., 2002, numerous group shows including most recently, exhibited in group shows at Fla. Atlantic U., Boca Raton, Fla., 2000, U. Ctrl. Ark., Conway, 2000, Ocean Grove Libr., Victoria, Australia, 2000, City Gallery, Szekesfehervar, Hungary, 2000, The Temple Judea, Elkins Park, Pa., 2001, Art Acad. Cin., 2002, Ohio State U. Librs., Columbus, 2002, Cuesta Coll. Art Gallery, San Luis Obispo, Calif., 2002, Pensacola (Fla.) Mus. Art, 2002, U. Indpls. (Ind.) Gallery, 2002, The Ctr. for Book Arts, N.Y.C., N.Y., 2003, Lowenstein Gallery, Miami, Fla., 2003, Starr Gallery, Newton Ctr., Mass., 2003, The Buddy Holly Ctr., Lubbock, Tex., 2003, Peck Arts Ctr. Gallery, Ctrl. Wyo. Coll., Riverton, 2003, Purdue U. Galleries, Lafayette, Ind., 2003, Wexford (Ireland) Arts Centre, Ellipse Art Ctr., Arlington, Va., 2003. Home: 67 Lakeview Ave W Cortlandt Manor NY 10567-6415

ROSENBERG, PAMELA, performing company executive, conductor; b. Los Angeles, Calif., 1945; m. Wolf Rosenberg (dec. 1996); 2 children. Diploma, London Opera Ctr.; B, U. Calif. at Berkely, 1966; M in Russian hist., Ohio State U. Various positions Frankfurt Opera, 1974—87; dir. of ops. Deutscher Schauspielhaus, Hamburg, Germany, 1987—88; mgr., artistic affairs Netherlands Opera, 1988—90; co-gen. dir. Stuggart Opera, 1990—2000; gen. dir. San Francisco Opera, 2001—. Office: San Francisco Opera 301 VanNess Ave San Francisco CA 94102

ROSENBERG, RUTH HELEN BORSUK, lawyer; b. Plainfield, N.J., Feb. 23, 1935; d. Irwin and Pauline (Rudich) Borsuk; children— Joshua Cohen, Sarah, Rebecca, Daniel, Miriam, Tziporah, Isaac AB, Douglass Coll., 1956; JD, U. Pa., 1963. Bar: Pa. 1964, N.Y. 1967, D.C. 1986, Md. 1987, Va 1994, Mass. 1995, U.S. Ct. Appeals (3d cir.) 1969, U.S. Supreme Ct. 1969, U.S. Ct. Appeals (4th cir.) 1994. Law clk. Ct. Common Pleas, Phila., 1963-64; assoc. Blank, Rudenko, Klaus & Rome, Phila., 1964-67; atty. Office Corp. Counsel, City of Rochester, 1967-68; assoc. Nixon, Hargrave, Devans & Doyle, Washington, 1968-74, ptnr., 1975-99, Nixon Peabody LLP, Washington, 1999—2003. Vice chairperson character and fitness com. Appellate divsn. 4th dept. 7th Jud. Dist. N.Y. Supreme Ct., 1976-80, mem. grievance com., 1981-84. Bd. dirs. Soc. Prevention Cruelty to Children, 1976-77, N.Y. Civil Liberties Union, 1972-85, v.p. 1976-85; bd. dirs. Jewish Home and Infirmary, 1978-83, pres., 1980-83; v.p. Jewish Fedn. Rochester, 1983, Yachad, Inc., Jewish Cmty. Housing Devel. Corp., 1990-94; bd. dirs. Jewish Cmty. Coun., Greater Washington, 1989-93, Leadership Washington, 1990-91, Libr. Theatre, 1994-97, Op. Understanding, D.C., 1994-95. Mem. ABA, D.C. Bar Assn., Md. Bar Assn., Va. Bar Assn., Phi Beta Kappa. Office: Nixon Peabody LLP 401 9th St NW Ste 900 Washington DC 20004-2128 E-mail: rrosenberg@nixonpeabody.com.

ROSENBERG, SARAH ZACHER, institute arts administration executive, humanities administration consultant; b. Kelem, Lithuania, Jan. 10, 1931; came to U.S., 1938; d. David Meir Zacher and Rachel Korbman; m. Norman J. Rosenberg, Dec. 30, 1950; children: Daniel, Alyssa. BA in History, U. Nebr., 1970, MA in Am. History, 1973. Rsch. historian U. Mid-Am., Lincoln, Nebr., 1974-78, program developer dept. humanities, 1978-79, asst. dir. div. acad. planning, 1980-81, dir. program devel., 1981-82; exec. dir. Nebr. Humanities Coun., Lincoln, 1982-87, Nebr. Found. for Humanities, Lincoln, 1984-87, Am. Inst. for Conservation Hist. and Artistic Works, Washington, 1987-97, exec. dir. found., 1991-97; program officer, spl. cons. mus. div. NEH, Washington, 1987, external reviewer, 1981, 89; cons. strategic planning for nonprofit cultural instns., 1997—. Lay participant long-range planning conf. Nebr. Bar Assn., Hastings, 1986. Co-editor: The Great Plains Experience: Readings in the History of a Region, 1978; contbr. articles to profl. jours. Action mem. Hadassah, Lincoln, 1961—87, Tifereth Israel Synagogue, Lincoln, 1961—87, Beth El Congregation, Bethesda, Md., 1988—2001, Kol Shalom Congregation, 2001—; bd. dirs. Sta. KUCV, affiliate Nat. Pub. Radio, Lincoln, 1986—87, Lincoln Cmty. Playhouse, Lincoln, 1986—87.

NEH grantee, 1981, 86, merit awards, 1983, 87; Humanities Resource Ctr. grantee, Peter Kiewit Found., 1984. Mem. Am. Hist. Assn., Western Hist. Assn., Alpha Theta. Democrat. Home: 8102 Appalachian Ter Potomac MD 20854-4050

ROSENBERG, SHELI Z. investment company executive; Degree, Tufts U., Northwestern U. Atty. Cotton, Watt, Jones & King, 1966—70; mng. ptnr. Schiff Hardin & Waite, 1976—80; from gen. coun. to vice-chmn. Equity Group Investments, LLC, Chgo., 1980—2000, vice-chmn., 2000—. Bd. dirs. CVS Corp., Capital Trust, Cendant Corp., Manufactured Home Communities, Inc., Equity Residential Properties Trust, Equity Office Properties Trust, Ventas, Inc.; adv. bd. J.L. Kellogg Grad. Sch. Bus. N.W. Univ. Trustee Rush Presbyn. St. Luke's Med. Ctr., exec. com.; co-founder, pres. Ctr. for Exec. Women, J.L. Kellogg Grad. Sch. Bus., 2001—. Office: Equity Group Investments LLC 737 North Michigan Ave Ste 1405 Chicago IL 60611 E-mail: szr312@aol.com.

ROSENBERG, SHELI ZYSMAN, lawyer, financial management executive; b. N.Y.C., Feb. 2, 1942; d. Stephen B. and Charlotte (Laufer) Zysman; m. Burton X. Rosenberg, Aug. 30, 1964; children: Leonard, Marcy. BA, Tufts U., 1963; JD, Northwestern U., 1966. Bar: Ill. 1966. Ptnr. Schiff, Hardin & Waite, Chgo., 1973-80; exec. v.p., gen. counsel Equity Fin. Mgmt., Chgo., 1980-90, Equity Group Investments, Inc., Chgo., 1988-94, pres., CEO, 1994—, Equity Fin. and Mgmt. Co., Chgo., 1994—; prin. Rosenberg & Liebentritt, P.C., Chgo., 1995—. Bd. dirs. Gt. Am. Mgmt. & Investment, Chgo., 1984—, v.p., gen. counsel, 1985-90, sec., 1983-90; bd. dirs. CVS Corp. Ill.; trustee Equity Residential Properties Trust, Manufactured Home Cmtys., Inc.; mem. bd. trust Equity Office Properties. Bd. dirs., pres. Chgo. Network.

ROSENBERG, TINA, international relations educator, writer; b. 1958; BS, Northwestern U., 1981, MS, 1982. Fgn. policy editl. writer The New York Times, freelance writer New York Times mag., 1983-96, fgn. policy editl. writer, 1996—, mem. editl. bd.; adj. prof. internat. rels. Columbia U., N.Y.C. Vis. fellow Nat. Security Archive; former sr. fellow World Policy Inst., New Sch. U. Author: Children of Cain: Violence and the Violent in Latin America, The Haunted Land:; Facing Europe's Ghosts After Communism (Pulitzer and Nat. Book award, 1996); contbr. articles to publs. Recipient MacArthur Fellowship "genius" award. Office: NY Times Editl Bd 229 W 43rd St New York NY 10036

ROSENBERGER, CAROL, concert pianist; b. Detroit, Nov. 1, 1935; d. Maurice Seiberling and Whilamet (Gibson) R. B.F.A., Carnegie-Mellon U., 1955; postgrad., Acad. Performing Arts, Vienna, 1956-59. In charge of artists and repertoire Delos Internat. Mem. artist faculty U. So. Calif., Calif. State U., Northridge, Immaculate Heart Coll.; vis. artist numerous colls. and univs. Internat. concert career, 1964—; New York debut, 1970; appeared several times at Carnegie Hall; soloist Am. Symphony, Nat. Symphony, Royal Philharmonic, San Diego Symphony, Detroit Symphony, Houston Symphony, St. Louis Symphony, Indpls. Symphony, Los Angeles Chamber Orch.; performed world premiere of Buenaventura; piano concerts with Philippine Philharmonic, 1977, Am. Symphony, 1977; recital series in Am., European, Asian music capitals; recordings include Hindemith's Four Temperaments with London Royal Philharm., Water Music of the Impressionists (one of 25 Best Classical CDs of All Time, Stereo Rev., Recording of Yr., Gramophone mag., All-time Gt. Recording, Billboard mag.), works of Beethoven, Schubert, Szymanowski, Night Moods, 1989, Perchance To Dream, Lullabys for Children and Adults, 1989, Reveries: Music of Chopin, Such Stuff as Dreams, Singing on the Water, Mozart Adagios, (with N.Y. Chamber Symphony) Fantasy Variations on a Theme of Youth (Howard Hanson), 1991 (Grammy nomination), Haydn D Major Concerto, Nights in the Gardens of Spain, Beethoven Concerto No. 4, (with Seattle Symphony) Burleske, Piano Concerto of Howard Hanson, (with L.A. Chamber Orch.) Shostakovich 1st Piano Concerto, others; prodr., co-prodr. Music for Young People Series, others; author script for narration of The Firebird (Stravinsky) (Notable Recording award ALA);contbr. articles to music publs. Recipient Steinway Centennial medal, 1954, Critics Choice award Gramaphone mag., 1980, 10/10 award CD Rev. Mem. Nat. Acad. Rec. Arts and Scis. Achievements include being chosen to represent Am. women musicians by Nat. Commn. on Observance Internat. Womens Year, 1976. Office: Delos Internat Inc 1645 Vine St Ste 340 Los Angeles CA 90028-8842

ROSENBERGER, MARGARET ADALINE, retired elementary school educator, writer; b. Micanopy, Fla., Oct. 30; d. Eugene David and Lillian Adeline (Bauknight) Rosenberger. Student, Stetson U., 1946—48; BA in Edn., U. Fla., 1949, MEd, 1952. Drama sec. Nat. Youth Adminstrn., Gainesville, Fla., 1939—40; civil svc. clk. U.S. Army, Camp Blanding, Fla., 1940—46; tchr. J.J. Finley, Gainesville, 1949—52; prin., tchr. Micanopy Jr. H.S., 1952—55; gen. supr. Alachua County Schs., Gainesville, 1955—57, elem. supr., 1958—59; tchr. U.S. Army Dependents' Sch., Heidelberg, Germany, 1957—58; prin. Littlewood Elem. Sch., Gainesville, 1959—73, Prairie View Elem. Sch., Gainesville, 1973—82, ret., 1982; owner Rose Hill Pubs. Mem. sch. adv. com. Prairie View Elem. Sch. 1975—82. Co-author: Reflections of Light, 1995; author: My God of Love, Mercy, Miracles and Angels, 1996, Secrets and Songs of Payne's Prairie, 1998, A Teacher's Odyssey, 2001, My Pets and I, 1999, Poems for Children, 2001, My Angels and I, 2001, Spiritual Interpretations of God's Truths, 2002, The Birth and Growth of the Village, 2003, Secrets & Songs at Payne's Prairie, 2004—; author, composer: St. Augustine Song; contbr. articles to The Gainesville Sun, to WLUS Radio Talk Show, 1992-95, poems to mags. & papers. Pres. Children's Commn., Gainesville, 1956—57; dir. The Village Chorus, Gainesville, 1987—; mem. Gainesville Schs. PTA, 1959—82; mem. PTA Micanopy, 1952—55; Dem. candidate Fla. House Rep., 1974; pianist/organist The Village Vespers on Sunday Evenings, 1990—; bd. dir. Foster Grandparents, Gainesville, 1974—76; chmn. bd. dir. No. Fla. Retirement Village, Inc., Gainesville, Fla., 1982—86, bd. rep. to residents, 1986—, v.p. bd. dir., 1981—82. Mem.: Internat. Soc. Poets, Am. Soc. Composers, Authors & Pub., Micanopy Hist. Soc., Altrusa Internat. Club Gainesville (chmn. internat. com., chmn. newsletter, spkr. for programs), Order of Eastern Star, Delta Kappa Gamma (internat. soc. 1959—). Democrat. Baptist. Avocations: stamp collecting, coin collecting, book collecting, post card collecting, creative writing. Home: 410 SW Wacahoota Rd Micanopy FL 32667 Mailing: 8015 NW 28th Pl B 110 Gainesville FL 32606

ROSENBLAD, HELEN VIOLA, social services coordinator; b. Hutchinson, Kans., Dec. 14, 1923; d. Raymond Grant Streeter and Edith May Hunter; m. Ralph Alexander Rosenblad, June 8, 1946; children: Signe Elizabeth, Eric Lee, Kirstin Patricia, Lars Jon. BA in Sociology, Baker U., 1945. Dir. girls work Kingdom House, St. Louis, 1945—46; youth worker Morgan Meml. Youth and Children's Ctr., Boston, 1946—50; pricer Goodwill Industries, Springfield, Mass., 1950—52; EMT Downs (Kans.) Ambulance Svc., 1985—87; coord. Mother-To-Mother Ministry, Hutchinson, Kans., 1987—91. Transp. cons. S.W. Kans. Area Agy. on Aging, Dodge City, 1970—79. Author: The Flitting of Rose Leaves, 1983, 1997. Leader Girl Scouts, Boston, Springfield, Lowell, Andover, Mass., 1946—60; clothing and foods leader 4H, Winfield, Bushton, Stafford, Kans., 1960—75; bd. mem. Area Agys. on Aging, Kans., 1970—87; founder, mem. Downs Sr. Citizens, Inc, 1983—87; dir. Fed. Commodity Distbn., Osborne County, Kans., 1984—87; founder, mem. Downs Hist. Soc., 1983—87; founder, bd. mem. Interfaith Housing Svcs., Hutchinson, 1990—2003; adv. bd. Youthbuild, Inc., Hutchinson, 1993—96; mem. Hutchinson Cmty. Improvement Commn., 1995—2001, Hutchinson Housing Commn., 1995—; founder, bd. mem. Stepping-Stones for Youth, Inc., Hutchinson, 1997—; delivery person Meals on Wheels, Hutchinson, 1997—; mem. Hutchinson Housing Authority Bd., 1998—. Named Vol. of the Cmty., Hutchinson News, 2002; grantee to establish Sr. Ctr., S.W. Kans. Area Agy. on Aging., Minneola, Kans., 1976, N.W. Kans. Area Agy. on Aging, Downs, 1984. Mem.: United Meth. Women, United Meth. Ch. (missions com. 1960—). Avocation: geneaology. Home: 814 E 30th 301 Hutchinson KS 67502

ROSENBLATT, ALICE F. health products executive; With New England, William M. Mercer, Inc., Mutual of NY; chief actuary, sr. v.p. Blue Cross HMO, 1987—89; sr. v.p., chief acutary Blue Cross/Blue Shield Mass., 1989—93; prin. health and welfare group Coopers & Lybrand, Boston; chief actuary, exec. v.p. integration planning and implementation Wellpoint Health Networks, Inc., 1996—. Commr. Medicare Payment Adv. Commn. Fellow: Soc. Actuaries (bd. dirs.); mem.: Am. Acad. Actuaries (bd. dirs.). Office: Wellpoint Health Networks Inc 1 Wellpoint Way Thousand Oaks CA 91362*

ROSENBLATT, JOAN RAUP, mathematical statistician; b. N.Y.C., Apr. 15, 1926; d. Robert Bruce and Clara (Eliot) Raup; m. David Rosenblatt, June 10, 1950. AB, Barnard Coll., 1946; PhD, U. N.C., 1956. Intern Nat. Inst. Pub. Affairs, Washington, 1946-47; statis. analyst U.S. Bur. of Budget, 1947-48; rsch. asst. U. N.C., 1953-54; mathematician Nat. Inst. Standards and Tech. (formerly Nat. Bur. Standards), Washington, 1955—, asst. chief statis. engring., 1963-68, chief statis. engring. lab., 1969-78, dep. dir. Ctr. for Applied Math., 1978-88; dep. dir. Computing and Applied Math. Lab., Gaithersburg, 1988-93, dir., 1993-95, guest rschr. Statis. Engring. Divsn., 1996—. Mem. com. on indsl. rels. Dept. Stats. Ohio State U., 1981-90; mem. adv. com. in math. and stats. USDA Grad. Sch., 1971—; mem. Com. Applied and Theoretical Stats., Nat. Rsch. Coun., 1985-88. Mem. editorial bd. Communications in Stats., 1971-79, Jour. Soc. for Indsl. and Applied Math., 1965-75, Nat. Inst. Stds. and Tech. Jour. Rsch., 1991-93; contbr. articles to profl. jours. Chmn. Com. on Women in Sci., Joint Bd. on Sci. Edn., 1963-64. Rice fellow, 1946, Gen. Edn. Bd. fellow, 1948-50; recipient Fed. Woman's award, 1971, Gold medal Dept. Commerce, 1976, Presdl. Meritorious Exec. Rank award, 1982. Fellow AAAS (chmn. stats. sect. 1982, sec. 1987-91), Inst. Math. Stats. (coun. 1975-77), Am. Statis. Assn. (v.p. 1981-83, dir. 1979-80, Founders award 1991), Washington Acad. Scis. (achievement award math. 1965); mem. AAUW, Royal Statis. Soc. London, Philos. Soc. Washington, Internat. Statis. Inst., Bernouilli Soc. Probability and Math. Stats., Caucus Women Stats. (pres. 1976), Assn. Women Math., Exec. Women Govt., Phi Beta Kappa, Sigma Xi (treas. Nat. Bur. Standards chpt. 1982-84). Home: 2939 Van Ness St NW Apt 702 Washington DC 20008-4628 Office: Nat Inst Stds and Tech 100 Bureau Dr Stop 8980 Gaithersburg MD 20899-8980 E-mail: jrr@nist.gov.

ROSENBLATT, KARIN ANN, cancer epidemiologist; b. Chgo., Apr. 22, 1954; d. Murray and Adylin Rosenblatt. BA, U. Calif., Santa Cruz, 1975; MPH, U. Mich., 1977; PhD, Johns Hopkins U., 1988. Postdoctoral fellow U. Wash., Seattle, 1987-89; staff scientist Fred Hutchinson Cancer Rsch. Ctr., Seattle, 1989-91; asst. prof. U. Ill., Champaign, 1991-97, assoc. prof., 1997—. Vis. scientist Fred Hutchinson Cancer Rsch. Ctr., 1999-2000; vis. scholar U. Wash., 1999-2000. Fellow Am. Coll. Epidemiology; mem. APHA (governing councilor epidemiology sect. 1988-2000), Internat. Epidemiologic Assn., Internat. Genetic Epidemiology Soc., Soc. for Epidemiologic Rsch. Office: Dept Cmty Health 120 Huff Hall MC 588 1206 S 4th St Champaign IL 61820-6920

ROSENBLOOM, NORMA FRISCH, lawyer; b. N.Y.C., Dec. 2, 1925; d. Jacob Frisch and Anna (Fox) Frisch Schwartz; m. Philip Rosenbloom, Oct. 31, 1946; children: David, James, Eric. BA, New Sch. Social Rsch., 1951; JD, Rutgers U., Newark, 1979. Bar: N.J. 1979, N.Y. 1980. Mem. faculty, head dept. music Ranney Sch., Tinton Falls, N.J., 1962-74; chief law clk. Monmouth County (N.J.) Prosecutor's Office, 1979-80; assoc. Karasic & Karasic, P.C., Oakhurst, N.J., 1980-82; ptnr. Abrams, Gatta, Rosen & Rosenbloom, Ocean Twp., N.J., 1982-90, Abrams, Gatta, Rosen, Rosenbloom & Sevrin, P.C., 1990-92; of counsel Abrams, Gatta, Falvo & Sevrin, P.A., 1992-99, Abrams Gatta Falvo LLP; legal adv. Epiphany House Inc., Asbury Park, N.J., 1999—. Asst. county counsel Monmouth County, 1987-88; mem. N.J. Supreme Ct. Family Part Practice Com., 1997-98. Sec., mem. exec. bd. Temple Beth Miriam, Elberon, N.J., 1969-74; mcpl. leader Monmouth Beach (N.J.) Dem. Com., 1973—; del. Dem. Nat. Conv., 1976; freeholder rep. to Monmouth County Cmty. Action Program, poverty program, 1975-76; bd. dirs. Cen. Jersey Regional Health Planning Bd., 1973-75; trustee search com. Brookdale C.c., Lincroft, N.J., 1984-85; trustee Planned Parenthood Monmouth County, 1981-88. Recipient award for cmty. involvement Asbury Park-Neptune Youth Coun., 1970. Fellow Am. Acad. Matrimonial Lawyers; mem. ABA, N.J. Women Lawyers Assn. (pres. 1994-95), N.J. State Bar Assn. (mem. legis. com., trustee women in the profession sect.), Women Lawyers Monmouth County. Democrat. Jewish. Avocation: classical pianist. Home: Channel Club Towers Monmouth Beach NJ 07750 Office: Epiphany House 300 4th Ave Asbury Park NJ 07712-6006

ROSENBLUM, ELLEN F. judge; b. 1951; m. Richard Meeker. BS, U. Oreg., 1971, JD, 1975. Bar: Oreg. 1975. Cir. ct. judge Multnomah County Ct., Portland, Oreg. Trustee Nat. Jud. Coll. Mem.: ABA (bd. govs., sec. 2002—). Office: Multnomah County Courthouse Rm 512 1021 SW 4th Ave Portland OR 97204

ROSENBLUM, MINDY FLEISCHER, pediatrician; b. Bronxville, N.Y., June 5, 1951; d. Herman and Muriel (Gold) Fleischer; m. Jay S. Rosenblum, June 22, 1971; children: Meira, Tamar, Rafi, Rachel. BA, Yeshiva U., 1972; MD, Albert Einstein Coll., 1976. Diplomate Am. Bd. Pediat., Am. Bd. Pediatric Endocrinology. Intern in pediat. Bronx Mcpl. Hosp. Ctr., 1976-77, residency in pediat., 1977-79; fellow in pediatric endocrinology Children's Hosp. of Phila., 1981; asst. prof. U. Pa., Phila., 1981—95; attending physician Bryn Mawr (Pa.) Hosp., 1981—, Lankenau Hosp., Wynnewood, Pa., 1983—; clin. assoc. Children's Hosp. of Phila., 1995—. Fellow Am. Acad. Pediat.; mem. Phila. Pediat. Soc. (bd. dirs. 1988-92), Am. Diabetes Assn., Lawson Wilkins Pediatric Endocrine Soc. Office Phone: 610-642-9200. E-mail: jmr101@comcast.net.

ROSENBLUM, SHARON, interior designer; b. Chgo., Aug. 9, 1945; d. Norman Benton and Sally (Lefstein) Rich; m. Jeffrey Arthur Rosenblum; children: Wendy, Jill, Deborah. BFA, Washington U., St. Louis, 1968. Cert. tchr. Mo. Office mgr., prin. designer Interior Design Studio, St. Louis, 1989—96; pres., prin. designer S. Rosenblum Interiors, St. Louis, 1996—. V.p. membership svcs. Jewish Hosp. Aux., St. Louis, 1987—89. Office: S Rosenblum Interiors Inc 9722 Bonhomme Estates Dr Saint Louis MO 63132 Office Phone: 314-432-8558.

ROSENFELD, SARENA MARGARET, artist; b. Elmira, N.Y., Oct. 17, 1940; d. Thomas Edward and Rosalie Ereny (Fedor) Rooney; m. Robert Steven Bach, June 1958 (div. 1963); children: Robert Steven, Daniel Thomas; m. Samson Rosenfeld III, June 5, 1976. Student, Otis/Parson Art Inst., L.A., 1994-98, Idyllwild Sch. Music and Arts, 1994-98. One-woman shows include Robert Dana Gallery, San Francisco, Gordon Gallery, Santa Monica, Calif., Hespe Gallery, San Francisco, Art Expressions, San Diego, L.A., La Jolla, Calif., Aspen, Colo., New Orleans, Honolulu, La Sierra U., Riverside, Calif., U. Enklinik, Bochum, Germany, Ruhr U., Germany, Universitatsklinikum Benjamin Franklin, Berlin, 2002, Gallery 444, San Francisco; artist (group shows) Ergane Gallery, N.Y.C., Orlando Gallery, Sherman Oaks, Calif., Bradford Gallery Blue Sq., Newport Beach, Calif., 2001, L.A., Soho, N.Y.C., Santa Barbara, Calif., Tanglewood, Mass., Johannesburg, South Africa, Coda Gallery, Palm Desert, Calif., Johnson Art Collection, Melrose Ave., L.A. Mem., vol., animal handler Wildlife Waysta., Angeles Nat. Forest, Calif.; vol. animal keeper L.A. Zoo, docent Simon Wiesenthal Mus. of Tolerance, L.A. Recipient Best of Show award Glendale Regional Arts Coun., 1984-85, 1st pl. awards Santa Monica Art Festival, 1982, 83, 84, 85, 86, Sweepstakes award and 1st pl., 1986, Purchase prize awards L.A. West C. of C., 1986-87, Tapestry in Talent Invitational San Jose Arts Coun., 1986, 1st pl. awards Studio City and Century City Arts Couns., 1976-84, 1st award Pacific Palisades Art Affair XII, 1997, Sherman Oaks Fall Arts Festival, 1997. Mem. Nat. Mus. of Women in the Arts. Republican. Home: 6570 Kelvin Ave Canoga Park CA 91306-4021

ROSENFIELD, RUTH, advertising executive; b. Santa Monica, Calif., Nov. 24, 1962; m. Thomas Andrew Rosenfield, 1989; childen: Charlotte Elyse, Oliver Cole. Student, UCLA, 1980-82; BFA with honors, Art Ctr. Coll. Design, 1985. Art dir. Oglivy & Mather, N.Y.C., 1985-86, Chiat/Day, N.Y.C., 1986-88, Venice, Calif., 1988-91; v.p., assoc. creative dir. Hill Holliday, L.A., 1991-93; freelance art dir. San Francisco and L.A., 1993-95; v.p., creative dir. Publicus & Hal Riney (formerly Hal Riney & Ptnrs.), San Francisco, 1995—. Recipient Comm. Arts award, Cannes awards, Obie awards, Belding awards, Andy awards. Office: Publicus & Hal Riney 2001 The Embarcadero San Francisco CA 94133-5200

ROSENHEIM, MARGARET KEENEY, social welfare policy educator; b. Grand Rapids, Mich., Sept. 5, 1926; d. Morton and Nancy (Billings) Keeney; m. Edward W. Rosenheim, June 20, 1947; children: Daniel, James, Andrew. Student, Wellesley Coll., 1943-45; JD, U. Chgo., 1949. Bar: Ill. 1949. Mem. faculty Sch. Social Service Adminstrn., U. Chgo., 1950—, assoc. prof., 1961-66, prof., 1966—, Helen Ross prof. social welfare policy, 1975-96, dean, 1978-83; lectr. in law U. Chgo., 1980-97. Vis. prof. U. Wash., 1965, Duke U., 1984; Helen Ross prof. emerita U. Chgo., 1996—; acad. visitor London Sch. Econs., 1973; cons. Pres.'s Commn. Law Enforcement and Adminstrn. Justice, 1966-67, Nat. Adv. Commn. Criminal Justice Stds. and Goals, 1972; mem. Juvenile Justice Stds. Commn., 1973-78; trustee Carnegie Corp. N.Y., 1979-87; trustee Children's Home and Aid Soc. of Ill., 1981—, chair, 1996-98; chair CHASI Sys. Inc., 1998-2001; dir. Nat. Inst. Dispute Resolution, 1981-89, Nuveen Bond Funds, 1982-97; mem. Chgo. Network, 1983—. Editor: Justice for the Child, 1962; contbr. 2d edit., 1977; editor: Pursuing Justice for the Child, 1976; editor: (with F.E. Zimring, D.S. Tanenhaus, B. Dohrn) A Century of Juvenile Justice, 2002; editor: (with Mark Testa) Early Parenthood and Coming of Age in the 1990s, 1992; contbr. articles to profl. jours. Home: 5805 S Dorchester Ave Chicago IL 60637-1730 Office: 969 E 60th St Chicago IL 60637-2677 E-mail: mrosenhe@midway.uchicago.edu.

ROSENKRANTZ, BARBARA GUTMANN, retired history educator; b. N.Y.C., Jan. 11, 1923; d. James and Jeanette (Mack) G.; m. David P. Bennett, Sept. 5, 1942 (div.); 1 child, Louise; m. Paul Rosenkrantz, Apr. 19, 1950 (dec. 1986); children: Judith, Deborah; m. J. Nathaniel Marshall, 1988. AB, Radcliffe Coll., 1944; PhD, Clark U., 1970. Rsch. assoc. Harvard U., Cambridge, Mass., 1970-71, lectr., 1971-73, assoc. prof. history of sci., 1973-75, prof., 1975-93, chmn. history of sci. dept., 1984-89, master Currier House, 1974-79, faculty adminstr. Author: Public Health and the State, 1972, (with William A. Koelsch) American Habitat, 1973; editor for history Am. Jour. Pub. Health, 1985-89. NIH research grantee, 1970-72; Rockefeller Found. fellow, 1979-80; Ctr. for Advanced Study in Behavioral Scis. fellow Stanford U., 1984, Inst. Medicine fellow; Sherman Fairchild Disting. Scholar, Calif. Inst. Tech., 1989. Fellow Am. Acad. Arts and Scis., Mass. Hist. Soc.; mem. Am. Hist. Assn., History of Sci. Soc., Am. Assn. for History of Medicine. Jewish. Office: Harvard U Dept History Sci Ctr 371 Cambridge MA 02138 Fax: 415-440-6152.

ROSENSAFT, JEAN BLOCH, university administrator; b. N.Y.C., Jan. 6, 1952; d. Sam E. and Lilly Bloch; m. Menachem Rosensaft, Jan. 13, 1974, 1 child, Joana Deborah. BA in Art History, Barnard Coll., 1973; postgrad., NYU, 1978. Gallery lectr. in spl. exhbns. Mus. of Modern Art, N.Y.C., 1977-80; NEA lectr. on collections Modern Art Edn. Dept., 1979-80, spl. asst. for ind. sch. program, 1980-83, spl. asst. for publs., 1983-84; coord. pub. programs The Jewish Mus., N.Y.C., 1984-86, asst. dir. of edn., 1986-89; sr. nat. dir. for pub. affairs and institutional planning Hebrew Union Coll.-Jewish Inst. of Religion, N.Y.C., 1989—, exhbns. dir., 1994—2000, mus. dir., 2000—. Author: Chagall and the Bible, 1987; editor: Ann Sperry: 30 Pieces/30 Years, 2003, The Art of Aging, 2003. Mem. collections and acquisitions com. U.S. Holocaust Meml. Mus., Washington, 1980—; mem. steering com. Coun. of Am. Jewish Mus., N.Y.C., 1995—; chair task force on the arts UJA/Fedn. Women's Task Force, N.Y.C., 1995—; v.p. Internat. Network of Children of Jewish Holocaust Survivors, N.Y.C., 1987—; chair Park Ave Synagogue H.S. Parents Assn., N.Y.C., 1993-96, sch. bd., 1993—, adv. bd. 1996—. George Welwood Murray fellow Barnard Coll., 1973. Home: 179 E 70th St New York NY 10021-5109 Office: Hebrew Union Coll-Jewish Inst Religion 1 W 4th St New York NY 10012-1105

ROSENSTEIN, MARY ELISABETH MALLORY, retired social worker; b. Los Gatos, Calif., Feb. 25, 1916; d. Merton Shannon and Mabel Beatrice (Penny) Mallory; m. Albert Rosenstein, Sept. 20, 1947; children: Nathan Stewart, Thomas Mallory. AB, U. Calif., Berkeley, 1937; MA in Social Work U. Chgo., 1950. Licn. clin. social worker, marriage, family and child counselor, Calif. Caseworker Calif. Relief Adminstrn., San Francisco, 1938-40, San Francisco Children's Agy., 1940-42; caseworker foster home placement Oakland (Calif.) Family Svc., 1942-44; psychiat. social worker ARC Hosp. Svc., Oakland and Long Beach, Calif., 1946-51, Calif. Dept. Mental Health, L.A., Long Beach, Santa Ana, Calif., 1950-51; dist. supr. Calif. Dept. Mental Health, L.A., 1951-53; caseworker, acting dir. Family Svc. Assn. Rio Hondo Area, Whittier, Calif., 1954-81; pvt. practice, 1981-91; ret., 1991. Chmn. mental health study LWV, Whittier, 1974-76; workshop leader Montebello (Calif.) Child Study Workshop; chmn. liaison com. San Gabriel Valley Regional County Mental Health, Pasadena, Calif., 1976-81; cons. dist. teen mothers Montebello Unified Sch. Dist. Mem. Whittier Area Coordinating Coun., 1960—; pres. Birney Elem. Sch. PTA, Pico Rivera, Calif., 1957; cellist Rio Hondo Symphony Assn. Orch., Whittier, 1970-97; v.p., membership chmn. UN Assn., Whittier, 1968-97. Recipient commendation Calif. Legislature, 1981, U.S. Ho. of Reps., 1981, County of L.A., 1981, spl. citation UN Assn. U.S.A., 1996. Fellow Soc. for Clin. Social Workers; mem. NASW (diplomate in clin. social work), Acad. Cert. Social Workers, AAUW (Las Distinguitas award 1979), LWV. Democrat. Unitarian Universalist. Avocations: music, gardening, swimming, river rafting, live theater.

ROSENSTOCK, LINDA, federal agency administrator, medical educator; b. N.Y.C., Dec. 20, 1950; AB in Psychology, Brandeis U., 1971; student, U. B.C., Vancouver, Can., 1971-72; MD, MPH, Johns Hopkins U., 1977. Diplomate Am. Bd. Internal Medicine, Am. Bd. Preventive Medicine; lic. physician and surgeon, Wash. Med. resident then chief resident U. Wash., Seattle, 1977-80, resident in preventive medicine, instr. medicine, 1980-82, asst. prof., 1982-83, 83-87, lectr. environ. health, 1982-83, adj. asst. prof., 1983-86, mem. grad. sch. faculty, 1985—, assoc. prof., 1987-93, prof. medicine and environ. health, 1993—, also dir. programs, 1994—; dir. Nat. Inst. Occupational Safety and Health, Washington, 1997—. Dir. Harborview Med. Ctr., Seattle, 1981-87, acting sect. head, 1992-94; dir. Nat. Inst. Occupational Safety and Health, Washington, 1994—. Assoc. editor Internat. Jour. Occupational Medicine and Toxicology, 1991—; mem. editorial bd. Am. Jour. Indsl. Medicine, 1985-94, Jour. Gen. Internal Medicine, 1987-90, Environ. Rsch., 1987—, Western Jour. Medicine, 1990—; contbr. numerous articles to profl. jours. Mem. exec. bd. Physicians for Human Rights, 1990—; mem. occupl. health adv. bd. United Auto Workers GM, 1990-94, chair, 1993-94; mem. task force on pneumoconioses Am. Coll. Radiology, 1991-94; mem. external adv. panel Agrl. Health and Safety Ctr., 1992-93; mem. adv. com. Ctrs. for Disease Control, 1992-94; mem. com. to survey health effects of mustard gas and lewisite Inst. Medicine, 1992, mem. bd. health promotion and disease prevention, 1993-94; mem. bd. sci. counselors HHS, 1993-94, mem. exec. com. nat. toxicology program, 1994—; mem. med. adv. bd. Teamsters Internat., 1993-94. Recipient Upjohn Achievement award Harborview Med. Ctr., 1978, Jean Spencer Felton MD award Western Occupational Med. Assn., 1988, Environ. and Occupational Medicine award Nat. Inst. Environ. Health Scis., 1991-94, Robert Wood Johnson scholar, 1980-82, Henry J. Kaiser scholar, 1984-89. Fellow ACP (health promotion subcom. 1989-90, clin. practice subcom. 1990-91), Collegium Ramazzini; mem. APHA (chair membership com. 1983-85, chairperson occupational helath and safety sect. 1985-86, gov. coun. 1986-88), Am. Coll. Occupational Medicine (mem. jud. com. 1989-94), Am. Thoracic Soc. (com. health care policy and clin. practice 1990-93), Internat. Commn. Occupational Health (sci. com. epidemiology in occupational health 1989—), Soc. Gen. Internal Medicine (program planning com. 1987, Glaser award com. 1993-94), Western Assn. Physicians, Pacific Interurban Clin. Club. Office: Nat Inst Occpl Safety and Health 200 Independence Ave SW Rm 715H Washington DC 20201-0004

ROSENSTOCK, SUSAN LYNN, orchestra administrator; b. Bklyn., Nov. 2, 1947; BS, SUNY, Cortland, 1969; MBA, So. Meth. U., 1977, MFA, 1978. Asst. mgr. Columbus (Ohio) Symphony Orch., 1978-82; grants program dir., info. officer Greater Columbus Arts Coun., 1982-83, asst. dir. grants and adminstrn., 1983-84; dir. ann. giving and spl. events Columbus Symphony Orch., 1984-86, dir. devel., 1986-90, orch. mgr., 1990-98, gen. mgr., 1998—. Panelist Ohio Arts Coun. Music Panel, 1986, 87, NEA, 2002, Challenge Grants Panel, 1991, J.C. Penney Gold Rule Award Judges Panel, 1993, 94. Mem. Am. Symphony Orch. League (devel. dirs. steering com. nat. conf. 1987, 88), Nat. Soc. Fund Raising Execs. (program com. Ctrl. Ohio chpt. 1988-94, chmn. program com. 1993, 94, bd. dirs. 1993-95, treas. 1995). Office: Columbus Symphony Orch 55 E State St Columbus OH 43215-4203 E-mail: susanr@columbussymphony.com.

ROSEN-SUPNICK, ELAINE RENEE, physical therapist; b. N.Y.C., May 7, 1951; d. Oscar Arthur and Sydell (Zimmerman) R.; m. Jed Supnick, Apr. 21, 1985. BS, CUNY, 1973; MS, L.I. U., Bklyn., 1977; D of Health Sci., U. St. Augustine, 1998. Cert. orthop. specialist/Am. Bd. Phys. Therapy Specialists. Phys. therapy cons. Lenox Hill Hosp. Home Care, N.Y.C., 1977-83, Group Health Ins., Queens, N.Y., 1977-83, Vis. Nurse Assn., Bklyn., 1977-83; sr. phys. therapist Bird S. Coler Hosp., Roosevelt Island, N.Y., 1973-77; assoc. prof. CUNY-Hunter Coll., 1977—; ptnr. Queens Phys. Therapy Assocs., Forest Hills, N.Y., 1982—. Fellow Am. Acad. of Orthop. Manual Phys. Therapists; mem. Am. Phys. Therapy Assn. (bd. cert. orthop. specialist, cert. phys. ther Democrat. Jewish. Office: Queens Phys Therapy Assocs 6940 108th St Flushing NY 11375-3851 E-mail: elaine.rosen@hunter.cuny.edu.

ROSENTHAL, DONNA MYRA, social worker; b. Rochester, NY, Feb. 23, 1944; d. Harry Lionel and Leila Estelle (Eber) Rosenthal; m. Thomas Robert Kolar, Aug. 5, 1979. BA, George Washington U., 1965; MS, Columbia U., 1967. Cert. social worker. Community organizer Health & Welfare Coun. Nassau County, Uniondale, N.Y., 1967-68; field rep. N.Y. State Office Aging, N.Y.C., 1968-73; asst. dir. United Neighborhood Houses, N.Y.C., 1973-84; exec. dir. Nat. Down Syndrome Soc., N.Y.C., 1984-94; exec. vice chmn. CLAL-The Nat. Jewish Ctr. for Learning and Leadership, N.Y.C., 1994—. Pres. Exec. Women in Human Svcs., N.Y.C., 1985-89. Pres. Congregation Beth Elohim, Bklyn., 1991-94; pres. Columbia U. Social Work Alumni, NYC, 1989-91; 3rd vice-chmn. adv. coun. Columbia U. Sch. Social Work, 1991-2000, co-chair centennial com., 1995-98, chmn. adv. coun. 2000—; treas. Alumni Fedn. Columbia U., 1995-97, sec., 1997-99, v.p., 1999-2001, pres. 2001-03. Recipient Alumni medal Columbia U., 1991; NIMH fellow Columbia U., 1966-67, Regents scholar, 1961. Avocation: music. Office: CLAL 440 Park Ave S New York NY 10016-8012

ROSENTHAL, HELEN NAGELBERG, county official, advocate; b. N.Y.C., June 6, 1926; d. Alfred and Esther (Teichholz) Nagelberg; m. Albert S. Rosenthal, Apr. 10, 1949 (dec.); children: Lisa Rosenthal Michaels, Apryl Meredith Rosenthal Stuppler. BS, CUNY, 1948; MA, NYU, 1950; postgrad., Adelphia U., L.I. U., Lehman Coll., 1975. Cert. early childhood and gifted edn. tchr., N.Y., N.J., elem. and secondary tchr., Fla. Tchr. gifted students N.Y. Bd Edn., Bklyn., 1949-77, 79-87, Baldwin (N.Y.) Pub. Schs., 1977-79; rep. community affairs County of Dade, Fla., 1988-92; ret., 1992; condo dir. Pembroke Pines, 1999—. Author: Criteria for Selection and Curriculum for the Gifted, 1977, Science Experiments for Young Children, 1982, Music in the Air...and in Our Minds. Dir. Condominium, 1989-91. Recipient Departmental award, 1948. Mem. Concerned Citizens for Educating Gifted and Talented (officer N.Y.C. chpt.), Assn. Gifted and Talented Edn. (N.Y. chpt.), Am. Inst. Cancer Rsch., Bklyn. Coll. Alumni Assn. (pres. Broward-Dade chpt. 1995-96, v.p. membership 1996—).

ROSENTHAL, JANE, film company executive; b. Providence, 1957; d. Martin and Ina; m. Craig Hatkoff; children: Juliana, Isabella. Student, Brown U.; BA, NYU, 1977. Rsch. staff CBS Sports, NY; editor program practices CBS Entertainment, 1977, program exec. miniseries, 1978, assoc. dir. motion pictures for TV, 1979; v.p. feature prodn. Universal Studios, 1984—85; v.p. in charge of motion pictures and TV Walt Disney, 1985—87; v.p. in charge of movies and miniseries Warner Bros. TV, 1987—88; co-founder Tribeca Films, N.Y.C., 1988—, Tribeca Film Festival, N.Y.C., 2002. Prodr.: (films) Thunderheart, 1992, Night and the City, 1992, A Bronx Tale, 1993, Faithful, 1996, Marvin's Room, 1996, Wag the Dog, 1997, Analyze This, 1999, Entropy, 1999, Flawless, 1999, The Adventures of Rocky & Bullwinkle, 2000, Meet the Parents, 2000, Prison Song, 2001, Showtime, 2002, About a Boy, 2002, Analyze That, 2002; (TV series) Tribeca, 1993; exec. prodr.: (films) Nine, 1996, The Repair Shop, 1998; (TV films) Witness to the Mob, 1998, Holiday Heart, 2000, Porn 'n Chicken, 2002. Office: Tribeca Prodns 6th Fl 375 Greenwich St New York NY 10013*

ROSENTHAL, LEE H. federal judge; b. Nov. 30, 1952; m. Gary L. Rosenthal; children: Rebecca, Hannah, Jessica, Rachel. BA in Philosophy with honors, U. Chgo., 1974, JD with honors, 1977. Bar: Tex. 1979. Law clk. to Hon. John R. Brown U.S. Ct. Appeals (5th cir.), 1977-78; assoc. Baker & Botts, 1978-86, ptnr., 1986-92; judge U.S. Dist. Ct. (so. dist.) Tex., 1992—. Vis. com. Law Sch. U. Chgo., 1983-86, 94-97, 99-2001; mem. Fed. Jud. Conf. Adv. Com. for Fed. Rules of Civil Procedure, 1996—; chair 1999 Fifth Cir. Jud. Conf. Mem. bd. editors Manual for Complex Litigation, 1999—. Mem. devel. com. Tex. Children's Hosp., 1988-92; pres. Epilepsy Assn. Houston/Gulf Coast, 1989-91; trustee Briarwood Sch. Endowment Found., 1991-92; bd. dirs. Epilepsy Found. Am., 1993-98, DePelchin Children's Ctr., 2000—. Fellow Tex. Bar Found.; Mem. ABA, Am. Law Inst. (consultative group for transnat. rules of civil procedure), Texas Bar Assn., Houston Bar Assn. Office: US Dist Ct US Courthouse Rm 11535 515 Rusk St Houston TX 77002-2600

ROSENTHAL, LUCY GABRIELLE, writer, educator, editor; b. N.Y.C. d. Henry Moses and Rachel (Tchernowitz) R. AB, U. Mich., 1954; MS in Journalism, Columbia U., 1955; MFA, Yale Sch. Drama, 1961; postgrad. Writers Workshop, U. Iowa, 1965-68. Asst. editor Radiology mag., Detroit, 1955—57; free-lance editl. cons. various pub. houses, lit. agts. N.Y.C., 1957—73; mem. admissions staff Writers Workshop U. Iowa, Iowa City, 1965—68; editor Book-of-the-Month Club, N.Y.C., 1973—74, mem. editl. bd. judges, 1974—79, sr. editl. advisor, 1979—87. Mem. biography jury Pulitzer Prize, 1980; mem. bd. Am. Book Awards, 1981-82; adj. prof. English, NYU, 1986—; mem. guest faculty in writing Sarah Lawrence Coll., 1988-96, regular faculty writing, 1996—; lectr., adj. asst. prof. writing program Columbia U., 1990-96, Humanities faculty, 92nd St. YM/YWCA, 1987; fiction workshop The Writer's Voice, West Side YMCA, summer 1991; adj. prof. NYU Sch. Continuing Edn., 1988; mem. faculty Sarah Lawrence Ctr. for Continuing Edn., 1989, 90; instr. fiction writing course Art Workshop Internat., Assisi, Italy, summer 1993. Plays produced at Eugene O'Neill Meml. Theater Ctr., 1966, 67; author: The Ticket Out, 1983; editor; Great American Love Stories, 1988, The World Treasury of Love Stories, 1995, The Eloquent Short Story: Varieties of Narration, 2004; contbr. articles and revs. to various mags. and periodicals including Washington Post and Chgo. Tribune Book World, Saturday Rev., Ms. mag., Mich. Quar. Rev., N.Y. Times Book Rev.; contbr. fiction to Global City Rev., 1995. Pulitzer fellow critical writing, 1968. Mem. Authors Guild, Authors League, Nat. Book Critics Circle, Women's Media Group (bd. mem. 1979-81), PEN, Phi Beta Kappa, Phi Kappa Phi. Office: Sarah Lawrence Coll Bronxville NY 10708 E-mail: lrosenth@slc.edu.

ROSENTHAL, LYOVA HASKELL See GRANT, LEE

ROSENTHAL, MARILYN, school librarian, educator; b. Cambridge, Mass., Oct. 8, 1941; d. Edward and Helen Ruth Goldman; m. Stephen Alan Rosenthal, Apr. 11, 1964; children: Diane Wood, David. AB, Vassar Coll., 1963; MA in French, NYU, 1965; MS in Libr. Sci., Palmer Sch. Libr. and Info. Sci., 1979. Reference trainee Post Ctr. for Bus. Rsch., Brookville, NY, 1978—79; adj. reference libr. North Bellmore (N.Y.) Pub. Libr., 1979—83; adj. libr. Nassau C.C. Libr., Garden City, NY, 1983—88, instr., 1988—93, asst. prof., 1993—98, assoc. prof., reference libr., 1998—2003, prof., 2004—. Mem. interlibr. loan com. L.I. Libr. Coun., 1988—, chmn., 1989—95; presenter in field.; mem. adv. panel on info. literacy Mid. States Commn. on Higher Edn., 2002—; v.chmn. academic senate Nassau C.C., 1997—2001. Contbr. chapters to books, articles, revs. to profl. publs. Del. SUNY Librs. Assn. Coun., 1990—2001. Recipient Chancellor's award for Excellence in Librarianship, SUNY, 1996. Mem.: Assn. Coll. Rsch. Librs. (symposium planning com.), Assn. Coll. and Rsch. Librs. (vice chmn. L.I. sect. 1992, membership sec. 1994—2000, v.p. 2000, mem. chpts. coun. 2000—02, pres. 2001, past-pres. 2002, L.I. sec. 2003), Women's Faculty Assn. Nassau C.C. (membership sec. 1993—96, pres. 1996—2000, past pres. 2000—02, recording sec. 2003—). Home: 4 Northwood Ct Woodbury NY 11797

ROSENTHAL, NAN, curator, educator, author; b. N.Y.C., Aug. 27, 1937; d. Alan Herman and Lenore (Fry) R.; m. Otto Piene (div.); m. Henry Benning Cortesi, Sept. 5, 1990. BA, Sarah Lawrence Coll., 1959; MA, Harvard U., 1970, PhD, 1976. Asst. prof. art history U. Calif., Santa Cruz, 1971-77, assoc. prof., 1977-84, prof., 1985-86, chair dept. art history, 1976-80; curator 20th-century art Nat. Gallery Art, Washington, 1985-92; sr. cons. dept. modern art Met. Mus. of Art, N.Y.C., 1993—; Lila Acheson Wallace vis. prof. fine arts NYU Inst. Fine Arts, N.Y.C., 1996, 2000. Vis. prof. art history Fordham U., Lincoln Ctr., 1981, 85; vis. scholar N.Y. Inst. for Humanities, NYU, 1982—83; vis. lectr. visual arts Princeton U., 1985, 88, 92; adj. prof. art history Columbia U., 2002. Author: George Rickey, 1977; also exhbn. catalogues, catalogue essays and articles; art editor Show, 1963-64; assoc. editor, then editor at large and contbg. editor Art in Am., 1964-70. Radcliffe Inst. fellow, 1968-69, scholar, 1970-71; travelling fellow Harvard U., 1973-74, rsch. fellow U. Calif., 1978, Ailsa Mellon Bruce curatorial fellow Nat. Gallery of Art, 1988-89; rsch. and travel grantee U. Calif., Santa Cruz, 1974, 77-80, 82-85. Office: Met Mus of Art Dept Modern Art 1000 Fifth Ave New York NY 10028-0113 E-mail: nan.rosenthal@metmuseum.org.

ROSENTHAL, SHIRLEY LORD, cosmetics magazine executive, novelist; b. London, Aug. 28; came to U.S., 1971; d. Francis J. and Mabel Florence (Williamson) Stringer; m. James Hussey; m. Cyril Lord; m. David Anderson; m. A. M. Rosenthal, June 10, 1987; children: Mark, Richard. Student, S.W. Essex Coll., London, 1948—50. Reporter London Daily Mirror; fiction editor Woman's Own, 1950-53; features editor Good Taste mag., 1953-56; features, fiction editor Woman and Beauty, 1956-59; women's editor Star Evening newspaper, 1959-60, London Evening Standard, 1960-63, London Evening News, 1963-68; beauty editor Harper's Bazaar, London, 1963-71, N.Y.C., 1971-73; beauty, health editor Vogue mag., Condé Nast Publs., N.Y.C., 1973-75; v.p. corp. rels. Colgate, Helena Rubinstein, N.Y.C., 1975-80; beauty dir. Vogue mag., 1980—95, contbg. editor, 1995—. Chairwoman media coun. The Am. Acad. Dermatology, 1995—; corp. v.p. content iBeauty.com, 1999—2002. Syndicated Field columnist on beauty, health; author 3 beauty books; also novels: Golden Hill, 1982; One of My Very Best Friends, (Lit. Guild Selection), 1985; Faces, 1989; My Sister's Keeper, 1993, The Crasher, 1998. City commr. Craigavon City, No. Ireland, 1963-68. Address: 131 E 66th St New York NY 10021-6129 E-mail: Shirlord3@aol.com.

ROSENTHAL, SUSAN R. pediatrician, educator; MD, Mount Sinai Sch. of Medicine, N.Y.C., 1977. Diplomate Pediatrics Am. Bd. Pediarics, 1981, Pediatric Gastroenterology Am. Bd. Pediatrics, 1990. Intern in Pediatrics Bronx Mcpl. Hosp., N.Y.C., 1977—78; resident Boston Children's Hosp. Med. Ctr., 1978—80; fellow in Pediatric Gastroenterology and Nutrition Mass. Gen. Hosp., Boston, 1980—82; physician dept. Pediatrics Robert Wood Johnson U. Med. Group, New Brunswick, NJ, 1995—. Clin. assoc. prof. Pediatrics Robert Wood Johnson Univ. Hosp., New Brunswick, 1998—, asst. dean of students, 1998—. Office: Clin Acad Bldg Se 6140 125 Paterson St New Brunswick NJ 08901-1977

ROSENWASSER, DONNA, management consulting company executive; CFO McKinsey & Co., Inc., N.Y.C. Office: McKinsey & Co Inc 55 E 52nd St Fl 18 New York NY 10055-0183

ROSENZWEIG, AMY, biochemist, educator; BA, Amherst Coll., 1988; PhD., MIT, 1992. NIH fellow Harvard Med. Sch., Dana Farber Cancer Inst.; asst. prof. of biochemistry, molecular Biology, and cell biology Northwestern U., 1997—2002, asst. prof. chem., 1997—2002, assoc. prof., 2002—. Recipient Camile and Henry Dreyfus Tchr - Scholar. award; fellow David and Lucile Packard, MacArthur Found., 2003. Office: Northwestern Univ Dept BMBCB Cook Hall 4162 2220 Campus Dr Evanston IL 60208

ROSENZWEIG, PEGGY A. state legislator; b. Detroit, Nov. 5, 1936; married; 5 children. BS, U. Wis., Milw., 1978; postgrad., Wayne State U. Wis. state assemblyman Dist. 98, 1982-92, Dist. 14, 1993; mem. Wis. Senate from 5th dist, Madison, 1993—. Former ranking minority mem. Health Com. Former dir. comty. rels. Milw. Regional Med. Ctr.; former pres. Med. Coll. Wis. Mem. LWV. Address: 6236 Upper Pkwy N Wauwatosa WI 53213-2430 Office: Wis State Senate State Capitol PO Box 7882 Madison WI 53707-7882

ROSETE, AMY RENEE, accountant, writer, editor; b. Valencia, Calif., Feb. 25, 1976; d. David Arthur Warner and Barbara Ann Pickleheimer; m. Andy Rosete, Apr. 29, 1995; 1 child, Amareese. Cert. chiropractic asst., L.A. Coll. Chiropractic, 1995. Chiropractic asst. High Desert Chiropractic, Lancaster, Calif., 1994—96; receptionist, asst. acct. Sheila Scott M.D., Lancaster, 1996—99; acctg. adminstr. Lance Camper Mfg., Lancaster, 2000—; writer, assoc. editor AV Woman Mag., Palmdale, Calif., 2003—. Author: (poetry chapbook) Times Passions and Destiny's Tears, 1994 (Honorable Mention, 1994, Pres. award, 1994). Avocations: wine tasting, reading, writing, cooking. Office: AV Woman Mag PO Box 902195 Palmdale CA 93590

ROSHONG, DEE ANN DANIELS, dean, educator; b. Kansas City, Mo., Nov. 22, 1936; d. Vernon Edmund and Doradell (Kellogg) Daniels; m. Richard Lee Roshong, Aug. 27, 1960 (div.). BMusEd., U. Kans., 1958; MA in Counseling and Guidance, Stanford U., 1960; postgrad., Fresno State U., U. Calif.; EdD, U. San Francisco, 1980. Counselor, psychometrist Fresno City Coll., 1961-65; counselor, instr. psychology Chabot Coll., Hayward, Calif., 1965-75, coord. counseling svcs. Livermore, Calif., 1975-81, asst. dir. student pers. svcs., 1981-89, Las Positas Coll., Livermore, Calif., 1989-91, assoc. dean student svcs., 1991-94, dean student svcs., 1991—2003, life coach, 2000—; counselor Experience Unltd., Pleasant Hill, Calif., 2004—. Writer, coord. I, A Woman Symposium, 1974, Feeling Free to Be You and Me symposium, 1975, All for the Family Symposium, 1976, I Celebrate Myself Symposium, 1978, Person to Person in Love and Work Symposium, 1978, The Healty Person in Mind and Spirit Symposium, 1980, Change Symposium, 1981, Sources of Strength Symposium, 1982, Love and Friendship Symposium, 1983, Self Esteem Symposium, 1984, Trust Symposium, 1985, Prime Time: Making the Most of This Time in Your Life Symposium, 1986, Symposium in Healing, 1987, How to Live in the World and Still Be Happy Symposium, 1988, Student Success is a Team Effort, Sound Mind, Sound Body Symposium, 1989, Creating Life's Best Symposium, 1990, Choices Symposium, 1991, Minding the Body, Mending the Mind Symposium, 1992, Healing through Love and Laughter Symposium, 1993, Healing Ourselves Changing the World Symposium, 1994, Finding Your Path Symposium, 1995, Build the Life You Want Symposium, 1996, Making Peace With Yourself and Your Relationships Symposium, 1997, Everyday Sacred Symposium, 1998, Wisdom of the Heart Symposium, 1999, Inner Wisdom Symposium, 2000, Second Half of Life Symposium, 2001, A Celebration of Life Symposium, 2003, Viewing Mental Health and Mental Illness From a Multi-Cultural Perspective Symposium, 2004, others; mem. cast TV prodns. Eve and Co., Best of Our Times, Cowboy; chmn. Falling Awake Symposium, 2002, Celebration of Life Symposium, 2003, Calif. C.C. Chancellor's Task Force on Counseling, Statewide Regional Counseling Facilitators, 1993-95, Statewide Conf. Emotionally Disturbed Students in Calif. C.C.s, 1982—, Conf. on the Under Represented Student in Calif. C.C.s, 1986, Conf. on High Risk Students, 1989. Author: Counseling Needs of Comunity College Students, 1980. Bd. dirs. Teleios Sinetar Ctr., Ctr. for Cmty. Dispute Resolution, 1998—, Pleasanton Youth Collaborative Bd., 1997-2002, Pleasanton Youth Master Plan Bd., 1998—; choir dir., 1996-99; pres. Tri-Valley Unity Ch. bd., 1998, Tri-Valley Haven bd., 2000—, Calif. State U. at Hayward Inst. of Mental Illness and Wellness Edn. bd., 2000—, Ellis Life Coach Tng., 1999—; title III activity dir. Las Positas Coll., 1995-99, dir. pace program, 1999-2003, dir. quest program, 2000-03. Mem.: Calif C.C. Counselors Assn. (svc. award 1986—87, award for Outstanding and Disting. Svc. 1986—87, Pleasanton Mayor's award 2000—01, 2002), Calif. Assn. C. C. (chmn. commn. on students svcs. 1979—84), Assn. Counseling and Devel., Nat. Assn. Women Deans and Counselors, Western Psychol. Assn., Assn. Humanistic Psychologists. Home: 1856 Harvest Rd Pleasanton CA 94566-5456 Office: 3033 Collier Canyon Rd Livermore CA 94550-9797 E-mail: deeroshong@comcast.net.

ROSILE, GRACEANN, business management educator; b. Bessemer, Pa., July 5, 1950; d. Philip Joseph and Carmela Madeline Rosile; m. John Collins Ryan, Mar. 17, 1978 (div. Apr. 15, 1994); m. David Michael Boje, Dec. 30, 1995. BA in English Lit., St. Francis U., 1972; MPH in Hosp. Adminstrn., U. Pitts., 1975, MBA in Bus. Adminstrn., 1978, PhD in Bus. Adminstrn. and Hosp. Adminstrn., 1981. Asst. prof. Ind. U. of Pa., 1980—95; rsch. specialist, asst. faculty bus. adminstrn. N.Mex. State U., Las Cruces, 1996—. Bd. dirs. Jour. Mgmt. Edn.; presenter in field. Contbr. articles to profl. jours. Roman Catholic. Avocation: horseback riding and training. Home: 2831 Buena Vida Ct Las Cruces NM 88011 Office: NMex State U MSC 3DJ Box 3001 Corner Solano and University Las Cruces NM 88003

ROSITA, ALMA See DAVIES, ALMA

ROSKEY, CAROL BOYD, social studies educator, dean, director; b. Columbus, Ohio, Mar. 9, 1946; d. Clarence Eugene and Clara Johanna (Schwartz) B.; m. Joseph Meeks, Aug. 17, 1968 (div. 1981) m. William Roskey, Nov. 16, 2003 ; children: Catherine Rachael, Tiffany Johannah. BS, Ohio State U., Mex., 1968; MS, Ohio State U., 1969, PhD, 1972. Rsch. asst., assoc. Ohio State U., Columbus, 1968-71; internship Columbus Area C. of C., Ohio, 1970; lectr. Ohio State U., Columbus, 1970, 72; asst. prof. U. Mass., Amherst, 1972-74, Cornell U., Ithaca, N.Y., 1974-78, assoc. prof., 1978-80; legis. fellow Senate Com. Banking, 1984; supr. economist, head housing section USDA, Washington, 1980-85; assoc. prof. housing and consumer econs. U. Ga., Athens, 1985-90, prof., 1990-97, head housing and consumer econs., 1992-97; dean Coll. Family and Consumer Scis. Iowa State U., Ames, 1997—2003, dir. Family Policy Ctr., 2003—. Rsch. fellow Nat. Inst. for Consumer Rsch., Oslo, Norway, 1992; cons. Yale U., 1976-77, HUD, Cambridge, Mass., 1978, MIT Ctr. for Real Estate Devel. Ford Found. Project on Housing Policy; del. N.E. Ctr. for Rural Devel. Housing Policy Conf. Reviewer Home Econ. Rsch. Jour., 1987—01, ACCI conf., 1987—; contbr. articles to profl. mags. Mem. panel town of Amherst Landlord Tenant Bd.; bd. dirs. Am. Coun. Consumer Interests; mem. adv. coun. HUD Nat. Mfg. Housing, 1978-80, 91-93; chair Housing Mfg. Inst. Consensus Commn. on Fed. Standards. Recipient Leader award AAFCS, 1996, Disting. Alumni award Ohio State U., 1999; named one of Outstanding Young Women of Am., 1979; Columbus Womens Chpt. Nat. Assn. Real Estate Bds. scholar, Gen. Foods fellow, 1971-72, HEW grantee, 1978, travel grantee NSF bldg. rsch. bd., AID grantee, USDA Challenge grant, 1995-98. Mem. Am. Assn. Housing Educators (pres. 1983-84), Nat. Inst. Bldg. Sci. (bd. sec. 1984, 85, 89-92, bd. dirs. 1981-83, 85, 87-93), Internat. Assn. Housing Sci., Com. on Status on Women in Econs., Nat. Assn. Home Builders (Smart House contract 1989, treas. bd. human sci. 2001-03), Epsilon Sigma Phi, Phi Upsilon Omicron, Gamma Sigma Delta, Phi Beta Delta, Kappa Omicron Nu (v.p. of programs 1995-96), Phi Kappa Phi, others. Office: Iowa State U 2354 Palmer Ames IA 50011-0001

ROS-LEHTINEN, ILEANA, congresswoman; b. Havana, Cuba, July 15, 1952; d. Enrique Emilio and Amanda (Adato) Ros; m. Dexter Lehtinen; 2 children, 2 stepchildren. AA, Miami (Fla.)-Dade C.C., 1972; BA, Fla. Internat. U., 1975, MS, 1987. Prin. Ea. Acad., from 1978; mem. Fla. Ho. of Reps., Tallahassee, 1983—86, Fla. Senate, 1986—89, U.S. Congress from 18th Fla. dist., 1989—; mem. govt. reform com., internat. rels. com. Recipient Nat. Legis. award LULACH, 1999. Republican. Roman Catholic. Office: US Ho of Reps 2160 Rayburn Ho Office Bldg Washington DC 20515-0918*

ROSMUS, ANNA ELISABETH, writer; b. Passau, Germany, Mar. 29, 1960; d. Georg Rudolf and Anna Johanna (Friedberger) R.; divorced; children: Dolores Nadine, Beatrice Salome Kassandra M Sociology, German Lit. and Fine Arts, U. Passau, 1994; PhD (hon.), U. S.C., 2000. Spkr. and organizer in field. Author: Resistance and Persecution, 1983 (Geschwister Scholl prize, 1984), Exodus in the Shadow of Mercy, 1988, Robert Klein A German Jew Looks Back, 1991, Wintergreen Suppressed Murders, 1993 (Conscience in Media award, 1994), Pocking End and Renewal, 1995, What I Think, 1995, Out of Passau, 1999, Against the Stream, 2002, Leaving a City Hitler Called Home, 2004; guest talk shows, including documentaries and features in Germany, Austria, Gt. Britain, Denmark, Holland, France, Italy, Sweden, Poland, Can., U.S., S.Am., Australia, 1983-. Fundraiser Anne Frank Found., Jewish Cmty. Ctrs., Holocaust Ctrs., others, 1992—. Recipient Immigrant Achievement award Am. Immigration Lawyers Assn., 1998; named Best German Writer, European essay Competition, 1980; Sarnat award Anti Defamation League, 1994; Anna Rosmus Day, City of Santa Cruz, 1994. Mem. PEN Internat. Avocations: environment protection, multicultural projects, minority programs. E-mail: researchaer@hotmail.com.

ROSOF, PATRICIA J.F. retired secondary school educator; b. N.Y.C., May 19, 1949; d. Sylvan D. and Charlotte (Fischer) Freeman; m. Alan H. Rosof, Sept. 13, 1970; children: Jeremy, Simon, Ali. BA, NYU, 1970, MA,

1971, PhD, 1978. Cert. tchr. social studies, N.Y. Instr. history Iona Coll., New Rochelle, N.Y., 1978-81; tchr. social studies Profl. Children's Sch., N.Y.C., 1981-82, Hunter Coll. H.S., N.Y.C., 1984—2003; ret., 2003. European history reader Advanced Placement Ednl. Testing Svcs.; adj. asst. prof. Sch. Edn., Pace U., 2003; coll. bd. cons. Co-editor Trends in History, 1978-84, Hunter Outreach, 1988-92; contbr. articles to profl. jours. Internat. Cultural Soc. Korea fellow, 1989; CUNY Women's Rsch. and Devel. Fund grantee, 1993-95. Mem. Am. Hist. Assn., Orgn. History Tchrs. Avocations: tennis, attending concerts, shows and dance performances.

ROSS, A. CATHARINE, biochemist, educator; Bachelor's, U. Calif., Davis; Master's, Cornell U., PhD, 1976. Prof. dept. biochemistry Med. Coll. Pa. State U., University Park, Dorothy Foehr Huck chair in nutrition, 1994—. Recipient Mead-Johnson award, Am. Inst. Nutrition. Mem.: NIH (mem. policy panel), AAAS, NAS (mem. policy panel), Fedn. Am. Socs. Exptl. Biology (mem. policy panel), Am. Soc. Cell Biology, Am. Soc. Nutritional Scis. (Osborne and Mendel award), Phi Kappa Phi, Sigma Xi. Office: Pa State U 126 Henderson South University Park PA 16802

ROSS, AUDREY, theatrical publicist; b. Chgo., Aug. 3, 1938; d. Hyman and Frieda (Tangul) R. Dancer Ballet Russe de Monte Carlo, 1959, Chgo. Opera Ballet, 1963; dancer with Camelot, 1963-64 Lyric Opera Chgo., 1963; dancer with Oklahoma! Lincoln Ctr., 1969; publicist Pentacle Mgmt., N.Y.C., 1980-82, Audrey Ross/Publicity, N.Y.C., 1982—. Cons. dance program N.Y. State Coun. on the Arts, N.Y.C., 1972—, dance program assoc., 1979-80. Jewish. Home: 205 W End Ave Apt 16E New York NY 10023-4811 Office: 130 W 56th St New York NY 10019-3803

ROSS, BERNADETTE MARIE-TERESA, librarian; b. New Orleans, Sept. 23, 1948; d. Arnold and Doris Learson. MLS, U. S.C., 1975. Cert. libr., N.C. Instr. Southern U., New Orleans, 1972-74; libr. S.C. State Atty. Gen. Office, Columbia, 1975; head outreach svcs. Forsyth County Pub. Libr. Systems, Winston Salem, N.C., 1975-77; head libr. Reid Ross Sr. High Sch., Fayetteville, N.C., 1977-85; reference libr. Fayetteville State U., 1989—; head libr. Terry Sanford Sr. High Sch., Fayetteville, 1985—, co-chair sch. renewal process, 1992—. Coord. student forum on sch. violence, 1992—; presenter Fayetteville State U. Ednl. Forum, 1999; dist. rep. Cumberland County Schs. Media Adv. Com., 1997—; cons. in field; mem. Supt.'s Roundtable, 1998; participant N.C. State Libr. Leadership Youth Svcs. Project, 1999-00; coord. Black Pearls: African Am. Films in Transition, 2000. Author: Educator's Guide to the Internet, 1995, Vocational Assessment and the Internet: A Beginner's Guide, 1997; editor newsletters From the Shelf, 1980-85, The Media Express, 1985-89; sect. editor N.C. Libr., 1976; book reviewer N.C. Materials and Evaluation Ctr., Raleigh, 1979. Sec. Cumberland County Friends of the Libr., Fayetteville, 1984-86, pres., 1986-88; adv. bd. arts coun. Umoja Cultural Arts Festival, Fayetteville, 1989; creater, organizer First Charles Chesnutt Film Festival, 1991. Fayetteville Jr. League grantee, 1989—, Florence Rogers Trust grantee, Innovation in Edn. grantee, 1999. Mem. ALA, N.C. Libr. Assn., N.C. High Sch. Libr. Assn. (s.e. dist. dir. 1981-82), N.C. Edn. Assn., N.C. Ctr. for Advancement of Tchg., Cumberland County Edn. Assn., Nat. Coun. Negro Women (charter mem. Fayetteville chpt.), Phi Alpha Theta, Delta Sigma Theta. Home: 502 Nottingham Dr Fayetteville NC 28311-1334 Office: Terry Sanford Sr High Sch 2301 Fort Bragg Rd Fayetteville NC 28303-7035

ROSS, BEVERLEY LONG, real estate broker; b. Reno, Sept. 1, 1940; d. John Clemons Long and Roma Lucille Barkman; m. Barry L. Ross, Oct. 2, 1959; children: J. Michael, Pamela Jo Ross Snodgrass. BS, Calif. State, Sacramento, 1970; grad., Realtors Inst. Cert. residential specialist, accredited buyer rep. Tchr. Washoe County Schs., Reno, 1961-64; homebound tchr. Prince Georges County, Oxon Hill, Md., 1972-73; kindergarten tchr. Raleigh Pre-Sch., N.C., 1974-75; owner Boise (Idaho) Pre-Sch., 1975-82; realtor United Realty, Boise, 1977-79; assoc. broker, ptnr. Treasure Valley Realty, Boise, 1979-92; broker, owner Bev Ross Realty, Boise, 1992—. Mem. foothill plans com. City of boise, 1990—92; mem. source water assessment adv. com. Idaho Dept. Environ. Quality, Boise, 1998; elder Southminster Presbyn. Ch., 1991—92, corp. pres., treas., 2001—. Recipient Tribute to Women in Industry, Women's and Children's Alliance, 1999. Mem.: Women's Coun. Realtors (pres. 2000), Ada County Assn. Realtors (chair legis. com. 1991, dir. Ada County Realtors Found. 1999—2001, v.p. 2002, pres.-elect 2003, pres. 2004, Disting. Svc. award 1993), Idaho Assn. realtors (chair legis. com. 1992, state dir. continuing edn. task force 1997—98), Nat. Assn. Realtors, Soroptimist Internat. Boise (pres. 1988—89). Avocations: singing, reading, walking, traveling. Office Phone: 208-345-7555. E-mail: bev@bevrossrealty.com.

ROSS, CATHERINE JANE, lawyer, social policy analyst; b. N.Y.C., Dec. 27, 1949; d. Alexander I. and Wilma (Saltzman) Ross; m. Jonathan Rieder, Mar. 14, 1981. BA, Yale U., 1971, PhD, 1977, JD, 1987. Postdoctoral fellow/rsch. assoc. Yale Bush Ctr. in Child Devel. and Social Policy, New Haven, 1977—79; asst. prof. Yale Child Study Ctr., New Haven, 1979—85; assoc. Paul, Weiss, Rifkind, Wharton & Garrison, New York, 1987—94; asst. prof. law, history and edn. Boston Coll. Law Sch., 1994—96; assoc. prof. George Washington U. Sch. Law, 1996—. Vis. prof. U. Pa. Law Sch., 2001; mem. HHS Expert Working Group Adoption, 02; cons. Adminstrn. for Children Youth and Families, HEW, 1979, Conn. Dept. Children and Youth Svcs., 1978—84, ednl. films and radio programs. Joint editor: Child Abuse: An Agenda for Action, 1980. Del. Conn. Task Force on Juvenile Justice, 1979—80; com. mem. Conn. Task Force on Foster Care, 1979—81. Grantee Edna McConnell Clark Found., 1981—82, Herman and Amelia Ehrmann Found., 1979—82, Ford Found., 1980—82, John and Catherine MacArthur Found., 1981; Mellon fellow, Aspen Inst. Humanistic Studies, 1983—84. Fellow: Am. Bar Found.; mem.: ABA (vice chair working group on unmet legal needs of Am.'s children and th 1993—94, steering com. unmet legal needs of children 1993—94, chair 1994—97, co-chair 1997—98, mem. sect. litigation task force children, chair com. children's rights 1999—), Coalition Justice. Jewish. E-mail: cross@law.gwu.edu.

ROSS, CHARLOTTE PACK, social services administrator; b. Oklahoma City, Oct. 21, 1932; d. Joseph and Rose P. (Traibich) Pack; m. Roland S. Ross, May 6, 1951 (div. July 1964); children: Beverly Jo, Sandra Gail; m. Stanley Fisher, Mar. 17, 1991. Student U. Okla., 1949-52, New Sch. Social Rsch., 1953. Cert. tchr. Exec. dir. Suicide Prevention and Crisis Ctr. San Mateo County, Burlingame, Calif., 1966-88; pres., exec. dir. Youth Suicide Nat. Ctr., Washington, 1985-93; exec. dir. Death with Dignity Edn. Ctr., San Mateo, Calif., 1994—; pres. Calif. Senate Adv. Com. Youth Suicide Prevention, 1982-84; speaker Menninger Found., 1983, 84; instr. San Francisco State U., 1981-83; conf. coord. U. Calif., San Francisco, 1971—; cons. univs. and health svcs. throughout world. Contbg. author: Group Counseling for Suicidal Adolescents, 1984, Teaching Children the Facts of Life and Death, 1985; mem. editorial bd. Suicide and Life Threatening Behavior, 1976-89. Mem. regional selection panel Pres.'s Commn. on White House Fellows, 1975-78; mem. CIRCLON Svc. Club, 1979—, Com. on Child Abuse, 1981-85; founding mem. Women for Responsible Govt., co-chmn., 1974-79. Recipient Outstanding Exec. award San Mateo County Coordinating Com., 1971, Koshland award San Francisco Found., 1984. Fellow Wash. Acad. Scis.; mem. Internat. Assn. Suicide Prevention (v.p. 1985—), Am. Assn. Suicidology (sec. 1972-74, svc. award 1990), bd. govs. 1976-78, accreditation com. 1975—, chair region IX, 1975-82), Assn. United Way Agy. Execs. (pres. 1974), Assn. County Contract Agys. (pres. 1982), Peninsula Press Club.

ROSS, CONNIE L. music educator; b. Pratt, Ks., Nov. 5, 1952; d. Eugene Haile and Alta Ross. BA, Mid-Am. Nazarene U., 1975; MusM in Edn., Fort Hays State U., 2003. Vocal music tchr. USD 483, 1975—82; elem. vocal music tchr. USD 443, Dodge City, Kans., 1982—2003. Pvt. piano tchr. Ch. pianist & accompanist. Mem.: NEA, Music Edn. Nat. Conf., Delta Kappa Gamma (co-chmn. music com.). Home: 2805 Buffalo Dr Dodge City KS 67801

ROSS, DEBORAH KOFF, lawyer, state legislator; b. Phila., June 20, 1963; d. Marvin S. and Barbara A. (Klein) Koff; m. Stephen J. Wrinn, July 30, 1994. BA, Brown U., 1985; JD, U. N.C., 1990. Adminstrv./legis. coord. Citizens' Campaigns, Washington, 1985-87; lawyer Hunton & Williams, Raleigh, N.C., 1990-94; exec./legal dir. ACLU of N.C., Raleigh, 1994—2002; mem. N.C. Ho. Reps., 2002—. Sr. lectr. Law Sch. Duke U.; cons. in field; mem. race rels. implementation com. N.C. Ho. Reps. Co-chair Betsy McCrodden for Judge, Raleigh, 1994; bd. dirs. N.C. Vol. Lawyers for Arts, Raleigh, 1991—96; mem. Women's Polit. Caucus, Raleigh, 1993—. Friday Fellow for Human Rels., 1995. Mem. N.C. Bar Assn. (mem., sec. constnl. rights and responsibilities 1995—, childrens rights com. 1996—), Wake County Bar. Democrat. Avocations: swimming, walking, reading, the arts. Home: 425 S Boylan Ave Raleigh NC 27603-1956

ROSS, DESHAN JACKSON, elementary school educator; d. Edward Nathaniel and Geneva Jackson; m. Elton Ross, June 20, 1998. Assoc., Sandhills C.C., Pinehurst, N.C., 1995; Bachelor, St. Andrews Coll., Lauringburg, N.C., 1998. Asst. tchr. Moore County Schs., Pinehurst, NC, 1995—98, kindergarten tchr. Vass, NC, 1998—99, 1st grade tchr. Aberdeen, NC, 1999—. Avocations: cross stitch, gospel choir, camping, reading, teaching. Office: Aberdeen Primary Sch 310 Keyser St Aberdeen NC 28315

ROSS, DIANA ERNESTINE EARLE, singer, actress, entertainer, fashion designer; b. Detroit, Mar. 26, 1944; d. Fred and Ernestine R.; m. Robert Ellis Silberstein, Jan. 1971 (div. 1976); children: Rhonda, Tracee, Chudney; m. Arne Naess, Oct. 23, 1985 (div. 2000, dec. 2004); children: Ross Arne, Evan Olaf. Pres. Diana Ross Enterprises, Inc., Anaid Film Prodns., Inc., RTC Mgmt. Corp., Chondee Inc., Rosstown, Rossville, music pub. Started in Detroit as mem. the Primettes, lead singer until 1969, Diana Ross and the Supremes; solo artist, 1969—; albums include Diana Ross, 1970, 76, Everything Is Everything, 1971, I'm Still Waiting, 1971, Lady Sings The Blues, 1972, Touch Me In The Morning, 1973, Original Soundtrack of Mahogany, 1975, Baby It's Me, 1977, The Wiz, 1978, Ross, 1978, 83, The Boss, 1979, Diana, 1981, To Love Again, 1981, Why Do Fools Fall In Love?, 1981, Silk Electric, 1982, Endless Love, 1982, Swept Away, 1984, Eaten Alive, 1985, Chain Reaction, 1986, Diana's Duets, 1987, Workin' Overtime, 1989, Red Hot Rhythm and Blues, 1987, Surrender, 1989, Ain't No Mountain High Enough, 1989, The Force Behind the Power, 1991, Stolen Moment: The Lady Sings... Jazz & Blues, 1993, Musical Memories Forever, 1993, The Remixes, 1994, A Very Special Season, 1994, Making Spirits Bright, 1994, Take Me Higher, 1995, Voice of Love, 1996, Gift of Love, 1996, The Greatest, 1998, The Real Thing, 1998, Every Day is a New Day, 1999; films include Lady Sings the Blues, 1972, Mahogany, 1975, The Wiz, 1978; NBC-TV spl., An Evening With Diana Ross, 1977, Diana, 1981, numerous others; TV movie Out of Darkness, 1994; author: Secrets of a Sparrow, 1993. Recipient citation V.P. Humphrey for efforts on behalf Pres. Johnson's Youth Opportunity Program, citation Mrs. Martin Luther King and Rev. Abernathy for contbn. to SCLC cause, awards Billboard, Cash Box and Record World as worlds outstanding singer, Grammy award, 1970, Female Entertainer Yr. NAACP, 1970, Cue award as Entertainer Yr., 1972, Golden Apple award, 1972, Gold medal award Photoplay, 1972, Antoinette Perry award, 1977, nominee as Best Actress Yr. Lady Sings the Blues Motion Picture Acad. Arts and Scis., 1972, Golden Globe award, 1972, BET (Black Entertainment Television) Walk Fame award, 1999, Heroes award, NARAS, NY Chpt., 2000; named to Rock and Roll Hall Fame, 1988. Office: c/o Motown Records 825 8th Ave New York NY 10019*

ROSS, ELLEN HARDMAN, graphic designer; b. Waynesboro, Va., Mar. 12, 1947; d. John Dewey and Betty Lou (Hardman) Ross; m. Warren Douglas Drumheller, June 7, 1969 (div. 1987); children: Amy Heather Drumheller, Warren Daniel Drumheller. BS, James Madison U., 1990. Cert. tchr. art K-12, Va. Graphic artist The News-Virginian, Waynesboro, 1990-92, advt. prodn./composing mgr., 1992-94; graphic designer The Humphries Press, Inc., Waynesboro, Va., 1994—. Recipient Distinction award Shenandoah Valley Art Ctr., 1989, 1st pl. award for design of newsletter Printing Industries of Va., 1995, 1st pl. for design of brochure, 1995, award of excellence for ann. report Vector Industries, 1996, award of excellence for letterhead & bus. cards WKDW/Oldies/WINF, 1997, 1st place award booklet process Turfgrass Quar. Jour., 1998. Mem. Va. Press Assn. (1st pl. color automotive advt. merit cert. 1991, 1st pl. color health, profl. svcs. advt. merit cert. 1991, 1st pl. color food and drugs, variety advt. merit cert. 1993). Methodist. Avocations: ceramics, watercolor, horseback riding. Home: 1830 S Talbott Pl Waynesboro VA 22980-2252 Office: NTELOS 1154 Shenandoah Dr Waynesboro VA 22980-1948

ROSS, ELLYN N. educational association administrator, consultant; b. Hackensack, N.J., Apr. 2, 1949; d. Peter Henry and June Ellyn Naclerio; m. David Bradley Ross, Mar. 16, 1996; children: Joshua David, Jesse Deacon, Janie Dianne, Jonathan Dwain. BS, Fla. State U., Tallahassee, Fla., 1971; MS, Fla. Internat. U., Miami, Fla., 1976, PhD, U. Pitts., Pitts, Pa., 2000. Cert. Orientation and Mobility Specialist Acad. for Cert. of Vision Rehab. and Edn., 1999, profl. tchr., visually impaired Commonwealth of Pa., 2001. Tchr. of students with visual impairment(s) Dade County Pub. Sch., Miami, Fla., 1971—76; ednl. specialist Dade-Monroe Diagnostic and Resource Ctr., Miami, Fla., 1976—77; tchr. of students with learning disabilities Dade County Pub. Sch., Miami, Fla., 1977—78, tchr. of students with visual impairment(s), 1978—88; coord., instrnl. resource svcs. Fla. Instrnl. Materials Ctr. for the Visually Impaired, Tampa, Fla., 1988—92; orientation and mobility specialist Susquehanna Assn. for the Blind and Vision Impaired, Lancaster, Pa., 1996—97; adj. faculty mem. Pa. Coll. of Optometry, Phila., 1996—2003; tchr. and orientation and mobility specialist/students with visual impairment(s) Lancaster-Lebanon Intermediate Unit 13, Lancaster, Pa., 1997—2000; ednl. cons. Pa. Tng. and Tech. Assistance Network, Harrisburg, Pa., 2000—. Orientation and mobility cert. bd. mem. Acad. for Cert. of Vision Rehab. and Edn. Profl., Tucson, 2001—02; profl. workshop presentation (invited speaker) Weekend with the Experts, Tampa, Fla., 2003; profl. presentation (juried) Coun. for Exceptional Children Ann. Conv., Charlotte, NC, 1999, Mpls., 98, Salt Lake City, 97, PA Spring Conf./Field of Visual Impairment, Grantville, Pa., 1996, numerous confs. in field. Author: (doctoral dissertation) Braille Reading Instruction for Beginning Readers: Perspectives Regarding Current Practice (Outstanding Disssertation of the Yr., 2000). Recipient Assoc. Master Tchr., State of Fla., 1984 - 1987, Superlative Academic Performance, U. Pitts., Honors Convocation, 1996; fellow Alumni Doctoral Fellowship, U. Pitts., 1995. Mem.: Coun. for Exceptional Children, Divsn. Visual Impairments (dir. exec. bd. 1991—93, student gov. 1993—95, dir. exec. bd. 1996—98, treas. 1998—2000, dir. exec. bd. 2000—02, pres.-elect 2004—), Internat. Dyslexia Assn., Assn. for Edn. and Rehab. of the Blind and Visually Impaired (south regional rep. (fla.) 1973—74), Coun. for Exceptional Children, Divsn. on Learning Disabilities. Avocations: piano, harp, travel, reading, needlecrafts. Home: 106 Stone Hedge Ct Lebanon PA 17042-7818 Office: PA Tng/Techl Assistance Network 6340 Flank Dr Ste 600 Harrisburg PA 17112-2764 Personal E-mail: ellynross@comcast.net.

ROSS, EUNICE LATSHAW, judge; b. Bellevue, Pa., Oct. 13, 1923; d. Richard Kelly and Eunice (Weidner) Latshaw; m. John Anthony Ross, May 29, 1943 (dec. Jan. 1978); 1 child, Geraldine Ross Coleman. BS, U. Pitts., 1945, LLB, 1951. Bar: Pa. 1952. Atty. Pub. Health Law Rsch. Project, Pitts., 1951-52; atty. jud. asst., law clk. Ct. Common Pleas Allegheny County, Pitts., 1952-70, dir. family divsn., 1970-72, judge, 1972-96, Commonwealth Ct. Pa., 1997—2004. Adj. law prof. U. Pitts., 1967-73; mem. Bd. Jud. Inquiry and Rev., Commonwealth of Pa., 1984-89, Gov's Justice Commn., 1972-78; mem. orphan's ct. rules com. Supreme Ct. Pa., 1998—. Author: (with others) Survey of Pa. Public Health Laws, 1952, Justice, 1995, Lötschers of Latterbach, Monnonite Heritage Mag., 2003; co-author: Will Contests, 1992; contbr. articles to law publs. Mem. exec. com. bd. trustees U. Pitts., 1980—86, bd. visitors Law Sch., 1985—, bd. visitors Sch. Health, 1986—98; mem. adv. bd. Animal Friends, Pitts., 1973—98; committeewoman for 14th ward, vice chmn. Pitts. Dem. com., 1972; bd. dirs. The Program, Pitts., 1983—87, Pitts. History and Landmarks Found., West Pa. Hist. Soc., West Pa. Conservancy. Named Girls Scouts Woman of Yr., Pitts. coun. Girl Scouts U.S.A., 1975, Alumni of Yr., U. Pitts. Law Sch., 2001; recipient Disting. Alumna award, U. Pitts., 1973, Medal of Recognition, 1987, Alumni award, U. Pitts. Sch. of Law, 2001, Susan B. Anthony award, Women's Bar Assn. Western Pa., 1993, Probate and Trusts award, 1994, cert. of achievement, Pa. Fedn. Women's Clubs, 1975, 1977. Mem.: ABA, Allegheny County Bar Assn. (vice chmn., exec. com. young lawyers sect. 1958—59), Pa. Trial Judges Conf., Scribes, Order of Coif. Home: 1204 Denniston Ave Pittsburgh PA 15217-1329

ROSS, JANE ARLENE, music educator; b. Uniontown, Pa., July 19, 1945; d. Earl Frank Diamond and Iva Jane Gower; m. Orval Jones Ross, June 17, 1967; 1 child, Elizabeth Jane. BS in Music Edn., Indiana U. of Pa., 1967; MusM in Music Edn., U. Akron, 1985, postgrad., Oberlin Coll., Ashland U. Music tchr. - elem. Fairview Park (Ohio) City Schs., 1967—70; music tchr.-jr. h.s. Medina (Ohio) City Schs., 1970—76, music tchr. - elem., 1979—2000; adj. prof. Ashland (Ohio) U., 2001—. Handbell choir cons. various area chs., Medina, 1994—99; guest clinician U. Akron, Ohio, 1986, Medina Coutny Schs., 1990; curriculum writer Medina City Schs., 1973. Contbr. articles to profl. jours. Organist, choir dir. United Ch. of Christ, Congl., Medina, 1972—79, Mt. Zwingli United Ch. of Christ, Wadsworth, Ohio, 1983—93; dir. music ministries First Christian Ch., Wadsworth, 2001—. Grantee, Rockefeller Bros. Fund, N.Y.C., 1984; scholar, Martha Holden Jennings Found., Cleve., 1988. Mem.: Am. Guild Organists, Am. Guild English Handbell Ringers, Music Educators Nat. Conf., Medina County Ret. Tchrs. Assn. (life), Ohio Ret. Tchrs. Assn. (life), Kappa Delta Pi, Delta Omicron (life) Democrat. Avocations: reading, collecting bells, old hymnals and music boxes, needlework, travel. Office: First Christian Ch 116 E Boyer St Wadsworth OH 44281 E-mail: jross@neo.rr.com.

ROSS, JEAN M. think-tank executive; Grad., U. Calif., Santa Cruz; M in City and Regional Planning, U. Calif., Berkeley. Asst. rsch. dir. Svc. Employees Internat. Union, Washington; sr. cons. Assembly Human Svcs.; prin. cons. Assembly Revenue and Taxation Com., exec. dir. Calif. Budget Project, Sacramento, 1994—. Mem. exec. com. Calif. Governance Consensus Project; bd. mem. Inst. on Taxation and Econ. Policy, Washington; mem. adv. com. Calif. Franchise Tax Bd.; spkr. in field. Contbr. articles to profl. jours. Sr. fellow, UCLA Sch. Pub. Policy and Social Rsch., 2000—01. Office: Calif Budget Project Ste 502 921 11th St Sacramento CA 95814-2820

ROSS, JOAN STUART, artist, art educator; b. Boston, Sept. 21, 1942; d. John Stuart and Lulu Margery (Nelson) Ross. BA, Conn. Coll., 1964; postgrad., Yale U., 1964-65; MA, U. Iowa, 1967, MFA, 1968; Advanced Cert. in Poetry, U. Wash., 1996. Cert. tchr. Wash. Instr. painting, printmaking Seattle Art Mus., 1992, Edmonds (Wash.) C.C., 1992-96, Pratt Fine Arts Ctr., Seattle, 1992-96, North Seattle C.C., 1996—. Mem. artist in city program Seattle Arts Commn., 1979—81; mem. new proposals program King County Arts Commn., 1977, 80. One-woman shows include Seattle Art Mus., 1981, 1982, Karl Bornstein Gallery, Sant Monica, 1982, Surrey (B.C., Can.) Art Gallery, 1982, Lawrence Gallery, Portland, Oreg., 1987, 1988, Foster/White Gallery, Seattle, 1981, 1983, 1985, 1987, 1989, 1990, Skagit Valley Coll., Mt. Vernon, Wash., 1990, Green River CC, Auburn, Wash., 1985, 1990, 1004 Gallery, Port Townsend, Wash., 1993, Grover/Thurston Gallery, Seattle, 1991, 1993, 1995, Friesen Gallery, 1997, others, exhibited in more than 200 group and juried shows. Mem. Bumbershoot Festival Commn., Seattle, 1985—91, Seattle Arts Commn., 1981—85; bd. dirs. N.W. Women's Caucus Arts. Recipient Bowen award, Seattle Art Mus., 1981. Mem.: N.W. Inst. Architecture and Urban Studies Italy (Rome fellow 1993), Book Arts Guild, Seattle Print Arts, N.W. Print Coun. Office Phone: 206-528-4536.

ROSS, JUNE ROSA PITT, biologist, educator; b. Taree, New South Wales, Australia, May 2, 1931; came to U.S., 1957; d. Bernard and Adeline Phillips; m. Charles Alexander, June 27, 1959. BSc with honors, U. Sydney, New S. Wales, Australia, 1953, PhD, 1959, DSc, 1974. Research assoc. Yale U., New Haven, 1959-60, U. Ill., Urbana, 1960-65, Western Wash. U., Bellingham, 1965-67, assoc. prof., 1967-70, prof. biology, 1970—, chair dept. biology, 1989-90. Pres. Western Wash. U. Faculty Senate, Bellingham, 1984-85; conf. host Internat. Bryozoology Assn., 1986. Author (with others): A Textbook of Entomology, 1982, Geology of Coal, 1984; editor (assoc.): Palaios, 1985—89; contbr. 130 articles to profl. jours. Recipient J. Wolfensohn Award of Excellence Sydney U. Grad. Union of N.Am., 1995, P. and R. Olscamp Outstanding Rsch. award Western Wash. U., 1986; NSF grantee. Mem.: Internat. Bryozoology Assn. (pres. 1992—95), The Paleontol. Soc. (councillor 1984—86, treas. 1987—93), Australian Marine Scis. Assn., U.K. Marine Biol. Assn. (life). Avocations: hiking, classical music. Office: Western Wash U Dept Biology Bellingham WA 98225-9160 Office Phone: 360-650-3634. E-mail: ross@biol.wwu.edu.

ROSS, KAREN, information technology executive; Founder, pres. Turn-Key Solutions, 1985—90; founder, prin. owner, CEO Sharp Decisions, N.Y.C., 1990—. Office: Sharp Decisions 55 W 39th St New York NY 10018

ROSS, KATHERINE, librarian; b. Glendale, Calif., Oct. 24, 1964; d. Homer and Maryella Bradley; m. Steven Ross, 2004. BA in English, Calif. State U., 1987; MLS, U. Az., 1990. Refrence libr. Kern Co. Libr., Bakersfield, Calif., 1990—. Staff assn. treas. Kern Co. Libr., Bakersfield, Calif., 1991, sec. libr. students orgn., U. Az., Tucson, 1990. Mem. Order Eastern Star. Republican. Avocations: sketching, sewing, basketball, hiking. Office: Kern Co Libr 701 Truxtun Ave Bakersfield CA 93301-4800

ROSS, KATHLEEN ANNE, academic administrator; b. Palo Alto, Calif., July 1, 1941; d. William Andrew and Mary Alberta (Wilburn) Ross. BA, Ft. Wright Coll., 1964; MA, Georgetown U., 1971; PhD, Claremont Grad. U., 1979; LLD (hon.), Alverno Coll. Milw., 1990, Dartmouth Coll., 1991, Seattle U., 1992; LHD (hon.), Whitworth Coll., 1992; LLD (hon.), Pomona Coll., 1993; LHD (hon.), Coll. of New Rochelle, 1998; LLD (hon.), U. Notre Dame, 1999, Gonzaga U., 1999; LHD (hon.), Carroll Coll., 2003. Cert. tchr., Wash. Secondary tchr. Holy Names Acad., Spokane, Wash., 1964-70; dir. rsch. and planning Province Holy Names, Wash. State, 1972-73; v.p. acads. Ft. Wright Coll., Spokane, 1973-81; rsch. asst. to dean Claremont Grad. Sch., Calif., 1977-78; assoc. faculty mem. Harvard U., Cambridge, Mass., 1981; pres. Heritage Coll., Toppenish, Wash., 1981—. Cons. Wash. State Holy Names Schs., 1971-73; coll. accrediting assn. evaluator N.W. Assn. Schs. and Colls., Seattle, 1975—; dir. Holy Names Coll., Oakland, Calif., 1979—; cons. Yakama Indian Nation, Toppenish, 1975—; speaker, cons. in field. Author: (with others) Multicultural Pre-School Curriculum, 1977, A Crucial Agenda: Improving Minority Student Success, 1989; Cultural Factors in Success of American Indian Students in Higher Education, 1978. Chmn. Internat. 5-Yr. Convocation of Sisters of Holy Names, Montreal, 1981, 96; TV Talk show host Spokane Coun. of Chs., 1974-76; mem. Nat. Congl. Adv. Com. on Student Fin. Assistance, 2002—. Named Yakima Herald Rep. Person of Yr., 1987, MacArthur fellow, 1997; recipient E.K. and Lillian F. Bishop Founds. Youth Leader of Yr. award, 1986, Disting. Citizenship Alumna award, Claremont Grad. Sch., 1986, Golden Aztec award, Wash. Human Devel., 1989, Harold W. McGraw Edn. prize, 1989, John Carroll awrd, Georgetown U., 1991, Holy Names medal, Ft. Wright Coll., 1981, Pres.'s medal, Estern Wash. U., 1994,

First Ann. Leadership award, Region VIII Coun. Advancement and Support Edn., 1993, Wash. State Medal of Merit, 1995, Lifetime Achievement award, Yakima YWCA, 2001, numerous grants for projects in multicultural higher edn., 1974—. Mem. Nat. Assn. Ind. Colls. and Univs., Soc. Intercultural Edn., Tng. and Rsch., Sisters of Holy Names of Jesus and Mary-SNJM. Roman Catholic. Office: Heritage Coll Office of Pres 3240 Fort Rd Toppenish WA 98948-9562 Office Phone: 509-865-8600.

ROSS, KATHRYN AMIE, psychologist; b. Miami Beach, Fla., Dec. 30, 1973; d. Nancy Lowenthal Ross-Bennett and Jonathan Michael Bennett(Stepfather), James Eli Ross; m. David Scully Jr., Apr. 6, 2002. BS with honors, U. of Fla., 1995; MS, Nova Southeastern U., Ft. Lauderdale, Fla., 1996; Psy. D., Nova Southeastern U., 2000. Lic. psychologist Fla., 2001. Psychology intern Dallas Child and Family Guidance Ctr., Dallas, 1999—2000; psychology resident Children's Psychology Assn., Weston, Fla., 2000—01, psychologist, assoc. dir., 2001—02; pvt. practice psychology Ft. Lauderdale, 2002—. Vol. Gilda's Club of South Fla., Ft. Lauderdale, Fla., 1997—99; mem. Pine Island Ridge Phase A-1 Condominiums, Davie, Fla., 2002—02. Recipient Hon. Mention, Gt. Women in Journalism, 1990. Mem.: APA (assoc.; mem. 1995—), Golden Key. Achievements include research in comparing symptoms of post-traumatic stress disorder and attention-deficit/hyperactivity disorder. Avocations: travel, exercise, yoga, sports. Office: Kathryn Ross PsyD PA PO Box 551363 Davie FL 33355 E-mail: drkathyross@yahoo.com.

ROSS, LESA MOORE, quality assurance professional; b. New Orleans, Jan. 25, 1959; d. William Frank and Carolyn West Moore; m. Mark Neal Ross, Nov. 30, 1985; children: Sarah Ann, Jacquelyne Caroline. BS in Engring., U. N.C., Charlotte, 1981; MBA in Quality and Reliability Mgmt., U. North Tex., 1991. Seismic qualification engr. Duke Power Co., Charlotte, N.C., 1981-82; quality assurance engr. Tex. Instruments Inc., Lewisville, Tex., 1982-91; compliance mgr. Am. Med. Electronics, Inc., 1992-93; owner Ross Quality Cons., 1993-95; customer quality assurance sect. mgr. Hitachi Semiconductor (Am.) Inc., 1995-96; v.p. quality Ross Networking Cons. Inc., Flower Mound, Tex., 1996—. Bd. dirs. Greater Lewisville YMCA, 2000—03. Recipient Nat. Sci. Found. Rsch. Grant, U. N.C., Charlotte, 1980. Mem. Am. Soc. Quality Control (cert. quality engr., quality auditor, reliability engr., cert. quality technician, cert. quality mgr., sec. Dallas sect. 1994-95, chair-elect Dallas sect. 1995-96, chair 1996-97), Zeta Tau Alpha (pres. 1984-85). Avocations: crafts, cross-stitching, reading, travel. Home and Office: 4925 Wolf Creek Trl Flower Mound TX 75028-1955 E-mail: Lross@rnc-inc.com.

ROSS, LISA SIMS, special education educator; b. Jackson, Miss., Feb. 14, 1952; d. Johnie Mack and Elizabeth Crane Sims; m. Richard C. Ross, Aug. 16, 1974 (div. Mar. 1996); children: Jason Conn, Robert Sims. BS, U. So. Miss., 1974, EdM, 1996. Cert. tchr. Miss. Spl. edn. tchr. Jackson County Sch., Wade, Miss., 1974—75, Holly Springs (Miss.) Sch., 1975—76, Lanar County Schs., Purvis, Miss., 1976—93, Richton (Miss.) City Sch., 1995—99; educator Ellisville (Miss.) State Sch., 1999—. Mem.: Miss. Assn. Educators, Kappa Delta Alumnae (pres. 1998—99), U. So. Miss. Alumni Assn. Baptist. Avocations: reading, exercise, shopping. Home: 2309 Adeline St Hattiesburg MS 39401 Office: Ellisville State Sch 1101 Hwy 11 South Ellisville MS 39437 Office Phone: 601-477-6245.

ROSS, LORETTA J. human rights association executive; Founder, exec. dir. Ctr. Human Rights Edn., Atlanta. Political commentator Good Morning Am., The Donahue Show, The Charlie Rose Show, CNN, BET. Office: Ctr Human Rights Edn PO Box 311020 Atlanta GA 31131-1020

ROSS, MADELYN ANN, newspaper editor; b. Pitts., June 26, 1949; d. Mario Charles and Rose Marie (Mangieri) R. BA, Indiana U. of Pa., 1971; MA, SUNY-Albany, 1972. Reporter Pitts. Press, 1972-78, asst. city editor, 1978-82, spl. assignment editor, 1982-83, mng. editor, 1983-93, Pitts. Post-Gazette, 1993—. Bd. dirs. PG Pub. Co.; instr. Community Coll. Allegheny County, 1974-81; Pulitzer Prize juror, 1989, 90. Mem. Task Force Leadership Pitts., 1985-92; v.p. Old Newsboys Charity Fund; bd. dirs. Dapper Dan Charity. Mem. Am. Soc. Newspaper Editors, Press Club of Western Pa. (pres.). Democrat. Roman Catholic. Avocations: tennis; piano; organ. Office: Pitts Post-Gazette 34 Blvd Of The Allies Pittsburgh PA 15222-1204

ROSS, MARILYN J. English and communications educator; BA in Am. Studies, U. Miami, Fla., 1969, MA in Am. Studies, 1971, PhD in Higher Edn. Leadership, 1995. Asst. prof. English Fla. Meml. Coll., 1971-84, assoc. prof. English and mass comm. arts, 1985-94, prof. higher edn., 1995—. Founder mass comm. arts program Fla. Meml. Coll., 1980, coord. modern langs., 1999—. Author: Success Factors of Young African American Males at a Historically Black College, 1998, Success Factors of Young African American Women at a Historically Black College, 2003; prodr. over 100 hrs. African Am., Caribbean and Hispanic programming, WLRN-TV. Recipient Outstanding Svc. award Vets. Club, 1979, Outstanding and Dedicated Svc. in Behalf of FMC award Miami Cable Access Corp., 1987, award Fla. Meml. Coll./Black Archives History and Rsch. Found. of South Fla., Inc., 1999. Mem. AAUW, Assn. Ednl. Leadership, Nat. Coun. Tchrs. of English, Epsilon Tau Lambda, Kappa Delta Pi, Phi Lambda Pi, Delta Theta Mu, Phi Kappa Phi, Phi Alpha Theta. Address: Unit F-602 1121 Crandon Blvd Apt F602 Key Biscayne FL 33149-2781

ROSS, MOLLY OWINGS, jewelry designer, sculptor, small business owner; b. Ft. Worth, Feb. 5, 1954; d. James Robertson and Lucy (Owings) R. BFA, Colo. State U., 1976; postgrad., U. Denver, 1978-79. Graphic designer Amber Sky Illustrators and Sta. KCNC TV-Channel 4, Denver, 1977-79; art dir. Mercy Med. Ctr., Denver, 1979-83, Molly Ross Design, Denver, 1983-84; co-owner Deltex Royalty Co., Inc., Colorado Springs, Colo., 1981—, LMA Royalties, Ltd., Colorado Springs, 1993—; art dir., account mgr. Schwing/Walsh Advt., Mktg. and Pub. Rels., Denver, 1984-87, prodn. mgr., 1987-88; jewelry designer Molly O. Ross, Gold and Silversmith, Denver, 1988—. Coun. mem. feminization of poverty critical needs area coun. Jr. League Denver, 1989—90, chmn. children in crisis/edn. critical needs area, 1990—91, chmn. project devel., 1991—92, co-chmn. Done in a Day Cmty. Project 75th Anniversary Celebration, 1991—93, bd. dirs., 1993—94, co-chmn. project IMPACT, 1994—95, exec. v.p. external affairs, 1995—96, co-chmn. cmty. coalitions com., 1996—98; mem. steering com. Denver Urban Resources Partnership, 1995—2002, steering com. chmn., 1996—99; pres.-elect Jr. League Denver, 1989—99, pres., 1999—2000; mem. steering com. Internat. Conf. on Vol. Adminstrn., 2001—02; bd. dirs. Environ. Def. Regional Adv. Bd., 2003—; pres. Four Mile Hist. Pk. Vol. Bd., 1985—86; bd. dirs. Four Mile Hist. Pk. Assn., 1985—86, Hist. Denver, Inc., 1986—87, Denver Emergency Housing Coalition, 1989—90; co-founder, bd. dirs. Ctr. Ethics and Social Responsibility/PREP, 1994—2001, pres. bd. dirs., 1997—99, treas. bd. dirs., 1999—2000; bd. dirs. Jr. League Denver Found., 1998—2002, Excelsior Youth Ctr. Found., 2001—, Friends of Warren Village, 2000—01, Art Reach, 2001—. Named Vol. of Month (March), Jr. League Denver, 1990, Vol. of Yr., Four Mile Hist. Pk., 1988; recipient Gold Peak Mktg. award-team design Am. Mktg. Assn., 1986, Silver Peak Mktg. award-team design Am. Mktg. Assn., 1986, Gold Pick award-art dir. Pub. Rels. Soc. Am., 1980-81, cert. Appreciation USDA, 1999, 2001. Mem. Natural Resources Def. Coun., Physicians for Social Responsibility, Am. Farmland Trust, Nat. Trust for Hist. Preservation, Environ. Def. Avocations: horseback riding, bicycling, hiking, backpacking, pastel drawing.

ROSS, NORA FAY, poet; b. Troy, Ala., Oct. 7, 1951; d. William Thomas and Elizabeth Nora M. Petty; m. Robert J. Ross, May 10, 1985 (div. June 21, 1997); children: H. Roy Ferrell, Linda F. Foster, William A. Ferrell, Tracey E. Guilott. Grad. h.s., Montgomery, Ala. Cashier retail bus., Gonzales, La., 1991—2001, Baton Rouge, 2001. Contbr. poetry to anthologies. Avocations: crafts, reading. Home: Apt 11-E Rte 2 Box 1 Evergreen AL 36401

ROSS, PATTI JAYNE, obstetrics and gynecology educator; b. Nov. 17, 1946; d. James J. and Mary N. Ross. B.S., DePauw U., 1968; M.D., Tulane, U., 1972; m. Allan Robert Katz, May 23, 1976. Asst. prof. U. Tex. Med. Sch., Houston, 1976-82, assoc. prof., 1982-98, prof., 1998—, dir. adolescent ob-gyn., 1976—, also dir. student edn., dir. devel. dept. ob-gyn.; cons. OrthoMcNeil and Wyeth-Pharm., 3M; speaker in field. Bd. dirs. Am. Diabetes Assn., 1982—; mem. Rape Coun. Diplomate Am. Bd. Ob-Gyn, Children's Miracle Network Hermann's Children's Hosp; Olympic torch relay carrier, 1996; founder Women's Med. Rsch. Fund, U. Tex. Med. Sch., Houston; bd. mem. Susan Komen Found. Appeared on Lifetime TV network. Mem. Tex. Med. Assn., Harris County Med. Soc., Houston Ob-Gyn. Soc., Assn. Profs. Ob-Gyn., Soc. Adolescent Medicine, AAAS, Am. Women's Med. Assn., Orgn. Women in Sci., Sigma Xi. Roman Catholic. Clubs: River Oak Breakfast, Profl. Women Execs. Contbr. articles to profl. jours. Office: 6431 Fannin St #3278 Houston TX 77030-1501

ROSS, RHODA, artist; b. Boston, Dec. 24, 1941; Student, Skowhegan Sch. Painting, 1986; BFA, RISD, 1964; MFA, Yale U., 1966. Art tchr. Emma Willard School, 1983-85, Nat. Found. For Advancement in Arts, 1985, Ocean County College, 1990, Chautauqua Sch. of Art, 1991, NYU, 1994-, The Lucy Moses School, 1987-; participant Art in Embassies Program Dept of State. One woman shows: Yale U., Pierson Coll., New Haven, 1967, Convent of the Sacred Heart, N.Y., 1976, Municipal Art Soc., N.Y., 1978, Long Island U., N.Y., 1981, Dietal Gallery, Emma Willard Sch., Troy, N.Y., 1983, Marymount Manhattan Coll., N.Y., 1985, N.Y.C. Landmarks Preservation Com. 25th Silver Anniversary, 1990, Frick Gallery, Maine, 1991; perm. collections include: Wilkie, Farr & Gallagher, N.Y., St. Louis Conservatory of Music, The Julliard School, Museum of The City of N.Y., Gracie Mansion, The White House; numerous other pvt. and pub. collections; artwork appears on New Sch. Social Rsch. catalog cover, Gifts and Decorative Accessories Mag. cover, UNICEF greeting card, The New York Times, The Chronicle, ABC-TV. Treas. R.I. Sch. Design Alumni Exec. Com. Fellow Va. Ctr. for Creative Arts; recipient Grumbacher Gold Medal, 1985. Mem. RISD Alumni Assn. (treas., mem. alumni exec. com.), Phi Tau Gamma. Home: 473 W End Ave New York NY 10024-4934 E-mail: rr18@nyu.edu.*

ROSS, SALLY PRICE, artist, painter; b. Cleve., Oct. 25, 1949; d. Philip E. and Mimi (Einhorn) Price; m. Howard D. Ross, Mar. 3, 1979; children: Sasha, Emily. BFA, Kent State U., 1971; MA, U. Iowa, 1974, MFA, 1975; student, Art Students League, N.Y.C., 1976-78. Art cons. Art Options, Cleve., 1990—94; 1st and only woman artist to paint murals U.S. Capital/Ho. of Reps. corridors, 1978—79. Exhibitions include, Cain Park Art Gallery, Cleve., 1967, Jewish Cmty. Ctr. Cleve., 1967, 1986, Canton (Ohio) Art Inst., 1969, Studio Theatre, Iowa City, 1973, The Cleve. Playhouse Art Gallery, 2000, Fairmount Art Ctr., Russell, Ohio, 2001 (Best in Show); designed and executed murals, Montefiore Nursing Home, Cleve., designed and executed 2 murals, Rainbow Babies and Children's Hosp. New Bldg., Cleve., 1996—97, Menorah Pk. Nursing Home, Cleve., 1997, (bibl. mural) Hartzmark Libr., 1999, The Temple, Cleve., 1999, (commd. works), Solon (Ohio) Libr., 1998—99, (4 commd. murals) Hilton Garden Inn, Cleve., 2002; mural, Univ. Hosps., Cleve., 2002, Hittor Garden, 2002. Scholar Edwin Abbey, 1975—77, Fresco, Skowhegan Sch. Painting and Sculpture, 1977. Home: 25 Millcreek Ln Chagrin Falls OH 44022-1265

ROSS, SELMA BELLE, retired not-for-profit fundraiser; b. N.Y.C., Feb. 20, 1924; d. Saul Irving and Sarah Leah Soble; m. Harold S. Davidow, Apr. 20, 1944 (dec. Jan. 5, 1974); children: Lauren Fitter, Gerald Davidow; m. Hyman Ross, Dec. 6, 1974 (dec. 1998). Student, Hunter Coll., 1942—43, City Coll., Manhattan, N.Y., 1943—44. Vol. USO Temple Emanuel, Manhattan, 1941; salesperson Jacowitz Bros. of Long Beach, N.Y., Lido Beach, 1960—63. Tchr. phonetic reading to slow achievers Ky. Mid. Sch., South Miami, Fla., 1998—2000. Author: (book of poetry) Things I Love to Do!, 1940. Pink lady, nurses' aid Long Beach Meml. Hosp., 1960—73; condr. vol. water aerobics class, 1996—99. Recipient several cert. of merit for svc., Long Beach Meml. Hosp., 1970, Washington County Hosp., Hagerstown, Md., 1974—86. Mem.: Brandeis Univ. Nat. Women's Com. (pres. 1991—94, fundraising and programming com. 1986—94, Justice Lousi D. Brandeis award 1991, Brandeis award 1994), Justice Louis D. Brandeis Soc. Democrat. Avocations: reading, swimming, playing piano, singing, volunteering. Home: Apt 1611 18151 NE 31st Ct Aventura FL 33160

ROSS, SHARON D. artist, art gallery owner; b. L.A., Feb. 27, 1960; d. Leonard Ross and Alice (Darling) Stoner. MA in Marital and Family Therapy/Clin. Art Therapy, Loyola Marymount U., 1995; BS in Math./Ops. Rsch. Research, SUNY, Old Westbury, 1988; attended, James Madison U., Va. Commonwealth U., Penland Sch. Arts Crafts. Artist, Dahlgren, Va., 1990—; mem. North Windsor Artists, King George, Va., 1995—; co-founder Blue Door Studio, Fredericksburg, Va., 1998—; founder, participating mem. ArtSpeaksGallery.com, Dahlgren, 1999—; co-founder, participating mem. North Windsor Gallery, Fredericksburg, 2001—03. Dir. mem. King George Art Guild, 1995—. Exhibitions include Capital Hill Art League, 1998, Ctrl. Rappahannock Reg. Libr., 1998, Fredericksburg Ctr. Creative Arts, 1998, Belmont Mus., 1998, Art First Gallery, 1998, No. Windsor Artists, 1999, Fredericksburg Ctr. Creative Arts, 1999, one-woman shows include Peppers Restaurant, 1999, exhibited in group shows at Art First Gallery, 1999, exhibitions include Capitol Hill Art League, 2001, King George Art Show, 2001, exhibited in group shows at Liberty Town Gallery, 2002, Art First Gallery, 2002, Six Twenty Three, 2003, exhibitions include Sawmill Gallery, 2002, one-woman shows include Bistro 309, 2002, exhibitions include Eyeclopes Studio and Gallery, 2002, one-woman shows include Fredericksburg Ctr. Creative Arts, 1999, 2003, exhibitions include Liberty Town Gallery, 2003; contbr. articles various profl. jours. Recipient Honorable Mention award, King George Art Show, 1997, Judge's Choice award, 1997, Honorable Mention award, Oils, 1998, Judge's Choice award, King George Art Show, 1999, Merit award, 2001. Personal E-mail: info@sharondross.com. Business E-Mail: info@sharondross.com.

ROSS, SUE, entrepreneur, author, fundraising executive; b. Chgo., Feb. 2, 1948; d. Irving and Rose (Stein) R. BA in Secondary Edn., Western Mich. U., 1971; postgrad., Northwestern U., Chgo. State U., U. Ill. Dir. youth employment Ill. Youth Svcs. Bur., Maywood, 1978-79; exec. dir. Edn. Resource Ctr., Chgo., 1979-82; asst. dir. devel. Art Inst. Chgo., 1982-83, mgr. govt. affair, 1983-84, dir. govt. affairs, 1984-85; v.p. devel. Spertus Inst. of Judaica, Chgo., 1985-90; mgmt. and fundraising counsel Sue Ross Enterprises, Chgo. and San Francisco, 1990—; founder, pres. Kid Angels Internat., San Francisco, 1994—. Lectr. Sch. Art Inst., Chgo., 1982-85, Episcopalian Archdioceses, Chgo., 1984, Nat. Soc. Fund Raising Execs., Chgo., 1984-90; instr. DePaul U. Sch. for New Learning, 1987-88, Columbia Coll., Chgo., 1980-91; dep. dir. devel. Lead Internat., 2000-01. Resident counsel for devel. The Joffrey Ballet, 1990-91; resident counsel for devel. The 1995 Children's World Peace Festival; adv. panelist Chgo. Office Fine Arts, 1981-82; v.p., bd. dirs. Lines Contemporary Ballet, 1995—; mem. adv. bd. Silkworm Peace Inst., 1996—; mem. Marin Coun. Agys., dev. dirs. Roundtable 1998—; co-chair Marin Estate Planning Seminar, 1999—; mem. adv. coun. Greater Chgo. Food Depository, 1984-85; exec. com. Chgo. Coalition Arts in Edn., 1981-82; mem. info. svcs. com. Donors' Forum Chgo., 1986-88; mem. Marin Devel. Dirs. roundtable, 1999-2001; mem. internationally renowned Gospel Choir of Glide Meml., 1991-93, San Francisco City Chorus, 1994; mem. com. Congregation Sherith Israel, 1996, San Francisco Angel Club, 1994; dir. devel. and comm. Osher Marin Jewish Cmty. Ctr., 1998-2001. Mem. Am. Fund Raising Profls. (Golden Gate chpt.)), World Affairs Coun. Democrat. Jewish. Avocations: community service, singing. Home and Office: 18 Arcangel Ct Fairfax CA 94930-1102

ROSS, THERESA MAE, secondary school educator; m. H. Richard Ross; 1 child, Gwendolyn Denise. BS, Eastern Mich. U., 1967, MS, 1970; PhD, U. Mich., 1981. Tchr. Jackson (Mich.) Pub. Schs., 1967—68, Ann Arbor (Mich.) Pub. Schs., 1968—69, 1971—; grad. intern Inkster (Mich.) Child Devel. Ctr., 1968—70. HEW Early Childhood fellow, 1969—70. Mem.: NEA, Internat. Platform Assn., Am. Bus. Women's Assn., Assn. Curriculum and Supervision (curriculum cons.), World Orgn. Early Childhood Edn., Mich. Edn. Assn., Ann Arbor Edn. Assn. (lang. arts rep., multicultural coord., motivational spkr., life coach), Delta Kappa Gamma, Beta Sigma Phi, Phi Delta Kappa. Home: 1835 N Franklin Ct Ann Arbor MI 48103-2444

ROSS, WENDY CLUCAS, newspaper editor, journalist; b. Balt., Apr. 15, 1942; d. Charles Max and Jean (Talbot) Clucas; m. David N. Ross, Sept. 5, 1964 (div. 1979). BA, Bradley U., 1964; MLA, Johns Hopkins U., 1999. Women's editor DeKalb Daily Chronicle, Ill., 1968-69; reporter Chgo. Tribune, Ill., 1969-70; copy editor, mag. editor Mpls. Tribune, Minn., 1970-72; copy editor Peoria Jour. Star, Ill., 1973-75, Miami Herald, Fla., 1975-77; asst. news editor Washington Post, 1977-83, dep. news editor, 1983-87, news editor, 1987-93, asst. mng. editor news desk, 1993-2000; design editor Internat. Herald Tribune, Paris, 1998—2003, Wash. Post, 2003. Recipient award of excellence Soc. Newspaper Design, 1985, 87-91, Disting. Alumnae award Bradley U. Centurion Soc., 1994; Nieman fellow Harvard U., 1983-84. Avocations: skiing, sailing, reading, travel. Home: 2735 Olive St NW 4 Washington DC United States Office: Washington Post 1150 15th St SW Washington DC 20071-0002 E-mail: rossw@washpost.com.

ROSSBACH, JANET B. art association administrator, not-for-profit fundraiser; b. N.Y.C., Mar. 17, 1971; BA cum laude, Georgetown U., 1993; MS in Nonprofit Mgmt., New Sch. U., 2002. Assoc. dir. Works of Art for Pub. Spaces, N.Y.C., 1993-95; acquisitions assoc. Voyager Co., N.Y.C., 1995-96; mktg. mgr. Kaufman Patric of Enterprises, N.Y.C., 1996; dir. devel. and alumni affairs Sch. of Visual Arts, N.Y.C., 1997-2001; dir. found. and govt. rels. Manhattan Theatre Club, N.Y.C., 2001—. Author, editor Visual Arts Jour., 1997-2001. Bd. dirs. Troika Ranch. Mem. Am. Assn. Museums, Blue Hill Troupe. Office: Manhattan Theatre Club 311 W 43d Club New York NY 10036

ROSSBACHER, LISA ANN, university president, geology educator, writer; b. Fredericksburg, Va., Oct. 10, 1952; d. Richard Irwin and Jean Mary (Dearing) R.; m. Dallas D. Rhodes, Aug. 4, 1978. BS, Dickinson Coll., 1975; MA, SUNY, Binghamton, 1978, Princeton U., 1979, PhD, 1983. Cons. Republic Geothermal, Santa Fe Springs, Calif., 1979-81; asst. prof. geology Whittier (Calif.) Coll., 1982-84, Calif. State Poly. U., Pomona, 1984-86, assoc. prof. geol. sci., 1986-91, assoc. v.p. acad. affairs, 1987-93, prof. geol. sci., 1991-93; v.p. acad. affairs, dean faculty Whittier (Calif.) Coll., 1993-95; dean of coll., prof. geology Dickinson Coll., Carlisle, Pa., 1995-98; pres. So. Poly. State U., Marietta, Ga., 1998—. Vis. rschr. U. Uppsala, Sweden, 1984. Author: Career Opportunities in Geology and the Earth Sciences, 1983, Recent Revolutions in Geology, 1986; (with Rex Buchanan) Geomedia, 1988; columnist Geotimes, 1988—; contbr. articles to profl. jours. Recipient scholarship Ministry Edn. of Finland, Helsinki, 1984; grantee Sigma Xi, 1976, NASA, 1983-94. Fellow AAAS (geol. nominating com. 1984-87, chair-elect geology and geography sect. 1997-98, chair 1998-99, past chair 1999-2000); mem. Geol. Soc. Am. Office: So Poly State U 1100 S Marietta Pkwy SE Marietta GA 30060-2855

ROSSEEL-JONES, MARY LOUISE, lawyer; b. Detroit, Apr. 19, 1951; d. Rene Octave and Marie Ann (Metcko) Rosseel; m. Mark Christopher Jones, Mar. 16, 1984; 1 child, Kathleen Marie. BA in French with honors, U. Mich., 1973, MA in French, 1976; JD, U. Detroit, 1981. Bar: Mich. 1982, U.S. Ct. Appeals (6th cir.) 1982, U.S. Dist Ct. (ea. dist.) Mich. 1982, U.S. Dist. Ct. (we. dist.) Mich. 1983. Tchg. fellow Wayne State U., Detroit, 1973—74; teaching asst. French U. Mich., Ann Arbor, 1974-76; law clk. Johnson, Auld & Valentine, Detroit, 1979-80; assoc. Monaghan, Campbell et al, Bloomfield Hills, Mich., 1981-82; lectr. law U. Clermont, Clermont-Ferrand, France, 1981-82; staff atty. Mich. Nat. Corp., Bloomfield Hills, 1983-85; litigation atty. Am. Motors Corp., Southfield, Mich., 1985-87; staff counsel Chrysler Corp., Auburn Hills, Mich., 1987-98; freelance designer, pvt. lang. and piano tutor, editor, writer; pvt. law counselor, 1998—; jr. h.s. homesch. tchr., 2002—. Editor: sequel One Life to Give. Recipient Mich. Competitive scholarship, 1969-70, Julia Emanuel scholarship, 1974-75, Henderson House scholarship, 1973; Wayne State U. fellow, 1973-74, U. Mich. fellow, 1974-76, U. Detroit fellow, 1981-82. Republican. Roman Catholic. Avocations: classical pianist, interior design.

ROSSER, ANNETTA HAMILTON, composer; b. Jasper, Fla., Aug. 28, 1913; d. Carlos Calvin and Jermai Reuben (Gilbert) Hamilton; m. John Barkley Rosser, Sept. 7, 1935 (dec. Sept. 1989); children: Edwenna Merryday, John Barkley Jr. BM, Fla. State U., 1932. Cert. tchr. Fla. Tchr. music Kirby-Smith Jr. High Sch., Jacksonville, Fla., 1932-35; 1st violinist Santa Monica (Calif.) Symphony, 1949-50; concertmaster Ithaca (N.Y.) Chamber Orch., 1948-56, Cornell Univ. Orch., Ithaca, 1948-56, soloist, 1957; 1st violinist Princeton (N.J.) Symphony, 1959-61; concertmaster Madison (Wis.) Symphony Orch., 1963-66, 1st violinist, 1967-82. Composer of over 100 vocal and instrumental compositions including Meditations on Cross, song cycle for 2 voices, flute and piano, 1976, An Offering of Song, book of 48 songs, 1977, Songs of a Nomad Flute, song cycle for soprano, flute and piano, 1978, Six Songs of the T'ang Dynasty for soprano and violin, 1983, Nocturne for violin and piano, 1989, Trio for flute, violin and piano, 1991, Scherzo for flute ensemble, 1991, (book of 21 songs) Another Offering of Song, 1998. Bd. dirs. Madison Opera Guild, 1972-86, Madison Civic Music Assn., 1983-85; past pres. Madison Symphony Orch. League, Ithaca Federated Music Club, Ithaca Composers Club; bd. dirs. Madison Art Ctr., 1979-83, Madison Woman of Distinction, 1980, Madison Civics Club, 1976-79, pres., 1977-78; pres. Art League Madison Art Ctr., 1980-82, Univ. League Scholarship Benefit Concert of Rosser Compositions, U. Wis., MMadison, 2003. Recipient Sr. Svc. award Rotary Club, 1994; original music manuscripts and programs were added to archives of U. Wis.-Madison Music Libr., 1996. Mem. AAUW, Wis. Acad. Scis., Arts, and Letters, Univ. League, Univ. League Bird Study Group, Madison Club, Wis. Acad. Scis., Arts, and Letters, PEO, Phi Kappa Phi, Pi Kappa Lambda, Sigma Alpha Iota. Republican. Presbyterian. Avocations: Chinese snuff bottles, English brass rubbings, birding. Home: 4209 Manitou Way Madison WI 53711-3703

ROSSER, SUE V. dean, educator; d. John E. Vilhauer and Elizabeth F. Brown; m. J. Barkley Rosser, Jr, Aug. 31, 1968 (div. Dec. 7, 1978); children: Meagan Rebecca, Caitlin Elizabeth. PhD, U. of Wisconsin-Madison, 1971—73. Post-doctoral fellow U. of Wis., 1973—76; dean, Ivan Allen coll. Ga. Inst. of Tech., Atlanta, 1999—, prof. of history, tech. and soc., 1999—; asst. prof. Mary Baldwin Coll., Staunton, Va., 1976—83, assoc. prof., 1983—86; dir., women's studies U. of SC., 1986—95, assoc. prof. of family, preventive medicine, 1986—90, prof. of family and preventive medicine, 1990—95; sr. program officer women's programs NSF, Washington, 1994—95; dir., ctr. for women's studies and gender rsch. U. of Fla., 1995—99, prof. of anthropology, 1995—99. Vis. prof. U. of Wis., 1976—86; vis. lectr. Towson State U., 1984; vis. disting. prof. U. of Wis. Sys., 1993; adj. prof. of biology Ga. Inst. of Tech., 1999—. Author: (book) The Sci. Glass Ceiling, Women, Sci., and Soc.: The Crucial Union, Re-engring. Female Friendly Sci., Tchg. the Majority: Sci., Math., and

Engring. Tchg. that Attracts Women, Women's Health: Missing from U.S. Medicine, Feminism and Biology, Female-Friendly Sci.: Applying Women's Studies Methods and Theories to Attract Students to Sci., Feminism in the Sci. and Health Care Professions: Overcoming Resistance, Tchg. Sci. and Health from a Feminist Perspective: A Practical Guide; contbr. articles to jours. Named one of Outstanding Women of Am., 1978—80; recipient Betty Vetter award for Rsch., Women Engring. Program Advocates, 2003, Choice Outstanding Academic Book award, ALA, 1993, Award for Outstanding Svc. to the Bd., SC Women in Higher Edn. Assn., 1990, S.C Women of Achievement award, 1990, Mortarboard Excellence in Tchg. award, Mortarboard, 1989—90. Fellow: AAAS, Am. Assn. for Women in Sci.; mem.: NY Acad. of Sciences, Nat. Women's Studies Assn., SE Women's Studies Assn., Sigma Epsilon Sigma, Omicron Delta Kappa, Tri Beta, Sigma Delta Epsilon, Signa Xi, Phi Beta Kappa. Avocations: travel, reading, cooking. Office: Georgia Inst of Tech Ivan Allen College 781 Marietta Street Atlanta GA 30332-0525 Business E-Mail: sue.rosser@iac.gatech.edu.

ROSSI, ALICE S. sociology educator, author; b. N.Y.C., Sept. 24, 1922; d. William A. and Emma (Winkler) Schaerr; m. Max Kitt, Dec. 1941 (div. Sept. 1951); m. Peter H. Rossi, Sept. 29, 1951; children: Peter Eric, Kristin Alice, Nina Alexis. BA, Bklyn. Coll., 1947; PhD, Columbia U., 1957; 9 hon. degrees. Rsch. assoc. Cornell U., Ithaca, N.Y., 1951-52, Harvard U., Cambridge, Mass., 1952-55, U. Chgo., 1961-67, Johns Hopkins U., Balt., 1967-69; prof. sociology Goucher Coll., Balt., 1969-74, U. Mass., Amherst, 1974-91, prof. emerita, 1991—. Author/editor: 11 books; contbr. numerous articles to profl. jours. Founder, bd. mem. NOW, 1966-70; pres. Sociologists for Women in Soc., 1971-72. Career grantee NIMH, 1965-69, rsch. grantee Rockefeller Found., Ford Found., NIH, NSF, others; CommonWealth Disting. Scholarship award, 1988. Mem. Am. Sociol. Assn. (pres. 1983-84), Ea. Sociol. Soc. (pres. 1973-74). Avocations: design, sewing, gardening, creative writing. Home: 34 Stagecoach Rd Amherst MA 01002-3527

ROSSI, MARIANNE, financial analyst; b. Jan. 20, 1960; BA, NYU, 1982. Chartered fin. analyst. Analyst Kidder Peabody, N.Y.C., 1983-88, Prudential Inst. Co., Newark, 1988-91, Credit Suisse Asset Mgmt., N.Y.C., 1991—. Office: High Yield Analyst Credit Suisse Asset Mgmt 153 E 53d St Fl 57 New York NY 10022-4611

ROSSI, NORMA J. not-for-profit executive, advocate; b. Melrose, Mass., Dec. 10, 1929; d. Andrew Steven and Marie Eleanor (Nordbo) Scott; m. Bruce A. Rossi (dec. Dec. 1992); children: Robert, Barry, Max. Degree in Nursing, Peter Bent Brigham Hosp., Boston, 1952; grad. mediation skills, S.D. Mediation Ctr., 1992; completion 4-Day Diversity tng., 1998. RN, Mass., Calif. Emergency rm. nurse various hosps., Boston, Modesto, Calif., 1953-75, San Diego, 1962-73. Founder, vol. exec. dir. San Diego Coalition for Homeless, 1988—; mem. Citizens Police Rev. Bd., San Diego, 1994—98; bd. dirs. City of San Diego Human Rels., 1991. Named hon. educator, St. Joseph's Indian Sch., 1997; recipient Leadership award, San Diego Hunger Coalition, 2000, Seahorse award, City of San Diego, 1992, Leadership award, Channel 10, 1999, 2000, Appreciation of Svc. award for serving homeless, poor and needy, Uptown Interfaith, 1995, Spl. Commendation for continued commitment to make San Diego a better place to live, City Coun., 2001, Say award for making a difference in families in San Diego, 2001, Outstanding Citizen of Yr., Iota Chi chpt. Sigma Chi, 1995, Ranger Run Buddy Grey award, 2002—03, Juvenille Justice Accomadation, 2003. Office: San Diego Coalition for Homeless 4101 University Ave San Diego CA 92105-1418 E-mail: Rossinorma@aol.com.

ROSSI, NORMA M. management consultant; b. N.Y.C., July 23, 1947; d. Attilio G. and Laura (Restani) R. BA, CCNY, 1970; Masters, New Sch. Social Rsch., 1988. Dir. corp. quality Met. Life Ins. Co., N.Y.C., 1970—. Sec. Internat. Svc. Quality Assn., 1991—. Co-author: At the Service Quality Frontier, 1993; author: (chpts.) Service Quality Handbook, 1993, Total Quality Management, 1994; contbr. articles to profl. jours. Recipient Cert. of Appreciation, QUIS, 1994. Mem. ASTD, Human Resources Planning Soc. Roman Catholic. Avocations: opera, theater. Home: 260 Garth Rd Apt 8b4 Scarsdale NY 10583-4053 Office: Met Life Ins Co 1 Madison Ave New York NY 10010-3603

ROSSI, RUTH HARRIS, special education educator; d. Everett Tomlinson Harris and Clora Ethel Stanley; m. Raymond Anthony Rossi, Feb. 26, 1977; children: Hillary Niles, Tess Virginia, Anthony John. BA, U. R.I., 1967, postgrad., 1973; EdM, Seattle U., 1995. Spl. edn. tchr. Lakota Mid. Sch., Federal Way, Wash., 1989—, spl. edn. dept. chair, 2002—. Mem. post-secondary transition adv. com. Federal Way Sch. Dist., 1999—. Treas. PTA, Woodmont East Sch., Federal Way, 1982, 1996, 1997; leader, membership facilitator CampFire, Kent, Wash., 1982—86; mem. customer adv. com. Puget Sound Power, Renton, Wash., 1983, 1984. Grantee, Federal Way Edn. Found., 2003. Mem.: ASCD, ACLU, Audubon Soc. Avocations: reading, walking, gardening, cooking, needlepoint. Office: Lakota Mid Sch 1415 SW 314th St Federal Way WA 98023

ROSSITER, EILEEN, Canadian senator; b. Souris, Prince Edward Island, Can., July 14, 1929; m. Linus J. Rossiter (dec. Mar. 1987); children: Philip, Leonard, Kevin, Patricia, Colleen, Mary. Student, Prince of Wales Coll. Senator, The Senate of Can., 1986. Progressive. Avocation: Avocations: reading, knitting, swimming. Office: 402 Victoria Bldg The Senate of Canada Ottawa ON Canada K1A 0A4

ROSS-LEE, BARBARA, dean, educator; BS Biology and Chemistry, M Tchr. Spl. Populations, Wayne State U.; grad., Mich. State U., 1973; DSc (hon.), N.Y. Coll. Osteo. Medicine; degree (hon.), Wilmington Coll., 2001. Legis. asst. Senator Bill Bradley; chmn. dept. family medicine, assoc. dean health policy Mich. State U. Coll. Medicine; dean Ohio U. Coll. Osteo. Medicine, 1993—2001; dean, v.p. health scis. and med. affairs N.Y. Coll. Osteo. Medicine, 2001—. Lectr. in field; dir. Osteo. Heritage Health Policy Fellowship Program ; exec. dir. Inst. Nat. Health Policy and Rsch., NOMA (the osteo. affiliate NMA) ; mem. bd. dirs. Assn. Acad. Health Ctrs., Nat. Fund Med. Edn., Nat. Health Svs. Corps' Assn. Clinicians Underserved ; trustee Found. Appalachian Ohio; participant confs. Contbr. more than 30 scholarly articles med. and health-care issues. Named to Ohio Women's Hall of Fame, 1998; recipient Magnificent 7 award, Bus. and Profl. Women/USA, 1993, Women's Health award, Blackboard African-Am. Nat. Bestsellers, Disting. Pub. Svc. award, Okla. State U. Coll. Osteo. Medicine, Walter F. Patenge medal pub. svc., Mich. State U. Coll. Osteo. Medicine, 2001. Fellow: Am. Osteo. Bd. Family Physicians; mem.: NIH (adv. com. rsch. on women's health), Future Primary Care (Inst. Medicine's com.), U.S. Dept. Health and Human Svs. (nat. adv. com. rural health), Appalachian Health Policy (Appalachian regional commn.'s adv. coun.), AACOM Bd. Govs. (chair-elect exec. coun.), AOA Bur. Profl. Edn., Trilateral Internat. Med. Workforce Group. Achievements include first to be an osteopathic physician to participate in the prestigious Robert Wood Johnson Health Policy Fellowship. Office: NY Coll of Osteopathic Med Old Westbury No Blvd Rockefeller Bldg Rm 107 Westbury NY 11568-8000 E-mail: brosslee@nyit.edu.

ROSSMAN, RUTH SCHARFF, artist, educator; b. Bklyn. d. Joseph and Elsie (Frankel) Scharff; m. Phillip Rossman; 1 dau., Joanne. Grad., Cleve. Inst. Art, 1934; BS, Case Western Res. U., 1934; postgrad., Kahn Inst. Art, 1947-50, UCLA, 1960. Art instr. Canton (Ohio) public schs., 1934-39, Canton Art Inst., 1937-45, Rustic Canyon Art Center, Los Angeles, 1978-81. One-woman shows at Heritage Gallery, L.A., 1963, 66, Canton (Ohio) Community Ctr., 1967, Marymount Coll., U. Judaism, 1980, L.A. Fedn. Bldg., 1981, 89, Platt Gallery, 1986, 93, 98, others; exhibited in group shows Mus. Modern Art, N.Y.C., Butler Mus., Washington and Jefferson Coll., Denver Mus., Space Mus., Mt. St. Mary's Coll., L.A., M.H. de Young Mus., San Francisco Mus. Art, Venice Art Walk, ann. 1981-94, 96-2000, Univ. Judaism, 1986, 93, Brand Art Gallery, 1987, Platt Gallery, 1998, others; represented in permanent collections Pa. Acad. Fine Arts, Phila., Brandeis-Bardin Inst., U. Redlands, Calif., Nat. Watercolor Soc., Ahmanson Collection, Rocky Mt. Nat., others; paintings included in book The California Romantics: Harbingers of Watercolor, 1987, Retrospective Art Exhibit U. Judaism Platt Gallery, 1998. Chair selection com. for Platt Gallery, U. Judaism, L.A., 1986—. Recipient purchase-cash awards Los Angeles All-City Art Exhbn. Mem. Nat. Watercolor Soc. (pres. 1974-75, juror 75th Ann. Exhbn. 1995).

ROSSO DE IRIZARRY, CARMEN (TUTTY ROSSO DE IRIZARRY), finance executive; b. Ponce, P.R., Feb. 9, 1949; d. Jorge Ignacio and Carmen Teresa (Descartes) Rosso Castain; m. Alfredo R. Irizarry Sile, Aug. 29, 1967. BBA, U. P.R., Rio Piedras. Vice pres. Alcay Inc., San Juan, P.R., 1972—, also bd. dirs.; v.p. J.I.C. Corp., M.I.C. Corp. Bd. dirs., now pres. bd. Construcciones Urbanas Inc., Internat. Fin. Corp.; organizer Best of Saks Fifth Avenue 1990-2000. Troop leader Girl Scouts U.S.A., 1977-80; bd. dirs. PTA, San Juan, 1978-81, 86-88; activities coord. Colegio Puertorriqueño Niñas, San Juan, 1987-88; judge Miss P.R. Pageant, San Juan 1987-88, 93, 94, 95, Miss World P.R. Pageant, San Juan, 1987-88, Miss World of P.R., 1990; pres. fundacion dept. Oncologia Pediatrica Hosp. Universitario Dr. Antonio Ortiz, 1990-2003; organizer Best of Saks Fifth Avenue Benefit, 1991, 92, 93, 94, 95, pres. 1992, 94, 96; com. mem. Make a Wish Found. Colleccion Alta Moda, 1994; mem. com. Muceo Ponce Gala, 1994; mem. com. Museo Ponce Coala, 1994; luminaria J.C. Penney, 1994; destellos de la Moda, 1994, 95-96; pres. Best of Saks 5th Avenue Benefit, 1990-96; organizer Fundacion Oncologica Escada Spring and Summer, 2003. Named to Ten Best Dressed List, San Juan Star, 1986-87, Hall of Fame of Ten Best Dressed, 1989; recipient luminaria J.C. Penney, 1994. Fellow Assn. Porcelanas; mem. Union Mujeres Americanas, Club de Leones (Garden Hills, P.R., Lady of Yr. award 1978), Club Avico Dama, Caparra Country Club (pres. 1985-86), Club de Presidentas, Altrusas, Bankers Club, Club Civicos Damas (judge hat show 1989, in charge spl. events 1992), Mu Alpha Phi. Republican. Roman Catholic. Avocations: china painting, boating, water skiing. Office: Internat Fin Corp PO Box 8486 Santurce San Juan PR 00910-0486

ROSSOTTI, BARBARA JILL MARGULIES, lawyer; b. Englewood, N.J., Feb. 28, 1940; d. Albert and Loretta (Jill) Margulies; m. Charles Ossola Rossotti; children: Allegra Jill, Edward Charles. BA magna cum laude, Mount Holyoke Coll., 1961; LLB, Harvard U., 1964. Bar: D.C. 1966. Assoc. Nutter McClennen & Fish, Boston, 1964-65, Covington & Burling, Washington, 1965-72, Shaw, Pittman, Potts & Trowbridge, Washington, 1972-73; ptnr. Shaw Pittman LLP (formerly Shaw, Pittman, Potts & Trowbridge), Washington, 1973—. Trustee Mt. Holyoke Coll., South Hadley, Mass., 1984-99, vice chmn., 1989-94, chmn., 1994-99; trustee Legal Aid Soc., D.C., 1979-92, pres. 1985-89, mem. pres. coun., 1992—; trustee Choral Arts Soc., Washington, 1989-96, 1997-2003, chair, 1993-95; bd. dirs. Washington Home, 1989-93, bd. govs., 1993-, chair, 2002—. Fellow Am. Bar Found.; mem. ABA, Am. Soc. Internat. Law, Internat. Law Assn., D.C. Bar, D.C. Bar Found. (adv. com.). Office: Shaw Pittman 2300 N St NW Fl 5 Washington DC 20037-1172

ROSTAD, LEE B. rancher, writer; b. Roundup, Mont., Oct. 28, 1929; d. Edward and Emma Gail (Haddock) Birkett; m. O. Phillip Rostad, June 29, 1952; children: Phillip, Carl Eric. BA with honors, U. Mont., 1951; LLD (hon.), Rocky Mountain Coll., Billings, Mont., 1995. Rancher Rostad and Rostad, Martinsdale, Mont., 1952—; tchr. Pub. Sch., Great Falls, Mont., 1953-54, White Sulphur Springs, Mont., 1967-68, Helena, Mont., 1968-72. Bd. dirs., fundraiser Mountainveiw Med. cTr., White Sulphur Springs, 1990—2000. Author: (novels) Honey Wine and Hunger Root, 1985, Fourteen Cents and Seven Green Apples, 1992, Mountains of Gold, Hills of Grass, 1994; illustrator, author Meagher County Sketchbook; newspaper columnist:. Trustee Mont. State Hist. Soc., 1997—, exec. bd.; pres. Mont. chpt. Nat. Mus. Women in the Arts, 1992—2000; mem. County Study Commn., Meagher County, 1975; bd. dirs. Mont. Com. Humanities. Recipient Gov.'s Humanities award, 2001; scholar Fulbright, 1952. Mem.: Meagher County Archives Assn. (charter), Meagher County Hist. Assn. (fundraiser 1960—), Mont. Watercolor Soc. Republican. Avocations: pottery, art, writing. Home and Office: Rostad and Rostad 169 Bozeman Fork Rd Martinsdale MT 59053

ROSTOW, ELSPETH DAVIES, political science educator; b. N.Y.C. d. Milton Judson and Harriet Elspeth (Vaughan) Davies; m. Walt Whitman Rostow, June 26, 1947 (dec. Feb. 2003); children: Peter Vaughan, Ann Larner. AB, Barnard Coll., 1938; AM, Radcliffe Coll., 1939; MA, Cambridge (Eng.) U., 1949; LHD (hon.), Lebanon Valley Coll.; LLD (hon.), Austin Coll., 1982, Southwestern U., 1988. Mem. faculty various instns. Barnard Coll., N.Y.C. and MIT, Cambridge, 1939-69; mem. faculty U. Tex., Austin, 1969—, dean div. gen. and comparative studies, 1975-77, prof. govt., 1976—, dean Lyndon B. Johnson Sch. Pub. Affairs, 1977-83, Stiles prof. Am. studies, 1985-88, Stiles prof. emerita, 1988—. Mem. Pres.'s Adv. Com. for Trade Negotiations, 1978-82, Pres.'s Commn. for a Nat. Agenda for the Eighties, 1979-81; rsch. assoc. OSS, Washington, 1943-45; Geneva corr. London Economist, 1947-49; lectr. Air War Coll., 1963-81, Army War Coll., 1965, 68, 69, 78, 79, 81, Nat. War Coll., 1962, 68, 74, 75, Indsl. Coll. Armed Forces, 1961-65, Naval War Coll., 1971, Fgn. Svc. Inst., 1974-77, Dept. of State, Europe, 1973; bd. dirs. U.S. Inst. of Peace, vice chmn., 1991, chmn. 1991-92; co-founder The Austin Project, 1991; mem. Gov.'s Task Force on Revenue, Tex., 1991. Author: Europe's Economy After the War, 1948, (with others) American Now, 1968, The Coattailless Landslide, 1974; editor (with Barbara Jordan) The Great Society: A Twenty-Year Critique, 1986; columnist Austin Am. Statesman, 1985-92; contbr. articles to revs., poems to scholarly jours., newspapers, and mags. Trustee Nat. Acad. Pub. Adminstrn., 1989—95, Sarah Lawrence Coll., 1952—59, So. Ctr. for Internat. Studies, 1990—; bd. visitors and govs. St. Johns Coll., 1986—89; bd. dirs. Barnard Coll., 1962—66, Lyndon Baines Johnson Found., 1977—83, Salzburg Seminar, 1981—89, co-chair sr. fellows, 1997—2001; vis. scholar Phi Beta Kappa, 1984—85; bd. adv. to pres. Naval War Coll., Newport, RI, 1995—99; nat. advisor Commn. on Deliberative Polling, 1999—2001. Decorated Order of St. Joan D'Arc; named Fulbright lectr.; recipient Top Hand award, U. Tex. Ex-Students Assn., 1996, Presdl. citation, U. Tex., 1998, Disting. Alumna award, Barnard Coll., 1998; grantee, USIA, 1983—84, 1990. Mem.: Tex. Philos. Soc. (trustee 1989—95, 1997—2001), Headliners Found. (vice-chmn. 1996—2002), Phi Beta Kappa, Omicron Delta Kappa, Mortar Bd. (hon.), Phi Nu Epsilon (hon.). Home: 1 Wildwind Pt Austin TX 78746-2434 Office: U Tex PO Box Y University Station Austin TX 78713

ROTBERG, IRIS COMENS, social scientist; b. Phila., Dec. 16, 1932; d. Samuel Nathaniel and Golda (Shuman) Comens; m. Eugene H. Rotberg, Aug. 29, 1954; children: Diana Golda, Pamela Lynn. BA, U. Pa., 1954, MA, 1955; PhD, Johns Hopkins U., Balt., 1958. Research psychologist Pres.'s Commn. on Income Maintenance Programs, Washington, 1968-69, Office Planning, Research and Evaluation, Office Econ. Opportunity, Washington, 1970-73; dep. dir. compensatory edn. study Nat. Inst. Edn., Washington, 1974-77, dir. Office Planning and Program Devel., 1978-82; program dir. NSF, Arlington, Va., 1985-87, 89-91, 1993-96; tech. policy fellow Com. on Sci., Space and Tech., U.S. Ho. of Reps., Washington, 1987-89; sr. social scientist RAND, Washington, 1991-93; rsch. prof. edn. policy Grad. Sch. Edn. and Human Devel. George Washington U., Washington, 1996—. NSF fellow, 1956-58. Home: 7211 Brickyard Rd Potomac MD 20854-4808 Office Phone: 202-994-2735. Business E-Mail: irotberg@gwu.edu.

ROTBLATT, JOY J. artist; d. Archie and Bertha Aron Rotblatt; children: Lauren M. Lasseur, Kimberly A. Baldwin. BA in Edn., Calif. State U., L.A., 1961; BFA in Painting, Otis Coll. Art and Design, 1983. Cert. tchr. L.A. Tchr. elem. edn. L.A. City Schs., 1961—64; painter Studio City, Calif., 1983—. Curator exhbns. Installations Gallery, Encino, Calif., 1988—91; leader art tours Mus. Contemporary Art, L.A., 1984—86; participant painting workshop, Italy, 1990, Otis Coll. Art and Design, Paris, 1985; participant painting workshop Painting and Beyond Calif. State U., Humboldt, 1990. Work published in exhbn. catalog, So. Calif. Women's Caucus for Art, 1988, Brand XXV, 1996 (Silver Anniversary award, 1996), 9 one-person exhbns., L.A. area, 1990—2004, over 50 selected group exhbns., 1983—2003. Recipient Bronze medal for painting, Art of Calif. Mag., 1992, artist-in-residence scholarship, Santa Fe Art Inst., 2000, Master Class scholarship, 1993. Mem.: Gallery 825 Art Assn. (exhibiting artist 1986—), Arroyo Arts Collective (exhibiting artist 1988—). Home and Studio: 11296 Dona Lisa Dr Studio City CA 91604 E-mail: joyartist@sbcglobal.net.

ROTE, NELLE FAIRCHILD HEFTY, management consultant; b. Watsontown, Pa, May 23, 1930; d. Edwin Dunkel and Phebe Hill (Fisher) Fairchild; m. John Austin Hefty, Mar. 20, 1948 (div. June 1970); children: Harry E. Hefty, John B. Hefty, Susan E. Hefty DeBartolo; m. Keith Maynard Rote, Dec. 16, 1983 (dec. Aug. 1985). Student, Bucknell U., 1961, Williamsport Sch. of Commerce, 1968-69, Pa. State U., 1971-72, 83, Susquehanna U., 1986. Typesetter, page designer Colonial Printing House, Inc., Lewisburg, Pa., 1970-76; account exec. Sta. WTGC Radio, Lewisburg, 1976-78; co-owner Colonial Printing Co., Lewisburg, 1978-83; temp. HATS-Temps, Lewisburg, 1986-89; artist, editor Create-A-Book, Inc., Milton, Fla., 1980-92; census crew leader, spl. svc. Dept. Commerce, Washington, 1990; cons. Create-A-Book, Inc., Gulf Breeze, Fla., 1991—99, 2002—. Children's Playmate Mag., 1942; author: McGruff and Me, 1999, My Christmas Wish, 1999, School Fun Book, 1999, My Fishing Adventure, 1999; co-author: Am. Nursing: A Biog. Dictionary, 2000; contbr. articles to profl. jours.; exhibitions include Union County Libr., Lewisburg, 2003. Proofreader Lewisburg Bicentennial Commn., Lewisburg, 1976; charter mem. Women's Art Mus., Washington; charter sponsor Women in Mil. Svc. Meml., Arlington, Va., 1991; founder, donor Nelle Fairchild Rote Book Fund, Union County Libr.; editor, poet Holiday Newspaper Bus. Assn., Lewisburg, 1987. Recipient Humanitarian recognition, Tri-County Fedn. Women's Clubs, Pa., 1965, Grand prize in Cooking, Milton Std., 1966, Most Profl. Photo award, Lewisburg Festival Arts, 1980, Hon. Mention award, Women in Arts, Harrisburg, Pa., 1981, Photo Contest award, Congressman Allen Ertel, 1981, 2d pl. Photo award, Union County Fair, 1981, 3d pl. Photo award, 1981, Hon. Mention Photo award, Susquehanna Art Soc., 1981, Silver award for Poetry, World of Poetry, 1990. Mem.: DAR (nat. def. reporter Shikelimo chpt. 1989—95, sec. 1992—95, regent 1995—2001, vice chmn. Pa. State Soc. DAR women vets com. 1998—2001, vice-regent 2001—, Prize for safety poster 1942), Soc. Profl. Journalists, Warrior Run Heritage Soc., Orgn. United Environment, Marine Corps League Aux. (life), Western Front Assn., Civic Club Lewisburg (v.p. 1994—97), Am. Legion Aux. (sgt. at arms 2003, Unit 182). Achievements include Initiator for renaming bridge in Watsontown, PA. to "Nurse Helen Fairchild Meml. Bridge" (a WWI Reserve Army Nurse relative), 2002. Home: 1015 St Paul St Lewisburg PA 17837-1213

ROTELL, CYNTHIA A. lawyer; BA, Barnard Coll., 1982; JD, Bklyn. Law Sch., 1990. Bar: Calif. 1990. With Latham & Watkins, L.A., 1990—, ptnr., 1997—. Mem.: L.A. County Bar Assn. (exec. com. bus. and corps. law sect.), State of Calif. Bar Assn. Office: Latham and Watkins LLC 633 W Fifth St Ste 4000 Los Angeles CA 90071*

ROTERT, TERESA LYNN, elementary and secondary school music educator; b. Sutherland, Nebr., Sept. 27, 1956; d. Jimmy Dale Colburn and Beverly Rae Colb urn; m. Donald James Rotert, Dec. 18, 1977; children: Brian David, Matthew James. BA in Music Edn., Kearney State Coll., 1978; postgrad. in music, speech and multicultural and middle sch. social studies, U. Nebr. at Kearney, 1985—. K-12 vocal and instrumental tchr. Paxton (Nebr.) Pub. Sch., 1978—80; K-8 vocal music tchr. Sutherland Pub. Sch., 1985—90; 9-12 vocal music tchr. Hershey (Nebr.) Pub. Sch., 1990, K-12 vocal music tchr., girls h.s. golf coach, 1991—. Dist. music coord. Dist. IV in Nebr., North Platte, 2001—; ch. organist, choir dir. United Meth. Ch., Sutherland, 1982—. Contbg. columnist The Nebr. Music Educator mag.1999, 1999. Pres., cmty. chair Lincoln County Home Ext. Coun., North Platte, 1986; dir. several 4-H Clubs, Sutherland, 1974—92. Mem.: Am. Choral Dirs. Assn., Nebr. Choral Dirs. Assn. (host Sing Around Nebr. 1998, 2000, 2002—04), Music Educators Nat. Conf., Sutherland Home Ext. Club (past pres., sec., treas.). Methodist. Avocations: reading, hunting, golf, cooking. Home: 1240 Locust Box 363 Sutherland NE 69165

ROTH, ANNE BROHMANN, journalist; b. Syracuse, N.Y., Jan. 10, 1933; d. Alfred Brohmann Roth and Agnes Helen Hurley; m. Noel Richard Hueber, July 4, 1955 (div. Feb. 12, 1990); children: Philip Brohmann, Peter Roth, Sara Stuart; m. Robert Ekman Cook, June 20, 1998. BS, Marywood U., 1954; MS, Syracuse U., 1974. Staff writer various newspapers, Syracuse, 1988—95, contbg. writer, 1981—85, cmty. writer, 1999—2001; editor Skaneateles Press, NY, 1985—88; copy editor Shanghai Star, 1995—96; contbg. writer The Citizen, Auburn, NY, 2001—; fgn. expert English Hangzhou U., 1996—98, prof., 1996—98. Tchr. writing Hanzhou U., Hangzhou, China, 1996—98. Author: The Best of Brohmann, 1985. Pres. Syracuse Repertory Theatre Guild, 1973—74; bd. dirs. Skaneateles Festival, 2001—. Mem.: AAUW, Syracuse Press Club, Irish Am. Cultural Inst. Roman Catholic. Avocation: sailing.

ROTH, CAROLYN LOUISE, art educator; b. Buffalo, June 17, 1944; d. Charles Mack and Elizabeth Mary (Hassel) R.; m. Charles Turner Barber, Aug. 4, 1991. Student, Art Student's League N.Y., 1965, Instituto Allende, San Miguel de Allende, Mex., 1966; BFA, Herron Sch. Art, 1967; MFA, Fla. State U., 1969. Asst. prof. art U. Tenn., Chattanooga, 1969-72; lectr. art So. Ill. U., Carbondale, 1973-75; asst. prof. art U. Evansville, Ind., 1975-80; lectr. art U. So. Ind., Evansville, 1984—. Exhbn. coord., gallery dir. Krannert Gallery, U. Evansville, 1977-79; exhbn. coord., conf. advisor Ind. Women in Arts Conf., Ind. Arts Commn., Evansville, 1978; reviewer in field. One-woman shows include Wabash Valley Coll., Mt. Carmel, Ill., 1994, So. Ind. Ctr. for Arts, Seymour, Ind., 1996, Zionsville (Ind.) Muncie Art Ctr., 1997, Oakland City (Ind.) U., 1998; exhibited in group shows Liberty Gallery, Louisville, 1992, Artlink Contemporary Art Gallery, Ft. Wayne, Ind., 1994, S.E. Mo. Coun. on Arts, Cape Girardeau, 1994, Lexington (Ky.) Art League, 1996, Mills Pond Horse Gallery, St. James, N.Y., 1996, SOHO Gallery, Pensacola, Fla., 1996, Indpls. Art Ctr., 1996, Artemesia Gallery, Chgo., 1997, DelMar Coll., Corpus Christi, Tex., 1998, La. State U., Baton Rouge, 1998, Woman Made Gallery, Chgo., 2002; works appeared in various publs.; represented by Creative Art Gallery, St. Louis, the New Harmony Gallery of Contemporary Art, New Harmony, Ind. Malone fellow visitor to Morocco and Tunisia, 1996. Mem. Nat. Mus. Women in Arts, Met. Mus. Art, Evansville Mus. Arts and Sci., New Harmony Gallery of Contemporary Art, Golden Key Honor Soc. (hon.). Democrat. Mem. Unity Ch. Avocation: travel to study art works in museums and galleries in europe and mex. Home: 10801 S Woodside Dr Evansville IN 47712-8422 Office: U So Ind 8600 University Blvd Evansville IN 47712-3534 E-mail: croth@usi.edu.

ROTH, DARYL, theater producer; b. NJ; m. Steven Roth, 1969; children: Amanda, Jordan. Student, NYU. Prodr., owner Daryl Roth Prodns., N.Y.C.; owner Daryl Roth Theater, 1998—, DR2 Theater, 2002—. Co-anchor PBS show N.Y. Theatre Rev.; spkr. in field; guest lectr. Columbia U., NYU, Harvard Club, Women's Art Coalition. Prodr.: (N.Y. and London prodn.) Three Tall Women (Pulitzer prize, 1994), (Broadway prodn.) Twilight. Los

Angeles.1992 (Tony nomination), Camping with Henry and Tom (Outer Critics Circle award, Lucille Lortel award), Defying Gravity, (off-Broadway) Snakebit, How I Learned to Drive (Best Play of Season, 1997, Pulitzer prize, 1998), Old Wicked Songs, 1996 (Pulitzer prize finalist for drama, 1996), Wit (Pulitzer prize for Drama, 1999), Bomb-itty of Errors; (plays) Closer Then Ever, 1987—1888, Nick & Nora, 1991, Proof, 2000—03 (Tony Award for Best Play, 2001), The Tale of the Allergist's Wife, 2000—02, Bea Arthur on Broadway, 2002, The Goat, or Who is Sylvia, 2002 (Tony Award for Best Play, 2002), Medea, 2002—03, Salome, 2003, Anna in the Tropics, 2003—04, Caroline, or Change, 2004—. Established (with husband) Roth Ctr. for Jewish Life, Dartmouth U., 1997; bd. dirs. Lincoln Ctr. Theater, Sundance Inst., Albert Einstein Coll. for Med. Rsch. Named award in her honor Daryl Roth Creative Spirit award, honored (with husband) with the Louis Marshall Award, Jewish Theological Seminary. Office: Daryl Roth Prodns 152 W 57th St Fl 21 New York NY 10019*

ROTH, GLADYS THOMPSON, retired early childhood and special education educator; b. N.Y.C., June 24, 1923; d. Meyer and Sarah (Siporin) Thompson; m. Martin Roth, Dec. 25, 1949; children: Jan Roth Hauptman, Lisa. BA, Bklyn. Coll., 1943; postgrad., Queens Coll., 1961-63; M in Spl. Edn., NYU, 1972. Cert. kindergarten tchr., health conservation tchr., tchr. grades K-6, N.Y.C. Bd. Edn. Tchr. Day Care Ctr. Mayor's Com., Bedford & Stuyvesant, N.Y., 1943-45; kindergarten tchr. N.Y.C. Bd. Edn., Red Hook, N.Y., 1945-62; spl. edn. tchr. N.Y.C. Bd. Edn.-St. Francis Hosp., 1962-64, N.Y.C. Bd. Edn.-Queens Gen. Hosp., 1964-65, N.Y.C. Bd. Edn.-St. Mary's Hosp., 1965-79; ednl. evaluator N.Y.C. Bd. Edn. Queens Dist., 1979-90; ret., 1990. Mem. exec. com. Coun. for Exceptional Children, Queens, 1962-64; spl. reading cons. St. Mary's Hosp., Queens, 1964-65. Contbr. articles to profl. jours.; exhibits stone and wood sculpture. Organizer parenting groups Pub. Sch. 84-Queens, Bayside, N.Y., 1979-90; dir. Womanspace in Great Neck, N.Y., 1989-96, dir. of outreach, 1996—; mem. adv. bd. Copay Hispanic Cmty., Inc., Great Neck, 1996—. Recipient Achievement award Soroptomist Soc., Nassau County, N.Y., 1992, Cmty. Achievement award Eleanor Roosevelt chpt. Am. Jewish Congress, Nassau County, 1992, Martin Fisher Post Harvest award Bklyn. Coll., 1997; named Outstanding Woman, Town of North Hempstead, 1994, Disting. Citizen, N.Y. State Assembly, Albany, 1995. Avocations: sculpture, tennis, music. Home: 13 Briar Ln Great Neck NY 11024-1720

ROTH, HARRIET STEINHORN, advocate, educator, public speaker; b. Lodz, Poland, Apr. 12, 1929; d. Pinkus Feldman and Brenda Rubinstein; m. Irving Hyman Steinhorn, Apr, 15, 1951 (dec. June 1981); children: Pauline-Sue, Allan Wrenn, Mark Paul; m. Marvin Roth, June 22, 1986; stepchildren: Linda Fern, Steve Howard. B in Hebrew Lit., Balt. Hebrew U., 1974. Tchr. Hebrew Shaare Tefila Hebrew Sch., Silver Spring, Md., 1964-84, ednl. dir., 1984-92. Author: Shadows of the Holocaust, 1983. Publicity chair Jewish Holocaust Survivors & Friends Greater Washington, Rockville, Md., 1990-99. Avocations: gardening, reading, swimming, theater, traveling. Home: 10411 Burnt Ember Dr Silver Spring MD 20903-1337

ROTH, IRMA DORIS BRUBAKER, editor; b. Lexington, Nebr., Dec. 7, 1914; d. Ralph H. and Hazel Louise (Lincoln) Brubaker; m. George Knox Roth, Dec. 18, 1933; children: Dana Lincoln, Mary Joan, John Knox, Diana Jean. AA, Pasadena City Coll., 1951. Editl. asst., office mgr. New Outlook Mag., L.A., 1955-59; supr. catalog clerical staff J.F.K. Libr., Calif. State Coll., L.A., 1960-68; rsch. editor Gen. Rsch. Cons., Las Vegas, San Diego, 1968-75. Editor: (book) Nevada Water Quality, 1969; contbr. articles to popular mag. Press rep. Dem. Nat. Conv., L.A., 1960; mem. campaign staff Humphrey for Pres., Las Vegas, 1968; treas. San Gabriel Valley Dem. Women, Los Angeles County, 1982—83, 1986—87, pres., 1984—85, 1988—94; bd. dirs. Conf. Christians and Jews, Las Vegas, 1968—70; rec. sec. Pacific S.W. dist. Unitarian-Universalist Women's Fedn., 1977—82; mem. L.A. Press Club, 1955—80. Named Woman Dem. of the Yr., 42d Assembly Dist. Com., 1991. Mem.: Coll. Women Pasadena (publicity chair 1996—98, mem. scholarship com. 1998—). Avocations: reading, knitting, children. Home: 440 N Madison Ave Apt 507 Pasadena CA 91101-1430

ROTH, JANE RICHARDS, federal judge; b. Philadelphia, Pa., June 16, 1935; d. Robert Henry Jr. and Harriett (Kellond) Richards; m. William V. Roth Jr., Oct. 9, 1965; children: William V. III, Katharine K. BA, Smith Coll., 1956; LLB, Harvard U., 1965; LLD (hon.), Widener U., 1986, U. Del., 1994. Bar: Del. 1965, U.S. Dist. Ct. Del. 1966, U.S. Ct. Appeals (3d cir.) 1974. Adminstrv. asst. various fgn. service posts U.S. State Dept., 1956-62; assoc. Richards, Layton & Finger, Wilmington, Del., 1965-73, ptnr., 1973-85; judge U.S. Dist. Ct. Del., Wilmington, 1985-91, U.S. Ct. Appeals (3d cir.), Wilmington, 1991—. Adj. faculty Villanova U. Sch. Law. Hon. chmn. Del. chpt. Arthritis Found., Wilmington; bd. overseers Widener U. Sch. Law; bd. consultors Villanova U. Sch. Law; trustee Hist. Soc. Del. Recipient Nat. Vol. Service citiation Athritis Found., 1982. Fellow Am. Bar Found.; mem. ABA, Fed. Judges Assn., Del. State Bar Assn. Republican. Episcopalian. Office: US Court of Appeals 3rd Circuit 844 King St Lock Box 12 Wilmington DE 19801-1790*

ROTH, JUDITH SHULMAN, lawyer; b. N.Y.C., Apr. 25, 1952; d. Mark Alan and Margaret Ann (Podell) Shulman; m. William Hartley Roth, May 30, 1976; children: Andrew Henry, Caroline Shulman. AB, Cornell U., 1974; JD, Columbia U., 1977. Bar: N.Y. 1978, U.S. Dist. Ct. (ea. dist.) N.Y. 1978, U.S. Dist. Ct. (so. dist.) N.Y. 1978, U.S. Ct. Appeals (2d cir.) 1993. Assoc. Phillips Nizer Benjamin Krim & Ballon, N.Y.C., 1978-87, ptnr., 1988—. Lectr. CLE Fordham Law Sch., N.Y.C., 1990. Mem. Cosmopolitan Club. Jewish. Avocations: reading, tennis, golf, art, gardening. Office: Phillips Nizer Benjamin Krim & Ballon 666 5th Ave New York NY 10103-0001 E-mail: jroth@phillipsnizer.com.

ROTH, LISA MAE, writer; b. Quakertown, Pa., Apr. 13, 1963; d. Willard Leon Stoneback, Pauline D Stoneback; m. William Andrew Roth; children: Alison, Andrew. BA cum laude, California U. Pa., 1985. Prodn. dir., copywriter WOVU-Radio Sta., Ocean View, Del., 1985—88; pub. rels. coord. Hist. Soc. Talbot County, Easton, Md., 1988—90; home day care provider Lisa Roth Daycare, McDaniel, 1990—2001; tchrs. aide St. Luke's United Meth. Ch. Pre-school, St. Michael's, 1999—2000; writer self-employed, McDaniel, 1998—. Author: (plays) Something to Chew On, 1999, Toying With History, 2000, The Golden Halo Awards, 2001, To Shine Or Not to Shine, 2001; actor(Tred Avon Players): (plays) Women and Children, 1992, Ten Little Indians, 1994, Habitat for Humanity/FOLLIES, 1996, The Man Who Came to Dinner, 1996, The Nerd, 1997, Later Life, 1997, Cat On a Hot Tin Roof, 1998, Neil Simon's Rumors, 2000, Royal Gambit, 2003, (audiotape) St. Mary's Square Mus., 1999; singer: (plays) Habitat for Humanity/Neviaser FOLLIES, 1999, 2001, 2003, Cabaret, 2000, Past to Present to Oxford: The Music of Broadway, 2003; asst. dir. : (plays) 1776, 1998; asst. state mgr. Twelve Angry Men, 2000. Bd. dirs. Tred Avon Players, 2001—02; dir., writer Christmas Pageants St. Luke's United Meth. Ch., St. Michael's, 1996—2002, comm. coord., 1997—98. Mem.: Ea. Shore Writer's Assn., Alpha Psi Omega (life). Avocations: acting, dance, swimming, boating, reading. Home: 23387 Sans Souci Dr McDaniel MD 21647 Personal E-mail: cooldeal@dmv.com.

ROTH, MARJORY JOAN JARBOE, special education educator; b. Ranger, Tex., May 24, 1934; d. James Aloysius and Dorothy Knight (Taggart) Jarboe; m. Thomas Mosser Roth, Jr., Dec. 22, 1959; children: Thomas Mosser III, James Jarboe. BA in English, Rice U., 1957; MEd in Ednl. Adminstrn., U. N.C., Greensboro, 1981. Cert. tchr.-specific learning disabilities, middle grades lang. arts and social studies, intermediate grades, adminstr.-prin., N.C. Tchr. 4th grade Houston Ind. Sch. Dist., 1957-60; specific lang. disabilities instr. Forsyth Tech. C.C., Winston-Salem, N.C., 1976-77; specific learning disabilities tchr. Forsyth Country Day Sch., Winston-Salem, 1977-80; tchr. 5th grade Winston-Salem/Forsyth County Schs., 1982-83, specific learning disabilities tchr. Mt. Tabor High Sch., 1983-86; part time instr. English and Learning Disabilities Forsyth Tech. C.C., 1986-90; founding pres., prin. Greenhills Sch., Winston-Salem, 1990—. Co-author, co-editor booklets. Sunday Sch. dir., tchr. Galloway Meml. Episcopal Ch., 1960-70, pres., treas., sec. Churchwomen, 1963-74; treas. Elkin Jr. Woman's Club, 1960, chmn. Elkin Heart Fund Drive, 1968; bd. dirs. Hugh Chatham Hosp. Auxillary, 1968, Friends of the Elkin Pub. Libr., 1968-74, chmn., 1970-72, chmn., exhibits chmn. summer reading program; pres. South Surry Heart Assn., 1969; mem. Churchwomen of St. Paul's Episcopal Ch., Winston-Salem, 1982—, Fiddle and Bow Folk Music Soc., Winston-Salem, 1992—. Recipient June Lyday Orton award for outstanding svc. in the field of dyslexia, 1997; Forsyth fellow NEH, 1985; grantee in field. Fellow Acad. Orton-Gillingham Practitioners and Educators; mem. ASCD, Children with Attention Deficit Disorder (profl. adv. bd. N.C. Triad chpt. 1990-96), Learning Disability Assn. N.C. (sec., bd. dirs. 1981-86), Internat. Dyslexia Assn. (sec., bd. dirs. Carolinas br. 1981-85, founding pres. N.C. br. 1987-91, bd. dirs. 1987-96, nat. nominating com. 1992-94), Internat. Multisensory Structured Lang. Edn. Coun., Inc. (bd.dirs. 2000-03, mem. coun. 1993—). Republican. Avocations: tennis, hiking, folk music. Home: 940 Fox Hall Dr Winston Salem NC 27106-4431 Office: Greenhills Sch 1360 Lyndale Dr Winston Salem NC 27106-9739

ROTH, NANCY LOUISE, former nurse, veterinarian; b. Cin., June 24, 1955; d. Jack Leopold Jr. and Elsie Harriet (Shemin) R. BS in Agr., U. Mo., 1977, DVM, 1989; BSN, Avila Coll., 1980. Critical care RN. Staff nurse St. Louis Univ. Hosp., 1980-81, Barnes Hosp., St. Louis, 1981-85, U. Mo. Hosp. and Clinic, Columbia, 1985-89; assoc. veterinarian Ill. Equine Field Svc., North Aurora, 1989-95; proprietor Cedar Ln. Equine Clinic, New Haven, Mo., 1995—. Contbr. articles to profl. jours. Vol. instr. U.S. Pony Club, Wayne, Ill., 1991-95, 4-H Club, Wheaton, Ill., 1991-95; bd. dirs. Ill. Dressage and Combined Tng. Assn; chmn. U.S. Combined Tng. Assn. Area 4, 1998—. Mem. AVMA, Am. Assn. Equine Practitioners (trails and events com.), U.S. Combined Tng. Assn. (area IV chmn. 1998-2000), Sigma Theta Tau, Phi Zeta. Avocations: horse show competitor, travel, drawing, painting, reading. Home: 3134 Highway E New Haven MO 63068-2301 Office: Cedar Ln Equine Clinic PO Box 108 New Haven MO 63068-0108

ROTH, PAMELA SUSAN, lawyer; b. N.Y.C., Nov. 23, 1961; d. Edward Abraham and Susan Violet (Castro) R. BS in Biology, Adelphi U., 1982, MBA, 1986; JD, Pace U., 1990. Bar: N.Y. 1991, U.S. Dist. Ct. (ea. and so. dists.) N.Y. 1991, U.S. Ct. Appeals (10th cir.) 1993, Colo. 1995, U.S. Dist. Ct. Colo. 1995, U.S. Supreme Ct. 1995. Asst. gen. counsel N.Y.C. Dept. Probation, Bklyn., 1990-91; asst. dist. atty. Kings County Dist. Atty., Bklyn., 1992-93; assoc. Law Firm of Portales & Assocs., Denver, 1993-95; pvt. practice N.Y.C., 1995—. Gen. counsel Hispano Crypto-Jewish Rsch. Ctr., Denver, 1994—. Mem. ABA, Am. Soc. Internat. Law, Hispanic Nat. Bar Assn., Bklyn. Bar Assn., Internat. Assn. Jewish Lawyers and Jurists, Kings County Criminal Bar Assn. Avocations: aerobics, skiing, roller blading, gourmet cooking. Office: 26 Court St Ste 2003 Brooklyn NY 11242-1120 Address: 2361 E 71st St Brooklyn NY 11234-6511

ROTH, SARAH EVE, occupational safety professional; b. W. Allis, Wis., Mar. 10, 1971; d. Douglas Fred and Rene'e Alice Roth. BS in Edn., U. of Wis., Whitewater, 1994. Sales assoc. K-Mart, Burlington, Wis., 1988—94; safety asst. Velvac, Inc., New Berlin, Wis., 1993; safety intern Johnson Controls, Inc, Milw., 1994; corp. safety adminstr. Schweiger Industries, Inc., Jefferson, Wis., 1994; tech./product specialist Lab Safety Supply, Janesville, Wis., 1994—; tax specialist H & R Block, Janesville, Wis., 1999—2003; comml. print model Janesville, Wis., 1997—. Program com. chairperson Jefferson County Area Safety Network, Jefferson, 1994. Author: (book) Moments in Time, 2000. Mem.: Am. Soc. Safety Engrs. (pub. comm. dir. 1992, social chair 1993). Non-Denominational. Avocations: writing, dance, piano, weightlifting, golf. Home: 1521 Excalibur Dr Janesville WI 53546 Office: Lab Safety Supply 401 South Wright Rd Janesville WI 53546 Personal E-mail: sarahroth310@hotmail.com. Business E-Mail: s.roth@labsafety.com.

ROTH, TERESA ANN, broadcast executive; b. Little Rock, July 13, 1961; d. Carl Henry and Peggy Joann (Hartsell) Habig; m. Paul Gerhardt Roth, July 15, 1989 (div. May 1990). BA in Comm., U. Ark., 1983. Camera operator Sta. KATV-TV, Little Rock, 1983-85, writer, prodr., 1985-87, Sta. WSB-TV, Atlanta, 1987-89; exec. prodr., mgr. St. WSB-TV, Atlanta, 1989—. Prodr., dir. documentary Jo's Town, 1998, Jo's Town Shown at ValleyFest, 2000, The Hot Springs Documentary Film Festival, 2000, The Memphis Film Festival, 2001, The N.Y. Internat. Film Festival, 2001, The Kan Film Festival, 2001. Vol. Habitat for Humanity, Atlanta, 1996—; co-founder NATAS Student Connection, Atlanta, 1997—. Recipient Addy award Ad Club, Little Rock, 1986. Mem. NATAS (bd. dirs. 1991—, sec. 1993-95, v.p. 1995-99, nat. trustee 1999—), Promotion and Mktg. Execs., Atlanta Press Club. Avocations: movies, painting, writing, travel. Office: WSB-TV 1601 W Peachtree St NE Atlanta GA 30309-2641

ROTHBARD, BARBARA, allergy and dermatology nurse; b. Miami, May 20, 1943; Diploma, Mt. Sinai Hosp. Sch. Nursing, N.Y.C., 1964. Staff nurse Group Health Assocs., Takoma Park, Md.; head nurse physician's office, Washington; staff nurse Washington Hosp. Ctr.; head nurse physicians' office, Silver Spring, Md. Recipient Guggenheim medal, 1964. Mem. Dermatology Nurses Assn., Am. Acad. Allergy and Immunology.

ROTHBARD, SUSAN KAYE, humanities educator; d. Gerald and Florence Schlesinger Kaye; m. Jeffrey Mark Rothbard, Aug. 24, 1980; children: Sarah Kaye, Barry Jacob. BA, Georgetown U., 1975—79; MBA, Columbia U., 1979—81. Cert. Tchr. NJ, 1994. Fin. analyst W.R. Grace and Co., NYC, 1981—84; tchr. of english Livingston Bd. of Edn., Livingston, NJ, 1994—. Office: Livingston High School 30 Robert Harp Dr Livingston NJ 07039 E-mail: srothbard@livingston.org.

ROTHBERG-BLACKMAN, JUNE SIMMONDS, retired nursing educator, psychotherapist, psychoanalyst; b. Phila., Sept. 4, 1923; d. David and Rose (Protzel) Simmonds; m. Jacob Rothberg, Sept. 7, 1952 (dec. Feb. 2001); children: Robert Rothberg, Alan Rothberg; m. Stanley F Blackman, May 27, 2002. Diploma in nursing, Lenox Hill Hosp., 1944; BS, N.Y. U., 1950, MA, 1959, PhD (NIH fellow), 1965; Diploma in Psychotherapy and Psychoanalysis, Adelphi U., Inst. for Advanced Psychol. Studies, 1987. USPHS traineeship N.Y. U., 1957-59; sr. public health nurse Bklyn. Vis. Nurse Assn., 1951-53; prin. investigator in nursing, homestead study project Goldwater Hosp. and N.Y. U., 1959-61; instr. N.Y. U., 1964-65, asst. prof., 1965-68, assoc. prof., 1968-69, project dir. grad. program rehab. nursing, 1964-69, prof., 1969-87, prof. emeritus, 1987—; dean Adelphi U., Garden City, N.Y., 1969-85, v.p. acad. adminstrn., 1985-86; pvt. practice West Hempstead, N.Y., 1993-97. Pres. David Simmonds Co. Inc., Med. Supply Co., 1982-89; dir., chmn. compensation com. Quality Care, Inc.; cons. to various ednl. and svc. instns.; cons. region 2 Bur. Health Resources Devel., HHS.; speaker on radio and TV; bd. dirs., mem. audit com. Ipco Corp. (formerly Sterling Optical Corp.), 1991. Contbr. articles to profl. jours. Mem. pres's coun. N.Y. U. Sch. Edn., 1973-75; treas. Nurses for Polit. Action, 1971-73; trustee Nurses Coalition for Action in Politics, 1974-76; bd. visitors Duke Med. Ctr., 1970-74; mem. governing bd. Nassau-Suffolk Health Systems Agy., 1976-79; leader People-to-People Internat. med. rehab. del. to People's Republic of China, 1981; mem. com. for the study pain disability and chronic illness behavior Inst. Medicine, 1985-86, com. on ethics in rehab. Hastings Ctr., 1985-87; trustee Paget's Disease Found., 1987-89. Recipient Disting. Alumna award NYU, 1974, recognition award Am. Assn. Colls. Nursing, 1976, Achievers award Ctr. for Bus. and Profl. Women, 1980 Fellow Am. Acad. Nursing (governing coun. 1980-82); mem. Nat. League Nursing (exec. com. coun. of baccalaureate and higher degree programs 1969-73), Am. Nurses Assn. (joint liaison com. 1970-72), Commn. Accreditation of Rehab. Facilities, Am. Congress Rehab. Medicine (pres. 1977-78, chmn. continuing edn. com. 1979-86, 34th Ann. John Stanley Coulter Meml. lectr. 1984, Gold Key award 1984, Edward W. Lowman award 1990), Am. Assn. Colls. Nursing (pres. 1974-76), [illegible] Women's Network (pres. 1980-81), Kappa Delta Pi, Sigma Theta Tau, Pi Lambda Theta. Achievements include having June S. Rothberg collection in Nursing Archives, Mugar Meml. Library, Boston U. Home and Office: 3941 Redondo Way Boca Raton FL 33487

ROTHENBERG, ELIZABETH JILL, editor; b. N.Y.C., Mar. 9, 1966; d. Jerry and Roslyn Diane (Rosenberg) R. BA, Colby Coll., 1989; M in Journalism, Northwestern U., Evanston, Ill., 1991; postgrad., U. Denver, 1992. Reporter, Washington corr. Madison (Wis.) Capital Times, 1991; reporter Sonora (Calif.) Union Democrat, 1991-92; sr. editor sociology, current affairs Westview Press/Perseus Books Group, Boulder, Colo., 1993—. Mem. Phi Beta Kappa. Avocations: running, hiking, tennis. Office: Westview Press Perseus Books Group 5500 Central Ave Boulder CO 80301-2877

ROTHENBERG, KAREN H. dean, law educator; BA, Princeton U., 1973, MPA, 1974; JD, U. Va., 1979. Dean law sch.'s law and health care program U. Md., 2001—, law educator, 2001—. Formerly practiced with Washington D.C. Law firm of Covington and Burling; worked with a variety of health and med. orgns. ; pres. Am. Soc. Law, Medicine and Ethics; lectr. on legal issues in health care; dir. law sch.'s law and health care program U. Md.; spl. asst. to dir., 1995—96. Co-editor-in-chief (jours.) Jour. Law, Medicine, and Ethics; co-editor: (book with Elizabeth Thompson) Women and Prenatal Testing: Facing the Challenges of Genetic Technology ; contbr. articles on AIDS, women's health, genetics, right to forego treament. Recipient Joseph Healey Health Law Tchr.'s award, Am. Soc. Law, Medicine and Ethics. Mem.: NIH (sect. on prenatal care, recruitment & ret. of women in clin studies, sect. on ethical, legal and social implications of genetics), Nat. Inst. Child & Human Develop. (adv. coun.), ABA (coordinating group on bioethics and the law), Nat. Action Plan Breast Cancer, Ethics in Reproduction (nat. adv. bd.), Inst. Medicine's Com. (sect. legal and ethical issues for inclusion of women in clin. stud.). Office: U Md Law Sch 515 West Lombard St Baltimore MD 21201 Business E-Mail: krothenberg@law.umaryland.edu.

ROTHENBERGER, DOLORES JANE, legal association administrator, actress, singer; b. Blue Island, Ill., July 19, 1932; d. Ervin Louis and Emily Lorraine (Karafa) R. Grad. h.s., Chgo. Sec. claims dept. Continental Casualty Co., Chgo., 1950-51; legal sec. Rlwy. Express Agy., Chgo., 1951-59, Slovacek and Galliani, Chgo., 1959-69; actress, singer various theaters, 1967—; asst. to exec. dir. Internat. Assn. of Def. Counsel, Chgo., 1982-98. Mng. editor company newsletter, 1985-98. Active campaign Gov. Otto Kerner, Ill.; dir. ch. choir, writer, prodr., choreographer ch. shows. Recipient 1st Joseph Jefferson award for Best Chgo. Actress, Joseph Jefferson Com., 1970, Svc. award Village of Calumet Park, 1983. Mem. Actors' Equity Assn. Roman Catholic.

ROTHERMICH, GAYLA, music educator, director; b. Denver, May 5, 1946; d. C. Stanley and Bessey Welsh; children: Stefan, Candace. B in Music Edn., Wichita State U., s, 1968; MusM, So. Ill. U., Edwardsville, 1973; student, Hamburg Musickhochschule, Germany, 1973—75. Cert. instrumental/vocal K-12. Dir. Rothermich Studio for violin and viola, Ballwin, Mo., 1976—, St. Louis Suzuki Edn. Program, 1976—81; dir. strings, Suzuki specialist Parkway Sch. Dist./Barretts, Manchester, 1983—; program dir. Barretts Voyage to Mars, Manchester, Mo., 1999—. Freelance spkr. Parkway Sch. Dist., St. Louis, 1997—, Barretts Voyage to Mars, 1999—2000, musician website design, 1999—, prodr. integrated arts and scis. program, 1999—. Named All-State Award winner, Nat. Federated Music Club, 1964. Mem.: NEA (workshop leader Mo. state convention 2001), Music Educators Nat. Conf. (curriculum coun.), Am. String Tchrs. Assn., Social Concerns Com. Presbyterian. Avocations: computer technology/graphic design, gardening, travel, research, exploring. Office: Barretts Elem Sch 1780 Carman Rd Ballwin MO 63021 Personal E-mail: GRothermic@aol.com. Business E-Mail: grothermich@pkwy.k12.mo.us.

ROTHERT, MARILYN L. dean, nursing educator; b. June 4, 1939; married; 3 children. BSN cum laude, Ohio State U., 1961; MA in Ednl. Psychol., Mich. State U., 1979, PhD in Ednl. Psychol., 1980. RN, Mich. Staff nurse Univ. Hosp., Columbus, Ohio, 1961; instr. sch. nursing Hurley Hosp., Flint, Mich., 1961-66; asst. instr. sch. nursing Mich. State U., East Lansing, 1967-77, grad. asst. dept. community health sci., 1977-80, asst. prof. Coll. Human Medicine, 1980-82, asst. prof., dir. lifelong edn. Coll. Nursing, 1982-84, asst. prof. Coll. Human Medicine, 1982-84, assoc. prof., dir. lifelong edn. Coll. Nursing, 1984-88, assoc. prof. Coll. Human Medicine, 1984-86, prof., dir. lifelong edn. Coll. Nursing, 1988-92, prof., assoc. dean outreach and profl. devel., 1992-96, prof., dean Coll. Nursing, 1996—. Cons. No. Ill. U., Ohio State U., Mich. State Dept. Natural Resources, Can. Nurses Assn., Mich. Judicial Inst., Med. Coll. Va., U. Wash., Kirtland Coll., Anderson Coll. Contbr. articles to profl. jours. Co-chmn. Capitol Health Event, 1987-88; mem. worksite health subcom. Mich. Dept. Pub. Health; mem. State 4-H Health Com. Coop. Extension Svc., 1972-75, 82—; mem. med. adv. com. Mich. Civil Svc. Health Screening Unit, 1984. Mem. ANA (mem. coun. continuing edn., nurse researchers), Mich. Nurses Assn. (chmn. continuing edn. adv. com. 1989), Soc. for Med. Decision Making, The Brunswik Soc., Soc. for Judgment and Decision Making, Soc. for Rsch. in Nursing Edn., Midwest Nursing Rsch. Soc., Am. Pub. Health Assn., Nat. Ctr. for Health Edn., Nat. League for Nursing, Mich. State U. Faculty/Profl. Women's Assn. (bd. dirs. 1989—), Capitol Area Dist. Nurses Assn. (mem. nom. com. 1984-86, continuing edn. com. 1984), Phi Kappa Phi. Office: Mich State U Coll Nursing A-230 Life Sci Bldg East Lansing MI 48824

ROTHFIELD, NAOMI FOX, physician; b. Bklyn., Apr. 5, 1929; d. Morris and Violet (Bloomgarden) Fox; m. Lawrence Rothfield, Sept. 18, 1954; children: Susan, Lawrence, John, Jane. BA, Bard Coll., 1950; MD, NYU, 1955. Intern Lenox Hill Hosp., N.Y.C., 1955-56; instr. N.Y. U. Sch. Medicine, 1956-62, asst. prof., 1962-68; assoc. prof. U. Conn. Sch. Medicine, Farmington, 1968-72, prof., 1972—, chief divsn. rheumatic diseases, 1972—99. Contbr. chpts. to books; contbr. articles to med. jours. Bd. dirs., Conn. Choral Artists, 1999—. Mem. Am. Soc. Clin. Investigation, Am. Rheumatism Assn., Assn. Am. Physics. Jewish. Home: 540 Deercliff Rd Avon CT 06001-2859 Office: U Conn Sch Medicine Div Of Rheumatic Diseases Farmington CT 06030-0001 E-mail: rothfield@nso.uchc.edu.

ROTHKIN, MARILYN MAE, psychotherapist; b. Bklyn., Aug. 24, 1940; d. Robert Isadore and Sally Sarah (Perlman) Glazer; m. Richard Murray Rothkin, Jan. 5, 1963; children: Stacey Rothkin Post, Sheryl Rothkin Deppisch. BS, Kent State U., 1961; MA, U. Akron, 1987; cert., Gestalt Inst. Cleve., 1993. Lic. profl. clin. counselor, Ohio; cert. chem. dependency counselor, Ohio. Tchr. Akron, Barberton and Cleve. pub. schs., Ohio, 1961-73; social worker Western Res. Coun. Girl Scouts U.S., Akron, 1974-76, Medina (Ohio) County Dept. Human Svcs., 1987-88; counselor Touchstone Counseling Ctr., 1986-87, YMCA Rape Crisis Ctr., Akron, 1985-89; program dir. Cmty. Drug Bd., Akron, 1988-93; psychotherapist N.E. Ohio Psychol. Assocs., Cuyahoga Falls, 1990—2000. Staff writer Village Views/West Side Leader, Akron, 1974-84; spkr., workshop presenter, dir. Rothkin Assocs., Copley, Ohio, 1993-2002; pres. Intertel, 2001— Co-editor newsletter Summit County AMI, 1992-95. Mem. adolescent comprehensive health care adv. bd. Children's Med. Ctr., Akron, 1991-93; mem. drug free schs. adv. bd. Akron Pub. Schs., 1988-93; mem. edn. alumni bd. U. Akron; mental health disaster svcs. vol. ARC, 1999—; mem. com. Healthy Cmtys.-Healthy Youth, Copley, Ohio. Mem. Intertel (bd. dirs. 1988-2000, regional dir. 1988-89, 95-99, gen. sec. 1990-95, 99-2000, editor newsletter 1988-89, 95-98, editor Intertel Inquiries column 1999-01, Svc. award 1991, pres. 2001—), Am. Soc. Clin. Hypnosis (sec. Akron-Cleve. br. 1995-97), Mensa (exec. com. East Ctrl. Ohio br. 1987-88, ombudsman 1990--), Phi Delta Kappa, Chi Sigma Iota. Avocations: gardening, reading. Office: Marilyn Rothkin LPCC Counseling Akron Gen's Wellness Ctr 4125 Medina Rd Akron OH 44333-2483 E-mail: mmg2440@aol.com.

ROTHLEUTNER, PHYLLIS HARRIET, rancher; b. Neligh, Nebr., Apr. 24, 1928; d. Ralph Leslie and Marguerite L. Carnes; m. Wesley M. Rothleutner (dec. Aug. 1992); children: Elise M. Douglas, Todd W. BA, Nebr. Wesleyan U., 1950. Ptnr. Rothleutner Family Ranch, Todd County, S.D., Cherry County, Nebr. Mem. Cattlemen's Beef Bd., 1987-95, nominating com., dubget, rsch., adminstrn. and fgn. mktg. coms. Bd. trustees Cherry County Hosp., chmn.; charter mem. Cozy Fireside Ext. Club, Kilgore; state ext. sec., 1977-78; leader 4-H. Recipient Alumni Loyalty award Nebr. Wesleyan U., 1973. Mem. Am. Nat. Cattlewomen (exec. com. 1983-84, 88-93, membership chmn. 1987, 88, 2d v.p. 1988, 1st v.p. 1989, budget com. chmn. 1989, regional meetings chmn. 1990, pres. 1991, chmn. nominating com. 1992, chmn. outstanding cattlewomen com. 1992, nat. beef cookoff com. 1988-91, Outstanding Cattlewoman of Yr. award 1995, San Antonio, 1996), Nat. Cattlemen's Beef Assn., N.E. Cattlemen, Nebr. Cattlewomen (chmn. 1977, 78, sec.-treas. 1978-79, 2d v.p., chmn. Beef for Fathersday 1979-80, 1st v.p., membership chmn. 1980-81, pres. 1981-82, beeferendum chmn. 1981-82, Outstanding CattleWoman of Yr. award 1994), Agrl. Women's Leadership Network (treas., v.p., pres. 1995-96), Order of Ea. Star (Worthy Matron 1970, 93, 94, grand rep. Wash. state 1994, 95), Beta Sigma Phi (pres.). Home and Office: PO Box 88 Kilgore NE 69216-0088

ROTHMAN, CAROL, theater director; BSS, Northwestern U.; MFA, NYU, 1973. Co-founder Second Stage Theatre, N.Y.C., artistic dir. Mem. nat. adv. bd. Sch. Speech Northwestern U. Dir.: (plays), Williamstown Theatre Festival. Nominee Best Dir. Tony award; recipient OBIE award, Rosamund Gilder award. Office: Second State Theatre 307 West 43rd St New York NY 10036*

ROTHMAN, SHEILA MILLER, public health educator; b. Phila., Jan. 25, 1939; d. Harry and Rose (Newman) Miller; m. David J. Rothman, June 26, 1960; children: Matthew S., Micol S. BS, Simmons Coll., 1960, MSW, 1963; PhD, Columbia U., 1989. Rsch. assoc. Ctr. for Policy Rsch., N.Y.C., 1972-78, Columbia U., N.Y.C., 1978-84; rsch. scholar Columbia Coll. Physicians and Surgeons, N.Y.C., 1984-95, sr. rsch. scholar, 1995—; prof. pub. health Mailman Sch. Pub. Health Columbia U., N.Y.C., 1999—. Bd. dirs. Asia Watch, N.Y.C.. Author: Woman's Proper Place, 1978, Living in the Shadow of Death, 1994, The Pursuit of Perfection, 2003; co-author: The Willowbrook Wars, 1984. Fellow NEH, 1987-90, NIH, 1996-98, 2003—; rsch. grantee, Rudin Family Found., 1984-97. Office: Columbia Coll Phys/Surgeons 630 W 168th St New York NY 10032 3702

ROTHMAN-BERNSTEIN, LISA J. occupational health nurse; b. Toledo, Dec. 29, 1949; 1 child, Daniel Karvinen. Diploma, Mercy Hosp. Sch. Nursing, Toledo, 1974; B Individualized Studies magna cum laude, Lourdes Coll., Sylvania, Ohio, 1989; AS in Bus., U. Toledo, 1970; cert. in Italian lang., history, art, U. Florence, Italy, 1972. Buyer Lamson's of Toledo, 1971; owner, designer FUNKtional Art, Inc., 1984—; owner, baker Tres Bon Cheesecakes, Inc., Margate, Fla., 1984; cruise ship nurse Costa Cruise Line, Miami, Fla., 1979; sales Chandris Cruise Line, Greece, 1980, Bahama Cruise Line, Miami, Fla., 1980; home health nurse Upjohn, Ft. Lauderdale, Fla., 1983; patient svcs. coord. Fla. Med. Ctr., Lauderdale Lakes, Fla., 1983; sales and entertainment Norwegian Cruise Line, Miami, Fla., 1984—87; vol. nurse in ob-gyn. Yoseftal Hosp., Eilat, Israel, 1976—78; staff nurse in ob-gyn. Mt. Sinai Med. Ctr., Miami Beach, Fla., 1974—76; staff nurse on eye svc., oper. rm. St. Vincent Mercy Med. Ctr., Toledo, 1990, nursing and healthcare recruiter, 1991—95, patient advocate, 1995—99. Co-chair Lourdes Coll. Red Cross Blood Drive, 1988, 89; publicity chair St. Vincent Med. Ctr. 1993 Nurses' Week. Mem. Phi Theta Kappa, Kappa Gamma Pi.

ROTHMAN-DENES, LUCIA BEATRIZ, biology educator; b. Buenos Aires, Feb. 17, 1943; came to U.S., 1967; d. Boris and Carmen (Couto) Rothman; m. Pablo Denes, May 24, 1968; children: Christian Andrew, Anne Elizabeth. Lic. in Chemistry, Sch. Scis., U. Buenos Aires, 1964, PhD in Biochemistry, 1967. Vis. fellow NIH, Bethesda, Md., 1967-70; postdoctoral fellow biophysics U. Chgo., 1970-73, rsch. assoc., 1973-74, from asst. prof. to assoc. prof., 1974-83, prof. molecular genetics and cell biology, 1983—. Mem. microbial genetics study sect. NIH, 1980-83, 93-96, chair, 1994-96, mem. genetic basis of disease study sect., 1985-89, mem. coun. Ctr. for Sci. Rev., 2000—; mem. Damon Runyon and Walter Winchell Sci. Adv. Com., N.Y.C., 1989-93; mem. biochemistry panel NSF, 1990-92. Contbr. articles to profl. jours. Fellow AAAS, Am. Acad. Microbiology (bd. govs. 2000-03); mem. Am. Acad. Arts and Scis., Am. Soc. Microbiology (divsn. chair 1985, divsn. group II rep. 1990-92, vice chair GMPC 1995-99, chair GMPC 1999-2001, chair meetings. bd. 2003-), Am. Soc. Virology (councilor 1987-90), Am. Soc. Biochemistry and Molecular Biology. Office: Univ Chgo 920 E 58th St Chicago IL 60637-5415 Office Phone: 773-702-1083. E-mail: lbrd@midway.uchicago.edu.

ROTHS, BEVERLY OWEN, environmentalist; b. Kansas City, Kans., Aug. 25, 1935; d. Edward Charles and Josephine Mary (Vogel) Owen; m. Robert L. Roths, Sept. 4, 1954; children: Karen Kay, Daniel Owen, Nancy Jo. AA with honors, Antelope Valley Coll., 1975. Sec. McDonnell Aircraft Co., St. Louis, 1955-58; exec. dir. Florissant (Mo.) Valley C. of C., 1976-86; pres. Poppy Reserve/Mojave Desert Interpretive Assn., Lancaster, Calif., 1988-2000. Pres. Soroptimist Internat., North St. Louis County, 1981-82; sec.-treas. St. Louis County League C. of C., Clayton, 1978; bd. dirs. Lake Shastina (Calif.) Cmty. Svcs. Dist., 2003—. Prodr. Small Bus. Profiles, condr. interviews Storer Cable TV, Florissant, 1983-86. Mem. Florissant City Coun., 1968-72; bd. dirs. Mo. Mcpl. League First Woman, Florissant, 1970-71; co-chair Bicentennial, Florissant, 1985-86, Police Bldg. Bond Issue, Florissant, 1980; dir. Lake Shastina Cmty. Svcs. Dist., 2003—. Recipient Woman of Achievement award, Florissant Bus. and Profl. Women, 1979, Superior Achievement award, State Calif. Dept. Parks and Recreation, 1999; Inst. Orgn. Mgmt. scholar, C. of C. Jefferson City, Mo., 1980. Mem. Lancaster Woman's Club, Wildflower Preservation Found. (bd. dirs., treas. 1991-2000), League Calif. State Park Non-Profit Orgns. (bd. dirs., sec. 1994-98), Poppy Res./Mojave Desert Interpretive Assn. (pres. 1988-2000). Roman Catholic. Avocations: bird watching, gardening, golf, reading, genealogy.

ROTHSCHILD, BARBARA, artist, educator; b. Chgo., Nov. 16, 1928; AA, Am. Acad. Art, Chgo., 1949; BA, Coll. New Rochelle, 1974, MA in Art Edn., 1978. Registered art tchr., N.Y. Instr. Ctr. for Continuing Edn., Mamaroneck, N.Y., 1974-81, Boca Mus. Art, Boca Raton, Fla., 1995—. Artist-in-residence New Rochelle, N.Y., 1974-85; adj. prof. Mercy Coll., Dobbs Ferry, N.Y., 1981-87; lectr. Pelham (N.Y.) Art Ctr., Coral Springs (Fla.) Art Guild, 1993, Women in Visual Arts, Boca Raton, 1994-96, Coconut Ctr. Art Guild, Fla., 1996; judge various orgns. Solo shows include Pelham Art Ctr., 1978, Mus. Gallery, White Plains, N.Y., 1979, MAG Gallery, Mamaroneck, N.Y., 1983, Lumen Winter Gallery, New Rochelle, 1987,Dover Gallery, Boca Raton, 1991, 93, Conservart Gallery, Boca Raton, 1993; group exhbns. include Gold Coast Watercolor Soc., Ft. Lauderdale, Bruce Mus., Greenwich, Conn., Hudson River Mus., Yonkers, N.Y., Nat. Arts Club, N.Y., Fla. Watercolor Soc., Broward Art Guild, Tallahassee Watercolor Soc. Ann., Mus. Fine Arts, St. Petersburg, Fla., Cornell Mus., Delray Beach, Fla., Boca Mus. Artists Guild, Boca Raton, LeMoyne Art Found., Tallahassee, Boca Museum of Art, Boca Raton; numerous pvt. and pub. collections. Recipient Artists Guild Norton Mus. award, 1990, Merit award, 1993, 2nd Pl. award Profl. Artists Guild, 1993-94, 96, Boca Mus. Artists Guild award, 1997-99. Mem. Gold Coast Watercolor Soc. (signature), Boca Raton Mus. Artists Guild (pres. 1991-93), Fla. Watercolor Soc. Avocations: singing, drama. Studio: 19577 Sedgefield Ter Boca Raton FL 33498-4644

ROTHSCHILD, JENNIFER ANN, artist, educator; b. Mesa, Ariz., Aug. 16, 1948; d. Joe Dean and Frances Ann (McFarland) Johnston; m. Harry Ronald Rothschild, Feb. 14, 1981. Diploma, El Camino Jr. Coll., 1968; BA in Art Edn., Calif. State U., 1970. Cert. secondary sch. tchr., Calif. Arts and crafts specialist City of Hawthorne (Calif.) Parks and Recreation, 1966-67; portrait artist Disneyland, Anaheim, Calif., 1970-74; secondary sch. art tchr. Orange (Calif.) Unified Schs., 1972-80; freelance custom apparel designer Honolulu, 1982-94; sculptor, artist, 1994—. One woman show at Roy's Honolulu, 2001, Art Centre Gallery, Honolulu, 1997, Studio 1 Gallery, 2004; corp. artist Arts of Paradise Gallery, Honolulu, 1997—; exhibited in show at City of Manhattan Beach, Calif., 1966, Assn. of Hawaii Artists, 1996—, in book Encyclopedia of Living Artists, 10th edit., 1997. Bd. dirs. Hawaii Tennis Patrons, Honolulu, 1996—, Assn. of Hawaii Artists Show chairwoman, 2002. Recipient scholarship Chouinard Sch. Art Inst., 1965-66, 1st Place Stamp Design award Easter Seals, 1995-96, Hokele Artists award Hawaiian Airlines, 1996, Most Unique Art award Assn. of Hawaii Artists Aloha Show, 1997. Fellow Nat. Mus. Women in Arts; mem. AAUW, Honolulu Art Acad., Assn. Hawaii Artists (v.p. 1996-97, pres. 1999-2000), Hawaiian Pacific Tennis Assn. (rules chmn. 1997), mem. Windward Art Guild, 2002, Nat. League of Am. Pen Women, Hon., chapter, Alpha Omicron Pi. Republican. Presbyterian. Avocations: tennis, reading, writing, painting, sculpting. E-mail: onoaloha@attglobal.net.

ROTHSTEIN, BARBARA JACOBS, federal judge; b. Bklyn., Feb. 3, 1939; d. Solomon and Pauline Jacobs; m. Ted L. Rothstein, Dec. 28, 1968; 1 child, Daniel. BA, Cornell U., 1960; LL.B., Harvard U., 1966. Bar: Mass. 1966, Wash. 1969, U.S. Ct. Appeals (9th cir.) 1977, U.S. Dist. Ct. (we. dist.) Wash. 1971, U.S. Supreme Ct. 1975. Pvt. practice law, Boston, 1966-68; asst. atty. gen. State of Wash., 1968-77; judge Superior Ct., Seattle, 1977-80, Fed. Dist. Ct. Western Wash., Seattle, 1980—, chief judge, 1987-94, dir. Fed. Jud. Ctr., 2003—. Faculty Law Sch. U. Wash., 1975-77, Hastings Inst. Trial Advocacy, 1977, N.W. Inst. Trial Advocacy, 1979—; mem. state-fed. com. U.S. Jud. Conf., chair subcom. on health reform; dir. Fed. Jud. Ctr. Recipient Matrix Table Women of Yr. award Women in Communication, Judge of the Yr. award Fed. Bar Assn., 1989; King County Wash. Women Lawyers Vanguard Honor, 1995. Mem. ABA (jud. sect.), Am. Judicature Soc., Nat. Assn. Women Judges, Fellows of the Am. Bar, Wash. State Bar Assn., U.S. Jud. Conf. (state-fed. com., health reform subcom.), Phi Beta Kappa, Phi Kappa Phi. Office: Fed Jud Ctr 1 Columbus Cir NE Washington DC 20002-8003

ROTHSTEIN, MARIAN, humanities educator; b. N.Y.C., Oct. 13, 1944; BA, U. Wis., 1965, MA, 1969, PhD, 1974. Faculty Grinnell Coll., 1987—91; prof. French Carthage Coll., Kenosha, Wis., 1991—. Author: (book) Reading in the Renaissance, 1999; contbg. editor: 1540: Charting a Change, —; editor (translator): Life in Renaissance France, 1978; mem. editl. bd. 16th Century Studies Jour., 2000—, Early Modern Studies, 2002—. Office: Carthage College 2001 Alford Dr Kenosha WI 53140-1994

ROTHWELL, ELAINE B. artist; b. Mpls., May 8, 1926; d. Frederick Roscoe and Stella Frances (LaVallee) Bartholomew; m. William Stanley Rothwell, May 10, 1946; children: Suzanne, Amy Verrett, Wendy Rothwell-Lopez, Bart. BFA, San Jose State U., 1966; pvt. study, Woodbury Graphic Studio, Los Altos, Calif., 1975-76, Amaranth Intaglio Workshop, Los Altos, 1985. One-woman shows include Triton Mus. Art, Santa Clara, Calif., 1976, Palo Alto (Calif.) Civic Ctr., 1977, Stanford (Calif.) Art Spaces, Stanford U., 1985, 1988, 1989, West Valley Art Mus., Surprise, Ariz., 1996, Roseville (Calif.) Arts Ctr., 2003, exhibited in group shows at Carnegie Art Ctr., North Tonawanda, N.Y., 1995, 1996, N.J. Ctr. Visual Arts Internat., Summit, 1997, 1998, Brand Libr. and Art Ctr., Glendale, Calif., 1996, Internat. Exhbn. Art League Manatee County, Fla., 1996, Nat. Soc. Artists, 1997, Am. Color Print Soc., 1997, Grand Exhbn. Nat. Competition, Akron, Ohio, 1998, Printwork '98, Barrett Ho., Poughkeepsie, N.Y., 1998, 73d Ann. Internat. Print Competition/Print Ctr., Phila., 1999, Manhattan Arts Internat., 1999, Chautauqua Nat. Exhbn. Am. Art, 1999, No. Colo. Ann. Nat. Exhbns., 1999, 2000, Stage Gallery, Merrick, N.Y., 2000, others, retrospective exhbns., Gallery 9, Los Altos, Calif., 2002, Gallery II, Nevada City, Calif., 2002, Represented in permanent collections Newberry Libr., Chgo., Triton Mus. Art, Santa Clara, West Valley Art Mus., Brand Libr. Art Ctr., Glendale. Mem.: Am. Color Print Soc., Nat. Mus. Women in Arts (charter), Auburn Old Town Gallery, Gallery II, Triton Mus. Art. Home and Office: 3030 Eagles Nest Auburn CA 95603-5918

ROTMAN, CARLOTTA HILL, physician; b. Chgo., Apr. 8, 1958; d. Clarence Kenneth and Vlasta (Cizek) Hayes; m. Chester James Hill III, June 10, 1967 (div. 1974); m. Carlos A. Rotman, July 31, 1980; children: Robin Mercedes. BA magna cum laude, Knox Coll., 1969; MD with honors, U. Ill., 1973. Diplomate Nat. Bd. Med. Examiners, Am. Bd. Dermatology. Intern Mayo Sch. Medicine, Rochester, Minn., 1973-74; resident U. Ill., Chgo., 1975-78, asst. prof. clin. dermatology Coll. Medicine, 1978-93, assoc. prof. clin. dermatology Coll. Medicine, 1993—. Sen. U. Ill. Senate, Chgo., 1986-91, 99-2002; councilor Chgo. Med. Soc., 1990-96, 99—. Contbr. articles to profl. jours. Bd. dirs. Summerfest St. James Cathedral, Chgo., 1986-91, YWCA, Lake Forest, Ill., 1995—, pres., 1998-00; master gardner Chgo. Botanic Garden, Glencoe, Ill., 1994-98; bd. dirs. Lake Bluff Open Lands Assn., 1997—. Recipient Janet Glascow award Am. Women's Med. Assn., 1973. Mem. AMA, Am. Acad. Dermatology, Herb Soc. Am. (ways and means No. Ill. unit 1992-94, treas. N. Ill. unit 1996-2000, vice chair 2000-02, chair 2002-), Ill. State Dermatologic Soc., Ill. State Med. Soc., Chgo. Med. Soc., Chgo. Dermatologic Soc., Phi Beta Kappa, Alpha Omega Alpha. Avocations: travel, cooking, gardening, reading. Office: Dept Dermatology 808 S Wood St Chicago IL 60612-7300 E-mail: chhill@uic.edu.

ROTOLO, SUSAN, artist; b. N.Y.C., Nov. 20, 1943; d. Joachim Peter and Mary Teresa Rotolo; m. Enzo Bartoccioli; 1 child, Luca. Tchr. bookmaking; workshop leader in field. Illustrator, designer textiles, compact disc cover art, scenery and props for theater, Laugh the Blues Away Cookbook, 2001; solo exhbns. at Jefferson Market Libr., N.Y.C., 1997, 98, 99, NYU Casa Italiana Gallery, 1998, Donnell Libr. Ctr., N.Y. Pub. Libr., 2000; exhibited at Galleria Todini, Perugia, Italy, 1992, AKA Artists Ctr., Saskatoon, Can., 1993, Ctr. for Book Arts, N.Y.C., 1994, 95, 96, 97, ARC Gallery, Chgo., 1995, Spring Studio, N.Y.C., 1996, Columbia Coll. Gallery, Chgo., 1996, C.A.C. Gallery, Cambridge, Mass., 1999, N.Y. State Mus., Albany, 1997, Left Bank Gallery, Bennington, Vt., 1996, 97, Art Acad. Cin., 1998, Nat. Guild Bookworkers Traveling Exhbn., 1998-99, Harper Collins Exhbn. Space, N.Y.C., 1999, Corcoran Gallery, Washington, D.C., Nat. Mus. Women in Arts, Washington, D.C., Core Gallery, Denver, Colo., many others; artist one-of-a-kind sculptural books; included in Book Arts Collection of L.I. U., Bklyn. Mus., Bklyn. N.Y., Nat. Mus. of Women in the Arts, Washington, Mus. of Modern Art, Franklin Fuurance, N.Y.C. Recipient Spl. Mention award for tech. expertise combined with creative risk, Appearances and West Village Coalition for Parks and Playgrounds, 1995, First Pl. Jury prize Valdosta (Ga.) Fine Arts Gallery, Valdosta (Ga.) U. Mem. Ctr. for Book Arts, Am. Craft Coun., Guild of Bookworkers. Avocations: art, music, books, good food, the ocean. Office: Suzart 682 Broadway New York NY 10012-2320 Office Phone: 212-254-5591. Personal E-mail: suzarte@earthlink.net.

ROTUNDO, MARGARET R. state legislator; b. Schenectady, N.Y., July 16, 1949; m. Loring Danforth; 2 children. BA, Mount Holyoke Coll., 1971. Devel. coord. Abington (Maine) Friends Sch., 1976-78; asst. dir. Office of Career Counseling Bales Coll., 1978-80, dir., 1980-86, assoc. dir. Ctr. for Svc. Learning, 1995—; mem. Maine Senate from 21st Dist., Augusta, 2001—, mem. edn. and cultural affairs, state/local govt. coms., 2001—. Bd. dirs. Head Start, 1999—, LA Arts, 1996—; co-chair Lewiston Asjurations Partnership, 1994—; chair Lewiston Sch. Com., 1999—. Mem. Androssoggin Valley C. of C. (bd. dirs. 1996—), Maine Sch. Bds. Assn. (past pres.). Home: 446 College St Lewiston ME 04240 Office: State House 3 State House Sta Augusta ME 04333 Office Fax: (207) 287-1585. E-mail: mrotundo@bates.edu.

ROUBIK, SUSANNE EILEEN, architect; b. Milw., Dec. 1, 1959; d. Joseph Rudolph and Gertrude Mae Brown. BS in Architecture, U. Wis., Milw., 1981, MArch summa cum laude, 1984; postgrad., Inst. of Architecture Studies, Paris, Barcelona, 1984, Taller de Architecture:, Ricardo Bofill. Registered architect, Ill. Archtl. photographer U. Wis., Milw., 1983-84, archtl. slide curator, 1983-84; sr. archtl. designer Skidmore, Owings & Merrill, Chgo., 1984-90; prin. S.E. Roubik & Assocs.-Design Cons., Chgo., 1990—; cons. KMR Group, Inc., Chgo., 1991-93, World Trade Ctr., Chgo., 1995; pres. Internat. Collaborations Group, Inc., Chgo., 1997—; sr. project mgr. McClier, Chgo., 1999-2000, svc. group dir., 2000-01; assoc., project mgr. Skidmore, Owings & Merrill, Chgo., 2001; pres., founder Feng Shui & Design Inst. Chgo., 2003—, Feng Shui & Design Inst. of Ill., 2003—. Design critic Notre Dame U., U. Wis. Mil., U. Ill. Chgo., Ill. Inst. Tech., Chgo., U. Ohio, Miami, Andrews U.; com. chairwoman CCAIA V.I.P./Protocol 1993 AIA/UIA World Congress Architects, 1991-93; founder, bd. dirs., exec. v.p. Newhouse Architecture Found., 1989-93, sec., 1987-88, dir. internships, 1984-93. Com. chairwoman CCAIA V.I.P./Protocol, 1991—93; bd. directors Rehab. Inst. Chgo., Health Resource Ctr. for Women with Disabilities, 1994—98. Recipient award Nat. Inst. Archtl. Edn., 1984, Piux XI H.S. Alumni award, Milw., 1994. Mem.: AIA (program coord. Chgo. chpt. 1987—89, chmn. real estate com. 1989—91, del. young architects forum 1990—92, steering com. young architects forum 1990—92, bd. dirs. 1990—95, program com. 1991—93, Chgo. award 1984, Chgo. chpt.-Chgo. Bar Assn. Young Arch. award 1987, Young Arch. award 1993), Urban Land Inst. (program com. 1999—2003), Crew: Comml. Real Estate Exec. Women, Women in Planning and Devel. (bd. dirs. 2003—, dir. 2003), Third Coast Design Coop. (v.p. bd. dirs. 1981—84), Third Coast Women in Arch. (founder, pres. 1983), Graphic Artists Guild, Am. Mktg. Assn., Internat. Women Assocs. (chair English group 1998—99, ofcl. photographer 1998—, Kent Coll. of Law-Ill. Inst. Tech. 1998—, libr. internat. rels., consular ball exec. com.), Mid Day Club Chgo. (assoc. bd. dirs. co-chair 1995—96, chair 1996—97). Office: Internat Collaborations Grp 421 W Melrose St Ste 15B Chicago IL 60657-5539

ROUGH, MARIANNE CHRISTINA, librarian, educator; b. Glen Cove, N.Y., June 27, 1941; d. Michael Anthony Scarangello, Ann Nancy (Kulka) Scarangello; m. Allan Conrad Rough; 1 child, William Johnson. AAS, SUNY, Farmingdale, 1976, BA, SUNY, Old Westbury, 1977; MLS, L.I. U., 1978; cert. in advanced librarianship, Columbia U., 1985. Art dir. Technamation, Inc., Port Washington, NY, 1962—68; dir. new product design Queens Lithography, Inc., L.I., NY, 1968—70; tech. specialist SUNY, Coll.at Farmingdale, 1970—78; dir. Libr. Learning Resources Ctr. SUNY, Coll. Old Westbury, 1978—82; prof., libr. Prince George's C.C., Largo, Md., 1983—. Mem. C.C. adv. group OCLC Online Computer Libr. Ctr., Inc., Dublin, 2001—. Contbr. chapters to books. Regional publicity coord. Audubon Soc., L.I., 1978—79, coordinating team mem. Sierra Club, Annual C&O Canal Hike, Washington, 1991—95; bd. dirs. Friends Pub. Libr., Port Washington, NY, 1980—81. Recipient award of merit, Md. Assn. Higher Edn., 1987; grantee Pathfinder grants, Prince George's C.C., 1999, 2001. Mem.: Assn. Coll. and Rsch. Librs. of ALA (sec. cmty. and jr. coll. sect. 2001—02, vice-chmn., chmn.-elect, past chmn. 2002—), Assn. Libr. Collections and Tech. Svcs. of ALA (sec. coun. regional groups 1999—2001, Md. rep. Potomac Tech. Processing Librs.). Methodist. Avocations: fine art, art history, history, historical preservation. Home: 1015 Danbury Dr Bowie MD 20721-3202 Office: Prince Georges CC 301 Largo Rd Upper Marlboro MD 20774-2199 Home Fax: 301-390-7824; Office Fax: 301-808-8847. Personal E-mail: mrough@pgcc.edu.

ROUKEMA, MARGARET SCAFATI, congresswoman; b. West Orange, N.J., Sept. 19, 1929; d. Claude Thomas and Margaret (D'Alessio) Scafati; m. Richard W. Roukema, Aug. 23, 1951; children[00bf] Margaret, Todd (dec.), Gregory. BA with honors in History and Polit. Sci, Montclair State Coll., 1951, postgrad. in history and guidance, 1951-53; postgrad. program in city and regional planning, Rutgers U., 1975. Tchr. history, govt., public schs., Livingston and Ridgewood, N.J., 1951-55; mem. U.S. Congress from 7th N.J. dist., Washington, 1981—83, U.S. Congress from 5th N.J. dist., Washington, 1983—2003; vice chair fin. svcs. com., chair housing and community opportunity subcom.; mem. banking com., edn. and the workforce com. Vice pres. Ridgewood Bd. Edn., 1970-73; bd. dirs., co-founder Ridgewood Sr. Citizens Housing Corp.; chairwoman Fin. Inst. and Consumer Credit Sub. Com. U.S. Congress; sponcer Family Med. Leave U.S. Congress, lectr. Rutgers Univ. Trustee Spring House, Paramus, N.J.; trustee Leukemia Soc. No. N.J., Family Counseling Service for Ridgewood and Vicinity; mem. Bergen County (N.J.) Republican Com.; NW Bergen County campaign mgr. for gubernatorial candidate Tom Kean, 1977; bd. mem. Children's Aid and Family Svcs., The Red Cross, Ramapo Coll. Mem. Bus. and Profl. Women's Orgn. Clubs: Coll. of Ridgewood, Ridgewood Rep. Republican.

ROULET, SISTER ELAINE, social services administrator; b. 1930; Family liaison Bedford Hills (N.Y.) Correction Ctr., 1970—; founder, exec. dir. Providence House, Inc., 1980; founder, dir. Children's Ctr. at Bedford Hills. Creator support programs for mothers and their babies in prison.

ROUMBOS, MARIA K. elementary school educator; b. Flushing, N.Y., Nov. 22, 1970; d. Kostas J. and Alexandra K. Roumbos; m. Mark A. Cichon, July 2, 1995; 1 child, Michael Roumbos Cichon. BS in Elem. Edn. summa cum laude, Adelphi U., 1991, MA in Secondary Edn. in Math. summa cum laude, 1993. Cert. tchr. early childhood edn., elem. edn., math. edn. Tchr. St. Nicholas Ch. Sch., Flushing, NY, 1986—, asst. dir., 1990—; tchr. Floral Park-Bellerose Sch. Dist., 1991—. Tutor in field, NY, 1991—2001. Recipient Pres.'s Achievement award, Queens Coll., 1989, Honors in Sci. and Math cert. merit, Soc. Women Engrs., 1991, Merit award, N.Y.C. Assn. Tchrs., 1988, Scholastic Achievement award, N.Y. Gov.'s Com., 1991, Merit award, Hellenic U. Club of N.Y., 1993, Outstanding Achievement award, Greek Lang. Inst., 1988, Internat. award for Striving for Peace on Earth, N.Y. Dist. of Kiwanis, 1987; Paul Douglas scholar, Empire State Challenger scholar, United Fedn. Tchrs. scholar, N.Y. State scholar. Mem.: Inst. for Math. and Sci. Studies (life), Internat. Baccalaureate Scholars (life), Nat. Honor Soc. (life; chpt. co-pres. 1987—88), Kappa Delta Pi (life). Democrat. Greek Orthodox. Avocations: reading, photography, painting, arts-n-crafts, gardening.

ROUNDS, BARBARA LYNN, psychiatrist; b. L.A., Mar. 17, 1934; d. Ralph Arthur and Florene V. (Heyer) Behrend; divorced 1962; children: Steve, Mike, Pamela, Ronald, Thomas. BA, Stanford U., 1964, MD, 1966; postgrad., San Francisco Psychoanalytic, 1973-81. Diplomate Am. Bd. Psychiatry and Neurology; cert. psychoanalyst. Intern New Orleans Pub. Health Svc., 1966-67; resident psychiat. Mendocino State Hosp., 1967-69, U. Calif. Davis, 1969-70; staff psychiatrist U. Calif. Davis Med. Sch., Sacramento, 1970-77, clin. instr., 1970-76; psychiatrist pvt. practice, Sacramento, 1971—; asst. clin. prof. U. Calif. Davis, Sacramento, 1976-84, assoc. clin. prof., 1984-94. Mem. Am. Psychiat. Assn., Am. Psychoanalytic

Assn., AMA, Cen. Calif. Psychiat. Soc. (pres.-elect 1990-91, pres. 1991-92). Democrat. Home: 8910 Leatham Ave Fair Oaks CA 95628-6506 Office: 1317 H St Sacramento CA 95814-1928

ROUNTREE, NEVA DIXON, public relations executive; b. Jacksonville, Fla., Dec. 13, 1943; d. Jarma E. and Helen (McIlvaine) Dixon; m. Don C. Rountree, Mar. 23, 1941; 1 child, Don C. III. AB in Journalism, U. Ga., 1964, MA, 1979. Press sec. Underwood for U.S. Senate, Atlanta, 1979-80; account exec. Cohn & Wolfe, Atlanta, 1980-81; v.p. Carl Byoir & Assocs., Atlanta, 1981-84; pres. Rountree Group, Inc., Atlanta, 1985—. Co-chmn. Leadership Sandy Springs, Ga., 1985-86, trustee, 1986—; adv. bd. Northside Found., 1994—; comm. com. Atlanta Com. for Olympic Games, 1990-92. Recipient 1 of 3 Best Run Agys. award Atlanta Bus. Chronicle, 1988, 89; named 25 Hot Smaller Pub. Rels. Agys. by Inside Pub. Rels., 1992, named Best Mktg. Driven Pub. Rels. by Atlanta Bus. Chronicle, 1991, 92. Mem. Pub. Rels. Soc. Am. (Counselors Acad., pres. Ga. chpt. 1994—, George Goodwin award 1992), Pub. Rels. Exch. (bd. dirs. 1987—), U. Ga. Journalism Alumni Assn. (v.p., pres. 1986-89).

ROUP, BRENDA JACOBS, nurse, retired army officer; b. Petersburg, Va., July 8, 1948; d. Eugene Thurman and Sarah Ann (Williams) Jacobs; m. Clarence James Roup, May 8, 1976. BSN, Med. Coll. Va., Richmond, 1970; MSN, Cath. U. Am., 1977; PhD, U. Md., 1995. Commd. 2d lt. U.S. Army, 1970, advanced through grades to lt. col., 1986; infection control cons. 7th MEDCOM, Fed. Republic Germany, 1982-83; chief infection control Brooke Army MEDCEN, San Antonio, 1983-86; chief infection control Walter Reed MEDCEN, Washington, 1986-92, ret., 1992; Johnson & Johnson postdoctoral fellow Johns Hopkins U. Sch. Nursing, Balt., 1995-97; nurse cons. in infection control Md. Dept. Health and Mental Hygiene, 1999—; nurse cons. in infection control to U.S. Army Surgeon Gen., 1986-92. Contbr. articles to profl. jours. Mem. Assn. Profls. in Infection Control, Sigma Theta Tau. Avocations: reading, gardening, cooking. Office: Md Dept Health & Mental Hygiene Baltimore MD 21201 E-mail: broup@dhmh.state.md.us.

ROURKE, ARLENE CAROL, publisher; b. N.Y.C. Pres. Rourke Publs., Vero Beach, Fla., 1984—. Author, pub. books for children on Native Am. people, western history, religion, the environment, animal care and personal relationships, science biographies. Active Ctr. for the Arts, 1985—, Riverside Theatre, Vero Beach, 1985—, Humane Soc. Vero Beach; bd. dirs. Dollars for Scholars.

ROUSE, DORIS JANE, physiologist, research administrator; b. Greensboro, N.C., Oct. 3, 1948; d. Welby Corbett and Nadia Elizabeth (Grainger) R.; m. Blake Shaw Wilson, Jan. 6, 1974; children: Nadia Jacqueline, Blair Elizabeth. BA in Chemistry, Duke U., 1970, PhD in Physiology and Pharmacology, 1980. Tchr. sci. Peace Corps, Tugbake, Liberia, 1970-71; research scientist Burroughs Wellcome Co., Research Triangle Park, N.C., 1971-76; sr. physiologist Rsch. Triangle Inst., Durham, 1976-83, ctr. dir., 1980-2000, also dir. NASA tech. application team, 1980-2000, dir. Tuberculosis Tech. Transfer Program, 1999—, dir. Global Health, 2001—; portfolio project mgr. Global Alliance for Tuberculosis Drug Devel., 2002—. Adminstr. ANSI Tech. Adv. Group for Wheelchairs, N.Y.C., 1982-86; adj. asst. prof. U. N.C. Sch. Medicine, 1983-92; chair Instl. Rev. Bd., Profl. Devel. Award com., chair salary com. Rsch. Triangle Inst.; mem. adv. bd. Assistive Tech. Rsch. Ctr., 1994-96; portfolio project mgr. Global Alliance for TB Drug Devel., 2002—. Mem. adv. bd. Assn. Retarded Citizens, Arlington, Tex., 1981—88, Western Gerontology Soc., San Francisco, 1982—85; bd. dirs. Simon Found., Chgo., 1983—95; mem. spl. rev. com. small bus. applications Nat. Forum on Tech. and Aging; mem. fund steering com. Academy Venture, 2000—. Recipient Group Achievement award NASA, 1979, 2000, President's award, RTI, 2003. Mem.: Am. Soc. Microbiology, Assn. Fed. Tech. Transfer Execs., Licensing Execs. Soc., Rehab. Engring. Soc. N.Am., Rehab. Engring. Soc. N.Am. (chmn. wheelchair com. 1981—86). Home: 2410 Wrightwood Ave Durham NC 27705-5802 Office: Research Triangle Inst PO Box 12194 Durham NC 27709-2194 Office Phone: 919-541-6980.

ROUSE, TERRIE S. museum administrator; b. Youngstown, Ohio; BA in Intercultural Studies, Trinity Coll., Hartford, Conn.; MA in African History, cert. in African studies, Columbia U. Sr. curator Studio Mus., N.Y.C.; dir. Calif. Afro-Am. Mus., L.A., N.Y. Transit Mus., N.Y.C.; exec. dir. Children's Mus. Maine; pres., CEO, African Am. Mus. (formerly Afro-Am. Hist.-Cult. Mus.), Phila. Vis. art coord. L.A. Festival, 1993. Avocation: collecting african american books and dolls. Office: AfricanAm Mus in Phila 701 Arch St Philadelphia PA 19106-1504 Fax: 215-574-3110.

ROUSE, TERRIE SUZITTE, former museum director; b. Youngstown, Ohio, Dec. 2, 1952; d. Eurad R. and Florence Wilcox; 1 child, Malcom Adam Rouse-West. BA, Trinity Coll., 1974; MS in Profl. Studies, Cornell U., 1977; certificate Internat. Affairs, MA, Columbia U., 1979. Mgr., curator Adam Clayton Powell St. Office Bldg., N.Y.C., 1979-81; sr. curator Studio Mus. Harlem, N.Y.C., 1981-86; dir. mus. N.Y. Transit Mus., Bklyn., 1986—91; dir. Calif. Afro-Am. Mus., 1991—93; artistic exec. dir. Atlanta Ballet, 2002—03. Advisor Bellevue Hosp. Art Bd., 1981—. Contbr. articles to profl. jours. Mem. Conf. Mil. Transp. Ofcls. Named Outstanding Young Women Am., 1981-83. Mem. Am. Assn. Museums (assessor 1981—). Avocations: sewing, reading, exploring harlem, doll collecting.*

ROUSEY, ANNE, social worker; b. Denison, Tex., Dec. 7, 1939; d. Lynden A. and Evelyn M. Hagans; m. Lelon M. Rousey (dec. Nov. 22, 1998); children: Sharon A. Rousey Ward, Lynda Lee Fields. BSE, Midwestern State U., Wichita Falls, TX, 1975. Editor The Frauen, USAF Officers Wives, Ramstein, Germany, 1970—70; art instr. Southside Girls Club Inc., Wichita Falls, Tex., 1973; organist St. Mark's United Meth. Ch., Wichita Falls, Tex., 1974, choir dir., 1975—77; exec. dir. Southside Girls Club Inc., Wichita Falls, Tex., 1975—2001. Sec. Bus. & Profl. Women, Wichita Falls, Tex., 1975; pres. Soroptimist Internat., Wichita Falls, Tex., 1981. Recipient Good Neighbor Award, TV Channel 3, 1990. Mem.: Family Self-Sufficiency Coordinating Com., Soroptimist Club Internat. (pres. 1981—2002). D-Liberal. Methodist. Achievements include Have helped approximately 20,000 deserving young children reach their potentials, many of whom have become nurses, teachers, social workers, business professionals, accountants and doctors. Avocations: piano, cooking, bridge. Home: 2249 Wranglers Retreat Wichita Falls TX 76310 Office: Southside Girls Club Incorporated 1205 Montgomery Wichita Falls TX 76302

ROUSH, SUE, newspaper editor; b. Mason City, Iowa., Dec. 26, 1957; BS in Journalism, Northwestern U., 1980. Mng. editor Universal Press Syndicate, Kansas City, Mo., 1995—. Office: Universal Press Syndicate 4520 Main St Ste 700 Kansas City MO 64111-7701

ROUSS, RUTH, lawyer; b. Des Moines, May 21, 1914; d. Simon Jacob and Dora (Goldin) R.; m. Dennis O'Rourke, Jan. 21, 1940; children: Susan Jerene, Kathleen Frances, Brian Jay, Dennis Robert, Ruth Elizabeth, Dolores Ann. BA, Drake U., 1934, JD, 1937. Bar: Iowa bar 1937, U.S. Supreme Ct. bar 1945, Colo. bar 1946, D.C. bar 1971. Legal counsel to Jay N. Darling, Des Moines, 1937-38; atty. Office of Solicitor, Dept. Agr., 1938-45, asst. to solicitor, 1940-45; practice law Colorado Springs, Colo., 1946—; mem. firm Williams & Rouss, 1946-50, individual practice law, 1950-69; of counsel firm Sutton, Shull & O'Rourke, Colorado Springs and Washington, 1969-72; mem. firm Rouss & O'Rourke, Colorado Springs and Washington, 1972-99, Colorado Springs, 2000—. Dir., sec.-treas. Man-Exec., Inc. Mem. cast chorus, Colo. Opera Festival, 1976, 78; mem., Colorado Springs Chorale, 1976— . Bd. dirs. Human Relations Commn. City Colorado Springs, 1968-73, chmn., 1971-72; bd. dirs., sec. Colorado Springs Community Planning and Research Council, 1972-78; bd. dirs. Logos, Inc., Colorado Springs, 1972-78, sec., 1976-77, v.p., 1977-78; bd. dirs. Colorado Springs Opera Festival, Colorado Springs World Affairs Council, Urban League of Pikes Peak Region; mem. com. protection human rights Penrose Hosp., adv. council Am. Lung Assn. of Colo., Pikes Peak region; dir., pres., Joseph Henry Edmondson Found.; adv. bd. Care Castle Divsn. Pikes Peak Seniors,El Paso County, Colo. Mem. El Paso County (Colo.) Bar Assn., Colo. Bar Assn., D.C. Bar Assn., Am. Law Inst. (life), Internat. Fedn. Women Lawyers, Women's Forum Colo., Phi Beta Kappa. Home: 8 Heather Dr Colorado Springs CO 80906-3114 Office: Box 572 231 E Vermijo Ave Colorado Springs CO 80903-2113

ROUSSAKIS, DOROTHY FERGUSON, artist; b. Danbury, Conn., Apr. 24, 1914; d. Daniel Odell and Flora Ellwood Ferguson; m. Charles Roussakis, Dec. 15, 1944 (dec. Sept. 25, 1990); 1 child, Peter. Student, Fed. Art Sch., 1932—36; studied with Karl Anderson, 1943—45. Fashion illustrator Leavitts Dept. Store, 1963—64; dir. Am. Artists Profl. League, NY, 1965—66; tchr. Nichols Cmty. Ctr., Conn., 1969. One-woman shows include Rochester (N.H.) Libr., 1998, Ind. U., Kokomo, 2001, Burlington (Ind.) Libr., 2001. Recipient Best Portrait, Contemporary Arts and Crafts, 1953, Best Portrait award, Milford Conn. Art League, 1955, 1966, award for graphics, Acad. Artists, 1981, Sheffield Mass. Art Assn., 1981, Kent Art Assn., 1988. Mem.: Am. Pen Women (pres. Conn. br. 1962—64, 1970—72, 1978—80, pres. Conn. state 1974—76, art chmn. Conn. state 1962—64, state sec. 1968—70). Home and Studio: 1101 S Jackson St Burlington IN 46915

ROUSSEAU, IRENE VICTORIA, artist; children: Douglas, Scott. BA, Hunter Coll., N.Y.C.; MFA, Claremont (Calif.) Grad. Sch., 1969; PhD, N.Y. U., 1977. Tenured prof. William Paterson Coll., Wayne, N.J., 1970-74. Invited spkr. Coll. Art Assn./Women Caucus on Art Conf., L.A., 1985, N.J. Ctr. for Visual Arts, Summit, N.J., 1985, Noyes Mus., 1994, Mus. African Art, 1994, Hillwood Art Mus.-C.W. Post/L.I. U., 2000, AIEMA IX Internat. Conf. on Antique and Medieval Mosaic Rsch., Rome, 2001, Sch. Arch., Weston Art Gallery NJIT, Newark, 2004; guest spkr. Internat. AIEMA Conf., Lausanne, Switzerland, 1997, invited guest spkr. Villeme Colloque Intl. de la Mosaique Antique, Univ. de Lausanne, Switzerland, 1997; spkr. Bridges: Math. Connections in Art, Music and Sci. Exhbns. include Betty Parsons Gallery, N.Y.C., Claremonte Colls., State Mus. Sci. and Industry, L.A., Morris Mus. Arts and Scis., Morristown, N.J., The Bronx Mus. of Art, Galleri Sci. Agnes, Copenhagen/Roskilde, Denmark, Sculptors 5, Madison, N.J., Edmund Sci. Co., Barrington, N.J., AT&T World Hdqrs., Basking Ridge, N.J., N.J. Ctr. for Visual Arts, The Brotherhood Synagogue Holocaust Meml. Gramercy Pk. (mosaic), N.Y.C., 1986, 1st Internat. Art Biennale, Malta, 1995, U. Lausanne (Switzerland), 1997, Internat. Biennale Malta, 1997 (awards), Am. Inst. Archs., N.Y., 1998, Southwestern Coll., Kans., 1999, Lausanne, Switzerland, 2001, BRIDGES, Internat. Joint Conf., 2003; artist in residence Program Greece, 2000; guest spkr. and exhibit Internat. Conf. Internat. Soc. Art, Math., Architecture, Frieburg, Germany, 2002, Internat. Conf. Connections in Math., Music, Art, Sci., and Arch., Granada, Spain, 2003, Internat. Soc. Arts, Math., and Arch. and BRIDGES (Math. Connections in Art, Music, and Sci.) Internat. Joint Conf., Granada, Spain; one person exhibits Weston Gallery Sch. Arch., Newark, N.J., 2003, N.J. Inst. Tech. Sch. Arch., 2003, Weston Art Gallery Sch. Arch. NJIT, Newark, 2004; author: Mathematical Connections in Art, Music & Science, 2003, Geometric Mosaic Tiling on Hyperbolic Sculptures, Granada, 2003, Mosaic Art as a Metaphor for Concepts of Science and Mathematics, Rome, 2003; contbr. articles and works of art. Recipient seven 1st prize awards for creative work in N.J., ER Squibb and Sons Sculpture award, AIA N.J. Presentation Design award, 1995, Internat. Art Biennale Malta Installatin award, 1997, Traveling Exhibit throughout Europe and Middle East and Africa of Winners of the 1997 Biennale in Malta, 1997-99. Mem. AIA (profl. affiliate N.J., N.Y., chmn. architecture dialogue com. Presentation award 1995), Internat. Sculptors Assn., Am. Abstract Artists (exhbn. chmn. 1978-79, pres. 1979-82), Fine Arts Fedn. (bd. dirs.), Coll. Art Assn., Women's Caucus on Art (conf. spkr.), Phi Delta Kappa. Home: 41 Sunset Dr Summit NJ 07901-2322 E-mail: mosiaicartforms@aolc.om.

ROUSSEAU, LILLIAN MCKIM See PULITZER, LILLY

ROUSSEAU-VERMETTE, MARIETTE, artist; b. Trois-Pistoles, Que., Can., Aug. 29, 1926; d. Joseph-Herve and Corrinne (Belanger) Rousseau; m. Claude Vermette, Nov. 29, 1952; children: Marc, Jerome. Student, Ecole des Beaux Arts du Que., 1944-48, Studio Dorothy Liebes, San Francisco, 1948-49, Oakland Coll. Arts and Crafts, 1948-49; studied different tapestry techniques in Europe, 1952, 58. Head dept. fibre, visual arts Banff (Alta.) Sch. Fine Arts, Canada, 1979—85. Solo exhbns. include: Musée des Beaux-Arts de Montréal, 1961, Galerie Camille Hébert, Montréal, 1964, New-Design Gallery, Vancouver, B.C., 1964, Galerie Godard-Lefort, Montréal, 1969, Musée du Québec, 1972, Marlborough-Godard Gallery, Toronto, 1974, Centre Culturel Canadien, Paris, 1974, Centre Culturel Canadien, Brussels, 1974, Winnipeg (Man.) Art Gallery, 1976, Grace Borgenicht Gallery, N.Y., 1977, Galerie Alice Pauli, Lausanne, Switzerland, 1978, Brown Grotta Gallery, Wilton, Conn., 1993-2001, Galerie Bernard, Montreal, Can., 2004—, numerous others; group shows include: Nat. Gallery of Can., 1959, Biennale Internationale de la Tapisserie, Lausanne, Switzerland, 1962, 65, 67, 71, 77, Triennale de Milan, 1968, Mus. Modern Art, N.Y.C., 1968-69, Art Gallery of Windsor, Ont., 1977, 81, Musée d'Art Contemporain, Montréal, Mus. Modern Art, Kyoto, Japan, 1977, Mus. Modern Art, Tokyo, 1978, Musée d'Art Contemporain de Montréal, 1979, Biennale, Lodz, Poland, 1981, numerous others; theatrical works include: Théâtre Maisonneuve, Place des Arts, Montréal, 1967, Theatre of the Can. Ctr. of Arts, Ottawa, 1965-68, The JFK Ctr. for Performing Arts, Washington, 1970, Group de la Place Royal, 1968, 69, 73; permanent collections include: Nat. Gallery of Can., Art Gallery of Charlottetown, Can. Pavilion, Osaka, Japan, Québec Pavilion, Osaka, Palais de Justice, Montréal, Mus. Modern Art, Kyoto, Met. Mus., N.Y.C., Chgo. Art Mus., numerous others. Decorated officer Order of Can.; Can. Coun. grantee, 1968; recipient Honor certificate la Conférence Canadienne des Arts, 1974. Subject of numerous articles and books. Office: 373 Rue Morin Saint-Adele QC Canada J8B 2P8

ROUSUCK, J. WYNN, theater critic; b. Cleve., Mar. 19, 1951; d. Morton I. and Irene Zelda (Winograd) R. BA summa cum laude, Wellesley Coll., 1972; MS, Columbia U., 1974. Assoc. editor, program guide, Sta. WCLV-FM, Cleve., 1972-73; theater and film reviewer Cleve. Press, 1973; gen. assignment arts reporter Balt. Sun, 1974-84, theater critic, 1984—. Instr. English Goucher Coll., Towson, Md., 1981; master critic O'Neill Critics Inst., Waterford, Conn., 1990—; theater critic Md. Pub. TV., 1986; spkr. in field. Recipient Dog Writers Assn. Am. awards 1977, 79, Md. chpt. 1st Place Arts Reporting award Soc. Profl. Journalists, 1993, Front Page award, Disting. Criticism Washington-Balt. Newspaper Guild, 1997, 99, 2002, Bill Pryor Meml. grand prize for writing, 1999, Bernie Harrison Meml. award for commentary, 2002; NEH journalism fellow U. Mich., 1979-80, fellow O'Neill Critics Inst., 1982. Mem. Balt. Bibliophiles (bd. dirs. 1982-83), Octavo Plus, Walters Art Gallery, Balt. Wellesley Club (pres. 1978-79). Jewish. Avocations: rare books, art, dogs. Office: The Baltimore Sun 501 N Calvert St Baltimore MD 21278-0001

ROUX, MILDRED ANNA, retired secondary school educator; b. New Castle, Pa., June 1, 1914; d. Louis Henri and Frances Amanda (Gillespie) R. BA, Westminster Coll., 1936, MS in Edn., 1951. Tchr. Farrell (Pa.) Sch. Dist., 1939-55; tchr. Latin, English New Castle (Pa.) Sch. Dist., 1956-76; ret., 1976. Chmn. sr. H.S. fgn. lang. dept. New Castle Sch. Dist., 1968-76, faculty sponsor sch. fgn. lang. newspapers, 1960-76, Jr. Classical League, 1958-76. Mem. Lawrence County Hist. Soc., Am. Classical League, 1958-76. Mem. AAUW (chmn. publicity, chmn. program com. Lawrence County chpt. 1992-96), Am. Assn. Ret. Persons, Nat. Ret. Tchrs. Assn., Pa. Assn. Sch. Retirees (chmn. cmty. participation com. Lawrence County br. 1976-81, telephone com. Lawrence County br. 1990-98), Coll. Club New Castle (chmn. sunshine com. 1989-91, mem. social com. 1991-92), Woman's Club New Castle (chmn. pub. affairs com. 1988-90, internat. affairs com. 1990-92, program com. 1990-92, telephone com. 1992-99). Republican. Roman Catholic. Avocations: church choir, reading, civic interests. Home: # 302 3345 Wilmington Rd New Castle PA 16105-1038

ROVE, FRANCES ANN, lawyer; b. Conroe, Tex., Jan. 28, 1960; d. James Vincent and Frances M. (Cashin) R. BS, U. Kans., 1981, JD, 1985. Bar: Kans. 1985, Mo. 1988. Jud. clk. Johnson County Ct., Olathe, Kans., 1984-85; rsch. atty. Nat. Inst. for Child Support Enforcement, Chevy Chase, Md., 1985-86; trust adminstr. United Mo. Bank, N.A., Kansas City, 1986-88; mem. Linde, Thomson, Langworthy, Kohn & Van Dyke, P.C., Kansas City, 1988-90; chief dep., counsel Jackson County Pub. Adminstr., Kansas City, 1990-94, pub. adminstr., 1994—. Mem. ABA, Kans. Bar Assn., Kansas City Met. Bar Assn., Johnson County (Kans.) Bar Assn., Arc of Friends, Mo. Pub. Adminstrn. Assn., Nat. Guardianship Assn. (charter mem., registered guardian), Alliance for Mentally Ill, Midwest Bioethics, Assn. Women Lawyers. Roman Catholic. Office: Pub Adminstr Office 415 E 12th St Kansas City MO 64106-2706

ROVELSTAD, MATHILDE V(ERNER), library science educator; b. Germany, 1920; came to U.S., 1951. m. Howard Rovelstad, 1970. PhD, U. Tubingen, 1953; MS in L.S, Catholic U. Am., 1960. Prof. libr. sci. Cath. U. Am., 1960-90, prof. emeritus, 1990—. Vis. prof. U. Montreal, 1969 Author: Bibliotheken in den Vereinigten Staaten, 1974; translator Bibliographia, an Inquiry into its Definition and Designations (R. Blum), 1980, Bibliotheken in den Vereinigten Staaten von Amerika und in Kanada, 1988; contbr. articles to profl. jours. Research grantee German Acad. Exch. Svc., 1969, Herzog August Bibliothek Wolfenbüttel, Germany, 1995. Mem. Internat. Fedn. Libr. Assns. and Instns. (standing adv. com. on libr. schs. 1975-81), Assn. for Libr. and Info. Sci. Edn. Home: Apt HR-T35 719 Maiden Choice Ln Catonsville MD 21228-6231 Office: Cath U Am Sch Libr & Info Sci Washington DC 20064-0001

ROVNER, ILANA KARA DIAMOND, federal judge; b. Riga, Latvia, 1938; arrived in U.S., 1939; d. Stanley and Ronny (Medalje) Diamond. AB, Bryn Mawr Coll., 1960; postgrad., U. London King's Coll., 1961, Georgetown U., 1961—63; JD, Ill. Inst. Tech., 1966; LittD (hon.), Rosary Coll., 1989, Mundelein Coll., 1989; DHL (hon.), Spertus Coll. of Judaica, 1992. Bar: Ill. 1972, U.S. Dist . (no. dist.) Ill. 1972, U.S. Ct. Appeals (7th cir.) 1977, U.S. Supreme Ct. 1981, Fed. Trial Bar (no. dist.) Ill. 1982. Jud. clk. U.S. Dist. Ct. (no. dist.) Ill., Chgo., 1972—73; asst. U.S. atty. U.S. Atty.'s Office, Chgo., 1973—77, dep. chief of pub. protection, 1975—76, chief pub. protection, 1976—77; dep. gov., legal counsel Gov. James R. Thompson, Chgo., 1977—84; dist. judge U.S. Dist. Ct. (no. dist.) Ill., Chgo., 1984—92; cir. judge U.S. Ct. Appeals (7th cir.), Chgo., 1992—. Mem. Gannon-Proctor Commn. on the Status of Women in Ill., 1982—84; mem. civil justice reform act adv. com. 7th Cir. Ct., Chgo., 1991—95, mem. race and gender fairness com., 1993—; mem. fairness com. U.S. Ct. Appeals (7th cir.), 1996—, mem. gender study task force, 1995—96; mem. jud. conf. U.S. Com. Ct. Adminstrn. Case Mgmt., 2000—. Ctrl. and East European law initiative vol. ABA, 1997—; trustee Bryn Mawr Coll., Pa., 1983—89; mem. bd. overseers Ill. Inst. Tech./Kent Coll. Law, 1983—; trustee Ill. Inst. Tech., 1989—; mem. adv. coun. Rush Ctr. for Sports Medicine, Chgo., 1991—96; bd. dirs. Rehab. Inst. Chgo., 1998—; bd. visitors No. Ill. U. Coll. Law, 1992—94; vis. com. Northwestern U. Sch. Law, 1993—98, U. Chgo. Law Sch., 1993—96, 2000—03; chair Ill. state selection com. Rhodes Scholarship Trust, 1998—2000. Named Today's Chgo. Woman of the Yr., 1985, Woman of Achievement, Chgo. Women's Club, 1986; named one of 15 Chgo. Women of the Century, Chgo. Sun Times, 1999; named to Today's Chgo. Women Hall of Fame, 2002; recipient Spl. Commendation award, U.S. Dept. Justice, 1975, Spl. Achievement award, 1976, Ann. Nat. Law and Social Justice Leadership award, League to Improve the Cmty., 1975, Ann. Guardian Police award, 1977, Profl. Achievement award, Ill. Inst. Tech., 1986, Louis Dembitz Brandeis medal for Disting. Legal Svc., Brandeis U., 1993, 1st Woman award, Valparaiso U. Sch. Law, 1993, ORT Women's Am. Cmty. Svc. award, 1987—88, commendation def. of prisoners com., Chgo. Bar Assn., 1987, Svc. award, Spertus Coll. of Judaica, 1987, Ann. award, Chgo. Found. for Women, 1990, Arabella Babb Mansfield award, Nat. Assn. Women Lawyers, 1998, award, Chgo. Attys. Coun. of Hadassah, 1999, 1st Woman award, Georgetown U. Law Ctr., 2001, Today's Chicago Woman Hall of Fame, 2002, Hebrew Immigrant Aid Soc. Chgo. 85th Anniversary honoree, 1996, Chgo. Hist. Soc. Trailblazers Award, 2003, First Woman award, Chgo. Bar Assn. Alliance for Women and Women's Bar Assn. Ill., 2000, Vanguard award, Chgo. Bar Assn. and Lesbian and Gay Bar Assn. Chgo., 2004. Mem.: Decalogue Soc. of Lawyers (citation of honor 1991, Merit award 1997), Chgo. Coun. Lawyers, Women's Bar Assn. Ill. (ann. award 1989, 1st Myra Bradwell Woman of Achievement award 1994, 1st Woman Award (in conjunction with Chicago Bar Assn. Alliance for Women) 2000), Fed. Judges Assn., Fed. Bar Assn. (mem. selection com. Chgo. chpt. 1977—80, treas. 1978—79, sec. 1979—80, 2d v.p. 1980—81, 1st v.p. 1981—82, pres. 1982—83, 2d v.p. 7th cir. 1983—84, v.p. 7th cir. 1984—85), Kappa Beta Pi, Phi Alpha Delta (hon.). Office: 219 S Dearborn St Ste 2774 Chicago IL 60604-1803

ROWAN, CYNTHIA L. REEVES, accountant; b. Pomona, Calif., Sept. 30, 1957; d. Jack Harding and Ruth Evelyn Reeves; m. Jeffrey Wayne Rowan, Dec. 21, 1985; children: Alexander Roy Harding, Kathryn Elizabeth. BS, Calif. Poly. State U., Pomona, 1980; MS, Golden Gate U., 1987. CPA, Colo., Calif. Tax mgr. Fleming and Co., San Bernardino, Calif., 1980-93, Fleming and Co. formerly Lester Witte & Co., Colorado Springs, Colo., 1993—. Fundraising chair Kiwanis, Redlands, Calif., 1990-93; bd. dirs. Kiwanis Found., Redlands, 1990-93. Named Rookie of the Yr., Kiwanis, Redlands, 1993. Mem. AICPA, Colo. Soc. CPAs. Republican. Methodist. Avocations: water-skiing, puzzles, snow skiing, kids activities. Office: Fleming and Co #203 2975 Broadmoor Valley Rd Colorado Springs CO 80906-4466

ROWE, AUDREY, paralegal; b. Albuquerque, June 26, 1958; d. James Franklin Ringold and Geneva Doris (Jennings) Robinson. A in Specialized Bus. in Acctg., ICS Ctr. for Degrees, Scranton, Pa., 1988, A in Specialized Bus. in Fin., 1989; BSBA, Century U., 1991, MBA, 1995, cert. paralegal studies, 1996, A in Specialized Bus. in Paralegal Studies, 1999. Svc. rep. Mountain and Southwestern Bell Telephone Co., Albuquerque, Houston, 1978-83; clk., carrier U.S. Postal Svc. PS05, Bellaire, Sugar Land, Tex., 1983-86; supr. mails U.S. Postal Svc. EAS15, Sugar Land, 1986-87; officer-in-charge U.S. Postal Svc. EAS 18, Rosharon, Tex., 1987; from supr. mails EAS 15 to gen. supr. mails EAS 17 U.S. Postal Svc., Houston, 1987-89; relief tour supt. U.S. Postal Svc. EAS 21 (Detail Assignment), Houston, 1989; mgr. gen. mail facility U.S. Postal Svc. EAS22 (Detail Assignment), Capitol Heights, Md., 1989-90; mgr. mail processing U.S. Postal Svc. EAS21, Charlottesville, Va., 1990-91; MSC dir. city ops. U.S. Postal Svc. EAS23 (Detail Assignment), Roanoke, Va., 1991; mgr. gen. mail facility U.S. Postal Svc. EAS24, Washington, 1991-96; plant mgr. U.S. Postal Svc. EAS25, Dulles, Va., 1992; pvt. contractor, paralegal, 1996-98; paralegal Lenox, Biddinger & Conrad, P.C., Woodbridge, Va., 1997-99, Wilson Strickland & Benson P.C., Atlanta, 1999-2000, Chamberlain, Hrdlicka, White, Williams & Martin, 2000—03, Holland & Knight, LLP, 2003—. Mem. Am. Soc. Notaries, Nat. Capital Area Paralegal Assn., Nat. Fedn. Paralegal Assn., Nat. Assn. Legal Assts. Avocations: piano, violin, reading.

ROWE, DIANE ELIZABETH, law clerk; b. Grove City, Pa. BS, Ind. U., 1981; M.Pub. Affairs, Ind. U., Gary, 1983; JD, Loyola U. Chgo., 2000. V.p. Ptnrs. in Contracting Corp., Hammond, Ind., 1983-85; energy conservation programs specialist U.S. Dept. Energy, Argonne, Ill., 1985-89, contracting officer Chgo., 1989-97; law clk. U.S. Dist. Ct. (no. dist.) Ill., Chgo., 2000—. Contbr. articles to profl. jours. Recipient Excellence for the Future award Ctr. for Computer-Assisted Legal Instrn., 1996. Mem.: ABA, Am. Soc. Pub. Adminstrn. (exec. coun. 1985—89, pub. rels. com. chair 1985—89), Fed. Bar Assn., Chgo. Bar Assn., Ill. State Bar Assn. Home: 1313 Azalea Dr Munster IN 46321 Office: US District Court 219 S Dearborn St Chicago IL 60604 E-mail: drowel@att.net., diane_rowe@ind.uscourts.gov.

ROWE, LISA DAWN, computer programmer/analyst, computer consultant; b. Kenton, Ohio, Feb. 2, 1966; d. Daniel Lee and Frances Elaine (Johnson) Edelblute; m. Jeffrey Mark Rowe, Feb. 13, 1982; children: Anthony David, Samantha Paige Elizabeth, Zane Thomas, Zachary Tyler. Student, Inst. of Lit., 1988-90, Acad. Ct. Reporting, 1988, Marion Tech. Coll., 1991-92; postgrad., Ohio State U., 1993—. Writer, model Newslife, Marion, Ohio, 1982-83; bookkeeper Nat. Ch. Residences, Columbus, Ohio, 1985, Insty-Prints, Columbus, 1985; asst. editor Columbus Entertainment, 1984-85; book reviewer, writer Columbus Dispatch, 1989-91; writer Consumer News, Delaware, Ohio, 1989-90; computer programmer, supr. Dyserv, Inc., Columbus, 1986-92; bookkeeper, acct., office mgr. Marion Music Ctr., Inc., 1990; computer programmer EBCO Mfg., Columbus, 1992-93; sr. programmer/analyst Borden, Inc., Columbus, 1993-94; computer cons. System X, Columbus, 1994-95, LDA Systems, Dublin, Ohio, 1995-96; pres. Rowe Techs. Inc., Marion, Ohio, 1996—. Editor newsletter Assn. System Users, 1989-90; contbr. articles and revs. to profl. jours. Mem. NAFE, MADD, DAV (chaplain 1990), Heart of Ohio Am. Cat Fanciers Assn. Cat Club (pres. 2002), Ragamuffin Cat Lovers Soc., Inc. (v.p. 2003). Republican. Mem. Lds Ch. Avocations: horseback riding, swimming, camping, fishing, reading. Home: 1150 Toulon Ave Marion OH 43302-6610 Office: Rowe Techs Inc 1150 Toulon Ave Marion OH 43302-6610 E-mail: Lisarowe@rowetech.com.

ROWE, MARIELI DOROTHY, media literacy education consultant, organization executive; b. Bonn, Germany, Aug. 13; came to U.S., 1939; m. John Westel Rowe; children: Peter Willoughby, William Westel, Michael Delano. BA, Swarthmore Coll.; postgrad., U. Colo., 1990; MA, Edgewood Coll., 1990. Interim exec. dir. Friends of Sta. WHA-TV, Madison, Wis., 1976; exec. dir. Nat. Telemedia Coun., Madison, 1978—. Project assoc. Loyola U., Chgo., 1989-92; bd. dirs. Sta. WYOU, Madison. Co-prodr., author TV documentary Kids Meet Across Space, 1983; editor Telemedium, Jour. of Media Literacy, 1980—. Co-founder, bd. dirs., pres. Friends of Pub. Stas. WHA-TV, radio, Madison, 1968-78; v.p. bd. Nat. Friends of Pub. Broadcasting, N.Y. and Washington, 1970-76; pres., v.p. bd. Wis. Coun. and Am. Coun. for Better Broadcasts, Madison, 1963-75; commr. Gov.'s Blue Ribbon Commn. on Cable Communications, Wis., 1971-73; bd. dirs. Broadband Telecommunications Regulatory Bd., Madison, 1978-81. Recipient Spl. Recognition award Am. Coun. Better Broadcasts, 1981, Spl. award Joint Congress and World Meeting on Media Literacy, Spain, 1995, Meritorious Svc. award Alliance for Media Literate Am., 2003, 50th Anniversary award "for Lighting the Way Toward a Media Wise World", Nat. Telemedia Coun., 2003. Mem. Soc. Satellite Profls. Internat. (charter), Internat. Visual Literacy Assn., Zeta Phi Eta (1st v.p. 1992, pres. 1993, Marguerite Garden Jones award 1989). Unitarian Universalist. Avocations: skiing, mountain hiking, travel, music. Home: 1001 Tumalo Trl Madison WI 53711-3024 E-mail: NTelemedia@aol.com.

ROWE, MARY P. organizational ombudsman, management educator; b. Chgo., Feb. 18, 1936; married; children: Katherine, Susannah, Timothy. BA in History, Swarthmore Coll., 1957; PhD in Econs., Columbia U., 1971; LLD (hon.), Regis Coll., 1975. With World Council of Chs./Office of UN High Commr. for Refugees, Salzburg and Vienna, Austria, 1957-58; research asst. Nat. Bur. Econ. Research, N.Y.C., 1961; economist planning bd. Office of Gov., V.I., 1962-63; free-lance cons. Nigeria, 1963-66, 1967-69; cons., sr. economist with Ctr. for Ednl. Policy Research, Harvard U. Harvard U., Cambridge, Mass., 1970, cons., sr. economist with Abt Assocs., 1970, tech. dir. early edn. project, 1971-72, cons. economist with Abt Assocs., 1971; dir. Carnegie Corp. Grant Radcliffe Inst., Cambridge, 1972; spl. asst. to pres., ombudsperson MIT, Cambridge, 1973—, adj. prof. Sloan Sch. Mgmt., 1985—. Mem. steering com., program on negotiations Harvard U., 1995—. Mem. editorial bd. Negotiation Jour., 1985—, Alternative Dispute Resolution Report, 1987-90; contbr. articles to profl. jours. Trustee Cambridge Friends Sch., 1969-75; mem. bd. advisors Brookline Children's Ctr., 1971-76; mem. Cambridge Friends Meeting and Com. on Clearness, 1971-78, New Eng. Concerns Com., 1973—, Mass. Policy Adv. Com. on Child Abuse/Neglect, 1977-79, Mass. State Youth Council, 1978-83; mem. Mass. State Employment and Tng. Council, 1975-83, chair, 1980-83; mem. nat. adv. Com. Black Women's Ednl. Policy and Research Network Project/Wellesley Coll. Ctr. for Research on Women, 1980-83; bd. dirs. Bay State Skills Commn., 1980-81, Wellesley Women's Research Ctr., 1984-87; sec. bd. dirs. Bay State Skills Corp., 1981-90; mem. panel on employment disputes Ctr. for Pub. Resources, 1986—. Recipient Meritorious Civilian Svc. award Dept. of Navy, 1993. Mem. Soc. Profls. in Dispute Resolution (chair com. on ombudspersons 1982-92, employment disputes), Calif. Caucus Coll. and Univ. Ombudsmen, Univ. and Coll. Ombudsman Assn., Ombudsman Assn. (pres. 1985-87, program on negotiation steering com. 1995—, Disting. Neutral Ctr. for Pub. Resources 1990—, covenor, presenter confs. 1982, 84, 85, 88, 89, 90-2003). Office: MIT 10-213 77 Massachusetts Ave Cambridge MA 02139

ROWE, MELINDA GRACE, public health service officer; b. Decatur, Ala., Aug. 18, 1953; m. Dana Calvin Craig Jr., Jan. 1, 1994. MD, U. Ala., 1978, MPH, 1985, MBA, 1987. Bd. cert. Am. Bd. Pediatrics, Am. Bd. Preventive Medicine. Pediatrics intern U. Ky., Lexington, 1978-79; pediatrics resident Lloyd Nolan Hosp., Fairfield, Ala., 1979-81; physician Columbus (Miss.) Children's Clinic, 1981, pvt. practice, Winfield, Ala., 1982-84; preventive medicine resident U. Ala., Birmingham, 1984-85; asst. state health officer Pub. Health Area III, Pelham, Ala., 1985-95; dir. health Jefferson County Health Dept., Louisville, 1995—2001; dist. health officer Savannah (Ga.) East Health, 2001—03; commr. of health Lexington Fayette County Health Dept., Lexington, Ky., 2003—. Asst. prof. U. Ala., Birmingham, 1988—, U. Louisville, 1995—. Bd. dirs. Cahaba River Soc., Birmingham, 1988—95, U. Ala.-Birmingham Nat. Alumni Soc., 1988—93, Health Ky., Goodwill Industries. Mem.: Ga. Med. Assn., Ky. Health Depts. Assn. (v.p.), Louisville/Jefferson County Primary Care Assn. (bd. dirs.), Jefferson County Med. Soc., Ky. Pediat. Soc., Ky. Pub. Health Assn. (pres.-elect), Ky. Med. Assn. Methodist. Avocations: reading, walking, travel, music. Home: 2006 Fontaine Rd Lexington KY 40502 Office Phone: 859-288-2300. E-mail: melinda.rowe@ky.gov.

ROWE, SANDRA MIMS, editor; b. Charlotte, N.C., May 26, 1948; d. David Lathan and Shirley (Stovall) Mims; m. Gerard Paul Rowe, June 5, 1971; children: Mims Elizabeth, Sarah Stovall. BA, East Carolina U., Greenville, N.C., 1970; postgrad., Harvard U., 1991. Reporter to asst. mng. editor The Ledger-Star, Norfolk, Va., 1971-80, mng. editor, 1980-82, The Virginian-Pilot and The Ledger Star, Norfolk, Va., 1982-84, exec. editor, 1984-86, v.p., exec. editor, 1986-93; editor The Oregonian, Portland, 1993—. Mem. Pulitzer Prize Bd., 1994-2003, chair, 2003. Bd. visitors James Madison U., Harrisonburg, VA., 1991-95; chair journalism adv. bd. Knight Found.; mem. adv. bd. The Poynter Inst., Medill Sch. Journalism, Northwestern U.; chair bd. visitors Knight Fellowships, Stanford U. Recipient George Beveridge Editor of Yr. award Nat. Press Found., 2003; named Woman of Yr. Outstanding Profl. Women of Hampton Rds., 1987; inducted into Va. Journalism Hall of Fame, 2000. Mem. Am. Soc. Newspaper Editors (pres., bd. dirs. 1992-99), Va. Press Assn. (bd. dirs. 1985-93). Episcopalian. Office: The Oregonian 1320 SW Broadway Portland OR 97201-3499

ROWE, SHERYL ANN, librarian; b. Stephenville, Tex., Sept. 29, 1946; d. Horace Milton and Letha Faye (Hensley) Hughes; m. Darrell Vanoy Rowe, Nov. 27, 1969; children: Jason Burt, Shelley Jean. BA in English, Tarleton State U., Stephenville, 1967; MS in Libr. Sci., Tex. Women's U., Denton, 1986. Cert. tchr. secondary edn. Tchr. Lake Worth (Tex.) H.S., 1967-69, Aledo (Tex.) H.S., 1967-73, 78-84, libr., 1984—. Mem. Aledo Children's Advocates. Mem. ALA, Tex. Libr. Assn., Region XI Librs. Assn. (treas. 1984—). Office: Aledo HS 1000 Bailey Ranch Rd Aledo TX 76008-4407 E-mail: srowe@aledo.k12.tx.us.

ROWE, TINA L. government official; b. Griffin, Ga., July 22, 1946; 1 child. Student, FBI Nat. Acad., 1981; AA, Aurora (Colo.) C.C., 1991; BA, Colo. Christian U., 1999. From patrol officer to comdr. patrol dist. 2 Denver Police Dept., 1969-94; U.S. marshal for Dist. Colo., U.S. Marshals Svc., Dept. Justice, Denver, 1994—. Trainer, spkr. cons. operational planning, motivation, leadership. Recipient various awards, including Woman of Yr. award Bus. and Profl. Women's Club, 1994; named Outstanding Law Enforcement officer, Am. Legion, 1999. Mem. FBI Nat. Acad. Assocs., Nat. Sheriffs Assn., Colo. Assn. Chiefs Police, Intenat. Assn. Chiefs of Police, Am. Coll. Forensic Examiners, Am. Bd. Law Enforcement Experts. Baptist. Office: US Marshals Svc Dept Justice 1929 Stout St Rm 324C Denver CO 80294-1929

ROWELL, BARBARA CABALLERO, retired academic administrator; b. New Orleans, Sept. 5, 1922; d. Albert Henry Wischnewske (stepfather) and Antoinette (Angelo) Caballero; m. J.C. Rowell, Dec. 17, 1941; children: Jerrie Carlene, Kerry Gene, Ricky Ray. AA in Bus. Adminstrn., Okaloosa Walton Jr. Coll., Niceville, Fla.; BA in Social Scis., U. West Fla. Exec. sec. Bishop Enterprises, Ft. Walton Beach; office mgr. and real estate property mgr. Fred Cooke Real Estate, Ft. Walton Beach, Fla.; adminstrv. sec. to v.p. Okaloosa Walton Jr. Coll., Niceville. Leader brownie scouts Girl Scouts U.S., cub scouts Boy Scouts Am.; bd. dirs., mem. curriculum com. U. West Fla. Ctr. for Life Long Learning; chair univ svc. com., pres., began Writing Lab; originator, implementor U. West Fla. Tutor Program, Career Fair, started scholarship program, Proctor Program; mem. curriculum com. U. West Fla.Ctr. for Lifelong Learning, presenter S.E. Conf. Insts. of Learning in Retirement, Charleston, S.C.; gov.'s campaign vol.; state legislature campaign vol.; mem. Sr. Ctr. Life Long Learning, U. West Fla. Mem. AAUW, DAV Aux., Order of Ea. Star (past matron). Avocations: education, travel, reading, gardening, dance, volunteering

ROWEN, RUTH HALLE, musicologist, educator; b. N.Y.C., Apr. 5, 1918; d. Louis and Ethel (Fried) Halle; m. Seymour M. Rowen, Oct. 13, 1940; children: Mary Helen Rowen, Louis Halle Rowen. BA, Barnard Coll., 1939; MA, Columbia U., 1941, PhD, 1948. Mgmt. ednl. dept. Carl Fischer, Inc., N.Y.C., 1954-63; assoc. prof. musicology CUNY, 1967-72, prof., 1972—, mem. doctoral faculty in musicology, 1967—. Author: Early Chamber Music, 1948, reprinted, 1974; (with Adele T. Katz) Hearing Gateway to Music, 1959, (with William Simon) Jolly Come Sing and Play, 1956, Music Through Sources and Documents, 1979, (with Mary Rowen) Instant Piano, 1979, 80, 83, Symphonic and Chamber Music Score and Parts Bank, 1996; contbr. articles to profl. jours. Mem. ASCAP, Am. Musicol. Soc., Music Library Assn., Coll. Music Soc., Nat. Fedn. Music Clubs (nat. musicianship chmn. 1962-74, nat. young artist auditions com. 1964-74, N.Y. state chmn. Young Artist Auditions 1981, dist. coord. 1983, nat. bd. dirs. 1989-2000, rep. UN 1991-2000), N.Y. Fedn. Music Clubs (pres.), Phi Beta Kappa Home: 115 Central Park West At 25D New York NY 10023-4153

ROWLAND, DIANE, health facility administrator, researcher; b. Bridgeport, Conn., Oct. 14, 1948; m. Brian L. Biles, Sept. 17, 1977. BA, Wellesley Coll., 1970; MPA, U. Calif., L.A., 1973; SCD, Johns Hopkins U., 1987. Mem. staff U.S. House Rep., Washington, 1983—91; assoc. dir. Commonwealth Fund Commn. on Elderly People Living Alone, Balt., 1985—91; assoc. prof. Johns Hopkins U., Balt., 1987—93; exec. v.p. Kaiser Family Found., Washington, 1993—. Exec. dir. Kaiser Commn. on Future of Medicaid, Washington, 1991—98, Kaiser Commn. on Medicaid & the Uninsured, Washington, 1998—; pres. Assn. Health Svc. Rsch., Washington, 2000; mem. Sec. Task Force on Infant Mortality, Washington, 2000—. Contbr. articles to profl. jours. Fellow Brookdale Nat. fellow, Brookdale Found., 1987. Greek Orthodox. Avocations: travel, reading, sailing. Office: Henry J Kaiser Family Found 1330 G Street NW Washington DC 20005

ROWLAND, ESTHER E(DELMAN), retired dean; b. N.Y.C., Apr. 12, 1926; d. Abraham Simon and Ida Sarah (Shifrin) Edelman; m. Lewis P. Rowland, Aug. 31, 1952; children: Andrew, Steven, Judith. BA, U. Wis., 1946; MA, Columbia U., 1948, MPhil, 1984; cert. in bioethics, Columbia U./Albert Einstein, 1996. Instr. in polit. sci. CCNY, 1947-51, Mt. Holyoke Coll., South Hadley, Mass., 1948-49; dir. health professions adv. bd. U. Pa., Phila., 1971-73; adviser to pre-profl. students Barnard Coll., N.Y.C., 1974-79, dean for pre-profl. students, 1980-93, assoc. dean studies, 1989-95; ret., 1995—. Proofreader Monthly Review, N.Y.C., 1997-2003. Mem. exec. com. Nat. Emergency Civil Liberties Com., N.Y.C., 1975-90; mem. exec. com. Women's Counseling Project, 1981-86. Mem. N.E. Assn. Health Professions Advisers (exec. com. 1973-74), N.E. Assn. Pre Law Advisors (exec. com. 1981-83, 85-86), Neurol. Inst. Aux., N.Y.C Found. Sr. Citizens (ombudsman 1997-99), Aux. Am. Acad. Neurologists (exec. bd. 1999-2001). Home: 404 Riverside Dr New York NY 10025-1861 E-mail: eerowland@aol.com.

ROWLAND, PLEASANT, publisher, toy company executive; m. Jerry Frautschi. Grad., Wells Coll., 1962. Elem. tchr. Mass., Calif., Ga. and N.J.; TV news reporter, anchor KGO-TV, San Francisco; v.p. Boston Ednl. Rsch. Co., 1971-78; pub. Children's Mag. Guide, 1981-89; founder, pres. Pleasant Co., 1986—; vice chmn. Mattell, 1998—. Named one of 12 Outstanding Entrepreneurs, Inst. Am. Entrepreneurs, 1990, one of Am.'s Top 50 Women Bus. Owners, Working Women mag., 1993-98; recipient Best and Brightest in Mktg. award Advt. Age, 1993, Mem. Intenrat. Women's Forum, Com. of 200. Office: Pleasant Co/Am Girl 8400 Fairway Place PO Box 998 Middleton WI 53562-0998

ROWLAND-RAYBOLD, ROBERTA, insurance agent, music educator; b. Utica, N.Y., Apr. 15, 1938; d. Robert Stanley and Mildred Celia (Easton) Rowland; children: Betsy Ross Raybold, Paul Robert Raybold. Bus. student, King's Coll., Briarcliff Manor, N.Y., 1957; student, Wittenberg U., Springfield, Ohio, 1998—. Organist Ch. of God, Moundsville, W. Va., 1969-71, Presbyn. Ch., Natrona Heights, Pa, Univ. Bapt. Ch., State College, Pa., 1981-98; sales rep. Am. Ch. Dirs., Havertown, Pa., 1972-76; ins. agt. Equitable of N.Y., State College, 1976-83, Allstate Ins. Co., State Collete, 1983-91; piano instr. pvt. practice, State College, 1987—97; ins. staff assoc. State Farm Ins., State College, 1997-98; dir. music U. Bapt. Ch., State College, 1981-98; music dir. Meml. United Presbyn. Ch., Xenia, Ohio, 1998—. Bd. dirs. Ctr. County Life Underwriters, State College, 1978—80; interim dir., staff piano instr. Ctr. for Musical Devel., Wittenberg U., 2001—. Composer-arranger music. various hymns, 1983—. Pres. Interfaith Singles, State College, Pa., 1982-86; active Nittany Valley Handbell Festival, Am. Cancer Soc., State College, 1994-98. Mem.: Suzuki Assn. Am., Music Tchrs. Nat. Assn., Palatine Hist. Soc. N.Y., Organ Historic Soc. U.S., Am. Guild of Organists (dean, pres. State College chpt. 1985—87, 1996—98, Svc. Organist status 1989). Republican. United Methodist. Home: 1420 Saint Paris Pike Apt C Springfield OH 45504-1651

ROWLANDS, GENA, actress; b. Cambria, Wis., June 19, 1936; d. Edwin Merwin and Mary Allen (Neal) R.; m. John Cassavetes (dec.); children: Nicholas, Alexandra, Zoe. Student, U. Wis., Am. Acad. Dramatic Art, N.Y.C. Theatrical appearance include The Middle of the Night, 1956; films include The High Cost of Loving, 1958, Lonely Are The Brave, 1962, A Child is Waiting, 1962, Spiral Road, 1962, Faces, 1968, At Any Price, 1970, Minnie and Moscowitz, 1971, Woman Under the Influence, 1973, Two Minute Warning, 1976, Opening Night, 1977, The Brinks Job, 1978, One Summer Night, 1979, Gloria, 1980, Tempest, 1982, Love Streams, 1983, Light of Day, 1987, Another Woman, 1988, Once Around, 1990, Ted and Venus, 1991, Night on Earth, 1992, Silent Cries, 1993, Parallel Lives, 1994, Anything for John, 1995, Something to Talk About, 1995, The Neon Bible, 1995, Enfants de Salaud, 1996, Unhook the Stars, 1996, Hope Floats, 1997, She's so Lovely, 1997, The Mighty, 1997, Paulie, 1998, The Weekend, 1999; TV movies A Question of Love, 1978, Strangers, 1979, Thurday's Child, 1983, Early Frost, 1986, The Betty Ford Story, 1987, Montana, Face of a Stranger, 1991 (Emmy award, Leading Actress in a Mini-Series or Special, 1992), Parallel Lives, 1994, Best of Friends for Life, 1996, Ljuset häller mig sällskap, 2000, Color of Love: Jacey's Story, 2000, Wild Iris, 2001, Hysterical Blindness, 2002, (Emmy award best supporting actress in TV movie, 2003), Charms for the Easy Life, 2002; numerous other TV appearances. Mem. Actors Equity Assn., Screen Actors Guild, AFTRA, Am. Guild Variety Artists.

ROWLEY, BEVERLEY DAVIES, medical sociologist; b. Antioch, Calif., July 28, 1941; d. George M. and Eloise Davies; m. Richard B. Rowley, Apr. 1, 1966 (div. 1983). BS, Colo. State U., 1963; MA, U. Nev., 1975; PhD, Union Inst., 1983. Social worker Nev. Dept. Pub. Welfare, Reno, 1963-65, Santa Clara County Dept. Welfare, San Jose, Calif., 1965-66; field dir. Sierra Sage coun. Camp Fire Girls, Sparks, Nev., 1966-70; program coord. divsn. health scis. Sch. Medicine U. Nev., 1976-78, program coord., health analyst office rural health, 1978-84, acting dir. office rural health, 1982-84; exec. asst. to pres. Med. Coll. of Hampton Rds., Norfolk, Va., 1984-87; rsch. mgr. Office Med. Edn. Info. AMA, Chgo., 1987-88, dir. dept. data systems, 1988-91; dir. med. edn. Maricopa Med. Ctr., Phoenix, 1991-99; pres. Med. Edn. and Rsch. Assocs., Inc., Phoenix, Chgo., 1999—, Med. Edn. & Rsch. Assocs., Tempe, Ariz., 1999—; vis. prof. Ariz. State U. East, Mesa, 1999-2000, profl. and personal coach, 2004—. Various positions as adj. prof. and lectr. in health scis. U. Nev. Sch. of Medicine, 1972-75, lectr. dept. family and cmty. medicine U. Nev., 1978-84, asst. dir., evaluator Health Careers for Am. Indians Programs, 1978-84; cons. Nev. Statewide Health Survey, 1979-84; interim dir. Health Max, 1985-86; asst. prof. dept. family and cmty. medicine Med. Coll. of Hampton Rds., Norfolk, Va., 1985-87. Editor of five books; contbr. numerous articles to profl. jours. Mem. Am. Sociol. Assn., Nat. Rural Health Assn. (bd. dirs. 1986-88), Assn. Behavioral Sci. and Med. Edn. (pres. 1986), Assn. Am. Med. Colls. (exec. coun. 1993-95), Coun. Acad. Scis. (adminstrv. bd. 1992-97), Assn. Hosp. Med. Edn. (bd. dirs. 1997—), Delta Delta Delta. Achievements include development of three computer systems including AMA-FREIDA; four internet-based educational programs for physicians. Avocations: hiking, skiing, gardening, sewing, ceramics. Office: MERA Inc 8850 S Los Feliz Dr Tempe AZ 85284-3430 E-mail: BRowley@MERAInc.com.

ROWLEY, JANET DAVISON, physician; b. NYC, Apr. 5, 1925; d. Hurford Henry and Ethel Mary (Ballantyne) Davison; m. Donald A. Rowley, Dec. 18, 1948; children: Donald, David, Robert, Roger. PhB, U. Chgo., 1944, BS, 1946, MD, 1948; DSc (hon.), U. Ariz., 1989, U. Pa., 1989, Knox Coll., 1991, U. So. Calif., 1992, St. Louis U., 1997, St. Xavier U., 1999, Oxford (Eng.) U., 2000, Lund U., Sweden, 2003. Diplomate Am. Bd. Med. Genetics. Rsch. asst. U. Chgo., 1949—50; intern Marine Hosp., USPHS, Chgo., 1950—51; attending physician Infant Welfare and Prenatal Clinics Dept. Pub. Health, Montgomery County, Md., 1953—54; rsch. fellow Levinson Found., Cook County Hosp., Chgo., 1955—61; clin. instr. neurology U. Ill., Chgo., 1957—61; USPHS spl. trainee Radiobiology Lab The Churchill Hosp., Oxford, England, 1961—62; rsch. assoc. dept. medicine and Argonne Cancer Rsch. Hosp. U. Chgo., 1962—69, assoc. prof. dept. medicine and Argonne Cancer Rsch. Hosp., 1969—77, prof. dept. medicine and Franklin McLean Meml. Rsch. Inst., 1977—84, Blum-Riese Disting. Svc. prof., dept. medicine and dept. molecular genetics and cell biology, 1984—, Blum-Riese Disting. Svc. prof. dept. human genetics, 1997—, interim dep. dean for sci. biol. scis. divsn., 2001—02. Bd. sci. counsellors Nat. Inst. Dental Rsch., NIH, 1972—76, chmn., 1974—76; mem. Nat. Cancer Adv. Bd., Nat. Cancer Inst., 1979—84, Nat. Adv. Coun. for Human Genome Rsch. Inst., 1999—; adv. com. Frederick Cancer Rsch. Facility, 1983—84; bd. sci. counsellors Nat. Human Genome Rsch. Inst., NIH, 1994—99, chmn., 1994—97; adv. bd. Howard Hughes Med. Inst., 1989—94, MD Anderson Cancer Ctr., 1998—; vis. com. dept. applied biol. scis. MIT Corp., 1983—86; bd. sci. cons. Meml. Sloan-Kettering Cancer Ctr., 1988—90; adv. com. Ency. Britannica U. Chgo., 1988—96; Bernard Cohen Meml. lectr. U. Pa., 1993; Katherine D. McCormick Disting. lectr. Stanford U., 1994; Donald D. Van Slyke lectr. Brookhaven Nat. Lab., 1994; Hilary Koprowski lectr. Thomas Jefferson U., 1994; W. Jack Stuckey Jr. lectr. Tulane Career Ctr., 1996; Presdl. Symposium Am. Soc. Pediatric Hematology/Oncology, 1995; Brit. Jour. of Haematology Plenary lectr. Brit. Soc. Haematology, 1997; Peacock Meml. lectr. in pathology U. Tex. Southwestern Med. Sch., 1997; Cosbie lectr. Royal Coll. Physicians and Surgeons Can., 1997; Richard Brunning lectr. U. Minn., 1999; Muriel Verder Millenium lectr. Evanston Hosp., 1999; Disting. Women in Medicine and Sci. lectr. Northwestern Med. Sch., 2000; Edward C. Hill lectr. U. Calif., San Francisco, 2000; Margaret Pittman lectr. NIH, 2000; plenary spkr. Spanish Soc. Hematology, 2000; plenary lectr. 10th Internat. Congress Human Genetics, Vienna, 2002, Soc. Hematology and Oncology of Germany, Austria and Switzerland, 2002; vis. McKusick lectr. Johns Hopkins U., 2003. Co-founder, co-editor: Genes, Chromosomes and Cancer, mem. editl. bd.: Oncology Rsch., Cancer Genetics and Cytogenetics, Internat. Jour. Hematology, Genomics, Internat. Jour. Cancer, Leukemia, past. mem. editl. bd.: Blood, Cancer Rsch., Hematol. Oncology, Leukemia Rsch.; contbr. chapters to books, articles to profl. jours. Adv. com. for career awards in biomed. scis. Burroughs Wellcome Fund, 1994—98; selection panel for Clin. Sci. award Doris Duke Charitable Found., 2000—02; mem. Pres.'s Adv. Coun. on Bioethics, 2001—; nat. adv. com. McDonnell Found. Program for Molecular Medicine in Cancer Rsch., 1988—98; adv. bd. Leukemia Soc. Am., 1979—84; selection com. scholar award in biomed. sci. Lucille P. Markey Charitable Trust, 1984—87; trustee Adler Planetarium, Chgo., 1978—; med. adv. bd. G&P Charitable Found., 1999—. Co-recipient Charles Mott prize, GM Cancer Rsch. Found., 1989; named Chicagoan of Yr., Chgo. mag., 1998; recipient First Kuwait Cancer prize, 1984, Esther Langer award, Ann Langer Cancer Rsch. Found., 1983, A. Cressy Morrison award in natural scis., N.Y. Acad. Scis., 1985, Past State Pres. award, Tex. Fedn. Bus. and Profl. Women's Clubs, 1986, Karnofsky award and lecture, Am. Soc. Clin. Oncology, 1987, Antoine Lacassagne Lique prize, Nat. Francaise Contre le Cancer, 1987, King Faisal Internat. prize in medicine (co-recipient), 1988, Katherine Berkan Judd award, Meml. Sloan-Kettering Cancer Ctr., 1989, Steven C. Beering award, U. Ind. Med. Sch, 1992, Robert de Villiers award, Leukemia Soc. Am., 1993, Kaplan Family prize for cancer rsch. excellence, Oncology Soc. Dayton, 1995, Cotlove award and lecture, Acad. Clin. Lab. Physicians and Scientists, 1995, Nilsson-Ehle lecture, Mendelian Soc. and Royal Physiographic Soc., 1995, The Gairdner Found. award, 1996, medal of honor, Basic Sci. Am. Cancer Soc., 1996, Nat. Medal of Sci., 1998, Lasker award for clin. scis., 1998, Woman Extraordinaire award, Internat. Women's Assocs., 1999, Golden Plate award, Am. Acad. Achievement, 1999, Women Achieving Excellence award, YWCA of Met. Chgo., 2000, Philip Levine award, Am. Soc. Clin. Pathology, 2001, Emile M Chamot award, State Microsurg. Soc. Ill., 2001, Mendel medal, Villanova U., 2003, Benjamin Franklin medal, Am. Philos. Soc., 2003, Dist. Alumni Award, U. Chgo., 2003. Fellow: AAAS (nominating com. 1998); mem.: NAS (chmn. sect. 41 1995—99), Inst. Medicine (coun. 1988—90), Cancer Rsch. (lectr. 2003, G.H.A. Clowes Meml. award 1989, Charlotte Friend award 2003), Am. Soc. Hematology (lectr. Millenium Symposium 1999, Presdl. Symposium 1982, Dameshek prize 1982, Ham-Wasserman award 1995), Genetical Soc., Am. Soc.

Human Genetics (pres.-elect 1992, pres. 1993, Allen award and lectr. 1991, Disting. Sci. lectr. 2003), Am. Philos. Soc., Am. Acad. Arts and Scis. (nominating com. 1998), Alpha Omega Alpha, Sigma Xi (William Proctor prize for sci. achievement 1989). Episcopalian. Home: 5310 S University Ave Chicago IL 60615-5106 Office: U Chgo 5841 S Maryland Ave Rm 2115 Chicago IL 60637-1463 Office Phone: 773 702-6117. Business E-Mail: jrowley@medicinebsd.uchicago.edu

ROWLEY, KARA DAWN, music educator; b. West Chester, Pa., July 11, 1974; d. Eileen and Carmen Battavio; m. Jason Rowley, July 27, 1996. BS in Music Edn., Elizabethtown (Pa.) Coll., 1996; MS in Music Edn., Towson U., 2003. Band and orch. dir. High Point HS, Beltsville, Md., 1996—97, Southampton Mid. Sch., Bel Air, Md., 1997—2002; orch. dir. Aberdeen Mid. Sch., Aberdeen, Md. Music dir. Southampton Mid. Sch. Spring Musical, Bel Air, Md.; performing mem. Susquehanna Symphony Orch., Bel Air, Md. Mem.: Md. Orch. Dirs. Assn. (exec. bd.), Md. Band Dirs. Assn. (exec. bd.), Md. Music Educators Assn. (exec. bd., state band chair, chief judge, All State Horn auditions). Avocations: yoga, travel, reading mysteries. Personal E-mail: kararowley@comcast.net.

ROWLING, J.K. (JOANNE KATHLEEN ROWLING), writer; b. Gloucestershire, England, July 31, 1965; d. Peter and Anne Rowling; m. Jorge Arantes, Oct. 16, 1992 (div. 1993); 1 child, Jessica ; m. Neil Murray, Dec. 26, 2001; 1 child, David. Attended, Exeter U.; degree (hon.), Napier U., 2000, Dartmouth Coll., 2000, Univ. of Exeter, 2000, Univ. of St. Andrews, 2000. Former rschr. Amnesty International; teacher Scotland, 1990—94. Author: (novels) Harry Potter and the Philosopher's Stone, 1997 (Children's Book of the Year, British Book Awards, 1998, Gold Winner, Smarties Book Prize, 1997, Birmingham Cable Children's Book Award, Young Telegraph Paperback of the Year, Sheffield Children's Book Award, Sorcieres Prix, 1999, Premio Cento per la Letteratura Infantile, 1998), Harry Potter and the Sorcerer's Stone (U.S. title), 1998 (Anne Spencer Lindbergh Prize in Children's Literature, 1998, ABBY Award, American Booksellers Assoc., 1999), Harry Potter and the Chamber of Secrets, 1998 (Gold Winner, Smarties Book Prize, 1998), Harry Potter and the Prisoner of Azkaban, 1999, Harry Potter and the Goblet of Fire, 2000, Quidditch Through the Ages, 2001, Fantastic Beasts & Where to Find Them, 2001, Harry Potter and the Order of the Phoenix, 2003. Named Officer of the Most Excellent Order of the British Empire (O.B.E.) by Charles, Prince of Wales. Office: Christopher Little Literary Agency 10 Eel Brook Studios 125 Moore Park Rd London SW6 4PS England*

ROWSE, CYNTHIA (CINDY) LYNN, writer; d. Mark David and Erma Louise Rowse; m. Thomas Kenneth Carter, June 5, 1993. BA in Radio, TV & Film, U. Md., College Park, MD, 1989—93; MA in Film and Video, Am. U., Washington, DC, 1993—95. Film reviewer Creative Screenwriting Mag., Los Angeles, Calif., 1995—2001, bd. script reviewers, 1998—2001; freelance writer Millsboro, Del.; screenplay writing cons. ScriptFix, Kensington, Md., 1999—2001. Author: (screenplays) Home (Hon. Mention Writer's Digest Writing Contest, 1995), The Willing Prey (aka The Cult) (Quarter Finalist Quantum Quest Screenplay Search, 1998, Semi-Finalist Lone Star Screenplay Competition, 1996, Quarter Finalist The Writer's Network Screenplay & Fiction Competition, 1997), The Actor (aka Smoke & Mirrors/In The Eye of the Beholder) (Quarter Finalist Lone Star Screenplay Competition, 1997, Semi-Finalist America's Best Screenplay Competition, 1997), (short stories) Lists. Named a Semi-Finalist, Nat. Merit Scholars, 1978. Mem.: Golden Key Nat. Honor Soc. (life). Personal E-mail: cindyrowse@aol.com.

ROY, ARUNDHATI, writer; b. Bengal, India, 1961; d. Mary Roy. Author (also actor): (films) In Which Annie Gives it Those Ones; author: (screenplays) Electric Moon, (book) The God of Small Things, 1997 (Man Booker prize for fiction, 1997), (essays) The End of Imagination, The Greater Common Good. Office: Random House Inc 201 E 50th St, 22nd Fl New York NY 10022

ROY, DARLENE, human services administrator; b. St. Louis, June 17, 1945; d. Robert and Ezora Gertrude Duncan; m. Lovell Swanson, June 17, 1967 (div. 1980); 1 child, Troy Anthony Swanson. BA, So. Ill. U., 1967; MSW, St. Louis U., 1971. Caseworker Ill. Dept. Pub. Aid, East St. Louis, 1967-72, supr., 1972-80, asst. adminstr. I, 1980-94, asst. adminstr. II, 1994-97, adminstr., 1997—. Mem., past pres. Child Care Resource and Referral Coun., Granite City, Ill., 1989—; mem. SIU Headstart Coun., East St. Louis, 1994—97, Social Svc. Task Force, East St. Louis, 1996—, St. Clair County Homeless Action Coun., 1996—. Assoc. editor: (literary jour.) Drumvoices Rev., 1994; contbr. articles to literary jours. Mem. Bi-State Arts in Transit, St. Louis, 1990; mem. Ct. Apptd. Spl. Advs. Bd. Dirs.; bd. dirs. Delta Child Devel. Ctr., v.p., 2001—. Recipient Black Women in Middlewest award Purdue U., 1986, Cmty. Svc. award Top Ladies of Distinction, 1987, Jail and Bail Fund Raising award Am. Cancer Soc., 1999. Mem.: NAACP, East St. Louis Pan Hellenic Coun. (v.p. 1999—), Arts Coun., Nat. Coun. Negro Women (charter), Sunday Jams Fund Raiser Club (v.p. 2001—), Eugene B. Redmond Writers Club (pres. 1986—), Delta Sigma Theta (life; pres. 1979—81). Baptist. Avocations: reading, modeling, dance. Home: 301 Winchester Pl Fairview Heights IL 62208-3829 Office: Ill Dept Human Svcs 225 N 9th St East Saint Louis IL 62201-1706

ROY, DELLA MARTIN, materials science educator, researcher; b. Merrill, Oreg., Nov. 3, 1926; d. Harry L. and Anna (Cacka) Martin; m. Rustum Roy, June 8, 1948; children: Neill R., Ronnen A., Jeremy R. BS, U. Oreg., 1947; MS, Pa. State U., 1949, PhD, 1952. Various rsch. pos. Pa. State U., University Park, 1952—60, sr. rsch. assoc. geochemistry, 1960—62, sr. rsch. assoc. materials sci. engring., 1962—69, assoc. prof. materials sci. engring., 1969—75, prof. materials sci. engring., 1975—. Cons. in field; chmn. status of cement, concrete materials adv. bd., Washington, 1977—80; spl. adv. concrete durability NRC, 1985—. Editor: Instructional Moduules in Cement Science, 1985, Jour. Cement & Concrete Rsch., 1971—; contbr. articles to profl. jours. Fellow: AAAS, Am. Concrete Inst. (Can. Ctr. Mineral and Energy Tech. award 1989, Keynote address 1980), Mineral. Soc. Am., Inst. Concrete Tech. (hon.), Am. Ceramic Soc. (trustee 1990—, Jeppson Medal award 1982, Copeland award 1987); mem.: NAS (exec. com., transp. rsch. bd. 1991—), Internat. Acad. Ceramics, Nat. Acad. Engring. (acad. adv. bd. 1989—, membership policy com. 2001—), Coun. Materials Rsch. Soc. (chmn. cement symposia 1980—81, 1986—88, trustee 1988—90). Democrat. Office: Pa State U Hastings Rd 110 Materials Rsch Lab State College PA 16802

ROYAL, NANCY B. primary school educator; b. Newnan, Ga., Mar. 27, 1949; d. Harold C. and Jewell (Stephens) Batchelor; m. Mayo H. Royal Jr., Aug. 15, 1970; children: Amanda Elizabeth, Molly Cole. BSEd, Ga. Coll., 1971; MEd, Ga. State U., 1978; EdS, West Ga. Coll., 1986. Cert. early childhood edn. Second grade tchr. Jo Wells Elem. Sch., Hapeville, Ga., 1970-71; kindergarten tchr. Columbia Drive Bapt. Sch., Decatur, Ga., 1972-75, Indian Creek Bapt. Sch., Stone Mountain, Ga., 1975-77, Meml. Drive Presbyterian Sch., Stone Mountain, 1978-80; first grade tchr. Elm St. Elem. Sch., Newnan, Ga., 1980-83, kindergarten tchr., 1980-96, prin., 1999. Active State Reading Textbook Adoption Com., 21st Century Consortium Edn.; presenter edn. workshops. Treas. Newnan Jr. Svc. League, chairperson selection com. christmas program; pre-sch. Sunday sch. tchr. Newnan First Bapt. Ch., 1980—, children's choir dir., mem. stewardship com., chair weekday ministries com. Recipient Presdl. Excellence in Math. award 1992, Disting. Alumni award Ga. State U., 1993; named Atlanta Jour.-Constitution's Honor Tchr., 1989, Ga. Tchr. of Yr., 1993, Nat. Educator award Milken Family Found., 1995. Mem. Alpha Delta Kappa, Phi Kappa Phi, Phi Delta Kappa, Ga. Coun. Tchrs. Math. Home: 6 Summit Ln Newnan GA 30263-5531 Office: Ruth Hill Elem Sch 57 Sunset Ln Newnan GA 30263-2836

ROYAL, SUSAN, classical musician, music educator; b. Phila., July 21, 1955; d. Douglas David and Bette (Caum) Royal; m. Wayne Arthur Jones, Aug. 13, 1988; children: Daria Jones, Ethan Jones. BMusic, Ithaca Coll., 1977; MMusic, Yale U., 1981; DMusical Arts, SUNY, Stony Brook, 1989. Instr. flute Tenn. Technol. U., Cookeville, 1981-83, flutist Erie (Pa.) Philharm., 1983—, Fredonia Chamber Players, 1983—; substitute flutist Buffalo Philharm., 1984—; prof. flute SUNY Coll., Fredonia, 1983—. Performer/clinician Fredonia Woodwind Quintet Summer Camp, 1994—, Fredonia Woodwind Quintet, 1983—; artist performer Armstrong/Artley Flutes, 1991—. Concert soloist; performances on CD include Opera Sacra, 1994, Piorkowski, 1998. Elder First United Presbyn. Ch., Dunkirk, N.Y., 1987—. Mem. Nat. Flute Assn. (performer/adjudicator/panelist 1977—), Niagara Frontier Flute Assn. Democrat. Avocations: sailing, running, gardening. Office: SUNY Coll at Fredonia Sch Music Fredonia NY 14063

ROYBAL-ALLARD, LUCILLE, congresswoman; b. Boyle Heights, Calif., June 12, 1941; d. Edward Roybal; m. Edward T. Allard; 4 children. BA, Calif. State U., L.A. Former mem. Calif. State Assembly; mem. U.S. Congress from 34th Calif. dist., 1993—; mem. appropriationscom.; mem. Ho. Com. on Standards of Official Conduct. Democrat. Office: Ho of Reps 2330 Rayburn Bldg Washington DC 20515-0533*

ROYCROFT, CHERYL, secondary school educator; b. Buffalo, N.Y., Mar. 11, 1961; d. Edward Stanley and Delphine Theresa Janusz; m. Henry Phillip Roycroft, Oct. 14, 1983. BS, Daemen Coll., 1993; MEd, Cambridge Coll., 2002. Cert. tchr. Payroll clerk Sellmore Industries, Buffalo, N.Y., 1984-85; acct. clerk Desiderio Produce, Buffalo, 1985-87, Fisher-Price, E. Aurora, 1987-90, Acme Electric, E. Aurora, 1993-94; tchr. Bryant & Stratton, Buffalo, 1994-96, Lake City H.S., S.C., 1996-97, Mt. Pleasant H.S., Elliott, S.C., 1997-2000, Lee Ctrl. H.S., Bishopville, S.C., 2000—. Mem. Assn. Career and Tech. Educators, S.C. Bus. Educators Assn., Coun. for Exceptional Children, Kappa Delta Pi (pres. 1992-95, historian 1991-92), Delta Mu Delta (v.p. 1991-92, pres. 1992-93), ASCD. Avocations: reading, swimming, dance. Office: Lee Ctrl HS 1800 Wisacky Hwy Bishopville SC 29010 E-mail: keyteacher77@hotmail.com.

ROYER, KATHLEEN ROSE, pilot; b. Pitts., Nov. 4, 1949; d. Victor Cedric and Lisetta Emma (Smith) Salway; m. Michael Lee Royer, June 6, 1971 (div. Aug. 1975). Student, Newbold Coll., 1968-69; BS, Columbia Union Coll., 1971; MEd, Shippensburg U., 1974; student, Lehigh U., 1974-75. Cert. tchr. Pa. Music. Music tchr. Harrisburg (Pa.) Sch. Dist., 1971-77; flight instr. Penn-Air, Inc., Altoona, Pa., 1977; capt., asst. chief pilot Air Atlantic Airlines, Centre Hall, Pa., 1977-80; capt., chief pilot Lycoming Air Svc., Williamsport, Pa., 1980-81; govs. pilot Commonwealth of Pa., Harrisburg, 1981-87; flight engr. Pan-Am, N.Y.C., 1987-91; pilot, 1st officer B737 United Airlines, Chgo., 1992-96, 1st officer B767 N.Y.C., until 1996, Washington, 1996-99; flight officer B747-400 JFK Internat. Airport, Jamaica, NY, 1999—2001, capt. Airbus 320, 2001—. Frist woman pilot/engr. crew mem. on 747 Pan Am. Airlines, 1989—91, chief pilot, cons. Mem.: UAL-Airline Pilot Assn. (coord. critical incident stress program 1994—96), Flight Engrs. Internat. Assn. (scheduling rep. 1989, scheduling dir. 1990, 1st vice chmn., mem. bd. adjustments 1989, v.p. dir. scheduling 1991—92), Internat. Soc. Women Airline Pilots, Whirley Girls (Washington), 99's (local chair Ctrl. Pa. chpt. 1987—92), Hershey Country Club. Republican. Avocations: owner/flying 1965 Cessna 180, golf, music, reading. Home: 34 Lazy Eight Dr Daytona Beach FL 32128 Office: San Francisco Intl Airport San Francisco CA

ROYLE, CYNTHIA, editor; Student, Brigham Young U.; B Comms., U. Del. Copy editor, reporter, bur. chief, state editor, city editor, city-state editor News Jour., Wilmington, Del.; enterprise editor Jour. News, White Plains, NY, 1995—97, mng. editor Rockland edit., 1997, now sr. mng. editor. Office: Jour News 1 Gannett Dr White Plains NY 10604*

ROYSTON, PAMELA JEAN, special education educator; b. Anchorage, Alaska, Sept. 26, 1958; d. Ralph Vedra Allen (Deceased) and Wilma Jean Daniels, Franklin Hicks Daniels (Stepfather); m. Randy Glenn Royston, June 23, 1977; children: Rusty Brandon, Bridgett Starr Vaughn. AA, Emmanuel Coll., Franklin Springs, Ga., 1990—91; BS edn., The U. of Ga., Athens, Ga., 1991—94. Severe/profound spl. edn. tchr. Madison County Mid. Sch., Danielsville, Ga., 1994—96; moderate/severe spl. edn. tchr. Hart County Mid. Sch., Hartwell, Ga., 1996—. Sch. beautification dir. Madison County Mid. Sch., Danielsville, Ga., 1994—96; peer tutor dir. Hart County Mid. Sch., Hartwell, Ga., 1996—, sch. beautification dir., 1996—, cmty.-based instrn. dir., 1996—. Rschr. (instrnl. procedures rsch.) Collaborated with Dr. Gast and Dr. Wall: Univ. of Ga., in conducting a rsch. study investigating the effectiveness of using constant time delay when tchg. leisure skills to students who are intellectually disabled. (Jour. of Devel. and Phys. Disabilities, 11, 193-218., 1999), presenter Gave presentation to the Ga. State Adv. Panel for Spl. Edn. about my Peer Tutor and Cmty.-Based Instn. Program., (rsch.) Mid. Sch. Students Tchg. Leisure Skills to Peer with Disabilities. Paper presented at the 2001 Ann. Meeting of the Am. Assn. on Mental Retardation, Denver, Colo., Presented rsch. paper at the Nat. Inst. for People with Disabilities' 20th Ann. Internat. Conf., NYC, NY, Gave Power Point presentation for the pre-svc. spl. edn. students at Ga. So. Univ. Focus: Cmty.-Based Instrn. and classroom set-up., Presented paper concerning using e-mail as a way of increasing written lang. skills at the Conf. of the Tchr. Edn. Divsn. of the Coun. for Exceptional Children, Dallas, Tex., Presented paper concerning teachers and researchers at he Conf. of the Tchr. Edn. Divsn. of the Coun. for Exceptional Children, Savannah, Ga., (research-instructional procedues) Poster session presented at the Ann. Conf. of the Assn. for Persons with Severe Handicaps, New Orleans, La., (rsrch.-instructional procedures) Presented paper at the Ann. Meeting of the Assn. for Persons with Severe Handicaps, San Francisco, Calif. Assist in fundraising activities Congressman Charles Taylor, Asheville, NC, 2002—03. Recipient Honor Special Education Teacher for the State of Georgia, Atlanta Journal-Constitution, 2000. Mem.: Ga. Assn. of Educators, Coun. for Exceptional Children, The Assn. for Persons with Severe Handicaps, Golden Key Honor Soc., Kappa Delta Pi Ednl. Honor Soc., PA of Ga. Educators. Meth. Avocations: houseboating, painting, travel. Home: 196 Dove Hill Road Royston GA 30662 Office: Hart County Middle School 176 Drive Powell Drive Hartwell GA 30643 Office Phone: 706-856-7234. Personal E-mail: pa1ra1@aol.com. E-mail: proyston@hart.k12.ga.us.

ROZANTINE, GAYLE STUBBS, clinical psychologist; b. Atlanta, Dec. 1, 1944; d. William L. and Louise (Cash) Stubbs; children: Kathryn Patricia, Webb Black III, Gregory William, Benjamin Stubbs, John Paul; m. Barry Rozantine. BA in Psychology, Agnes Scott Coll., 1965; MA in Tchg., Emory U., 1966; MA in Clin. Psychology, Western Carolina U., 1990; PhD, U. Tenn., 1995. Lic. psychologist, Ga.; diplomate Am. Acad. of Experts in Traumatic Stress; cert. domestic violence counselor. Tchr. Fulton Co. Bd. Edn., Ga., 1967-68; psychology resident Med. Coll. of Ga., Augusta, 1994-95, clin. fellow, 1995-96; rsch. psychologist Pain Evaluation and Intervention Program Dept. of VA Med. Ctr., Augusta, 1995-98; staff psychologist Compass Health Systems, Miami Beach, Fla., 1998, Charter Savannah Bevioral Health System, Ga., 1999-2000; CEO Ctr. Health and Well-Being, 2000—. Mem. critical incident stress debriefing team Med. Coll. Ga.; disaster mental health response team ARC; presenter in field. Mem. Am. Psychol. Assn., Coastal Area Psychologists, Ga. Psychol. Assn., Ga. Breast Cancer Coalition and Fund, Nat. Assn. of Forensic Counselors, Nat. Register Health Svc. Providers in Psychology. Office: The Ctr for Health and Well-Being PC 400 Commercial Ct Savannah GA 31406

ROZOF, PHYLLIS CLAIRE, lawyer; b. Flint, Mich., Aug. 3, 1948; d. Eugene Robert and Loveta Lucille Greenwood; m. Robert James Rozof, July 17, 1970 (dec. Oct. 1995); children: Nathan, Zachary. AB with high distinction, U. Mich., 1970, JD magna cum laude, 1977. Bar: Mich. 1977, Fla. 1978. Assoc. Honigman Miller Schwartz and Cohn, Detroit, 1977-81, ptnr., 1982—. Mem. Comml. Real Estate Women Detroit (pres. 1992-93). Office: Honigman Miller Schwartz & Cohn 2290 1st National Bldg Detroit MI 48226

RUBEN, IDA GASS, state senator; b. Washington, Jan. 07; d. Sol and Sonia E. (Darman) Gass; m. L. Leonard Ruben, Aug. 29, 1948; children: Garry, Michael, Scott, Stephen. Del. Md. Ho. of Dels., Annapolis, 1974-86; mem. Md. Senate, Annapolis, 1986—, majority whip, 1995-99, pres. pro-tem, 2000—. Chair Montgomery County House Delegation, 1981-86, Montgomery County Senate Delegation, 1987—; mem. house econ. matters com., 1974-85, house ways and means com., 1985-86, legis. policy com., 1991—, vice-chair senate budget and taxation com., 1997-99, joint budget and audit com., 1991—, exec. nominations com., 1991—, joint protocol com., 1991—, chair, senate budget and tax., subcom. on pub. safety, transp., econ. devel. and natural resources, 1995-99, mem. joint com. on spending affordability, 1995—, mem. capital budget subcom., 1995—; mem. Gov.'s Motor Carrier Task Force, 1989—; conv. chair Nat. Order Women Legislators, 1980. Chair Women Legislators Caucus Md., 1982-84; trustee Adventist Health Care Mid-Atlantic, Takoma Park, Md.; bd. dirs. Ctrs. for Handicapped, Silver Spring, Md.; former internat. v.p. B'nai Brith Women. Recipient Cert. Appreciation Ctrs. for Handicapped, 1987, Meritorious Svc. award Safety and Survival, 1989, Cover Those Trucks award AAA Potomac, 1989, Leadership Laurel award Safety First Club Md., 1989, Woman of Valor award B'nai B'rith Women, 1991, Pub. Affairs award Planned Parenthood Md., 1992, ESOL support recognition Montgomery County Pub. Schs., 1992, Appreciation award Fraternal Order Police, 1992, John Dewey award Montgomery County Fedn. Tchrs., 1992, ARC of Md., 1992, Safety Leader award Advocates for Hwy. and Auto Safety, 1993, Disting. Svc. award Gov.'s Commn. Employment of People with Disabilities, 1993, award Faculty Guild U. Md. for support of faculty and univ., 1993, Sincere Appreciation award for commitment to Md.'s youth Md. Underage Drinking Prevention Coalition, 1994, Faithful Svc. to citizens Montgomery County award Montgomery County Assn. of Realtors, 1994; named Most Effective Pub. Ofcl. by residents of Silver Spring, 1990, one of 100 Most Powerful Women in Washington Metro Area by Washingtonian Mag., 1994, 97, Legislator of Yr. award Nat. Commn. Against Drunk Driving, 1995, Legislator of Yr. award Montgomery County Med. Soc., 1995, Carmen S. Turner Achievement in Cmty. Svc. award Montgomery County Dept. Transp., 1995, Safety Leader award Advocates for Hwy. and Auto Safety, 1996, Legislator of Yr. award AAA, Potomac, Md., 1997, Vince and Larry award Md. Com. for Safety Belt Use, 1997, Legislative Leadership award Montgomery County, 1998, Leadership award Olney Theater Ctr., 1998, Legislator of Yr. award Greater Montgomery County C. of C., 1999, Hwy. Safety Herd award Advocates for Hwy. and Auto Safety, 1999, One of Md.'s Top 100 Women, The Daily Record, 1994, 97, 2001, Am. Lung Assn. Appreciation award in protecting youth from tobacco industry, 2000, Olney Theater honoree contbns. Olney Theatre and arts in Md., 2000, Pub. Policy Leadership award Am. Cancer Soc., 2002; M.A.D.D. Award of Exellence, 2002, Disting. Pub. Svc. award Am. Lung Assn., 2003, others; named to Washington, Md., Del., Pa. Svc. Sta. Assn. Hall of Fame, 1994, Suburban Md. Transp. Priorities outstanding leadership in transp. pub. policy adminstrn., 2000; Md. Coll. Art and Design honoree, 2000. Mem. Com. State Govts. (com. on suggested legislation), Hadassah. Democrat. Jewish. Home: 11 Schindler Ct Silver Spring MD 20903-1329 Office: Md State Senate 422 Miller Senate Office Bldg 11 Bladen St Annapolis MD 21401-8012

RUBENSTEIN, ATOOSA BEHNEGAR, editor-in-chief; b. Iran, 1973; arrived in U.S., 1978; m. Ari Rubenstein, 1998. BA in Polit. Sci., Barnard COll., 1993. Fashion asst., assoc. fashion editor, fashion edit to sr. fashion editor Cosmopolitan Mag., 1993—95, editor-in-chief, 1998—2003, Seventeen Mag., 2003—. Office: Seventeen Mag 1440 Broadway 13th Fl New York NY 10018

RUBENSTEIN, PAMELA SILVER, manufacturing executive; b. Lansing, Mich., May 12, 1953; d. Neil M. and Leah Rebecca (Coffman) Silver; m. Alec Robert Rubenstein. BA in Linguistics, U. Mich., 1974; MA in teaching English to spkrs. of other langs., Columbia U. Tchrs. Coll., 1976; MA in Linguistics, U. Ill., 1978, doctoral studies in linguistics, 1978-80. Instr. Columbia U. Tchrs. Coll., N.Y.C., 1976, U. Ill., Urbana, 1978, libr. Linguistic Dept., 1978-79; asst. libr. Ill. State Geol. Survey, 1979-80; tchr. Congregation Temple Israel, Springfield, Ill., 1980-81; adminstr., tchr. Springfield Bd. Jewish Edn., 1981-82; instr. Comm. Divsn. Lincoln Land C.C., Springfield, 1981-82; tchr. Cmty. Hebrew Sch., Charleston, SC, 1982-83; instr. The Citadel and Coll. of Charleston, 1983; legal sec. Gibbs & Holmes, Charleston, 1984, May, Oberfell & Lorber, South Bend, Ind., 1984-88; instr. U. Notre Dame, Ind., 1987; tchr. Triton Sch. Corp., Bourbon, Ind., 1988-89; v.p., asst. treas. Allied Splty. Precision, Inc., Mishawaka, Ind., 1989—. Mem. next generation team Nat. Tool and Machining Assn., 2003—. Contbr. articles to profl. jours. Mem. Temple Beth-El Sisterhood, South Bend, 1987—, Hadassah (life mem.). Mem. Michiana Gem and Mineral Soc. (treas. 1995-98, 2004). Office: Allied Splty Precision Inc 815 E Lowell Ave Mishawaka IN 46545-6480 Business E-Mail: pamr@aspi-nc.com.

RUBENSTEIN, SHARON LYNN, poet; b. L.A., Aug. 30, 1945; d. Harry and Sylvia Rubenstein; m. John Svehla, Nov. 12, 1976 (div. 1991). Student, Pierce Coll.; grad., Ross Bus. Inst. Contbr. poetry to profl. jours. Recipient Featured Poet award, The Poet, 1984, Broken Streets, 1983, 1985, 1987, Poetry Excellence award, Fine Arts Press, 1988, Poet Laureate award, Poetry Ctr., 1988, Poetic Achievement award, Am. Poetry Assn., 1989, Editor's Choice award for Outstanding Poetic Achievement, Poetry Ctr., 1990, Editor's Choice award, Internat. Libr. Poetry, 2000. Avocations: crafts, drawing, jewelry creations.*

RUBICO-JAMIR, SONIA MENDOZA, sensory/food scientist, consumer researcher; b. San Pablo, The Philippines, June 8, 1958; came to U.S., 1988; d. Pedro Rubico and Florentina Mendoza; m. Tomas Vergel Cervania Jamir, June 10, 1994; 1 child, Sierra Mari Jamir. MS in Food Sci., U. The Phillipines, Los Baños, 1983; postgrad. in food sci., U. Ga., Athens, 1987; PhD in Food Sci., Oreg. State U., 1993, MBA, 1996. Rsch. assoc. Inst. Food Sci. and Tech. U. The Philippines, 1978-86; grad. rsch. asst. U. Ga., 1986-87; sensory lab. mgr., rsch. assoc. dept. food sci. Oreg. State U., Corvallis, 1993-97; sensory rsch. analyst SC Johnson Wax Co., Racine, Wis., 1997—. Co-author: Peanut Consumption, 1988; contbr. articles to profl. jours. Grantee Japan Soc. Promotion Sci., 1983, USAID, Athens, 1986-87, Corvallis, 1994-96; Haarman & Renier Co. fellow, 1989-92. Mem. Am. Mktg. Assn., Inst. Food Technologists, Toastmasters' Internat., Oreg. State Alumni Assn. Avocations: reading, bowling, watching tv, listening to music. Office: SC Johnson Wax 1525 Howe St Racine WI 53403-2236

RUBIN, CATHY ANN, retired educator; b. Denver, July 17, 1948; d. Harry Phillip and Charlotte Ruth (Brinig) R. BA, Colo. State U., 1970; MA, U. No. Colo., 197l. Cert. tchr., Colo. Tchr. Adams County Dist. 50 Schs., Westminster, Colo., 1971-72; tchr. educationally handicapped Jefferson County Pub. Schs., Golden, Colo., 1972-98. Typist, bookkeeper Kenmark-Shaw's Jewelers, Denver, 1966—. Sec.-treas. Hillel Found., Denver, 1979-81; fundraiser Women's Am. Orgn. for Rehab. through Tng., Denver, 1979—; bookkeeper Religious Coalition for Abortion Rights, Denver, 1982-90; vol. TV PBS sta., Denver, 1978, Muscular Dystrophy Assn., Colo. AIDS Project; vol. usher DCTC, 1999—. Democrat. Jewish. Avocations: music, reading, sailing, knitting, needlepoint. Home: 3500 S Ivanhoe St Denver CO 80237-1123

RUBIN, CHANDA, professional tennis player; b. Lafayette, La., Feb. 18, 1976; d. Edward and Bernadette Rubin. Grad., Episcopal Sch. Acadiana, 1993. Mem. USTA Jr. Devel. Team, 1989, USTA Nat. Team, 1990; prof. tennis player, 1991—. Mem. U.S. Pan Am. Team, 1995, U.S. Fed Cup Team, 1995—97, 1999, 2003, U.S. Olympic Team, Atlanta, 1996. Founder The Chanda Rubin Found. Recipient 3 U.S. Jr. Titles; winner U.S. nat. title and Rolex Orange Bowl 12s crown, 1988; named Most Improved Female Player, Tennis Mag., 1995, Female Athlete of Yr., U.S. Tennis Assn., 1995, Most Caring Athlete, USA Weekend Mag., 1997; singles winner Hobart, 1999; finalist (with Testud) U.S. Open.; winner 7 Career Singles titles and 10 Career Doubles titles, WTA Tour. Office: USTA 70 W Red Oak Ln White Plains NY 10604-3602 also: Advantage International 1751 Pinnacle Dr Ste 1500 Mc Lean VA 22102-3833

RUBIN, LOIS S. lawyer; d. Joseph Louis and Ruth Sylvia Speyer; m. Ronald P. Rubin, Aug. 21, 1955; children: Judith, Ellen, Lawrence. BSc, Tufts U., 1955; MA, Adelphi U., 1971; PhD, U. Va., 1985; JD, SUNY, 1994. Bar: N.Y. 1995. Tchr. Valley Stream (N.Y.) Pub. Sch., 1969—74, Henrico (Va.) Pub. Schs., 1975—80; from testing specialist to dir. rsch. and testing Va. Dept. Edn., Richmond, Va., 1980—88, dir. rsch. and testing, 1988—90; adj. faculty Niagara U., NY, 1991; pvt. practice Buffalo, 1996—; assoc. atty. Pusatier, Sherman, Abbott & Sugarman, Kenmore, NY, 1997—. Mem. bd. ethics Town of Clarence, NY, 1995—98. Mem.: ABA, Bar Assn. N.Y. State, N.Y. State Coun. Divorce Mediation, Bar Assn. Erie County, N.Y. Bar Assn. Office: Law Office Lois S Rubin 3517 Genesee St Buffalo NY 14225 Office Phone: 716-634-6111.

RUBIN, PATRICIA, internist; b. Apr. 27, 1962; MD, Wright State U., 1988. Cert. internal medicine. Resident in internal medicine U. Cin., 1988-91; fellow in cardiology U. Hosp., Cleve., 1991; rsch. fellow in cardiology U. Wash. Sch. Medicine, Seattle, 1993—; pvt. practice Cardiology One, Kent, Ohio. Recipient Clinician Scientist award Am. Heart Assn., 1995-96. Mem. ACP, AMA, ACC. Office: Cardiology One Box 8086 1330 Mercy Dr NW Ste 200 Canton OH 44708-2624

RUBIN, PHYLLIS GETZ, health association executive; b. N.Y.C., Aug. 6, 1937; d. Joseph and Sylvia (Rosenberg) Getz; m. James Milton Rubin, Oct. 28, 1961; children: Felicia Sue, Andrea Faith. BA, Syracuse U., 1959; MA, Columbia U., 1961, Adelphi U., 1975. Physical edn. tchr. Hicksville (N.Y.) Pub. Schs., 1959-93; bd. dirs., pres. Assoc. Am. Acad. Allergy, Asthma and Immunology. Producer: (video) Aerobic Dancercise for Children, 1987. Bd. dirs. COPAY, Great Neck, N.Y., 1986-91; v.p., sec. Pierpont Condominium Bd., 1986-90. Recipient Founder's Day award PTA, 1986. Mem.: N.Y. State Alliance for Health, Phys. Edn., REcreation and Dance (program spkr. 1984, 85, 93, v.p. Nassau zone 1987—2000, Zone Svc. award 1993). Avocations: tennis, reading, meditation, golf.

RUBIN, ROBERTA GAIL, pathologist; b. Bklyn., Apr. 2, 1934; d. Victor and Pearl Berger Rubin; m. Walter D'Ull; children: Leon Jesse, Victoria Roslyn. MD, SUNY, Bklyn., 1958. Pathologist Chilton Meml. Hosp., Pompton Plains, N.J., 1968-98; dir. lab. Livingston (N.J.) Cmty. Hosp., 1987-88; assoc. pathologist Bronx Lebanon Hosp. Ctr., 1967-68; staff pathologist Maimonides-Coney Island Med. Ctr., Bklyn., 1964-67; dir. MDS Lab., Wayne, N.J., 1973-89. Clin. instr. pathology SUNY, Bklyn., 1964-67, Albert Einstein Sch. Medicine, Bronx, 1967-68. Sec., treas. bd. Morris Area Cmty. Fedn., Whippany, N.J., 1989—. Fellow: Coll. Am. Pathologists; mem.: N.J. Soc. Pathologists (bd. dirs. 1989—2001), Found. Am. Med. Women's Assn. (treas. 2001—), Nat. Coun. Women's Health (pres. 1999—2001), Am. Women's Hosp. Assn. (chmn. 1993—), Am. Med. Women's Assn. (v.p. fin. 1993, Camille Mermod award 1995). Avocations: doll art collector, cosmology, reading. Home: 10 Woodland Ave Glen Ridge NJ 07028

RUBIN, SANDRA MENDELSOHN, artist; b. Santa Monica, Calif., Nov. 7, 1947; d. Murry and Freda (Atliss) Mendelsohn; m. Stephen Edward Rubin, Aug. 6, 1966. BA, UCLA, 1976, MFA, 1979. Instr. Art Ctr. Coll. Design, Pasadena, Calif., 1980, UCLA, 1981. One-woman exhbns. include L.A. Louver Gallery, 1982, L.A. County Mus. Art, 1985, Fischer Fine Arts, London, 1985, Claude Bernard Gallery, N.Y.C., 1987, L.A. Louver Gallery, L.A., 1982, 92, 2003; group exhbns. include L.A. County Mus. Artm 1977, 82, 83, L.A. Mcpl. Art Gallery, 1977, 83, 93, L.A. Contemporary Exhbns., 1978, L.A. Inst. Contemporary Arts, 1978, Newport Harbor Art Mus., Newport Beach, Calif., 1981, Odyssia Gallery, N.Y.C., 1981, Nagoya (Japan) City Mus., 1982, Long Beach (Calif.) Mus. Art, 1982, Brooke Alexander Gallery, N.Y.C., 1982, Laguna Beach (Calif.) Mus. Art, 1982, Jan Baum Gallery, L.A., 1984, San Francisco Mus. Art, 1986, Claude Bernard Gallery, N.Y.C., 1986, Struve Gallery, Chgo., 1987, Boise (Idaho) Mus., 1988, Judy Youen's Gallery, London, 1988, Tatistscheff Gallery, Inc., Santa Monica, Calif., 1989, Tortue Gallery, Santa Monica, 1990, Contemporary Arts Forum, Santa Barbara, Calif., 1990, San Diego Mus. Art, 1991, Fresno (Calif.) Met. Mus., 1992, Jack Rutberg Fine Arts, L.A., 1993, San Jose Mus. Art, 2003, Pasadena Mus. Calif. Art, 2004. Recipient Young Talent Purchase award L.A. County Mus. Art, 1980; Artist's Fellowship grant NEA, 1981, 91. Avocations: gardening, exercise, reading, singing E-mail: smr@pacific.net.

RUBINSTEIN, EVA (ANNA), photographer; b. Buenos Aires, 1933; d. Arthur and Aniela (Mlynarska) R.; m. William Sloane Coffin Jr., 1956 (div. 1968); children: Amy, Alexander (dec.), David. Ballet tng., Paris, N.Y.C., Calif., 1938-53; student, Scripps Coll., 1950-51, UCLA, 1952-53; student in photography, Lisette Model, 1969, Jim Hughes, 1971, Ken Heyman, 1970, Diane Arbus, 1971. Lectr. numerous workshops, seminars, confs.; instr. photo seminars Lodz Film Sch., Poland, 1986, 86-87. Dancer, actress: off-Broadway and Broadway, including original prodn. The Diary of Anne Frank, 1955-56; European dance tour, 1955; one-person shows of photographs include Underground Gallery, N.Y.C., 1972, Dayton Art Inst., Ohio, 1973, Arles Festival, France, 1975, Canon Photo Gallery, Amsterdam, 1975, Neikrug Gallery, N.Y.C., 1975, 79, 81, 82, 85, La Photogalerie, Paris, 1975, Friends of Photography, Carmel, Calif., 1975, Galerie 5.6, Ghent, Belgium, 1976, Gallery Trochenpresse, Berlin, 1977, Frumkin Gallery, Chgo., 1977, Galeria Sinisca, Rome, 1979, Hermitage Found. Mus., Norfolk, Va., 1982, Photographers Gallery, London, 1983, Galerie Forum Labo, Arles, France, 1983, Galerie Nicephore, Lyon, France, 1983, Image Gallery, Madrid, 1984, Muzeum Sztuki, Lodz, Poland, 1984, Il Diaframma/Canon Gallery, Milan, 1984, A.R.P.A. Gallery, Bordeaux, 1984, Chateau d'Eau, Toulouse, France, 1985, Galerie Demi-Teinte, Paris, 1985, Associated Artist Photographers galleries in Warsaw, Krakow, Lodz, Katowice and Gdansk, Poland, 1985-86, Foto/Medium/Art Gallery, Wroclaw, Poland, 1986, Visions Gallery, San Francisco, 1986, Canon Galerie, Paris, 1986, Salone Internat. SICOF, Milan, 1987, St. Krzysztof Gallery, Lodz, 1987, L'Image Fixe, Lyon, 1988, Artotheque, Grenoble, 1988, Neikrug Photographica, N.Y.C., 1989, Heuser Art Ctr. Gallery, Bradley U., Peoria, Ill., 1989, 3-os Encontros da Imagem, Braga, Portugal, 1989, Bibliotheque Nat. Galerie Colbert, Paris, 1989, Galerie Picto-Bastille, Paris, 1989-90, Portfolio Gallery, London, 1990, Vaison-La-Romaine, France, 1990, Hist. Mus. of City of Lodz, 1990, Galerie Artem, Quimper, France, 1993, Galerie F.N.A.C. Etoile, Paris, 1994, other F.N.A.C. galleries (France, Belgium, Spain), 1994-97, Galerie Augustus, Berlin, 1995, L'Imagerie, Lannion, France, 1995, Zacheta Gallery, Warsaw, 1996, Salon of Modern Art B.W.A., Bydgoszcz, Poland, 1997, Galleries of Polish Insts., Sofia, Bulgaria, Berlin, Moscow, Bratislava, Slovakia, I. Beszkova Gallery, Plewen, Bulgaria, 1997, Hungarian Mus. Photographic Art, Budapest, 1997, LTF Gallery, Lodz, Poland, 1998, Konfrontacje Fotograficzne, Gorzow Wielopolski, Poland, 1998, Centrum Kultury Zamek, Poznan, Poland, 1998, Mus. Regionalny, Wrzesnia, Poland, 1998, Galeria Korytarz, Jelenia Gora, Poland, 1998, Galeria Foto-Medium-Art, Wroclaw, Poland, 1998, Galeria Pusta, Centrum Kultury, Katowice, Poland, 1998, Teatr Wielki, Lodz, Poland, 2000, Gallery Europa Club, NY, 2003; group shows include, Internat. Salon, Krakow, Poland, 1971, Delgado Mus., New Orleans, 1972, Neikrug Gallery, 1972, 73, 75, Salone Internazionale, Milan, Italy, 1973, Photo-OVO, Montreal, Que., Can., 1974, Nat. Portrait Gallery, London, 1976, Hera Gallery, R.I., 1977, Musee National d'Art Moderne Georges Pompidou, Paris, 1977, Centre Culturel de l'ouest Aquitain, Bordeaux, France, 1978, Fotografiska Museet, Stockholm, 1978, Nat. Arts Club, N.Y.C., 1979, Chrysler Mus., Norfolk, 1979, Maine Photog. Gallery, 1981, Floating Found. Photography, N.Y.C., 1970, 71, 72, 73, 79, 82, Ffoto Gallery, Cardiff, Wales, 1983, Musée d'Art Moderne de la Ville de Paris, 1987-88, Boca Raton (Fla.) Mus., 1989, Galerie PICTO Bastille, Paris, 1989, Galerie Arena, Arles, 1989-90, Settimana della Fotografia, Palermo, 1990, Festival de l'Image, Le Mans, France, 1993, Quimper (France), 1995, Galerie Camera Obscura, Paris, 1996, Zacheta Gallery, Warsaw, 2002, Lodz Photographic Soc., 2002, Polish/Am.Photographers, Polish Consulate, NY, 2003, Gutman Libr., Harvard, 2003; represented: in permanent collections Library of Congress, Washington, Met. Mus. Art, N.Y.C., Bibliotheque Nationale, Paris, Musee Reattu, Arles, France, Kalamazoo Inst. Arts, Israel Mus., Jerusalem, Fotografiska Museet, Stockholm, Muzeum Sztuki, Lodz, Poland, Histo Mus. of City of Lodz, others; author: Eva Rubinstein, 1974, Eva Rubinstein, I Grandi Fotografi, 1983, 2 ltd. edit. portfolios with introductions by John Vachon and André Kertész, Lodz: Brief Encounters, 1998, Eva Rubinstein: Fotografie, 1967-1990; contbr. photographs in various books, mags., profl. jours.

RUBINSTEIN, PHYLLIS M. lawyer; BA in English, Pa. State U., 1966; JD, Temple U., 1977. Bar: Pa. 1977, D.C. 1980, Va. 1982. Jud. clk. to Hon. Israel Packel Phila. Supreme Ct., 1977-78; with Samuel B. Hornstein & Assocs., Doylestown, Pa., 1978-79; adj. instr. Inst. Paralegal Tng., Phila., 1979; counsel Hunton & Williams, Richmond, Va., 1981-95; dir. McCandlish Kaine & Grant, Richmond, 1995—. Speaker in field. Past condominium adv. bd. Commonwealth of Va.; exec. bd. Comml. Real Estate Women, Jewish Family Svcs.; past bd. dirs. B'Nai B'rith Youth Orgn., Beth Sholom Home Ctrl. Va. Mem. ABA (coun., real property, probate and trust law sect. 1993-99, chair diversity com., past chair com. ethics and professionalism, past task force on Applying Fed. Legis. to Congress, past standing com. on membership of real property, probate and trust law sect., past vice-chair com. on significant decisions of real property, probate and trust law sect., former mem. real estate fin. com., liaison to ethics 2000 commn.), Va. Bar Assn., Va. State Bar, Met. Richmond Women's Bar Assn. Home: 1905 Oakway Dr Richmond VA 23233-3513

RUBINSTEIN, ROSALINDA, allergist, medical association administrator; b. Buenos Aires, Jan. 3, 1942; came to U.S., 1967; MD, U. Buenos Aires, 1965. Residence Beth Israel Hosp., 1968-70; fellow in allergy-asthma Harvard Med. Sch., Boston, 1970-71; allergy-asthma asst. pediatrician Columbia Presbyn., N.Y.C., 1971—, Mt. Sinai Med. Ctr., N.Y.C., 1972—. Bd. dirs. N.Y. Women's Agenda, Argentina Am. Med. Soc.; pres. elect Nat. Coun. Women's Health, 1998-2000, pres., 2000-2002; pres. Women's Med. Assn., N.Y.C., 1995-97. Recipient Recognition award N.Y. Women's Agenda, 1997, Women's Med. Assn., N.Y.C., 1996, Community award Am. Med. Women's Assn., 1998. Mem. AMA, Am. Coll. Allergy-Asthma, Am. Acad. Allergy-Asthma, N.Y. County Med. Soc., Columbia Presbyn. Club, N.Y. Harvard Club. Avocation: women's health issues. Home and Office: 1016 5th Ave New York NY 10028-0132

RUBISOFF, DEBORAH L. state agency administrator; b. Hayti, Mo., Jan. 16, 1955; m. Charles T. Rubisoff, May 15, 1976; children: Charlie, Haley, John. BBA in Acctg., Delta State U., 1976. Budget analyst Commn. Budget & Acctg., Jackson, Miss., 1980—86, Legis. Budget Office, Jackson, 1986—2000, dep. dir., 2000—02. Bd. dirs. Miss. Girlchoir, Jackson, 2000—02. Office: 501 N West St Ste 201B Jackson MS 39201-1008 Business E-Mail: drubisoff@mail.lbo.state.ms.us.

RUBLEY, CAROLE A. state legislator; b. Bethel, Conn., Jan. 18, 1939; d. George B. and Evelyn M. (Maloney) Drumm; m. C. Ronald Rubley, Aug. 25, 1962; children: Lauren M. Rubley Simpson, Stephen R., Kristin Rubley Vaughan. BA in Biology, Albertus Magnus Coll., 1960; MS in Environ. Health, West Chester U., 1988. Tchr. biology Danbury (Conn.) High Sch., 1960-62, Waltham (Mass.) High Sch., 1962-63; real estate salesperson Henderson-Dewey, Wayne, Pa., 1976-81; solid waste coord. Chester County Health Dept., West Chester, Pa., 1981-88; environ. cons. Environ. Resources Mgmt., Exton, Pa., 1988-92; mem. Pa. Ho. Reps., Valley Forge, 1992—. Mem. environ. resources, energy, consumer affairs, fin. and children and youth com. House of Reps.; mem. Pa. 21st Century Environ. Commn.; vice-chair environ. com. NCSL, task force on protecting Democracy, chair environ. and natural resources com. Author: (with others) Leading Pennsylvania into 21st Century, 1990. Chmn. Ea. Chester County Regional Planning Commn., 1976-85; vice chmn. planning commn. Tredyffrin Twp., Berwyn, Pa., 1976-86, mem. bd. suprs., 1987-92; bd. dirs. Pa. Resources Coun., exec. v.p., 1988-92. Mem. LWV (pres. Upper Main Line chpt. 1976-78, Involved Voter of Yr. award 1993), Pa. Environ. Coun., Green Valleys Assn., Open Land Conservancy. Republican. Roman Catholic. Avocations: aerobics, tennis, hiking, reading, traveling. Home: 621 Vassar Rd Wayne PA 19087-5312

RUBRIGHT, BEVERLY JEAN, music educator; b. Greenburg, Pa., Aug. 6, 1954; d. Donald Eugene and Helen Elizabeth Lawther; m. Keith Alan Rubright, Sept. 16, 1978; children: Karrie Alana, Kevin Alan, Karlee Ann. BA Music Edn., West Liberty State Coll., 1976; MEd, Indiana U. Pa., 1982. Tchr. Penn Trafford Sch. Dist., Harrison City, Pa., 1979—. Sponsor, producer high sch. musical Penn Trafford Sch. Dist., 1994—, coach girls tennis team, 1999, prodr. fall play, 2003—. Children's choir dir. Markem Prodns., Trafford, 1998—; organist First Bapt. Ch., Jeannette, Pa., 1990—. Mem.: Music Educators Nat. Conf., Pa. Music Educators Assn., Westmoreland County Music Educators Assn. (v.p. 2002, pres. 2003—). Democrat. Baptist. Avocations: tennis, softball, sewing, cross stitch. Home: 1127 Harrison City-Export Rd Jeannette PA 15644 Office: Penn Trafford Sch Dist Rt 130 Harrison City PA 15636

RUBRUM, ERICA COURTNEY, family therapist, school counselor; b. N.Y.C., Feb. 20, 1965; d. Walter and Rhoda (Metviner) R.; m. Todd Schaffhauser, Sept. 29, 1996, c. Olivia Morgan. BA, U. Mass., 1987; MS in Edn., L.I. U., 1990; MS in Counseling, Queens Coll., 1992. Registered sch. counselor, N.Y. Mgr. Am. Leisure, N.Y.C., 1988-90; family therapist Counseling and Psychotherapy Group, Merrick, N.Y., 1990-94; sch. counselor Herricks Pub. Schs., New Hyde Park, N.Y., 1992-94; pvt. practice family therapy Roslyn, N.Y., 1994—; social worker Big Bros./Big Sisters, Levittown, N.Y., 1995-96; supervising therapist New Image Med., Huntington, N.Y., 1995-96; sch. counselor Carle Place Pub. Schs., 1996-2000, Hollow Hills Pub. Schs., 2000. V.p. One to One: L.I.'s Disability Support and Outreach Group, Islip, N.Y., 1993—; family therapist Family Wellness Ctr., Smithtown, N.Y., 2000—. Mem. ACA, Am. Assn. Marriage and Family Therapists, Am. Psychotherapy Assn., Nassau Counselors Assn. (exemplary practice award 1992, 95). Office: 56 Sherrard St Roslyn Heights NY 11577-1713

RUBY, LINDA ANNA, pre-school educator, music educator; b. Chgo., Dec. 17, 1964; d. George and Helga Ruby. BA, BSc, Mundelein Coll., 1987. Cert. tchr. Tchr. music NCA, Chgo., 1992—2003; tchr. kindergarten St. Mary Sch., Griffith, Ind., 2003—. Mem.: Music Educators Nat. Conf. Avocations: music, theater.

RUCK, ROSEMARIE ULISSA, retired social worker, freelance/self-employed writer; b. Buffalo, Aug. 24, 1939; d. Stanley Joseph Ren and Bertha Sosnowski; m. Donald Neal Ruck, Nov. 8, 1958; children: Theresa Dorene Ruck Novak, Donna Rose Ruck Seyler, Michael Donald. AS, Genesee C.C., 1970—72; BS, SUNY Brockport Coll., 1972—75. Chemical Dependency Counselor Pk. Ridge Unity Health Sys. & Brockport Coll., NY, 1999, Basic Reading and ESL Tutor Literacy Volunteers of Am., Inc., NY, 1984. Sr. caseworker/counselor Assn. for Retarded Citizens, Batavia, NY, 1975—79; dir. Literacy Volunteers of Am. - Genesee County Chpt., Batavia, NY, 1983—89. Exec. dir. Literacy Volunteers of Am. - Orleans County Chpt., Albion, NY, 1989—98; chem. dependency counselor Pk. Ridge- Unity Health Sys., Rochester, NY, 1998—99; social worker Lakeside Beikirch Care Ctr., Brockport, NY, 1999—2002; writer Freelance -, Holley, NY, 2002—. Mem. of Genesee c.c. steering com. Genesee County Legislature, Batavia, NY, 1967—68; mem. of com. responsible for devel. of Genesee county registry Genesee County Inter-Agy. Coun., Batavia, NY, 1975—77; grant writer & mem. of program com. for domestic violence program YWCA, Batavia, NY, 1980—81; mem. of steering com. for regional action phone Genesee County Inter-agency Coun., Batavia, NY, 1985—86; mem. of steering com. for vol. connection registry United Way of Genesee County, Batavia, NY, 1983—84; program chair person YWCA, Batavia, NY, 1980—82; voluneer leadership chairperson Young Women's Christian Associaiton, Batavia, NY, 1983—84; strategic planning com. chairperson United Way of Ea. Orleans County, Albion, NY, 1999—2001. Recipient Friends of Edn., Albion Ctrl. Sch. Bd. of Edn., 1991, Recognition of Outstanding Leadership, Literacy Volunteers of Am. - Genesee County Chpt., 1989, Literacy Volunteers of Am. - Orleans County Chpt., 1992, 1993, 1994, 1995, 1996, 1997, 1998, Genesee County Chpt. of Assn. for Retarded Citizens, 1979, Quality Recognition award, Lakeside Beikirch Care Ctr., 2001. Mem.: Literacy Volunteers of Am., Holley's Writers Club. Catholic. Achievements include Revived rural literacy organization and became number one in national organizations from over 450 affiliates; development of first workplace literacy program in Western NY state. Avocations: reading, writing, travel, art, exercise. Home: 5314 Upper Holley Rd Holley NY 14470 Personal E-mail: tutuck@juno.com.

RUCKER, BRONWYN, actress, writer, social worker; b. Ithaca, N.Y., Mar. 18, 1951; d. James Charles and Mary Elizabeth (Costello) R.; m. Rick Russo, Dec. 31, 1984. BA in Theatre Arts, Point Park Coll., Pitts., 1973; MSW, Hunter Coll., 1993. Cert. Social Worker NYU Edn. Dept., 1993. Profl. actress various theatres, N.Y., N.J., 1969-80; artistic dir./co-founder not-for-profit social svc. arts co. Meltdown Inc., Bklyn., 1993—; med. social worker Bklyn. Hosp. Ctr., 1993-95; therapist New Hope Guild, N.Y.C., 1997; theatre dir. Madison Hamilton Settlement, N.Y.C., 1997; prof. human svcs. N.Y.C. Tech. Coll., 1998—. Bd. dirs. Women in Limbo, N.Y.C., 1992—. Prodr. John Cage Meets Sun Ra Concert and album, Bklyn.-Coney Island, 1986; actress, writer (one-woman show) Subway Named Desire, 1980, (plays) Brooklyn Boys, 1980, Angela Plays, 1980, The Radon Daughters, 1984, The True Story, 1986, Voices of the Armory, 1992, Teen Scenes, 1993, (autobiography) White Lady, 1999; performer, songwriter (CD) Inclines, 1996. Vol. staff, dir. teen program, YWCA Bklyn., 1993—. Recipient Most Creative Painting award Associated Artists Pitts., 1979, Woman of Influence award YWCA Bklyn., 1993, commendation N.Y.C. Office Comptroller Violence Prevention Work, 1995, Racial Harmony and Diversity award Chase Manhattan Bank, N.Y.C., 1996, Dr. Harold Diner Meml. Lectr. award Albert Einstein Coll. Medicine, 1999; grantee N.Y.C. Mayor's Stop The Violence program, 1994. Mem. AFTRA, SAG, NASW, Actors Equity Assn., Assn. Advancement Social Work with Groups, The Players Club, Bklyn. C. of C. Democrat. d Office: Meltdown Inc 346 Flatbush Ave Brooklyn NY 11238-4902

RUCKERT, ANN JOHNS, musician, singer; b. N.Y.C., Mar. 12, 1945; d. G. Wallace and Elizabeth (Johns) R. Student, Julliard Sch., 1961-69, NYU, 1969-70, Royal Acad. Music, London, 1972; studies in composition with Nadia Boulanger, Paris, 1972-73; studies with Helen Hobbs Jordon, N.Y.C., 1973-75; studies with David Sorin Collyer, 1975-78. Profl. musician over 3,000 commercially released records, 1960—; owner, pres. Ann Ruckert Music, N.Y.C. and Los Angeles, 1980—. Cons., spkr. Platinum Record Industry seminars; chairperson N.Y. Jazz Mus., N.Y.C., 1977-79; bd. dirs. Jazzmobile, N.Y.C., 1983-89, 92—; TV com. Grammy awards, 1985-87; mem. creative staff Lifetime Achievement awards show, 1987; adv. Universal Jazz Coalition, N.Y.C., 1979-87; cons. rec. industry including: Zero House Records, Warner Group, bd. dirs. ASCAP; also individual artists: Roberta Flack, Diane Schnur, Morgan Ames, over 300 clients; performance Ann Ruckert Choir, Macy's 4th of July Show, 1996; lectr. NYU, SUNY, Harvard, 1996-97. Musician, singer: (recs.) Strawbs, Greatest Hits (Gold Record award, 1975); music contractor: (film) Housesitter, 1993, Boys on the Side, 1994; performed at Hudson Theatre, 1994, Shea Stadium, 1994, Lincoln Ct., 1994; producer albums: Jane Jarvis, Jazz, Mike Longo, Jazz, 1996-97. Commr. Deed, N.Y., 1986—, Schomberg Collection N.Y.C. Pub. Library; mem. county com. Westside Manhattan, 1980-89; co-chair and chair edn. com. Grammys in the Schs., N.Y.C. Mem. NARAS (Named Most Valuable Player 1982, 89, trustee, gov., v.p. N.Y. chpt., bd. trustees 1989—, bd. dirs. World Hunger Yr.), Soc. Singers (bd. dirs. N.Y.C. chpt.), Songwriters Guild Am. (bd. dirs., concert, Pres.'s award 1997). Democrat. Episcopalian. Avocations: arts, music, visual arts. Home and Office: 119 W 71st St New York NY 10023-3876

RUDACILLE, SHARON VICTORIA, medical technologist; b. Ranson, W. Va., Sept. 11, 1950; d. Albert William and Roberta Mae (Anderson) R.; BS cum laude, Shepherd Coll., 1972. Med. technologist VA Ctr., Martinsburg, W.Va., 1972—, instr. Sch. Med. Tech., 1972-76, assoc. coord. edn., 1976-77, edn. coord., 1977-78, quality assurance officer clin. chemistry, 1978-80, lab. svc. quality assurance and edn. officer, 1980-84, clin. chemistry sect. leader, 1984-86, staff med. technologist, 1986-94, supervisory med. technologist, 1994-95, sr. med. technologist, 1995—; adj. faculty mem. Shippensburg (Pa.) State Coll., 1977-78, Shepherd Coll., 1977-78. Mem. Am. Soc. Med. Tech., Am. Soc. Clin. Pathologists, W.Va. Soc. Med. Technologists, Shepherd Coll. Alumni Assn., Sigma Pi Epsilon. Baptist. Home: PO Box 14 Ranson WV 25438-0014

RUDD, SUSAN, retail executive; b. Rolla, Mo., Jan. 25, 1961; d. Wayne LeRoy and Chie Owada Schwatka; m. Edward Thomas Rudd, Oct. 27, 1947. BBA, Fontbonne U., 1999, postgrad., 2002—. Exec. sec. McDonnell Douglas Astronautics, St. Louis, 1981—90; sr. exec. office adminstr. Anheuser-Busch Cos. Inc., St. Louis, 1990—2000, corp. rels. mgr. Asian Pacific Am. market, 2000—03; mgr. nat. retail sales Anheuser-Busch Inc., St. Louis, 2002—. Bd. dirs. Asian Pacific Am. Women's Leadership Inst., Denver. Recipient Women's Bus. Leadership award, Columbia Coll.-Ctr. Asian Arts and Media, 2001. Mem.: NAFE. Office: Anheuser-Busch Inc One Busch Pl Saint Louis MO 63118 Home: 40804 North Nobel Hawk Way Anthem AZ 85086-1816 Business E-Mail: susan.rudd@anheuser-busch.com.

RUDDEN, MARIE GEORGINE, psychiatrist; b. Bklyn., Aug. 22, 1951; d. Francis Joseph and Georgette (Heinecke) R.; m. Howard B. Levy (div. 1984); 1 child, Daniel; m. Peter Michael Lazes; 1 child, Adrienne. BA, Yale Coll., 1973; MD, NYU Sch. Medicine, 1977; grad., N.Y. Psychoanalytic Inst., 1994. Diplomate Am. Bd. Psychiatry and Neurology, 1984. Intern Meml. Sloan Kettering Cancer Ctr. and N.Y. Hosp., 1977-78; resident Payne Whitney Clinic/Cornell Med. Sch., 1978-82; clin. instr. Cornell U. Sch. of Medicine, N.Y.C., 1982-92; clin. asst. prof. Cornell U. Sch. Medicine, N.Y.C., 1992—. Contbr. articles to profl. jours. Recipient Rock Sleyster Meml. scholarship AMA, 1976. Mem. Am. Psychiat. Assn., Am. Psychoanalytic Assn., Internat. Psychoanalytic Assn. Avocations: reading, hiking, horseback riding. Home and Office: 55 Hawthorne St Lenox MA 01240-2801

RUDDLE, NANCY HARTMAN, microbiology educator, microbiologist, researcher; b. St. Louis, Apr. 3, 1940; d. David Eugene and Josephine (Odell) Hartman; m. Francis Hugh Ruddle, Aug. 1, 1964; children: Kathlyn,

Amy. BA, Mt. Holyoke Coll., 1962; PhD, Yale U., 1968. Rsch. assoc. Yale U., New Haven, 1968-71, postdoctoral fellow, 1971-74, rsch. assoc., 1974-75, asst. prof., 1975-80, assoc. prof., 1980-91, prof. epidemiology and immunobiology, 1991—, head divsn. epidemiology of microbial diseases, 1990—. Panel mem. Am. Cancer Soc., 1987-91; study sect. mem. NIH, 1991—. Contbr. articles to profl. jours. Recipient Am. Cancer Soc. Faculty Rsch. award; fellow Am. Cancer Soc. postdoctoral fellow, Damon Runyon postdoctoral fellow; grantee NIH grantee, Am. Cancer Soc. grantee, Multiple Sclerosis Soc. grantee. Office: Yale Univ Sch Medicine 60 College St New Haven CT 06510-3210

RUDDOCK, ELLEN SYLVES, business consultant; b. Pitts., May 9, 1944; d. Clyde Lysle and Margaret Beck (Tilley) Sylves; m. Rodney David Ruddock, Apr. 2, 1966; children: Dana William, Darin Willis. BS, Indiana U. Pa., 1966; cert. in entrepreneurial mgmt., Carnegie Mellon U., 1995. Lic. real estate agt., Pa.; cert. facilitator, Leadership Mgmt. Inc. Tchr. Penn Hills H.S., Pitts., 1966; adminstrv. asst. Utah-Martin-Day, Bangkok, 1967-68, Comusmachthai, Bangkok, 1968-69; tchr. United H.S., Armagh, Pa., 1969-70; owner Swing Set Children's Store, Indiana, 1975-80; radio cons. RMS Media Mgmt., Indiana, 1980-89; owner Career Dynamics, Pitts., 1989—2002. Bd. dirs. PowerLink, Pitts., pres., 2000-01; initiator partnership between PowerLink and Athena Found. to aid women-owned businesses. Initiator 100-mem. vol. strategic planning group Indiana County for 2020, revitalization program Indiana for the 80s, also fundraisers; chairperson New Growth Arts Festival, Indiana, 1984—85, 1995—2001, Greater Indiana Strategic Planning Commn.; bd. dirs. PNC Adv. Bd., Indiana, 1986—2000; chmn. bd. dirs. ATHENA Found., Lansing, Mich., 2003—; bd. dirs., now emeritus Downtown Indiana, 1975—, pres., 1979—81; campaign mgr. Found. Indiana U. Pa., 2001—; bd. dirs. Indiana U. Pa. Alumni Assn., 2001—. Named World Sales Leader of Assessments, Leadership Mgmt. Inc., 2000, 2001, Retailer of Yr., Kids Mag., N.Y.C., 1978, Ind. County Civic Leader of Yr., 2000; named one of Pa. 50 Best Women in Bus., 1999; recipient Athena award, ATHENA Found., 1987, Svc. award, Alice Paul Ho., Ind., Pres.'s Club award, Leadership Mgmt., Inc., Waco, Tex., 1997, Golden Eagle award, 1997, Distbr. of Yr. award, Leadership Mgmt. Inc., 2000, Outstanding Civilian Svc. award, USAR, Pitts., 1997, 2000, Distbr. of Yr. award, Leadership Mgmt. Inc., 2001. Mem. Indiana County C. of C. (chairperson task force 1975-97, bd. dirs. 1997—), Quota Club (pres. 1986-88, Svc. award 1986). Republican. Methodist. Avocations: reading, walking, community service. Home: 465 Edgewood Ave Indiana PA 15701 E-mail: eruddock@adelphia.net.

RUDER, DIANE G. fund raising executive; b. Pasadena, Tex., Feb. 3, 1941; d. David A. and Gladys S. (Cook) Garrett; m. Melvin P. Ruder, Nov. 11, 1961; children: N. Christine, M. Shawn, M. Kirk, Heather M., Eric R. AB, Miami U., Oxford, Ohio, 1984; MBA, Xavier U., Cin., 1992. News writer The Jour. News, Hamilton, Ohio, 1972-76; alumni dir. Wilmington (Ohio) Coll., 1985-88, dir. alumni rels. and ann. fund progs., 1988-89, dir. ann. fund, 1989-90; exec. dir. Middletown (Ohio) Regional Hosp. Found., 1990-92; asst. dir. devel. Episcopal Retirement Homes, Cin., 1992-93; dir. devel. United Cerebral Palsy of Cin., 1993-94, Otterbein Retirement Living Cmtys., Lebanon, Ohio, 1994—. Mem. Ctrl. Com., Rep. Party, 1968-84; bd. dirs. Am. Heart Assn. Butler County; bd. dirs. Sr. Citizens Assn. Middletown, Friends of Chrisholm; dir. devel. Otterbein Retirement Living Communities, Lebanon, Ohio, 1994—. Recipient May Cup award of spl. recognition, Am. Mktg. Assn., 1989, Cert. of Merit, Admissions Mktg. Report, 1989. Mem. Ohio Assn. Hosp. Devel., Nat. Assn. Hosp. Devel., Nat. Soc. Fund Raising Execs. (cert. fund raising exec.), Nat. Assn. Fundraising Profls., Leadership Middletown, Nat. Planned Giving Coun. Roman Catholic. Home: 5660 Headgates Rd Hamilton OH 45011 Office: Otterbein Homes 580 N St Route 741 Lebanon OH 45036-8839 E-mail: ruder@otterbein.org., lmcfre@aol.com.

RUDERMAN, ELLEN G. psychotherapist, consultant, psychoanalyst; b. N.Y.C., July 12, 1937; d. Joseph and Sarah (Ornstein) Bassin; m. Herbert Charles Ruderman, Aug. 14, 1965; 1 child, Adam Scott. BA, UCLA, 1959; MSW, U. So. Calif., 1963; PhD, Calif. Inst. Clin. Social Work, Berkeley, 1983; PsyD, Inst. Contemp. Psychoanalysis, L.A., 1995. Diplomate Am. Bd. Examiners in Social Work, Nat. Assn. Social Workers; lic. clin. social worker, Calif. Casework specialist Jewish Big Bros., L.A., 1963; psychotherapist, supr. Cedars-Sinai Med. Ctr., L.A., 1963-81; cons., coord. spl. edn. projects Ctr.-Thalians Clinic, L.A., 1963-81; pvt. practice psychoanalytic psychotherapy/psychoanalysis Encino, West Los Angeles, Calif., 1966—. Adj. faculty div. psychiatry Cedars Sinai Med. Ctr./Thalians Clinic, 1981—; part-time clin. faculty UCLA Grad. Sch. Social Welfare, 1988-94; psychoanalytic cons. to pvt. groups, 1978—; faculty, tng. and supervising analyst Inst. Contemporary Psychoanalysis, L.A., 1995—; mem. adv. bd. Calif. Inst. for Clin. Social Work, Berkeley, 1984—, cons. clin. faculty, 1983—; assoc. Stone Ctr./Wellesley U., 1985—. Cons. editor Jour. Clin. Social Work; contbr. articles to profl. jours. NIMH fellow, 1961-62, 62-63. Fellow Calif. State Soc. for Clin. Social Work; mem. So. Calif. Area Com. on Psychoanalysis (chair 1990—), Acad. Cert. Social Workers. Democrat. Office: 16055 Ventura Blvd Ste 1110 Encino CA 91436-2612

RUDIGIER, ROBERTA LYNN, librarian; b. Honolulu, HI, June 3, 1947; d. James Philip Carbaugh and Doris Ida Clements; m. Gregory Charles Rudigier, Jun. 8, 1968; children: Darcy, Holly. BA, St. Mary's Coll. of Md., 1972. Art tchr., 1973-74; home sch. pioneer, 1984—92; reference libr. St. Mary's Meml. Libr., Leonardtown, Md., 1997—. Editor: Where Maryland Began, 2000. Mem. Md. Libr. Assn. Avocation: travel. Office: St Marys County Meml Library 23250 Hollywood Rd Leonardtown MD 20650 E-mail: lrudigier@somd.lib.md.us.

RUDIN, ANNE, retired mayor, nursing educator; b. Passaic, N.J., Jan. 27, 1924; m. Edward Rudin, June 6, 1948; 4 children BS in Edn., Temple U., 1945, RN, 1946; MPA, U. So. Calif., 1983; LLD (hon.), Golden Gate U., 1990. RN, Calif. Mem. faculty Temple U. Sch. Nursing, Phila., 1946-48; mem. nursing faculty Mt. Zion Hosp., San Francisco, 1948-49; mem. Sacramento City Council, 1971-83; mayor City of Sacramento, 1983-92; ind. pub. policy cons. Pres. LWV, Riverside, 1957, Sacramento, 1961, Calif., 1969-71, Calif. Elected Women's Assn., 1973—; trustee Golden Gate U., 1993-96; mem. adv. bd. U. So. Calif., Army Depot Reuse Commn., 1992-94; bd. dirs. Sacramento Theatre Co., 1992-99, Japan Soc. No. Calif., Sacramento Symphony, 1993-96, Calif. Common Cause, 1993 -96, Sacramento Edn. Found., 1993-2004; v.p. Sacramento Traditional Jazz Soc. Found.; pres. bd. dirs. Natomas Basin Conservancy; foreman Sacramento County Grand Jury, 2000-01. Recipient Women in Govt. award U.S. Jaycee Women, 1984, Woman of Distinction award Sacramento Area Soroptimist Clubs, 1985, Civic Contbn. award LWV Sacramento, 1989, Woman of Courage award Sacramento History Ctr., 1989, Peacemaker of Yr. award Sacramento Mediation Ctr., 1992, Regional Pride award Sacramento Mag., 1993, Humanitarian award Japanese Am. Citizen's League, 1993, Outstanding Pub. Svc. award Am. Soc. Pub. Adminstrn., 1994; named Girl Scouts Am. Role model, 1989, Cmty. Svc. Recognition award, Japanese Am. Citizens League, 1999, Sacramento Traditional Jazz Soc. Hall of Fame, 2000.

RUDNER, SARA, dancer; b. Bklyn., Feb. 16, 1944; d. Henry Nathaniel and Jeannette (Smolensky) R.; 1 child, Edward Eli Rudner Marschner. AB in Russian Studies, Barnard Coll., 1964; MFA in Choreography, Bennington Coll., 1999. Dancer Sansardo Dance Co., N.Y.C., 1964-65, Am. Dance Co. at Lincoln Ctr., N.Y.C., 1965, Shakespeare Festival Touring Children's Show, N.Y.C., 1966; featured dancer Twyla Tharp Dance Found., N.Y.C., 1966-85; artistic dir., dancer Sara Rudner Performance Ensemble, N.Y.C., 1977—; guest dancer Joffrey Ballet, N.Y.C., 1973, Pilobolus Dance Theatre, N.Y.C., 1975, Lar Lubovitch Dance Co., N.Y.C., 1975-76; guest lectr., choreographer grad. dance dept. UCLA, 1975. Dir. dance Sarah Lawrence Coll.; tchr. master workshop NYU Theater Program, 1988-90; pres., artistic dir. Heart Dance, Inc. Choreographer: Palm Trees and Flamingoes, 1980, Dancing for an Hour or So, 1981, Minute by Minute, 1982, Eight Solos, 1991, Heartbeats, Inside Out, 1993; (with Jennifer Tipton and Dana Reitz) Necessary Weather, 1994; (with Rona Pondick, Robert Feintuch and Jennifer Tipton) Mine, 1996, Alley Theater-The Greeks part I and II, 1997, Heartbeat/mb with Christopher Janney and Mikhail Barysnikov, 1998. Choreographer Dancing-on-View St. Mark's Ch., N.Y.C., 1999, Santa Fe Opera. Grantee Creative Artists Pub. Svc. Program, N.Y., 1975-76, N.Y. State Coun. on Arts, 1975-78, Nat. Endowment for Arts, 1979-81, 91-92, 94-97; Guggenheim fellow, 1981-82; recipient N.Y. Dance and Performance award, 1984.

RUDNICK, ELLEN AVA, healthcare executive; b. New Haven; d. Harold and C. Vivian (Soybel) R.; children from previous marriage: Sarah, Noah; m. Paul W. Earle. BA, Vassar Coll., 1972; MBA, U. Chgo., 1973. Sr. fin. analyst Quaker Oats, Chgo., 1973-75; from with to pres. Baxter Internat., Deerfield, Ill., 1975—83; pres. Baxter Mgmt. Svcs., 1983-1990, HCIA, Balt., 1990-92, CEO Advs., Northbrook, Ill., 1992—; prin., chmn. Pacific Biometrics, Lake Forest, Calif., 1993-99; exec. dir., clin. prof. Polsky Ctr. for Entrepreneurship U. Chgo., 1999—. Bd. dirs. Liberty Mut. Ins., Oxford Health Plans, Pattrson Dental Co. Chief crusader Met. Chgo. United Way, 1982—85; mem. cir. friends Chgo. YMCA, 1985—89; bd. dirs. Evanston Northwestern-Highland Park Hosp., 1990—99, 2003—, Health Mgmt. Sys., 1997—, Evanston-Northwestern Hosp., 2000—02; pres. coun. Nat. Coll. Edn., Evanston, Ill., 1983—93. Office: Univ Chgo Grad Sch Bus 1101 E 58th St Chicago IL 60637-1511

RUDNICK, IRENE KRUGMAN, lawyer, former state legislator, educator; b. Columbia, S.C., Dec. 27, 1929; d. Jack and Jean (Getter) Krugman; m. Harold Rudnick, Nov. 7, 1954 (dec.); children: Morris, Helen Gail. AB cum laude, U. S.C., 1949, JD, 1952. Bar: S.C. 1952. Individual practice law, Aiken, SC, 1952—; now ptnr. Rudnick & Rudnick; instr. bus. law U. S.C., Aiken, 1962—; tchr. Warrenville Elem. Sch., 1965-70; supt. edn. Aiken County, 1970-72; mem. S.C. Ho. of Reps., 1972—78, 1980—84, 1986—94. Pres. Adath Yeshurun Synagogue; active Aiken County Dem. Party, S.C. Dem. Party; hon. mem. Aiken Able-Disabled. Recipient Citizen of Yr. award, 1976-77, Bus. and Profl. Women's Career Woman of Yr., 1978, 94, Aiken County Friend of Edn. award, 1985, 93, Outstanding Legis. award Disabled Vets., 1991, Citizen of Yr. award Planned Parenthood, 1994, Sertoma Svc. to Mankind award, 1996. Mem. AAUW, Aiken Able-Disabled (hon.), Aiken Hist. Soc., Hist. Aiken Found., Alpha Delta Kappa, Order Eastern Star, Hadassah Sisterhood, Am. Legion Aux. Office: PO Box 544 135 Pendleton St NW Aiken SC 29801-3859

RUDOLPH, LISA BETH, news correspondent; b. Oceanside, Calif., Dec. 7, 1957; d. Jerome Howard and Suzanne (Garber) R.; m. Richard Hurwitz, Sept. 23, 1989; children: Kyra Rachael, Gabriel Jerome. BA in History, Wellesley (Mass.) Coll., 1979; MA in Internat. Affairs, Columbia U., 1984. Children's news show writer WXXI-TV PBS, Rochester, N.Y., 1979-80; reporter WOKR-TV, ABC affiliate, Rochester, 1979-82; news writer WCBS-TV, CBS affliate, 1983-86; anchor, reporter KSAT-TV, ABC affiliate, San Antonio, 1986-87, WCBS-TV, CBS affiliate, N.Y.C., 1987-93; corr. Dateline NBC, N.Y.C., 1994—. Recipient 3 Emmys, 1990-92, Media award N.Y. State Bar Assn., 1991, 19th Ann. Eddy award, 1992, Clarion, Gabriel awards, 1997, 98. Mem. Phi Beta Kappa. Office: Dateline NBC 30 Rockefeller Plz Fl 2 New York NY 10112-0044

RUDOLPH, MAYA, actress, comedienne; b. Gainesville, Fla., July 27, 1972; d. Richard and Minnie (Riperton) Rudolph. BA in photography, U. Calif., Santa Cruz, 1994. Former backup singer The Rentals. Actor: (TV series) Saturday Night Live, 2000—, City of Angels, 2000, (guest star) Chicago Hope, 1996—97, : (TV films) The Devil's Child, 1997; (films) Gattaca, 1997, Chuck & Buck, 2000, Duets, 2000, Duplex, 2003, 50 First Dates, 2004. Office: 30 Rockefeller Plaza New York NY 10112*

RUDOLPH, WANDA, art educator; b. Kirksville, Mo., June 26, 1954; d. Stephen William and Martha Marie Vose; m. Robert Lee McGhee, Sept. 3, 1976 (div.); 1 child, Jeremiah Shoji McGhee ; m. Kevin Lynn Rudolph, May 28, 1988; stepchildren: Christina Lynn, Jeromy Scott. BS in edn., Southwest Mo. State U., 1977; MA, Truman U., 1987; degree in lib., Southwest Mo. State U., 1996. Art tchr. Evangel U., Springfield, Mo., 1982—87, Mansfield (Mo.) Sch., 1983—88, Niangua (Mo.) Sch., 1988—89, Drury U., Cabool, Mo., 1990; lib. Springfield (Mo.) Art Mus., 1990—94; art tchr. Galena (Mo.) Sch., 1994—95, Fordland (Mo.) Sch., 1995—96, Seymour (Mo.) R II Sch., 1996—. One-man shows include various mixed media shows. Prison ministry leader James River Assembly of God, Ozark, Mo., 2000—; prison vol. Mo. Dept. Corrections, 2000—; prison fellowship vol. Prison Fellowship, Jefferson City, Mo., 2000—. Mem.: Ava Art Guild, Southeast Dist. Art Tchrs. Assn., Mo. Art Edn. Assn., Mo. State Tchrs. Assn., Springfield Lib. Assn., Webster County Rep. Ctrl. Com. (I Dare You award, Qualities of Leadership 1972), Tri-M (hon.). Republican. Avocations: piano, genealogy, reading, singing, writing. Home: 1392 S Diggins Main St Seymour MO 65746 Office: Seymour R-II Sch Seymour MO 65746 E-mail: wandajoy12@yahoo.com.

RUDY, ELLEN BEAM, nursing educator; b. Moundsville, W.Va., May 5, 1936; d. William Henry and Mary Ellen Beam; m. Theodore Rudy, June 13, 1959; children: Richard, Alan, William. BSN, Ohio State U., 1958; MPA, U. Dayton, 1974; MSN, U. Md., 1977; PhD, Case Western Res. U., 1980. Cmty. health staff nurse Columbus (Ohio) Pub. Health Nursing Svc., 1958-60; supr. in-svc. instr. Henry County Hosp., New Castle, Ind., 1960-66; emergency room staff nurse St. Elizabeth Med. Ctr., Dayton, Ohio, 1970-73; instr. critical care Johns Hopkins Hosp., Balt., 1975-76; assoc. prof., program dir. Kent (Ohio) State U. Adult Program, 1978-84; adminstrv. assoc. U. Hosp. Cleve., 1985-90; assoc. prof., chmn. MSN Case Western Res. U., Cleve., 1985-88, prof., chair acute care nursing, 1988-90, assoc. dean rsch., 1990-91; dean, prof. U. Pitts. Sch. Nursing, 1991—. Author: (with others) Critical Care Nursing, 1992 (Am. Jour. Nursing Book of Yr. 1993); contbr. articles to profl. jours. Grant reviewer NIH Nursing Student Sect., Washington, 1990-93; provider expert testimony Senate Appropriations Com., Washington, 1993, Health Care Forum, Washington, 1993. Edward J. and Louise Mellen Endowed Chair in Acute Care Nursing, 1989-91; fellow Am. Acad. Nursing, 1988; rsch. grantee NIH Nat. Ctr. for Nursing Rsch., 1989-91, 91-94. Mem. ANA, AACN, Am. Heart Assn., Nat. Kidney Found. (co-chair critical care task force 1988-91), Coun. Nurse Researchers. Office: Univ Pitts Sch Nursing 350 Victoria Building Pittsburgh PA 15261-2403 Home: 7815 Lydia Dr Lewis Center OH 43035-8076

RUDY, KATHLEEN VERMEULEN, small business owner; b. Grand Rapids, Mich., Dec. 29, 1931; d. John Weston and Geneva (Swiet) Vermeulen; m. Fredrick Albers Yonkman, June 9, 1953 (div. Sept. 1980); children: Sara Yonkman Davis, Margriet Yonkman Finnegan, Nina Tower; m. Raymond Bruce Rudy, Nov. 14, 1981. BA, Hope Coll., Holland, Mich., 1953. Owner Kate's Antiques, 1974-2000. Editor mag. Jr. League of Boston, 1960's, Scarsdale Jr. League, 1960's. Bd. dirs. Jr. League of Boston, 1960s, Greenwich Cmty. for Human Svcs., 1970s-80s, Neighbor to Neighbor, Greenwich, 1980-98; trustee Hope Coll., 1986-96; chmn. Mary Fund com. Ladies Golf Tournament, 1985; mem. Women's Nat. Rep. Club, N.Y.C., 1995—, bd. govs., 1997—; mem. Hope Coll. Pres.'s Task Force, 1997-99; treas. Women's Nat. Rep. Club, 2000-2002, chmn. nominating com. 2000—, 2d v.p., 2002-. Mem. Jr. League of Phoenix, Greenwich Country Club, Dorset Field Club, Kappa Alpha Theta. Republican. Congregationalist. Avocations: tennis, golf, antiques, travel. Home and Office: 37 Lismore Ln Greenwich CT 06831-3741 E-mail: RayRudy@worldnet.att.net.

RUDY, RUTH CORMAN, former state legislator; b. Millheim, Pa., Jan. 3, 1938; d. Orvis E. and Mabel Jan (Stover) Corman; m. C. Guy Rudy, Nov. 21, 1956; children: Douglas G., Donita Rudy Koval, Dianna F. Degree in x-ray tech., Carnegie Inst., 1956; student, Pa. State U., 1968-71. Clk. of cts. County of Centre (Pa.), Bellefonte, 1976-82; rep. Pa. Gen. Assembly, Harrisburg, 1982-96. Mem. Dem. Nat. Com., 1980—, chair women's caucus, 1989-91; past pres. Pa. Fedn. Dem. Women, Harrisburg; pres. Nat. Fedn. Dem. Women, 1987-89; mem. exec. com. Dem. Nat. Com., 1987-89; candidate U.S. Congress, 5th Dist., 1995-96; rep. Nat. Dem. Inst. for Internat. Affairs, 1997—; rep. to Yemen, 1997. Granted U.S. Patent on hair spray face shield 1995. Named Woman of Yr. Pa. Fedn. dem. Women, 1982, Centre County Living Legend, 2000. Mem.: Gov. Rendells's Transition Team on Agr. (Pa. office 2003). Methodist.

RUDY, SANDRA ROBERSON, photographer; b. Amarillo, Tex., Dec. 26, 1941; d. Deward Belmont and Tiny Lee (Springer) Roberson; m. Steven Jay Rudy, July 27, 1974. BA, Baylor U., 1964, MA, 1968. Cert. tchr. Tex. Tchr. Lubbock (Tex.) Pub. Schs., 1964—69, Clear Creek Pub. Schs., Clear Lake, Tex., 1969—72, Houston Ind. Sch. Dist., 1972—76; mktg. dir. Creative Restoration, Houston, 1976—79; owner, dir. S. Rudy Gallery, Santa Fe; photographer, designer S. Rudy Photography, Santa Fe, 1984—87, Crested Butte, Colo., 1988—2001, Alcalde, N.Mex., 2002—. Editor: Los Descansos, 2002; photographer, book artist: The Color Red, 2003. Pres. Crested Butte (Colo.) Ctr. for the Arts, 1990—93; bd. mem. Santa Fe Festival of the Arts, 1982—85, Crested Butte Soc. for the Arts, 1998—2001. Mem.: Vecinos del Rio. Avocations: gardening, reading, piano.

RUDZIK, MARCIA ANN, music educator; b. Booneville, Miss., May 21, 1947; d. Charles Howard Shackelford and Bama Sue Rowland; m. Francis John Rudzik, Aug. 18, 1972; 1 child, Sara Elizabeth. MusB, Union U., 1969; MA, George Peabody Coll., 1972; student in Orff Tng., U. South Fla. Tchr. East End Elem. Sch., Humboldt, Tenn., 1969—70, St. Mark's Episc. Day Sch., Cocoa, Fla., 1972—74, Sunwood Acad., Merritt Island, Fla., 1981—86, Spring Grove Acad., Titusville, Fla., 1987—90; youth min. St.Gabriel's Episc. ch., Titusville, 1990—93; dir. Before/After Sch. Program Child Care Assn., Cocoa, 1993—97; tchr. music St. Mark's Acad., Cocoa, 1997—. Organist St. Luke's Episc. Ch., Merritt Island, 1975—87; choir dir., organist St. Gabriel's Episc. Ch., Titusville, 1997—, handbell choir dir., 1998—. Vol. Canaveral Nat. Seashore, Cape Canaveral, Fla., 1993—95; accompanist Titusville (Fla.) Playhouse, 1993—98. Mem.: Music Educators Nat. Conf., Ctrl. Fla. Orff Chpt., Chi Omega Space Coast Alumnae. Democrat. Episc. Avocations: quilting, reading, music, hiking, bicycling. Home: 4241 Longbow Dr Titusville FL 32796 Office: St Marks Acad 2 Church St Cocoa FL 32922

RUECKER, MARTHA ENGELS, retired special education educator; b. South Gate, Calif., Sept. 22, 1931; d. Eugene and Minna (Wilhelm) Engels; m. Gert Frank Ruecker, Aug. 10, 1959 (div. 1964); 1 child, Ann. MusB, U. So. Calif., 1954, Calif. tchr. credential, 1955. Cert. tchr. for non-English speaking students, Calif. Tchr. educationally handicapped Downey (Calif.) Unified Schs., 1964-92; tchr. 2d grade Lynwood (Calif.) Unified Schs., 1992-97, 1997—2001. Recipient award for work with mentally gifted Johns Hopkins U., 1992; South Gate Kiwanis scholar U. So. Calif., 1949-54. Mem. NEA (life), Los Angeles County Art Mus. Republican. Methodist. Avocations: interior design, gardening, music, travel. Home: PO Box 630 Downey CA 90241-0630

RUEDA, DEBORAH JEAN, music educator; b. Tulsa, Okla., June 24, 1956; d. Charles Wallace and Veda Ruth Harmon; m. Carlos R. Rueda, July 19, 2000; children: Jason Charles Yeargin, Megan Elizabeth Yeargin. Bof Music Edn., Okla. State U., Stillwater, 1978. Tchr. Pub. Sch., Okla., 1981—98, 1998—. Moderator Internat. Baccelaurate, Colorado Springs, 2001—; corrective reading instr.; contest and honor choir judge. Dir. music, Okla., 1998—. Republican. Assembly Of God. Avocations: music, travel, cooking, religious studies. Office: North Mid Sch 612 E Yampa Colorado Springs CO 80903 Office Phone: 719-328-2476. Office Fax: 719-448-0268. Personal E-mail: mamamusic1@aol.com. Business E-Mail: ruedadj@d11.org.

RUELLAN, ANDREE, artist; b. N.Y.C., Apr. 6, 1905; d. André and Louise (Lambert) R.; m. John W. Taylor, May 28, 1929. Student, Art Students League, 1920-22; art schs., France and Italy. Guest instr. Pa. State Coll., summer 1957 One-man shows include Paris, 1925, Weyhe Galleries, N.Y.C., 1928, 31, Maynard Walker Galleries, 1937, 40, Kraushaar Galleries, 1945, 52, 56, 63, 80-81, Phila. Art Alliance, 1955, S.I. Mus., 1958, nat. exhbns., Carnegie Inst., Whitney Mus., Art Inst. Chgo., Corcoran Gallery, Internat. Expn., San Francisco, Artists for Victory Exhbn., N.Y.C., other cities U.S.; retrospective exhbns., Storm King Art Ctr., Mountainville, N.Y., 1966, Lehigh U., 1965, Woodstock Artists Assn., 1977, Ga. Mus. of Art, 1993, Hyde Collection, Glens Falls, N.Y., 1993, Gibbs Mus of Art, Charleston, S.C., 1993, Prints Gallery at Parkbest, Kingston, N.Y., 1995; drawing retrospective Kaushaar Galleries, 1990, 93, Ga. Mus. Art, Athens, 1993, The Hyde Collection, Glen Falls, N.Y., 1993, Gibbs Mus. Art, Charleston, S.C., 1993, Butler Inst., 1996, Grolier Club, 1996-97; executed murals in Emporia, Va., Lawrenceville, Ga.; represented in permanent collections at Met. Mus. Art, Whitney Mus. Am. Art, N.Y.C., Fogg Mus., Harvard U., Phila. Mus., Storm King Art Ctr., William Rockhill Nelson Mus., Kansas City, Mo., Duncan Phillips Gallery, Washington, Springfield Mus., Norton Gallery, Art Mus., New Britain, Conn., Libr. of Congress, Ency. Brit., IBM Collections, Art Inst., Zanesville, Ohio, U. Ga., S.I. Mus., Butler Inst., Pa. State U., Lehigh U., Columbia (S.C.) Mus. Art, The Whatcom Mus., Washington, Springville (Utah) Mus. Art, S.C. State Mus., Wichita Art Mus., Telfair Mus., Savannah, Ga., drawing retrospective Butler Inst. Am. Art, 1996; also numerous pvt. collections. Recipient 3d prize for painting Charleston Worcester Mus. Biennial, Jan. 1938; 1,000 grant in arts Am. Acad. and Inst. Arts and Letters, 1945; Pennell medal Pa. Acad., 1945; medal of Honor and purchase Pepsi-Cola Paintings of Year, 1948; Dawson Meml. medal Pa. Acad., 1950; Purchase award N.Y. State Fair, 1951; Drawing award Ball State Tchrs. Coll.; Guggenheim fellow, 1950-51; recipient Kuniyoshi award, 1994. Mem. Woodstock Artists Assn. (Sally Jacobs award 1981), Art Students League (life), Nat. Mus. Women in Arts Home: 54 Garrison Rd Bearsville NY 12409-9510

RUESINK, LINDA JOAN, music educator; b. Milw., Dec. 28, 1963; d. Edward Ronald Hallisch and Rosita Panetti; m. Mitchell Kevin Ruesink, July 9, 1988; 1 child, Samuel Phillip. MusB, U. Wis., Whitewater, 1987, EdM in Profl. Devel., 1994. Cert. Music Edn. Ec-12, Vocal Music Ec-12 State Wis., 1987, Adaptive Edn. State Wis., 1994. Music tchr. St. Jerome Sch., Oconomowoc, Wis., 1987—88, Watertown (Wis.) Unified Sch. Dist., 1988—. Author: (booklet series) I Can Read Music, 1999; composer: The Shepherd, 1994, Reflections, 1996, Solace, 1996, Asleep in Jesus, 2000. Mem.: Watertown Concert Assn., Watertown Mcpl. Band, Wis. Music Educators' Assn., Music Educators' Nat. Conf. Avocations: music, reading, gardening, swimming, walking. Home: 875 Briar Ct Watertown WI 53094 Office: Watertown Unified Sch Dist 111 Dodge St Watertown WI 53094

RUFF, CHERYL ANDERSON, health facility administrator; BS, U. S.C., 1981. Intern U. S.C. Sch. Pharmacy, 1978-81; sr. student extern, relief pharmacist, cons., clin. ptnr. John Nates Pharmacy, Columbia, S.C., 1981-96; office coord., mgr., co-owner, clin. office-base pharmacist John M. Woodward M.D., Columbia, 1983-94; staff pharmacist S.C. Dept. Mental Health/Bryan Psychiat. Hosp., Columbia, 1994; dir. pharmacy D.T.E.C., Inc., Germantown, Tenn., 1994-96, Charter Rivers Behavioral Health Sys., West Columbia, S.C., 1994-96; cons. pharmacist Luth. Svcs., White Rock, S.C., 1996; adminstr., chief drug inspector S.C. Dept. Labor, Licensing and Regulation Bd. Pharmacy, Columbia, 1996—; assoc. prof. Sch. Pharmacy U. S.C. Mem. pharmacy adv. com. Midlands Tech. Coll. Active St. Joseph's

Cath. Ch., Crayton Mid. Sch. PTO. Mem. Nat. Assn. Bds. Pharmacy Bd. (multi-state pharmacy jurisprudence examination program, item writer, examiner, com. on constn. and bylaws 1998), S.C. Pharm. Assn., 5th Dist. Pharm. Assn., S.C. Soc. Health Care Pharmacists, Med. Reps. Columbia. Address: PO Box 11927 Columbia SC 29211-1927

RUFF, L. CANDY, state legislator; m. Gregory W. Ruff. Student, U. Kans. Rep. dist. 40 State of Kans., 1993—. Democrat. Home: 321 Arch St Leavenworth KS 66048-3421 Office: Kans Ho of Reps State Capitol Topeka KS 66612

RUFFALO, MARIA THERESE, secondary school educator; b. Seattle, Feb. 26, 1963; d. Patrick and Helen (Eckhardt) R.; m. Joseph Patrick Otterbine, May 5, 1987. BS in Mech. Engring., U. Rochester, 1985. Proj. engr. Polycast Tech. Corp., Hackensack, N.J., 1985-86, sr. project engr., 1986-87, cons., 1987; project engr. ink divsn. J.M. Huber Corp., Edison, N.J., 1987-89; sr. engr. Himont USA, Inc., East Brunswick, N.J., 1990-93; engring. team leader Anchor Glass Container, Cliffwood, N.J., 1993-95; real estate developer, 1995—2001; tchr. math. Lacey Twp. H.S., NJ, 2002—. Avocations: reading, women's issues. Home: 11 Penn Pl Forked River NJ 08731

RUFFENACH, ROSEMARY ANNE, English and writing educator; d. Peter Joseph Ruffenach and Mary Catherine Polson Ruffenach; m. John James Sommerville (div. 1987); children: Patrick Michael, Mary Jane, Robert Sommerville. MA in English, Northwestern U., 1969; BS in Edn., U. Minn., 1968, EdD in Ednl. Adminstrn., 1979; MA in Theology, U. St. Thomas, 1994. Cert. tchr. secondary lang. arts Minn. Mayoral aide Mpls. Office of Mayor, 1983; com. adminstr. Minn. Ho. of Reps., St. Paul, 1985—87; lobbyist New Brighton, Minn., 1988—96; coord. West Metro Edn. Program, Edina, Minn., 1996—2000; writer, editor, co-owner Many Arts Collaborative, St. Paul, 2000—; instr. English Ind. Sch. Dist. # 287, Plymouth, Minn., 2002—; writing instr. Anoka-Ramsey C.C., Coon Rapids, Minn., 2003—. Co-chair strategic planning com. St. Francis Cabrini Comty., Mpls., 2002—03. Contbr. essay to book Voices for the Land, 2002 (Minn. Book award, 2003), essay to web publ. Voices for the City, 2003, editl. to newspaper Camden News, 1990 (Best Editl. in Neighborhood Newspaper). Commr. City Planning Commn., Mpls., 1980—83, campaign coord. Mpls. Sch. Bd. candidate, 1993—94; active Minn. Acad. Excellence Found., St. Paul, 1985—86. Recipient Disting. Svc. award, Archdiocese of St. Paul/Mpls., 1986, Resolution of Appreciation, City of Mpls., 1983, study fellowship, U. St. Thomas, 1991—93, rsch. grant, Dept. Edn. Minn., 1978. Mem.: Archdiocesan Com. on Intimacy Violence and Abuse, Profl. Editor's Network. Democrat. Roman Catholic. Avocation: watercolor and oil painting. Home: 120 Juno Ave Saint Paul MN 55116 Office: Prairie Ctr Alternative Sch 9955 W 69th St Eden Prairie MN 55344 E-mail: r.ruffenach@att.net.

RUFFER, JOYCE SELLARS, poet, artist; b. Cairo, Ga. children: Charles Scott Mason, Jeffrey Dewayne Mason. Artist, all mediums. Author: (poetry) Rose Moon. Named Best Poet 1994, Nat. Libr. Poetry, Poet of Yr., Internat. Soc. Poets, 1996; recipient Editor's Choice award Nat. Libr. Poetry, Poetic Achievement award, Am. Poetry Soc. Avocations: spiritual enhancement, birding, nature photography, marine ecology, feline appreciation. Home: Sea Lily 2426 Maher Ave Crescent City CA 95531-9137 Fax: 707 464-7557. E-mail: Jpolli@cc.northcoast.com.

RUFFING, ANNE ELIZABETH, artist; b. Bklyn. d. John Paul and Ruth Elizabeth (Price) Frampton; m. George W. Ruffing, Mar. 29, 1967; 1 dau., Elizabeth Anne. BS, Cornell U., 1964; postgrad., Drexel Inst. Tech., 1966. One-woman exhbns. include, IBM, 1966, Hall of Fame, Goshen, N.Y., 1971, group exhbns. include, Internat. Women's Arts Festival, World Trade Center, N.Y.C., 1975-76, Berkshire Mus., Pittsfield, Mass., 1965, 76, Cooperstown (N.Y.) Mus., 1969; represented in permanent collections, Met. Mus. Art, Bklyn. Mus., Library of Congress, Harvard U., Smithsonian Instn., N.Y. Hist. Soc. Johnston Hist. Mus., Atwater Kent Mus., Albany Inst. History and Art, Whitney Mus. Am. Art, Boston Public Library. Recipient 1st place Eric Sloane award, 1974; Internat. Women's Year award Internat. Women's Art Festival, 1976 Address: 1031 Lewis Farm Rd Zebulon NC 27597

RUFFING, EILEEN MARY, elementary school educator, music educator; b. Sandusky, Ohio, Nov. 8, 1955; d. Francis A. and Evelyn A. Ruffing. B of Mus. Edn., Bowling Green State U., 1978, M of Music Edn., 1983. Cert. permanent tchg. cert. Ohio. Elem. music tchr. K-6 Highland Local Schs., Sparta, Ohio, 1978—81; tchg. asst. instrumental music Bowling Green State U., 1981—83; tchr. instrumental music 5-8 St. Patrick of Heatherdowns, Toledo, 1981—83; tchr. instrumental music 5-12 Highland Local Schs., Sparta, 1983—. Lead mentor tchr. Highland Local Schs., Sparta, 2001—; music camp instr. Wooster (Ohio) Music Camp, 2002—; performing mem. clarinetist Mt. Vernon (Ohio) U. Wind Ensemble, 1993—. Bldg. rep. Highland Edn. Assn., Sparta, 1998—2000; local profl. devel. com. Highland Local Schs., Sparta, 1998—2001. Mem.: Am. Sch. Band Dirs. Assn., Music Educators Nat. Conf., Ohio Music Edn. Assn. (adjudicator 2001—, dist. sec.-treas. 1992—2002). Roman Catholic. Avocations: cross stitch, reading, baking, baseball, attending concerts and theater. Home: 1103 A Beech St Mount Vernon OH 43050 Office: Highland Mid Sch PO Box 68 1250 Township Rd 16 Sparta OH 43350

RUFFING, JANET KATHRYN, spirituality educator; b. Spokane, Wash., July 17, 1945; d. George Benjamin and Dorothy Edith (Folsom) R. BA, Russell Coll., 1968; M of Applied Spirituality, U. San Francisco, 1978; lic. in Sacred Theology, Jesuit Sch. Theology, 1984; PhD in Christian Spirituality, Grad. Theol. Union, 1986. Joined Sisters of Mercy Congregation, Roman Cath. Ch., 1963. Tchr. reading and English Mercy High Sch., Burlingame, Calif., 1968-72, 75-77, San Francisco, 1972-75; tchr., dept. head Marian High Sch., San Diego, 1978-80; faculty and originating team mem. Fully Alive, Burlingame, 1980-86; faculty, facilitator Permanent Diaconate Formation Program, Oakland, Calif., 1984-86; faculty Internship in Art of Spiritual Direction, Burlingame, 1984, 85, 87; prof. spirituality and spiritual direction Fordham U., Bronx, NY, 1986—, prof., 2000—. Spkr. Villanova Theol. Inst., 1995, Roger Williams Symposium, Pullman, Wash., 1985; vis. faculty Australian Cath. U., Brisbane, summer 1994, San Francisco Theol. Sem., summer 1993, U. San Francisco, summer 1991, St. Michael's Coll., Vt., summer 1990, Fordham at Limerick, Ireland, 1996-97, Colston Symposium, Bristol, Eng., 2000, San Francisco Theol. Sem., 2001, Gettysburg Luth. Sem., 2001, Inner Sabbath, Leuven, Belgium, 2002; Holy Wisdom lectr. Washington Theol. Union, 2003; presenter in field. Author: Uncovering Stories of Faith, 1989, Spiritual Direction: Beyond the Beginnings, 2000; contbg. author, editor: Mysticism and Social Transformation, 2001; assoc. editor The Way; contbr. articles to profl. jours. Mem. Cath. Theol. Soc. Am. (seminar moderator 1987-90), Am. Acad. Religion (chairperson mysticism group 1994-98), Mercy Assn. in Scripture and Theology (treas. 1987-96, mem. editorial bd. MAST jour.), Spiritual Dirs. Internat. (founding coord. com. mem. 1990-93, coord. of regions 1990-93), Women's Ordination Conf. Democrat. Avocations: cooking, hiking, swimming. Office: Fordham U Grad Sch Religion and Religious Bronx NY 10458

RUGEN, KAREN, manufacturing executive, corporate communications specialist; Head corp. comms. Hyatt Hotels Corp., 1978—94; chief comm. officer Boston Chicken Co., Boston, 1994—98; sr. v.p. corp. comms. and pub. affairs Rite Aid Corp., Camp Hill, Pa., 1999—. Office: Rite Aid Corp 30 Hunter Ln Camp Hill PA 17011

RUGERS, TATIANA YURIEVNA, computer programmer, consultant; b. Kr. Gorodischi, USSR, Nov. 17, 1954; came to U.S., 1994. d. Yuriy Alexandrovich and Claudia Dmitrievna (Diagileva) Scherbakov; m. Michael Alan Rugers, Sept. 11, 1994; 1 child, Anthony. M in Computer Engring. and Maths., U. Power Engring., Moscow, 1977. Software engr. Ctrl. Aero-Hydra-Dynamic Inst., Moscow, 1977-82; sr. software engr. Moscow Inst. Computer Scis., 1982-86, Chasprom, Moscow, 1986-89; head computer dept. Moscow Pub. Schs., 1989-94; computer programmer, cons. Decision Cons. Inc., Tampa, 1995-96, Structured Logic, Atlanta, 1996-97, Career Concepts Techs. Inc., Winter Park, Fla., 1997—. Contbr. articles to profl. jours. Avocations: fine wine, travel, theater, literature, fitness. Home: 2507 W Morrison Ave Tampa FL 33629-5328

RUHL, MARY B. lawyer; BA, Wilson Coll., 1971; MA, U. Wis., 1973, JD, 1977. Bar: Calif. 1977, Wis. 1977. With Latham & Watkins, L.A., 1977—, ptnr. Mem.: Wis. State Bar Assn., Calif. State Bar Assn. Office: Latham and Watkins LLP 633 W Fifth St Ste 4000 Los Angeles CA 90071*

RUIZ, COOKIE, performing company executive; BA in English, Spanish, Wright St. U., Dayton, Ohio. Cert. Fund Raising Executive, 2002. Pres. Jr. League, Austin, Tex.; dir. fund devel. Ballet Austin, 1996-97, gen. mgr., 1997—99, exec. dir., 1999—. Recipient American Red Cross Clara Barton Medal of Honor. Mem.: bd. Austin Convention & Visitors Bureau, Assoc. of Fundraising Professionals, bd. trustees, Dance USA. Office: Ballet Austin 3002 Guadalupe St Austin TX 78705-2818*

RUIZ, MICHELE, newscaster; Anchor, reporter KTLA, Los Angeles, 1991—98; gen. assignment reporter NBC4, Los Angeles, 1998—99, co-anchor, Channel 4 News at 6, 1999—. Recipient LA Press Club Award, 2002, Local Emmy Award, 2003. Mem.: Nat. Assn. of Hispanic Journalists, Radio TV News Dirs. Assn., Investigative Reports and Editors Inc. Office: NBC4 3000 W Alameda Ave Burbank CA 91523*

RUIZ, MICHELE ILENE, lawyer; b. Washington, Nov. 3, 1969; BS, Cornell U., 1991; JD, U. Chgo., 1994. Bar: U.S. Dist. Ct. (no. dist.) Ill. 1994. Assoc. McDermott, Will & Emery, Chgo., 1994—96; ptnr. Sidley Austin Brown & Wood, LLP, Chgo., 1996—. Office: Sidley Austin Brown & Wood LLP Bank One Plz 10 S Dearborn Chicago IL 60603 E-mail: mruiz@sidley.com.

RUIZ, VANESSA, federal judge; b. San Juan, P.R., Mar. 22, 1950; d. Fernando and Irma (Bosch) Ruiz-Suria; married; m. David E. Birenbaum, Oct. 22, 1983; stepchildren: Tracy, Matthew. BA, Wellesley Coll., 1972; JD, Georgetown U., 1975. Bar: D.C. 1972. Assoc. Fried, Frank, Harris, Shrives & Kampelman, Washington, 1975—83; sr. mgr., counsel Sears World Trade Inc., Washington, 1983—87; founding ptnr. Sloan, Lehner & Ruiz, Washington, 1987—89; ptnr. Pepper, Hamilton & Scheetz, Washington, 1989—91; dep. corporation counsel, legal counsel div. D.C., Washington, 1991—93, prin. dep. corporation counsel, 1993—94, corporation counsel, 1994; assoc. judge D.C. Ct. of Appeals, Washington, 1994— . Spkr. in field. Recipient Judge of the Year award, Hispanic Bar Assoc., 2001. Mem.: ABA, Inter-Am. Bar Assn. Office: DC Ct of Appeals 500 Indiana Ave NW Fl 6 Washington DC 20001-2131*

RUIZ, VICKI LYNN, history educator; b. Atlanta, May 21, 1955; d. Robert Paul and Erminia Pablita (Ruiz) Mercer; m. Jerry Joseph Ruiz, Sept. 1, 1979 (div. Jan. 1990); children: Miguel, Daniel; m. Victor Becerra, Aug. 14, 1992. AS in Social Studies, Gulf Coast Community Coll., 1975; BA in Social Sci., Fla. State, 1977; MA in History, Stanford U., 1978, PhD in History, 1982. Asst. prof. U. Tex., El Paso, 1982-85, U. Calif., Davis, 1985-87, assoc. prof., 1987-92; Andrew W. Mellon prof. Claremont (Calif.) Grad. Sch., 1992-95, chmn. history dept., 1993-95; prof. history Ariz. State U., Tempe, 1995—, chair dept. Chicano studies, 1997—. Dir. Inst. of Oral History, U. Tex., El Paso, 1983-85, minority undergrad. rsch. program U. Calif., Davis, 1988-92. Author: Cannery Women, Cannery Lives, 1987, From Out of the Shadows, 1998 (Choice Outstanding Book of 1998); editor: Chicana Politics of Work and Family, 2000; co-editor: Women on U.S.-Mexican Border, 1987, Western Women, 1988, Unequal Sisters, 1990, 3d edit., 1999. Mem. Calif. Coun. for Humanities, 1990-94, vice chmn., 1991-93. Fellow Univ. Calif. Davis Humanities Inst., 1990-91, Am. Coun. of Learned Socs., 1986, Danforth Found., 1977. Mem. Orgn. Am. Historians (chmn. com. on status of minority history 1989-91, nominating com. 1987-88, exec. bd. 1995-98), Immigration History Soc. (exec. bd. 1989-91), Am. Hist. Assn. (nat. coun. 1999—), Am. Studies Assn. (nominating bd. 1992-94, nat. coun. 1996-99), Western History (nominating bd. 1993-95). Democrat. Roman Catholic. Avocations: walking, needlework. Office: Ariz State U History Dept Tempe AZ 85287

RUIZ-VALERA, PHOEBE LUCILE, law librarian; b. Barranquilla, Colombia, Jan. 27, 1950; d. Ramon and Marion (Mehlman) Ruiz-Valera; m. Thomas Patrick Winkler, Mar. 27, 1981. BA cum laude, Westminster Coll., 1971; MLS, Rutgers U., 1974; MA, NYU, 1978. Libr. trainee Passaic (N.J.) Pub. Libr., 1973-74, reference libr., 1974; libr. assoc. cataloger NYU Law Libr., N.Y.C., 1974-79, asst. curator, cataloger, 1979-81; libr. III, cataloger Rutgers U. Libr., New Brunswick, N.J., 1981-82; chief cataloger Assn. Bar City N.Y., 1982-85, head tech. svcs., 1985-99; tech. svcs. libr. Cleary, Gottlieb, Steen and Hamilton, N.Y.C., 1999—. Mem. Am. Assn. Law Librs., Am. Translators Assn. (cert. translator English to Spanish), Law Libr. Assn. Greater N.Y., Reforma, Salalm. Democrat. Presbyterian. Office: 1 Liberty Plz Fl 43 New York NY 10006-1404 E-mail: pruiz-valera@cgsh.com.

RULE, MARY SHAND (MARY SHAND), artist, educator; b. Columbia, SC, Aug. 8, 1929; d. Gadsden Edwards and Mary Boykin (Heyward) Shand; m. Julian Cowden Rule, June 24, 1950 (dec. Mar. 1967); children: Robert Stafford, Gadsden Edward, Julia Rule Edelen. BS, U. S.C., 1950; postgrad., Stratford Coll., U. Va., 1964-66, Corcoran Sch. Art. Art tchr. Dormont Pub. Schs., Pitts., 1953-54, Arlington (Va.) Pub. Schs., 1966-87, art curriculum cons., 1987-91. Asst. tchr. vol. Freedom Hill Elem. Sch., Fairfax, Va., 1990-91, Rockhill Elem. Sch., Stafford, Va., 1996-98. One-woman shows include Spartanburg (SC) Arts Ctr., 1986; groups shows include Va. Mus., 1967, Studio 10, Washington, 1989, Metro Gallery, Arlington, Va., 1984, Ellipse Arts Ctr., 1994-95, 99, Abney Gallery, N.Y.C., 1996. Vol. worker Opera Theater No. Va., 1994—2003; bd. dirs. Opera Guild N.Va., chmn. children's opera poster contest, 1995—2003. Recipient Biennial award Corcoran Gallery, 1968, Best Painting award Kean Mason Gallery, 1981; honored by Arlington County Bd., 2000. Democrat. Episcopalian.

RUMFOLO, MARILU, financial analyst, non-profit corporation executive; b. Houston, July 19, 1953; d. Walter John and Lucille (Jones) R. Grad., Arrons Sch. Real Estate, 1978; student, U. Houston, 1979. Lic. real estate agt. Jr. acct. Gen. Leisure Corp., Houston, 1973-75; security cons. Burns Internat. Security, Houston, 1975-77; founder, dir. govt. affairs Time Energy Systems, Inc., Houston, 1977-83; founder, exec. dir., chmn. bd. trustees The Children's Drug Abuse Network, Houston, 1983—; founder, pres. Sun Am. Fin., LLC, 2000; general securities, principal, pres. founder Rumfolo & Assocs., Securities, LP, 2000—; founder, pres. Tex. Capital Securities, LLC, 2002. Bd. dirs. Eliza Johnston Home for Aging, Houston, 1981-82; chmn. bd. Citizens United for Pub. Edn., Houston, 1980-82; candidate city council, Houston, 1981, 83; team capt. Am. Heart Assn. Houston, 1982. Recipient Drugbuster award Children's Drug Abuse Network, 1985; honoree ann. appreciation breakfast for outstanding work in community, County Commr. Houston, 1986; named Rep. of Yr., Tex., 2001. Mem.: Order Eastern Star (officer 1986-87). Republican. Avocations: swimming, reading, writing poetry, walking. Office: Rumfolo & Assocs Securities LP 4708 Tamarisk Bellaire TX 77401

RUMP, MARJORIE, library director; b. St. Joseph, Mo., Jan. 19, 1919; d. Edward August and Adeline Amelia Gummig; m. John S. Rump, July 25, 1943 (dec. Sept. 29, 1996); children: Jack, Susan, Marilyn. BA, U. Redlands, 1941; MLS, U.So. Calif., L.A., 1957. Book buyer Sierra Book Store, Bakersfield, Calif., 1953—66; libr. Kern County Libr., Bakersfield, 1961—66, Ea. Bakersfield H.S., Bakersfield, 1966—68; from br. supr. to dep. dir. Kern County Libr., 1968—88, dep. dir., 1988—2001. Mem. adv. bd. Kern County Cmty. Found., Bakersfield, 1995—; trustee Conf. of Calif. Hist. Socs. Trust, Stockton, Calif., 1998—; mem. Rocky Hts. LLC, 2001—, Easter Hill Assn., 1996. Editor: Inside Historic Kern, 1982; contbr. articles California Historian, 1997. Recipient Citizen's Recognition award, City of Bakersfield, 1983, Jubilee medallion, U. Redlands, 1984, Soroptimist Woman of Distinction award, Soroptimist Internat., 1990. Mem.: Am. Soc. Pub. Adminstrs. (pres. 1980, Doubenmeir award for Pub. Adminstrn. 1979), Kern County Hist. Soc. (pres. 1981), Soroptimist Internat. Bakersfield (pres. 1978—79, Soroptimist Woman of Distinction award 1990), Greater Bakersfield C. of C., Wakayama Sister City (treas. 1984—94). Presbyterian. Avocations: gardening, travel. Home: 3000 Elmwood Bakersfield CA 93305

RUMRILL ZULLO, PATRICIA ROBBIN, music educator; b. Gloversville, June 18, 1951; d. Robert Ellsworth and Elsie Patricia Rumrill; children: Amanda Jane, Molly Ann. MusB in Edn., SUNY, Potsdam, 1973; M of Music Edn., Temple U., 1975. Cert. tchr. music (permanent) N.Y. Tchr. elem. vocal music Greater Johnstown Sch. Dist., Gloversville, NY, 1976—; music dir. summer children's prodn. Glove Theater, Gloversville, 1998—; vocal music adjudicator N.Y. State SMA, 1999—. Chairperson music dept. Greater Johnstown Sch. Dist., 2000—. Actor: (theatrical prodns.) Mame; dir.: (plays) Alice in Wonderland; actor: (theatrical prodns.) Nine, Fiddler on the Roof, Music Man; dir.: (plays) Peter Pan, Beauty and the Beast, Mary Poppins; asst. music dir.: plays Wizard of Oz. Music dir., musician, sch. dist. devel. programs, Fulton County First Night Com., Gloversville and Johnstown, 1975. Mem.: Fulton County Music Educators Assn. (assoc.; historian 1999). Liberal. Methodist. Home: 184 First Ave Gloversville NY 12078 Office: Greater Johnstown Sch Dist Wright Dr Johnstown NY 12095 Personal E-mail: patriciarz@hotmail.com.

RUNBECK, LINDA C. state legislator; b. June 11, 1946; m. Richard Runbeck; 1 child. BA, Bethel Coll., 1968. Former mem. Minn. Ho. of Reps., St. Paul; mem. various coms.; U.S. senator from Minn., 1993—. Mem. govt. ops. and reform com., mem. jobs, eneregy and cmty. devel com., others; advt. exec. Mem. League Women's Voters. Home: 48 E Golden Lake Rd Circle Pines MN 55014-1725 Office: Minn State Senate State Capitol Building Saint Paul MN 55155-0001

RUNDIO, JOAN PETERS (JO RUNDIO), public administrator; b. Dearborn, Mich., Mar. 17, 1941; d. Joe and Donna (Sells) Peters; m. Florian (Pug) Frank Rundio Jr., Sept. 8., 1971; children: Jeffrey Daniel, David Eric. Diploma, Bronson Meth. Sch. Nursing, 1962; BA, U. Redlands, 1978; MPA, U. South Ala., 1987. RN, Mich. Emergency nurse Bronson Meth. Hosp., Kalamazoo, 1962-63, The Queen's Med. Ctr., Honolulu, 1963-65; orthopaedic nurse The Honolulu Med. Group, 1965-72; sch. nurse Corpus Christi (Tex.) Sch. Dist., 1979-81; pub. health nurse Tri-County Health Dept., Traverse City, Mich., 1983-85; adminstrv. intern City of Troy (Mich.), 1987-88; acting econ. devel. dir. City of Traverse City, 1988-89; mgr. personal health svcs. Tri-County Health Dept., Traverse City, 1989; asst. city mgr. City of Traverse City, 1990-98. Mediator Conflict Resolution Svc., 1998—, pres., 2000—02, exec. com., 2002—. V.p. Women's Econ. Devel. Orgn., Traverse City, 1993-95, mem., 1984-2002; mem. Traverse City Planning Commn., 1995-97; rep. Traverse City Schs. Adv. Com., 1982-85, 88-89; trustee Nat. Cherry Festival, 1996-98; bd. mem. Conflict Resolution Svc., 1999—. Recipient James H. Boyd award U. South Ala., Mobile, 1987. Mem. AAUW (sec. Traverse City br. 2000—02), NOW (founding mem. Meridian, Miss. chpt. 1973), Michigan City. Mgmt. Assn. (bd. dirs. 1996-98), Internat. City Mgmt. Assn., Cherryland Humane Soc., Pi Sigma Alpha. Avocations: travel, reading, canoeing, cross-country skiing.

RUNDLE, KATHERINE FERNANDEZ, state's attorney; b. Washington, 1951; BEd, U. Miami, Fla., 1973; MA, U. Cambridge, Eng., 1976. Asst. state's atty. Dade County, Miami, Fla., dep. chief, chief, state's atty. 11th Jud. Cir., 1993—. Office: Dade County 11th Judicial Cir 1350 NW 12th Ave Miami FL 33136-2102

RUNER, EVELYN ROSARIO, endocrinologist; b. Staten Island, NY, June 5, 1969; d. George and Evelyn (Yañez) R.. BS, Temple U., 1991; MD, Mt. Sinai Sch. Medicine, 1995. Diplomate Am. Bd. Internal Medicine. Resident in gen. surgery Robert Packer Hosp., Sayre, Pa., 1995—96, Waterbury (Conn.) Hosp., 1996—97; resident in internal medicine Lehigh Valley Hosp., Allentown, Pa., 1997—2000; fellow in endocrinology U. S.C., Columbia, 2000—02. Mem.: ACP, AMA, Women in Endocrinology, Am. Assn. Clin. Endocrinologists, Endocrine Soc., Am. Soc. Internal Medicine. Democrat. Roman Catholic. Avocations: martial arts, medical history, military history, science fiction, guitar. Office: Ctr for Women's Health 600 Fitch St Ste 203 Elmira NY 14905

RUNFOLA, SHEILA KAY, nurse, b. Canton, Ohio, Feb. 8, 1944; d. Benjamin and M. Suzanne (deBord) Suarez; m. Steven Joseph Runfola, Aug. 17, 1968; children: Michael, Janine, Christine; stepchildren: Stephanie Bufalini, Darlene Teran. BS in Nursing, St. John Coll. Cleve., 1966; teaching credential jr. coll. nursing, UCLA Ext., San Diego, 1973. RN, Calif.; cert. occupational health nurse, cert. pub. health nurse. Staff nurse emergency rm. Leland Meml. Hosp., Riverdale, Md., 1966-67; staff nurse/team leader med./surg. Mercy Hosp., San Diego, 1967-68; staff nurse, charge nurse emergency dept., dept. radiology U. Calif.-San Diego Med.Ctr., 1968-76; staff devel./asst. dir. nurses TLC Nursing Home, El Cajon, Calif., 1978-80; staff nurse/charge nurse emergency dept. Kaiser Permanente Hosp., San Diego, 1980-89, staff nurse emergency dept. Sacramento, Calif., 1989-90, house supr., 1992-94, case mgr. occupational medicine, 1995—; health svcs. nurse U.S. Automobile Assn., Sacramento, 1990-95. Contbr. articles to profl. jours. Leader Girls Scouts Am., San Diego and Sacramento, 1982-91, treas., local svc. team, 1986-89, 90; parent rep. Elk Grove (Calif.) Sch. Bd. for Elk Grove H.s., 1994, co-chair Sober Grad. Night, 1993-95. Mem. Sacramento Valley Occupational Health Nurses (v.p. 1992-95, sec. 1998—, election chair 1998), Newcomers Club, Calif. State Assn. Occupl. Health Nurse (bd. dirs. 1998—, newsletter editor). Democrat. Roman Catholic. Avocations: crafts (quilting), piano, reading, cooking, boating. Office: Kaiser Permanente Dept Occupl Med 6600 Bruceville Rd Sacramento CA 95823-4671 Home: 260 Tall Spruce Cir Brighton CO 80601-5356

RUNGE, KAY KRETSCHMAR, library director; b. Davenport, Iowa, Dec. 9, 1946; d. Alfred Edwin and Ina (Paul) Kretschmar; children: Peter Jr., Katherine. BS in History Edn., Iowa State U., 1969; MLS, U. Iowa, 1970. Pub. svc. libr. Anoka County Libr., Blaine, Minn., 1971-72; cataloger Augustana Coll., Rock Island, Ill., 1972-74; dir. Scott County Libr. Sys., Eldridge, Iowa, 1974-85, Davenport (Iowa) Pub. Libr., 1985—2001, Des Moines Pub. Libr., 2001—. V.p. Quad-Cities Conv. and Visitors Bur., 1992—97, Quad-Cities Grad. Study Ctr., 1992—2001, Downtown Davenport Devel. Corp., 1992—2000, Hall of Honor Bd., Davenport Ctrl. H.S., 1992—95, Brenton Bank Bd., 1995—2001, Wells Fargo Bank Bd., 2001; steering com. Quad-Cities Vision for the Future, 1987—91, Humanities Iowa, 1993—2000, chair, 1998—99; bd. govs. Iowa State U. Found., 1991—; citizens adv. coun. Iowa State U., 1998—2000, Leadership Iowa, 1998—99; adv. bd. U. Iowa Sch. Libr. Sci., 1999—, adj. prof., 2000—01; devel. bd. Iowa State U. Found., 2000—; mem. Greater Des Moines Leadership, 2002—03; bd. dirs. River Ctr. for Performing Arts, Davenport, 1983—97, Iowa State U. Rsch. Pk., 1998—2000, Quest Ednl. Corp.,

1999—2002, Hamilton/Kaplan U., 2002—, Davenport One, Downtown Devel., 2000—01; chmn. bd. dirs. Am. Inst. Commerce, 1989—98. Recipient Svc. Key award Iowa State U. Alumni Assn., 1979, ALA/ALTA Nat. Advocacy Honor Roll award, 2000; named Quad City Panhellenic Woman of Yr., 1998. Mem. ALA (chmn. libr. adminstrs. and mgrs. div., fundraising sect. 1988, bd. dirs., Exhibits Round Table 2003-), Iowa Libr. Assn. (pres. 1983, Mem. of Yr. award 2000), Pub. Libr. Assn. (bd. dirs. 1990-99, pres. 2000-01), Iowa Edn. Media Assn. (Intellectual Freedom award 1984), Alpha Delta Pi (alumni state pres. 1978). Lutheran. Office: Pub Libr of Des Moines 100 Locust St Des Moines IA 50309-1791

RUNNER, SHARON, state representative; m. George Runner; children: Micah, Rebekah. Student, Antelope Valley (Calif.) Coll. Dir. pub. rels. Desert Christian Schs., 2002—; realtor Red Carpet Real Estate Co.; owner Runner Group; mem. Calif. Assembly, 2002—. Del. Rep. Nat. Conv., 1996, 2000; chair heartwalk Am. Heart Assn.; dir. Antelpe Valley Crime Task Force; dir. gift found. Antelope Valley Hosp.; dir. Antelope Valley Vols., CareNet Pregnancy Resource Ctr. Antelope Valley, Friends in Action; dir. adv. coun. Healthy Homes; dir. bd. dirs. United Way. Mem.: Lancaster C. of C. (bd. dirs.). Reform. Baptist. Office: PO Box 942849 Rm 2174 Sacramento CA 95814 Address: 747 W Lancaster Blvd Lancaster CA 93534

RUNOLFSON, MARILYN DOLORES, special education educator; d. Frances (Baier) MacDonald, Margaretta MacDonald (Stepmother), Clifford MacDonald; m. Randall Runolfson, Aug. 8, 1981; children: Samuel, Simon, Shaina. BS in Elem. Edn., Weber State U., 1995; MEd in Spl. Edn., Utah State U., 2001. Cert. tchr. spl. edn. Utah State Office of Edn., 1995. Reading specialist Ogden (Utah) City Sch. Dist., 1996; spl. edn. tchr. Weber County Sch. Dist., Ogden, Utah, 1996—2002, mentor, cooperating tchr., behavior specialist, 2000—03, spl. edn. coord., 2003—. Mem mentor and induction com. Weber County Sch. Dist., Ogden, Utah, 2002—; mem. mentor and induction com. Utah Signal Project, Mentor and Induction Com., Salt Lake City, 2002—; presenter in field. Author: A Mentor's Handbook, (calendar) The Art and Soul of Tching.: A Weekly Calendar for New Spl. Edn. Tchrs., 2003. Mem.: Coun. for Exceptional Children. Roman Catholic. Avocations: reading, gardening, needlework. Office: Weber School District 5320 S Adams Avenue Ogden UT 84405 E-mail: mrunolfson@weber.k12.ut.us.

RUNQUIST, LISA A. lawyer; b. Mpls., Sept. 22, 1952; d. Ralf E. and Violet R. BA, Hamline U., 1973; JD, U. Minn., 1976. Bar: Minn. 1977, Calif. 1978, U.S. Dist. Ct. (ctrl. dist.) Calif. 1985, U.S. Supreme Ct. 1995. Assoc. Caldwell & Toms, L.A., 1978-82; ptnr. Runquist & Flagg, L.A., 1982-85; pvt. practice Runquist & Assocs., L.A., 1985-99, Runquist & Zyback LLP, L.A., 1999—. Mem. adv. bd. Exempt Orgn. Tax Rev., 1990—, Calif. State U. L.A. Continuing Edn. Acctg. and Tax Program, 1995—. Mem. editl. bd. Bus. Law Today, 1994—2002. Mem. ABA Bus. Law Today, (bus. law sect.com. on nonprofit corps. 1986—, chair 1991-95, coun. mem. 1995-99, subcom. current devels. in nonprofit corp. law 1989—, chair 1989-91, subcom. rels. orgns. 1989—, chair 1987-91, 95-98, subcom. legal guidebook for dirs. 1986—, ad hoc com. on info. tech., 1997—, chair 1997-98, co-chair, 1998—2002, sect. liaison to ABA tech. coun. 1997-2000, subcom. model nonprofit corp. act, partnerships and unincorp. bus. orgns. com. 1987—, state regulation of securities com. 1988-99, corp. laws com. 1999-, subcom. guidebook for dirs. of closely held corps. chair 2000—, sec. of taxation exempt orgns. com. 1987—, tax), Calif. Bar Assn. (bus. law sect., nonprofit and unincorp. orgns. com. 1985-92, 93-96, 97—, chair 1989-91), Christian Legal Soc., Ctr. Law and Religious Freedom, Christian Mgmt. Assn. (dir. 1983-89). Office: 10821 Huston St North Hollywood CA 91601 E-mail: lisa@runquist.com.

RUNTE, ROSEANN, academic administrator; b. Kingston, N.Y., Jan. 31, 1948; arrived in Can., 1971, naturalized, 1983; d. Robert B. and Anna Loretta (Schorkopf) O'Reilly; m. Hans-Rainer Runte, Aug. 9, 1969. BA summa cum laude, SUNY, New Paltz, 1968; MA, U. Kans., 1969, PhD, 1974; DLitt (hon.), Acadia U., 1989, Meml. U., 1990, U. Vest Timisoara, 1996, U. Arad, 2001; Assoc. (hon.), Moraine Valley C.C., 2003. Lectr. Bethany Coll., W.Va., 1970—71; lectr. adult studies St. Mary's U., Halifax, Canada, 1971—72; from lectr. to assoc. prof. Dalhousie U., Halifax, Canada, 1972—83, asst. dean, 1980—82, chmn. dept. French, 1980—83; pres. U. Sainte-Anne, Pointe-de-l'Eglise, Canada, 1983—88; prin. Glendon Coll., Toronto, Canada, 1988—94; pres. Victoria U., 1994—2001, Old Dominion U., 2001—. Bd. dirs. Banque Nationale, Va. Advanced Carrier and Shipbldg. Integration Ctr. Author: Brumes Bleues, 1982, Faux-Soleils, 1984, Birmanie Blues, 1993; editor: Studies in 18th Century Culture, vols. VII, VIII, IX, 1977—79, A Canadian in Love, 2000, The Passionate Mind, 2000; lit. rev. editor: French Rev., 1988—94; editor: Lit. Rsch., 1994—97; co-editor: Man and Nature, 1982, Le Development Regional, 1986—87, From Orality to Literature, 1991, Lectures Canadiennes, 1993, Visions of Beauty, 1995, The Foundation for International Training: 25 Years of International Development, 2001; co-translator: Local Development, 1987; mem. editl. bd. Purdue Romance Lang. Series, 2001—. V.p. Can. commn. UNESCO, 1991—92, pres., 1992—96; vice-chair exec. bd. Found. for Internat. Tng., 1994—95, chair bd., 1995—2000; internat. adv. bd. Expo 2000, 1995—2000; v.p. Assn. Internat. des études québecoises, 1999—2001; mem. Internat. Women's Forum, 1998—; chair comm. internat. edn. Am. Coun. on Edn., 2004—; chair accreditation com. visit NCAA, 2004—; commr. Southeastern Accreditation Commn., 2004—; chair Gottschalk Prize Com., 1994; chair publs. com. Hannah Found., 1989—92; vice-chair bd. Gardiner Mus., 1994—2001; mem. Commn. Langs. Instrn., Ontario, Canada, 1999—2001; chair prix du salon Livre Com., 1998; hon. life mem. UNESCO, 2003; bd. dirs. Assn. Med. Svcs., 1989—92; adv. bd. Nat. Libr., 1984—91; bd. dirs. Urban League, United Way. Decorated Order of Can., Ordre du Mérite France, Order Acad. Palmes; recipient Fr. Coppée award, French Acad., 1989, Queen Elizabeth Jubilee medal, 2002, Zonta award, 2004; Regents scholar, SUNY, 1965, Title IV grantee, NDEA, 1968. Fellow: Royal Soc. Can., Soc. Study Values in Edn., World Acad. Arts and Scis.; mem.: Royal Coll. Physicians and Surgeons (exec. com.), Soc. for Study Higher Edn. (bd. dirs. 1988—90), Can. Soc. 18th Century Studies (pres. 1975—76), Atlantic Soc. 18th Century Studies (pres. 1972—76), Can. Fedn. Humanities (pres. 1982—84), Internat. Assn. of Comparative Lit. (treas. 1985—91, sec. 1991—94), Internat. Soc. 18th Century Studies (assoc. treas. 1983—87), World Parliament of Cultures, Club of Rome (exec. com. 1999—), Knights of Malta (grande dame 1991—), Phi Delta Kappa, Delta Kappa Gamma. Home: 5000 Edgewater Dr Norfolk VA 23508 Office: Old Dominion U Norfolk VA 23529 Office Phone: 757-683-3159. E-mail: rrunte@odu.edu.

RUNYAN, ANNE SISSON, political science educator; b. Cin., Mar. 30, 1955; d. Richard Van Pelt and Margery Wing (Sisson) R.; m. Albert Adrian Kanters, Nov. 8, 1976. BA, U. Windsor, Ont., Can., 1976; MS, Am. U., 1979, PhD, 1988. From. asst. prof. to assoc. prof. politics dept. SUNY, Potsdam, 1988-96, chair politics dept., 1990-95, women's studies dir., 1992-96; assoc. prof. polit. sci. dept. Wright State U., Dayton, Ohio, 1996—2001, women's studies dir., 1996—2001; head, assoc. prof. women's studies dept. U. Cin., 2001—. Vis. scholar U. Amsterdam, The Netherlands, 1994-95; rsch. cons. Capital Counselors, Washington, 1978-80, Inst. Govt. Pub. Info. Rsch., Am. U., 1980-81, Alta. Soc. Women Against Violence, Edmonton, 1983-84, Soc. Svcs. Dept. Niagara Regional Municipality, St. Catharines, Ont., 1985; rsch. project dir. Status of Women in Miami Valley, Wright State U., 2000-01, Women's Studies in N.Am. Context, 2002-03. Co-author: Global Gender Issues, 1993, 99; contbg. author: Gendered States, 1992, Women, Gender & World Politics, 1994, Globalization Theory & Practice, 1996, 2001; co-editor: Gender and Global Restructuring; contbr. articles to profl. jours. including Internat. Feminist Jour. of Politics, Internat. Politics Jour. Bd. dirs. Alta. Status Women Action Com., Edmonton, 1982-83, Canadian Voice Women Peace, Toronto, Can., 1985-86; mem. Friends of Women's Studies, 2001—. Rsch. fellow Rsch. Ctr. Socs. Internat. Polit. Economy, U. Amsterdam, 1995. Mem. Am. Polit. Sci. Assn. (rsch. grantee 1994), Nat. Women's Studies Assn., Internat. Studies Assn. (sect. chair, bd. dirs. 1990-95). Democrat. Avocations: travel, tennis. Office: Univ of Cincinnati Dept Women's Studies Cincinnati OH 45221-0164 E-mail: anne.runyan@uc.edu.

RUNYAN, CAROL REID, audiologist; b. Niagara Falls, N.Y., May 2, 1961; d. Harold James Reid and Gudrun Ann Hildebrandt; m. Troy Scott Runyan, Apr. 14, 1993; children: Jamie, Jessica, Mason. BS magna cum laude, Ithaca (N.Y.) Coll., 1983; MA, U. No. Colo., 1985; D in Audiology, Ariz. Sch. Health Scis., 2002. Lic. audiologist Tenn., clin. cert. of completence in audiology Am. Speech, Lang., and Hearing Assn., 1987, cert. Am. Bd. Audiology, 1999. Clin. audiologist Hearing & Speech Svcs., Glenwood Springs, Colo., 1985—89, West Seneca (N.Y.) Devel. Ctr., 1989—90, Buffalo (N.Y.) Speech & Hearing Ctr., 1989—91, Cape Fear Valley Med. Ctr., Fayetteville, NC, 1991—93; ednl. audiologist Cooperative Ednl. Svcs. Assn., Milton, Wis., 1993—95; clin. audiologist Profl. Hearing Svcs., Waukesha, Wis., 1994—96, Ear Nose and Throat Assocs., Kingsport, Tenn., 1996—. Mem. adv. bd. Maintain Regin Speech & Hearing Ctr., Kingsport, 1998—2000. Fellow: Am. Acad. Audiology; mem.: Am. Auditory Soc., Am. Tinnitus Assn., Tenn. Acad. Audiology, Am. Speech Hearing Assn. Office: Ent Assoc of Kingsport PC 2204 Pavilion Dr Ste 105 Kingsport TN 37660 Office Phone: 423-246-8155.

RUNYAN, MARY LYNN, music educator; b. Worland, Wyo., Aug. 7, 1957; d. Woodrow W. and Lois L. Harris; m. Dewey R. Runyan, Aug. 1, 1987; 1 child, Preston T. B in Music Edn., U. Okla., 1979; M in Music Edn., Southwestern Okla. State U., 1987. Nat. bd. cert. tchr. 2003. Band dir. Velma (Okla.)-Alma Pub. Schs., 1980—84, Altus (Okla.) Pub. Schs., 1984—. Workshop presenter Midwest Internat. Band Clinic, Chgo., 2000. Mem.: Okla. Bandmaster's Assn., Phi Beta Mu (pres. 1999—2001). Home: 804 Jamestown Dr Altus OK 73521 Office: Altus High Sch 400 N Park Ave Altus OK 73521

RUPERT, DOROTHY, state legislator; b. Meadow Grove, Nebr., Oct. 20, 1926; m. Richard Rupert. BA, Nebr. Wesleyan U., 1948; MA, U. Colo., 1967; postgrad., Harvard U., 1993. Tchr., counselor various high schs., 1948-96; dir. counseling svcs. statewide Colo., 1977-78; developer, dir. Displaced Homemaker Program, 1979-80; mem. Colo. Ho. of Reps., Denver, 1986-94, Colo. Senate, Denver, 1994—, mem. health, environment, welfare and instns. com., mem. jud. com., mem. state local govt. com. Attendee UN Beijing Conf., 1995, Peace & Justice Internat. Conf., Bolivia, 1992, Helsinki, 1995. Mem. Thornton City Coun., 1958-61. Mem. Colo. Counselors Assn. (past pres.), Nat. Human Rights Commn. for Counselors, Nat. Order Women Legislators (bd. dirs.), NOW, Nat. Abortion Rights Action League, AAUW, Amnesty Internat., World Internat. League for Peace and Freedom. Democrat. Office: State Capitol 200 E Colfax Ave Ste 274 Denver CO 80203-1716

RUPERT, ELIZABETH ANASTASIA, retired dean; b. Emlenton, Pa., July 12, 1918; d. John Hamilton and Eva Blanche (Elliott) R. Diploma, Altoona Sch. Commerce, 1936; BS in Edn., Clarion State Coll., 1959; MSLS, Syracuse U., 1962; PhD, U. Pitts., 1970. Sec. Quaker State Oil Refining Corp., 1939-56; tchr., libr. Oil City Area Schs., 1959-61; libr. Venango campus Clarion (Pa.) U., 1961-62, prof. Coll. Libr. Sci., 1962-70, dean Sch. Libr. Sci., Coll. Libr. Sci., 1971-85; prof. emeritus, 1994. Interim pres. Clarion U., spring 1977; acct. William Rupert Mortuary, Inc., 1948-88. Author: Pennsylvania Practicum Program for School Librarians: An Appraisal, 1970; mem. ad hoc edit. com. Pa. Media Guidelines, Pa. Dept. Edn., 1976, author (with others) Encylopedia of Library and Information Science, 1984. Bd. dirs. Knox Pub. Libr., 1991-97; mem. Abscurf; mem. numerous bds. and couns. Church of God. Recipient Disting. Faculty award Clarion U. Alumni Assn., 1976, Disting. Svc. award, 1986, Disting. Alumni award, 1987, Zonta Internat. Women of Achievement award, 1987. Mem. Beta Phi Mu, Pi Gamma Mu. Republican. Home: PO Box H Knox PA 16232-0608

RUPINSKI, JANETTE MARIE, banker; b. Sheboygan, Wis., Jan. 7, 1946; d. Reuben Roy and Marie (Horn) Friedel; m. Albin Michael Hoffart, June 24, 1967 (div. Feb. 1993); children: Craig Michael, Curtis Marc.; m. Michael A. Rupinski, July 29, 1996. BS in Bus. Adminstrn., Cardinal Stritch Coll., Milw., 1992. Sec.-treas. Cmty. Fin. Svcs., Inc., Port Washington, Wis., 1979-84; teller Port Washington Savs. & Loan, 1977-79, asst. v.p., 1984-86, v.p., br. mgr., 1986-88, Port Savs. Bank, S.A., Grafton, Wis., 1988-90; asst. v.p., mgr. St. Francis Bank, FSB, Thiensville, Wis., 1990-94; ops. mgr. Horizon Credit Union, Racine, Wis., 1994—. Bd. dirs. Inst. Fin. Edn., Milw., 1984-90, membership chair, 1986-88, chpt. excellence chair, 1988-90. Vol. Port Washington Pub. Schs., 1976-79, Advocates for Victims of Abuse, Ozaukee County, Wis., 1992-94; bd. dirs. Ozaukee County Vol. Ctr., Port Washington, 1993-94; asst. cubmaster Boy Scouts Am., Port Washington, 1977-79. Mem. Wis. Credit Union League. Avocations: russian folk dance (kavkaz dance troup), reading, needlepoint. Office: Horizon Credit Union 1931 Grove Ave Racine WI 53405-3841

RUPNOR, JENNIFER, journalist; BA in Broadcast Journalism, U. Wis., Eau Claire, 2000. Mem. radio news staff WAXX-WAYY, 1997—2000; reporter, prodr. WEAU-TV, Eau Claire, Wis., 2000, anchor NewsCenter 13 sunrise and noon, 2000—. Avocations: baseball, mysteries. Office: WEAU-TV P oBox 47 Eau Claire WI 54702

RUPP, JOYCE M. nun, writer; b. Cherokee, Iowa, June 8, 1943; d. Lester P. Rupp and Hildegard A. Wilberding. BA in Elem. Edn., Duchesne Coll., 1965; MRE, St. Thomas U., 1975; MTP, Inst. Transpersonal Psychology, 1993; postgrad., Creighton U., Notre Dame U. Joined Servants of Mary Order. Author: Fresh Bread, 1985, Praying Our Goodbyes, 1988, The Star in My Heart, 1990, May I Have This Dance?, 1992, Little Pieces of Light, 1994, Dear Heart, Come Home, 1996, The Cup of Our Life, 1997; author: (with Joyce Hutchison) May I Walk You Home?, 1999; author: Your Sorrow is My Sorrow, 1999, Out of the Ordinary, 2000, Prayers to Sophia, 2000, Inviting God In, 2001, The Cosmic Dance, 2002, Rest Your Dreams on a Little Twig, 2003.*

RUPP, SHERON ADELINE, photographer, educator; b. Mansfield, Ohio, Jan. 14, 1943; d. Warren Edmund Rupp and Frances Adeline (Hanson) Christian. BA in Sociology and Psychology, Denison U., 1965; MFA in Photography, U. Mass., 1982. Teaching asst. in photography Hampshire Coll., Amherst, Mass., 1981; instr. photography Northfield (Mass.) Mt. Hermon Sch., 1982-83, U. Mass., Amherst, 1984, Holyoke (Mass.) Community Coll., 1986, 87-88; vis. asst. prof. photography Hampshire Coll., 1985, 87; vis. lectr. photography Amherst (Mass.) Coll., 1994. Guest artist, lectr. Boston Mus. Sch., Portland (Maine) Sch. Art, NYU, U. Mass., Deerfield (Mass.) Acad., Hartford Sch. Art/U. Hartford-Conn., Springfield Mus. Fine Arts, Mass., Bard Coll, N.Y., Mass. Coll. Art, Boston, others; guest lectr. Carpenter Ctr., Harvard U., Cambridge, Mass., 2000. One-woman shows include Tisch Sch. Arts NYU, 1987, Portland Sch. Art, 1989, Hart Gallery, Northampton, Mass., 1992, O.K. Harris Gallery, N.Y.C., 1992, Cleve. Mus. Art, 2000; two-person shows include Columbus (Ohio) Mus. Art, 1997—98, Springfield (Mass.) Tech. C.C., 1997; Exhibited in group shows at Mus. Modern Art, N.Y.C., 1991, 1999—, Springfield Mus. Fine Art, 1993, U. Mass., Amherst, 1993, Dirs. Guild, L.A., 1994, Manchester (N.H.) Inst. Arts and Scis., 1995, Weber State U., Utah, 1995, Grand Ctrl. Terminal, N.Y.C., 1995, Photog. Resource Ctr. 3d Biennial, Boston, 1995, DeCordova Mus., Lincoln, 2000—, Smithsonian Arts and Scis., Washington, 2001, Denison U. Art Gallery, Granville, Ohio, 2002, Around the House, A.N. Bush Gallery, Salem, Oreg., 2002, Boston Mus. Fine Arts, 2002—03, Guild Hall, East Hampton, N.Y., 2003, Smith Coll. Mus. Art, Northampton, Mass., 2004, Represented in permanent collections De Cordova Mus., Mus. Modern Art, N.Y.C., Fogg Art Mus. at Harvard U., Hallmark Collection of Photography, Kansas City, Columbus Mus. Art, Mus. Fine Arts, Boston, Rose Art Mus. Brandeis U., Mead Art Mus. Amherst Coll., Smith Coll. Mus. Art, Danforth Mus. Art, Springfield Tech C.C. Found., Carpenter Ctr. for Visual Arts Harvard U., The Smithsonian; photographs (including cover photo) in Double-Take Mag., winter 1998. Bd. dirs. Zone Art Ctr., 1987-94. Recipient Mass. Fellowship award in photography Artist Found., 1984, 87; visual artist fellow Nat. Endowment for the Arts, 1986, 94, Guggenheim fellow, 1990. Avocations: hiking, bicycling, writing. Home and Office: 364 Hatfield St Apt C Northampton MA 01060-1541 E-mail: sheron@crocker.com.

RUPPRECHT, NANCY ELLEN, historian, educator; b. Coeur d'Alene, Idaho, Sept. 23, 1948; d. George John and Nancy Berneeda (Baird) R. BA with honors, U. Mo., 1967, MA, 1969; PhD, U. Mich., 1982. Acad. dir. pilot program U. Mich., Ann Arbor, 1971-73, lectr. in women studies, 1973-75; vis. lectr. history U. Mo., St. Louis, 1976-77; vis. instr. of history Wash. U., St. Louis, 1977-79, Grinnell (Iowa) Coll., 1979-81; asst. prof. Oakland U., Rochester, Mich., 1981-83; asst. prof. of history Mid. Tenn. State U., Murfreesboro, 1985-91, assoc. prof., 1991-97, prof. history, 1997—. Dir. women's studies program Middle Tenn. State U., 1988—, publicity dir. women's history month, 1989-92, mem. faculty senate, 1992-95; bd. dir. Remember the Women. Mem. editl. bd. German Studies Rev., 1999—; contbr. articles to profl. jours. Bd. adv. Remember the Women Found. Mem.: NOW, AAUW, AAUP (chpt. v.p. 1988—89, pres. 1989—93), Remember the Women (bd. mem.), Assn. Faculty and Adminstrv. Women (chpt. pres. 1995—), Concerned Faculty and Adminstrv. Women (chpt. v.p. 1993—95, chpt. pres. 1995—96), Women in Higher Edn. in Tenn., German Studies Assn., Mid Tenn. Women's Studies Assn., Holocaust Studies Assn., So. Humanities Assn., So. Hist. Assn. (chair nominating com. European divsn. 1996—97, mem. exec. com. 1996—, mem. program com. 1997—2000, chmn. program com. 2001—02, vice chair European divsn. 2002—03, chair European divsn. 2003—), S.E. Women's Studies Assn., Am. Hist. Assn. Home: 1106 Jones Blvd Murfreesboro TN 37129-2310 Office: Middle Tenn State U 275 Peck Hall Murfreesboro TN 37132-0001

RUPP-SERRANO, KAREN, school librarian; b. WaKeeney, Kans., May 18, 1962; d. Marcus and Julia Rupp; m. Gabriel Serrano, Jan. 6, 1990; 1 child, Augustin Serrano. BA in Interdisciplinary Social Scis., Kans. State U., Manhattan, 1984; MLS, Emporia State U., 1988; MPA, U. Okla., Norman, 1996. Head, collection devel. U. Okla. Librs., Norman, Okla., 2000—. Mem.: ALA, Assn. Coll. and Rsch. Librs. Office: U Okla Libraries 401 W Brooks Norman OK 73019

RUSAW, SALLY ELLEN, librarian; b. Potsdam, N.Y., Apr. 24, 1939; d. Ralph Clinton and Marion Ellen (Jenack) R. BS in Edn., Potsdam Coll., 1964; MLS, SUNY, Albany, 1975. Cert. libr. media specialist, pub. libr., permanent tchr. N-6, N.Y. Tchr. grade 7th-9th Diocese of Ogdensburg, N.Y., 1960-74, cons. office edn., 1975-78; assoc. libr. Mater Dei Coll., Ogdensburg, 1974-89, head libr., 1989-99, SUNY, Potsdam, 2000—. Vol. Ogdensburg Correctional Facility, 1982-95, Riverview Correctional Facility, Ogdensburg, 1987—; lector, Eucharistic min. Rite for Christian Initiation of Adults catechist St. Mary's Cathedral; vol. Ogdensburg Cath. Ctrl. Sch., sch. bd., 1995-2000. Named Vol. of Yr. Ogdensburg Correctional Facility, 1985, Outstanding Vol. Riverview Correctional Facility, 1991; Nat. Def. Edn. Act grantee, 1965. Mem. ALA, N.Y. Libr. Assn., North Country 3Rs Coun., North Country Ref. and Rsch. Resources Coun. (trustee 1994-99). Roman Catholic. Avocations: music, reading, berrying, outdoor activities, swimming.

RUSH, JULIA ANN HALLORAN (MRS. RICHARD HENRY RUSH), artist, writer; b. St. Louis, Oct. 25, 1927; d. Edward Roosevelt and Flavia Hadley (Griffin) Halloran; m. Richard Henry Rush, Aug. 15, 1956; 1 child, Sallie Haywood. Student Washington U., St. Louis, 1945-47; B.A., George Washington U., 1949. One-woman shows: Fort Amador Officers Club, Panama Canal Zone, El Panama Hotel, Panama, George Washington U., Statler Hotel, Roosevelt Hotel, Washington, Newspaper Women's Club, Washington, Waukegan Library, Ill., Epworth Heights Hotel, Ludington, Mich.; exhibited in group shows: Panama Art League, Corcoran Gallery; represented in permanent collections: U. Panama; also pvt. collections; model John Robert Powers Agy., 1950; sec.-treas., dir. N.Am. Acceptance Corp., 1956-58; v.p. Rush and Halloran, Inc., 1957-58, ptnr., 1954-57; research asst. to husband's bi-weekly newsletter Art/Antiques Investment Report, 1973—, articles in Wall St. transcript, 1971—. Illustrator: Antiques As An Investment (author Richard H. Rush), 1968; research asst.: Investments You Can Live With and Enjoy (author: Richard H. Rush), 1974, 2d, edit., 1975, 3d edit., 1976; Photographer: Automobiles as an Investment, 1982; Investing in Classic Cars, 1984. Recipient 1st prize (Panama) Newspaper Women's Club, 1953; First Prize Panama Art League, 1953. Mem. DAR, Nat. League Am. Penwomen, Florence Crittenton Circle (rec. sec. 1968-69), Kappa Kappa Gamma. Club: Washington, Royal Palm Yacht (No. Ft. Myers, Fla.), Boca West Golf and Country (Boca Raton, Fla.)

RUSHING, DOROTHY M. retired historian, writer; b. Bonham, Tex., Aug. 28, 1925; d. Van Bain and Ada (Price) Hawkins; m. J. E. Rushing, Aug. 6, 1960 (dec. 1985); children: Charles Maret, Bill Maret, Bob Maret, Charles Rushing, Martha Rushing Sosebee. BA, Tex. Woman's U., 1972; MA, Tex. A&M Commerce, 1974; PhD, U. North Tex., Denton, 1981. Instr. Tex. A&M Commerce, Commerce, 1972-74, 80-81, U. North Tex., Denton, 1975-76; prof. Richland Coll., Dallas, 1975-98, Collin County Community Coll., McKinney, Tex., 1985-88; historian-archivist J.C. Penney, Inc., Dallas, 1988-95. Vis. prof. Johns Hopkins U., 1985, U. Va., 1989; statis. analyst Dallas County C.C., 1982; lay rep. N.E. Tex. Libr. System, 1982-90. Contbg. author: Handbook of Texas, 1986. Named Outstanding Instr., Richland Coll., 1987, Disting. Alumni, Denison H.S., 2001; postdoctoral fellow NEH, 1985, 89. Mem. Phi Kappa Phi, Sigma Tau Delta, Phi Alpha Theta. Avocations: genealogy, literacy, history. Home: 498 Lockloma Ct Denison TX 75020-3668

RUSIE, RUTH LOUISE, literacy educator; b. Russiaville, Ind., Oct. 13, 1918; d. Volna Ernest and Mamie Audrey (Gallion) Ritz; m. Horace Robert Rusie, June 28, 1941; children: James Frederick, David Robert, John Lindley. BA, DePauw U., 1940; MS, Ind. U., 1972. Elem. sch. tchr. Met. Sch. Dist. Martinsville (Ind.), 1958-72, spl. reading tchr., 1972-80; coord. Martinsville Literacy Coalition, 1982—. Mem. Ind. Right-to-Read Com., 1975-78; mem. adv. bd., participant Reading is Fundamental, Martinsville, 1992-96. Composer music for elementary students The Stupid Thief, 1972. Bd. dirs. Martinsville Edn. Found., 1991—, Cmty. Found. of Morgan County, 2001—, People Respecting Individuality and Diversity in Everyone (P.R.I.D.E.), 1997—, co-pres., 2002—, Cmty. Concerts N.Y.C., 1994—, co-pres., 2003-2004; bd. dirs., treas. Morgan County Pub. Libr., Martinsville, 1984-2001; mem. com. on food Habitat for Humanity, Martinsville, 1997—; mem. Martinsville Arts Coun., 1981—, dir., 1981—; driver cancer patients ARC, Martinsville, 1981-2000, dir., 1986-92; dir. vol. desk Morgan County Meml. Hosp., Martinsville, 1982-94; driver Meals-On-Wheels, Martinsville, 1985—; grand marshall Morgan County Fall Foliage Festival Parade, Martinsville, 1993; adv. bd. United Way Ctrl. Ind., 2003-2004; elder Presby. Ch., 2004-2006. Named Citizen of Yr., Kiwanis, 1990, Rotary, 1993; recipient Cmty. Spirit award, H.S. Nat. Honor Soc., 1992, Mayor's award for literacy, Mayor and City Ofcls., 1993, Excellence of Cmty. Svc. award, DAR, 1995, Ind. Jefferson award, Am. Inst. Pub. Svc./Indpls. Star, 1996, Svc. to Mankind award, Morgan County Sertoma Club, 2002, S.W. Ind. Dist. Sertoma Internat., 2003. Mem. Martinsville Woman's Club (pres. 1957-59), Martinsville Literary Club, Coterie (pres. 1986-88), Monday Afternoon Art Club, Foxcliff Golf Club (pres. 1981-82), Kappa Kappa Kappa (pres. 1956-57, province officer 1957-59). Presbyterian. Avocations: reading, bell and singing ch. choirs, bridge, opera, theater.

RUSS, JOANNA, author; b. N.Y.C., Feb. 22, 1937; d. Evarett and Bertha (Zinner) R. BA in English with high honors, Cornell, U., 1957; M.F.A. in Playwriting and Dramatic Lit, Yale U., 1960. Lectr. in English Cornell U., 1967-70, asst. prof., 1970-72; asst. prof. English, Harpur Coll., State U. N.Y. at Binghamton, 1972-75, U. Colo., 1975-77; asso. prof. English, U. Wash., 1977-90, prof., 1984-90. Author: Picnic on Paradise, 1968, And Chaos Died, 1970, The Female Man, 1975, We Who Are About To, 1977, Kittatinny: A Tale of Magic, 1978, The Two of Them, 1978, On Strike Against God, 1980, The Adventures of Alyx, 1983, The Zanzibar Cat, 1983, How To Suppress Women's Writing, 1983, Extra (Ordinary) People, 1984, Magic Mommas, Trembling Sisters, Puritans and Perverts: Feminist Essays, 1985, The Hidden Side of the Moon, 1987, To Write Like a Woman, 1995, (nonfiction) What Are We Fighting For, 1998; also numerous short stories. Mem. Sci. Fiction Writers Am. (Nebula award for best short story 1972, Hugo award for best novella 1983).

RUSSELL, ANNE M. editor-in-chief; Editor book divsn. Billboard Publ.; editor Photo Dist. News; reporter Adweek; assoc. editor Am. Photographer; sr. editor Working Women; exec. editor Folio: Pub. News, editor-in-chief, 1992—97, Living Fit, 1997—99, Vegetarian Times, 1999; editl. dir. Fox TV's Health Network, Shape mag., 2001—03, editor-in-chief, 2003—. Office: Shape 21100 Erwin St Woodland Hills CA 91367*

RUSSELL, ANNE WRENN, property manager; b. Greensboro, NC, Mar. 2, 1934; d. Oscar Ivey and Lucy (Lula) Elinor (Wright) Wrenn; children: Elinor Russell Ball, Martha Anne Russell Martin, John Leon, Barbara Russell Richardson. BA in French, U. NC, Chapel Hill, 1956. Cert. N.C. Real Estate Bd., paralegal Atlanta Paralegal Inst., 1991. Camp counselor, Mass., 1954; with acctg. dept. Bank Greensboro, 1955; sec. Meth. Bd. Edn., Durham, NC, 1957—59; real estate sales person Geraci and Preston, Greensboro, 1991—92; property mgr. Wrenn-Zealy Properties, Inc., Greensboro, 1992—. Active Greensboro Opera Guild, Greensboro Opera Co., 1981—90; opera chorus mem. Greensboro Opera Co., 1981—85; active Greensboro Symphony Guild, 1981—90; bd. mem. Ea. Music Festival, Greensboro, 1985—86. Mem.: U. N.C. Greensboro Musical Arts Guild (bd. mem. 2003—), English Speaking Union, Greensboro Choral Soc. (mem. steering com.), U. N.C. Chapel Hill Alumni Assn. (life), Greensboro Hist. Book Club (life). Republican. Methodist. Avocations: piano, singing, painting, sewing, tennis. Office: Wrenn-Zealy Properties 1403 Sunset Dr Greensboro NC 27408

RUSSELL, ANNIKA RENEE, secondary school educator, financial consultant; d. Sondra Kay and Steve Lynn Russell. BA, Dakota Wesleyan U., Mitchell, SD, 1992—96; MEd, U. Nebraska-Lincoln, 2000—02. Lic. Securities SD, 2003. Hs tchr., coach Artesian-Letcher Schools, Artesian, SD, 1996—; fin. rep. Primerica Fin. Services, Mitchell, SD, 2000—. Tech. instr. cons. State of SD, Spearfish, SD, 1998—99; sd team coach Internat. Sports Specialist, Inc., North Logan, Utah, 1999—. Youth group leader United Meth. Ch., Mitchell, SD, 1999—2001. Mem.: SD Edn. Assn./Nat. Edn. Assn., SD Volleyball Coaches Assn., SD Coaches Assn., Nat. Bus. Edn. Assn., ASCD. Methodist. Avocations: running, reading, crafts, skiing, biking. Home: 301 W 12th Ave Mitchell SD 57301

RUSSELL, ATTIE YVONNE, academic administrator, pediatrics educator, dean; b. Washington, Aug. 10, 1923; d. George and Kathleen L. (Milliner) Werner; m. Rex Hillier, Apr. 19, 1954 (dec.); m. Henry J. Russell, 1960 (div. 1971); children: Richard Russell, Margaret Jane Russell-Harde; m. Harry F. Camper, Sept. 2, 1984. BS, Am. U., 1944, PhD, State U. Iowa, 1952; MD, U. Chgo., 1958. Intern Phila. Gen. Hosp., 1958-59; resident in pediatrics Bronx (N.Y.) Mcpl. Hosp., 1960-61, Del. Hosp., Wilmington, 1962-63; dir. maternal and child health, crippled children's svcs. Del. State Bd. Health, Dover, 1963-68; asst. dean community health affairs, assoc. prof. pediatrics U. Cin. Coll. Medicine, 1968-71; clin. assoc. prof. pediatrics Med. Coll. Pa., Phila., 1966-68, 71-74; dep. dir. div. pub. health State of Del., Dover, 1971-74; dir. Santa Clara Valley Med. Ctr., San Jose, Calif., 1974-79; assoc. dean, clin. prof. pediatrics, family medicine Stanford (Calif.) U. Sch. Medicine, 1974-79; dir. USPHS Hosp., Boston, 1979-81, Balt. City Hosps., 1981-82; asst. v.p. community affairs, prof. pediatrics U. Tex. Med. Br., Galveston, 1982-87, asst. v.p. student affairs, dean students, prof. pediatrics, 1987-92, clin. prof. pediatrics, 1992—. Reviewer Coun. for Internat. Exchange of Scholars, Washington, 1987-94; dir. III Symposium on Health and Human Svcs. in the U.S.-Mex., Brownsville, 1988; mem. sci. coun. Am. Fedn. for Aging Rsch., Inc., 1983-86. Contbr. articles and abstracts to profl. jours. Mem. budget com. United Way, Galveston, 1982-84; mem. Mayor's Adv. Com. for Sr. Citizens and Handicapped Persons for the City of Galveston, 1983-85; bd. dirs. Galveston County Coordinated Community Clinics, 1983-87; bd. advisors Galveston Hist. Found., 1983-88; mem. Com. for Coop. Action Planning, 1983-88, Houston-Galveston Health Promotion Consortium, 1983-88, Injury Control Prevention (Houston), 1984-89, aging programs adv. com. Houston-Galveston Area Coun., 1985-92. Recipient Disting. Alumni award Am. U., 1984. Fellow Am. Acad. Pediatrics, Am. Pub. Health Assn.; mem. AMA, Am. Coll. Preventive Medicine, Am. Physiol. Soc., Mass. State Med. Soc., Tex. Med. Assn., Galveston C. of C. (legis. com. 1983-88), Order of Eastern Star, Sigma Xi, Alpha Omega Alpha.

RUSSELL, BEVERLY ANN, librarian, writer; b. Riverside, Calif., Jan. 15, 1947; d. James and Hazel M. Russell. BA in Polit. Sci., Calif. State U., 1971, MLS, 1973. Libr. asst. Riverside Pub. Libr., 1974—75; asst. libr. U. Calif., 1975—76; office asst. Calif. State Dept. Rehab., L.A., 1976—77; libr. technician Magnavox Rsch. Labs., Torrance, Calif., 1976—83; libr. asst. Burbank (Calif.) Unified Sch. Dist., 1985—86; office technician Social Svcs. Dept., Van Nuys, Calif., 1988—92; libr. Pleasant Valley State Prison, Coalinga, Calif., 1994—. Co-author (poetry): Roots & Wings, 1986, Three Women Black, 1988. Mem.: Alpha Kappa Alpha. Avocations: writing, poetry. Home: 250 Truman St #250 Coalinga CA 93210 Office: Pleasant Valley State Prison 24863 W Jayne St Coalinga CA 93210

RUSSELL, CAROL ANN, personnel service company executive; b. Detroit, Dec. 14, 1943; d. Billy and Iris Koud; m. Victor Rojas (div.). BA in English, CUNY-Hunter Coll., 1993. Registered employment cons. Various positions in temp. help cos., N.Y.C., 1964-74; v.p. Wollborg-Michelson, San Francisco, 1974-82; co-owner, pres. Russell Staffing Resources, Inc., San Francisco and Sonoma, 1983-98; ret.; co-founder HR 24/7, 1999—. Media guest, spkr., workshop and seminar leader in field; host/cmty. prodr. Job Net program for TCI Cable T.V. Pub. Checkpoint Newsletter; feature writer/columnist The Slant; contbr. articles to profl. publs. Founding v.p. The Friends of the Frank Lloyd Wright Civic Ctr. Libr. Marin County; mem. Sonoma County Commn. on Status of Women, 2003—; bd. dirs. Sonoma County Libr. Found., 2003—; mem. cmty. action com. Sonoma County Commn. on Human Rights. Named to Inc. 500, 1989—90. Mem. Am. Women in Radio and TV, No. Calif. Human Resources Coun., Soc. Human Resource Mgmt., Calif. Assn. Pers. Cons. (pres. Golden State chpt. 1984-85), Calif. Assn. Temp. Svcs., Bay Area Pers. Assn. (pres. 1983-84), Pers. Assn. Sonoma County, Scrowers and Molly Maguires (bd. dirs.), Sherlock Holmes Soc. London, Nat. Women's Polit. Caucus (comms. chair Marin chpt. 2002, pres. Marin chpt. 2003). E-mail: incloverdale@comcast.net.

RUSSELL, CAROLYN B. state legislator; b. Greenville, N.C., June 19, 1944; d. Oscar Dixon and Naomi (Grey) Barnes; m. Douglas M. Russell; children: Susannah, Douglas, Meredith. B, M in Clin. Psychology, East Carolina U. Psychologist, Fla., S.C.; pers. dir. O'Berry Ctr., Goldsboro, N.C.; mem. N.C. Ho. of Reps., 1991—. Bd. dirs. Green Lamp Bd.; bd. dirs. Smart Start early childhood devel. program Avocations: baking bread, gourmet cooking, reading, boating. Office: State Legislative Bldg Raleigh NC 27603

RUSSELL, CHARLOTTE SANANES, biochemistry educator, researcher; b. N.Y.C., Jan. 4, 1927; d. Joseph and Marguerite (Saltiel) Sananes; m. Joseph Brooke Russell, Dec. 20, 1947; children: James Robert, Joshua Sananes. BA, Bklyn. Coll., 1946; MA, Columbia U., 1947, PhD, 1951. Asst. prof. chemistry CCNY, N.Y.C., 1958-68, assoc. prof., 1968-72, prof., 1972—, prof. emerita, 2001—. Peer reviewer NSF, NIH; ad hoc reviewer sci. jours. including Jour. Bacteriology, Biochemistry. Contbr. articles to profl. jours. Mem. AAAS, AAUP, AAUW (internat. fellowship panel 1986-89), Am. Soc. Biochemistry and Molecular Biology, Am. Chem. Soc., Amnesty Internat., Urgent Action Network, Sigma Xi. Office: CCNY Dept Chemistry 138th St & Convent Ave New York NY 10031 E-mail: chrcc@mail.sci.ccny.cuny.edu.

RUSSELL, CHRISTINE R. music educator; d. Glenn B. and Bonnie B Russell. MusB in Edn., DePauw U., Greencastle, IN, 1997; MusM, Bowling Green State U., Ohio, 2002. Cert. tchr. Ind., 1998. Edn. intern Nat. Symphony Orch., J.F. Kennedy Ctr. for the Performing Arts, Washington, 1997—97; substitute tchr. Fairfax County Pub. Schs., Va., 1998—2000; grad. asst. Bowling Green State U., Ohio, 2000—02; dir. of bands and orch. Bishop Dwenger H.S., Ft. Wayne, Ind., 2002—. Iterim music dir. Kirkwood Presbyn. Ch., Springfield, Va., 1999—2000; music dir. Encore Theater, Lima, Ohio, 2001, Bowling Green U. Theater, Ohio, 2001—02. Second author (journal) Journal of Research in Music Education, music director (musical theater) Into the Woods. Mem.: Ind. Bandmasters Assn., Ind. Music Educators Assn., MENC, Pi Kappa Lambda, Phi Kappa Phi. Office: Bishop Dwenger HS 1300 E Washington Center Rd Ft. Wayne IN 46825 Personal E-mail: c_russell@earthlink.net.

RUSSELL, CYNTHIA M. college president; Pres. Clinton Jr. Coll., Rock Hill, S.C., 1994—. Office: Clinton Jr College 1029 Crawford Rd Rock Hill SC 29730-5152

RUSSELL, DAWN ANN, dean; BA, St. Thomas U., 1977; LLB, Dalhousie U., 1981; LLM, Cambridge U., 1985. Bar: N.B. 1982, Nova Scotia 1983. Assoc. lawyer Halifax (Can.) Stewart McKelvey Stirling Scales, 1983-87, part-time assoc., 1987-95; asst. prof. law Dalhousie Law Sch., Halifax, 1987-92, assoc. prof., dean, 1992—. Pres. Nova Scotia Law Reform Commn., 1995-2002; bd. dirs. Oxford Frozen Foods Ltd., The Canadian Investors Protection Fund, Canadian Inst. Resources Law. Contbr. articles to profl. jours. Mem.: N.S. Barristers Soc., Bar Coun. Office: Dalhousie U Law Sch 6061 University Ave Halifax NS Canada B3H 4H9

RUSSELL, DIANE ELIZABETH HENRIKSON, career counselor; b. Chgo., July 18, 1952; d. Arthur Allen and Lois Elizabeth (Wessling) H.; m. Darrell Lee Slider, May 31, 1975 (div. Dec. 1992); m. Thomas Lee Russell, July 27, 1999. BA in Spanish, U. Ill., 1974; MA in Counselor Edn., U. South Fla., 1996. Employment counselor Crown Personnel Inc., Mt. Prospect, Ill., 1974-75; bilingual tchr.'s aide Sch. Dist. #21, Wheeling, Ill., 1975; sec., asst. registrar Yale U., New Haven, 1975-77; asst. to personnel dir., personnel coord. Housing Authority New Haven, 1977-79; benefits specialist Profl. Pensions Inc., New Haven, 1980-81, Chloride Inc., Tampa, Fla., 1981-83; personnel technician II human resources dept. U. South Fla., Tampa, 1984-86, personnel technician III, personnel svcs. specialist, 1986-90, coord. human resources dept., 1990-96, career specialist career ctr., 1996—2002, counselor, advisor honors coll., 2002— . Mem. choirs St. Mark United Ch., Valrico, Fla., 1987-99, 2003-, dir. Caregivers, 2001—; mem. chorus U. South Fla., 1986-88, women's chorale, 1993-95. Mem. AAUW (treas. 1976-78, 80-81), Am. Assn. Employment in Edn., Fla. Coop. Edn. and Placement Assn., Phi Kappa Phi, Phi Beta Kappa, Alpha Lambda Delta. Avocations: singing, theater, going to theme parks, traveling. Home: 723 Herlong Ct Brandon FL 33511-7920 Office: U South Fla Honors Coll 4202 E Fowler Ave Stop FA0274 Tampa FL 33620-6930 E-mail: dhenrik718@aol.com.

RUSSELL, ELEANOR M. retired technologist; b. Springfield, Mass., Dec. 3, 1335; d. William Albert and Elvie Agnes Russell. BS in med. tech., Colby Sawyer Coll., 1957; MS in med. tech., U. of Vt., 1976. Cert. medical technologist Am. Soc. of Clin. Pathology, 1957, clin. lab. sci. Nat. Cert. Agy. for Med. Lab. Pers., 1979, clin. lab. dir. Nat. cert. Agy. for Med. Lab. Pers., 1985. Med. technologist New Eng. Bapt. Hosp., Boston, 1958—63, Huntington Meml. Hosp., Pasadena, Calif., 1957—58; supr., chemistry lab. DeGoesbriand Meml. Hosp., 1963—67; adminstrv. dir. of lab. Fletcher Allen Health Care, 1967—92, interim v.p. for profl. svcs., 1989, sr. mgr. for clin. support svcs., 1989—92; instr. U. Vt., 1967—82, asst. prof., 1982—93, chmn. dept. med. tech., 1990—93. Reach to recovery vol. Am. Cancer Soc., 1987—93; vol. Milw.-Wis. Zoo, 1996—97, Charlotte News, 1998—, Green Mountain Audubon Soc., 1998—99; rd. to recovery regional coord. Am. Cancer Soc., 1999—, reach to recovery vol., 1999—; conservation commn. edn. com. Charlotte, Vt., 1999—2002; selectboard Town of Charlotte, Vt., 2002—; Thorp Barn preservation com. Charlotte, Vt., 2000—02. Recipient grant to evaluate med. tech. edn. in Egypt, Nat. Assn. of Student Affairs, 1965. Avocations: gardening, bicycling, skiing, reading, music. Home: 528 Cloflin Farm Rd Charlotte VT 05445

RUSSELL, ELISE BECKETT, piano teacher; b. Misawa AFB, Japan, June 16, 1955; d. George Stanley and Jettie Louise (Thomas) Beckett; m. Michel Gene Russell, Jan. 31, 1981; 1 child, Sean Michael. BMusic, U. Miss., 1976. Tchr. English and music Millington (Tenn.) H.s., 1977-79; tchr. music Port Sulphur (La.) Elem., Middle and High Schs., 1979-80; piano lab., pvt. piano tchr., accompanist self employed, Bay St. Louis, Miss., 1980-81, pvt. piano tchr. Kenner, La., 1981-86, Sugar Land, Tex., 1987—. Adjudicator Nat. Guild Piano Tchrs. Co-author: The Piano Lesson, 2003. Asst. youth councilor United Meth. Ch., Bay St. Lois, 1980; PTO bd. dirs. Colony Bend Elem. Sch., Sugar Land, 1989-90; founder Bay St. Louis Fine Arts Coun., mem., dir. players; soloist St. Charles Christian Ch. Named to Outstanding Young Women of Am., 1981. Mem. Tex. Music Tchrs. Assn. (theory coord., presenter, nominations mem., dist. asst., bd. dirs. 2001, chmn. cmty outreach and edn., 2001, pres. ind. music tchrs. assn., 2002), Ind. Music Tchrs. Assn. (founder, charter mem., pres. 2001). Methodist. Avocations: gardening, sewing, home renovation.

RUSSELL, FRANCIA, ballet director, educator; b. Los Angeles, Jan. 10, 1938; d. W. Frank and Marion (Whitney) R.; m. Kent Stowell, Nov. 19, 1965; children: Christopher, Darren, Ethan. Studies with, George Balanchine, Vera Volkova, Felia Doubrouska, Antonina Tumkovsky, Benjamin Harkarvy; student, NYU, Columbia U.; degree (hon.), Seattle U., 2003. Dancer, soloist N.Y.C. Ballet, 1956-62, ballet mistress, 1965-70; dancer Ballets USA/Jerome Robbins, N.Y.C., 1962; tchr. ballet Sch. Am. Ballet, N.Y.C., 1963-64; co-dir. Frankfurt (Fed. Republic Germany) Opera Ballet, 1976-77; dir., co-artistic dir. Pacific N.W. Ballet, Seattle, 1977—; dir. Pacific N.W. Ballet Sch., Seattle. Affiliate prof. of dance U. Wash. Dir. staging over 100 George Balanchine ballet prodns. throughout world, including Russia and China, 1964—. Named Woman of Achievement, Matrix Table, Women in Comm., Seattle, 1987, Gov.'s Arts award, 1989, Dance Mag. award, 1996, Brava award Women's U. Club, 2003. Mem. Internat. Women's Forum. Home: 2833 Broadway E Seattle WA 98102-3935 Office: Pacific NW Ballet 301 Mercer St Seattle WA 98109-4600*

RUSSELL, HARRIET SHAW, social worker; b. Detroit, Apr. 12, 1952; d. Louis Thomas and Lureleen (Hughes) Shaw; m. Donald Edward Russell, June 27, 1980; children: Lachante Tyree, Krystal Lanae. BS, Mich. State U., 1974; AB, Detroit Bus. Inst., 1976; BA in Pub. Adminstrn., Mercy Coll., Detroit, 1988; MSW, Wayne State U., 1992. Factory staff Gen. Motors Corp., Lansing, Mich., 1973; student supr. tour guides State of Mich., Lansing, Mich., 1974; mgr. Ky. Fried Chicken, Detroit, 1974-75; unemployment claims examiner State of Mich. Dept. Labor, Detroit, 1975-77, asst. payment worker, 1977-84, social svcs. specialist, 1984-90; pres. Victory Enterprises, 1991; social worker Detroit Bd. Edn., 1992—. Ind. contractor Detroit Compact; moderator Mich. Opportunity Skills and Tng. Program, 1985-86. Vol. Mich. Cancer Soc., East Lansing, 1970-72, Big Sisters/Big Bros., Lansing, 1972-73; elected rep. Mich. Coun. Social Svcs. Workers; spkr. Triumphant Bapt. Ch., Detroit, 1976-80; chief union steward Mich. Employees Assn., Lincoln Park, 1982-83; leader Girl Scouts U.S.; area capt. Life Worker Project Program; bd. dirs. Neighborhood Found., 1995-97. Wayne State U. scholar, 1990-91, Deans scholar, 1991-92; recipient Outstanding Work Performace Merit award Mich. Dept. Social Svcs., 1979, Unsung Hero award Neighborhood Found., 1995; elected to Wayne State Sch. Social Work Bd., 1992-98. Mem. NAFE, Am. Soc. Profl. and Exec. Women, Assn. Internat. Platform Spkrs., Mich. Coun. Social Svcs. Workers, Nat. fedn. Bus. and Profl. Womens Clubs Inc. U.S.A. (elected del. to China), Nat. Assn. Black Social Workers, Wayne State U. Social Work Alumni Assn. (bd. dirs. 1992-98), Delta Sigma Theta. Democrat. Baptist. Office: PO Box 361 Lincoln Park MI 48146-0361

RUSSELL, HEATHER FLYNN, psychologist, researcher; b. New Haven, Oct. 13, 1969; d. Glenn and Donna Ellen (Matthews) Whittaker; m. John Patrick Russell, Mar. 17, 2000. AB, Smith Coll., 1991; MA, LaSalle U., Phila., 1995; PhD, Temple U., 2000. Lic. psychologist Pa. Rsch. technician Children's Hosp. of Phila., 1991—2000; intern duPont Hosp. Children, Wilmington, Del., 1997—98; postdoctoral fellow Children's Hosp. of Phila., 2000—01; rsch. psychologist NIH, Bethesda, Md., 2001—02; clin. psychologist Shriner's Hosp. Children, Phila., 2001—. Pvt. practice Clearings, Inc., Bala Cynwyd, Pa., 2002—. Contbr. articles to profl. jours. Mem.: APA, Soc. of Pediat. Psychology, Am. Pain Soc. Avocations: tennis, skiing. Office: Shriners Hosp Children 3551 N Broad St Philadelphia PA 19140

RUSSELL, HELEN DIANE, retired museum curator, educator; b. Kansas City, Mo., Apr. 8, 1936; d. Harry Fay Russell and Georgia Mae (Canfield) Haeberle. AB, Vassar Coll., 1958; PhD, Johns Hopkins U., 1970; postgrad., Inst. for Advanced Study, Princeton, N.J., 1980-81. Mus. curator Nat. Gallery Art, Washington, 1964-90, curator of Old Master Prints, 1990-98. Professorial lectr. The Am. U., Washington, 1966-82, adj. prof. Art History, 1982—. Author: Rare Etchings of G.B. and G.D. Tiepolo, 1972, Jacques Callot, 1975, Claude Lorrain, 1982 (Barr award 1984), EVA/AVE: Woman in Renaissance and Baroque Prints, 1990. Woodrow Wilson Foun. fellow, 1958-59; Univ. fellow, Johns Hopkins U., 1961-63; Kress Found. fellow, 1973; Nat. Endowment for Arts fellow, 1980-81. Mem. Coll. Art Assn., Renaissance Soc. Am., Print Coun. Am., Vassar Club. Avocations: poodles, photography.

RUSSELL, JOYCE ANNE ROGERS, librarian; b. Chgo., Nov. 6, 1920; d. Truman Allen and Mary Louise (Hoelzle) Rogers; m. John VanCleve Russell, Dec. 24, 1942; children: Malcolm David, John VanCleve. Student, Adelphi Coll., 1937; BS in Chemistry, U. Ky., 1942; M.L.S., Rosary Coll., 1967; postgrad., Rutgers U., 1970-71. Research chemist Sherwin Williams Paint Co., Chgo., 1942-45; reference librarian Chicago Heights (Ill.) Pub. Library, 1959-61; librarian Victor Chem. Works, Chicago Heights, 1961-62; lit. chemist Velsicol Chem. Corp., Chgo., 1964-67; chemistry librarian U. Fla., Gainesville, 1967-69, interim assoc. prof., 1967-69; librarian Thiokol Chem. Corp., Trenton, N.J., 1969-73; supr. library operations E.R. Squibb Co., Princeton, N.J., 1973-80, sr. research info scientist, 1980-91. Mem. library adv. commn. Mercer Community Coll., 1979— ; adv. asso. Rutgers U. Grad. Sch. Library and Info. Scis., 1978— Editor: Bibliofile, 1967-69; contbr. articles to profl. jours. Mem. PTA, 1950-66; den mother Cub Scouts, 1952-59. Mem. Spl. Libraries Assn. (sec., dir., v.p., pres. Princeton-Trenton 1971, 75-80), Am. Chem. Soc. (bus. mgr., sec., dir. Trenton sect. 1969-78), AAUW, Mortar Board, Beta Phi Mu, Sigma Pi Sigma, Chi Delta Phi, Pi Sigma Alpha. Home: 1189 Parkside Ave Trenton NJ 08618-2625

RUSSELL, JUDY C. government agency administrator; children: Christopher, Michael, Catherine. BA cum laude, Dunbarton Coll. of the Holy Cross, Washington; MLIS, Cath. U. Am., Washington. Libr. Office of Tech. Assessment; staff mem. program of policy studies in sci. and tech. George Washington U., Washington; staff mem. COMSAT Labs.; dir. fed. depository libr. program Govt. Printing Office, Washington, dir. office of electronic info. svcs., 1991—96, supt. documents, 2003—; dir. govt. svcs. divsn. IDD Ent., 1996—98; dep. dir. Nat. Commn. on Librs. and Info. Scis., 1998—2003. Cons. in field. Recipient Spl. award, Fed. Computer Week's Fed. 100: The Readers' Choice awards, 1993. Office: Govt Printing Office 732 N Capitol St NW Washington DC 20401*

RUSSELL, KERI, actress; b. Fountain Valley, Calif., Mar. 23, 1976; Actress in films: Honey, I Blew Up the Kid, 1992, The Curve, 1998, Mad About Mambo, 1999, We Were Soldiers, 2002; TV series include: MMC, 1989, Mickey Mouse Club, 1991-93, Emerald Cove, 1993, Daddy's Girls, 1994, Malibu Shores, 1996, Roar, 1997, Felicity, 1998-2002; TV films include: MMC in Concert, 1993, The Babysitter's Seduction, 1995, The Lottery, 1996, When Innocence is Lost, 1997, Eight Days a Week, 1997, Cinderelmo, 1999; TV guest appearances include: Boy Meets World, 1993, Married...with Children, 1987, 7th Heaven, 1996. Winner Golden Globe for best performance by an actress in a TV series for Felicity, 1999. Office: The Gersh Agy 232 N Canon Dr Beverly Hills CA 90210-5302*

RUSSELL, LIANE BRAUCH, retired geneticist; b. Vienna, Aug. 27, 1923; came to U.S., 1941; d. Arthur and Clara (Starer) Brauch; m. William Lawson Russell (dec.), Sept. 23, 1947; children: David Lawson, Evelyn Ruth. AB, Hunter Coll., 1945; PhD, U. Chgo., 1949; ScD (hon.), Hunter Coll., N.Y.C., 1999. Fellow U. Chgo., 1945-46, teaching asst., 1946-47; rsch. asst. Jackson Lab., Bar Harbor, Maine, 1945-46; rsch. staff mem. Oak Ridge (Tenn.) Nat. Lab., 1947-75, sect. head., 1975-95, sr. rsch. fellow, 1988—2001; ret., 2002. Sci. advisor U.S. Del. at 1st Atoms for Peace Conf., Geneva, Switzerland, 1955; mem. numerous sci. bds. including Nat. Research Council com. on energy and environment, 1975-77, com. on biol. effects of ionizing radiation, 1977-80, bd. on environ. studies and toxicology, 1981-90, Nat. Council on Radiation Protection and Measurement Task Group, Washington, 1975-77, Genetox Program EPA, Washington, 1979—, Internat. Com. for Protection Against Environ. Mutagens and Carcinogens, Lausanne, Switzerland, 1977-83, Internat. com. on standardized genetic nomenclature for mice, 1977-91, office of tech. assessment, scientific adv. panel, 1985-86; mem. task group Internat. Agy. for Research on Cancer, Hanover, Fed. Republic of Germany, 1979, EPA review panel on mutagenicity guidelines, 1985-86; adj. faculty U. Tenn., 1980-. Assoc. editor Mutation Rsch., 1976-96, Environ. Mutagenesis, 1980-83; editor TCWP Newsletter, 1966—; editor: (book) Genetic Mosaics and Chimeras, 1979; contbr. more than 165 articles to profl. jours. Founder Tenn. Citizens for Wilderness Planning, Oak Ridge, 1966, pres. 1967-70, 86-87; active numerous environ. groups. Corp. fellow Union Carbide, 1983; corp. fellow Martin Marietta, 1985, sr. corp. fellow, 1988; recipient Merit award Mademoiselle, 1955, Roentgen medal City of Remscheid-Lennep, 1973, Disting. Assoc. award U.S. Dept. Energy, 1987; named to Hunter Coll. Hall of Fame, 1979, Sol Feinstone Environ. Achievement award SUNY, 1987, Lifetime Achievement award Tenn. Environ. Coun., 1990, Vocational Svc. award Oak Ridge Rotary, 1992, Marjorie Stoneman Douglas award Nat. Parks Conservation Assn., 1993, Enrico Fermi award U.S. Dept. Energy, 1993, Lifetime Environ. Conservation award Tenn. Dept. Environ. & Conservation, 2000. Fellow AAAS, Environ. Health Inst.; mem. Nat. Acad. Scis., Environ. Mutagen Soc. (pres. 1984-85, EMS award 1993), Genetics Soc. Am., Tenn. Environ. Honor Soc. Avocation: environ. acitivism.

RUSSELL, LOUISE BENNETT, economist, educator; b. Exeter, N.H., May 12, 1942; d. Frederick Dewey and Esther (Smith) B.; m. Robert Hardy Cosgriff, May 3, 1987; 1 child, Benjamin Smith Cosgriff. BA, U. Mich., 1964; PhD, Harvard U., 1971. Economist Social Security Adminstrn.,

Washington, 1968-71, Nat. Commn. on State Workmen's Compensation Laws, Washington, 1971-72, Dept. Labor, Washington, 1972-73; sr. economist Nat. Planning Assn., Washington, 1973-75; sr. fellow Brookings Instn., Washington, 1975-87; rsch. prof. Inst. for Health, Health Care Policy and Aging Rsch. Rutgers U., New Brunswick, N.J., 1987—, prof. econs., 1987—. Chmn. health care policy divsn. Rutgers U., 1988—. Author: Technology in Hospitals, 1979, The Baby Boom Generation and the Economy, 1987, Is Prevention Better Than Cure, 1986, Evaluating Preventive Care: Report on a Workshop, 1987, Medicare's New Hospital Payment System: Is It Working, 1989, Educated Guesses: Making Policy About Medical Screening Tests, 1994, (with MR Gold, JE Siegel and MC Weinstein) Cost-Effectiveness in Health and Medicine, 1996; also numerous articles. Mem. U.S. Preventive Svcs. Task Force, 1984-88; co-chair Panel on Cost Effectiveness in Health and Medicine DHHS, USPHS, 1993-96. Mem. Inst. Medicine of NAS (com. to study future pub. health 1986-87, bd. on health scis. policy 1989-91, com. on clin. practice guidelines 1990-91, com. on setting priorities for practice guidelines 1994, nat. cancer policy bd. 2001—). Office: Rutgers U Inst for Health Care Policy 30 College Ave New Brunswick NJ 08901-1283

RUSSELL, MARY ANN, secondary school educator; b. Murray, Ky., Oct. 12, 1932; d. Elginn Newton Underwood and Mary Louise Orr Underwood; m. Allen Wells Russell, Aug. 6, 1953; children: Mark Allen, Lisa Louise. BA, Murray State U., 1954, MA, 1956; cert. Rank 1, U. Colo., 1958; PhD, Vanderbilt U., 1970. Cert. Tchr. Ky. Dept. Edn., 1955. Tchr. English Murray City Sch., Murray, Ky., 1955—65, Paducah C.C., Paducah, Ky., 1965—66, Martin Jr. Coll., Pulaski, Tenn., 1968, Murray H.S., Murray, 1970—95; ret., 1995. Com. mem. Cmty. Edn., Murray, 1999—2000, Calloway 2020, Murray, 1999—2002, Cmty. United Benevolance Svc., Murray, 2001—02. Recipient Ky. Shakespeare Tchr. of Yr. award, State Shakespeare Festival, 1987, Golden Tchr. award, Ashland Oil, 1992, Tchr. of Yr. award, Kiwanis Club, 1992. Mem.: Calloway County Tchrs., Ky. Retired Tchrs., Murray Women's Club (pres. 1999—2002, Outstanding Clubwoman award 2001). Republican. Baptist. Avocations: reading, bridge, travel, cooking. Home: 1503 Sycamore Street Murray KY 42071

RUSSELL, MARY WENDELL VANDER POEL, non-profit organization executive; b. N.Y.C., Feb. 6, 1919; d. William Halsted and Blanche Pauline (Billings) Vander Poel; m. George Montagu Miller, Apr. 5, 1940 (div. 1974); children: Wendell Miller Steavenson, Gretchen Miller Elkus; m. Sinclair Hatch, May 14, 1977 (dec. July 1989); m. William F. Russell, June 24, 1995 (dec. Apr. 1996). Pres. Miller Richard, Inc., Interior Decorators, Oyster Bay, NY, 1972—2000; bd. dirs. Eye Bank Sight Restoration, N.Y.C., pres., 1980-88, hon. chair, 1988—2002; v.p. Manhattan Eye Ear and Throat Hosp., N.Y.C., 1978-90; sec. Cold Spring Harbor Lab., N.Y., 1985-89, 92-97; mem. DNA Learning Ctr. Bd., 1991-97; bd. dirs. DNA Learning Ctr., 1997-2000; sec. Cold Spring Harbor Lab, 1992-97, hon. trustee, 1998—. V.p. North Country Garden Club, Nassau County, N.Y., 1979-81, 1983-85; dir. Planned Parenthood Nassau County, Mineola, N.Y., 1982-84, Hutton House C.W.Post Coll.,Greenvale, N.Y., 1982—; chair Hutton House, 1992-94. Recipient Disting. Trustee award United Hosp. Fund, 1992. Mem. Colony Club (N.Y.C.), Church Club (N.Y.C.), Piping Rock Club (Long Island), Order St. John Jerusalem (N.Y.C.). Republican. Episcopalian. Home: Mill River Rd # 330 Oyster Bay NY 11771-2733 E-mail: ydnewr@aol.com.

RUSSELL, MARYANNE, photographer; Grad., NYU; student, Internat. Ctr. Photography. Staff photographer Time Inc.; owner Maryanne Russell Photography Inc., 1986—. Photographer (works appeared at) Acad. Art Coll., San Francisco, Lobet Gallery, NYC, Grant Gallery, Chelsea Art Gallery, (group exhbns.) Sephora's Flagship store. Mem.: Am. Soc. Media Photographers, NY Women in Comm. (Liz Hoover award 1994). Achievements include photography clients AT&T, Christian Dior, HBO, NY Giants, Paramount Pictures, People mag., Time Warner Inc., Viacom, and many others. Office: Maryanne Russell Photography Inc 230 E 52nd St Ste 1B New York NY 10022 Office Phone: 212-308-8722.*

RUSSELL, MAXINE, poet, writer; b. St. Paul, Feb. 17, 1912; d. Maximilian Karl Kaiser and Klara Treubert; m. Robert Lee Russell, Oct. 2, 1946; children: James Max, Roberta Russell Fraser. BA, U. Minn., 1932. Retail mgr. Merriam Pk. Floral, St. Paul, 1932—46. Poetry reader, spkr. Career Day Cmty. Leaders, 1990; poetry reader Arts in the Pk., Brainerd, Minn., 1995—99. Author: (book) Leaves from a Greenhouse, 1984, Honey in the Heart, 1987, Jungle Angel: Bataan Remembered, 1988, (poems) Searching for Star Trillium, 1997, Crossing Wild Moccasin Trails, 2001; contbr. articles and poems to local mags. and newspapers. Chmn. UNICEF Halloween Dr., Brainerd, 1973—76. Recipient Appreciation cert., U. Minn. Alumni Assn., 1980, 1981, award of Merit, Minn. State Horticulture Soc., 1990. Mem.: AAUW, Heartland Poets, League Minn. Poets (Minn. Poet laureate 2001—), Nat. Fedn. State Poetry Socs. Republican. Roman Catholic. Avocations: gardening, beekeeping. Home: 15277 Russell Rd N Brainerd MN 56401

RUSSELL, MELINDA FARRAR, music educator; b. Arlington, Va., Oct. 30, 1954; d. Wallace and Kathryn Farrar; m. John Wallace Russell Jr., July 9, 1977; children: John, Charles, Elizabeth. MusB in Edn., Shenandoah Conservatory Music, 1976; MusM in Music Edn., Shenandoah U., 1994. Tchr. music Page County Pub. Schs., Luray, Va., 1979—83; youth choir dir. Front Royal United Meth. Ch., 1983—87; dir. music and choral Rappahannock County Pub. Schs., Sperryville, Va., 1990—96, Frederick County Pub. Schs., Winchester, Va., 1996—; dir handbell First United Meth. Ch., 2001—. Mem.: NEA, Frederick County Edn. Assn., Va. Edn. Assn., Music Edn. Nat. Conf., Va. Music Educators Assn. Avocations: reading, gardening. Home: 820 Parishville Rd Gore VA 22637 Office: Redbud Run Elem Sch 250 First Woods Dr Winchester VA 22603

RUSSELL, PAMELA REDFORD, writer, film documentarian; b. Long Beach, Calif., June 11, 1950; d. George Martin and Helen Glyn (Brewen) R.; children: Caitlin, Maggie, Tess. Student, UCLA, 1970-74. Field prodr. Santa Fe Comm., L.A., 1983-84; exec. prodr. Guiding Star Prodns., L.A., 1994-96. Author: The Woman Who Loved John Wilkes Booth, 1978, Wild Flowers, 1982, (screenplay) Am American Woman, 1993; writer for Mary Tyler Moore Show, 1974, Touched By An Angel, 1997, also 14 scripts for Sears and Mut. Radio Theater, 1980-81, (TV show) Touched by An Angel, 1997, (teleplay) Have You Seen Me, 1998. Mem. Nat. Trust for Hist. Preservation, Civil War Trust., Pacific Grove Heritage Soc. Mem. PEN, Authors Guild, Writers Guild Am. West, PEN Ctr. USA West. Avocation: historic preservation.

RUSSELL, PEGGY TAYLOR, soprano, educator; b. Newton, N.C., Apr. 5, 1927; d. William G. and Sue B. (Cordell) Taylor; m. John B. Russell, Feb. 23, 1953; children: John Spotswood, Susan Bryce. MusB in Voice, Salem Coll., 1948; MusM, Columbia U., 1950; postgrad., U. N.C., Greensboro, 1977; student, Am. Inst. Music Studies, Austria, 1972, student, 1978; student of Clifford Bair, Nell Starr (hon.), Salem Coll., Winston-Salem, N.C.; student of Edgar Schofield, Chloe Owen, N.Y.C.; student operadramatics, Boris Goldovsky, Southwestern Opera Inst.; student of Ande Andersen, Max Lehner, Graz, Austria. Mem. faculty dept. voice Guilford Coll., Greensboro, NC, 1952—53, Greensboro Coll., 1971—72; pvt. tchr. voice Greensboro, 1963—. Co-founder, v.p. sales, mktg. Russell Textiles, Inc., Greensboro, 1988; vis. instr. in voice U. N.C., Chapel Hill, 1973—77; founding artistic dir., gen. mgr. Young Artists Opera Theatre, Greensboro, 1983, staged and produced 18 operatic prodns., 1983—91; gues lectr. opera workshop U. N.C., Greensboro, 1990—91; lectr. opera Friends of Weymouth, Southern Pines, NC, 1994; lectr. on music history and opera, High Point, NC, Ctr. Creative Leadership, Greensboro, 1979—80, 1st Presbyn. Ch., 1982. Singer: debut in light opera as Gretchen in The Red Mill, 1947; singer: (debuts) Rosalinda in Die Fledermaus, 1949, Lola in Cavalleria Rusticana, 1951, Violetta in La Traviata, 1953, Fiordiligi in Cosi fan Tutte, 1956; singer: Marguerite in Faust, 1967, First Lady in The Magic Flute, 1972, mem. Greensboro Orotario Soc., 1955—59; singer: (soprano soloist) The Messiah, 1952, 1958, The Creation, 1955, Solomon, 1958, Presbyn. Ch. of the Covenant, 1958—71; singer: guest appearances Sta. WFMY TV, 1958—62; singer: (soprano soloist) Greensboro Symphony Orch., 1964, 1980, Ea. Music Festival Orch., 1965, Greensboro Civic Orch., 1980; singer: (soloist in numerous recitals). Judge Charlotte Opera Guild Auditions, 1994; mem. Friendship Force of Guilford County, Netherlands, 1985, 1987; bd. dirs. Music Theater Assocs., Greensboro Friends of Music, N.C. Lyric Opera, Piedmont Opera Theatre. Grantee N.C. Arts Coun. and NEA, 1991. Mem.: Piedmont Triad Coun. Internat. Vis. (Appreciation award Nat. Coun. Internat. Visitors 1994), N.C. Symphony Soc., Civic Music Assn. (chmn. 1963—64), Atlanta Opera Guild, Broadway Theater League (chmn. 1961—63), Symphony Guild (dir. 1977—78), Greensboro Music Tchrs. Assn. (pres. 1966—67), Music Educators Nat. Conf., N.C. Fedn. Music Clubs (dir. 1956—58), Nat. Assn. Tchrs. of Singing (state gov. 1976—82, coord. Regional Artist Contest 1982—84), Ctrl. Opera Svc., Nat. Opera Assn. (chmn. regional opera cos. com. 1985—91, judge vocal competition auditions 1991, 1992, 1994, chmn. trustees Cofield Endowment 1991), Weatherspoon Art Mus. Guild, English Speaking Union (bd. dirs. Greensboro chpt., chmn. Shakespeare competition 1995), Guilford County Planning/Devel. Office (Forecast 2015 com.), Greensboro Preservation Soc., Greensboro City Club. Home: 3012 W Cornwallis Dr Greensboro NC 27408-6730

RUSSELL, RHONDA CHERYL, piano educator, recording artist; b. Ada, Okla., May 19, 1947; d. Joe Roy and Vina Olive (McEntire) Sammons; m. James Michael Davis, June 1, 1973 (div. Mar. 1986); m. Joel Reed Russell, Apr. 2, 1989; 1 child, Christopher Nathaniel. BFA in Music, U. Okla., 1969, postgrad., 1970-71; M of Ch. Music, Performance, Golden Gate Bapt. Theol. Sem., 1984; postgrad., U. Ariz., 1986. Piano tchr., various states, 1969—; music evangelist So. Bapt. Conv., nationwide, 1969—; asst. choral dept. Elk City (Okla.) H.S. Elk City Pub. Schs., 1975-78; supr. banking ops. Alaska Statebank, Anchorage, 1978-82; tchg. asst. to piano prof. Golden Gate Bapt. Theol. Sem., Mill Valley, Calif., 1982-83, mem. adj. faculty, 1984-85, mem. music adv. coun., 1998-01; touring accompanist, ednl. tutor Tucson Ariz. Boys Chorus, 1985; choral dir., program founder fine arts dept. Buckingham Charter Sch., Vacaville, Calif., 1994-2001; rec. artist, 2002. State music cons. Calif. Bapt. Conv., Fresno, 1984-01; music dir., artistic dir. Solano Childrens Chorus, Fairfield, Calif., 1993-94; music dir. Playground Prodns. Theatre, Vacaville, 1994-96; music conf. clinician Nev. Bapt. Conv., Reno and Las Vegas, 1995, 96; con. pianist N.Am. Mission Bd., So. Bapt. Conv., Santa Clara, Calif., 1995; accompanist Anchorage Civic Opera, 1979-81, So. Ariz. Light Opera Co., 1985; minister of music Internat. Bapt. Ch., 1999-2000, Garland Rd. Bapt. Ch., Enid, Okla., 2001-. Contbr. poetry to anthologies, 4 original songs to CD You're Not Alone, 2003. Pres. Decent Lit. Coun., Ponca City, Okla., 1977-78; campaign office helper Dem. Party of Okla., Oklahoma City, 1968; music dir. nursing home; beauty pageant coach, cons. Miss Am. Pageant Scholarships, Okla. and Calif., 1969—. Scholar Calif. Singing Churchwomen and Calif. Bapt. Conv., 1983. Mem. Nat. Guild Piano Tchrs., Music Ednl. Nat. Conf., Music Tchr. Assn. of Calif. (past treas. 1987-89), Calif. Profl. Music Tchrs. Assn. (program chair 1996), Tau Beta Sigma (life mem., treas., v.p., pres. 1965-69, Outstanding Mem. 1965). Democrat. Southern Baptist. Avocations: writing, composing, traveling, reading. Home and Office: 1710 E Locust Ave Enid OK 73701-2618

RUSSELL, SOFIA, writer; b. Tucson, Ariz., Dec. 4, 1943; d. Nick and Zalota Mary (Sexton) R.; m. Khalid Saleh Mohammad Al Najdi, Aug. 3, 1968 (dec. Oct. 1982). BA, Nat. U., 1990. Author: (novel) Whiskey Trail, 1997, (poems) The Artist and the Dreamer, 1997; contbr. hist. fiction, poetry, essays, philosophy and short stories to publs. Avocations: photography, oil painting, pencil sketches, hiking, sports.

RUSSETT, MARGARET E. language educator; b. New Haven, Conn., May 10, 1961; d. Bruce Martin and Cynthia (Eagle) Russett. BA, Yale U., 1983; MA, Johns Hopkins U., Balt., 1986; PhD, Johns Hopkins U., 1992. Asst. prof. U. So. Calif., L.A., 1990—96, assoc. prof., 1996—, dir. undergrad. studies in English, 1998—2001. Fulbright sr. lectr. Bozazici U., Istanbul, Turkey, 2002; bd. dirs. Soaring Apple, 2001—. Author: Dr. Quincey's Romanticism, 1997. Recipient Fulbright AIA award, CIES, 2003—, Fulbright lectureship, 2002; fellow, Guggenheim Found. fellow, 2001—02. Avocations: travel, hiking, yoga, marathon running. Office: Univ of Southern Calif Dept English Los Angeles CA 90089-0354 Office Phone: 213-760-3749.

RUSSMAN, IRENE KAREN, artist; b. Chgo., Mar. 10, 1942; d. Andrew Earl and Irene Margaret Kane (Barthley) James; m. James Ora Duffy, Jan. 27, 1963 (div. Oct. 20, 1993); children: Dawn Ann Duffy, James Sean Duffy, Maureen Marie Duffy; m. Stephen George Russman, Aug. 10, 2002. BA, Wash. State U., 1985, MFA, 1989; student summer workshops, Red Deer Coll., 2001, Pitchuk Sch. of Glass, 2001. Exhibitions include Galeria 5, Caracas, Venezuela, 1989, Acad. Arts, Riga, Latvia, 1990, Union Gallery, Pullman, Wash., 1991, Chase Gallery, Spokane, Wash., 1992, Virginia Inn, Seattle, 1993, Wash. State U./U. Ill., 1994, Gallery X "Out of the Box", Art Inst. Chgo., 1995, juried summer workshop, Pilchuck Glass Sch., Seattle, 2001, Represented in permanent collections Johanna Bur. Handicapped, Chgo., Gordon Gilkey Collection, Portland Art Mus., Modern Art Gallery, Leningrad, Russia, Neill Pub. Libr., Vetreria 2001, S.R.L., Murano, Italy, The Nat. Marble Mus., Yreka, Calif., The National Marble Museum. Bd. dirs. Pullman/Moscow Regional Airport; mem. Global Vols. Project, Ostuni, Italy, 1998, Passport Time Forest Svc., 2000. Recipient Civic Appreciation award, City of Pullman Mayor Pete Butkus, 1984. Mem.: Red Hat Soc., Palouse Folklore Soc., Bella Vita Lodge Number 2285. Avocations: folk dancing, flying, travel, gardening. Home: 3014 Lorne St SE Olympia WA 98501 Personal E-mail: irussman@hotmail.com.

RUSSO, IRMA HAYDEE ALVAREZ DE, pathologist; b. San Rafael, Mendoza, Argentina, Feb. 28, 1942; came to U.S, 1972; d. Jose Maria and Maria Carmen (Martinez) de Alvarez; m. Jose Russo, Feb. 8, 1969; 1 child, Patricia Alexandra. BA, Escuela Normal MTSM de Balcarce, 1959; MD, U. Nat. of Cuyo, Mendoza, 1970. Diplomate Am. Bd. Pathology. Intern Sch. Medicine Hosps., Argentina, 1969-70; resident in pathology Wayne State U. Sch. Medicine, Detroit, 1976-80. Rsch. asst., instr. Inst. Histology and Embryology Sch. Medicine U. Nat. of Cuyo, 1963-71, assoc. prof. histology Faculty Phys., Chem. and Math. Scis., 1970-72; rsch. assoc. Inst. Molecular and Cellular Evolution U. Miami, Fla., 1972-73; rsch. assoc. exptl. pathology lab. divsn. biol. scis. Mich. Cancer Foun., Detroit, 1973-75, rsch. scientist, 1975-76, vis. rsch. scientist, 1976-82, asst. mem., pathologist, 1982-89, assoc. rsch. mem., 1989-91, co-dir. pathology reference lab., 1982-86, chief exptl. pathology lab., 1989-91; co-dir. Mich. Cancer Found. Lab. Svcs., 1986-91; mem. Fox Chase Cancer Ctr., 1991—; dir. anatomic pathology Am. Oncologic Hosp. Dept. Pathology, 1991-92; dir. Lab. Svcs., 1992-94; chief molecular endocrinology sect. Breast Cancer Rsch. Lab. Fox Chase Cancer Ctr., 1994—; chief resident physician dept. pathology Wayne State U. Sch. Medicine, 1978-80, asst. prof., 1980-82; mem. staff Harper-Grace Hosps., Detroit, 1980-82; adj. prof. Pathology and Cell Biology Jefferson Sch. Medicine/Thomas Jefferson U., 1992—, chairperson Basic Breast Biology Study Sect. U. Calif. Breast Cancer Program, 1997, mem. endocrinology panel peer rev. com. breast cancer rsch. program U.S. Army R & D Command, 1994, 95, 96, 2002, 03, chairperson endocrinology peer rev. com., 1996; ad-hoc mem. biochem. endocrinology study sect. NIH, DHHS, 1994, metabolic pathology study sect., 1996-97; mem. European Commn. Cancer Prevention, 1994—; mem. bd. sci. counselor, sec. health and human svcs. Nat. Toxicology Program Bd., 1994-98; mem. Internat. Life Scis. Inst.-Risk Sci. Inst. Mammary Working Group, 1992—; pres., founder League of Women Against Cancer, Rydal, Pa., 1994—; guest lectr. dept. obstetrics Sch. Medicine U. Nat. of Cuyo, 1965-71; mem. resource devel. subcommittee of the profl. advisory com., Latinas Living Beyond Breast Cancer, 2000—; mem. Breast Cancer Res. Fdn. Review Panel, N.J.commr. on cancer rsch., Trenton, N.J., 1997, 2000. Editor-in-chief Jour. Women's Cancer, 1997—; contbr. articles to profl. jours. Rockefeller grantee, 1972-73; Nat. Cancer Inst. grantee, 1978-81, 84-87, 94-99, 2003—, Am. Cancer Soc. grantee 1988-89, 91-94, U.S. Army Med. R&D Command grantee, 1994-99, 2003—; recipient Shannon award Nat. Cancer Inst./NHHSS, 1992-94, Gold medal Inst. U. Dexeus, Barcelona, Spain, 2000. Mem. AAAS, Soc. Española Senología y Patología Mamaria, Nat. Cancer Inst. (breast cancer working group, breast cancer program 1984-88), Nat. Alliance Breast Cancer Orgns. (med. adv. bd. N.Y.C. chpt. 1986—), Ea. Coop. Oncology Group, Coll. Am. Pathologists, Am. Soc. Clin. Pathologists, Am. Assn. Cancer Rsch., Am. Assn. Clin. Chemistry, Internat. Coll. Physicians and Surgeons, Women in Cancer Rsch., The Endocrine Soc., Internat. Assn. Against Cancer, Sigma Xi, Food Quality Protection Act, Sci. Review Bd., Fed. Insecticide Fungi and Rodenticide Act, Adivsory Panel, EPA. Roman Catholic. Office: Fox Chase Cancer Ctr 333 Cottman Ave Philadelphia PA 19111 E-mail: I_Russo@fccc.edu., Lowac@msn.com.

RUSSO, JOAN MILDRED, special education educator; b. New Haven, Aug. 23, 1933; d. Stanley Alfred and Mildred Mary (Burns) Marcotte; div.; children: David C., Thomas E., Mary Russo Herrmann, Elizabeth Russo Sant, Robert J., James E. Goeth. AA, Coll. DuPage, 1975; BS in Edn., No. Ill. U., 1977; MEd, Lewis U., Evanston, Ill., 1985. Cert. K-12 educable mentally handicapped, K-12 learning disabilities, K-12 Trainable mentally handicapped, K-9 elem tchg., Ill. Tchrs. aid Pioneer Sch., West Chgo., 1977-78; pvt. practice Wheaton, Ill., 1978—. Co-editor: Yes, You Can, 1994. Active Dem. political campaigns, Ill., 1960—; sec. Winfield Libr. Assn., 1963-68; bd. dirs. Orton Dyslexia Soc., Ill., 1980-81, sec., 1981-82. Mem. LWV (con-con com., 1972), Orton Dyslexia Soc. (bd. dirs. 1980-81, sec. 1981-82), Nat. Assn. Learning Disabilities, Nat. Ctr. Learning Disabilities. Avocations: music, theater, reading, art, travel. Home and Office: 10 Old Blue Point Rd Scarborough ME 04074-7600

RUSSO, JONI K. director; b. Boston, June 1, 1956; d. Leonard and Eleanor Holbrook; m. Lester Greene, Apr. 4, 1982 (div. July 1993); 1 child, Jonathan Greene ; m. Clifford R. Russo, Aug. 8, 1993; children: C. J., Alex. MusB, Berklee Coll. Music, 1978; MA, Hofstra U., 1988, postgrad., 1996—97. Tchr. Lawrence Country Day Sch., NY, 1988—90, Rockville Ctr. Sch. Dist, 1990—91, Wantagh Pub. Sch. Dist., 1991—98; dir. music Carle Pl. Sch. Dist., 1998—2003. Chair fine and performing arts Carle Pl. Sch. Dist., 1998—. Mem.: ASA, NYSSMA (sec. 2001—03), MENC, MNEA. Home: 211 Berry Hill Rd Syosset NY 11791 Office: Carle Pl Sch Dist 168 Cherry Ln Carle Place NY 11514

RUSSO, KRISTEN DANIELLE, music educator; b. Manchester, Conn., Apr. 19, 1976; d. Sebastian and Linda Russo. MusB in Edn., Anna Maria Coll., 1999. Initial educator cert. music Conn., 2002. Cantor Immaculate Conception Ch., Terryville, Conn., 1997—2000; vacation bible sch. music tchr. Zion Evang. Luth. Ch., Bristol, Conn., 1998—; children's handbell choir dir. St. Joseph Ch., Bristol, 1999—2000; music dir. St. Paul Cath. H.S., Bristol, 1999—2000; music tchr. Sterling Meml. Sch., Oneco, Conn., 2000—01, North St. Sch., Windsor Locks, Conn., 2001—02, Broadview Mid. Sch., Danbury, Conn., 2002—03; handbell dir. Unitarian Universalist Ch., West Hartford, Conn., 2003—. Musician: New England Ringers; singer: Gaudeamus. Mem.: CMEA, MENC, AGEHR. Roman Catholic. Avocations: singing, handbell ringer, reading.

RUSSO, LISA ANN, registrar; b. Encino, Calif., Dec. 20, 1961; d. Edmund Severo and Lucille Delores Russo. AA in Politics, Coll. San Mateo; BS, UCLA, 1985, postgrad. Fin. dir. So. Calif. Inst. Architecture, Santa Monica, 1988-92, registrar L.A., 1992—, chief adminstrv. officer, 2003—. Con. Exec. Search Solutions, Newport Beach, Calif., 1999—. Mem. Chgo. Art Inst., 1996—; activist World Wildlife Fund, 1997—, Nature Conservancy, 1998—, Nat. Mus. Women Arts, 1998—, Natural Resources Def. Coun., 1999—. Mem. AAUW, Am. Assn. Collegiate Registrars and Admissions Officers, Nat. Assn. Fgn. Student Admin. Roman Catholic. Avocations: skiing, mountain biking, travel, language, politics. Office: So Calif Inst Architecture 970 E Third St Los Angeles CA 90013 E-mail: lisarusso@sciarc.edu., lrusso3626@earthlink.net.

RUSSO, MELISSA, reporter; BA, Tufts U., Boston; MS in Journalism, Columbia U., N.Y.C. Intern Office Media Rels. White House, Washington; assoc. producer, video journalist Time Inc. Mag. Group, 1987—92; polit. reporter N.Y, News 1, N.Y.C., 1992—98, NewsChannel4 NBC, N.Y.C., 1998—. Recipient Gold Typewriter award, N.Y. Press Club, 1997. Mem.: The Inner Circle. Office: NBC 30 Rockefeller Plz New York NY 10112

RUSSO, PATRICIA F. communications executive; BA, Georgetown U.; postgrad. in advanced mgmt., Harvard U., 1989. Sales and mktg. mgmt. exec. IBM, 1973-81; with AT&T (now Lucent Techs. Inc.), 1981—; pres. bus. unit Bus Comm. Sys., 1992-96; exec. v.p. strategy bus. devel. and corp. ops. Lucent Techs., Inc., Murray Hill, NJ, 1997-99, exec. v.p., CEO svc. provider networks Warren, NJ, 1999—2000; pres., CEO Lucent Techs. Inc., Murray Hill, 2002—, chmn., 2003—; pres., COO Eastman Kodak, 2000—02. Bd. dirs. Xerox Corp., Schering-Plough Corp., N.J. Mfrs. Ins. Co., Georgetown U. Office: Lucent Techs 600 Mountain Ave New Providence NJ 07974*

RUSSO, ROSALIE J. social worker, vocational rehabilitation counselor, educator; MSW, Yeshiva U., 1995; BA in Sociology summa cum laude, CUNY, 1993, postgrad. cert. in social work adminstrn., 1998, DSW, 2002. Cert. social worker N.Y. Social worker, admissions coord. Assn. Children Retarded Mental Devel./Lifespire/Day Treatment and Workshop, N.Y.C., 1995—98; vocat. rehab. counselor N.Y. State Edn. Dept./Vocat. Ednl. Svcs. Individuals with Disabilities, Bklyn., 1998—. Adj. asst. prof. human svcs. dept. N.Y.C. Tech. Coll., CUNY, Bklyn., 2002. Contbr. articles to profl. jours.; author: (book chpt.) Integrating Disability in Social Work Education. Mem.: NASW, Coun. on Social Work Edn., Am. Assn. on Mental Retardation. Home: Apt #2-C 201 W 70th St New York NY 10023 Personal E-mail: rosedsw@aol.com.

RUST, LOIS, food company executive; Pres. Rose Acre Farms, Seymour, Ind., 1989—. Office: Rose Acre Farms PO Box 1250 Seymour IN 47274-3850

RUSZKIEWICZ, CAROLYN MAE, newspaper editor; b. Tucson, Nov. 10, 1946; d. Robert Frank and Charlotte Ruth (Hadley) Knapton; m. Joseph Charles Ruszkiewicz, July 11, 1969. BA, Calif. State U., Long Beach, 1971, MA, 1973. Reporter Long Beach (Calif.) Press-Telegram, 1968-85, consumer editor, 1985-86, lifestyle editor, 1986-89, regional news editor, 1989-91, city editor, 1991-95, asst. mng. editor, 1995-97, mng. editor, 1997—. Avocations: swimming, walking, reading. Office: Long Beach Press Telegram 604 Pine Ave Long Beach CA 90844-0003

RUT, WANDA E. artist, educator, writer; b. Lwow, Poland, Jan. 5, 1923; arrived in U.S., 1976, naturalized; d. Adam Edmunt and Langmoier Anna Binder; m. Roman Smoleniec, 1977 (dec. 1979); m. Tadewsz Rut, 1958 (div. 1968); 1 child, Tomasr. BA in Textile Design, Inst. Indsl. Arts, Lwow, Poland, 1943; BA in Econs., Sch. Higher Edn. in Econ., Wroclaw, Poland, 1950; MFA, Acad. Fine Arts, Warsaw, Poland, 1957; student, Polish Acad. Scis., 1975. Chmn. Art Tchg. Divsn. Polish Assn. Artists and Designers,

Warsaw, 1966—75; coord. Tailoring Mus. Fashion and Modeling Sch., Warsaw, 1975; editor art column Polish-Am. Weekly Newspaper, N.Y., 1978—80; art dir. Polish Inst. Arts and Scis., N.Y., 1983; cons. Polish Mus. Found., Port Washington, NY, 1984; art therapist N.Y., NY, 1984—85; freelance clothing designer. Tchr. various schs., Poland; costume designer Motion Picture Studios, Wroclaw, Opera House, Prague, Czech Republic; bd. jurors Artist Craftsmen of N.Y., 1980—82. One-woman shows include 40 shows in various international cities including, Avery Fisher Hall Lincoln Ctr., N.Y.C., N.Y., 1977, Suffolk County Hist. Mus., Riverhead, L.I., N.Y., 1978, Mus. of Sci. and Industry, LA, Calif., 1979, Guild Hall Mus., Moran Gallery, East Hampton, N.Y., 1977, Cepelia Salons, San Francisco, Calif., 1977, Interchurch Ctr., N.Y.C., N.Y., 1980, Pen & Brush Club, 1980 (1st prize, 1980), Donnell Libr., 1984, exhibited in group shows at Student Art Show, Moscow, Russia, 1953 (award, 1953), numerous others totalling near 100, exhibitions include Polish Art Weaving, Dresden, East Germany, 1969 (award, 1969), Tchrs. Head Club, Warsaw, Poland, 1973 (award, 1973), Internat. Book & Press Clubs, Poland, 1974 (award, 1974), Womanart Gallery, N.Y.C., N.Y., 1978 (1st prize, 1978), Slavic-Am. Cultural Assn., 1983 (award, 1983), numerous others, Represented in permanent collections Polish Inst. Arts and Scis., N.Y.C., N.Y., Old Warsaw (Poland) Gallery, Alexandria, Va., Polish Mus. Found., Port Washington, N.Y., Slavic Gallery, Glen Cove, N.y., Mus. Textile Industry, Lodz, Poland, Sport Mus., Warsaw, Poland, Brno, Czech. Republic, Stockholm, Sweden, Parliament of Polish People's Republic, Warsaw, Poland, Phys. Edn. Ctr., Cairo, Egypt, City Coun. of Warsaw and Wroclaw, Nat. Tchrs. Club, Warsaw, Poland, Forum Hotel. Recipient 1st prize, Cepelia Art Contest, Warsaw, Poland, 1976, Polish Art Competition, Doylestown, Pa., 1977. Achievements include invention of cylindrical loom enabling weaving in the round. Avocations: poetry, writing. Home: 1660 NE 191 St Apt 402 North Miami Beach FL 33179 Office: Am Inst Polish Culture 1440 79th St Causeway Ste 117 Miami Beach FL 33141

RUTH, SHIELA GRANT, music educator; b. Sagamiono, Japan, May 12, 1955; came to U.S., 1957; d. Allan Francis and Eiko (Nagasawa) Grant; m. Terrence Allan Ruth, Sept. 8, 1979. BA, Frostburg State Coll., 1977. Health care asst. Deaton Med. Ctr., Balt., summer 1974, 75, Nursing Staff, Annapolis, Md., 1977; sub. tchr. Anne Arundel County Schs., Md., 1977-78; tchr. piano/organ Jordan Kitts, Glen Burnie, Md., 1978-79; music asst. Lindale Jr. H.S., Ferndale, Md., 1986-90, Harundale Presbyn. Ch., Glen Burnie, 1990—; tchr. piano/organ Severn, Md., 1977—. Mem. Md. State Music Tchrs. Assn., Music Tchrs. Nat. Assn., Anne Arundel Music Tchrs. Assn. (corr. sec. 1997—), Delta Omicron (warden 1975-77), Sigma Delta Pi. Republican. Presbyterian. Avocations: playing piano, touring civil war battlefields, ice skating. Home: 753 Rosewood Rd Severn MD 21144-2069 Office: Harundale Presbyn Ch 1020 Eastway Glen Burnie MD 21060-7303

RUTHERFOORD, REBECCA HUDSON, computer science educator; b. Elkhart, Ind., Feb. 24, 1948; d. Charles Melvin Hudson and Eunice Klaire (Lund) Edmonds; m. James Kincanon Rutherfoord, Aug. 31, 1968; children: James Kincanon Jr., Charles Penn. BS, Ind. State U., 1971, MS, 1972, EdD, 1975; MS in Computer Sci., So. Poly State U., Marietta, Ga., 1995. Cert. data processor. Staff asst. Ind. State U., Terre Haute, 1969-71; vocal music tchr. S.W. Parke Schs., Rockville, Ind., 1971-73; fellowship asst. Ind. State U., Terre Haute, 1974-75; vocal music tchr. Slidell (La.) H.S., 1977 78; programmer, analyst La. State U., Baton Rouge, 1978-79, dir. computer rehab. program, 1979-80; programmer, analyst Hanes Corp., Atlanta, 1980-81; asst. prof. Devry Inst., Atlanta, 1981-83; acting dept. chair So. Poly. State U., Marietta, Ga., 1989-92, prof. computer sci., 1983—, computer sci. grad. program coord., 1996-97, asst. to pres., 1997-98, interim dean arts and scis., 1998-99, chair MSIT program, 1999—, acting head dept. computer sci., 2000-01, dept. chair, info. tech., 2001—. Cons. The Assocs. Group, Inc., Roswell, Ga., 1986-88, Crawford Comm., Atlanta, 1987; adj. prof. Cobb County Bd. Edn., Marietta, 1985-87, Joseph T. Walker Sch., Marietta, 1985-86; vis. prof. Leicester (U.K.) Poly., 1990. Choir dir. St. Peter and Paul Episcopal Ch., Marietta, 1981—85, choir mem., 1992—2001, bd. dirs., 1998—2001; Christian edn. dir. St. Francis Episcopal Ch., Denham Springs, La., 1978—80; choir mem. St. David's Episcopal Ch., Roswell, 1985—92; choir dir. Ch. of the Messiah, 2001—; bd. dirs., mem. Cherokee Cmty. Habitat for Humanity, 1994—98. Mem. Data Processing Mgmt. Assn., Assn. Computing Machinery, Nat. Assn. Women in Edn., Computer Sci. Edn. (spl. interest group), Nat. Assn. Women Edn., Delta Kappa Gamma, Sigma Alpha Iota. Republican. Avocations: boating, reading. Office: So Poly State Univ 1100 S Marietta Pky Marietta GA 30060-2855

RUTHERFORD, DOREEN, artist, excavating company executive; b. Newton, N.J., Dec. 12, 1966; m. Daniel Grey Rutherford, Aug. 30, 1986; children: Lillian, Julia. Diploma in computer programming, Warren Vocat. Sch., N.J., 1986; pvt. studies in art, with Howard Carr and Charles Slovek. CEO, Rutherford's Excavating, Bend, Oreg., 1992—. Art cons. Gallery Haleiwa, Hawaii, 1988-89, Fettiq Gallery, Haleiwa, 1989-90, Where Eagles Soar Gallery, Sun River, Oreg., 1991-92; mem. adv. bd. Humane Soc. Art Show, Bend, 1992, distbr. lit. Living Waters Beijing and Canton, 1987, Taipei, Taiwan, 1987. Illustrator: (book) Bend Business Woman's Association, 1994; one-woman shows Rix of Hawaii, Haleiwa, Oahu, 1987, Sun River (Oreg.) Coffee Co., 1999, Wind River Gallery, Bend, Oreg., 1997, Charlotts Fine Art Gallery, 2001. Contbr. Sara Fisher Cancer Rsch. Auction, Bend, Oreg.; sole contbr. SunRiverDance Acad. Ann. Presentation, 2002. Mem. Oreg. C. of C. Avocations: skiing, equestrian sports, antiquing, writing, plein air painting.

RUTHERFORD, GUINEVERE FAYE, surgical technician; b. Cleve., Sept. 17, 1955; d. Alex and Alice Rose Watson; m. La Juane Edward Rutherford, Apr. 23, 1999. Grad. liberal arts, Highland Park C.C., Highland Park, Mich., 1981; BS Allied Health, Madonna U., 1983; MA Bus. Sci., Ctrl. Mich. U., 1991. Surg. technologist Children Hosp. Mich., Detroit, 1981—85; clin. and classroom instr. Madonna U., Livonia, Mich., 1983; surg. unit specialist Botsford Gen. Hosp., Farmington Hills, Mich., 1985—87, surg. technologist, 1985—95; clin. and classroom instr. Detroit Bd. Edn., 1986, Highland Park (Mich.) C.C., 1992—94; surg. technologist various hosps., 1995—, St. John Hosp., Detroit, 1998—99. Mem.: Am. Bus. Women Assn., Assn. Surg. Tech. Office: Surg Helping Hand Inc PO Box 47317 Oak Park MI 48237

RUTHERFORD, VICKY LYNN, special education educator; b. Florence, S.C., Sept. 12, 1947; BS, Hampton U., 1969, MA, 1971; PhD, Mich. State U., 1991. Cert. tchr. French, spl. edn., reading specialist, Va., tchr. spl. edn., S.C. Social worker day care Hampton (Va.) Dept. Social Svc., 1970-72; reading therapist, asst. dir., dir. Bayberry Reading Clinic, Hampton, 1973-77; tchr. reading, English, counselor York County Schs., Yorktown, Va., 1977-85; staff advisor, asst. to course coord. Mich. State U., East Lansing, 1985-90; tchr. autism Florence (S.C.) Dist. 1 Sch. Sys., 1992-96, tchr. emotionally impaired, 1996—. Instrnl. designer: Addiction Severity Index #1, 1987, #2, 1988, Managing a Diverse Workforce, 1990; designer, trainer: Project Teach, 1991; designer, developer: (video) Camp Takona Summer Experience, 1992. Bass guitarist, Sun. sch. sec., youth worker, Sun. sch. supt. Progressive Ch. of Jesus, Florence, 1992-98, Greater Zion Tabernacle Apostolic Ch., Florence, 1998—. Fellow Mich. Dept. Edn., 1987-89. Mem. Internat. Reading Assn. Office: Delmae Heights Elem Sch 1211 S Cashua Dr Florence SC 29501-6399 E-mail: v_rutherford@fsdl.org.

RUTLEDGE, DEBORAH JEAN, secondary school educator, music educator; b. St. Louis, Mar. 13, 1954; d. George Roosevelt and Morie Louise Albin; m. Mark H. Rutledge, Mar. 12, 1978 (div. July 28, 1997); children: Mary-Esther, Martha-Ann, Joanna-Ruth, Susanna-Rachel, Sarah-Naomi. MusB, So. Meth. U., 1976; MEd, U. No. Tex. Cert. tchr. reading, elem., ESL, music, English lang., arts and English Tex. Reading tchr.'s aide Sam Houston Mid. Sch., Irving, Tex., 1994—95; reading tchr. Irving H.S., 1995—2002; reading and ESL tchr. Lorenzo de Zavala Mid. Sch., Irving, 2002—03, counselor, 2002—03. Reading tutor, Irving; piano tchr., Irving. Pianist The Ch. in Oklahoma City, 1976—81. Grantee, Irving Schs. Found., Tex. Pub. Edn., U. North Tex. Mem.: Irving Music Tchrs. Assn., Internat. Reading Assn., Assn. Tex. Profl. Educators, Tex. Counselling Assn., Tex. Music Tchrs. Assn., Nat. Guild Piano Tchrs., Nat. Music Tchrs. Assn., Phi Delta Kappa. Home: 2008 Addington St Irving TX 75062

RUTLEDGE, JOANNE, artist, consultant; b. Indpls., Dec. 17, 1941; d. Edward John and Dorothy Louise (Bachelor) Underwood; m. Kenneth Clay Smith, Sept. 7, 1963 (div. May 1990); children: Elizabeth, Kenneth Clay, Jr., Andrew; m. Mark Alan Rutledge, July 31, 1993. RN, St. Vincent's Sch. Nursing, Indpls., 1962; BSN, Ind. U., 1979. Staff RN Children's Hosp., Washington, 1962—63, St. Vincent's Hosp., Indpls., 1963—64, Women's Hosp. Spl. Care Nursery, Indpls., 1990—97; nurse cons. Hosp. Care for Indigent Ind. State Program, Indpls., 1995—. Ptnr. Collective Art Gallery, Indpls., 2003—. Exhibitions include Ind. State Fair, Ind. Heritage Arts, Southside Art League Regional Show. Docent Indpls. Mus. Art, 1983—; reading tutor Kiwanis Project, 2002—; active various coms. Children's Mus. Guild, 1975—; v.p. Indpls. Athletic Club Art Bd. Found., 1990—. Recipient Billy Cothran Landscape award, Indpls. Art Ctr., 1985. Mem.: Ind. Plein Art Painters Assn., Stutz Artist's Assn., Ind. Artist's Club (assoc.), Proctor Club (pres. 1994—95). Roman Catholic. Avocations: travel, photography, hiking, canoeing, attending concerts and theater. Home: 1019 W 75th St Indianapolis IN 46260-3408 Office: Ind Hosp Care for the Indigent 402 W Washington St Indianapolis IN 46204

RUTLEDGE, KATHERINE BURCK, artist; b. La., Mar. 16, 1949; d. Cyril Büsing and Sarah Marlette Burck; m. Clayton Fenton Rutledge, Apr. 24, 1982. BFA, La. State U., 1971; postgrad., New Orleans Acad. Fine Arts, 1988—90. Represented in permanent collections McIlhenny Collection of Natural Sci., La. State U., New Orleans Zoo. Fellow La. State Mus. Natural Sci., Baton Rouge, 1979—82. Scholar, Audubon Soc., Baton Rouge Chpt., 1980. Mem.: The Pocahontas Found., Magna Carta Dames, Jamestown Soc. (life). Republican. Avocations: gardening, birdwatching. Home: 238 Ship Dr Baton Rouge LA 70806

RUTSCHKE, ANNAMARIE, artist; b. Santa Barbara, Calif., June 29, 1965; d. Benjamin Wiley Jordan and Jeannette Irene Rutschke; m. Robert Allan Bryant, July 31, 1988 (div. 1996). File clk. San Luis Welding Supply, San Luis Obispo, Calif., 1983; customer svc. clk. The Living Picture, Alameda, Calif., 1984, 7-11, Alameda, 1985-86; clk. Def. Subs. Reg. Pacific, Alameda, 1987-88; pers. clk. Def. Depot Tracy, Alameda, 1988-90; adminstrv. clk. Gen. Svcs. Adminstrn., San Francisco, 1990, purchasing agt., 1990-96, adminstrv. technician, 1996-99; legal clk. IRS Dist. Counsel, San Francisco, 1999-2000. Freelance artist. Co-coord. Fed. Recycling Coun., 1992, 93; operator Muscular Dystrophy Assn., Arroyo Grande, Calif., 1980. Republican. Lutheran. Avocations: art, writing, computer programming, web design, cooking. E-mail: ldrsnewswolfe@aol.com.

RUTSTEIN, SEDMARA ZAKARIAN, piano educator, concert pianist; b. Kazan, Russia, Oct. 18, 1937; came to U.S., 1974; d. Suren and Ekaterina (Todorovskaya) Zakarian; m. Alexander Rutstein, Aug. 29, 1958; 1 child, Alla. D in Music, Leningrad State Conservatory, USSR, 1961, diploma (hon.), 1959. Prof. Leningrad State Conservatory, 1961-73; artist-in-residence Grinnell (Iowa) Coll., 1974—76; prof. Oberlin (Ohio) Conservatory, 1976—. Recording artist, classical piano music XVIII through XX centuries, 1972—. Grantee Oberlin Coll., 1984-98. Mem. Am. Music Tchrs. Assn. Avocations: reading, music, travel. Home: 226 N Prospect St Oberlin OH 44074-1035 Office: Oberlin Coll Conservatory of Music Oberlin OH 44074 Office Phone: 440-775-8250. E-mail: sedrut@oberlin.net.

RUTTENBERG, RUTH A. economist; b. Washington, D.C., Feb. 16, 1948; d. Stanley Harvey and Gertrude Leah Bernstein Ruttenberg; children: Estye Ross, Jack Ross. BA in Econs. with honors, U. Wis., 1969; M in City Planning, U. Pa., 1971, PhD in City Planning, 1981. Prof. Bradford Coll., 1972—73; sr. assoc. Ruttenberg, Kilgallon & Assocs., Inc., Washington, 1973-86; pres. Ruth Ruttenberg & Assocs., Bethesda, Md., 1986—; sr. staff assoc. George Meany Ctr. for Labor Studies, Nat. Labor Coll., 2001—. Sr. lectr. Am. U., Washington, 1973—75; asst. prof. Howard U., Washington, 1975—82; adj. faculty U. Md., College Park, Md., 1974—; mem. Bd. Equalization and Rev., Washington, 1981—82; sr. economist Occupl. Safety and Health Adminstrn., Washington, 1979—80; dir. Nat. Clearinghouse for Worker Safety and Health Tng., Bethesda, 1995—2000; co-chair Instnl. Rev. Bd., Ctr. to Protect Workers Rights, Washington, 1996—; peer rev. mem. U.S. Dept. Energy, Washington, 1996, 97. Author: Occupational Safety and Health in the Chemical Industry, 1981; mem. editl. rev. bd. Indsl. Rels. Rsch. Assn., 2002—. Bd. dirs. Group Health Assn., Washington, 1982-88, 90-94; bd. dirs., Consumer Health Found., Washington, 1994—; bd. dirs. Children's Internat. Summer Villages, Washington, 1994—. Woodrow Wilson fellow, 1969-70; Bicentennial grantee Govt. Sweden, 1978. Democrat. Avocations: reading, kayaking, traveling. Office: Ruth Ruttenberg & Assocs Inc 5107 Benton Ave Bethesda MD 20814-2807 E-mail: rruttenberg@comcast.net., rruttenberg@georgemeany.org.

RUTTENBERG, SUSANN I. health sciences administrator; b. Chgo., Apr. 7, 1943; d. William and Audrey A. Kray; m. Harold Seymour Ruttenberg, Aug. 11, 1963 (div. Oct. 1977); children: Adam, Michael, Leslie. BS, Northwestern U., 1964; MBA, U. Calif., Irvine, 1993. Writer, prodr. Kragie Newell & Assocs., Des Moines, 1977-80, Nat. Cable Prodns. and Telesshopper, 1980-81; owner, mgr. Rib Joint, Des Moines, 1978-81; gen. mgr. Stuart Anderson's Black Angus, Ariz. and Calif., 1982-87; various adminstr. positions in pediats. U. Calif., Irvine, 1988-93, adminstr. child devel. ctr., 1997-98, adminstr. dermatology, 1996—, adminstr. phys. medicine and rehab., 1999—. V.p. U. Calif. Irvine GSM Healthcare Alumni, 1995—2002; mem. exec. bd. Acad. Bus. Officers Group, 2000—03, chair exec. bd., 2000—01, ADA/M bd. dirs., 2000—04, chair IT com., 2003—04. Editor, contbr.: (cookbook) Child's Play, 1989; editor, writer newsletter UCInsights on Pediatrics, 1995; author: Never Let'em Catch You With Your Bed Rails Down, 2003; contbr. Executive Decisions in Dermatology, 2000—04. Women's chair United Jewish Appeal, Des Moines, 1975; bd. dirs. Child Guidance Ctr., Des Moines, 1976-77, Cmty. Telephone Coun., Des Moines, 1978-81; mem. dir.'s coun. U. Calif. Irvine Chao Family Comprehensive Cancer Ctr., 1998—; vol. rep., sec. bd. dirs. Rancho Mirage, Calif. C. of C., 1984-86. Northwestern U. scholar, 1963-64; U. Calif. Irvine Coll. Medicine Career Devel. award, 1992-93, Healthsci. Adminstr. of Yr. award, U. Calif. Chancellor. Mem.: Assn. Dermatology Adminstrs./Mgrs. (chair newsletter com. 2001, chair comms. com. 2002—03, bd. dirs. 2002—), Assn. Profs. Dermatology, Med. Group Mgmt. Assn. Avocations: cooking, reading, literacy tutoring, dance, travel. Office: U Calif Irvine C340 Med Scis I Irvine CA 92697-0001

RUTTER, FRANCES TOMPSON, publisher; b. Arlington, Mass., Apr. 12, 1920; d. Harold F. and Mildred F. (Wheeler) Tompson; m. John H. Ottemiller, Mar. 24, 1943; children: Joan Tompson Gillum, John Tompson; m. William D. Rutter, Oct. 26, 1970. AB magna cum laude, Pembroke Coll., Brown U., 1941; postgrad., Mt. Holyoke Coll., 1942-43. Res. book librarian Brown U., 1941-42; annotator ship's papers John Carter Brown Library, Providence, 1943-44; librarian Sci. Service, Washington, 1944-45; ptnr. Shoe String Press, Hamden, Conn., 1952-58; sec., treas. Shoe String Press, Inc., 1958-68, pres., treas., 1968-80, also bd. dirs.; sec.-treas., dir. Tompson-Malone, Inc., book mfrs., 1967-80; pres., treas., dir. Tompson & Rutter, Inc., 1980-89. V.p. class 1941 Pembroke Coll., 1967-73, 76-91, pres., 1973-76, head class agt., 1979-85, bequests and trust chmn., 1979-90, 40th reunion gift com., 1980, co-chair 50th reunion gift com., 1990-91, 55th reunion gift com., 1995-96; spl. projects adv. panel N.H. Commn. on Arts, 1980-84; mem. natural resources com. Grantham, 1980; mem. Grantham Planning Bd., 1981-87, sec., 1981-83, chmn., 1985-87; chmn. Grantham Recycling Com., 1988-89, Grantham Hist. Soc., 1992-96, Habitat for Humanity-Kearsarge/Sunapee chpt., 1989-94; mem. Diocesan Altar Guild Bd., 1990-93, sec., 1991-92; vol. Mary Hitchcock Meml. Hosp. Aux., 1991-2003; mem. vestry St. Paul's Episc. Ch., 1997-2000, jr. warden, 1998-2000; assoc. Holy Cross Monastery, West Park, N.Y. Mem. Friends of Fernald Libr. of Colby-Sawyer Coll., ACLU (life), LWV (editor newsletter 1987-89), Assoc. Alumni Brown U. (bd. dirs. 1981-83), Nicholas Brown Soc., Pembroke Ctr. Assocs. (coun. 1984-86), Soc. for Preservation N.H. Forests, Episcopal Peace Fellowship, Phi Beta Kappa. Episcopalian. Home: 80 Azalea Cir # 19 White River Junction VT 05001 E-mail: franbill@valley.net.

RUTTER, MARIE E. music educator; b. Bklyn., Nov. 6, 1939; d. Edward George de Beaumont and Lela Dean Graham; m. Stuart Mishler Rutter, Aug. 26, 1961; children: Deborah Gulliver, Jeanne Meister, Suzanne Cook, Caryn Einsweiler. BA, Albion Coll., 1961. Profl. cert. in piano Music Tchrs. Nat. Assn. Pub. sch. music tchr. Mona Shores Sch. Dist., Muskegon, Mich., 1961-63; pvt. piano tchr. Muskegon, 1962-63, Ft. Wayne, Ind., 1963-73, Lincoln, Nebr., 1973-74, Elk Grove Village, Ill., 1974-76, Hickory, N.C., 1976-84, Schaumburg, Ill., 1984—. Elder Ch. of the Cross, Hoffman Estates, Ill., 1995—96, mem. Christian edn. com., 1996—2000, dir. handbell choir, 2002—. Mem. Ill. State Music Tchrs. Assn. (profl. cert. in piano, state syllabus performance chair 1994—), N.W. Suburban Music Tchrs. Assn. (syllabus chair, 2nd v.p., 1st v.p., pres.). Presbyterian. Avocations: quilting, reading, sewing, gardening.

RUTTINGER, JACQUELYN, director of exhibitions; b. Great Falls, Mont., July 21, 1940; d. Robert Muir and Amy Rosalie (Kernaghan) R.; m. Lee Alan Boye, July 1961 (div. 1969); 1 child, Richard William. BFA, Sch. of Art Inst. Chgo., 1963; MA, No. Ill. U., 1976, MFA, 1977. Instr. art Kankakee (Ill.) C.C., 1977-79, Prairie State Coll., Chicago Heights, Ill., 1977-81; cmty. prof. Govs. State U., University Park, Ill., 1982; chair dept. art St. Mary of the-Woods (Ind.) Coll., 1983-85; dir. exhbns. Western Mich. U., Kalamazoo, 1986—. One woman shows include Freeport (Ill.) Art Mus., 1979, Jesse Besser Mus., Alpena, Mich., 1987, Saginaw (Mich.) Art Mus., 1988, Kalamazoo Inst. of Arts, 1990; exhibited in group shows at Mitchell Mus., Mt. Vernon, Ill., 1981, Millikin U., Decatur, Ill., 1982 (Purchase award), No. Ill. U., DeKalb (Purchase award State of Ill.), Ea. Ill. U., Charleston (Purchase award State of Ill.), Western Mich. U., Kalamazoo (2 Purchase awards State of Mich.); represented in permanent collections Ill. State Mus., Springfield, Freeport Art Mus., Sheldon Swope Art Mus., Terre Haute, Ind., Jesse Besser Mus. Project Completion grantee Ill. Arts Coun., 1981; Rsch. grantee Coll. Fine Arts, Western Mich. U., 1986, 87, 88-89, 90-91; recipient Best of Show award Jackson Area Juried Show, Ella Sharp Mus., Jackson, Mich., 1996; Creative Artists grantee Arts Found. of Mich and Mich. Coun. for Arts and Cultural Affairs, 1996-97. Mem. Assn. Coll. and Univ. Museums and Galleries, Mich. Mus. Assn., Arts Coun. Greater Kalamazoo (Mini grantee 1987-88), Detroit Inst. Arts, Kalamazoo Inst. Arts. Avocations: gardening, canoeing, environmentalism. Home: 1110 Dwillard Dr Kalamazoo MI 49048-2259 Office: Western Mich U Sch Art 1903 W Michigan Ave Kalamazoo MI 49008

RUVIELLA-KNORR, JEANNE L. music educator, consultant, clinician; d. Jean and Marion Post Ruviella; m. H. Richard Knorr, May 26, 1962 (div. Dec. 24, 1993); children: Richard Post Knorr, Michelle Renee Mitchell. MusB, Boston U., 1962; MA, U. So. Calif., 1966; PhD, U. Md., 2004. Cert. advanced profl. cert. tchg. Md., Dalcroze cert. Longy Sch., Dalcroze Orff Kodaly cert. Manhattan Sch. Music. Music tchr. L.A. Pub. Schs., 1962—66, Burlington (Vt.) Pub. Schs.; prof. music edn. Shelton Coll., Cape Canaveral, Fla., 1968—74; music tchr., cons. Anne Arundel County Pub. Schs., Severna Park, Md., 1974—79; prof. music edn. Towson (Md.) U., 1979—97, prof. emerita, 1997—; prof. music edn. Frostburg (Md.) State U., 1999—2000; tchr. music Harford County Schs., Abingdon, Md., 2000—. Cons., clinician pub. sch. sys., Md., Va., Pa., N.J., 1983—; clinician Towson U., 1994—2004, developer Grad. Dalcroze-Orff-Kodaly Cert. Program, co-dir. Dalcroze-Orff-Kodaly Cert. Program, 1981—97, adj. faculty, 1997—. Contbg. author: music series Share the Music, Grades 7-8, 1996—2003, Music and You, Grades 7-8, 1989—95, co-compiler: keyboard proficiency packet for Towson U., rev. Leader women's support groups Chapelgate Ch., Marriottsville, Md., 2000—. Mem.: Md. Music Educators Assn., Music Educators Nat. Conf. (clinician 1983—87, 2000). Avocations: travel, music.

RUWITCH, ANN RUBENSTEIN, urban planner; b. Bayonne, N.J., Nov. 17, 1939; d. Eli and Miriam (Cooper) Rubenstein; children: Michael, Thomas. BA, Conn. Conn., 1961. Dir. St. Louis Currents, 1983-87, Arts in Transit, St. Louis, 1987-94; pres., CEO Grand Ctr., Inc., St. Louis, 1994—. Trustee St. Louis Art Mus., 1987-91; bd. dirs. Forum for Contemporary Art, St. Louis; chmn. bd. Dow Screw Products, St. Louis. Participant Leadership St. Louis, 1978-79; mem. St. Louis County Bd. Election Commrs., 1981-85; mem. exec. com. Bar Assn. Fee Dispute Com., St. Louis, 1987-91. Mem. Women's Dem. Forum (exec. com. 1990—), Mo. Womens Forum. Jewish. Avocations: travel, gardening, bridge. Office: Grand Ctr Inc 634 N Grand Blvd Ste 10A Saint Louis MO 63103-1025

RUYLE, JULIE MARIE, marketing professional; b. Houston, July 11, 1979; d. Donald Charles and Helen Ruth Anderson; m. Chad Rollins Ruyle. B in Mktg./Comm., Baylor U., 2001. Mktg. rep. Baylor U. Athletics, Waco, Tex., 2000—01; recruiting supr. Pro Staff, San Diego, 2001—02; mktg. project mgr. PeopleFirst.com, San Diego, 2002—. Co-chair student recruitment Baylor U., Waco, 1999—2001. Recruiter, team leader Vol. San Diego, 2002—. Mem.: Direct Mktg. Assn. (assoc.), Am. Mktg. Assn. (assoc.; dir. publicity 2002), Evening Edit. (assoc.; co-chair promotions 2003). Republican. Avocations: volunteer, youth director/mentor. Business E-Mail: julie.ruyle@peoplefirst.com.

RUYLE-HULLINGER, ELIZABETH SMITH (BETH RUYLE), consultant, municipal financial advisor; b. Oct. 26, 1946; d. Daniel Lester and Mae (Coley) Smith; m. Craig Harlan Hullinger, Oct. 24, 1985; children: Leigh Ann Ruyle, Clint (dec.), Bret. AA, St. Petersburg Jr. Coll., 1966; BA in English, U. Fla., 1968; MPA, U. Ga., 1975. Rsch. asst. Emory U., Atlanta, 1969—70; health planner Met. Coun. for Health, Atlanta, 1970-72; govtl. rels. coord. Atlanta Regional Commn., 1972-76, govtl. affairs coord., 1976-78; exec. dir. South Suburban Mayors' and Mgrs. Assn., East Hazel Crest, Ill., 1978-2000; pres. Chgo. Southland Econ. Devel. Alliance, 1999-2000; exec. v.p., dir. Ehlers & Assocs., Naperville, Ill., 2000—. Exec. dir. South Towns Agy. Risk Mgmt., 1980-98, South Towns Area Benefits Coop., 1983-89, South Towns Bus. Growth Corp., 1983-90; cons. Planning Devel. Svc., Tinley Park, Ill., 1986—. Contbr. articles to profl. and devel. mags. Mem. World's Fair Adv. Com., Chgo., 1986, Met. Planning Coun., 1990-2000, Cook County Tax Reform adv. coun., South Suburban Arts Coun., 1987, Coun. Urban Econ. Devel., 1986; adv. coun. Urban Innovations, Chgo., Chgo. Assembly Project; mem. Regional Partnership, 1985-2000; bd. dirs. South Suburban Hosp., 1987-96, mem. governing coun., 1999—; bd. dirs. Fin. Cmty. Devel. Corp., 1998-2000; mentor U. Chgo. Sch. Pub. Policy. Mem. Internat. City Mgmt. Assn., Ill. City Mgmt. Assn., Met. City Mgrs. Assn., Ill. Govtl. Fin. Officers Assn., Ill. Tax Increment Assn., Plank Road Trail Assn., Lambda Alpha. Methodist. Home: 17255 66th Ct Tinley Park IL 60477-3501 Office: Ehlers & Assocs 1001 E Chicago Ave Ste 135 Naperville IL 60540-5500 Office Phone: 630-355-6100. E-mail: bruyle@ehlers-inc.com.

RUYTER, NANCY LEE CHALFA, dance educator; b. Phila., May 23, 1933; d. Andrew Benedict Chalfa and Lois Elizabeth (Strode) McClary; m. Ralph Markson (div.); m. Hans C. Ruyter, Dec. 7, 1968 (dec. Jan. 1998).

BA in History, U. Calif., Riverside, 1964; PhD in History, Claremont Grad. Sch., 1970. Tchr. theater dept. Pomona Coll., 1965-72; instr. dance program U. Calif., Riverside, 1972-76, acting chair dance program, 1974-75; instr. dance dept. UCLA, 1976; instr. phys. edn. dept. Orange Coast Coll., 1976-77; asst. prof. dept. phys. edn. and dance Tufts U., 1977-78; asst. prof. phys. edn. dept. Calif. State U., Northridge, 1978-82; from asst. prof. to full prof. dance dept. U. Calif., Irvine, 1982—, assoc. dean Sch. Fine Arts, 1984-88, 95-96, chair dept. dance, 1989-91. Presenter in field. Appeared with Jasna Planina Folk Ensemble, 1972-77, 78-79, Di Falco and Co., 1955-57; choreographer, dir. numerous coll. dance prodns.; contbr. articles, revs. to profl. publs.; author: Reformers and Visionaries: The Americanization of the Art of Dance, 1979, The Cultivation of Body and Mind in Nineteenth-Century American Delsartism, 1999. Mem. Am. Soc. Theatre Rsch., Bulgarian Studies Assn., Congress on Rsch. in Dance (bd. dirs. 1977-80, pres. 1981-85), Folk Dance Fedn., Internat. Fedn. Theatre Rsch., Soc. Dance Rsch., Soc. Ethnomusicology, Soc. Dance History Scholars (steering com. 1980-81), Spanish Dance Soc., Theatre Libr. Assn. Office: U Calif-Irvine Dept Dance Irvine CA 92697-0001 E-mail: nlruyter@uci.edu.

RYALL, JO-ELLYN M. psychiatrist; b. Newark, May 25, 1949; d. Joseph P. and Tekla (Paraszczuk) R. BA in Chemistry with gen. honors, Rutgers U., 1971; MD, Washington U., St. Louis, 1975. Diplomate Am. Bd. Psychiatry and Neurology. Resident in psychiatry Washington U., St. Louis, 1975-78, psychiatrist Student Health, 1978-83, asst. prof. clin. psychiatry, 1983—2003, assoc. prof. clin. psychiatry, 2003—. Inpatient supr. Malcolm Bliss Mental Health Ctr., St. Louis, 1978-80, pvt. practice medicine specializing in psychiatry, St. Louis, 1980—. Bd. dirs. Women's Self Help Ctr., St. Louis, 1980. Fellow: APA (pres. ea. Mo. dist. br. 1983—85, sect. coun. AMA 1986—99, dep. rep. to assembly 1994—97, rep. 1997—2001, chair bylaws com. 2000—03, dep. rep. area 4 2001—); mem.: AMA (alt. del. Mo. 1988—90, 1993—94, del. 1995—, mem. coun. on constn. bylaws 1998—, vice chair 2002—04, chair 2004—), Manic Depressive Assn. St. Louis (chmn. bd. dirs. 1985—89), Mo. State Med. Assn. (vice spkr. ho. of dels. 1986—89, spkr. 1989—92), St. Louis Met. Med. Soc. (del. to state conv. 1981—86, councilor 1985—87, v.p. 1989, del. to state conv. 1993—), Am. Med. Women's Assn. (pres. St. Louis dist. br. 1981—82, regional gov. VIII 1986—89, pres. St. Louis dist. br. 1992, spkr. ho. of dels. 1993—96), Washington U. Faculty Club. Office: 9216 Clayton Rd Ste 105 Saint Louis MO 63124-1515

RYALLS, BARBARA TAYLOR, freelance/self-employed editor, critic; b. Akron, Ohio, Apr. 13, 1940; d. Robert Hull and Rosemary Resch Taylor; m. Frederick Ryalls, Sept. 14, 1963; children: Christopher Hull, Jordan Lee. BA, Beaver Coll. (now Arcadia U.), 1962. Food critic Bucks County Courier Times, Bristol, Pa., 1976—; project editor Lippincott Williams & Wilkins, Phila., 1992—96, mng. editor, 1996—2001; freelance editor, 2001—. Author: Dining Out in Bucks County, 1984; co-author: $ave Bucks in Buck$, 1977, 1979. Pres. LWV, Newtown, Pa., 1970—72; tour guide Walk Phila.; bd. mem. Famly Svcs., Bucks County, 1977—79, Delaware Valley Philharm. Orch., Bucks County, 1993—95. Avocations: architecture, gardening, travel. Home: 490 Rocksville Rd Holland PA 18966

RYAN, CATHLEEN RENEER, management consultant; b. Bountiful, Utah, June 1, 1962; d. Philip John and Isabel Faye (McPhee) R. BA, Assumption Coll., 1984. Adminstrv. analyst and various entry adminstrv. positions IBM, Mt. Pleasant, N.Y., 1984-89, office systems adminstrv. mgr. Somers, N.Y., 1989-92, office systems and site ops. mgr., 1992-94, resource devel. mgr., 1994—. Baptist. Avocations: skiing, horseback riding, reading, crafts. Home: 122 Shell Ave Milford CT 06460-6322 Office: IBM Rt 100 Somers NY 10589

RYAN, CHRISTINE BRETT, music educator; b. York, Pa., Mar. 27, 1965; d. James Joseph and Dorothy Regina (Wirtz) Brett; m. Donald Lee Ryan, Aug. 4, 1990; children: Cecily Anna, Michaela Brett. Bachelor of Music Edn., Westminster Choir Coll., 1987; Master of Music Edn., Fla. State U., 1990. Elem. music tchr. Hillsborough Pub. Schs., NJ, 1987—88; elem. and secondary music tchr. Ewing Twp. Pub. Schs., NJ, 1990—93; elem. music tchr. Hamburg Area Sch. Dist., Pa., 1993—95, secondary music tchr., 1996—. Mem. nat. devel. team and trainer Nat. Bd. Profl. Tchg. Stds., San Antonio, 2000—. Condr.: Hamburg Cmty. Childrens Chorus, 2000—, St. Johns UCC/Kutztown Handbell Choir, 2003—. Mem. Albany Twp. Hist. Soc., 2001—. Mem.: Music Educators Nat. Conf. Avocations: cooking, gardening, farming. Home: 1691 Old 22 Lenhartsville PA 19534

RYAN, CYNTHIA RHOADES, lawyer; b. Wilmington, Del., Feb. 6, 1954; d. Harry Edris and Patricia Irene (Dux) Rhoades; m. John G. Christfield, Aug. 6, 1977 (div. 1984); m. Matthew C. Ryan, Oct. 10, 1993. BA in Polit. Sci., U. Del., 1976; JD, Widener U., 1979. Bar: Del. 1979, U.S. Supreme Ct. 1989. Dep. atty. gen. State of Del., Wilmington, 1979-85; staff counsel permanent subcom. investigations U.S. Senate, Washington, 1985-87; trial atty. criminal div. U.S. Dept. Justice, Washington, 1987-88, sr. atty. DEA, 1988-91, assoc. chief counsel internat. law sect., 1991-96; chief counsel Office of the Chief Counsel, Drug Enforcement Adminstrn., 1996—. Mem. ABA, Del. Bar Assn., Internat. Assn. of Chiefs of Police, Alpha Sigma Alpha. Avocations: sports, gardening, gourmet cooking, piano, tenor banjo.

RYAN, ELLEN BOUCHARD, psychology educator, gerontologist; b. Holyoke, Mass., 1947; emigrated to Can., 1982; d. Raoul Rosario and Etiennette Marie Bouchard; m. Patrick J. Ryan, July 12, 1969; children: Lorraine Yvette, Dennis Patrick, Kevin Myles. BA, MA, Brown U., 1968; PhD, U. Mich., 1970. Asst. prof. psychology U. Notre Dame, 1970-76, assoc. prof., 1976-81, prof., 1981-82, chmn. dept., 1978-82; prof. psychiatry McMaster U., Hamilton, Ont., Can., 1982—, dir. Ctr. for Gerontol. Studies, 1985-95, prof. gerontology, 1987—. Editor: Attitudes Toward Language Variation, 1982, Language Communication and The Elderly, 1986, Intergenerational Communication, 1994, Language Attitudes, 1994, Communication, Aging and Health, 1996. Grantee NICHD, 1972-75, NSF, 1976-79, Nat. Inst. Edn., 1979-82, Natural Scis. and Engring. Rsch., 1983-89, Gerontol. Rsch. Coun. of Ont., 1983-85, Ont. Ministry Health, 1986-89, Soc. Sci. and Humanities Rsch. Coun., 1986—. Fellow APA, Gerontol. Soc. Am., Can. Psychol. Assn.; mem. Internat. Assn. of Lang. and Social Psychology, Can. Assn. Gerontology. Roman Catholic. Home: 346 Brookview Ct Ancaster ON Canada L9G 4C2 Office: McMaster U Dept Psychiatry 1200 Main St W Hamilton ON Canada L8N 3Z5 E-mail: ryaneb@mcmaster.ca.

RYAN, EVONNE IANACONE, capital management company executive; b. Buffalo, N.Y., Aug. 30, 1949; d. Raphael and Mary (Silvaroli) Ianacone; m. Thomas William Ryan, July 11, 1981; children: Christine Irving, Thomas William IV. Student, U. Buffalo, 1970-72; BS in Edn., So. Ill. U., 1974, postgrad., 1975-78, U. Mo., 1989-91; MBA, Harrington U., 1993. Registered securities prin.; cert. estate planner; cert. sr. adv. Spl edn. tchr. Belleville (Ill.) Pub. Sch., 1974-78; rsch. dir. Mo. Pub. Interest Rsch. Group, St. Louis, 1978-79, exec. co-dir., 1979-83; corp. trainer, producer, dir. cmty. access coordination Storer Cable Comms., Florissant, Mo., 1983-85, prodn. mgr., 1985-86; employee devel. and cmty. rels. dir. Cencom Cable TV, St. Louis, 1987-88; stockbroker Edward D. Jones & Co., Littleton, Colo., 1989-93, SunAmerica Securities, Littleton, Colo., 1993-97, ProEquities, Inc., Littleton, Colo., 1997—; co-founder Fin. & Tax Strategies, Inc., Littleton, 1994; CEO FTS Capital Mgmt., 1997—, NFP Securities, Inc., 2000—. Co-founder Life Transition Planners, Inc., 2000, Fin. and Tax Strategies, 1994. Contbr. articles to profl. publs. Recipient ACE award for cable excellence Nat. Acad. Cable Programming, 1988, Emmy award, 1988. Home: 144 Willowleaf Dr Littleton CO 80127-3572 Office: 5944 S Kipling St Ste 350 Littleton CO 80127-5557 E-mail: proadvisor@msn.com.

RYAN, IONE JEAN ALOHILANI RATHBURN, retired educator, counselor; b. Honolulu, Oct. 18, 1926; d. William Alexander and Lilia (Nainoa) Rathburn; m. Edward Parsons Ryan, June 23, 1962 (dec.); children: Ralph M., Lilia K. BEd, U. Hawaii, 1948; MS in Pub. Health, U. Minn., 1950; EdD, Stanford U., 1960. Lic. marital and family therapist, N.C. Tchr. W.R. Farrington High Sch., Honolulu, 1948; instr. to asst. prof. U. Hawaii, Honolulu, 1950-66; assoc. prof. to prof. East Carolina U., Greenville, 1966-90, prof. emerita, 1990—. Contbr. articles to profl. publs. Recipient first scholarship Honolulu C. of C., 1948-50.

RYAN, JANE FRANCES, corporate communications executive; b. Bronxville, N.Y., Nov. 1, 1950; d. Bernard M. and Margaret M. (Griffith) R.; m. Kevin Horan, Dec. 26, 1982; 1 child, Kevin. BS in Journalism, Ohio U., 1972; MBA in Mktg., Golden Gate U., 1990. Asst. promotion mgr. Fawcett Publs., Greenwich, Conn., 1972-75; mktg. coordinator Fawcett Mktg. Services div. CBS, Greenwich, Conn., 1975-78; dist. sales mgr. CBS Publs., San Francisco, 1978; prodn. mgr. Cato Inst., San Francisco, 1979-81; account supr. Bus. Media Resources, Mill Valley, Calif., 1981-90, dir. mktg. svcs., 1990-93; dir. publs. RAND Corp., Santa Monica, Calif., 1993—. Office: RAND 1700 Main St Santa Monica CA 90401-3297

RYAN, JOAN, food company executive; BS in Acctg., U. Ill. CPA, Ill. With Price Waterhouse Co., Baxter Healthcare Corp., Kewaunee Sci. Corp.; divsn. contr., CFO NutraSweet Co.; v.p. fin., CFO Ameritech Small Bus. Svcs., 1995-98, Alliant Foodservice, Inc., Deerfield, Ill., 1998-2000; CFO, Tellabs, Inc., Lisle, Ill., 2000—03; sr. v.p., CFO SIRVA, Inc., Westmont, Ill., 2003—. Bd. dirs. Fed. Signal Corp. Bd. dirs. Boys and Girls Club Chgo. Office: SIRVA Inc 700 Oakmont Ln Westmont IL 60559

RYAN, JOYCE ETHEL, artist, author; b. Atlanta, Aug. 29, 1949; m. Jim Cyril Klar, Apr. 5, 1975. BFA, U. Ga., 1972. Instr. Marsh Draughon Coll., Atlanta, 1972-73; retail store mgr. Army & Air Force Exch. Svc., Dallas, 1974; illustrator U.S. Army Logistics Ctr., Ft. Lee, Va., 1975-77; graphics mgr. Ecosystems Internat., Millersville, Md., 1980-82; freelance art studio dir. Seoul, 1983-85; pres. Butterfly Books, Ariz., 1985—. Instr. Cochise Coll., Sierra Vista, 1986. Illustrator, author: Seoul Sketches, 1985, Scenes of Southern Arizona, 1986, Seoul Travel Guide, 1987, Traveling with Your Sketchbook, 1990, The Happy Camper's Gourmet Cookbook, 1992, Calligraphy: Elegant and Easy, 1994, Drawing at Home, 1996, America's Best Cheesecakes, 1998, Fifty Years of Excellence: Texas Watercolor Society, 1999, America's Best RV Cookbook, 2003. Mem.: Art Ctr. Corpus Christi, San Antonio Watercolor Group. Avocations: drawing, painting. E-mail: texaswavelady@hotmail.com.

RYAN, JUDITH W. geriatrics consultant, adult nurse practitioner, educator, researcher; b. Waterbury, Conn., Dec. 8, 1943; d. James Patrick Ryan and Edna (Swanson) Billings. BS, U. Conn., 1965; MS, Boston U., 1967; PhD, U. Md., 1984. RN, Md., Conn.; cert. adult nurse practitioner ANCC. Instr. U. Conn., Storrs, 1967-69; asst. prof. Ind. U., Purdue U., Indpls., 1969-73, U. Md., Balt., 1973-82, dir. primary care adult nurse practitioner cert. program, dept. medicine, supportive care project, 1985-87, asst. prof. sch. nursing, 1987-95, asst. prof., 1976-82; clin. dir. EverCare, Balt., 1995-99; pres. Nurse Practitioners and Cons., P.C. of Prime Health Group, 2000—. Arbitrator Health Claims Arbitration Program, Md., 1976—; bd. mem. Md. Bd. Nursing, Balt., 1991-98, pres., 1993-96; trustee Md. Nurses Assn. Polit. Action Com., Balt., treas., 1989-91. Contbr. articles to profl. jours. Named Distinguished Practitioner Nursing, Nat. Acad. Practice, 1984-99. Mem. Am. Coll. Nurse Practitioners, Md. Nurses Assn. (2d v.p. 1986-88), Nurse Practitioner Assn. Md., Sigma Theta Tau, Phi Kappa Phi. Home: 622 Lucia Ave Baltimore MD 21229-4516 Office: 20 New Plant Ct Ste 204 Owings Mills MD 21117 E-mail: jwryan@starpower.net.

RYAN, KELLY, lawyer; b. N.Y.C., July 18, 1963; d. Robert Gerard and Edith Shaffer Ryan. BA, Tulane U., New Orleans, 1985; JD, Georgetown U., Washington, 1988; LLM, Cambridge U., Eng., 1989. Bar: N.Y. 1990, Wash. 1992. Assoc. gen. counsel Office of Gen. Counsel, INS, Washington, 1992—98, chief refugee and asylum law divsn., 1998—2002; dep. asst. sec. Dept. of State Bur. Population, Refugees and Migration, 2002—. Recipient Commrs. award for meritorious svc., INS, 1998, 2000. Roman Catholic.

RYAN, MARLEIGH GRAYER, language educator; b. N.Y.C., May 1, 1930; d. Harry and Betty (Hurwick) Grayer; m. Edward Ryan, June 4, 1950; 1 child, David Patrick. BA, NYU, 1951; MA, Columbia U., 1956, PhD, 1965; Cert., East Asian Inst., 1956; postgrad., Kyoto U., 1958-59. Research assoc. Columbia U., N.Y.C., 1960-61, lectr. Japanese, 1961-65, asst. prof., 1965-70, assoc. prof., 1970-72; vis. asst. prof. Yale U ., New Haven, 1966-67; assoc. prof. U. Iowa, Iowa City, 1972-75, prof., 1975-81, chmn. dept., 1972-81; prof. Japanese SUNY, New Paltz, 1981-98, dean liberal arts and scis., 1981-90, prof. emeritus, 1999—; assoc. in rsch. Reischauer Inst. for Japanese Studies, Harvard U., Cambridge, Mass., 1999—, chair study group on Asian Am. Lit., 2000—02. Vice chmn. seminar on modern Japan, Columbia U., 1984-85, chmn., 1985-86; co-chmn. N.Y. State Conf. on Asian Studies, 1986, editor, 1993-99, mem. exec. com., 1993-96, sec., 1993-99, co-chmn., 1998. Co-author: (with Herschel Webb) Research in Japanese Sources, 1965; author: Japan's First Modern Novel, 1967, The Development of Realism in the Fiction of Tsubouchi Shoyo, 1975; assoc. editor: Jour. Assn. Tchrs. Japanese, 1962-71, editor, 1971-75. East Asian Inst. fellow Columbia U., 1955; Ford Found. fellow, 1958-60; Japan Found. fellow, 1973, Woodrow Wilson Ctr. Internat. Scholars fellow, 1988-89; recipient Van. Am. Disting. Book award Columbia, 1968 Mem. MLA (sec. com. on teaching Japanese Lang. 1962-68, mem. del. assembly 1979-87, mem. exec. com. div. Asian lit. 1981-86), Assn. Tchrs. Japanese (exec. com. 1969-72, 74-77), Assn. Asian Studies (bd. dirs. 1975-78, N.E. asian coun. 1975-78, coun. of confs., 1993-96), Midwest Conf. Asian Studies (pres. 1980-81)

RYAN, MARY A. diplomat; b. New York, N.Y., Oct. 1, 1940; BA, St. John's Univ., 1963, MA, 1965. With Foreign Service, Dept. of State, 1966—; consular and adminstrv. officer, 1966-69; personnel officer Am. Embassy, Tegucigalpa, Honduras, 1970-71; consular officer Am. Consulate Gen., Monterrey, Mexico, 1971-73; adminstrv. officer Bur. of African Affairs, Dept. of State, Washington, 1973-75, post mgmt. officer, 1975-77; career devel. officer Bur. of Personnel, Dept. of State, 1977-80; adminstrv. counselor Abidjan, Ivory Coast, 1980-81, Khartoum, Sudan, 1981-82; inspector, Office of Insp. Gen. Dept. of State, Washington, 1982-83, exec. dir. Bur. of European and Can. Affairs, 1983-85, exec. asst. to Under Sec. of State for Mgmt., 1985-88; ambassador to Swaziland, 1988-90; dep. asst. sec. Bur. of Consular Affairs, Washington, 1990; dir. Kuwait task force, 1990-91; ops. dir. UN spl. commn. on elimination of Iraqi weapons, 1991; dep. asst. sec. Bur. European & Can. Affairs, Washington, 1991-93; asst. sec. Bur. of Consular Affairs, Washington, 1993—, career amb., 1999. Office: Dept State Bureau of Consular Affairs 2201 C St NW Washington DC 20520-0001

RYAN, MARY ESTHER, music educator; b. Zanesville, Ohio, Oct. 3, 1946; d. Clovis Dubois Fritter and Florence Estelle Weigand Fritter; m. Dale Vernon Ryan, Dec. 25, 1966; children: Scott Dana, Brenda Sue, Randy Alan, Pamela Jean. BA in Music Edn., Muskingum Coll., 1968. Gen. music tchr. Caldwell (Ohio) Exempted Village Sch. Dist., 1968—69; substitute tchr. Tri-Valley Schs., Concord, Ohio, 1978—81, East Muskingum Schs., Adamsville, Ohio, 1978—81, tchr. New Concord, Ohio, 1981—98, music tchr., 1998—. Song writer East Muskingum Schs., 1981—. Mem. worship com. New Concord (Ohio) United Meth. Ch., 1988—, mem. handbell choir. Mem.: PEO. Avocations: latch hook rug making, gardening, fishing, Nascar, poetry. Home: 64646 Haught Rd Cambridge OH 43725-9727

RYAN, SISTER MARY JEAN, health facility executive; LHD, Webster U., 1994, U. Mo., St. Louis, 2003, Lindenwood U., 2003. Pres., CEO SSM Health Care, 1986—. Presenter in field. Co-author: CQI and the Renovation of an American Health Care System: A Culture Under Construction, 1997. Mem. Excellence in Mo. Found.; chair Taking Care/A Health Forum for Women Religious, Madison, Wis.; bd. dirs. Inst. for Healthcare Improvement, United Way of Greater St. Louis; sec. Hawthorn Found. of Mo.; mem., treas., bd. dirs. St. Louis Regional Chamber and Growth Assn.; bd. dirs. SSM Health Care of Okla., SSM Health Care of Wis., SSM Health Care-St. Louis. Named one of 20 Disting. Women/St. Louis Area, 25 Most Influential Women in Bus. in St. Louis; recipient Brotherhood/Sisterhood award, Nat. Conf. Cmty. and Justice, Gov.'s Quality Leadership award, State of Mo., Corp. that Makes a Difference award, Internat. Women's Forum. Office: SSM Health Care Sys Inc 477 N Lindbergh Blvd Saint Louis MO 63141

RYAN, MEG, actress, film producer; b. Fairfield, Conn., Nov. 19, 1961; m. Dennis Quaid, 1991 (div. 2001); 1 child, Jack Henry. Student, NYU. Appearences include (TV) One of the Boys, 1982, As The World Turns, 1982-84, Wild Side, 1985, (films) Rich and Famous, 1981, Amityville 3-D, 1983, Top Gun, 1986, Armed and Dangerous, 1986, Innerspace, 1987, Promised Land, 1987, D.O.A., 1988, The Presidio, 1988, When Harry Met Sally, 1989, Joe Versus the Volcano, 1990, The Doors, 1991, Prelude to a Kiss, 1992, Sleepless in Seattle, 1993, Flesh and Bone, 1993, When a Man Loves a Woman, 1994, Restoration, 1994, I.Q., 1994, French Kiss, 1995, Two for the Road, 1996, Courage Under Fire, 1996, Addicted to Love, 1997, Anastasia (voice), 1997, City of Angels, 1998, Hurlyburly, 1998, You've Got Mail, 1998, Hanging Up, 1999, Proof of Life, 2000, Kate & Leopold, 2001, In the Cut, 2003, Against the Ropes, 2004; owner Prufrock Pictures movie prodn. co.; prodr.: French Kiss/Paris Match, 1995, Two for the Road, 1997, Northern Lights, 1997 (TV, exec. prodr.), Lost Souls, 2000, The Wedding Planner, 2001, Desert Saints, 2002. Recipient Golden Apple award Hollywood Women's Press Club, 1989, Woman of Yr. award Hasty Pudding Theatricals, 1994, ShoWest Conv. Actress of Yr. award, 1999, Am. Comedy Award, 1990, 1994, Women in Film Crystal Award, 1995. Office: care ICM c/o Steve Dontanville 8942 Wilshire Blvd Beverly Hills CA 90211-1934

RYAN, MELBAGENE T. retired food and nutrition service director; b. Arkadelphia, Ark., Jan. 6, 1927; d. Horace Samuel and Eunice Bridges (Moorman) Tull; m. Wayne Stuart Ryan, Dec. 26, 1954. BS in Edn., Henderson U., 1948; M in Edn., Tex. Women's U., 1951. Tchr. Eudora (Ark.) Pub. Schs., 1948-52; dir. food services Tex. Christian U., Ft. Worth, 1952-53, Tex. Women's U., 1953-58; dir. food and nutriton service Irving (Tex.) Ind. Sch. Dist., 1958-85. Project dir. to develop stds. excellence with a self study and evaluation Tex. Sch. Food Svc. Assn., 1985-88; cons. in field. Co-author and project dir.: (with others) Youth Advisory Council Resource Manual, 1978-79, Effective Food Service Management Using Computers, 1982. With child nutrition Tex. Sch. Food Svc. Assn., Washington, 1974-79; with legis. Am. Sch. Food Svc. Assn., Irving, 1980-85; mem. Denton Co. Hist. Commn., 1997—, Denton Co. Courthouse-on-the Square Mus., chmn. 1998—; mem. adv. bd. Lake Forest Good Samaritan Village, 1998—, Tex. Woman's U. Centennial Celebration, 2001, planning com., 1998-99, Denton Good Samaritan Village, 2003; chmn. Bayless Selby House Mus., 2002—. Recipient Food Facilities Design award Instns. Volume Feeding Awards Program, New Orleans, 1977, Trend Setter award, North Tex. Brokers Assn., Dallas, 1978; Melbagene Ryan Scholarship named in her honor by Dallas Profl. Friends, 1985. Mem. Denton Dietetic Assn. (pres. 1977-78), Tex. Dietetic Assn., Am. Dietetic Assn. (chmn. joint com. 1979-82), Tex. Sch. Food Svc. Assn. (pres. 1975-76, nutrition edn. 1975), Am. Sch. Food Svc. Assn. (conf. com. 1977-78, 1982-83), Tex. Women's U. Alumni Assn. Methodist. Home and Office: 1121 Ryan Rd Denton TX 76210-5539

RYAN, MICHELE KING, marketing professional; b. Connellsville, Pa., Nov. 25, 1939; d. Francis Joseph and Ella Elizabeth (Hoffman) King; m. Charles Joseph Ryan Jr. (dec Jan. 1994); children: Charles J. Ryan III, Kimberly Ryan Winchester; m. Ernest Bayard Crofoot, Jan. 6, 1996; 6 stepchildren. Student, Georgetown U., 1958. Lic. real estate broker, Md. Adminstr. Corridor Info. Ctrs., Laurel, Md., 1977; devel. dir. Resource Realty, Inc., Laurel, 1977-81, v.p., 1981-88; exec. v.p. Resource Enterprises LLC, 1988-95; dir. mkgt. Balt./Washington Corridor C. of C., 1997-2000; pres. The Ryan Group, Annapolis, Md., 2000—. Bd. dirs. Citizens Nat. Bank, Laurel; commr. Md. Aviation Commn., Annapolis, 1995—, Md. Commn. on Transp. Investment, Annapolis, 1999; v.p. Gtr. Laurel Nursing Home, 1980-93 Author, co-editor: Travel Patterns in Baltimore/Washington Corridor, 1977. Bd. dirs. Balt./Wash. Internat. Airport Devel. Coun. Named Bus. Woman of Yr. Bowie Crofton BPW, 1981. Mem.: Balt.-Washington C. of C. (chmn. bd. 1991—92), Soroptimist Internat. (treas. 1976), Bowie Women's Club (pres. 1966—68), Bowie Bus. Profl. Women's Club (pres. 1976). Roman Catholic. Avocations: music, reading, travel. Home: 910 Boom Way Annapolis MD 21401-6889 Office: The Ryan Group 910 Boom Way Annapolis MD 21401

RYAN, PAMELA JEANNE, guidance director; b. Evergreen Park, Ill., Jan. 16, 1955; d. Harold C. and Marilyn J. (Wales) Holck; m. Philip J. Ryan, July 15, 1983. BA, Coll. of St. Francis, Joliet, Ill., 1976; MA, Govs. State U., University Park, Ill., 1984; postgrad., Lewis U., Romeoville, Ill. Tchr. Providence Cath. H.S., New Lenox, Ill., 1976-88, dir. guidance, 1988—, coord. student assistance program, 1993—. Mem. critical incident stress debriefing team St. Joseph's Med. Ctr., Joliet, 1993—; conf. presenter in field. Mem. ACA, Am. Sch. Counseling Assn., Ill. Sch. Counseling Assn. Democrat. Roman Catholic. Avocations: reading, walking, flower gardening. Office: Providence Cath HS 1800 W Lincoln Hwy New Lenox IL 60451-3533

RYAN, PRISCILLA E. lawyer; AB, Marquette U., 1969; JD, Loyola U., Chgo., 1982. Bar: Ill. 1982. With IRS, 1986-87; atty.-advisor Office Tax Policy, U.S. Treasury Dept., Washington, 1988-89; ptnr. Sidley & Austin, Chgo. Frequent spkr. on employee benefits. Contbr. articles to profl. jours. Mem. ABA. Office: Sidley & Austin 1 S First National Plz Chicago IL 60603-2000 Fax: 312-853-7036.

RYAN, RANDA CATHERINE, university administrator, business owner; b. Austin, Tex., Jan. 25, 1955; d. James Prewitt and Susan Farrington Holt; m. Steve Klepfer; children: Seth, Rhett, Kasey, Shea. BA, Schreiner Coll., Kerrville, Tex., 1984; MA, U. Tex., 1989, PhD, 1996. Asst. to nat. team swim coach U.S. Swim, Colorado Springs, Colo., 1984-88; asst. swim coach U. Tex., Austin, 1984-88, performance team dir., 1988-92, asst. athletic dir., 1992—. Meet dir. Olympic trials-swimming U. Tex., 1988. Writer Performance Team Newsletter, 1988-91; contbr. chpt. to book, articles to profl. jours. Mem. AAUW, Am. Coll. Sports Medicine, Am. Assn. Phys. Edn., Nat. Assn. Coll. Athletic Dirs. Office: Women's Athletics 718 Belmont Hall Austin TX 78712-1201

RYAN, SHEILA A. nursing educator, former dean; Diploma in nursing, Creighton Meml. St. Joseph's Hosp. Sch. Nursing, 1967; BSN, U. Nebr., 1969; MSN in Psychiat. Nursing, U. Calif., San Francisco, 1971; PhD in Clin. Nursing Rsch., U. Ariz., 1981. Asst. prof. nursing Creighton U., Omaha, 1971—76, dean nursing, 1977—86; dean Sch. Nursing, dir. Med. Ctr. Nursing U. Rochester, NY, 1986—99; prof., Charlotte Peck Lienemann and Alumni Disting. Chair Coll. Nursing U. Nebr. Med. Ctr., Omaha. Fellow: Am. Acad. Nursing; mem.: Inst. for Healthcare Improvement, Nat. League Nursing (treas. 1993, pres. 1996—97), Inst. Medicine (treas.-sec.), Am. Internat. Health Alliance (bd. dirs. 1999—). Office: UNMC Coll Nursing Rm 4030 985330 NE Medical Ctr Omaha NE 68198-5330*

RYAN, SUSAN MAGNESS, librarian, educator; b. Takoma Park, Md., May 27, 1958; d. Donald Eaton and Shirley Anne (Lusby) Magness; m. Edward Timothy Ryan, Sept. 1, 1984; 1 child, Shannon Kelsey. BS, Fla. State U., 1981, MS, 1982; MLS, UCLA, 1989. Intelligence officer CIA, Washington, 1983-84; assoc. dir. libr. Stetson U., DeLand, Fla., 1989—. Author: Downloading Democracy: Government Information in an Electronic Age, 1996; contbg. author: Government CD-ROMs: A Practical Guide to Searching Electronic Databases, 1994; series and cons. editor Librs. Unltd., 1994-96; mem. editl. bd. Jour. Govt. Info., 1993-96, column editor, 1994-96; contbr. numerous articles to acad. jours. Bd. dirs. coun. advisors for Sch. Libr. and Info. Studies, Fla. State U., Tallahassee, 1995-97. Mem. ALA (Catharine J. Reynolds award for rsch., govt. docs. round table 1996), Fla. Libr. Assn. (chairperson govt. docs. caucus 1992-93), Ctrl. Fla. Libr. Consortium (chairperson govt. docs. interest group 1991-92), Fla. Assn. Coll. and Rsch. Librs. (exec. bd. 2002—). Office: duPont-Ball Libr Campus Unit 8418 Deland FL 32723

RYAN, SUZANNE IRENE, nursing educator; b. Yonkers, NY, Mar. 13, 1939; d. Edward Vincent and Winifred E. (Goemann) R. BA in Biology, Mt. St. Agnes Coll., Balt., 1962; BSN, Columbia U., 1967, MA in Nursing Svc., 1973, MEd in Nursing Edn., 1975, MS in Oncology, 1982, EdD in Nursing Edn., 1997. RN, N.Y.; cert. AIDS educator, N.Y. Prof. nursing Molloy Coll., Rockville Centre, N.Y., 1970—, co-dir. health svcs., dir. ednl. programs, 1987-94, dir. health svcs., 1994—, health educator, 1992—, co-dir. mobile health van, adminstr. health edn., 1992—; pres., CEO SIR Enterprises, Inc., 1982—; photographer Molloy Coll. Pubs., 1991—. Photographer dir. Bali-Art, Inc., 1992—; mem. N.Y. State AIDS Coun., 1987—, L.I. Alcohol Consortium, 1987—; educator Nassau County Dept. Sr. Citizens Health, 1991—; photographer-in-residence Molloy Coll., 1992—; lectr. on landscape, wildlife and flower photography, L.I., N.H., Can., 1993—. Represented in permanent collections in photographic galleries in Carmel, Calif., Laconia, Wolfboro and Moultonboro, N.H., 1963—; one-woman shows include Mollay Coll., Rockville Ctr. Library; photographer 4 books on Monterey Peninulsa, New Eng. and N.H.; writer, editor Health News Letter Molloy Coll., 1990—. Health educator Nassau County Dept. of Sr. Citizens Outreach Program, Molloy Coll., AIDS educator, 1991—; adminstr., chief AIDS counselor Interaction AIDS Counseling, Babylon, N.Y., 1992—; lic. AIDS educator N.Y. Metro Area; chairperson of grants com. in higher edn. Nassau U.; dir. AIDS Outreach Program, Episcopal Diocese of L.I., 1997—; dir. photography Visual Graphics N.H., 1997—; co-chair AIDS Outreach Cathedral of the Incarnation, 1998—. USPHS fellow, 1962, Nat. Cancer Inst. fellow, 1981-82. Mem. AAUP, AAUW, Nat. Congress Oncology Nurses, N.Y. State Fedn. Health Educators, Inc., Nurses Assn. Counties L.I. Dist. 14, N.Y. State Nurses Assn., World Wildlife Orgn., Audubon Soc., Internat. Ctr. Photography, Nature Conservancy, Sierra Club, Cathedral Womens Club, Alter Guild, Sigma Theta Tau (Epsilon Kappa chpt., rsch. grantee 1985, 87), Zeta Epsilon Gamma. Episcopalian. Avocations: writing, photography. Home: 16 Walker St Malverne NY 11565

RYAN, THERESA ANN JULIA, accountant; b. N.Y.C., Mar. 1, 1962; d. John Patrick and Diane Elizabeth Ryan. BA in Math. and Econs., Fordham U., 1984, MBA in Profl. Acctg., 1989. CPA, N.Y., F.L.M.I. With sales dept. Abraham & Straus, White Plains, N.Y., 1980-84; adminstrv. asst. Companion of N.Y., Rye, 1984-86, asst. fin. analyst, 1986-87; with tech. ctr. Fordham U., N.Y.C., 1987-88; staff acct. Konigsberg Wolf & Co., N.Y.C., 1989-91; sr. audit assoc. Coopers & Lybrand, L.L.P., N.Y.C., 1992-95; internal auditor N.Y. Power Authority, White Plains, 1996-99; circulation acctg. analyst Gannett Corp., White Plains, 2000-2001; sr. accountant Time Warner Cable, 2001- . Mem. Inst. Internal Auditors (cert.), Beta Gamma Sigma. Avocations: music, biking, writing, travel, psychology. Home: 5 Clare Ter Yonkers NY 10707-3201 Office: Time Warner Cable 290 Harbor Drive Stamford CT 06902-7441

RYAN, UNA SCULLY, health sciences professional, medical educator; b. Kuala Lumpur, Malaysia, Dec. 18, 1941; d. Henry and Amy (Yee) Scully; m. Allan Dana Callow, May 26, 1989; children: Tamsin Randlett, Amy Jean Susan Ryan. BSc in Zoology, Chemistry & Microbiology, Bristol (Eng.) U., 1963; PhD in Cell Biology, Cambridge (Eng.) U., 1968. Fellow dept. biology U. Va., Charlottesville, 1964-66; fellow dept. medicine U. Miami, Fla., 1966-67, adj. asst. prof. biology, 1968-71; dir. lab. for ultrastructure studies Howard Hughes Med. Inst., Miami, 1967-71; from instr. to assoc. prof. medicine U. Miami Sch. Medicine, 1967-80, prof. medicine, 1980-89; sr. scientist Papanicolaou Cancer Rsch. Inst., Miami, 1972-77; rsch. prof. surgery Washington U. Sch. Medicine, St. Louis, 1990—; dir. health scis. Monsanto Co., St. Louis, 1990-93; pres., CEO T Cell Scis., Needham, Mass., 1993-98; rsch. prof. medicine Boston U. Sch. Medicine, 1993—; pres., CEO AVANT Immunotherapeutics, Needham, Mass., 1998—. Dir. course W. Alton Jones Cell Sci. Ctr., 1979-81; dir. Hybridoma Facility, U. Miami, 1986-89; chair local organizing com. Internat. Coun. on Thrombosis and Hemostasis, 1984; chair Rev. Com. for Extracellular Matrix Interactions in Lung, 1983; chair various revs. NHLBI; mem. various rev. and adv. coms. Author: J. Tissue Culture Methods, 1987, Pulmonary Endothelium in Health Disease, 1987, Endothelial Cells, 1988, Vascular Endothelium: Receptors and Transduction Mechanisms, 1989; editor: Tissue & Cell, 1981-87; rev. editor: In Vitro, 1986; reviewer profl. jours., contbr. articles to profl. jours. UK state scholar, 1960, Country Major scholar, 1960; D.S.I.R. rsch. fellow, 1964, 65, Ethel Sargant Rsch. fellow, 1964-65, Sci. Rsch. Coun. fellow, 1966; recipient Louis and Artur Lucian award for rsch. in circulatory diseases, 1984, Merit award Nat. Heart, Lung and Blood Inst., 1986, Lillie award Woods Hole, Marine Bill, Lab., 1989, Order of Brit. Eagle, 2002. Mem. Am. Soc. Cell Biology, Soc. Neurosci., Tissue Culture Assn., Internat. Soc. Heart Rsch., Am. Heart Assn. (coun. on basic rsch., coun. on circulation, cardiopulmonary coun.), Am. Physiol. Soc., Am. Microcirculatory Soc., European Soc. Microcirculation, Am. Thoracic Soc. (dir. course on culture of pulmonary endothelial cells), Internat. Soc. Applied Cardiovascular Biology, N.Y. Acad. Scis., Fla. Soc. Electron Microscopy, Sigma Xi. Office: AVANT Immunotherapeutics 119 4th Ave Needham MA 02494-2725

RYAN-GRIFFITH, MARY KATE, special education educator; b. Balt., Oct. 9, 1957; d. Charles Ambrose Ryan and Elizabeth Joan Ebert; m. George Vintin Griffith Jr., June 29, 1991; 1 child, Virginia Elizabeth Griffith ; m. Ronald Hemmerick, Apr. 24, 1982 (div. 1988). BS, Vanderbilt U., 1980; MA, Gallaudet U., Washington, 1984. Cert. advanced profl. tchr. Md. Interpreter, tutor Montgomery County Pub. Schs., Wheaton, Md., 1986—87, spl. edn. instrln. asst. Rockville, Md., 1987—89, 3d-4th gr. tchr. Tacoma Park, Md., 1989—91, spl. edn. tchr. Gaithersburg, Md., 1991—. Presenter in field. Contbr. Exceptional Children-An Introduction to Special Education, 2003. Pres. Lovettsville Cmty. Ctr., Va., VSA Arts Bd., 2000; mem. Lovettsville ES PTO, Va., Resnik E.S. PTA, Gaithersburg, Va. Named Outstanding Woman of Loudoun County, Loudoun Commn. on Women, 2003, Outstanding Spl. Educator, PTA Mont. chpt. Mem.: NEA, Coun. for Exceptional Children, Md. State Tchr.'s Assn., Delta Kappa Epsilon. Achievements include being named Ms. Wheelchair, Md., 1987. Avocations: performing with very special arts, drawing, making jewelry, writing, stained glass. Home: 12942 Axline Rd Lovettsville VA 20180

RYAN-HALLEY, CHARLOTTE MURIEL, oncology clinical specialist, family nurse practitioner; b. Beedeville, Ark., Sept. 2, 1939; d. Eugene Sanford and Edith Elizabeth (Goforth) Breckenridge; m. Alexander Halley; children: Russell Kent Ryan, Cary Randall Ryan, Molly Reneé Ryan Nankervis. BSN cum laude, Calif. State U., Fresno, 1991, MSN, clin. specialist, 1997. RN Calif., nat. cert. oncology nurse, cert. pub. health nurse, sch. nurse, nat. cert. advanced oncology nurse. Psychiat. technician Porterville (Calif.) State Hosp., 1959-67; tchr. developmentally disabled Ariz. Tng. Ctr., Coolidge, 1967-71; Montessori tchr. Tucson, 1972-77; tchr. developmentally disabled Heartland Opportunity Ctr., Madera, Calif., 1977-79; med. office mgr. office of orthopedic surgeon, Madera, 1979-83, office mgr., x-ray technician, 1983-87; staff nurse in oncology St. Agnes Med. Ctr., Fresno, 1991—99; oncology clin. nurse specialist Kaweah Delta Hosp., Visalia, Calif., 1999—2002. Instr. nursing dept. Calif. State U., Fresno, 1992-93, 95-98; clin. instr., Fresno City Coll. Paradigm Nursing Program, Fresno, Calif., 2003. Treas. Hospice of Madera County, 1990-92, bd. dirs., 1992; peer counselor Calif. State U., Fresno, 1989-91; pres. bd. dirs. Easter Seals Soc., Madera, 1981. Mem. Nat. Oncology Nursing Soc. (on-line forum moderator, item writer cert. test 1998), Nightingale Soc., Golden Key, Sigma Theta Tau (chmn. pub. com., editor MUNEWS newsletter 1994-95). Republican. Avocations: reading, improving quality of life for cancer patients. Home: 2235 S Virmargo St Visalia CA 93292-1311

RYAVEC, ISABEL SEATON, librarian, media specialist; b. Cin., June 2, 1936; d. John Thomas and Isabella (Seaman) Seaton; m. Karl William Ryavec, Aug. 24, 1957; children: Karen Lenore Ryavec, Karl Ernest Ryavec. MSLS, Simmons Coll., 1971; BS in Edn., Miami U., 1957. Cert. sch. libr., Mass. Desk asst. Jones Libr., Amherst, Mass., 1968-70; sch. libr. Minnechaut H.S., Wilbraham, Mass., 1971-73, Amherst Regional H.S., 1973-95; ret., 1995. Mem. Media Coun., Amherst, 1973-95; co-chair, founder Joint Tech. Com., Amherst, 1992-95. Recipient Sonia Wexler award Multi-Cultural Edn. Com., 1986. Democrat. Avocations: herb gardening, hiking, photography.

RYCHLAK, BONNIE LEE, artist, museum curator; b. Culver City, Calif., July 7, 1951; d. Walter Arthur and Margaret Rychlak; m. Brian Stewart Gayman, Dec. 23, 1973. BA, UCLA, 1973; MFA, U. Mass., 1976. Dir. collections, curator Isamu Noguchi Found., LI. Solo exhbns. include St. Peter's Ch., NYC, 1986, Rastovsky Gallery, NYC, 1989, Shoshana Wayne Gallery, Santa Monica, Calif., 1991, The Sculpture Ctr., NYC, 1993, Gallery Three Zero, NYC, 1994; exhibited in group shows at Artists' Space, NYC, 1986, White Columns, NYC, 1986, Bess Cutler Gallery, NYC, 1986, Mission Gallery, NYC, 1987, A.I.R. Gallery, NYC, 1988, Space III, Birmingham, Ala., 1988, Longwood Gallery, Bronx, 1987, Rastovsky Gallery, 1988, Shoshana Wayne Gallery, 1989, Stux Gallery, NYC, 1990, Penine Hart Gallery, NYC, 1990, Emily Sorkin Gallery, 1990, Sue Spaid Fine Art, LA, 1990, Hallwalls, NY, 1991, Internat. House, NYC, 1992, 55 Ferris St., Bklyn., 1992, Wyn Kamarsky Inc., NYC, 1993, T'zart Test Wall, NYC, 1993, No. Ill. U., DeKalb, 1994, K & E Gallery, NYC, 1994, Adam Baumgold Gallery, NYC, 1994, Ota Fine Arts, Tokyo, 1996, Basilico Fine Arts, NYC, 1996, Silverstein Gallery, 1998, R&F, Kingston, NY, 1999, Momenta, Bklyn., 2000, Williamsburg Art and Hist. Ctr., Bklyn., 2000, 02, Parrish Art Mus., Southampton, NY, 2000, others; work in pub. collection of Harvard U. NEA grantee, 1976; Bellagio residency Rockefeller Found., 1985; recipient Prix de Rome, Am. Acad. in Rome, 1990. Home: 248 Lafayette St New York NY 10012-4030 Office: The Isamu Noguchi Found 32-37 Vernon Blvd Long Island City NY 11106

RYDALCH, ANN, federal agency administrator, former state senator; m. Vernal Rydalch. BS in Business Educ., Idaho State U. Mem. Idaho Senate, 1983—1990, chmn. Fed. Lab. Consortium Tech. Transfer, 2001- . Past mem. Idaho Bicentennial Commn.; former vice chmn. Idaho Republican Com. Office: ID Natl Energy & Envrn Lab PO Box 1625 MS 3810 2525 N Fremont Ave Idaho Falls ID 83415-3810

RYDELL, CATHERINE M. former state legislator; b. Grand Forks, N.D., May 8, 1950; d. Hilary Harold and Catherine F. (Ireland) Wilson; m. Charles D. Rydell, 1971; children: Kimberly, Jennifer, Michael. BS, U. N.D., 1971. Mem. N.D. Ho. of Reps., 1985—, mem. supreme ct. judicial planning, govt., vet. affairs com., past rep. caucus leader; exec. dir. Am. Acad. Neurology, St. Paul. Coord. cmty. svc. Bismarck Jr. Coll.; bus. mgr. surg. svc. St. Alexius Med. Ctr. Bd. dirs. Mission Valley Family, YMCA, N.D. Early Childhood Tng. Ctr., Ronald McDonald Found., CHAND; mem. state adv. bd. Casey Family Program, Juvenile Justice; mem. lay adv. bd. St. Alexius; mem. regional adv. bd. Luth. Social Svcs.; mem. N.D. State Centennial Com., N.D. State Mus. Art. Recipient Outstanding Svc. award Tobacco Free N.D., Legislator of Yr. award Children's Caucus, Guardian of Bus. award Nat. Fedn. Ind. Bus. Mem. Philanthropic and Edn. Orgn. Sisterhood, N.D. Med. Assn. (v.p.), Gamma Phi Beta. Office: Am Acad Neurology 1080 Montreal Ave Saint Paul MN 55116-2386

RYDER, BEVERLY, utilities executive; BA in Econs., Stanford (Calif.) U.; MBA in Fin., U. Chgo. From dir. strategic alliances So. Calif. to corp. sec. Edison Internat., Rosemead, Calif., 1972—96, corp. sec., 1996—, v.p. cmty. involvement, 2000—. Trustee Stanford (Calif.) U.; commr. LA (Calif.) City Employees' Retirement Bd. Bd. dir. United Way, LA. Office: Edison International 2244 Walnut Grove Ave Rosemead CA 91770

RYDER, MICHELE CAIN, counselor, speech therapist; b. McKeesport, Pa., Aug. 12, 1946; d. Michael Patrick and Rose Elizabeth (Keddie) Cain; m. Dennis E. Ryder, May 26, 1973; children: Patrick Cain, Christian Cain. BS, Indiana U. Pa., 1968; MEd, Shippensburg U., 1972. Speech therapist Capital Area Intermediate Unit, Lemoyne, Pa., 1968-73; vol. in speech programs various pub. schs., Hawaii and, Germany, 1975-82; tchr. U. Md. European Divsn., Stuttgart, Germany, 1982; supr. child care ctr. Dept. Army, Moehringen, Germany, 1982-83; counselor Manassas Park (Va.) City Schs., 1987-89, Arlington (Va.) County Pub. Schs., 1989—. Sec. Kings Park West Civic Assn., Fairfax, Va., 1986, mem. cmty. affairs, 1988. Fellow Pa. State U., 1969, Gallaudet Coll., 1973. Mem. ACA, NEA, Va. Counseling Assn., Am. Sch. Counselor Assn., Va. Sch. Counselor Assn., No. Va. Sch. Counselor Assn. Avocations: reading, dance, cooking. Home: 4910 Orkney Ct Fairfax VA 22032-2327

RYDER, WINONA (WINONA LAURA HOROWITZ), actress; b. Winona, Minn., Oct. 29, 1971; d. Michael and Cynthia (Istas) Horowitz. Films include: Lucas, 1986, Square Dance, 1987, Beetlejuice, 1988, Great Balls of Fire, 1989, Heathers, 1989, Edward Scissorhands, 1990, Mermaids, 1990, Welcome Home, Roxy Carmichael, 1990, Night On Earth, 1992, Bram Stoker's Dracula, 1992, Age of Innocence, 1993 (Golden Globe for Best Supporting Actress, 1994, Academy award nominee, Best Supporting Actress, 1993), The House of the Spirits, 1994, Reality Bites, 1994, Little Women, 1994 (Acad. Awd. nom., Best Actress), How to Make An American Quilt, 1995, Looking for Richard, 1995, The Crucible, 1996, Boys, 1996, Alien Resurrection, 1997, Celebrity, 1998, Girl, Interrupted, 1999, Autumn in New York, 1999, Lost Souls, 2000, Mr. Deeds, 2002, S1mOne, 2002, The Day My God Died (narrator), 2003 Hollywood Walk of Fame-2000.

RYERSON, LISA M. academic administrator; BA in English cum laude, Wells Coll., Aurora, N.Y., 1981; MS, SUNY. Asst. dir. admissions Wells Coll., Aurora, NY, 1981—84, assoc. dean of students, 1984—87, dean of students, 1991—94, v.p. to exec. v.p., 1994—95, pres., 1995—. Vice chair bd. of mng. dir. Ind. Coll. Funf of N.Y.; chair exec. bd. Pub. Leadership Edn. Network, Washington; bd. mem. Women's Coll. Coalition, Washington. Mem. exec. com. Cayuga County C. of C., Auburn, NY. Office: Wells Coll 170 Main St Aurora NY 13026*

RYG, KATHLEEN SCHULTZ, municipal government official; b. Evanston, Ill., Aug. 6, 1952; d. Robert Coyne and Sheila (Hogan) Schultz ; m. Martin Lee Ryg, Sept. 21, 1974 (div. Apr. 1986). BS, No. Ill. U., 1974; MA, Roosevelt U., 1979. Tng. counselor Clearbrook Ctr., Elk Grove Village, Ill., 1974-77, dir. residential services Arlington Heights, Ill., 1977-79; employment supr. Condell Hosp., Libertyville, Ill., 1979-80; dir. residential program NW Mental Health Ctr., Arlington Heights, Ill., 1985-89, asst. dir., 1985-89; village clk. Village of Vernon Hills (Ill.), 1989—. V.p. Career Guidance Ctr., Grayslake, Ill., 1980-82, v.p. summer celebration com., Vernon Hills, 1986-89, bd. dirs., 1986; co-chmn. Programs for Alternative Living, Chgo. area, 1984-86. Mem. Lake County Mcpl. Clks., Ill. Mcpl. Clks., Internat. Inst. Mcpl. Clks., Community Alliance Project, Nawthorn Sch. Drug and Alcohol Awareness Com., Jaycees. Roman Catholic. Avocations: tennis, horseback riding. Home: 307 Onwentsia Rd Vernon Hills IL 60061-2120 Office: Village of Vernon Hills 290 Evergreen Dr Vernon Hills IL 60061-2904

RYLANT, CYNTHIA, author; b. Hopewell, Va., June 6, 1954; d. John Tune and Leatrel (Rylant) Smith; 1 child, Nathaniel. BA, U. Charleston, 1975; MA, Marshall U., 1976; MLS, Kent State U., 1981. English instr. Marshall U., Huntington, W.Va., 1979-80, U. Akron, Ohio, 1983-84; children's libr. Akron (Ohio) Pub. Libr., 1983. Part-time lectr. Northeast Ohio Univs. Coll. Medicine, Rootstown, Ohio, 1991—. Author: (picture books) When I Was Young in the Mountains, 1982 (Caldecott Honor book, 1983, English Speaking Union Book-Across-the-Sea Amb. of Honor award, 1984, Am. Book award nom., 1983), Miss Maggie, 1983, This Year's Garden, 1984, Waiting to Waltz: A Childhood (verse), 1984 (Nat. Coun. for Social Studies Best Book, 1984), A Blue-Eyed Daisy (in U.K. as Some Year for Ellie), 1985 (Children's Book of Yr., Child Study Assn. Am., 1985), The Relatives Came, 1985 (Horn Book Honor book, 1985, Children's Book of Yr., Child Study Assn. Am., 1985, Caldecott Honor book, 1986), Every Living Thing (stories), 1985, A Fine White Dust, 1986 (Newbery Honor Book, 1987), Night in the Country, 1986, Birthday Presents, 1987, Children of Christmas (in U.K. as Silver Packages and Other Stories), 1987, All I See, 1988, A Kindness, 1989, Mr. Grigg's Work, 1989, Soda Jerk (verse)1990, A Couple of Kooks (stories), 1990, Appalachia: The Voices of Sleeping Birds, 1991 (Boston Globe/Horn Book Honor book for nonfiction, 1991), Best Wishes, 1992, An Angel for Solomon Singer, 1992, Missing May, 1992 (Newbery Medal, 1992), The Dreamer, 1993, I Had Seen Castles, 1993, The Everyday Books, 1993, The Old Lady Who Named Things, 1996, Whales, 1996, Bookshop Dog, 1996, Blue Hill Meadows, 1997, Poppleton, 1997, Poppleton and Friends, 1997, Cat Heaven, 1997, Blue Hill Meadows and the Much-Loved Dog, 1997, Scarecrow, 1998, Bear Day, 1998, Tulip Sees America, 1998, Poppleton Everyday, 1998, Poppleton Forever, 1998, Bird House, 1998, Islander, 1998, Bless Us All, 1998, Cobble Street Cousins in Aunt Lucy's Kitchen, 1998, Bunny Bungalow, 1999, Cookie-Store Cat, 1999, Poppleton in Spring, 1999, Cobble Street Cousins: Some Good News, 1999, Cobble Street Cousins: Special Gifts, 1999, Poppleton in Fall, 1999, Give Me Grace, 1999, Heavenly Village, 1999, Poppleton Through and Through, 2000, Wonderful Happens, 2000, Thimbleberry Stories, 2000, Let's Go Home, 2000, Little Whistle, 2000, In November, 2000, Poppleton Has Fun, 2000, Little Whisule's Dinner Party, 2001, Little Whistle's Medicine, 2001, Ticky-Tacky Doll, 2001, The Great Gracie Chase, 2001, Poppleton in Winter, 2001, Summer Party, 2001, Good Morning Sweetie Pie and Other Poems for Little Children, 2002, Old Town in the Green Groves, 2002, Wedding Flowers, 2002, (Mr. Putter and Tabby series) Walk the Dog, 1994, Bake the Cake, 1994, Pour the Tea, 1994, Pick the Pears, 1995, Fly the Plane, 1997, Row the Boat, 1997, Toot the Horn, 1998, Take the Train, 1998, Paint the Porch, 2000, Feed the Fish, 2001, (The High-Rise Private Eyes series) Case of the Climbing Cat, 2000, Case of the Missing Monkey, 2000, The Case of the Puzzling Possum, 2001, The Case of the Troublesome Turtle, 2001, (Henry and Mudge Series) Henry and Mudge, 1987, Henry and Mudge in Puddle Trouble, 1990, Henry and Mudge Take the Big Test, 1991, Henry and Mudge in the Green Time, 1992, Henry and Mudge under the Yellow Moon, 1992, Henry and Mudge in the Sparkle Days, 1993, Henry and Mudge and the Forever Sea, 1993, Henry and Mudge Get the Cold Shivers, 1993, Henry and Mudge and the Happy Cat, 1994, Henry and Mudge and the Bedtime Thumps, 1991, Henry and Mudge and the Long Weekend, 1992, Henry and Mudge and the Wild Wind, 1992, Henry and Mudge and the Careful Cousin, 1994, Henry and Mudge and the Best Day of All, 1995, Henry and Mudge in the Family Trees, 1997, Henry and Mudge and the Sneaky Crackers, 1998, Henry and Mudge and the Starry Night, 1998, Henry and Mudge and Annie's Good Move, 1998, Henry and Mudge and the Snowman Plan, 1999, Henry and Mudge and Annie's Perfect Pet, 1999, Henry and Mudge and the Funny Lunch, 1999, Henry and Mudge and the Tall Tree House, 1999, Henry and Mudge and Mrs. Hopper's House, 1999, Henry and Mudge and the Great Grandpas, 1999, Henry and Mudge and a Very Special Merry Christmas, 1999, Henry and Mudge and the Wild Goose Chase, 1999, Henry and Mudge and the Big Sleepover, 1999, Henry and Mudge and the Tumbling Trip, 1999, Henry's Puppy Mudge Has a Snack, 2001, Henry's Puppy Mudge Takes aBath, 2001. Office: Simon & Schuster Children's 4th Floor 1230 Ave of The Americas New York NY 10020*

RYLEE, GLORIA GENELLE, music educator; b. Commerce, Ga., Nov. 26, 1947; d. John Otis Sr. and Genelle Byrd Rylee. BS in Edn., Ga. So. Coll., 1969; MusM, Southwestern Bapt. Theol. Sem., 1973. Tchr. Banks County Bd. Edn., Homer, Ga., 1969-71; piano tchr. Ft. Worth, 1972-73; min. music, ch. sec. Mt. Olive Bapt. Ch., Commerce, Ga., 1974-81; sec. Ga. Bapt. Conv., Atlanta, 1981-86; parapro Banks County Bd. Edn., Homer, 1986-87, tchr. music, 1987—. Tchr. piano, Homer, 1975-81, 89-96; staff mem. Youth II Music Camp, Norman Park, Ga., 1996-98. Pianist Webbs Creek Bapt. Ch., Commerce, 1991—. Active Grassroots Arts Coun., Gainesville, Ga., 1994—, State Bapt. Women's Choral Group, 1979-86, 1996-2001, Messiah Singers, Khabarovsk, Russia, 2003; team mem. Vol. Missions Ga. Bapt. Conv., Seoul, Korea, 1998-2000; mem. Messiah singers Kahbarovsk, Russia, 2003. Mem. Nat. Mus. Educators Assn., Music. Tchrs. Nat. Assn., Ga. Music Educators Assn., Profl. Assn. Ga. Educators. Home: 1785 Wilson Bridge Rd Homer GA 30547-2911 Office: Banks County Elem Sch 335 Evans St Homer GA 30547

RYMER, ILONA SUTO, artist, retired art educator; b. N.Y.C., Dec. 1, 1921; d. Alexander and Elizabeth (Komaromy) Suto; m. Robert Hamilton Rymer, Mar. 27, 1944 (dec. Dec. 1999); children: Thomas Parker, Shelley Ilona. BA, Long Beach State U., 1953, MA, 1954. Tchr., cons. Long Beach (Calif.) Sch. Dist., 1953-56; tchr. Orange (Calif.) Sch. Dist., 1956-58; tchr., cons. Brea (Calif.)-Olinda Sch. Dist., 1958-80; ind. artist, designer Graphic Ho. Studio, Santa Ynez, Calif., 1980—, Stampa-Barbara, Santa Barbara, Calif., 1990—. Lectr. folk art Brea Sch. Dist., 1975—80. Author: (instrn. book) Folk Art U.S.A., 1975 (Proclamation City of Brea, 1975); art editor, feature writer, illustrator: Arabian Conneciton mag., 1985—86; needlepoint designer Backsticth Store, Solvang, Calif., 1982—83; one-woman shows include Liberty Bell Race Track, Pa., exhibited in group shows, 1970—, exhibitions include Dennas Mus. Ctr., Northwestern Mich. Coll., 2001, exhibited in group shows at Nat. Exhbn. Am. Watercolor, 2002, Adirondack's Nat. Exhbn. of Am. Watercolors, Old Forge, N.Y., 2002—, commission, Pres. Regan's portrait on his stallion, Reagran Libr., Simi Valley, Calif., Khemosabi and Ruth, 1995. Co-founder, mem. Gallery Los Olivos, pres., 1993—. Recipient 1st pl. Seminar award, Rex Brandt, 1961, Affiliate award, Laguna Art Mus., 1967, Best of Watercolor award, Orange County Fair, 1969, Bicentennial trip to France, Air France, 1975, Proclamation for Tchg., City of Brea, 1980, Theme award, Santa Barbara County Fair, 1991. Mem.: Artist Guild Santa Ynez Valley, Ctrl. Coast Art Assn., Santa Barbara ARt Assn., Calif. Gold Coast Watercolor Soc. (signature). Presbyterian. Studio: PO Box 822 Santa Ynez CA 93460-0822 Personal E-mail: ilonarymer@aol.com.

RYMER, PAMELA ANN, federal judge; b. Knoxville, Tenn., Jan. 6, 1941; AB, Vassar Coll., 1961; LLB, Stanford U., 1964; LLD (hon.), Pepperdine U., 1988. Bar: Calif. 1966, U.S. Ct. Appeals (9th cir.) 1966, U.S. Ct. Appeals (10th cir.), U.S. Supreme Ct. Dir., polit. rsch. and analysis Goldwater for President Com., 1964; v.p. Rus Walton & Assoc., Los Altos, Calif., 1965—66; assoc. Lillick McHose & Charles, L.A., 1966—75, ptnr., 1973—75, Toy and Rymer, L.A., 1975—83; judge U.S. Dist. Ct. (cen. dist.) Calif., L.A., 1983—89, U.S. Ct. Appeals (9th cir.), L.A., 1989—. Faculty The Nat. Jud. Coll., 1986-88; mem. com. summer edn. programs Fed. Jud. Ctr., 1987-88, mem. com. appellate judge edn., 1996-99; chair exec. com.

9th Cir. Jud. Conf., 1990; mem. com. criminal law Jud. Conf. U.S., 1988-93, Ad Hoc com. gender-based violence, 1991-94, fed.-state jurisdiction com., 1993-96; mem. commn. on structural alternatives Fed. Cts. Appeals, 1997-98. Mem. editorial bd. The Judges' jour., 1989-91; contbr. articles to profl. jours. and newsletters. Mem. Calif. Postsecondary Edn. Commn., 1974-84, chmn., 1980-84; mem. L.A. Olympic Citizens Adv. Commn.; bd. visitors Stanford U. Law Sch., 1986-99, trustee, 1991-2001, chair, 1993-96, exec. com., chmn. bd. trustees com. acad. policy, planning and mgmt. and its ad. hoc. com. athletics., chmn. bd. visitors Sch. Law, 1987—; bd. visitors Pepperdine U. Law Sch., 1987—; mem. Edn. Commn. of States Task Force on State Policy and Ind. Higher Edn., 1987-89, Carnegie Commn. Task Force Sci. and Tech. Jud. and Regulatory Decisionmaking, 1990-93, Commn. Substance Abuse Coll. and Univ. Campuses, 1992-94, commn. substance abuse high schs. Ctr. Addiction and Substance Abube Columbia U.; bd. dirs. Constnl. Rights Found., 1985-97, Pacific Coun. Internat. Policy, 1995—, Calif. Higher Edn. Policy Ctr., 1992-97; Jud. Conf. U.S. Com. Fed.-State Jurisdiction, 1993, Com. Criminal Law, 1988-93, ad hoc com. gender based violence, 1991-94; chair exec. com. 9th cir. jud. conf., 1990-94. Recipient Outstanding Trial Jurist award L.A. County Bar Assn., 1988; named David T. Lewis Disting. Jurist-in-Residence U. Utah, 1992. Mem. ABA (task force on civil justice reform 1991-93, mem. coord. com. agenda civil justice reform in Am. 1991), State Bar Calif. (antitrust and trade regulation sect., exec. com. 1990-92), L.A. County Bar Assn. (chmn. antitrust sect. 1981-82, mem. editl. bd. The Judges Jour. 1989-91, mem. com. professionalism 1988—, numerous other coms.), Assn. of Bus. Trial Lawyers (bd. govs. 1990-92), Stanford Alumni Assn., Stanford Law Soc. Soc. Calif., Vassar Club So. Calif. (past pres.). Office: US Ct Appeals 9th Cir US Court of Appeals Bldg 125 S Grand Ave Rm 600 Pasadena CA 91105-1621*

RYPCZYK, CANDICE LEIGH, employee relations executive; b. Norman, Okla., Apr. 24, 1949; d. John Anthony and Lee (Brunswick) Wirth; m. Peter Charles Rypczyk, Nov. 27, 1976. BA, Kalamazoo Coll., 1971; cert. labor studies extension program, Cornell U., N.Y. Sch. Indsl., Labor Relations, Middletown, 1985. Personnel asst. PFW divsn. Hercules Inc., Middletown, 1973-77, asst. personnel mgr., 1977-79, mgr. employee relations, 1979-92; mgr. human resources Huck Internat., Kingston, N.Y., 1992-2000; human resources cons., 2000—. Mem. DAR, Soc. for Human Resource Mgmt. (v.p. Mid-Hudson Valley chpt. 1985, pres. 1986, treas. N.Y. State coun. 1986, dist. bd. dirs. 1988-90, cert.). Avocations: photography, reading, genealogy.

RYPSTRA, ANN, zoology educator; PhD, Pa. State U., 1982. Prof. zoology Miami U., Oxford, Ohio; also dir. Ecology Rsch. Ctr., Oxford, Ohio. Reviewer NSF. Contbr. articles to sci. jours., including Animal Behaviour, Jour. Arachnology, Oikos. Rsch. grantee NSF. Office: Miami U Dept Zoology Oxford OH 45056

RZESZOTARSKI, PAMELA SUE (PAMELA SUE DOUGHERTY), banker; b. Denver, Nov. 11, 1964; d. John Patrick and Marion Alexine (Denison) D. BS, Colo. State U., 1987. Dist. loan underwriting mgr. World Savs. & Loan, Melville, N.Y., 1981-89; asst. v.p. underwriting mgr. Citibank N.A., Bklyn., 1989-92; mgr. audit processing Mortgage Monitor, N.Y.C., 1992; ops. mgr. RPI Profl. Alternatives, N.Y.C., 1992-94; asst. v.p. vendor mgr. NatWest Home Mortgage, Wall Township, N.J., 1994-96; divsn. mgr. fin. CIGNA Healthcare, Bristol, Conn., 1996—99; contr. Cmty. Premier Plus, N.Y.C., 1999—. Mem. Appraisal Found. Avocations: reading, team sports, golf, arts, classic movies. Office: 534 W 135th St New York NY 10031 Office Phone: 212-491-2320.

RZEWNICKI, JANET C. state official; b. May 21, 1953; d. Robert Myers; m. Victor Rzewnicki, June 3, 1972. BS in Acctg. and Fin. with distinction, U. Del. CPA. Sr. acct. KPMG Peat Marwick, Wilmington, Del., 1978-80; corp. acct. internat. sect. Hercules Inc., Wilmington, 1980-81; acctg. instr. U. Del., Newark, 1980-82; pvt. practice acctg. Wilmington, 1981-82; state treas. State of Del., Dover, 1983-97; dir. investments banking Am. Fronteer, N.Y.C., 1998-99. Mem. Del. Econ. Adv. Coun. Leader People to People Del., China, 1985; treas., bd. dirs. March of Dimes, Newark, 1979—; former bd. dirs. United Way of Del., Wilmington, 1980-82; active Gov.'s Coun. on Devel. Fin., 1982-95. Mem. AICPA, Nat. Assn. State Treas. (pres. 1989), Nat. Assn. State Auditors, Contrs. and Treas. (pres. 1998), Del. Soc. CPAs, Pa. Inst. CPAs, Am. Soc. Women Accts. (bd. dirs. 1981), Beta Gamma Sigma. Republican. Office: Am Fronteer 10th Fl 30 Wall St Fl 10 New York NY 10005-2201

SA, JULIE, councilwoman; b. Korea, Dec. 15, 1950; came to U.S., 1973, naturalized, 1982; married. Degree in Polit. Sci., Dong-A U., Korea. Owner restaurant chain; councilwoman City of Fullerton, Calif., 1992-94, 96-99, mayor, 1994-95. Rep. bd. Orange County Sanitation Dists.; rep. to Tri-City Park Authority, City of Fullerton. Mem. Fullerton C. of C., Orange County Korean C. of C., Orange County Chinese C. of C. Office: Office of City Council 303 W Commonwealth Ave Fullerton CA 92832-1710

SAAB, DEANNE KELTUM, real estate appraiser, real estate broker; b. Allentown, Pa., Jan. 27, 1945; d. James A. and Agnes G. (Hanzlik) S. BA, Cedar Crest Coll., 1966; MS, U. Calif., Santa Barbara, 1973; realtors cert., Pa. State U., 1978. Cert. appraiser Assoc. Appraisal Inst., Pa., 1991; cert. sales profl. Nat. Assn. Home Builders, 1994. Tchr. Ojai (Calif.) Unified Sch. Dist., 1966-74; pvt. practice Allentown, Pa., 1978—; pres./treas. DeAnne & Assoc., Inc., Allentown, Pa., 1987—; owner Heritage Gardens, Allentown, Pa., 1981—. Co-founder, treas. performance group Lehigh Valley Folk Music Soc., 1996. Mem. AAUW (various offices, Best State Newsletter award 1987), Nat. Assn. Realtors, Pa. Assn. Realtors, Allentown Lehigh Valley Assn. Realtors, Cedar Crest Coll. Alumnae Assn. (class rep., various offices), Lehigh Valley Guild Craftsmen (various offices). Avocations: gourd, herbal crafting, painting, folk music performance. Home and Office: 1360 Dorney Ave Allentown PA 18103-9731 Office Phone: 610-820-9529.

SAARI, JOY ANN, family nurse practitioner, geriatrics medical and surgical nurse; b. Chippewa Falls, Wis., July 14, 1953; d. Harry R. and Hilda R. (Christianson) Harwood; m. Allan A. Saari, Dec. 31, 1973 (dec.); children: Christopher, Erik. BSN summa cum laude, U. Wis., Eau Claire, 1978; postgrad., Blue Ridge Community Coll., Verona, Va., 1987; MSN, FNP, George Mason U., 1995; MSN. RN, Mich., Wis., Va.; FNP, Va.; cert. BLS instr., ACLS. Staff nurse Portage View Hosp., Hancock, Mich., 1979-80; evening supr., asst. dir. nursing Chippewa Manor, Chippewa Falls, 1980-86; staff nurse Bridgewater (Va.) Home, Inc., 1986-90; p.m. charge nurse Medicalodge Leavenworth, Kans., 1990-91; outdoor edn. nurse Montgomery County (Md.) Schs., 1991-93; FNP Leesburg/Sterling Family Practice, 1995—; affiliate faculty George Mason U., 2002—. Affiliate faculty George Mason U., 2003—. Maj. USAR Nurse Corps, 1989—. Mem. Am. Acad. Nurse Practitioners, Nat. League of Nursing, No. Va. Nurse Practitioner Assn., Res. Officer Assn., Am. Legion Aux., Phi Kappa Phi. E-mail: saarin@aol.com.

SAAS, DEBORAH ANNE, investment advisor, securities broker; b. Cleve., Mar. 17, 1955; d. Efrom Youngstein and Gerda Lillian (Klipper) Levine; m. Henry Ivan Saas, Jan. 8, 1977; children: Tyler Reed, Jonathan David, Jordan Peter. BS, Miami U., Oxford, Ohio, 1977. Cert. fin. mgr., registered prin. br. mgr., investment advisor. Asst. buyer May Co., Cleve., 1977-79; buyer Diamonds, Tempe, Ariz., 1979-84; retail buyer Broadway Southwest, Mesa, Ariz., 1984-86; fin. cons. Merrill Lynch, Mesa, Ariz., 1986-91; br. mgr. Linsco/Pvt. Ledger, Oxford, Ohio, 1991—. Office: 193 Shadowy Hills Dr Oxford OH 45056-1440

SABAAN, OTDRIA, finance company executive; b. Atlanta, Oct. 23, 1961; d. William Hershel Glenn and Claudia Jacqueline Gordon; children: Marcus Darielle Hutcherson, Maurice Lashaun Hutcherson. BA, Southwestern Bus. Tech., Lockland, Ohio, 1994; MBA, Oglethorpe U., 1998. Mgr. acctg., Atlanta, 1991—96; payroll acct., 1997—98; acctg. mgr. San Francisco, 1998—2001; adminstrn. mgr. Atlanta, 2001—02, 2002—. Civil rights ptnr. NAACP, Atlanta, 2002; state rep. assoc. State Dept., Atlanta, 2003. Mem.: L.A. Fitness Club. Avocations: running, bicycling, kickboxing, theater, music. Home: PO Box 12033 Atlanta GA 30355 Office: ADP Business Technology 2575 Westside Pky Alpharetta GA 30004

SABAJ, NANCY J. secondary school educator; b. Chgo., Mar. 23, 1969; d. Eugene A. and Florence M. Sabaj. BS in Music Edn., U. Ill., 1992; M in Music Edn., Vander Cook Coll. Music, Chgo., 1997. Cert. tchr. Ill. Band dir. St. John Luth. Sch., Champaign, Ill., 1992—94, Iuka (Ill.) Cmty. Consolidated Dist. 7, 1994—96, Odin (Ill.) Pub. Schs., 1997—2000, Roxana (Ill.) Cmty. Unit Sch. Dist. 1, 2000—. Mem.: Madison County Band Dirs. Assn., Ill. Music Educators Assn., Music Educators Nat. Conf. Avocations: church, fitness, sports. Home: 608 Hillside Bethalto IL 62010

SABATINI, SANDRA, physician; b. N.Y.C., Dec. 1, 1940; BS in Chemistry, Millsaps Coll., 1962; MS in Pharmacology, Marquette U., 1966; PhD in Pharmacology, U. Miss., 1968; MD in Internal Medicine, Tex. Med. Sch., 1974. Lic. physician, Ill., Tex. Intern in medicine U. Ill. Hosp., Chgo., 1974-75; asst. prof. U. Tex. Med. Sch., San Antonio, 1968-70; assoc. dir. U. Ill. Hosp., Chgo., 1977-78; asst. prof. U. Ill. Coll. of Medicine, Chgo., 1977-83, assoc. prof. medicine and physiology, 1983-84; attending physician in nephrology VA, Chgo., 1977-84; med. dir. Dialysis Unit U. Ill., Chgo., 1978-84; prof. internal medicine and physiology Tex. Tech. U. Health Sci. Ctr., Lubbock, 1985—, chmn. dept. physiology, 1993-96; attending physician in nephrology U. Med. Ctr., Lubbock, 1985—. Lab. instr. Millsaps Coll., Jackson, Miss., 1961-62; instr. pharmacology Bapt. Hosp. Sch. Nursing, Jackson, 1966-68; merit rev. mem. NSF, 1987, 91, 92; rev. mem. several orgns. including Chgo. Heart Assn., 1984, NIH, 1983, 86, 89-93, 96, Nat. Kidney Found., 1987, 89—, Am. Heart Assn., 1981-84, others; cons. U.S. Med. Licensing Exam/Nat. Bd. Med. Examiners, Step 1 Physiology Test Com., 1996-99. Editl. referee Am. Jour. Kidney Disease, Am. Jour. Physiology, Am. Jour. Nephrology, Annals of Internal Medicine, others; mem. editl. bd. Am. Jour. Nephrology, 1989-93, Seminars in Nephrology, 1984—; co-editor Am. Jour. Kidney Diseases, 1997—; author numerous publs. and abstracts in field; contbr. articles to profl. jours. Bd. dirs. YWCA of Lubbock, 1994-99; mem. Leadership Tex., 1994. Predoctoral fellowship grantee Marquette U., 1963-66; pub. health predoctoral fellow U. Miss. Med. Sch., 1967-69, gen. medicine sci. rsch. grantee U. Tex. Med. Sch., 1968-70, post-grad. fellow Karolinska Inst., Swedish Med. Coun., 1971, 73, NIH grantee, 1979-82, 84-99, Chgo. Heart Assn. grantee-in-aid, 1979-85, 99; grantee Nat. Eye Inst., 1979-80; recipient Banes Charitable trust award U. Ill., 1984-85, U.S. Olympic com. Rsch. Foudn., 1986-87; recipient Outstanding Alumnus award Tex. Med. Sch., 1994, numerous other awards in field. Fellow: ACP; mem.: AAUP, AAAS, ADA (hon.), Nat. Kidney Found. West Tex. (bd. dirs. 1993—99, Outstanding Vol. 1995, 2001, Disting. Svc. award 1996), Nat. Kidney Found. (numerous offices including chmn. several coms.), Italian-Am. Nephrologists, Inc., Internat. Soc. Nephrology, Ill. Kidney Found., Ctrl. Soc. Clin. Rsch., So. Soc. Clin. Rsch. (councillor 1997—99, pres.-elect 1999, pres. 2000), Assn. Chairs Dept. Physiology (councillor 1995—97), Am. Soc. Renal Biochemistry and Metabolism (pres.-elect 1994), Am. Soc. Pharmacology and Exptl. Therapeutics, Am. Soc. Nephrology, Am. Physiol. Soc., Am. Heart Assn., Am. Fedn. Med. Rsch. Office: Tex Tech U Health Sci Ctr 3601 4th St Lubbock TX 79430-0001

SABELHAUS, MELANIE R. government agency administrator; b. Cleve. m. Bob Sabelhaus; 2 children. BS in Journalism, Ohio U. With IBM, 1972—86; founder, CEO Exclusive Interim Properties Ltd., Balt., 1986—97; v.p. global sales Bridgestreet Accommodations, 1997—98; dep. adminstr. SBA, Washington, 2002—. Co-chair Nat. Summit on Women in Philanthropy; bd. dirs. United Way, Alzheimer's Assn. of Ctrl. Md. Recipient Outstanding Vol. Fundraiser of the Yr. award for Md., Assn. of Fundraising Profls., 2002. Office: Small Bus Adminstrn 409 Third St SW Washington DC 20024-3203*

SABER, LISA MARIE, insurance agent; b. Lowell, Mass., Aug. 8, 1974; d. Walter James and Carol Ann Saber. AA, Middlesex C.C., 1994. Customer svc. rep. Wilkens Ins. Agy., Tewksbury, Mass., 1991—2000; from customer svc. rep. to asst. v.p. Risman Ins. Agy., Medford, Mass., 1996—.

SABILI, ERLINDA ASA, internist, psychiatrist, pastoral care minister; b. San Juan, Batangas, The Philippines, Sept. 27, 1959; came to U.S., 1991; d. Marciano Acorda and Rita Lalvces (Asa) S. BS in Med. Tech., U. Santo Tomas, Manila, 1976, MD, 1982. Registered med. technician, The Philippines. Intern U. Santo Tomas Hosp., 1982-83, pre-resident and resident dept. internal medicine, 1987-90; physician Antipolo (Rizal, The Philippines) Rural Health Clinic, 1983; missionary physician Sister of St. Paul, Manila, 1984-87; physician-in-charge Patronato de Sra. de Lourdes Free Clinic, Manila, 1984-95, 90-91; pastoral care vol. St. Elizabeth's Hosp., Elizabeth, N.J., 1991-93; sr. resident in internal medicine and psychiatry Albert Einstein Med. Ctr., Phila., 1993—. Presenter in field. Contbr. articles to med. jours. Vol. physician Archdiocese of Bulacan, The Philippines, 1985-86, San Antonio Feeding Ctr. for Malnourished Children, Manila, 1989-91; vol. Homeless Shelter Dwelling Place, N.Y.C., 1991-93; pastoral care vol. Albert Einstein Healthcare Network, Phila., 1993—; choir leader, pastoral care vol. to Filipino cmty. St. Mary's Cath. Ch., Elizabeth, 1991-93. Recipient young investigator's award Philippine Coll. Cardiology, 1990; Laughlin fellow Faughlin Found., 1997. Mem. AMA, ACP, Am. Psychiat. Assn., Am. Assn. Medicine and Psychiatry, Philippine Med. Assn., U. Santo Tomas Med. Alumni Assn., U. Santo Tomas Med. Mission. Avocations: playing guitar, writing poetry, singing, cooking, gardening. Home: 3207 Friendship St Philadelphia PA 19149-1516 Office: Albert Einstein Med Ctr 5501 Old York Rd Philadelphia PA 19141-3018

SABINI, BARBARA DOROTHY, artist, educator; b. Bklyn., June 11, 1939; d. Joseph and Fannie (Ciazzia) Gugliucci; m. John Sabini Jr., June 22, 1957 (div. 1982); children: Michael, John, Gerald, Barbara-Jo. AAS in Psychology, Orange County C.C., Middletown, N.Y., 1979; BFA in Painting, SUNY, New Paltz, 1984, MFA in Painting, 1988. Cert. tchr. art edn. Tchg. asst. drawing and design SUNY, New Paltz, 1986; art tchr. Newburgh (N.Y.) Free Acad. H.S., 1987—. Lectr. freshman drawing SUNY, NW Paltz, 1990; painting instr. Orange County C.C., 1991; instr. collage Coll. New Rochelle, N.Y., 2001; faculty supr. teen art projects Newburgh Free Acad. H.S., 1990-99; instr. Kosciuszko Found./UNESCO, Poland, 1995, 96, 97; mem. China Study Tour, 1998; lead tchr. Travel & Tourism Acad., 1999. One-woman shows include White Herron Lounge, Virginia Beach, Va., 1986, Ave. A Cafe, N.Y.C., 1987, Pumpkin Eater, N.Y.C., 1989, Painters Tavern, Cornwall-on-Hudson, N.Y., 1992; exhibited in group shows including Hammerquist Gallery, N.Y.C., 1984, Ariel Gallery, N.Y.C., 1985, James Callahan Gallery, Palm Springs, Calif., 1985, The Real Gallery, Cornwall, N.Y., 1986, Cork Gallery, Lincoln Ctr., N.Y.C., 1986, Mid Hudson Arts and Sci. Ctr., Poughkeepsie, N.Y., 1986, Ledo Gallery, N.Y.C., 1987, Outer Space Gallery, N.Y.C., 1989, 91, Wall Gallery, N.Y.C., 1989, 90, Women in the Arts Found. Gallery, N.Y.C., Ledger DeMain Gallery, N.Y.C., China Phoenix Gallery Store, Albuquerque, 1995. Recipient Appreciation cert. N.Y. State Art Tchrs. Assn., 1st pl. award Most Creative Olympics of Visual Arts. Mem. Nat. Art Tchrs. Assn., N.Y. State Tchrs. Assn., N.Y. State Art Tchrs. Assn. Avocations: travel, cross country skiing, reading, arts. Home: 27 Manor Dr Cornwall NY 12518-1474 Office: Newburgh Free Acad 201 Fullerton Ave Newburgh NY 12550-3798

SABINO, CATHERINE ANN, magazine editor; b. N.Y.C., May 6, 1952; d. Joseph A. and Frances (Phelan) S. AB, Barnard Coll., 1973. Beauty editor, editor-at-large Harper's Bazaar, Italia, Men's Bazaar, 1976-79; beauty editor Seventeen mag. Triangle Comms., 1979-83; N.Y. editor Linea Italiana Mondadori, 1983-85; N.Y. editor Moda RAI, 1985-86; editor in chief Worldstyle The Aegis Venture Group, 1987-88; editor in chief In Fashion Murdoch Mags., 1988-89; editor mag. devel. European Home, 1989-91; cons. Hachette Mags., 1992; editor in chief Woman's Day Beauty Hachette Mags., 1993; editor-in-chief, group editor N.Y. Times Custom Pub., N.Y.C., 1993-97; editor-in-chief, group editor, v.p. Forbes Spl. Interest Publs. Group, N.Y.C., 1997—; editor-in-chief Brit. Living and Style, 2000—, Forbes Finest Luxury Real Estate, Four Seasons Mag., 1995—. Author: Italian Style, 1985, Italian Country, 1988. Recipient Folio award 1994, Clarion award 1998-2000, 2002. Mem. Am. Soc. Mag. Editors, Barnard-Columbia Club N.Y. (dir. at large 1991-93), Yale Club. Office: 28 W 23d St New York NY 10010-7629 E-mail: csabino@forbes.com.

SABLE, BARBARA KINSEY, retired music educator; b. Astoria, L.I., N.Y., Oct. 6, 1927; d. Albert and Verna (Rowe) Kinsey; m. Arthur J. Sable, Nov. 3, 1973. BA, Coll. Wooster, 1949; MA, Tchrs. Coll. Columbia U., N.Y.C., 1950; DMus, U. Ind., 1966. Office mgr., music dir. Sta. WCAX, Burlington, Vt., 1954; instr. Cottey Coll., 1959-60; asst. prof. N.E. Mo. State U., Kirksville, 1962-64, U. Calif., Santa Barbara, 1964-69; prof. music U. Colo., Boulder, 1969—, prof. emeritus, 1992—. Author: (novels) The Vocal Sound, 1982; contbr. poetry and short stories to lit. jours. Mem.: Colo. Music Tchrs. Assn., AAUP, Nat. Assn. Tchrs. Singing (past state gov., assoc. editor bull.). Democrat. Avocation: poetry. Home: 3430 Ash Ave Boulder CO 80305-3432 Office: U Colo PO Box 301 Boulder CO 80309-0301 Business E-Mail: bks@sable-boulder.com.

SABO, CORINNE MAE, volunteer; b. San Antonio, Tex., Apr. 23, 1948; d. James Beard and Mary Rita (Veer) S. Contbr. articles to various jours. Bd. dirs., co-chair advocacy com. Alamo Breast Cancer Coalition and Found.; co-founder Valley Info. of AIDS Svc. for Lower Rio Grande Valley; mem. nat. adv. coun. Pastors For Peace; mem. Poverty and Race Rsch. Action Coun.; del. Tex. State Dem. Party Conv., 1996, 98, 26th Senatorial Convention Dem. Party; active Nat. Ctr. for Lesbian Rights, Tex. Dem. Women, 21st Century Democrats, Liberty Tree, Bexar County Women's Polit. Caucus, Tex. Freedom Network, Women's Inst. for Freedom of the Press, Texans for Pub. Schs., Coalition for Pub. Schs., Caths. for a Free Choice, Religious Coalition for Reproductive Choice, Christians for Bibl. Equality, Tex. Women's Polit. Caucus, Nat. Women's Polit. Caucus, Fairness and Accuracy in Reporting, Nat. Abortion and Reproductive Rights Action League, Tex. Abortion and Reproductive Rights Action League; parliamentarian Tex. Dem. Party; mem. citizens oversight com., San Antonio (Tex.) Ind. Sch. Dist., mem. roofing task force, mem. early childhood edn. sub-com., parliamentarian state conv., 2000, 02, 04. Recipient Hermine Tobolowsky award, Tex. Bus. and Profl. Women, 2001. Mem. NAACP, INFACT, MADRE, Nat. Assn. Parliamentarians, Tex. Assn. Parliamentarians, Mission City Bus. and Profl. Women, Tejano Dems., Human Rights Campaign. Democrat. Roman Catholic. Home: PO Box 12212 San Antonio TX 78212-0212

SABOL, CAROLYN A. lawyer, government official; b. Pitts., Nov. 5, 1957; m. Gerald Kirschner, Mar. 15, 1986; 2 children. BA magna cum laude, U. Dayton, 1979; JD with honors, George Washington U., 1982. Bar: Pa. 1982, D.C. 1983, U.S. Supreme Ct. 1991. Dep. gen. counsel Fed. Bur. Prisons, Dept. Justice, Washington, 1982—. Com. chmn. pack 1250 Cub Scouts Am. Mem. Psi Chi. Roman Catholic. Office: Dept Justice Fed Bur Prisons 320 1st St NW Rm 754 Washington DC 20534-0002

SACERDOTE, FRANCES ARLENE, executive recruiter; b. Hartford, Conn., Oct. 30, 1921; d. Francis Edward McCarthy and Edith Mae Marsh; m. Marlowe Joseph Sacerdote, May 31, 1940 (div. Jan. 20, 1961); children: Susan, Marlene, Frances, Denise, Marlowe. BA in Psychology, U. Hartford, 1977; MA, Wesleyan U., 2003. Cert. paralegal: St. Joseph Coll. 2004; cert. life ins. sales Life Office Mgmt. Assn. Inst., 1981. Benefits supr. CIGNA Corp., Bloomfield, Conn., 1959—77; sr. contract analyst Unum Corp., Portland, Maine, 1980—85, CIGNA Corp., Bloomfield, 1986—90; telemarketing recruiter Conn. Region Am. Red Cross, Farmington, Conn., 1991—. Treas. Cerebral Palsy Orgn., Hartford, 1970—72; mem. Immanuel Ch. Women, 1999—. Republican. Congl. Avocations: reading, running, swimming, dance, stamp collecting. Office: American Red Cross Ct Region Blood Svcs Farmington Ave Farmington CT 06032

SACHAROW, BEVERLY, gerontologist; b. N.Y.C. d. Jules and Mary (Trupine) Levy; m. Stanley Sacharow, June 18, 1961; children: Scott Hunter, Brian Evan. BA, Rutgers U., 1980, M in Gerontology Edn., cert. ednl. gerontology, Rutgers U., 1983. Rschr. U. Pa., Robert W. Johnson Hosp., New Brunswick, N.J., 1976-81; dir. Gerontology Inst. N.J., Milltown, 1983—, Gerontology Inst. N.J., Pa., N.Y., Milltown, 1996—. Tour guide, rsch. leader, del. on tour of geriatric facilities, Moscow, Kiev and St. Petersburg, Russia, 1992; invited reporter White House Conf. on Aging, Washington, 1996; conf. planner in gerontology and social work issues and health; cons. assisted living industry, long term care nursing homes. Editor (newsletter) Update on Aging, 1983; video prodr. over 300 gerontology video catalog, 1998—. Mem. adv. com. Gov. Conf. on Aging, Trenton State Coll., 1981; mem. adv. bd. East Brunswick (N.J.) Office on Aging, 1982; planner Brandeis U. Women Study Group. Mem. Am. Soc. on Aging, Nat. Coun. on Aging (mem. press for nat. conf.), Sigma Phi Omega. Avocations: travel, golf. Office: Gerontology Inst PO Box 345 Milltown NJ 08850-0345 E-mail: geronusa@aol.com.

SACHS, MARILYN STICKLE, author, lecturer, editor; b. N.Y.C., Dec. 18, 1927; d. Samuel and Anna (Smith) Stickle; m. Morris Sachs, Jan. 26, 1947; children: Anne, Paul. BA, Hunter Coll., 1949; MSLS, Columbia U., 1953. Children's libr. Bklyn. Pub. Libr., 1949-60, San Francisco Pub. Libr., 1961-67. Author: Amy Moves In, 1964, Laura's Luck, 1965, Amy and Laura, 1966, Veronica Ganz, 1968, Peter and Veronica, 1969, Marv, 1970, The Bears' House, 1971 (Austrian Children's Book prize 1977, Recognition of Merit award George C. Stone Ctr. for Children's Books 1989), The Truth About Mary Rose, 1973 (Silver Slate Pencil award 1974), A Pocket Full of Seeds, 1973 (Jane Addams Children's Book Honor award 1974), Matt's Mitt, 1975, Dorrie's Book, 1975 (Silver State Pencil award 1977, Garden State Children's Book award 1978), A December Tale, 1976, A Secret Friends, 1978, A Summer's Lease, 1979, Bus Ride, 1980, Class Pictures, 1980, Fleet Footed Florence, 1981, Hello...Wrong Number, 1981, Call Me Ruth, 1982 (Assn. Jewish Librs. award 1983), Beach Towels, 1982, Fourteen, 1983, The Fat Girl, 1984, Thunderbird, 1985, Underdog, 1985 (Christopher 1986), Baby Sister 1986, Almost Fifteen, 1987, Fran Ellen's House, 1987 (award Bay Area Book Reviewers Assn. 1988, Recognition of Merit award George C. Stone Ctr. for Children's Books 1989), Just Like A Friend, 1989, At the Sound of the Beep, 1990, Circles, 1991, What My Sister Remembered, 1992, Thirteen, 1993, Ghosts in the Family, 1995, Another Day, 1997, Suprise Party, 1998, Jo Jo & Winnie, 1999, Jo Jo & Winnie Again, 2000, The Four Ugly Cats in Apartment 3D, 2002; co-editor: (with Ann Durell) Big Book for Peace, 1990 (Calif. Children's Book award 1991, Jane Addams Children's Book prize 1991); reviewer books N.Y. Times, San Francisco Chronicle, 1970—. Mem. PEN, ACLU, Sierra Club, Authors' Guild. Democrat. Jewish. Avocations: reading, walking, baseball. Home: 733 31st Ave San Francisco CA 94121-3523

SACHS, ROMAYNE LIEBER, education administrator; b. Scranton, Pa., Feb. 20, 1931; d. Samuel and Anna (Ouslander) Lieber; m. David Morton Sachs, July 15, 1958; children: Paul, Jean. BA, U. Pa., 1952. Exec. sec. Civil Svc. Commn., Phila., 1954-61; vol. resource group Lower Merion Sch. Dist., Ardmore, Pa., 1974-77; admissions dir. Oak Lane Day Sch.,

Bluebell, Pa., 1980-84; program coord. Phila. Futures, 1988-96. Dem. committeewoman Lower Merion Dem. Party, Ardmore; mem. intersch. coun. Lower Merion Sch. Dist., Ardmore, 1970-80; mem. adv. bd. Moore Coll.-Levy Gallery, Phila., 1994—; bd. dir. Clay Studio, 2000—; mem. citizens adv. bd., 2001—, chmn., 2003. Jewish.

SACKETT, DIANNE MARIE, city treasurer, accountant; b. Oil City, Pa., Dec. 29, 1956; d. Clarence Benjamin and Donna Jean (Grosteffon) Knight; m. Mark Douglas Sackett, May 26, 1984; children: Jason Michael, Cory James. BBA, Ea. Mich. U., 1979, MBA, 1986. Cert. mcpl. fin. adminstr. Accounts payable supr. Sarns, Inc., Ann Arbor, Mich., 1979-81; cost acct. Simplex Products Divsn., Adrian, Mich., 1981-83, gen. acctg. supr., 1983-88; city treas. City of Tecumseh, Mich., 1991—. Mem. Mich. Mcpl. Treas.' Assn., Mich. Mcpl. Fin. Officers Assn., Mcpl. Treas.' Assn. of the U.S. and Can. Pentecostal. Office: 309 E Chicago Blvd Tecumseh MI 49286-1550 E-mail: treasur@tecumseh.mi.us., dsackett@msn.com.

SACKETT, SUSAN DEANNA, film and television production associate, writer; b. N.Y.C., Dec. 18, 1943; adopted d. Maxwell and Gertrude Selma (Kugel) S. BA in Edn., U. Fla., 1964, MEd, 1965. Tchr. Dade County Schs., Miami, Fla., 1966-68, L.A. City Schs., 1968-69; asst. publicist, comml. coord. NBC-TV, Burbank, Calif., 1970-73; asst. to Gene Roddenberry, creator Star Trek, 1974-91; prodn. assoc. TV series Star Trek: The Next Generation, 1987-91, writer, 1990-91. Lectr. and guest spkr. Star Trek convs. in U.S., Eng., Australia, 1974-. Author, editor: Letters to Star Trek, 1977; co-author: Star Trek Speaks, The Making of Star Trek--The Motion Picture, 1979, You Can Be a Game Show Contestant and Win, 1982, Say Goodnight Gracie, 1986; author: The Hollywood Reporter Book of Box Office Hits, 1990, 2d edit., 1996, Prime Time Hits, 1993, Hollywood Sings, 1995, Inside Trek: My Secret Life with Star Trek Creator Gene Roddenberry, 2002. Mem. ACLU, Writers Guild Am., Nat. Writers Union, Am. Humanist Assn., Humanist Soc. Greater Phoenix (pres. 2000—), Mensa, Sierra Club. Democrat.

SACKIN, CLAIRE, retired social work educator; b. N.Y.C., Oct. 1, 1925; d. Harry and Diana (Mednick) Gershfeld; m. Milton Sackin, Feb. 4, 1955; children: William, Daniel, David. BA, Hunter Coll., 1946; MEd, U. Pitts., 1968, MSW, 1972, PhD, 1976. Tenured tchr. jr. high sch., Bronx, N.Y., 1947-57; rsch. asst. U. Pitts., 1973, instr. dept. urban mgmt., 1974, rsch. assoc. U. Pitts. Sch. of Social Work, 1975-76, Health & Welfare Planning Assn., 1974; prof. social work, dir. social work program St. Francis U., Loretto, Pa., 1976-97, prof. emerita, 1997—. Registered trainer alcoholism specialists cert. program; mem. adv. bd. Cedar Manor Treatment Ctr., Cresson, Pa., 1994-95; mem. Pa. Gov.'s Coun. Alcoholism, 1980, Nat. Assn. People with AIDS; presenter in field. Contbr. articles to jours. Mem. NASW (social action com. Pa. chpt. 1983-85, mem. Del. Assembly 1984, eastern regional coalition liaison 1984), Coun. on Social Work Edn., Amyotrophic Lateral Sclerosis Assn., Alpha Delta Mu (nat. bd. dirs.). Avocations: reading, crossword puzzles, opera, gardening, travel. Home: 531 Sandrac Dr Pittsburgh PA 15243-1727 Office: St Francis U Loretto PA 15940 E-mail: sackin@worldnet.att.net.

SACKS, PATRICIA ANN, librarian, consultant; b. Allentown, Pa., Nov. 6, 1939; d. Lloyd Alva and Dorothy Estelle (Stoneback) Stahl; m. Kenneth LeRoy Sacks, June 27, 1959. AB, Cedar Crest Coll., 1959; MS in Libr. Sci., Drexel U., 1965. News reporter Call-Chronicle, Allentown, 1956-59, 61-63; reference libr. Cedar Crest Coll., Allentown, 1964-66, head libr., 1966-73; dir. librs. Muhlenberg and Cedar Crest Colls., Allentown, 1973-94; dir. libr. svcs. Cedar Crest Coll., 1994; sr. fellow Lehigh Valley Assn. Ind. Colls., 1994-97, Ctr. Agile Ptnrs. in Edn., 1997-98; info. svcs. cons., 1998—. Del. On Line Computer Library Ctr. Users Council, Columbus, Ohio, 1977-84; cons. colls./health care orgns., libr. orgns. 1981—. Author: (with Whildin Sara Lou) Preparing for Accreditation: A Handbook for Academic Librarians, 1993; mem. editl. bd. Jour. Acad. Librarianship, 1982-84. Mem. United Way Lehigh Valley Coms., 1993—97; trustee Cedar Crest Coll., 1985—89; bd. dirs. John and Dorothy Morgan Cancer Ctr., 1994—96. Named Outstanding Acad. Woman, Lehigh Valley Assn. for Acad. Women, 1984, Muhlenberg Coll. Outstanding Adminstr., 1987, Alumni Tricorn awrd Muhlenberg Coll., 1989, Alumnae Achievement award Cedar Crest Coll., 1994. Mem. ALA (chmn. copyright com. 1985-87), Assn. Coll. and Rsch. Librs. (chmn. stds. and accreditation com. 1976-78, 81-84), Lehigh Valley Assn. Ind. Colls. (chmn. librs. sect. 1967-81, 88-92), AAUW, LWV, Wildlands Conservancy, Appalachian Mountain Club, Phi Alpha Theta, Phi Kappa Phi, Beta Phi Mu. Democrat. Home: 2997 Fairfield Dr Allentown PA 18103-5413

SACKS, TEMI J. public relations executive; b. Phila. d. Jule and Adeline (Levin) S. BA, Temple U. Pubs. editor Del. Valley Regional Planning Commn., Phila.; comms. assoc. Fedn. Jewish Agys., Phila.; exec. v.p., mng. dir. healthcare div. Lobsenz-Stevens Inc., N.Y.C.; exec. v.p., dir. nat. healthcare practice Shandwick, N.Y.C.; sr. v.p. Noonan-Russo, N.Y.C.; pres. T.J. Sacks & Assocs. Inc., N.Y.C. Mem. Healthcare Businesswomen's Assn., Healtcare Mktg. Assn., Women Execs. in Pub. Rels. Avocations; painting, skiing, americana antiques, jewelry design.

SACKSTEDER, ELIZABETH M. lawyer; AB summa cum laude, Princeton U., 1980; JD, Yale U., 1988. Bar: N.Y. 1989, U.S. Dist. Ct. (so. and ea. dists.) N.Y. 1989, U.S. Ct. Appeals (2d cir.) 1994. Law clk. to Hon. Eugene H. Nickerson, U.S. Dist. Ct. for Ea. Dist. N.Y., N.Y.C., 1988-89; ptnr. Sidley & Austin, N.Y.C., 1995—. Mediator U.S. Dist. Ct. for So. Dist. N.Y. Coordinating articles editor Yale Law Jour., 1988. Mem. Am. Arbitration Assn. (arbitrator, mediator). Office: Sidley & Austin 875 3d Ave New York NY 10022 Fax: 212-906-2021. E-mail: esackste@sidley.com.

SACKSTEIN, ROSALINA GUERRERO, music educator, consultant; b. Camaguey, Cuba, Mar. 5, 1923; came to U.S., 1948; d. Luis and Rosalina (Santana) Guerrero; m. Louis Aguirre, Jan. 1, 1939 (div. June 1946); 1 child, Louis Aguirre Jr.; m. Harold C. Sackstein, Apr. 19, 1952; children: Rosalin R., Robert. B in Arts and Scis., Inst. Camaguey, 1941; prof. piano, violin theory, solfege, Conservatory of Music, Camaguey, 1944; D in Pedagogy, U. Havana, Cuba, 1947; M in Secondary Edn., U. Miami, Coral Gables, 1964. Music tchr. Abraham Lincoln Jr. H.S., Havana, 1944-47; psychology of music tchr. Tchrs. Coll., Havana, 1953-59; tchr. music theory, ear tng., solfege U. Miami Sch. Music, Coral Gables, 1963-65, asst. prof. to assoc. prof., 1963-78, prof. music, 1978—. Faculty advisor Sigma Chi chpt. U. Miami, 1970-90; founding mem. women's adv. com. acad. affairs, U. Miami, 1972—. Concert pianist, Cuba, 1944-48, U.S., 1952—; various solo recitals and orch. solos, U.S. and abroad; also appearances on radio and T.V. Chair of judges, Fla. Fedn. Music Clubs, Royal Poinciana, 1980—; mem. bd. Chopin Found. Miami, 1998. Recipient Gold medal, concerto competition, Havana, 1947; recipient Baldwin Keyboard award, 1977-78, 83-84; recipient Cmty. Svc. award B'nai B'rith, 1992. Mem. Am. Coll. Musicians (judge 1964—), Nat. Music Tchrs. Assn., Fla. State Music Tchrs. Assn. (pres. dist. 6 1969-71, pub. sch. liaison dist. 1971-73), Miami Music Tchrs. Assn. (pres. 1991-93, bd. dirs. 1993—), Young Performers Music Club (advisor 1970—), Miami Civic Music Assn. (v.p. 1981-83, pres. 1983—), Sigma Alpha Iota (advisor, v.p. 1964—, sword of honor 1975), Pi Kappa Lambda. Avocations: sports, games. Office: U Miami Sch Music PO Box 248165 Coral Gables FL 33124-8165

SADAK, DIANE MARIE, performing arts educator; d. John Charles and Dolores Hope (Salvi) Sadak; m. Barry Kendall Smith, Oct. 18, 1999; children: Noel Kendall Smith-Sadak, Sage Noelle Smith-Sadak. MFA in Directing, Fla. State U., 1989; BA in Polit. Sci. and Econs., Union Coll., 1985. Head of the acting program, asst. prof. of acting and directing Dept. Theatre Arts Towson U., Md., 1999—; guest artist Union Coll. and Schenectady County C.C., Schenectady, NY, 1998—99; vis. prof. voice and acting Korean Nat. U. of Arts, Seoul, Republic of Korea, 1997—98; artist-in-residence, Calif. Arts Coun. Laurel Elem. Sch., San Diego, 1990—92; staff artist Calif. Young Playwrights Project, San Diego, 1989—93; artist-in-residence Comprehensive Adolescent Treatment Ctr. Ensemble Arts Theatre, San Diego, 1991—91; adj. faculty Grossmont Coll., Calif., 1992. Consulting, inservices and workshop leader Self-Employed, Joppa, Md., 1991—; presenter workshop, St. Petersburg, Russia, 2004. Actor(Janis Joplin): (theatre) LEGENDS; author: (playscript: one-woman show) It's Not Funny, I'm Only Laughing; contbr. mgmt., prodr. Actors Alliance of San Diego; singer: (cabaret show) You're Gonna Hear From Me; actor(Lula): (theatre) Dutchman; dir.: The Cultural Hyphen; actor: A Cave In The Sky; dir.: Cabaret, Evita, Three Sisters, Hot 'N Throbbing, (theatre production) How To Succeed In Business Without Really Trying, (theatrical prodn.) Our Country's Good; actor: (indsl. video series) ACT Training Series; prodr.(dir. pub. rels.): San Diego Actors Festival; contbr. chapter to book. Grantee Artist-In-Residence Funding, Calif. Arts Coun., 1990—92. Mem.: Internat. Alliance of Tchrs. and Scholars, Actors Equity Assn., Internat. Fedn. of Theatre Rsch. (convener of working group 2002—03). D-Liberal. Buddhist. Achievements include Research Grant Award for Integration of Extended Voice work with Current Movement Techniques of Western Theatre Training; Travel Grant to Australia to teach workshop on using Anne Bogart's Viewpoints as a tool in Directing to the Graduate Students at the National Institute of Dramatic Arts, Sydney; Travel Grant to India to Teach Viewpoints and Roy Hart Extended Voice Technique to Students at Jawal-Kala Kendra College and the University of Rajasthan; research in Banff Centre for the Arts Advanced Voice Intensives (2001 and 2003) with Richard Armstrong; Month-long intensives with the SITI Company in 1993, 1994 and 1995. Avocations: gourmet cooking, herb gardening, travel, yoga and fitness, reading. Office: Towson University Theatre Dept 8000 York Rd Rm 339 Towson MD 21252 E-mail: dsadak@towson.edu.

SADDLEMYER, ANN (ELEANOR SADDLEMYER), humanities educator, critic, theater historian; b. Prince Albert, Sask., Can., Nov. 28, 1932; d. Orrin Angus and Elsie Sarah (Ellis) S. BA, U. Sask., 1953, DLitt, 1991; MA, Queen's U., 1956, LLD (hon.), 1977; PhD, U. London, 1961; DLitt (hon.), U. Victoria, 1989, McGill U., 1989, Windsor U., 1990, U. Toronto, 1999, Concordia U., 2000. Lectr. Victoria (B.C.) Coll., 1956-57, instr., 1960-62, asst. prof., 1962-65, assoc. prof. U. Victoria, 1965-68, prof. English, 1968-71, Victoria Coll. U. Toronto, 1971-95; prof., dir. Grad. Ctr. for Study of Drama, U. Toronto, 1972-77, 85-86; prof. emerita Dept. English, Comparative Lit. Grad Ctr. for Study of Drama, U. Toronto, 1995—; sr. fellow Massey Coll., 1975-88, master, 1988-95, master emerita, 1995—; Berg prof. NYU, 1975. Adj. prof. U. Victoria. Dir. Theatre Plus, 1972-84; dir. Colin Smythe Pubs.; author: (with Robin Skelton) The World of W.B. Yeats, 1965, In Defence of Lady Gregory, Playwright, 1966, Synge and Modern Comedy, 1968, J.M. Synge Plays Books One and Two, 1968, Lady Gregory Plays, 4 vols., 1970, Letters to Molly: Synge to Maire O'Neill, 1971, Letters from Synge to W.B. Yeats and Lady Gregory, 1971, Collected Letters of John Millington Synge, Vol. 1, 1983, vol. II, 1984, Theatre Business, The Correspondence of the First Abbey Theatre Directors, 1982, (with Colin Smythe) Lady Gregory Fifty Years After, 1987, Early Stages: Theatre in Ontario, 1980-1914, 1990, J.M. Synge: The Playboy of the Western World and Other Plays, 1995; (with Richard Plant) Later Stages: Theatre in Ontario, 1914-1970s, 1997, Becoming George--The Life of Mrs. W.B. Yeats, 2002; co-editor Theatre History in Canada, 1980-86; editorial bds. Modern Drama, 1972-82, English Studies in Can., 1973-83, Themes in Drama, 1974-93, Shaw Rev., 1977—, Research in the Humanities, 1976-90; Irish Univ. Rev., 1970—, Yeats Ann., 1982-86; Studies in Contemporary Irish Lit., 1986—, Irish Studies Rev., 1997; contbr. articles to profl. jours. Recipient Brit. Acad. Rose Mary Crawshay award, 1986, Disting. Svc. award Province of Ont., 1985, U. Toronto Alumni award of excellence, 1991, award yeats Soc. N.Y. 2001; named Disting. Dau. of Pa., 1992, Woman of Distinction in Letters, Toronto, YWCA, 1994; Officer of Order of Can., 1995; Can. Coun. scholar, 1958-59, fellow, 1968, Guggenheim fellow, 1968, 77, sr. rsch. fellow Connaught, 1985. Fellow Royal Soc. Can., Royal Soc. Arts; mem. Internat. Assn. Study Anglo-Irish Lit. (chmn. 1973-76), Assn. Can. Theatre Rsch. (pres. 1976-77), Can. Assn. Irish Studies, Assn. Can. Univ. Tchrs. English. Home: 10876 Madrona Dr Sidney BC Canada V8L 5N9 E-mail: saddlemy@uvic.ca.

SADDLER, PEGGY CHANDLER, counselor; b. Paducah, Ky., June 16, 1955; d. Joe Paul and Nell (Garrett) Chandler. BS in Psychology and Sociology, Union Coll., Barbourville, Ky., 1977; M of Pub. Svc. in Counseling, Western Ky. U., 1977; postgrad., U. South Fla. Cert. in guidance and counseling Fla. Dept. Edn., in secondary guidance and counseling Va. Dept. Edn. Instr. U. Ky. S.E. C.C., Cumberland, 1979; guidance counselor Northampton H.S., Eastville, Va., 1980-85; dist. intake counselor Dept. Health and Rehabilitative Svcs., Wauchula, Fla., 1986; guidance counselor McLaughlin Jr. H.S., Lake Wales, Fla., 1986-87, Hardee Sr. H.S., Wauchula, 1987—. Acad. team coach Northampton H.S., Eastville, 1981-85, Hardee Sr. H.S., Wauchula, 1992—; counselor summer youth employment program Ea. Shore C.C., Melfa, Va., 1982-85; bd. mem., exec. com. mem. Hardee County Juvenile Justice Bd., Wauchula, 1993-98; mem. adv. bd. Hardee County 4-H, Wauchula, 1993-98. Editor: Food for Thought, 1985. Coun. mem. Alcohol, Drug Abuse and Mental Health Planning Coun., 1991-93; vice-chmn. Dist. 14 Health and Human Svcs. Bd., 1992-96; chmn. strong families and cmtys. com. Health and Human Svcs. Bd., 1993-96, mem. dist. 14 Ptnr. in Crisis Bd., 2000-. Recipient Vol. Svc. award Fla. Dept. Corrections, Wauchula, 1993, Cmty. Svc. award Ctrl. Fla. Human Svcs. Ctrs., Lakeland, 1994; named Outstanding Young Women of Am., Jaycees, 1984. Mem. Fla. Counselor's Assn., Fla. Sch. Counselor's Assn., Fla. Assn. for Humanistic Edn. and Devel., Hardee Optimist Club (bd. dirs. 1995-96). Democrat. Avocations: audiophile, ailurophile, bibliophile. Home: PO Box 172 Wauchula FL 33873-0172 Office: Hardee Sr HS 830 Altman Rd Wauchula FL 33873-9453 Office Phone: 863-773-3181. E-mail: saddlep@hotmail.com.

SADER, CAROL HOPE, former state legislator; b. Bklyn., July 19, 1935; d. Nathan and Mollie (Farkas) Shimkin; m. Harold M. Sader, June 9, 1957; children: Neil, Randi Sader Friedlander, Elisa Sader Waldman. BA, Barnard Coll., Columbia U., 1957. Sch. tchr. Bd. Edn., Morris, Conn., 1957-58; legal editor W. H. Anderson Co., Cin., 1974-78; freelance legal editor Shawnee Mission, Kans., 1978-87; mem. Kans. Ho. of Reps., 1987-94. Chair Ho. Pub. Health and Welfare Com., 1991-92; chair Joint Ho. and Senate Com. on Health Care Decisions for the 90's, 1992; vice chair Ho. Econ. Devel. Com., 1991-92; policy chair Ho. Dem. Caucus, 1993-94; appointee Kans. jud. qualifications commn. Kans. Supreme Ct., 1995—; apptd. Kans. Racing and Gaming Commn., 2003—, Kans. State Bd. Healing Arts, 2003—. Pres. LWV, Johnson County, 1983—85; mem. State of Kans. LWV Bd., 1986—87; pres. Johnson County Found. Aging, 2002—; mem. Johnson County Charter Commn., 1999; mem. exec. bd. Johnson County C.C. Found., 2000—03; mem. adv. group Kans. Gov.'s B.E.S.T. Team, 2002—; dem. candidate for Kans. Lt. Gov., 1994; mem. Jewish Cmty. Rels. Bd., 1999—; chmn. bd. trustees Johnson County C.C., Overland Park, Kans., 1984—86, trustee, 1981—86; bd. dirs. United Cmty. Svcs. of Johnson County, Shawnee Mission, 1984—92, Jewish Vocat. Svc. Bd., 1983—92, House of Menuha, 1998—99, Appleseed Found. Kans., 1999—2001; bd. dirs., exec. bd. Midwest Ctr. Holocaust Edn., 1999—; chmn. Kans. State Holocaust Commn., 1991—94; pres. MAINstream Coalition, 1995—97, vice chair, 1998—2003; v.p. Kans. Advocates for Better Care, 1998—2001. Recipient Trustee award Assn. of Women in Jr. and C.C., 1985, awards Kans. Pub. Transit Assn., 1990, AARP, 1992, Assn. Kans. Theater, 1992, Nat. Coun. Jewish Women, 1992, Kans. Assn. Osteo. Medicine, 1992, Kans. Chiropractic Assn., 1992, United Com. Svcs. Johnson County, 1992, Disting. Pub. Svcs. award Johnson County, 1993, Hallpac Kans. Pub. Svc. award Hallmark Cards, Inc., 1993, Eddie Jacobsen award B'nai B'rith, 1994, Cmty. Svc. award House of Menuha, 1998, The Pillar award Greater K.C. Women's Political Caucus, 2003, Stand-Up, Speak-Out award Mainstream Coalition, 2003. Mem. Coun. Women Legislators, Phi Delta Kappa. Democrat. Avocations: grandparenting, lakehouse, theater, travel. Home: 8612 Linden Dr Shawnee Mission KS 66207-1807

SADIK, NAFIS, United Nations administrator; b. Jaunpur, India, Aug. 18, 1929; d. Iffat Ara and Mohammad Shoaib; m. Azhar Sadik, 1954; 5 children. Student, Loretto Coll., Calcutta, India, Dow Med. Coll., Karachi, Pakistan, Johns Hopkins U., LHD (hon.), 1989, Brown U., 1993, Duke U., 1995; LLD, Wilfrid Laurier U., 1995; DSc (hon.), U. Mich., 1996, Claremont U., 1996; LHD (hon.), Philippines U., 1997; DSc (hon.), Long Island U., 1997; LHD (hon.), Nepal Tribhuvan U., 1998; DSc, Tulane U., 1999. Intern ob-gyn. City Hosp., Balt., 1952-54; civilian med. officer in charge of women's and children's wards various Pakistani armed forces hosps., 1954-63; resident physiology Queens U., Kingston, Ont., Can., 1958; head health sect. Planning Commn. on Health and Family Planning, Pakistan, 1964; dir. planning and tng. Pakistan Ctr. Family Planning Coun., 1966-68, dep. dir.-gen., 1968-70, dir.-gen., 1970-71; tech. advisor UN Fund for Population Activities, 1971-72, chief programme divsn., 1973-77, asst. exec. dir., 1977-87, exec. dir., 1987—; under-sec.-gen. UN, 1987—. Sec.-gen. Internat. Conf. on Population and Devel., 1994, Soc. for Internat. Devel. (pres. 1994-97). Writings include: Population: National Family Planning Programme in Pakistan, 1968, Population: the UNFPA Experience, 1984, Population Policies and Programmes: Making a Difference: Twenty-five Years of UNFPA Experience, 1994, Lessions learned from Two Decades of Experience, 1991, Making a Difference: Twenty-Five Years of UNFPA Experience, 1994; contbr. articles to profl. jours. Recipient Hugh Moore award; Paul Harris fellow Rotary, 1997. Fellow Royal Coll. Ob-Gyn. Avocations: bridge, reading, theatre, travel. Office: UN Population Fund 220 E 42nd St Fl 19 New York NY 10017-5806

SADOWSKI, CAROL JOHNSON, artist; b. Chgo., Mar. 20, 1929; d. Carl Valdamar Johnson and Elizabeth Hilma (Booth) Johnson Chellberg; m. Edmund Sadowski, July 9, 1949; children: Lynn Carol Mahoney, Christie Sadowski Cortez. AAS, Wright Coll., Ill., 1949. Tchr. art Malverne H.S., NY, 1968-69; artist Valley Stream, NY, 1968-76, Hollywood, Fla., 1976—. Guest spkr. Mus. Art, Ft. Lauderdale, Fla., 1991; Libr. League, Oakland Park, 1985; Boca Raton, Fla. Mus., others, TV appearances on WCGB, Gainesville; WSVN, Miami; Storer and Hollywood Cable; Artist Guild, Boca Raton Mus.; Broward C.C., Hollywood, Fla. One woman shows include Mus. Fla. History, Tallahassee, 1984-85, 87; Hist. Mus. South Fla., Miami, 1986; Thomas Ctr. Arts, Gainesville, Fla., 1985, 87; Elliott Mus., Stuart, Fla., 1987; Hemingway Mus. and Home, Key West, Fla., 1986; I.G.F.A. Fishing Hall of Fame Mus., Dania, Fla., 1999, Alliance Francaise de Miami, 1995; commd. painting St. Agustin Antigua Found., St. Augustine, Fla., 1985, Atlantic Bank, Ft. Lauderdale, Fla., Bonnet House Fla. Trust, Ft. Lauderdale, Hollywood Art & Culture Ctr., Hemingway Mus., San Francisco de Paula, Presdl. Palace, Havana, Tropical Art Gallery, Naples, Fla., 1981-83, Tequesta (Fla.) Art Gallery, 1985-89, Gingerbread Square Gallery, Key West, 1990—, Wally Findlay Galleries, Inc., Palm Beach and N.Y.C., DeBruyne Fine Arts Gallery, Naples, 1998—, Patricia Cloutier Gallery, Tequesta, Fla., 1992-2003. Mem. Ft. Lauderdale Mus. Art; Hollywood Art and Culture Ctr. Recipient Hemingway medal, Ernest Hemingway Mus., Cuba, 1990; appreciation award City of Hollywood; Chgo. Art Inst. scholar; Salmagundi Club N.Y. scholar. Mem. Internat. Platform Assn.; Broward Art Guild; Fla. Hist. Assn.; Ernest Hemingway Soc.; Chopin Found.; Am. Inst. for Polish Culture; Alliance Francaise de Miami; Women in the Arts Nat. Mus. (charter mem.). Avocations: travel, bicycling, swimming, reading. Home: 1480 Sheridan St Apt B 17 Hollywood FL 33020-2295 Personal E-mail: esadowski@msn.com.

SAEGESSER, MARGUERITE M. artist; b. Bern, Switzerland, May 27, 1922; came to U.S., 1974; d. Wilhelm and Fanny (Kuepfer) Ruefenacht; m. Max Saegesser, May 27, 1952; 1 child, Francisca Marguerite; stepchildren: Anne-Marie Logan, Elisabeth, Barbara, Ursula L'Eplattenier. Solo exhbns. include De Saisset Mus., Santa Clara, Calif., 1995, Smith Andersen Gallery, Palo Alto, Calif., 1981, 85, 89, 91, 92, 95, Galerie Schindler, Bern, 1968, 90, Art Fair, Basel, Switzerland, 1990, many others; group exhbns. include Long Beach, Calif., 1971, Bienne Open Air Sculpture Show, Switzerland, 1958, 62, 66, Soc. Painters & Sculptors, Bern, 1945-46, 52, 56. Grantee Swiss Endowment Arts, 1995. Mem. South Bay Area Women's Caucus for Arts. Democrat. Home: 840 Mesa Ave Palo Alto CA 94306-3709

SAELER, PENELOPE, music educator; b. Clarksburg, W.Va., Apr. 21, 1948; d. Emma June Luzader and Charles Woodrow Saeler; m. Kenneth James Claudio, May 30, 1999. PhD music edn., W.Va. U., Morgantown, W. Va., 1996, MA, 1973—74. Cert. Level 3 Orff Memphis State U., 1993. Choral music Wash. Irving H.S., Clarksburg, W.Va., 1970—72; choral and gen. music Sabraton Jr. H.S., Morgantown, W.Va., 1972—73; music tchr. Monongalia County Bd. Of Edn., Morgantown, W.Va., 1974—78; gen. music and choral music North Elem., Morgantown, W.Va., 1978—87; choral music and drama U. H.S., Morgantown, W.Va., 1988—; grad. asst. W. Va. U., Morgantown, W.Va., 1987—88, adj. instr., 1989—92. Music min. Drummond Chapel United Meth. Ch., Morgantown, W.Va., 1984—94; website coord. W. Va. Am. Choral Director's, W.Va., 2000—03; pres. W. Va. Am. Choral Director's Assn., W.Va., 1995—97. Author: (paper presented) Left And Right Hemispheric Integration: Music Education Provides A Model; dir.: (production of a play) Rumors By Neil Simon, (production of a musical) Pajama Game, Hello Dolly, Footloose. Directed performances staged for nursing homes and civic organizations Impact Show Choir, Morgantown, W.Va., 1988—2003, directed sponsorship of angel children at Christmas, 2000—01; pres. W. Va. Am. Choral Dir. Assn., 2000—03; mem. com. for curriculum W. Va. State Dept., 1994—95; selected State participant Soc. for Gen. Music, Reston, W.Va., 1993. Recipient Sylvia Suppart Award, Monongalia County Schools, 2002, Bus. Woman of the Yr., Morgantown Young Profl. Bus. Women, 1986. Mem.: W. Va. Vocal Assn., Music Educator's Nat. Conf., Am. Choral Director's Assn. (assoc.). Methodist. Avocations: walking, aerobics. Office: University High School Price Street Morgantown WV 26505 Personal E-mail: psaeler@verizon.net. E-mail: psaeler@access.k12.wv.us.

SAENZ, RUTH E. missionary; b. Columbus, Ind., Nov. 26, 1952; d. A. Allen and Eunice J. McVey; m. Leon Saenz, Jan. 31, 1989; children: E. Rose, Jonathan A. BA in Religious Edn., Carolina Christian Coll., 1981. Tchr., Bermudian Springs, Pa., 1971—74, Immanual Missionary Christian Sch., Spring Grove, Pa., 1975—78; pastor Wesley Holiness Chapel, Spencer, Ind., 1974—75; missionary Latin Holiness Mission, San Ildefonso, Mexico, 1983, Immanuel Missionary Church Bolivian Mission, Sucre, 1984—97; mission fund raiser Emmanuel Mission of Bolivia, Shoals, Ind., 1997—2003. Dist. sec. Immanuel Missionary Ch., Shoals, 1974—82, Shoals, 1997—99; founding missionary, sec. Iglesia Evangelica Emanuel, Sucre, Bolivia, 1984—97. Contbr. articles, poems IMC Bolivian Mission News. Avocations: writing, health and nutrition, especially cancer cure, music, sewing. Home: Rte 2 Box 280 Shoals IN 47581-9673 E-mail: ruthmcveydesaenz@hotmail.com.

SAFFER, AMY BETH, foreign language educator; b. N.Y.C., Apr. 19, 1950; d. William and Evelyn (Yankowitz) S. BA, Fairleigh Dickinson U., 1972, MA, 1983; postgrad., Jersey City State Coll., 1983-84. Cert. tchr. Spanish K-12, N.J. Tchr. Madison (N.J.) High Sch., 1973, Livingston (N.J.) High Sch., 1973—. Mem. faculty and dist. coms. Livingston Sch. Dist., 1975—; advisor to class of 1977, Livingston High Sch., 1975-77, chair mid. states subcom., 1990; tchr. mentor. Inducted Livingston H.S. Alumni Hall of

Fame, 1993. Mem. NEA, Am. Assn. Tchrs. of Spanish and Portuguese, N.J. Edn. Assn., Fgn. Lang. Educators of N.J., Livingston Edn. Assn. (negotiations rep. 1980—), Essex County Edn. Assn. Office: Livingston High Sch Livingston NJ 07039

SAFFORD, FLORENCE VIRAY SUNGA, travel agent, consultant; b. Masantol, Pampanga, Luzon, Philippines, Mar. 19, 1932; came to U.S., 1953; d. Filomena Garcia and Dominga (Viray) Sunga; m. Francis Ingersoll Safford, Aug. 4, 1979; children: H. Robert, Erlinda Ann, Ruben Michael. BS in Edn., Adamson U., Manila, 1952; student Hotel Mgnt., Political Sci., Kapiolani C.C., Honolulu, 1975; student, Am. Travel Sch., Honolulu, 1977. Tchr. Cecilio Apostles Elem. Sch., Manila, 1949-51, St. Michael Acad., Masantol, 1951-52; social worker Cath. Social Svc., Honolulu, 1970-77; cons. Travel Cons. of the Pacific, Honolulu, 1977—. Exec. bd. dirs. Oahu Cmty. Coun., 1994—; elected to Neighborhood Bd., 1982-84, 93-95; apptd. by mayor of Honolulu to Ethics Commn., 1986-95. Named Most Outstanding Leader of the Community, Filipino Jaycees of Honolulu, 1976. Mem. Women's Cmty. Action League of Hawaii (pres. 1972-98, Outstanding Pres. 1992), Filipino C. of C. of Hawaii (treas., bd. dirs. 1994, Outstanding award 1991-92), Aloha Bus. and Profl. Women's Club (treas., Outstanding award 1981-89). Republican. Roman Catholic. Avocations: counseling, dance. also: 10849 Carbonia Ct Las Vegas NV 89144-4508 Office: 10849 Carbonia Ct Las Vegas NV 89144-4508

SAFIAN, GAIL ROBYN, public relations executive; b. Bklyn., Dec. 12, 1947; d. Jack I. and Harriet S.; m. Jay Mark Eisenberg, Jan. 6, 1979; children: Julia, Eric. BA, SUNY, Albany, 1968; MBA, NYU, 1982. Reporter Albany (N.Y.)-Knickerbocker News/Times-Union, 1969, Athens (Ohio) Messenger, 1969-71; pub. relations asst. Mountainside Hosp., Montclair, N.J., 1971-74; dir. pub. relations Riverside Hosp., Boonton, N.J., 1974-78; consumer affairs coordinator Johnson & Johnson Personal Products Div., Milltown, N.J., 1978-79; v.p., group mgr. Harshe Rotman & Druck, N.Y.C., 1979-82; exec. v.p., dir. Health Care Div. Ruder Finn & Rotman, N.Y.C., 1982-84; v.p., mgr. client services Burson-Marsteller, N.Y.C., 1984-86; v.p., group mgr. health care Cohn & Wolfe, N.Y.C., 1986-90; exec. v.p., gen. mgr. MCS, Summit, N.J., 1990-94; pres. Safian Comm. Inc., Maplewood, N.J., 1994—. Mem. devel. com. Cancer Care, N.Y.C., 1985—. Recipient MacEachern award Am. Hosp. Assn., 1974, Communications Award Internat. Assn. Bus. Communicators, 1976, Creativity in Pub. Rels. award Inside PR, 1992, 93. Mem. Healthcare Businesswomen's Assn. (mem. bd. dirs.), N.Y. Acad. Scis., Women in Comm. (Clarion award 1974). Jewish. Home and Office: Safian Comm Inc 31 Hickory Dr Maplewood NJ 07040-2107 E-mail: gsafian@safianhealth.com.

SAFIAN, SHELLEY CAROLE, advertising executive; b. Bklyn., May 29, 1954; d. Jack Israel and Harriet Sara (Cohen) S. BFA, Parsons Sch. Design, 1975. Asst. art dir. Axelrod and Assocs., N.Y.C., 1975-77; art dir. Sta. WDBO-TV-AM/FM, Orlando, Fla., 1978-80; owner, pres. Safian Comm. Svcs., Inc., Winter Park, Fla., 1981—, Bonté Sportswear, Winter Park, Fla., 1993-97. Mem. adv. com. Career Edn., Orange County, Fla., 1981—88, 1996—98; adj. prof. Internat. Acad. Design and Tech., 2000—; adj. prof. City Coll., Casselberry, Fla., 2000—. Exec. producer/dir. March of Dimes Telethon, Orlando, 1984; bd. dirs. Boy Scouts Am., 1987-91; exec. dir. United Cerebral Palsy Telethon, Orlando, 1982-83; pub. rels. liaison United Cerebral Palsy, Orlando, 1983-84; founder Career Dir. for Deaf, Orlando, 1985; trustee, pub. rels. chair Nat. Multiple Sclerosis Soc., 1991-92, bd. dirs., 1990, 91. Recipient 1st pl. Addy awards Orlando ADvt. Fedn., 1981, 87, 88, 89, 1st pl. Addy award, 2d pl. awards, merit awards, 1982, 84, 85, 87, 88, Nat. Telly award Bronze Statue, 1988, Up and Coming award Price Waterhouse/Orlando Bus. Jour., 1988, Pro-Mark 1st pl. awards Fla. Coun. Shopping Ctrs., 1989, 90, merit award, 1990, Telly award Bronze finalist, 1989, 91; named Tchr. of the Quarter, 2001. Mem. Broadcast Promotion and Mktg. Execs. Assn. (Silver Medalion 1983, nat. finalist 2 Silver Microphone awards 1986, 87), Broadcast Designer's Assn. (bd.d irs. 1980-82), Am. Women in Radio and TV (bd. dirs. 1980-81). Republican. Avocation: horseback riding. Office: Safian Communications Svcs PO Box 1016 Winter Park FL 32790-1016

SAFRIT, MARGARET, physical education educator; Chair dept. phys. edn. U. Wis., Madison; chair dept. health and fitness Am. Univ., Washington, prof. emeritus. Presenter in field. Author several books; editor Rsch. Quarterly. Mem. AAHPERD (chair measurment and evaluation coun., Gulick award 1994), Am. Acad. Phys. Edn. Higher Edn. (pres.), Internat. Soc. Measurement and Evaluation (founder, pres.).

SAFRO, MILLICENT, small business owner, decorative arts scholar, writer; Co-owner Tender Buttons, N.Y.C. and Chgo., 1964—. Lectr., appraiser in field. Co-author: Buttons, 1991; contbr. articles to mags., periodicals; exhibitions include Cooper-Hewitt Mus., N.Y.C., Smithsonian Instn., Washington, Atheneum, La Jolla, Calif., L.A. County Mus. Art, Henry Flagler Mus., Palm Beach, Fla., Shiseido Art Gallery, Tokyo. Office: Tender Buttons 143 E 62d St New York NY 10021

SAGAWA, SHIRLEY SACHI, lawyer; b. Rochester, N.Y., Aug. 25, 1961; d. Hidetaka H. and Patricia (Ford) S.; m. Gregory A. Baer; children: Jackson Ford Baer, Matthew Sagawa Baer, Thomas Arthur Baer. AB, Smith Coll., l983; MSc, London Sch. Econs., l984; JD, Harvard U., 1987. Bar: Md. l988. Chief counsel youth policy, labor and human resources com. U.S. Senate, Washington, l987-91; sr. counsel and dir. family and youth policy Nat. Women's Law Ctr., Washington, 1991-93; spl. asst. to Pres. Clinton for domestic policy, 1993; exec. dir., mng. dir., exec. v.p. Corp. for Nat. and Comty. Svc., Washington, 1993-97; exec. dir. Learning First Alliance, Washington, 1997-98; dep. asst. Pres. Clinton, dep. chief staff First Lady The White House, Washington, 1998-2001; ptnr. sagawa/jospin, 2001—. Co-author: Common Interest, Common Good, Creating Value Through Business and Social Sector Partnership, 1999. Mem. exec. bd. Orgn. for Pan-Asian Am. Women, Washington, 1987-89; mem. Women of Color Leadership Coun., 1991-92; vice chair, bd. dirs. Nat. Community Svc. Commn., 1991-93; trustee Am. Folklife Ctr., Libr. Congress, 1996-97; commr. Head Start Fellowships Commn., 1996-97; bd. dirs. My Sister's Place, 1996-98, Jumpstart, 1998, Campus Outreach Opportunity League, 1997-98, Nat. Inst. Dispute Resolution, 1997-98. Recipient Philip V. McGance award Coun. for Advancement of Citizenship, 1991, cert. of recognition Nat. Coun. Jewish Women, 1989, Alexandrine medal Coll. St. Catherine, St. Paul, 1995, Alec Dickson Servant Leader award Nat. Youth Leadership Coun., 2002; named one of 25 most influential working women Working Mother Mag., 1999; recipient Alec Dickson Servant Leader award, National Youth Leadership Council, 2002; Harry S. Truman scholar, 1981; Smith Coll. Alumnae Assn. fellow, 1983, AAUW fellow, 1986. Mem. Md. Bar Assn. Democrat. Episcopalian. Home: 3000 Greenvale Rd Chevy Chase MD 20815 E-mail: ssagawa@sagawajospin.com.

SAGE-GAVIN, EVA MARIE, retail executive; b. Boston, Sept. 26, 1958; d. Ross Francis and Theresa Veronica (Bufalo) S.; m. Dennis Gavin. BS in Indsl. Relations, Cornell U., 1980. Affirmative action personnel specialist Xerox Corp., Washington, 1980-81; compensation analyst Xerox Corp, Rochester, N.Y., 1981-82, sales recruiter Boston, 1982, employment mgr., 1983, systems mktg. rep., 1983-85; personnel mgr. Xerox Corp., L.A., 1985—86; human resources mgr. Xerox Corp, Irvine, Calif., 1986; dir. human resources Pepsi Co., 1991, v.p. corp. human resources, Taco Bell; sr. v.p. human resources Disney Consumer Products, 1997—2000, Sun Microsystems, Inc., 2000—03; exec. v.p. human resources Gap Inc., 2003—. Mem. career adv. bd. Emmanuel Coll., Boston, 1983-85. Mem. Am. Soc. Personnel Adminstrn., Women in Mgmt., Xerox Women's Network (edn. com. l988), Kappa Kappa Gamma. Democrat. Roman Catholic. Avocations: skiing, travel, boating, sailing, aerobics. Office: Gap Inc 2 Folsom St San Francisco CA 94105

SAGEN, JUDY, secondary education choral director; b. Virginia, Minn., Apr. 29, 1953; d. Earl and Barbara Sagen; m. Michael J. Atherton, May 25, 1980; children: Brent, Amy. B in Music Edn., 1975; BMus, Drake U., 1975; MA U. Minn., 1991. Choral dir. Valley Middle Sch., Apple Valley, Minn., 1975—80, Rosemount (Minn.) H.S., 1980—89, Eagan (Minn.) H.S., 1989—98, Eastview H.S., Apple Valley, 1999—. Dir. Bravo! Musical Extravaganza, Apple Valley, 1975—; mus. dir. sch. musicals, Apple Valley, 1975—. Vol. coord. World Choral Symposium, Mpls., 2002; vol. Relay for Life, Mpls., 2002. Mem.: Minn. Music Edn. Assn. (choral v.p.), Am. Choral Dirs. Assn. (bd. dirs. Met. East chpt., Minn. Choral Dir. of Yr. 2004), Mu Phi Epsilon, Phi Lambda Delta. Home: 13650 Elkwood Dr Apple Valley MN 55124 Office: Eastview HS 6200 140th St W Apple Valley MN 55124 E-mail: Judy.Sagen@district196.org.

SAGER NEIL, THERESA LOUISE, poet, author of children's books; b. Vallejo, Calif., Feb. 5, 1955; d. Lavern Irvan and Loretta Theresa (Linneman) S.; married; children: Ian Stover, Andrea Stover. Student, Inst. Children's Literature, 1990-91. Book-keeping clk. No. Propane Gas Co., Des Moines, 1977-79; various postions with Home Health Aid, 1980-89; self-employed home health aide, 1989—; babysitter; author of children's books. Recipient Golden Poet award World of Poetry, 1990, 91, Editor's Choice award Nat. Libr. Poetry, 1993. Mem. Found. For Christian Living, Arbor Day Found., World Wildlife Fund, Audubon Soc. Democrat. Avocations: poetry, plants, herbology. Home: # 1 316 N Court St Ottumwa IA 52501-2642

SAGO, JANIS LYNN, photography educator; b. St. Louis, Nov. 27, 1948; d. Bernard William and Eunice Alberta (Henry) Osthof; m. William Leo Sago Jr., Feb. 18, 1967 (dec. Mar. 1989); children: Brian William, Shelley Lynn, Carrie Renee. AA, St. Louis C.C., 1990; BA cum laude, Webster U., 1993. Office mgr. C.B. Smith Co., St. Louis, 1989—; free-lance photographer St. Louis, 1990—; adj. faculty photography St. Louis C.C., 1993—, St. Charles County C.C., 1998—. Interim staff photographer St. Louis C.C., 1990; gallery asst. Webster U., St. Louis, 1993; adj. faculty photography St. Louis C.C., 1993—, St. Charles County C.C., 1998—; photography instr. Mo. Bot. Gardens, 1999—. Photographer The Webster Jour., 1992-93; photo's exhibited at May Gallery, 1993, Campus Gallery, 1996—, Martin Schweig Gallery, 1996, St. Charles County C.C., 1998—, St. Peters Cultural Art Ctr., 2002—. Mem. St. Louis Art Mus., 1994—, St. Louis Sci. Ctr., 1996-97, Mo. Bot. Gardens, 1997—; officer, asst. chief YMCA Indian Guides, St. Louis, 1989-97; vol./chair Mothers' Club, Lindbergh Schs., St. Louis, 1974-90, PTO, 1974-90. Mem. AAUW, Greater St. Louis Orchid Soc., Phi Theta Kappa. Avocations: gardening, reading, travel, music. Office: St Louis C C 11333 Big Bend Rd Saint Louis MO 63122-5720

SAHAGIAN, LUCILLE BEDROSIAN, gasoline company executive; b. Chgo., Mar. 27, 1927; d. KEsrow and Rebecca (Babian) Bedrosian; m. John Sahagian, Jan. 10, 1953 (dec. Sept. 1993); 1 child, Rebecca Jan. Grad. exec. sec. and bus. acctg., Bryant and Stratton Bus. Sch., Chgo., 1944. Exec. sec. William Morris Theatrical Agy., Chgo., 1944-46, Goldblatts Dept. Store/Retail Advt., Chgo., 1946-53, Ross Roy Advt. Agy., Chgo., 1953-54; dealer, ptnr. John Sahagian Svc. Stas., Conn. Turnpike East, Fairfield, 1958-64, Darien, 1966-72, lessee, ptnr. East and West, 1972-84; treas., owner John Sahagian, Inc., Fairfield, Conn., 1976-85; lessee, ptnr. N.Y. State Thruway Authority John Sahagian Svc. Stas., Ramapo, Sloatsburg, N.Y., 1978-84, lessee, ptnr. Paliades Pkwy., N. & S. Interstate Pkwy. Englewood Cliffs, N.J., 1981-86; account exec. Sebastian Gangemi Svc. Stas., Conn. Turnpike, Darien, 1984-88, Trumbull (Conn.) Shell, 1988—; travel cons. Etna Travel Bur., Inc., Stratford, Conn., 1944—. Treas. Ladies Prelacy Guild of Armenian Apostolic Ch., N.Y.C., 1981—; dir. Fairfield County Charity for Austic Children, 1961-64; pres., treas. Armenian Relief Soc., 1970. Mem. Gasoline Retailers Assn., Internat. Airlines Travel Agt. Network, Shorehaven Golf Club (bd. mem. 1966, treas. ladies golf 1990). Avocations: golf, travel, music and religious studies. Home: 168 Spring Hill Rd Fairfield CT 06430-1949 Office: Etna Travel Bur Inc 5 Sanford Pl Stratford CT 06614-2832

SAHATJIAN, MANIK, nurse, psychologist; b. Tabris, Iran, July 24, 1921; came to U.S., 1951; d. Dicran and Shushanig (Der-Galustian) Mnatzaganian; m. George Sahatjian, Jan. 21, 1954; children: Robert, Edwin. Nursing Cert., Am. Mission Hosps.-Boston U., 1954; BA in Psychology, San Jose State U., 1974, MA in Psychology, 1979. RN, Calif. Head nurse Am. Mission Hosp., Tabris, 1945-46; charge nurse Banke-Melli Hosp., Tehran, 1946-51; vis. nurse Vis. Nurse Assn., Oakland, Calif., 1956-57; research asst. Stanford U., 1979-81, Palo Alto (Calif.) Med. Research Found., 1981-84; documentation supr. Bethesda Convalescent Ctr., Los Gatos, Calif., 1985-86; sr. outreach worker City of Fremont (Calif.) Human Svcs., 1987-90, case mgr., 1990-97; ret., 1997. Guest rsch. asst. NASA Ames Lab., Mountain View, Calif., summers 1978, 79. Author (with others) psychol. research reports. Mentor elem. sch. children, 1997-2002; pro bono tchg./counseling for srs. who are home bound, Bay Area, Calif., 1999—; pro bono tchr. peer counseling trainers for srs. Armenian Cmty. Santa Clara, Calif., St. Andrew Ch. Fulbright scholar, 1951; Iran Found. scholar, 1953; Morgan-Segal scholar for peer counseling tng., 1998. Mem. AAUW, Western Psychol. Assn., Am. Assn. Sr. Counseling. Democrat. Mem. St. Andrew Armenian Church. Achievements include fluency in Armenian, Farsi, Turkish; familiarity in Spanish, Russian, French langs. Avocations: oil painting, classic dance. Home: 339 Starlite Way Fremont CA 94539-7642

SAHLSTROM, JILL LOUISE, elementary school educator; d. Warren A. and Sylvia J. Trepp; m. Kenneth P. Sahlstrom, Jan. 2, 1977; children: Brooke, Jonathan, Matthew. AS, Sheldon Jackson Coll., 1977; BA, Seattle Pacific U., 1981. Tchr. English as 2d lang. Griffin Bus. Coll., Seattle, 1980; tchr. art, English as 2d lang. Seattle Sch. Dist., 1984—93; substitute tchr. various sch. dists., 1994—2004. Sec., founder Coop. S.E. Asian Design, Seattle, 1979—80; owner A Childs Easel & Co., Snohomish, 1989—2003. Sculpture, An. American David, Vietnam Vet, 1994, Represented in permanent collections N.W. Hosp. Lobby. Bd. dirs. Pacific Arts Ctr., Seattle, 1996; tchr. Domican Reflection Ctr., Edmonds, 2001—03. Grantee, Snohomish Edn. Found., 2003. Mem.: Northwest Coll. Soc., Arts of Snohomish, Artamous (founder 1994). Presbyterian. Avocations: hiking, writing, poetry, swimming, travel, photography. Home: PO Box 1094 Snohomish WA 98291

SAIA, DIANE PLEVOCK DIPIERO, nutritionist, educator, legal administrator; b. Oct. 2, 1941; d. Charles and Monica (Alexandravich) Plevock; married; 1 child, David. BS, Framingham (Mass.) State Coll., 1962; MS, Simmons Coll., Boston, 1969; doctoral candidate, U. Mass., 1974—75. Field nutritionist Mass. Dept. Edn., Boston, 1962—64; sch. program coord. New Eng. Dairy and Food Coun., Boston, 1964—67, sr. staff Springfield, Mass., 1970—83; tchr. Weymouth (Mass.) Schs., 1967—70; adj. prof. Springfield Coll., 1970—80. Nutrition tchr. Baystate Med. Ctr., Springfield; adj. faculty Western New Eng. Coll., 1982—84; legal adminstr. SAIA Law Offices, 1984—; host radio show Law Talk, 1997—; prodr. TV shows, radio and consumer edn. programs. Fund raiser Am. Heart Assn., 2000—02. Mem.: ATLA, Assn. Legal Adminstrs., Sales and Mktg. Execs., Assn. Family and Consumer Econs. (exec. bd. 1972—, pres. 1978—79), New Eng. Pub. Health Assn., Mass. Bar Assn., Valley Press Club (assoc. dir. 1976—79, chmn. scholarship ball 1977—79). Roman Catholic. Home: 502 Frank Smith Rd Longmeadow MA 01106-2928 Office: 106 State St Springfield MA 01103-2034

SAIBLE, STEPHANIE IRENE, magazine editor; b. Mobile, Ala., Sept. 11, 1954; d. Lewis J. Slaff and Phoebe-Jane (Berse) Meiss. Student, Va. Commonwealth U., 1972—75. Editorial asst. Woman's World Magazine, Englewood, NJ, 1980—81, service copywriter, 1981—83, assoc. articles editor, 1983—84, articles editor, 1984—85, sr. editor features dept., 1985—86, sr. editor services dept., 1986, now editor-in-chief, 1994—. Contbr. articles to Woman's World, Modern Bride, New Body, Celebrity Beauty, Trim and Fit, Ladies Home Jour. Named Wonder Woman of the Yr., Bus. Jour., N.J., 1986. Mem.: Women in Comms. Office: Woman's World Mag 270 Sylvan Ave Englewood Cliffs NJ 07632-2521

SAIDENS, SUSAN M. accountant, consultant; d. Julius and Bella Mendick; m. Gary L. Saidens, June 3, 1979; 1 child, Lindsay. BA, Douglass Coll., New Brunswick, 1973. CPA Pa. Inst CPAs, 1991, cert. valuation analyst, Nat. Assn. Cert. Valuation Analysts, 2000, info. tech. profl., Am. Inst. CPAs, 2001. Sportswear buyer Macy's, N.Y.C., 1973—78; divsional mdse. mgr. Abraham and Straus, Bklyn., 1978—80; auditor KPMG, Phila., 1989—94; asst. contr. Home Health Corp. of Am., King of Prussia, Pa., 1994—96; dir. Smart & Assocs., LLP, Paoli, Pa., 1996—2000; dir., shareholder Asher & Co., Ltd., Phila., 2000—. Bd. mem. adv. bd. Chester County Mental Health/Mental Retardation, West Chester, Pa., 1999—2001. Author: The Challenge: Educating Clients on the Valuation Process, 2002. Steering com. United Way of Chester County, West Chester, Pa., 1995—2001; vol. Pew Charitable Trusts. Mem.: Appraisal Issues Task Force, Assn. Cert. Fraud Examiners, Nat. Assn. Female Execs., Pa. Inst. CPAs. (com. mem. 1998—), Am. Inst. CPAs., Nat. Assn. Cert. Valuation Analysts (mentor 2000—, chair valuation edn. and credentialing bd., bd. mem. 2002—). Avocations: music, reading. E-mail: smssaid@comcast.net.

SAIDI, PARVIN, hematologist, medical educator; b. Teheran, Iran, Mar. 21, 1932; came to U.S., 1946; d. Ahmad and Fatemeh (Ashouri) S.; m. Allahverdi Farmanfarmaian, May 27, 1958; children: Dellara Farmanfarmaian Terry, Kimya Farmanfarmaian Harris. BS, Smith Coll., Northampton, Mass., 1952; MD, Harvard U., 1956. Diplomate Am. Bd. Internal Medicine, subspecialty hematology and med. oncology. Intern medicine UCLA Med. Ctr., 1956-57; resident internal medicine U. Calif., San Francisco, 1957-59; NIH rsch. fellow hematology U. Calif. Hosps. and Children's Med. Ctr., San Francisco, 1959-61, 63-64; asst. prof. medicine U. Medicine & Dentistry N.J.-Rutgers Med. Sch., New Brunswick, 1968-71, assoc. prof., 1971-74; prof. U. Medicine & Dentistry N.J.-Robert Wood Johnson Med. Sch., New Brunswick, 1974—, chief divsn. hematology and oncology, dept. medicine, 1972—, Robert Wood Johnson U. Hosp., New Brunswick, 1981—. Cons. internist, hematologist, oncologist St. Peter's Med. Ctr., New Brunswick, Douglass Coll., Rutgers U., New Brunswick, VA Hosp., Lyons, N.J., Muhlenberg Hosp., Plainfield, N.J., Princeton (N.J.) Med. Ctr.; dir. Melvyn H. Motolinsky Lab. Hematology Rsch., N.J. Regional Comprehensive Hemophilia Care Program; mem. Gov.'s Adv. Coun. on AIDS; chmn. N.J. Regional Comprhensive Hemophilia Care Program Adv. Bd.; chmn. HHS region II Comprehensive Hemophilia Diagnostic and Treatment Ctrs., 1984-85, 89-90, 94-95, 99-2000; chmn. med. adv. bd. Hemophilia Found. N.J.; mem. med. adv. exec. com. N.J. Blood Svcs. Cons. editor Am. Jour. Medicine; contbr. articles to profl. jours. Recipient disting. svc. award for rsch. in leukemia Melvyn H. Motolinsky Rsch. Found., 1977, Humanitarian award Hemophilia Assn. No. N.J., 1978. Fellow ACP (mem. sci. program com. N.J. region), Acad. Medicine N.J.; mem. Am. Soc. Hematology (edn. com.), N.J. Hemophilia Assn. (chmn. med. adv. com., spl. award, Dr. L. Michael Kuhn Meml. award 1996), Coop. Oncology Group N.J. (exec. com., chairperson subcom. on lymphoma), Am. Heart Assn. (coun. on thrombosis), Am. Fedn. Clin. Rsch., Royal Soc. Medicine (affiliate), Am. Soc. Clin. Oncology, World Fedn. Hemophilia, Alpha Omega Alpha, Phi Beta Kappa, Sigma Xi. Office: Robert Wood Johnson Med Sch 1 Robert Wood Johnson Pl New Brunswick NJ 08901-1928

SAIF, LINDA J. animal scientist; Bachelor's, Coll. Wooster, 1969; master's, Ohio State U., 1971, doctorate in Microbiology/Immunology, 1976; doctorate (hon.), Ghent U., Belgium, 2003. Prof. OARDC Ohio State U., Wooster, 1979—, disting. univ. prof., 2002—. Contbr. articles to profl. jours. Mem.: NAS. Office: Food Animal Health Rsch Program OARDC 118 Food Animal Health Bldg Wooster OH 44691

SAIKEVYCH, IRENE A. pathologist; b. Perth Amboy, N.J., Oct. 16, 1950; d. Victor C. and Maria (Shomber) S.; divorced; 1 child, Natalie S. White. BA in Chemistry, U. Ill., 1972; MD, Northwestern, 1976. Diplomate Am. Bd. Med. Genetics; cert. pathologist. Resident Northwestern U., Honolulu, 1976-81; fellow in cytogenetics U. Hawaii, Honolulu, 1982-84, dir. cytogenetics rsch. lab., 1985-92, asst. prof. to assoc. prof. Dept. Pathology, 1982-92; med. dir. clin. cytogenetics Dept. Pathology St. Francis Hosp., Honolulu, 1988-92; staff pathologist Presbyn. Hosp., Charlotte, N.C., 1993—, dir. genetic svcs., 1993—. Contbr. numerous articles to profl. jours. Fellow Am. Coll. Med. Genetics (founder); mem. AAAS, AMA, Coll. Am. Pathologists (cytogenetics resource com. 1987—), Am. Soc. Human Genetics, Am. Soc. Hematology. Avocations: classical music, hiking, dance, painting, reading. Office: Presbyn Hosp Path Lab Med 200 Hawthorne Ln Charlotte NC 28204-2515

SAIKI, PATRICIA (MRS. STANLEY MITSUO SAIKI), former federal agency administrator, former congresswoman; b. Hilo, Hawaii, May 28, 1930; d. Kazuo and Shizue (Inoue) Fukuda; m. Stanley Mitsuo Saiki, June 19, 1954; children: Stanley Mitsuo, Sandra Saiki Williams, Margaret C., Stuart K., Laura H. BA, U. Hawaii, 1952. Tchr. U.S. history Punahou Sch., Kaimuki Intermediate Sch., Kalani High Sch., Honolulu, 1952-64; sec. Rep. Party Hawaii, Honolulu, 1964-66, vice chmn., 1966-68, 82-83, chmn., 1983-85; rsch. asst. Hawaii State Senate, 1966-68; mem. Hawaii Ho. of Reps., 1968-74, Hawaii State Senate, 1974-82, 100th-101st Congresses from 1st Hawaii dist., Washington, 1987-91; adminstr. SBA, Washington, 1991-93. Mem. Pres.'s Adv. Coun. on Status of Women, 1969-76; mem. Nat. Commn. Internat. Women's Yr., 1969-70; commr. We. Interstate Commn. on Higher Edn.; fellow Eagleton Inst., Rutgers U., 1970; fellow Inst. of Politics, Kennedy Sch. Govt., Harvard U., 1993; bd. dirs. Bank of Am.-Hawaii, Landmark Systems Corp., Internat. Asset Recovery Corp.; mem. nat. selection com. Innovations in Am. Govt., Ford Found., Harvard U., 1999-2002. Mem. Kapiolano Hosp. Aux.; sec. Hawaii Rep. Com., 1964-66, vice chmn., 1966-68, chmn., 1983-85; del. Hawaii Constl. Conv., 1968; alt. del. Rep. Nat. Conv., 1968, del., 1984, Rep. nominee for lt. gov. Hawaii, 1982, for U.S. Senate, 1990, for. gov. Hawaii, 1994; mem. Fedn. Rep. Women; trustee Hawaii Pacific Coll.; past bd. govs. Boys and Girls Clubs Hawaii; mem. adv. coun. ARC; bd. dirs. Nat. Fund for Improvement of Post-Secondary Edn., 1982-85; past bd. dirs. Straub Med. Rsch. Found., Honolulu, Hawaii's Visitors Bur., Honolulu, Edn. Commn. of States, Honolulu, Hawaii Visitors Bur., 1983-85; trustee U. Hawaii Found., 1984-86, Hawaii Pacific Coll., Honolulu; bd. govs. East West Ctr., 2003—. Republican. Episcopalian. Avocation: golf. Home: 784 Elepaio St Honolulu HI 96816-4710

SAILORS, EMMA LOU, pediatrician; b. Lincolnville, Ind., Aug. 21, 1923; d. Lee J. and Ethel Lavonne (Wingard) S.; m. Thomas E. Louis (dec.), Mar. 16, 1957; children: Susan, Julie, Tracy, Hilarie. BA, Manchester Coll., North Manchester, 1944; MD, Ind. U., Indpls., 1949. Diplomate Am. Bd. Pediat. Intern U. Ill., Chgo., 1949-50; resident in pediat. N.E. Med. Ctr.-Tufts, Boston, 1950-51; resident, then fellowship La. State U., New Orleans, 1951-54; instr. Tulane U. Sch. Med. dept. pediat., New Orleans, 1954-57, asst. prof., 1957-61, assoc. clin. prof., 1961-67; sch. physician Yonkers (N.Y.) Pub. Schs., 1971-77, chief sch. physician, 1977—2000; clinician Westchester County (N.Y.) Dept. Health, 1971-95. Mem. task forces (adolescent pregnancy, immunization), Yonkers. Contbr. articles to prof. jours. Bd. mem. 1st Unitarian Ch., New Orleans, 1955-57, Cmty.

Unitarian Ch., White Plains, N.Y., 1967-, Youth Svcs. Coun. former chair, Dobbs Ferry, N.Y., 1975-, sch. bd. nominating com., Dobbs Ferry, 1970's, 1980's, Sheltering the Homeless is Our Responsibility, White Plains, 1993-99; ch. sch. tchr. Unitarian Chs., New Orleans, 9 yrs. Mem. Med. Soc. N.Y. State, Am. Sch. Health Assn., LWV. Democrat. Avocations: painting, crafts, sewing, writing. Home: 125 Bellair Dr Dobbs Ferry NY 10522-3503

SAINT, EVA MARIE, actress; b. Newark, July 4, 1924; d. John Merle and Eva Marie (Rice) S.; m. Jeffrey Hayden, Oct. 28, 1951; children: Darrell, Laurette. BA, DFA, Bowling Green State U., 1946; student, Actors Studio, after 1950. Appeared in various radio and TV dramatic shows, N.Y.C., 1947—; theater roles include The Trip to Bountiful, 1953 (Outer Circle Critics award, N.Y. Drama Critics award 1953), The Rainmaker, 1953, Winesburg, Ohio, 1970, The Lincoln Mask, 1972, Summer and Smoke, 1973, Desire Under the Elms, 1974, The Fatal Weakness, 1976, Candida, 1977, Mr. Roberts, First Monday in October, 1979, Duet for One, 1982-83, The Country Girl, 1986 (L.A. Dramalogue award 1986), Death of a Salesman, 1994, Love Letters, 1994-2004, On the Divide, 1994-2004; appeared in films On the Waterfront, 1954 (Acad. Award for best supporting actress 1955), That Certain Feeling, 1956, Raintree Country, 1957, A Hatful of Rain, 1957, North by Northwest, 1959, Exodus, 1961, All Fall Down, 1962, 36 Hours, 1963, The Sandpiper, 1964, The Russians are Coming, The Russians are Coming!, 1965, Grand Prix, 1966, The Stalking Moon, 1969, Loving, 1970, Cancel My Reservation, 1972, Nothing in Common, 1986, Mariétté in Ecstacy, 1995, I Dreamed of Africa, 2000, Because of Winn-Dixie, 2003; TV dramas include The Macahans, 1976 (Emmy nom.), The Fatal Weakness, 1976, Taxi!!, 1978 (Emmy nom.), A Christmas to Remember, 1978, When Hell Was in Season, 1980, The Curse of King Tut's Tomb, The Best Little Girl in the World, 1981, Splendor in the Grass, 1981, Love Leads the Way, 1983, Jane Doe, 1983, Fatal Vision, 1984, The Last Days of Patton, 1986, A Year in the Life, 1986, Breaking Home Times, 1987, I'll Be Home for Christmas, 1988, Voyage of Terror: The Achille Lauro Affair, 1990, People Like Us, 1990 (Emmy award 1990), Palomino, 1991, Kiss of the Killer, ABC, 1992, My Antonia, 1994, After Jimmy, 1996, Time to Say Goodbye, 1997, Titanic, 1997; (documentary) Primary Colors: The Story of Corita, 1991; (with Bill Moyers) Children in America's Schools, 1997, Papa's Angels, 2000, Open House, TV-CBS, 2003; (feature film) Because of Winn-Dixie, 2003.

ST. AMAND, JANET G. government relations lawyer; b. N.Y.C., Feb. 27, 1953; d. Leonard Marsh and Glenda Weaver St. A.; children: Nikolai, Peter. BA, Arcadia U., 1975; JD, Georgetown U., 1980. Bar: D.C. 1981, N.Y. 1989. Legis. counsel Congressman Jim Coyne, Washington, 1981-83, Congressman Tom Carper, Washington, 1983-85, Sen. John Heinz, Washington, 1985-86, Am. Bankers Assn., Washington, 1986-87; asst. resident counsel J.P. Morgan, N.Y.C., 1987-90; counsel Fin. Svcs. Coun., Washington, 1990-93; fed. dir., counsel Household Internat., Washington, 1993—. Mem. Leadership Coun., Salvation Army, 1994—, trustee Arcadia U. (formerly Beaver Coll.), Glenside, Pa., 1999—, alumni bd. dirs., 1995—; trustee Womenin Housing and Fin. Found.; mem. Tax Coalition, 1999—. Recipient Mary Armstrong Wolf award Arcadia U., 1999. Mem. Women in Housing & Fin. (bd. dirs. 1991-95, mem. of yr. 1993), Univ. Club, Columbia Country Club, Exchequer Club, Tax Coalition. Presbyterian. Avocations: reading, traveling, jogging, politics. Home: 5423 33rd St NW Washington DC 20015 Office: Household Internat 1401 I St NW # 520 Washington DC 20005 E-mail: jgst.amand@household.com.

ST. FLEUR, MARIE P. state representative, state legislator; Degree, Univ. Mass. at Amherst; JD, Boston Coll. Law Sch., 1987. State rep. legis., 1999—. Ho. vice chairperson Counties; com. mem. Edn., Arts and Humanities, Housing and Urban Devel. Democrat. Office: State Ho Rm 33 Boston MA 02133

ST. GEORGE, JUDITH ALEXANDER, author; b. Westfield, N.J., Feb. 26, 1931; d. John Heald and Edna (Perkins) Alexander; m. David St. George, June 5, 1954; children: Peter, James, Philip, Sarah Anne. BA, Smith Coll., 1952. Author: Turncoat Winter, Rebel Spring, 1970, The Girl with Spunk, 1975, By George, Bloomers!, 1976, The Chinese Puzzle of Shag Island, 1976, The Shad Are Running, 1977, The Shadow of the Shaman, 1977, The Halo Wind, 1978, The Halloween Pumpkin Smasher, 1978, Mystery at St. Martin's, 1979, The Amazing Voyage of the New Orleans, 1980, Haunted, 1980, Call Me Margo, 1981, The Mysterious Girl in the Garden, 1981, The Brooklyn Bridge: They Said It Couldn't Be Built, 1982 (Am. Book award, N.Y. Acad. of Sci. award), Do You See What I See?, 1982, In The Shadow of the Bear, 1983, What's Happening to My Junior Year?, 1983, Who's Scared? Not Me!, 1984, The Mount Rushmore, 1985 (Christopher award), Panama Canal: Gateway to the World, 1989 (Golden Kite award), The White House, 1990, Mason and Dixon's Line of Fire, 1991, Dear Dr. Bell...Your Friend Helen Keller, 1992, Crazy Horse, 1994, To See With the Heart: The Life of Sitting Bull, 1996, Betsy Ross: Patriot of Philadelphia, 1997 (N.Y. Sons of the Am. Revolution award), Sacagawea, 1997, In the Line of Fire: President's Lives at Stake, 1999, So You Want To Be President?, 2001 (Caldecott medal, 2001), John and Abigail Adams: An American Love Story, 2001, So You Want to be an Inventor?, 2002, You're On Your Way, Teddy Roosevelt, 2004. Adv. coun. on children's lit. Rutgers U., 1977-94; chmn. ednl. com. Bklyn. Bridge Centennial Commn., 1981-83; tchr. creative writing York Correctional Instn., Niantic, Conn. Mem. Soc. Children's Book Writers, Author's Guild. Episcopalian. Avocations: tennis, hiking, travel. Home: 8 Binney Rd Old Lyme CT 06371-1445

ST. GERMAIN, JEAN MARY, medical physicist; b. N.Y.C. d. Herbert and Mary J. St. Germain. BS, Marymount Manhattan Coll.; MS, Rutgers U. Cert. Am. Bd. Med. Physics; lic. med. physicist, N.Y.; cert. Am. Bd. Medical Physics. USPHS fellow radiol. health Rutgers U., New Brunswick, N.J.; fellow dept. med. physics Meml. Hosp., N.Y.C.; asst. physicist Cornell U. Med. Coll., N.Y.C., 1968-71, instr. radiology (physics), 1971-78, clin. asst. prof., 1979-94, assoc. prof. clin. radiology, 1996—; assoc. attending physicist Meml. Sloan-Kettering Cancer Ctr., 1993—. Trustee Am. Bd. Med. Physics, 2003—, chair panel med. health physics, 1993-2000; cons. in field. Author: The Nurse and Radiotherapy, 1978; contbr. articles, chpts. to med. jours. Fellow: Health Physics Soc. (Failla Meml. lectr. 1999, pres. N.Y. chpt., pres. med. health physics sect.), Am. Assn. Physicists in Medicine (sec., bd. dirs.); mem.: Nat. Soc. Arts and Letters (regional dir., pres. N.Y. chpt., nat. music chair, nat. career awards chair), Radiol. and Med. Physics Soc. N.Y. (past pres.), Am. Acad. Health Physics (treas. 1996—99), Am. Inst. Physics (govs. bd.), Iota Sigma Pi (treas., pres. V chpt.). Office: 1275 York Ave New York NY 10021-6007

ST. GERMAIN, SHARON MARIE, writer; b. Mpls., Nov. 14, 1938; d. John Benjamin and Esther Lenoria Vandermyde; m. Donald Joseph St. Germain, June 17, 1961; children: Kim, Michael, Beth. BE, Hamline Univ., St. Paul, Minn., 1960. Co-dir. Writers Unlimited, White Bear Lake, Minn., 1969—; writing tchr. Hamline Univ., St. Paul, 1978—84, Mpls. Cmy. & Tech. Coll., Mpls., 1981—, Century Coll., White Bear Lake, Minn., 1994—, Cmty. Edn. programs, Mpls., St. Paul, Rochester Cmty. Edn., Minn., 1997—, St. Cloud Cmty. Edn., Minn., 1997—. Writer-in -the-sch. Mid. Sch., Mpls., St. Paul, 1980—85; faculty presenter Midwest Writers Conf., River Falls, Wis., 1979; guest spkr. pub. sch., libr. and writing organizations, Mpls., St. Paul, 1980—. Author: (childrens book) The Terrible Fight, 1990, several children's books; contbr. mag. story Boys' Life, 1975, sport series book Highlights for Children, 1975, articles to numerous profl. jours. Mem.: So. of Children's Book Writers and Illustrators, Writers Unlimited, World Wildlife Fund, Minn. Sr. Fedn., Am. Assn. of Retired People. Avocations: reading, travel, bicycling, swimming, family activities. Home: 2555 Upper Afton Rd Maplewood MN 55119

ST. HILAIRE, CAROLINE, member of parliament; b. Longueuil, Can., Nov. 16, 1969; children: Etienne, Louis-Félix. BA in Adminstrn., U. Québec, 1993. With Soc. du droit de reproduction des auteurs, compositeurs et éditeurs du Can.; M.P. for Bloc Quebecois House of Commons, asst. house leader and spokesperson for amateur sport. Founder Soc. de Promotion Pour La Releve Musicale de l'espace Francophone. Avocation: competitive figure skating. Office: House of Commons 647-S Centre Block Ottawa ON Canada K1A 0A6

ST. JOHN, JENNIFER KATHLEEN, gifted and talented educator; b. Washington, June 21, 1969; d. James E. and Carolin M. G. St. John. BA, M in Tchg., U. Va., 1992. Postgrad. profl. lic. Va., 1992. Classroom tchr. Fairfax County Pub. Schs., Centreville, Va., 1992—96, gifted and talented specialist Fairfax Station, Va., 1996—. Mem.: NEA, ASCD, Fairfax Edn. Assn., Va. Edn. Assn., Nat. Assn. for Gifted Children, U. Va. Alumni Assn. (life), Kappa Delta Pi, Alpha Delta Pi (life; guard 1988—89). Roman Catholic. Home: 6019 Selwood Pl Springfield VA 22152 Office: Silverbrook Elem - FCPS 9350 Crosspointe Dr Fairfax Station VA 22039 Personal E-mail: jkstjohn@prodigy.net. E-mail: jennifer.st.john@fcps.edu.

ST. JOHN, JULIE, mortgage company executive; BA in English, U. Mich.; MBA, Fla. State U. CPA, Fla. Prin. Arthur Young & Co.; v.p. info. sys. Residence Inn divsn. Marriott; sr. v.p. transaction processing and mgmt. sys. Fed. Nat. Mortgage Assn., Washington, 1990—. Office: Fed Nat Mortgage Assn 3900 Wisconsin Ave NW Washington DC 20016-2806

ST. JOHN, KATHERINE IVA, artistic director, dance educator; b. St. Paul, Nov. 18, 1948; d. Arthur E. and Lillian Faye (Teetsell) Tester; m. Curtis St. John (div.). BA, U. Utah, 1989; MA, Brigham Young U., 1994, U. Utah, 1994; postgrad., U. Calif., Riverside. Instr. U. Utah, Salt Lake City, 1989-94; dir. Ea. Arts, Salt Lake City, 1989—; artistic dir. Internat. Dance Theatre, Salt Lake City, 1993—. Author, choreographer: Radif E Raos; author: Afghan Dance: A Cultural and Historical Study; contbr. articles to profl. publs. Vol. Salt Lake Ethnic Arts Coun.; bd. chair Assn. Students Univ. Utah, 1992; speaker Utah Humanities Coun. Grantee Utah Arts Coun., Salt Lake City Arts Coun. Mem. Internat. Orgn. of Folk Arts, Mid. East Studies Assn., Soc. Ethnomusicology, Congress on Rsch. in Dance, Dance and the Child Internat., Phi Kappa Phi. Home: PO Box 526362 Salt Lake City UT 84152-6362 Office: Eastern Arts Ethnic Dance Co PO Box 526362 Salt Lake City UT 84152-6362

ST. JOHN, MARIA ANN, nurse anesthetist; b. Rochester, Pa., Dec. 15, 1953; d. James Edward and Evelyn Marie (Sayers) St. J.; m. Paul David Dworsky, Aug. 19, 1978 (div. Dec. 13, 1991); children: Lauren Marie Dworsky, Michael David Dworsky. BSN, U. Pitts., 1975; cert. reg. nurse anesthetist, U. Health Ctr. Pitts. Sch. Anesthesia for Nurses, 1984. Advanced RN practitioner Fla., Ohio; cert. RN anesthetist, Pa., Ohio, N.C., Ky. Nurse Presbyn. U. Hosp., Pitts., 1975-77, VA Hosp., Pitts., 1977-82; nurse anesthetist Anesthesia Assocs. of Hollywood, Fla., 1984-87, North Hills Anesthesia Assocs., Pitts., 1987-98, Queen City Anesthesiologists, Inc., Cin., 1998—. Vol. tchr. art history, fundraiser St. Alexis Sch., Wexford, Pa., 1991-97, recording sec. PT6 Bd., 1996-97, v.p. PT6 Bd., 1997-98; mem. Cranberry Twp. Athletic Assn., 1991-98, Oak Hills PTA, Cin., 1998-99, Oak Hills Athletic Boosters, 1999, PTG Springmeyer Sch. and Bridgetown Jr. H.S., Cinn., 1998-99, PTG and Athletic Boosters, Bridgetown Middle Sch., 1999—. Recipient scholarship March of Dimes, Beaver County, Pa., 1971, Pitt. scholarship, 1971-75. Mem. DAR, Am. Assn. Nurse Anesthetists, Pa. Assn. Nurse Anesthetists, Ohio Assn. Nurse Anesthetists, Fla. Assn. Nurse Anesthetists, Ky. Nurse Anesthetists, N.C. Nurse Anesthetists. Avocations: playing piano, reading, traveling, school volunteering, swimming. Home: 6073 Werk Rd Cincinnati OH 45248-4043

ST. JOHN, PATRICIA ANNE, art educator; b. Johnson City, N.Y., Dec. 6, 1943; d. Michael and Helen (Gordan) Wovkulich; m. Mark Gregory St. John, Aug. 28, 1966 (div. Nov. 1970); m. Jack Tager, Dec. 4, 1987. BS, SUNY, Buffalo, 1964; MA, Ohio U., 1968; EdD, Columbia U., 1978; MA, NYU, 1986. Registered art therapist (A.T.R.), bd. cert. art therapist. Art tchr. Bd. Coop. Ednl. Svcs., Potsdam, N.Y., 1964-65, Gouverneur (N.Y.) Pub. Schs., 1965-66; therapeutic art specialist Wellesley (Mass.) Pub. Schs., 1969-73; pvt. practice Amherst, 1984—; art edn. instr. Kean Coll., Union, N.J., 1974-79; asst. prof. art U. Mass., Amherst, 1979-86; dir. grad. art programs Coll. New Rochelle, N.Y., 1986-94, div. head grad. art, comm. arts, 1994—. Cons. editor Davis Publs., Inc. Worcester, Mass., 1989-90, Magnolia Pubs., Inc. Chgo., 1995—. Assoc. editor: Art Therapy, 1991-95; contbr. articles to profl. jours. N.J. state rep. Nat. Com. Arts for the Handicapped (ea. divsn.), Washington, 1976; co-dir. Western Mass. Scholastic Art awards, Amherst, 1982, 83; exhibit coord. Western Mass. Youth Art Month Exhibit, Chicopee, 1984, 85. Recipient 2d prize exptl. weaving, Midwest Weavers Conf., 1967; rsch. grantee Kean Coll. N.J., 1978. Fellow Am. Soc. Psychopathology Expression; mem. Nat. Art Edn. Assn. (rev. panelist, 1990-97), Am. Art Therapy Assn. (chair long range planning com., bd. dirs. 1999-2001, book rev. editor 2001—, edn. com. 2001—), New Eng. Assn. Art Therapists (hon. life mem., pres. 1984-86), Mass. Art Edn. Assn. (v.p. 1985). Avocations: travel, classical music, gourmet cooking. Office: Coll New Rochelle 29 Castle Pl New Rochelle NY 10805-2338 E-mail: pstjohn@cnr.edu.

ST. JOHN, SUZAN, astrologer, illustrator, writer, vocalist; b. N.Y.C., Nov. 28, 1948; d. John Lo Nigro and Gilda De Luca; AAS in Hotel and Restaurant Mgmt., N.Y.C. Tech. Coll., 1973; BA in Anthropology, Religion, NYU, 1984. Wine capt. Sommelier Soc. Am., 1972. Transformative counselor, N.Y.C., 1970—; radio prodr., host, writer WBAI-FM 99.5, N.Y.C., 1984—2000; illustrator N.Y.C., 1985—; singer, 2001—. Astrologer, N.Y.C., 1995—. Co-author: In the Footsteps of the Goddess, 1988; author (publisher, illustrator): Lotus Speaks Mag. Vol. Project Liberty, St. Vincent's Hosp., N.Y.C., 2003. Mem.: Nat. Ctr. for Geocosmic Rsch. (lectr. 1997—2003). D-Liberal. Nigmapa Buddhist/Tibet. Avocations: poetry, martial arts, clarinet, saxophone, dance. Home and Office: 82 Horatio St 4A New York NY 10014-1587 Personal E-mail: suereal8@hotmail.com.

ST. LIFER KENNEDY, JANE, art appraiser, curator; b. N.Y.C., Apr. 19, 1956; d. Martin R. and Marcia Simon St. Lifer; m. Steven J. Kennedy, Aug. 26, 2001. BFA, Syracuse U., N.Y., 1978; postgrad., New Sch. of Social Rsch., N.Y.C., 1979, Ariz. State U., 1980; MA, New Jersey City U., Jersey City, 1996; Cert. in Appraisal Studies, George Washington U., 2002. Cert. appraiser. Curatorial asst. Everson Mus., Syracuse, 1978; framer Graphic Image, Milburn, NJ, 1978—79; asst. dir. Trailside Galleries, Scottsdale, Ariz., 1979—80, John Douglas Cline Gallery, Phoenix, 1980—81; weekend sales mgr. Circle Fine Art, Chgo. and N.Y.C., 1981; dir. Hammer Graphics and Hammer Pub. Hammer Galleries, N.Y.C., 1981—86; sales mgr. Gallery Urban, Nagoya, Japan and N.Y.C., 1986—88; asst. dir. 19th and 20th century Am. impressionist and realist paintings and sculpture Grand Ctrl. Art Galleries, N.Y.C., 1993—94; pres. Jane St. Lifer Art, Inc., N.Y.C., 1988—; dir., curator Digital Sandbox Network Gallery, N.Y.C., 1999—. Lectr. Parsons Sch. Design, N.Y.C. Mem.: Nat. Mus. of Women in the Arts, Nat. Arts Club, Internat. Found. of Art Rsch., Auctioneers Assns., Inc. (v.p.), Am. Soc. Appraisers (assoc.), Dog Fanciers Club (photography competition chair). Avocations: theater, culinary art. Office: 140 Riverside Blvd #323 New York NY 10069

ST. MARIE, JUDY See DAILEY, JUDY

SAINT-OUEN LEUNG, BRIGITTE, art dealer, consultant; arrived in U.S., 1993; d. Rene-Gerard Saint-Ouen and Christiane; m. John Leung, May 31, 1999. BA of Bus., Paris VIII, 1984; degree in art history, The Louvre, Paris, 1993. Mktg. dir. Wally Findlay, Paris, 1989—93; mktg. dir., art cons. Wally Findlay Galleries, N.Y.C., 1993—2000; pres., owner Gramercy 32 Fine Arts, N.Y.C., 2000—; art, art cons. 19th Century to Outsider and Photography, European and Am. artists. Office: Gramercy 32 Fine Arts Ste 15 D-B 32 Gramercy Park S New York NY 10003 E-mail: gramercy@32finearts.com.

ST. VINCENT, KATHARINE NEYMAN, secondary school educator; b. Vallejo, Calif., Nov. 8, 1946; d. Robert Leslie and Rosalind Smith Neyman; m. Bernard Schwartzberg, June 28, 1981; children: Robert Jordan Schwartzberg, Steven Eliot Schwartzberg. BA in Romance Langs., Pomona (Calif.) Coll., 1968; MA in Tchg., Johns Hopkins U., 1969; MSW, Fordham U., 1992; EdM in Adminstrn., Coll. of New Rochelle, N.Y., 2000. Cert. tchr. ESL, Spanish, French N.Y., sch. dist. adminstr. N.Y. State Edn. Dept., sch. adminstrn. and supervision N.Y. State Edn. Dept. Spanish tchr. Paint Br. H.S., Burtonsville, Md.; tchr. ESL, spanish K-12 Pub. Schools of the Tarrytowns, Tarrytown and Sleepy Hollow, NY, 1971—; ESL chairperson Sleepy Hollow Mid. and H.S., 1998—. Presenter, spkr. N.Y. State TESOL and SABE, 1974—. Author: (short stories) The Yr. I Met Santa, Good Housekeeping, 1988, Other Grandpa, Chicken Soup for the Grandparents Soul, 2002. Finalist Tchr. of the Yr., N.Y. State Lottery and the Jour. News, 2001; recipient award in Romance langs., Bank of Am., 1964, Hermann Fischer Meml. prize in Latin Am. lit., U. Toronto, 1978, Brazilian Embassy award, U. of Toronto, 1978. Mem.: N.Y. State Assn. Bilingual Educators, N.Y. State Tchrs. of English to Spkrs. of Other Langs. Office: Pub Schs of the Tarrytowns 200 N Broadway Sleepy Hollow NY 10591

SAIZ, LEONOR, physicist, researcher; b. Barcelona, Jan. 17, 1969; d. Jesus Saiz and Leonor Ardanaz. BSc in Physics, U. Barcelona, 1992, PhD in Physics, 1998. Postgrad. rsch. asst. U. Barcelona and SOCIMAG S.A., Barcelona, 1992—93; postdoctoral Fellow U. Manchester Inst. Sci. and Tech., England, 1998; postdoctoral fellow U. Pa., Phila., 1999—2002; physicist, guest scientist Ctr. for Neutron Rsch., Nat. Inst. Standards and Tech., Gaithersburg, Md., 2002—. Sr. rsch. assoc. U. Pa., Phila., 2002—. Reviewer European Phys. Jour.-E Soft Matter, Biophys. Jour., Chem. Physics Letters, Chem. Physics, Molecular Pharmacology, Jour. Am. Chem. Soc.; contbr. articles to profl. jours., DGICYT fellow Spanish Govt., 1993—96. Mem.: AAAS, Am. Phys. Soc. Avocations: hiking, music, dance, reading, travel. Office: U Pa 231 S 34th St Philadelphia PA 19107 also: NIST NCNR 100 Bureau Dr Stop 8562 Gaithersburg MD 20899-8562

SAIZAN, PAULA THERESA, oil company executive; b. New Orleans, Sept. 12, 1947; d. Paul Morine and Hattie Mae (Hayes) Saizan; m. George H. Smith, May 26, 1973 (div. July 1976). BS in Accts. summa cum laude, Xavier U., 1969. CPA Tex. Systems engr. IBM, New Orleans, 1969-71; acct., then sr. acct. Shell Oil Co., Houston, 1971-76, sr. fin. analyst, 1976-77, fin. rep., 1977-79, corp. auditor, 1979-81, treasury rep., 1981-82, sr. treasury rep., 1982-86; asst. treas. Shell Credit Inc., Shell Leasing Co., Shell Fin. Co., Houston, 1986-88, sr. pub. affairs rep., 1988-89, sr. staff pub. affairs rep., 1990-91, program mgr., 1991-96, sr. program mgr., 1996-97, mgr. constituent rels. and edn. support, 1997-2000, mgr. nat. and cmty. outreach, 2000—03, mgr. stakeholder mgmt., 2003—04, sr. advisor, corp. diversity, 2004—. Bd. dirs. Houston Downtown Mgmt. Dist., Greater Houston Conv. and Visitors Bur., United Negro Coll. Fund; vice-chair Nat. Coun. Negro Women, Inc.; found. adv. coun. Links, Inc.; adv. bd. Sch. Engring, Tex. So. U.; del. White House Conf. on small bus., 1995. Mem. AICPA, NAACP (life, bd. dir., spl. contbn. fund, trustee), Tex. Soc. CPAs, Leadership Houston, Greater Inwood Partnership, LWV of Houston, Xavier U. Alumni Assn., Nat. Coun. LaRaza, Nat. Assn. Black Accts., Links Inc., Nat. Coun. Garden Clubs (life), Nat. Congress of Black Women, Alpha Kappa Alpha, Phi Gamma Nu, Kappa Gamma Pi. Roman Catholic. Home: 5426 Long Creek Ln Houston TX 77088-4407 Office: Shell Oil Co PO Box 2463 Houston TX 77252-2463 E-mail: paulusinv@aol.com.

SAKAC, SISTER ANN, college administrator. Pres., Mount St. Mary Coll., Newburgh, N.Y. Office: Mt St Mary Coll Office of the President Powell Ave Newburgh NY 12550-3494

SAKAI, KIYOKO, artist; b. Osaka, Japan, Oct. 24, 1938; Osaka, Japan, m. Keizo Sakai, Nov. 7, 1965; children: Miyako, Alisa. BA, Doshisha U., Kyoto, Japan, 1961; postgrad., Art Students League, N.Y.C., 1973—78. Exhibited in one woman shows at Cottage Gallery, N.J., Move 21, Osaka, Japan, Kanner Kurzan Mus., N.Y., Myung Sook Lee Gallery, N.Y., Osaka Prefecture Comtemporary Art Ctr., Japan, Drew U., N.J., Permanent Collection: Deloitte, Haskins and Sells, N.J., The Zen Studies Soc., N.Y., The New York Stock Exchange, N.Y.; group exhbn. Bergen Mus. of Art and Sci., N.J., Instituto Superiore Per Industrio Artistiche, Urbino, Italy, Newark Mus. Recipient award Bergen Mus. Juried Show, Ramapo Coll. Juried Show, Art Showcase award, Manhattan Art Internat., Manhattan Art Internat.; Kenneth Hayes Miller Meml. scholar Art Student League of N.Y. Life mem. Art Student League of N.Y. Avocations: music, dance, literature.

SAKS, JUDITH-ANN, artist; b. Anniston, Ala., Dec. 20, 1943; d. Julien David and Lucy-Jane (Watson) S.; m. Haskell Irvin Rosenthal, Dec. 22, 1974; 1 child, Brian Julien. Student, Tex. Acad. Art, 1957-58, Mus. Fine Arts, Houston, 1962, Rice U., 1962; BFA, Tulane U., 1966; postgrad., U. Houston, 1967. Curator student art collection U. Houston, 1968-72; artist Am. Revolution Bicentennial project Port of Houston Authority, 1975-76. Solo shows include Alley Gallery, Houston, 1969, 2131 Gallery, Houston, 1969; group shows include Birmingham (Ala.) Mus., 1967, Meinhard Galleries, Houston, 1977, Galeire Barbizon, Houston, 1980, Park Crest Gallery, Austin, 1981; represented in permanent collections including L.B. Johnson Manned Space Mus., Clear Lake City, Tex., Harris County Heritage Mus., Windsor Castle, Smithsonian Instn.; commns. include Pin Oak Charity Horse Show Assn., Roberts S.S. Agy., New Orleans, Cruiser Houston Meml. Rm., U. Houston. Recipient art awards including 1st prize for water color Art League Houston, 1969, 1st prize for graphics, 1969, 1st prize for sculpture, 1968, Nat. 1st place award for original print DAR/Am. Heritage Com., 1987, Nat. 1st place award for acrylic painting, DAR, 2000, Tex. award for Acrylic, 2003, Nat. 3rd place award for painting, 2003, Tex. State 1st prize for drawing DAR, 2002, Shofar award, 2003. Outstaind Svc. awrd Boy Scout Troop 806, 2002. Mem. Art League Houston, Houston Mus. Fine Arts, DAR (Lady Washington chap., curator 1983-85, 93-95, contbr. Tex. sesquicentennial drawing for DAR mag., recording sec. 2001-03, libr. 2003—, Tex. Best Chpt. Chmn. award 2003, Tex. award for art 2003, Tex. State 1st prize acrylic 2004), Daus. Republic of Tex., Magna Charta Dames.

SALAMAN, MAUREEN KENNEDY, writer, nutritionist; b. Glendale, Calif., Apr. 4, 1937; d. Ted and Elena (Peters) Kennedy; 1 child, Sean. With Making Healthy Choices, 1980—; hostess Le Sea Broadcasting, Sky Angel Satellite Worldwide Direct TV with Maureen Kennedy Salaman; pres. Nat. Health Fedn., Monrovia, Calif., 1982—. Cons., lectr., rschr. on cancer rsch. and metabolic medicine, nutrition; lobbyist for freedom of choice. Author: Foods That Heal, Nutrition: The Cancer Answer, 1983, 2d edit., The Diet Bible, The Light at the End of the Refrigerator, All Your Health Questions Answered, Naturally I and II, Achieving Super Immunity, How to Renew You; editor: Nosy News, Health Freedom News, 1982—2004; contbr. articles to profl. jours. Office: Nat Health Fedn PO Box 688 Monrovia CA 91017-0688 also: Maureen Kennedy Salaman Inc 1259 El Camino Real Ste 1500 Menlo Park CA 94025-4227

SALAMON, LINDA BRADLEY, English literature educator; b. Elmira, N.Y., Nov. 20, 1941; d. Grant Ellsworth and Evelyn E. (Ward) Bradley; divorced; children: Michael Lawrence, Timothy Martin. BA, Radcliffe Coll., 1963; MA, Bryn Mawr Coll., 1964, PhD, 1971; Advanced Mgmt. Cert., Harvard U. Bus. Sch., 1978; D.H.L., St. Louis Coll. Pharmacy, 1993.

Lectr., adj. asst. prof. Eng., Dartmouth Coll., Hanover, N.H., 1967-72; mem. faculty lit. Bennington Coll., Vt., 1974-75; dean students Wells Coll., Aurora, N.Y., 1975-77; exec. asst. to pres. U. Pa., Phila., 1977-79; assoc. prof. English, Washington U., St. Louis, 1979-88, prof., 1988-92, dean Coll. Arts and Scis., 1979-92; prof. English, George Washington U., Washington, 1992—; dean Columbia Coll. Arts and Sci., Washington, 1992-95; interim v.p. for acad. affairs George Washington U., Washington, 1995-96. Mem. faculty Bryn Mawr Summer Inst. for Women, 1979-99. Author, co-editor: Nicholas Hilliard's Art of Limning, 1983; co-author: Integrity in the College Curriculum, 1985; contbr. numerous articles to literary and ednl. jours. Bd. dirs. Assn. Am. Colls., vice chmn., 1985, chmn., 1986; bd. dirs. Greater St. Louis council Girl Scouts U.S.A.; trustee Coll. Bd., St. Louis Coll. Pharmacy. Fellow Radcliffe Inst., 1973-74, Fulbright fellow, Taiwan, 2003, Ringler fellow Huntington Libr, 2004; Am. Philos. Soc. Penrose grantee, 1974; fellow Folger Shakespeare Libr., 1986, NEH Montaigne Inst., 1988. Mem. MLA, Renaissance Soc. Am., Cosmos Club, Phi Beta Kappa. Office: George Washington U Dept of Eng Rome Hall 760 801 22D St NW Washington DC 20052-0001

SALAMON, RENAY, real estate broker; b. N.Y.C., May 13, 1948; d. Solomon and Mollie (Friedman) Langman; m. Maier Salamon, Aug. 10, 1968; children: Mollie, Jean, Leah, Sharon, Eugene. BA, Hunter Coll., 1969. Licensed real estate borker, N.J. Mgr. office Customode Designs Inc., N.Y.C., 1966-68; co-owner Salamon Dairy Farms, Three Bridges, N.J., 1968-86; assoc. realtor Max. D. Shuman Realty Inc., Flemington, N.J., 1983-85; pres., chief exec. officer Liberty Hill Realty Inc., Flemington, N.J., 1985—. Cons. Illva Saronna Inc. (Illva Group), Edison, N.J. 1985—; real estate devel. joint venture with M.R.F.S. Realty Inc. (Illva Group), 1986—; bd. dirs. Anderson House. Mem. Readington twp. Environ. Commn., Whitehouse Sta., N.J., 1978-87, N.J. Assn. Environ. Commrs., Trenton, 1978—; fundraiser Rutgers Prep. Sch., Somerset, N.J., 1984-95; bd. dirs. Hunterdon County YMCA, 1987-95, Anderson House, 2000-; mem. N.J.-Israel Commn., 1998—; bd. trustees Rutgers Prep. Sch., 2000—; chair Hunterdon County Bd. Social Svc., 2002-; vice-chair Hunterdon County Health and Human Svcs. Commn., 2002-. Named N.J. Broker Record, Forbes Inc., N.Y.C. 1987. Mem.: Realtors Land Inst. Republican. Jewish. Office: Liberty Hill Realty Inc 415 US Highway 202 Flemington NJ 08822-6021

SALAMONE-KOCHOWICZ, JEAN GLORIA, retired bank executive; b. White Deer, Pa., Dec. 28, 1929; d. Dewey and Pearl Viola (Bastian) Smith; m. Daniel W. Salamone, Nov. 2, 1946 (div. 1977); children: Daryl Joseph, John Daniel; m. John T. Kochowicz, Feb. 10, 1990 (dec. 1993). Student, Bloomsburg State Coll., 1946, Am. Inst. Banking, 1974-85. Sec. Chef Boy-ar-Dee Foods, Milton, Pa., 1946-48, Arthur Andersen & Co., Washington, 1948-58; exec. sec. Citizens Bank and Trust Co., Riverdale, Md., 1970-74, asst. treas., 1974-77, asst. v.p., 1977-84; v.p. Citizens Bank, Laurel, Md., 1984-97; corp. sec. Citizens Bancorp (holding corp. for Citizens Bank), Laurel, 1982-96; ret. CRESTAR, 1997. Trustee Prince George's Arts Coun., Riverdale, 1983-98, treas., 1983-89, pres. 1990-91. Mem. Fin. Women Internat. (pres. met. Md. group 1977-78). Roman Catholic. Avocations: travel, photography, art collecting, volunteering. E-mail: salakoch@aol.com.

SALAND, DEBORAH, psychotherapist, educator; b. Val Dosta, Ga., July 25, 1954; d. Charles and Audrey (Horan) Gianniny. B in Profl. Studies, Barry U., 1990, MSW, 1992; D in Psychology, So. Calif. Sch. Profl. Studies, 1996. Lic. clin. social worker, Fla. Substance abuse counselor Spectrum Programs, Ft. Lauderdale, Fla., 1974-79; owner Obsession in Time, Miami, Fla., 1984-88; asst. clin. dir. Interphase Recovery, Miami, 1988-89; substance abuse counselor Transitions Recovery, Miami, 1989-91; clin. dir. level II Pathways Treatment, Miami; pvt. practice Inst. Human Potential, Miami, 1993—; founder Eating Disorder Tex. Program, 1997—. Lectr. Addiction Traingin Inst. U. Miami, 1992, mem. faculty, 1993—; clin. supr. Transitions Recovery, Miami, 1993—, Treatment Resources, Miami, 1993-94; adj. faculty N.Y. Inst. Tech., Boca Raton, Fla., 1997—; dir. Am. Family Eating Disorder Tract, 1997-98. Contbr. articles to profl. jours. Named Spl. Alumni Barry U., 1996. Mem. NASW, APA, Am. Group Psychotherapy Assn. (clin.), Med. Psychotherapist Am. (assoc. clin.) Nat. Bd. Cert. Counselors (counselor), Broward County Mental Health Assn. Office: Inst Human Potential 19501 NE 10th Ave Ste 305 Miami FL 33179-3502

SALAND, LINDA CAROL, anatomy educator, neuroscience researcher; b. N.Y.C., Oct. 24, 1942; d. Charles and Esther (Weingarten) Gewirtz; m. Joel S. Saland, Aug. 16, 1964; children: Kenneth, Jeffrey. BS, CCNY, 1963, PhD in Biology, 1968; MA in Zoology, Columbia U., 1965. Rsch. assoc. dept. anatomy Columbia U. Coll. Physicians and Surgeons, N.Y.C., 1968-69; sr. rsch. assoc. dept. anatomy Sch. Medicine U. N.Mex., Albuquerque, 1971-78, asst. prof. anatomy, 1978-83, assoc. prof., 1983-89, prof., 1989-97, prof. dept. neuroscis., 1997—. Ad hoc reviewer study sect. NIH, 1994, 95, 97, 2000, mem. site visit team. Mem. editl. bd. Anat. Record, 1980-98; contbr. articles to profl. jours. Recipient Khatali Tchg. Excellence award, U. N.Mex. Med. Class of 2001; fellow NDEA, 1966—68. Mem. AAAS, Soc. for Neurosci., Women in Neurosci. (chmn. steering com. 1991-93). Office: U New Mex Sch Medicine Dept Neuroscis MSC 084740 Albuquerque NM 87131-0001 E-mail: lsaland@salud.unm.edu.

SALAT, CRISTINA, writer; b. N.Y.C. Student, L.I. U. Freelance editor, 1987—; author, editor, manuscript cons., workshop facilitator, 1985—. Author: Living in Secret, 1993, Alias Diamond Jones, 1993, Min Mors Koereste hedder Janey, 1995, Defending the Dreamcatchers, 1999, Robin, Romeo & Juliette, 1999, Peanut's Emergency, 1999; contbr. to anthologies including Sister/Stranger, 1993, Am I Blue, 1994, Once Upon A Time, 1996; contbr. to popular publ. Home: PO Box 13214 Pahoa HI 96778

SALAY, CINDY ROLSTON, systems engineer; b. Roanoke, Va., July 18, 1955; d. Gilbert Wilson and Ellnor Patterson (Sandridge) Rolston; m. John Matthew, July 7, 1988; 1 child, David. AAS, Va. Western Community Coll., 1976; AS, J. Sargeant Reynolds Community Coll., 1982; BS, Va. Commonwealth U., 1984. RN. Operating room RN Henrico Doctors Hosp., Richmond, Va., 1979-80; nursing supr. Johnston Willis Hosp., Richmond, 1980-87; systems analyst, coord. Health Corp Va., Richmond, 1983-87, sr. project leader, 1987-88; sr. systems analyst Hosp. Corp. Am., Nashville, 1987; sr. systems cons. IBAX Healthcare Systems, Reston, Va., 1988-94; sys. analyst MCV Hosps. Info. Sys., Richmond, Va., 1994-95; sr. sys. engr. McKesson, Atlanta, 1995—. Methodist. Avocations: reading, plants, pets, exercising. Home: 13800 Sunrise Bluff Rd Midlothian VA 23112-2512 Office: McKesson 5995 Windward Pkwy Alpharetta GA 30005-4184 E-mail: cindy.salay@mckesson.com.

SALAZAR, LAURA ALICE GARDNER, retired theater educator; b. Gilbert, Minn., Feb. 22, 1935; d. Lloyd William and Isabel Mary (Aldrich) Gardner; m. Hugo Salazar, June 12, 1962; children: Anthony, Catherine. BS, U. Wis., River Falls, 1957; MA, Kent State U., 1960; PhD, U. Mich., 1984. H.s. tchr. various pub. schs., Wis., 1957-59, 1960-64; instr. Mich. State U., East Lansing, 1964-65; prof. Grand Valley State U., Allendale, Mich., 1996—2002, emerita, 2002—. Cons., writer, Mich. 4H, East Lansing, 1995—; cons. Goals 2000, U.S. Dept. Edn. and MENC, Reston, Va., 1992-95; founder, exec. dir. Fabulous African Fabrics: Supporting AIDS Widows and Orphans, 1999. Author: Teaching Dramatically: Learning Thematically, 1995 (Ann. Disting. Book award Am. Alliance for Theatre and Edn. 1996), Making Performance Art, 1999; co-author (with S. Harbin): International Theatre Events, 1991; writer, creator performance art pieces performed in Europe, the Caribbean, Australia, and the U.S., 1992-96; dir. over 60 stage plays, mostly at Grand Valley State U., 1966—; contbr. over 30 articles to profl. jours. Leader Theatre for At-Risk Youth, Grand Rapids/Trinidad, Mich., 1985—; pres. Coun. of Performing Arts, Children, Grand Rapids, 1976-77; cons. Leadership Grand Rapids, 1993, 95; team mem. Kent County Jail Ministry, Grand Rapids, 1995—; bd. mem. Grand Rapids Ballet, 1994-97. Recipient Fulbright rsch. grant, 1992, Australia-Am. Edn. Found. grant, 1995 Mem. Internat. Amateur Theatre Assn. N.Am. (mem. bd. 1990—), Internat. Theatre for Youth (six internat. offices), Internat. Amateur Theatre Assn. (editor, info. officer, 1991—), Am. Alliance for Theatre and Edn. (pres. 1993-95, bd. dirs. 1987—, Presdl. award 1989), Internat. Drama in Edn. Assn. (U.S. rep. 1993-95). Democrat. Methodist. Avocation: surface design. Office: Grand Valley State Univ 1 Campus Dr Allendale MI 49401-9403

SALAZAR, SHIRLEY ANN, music educator; b. Chgo., Feb. 7, 1957; d. Jacobus Van Yzendoorn and Sarai VanderLip; m. Gabriel Salazar, May 12, 1984; children: Sarah, Hannah. BA, Northeastern Ill. U., 1981. Headmistress Mueller Acad., Peoria, Ill., 1982—84; adj. prof. Eureka Coll., Eureka, Ill., 1990—91, Bradley U., Peoria, 1991—; dir. of choirs Peoria Coop. Acad., Peoria, 1997—. Music worship dir. Peoria (Ill.) Christian Fellowship, 1992—; adj. Nat. Assn. of Tchrs. of Singing, 1995—; artist in residence Peoria Area Civic Choral Choir Camp, Eureka, Ill., 2001—. Singer: (soprano soloist) Handel's Messiah, Peoria Bachfest, Peoria Symphony Orch., Bradley Cmty. Chorus, Western Ill. U. Mem.: Music Educators Nat. Conf., Ill. Music Educators Assn., Nat. Assn. of Tchrs. of Singing. Avocations: reading, swimming, water sports. Home: 800 E Seneca Pl Peoria IL 61603-1948 Office: Bradley U Peoria IL 61603

SALBEC, PATRICIA R. emergency medical technician; Emergency physician. Co-author: (book) the Physician's Guide to Domestic Violence: How to ask the right questions and recognize abuse. Mem. Atty. Gen.'s Policy Coun. on Violence Prevention; pres. Physicians for a Violence-free Soc., San Francisco. Mem.: Am. Coll. Emergency Physicians (chpt. pres.). Office: Physicians for a Violence-Free Soc 160 14th St San Francisco CA 94103

SALCETTI, MARIANNE, newswriter, educator; d. Robert Anthony Salcetti and Mary Jane Lusher; m. Michael Mrkvicka, May 21, 1977 (div. Mar. 1985); 1 child, Jacob Gene Mrkvicka ; m. Dale Rhines, Mar. 18, 1989 (div. June 1995); 1 child, Amalia Margaret Rhines. BA in Polit. Sci., Ohio State U., 1972, MA in Journalism, 1975; PhD in Mass. Comm., U. Iowa, 1992. Editor Franklinton News, Columbus, Ohio, 1974—76; beat reporter Chillicothe (Ohio) Gazette, 1976—77; investigative and health reporter Colorado Springs Gazette Telegraph, 1977—78; editor, co-owner The Weekly News, Johnson County, Iowa, 1980—82; instr. U. Iowa Sch. Journalism and Mass Comm., Iowa City, 1982—87; adj. faculty John Carroll U. and Ursuline Coll., Cleve., 1988—89; asst. prof. dept. comm. John Carroll U., Cleve., 1990—2000; contbg. writer The Cleve. Free Times, 1995—98; spl. projects editor The Garden City (Kans.) Telegram, 2000—02; comm. cons. Water Preservation Com., Finney County, Kans., 2002; investigator-rschr. Rebein & Bangerter, Attys. at Law, Dodge City, 2002—. Editl. radio commentator KSUI/WSUI, 1984—87; Presdl. election commentator WHK, Cleve., 1992; legis. prodr.-reporter State Capitol Update High Plains Pub. Radio, 2003; asst. prof. journalism Keene (N.H.) State Coll., 2003—; lectr. and presenter in field. Contbr. articles to profl. jours. V.p. Greater Cleve. Labor History Soc., 1997—99. Recipient Investigative Reporting award, Inland Daily Press Assn., 1977, Best News Story of the Yr. award, Iowa Press Assn., 1980, Silver Gavel award, ABA, 1981, Nat. Scholar award, Gannett Found., 1986, 1st pl. consumer reporting, Ohio Soc. Profl. Journalists, 1998, 2nd pl. best explanatory journalism, 1998, two honorable mentions, Enterprise News, 2001, honorable mention, Spot News, 2001, Bus. Reporting, 2002; Grauel Faculty fellow, John Carroll, 1995, John F. Murray Dissertation Rsch. grantee, George Meany Meml. Archives, AFL-CIO, 1987. Mem.: Kappa Tau Alpha. Avocations: reading, kayaking, gardening. Home: #2 43 S Main St Troy NH 03465 Office: Keene State Coll 229 Main St Keene NH 03435 Office Phone: 603-358-2724.

SALCUDEAN, MARTHA EVA, mechanical engineer, educator; b. Cluj, Romania, Feb. 26, 1934; arrived in Can., 1976, naturalized, 1979; d. Edmund and Sarolta (Hirsch) Abel; m. George Salcudean, May 28, 1955; 1 child, Septimiu E. BEng, U. Cluj, 1956, postgrad., 1962; PhD, U. Brasov, Romania, 1969; DSc (hon.), U. Ottawa, Ont., Can., 1992, U. B.C., 2001. Mech. engr. Armatura, Cluj, 1956-63; sr. rsch. officer Nat. Rsch. Inst. Metallurgy, Bucharest, 1963-75; part-time lectr. Inst. Poly., Bucharest, 1967-75; sessional lectr. U. Ottawa, 1976-77, from asst. prof. to assoc. prof. to prof., 1977-85; prof., head dept. mech. engring. U. B.C., Vancouver, Can., 1985-93, assoc. v.p. rsch., 1993-96, acting v.p. rsch. pro-tem, 1995, Weyerhausen Indsl. Rsch. chair computational fluid dynamics, 1996—2002, prof., Weyerhausen indsl. chair emerita dept. mech. engring., 2002—. Mem. grant selection com. for mech. engring. Natural Scis. and Engring. Rsch. Coun. Can.; mem. Nat. Adv. Panel to Min. Sci. and Tech. on advanced indsl. materials, Can., 1990; mem. governing coun. Nat. Rsch. Coun.; mem. defense science adv. bd. Dept. Nat. Def.; chair Sci. Coun. B.C. Contbr. numerous articles to profl. jours. Decorated Order of B.C., 1998; recipient Gold medal B.C. Sci. Coun., Killam Rsch. prize U. B.C. Rsch. Coun. Can. grantee, 1978—, Commemorative medal 125th anniversary Can. Confederation, 1993, Julian C. Smith medal Engring. Inst. Can., 1994-95, Meritorious Achievement award Assn. Profl. Engrs. & Geoscientists B.C., 1996, Killam Meml. prize engring., 1998, Order of B.C., 1998. Fellow CSME, Can. Acad. Engring., Royal Soc. Can.; mem. ASME, Assn. Profl. Engrs. Ont. Home: 1938 Western Pkwy Vancouver BC Canada V6T 1W5

SALE, DOROTHY O. psychotherapist; b. Boston, May 30, 1942; d. Michael Joseph O'Neil and Dorothy Mary Hommel-O'Neil; m. George Edgar Sale, June 4, 1970 (div. June 1978); m. James Trevitt Peterson, Feb. 14, 1988. BA in English Lit., Stonehill Coll., North Easton, Mass., 1963; MA in English Lit., N.Mex. State U., Las Cruces, 1969; MSW, U. Wash., Seattle, 1974; MA in Pastoral Studies, Seattle U., 2000. LCSW Wash., 1983, cert. social worker Wash., 1983. Child welfare worker Dept. Health and Social Svcs., Las Cruces and Bernalillo, N.Mex., 1964—69; alcoholism therapist Puget Sound Hosp., Tacoma, 1976—80; psychotherapist Seattle and Tacoma, Wash., 1980—2002; instr. Seattle U., 1982—85; tchr., trainer State of Wash., 1979—85; guest instr. U. Wash., Seattle, 1979—86; psychotherapist, spiritual dir. Republic, Wash., 2003—. Workshop presenter various agencies, Wash., 1979—86; vol. therapist Seattle Counseling Svcs., 1983—84; cons. Lakeside Recovery, Kirkland, Wash., 1984. Mem.: NASW. Achievements include helped found field dealing with adult children of alcoholics; development of first Native Am. foster homes on N.Mex. pueblos. Avocations: reading, music, writing, yoga, meditation. Home: PO Box 1224 83 Barrett Creek Rd Republic WA 99166

SALÉ, JAMIE, Olympic athlete, ice skater; b. Calgary, Alta., Can., Apr. 21, 1977; Profl. ice skater, Canada. Recipient (with David Pelletier) 2d pl. pairs, Can. Nat. Championships, 1999, 1st pl., 2000, 2001, 2002, ISU Four Continents, 2000, 2001, Skate Am., 2000, 2001, Skate Can., 2000, 2001, Sears Figure Skating Open, 2000, ISU Grand Prix Final, 2001, 2002, World Championships, 2001, Gold medal, 2002 Olympic Games, (with David Pelletier) Ptnrs. of the Yr. award, 30th Ann. Can. Sports awards, 2003. Office: Skate Canada 865 Shefford Rd Gloucester ON K1J 1H9 Canada

SALEM, KAREN E. information technology executive; BS in indsl. engring., Penn. State U.; MBA, U. Cin. Sr. cons. Anderson Consulting; dir. bus. solutions Burger King; v.p. info. tech. Rexall Sundown; IT head AFC Enterprises; sr. v.p. and CIO Corning Cable Sys., Winn-Dixie Stores, Inc., Jacksonville, Fla., 2002—. Office: Winn Dixie Stores Inc 5050 Edgewood Ct Jacksonville FL 32254-3699*

SALEMBIER, VALERIE BIRNBAUM, publishing executive; b. Teaneck, N.J. d. Jack and Sara (Gordon) Birnbaum; m. Paul J. Block, Dec. 9, 1990. BA, Coll. New Rochelle, 1973. Advt. dir. Ms. Mag., N.Y.C., 1976-79, assoc. pub., 1979-81; pub. Inside Sports Mag., N.Y.C., 1982; sr. v.p. advt. USA Today, 1983-88; pub. TV Guide, Radnor, PA, 1988-89; pres. N.Y. Post, N.Y.C., 1989-90, pub. Family Circle Mag., N.Y.C., 1991-93; v.p. advt. N.Y. Times, 1993-95; v.p., pub. Esquire Mag., 1996—2003; sr. v.p., pub. Harper's Bazaar, N.Y.C., 2003—. Lectr. in field. Author: (book) Rotissereie League Baseball, 1982; freelance mag. writer:. Vice chair N.Y.C. Police Found.; bd. dirs., past pres. Nat. Alliance Breast Cancer Orgns., former bd. dirs.; bd. dirs., past pres. Beneficial Orgn. Aid Ex-Fighters; former trustee Ctrl. Synagogue, Coll. New Rochelle; trustee N.Y.C. Sports Devel. Corp. Mem.: Women in Comm., Com. 200, Womens Forum. Office: Harpers Bazaar 1700 Broadway New York NY 10019

SALERNO, AMY, state legislator; m. Joe Armeni. BA, Youngstown State U., 1979; JD, Ohio State U., 1982. Bar: Ohio. Lawyer, small bus. owner, Columbus, Ohio; mem. Ohio Ho. of Reps., Columbus. Past chmn. Italian Village Commn; former mem. bd. dirs. St. Mark's Comty. HealthCtr.; former mem. Victorian Village Commn., Downtown Housing Task Force, Columbus. Recipient Appreciation cert. Italian Village Commn, Victorian Village Commn., Columbus City Coun., Outstanding Orgn. award Short North Bus. Assn.

SALERNO, CHERIE ANN (C. S. MAU), artist; b. Chgo., Nov. 21, 1948; d. Henry Jasper and Helen (Polyak) Mau; m. Kenneth Daniel Salerno; children: Nick Anthony, Brittney Ann. AAS in Advertising, Triton Coll., 1985; BFA, Art Inst. Chgo., 1999. Freelance comml. artist, Chgo., 1986-90, 2000—; artist Chgo. Fine Arts Exch., 1994-98; artist, owner C.S. Mau Studio, River Grove, Ill., 1992—; art dir., bd. dirs. Harrison St. Coop. Gallery, Oak Park, Ill., 1999—2002; art tchr. grades 3-7, 2000—03, Bethlehem Luth. Sch., River Grove, Ill., 2002—. Designer Centennial Quilt, River Grove Libr., 1988; logo designer, River Grove Sch., 1984. Designer stained glass window Bethlehem Luth. Ch., River Grove, Ill., 1999, Celebrating Diversity art exhibit, Chgo., 2002; cover designer Louie Records, Corvallis, Oreg., 1998-99, MSS Pub., Jefferson, Oreg., 2002, A440 Music Group, Chgo., for Henry Johnson and Nancy Wilson, 2003; cover artist Aim Mag., 2003-04. Vol. tchr. art Bethlehem Luth. Sch., River Grove, Ill., 1996-2002; vol. ElderCare, 1990-94. Fellow: West Suburban Art League (excellences honor 1990—2003, excellences awards 1990—), Glenview Art League (Excellence award 1996), Chgo. Artist Coalition; mem.: Oak Park Art League (bd. dirs. 1989—, arts and stds. judge 1991—93, sch. bd. 1993—94, active fundraising 1994, stds. judge 2000—, juror of artist stds., excellences merit 1990—94). Lutheran. Avocations: Japanese patio gardening, reading, aerobics and weight-lifting, sewing, gourmet cooking. Personal E-mail: cheriesart@salerno.com.

SALERNO-SONNENBERG, NADJA, violinist; b. Rome, Jan. 10, 1961; came to U.S., 1969; d. Josephine Salerno-Sonnenberg. Grad., Curtis Inst. Music, 1975, Juilliard Sch., 1982; doctorate (hon.), N.Mex. State U., 1999. Profl. debut with Phila. Orch., 1971; appearances include Am. Symphony Orch., Balt., Chgo., Cin., Detroit, Houston, Indpls., Milw., Montreal, N.Y., Pitts. symphonys, Boston Symphony Orch., Cleve., L.A. Chamber, Phila., Minn. orchs., New Orleans, N.Y., L.A. philharms.; festival appearances include Mostly Mozart Festival, Ravinia, Blossom, Meadow Brook, Gt. Woods, Caramoor, Aspen, Hollywood Bowl; internat. orchestral appearances include Vienna, Munich, Stuttgart, Frankfurt, Geneva, Rotterdam, Lisbon, Tokyo; featured on 60 Minutes, CBS, CBS Sunday Morning, NBC Nat. News, PBS Live from Lincoln Ctr., CNN Newsstand, Charlie Rose Show, Sesame Street; numerous appearances on The Tonight Show with Johnny Carson; rec. artist Capitol Classics and Jazz Records, 1987—, Nonesuch, 1996—; subject of documentary: Speaking in Strings, 1999 (film nominated for Oscar 2000). Recipient 1st prize Naumburg Violin Competition, N.Y.C., 1981; Avery Fisher Career grantee., N.Y.C., 1983, Avery Fisher prize, N.Y.C., 1999. Mem. AFTRA, Screen Actors Guild. Office: care M L Falcone Pub Rels 155 W 68th St Ste 114 New York NY 10023-5808

SALES, CATHERINE, special education educator; b. N.Y.C., July 30, 1966; d. Nicholas Sales and Carol Ann Romano. BS in Spl. Edn. magna cum laude, Manhattan Coll., 1988; MS in Spl. Edn., Fordham U., 1991; EdM in Instrnl. Practices, Columbia U., 1997, EdD in Spl. Edn., 1998. Cert. spl. edn. tchr. Sch. Adminstrn. and Supervision, behavior analyst. Spl. edn. tchr. Fred S. Keller Sch., Yonkers, N.Y., 1988-92, asst. behavior analyst, 1992-93, curriculum coord., 1993-94, individualized edn. plan coord., 1994-97, spl. edn. hinerant tchr. coord., 1997—. Mem. Internat. Soc. for Behaviorology (chair student support com. 1997-98), Assn. for Behavior Analysis, Calif. State Assn. for Behavior Analysis, N.Y. State Assn. for Behavior Analysis, Epsilon Sigma Pi, Kappa Delta Pi. Democrat. Avocations: photography, Okinawan karate (1st deg. black belt). Fax: 914-965-1419. E-mail: dancingcat@msn.com.

SALETTA, MARY ELIZABETH (BETTY SALETTA), sculptor, rancher; b. Miami, Fla., Sept. 30, 1941; d. Earl Robert and Alta Florence Cotner; m. Albert Michael Saletta, July 1, 1959; children: Tia Suzanne, Kamber Ann. Graphic artist Moore Bus. Forms Inc., Modesto, Calif., 1960-67, Live Oak Pub. Co., Oakdale, Calif., 1977-80; freelance artist U.S. Forest Svc., Modesto Irrigation Dist., Stanislaus Schs., New Don Pedro Dam Project, Calif., 1967-77; sculptor Saletta Sculpture, Oakdale, 1980—. Mem. adv. bd. Calif. State U. Coll. Arts, Letters and Sci., Turlock, 1999-2002; charter mem., dir. Downtown Arts Project, Modesto, 1992-96. One-woman shows City of Oakdale Redevel. Agy., 1990, Modesto C. of C., 1996; group shows include Calif. State U. Stanislaus, Turlock, 1986, Cowboy Artist Am. Mus., Kerrville, Tex., 1988, Benson Park Sculpture Garden, Loveland, Colo., 1989, 90, 93, Danada Sculpture Garden, Chgo., 1991, 93, Tucson Mus. Art, 1995; represented in permanent collections Tucson Mus. Art, Buckaroo Hall of Fame, cities of Modesto, Oakdale, Ripon, Calif., Stockton, Calif.; sculptures include life-size pub. sculptures Yesterday Is Tomorrow, 1991, Am. Graffiti, 1997, Stockton Firefighters Meml., 1998, World War II Meml., 1999, Nursing, the Finest Art, 2001, Chief Estanislao, 2001, Firefighter Sculpture produced at Laguna Beach Pageant of the Masters, 2002. Recipient Excellence in Fine Art award Bank Am., Stockton, Calif., 1959, Best of Show award Western Art Roundup, Winnamucca, Nev., 1987, 88, Excellence in Visual Arts award Stanislaus Arts Coun., Modesto, 1999. Mem. Nat. League Am. Pen Women, Ctrl. Calif. Art League (advisor 1991, Best of Show award 1987), Rotary (bd. dirs. Oakdale 1997-99). Democrat. Avocations: horses, skiing, mountain climbing, fishing. Home: 4255 Wellsford Rd Oakdale CA 95361-7930 Fax: 209-572-4089. E-mail: salettasculpture@aol.com.

SALGADO, SUSANA, musicologist, researcher, consultant; b. Montevideo, Uruguay, June 14, 1927; d. Juan Andres Salgado, Amelia Gomez-Eirin; m. Roberto O. Morassi. Musicologist, School of Humanities (Dept. of Musicology), Montevideo, Uruguay, 1954—65. Chair Uruguayan Music Rsch. Sch. Humanities, Dept. Musicology, Montevideo, Uruguay, 1965—71; cons., music divsn. Libr. Congress, Washington, 1994—. Mem. bd. advisors Garland Publishing for Opera performances, New York, 1992—; lectr. in field. Author: (Scholarly Book) The Teatro Solis, 150 Years of Opera, Concert and Ballet in Montevideo, 2003, Breve Historia de la Musica Culta en el Uruguay, Montevideo, 1971, 1980; contbr. 5 Grove Dictionaries including Opera, Music and Musicians, Women Composers, Am. Composers, 1980, 5 Grove Dictionaries including Opera, Music and Musicians, Women Composers, Am. Composers 2d edit., 2001, articles to profl. jours. N/A. N/A. Mem.: Women National Book Association. Avocation: Traveling, swimming, walking. E-mail: saisalgado@aol.com.

SALHANY, LUCILLE S. broadcast executive; Formerly with Paramount Pictures; pres. Paramount Domestic Television, from 1985; chmn. Twentieth Television, a unit of Fox Inc., 1991-92, Fox Broadcasting Co., Beverly Hills, Calif., 1993-94; pres. United ParamountNetwork, 1994-97; pres., CEO JH Media, Boston, 1998—, HJ Media. Office: JH Media 34 Strawberry Hill St Dover MA 02030-2250

SALIS, JEANNE ELAINE, artist; b. Phila., Pa., Apr. 19, 1946; d. Herbert and Gladys Diane (Fomalont) Salis; m. Robert B. Hurwitz, June 29, 1969 (div. Dec. 1991); children: Joshua, Zachary; m. Agustín Reyna, Aug. 1, 2003. BA, U. Pa., 1968; MA, Ind. U., 1971, MS, 1974; MFA, Art Inst. Chgo., 1986. Adj. faculty Moraine Valley C.C., Palos Hills, Ill., 1986—92; from assoc. & program developer to v.p. cmty. svcs. Chgo. Children's Mus., Chgo., 1991—2001, v.p. cmty. svcs., 2001—02. Cons. Shanti Found., Evanston, Ill., 1997—2002, Cuentos Found., Chgo., 1997—2003. One-woman shows include A.R.C. Gallery, Chgo., 1989, McHenry C.C., Crystal Lake, Ill., 1989, Oakton C.C., Des Plaines, Ill., 1989, St. Xavier Coll., Chgo., 1990, Casa de Cultura Jesus Reyes Heroles, Coyoacan, Mexico City, 2003, exhibited in group shows at Judith Racht Gallery, Lakeside, Mich., 1989, Beverly Art Ctr., Chgo., 1996, Brickton Gallery, Pk. Ridge, Ill., 1998, SAIC Gallery, Chgo., 1998, 1999, Polvo Gallery, 1999, ARC Gallery, 1999, pvt. collections. Adv. com. Bethel Culural Arts Ctr., Chgo., 1999—2002; bd. dir. Onward Neighborhood House, Chgo., 1998—2001. Grantee Cmty. Arts Assistance Program grant, Chgo., 1999, 2000, 2001; Ragdale Found. fellowship, Lake Forest, Ill., 1988, 1989. Mem.: Chgo. Cultural Inst. Outreach Network (chmn. 1995—2002), Ill. Alliance for Art Edn. (exec. bd. 2000—02, sec. 2000—02). Avocations: guitar, Spanish language. Mailing: Ahuehuetes 55 Jardines de San Mateo Naucalpan Edo de México 53420 Mexico E-mail: j_salis@yahoo.com.

SALISBURY, ALICIA LAING, state senator; b. N.Y.C., Sept. 20, 1939; d. Herbert Farnsworth and Augusta Belle (Marshall) Laing; m. John Eagan Salisbury, June 23, 1962; children: John Eagan Jr., Margaret Salisbury La Rue. Student, Sweet Briar Coll., 1957-60; BA, Kans. U., 1961. Mem. Kans. Senate, 1985—, v.p., chmn. commerce com., telecomm. stragegic planning, 1995, vice chmn. ways and means com., mem. utilities com., jt. com. on econ. devel., mem. orgn. and calendar rules com., mem. jt. com. corrections and juvenile justice, mem. confirmations oversight com. Elected mem. State Bd. Edn., Topeka, 1981-85, Kans.; past pres. Jr. League of Topeka; trustee Leadership Kans., 1982-89; bd. dirs. Topeka Cmty. Found., 1983—, Topeka Pub. Sch. Found., 1985-89, Capitol Area Pla. Authority, 1989—, Kans. Inc., 1996—, Mid-Am. Mfg. Tech. Ctr., 1994-96, mem. workers' compensation fund oversight com., 1993— Stormont-Vail Hosp. Aux.; mem. adv. commn. Juvenile Offenders Program, Kans., 1985-95; mem. adv. bd. Topeka State Hosp., Kans. Action for Children, 1982—, Kans. Ins. Edn. Found., 1984-95, Youth Ctr. at Topeka, 1987—; steering com. One Stop Career Ctr., 1996, Interstate Cooperation Com. Coun. State Govts.; mem. Nat. Fedn. Rep. Women; past bd. mem. United Way Greater Topeka, ARC, Family Svc. and Guidance, Topeka, Shawnee County Mental Health Assn., Florence Crittenton Svcs., Topeka, Topeka City Commn. Govtl. Adv. Com.; chmn. Topeka State Hosp. Grounds Adv. Com.; mem. Kans. Workforce Investment Partnership Coun. Recipient Woman of Yr. award Topeka Panhellenic Coun., 1997. Mem. Nat. Conf. State Legislators (exec. com.), Nat. Rep. Legislators' Assn. (Nat. Rep. Legislator of Yr. 1993, Gold Rose award 1992, Bus. Guardian award 1990, 99, Outstanding Individual Legis. Achievement award 1989), Shawnee County Rep. Women, Kans. State Hist. Soc. (exec. com.), Kappa Kappa Gamma. Episcopalian. Avocations: tennis, downhill skiing, water sports, horseback ridng, gardening. Office: Kans State Senate State Capital Topeka KS 66612

SALISBURY, HOLLY BUCKNER, university arts director; b. Paris, Ky., Apr. 29, 1945; d. Catlett Lockhart and Marjorie Witherspoon (Routt) Buckner; m. William Benson Salisbury III, Aug. 24, 1967 (div. 1980); children: Leila Witherspoon, Brent Buckner. Student, L'Acad. de Belle Arte, Florence, Italy, 1965-66; BA, George Washington U., 1967. Art tchr. Charles County (Md.) Pub. Schs., 1967-70, Pks. and Recreation Dept., Prince George County, Md., 1970-73; dir. Singletary Ctr. for Arts U. Ky., Lexington, 1979—. Pres. Cen. Ky. Youth Orch., Lexington, 1986-88; site coord. Gov's. Sch. for Arts Lexington, 1988—. Editor (booklet) Artworks, 1983. Active Lexington Forum, 1986—; bd. dirs. Lexington Arts and Cultural Coun., 1989-90, Opera Cen. Ky., 1989—, Ky. Citizens for Arts, 1989—. Mem. Am. Bus. Women's Assn., Assn. Performing Arts Presenters (membership com.), U. Ky. Faculty Club, Lexington Arts Cultural Coun., Jr. League Lexington. Episcopalian. Avocation: painting. Home: 30 Mentelle Park Lexington KY 40502-1512

SALISBURY, TAMARA PAULA, foundation executive; b. N.Y.C., Dec. 14, 1927; d. Paul Terrance and Nadine (Korolkova) Voloshin; m. Franklin Cary Salisbury, Jan. 22, 1955; children: Franklin Jr., John, Elizabeth, Elaine, Claire. BA, Coll. Notre Dame, 1948; postgrad., Am. U., George Washington U. Chemist depts. pathology and chemotherapy NIH Cancer Inst., Bethesda, Md., 1946-52; asst. to chief of Chemistry Br. Office of Naval Rsch., Bethesda, 1953-55; v.p., COO Nat. Found. Cancer Rsch., Bethesda, 1973—. Mem. Assn. Internat. Cancer Rsch., 1995. Decorated d'Officier De L'Ordre De Leopold II; outstanding contbns. award Internat. Soc. Quantum Biology, 1983, award of appreciation Beth Israel Hosp., Harvard Med. Sch., Brigham & Women's Hosp., 1993. Mem. AAAS, Am. Chem. Soc., N.Y. Acad. Scis., Inst. Phys. and Chem. Biology (fgn.), Krebforschung Internat., Nat. Liberal Club. Home: 10811 Alloway Dr Potomac MD 20854-1504 Office: Nat Found Cancer Rsch 4600 E West Hwy Ste 525 Bethesda MD 20814-6900

SALLEE, MARGUERITE, association executive; m. Knox Sallee; 4 children. Grad., Duke U. Commr. Tenn. Dept. Hunan Svcs.; co-chmn., co-founder, pres., CEO CorporateFamily Solutions; co-chmn. Bright Horizons Family Solutions (formerly CorporateFamily), Cambridge, Mass. Dir. MagneTek, Inc., Bank Am., Tenn. and Ky., Ladies Profl. Golf Assn. Mem. Acad. Women of Achievement (Corp. Leadership award), Nashville Area C. of C. (chair). Office: Bright Horizons Family Solutions One Kendall Sq Bldg 200 Cambridge MA 02139

SALLEE, MARY LOU, state legislator; Mem. Mo. State Ho. of Reps. Dist. 144. Home: PO Box 128 Ava MO 65608-0128 Office: Mo Ho of Reps State Capitol Building Jefferson City MO 65101-1556

SALLOWAY, JOSEPHINE PLOVNICK, psychologist, educator, marriage and family therapist; b. Brookline, Mass., July 30, 1944; d. Isadore B. and Gladys J. (Press) Plovnick; m. Richard B. Salloway, July 4, 1967; 1 child, Matthew. AB in History, Boston U., 1965, EdM in Counseling, 1966; cert. in human resource mgmt., Bentley Coll., 1980. Cert. sch. psychologist, sch. adjustment counselor, history and social studies tchr.; clinically cert. forensic counselor, domestic violence counselor; lic. mental health counselor, marriage and family therapist; cert. psychologist. Counselor Boston Pub. Schs., 1966-78; counselor, psychologist ednl. enrichment program Milton (Mass.) Acad., 1970-71; psychologist Braintree (Mass.) Pub. Schs., 1983-89; psychologist, adjustment counselor Norwood Pub. Schs., 1990-92; sch. adjustment counselor Stoughton, Mass., 1993-94; cons. psychologist Waltham (Mass.) Schs., 1997—2000; pvt. practice Braintree, 1997—. Faculty psychology and child devel. Quincy (Mass.) Coll., 1997—, head counselor student support advisor, 1997-2003; faculty psychology and early childhood edn. and devel., faculty advisor Massasoit C.C., 1999—; faculty Program for Advancement of Learning Curry Coll., 1999, faculty psychology, 2000—, diagnostic tchr. Edn. and Diagnostic Ctr., 1999-00; field supr. dept. counselor edn. Harvard U., Cambridge, Mass., Northeastern U., Boston; del. Coastline Coun. for Children, Mass., 1985-2000, del. Mass. Soc. for Prevention of Cruelty to Children, 1998—; psychometrist Mass. Gen. Hosp., Boston; asst. coord. Boston U. Counseling Clinic; diagnostic tchr. Braintree, Mass., 1999-2002, Mass. Edn. Reform, Tutor, Canton Pub. Schs., 2000; mem. edn. reform Mass. Comprehensive Assessment Sys., 2000; commn. on child advocacy and domestic violence Dist. Atty.'s Office, 2000-02; lectr., presenter in field. Pub. dir. Curtain Call Theatre, 1997; contbg. editor Gazette newsletter, 1996— Class agt. Boston U. Alumni Assn., 1996—; ednl. dir. House of Worship, Braintree, 1994—; del. Braintree Fair Housing Commn., 1994-2000, Braintree Multicultural Com., 1994-2000; pres., bd. chmn. Cmty. Friends for Human Svcs., Inc., Boston, 1995—, chmn. edn. bd.; vol. Genesis Fund Telethon. Recipient Presdl. award Cmty. Friends for Human Svcs., Inc., 1996-97, 2001, Svc. award, 1998, 99, 2001, 03, Senatorial award, 1998; award for contbn. to svcs. for children Mass. Soc. for Prevention Cruelty to Children, 1998, 99, Senatorial award for outstanding contbn. to mental health Mass. Senate, 1998, award for contrbn. to Adult and Family Edn., 2003, Award for Contbr. Edn. N.E. Educators Assn., 2003. Mem. APA, AAUP, ACA (clin.), NASP, NAMP, Nat. Assn. Cert. Forensic Counselors, Am. Assn. Marriage and Family Therapists (clin.), N.E. Assn. Coll. Educators, Mass. Assn. Sch. Adjustment Counselors, Mass. Assn. Marriage and Family Therapists, Mass. Assn. Mental Health Counselors, Mass. Tchrs. Assn., Pi Lambda Theta, Scarlet Key. Avocations: antique collecting, reading, travel, volunteer work, theater. Home: 57 Cochato Rd Braintree MA 02184-4628 E-mail: jsalloway@aol.com.

SALMELA, LYNN MARIE, clinical nurse specialist; b. Albert Lea, Minn., Mar. 29, 1960; d. Melvin Raymond and Patricia Lou (Bushey) Salmela. BSN, Winona State U., 1982; MSN, Coll. St. Scholastica, 2000; compliant documentation mgmt. course, J.A. Thomas & Assocs., 2000; attended for ambulatory electronic med. record tng., Epic Sys., Corp., 2003. RN Minn., Wis., cert. pub. health nurse, Minn., intravenous therapy nurse. Staff nurse Milw. Children's Hosp. (now Children's Hosp. of Wis.), 1982—83, Mpls. Children's Hosp., 1983—86, St. Mary's Duluth (Minn.) Clinic, 1986—2001; adj. faculty mem. Coll. of St. Scholastica, Duluth, 1998—99; compliant Documentation Mgmt. Coord. St. Luke's Hosp., Duluth, 2000—03; Epicare edn. specialist St. Mary's Duluth Clinic Health Sys., 2003—. Author: (newsletter) Volunteer Link, St. Mary's Grief Support Ctr., 1993, 1995—96; contbr. articles to profl. publs. and newspapers. Vol. presch. screening programs, Winona, Minn., 1981—82; vol. blood screening clinic, Milw., 1982; vol. med. staff Grandma's Marathon, Duluth, 1989; vol. St. Mary's Grief Support Ctr., Duluth, 1993—97. Recipient 1st Pl. award, Amateur Still Life Category, photography contest, 2001, 1st Pl. award portrait category, Photography Contest, 2002; scholar Presdl. scholar, Winona State U., 1978. Mem.: Intravenous Nurses Soc., Nat. Assn. Clin. Nurse Specialists, Sigma Theta Tau. Republican. Avocations: walking, music, photography, writing, cooking. Home: 110 S 58th Ave E Duluth MN 55804

SALMON, BETH ANN, magazine editor in chief; b. Syracuse, N.Y., Oct. 1, 1969; d. Richard George and Sharon Dian (Clark) S. BFA, Emerson Coll., 1991. Edtl. asst. Let's Live mag., L.A., 1994, asst. editor, 1994-95, editor in chief, 1995—. Author: (screenplays) Postcards, 1994, Watch Me, 1995. Office: Lets Live Magazine 11050 Santa Monica Blvd Los Angeles CA 90025-3594

SALMON, MARGARET BELAIS, nutritionist, dietitian; b. N.Y.C. m. Douglas A. Salmon; children: Robert, Betty Lynn, Donald. BS in Food Chemistry, Dietetics and Nutrition, U. Calif., Berkeley, 1941; MS in Human Nutrition, Columbia U., 1964, MS in Sci. Nutrition, 1982. cert. Hosp. Dietetics, Duke U. Hosp., 1943; specialist Nutrition Edn., Columbia U., 1967. Clin. dietitian Columbia-Presbyn. Med. Ctr., N.Y.C., 1943-44, research dietitian, 1956-66; teaching and therapeutic dietitian Englewood (N.J.) Hosp., Hackensack (N.J.) Hosp. and Holy Name Hosp., 1954-57; adminstrv. and therapeutic dietitian St. Luke's Hosp. Ctr., N.Y.C., 1966-70; chief dietitian, dir. dietetic traineeship program St. Joseph's Hosp. and Med. Ctr., Paterson, N.J., 1971-82; pres. Salmon Cons., Harrington Park, N.J., 1970—. Assoc. dir. dietary dept. Bronx (N.Y.)-Lebanon Hosp. Ctr., 1970-71; lectr. in field. Author: Soy Discoveries: Over 700 Quick Soy Recipes, 2001, Diabetic Diet Handbook, 1998, Food Facts for Teenagers, 1965, 2d edit., 2003, (with A. Colby) Physician's Diet Handbook, 1975, rev., 1978, The Joy of Breastfeeding, 1977, 2d rev. edit., 1979, Diabetic Diet Handbook, 1977, Dieta Diabetica Para Buena Salud, 1979, Diabetic Diet Handbook for Low Sodium Diets, 1980, Breast Milk: Nature's Perfect Formula, 1994, Soy Expressions: Common Sense Way to Small Food Bills, 1999, Soy Discoveries: Over 700 Quick Soy Recipes, 2001; editor: Enjoying Your Restricted Diet, 1972, St. Joseph's Hosp. & Med. Ctr. Diet Man., 1977, rev., 1981; contbr. Career Guidance for Young Women, 1974, Easy and Delicious Rice Flour Recipes, 1974, A Professional Dietitian's Natural Fiber Diet, 1987, La Alegria De Alimentacion A Pecho (Joy of Breastfeeding, in spanish), 1987; contbr. articles profl. books and jours.; numerous TV appearances. Mary Swarz Rose scholar, 1961. Mem. Am. Dietetic Assn., Pi Lambda Theta, Omicron Nu, Kappa Delta Pi. Home: 435 Lynn St Harrington Park NJ 07640-1131 Office: Salmon Cons 435 Lynn St Harrington Park NJ 07640-1131

SALMON, MARLA E. nursing educator, dean; b. Vermillion, S.D., May 2, 1949; d. Everett Lloyd and Marceline Louise (Adamson) S.; m. Jerry Steven Anderson, Aug. 1, 1984; children: Jessica Louise White, Matthew Lawrence White. BA cum laude, U. Portland, 1971, BSN cum laude, 1972; MSN, 1999; ScD, Johns Hopkins U., 1977; DSc (hon.), UNMC, 2003. Dir. patient advocacy program Johns Hopkins U., Balt., 1974-75, instr., 1975-78; asst. prof. U. Minn., Mpls., 1978-82, asst. dir. PRONA, 1978-79, acting dir. PRONA, 1978-80, dir. pub. health nursing programs, 1980-85, assoc. prof., 1982-86; prof. pub. health nursing, chmn. dept. U. N.C., Chapel Hill, 1986-92; dir. nursing div., Bureau Health Professions HHS, Rockville, 1991-97; prof., dean Grad. Sch. Nursing U. Pa., Phila., 1997-99, dir. grad. studies; dean, prof. Nell Hodgson Woodruff Sch. Nursing Emory U., 1999—. Trustee Robert Wood Johnson Found., 2002—; mem. Presdl. Task Force Health Care Reform, Washington, 1993; U.S. del. WHO, Geneva, 1995; cons. in field. Co-editor News Outlook, 1989-91; contbr. articles to profl. jours. Fulbright scholar, 1972-73; W.K. Kellogg fellow, 1984-87, Reflective Leadership fellow, 1985-86; Rsch. grantee, 1975-78; recipient Recognition award Assn. State Territorial Dirs. of Nursing, 1993, Achievement award Nat. Black Nurses Found., 1994, Presdl. award for meritorious exec. The White House, 1995. Mem. ANA (v.p. coun. community health nursing, 1988—, task force credentialing 1989), Am. Acad. Nursing, Am. Pub. Health Assn., Am. Tae Kwon Do Assn., Nat. League Nursing, N.C. League Nursing, N.C. Pub. Health Assn., N.C. Nurses Assn., Assn. Community Health Nurses Educators, Women's Health Leadership Trust, Sigma Theta Tau, Sigma Xi, Delta Omega. Avocations: athletics, gardening. Office: Emory U Nell Hodgson Woodruff Sch 1520 Clifton Rd Ste 402 Atlanta GA 30322-4207

SALNY, ABBIE FEINSTEIN, psychologist; b. N.Y.C., July 3, 1926; d. Carl and Edith (Cooperman) Feinstein; m. Jerome E. Salny, July 12, 1973. BA, NYU, 1949; MA, Montclair State U., 1953; EdD, Rutgers U., 1966. Lic. psychologist, N.J.; diplomate Am. bd. Profl. Psychology. Sch. psychologist Bd. of Edn., Parsippany, N.J., 1959-66; prof., dep. chair, acting chair psychology dept. Montclair State U., 1966-79; supervisory psychologist Am. and Internat. Mensa, 1979—; trustee Mensa Edn. and Rsch. Found., 1971-96. Chmn. scholarship com. Mensa Edn. and Rsch. Found., 1973-82, dir. sci. and edn. Am. Mensa com., 1983-87, dir. rsch. rev. com., 1984-88. Co-author: Mensa Genius Quiz Book, 1981, Mensa Genius Quiz Book II, 1983, Mensa Think Smart Book, 1985; author: Quiz-A-Day Book, 1986, Book of Literary Quizzes, 1988, Page-A-Day Puzzle Calendar, 1995—, others; contbr. articles to profl. jours. Fellow Am. Acad. of Sch. Psychologists; mem. Am. Psychol. Assn., N.J. Psychol. Assn., British Psychol. Soc., Am. Soc. of Journalists and Authors, Am. Mensa Ltd. Avocations: travel, cooking. Home and Office: 407 Breckenridge Wayne NJ 07470-4072

SALO, ANN SEXTON DISTLER, lawyer; b. Indpls., Sept. 2, 1947; d. Harry W. and Ann (Malloy) Distler; m. Donald R. Salo, June 3, 1972 (div. Feb. 1983); 1 child, Eric V. Salo; m. Phillip G. Clark, May 5, 1990; children: Ann Potter Clark, Philip Gray Clark. BA, Purdue U., 1969; JD, George Washington U., 1972; LLM in Taxation, Emory U., 1976. Bar: Ga. 1973, U.S. Dist. Ct. (no. dist.) Ga. 1974. Assoc. Hansell & Post, Atlanta, 1972-78, mng. ptnr., 1978-89; ptnr. Grenwald and Salo, Atlanta, 1989-92, Long, Aldridge & Norman, Atlanta, 1992-95, Salo & Walker, Atlanta, 1995—. Adj. prof. law Emory U., 1983-86; mem. fin. planning adv. bd. Warren Gorham & Lamont, 1988-2000. Author: Estate Planning, 1988. Bd. dirs. Auditory Edn. Ctr., Atlanta, 1987-93, 98-2001; pres. Planned Parenthood of Atlanta, 1984-86; pres. Atlanta Humane Soc., 1990-93. Fellow Am. Coll. Trust and Estate Counsel (state chair 2001—); mem. Atlanta Estate Planning Coun., Atlanta Tax Forum. Office: Salo & Walker 2968 Lookout Pl NE Atlanta GA 30305-3272 E-mail: adsalo@bellsouth.net.

SALOMON, MARILYN, artist; b. Ann Arbor, Mich., Jan. 30, 1943; d. William Iane and Sarah Sheon; m. Charles Sam. Salomon, Dec. 22, 1962; children: Teri(dec.), Alicia, Cliff. BA, UCLA, 1965; postgrad., Calif. State U., Northridge, 1969-70, 88, Miriam Ariav, Israel, 1970. Elem. edn. tchr., Simi Valley, Calif., 1966-69; artist, 1970—. Guest lectr. Internat. Batik Conf., Ghent, Belgium, 1999, Scottsdale Art League, 2003; asst. art curator mus. show, Lancaster, Calif., 1993; leader workshop Surface Designer Nat. Conf., Calif. State U., Northridge, 1988; represented by Horizon Fine Arts, Jackson, Wyo., Judith Hale Gallery, Los Olivos, Calif., Studios Gallery, La Quinta, Calif., Feats of Clay, Idyllwild, Calif., Pepper Tree Show, Santa Ynez, Calif., 2003; participant Internat. Batik Exhibit, Hanover, Germany, 2002, Internat. Batik Exhibit, Cologne, Germany, 2002, Internat. Batik Exhibit, Dortmund, Germany, 2002, Ryman Found. show, 2000-03, Koln, Germany, 2002, Dortmund, 2003; lectr. in field; subject of TV interview Process of Batik, 2001. One-woman shows include Ranch House, Ojai, Calif., 1975-78, Gallerie 507, Carlsbad, Calif., 1984, Sun West Gallery, Prescott, Ariz., 1986, Art Beat Gallery, Agoura, Calif., 1987, Jewish Cmty. Ctr., Long Beach, Calif., 1985; exhibited in group shows at Cygnet Gallery, Santa Rosa, Calif., 1981, Jewish Fedn. Bldg., Olympic Exhbn., L.A., 1984, La Quinta Arts Found., 1985-91, Thousand Oaks Mus., 1988-89 (1st pl. 1988, Purchase award 1989), Calif. Luth. U., 1989, Nat. Mus. History, Santa Barbara, Calif., 1990, City of La Quinta, 1991 (Purchase award), Lancaster Mus., 1992-93, 98, Conejo Valley Mus., 1992 (2d pl. award), Riverside Mus. Art, 1998, Walt Disney Ryman Found., Burbank, Calif., featured artist, 1997-99, Horizen Fine Arts, Jackson, 2002; represented in permanent collections City of Tempe, City of Thousand Oaks, City of La Quinta, Taft Entertainment, 1983, Cancer Inst. Ariz., 1983; featured in TV interview KTVK, Ariz., 2000; works appear in Batik for Artists & Quilters, 2000. Workshop leader Surface Designer's Nat. Conf., Calif. State U., Northridge, 1988; studio home tour Westlake Art Guild, Calif., 1989, Pan Hellenic Home Tour Riverside featured Salomon's Art, 1986. Recipient purchase award City of Tempe, Ariz., 1983, City of Thousand Oaks, Calif., 1989, City of La Quinta, 1991. Mem. (elected charter mem.) Women's Nat. Mus., Phoenix Art Mus. Avocations: hiking, yoga, reading, music. Home: HC 2 Box 261D Payson AZ 85541-9418

SALONGA, LEA, actress, singer; b. Manila, Feb. 22, 1971; d. Feliciano Genuino and Maria Ligaya (Imutan) S. Attended, Ateneo De Manila U., 1988-89. Actress, singer The King and I, Manila, 1978, Annie, Manila, 1980, The Rose Tattoo, Manila, 1980, The Bad Seed, Manila, 1981, The Goodbye Girl, Manila, 1982, Paper Moon, Manila, 1983, The Fantasticks, Manila, 1988, Miss Saigon, London, 1989-90 (Outstanding Performance by Actress in Musical Olivier award 1990), Broadway, 1991-92 (Best Actress in Musical Tony award 1991, Best Actress in Musical Drama Desk award 1991, Best Actress in Musical Outer Critics Circle award 1991, Outstanding Debut Theatre World award 1991), Les Miserables, Broadway, 1993, My Fair Lady, Manila, 1994, Into the Woods, Singapore, 1994, Les Miserables, London, 1996, 3rd nat. tour, 1996, also The Sound of Music, Manila, Fiddler on the Roof, Manila, Cat on a Hot Tin Roof; Philippine films include Bakit Labis Kitang Mahal?, Dear Diary, Pik Pak Boom, Captain Barbell, Ninja Kids, Like Father, Like Son, Tropang Bulilit; Philippine TV: (host) Kulit Bulilit, Love Lea, Naku, Ha!, Sunday Special, Iba Ito!, That's Entertainment!, This is It!, (co-host) Patok Na Patok!; opening act for Stevie Wonder, Menudo; concerts: The Filipinos of Miss Saigon, A Miss Called Lea, Lea Salonga in Concert, L.A., San Francisco, Les Miserables 10th Anniversary Concert, London, 1995; recs. include Small Voice, 1981 (gold record), Lea, Happy Children's Club, Christmas Album, We are the World, (debut album) Lea Salonga, 1993, Miss Saigon original London cast rec. (gold record), The King and I, Aladdin, 1992 (singing voice Princess Jasmine, motion picture soundtrack), Les Miserables 10th Anniversary Concert Album, 1996, Royal Couyabyab: The Silver Album, 1996, The Little Tramp, (singing voice) Mulan, 1998, (Broadway) Flower Drum Song, 2002; TV films include: Redwood Curtain, 1998, (TV series) As the World Turns, 2001, 03. Recipient AWIT award outstanding svc. Philippings Recording Industry, 1993, ASEAN Industry award performing arts, 1992, Ten Outstanding Young Men award outstanding debut, 1991, AWIT award outstanding performer, 1990, Presdl. Award of Merit Pres. Aquino, 1990, Laurence Olivier award best actress musical, 1990, Cecil award best recording by a child, 1984, Tinig award one of 10 outstanding singers, 1983, 94, 92, ALIW award best child performer, 1980, 81, 82; named Outstanding Manilan by Govt. City of Manila, 1990. Mem. AFTRA, Actors' Equity Assn., Screen Actors' Guild. Roman Catholic. Avocations: music, reading, collecting raised-trunk elephants, collecting swatches, working on computers. Office: c/o Jeff Hunter 1325 Avenue Of The Americas New York NY 10019-6026 Address: 205 W 54th St Apt 9C New York NY 10019-5532

SALSITZ, ELENA L. city official; married. Chief of protocol NASA/Johnson Space Ctr., Houston, 1989—90, 1990—95, Office of the Mayor, San Diego, 2000—; spl. asst. to the social sec. The White House, Exec. Office of the Pres., Washington, 1994. Mem. exec. com., bd. dirs. Japan Soc. of San Diego & Tijuana, 2001—.

SALTER, LINDA LEE, security officer; b. Garden City, Mich., Oct. 10, 1953; d. Bertram Edward Salter and Gertrude Thersa (Barnes) Honeycutt; children: Korina Reshell Irene Miller, Terry Wayne Tomlin II. Grad., Henry Ford C.C., 1998; student, U. Detroit, 1999. Security supr. Guardsmark, Memphis, 1979-86, security officer, 1986-96, Detroit, 1998—, Detroit Newspapers, 1986-96, advt. officer, 1996—. Emergency first aid specialist ARC, Dearborn, Mich., 1993—. Mem. St. Anne's Cath. Ch.; pres. Downriver/Monroe County Women Involved Wings, South Rockwood, Mich., 1991—; mem. Lupus Found., 1995—, Monroe County Humane Soc., 1993—, Ladies Aux., 1971—; reunion class tchr. Carlson HS, Gibraltar, Mich., 1971. Mem.: Humane Soc. Warren County Tenn., Mich. Humane Soc., C. of C. Huron Twp. Roman Catholic. Avocations: reading, travel, horses, sports, gardening. Home: 22033 Verdun St Romulus MI 48174-9533 Office: Detroit Newspapers 615 W Lafayette Blvd Detroit MI 48226-3197 E-mail: llsalt@prodigy.net.

SALTER, MARY JO, poet; b. Grand Rapids, Aug. 15, 1954; d. Albert Gregory and Lormina (Paradise) S.; m. Brad Leithauser, 1980; children: Emily Salter, Hilary Garner. BA cum laude, Harvard U., 1976; MA, Cambridge U., 1978. Instr. Harvard U., 1978-79; instr. English conversation Japan, 1980-83; lectr. English Mt. Holyoke Coll., South Hadley, Mass., 1984—, Emily Dickinson sr. lectr. in humanities, 1995—. Staff editor Atlantic Monthly, 1978-80; poet-in-residence Robert Frost Place, 1981; poetry editor The New Republic, 1992-95. Author: Henry Purcell in Japan, 1985, Unfinished Painting, 1989 (Lamont prize in poetry 1988), The Moon Comes Home, 1989, Sunday Skaters: Poems, 1994 (Nat. Book Critics Circle award nomination 1994), A Kiss in Space: Poems, 1999, Open Shutters: Poems, 2003; co-editor: Norton Anthology of Poetry, 4th edit., 1996; contbr. to periodicals including New Yorker, New Republic, Kenyon

Rev. Amy Lowell scholar, 1995; recipient Discovery prize Nation, 1983; Nat. Endowment for Arts fellow, 1983-84, Guggenheim fellow, 1993. Mem. Internat. P.E.N. Office: care Alfred A Knopf Inc 1745 Broadway New York NY 10019 E-mail: njsalter@mtholyoke.edu.

SALTUS, PHYLLIS BORZELLIERE, music educator; b. Rochester, N.Y., Jan. 17, 1931; d. Nicholas and Sadie Veronica (Leone) Borzelliere; m. William Thomas Saltus, Aug. 21, 1965 (div. Apr. 1991); children: Julie Marie Nicole, William Nicholas. AA, Burlington County Coll., Pemberton, N.J., 1987; MEd in Measurement and Guidance, U. Maine, Orono, 1963; BS in Music Edn., SUNY, 1953, MS, 1957. Cert. student personnel svcs., music and guidance, N.J., N.Y., Me. Music tchr., choral dir. Rochester Pub. Schs., 1953-56, 62-63, 1969-70, high sch. guidance counselor, 1963-65; asst. prof. music edn. SUNY, Geneseo and Fredonia, 1956-62; music tchr, choral dir. Concord (Mass.) Pub. Schs., 1965-66; owner, dir. Saltus Music Studio, Medford, N.J., 1982-94. Music tchr., choral dir. Delanco (N.J.) Pub. Schs., 1984-86; prof. voice N.J.Dept. Edn. Sch. Arts, Rowan Univ., Glassboro (N.J.) State Coll., 1987-89; sr. adj. prof. & coordn., piano lab Burlington County Coll., Pemberton, N.J. and Ft. Dix Mil. Post, Cmty. Coll. of the Air Force at McGuire AFB, 1989—, Interactive Classroom Program, 1995—, Power Package Accelerated Program, 1995—, Telecourse for Distance Learners Program WBZC, 1995—; music coord., dist. tchr. for gifted and talented program Mt. Laurel (N.J.) Pub. Schs., 1989-94; music dir., founding mem. Triple Threat Prodns., Cherry Hill, N.J., 1991—, Burlington County Cmty. Chorus, N.J., 1995—, Kosciusko Boys Choir, Rochester, 1959-60, Young Adults Cath. Youth Orgn. Choir, Dunkirk, N.Y., 1960-62; faculty adv. N.Y. Province of Newman Clubs Fedn. SUNY, 1957-62, lectr., researcher in field. Artist: The Fredonia Main Street Diner, 1952-53, Clarence Welcome Wagon Gourmet Cook Book, N.Y., 1973; contbr. poems to various publs.; soloist Rochester Philharm. Orch. Concert Series, Songsters, Inc., 1953-59. Choir dir., organist, soloist St. Philip Neri R.C. Ch., Rochester, 1949-65, St. Peter's Episc. Ch., Medford, 1989-90; choir dir., accompanist Thessalonia Baptist Ch. Sr. and Jr. Choirs, Willingboro, N.J., 1990-91; vocal dir., accompanist Pineland Players of South Jersey Community Theatre, Medford, 1987-89, Cherry Hill East High Sch., N.J., 1991—; team capt. United Way, Rochester, 1953-56; membership chair Rochester Community Theater, 1955-56; founding mem. Sta. WCVF, 1952-58; bd. dirs., founding mem. Rochester Chamber Orch., 1964-65, Medford (N.J.) Newcomers Club, 1977—; vol. Cmty. Companions of Erie County Office of the Aging, N.Y., 1972-76, Medford PTO, 1976-85; judge preliminary Miss Am. contest Jr. C. of C., Jamestown, N.Y., 1962, vocal dir., accompanist Miss Dunkirk (N.Y.) pageant, 1962, vocal coach Miss Burlington County Pageant, Jr. C. of C., 1989,97-99; active Welcome Wagon, Inc., Clarence, N.Y., pres., 1974, historian, 1981; chair Medford (N.J.) Evening Book Review Group, 1978-80; mem. Medford Morning Book Review Group, 1980—; active Meml. Health Alliance, Burlington County Women's Health Network. NDEA grantee, 1964; EEOC scholar, 1986-87; recipient Jr. County Rifle Championship award Monroe County Dept. Health and Recreation, 1948, Womens Student Table Tennis Championship award SUNY, 1952, Outstanding Scholarship award Charlotte Putnam Landers Outstanding Scholarship award SUNY, 1953. Mem. AAUP (treas. 1960-62, state del. 1961), Music Educators Nat. Conf., Am. Personnel and Guidance Assn., South Jersey Music Tchrs. Assn., Meml. Health Alliance, Women's Health Network, AARP Medford chpt. of Deborah heart & lung hosp. foudn.,Red Lion wildlife Refuge, Vincetown, N.J., Cedar Run Wildlife Refuge, Medford, N.J., Order Sons of Italy in Am., Kappa Delta Pi (del. Barnard Coll., N.Y., 1952, state del., Atlantic City, N.J., 1953). Roman Catholic. Avocations: reading and research, creative writing, golf, painting, crossword puzzles, gourmet cooking. Home: 112 Pine Valley Dr Medford NJ 08055-9214

SALTZBERG, JOANNE MARIA, company executive; b. Yonkers, N.Y., July 24, 1945; d. John Salvatore and Josephine Pauline (Aiello) Vasile; m. Jerald Stanley Saltzberg, Dec., 1971 (div. Mar. 1981). BS, Univ. Coll. Md., 1997. CLU; ChFC. Adminstr. Security Brokerage, Balt., 1970-79; adminstrv. mgr. The Phoenix Cos., Bethesda, Md., 1979-85, fin. planner, 1985-92; exec. dir. Md. Commn. for Women, Balt., 1992-99; COO Women Entrepreneurs of Balt., 1999—. Editor: Gender Composition of Maryland Boards and Commissions, 1965-93, 1994. Bd. dirs. Women's Alliance of Md., Balt., 1995—, Girl Scouts U.S., Ctrl. Md. Coun., Balt., 1996—; mem. Child Care Adv. Bd., Balt., 1994—, Equal Opportunity Coun., Balt., 1996—, Family Violence Coun., Annapolis, 1997, YWCA of Greater Balt., 1998—. Named Legis. Leader, Md. Network Against Domestic violence, 1995, Md.'s Top 100 Women, 1997, 99. Mem. NOW (sec. 1990-91). Democrat. Office: Women Entrepreneurs of Baltimore 1118 Light St Ste 202 Baltimore MD 21230-4135

SALTZMAN, IRENE CAMERON, consumer products company executive; b. Cocoa, Fla., Mar. 23, 1927; d. Argyle Bruce and Marie T. (Neel) Cameron; m. Herman Saltzman, Mar. 23, 1946 (dec. May 1986); children: Martin Howard (dec.), Arlene Norma Hanly. Owner Irene Perfume and Cosmetics Lab., Jacksonville, Fla., 1972—. Mem. Cummer Mus. Art, Jacksonville, 1972-. Mem. Ret. Judge Advocates Assn. of USAF (hon.), Mil. Officers Assn. Am., Aircraft Owners and Pilots Assn., Trade, Cosmetic, Toiletry and Fragrance Assn., Ret. Officers Assn., Ponte Vedra Club. Democrat. Episcopalian. Avocations: aviation, painting, travel, swimming, golf. Home: 2701 Ocean Dr S Jacksonville Beach FL 32250 E-mail: irene@ireneparfums.com.

SALTZSTEIN, SUSAN L. lawyer; b. N.Y., 1965; BA, U. Pa., 1987; JD magna cum laude, Columbia U., 1991. Bar: N.Y. 1992. Atty. Skadden, Arps, Slate, Meagher & Flom LLP, N.Y., 1992—. Office: Skadden Arps Slate Meagher & Flom LLP Four Times Sq New York NY 10036*

SALVATORE, DIANE J. editor; BA, Pa. State U.; MA, NYU. Rschr., reporter The Soho News, N.Y.C.; editl. asst. Met. Home, N.Y.C., Cosmopolitan, N.Y.C.; assoc. editor Ladies' Home Jour., N.Y.C.; articles assoc. Glamour, N.Y.C.; articles sr. editor Redbook, N.Y.C.; dep. editor Good Housekeeping, N.Y.C., exec. editor, 1998—99; editor in chief YM, 1999—2002, Ladies Home Jour., N.Y.C., 2002—. Mem.: Am. Soc. Mag. Editors.

SALVESEN, B. FORBES, artist; b. Elgin, Ill., Nov. 6, 1944; d. Donald Behan and Helen Elaine (Krajacik) Forbes; m. Bruce Michael Salvesen, Sept. 3, 1966. Studied with Elvira Spivey, Barrington, Ill., 1972-74; studied with Peter Schoelch, Cary, Ill., 1975-82; student, Am. Acad. Art, 1976, Sch. Art Inst. Chgo., 1980-82, Kulick-Startk Byzantine Jewelry Sch., 1983. Asst. to purchasing agt. Harnischfeger, Crystal Lake, Ill., 1962-64; rec. sec. Electric Mfrs. Credit Bur., Cary, Ill., 1964-66; student and practicing artist, 1968—. Illustrator: (book) There were Reasons, 1983. Recipient Award of Excellence, Ill.-Arlington Heights Fine Arts Festival, 1995, Best of Show award 20th Ann. Cambridge Art Fair, 1995, 19th Ann. Fine Arts Festival, Downers Grove, Ill., 1995. Democratic. Roman Catholic. Avocations: writing, poetry, jewelry crafting, cross-country skiing, hiking. Home: 1312 Whippoorwill Dr Crystal Lake IL 60014-2614 Studio: 1311 Behan Rd Crystal Lake IL 60014

SALZ, SUE, music educator; b. Cedar Rapids, Iowa, Apr. 12, 1954; d. Lois Ann Prochaska and Norbert John Salz. MusB, Morningside Coll., 1972—76; MusM, U. of Colo., 1977—78. Strings instr. Sheridan County Schools, Wyo., 1976—77; grad. asst. U. of Colo., Boulder, 1976—77; orch. dir. Sheridan Collge, Sheridan, Wyo., 1976—77; strings tchr. Natrona County Sch. Dist. #1, Casper, Wyo., 1978—; grad. asst. U. of Tex., 1985—86. Mem.: Nation Edn. Assn., Music Educators Nat. Conf., Am. String teachers Assn. (state treas. 1988—2003), Phi Delta Kappa. Avocations: travel, reading, gardening, music, theater.

SALZGEBER, KAREN A. secondary school educator; b. Cleve., Ohio, Oct. 19, 1953; d. Frederick Robert and Carol Grace Petersen; m. Alan Joseph Salzgeber, May 6, 1978; children: Kristen, Kurt. BE cum laude in Math., Kent State U., 1976; MEd in Curriculum & Instr., Cleve. State U., 1993. Permanent cert. tchr. Ohio, 1998. Tchr. math. & journalism Cleve. Pub. Schs., Cleve., 1976—79; presch. tchr. Ridgewood Presch., Parma, Ohio, 1989—91; tchr. H.S. math. Parma City Sch., Parma, 1991—. Math. chairperson Parma Sr. H.S.; co-chmn. Action Com. for Essential Schs., Parma, 1999—; mem. various coms. Parma City Schs. Mem.: Parma Edn. Assn., Ohio Edn. Assn., Nat. Edn. Assn., Ohio Coun. Tchrs. Math., Nat. Coun. Tchrs. Math. Avocations: reading, travel, counted cross stitch, skiing, gardening. Office: Parma Sr High School 6285 W 54th St Parma OH 44129 E-mail: alkare@aol.com.

SALZMAN, JOANNA MICHELE, special education educator; b. N.Y.C., May 15, 1969; d. Robert and Janet Miriam (Weiler) S. BS, James Madison U., 1991; MA, Am. U., Washington, 1992; cert. edn. specialist, George Washington U., 1997. Cert. elementary tchr., K-12 learning disabled tchr. Sub. tchr. The Lab. Sch. Washington, 1991-92; spl. edn. resource tchr. Prince Georges County Pub. Schs., Mt. Rainier, Md., 1992-96, spl. edn. self-contained tchr. Takoma Park, Md., 1996-98. Camp counselor Lane Robbins II, Newton, N.J., summers 1989-91; pvt. tutor The Lab. Sch., 1993—; chmn. social com. Mt. Rainier Elem. Sch., 1995-96. Campaign mgr. Bd. Edn., Somerset, 1981; vol. Sean Williard Liver Transplant Fund, Somerset, 1983, Salvation Army, Somerset, 1985. Recipient Acad. grant George Washington U., 1995. Mem. Prince George's County Edn. Assn., Coun. Exceptional Children. Jewish. Avocations: working out at the gym, movies, reading, exploring the internet, spending time with friends. Office: Twinbrook Elem Sch 5911 Ridgeway Ave Rockville MD 20851-1931 Home: 2123 Darcy Green Pl Silver Spring MD 20910-1170

SAMANIEGO, JULIA ROSE, elementary school educator; b. El Paso, Tex., Aug. 19, 1930; d. Josefino and Josefina (Gomez) Bencomo; m. Henry Samaniego, June 24, 1950; children: Sylvia Mae Howell, Robert Edward, Cynthia R. Heitzman. BA, U. Tex., 1949. Cert. elem. tchr., N.Mex., Tex. Tchr. El Paso Ind. Schs., 1949-50, 52-58, 71-93, parent and cmty. liaison, 1993-94; tchr. Dallas Ind. Sch. Dist., 1950-52, Farmington (N.Mex.) Mcpl. Schs., 1968-71; kindergarden tchr. Gadsden Ind. Sch. Dist., Anthony, N.Mex., 1995-97, tchr., 1997—. Pres. El Paso Ind. Sch. Dist. PTA, 1986-87, 93-95; v.p. Tex. State PTA, 1995-96; active U. Tex. Womens Aux., El Paso, 1966—; active womens dept. El Paso C. of C., 1992-96; tchr. St. Patricks Confraternity of Christian Doctrine, El Paso, 1958-68, Queen of Peace Cath. Ch., El Paso, 1974-94. Named Outstanding Tchr., El Paso Pilot Club, 1966, Tchr. of Yr., Mesita Sch., El Paso, 1967, one of Outstanding Elem. Tchrs. Am. El Paso Ind. Sch. Dist., 1974; Tchr. scholar Delta Kappa Gamma, 1969; recipient Extended Svc. award Tex. State PTA, 1992, Outstanding Achievement award Chaparral Sch., 1995. Mem. AAUW (pres. 1985-86), Assn. for Childhood Edn. (pres. 1967-68), El Paso Tchrs. Assn. (pres. 1977-78), Delta Kappa Gamma (pres. 1966-68, Outstanding Achievement award 1986). Roman Catholic. Avocations: travel, swimming, dance, children, grandchildren. Office: 1002 Muirfield Dr Mansfield TX 76063-6635

SAMELSON, JUDY, editor; Editor Playbill, N.Y.C., 1993—. Office: Playbill 52 Vanderbilt Ave Fl 11 New York NY 10017-3870

SAMET, DEE-DEE, lawyer; b. Greensboro, N.C., Sept. 18, 1940; BA, U. Ariz., 1962, JD, 1963. Bar: Ariz. 1964. Ptnr. Samet & Gage, P.C., Tucson, 2001; pvt. practice Tucson, 2001—. Arbitrator U.S. Dist. Ct. Ariz., Gender Equality Task Force, 1993; judge pro tem Pima County Superior Ct., 1985—; Ninth Cir. Lawyer rep., 1990-93; mem. Jud. Performance Rev. Commn., 1996-99. Mem. State Bar Ariz. (family law sect., workers compensation sect., trial law sect., co-chair worker's compensation sect. 1988-89, gender bias task force, bd. govs. 1994-97, pres.-elect, pres. 1999-2000), Nat. Panel Arbitrators, Am. Arbitration Assn. (com. on exams., supreme ct. state Ariz. 1984-91), Pima County Bar Assn. (bd. dirs. 1994—), Nat. Assn. Coun. for Children, Ariz. Assn. Coun. for Children, So. Ariz. Fed. Bar Assn. (exec. com. 1995—, pres.-elect 2004), So. Ariz. Women Lawyers Assn. (bd. dirs. 1990, pres. 1994-95), Nat. Orgn. Social Security Claimants' Reps. Office: Dee-Dee Samet PC 717 N 6th Ave Tucson AZ 85705-8304

SAMIMI, SANDRA, lawyer; b. Wooster, Ohio, Sept. 20, 1959; d. Kenneth Earl and June Eileen (Miller) Weaver; m. Kenneth J. Murphy; children: Daniel Abraham, Elizabeth Mariam, Sarah Catherine, Eve Alison. BA, Miami U., 1980; JD, U. Mich., 1983. Bar: N.Y. 1984. Ct. atty. State of N.Y. Supreme Ct., N.Y.C., 1984-92; pvt. practice Spring Valley, N.Y., 1992-94; ptnr. Samimi & Murphy, New City, N.Y., 1995—. Surrogate decision making com. N.Y. State Commn. on Quality of Care for the Mentally Disabled, 1993—. Author: (with others) Criminal Defense Techniques, 1991. Bd. dirs. Rockland Parent-Child Ctr., N.Y.C., Nyack, 1994-96, Hudson Valley Children's Mus., Nyack, 1993-96, Chestnut Rotary, Chestnut Ridge, N.Y., 1993-96; mem. New City United Meth. Ch., 1990—. Mem. Rockland County Bar Assn., Rockland County Women's Bar Assn., N.Y. State Bar Assn., Tappan Zee Bus. and Profl. Women. Avocations: gardening, swimming. Office: Samimi & Murphy 616 S Main St New City NY 10956-2922

SAMMET, JEAN E. computer scientist; b. N.Y.C. d. Harry and Ruth S. BA, Mt. Holyoke Coll., Sc.D. (hon.), 1978; MA, U. Ill. Group leader programming Sperry Gyroscope, Great Neck, N.Y., 1955-58; sect. head, staff cons. programming Sylvania Electric Products, Needham, Mass., 1958-61; with IBM, 1961-88; adv. program mgr. Boston, 1961-65; program lang. tech. mgr. IBM, 1965-68; programming tech. planning mgr. Fed. Systems div., 1968-74, programming lang. tech. mgr., 1974-79, software tech. mgr., 1979-81, div. software tech. mgr., 1981-82, programming lang. tech. mgr., 1983-88; programming lang. cons. Bethesda, Md., 1989—. Chmn. history of computing com. Am. Fedn. Info. Processing Socs., 1977-79; mem. exec. com. Software Patent Inst., 1991—, edn. com., 1992—, chair edn. com., 1992-93; bd. dirs. Computer Mus., 1983-93. Author: Programming Languages: History and Fundamentals, 1969; editor-in-chief: Assn. Computing Machinery Computing Revs, 1979-87; contbr. articles to profl. jours. Fellow Assn. for Computing Machinery, 1994, (charter, pres. 1974-76, Disting. Svc. award 1985), Computer History Mus.; mem. NAE, Upsilon Pi Epsilon. Home and Office: 3124 Gracefield Rd Apt 311 Silver Spring MD 20904-5818

SAMMONS, ELAINE D. corporate executive; m. Charles A. Sammons (dec. 1988). Chmn. Sammons Enterprises, Inc., Dallas, 1988—. Chmn. bd. Sammons Ctr. for the Arts, Dallas, 1988—. Office: Sammons Enterprises Inc 5949 Sherry Ln Ste 1900 Dallas TX 75225-8015

SAMMONS, MARY F. retail executive; b. Portland, Oreg., Oct. 12, 1946; d. Lee W. and Ann (Cherry) Jackson; m. Nickolas F. Sammons, Sept. 12, 1967; 1 child, Peter. BA, Marylhurst Coll., 1970. Buyer Fred Meyer Inc., Portland, 1975-80, v.p., merchandiser, 1980-85, sr. v.p., softgoods div. mgr., from 1986, sr. v.p., apparel & home electronics group, 1996, exec. v.p., apparel, home & home electronics group, 1997—98; pres. Fred Meyer Stores, Portland, 1998, pres., CEO, 1999; pres., COO Rite Aid Corp., Camp Hill, Pa., 1999—2003, pres., CEO, 2003—. Chmn. Nat. Assoc. Chain Drug Stores. Named Woman of Achievement, YWCA, Portland, 1987. Mem. Am. Mgmt. Assn. Office: Rite Aid Corp 30 Hunter Ln Camp Hill PA 17011*

SAMMONS, ROSE ANN, special education educator; b. Little Falls, N.Y., Oct. 27, 1963; d. Fiorino Peter and Adelaide Agnes (LaCoppola) Battisti; m. John Paul Sammons, Oct. 20, 1990; children: Nathan, Andrew, Matthew. AA, Hudson Vly. C.C., 1983; BS Edn., SUNY, Oneonta, 1985; M Spl. Edn., Coll. St. Rose, 1988.

SAMPAS, DOROTHY MYERS, retired government official; b. Washington, Aug. 24, 1933; d. Lawrence and Anna Cornelia (Henkel) Myers; m. James George Sampas, Dec. 8, 1962; children: George, Lawrence James. AB, U. Mich., 1955; postgrad., U. Paris, 1955-56; PhD, Georgetown U., 1970; cert., Nat. War Coll., Washington, 1987, Naval Post Grad. Sch., 1993. With Bur. Pub. Affairs Dept. State, Washington, 1958-60, analyst Bur. of Adminstrn., 1973-75, div. chief, dep. chief Office of Position and Pay Mgmt., 1979-83, div. chief Office of Mgmt., 1983-84, dir. Office of Mgmt., 1984-86; vice consul Am. Consulate Gen., Hamburg, Fed. Republic Germany, 1960-62; cons. Trans Century Corp., Washington, 1972; gen. svcs. officer Am. Embassy, Brussels, 1975-79, embassy minister-counselor Beijing, 1987-90; minister-counselor U.S. Mission to UN, N.Y.C., 1991-94; Am. ambassador to Islamic Republic of Mauritania, 1994-97; ret., 1998. Presbyterian.

SAMPERE, ROBERTA LYNN, English language educator, consultant; b. South Amboy, N.J., June 12, 1954; d. Wilbur and Betty Ruth (Wyckoff) Farley; m. Charles Rogers Curran II, Jan. 16, 1971 (div. Feb. 1978); 1 child, Jason Samuel Curran; m. Michael Sampere, Aug. 3, 1991; 1 child, Katharine Rose. BS in English, Emporia State U., 1988, MA in English, 1991. Homemaker, 1971-75, 79-86; adminstrv. specialist US Army, 1975-79; grad. asst. Emporia (Kans.) State U., 1988-91; adminstrv. asst. The Farm, Inc., Emporia, Kans., 1990-91; adj. faculty Brevard C.C., Melbourne, Fla., 1991—2000, learning specialist Computer Assisted Instrn. Lab., 1997—2000, asst. prof. devel. comms. Palm Bay, Fla., 2000—. Exec. dir. Women's Wisdom, Palm Bay, 2001—02; presiding ptnr. Practical Women's Investment Club, 2000—. Contbr. article to The Body Politic mag.; contbg. editor Space Coast Review; guest editor Florida Today newspaper. Co-dir. Clinic Def. Project, Melbourne, Fla., 1993-98; exec. dir. Brevard County Voters' Alliance, Melbourne, 1995-96; coord. Mainstream Voters' Alliance, Melbourne, 1996-98. Mem. NOW, Nat. Audubon Soc., Nature Conservancy. Avocations: birdwatching, reading, motor sports, travel, theater. Home: 891 Charcoal Ave SE Palm Bay FL 32909-4630 Office: Brevard C C 250 Community College Pkwy Palm Bay FL 32909

SAMPEY, DEBRA A. middle school principal; b. Chgo., Apr. 10, 1961; d. John Francis and Geri Ann Sampey; m. Timothy Collins Cronister, July 1, 1995; 1 child, Catherine Taylor Cronister. BS, George Williams Coll., Downers Grove, Ill., 1983; MS, U. Wis., 1985. Tchr. phys. edn., athletic dir. St. Teresas and St. Priscillas, 1985-86; tchr. phys. edn./health, coach track, volleyball, basketball Latin Sch., Chgo., 1986—, also Middle Sch. dean of students, Middle Sch. prin., varsity volleyball coach. Named Coach of Yr., Ind. Sch. League, 1995, 97; Klingenstein summer fellow, 1989. Mem. AAUW, Nat. Mid. Sch. Assn., Nat. Assn. Ind. Schs., Nat. Assn. Secondary Sch. Prins., Phi Beta Kappa. Democrat. Roman Catholic. Avocations: ethnic cooking, reading, tennis. Office: Latin Sch Chgo 59 W North Blvd Chicago IL 60610-1403

SAMPITE, SHARON, academic administrator; b. Shreveport, La., Apr. 19, 1961; d. Joe and Hazel Sampite; children from previous marriage: John Van Hoof, Allison Van Hoof. BS in Computer Info. Systems, 1985, BSBA U. La., 1986. Lic. life, health and accident ins.; Series 7 and 63 securities dealer Nat. Assn. Securities Dealers, cert. Notary, lic. variable annuities. Mgr. Fidelity Investments, Dallas, 1986—94; benefits mgr. BRC Corp, Dallas, 1995—96; investment rep. A.G. Edwards & Sons, Natchitoches, La., 1998—2002; dir. instl. investment Northwestern State U., 2002—. Spkr. Elem. Lab. Sch., Northwestern State U., Natchitoches, 2000, mem. dean's exec. adv. bd. Coll. Bus., 2000—, co-instr. continuing edn.; spkr. Natchitoches Ctrl. H.S. Bd. dirs. Am. Heart Assn., Natchitoches, 1999—2000, Northwestern State U. Athletic Assn., Natchitoches Domestic Violence; bd. dirs., pub. rels. chair, 2d v.p. Natchitoches Are C. of C.; bd. dirs. Dixie Youth Softball/Baseball, Natchitoches, Assn. for Preservation of Hist. Natchitoches. Named one of Outstanding Young Women of Am., 1987. Mem.: Bus. and Profl. Women (pres. 2001—), Krewe of Dionysis, Les Amies of Natchitoches (pres. 1998—99), Rotary (pres. 2000—01). Avocations: photography, in-line skating, reading, community service, childrens activities.

SAMPSON, EARLDINE ROBISON, education educator; b. Russell, Iowa, June 18, 1923; d. Lawrence Earl and Mildred Mona (Judy) Robison; m. Wesley Claude Sampson, Nov. 25, 1953; children: Ann Elizabeth, Lisa Ellen. Diploma, Iowa State Tchrs. Coll., 1943, BA, 1950; MS in Edn., Drake U., 1954; postgrad., No. Ill. U., Iowa State U., 1965-66, 74. Cert. tchr., guidance counselor, Iowa. Tchr. elem. sch. various pub. sch. sys., 1943-48; cons. speech and hearing Iowa Dept. Pub. Instrn., Des Moines, 1950-52; speech therapist Des Moines Pub. Schs., 1952-54, 55; lectr. spl. edn. No. Ill. U., DeKalb, 1964-65; tchr. of homebound Cedar Falls (Iowa) Pub. Schs., 1967-68; asst. prof. edn. U. No. Iowa, Cedar Falls, 1968; asst. prof., counselor Wartburg Coll., Waverly, Iowa, 1968-70; instr. elem. edn., then head of advising elem. edn. Iowa State U., Ames, 1972-82; field supr. elem. edn. U. Toledo, 1988, 89; ind. cons. Sylvania, Ohio, 1989—. Cons. Des Moines Speech and Hearing Ctr., 1958-59; cons. Sartori Hosp., Cedar Falls, 1967-69. Fellow, NDEA, 1965. Methodist. Avocations: public speaking on preservation of prose and poetry, reading, music, photography. Home: 4047 Newcastle Dr Sylvania OH 43560-3450

SAMS, ANN GRASTY, artist, educator; b. Henderson, Ky., Mar. 11, 1929; d. Claire and Nancy Nicholson Mendel; m. Francis Sams (dec.); children: Nancy Nicholson, Bradley. BA, Vanderbilt U., 1950; MFA, U. Miami, 1978; postgrad., Pratt U. Art tchr. St. Stephen's Sch., Miami, 1967—72; rug designer Regal Rugs, Columbus, Ind., 1970—85; designer, curator Miami, 1972—; art tchr.; owner, oper. River Ridge Ranch, Millboro, Va. Mem. Jr. League Miami, 1961—; organizer pub. TV, 1958—. Democrat. Avocations: tennis, horseback riding. Home: Rt 1 Box 119-1 Millboro VA 24460-9528 Office: River Ridge Ranch Rt 1 Box 119-1 Millboro VA 24460-9528

SAMSAMI, SOONA, advocate; b. Isfahan, Iran, Nov. 14, 1959; came to U.S., 1979; d. Mohammad Ali Samsami and Mohtaram Sohrabi. BS, Mich. State U., 1982. Mem. fgn. affairs com., parliament in exile Nat. Coun. Resistance Iran, Washington and France, 1993—, mem. women's com., parliament in exile, 1994-96. Spkr. human rights commn. UN, Geneva, 1994; coord. exiled women orgns., Iran, 1994—; coord. exiled women orgns. World Conf. Women, 1996; spkr., coord. frontline feminists U. Calif., Riverside, 1997. Moslem. Avocations: the internet, women activities, soft rock music, drawing. Home: 7460 Towchester Ct Alexandria VA 22315-3836 Office: Nat Coun Resistance Iran 1051 National Pren Bldg Washington DC 20045

SAMSON, LEONA D. biological engineering educator, research center director, researcher; BSc in Biochemistry, Aberdeen (Scotland) U., 1974; PhD, London U., 1978. Postdoctoral rschr. U. Calif., San Francisco, Berkeley; from asst. prof. to full prof. dept. molecular and cellular toxicology Harvard Sch. Pub. Health, 1983—2001; prof. biol. engring. and toxicology MIT, 2001—, dir. MIT Ctr. for Environ. Health Scis., MIT Toxicogenomics Rsch. Program, 2001—. Mem. exec. com. Computational and Systems Biology Initiative MIT; mem. bd. sci. counselors NIEHS; mem. coun. for extramural grants ACS. Named Am. Cancer Soc. Rsch. Prof., 2001; recipient Burroughs Wellcome Toxicology Scholar award,

1993, Charlotte Friend Women in Cancer Rsch. award, 2000. Mem.: Inst. Medicine. Office: Ctr for Environ Health Scis MIT Bldg 56-235 Cambridge MA 02139 Business E-Mail: lsamson@mit.edu.*

SAMS SCHREIBER, CAROL MARIE HOUSER, artist, graphic designer; b. Knoxville, Tenn., Sept. 28, 1952; d. Harrison Barton Houser and Doris Marie McFarland; m. Richard Vernon Sams (div. 1980); m. Robert William Schreiber, 1990. BFA, U. Tenn., 1973. Prodn. artist Cope Studios, Memphis, 1973-75, Brunner Printing Co., Memphis, 1975-76; graphic designer Smith & Nephew Richards, Memphis, 1976-78, art mgr., designer, 1978-87, creative svcs. coord., 1987-89; owner, electronic designer, illustrator, free-lancer Square One Studio, Memphis, 1989-95, artist, illustrator St. Louis, 1995—2000. One-woman shows include The Bell Gallery, Memphis, 1993—95, Creative Resources Gallery, Birmingham, Mich., 1995—98, David Lusk Gallery, 2000—03, exhibitions include Nat. Watercolor Soc. Ann., 1980, Tenn. Watercolor Soc., 1974—82, Maple Art Gallery, Evanston, Ill., 1995—2004. Office: Square One Studio 656 Madison Ave 1B Memphis TN 38104

SAMUELS, CYNTHIA KALISH, communications executive; b. Pitts., May 21, 1946; d. Emerson and Jeanne (Kalish) S.; m. Richard Norman Atkins, Sept. 12, 1971; children: Joshua Whitney Samuels Atkins, Daniel Jonathan Samuels Atkins. BA, Smith Coll., 1968. Press aide McCarthy for Pres. Campaign, Washington, 1968; assoc. prodr. Newsroom program Sta. KQED, San Francisco, 1972-73; with CBS News, 1973-80, rschr., Washington, 1969-71, documentary rschr., N.Y.C., 1973-74, asst. fgn. editor, 1973-76, asst. N.Y. bur. chief, 1976-80; writer, field prodr. Today program NBC News, N.Y.C., 1980-84, polit. prodr. Today program, 1984-89; polit. and planning prodr., 1988-89; sr. prodr. Main Street program NBC News, N.Y.C., 1987; founding exec. prodr. Channel One Program, 1989-92; exec. v.p. Whittle Comms., N.Y.C., 1989-94; internet cons., developer TV and multimedia prodn. exec., 1994—; pres., CEO Cobblestone Prodns.: Online and On TV, 1996—. Cons. spl. projects iVillage.com The Women's Network, 1997—. Author: It's A Free Country!: A Young Person's Guide to Politics and Elections, 1988; editor Excite, 1995-96; contbg. editor Women's Wire, 1996-98; prodr. 3d Ann. Childrens Interactive Media Festival, 1996, Village, 1997—, Global Information Infrastructure awards, 1997-98, Education Central at Parent Soup Web site; contbr. book revs. to N.Y. Times Book Rev., Washington Post Book World; children's book editor Amazon-.com, 1997-98; spl. projects cons. Village.com, 1997—; contbg. editor children's books, Barnesandnoble.com, 1998—; sr. nat. editor Washington Nat. Pub. Radio, 1999—. Recipient Emmy award No. Calif. Acad. TV Arts and Scis., 1974, Columbia DuPont citation, 1975, Media Access award Calif. Office of Handicapped, 1991, Silver award Nat. Mental Health Assn., 2 Bronze awards Nat. Assn. Edn. in Film and TV, 1993. Mem. Women in New Tech., Internat. Interactive Comms. Soc. Office: 635 Massachusetts Ave Washington DC 20001 E-mail: csamuels@earthlink.net.

SAMUELS, DIANE, public information officer, real estate appraiser; d. Edward Johnson and Margeret Brandon; children: Earl Tyson Jr., Tiffany Tyson, Delonte Tyson, Darius Tyson. Student, Chgo. State U., 1992, Prince George C.C., 1999—2003. Data processing operator Planning Rsch. Corp., Arlington, Va., 1975—78; libr. aid Health, Edn. and Welfare, Washington, 1978—79; postal clk. U.S. Postal Svc., Washington, 1980—, svc. improvement, 1985—92, safety capt., 1988—94. Clk. typist Lic., Cert. and Cons., Washington, 1979—84; gen. clk. White House, Washington, 1983; cons. C C Quest Ednl. Supplies, Bowie, Md., 2000—. Vol. Rick Snyders, Washington, 1979, House of Ruth, Washington, 1986, Martha's Kitchen, Washington, 1988. Named to Wall of Tolerance, Nat. Campaign for Tolerance, Montgomery, Ala., 2003. Mem.: NAACP (assoc.), Am. Women Econ. Develop., Nat. Assn. Female Exec. Avocations: reading, swimming, chess, checkers. Home: PO Box 47504 Forestville MD 20753 Office: US Postal Svc 900 Brentwood Rd NE Washington DC 20066

SAMUELS, DOROTHY J. journalist, writer; b. N.Y.C., N.Y., May 15, 1951; d. Herman and Roz Silver; m. Peter G. Samuels, Dec. 26, 1971; children: Laurah, Tom, Jenny. AB, Bryn Mawr Coll., 1972; JD, Northeastern U., 1975. Bar: N.Y. Atty. Brown & Wood, N.Y.C., 1975—76; exec. dir. Com. for Pub. Justice, N.Y.C., 1976—79, N.Y. Civil Liberties Union, N.Y.C., 1979—81; cons. Ford Found., N.Y.C., 1981—83; mem. editl. bd. N.Y. Times, N.Y.C., 1985—. Author: (novels) Filthy Rich, 2001; contbr. book Then and Now, 2000, articles to mags. Office: NY Times 229 W 43d St New York NY 10036 E-mail: dosamu@aol.com.

SAMUELS, FERN JACQUELINE, artist, educator; b. Chgo., Feb. 16, 1931; d. Noah S. and Ann (Zager) Andrews; m. Howard Stanley Samuels, Sept. 17, 1950; children: Mitchell, Paul, David. BFA, Loyola U., 1973; MFA, Sch. Art Inst. Chgo., 1983. Instr.-coord. Mundelein Coll., Chgo., 1976-83; faculty Columbia Coll., Chgo., 1978-2000. Instr. workshops Field Mus., Chgo., 1976, Lake Forest Coll., Chgo., 1976, Lincoln Park Cultural Ctr., Chgo., 1973, Ill. Inst. Tech., Chgo., 1980—, Latin Sch., Chgo., 1976; juror St. Louis Arts Guild, 1998. One-women shows include Northwestern U., 1988, Ne. Ill. U., Chgo., 1989, Countryside Gallery, 1988, Upstart Gallery, 1990, Soho 20, N.Y.C., 1993, Loyola U., 1995, Morraine Valley Coll., 1995, McDonough Mus. Art, 1997, Fyr Place Gallery, 2000, Gallery on Azeele, 2000, Mos Art Gallery, Lake Park, Fla., 2004, Cornell Mus., Del Ray, Fla., 2004; exhibited in group shows including Smithsonian Air and Space Mus., 1983, Freeport Mus., 1995, Rockford Mus., 1996, Butler Inst. Am. Art, 1998, Lafayette Mus., 1999, Columbus Mus. Art, 2000, So. Ohio Mus., 2000, South Bend Regional Mus., 2000, Univ. Mus. S.D., 2001, Gallery 228, N.Y., N.Y., 2003. Mem. LWV, Chgo., 1969—; founding mem. Alternative Fibers, Chgo., 1982; chairperson, coord. Seven Ethnic Museums, Chgo., 1986; membership chmn. ARC Gallery, Chgo., 1983-86, pres. 1988-90; bd. dirs. Artist Book Works, Chgo., 1992-93. Recipient Best of Show award Women in the Visual Arts, Boca Raton, Fla., 2001, Judges Recognition award, Boca Raton, 2001, 2nd prize Boca Mus. Artists Guild, 2001, 1st prize, 2002, 1st prize Women in Visual Arts, Del Ray, Fla., 2002, Mus. Exhibits, 2002, Jewish Mus., Miami, Norton Mus., West Palm Beach, Fla., 2002, 2004, Cornell Mus. of Art and Sci., Del Ray, 2002, Art Club Chgo., 2003, Permanent Collection,, Rutgers U., 2003, 1st prize Northwood U., West Palm Beach, Fla., 2003, 1st prize Boca Mus. Artist Guild, 2003; grantee Columbia Coll., 1981; Fern Samuels Scholarship Fund est. Columbia Coll., Chgo., 1st prize Milagro Art Ctr., Del Ray Fla., 2003, 1st prize Boca Mus. Artist Guild, 2003. Mem. Nat. Assn. Women Artists, Internat. Soc. Exptl. Artists, Nat. Collage Soc., Arts Club Chgo., Chgo. Soc. Arts, City of Hope (Bobby Blechman chpt. founding mem.), Sch. Art Inst. Chgo. Alumni (2d prize 2002). Democrat. Avocations: reading, music, theater, exercise. Home: 84 Saint James Ct Palm Beach Gardens FL 33418 E-mail: ucars1@aol.com.

SAMUELS, HANNA, artist; b. Buffalo, Apr. 26, 1908; d. Emil and Rachel (Span) S. Student, Art Inst. Buffalo, 1937-54. Sr. clk. in charge of catalog Buffalo State Coll., 1966-73, vol. cons. on art. Represented in permanent collections at Erie County Hist. Soc., Vincent Price Collection, Judaic Mus., Temple Beth Zion, Buffalo, Butler Libr., Buffalo State Coll., Cox Conv. Hall, Pentecostal Temple Ch., Buffalo, Burchfield-Penney Art Ctr., Buffalo; exhibited in group shows Smithsonian Instn., Kenan Ctr., Lockport, N.Y.; exhbns. of sculpture include Burchfield-Penney Art Ctr., Buffalo, Albright-Knox Art Gallery, Memphis, Jr. League, Smithsonian Instn., Washington, Castellani Art Mus., Smithsonian Assocs. Nat. Mem. The Libr. of Congress. Vol. USO, Buffalo, 1942-45. Mem. Patteran Artists (rec. sec.), Castellani Art Mus. Niagara U., Libr. Congress (nat.), Smithsonian Inst. (assoc.). Democrat. Avocations: painting, music. Address: 1190 Amherst St Buffalo NY 14216-3624

SAMUELS, LINDA S. science administrator; b. Mansfield, Ohio, Feb. 15, 1947; d. Robert Lloyd and Esther Sophia (Schwob) Garber; children: Marilyn L., Charles L. AB in Biology-Zoology, U. Cin., 1969, MS in Population Biology, 1971; MBA, Suffolk U., 2003. Anatomy and physiology instr. U. Cin., 1969—70; biology, chemistry, physics, algebra instr. Cambridge (Mass.) Acad., 1971—72; instr. biology Simmons Coll., Boston, 1972—73; instr. advanced biology, life sci., dance sci. Dana Hall Sch., Wellesley, Mass., 1972—2002; CEO Sci. of Learning Ctr., Boston, 2002—; v.p. Hobson Sleep Sch., Winthrop, Mass., 2003—. Rap Around: Discussion Dissection in the Classroom, WBZ-TV, Boston, 1996-97; liaison com. to head of sch. Dana Hall Sch., Wellesley, Mass., 1995-98, developer dance sci. curriculum, 1998—; cons. NSF summer project Girls in Engring. engring. adv. com. Tufts U., 1997; mem. com. to study physiology of learning Harvard Med. Sch, 1998—; mem. neurosci. com. minority faculty devel. program, 1995 Author: Girls Can Succeed in Science, 1999; contbr. articles to sci. jours. Mem. Bar/Bat Mitzah Com. Temple Israel, Boston, 1995, adult choir, 1997; parent rep., Buckingham, Browne and Nichols Sch., Cambridge, 1995-98; mem. parking com. Back Bay Assn. Recipient Sci. Tchr. of Yr. award Norfolk County, 1994, sabbatical grant Dana Hall Sch., 1995, Disting. Alumni award U. Cin., McMicken Coll. Arts and Scis., 1996, H. Dudley Wright Fellowship for Innovative Sci. Edn. Tufts U., Medford, Mass., 1996-97; dedication of Linda S. Samuels Animal Behavior Lab. at Dana Hall; inductee Mass. Hall of Fame Educators, Boston, 1999. Mem. Nat. Assn. Biology Tchrs. (presenter 1986—, award for excellence in encouraging equity sect. on women 1997-98, Outstanding Biology Tchr. Mass. 1994), Nat. Sci. Tchrs. Assn. (presenter 1986—, Tchr. of Yr. award 1994), New Eng. Sci. Tchrs., Mass. Assn. Biology Tchrs. (v.p. 1997, pres. 1998), Mass. Assn. Sci. Tchrs. (presenter 1986-95, 99, Presdl. award state finalist Sec. Sch. Sci., Mass). Avocations: science business consulting, exercise.

SAMUELS, YVONNE JAMES, retired special education educator; b. Soc. Hill, S.C., Jan. 2, 1943; d. Woodrow and Edna Thomas James; m. Hayes Samuels, Feb. 18, 1967; 1 child, Yvette C. BA, Benedict Coll.; MEd, S.C. State U. Tchr. English Greeleyville (S.C.) Sch. Sys.; tchr. spl. edn. Manning (S.C.) Sch. Sys.; pvt. practice speech instr. Manning; dir. Trinity AME, Manning. Speech writer S.C. Jr. Academic, Greenville, 1997—, S.C. Miss Homecoming, Columbia, SC, 1998; coach S.C. Jr. Miss Competition. Author: PRIDE Handbook, 1997. State judge Clemson (S.C.) U., 1993—99. Named Woman of Yr., Over All Youth Activities, 1999; recipient 21 awards. Mem.: Nat. Female Execs., Alpha Kappa Alpha (chmn. call me mister 1995). Democrat. Meth. Home: 114 North Church St Manning SC 29102

SAMUELSON, BILLIE MARGARET, artist; b. Long Beach, Calif., Apr. 11, 1927; d. William Christian and Gladys Margaret (Caffrey) Newendorp; m. Fritz Eric Samuelson, Aug. 12, 1950 (div. 1985); children: Craig Eric, Clark Alan, Dana Scott. Student, Long Beach City Coll., 1945—46. Pvt. art tchr., Wycokoff/Allendale, NJ, 1985. Workshop instr. Jane Law Studio, Long Beach Island, N.J., 1990—. Exhibited in solo show at Ridgewood (N.J.) Art Inst., 1985, West Wing Gallery, 1991, Chas. Austin Gallery, Saddle River, N.J., 1997; group shows include Craig Gallery, Ridgewood, 1979, Charisma Gallery, Englewood, N.J., 1981-83, Custom Gallery, Waldwick, N.J., 1985, Wyckoff (N.J.) Gallery, 1987-90, West Wing Gallery, Ringwood State Park, N.J., 1991, Union Camp Corp., 1992, Eisenhauer Gallery, Block Island, R.I., 1996—; featured in Am. Artists Mag., 2001. Recipient 1st in State N.J. Womens Clubs, 1978-80, Watercolor award N.J. Painters and Sculptors, 1981. Mem. DAR, Community Arts Assn. (pres. 1978-79), Am. Artists Profl. League (bd. dirs. 1985-87, watercolor prize 1992), Ringwood Manor Arts Assn. (sr. profl.), Catherine Lorillard Wolfe Art Club (cash award 1993), Salute to Women in the Arts, Art Ctr. Watercolor Affiliates, Nat. Mus. of Women in the Arts. Avocations: bridge, travel, museums, theatre, reading. Home: 1-3 Chestnut Pl Waldwick NJ 07463-1113

SAMUELSON, CYNTHIA, information technology executive; b. N.C. m. Lawrence Samuelson. BA in Math., Hampton U.; MS in Computer Sci., Fairleigh Dickinson U.; postgrad., U. So. Calif. Mathematician Westinghouse R&D Ctr., Pitts.; with FTC, Washington, U.S. Dept. Commerce, Washington, Nat. Edowment for the Arts; info. resource mgmt. dir. Dept. of Transp.; prin. dir. info. mgmt. Office of the Asst. Sec. of Def. for Command, Control, Comm. and Intelligence, Washington; bus. devel. dir. Lucent Technologies Govt. Solutions (now Avaya), Basking Ridge, NJ, v.p. mktg., telesales and svcs. Mem. Aero. and Space Engring. Bd., NAS. Bd. dirs. Sch. Engring., Hampton U.; mentor Boy Scouts Am.; mentor various pub. and pvt. sector orgns. Named one of Fed. Computer Week's Top 100 Fed. Info. Tech. Execs.; recipient Bronze medal, Dept. Transp., Medal for Meritorious Civilian Svc., Dept. of Def., Exceptional Civilian Svc. award, Tech. award, Black Engr.'s Women of Color. Mem.: Armed Forces Comm. and Electronics Assn. (bd. dirs.). Office: Avaya 211 Mount Airy Rd Basking Ridge NJ 07920

SAMUELSON, JOAN BENOIT, professional runner; b. Cape Elizabeth, Maine, May 16, 1957; d. André and Nancy Benoit; m. Scott Samuelson; children: Abigail, Anders. Student, Bowdoin Coll., N.C. State U. Long-distance coach Boston U.; runner; Runner 10K L.L. Bean Run, July 4, 1997. Bd. dirs. Gulf of Maine Aquarium, Found. for Advancement Edn., Internat. Amateur Athletic Fedn. Coun.; active Maine Lung Found., Natural Resources Coun. Main, Alzheimer's Found., Multiple Sclerosis Soc., Spl. Olympics. Recipient Gold medal Olympic Games, 1984 (set world record); won Boston Marathon, 1983 (set world record). Office: Edwin P Whittemore 114A Massachusetts Ave Arlington MA 02474-8624 also: Roadrunners Club of America 1150 S Washington St Ste 205 Alexandria VA 22314-4493

SAMUELSON, PAMELA ANN, law educator; b. Seattle, Aug. 4, 1948; d. Peter David and Margaret Susanne (Green) S.; m. Robert J. Glushko, May 7, 1988; 1 child, Robert M. BA in History, U. Hawaii, 1971, MA in Polit. Sci., 1972; JD, Yale U., 1976. Bar: N.Y. 1977, U.S. Dist. Ct. (so. dist.) N.Y. 1977. Rsch. assoc. Vera Inst. of Justice, N.Y.C., 1976-77; assoc. Willkie Farr & Gallagher, N.Y.C., 1977-81; prin. investigator Software Engring. Inst., Pitts., 1985-86; asst. prof. Law Sch. U. Pitts., 1981-84, assoc. prof. Law Sch., 1984-87, prof. Law Sch., 1987-96; prof. law and info. mgmt. U. Calif. Law Sch./Sch. Info. Mgmt. and Sys., Berkeley, 1996—. Bd. dirs. Berkeley Ctr. for Law and Tech./U. Calif., Berkeley; vis. prof. Emory Law Sch., Atlanta, 1989-90, Cornell Law Sch., Ithaca, 1995-96; mem. Nat. Rsch. Coun. Study Com. on Intellectual Property Rights and Info. Infrastructure, 1998-2000. Contbr. articles to profl. jours. Bd. dirs. ACLU Greater Pitts., 1983-88, Electronic Frontier Found., 2000—. John D. and Catherine T. MacArthur Found. fellow, 1997, Pub. Policy fellow Electronic Frontier Found., 1997—; recipient Disting. Alumni award U. Hawaii, 2000. Mem. ABA (sci. and tech. sect.), Am. Intellectual Property Law Assn. (subcom. chair 1988-89), Assn. Am. Law Schs. (intellectual property sect.). Democrat. Avocations: gardening, reading. Office: U Calif Berkeley Sch Info Mgmt and Sys 102 South Hall #4600 Berkeley CA 94720-4600 E-mail: pam@sims.berkeley.edu.

SAN AGUSTIN, MUTYA, pediatrician; b. Manila, Nov. 25, 1934; d. Dionisio and Trinidad (Tolentino) San A.; m. Barry Shaw, July 27, 1969; children: Noel, Ariel, Angela, Joanna. MD, U. Philippines, 1957. Diplomate Am. Bd. Pediats. Intern, resident Sinai Hosp., Balt., 1960, chief resident in pediats., 1961; chief phys. devel. rsch. divsn. Nat. Coordinating Rsch. Ctr., Philippines, 1962-64; dir. Montefiore-Morrisania Comprehensive Health Care Ctr., Bronx, N.Y., 1968-76; dir. ambulatory care medicine North Ctrl. Bronx Hosp.- Montefiore Med. Ctr., Bronx, 1976-97; dir. dept. primary care medicine Montefiore Med. Ctr., Bronx, 1997—. Cons. internat. ednl. br. HEW, 1969-74; cons. health com. U.S. China People's Friendship Assn., 1975-81; cons. to pres. N.Y.C. Health and Hosps. Corp., 1979-89;dir. primary care residency in pediats. and internal medicine Albert Einstein Coll. Medicine, 1979-92, prof. pediat.- clin. epidemiology and social medicine, 1993; vis. prof. UCLA, 1985, Ben-Gurion U., Beer-Sheva, Israel; mem. N.Y. State Coun. Grad. Med. Edn., 1988-90, N.Y. State Hosp. Rev. and Planning Coun., 1990-95, N.Y. State Gov.'s Health Adv. Bd., 1991-95; mem. residency tng. rev. com. divsn. medicine Bur. Health Profls., HHS, 1990-94; project dir. internat. pediat. fellowship program Montefiore Med. Ctr., Albert Einstein Coll. Medicine, 1989—; lectr. in field. Pediats. fellow John Hopkins U., 1960-61; Grantee NIH, 1967, NIMH, 1990-92; Atram Found. scholar, 1980; recipient Hon. Fellow award Philippine Pediat. Soc., Inc., 1996. Mem. APHA, Am. Acad. Pediat., Am. Pediat. Soc., Royal Soc. Medicine, Soc. Gen. Internal Medicine, Ambulatory Pediat. Assn., N.Y. Acad. Medicine, Philippine Ambulatory Pediat. Assn. (founding pres. 1995). Office: Montefiore Med Ctr 111 E 210th St Bronx NY 10467-2401

SANBORN, ANNA LUCILLE, pension and insurance consultant; b. Bklyn., Mar. 29, 1924; d. Peter Francis and Matilda M. (Stumpp) Galligen; 1 son, Dean Sanborn. BA, Bklyn. Coll., 1945. Head dept. benefit and estate planning Union Ctrl. Life Ins. Co., N.Y.C., 1949-51; adminstr. employee benefits Seaboard Oil Co., N.Y.C., 1952-56; with Frank J. Walters Assocs., Inc., N.Y.C., 1957—, pres., 1970—. Bd. dirs. Archdiocesan Svc. Corp. Mem. Am. Acad. Actuaries. Republican. Roman Catholic. Home: 58-11 Seabury St Elmhurst NY 11373-4825 Office: Frank J Walters Assocs 58-13 Seabury St Flushing NY 11373-4825 Office Phone: 718-779-8404. E-mail: fjwainc@aol.com.

SANBORN, DOROTHY CHAPPELL, retired librarian; b. Apr. 26, 1920; d. William S. and Sammie Maude (Drake) Chappell; m. Richard Donald Sanborn, Dec. 1, 1943; children: Richard Donald, William Chappell. Asst. cataloger El Paso (Tex.) Pub. Libr., 1954-55, 57-59, Stanford Rsch. Inst., Menlo Park, Calif., 1955-57; libr. Auburn (Calif.) Pub. Libr., 1959-62; cataloger Sierra Coll., Rocklin, 1962-64; reference libr. Sacramento (Calif.) City Libr., 1964-66; county libr. Placer County (Calif.), Auburn, 1966-89, ret., 1989. Chmn. Mountain Valley Libr. Sys., 1970-71, 75-76, 1984-85; cons. county libr. Alpine County Libr., Markleeville, Calif., 1973-80. Pres. Auburn Friends of Libr., 1995-97; vol. Peace Corps., Thailand, 1991-93. With WAVES, 1944-46. Mem. AAUW (pres. chpt. 1982-84), Calif. Libr. Assn., Soroptimists. Democrat. Mem. United Ch. Christ. Home: 135 Midway Ave Auburn CA 95603-5415

SANBORN, KATHY, career planning administrator, consultant; BA in Psychology, Calif. State U., Sacramento, 1989. Founder Life and Career Coaching, Sacramento, 2001. Keynote spkr., trainer, workshop presenter in field. Author: (book) Grow Your Own Love, 2001, The Seasons of Your Career, 2003; singer (composer): (CD) Critical Mass, 1996; contbr. articles to profl. jours.; columnist: various web sites. Mem.: Golden Key Honor Soc. (life). Office: Life and Career Coaching PO Box 215664 Sacramento CA 95821 Office Phone: 916-502-5770. Business E-Mail: kathy@lifeandcareercoaching.com.

SANCHEZ, BEATRICE RIVAS, art institute executive, artist; b. San Antonio, June 17, 1941; MFA, U. Mass., 1975. Artist in residence Trinity U., San Antonio, 1976; coord. fine arts program Fla. Sch. Art, Palatka, 1976-78; acad. dean, assoc. dean Md. Coll. Art & Design, 1978-82; dean Cranbrook Acad. Art, 1982-87; pres. Kansas City Art Inst., 1987—. Exhibited in group shows Women's Nat. Exhbn., Washington, 1980, Montgomery County (Md.) Regional Juried Exhbn., 1981, Greater Reston (Va.) Art Ctr., 1981, Alternative Space Gallery, Kansas City, Mo., 1991. Trustee Native Am. and Alaskan Indian Culture Inst., Santa Fe. Mem. Nat. Assn. Schs. of Art and Design (bd. dirs.). Office: Kansas City Art Inst Office of the President 4415 Warwick Blvd Kansas City MO 64111-1820

SANCHEZ, BERNADETTE M. state senator; BA in Psychology, MA in Counseling and Family Studies, U. N.Mex. Clin. mental health and sch. counselor; Dem. senator dist. 26 N.Mex. State Senate. Mem. edn. com. N.Mex. State Senate, vice chair corps. and transp. Home: 7712 Ranchwood NW Albuquerque NM 87120 Office: NMex State Senate State Capitol Mail Rm Dept Santa Fe NM 87503 E-mail: senate@state.nm.us.

SANCHEZ, HAZEL, reporter; BA in Broadcasting and Electronic Comm., Marquette U. Asst. prodr., news anchor Sta. WISN-TV, Milw.; host, moderator Teen Connection Wis. Pub. TV, Green Bay; reporter, weekend anchor Sta. WBAY-TV; gen. assignment reporter Sta. WCBS-TV, N.Y.C., 2000—. Recipient Golden Eagle, 1997, CINE award, 1997, award, Wis. Broadcast Assn., 1997, Midwest Emmy, 1997. Office: CBS 524 W 57th St New York NY 10019

SANCHEZ, LINDA T. congresswoman; b. Orange, Calif. m. Mark Sanchez. BA in Spanish Lit., U. Calif., Berkeley; JD, UCLA, 1995. Bar: Calif. 1995. Clk. to Hon. Chief Justice Terry Hatter, Jr. Ctrl. Dist. Ct., Calif.; compliance officer Nat. Elec. Contractors Assn. and Internat. Brotherhood Elec. Workers, 1998—2002; mem. from 39th Calif. dist. U.S. Ho. of Reps., 2002—; mem. judiciary com.; mem. govt. reform com., small bus. com. Lectr. Nat. Assn. Elected and Apptd. Ofcls., 1998—. Exec. sec.-treas. Orange County ctrl. labor coun. AFL-CIO; campaign worker Loretta Sanchez for U.S. Congress, 1996, 1998. Mem.: Internat. Brotherhood Elec Workers (Local 441). Office: 1007 Longworth Bldg Washington DC 20515 also: 4007 Paramount Ste 106 Lakewood CA 90712

SANCHEZ, LORETTA, congresswoman; b. Anaheim, Calif., Jan. 7, 1960; BA, Chapman U., 1982; MBA, Am. U., 1984. With Orange County Transp. Authority, 1984-87, Fieldman Rolapp & Assocs., 1987-90; strategic mgmt. cons. Booz Allen & Hamilton; owner, operator AMIGA Advisors Inc.; mem. U.S. Congress from 47th Calif. dist., 1997—; former mem. edn. and the workforce com., mem. armed svcs. com.; mem. House Select Com. on Homeland Security, House of Blue Dogs. Mem. Anaheim Rotary Club. Democrat. Office: US Ho of Reps 1230 Longworth Ho Office Bldg Washington DC 20515-0001*

SANCHEZ, MARLA RENA, retired controller; d. Tomas Guillermo and Rose Sanchez; m. Bradley D. Gaiser. BS, MS, Stanford U., 1979; MBA, Santa Clara U., 1983. Rsch. biologist Syntex, Palo Alto, Calif., 1980-81; fin. analyst Advanced Micro Devices, Sunnyvale, Calif., 1983-85; fin. mgr. ultrasound divsn. Diasonics, Inc., Milpitas, Calif., 1985-86, contr. therapeutic products divsn., 1989-93, contr. internat. divsn., 1992-93; contr. Ridge Computers, Santa Clara, Calif., 1986-88; dir. fin. VLSI Tech., Inc., San Jose, Calif., 1993-98; corp. contr. SDL, Inc., San Jose, 1999—2001, ret., 2001. Home: 1234 Russell Ave Los Altos CA 94024-5541

SANCHEZ, PAULINE STELLA, artist; MFA, UCLA. Artist and mem. faculty Art Ctr. Coll. of Design, 1989—. One-woman shows include Rosamund Felsen Gallery, Angeles Gallery, ACME, Ace Gallery, Marc Jancou Galerie, Zurich, Froment y Putman Galerie, Paris, exhibited in group shows at MOCA, Santa Monica Mus., The Drawing Ctr., N.Y., Galerie Krinzinger, Vienna, Monash U. Gallery, Australia, Kulturzentrum bein den Minoriten, Austria, New Langton Arts, San Francisco, Fotouhi Cramer Gallery, N.Y., Auckland Art Mus., New Zealand, Los Angeles Contemporary Exhibitions, Museu de Arte de Sao Paulo, Brazil. Recipient Credac Artist award, France-Europe;, John Simon Guggenheim Meml. Found. fellow, 2003, Foundation Cartier pour l'Art fellow, Nat. Endowment of Arts fellow. Office: Art Ctr Coll of Design 1700 Lida St Pasadena CA 91103

SANCHEZ, SONIA, English literature educator; Laura Carnell prof. English, Temple U., Phila., chmn. women's studies program. Lectr. on black culture and lit., women's rights and social justice at over 500 univs. colls. in U.S.; reader her poetry worldwide. Author 16 books, including We

A BaddDDD People, Under a Soprano Sky, Homegirls and Handgrenades (Am. Book award 1985), Like the Singing Coming off the Drums, 1999; contbg. editor Black Scholar, Jour. African Studies; editor 2 books black lit. Bd. dirs. MADRE. Recipient Lucretia Mott award, 1984, cmty. svc. award Nat. Black Caucus State Legislators; Pew fellow in arts, 1992-93. Mem. Women's Internat. League for Peace and Freedom (sponsor, Peace and Freedom award 1989). Office: Temple U Dept English 10th Fl Anderson Hall 1114 W Berks St Philadelphia PA 19122-6007

SANCHEZ, SUSIE RIOJAS, elementary school educator; b. San Antonio, Dec. 25, 1937; d. Lorenzo and Juanita (Cisneros) Riojas; m. Edward R. Sanchez, Aug. 28, 1960; six children. BA, St. Mary's U., San Antonio, 1984; cert., Our Lady of the Lake, 1985; MS, A&I U., 1990. Tchr. San Antonio Ind. Sch. Dist.; ret. Mem. PTC bd. Ursuline Acad. Mem. NEA, ASCD, San Antonio Tchrs. Coun., Tex. Tchrs. Assn. Home: 206 Inspiration Dr San Antonio TX 78228-1951 Office Phone: 210-977-9301.

SANCHEZ-WAY, RUTH DOLORES, health services administrator; b. N.Y.C., Aug. 8, 1940; d. Manuel and Cruz Maria (Rivera) Sanchez; m. Harley Milton Dirks, Feb. 9, 1974 (dec. Aug. 1986); stepchildren: Timothy, Darcy Kimmel, Marcine Thomas, James, David, Dale; m. David Vincent Way, Apr. 16, 1988. BS, St. John's U., 1962; MSW, Fordham U., 1965; PhD, NYU, 1978; postgrad., Emory U., Geroge Washington U. Cert. social worker, Md. Spl. asst. to dir. Nat. Inst. Alcohol Abuse and Alcoholism, U.S. Dept HEW, Rockville, Md., 1971-79; assoc. dep. adminstr. EEO Office Asst. Sec. Health, U.S. Dept. HEW, 1979-83; dep. dir. Office Adolescent Pregnancy Programs HHS, Washington, 1983-91; assoc. adminstr. minority health concerns Substance Abuse & Mental Health Svcs. Adminstrn., HHS, Rockville, 1993-96, divsn. dir. Ctr. for Substance Abuse Prevention, 1991-96, acting dep. dir. Ctr. for Substance Abuse Prevention, 1997, acting dir., 1997—2000, dir., 2000—02; assoc. dir. Ctr. for Faith-Based and Cmty. Initiatives, HHS, 2002—03; v.p. health and cmty. initiatives Mgmt. Scis. for Devel., 2003—. Bd. dirs. Nat. Health Coun., Washington, 1987-94, Nat. Coun. on Alcoholism and Drug Dependence, N.Y.C., 1979-91, Nat. orgn. ADOL Pregnancy Parenting and Prevention, Washington, 1991-93. Vol. Girl Scouts U.S.A., N.Y.C., 1996—. Recipient Excellence in Govt. Svc. award Mex.-Am. Legal Def. and Ednl. Fund, 2000, Presdl. Meritorious Exec. Rank award SES, 1998, Sec.'s award for disting. svc. HHS, 2001; primary care policy fellow USPHS. Mem. NASW, APHA, Chesapeake Crusing Multihull Assn. (past commodore, Kilmon award 1996). Roman Catholic. Avocations: sailing, skiing, jazzercise. Office: 4455 Connecticut Ave NW Ste A100 Washington DC 20008

SANDAHL, BONNIE BEARDSLEY, health services executive and provider, educator; b. Washington, Jan. 17, 1939; d. Erwin Leonard and Carol Myrtle (Collis) B.; m. Glen Emil Sandahl, Aug. 17, 1963; children: Cara Lynne, Cory Glen. BSN, U. Wash., 1962, MN, 1974; cert. pediat. nurse practitioner, 1972. Dir. Wash. State Joint Practice Commn., Seattle, 1974-76; instr. pediatric nurse practitioner program U. Wash., Seattle, 1976, course coord. quality assurance, 1977-78; pediatric nurse practitioner/health coord. Snohomish County Head Start, Everett, Wash., 1975-77; clin. nurse educator (specialist), nurse mgr. Harborview Med. Ctr., Seattle, 1978-97, dir. child abuse prevention project, 1986-97; mgr. Children's Ctr., Providence Health Sys. Northwest, 1997-2000; v.p. clin. svcs. and ops., COO Seattle Children's Home, 2000—03, exec. dir., 2003—. Spkr. legis. focus on children, 1987; clin. assoc. dept. pediatrics U. Wash. Sch. Medicine, 1987—; clin. faculty U. Wash. Sch. Nursing, 1987—97; mgr. Providence Gen. Children's Ctr., Everett, 1997—2000; gov. appointee State Interagy. Coord. Coun., 1998—, gov. appointee chair, 2004. Mem. Task Force on Pharmacotherapeutic Courses, Wash. State Bd. Nursing, 1985-86; Puget Sound Health Sys. Agy., 1975-88, pres., 1980-82; mem. child devel. project adv. bd. Mukilteo Sch. Dist., 1984-85; mem. parenting adv. com. Edmonds Sch. Dist.; chmn. hospice-home health task force Snohomish County Hospice Program, Everett, 1984-85, bd. dirs. hospice, 1985-87, adv. com. 1986-88; mem. Wash. State Health Coordinating Coun., 1977-82, chmn. nursing home bed projection methodology task force, 1986-87; mem. interim chair Nat. Coun. Health Planning and Devel., HHS, 1980-87; mem. adv. com. on uncompensated care Wash. State Legislature, 1983-84; mem. Joint Select Com., Tech. Adv. Com. on Managed Health Care Sys., 1984-85; pres., Alderwood Manor Cmty. Coun., 1983-85; treas. Wash. St. Women's Polit. Caucus, 1983-84; mem. com. to examine changes in Wash. State Criminal Sex Law, 1987; appointee county needs assessment com. Snohomish County Govt. United Way, 1989, 94; chair human svcs. adv. coun. Snohomis County Human Svcs. Dept., chair adv. com., 1998-; gubernatorial appointee State Interagency Coordinating coun. Health Svcs. Adv. Com. for Wash. State, 1995-97; apptd. Snohomish County Children's Commn., 1997—; apptd. by gov. State Interagy. Coordinating Coun., 1998—. Recipient Golden Acorn award Seattle-King County PTA, 1973, Katherine Rickey Vol. Participation award, 1987. Mem. ANA (chmn. pediatric nurse practitioner subcom. Com. Examiners Maternal-Child Nursing Practice, 1986-92, chair Com. Examiners Maternal-Child Nursing Practice 1988-90), Wash. State Nurses Assn. (hon. leadership award 1981, chair healthcare reform task force 1992-96), King County Nurses Assn. (Nurse of Yr. 1985, 1st v.p. 1992-96, pres. 1996-97), Sigma Theta Tau. Home: 1814 201st Pl SW Lynnwood WA 98036-7060 Office: Seattle Childrens Home Seattle WA 98119-2899

SANDBERG-MORGAN, BARBARA, retired communication and women's studies educator; b. McAllen, Tex., Dec. 19, 1934; d. Dean M. and Katherine (Hurlbert) Baer; m. Robert Morgan, July 31, 1976 (dec. Nov. 1994); 1 chld, Allison Morgan. BS, Ind. U., 1959; MA, Columbia U., 1963, EdD, 1974. Registered drama therapist. Prof. William Paterson U., Wayne, N.J., 1963-2000, prof. emerita, 2000—. Instr. Tchrs. Coll./Columbia U., N.Y.C., 1971-77; drama therapist, 1979—; mem. adv. bd., drama cons. Jersey Shore Arts Ctr., Ocean Grove, N.J., 1996—; dir. edn. Inner City Ensemble, Paterson, N.J., 1984-89; dir. Washington St. Gallery, Paterson, 1989-93. Dir. Paterson Bicentennial Pageant, Hist. Commn., 1992; dir. Washington St. Cultural Activities Assn., Paterson, 1990-93. Recipinet Heritage Citizen award Paterson, 1993, citation for tchg. excellence William Paterson U., 1994; named Woman of Yr., World of the Arts-Girl Scout Coun., 1995. Mem. Nat. Assn. for Drama Therapy (founding; bd. dirs.). Avocations: acting, directing, gardening. E-mail: millik@sedona.net.

SANDBURG, HELGA, author; b. Maywood, Ill., Nov. 24, 1918; d. Carl and Lilian (Steichen) S.; m. George Crile, Jr., Nov. 9, 1963; children by previous marriage: John Carl Steichen, Paula Steichen Polega. Student, Mich. State Coll., 1939-40, U. Chgo., 1940. Dairy goat breeder, also personal sec. to father, 1944-51; sec. manuscripts div., also for keeper of collections Library of Congress, 1952-56; adminstrv. asst. for papers of Woodrow Wilson, 1958-59; writer, lectr., 1957—. Author: (novels) The Wheel of Earth, 1958, Measure My Love, 1959, The Owl's Roost, 1962, The Wizard's Child, 1967; (non-fiction) Sweet Music, A Book of Family Reminiscence and Song, 1963; (with George Crile, Jr.) Above and Below, 1969; (poetry) The Unicorns, 1965; To A New Husband, 1970, The Age of the Flower, 1994; (young adult novels) Blueberry, 1963; Gingerbread, 1964; (juveniles) Joel and the Wild Goose, 1963; Bo and the Old Donkey, 1965, Anna and the Baby Buzzard, 1970; Children and Lovers: 15 Stories by Helga Sandburg, 1976; (biography) A Great and Glorious Romance: The Story of Carl Sandburg and Lilian Steichen, 1978; "...Where Love Begins", 1989, (recorded poems) From in the Dream: Helga Sandburg Reads her Poems, 2001; also numerous short stories; rep. in collections.; contbr.short stories, poems, articles to popular mags. including Seventeen. Recipient Va. Quar. Rev. prize for best short story, 1959, Borestone Mountain poetry award, 1962, Poetry award Chgo. Tribune, 1970; 2d prize 7th Ann. Kans. Poetry Contest, Florence Roberts Head Ohioana Book award, 1990; grantee Finnish Am. Soc. and Svenska Inst., 1961 Mem. Authors Guild, Poetry Soc., Am. Milk Goat Record Assn., Am.-Scandinavian Found., Nat. Nubian Club, Coun. Save the Dunes, Am. Luxembourg Soc., Acad. Am. Poets. Address: 2060 Kent Rd Cleveland Heights OH 44106-3339 E-mail: helgacrile@aol.com.

SANDER, ALISON BISHOP, international consultant; b. Boston, July 28, 1959; d. Frank E.A. and Emily (Jones) S. BA, U. Chgo., 1983; JD cum laude, MBA, Harvard U., 1987. Assoc. Goldman Sachs, N.Y.C., 1987—89; pres., CEO Cambridge Transnat. Assocs., Boston, 1990—97; mgr., globalization topic leader Boston Cons. Group, 1997—. Mem. bd. mgrs. N.E. Yearly Meeting of Friends, Boston, 1992-94; bd. dirs. Lisle Fellowship, Mich., 1990-94, Harvard Coop., Cambridge, Mass., 1984-87, Boston Ctr. for Internat. Visitors, 1993-94; overseer Boston Sci. Mus., 1998-; globalization commr. State of World Forum, 1998-. Recipient Perry S. Herst prize U. Chgo., 1981. Mem. UN Assn. N.Y. (panel), Coun. Fgn. Rels., Asia Soc., World Affairs Coun., Harvard Bus. Sch. Club of Boston, Phi Beta Kappa. Avocations: running, ballet, playing the dulcimer. Home: 74 Buckingham St Cambridge MA 02138-2229 Office: Boston Cons Group Exch Pl Boston MA 02109

SANDER, DOROTHY E. manufacturing executive; V.p. adminstrn. and benefits Hanson Industries, 1984-95; assoc. dir. Hanson PLC, 1993-95; v.p. adminstrn. U.S. Industries, Inc., Iselin, NJ, 1995—98, sr. v.p. adminstrn., 1998—, West Palm Beach, Fla., 2000—. Mem. adv. bd. Bank of N.Y. Bd. editors HR-Law and Practice mag., Feminist Press. Office: US Industries Inc 777 S Flagler Dr Ste 1112 West Palm Beach FL 33401

SANDERS, BARBARA FAYNE, artist, educator; b. Draper, N.C., Apr. 20, 1936; d. Elwood Oris and Gladys (Martin) Fayne; m. Joseph J. Sanders, June 11, 1960; children: J. Gregory, Kimberly Ann. Student ., Rockingham C.C., Wentworth, N.C., 1970—92. Jr. designer Design Dept., Karastan Rug Mill, Eden, NC, 1954—60; art instr. Rockingham C.C., Wentworth, 1985—2000; pvt. instr./condr. workshops, 1985—. Art coord. Eden Pub. Libr., 1985—90, Eden City Hall, 1995—. One-woman shows include Eden (N.C.) Pub. Libr., Eden City Hall Gallery, Rockingham County Govtl. Ctr., Wentworth, N.C., Forum VI, Greensboro, N.C., Stokes County Arts Coun. Gallery, Danbury, N.C., Chinqua Penn Plantation, Reidsville, N.C., Women's Club Gallery, Reidsville, Mt. Airy (N.C.) Art Guild, others, exhibited in group shows at Rockingham County Fine Arts Festival, Wentworth, Arts Davidson County Mus., Lexington, N.C., Carolina Craftsmen, Greensboro, Southeastern Artists Assn., Benton Conv. Ctr., Winston-Salem, N.C., Sawtooth Gallery, Winston-Salem, Art in the Pk., Blowing Rock, N.C., High Point (N.C.) Theatre Art Galleries, Carolina St. Scene, Winston-Salem, Arts Coun. Gallery, Cary, N.C., Piedmont Arts Assn. Gallery, Martinsville, Va., Danville Mus. History and Art, Capt.'s Ho. Gallery, others, Represented in permanent collections NationsBank, Wachovia Bank, First Nat. Bank, Home Savs. Bank., Miller Brewing Co., RJR Nabisco, Gem Dandy, Inc., Rockingham Arts Coun., Rockingham CC, Rockingham County Pub. Libr., Morehead Meml. Hosp., Steamway Internat., Gov. James Martin, N.C. U.S. area dir. Y's Menettes YMCA, Geneva, 1995—96, regional dir. Kannapolis, NC, 1993—95; pres. Draper Y's Menettes, Eden, 1978—2001. Named Y's Menette of the Yr., Draper Y's Menettes, 1984; recipient Vis.'s Favorite award, Fine Arts Festival Rockingham County, 1975, Best in Show, Rockingham County Fine Arts Festival, 1980, 1st pl., Sr. Art Expo, 1996, award of distinction, Danville Artists League, 1998, Piedmont Arts Assn., 2000, 2001, others. Mem.: Studio Group of Rockingham County (pres. 1996—97), High Point Art Guild (RECEPTION COORD. 1992—), Watercolor Soc. N.C. Avocations: reading, music, writing poetry and stories. Home: 135 River Ridge Rd Eden NC 27288-8004

SANDERS, CALLI THEISEN, athletics administrator; b. Great Falls, Mont., Oct. 11, 1964; d. Clifford Matthew and Theresa Eileen Theisen; m. Rick G. Sanders, July 14, 1966; children: Theisen Richard, Jack McDonnell, Molly Theresa. BA, U. Mont., 1986; MA, U. Ala., Birmingham, 1990; EdD, Mont. State U., 2004. Assoc. sports info. dir. U. Ala., Birmingham, 1988—90, asst. athletics dir., 1990—92, assoc. athletics dir., 1992—97, Mont. State U., Bozeman, 1997—2001; assoc. dean students U. Maine, Orono, 2001—03; assoc. athletics dir. Iowa State U., Ames, 2003—. Mem. athletics certification peer rev. team NCAA, Indpls., 1995—, mem. Divsn. 1 women's basketball com., 1999—2001; grad. Sports Mgmt. Inst., 2001—02. Mem. editl. bd.: Athletic Mgmt. Mag., 2001—. Bd. mem. Valley View Golf Club, Bozeman, 1998—98. Scholar, Mont. Bd. Regents, 1982. Mem.: Nat. Soc. Collegiate Scholars, Nat. Assn. Student Pers. Adminstrs., Nat. Assn. Collegiate Dirs. Athletics. Roman Catholic. Office: Iowa State Univ 1800 S 4th St Ames IA 50011

SANDERS, CATHARINE DOWNER, retired adult educator, historical researcher; b. Reno, Aug. 6, 1935; d. Robert Carpenter and Alice Marie (Gottschalk) Downer; m. Archable O'Neill Sanders, May 1, 1955; children: Christopher O'Neill, Eric Downer, Scott Carpenter. BA in Elem. Edn., U. Nev., 1975, MEd in Edn. Adminstrn. and Higher Edn., 1984. Cert. elem. tchr. grades K-8, Nev. Dir. ind. study by correspondence U. Nev., Reno, 1984-95; ret., 1995. Mem. Nat. Univ. Continuing Edn. Assn. (emeritus, Devoted Svc. award 1996), Nev. Adult Edn. Assn. (pres. 1989-90, Commendation award 1991), Nev. Women's History Project (no. Nev. vice chair 1996-98, state bd. chair 1997-98, co-chair conf. 1997, 98), Mountain Plains Adult Edn. Assn. (emeritus, co-editor newsletter 1994-96, award of merit 1996). Democrat. Presbyterian. Avocations: hiking, skiing, reading, music, traveling.

SANDERS, CHERYL ANN, special education educator, medical/surgical nurse; b. Balt., Dec. 22, 1958; d. Frederick William, Jr. and Addie Pearl Heinicken; m. Danny Glenn Sanders, July 17, 1977; children: Christina Lynn Ledbetter, Joshua Ryan. AS, San Jacinto Coll., Pasadena, TX, 1984; BS summa cum laude, U. of Houston - Clear Lake, 2003. RN Tex., 1984, cert. operating rm. nurse, Tex., 1991; tchr. Tex., 2003. Oper. rm. nurse The Meth. Hosp., Houston, 1984—93, St. Lukes Episcopal Hosp., Houston, 1994—95, Meml. Hermann SE Hosp., Houston, 1995—2002, M. D. Anderson Cancer Ctr., Houston, 1997—98, Clear Lake Regional Med. Ctr., Webster, 2002—; spl. edn. tchr. Deer Pk. (Tex.) Ind. Sch. Dist., 2003—. V.p. student coun. for exceptional children Clear Lake chpt. U. of Houston, 2002—02. Mem.: Coun. for Exceptional Children, Alpha Chi, Delta Kappa Phi. Home: 10914 Longren Houston TX 77089 Office: Deep Water Elem Sch 309 Glenmore Pasadena TX 77503

SANDERS, DAWN MARIE, special education educator; b. Calif., Oct. 1, 1977; d. Glen Verdale Sanders and Diane Catherine Simpson. BS in Edn., U. Ctrl. Ark., 1999, MS in Edn., 2001. Dir., tchr. Rainbow Child Care, Calico Rock, Ark., 2000; early childhood spl. edn. tchr. North Ctrl. Ark. Edn. Svc. Ctr., Melbourne, Ark., 2001—. Cons. Ark. Sch. for Blind/Deaf Children/Families with Multidiscipline Children, 1971. Asst. coach peewee basketball Calico Rock Sch., 2000, ofcl. score keeper basketball, 2001—. Baptist. Avocations: golf, reading. Home: PO Box 110 Pineville AR 72566 Office: North Ctrl Ark Edn Svc Ctr PO Box 739 Melbourne AR 72556

SANDERS, ELIZABETH ANNE WEAVER (BETSY SANDERS), management consultant; b. Gettysburg, Pa., July 25, 1945; Student, Gettysburg (Pa.) Coll., 1963-65; BA in German Lang. and Linguistics, Wayne State U., 1967; MEd, Boston U., 1970; postgrad., U. Wash., 1976-78. Prin. The Sanders Partnership, Sutter Creek, Calif., 1971-90; founder, dir. Nat. Bank So. Calif., 1971-90; v.p., gen. mgr. Nordstrom Inc.; prin. The Sanders Partnership, Sutter Creek, Calif. Bd. dirs. Wal Mart Stores, Inc., Washington Mut., Wellpoint Health Sys., Inc., Wolverine Worldwide, Inc., Denny's Inc., H.F. Ahmanson Co., Carl Karcher Enterprises, Sport Chalet, St. Joseph Health Sys. Author: Fabled Service. Trustee Gettysburg Coll. Recipient Woman of Achievement in Bus. award YWCA South Orange County, Director's Choice award, 1997; named Woman of Yr. Bus. and Industry YWCA North Orange County, Humanitarian of Yr. NCCJ, Author of Yr., 1996, Dir. of Yr., Corp. Gov. Forum for Corp. Dirs., 2002. Mem. Internat. Women's Forum. Office: The Sanders Partnership PO Box 14 Sutter Creek CA 95685-0014 Office Phone: 209-267-5400. E-mail: BetSanders@aol.com.

SANDERS, JACQUELYN SEEVAK, psychologist, educator; b. Boston, Apr. 26, 1931; d. Edward Ezral and Dora (Zoken) Seevak; 1 child, Seth. BA, Radcliffe Coll., 1952; MA, U. Chgo., 1964; PhD, UCLA, 1972. Counselor, asst. prin. Orthogenic Sch., Chgo., 1952—65; rsch. assoc. UCLA, 1965—68; asst. prof. Ctr. for Early Edn., L.A., 1969—72; assoc. dir.. Sonia Shankman Orthogenic Sch., U. Chgo., 1972—73, dir., 1973—93, dir. emeritus, 1993—; curriculum cons. day care ctrs. L.A. Dept. Social Welfare, 1970—72; instr. Calif. State Coll., L.A., 1972; lectr. dept. edn. U. Chgo., 1972—80, sr. lectr., 1980—93, clin. assoc. prof. dept. psychiatry, 1990—93, emeritus, 1993—; instr. edn. program Inst. Psychoanalysis, Chgo., 1979—82. Cons. Osawatomie State Hosp. (Kans.), 1965—68; reading cons. Foreman H.S., Chgo.; treas. Chgo. Inst. Psychoanalysis, 2003—. Author: Greenhouse for the Mind, 1989; editor (with Barry L. Childress): Psychoanalytic Approaches to the Very Troubled Child: Therapeutic Practice Innovations in Residential & Educational Settings, 1989; editor: Severely Disturbed Children and the Parental Alliance, 1992; editor: (with Jerome M. Goldsmith) Milieu Therapy: Significant Issues and Innovative Applications, 1993; editor: The Seevak Family, The Zoken Family; contbr. articles to profl. jours. Mem. vis. com. univ. sch. rels. U. Chgo.; bd. dirs. KAM Isaiah Israel Congregation, 1997—2001, Chgo. Inst. for Psychoanalysis. Recipient Alumna award, Girls' Latin Sch., Boston, Bettelheim award, Am. Assn. Children's Residential Ctrs., Disting. Svc. award, Radcliffe Assn., 2002; scholar Radcliffe Coll. scholar, 1948—52; Univ. fellow, UCLA, 1966—68. Mem.: Chgo. Inst. for Psychoanalysis, Assn. Children's Residential Ctrs. (past pres.), Harvard Club (bd. dirs. 1986—2001, Chgo.), Radcliffe Club (sec.-treas. 1986—87, pres. 1987—89, Chgo.). Home: 5842 S Stony Island Ave Apt 2G Chicago IL 60637-2033 E-mail: jsand09@attglobal.net.

SANDERS, JOAN SKOGSBERG, artist; b. Portland, Oct. 18, 1930; d. George and Dorothy (Myers) Skogsberg; m. Milford P. Cooper, Oct. 17, 1953 (div. 1972); children: Chapman J., Kristin D. Cooper-Segal; m. Salvador L. Sanders, June 12, 1983. BA, Calif. State U., 1988. One-woman shows include World Trade Ctr., Long Beach, Calif., 1994; group shows include Legal Aid Found., 1995, Long Beach Mus. Art, 1996, Goldenwest Coll. Fine Arts Gallery, 1997, JCC Gallery, Long Beach, 1997, 98, Art Auction 6, Long Beach, 1998, MWP Prodn. House, L.A., 1998, Orlando Gallery, Sherman Oaks, Calif., 1999, Macy Gallery, Valhalla, N.Y., 1999, Black Sheep Gallery, England, 1999, others; represented in permanent collections Mr. and Mrs. George Ryder, Ont., Can., Mr. and Mrs. Robert Kendrick, Ashland, Oreg., Mr. and Mrs. Elliot Segal, Laguna Hills, Calif., Mrs. Donna Lemmon, Las Vegas, Mr. and Mrs. Paul Casselman, San Juan Capistrano, Calif., Mr. Howard Harris, Mercer Island, Wash., Mr. William Beahm, Rolling Hills Estates, Calif., Mr. Chap Cooper, Long Beach, Calif., Mr. and Mrs. Henry Trujillo, Pueblo, Colo., Mr. and Mrs. Rich Darling, Long Beach, Ms. Barbara Ross, Hermosa Beach, Calif., Ms. Jacqueline Thompson, Manhattan Beach, Calif., Mr. and Mrs. Robert Langslet, Long Beach. Republican. Home: 3156 Stevely Ave Long Beach CA 90808-4439

SANDERS, KIM THERESA, marketing professional, consultant; d. Millard Wade Sanders and Louise Allen Davies; m. Robert Nelson Holden, Oct. 31, 1985. BA in English, Cabrini Coll., Radnor, Pa., 1977; MA in Adminstrn., Antioch U., 1983; PhD in Mktg. and Bus. Adminstrn., Rochville U., 2004. AVP dir. mktg. Beneficial Corp., 1985—87; sr. mktg. dir. Clement Comm., Inc., Concordville, Pa., 1987—94; group account mgmt. supr. MBNA, Wilmington, Del., 1994—96; dir., new bus./acct. mgt. Devon Direct Euro RSG, Berwyn, Pa., 1996—97; v.p. credit card mktg. PNC Bank, Wilmington, Del., 1997—99; sr. mng. dir. product and mktg. Bank One, Milw., 1999—2003; pres./mng. ptnr. Phaedeaux LLC, Oconomowoc, Wis., 2003—. Office Phone: 262-965-4832. Personal E-mail: ksanders@wi.rr.com.

SANDERS, MARION YVONNE, retired geriatrics nurse; b. St. Petersburg, Fla., Dec. 4, 1936; d. Ira Laurey and Maude Mae Cherry Sanders; children: Dwayne Irwin, Princess Charrie. BS, Fla. A&M U., 1959; MS, Nova U., Ft. Lauderdale, Fla., 1992. RN, Fla. Staff nurse Lantana (Fla.) TB Hosp., 1960-61, Mercy Hosp., St. Petersburg, 1961; gen. duty nurse VA, Tuskegee, Ala., 1961-62; staff nurse John Andrews Hosp., Tuskegee, 1962-63; gen. duty staff nurse Brewster Meth. Hosp., Jacksonville, Fla., 1963-65, Duval Med. Ctr., Jacksonville, 1965-66; pvt. duty nurse Dist. 2 Registry, Jacksonville, 1966-70; supr. Eartha White Nursing Home, Jacksonville, 1970; staff nurse Bapt. Hosp., Jacksonville, 1971-73, City-County Methadone Clinic, Jacksonville, 1976-78; pvt. duty nurse Home Nursing, Jacksonville, 1982-86, pvt. duty geriatric nursing and gerontology specialist, 1995—2001, Sr. Companion Svc. Corp., 1997-98; ret., 2001. Respite and relief sr. companion vol. Urban Jacksonville Cathedral Found., 1996-98. Mem. Ideas for Am.'s Future, 1997, 1998, NAACP, 1997—98; vol. shelter mgr. ARC, Miami, Fla., 1992—94; vol. cmty. activist, 1994; vol. Jacksonville Cmty. Rels. Bd., 1996, Jacksonville Inc. Cathedral Found., 1997—; sr. companion Svc. Corp., 1997—98, 1999; mem. Brewseter's and Cmty. Nurses Alumni, 1998—2000, 2001—02; vol. Rep. Senatorial Com., 1999; vol. cmty. svcs., elem. grades tutor, polit. campaigns, tchr. health edn.; vol. Rep. Nat. Com., 1997—2000, 2001—02, Rep. Com. Fla., 1997—98, Northside Rep. Club, 1997, 1998, 1999; active St. Stephen AME Ch., Jacksonville, tch. Bible studies for youth, advocate for poor, homeless and prisoners. Recipient Cert. of Recognition, Rep. Party, Fla. and Wash., 1990, Rep. Congl. Orgn., 1988, 90, 91. Mem. ANA (mem. polit. action coms.), Fla. Nurses Assn., Women's Missionary Soc. (life). Republican. Methodist. Avocations: reading the holy bible, teaching sunday school, volunteer work. Home: 4832 N Main St Apt 14 Jacksonville FL 32206-1458

SANDERS, MARLENE, anchor, journalism educator, news correspondent; b. Cleve., Jan. 10, 1931; d. Mac and Evelyn (Menitoff) Sanders; m. Jerome Toobin, May 27, 1958 (dec. Jan. 1984); children: Jeff, Mark. Student, Ohio State U., 1948—49. Writer, prodr. Sta. WNEW-TV, N.Y.C., 1955-60, P.M. program Westinghouse Broadcasting Co., N.Y.C., 1961-62; asst. dir. news and pub. affairs Sta. WNEW, N.Y.C., 1962-64; anchor, news program ABC News, N.Y.C., 1964-68, corr., 1968-72, documentary prodr., writer, anchor, 1972-76, v.p., dir. TV documentaries, 1976-78; corr. CBS News, N.Y.C., 1978-87; host Currents Sta. WNET-TV, N.Y.C., 1987-88; host Met. Week in Rev., 1988-90; host Thirteen Live Sta. WNET-TV, 1990-91; prof. dept. journalism NYU, N.Y.C., 1991-93; adj. prof. journalism, adminstr. Columbia U. Grad. Sch. Journalism, N.Y.C., 1994-95; adj. prof. journalism NYU, 1996—. Profl.-in-residence Freedom Forum Media Studies Ctr., 1997-2000; freelance broadcaster, narrator; chmn. bd. womensenews.org, chair RSVP, Inc., 1997-. Co-author: Waiting for Prime Time: The Women of Television News, 1988. Mem. N.Y.C. Commn. on Women's Issues, NY, 2003—. Recipient award N.Y. State Broadcasters Assn., 1976, award Nat. Press Club, 1976, Emmy awards, 1980, 81, others. Mem. Am. Women in Radio and TV (Woman of Yr. award 1975, Silver Satellite award 1977), Women in Comm. (past pres.), Coun. Fgn. Rels. Personal E-mail: sanders110@aol.com.

SANDERS, MARY MARGARET, personnel director, dancer; b. Denver, Colo., July 22, 1948; d. Theron Eldrige Green and Bernice Myrtle Reed; life ptnr. Paul N. Owens; m. Larry Lee Russell Sanders (dec.); children: Larry Lee Russell, Dereck Leon; children: Clinton Edward Chisolm, Asenath Evett Chisolm. AA in Bus., Denver Free U., 1999; BA in Bus., Harvard U.

Caregiver Excellent Personnel, Denver, 1972—81. Sales exec. Amway Corp., Denver, 1989—; model Colo. U., Denver, 1973—; mgr. Female Exec., Denver, 1981. Mem. Women's Action Coun. Mem.: LWV, Nat. Assn. Female Exec., Nat. Mus. Women in Arts. Republican. Home: 250 W 14th Ave 706 Denver CO 80204

SANDERS, MELANIE, newscaster; b. Dayton, Ohio; m. Troy Carter Sr.; 2 children. Grad. in Journalism, Ohio U. Reporter WTVY, Panama City, Fla., weekend anchor Dothan, Ala.; noon anchor WKRG, Mobile, Ala.; news anchor WDSU News Channel 6, New Orleans, 1997—. Active Links, House of Ruth, Soc. for Prevention of Cruelty to Animals. Office: WDSU News Channel 6 846 Howard Ave New Orleans LA 70113

SANDERS, NANCY IDA, writer; b. Everett, Pa., May 17, 1960; d. Richard J. and Phyllis (Harden) Hershberger; m. Jeffrey L. Sanders, May 23, 1982; children: Daniel M., Benjamin L. Freelance writer, 1985—. Editor TCC Manuscript Svc.; contbg. editor The Christian Communicator, 1992-2000; asst. editor Trails 'N Treasure, Christian Mag. for Kids, 1998-99; leader Chino Hills Writers Critique Group. Author: Favorite Bible Heroes: Activities for Ages 4 and 5, 1993, Bible Crafts on a Shoestring Budget for Grades 3 and 4, 1993, Amazing Bible Puzzles: Old Testament, 1993, Amazing Bible Puzzles: New Testament, 1993, Jumbo Bible Bulletin Boards: More Bible Stories for Preschool and Primary, 1994, Jumbo Bible Bulleton Boards: Fall and Winter, Preschool and Primary, 1994, Jonah: Six Fun Surprises, 1994, Moses: Six Fun Surprises, 1994, My Book About Ben and Me, 1994, My Book About Sara and Me, 1994, Cents-ible Bible Crafts, 1995, The Fall into Sin, 1995, Jesus Walks on the Water, 1995, WA-A-A-AY COOL Bible Puzzles, 1996, Red Hot Bible Puzzles, 1996, Marshal Matt and the Slippery Snacks Mystery, 1996, Marshal Matt and the Case of the Secret Code, 1996, Marshal Matt and the Topsy-Turvy Trail Mystery, 1996, Marshal Matt and the Puzzling Prints Mystery, 1997, Marshall Matt and the Case of the Freezing Fingers, 1997, Archy's Adventures with Colors, 1998, Archy's Adventure with Numbers, 1998, Archy's Alphabet Adventure, 1998, Unforgettable Edible Bible Crafts, 1999, Old Testament Days, 1999, Bible Crafts and More, 1999, Lost and Found, 2000, Hidden Treasure, 2000, Comet Campout, 2000, Moon Rocks and Dinosaur Bones, 2000, 15 Irrestible Mini-Plays for Teaching Math, 2000, Can't Catch Me!, 2000, Off to the Fair, 2000, Cooks, Cakes, and Chocolate Milkshakes, 2000, The Super Duper Seed Surprise, 2000, A Kid's Guide to African American History, 2000, Just Right Science Plays for Emergent Readers, 2001, (with Jeff Sanders) American History Mini-Books, 2001, 25 Read and Write Mini-Books That Teach Word Families, 2001, Fresh and Fun: November, 2001, The Pet I'll Get, 2001, My Many Hats, 2001, Kingdom Kidz: Noah, 2001, Kingdom Kidz: Solomon, 2001, Kingdom Kidz: Zacchaeus, 2001, Kingdom Kidz, Martha and Mary, 2001, To Follow Yahweh's Plan, 2001, 15 Easy to Read Mini-Book Plays, 2002, Math Mystery Mini-Books, 2002, Munch and Learn Math Story mats, 2002, 15 Easy and Irresistible Math Mini-Books, 2002, Holiday and Seasonal Plays, 2002. Mem. Soc. Children's Book Writers and Illustrators. Home: 15212 Mariposa Ave Chino Hills CA 91709-2703

SANDERS, ROBIN RENEE, diplomat; b. Hampton, Va., July 5; d. Robert M. and Geneva (Machoney) Sanders. B.A., Hampton Inst.; M.A., Ohio U., 1979; M.S., 1979. Broadcast lic. FCC 3d class. Editoral assts. Essence Mag., N.Y.C., 1974-76, Fgn. Broadcast Info. Service, Washington, 1976-77; intern account exec. Burson-Marsteller Co., N.Y.C., 1977-78; pub. relations assoc. Seventeen mag., N.Y.C., 1979-80; polit. and counselor officer Am. embassy, Dominican Republic, 1980-83, consular officer Am. consulate, Oporto, Portugal, 1983-86, dep. polit. sect. chief Am. Embassy Khartoum, Sudan, 1986-88; spl. asst. AF Bur., 1989; dir. for pub. diplomacy for Africa, State Dept.; dir. for Africa, Nat. Security Coun. at the White House, 1988-89, 97-99; spl. asst. for L.Am., Africa and internat. crime for the under sec. for polit. affairs Dept. State, Washington; chief of staff, sr. fgn. policy Mem. Ho. Internat. Rels. Com.; U.S. amb. to Republic of Congo, 2002—; cons. Profl. Women's Seminar, 1983, 84; speaker U. Oporto, 1983; researcher dept. internat. relations Ohio U., 1978; TV producer dept. gerontology Hampton Inst., 1976-77. Recipient 1st place award for painting Two Faces, Scholastic Art Bd., 1981, Dept of State Meritorious award, 1989, three State Dept. Superior Honor awards, three State Dept. Meritorious Honor awards; journalism scholar Syracuse U, 1970. Dir. Nat. Security Coun., 1989; political Econ. Officer Namibia, 1989. Mem. Women in Communications, Pub. Relations Soc. Am., Am. Fgn. Service Assn., Nat. Council Negro Women, Black Caucus, Mus. African Art, Coun. on Fgn. Rels., D.C. C. of C.; Alpha Kappa Alpha, Alpha Kappa Mu. Consular Corps (Oporto); Diplomatic (Santo Domingo), Thursday Luncheon Group, Capital Press (Washington). Home: 110 E Bloomfield St Rome NY 13440-4339 Address: Embassy Republic of the Congo 310 Avenue des Aviateurs Kinshasa Gombe Republic of the Congo*

SANDERS, SUMMER, Olympic athlete, news correspondent, newscaster; b. 1972; d. Bob and Barbara Sanders. Plumpic swimmer, Barcelona, 1992; ret. from profl. swimming, 1993; host game show for children Figure It Out Nickelodeon, 1997—; broadcaster WNBA Lifetime TV, 1997—98; co-host NBA Inside Stuff, 1998—. Recipient Gold medal, 200m Butterfly, Barcelona Olympic Games, 1992, Silver medal, 200m Individual Medley, 1992, Bronze medal, 400m Individual Medley, 1992. Office: care Nickelodeon/Figure It Out 1515 Broadway Fl 38 New York NY 10036-8901 also: NBA Inside Stuff care NBA Entertainment Inc 450 Harmon Meadow Blvd Secaucus NJ 07094-3618

SANDERSON, HOLLADAY WORTH, priest; b. Raleigh, N.C., May 17, 1950; d. Hal Venable Jr. and Mary Simmons (Andrews) W.; m. Glen Wessel Potter, Apr. 15, 1978 (div. Sept. 1980); m. Stanley McNaughton Sanderson, July 2, 1984. AB in Music and French, U. N.C., 1972; MMEd, East Carolina U., 1975; cert. advanced acctg./data processing, Kinman Bus. U., 1985; MDiv, Va. Theol. Sem., 2001. Ordained deacon Episcopal Ch., 2001, ordained priest 2001. Orch. tchr. New Hanover County Schs., Wilmington, N.C., 1972-74, 75-78, Fairfax (Va.) County Schs., 1978-80, 86-89, Missoula (Mont.) Elem. Sch. Dist., 1983-84; musician, music tchr. Coeur d'Alene, Idaho, 1980-83, 84-86, 1989-91; adj. music faculty, violin, viola, chamber music North Idaho Coll., Coeur d'Alene, 1980-83, 84-86; organist, choir dir. St. Luke's Epsicopal ch., Coeur d'Alene, 1980-83, 84-86, St. Luke's Episcopal Ch., Coeur d'Alene, 1989-95; gen. mgr., artistic dir. Coeur d'Alene Summer Theatre, Coeur d'Alene, 1991-92; bookkeeper, adminstrv. asst. Women's Ctr., Coeur d'Alene, 1993-95, exec. dir., 1995-98; rector St. Martin's Episcopal Ch., Moses Lake, Wash., 2001—; mem. diocesan coun., 2001—03; sec. Episcopal Diocese of Spokane, 2002—03, mem. commn. on ministry, 2002—, chair com. on sexual ethics in conduct and ministry, 2001—; developer Episcopal Diocese of Spokane, Mission Imperatives, 2003—. Sec. Idaho Coalition Against Sexual and Domestic Violence, 1995-98; sec.-treas. North Idaho Coalition on Domestic Violence, 1995-98; bd. dirs. Idaho Women's Network, 1997-98; mem. vestry St. Luke's Episcopal Ch., 1995-97, chair audit com., 1992-95, lay reader, chalice bearer, 1992-98, parliamentarian, 1996, sr. warden, 1997; orch. dir. Pend Oreille Chamber Orch., Sandpoint, Idaho, 1994-95, North Idaho Symphony, 1991, Coeur d'Alene Summer Theatre, 1982-85; cert. QPR suicide prevention gatekeeper instr. Greentree Behavioral Ctr., Spokane, 1996—; mem. Nat. Coalition Against Domestic Violence, Washington State Coalition Against Domestic Violence, NOW, NARAL, Emily's List. Democrat. Avocations: reading, cross-stitch, feminist theology. Home: 3805 Sherwood Dr Coeur D Alene ID 83815-7834 Address: 415 E State St Moses Lake WA 98837 Office: St Martins Episcopal Ch 416 E Nelson Rd Moses Lake WA 98837

SANDERSON, JANET A. ambassador; b. Tucson, Ariz., Apr. 1955; Diploma, Coll. of William and Mary, 1977; MA in Nat. Security Studies, Naval War Coll., 1993. Econ. officer U.S. Fgn. Svc., 1978; various govt. positions, including energy and petroelum advisor Bur. of European Affairs (OECD), 1986—88; various state dept. positions to dept. econ. counselor to min./counselor for econ. affairs U.S. Embassy, Cairo, dept. chief of mission Amman, Jordan, 1997—2000; U.S. amb. to Algeria, 2000—. Recipient Herbert A. Salzman award for Internat. Econ. Performance, U.S. Dept. of State, 1996, numerous honor awards. Office: DOS Amb 6030 Algiers Pl Washington DC 20521

SANDERSON, MARY LOUISE, medical association administrator; b. Fairmont, W. Va., Oct. 29, 1942; d. Lawrence Oliver and Frances Evelyn (Shuttleworth) Shingleton; m. William W. Olmstead III, Dec. 1966 (div. June 1974); children: William W. IV, Happy; m. Lester F. Davis, III, Oct. 1979 (div. Dec. 1986); m. David S. Sanderson, Sept. 1992. Student, Vassar Coll., 1960-62, Carnegie Mellon, 1962-63. Real estate broker, N.C. Exec. sec. Creative Dining, Raleigh, N.C., 1980-83, Sea Pines Plantation Co., Hilton Head, S.C., 1973-79; adminstr. Am. Bd. Neurological Surgery, Houston, 1983—. Vol. Interact, Raleigh, 1984-86, M.D. Anderson Cancer Ctr./Camp Star Trails, 1994—; docent Mordicai House Hist. Preservation, Raleigh, 1981-83; mem. Reach to Recovery, 1995—. Recipient Vol. award N.C. State Gov., 1986. Mem. Am. Soc. Assn. Execs. Democrat. Episcopalian. Office: Am Bd Neurol Surgery 6550 Fannin St Ste 2139 Houston TX 77030-2718

SANDERS-SELF, MELISSA LYNN, author; b. Murfreesboro, Tenn., Dec. 8, 1962; d. David Self and Sharon Mayes; m. Nigel Sanders, Nov. 5, 1982; children: Dylan, Luke. BA, U. Calif., Santa Cruz, 1987. Author: (novel) All That Lives, 2002; dir., prodr. (CD-ROM) Writing Women's Lives, 1997, (films), 1995. Avocations: gardening, animals.

SANDFORD, BRENDA LYNNE, executive secretary; b. Hawthorne, Calif., Dec. 7, 1965; d. Buddy Lee and Karen Sue (Smith) Richards; m. Michael Burdette Sandford, Aug. 28, 1992; children: Hannah, Haley. Grad. high sch., Joplin, Mo. Cert. Prof. Secretary, Okla. Contracts adminstr. Mimix Corp., Tulsa, Okla., 1988-91, Word Industries, Tulsa, Okla., 1991-93; exec. sec. Williams Energy Group, Tulsa, Okla., 1993—. Active local United Way. Mem. Profl. Secretaries Internat., Nat. Assn. Female Execs., Nat. Notary Assn., Williams Office Network (pres. 1997—). Republican. Baptist. Avocations: native american heritage, singing, piano, violin, gardening. Home: 305 N Dogwood St Owasso OK 74055-2823

SANDFORD, JUANITA DADISMAN, sociologist, educator, writer; b. Wichita, Kans., June 20, 1926; d. Carl Orville and Mabel Bernice (Stearman) Dadisman; m. Herman Prestridge Sandford, Dec. 22, 1946; children: Susan Jane, Linda Ann, Mary Kaye. BA, Baylor U., 1947, MA, 1948; LLD (hon.), Hendrix Coll., 1991. Instr. sociology Wayland Bapt. Coll., Plainview, Tex., 1948-49, Ft. Smith (Ark.) Jr. coll., 1959, Ouachita Bapt. U., Arkadelphia, Ark., 1960-68, adj. prof., 1996—; asst. prof. sociology Henderson State U., Arkadelphia, Ark., 1968-89, coord. women's studies, 1975-89; ret., 1989; adj. tchr. Ouachita Bapt. U., 1996—. Chmn. bd. Coll. Cmty. Action, Inc., 1974-78; cons. human rels. Ark. Tech. Assistance & Consultative Ctr., 1964-78; mem. Gov. Ark. Commn. on Status of Women, 1975-80, Atty. Gen. Consumer Adv. Bd., 1977-79. Author: I Didn't Get a Lot Done Today, 1974, Poverty in the Land of Opportunity, 1978, Sunbonnet Sue: The Crone, 1996; contbg. author Women & Religion: Images of Women in the Bible, 1977, Arkansas: State in Transition, 1981, Arkadelphia: 2000 AD, 1982. Bd. dirs. Ctrl. Ark. Devel. Coun., 1975-80, Ark. Hunger Project, 1983-86, Ark. Advs. for Children and Families, 1986-89. Recipient Ark. Woman of Achievement award Ark. Womens Polit. Caucus, 1975. Mem. NOW, Ark. Sociolog. & Anthropolog. Assn. (pres. 1991-92), Inst. Noetic Sci. Avocations: quilting, flower gardening. Home: 959 N 8th St Arkadelphia AR 71923-3201 E-mail: sandford@ezclick.net.

SAND LEE, INGER, artist; came to U.S., 1960; d. Inge Sigvald and Johanne Elise (Hamre) Sand; m. Charles Allen Lee, Aug. 28, 1981. Cert. in decorative art, N.Y. Sch. Interior Design, 1968; BFA, Marymount Manhattan Coll./N.Y. Sch. Interior Design, 1980; cert. completion, Art Students League, 1993; postgrad., Nat. Acad. Design, 1993-94. Auction benefit ASID 85th Anniversary, 2001; juror small works Wash. Sq. East Galleries Dept. or N.Y.U., 2002. One-woman shows include Art 54, N.Y.C., 1988, Pyramid Gallery, 1990, Exhbn. Space, 1991, Denise Bibro Fine Art, 1993, 1995, 1997, 1998, 1999, 2000, 2001, DYN-CORP, Oak Ridge, Tenn., 1998, En Vogue Gallery, Knoxville, 1999, exhibitions include Lincoln Ctr., N.Y.C., 1988, Avery Fisher Hall, 1988, Mus. Atheism and Realism, Lviv, USSR, 1990, Lever House, N.Y.C., 1991, Nat. Acad. Mus., 1994, Albright-Knox Mus., Buffalo, N.Y., 2000, group exhbns., Pyramid Gallery, N.Y.C., 1989, 1990, 1991, Ariel Gallery, 1991, Broome St. Gallery, 1992, 1993, Ward-Nasse Gallery, 1992, Hudson Guild Art Gallery, 1992, Denise Bibro Fine Art, 1992, 1994, 1995, 1997, 1999, 2000, 2001, Frank Bustamante Gallery, 1993, So. Alleghenies Mus. Art, Loretto, Pa., 1994, Edward William Gallery, 1996, Knoxville (Tenn.) Opera Guild, 1996, Fairleigh Dickinson U., 1996, N.Y. Internat. Film and Video Festival, 1998, Gramercy Pk. Armory, N.Y.C., 1998, Jacob K. Javits Conv. Ctr., 1998, DYN Corp., Oakridge, Tenn., 1998, Cambridge Fin., Knoxville, 2000, exhibited in group shows at En Vogue Gallery, Knoxville, Tenn., 1999, Art at the Mill, Millwood, Va., 1999, Adventures in Art, The Women's Nat. Rep. Club, 2001, Invitational Group Show, Denise Bibro Fine Art, N.Y.C., 2003. Mem. presdl. victory team Republican Nat. Com., 2001. Grantee Cork Gallery, Lincoln Ctr., N.Y.C.; recipient Alumni award N.Y. Sch. Interior Design, 1979; merit scholar Art Student's League, 1991. Mem. Archtl. League N.Y., Friends N.Y. Libr., Ams. Soc. (N.Y.), Nat. Geog. Soc., Nat. Mus. Women in the Arts, Pres.'s Cir. Smithsonian Nat. Mus. Am. History (charter, name inscribed on wall of Am. history patrons), Frick Mus., Guggenheim Mus, The Women's Nat. Republican Club. Address: PO Box 2036 New York NY 10021-0051

SANDLER, BERNICE RESNICK, women's rights specialist; b. N.Y.C., Mar. 3, 1928; d. Abraham Hyman and Ivy (Ernst) Resnick; children: Deborah Jo, Emily Maud. BA cum laude, Bklyn. Coll., 1948; MA, CCNY, 1950; EdD, U. Md., 1969; LLD (hon.), Bloomfield Coll., 1973, Hood Coll., 1974, R.I. Coll., 1980, Colby-Sawyer Coll., 1984; LHD (hon.), Grand Valley State Coll., 1974; Dr. Pub. Service (hon.), North Adams State Coll., 1985; LLD (hon.), Goucher Coll., 1991; LHD (hon.), Plymouth State Coll., 1992, Wittenberg U., 1993, Ripon Coll., 1998. Research asst., nursery sch. tchr., employment counselor, adult edn. instr., sec.; psychologist HEW, 1970; tchr. psychology Mt. Vernon Coll., 1970; head Action Com. for Fed. Contract Compliance, Women's Equity Action League, 1970-71; edn. specialist U.S. Ho. Reps., Washington, 1970; dep. dir. Womens Action program, HEW, Washington, 1971; dir. project on status and edn. of women Assn. Am. Colls., Washington, 1971-91; sr. assoc. Ctr. for Women Policy Studies, 1991-94; sr. scholar in residence Nat. Assn. Women in Edn., Washington, 1994—2000; sr. scholar Women's Rsch. and Edn. Inst., 2000—. Cons., 1991—; expert witness, 1990—; writer, 1971—; vis. lectr. U. Md., 1968-69; adv. bd. Women's Equity Action League Ednl. and Legal Def. Fund, 1980—, trustee, 1974-80, Women's Equity Action League, 1971-78; adv. com. Math./Sci. Network, 1979, Wider Opportunities for Women, 1978-85, Women's Legal Def. Fund, 1978-84; Nat. Coun. for Alternative Work Patterns Inc., 1978-85, Women's Hdqs. State Nat. Bank for Women's Appointments, 1977-78, and others. Mem. adv. bd. Jour. Reprints Documents Affecting Women, 1976-78, Women's Rights Law Reporter, 1970-80; editor: (newsletters) On Campus With Women, 1971-91, About Women on Campus, 1991-99; contbr. articles. Mem. bd. overseers Wellesley Coll. Ctr. for Rsch. on Women, 1975-87; bd. dirs. Ctr. for Women's Policy Studies, 1972-75; mem. exec. com. Inst. for Ednl. Leadership, 1982-87, mem. program adv. com., 1987-88, chair bd. dirs., 1981, chair adv. com., 1975-81; mem. affirmative action com., task force on family, nat. affairs commn. Am. Jewish Com., 1978, bd. dirs. D.C. chpt.; tech. adv. com. Nat. Jewish Family Ctr., 1980-89; adv. coun. Ednl. Devel. Ctr., 1980-85; adv. bd. Urban Inst., 1981-85, Women Employed Inst., 1981-84, Ex-New Yorkers for N.Y., 1978-79; mem. adv. com. Arthur and Elizabeth Schlesinger Libr. History of Women in Am., 1981-85; nat. adv. com. Shelter Rsch. Inst., Calif., 1980-82; chair adv. panel project on self-evaluation Am. Insts. for Rsch., 1980-82; bd. dirs. Equality Ctr., 1983, Evaluation and Tng. Inst., Calif., 1980, Inst. for Studies in Equality, 1975-77; exec. v.p. Bd. Women for Women, 1997—. Recipient Athena award Intercollegiate Assn. Women Students, 1974, Elizabeth Boyer award Women's Equity Action League, 1976, Rockefeller Pub. Svc. award Princeton U., 1976, Women Educators award for activism, 1987, Anna Roe award Harvard U., 1988, Readers Choice honors Washington Woman Mag., 1987, Woman of Distinction award Nat. Assn. Women in Edn.., 1991, Georgina Smith award AAUP, 1992, Woman of Achievement Turner Broadcasting System, 1994; named one of 100 Most Powerful Women Washingtonian Mag., 1982, one of the nation's 100 Most Important Women, Ladies Home Jour., 1988, Leadership Matters award Inst. Ednl. Leadership, 1997, Medal of Honor, Vet. Feminists, 2001, Donna Shavlik award Am. Coun. Edn., 2003, Mary Keetz award Women's Consortium Pa. State Sys. Higher Edn. Mem. Assn. for Women in Sci. Found. (bd. dirs. 1977—), Am. Soc. Profl. and Exec. Women (adv. bd. 1980). Avocations: birding, music, swimming, hiking. Office: Women's Rsch and Edn Inst 1350 Connecticut Ave NW Ste 850 Washington DC 20036-1740

SANDLER, DEBORAH, performing company executive; married; children: Shira, Benjamin. Degree, Temple U.; MA in Musicology, NYU. Exec. dir. Opera Festival N.J., Princeton, NJ, 1981—92, gen. dir., 1992—98, Ky. Opera, Louisville, 1998—. Office: Kentucky Opera 101 S Eighth St Louisville KY 40202*

SANDLER, LUCY FREEMAN, art history educator; b. N.Y.C., June 7, 1930; d. Otto and Frances (Glass) Freeman; m. Irving Sandler, Sept. 4, 1958; 1 child, Catherine Harriet. BA, Queens Coll., 1951; MA, Columbia U., 1957; PhD, NYU, 1964. Asst. prof. NYU, 1964-70, assoc. prof., 1970-75, prof. fine arts, 1975-86, Helen Gould Sheppard prof. art history, 1986—2003, chmn. dept., 1975-89; editorial cons. Viator, UCLA, 1983-97; Helen Gould Sheppard prof. emerita, 2003—. Author: The Peterborough Psalter in Brussels, 1974, The Psalter of Robert De Lisle in the British Library, 1983, new edit., 1999, Gothic Manuscripts 1285-1385, 1986, 'Omne Bonum': A Fourteenth-Century Encyclopedia of Universal Knowledge, 1996, The Ramsey Psalter, 1999, Der Ramsey-Psalter (Glanzlichter der Buchkunst 12), 2003, Der Bestiarium aus Peterborough/The Peterborough Bestiary, 2003, The Lichtenthal Psalter and the Patronage of the Bohun Family, 2004; editor: Essays in Memory of Karl Lehmann, 1964, Art the Ape of Nature: Studies in Honor of H.W. Janson, 1981, Coll. Art Assn. Monograph Series, 1970-75, 86-89, Gesta, 1991-94; asst. editor Art Bull., 1964-67, mem. editl. bd., 1994; mem. editl. bd. Jour. Jewish Art, 1978, Speculum, 1994. Trustee Godwin-Ternbach Mus., Queens Coll., 1982-94; chair dels. exec. com. Am. Coun. Learned Socs., 2002-04. NEH fellow, 1967-68, 77; fellow Pierpont Morgan Library; Guggenheim fellow, 1988-89. Fellow Medieval Acad. Am. (councillor 2002—), Soc. Antiquaries (London); mem. AAUP, Coll. Art Assn. (pres. 1981-84), Internat. Ctr. Medieval Art (adv. bd., bd. dirs. 1976-80, 84-87, 89-92, 1995-2001). Home: 100 Bleecker St Apt 30A New York NY 10012-2207 Office: NYU Dept Fine Arts New York NY 10003 Office Phone: 212-998-8181.

SANDLER, MARION OSHER, savings and loan association executive; b. Biddeford, Maine, Oct. 17, 1930; d. Samuel and Leah (Lowe) Osher; m. Herbert M. Sandler, Mar. 26, 1961. BA, Wellesley Coll., 1952; postgrad., Harvard U.-Radcliffe Coll., 1953; MBA, NYU, 1958; LLD (hon.), Golden Gate U., 1987. Asst. buyer Bloomingdale's (dept. store), N.Y.C., 1953-55; security analyst Dominick & Dominick, N.Y.C., 1955-61; sr. fin. analyst Oppenheimer & Co., N.Y.C., 1961-63; sr. v.p., dir. Golden West Fin. Corp. and World Savs. & Loan Assn., Oakland, Calif., 1963-75, vice chmn. bd. dirs., CEO, mem. exec. com., dir., 1975-80, pres., co- chief exec. officer, dir., mem. exec. com., 1980-93, chmn. bd. dirs., CEO, mem. exec. com., 1993—; pres., chmn. bd. dirs., CEO Atlas Assets, Inc., Oakland, 1987—, Atlas Advisers, Inc., Oakland, 1987—, Atlas Securities, Inc., Oakland, 1987—. Mem. adv. com. Fed. Nat. Mortgage Assn., 1983-84. Mem. Pres.'s Mgmt. Improvement Coun., 1980, Thrift Insts. Adv. Coun. to Fed. Res. Bd., 1989-91, v.p., 1990, pres., 1991; mem. policy adv. bd. Ctr. for Real Estate and Urban Econs. U. Calif., Berkeley, 1981—, mem. exec. com. policy adv. bd., 1985—; mem. ad hoc com. to rev. Schs. Bus. Adminstrn. U. Calif., 1984-85; vice chmn. industry adv. com. Fed. Savs. and Loan Ins. Corp., 1987-88, Ins. Corp., 1987-88; bd. overseers NYU Schs. Bus., 1987-89; mem. Glass Ceiling Commn., 1992-93. Mem. Phi Beta Kappa, Beta Gamma Sigma. Office: Golden W Fin Corp 1901 Harrison St Fl 6 Oakland CA 94612-3588*

SANDLER, MICHELLE GAIL, librarian; b. Long Beach, Calif., Oct. 22, 1956; d. Arthur Nelson and Annabelle (Marks) S. AA in History, Cypress C.C., 1977; BA in History, U. Ariz., 1979; cert. in cartography, Calif. State U., Long Beach, 1983; MLS, San Jose State U., 1993. Cartographer Teledyne Geotronics, Long Beach, 1983-84; tech. illustrator Oldershaw Engring., Anaheim, Calif., 1984-85, Cons. and Designers, Anaheim, 1985-86; sales clk. Aaron Bros. Art Marts, Garden Grove, Calif., 1987-90, libr. asst. County of Orange Environ. Mgmt. Agy., Santa Ana, Calif., 1990-93, County of Orange-Orange County Pub. Libr., Santa Ana, 1993; libr. Jewish Cmty. Ctr., Costa Mesa, Calif., 1992-94, Morasha Day Sch., Aliso Viejo, Calif., 1993—99, Temple Bat Yahm, Newport Beach, Calif., 1994—2001, Westwood Coll. Tech., Anaheim, Calif., 2000—. Profl. genealogist, Calif., 1986-90. Environ. educator Sierra Club, Tucson, 1977-79. Mem. Assn. Jewish Librs., Jewish Genealogy Soc. (pres. 1987-94). Democrat. Avocations: international folk dancing, genealogy, theater, museums, big band music. Home: 5773 Centerstone Ct Westminster CA 92683-9517 Office: Westwood Coll Tech 2461 West La Palma Ave Anaheim CA 92801-2610

SANDLIN, DEBBIE CROWE, critical care nurse; b. Columbia, Tenn., Oct. 1, 1953; d. William Taylor and Jean (Burns) Crowe; divorced; 1 child, Ashley Taylor. AS cum laude, Columbia State Coll., 1973; student, U. Tenn., Nashville, 1974-76. RN, Tenn.; cert. post anesthesia nurse; cert. ACLS, BCLS, U. Tenn. critical care curriculum. Charge nurse surg. unit Maury Regional Med. Ctr., Columbia, 1973-74; charge nurse surg. ICU HCA Pk. View Med. Ctr., Nashville, 1974-76; staff nurse post anesthesia care unit HCA Westside Hosp., Nashville, 1976-79; head nurse Columbia Centennial Surgery Ctr., Nashville, 1979-85; nurse mgr. Columbia So. Hills Med. Ctr., Nashville, 1985—, post anesthesia care unit nurse, 1985—; post anesthesia nurse Southern Hills Med. Ctr. Hosp., Nashville, 2000—. Mem. Am. Bd. Peri-Anesthesia Nursing Certification Appeals Bd. Surg. missionary Chocola, Guatemala, 1998. Recipient Excellence Critical Care Nursing award U. Tenn.; Maury Regional Med. Ctr. Aux. scholar, 1971; Dr. Frist Humanitarian award nominee, 1989, 95, 96, 97. Mem. Am. Bd. Peri Anesthesia Nursing (cert. rev. task force 1998-99), Mid. Tenn. Soc. Post Anesthesia Nurses (founder, pres. 1986, bd. dirs. 1986-88, Outstanding Svc. award 1986-87, pub. newsletter, editor 1986-87, various coms.), Tenn. Soc. Post Anesthesia Nurses (v.p. 1986-87, pres. 1987-88, bd. dirs. 1986-93, state seminar com. chairperson 1993-94, congl. rep. Point Sys. Winner 1987, 88, chair edn. com. 1994-98, chair TSPAN mid-yr. seminar 1996, various coms.), Am. Soc. Post Anesthesia Nurses (Tenn. dir. 1990-93, membership com. 1993-95, 2000-2001, ethics com. 1993-94, new products com., exec. com. 1992-93, chair bylaws com. 1992-93, nat. conf. com. 1991-92, amb. to Nat. Assn. Orthopaedic Nurses 1994, Pres. Appreciation award 1992, 93, 94, Amb. award 1995, 96, product evaluation com. 1995-96, edn. approver com. 1997-98, liasion to emergency nurses assn. nat. conf. 1995, scholar 1997, standards guidelines com. 1998-99, 99-2000, mktg. com. 1998-99, 2000-02, computer tech. com., computer tech. com. 1998-99, 2000-2001; editl. bd. dirs., columnist Jour. PeriAnesthesia Nursing 2000-), Am. Assn. Oper. Rm. Nurses (publ. com. 2001-02, mem. mktg. com. 2001—, editl. bd. jour. peri-anesthesia nursing 2000-03, resource guide columnist jour. peri-anesthesia nursing 2000—). Home: 508 Michele Dr Antioch TN 37013-4109

SANDMEYER, E. E. toxicologist, consultant; b. Winterthur, Zurich, Switzerland, Aug. 9, 1929; came to U.S., 1955; BSChemE, Technikum, Winterthur, 1951; MS in Organic Chemistry, Ohio State U., 1960, PhD in Biochemistry, 1965. Cert. civil svc. chemist II, Nev., biochemist II, Pa., clin. lab. dir. Ctrs. for Disease Control. Asst. prof. sci., gen. chemistry, organic chemistry Friends U., Wichita, 1965-66; asst. prof. biochemistry, labs., and rsch. U. Nev., Reno, 1966-71; head corp. toxicology Gulf Oil Corp., Pitts., 1971-76; divsn. head organic analysis Barringer Labs., Denver, 1987-88; pres., toxicologist, owner Transcontec, Inc., Kelseyville, Calif., 1976—. Div. head organic analysis Barringer Labs., Denver, 1986-88. Contbg. author: Patty's Industrial Hygiene and Toxicology, 1981, A Guide to General Toxicology, 1983. Mem. AAAS, Am. Chem. Soc., Soc. Environ. Health, Sigma Xi, Sigma Delta Epsilon. Office: Transcontec 7305 Live Oak Dr Kelseyville CA 95451-7862 Office Phone: 707-279-2821.

SANDOR, JOCELYN R. artist; b. Stamford, Conn., Mar. 4, 1957; d. Edward Albert and Rita Malyndziak Sandor; m. Richard Bruce Urban, Dec. 30, 1989; 1 child, Nicholas Vincent. BS in Fine Art, Skidmore Coll., 1979; MFA, U. Mass., 1981. Owner Jocelyn Sandor Fine Animal Portraits, Sherman, Conn., 1982—; v.p. FurSure Enterprises, Inc., Sherman, 1989-94, pres., 1994—. Artist Sherman Sentinel/Hist. Soc., 1999—. Selected exhbns. include N.C. Print and Drawing Soc., Charlotte, 1983, John Cusano Fine Art, South Norwalk, Conn., 1984, 86, 88, Mary Ryan Gallery, N.Y.C., 1985, Wenniger Graphics, Boston, 1985, Miriam Perlman Gallery, Chgo., 1985, Gallery on the Green, Lexington, Mass., 1987, U. Mass. Med. Ctr. Gallery, Worcester, 1987, Jocelyn Sandor/Cathrin Cammett/James Leslie Parker, Clayton and Liberatore Gallery, Bridgehampton, N.Y., 1991, Burnham Libr., Bridgewater, 1994, No. Westchester Ctr. for the Arts, Mt. Kisco, N.Y., 1998, 99, Sherman Libr., 1999, Hartford (Conn.) Fine Art and Framing, 1999, Bruce Mus., Greenwich, Conn., 1999; represented in permanent collections E.F. Hutton & Co., Inc., N.Y.C., Am. Nat. Bank and Trust, Chgo., Reader's Digest Assn., Inc., Pleasantville, N.Y., Exxon Corp., N.Y.C., World's Finest Chocolate, Inc., Chgo., Irving Trust, Westport, Conn., Ill. Bell Tel., Chgo., Ency. Brittanica, Chgo., Skadden, Arps, Meagher and Flom, N.Y.C., Skidmore Coll., Saratoga Springs, N.Y., Ky. Derby Mus., Louisville, Shearson Lehman, Chgo., Salomon Bros., Inc., N.Y.C., Chgo., Conn. Bank and Trust Co., Mktg. Corp. Am., Westport, Prudential Ins. Co., Boston, Mfrs. Bank Detroit, Reliance Nat. Ins. Co., N.Y.C., Westinghouse Corp., Chgo., Stonebridge Ptnrs., N.Y.C., others. Mem. varsity tennis team Skidmore Coll., 1975-79. Named Best in Show, Bruce Mus. Outdoor Art Festival, Greenwich, Conn., 1988; Rotary Found. fellow Rotary Club Fairfield, Conn., 1981. Mem. Quaker Hill Country Club (Pawling, N.Y.). Republican. Roman Catholic. Home and Office: PO Box 546 Sherman CT 06784-0546

SANDOVAL, AMADA, education program director; Interim dir. women's ctr. Princeton U., NJ. Mem.: Modern Lang. Assn. Am. (exec. coun. 2002—). Office: Princeton Univ 243 Frist Campus Ctr Princeton NJ 08544-2142 E-mail: sandoval@princeton.edu.

SANDOVAL, PAULA E. state senator; m. Paul Sandoval; 5 stepchildren. BA in Comm., MPA. State sen., dist. 34 Colo. Senate, Denver, 2002—. Mem. Finance Com. Bd. govs. Colo. State U.; mem. Denver Welfare Reform Bd.; bd. mem. Greenway Found.; mem. Hispanic Edn. Adv. Coun., Colo. Healthy Kids Coalition. Democrat. Office: State Capitol 200 E Colfax Ave Denver CO 80203

SANDROCK, DONNA, gallery director; b. Coon Rapids, Iowa, July 27, 1948; d. Forrest Orrie and Eleanor Caroline (Sieg) S. BA, Calif. State U., 1987. Curatorial asst. Calif. State U. Art Mus., Long Beach, 1985—86; asst. curator Long Beach Art Mus., 1986—90; asst. to registrar Laguna Art Mus., Laguna Beach, Calif., 1990—; dir., curator Fine Arts Gallery Golden West Coll., Huntington Beach, Calif., 1992—. Address: Fine Art Gallery PO Box 2748 Huntington Beach CA 92647-0748

SANDS, CHRISTINE LOUISE, English educator; b. Johnstown, Pa., Oct. 13, 1947; d. Joseph and Margaret (Kocsis) Migut; m. Angelo Joseph Sands, Dec. 28, 1968 (div. Nov. 1989); children: Vincent, Linda. BS in German, Indiana U. Pa., 1969, BS in English, 1975; postgrad., Slippery Rock U., 1971-76. Tchg. cert. Pa. Educator New Castle (Pa.) Schs., 1969—. Student advisor, judge Forensics, New Castle, 1981-96, Youngstown (Ohio) Reading Festival, 1981-95. Pres. New Castle City Coun., 1996; parish coun. St. Vitus Ch., New Castle, 1986-92; basketball referee PIAA, Mechanicsburg, Pa., 1972-91; coach New Castle H.S. Bowling, 1986-97. Democrat. Roman Catholic. Avocations: reading, traveling, sports, cooking, politics. Home: 819 E Hillcrest Ave New Castle PA 16105-2256 Office: New Castle HS 230 N Jefferson St New Castle PA 16101-2274

SANDS, CORI EILEEN, artist; b. Balt., Nov. 15, 1959; d. Reginald and Phyllis Emily (Johnson) S. Exhbns. include American Dream Festival, L.A., 1987, Currents, Balt., 1989, 4th Annual Am. Artist With Disabilities Lincoln Ctr., N.Y.C., 1990, City Hall Galleries, Balt., 1990, African Am. Artist With Disabilities, N.Y., 1992, Towson Town Art Festival, 1992, 94, Artscape, Balt., 1993, 95, 96, Out of Order Md. Art Place, Balt., 1995, Arena Playhouse, Balt., The Adler Gallery, 1996, Eubie Blake Mus., Balt., 1997. Served in U.S. Army, 1979-83. Democrat. Roman Catholic. Avocations: bicycling, billiards, bird breeding. Home: 912 Lenton Ave Baltimore MD 21212-3209

SANDS, DEANNA, editor; Mng. editor Omaha World Herald, 95—. Office: Omaha World-Herald World-Herald Sq Omaha NE 68102-1138

SANDS, DOLORES S. dean; BSN, MSN, Wayne State U.; PhD, Ariz. State U. Prof., dir. Ctr. Health Care Rsch. and Evaluation U. Tex., Austin, 1984-89, dir. grad. program nursing adminstrn., 1989—, former acting dean, asst. dean rsch. and resources, asst. dean baccalaureate program, now dean, Laura Lee Blanton chair in nursing, also now Joseph H. Blades Centennial Meml. prof. in nursing. Mem. nursing sci. rev. com. Exploratory Rsch. Ctr. Grants; mem. adv. coun. on nurses edn. and practice divsn. nursing Health Resources and Svcs. Adminstrn. U.S. Dept. Health and Human Svcs., 1991-93, co-chair adv. coun., 1993-95, mem. adv. group nat. task force for workforce projections of nurse practitioners and nurse-midwives, 1993, now mem. joint coun. primary care workforce workgroup; active Nat. Ctr. for Nursing Rsch., NIH. Contbr. articles to profl. jours. Grantee USPHS, 1986-89; recipient Alumni Achievement award Ariz. State U., 1987. Mem. ANA, Coun. Nurse Rschrs., Soc. Rsch. in Nursing Edn., Phi Kappa Phi, Sigma Theta Tau. Office: U Tex Austin Sch Nursing Office Dean 1700 Red River St Austin TX 78701-1412

SANDS, ROBERTA ALYSE, real estate investor; b. N.Y.C., Oct. 7, 1937; d. Harry and Irene (Mytelka) S. BEd, U. Miami, 1960; postgrad., U. Oslo, 1960. Cert. secondary educator biology, Mass. Phys. edn. instr. Key Biscayne and Ludlam Elem. Sch., Miami, 1961-63; sci. tchr. Plantation (Fla.) Mid. Sch., 1969-71, Rickards Middle Sch., Ft. Lauderdale, Fla., 1972-76. Founder U. Miami Diabetes Rsch. Inst., 1989. Author: Biology on the Secondary Level, 1970. Vol. Douglas Garden Retirement Home, Miami, 1988-92, Mus. of Art, Ft. Lauderdale, 1988-92, Imperial Point Hosp., Ft. Lauderdale, 1981-83. Mem. AAUW (rec. sec. 1988-92, cultural chair 1993-94, legis. chair Ft. Lauderdale br. 1994-95, women's issue chair Ft. Lauderdale 1994—, edn. chair Pompano Beach br. 1994-96, Recognition of Significant Svc. award 1983). Avocations: oil painting, golf, embroidery, travel. Home: 4250 Galt Ocean Dr Apt 8S Fort Lauderdale FL 33308-6113

SANDS, SHARON LOUISE, graphic design executive, art publisher, artist; b. Jacksonville, Fla., July 4, 1944; d. Clifford Harding Sands and Ruby May (Ray) MacDonald; m. Jonathan Michael Langford, Feb. 14, 1988. BFA, Cen. Washington U., 1968; postgrad, UCLA, 1968. Art dir. East West Network, Inc., L.A., 1973-78, Daisy Pub., L.A., 1978; prodn. dir. L.A. mag., 1979-80; owner, creative dir. Carmel Graphic Design, Carmel Valley, Calif., 1981-85; creative dir., v.p. The Video Sch. House, Monterey, Calif., 1985-88; graphic designer ConAgra, Omaha, 1988; owner, creative dir. Esprit de Fleurs, Ltd., Carmel, Calif., 1988-99; owner Sweden by the Sea, Carmel, Calif., 1999—2001; owner, dir. Sands Studios, 1999—. Lectr. Pub. Expo, L.A., 1979, panelist Women in Mgmt., L.A., 1979; redesign of local newspaper, Carmel, Calif., 1982. Contbr. articles to profl. mags. Designer corp. ID for Carmel Valley C. of C., 1981, 90. Recipient 7 design awards Soc. Pub. Designers, 1977, 78, Maggie award, L.A., 1977, 5 design awards The Ad Club of Monterey Peninsula, 1983, 85, 87, Design awards Print Mag. N.Y., 1986, Desi awards, N.Y., 1986, 88, Oil Painting awards Jazz Festival, 1999. Mem.: Soc. for Prevention of Cruelty to Animals. Democrat. Avocations: oil painting, interior decorating, gardening. Home and Office: 175 Ford Rd Carmel Valley CA 93924-9621

SANDSTROM, ALICE WILHELMINA, accountant; b. Seattle, Jan. 6, 1914; d. Andrew William and Agatha Mathilda (Sundius) S. BA, U. Wash., 1934. CPA, Wash. Mgr. office Star Machinery Co., Seattle, 1935-43, Howe & Co., Seattle, 1943-46; pvt. practice acctg. Seattle, 1945-85. Controller Children's Orthopedic Hosp. and Med. Ctr., Seattle, 1948-75, assoc. adminstr. fin., 1975-81; lectr. U. Wash., Seattle, 1957-72. Mem. Wash. state Title XIX Adv. Com., 1975-82, Wash. State Vendors Rate Adv. Com., 1980-87, Mayor's Task Force for Small Bus., 1981-83; bd. dirs. Seattle YWCA, 1981—, pres., 1986-88; bd. dirs. Sr. Svcs. Seattle King Co., 1989-95, 2003, bd. dirs. Sr. Svcs. Seattle/King County, 1985, treas., 1986, pres., 1988-90; bd. dirs. Children's Orthopedic Hosp. Found., 1982-90; mem. LWV, 1997. Recipient Jefferson award for vol. svcs., 1997, Alumnus award, U. Wash. Bus. Sch., 2002, Leadership award, 2002—03, Isabel Coleman Pierce award, YWCA, 2003. Fellow Hosp. Fin. Mgmt. Assn. (charter, state pres. 1956-57, nat. treas. 1963-65, Robert H. Reeves merit award 1970, Frederick T. Muncie award 1985; mem. Wash. State Hosp. Assn. (treas. 1956-70), Am. Soc. Women Accts. (pres. Seattle chpt. 1946-48), Am. Soc. Women CPAs, Wash. Soc. CPAs, Seattle Women's Voters League, Women's Univ. Club (Seattle), City Club (Seattle, charter mem.), Beta Alpha Psi (Outstanding Alumnus award 2001). Home and Office: 5725 NE 77th St Seattle WA 98115-6345 E-mail: sandstromaw@hotmail.com.

SANDVIG, SALLY, state legislator; m. Henry David Sandvig; 3 children. Student, N.D. State U. Sales rep. Avon; rep. Dist. 21 N.D. Ho. of Reps., mem. human svc. and govt. and vet. affairs coms. Precinct chmn., dist. sec. Dist. 21, Cass, N.D.; 4-H leader; client coun. mem. LAND; mem. Dem. Women. Soroptimist Internat. Tng. Awards scholar, 1988. Mem. Avon Pres.'s Club. Office: ND Ho of Reps State Capitol Bismarck ND 58505 Address: 201 11th St N Fargo ND 58102-4652

SANDVIK, HELVI, state agency administrator; BS Econs., Kalamazoo Coll.; MBA, U. Alaska. From transportation planner to dep. commr. State of Alaska Dept. Transportation; bd. dirs. Alaska Indsl. Devel. & Export Auth.; pres. NANA Devel. Corp. Office: AIDEA 813 W Northern Lights Blvd Anchorage AK 99503

SANDWEISS, MARTHA A. author, American studies and history educator; b. St. Louis, Mar. 29, 1954; d. Jerome Wesley and Marilyn Joy (Gilk) S. BA magna cum laude, Radcliffe Coll., 1975; MA in History, Yale U., 1977, MPhil in History, 1981, PhD, 1985. Smithsonian-Nat. Endowment Humanities fellow Nat. Portrait Gallery, Washington, 1975-76; curator photographs Amon Carter Mus., Ft. Worth, 1979-86; adj. curator photographs, 1987-89; dir. Mead Art Mus. Amherst Coll., 1989-97, adj. assoc. prof. of fine arts and Am. studies, 1989-94, assoc. prof. Am. studies, 1994-97, assoc. prof. Am. studies and history, 1997-2000, prof. Am. studies and history, 2000—. Author: Carlotta Corpron: Designer with Light, 1980, Masterworks of American Photography, 1982, Laura Gilpin: An Enduring Grace, 1986, (catalogue) Pictures from an Expedition: Early Views of the American West, 1979, Print the Legend: Photography and the American West, 2002; co-author: Eyewitness to War: Prints and Daguerreotypes of the Mexican War, 1989; editor: Historic Texas: A Photographic Portrait, 1986, Contemporary Texas: A Photographic Portrait, 1986, Denizens of the Desert, 1988, Photography in Nineteenth Century America, 1991; co-editor: Oxford History of the American West, 1994. Fellow Ctr. for Am. Art and Material Cultures, Yale U., 1977-79, NEH, 1988, 2000-01, Am. Coun. Learned Socs., 1996-97, Weatherhead, 2000-2001. Office: Amherst Coll Am Studies Dept Box 2225 Amherst MA 01002-5000

SANDWELL, KRISTIN ANN, special education educator; b. Topeka, Kans., Jan. 13, 1955; d. Edwin C. and E. Maxine (Nelson) Henry; m. Steve Sandwell, Dec. 27, 1997; children: Dustin Grimm, Chris Creek, Brandon Grimm, Sarah Sandwell, Paul Sandwell. AA, Hutchinson (Kans.) C.C., 1986; BS, McPherson (Kans.) Coll., 1989; MEd, Wichita State U., 1992. Cert. tchr. elem., gifted. Math/parenting tchr. Flint Hills Job Corps Ctr., Manhattan, Kans., 1992; gifted facilitator Unified Sch. Dist. 353, Wellington, Kans., 1993-94, Unified Sch. Dist. 260, Derby, Kans., 1995-97; tchr. City of Wichita Summer Youth Employment Program-Edn., 1997—98; gifted facilitator Unified Sch. Dist. 259, 1998—. Head injury counselor, life skills trainer Three Rivers Ind. Living Ctr., Wamego, Kans., 1992; facilitator Summer Youth Employment Edn. Program, 1997-98. Epiphany Festival prodr. Trinity Luth. Ch., McPherson, 1991, 93; CASA organizer McPherson Coll., 1988-89; vol. Coun. on Violence Against Persons, McPherson, 1990-92. Mem. ASCD. Avocations: reading, travel, working with disability issues. Office Phone: 316-973-6450. E-mail: ksandwell@yahoo.com., ksandwell@usd259.net.

SANDY, CATHERINE ELLEN, librarian; b. Italy; d. Felice Antonio and Guglielma Elena Santaniello; student Rosary Coll., 1933-34, U. Florence, Italy, 1951; B.S., Columbia U., 1953. Librarian, Port Washington (N.Y.) Pub. Library, 1926-73. Bd. dirs. Art Adv. Council, Port Washington Pub. Library; trustee, charter mem. Cow Neck Peninsula Hist. Soc. Recipient Alumni medal Columbia, 1970. Mem. Am., N.Y., N.C. library assns., UN Assn., Gen. Studies Alumni Assn. Columbia. Catholic. Editor: Cow Neck Peninsula Hist. Jour. Home: 2979 VT Route 22A Vergennes VT 05491-9092

SANFACON, MARY ELIZABETH, French educator; b. Worcester, Mass., Apr. 29, 1967; d. Michel Joseph and Phyllis Mary LeMay; m. Stephen Philip Sanfacon, Oct. 14, 2000. BA, Boston Coll., 1987; M French, Middlebury Coll., 1993. French tchr. Wachusett Regional H.S., Holden, Mass., 1987—. Drama dir. Wachusett Theatre, Holden, 1992—94; French exch. leader Wachusett and Dreux, France, 1997—99. Tchr. ESL course Cath. Charities, Worcester, Mass., 1988—90. Recipient Fulbright scholarship, NESDAC, Washington, 1995—96. Mem.: Mass. Assn. Fgn. Langs., Assn. Tchrs. French. Avocations: travel, cuisine, kickboxing. Home: 4 Mason Dr North Grafton MA 01536 Office: Wachusett Regional HS 1401 Main St Holden MA 01520 E-mail: mary_sanfacon@wrsd.net.

SANFORD, CAROLYN ANN, music educator; b. Corry, Pa., Aug. 1, 1944; d. Arthur John and Mildred Florence Brundage; m. James Irwin Sanford, Nov. 29, 1986; m. Frank Newton Bull, Aug. 20, 1966 (div. Jan. 1986); children: Jeremiah Jay Bull, Sarah Marie Bull. BS in Music Edn., SUNY, Fredonia, 1966; MEd, Gannon U., Erie, Pa., 1997. Cert. tchr. Pa. Music tchr. Ramstad Mid. Sch., Minot, ND, 1967—68, Burger Mid. Sch., Rush-Henrietta, NY, 1968—69, Robert Jackson Elem. Sch., Frewsburg, NY, 1969—70, Fairview Elem. Sch., Pa., 1970—. Mem. Lakeshore Railway Hist. Soc.-N.E.; organist, choir dir. Congl. Ch., Spring Creek, Pa., 1956—62, Minot Congl. Ch., ND, 1966—68, St. Stephens Episcopal Ch., Fairview, Pa., 1970—75, St. Paul's Luth. Ch., Erie, Pa., 1976—77, St. Stephens Episcopal Ch., Fairview, Pa., 1982—84, St. John's Luth. Ch., Girard, Pa., 1977—2002, youth group leader, 1988—99. Recipient Salute to Tchg. award, State of Pa., 1990. Mem.: Erie Music Tchrs. Assn. (v.p. 1984—85, sec. 1985—87, v.p. 1998—2000, pres. 2000—), Music Educators Nat. Conf., Kappa Gamma Pi, Sigma Alpha Iota. Republican. Lutheran. Avocations: travel, reading, gardening, theater, family. Home: 1314 Morrison Dr Erie PA 16505 Office: Fairview Sch Dist McCray Rd Fairview PA 16415

SANFORD, GLENDA LEVONNE, educational administrator; b. Mpls., Apr. 3, 1935; d. Robert Emmanuel and Stella Glendora (Larson) Carlson; m. Reed Ellis Sanford, June 17, 1955 (div. June 1979); children: Kenneth, Paul, Sheryl Sanford Vanscoy; m. Vernon Edward Almlie, Aug. 12, 1995; stepchildren: Jurgan, William, Ann Almlie Iglehart. AA, U. Minn., 1955; BA, Moorhead (Minn.) State U., 1979; MS, N.D. State U., 1986. Bus. office mgr. U. Minn. Health Svc., Mpls., 1955-58; office mgr. Reed E. Sanford Inc., Fargo, 1958-77; exec. dir. YWCA of Fargo-Moorhead, 1979-85; owner, mgr. farm and rental properties, Fargo, 1981-89; pres. Sanford Money Mgmt. Inc., Fargo, 1987—; program coord. Early Childhood Tracking Sys. State of N.D., Bismarck, 1989-98; spl. pub. adminstr. Cass County, Fargo, 1988-89; tax preparer H&R Block, Fargo, 1999—. Spkr. Women in Leadership N.D. State U. and KFME, Fargo, 1975-76; advisor N.D. Office Vol. Svcs., Bismarck, 1984-86. Mem. bds. YWCA, LWV, AAUW, Fargo, 1989-92; pres., treas. Jr. League Fargo-Moorhead, 1971-75; pres., bd. mem. Hot Line, Inc., Fargo, 1970-76, United Way of Cass County, Fargo, 1983, N.D. Dental Aux., Fargo, 1975-77; del. White House Conf. on Family, L.A., 1981. Recipient Women Helping Women award Soroptomist Internat., Moorhead, 1984. Mem. AAUW, LWV (treas. 1990-92), Women's Polit. Caucus (fundraising chair 1989-94), N.D. Mental Health Assn. Republican. Lutheran. Avocation: reading. Home and Office: 2101 10th St S Fargo ND 58103-5307

SANFORD, ISABEL GWENDOLYN, actress; b. N.Y.C., Aug. 29; d. James Edward and Josephine (Perry) S.; m. William Edward Richmond (dec.); children: Pamela (Mrs. Eddie Ruff), William Eric, Sanford Keith. Ed. pub. schs. Stage appearances in off-Broadway prodns., also in L.A.; Broadway appearance in Amen Corner; film appearances include Guess Who's Coming to Dinner, 1968, Pendulum, 1969, Stand Up and Be Counted, 1972, The New Centurions, 1972, Love at First Bite, 1979, Original Gangstas, 1996, Sprung, 1997, Mafia!, 1999, Jackie's Back, 1999, Click Three Times, 1999; appeared in TV film The Great Man's Whiskers, 1973, series All in the Family, numerous guest appearances various series, The Carol Burnett Show; co-star: TV series The Jeffersons, 1974-85, Hearts Are Wild, 1992, South Beach, 1992, Living Single, 1994, Hangin' with Mr. Cooper, 1994, The Fresh Prince of Bel Air, Cybill, Lois & Clark: The New Adventures of Superman, Roseanne, The Parkers, 2000. Mem. Kwanza Found. Address: Lemack & Co Mgmt 221 S Gale Dr Ste 403 Beverly Hills CA 90211

SANFORD, JO ANNE, state agency administrator; b. Laurinburg, N.C., Oct. 18, 1950; m. William E. Brewer, Jr.; 1 child, Charlotte Brewer. BA Polit. Sci., N.C. State U., 1972; JD, U. N.C. Sch. Law, 1975. Spl. deputy atty. gen. N.C. Atty. Gen.'s Office, 1975—95; chair N.C. Utilities Commn., Raleigh, 1995—2001; bd. dirs. USAC, 2001—. Apptd. to N.Am. Numbering Coun. FCC; bd. dirs. Nat. Regulatory Rsch. Inst. Master: N.C. Bar Assn.; mem.: Women Execs. in State Govt., Wake County Bar Assn. Office: 4325 Mail Svc Ctr Raleigh NC 27699-4325

SANFORD, LINDA S. information technology executive; b. Jan. 21, 1953; d. William J. and Catherine A. Sanford; 2 children. BA, St. John's U.; MS in Ops. Rsch., Rensselaer Poly. Inst. From mem. staff to sr. v.p. IBM, Westchester, NY, 1975—2003, sr. v.p. enterprise on demand transformation and info. tech. Somers, 2003—. Bd. dirs. ITT Industries. Bd. dirs. St. John's U., Rensselaer Poly. Inst. Named one of 50 Most Influential Women in Bus., Fortune Mag., Top 10 Innovators in Tech. Industry, Info. Week Mag., 10 Most Influential Women in Tech., Working Woman Mag.; named to Women in Tech. Internat. Hall of Fame. Mem.: NAE. Office: IBM Corp Rte 100 Somers NY 10589

SANFORD, SARAH J. healthcare executive; b. Seattle, July 20, 1949; d. Jerome G. and Mary L. (Laughlin) S. BS in Nursing, U. Wash., 1972, MA in Nursing, 1977. Cert. in advanced nursing adminstrn. Critical care staff nurse Valley Gen. Hosp., Renton, Wash., 1972-75, Evergreen Gen. Hosp., Kirkland, Wash., 1975-76; instr. nursing Seattle Pacific U., 1977-79; with Overlake Hosp. Med. Ctr., Bellevue, Wash., 1979-88, critical care coord., 1979-80, dir. acute care nursing, 1980-82, assoc. adminstr., 1982-83, sr. v.p. patient care, 1983-88; exec. dir. AACN, Aliso Viejo, Calif., 1988-90, CEO, 1990-99. Bd. dirs. Partnership for Organ Donation, Boston, Am. Soc. of Assn. Execs. Found., Washington. Co-editor: Standards for Nursing Care of the Critically Ill, 1989; contbr. articles to books and jours. Fellow Am. Acad. Nursing; mem. AACN (pres. 1984-85, bd. dirs. 1981-83), ANA, Am. Coll. Healthcare Execs., Soc. for Critical Care Medicine, Am. Orgn. Nurse Execs., Sigma Theta Tau.

SANFORD-HUGUS, BARBARA, geneticist, consultant; b. Brockton, Mass., Oct. 7, 1927; d. Arthur A. and Grace Brennan Hendrick; m. George R. Sanford, Nov. 25, 1950 (div. Jan. 15, 1971); children: Arthur, Jane, Brian, Paul; m. J. Edward Hugus, Apr. 14, 1992. BS, BA, Boston U., 1949; MA, Brown U., 1960, PhD, 1963; DSc (hon.), Bates Coll., 1986. Assoc. biologist Mass. Gen. Hosp., Boston, 1963—73; br. chief biology br. Nat. Cancer Inst., Bethesda, Md., 1973—78; assoc. prof. pathology Harvard Med. Sch., Boston, 1978—81; rsch. dir. Dana Farber Cancer Ctr., Boston, 1978—81; dir. Jackson Lab., Bar Harbor, Maine, 1981—88. Trustee U. Maine, Bangor, 1983—88, Jackson Lab., Bar Harbor, 1988—, Dana Farber Cancer Inst., Boston, 1981—. Contbr. numerous articles to sci. jours. Grantee, NIH, 1963—88. Mem.: Am. Assn. for Cancer Rsch. Home: 1090 Mission Rd Pebble Beach CA 93953 Personal E-mail: barbarahugus@hotmail.com.

SANGER, HAZEL A D, investment company executive; b. Glasgow, United Kingdom, Feb. 1, 1941; came to U.S. 1966; d. Paul Cedric Douglas Archer and Marian Reid Carmichael; m. Paul Weldon Sanger, Jul. 23, 1965; children: Georgina, Christopher. MA, Oxford U., England, 1962. CFA. With JF Chown & Co., London, 1963-66; v.p. TDP & L (name now Wellington Mgmt.), Atlanta, 1967-83; dir., managing dir. Atlanta Capital Management, 1983-93; dir. The Arden Group, Inc., Atlanta, 1994—2003; sr. dir. account mgmt. Mellon Pvt. Health Mgmt., 2003—. Co-author (with Prof. J. Peter Williamson): section on endowment fund mgmt., Investment Manager's Handbook, 1980. Hon. mem. adv. bd. dirs. Trust for Pub. Lands, Ga.; chmn. adv. coun. Lady Margaret Hall, Oxford U.; hon. bd. dirs. Atlanta Opera; bd. visitors, vice-chmn. fin. com. CDC Found., Atlanta. Fellow Royal Soc. Arts and Commerce, London, U.K.; mem. Assn. for Investment Mgmt. and Rsch. Avocations: reading, travel, opera, theater, countryside. Office: The Arden Group Inc 3495 Piedmont Rd NE Atlanta GA 30305-1773

SANGIULIANO, BARBARA ANN, tax consultant; b. Bronx, N.Y., Dec. 28, 1959; d. Patrick John and Mildred (Soell) Gallo; m. John Warren Sangiuliano, Aug. 28, 1982. BA, Muhlenberg Coll., 1982; MST, Seton Hall U., 1989, JD, 1997. Bar: N.J. 1997; CPA, N.J., 1987; CMA. Sr. tax mgr.

KPMG Peat Marwick, Short Hills, N.J., 1988-92; sr. tax analyst Allied Signal, Morristown, N.J., 1992-93; tax mgr. AT&T, Morristown, 1993-96, Lucent Techs., Morristown, 1996-97; tax atty. Witman, Stadtmauer & Michaels, Florham Park, NJ, 1997-98; tax cons. Ernst & Young LLP, Iselin, NJ, 1998—2003, Deloitte & Touche, Parsippany, NJ, 2003—. Mem. AICPA, ABA, N.J. Soc. CPAs (past pres. Union County chpt.), N.J. Bar Assn., Inst. Mgmt. Accts., Mensa, Omicron Delta Epsilon, Phi Sigma Iota. Republican. Roman Catholic. Avocations: reading, bicycling, fencing. Home: 340 William St Scotch Plains NJ 07076-1430 Office: Deloitte & Touche Two Hilton Ct Parsippany NJ 07054-4410 Personal E-mail: pudd__bear@msn.com.

SANKARAN, SHUBHA SILVER, musician, music educator, consultant; b. Calcutta, India, Dec. 18, 1948; came to U.S., 1979; d. Ganapathi and Sachi (Iyengar) S.; m. Brian Quayle Silver. BS with honors, Jadavpur U., Calcutta, 1969. Comml. model J. Walter Thompson, Calcutta, 1971-73; furniture designer Calcutta, 1971; accounts/programmer analyst Union Carbide, Calcutta, 1972-79; sr. prin. programmer analyst Digital Equip. Corp., Maynard, Mass., 1979-84, info. systems mgr., 1984-88, Washington, 1988-97; artistic dir. Internat. Music Assocs., Washington, 1988—. Tchr. Indian classical instrumental and vocal music, U.S., 1979—; lectr. Indian music U. Pa., 1998-99. Composer, performer (Indian instrumental and vocal music) Nat. Pub. Radio series, 1992 (Best sound award Internat. Radio Festival N.Y. 1991, Cindy Awards citation 1991), (Indian music on surbahar) Lincoln Ctr. for Performing Arts, N.Y., 1995, for Indian Pres. Narayanan, Peruvian Pres. Fujimori, 1998, Nat. Mus. Women in Arts, Washington, 1999, India, Pakistan, Bangladesh, Morocco, Rumania, Peru, Guatemala, Great Britain, U.S., 1988; composer, dir., performer (Indian ballet) Dasavatar, 1991/92; composer, dir., arranger, performer (BBC Radio Documentary) Monsoon, 1997. Recipient Gold medal All Pakistan Music Conf., 1990, Apprenticeship grant D.C. Commn. for Arts and Humanities, 1990, 92, 94, Grant-in-Aid, D.C. Commn./Arts and Humanities and Nat. Endowment for Arts, 1994, 99, Saeeda Khan Meml. award and Gold medal All Pakistan Music Conf., 1997, Travel grant to Pakistan, Sanjan Nagar Inst. Philosophy and Arts, 1997. Mem. Nat. Mus. Women in Arts. Democrat. Avocations: cooking, gardening, sports, reading. Home: 1730 C St NE Washington DC 20002-6661 Office: Internat Music Assocs PO Box 15526 Washington DC 20003-0526 E-mail: surbahar@aol.com.

SAN MIGUEL, LOLITA, artistic director; Student, Sch. Am. Ballet. Performer Robert Joffrey Co., Benjamin Harkarvy Co., Slavenska-Franklin Ballet; soloist Met. Opera Ballet; founder Puerto Rican Dance Theatre, N.Y., 1970; artistic dir., founder Ballet Concierto de P.R., Santurce, 1978—. Tchr., ballet mistress Ballet Hispánico, N.Y.; tchr. Dance Theatre Harlem, Performing Arts H.S., Adelphi Coll., Hofstra U., L.I. U., Clark Ctr., Met. Opera. Office: Ballet Concierto de PR PO Box 13245 San Juan PR 00908 3245*

SANNA, CATHERINE LEE, special education educator; b. Anchorage, Dec. 11, 1951; d. Julius Anthony and Willa Lee Sanna. BA in Elem. Edn., SUNY, Stony Brook, 1974; MS in Edn. and Spl. Edn., Hofstra U., 1978. Remedial math tchr. South Huntington (N.Y.) Pub. Schs., 1978; resource rm. tchr. Lindenhurst (N.Y.) Pub. Schs., 1978—80; health conservation tchr. Flushing Queens N.Y.C. Pub. Schs., NY, 1980—83. Host Spl. People show Radio Sta. WNYG, Babylon, NY, 1980—83. Author: A Forest Christmas: Campfire Girls, 1963 (award, 1965); music writer: Liar Rainbow Records, We are the World, The Rose, and many others; (sold paintings), 2003; song writer I Am Woman; song writer I Just Called to Say I Love You. Founder Police Survivors; active WWII Vet. Meml., British Am. & Am. Air Mus. Named Distinguished Alumni Broadcasting Civil Rights Activist for Disabled, SUNY at Stony Brook, 1992; recipient Internat. Poet of Merit award, 2003. Mem.: DAV, Am. Legion. Republican. Roman Catholic. Home: 161 S 6th St Lindenhurst NY 11757 Address: Gurwin Jewish Geriatric Ctr Ventilator Resident 68 Hauppauge Rd Commack NY 11725

SANO, EMILY JOY, museum director; b. Santa Ana, Calif., Feb. 17, 1942; d. Masao and Lois Kikue (Inokuchi) S. BA, Ind. U., 1967; MA, Columbia U., 1970, MPhil, 1976, PhD, 1983. Lectr. Oriental Art Vassar Coll., Poughkeepsie, N.Y., 1974-79; curator Asian Art, asst. dir. programs Kimbell Art Mus., Ft. Worth, 1979-89; dep. dir. collections and exhbns. Dallas Mus. Art, 1989-92; dep. dir., chief curator Asian Art Mus., San Francisco, 1993-95, dir., 1995—. Author: Great Age of Japanese Buddhist Sculpture, 1982; editor: The Blood of Kings, 1986, Weavers, Merchants and Kings, 1984, Painters of the Great Ming, 1993. Active Assn. Art Mus. Dirs.; vis. com. Harvard U. Art Mus. Woodrow Wilson Fellow, 1966-67; grantee Carnegie, 1963-64, Fulbright-Hays, 1977-78. Office: Asian Art Museum 200 Larkin St San Francisco CA 94102-4734 E-mail: esano@asianart.org.

SANQUIST, NANCY JOHNSON, facitliy management consultant, real estate consultant; b. Muncie, Ind., Aug. 31, 1947; d. Charles Elof and Pauline Lydia (Murphy) S.; m. James M. Johnson, Dec. 1988. BA, UCLA, 1970; MA, Bryn Mawr Coll., 1973; MS, Columbia U., 1978. Cert. facilities mgr. Instr. Lafayette Coll., Easton, Pa., 1973—74, Muhlenberg Coll., Bethlehem, Pa., 1974—75, Northampton Area CC, Bethlehem, 1974—75; dir. Preservation Office City of Easton, 1977—78; cons. El Pueblo de Los Angeles State Hist. Pk., 1978—79; dir. restoration Bixby Ranch Co., Long Beach, Calif., 1979-82; mgr. computer applications Cannel-Heumann & Assoc., L.A., 1982—84; dir. Computer-Aided Design Group, Marina del Rey, Calif., 1984-93; v.p. PAE Facility Mgmt. Svcs., L.A., 1993—97, Vanderweil Facility Advisors, Boston, 1997—99; dir. strategic initiatives Peregrine Sys., San Diego, 1999—2002; strategic asset mgmt. adv. Autodesk, San Rafael, Calif., 2003—. Adj. instr. UCLA, 1979-86, Grad Sch. Calif. State U., Dominguez Hills, 1981. Author numerous tech. articles and manuals. Bd. dirs. Historic Easton, Inc., 1977-78, Simon Rodia's Towers in Watts, Los Angeles, 1979-81, Los Angeles Conservancy, 1982-86, Friends of Schindler House, West Hollywood, Calif., 1978—, pres., 1982-85. Recipient Outstanding Contbn. award Nat. Computer Graphics Assn., 1987. Fellow Internat. Facility Mgmt. Assn. (seminar leader, lectr. N.Am., Asia, Australia, Europe and Mid. East 1987—); mem. AIA (assoc.). Avocations: travel, art and architecture, photography. Office Phone: 858-699-0827.

SANTAELLA, IRMA VIDAL, retired state supreme court justice; b. N.Y.C., Oct. 4, 1924; d. Rafael and Sixta (Thillet) Vidal; children: Anthony, Ivette. Acctg. degree, Modern Bus. Coll., 1942; BA, Hunter Coll., 1959; LLB, Bklyn. Law Sch., 1961, JD, 1967; LLD, Sacred Heart U., Conn., 1990. Bar: N.Y. 1961. Sole practice, N.Y.C., 1961-63; with ptnr., 1966-68; dep. commr. N.Y.C. Dept Correction, 1963-66; mem. N.Y. State Human Rights Appeal Bd., N.Y.C., 1968-83, chmn., 1975-83; justice N.Y. State Supreme Ct., N.Y.C., 1983-94, ret., 1994. Mem. N.Y.C. Adv. Council on Minority Affairs, 1982—, N.Y.C. Commn. on Status of Women, 1975-77. Founder, chmn. Legion of Voters, 1962-68; nat. del. Presdl. Democratic Convs., 1968, 72, 76, 80; vice chmn. N.Y. State del. 1976 Conv.; founder Nat. Assn. for Puerto Rican Civil Rights, 1962, Hispanic Community Chest Am., 1972; chmn. bd. dirs. Puerto Rican Parade, 1962-67; bd. dirs. Catholic Interracial Council, 1968-81; nat. co-chmn. Coalition Hispanic People, 1970; fund raiser Boy Scouts Am., 1962-63; chmn. Children's Camp, South Bronx (N.Y.) 41st Police Precinct, 1967; active City-Wide Steering Com. for Quality Edn., 1962-64, Community Service Soc., 1972-74, Talbott Perkins Children's Services, 1973-75, Planned Parenthood Assn., 1968-69, Puerto Rican Crippled Children's Fund, 1965-69; founder N.Y. chpt. Clinica Grillasca, P.R. Cancer Assn., 1974—. Recipient citations for civic work Gov. Rockefeller, 1972, Gov. Carey, 1982, First Puerto Rican woman to be elected to the N.Y. State Supreme Ct., County of Bronx, 1983; recipient Recognition award Gov. Mario M. Cuomo, 1990, Nat. Puerto Rican Coalition Life Achievement award, 1990, Life Achievement award Pres. of Dominican Republic, 1991, Life Achievement award Nat. Coun. Hispanic Women, 1991, others; inducted to N.Y. City Hunter Coll. Hall of Fame, 1998. Mem. Am. Judicature Soc. Roman Catholic. Home: 853 7th Ave New York NY 10019-5215

SANTAMARIA, ROSE, real estate agent; b. Kansas City, Mo., Dec. 5, 1955; d. Anthony and Minnie Mae (Sickler) S. Cert. residential specialist; accredited buyers rep.; cert. previews property specialist. Exec. sec. Russell Stover Candies, Inc., Kansas City, 1974-76; mgr. Land Banque Enterprises, Inc., Kansas City, 1977-80; mktg. sec. Sperry Univac, Kansas City, 1980-81; mktg. mgr. U.S. Devel. Corp., Hurst, Tex., 1984-94; real estate agt. Coldwell Banker Residential Brokerage, Dallas, 1994—, advisor new home divsn., 1996—. Bd. dirs., mem. archtl. control com. WoodBridge Devel. Corp., Hurst, 1985-87. Mem. Tex. Assn. Realtors, Greater Dallas Assn. Realtors, Internat. Pres. Elite (Multi Million Dollar Prodr. 1995, 96, 97, 98, 99, Top Office Prodr. award 1998). Office: Coldwell Banker Residential Brokerage 17101 Preston Rd Ste 110 Dallas TX 75248-1374

SANTI, KRISTI L. special education educator, researcher; b. Des Moines, Apr. 16, 1969; d. Joseph L. and Lois A. Santi. PhD, Fla. State U., 2002; M in Spl. Edn., Drake U., 1995, MA, 1993. Tchg. Cert. Iowa, 1993. Asst. prof. U. Tex. Houston, 2001—; adj. prof. Fla. State U., Tallahassee, 2000—02. Author: (jour. article) Remedial and Spl. Edn. (Publ., 2004). Mem.: Am. Ednl. Rsch. Assn., Coun. for Exceptional Children. Home: PO Box 20766 Houston TX 77225 Office: University of Texas Houston 7000 Fannin Street UCT 2443 Houston TX 77030 Personal E-mail: kristisanti@netscape.net.

SANTIAGO, MAYUMI-MAE LACAYA, marriage therapist; b. Manila, Feb. 15, 1966; came to U.S., 1969; d. Marciano B. and Eleanor (Lacaya) S. BS, Andrews U., Berrien Springs, Mich., 1989; MS, Loma Linda (Calif.) U., 1991. Registered marriage and family counselor, Calif.; cert. marriage and family therapist, Ariz. Intern marriage and family therapist Child Adolescent Treatment Svcs., San Bernardino, Calif., 1989-90, Loma Linda U. Marriage & Family Clinic, 1990-91; sr. intern marriage and family therapist Family & Child Therapy Program, Loma Linda, 1991-95; asst. dir., social worker Inland Empire Residential Ctrs., Redland, Calif., 1995-96; family preservation therapist Our Town Family Ctr., Tucson, Ariz., 1996-97, child and family counseling coord., 1997—. Mem. faculty U. Phoenix, Tucson, 1997—, faculty curriculum coord. marriage and family program, 1997—. Contbr. articles to profl. jours. Mem. Am. Assn. Marriage and Family Therapy. Seventh-Day Adventist. Home: 321 Bill Bean Cir Sacramento CA 95835-1703

SANTIAGO, THERESA MARIE, special education educator; b. Bronx, N.Y., Dec. 30, 1970; d. Louis C. and Maria M. (Rodriguez) Berrios; m. Mark C. Santiago, Aug. 19, 1995; 1 child, Louis Anthony. BS, St. John's U., 1992, MS, 1996. Cert. elem. tchr., tchr. of handicapped, N.Y. Elem. tchr. Leif Ericson Day Sch., Bklyn., 1992-93; tchr. handicapped Perth Amboy (N.J.) Pub. Schs., 1993—. Contbr. articles to profl. jours. Vol. Multicultural Fun Day, Perth Amboy, 1994—. Recipient Prin.'s award, Humane Educator of Yr. N.J. Humane Edn. Soc., 1996, Good Neighbor award Farmers Ins., others; subject of mag. articles for work in tchg. field. Mem. Coun. Exceptional Children, Alliance N.J. Environ. Educators (Educator of Yr. 1998). Democrat. Roman Catholic. Avocations: travel, computers, golf, arts and crafts. Home: 13 Kirschman Dr Matawan NJ 07747-6667 Office: Perth Amboy Pub Schs 178 Barracks St Perth Amboy NJ 08861-3402

SANTIN, JEAN, cosmetic company executive, consultant; b. Trenton, N.J., May 31, 1938; d. Joseph and Angeline (Parziale) Inverso; m. Louis Santin, Apr. 12, 1958; children: Renee, Scott. Grad. high sch., Trenton. Self employed jewelry bus., Hamilton Square, N.J., 1967-71; credit mgr. Lenape Products, Inc., Pennington, N.J., 1971-80; sales dir. Mary Kay Cosmetics, Ringoes, NJ, 1980—2003, fashion, beauty and color analysis cons., 1980-91, nat. sales dir., 2003—. Motivational speaker, Christian and secular in spiritual guidance, drug rehab. and eating disorders, 2001—. Beauty cons. for drug and alcohol rehab. area hosps., 1980-91; organizer of Christmas gifts for the underpriviledged, Hunterdon County, 1989, 90. Mem. Hunterdon County C. of C. Avocations: cycling, walking, traveling, fine dining, aerobics. Home and Office: Mary Kay Cosmetics 23 Runyon Mill Rd Ringoes NJ 08551-1514

SANTINA, DALIA, nutritionist, writer, skin care specialist; b. Amman, Jordan, Sept. 24, 1954; d. Mahmoud Dauod Abbasi, Widad Abbasi; m. Mohammed Shafiq Santina. BA in English Lit., U. Riyadh, Saudi Arabia, 1977; diploma in computer programming, Western Bus. Coll., 1980; diploma in Skin Aesthetics, Career Acad. Beauty, 1989; PhD in Holistic Nutrition, Clayton Coll. Natural Health, 1994. Cert. paramedical acne 1990, glycolic acid services 1991, mgmt. aging and sun-damaged skin 1992, natural pharmacology 1992, aesthetic peeling 1992, oxygenation of the skin 1993, lymphatic drainage massage techniques 1994, homeopathic esthetiocology 1994, iridology diploma 1995, cert. chem. peels 1996, hydrotherapy 1997, glycolic treatments 1998, diploma in iridology 2003, cert. in herbology 2003. Exec. asst. to v.p. Am. Health Ctr., Newport Beach, Calif., 1988—89; skin care co. Skinclub, Huntington Beach, Calif., 1991—96; lectr. holistic nutrition/skin health issues, 1999—. Translator computer sys. tng. manuals, Dallas, 1983—84; tech. translator England and No. Ireland, 1984. Author: Holistic Skin Is...In, 2001, Super Supplements for Skin, Body & Mind, 2003; contbr. articles to profl. jours. Recipient Gold medal in Table Tennis, Sports Bd., Kuwait, 1972. Avocations: horseback riding, reading, antiques. E-mail: dalia4skin@msn.com.

SANTINI, DEBRAH ANN, art educator, artist; BFA in Painting, U. Mass., 1983, MFA in Printmaking, 1994; postgrad., Pratt Inst., 1983-84; MEd in Printmaking, U. Hartford, 1988. Cert. tchr. 5-12, Mass., K-12 (provisional), Conn. Art tchr. Granby (Conn.) Meml. H.S., 1989-90, Suffield (Conn.) H.S., 1990-91; tchr. U. Mass, Amherst, 1991-93; asst. prof. State U. West Ga., Carrollton, 1994—. Artist-in-residence Bridgeport Mus. Art, Sci. and Industry, 1988, Lit. Showcase, Bristol, R.I., 1990, Connecticut Loves to Read, Windsor, Conn., 1991, Internat. Reading Assn., San Antonio, 1993, Am. Book Sellers Assn., Chgo., 1995, 96, Southeastern Book Sellers Assn., Nashville, 1996, So. Festival Books: Tenn. Humanities Coun., 1996, Westside Magnet Sch., LaGrange, Ga., 1997, 5th Annual Children's Storytelling Festival, Mableton, Ga., 1997; adj. prof. U. Hartford, Conn., 1991-92; lectr. in field. One-woman shows include Josoloff Gallery, U. Hartford, 1987, Springfield (Mass.) Ctrl. Gallery, 1988, Western New England Coll., Springfield, 1989, Fitchburg (Mass.) Mus. Fine Arts, 1993, Am. Internat. Coll., Springfield, 1993; group shows include Taipei Mus. Arts, 1988, 90, New Britain (Conn.) Mus. Art, 1989, U. Wis., Kenosha, 1991, Okla. State U., Stillwater, 1991, Associated Artists, Winston-Salem, N.C., 1992, San Jacinto Coll., Houston, 1993, Print Club Albany, Schenectady, N.Y., 1995, Arno Maris Gallery, Westfield, Mass., 1995, Artlink, Fort Wayne, Ind., 1996, Rolling Stone Press, Atlanta, 1996, 97, Appalachian State U., Boone, N.C., 1997, Rutgers U., New Brunswick, N.J., 1997, Cultural Ctr. Recoleta, Buenos Aires, 1997, Cultural Ctr. Trapalanda, Rio Cuarto, Cordoba, 1997, Contemporary Art Ctr., Mendoza, 1997, U. Minn., Mpls., 1998, Woman Made Gallery, Chgo., 1998, Visual Arts Alliance Nashville Am. Pop Culture Gallery, 1998, Museao Emilio Caraffa, Cordoba, 1998, Nat. U. Chaco, 1998, Columbus (Ga.) Mus., 1998; represented in permanent collections Gardiner Art Gallery, Okla. State U., Agawam (Mass.) Pub. Libr., Smith Coll. Rare Book Room, Neilson Libr., Northampton, Mass., Cultural Arts Ctr., Douglasville, Ga., Ga. Coll., Milledgeville, Chattahoochee Valley Art Mus., LaGrange; illustrator: The Baby Who Would Not Come Down, 1989, Santa's Secret Helper, 1990, Tulips, 1992, 96, Cinderella, 1994, The Last Dance, 1996, Wishing, 1996, When Young Melissa Sweeps, 1998, Oh, Georgia, Too!, 1998, (mags.) US KIDS, 1991, CRICKET, 1991, READ, 1993, POCKETS, 1998, 99. Recipient Purchase award Cimarron Nat. Works on Paper, 1991, Douglas County Regional Juried Fine Arts Show, 1994, Pressed & Pulled IV, 1995, XIX LaGrange Nat. Biennial Exhbn., 1996, Merit award Springfield Art League 76th Nat. Exhbn., 1995, Overall Excellence award Southeastern Libr. Assn., 1996; Don Freeman Meml. grantee Soc. Children's Book Writers Illustrators, 1987, Mass. Arts Lottery grantee, 1988, Nat. Endowment Arts/Southern Artists Fedn. grantee, 1996.

SANTINI, ROSEMARIE, writer; Lectr. in field. Author: (fiction) The Disenchanted Diva, A Swell Style of Murder, Ask Me What I Want, Beansprouts, (non-fiction) The Secret Fire, (novelization) All My Children; contbr. articles to numerous mags., anthologies; poetry performances include ATA Theater, Westbeth Cabaret, Greenwich Music Sch., St. Peter's Ch., Greenwich Ho. Mem.: NATAS, PEN, Sisters in Crime, Internat. Assn. Crime Writers, Dramatists Guild, Soc. Am. Journalists and Authors, Poetry Soc. of Am., Poets & Writers, Authors Guild, Mystery Writers of Am. (N.Y. bd.).

SANTO, MELISSA MARIE, chemist; b. Phila., Oct. 2, 1980; d. James Philip and Jennifer Brady Santo. BA, La Salle U., 2002. Writing fellow La Salle U., Phila., 2000—02; lab analyst Drug Control Centre, London, 2001—01; clin. receiving specialist Merck & Co., Inc., Wayne, Pa., 2002—. Mem.: Am. Chem. Soc. Home: 1152 Medway Rd Philadelphia PA 19115-2006 Office: Merck & Co Inc 466 Devon Park Dr Wayne PA 19087 Personal E-mail: melissamsanto@aol.com.

SANTONA, GLORIA, lawyer; b. Gary, Ind., June 10, 1950; d. Ray and Elvira (Cambeses) S.; m. Douglas Lee Frazier, Apr. 12, 1980. BS in Biochemistry, Mich. State U., 1971; JD, U. Mich., 1977. Bar: Ill. 1977. Atty. McDonald's Corp., Oak Brook, Ill., 1977-82, dir., 1982-86, assoc. gen. counsel, 1986-92, asst. v.p., 1989-93, v.p., sec., dep. gen. counsel, 1996-99, v.p., U.S. gen. counsel, sec., 1999-2001, sr. v.p., gen. counsel, sec., 2001—. Mem. ABA, Chgo. Assn., Am. Corp. Counsel Assn., Am. Soc. Corp. Secs. Office: McDonalds Corp 1 Mcdonalds Plz Oak Brook IL 60523-1911

SANTORE, MARCIA LUCINDA GREEN, editor, artist; b. Hartford, Conn., Nov. 25, 1960; d. Douglass Marshall Green and Marquita Yvonne Dubach; m. Jonathan Conrad Santore, May 30, 1987; children: Peter Douglass, Thomas Marshall. BFA, U. Tex., 1982. Devel. asst. Mount St. Mary's Coll., LA, 1987-91, alumni coord. physics dept. UCLA, 1991-93; gen. mgr. Minnetonka (Minn.) Orchestral Assn., 1994; advancement coord. Coll. Lifelong Learning, Concord, 1995-98; devel. assoc. Holderness Sch., Plymouth, NH, 1998—2000; editor Plymouth Mag. Plymouth (N.H.) State U. (formerly Plymouth State Coll.), 2000—. Tchr. Batchelder Artist Studios, Plymouth, N.H., 1995—; lectr. Plymouth (N.H.) State Coll., 2001-02. One-woman shows include Boyd Sci. Ctr./Plymouth State U., Silver Cultural Arts Ctr./Plymouth State Coll., UCLA Kerckhoff Gallery, North Country Ctr. for the Arts, Lincoln, N.H., Borders, Concord, N.H.; numerous group exhbns. Coun. Advancement and Support Edn. Newcomer scholar, 1991. Mem.: Women's Caucus for Art. Democrat. Episcopalian. Avocation: child rearing. Office: MSC 24 Plymouth State U 17 High St Plymouth NH 03264

SANTOS, ADELE NAUDE, architect, educator; b. Cape Town, South Africa, Oct. 14, 1938; came to U.S., 1973; d. David Francois Hugo and Aletta Adèle Naudé. Student, U. Cape Town, South Africa, 1956-58; diploma, Archtl. Assn., London, 1961; MArch in Urban Design, Harvard U., 1963; MArch., M in City Planning, MArch, U. Pa., 1968. Registered arch., Pa., Mass. Pvt. practice architecture with Antonio de Souza Santos, 1966-73; ptnr. Interstudio, Houston, 1973-79; assoc. prof. architecture Rice U., Houston, 1973-78, prof., 1979; prof. architecture and urban design, dept. architecture U. Pa., Phila., 1981-90; founding dean Sch. Architecture U. Calif., San Diego, 1990-94; pvt. practice architecture and urban design Adele Naude Santos, Arch., Phila., 1979-90, Adele Naude Santos and Assocs., San Diego and Phila., 1991—2002; prof. architecture Coll. Environ. Design U. Calif., Berkeley, 1994—2003; dean Sch. Architecture and Planning, MIT, 2004—. Project dir., co-filmmaker for 5 part series, 1979-80; works include Albright Coll. Ctr. for the Arts, Reading, Pa., 1991, Franklin-LaBrea Housing, Hollywood, Calif., 1995, Inst. of Contemporary Art, Phila., 1991, Yerba Buena Gardens, San Francisco, 1998. Wheelwright Travelling fellow, Harvard U., 1968; NEA grantee, 1976, Tex. Com. for Humanities grantee, 1979; recipient (with Hugo Naudé) Bronze medal for House Naudé Capt. Inst. South African Architects, 1967, award for public TV program So. Ednl. Communications Assn., 1980, 3d place award Inner city Infill Competition, 1986; winner Internat. Design Competition, Hawaii Loa Coll., hon. mention Cin. Hillside Housing Competition and City Visions, Phila., 1986; winner competition for Franklin/La Brea Affordable Housing Project Mus. Comtemporary Art and Community Redevel. Agy. City L.A., 1988, Pa. Soc. Architects design award for Franklin/La Brea Multi-Family Housing, 1988; winning entry collaborative competition for amphitheater, restaurant and natural history mus., Arts Pk., La., 1989; winner competition for 24-unit residential devel., City of Camden, N.J., 1989, for New Civic Ctr., City of Perris, Calif., 1991, children's mus. The Zoum, 1998, child care facility Yerba Buena Gardens, San Francisco, 1998, Please Touch Mus., Phila., 1998, winner design competition ChildCare Ctr. U. Pa., 1999. Fellow Am. Inst. Archs.; mem. Pa. Soc. Archs., Archs. Registration Coun. (U.K.). Office: 2527 South St Philadelphia PA 19146-1037 also: Santos Prescott & Assocs 33 Zoe St San Francisco CA 94107-1709

SANTOS, KAREY MICHALE, elementary school educator; b. Paramus, N.J., Oct. 3, 1956; d. Donald James Keeney and Barbara Jean (Wilson) Alderman; m. Joseph Karl Santos, Aug. 28, 1976; children: Sonya Rae, Donald Wesley. BA, U. S.C., Aiken, 1989, Interdisciplinary MA in Natural Sci., 1995. Math./sci. specialist Millbrook Elem. Sch., Aiken, SC, 1989—. Tchr., sponsor math. and sci. acad. teams, 1992—; mem. State Curriculum Standards Revision Team and Assessment Coms., 1999—. Recipient Sci. Scope award NASCO, 1992, Palmetto Cablevision Tchr. of Yr., 1992, Am. Nuclear Soc. Achievement award, Nat. Presdl. award for excellence in math. and sci. tchg., 2000; grantee Westinghouse, 1992-2002 EIA, So. Bell, Project Wild, Bryan Foods, Am. Chem. Soc. Mem. NSTA (Optical Data Corp. Videoisk award 1992, 93), S.C. Coun. Tchrs. Math., Soc. Elem. Pres. Awardees, S.C. Marine Edn. Assn., Environ. Edn. Assn. S.C. Home: 13 Normandy Ln Aiken SC 29801-2852 Office: Millbrook Elem Sch 225 E Pine Log Rd Aiken SC 29803-7613

SANTOS, WILMA, missionary; b. Cayey, P.R., Apr. 15, 1945; d. Faustino Escalera, Isabel Ortiz; m. Eugenio Santos, Nov. 22, 1964; children: Carlos Eugenio, Joann Lisa, Luis Ricardo, Hector. Missionary, Theol. Inst. Assemby of Christian Chs. Inc., Rochester, N.Y., 1975; BA, SUNY, Brockport, 1982. Cert. tchr. N.Y. Consumer educator Rochester (NY) City Sch. Dist., 1968—77, coord. CommUniv. program, 1977—78, elem. tchr., 1982—84, translator, 1985—86, lang. assessor, placement ctr., 1985—90; Spanish tchr. Cath. Diocese of Rochester, 1988—90, Charles Finney H.S., 1996—98; tutor Integrated Learning Ctr. Monroe C.C., 1998—. Tchr. God's Work Pentecostal Ch., Rochester, 1975—; missionary to Mex.; tchr. Bible studies; prodr. tchg. tapes; facilitator confs. various locations. Author: (book of poetry) Rayitos de Inspiración; contbr. Founder Spanish Christian Svc. Monroe County Jail; vol. Albion Correctional Facilities. Office: To God be the Glory Ministry PO Box 13225 Rochester NY 14613

SANTOSO, MICHELLE JO, music educator, pianist; b. Surabaya, Indonesia, Sept. 8, 1968; arrived in U.S., 1993; d. Kim Man Jo and Kiem Ing Tio; m. Peter Santoso, July 10, 1994; children: Hillary Lin, Herbert Lin. BA cum laude, IKIP, Jakarta, Indonesia, 1992; MA, Calif. State U., L.A., 1998. Music dir. Yip's Children Choir, San Marino, Calif., 1994—96; dir., tchr. piano Master Artists Piano Performing Studio, Alhambra, 1996—. Performer: Chopin's Nocturne, 1992 (Best Performance and Interpretation award, 1992), Bratislava Chamber Orch., Austria, 2001, Internat. Chamber Music Festival, Italy, 2002, Internat. Chamber Music Festival, Prague, 2003. Vol. Tiu Chi Orgn. Recipient prize, Yamaha Piano Competition, 1992, L.A. Liszt Piano Competition, 2000; scholar Inez Schubert scholarship, Calif. State U., L.A., 1996. Mem.: Southwestern Youth Music Festival, Nat. Guild Piano Tchrs., Calif. Assn. Profl. Music Tchrs., Music Tchrs. Assn. Calif., Nat. Fedn. Music Clubs. Home: 1475 Rubio Dr San Marino CA 91108

SANTUCCI, ANGELA MARIA, performing arts educator, actress, singer; b. Aurora, Colo., Feb. 25, 1976; d. Phillip John and Carolyn Louise Santucci. BA, No. Ariz. U., 1994—97. Asst. dir. Ctrl. Tex. Coll. Prep. Fine Arts Program, Killeen, 1998—2000; music, theatre tchr. Ravenscroft Sch., Raleigh, NC, 2001—; music instr. Spoleto Study Abroad, Spoleto, Italy, 2001; adminstrv. mgr. Chamber Orch. of the Triangle, Raleigh, NC, 2002—; asst. dir. of youth music Hillyer Meml. Christian Ch., Raleigh. Singer: (choral performances including) NC Master Chorale and Hillyer Cmty. Chorus; actor: (play) The Crucible by Arthur Miller, A Midsummer's Night Dream. Mem.: NC Music Educators Assn., Golden Key Nat. Honor Soc., Phi Alpha Theta Honors History Frat., Sigma Alpha Iota Music Frat. for Women (life). Office: Ravenscroft Sch 7409 Falls of Neuse Rd Raleigh NC 27615

SANTUCCI, L. MICHELLE, adult nurse practitioner, nutrition consultant; b. Denville, N.J., Oct. 11, 1956; d. Anthony Jr. and Raymonde (Cloitre) Santucci. BS in Biology, U. Bridgeport, 1977; AAS, Cumberland County Coll., Vineland, N.J., 1982; MSN, U. Medicine/Dentistry N.J., 1997; PhD in Holistic Nutrition, Clayton Coll. Natural Health, Birmingham, Ala., 1998. RN; cert. critical care nurse, intravenous therapy nurse, adult nurse practitioner. Staff nurse South Jersey Hosp. System, Bridgeton Divsn., N.J., charge nurse Bridgeton, N.J., nurse educator, adminstrv. nursing supr. Millville, N.J.; adult nurse practitioner Regional Med. Assocs., Millville, N.J., 1997-99; adult nurse practitioner, nutrition cons. Cumberland Med. Assocs., Millville, NJ, 1999—2001; prin., owner The Wholistic Ctr. for Wellness, Inc., 2001—. Clin. faculty assoc. U. Medicine and Dentistry N.J., Wilmington Coll. Mem. Am. Acad. Nurse Practitioners, N.J. State Nurses Assn., Coalition for Natural Health, Complementary Healthcare Consortium South Jersey. Home: 3284 Swan Dr Vineland NJ 08361-7367 Personal E-mail: lmsnp@aol.com.

SANZONE, DONNA S. publishing executive; b. Bklyn., Apr. 4, 1949; d. Joseph J. Seitz and Faye (Brooks) Rossman; m. Charles F. Sanzone, Jan. 2, 1972; children: Danielle, Gregory. BA magna cum laude, Boston U., 1970; MA, Northeastern U., 1979. Grad. placement specialist Inst. Internat. Edn., N.Y.C., 1970-72; adminstr. AFS Internat. Scholarships, Brussels, 1972-74; editor Internat. Ency. Higher Edn., Boston, 1974-76, G.K. Hall & Co., Pubs., Boston, 1977-81, exec. editor, 1981-91, editor-in-chief, 1991-96; v.p. Oryx Press, Boston, 1996-2000; editor-in-chief Grolier Acad. Reference, Danbury, Conn., 2000—. Contbg. author: Access to Power, 1981. Mem.: ALA, Libr. and Info. Tech. Assn., Assn. Coll. and Rsch. Librs., Soc. for Scholarly and Profl. Pub., Assn. Am. Pubs. Office: Grolier Acad Ref 18 Pine St Weston MA 02493-1116

SAPP, GINA LEANN, music educator; b. Chillicothe, Mo., Dec. 6, 1964; d. Marvin Lee and Shirley Ann Arbuckle; m. Jeffrey Dean Sapp, Sept. 7, 1991. B in Music Edn., Mid Am. Nazarene U., Olathe, Kans., 1989; M in Music Edn., U. Mo., Kansas City, 2004. Cert. K-12 vocal/instrumental music tchr. Kans., Mo. Music educator K-5 Kans. City (Mo.) Sch. Dist., 1990—94; music educator K-6 Shawnee Mission Sch. Dist., Prairie Village, Kans., 1994—. Mem. faculty adv. com., student coun. sponsor Leroy Satchel Paige Classical Greek Magnet, Kansas City, 1992—93; AAA safety patrol sponsor Briarwood Elem., Prairie Village, 1994—99, mem. quality performance accreditation reading com., 6th grade musical co-dir., 5th and 6th grade choral dir., 1994—; East Area Choral Festival chairperson Shawnee Mission Sch. Dist., 2000; Lyric Opera Express in conjunction with 5th grade choir participants Lyric Opera, Kansas City, Mo., 1994—. Mem. Project WILD, Pratt, Kans., 1997; participant Borders Book Benefit for Edn., Overland Park, Kans., 2002, Johnson County and Shawnee Mission East H.S. Earth Day Fair, Prairie Village, 2003; worship team soprano singer Westside Family Ch., Shawnee, Kans., 2001—03. Recipient Outstanding United Way Student Campaign award tchr. sponsor, 2003; grantee Shawnee Mission Sch. Dist., 2003. Mem.: NEA, Music Educators Nat. Conf., Nat. Riviera Owners Assn., Nat. Gran Sport Club Am., Nat. Buick Club Am., Phi Delta Lambda, Phi Theta Kappa, Pi Kappa Lambda. Avocations: antiques, Victorian architecture photography, classic automobiles, motorcycling, travel.

SAPP, LAUREN B. librarian, educator; b. Smithfield, N.C., Aug. 22; d. Lee and Senoria Burnette Sapp; m. Chester L. Williams, June 22, 1968 (div. Aug. 1990); children: Corey T., Christopher J., Cheston L. Williams. BA, N.C. Ctrl. U., 1967; MLS, U. Mich., 1971; advanced masters, Fla. State U., 1979, PhD, 1984. Instr. libr. Voorhees Coll., Denmark, S.C., 1971-74; libr. Fla. State U., Tallahassee, 1974-84, Duke U., Durham, N.C., 1984-96; libr. dir. Fla. A&M U., Tallahassee, 1996—. Vis. lectr. U. N.C. Sch. Libr. and Info. Sci.; adj. assoc. prof. N.C. Ctrl. Univ. Sch. Libr. and Info. Sci., 1995-96. Bd. dirs. Durham Vol. Ctr., 1995-96; chair Lit. Program Long Range Planning, Leon County Pub. Libr., Tallahassee, 1999. Fellow U. Mich., 1970-71, Bd. Regents-Fla., 1978-79, 82. Mem. ALA, Assn. Coll. and Rsch. Libr. (mem. internat. rels. com. 1994-99), Libr. Adminstrn. and Mgmt. (mem. cultural diversity com. 1997—), Black Caucus-ALA, 1890 Libr. Dirs. Assn. (treas. 1997—), Beta Phi Mu. Democrat. Episcopalian. Home: PO Box 6326 Tallahassee FL 32314-6326 Office: Fla A&M U Coleman Libr 1500 S Martin Luther King Tallahassee FL 32307 E-mail: lauren.sapp@famu.edu.

SAPP, NANCY L. educational administrator; b. Joplin, Mo., July 22, 1951; d. Jim L. and Leah (Smith) Hayes; children: Michael A., Julie D. B in Music Edn., Pittsburg (Kans.) State U., 1973; MEd in Psychology, Wichita State U.; cert. in elem./secondary sch. adminstrn., Emporia State U., 1994. Cert. elem./secondary vocal/instrumental music tchr., learning disabled tchr., behavior disorder tchr., adminstr., dist. level adminstrn. dir. spl. edn. Vocal and instrumental music instr., Cherokee, Kans., 1973-75, Holy Cross Grade Sch., Hutchinson, Kans., 1980-85, Trinity H.S., Hutchinson, 1980-82; learning disabilities tchr. Unified Sch. Dist. # 308, Hutchinson, 1987-89, behavior disorder tchr., 1989-95, behavior cons., 1990-95; asst. sch. prin. Unified Sch. Dist. 308, Hutchinson, 1995-97; prin., coord. student svcs. Unified Sch. Dist. 443, Dodge City, Kans., 1997-99; asst. dir. spl. edn. Southwest Kans. Area Coop. Dist., Dodge City, 1999—. Prin. second violin Hutchinson Symphony, 1991-97; pres. exec. bd. Hutchinson Regional Youth Symphony, 1994-95; bd. dirs. Reno Choral Soc., Kans. Youth Soc. Grantee Southwestern Bell Tel., Hutchinson, 1992. Mem. Internat. Reading Assn., NEA, Kans. NEA, Kans. Reading Assn., Hutchinson NEA (bldg. rep. 1992-94), Ark Valley Reading Assn. (pres. 1994-95), Phi Delta Kappa. Republican. Methodist. Avocations: theater, music, cross stitch, quilting. Home: 108 La Vista Blvd Dodge City KS 67801-2848

SAPPENFIELD, MAEDEANE L. piano and organ educator; b. Belmond, Iowa, Nov. 1, 1927; d. Henry Gerhard and Lucille Bernice (Legge) Mennenga; m. David Reddick Sappenfield, May 14, 1948 (dec. Apr. 1997); children: Valoris Jane, Linda Jo-Anne, David Clark. Lic. pvt. pilot. Sec. at airport Bram Air Svc., Clarion, Iowa, 1947-48; sec. to sec. C. of C., Clarion, 1948-49; sales, demonstrator, tchr. Jones Piano and Organs, Mason City, Iowa, 1970-85. Tchr. piano and organ. Composer organ solo (state winner Adult Composer, Fed. Music Club 1987). Leaders chair Campfire Girls Am., Belmond, 1959-61; pres. Women's Missionary Fedn., Belmond, 1963-64; pres. Luth. Ch. Women, Osage, Iowa, 1967-69, sec. Mason City conf., 1970-75; organist various chs., presently at Ch. of Christ Scientist, Clear Lake, Iowa. Mem. Music Tchrs. Nat. Assn., North Iowa Music Tchrs., Matinee Musicale Club (pres. 1989-90), Am. Guild Organists (dean 1975-78). Avocations: creative design/sewing, composing, photography, gourmet cooking. Home: One S Taylor Mason City IA 50401

SAPPINGTON, SHARON ANNE, retired school librarian; b. West Palm Beach, Fla., Sept. 15, 1944; d. A.D. and Laura G. (Jackson) Chambless; m. Andrew Arnold Sappington III, June 11, 1966; children: Andrew Arnold IV, Kevin Sean. Student, Fla. So. coll., 1962-64; BA in Edn., U. Fla., 1966; media specialist, U. Ala., 1980. 5th grade tchr. Tates Creek Elem., Lexington, Ky., 1966-68; 4th grade tchr. Sadieville (Ky.) Elem., 1968-69; libr. media specialist A.H. Watwood Elem., Childersburg, Ala., 1980-98; ret. Guest storyteller Young Author's Conf., Winterboro, Lincoln, Sylacauga, and Fayetteville, Ala., 1982-94; vis. com. mem. Southeastern Accreditation Assn.; program presenter Internat. Reading Assn., Birmingham, Ala., 1983; guest speaker rare children's books "By the Way" TV talk show, 1983; pres. Tale Tellers of St. Augustine, 2003—; chmn. RSVP Read Aloud Program, 2002—. Creator, presenter: (slide presentation) Tellers of Tales and Sketchers of Dreams, 1983, (multimedia programs) Dinosaurs, Teddy Bears, and Wild Things, 1990, Shanghaied in the Beijing Airport, 1994. Circle chmn., Sunday tchr. Grace United Meth. Ch., Birmingham, 1973, 92-95; delivery mem. Meals on Wheels, Birmingham, 1975-76; radio reader for the blind WBHM Pub. Broadcasting, Birmingham, 1980; guest speaker, program presenter Jaycees, Kiwanis, and C. of C., Childersburg, 1993-94; chmn. Nat. Librl Week Ala, 1993-94. Title I grantee, 1991, Stutz Bearcat grantee, 1992. Mem. AAUW, ALA, Internat. Platform Assn., Am. Assn. Sch. Librs., Ala. Libr. Assn. (children's and sch. divsn. publicity chmn. 1991-93, chmn. Nat. Libr. Week in Ala. 1993-94, Outstanding Youth Svcs. award 1989), People to People Internat. (libr. del. to China 1993), Kappa Delta Pi, Internat. Platform Assoc., 1997-98. Democrat. Methodist. Avocation: collector of 19th century illustrated children's literature. Home: 5131 Shore Dr Saint Augustine FL 32086-6473

SARACENO, JUNE SYLVESTER, literature educator, department chairman; b. Elizabeth City, N.C., Sept. 23, 1958; d. Dwight and Mary Gray Sylvester; m. Anthony Nicholas Saraceno, July 11, 1998; 1 child, Dylan Victor. BA in English, East Carolina U., 1980; MFA in Creative Writing, Bowling Green State U., 1982. Adj. prof. U. Nev., Reno, 1995—96; asst. prof. Sierra Nevada Coll., Incline Village, Nev., 1997—2000, assoc. prof., 2000—, chair English program, 2002—. Editor: (lit. mag.) Sierra Nevada Coll. Rev., 1990—. Office: Sierra Nevada Coll 999 Tahoe Blvd Incline Village NV 89452

SARACHIK, MYRIAM PAULA MORGENSTEIN, physics educator; b. Antwerp, Belgium, Aug. 8, 1933; came to U.S., 1947; d. Solomon and Sarah (Segal) Morgenstein; m. Philip Sarachik, Sept. 6, 1954; 1 child, Karen Beth. AB, Barnard Coll., 1954; MS, Columbia U., 1957, PhD, 1960. Rsch. assoc. IBM Watson Labs., Columbia U., N.Y.C., 1960-61; mem. tech. staff Bell Telephone Labs., Murray Hill, N.J., 1962-64; asst. prof. physics CCNY, 1964-67, assoc. prof., 1967-70, prof., 1971—, Disting. prof., 1995—. Advisor NSF, NRC. Contbr. articles to profl. jours. Recipient N.Y.C. Mayor's award for excellence in sci. and technology, 1995. Fellow AAAS, Am. Phys. Soc. (v.p. 2001, pres.-elect 2002, pres. 2003), N.Y. Acad. Scis.; mem. NAS, Am. Acad. Arts and Scis. Office: CCNY Physics Dept Convent Ave and 138 St New York NY 10031 E-mail: sarachik@sci.ccny.cuny.edu.

SARANDON, SUSAN ABIGAIL, actress; b. N.Y.C., Oct. 4, 1946; d. Phillip Leslie and Lenora Marie (Criscione) Tomalin; m. Chris Sarandon, Sept. 16, 1967 (div. 1979); children: Eva Maria Livia Amurri, Jack Henry Robbins, Miles Guthrie Robbins. BA in Drama and English, Cath. U. Am., 1968. Actress: (plays) include An Evening with Richard Nixon, 1972, A Coupla White Chicks Sittin' Around Talkin', 1980-81, A Stroll in the Air, Albert's Bridge, Private Ear, Public Eye, Extremities, 1982, (films) Joe, 1970, Lady Liberty, 1972, The Rocky Horror Picture Show, 1975, Lovin' Molly, 1974, The Front Page, 1974, The Great Waldo Pepper, 1975, Dragon Fly, 1976, Crash, 1976, The Other Side of Midnight, 1977, The Last of the Cowboys, 1978, Checkered Flag or Crash, 1978, Pretty Baby, 1978, King of the Gypsies, 1978, Something Short of Paradise, 1979, Loving Couples, 1980, Atlantic City, 1980 (Prix Genie Best Fgn. Actress award 1981, Acad. award nominee 1981), Tempest, 1982 (Best Actress award Venice Film Festival 1982), The Hunger, 1983, Buddy System, 1984, Compromising Positions, 1985, The Witches of Eastwick, 1987, Bull Durham, 1988, Sweet Hearts Dance, 1988, A Dry White Season, 1989, The January Man, 1989, White Palace, 1990, Thelma and Louise, 1991 (Acad. award nominee for best actress 1992, Golden Globe award nominee 1992), The Player, 1992, Light Sleeper, 1992, Bob Roberts, 1992, Lorenzo's Oil, 1992 (Acad. award nominee 1993), The Client, 1994 (Acad. award nominee for best actress), Little Women, 1994, Safe Passage, 1994, Dead Man Walking, 1995 (Golden Globe award nominee for best actress 1996, Acad. award for best actress 1996), James and the Giant Peach (voice), 1996, 187 (voice), 1997, Illuminata, 1998, Twilight, 1998, Stepmom (also producer), 1998, Joe Gould's Secret, 1999, Baby's in Black, 1999, Cradle Will Rock, 1999, Anywhere But Here, 1999, (voice) Rugrats in Paris: The Movie - Rugrats II, 2000, Moonlight Mile, 2002 (also exec. prodr.), The Banger Sisters, 2002, Igby Goes Down, 2002, Ice Bound, 2003, Moonlight Mile, 2003; TV appearances The Haunting of Rosalind, 1973, F. Scott Fitzgerald and The Last of the Belles, 1974, Who Am I This Time, 1982, A.D., 1985. Mussolini: The Decline and Fall of Il Duce, 1985, Earthly Possessions, 1999, (TV series) A World Apart, 1970-71, Search for Tomorrow, 1972-73; TV appearances: Friends, 2001 (Emmy nominee), Malcolm in the Middle, 2002 (Emmy nominee). Mem. AFTRA, Screen Actors Guild, Actors Equity, Acad. Motion Picture Arts and Scis., NOW, MADRE, Amnesty Internat., ACLU Office: Internat Creative Mgmt care Samuel Cohen 40 W 57th St New York NY 10019-4001*

SARD, SUSANNAH ELLEN, non-profit executive; b. Boston, May 10, 1944; d. Russell Ellis and Miriam Clark Sard. AB, Bryn Mawr Coll., 1966. Devel. adminstr. Ky. Ednl. TV, Lexington, 1978—88; dir. found. and corp. rels. Sarah Lawrence Coll., Bronxville, NY, 1991—96; dir. devel. The Town Hall, N.Y.C., 1998—2002; exec. dir. Women's City Club of N.Y., 2002—04; program officer R.J. & S.H. Kaplan Family Found., N.Y.C., 2004—. Alumni bd. Rippowam Cisqua Sch. Mem.: Women in Devel., Blue Hill Troupe. Office: Kaplan Family Found 866 UN Plz Ste 306 New York NY 10017 E-mail: owlkap@aol.com.

SARFATY, SUZANNE, internist, educator; b. Irvington, N.Y., Apr. 11, 1962; d. Sam and Pat (Petrovich) S. BS, Boston U., 1984, MD, 1988, MPH, 1994. Diplomate Am. Bd. Internal Medicine. Intern and resident Boston City Hosp., 1988-91; asst. prof. medicine Boston U., 1991-93, asst. prof. medicine and pub. health, 1995—, asst. dean of student affairs, 1995—. Mem. prof. com. Am. Cancer Soc., Boston, 1991—; mentor Boston Ptnrs. for Edn., 1991—. Recipient Cmty. Svc. award CIBA Geigy, 1986; Dana Farber cancer prevention fellow, 1993-94. Fellow ACP. Avocations: cooking, travel, reading, spanish language. Home: 11 Verndale St Brookline MA 02446-2415

SARGENT, DIANE ROBERTSON, mathematician, educator; b. Savannah, Ga., Jan. 9, 1942; d. Augustus John Robertson III and Jayne Evelyn (Winter) Robertson; m. George Blackburn Sargent, Aug. 14, 1976; 1 child, Debra Paige. AA, Orlando Jr. Coll., 1962; B in Gen. Studies, Rollins Coll., 1970; specialist in Edn., Ga. Coll. & State U., 1991, MEd, 1977. Cert. Tchr. Ga., 1963. Tchr. St. Mary Magdalen, Altamonte Springs, Fla., 1963—72, Lakeview Acad., Gainesville, Ga., 1972—76; middle sch. sci. tchr. Gatewood Acad., Eatonton, Ga., 1976—85; 7th grade math. & sci. tchr. John Millege Acad., Milledgeville, Ga., 1985—87; 6th grade math. tchr. Ga. Military Coll., Milledgeville, 1987—. Instr. Ga. Coll. & State U., Milledgeville, 1991—2000; mem. Ga. Coun. Math. Tchrs., 1995—. Pres. Am. Heart Assn., Baldwin County, Ga., 1983—85, Pink Ladies Baldwin County Hosp., Milledgeville, 1978—82. Dem. Women, Baldwin County, 1980—. Named Tchr. of the News, Channel One News, N.Y., 1999. Mem.: AAUW (pres. 1988—2001, state sec. 1988—2001), Delta Kappa Gamma (treas. 1995—2000). Democrat. Roman Catholic. Avocations: reading, travel, volunteer work. Home: 215 Lakeshore Dr Milledgeville GA 31061 Office: Ga Military Coll Middle School 201 E Greene Str Milledgeville GA 31061

SARGENT, JAN, art appraiser; b. Plant City, Fla., Apr. 20, 1958; d. Floyd and Carolyn Johnson; m. Frank Charles Sargent. BBA, Stetson U., 1980. Bd. dirs. Jr. League, Miami, 1990, Asheville, N.C., 1993, Asheville Art Mus., 1994. Republican. Avocations: gardening, needlepoint, museums, travel. Home: 3850 Galt Ocean Dr Apt 1204 Fort Lauderdale FL 33308-7648 Office: 6203 Bay Club Dr Fort Lauderdale FL 33308-1520

SARGENT, LIZ ELAINE (ELIZABETH SARGENT), safety consulting executive; b. Meadville, Pa., Apr. 17, 1942; d. Melvin Ellsworth and Roberta Jean (Beach) Taylor; m. Lawrence Sargent, Sept. 6, 1969; 1 child, Kathy-Dawn. AA cum laude, Cuyahoga C.C., Cleve., 1987, Assoc. in Transp. cum laude, 1989. Car distbr. Norfolk and Western R.R., Cleve., 1963-69; account mgr. Ill. Cen. R.R., Cleve., 1970-73; traffic coord. Carlon Pipe, Mantua, Ohio, 1973-75; chief dispatcher X.L. Trucking, Coshocton, Ohio, 1975-77; corp. log auditor Anchor Motor Freight, Beachwood, Ohio, 1977-78; cons. Saf-T, Parma, Ohio, 1978-84, v.p. safety Shaker Heights, Ohio, 1987-91; dir. safety Sherwin Williams, Cleve., 1984-87; pres. Safety Advisors for Transp., Inc., Beachwood, Ohio, 1991—; founder Love Keepers, 1996. Spkr. Coshocton (Ohio) Traffic Club, 1984, Am. Indsl. Hygiene, Cleve., 1985, All-Ohio Safety and Health Congress, 1996. Author: Hall Chemical-Safety Procedures, 1983-84, Progressive Insurance, 1987, RL Lipton Co. manual, 1995; contbr. articles to profl. jours. Chair intergenerational com. Ch. in Aurora, Ohio, 1984-86, Valley View Village Ch. libr. chair The Friends Ch. Choir; bd. dirs. Shaker Heights Teen Recreational Com., 1984-87. Delta Nu Alpha scholar, 1977. Mem. Ohio Trucking Assn. (nat. safety coun.), Cleve. Bd. Realtors, Motor Fleet Safety Suprs. (nat. com.), Fleet Maintenance Coun., Phi Theta Kappa. Republican. Avocations: interior design, painting, writing poetry and short stories, dried floral arrangements, hiking. Office: Saf-T 14716 Rockside Rd Maple Heights OH 44137-4016 E-mail: sargentee@yahoo.com.

SARGENT, PAMELA, writer; b. Ithaca, N.Y., Mar. 20, 1948; BA, SUNY, Binghamton, 1968, MA, 1970. Mng. editor, Binghamton, 1970-73; asst. editor, 1973-75; Am. editor Bull. Sci. Fiction Writers Am., Johnson City, NY, 1983-91. Author: Cloned Lives, 1976, Starshadows, 1977, The Sudden Star, 1979, Watchstar, 1980, The Golden Space, 1982, The Alien Upstairs, 1983, Earthseed, 1983, Eye of the Comet, 1984, Homesmind, 1984, Venus of Dreams, 1986, The Shore of Women, 1986, The Best of Pamela Sargent, 1987, Alien Child, 1988, Venus of Shadows, 1988, Ruler of the Sky, 1993 (Nebula best novelette award 1992, Locus best novelette award 1993, Electric Sci. Fiction award 1993), Climb the Wind: A Novel of Another America, 1999, (with Ron Miller) Firebrands: The Heroines of Science Fiction and Fantasy, 1998, Child of Venus, 2001, Behind the Eyes of Dreamers and Other Short Novels, 2002, The Mountain Cage and Other Stories, 2002, Eye of Flame: Fantasies, 2003; editor: (anthology) Women of Wonder, 1975, Bio-Futures, 1976, More Women of Wonder, 1976, The New Women of Wonder, 1978, (with Ian Watson) Afterlives, 1986, Women of Wonder, The Classic Years, 1996, Women of Wonder, The Contemporary Years, 1995, Nebula Awards 29, 1995, Nebula Awards 30, 1996, Nebula Awards 31, 1997, Conqueror Fantastic, 2004. Office: care Richard Curtis Assocs Inc 171 E 74th St New York NY 10021-3221

SARICKS, JOYCE GOERING, librarian; b. Nov. 8, 1948; d. Joe W. and Lovella Goering; m. Christopher L. Saricks, Aug. 21, 1971; children: Brendan James, Margaret Katherine. BA with highest distinction in English and German, U. Kans., 1970; MA in Comparative Lit., U. Wis., 1971; MA/MAT in LS, U. Chgo., 1977. Reference librarian Downers Grove (Ill.) Pub. Library, 1977-80, head tech. svcs., 1980-83, coord. lit. and audio svcs., 1983—. Presenter workshops in field. Author: (with Nancy Brown) Readers' Advisory Service in the Public Library, 1989, revised edit., 1997, The Readers' Advisory Guide to Genre Fiction, 2001. Mem. Read Ill. adv. com., 1990-91. Woodrow Wilson fellow, 1970; recipient Allie Beth Martin award Pub. Library Assn., 1989, No. Ill. Libr. of Yr. award Windy City Romance Writers, 1995, Libr. of the Yr. award Romance Writers of Am., 2000. Mem. ALA, Ill. Library Assn., Adult Reading Round Table (founder), Phi Beta Kappa, Delta Phi Alpha, Pi Lambda Theta, Beta Phi Mu. Home: 1116 61st St Downers Grove IL 60516-1819 Office: Downers Grove Pub Library 1050 Curtiss St Downers Grove IL 60515-4606 E-mail: saricksj@juno.com.

SARIS, PATTI BARBARA, federal judge; b. 1951; BA magna cum laude, Radcliffe Coll., 1973; JD cum laude, Harvard U., 1976. Law clerk to Hon. Robert Braucher Mass. Supreme Judicial Ct., 1976-77; atty. Foley Hoag & Eliot, Boston, 1977-79; staff counsel U.S. Senate Judiciary Com., 1979-81; atty. Berman Dittmar & Engel, Boston, 1981-82; chief civil divsn. U.S. Atty.'s Office, 1984-86; U.S. magistrate judge U.S. Dist. Ct. Mass., 1986-89; assoc. justice Mass. Superior Ct., 1989-94; dist. judge U.S. Dist. Ct. Mass., 1994—. Bd. overseers, chair com. on defender svcs. judicial conf. Harvard. Bd. trustees Beth Israel Hosp.; active Wexner Heritage Found. Recipient award Haskell J. Cohn Disting. Jud. Svc. award Boston Bar Assn.; Nat. Merit scholar, 1969. Mem.: Phi Beta Kappa. Office: US Courthouse Courthouse Way Ste 6130 Boston MA 02210

SARKISIAN, CHERILYN **See CHER**

SARKISIAN, PAMELA OUTLAW, artist; b. Spokane, Sept. 26, 1941; d. Willard Clinton and Frances (Montieth) Outlaw; m. Ronald Edward Sarkisian, Nov. 11, 1960; children: Ronald Abraham, Michelle Suzanne. Grad. high sch., Stockton, Calif. Art student, Oceanside, Calif., 1972-80; founder Palette 'N Easel Studio, Oceanside, Calif., 1980—, operator, mgr., 1980—, art tchr. in residence, 1985—. Publisher greeting cards Polytint, Ltd., England, 1995, 96; fine art prints pub. by Bentley House, Ltd., Walnut Creek, Calif., 1994-97. Designer collector plate series Danbury Mint/MBI, Inc., gift items Enesco Internat. Gift Co.; represented by Casay Gallery, Kailau, Kona, Hawaii, 1991, Galeria Jean Lammelin, Paris, 1991, 2d St. Gallery, Encinitas, Calif., 1991, Blondes Gallery, San Diego, 1992, Valentine-Owens Gallery, Santa Monica, Calif., 1992, Sodarco Gallery, Montreal, 1993, Surtex, 1993, Jacob G. Javity Conv. Ctr., N.Y.C., 1993, Laura Larkin Gallery, Del Mar, Calif., 1993-94, Charles Hecht Galleries, Tarzana and Palm Desert, Calif., 1993-96, Lou Martin Gallery, Laguna Beach, Calif., 1994, Charles Hecht Gallery, La Jolla, Calif., 1995-96, Calif. Art Gallery, Laguna Beach, 1996, Hunter Gallery, Tucson, 1996, Cottage Gallery at Carmel, Calif., 1996, Dy'ans-Branham Gallery, Laguna Beach, 1997-99, Aka'mai Gallery, Del Mar, 1998-99, Gallery Adrienne, La Jolla, 1998, Cosmopolitan Gallery, La Jolla, Calif., 1998-99, The Lillian Berkley Collection, Escondido, Calif., 1999-2003, Waters Edge Gallery, Rancho Mirage, Calif., 2003; one-woman shows include AKA Mai Gallery, 1999, Lillian Berkeley Collection, 2001, Four Seasons-Aviara, La Costa, Calif., 2001, Waters Edge Gallery, Rancho Mirage, Calif., 2003. Pres. Zonta Internat., Oceanside, 1980-81; mem. Emblem Club #177, Oceanside, 1971-2003; princess Daughters of the Nile, San Diego, 1974; bd. dirs. Oceanside Girls Club, 1980. Recipient 1st Pl. award San Dieguito Art Guild, 1978, 85, 2nd Pl. award, 1983, 89, 3rd Pl. award, 1983, 1990; winner People's Choice award Internat. Show of Women Artists of the West, Las Vegas, 1992. Mem. North County Art Assn. (founder), Carlsbad Oceanside Art League, 1978, San Dieguito Art Guild, Fallbrook Art Assn., San Diego

Art Inst., Assn. pour Promotion Artiste Français, Artisphere. Avocations: ceramics, sculpture, swimming. Office: Palette 'N Easel Studio 1021 S Coast Hwy Oceanside CA 92054-5004 E-mail: pamiwigle@msn.com.

SARKISSIAN, NAVER AGOP, pathologist; arrived in U.S., 1994; d. Yuhaper Garabed and Agop Sarkis Hazarosyan; m. Assen Petrov Bogdanov, Sept. 21, 1995; children: Mark Alan Bogdanoff, Marie Juliette Bogdanoff. BS, Med. Coll., Varna, Bulgaria, 1980; MD, Med. Sch., Varna, Bulgaria, 1987; PhD, Med. Acad., Moscow, 1993. Lab. technologist dept. microbiology, virology and immunology Sch. of Medicine, Varna, 1980—81; clin. pathologist divsn. med. microbiology and virology Inst. of Epidemiology, Varna, 1987—89; post-doctoral rsch. assoc. St. Jude Children's Rsch. Hosp., Memphis, 1994—96; rsch. scientist Columbia U. Coll. of Physicians and Surgeons, N.Y.C., 1996—98, Cornell U. Med. Coll., N.Y.C., 1998—99. Recipient fellowship in med. virology, Bulgarian Ministry of Edn., 1989—93. Mem.: Union of Bulgarian Physicians, Internat. Med. Assn., Bulgaria, Am. Soc. for Virology. Avocations: travel, music, crafts, reading, cooking. Home: 31-11 Crescent St Apt C-5 Astoria NY 11106 Office Phone: (212). Personal E-mail: n_sarkissian@hotmail.com.

SARMIENTO, SHIRLEY JEAN, counselor, court advocate; b. Buffalo, Nov. 28, 1946; d. John Clyde and Claudia Mary (Hall) Laughlin; divorced; 1 child, Tolley C. BS in Liberal Studies and Social Sci., Medaille Coll., 1980; M Arts and Scis., SUNY, Buffalo, 1996. Cmty. health worker Jesse Nash Health Ctr., Buffalo, 1979-83; educator Western N.Y. Peace Ctr., Buffalo, 1984-89; substitute tchr. Buffalo Bd. Edn., 1990-91; counselor, ct. advocate LHI, Buffalo, 1990—; family advocate, educator to hearing disabled WNY LDA, 1997—. Narrator fundraising video, 1993; editor: Drum Beats, 1996. Mem. Art Space, 1995—; founder Urban Arts, Buffalo, 1994—; vol. Burchfield/Penny Art Gallery, Buffalo, 1994—; bd. dirs. Jubilee Fund, Buffalo, 1989-91; vol. MLK Com., 1993, Movin On Residential House, 1995-96. Avocations: writing, travel, theater, movies, art galleries. Home: 205 Marine Dr Apt 4D Buffalo NY 14202-4215

SARNOFF, LILI-CHARLOTTE (LOLO SARNOFF), artist; b. Frankfurt, Germany (as Swiss citizen), Jan. 9, 1916; arrived in U.S., 1940; d. Willy and Martha (Koch von Hirsch) Dreyfus; m. Stanley Jay Sarnoff, 1948; children: Daniela Martha Bargezi, Robert L. Grad, Reimann Art Sch., Germany, 1936, U. Berlin, 1938; student, U. Florence, Italy, 1948-54; DFA (hon.), Corcoran Coll. Art & Design, 2003. With Red Cross Swiss Motor Corps, 1939—40; Red Cross nurse Bellevue Hosp., N.Y.C., 1942—47; rsch. asst. Harvard Sch. Pub. Health, 1950-54; rsch. assoc. cardiac physiology Nat. Heart Inst., Bethesda, Md., 1954-59; pres. Rodana Rsch. Corp., Bethesda, 1959—61; v.p. Catrix Corp., Bethesda, 1959—61. Inventor Flolite light sculptures under name Lolo Sarnoff, 1968—; one-woman shows include Agra Gallery, Washington, 1969, Corning (N.Y.) Glass Ctr. Mus., 1970, Gallery Two, Woodstock, Vt., 1970, Gallery Marc, Washington, 1971, 1972, Franz Bader Gallery, 1976, Gallery K, 1978, 1981, 1985, 1987, 1991, Retrospective Show, 1995, Alwin Gallery, London, 1981, Galerie von Bartha, Basel, Switzerland, 1982, La Galerie L'Hotel de Ville, Geneva, 1982, Pfalzgalerie, Kaiserslautern, Germany, 1985, Galerie Les Hirondelles, Geneva, 1988, Represented in permanent collections. Founder, pres. Arts for Aging, Inc., Bethesda, 1988—; pres. Dara's Canine Found., Inc., 1999—. Recipient Golda Meir award, 1995, Life Commitment to Arts award, Swiss Am. Cultural Exch., 1999, Path of Achievement award for Arts and Humanities, Montgomery County, Md., 2000, Outstanding Citizen award, Iona Sr. Citizen Svcs., Washington, 2002. Home: 7507 Hampden Ln Bethesda MD 20814-1331 E-mail: lolos@erols.com.

SARNOFF, SUSAN KISS, social worker, educator; d. Stephen Paul and Theresa Marakowski Kiss; m. Jerome Thomas Sarnoff, Sept. 23, 1990; children: Kristina Mott Stevens, Stephen Durand Mott. BA in Sociology, Adelphi U., 1982, MSW, 1984, DSW, 1992. Author: (book) Paying for Crime: The Policies and Possibilities of Crime Victim Reimbursement, Sanctified Snake Oil: The Effect of Junk Science on Public Policy. Mem.: NASW (v.p. of profl. stds. 2003—, cert.). Home: P O Box 71 Athens OH 45701 Office: Ohio U Dept Social Work Morton Hall 416 Athens OH 45701 Office Phone: 740-593-1301. Personal E-mail: sarnoff@ohio.edu. E-mail: sarnoff@ohio.edu.

SARPY, SUE ANN CORELL, environmental health sciences educator; b. Roanoke, Va., June 24, 1965; d. Gaylord Stafford and Betty Frances (Spangler) Corell; m. Christopher Alexis Sarpy, Feb. 18, 1995. BA in Psychology, U. Richmond, 1987; MS in Indsl. and Orgnl. Psychology, Tulane U., 1990, PhD in Indsl. and Orgnl. Psychology, 1996. Tchg. asst. dept. psychology Grad. Sch., Tulane U., New Orleans, 1988-94, rsch. assoc. Hammer rsch. project, 1995-96, tng. evaluation coord., 1996—, rsch. asst. A.B. Freeman Sch. Bus., 1989-90, rsch. asst. dept. psychology, 1992, tutor, 1993-94; clin. asst. prof. dept. environ. health scis. Tulane U. Med. Ctr., 1996—. Psychometrician Test Devel. and Validation Unit, New Orleans, 1990-92; asst. prof. Loyola U. Coll. Bus. Adminstrn. New Orleans, part-time 1994095 Advocate New Orleans Mus. Art, 1994—; mem. Heritage Club, Preservation Resource Ctr. New Orleans, 1996—. Scholar Tulane U., 1987. Mem. APA, ASTD, Soc. Indsl. and Orgnl. Psychologists, Audubon Inst. (charter), Psi Chi. Avocations: skiing, walking, photography, classical music. Home: One River Pl 244 Arlington Dr Metairie LA 70001-5510 Office: Tulane U Med Ctr Environ Health Edn-Tng Proj 1440 Canal St Ste 800 New Orleans LA 70112-2793

SARRAF, SHIRLEY A. secondary school educator; BA in polit. sci., U. Calif., Davis, 1968; MEd, Idaho State U., 1976, postgrad., 1976—. Cert. Educator Nat. Bd. Edn., 2001. Asst. psychometrist U. Wash., 1969-72; asst. prof. dept. fgn. lang. Farah Pahlavi U., Teheran-Vanek, Iran, 1978-79; tchr. presch. program T.L.C. Child Care Ctr., Pocatello, Idaho, 1980-82; dir. of curriculum for English as a second lang. Idaho State U., Pocatello, Idaho, 1982-85; tchr. English, Math, History, Computers Highland High Sch. Sch. Dist. 25, Pocatello, Idaho, 1986—2001; tchr. English Folsom H.S., Folsom, Calif., 2001—. Infant and child stimulation workshops Idaho State U. Pocatello, Idaho, adj. prof. U. Teheran, Iran, 1978-79. Recipient Tchr. of the Year award State of Idaho, 1994-95. Home: PO Box 6001 Folsom CA 95763-6001

SARREALS, SONIA, data processing consultant; b. NYC, Sept. 17, 1938; d. Espriela and Sadie Beatrice (Scales) Sarreals; m. Waldro Lynch, Sept. 18, 1981 (div. Oct. 1983). BA in Langs. summa cum laude, CCNY, 1960; cert. in French, Sorbonne, Paris, 1961. Systems engr. IBM, N.Y.C., 1963-69; cons. Babbage Systems, N.Y.C., 1969-70; project leader Touche Ross, N.Y.C., 1970-73; sr. programmer McGraw-Hill, Inc., Hightstown, N.J., 1973-78; staff data processing cons. Cin. Bell Info. Systems, 1978-89; sr. analyst AT&T, 1989-92; lead tech. analyst Automated Concepts Inc., Arlington, Va., 1992-96; tech. cons. Teksystems, Reston, Va., 1996—. Elder St. Andrew Luth. Ch., Silver Spring, 1992-96. Downer scholar CUNY, 1960; Dickman Inst. fellow Columbia U., 1960-61. Mem. Assn. for Computing Machinery, Phi Beta Kappa. Democrat. Avocations: needlework, sewing. Home: 13705 Beret Pl Silver Spring MD 20906-3030 Office: Teksystems 12343 Sunrise Valley Dr Reston VA 20191 Business E-Mail: ssarreals@teksystems.com.

SARRY, CHRISTINE, ballerina; b. Long Beach, Calif., May 25, 1946; d. John and Beatrice (Thomas) S.; 1 child, Maximilian Sarry Varriale. With Joffrey Ballet, 1963—64, Am. Ballet Theatre, 1964—68, prin. dancer, 1971—74; leading dancer Am. Ballet Co., 1969—71; ballerina Eliot Feld Ballet, 1974—81. Dir. faculty Ballet Tech. Upper Sch., N.Y.C., also freelance guest tchr. Performed ballets for Agnes DeMille, Antony Tudor, Jerome Robbins, Eliot Feld; appeared at White House, 1963, 67; U.S. Dept. State tours include, Russia, 1963, 66, S.Am., 1964, 76, various tours of N.Am., Orient, Europe, various appearances U.S. nat. TV; partnered by Mikhail Baryshnikov.

SARUTTO, ANNE MARIE RITA, research scientist; b. Bklyn., Feb. 13, 1950; d. Michael Robert and Margaret Lorraine Sarutto. BA in Meteorology, U. St. Thomas, 1994. Interviewer Pa. State U., Phila., 1973—74; biol. aid U.S. Wildlife Fisheries, NOAA, Galveston, 1974—75; cen. supply technician Pub. Health Hosp., Galveston, Tex., 1975—76, phys. therapy aid, 1976—81; med. asst. Army Reentry Examining Unit, Houston, 1981—82; rsch. asst. CCNY, N.Y.C., 1995—97, weather technician, 1995—96, sch. asst., 1997—99, with Peer Mentor Program, 2002—. Mentor grad. intern program NOAA/NEDSIS, N.Y.C., 2003; student sen. CCNY, N.Y.C., 1995—96, Colin Powell assoc., 2003—04. Contbr. poetry to anthologies. Recipient Petroleum award, Exxon Corp., 1978—79; minority rsch. grantee, Geol. Soc. Am., 1993—94. Mem.: Math. Soc. Am., Am. Geophys. Soc., Am. Meteorol. Soc., Alpha Phi Delta, Phi Delta Kappa, Phi Theta Kappa. Achievements include having name written on Wall of Tolerance. Avocations: walking, weather observing, astronomy, creative and poetry writing. Home: 202 Bay 17th St Brooklyn NY 11214 Personal E-mail: AMSARUTTO@AOL.COM.

SARWAR, BARBARA DUCE, education consultant; b. Mpls., Aug. 9, 1938; d. Harold Taylor and Barbara (Thayer) Duce; m. Mohammad Sarwar, Dec. 28, 1972; 1 child, Barbara Sarah Franklin. BS, U. Colo., 1972; M Spl. Edn., Ea. N.Mex. U., 1975, Edn. Specialist, 1979. Cert. tchr., adminstr., N.Mex. Tchr. 2d grade, English as 2d lang. Lake Arthur (N.Mex.) Mcpl. Schs., 1972-74; tchr. spl. edn. Artesia (N.Mex.) Pub. Schs., 1974-79, ednl. diagnostician, 1979-88, dir. spl. edn., 1988-97; cons. Edn. Diagnosis, Artesia, 1998—; owner Barbara's Diagnostic Svcs., Artesia, 1998—. Contbr. to profl. publs. Pres. Altrusa Club Artesia, 1981-82, 86-87, The Arc of Artesia, 1990-92; bd. dirs. Zia Girl Scout Coun., 2002 . Named Employee of Yr. Arc of N.Mex., 1994. Mem.: Coun. for Exceptional Children (professionally recognized spl. educator in ednl. diagnosis), Nat. Assn. Sch. Psychologists, Internat. Reading Assn. (pres. Pecos Valley chpt. 1975—76, sec. N.Mex. unit 1977—78), Artesia Edn. Assn. (pres. 1978—79), Phi Delta Kappa, Phi Kappa Phi. Avocations: reading, sewing, golf. Home and Office: 16541 E Lwo Dr Fountain Hills AZ 85268-6530 E-mail: bsarwar@bulldogs.org.

SASEK, GLORIA BURNS, English language and literature educator; b. Springfield, Mass., Jan. 20, 1926; d. Frederick Charles and Minnie Delia (White) Burns; m. Lawrence Anton Sasek, Sept. 5, 1960. BA, Mary Washington Coll. of U. Va., 1947; student, U. Paris, 1953, U. Stranieri, Perugia, Italy, 1955; MA, Radcliffe Coll., 1954; EdM, Springfield Coll., 1955. Tchr., head dept. jr. and sr. hs English, Pub. Schs., Somers, Conn., 1947—59; tchr. English, Winchester (Mass.) Pub. Schs., 1959—60; mem. faculty La. State U., Baton Rouge, 1961—, asst. prof. English, 1971-96, chmn. freshman English, 1969-70. Named La. State U. Yearbook Favorite Prof., 1978; recipient George H. Deer Disting. Tchg. award, La. State U., 1977, Disting. Undergrad. Tchg. award, Amoco Found., 1994, commendation, La. Ho. of Reps., 1996. Mem. MLA, AAUP (chpt. v.p. 1981-84), South Ctrl. MLA, South Ctrl. Renaissance Soc., South Ctrl. Conf. on Christianity and Lit. Office: Dept English La State U Baton Rouge LA 70803 E-mail: glsasek@worldnet.att.net.

SASKO, NANCY ANN, insurance agent; b. Camp Lejuene, N.C., Nov. 22, 1956; d. George Michael Jr. and Margaret (Simons) S. BA in English Lit., Ind. U., 1981. Customer svc. rep. Apple Computer, Inc., Denver, 1982-84; owner Monitor Systems, Inc., Denver, 1984—89; long term care ins. sales rep. Sr. Ins. Svs. Episcopalian. Avocations: classical music, art, reading, gardening, cooking. Address: 2427 Loganberry Cove Fort Wayne IN 46818 E-mail: nancysasleo@aol.com.

SASMAN, IRENE DEAK HANDBERG, educational publishing executive; b. Jamaica, N.Y. d. Paul and Irene (Dyroff) Deak; children: Roger B. Handberg III, Ryan Paul Handberg; m. Timothy Carl Sasman. BS, Fla. State U.; MEd, U. N.C., 1970. Cert. tchr. in reading and math., N.C. Lead tchr., reading specialist Chapel Hill (N.C.) City Schs., 1966-69; dir. learning lab. Seminole Community Coll., Sanford, Fla., 1974-78; basic skills cons. EDL/McGraw-Hill Book Co., Orlando, Fla., 1978-82; regional dir. EDL/Arista Pub., Orlando, 1982-84; mktg. mgr., product mgr. Arista/Regents/EDL-Hachette, N.Y.C., 1984-85; v.p. mktg. and sales Raintree Pubs., Milw., 1985, gen. mgr., pub., 1985-87; dir. spl. projects Simon & Schuster, Englewood Cliffs, N.J., 1987-88, v.p. corp. devel. N.Y.C., 1988-90, sr. v.p., 1990-91; chmn. Irene Handberg Internat., N.Y.C., 1991—; pres. The Learning Connection, New York, N.Y., 1991—. Co-author: EDL/McGraw-Hill Teacher's Guide. Elected precinct woman com. Dem. County Com., Fla.; capt. Nat. Cancer So., Fla., chmn. Sch. Adv. Com., Fla. NSF fellow U. N.C., 1969; recipient Svc. award Jr. Achievement. Mem. Chief Exec. Officers Group (coun. small bus. execs.), Sales and Mktg. Execs., Profl. Dimensions, Chief Exec. Officers Club. Lutheran. Avocations: spectator sports, art, music, skiing. Office: The Learning Connection 300 E 93rd St Apt 29C New York NY 10128-6109

SASS, CANDACE ELAINE, research associate; b. Mar. 16, 1960; d. Robert Ernest and Dolores LaRue Truscott; m. Craig Steven Sass, May 5, 1959; 1 child, Christine Elizabeth. BSChem, Muskingum Coll., 1982; MSChem, PhDChem, U. Cin., 1986. Postdoctoral fellow U. Houston, 1986-88; rsch. chemist Eastman Chemical Co. Rsch., Kingsport, Tenn., 1988-91; sr. chemist Tenn. Eastman Divsn., Kingsport, 1991-94; principal chemist Eastman Chemical Co., Kingsport, 1994-98, rsch. assoc., 1998—. Contbr. to profl. jours. Bd. dir. Waverly Road Child Care Ctr. (v.p., 1997, sec., 1996); mem. Am. Chemical Soc., An. Lab. Mgrs. Assocs. Home: 430 Harding Rd Kingsport TN 37663-2557 Office: Eastman Chemical Co PO Box 1972 Kingsport TN 37662-1972

SASSO, ELEANOR CATHERINE, state senator; b. Fall River, Mass., Dec. 9, 1934; d. Robert Charles and Ellen (O'Hare) Ashworth; m. Louis Anthony Sasso, 1957; children— Ellen Marie, Ann Marie, Robert. BS, Immaculata Coll., Pa., 1957. Mem. R.I. State Senate, 1979— ; researcher Bur. Nat. Affairs, from 1978. Chmn. Cranston Recycling Commn., 1972-73; mem. Cranston Transvan Com., from 1973; mem. Spl. Gov.'s Commn. To Study Entire Election Process, 1977-78. Mem. LWV, Met. Nursing and Health Assn. (bd.), Common Cause, Save the Bay. Democrat. Roman Catholic. Home: 60 Glenmere Dr Cranston RI 02920-6148 Office: Senate Chamber State House Providence RI 02903

SASTROWARDOYO, TERESITA MANEJAR, nurse; b. Iloilo, Philippines; came to U.S., 1960; d. Timoteo and Monica (Casianan) Manejar; m. Sumarsongko H. Sastrowardoyo, June 8, 1962; children: Timoteo, Daniel (dec.), Benjamin. BSN, Ctrl. Philippine U., Iloilo, 1957; cert. operating rm. and surgical nursing, St. Luke's Hosp Ctr., N.Y.C., 1960-61. Head nurse med. unit Emmanuel Hosp., Roxas City, Philippines, 1957-58; supr. oper. rm. Brent Hosp., Zamboanga City, Philippines, 1958-60; staff nurse oper. rm. Jewish Meml. Hosp., N.Y.C., 1961-62; evening staff nurse oper. rm. Flower and Fifth Ave Hosp., N.Y.C., 1963-65; staff nurse oper. rm., charge nurse night shift St. Lukes Hosp. Ctr., N.Y.C., 1966-76; staff nurse oper. rm. South Side Hosp., Bayshore, N.Y., 1976—, asst. head nurse operating room, 2003—. Mem.: N.Y. State Nurses Assn., Ctrl. Philippine U. Alumni Assn. N.Y., N.J. and Conn. (bd. dirs. 1994—95, 1995—97). Baptist. Avocations: gardening, reading.

SATCHER, CATHERINE LEA, pre-school educator; b. Jasper, Ala., Dec. 18, 1959; d. Hester Guy Able Sr. and Sara Earnest Able; m. Roger Dale Satcher, July 7, 1997. BS in Home Econs., U. Montevallo, 1984, MS, 1991. Sec. First Christian Ch., Jasper, deacon. Mem.: AAUW (pres. Jasper chpt. 2001—02), Walker Coll. Alumni Assn. (pres.), Delta Kappa Gamma. Mem. Christian Ch. (Disciples Of Christ). Avocations: reading, gardening.

SATER, DENISE M. journalist, editor; b. Spangler, Pa. d. Harry Edward Murphy and Mary Louise Valeria. BA, Pa. State U., 1974. Counselor Devereaux, Devon, Pa., 1974-75; editor Antiques & Auction News, Marietta, Pa., 1975-82, Mount Joy, Pa., 1995—. Mem. Phi Beta Kappa. Avocation: antiques. Office: Antiques & Auction News PO Box 500 Mount Joy PA 17552-0500

SATHER, VOLEEN ROTUNDA, coroner; b. Jan. 18, 1940; d. Cameron and Glenda Sather; m. Gregor Thomas Sather, July 26, 1965; children: Kathryn Marie, Jeffrey Adam, Jonah Bradley. MD, Harvard Med. Sch., 1968. Coroner County Gen. Hosp., Chgo., 1970—94, Bronx Med. Ctr., 1995—98, Meriks Meml. Hosp., Selden, NY, 1998—. Author: The Living Dead, 1999, I See Dead People, 2000; contbr. articles to med. jours. Republican. Avocations: thimble collecting, yodelling, Monopoly. Office: Meriks Meml Hosp 131 Berkley Ave Selden NY 11784-1903

SATIN, CLAIRE JEANINE, sculptor, book artist; b. Bklyn., Jan. 9, 1942; BA, Sarah Lawrence Coll., 1956; MFA, Pratt Inst., 1968. Instr. art edn. dept. edn. Bklyn. Mus., 1958-59; instr. dept. edn. and dept. Fine Arts Broward Cmty. Coll., Ft. Lauderdale, Fla., 1971-83; dir. Broward Cmty. Coll. Gallery, Ft. Lauderdale, 1975-76. Artist rep. Vorpal Gallery, Soho, N.Y.C., Jan van der Donk Gallery, Chelsea, N.Y.C. Collections include Victoria and Albert Mus., London, Getty Ctr. Hist. Art and Humanities, L.A., Mus. Modern Art, N.Y.C., Mus. Art, Ft. Lauderdale, King Stephen Mus., Szekesfeherdr, Hungary, Ruth and Marvin Sackner Archive of Concrete and Visual Poetry, others; commd. works include: Chapman Chronicles, State of Alaska, U. Alaska, Fairbanks, 1992, Alphawalk, New Tampa Regional Libr., Hillsborough County, Tampa, Fla., 1997 (catalog); Alphastory, Pembroke Pines Libr., Pembroke Pines, Fla., Broward County Art in Pub. Places Program (brochure), Am. Ctrs., New Delhi, Bombay, India. Bd. dirs. Broward County Cultural Affairs Coun., Ft. Lauderdale, 1975-83, hon. chair, 1981—. Recipient S. Fla. Cult Consortium award Miami Art Mus., Fla., 1997-98; So. Arts Fedn./NEA Regional Visual Arts fellow, 1996; Fla. State Individual Artist fellow Statewide Exhbn., 1978, 97-98; Cult Consortium fellow Miami Art Mus., 1997-98; Tiffany Found. grantee, 1968-69, Meml. Found. for Jewish Culture, 2001-02. Mem. Internat. Sculpture Ctr., Am. Craft. Coun., Ctr. Book Arts, Fonteneda Soc. (bd. dirs. 1997—). Office: care ARTWORKS/ARTSPACE 101 SW 1st St Dania FL 33004-3628

SATIR, BIRGIT H. medical educator, medical researcher; b. Copenhagen, Mar. 22, 1934; Magistra in Biochemistry, U. Copenhagen, 1961. Rsch. assoc. dept. zoology U. Chgo., 1962-66, asst. rsch. physiologist U. Calif Dept. Physiology-Anatomy, Berkeley, 1967-74, assoc. rsch. physiologist, 1974-76, adj. assoc. prof., 1976-77; sci. dir. Analytical Ultrastructure Ctr., Cancer Rsch. Inst. Albert Einstein Coll. of Medicine, Bronx, N.Y., 1977-84, prof. dept. anatomy and structural biology, 1977—. Rschr. Phys.- Chem. Inst. Copenhagen, 1956-57, Biol. Inst., Copenhagen, 1958-61; mem. Cellular and Molecular Basis of Disease Rev. Com., Nat. Inst. Gen. Med. Scis., 1977-79; vis. prof. divsn. biology Calif. Inst. Tech., 1984-85. Mem. editl. bd. Jour. Ultrastructural Rsch., 1975-80, Jour. Cell Biology, 1979-81, Modern Cell Biology, 1980-90, Jour. Eukaryotic Microbiology, 1989-95. Rsch. fellow U. Geneva, 1965-66, Spl. fellow USPHS, 1972-73; recipient Outstanding Women Scientist award N.Y. chpt. Assn. Women in Sci., 1990, Rsch. award Am. Diabetes Assn., 1995. Fellow AAAS, Royal Danish Acad. Sci. and Letters; mem. Am. Soc. Cell Biology (coun. 1975-78, minority affairs com. 1987-90, fin. com. 1993—), Am. Assn. Anatomists, Am. Soc. Biochemistry and Molecular Biology, Electron Microscopy Soc. Am. (program vice-chairperson 38th Meeting 1980, program chairperson 39th Meeting 1981), NYSEM (pres. 1979-80), N.Y. Acad. Sci., Biophys. Soc. Office: Albert Einstein Coll of Medicine Dept Anatomy & Structural Biology 1300 Morris Park Ave Bronx NY 10461-1926

SATKOWSKI, SHARON KATHLEEN KENNEDY, elementary school educator; b. Goshen, N.Y., Sept. 1, 1957; d. Michael Joseph Kennedy and Nancy Elizabeth Henry; m. Paul Thomas Satkowski, July 7, 1979; children: Justin, Jonathan. BS in Music Edn., SUNY, Fredonia, 1979; MS in Music Edn., Western Conn. State Coll., 1983. Tchr. Valley Ctrl. Mid. Sch., Montgomery, NY, 1979—83, Walden Elem. Sch., Montgomery, 1983—. Address: PO Box 272 Salisbury Mills NY 12577

SATO, EUNICE NODA, former mayor, consultant; b. Livingston, Calif., June 8, 1921; d. Bunsaku and Sawa (Maeda) Noda; m. Thomas Takashi Sato, Dec. 9, 1950; children[00bf] Charlotte Patricia, Daniel Ryuichi and Douglas Ryuji (twins). AA, Modesto Jr. Coll., 1941; BA, U. No. Colo., 1944; MA, Columbia U., 1948. Pub. sch. tchr. Mastodon Twp. Schs., Alpha, Mich., 1944-47; ednl. missionary Reformed Ch. Am., Yokohama, Japan, 1948-51; coun. mem. City of Long Beach, Calif., 1975-86; mayor, 1980-82. Sec. corp. bd. Los Angeles County Health Systems Agy., 1978-79 Monthly contbr. articles to 2 neighborhood papers, 1975-86. Bd. dirs. Long Beach chpt. ARC, 1975-2000, mem. exec. com., 1978-91, 93-99, past pres. and v.p., mem. Calif. state svc. coun., A.R.C., 1995-2001; bd. dirs. Goodwill Industries, 1978-82 ; trustee St. Mary's Bauer Med. Ctr., 1977—; pres. Industry Edn. Coun., Long Beach, 1984-86, mem. exec. bd., 1984—; bd. dirs. Industry Edn. Coun. of Calif.; treas. So. Calif. Consortium of I.E.C., 1984-86, pres., 1988-89; mem. State Adv. Group on Juvenile Justice and Delinquency Prevention, 1983-91, Calif. Coun. Criminal Justice, 1983-92, legis. com. Girl Scout coun. Calif., 1986-92, chair, 1991-92; bd. dirs. Long Beach coun. Girl Scouts U.S., 1986-92, Region III United Way, 1974-88; mem. Asian Pacific adv. com. Calif. Dept. Rehab., 1985-87, recreation commn. City of Long Beach, 1985-86, pub. safety policy com. League Calif. Cities, 1981-86, cmty. econ. and housing devel. com. So. Calif. Assn. Govts., 1976-86, Calif. Task Force to Promote Self-Esteem and Personal and Social Responsibility, 1987-90; Long Beach chpt. pres. NCCJ, 1987-88; pres. Internat. Cmty. Coun., 1986-87, bd. dir. 1986-2001, pres. Japanese Am. Reps., 1987, 88, exec. bd. mem. 1987-2003; presdl. appointee Nat. Adv. Coun. Ednl. Rsch. and Improvement, 1991-94; pres. Aux. to Sch. Theology, Claremont, 1990-91, exec. bd. 1989-91, nat. selective svc. sys. local bd. 138, 1990-2001, SCA Edison Co. Equal Opportunity adv. coun., 1990-94; chair selection com. Leadership Long Beach, 1990-91, sec. exec. bd., 1991-92; chair adv. bd. AIESEC, 1990-92; chmn. Long Beach Area Rep. Party, 1990-92; asst. sec. gen. com., L.A, 1990-92; sec.-gen. coun. on fin. and adminstrn. United Meth. Ch., 1992-2000; appointed by Gov. to commn. on tchr. credentialing State Calif., 1994, L.A. coun. svc. coun. A.R.C., 1995-99; chair adminstrv. bd. Leisure World Cmty. Ch., 1996-2002; rep. to South Coast Ecumenical Coun., 1993-2002, chair pastor parish rels. com., 2000; chair Parents Day Festival com. greater L.A. county, 1996-2000, Blue Ribbon Com. for Effective Parenting in Long Beach, 1997-99. Recipient Outstanding Svc. award Long Beach Coord. Coun., 1969, Mother of Yr. award Silverado United Meth. Ch., 1973, Hon. Svc. award Calif. PTA, 1963, Continuing Svc. award, 1974, hon. life membership award Nat. PTA, 1974, Outstanding Laywoman of Yr. award Long Beach Area Coun. Chs., 1976, Woman of Yr. award State Women's Coun.-C. of C., 1979, Long Beach Internat. Bus. and Profl. Women's Club, Nat. Merit award DAR, 1982, Citizen of Yr. award Los Altos YMCA, 1982, Calif. Cmty. Pool for Handicapped, 1982, Outstanding Citizen award Torch Club of Long Beach, 1983, W. Odie Wright award Industry Edn. Coun., 1990, Humanitarian award NCCJ, 1992, Vol. of Yr. award ARC, 1995, 1st Life Membership award Long Beach chpt. UN Assn., Kunsho award of Order of the Sacred Treasure, Gold Rays with rosette from Japanese Govt., 1996, Sr. Vol. of Yr. Long Beach C.C., 1999, Al Taucher Rep. of Yr. award, 2001.

Mem. Industry Edn. Coun. Long Beach (hon. life), Long Beach C. of C. (Dewey Smith cmty. svc. award), Lions (hon. life), Soroptimist Interant. (Woman of Distinction in Econ. and Social Devel. 2001), Alpha Iota. Republican. Presbyterian. Home: Bixby Village 551 Pittsfield Ct Unit 101 Long Beach CA 90803-6355

SATTERFIELD-HARRIS, RITA, workers compensation representative; b. Bklyn, Oct. 14, 1949; d. Wilton Anthony and Hattie Eva (Tunstall) Satterfield; m. Sidney Harris, Jan. 5, 1973; 1 child, Marcial A.H. BA in Psychology, Bernard Baruch Coll., N.Y.C., 1983; student, CCNY, 1971-74; Cert. in Paralegal Studies, L.I. U., Bklyn., 1982; cert. unemployment ins. benefits law, Cornell U., 1984. Lic. workers' compensation rep. N.Y.; registered agt. N.Y. State Unemployment Ins. Dir. social svcs. Lincoln Sq. Neighborhood Ctr., N.Y.C., 1979-88; pvt. practice N.Y.C., 1988—. Writer of proposals funded by N.Y.C. Dept. for Aging Inc., 1980-82, and N.Y.C. Cmty. Devel. Agy., 1984-88. Recipient Cert. of Appreciation for participation in vol. income tax assistance program Dept. Treasury, IRS, 1985, 86, Ptnrs. in Change award Nat. Displaced Homemakers Network, 1991. Mem. Workers' Def. League, Nat. Orgn. Social Security Claimant's Reps. Avocations: rollerskating, music, gourmet cooking. Office: 141 Livingston St Brooklyn NY 11201-5133 Office Phone: 718-403-9041.

SATTERLEE, TERRY JEAN, lawyer; b. Kansas City, Mo., Aug. 28, 1948; d. Charles Woodbury and Francis Jean (Shriver) S.; m. William W. Rice, Jan. 9, 1982; children: Cassandra Jean Rice, Mary Shannon Rice. BA, Kans. U., 1970; JD, U. Mo., 1974. Bar: Mo. 1974. Lawyer Arthur Benson Assocs., Kansas City, Mo., 1974-77, Freilich & Leitner, Kansas City, 1977-78, U.S. Environ. Protection Agy., Kansas City, 1978-83; of counsel Lathrop & Norquist, Kansas City, 1985-87, ptnr., 1987—, mem. exec. com., 1997-2001. Contbr. articles to profl. jours. Chmn. Bd. Zoning Adjustment, Kansas City, 1983-87, Mo. State Parks Adv. Bd., 1997-2002; Kansas City Hazardous Materials com; steering com. COMPASS Met. Planning, Kansas City, 1990-93. Mem. Mo. Bar Assn. (chair environ. com. 1990-93), Kansas City Bar Assn. (environ. com. chmn. 1986-90, chair 2001), Mo. C. of C. (natural resource coun. 1990-2002, bd. dirs. 1999-2002, chair 1998-2002), Kansas City C. of C. (environ. com. chmn. 1992), Women's Pub. Svc. Network (named Top 25 US Women in Bus. 2000), Am. Met. Sewerage Assn. (legal affairs com. 1992—). Democrat. Episcopalian. Office: Lathrop & Gage 2345 Grand Blvd Kansas City MO 64108-2612 Office Phone: 816-292-2000.

SATTERTHWAITE, HELEN FOSTER, retired state legislator; b. Blawnox, Pa., July 8, 1928; d. Samuel J. and Lillian (Schreiber) Foster; m. Cameron B. Satterthwaite, Dec. 23, 1950 (div. July 1979); children: Mark Cameron, Tod Foster, Tracy Lynn, Keith Alan, Craig Evan (dec.). BS in Chemistry, Duquesne U., 1949. Biol. technician USDA, 1967-68; lab. technician U. Ill. Coll. Agr., 1968-70; rsch. asst. Iowa State U. Coll. Agr., 1971, Gulf R & D, Harmarville, Pa., 1950; rsch. chemist E.I. duPont de Nemours & Co., Wilmington, Del., 1951-53; technician Nat. Sci. Lab., U. Ill. Coll. Vet. Medicine, 1971-74; rep. Ill. Ho. of Reps., Springfield, 1974-92, majority leader, 1991-92, mem. sch. fin. task force, 1990-92, chmn. com. on higher edn., 1983-91, vice chmn. elem. and secondary edn., 1983-91; ret., 1993. Mem. Commn. on Mental Health and Devel. Disabilities, 1975-85, mem. exec. com., 1977-85, vice chmn., 1979-85; mem. Commn. to Visit and Examine State Instns., 1977-85, Ill. Coun. Mental Health, 1992-95, Task Force on Global Climate Change, 1991-96; treas. LWV, 1995-98, sec., 1998-2001; treas. Bus. and Profl. Women's Club, 1993-94, sec., 1994-95; bd. dirs. East Ctrl. Ill. Health Sys. Agy., 1977-79, Champaign County Mental Health Ctr., 1993-2002, Univ. YWCA, U. Ill., 1987—, Girls Inc., 1992-96; bd. dirs. Champaign County United Way, 1970-74, mem. budget com., 1973-74, mem. joint rev. com. on funding Champaign County mental health programs, 1973; co-chmn. task force on mental retardation Champaign County Mental Health Bd., 1973; mem. Ill. Devel. Disability Advocacy Authority, 1977-85, vice chmn., 1979-80; chmn. Ill. House Dem. Study Group, 1979-81; mem. Edn. Commn. on States, 1985-92, Nat. Conf. State Legis. Commn. on Labor and Edn., 1985-92; bd. govs. U. YMCA, 1995-2003. Recipient Freshman Legislator of Yr. award Ill. Edn. Assn., 1975, commndation Ill. State's Attys. Assn., 1975, Best Legislator award Ind. Voters Ill., 1976, 78, 80, 82, 84, 86, 88, 90, cert. of honor Assn. Student Govts., 1977, Disting. Svc. cert. AMVETS, 1977, Environ. Legislator of Yr. award Ill. Environ. Coun., 1977, 79, 81, 83, Meritorious Svc. award Champaign County Coun. on Alcoholism, 1978, Ill. C.C. Trustees ASsn., 1986, Perfect Voting Record award Ill. Credit Union League, 1979, Ill. Wildlife Fedn., 1979, cert., of spl. recognition Ill. Women's Polit. Caucus, 1979, 80, Pub. Svc. award Izaak Walton League, 1980, Friend of Edn. award Ill. Bd. Edn., 1985, cert. of appreciation Champaign County Urban League, 1987, Resolution of Honor, Ill. Libr. Assn., 1987, 100 Percent award Ill. Coun. Sr. Citizens Orgns., 1989, Dare To Be Great award Ill. Women Adminstrs., 1989; named Person of Yr., Champaign County Mental Health Assn., 1981, Pub. Citizen of Yr., Illino Dist. and Ill. chpt. NASW, 1981, Legislator of Yr., Ill. Assn. Sch. Social Workers, 1989. Mem. Ill. Conf. Women Legislators (co-convenor 1981-83), Nat. Order Women Legislators (bd. dirs. region IV 1982, treas. 1983-84), Champaign County League Women Voters, Delta Kappa Gamma. Mem. Soc. Of Friends.

SATTLER, NANCY JOAN, educational administrator; b. Toledo, July 14, 1950; d. Thomas Joseph and Margaret Mary (Linenkugel) Ainsworth; m. Rudolph Henry Sattler, June 17, 1972; children: Cortlund, Clinton, Corinne. BS, U. Toledo, 1972, MEd, 1988, PhD, 2004. Office worker/bookkeeper Gilbert Mail Svc., 1967-71; computer typesetter Quality Composition, Toledo, 1971-89; instr. Terra Tech. Coll. (now Terra C.C.), Fremont, Ohio, 1988-89; dept. head Terra Tech. Coll., Fremont, Ohio, 1989-95, curriculum chair bus., social scis., math. and arts, 1995-99, assoc. dean curriculum, 1999—2003, dean arts and scis., 2003—. Adj. instr. Terra Tech. Coll., Fremont, 1982-88, Terra Cmty. Coll., 1998—, U. Toledo, 1988, Lucas County Bd. Edn. Gifted Program, Toledo, 1988-92; computer coord. St. Joseph Elem. Sch., Fremont, 1987-94, coord. quiz bowl, 1993; extern in quality control Atlas Crankshaft, Fostoria, Ohio, 1990; instr. devel. math. A.O. Smith, Bellevue, Ohio, 1991, 93, 94; adult edn. computer instr. St. Joseph Ctrl. Cath. Sch., Fremont, 1990-92, sec. sch. bd., 1989-94, pres., 1991-94; instr. devel. math. and sci. Whirlpool Corp., Findlay, Ohio, 1992; presenter Am. Math. Assn. Two-Yr. Colls., 1991-2003, Nat. Coun. Tchrs. Math. Conf., 1993, 95, 98, 99; co-presenter Continuous Improvements Through Faculty Externship, League for Innovation, 1992; co-chmn. Ohio Gt. Tchrs. Seminar, 1993-; chmn. Kids Coll., Fremont, 1993-95; facilitator Mo. Gt. Tchrs. Seminar, 1993, Ohio Gt. Tchrs. Retreat, 1994-2004, N.Y. Gt. Tchrs. Seminar, 1994, Inventing Our Future, 1995-2002; co-chmn., presenter Ohiomatyc Winter Inst., 1994-98, 2000, 02, 03; TOM trainer Terra C.C., 1994-96. Author: The Implication of Math Placement Testing in the Two Year College, 1988, Applied Math for Industrial Technology, 1989; co-author: Math and Science Made Easy, 1992, The Metric System, Preparing for the Future, 1992, Workplace Literacy, 1994, The Basics of Using the TI-85 Graphing Calculator, 1995, Using the TI-85 Calculator to Solve Practical Application Problems for Business and Engineering Technologies. Sec. St. Joseph Ctrl. Cath. Sch. Bd., 1989-94, pres., 1991-94; Sunday sch. dir. St. Joseph Ch., Fremont, 1977-87; pres. Plant 'N Bloom Garden Club, Fremont, 1977-79, 2004—; clk. Sandusky County Fair, 1977—; rep. for deanery Early Childhood Devel., 1982-84; parliamentarian Welcome Wagon, 1980; Eucharistic min., 1991—; chair communications Inventing Our Future, 1996-; mem. adv. bd. Ohio Resource Ctr.; advisor Distributed Learning Workshop, 2001—; coun. bd. mem. Family and Children First, 2002—, Prevention Partnership, 2000—. Mem. Ohio Math. Assn. Two-Yr. Colls. (pres. 1992-95, historian 1997-, NSF grant com. 1992), Am. Math. Assn. Two-Yr. Colls. (assessment com. 1990—, chmn. 1993-97, program com. 1993, chmn. distance edn. task force 1998-2000, chmn. distance learning com. 2001—), Nat. Coun. Tchrs. Math., Ohio Coun. Tchrs. Math., chair, Distance Learning Com., 2000-, Ohio Assn. Garden Clubs, Alumni and Friends (bd. dirs. 1995-98, bd. visitors 1995—), Ohio Math. and Sci. Coalition (co-chmn. collaboration com. 1996-98, chmn. 1998—, mem. exec. bd. 1998—, chmn.-elect 2003). Democrat. Roman Catholic. Avocations: quilting, gardening, canning, sewing. Home: 712 Hayes Ave Fremont OH 43420-2914 Office: Terra Cmty Coll 2830 Napoleon Rd Fremont OH 43420-9611 Office Phone: 419-334-8400.

SAUBEL, KATHERINE SIVA, Indian culture consultant, educator; b. Los Coyotes Indian Reservation, Calif., Mar. 7, 1920; d. Juan C. and Melana Sewaill; m. Mariano Saubel, Oct. 2, 1940 (dec.); 1 child, Allen. Grad. high sch., Palm Springs, Calif. Tchr.'s asst. dept. anthropology UCLA, 1959-60; cons. to Dr. Hansjakob Seiler, U. Cologne, Banning, Calif., Germany, 1964-74; on Cahuilla Indian culture throughout U.S., 1960—; pres., editor press Malki Mus., Banning, 1964—. Lectr. U. Cologne, 1971; vis. lectr. U. Calif., Riverside, 1990; lectr. to sch. classes, Indian gatherings, 1958—. Author: Kunvachmal: A Cahuilla Tale, 1969; co-author: Temelpakh: Cahuilla Knowledge and Use of Plants, 1972, Chem'villu' (Lets Speak Cahuilla), 1981. Mem. Native Am. Heritage Commn., Calif.; speaker to various orgns. fighting nuclear and hazardous waste dumps in areas significant to Native Ams.; keynote spkr. Symposium on Am. Indian Religious Freedom, UCLA, 1992. Named County Historian of Yr., Riverside County Hist. Soc., 1986; named to Nat. Women's Hall of Fame, 1993. Home: PO Box 373 Banning CA 92220-0003 Office: Malki Mus Morongo Indian Reservation PO Box 578 Banning CA 92220-0017

SAUCIER, BONNIE L. dean, pediatrics nurse; b. Alton, Ill., Oct. 12, 1945; d. Robert E. and Laura L. (Rice) Powers; children: Michelle Marie, Kent Lawrence. Diploma, St. Johns Hosp. Sch. Nursing, Springfield, Ill., 1966; BA, Stephens Coll., 1976; MEd, U. Mo., 1977; MSN, U. Mo., Kansas City, 1983; PhD in nursing, Tex. Womans U., 1986. RN, Calif., Tex. Pedriatric staff nurse St. Johns Hosp., St Louis, 1966-69; asst. head nurse pediatrics North Kansas City (Mo.) Meml. Hosp., 1969-71; instr. nursing Trenton (Mo.) Jr. Coll., 1974-81; asst. prof. Mo. Western State Coll., St. Joseph, Mo., 1981-84; Inst. Cook County Coll., Gainesville, Tex., 1984-85; dir. health scis. Midwestern State U., Wichita Falls, Tex., 1986-92; prof., chair dept. nursing Calif. State U., Bakersfield, 1992—. Adj. inst. U. Tex., Arlington, 1985-86; bd. dirs. ARC. Wichita Falls, 1988-92; adv. bd., cons. Vernon (Tex.) Regional Jr. Coll., 1987-92; trustee Red River Hosp. Wichita Falls, 1989-92. Contbr. articles to profl. jours. Adv. bd. Care Team Healtha Care Svcs. Wichita Falls, 1991-92; bd. dirs. March of Dimes, 1989, Nat. Kidney Found., 1989-90; mem. Midwestern Div. Tex. Hosp., 1987-92; Tex. Orgn. of Baccalaureate Nursing Programs, 1989-92, Tex. Outstanding Rural Scholars Adv., 1989-92, Tex. Nurses Edn. Adv., 1989-90. Profl. Nursing Shortage grant, Office of Gov., 1991, Profl. Nursing Retention grantee Coordinating Bd., 1991; named to Women's Hall of Fame, Mayors Commn., 1991. Mem. Tex. Nurses Assn. (coun. edn. 1991-92), Tex. Nurses Assn. #11 (pres. 1990-91, bd. dirs. 1991-92), Calif. Nurses Assn. (state adv. com. for nursing manpower study 1992), Calif. Assn. Colls. of Nursing (health care adv. com., MSA program 1992-93, acad. senator), Tex. League for Nursing (bd. dirs. 1985-92), So. Coun. on Collegiate Edn., Sigma Theta Tau. Republican. Roman Catholic. Avocations: walking, travel, racquetball, reading. Office: Calif State U 9001 Stockdale Hwy Bakersfield CA 93311-1022

SAUCIER, GUYLAINE, corporate director; b. Noranda, Que., Can., June 10, 1946; d. Gérard and Yvette (Thiffault) S. Chartered acct., École Hautes Etudes Commls., Montreal, Can., 1971. Formerly chair Joint Com. on Corp. Governance. Bd. dirs. Petro-Can., Bank Montreal, Nortel Networks Corp., Tembec Inc., Altran Techs.; mem. Commn. Inquiry Unemployment Ins. Fellow Inst. Chartered Accts.; mem. Order Can. Avocation: tennis. E-mail: gusauci@attglobal.net.

SAUER, ELISABETH RUTH, lawyer; b. Charleston, W.Va., July 27, 1948; d. Gordon Chenoweth and Mary Louise (Steinhilber) S. B.A., Northwestern U., 1970; J.D., U. Mo., 1975. Bar: Mo. 1975. Assoc. Campbell, Erickson, Cottingham, Morgan & Gibson, Kansas City, Mo., 1975-80, ptnr., 1980-88; ptnr. Lashly Baer & Hamel, P.C., 1989-91; of counsel Swanson, Midgley, Gangwere, Clark & Kitchin, 1991-93; mem., owner Elisabeth R. Sauer, P.C., Kansas City, 1994—. Bd. dirs. Kansas City Met. Regional Com. on Status of Women, 1976-78; trustee UMKC Conservatory for Music. Mem. ABA, Mo. Bar Assn., Kansas City Bar Assn., Assn. Women Lawyers of Greater Kansas City, Nat. Women's Law Ctr., Internat. Assn. Ins. Receivers, Rockhill Tennis-Kenwood Club. Office: 802 Broadway St Fl 2D Kansas City MO 64105-1598

SAUER, ELISSA SWISHER, nursing educator; b. Williamsport, Pa., Jan. 9, 1935; d. Oliver S. and Emily Louisa (Gehron) Swisher; m. Raymond James Sauer, Nov. 27, 1964. Diploma, Reading Hosp. Sch. Nursing, Pa., 1957; BS, Albright Coll., Reading, 1958; MSN, U. Pa., 1964. Nurse Cmty. Health and Civic Assn., Ardmore, Pa., 1966-67; pub. health coord. Albert Einstein Med. Ctr., 1967-68; pvt. duty nurse, 1968-73; clin. faculty Schuylkill County AVTS, 1973-74; prof. nursing Reading (Pa.) Area C.C., 1975-80; oncology nurse adminstr.-educator Comprehensive Cmty. Cancer Ctr., Allentown, Pa., 1981-85; exec. dir. Holy Family Home Health Care, Orwigsburg, Pa., 1985-89; dir. nursing programs, asst. dean health svcs. Reading Area C.C., 1989-2000, asst. dean emerita, 2001—. Cons. nursing edn. and continuing edn.; evaluator for nat. nurse aide cert. assessment program, 2000—. Author: Procedure Manual to accompany Fundamentals of Nursing: Human Health and Function, 3d edit., 2003. Mem.: Sigma Theta Tau. Home: 1114 Pepper Ridge Dr Reading PA 19606-3803 E-mail: esauer@ptd.net.

SAUER, ELIZABETH MASON, school social worker; b. Chgo., Aug. 1, 1933; d. George Allen Jr. and Louise Townsend (Barnard) Mason; m. Louis Sauer, June 7, 1956 (div. Aug. 1990); children: Christopher G., Kathryn Sauer Chandler. BS in Speech/Theatre, Northwestern U., Evanston, Ill., 1955; MSW, U. Pa., 1961; Diploma in Edn. for Ministry, Theol. Sch. of the South, Sewanee, Tenn., 1992. Lic. social worker, Pa.; cert. home and sch. visitor, Pa. Social worker, supr. Dept. of Welfare City of Phila., 1958-65; social work supr. Child Care Ctrs. Sch. Dist. of Phila., 1965-69; social worker St. Peter's Child Devel. Ctrs., Pitts., 1982-84; supr. run-away-youth program Youth Emergency Svcs./Youth Svc., Inc., Phila., 1984-87; foster care social worker Residential Treatment/Silver Springs-Martin Luther Sch., Plymouth Meeting, Pa., 1987-89; sch. social worker Martin Luther Sch., Plymouth Meeting, Pa., 1989—. Cons. Child Care Ctrs., Phila., 1970-72. Actor The Playhouse, Eagles Mere, Pa., 1954, 55. Bd. dirs. Northwest Cmty. Coun., Phila., 1976-79; mem. outreach com. Ch. of St. Martin's In the Fields, Phila., 1993-96, Litergist, 1995-2002; mem. Phila.-Chestnut Hill Cmty. Assn., 1970-79, 84—. Mem. Pa. Assn. Sch. Social Work Personnel, NASW, ACSW. Democrat. Episcopalian. Avocations: domestic gardening, reading, quilting, spiritual growth, vacationing in the thimble islands, long island sound. Office: Martin Luther Sch 512 Township Line Rd Plymouth Meeting PA 19462-1001

SAUER, MARY JULIA, special education educator; b. Pitts., Oct. 10, 1949; d. Edward Henry and Julia Ann (Polkabla) Sauer; 1 child, Jason Michael Sauer; m. John Harold Moore, Oct. 27, 1990 (div.); 1 adopted child, Jocelyn Quan. BS in Art Edn., Edinboro State Coll., 1971; MS in Spl. Edn., Clarion State Coll., 1980; postgrad, U. Pitts., 1988—. Cert. art tchr., spl. edn. tchr. for mentally retarded. Tchr. Polk (Pa.) State Sch. & Hosp., 1971-72; vol. VISTA, Bath, N.Y., 1972-73; tchr. Polk Ctr., 1973-80, program specialist, 1980-92; residential svc. supr., qualified mental retardation profl. Polk (Pa.) Ctr., 1992—. Lectr., speaker, video on local TV on history of Polk Ctr., 1987. Patentee beer bottle shaped cake pan; cakes displayed in TV videos and in various mags.; creator history video Polk Ctr., Some Leaky Boot Statues, Polk Center--100 Years; creator video A Century of Care-The History of the Evolution of Institional Care of the Devlopment Disabled. Past vol. Big Bros./Big Sisters. Democrat. Roman Catholic. Avocations: cake decorating, reading. Home: PO Box 97 Franklin PA 16323

SAUERBREY, ELLEN ELAINE RICHMOND, diplomat; b. Balt., Sept. 9, 1937; d. Edgar Arthur and Ethel Frederika (Landgraf) Richmond; m. Wilmer John Emil Sauerbrey, June 27, 1959. AB summa cum laude in Biology and English, Western Md. Coll., 1959. Biology instr., chmn. sci. dept. Baltimore County Sch. System, 1959-64; dist. mgr. Baltimore County U.S. Census, 1970; Md. Ho. of Dels., Annapolis, 1978-94, minority leader, 1986-94; radio talk show host Sta. WBAL, Balt., 1996; U.S. rep. com. status women UN, 2002—; amb. to UN Commn. on the Status of Women, 2002—. Rep. nominee for Gov., 1994; Rep. nominee for Gov., 98; bd. dirs. BBB; U.S. del. to UN Commn. on Human Rights, 2001, 03; U.S. rep. to UN Commn. on Status of Women, 2002—; head U.S. Del. to Baltic States Conf., 2003. Nat. chmn. Am. Legis. Exec. Coun., 1990—91; trustee Md. Coun. Econ. Edn., Franklin Sq. Hosp.; founder United Citizen's for Md.'s Future; bd. advisors Yorktown University; Rep. Nat. Com. Woman Md., 1996—2003; Rules com., 1996; del. Rep. Nat. Convs., 1968, 1976, 1984, 1988, 1992, 1996, 2000, platform com., chmn. subcom. on economy, 1977; nat. adv. bd. Nat. Conservative Campaign Fund; mem. credentials com. Rep. Nat. Convs., 1984; vice chmn. Rep. State Ctrl. Com. of Balt. County, 1966—71; state chmn. Md. chpt. George W. Bush for Pres., 1999—2000. Recipient Pvt. Property award Greater Balt. Bd. Realtors, 1984; named Legislator of Yr., Md. Assn. Builders and Contractors, 1982, Am. Legis. Exec. Coun., 1986, Western Md. Coll. Alum of Yr., 1988, Outstanding Legis. Leader, Am. Legis. Exec. Coun., 1992, Rep. Woman of Yr., Md. Rep. Party, 1995, Nat. Fedn. Ind. Bus., Guardian of Small Bus. award, 1989, Lifetime Svc. award Baltimore County Rep. Party, 2003, Md. State of Mind award, 2004; named one of top 100 Md. Women, The Daily Record, 1998. Mem. DAR, Nat. Fedn. Rep. Women (Margaret Chase Smith award 1995, Lifetime Svc. award Balt. chpt., 2003, Md. State of Mind award 2004), Md. Fedn. Rep. Women, Am. Legis. exch. Coun. (chmn. emeritus), Md. Farm Bur., Md. Conservative Union, Beta Beta, Beta, Phi Beta Kappa. Presbyterian. Avocations: gardening, travel. E-mail: Ellen99@erols.com.

SAUERBRUN, SUSAN JO, artist; b. Warren, Ohio, Mar. 9, 1949; d. Jack Edward and Mary Colette (Lins) S. AA, Stephens Coll., Columbia, Mo., 1969, BFA, 1971; student, Sir John Cass Sch. Art, London, 1973-75, Johnson Atelier, Princeton, N.J., 1980; MFA Mason Gross Sch. of Art, Rutgers U., 1979; MFA, Pratt Inst., N.Y.C., 2001. Lectr. painting Havering Coll., Hornchurch, Eng., 1976-77; vis. artist Queens Coll. CUNY, N.Y.C. 1983; adj. prof. art Manhattanville Coll., Purchase, N.Y., 2003; exch. scholar Am. Field Svc. Austria, 1966; artist in residence Henry St. Settlement, N.Y.C., 1981-82, Bronx (N.Y.) Coun. on Arts, 1984-90; one on one program Air Gallery, N.Y.C., 1982, 84; bd. dirs. Acme Gallery, London, 1973-78, curator exhbn. 1973-76; founder, bd. dirs. Acme Housing Assn., London, 1973-78; head animator Elm St. Studio, 1999--. One-person show include Amp Gallery, London, 1973, Maynard Gallery, Herts, Eng., 1975, Brownson Art Gallery, Manhattanville Coll., Harrison, N.Y., 1991; exhibited in group shows at White Chapel Art Gallery, London, 1977, Westbeth Gallery, N.Y.C., 1982, Morivioi Gallery, N.Y.C., 1983, Inter Art Gallery, N.Y.C., 1985, Longwood Art Gallery, Bronx, N.Y., 1986, 87, The City Gallery, N.Y.C., 1981, 89, Bronx Mus. Art, 1991, The Time Sq. Hotel, N.Y.C., 1993, The Water Book Show, Abiquiu, 1996, Art Between the Bridges, 1997. Recipient Artist's Grant Artist's Space, N.Y.C., 1991, Am. Drawing Biennial prize, 2000, Pollack-Krasner award 2001. Mem.: Coll. Art Assn. Avocations: t'ai chi chuan, swimming, bicycling, needlework, reading.

SAUERWEIN, AMANDA MARIE, small business owner; b. St. Louis, Mo., Nov. 10, 1977; d. Linda Marie Hosack; 1 child, Eli Jewell. MA in Tchg., Webster U., St. Louis, 2003. Cert. tchr. gifted K-12 Mo., 2003. Gifted edn. coord. Newburg (Mo.) R-2 Schs., 1999—2003; sole propr. Violet Sunshine Books and Beads, Rolla, Mo., 1999—. Mem.: Jaycees (assoc.). Office: Violet Sunshine Books and Beads 1007a North Pine St Rolla MO 65401 Personal E-mail: amsauerwein@excite.com.

SAUFLEY, LEIGH INGALLS, judge; m. William Saufley; 2 children. Grad., Maine Sch. Law. Pvt. practice, Ellsworth; asst. counsel U.S. VA; asst., then dep. atty. gen. Maine, 1981-90; judge Maine Dist. Ct., 1990—93; justice Maine Superior Ct, 1993—97; assoc. justice Maine Supreme Judicial Ct., 1997—2001, chief justice, 2001—. Office: Cumberland County Courthouse PO Box 368 142 Federal St Portland ME 04112-0368 E-mail: amanda.j.martin@state.me.us.

SAUL, APRIL, photographer; b. Bklyn., May 27, 1955; children: Amy, Nicholas. BA in English, Tufts U.; MA in Mass Comm., U. Minn. Staff photographer Balt. Sun, 1980, Phila. Inquirer, 1981—. Co-recipient Pulitzer Prize for exploratory journalism, 1997; named Photography of the Yr., Soc. Newspaper Design, 1994; recipient Robert F. Kennedy Journalism award, 1983, Budapest award, World Press Photo, 1991, Gold medal, best in show award, Soc. Newspaper Design, 1994; Nikon/NPPA Documentary Sabbatical grantee, 1985. Office: Phila Inquirer PO Box 8263 Philadelphia PA 19101-8263

SAUL, STEPHANIE, journalist; b. St. Louis, Jan. 28, 1954; d. Elmer William and Nancy (Cromer) Saul; m. Walt Bogdanich, Jan. 2, 1982; children: Nicholas Walter Bogdanich, Peter Eric Bogdanich. BA, U. Miss., 1975. Reporter New Albany (Miss.) Gazette, 1974, Clarion-Ledger, Jackson, Miss., 1975—80, The Plain Dealer, Cleve., 1980—84; nat. corr. Newsday, Melville, NY, 1984—. Adj. prof. journalism Columbia U., N.Y.C., 1999—. Named Journalist of Yr., Times Mirror Co.; recipient Silver Gavel award, ABA, 1980, George Polk award for regional reporting, 1981, Nat. Press Club award, 1990, IRE award, Investigative Reporters and Editors, 1995, Headliner award, Atlantic City Press Club, 1995, Roy Howard award, Scripps Howard Found., 1995, Pulitzer Prize for investigative reporting, 1995, Golden Typewriter award for pub. svc. journalism, N.Y. Press Club, 1995, Silver Em Miss. Scholastic Press Assn., 1997, N.Y. Assn. of Black Journalists award, 1998, James Aronson award for social justice journalism, Hunter Coll., N.Y., 1999. Office: Newsday 235 Pinelawn Rd Melville NY 11747-4250

SAULMON, SHARON ANN, college librarian; b. Blackwell, Okla., June 13, 1947; d. Ellis Gordon and Willa Mae Overman; 1 child, John Henry. AA, No. Okla. Coll., 1967; BA, Ctrl. State U., 1969, MBA, 1987; MLS, U. Okla., 1974; postgrad., Okla. State U., 1982. Children's libr. Met. Libr. Sys., Oklahoma City, 1969-74, coord. pub. svcs., 1974-77, asst. chief ext. svcs., 1977-80; reference/special projects libr. Rose State Coll., Midwest City, Okla., 1980-91, head libr., 1991—2003; dir. LRC, 2004—. Adj. faculty Rose State Coll., 1983—; program chair Global Okla. Multi-Cultural Festival, 1993; mem. Nat. Adv. Panel for Assessment of Sch. and Pub. Librs. in Support of Nat. Edn. Goals, 1995—96, project dir. internet tng., 1997, chair website com., 1996—98, v.p. profl./adminstrv. staff, 1998—99, pres., 1999—2000; vice chair Okla. Coun. Acad. Libr. Dirs., 2001—03, chair, 2003—05; spkr. in field. Contbr. articles to profl. jours. Bd. dirs. Areawide Aging Agy., 1974-77; chair Met. Libr. Commn., 1990-98, disbursing agt., chair fin. com., 1986-88, long-range planning com., 1985-87; chair bd. dirs. Met. Librs. Network Ctrl. Okla., 1989-90, chair alternative funding com., 1990-98, newsletter editor, 1987-89, chair electronic media com., 1987-89, chair bd. dirs., 1997-98, Webmaster, 1997-2000. Recipient Outstanding Contbn. award Met. Libr. Sys., Friends of the Libr., 1990, Disting. Svc. award Okla. Libr. Assn., 1995, OLA/SIRS Intellectual Freedom award 1999. Mem. ALA (mem. legis. com. 1996-98, adv. bd. 1996-98, Cited Trustee award 1999), Am. Libr. Trustee Assn. (bd. dirs. 1997-98, 2000-04, pres. 1994-95, 1st v.p., pres. elect 1993-94, newsletter editor 1989-93, 99-2003, chair publs. com. 1987-92, regional v.p. 1985-88, chair speakers bur. com. 1991-92, chair awards com. 1998-99, chair pres. program com. 2000-03), Assn. Coll. and Rsch. Librs. (Cmty. and Jr. Coll. sect.), Pub. Libr. Assn., Okla. Libr. Assn. (conf. preview editor 1990-91, chair trustees divsn. 1989-90, com. mem., disting. svc. award 1995, chair divsn. univ. colls. 1996-97, chair program com. 1998-99, v.p. 1999-2000, pres. 2000-01, budget com. chair 2001-02, navigating info. chair 2002-03, career recruit, ret. chair 2003-04). Democrat. Methodist. Office: Rose State Coll Libr 6420 SE 15th St Midwest City OK 73110-2704 E-mail: ssaulmon@yahoo.com.

SAUNDERS, DEBRA J. columnist; b. Newton, Mass., Dec. 8, 1954; BA in Latin and Greek, U. Mass., Boston, 1980. Asst. dir. Arnold Zenker Assocs., 1982-83; writer/rschr., account exec. Todd Domke Assocs., Sacramento, 1983-84, Russo Watts & Rollins, Sacramento, 1985-86; asst. to Rep. Leader Calif. Assembly, Sacramento, 1987-88; columnist, editl. writer L.A. Daily News, 1988-92; columnist San Francisco Chronicle, 1992—. Leader study group on polit. speechmaking Harvard U., Cambridge, Mass., 1984; tchr. editl. and column writing UCLA Ext., 1992. Published in Wall St. Jour., Nat. Review, Weekly Std., Reason mag.; syndicated nationally via Creators Syndicate; appeared on Politically Incorrect, CNN and BBC radio. Office: San Francisco Chronicle 901 Mission St San Francisco CA 94103-2905

SAUNDERS, DONNA M. accountant; b. Washington, July 23, 1969; d. Ellridge Everette Carey and Joyce Bernice Ramey; m. Gary Roland Saunders, June 10, 2000. BS, U. Md., 1991. Market rschr. Nat. Rsch. Inc., New Carrollton, Md., 1986-87; clk.-typist USN, Washington, 1987; student asst. U. Md. College Park, Washington, 1987-91; sr. acct. Bert Smith & Co., Washington, Va., 1992-94; staff acct. Arrow Gen., Alexandria, Va., 1994; accts. payable supr. Franklin Acceptance, Greenbelt, Md., 1994-96; acctg. mgr. Rental Tools, Upper Marlboro, Md., 1996-99; sr. acct. FTI Cons., Annapolis, Md., 1999; acctg. mgr. Safeware, Inc., Largo, Md., 1999 . Bd. dirs., asst. sec./treas. Safeward, 2003. Mem. AICPAs, Md. Assn. CPAs. Democrat. Baptist. Avocation: missionary youth work.

SAUNDERS, JOANNE HINES, elementary school educator; b. Yonkers, N.Y., Mar. 5, 1952; d. Bernard L. and Jean (Filippone) Hines; m. Earl Duston Saunders, June 2, 1973. BA, Marymount Coll., 1973; EdM, Boston U., 1981; cert. in gifted edn., Coll. New Rochelle, 1990. Cert. tchr., N.Y., Ky., N.J.; cert. in gifted edn., N.Y. Tchr. Marshall Elem. Sch., Ft. Campbell, Ky., 1974-77; adult tchr. Dept. of Def. Schs., Vicenza, Italy, 1978-81; elem. tchr. Little Britain Sch., Newburgh, N.Y., 1982—. Co-author: Beyond the Book, 1997; appearances include (TV) Good Morning America, 1996; contbr. articles to profl. jours. Recipient Excellence in Teaching award Springhouse Corp., 1990. Mem. Nat. Assn. Gifted Children, Cath. Women of Chapel, Nat. Honor Soc. Avocations: reading, racquetball, tennis, cross-stitch, drawing, photography, fitness. Office: Little Britain Sch 1160 Little Britain Rd New Windsor NY 12553-5906

SAUNDERS, KATHRYN A. retired data processing administrator; b. Elgin, Minn., Apr. 12, 1920; d. William P. and Mathilda M. (Mielke) Hagner; m. James L. Saunders, June 14, 1952 (dec. 1992); children: Gary, Wade, Brian. BA, U. Calif., Berkeley, 1941; cert., Coll. of Marin, Kentfield, Calif., 1948. Mem. gen. staff Fed. Res. Bank, San Francisco; with civilian pers./payroll dept. USAF, Hamilton AFB, Calif.; coord. data processing Sir Francis Drake High Sch., San Anselmo, Calif. Sec. program resource United Meth. Women, 1988—, treas., 1994-99; mem. decorations guild Marin Art and Garden Ctr., 1996—. Mem. AAUW, Calif. Sch. Employees Assn., Calif. Scholarship Fedn. (life), Nat. Assn. Ret. Fed. Employees, Coll. of Environ. Design Alumni Assn. of U. Calif. Berkeley, Order of Golden Rose of Delta Zeta, Commonwealth Club of Calif., Sierra Club. Avocations: sewing, knitting, art work, piano, volunteer work. Address: 118 Tamal Vista Dr San Rafael CA 94901-1646

SAUNDERS, KENDRA J. psychologist, educator; b. Hinsdale, Ill., Mar. 2, 1974; d. Gerald Wilson and Olivia Jean Saunders. BS in Psychology, U. Ill., 1996; MA in Psychology, Tex. Tech. U., 1999, PhD in Counseling Psychology, 2002. Clin. asst. Montford Psychiatric Prison, Lubbock, 2000—01; intern in psychology Ariz. State U., Tempe, Ariz., 2001—02; asst. prof. Millersville (Pa.) U., 2002—, psychologist, 2002—. Rsch. asst. Tex. Tech. U., Lubbock, 1997—99, tchg. asst., 1999—2000. Author: (chpt.) Management of Stress and Eating Disorders in Women and Children, 2000. Mem.: Am. Psychol. Assn. Avocations: horseback riding, dance, hiking. Office: Millersville U PO Box 1002 Millersville PA 17551 Home: 527 E Chestnut St Lancaster PA 17602-3018

SAUNDERS, LONNA JEANNE, lawyer, newscaster, talk show host; b. Cleve. d. Jack Glenn and Lillian Frances (Newman) Slaby. Student, Dartmouth Coll.; AB in Polit. Sci. with honors, Vassar Coll.; JD, Northwestern U., 1981; cert. advanced study in Mass Media, Stanford U., 1992. Bar: Ill. 1981. News dir., morning news anchor Sta. WKBK-AM, Keene, NH, 1974-75; reporter Sta. KDKA-AM, Pitts., 1975; pub. affairs dir., news anchor Sta. WJW-AM, Cleve., 1975-76; helicopter traffic reporter WERE-AM Radio, Cleve., 1976-77; morning news anchor Sta. WBBG-AM, Cleve., 1978; talk host, news anchor Sta. WIND-AM, Chgo., 1978-82; atty. Arvey, Hodes, Costello & Burman, Chgo., 1981-82; host, "The Stock Market Observer", news anchor WCIU-TV, Chgo., 1982-85; staff atty. Better Govt. Assn., Chgo., 1983-84; news anchor, reporter Sta. WBMX-FM, Chgo., 1984-86; pvt. practice Chgo., 1985—; news anchor Sta. WKQX-FM, Chgo., 1987. Instr. Columbia Coll., Chgo., 1987-90; guest talk host Sta. WMCA, N.Y.C., 1983, Sta. WMAQ, Chgo., 1988, Sta. WLS, Chgo., 1989, Sta. WWWE, Cleve., 1989, Sta. KVI, Seattle, 1994, WCBM-AM, Balt., 1996, WRC-AM, Wash., D.C., 1997; host, prodr. The Lively Arts, Cablevision Chgo., 1986; talk show host The Lonna Saunders Show, Sta. KIRO-AM, Seattle, 1995-96; news anchor, WTOP-AM Radio, Washington, D.C., 1996-97; talk host, "Today and Tomorrow show", WMAL-AM radio, Washington, D.C., 1997, freelance reporter, CBS Radio Network, N.Y.C., 1975—; writer, General Media, N.Y.C., 1996—; atty. Lawyers for Creative Arts, Chgo., 1985-91; guest columnist Gainesville (Fla.) Sun Newspaper, 1998-99, Rockford (Ill.) Register Star Newspaper, 1998—; freelance writer Indians Ink mag., 1998—. Columnist Chgo. Life mag., 1986—; editl. bd. Jour. Criminal Law and Criminology, 1979-81; contbr. articles to profl. jours.; creator pub. affairs program WBBM-AM, Chgo., 1985. Mem. women's action coun. Amnesty Internat., 2000—. Recipient Akron Press Club award for best pub. affairs presentation, 1978; grantee Scripps Howard Found., 1978-81; AFTRA George Heller Meml. scholar, 1980-81. Fellow Am. Bar Found.; mem. ABA (mem. exec. coms. Lawyers and the Arts, Art Law and Media 1986-92, chmn. exec. com. Law and Media 1990-91, 91-92, Young Lawyers divsn. liaison to Forum Com. on Comm. Law 1991-93, Commn. for Partnership Programs 1993-94, regional divsn. chair Forum on Comm. Law 1995-96). Roman Catholic. Avocations: theater, piano, baseball. E-mail: lonna2@aol.com.

SAUNDERS, MARI PITTMAN, psychologist; b. Newark, May 13, 1935; d. Tillmon Ulysses Pittman and Christine Lisabeth Von Heiskell; m. David Milton Saunders Jr., Apr. 10, 1960; children: Phillip Michael, Leslie Beth. BS, CUNY, 1958, MA, 1962, MS, 1964; Doctorate, Fordham U., 1976. Cert. tchr., guidance counselor, N.Y.; Nat. Assn. Forensic Counselors cert. psychopathologist, psychotherapist, and addictions counselor. Tchr. elem. edn. Pub. Sch. 161, N.Y.C., 1961-62; tchr. jr. h.s. Jr. H.S. 43, N.Y.C., 1962-65; tchr. h.s. English, guidance counselor Taft H.S., Bronx, N.Y., 1965-70; clin. counselor H.H. Lehman, CUNY, Bronx, 1970-75; psychologist, therapist Edupsych Assocs., N.Y.C., 1975—; pvt. practice Urban League, Bklyn. and N.Y.C., 1981—, Addicts Rehab. Ctr., N.Y.C., 1984—. Clin. supr. Samaritan Women's Project, Rikers Island, N.Y., 1988-90; therapy cons. Assn. for Interpersonal Dynamics, N.Y.C., 1980-88; asst. supr. for cmty. guidance and edn. Bd. Edn., Bklyn., 1970-73; social worker NY Dept. Welfare N.Y.C. Social Svcs., Bronx, 1959-60. Author: (book) Marry Yes, Marry No, 1999; contbr. articles and book revs. to profl. publs. Psychologist, treas. Inst. for Interracial Harmony, Bklyn., 1982—; host telequest radio program WMCA, N.Y.C., 1983; appeared on several TV shows. Mem. Les Vivantes Noires (v.p. 1978, 2000—, pres.), Vanguard Coalition (psychologist 1999, 2000—).

SAUNDERS, MARY L. career officer; BS in Social Work, Tex. Woman's U., 1970; grad., Squadron Officer Sch., 1973; MA in Guidance and Counseling, Rider Coll., 1978; grad., Air War Coll., 1993; nat. security leadership course, Johns Hopkins U., 1997. Commd. 2d lt. USAF, 1971, advanced through grades to brigadier gen., 1997; air terminal ops. officer 610th Mil. Airlift Support Squadron, Yokota Air Base, Japan, 1973-75; dep. comdr., comdr. Mil. Air Traffic Coordinating Office Mil. Traffic Mgmt. Command, McGuire AFB, N.J., 1976-79; chief of transp. 6168th Combat Support Squadron, Taegu Air Base, South Korea, 1982-83; comdr. 475th Transp. Squadron, Yokota Air Base, Japan, 1983-84; transp. staff officer Joint Deployment Agy., MacDill AFB, Fla., 1986-88, J-5, U.S. Transp. Command, Scott AFB, Ill., 1988-90; chief contingency plans divsn. J-5, U.S. So. Command, Quarry Heights, Panam, 1990-92; chief logistic plans Hdqs. Air Force Res., Robins AFB, Ga., 1993-96; dir. transp. Office Dep. Chief Staff Installations/Logistics Hdqs. USAF, The Pentagon, Washington, 1996-98; comdr. Def. Supply Ctr. Columbus Def. Logistics Agy., Columbus, Ohio, 1998—. Decorated Legion of Merit, Def. Meritorious Svc. medal with oak leaf cluster, Meritorious Svc. medal with 2 oak leaf clusters. Mem. AAUS, NAFE, Air Force Assn., Nat. Def. Transp. Assn. Office: Def Supply Ctr Columbus PO Box 3990 Columbus OH 43216-5000

SAUNDERS, MYRA KATHLEEN, dean, law librarian, educator; b. San Francisco, 1950; BA, U. Calif., Berkeley, 1972; MLS, U. So. Calif., 1973; JD, U. San Diego, 1979. Law libr. U. San Diego, Whittier Coll. Sch. Law, U. Calif., Berkeley; assoc. law libr. for pub. svcs. UCLA, 1983—89, law libr., prof. law in residence, 1989—, assoc. dean Hugh and Hazel Darling Law Libr., 1989—. Contbr. articles to profl. jours. Office: 1112 Law Bldg 405 Hilgard Ave Los Angeles CA 90095-1458

SAUNDERS, PATRICIA GENE KNIGHT, freelance writer, editor; b. Tulsa, Okla., Nov. 29, 1946; d. Eugene Merritt and Patricia May (Hough) Knight; m. Joseph Eugene Saunders, June 24, 1989. BA, Baylor U., 1969. Nat. advt. sec. KTVT-TV, Ft. Worth, 1969-71; tchr. Arlington (Tex.) Ind. Sch. Dist., 1971-77, Garland (Tex.) Ind. Sch. Dist., 1977-79; payroll, spl. projects assoc. Electronic Data Systems, Dallas, 1979-81; adminstrv. asst. Diversifield Innovators, Dallas, 1981-82; system ops. mgr. Span Instruments, Plano, Tex., 1982-86; data processing mgr. Claire Mfg., Addison, Ill., 1986-87, Everpure, Inc., Westmont, Ill., 1987-88; software cons. Software Alternatives, Inc., Downers Grove, Ill., 1988-89; sys. ops. asst., cons. J&J Maintenance, Inc., Austin, Tex., 1989-90; pres., computer cons. Cardinal Software Solutions, Inc., Austin, 1990-93; editor Holt, Rinehart & Winston, Austin, 1993-99. Mem.: Writers' League of Tex., Soc. of Children's Book Writers and Illustrators, N.Y. Met. Mus. Fine Art, Smithsonian Instn., Nat. Mus. Women in the Arts, Nat. Arbor Day Found., Lady Bird Johnson Wildflower Ctr. Republican. Baptist. Avocations: gardening, travel, reading, movies, cats. Home: 410 Teal Ln Kyle TX 78640-8888

SAUNDERS, SALLY LOVE, poet, educator; b. Bryn Mawr, Pa., Jan. 15, 1940; d. Lawrence and Dorothy (Love) S. Student, Sophia U., Tokyo, Japan, 1963, U. Pa., Columbia; BS, George Williams Coll., 1965. Tchr. Shipley Sch., Bryn Mawr, 1962-65, Agnes Irwin Sch., Wynnewood, Pa., 1964-65, Montgomery County Day Sch., Wynnewood, 1962, Miquon (Pa.) Sch., Waldron Acad., Merion, Pa., 1965-66, Phelps Sch., Malvern, Pa., 1965-70, Frankford Friends Sch. Phila., 1965-66, Haverford (Pa.) Sch., 1965-66, Friends Sem. Sch., N.Y.C., 1966-68, Ballard Sch., N.Y.C., 1966-67, Lower Merion Sch., Ardmore, Pa., nights 1967-71, Univ. Settlement House, Phila., 1961-63, Navajo Indian Reservation, Fort Defiance, Ariz., 1963, Young Men's Jewish Youth Center, Chgo., 1964-65, Margaret Fuller Settlement House, Cambridge, Mass., 1958-61; poetry therapist Pa. Hosp. Inst., 1969-74, also drug rehab. house; poet in residence Tyrone Guthrie Ctr., Newbliss, Ireland, Aug. 1988; poetry workshop leader Pendle Hill Quaker Ctr., Wallingford, Pa., Apr. 1988; poetry week leader Ferry Beach, Saco, Maine, summer 1988. Pioneer in poetry therapy. Poet, 1946—; poems pub. in periodicals including others; author: Past the Near Meadows, 1961, Pauses, 1978, Fresh Bread, 1982, Random Thoughts, 1992, Patchwork Quilt, 1993, Quiet Thoughts and Gentle Feelings, 1996, Word Pictures, 1998; contbr. poems to newspapers. Mem. Acad. Am. Poets, Nat. Fedn. State Poetry Socs., Am. Poetry League, Nat. League Am. Pen Women, Poetry Therapy Assn. (v.p.), Avalon Orgn., Authors Guild, Nat. Writers Club, Pen and Brush Club, N.H., Pa. poetry socs., Cath. Poetry Soc. (asso.), Fla. State Poetry Soc. (asso.) Episcopalian. Home: 2030 Vallejo St Apt 501 San Francisco CA 94123-4854 Office: 609 Rose Hill Rd Broomall PA 19008-2254

SAUSMAN, KAREN, zoological park administrator; b. Chgo., Nov. 26, 1945; d. William and Annabell (Lofaso) S. BS, Loyola U., 1966; student, Redlands U., 1968. Keeper Lincoln Park Zoo, Chgo., 1964-66; tchr. Palm Springs (Calif.) Unified Sch., 1968-70; ranger Nat. Park Svc., Joshua Tree, Calif., 1968-70; zoo dir. The Living Desert, Palm Desert, Calif., 1970—. Natural history study tour leader internat., 1974—; part-time instr. Coll. Desert Natural History Calif. Desert, 1975-78; field reviewer conservation grants Inst. Mus. Svcs., 1987—, MAP cons., 1987—, panelist, 1992—; internat. studbook keeper for Sand Cats, 1988-2001, for Cuvier's Gazelle, Mhorr Gazelle, 1990-2000; co-chair Arabian Oryx species survival plan propogation group, 1986-95; spkr. in field. Author Survival Captive Bighorn Sheep, 1982, Small Facilities- Opportunities and Obligations, 1983; wildlife illustrator books, mags, 1970—; editor Fox Paws newsletter Living Desert, 1970—, ann. reports, 1976—; natural sci. editor Desert Mag., 1979-82; compiler Conservation and Management Plan for Antelope, 1992; contbr. articles to profl. jours. Past bd. dirs., sec. Desert Protective Coun.; adv. coun. Desert Bighorn Rsch. Inst., 1981-85; bd. dirs. Palm Springs Desert Resorts Convention and Visitors Bur., 1988-94; bd. dirs., treas. Coachella Valley Mountain Trust, 1989-92. Named Woman Making a Difference Soroptimist Internat., 1989, 93, 97, Woman of Distinction, Riverside Bus. Press, 2000. Fellow Am. Assn. Zool. Parks and Aquariums (bd. dirs., accredation field reviewer, desert antelope taxon adv. group, caprid taxon adv. group, felid taxon adv. group, small population mgmt. adv. group, wildlife conservation and mgmt. com., chmn. ethics com. 1987, mem. com., internat. rels. com., ethics task force, pres'. award 1972-77, outstanding svc. award 1983, 88, editor newsletter, Zool. Parks and Aquarium Fundamentals 1982); mem. Internat. Species Inventory System (mgmt. com., policy adv. group 1980-96), Calif. Assn. Mus. (v.p. 1992-96), Calif. Assn. Zoos and Aquariums, World Assn. Zoos and Aquariums (coun. 2002—, governing coun. 2002—, pres.-elect 2003—), Western Interpretive Assn. (so. Calif. chpt.), Am. Assn. Mus., Arboreta and Botanical Gardens So. Calif. (coun. dirs.), Soc. Conservation Biology, Nat. Audubon. Soc., Jersey Wildlife Preservation Trust Internat., Nature Conservancy, East African Wildlife Soc., African Wildlife Found., Kennel Club Palm Springs (past bd. dirs., treas. 1978-80), Scottish Deerhound Club Am. (editor Scottish Deerhounds in N.A., 1983, life mem. U.K. chpt.), Internat. Bengal Cat Soc. (pres. 1994-96). Avocations: pure bred dogs, cats, dressage, painting, photography. Office: The Living Desert 47 900 Portola Ave Palm Desert CA 92260 E-mail: kastld@aol.com.

SAUTNER, ZENOBIA ZOE, office manager; b. Phillipsburg, N.J., June 2, 1972; d. Alfred Carl Sautner Jr.and Vanessa Amy (Fleming) Thatcher. AS in Chemistry, Raritan Valley C.C., 1998; student, Rutgers U., 1998—. Tax adminstr. Chapman, Bird & Grey, L.A., 1990-94; exec. asst. Yale Materials Handing Corp., Flemington, N.J., 1994-97; office manager Payback Tng. Systems, Morristown, N.J., 1997—. Mem. Phi Theta Kappa (v.p. fundraising), Alpha Epsilon Pi. Baptist. Avocations: hiking, biking, foreign films, theater, fine music. Home: 505 Spring Mills Rd Milford NJ 08848-1949

SAUVÉ, CAROLYN OPAL, writer, journalist, poet; b. Columbus, N.C., Apr. 30, 1934; d. Anthony Floyd and Nina Morris Pittman; m. Joseph Ernest Sauvé, Mar. 31, 1953; children: Floyd, Kenneth, Timothy. Student, Spartanburg Meth. Coll., 1952-53; AAS, Isothermal C.C., 1976. Editor, author, photographer: History of Polk County, 1983; author, photograph APP Jour., 1999; author: Spirit of the Age, 1996. Trustee Isothermal C.C., Spindale, N.C., 1985-93; bd. dirs. Area Mental Health Bd., Spindale, 1985-91; v.p., sec., edn. chmn. Am. Cancer Soc., Polk County, N.C., 1975-79; bd. dirs. Juvenile Justice Bd., Rutherfordton, N.C., 1978-82; chmn. Polk County Commn., Columbus, 1978-82; chmn. Polk County Rep. Party, Columbus, 1984-86, 95-98; vice chmn., dist. chmn. N.C. Rep. Women's Club, Raleigh, 1975-79; chmn. World Missions Com., 1994-2000; chmn. bd. Polk County Dept. Social Svcs., 2003—. Mem. Polk County Hist. Assn. (pres. 1984-86, v.p. 1996-2000). Presbyterian. Avocations: creative writing, boating, cake decorating, grandchildren. Home: 165 Landrum Rd Columbus NC 28722-9545

SAVAGE, CARLA LEE, insurance agent; b. Howell, Mich., Dec. 12, 1963; d. Evert and Gloria Jean (Andrews) Van Raden; m. Matthew Paul Savage, Apr. 9, 1994; 1 child, Trevor MacKenzie. AA, Yakima Valley C.C., Yakima, Wash., 1984; BA cum laude, Ctrl. Wash. U., 1986. Asst. mgr. Jay Jacobs, Yakima, Wash., 1983-85; probation counselor Kittitas Co. Probation Svc., Ellensburg, Wash., 1985-86; staff asst. N.W. Adminstr., Inc., Seattle, 1986-89; svc. rep., agent Sedgwick Noble Lowndes, Yakima, 1989-94; sales exec., agent Marsh Advantage America/Seabury & Smith, Yakima, 1995—. Mem. adv. bd. health care reform Yakima Herald Republic, 1996. Vol. phone lines Crisis Line, Ellensburg, 1985, ARC, YMCA, Yakima Greenway, Pub. TV, Yakima C. of C., Kiwanis. Recipient Bus. Edn. award U.S. Achievement Acad., 1982. Avocations: boating, fishing, camping, sewing, furniture refinishing. Office: Marsh Advantage Amer/Seabury & Smith Lake Aspen Office Park 1430 N 16th Ave Yakima WA 98902-1381 E-mail: carla.l.savage@seabury.com.

SAVAGE, CHRISTINE R. state legislator; b. Union, Maine, Aug. 5, 1931; m. Elmer Savage, four children. Town ofc. mgr. Town of Union, 1975-90, acting mgr., municipal mgmnt., 1990-91, town mgr., 1991-95, mem. Dist. 60 Maine Ho. of Reps., Augusta, 1994-99; mem. Dist. 12 Maine Senate, Augusta, 2000—. Home: 504 Barrett Hill Rd Union ME 04862 Office: Maine Senate 3 State House Station Augusta ME 04333

SAVAGE, ELAYNE R. communications educator, counselor, psychotherapist; b. Washington, Nov. 3, 1941; d. Mike Raskin and Goldie Wolfson; 1 child, Jocelyn Laura. BA, U. of Ala., Tuscaloosa, 1963; M.Psychology, John F. Kennedy U., Orinda, Calif., 1981; PhD, Calif. Grad. Sch. of Family Psychology, San Rafael, 1989. Lic. marriage and family therapist Bd. of Behavioral Scis., 1982, cert. hypnosis Bd. of Behavioral Scis., 1990. Med. social worker Balt. City Hosps., 1964—65; social worker City and County of San Francisco, 1965—84; comm. counselor, psychotherapist Berkeley, Calif., 1982—. Lectr. in field. Author: (relationship books) Don't Take It Personally! The Art of Dealing with Rejection, Breathing Room-Creating Space to Be a Couple. Cons. Alameda County Superior Ct., Oakland, Calif., 1987—90. Mem.: Authors Guild, Am. Assn. of Marriage and Family Therapists, Am. Profl. Soc. on the Abuse of Children (task force 1989—95), Calif. Assn. of Marriage and Family Therapists (bd. of directors E. Bay chpt. 1987—93), Nat. Spkrs. Assn. (profl. acad. com. 2001—03). Office: Elayne Savage Assocs 2607 Alcatraz Ave Berkeley CA 94705 Office Phone: 510-540-6230. Personal E-mail: elayne@elaynesavage.com. E-mail: elayne@elaynesavage.com.

SAVAGE, JILL A. music educator; b. Dunkirk, N.Y., Sept. 8, 1968; d. Edmund J. and Kathleen E. Zielinski; m. Timothy L. Savage, Aug. 21, 1992; children: Kaitlin, Abigail. MusB in Music Edn., SUNY, Fredonia, 1990; MusM in Violin Performance, SUNY, Potsdam, 1996. Cert. music tchr. grades K-12 N.Y. Orch. dir. Indian River Ctrl. Schs., Philadelphia, NY, 1990—93; string tchr. Gouverneur (N.Y.) Ctrl. Schs., 1998, Canton (N.Y.) Ctrl. Schs., 1999; orch. dir. Potsdam Ctrl. Schs., 2000—03; string tchr. West Genesee Ctrl. Schs., Camillus, NY, 2004. Violinist Orch. No. N.Y., Potsdam, 1992—. Mem.: Am. String Tchrs. Assn., St. Lawrence County Music Educators Assn., Music Educators Nat. Conf., N.Y. State Sch. Music Assn.

SAVAGE, LINDA EILEEN, psychologist; b. Boston, Apr. 18, 1945; d. E. Linwood and Helen (Mills) Savage; m. Jerry Allen Spiegel, Jan. 26, 1973 (div. Aug. 29, 1979); 1 child, Sarah Orion ; m. Gary Lee Reinhardt, Mar. 23, 1986; 1 child, Jamie Linn Reinhardt. BA, Mount Holyoke Coll., 1967; MA, U. Mass., Amherst, 1970; PhD, Internat. Coll., L.A., 1983. Lic. marriage and family therapist Calif., psychologist Calif., cert. Am. Bd. Sexology. Tchg. asst. U. Mass., Amherst, 1967—69; counselor Miami Dade C.C., Fla., 1970—72; co-dir., cons. Lakeview Ednl. Assn., Chgo., 1973—79; clin. dir. Asterte Comm. Ctr., Leucadia, Calif., 1983—85, pvt. practice clin. psychologist Linda E. Savage PhD, Vista, Calif., 1985—. Speaker, seminar leader Goddess Seminars, 1999—. Author: (Book) Reclaiming Goddess Sexuality, 1999. Mem. Found. for Women, San Diego, 2001—. Mem.: Soc. for Sci. Study of Sexuality, Am. Assn. Marriage and Family Therapists, Am. Assn. Sex Educators, Counselors and Therapists (cert. sex educator 2000), Phi Beta Kappa. Office: Family Counseling Ctr 630 Alta Vista Ste 206 Vista CA 92084 Office Phone: 760-758-3308. E-mail: lindasavagephd@goddesstherapy.com.

SAVAGE, RUTH HUDSON, poet, writer, speaker; b. Childress, Tex., Apr. 29, 1932; d. John Floyd and Eula Jemima (Cornelius) Hudson; m. Robert Berkes, Nov. 6, 1950 (div. June 1963); children: Donna, Mike, Kelly, Rex; m. Martin Thomas Savage, Sept. 18, 1965. Pres. Poets of Tarrant County, 1992—94; founder, pres. New Millennium Poets, Arlington, Tex., 2000; judge local, nat. and state poetry contests; featured spkr., writer, Tex.; sponsor poetry contests; cores. poet Arlington Arts Advocate. Author: (poetry) Voices in the Wind, 1982, (CD) Savage Whispers, 1999, Texas Tuff, 2001, (plays) Tumbleweed Christmas, 1989, (cassette) Simply Savage, 1992, numerous poems. Judge various chpts. Poetry Soc. Tex. and Tex. Students, 1987—. Recipient numerous awards for poetry. Mem.: New Millennium Poets (founder), Poetry Soc. Tex. (judge various chpts. 1987—, councilor 2000—, sch. liaison 2000—, rec. sec. 2000—, sec. 2000—, monthly contest chair), Nat. Fedn. State Poetry Socs. Avocations: art, speaking, writing. Home: 1700 Ocho Rios Ct Arlington TX 76012-2023 E-mail: nmpoetRHS@comcast.net.

SAVAGE, SONDRA L. finance educator; b. McMinnville, Tenn., Mar. 4, 1964; d. Fred D. and Eva L. Savage. BS, U. Tenn., 1987, BA, 1988; MS, Nova Southeastern U., 1996; postgrad., Nova Southwestern U., 1998—. Fin. adviser Nova Southeastern U., Ft. Lauderdale, Fla., 1994—98, Herzing Coll., Atlanta, 1998—99, asst. prof., 1999—2000; prof. DeVry U., Alpharetta, Ga., 2000—. Mem.: ACA. Avocations: reading, meditation, music, creative writing, swimming.

SAVAGE, SUSAN M. state official, former mayor; b. Tulsa, Okla., 1936; married; 2 children. Student, U. Aix-Marseilles, Aix-en-Provence, France, 1969, City of London Poly., Eng., 1972; BA in Sociology with honors, Beaver Coll., 1974. Pre-trial rep. Phila. Ct. Common Pleas, 1974-75; criminal justice planner Montgomery County Criminal Justice Unit, 1975-77; exec. dir. Met. Tulsa Citizens Crime Com., 1977-87; vol. coord. Vote Yes For Tulsa, 1987; chief of staff to mayor City of Tulsa, 1988-92, mayor,

1992—2002; sec. of state State of Okla., Oklahoma City, 2003—. Active Lee Elementary Sch. PTA; bd. dirs., treas. Okla. Crime Prevention Assn.; bd. dirs. Youth Svcs. of Tulsa County, 1984-88, pres., 1986-87; co-chair Safe Streets/Enhanced 911 Steering Com., 1987; mem. C. of C. Task Force/Community Edn. Network, 1983. Mem. U.S. Conf. Mayors (chmn. com. energy and environment). Office: State Capitol Rm 101 Oklahoma City OK 73105 Home: 224 NW 33rd St Oklahoma City OK 73118 8614

SAVAGE, TERRY, television personality, journalist, stockbroker; Grad., U. Mich. Registered investment advisor stocks and commodity futures. Founding mem., 1st woman trader Chgo. Bd. Options Exch.; mem. Internat. Monetary Market; columnist Chgo. Sun Times, Chgo.; personal fin. columnist Barron's Online; featured columnist MSN Money website; columnist pvt. website www.TerrySavage.com. Bd. dirs. McDonald's Corp, Pennzoil Quaker State Co., Devon Energy, Broadway Stores; spkr. in field. Host Money Talks; author: Terry Savage's New Money Strategies for the 90s, Terry Savage Talks Money: The Common-Sense Guide to Money Matters, The Savage Truth on Money; columnist Chgo. Sun-Times. Dir. Chgo. Mus. Sci. and Industry, Northwestern Meml. Hosp. Found., Econ. Club Chgo., Execs. Club Chgo., Jr. Achievement Ill., Ill. Coun. on Econ. Edn., Women's Bus. Devel. Ctr. Recipient Outstanding Consumer Journalism award Nat. Press Club, 1987, Dir.'s Choice award, 1994, Emmy award; Woodrow Wilson fellow in Am. history and econs. Mem. Phi Beta Kappa. Office: Chgo Sun-Times Hollinger Inc 401 N Wabash Ave Chicago IL 60611-5642 also: Terry Savage Productions 676 N Michigan Ave Ste 3610 Chicago IL 60611 E-mail: savage@suntimes.com.

SAVAGE, VERONICA RIVERA, social worker, educator; b. N.Y.C., Oct. 15, 1972; d. Edward Rivera and Maria Parrilla; m. Israel Toren Savage, Mar. 30, 2002. BS in Psychology, BS in Human and Orgnl. Devel., Vanderbilt U., 1994; MSW, Fordham U., 2003. LCSW 2004. Drop-out prevention counselor Henry St. Settlement, N.Y.C., 1994—95; rsch. asst. John Jay Coll. Criminal Justice-CUNY, N.Y.C., 1995—98; cmty. rels. coord. CityKids Found., N.Y.C., 1998—99; tchr. Sch. Social Work N.Y.C. Dept. Edn., 1999—. Cons. Peer Influence, N.Y.C., 1999. Cmty. svc. worker, India, Guatemala, Costa Rica, Africa; youth ministry worker N.Y.C. Ch. Christ, 1998—2001. Recipient Posse scholarship, Posse Found., 1990—94, Dean Select scholarship, Vanderbilt U., 1990—94. Mem.: NASW, United Fedn. Tchrs. Avocations: internat. travel, yoga, dance, flowers, dramatic movies. Home: 25 Hillside Ave #6J New York NY 10040 Office: City-As-School HS 16 Clarkson St New York NY 10014

SAVAN, JAKKI L. lawyer, writer; b. St. Louis, Oct. 14, 1950; d. Joseph Paul and Edythe Breadman Savan; m. Sheldon L. Zide, July 23, 1972 (div. Nov. 10, 1980). Student, U. Mo., 1968—70; BA, Wash. U., 1972; JD, U. Denver, 1987. Bar: Colo. 1988, U.S. Ct. Appeals (10th cir.) 1989. Jud. clk. for Hon. Jim R. Carrigan U.S. Dist. Ct., Denver, 1989—89, staff atty., 1989—. Owner Savan Associ. Pub. Rels., Denver, 1979—88; internship Denver County Ct., 1986; faculty panel mem. Fed. Jud. Ctr., Washington, 1990—93; adj. Eng. composition prof. Met. State Coll., Denver, 1992—93; adj. legal rsch. instr. Arapahoe C.C., Denver, 1991; contbg. writer, editor St. Louis Post-Dispatch, St. Louis Jewish Light, Boulder Daily Camera, Rocky Mountain News, Colo. Bus., Colo. Mag., 1972—89. Interviewer (of Holocaust survivors) William E. Wiener Oral History Libr.; asst. editor: Annual Survey of Colo. Law, 1988—89. Pres. Georgetown Ct. Condominium Assn., Denver, 1993—94. Recipient Smolar Award for Excellence in N.Am. Jewish Journalism, Coun. of Jewish Fedn., 1974—76. Mem.: Denver Bar Assn., Colo. Bar Assn., Phi Beta Kappa. Office: US Dist Ct 901 Nineteenth St Denver CO 80294

SAVEDRA, JEANNINE EVANGELINE, artist, educator, art educator; b. Montebello, Calif., Dec. 21, 1965; d. Robert Anthony Savedra and April Elizabeth (Sanchez) Baroth. Student, Pasadena C.C., Calif., 1985-87, Otis Art Inst./Parsons Sch., 1987-88; BA in Studio Art, Calif. State U., L.A., 1991; postgrad., 1992-93; MA in Art/Humanities, Calif. State U., Dominguez Hills, 1999; postgrad. IMMEX Inst., UCLA, 1999; postgrad., Getty Edn. Inst. for Arts. Cert. art tchr., Calif. Children's counselor Salvation Army, Pasadena, Calif., 1987-88; graphic artist Calif. State U., L.A., 1989; pvt. investigator Larry J. Larsen Investigations and Trial Preparations, L.A., 1990-93; art instr. Pasadena Unified Sch. Dist., 1994-95; studio art instr. Visual Arts and Design Acad., Pasadena, 1995—, coord./lead tchr., 1999-00. Supr. mural Pasadena Playhouse Improvement Assn., 1995-96; mentor Puente program U. Calif., Berkeley, 1995—; educator Nat. Conf. Human Rels., Temescal Canyon, Calif., 1996, Annenberg Inst. Sch. Reform, Brown U., 1998—; apptd. to ednl. adv. com. Jack Scott, mem. Assembly, Calif. State Legislature, 1997—; apptd. to Sierra Madre Arts Commn., 1999; artist exch. program Cultural Min., Havana, Cuba, 2000. Co-author interactive multi-media ednl. CD-ROM. Appt. to Sierra Madre Downtown Improvement Com., 2000; founding mem. Nat. Campaign for Tolerance, Montgomery, Ala. Calif. Partnership Acad. grantee, 1996—; recipient Excellence in Visual Arts award Calif. State U., 1990. Mem. Nat. Art Edn. Assn., L.A. County Mus. Art, Mus. Contemporary Art, Nat. Soc. Women Artists, Mus. Tolerance, Pasadena Armory Ctr. for Arts, Armand Hammer Art Mus.

SAVELLO, CHERYL ADAMSON, secondary school educator; b. Twin Falls, Idaho, Aug. 17, 1946; d. Robert Calvin and Lois LaVern (Timm) Adamson; m. Paul Alexander Savello, June 29, 1974; children: Denise, Robert Alexander, Catherine Jane Allison. BFA, U. Utah, 1970, MEd, 1975. Tchr. art Granite Sch. Dist., Salt Lake City, 1972-75, Jordan Sch. Dist., Sandy, Utah, 1977-80, Cache County Sch. Dist., North Logan, Utah, 1989-90, Marsh Valley Sch. Dist., Arimo, Idaho, 1990-91, West Side Sch. Dist. 202, Dayton, Idaho, 1992—2000, Clark County Sch. Dist., Las Vegas, Nev., 2000—. Tchr. Peace Corps, Saipan, Mariana Islands, 1970-72. Mem. NEA, Idaho Art Edn. Assn., Utah Art Edn. Assn., Nat. Art Edn. Assn., Art Educators Nev., Art Educators So. Nev., Logan Golf and Country Club. Mem. Ch. LDS. Avocations: artist, choir, church duties. Office: JO Smith Mid Sch 1301 E Tonopah Ave North Las Vegas NV 89030 Home: 940 Sitting Bull Dr Henderson NV 89014-0804 E-mail: image-a-nation@cox.net.

SAVENOR, BETTY CARMELL, painter, printmaker; b. Boston, Sept. 2, 1927; d. Harry Hyman and Sally Carmell; m. Jack Savenor, June 1, 1948; children: Alan, Barry, Ronald. Student, Jackson Van Ladau Sch. Fashion, Brandeis U., DeCordova Mus.; BFA, Mass. Coll. Art, 1993. Represented by Art 3, Inc., Manchester, NH, Diane Levine, Boston, Gallery 333, Falmouth, Mass., So.Watercolor Soc. Exhibited in group shows at Guild of Boston Artists, Salmagundi Club, N.Y., Boston Printmakers, U. Mass., Harvard U., Okla. U., Brandeis U., Purdue U., Ind., Attleboro (Mass.) Mus., Western N.Mex. U., Montclair Art Mus., N.J., Duxbury Art Complex, Mass., Morris Mus. Arts & Scis., N.J., George Walker Vincent Smith Mus., Mass., Nat. Gallery, N.Y., Fairleigh Dickinson U., N.J., Fitchburg Art Mus., Mass., Boston C. of C., Fed. Res. Bank of Boston, Adelphi U., N.Y., Stonehill Coll., Cahoon Mus. Am. Art, Midwest Mus. Art, Ind., Allied Artists Am., N.Y., Bentley Coll., Mass.; represented in permanent collections Fairfield Med. Assn., Vackerville, Calif., Bank of Boston, Data Products, NEC Info. Sys., Inc., Skowhegan Bank, Maine, Sheraton Corp., Hollywood, Calif., Tex. A&M U., and New Orleans, Meadows Country Club, Fla., U. Tampa, First Bank of Concord, N.H., Indian Head Bank, N.H., New Eng. Life Ins. Co., Conn. Mut. Ins. Co., Liberty Mut. Ins. Co., Velcro Mgmt., Jo-Ann Fabrics, Tampa Energy Corp., Fla., Weisner Assocs., Fla.; pubs. include Collograph Printmaking, Best of Watercolor, Painting Textures, Best of Watercolor, The Collected Best of Watercolor. 2002. Juror for numerous art shows, Mass.; demonstrator for many art socs. Recipient Nicholas Reale Meml. award for graphics Allied Artists Am., First Frontier Collage Soc., Guiller Gall. Awd., TX, 1999, Sarasota Visual Art Ctr., First Prize, 1999-00, FL, Art League of Manatee, FL, Printmaker Awd., 2000. Mem. Nat. League of Am. Pen Women (award of excellence 1998), New Eng. Watercolor Soc. (sec. 1983-93, Best Contemporary Watercolor prize 1990, Pelikan Disting. award 1997, Bronze medal 1998), New Eng. Watercolor Soc. (Excellence in Abstraction 2002), Nat. Assn. Women Artists (prize 1982, 87, 89, 1st prize 2002), Northwest Watecolor Soc. (signature mem.), Cape Cod Art Assn. (Jurors Merit award 1992-94, 1st prize in graphics 1993-95, 97, 2002), Nat. League Am. Pen Women (Best in State award 1983-95, 39th Nat. Exhbn. award of excellence 1998), Concord Art Assn. (Gold medal 1985, 1st prize 1991, Yarmouth Art award 1998), Falmouth Art Guild (best in show 1997), Catamet Art Ctr. (1st prize 2002), Teco Co. (Hon. Mention 2003), Tampa, Women's Contemporary Artists, Art Ctr., Long Boat Key Art Ctr., N.W. Watercolor Soc., So. Watercolor Soc., New Eng. Watercolor Soc. Democrat. Jewish. Avocations: tennis, swimming, decorating. Home: 4305 Highland Oaks Cir Sarasota FL 34235-5173

SAVERCOOL, SUSAN ELISABETH, elementary school educator; b. La Grande, Oreg., Aug. 1, 1947; d. Edwin Gilbert and Francis Gwynne Kirby; m. Niles Seymour Duncan, June 21, 1971 (div. Sept. 1976); m. Lawrence Yeldham Savercool, Aug. 6, 1983; 1 child, David R. BA in Theater/English, Calif. State U., Northridge, 1969; MA in Elem. Edn., No. Ariz. U., 1988. Cert. elem. tchr. Calif., Ariz. Elem. tchr. St. Catherine of Siena Sch., Reseda, Calif., 1969—71; presch. tchr. La Palma E. Preschool, Anaheim, Calif., 1973—74; elem. tchr. Egremont Sch., Encino, Calif., 1977—80, Ganado Intermediate, Ariz., 1980—84, Blue Ridge Elem., Lakeside, Ariz., 1986—98; freelance writer Penn Yan, NY, 2000—. Presenter poetry for tchrs. workshop Blue Ridge Elem., Lakeside, 1991—96; instr. elem. lang. arts No. Ariz. U., Flagstaff, 1992; creatorArs Poetica. Editor: (books) Mountains of Time, vols. 1-5, 1992—97, Saint Bobo and Other Contemporary Short Stories, 1994; Ars Poetica. Actress, make-up head Theater Mountain, Lakeside, 1993—97; contbg. author Oliver House Mus., Penn Yan, 2000—. Scholar, Arts Coun., 1968. Mem.: Nat. Acad. Songwriters, Nat. Homer Poet Famoun Poets Soc., Loyal Order Moose, Phi Kappa Phi. Democrat. Roman Catholic. Achievements include development of Ars Poetica gift line. Avocations: reading, fishing, community chorus, community theater.

SAVERI, FRANCESCA, humanities educator, consultant; b. San Francisco, Dec. 1, 1958; d. Guido and Catherine Saveri. BA in Fine Arts, U. Calif., Berkeley, 1981; MS in Edn., Calif. State U., Hayward, 1993. Cert. tchr. Calif., 1986, tchr. cons. Bay Area Writing Project, Calif., 1993, trainer Western Assessment Collaborative, Calif., 1998. Tchr. Oakland Unified Sch. Dist., Calif., 1986—99; voorhaus fellows project coord./leader Interactive U., U. Calif., Berkeley, 2001—02. Facilitator Bay Area Sch. Reform Collaborative, San Francisco, 1996—98; reform coord. Arts Sch., Oakland Unified Sch. Dist., Calif., 1996—99; program designer/facilitator Founds.-Oakland Unified Sch. Dist., Calif., 1999—2001. Illustrated folding book poem, Plain Geometry A Theory (Juried Exhbn.); author: (digital storytelling) A Map of the Future; etching/aquatint, (Juried Exhbn. Artisan Gallery); author: (short story) Running Out of Gas: Lessons from Strike School about Adult Interaction. Recipient Resolution from East Bay Regional Parks, Bd. of Edn., Oakland & EBRP, 1989, Calif. Outstanding Educator Awards Program, Johns Hopkins U. Inst. for the Academic Advancement of Youth, 1996, Mentor Tchr., Oakland Unified Sch. Dist., 1990-1999; grantee, Bay Area Sch. Reform Collaborative, 1996-1999, SB 1510 Tech. Grant, 1997. Mem.: Bay Area Writing Project (life). Personal E-mail: fsaveri@earthlink.net.

SAVICK, CECILY BIANCA SIMON, secondary school educator; b. N.Y.C., May 3, 1945; d. Martin Sebastian and Adelaide Virginia Simon, Pearl Levin Simon (Stepmother); m. David Stanley Savick, July 29, 1989; children: Bryan Andrew Becker, Alan Jared Becker, Dania Simone Becker. AB, U. Mich., 1967, AM in Social Scis. Edn., 1969. Tchr. K-12 Mich., 1971. 6th grade tchr. Michigan Center (Mich.) Schs., 1969—, 5th grade tchr., 1969—2003. Campaigner Dem. Party, Jackson, Mich., 1970—2003. Recipient Dem. of the Yr. award, Jackson County Dem. Party, 1998. Mem.: Michigan Center Edn. Assn. (pres. 1997—). Office: Michigan Center Schs 400 S State St Michigan Center MI 49254

SAVILLE, PAT, state senate official; b. Marysville, Kans., Sept. 10, 1943; Sec. Kans. Senate, Topeka, 1991—. Mem.: Nat. Conf. State Legis. Exec. Com., Am. Soc. Legis. Clks. and Secs. (past pres.). Office: Kans Senate State House 360 East Topeka KS 66612 E-mail: pats@senate.state.ks.us.

SAVIO, FRANCES MARGARET CAMMAROTTA, music educator; b. Phila., Oct. 2, 1936; d. Frank Cammarotta and Margaret Eleanor Cammarotta Parilla; m. Savio, Sept. 12, 1959; 1 child, Margaret Mary. B Music Edn., Immaculata Coll., 1958; M Music Edn., Trenton State U., 1976. Music and English tchr. East Lansdowne (Pa.) schs., 1958—59; music tchr. Mary Calcott Elem. Sch., Norfolk, Va., 1959—61; music and English tchr. Northside Jr. High, Va., 1961—63; kindergarten tchr. Bar H. Crocker Country Day Sch., Oceanside, NY, 1965—68; gen. music tchr. K-8, drama dir. St. Bartholomew Sch., NJ, 1968—. Leader Girl Scouts U.S.A.; music dir., counselor, music coord. summer camps, Pa., N.J., Va.; organist, pastoral musician St. Bartholomew Ch., East Brunswick, 1968—90; mem. curriculum com. Diocese of Trenton, 1977; organist adult choir, dir. folk group St. Bartholomew Ch., East Brunswick, NJ; mem. profl. day com., mem. com. for outstanding Cath. educator Metuchen Diocese; mem. Altar Rosary Soc. Named Tchr. of Excellence, Diocese of Metuchen, 1995. Mem.: Nat. Music Honor Soc., Pi Kappa Lambda. Home: 14 Hershey Rd East Brunswick NJ 08816

SAVITRIPRIYA, SWAMI, Hindu religious leader, author; b. Apr. 1, 1930; Ordained Hindu nun, Holy Order of Sannyas, 1975. Psychotherapist, 1970-75; founder, spiritual dir. Shiva-Shakti Kashmir Shaivite Hindu Ch., Ashram, Marin County, Calif., 1975-77, Shiva-Shakti Ashram, Oakland, Calif., 1978, Convent of the Divine Mother, Kona, Hawaii, 1979-80, Holy Mountain Monastery and Retreat Ctr., Groveland, Calif., 1984-92, Holy Mountain U., Groveland, Calif., 1985-92, Inst. for New Life, Groveland, Calif., 1990-92, Santa Cruz, Calif., 1993, Shiva-Shakti Ananda Ashram, Guadalajara, Mexico, 1995—, Bangalore, Karnataka, India, 1997—. Author (books) Kundalini-Shakti: From Awakening to Enlightenment, 1980, The Psychology of Mystical Awakening: The Yoga Sutras, 1991, The Cloud of the Universe, 1986, The Worlds of the Chakras, 1987, Arising Woman, 1988, Arising Man, 1988, Tantras of Personal and Spiritual Unfoldment, 1989, New World Hinduism, 1990, others; translator: Bhagavad Gita, 1974, Narada Bhakti Sutras, 1976, Upanishads, 1981, Shiva Sutras, 1984, Pratyabhijnahridayam, 1987, Vijnana Bhairava, 1989, others. E-mail: savitripriya_sw@hotmail.com.

SAVITT, SUSAN SCHENKEL, lawyer; b. Bklyn., Aug. 21, 1943; d. Edward Charles and Sylvia (Dlugatch) S.; m. Harvey Savitt, July 2, 1969 (div. 1978); children: Andrew Todd, Daniel Cory. BA magna cum laude, Pa. State U., 1964; JD, Columbia U., 1968. Bar: N.Y. 1968, U.S. Dist. Ct. (so. and ea. dists.) N.Y. 1973, U.S. Tax Ct. 1973, U.S. Ct. Appeals (2d cir.) 1981, U.S. Supreme Ct. 1980, U.S. Dist. Ct. (we. dist.) N.Y. 1996. Atty. Nassau County Legal Svcs., Freeport, N.Y., 1973-74; asst. corp. counsel City of Yonkers, 1977-78; from assoc. to ptnr. Epstein, Becker & Green, P.C., N.Y.C., 1978-94; ptnr. Winston & Strawn, N.Y.C., 1994—. Adj. prof. Elizabeth Seton Coll., Yonkers, 1982-83; mem. NYU exec. coun. Met. Ctr. for Ednl. Rsch. Devel. and Tng., 1987-90; mediator Vol. Mediation Panel, U.S. Dist. Ct. (so. dist.) N.Y., 1997—, U.S. Dist. Ct. (ea. dist.) N.Y., 1999—. Mem. Hastings-on-Hudson (N.Y.) Sch. Bd., 1984-93, v.p., 1986, 87-88, pres., 1989-90, 92-93; bd. dirs. Associated Blind, 1993-95, Nat. Child Labor Com., 2001—, Liberal Arts Alumni Coun., Pa. State U., 2001—; bd. dirs. Search for Change, 1996—2002, sec., 1998—2002; bd. dirs. Pa. State Profl. Women's Network of N.Y., 1996—, pres., 1998-2000. Mem. ABA (internat. law sect., litigation and labor law sect.), N.Y. State Bar Assn. (labor law sect., comml. litigation sect.), Women's Bar Assn., Fed. Bar Coun., Pa. State Alumni Club (v.p. Westchester County 1985-87), Phi Beta Kappa, Alpha Kappa Delta, Phi Gamma Mu, Pi Kappa Phi. Office: Winston & Strawn 200 Park Ave New York NY 10166-0005 Office Phone: 212-294-4772. Business E-Mail: ssavitt@winston.com.

SAVITZ, MAXINE LAZARUS, aerospace company executive; b. Balt., Feb. 13, 1937; d. Samuel and Harriette (Miller) Lazarus; m. Sumner Alan Savitz, Jan. 1, 1961; children: Adam Jonathan, Alison Carrie. BA in Chemistry magna cum laude, Bryn Mawr Coll., 1958; PhD in Organic Chemistry, MIT, 1961. Instr. chemistry Hunter Coll., N.Y.C., 1962-63; sr. electrochemist Mobility Equipment Rsch. and Devel. Ctr., Ft. Belvoir, Va., 1963-68; prof. chemistry Federal City Coll., Washington, 1968-72; program mgr. NSF, Washington, 1972-74; dir. FEA Office Bldgs. Policy Rshc. U.S. Dept. Energy, Washington, 1974-75, dir. div. indsl. conservation, 1975-76, from dir. div. bldgs. and community systems to dep asst sec., 1975-83; pres. Lighting Rsch. Inst., 1983-85; asst. to v.p. engring. Ceramic Components div. The Garrett Corp., 1985-87; gen. mgr. ceramic components divsn. AlliedSignal Inc., Torrance, Calif., 1987-99; gen. mgr. tech. partnerships Honeywell, Torrance, Calif., 1999—2001, ret., 2001. Bd. dirs. Am. Coun. for Energy Efficient Economy, Draper Corp.; bd. dirs. divsn. engring. and phys. sci. NRC; cons. State Mich. Dept. Commerce, 1983, N.C. Alternative Energy Corp., 1983, Garrett Corp., 1983, Energy Engring. Bd., Nat. Rsch. Bd., 1986—93, Office Tech. Assessment, U.S. Congress Energy Demand Panel, 1987—91; nat. materials adv. bd. NRC, 1989—94, adv. bd. on energy and environ. systems, divsn. of engring. and physical sci., 2002—; chmn. U.S. Advanced Ceramic Assn., 1992; adv. com. divsn. ceramics/materials ORNL, 1989—92, adv. com. dir., 1992—96; mem. lab. adv. com. Pacific N.W. Nat. Lab., 2000—; adv. bd. Sec. Energy, 1992—2002; mem. Def. Sci. Bd., 1993—96; vis. com. adv. tech. Nat. Inst. Stds. and Tech., 1993—98, Nat. Sci. Bd., 1999—; mem. bd. on energy and environ. sys. NRC, 2002—, mem. divsn. on engring. and phys. sci., 2003—. Editor Energy and Bldgs.; contbr. articles to profl. jours. Mem. policy com. NAE, 1994-98. NSF postdoctoral fellow, 1961, 62, NIH predoctoral fellow, 1960, 61. Mem. Nat. Acad. Engring. E-mail: maxinesavitz@aol.com.

SAVOCCHIO, JOYCE A. former mayor; b. Erie, Pa. d. Daniel and Esther Savocchio. BA in History, Mercyhurst Coll., 1965; MEd, U. Pitts., 1969; cert. secondary sch. adminstrn., Edinboro U., 1975; LLD (hon.), Gannon U., 1990. Tchr. social studies Erie Sch. Dist., 1965-85, asst. prin. Strong Vincent High Sch., 1985-89, tchr. coord. high sch. task force, 1971-75; pres. Erie Edn. Assn., 1975-76; mem. coun. City of Erie, 1981-90, pres. coun., 1983, mayor, 1990—2001. Mem., past pres. Pa. League of Cities and Municipalities, Northwestern Pa. Mayors' Roundtable; mem. subcoms. on transp. and comms. U.S. Conf. of Mayors; mem., sec. Electoral Coll. for Commonwealth of Pa.; v.p. Christopher Columbus Found.; past pres., mem. Coun. of Govts. of the Greater Erie Area. Past pres. Erie Hist. Mus.; mem. Pa. Gov.'s Flagship Commn., Cmty. Task Force on Drug and Alcohol Abuse; treas., v.p., pres. Erie Area Job Partnership Tng., Inc. Named Woman of Yr., Dem. Women Erie, 1981, Italian Am. Women's Assn., 1987, Outstanding Citizen of Yr., MECA United Cerebral Palsy, 1991; recipient Disting. Alumna award Mercyhurst Coll., 1990, Disting. Citizen award French Creek coun. Boy Scouts Am., 1991, Tree of Life award Jewish Nat. Fund, 1995; named to Pa. Honor Roll of Women. Roman Catholic.

SAVOIA, MARIA CHRISTINA, vice dean; BA with highest honors, Wellesley Coll., 1972; MD, Harvard U., 1976. Diplomate Am. Bd. Internal Medicine. Med. intern U. Calif., San Diego, 1976-77, med. resident, 1977-79, fellow divsn. infectious diseases, 1980-84, clin. instr. medicine, 1980-84, asst. adj. prof. medicine, 1984-90, acting vice-chair dept. medicine, 1987-89, assoc. prof. clin. medicine, 1990-96, assoc. dean curriculum and student affairs sch. medicine, 1990—2003, vice dean med. edn., 2003—, acting dir. office learning resources sch. medicine, 1991-95, acting assoc. dean admissions sch. medicine, 1991, chief acad. officer sch. medicine, 1994—, prof. clin. medicine, 1996—; sr. fellow in med. edn. Harvard Macy Inst., Boston, 1996-97; assoc. investigator VA Med. Ctr., San Diego, 1981-84, asst. chief to acting chief med. svc., 1984-90, 87-89. Author: (with others) Medical Microbiology and Infectious Diseases, 1986, Infectious Disease, 1986, Principles and Practice of Infectious Diseases, 1989, Infections in Urology, 1990, Medical Complications During Pregnancy, 1995, and others; contbr. numerous articles and abstracts to profl. jours. Recipient Calif. Women in Govt. award, 1987; NSF grantee, 1972; Durant scholar Wellesley (Mass.) Coll., 1968-72. Fellow Infectious Diseases Soc. Am.; mem. Am. Soc. Microbiology. Office: Univ Calif Sch Medicine Assoc Dean Student Affairs 9500 Gilman Dr La Jolla CA 92093-0606

SAVOY, SUZANNE MARIE, advanced practice nurse; b. N.Y.C., Oct. 18, 1946; d. William Joseph and Mary Patricia (Moclair) S. BS, Columbia U., 1970; M in Nursing, UCLA, 1978. RN, cert. clin. nurse specialist, cert. critical care nurse. Staff nurse MICU, transplant Json Meml. Hosp., Miami, 1970-72; staff nurse MICU Boston U. Hosp., 1972-74, VA Hosp., Long Beach, Calif., 1974-75; staff nurse MIRU Cedars-Sinai Med. Ctr., L.A., 1975-77; critical care clin. nurse specialist Anaheim (Calif.) Meml. Hosp., 1978-81; practitioner, instr. Rush-Presbyn.-St. Luke's Med. Ctr. Coll. Nursing, Chgo., 1982-88; rsch. assoc. dept. neurosurgery Rush U., 1984-88; clin. rsch. assoc. Medtronic, Inc. Drug Adminstrn. Sys., Mpls., 1988-91; staff nurse crit. care Harper Hosp., Detroit, 1992-93; clin. nurse specialist, surg./trauma crit. care Detroit Receiving Hosp., 1993-95; clin. instr. Wayne State U. Coll. of Nursing, Detroit, 1991-96, adj. faculty staff, 1996-98. Program coord. Crit. Care ACNP-CC MSN, Wayne State U., 1993-96; adult crit. care clin. nurse specialist Saginaw Gen. Hosp., 1996-98; card. clin. nurse specialist Covenant Healthcare Sys., Saginaw, 1998—; neurosci. clinician acute stroke unit Harper Hosp., Detroit, 1989; edn. cons. Crit. Care Svcs., Inc., Orange, Calif., 1979-81. Co-author articles for profl. jours. Mem. Am. Assn. Neurosci. Nurses (treas. Ill. chpt. 1983-85, pres. 1986-87, SE Mich. chpt. 1992-98, bd. dirs., treas., program chair), Am. Assn. Crit. Care Nurses (bd. dirs. Long Beach chpt. 1981-82, treas. NEMC chpt. 1999-2001), Assn. Healt Care Quality (treas. 2002—, Am. Assn. Spinal Cord Injury Nursing (mem. rsch. com. 1993-95), Lambda and Gamma Phi (bd. dirs. 1994-96), Sigma Theta Tau. Roman Catholic. Office Phone: 989-583-6532. Business E-Mail: ssavoy@chs-ml.com. E-mail: ssavoy@chs-mi.com.

SAVVA, ANDREA, financial consultant; b. Nicosia, Cyprus, Apr. 30, 1955; arrived in U.S., 1964; d. Michael and Efrosine Savva; children: Paul E. Papapetrou, Michael G. Papapetrou. A in Occupl. Studies, Lab. Inst. Merchandising, N.Y.C., 1976. Lic. Series 7, 6, 63 Nat. Assn. Securities Dealers, life and health lic./prodr. N.J., N.Y., Fla. Account rep., broker Mokrynsky & Assocs., Hackensack, NJ, 1993—97; fin. cons. Fin. Network Investment Corp., Florham Park, NJ, 1997—98, Hudson Trader Investment Svcs., Clifton, NJ, 1998—2001; sr. fin. cons. Quick & Reilly/Fleet Fin., Hackensack, NJ, 2001—. Greek Orthodox. Avocations: gardening, reading, physical activities, music, movies. Home: 2 Violet Ct Bergenfield NJ 07621 Office: Quick & Reilly 152 Blvd Hasbrouck Heights NJ 07604 Office Phone: 201-288-0216.

SAWAI, DAHLEEN EMI, language educator; b. Honolulu, Mar. 13, 1954; d. Kiyoto and Aiko Sawai. BA, U. Hawaii, Manoa, 1975, diploma in elem. edn., 1977, diploma in secondary edn., 1981, MEd, 1984. Cert. tchr. Hawaii. English tchr. Tokyo Family Court, 1977—78; Japanese tchr. Kailua H.S., Honolulu, 1978—80; English tchr. Family Ct. Probation Officer Tng. Sch., Tokyo, 1983—84; Japanese tchr. W. R. Farrington H.S., Honolulu, 1985—; educator Consortium for Tchg. Asia and the Pacific in the Schs., Honolulu, 1989—95; tchr. Family Court Probation Officer Training Sch., Tokyo. Instr. Sch. Cmty. Based Mgmt., Honolulu, 2000—; interpreter Star Tanjo, 1976; chmn. Dept. World Langs. W.R. Farrington H.S., Honolulu,

2001—. Dir. Moanalua Gardens Cmty. Assn., Honolulu, 1976—77, sec., 1978—80. Scholar, Keio Gijuku Daigaku, 1982—84. Mem.: Nat. Coun. Japanese Lang. Tchrs., Farrington Alumni and Cmty. Found., Japanese Cultural Ctr. Hawaii, Alliance Drama Edn., Temari Ctr. for Asian and Pacific Arts, Pi Lambda Theta.

SAWH, RUTH, English educator, writer; b. Port-of-Spain, Trinidad, July 25, 1947; arrived in U.S., 1967; m. Prettilal Sawh, Sept. 3, 1967; children: Keith, Ian. BA, Union Coll., 1970; MA, U. Nebr., 1978; PhD, Fla. State U., 1994. Sec. sociology U. Nebr., Lincoln, 1971—72; tchr.-sec. Andrews H.S., San Juan, Trinidad and Tobago, 1973—75; sec. Malone C.C., Lincoln, 1976—78; asst. prof. Caribbean Union Coll., Maracas, Trinidad and Tobago, 1979—88; instr. U. of W.I., St. Augustine, Trinidad and Tobago, 1984—88; asst. prof. Fla. A&M U., Tallahassee, 1988—98, assoc. prof., 1998—. Editor Tallahassee Caribbean Assn., 1997—98; lit. judge Caribbean Student Assn., Fla. A&M U., Tallahassee, 2003. Author: (creative nonfiction) Seven Hills Fiction, 2002 (Hon. Mention, 2002); co-author: (textbook) Writing from the Ground Up, 1998 (Pub.'s award, 2000). Mem.: NEA, Coll. Lang. Assn., Tallahassee Writers' Assn. Avocations: reading, writing, thimble collecting, watching documentaries and game shows on TV. Office: Fla A&M U Wahnish Way Tallahassee FL 32307

SAWHILL, ISABEL VAN DEVANTER, economist; b. Washington, Apr. 2, 1937; d. Winslow B. and Isabel E. Van Devanter; m. John C. Sawhill, Sept. 13, 1958; 1 son, James W. BA, NYU, 1962, PhD, 1968. Asst. prof. econs. Goucher Coll., Balt., 1969—73; sr. rsch. assoc. Urban Inst., 1973—77, program dir., sr. fellow, 1980—93; dir. Nat. Commn. Employment Policy, Washington, 1977—79; program assoc. dir. Office Mgmt. and Budget, 1993—95; sr. fellow and Arjay Miller chair in pub. policy Urban Inst., 1995—97; sr. fellow Brookings Instn., Washington, 1997—2003, v.p., dir. econ. studies, 2003—. Vis. prof. Georgetown U. Law Ctr., 1990-91; chairperson rsch. adv. bd. Com. for Econ. Devel., 1995-98. Author: Getting Ahead, 1998, Updating America's Social Contract, 2000, Restoring Fiscal Sanity, 2004. Bd. dirs. Manpower Demonstration Res. Corp.; pres. Nat. Campaign Prevent Teen Pregnancy, 1996—. Mem. Am. Econ. Assn., Assn. Pub. Polit. Analysis and Mgmt. (pres. 1988), Phi Beta Kappa. Office: Brookings Inst 1775 Massachusetts Ave NW Washington DC 20036-2103

SAWYER, CHERYL LYNNE, foundation administrator, consultant; b. Balt., Mar. 8, 1954; d. Carolyn (Brooks) Bulcken; m. Gary W. Sawyer, July 16, 1976; children: Jesse, Stacy. BA in English, Sam Houston State U., 1976; MA in Behavioral Scis., U. Houston, Clear Lake, 1984; EdD in Adminstrn. and Supervision, U. Houston, University Park, 1993. Lic. psychol. assoc., Tex.; cert. trauma cons.; cert. English, history, psychology, learning disabilities tchr., Tex.; cert. diagnostician, counselor, spl. edn. counselor, assoc. sch. psychologist, Tex.; lic. specialist sch. psychology. Tchr. Alvin (Tex.) Ind. Sch. Dist., 1976-84, LaMarque (Tex.) Ind. Sch. Dist., 1985-90; ednl. cons. Dickinson, Tex., 1992—; from vis. asst. prof. to adj. prof. U. Houston, 1990—99; dir. acute children's programs Devereux Found., League City, Tex., 1994-97; counselor LaMarque (Tex.) Ind. Sch. Dist., 1997-98; tchr. Dickinson Ind. Sch. Dist., 1998—2000; asst. prof. counselor edn. U. Houston, Clear Lake, 2000—, coord. counselor edn., 2000—. Mem. adv. bd. spl. edn. Santa Fe Sch. Dist., 1993, 94, 95; mem. adv. bd. drug and alcohol prevention LaMarque Sch. Dist., 1989, 90, 91, 92; spkr. child-related psychol. issues; presenter in field. Contbr. articles to profl. jours. Mem. Am. Counseling Assn., Tex. Counseling Assn., Nat. Assn. for Gifted, Coun. for Exceptional Children, Dickinson Civic Assn. (bd. dirs. 1996-99, 2002—), Beta Sigma Phi, Phi Delta Kappa, Chi Sigma Iota. Home: 12308 Marion Ln Dickinson TX 77539-9224

SAWYER, DIANE (L. DIANE SAWYER), newscaster, journalist; b. Glasgow, Ky., Dec. 22, 1945; d. E. P. and Jean W. (Dunagan) Sawyer; m. Mike Nichols, Apr. 29, 1988. BA, Wellesley Coll., 1967. Reporter Sta. WLKY-TV, Louisville, 1967—70; adminstr. press office White House, 1970—74; rschr. Richard Nixon's memoirs, 1974—78; gen. assignment reporter, then Dept. State corr. CBS News, 1978—81; co-anchor Morning News CBS, 1981—, co-anchor Early Morning News, 1982—84; corr., co-editor 60 Minutes CBS-TV, 1984—89; co-anchor Prime Time Live (now known as 20/20) ABC News, 1989—; co-anchor Day One, 1995, Turning Point, 1996, Good Morning Am. ABC News, N.Y.C., 1999—. Named to TV Hall of Fame, 1997; recipient 2 Peabody awards for pub. svc., 1988, Robert F. Kennedy award, 13 Emmy awards, 2 Dupont awards (one Spl.), IRTS Lifetime Achievement award. Office: Good Morning America Fl 10 147 Columbus Ave New York NY 10023-5900

SAWYER, DOLORES, motel chain executive; b. Shreveport, La., Oct. 16, 1938; d. Orlan B. Greer and Doris Lucile (Sanders) Eckman; m. Raymond Lee Sawyer Jr., June 11, 1960; children: Lisa Kay, Linda Faye. BSN, Northwestern State Coll., 1960; MSN, Tex. Woman's U., 1975. Supr. obstetrics dept. Highland Hosp., Shreveport, La., 1962-64; head nurse (3-11 shift) Scott and White Meml. Hosp., Temple, Tex., 1966-71, dir. of nursing edn., 1975-76; sch. nurse Temple Ind. Sch. Dist., 1971-72; instr. Mary-Hardin Baylor Coll., Belton, Tex., 1972-74; asst. prof., clin. specialist U. Tex. Arlington, 1976-86; v.p. Budget Host Internat., Arlington, Tex., 1986-96, sr. v.p., 1996—, also bd. dirs. Recipient Amoco Outstanding Tchg. award, 1981. Mem. Sigma Theta Tau. Republican. Methodist. Avocations: reading, tole painting, gardening, crafts, piano. Office: Budget Host Internat Ste B 2307 Roosevelt Dr Arlington TX 76016-5865 Office Phone: 817-861-6088. Personal E-mail: rsawyerl@airmail.net. Business E-Mail: dsawyer@budgethost.com.

SAWYER, LINDA, advertising executive; Exec. v.p., group acct. dir. Deutsch, Inc., N.Y.C., gen. mgr., 1997—. Office: Deutsch Dworin 215 Park Ave S Fl 8 New York NY 10003-1603

SAWYER, MARGO LUCY, artist, educator; b. Washington, May 6, 1958; d. Eugene Douglas and Joan Imogen (Alford) S. BA hons., Chelsea Sch. Art, London, 1980; MFA, Yale U., 1982. Prof. U. Tex., Austin, 1988—. Vis. artist Chelsea Sch. Art, London, 1982—. One-person shows include Brit. Coun., Bombay, India, 1983, Barbara Toll Fine Arts, N.Y.C., 1989, 91, Sagacho Exhibit Space, Tokyo, 1996, Gallery Gallery, Kyoto, Japan, 1996, Internat. House of Japan, Tokyo, 1996, Austin (Tex.) Mus. Art, 1998, Artplace, 2000, Mattress Factory, Pitts., 2003, others; group shows include Whitechapel Gallery, London, 1979, ICA, London, 1979, 80, Leo Castelli Gallery, N.Y.C., 1986, Portland (Maine) Mus. Art, 1987, U. Md. Art Gallery, Balt., 1988, Meyers/Bloom Gallery, Santa Monica, Calif., 1989, Archer M. Huntington Art Gallery, Austin, Tex., 1990, 91, 92, 93, 94, Harn Mus. Art, Gainesville, Fla., 1992, Laguna Gloria Art Mus., Austin, 1994, Abilene (Tex.) Outdoor Sculpture exhbn., 1995-96, Artspace A Found. for Contemporary Art, 2000, Finesilver Gallery, San Antonio, 2002; permanent collections include Hyde Park, London, Cityarts Workshop, Portland Mus. Art, Samuel O. Harn Mus. Art, U. Fla., Prudential Ins., Chem. Bank, Champion Paper, and various pvt. collections. Recipent Louis Comfort Tiffany Found. award, 2001; Am. Acad. Rome fellow, 1986-87, Japan Found. visual arts fellow, 1996; Travel grantee Ford Found., 1981, Fulbright rsch. grantee, India, 1982-83, Japan, 1995-96, N.Y. State Coun. on Arts grantee, 1987, Travel grantee NEA, 1994. Office: U Tex Dept Art and Art History Austin TX 78712-1104

SAWYER, PAMELA Z. state legislator; b. Providence; BA, U. R.I. Mem. Bolton (Conn.) Bd. Edn., 1981-93; justice of peace City of Bolton, 1983—; mem. Conn. Ho. of Reps., Hartford, 1993—, asst. minority leader, 1997—. Mem. Edn. Transp. Exec. Nominations coms. Office: Legis Office Bldg 300 Capitol Ave Hartford CT 06106-1553

SAWYER-MORSE, MARY KAYE, nutritionist, educator; b. Ft. Stockton, Tex. BA in Psychology, S.W. Tex. State U., 1978; MS in Nutrition, Incarnate Word Coll., 1987; PhD, U. Tex., 1997. Lic. dietitian. Nutrition svcs. con. Christian Sr. Svcs., 1985-87, exec. dir., 1987-90; nutrition svcs. cons. Alternative Adult Day Care Ctr., 1989-90; pvt. cons. dietitian, 1990—; cmty. dietitian Health Enhancement Ctr. Humana Hosp. Met., 1990-91; assoc. prof., dietetic program dir. U. Incarnate Word, San Antonio, 1991—. Presenter Innovative Nutrition Svc. Model S.W. Tex. Gerontol. Soc. Ann. Meeting, 1988, Diabetic Homebound Svcs. Nat. Conf. Meals-On-Wheels Am., 1989; spkr. in field. Contbr. articles to profl. jours. Named Tex. Dietetic Educator, 2003; recipient Disting. Rsch. award, 1977, 1978, Acad. Excellence award, 1978, Women's Leadership award, YWCA, 1988, Creative Tchg./Rsch. award, 1994; grantee, U.S. Dept. Edn., 1997—2000; Carnation Corp. scholar, 1995. Mem.: Nat. Spkrs. Assn. (devel. dir. 2000—01, Tex. Dietetic Educator of the Yr. 2003), San Antonio Dist. Dietetic Assn., Tex. Dietetic Assn., Am. Dietetic Assn. (sec. 1990—92, mem. nominating com. 1993—94, dietetic educators practice group). Personal E-mail: morsemk@msn.com.

SAWYERS, CLAIRE ELYCE, arboretum administrator; b. Maryville, Mo., May 30, 1957; d. Scott Kirkir and Betty Jane (Alexander) S. BS with distinction, Purdue U., 1978, MAg., 1981; MS, U. Del., 1984. Dir. Scott Arboretum of Swarthmore (Pa.) Coll., Swarthmore, Pa., 1990—. Recipient Disting. Alumna award, U. Del., 2001, Purdue U. Dept. Horticulture, 1999. Office: Scott Arboretum 500 College Ave Swarthmore PA 19081-1306 E-mail: csawyer1@swarthmore.edu.

SAWYERS, ELIZABETH JOAN, librarian, administrator; b. San Diego, Dec. 2, 1936; d. William Henry and Elizabeth Georgiana (Price) S. AA, Glendale Jr. Coll., 1957; BA in Bacteriology, UCLA, 1959, M.L.S., 1961. Asst. head acquisition sect. Nat. Library Medicine, Bethesda, Md., 1962-63, head acquisition sect., 1963-66, spl. asst. to chief tech. services div., 1966-69, spl. asst. to assoc. dir. for library ops., 1969-73; asst. dir. libraries for tech. services SUNY-Stony Brook, 1973-75; dir. Health Scis. Library Ohio State U., Columbus, 1975-90, spl. asst. to dir. Univ. librs., 1990—. Mem. Assn. Acad. Health Scis. Library Dirs. (sec./treas. 1981-83, pres. 1983-84), Med. Library Assn., Am. Soc. for Info. Sci., Spl. Libraries Assn., ALA Office: Ohio State Univ Librs 1858 Neil Ave Columbus OH 43210-1225

SAWYER-SCHLAEPFER, COLENE, marriage and family therapist, writer; b. Weisser, Idaho, June 12, 1930; d. Herlan Isaiah and Florence Starr (Knight) Sawyer; m. John Johnathan Tangney, Sept. 2, 1951 (div. Nov. 1976); children: Steven M., Eileen M., Lauren L., Daniel B.; m. Fred S. Schlaepfer, Oct. 10, 1993. BA in Social Welfare, U. Calif., Berkeley, 1952; MS in Counseling, Calif. State U., Hayward, 1973; PhD in Counseling Psychology, Ryokan Coll., 1990. Lic. marriage and family therapist, Calif. Dir. parent nursery sch. Castro Valley (Calif.) Adult Sch., 1968-74, parent cons., 1974 77; instr. St. Mary's Coll., Chabot Coll., Moraga and Hayward, Calif., 1978-80; pvt. practice marriage and family counselor, workshop leader L.A. and Lafayette, Calif., 1976-92; pvt. practice marriage and family counseling, San Jose, Calif., 1992—. Lectr. U. So. Calif., 1981-82; workshop leader, speaker on radio and TV Author: Fishing by Moonlight, the Art of Choosing Intimate Partners, 1996. Mem. AAUW, Am. Assn. Marriage and Family Therapists, Internat. Family Therapy Congress, Calif. Assn. Marriage and Family Therapists (Clark Vincent award for contbn. to profession 1996), Toastmasters. Avocations: gardening, dance, grandmothering, cooking. Office: Associated Counselors 1101 S Winchester Blvd Ste A101 San Jose CA 95128-3914

SAX, MARY RANDOLPH, speech and language pathologist; b. July 13, 1925; d. Bernard Angus and Ada Lucile (Thurman) TePoorten; m. William Martin Sax, Feb. 7, 1948. BA magna cum laude, Mich. State U., 1947; MA, U. Mich., 1949. Cert. clin. competence in speech and lang. pathology. Supr. speech correction dept. Waterford Twp. Schs., Pontiac, 1949-69; lectr. Marygrove Coll., Detroit, 1971-72; pvt. practice in speech and lang. pathology Wayne and Oakland Counties, Mich., 1973—. Co-investigator Support Pers. Profl. Practice of Speech-Lang. Pathology; mem. stroke com. Mich. Heart Assn., 1982—99; counselor to divsn. stroke liaisons Am. Heart Assn. Mich.; stroke advisor for Midwest affiliate Am. Heart Assn., 1999—, advocacy com. for Midwest affiliate of Ill., Ind. and Mich., 1999—; liaison between Am. Heart Assn. of Mich. and Am. Heart Assn., Dallas, 1996—98; adj. speech pathologist, Southfield, Mich.; lectr. on stroke Mich. Spkrs. Bur., Am. Heart Assn., 1990—; pub. spkg. coach, 1989—; mem. adj. faculty SS Cyril and Methodius Sem., Orchard Lake, Mich., 1989—90; adj. St. Mary's Prep. Sch., Orchard Lake, 1990—; mem. Met. Detroit Operation Stroke com. Am. Stroke Assn., 1999—, mem. med. subcom. to move area hosps. to become primary stroke ctrs. with acture stroke teams, 2001—; founder, mem. Stroke Project Task Force for Detroit, 1993—98; com. mem. Charette, study Arch. and Design for phys. restructuring Franklin, Mich., 1993; invited speech pathology del. Internat. Health Programs People to People Citizen Amb. Program, 1996; mem. sci. coun. on stroke Am. Heart Assn., 1980—2002; invited U.S. rep. speech and lang. pathology (cancelled because of 9/11) Med. People to People Amb. Program, neurol. ctrs., Czech Republic, Hungary and Austria. Contbr. articles to profl. jours. including Lang. and Lang. Behavior Abstracts, Lang. Speech and Hearing Svcs., Speech Lang. Hearing Jour. Active Franklinites for Responsible Govt. Recipient Svc. Recognition award Coll. Edn. Mich. State U.; grantee Inst. Articulation and Learning, 1969, others; Christian svc. commn. St. Owen, Birmingham co-chmn. blood dr. Red Cross, Franklin, Mich., 1991—. Mem.: Am. Stroke Assn. (Metro Detroit Operation Stroke com.), Founders Soc. of Detroit Inst. Arts, Franklin Found. (mem. natural resources adv. coun. 1991—99, bd. dirs. 1994—98), Pvt. Practitioners Speech-Lang. Pathology (co-founder), Internat. Assn. Logopedics and Phoniatrics (Switzerland), Am. Heart Assn. Mich. (mem. stroke awareness seminars, continuing edn. for physicians and other profls., planning and operation edn.), Mich. Speech-Lang.-Hearing Assn. (pvt. practitioner liaison 1991—, developer structural parameters for State Clin. Svc. award 1999—, com. comty. and hosp. svcs., mem. state award selection com.), Am. Speech-Lang.-Hearing Assn. (clin. competence cert.), Mich. Humane Soc., Gamma Phi Beta, Kappa Delta Pi, Phi Kappa Phi, Theta Alpha Phi. Achievements include research in language and speech acquisition in children in reference to the development of and prediction of biological speech change; research interests in developmental phonatory voice disorders, and in adult acquisition of language and speech relative to central and autonomic nervous systems. Office: 31320 Woodside Dr Franklin MI 48025-2027

SAXE, DEBORAH CRANDALL, lawyer; b. Lima, Ohio, July 23, 1949; d. Robert Gordon and Lois Barker (Taylor) Crandall; m. Robert Saxe, June 3, 1989; children: Elizabeth Sara, Emily Jane. BA, Pa. State U., 1971; MA, UCLA, 1973, JD, 1978. Bar: Calif. 1978, D.C. 1979, U.S. Dist. Ct. D.C. 1979, U.S. Dist. Ct. (ea. dist.) Calif. 1981, U.S. Dist. Ct. (ctrl. dist.) Calif. 1982, U.S. Dist. Ct. (no. and so. dists.) Calif. 1987, U.S. Ct. Appeals (4th and D.C. cirs.) 1979, U.S. Ct. Appeals (6th cir.) 1985, U.S. Ct. Appeals (8th and 9th cirs.) 1987, U.S. Ct. Appeals (2nd cir.) 1990, U.S. Supreme Ct. 1982, U.S. Dist. Ct. (no. dist.) Ill. 2001, U.S. Ct. Appeals (7th cir.) 2001. Assoc. Seyfarth, Shaw, Fairweather & Geraldson, Washington, 1978-83, Jones, Day, Reavis & Pogue, Washington, 1983-85, L.A., 1985-87, ptnr., 1988-97; shareholder Heller Ehrman White & McAuliffe LLP, 1997—. Judge pro tem, Small Claims Ct., L.A., 1985-88. Co-author: Advising California Employers, 1990, 2d edit., 1995; contbg. editor Employment Discrimination Law, 1989. Bd. dirs. Constitutional Rights Found., 1997—2002; chair Eisner Pediatric and Family Med. Ctr., 1996—98, bd. dirs., 1990—2003, L.A. County Bar Found., 1997—99. Fellow: Coll. Labor and Employment Lawyers; mem.: ABA (labor law sect. 1978—), L.A. County Bar Assn. (labor and employment law sect. 1985—, mem. exec. com. 1988—, chair 2002—03), Calif. Bar Assn. (labor law sect. 1985—), Phi Beta Kappa, Pi Lambda Theta. Office: Heller Ehrman White & McAuliffe 601 S Figueroa St Fl 40 Los Angeles CA 90017-5704 Fax: 213-614-1868. E-mail: dsaxe@hewm.com.

SAXE, THELMA RICHARDS, secondary school educator, consultant; b. Ogdensburg, N.J., Apr. 21, 1941; d. George Francis and Evelyn May (Howell) Richards; m. Kenneth Elwood Meeker, Jr., June 22, 1957 (div. 1965); children: Sylvia Lorraine Meeker Hill, Michelle Louise Meeker Aromando, David Sean (dec.); m. Frederick Ely Saxe, Feb. 18, 1983 (dec. Oct. 9, 2003); stepchildren: Jonathan Kent, Holly Harding Schenker. BA, William Paterson Coll., Wayne, N.J., 1972, MEd, 1975, postgrad., 1983-84; Dyslexia cert., Fairleigh Dickinson U., 1994; organ student with, Rick Roberts; voice student, Dr. Roberta Moger. Cert. paralegal. Tchr. handicapped Sussex (N.J.)-Wantage Regional Sch. Dist., 1972-75; resource rm. tchr. Sussex County Vo-Tech Sch., Sparta, N.J., 1975-77, learning cons., 1977-83; learning specialist Bennington-Rutland Supervisory Union, Manchester, Vt., 1986-87; learning cons. Stillwater (N.J.) Twp. Sch., 1987-88, Independence Twp. Cen. Sch., Great Meadows, N.J., 1989; learning cons., tutor in pvt. practice specializing dyslexia Sparta, 1986-97; asst. prin. Harmony Twp. Sch., Harmony, N.J., 1989-92; learning cons. Montague (N.J.) Elem. Sch., 1996-98; coord. gifted/talented Sussex Vo-Tech, 1980-83; coord. child study team Stillwater Twp. Sch., 1987-88, Montague Twp. Sch., 1996-98; ret., 1998; learning cons. Sandyston-Walpack Consolidated Sch., 1997-98. Soprano mem. Nature Coast Festival Singers, Spring Hill, Fla. Mem.: Kappa Delta Pi. Democrat. Presbyterian. Avocations: piano, organ, travel. Home: 3029 N Annapolis Ave Hernando FL 34442-4718

SAXL, JANE WILHELM, state legislator; b. N.Y.C., Aug. 26, 1939; d. Seymour F. and Doris (Fuld) Wilhelm; m. Joseph Saxl, Nov. 17, 1957; children: Susan S., Ruth L., Mary-Anne, Michael V. BA, U. Ill., Springfield, 1973, MA, 1974. City councilor City of Bangor, Maine, 1987-93; mem. Maine Ho. Reps., Augusta, 1992—, chair banking and ins. com. Sec./treas. Penobscot Valley Coun. Govts., 1988-91. Mem. Bangor Sch. Bd., 1984-87, Family Planning Maine, Natural Resources Coun., Penobscot Dem. Com.; bd. dirs. Bangor Beautiful, Bangor Conv. and Visitors Bur.; past chmn. Bangor Recycling. Recipient 1st Maine Waste Mgmt. award, 1995, Toll Fellow Scholarship award, 1996. Mem. LWV (pres. Maine chpt. 1987-93), Nat. League State Legislators, E./W. Hwy Assn., Maine Women's Lobby, Friends of Bangor Pub. Libr., Spruce Run Assocs., Maine Audubon Soc. (award 1999), Tuesday Forum, Maine Women's Legis. Lobby. Democrat. Jewish. Avocations: bird watching, fly fishing. Office: Maine Legislature 2 State House Sta Augusta ME 04333-0002 Home: 196 Norway Rd Bangor ME 04401-5851

SAXMAN, ANNA ESTHER, lawyer; b. Latrobe, Pa., May 14, 1949; d. Harry Suydam and Eleanor Ruth S.; m. Robert Halpert, Feb. 18, 1989. BS magna cum laude, U. Vt., 1978, JD magna cum laude, 1985. Clk. to presiding justice Vt. Supreme Ct., Montpelier, 1985-86; assoc. Langrock, Sperry, Parker & Wool, Burlington, Vt., 1986—; atty. Vt. Defender Gen., dep. defender gen., 2000—. Mem. Task Force on Gender Bias in the Legal System, Montpelier, 1988—. Editor U. Vt. Law Rev. Pres., bd. trustees Vt. Assn. for Mental Health, Montpelier, 1989—. Mem. ABA, ATLA, Vt. Bar Assn. (chmn. women's sect. 1989—, chmn. com. on rights of the mentally and physically handicapped, 1988-89, pres. 2003-04). Office: Vermont Def Gen Office 120 State St Montpelier VT 05620-3301

SAXTON, CAROLYN VIRGINIA, fund raising executive; b. Charleston, W.Va., June 24, 1948; d. Robert Everett and Jo Ann (Rader) S.; children: Jon Hamilton Rickey Jr., Leigh Ann Rickey; m. Harlow William Gregory Jr., May 27, 1989. BA, W.Va. Wesleyan Coll., 1971; postgrad., Loma Linda U., 1989-91. Cert. Fund Raising Exec. Counselor Open Door, Annapolis, Md., 1971-73; social worker Salvation Army, Charleston, 1977-79; patient educator Womens Health Ctr., Charleston, 1979-83; community edn. specialist Shawnee Hills Mental Health, Charleston, 1983; exec. dir. W.Va. Nat. Abortion Rights Action League, Charleston, 1983-86; lobbyist Charleston, 1986; exec. dir. Community Hospice, Ashland, Ky., 1986-89; dir. home hospice Home Hospice VNA North, Evanston, Ill., 1989-90; exec. dir. Community Chest Oak Park/River Forest, Ill., 1990—. Oak Park/River Forest Cmty. Found., 1993—. Mem. Ky. Cancer Program Network, Ashland, 1986—89, Citizens Coun. Oak Park/River Forest H.S., 1991—93, W.Va. Task Force on Adolescent Residential Treatment Ctr./Drug Abuse, 1983, Jr. League Charleston, 1982—86; chmn., usher com. Paramount Women's Assn., Ashland, 1988—89; mem. Nat. Abortion Rights Task Force on Minor's Access, 1986—87; mem. com. on minor's access W.Va. Dept. Health, 1986—87; mem. choir 1st Presbyn. Ch., Ashland, 1986—89, Sunday sch. tchr., 1988—89; mem. choir Fair Oaks Presbyn. Ch., 1990—92, bd. deacons; mem. First United Meth. Ch., chair adminstrn. coun., 1997—99. Mem. Assn. Fundraising Profls. (programming com. 1991-93, internat. conf. com. 1994-95, scholarship com. 1994-95, bd. dirs. 1995-97, spl. interest group com. chair 1995, 96), Nat. Hospice Orgn. (award of excellence 1988), Ky. Assn. Hospice (bd. dirs., mem.-at-large 1989, chmn. nominating com. 1988-89), Coun. for Non-Profits (vol. action com. 1988-89, co-chmn. cmty. support com. 1989), Zonta (status of women com., program com.), Women in Mgmt. (treas. 1993-95), Rotary (program co-chair, bd. dirs. 1993-93, co-chair spl. events 1994-95, sec. 1996-98, sgt.-at-arms 1998-2002, v.p. 2002), Cmty. Founds. Advancement Network. Democrat. Avocations: traveling, reading, collecting miniatures and antique valentines, duplicate bridge. Home: 11 Skyline Dr Portage IN 46368 Office: Community Chest Oak Park River Forest 1042 Pleasant St Oak Park IL 60302-3002

SAXTON, CATHERINE PATRICIA, public relations executive; b. Sheffield, Eng., July 5, 1944; d. Clifford and Kate Ann Saxton. BA cum laude, Fordham U., 1978. Mgr. corp. comms. Westinghouse Broadcasting & Cable Co., N.Y.C., 1981-82; prin., pres. Saxton & Assocs., N.Y.C., 1983—; CEO Potter/Saxton Assocs., Inc., N.Y.C., 1985-90, The Saxton Group Ltd., 1990—, co-founder, co-chair A-List Strategic affiliate, 2003—. Prof. pub. speaking Katharine Gibbs Coll., N.Y.C., 1977—. Mem. exec. com. Mayor's Commn. for a Vietnam Vets. Meml., 1982-90. Roman Catholic. Home: 325 E 90th St New York NY 10128-5260

SAXTON, MARY JANE, management educator; b. Syracuse, N.Y., Mar. 3, 1953; d. John Cook and Florence (Cooper) S.; m. Paul Hood. BA, SUNY, Cortland, 1975; MBA, U. Pitts., 1979, PhD, 1987. Counselor Methadone Mgmt. Svcs., Inc., N.Y.C., 1975-76; resident mgr. Crossroads Svcs., Inc., Jackson, Miss., 1976; outreach worker Jackson Mental Health Ctr., 1977-78; cons. Organizational Design Cons., Inc., Pitts., 1982-83, mktg. dir., 1984-86; asst. prof. mgmt. U. Houston, 1988-93; lectr. mgmt. U. Colo., Denver, 1994-97, U. Denver, 1994-96, Colo. Christian Coll., Denver, 1996; lectr. Met. State Coll., Denver, 1996-97; vis. assoc. prof. in strategy Norwegian Sch. Mgmt., Oslo, 1997-98, vis assoc. prof. in knowledge mgmt., 1999; orgnl. cons. Internat. Petroleum Cons. Assn., Inc., Evergreen, Colo., 1999—; vis. instr. U. Colo., Denver, 2000. Sabbatical researching Arab culture, Abu Dhabi, United Arab Emirates, 2001—01; cons. Wessex, Ctr. for Creative Comm., Kodak, Children's Hosp., Pullman Swindell, Westinghouse Elec. Corp., IPCA, Inc., Bergen, Norway, 2002—03; lectr. in field. Co-editor: Gaining Control of the Corporate Culture, 1985; co-author: The Kilmann-Saxton Culture-Gap Survery, 1983; contbr. articles to profl. jours. Active Greater Houston Women's Found., 1991-93. U.S.-Soviet Joint Ventures grantee U. Houston, 1990. Mem. ASTD, Acad. of Mgmt., Inst. Ops. Rsch. and Mgmt. Svcs. Avocations: flying, sailing, reading, biking, movies. Home and Office: PO Box 1657 Evergreen CO 80437-1657 E-mail: ipcainc@attglobal.net.

SAYLES BELTON, SHARON, former mayor; b. St. Paul, Minn., May 13, 1951; m. Steve Belton, Aug. 29, 1981; 3 children. Student, Macalester Coll.,

1969-1973; Doctorate (hon.), Walden U. Asst. dir. Minn. Program for Victims of Sexual Assault; parole officer Minn. Dept. Corrections; city coun. mem., 1983-93; coun. pres., 1989-93; mayor City of Mpls., 1994—2001; sr. fellow Roy Wilkins Ctr. Human Rels. and Social Justice U. Minn., 2001—. Pres., co- founder Nat. Coalition Against Sexual Assault; co-founder, pres. Harriet Tubman Shelter for Battered Women; trustee U.S. Conf. of Mayors, chair Youth Violence Task Forum; bd. dirs. Bush Found., Search Inst., Youth Coordinating Bd., Neighborhood Revitalization Program, Clean Water Partnership, Children's Healthcare and Hosp., Bush Found., U.S. Conf. Mayors, Nat. League Cities. Recipient Gertrude E. Rush Disting. Svc. award, Nat. Bar Assn., Rosa Parks award, Am. Assn. Affirmative Action . Office: U Minn Herbert Humphrey Inst Pub Affairs 301 19th Ave S Minneapolis MN 55455 E-mail: ssayles-belton@hhh.umn.edu.*

SAYWARD, TERESA R. state representative; m. Kenneth Sayward; 4 children. Lic. Realtor N.Y. N.Y. state rep., 2002—. Apptd. Assembly Minority Task Force on State of N.Y. Agrl.; owned, operated Holstein Cattle Dairy Farm, Wilsboro; chairwoman Willsboro's Zoning Bd. of Appeals; town supr., Willsboro, NY; bd. of suprs. Essex County, chairwoman bd. suprs.; chairwoman Econ. Devel., Planning and Publicity Com., Essex County Bd. of Suprs. Legis. Com.; lobbyist in Albany for Essex County. Minority mem. Corrections Com.; standing com. Edn., Environ. Conservation and Tourism; chairwoman Inter-Govtl. Affairs Com. at N.Y. State Assn. of Counties, North County Adv. Coun. for N.Y. State Divsn. for Women; dir. Adirondack Assn. of Towns and Villages, Plattsburgh North Country Regional C. of C.; bd. dirs. Smith House Health Care Ctr., Cornell Coop. Ext. Soil and Water Conservation Dist., Adirondack North County Assn., Willsboro Devel. Corp.; mem. Corp. of the Champlain Valley Physicians Hosp. Med. Ctr. Avocations: gardening, art, golf. Office: 7559 Court St Rm 203 Elizabethtown NY 12932 Address: LOB 633 Albany NY 12248 E-mail: saywart@assembly.state.ny.us.

SAZAMA, KATHLEEN, pathologist, lawyer; b. Sutherland, Nebr., May 8, 1941; d. Roger William and Esther Mary (Reitz) Paulman; m. Franklin Jed Sazama, Aug. 26, 1962; children: Clare Ann, Jill Patrice. BS, U. Nebr., 1962; MS, Am. U., 1969; MD, Georgetown U., 1976; JD, Cath. U. Am., 1990. Diplomate Am. Bd. Pathology; lic. pathologist Mich., Va., Md., D.C., Calif., Pa., Tex.; bar: Md. Intern and resident Georgetown U. Med. Ctr., Washington, 1976-78; resident NIH, Bethesda, Md., 1978-79; clin. asst. prof. pathology Uniformed Svcs. U. Health Scis., Bethesda, 1981-89; clin. affiliate Ferris State Coll., Big Rapids, 1985-86; chief lab. of blood bank practices FDA Ctr. for Biologics Evaluation and Rsch., Bethesda, 1986-89; cons. Ober, Kaler, Grimes & Shriver, Balt., 1989-90; assoc. med. dir. Sacramento (Calif.) Med. Found. Blood Ctr., 1990-92; asst. clin. prof. pathology U. Calif., Davis, 1990-92, assoc. prof., dir. clin. pathology, 1992-93; prof. pathology and lab. medicine Allegheny U. of the Health Scis., Phila., 1994—99; v.p. for faculty acad. affairs U. Tex./M.D. Anderson Cancer Ctr., Houston, 2000—02, prof. lab. medicine, 2000—. V.p. bd. Met. Washington Blood Banks, Inc., 1981-84; pres. bd. Am. Assn. Blood Banks, 2003-04; spkr. in field. Author: (with others) Stat: The Laboratory's Role, 1986; contbr. numerous articles to profl. jours. Comdr. USPHS, 1986-89. Fellow Coll. Am. Pathologists, Am. Soc. Clin. Pathologists; mem. AMA, ABA, Am. Assn. Blood Banks (bd. dirs.), Nat. Health Lawyers Assn., Phi Kappa Phi, Beta Beta Beta. Avocations: tennis, playing bridge. Address: Univ of Texas MD Anderson Cancer Center 1515 Holcombe Blvd # 800 Houston TX 77030-4009 E-mail: ksazama@midanderson.org.

SCAFFIDI, JUDITH ANN, academic administrator; b. Bklyn., Aug. 2, 1950; d. Anthony William and Rose Virginia (Nocera) S. BA, SUNY, Plattsburg, 1972, MS, 1973; postgrad., Einstein Coll. Medicine, 1983; PhD (hon.), Internat. U. Bombay, 1993; HHD (hon.), London Inst. Applied Rsch., 1993. Cert. secondary edn. English. VISTA mem. ACTION, N.Y.C., 1976-77; coord. cultural resources Learning Leaders, N.Y.C., 1977-80, tng. splst. in Bklyn., 1980—. Field supr., adj. faculty Coll. for Human Svcs., N.Y.C., 1984-86; adv. coun. chair Ret. Sr. Vol. Program in Bklyn., 1983-86; adv. bd. Ret. Sr. Vol. Program in N.Y.C., 1983-86. Acvive Am. Friends Svc. Com., 1994—. Recipient award for svcs. in promotion literacy Internat. Reading Assn. and Bklyn. Reading Coun., 1986, award for outstanding leadership Ret. Sr. Vol. Program, 1986, cert. of appreciation Mayor City of N.Y., 1991, cert. of appreciation for exceptional support and encouragement of volunteerism, 1998. Mem. NAFE, Cath. Tchrs. Assn. Bklyn. (del. sch. dist. 18, 1982-91), Internat. Platform Assn., World Found. Successful Women, Am. Biog. Inst. (rsch. bd. advisors 1992-93), Am. Biog. Inst. Rsch. Assn. (bd. govs. 1992—), Internat. Parliament for Safety and Peace (dep. mem. and diplomatic passport), Maisson Internat. de Intellectuels (Acad. MIDI), Cath. Alumni Club N.Y., Amnesty Internat. Roman Catholic. Avocations: foreign and domestic travel, reading, walking. Home: 2330 Ocean Ave Apt 3H Brooklyn NY 11229-3036 Office: Learning Leaders 352 Park Ave S Fl 13 New York NY 10010-1709

SCALES, FREDA S. dean, nursing educator; BSN, Okla. Bapt. U., 1965; MSN, Ind. U., 1970; PhD, Purdue U., 1977. Mem. staff faculty Sch. Nursing Ind. U., Inpls., 1970-82; dean Coll. Nursing Valparaiso (Ind.) U., 1982—. Mem. ANA, Am. Assn. Coll. Nursing, Nat. League Nursing. Office: Valparaiso U Coll Nursing Valparaiso IN 46383 Fax: 219-464-5425.

SCALES, PATRICIA KATHLEEN, psychological therapist; b. Guam, Feb. 11, 1948; d. James Lawrence Sr. and Mary Helen (Keefe) Seale; married; children: Robert Wade Scales, Steven Pryor Scales. BS, U. Tenn., Martin, 1970, MS, 1974; EdD, U. Memphis, 1994. Alcohol and drug counselor, trainer Memphis Fed. Correctional Instn., 1992-94; pvt. practice Bartlett (Tenn.) Family Counseling Ctr., 1994-95; exec. counselor Second Chance Ministries, Memphis, 1994-95; mental retardation program specialist Peabody Residential Treatment Ctr., Memphis, 1994—2000; domestic violence counselor Memphis Police Dept., 1996—2001; therapist Midtown Mental Health, Memphis, 1996—2001; lead therapist Youth Diagnostic Assessment Ctr., 2001—. Expert witness Memphis Juvenile Ct., 1995; mem. student adv. com. Office of Dean of Edn., U. Memphis, 1992-93, mem. grad. student assn. com., 1991-93; presenter in field. Active local PTA, Memphis, 1992—. Mem. NAFE, ACA, Tenn. Assn. for Gifted (v.p. 1996-97), Am. Correctional Assn., Scottish Soc.(v.p. 2003), Nigel Tranter Book Club, Sovreign Mil. Order Temple Jerusalem (commandary sec. 2002—), Tenn. State Guard (major, family assistance officer 1999-2002, civilian mil. affairs officer 2002—), U. Memphis (Tenn.) Alumni Assn., Kappa Delta Pi. Avocations: bridge, swimming, dance, tennis, walking. Home: 3610 Englishill Dr Memphis TN 38135-2307 Office: Youth Diagnostic Assessment Center 450 Pontotoc Ave Memphis TN 38126-2023

SCALETTA, HELEN MARGUERITE, volunteer; b. Sioux City, Iowa, Apr. 13, 1927; d. Ralph J. and Ruth Cora (Coyle) Beedle; m. Phillip Jasper Scaletta, May 21, 1946; children: Phillip Ralph, Cheryl Diane Kesler. AA in Bus., Edwards Coll. Bus., Sioux City, 1946. Acct. Towners Dept. Store, Iowa City, 1947-48; legal sec. Phillip Scaletta, Sioux City, 1950-74; service chmn. Easter Seal Soc., Lafayette, Ind., 1970-88; recording sec. Home Hosp. Aux., Lafayette, 1989. Danced in Civic Theatre Follies, 1962. Orch. mem. June's All-Girl Ensemble, 1943-50. Pres. Newcomers club YWCA, Lafayette, 1967-68, mem. chmn., bd. dirs., 1979; leader Girl Scouts Am., Ft. Wayne, Ind., 1960-63; chmn. Mental Health Inc., Ft. Wayne, 1960-61, Cancer Crusade, West Lafayette, 1973-74; precinct worker Rep. Cen. Com., West Lafayette, 1974-76; Nat. Missions sec. 1st Presbyn. Ch., 1957. Recipient Citation Easter Seal Soc., 1981, Ernestine Duncan Collins Pearl Ct. award Sigma Kappa, 1997. Mem. Purdue U. Women's Club (pres. 1973-74), Lafayette Country Club (golf chmn. 1971, 90, bowling pres. 1992-93, golf co-chair Battleground 9-hole group 1996), Purdue Women's Bowling League (treas. 1978-79), Cosmopolitan Club, Sigma Kappa (corp. bd., sec., treas. 1971-99), Kappa Kappa Sigma (pres. 1972), Sigma Kappa Lafayette Alumnae (pres. 1970, 1988-93, Ernestine Duncan Collins Pearl Court award 1997). Avocations: collecting dolls, bowling, golf, sports, activities with grandchildren. Home: One Via Verde Lafayette IN 47906

SCALETTAR, ELLEN, state legislator; b. N.Y.C. BA cum laude, CCNY; JD, U. Md. Hearing officer City of Woodbridge; mem. Conn. Ho. of Reps., Hartford, 1993-98; asst. treas. govtl., corp., and cmty. rels. Hartford, Conn., 1999—. Office: Office of the Treas 55 Elm St Hartford CT 06106-1746

SCANLON, DOROTHY THERESE, history educator; b. Bridgeport, Conn., Oct. 7, 1928; d. George F. and Mazie (Reardon) Scanlon. AB, U. Pa., 1948, MA, 1949, Boston Coll., 1953; PhD, Boston U., 1956; postdoctoral scholar, Harvard U., 1962—64, postdoctoral scholar, 1972. Tchr. history and Latin Marycliff Acad., Winchester, Mass., 1950—52; tchr. history Girls Latin Sch., Boston, 1952—57; prof. Boston State Coll., 1957—82, Mass. Coll. Art, Boston, 1982—95, prof. emerita, 1995—; lectr. Cape Mus. Fine Arts, Dennis, Mass., 1997—. Author: Instructor's Manual to Accompany Lewis Hanke, Latin America: A Historical REader, 1974; contbr. Biographical Dictionary of Social Welfare, 1986. Recipient Disting. Svc. award, Boston State Coll., 1979, Faculty award of excellence, Mass. Coll. Art, 1985, Faculty Disting. Svc. award, 1987. Mem.: AAUW, AAUP, History of Sci. Soc., Am. Assn. History of Medicine., Am. Studies Assn., Orgn. Am. Historians, Am. Hist. Assn., L.Am. Studies Assn., Pan-Am. Soc., Delta Kappa Gamma, Phi Alpha Theta. Home: 23 Mooring Ln Dennis MA 02638-2321 Office: Mass Coll Art Dept History 621 Huntington Ave Boston MA 02115-5801

SCANLON, ELIZABETH C. poet, editor; b. Washington, Oct. 6, 1973; d. Catherine Mary Sullivan and Robert Lawrence Scanlon. BA, Bryn Mawr Coll., 1999. Assoc. editor The Am. Poetry Rev., Phila. Individual Artist fellow, Pa. Coun. on the Arts, 2002. Office: The Am Poetry Rev 117 S 17th St Ste 910 Philadelphia PA 19103 E-mail: escanlon@aprweb.org.

SCANLON, GAIL GRETCHEN, librarian, nurse; b. Holyoke, Mass., Aug. 2, 1955; d. Rudy John and Josephine Sophia (Burek) Wojnarowski; m. Michael John Scanlon, June 5, 1976; children: Jonathan Spencer Scanlon, Douglas Todd, Abigail Jillian. Diploma in Nursing, Framingham Union Hosp. Sch. Nursing, Mass., 1976; BA, Mount Holyoke Coll., So. Hadley, Mass., 1995; MLS, U. Albany, 1999; grad. student, Frye Institute, Emory Univ., 2002. RN; lic. real estate agent. Nurse Seaside Nursing Home, Portland, Oreg., 1979-80, Upjohn Health Care, Torrance, Calif., 1983-85; real estate sales agt. Chestnut Hill Real Estate, South Hadley, Mass., 1987—; nurse Meadowood Nursing Home, 1988-91; owner The Elegant Basket, 1988-91; libr. circulation asst. Mt. Holyoke Coll., 1993—96; dir. access svcs. Mt. Holyoke Coll. Libr., 1996—2003, dir. access, tech. svcs., 2003—. Creator: (mus. exhibit) Past, Present and Future: Women Making a Difference in South Hadley, 1995. Mem., bd. dirs. So. Hadley Swim Club, Mass., 1988—94; libr. trustee So. Hadley Pub. Library, 1989—2004; mem. town mtg. Town South Hadley, 1990; dir. South Hadley Youth Ctr., 1994. Mem. ALA, ACRL, Mass. Library Trustees Assn., Mass. Friends of Libraries Assn., Know Your Town, Mass. State Adv. Coun. for Libraries, 2002-04. Home: 20 Mary Lyon Dr South Hadley MA 01075 Office: Mount Holyoke Library South Hadley MA 01075 Business E-Mail: gscanlon@mtholyoke.edu.

SCANLON, JANE CRONIN, mathematics educator; b. N.Y.C., July 17, 1922; d. John Timothy and Janet Smiley (Murphy) Cronin; m. Joseph C. Scanlon, Mar. 5, 1953 (div.); children: Justin, Mary, Anne, Edmund. Student, Highland Park Jr. Coll., 1939-41; BS, Wayne State U., 1943; MA, U. Mich., 1945, PhD, 1949. Mathematician Air Force Cambridge Research Center, 1951-54; instr. Wheaton Coll., Norton, Mass., 1954-55; asst. prof. Poly. Inst. Bklyn., 1957-58, asso. prof., 1958-60, prof., 1960-65; prof. math. Rutgers U., New Brunswick, N.J., 1965-91, prof. emerita, 1991—. Cons. Singer-Kearfott Div., Naval Research Lab. Office Naval Research Fellow Princeton, 1948-49; Horace H. Rockham Postdoctoral fellow U. Mich., 1950-51, Rutgers Research Council fellow, 1968-69, 72-73; NSF vis. professorship for women Courant Inst., NYU, 1984-85. Author: Fixed Points and Topological Degree in Nonlinear Analysis, 1964, Advanced Calculus, 1967, Differential Equations: Introduction and Qualitative Theory, 1980, 2d edit., 1994, Mathematics of Cell Electrophysiology, 1980, Mathematical Aspects of Hodgkin-Huxley Neural Theory, 1987; editor: Analyzing Multiscale Phenomena Using Singular Perturbation Methods, 1999. Mem. Am. Math. Soc., Soc. for Indsl. and Applied Math., Internat. Soc. Chronobiology. Home: 110 Valentine St Highland Park NJ 08904-2106 Office: Rutgers U Dept Math New Brunswick NJ 08903 E-mail: croninscanlon@erols.com.

SCANLON, ROSEMARY, economist; b. Dec. 25, 1939; d. Donald Angus and Mary Agnes (MacDonald) MacLellan; m. Michael Scanlon, Apr. 24, 1965 (div. 1979); children: Sean Donald, Jennifer. AB, St. Francis Xavier U., N.S., 1959; MA (Ford Found. scholar), U. New Brunswick, 1960; PMD, Harvard Bus. Sch., 1981. Instr. econs. Coll. of William and Mary, Williamsburg, Va., 1960—63; asst. prof. Old Dominion U., Norfolk, Va., 1963—65; econ. analyst Port Authority of NY and NJ, 1969—93, sr. economist for regional rsch., 1977—80, mgr. econ. devel. planning, 1980—83, chief economist, 1983—. Asst. dir. Planning and Devel. Dept., 1985; apptd. dep. state contr., NYC, 1993—97; vis. rsch. fellow London Sch. Econ., 1997—2000; cons. urban and regional econs., 2000—; assoc. prof. econs. Real Estate Inst. NYU, 2001—; bd. dirs. Emera, Inc. Author (with others): Cities in a Global Society, 1989; author: The Arts as an Industry, 1993, The Regional Economy, 1993; editor: (project) The London-NY Study, 2000; author: Bldg. for Growth, A development strategy, 2002. Recipient Outstanding Achievement award, Exec. Dirs. award, 1987, de Luca award for lifetime achievement in econ. devel., 1999, Disting. Alumnus award, St. Francis Xavier U., 2001. Mem.: Nat. Coun. for Urban Econ. Devel. (bd. dirs. 1982—88). Home: 10 Clinton St Apt 9T Brooklyn NY 11201-2710 Office: 11 W 42nd St New York NY 10036 Office Phone: 917-922-8268. E-mail: rosemaryscanlon@msn.com.

SCANLON, VICKI E. secondary school educator; b. Atlanta, Oct. 25, 1950; d. William Windsor and Martha King Evans; m. Stephen William Scanlon, June 18, 1971. BA, U. Kans., 1974, MA, 1981. Cert. tchr. Kans. Art tchr. K-6 Shawnee Mission (Kans.) Schs., 1974—89, art tchr. 7-8, 1989—2000, art tchr. 9-12, 2000—. Excellence in tchg. mentor Avila Coll., Kansas City, Mo., 1993—; mem. curriculum coun. Shawnee Mission Schs. Kans. Cow: Grazing, 2000. Pres. Morningside Homes Assn., Kansas City, 1989—93; v.p. Countryside Homes Assn., Kansas City, 1987—89; vol. Salvation Army, Kansas City, 1999—; art cons. Friends of Children's Ctr. for Visually Impaired, 2001—. Recipient Purchase award for painting, McEachen Adminstrn. Ctr., 1986, Mayor's Proclamation for cmty. improvements, 1993; scholar, Pi Beta Phi, 2000, Kansas City Art Inst., 2003; Tchr. Inst. scholar, Sch. of Art Inst. Chgo., 2003, Excellence in Edn. grantee, Southwestern Bell, 1988. Mem.: NEA (rep. 1974—2000), Friends of Art, Delta Gamma (scholarship chmn. 1969—72). Democrat. Avocations: piano, drawing, painting, gardening, hiking. Home: 2012 W 96th St Leawood KS 66206 Office: Shawnee Mission NW HS 12701 W 67th St Shawnee KS 66216 Business E-Mail: vickiscanlon@smsd.org.

SCANLON HOBBS, LAURIE ANN, public relations professional; b. Flint, Mich., Jan. 6, 1961; d. James Francis and Angeline (Lubinski) Scanlon; m. William Walter Hobbs, Aug. 1994; 1 child, William James Hobbs. BA in Journalism, No. Ill. U., 1983. Asst. v.p. Fin. Shares Corp., Chgo., 1984-85; account exec., then sr. account exec. Edelman Pub. Rels. Worldwide, Chgo., 1985-87, account supr., then sr. account supr., 1987-90, v.p., 1991-96, prin. Milw., 1996—98; cons. GE Med. Sys. a unit of Gen. Electric Corp., 1999—. Mem. adv. coun. Early Childhood Family Edn.; lectr. on pub. rels. Mem. Chgo. Symphony Orch. Bus./Profl. Orgn., 1990—93. Recipient Silver Trumpet award Publicity Club Chgo., The Tower award The Bus. Profl. Adv. Assn., Golden Bell award The Hotel Sales and Mktg. Assn., Clarion award Women in Comms. Mem. Pub. Rels. Soc. Am. (com.), Northern Ill. U. Exec. Club (charter). Roman Catholic. Avocation: teaching figure skating. Home: 685 Tanager Rd Waconia MN 55387-9778 E-mail: lhobbs@execpc.com.

SCANNELL, ANN ELIZABETH, nurse, educator; b. Evanston, Ill., Sept. 23, 1953; BSN, Villanova U., 1975; MS in Community Health, Cath. U., 1977; ND, Case Western Reserve U., 1996. Staff nurse emergency rm. Rahway (N.J.) Hosp., 1975-76; staff nurse med. ICU Georgetown U. Med. Ctr., Boston, 1977-78; continuing care nurse Mass. Rehab. Hosp., Boston, 1977-78; skills coord. dept. nursing Coll. Health Professions U. Lowell, Mass., 1978-79; clin. supr. Melrose (Mass.) Vis. Nurse Svc., 1979-80, exec. dir., 1980-87; dir. coords. and continuing care VNA of Greater Lowell, 1988-89; child and adolescent psychiat. nurse Brookside Hosp., Nashua, N.H., 1989-93; instr. community health nursing St. Anselm Coll., Manchester, N.H., 1991-96; asst. prof., comm. health nurse Fitchburg State Coll., Fitchburg, Mass., 1996—. Mem. ANA (cert. community health, home health and nursing adminstrn.), Sigma Theta Tau (treas. Eta Omega chpt.). Home: 271 Sanders Ave Lowell MA 01851-3418 Office: Dept Nursing Fitchburg State Coll 160 Pearl St Fitchburg MA 01420-2631 E-mail: ascannell@fsc.edu.

SCARANO-ILUTZI, DONNA LEE, community and business development executive; b. Newark, Apr. 23, 1952; d. Joseph and Rose (Giorella) Scarano; m. Anthony P. Ilutzi, June 20, 1993; 1 child, Liana. BA in Econs. and Acctg., Rutgers U., 1974; postgrad., U. Va., 1984. Asst. v.p., dept. mgr. Fidelity Union Bank, Newark, 1974-82; v.p. corp. and retail mktg. Core States, Pennington; v.p. cmty. devel. Nat. West/Fleet Bank, N.A., Jersey City, 1987-96; owner, cons. D. Scarano & Assocs., Livingston, N.J., 1996—. Mem. Gov.'s Cmty. Fin. Svcs. Adv. Bd. Dept. Banking; trustee, exec. com., mem. small and affordable housing loan com. N.J. Cmty. Loan Fund; bd. dirs. Bergen County Cmty. Action Program, The Cathedral Cmty. Devel. Corp.; bd. dirs., co-chair corp. adv. bd. State of N.J. Hispanic Ctr. for Policy, Rsch. and Devel.; mem. adv. coun. SBA, 1985. Scholar Rutgers U.; recipient Tribute to Women in Industry award YWCA, 1985, Nat. Bank Mktg. award, 1986, Excellence in Affordable Housing Financing award N.J. Gov. Whitman, 1995, Individual Housing Advocate of Yr. award N.J. Gov. Whitman, 1996, Leadership Am. award, 1998. Mem. Nat. Assn. Affordable Housing Lenders (bd. dirs.), Nat. Econs. Honor Soc., Nat. Journalism Honor Soc., Phi Beta Kappa. Avocations: public speaking, stock market, art collecting, europe, gourmet cooking and entertaining. Office: D Scarano & Assocs 7 Vanderbilt Dr Livingston NJ 07039-6132

SCARBROUGH, SARA EUNICE, librarian, archivist, consultant; b. Houston, Jan. 8, 1933; d. George Washington Johnson and Frances Elizabeth Evans; m. Henry Lester Scarbrough Sr., July 5, 1953 (dec. Mar. 1993); children: Henry Lester Jr., Sarita. BA, Talladega Coll., 1953; MLS, U. Tex., 1968; PhD, Columbia State U., 1998. Cert. tchr., libr., media specialist, adminstr. Music tchr. Brazos County Pub. Schs., Bryan, Tex., 1954-58; English tchr. Edgewood Sch. Dist., San Antonio, 1958-62; head libr. Houston Ind. Sch. Dist., 1962-92; dir. Hope Resource Ctr., Houston, 1992—. Exec. bd. Friends of the Houston Pub. Libr., 1994-99. Author: History of a Black Family on the Brazos, 1998. Treas. West McGregor Civic Assn., Houston, 1995—96; pres. Women's Missionary Soc., Houston, 1994—97, pres. Sr. Adult Ministry, 1999. Named Churchman of the Yr., Good Hope Ch., Houston, 1993. Mem. AAUW, Tex. Libr. Assn., U. Tex. Alumni Assn., Order of the Ea. Star (worthy matron, Outstanding Contbn. award 1995), Zeta Phi Beta (Lambda Zeta chpt. exec. bd., sec., chmn. econ. devel. 1998, Outstanding Contbn. to Econ. Devel. award 1999). Avocations: music, traveling, genealogical research, bibliotherapy. Home: 3901 Fernwood Dr Houston TX 77021-1521

SCARCELLA, KARYN ALLEE, coach, special education services professional; b. Riverside, N.J., Mar. 26, 1972; d. Roger Gene and Kathleen Karen Allee; life ptnr. Lisa Anne Scarcella. BA in Edn., U. Fla., 1993, EdM, 1994. Cert. early childhood generalist Nat. Bd. Profl. Tchg. Stds., cert. primary (K-3), elem. (1-6), and ESOL (K-12) tchr. Fla. Early childhood, primary grades tchr. Orange County Pub. Schs., Orlando, Fla., 1995—2003, instrnl. coach, 2001—. Nat. bd. candidate mentor, mem. mentor adv. coun. Orange County Pub. Schs., 2000—, trainer Gt. Beginnings (new tchr. induction tng.), 2002—; supervising tchr. for pre-svc. coll. intern Orange County Pub. Schs./U. Ctrl. Fla., Orlando, 2001. Mem. Rainbow Dem. Club, Orlando, 2001. Mem.: ASCD, NEA, U. Fla. Sch. Tchg. and Learning Alumni Assn. (life), Pi Lambda Theta. Episcopalian. Avocations: travel, gourmet cooking, outdoor leisure activities, reading. Home: 629 Dory Ln #101 Altamonte Springs FL 32714 Office: Orange County Pub Sch McCoy Elem 5225 S Semoran Blvd Orlando FL 32822 Personal E-mail: halcyongrl@aol.com. E-mail: scarcek@ocps.net.

SCARDINO, MARJORIE MORRIS, publishing company executive; b. Flagstaff, Ariz., Jan. 25, 1947; d. Robert Weldon and Beth (Lamb) Morris; m. Albert James Scardino, Apr. 19, 1974; children: Adelaide Katherine Morris, William Brown, Albert Henry Hugh. BA, Baylor U.; JD, U. San Francisco. Ptnr. Brannen Wessels & Searcy, Savannah, Ga., 1976-85; pub. Ga. Gazette Pub. Co., Savannah, 1978-85; pres. The Economist Newspaper Group, Inc., N.Y.C., 1985-93; chief exec. The Economist Group, London, 1993-97, Pearson P.L.C., London, 1997—. Non-exec. dir. Nokia Corp. Bd. dirs. Carter Ctr., The Bus. Coun.; trustee others, Victoria and Albert Mus. Office: Pearson PLC 80 Strand London WC2R ORL England

SCARF, MARGARET (MAGGIE SCARF), author; b. Phila., May 13, 1932; d. Benjamin and Helen (Rotbin) Klein; m. Herbert Eli Scarf, June, 1953; children: Martha Samuelson, Elizabeth Stone, Susan Merrell. BA, South Conn. State U., 1989. Contbg. editor New Republic, Washington, 1978—, Self Mag., N.Y.C., 1991—; writer-in-residence Jonathan Edwards Coll., 1995—. Assoc. fellow Jonathan Edwards Coll. Yale U., New Haven, 1979—; sr. fellow Bush Ctr. in Child Devel. and Social Policy, Yale U., 1991—; mem. adv. bd. Am. Psychiat. Press, Poynter Fellowship Journalism Yale U., 1995-96. Author: Meet Benjamin Franklin, 1968, Antarctica: Exploring the Frozen Continent, 1970, Body, Mind, Behavior, 1976 (Nat. Media award Am. Psychological Assn. 1977), Unfinished Business: Pressure Points in the Lives of Women, 1981, Intimate Partners: Patterns in Love and Marriage, 1987, Intimate Worlds: Life Inside the Family, 1996; contbr. numerous articles to jours. including N.Y. Times mag. and book rev., Psychology Today; TV appearances include: David Letterman Show, Oprah Winfrey Show, CBS News, Good Morning Am., Today Show, Phil Donahue, numerous others. Recipient Nat. Media award Am. Psychol. Found., 1971, 74, 77, Conn. UN award Outstanding Conn. Women, 1987, cert. commendation Robert T. Morse Writers Competition Am. Psychiat. Assn., 1997, Disting. Svc. award Am. Psychiat. Assn., 1999, cert. of recognition N.Y. State Soc. Clin. and Social Work, 1998 ; grantee Smith Richardson Found., 1991-94; Ford Found. fellow, 1973-74, Neiman fellow Harvard U., 1975-76, Ctr. Advanced Study in Behavioral Scis. fellow, 1977-78, 85-86, Alicia Patterson Found. fellow, 1978-79. Mem. Conn. Soc. Psychoanalytic Psychologists, Am. Psychiat. Press (mem. adv. bd. 1992), Lawn Club, Elizabethans, PEN Writer's Assn. Avocations: reading, hiking, swimming. Office: Jonathan Edwards Coll Yale U 68 High St New Haven CT 06511-6643

SCARLETT, NOVLIN ROSE, public health nurse, educator; b. Jamaica, West Indies, Jan. 11, 1938; d. Cyrus Freeman and Sylvia Belafonte; m. Sherlock Anthony Scarlett, Dec. 19, 1964 (dec. Jan. 8, 1970); children:

Douglas, Anne. Nursing degree, Queensboro C.C., 1978, York Coll., 1984. RN N.Y. Staff nurse City Hosp., Elmhurst, NY, 1978—82; asst. head nurse Margaret Tietz, NY, 1982—86, head nurse, 1986—97; public health nurse City of N.Y., 1997—.

SCARLETT, P. LYNN, foundation administrator, writer; b. Pitts., Dec. 8, 1949; d. James Miles and Virginia (Young) S.; m. James R. Trotter, May 6, 1978; 1 child, Rachel Scarlett Trotter. BA, U. Calif., Santa Barbara, 1970, MA, 1972. Vis. lectr. U. Calif., Santa Barbara, 1980-81; book rev. editor Reason Mag., Santa Barbara, 1982-85; dir. rsch. Reason Found., Santa Monica, Calif., 1985-89, v.p. rsch., 1990—. Mem. task force Calif. Joint Legis. Com. on Surrogate Parenting, Calif., 1989-90; panel reviewer Project 88 Phase II, 1990; chmn. issues com. Citizens for Balanced Community, Santa Barbara, 1989—; bd. dirs. Laguna Blanca Sch., Santa Barbara. Author: (chpt.) Food Politics, 1982; contbr. articles to profl. jours. Chmn. Jim Trotter for City Coun., Carpinteria, Calif., 1990—; mem. parents aux. Laguna Blanca, 1986-88. Geneva Inst. of Internat. Studies fellow, 1974-75. Mem. Friends of Girls Club Corp. (2d v.p. 1986-87). Avocations: bird watching, illustrator, swimming. Office: Reason Found 3415 S Sepulveda Blvd Ste 400 Los Angeles CA 90034-6014

SCARLETT, PATRICIA LYNN, federal agency administrator; BA, MA in Polit. Sci., U. Calif., Santa Barbara. Joined Reason Pub. Policy Inst., 1979—, dir. rsch., 1985, mgr., 1989, exec. dir., v.p. rsch., pres., 2001—; asst. sec. policy, mgmt. and budget U.S. Dept. Interior, Washington, 2001—. Chair Inspection and Maintenance Rev. Com.; panelist Pay-as-You-Throw project EPA, 1995; tech. advisor N.Am. Integrated Waste Mgmt. Project Solid Waste Assn., 1995—96; bd. dirs. EarthShell Corp.; com. mem. Nat. Environ. Policy Inst.; sr. fellow Found. for Rsch. on Econs. and the Environment; environ. campaign advisor to George W. Bush; mem. Bush transition adv. team EPA. Contbr. articles to profl. jours. Bd. mem. Thoreau Inst. Republican. Office: US Dept Interior Policy Mgmt and Budget 1849 C St NW Washington DC 20240

SCAROLA, SUSAN MARGARET, lawyer; b. Elizabeth, N.J., Mar. 19, 1948; d. Anthony and Ruth (Cohen) S. BA cum laude, Thiel Coll., 1970; JD, Rutgers-State of U. of N.J., 1976. Bar: N.J. 1976, N.Y. 1985, Fla. 1993; cert. criminal trial atty., matrimonial law atty. Law sec. to Judge Triarsi, Superior Ct. of N.J., Elizabeth, 1976-77; asst. prosecutor Union County Prosecutor's Office, Elizabeth, 1997-88; non-equity ptnr. Lomurro Davison Eastman & Munoz, Freehold, N.J., 1988-97; ptnr. Newman Scarola & Assoc., Freehold, N.J., 1997—. Judge Mcpl. Ct., Twp. of Old Bridge, 1999—. Trustee Legal Aid Soc. of Monmouth County, 1992—, sec., 1998-2000, v.p. 2000—; committeewoman Old Bridge Dem. Com., 1995-99. Named Women of Yr. Women Lawyers in Monmouth County, 1994. Mem. Monmouth Bar Assn. (chair family law com. 1995-97), N.J. Bar Assn., Fla. Bar Assn., Middlesex County Bar Assn., Rutgers (Newark) Law Sch. Alumni (trustee 2000). Office: Newman Scarola & Assocs 64 W Main St Freehold NJ 07728-2142 E-mail: sscarola@monmouthlaw.com.

SCARPETTI, ANGELINA (LEE SCARPETTI), state legislator; b. Faeto Fogga, Italy; d. Carmine & Giovianina Capozziello, four children, four grandchildren. Grad., Bridgeport (Conn.) Ctrl. H.S. Restaurant cons., Trumbull, Conn., mem. Conn. State Senate, 1985—. Mem. environ. com., housing com. and transp. com., asst. majority leader Conn. State Senate; mem. Rep. Town Com.; sec. Greater Bridgeport Transit Dist. Address: Senate Rep Ofc LOB Rm 3400 Hartford CT 06106 Office: 80 Hill Pkwy Middlebury CT 06762-3328

SCARR, SANDRA WOOD, psychology educator, researcher; b. Washington, Aug. 8, 1936; d. John Ruxton and Jane (Powell) Wood; m. Harry Alan Scarr, Dec. 26, 1961 (div. 1970); children: Phillip, Karen, Rebbecca, Stephanie; m. James Callan Walker, Aug. 9, 1982 (div. 1994). AB, Vassar Coll., 1958; AM, Harvard U., 1963, PhD, 1965. Asst. prof. psychology U. Md., College Park, 1964-67; assoc. prof. U. Pa., Phila., 1967-71; prof. U. Minn., Mpls., 1971-77, Yale U., New Haven, 1977-83; Commonwealth prof. U. Va., Charlottesville, 1983-95, chmn. dept. psychology, 1984-90; CEO, chmm. bd. dirs. KinderCare Learning Ctr., Inc., 1995-97; ret., 1997. Mem. nat. adv. bd. Robert Wood Johnson Found., Princeton, N.J., 1985-91; coord. coun. psychology SUNY Bd. Regents, N.Y.C., 1984-92; prof. Kerstin Hesselgren, Sweden, 1993-94. Author: Race, Social Class and Individual Differences in IQ, 1981, Mother Care/Other Care, 1984 (Nat. Book award APA 1985), Caring for Children, 1989; editor Jour. Devel. Psychology, 1980-86, Current Directions in Psychol. Sci., 1991-95. Fellow Ctr. for Advanced Studies, Stanford U., Calif., 1976-77; grantee NIH, NSF, others, 1967-95. Fellow AAAS, APA (chmn. com. on human rsch. 1980-83, coun. of reps. 1984-89, bd. dirs. 1988-90, Award for Disting. Contbn. to Rsch. on Pub. Policy 1988), Am. Psychol. Soc. (bd. dirs. 1992—, pres. 1996-97, James McKeen Cattell award 1993); mem. Am. Acad. Arts and Scis. (coun. mem. 1995-2000), Behavior Genetics Assn. (pres. 1985-86, mem. exec. coun. 1976-79, 84-87), Soc. for Rsch. in Child Devel. (governing coun. 1974-76, 87-93, chmn. fin. com. 1987-89, pres. 1989-91) Internat. Soc. for Study of Behavioral Devel. (exec. bd. 1987-94). Avocations: dogs, gardening. Home: 77-6222 Kaumalumalu Dr Holualoa HI 96725-9757 E-mail: SandraScar@aol.com.

SCARSE, OLIVIA MARIE, cardiologist, consultant; b. Chgo., Nov. 10, 1950; d. Oliver Marcus and Marjorie Ardis (Olsen) S. BS, North Park Coll., 1970; MD, Loyola U., Maywood, Ill., 1973. Diplomate Am. Bd. Internal Medicine, Am. Bd. Cardiovascular Diseases. Surg. intern Resurrection Hosp., Chgo., 1974; resident in internal medicine Northwestern U., Chgo., 1974-77; cardiovascular disease fellow U. Ill., Chgo., 1977-80; dir. cardiac catherization lab. Cook County Hosp., Chgo., 1981; dir. heart sta. MacNeal Hosp., Berwyn, Ill., 1983; dir. electrophysiology Hines VA Hosp., Maywood, Ill., 1984-85; dir. progressive care Columbus Hosp., Chgo., 1985-88, pvt. practice, 1984—, Ill. Masonic Hosp., Chgo., 1989-96. Founder Physician Cons. for Evaluation of Clin. Pathways, Practice Parameters and Patient Care Outcomes, 1991—. Dir. continuous quality improvement Improvement Columbus, 1990-95; mem. presdl. ad hoc com. on prevention and treatment of domestic violence Chgo. Med. Soc., 1997—. Pillsbury fellow Pillsbury Fund, 1980. Fellow Am. Coll. Cardiology; mem. AMA, ACP, Chgo. Med. Assn., Ill. State Med. Assn., Am. Heart Assn. (coun. on clin. cardiology), Crescent Countries Found. for Med. Care, Physicians Health Network, Cen. Ill. Med. Rev. Orgn. Avocations: musician, ballet and tap dancer, actress, model, singer. Home and Office: 2650 N Lakeview Ave Apt 4109 Chicago IL 60614-1833 Fax: (773) 935-1039.

SCARWID, DIANA ELIZABETH, actress; b. Savannah, Ga. d. Anthony and Elizabeth Scarwid. Grad., Am. Acad. Dramatic Arts, 1975; degree in Theater Arts, Acting, Pace U., 1975. Appeared in films including Pretty Baby, Honeysuckle Rose, Inside Moves, (Oscar award nomination Best Supporting Actress), Mommie Dearest, Rumble Fish, Strange Invaders, Silkwood, Psycho III, Extremeties, Heat, Neon Bible, The Cure, Gold Diggers: The Secret of Bear Mountain, What Lies Beneath, The Angel Doll, A Guy Thing, 2002, Party Monster, 2002; TV films include Thou Shalt Not Kill, Studs Lonigan, Guyana Tragedy: The Story of Jim Jones, Desperate Lives, A Bunny's Tale, After the Promise, Night of The Hunter, Critical Choices, Bastard Out of Carolina, Angel of Pennsylvania Avenue, Truman (Emmy nomination 1996), If These Walls Could Talk, Ruby Bridges Story, also mini-series From the Earth to the Moon, Before He Wakes; theater prodns. include Key Exchange, Toronto, Can., A Thousand Clowns, Jupiter, Fla., Gethsamanie Springs, Mark Taper Forum, L.A., Spoon River Anthology, Ring 'round the Moon, N.Y.C., Nat. Shakespeare Conservancy, NY; (TV films) Down Will Come Baby, 1999, Dirty Pictures, 2000, Path to War, 2002 Avocations: reading, bicycle riding, crabbing from row boat, walking.

SCATENA, LORRAINE BORBA, retired rancher, women's rights advocate, retired advocate; b. San Rafael, Calif., Feb. 18, 1924; d. Joseph and Eugenia (Simas) de Borba; m. Louis G. Scatena, Feb. 14, 1960; children: Louis Vincent, Eugenia Gayle. BA, Dominican Coll., San Rafael, 1945; postgrad., Calif. Sch. Fine Arts, 1948, U. Calif., Berkeley, 1956-57. Cert. elem. tchr., Calif. Tchr. Dominican Coll., 1946; tchr. of mentally handicapped San Anselmo (Calif.) Sch. Dist., 1946; tchr. Fairfax (Calif.) Pub. Elem. Sch., 1946-53; asst. to mayor Fairfax City Recreation, 1948-53; tchr., libr. U.S. Dependent Schs., Mainz am Rhine, Fed. Republic Germany, 1953-56; translator Portugal Travel Tours, Lisbon, 1954; bonding sec. Am. Fore Ins. Group, San Francisco, 1958-60; rancher, farmer Yerington, Nev., 1960-98. Hostess com. Caldecott and Newbury Authors' Awards, San Francisco, 1959; mem. Nev. State Legis. Commn., 1975; coord. Nevadans for Equal Rights Amendment, 1975-78, rural areas rep., 1976-78; testifier Nev. State Senate and Assembly, 1975, 77; mem. adv. com. Fleischmann Coll. Agr. U. Nev., 1977-80, 81-84; speaker Grants and Rsch. Projects, Bishop, Calif., 1977, Choices for Tomorrow's Women, Fallon, Nev., 1989. Poetry presenter World Congress on Arts and Comm., Lisbon, Portugal, 1999, Washington, 2000, St. John's Coll.-Cambridge U., 2001, Vancouver, B.C., Can., 2002. Trustee Wassuk Coll., Hawthorne, Nev., 1984-87; mem. Lyon County Friends of Libr., Yerington, 1971—, Lyon County Mus. Soc., 1978—; sec., pub. info. chmn. Lyon County Rep. Women, 1968-73, program v.p., 1973-75; mem. Lyon County Rep. Ctrl. Com, 1973-74, Marin County Soc. Artists, San Anselmo, Calif., 1948-53; charter mem. Eleanor Roosevelt Edn. Fund for Women and Girls, 1990, sustaining mem., 1992—; Nev. rep. 1st White House Conf. Rural Am. Women, Washington, 1980; participant internat. reception, Washington, 1980; mem. pub. panel individual presentation Shakespeare's Treatment of Women Characters, Nev. Theatre for the Arts, Ashland, Oreg., Shakespearean Actors local performance, 1977; mem. Nev. Women's History Project, U. Nev., 1996—; mem. pres.'s circle Dominican U. Calif., 1997-; mem. Bancroft Libr.'s coun. U. Calif., Berkeley, 2002-. Recipient Outstanding Conservation Farmer award Mason Valley Conservation Dist., 1992, Soroptimist Internat. Women Helping women award 1983, invitation to first all-women delegation to U.S.A. from People's Republic China, U.S. House Reps., 1979; Public Forum Travel grantee Edn. Title IX, Oakland, Calif., 1977; Internat. Biog. Ctr. (Cambridge) fellow World Lit. Acad., 1993. Mem. AAUW (life mem. nat. br. 1975—, Leaders Circle 1998-), Lyon County Ret. Tchrs. Assn. (unit pres. 1979-80, 84-86, v.p. 1986-88, Nev. State Outstanding Svc. award 1981, state conv. gen. chmn. 1985), Rural Am. Women Inc., AAUW (br. pres. 1972-74, 74-76, chair edn. found. programs 1983—, state conv. gen. chmn. 1976, 87, state sec. 1970-72, state legis. program chmn. 1976-77, state chmn. internat. rels. 1979-81, state pres. 1981-83, br. travelship, discovering women in U.S. history Radcliffe Coll. 1981, State Humanities award 1975, Future Fund Nat. award 1983, Lorraine Scatena endowment gift named in her honor for significant contbns. to AAUW Ednl. Found. 1997), Mason Valley Country Club, Italian Cath. Fedn. (pres. 1986-88), Uniao Portuguesa Estado da Calif., Nat. Mus. of Women in the Arts (charter mem., 1987, assoc., mem. mus. coun. 2000—). Roman Catholic. Avocations: writing, photography. Home: PO Box 247 Yerington NV 89447-0247

SCATES, ALICE YEOMANS, former government official, consultant; b. Pitts., Jan. 21, 1915; d. William E. and Georgiana L. (Lloyd) Yeomans. BS, State Tchrs. Coll., Glassboro, N.J., 1936; MEd, Duke U., 1949; EdD, George Washington U., 1963. Tchr. elem. sch., Haddon Heights, N.J., 1937-43; civilian personnel officer Sedalia Army Airfield, Mo., Greenfield Army Airfield, S.C., 1944-46; pers. tng. officer VA Ctr., Dayton, Ohio, 1947—48; rsch. assoc., dir. Am. Coun. on Edn. Staff for Office Naval Rsch. Projects, 1949-53; asst. dir. Nat. Home Study Coun., 1954; editor, rsch. asst. Office of Edn. HEW, 1955, rsch. analyst, coord. coop. rsch. program, 1956-64, program planning officer occupl. rsch. program, 1965-66, dir. basic rsch. br. secondary edn., 1967-69; program planning and eval. officer Nat. Ctr. Ednl. R & D, 1969-71; eval. specialist Office Program Eval., 1971-80; eval. officer Office of Mgmt. U.S. Dept. Edn., 1980-82, cons., 1982-91; mem. continuing care adv. com. Md. State Office on Aging, 1994-99. Contbr. articles to profl. jours.; editor: Life Line, 1998—. Mem. Nat. Continuing Care Residents Assn.; bd. dirs. Town Ctr. Cmty. Assn., Columbia, Md., 1997-2001. Capt. U.S. Army, 1943-46. Fellow AAAS; mem. LWV, Am. Sociol. Assn., Am. Ednl. Rsch. Assn., Adult Edn. Assn., Kappa Delta Pi, Phi Delta Gamma. Home and Office: Vantage House # 1006 5400 Vantage Point Rd Columbia MD 21044-2667 E-mail: ayscates@msn.com.

SCEERY, BEVERLY DAVIS, genealogist, writer, educator; b. Hartford, Conn. d. Howard Coe and Gladys (Cotton) Davis; m. Walter Raymond Sceery; children: Nancy Bazar, Edward Sceery, Walter Sceery Jr., Martha Creed, Mary Heaton. BS magna cum laude, U. Md., 1975, MS, 1977, postgrad., 1977-82. Fin. counselor U. Md., College Park, 1975-77, lectr., 1977-82; realtor Washington, 1982-95; genealogist DAR, Washington, 1992—. Dir. handicapped program U. Md., College Park, 1975-77. Editor Capital Gardener mag., 1980-84; contbr. articles to profl. jours. Leader Girl Scouts Am., Potomac, Md., 1963—73, chmn., 1970—73; dir. Camp Tuckerman, Bethesda, Md., 1973; stephen min. Warner Meml. Presbyn. Ch., 2001—, deacon, 2004—. Mem.: DAR (mus. docent Nat. Soc. 1989—, chmn. Am. History 1991—94, mem. speakers staff, organizing regent Potomac Hundred chpt. 1992—, state registrar 1994—97, hon. regent Great Falls chpt. 1996—, nat. vice chmn. vol. genealogists, state chmn. 1997—2000, regent 2000—, historian Mary Washington chpt. 2001—, regent Mary Washington chpt. 2002—, D.C. state chaplain 2004—), AAUW (chmn. nomination com. 1991), Hereditary Order Descs. Colonial Govs., Nat. Soc. New Eng. Women (Va. Couny pres. 1999—2002, registrar gen. 2002—), Colonial Dames 17th Century (registrar Va. Colony chpt. 1997—99, genealogist Nat. Soc. 1997—, parliamentarian 2002—), Nat. Soc. Old Plymouth Colony Descs., Nat. Soc. Women Descs. Ancient and Hon. Arty. Co. (Va. sec. 1999—, nat. registration and credentials chmn., recording sec. gen.), Women's Club Chevy Chase (chmn. thrift shop 1997—), Fernwood Garden Club (pres. 1996—98), Nat. Capital Area Fedn. Garden Clubs (master judge flower shows, landscape design 1972—, chmn. flower show sch. 1989—91), Omicron Nu, Alpha Lambda Delta, Phi Kappa Phi. Avocation: genealogy and historical research. Home: 10307 Riverwood Dr Potomac MD 20854-1539

SCHAAB, NANCY A. education educator, consultant; d. Aloysius Robert Schaab and Mary Catherine Topper; m. Arthur J. Tselepis, Jan. 15, 1983; children: Nicholas Arthur, Natalie Mary. BS, U. Pitts., 1978; MA, Ohio State U., 1980, PhD, 1985. Cons. Devel. Dimensions Internat., Pitts., 1982—86, pvt. practice, Midland, Mich., 1987—2001; adj. instr. Saginaw Valley State U., Univ. Ctr., Mich., 1989—2001; instr. Delta Coll., Univ. Ctr., Mich., 2001—. Text reviewer (book) Psychology, 2003. Mem. PTA Siebert Sch., Midland, Mich., 1996; mgr. Dow Libr. Battle of the Books, Midland, Mich., 1997—; vol. Big Brothers/Big Sisters, Midland, Mich., 2002—. Mem.: Soc. for Tchg. of Psychology, Soc. for Indsl. Orgnl. Psychology, Am. Psychol. Assn. Avocations: reading, interior decorating, writing, dog training. Home: 312 Mayfield Ln Midland MI 48640 Office: Delta Coll J-140 University Center MI 48710 Office Phone: 989-686-9050. Business E-mail: naschaab@alpha.delta.edu.

SCHAAL, BARBARA ANNA, evolutionary biologist, educator; BS in Biology with honors, U. Ill., Chgo., 1969; MPhil in Population Biology, Yale U., 1971, PhD in Population Biology, 1974. spkr. in field. Assoc. prof. biology Washington U., St. Louis, 1980-86, prof., 1986—; prof. genetics Wash. U. Sch. Medicine, Spencer T. Olin prof. biology in arts and scis., chair dept. biology, 1993-97, mem. various coms. Assoc. editor Molecular Biology and Evolution, Am. Jour. Botany, Molecular Ecology, Conservation Genetics. Trustee St. Louis Acad. Scis. Fellow AAAS; mem. NAS, Bot. Soc. Am. (pres. 1995-96, Merit award 1999), Nature Conservancy (trustee Mo. chpt.). Achievements include research on the evolutionary process within plant populations. Office: PO Box 1137 Saint Louis MO 63188-1137

SCHAAR, SUSAN CLARKE, state legislative staff member; b. Lawrenceville, Va., Dec. 21, 1949; d. Garland Lewis and Frances Virginia (Matthews) Clarke; m. William Berkley Schaar Jr., Nov. 24, 1990. BA, U. Richmond, 1972. Engrossing clk. Senate Va., Richmond, 1974, legis. rsch. analyst, 1974-77; asst. to the clk. Senate of Va., Richmond, 1977-83; asst. clk. Senate Va., Richmond, 1983-90, clk. of the Senate, 1990—. Exec. com. Nat. Conf. State Legis., 1999—2001, Mason's Manual Commn.; staff vice chmn. standing com. Nat. Conf. State Legis., 2002. Mem. YMCA Model Gen. Assembly Adv. com., Richmond, 1990—; trustee U. Richmond, 1990-94; pres. Richmond Club of Westhampton, 1988-90; mem. Spider Club Athletic Bd., Richmond, 1988-90; bd. assocs. U. Richmond, 1995—; govt. counselor Va. Girls State, bd. dirs., 2001—; staff vice chair legis. effectiveness com. Nat. Conf. of State Legislatures, 1996-98, chair, 1998-99. Mem. Am. Soc. Legis. Clks. and Secs. (mem. exec. com. 1995-99, sec.-treas. 1996, pres.-elect 1997, pres. 1997-98, past pres., 1998-99), Coun. on Preservation of Capitol Sq., Omicron Delta Kappa, Pi Sigma Alpha. Baptist. Office: Senate of Va PO Box 396 Richmond VA 23218-0396 E-mail: sschaar@sov.state.va.us.

SCHABNER, DAWN FREEBLE, art educator, artist; b. Mercer, Pa., Jan. 30, 1933; d. Benjamin Frederick and Mary Emma (McElheny) Freeble; m. Donald Russell Schabner, Jan. 5, 1954; children: Donald Russell Jr., Dean Aaron. Student, Phila. Mus. Sch. Art, 1950-52; BA in Fine Arts with honors magna cum laude, Hofstra U., 1971; student, Cleve. Inst Art., 1952-53; MA in Liberal Studies, SUNY, Stony Brook, 1976. Designer Am. Greetings, Cleve., 1953; art educator Islip (N.Y.) Pub. Schs., 1967-95, Dowling Coll., Oakdale, N.Y., 1991—. One-woman shows include East Islip (N.Y.) Pub. Libr., 1977, 1988, Unitarian Bay Gallery, Bellport, N.Y., 1997, L-Art Gallery, Kiev, Ukraine, 1999, exhibited in group shows at Hofstra U., 1970, Patchogue-Medford Pub. Libr., 1983, East End Arts & Humanities Coun., Riverhead, N.Y., 1984, Islip Art Mus. Juried Exhibit, 1985, 1987, 1988, 1999, 2000, 2002, Suffolk County Legis. Bldg., Hauppage, N.Y., 1988, Bennington Coll., 1989, Goat Alley Gallery, Sag Harbor, N.Y., 1989, Canio's Books, Sag Harbor, 1990, South County Libr., Bellport, N.Y., 1991, The Parrish Art Mus., Southampton, N.Y., 1999, Stage Gallery, Merrick, N.Y., 2001; featured artist East End Arts and Humanities Coun., Riverhead, 1986, Clayton Liberatore Art Gallery, Bridgehampton, N.Y., 1994, 1995, 1997, 2001, 2002. Mem. Nat. League Am. Pen Women Inc., Met. Mus. Art, East End Arts Coun., Smithtown Twp. Arts Coun., Guild Hall., Parrish Art Mus. Avocations: golf, bicycling, weight training, reading, attending concerts & ballet.

SCHABOW, NANCY A. DEXTER, music educator; b. Green Bay, Wis., Feb. 1, 1970; d. David John and Dianne Marie (Hein) Dexter; m. Jeremy Jon Schabow, July 31, 1993. MusB, Alverno Coll., 1992. Registered music therapist, Wis. Music therapist Kindcare, Inc., Milw., 1993-94; music therapist in pvt. practice Hartland, Wis., 1993-98; owner, dir. Music Therapy Svcs. Waukesha County LLC, Hartland, 1999—. Bd. dirs. Wis. Dept. Regulation and Licensing: Music Art Dance Therapy, Madison. Mem. Am. Music Therapy Assn. (treas. Wis. chpt. 1994-96, govt. rels. 1996—; Gt. Lakes regional chpt. alt. del. 1999—). Avocations: cooking, reading, movies. Office: Music Therapy Assn Waukesha County LLC Hartland WI 53029

SCHACHTEL, BARBARA HARRIET LEVIN, epidemiologist, educator; b. May 27, 1921; d. Lester and Ethel (Neiman) Levin; m. Hyman Judah Schachtel, Oct. 15, 1941 (dec. Jan. 1990); m. Louis H. Green, Feb. 26, 1995; children: Bernard, Ann Mollie. Student, Wellesley Coll., 1939-41; BS, U. Houston, 1951, MA in Psychology, 1967; PhD, U. Tex., Houston, 1979. Psychol. examiner Meyer Ctr. for Devel. Pediat., Tex. Children's Hosp., Houston, 1967-81; instr. dept. pediat. Baylor Coll. Medicine, Houston, 1967-81, asst. prof. dept. medicine, 1982—. Asst. dir. biometry and epidemiology Sid W. Richardson Inst. for Preventive Medicine, Meth. Hosp., Houston, 1981-88, dir. quality assurance, 1988-93; ret., 1993; mem. instl. rev. bd. for human rsch. Baylor Coll. Medicine, Houston, 1981-87, 97—; mem. devel. bd. U. Tex. Health Sci. Ctr., Houston, 1987-97; mem. dean's adv. bd. Sch. Arch., U. Houston, 1987-89. Contbr. articles to profl. jours. V.p., bd. dirs. Houston-Harris County Mental Health Assn., 1966—67; vice-chmn. bd. mgrs. Harris County Hosp. Dist., Houston, 1974—90, chmn., 1990—92, bd. dirs., 1970—93; trustee Inst. Religion in Tex. Med. Ctr., 1990—, vice chmn., 2000—; sec. Bo Harris County Hosp. Dist. Found. Bd., 1993—; bd. dirs. Congregation Beth Israel, 1993—95, Planned Parenthood of Houston, Inc., 1994—2000, Houston Ind. Sch. Dist. Found., 1993—2001, Crisis Intervention, 1994—96. Named Great Texan of Yr., Nat. Found. for Ilietis and Colitis, Houston, 1982, Outstanding Citizen, Houston-Harris County Mental Health Assn., 1985; recipient Good Heart award B'nai Brith Women, 1984, Women of Prominence award Am. Jewish Com., 1991, Mayor's award for outstanding vol. svc., 1994. Mem. APA, APHA, Wellesley Club of Houston (pres. 1968-70). Avocations: golf, tennis, books. Home: 2527 Glen Haven Blvd Houston TX 77030-3511

SCHACHTER, BERNICE, sculptor, educator, writer; b. Elizabeth, N.J., Jan. 21, 1925; d. Samuel Naiman and Nettie (Cohen) Nodelman; m. Saul Schachter, Dec. 22, 1946 (dec. Nov. 1993); children: Shari E. Schachter Canepa, Steven M. BS, Goddard Coll., 1973, MA, 1974; postgrad., UCLA, 1974. Art dir. Artist and Craftsmen Guild, Cranford, N.J., 1966-73; instr. sculpture Everywoman's Village, Van Nuys, Calif., 1973-99; owner, dir. Sculpture Source, Culver City, Calif., 1975—. Dir. Summer Stone Carving Workshop, Pietrasanta, Italy, 1973-97. Author: 20th Century American Sculpture, 1974, Masks of the Muses, 1986, (screenplays) Morris, 1980, 100 Years from Now, 1995. Recipient Carducci Cultural medal Commune of City, Pietrasanta, 1990. Mem. AAUW, Internat. Sculptures Soc., Nat. Sculptors Soc., Golden West Sculptors, Am. Pen Women (pres. 2000). Democrat. Jewish. Avocations: golf, bridge, lawn bowling, travel. Home: 5263 Miembro Laguna Hills CA 92653-1821

SCHADENFROH, JOANN, secondary school educator; b. Sumpter, SC, July 3, 1971; d. John Joseph Schadenfroh and Cynthia Ann Krug. AA, Daytona Beach C.C., 1993; BA in Spanish, U. Fla., 1996; MEd in Ednl. Leadership, U. Ctrl. Fla., 2001. Spanish tchr. Stetson Christian Bapt. Sch., Deland, Fla., 1996—97, Pine Ridge H.S., Deltona, Fla., 1997—. Mem. Contbl. for Sch. Need for Subs.; vol. Jr. League, Daytona Beach, Fla., 1999—, Young Rep. Club, Ormond Beach, Fla., 2001. Recipient Excellence award, Contbn. to Sch. Need for Subs., 1999. Mem.: NEA, Tchr.'s Union, Am. Assn. Tchrs. Spanish. Republican. Roman Catholic. Avocations: reading, walking, swimming, Spanish, studying other cultures. Office: Pine Ridge HS 925 Howland Blvd Deltona FL 32725

SCHADLER, CYNTHIA K. accountant; b. Owensboro, Ky., Nov. 29, 1974; d. Eugene Francis and Mary Kareen Schadler. BS in Acctg., Ky. Wesleyan Coll., Owensboro, 1996; MS in Mgmt., Oakland City U., 2003. Staff acct. Wax Works, Inc., Owensboro, 1996—98; acct. Kindill Mining, Inc., Owensboro, 1998—; asst. contr. corp. acct. Brenntag Mid-South Inc., Henderson, Ky., 2002—. Avocations: golf, boating, walking. Home: 427 Newbury Ct Owensboro KY 42301 Office: 1405 Hwy 136W Henderson KY 42420

SCHADOW, KAREN E. public speaking trainer/educator; b. Mar. 1949; 1 child, Kelby. BA in comm. and humanities magna cum laude, Fla. State U., 1971, MA in theatre magna cum laude, 1973. Previous cameraperson numerous programs, ABC TV, previous prodn. staff mem.; pres. The Voice of Success!, NYC. Adh. asst. prof. NYU, 1990—; instr. Bergen Cmty. Coll.,

NJ; creator, presenter various lectures and seminars for sch. and orgn. including Nat. Acad. TV Arts & Scis., NY Coalition Women in Arts and Media, high sch., nationwide. Mem.: Nat. Acad. TV Arts & Scis. (past mem. bd. govs., Emmy award 1984), Fla. State U. Theatre Project, New England Soc., Univ. Film & Video Assn., Screen Actors Guild, Actors' Equity, NY Women in Comm. (v.p. student affairs).*

SCHAEFER, CHRISTINA KASSABIAN, writer, genealogist; b. Meriden, Conn., May 31, 1954; d. Levon Harry and Lareine Alice (Kinstler) Kassabian; m. Douglas Eric Schaefer, May 1, 1981; children: Eric, Alice. BA in English, So. Conn. State Coll., 1975. V.p. Blue Sales, Inc., Guilford, Conn., 1977-81. Dir. Family Hist. Ctr., Annandale, Va., 1994-97. Author: The Center: Guide to Research in the National Capital Area, 1996, Guide to Naturalization Records of the United States, 1997, The Great War: Guide to the Service Records of All the World's Fighting Men and Volunteers, 1998, Genealogical Encyclopedia of the Colonial Americas: A Complete Digest of the Records of All the Countries of the Western Hemisphere, 1998, The Hidden Half of the Family: A Sourcebook for Women's Genealogy, 1999, Instant Information on the Internet/ A Genealogist's No-Frills Guide to the 50 States and the District of Columbia, 1999, Instant Information on the Internet: A Genealogist's No-Frills Guide to the British Isles, 1999. Vol. Boys Scouts Am., Springfield, Va., 1991—. Recipient 1st pl. literary award Conn. Soc. Genealogists, 1997, 1998; Selected for inclusion in Authors' Room of Libr. Va., 2000. Mem.: Bd. Cert. Genealogists.

SCHAEFER, ELZBIETA A. music educator; b. Warsaw, May 8, 1938; came to the U.S., 1967; d. Roman and Janina Pierzchalski; m. Vladimir S. Levitski, 1962 (div. 1981); children: Konstanzia, Teresa, Alexander; m. Dean H. Schaefer, June 27, 1998. MusM, Warsaw Conservatory Music, 1963. Choir dir. Holy Cross ch., Mpls., 1990—. Author: (musical programs) Fr. Chopin in His Music and Letters, R. Schumann and His Letters. Mem. Minn. Music Tchrs. Assn. Roman Catholic. Avocations: tennis, skiing, cooking, gardening, art. Home: 4364 Dunrovin Ln Saint Paul MN 55123-1728

SCHAEFER, MARILYN LOUISE, artist, writer, educator; b. Cedar Rapids, Iowa, Apr. 22, 1933; d. Henry Richard and Maria Augusta (Dickel) S. AA, Monticello Coll. for Women, 1953; BFA, Cranbrook Acad. Art, 1956, MFA, 1960; MA cum laude, U. Chgo., 1958; MA, St. John's Coll., Santa Fe, 1979. Rsch. asst. editor Encyclopaedia Britannica, Chgo., 1960-63; humanities editor Encyclopedia Americana, N.Y., 1964-68; acquisitions editor Litton Ednl. Pub., N.Y., 1968-70; from instr. to prof. emeritus art and advt. design dept. N.Y.C. Tech. Coll. CUNY, 1970—. Contbg. editor Encyclopedia Americana, 1979—, Coll. Teaching jour., 1979. Contbr. articles to profl. publs. including Art and Auction mag., Art and Antiques mag., Am. Artist mag., Encyclopedia Americana, 1970—. Luce Found. postgrad. study fellow St. John's Coll., 1976-79; Ingram Merrill Found. grantee, 1983-84. Mem. AAUW, CUNY Acad. Arts and Scis. Home: 306 W 76th St New York NY 10023-8065 Office: NYC Tech Coll CUNY 300 Jay St Brooklyn NY 11201-1909

SCHAEFER, PATRICIA, librarian; b. Ft. Wayne, Ind., Apr. 23, 1930; d. Edward John and Hildegarde Hartman (Hormel) S. MusB, Northwestern U., 1951; MusM, U. Ill., 1958; AMLS, U. Mich., 1963; DLS (hon.), Ind. Inst. of Tech., 2003. With U.S. Rubber co., Ft. Wayne, 1951-52; sec. to promotion mgr. Sta. WOWO, Ft. Wayne, Ind., 1952, sec. to program mgr., 1953-55; coord. publicity and promotion Home Telephone Co., Ft. Wayne, 1955-56; sec. Fine Arts Found., Ft. Wayne, 1956-57; libr. asst. Columbus (Ohio) Pub. Libr., 1958-59; audio-visual libr. Muncie (Ind.) Pub. Libr., 1959-86, asst. libr. dir., 1981-86, libr. dir., 1986-95. Chmn. Ind. Libr. Film Cir., 1962-63; treas. Ind. Libr. Film Svc., 1969-70, 83-85; mem. trustee adv. coun. Milton S. Eisenhower Libr., Johns Hopkins U.; mem. presdl. counsellors Johns Hopkins U., 1994—; bd. dirs. Franklin Elec. Co., Inc. Weekly columnist Libr. Lines, Muncie Evening Press, 1981-83; program annotator Muncie Symphony Orch., 1963-2003, Masterworks Chorale, 1982-2003; contbr. articles to profl. jours. Bd. dirs. Muncie Symphony Assn., 1964-74, 85-91, Ctrl. City Bus. Assn., 1986-92, Ind. Inst. Tech., Ind. Humanities Coun., 1996-2002, Sta. WIPB-TV, 1996-2002, Muncie Ctr. for the Arts, 1999-2001; adv. coun. Coll. Fine Arts, Ball State U.; adv. com., bookshop dir. Midwest Writers Workshop, 1976-77; sec. Del. County Coun. for the Arts, 1978-79, pres., 1979-81, bd. dirs., 1985-86; pres.'s coun. Berea Coll., 1990-2001; bd. dirs. Muncie YWCA, 1977-82, 85-89, 95-2001, treas. 1981-82, 88-89; bd. govs. Minnetrista Cultural Ctr., 1998-2001; gen. chmn. Ind. Renaissance Fair, 1978-79; pres. Muncie Matinee Musicale, 1965-67; past pres. Ind. Film and Video Coun.; adv. bd. Cmty. Found. Muncie and Delaware County; bd. dirs. Wapehani coun. Girl Scouts U.S., 1989-96, ARC Hoosier Heartland chpt., 1997-2003. Named Woman Achievement Pub. Svc., 1986; recipient Sagamore of the Wabash award Gov. State of Ind., Outstanding Libr. award Ind. Libr. Fedn., 1995, Cert. of Congrl. Recognition, 1995, Cert. of Achievement, Women's Coalition, 1996, Cert. of Appreciation, Masterworks Chorale, 1998. Mem. ALA, Ind. Libr. Assn. (pres. 1987-88), Nat. League Am. Pen Women (pres. Muncie br. 1974-78), Altrusa (pres. 1986-87, cmty. svc. award 2000), Art Students League, Del. Country Club, Delta Zeta, Mu Phi Epsilon. Republican. Roman Catholic. Home: 5400 W Deer Run Ct Muncie IN 47304-5775

SCHAEFER-WICKE, ELIZABETH, reading consultant, educator; b. Bridgeport, Conn., Mar. 30, 1941; d. William Joseph and Loretta Schaefer; m. Frederick Paul wicke, July 3, 1976. BS, U. Conn., 1963; MA, Columbia U., 1966; 6th yr. profl. diploma, U. Bridgeport, 1975. Cert. reading cons. Elem. sch. tchr. Miles Ave. Sch., Huntington Park, Calif., 1963-64, Eli Whitney Sch., Meriden, Conn., 1966-68; supr. student tchg. interns Tracey Sch., Norwalk, Conn., 1968-70; reading splst. Wolfpit Sch., Norwalk, 1970-81; remedial reading and math tchr., cons. Rowayton (Conn.) Sch., 1981—2003. Mentor tng. program BEST, 1987-94, tchr. reading recovery, 1994-2003. Grantee Norwalk Fund for Excellence, 1986-87; named to honor roll, Conn. Fedn. Ednl. Employees, 2003. Mem. Norwalk Fedn. Tchrs. (bldg. steward 1981-2003), Internat. Reading Assn., Reading Recovery Coun. Am., Delta Kappa Gamma, Phi Delta Kappa, Pi Beta Phi. Democrat. Roman Catholic. Avocations: writing short stories, worldwide ednl. rsch., photography, scuba diving. Home: 41 Lakeview Dr Norwalk CT 06850-2003 also: 535 Broad Ave S Naples FL 34102-7159

SCHAEFFER, BARBARA HAMILTON, retired rental leasing company executive, writer; b. Newton, Mass., Apr. 26, 1926; d. Peter Davidson Gunn and Harriet Bennett (Thompson) Hamilton; m. John Schaeffer, Sept. 7, 1946; children: Laurie, John, Peter. Student, Skidmore Coll., 1943-46; AB in English, Bucknell U., 1948; postgrad., Montclair State U., 1950-51, Bank St. Coll. Edn., 1959-61, Yeshiva U., 1961-62. Cert. primary, secondary tchr. N.J. Dir. Pompton Plains Sch., N.J., 1959-62; adviser Episcopal Sch., Towaco, N.J., 1968-70; v.p. Deltona-DeLand Trolley, Orange City, Fla., 1980-81; pres. Monroe Heavy Equipment Rentals, Inc., Orange City, 1981—; also Magic Carpet Travel, 1985-88. Cons., founder, pres. TLC Travel Club, Orange City, 1981-88; lectr. on children's art, 1959-70. Contbr. articles to profl. jours. Mem. Small Bus. Devel. Regional Ctr. (Stetson U. chpt.), Nat. Trust Historic Preservation. Episcopalian. Avocations: restoring old homes, oil painting, piano, writing. Home: 400 Foothill Farms Rd Orange City FL 32763-5502

SCHAEFFER, BETH BOLIN, pre-school educator, consultant; b. Tuscola, Ill., Mar. 8, 1962; d. Louise Arlene and Frank Fortner Bolin; m. James R. Schaeffer, Apr. 18, 1957; 1 child, Grace Elizabeth. MA in Edn., We. Ky. U. Tchr. Cert. Ky. Profl. Stds. Bd., 1996. Pre-sch. cons. Warren County Pub. Schools, Bowling Green, Ky., 1998—; devel. interventionist LifeLine Pvt. Duty, Bowling Green, 2000—03. Adj. faculty, cons. We. Ky. U., Bowling Green, 1995—. Chair Early Intervention Coun. Barren River Area Devel. Dist., Bowling Green, 1995—2003. Recipient Rose C. Engel Award for Excellence in Profl. Practice, Internat. Divsn. for Early Childhood of Coun. for Exceptional Children, 1999. Mem.: Nat. Assn. for Edn. of Young Children (local affiliate chair 2002—03). Democrat-Npl. Roman Catholic. Avocations: family, community involvement, professional networking. Home: 329 Wesley Way Bowling Green KY 42104 Office: Warren County Public Schools PO Box 51810 Bowling Green KY 42102 E-mail: bschaeffer@warren.k12.ky.us.

SCHAEFFER, NANCY ELLEN, liberal arts educator; d. Oliver Adam and Alice Viola Schaeffer; m. Richard Edward Schaedel, July 14, 1979; children: Sergio Adam Schaedel, Cedric Alexis Schaedel. PhD, U. Tex., Austin, 2003. Rsch. and computer designer CHICO Musical Heritage Network, Ann Arbor, Mich., 1989—99; asst. prof. liberal arts St. Edward's U., Austin, Tex., 1999—. Asst. editor Latin Am. Music Rev., Austin, Tex., 1994—95. Dir.: (workshop) Spirituality and Sacred Music; computer designer (computer virtual tour) Peruvian Music and Culture, field researcher (anthropology) Festival Cycle on Northwest Peru- Mochica/Chimu (Fulbright, 1995); author: (article) IASPM Turku Congressional Proceedings; dir.: (music) Andean Ensemble. Mem. Hilde Girls (sing Hildegard music to terminally ill), Austin, Tex., 1997—2003. Rsch. grant, NSF, 1974-1976. Mem.: Soc. for Ethnomusicology (assoc.), Ali Akbar Coll. of Music (assoc.), Am. Anthrop. Assn. (assoc.). Avocations: photography, video recorder, musician, piano, zamponas, travel, Chinese medicine. Office: St Edward's Univ 3001 S Congress PO 881 Austin TX 78704 E-mail: nancys@admin.stedwards.edu.

SCHAFER, DONNA RENEE, special education educator; b. Glendale, Calif., Dec. 19, 1954; d. Esther Ellen Adams-Arvizu and Carroll Dean Adams; m. Gary Ray Schafer, July 7, 1973; 1 child, Sean Michael. BS, U. So. Miss., Long Beach, 1998; MEd, William Carey Coll., Hattiesburg, Miss., 1999. Lic. educator A Miss., 1998, educator AA Miss., 1999, nat. bd. cert. tchr. Nat. Bd. for Profl. Tchg. Standards, 2002. Spl. edn. tchr. Vancleave (Miss.) Mid. Sch., 1998—2000, Biloxi (Miss.) Jr. HS, 2000—. LSC chairperson Biloxi Jr. HS, 2000—, student coun. advisor, 2001—. Grantee Beautify Biloxi, Shoebox Sci., Biloxi 1st, 2001—03, Beautify Biloxi, Coun. for Exceptional Children, 2002—03. Mem.: Am. Fedn. Tchrs., Coun. for Exceptional Children, Delta Kappa Gamma. Republican. Baptist. Avocations: reading, crafts, sports, travel.

SCHAFER, ELIZABETH DIANE, historian, writer; b. Opelika, Ala., Sept. 26, 1965; d. Robert Louis and Carolyn Louise (Henn) S. BA in History cum laude, Auburn U., 1986, MA in History of Sci. magna cum laude, 1988, PhD in History of Tech. magna cum laude, 1993; postgrad., Hollins Coll., 1996—2003. Archivist Lee County Hist. Soc. Mus., 1988—. Ind. scholar, 1993—; presenter in field. Author: Beacham's Sourcebooks for Teaching Young Adult Fiction: Exploring Harry Potter, 2000, Lake Martin: Alabama's Crown Jewel, 2002, Auburn: Plainsmen, Tigers and War Eagles, 2003; co-author: Women Who Made A Difference in Alabama, 1995; cons. editor Ency. of Sci., 1998; freelance editor various tech. docs.; editl. asst. Proceedings of the We. Soc. for French History, 1988-91, Nat. Forum: The Phi Kappa Phi Jour., 1990-91; contbr. History News Svc.; contbr. articles to profl. jours., encys., mags., chpts. to books. Recipient hon. mention poetry Writer's Digest, 1994 hon. mention children's non-fiction, 1997, children's non-fiction and fiction, 1998, Writer's Digest, Shirley Henn Meml. award Critical scholar, Hollins Coll., 1998. Mem. AAAS, AAUW, Am. Hist. Assn., Orgn. Am. Historians, Soc. History Tech., History Sci. Soc., Women's History Network, N.Y. Acad. Scis., So. Hist. Assn., Soc. Children's Book Writers and Illustrators, Children's Lit. Assn., Ala. Writer's Forum, Assn. Gravestone Studies, Lancaster Mennonite Hist. Soc., Lee County Hist. Soc. (life mem.), Auburn U. Alumni Assn. (life mem.), Descendants Mexican War Vets., United Daus. of the Confederacy, DAR (chmn. Light Horse Harry Lee's geneal. records com.), Daus. of Union Vets., Phi Alpha Theta (history hon.). Home and Office: PO Box 57 Loachapoka AL 36865-0057 E-mail: edschafer@reporters.net.

SCHAFER, LORRAINE, psychologist, researcher; b. Glendive, Mont., July 2, 1957; d. Ryland Norris and Marlene Joanne Chaska; m. David James Schafer, Aug. 24, 1979; 1 child, Daniel Rylie. BS in Psychology/Sociology, N.D. State U., 1979, MS in Clin. Psychology, 1981; PhD in Counseling Psychology, Colo. State U., 1989. Rsch. assoc. N.D. State U., U. N.D., Fargo, 1981-84; assoc. cons., asst. prof. psychology Mayo Clinic, Rochester, Minn., 1991-92; lic. psychologist Marshfield (Wis.) Clinic, 1992—. Reviewer Diabetes Care, 1990—; mem. instnl. rev. bd. Marshfield Clinic, 1994—. Contbr. articles to profl. jours. Biomed. Rsch. Support grantee Colo. State U., 1984, Outstanding Grad. scholar, 1986, Mayo Clinic grantee, 1990, Postdoctoral fellow in Med. Psychology, 1991. Mem. APA (lic., Dissertation Rsch. award 1988), Am. Diabetes Assn. (profl., behavioral scientists rep. nonperiodical pubs. com. Alexandria, Va. 1990-92), Soc. Pediatric Psychology, Soc. Tchrs. Family Medicine (assoc.). Roman Catholic. Office: Marshfield Clinic 1000 N Oak Ave Marshfield WI 54449-5702 E-mail: schafer@mfldclin.edu.

SCHAFER, SHARON MARIE, anesthesiologist; b. Detroit, Mar. 23, 1948; d. Charles Anthony and Dorothy Emma (Schweitzer) Pokriefka; m. Timothy John Schafer, Nov. 12, 1977; children: Patrick Christopher, Steven Michael. BS in Biology, Wayne State U., 1971, MD, 1975; MBA in Practice Mgmt., Madonna U., 2000. Diplomate Am. Bd. Anesthesiology. Intern, resident Sinai Hosp. Detroit, 1975-78; pvt. practice anesthesiology Troy, Mich., 1988—. Mem. AMA, Am. Soc. Anesthesiologists. Roman Catholic. Home and Office: 5741 Folkstone Dr Troy MI 48085-3154

SCHAFER, YVONNE A. human resources specialist; d. Theodore Grant Jenkins and Sharon Louise Van Cleve; m. Charles Joseph Schafer, Sept. 23, 2000; 1 child, Mason Charles. BA in Applied Cultural Anthropology, Ind. U., Indpls., 1999. Cert. Human Resources Concepts Brainbrench, 2003. Internet recruitment cons., human resource specialist Monster, Indpls., 2000—03. Vol. MDFF, Indpls., 1998. Roman Catholic. Avocations: travel, interior design, culture and the arts, reading. Office: Emmis Communications One Emmis Plz 40 Monument Circle 500 Indianapolis IN 46204 E-mail: yschafer@emmis.com.

SCHAFF, BARBARA WALLEY, artist; b. Plainfield, N.J., May 6, 1941; d. Miron M. and Silvia S. (Solott) Walley; m. John A. Schaff, Apr. 10, 1963 (div. 1992); children: Elizabeth A., Joshua L. BA, Syracuse U., 1963; cert., Pa. Acad. Fine Arts, 1994; grad., China Nat. Acad. Fine Art, Hangzhou, 1994. Clay artist, Stockton, N.J., 1968-88; advisor to faculty BFA program Kean Coll., Union, N.J., 1987—; painter Phila., 1990—. Mem. adv. bd. Hunterdon Art Ctr., Clinton, N.J., 1988, 89; workshop leader, U.S. and Can. One-man shows include NJ State Mus, Trenton, 1985, Lee Sclar Gallery, Morristown, NJ, 1986, Howe Gallery, Kean Coll., Union, 1989, ITT Boston Sheraton, 1995, Thos. Moser Cabinetmakers, Phila., 1995, Ciboulette, 1997, So. Vt. Art Ctr., Manchester, 1997, NJ State Mus., Trenton, 1997, Questar Libr., New Hope, Pa., 1998, Restaurant Phila. Mus. Art, 1999, Cafe Gallery, Phila., 1999, Grounds for Sculpture, Hamilton, N.J., 2003, exhibited in group shows at Newark Mus., 1973, 1977, Morris Mus., Morristown, NJ, 1973, 1977, Carnegie Ctr., Princeton, NJ, 1984, Newman Galleries, Phila., 1986, Ednl. Testing Svc., Princeton, 1987, Monarch Title Nat. San Angelo Mus. Art, Tex., 1989, US Artists, Phila., 1992, 1993, China Nat. Acad. Fine Art, 1994, Morris Gallery Mus. Am. Art., Phila., 1994, Am. Drawing Biennial V Muscarelle Mus. Art, Williamsburg, Va., 1996, Restaurant Phila Mus. Art, 1996, 1999, Fellowship of Pa. Acad. Fine Arts, Woodmere Mus., 1996, Peng Gallery, Phila., 2000, Carspecker-Scott Gallery, Wilmington, Del., 2001—, Walker-Kornbluth Gallery, Fair Lawn, N.J., 2003, Wayne (Pa.) Art Ctr., 2003, Represented in permanent collections Linda Lee Aeter collection Art by Women, NJ State Mus, Trenton, Fuller Meml. Art Mus., Brockton, Mass., Pfizer Internat., NYC, Atlantic Richfield Corp., Phila., Towers Perrin, NYC, Independence Found., Phila., Temple U. Sch. Law, McGraw Hill, NYC, Chubb Corp., Warren, NJ, Sta. WHYY and WHYY-TV, Phila., Marriott Corp., Princeton, NJ, Prince Music Theater, Phila., BristolMeyers Squibb Co., Hopewell, NJ, Va. Ctr. for the Creative Arts, Sweet Briar, Va., commns., NJ Natural Gas, Wall, 1983, Bell Comms. Rsch., Red Bank, NJ, 1985, Kenneth Endick, Boca Raton, Fla., 1987, McGraw Hill, 1990, works featured in, NJ Mag., Star Ledger, NY Times, Am. Artists, An Illustrated Survey of Leading Contemporaries, 2000 Outstanding artists and designers of the 20th Century. Recipient Medal of Excellence for promotion and design Art Dirs. Club N.J., 1986, medal for Outstanding Achievement, Long Beach Island Found. of the Arts and Scis., Harvey Aders, N.J., 1998, 99, Gold award Appleton Paper Corp., 2003; fellow N.J. State Coun. on Arts, 1984-85, resident fellow Va. Ctr. Creative Arts, 1996, 98, 99, 2001, 03. Mem. Fellowship of Pa. Acad. of Fine Arts (com. mem., exhibitor 1986, 87, 94, Mable Wilson Woodrow Meml. award 1994), Artist Equity, Nat. Arts Club. Avocations: gardening, cooking, music, sailing. Home: 1520 Spruce St Apt 906 Philadelphia PA 19102-4507 Office: Barbara Schaff Studio 314 Brown St Philadelphia PA 19123-2202 Office Phone: 215-829-0480. E-mail: babascha@aol.com.

SCHAFFNER, KAREN ANN *See* **FIELD, KAREN ANN**

SCHAFFNER, ROBERTA IRENE, retired medical, surgical nurse; b. Vero Beach, Fla., Oct. 5, 1926; d. Robert Wesley and Harriett Louise (Davis) Routh; m. David Leonard Schaffner, Apr. 25, 1947 (div. July 1975; dec.); children: Penny Routh S. (dec. July 1999), David Leonard II (dec. Jan. 1999). Mem. cadet nurse corps, Charity Hosp., New Orleans, La., 1944-45; ADA, Montgomery County C.C., Blue Bell, Pa., 1978; BSN, Gwynedd (Pa.) Mercy Coll., 1982, MSN, 1984. RN Pa. Med.-surg. nurse Chestnut Hill Hosp., Phila., 1978-2000, ret., 2000. Mem. delegation to study health care delivery sys., Moscow, Tbillisi, Azerbeijan, Kiev, 1981, Shanghai, Beijing, Nanjing, Hong Kong, 1984, Milan, Pisa, Bologna, Florence, Rome, Sorento, Naples, 1985. Cadet U.S. Nurse Corps, 1945. Mem. Oncology Nursing Soc., Sigma Theta Tau. Republican. Home: 1600 Church Rd Apt A214 Wyncote PA 19095-1929 E-mail: robertars4@aol.com.

SCHAFFNER-IRVIN, KRISTEN, oil executive; b. Seattle; m. Jeff Irvin; 4 children. B. in public relations, Ariz. State U. Sales mgr., fuel distributor Petro Am., 1987—92; owner Team Petroleum (formerly Kristin Schaffner Petroleum), Huntington Beach, Calif., 1992—. Office: Team Petroleum PO Box 659 Huntington Beach CA 92648-0659

SCHAGH, CATHERINE, federal agency administrator; Dir. impact aid program US Dept. Edn., Off Elem. Secondary Edn., Wash., DC, 1995—; analyst US Dept. Edn., Budget Off., divsn. dir. to program dir. Team leader US Dept. Edn., Class-Size Reduction Program, 1998—2000; co-pres. Annandale Bus. and Profl. Women, Va. Mem.: Annandale Bus. and Profl. Women Investment Club (treas.). Office: US Dept Edn Elem Secondary Edn 400 Maryland Ave SW FB-6 Rm 3E105 Washington DC 20202

SCHAIBLE, STACIE, newscaster; m. Mike Schaible; 1 child, Cade Michael. Student, Poynter Inst. for Media Studies; grad., U. Minn. Anchor WDAY-TV, Fargo, ND, KDLH-TV, Duluth, Minn., KXAN-TV, Austin, Tex., WFLA-TV, Tampa, Fla., 2000—. Recipient Katie award for Best Major Market Newscast. Avocations: golf, reading, travel. Office: WFLA-TV PO Box 1410 Tampa FL 33601

SCHAKOWSKY, JANICE, congresswoman; b. Chgo., May 26, 1944; d. Irwin and Tillie (Cosnow) Danoff; m. Harvey E. Schakowsky, Feb. 17, 1965 (div. 1980); children: Ian, Mary; m. Robert B. Creamer, Dec. 6, 1980; 1 stepchild, Lauren. BS, U. Ill., 1965. Cert. elem. tchr., Ill. Tchr. Chgo. Bd. Edn., 1965-67; organizer Ill. Pub. Action Coun., Chgo., 1976-85; exec. dir. Ill. State Coun. Sr. Citizens, Chgo., 1985-90; mem. Ill. Ho. Reps., 1990-98, U.S. Congress from 9th Ill. dist., 1999—; mem. banking and fin. svcs. com., 1999—2000; mem. govt. reform com., 1999—2000; ho. dem. leadership team-deputy whip; mem. Energy and Commerce Com. Bd. dirs. Ill. Pub. Action, 4 C's Day Care Coun., Evanston, Ill.; steering com. mem. Cook County Dem. Women, 1986-90; del. Nat. Dem. Conv., 1988; governing coun. Am. Jewish Congress, 1990—. Named Outstanding Legislator Interfaith Coun. for Homeless, 1993, Legislator of Yr. Ill. Nurses Assn., 1992, Ill. Assn. Cmty. Mental Health Agys., 1994, Coalition of Citizens with Disabilities and Ill. Coun. Sr. Citizens, 1993, Cmty. Action Assn., 1991, Champaign County Health Care Assn., 1992, Rookie of Yr. Ill. Environ. Coun., 1991. Mem. ACLU, NOW, Nat. Coun. Jewish Women, Ill. Pro-Choice Alliance, Evanston Mental Health Assn., Evanston Hist. Soc., Evanston Friends of Libr., Rogers Park Hist. Soc. Democrat. Jewish. Avocations: travelling, horsebackriding, reading. Office: Ho of Reps 515 Cannon Ho Office Bldg Washington DC 20515-1309*

SCHALLENKAMP, KAY, academic administrator; b. Salem, S.D., Dec. 9, 1949; d. Arnold B. and Jennie M. (Koch) Krier; m. Ken Schallenkamp, Sept. 7, 1970; children: Heather, Jenni. BS, No. State Coll., 1972; MA, U. S.D., 1973; PhD, U. Colo., 1982. Prof. No. State Coll., Aberdeen, S.D., 1973-88, dept. chair, 1982-84, dean, 1984-88; provost Chadron (Nebr.) State Coll., 1988-92, U. Wis., Whitewater, 1992-97; pres. Emporia (Kans.) State U., 1997—. Cons. North Ctrl. Assn., nursing homes, hosps. and ednl. instns. Contbr. articles to profl. jours. Commr. North Ctrl. Assn., 1995-99. Bush fellow, 1980; named Outstanding Young Career Woman, Bus. and Profl. Women's Club, 1976. Mem. NCAA (pres.'s coun. 2000—), Kans. C. of C. (bd. dirs. 2000—), Am. Speech and Hearing Assn. (cert.), Rotary. Avocation: martial arts. Office: Emporia State U 1200 Commercial St Emporia KS 66801-5087 E-mail: schallka@emporia.edu.

SCHALLER, JANE GREEN, pediatrician; b. Cleve., June 26, 1934; d. George and May Alice (Wing) Green; children: Robert Thomas, George Charles, Margaret May. AB, Hiram (Ohio) Coll., 1956; MD cum laude, Harvard U., 1960. Diplomate Am. Bd. Pediat., Am. Bd. Med. Examiners. Resident in pediat. Children's Hosp.-U. Wash., Seattle, 1960-63; fellow immunology Children's Hosp. U. Wash., 1963-65; faculty U. Wash. Med. Sch., 1965-83, prof. pediat., 1975-83; head divsn. rheumatic diseases Children's Hosp., Seattle, 1968-83; prof., chmn. dept. pediat., pediatrician-in-chief Tufts U. Sch. Medicine/New Eng. Med. Ctr., 1983-98; Karp prof. pediat. Tufts U. Sch. Medicine, Boston, 1983—, disting. prof., 1995—. Vis. physician Med. Rsch. Coun., Taplow, Eng., 1971-72; adj. prof. diplomacy The Fletcher Sch. Law and Diplomacy, Tufts U., 1998-2000. Contbr. articles to profl. jours. Bd. dirs. Seattle Chamber Music Festival, 1982-85; trustee Boston Chamber Music Soc., 1985—; mem. Boston adv. coun. UNICEF, tech. advisor UN Study on the Impact of Armed Conflict on Children, 1995-97; chmn., adv. com. children's rights divsn. Human Rights Watch, 1995—; mem. adv. com. Middle East divsn., 1998—; exec. com. Women's Commn. for Refugee Women and Children Internat. Rescue com., 1989-94, adv. coun. 1994—. Mem.: AAAS, Royal Coll. Pediats. U.K., Internat. Women's Forum, Mass. Women's Forum, Harvard U. Med. Sch. Alumni Coun. (v.p. 1977—80, pres. 1982—83), Physicians for Human Rights (exec. com. 1986—, founding pres. 1986—89), Com. Health in So. Africa (exec. com. 1986—92), Assn. Med. Sch. Pediat. Chmn. (exec. com. 1986—89, rep. to coun. on govt. affairs and coun. acad. socs.), New Eng. Pediat. Soc. (pres. 1991—93), Am. Coll. Rheumatology, Internat. Pediat. Assn. (pres.-elect 1998—2001, pres. 2001—04), Am. Acad. Pediat. (exec. com. sect. on internat. child health, head children's rights program, rep. to UNICEF), Am. Pediat. Soc., Soc. Pediat. Rsch., Inst. Medicine of NAS, Saturday Club, Tavern Club, Aesculapian Club (pres. 1988—89). Office: Floating Hosp for Children 750 Washington St # 8683 Boston MA 02111-1526

SCHANDELMEIER, LINDA ANN, elementary school educator; b. Anchorage, Alaska, Apr. 12, 1949; d. John Daniel and Nell Tressie S.; m. Grant E.M. Matheke, Mar. 29, 1975 (div. 1992); children: Lauren, Mara; m. John Norman Davies, July 17, 1993. BS in Biol. Sics., U. Alaska, Fairbanks, 1991. Creative writing tchr. Fairbanks (Alaska) Correctional Ctr., 1989—97, Summer Fine Arts Camp, Fairbanks, 1994—98; tchr. Fairbanks North Star Borough Sch. Dist., Fairbanks, 1995—. Author: poems. Recipient Presdl. award for excellence in math. and sci. tchg., NSF, 2000; Individual Artist fellow, Alaska State Coun. Arts, 1985. Mem.: NEA, Alaska State Literary Assn., Interior Democrats, Fairbanks Edn. Assn., Nat. Sci. Tchrs. Assn., LWV. Home: 1998 Kittiwake Dr Fairbanks AK 99709

SCHANSTRA, CARLA ROSS, technical writer; b. Berwyn, Ill., Sept. 4, 1954; d. Caroles Schanstra and Heather Millar (Thomson) Alonso. BA, Western Ill. U., 1976; postgrad., U. Ill. Circle, Chgo., 1980-81. Assoc. editor Hitchcock Pub., Wheaton, Ill., 1976-80; assoc. product mgr. Advanced Systems, Inc., Elk Grove Village, Ill., 1980-81; tech. writer Profl. Computer Resources, Oak Brook, Ill., 1982; sr. tech. writer Lucent Techs. (formerly AT&T Bell Labs.), Naperville, Ill., 1982-99; info. devel. Visual Insights, Naperville, 1999-2001; knowledge engr. ABN-AMRO Info. Tech. Svcs. Co., Chgo., 2001—02; freelance writer, 2002—; printed music mgr. Brookdale Music, Naperville, Ill., 2003—. Author: (plays) A Little Bit of Both, The Reversible Play, Survivors, Snakes and Apple Pie, It Should Be Obvious, Pastiche, The Model Home; contbr. articles. Violist DuPage Symphony, Glen Ellyn, Ill., 1984-87, 90-93, Elgin (Ill.) Symphonette, 1985-87. Mem. So. Tech. Comm. Assn. (award of excellence 1985), Dramatists Guild, Feminist Writers Western Suburbs (founder), Feminist Writers Guild Chgo. (adv. panel), Internat. Soc. Dramatists, Ill. Theatre Assn., Writers Workshop (co-founder), Village Theatre Guild. E-mail: laross98@aol.com.

SCHAPIRO, KAREN LEE, language educator; b. Cleve., June 11, 1947; d. George and Lena Keserich; m. Ross Harley Schapiro, Aug. 17, 1991; 1 child, Trevor Ross. BA in Span. and French, Oberlin Coll., 1969; MA in Span. Lang. Lit., Ohio State U., 1971; doctoral studies, U. Mass., 1971—73; attended, U. Calif. Berkeley, 1975, U. de Guadalajara, Mex., 1985. Tchg. asst. Ohio State U., Columbus, 1969—71; assoc. tchr. U. Mass., Amherst, 1971—73; lang. and dance tchr. Wooster Sch., Danbury, Conn., 1973—76, Carmel (Calif.) HS, 1976—81, Soledad (Calif.) Union Sch. Dist., 1981, Pacific Grove (Calif.) HS, 1981—. Named Calif. Span. Tchr. of Yr., Span. Heritage, 1986; recipient Travel Scholarship award, Mary Dufort, 1988. Avocations: travel, films, theater, reading, dance. Office: Pacific Grove HS 615 Sunset Pacific Grove CA 93950

SCHAPIRO, MARY, federal agency administrator, lawyer; b. N.Y.C., June 19, 1955; d. Robert D. and Susan (Hall) S.; m. Charles A. Cadwell, Dec. 13, 1980. BA, Franklin and Marshall Coll., 1977; JD, George Washington U., 1980. Bar: D.C. 1980. Trial atty., 1980-81; counsel to chmn. Commodity Futures Trading Commn., 1981-84; sr. v.p. Futures Ind. Assn., 1984; gen. counsel Futures Industry Assn., 1984-88; commr. SEC, Washington, 1988-94; chmn. Commodity Futures Trading Commn. (CFTC), Washington, 1994-96; pres. Nat. Assn. Securities Regulation, Inc., Washington, 1996—; vice chmn., pres., regulatory policy oversight Nat. Assn. of Securities Dealers, 1996—. Mem. Tech. Com. and the Develop. Markets Com. of the Internat. Org. of Securities (IOSCO); chmn IOSCO Cons. Com., 2001—. Mem. bd. trustees, vice chmn. audit com. Franklin and Marshall Coll.; bd. dirs. Cinergy Corp., 1999—, Kraft Foods. Named Fin. Women's Assn. Pub. Sector Woman of the Yr., 2000. Office: Nat Assn Securities Regulation Inc 1735 K St NW Washington DC 20006-1516

SCHAPP, REBECCA MARIA, museum director; b. Stuttgart, Fed. Republic Germany, Dec. 12, 1956; came to U.S., 1957; d. Randall Todd and Elfriede Carolina (Scheppan) Spradlin; m. Thomas James Schapp, May 29, 1979. AA, DeAnza Coll., 1977; BA in Art, San Jose State U., 1979, MA in Art Adminstrn., 1985. Adminstrv. dir. Union Gallery, San Jose, Calif., 1979-82; from mus. coordinator to dep. dir. de Saisset Mus. Santa Clara (Calif.) U., 1982-92, dir., 1993—. Mem. San Francisco Mus. Modern Art; bd. dirs. Works of San Jose, v.p. 1983-85. Mem. Non-Profit Gallery Assn. (bd. dirs.). Democrat. Avocations: racquetball, walking, bicycling, camping. Office: De Saisset Mus Santa Clara U 500 El Camino Real Santa Clara CA 95050-4345

SCHAPPELL, ABIGAIL SUSAN, speech, language, hearing and massage therapist; b. York, Pa., May 25, 1952; d. Felix and Ann (Getty) DeMoise; m. Gery Mylan Schappell, Oct. 20, 1979; 1 child, Jonathan Michael. BS with Master's equivalency, Longwood Coll., 1974; postgrad., Bloomsburg U., 1975-77; cert., Lehmann Sch Massage and Muscle, 1991, East-West Sch. Massage Therapy, 1995—. Lic. speech-lang. pathologist, Pa. Speech-lang.-hearing specialist dept. pub. welfare Hamburg (Pa.) Ctr., 1975—. Judge deaf posters and essays Virginville (Pa.) Grange, 1990—, judge Pa. State Grange Conv., 1997, tchr. emergency pers. on communicating with deaf and hard of hearing, 1991, 92; leader demonstrations and workshops on sign lang. and dysphagia, non verbal comms., active listening to various orgns., 1978—; massage therapy; bd. dirs. Berks Deaf and Hard of Hearing Svcs., 2000—; presenter in field. Pub: (Boy Scouts Coun. manual), Scouting for the Handicapped, Hawk Mountain, 1981-82. Sign/del. to conf. Bible Sch. dir., mem. Zion's United Ch. of Christ, Windsor Castle, Pa., 1985—; rep. nat. triann. conv. Penn Laurel coun. Girl Scouts U.S., 1975; instr. ARC, 2002; vol. residential monitoring project Berks County ARC, 1998-99. Named Virginville Grange Cmty. Citizen of Yr., 1994—95, Outstanding Young Women of Am., 1984. Mem.: AAUW, Schuykill Haven Bus. and Profl. Women (Young Careerist local, dist. and state honors 1980—81, pres. 1983—84, asst. dir. dist. 9 Pa. 1997—99, dist. 9 dir. 1999—2001, state mentoring com. 2001—03, dist. 9 parliamentarian 2002—, involvement on dist. and state level, presenter local, dist. and state level workshops, state edn. and svc. funds com. 2003—, Eleanor Briner award as dist. 9 dir. 2000), Pa. Speech and Hearing Assn., Am. Assn. Mental Retardation (mem. Region 9 core com. for speech 1976, presenter at state conf. 1994, regional conf. 1995), Yorktown chpt. DAR, Young Careerist Alumni Assn. (life), Hamburg Area Soccer Assn. (sec. 1989—94), Order Ea. Star (mem., chaplain Blue Mountain chpt. 1981, 1982). Republican. Avocations: massage, signing, music. Home: 531 S 4th St Hamburg PA 19526-1307 Office: Hamburg Ctr Old RR 22 PO Box 1000 Hamburg PA 19526

SCHARFENBERG, MARGARET ELLAN, retired elementary school educator; b. Lansing, Mich., Mar. 22, 1924; d. John Milton and Florence Lucille (Craig) Amiss; m. Howard Edward Scharfenberg, June 29, 1946; children: Ann Derr Scharfenberg White, Joan Carol Scharfenberg Anderson, John Howard Scharfenberg. Student, Oberlin Coll., 1942-44; BA, Mich. State U., 1946; MA in Teaching, Rollins Coll., 1966. Cert. tchr., elem. supr., Fla. Tchr. Hill Elem. Sch., Maitland, Fla., 1964-65, Cheney Elem. Sch., Orlando, Fla., 1965-66; reading lab. tchr. Richmond Heights Elem. Sch., Orlando, 1966-68; supr. perceptual planning, oral clinician Orange County Schs., Orlando, 1968-69; reading lab. tchr. Winter Park (Fla.) H.S., 1969-72; from perceptual trainer to exptl. reading lab. tchr. Gateway Sch., Orlando, 1972-74; tchr. of migrant children Zellwood (Fla.) Elem. Sch., 1974-93; ret., 1993. Pioneer white/black sch. staffing Richmond Heights Elem. Sch., 1966-68; dir. Learning Skills Profl. Ctr., Orlando, 1971-74; speaker numerous symposia and convs. in field, 1968—; cons. in field. Author, editor (newsletter) Paper Meeting, 1968-69, (perception package) Patterns for a Purpose, 1968-69; producer films on perceptual tng., 1968-69. Chaplain, Oleander Garden Cir.; chaplain, past sec., Lakes and Hills Garden Club; sec. Tangerine Garden Club; chaplain, historian, past v.p. and pres. Women's Soc., Tangerine Cmty. Ch.; vol. Women of Hospice, Hospice Hope Chest; mem. Humane Soc. U.S.A.; mem. Congl. Ch. of Mt. Dora. Named Tchr. of Yr., Zellwood Elem. Sch., 1993. Mem.: NEA, AAUW, Internat. Reading Assn. (sec. Orange County coun. 1965, pres. 1969), Rosicrucian Order (A.M.O.R.C.), Lions (staff mem. seminars on perception, recipient various certs. and plaques), Gamma Phi Beta (past pres. alumna group). Republican. Congregationalist. Avocations: reading, boating, gardening, animal study. Home: 6492 Dora Dr Mount Dora FL 32757-7064

SCHAROLD, MARY LOUISE, psychoanalyst, educator; b. Mar. 3, 1943; d. Walter John and Louise Helen (Hartmann) Baumgartner; m. William Ballew McCollum, Aug. 23, 1964 (div. 1981); m. Harry Karl Scharold, June 19, 1982; children: Margaret Louise, Walter Ballew. BA with highest distinction, U. Kans., 1964; MD, Baylor Coll. Medicine, 1968; postgrad., Topeka Inst. Psychoanalysis, 1981. Diplomate Am. Bd. Psychiatry and Neurology. Intern Meml. Bapt. Hosp., Houston, 1968-69; resident in psychiatry Baylor Coll. Medicine, Houston, 1969—72, chief resident, 1971-72; psychoanalyst Houston, 1972—. Asst. prof. Baylor Coll. Medicine, Houston, 1973-76, asst. clin. prof., 1981-84, assoc. clin. prof., 1984—; dir. Baylor Psychiat. Clinic, Houston, 1973-76; co-dir. Rice U. Psychiat. Svc., Houston, 1981-82; asst. clin. prof. U. Kans. Sch. Medicine, Kansas City, 1977-81; tchg. assoc. Topeka Psychoanalytic Inst., 1984-86; tchg. analyst, Houston-Galveston Psychoanalytic Inst., 1986-90, tng. and supervising analyst, 1990—, v.p., 1994-96, pres., 1996-2001, bd. dirs., 2001—. Adv. bd. Leavenworth (Kans.) Mental Health Assn., 1977-81. Watkins scholar U. Kans., 1961-64. Fellow Am. Psychiat. Assn. (disting., mem. com. quality assurance 1986-87, chair Tex. peer rev. 1984-88), Am. Coll. Psychoanalysts; mem. Am. Psychoanalytic Assn. (cert. 1982, peer rev. com. 1985-90, prof. ins. commn. 1986-93, bd. profl. stds. 1994-2001, CME com. 1994-96, exec. coun. 1994-96, cert. com. 1995-98, preparedness and progress com. 1998—, chair preparedness and progress com. 2000—, coordinating com. bd. profl. stds. 2000—, bylaws com. 2001—, fin. com. 2003—), Am. Group Psychotherapy Assn., Ctr. Advanced Psychoanalytic Studies, Houston Psychiat. Soc. (v.p. 1984-85, pres.-elect 1985-86, pres. 1986-87), Houston-Galveston Psychoanalytic Soc. (sec.-treas. 1984-86, pres.-elect 1986-88, pres. 1988-90, alt. councillor 1994-96), Houston Group Psychotherapy Soc. (adv. bd. 1984-85), Hilltoppers, Mortar Bd., Phi Beta Kappa, Delta Phi Alpha, Alpha Omega Alpha, Pi Beta Phi Alumni Assn. Republican. Lutheran. Office: 2301 Westheimer Rd Houston TX 77098-1317 E-mail: mlscharold@mindspring.com.

SCHARP-RADOVIC, CAROL ANN, choreographer, classical ballet educator, artistic director; b. Ypsilanti, Mich., Aug. 9, 1940; d. John Lewis and Mary Vivien (Alther) Keeney; m. Jack Laurel Scharp, July 28, 1958 (div. July 1970); children: Kathryn E., Mark A.; m. Srecko Radovic, Nov. 15, 1989. Studied with Pereslavic, Danilova; student, Harkness Ballet, N.Y.C., Joffrey Ballet, Eglevsky Ballet, Briansky Ballet, Darvesh Ballet, N.Y.C.; studied with Jurgen Schneider, Am. Ballet Theatre, 1983-93; studied with Janina Cunova, Luba Gulyeava, Australian & Kirov ballet cos., 1983-93; studied with Ninel Kurgapkina, Ludmila Synelnikova, Genhrich Mayorov, Kirov Ballet, 1987-89; studied with Ludmila Sakharova, Perm Ballet, 1993; studied with Ludmila Synelnikova, Bolshoi Ballet Sch., Moscow, 1989; studied with Inna Zubkhovskaya, Alex. Stiopin, Lydia Goncharova, Valentina Chistova and Mararita Zagurskaya, studied with Mdm. Trafimova, Nina Sakhrouskaya and Valentina Rumyantsema, Vaganova Ballet Acad., St. Petersburg, Russia, 1993. Ballet mistress Adrian (Mich.) Coll., 1982-84; founder, artistic dir. Ann Arbor (Mich.) Ballet Theatre, 1980—. Former regional field judge Nat. Ballet Achievement Fund; dir. seminars Marygrove Coll., Detroit. Choreographer Cinderella, 1980, Nightingale, 1980, Nutcracker, 1984, Carnival of the Animals, 1981, Carmen, 1983, Midsummer Nights Dream, 1982, Vivaldi's Spring, 1990, Opulence, 1984, La Boutique Fantasque, 1995, Handel's Alcina, 1985, Gymnopedie, 1985, Gershwin's Preludes, 1996, Ravel's Bolero, 1997, Dracula, 1997, others. Ruth Mott grantee for choreography, 1982. Mem. Mich. Dance Assn. Avocations: gardening, reading, writing. Home: 6476 Huron River Dr Dexter MI 48130-9796 Office: CAS Ballet Theatre Sch Ann Arbor Ballet Theatre 548 Church St Ann Arbor MI 48104-2563

SCHATKEN, NANCY LEAH, medical editor; b. N.Y.C., Jan. 7, 1938; d. Robert V. and Lillian Belle (Neff) S. BS, U.N.C., 1959; cert. med. tech., Albany Sch. Med. Tech., 1960. Med. tech., instr. various orgns., 1960-66; acting mng. editor med. jours. Harper & Row, N.Y.C., 1966-69; assoc. editor Med. World News-McGraw-Hill, N.Y.C., 1969-70; owner, founder Mostly Med., N.Y.C., 1970—, St. James, Barbados, 1978-98. Avocations: travel, reading, swimming, entertaining. Address: 2677 Parkview Dr Hallandale FL 33009 Office Phone: 954-455-0039. E-mail: schatken@bellsouth.net.

SCHATTSCHNEIDER, DORIS JEAN, retired mathematics educator; b. N.Y.C., Oct. 19, 1939; d. Robert W. Jr. and Charlotte Lucile (Ingalls) Wood; m. David A. Schattschneider, June 2, 1962; 1 child, Laura E. AB, U. Rochester, 1961; MA, Yale U., 1963, PhD, 1966. Instr. in math. Northwestern U., Evanston, Ill., 1964—65; asst. prof. U. Ill., Chgo., 1965—68; prof. Moravian Coll., Bethlehem, Pa., 1968—2002, prof. emerita, 2003—. Project dir. Fund for the Improvement of Post-Secondary Edn. U.S. Dept. Edn., 1991—93, 1995—97; vis. scholar U. V.I., 2004. Author (with W. Walker): (books and models) M.C. Escher Kaleidocycles, 1977, 1987; co-author: (videos and activities) Visual Geometry Project, 1986—91; author: Visions of Symmetry, 1990, 2d edit., 2004; co-author: (videos and activities) A Companion to Calculus, 1995; editor: Geometry Turned On, 1997, M.C. Escher's Legacy, 2003. Exhbn. curator Allentown Art Mus., 1979, Payne Gallery, 1987. Grantee NEH rsch. grantee, 1988—90. Mem.: Assn. for Women in Math., Am. Math. Soc., Math. Assn. Am. (editor 1980—85, gov. 1980—89, 1st v.p. 1994—96, Allendoerfer award 1979, Meritorious Svc. award 1991, Dist. Math. Tchg. award 1993), Pi Mu Epsilon (councillor 1990—96). Mem. Moravian Ch. Office: Moravian College Math Dept PPHAC 1200 Main St Bethlehem PA 18018-6650 E-mail: schattdo@moravian.edu.

SCHAUB, MARILYN MCNAMARA, religion educator; b. Chgo., Mar. 24, 1928; d. Bernard Francis and Helen Katherine (Skehan) McNamara; m. Thomas Schaub, Oct. 25, 1969; 1 child, Helen Ann. BA, Rosary Coll., 1953; PhD, U. Fribourg, Switzerland, 1957; diploma, Ecole Biblique, Jerusalem, 1967. Asst. prof. classics and Bibl. studies Rosary Coll., River Forest, Ill., 1957-69; prof. Bibl. studies Duquesne U., Pitts., 1969-70, 73-01. Participant 8 archeological excavations, Middle East; hon assoc Am Schs Oriental Research, 1966—67, trustee, 1986—89; Danforth assoc, 1972—80; admin dir expedition to the Southeast Dead Sea Plains, Jordan, 1989—. Author: (book) Friends and Friendship for St. Augustine, 1964; translator (with H Richter): Agape in the New Testament, 3 vols, 1963—65. Mem.: Am Acad Religion, Cath Biblical Asn, Soc Biblical Literature. Democrat. Home: 25 Mckelvey Ave Pittsburgh PA 15218-1452

SCHAUB, THERESA MARIE, early childhood educator; b. Milw., Oct. 12, 1951; d. Joseph and Mary (Huberty) S. BS in Early Childhood, U. Wis., 1975. Cert. exceptional-edn.-early childhood, Wis. Kindergarten tchr. Sacred Heart, Milw., 1981-82, Ebenezer Child Care, Milw., 1982-83; presch.-head tchr. Ragamuffin Child Care, Milw., 1984-85, 86-87; asst. dir., head tchr. Country Kare, Albuquerque, 1985-86; kindergarten tchr. Holy Angels Sch., Milw., 1987-90, St. Rose Sch., Milw., 1990-94; head start tchr. Children's Outing Assn., Milw., 1994-96, Parkman Sch., Milw., 1996, Andrew S. Douglas Sch., Milw., 1996-97; kindergarten tchr. Sage program Maple Tree Sch., 1997—2000, Burbank Sch., 2000—. Supportive cons. St. Rose Sch., Milw., 1990-94, peer mediation supr., 1991-94, AV coord., 1990-94; parent vol. com. Children's Outing Assn., 1995-96 Author: ABC's of Peace, 1990. Pres. Young Dems.; vol. Homeless Shelter Casa Maria Hospitality, Milw., 1975-80; vol. tchr. Peacemakers Camp, Milw., 1992; bd. dirs. Clear Horizons Food Coop., Milw., 1978. Mem. Milw. Peace Ctr., NAEYC, Sierra Club, NOW, Nat. Audubon Soc., Wis. Edn. for Social Responsibility, Habitat for Humanity. Avocations: hiking, snowshoeing, traveling, listening to music, aerobics. Office: Burbank Sch 6035 W Adler Milwaukee WI

SCHAUENBERG, SUSAN KAY, retired counseling administrator; b. Taylor Ridge, Ill., Oct. 23, 1945; d. Albert George and Elizabeth (Stedman) Grill; m. Robert Dale Schauenberg Jr.; 1 child, Trevor Alan. BA, Marycrest Coll., 1967; MA, U. Iowa, 1968. Prof. Black Hawk Coll., Moline, Ill., 1971—, prof. emerita, 2001—. Bus. cons., Taylor Ridge, 1984—; v.p. faculty senate Black Hawk Coll., 1980-82. Author: Career Bingo, 1999. Planning com. United Way Orgn., Quad-Cities, Ill., 1981-84, agy. rels. com., 1981-82, allocations com., 1980-82; den mother Rock Island chpt. Boy Scouts Am., 1978-79; sponsor Christmas fundraiser for 100 children, yearly. Named one of Most Admired Women of the Quad-Cities, 1975; won L.I.V.E. Volunteerism honor for peer counselor-aide program, 1991. Mem. Am. Fedn. Tchrs., Ill. Guidance and Personnel Assn. (Black Hawk chpt.), U. Iowa Alumni Assn., Phi Gamma Delta (mem. Parents Assn.). Avocations: stained glass window designer, travel. Home: 8428 104th Ave W Taylor Ridge IL 61284-9210 Office: Black Hawk Coll 6600 34th Ave Moline IL 61265-5870

SCHAUER, CATHARINE GUBERMAN, public affairs specialist; b. Woodbury, N.J., Sept. 24, 1945; d. Jack and Anna Ruth (Felipe) Guberman; m. Irwin Jay Schauer, July 4, 1968; children: Cheryl Anne Schauer Crabb, Marc Cawin. AB, Miami-Dade Jr. Coll., 1965; BEd, U. Miami, 1967; postgrad., Mercer U., 1968; MPA, Troy State U., 1995. Writer Miami (Fla.) News, 1962-63; tchr. Dade County Schs., Miami, 1967-68; coord. pub. info. Macon (Ga.) Jr. Coll., 1968-69; writer Atlanta Jour., 1969-72; editor Ridgerunner, newspaper, Woodbridge, Va., 1973-75; pub. info. specialist U.S. Dept. Interior, Washington, 1980-82; writer Dept. Army, Ft. Belvoir, Va., 1982-84, chief prodn., design and editl. publs. divsn., 1984-85; head writer-editor S.E. region U.S. Naval Audit Svc., Virginia Beach, Va., 1986; pub. affairs specialist, tech. rep. for vis. ctr. ops. NASA Langley, 1986-90, project mgr., chmn. 75th anniversary yr., 1991-92; with NASA Langley Rsch. Ctr., Hampton, Va., 1987-89, acting head Office Pub. Svcs., 1989, pub. affairs officer for space, 1993—2002, interpers. govt. assignment to prof. Embry Riddle Aero U. Daytona Beach, Fla., 2001—03; prof. commn. Embry-Riddle Aeronautical U., Daytona Beach, Fla., 2003—. Columnist, writer Potomac News, Woodbridge, 1972-85; guest lectr. George Washington U. Grad. Sch.; apptd. mem. comm. program industry adv. bd. Embry-Riddle Aero. U., Dayton Beach, Fla., 2001—, bd. dirs. Sch. Comm. Contbr. articles to profl. jours. Historian, publicity chmn. PTO, Woodbridge, 1974; publicity chmn. Boy Scouts Am., Woodbridge, 1974-83, Girl Scouts U.S.A., Woodridge, 1974-79; bd. dirs. Congregation Ner Tamid, Woodbridge, 1984-85. Recipient Outstanding Tng. Devel. Support award U.S. Army, 1983, 1st place news writing award and 1st place for advt. design Fla. Jr. Coll. Press Assn., 1964, 1st place feature writing award, 1964, 1st place news writing award Sigma Delta Chi, 1965, 70th anniversary team NASA, 1988, Long Duration Exposure Facility Team award NASA, Combined Fed. Campaign Spl. award for Outstanding Svc. to Va. Peninsula, 1996, Discovery Team Excellence award NASA, 1998. Mem. Va. Press Women (1st place govt. mags. award 1991, 3d place govt. brochures award 1993, 1st place govt. media campaign award 1993, 2d place pub. svc. campaign award 1996, 1st place govt. pub. svc. campaign award 1996, 1st place pub. svc. campaign award 1997), Women in Comm., Nat. Fedn. Press Women (life, 1st place govt. mag. award 1991, 1st place govt. media campaign award 1993, 96, 1st place govt. internal comm. campaign award 1996, 3d place pub. svc. campaign award 1997, 1st pl. feature writing award 2003, 1st Place Pub. Svc. award 2003, Nat. award), Fla. Press Women (2d Pl. photography 2004, 2d Pl. feature mag. 2004, 3d Pl. newspaper article 2004), Internat. Assn. Bus. Communicators (1st place mktg. campaign award 1996, 1st place award of excellence for pub. svc. campaign 1996). Democrat. Office: Embry-Riddle Aero U Humanities and Social Scis Dept Rm A-210 600 S Clyde Morris Blvd Daytona Beach FL 32114-3900 E-mail: catharine.schauer@erau.edu.

SCHAUF, VICTORIA, pediatrician, educator, infectious diseases consultant; b. N.Y.C., Feb. 17, 1943; d. Maurice J. and Ruth H. (Baker) Bisson; m. Michael Delaney; 2 children. BS in Microbiology with honors, U. Chgo., 1965, MD with honors, 1969. Intern in pediat. U. Chgo. Hosp., 1969-70; resident in pediat. Sinai Hosp. of Balt., 1970-71; chief resident pediat. Children's Hosp. Nat. Med. Ctr., Washington, 1971-72; rsch. trainee NIH, Bethesda, Md., 1972; asst. prof. microbiology Rush Med. Coll., Chgo., 1972-74; prof. pediat., head pediatric infectious diseases U. Ill., Chgo., 1974-84, med. officer FDA, Rockville, Md., 1984-86; chmn. dept. pediat. Nassau County Med. Ctr., East Meadow, NY, 1986-90; prof. pediat. SUNY, Stony Brook, 1987-94. Vis. prof. Rockefeller U., 1990-92; mem. vis. faculty Chiang Mai (Thailand) U., 1978; mem. ad hoc com. study sects. NIH, Bethesda, 1981-82; bd. dirs. Pearl Stetler Rsch. Found., Chgo., 1982-84; cons. FDA, 1987-88, 93-95, Can. Bur. Human Prescription Drugs, Ottawa, 1990—, Biotech. Investors, 1993-95; course dir. pediat. infectious diseases rev. course Cornell U. Med. Coll., N.Y.C., 1994, faculty, 1995. Co-author: Pediatric Infectious Diseases: A Comprehensive Guide to the Subspecialty, 1997; prodr. radio and TV programs in field; contbr. articles to profl. jours., chpts. to books. Vol. physician Cook County Hosp., Chgo., 1974-84; mem. adv. com. Nat. Hansen's Disease Ctr., La., 1986, Nassau County Day Care Coun., N.Y., 1988-90; mem. adv. bd. Surg. Aid to Children of World, N.Y., 1986-90; commr., sec. Kern County Children and Families Commn., 1999-2002; sec., bd. dirs. Indian Wells Valley Cmty. Found., 2001-. Am. Lung Assn. grantee U. Ill., 1977; recipient contract NIH, U. Ill., 1978-81, grantee, 1979-84. Fellow Infectious Diseases Soc. Am.; mem. Pediatric Infectious Diseases Soc. (exec. bd.), Soc. Pediatric Rsch., Am. Pediatric Soc., AAAS, Am. Soc. Microbiology, Am. Acad. Pediat., Phi Beta Kappa, Alpha Omega Alpha. Avocation: walking.

SCHEALL, NORMA, writer, editor; b. Saginaw, Mich., Feb. 22, 1924; d. Frank August Leitow and Alma Lena Nickodemus-Leitow; m. Jack James Scheall, Oct. 11, 1941 (dec. May 9, 2003); 1 child, Theodore J. Grad., Famous Writers Correspondence Sch., 1970; BS, Ind. No. U., Gas City, 1972. Freelance editor Morris Harvey Coll., Charleston, W.Va., 1960—62; reporter Maysville Ledger, Ky., 1962—64; newsletter editor Blue Cross of S.W. Ohio, Cin., 1964—66; asst. dir. info. svcs. Ind. Vocat. Tech. Coll., Indpls., 1971—73; alumni editor Wichita State U., Kans., 1974—75; area rep. Dale Carnegie, Wichita, Kans., 1975—76; owner, pres. Air Purification Kans., Wichita, 1976—89; contbg. editor Thousand Trails Mag., Frisco, Tex., 1990—. Pub. Hoot Newsletter for Escapees-North Ranch, Congress, Ariz., 1998—. Author: (novels) Kepayshowink-The History of Camp Rotary, 1967, The Basham House Story, 1986. Mem.: Penwheels. Avocations: oil painting, RV travel, dogs, cooking, history. Home: 21250 Obsidian Congress AZ 85332

SCHEAR, BETTY Z. engineering executive, consultant; b. Dayton, Ohio, Dec. 17, 1925; d. Jacob Zukerman and Esther (Groban) Litwack; m. Burt E. Schear, July 4, 1948; children: Abe, Martin, Edith, Jesse. BS in Engring., U. Cin., 1948; MBA, U. Dayton, 1968. Assoc. editor Gardner Pubs., Cin., 1948-50; adminstrv. mgr. Schear Family Practice, Dayton, 1952-85; cons. Dayton, 1985—. Cons. Health Power, Inc., Columbus, Ohio, 1984-2000. One woman show U. Dayton, 1972. Mem. NSPE, NAFE, Nat. Mus. Women in the Arts (charter), Soc. Women Engrs., Am. Mgmt. Assn. Avocations: reading, art, travel, theater, music. Home: 4300 N Ocean Blvd # 8AB Fort Lauderdale FL 33308-5944 Home (Summer): Apt 4 927 Far Hills Ave Dayton OH 45419-3419

SCHECHTER, GERALDINE POPPA, hematologist; b. N.Y.C., Jan. 16, 1938; d. Josif and Victoria (Nosi) P.; m. Alan Neil Schechter, Feb. 6, 1965; children: Daniele Malka, Andrew M.R. AB, Vassar Coll., Poughkeepsie,

N.Y., 1959; MD, Columbia U., 1963. Diplomate Am. Bd. Internal Medicine (bd. dirs. 1990-95, mem. hematology com. 1985-91). Intern, then resident Presbyn. Hosp., N.Y.C., 1963-65; resident, fellow, rsch. assoc. VA Med. Ctr., Washington, 1965-70, staff physician, 1970-74, chief hematology, 1974—; asst., assoc. prof. medicine George Washington U., Washington, 1971-81, prof. medicine, 1981—. Residency rev. com. internal medicine Am. Coun. for Grad. Med. Edn., 1996—. Mem. editl. bd. Blood, 1985-89; contbr. articles to hematologic jours. Office: VA Med Ctr Hematology Sect 50 Irving St NW Washington DC 20422-0001

SCHECHTER, LYNN RENEE, psychologist; b. N.Y.C., July 7, 1969; d. Joel David and Sandra Bauman Schechter; m. Issam E. El-Zahr, July 8, 2001; 1 child, Leah Joy El-Zahr. BS, Cornell U., 1991; MA, Columbia U., 1992, EdM, 1996, PhD, 2001. Lic. psychologist N.Y. Sch. psychologist Reece Sch., N.Y.C., 1997—2000; psychologist Albert Einstein Coll. Medicine, Bronx, NY, 1997—2002; neurodevelopmentalist Jacobi Med. Ctr., Bronx, 2000—02; child behavior specialist The Drusilla Clinic, Baton Rouge, 2003—. Creator, dir. tutoring and mentoring program for children with HIV Jacobi Med. Ctr., Bronx, 2001—02. Mem.: APA (divsn. 16 sch. psychology), Golden Key, Kappa Delta Pi, Omicron Nu. Avocations: reading, music, sports. Office: The Drusilla Clinic 2356 Drusilla Ln Baton Rouge LA 70809

SCHECTER, ELLEN L. scriptwriter, television producer, educational consultant; b. Phila., Mar. 6, 1944; d. George and Pearl (Grossman) S.; m. James M. Altman, Sept. 27, 1980; children: Alexander, Anna. BA in English and Philosophy, Beaver Coll., 1966; MA in English and Comparative Lit., Hunter Coll., 1969. Head writer, assoc. prodr. Reading Rainbow PBS/Lancit Media, N.Y.C., 1979-86; co-writer, co-prodr. Miracle at Moreaux PBS/WQED, Washington, Pitts., 1983-85; writer, ednl. cons. TV series The Magic Schoolbus Scholastic/PBS, N.Y.C., 1989-90; ednl. cons., scriptwriter TV series Allegra's Window Topstone Prodn. & Nickelodeon, N.Y.C., 1992-96; exec. prodr. video Voices of Lupus Hosp. For Spl. Surgery, N.Y.C., 1991; dir. pub. and media Bank Street Coll. of Edn., N.Y.C., 1990—98. Tchr. Rhodes Sch., N.Y.C., 1967-69, Upward Bound, U. Mass., Boston, 1968-70; cons., writer CD-Roms Virgin Sound & Vision, L.A., 1995-96; cons. I Can Read CD-Roms HarperCollins Interactive, N.Y., 1994-95; ednl. adv. TV series Salty's Lighthouse, PBS and Discovery Channel; ednl. cons. Out of the Box TV series, Disney Channel, 1997-98 Author: (books) Career Connections, 1976, Work or Play?, 1976, Who? What? When?, 1976, Television Critikit, 1980, Voyage of the MIMI, 1985, Hide and Seek, 1986, Starting Free, 1987, The Warrior Maiden: A Hopi Legend, 1992, I Love to Sneeze, 1992, Sim Chung and the River Dragon, 1993, The Town Mouse and the Country Mouse, 1994, Sleep Tight, Pete, 1994, (with Doris Orgel and Emily Coplon) She'll Be Coming Round the Mountain, 1994, Diamonds and Toads, 1994, The Boy Who Cried Wolf, 1994, (with Orgel) The Flower of Sheba, 1994, (as Suzanne Altman with Orgel) My Worst Days Diary, 1995, Real-Live Monsters!, 1995, The Big Idea, 1996, The Pet-Sitters, 1996, Swim Like a Fish, 1997, The Family Haggadah, 1999, About Face, 2001, (online) Praxis Post: Bloodwork, 0502, Letter to My Son, 2001, Ducts.org, 2002, 03, Christian Science Monitor, Vaarwel, Vermeer: Men With Red Voices, At The Beginning, Movie In My Mind; cons., writer: Get Ready for School, Charlie Brown, Snoopy's Campfire Stories, Virgin Sound & Vision; scriptwriter (ednl. TV); exec. prodr., writer: (TV program) We're Here! (Nat. Endowment for Children's Ednl. TV 1997); scriptwriter David and Goliath video series The Children's Bible, Jumbo Pictures, N.Y.C., 1996. Mem. patient adv. bd. Hosp. for Spl. Surgery, N.Y.C.; dir. Bank Street Writers' Lab., N.Y.C., 1990—. Mem. ASCAP, PEN, Writer's Guild of Am., N.Y. Women in Film, Soc. of Children's Book Writers/Illustrators. Democrat. Jewish. Avocations: reading, window gardening, singing, swimming.

SCHECTER, KATE SARA, healthcare development executive; b. Montclair, NJ, Apr. 1, 1959; d. Jerrold and Leona Schecter; m. Ari Roth, June 30, 1985; children: Isabel, Sophie. BA, U. Mich., 1981; MA, Harvard U., 1986; PhD, Columbia U., 1992. Prof. U. Mich., Ann Arbor, 1993—97; cons. World Bank, Washington, 1997—2000; rschr. Carnegie Corp., NY, 1999—2003; program officer Am. Internat. Health Alliance, Washington, 2000—. Author: Boris Yeltsin, 1993; co-editor (with J. Twigg): Social Capital and Social Cohesion in Post-Soviet Russia, 2003. Mem. sch. bd. Jewish Primary Day Sch., Washington, 2000. Grantee, Nat. Coun. for Soviet and East European Rsch., Washington, 1997. Avocations: swimming, tennis, reading, gardening. Office: AIHA 1212 New York Ave Washington DC 20005

SCHEEL, KAREN RAE, psychologist; b. Dayton, Ohio, Feb. 12, 1964; d. Kenneth Richard and Julie (Johnson) Scheel; m. Loreto Richard Prieto, Dec. 19, 1998; 1 child, Indelisio Scheel. BA with honors, U. Calif., 1987; PhD, U. Iowa, 1999. Social svc. coord. Head Start, Omaha, 1988—92; adj. faculty Kirkwood C.C., Iowa City, 1994; pschology intern U. Counseling and Cons. Svcs. U. Minn., Mpls., 1996—97; asst. prof. U. Okla., Norman, Okla., 1998—2000, U. Akron, 2000—. Mem. editl. bd.: Jour. Mental Health Counseling, 2002—, Jour. Suicide and Life Threatening Behavior, —; contbr. articles to profl. jours. Scholar, U. Iowa, 1997, Iowa Psychol. Assn., 1997. Mem.: APA, Am. Mental Health Counselors Assn., Am. Assn. Sociology. Office: U Akron Collab Program Counseling Psychol Dept Counseling 127 Carroll Hall Akron OH 44325-5007 Office Phone: 330-972-8156.

SCHEETZ, SISTER MARY JOELLEN, English language educator; b. Lafayette, Ind., May 20, 1926; d. Joseph Albert and Ellen Isabelle (Fitzgerald) S. AB, St. Francis Coll., 1956; MA, U. Notre Dame, 1964; PhD, U. Mich., 1970. Tchr. English, Bishop Luers High Sch., Fort Wayne, Ind., 1965-67; acad. dean St. Francis Coll. (now U. St. Francis), Fort Wayne, 1967-68, pres. Ft. Wayne, Ind., 1970-93, pres. emeritus, English lang. prof., 1993—. Mem.: Delta Epsilon Sigma. Office: U St Francis 2701 Spring St Fort Wayne IN 46808-3939 E-mail: jscheetz@sf.edu.

SCHEFFEL, DONNA JEAN, elementary school educator; b. Balt., Sept. 20, 1953; d. G. Donald Scheffel and Mary LaVerne (Perry) Jones; 1 child, Amanda Lynne. BS, Salisbury (Md.) State Coll.; Cert., Baldwin-Wallace Coll., Berea, Ohio, 1983. Tchr. Wadsworth (Ohio) city schs., 1984-85, Parma (Ohio) city schs., 1984-85; elem. tchr. St. Leo the Great Sch., Cleve., 1985-91. Mem. team Early Prevention Sch. Failure; faculty rep. bd. dirs. Parent Tchr. Unit. Parma city schs., 1997—; 1st aux. svcs. computer sci. tchr. Bethel Christian Acad., Parma. Named one of Outstanding Young Women of Am., 1986. Mem.: ASCD, PEA, NEA, NAFE, Ohio Edn. Assn., N.E. Ohio Edn. Assn. Office: Bethel Christian Acad 12901 W Pleasant Valley Rd Parma OH 44130-5702

SCHEFFING, DIANNE ELIZABETH, special education educator; b. St. Louis, Mar. 17, 1963; d. Eugene Shibley Scheffing Jr. and Sarah Ann (Lukens) Scheffing. BS, Mo. Bapt. Univ., 1988; MA, Fontbonne Univ., St. Louis, 1999; postgrad., Webster U., St. Louis, 2002. Cert. elem. edn. grades 1-8 Mo., mild/moderate cross-category grades K-12 Mo., severely developmentally delayed 2002. Kindergarden tchr. asst. Andrews Acad., St. Louis, 1989—91; sci. tchr. edn. dept. St. Louis Sci. Ctr., 1994—96; tchr. asst. multi-handicapped Kehrs Mill Elem./Rockwood Sch. Dist., St. Louis, 1996—2000; tchr. spl. edn. Gateway/Hubert Wheeler State Sch. for Severely Handicapped, St. Louis, 2000—. Mem., sec. St. Louis Young Reps. Club, 1988—94; majority mem. Bethel #44 Internat. Order of Job's Daughters, Ballwin, 1978—84. Named Woman of Yr., St. Louis Young Reps. Club, 1992, 1994. Mem.: Am. Cancer Soc. Methodist. Avocations: Olympic supporter, bowling, traveling. Office: Gateway/Hubert Wheeler State Sch 100 S Garrison Saint Louis MO 63103

SCHEIBERG, SUSAN L. librarian; b. Chgo., Dec. 19, 1962; d. Steven M. Scheiberg, Margo Scheiberg. BA(hon.), Ind. U., 1984; MA, UCLA, 1986; MS in Libr. Sci., U. Ky., 1997. Grad. rsch. libr. U. So. Calif., 1997—98, team leader, serials acquisitions, 1998—2001; head acquisitions and serials, coord. outreach and cost-ctr. svcs. RAND Corp., Santa Monica, Calif., 2001—, assoc. dir., 2002—. Editor: (book) NASIG 2001: A Serials Odyssey, 2002, Transforming Serials: The Revolution Continues, 2003; contbr. articles to profl. jours. Fellow Univ., UCLA, 1984-1987; grantee Bardin Endowment Rsch., U. So. Calif., 1998, 1999, 2000. Mem.: ALA (Tony B. Leisner grantee 1996), Reference and User Svcs. Assn., Assn. Coll. & Rsch. Librs., N.Am. Serials Interest Group (proceedings editor 2000—), Libr. Adminstrn. and Mgmt. Assn., Assn. Libr. Collections and Tech. Svcs., Am. Folklore Soc., Spl. Librs. Assn., Beta Phi Mu, Phi Beta Kappa. Office Phone: 310-939-0411 x 6493.

SCHEID, ANN FRANCES, preservation planner, consultant; b. Rochester, Minn., Jan. 30, 1940; d. Joseph Frank and Clara Josephine (Larson) Underleak; m. John Allen Scheid, Dec. 24, 1977. AB in German, Vassar Coll., 1962; MA in Germanic Langs., U. Chgo., 1963, postgrad., 1964-68; M in Design Studies, Harvard U., 1993. Fgn. svc. officer USIA, Stockholm, 1963-65; sr. planner City of Pasadena, Calif., 1977-91; assoc. planner City of Redlands, Calif., 1991-92; archtl. historian Calif. Dept. Transp., L.A., 1992-95; prin. Ann Scheid, Pasadena, 1995—. Tchg. assoc. UCLA, 1975-76; adj. prof. Pasadena (Calif.) City Coll., 1978; archivist Greene and Greene Archives, U. So. Calif., 2000—; lectr. in field. Author: Pasadena: Crown of the Valley, 1986, The Valley Hunt Club: 100 Years, 1988, Historic Pasadena, 1999; contbr. chpts. to books and articles to profl. jours. NDEA fellow, 1966-68, Fulbright-Hays fellow, 1968-69. Mem. Am. Planning Assn., Nat. Trust Hist. Preservation, Soc. Archtl. Historians (bd. dirs. So. Calif. chpt. 1988-93), Soc. Am. City and Regional Planning History, Calif. Preservation Found., Calif. Coun. Promotion History, Hist. Soc. So. Calif. Home: 500 S Arroyo Blvd Pasadena CA 91105-2403 Office: Huntington Libr 1151 Oxford Rd San Marino CA 91108

SCHEID, CYNTHIA LOIUSE, music educator; b. Warren, Pa., Feb. 21, 1963; d. Stewart Raymond and Kay Van Ord; m. Eric Matthew Scheid, Oct. 11, 1986. MusB, Westminster Coll., 1985; MusM, Mansfield Univ. of Pa., 1986. Dir. Instrumental music Youngsville (Pa.) Midde Sch. HS, 1991—; orch. dir. All County Band, Warren, Pa., 2001, 2003; guest condr. Wilminton Menier Combined Concert, New Wilmington, Pa., 2002; flute instr.,ensemble dir., theory tchr. The Clarion Univ. Summer Band Clinic. Female mem. Phi Beta Mu Chpt. of The Am. Band Masters Assn., 2003; band performance St. Patricks Cathedral and St. Patricks Day Parade, Dublin. Host Pa. Music Edcators Assn. Dist. 2 Band Festival, Youngswille, Pa., 2000, 2002. Recipient Music Tchr. of The Yr., Philamel Club, 2003, Outstanding Women Educator, Delta Kappa Gamma Soc. Internat., 2001, nom., Phi Beta Mu Chpt. of the Am. Band Masters Assn., 2002, graduate asstantship, Mansfield Univ. of Pa. Mem.: lakeshore Marching Band Assn., Pa. Music Educators Assn., Order Of The Eastern Star. Home: 179 Buena Vista Blvd Warren PA 16365 Office: Youngsville Middle/HS 227 College Street Youngsville PA 16371

SCHEID, LINDA J. state legislator; b. June 16, 1942; 2 children. BA, Coe Coll.; JD, William Mitchell Coll. Law. Bar: Minn. Mem. Minn. Ho. of Reps., 1976, 82-90; mem. 47th dist. Minn. Senate, St. Paul, 1996—. Home: 6625 81st Ave N Brooklyn Park MN 55445-2513 Office: 317 Capitol 75 Constitution Ave Saint Paul MN 55155-1601

SCHEIDLER, ELANA DAWN, elementary school educator, art educator; b. Marquette, Mich., May 16, 1964; d. Roy James and Jessie Marie Woods; m. David Michael Scheidler, May 21, 1988; children: Whitney Marie, Michaela Nicole. BA in Instrumental Music Performance cum laude, Spring Arbor Coll., 1986, Secondary Music Edn. k-12, 1990, tchg. cert. in secondary music edn. K-12. Cert. secondary profl. tchr. Western Mich. U., 1999. Band dir. Coldwater (Mich.) Cmty. Schs., 1991—95, elem. music tchr., 1995—2003, elem. art tchr., 1999—. Pvt. instrumental instr., Coldwater, 1982—; colorguard instr. Coldwater H.S. Band, 1990—96, 2002—03. Participant Relay for Life/Walk for the Cure, Coldwater, 2003; co-dir. Power of Love Teen Group, Coldwater, 2002—03. Mem.: Coldwater Edn. Assn. (assoc.; elem. rep. 2002—03), Mich. Edn. Assn. (assoc.), Nat. Art Edn. Assn. (assoc.). Avocations: painting, perform in a christian rock band, performing with a family trio, dancing- tap and jazz, quilting. Home: 765 Tomahawk Trail Coldwater MI 49036 Office: Coldwater Cmty Schs Michigan Ave Coldwater MI 49036 Personal E-mail: scheidlered@cbpu.com.

SCHEIDT, REBECCA LYNNELL, psychologist, educator; b. Escondido, Calif., June 25, 1972; d. Charlene Johnston, James Preston Johnston; m. Billy Clayton Scheidt. MA in Psychology and Counseling, La. Bapt. U., PhD in Psychology and Counseling, 2001. Cert. sch. counselor Assn. Christina Schs. Internat. Visual merchandiser, sSales Barsa, El Centro, Calif., 1987—88; merchandiser, mgr. The Wet Seal, San Diego, 1989—93; counselor, sch. psychologist The Acad. of San Antonio, 1994—98; sch. psychologist, tchr. The Christian Academy, Shelbyville, Ky., 1998—. Counselor Charlie Home Foster Care, El Centro, 1988—90. Author: A Handbook for Parents of Teenagers, 2001. Mem.: Ky. Assn. Christian Counselors. Baptist. Avocations: orchid breeding, reading. Office: Cornerstone Christian Acad 5425 Frankfort Rd Shelbyville KY 40065 Office Phone: 502-633-4070. Home Fax: 502-633-9257.

SCHEIERMAN, MINDY, music educator, consultant; b. Bklyn., Aug. 20, 1964; m. Christopher J. Tarantino, June 30, 1996. MusB, Ithaca Coll., N.Y., 1986, MusM, 1987. Cert. tchr. k-12 instrumental music N.J., 1986, N.Y., 1986. Adj. prof. of music William Paterson U., Wayne, NJ; dir. of bands Millburn HS, 1998—. Clinician and regional artist Yamaha Corp. of Am.; guest condr. bands. Contbr. articles Tempo mag. of N.J. Music Educators Assn. (Tchg. Excellence Chamber Music Am., 2001). Band divsn. and festival chair Njmea, Njsma, NJ, 1990—2003. Mem.: CBDNA, WASBE, N.J. Music Educators Assn., Music Educators Nat. Conf., Am. Fedn. Musicians. Home: 14 Normandy Blvd West Convent Station NJ 07961 Personal E-mail: minchris@aol.com.

SCHEIN, VIRGINIA ELLEN, psychologist, editor; b. June 23, 1943; d. Jacob Charles and Anne Schein; m. Rupert F. Chisholm; 1 child, Alexander Nikos. BA cum laude, Cornell U., 1965; PhD, NYU, 1969. Lic. psychologist, Pa. Sr. rsch. assoc. Am. Mgmt. Assn., N.Y.C., 1969-70; mgr. personnel rsch. Life Office Mgmt. Assn., N.Y.C., 1970-72; dir. personnel rsch. Met. Life Ins. Co., N.Y.C., 1972-75; assoc. prof. Sch. Mgmt. Case Western Res. U., Cleve., 1975-76; vis. assoc. prof. Sch. Orgn. and Mgmt. Yale U., New Haven, 1977-80; mgmt. cons. Va. E. Schein, PhD, P.C., 1975—; assoc. prof. psychology Bernard M. Baruch Coll. CUNY, 1982-85; prof. mgmt. and psychology Gettysburg Coll., Pa., 1986—, chair mgmt. dept., 1993-95. Co-author: Power and Organization Development, 1988; author: Working from the Margins, 1995; mem. editl. rev. bds. Women Mgmt. Rev., Acad. Mgmt. Execs.; contbr. articles to profl. jours. Bd. dirs. Family Planning Ctr., 1988-91, Pvt. Industry Coun., 1990-93, Keystone Rsch. Ctr., 1996-98, Women Cmty. Svc., 1997-2003; bd. dirs. Survivors, Inc., pres. bd. dirs., 1991-92, Adams County Children and Youth Adv. Bd., 2003—. Mem.: APA (coun.rep. 1978—80, com. women 1980—83), Internat. Assn. Applied Psychology (divsn. orgnl. psychology chair sci. program com. 1995—98, pres.-elect 1998—2002, pres. 2002—), Acad. Mgmt. (rep. orgn.devel. divsn. 1979—81, exec. com. women mgmt. divsn.), Met. Assn. Applied Psychology (pres. 1973—74), Psi Chi. Office: Gettysburg Coll Dept Mgmt Gettysburg PA 17325 Office Phone: 717-337-6653.

SCHELL, JOAN BRUNING, information specialist, business science librarian; b. N.Y.C., June 9, 1932; d. Walter Henry and Gertrude Emily (Goossen) Bruning; m. Harold Benton Schell, Aug. 27, 1955 (div. 1978); children: Jeffrey Mark, Sue Lynne. AB, Wittenberg U., 1954; postgrad., Syracuse U., 1963, U. Md., 1965 66; MLS, U. Pitts., 1968. Actuarial, claims asst. Nationwide Ins., Columbus, Ohio, 1954-57; tech. report typist Cornell U., Ithaca, N.Y., 1957; bus. libr. asst. U. Pitts., 1969; bus. reference libr. Dallas Pub. Libr., 1971-73, Pub. Libr. Cin. and Hamilton County, Cin., 1973-79; book selection coord. Pub. Libr. Cin. & Hamilton County, Cin., 1979-83, asst. to main libr., 1983-85; literacy tutor Cin. LEARN, 1985-89; recorder feminist lit. Womyn's Braille Press, Mpls., 1985-89; wellness program asst. Times Pub. Co., St. Petersburg, Fla., 1989-96, Taoist Tai Chi Soc., 1995-99. Dir. Wittenberg U., Springfield, Ohio, 1988-2000, emeritus, dir., 2000; bd. dirs. Crazy Ladies Ctr. Inc., Cin., 1989-93; sec., trustee Clio Found., Inc., 1995-98, seniornet, 1998—; docent Fla. Internat. Mus., 1994-2000. Compiler: (reference source) Greater Cincinnati Business Index, 1975-79; editor: New Reference Materials, 1983, 84. Mem. Tampa Bay YWCA Women's Guild, St. Petersburg, 1991-95; vol. NOW Elect Women Campaign, St. Petersburg, 1990-92, Senator Helen G. Davis Reelection, St. Petersburg, 1992; mem. Fla. Internat. Mus., 1994-2000; choir mem. First Unity Ch., libr. com. Mem. ALA, Spl. Librs. Assn. (treas., archivist 1974-83), Beta Phi Mu Libr. Sci. Hon., Phi Delta Gamma Grad. Women Hon. Avocations: travel, reading, figure skating fan, yoga, swimming. Address: PO Box 7472 Saint Petersburg FL 33734-7472

SCHELL, MARY ELIZABETH, secondary school educator; b. Ft. Worth, Tex., May 13, 1922; d. Walter John and Marie Magdalene (Connelly) Nobles; m. James Hays Schell, Sept. 8, 1943; children: James Schell Jr., Elizabeth Jean. BS, North Tex. State U., 1941, MS, 1943. Cert. counselor coord., dir., Tex.; cert. tchr., Tex., Fla., Okla. Tchr. h.s., Peaster, Tex., 1941-42, Andrews, Tex., 1942-43, Lawton, Okla., 1943-44; supr. North Tex. State U., Denton, 1945-47; tchr., writer, coord., dir. Houston Ind. Sch. Dist., 1960-86; owner Schell Puppet Prodns., Houston, 1986—. Writer U.S. Army, Ft. Monmouth, N.J., 1945-46. Author: (radio programs) Texas School of the Air, 1946, (book series) The Adventures of Mrs. Sea Shell. Vol. leader Cub Scouts, Houston, 1955-57, Brownies, Houston, 1958-59; vol. ch. tchr., Houston, 1970-73; dir. Citizens Patrol, Houston, 1988-94; vol. dir. summer workshops, Houston, 1994-95. Nominee Nat. Contest for Outstanding Tchr., 1947; named Area II Outstanding Tchr., Iota Lambda Sigma, 1979-80. Mem. Delta Kappa Gamma (v.p. 1973—). Avocations: writing, directing plays, music. Home and Office: Schell Puppet Prodns 4402 Lorinda Dr Houston TX 77018-1113

SCHELLING, JOYCE ELAINE, communications executive, educator; b. Fort Wayne, Ind., Oct. 14, 1937; d. George Martin and Lucille Alice (Schuckel) Schelling. BA, St. Francis Coll., 1962; MA, Catholic U., 1968; PhD, NYU, 1987. Lic. tchr., Ind., N.J. Dir. drama St. Francis Coll., Ft. Wayne, 1966-70; instr. South Plainfield (N.J.) High Sch., 1970-80, NYU, N.Y.C., 1980-82; account exec. On-Line Software, Fort Lee, N.J., 1982-86, SDI, Hackensack, N.J., 1986-88, Microbank Software, Inc., N.Y.C., 1988-91, Performance Mgmt., Inc., N.Y.C., 1991-95, BBN Planet, Inc., N.Y.C., 1995-96, AT&T, N.Y.C., 1996—2002. Mem. NAFE, NOW. Women's Health Initiative Democrat. Avocations: literature, languages, theater, sports, horses. Home: 2100 Linwood Ave Apt 15R Fort Lee NJ 07024-3159

SCHELLINGER, ANN GOODWIN, medical manager; b. Miami, Fla., Mar. 11, 1945; d. Lynn Banks and Annabel (Weems) Goodwin; m. Robert Paul Schellinger, July 29, 1967; children: Anastasia, Robert Lynn, Ashley Miles. BS, U. Miami, Coral Gables, Fla., 1965. Med. bus. mgr., cons. numerous physicians Humble (Tex.) med. cmty., 1985—. Mem. NAFE, Nat. Assn. Profl. Women, Nat. Assn. Health Care Profls. (pres. Jackson, Miss. chpt. 1990-91; v.p. Spring, Tex. chpt. 1992). Presbyterian. Avocations: painting, collecting raggedy ann dolls, antiques, attending flea markets. Home: 3622 Postwood Dr Spring TX 77388-5061 Office: Sam Governale MD 20202 Highway 59 N Ste 350 Humble TX 77338-2403

SCHEMMEL, RACHEL ANNE, food science and human nutrition educator, researcher; b. Farley, Iowa, Nov. 23, 1929; d. Frederic August and Emma Margaret (Melchert) Schemmel. BA, Clarke Coll., 1951; MS, U. Iowa, 1952; PhD, Mich. State U., 1967. Dietitian Children's Hosp. Soc., L.A., 1952-54; instr. Mich. State U., East Lansing, 1955-63, from asst. prof. to prof. food sci., human nutrition, 1967—. Author: Nutrition Physiology and Obesity, 1980; contbr. articles to profl. jours. Recipient Disting. Alumni award Mt. Mercy Coll., 1971, Borden award, 1986, Outstanding Alumni award U. Iowa, 1996, Mich. State U., 2002, Outstanding Achievement award Clarke Coll., 1997. Fellow: Am. Soc. Nutrition Scis.; mem.: Soc. for Nutrition Edn., Brit. Nutrition Soc., Am. Diet Assn. (pres. Mich. 1976—77, pres. Lansing 1960, Outstanding Dietetic Educator award 1988), Inst. Food Technologists, Am. Assn. Family and Consumer Scis. (chair nutrition health and food mgmt. divsn. 1995—97, Outstanding Leader award 1998), Phi Kappa Phi (pres. 1994—95), Sigma Xi (pres. Mich. State U. chpt. 1983—84, Sr. Rsch award 1986). Roman Catholic. Home: 1341 Red Leaf Ln East Lansing MI 48823-1339 Office: Mich State U Dept Food Sci Nutrit East Lansing MI 48824 E-mail: schemmel@msu.edu.

SCHENDEL, KELLY RYAN, literature educator, writer; b. Phila., Dec. 5, 1950; d. James and Beatrice Elizabeth (Brown) Wobensmith, Charles W. Kelly (Stepfather); m. Ronald L. Schendel, Aug. 22, 1992; 1 child, Amy J. AA English, El Camino Coll., Torrance, Calif., 1998; BA English, Calif. State U., Long Beach, Calif., 2001, MFA English, creative writing, 2003. Cert.: U. of So. Calif. Law Ctr. (Law Practice Mgmt.) 1988; Transportation Demand Mgmt. UCLA, 1994. Legal adminstr. Ball, Hunt, Hart, Brown & Baerwitz, Los Angeles, Calif., 1988—90, Arter, Hadden, Lawler, Felix & Hall, Los Angeles, Calif., 1990—92; freelance writing/editing Kelly Schendel & Associates, Manhattan Beach, Calif., 1992—; faculty, English Calif. State U., Long Beach, Calif., 2001—, Orange Coast Coll., Costa Mesa, Calif., 2002—. Human resources cons. Sitag USA, Inc., Irvine, Calif., 1994—2001, Michael Devine & Associates, Manhattan Beach, Calif., 1994—2001; freelance writer City of Torrance, Torrance, Calif., 1996—; freelance editor Stephen Decker & Associates, Culver City, Calif., 2000—; human resources cons. dTank, Inc., Los Angeles, Calif., 2002—. Author: (humor columns) Daily Breeze Newspaper; author: (magazine) (articles) Women's World; mng. editor (lit. jour.) Rip Rap. Recipient Long Beach Professional Writer's Award for Best Novel in Progress, Long Beach Professional Writer's Assn., 2001; scholar Phi Kappa Phi Scholarship, Phi Kappa Phi Honor Soc., 2001. Mem.: Phi Kappa Phi (Phi Kappa Phi Scholarship 2001), Golden Key Honor Soc. (life), Nat. Honor Soc. (life), Sigma Tau Delta, English Honor Soc. (life). D-Liberal. Avocations: travel, cooking, entertaining.

SCHENK, SUSAN KIRKPATRICK, nursing educator, consultant, small business owner; b. New Richmond, Ind., Nov. 29, 1938; d. William Marcius and Frances (Kirkpatrick) Gaither; m. Richard Dee Brown, Aug. 13, 1960 (div. Feb. 1972); children: Christopher Lee, David Michael, Lisa Catherine; m. John Francis Schenk, July 24, 1975 (widowed Apr. 1995). BSN, Ind. U., 1962; postgrad., U. Del., 1973-75. RN, PHN, BCLS; cert. community coll. tchr., Calif.; cert. vocat. edn. tchr., Calif. Staff nurse, then asst. dir. nursing Bloomington (Ind.) Hosp., 1962-66; charge nurse Newark (Del.) Manor, 1967-69; charge nurse GU Union Hosp., Terre Haute, Ind., 1971-72; clin. instr. nursing Ind. State U., Terre Haute, 1972-73; clin. instr. psychiatric nursing U. Del., Newark, 1974-75; psychiatric nursing care coord. VA Med. Ctr., Perry Point, Md., 1975-78; from nurse educator to cmty. rels. coord. Grossmont Hosp., La Mesa, Calif., 1978—91; dir. psychiat. svcs. Scripps Hosp. East County, El Cajon, Calif., 1991-97; nursing instr., adult edn. Grossmont Union H.S. Dist., La Mesa, 1996—. Tech. advisor San Diego County Bd. Supervisors, 1987; tech. cons. Remedy Home and Health Care, San Diego, 1988; expert panelist Srs. Speak Out, KPBS-TV, San Diego,

1988; guest lectr. San Diego State U., 1987. Editor: Teaching Basic Caregiver Skills, 1988; author, performer tng. videotape Basic Caregiver Skills, 1988. Mem. patient svcs. com. Nat. Multiple Sclerosis Soc., San Diego, 1986-89; bd. dirs. Assn. for Quality and Participation, 1989. Adminstrn. on Aging/DHHS grantee, 1988. Mem. Ind. U. Alumni Assn. (life), Calif. Coun. Adult Edn., Mensa, Sigma Theta Tau. Avocations: piano, gardening, reading. Home and Office: 9435D Carlton Oaks Dr Santee CA 92071-2582 E-mail: susansks@aol.com.

SCHENKEL, SUZANNE CHANCE, retired natural resource specialist; b. Phila., Mar. 12, 1940; d. Henry Martyn Chance II and Suzanne (Sharpless) Jameson; m. John Lackland Hardinge Schenkel, June 15, 1963 (div. 2002); children: John Jr., Andrew Chance. BS in Edn., Tufts U., 1962. Tchr. Roland Pk. Country Sch., Balt., 1962-65; exec. dir. Mass. Citizens' Com. for Dental Health, Springfield, 1981-83; pub., editor Women's Investment Newsletter, Longmeadow, Mass., 1985-89; pub. affairs officer USDA's Soil Conservation Svc., Amherst, Mass., 1990-93; resource conservationist conservation & ecosys. assistance divsn. USDA's Natural Resources Conservation Svc., Washington, 1993-97; ops. partnership liaison East Regional Office, Beltsville, Md., 1997—2002; ret., 2002. Staff Merchant Marine and Fisheries com. U.S. Ho. of Reps., Washington, 1993. Author Wetlands Protection and Management Act. Chmn. Longmeadow (Mass.) Conservation Commn., 1984-90; supr. Hampden County (Mass.) Conservation Dist., 1985-90; bd. dirs., v.p. League of Women Voters of Mass., Boston, 1974-85; exec. com. Water Supply Citizens' Adv. Com.; adv. bd. Water Resources Authority, Mass., 1979-90; bd. dirs. Alliance for Chesapeake Bay, 2001. Mem. Soil and Water Conservation Soc., Nat. Assn. Conservation Dists. Episcopalian. Avocations: golf, tennis, sailing. Home: 304 W Coral Trace Cl Delray Beach FL 33445 Personal E-mail: sschenke@adelphia.net.

SCHENKENBERG, MARY MARTIN, principal; b. Oakland, Calif., Nov. 29, 1944; d. Leo Patrick and Florence Kathryn (Brinkoetter) Martin; m. Philip Rawson Schenkenberg III, Aug. 20, 1966; children: Philip Rawson IV, Amy Lynn, Stephen Patrick. BA in English, Fontbonne Coll., 1966; MA Teaching in English, St. Louis U., 1975, PhD in English, 1991. Cert. tchr., Mo. Asst. prof. Fontbonne Coll., St. Louis, 1978-85; English dept. chair Nerinx Hall High Sch., St. Louis, 1979-89; asst. prof. Webster U., St. Louis, 1986-89; co-prin. Nerinx Hall High Sch., St. Louis, 1989-92, prin., 1992—. Adj. prof. St. Louis U., 1985-89; advanced placement reader Ednl. Testing Svc., Princeton, N.J., 1986-89. Author: (with others) The English Classroom in the Computer Age, 1991. Bd. pres. Mary, Queen of Peace Sch., St. Louis, 1977. Mem. ASCD, Nat. Coun. Tchrs. English, Greater St. Louis Tchrs. English (bd. dirs. 1989—). Roman Catholic. Avocations: tennis, theater, travel. Office: Nerinx Hall High Sch 530 E Lockwood Ave Webster Groves MO 63119-3278

SCHEPARTZ, ALANNA, biochemist, educator; b. N.Y.C., Jan. 9, 1962; m. Thomas E. Schrader; 1 child, Abigail BS, SUNY, Albany, 1982; PhD in Chemistry, Columbia U., 1987. NIH fellow Calif. Inst. Tech., 1988; asst. prof. Yale U., New Haven, Conn., 1988-92, assoc. prof. chemistry, 1992-94, Milton Harris assoc. prof. chemistry, 1994-95, prof., 1995—. Contbr. numerous articles to profl. jours. Recipient Presdl. Young Investigator award NSF, 1991, Camille and Henry Dreyfus Teacher-Scholar award, 1993; David and Lucille Packard Found. fellow, 1991, Eli Lilly Biochemistry fellow, 1991, Alfred P. Sloan Rsch. fellow, 1994. Mem. Am. Chem. Soc. (Arthur C. Cope Scholar award 1995, Eli Lilly award 1997). Achievements include research in bioorganic chemistry.

SCHER, LAURA SUSAN, financial company executive; b. Passaic, N.J., Jan. 18, 1959; d. Alan E. and Frances Scher; m. Ian H. Altman, May 28, 1984. BA in Econs., Yale U., 1980; MBA, Harvard U., 1985. Assoc. cons. Bain & Co., Boston, 1981-83; chief exec. officer Working Assets Funding Service, San Francisco, 1985—. Named Baker Scholar, Harvard U., 1985.

SCHERBER, AMY, food service executive; Degree, N.Y. Restaurant Sch. Line cook, pastry cook Bouley Restaurant; bread baker Mondrian restaurant; pastry chef, owner Amy's Bread, N.Y.C., 1992—; owner 3 retail cafes, N.Y.C., store, N.Y.C., 2001—. Tchr. baking various local culinary schs.; bd. dirs. Bread Bakers Guild Am., Women Chefs and Restauranteurs. Author: (books) Amy's Bread cookbook; appeared (TV series) Food Network, guest appearances (numerous TV cooking shows). Named Amy's Bread one of top bread bakeries, N.Y. Times, N.Y. Mag., Time Out N.Y., Gourmet, Food and Wine, Amy's Bread 3rd in Top 100 Bangs for the Buck in N.Y.C., Zagat Survey Restaurants, 2001, Amy's Bread Top 100 favorite cafes and restaurants in N.Y., 2001, N.Y. Woman Bus. Owner of Yr., Nat. Assn. Women Bus. Owners, 1999, Woman of Yr., Profl. Women's Exchange, 2001, N.Y.'s Woman of Power and Influence, 2001; named one of 30 Rising Bus. Owners in Young Millionaires article, Entrepreneur Mag.; named to 40 Under 40 Rising Stars in Bus., Crain's N.Y. Bus., 1997. Office: Amy's Bread 75 Ninth Ave New York NY 10011

SCHERMAN, CAROL E. human resources professional; married; three children. BS in Orgnl. Behavior, U. San Francisco. With Bergen Brunswig Corp., exec. v.p. human resources. CEO Medi-Mail, Inc. subs. Bergen Brunswig Corp., Las Vegas. Active Human Resources Exec. Forum of Orange County; mem. human resources adv. com. Chapman U., Orange. Office: Bergen Brunswig Corp 4000 W Metropolitan Dr Orange CA 92868-3510

SCHERSTEN, KATHERINE ANNE, volunteer; b. Eau Claire, Wis., Sept. 22, 1941; d. Robert John Conley and Bettie Margaret Conley (Jobs) Helis; m. H. Donald Schersten, Jan. 20, 1973. Student, Nat. U. Mex., Mexico City, 1962; BA, St. Mary's Dominican Coll., New Orleans, 1964. Cert. tchr. La., Fla. Tchr. Orleans Sch. Bd., New Orleans, 1964; tchr. 5th grade Colegio Karl Parrish, Barranquilla, Colombia, 1964-65; tchr. Academia La Castellana, Caracas, Venezuela, 1965-67; ESOL tchr. Lang. Inst., Madrid, 1967-68, ESOL tchr., owner Caracas, 1968-69; tchr. Colegio Internacional de Caracas, 1968-73. Acad. olympics moderator Edn. Found., Sarasota, 1984—; mem. appeals bd. Sarasota County Sch. Bd., 1984—85. Mem. Sarasota Civic League, 1984—; campaign mgr. Tax Collector, Sarasota, 1984, 1988, 1992; bd. dirs. Edn. Found., Sarasota, 1996—2002, chmn. bd. dirs., 2001—02; chmn. bd. govs. Sr. Friendship Ctrs., 1997—99; chmn. adv. bd. Van Wezel Performing Arts Hall, 1990; pres. Women's Resource Ctr., 1985—90. Named to Hall of Fame, Cmty. Video Archives, 2001; recipient Cert. of Recognition, County of Sarasota, 1992, 1994. Mem.: AAUW (pres. 1982—84), Hispanic Am. Assn. (pres. bd. dirs. 1986—87, Cmty. award 1985), Sr. Friendship Ctrs. Found. (trustee 1995—2000), Exxon Annuitants Club (pres. bd. dirs. 1992—94). Roman Catholic. Avocations: volunteering, reading.

SCHETLIN, ELEANOR M. retired university official; b. NYC, July 15, 1920; d. Henry Frank and Elsie (Chew) Schetlin. BA, Hunter Coll., 1940; MA, Tchrs. Coll., Columbia U., 1942, EdD, 1967. Playground dir. Dept. Parks, N.Y.C., 1940-42; libr. Met. Hosp. Sch. Nursing, N.Y.C., 1943-44, dir. recreation and guidance, 1945-58, historian Alumnae Assn., 2000—03; coord. student activities SUNY, Plattsburgh, 1959-63, asst. dean students, 1963-64; asst. prof., coord. student personnel svcs. CUNY, Hunter Coll., 1967-68; asst. dir. student personnel Columbia U., Coll. Pharm. Scis., N.Y.C., 1968-69, dir. student personnel, 1969-71; assoc. dean students Health Scis. Ctr. SUNY, Stony Brook, 1971-73, asst. v.p. student svcs., 1973-74, assoc. dean students, dir. student svcs., 1974-85. Founding mem. Sea Cliff unit 300 Nassau County Aux. Police; founding mem. Nassau NOW Women of Color Task Force. Contbr. articles to profl. jours.; author: Myths of the Student Personnel Point of View. Recipient NOW Alliance PAC award, 1991, 1999, Lifetime Achievement award, Nassau NOW, 1992, Task Force Women of Color award, NOW, 1994. Mem.: So. Poverty Law Ctr., Wellesley Ctrs. Rsch. Women, Nat. Women's History Project, Women's Environment and Devel. Orgn., Nat. Women's Studies Assn., Nat. Assn. Women Edn., Nat. Mus. Women in the Arts. Home: 60 Hildreth Pl East Hampton NY 11937

SCHEU, LYNN MCLAUGHLIN, scientific publication editor, secondary school educator; b. Lancaster, Ohio, July 9, 1942; d. Franklin Neil and Carol Lois (Bigham) McLaughlin; m. Richard V. Scheu, Apr. 16, 1966; children: David Edward, Michael Patrick. BS, Auburn U., 1964; postgrad., Ohio State U., 1964-66. English, French tchr. Reynoldsburg (Ohio) H.S., 1966-70; adj. curator mollusks Mus. History & Sci., Louisville, 1978-85; editor Am. Conchologist, Louisville, 1987—; tchr. English, French and humanities Franklin H.S., Frankfort, Ky., 2000—. Chairperson Lambis Group, 1996; mem. editl. adv. bd. Bailey Matthews Shell Mus. and Ednl. Found., Sanibel, Fla., 1988—. Editor (website) The Conchologist's Information Network (ConchNet). Mem. exec. bd. Friends of Libr., Louisville, 1989-95; mem. Mayor's Task Force on Librs., Louisville, 1988-89. Mem. Conchologists Am. (bd. dirs. 1987—). Avocations: shell collecting, fossils, landscape gardening, genealogy. Home and Office: 1222 Holsworth Ln Louisville KY 40222-6616 E-mail: amconch@mindspring.com.

SCHEUBLE, KATHRYN JEAN, social worker, family therapist; b. Pitts., Sept. 4, 1951; d. Charles Joseph and Ann Mary (Powers) S. BA in Social Work, Pa. State U., 1973; MSW, Ohio State U., 1982; postgrad. cert., U. Pitts., 1997. Lic. social worker, Pa.; cert. home and sch. visitor, Pa. Foster care caseworker Family and Children's Svcs., Pitts., 1973-80; clin. instr. child psychiatry Ohio State U. Dept. Psychiatry, Columbus, 1982-86; chief social worker Western Psychiat. Inst., U. Pitts. Med. Ctr., 1986—. Vol. Carnegie Museum, Pitts., 1992-93, Columbus Ensemble Theater, 1985-86. Mem. NASW, Nat. Alliance for the Mentally Ill, Pa. Assn. Social Workers. Avocation: travel. Office: Western Psychiat Inst & Clinic 3811 Ohara St Pittsburgh PA 15213-2593

SCHEUERER, DIANE THOMSPON, home economics educator; b. Stuart, Fla., Jan. 23, 1943; d. Frances Earl Thomspon and Ida Ann (Minschke) Nall; m. Daniel Thomas Scheuerer, June 11, 1966; children: Daniel "Todd", David W. BS, Barry Coll., 1965. cert. vocat. home econ. tchr., Fla. Tchr. Melbourne (Fla.) High Sch., 1965-66, Southwest Jr. High, Melbourne, 1966-67, Cen. Cath. High Sch., Melbourne, 1971-79; tchr. edn. of teenage parents Brevard County Sch. Bd., Melbourne, 1979—. Adv. bd. mem. Child Care Aide Adv. Com., South Brevard, Fla., 1990—. Active West of EauGallie Civic Assn., Melbourne, 1986—, Ascension Cath. Women's Guild, Melbourne, 1990—. Recipient Nat. Second Place award Nat. FEdn. Indep. Bus., Washington, 1990, Second Place Entrepreneurship award Fla. Coun. on Econ. Edn., Tapma, 1991, Martha Schenck Priv. Enterprise Edn. award U. Cen. Fla., Orlando, 1992, Nat. Hon. Mention award Joint Coun. on Econ. Edn., New Orleans, 1992, Burps, Bibs, Bonnets Leavey award Freedoms Found., Beverly Hills, 1992. Mem. Am. Home Econ. Assn. (local arrangements com.), Fla. Vocat. Assn., Fla. Home Econs. Assn., Cen. Fla. Home Econs. Assn. (sec. 1992—), Brevard Vocat. Assn. Roman Catholic. Avocations: gardening, sewing, club work. Office: Sch Bd Brevard County 1400 Commodore Blvd Melbourne FL 32935-4122

SCHEUERLE, ANGELA ELIZABETH, geneticist; b. Syracuse, N.Y., Aug. 13, 1962; d. William Howard and Jane Frances (Walker) S.; m. Alan Joseph Eynon. BS in Biology magna cum laude, U. of the South, 1984; MD, U. South Fla., 1988. Resident in pediatrics Children's Hosp. Med. Ctr., Cin., 1988-91; fellow Inst. for Molecular and Human Genetics Baylor Coll. Medicine, Houston, 1991-95; asst. prof. pediat. divsn. med. genetics U. Tex. Med. Sch., Houston, 1995-98; fellow U. Chgo. Ctr. for Med. Ethics, 1998-99; adj. faculty U. Tex. Sch. Pub. Health, Houston, 2000—. Clin reviewer Tex. Birth Defects Registry, 1994—; med. dir. Tex. Birth Defects Rsch. Ctr., 1998—; mem. ethics in sci. and medicine program U. Tex. Southwestern Med. Sch., 1999—. Vol. Big Bros./Big Sisters, Tampa, Fla., 1978-82, Girl Scouts Am., Dallas; trustee St. Mark's Episcopal Sch., 1995-98; bioethics com. Episcopal Diocese of Tex. Fellow Am. Acad. Pediatrics, Am. Coll. Med. Genetics; mem. Am. Soc. Human Genetics, Phi Beta Kappa, Sigma Xi, Alpha Epsilon Delta. Democrat. Avocations: horseback riding, photography, crossword puzzles.

SCHEVE, MAY E. state legislator, political organization worker; b. St. Louis, June 27, 1964; d. Robert Anthony and May Ellen (Braun) S. BA, St. Louis U., 1987; postgrad., Webster U. Rep. Mo. State Ho. Reps. Dist. 98, 1991—2002; adminstr. Dem. Party, Jefferson City, Mo., 2002—. Committeewoman Gravois Twp. Dem. Club; chair, Mo. Dem. Party, 2002-. Mem. Women Legislators, Third Congl. Women's Club (sec.), Women's Dem. Forum, Alpha Gamma Delta, Kappa Beta Phi. Democrat. Office: Mo Democratic Party 419 E High St PO Box 719 Jefferson City MO 65102

SCHEVILL, MARGOT BLUM, anthropologist; b. Stockton, Calif., Aug. 15, 1931; d. Gay Frederick Helmuth and Ruth Carolyn (Zuckerman) Hartmann; m. Robert C. Blum, Sept. 9, 1951 (div. June 1965); children: Sherifa Zuhur, Paul Helmuth Blum; m. James Erwin Schevill, Aug. 2, 1966. BA, Brown U., 1972, MA, 1981. Rsch. assoc. Haffenreffer Mus. Anthropology, Brown U., Bristol, R.I., 1982-97, P. Hearst Mus. Anthropology, U. Calif., 1995-97, guest curator, 1996-97; asst. curator Haffenreffer Mus. Anthropology, Brown U., Bristol, R.I., 1987-91; sr. mus. scientist P. Hearst Mus., U. Calif., Berkeley, 1988-93; guest curator M.H. de Young Meml. Mus., San Francisco, 1995-96; asst. curator exhbns. San Francisco Airport Museums, 1998—2003. Author: Evolution in Textile Design, 1985, Costume as Communication, 1986, Maya Textiles of Guatemala, 1993; editor: Textile Traditions of Mesoamerica and the Andes, 1996; editor, contbr. The Maya Textile Tradition, 1997, Traditional Textiles of the Andes. Bd. dirs. Composers, Inc., San Francisco, 1993-96, Music in Schs. Today, San Francisco, 1991-93; pres. New Music Ensemble, Providence, 1968-84. Grantee NEA, 1984, 88, 90, 95-96, NEH, 1991-93. Mem. Am. Anthropol. Assn., Native Am. Art Studies Assn., The Textile Soc. Am. (bd. dirs. 1998—), Textile Arts Coun., Coun. Mus. Anthropology (v.p. 1981—, sec. 1986-89). Avocations: music, weaving, gardening, collector of textiles. Home: 1309 Oxford St Berkeley CA 94709-1424

SCHEWEL, ROSEL HOFFBERGER, education educator; b. Mar. 1, 1928; d. Samuel Herman and Gertrude (Miller) Hoffberger; m. Elliot Sidney Schewel, June 12, 1949; children: Stephen, Michael, Susan. AB, Hood Coll., 1949; MEd, Lynchburg Coll., 1974, EdS, 1982, EdD (hon.), 2000. Reading resource tchr. Lynchburg Pub. Schs., Va., 1967-75; adj. prof. edn. Lynchburg Coll., 1973-79, assoc. prof. edn., 1980-92. Cons., seminar leader Woman's Resource Ctr., Lynchburg, 1980-92. Trustee, chair bd. trustees Lynchburg Coll., Va., 1992-98, 99—; bd. dirs. Va. Found. for Humanities and Pub. Policy, 1985-90, New Vistas Sch., Lynchburg Human Rights Commn., 1992-2000, Lynchburg Youth Svcs., 1993-97; bd. dirs. Venture Enterprising Women, Planned Parenthood of the Blue Ridge; trustee Va. Mus. of Fine Arts, 1985-90; apptd. Commn. on Edn. for All Virginians, 1990; bd. dirs. Action Alliance for Virginia's Children and Youth, 1995-2002; trustee Amazement Sq. Children's Mus., 1996—; vol. Ct. Apptd. Spl. Advocate, Riverviews Art Space Bd., 2002—. Recipient Disting. Svc. award NCCJ, 1973, Outstanding Woman in Edn. award YWCA, 1988, Disting. Alumni award Lynchburg Coll., 1993. Mem. Phi Kappa Phi. Democrat. Jewish. Address: 4316 Gorman Dr Lynchburg VA 24503-1948

SCHEXNAYDER, CHARLOTTE TILLAR, state legislator; b. Tillar, Ark., Dec. 25, 1923; d. Jewell Stephen and Bertha (Terry) Tillar; m. Melvin John Schexnayder Sr., Aug. 18, 1946; children: M. John Jr., Sarah Holden, Stephen. BA, La. State U., 1944, postgrad., 1947-48. Asst. editor La. Agrl. Extension, Baton Rouge, 1944; editor The McGehee (Ark.) Times, 1945-46, 48-53; editor, co-publisher The Dumas (Ark.) Clarion, 1954-85, pub., 1985-99; mem. Ark. Ho. of Reps., Little Rock, 1985-99, asst. speaker pro tem, 1995—. Pres. Ark. Assn. Women, 1955, Nat. Newspaper Assn., Washington, 1991-92, Ark. Press. Assn., Little Rock, 1982, Nat. Fedn. Press Women, Blue Springs, Mo., 1977-78, Litte Rock chpt. Soc. Profl. Journalists, 1973; mem. pres.'s coun. Winrock Internat., 1990—; chmn. Dumas Area Cmty. Found., 2000-02. Editor: Images of the Past, 1991. 1st woman mem. Ark. Bd. Pardons and Parole, 1975-80; mem. Ark. Legis. Coun., 1985-92; bd. dirs. Women's Found. Ark., sec. 1999—; bd. dirs. Chicot-Desha Port Indsl. Com.; v.p. Desha County Mus., 1989—; dir. Dumas Indsl. Found., 1986—; mem. exec. com. Ark. Ctrl. Radiation Therapy Inst., 1991-92; mem. adv. bd. Ark. Profl. Women Achievement, 1992—; vice chair Ark. Rural Devel. Commn., 1991-96, chair 1996-97; mem. Winrock Internat. Adv. Coun., 1991—; founding incorporator Ark. Waterways Commn., 1996—, bd. dirs.; bd. visitors Manship Sch. Comm., La. State U., 1998—; bd. dirs. Main Street Ark., Hist. Preservation Alliance Ark.; mem. Ark. Transitional Employment Coun., 1999—; sec. Dumas Area Cmty. Fund, 2000—; bd. dirs. Enterprise Corp. for the Delta, 1999-2002, Dumas Main St., v.p.; bd. dirs. Historic Preservation Alliance Ark, 2000—; mem. Ark. Transitional Employment Assistance Bd., 2000; outstanding bd. mem. Ark. Main St., 2002; outstanding bd. chair Ark. Cmty. Found., 2003. Named Disting. Alumnus Ark. A&M Coll., 1971, Woman of Achievement Nat. Fedn. Press Women, 1970, Outstanding Arkansan C. of C., 1986; recipient Ark. Profl. Women of Distinction award No. Bank, Little Rock, 1990, Emma McKinney award Nation's Top Cmty. Newspaper Woman, 1980, Journalist award Nat. Conf. of Christians and Jews, 1989, Lifetime Achievement award Nat. Fedn. Press Women, 1992, Outstanding Svc. award Ark. Assn. Elem. Prins., Disting. Svc. award Ark. Press Assn., 1993; named to La. State U. Alumni Hall of Distinction, 1994, Disting. Svc. award Internat. Soc. Weekly Newspaper Editors, 1996, Golden Svc. award Ark. Press Assn., 1996, State Leadership award Ark. Waterways Commn., 1996, Horizon award League Women Voters Ark., 1998; named one Top 100 Ark. Women, Ark. Bus., 1995, 96, 97, 98; named to Journalism Hall of Fame La. State U., 1998; named Outstanding Bd. Mem. of Yr., Main Street Ark., 2002, Outstanding Bd. Mem., Puns. of Ark. Cmty. Found., 2003; honored Outstanding Svc. Women's Found. Ark., 2003. Mem.: Ark. Delta Coun. (chmn. emeritus, v.p. Dumas Main St., mem. Main St. Ark. adv. bd.), Pi Beta Phi (Crest award 1992). Democrat. Roman Catholic. Home: 322 Court St Dumas AR 71639-2718 Office: PO Box 160 Dumas AR 71639-0160 E-mail: cts@seark.net.

SCHGIER, LINDA PRIEST, musician, educator; b. Cullman, Ala., Nov. 16, 1942; d. Isaac Columbus and Frances Elene (Woodall) Priest; m. William Meyer Schgier, July 12, 1969. AA, Sacred Heart Coll., 1962; BS, U. N. Ala., 1965; postgrad., U. Ala., 1967-68. Tchr. Annapolis (Md.) Jr. H.S., 1965-66, Whitesburg Elem., Huntsville, Ala., 1966-69, West Elem. Sch., Cullman, 1970-83; music assoc., pianist 1st Bapt. Ch., Cullman, 1970—2000; music asst., pianist, dir. children's choir, dir. youth and children's handbells St. John's Evang. Protestant Ch., 2001—. Tchr. music summer camps, Older Children's Music Week Shocco Springs Bapt. Assembly, Talladega, Ala.,. 1982—; pvt. piano and organ tchr. Mem. Am. Music Tchrs. Assn., Cmty. Concerts Assn. (bd. dirs. 1972—), Coterie (historian 1997-98), Symphony Club (pres. 1996-97), DAR. Avocations: reading, music, travel, puzzles, model trains. Home: 166 County Road 1473 Cullman AL 35058-0792

SCHIEROW, LINDA-JO, environmental policy analyst; b. Milw., Aug. 17, 1947; d. Joseph August Schierow and Ruth Eleanore (Beyersdorff) Heuer; 1 child, Katherine Irene. BS in Edn. with honors, U. Wis., 1969, MS in Land Resources, 1980, PhD in Land Resources, 1983. Cert. tchr., Wis. Tchr. elem. Cedarburg (Wis.) Pub. Schs., 1972-78; project assoc. Water Resources Ctr. U. Wis., Madison, 1985; asst. prof. U. Okla., Oklahoma City, 1985-88, rsch. fellow Norman, 1988; rsch. assoc. MIT, Cambridge, 1989-90; pvt. practice cons., 1990-91; policy analyst resources, sci. & industry U.S. Congress Congl. Rsch. Svc., Libr. of Congress, Washington, 1991-95, policy specialist resources, sci. & industry, 1995—. Cons. U.S.-Can. Internat. Joint Commn., Windsor, Ont., Can., 1985. Mem. editl. bd. RISK: Health, Safety & Environ., 1990—. Mem. Okla. State Groundwater Protection Strategy Com., Oklahoma City, 1985-88; bd. dirs. Ctr. for Cmty. Tech., Madison, 1983-84. Mem. Risk Assessment and Policy Assn. (pres. 2003—). Democrat. Avocations: gardening, cooking. Office: Congl Rsch Svc Libr Of Congress Washington DC 20540-7450 E-mail: lschierow@crs.loc.gov.

SCHIESS, BETTY BONE, priest; b. Cin., Apr. 2, 1923; d. Evan Paul and Leah (Mitchell) Bone; m. William A. Schiess, Aug. 28, 1947; children: William A. (dec.), Richard Corwine, Sarah. BA, U. Cin., 1945; MA, Syracuse U., 1947; MDiv, Rochester Ctr. for Theol. Studies, 1972. Ordained priest Episcopal Ch., 1974. Priest assoc. Grace Episc. Ch., Syracuse, NY, 1975; mem. NY Task Force on Life and Law (apptd. by gov.), 1985—; chaplain Syracuse U., 1976-78, Cornell U., Ithaca, NY, 1978-79; rector Grace Episc. Ch., Mexico, NY, 1984-89. Cons. Women's Issues Network Episc. Ch. in US, 1987—; writer, lectr., cons. religion and feminism, 1979—. Author: Take Back the Church, Indeed The Witness, 1982, Creativity and Procreativity: Some Thoughts on Eve and the Opposition and How Episcopalians Make Ethical decisions, Plumline, 1980, Send in the Clowns, Chrysalis, Journal of the Swedenborg Foundation, 1994, Cassandra in the Temple, Chrysalis, Journal of the Swedenborg Foundation, 1998, Why Me, Lord?, 2003; contbr. forward to book, A Still Small Voice! Women Ordination and the Church, Frederick W. Schmidt Jr., 1996. Bd. dir. People for Pub. TV in NY, 1978, Religious Coalition for Abortion Rights; trustee Elizabeth Cady Stanton Found., 1979; mem. policy com. Coun. Adolescent Pregnancy; mem. NY State Task Force Life and the Law, 1983-96. Recipient Gov. award Women of Merit in Religion, 1984, Ralph E. Kharas award ACLU Ctr., NY, 1986, Goodall disting. alumna award & Hills Sch., 1988, Human Rightes award Human Rights Commn. of Syracuse and Onondaga County, NY, 1989; inducted into Nat. Women's Hall of Fame, 1994. Mem. NOW (Syracuse), Internat. Assn. Women Ministers (dir. 1978 pres. 1984-87), Na'amat US (hon. life), Mortar Bd., Theta Chi Beta. Democrat. Home and Office: 6987 Van Antwerp Dr Cicero NY 13039-9739 E-mail: bschies1@twcny.rr.com.

SCHIFF, JAYNE NEMEROW, underwriter; b. N.Y.C., Aug. 8, 1945; d. Milton E. Nemerow and Shirley (Kaplan) Wachtel; m. Albert John Schiff, Mar. 7, 1971; children: Matthew Evan, Kara Anne. BS in Bus., Marymount Coll., 1981; M in Profl. Studies in Elem. and Spl. Edn., Manhattanville Coll., 1995. Corporate sec., treas. Albert J. Schiff Assocs., Inc., N.Y.C., 1970-78; field underwriter Mut. N.Y. Fin. Svcs., Greenwich, Conn., 1973-90; freelance employee benefit cons. Greenwich, 1990-99; sr. account exec., contr. Nylex Benefits, Stamford, Conn., 1999—. Regional dir. mktg., MONY Fin. Services, N.Y.C., 1978-79; tutor HELP program Manhttanville Coll., 1996-2000. Bd. dirs. N.Y. League Bus. and Profl. Women, 1976-78, Temple Sinai, Stamford, Conn., 1979-84, N.Y. Ctr. Fin. Studies; leader Webelos Cub Scouts, 1977-78; treas. Ann. Mothers Bd. Benefit Greenwich Acad., 1988, upper sch. acquisitions chmn., 1989, chmn. spl. acquisitions Greenwich Acad. Benefit, 1990-91, chmn. advt., 1992; ESL tutor Lit. Vols. Am., ESL tutor, trainer, 1993; co-chair U. Rochester Parents Coun., 1993-96. Named Conn.'s Outstanding Young Woman, 1979. Mem. LWV, Am. Soc. Chartered Life Underwriters, N.Y. Ctr. Fin. Studies (bd. dirs.), N.Y.C. Life Underwriters Assn. (bd. dirs. 1977-78). Jewish. Avocations: sailing, knitting, playing piano, reading. Office: Nylex Benefits 301 Tresser Blvd Stamford CT 06901-3284

SCHIFF, LAURIE, lawyer; b. Newark, Apr. 24, 1960; d. Norman Nathan and Claire Jane (Schott) Schiff. BS in Law, Western State U., Fullerton, Calif., 1987, JD, 1988. Bar: Calif. 1989. Ptnr. Schiff Mgmt., Newport Beach, Calif., 1983-89; pvt. practice Schiff & Assocs., Irvine, Calif.,

1989-91; ptnr. Schiff & Shelton, Newport Beach, 1991—, Attys. Equity Law Group, LLP, 2001—. Probation monitor State Bar Ct. Calif., 1991—97, spl. prosecutor, 1997—. Prodr.: (Albums) Boys Just Want to Have Sex, 1984. Bd. dirs. Jewish Family Svcs. Orange County, 1994—99. Mem.: Orange County Bar Assn. (arbitrator 1995—), Am. Quarterhorse Assn., Am. Mensa, Online Feline Fanciers (v.p. 1995—97, bd. dirs. 1997—), Internat. Cat Assn. (chair legis. com. 1995—97, 1998—99, legal counsel 1999—, lic. splty. judge 2001—), Am. Polocrosse Assn., Saddlebrook Polocrosse (treas. 1991), Tonks West (v.p. 1994—96, pres. 1996—97), Tonkinese Breed Assn., Internat. Politically Correct Cat Club (v.p. 1996—). Democrat. Jewish. Office: Schiff & Shelton 3700 Campus Dr Ste 202 Newport Beach CA 92660-2603 E-mail: lschiff@schiff-shelton.com.

SCHIFF, MARGARET SCOTT, newspaper publishing executive; V.p., controller, personnel adminstr. Washington Post. Office: The Washington Post 1150 15th St NW Washington DC 20071-0002

SCHIFF, STACY, writer; b. Adams, Mass., 1960; BA, Williams Coll. Sr. editor Simon and Schuster. Author: Saint-Exupery: A Biography, 1994, Véra (Mrs. Vladimir Nabokov): Portrait of a Marriage, 1999 (Pulitzer prize for Biography, 2000); contbr. The New Yorker, The N.Y. Times Book Rev., The Times Literary Supplement, others. Fellow, Guggenheim Found., Nat. Endowment for the Humanities.*

SCHIFFER, CLAUDIA, model; b. Germany; Model Guess? jeans, 1989—, Revlon cosmetics, Chanel; amb., internat. spokesperson L'Oréal. Ptnr. Fashion Cafe, N.Y.C., London, New Orleans, Barcelona, Jakarta, Manila, others; host World Music Awards with Luke Perry, Monte Carlo, 1995. Runway debut in Chanel fashion show, 1990; appeared on covers of Mademoiselle, Cosmopolitan, Vogue, and over 100 others; creator series of exercise videos (with Kathy Kaehler) Claudia Schiffer's Perfectly Fit, 1996; pub.: (pictorial book) Memories. Hon. bd. dirs. Dishes AIDS; spokesperson Nat. Breast Cancer Coalition.

SCHIFFER, LOIS JANE, lawyer; b. Washington, Feb. 22, 1945; d. Benjamin and Clara (Goldberg) S. BA, Radcliffe Coll., 1966; JD, Harvard U., 1969. Bar: Mass. 1969, D.C. 1971, U.S. Supreme Ct. 1973. Legal svcs. lawyer Boston Legal Assistance Project, 1969-70; ct. law clk. D.C. Circuit Ct., Washington, 1970-71; assoc. Leva, Hawes, Symington, Martin, Oppenheimer, Washington, 1971-74; lawyer Ctr. for Law and Social Policy, Washington, 1974-78; chief gen. litigation sect. Land and Natural Resources div. U.S. Dept. Justice, Washington, 1978-81, spl. litigation counsel, 1981-84; gen. counsel Nat. Pub. Radio, Washington, 1984-89; ptnr. Nussbaum & Wald, Washington, 1989-93; acting asst. atty. gen. environ. and natural resources divsn. U.S. Dept. Justice, Washington, 1993-94, asst. atty. gen. environ. and natural resources divsn., 1994-2001; sr. v.p. for pub. policy Nat. Audubon Soc., 2001—02; ptnr. Baach, Robinson & Lewis, Washington, 2002—. Adj. prof. environ. law Georgetown U. Law Ctr., Washington, 1986—; lectr. Harvard Law Sch., 2004. Bd. dirs. Women's Legal Def. Fund, 1975-86, Am. Rivers, 1989-93, Keystone Ctr.; bd. dirs. ACLU/NCA, 1982-93, pres., 1988-90. Fellow Am. Bar Found.; mem. ABA, Am. Law Inst., Keystone Ctr. (bd. dirs.), Am. Bar Assn., Phi Beta Kappa. Democrat. Jewish. Avocations: reading, movies, hiking. Home: 4640 Brandywine St NW Washington DC 20016-4449 E-mail: lois.schiffer@baachrobinson.com.

SCHIFFMAN, SUSAN STOLTE, medical psychologist, educator; b. Chgo., Aug. 24, 1940; d. Paul R. and Mildred (Glicksman) Stolte; m. Harold Schiffman (div.); 1 child, Amy Lise; m. H. Troy Nagle, July 22, 1989. BA, Syracuse U., 1965; PhD, Duke U., 1970. Lic. psychologist, N.C. Postdoctoral fellow Duke U., Durham, N.C., 1970-72, asst. prof., 1972-77, assoc. prof., 1978-83, full prof., 1983—. Cons., mem. adv. bd. Nestle, Vevey, Switzerland, 1990-98, Sense of Smell Inst., N.Y.C., 1986—, and others. Author: Introduction to Multidimensional Scaling: Theory, Methods and Applications, 1981, Flavor Set-Point Weight Loss Cookbook, 1990. Nat. Inst. Aging grantee, 1972—. Mem. Assn. Chemoreception Scis., Internat. Behavioral Neurosci. Soc., Soc. for Neurosci. Office: Duke U Med Sch PO Box 3259 Durham NC 27710-3259 E-mail: sss@duke.edu.

SCHILD, SYLVIA G. retired elementary school educator, realtor; b. L.A., Nov. 3, 1925; d. Harry Bernstein and Eva Chaden; 1 child, Rachelle Hilmer Heartte. AA, L.A. City Coll., 1947; BA, U. Calif., Berkeley, 1950. Tchr. Berkwood Coop. Sch., Berkeley, Calif., 1957—63, Oakland (Calif.) Pub. Schs., 1963—76; ret.; realtor Crump & Jones, Berkeley, 1976—82. Founder, pres. Point Isabel Dog Owners, Richmond-East Bay, 1985—2003; mem. Cal Dog, Calif., 2002—03. Named Sylvia Schild Day named in her honor, City of Berkeley, 2000; named one of Outstanding Berkeley Women, Commn. on Status of Women, 2002. Mem.: Calif. Ret. Tchrs. Assn. Democrat. Jewish. Avocations: animal welfare, children's education and stories, travel, music. Home: 1321 Carlotta Ave Berkeley CA 94703

SCHILLING, BRENDA GAIL, music educator; b. Wolf Point, Mont., May 8, 1967; d. Gale Irvin and M. Beulah Peterson; m. Paul Robert Schilling, Aug. 3, 1991; children: Austin Paul, Alexandra Gail. B in Music Edn., Mont. State U., 1990. Music tchr. Cut Bank (Mont.) Schs., 1990—. Mem.: PEO, Cut Bank Edn. Assn., Mont. Choral Dirs. Assn., Mont. Music Educators Assn. Avocations: gardening, singing, piano, scrapbooks. Home: 409 Mountain View Blvd Cut Bank MT 59427 Office: Cut Bank Schs 101 3d Ave SE Cut Bank MT 59427

SCHILLING, EMILY BORN, editor, association executive; b. Lawton, Okla., Oct. 2, 1959; d. George Arthur and Sumiko (Nagamine) Born; m. Mark David Schilling, June 26, 1995. BS, Ball State U., 1981. Cert. coop. communicator Nat. Rural Electric Coop. Assn. Feature writer The News-Sentinel, Fort Wayne, Ind., 1981-83; wire editor The Noblesville (Ind.) Daily Ledger, 1983; staff writer Ind. Statewide Assn. Rural Electric Coops., Indpls., 1983-84, mng. editor, 1984-85, editor, 1985—. Author: Power to the People, 1985. Mem. Coop. Communicators Assn. (Michael Graznak award 1990), Internat. Assn. Bus. Communicators (award of excellence dist. 7 1985), Women's Internat. Network of Utility Profls. (pres. 1999, Mem. of Yr. 1999, Power award 1994), Nat. Electric Coops. Statewide Editors Assn. Office: Ind Statewide Assn RECs 720 N High School Rd Indianapolis IN 46214-3756

SCHILLING, JANET NAOMI, nutrition consultant; b. North Platte, Nebr., Mar. 1, 1939; d. Jens Harold and Naomi Frances (Meyer) Hansen; children: Allan Edward III, Karl Jens. BS, U. Nebr., 1961; MS, Ohio State U., 1965; MPH, U. Calif., Berkeley, 1991. Registered dietitian. Tchr. home econs. Peace Corps., Dimbokro, Ivory Coast, 1962-64; cons. nutrition Wis. Divsn. Health, La Crosse, 1966-67, 69; dietary cons. Cozad Cmty. Hosp., Nebr., 1968; instr. Viterbo Coll., La Crosse, 1974-81; lectr. U. Wis., La Crosse, 1982-84; teaching asst. ESL, Sch. Dist. La Crosse, 1984-87; nutrition educator Women, Infant, and Children Program, 1988-89; nutrition cons. Vis. Nurses, LaCrosse, 1987-89; dietitian Merrithew Meml. Hosp., Martinez, Calif., 1992; tutor Lafayette Elem. Sch., 2000—. Nutrition cons. Wis. Winnebago Nation, 1991; pediatric dietitian in Romanian Orphanges thru World Vision, 1993; nutritionist Contra Costa Head Start & Child Devel., 1994; pub. health nutrition cons. Women Infant & Children's Nutrition Support and Policy Unit, Sacramento, 1995-2000; pub. health nutrition cons. III, Calif. Childhood Lead Poisoning Prevention Br., 2000—; tutor Lafayette Sch., Oakland, Calif., 2000--. Author: Life in the Nutrition Cmty., 1980, Life in the Nutrition Cycle II, 1980; co-author: Nutrition Activities, 1984, Recipe Book of Nutritious Snacks, 1985; editor: 100 Winning Winnebago Recipes '91. Mem. LaCrosse Sch. Dist. Nutrition Task Force, 1976-88; Sunday sch. tchr., supr. Our Savior's Luth. Ch., 1975-86, chmn. Mobile Meals, 1982-86; v.p. membership booster club Ctrl. HS LaCrosse, 1985-87, pres., 1987-88; bd. dirs. YMCA, LaCrosse, 1982-88; mem. No. Calif. Returned Peace Corps vols., 1990—; mem. Glide Ch. Housing Task Force, 1995-99; trustee East Bay Habitat for Humanity, 1995-98, bd. dirs. 1998-2003; co-chair Calif. InterAgency Nutrition Coord. Coun., 2001—. Mem. AAUW (pres. 1978-80, named grant scholar 1981), APHA, LaCrosse Area Dietetic Assn. (1st pres. 1968-69, Outstanding Dietitian Yr. 1985), Wis. Dietetic Assn. (chmn. educators 1983-85), No. Wis. Dietetic Assn. (pres. 1982), Am. Dietetic Assn. (educators practice group 1978-90), LaCrosse Jaycettes (Carol award 1973), Calif. Dietetic Assn. (chmn. pediat. practice group chmn. 1997-98, del. 1998—, del.-at-large 1998-2001, sec.-treas. 2004-), PEO (sec. chpt.). Democrat. Avocations: running, swimming, biking, gardening. Home: 1604 Roger Ct El Cerrito CA 94530-2028

SCHIMBERG, BARBARA HODES, organizational development consultant; b. Chgo., Nov. 30, 1941; d. David and Tybe Zisook; children from previous marriage: Brian Hodes, Valery Lodato; m. A. Bruce Schimberg, Dec. 29, 1984. BS, Northwestern U., 1962. Ptnr. Just Causes, cons. not-for-profit orgns., Chgo., 1978-86. Cons. in philanthropy, community involvement, and organizational devel., 1987—; Chgo. cons. Population Resource Ctr., 1978-82. Mem. women's bd. dirs. Mus. Contemporary Art; bd. dirs., vice chmn. Med. Rsch. Inst. Coun., Michael Reese Med. Ctr.; bd. dirs., chmn. Midwest Women's Ctr.; trustee Francis W. Parker Sch.; bd. dirs. Women's Issues Network Found., 1991-98, pres., 1993-94; mem. adv. bd. Med. Rsch. Inst. Coun., Children's Meml. Hosp. Mem. ACLU (adv. com.), Women's Bd. U. Chgo. Office: 132 E Delaware Pl Apt 5002 Chicago IL 60611-4944 Office Phone: 312-944-2468.

SCHIMEK, DIANNA RUTH REBMAN, state legislator; b. Holdrege, Nebr., Mar. 21, 1940; d. Ralph William and Elizabeth Julia (Wilmot) Rebman; m. Herbert Henry Schimek, 1963; children: Samuel Wolfgang, Saul William. AA, Colo. Women's Coll., 1960; student, U. Nebr., Lincoln, 1960-61; BA magna cum laude, U. Nebr., Kearney, 1963. Former tchr. and realtor; mem. Nebr. Legislature from 27th dist., Lincoln, 1989—; chmn. govt., mil. and vets. affairs com. Nebr. Legislature, Lincoln, 1993-94, 99—, vice chair urban affairs com., 1995-98. Dem. Nat. committeewoman, 1984-88; chmn. Nebr. Dem. Com., 1980-84, mem. exec. com., 1987-88; past pres., sec. bd. dirs. Downtown Sr. Ctr. Found., 1990-96; mem. exec. bd. Midwestern Legis. Conf., 1995—, co-chair health and human svcs. com., 1995-96; exec. dir. Nebr. Civil Liberties Union, 1985; former bd. dirs. Nebr. Repertory Theater, Exon Found., 1997-2000; mem. adv. bd. Martin Luther Home, 1997—; chair Midwestern Legis. Conf. Coun. of State Govts., 2000-01; mem. Midwest Interstate passenger Rail Commn., 2001—; mem. exec. bd. Coun. State Govts., 2000—; chair NCSL Task Force on Initiative and Referendum, 2001-02. Toll fellow, 1999; recipient Outstanding Alumni award U. Nebr., 1989, Tribute award YWCA, 1992, Friend of Psychology award N.E. Psychol. Assn., 1998, Woman of Yr. award Nova Chpt. Bus. & Profl. Women, 1999, Disting. Svc. award Nat. Guard Assn., 2000, Woman of Distinction award Soroptomists, 1999, Legis. of Yr. award N.E. Dental Hygienists Assn., 2001, Disting. Svc. award N.E. League of Municipalities, 2002, Lincoln Interfaith Leadership award, 2003, Harold Steck award ARC of N.E., 2004, others. Mem. Nat. Conf. State Legislators Women's Network (bd. dirs. 1993-96, 1st vice chmn.), PEO, Soroptomists, Delta Kappa Gamma (hon.), Mortar Bd. (cmty. advisor 1998, hon.). Democrat. Unitarian Universalist. Home: 2321 Camelot Ct Lincoln NE 68512-1457 Office: Dist # 27 State Capital Lincoln NE 68509

SCHIMENTI, CHERYL D. retired research scientist; b. Ft. Worth, Oct. 1, 1951; d. Curtis Leroy and Ella Catherine (Patterson) Love; m. Scott Micheal Shelley, Oct. 27, 1972 (div. May 1974); m. Dan Schimenti, July 21, 1979. BS in Cell & Molecular Biology, San Francisco State U., 1985; PhD in Biomed. Scis., U. Tex., 1993. Rsch. asst. Medi-Physics, Emeryville, Calif., 1985-86; staff rsch. assoc. VAMC, San Francisco, 1986-89; postdoctoral fellow U. Calif., San Francisco, 1994, postgrad. rschr., 1998; postdoctoral fellow U. Calif. VA Med. Ctr., San Francisco, 1994—98; ret., 1998. Contbr. articles to profl. jours. NCI Tng. grantee NIH, 1990, 91, 92; postdoctoral fellow U.S. Army Breast Cancer Rsch. Program, 1996—. Avocations: yoga, reading, painting, cats. Home: 16 28th St San Francisco CA 94110-4909

SCHINDEL, ALICE, social worker; b. Chgo., Sept. 26, 1936; d. Leonard Earl and Mina Hecht Andrews; m. Donald M. Schindel; children: Susan Yost, Judi Harris, Andrea Glickman. BS in Edn., U. Ill., 1958, MSW, 1977. LCSW Ill. Tchr. Chgo. Pub. Schs., 1958—62; social worker Counsel for Jewish Elderly, Chgo., 1977—82; social worker home health Highland Park (Ill.) Hosp., 1982—83; social worker Family Svc. South Lake County, Highland Park, 1985—. Michal Reese Hosp. fellow, 1983—85, Family Inst. Chgo. fellow, 1985—87. Mem.: NASW, Am. Assn. Marital Family Therapists (cert.). Avocations: reading, swimming, bridge. Home: 636 Rice Highland Park IL 60035 Office: Family Svc South Lake County 777 Central Highland Park IL 60035

SCHINDLER, HOLLY SUZANNE, freelance/self-employed writer; b. Springfield, Mo., Jan. 10, 1977; d. John Whitmore and Edith Joanne (Jackson) Schindler. BA in English, S.W. Mo. State U., 1999, MA in English, 2001. Instr. S.W. Mo. State U., Springfield, 1999—2000, tutor, 2001; freelance writer Springfield, 2001—.

SCHINDLER, JUDI(TH) (JUDITH KAY SCHINDLER), public relations executive, marketing professional, consultant; b. Chgo., Nov. 23, 1941; d. Gilbert G. and Rosalie (Karlin) Cone; m. Jack Joel Schindler, Nov. 1, 1964; 1 child, Adam Jason. BS in Journalism, U. Ill., 1964. Assoc. editor Irving Cloud Publs., Lincolnwood, Ill., 1963-64; asst. dir. publicity Israel Bond Campaign, Chgo., 1965-69; v.p. pub. relations Realty Co. of Am., Chgo., 1969-70; dir. pub. relations Pvt. Telecomm., Chgo., 1970-78; pres. Schindler Comm., Chgo., 1978—. Del. White House Conf. on Small Bus., Washington, 1980, 86; mem. adv. bd. Entrepreneurship Inst., Chgo., 1988—92. Mem. Leadership Ill., 2003; appointee small bus. com. Ill. Devel. Bd., 1988—89; bd. dirs. Family Matters Cmty. Ctr. Named Nat. Women in Bus. Adv. SBA, 1986, Chgo. Woman Bus. Owner of Yr., Continental Bank and Nat. Assn. Women Bus. Owners, 1989, Ill.; named to Hall of Fame, Nat. Assn. of Women Bus. Owners, 2003. Mem. Nat. Assn. Women Bus. Owners (pres. Chgo. chpt. 1980-81, nat. v.p. membership 1988-89), Publicity Club Chgo., Alpha Epsilon Phi. Office: Schindler Comm 500 N Clark St Chicago IL 60610-4288 Office Phone: 312-464-9660. Business E-Mail: jschindler@schindlercommunications.com.

SCHINDLER, LAURA ANN, piano teacher, accompanist; b. St. Louis, Aug. 17, 1943; d. Francis Joseph and Alice Binkley (Hurtgen) Schindler; m. John Charles Noto, Dec. 27, 1986. BM cum laude, Fontbonne Coll., St. Louis, 1970; MAT, Washington U., St. Louis, 1972; student, Ecole Normale de Musique, Paris, 1973-74. Nat. cert. tchr. of music; cert. Orff Schulwerk, Mozarteum Acad., Salzburg, Austria. Organist, choir dir. St. John's Basilica, St. Louis, 1971-73; piano tchr. Cmty. Music Sch., St. Louis, 1971-73, St. Louis Inst. Music, 1972-73; accompanist Robert McFerrin, Sr., N.Y.C., Chgo.,Springfield, St. Louis, 1974-77; piano tchr., Orff instr. St. Louis Conservatory, 1974-82; pvt. piano tchr. and accompanist St. Louis, 1982—. Vocal accompanist Affiliate Artist Program, St. Louis, 1977; accompanist MTNA West. Ctr. Divsn. Auditions, St. Louis, 1979, Forest Park C.C. Chorus, 1980-82, Ethical Soc. Chorus, 1980-83, Washington U. Music Sch., 1970-72; adjudicator piano competitions, Mo. and Ill., 1978—; clinician Piano Tchr. Workshops, Mo./Ill., 1979—. Contbr. articles to profl. jours.; performer Today Show, NBC, 1976, Capella Soloists Sunset concerts, 1976, Bicentennial Horizons of Am. Music, 1976, Rubinstein Music Club Meetings, 1997—, Benefit for Mo. Com. for Firearms Safety, 1982; performer, composer Am. Composers Concert, 1976. Recipient Mid-Am. Disting. Ind. Piano Tchr. award N.W., 1997, Disting. Piano Tchr. award Cedarhurst Chamber Music and Beethoven Soc., 1992; Acad. fellow Washington U., 1970-72. Mem.: Piano Tchrs. Round Table (pres. 1999—2001, exec. bd. mem. 2003—), Musical Diversions Soc. (bd. dirs. 1995—), St. Louis Area Music Tchrs. Assn. (v.p. for programs 1986—88, pres. 1988—92, chair nominating com. 1996—2000), Rubinstein Music Club. Democrat. Mem. Ethical Soc. Avocations: travel, walking, reading, eastern european folk dancing, ballroom dancing. Home: 7567 Lindbergh Dr Saint Louis MO 63117-2173

SCHINDLER, TERI, sports association executive; m. Mike Gorman, 1988. Grad. summa cum laude, U. Notre Dame, Ind., 1983. News/sports desk runner 1984 Summer Olympic Games, 1984; prodr. Milw. Bucks telecasts/WVTV; exec. prodr. women's basketball Conn. Pub. TV; mgr. Big East TV Network; dir. broadcasting NBA Entertainment, 1997—99; v.p. broadcasting and sr. coord. prodr. Women's Nat. Basketball Assn., N.Y.C., 1999—. Freelance writer specializing in women's and environ. issues. Contbr. articles to newspapers including the Boston Globe. Nominee 8 Emmoy awards for basketball, football; recipient Emmy award (New Eng. region), 1993; scholar, Rotary scholar, 1983. Mem.: Phi Beta Kappa. Office: Women's Nat Baksetball Assn Olympic Tower 645 Fifth Ave New York NY 10022*

SCHINE, CATHLEEN, writer; b. Westport, Conn., 1953; m. David Denby, 1981; children: Max, Thomas. Student, Sarah Lawrence Coll., Barnard U., U. Chgo. Author: Alice in Bed, 1983, To the Birdhouse, 1990, Rameau's Niece, 1993 (one of best books of 1993 N.Y. Times, Voice Literary Supplement, finalist Book prize L.A. Times 1992-93), The Love Letter, 1995, The Evolution of Jane, 1998; contbr. articles, reviews, columns to popular publs. including N.Y. Times Mag., N.Y. Times Book Review, Village Voice, Vogue. Office: care Candida Donadio Donadio & Ashworth Inc 121 W 27th St Ste 704 New York NY 10001-6207

SCHINZEL, SUE MADELINE, registered nurse; b. Oct. 16, 1938; d. Richard Bernard and Madeline (Helmer) Nalty; m. Donald Lee Schinzel, Oct. 20, 1962; children: David, Denise, Daniel. Diploma, St. Josephs Hosp., Omaha, Nebr. Cert. RN. Office RN Prairie Clin., Omaha, Nebr., 1960-64; staff RN St. Joseph's Hosp., Omaha, 1961-62; pm team leader Doctors Hosp., Omaha, 1968-72; office RN Specialist Clin., Omaha, 1972-82; health clin. RN Interim Health, Omaha, 1989—. Vol. RN ARC, Omaha, Nebr., 1980-89, Democratic Party, 1958-61, Redcross, 1988. Recipient Hon. plaque West YMCA, 1986. Avocations: sewing, tennis, basketball. Office: Interim Health 7604 Pacific St Omaha NE 68114-5421

SCHIRMER, HELGA, retired chiropractor; b. Stavanger, Norway, Oct. 7, 1923; came to U.S., 1927; DC, Palmer Coll., Davenport, Iowa, 1964. Lic. chiropractor, N.Y., N.J., Mass., P.R., N.H., Fla. Practiced chiropractic, N.Y.C., 1965-96. Mem. N.Y. State Chiropractic Assn., Internat. Chiropractic Assn., Garden State Chiropractic Soc., N.J. Coun. Chiropractic. Address: 2200 N Central Rd Ste 12 Fort Lee NJ 07024-7557

SCHIRMER-SMITH, SARA JANE (SALLY SCHIRMER-SMITH), dean, director student activities; b. Saginaw, Mich., June 5, 1963; d. Charles Albert and Jeanne Marie (Ashbaugh) Schirmer; m. Steven John Smith, June 20, 1992; 1 child, Katherine Margaret. BS, Ctrl. Mich. U., 1985; MEd, Springfield Coll., 1989. Dir. student activities Bay Path Coll., Longmeadow, Mass., 1989—. Mem. AAUW, NAFE, Zonta Internat. Avocations: tennis, golf, art, reading, travel. Home: 33 Farmlea Rd Longmeadow MA 01106-1837 Office: Bay Path Coll 588 Longmeadow St Longmeadow MA 01106-2212 E-mail: salsmith@baypath.edu.

SCHIRN, JANET SUGERMAN, interior designer; b. Jersey City, N.Y. d. Oscar H. and Mary (Lustig) S.; 1 child, Martha. BFA, Pratt Inst.; MFA, Columbia U.; postgrad. in Architecture, U. Ill. Tchr. N.Y.C. Bd. Edn.; dir. N.Y.C. Bd. Adult Edn.; pres. Janet Schirn Design Group, Chgo., N.Y.C., 1950—; prin. The J S Collection, N.Y.C., 1978—. Adj. prof. So. Ill. U., 1991-92; mem. adv. bd. Du Pont Co., Monsanto, 1981-89, Masland, So. Ill. U., 1990-95; mem. adv. bd. interior arch. dept. Columbia Coll., Iowa State U., Mundelein Coll., 1978. Contbr. articles to interior design mag. Bd. dirs. Washington Archtl. Forum, 1992-96, Chgo. Archtl. Assistance Ctr., 1975, pres., 1982; mem. Met. Planning Coun., Chgo., 1980—, Art Resources Tchg., 1984-95—; mem. aux. bd. Sch. of Art Inst., Ill. Arts Alliance, 1992—. Recipient award Chgo. Lighting Inst., 1989, 92, 93, 95, 97, 98, Villeroy and Boch gold award, 1990, Designer mag. residential award, 1990, Edward Fields 1st prize Rug Design, 1981, 91, 1st prize project awards ASID, 1993, 95, 96, 98, 99, 2000, 01, named Designer of Distinction, 1998. Mem. UNESCO (steering com. tall bldgs. and urban habitat coun.), Am. Soc. Interior Designers (nat. pres. 1986, nat. treas. 1984, regional v.p. 1981, pres. Ill. chpt. 1977-78, nat. dir. 1979-83, chmn. pub. affairs 1989), Illuminating Engring. Soc., Am. Inst. Architects (nat. urban planning and design com. 1981-85), Chgo. Network, Internat. Fedn. Interior Designers (exec. bd. dirs. 1992-96). Home: 220 E Walton St Chicago IL 60611-1507 Office: Janet Schirn Design Group 401 N Franklin St Chicago IL 60610-4400 also: 521 5th Ave New York NY 10175-0003

SCHISLER, AMY MACWILLIAMS, school librarian, graphics designer; b. Washington, Mar. 15, 1970; d. James Richard and Judith Ann MacWilliams; m. Kenneth David Schisler, Oct. 16, 1993; children: Rebecca Kathleen, Katie Ann, Morgan Christina. BA in History, BA in Polit. Sci., Salisbury State U., 1992; MLS, U. Md., 1995. Children's libr. Calvert County Pub. Libr., Owings, Md., 1992—93; sch. libr. media specialist Talbot County Pub. Schs., Easton, Md., 1993—96; instrnl. libr. Chesapeake Coll., Wye Mills, Md., 1995—, libr. webmaster, 1999—; graphic designer Bozman, Md., 2000—. Author, editor: web page Chesapeake Coll. Libr., 1999—. Membership chair PTA St. Michaels (Md.) Elem., 2001—03, sec., 2003—; mem. Rep. Women Talbot County, Easton, 1993—; treas. Eckardt-Schisler Com., Bozman, 2001—03. Mem.: Md. Libr. Assn. Roman Catholic. Avocations: reading, sewing, photography. Home: 7604 Cooper Point Rd Bozman MD 21612 Office: Chesapeake Coll Learning Resource Ctr Rt 50/213 Wye Mills MD 21679

SCHIZAS, JENNIFER ANNE, law association administrator; b. Grand Island, Nebr., Aug. 18, 1959; d. John Delano and Jacqueline May (Pieper) S. BJ, U. Nebr., 1982. Rschr. U.S. Senator Carl T. Curtis, Washington, 1978; pub. rels. dir. Nebr. Solar Office, Lincoln, 1979; reporter Sta. WOWT-TV, Omaha, 1980-83; bur. chief Sta. KHAS-TV, Hastings, Nebr., 1983-84; divsn. dir. March of Dimes, Lincoln, 1986-90; exec. dir. Lincoln Arts Coun., 1990-92, Nebr. Food Industry Assn., Lincoln, 1992-93; dir. comm. Nebr. Bar Assn., Lincoln, 1993—. Mem. editor's exch. adv. bd. West Pub. CO., Eagan, Minn., 1995. Mem. Am. Soc. Assn. Execs., Nat. Assn. Bar Execs. (pub. rels. cons. 1995), Nebr. Soc. Assn. Execs. Sertoma Club (v.p.). Democrat. Greek Orthodox. Avocations: running, painting, antique collecting and refinishing. Office: Nebr Bar Assn 635 S 14th St Lincoln NE 68508-2700 Home: 4 Lake Hill Dr Durham NC 27713-8954 E-mail: jschizas@nebar.com.

SCHLAFLY, PHYLLIS STEWART, writer; b. St. Louis, Aug. 15, 1924; d. John Bruce and Odile (Dodge) Stewart; m. Fred Schlafly, Oct. 20, 1949; children: John F., Bruce S., Roger S., Phyllis Liza Forshaw, Andrew L., Anne V. BA, Washington U., St. Louis, 1944, JD, 1978; MA, Harvard U., 1945; LLD, Niagara U., 1976. Bar: Ill. 1979, DC 1984, Mo. 1985, U.S. Supreme Ct. 1987. Syndicated columnist Copley News Svc., 1976—. Broadcaster Spectrum, CBS Radio Network, 1973—78; commentator Matters of Opinion sta. WBBM-AM, Chgo., 1973—75, Cable TV News Network, 1980—83; pres. Eagle Forum, 1975—. Author, pub.: Phyllis Schlafly Report, 1967—; author: A Choice Not an Echo, 1964, The

Gravediggers, 1964, Strike From Space, 1965, Safe Not Sorry, 1967, The Betrayers, 1968, Mindszenty The Man, 1972, Kissinger on the Couch, 1975, Ambush at Vladivostok, 1976, The Power of the Positive Woman, 1977, First Reader, 1994, Turbo Reader, 2001, Feminist Fantasies, 2003; editor: (book) Child Abuse in the Classroom, 1984, Pornography's Victims, 1987, Equal Pay for Unequal Work, 1984, Who Will Rock the Cradle, 1989, Stronger Families or Bigger Government, 1990, Meddlesome Mandate: Rethinking Family Leave, 1991. Del. Rep. Nat. Conv., del., 1964, 1968, 1984, 1988, 1992, 1996, alt., 1960, 1980, 2000; 1st v.p. Nat. Fedn. Rep. Women, 1964—67; nat. chmn. Stop ERA, 1972—; mem. Ronald Reagan's Def. Policy Adv. Group, 1980, Commn. on Bicentennial of U.S. Constn., 1985—91, Adminstrv. Conf. U.S., 1983—86; pres. Ill. Fedn. Rep. Women, 1960—64; mem. Ill. Commn. on Status of Women, 1975—85. Named Woman of Achievement in Pub. Affairs, St. Louis Globe-Democrat, 1963; named one of 10 Most Admired Women in World, Good Housekeeping poll, 1977—90, 100 Most Important Women of 20th Century, Ladies Home Jour., 1998; recipient 10 Honor awards, Freedom Found., Brotherhood award, NCCJ, 1975. Mem.: DAR (nat. chmn. Am. history 1965—68, nat. chmn. bicentennial com. 1967—70, nat. chmn. nat. def. 1977—80, 1983—95), ABA, Ill. Bar Assn., Phi Beta Kappa, Pi Sigma Alpha. Office: Eagle Forum 7800 Bonhomme Ave Saint Louis MO 63105-1906 E-mail: phyllis@eagleforum.org.

SCHLAIN, BARBARA ELLEN, lawyer; b. N.Y.C., May 28, 1948; d. William and Evelyn (Youdelman) S. BA, Wellesley Coll., 1969; MA, Columbia U., 1970; JD, Yale U., 1973. Bar: N.Y. 1974, U.S. Dist. Ct. (so. dist.) N.Y. 1974, U.S. Ct. Appeals (2d cir.) 1975, U.S. Dist. Ct. (ea. dist.) N.Y. 1977. Assoc. firm Donovan Leisure Newton & Irvine, N.Y.C., 1973-76, Graubard Moskovitz McGoldrick Dannett & Horowitz, N.Y.C., 1976-79; atty. McGraw-Hill, Inc., N.Y.C., 1979-80, asst. gen. counsel, 1980-86, v.p., assoc. gen. counsel, asst. sec., 1986—. Sec. proprietary rights com. Info. Industry Assn., 1982-83. Author: outlines Practicing Law Inst., 1983, 84, 85, 86, 88; contbr. numerous articles to profl. jours. Bd. dirs., v.p., sec. Dance Rsch. Found., N.Y.C., 1983-86, chmn., 1986-98. Phi Beta Kappa scholar, Durant scholar Wellesley Coll., 1967-69. Mem. ABA, Assn. Am. Pubs. (lawyers com. 1979—), Assn. Bar City N.Y. (comm. law com. 1985-88). Office: The McGraw-Hill Companies Inc 1221 Avenue Of The Americas New York NY 10020-1095

SCHLATTER, ELIZABETH, museum administrator; b. Houston, Tex., Nov. 17, 1967; d. E. D. and Nancy Schlatter. BA, S.W. U., 1989; MA, George Washington U., 1996. Devel. asst. Contemporary Arts Mus., Houston, 1990—93; project dir. Travelling Exhibn. Svc. Smithsonian Inst., Washington, 1996—2000; asst. dir. U. Richmond (Va.) Mus., 2000—. Author: Structures of Nature: Photographs by Andreas Feininger, 2002, Become an Art Curator, 2003; contbr. articles to profl. jours. Mem.: Coll. Art Assn., ArtTable, Am. Assn. Mus. (curator's com. 2000—). Home: 105 N Allen Ave Richmond VA 23220-4501 Office: Univ Richmond Museums Richmond VA 23173

SCHLEGEL, AMY INGRID, curator, art historian; b. Phila., 1965; m. Thomas K. Standish. BA, U. Vt., 1986; MA, U. Chgo., 1990; PhD, Columbia U., 1997. Curatorial asst. Mus. Contemporary Art, Chgo., 1988; visual arts fellow Nat. Endowment for the Arts, Washington, 1992; vis. asst. prof. U. Vt., Burlington, 1996—97; curatorial fellow Hood Mus. Art, Dartmouth Coll., Hanover, NH, 1997—98; curator, dir. exhbns. Phila. Art Alliance, 1999—2003; dir. galleries and collections Tufts U., 2004—. Adj. faculty Moore Coll. Art, Phila., 2003. Author, editor: catalog An Unnerving Romanticism: Sylvia Sleigh and Lawrence Alloway, 2001. Mem.: Am. Assn. Museums, Coll. Art Assn. (Profl. Devel. fellow 1995—98), ARTTABLE. Avocation: hiking. Home: 15 Capen St # 303 Medford MA 02155 Office: Aidehman AAS Ctr 40R Talbot Ave Medford MA 02155 Office Phone: 617-627-3505. Personal E-mail: amyingridschlegel@hotmail.com.

SCHLEICHER, NORA ELIZABETH, banker, treasurer, accountant; b. Balt., Aug. 10, 1952; d. Irvin William and Eleanor Edna S.; m. Ray Leonard Settle Jr., July 27, 1985. AA cum laude, Anne Arundel Community Coll., 1972; BS summa cum laude, U. Balt., 1975. CPA, Md. Staff auditor Md. Nat. Bank, Balt., 1975-76, sr. staff auditor, 1976-77, supr. auditing dept., 1977-78; full charge acct. Wooden & Benson, CPA's, Balt., 1978-81; asst. to treas. First Fed. Savs. & Loan Assn., Annapolis, Md., 1981, asst. treas., 1982-83, v.p., 1984; v.p., treas. First Fed. Savs. & Loan Assn. (now First Annapolis Bank), 1984—. Bd. dirs., treas. Coll. Manor Community Assn. Mem. AICPA, Md. Assn. CPA's, Fin. Mgrs. Soc., Coll. Manor Community Assn. (bd. dirs., treas.). Methodist. Office: First Annapolis Savs Bank 1832 George Ave Annapolis MD 21401-4103

SCHLEIN, MIRIAM, author; children: Elizabeth Weiss, John Weiss. BA in Psychology, Bklyn. Coll., 1947. Author over 95 books for children, natural sci. books, concept books, story books, picture books, including: A Day at the Plygound, 1951, The Four Little Foxes, 1952 (Jr. Lit. Guild selection), Shapes, 1952, Go with the Sun, 1952, Tony's Pony, 1952, Fast is Not a Ladybug, 1953 (Boys' Club Am. Jr. Book award 1953), When Will the World Be Mine?, 1953 (Caldecott Honor Book, Am. Libr. Assn. 1954), The Sun Looks Down, 1954, How Do You Travel?, 1954, Heavy is a Hippopotamus, 1954, Elephant Herd, 1954 (Jr. Lit. Guild selection, Herald Tribune Honor Book award 1954), Oomi, the New Hunter, 1955, Little Red Nose, 1955, It's About Time, 1955, City Boy, Country Boy, 1955 (Jr. Lit. Guild selection), Puppy's House, 1955, Big Talk, 1955, Lazy Day, 1955, Henry's Ride, 1956, Something for Now, Something for Later, 1956, Deer in the Snow, 1956, The Big Cheese, 1957 (Jr. Lit. Guild selection), Little Rabbit, The High Jumper, 1957, Amazing Mr. Pelgew, 1957, A Bunny, A Bird, A Funny Cat, 1957, Here Comes Night, 1957, The Bumblebee's Secret, 1958, Home: The Tale of a Mouse, 1958, Herman McGregor's World, 1958, The Raggle Taggle Fellow, 1959, Little Dog Little, 1959, The Fishermans' Day, 1959, Kittens, Cubs and Babies, 1959, My Family, 1960, The Sun, the Wind, the Sea and the Rain, 1960, Laurie's New Brother, 1961, Amuny, Boy of Old Egypt, 1961, The Pile of Junk, 1962 (Jr. Lit. Guild selection), Snow Time, 1962, The Snake in the Carpool, 1963, Who?, 1963, The Big Green Thing, 1963, The Way Mothers Are, 1963, Big Lion, Little Lion, 1964, Billy, the Littlest One, 1966, The Best Place, 1968 Mem. Authors Guild, PEN Am. Ctr. (children's book com.), Nat. Writers Union. Home and Office: 19 E 95th St New York NY 10128-0710

SCHLESINGER, DEBORAH LEE, librarian; b. Cambridge, Mass., Sept. 13, 1937; d. Edward M. and Edith D. (Schneider) Hershoff; divorced; children: Suzanne, Richard. BA, U. Mass., 1961; MS, Simmons Coll., 1974; postgrad., U. Pitts., 1983. Reference librarian Bently Coll., Waltham, Mass., 1964-65; dir. Carnegie Library, Swissvale, Pa., 1973-77, South Park Twp. Library, Library, Pa., 1977-81, Monessen (Pa.) Library, 1981-82, Lewis & Clark Library, Helena, Mont., 1983-88, 89—; state librarian Mont. State Library, Helena, Mont., 1988-89. Vis. scholar Pitts. Regional Library Ctr., 1982-83. Editor Pa. Union List, 1982-83. Mem. exec. bd. Mont. Cultural Advocacy, 1983—. Mem. Mont. Library Assn. (chmn. legis. com. 1984-92, MLA lobbyist 1992—), Mont. Assn. Female Execs. (fin. com. 1986—), AAUW (exec. com. 1985-86). Clubs: Montana (Helena). Democrat. Avocations: flying, painting, reading, rafting, travel. Home: 2 Washington Pl Helena MT 59601-6283 Office: Lewis & Clark Libr 120 S Last Chance Gulch St Helena MT 59601-4165

SCHLESS, PHYLLIS ROSS, investment banker; d. Lewis H. and Doris G. Ross; m. Aaron Backer Schless, July 7, 1970; 1 son, Daniel Lewis Ross. Cert., Neighborhood Playhouse Sch. of Theatre, 1962, N.Y. Sch. Interior Design, 1964; BA in Econs., Wellesley Coll., 1964; MBA, Stanford U., 1966. Cert. theater prodns. Am. League Theater Owners and Prodrs. Assoc. internat. fin. Kuhn Loeb & Co., N.Y.C., 1966-70; fin. cons., 1971-73; sr. fin. analyst Trans World Airlines, N.Y.C., 1974-75; corp. fin., mergers and acquisitions Lazard Freres & Co., 1976-79; dir. mergers and acquisitions Am. Can Co., Greenwich, Conn., 1979-82; v.p. mergers and acquisitions Bear, Stearns & Co., N.Y.C., 1982-84; sr. v.p. corp. acquisitions Integrated Resources, 1984-85; chmn., chief exec. officer Ross Fin. Svcs. Group Inc., 1985—; supervisory dir. Merrill Lynch HYTS Funds, 1991-96. Bd. dirs. Calvary Hosp. Fund Bd., 1990-2000, chair investment com., 1995-99; trustee A.R. Tinker Fund, 1993—; trustee Nat. Child Labor Com., 1981-95, chmn., 1992-94; trustee New World Found., 1986-92, chair fin. com., treas. 1988-92; bd. dirs. Stanford Bus. Sch. Assn., N.Y., 1994—; adj. asst. prof. NYU, 1996—, Columbia U. Sch. Bus., 2001—; bd. dirs. Nat. Found. Tchg. Entrepreneurship, 1998—, metro. N.Y. chair, 2000—. Pres. Greater Bridgeport Nat. Coun. Jewish Women, 1971-73, bd. dirs., 1974-75; bd. dirs. Girls Clubs Am., 1975-89, mem. exec. com., 1982-89, pres., 1984-86; bd. dirs. Pauline Koner Dance Co., 1979-81, So. Conn. Child Guidance Clinic, 1981-83, New Canaan United Way, 1981-83; treas. Wellesley Class '64, 1984-89. Mem. Univ. Club. Office: Ross Fin Svcs Group Inc 6th Fl 689 5th Ave Fl 6 New York NY 10022-3133 also: PO Box 1986 East Hampton NY 11937-0908

SCHLESSINGER, LAURA, radio talk show host; b. Brooklyn, Jan. 16, 1947; d. Monroe and Yolanda Schlessinger; m. Lewis G. Bishop, 1982; 1 child, Deryk. BS in Biological Sciences, SUNY, Stonybrook; MS in Physiology, M Phil in Physiology, PhD in Physiology, Columbia U. Lic. in marriage and family therapy; cert. marriage, family and child counseling, U. So. Calif. Psychotherapist in private practice, Los Angeles, Calif., 1980—90; nat. syndicated radio talk show host The Dr. Laura Schlessinger Program, 1990—. Past mem. faculty U. So. Calif., Pepperdine U, instr. UCLA, UC Irvine; pres. Dr. Laura Schlessinger Foundation. Author: Ten Stupid Things Women Do to Mess Up Their Lives, 1994, How Could You Do That?! The Abdication of Character, Courage and Conscience, 1996, Ten Stupid Things Men Do To Mess Up Their Lives, 1997, The Ten Commandments: The Significance of God's Law in Everyday Life, 1998, Damsels, Dragons, and Regular Guys, 2000, Parenthood by Proxy; Don't Have Them If You Won't Raise Them, 2000, Ten Stupid Things Couples Do To Mess Up Their Relationships, 2002 The Proper Care & Feeding Of Husbands, 2004; books for children Why Do You Love Me?, 1999, But I Waaannt It!, 2000, Dr. Laura Schlessinger's Growing Up is Hard, 2001, I Hate My Life!, 2001, Dr. Laura Schlessinger's Where is God?, 2003; featured on The Oprah Winfrey Show, A&E Biography, Larry King Live, Lifetime's Intimate Portrait, 20/20, The Today Show, PBS, Hannity & Colmes, CBS This Morning, 48 Hours, Meet the Press with Tim Russert, Crier Today, Eye to Eye with Connie Chung, ABC This Week, Dateline; featured in Time, U.S. News and World Report, People, USA Today, The New York Times Magazine, The Los Angeles Times, The Wall Street Journal and others; featured spkr. Nat. Congressional Prayer Breakfast, Mus. Radio and Television, Claremont Inst., PBS, Nat. Religious Broadcasters, Country Radio Seminar. Recipient Marconi Award for Network/Syndicated Personality of the Yr., 1997, Genii Award, American Women in Radio & Television, 1998, Israel 50th Anniversary Tribute award, 1998, Crystal Cathedral Academy award, 1998, Love of a Child award, Childhelp USA, 1998, Chairman's award, Nat. Religious Broadcasters, 2000, Nat. Heritage award, Nat. Council of Young Israel, 2001, Conservative Leadership award, Clare Booth Luce Institute, 2001, Woman of the Yr. award, 2002. Mem.: AFTRA, SAG, Nat. Assn. At-Home Mothers (bd. adv.). Achievements include being broadcasted on approximately 300 stations with 12 million listeners; the second most popular talk show host in the country; show syndicated since June 1994; on air radio career for more than 25 years. Office: Premire Radio Networks 15260 Ventura Blvd Ste 300 Sherman Oaks CA 91403-5337*

SCHLICHTING, CATHERINE FLETCHER NICHOLSON, librarian, educator; b. Huntsville, Ala., Nov. 18, 1923; d. William Parsons and Ethel Loise (Breitling) Nicholson; m. Harry Fredrick Schlichting, July 1, 1950 (dec. Aug. 1964); children: James Dean, Richard Dale, Barbara Lynn. BS, U. Ala., 1944; MLS, U. Chgo., 1950. Asst. libr. U. Ala. Edn. Libr., Tuscaloosa, summers 1944-45; libr. Sylacauga (Ala.) H.S., 1944-45, Hinsdale (Ill.) H.S., 1945-49; asst. libr. Centre for Children's Books, U. Chgo., 1950-52; instr. reference dept. libr. Ohio Wesleyan U., Delaware, 1965-69, asst. prof., 1969-79, assoc. prof., 1979-85, prof., 1985—, curator Ohio Wesleyan Hist. Collection, 1986—, student pers. libr., 1966-72. Author: Introduction to Bibliographic Research: Basic Sources, 4th edit., 1983, Checklist of Biographical Reference Sources, 1977, Audio-Visual Aids in Bibliographic Instruction, 1976, Introduction to Bibliographic Research: Slide Catalog and Script, 1980; info. cons. (documentary) Noble Achievements: The History of Ohio Wesleyan 1942-1992, 1992, 150 Years of Excellence: A Pictorial View of Ohio Wesleyan University, 1992. Mem. adminstrv. bd. Meth. Ch., 1973-81, chmn. adminstrv. bd., 1985—, mem. coun. on ministries, 1975-81, chmn., 1975-77, trustee, 1999—2003. Recipient Algernon Sidney Sullivan award U. Ala., 1944, Hon. Alumna award Ohio Wesleyan U., 1997; Ohio Wesleyan U.-Mellon Found. grantee, 1972-73, 84-85; GLCA Tchg. fellow, 1976-77. Mem. ALA, Ohio Libr. Assn., Midwest Acad. Libr. Conf., Acad. Librs. Assn. Ohio (dir. 1984-86), AAUP (chpt. sec. 1967-68), United Meth. Women (pres. Mt. Vernon dist. 1994-97, newsletter editor 1998—), Ohio Wesleyan Woman's Club (exec bd. 1969-72, 77-79, 81-84, pres. 1969-70, sec. 1977-78), History Club (pres. 1971-72, v.p. 1978-79, 2003-04) Fortnightly Club (pres. 1975-76, 87-88, 2003-04), Am. Field Svc. (pres. Delaware chpt. 1975-76), Kappa Delta Pi, Alpha Lambda Delta. Democrat. Home: 57 Willow Brook Way S Delaware OH 43015 Office: Ohio Wesleyan U La Beeghly Library Delaware OH 43015

SCHLICKAU, LOIS MARIE, farmer; b. Arlington, Kans., Sept. 18, 1933; d. Otto W. and Maria Edna (Goering) Ritthaler; m. George Hans Schlickau, Apr. 26, 1955; children: Bruce, Susan Russell, James, Nancy Bernard. AA, Hutchinson C.C., 1953. Treas., v.p., pres. Kans. State Bd. Agr., 1986—93, Kans. State Fair Bd., 1986—94, pres., 1992; treas., v.p. women's exec. com. Kans. Electric Coop., 1991—95; mem. Kans. Value Added Ctr. Bd., 1994—96, vice-chmn., 1995—96, Kans. Fairs Assn. Bd., mem., 1994—96, v.p., 1995—96; mem. Cong. Sam Brownback's Agrl. Adv. Bd., 1995—97, Senator Sam Brownback's Agrl. Adv. Bd., 1997—99, Cong. Jerry Moran's Exec. Adv. Bd., 1996—, Reno County Ext. Coun. Bd., sec., Reno County Farm Bd.; mem. Nat. Cattle Women Bd.; mem. internat. agr. project adv. com. Kans. State U., mem. adminstrv. structure task force; mem. Kans. Vocat. Agr. Edn. Task Force. Charter mem., dir., parliamentarian, com. mem., v.p. Am. Hereford Aux. Bd., pres., 1980—81; charter mem., dir., com. mem., v.p., pres. Kans. Hereford Aux. Bd.; project leader Haven 4-H and Lucky H 4-H; past pres. Ladies of Congregation, past Sunday Sch. tchr., choir St. Paul's Luth. Ch.; former parent/tchr. league chmn. St. Paul's Luth. Sch.; local soc. pres. Luth. Women's Missionary League, 1994—96, local soc. sec., 2001—03, com. chmn., zone v.p., sec., state bd. mem., v.p., parliamentarian, nat. bylaws com., 1995—99; bd. dirs. Hutchinson Cmty. Found., 1996—2001, mem. exec. com., 1999—2001, chair grants com.; mem. Hutchinson C.C. Leadership Adv. Com., 1999—; bd. dirs. Bank Haven Adv. Bd., 2001—. Named Outstanding Woman, Am. Hfd. Aux., 1985, Friend of Extension, Kans. Extension Svc., 1993; named to Hall Fame, Kans. Fairs Assn., 1997, Wall of Hon., Hutchinson HS, 2004; recipient Outstanding Woman award, Kans. Hereford Aux., 1976, Achievement award, Kans. State Grange, 1993. Mem.: Kans. Agr. Women (pres. 1998—2000, v.p., parliamentarian, coms. mem., nat. legis. rep. 2001—), Am. Agri-Women (chmn. nat. conv. com. 1996, mem. com., Leaven award), Hutchinson Hosp. Corp. Bd. (bd. mem. 1998—2003, chmn. 2002, 2003), Kans. Tech. Enterprise Corp. Bd. (bd. dir. 1989—91, vice chmn. 1990—91), Reno County Hist. Soc. (dir. 1985—90, pres. 1988, dir. 1996—, v.p., sec., dir. 2000—), Hutchinson/Reno County C. of C. (mem. agri-bus. com.). Avocations: reading, cooking, traveling. Home and Office: 14506 S Victory Rd Haven KS 67543 Office Phone: 620-465-7749.

SCHLISSEL, LILLIAN, English educator, writer; b. N.Y.C., Feb. 22, 1930; d. Abraham and Mae (Isaacson) Fischer; children: Rebecca Claire, Daniel. BA, Bklyn. Coll., 1951; PhD, Yale U., 1957. From asst. prof. to prof. English Bklyn. Coll. and Grad. Ctr., CUNY, 1957—; dir. Am. studies program Bklyn. Coll., CUNY, 1974-97. Guest lectr. Am. studies U. N.Mex., Albuquerque, 1981, 83, 89; guest lectr. English U. Santa Clara, Calif., 1971. Co-editor: The Western Women's Reader, 2000-; author: Women's Diaries of the Westward Journey, 1982, Black Frontiers, 1995, Introduction to Covered Wagon Women, 1996; editor: Conscience in America, 1968, World of Randolph Bourne, 1970, Journals of Washington Irving, Vol. II, 1981, Three Plays by Mae West, 1997; co-editor: Western Women: Their Land, Their Lives, 1988, Far From Home, Families of Westward Journey, 1989. Mem. Am. Studies Assn., Orgn. Am. Historians, Western Hist. Assn., Western Lit. Assn. Avocation: painting. Office: Bklyn Coll Dept Am Studies Brooklyn NY 11210

SCHLITT, LYN M. lawyer; Gen. counsel Internat. Trade Commn., Washington, 1978—. Office: Internat Trade Commn 500 E St NW Washington DC 20436-0003

SCHLOSS, HADASSAH, open records program administrator; b. Buenos Aires, Nov. 18, 1950; came to US, 1977; d. Moises Zysman and Sofia (Zack) Kuperwasser; m. Peter Gordon Schloss, Mar. 27, 1977; 1 child, Merav Karen. BBA in Acctg., U. Tex., Austin, 1993. Clk. State of Tex., Austin, 1990-93; adminstrv. tech. III, 1993; internal auditor I, 1993-94; internal auditor II, 1994-95; program adminstr. open records sect., 1995—. Chair Open Records Steering Com., Austin, 1993—; mem. Freedom of Info. Found. Tex.; mem. Electronic Recording Adv. Com., Austin. Recipient James Madison award Freedom Info. Found. Tex., 1996. Mem. Nat. Assn. Govt. Communicators. Jewish. Avocations: reading mystery, suspense, biographies, sewing, cooking. Home: 6704 Roseborough Dr Austin TX 78747-4023 Office: Tex Bldg and Procurement Commn 1711 San Jacinto Blvd Austin TX 78701-1416 also: PO Box 13047 Austin TX 78711-3047

SCHLOSSBERG, CAROLINE BOUVIER KENNEDY (CAROLINE KENNEDY), writer, lawyer; b. Nov. 27, 1957; d. John Fitzgerald and Jacqueline Bouvier; m. Edwin A. Schlossberg, July 19, 1986; children: Rose, Tatiana, John (Jack) Bouvier Kennedy. Grad., Radcliffe Coll. (now part of Harvard), 1979; JD, Columbia Law Sch. Intern NY Daily News, 1977, Metropolitan Mus. Art, 1980; pres. John F. Kennedy Libr. Found.; chief exec. NYC Dept. Edn. Office Strategic Partnerships, 2003—. Author: In Our Defense- The Bill of Rights in Action, 1990; co-author: The Right to Privacy, 1995. Co-founder Profiles in Courage Awards, 1989; hon. chairwoman Am. Ballet Theatre.*

SCHLOSSER, ANNE GRIFFIN, librarian; b. N.Y.C., Dec. 28, 1939; d. C. Russell and Gertrude (Taylor) Griffin; m. Gary J. Schlosser, Dec. 28, 1965. BA in History, Wheaton Coll., Norton, Mass., 1962; MLS, Simmons Coll., 1964; cert. archives adminstrn., Am. U., 1970. Head UCLA Theater arts Libr., 1964-69; dir. Louis B. Mayer Libr., Am. Film Inst., L.A., 1969-88, dir. film/TV documentation workshop, 1977-87; head Cinema-TV Libr. and Archives of the Performing Arts, U. So. Calif., L.A., 1988-91; dir. Entertainment Resources Seminar, 1990; dir. rsch. libr. Warner Bros., 1991—. Project dir. Motion Pictures, Television, Radio: A Union Catalogue of Manuscript and Special Collections in the Wesern U.S., 1977. Active Hollywood Dog Obedience Club, Calif. Recipient numerous grants for script indexing, manuscript cataloging, libr. automation. Mem. Soc. Calif. Archivists (pres. 1982-83), Theater Libr. Assn (exec. bd. 1983-86), Spl. Librs. Assn. Democrat. Episcopalian. Avocations: running, swimming, reading, dog obedience training. Office: Warner Bros Rsch Libr 5200 Lankershim Blvd Ste 100 North Hollywood CA 91601-3100

SCHLOTFELDT, ROZELLA MAY, nursing educator, educator; b. DeWitt, Iowa, June 29, 1914; d. John W. and Clara C. (Doering) Schlotfeldt. BS, State U. Iowa, 1935; MS, U. Chgo., 1947, PhD, 1956; DSc (hon.), Georgetown U., 1972, Adelphi U., 1979, Wayne State U., 1983, U. Ill., Chgo., 1985, Kent State U., 1987, U. Cin., 1989, Case Western Res. U., 1996; LHD (hon.), Med. U. S.C., 1976. Staff nurse State U. Iowa, VA Hosp., 1935—39; instr., supr. maternity nursing (State U. Iowa), 1939—44; asst. prof. U. Colo. Sch. Nursing, 1947—48; asst., then asso. prof. Wayne State U. Coll. Nursing, 1948—55; prof., asso. dean Wayne State U. Coll. Nursing (Coll. Nursing), 1957—60; dean Frances Payne Bolton Sch. Nursing, Case Western Res. U., 1960-72, prof., 1960—82, prof., dean emeritus, 1982—95. Vis. prof. Rutgers U., 1984—89, 1990—95, U. Pa., 1985—86; spl. cons. Surgeon Gen.'s Adv. Group on Nursing, 1961—63; mem. nursing rsch. study sect. USPHS, 1962—66; mem. com. on nursing edn. facilities Nat. League for Nursing-USPHS, 1962—64; mem. com. on health goals Cleve. Health Coun., 1961—66; mem. Cleve. Health Planning and Devel. Commn., 1969—72; adv. com. divsn. nursing W.K. Kellogg Found., 1959—67; v.p. Ohio Bd. Nursing Edn. and Nurse Registration, 1970—71, pres., 1971—72; mem. Nat. Health Svcs. Rsch. Tng. Com., 1970—71; mem. supply and edn. panel Health Manpower Com., 1966—67; rev. com. Nurse Tng. Act, 1967—68; bd. visitors Duke U. Med. Ctr., 1968—70; mem. coun., exec. com. Inst. Medicine of NAS, 1971—75; mem. nat. adv. health svcs. coun. Health Svcs. and Mental Health Adminstrn., 1971—75; mem. def. adv. com. on women in svcs. Dept. of Def., 1972—75; bd. dirs. trean. Nursing Home Adv. and Rsch. Coun., 1975—96; mem. adv. panel Health Svcs. Rsch. Commn. on Human Resources, NAS, 1977—85; cons. Walter Reed Army Inst.; adv. coun. on nursing U.S. VA, 1965—69, chmn., 1966—69; mem. Yale U. Coun. Com. on Med. Affairs, 1981—86; mem. adv. bd. Scholarly Inquiry for Nursing Practice, 1987—96. Mem. editl. bd. Advances in Nursing Sci., Inquiry, 1982—85, Jour. Nursing Edn., 1982—91; contbr. articles to profl. jours. Bd. visitors Syracuse U., 1990—97. 1st lt. Nurse Corps U.S. Army, 1944—46. Named Living Legend, Am. Acad. Nursing, 1995; recipient Disting. Svc. award, U. Iowa, 1973, Case Western Res. U., 1991, N. Watts Lifetime Achievement award, 1995. Fellow: Nat. League Nursing, Am. Acad. Nursing (v.p. 1975—77); mem.: ANA (chmn. commn. on nurse edn. 1967—70, mem. com. for studying credentialling 1976—79, adv. com. W.K. Kellogg Nat. Fellowship program 1981—85), Sigma Theta Tau (nat. v.p. 1948—50, selection com., disting. lectr. program 1986—87, Founders award for creativity 1985, Henderson fellow 1985), Pi Lambda Theta. Home: Judson Manor 1089 E 107th St #318 Cleveland OH 44106*

SCHLUB, TERESA RAE, minister; b. Oak Park, Ill., July 11, 1946; d. Robert Carl and Shirley Rae (Listhartke) Grupe. BA, Westmar Teikyo U., 1971; MDiv, Garrett Evangel. Seminary, Evanston, Ill., 1974. Ordained deacon United Meth. Ch., 1973, elder, 1978. Asst. minister First United Meth. Ch., Morris, Ill., 1974-76; minister Leaf River (Ill.) German Valley United Meth. Ch., 1976-82, East Jordan United Meth. Ch., Sterling, Ill., 1982-86, Paw Paw (Ill.) United Meth. Ch., 1986-89, Community United Meth. Ch., LaMoille, Ill., 1989-95, Capron (Ill.) United Meth. Ch., 1995—2000, North Boone Coop. Ministries, Poplar Grove, Ill., 1998—2000. Mem. alumni coun., sec. Garrett Evangel. Theol. Seminary, Evanston, 1974-76; mem. Conf. Bd. of Evangelism, 1974-76, founder, Schlub Ministries. Bd. dirs. Green Hills coun. Girls Scouts U.S., Freeport, Ill., 1986-88, Lee County Red Cross, Dixon, Ill., 1986-89, Crossroads Counseling Ctr., Mendota, 1989-91; bd. dirs. Quad County Counseling Ctr., Princeton, 1991—, treas., 1993-94; mem. Ill. Home Extension Assn., Grundy, Ogle, Whiteside and Lee Counties, 1974-89; sec. DeKalb Dist. Com. Ordained Ministry; mem. Boone County Coun. Aging, 1997-2000, Boone County Planning Commn., 1998-2000; founder Schlub Ministries; cert. in spiritual formation United Meth. Ch., 2003. Home: 5813 Beechwood Dr Apt B Loves Park IL 61111-1543

SCHLUETER, JUNE MAYER, English educator, author; b. Passaic, N.J., Nov. 4, 1942; m. Paul Schlueter. BA in English magna cum laude, Fairleigh

Dickinson U., 1970; MA in English, Hunter Coll., CCNY, 1973; PhD in English and Comparative Lit., Columbia U., 1977. Asst. prof. Lafayette Coll., Easton, Pa., 1977-84, assoc. prof., 1984-91, prof., 1991-92, Charles A. Dana prof., 1992—, head English dept., 1992-93; asst. to provost, 1986-90; acting provost., 1993-94; provost Lafayette Coll., Easton, Pa., 1994—. Fulbright prof. Gesamthochschule Kassel Univ., Fed. Republic Germany, 1978-79; chmn. Shakespeare Seminar Columbia U., 1989-91, exec. bd., 1989—; active NEH summer seminar for coll. profs., 1981, lectr. Commonwealth Partnership Summer Lit. Inst., 1985-87, dir. summer seminar for sch. tchrs., 1988, selection panel, 1989, 91, evaluator Instl. Grant Program, 1990. Author: Metafictional Characters in Modern Drama, 1979, The Plays and Novels of Peter Handke, 1981; (with James K. Flanagan) Arthur Miller, 1987; (with James P. Lusardi) Reading Shakespeare in Performamce: King Lear, 1990, Dramatic Closure: Reading the End, 1995; editor: Feminist Rereadings of Modern American Drama, 1989, Modern American Drama: The Female Canon, 1990, Critical Essays: The Two Gentlemen of Verona, 1995; (with Paul Schlueter) The English Novel: Twentieth Century Criticism, Vol. 2: Twentieth Century Novelists, 1982, Modern American Literature, Supplement II, 1985, An Encyclopedia of British Women Writers, 1988; (with Enoch Brater) Approaches to Teaching Beckett's Waiting for Godot, 1991; editor Shakespeare Bull., 1984—; assoc. editor States, 1984-90; editl. bd. Studies in Am. Drama, 1945-Present, 1989—; editl. cons. Modern Drama, Theatre Jour., PMLA, Studies in Twentieth Century Lit., others; contbr. revs., essays to profl. jours. Bd. govs. Fairleigh Dickinson U., Rutherford, N.J., 1985—; adv. com. Lehigh Valley Ednl. Coop., 1988-90; selection panel German Acad. Exch. Svc., Bonn, 1979. Rsch. grantee Lafayette Coll., 1977-93, NEH summer rsch. grantee, 1990, DAAD summer rsch. grantee, 1991. Mem. MLA, Shakespeare Assn. Am., Internat. Shakespeare Assn., Coll. English Assn., Samuel Beckett Soc., AAUP, Columbia Shakespeare Seminar. Home: 123 High St Easton PA 18042-1609 Office: Lafayette Coll Lafayette College Easton PA 18042

SCHLUETER, SHERRY, protective services official; Sect. supr. Spl. Victioms and Family Crimes Sect./Criminal Investigations Broward County Sheriff's Office, Ft. Lauderdale, Fla. Spl. appearances on Opra, Leeza, and Montel on behalf of prevention of cruelty to animals, children and the elderly; tchr. nationwide law enforcement classes on subject of correlation between animal cruelty and human violence. Office: Sheriffs Office/Broward Cty 2601 W Broward Blvd Fort Lauderdale FL 33312

SCHMANDT-BESSERAT, DENISE, archaeologist, educator; b. Ay, France, Aug. 10, 1933; came to U.S., 1965, naturalized, 1970; d. Victor and Jeanne (Crabit) Besserat; m. Jurgen Schmandt, Dec. 27, 1956; children: Alexander, Christopher, Phillip. Ed., Ecole du Louvre, 1965. Rsch. fellow in Near Eastern Archaeology Peabody Mus. Harvard U., Cambridge, Mass., 1969-71; fellow Radcliffe Inst., Cambridge, 1969-71; asst. prof. Middle Eastern studies U. Tex., Austin, 1972-81, assoc. prof., 1981-88, prof., 1988—; acting chief curator U. Tex. Art Mus., 1978-79. Vis. assoc. prof. U. Calif., Berkeley, 1987-88; curator Legacy of the Middle East exhbn. Jeddah (Saudi Arabia) Hist. Preservation Dept. Author: Before Writing, 1992, How Writing Came About, 1996, History of Counting, 1999; adv. editor Tech. and Culture, 1978-92; editl. adv. bd. Archaeology Odyssey, 2003—; mem. editl. bd. Written Communication, 1993-95, Visible Lang., 1985—, Explorations in Media Ecology, 2001, Ancient Adminstrn., 2001; contbr. articles to profl. jours. Recipient Kayden Nat. U. Press Book award, 1992, Robert W. Hamilton Author award, 1998; named in Am. Scientist, 1999; Wenner-Gren Found. grant, 1970-71, NEA grant, 1974-75, 77-78, ACLS grant, 1984, Deutscher Akademischer Austauschdienst grant, 1986, NEH grant, 1992; NEH fellow, 1979-80, U. Wis. Inst. for Rsch. in Humanities fellow,, 1984-85, USIA, Am. Ctr. Oriental Rsch. fellow, 1994-95, 97, 2001, Malone fellow 1997, 99, fellow Humanities Rsch. Ctr. Stanford U., 2003—. Mem. Am. Oriental Soc., Archeol. Inst. Am. (governing bd. 1983-89), Am. Anthropol. Assn., Am. Schs. of Oriental Rsch., Centro Internat. Rsch. Archeologiche Anthropologiche e Storiche (Rome). Business E-Mail: dsb@mail.utexas.edu.

SCHMEDLEN, JEANNE HEARN, writer, legislative staff member, consultant; b. Darby, PA, May 23, 1947; d. Robert Francis and Jean McCaffrey Hearn; m. Daniel George Schmedlen; children: Daniel G. Jr., Michael J. Newspaper reporter, women's editor AP, Dodge City, Kans., 1974—78, Dodge City Daily Globe, Dodge City, 1974—78, Hutchinson News, Kansas, Dodge City, 1974—78; press sec., legis. liaison Pa. Coun. Arts, Harrisburg, Pa., 1978—83; dep. press sec. to Gov. Dick Thornburgh Gov. Office, Harrisburg, 1982—87; chief staff, press sec. First Lady of Pa., Harrisburg, Pa., 1987—95; dir. spl. projects and chief of protocol Office of the Spkr. of the House, Harrisburg, Pa., 1995—. Bd. dirs. MetroArts Capital Region, Harrisburg, 1994—97; spkr. rep. Pa. Coun. Arts, Harrisburg, 1995—2003; bd. mem. Theatre Harrisburg, Harrisburg, 1995—2001; commr. Lemoyne Borough Planning Commn., Lemoyne, 1996—2001; bd. mem. Susquehanna Art Mus., Harrisburg, 1997—; sr. ptnr. Women's Investment Network, Harrisburg, 1999—2000; bd. mem. State Mus. Pa., Harrisburg, 2000—, Art Assn. Harrisburg, Harrisburg, 2000—; chmn. Pa. Humanities Coun., Phila., 2001—03, vice chmn., 2003—; ski instr. Ski Roundtop, 1990—. Author: Wisdom, Vision & Diplomacy: Speakers of the Pennsylvania House, 1999, (Book) At the Dawn of the Millennium. The Pennsylvania Capitol: A Building for All Time, 1999, The Women of the Pennsylvania House of Representatives 1923, 2001, 103 Years of Leadership: Pennsylvania House of Representatives' Caucus Officers 1099 until Today, 2003, The Capitol, 2003; prodr.: (Videotape) The Arts... The Humanities... Older Pennsylvanians, 2001. Pres. Civic Club Harrisburg Affiliates, Pa., 2001—03; mem. adv. bd. Pa. Excellence Pub. Svc. Series, Harrisburg, 2001—02. Recipient friend art ed. award, Pa. Art Educators Assn., 2001, citizen diplomacy award, Internat. Visitors Coun., 2000, bd. govs. recognition, Pa. State Sys. Higher Ed., 1999, Legis. award, Pa. Assn. Health, Phys. Edn. and Dance, 2003. Roman Catholic. Avocations: sailing, travel, skiing. Home: 913 Woodland Dr Lemoyne PA 17043 Office: PA House of Reps 332 Ryan Office Bldg Harrisburg PA 17120-2020

SCHMERTZ, MILDRED FLOYD, editor, writer; b. Pitts., Mar. 29, 1925; d. Robert Watson and Mildred Patricia (Floyd) S. B.Arch., Carnegie Mellon U., 1947; M.F.A., Yale U., 1957. Archtl. designer John Schurko, Architect, Pitts., 1947-55; assoc. editor Archtl. Record, N.Y.C., 1957-65, sr. editor, 1965-80, exec. editor, 1980-85, editor-in-chief, 1985-90. Vis. lectr. Yale Sch. Architecture, 1979— Editor, contbr.: New Life for Old Buildings, other books on arch. and planning; contbg. writer: Architectural Digest, 2000—. Bd. mgrs. Jr. League, City of N.Y., 1964-65; commr. N.Y. Landmarks Preservation Commn., 1988-91. Fellow AIA; mem. Mcpl. Art Soc. N.Y., Century Assn. (N.Y.C.) Home and Office: 310 E 46th St New York NY 10017-3002

SCHMID, LYNETTE SUE, child and adolescent psychiatrist; b. Tecumseh, Nebr., May 28, 1958; d. Mel Vern John and Janice Wilda (Bohling) S.; m. Vijendra Sundar, June 13, 1987; children: Jesse Christopher Mikaéle, Eric Lynn Kalani, Christina Elizabeth Ululani. BS, U. Nebr., 1979; MD, U. Nebr., Omaha, 1984; postgrad., U. Mo., 1984-89. Diplomate Am. Bd. Med. Examiners, Am. Bd. Psychiatry and Neurology. Child and adolescent psychiatrist Fulton (Mo.) State Hosp., 1990-91, Mid-Mo. Mental Health Ctr., Columbia, Mo., 1991-96; owner Fairview Motel, Kemmerer, Wyo., 1996—. Clin. asst. prof. psychiatry U. Mo., Columbia, 1990-96. Contbr. articles to profl. jours. Mem. Am. Psychiat. Assn., Am. Acad. Child and Adolescent Psychiatry, Ctrl. Mo. Psychiat. Assn. (sec.-treas. 1992-93, pres.-elect 1993-94, pres. 1994-95), U. Nebr. Alumni Assn., Phi Beta Kappa, Alpha Omega Alpha. Republican. Avocations: walking, reading, studying scripture. Office Phone: 307-877-3938.

SCHMIDER, MARY ELLEN HEIAN, American studies educator, academic administrator; b. Chippewa Falls, Wis., Apr. 17, 1938; d. A. Bernard and Ellen Dagmar (Gunderson) Heian; m. Michael Heaton Leonard, June 16, 1962 (div. Oct. 1969); 1 child, William Gunerius Leonard; m. Carl Ludwig Schmider, June 17, 1970; 1 child, Dagmar Heian (née Schmider) Meinders. BA in English Lit. magna cum laude, St. Olaf Coll., Northfield, Minn., 1960; MA in English Lit., U. So. Calif., 1962; PhD in Am. Studies, U. Minn., 1983. Mem. founding faculty in English, Calif. Luth. Coll., Thousand Oaks, Calif., 1961-64; instr. dept. English U. Vt., Burlington, Vt., 1964-70; instr. Univ. writing program U. RI, South Kingston, RI, 1973-77; grad. asst. dept. rhetoric U. Minn., Mpls., 1975-76; dir. continuing edn./cmty. svc. Moorhead State U., Minn., 1977-86, dean grad. studies and grad. faculty, 1983-95; US Fulbright lectr. Lanzhou U., China, 1997. Mem. bd. pensions Luth. Ch. in Am., Mpls., 1982—87; mem. bd. higher edn. and schs. Evang. Luth. Ch. in Am., Chgo., 1987—95; cert. coll. mgmt. Carnegie Mellon U., 1987; lectr. USIA in Austria, Italy, Japan, Iceland; bd. dirs. Luth. Brotherhood, Mpls., 1988—2001; collegiate full prof. U. Md., U. Coll., Europe, Heidelberg, Germany, 2000—. Author: (biog. sketches) Biog. Dictionary of Social Welfare, esp. Jane Addams. Mem. exec. comm. Minn. Humanities Commn., St. Paul, 1983-89, chair, 1987-88. Bush Leadership fellow, 1987. Mem. US Fulbright Assn., Am. Studies Assn., Phi Beta Kappa, Phi Kappa Phi. Lutheran. Avocation: swimming, design, music, internat. travel, family activities.. Home: 7701 180th St Chippewa Falls WI 54729-6440 E-mail: mehscls@yahoo.com.

SCHMIDT, ANGELA MARIE, music educator, musician; b. Columbus, Ohio, Dec. 28, 1973; d. Frederick Owen and Heather Anne Schmidt; m. Daniel Edward Maske, July 26, 1997. BFA in Music Edn., U. Wis., Milw., 1997; MusM in String Devel., U. Wis., Madison, 2002. Cellist Green Bay (Wis.) Symphony Orch., 1991—96, Watertown (Wis.) Area Chamber Orch., 2000—; cellist, founding mem. Lakeside String Quartet, Milw., 1994—2000; orch. dir. grades 4-12 Lake Mills (Wis.) Sch. Dist., 1997—; cello instr. Marantha Bapt. Bible Coll., Watertown, 1999—2000; string methods instr. St. Norbert Coll., DePere, Wis., 2002. Cello coach, rehearsal condr. Milw. Youth Symphony Orch., 1995—97; adjudicator music festivals Wis. Sch. Music Assn., 1999—; counselor summer camp, chamber ensemble coach Wis. Youth Symphony Orch., Milw., 1999, Milw., 2001. Performer: (CD rec.) Age of Balance, Far Corner. Music Merit scholar, U. Wis.-Milw., 1995—97. Mem.: Wis. String Tchrs.' Assn., Wis. Cello Soc., New Directions Cello Soc., Am. String Tchrs.' Assn., Collegiate Music Educators' Nat. Conf. (v.p.). Avocations: hiking, bicycling, progressive rock, Siberian huskies, drawing.

SCHMIDT, CATHERINE ANN, psychologist; d. Walter A. and Diann C. Schmidt. BA magna cum laude, Beaver Coll. (name now Arcadia U.), Glenside, Pa., 1993; MA in Clin. Psychology, MCP Hahnemann (name now Drexel U.), Phila., 1996, PhD in Clin. Psychology, 2000. Lic. clin. psychologist Pa., cert. sexual assault counselor Network of Victims Assistance, 1992. Therapist, clin. psychology practicum MCP Hahnemann U. Student Counseling Ctr., Phila., 1992—98; diagnostic interview and group therapy leader Ea. Pa. Psychiat. Inst., Phila., 1996—99; pre-doctoral intern in psychology Norristown (Pa.) State Hosp., 1999—2000; clin. dir. anger mgmt. program U. Chgo. Clin. Neuroscience Rsch. Unit, Chgo., 2000—01; diagnostic assessor U. Pa., Phila., 2002—03; counselor and disabilities coord. Drexel U., Phila., 2002—03; clin. psychologist Southampton Psychiat. Assocs., Pa., 2003—. Statis. cons., Phila., 2003—. Contbr. chapters to books. Mem.: Pa. Psychol. Assn., Am. Psychol. Assn., Bucks County C. of C., Lambda Delta Alpha. Achievements include development of Lifetime History of Impulsive Behavior and Self Report (psychological assessment instruments). Avocations: yoga, bicycling, gardening. Office: Southampton Psychiat Assocs Ste 312 1111 Street Rd Southampton PA 18966

SCHMIDT, DIANE JOY, photographer, author, educator; b. Lake Forest, Ill., Oct. 10, 1953; d. John and Miriam (Friedman) S. BA in Lit., Prescott (Ariz.) Coll., 1974; BFA, R.I. Sch. Design, 1976; MA, U. N.Mex., 2002. Pvt. practice, Chgo., 1977—, Chgo. and Ariz., 1992—, Chgo., Ariz., N.Mex., 1998—; grad. fellow U. N.Mex., 1999, instr. English creative writing and composition, 2000—02. Photography dept. adj. faculty Columbia Coll., 1991-92; photographer Northwestern U., U. Ariz., U. Chgo.; founder, pres., CEO Secure Magic Cane, Inc., 2000. Author, photographer: Night Moves, 1984, Amen Corners: Chgo.'s Storefront Churches, 1987, Mother's Table, 1989, I Am a Jesse White Tumbler, 1990, WISE, 1996, Collected Stories of Ernestine the Bad, 2002; exhibitions include Abstract Rels., 1980, Chgo. Exhbn., 1985, Where's Chimpy, 1988, Navajo Psychology, 1997, Diné Terminology, 2003; co-dir.: Elders Album Project, 1994; contbr. articles to profl. jours. Organizer Operation Family Photo, USO, 1991. Recipient Childrens Reading Round Table, 1988, 89, IABC Silver Quill award, 1994, PIX Photo Dist. News Digital Photo award, 1996, Arts Genesis Vol. of Yr. award, 1994, Health Edn. Sci. Comm. award, 1996; Arts Midwest fellow Nat. Endowment for Arts, 1988.

SCHMIDT, GRETCHEN ERIKA, special education educator; b. Waterbury, Conn., Nov. 14, 1969; d. Carolyn Alice and Samuel Brown(Stepfather), Donald Joseph Schmidt; m. Jonathan Daniel Neuhausel, Mar. 15, 2003. DEd, No. Ariz. U., 1999, M in Adult Edn., 1995; BBA, George Wash. U., 1991. State articulation facilitator Ariz. Bd. Regents Ariz. C.C. Assn., Phoenix, 1999—; prof. No. Ariz. U., Flagstaff, 1995—. Mem. Ariz. Profl. Devel. Leadership Acad., Phoenix, 1999—2003, Univ. Career Women, Flagstaff, 1997—2003. D-Liberal. Avocations: backpacking, travel, snowboarding, biking. Office: Ariz Board of Regents No Ariz Univ Box 6052 Flagstaff AZ 86011 E-mail: gretchen.schmidt@nau.edu.

SCHMIDT, JEAN, state representative; b. Cin., Nov. 29, 1951; married; 1 child. BS in Polit. Sci., BA in Social Studies-Secondary Edn., U. Cin. State rep. dist. 66 Ohio Ho. of Reps., Columbus, vice chair, human svcs. subcom., mem. banking pensions and securities, fin. and appropriations, human svcs. and aging, and pub. utilities coms. Chair, founder Sauls Found. 5K Race; mem. exec. com., econ. devel. com., 2001 com. Clermont County Ctrl. Com., Ohio; bd. trustees Clermont County Libr.; bd. dirs. Clermont County Mercy Hosp. Mem.: Milford-Miami Twp. Coalition on Aging, Coalition of Large Ohio Urban Twps., Clermont County and Southwest Twp. Assns., Clermont County Agrl. Soc., Ohio Twp. Assn., Clermont County LWV, Clermont County and Milford Miami Twp. Cs. of C., Leukemia Soc. Team in Tng., Clermont Northwest Rotery, Clermont and Hamilton Counties Rep. Clubs. Republican. Office: 77 S High St 11th fl Columbus OH 43215-6111

SCHMIDT, JENNIFER ANNE, education educator; b. Indpls., Sept. 25, 1970; d. Thomas Charles and Mary Adelle (Galli) Schmidt; m. Anthony James Krolak, Nov. 22, 1996; 1 child, Nathaniel Schmidt Krolak (dec.). BA, Lawrence U., Appleton, Wis., 1992; PhD, U. Chgo., 1998. Rsch. dir. U. Chgo., 1998—2001; asst. prof. No. Ill. U., DeKalb, 2001—. Cons. Sloan Ctr. Parents, Children and Work, U. Chgo., 2001—. Contbr. articles to profl. jours., chpts. to books. Fellow Social Sci. Rsch. Inst., DeKalb, Ill., 2002—03, Rsch. fellow, William T. Grant Found., 1996—98. Mem.: Soc. for Rsch. Adolescence, Soc. for Rsch. Childhood Devel., Am. Ednl. Rsch. Assn. Office: No Ill U Leadership Ednl Psych & Found Dekalb IL 60115

SCHMIDT, JENNIFER SHAW, social sciences educator; b. Kansas City, Mo., Sept. 20, 1966; d. John and Melinda Shaw; m. Derek L. Schmidt. BA, Tex. Christian U., 1989; JD, U. Kans., 1994. Bar: D.C. 1995. Legis. corr. Senate Minority Leader Bob Dole, Washington, 1989—90; legis. asst. Congressman Jack Fields, Washington, 1990—91; law clk. Legal Aid Soc. Topeka, 1992, Orgn. of Am. States, Washington, 1993; assoc. Dyer Ellis & Joseph, Washington, 1994—96; counsel U.S. Senate Jud. Subcom. on Cts., Washington, 1996—98; sr. counsel U.S. Sen. Chuck Grassley, Washington, 1998—2000; chief of staf Kans. House Maj. Leader, Topeka, 2000—01, Kans. House Spkr., Topeka, 2001—03; instr. Pittsburg (Kans.) State U., 2003—. Gov. Kans. U. Law Sch. Bd. Govs., 2002—; Rep. precinct committeewoman Independence, 2002—; bd. dirs. Habitat for Humanity Montgomery County, Independence, Kans., 2002—, Kidsvoting Kans., 2003—; legis. com. mem. SEK, Inc., Kans., 2002—. Mem.: PEO, Rotary Internat. Office: Pittsburg State U Dept Social Scis Russ Hall Rm 327 D 1701 S Broadway Pittsburg KS 66762-7546

SCHMIDT, KAREN LEE, marketing professional, sales executive; b. Milw., Oct. 14, 1953; d. Walter K. and Marilyn V. Schmidt. BSBA, Colo. State U., 1975; postgrad., U. Louisville, 1978-79. Fin. analyst FICB of Louisville, 1975-79; sales rep. STSC, Inc., Chgo., 1979-81; regional software sales mgr. Xerox, Chgo., 1981-85; cen. region mgr. Datext, Inc., Chgo., 1985-87; regional mgr. Systems Software Assocs., Chgo., 1987-88; dir. bus. devel. Andersen Cons., Chgo., 1988-94; nat. dir. mktg. fin. svcs. KPMG, Chgo., 1994-95; chief mktg. officer Quantra Corp., Chgo., 1995-97; ptnr. in charge mktg. and sales BDO Seidman, Chgo., 1997—2000; exec. v.p. markets Land America, Richmond, Va., 2001—. Bd. trustees Theatre Va., 2002—. Home: 2905 E Stony Hill Ct Apt 1A Richmond VA 23235-6841

SCHMIDT, LEEANNE, artist; b. Dayton, Ky., June 13, 1940; d. Douglas Walter and Marian Brown; m. Edward Schmidt; children: Douglas, Eric. BS, U. Cin., 1962, MFA, 1992. Tchr. Gov.'s Inst. for Talented and Gifted, Miami U., 1997, U. Cin., 1991-92, 94, 96, 97, No. Ky. U., Highland Heights, 1992-96, Cairo Am. Coll., 1998, U. Calif., San Diego, 1999; vis. artist Art Acad. Cin., 1997, instr., 1998; vis. artist Morehead State U., 1997, U. Louisville, 1996, Thomas More Coll., Crestview Hills, Ky., 1996, U. Cin., 1996, numerous others; curator Summerfair, Inc., Cin., 1997, Images Gallery, Cin., 1995, others. One-person shows linclude: The Marta Hewett Gallery, Cin., 1997, Morehead State U., Ky., 1997, Gallery 292, N.Y.C., 1997, Gallery of So. Photographers, New Orleans, 1996, Miami U., Oxford, Ohio, 1996, U. Louisville, 1996, Lycoming Coll., Williamsport, Pa., 1996, others; groups exhbns. include Huntington Mus. Art, W.Va., 1997, Swann Galleries, N.Y.C., 1997, Wellington B. Gray Art Gallery, E. Carolina U., Greenville, 1997, Bank One Gallery, Louisville, 1997, Art Acad. of Cin., 1997, Marta Hewett Gallery, Cin., 1992-96, Gallery for So. Photographers, New Orleans, 1996, U. Minn., Mpls., 1996, numerous others; selected books and catalogues include: Nudes 2, 1997, Signs, 1997, Eros, 1996, Love, Flesh, and Water, 1996, Horizons, 1996, Body of Evidence, 1995, The Myth and Madness of Ophelia, 2001, others; corp. commns. include No. Ky. U., 1993; selected pub. collections include: The Bibliotek Nationale, Paris, J.B. Speed Art Mus., Louisville, Ogden Coll., New Orleans, Dayton Art Inst., Ohio, Cin. Art Mus., Cin. Bell Corp. Collections, U. Louisville; works collected in numerous pvt. collections; represented by Gallery 292, N.Y.C. Artist Profl. Devel. grantee Ky. Arts Coun., Frankfort, 1997, 98; recipient scholarships U. Cin., 1990-92, Kodak Educator scholarship, Palm Beach Workshops, Boca Raton, Fla., 1994, fellowships Ky. Found. for Women, Louisville, 1996, Al Smith Artist Fellowship, Frankfort, 1994, Wolfstein Travel fellowship U. Cin., 1991, others; recipient exhbn. awards that include: Inst. Nacional de Bellas Artes, San Miguel de Allende, Mexico, 1995, Hunter Mus. of Am. Art, Chattanooga, 1995, Louisville Visual Art Assn., 1993, 94, others. Home: 1071 Celestial St Apt 2000 Cincinnati OH 45202 E-mail: clestialee@fuse.net.

SCHMIDT, LYNDA WHEELWRIGHT, psychotherapist; b. Beijing, July 29, 1931; came to the U.S., 1931; d. Joseph Balch and Jane Byers (Hollister) Wheelwright; m. Klaus Dieter, May 8, 1930; children: Karen Calley, Claudia Lewis. BA, U. Calif., Berkeley, 1965, MSW, 1968. Cert. Jungian analyst; bd. cert. diplomate Am. Bd. Examiners Clin. Social Work. Staff psychiat. social worker Pacific Med. Ctr., San Francisco, 1968-71; pvt. practice psychotherapy and Jungian analysis San Francisco, 1971-87, Brooklin, Maine, 1985—. Tng. analyst CG Jung Inst., San Francisco, 1978—; mem. certifying com. CG Jung Inst., San Francisco, 1980-84; cons. and lectr. in field. Author: Time Out of Mind: Trekking the Hindu Kush, 1978, The Long Shore, A Psychological Experience of the Wilderness, 1991; contbr. articles to profl. jours. Fellow Calif. Soc. Clin. Social Workers; mem. NASW, Acad. Cert. Social Workers, Inc., CG Jung Inst. (chair certifying com. 1980-84), Alpha Phi Sorority. Democrat. Avocations: reading, horseback riding, travel, music. Home and Office: PO Box 269 Brooklin ME 04616-0269

SCHMIDT, MARTHA BUBECK, social sciences educator; b. Cadott, Wis., Sept. 28, 1912; d. Karl Christian and Lydia Sarah (Keller) Bubeck; m. Eugene Milton Schmidt, Sept. 11, 1943; children: Eugene Karl, Fredric John. BS, U. Wis., Stout, 1934; MPhil, U. Wis., Madison, 1947, M in Psychology and Behavioral Studies, 1959. Tchr. home econs. Barron (Wis.) High Sch., 1934-37; supr. student teaching U. Wis., Stout, 1937-38; state supr. home econs. edn. Wis. State Bd. Vocat. Edn., Madison, 1938-48; instr. adult evening sch. Madison Area Tech. Coll., 1949-69; guidance counselor Madison Met. Schs., 1959-79; coord. AARP and Wis. Ret. Tchrs. Assn., Madison, 1986-90; state chmn. health/long term care action group AARP, Wis., 1990-99, coord. health advocacy svcs., 1991-2001. Founder Future Homemakers of Am., 1943, past advisor; condr. fgn. study programs, Europe, Asia, Australia, 1971-88. Bd. dirs. Madison Oakwood Retirement Ctr., 1983-89, mem. resident care com., 1992—; com. mem. Wis. Legis. Study Elderly Abuse, 1985-88. Recipient Disting. Educator award, U. Wis., Stout, 1998. Mem.: AAUW, AARP, Mental Health Assn./Wis. Coalition Aging Groups (regional bd.), Valparaiso U. Guild (state pres. 1981—85), Luth. Women Missionary League, Nat. Honor Soc. Home Econs., Wis. Ret. Tchrs. Assn. (rec. sec. 1983—89, bd. dirs. 1990—2002), Madison Civics Club, Rotary (Sr. Svc. award 1998). Lutheran. Avocation: volunteering. Home: 6209 Mineral Point Rd Apt 1103 Madison WI 53705-5229

SCHMIDT, MARY LOUISE DONNEL, bank officer; b. Glendale, Calif., Mar. 1, 1957; d. Roscoe John and Esther Maria Donnel; m. Jack H. Schmidt, Apr. 21, 1984 (div.); 1 child, Alexandra Louise ; m. Tracy Forrest Robbins. Cert. in Spanish, U. Guadalajara, Mex., 1977; AA, Glendale Coll., 1982; BS, LaVerne U., 1989. Cert. broker Calif. Optical engr. Aerojet Electro Systems, Azusa, Calif., 1983—91; sr. loan officer Western Cities Mortgage, Carlsbad, Calif., 1991—93; sr. loan specialist Prudential Fin., Del Mar, Calif., 1993—95; sr. loan rep. Coastal Cities Mortgage, Del Mar, Calif., 1995—2001; v.p. Keller Williams, Carlsbad, 2001, MLS Fin. Group, Carlsbad, 2001—. Spkr. in field, 1993—. Mem.: Mortgage Bankers Assn., Better Bus. Bur., Alpha Gamma Sigma. Office: MLS Financial Group 5620 Paseo del Norte # 127-434 Carlsbad CA 92008 E-mail: mdonnel@hotmail.com.

SCHMIDT, MARY TERESA, retired elementary school educator; b. Detroit, May 12, 1926; d. Philip Schmidt and Angela Mary Bauer. BA, Emmanuel Coll., 1967; MFA, Boston U., 1979. Cert. lifetime tchg. cert. Mich., Tex., Mass. Tchr. Montessori sch., Providence, 1948—54; tchr. grades 1-4 Stella Maris Internat. Sch., Kobe, Japan, 1954—64, tchr. grade 1, 1967—75; tchr. grade 5 Rio Grande City (Tex.) Consol. Sch. Dist., 1979—83; tchr. primary grades Marle Montessori Ctr., Inc., Farmington Hills, Mich., 1984—95; tchr. grade 1 St. Annes Sch., Columbus, Ga., 1983—84; ret. Tutor 3-D drawing for children, 1998—. Exhibitions include (Top Ten award, 1998), pvt. collections. Mem.: NEA, Farmington Artists Club, Pi Lambda Theta. Roman Catholic. Avocations: hiking, walking, drawing, painting, photography. Address: 24138 Civic Center Dr Southfield MI 48034-5269 Office Phone: 248-827-7227.

SCHMIDT, RITA, retired library media specialist; b. Tacoma, Wash., Aug. 9, 1947; d. Robert V. and Ann Regine (Minette) Westermark; m. Guy Douglas Schmidt, June 29, 1972. BA, Knox Coll., 1969; MSLS, Case Western Res. U., 1970. Cert. tchg., sch. adminstrn., Mont. Libr. cataloger Trenton Pub. Libr., 1970-71; libr. media specialist Great Falls (Mont.) Pub. Schs., 1971—2001; part-time libr. Mont. State U., Coll. Tech., Great Falls,

2002—. Part-time instr. Coll. Great Falls, 1973-76. Chair, mem. Mont. Libr. Svcs. Adv. Coun., Helena, Mont., 1983-84, 85-89; mem. Project Excellence Sch. Accreditation Stds., Helena, 1988-89. Recipient scholarship Mountain Plains Libr. Assn., 1985. Mem. ALA (coun. 1986), Mont. Edn. Assn. (bd. dirs. 1989-90), Great Falls Edn. Assn. (v.p. 1988-90, Silver Key award 1983, 84, 85, 89, 90, 94, 98), Mont. Libr. Assn. (pres. 1983-84). Democrat. Home: 3721 7th Ave N Great Falls MT 59401-2222

SCHMIDT, RUTH ANN, retired academic administrator; b. Mountain Lake, Minn., Sept. 16, 1930; d. Jacob A. and Anna A. (Ewert) S. BA, Augsburg Coll., Mpls., 1952; MA, U. Mo., 1955; PhD, U. Ill., 1962; LLD, Gordon Coll., 1987. Asst. prof. Spanish Mary Baldwin Coll., Staunton, Va., 1955-58, SUNY-Albany, 1962-67, assoc. prof., 1967-78, dean of humanities, 1971-76; prof. and provost Wheaton Coll., Norton, Mass., 1978-82; pres. Agnes Scott Coll., Decatur, Ga., 1982-94, pres. emerita, 1994—. Interim pres. Lyon Coll., 1998; chair Women's Coll. Coalition, 1986-88. Author: Ortega Munilla y sus novelas, 1973, Cartas entre dos amigos del teatro, 1969. Trustee Gordon Coll., Wenham, Mass., 1980-86, Lyon Coll., 1993-2001; bd. dirs. DeKalb C. of C., 1982-85, Atlanta Coll. Art, 1984-94; mem. exec. com. Women's Coll. Coalition, 1983-88; v.p. So. Univ. Conf., 1993. Named Disting. Alumna Augsburg Coll., 1973 Mem. Assn. Am. Colls. (dir. 1979-82, treas. 1982-83), Soc. Values in Higher Edn., Am. Coun. Edn. (commn. on women in higher edn. 1985-88), AAUW, Assn. Pvt. Colls. and Univs. Ga. (pres. 1987-89), Internat. Women's Forum, Young Women's Christian Assn. Acad. Women Achievers. Democrat. Presbyterian. E-mail: ruthschmidt@mindspring.com.

SCHMIDT, RUTH A(NNA) M(ARIE), geologist; b. Bklyn., Apr. 22, 1916; d. Edward and Anna M. (Range) S. AB, NYU, 1936; MA, Columbia U., 1939, PhD, 1948. Cert. profl. geologist. Geologist U.S. Geol. Survey, Washington, 1943-56, dist. geologist Anchorage, 1956-63; prof., chmn. geology dept. U. Alaska, Anchorage, 1959-84; cons. geologist Anchorage, 1964—. Lectr. Elder Hostels Alaska Pacific U., Anchorage, 1988—89, U. Alaska, Anchorage, 1994; coord. Engring. Geol. Evaluation Group, Alaskan 1964 Earthquake, Anchorage, 1964; environ. cons. Trans Alaska Pipeline Office of Gov., Anchorage, 1975—76. Editor: Alaska geology field trip guide books, 1984, 89; contbr. articles to profl. jours. Trustee, pres. Brooks Range Libr., Anchorage, 1979-91; bd. dirs., com. chmn. Anchorage Audubon Soc., 1989-98; mem. exec. bd., chmn. various coms. Alaska Cen. Environment, Anchorage, adv. coun. Alaska Mus. Natural History, 1999-2001, bd. dirs., 2001—. Fellow AAAS, Arctic Inst. N.Am. (bd. govs. 1983-94), Geol. Soc. Am.; mem. Am. Inst. Profl. Geologists (charter), Am. Assn. Petroleum Geologists, Internat. Geol. Congress (del.), Alaska Geol. Soc. (hon. life mem., bd. dirs. 1993-95), Sigma Xi. Avocations: photography, gardening, hiking.

SCHMIDT, SANDRA JEAN, secondary school educator; b. Limestone, Maine, Mar. 21, 1955; d. Dale Laban and Marie Audrey (Bailey) Winters; m. Lee Lloyd Schmidt, Oct. 20, 1973; children: Colby Lee, Katrina Leesa. AA summa cum laude, Anne Arundel Community Coll., 1987; BS summa cum laude, U. Balt., 1990; MAT, Johns Hopkins U., 2003. CPA, Md. Enlisted U.S. Army, 1973, traffic analyst, 1973-85, resigned, 1985; auditor Md. State Office of Legislative Audits, Balt., 1990-93; fin. analyst Md. Ins. Adminstrn., Balt., 1993-2000; tchr. math. Baltimore City Pub. Schs., 2000—. Tutor Anne Arundel County Literacy Coun., Pasadena, Md., 1990-97; mentor U. Balt., 1991; host family Am. Intercultural Student Exchange, 1992-98. Named Tchr. of Yr., Balt. City Coun. of PTAs, 2001. Mem.: Md. Coun. Tchrs. Math., Nat. Coun. Tchrs. Math., U. Balt. Alumni Assn., Phi Theta Kappa, Beta Gamma Sigma, Alpha Chi. Republican. Baptist. Home: 7716 Pinyon Rd Hanover MD 21076-1585 E-mail: beadmaniac@hotmail.com.

SCHMIDT, SHERI LYNN, band director; b. Kalamazoo, Mich., Dec. 21, 1969; d. Robert LaDuke and Judith LaDuke; m. Darin Schmidt, Mar. 29, 1993. B Music Edn., Western Mich. U., 1992; M Music Edn., VanderCook Coll. of Music, 1999. Cert. tchr. Asst. dir. bands Pennfield Schs., Battle Creek, Mich., 1992—98; dir. bands Shakamak Schs., Jasonville, Ind., 1998—2001; band dir. Lakeview Schs., Battle Creek, Mich., 2001—. Flute tchr., Battle Creek, 1985—2001. Mem.: Music Educator's Nat. Conf., Mich. Sch. Band and Orch. Assn. (treas. Dist. 8 1995—98). Presbyterian. Avocations: photography, yoga.

SCHMIDT, VIVIEN ANN, political scientist, educator; b. N.Y.C., Nov. 19, 1949; d. Edith Diane Kurzweil and Charles Schmidt, Robert Kurzweil (Stepfather); m. Jolyon Michael Howorth. BA, Bryn Mawr Coll., 1971; MA, U. Chgo., 1973; postgrad., Institut d'Etudes Politiques, Paris, 1973—74; PhD, U. Chgo., 1981. Prof. U. Mass., Boston, 1979—98, Boston (Mass.) U., 1998—2002. Vis. prof. Institut d'Etudes Politiques, Paris, 2000—03; Fulbright fellow Nuffield Coll., Oxford U., England, 2001—02; vis. prof. Max Planck Inst. for the Study of Societies, Cologne, Germany, 1998—99, European U. Inst., Florence, Italy, 1999—2000, U. Lille, France, 1995—96; dir. Ctr. for Democracy and Devel., McCormack Inst., U. of Mass., Boston, 1994—98, European Studies Program, U. of Mass., Boston, 1993—98, Jean Monnet prof. European Union Commn., 2001—; Rockefeller Found. residency grantee, Bellagio, Italy, 2003. Author: The Futures of European Capitalism, 2002; co-editor Welfare and Work in the Open Economy, 2 vols., 2000; author: From State to Market? The Transformation of French Business and Government, 1996, Democratizing France, 1990 (Mention d'Honneur, Gaston Defferre Prize Ceremony, 1992). Decorated chevalier Order Palmes Académiques; recipient Fulbright European Union Rsch. Award, 2001—02; grantee Rockefeller Found., 2003; Fulbright sr. rsch. scholar, Paris, 1991. Mem.: Internat. Polit. Sci. Assn., Am. Polit. Sci. Assn. (exec. com. European sect. 2000—03), European Union Studies Assn. (chair exec. com. 1999—2001). Avocations: photography, skiing, travel. Office: Boston U 152 Bay State Rd Boston MA 02215 Office Phone: 617-358-0192.

SCHMIDT-NIELSEN, BODIL MIMI (MRS. ROGER G. CHAGNON), physiologist, educator; b. Copenhagen, Nov. 3, 1918; came to U.S., 1946, naturalized, 1952; d. August and Marie (Jorgensen) Krogh; m. Knut Schmidt-Nielsen, Sept. 20, 1939 (div. Feb. 1966); children: Astrid, Bent, Bodil; m. Roger G. Chagnon, Oct. 1968. DDS, U. Copenhagen, 1941, DOdont, 1946, DPhil, 1955; DS (hon.), Bates Coll., 1983; MD (hon.), U. Aarhus, Denmark, 1997. Mem. faculty Duke U., Durham, NC, 1952-64; prof. biology Case Western Res. U., Cleve., 1964-71, chmn. dept., 1970-71, adj. prof., 1971-74; trustee Mt. Desert Island Biol. Lab., Maine, rsch. scientist, 1971-86, exec. com., 1978-85, v.p., 1979-81, pres., 1981-85. Adj. prof. Brown U., Providence, 1971-75, dept. physiol. U. Fla., Gainesville, 1986—; mem. tng. grant com. NIGMS, 1965-71. Author: August and Marie Krogh, Lives in Science, 1995, Danish edit., 1997; editor: Urea and the Kidney, 1970; assoc. editor Am. Jour. Physiology: Regulatory, Integrative and Comparative Physiology, 1978-81. Trustee Coll. of Atlantic, Bar Harbor, Maine, 1972-92. Recipient Career award NIH, 1962-64, John Simon Guggenheim Meml. fellow, 1952-53; Bowditch lectr., 1958, Jacobaeus lectr., 1974. Fellow AAAS (del. coun. 1977-79), N.Y. Acad. Scis., Am. Acad. Arts and Scis.; mem. Am. Physiol. Soc. (coun. 1971-77, pres. 1975-76, Ray G. Daggs award 1989, Orr Reynolds award 1994, August Krogh lectr. 1994, Berliner award 1998), Soc. Exptl. Biology and Medicine (coun. 1967-71). Achievements include research, publications on biochemistry of saliva, water metabolism of desert animals, urea excretion, peristalsis of renal pelvis and concentrating mechanism, comparative kidney physiology, comparative physiology of excretory organs. Office: U Fla Dept Physiology Gainesville FL 32605 Home: Apt 3033 2431 NW 41st St Gainesville FL 32606-7406 E-mail: Bodimi@aol.com.

SCHMIEDING, REBECCA SUE, information technology manager; b. Lincoln, Nebr., Apr. 4, 1956; d. Trudy Schmieding. Bachelors degree, S.D. State U., 1978. Product mgr. IBM Asia Pacific, Rochester, Minn., 1993—96; project mgr. IBM eServer iSeries, Rochester, 1996—2004. Programmer IBM S/3 & S/36, Rochester, 1978—84; mgr. IBM AS/400, Rochester, 1984—86, project office, 1986—88; program mgr. IBM EMEA, Greenford, Middlesex, 1988—93; prodr., spkr. tech. presentations. Contbr. tech. articles to profl. jours. Lay evangelism advisor Covenant Ch. N.W. Conf., Minneapolis, 2000—03. Recipient COMMON Silver Medal Spkr., 2001—03, Bronze medal, 2003—04. Mem.: Phi Kappa Phi (life). Avocations: golf, officiating basketball, biking, travel, reading. Office: IBM 3605 Hwy 52 N Rochester MN 55901

SCHMITT, DIANA MAE, elementary school educator; b. Dubuque, Iowa, Jan. 19, 1950; d. Raymond J. and Marie Arlen Schmitt. BA, U. Iowa, 1972; MA, Clarke Coll., Dubuque, 1981; postgrad., U. Wyo. 6th grade tchr. Shelby County Sch. Dist., Shelby, Iowa, 1972-73; 4th and 5th grade tchr. Dist. 200, Woodstock, Ill., 1973-76; rural sch. tchr. Albany County Sch. Dist., Laramie, Wyo., 1976-83, 1st, 3d, 5th and 6th grade tchr., 1983-98; chmn. outdoor classrm. devel. Indian Paintbrush Elem., 1992—. Mem. rev. com. for excellence in sci. edn., adv. com. Western Edn. Adv. Com. for Wyo., 1989; tchr. sci. methods for elem. sch. U. Wyo., 1990-91; mem. Higher Edn. Grant Reading State Com., 1994; participant Sci. Grasp, 1990, Inst. Chemical Edn. Fundamental, 1992; presenter 1st Soviet-Am. Sci. Conv., Moscow, 1991; mem. workshop on water, Nat. Geog. Soc., 1993; presenter NSTA nat. and regional convs., state Wyo. Interdisciplinary Conf. convs., No. Iowa Beginning Reading conf. Recipient Delta award, 1993; named Dist. Exemplary Sci. Tchr., 1986-87; Wyo. Game and Fish grantee, 1993-95, Nat. Geog. Soc. grantee, 1997. Mem. NEA, Internat. Reading Assn., Nat. Sci. Tchrs. Assn., Wyo. Sci. Tchrs. Assn. (sec.), Alpha Delta Kappa (pres.). Home: 5737 Southview Rd Laramie WY 82070-6801 Office: Indian Paintbrush 1653 N 28th St Laramie WY 82072-9200 E-mail: msdmschmitt@yahoo.com.

SCHMITT, ELIZABETH MARIE, music educator; b. Naperville, Ill., Mar. 28, 1977; d. R. L. and C. A. Schmitt. B in Music Edn., U. Ill., 1999; M in Music Edn., Vandercook Coll. Music, 2003. Cert. tchr. Ill. Band dir. Peotone (Ill.) CUSD, 1999—. Music dir. Immanuel United Ch. of Christ, Peotone, 2001—; pit orch. mem. Kankakee (Ill.) Valley Theatre, 2003—. Mem.: Mu Phi Epsilon (pres. 1997—98). Avocations: camping, boating, cooking, reading.

SCHMITT, JOHANNA MARIE, plant population biologist, educator; b. Phila., Mar. 12, 1953; d. William Francis and Laura Belle (Wear) S.; m. Darrell Marion West, Aug. 6, 1983. BA, Swarthmore (Pa.) Coll., 1974; PhD, Stanford U., 1981. Postdoctoral rsch. assoc. Duke U., Durham, N.C., 1981-82; asst. prof. Brown U., Providence, 1982-87, assoc. prof. biology, 1987-94, prof., 1994—. Mem. R.I. Task Force, New Eng. Plant Conservation program, 1991—; mem. regional advisory com. New Eng. Plant Conservation program, 2000—. Assoc. editor Evolution, 1990-92, Am. Naturalist, 2000-2001; contbr. articles to profl. jours. including Evolution, Ecology, Am. Naturalist, Genetics, Nature. Bd. dirs. Sojourner House, Providence, 1989-92. NSF grad. fellow, 1974, mid. career fellow, 1992-93; rsch. grantee, 1984—; recipient faculty award for women, 1991—. Mem. Soc. for Study of Evolution (coun. mem. 1990-92, exec. v.p. 1994-95, v.p. 1999), Bot. Soc. Am., Ecol. Soc. Am., Am. Soc. Naturalists (v.p. 1997, pres. 2002). Achievements include research on ecological genetics and genomics of natural plant populations: density-dependent phenomena, gene flow and population structure, inbreeding depression, the evolution of sex, maternal effects, seed ecology, natural selection, evolution of plasticity, adaptive significance of phytochrome, ecological risks of transgenic plants. Office: Brown Univ Dept Ecology & Evolution Providence RI 02912-0001

SCHMITZ, BARBARA, art preservationist; b. Cin., 1936; AM, U. Chgo., 1960; MA, PhD, NYU, 1981. Contbr.: illustrated catalogs of Islamic paintings Islamic Manuscripts, N.Y. Pub. Libr., 1992, Islamic and Indian Manuscripts and Paintings, Pierpont Morgan Libr., 1996; co-author (with Z.A. Desai): Mughal and Persian Painting and Illustrated Manuscripts in the Raza Library, Rampur (U.P.), 2004; editor, contbr.: After the Great Mughals: Painting in Delhi and the Regional Courts in the 18th-19th Centuries, 2004. Fulbright grantee, 1992—93, 1997—98, Indira Gandhi Nat. Ctr. for the Arts grantee, New Delhi, 1995, Am. Inst. Indian Studies grantee, 1998—99. E-mail: barbaraschmitz65016@yahoo.com.

SCHMITZ, CAROL ANN, speech pathology/audiology services professional; d. James Norman and Edna Anna (Kiss) Wood; m. Hermann William Schmitz, IV, Mar. 28, 1981; children: Brooke, Lindsey, Ashlyn. BS, Mich. State U., 1977; MA, Ea. Mich. U., 1979, specialist, 2001. Cert. clin. competence in speech and lang. pathology. Speech pathologist Tri County Home Health Care, Southfield, Mich., 1980—83; pvt. practice Commerce, Mich., 1983—87; speech pathologist Heartland Rehab., Livonia, Mich., 1993—94, Walled Lake (Mich.) Schs., 1995—. Pres. PTA, Walled Lake, 1993—95; leader Girl Scouts Am., Commerce, 1988—2000. Mem.: Am. Speech Hearing and Lang. Assn., Mich. Canoe Racing Assn. (pres., treas. 1985—92). Avocations: reading, running, bicycling, hiking. Home: 2140 Sunnybrook Commerce Township MI 48382 Office: Walled Lake Schs Bldg D 850 Ladd Rd Walled Lake MI 48390 E-mail: cschmitz3@excite.com.

SCHMITZ, DOLORES JEAN, primary education educator; b. River Falls, Wis., Dec. 27, 1931; d. Otto and Helen Olive (Webster) Kreuziger; m. Karl Matthias Schmitz Jr., Aug. 18, 1956; children: Victoria Jane, Karl III. BS, U. Wis., River Falls, 1953; MS, Nat. Coll. Edn., 1982; postgrad., U. Minn., Mankato, 1969, U. Melbourne, Australia, 1989, U. Wis., Milw., 1989, Carroll Coll., 1990, Cardinal Stritch Coll., 1990. Cert. tchr., Wis. Tchr. Manitowoc (Wis.) Pub. Schs., 1953-56, West Allis (Wis.) Pub. Schs., 1956-59, Lowell Sch., Milw., 1960-63, Victory Sch., Milw., 1964, Palmer Sch., Milw., 1966-84, 86-94, unit leader, 1984-86; ret., 1994. Co-organizer Headstart Tchg. Staff Assn., Milw., 1968; insvc. organizer Headstart and Early Childhood, Milw., 1969-92; pilot tchr. for Whole Lang., Hi-Scope and Math. Their Way, 1988-93; bd. dirs. Curriculum Devel. Ctr. of Milw. Edn. Ctr., 1993-94. Author: (curriculum) Writing to Read, 1987, Cooperation and Young Children (ERIC award 1982), Kindergarten Curriculum, 1953. Former supporter Milw. Art Mus., Milw. Pub. Mus., Milw. County Zoo, Whitefish Bay Pub. Libr., Riveredge Nature Ctr.; vol. fgn. visitor program Milw. Internat. Inst., 1966-94, holiday folk fair, 1976-94, Earthwatch, 1989; lobbyist Milw. Pub. Sch. Bd. and State of Wis., 1986-93; coord. comty. vols., 1990-94. Grantee Greater Milw. Ednl. Trust, 1989. Mem. NEA (life), ASCD, Milw. Kindergarten Assn. (rec. sec. 1986-93), Nat. Assn. for Edn. of Young Children, Tchrs. Applying Whole Lang., Wis. Early Childhood Assn., Milw. Tchrs. Ednl. Assn. (co-chmn. com. early childhood 1984-86), Assn. for Childhood Edn. Internat. (charter pres. Manitowoc chpt. 1955-56), Milw. Educating Computer Assn., Alpha Psi Omega. Roman Catholic. Avocations: bicycling, nature, world travel. Home: 1355 Pinellas Bayway S Apt 22 Tierra Verde FL 33715-2140 E-mail: dolintv@aol.com.

SCHMITZ, JENNIFER DAWN, art educator; b. Houston, Dec. 24, 1974; d. George O. and Sharon M. Puig; m. Stacey Daniel Schmitz, May 30, 1998. B of Art Edn., U. Kans., 1998. Cert. art tchr. K-12 Kans. State Bd. Edn., 1998, State Mo. Bd. Edn., 2000. Tchr. art J. A. Rogers Acad., Kansas City, 1998—. Yearbook advisor J. A. Rogers Acad., 1999—, exploratory team leader, 2002—. Dir.: (arts festival) J. A. Rogers Acad. Spring Arts Festival. Dir. crafts and decorations South-Broadland Presbyn. Ch., Kansas City, 2003—03. Gt. IDEAS grantee, Kauffman Found., 2001—02. Mem.: Mo. Art Edn. Assocation, Nat. Art Edn. Assn. Achievements include research in the implementation of Discipline-Based Art Education. Home: 2223 W 72nd Terr Prairie Village KS 66208

SCHNAKENBERG, LORI ANN, secondary school educator; b. Carbondale, Pa., Jan. 2, 1976; BS in English Edn., Pensacola Christian Coll., 1998, MS in English Edn., 2001. Tchr. English, bus. Twin Tiers Bapt. High Sch., Breeseport, NY, 1998—99; tchr. English, computer sci. Twin City Christian Sch., Lunenburg, Mass., 2001—. Mem.: English First, Internat. Reading Assn., Nat. Coun. Tchrs. of English, Ronald Reagan Presdl. Found., Nat. Trust for Hist. Preservation, Arcaeological Conservancy, Acad. Am. Poets, Internat. Soc. Poets. Office: Twin City Christian Sch 194 Electric Ave Lunenburg MA 01426

SCHNALL, EDITH LEA, microbiologist, educator; b. N.Y.C., Apr. 11, 1922; d. Irving and Sadie (Raab) Spitzer; m. Herbert Schnall, Aug. 21, 1949; children: Neil David, Carolyn Beth. AB, Hunter Coll., 1942; AM, Columbia U., 1947, PhD, 1967. Clin. pathologist Roosevelt Hosp., N.Y.C., 1942-44; instr. Adelphi Coll., Garden City, N.Y., 1944-46; asst. med. mycologist Columbia Coll. Physicians and Surgeons, N.Y.C., 1946-47, 49-50; instr. Bklyn. Coll., 1947; mem. faculty Sarah Lawrence Coll., Bronxville, N.Y., 1947-48; lectr. Hunter Coll., N.Y.C., 1947-67; adj. assoc. prof. Lehman Coll., City U. N.Y., 1968; hon. curator N.Y. Botanical Garden, 1968; asst. prof. Queensborough Community Coll., City U. N.Y., 1967, assoc. prof. microbiology, 1968-75, prof., 1975—; adminstr. Med. Lab. Tech. Program, 1985—. Vis. prof. Coll. Physicians and Surgeons, Columbia U., N.Y.C., 1974; advanced biology examiner U. London, 1970—. Editor: Newsletter of Med. Mycology Soc. N.Y., 1969-85; founder, editor Female Perspective newsletter of Queensborough Community Coll. Women's Club, 1971-73. Mem. Alley Restoration Com., N.Y.C., 1971—; mem. legis. adv. com. Assembly of the State of N.Y., 1972; mem. Cmty. Bd. 11, Queens, N.Y., 1974-98, 3d vice-chmn., 1987-92, 2d vice chmn., 1992-97; public dir. of bd. dirs. Inst. Continuing Dental Edn. Queens County, Dental Soc. N.Y. State and ADA, 1973-97. Rsch. fellow NIH, 1948-49; faculty rsch. fellow, grantee-in-aid Rsch. Found. of SUNY, 1968-70; faculty rsch. grant Rsch. Found. City U. N.Y., 1971-74. Mem. AAAS, Internat. Soc. Human Animal Mycology, Am. Soc. Microbiology (coun., N.Y.C. br. 1981—, co-chairperson ann. meeting com. 1981-82, chair program com. 1982-83, v.p. 1984-86, pres. 1986-88), Med. Mycology Soc. N.Y. (sec.-treas. 1967-68, v.p. 1968-69, 78-79, archivist 1974—, fin. advisor 1983-97, pres. 1969-70, 79-80, 81-82), Bot. Soc. Am., Med. Mycology Soc. Americas, Mycology Soc. Am., N.Y. Acad. Scis., Torrey Bot. Club (N.Y. State), Queensborough Community Coll. Women's Club (pres. 1971-73, N.Y.C.), Sigma Xi, Phi Sigma. Home: 21406 29th Ave Flushing NY 11360 2622

SCHNEEMAN, BARBARA OLDS, nutritionist, educator; m. Paul Schneeman; 1 child, Eric. BS in Food Sci. and Tech., U. Calif., Davis, 1970; PhD in Nutrition, U. Calif., Berkeley, 1974. NIH postdoctoral fellow gastrointestinal physiology Children's Hosp., Oakland, Calif., 1974-76; faculty mem. nutrition dept. nutrition and food sci. & tech. U. Calif., Davis, 1976—, prof. dept. internal medicine divsn. clin. nutrition, 1986—, assoc. dean Coll. Agrl. and Environ. Scis., 1985-88, chair dept. nutrition, 1988-93, dean Coll. Agrl. and Environ. Scis., 1993-99. Pres., bd. dirs. Dannon Inst., 1996—; vis. scientist Cardiovascular Rsch. Inst., U. Calif., San Francisco, 1991-92; lectr. women in sci. series Coll. St. Catherine, St. Paul, 1987; adv. dir. Blue Cross Calif., 1992-95; mem. dietary guidelines for Ams. adv. com. to Secs. of Agr., Health and Human Svcs., 1989-90, 94-95; mem. expert panel on food safety and nutrition Inst. Food Technologists, 1985-91; mem. external adv. bd. Post Ctr. for Nutrition and Health, 1989-90; councilor Soc. for Exptl. Biology and Medicine, 1988-91. Assoc. editor Jour. Nutrition, 1991-94; contbg. editor Nutrition Revs., 1982-90; editl. bd. Jour. Nutrition, 1982-87, Procs. for Soc. Exptl. Biology and Medicine, 1985-91, Acad. Press: Food Sci. and Nutrition, 1988-2001. Fellow NDEA, U. Calif., Berkeley; recipient Outstanding Cmty. Svc. award Tierra del Oro coun. Girl Scouts U.S., 1995, Future Leaders award for rsch. Nutrition Found., 1978-80, Samuel Cate Prescott award for rsch. Inst. Food Tech., 1985, Farma Food Internat. Fibre prize, Copenhagen, 1989, Ethel Austin Martin disting. lectr. on Human Nutrition, S.D. State U., 1999. Fellow AAAS; mem. Inst. Food Technologists (sec.-treas. nutrition divsn. 1988-89), Am. Physiol. Soc., Am. Inst. Nutrition (treas. 1989-92), Am. Heart Assn. (fellow arteriosclerosis coun.), Food and Nutrition Bd. IOM, 2001—. Office: U Calif Davis Dept Nutrition Davis CA 95616

SCHNEIDER, ADELE SANDRA, clinical geneticist; b. Johannesburg, Mar. 21, 1949; came to U.S., 1976, naturalized, 1981; d. Michael and Annette (Sive) S.; m. Gordon Mark Cohen, July 2, 1978; children: Jeffrey, Brian, Adrienne. MB, BChir, Witwatersrand U., Johannesburg, South Africa, 1973. Intern in internal medicine Baragwanath Hosp., Johannesburg, 1974, intern in gen. surgery, 1974; sr. house officer in pediatrics Coronation Hosp., Johannesburg, 1975; sr. house officer in radiation therapy Johannesburg Gen. Hosp., 1975-76; resident in pediatrics Wilmington (Del.) Med. Ctr., 1976-78; fellow in clin. genetics and metabolic diseases Children's Hosp. of Phila., 1978-81, staff physician Cystic Fibrosis Clinic, 1987-88; staff pediatrician Children's Rehab. Hosp., Phila., 1981-82, dir. pediatrics, 1982-87, acting med. dir., 1984-85; clin. instr. dept. pediatrics Jefferson Med. Coll., Phila., 1982-84, clin. asst. prof. dept. pediatrics, 1984—, clin. assoc. prof. pediats., 2002—; clin. geneticist Hahnemann Univ. Hosp., Phila., 1987-90, asst. clin. prof. dept. pediatrics and neoplastic diseases, 1987-90, clin. geneticist Albert Einstein Med. Ctr., Phila. 1990-92, acting dir. med. genetics, 1992-93, dir. clin. genetics program, 1993—. Mem. courtesy faculty Sch. Medicine Temple U., Phila., 1987; clin. geneticist St. Christopher's Hosp. for Children, Phila., 1987; genetics cons. dept. pediatrics Bryn Mawr (Pa.) Hosp.; genetics cons. Lankenan Hosp., Thomas Jefferson U. Hosp.; presenter, lectr. in field. Contbr. articles to profl. jours. Bd. dirs. Phila. Parenting Associates, 1986-93. Fellow Am. Coll. Med. Genetics; mem. Am. Soc. Human Genetics, Am. Chem. Soc. Office: Albert Einstein Med Ctr Dept Pediatrics 5501 Old York Rd Philadelphia PA 19141-3018

SCHNEIDER, CAROL ANN, staffing services company executive; d. Glenn William and Beatrice Helen Kluth; m. Leon A. Schneider, Feb. 4, 1961; children: Paul, Joel, Neil. BEd in Bus. Edn., U. Wis., Whitewater, 1958; postgrad., U. Wis., 1971-74. Lic. secondary bus. educator, Wis., vocat. bus. educator, Wis.; cert. pers. cons.; sr. prof. in human resources. Bus. divsn. chair Milw. Area Tech. Coll.-North, Mequon, Wis., 1969-80, Port Washington (Wis.) Vocat., Tech. and Adult Sch., 1969-80; founder, CEO, chair of the bd. SEEK, Inc., Grafton, Wis., 1971—. Founder, mgr. The Schneider Co., LLC, Grafton, 1996—, ITech Profls., LLC, Grafton, 1998—, Guardian HealthStaff, LLC, 2002; past pres. Wis. Assn. Staffing Svcs.; presenter in field. Fund raising chair St. Joseph's Ch.; founder, past co-chair Workforce 2010; founder, co-chair Ozaukee County Transp. Mgmt. Assn.; former bd. mem. Ozaukee County Econ. Devel. Corp.; bd. mem., capitol campaign mem. B.A.B.E.S. Recipient Celebrate Success award Wis. Women Entrepreneurs, 1993, named Outstanding Citizen, Grafton C. of C., Nat. Employer of Yr., Coun. for Exceptional Children Divsn. on Career Devel. and Transition, 1998, Outstanding Bus. of Yr., Grafton Area C. of C., 1998, Wis. Welfare-to-Work Small Bus. Person of Yr., U.S. Small Bus. Adminstrn., 1999; named Woman of Yr. Wis. Women Entrepreneurs, 2000. Mem. FOCUS (founder, past pres., past v.p.), Am. Staffing Assn. (nat. temporary help week regional chair), Exec. Women's Orgn. (v.p. Envision program), Wis. Assn. Pers. Svcs. (past pres.), Washington/Ozaukee County Pers. Mgmt. Assn. (past pres.), Ind. Bus. Assn. Wis. (past bd. dirs., past pres., past v.p. state programs, past welfare reform chair, Mem. of Yr. award 1999). Republican. Roman Catholic. Avocations: community service, playing piano, reading, politics. Office: SEEK Inc PO Box 148 Grafton WI 53024-0148

SCHNEIDER, CAROL GEARY, educational association administrator; B in History magna cum laude, Mount Holyoke Coll.; postgrad., U. London; PhD in History, Harvard U. Instr. U. Chgo., DePaul U., Chgo. State U.,

Boston U.; exec. v.p. Assn. Am. Colls. and Univs., Washington, 1988—98, pres., 1998—. Contbr. articles to profl. jours. Woodrow Wilson fellow, Harvard U., Kent fellow, Harvard Prize fellow, Mina Shaughnessy fellow, U.S. Dept. Edn., 1982. Mem.: Phi Beta Kappa. Office: Am Assn Colls and Univs 1818 R St NW Washington DC 20009

SCHNEIDER, CHRISTINE LYNN, customs inspector; b. Staten Island, N.Y., Feb. 3, 1960; d. Howard Thomas and Ina Elise (Beyer) S. BS, SUNY Maritime Coll., Bronx, 1984. Lic. 3d mate, U.S. Mcht. Marine; cert. U.S. customs firearms instr. Chief inspector Customs and Border Protection, San Diego, 1989—. Served to lt. comdr. USNR, 1984-87, 91—. Democrat. Lutheran. Avocations: photography, coin collecting/numismatics, pistol shooting, archery. Home: 2940 Alta View Dr Apt F107 San Diego CA 92139-3363 Office: Customs and Border Protection 720 E San Ysidro Blvd San Ysidro CA 92173-3115 Office Phone: 619-690-8800. Personal E-mail: cschne6548@aol.com.

SCHNEIDER, CINDY E. GOWER (LONES), financial advisor; b. Springfield, Ohio, Nov. 27, 1960; d. James K. Lones and Catherine May (Dellinger) Oldfield; children: Natasha May, Matthew W.; m. Brian J. Schneider, Nov. 27, 1999. AAS in Electronic Engring., AAS in Acctg., Columbus State C.C., 1993. HVAC electronic control tech. Creative Control Designs, Inc., Columbus, 1993—96. Owner Schneider's Tax and Bookkeeping Svc., Columbus, 1992—. Mem. Nat. Assn. Tax Profls., Am. Inst. Profl. Bookkeepers, WIBC. Republican. Avocations: pencil drawing, reading, bowling, electronics, philosophy. Home and Office: 1933 Westfield Dr S Columbus OH 43223-3768 Office Phone: 614-351-2697. E-mail: taxprocindy@aol.com.

SCHNEIDER, CYNTHIA PERRIN, art historian, educator; b. Pa., Aug. 16, 1953; m. Thomas J. Schneider; 2 children. BA in Fine Arts magna cum laude, Harvard U., 1977, PhD in Fine Arts, 1984. Asst. curator European paintings Mus. Fine Arts, Boston, unitl 1984; asst. prof. art history Georgetown U., Washington, 1984-90, assoc. prof., 1990—; amb. to The Netherlands Am. Embassy, The Hague, 1998-2001; dir., life sciences & society initiative Georgetown U., Washington, 2003—. Lectr. on Rembrandt and Dutch art in U.S. and Europe. Author: Rembrandt's Landscapes, 1990; organizer, writer (catalog) Rembrandts Landscapes: Drawings and Prints, Nat. Gallery Art, Washington, 1990; contbr. articles to profl. jours. Former vice-chmn. President's Com. on Arts and Humanities, mem. steering com. for Creative Am. and millenium planning group, also chmn. fed. design subcom.; corrd. arts policy Clinton-Gore Campaign, 1992; past bd. dirs. Nat. Mus. Women in Arts, Australian-Am. Leagership Dialogue. Office: Georgetown U Dept Art Music & Theatre 37th and O St NW Washington DC 20057 E-mail: cpschneider@restructassoc.com.

SCHNEIDER, DAWN, chemist; d. Norbert Ray Schneider and Liesbeth Burgess. BS, Angelo State U., San Angelo, Tex., 1997; MS, SW Tex. State U., San Marcos, Tex., 2000. Lab asst. Angelo State U., San Angelo, Tex., 1994—97; rsch. asst./tchg. asst. SW Tex. State U., San Marcos, Tex., 1997—2000; quality assoc. Kimberly Clark, San Antonio, 2000—01; scientist Johnson & Johnson, Sherman, Tex., 2001—. Mem.: Am. Soc. for Quality, Am. Chem. Soc. Achievements include research in publ. assay devel. purification of HPBS desulfinase. Avocation: photography.

SCHNEIDER, ELAINE CAROL, lawyer, researcher, writer; b. Mpls., Aug. 28, 1957; d. Allan William and Deborah G. Schneider; m. William Mack Olivé, Oct. 10, 1987 (div. July 1996); 1 child, Vanessa Inez Olivè ; m. G.R. Smith, Jan. 2, 2002. BA, U. Minn., 1979; JD, William Mitchell Coll. Law, St. Paul, 1982. Bar: N.Mex. 1984, Minn. 1998, D.C. 1999. Assoc. Settles, Kalamarides & Assocs., Anchorage, 1982, Dickson, Evans & Esch, Anchorage, 1982; legal rschr. John Hanson, Anchorage, 1983; acct. rep. Westlaw Svcs., Inc., Albuquerque, 1984, sales rep. New Orleans, 1985-86; libr. sales rep. West Pub. Co., Spokane, Wash., 1986-87, reference atty. St. Paul, 1988-97, product mgr., 1997-2001; pvt. practice Mpls.; CEO, mem. Coeur a Coeur Fashion Beauty Products, LLC, Minn., 2004. Ethics adv. bd. N.Mex. Bar, Albuquerque, 1984-85; midwest regional conf. com. Am. Immigration Lawyers Assn., 2000. Author: Substantive Judicial Law Outline of Habeas Corpus, 1984, What They Don't Teach You in the Bar Review Course, 1991, Challenging an Incredibility Finding on Appeal, An Incredibility Paradigm, 2001; mem. law rev. staff : William Mitchell Coll. Law, 1980—81. Atty. immigration and naturalization law Minn. Advocates for Human Rights, Refugee and Immigrant Project. Recipient Vol. Pro Bono Atty. award, 15th Ann. Minn. Advocates for Human Rights, 1999. Mem. Phi Beta Kappa. Avocations: ventriloquism, skiing, swimming, travel, languages. Office: 701 4th Ave S Ste 500 Minneapolis MN 55415-1810 E-mail: avocatecs@aol.com.

SCHNEIDER, GRETA, economist, speaker, author, security consultant; b. Bklyn. Student, Bklyn. Conservatory of Music, 1961—66; BA, MA, CUNY, 1975, MA, 1976. Writer, cons., Pitts., 1972-73; cons. Flushing, N.Y., 1973-85; sr. writer, cons. Buck Cons. Inc., N.Y.C., 1985-86; chmn., CEO Schneider Cons. Inc., N.Y.C., 1986-90; pvt. cons. Greta Schneider Cons., N.Y.C., 1991—; prin. Schneider Consulting Group, 1996—. Lectr. The Learning Annex, 1995-96, 2002, Seminar Ctr., N.Y.C., 1998-, others; advisor Am. Women's Econ. Devel. Corp., 1988—; adv. bd. Women's Profl. Coun., 1998; guest mem. discussion Reuters Bus. Report, 1998; mem. Women's Econ. Round Table, 1998; mem. Profl. Women's Adv. Bd., 1998; spkr. in field. Author: Exploding the Bankruptcy Mystique, 1993, Holistic Bankruptcy, 1998, 2002. Mem. Little Theatre Group, Marathon Cmty. Ctr., Little Neck, N.Y., 1980-83; founder, pres. Bankruptcy Anonymous, 1996; mem. Bklyn. Conservatory of Music, 1961-66. Cambridge Biographical Inst. fellow, 1993. Mem. AFTRA, Nat. Assn. Women Bus. Owners, Nat. Assn. Bus. Communicators, Internat. Platform Assn. (spkr. 2001), Employee Assistance Profls. Assn., Soc. Human Resource Mgmt., U.S. C. of C., Writers Guild Am., Rotary. Avocations: chef, pilot, tennis, chess, speech coach. Office: c/o Manhasset Properties Inc 403 Main St #4 Port Washington NY 11050

SCHNEIDER, HILARY A. publishing executive; BA in Econs., Brown U., 1982; MBA, Harvard Bus. Sch., 1986. Dir. devel. The Balt. Sun Co., 1992—94, v.p. new bus. devel., 1994—95, v.p. sales, 1996—97, v.p. sales and mktg., 1997—98, gen. mgr., 1998—99; v.p. corp. fin. Drexel Burnham Lambert Inc., 1986—90; dir. bus. devel. Times Mirror Corp., 1990—92; pres., CEO Times Mirror Interactive, Balt., 1999—2000; CEO Red Herring Comm., 2000—02; v.p. Knight Ridder Digital, 2002—, pres., CEO, 2002—. Office: Knight Ridder Digital 50W San Fernando St San Jose CA 95113

SCHNEIDER, JANE HARRIS, sculptor; b. Trenton, N.J., Jan. 2, 1932; d. Leon Harris and Dorothy (Perlman) Rosenthal; m. Alfred R. Schneider, July 25, 1953; children: Lee, Jeffry, Elizabeth. BA, Wellesley Coll.; postgrad., Columbia U., Coll. New Rochelle. Exhibitions include numerous group and solo shows June Kelly Gallery, 1988, 1990, 1993, 1995, 1997, 2000, 2001, exhibitions include, 2003, exhibitions include in numerous group and solo shows Collaborative Concepts, Cold Spring, N.Y., 1998—99, 2001, Nassau County Mus. Fine Art, Roslyn, N.Y., 1988, Alternative Mus., N.Y.C., 1985, Phila. Art Alliance, 1984, Atrium Gallery, St. Louis, 1993, 1996, 1997, 1999, 2001, Bill Bace Gallery, 1992, Triplex Gallery, N.Y.C., 1991, Rockland Ctr. for Arts, West Nyack, N.Y., 1990, Hudson River Mus., Yonkers, N.Y., 1989, Sculpture Ctr., N.Y.C., 1988, Quietude Gardens Gallery, East Brunswick, N.J., 1997, 1998, Isis Conceptual Lab., West Branch, Iowa, 1997, 1998, Interch. Ctr., 2001, Gallery 128, N.Y.C., 1999—2001, many others, Represented in permanent collections Fine Arts Mus. L.I., Davis Mus. and Cultural Ctr., Wellesley, Mass., Paterson (N.J.) Mus., N.J. State Mus., Trenton, Ark. Art Ctr., Little Rock, Neuberger Mus., Purchase, N.Y., Kutztown (Pa.) U., Munson-Williams Proctor Inst., Utica, N.Y. Avocations: swimming, gardening, fabricating furniture. Studio: 75 Grand St New York NY 10013-2235 E-mail: jhsart@earthlink.net.

SCHNEIDER, JANET M. arts administrator, curator, painter; b. N.Y.C., June 6, 1950. d. August Arthur and Joan (Battaglia) S.; m. Michael Francis Sperendi, Sept. 21, 1985. BA summa cum laude, Queens Coll., CUNY, 1972; spl. study fine arts Boston U. Tanglewood Inst., 1971. With Queens Mus., Flushing, N.Y.C., 1973-89, curator, 1973-75, program dir., 1975-77, exec. dir., 1977-89. Collections arranged include: Sons and others, Women Artists See Men (author catalog), 1975, Urban Aesthetics (author catalog), 1976, Masters of the Brush, Chinese Painting and Calligraphy from the Sixteenth to the Nineteenth Century (co-author catalog), 1977, Symcho Moszkowicz: Portrait of the Artist in Postwar Europe (author catalog), 1978, Shipwrecked 1622, The Lost Treasure of Philip IV (author catalog), 1981, Michaelangelo: A Sculptor's World (author catalog), 1983, Joseph Cornell: Revisited (author catalog), 1992, Blueprint for Change: The Life and Times of Lewis H. Latimer (co-author catalog), 1995. Chmn. Cultural Instns. Group, N.Y.C., 1986-87; mem. N.Y.C. Commn. for Cultural Affairs, 1991-93; bd. dirs. N.Y.C. Partnership, 1987-88, Gallery Assn. N.Y. State 1979-81; exec. dir. Cultural Inst. Group, 1995—. Mem. Artists Choice Mus. (trustee 1979-82), Am. Assn. Mus., Phi Beta Kappa.

SCHNEIDER, JAYNE BANGS, school librarian; b. Cin., Nov. 9, 1950; d. Neil Kendrick and Edith (Dilworth) Bangs; m. James R. Bronn, June 9, 1973 (div. 1979); m. Arthur Schneider, July 11, 1986; 1 stepdaughter, Heather. BS in Elem. Edn., Ea. Ky. U., 1973; MA in Libr. Sci., Spaulding U., 1978. Tchr. 1st and 2d grades Ruth Moyer Elem. Sch., Fort Thomas (Ky.) Pub. Schs., 1973; libr. Lassiter Middle Sch., Ky., 1973-2000; part-time libr. Jefferson County Pub. Schs.; profl. libr. Gheens Acad. Presenter in field. Co-capt. Block Watch; tree bd. mem. City of Kingsley; mem. Ky. Hist. Soc., Friends of the Libr. Recipient Outstanding Media Librarian award Jefferson County, 1998; named Superstar Ky. Ednl. TV; Owen Badgett grantee Louisville Community Grant, 1988. Mem. NEA, ALA, AASL, PTSA (life), Nat. Mid. Sch. Assn., Jefferson County Sch. Media Assn. (treas. 1982-83, sec. 1991-92, newsletter editor 1992-93, pres.-elect 1993-94, pres. 1994-95, nomination chairperson 1996-97, bd. dirs. 1997-2000, named Jefferson County's Outstanding Sch. Media Librarian 1998), Ky. Sch. Media Assn. (bd. dirs. 1994-95, 97-98). Presbyterian. Avocations: genealogy, collecting antique glass, knitting. Home: 2553 Kings Hwy Louisville KY 40205-2646 E-mail: jaynesch@aol.com.

SCHNEIDER, JOAN, public relations company owner; BS, Boston U., 1972; postgrd., Harvard U. Pres. Schneider & Assocs., 1980—. Office: 240 Newbury St Boston MA 02116-3609

SCHNEIDER, JOANNE, artist; b. Lima, Ohio, Dec. 4, 1919; d. Joseph and Laura (Office) Federman; m. Norman Schneider, May 15, 1941; children— Melanie Schneider Tucker, Lois Schneider Oppenheim. B.F.A., Syracuse U., 1941. One-man shows John Heller Gallery, N.Y.C., 1954, 55, 57, 58, Tirca Karlis Gallery, Provincetown, Mass., 1963, Frank Rehn Gallery, N.Y.C., 1965, 66, 69, 72, 75, Elaine Benson Gallery, Bridgehamton, N.Y., 1972, 74, 79, 85, St. Mary's Coll., St. Mary's City, Md., 1978, Alonzo Gallery, N.Y.C., 1978, Discovery Art Gallery, Clifton, N.J., 1978; group shows include Whitney Mus., N.Y.C., Pa. Acad. Arts, Corcoran Galleries, Washington, Toledo Mus., U. Nebr., Everson Mus., Syracuse, N.Y.; represented in permanent collections Met. Mus. Art, N.Y.C., Colby Coll., Syracuse U., Butler Inst., St. Mary's Coll., U. Notre Dame, Guild Hall, East Hampton, N.Y. Recipient Audubon Artists Stanley Grumbacher Meml. award, 1972 Address: 35 E 75th St New York NY 10021-2761

SCHNEIDER, JULIA, library director; b. St. Joseph, Mo., Feb. 17, 1947; d. Lewis Wilber and Rosella Thompson; m. Thomas Edwin Schneider, Jan. 31, 1975; children: Jedd Christian, Jeremy Adam, Jacob Martin. AA, Mo. Western State Coll., 1967; BA, N.W. Mo. State U., 1969; MA, U. Mo., 1971. Cataloger St. Joseph Pub. Libr., 1969-70; acquisitions libr. Mo. Western State Coll., St. Joseph, 1971-75, tech. processes libr., 1975-83, coord. tech. svcs., 1983-90, libr. dir., 1990—. Pres. Mo. Libr. Assn., 1994; bd. dirs. Mo. Libr. Network Corp., v.p., 1998—2001, pres., 2001—04; treas. MOBIUS Consortium, Columbia, Mo., 1998—2001. Mem. St. Joseph Area Literacy Coalition, 1994—; mem. fund drive steering com. Allied Arts Assn., St. Joseph, 1991—; vol. United Way, St. Joseph, 1990—. Mem.: ALA, Mo. Libr. Assn. (pres. 1994, bd. dirs. 1995—), Bus. and Profl. Women (pres. 1998, 1999), The Runcie Club, Delta Kappa Gamma, Beta Phi Mu. Methodist. Avocations: antiques, music, organ. Home: 4908 NE County Line Rd Saint Joseph MO 64505-9329 Office: Mo Western State Coll 4525 Downs Dr Saint Joseph MO 64507-2246

SCHNEIDER, MARGARET PERRIN, writer; b. N.Y.C., Dec. 31, 1923; d. Sam and Peggy (Flood) Perrin; m. Paul Schneider, Apr. 10, 1950; children: Peggy Lee, Peter-Lincoln, Ann Rose. BA in Psychology and Edn., UCLA, 1949. Gen. elem. tchg. credential, Calif. Tchr. L.A. City Schs., North Hollywood, 1944-55; script writer MGM Studios, 1957-75; staff writer Universal Studios, 1957-75; head writer CBS Studios, N.Y.C., 1975-76. Participant Women in Film, L.A., 1975; chmn. Writers Craft Conf., Arrowhead, Calif., 1975. Mem. Writers Guild Am. (freelance writers com. 1985), Dems. for Action. Avocations: wild flower photography, birding, gardening, traveling. Home: PO Box 65 54386 Village View Idyllwild CA 92549

SCHNEIDER, MARY ETTA, finance company executive; m. John Beardsley. Grad. cum laude, SUNY, Oswego; grad., Coll. Europe, Brugge, Belgium, Center Latin Am. Studies, Mex. City. Mng. dir., head loan syndications BankBoston, 1996—97, mng. dir., investment bank, 1997—98; exec. VP, specialized fin. Bank Boston Corp.; exec. VP, corp. banking group FleetBoston Fin. Corp., exec. VP, capital markets, 2002—. Mem. adv. bd. Metropolitan Opera; bd. dirs. Boys & Girls Club Boston. Office: FleetBoston Fin Corp 100 Federal St Boston MA 02110

SCHNEIDER, MARY LEA, college administrator; Student, Cardinal Stritch Univ., 1960-63; BA in Theology and Philosophy, Marquette U., 1966, MA in Theology, 1969, PhD in Religious Studies, 1971. Asst. prof. dept. religious studies Mich. State U., 1971-79, assoc. prof., 1979-84, prof., 1984-90, acting chair dept. religious studies, 1988-90; pres. Cardinal Stritch Coll., Milw., 1990—. Vis. instr. theology dept. U. San Francisco, summer 1969, Creighton U., summers 1974-77; spkr., presenter papers, mem. seminars in field; cons. Lilly Endowment, 1988; various TV and radio interviews, 1985— Contbr. articles, revs. to profl. publs. Trustee Pub. Policy Forum, Mt. St. Clare Coll., Clinton, Iowa, 1995—; mem. program Peter Favre Forum; mem. Greater Milw. Com. NEH travel grantee, 1986-87, 1990, rsch. grantee Coll. Arts and Letters Mich. State U., 1987-88. Mem. Am. Acad. Religion (chair Thomas Merton consultation 1979-81), Coll. Theology Soc. (chair Detroit-Cleve. region 1975-77, mem. com. on membership and objectives 1977-79, program dir., chair ann. conv. 1981-84, 88, convenor ecclesiology sect. ann. conv. 1984-87, pres. 1988-90, bd. dirs. 1990-92), Cath. Theol. Soc. Am., Am. Cath. Hist. Soc., History of Women in Religious Network, Tempo (Greater Milw. com.), Wis. Assn. Ind. Colls. and Univs. (exec. com. 1995—, chair, 1997—). Home: 225 W Bradley Rd Milwaukee WI 53217-3154 Office: Cardinal Stritch Univ 6801 N Yates Rd Milwaukee WI 53217-3945

SCHNEIDER, MARY LOUISE, retired elementary education educator; b. Waterville, Wash., Oct. 17, 1918; d. John Steve and Alice Ray (Jones) S. BA in Edn., Holy Names Coll., 1940. Cert. elem. tchr. Wash., 1940. Tchr. Mud Springs/Douglas County, Mansfield, Wash., 1941-42; elem. tchr. Mansfield Sch. dist., Douglas County, Wash., 1942-43, Waterville (Wash.) Sch. Dist., Douglas County, Wash., 1943-49, Lewis and Clark Elem. Sch., Wenatchee, Wash., 1949-60; spl. reading tchr. H.B. Ellison Jr. High, Wenatchee, 1960-62, Orchard Jr. High, Wenatchee, 1962-67; lang. arts tchr. Pioneer Jr. High, Wenatchee, 1967-77; retired, 1977. Author lang. arts learning packages for students, 1967; co-author: Name on the Schoolhouse, 1989. Vol. Am. Heart Assn., Wenatchee, 1975-90, Am. Cancer Soc., Wenatchee, 1975-88. Recipient Cert. of Recognition, Wash. State Ct. Cath. Daus. of the Ams., 1970, 72, 74. Mem.: AAUW (treas. 1973—75), PEO (pres. 1980—82, 1988—90), Chelan-Douglas County Sch. Retirees Assn. (com. chmn. 1989—90), Cath. Daus. of the Ams. (state pres. 1984—86, nat. evangelization chmn. 1986—88, local ct. pres. 1958—60, 1999—2001, author Wash. State Ct. of Cath. Daus. 1988). Avocation: sewing.

SCHNEIDER, MICHELLE G. state representative; b. 1954; 2 children. Student, Ohio State U., U. Cin. Small bus. owner; mayor, 1997—99; state rep. dist. 35 Ohio Ho. of Reps., Columbus, 2000—, chair, human svcs. and aging com., mem. banking pensions and securities, health, and pub. utilities coms. Councilwoman Madeira City Coun., 1993—. Mem.: Am. Coll. Health Care Adminstrn. (Disting. Health Care Adminstr. Yr. 1989), Madeira Alumni Assn., Madeira Sch. Found. Office: 77 S High St 11th fl Columbus OH 43215-6111

SCHNEIDER, NANCY REYNOLDS, pathologist, educator; b. Schenectady, N.Y., July 27, 1942; d. Charles Philip Jr. and Ruth Louise (Taylor) Reynolds; m. John Stanley Schneider, July 13, 1968. BA, Ohio Wesleyan U., 1963; MA, U. Mich., 1964; MD, PhD, Cornell U., 1981. Diplomate Am. Bd. Pathology, Am. Bd. Med. Genetics; lic. Tex. Bd. Med. Examiners. Resident in pathology U. Tex. Southwestern Med. Ctr., Dallas, 1982-85, asst. instr. pathology, 1986, instr. pathology, 1986-87, asst. dir. hemotherapy dept., 1986-87, asst. prof. pathology, 1987-92, dir. cytogenetics lab., 1987—, assoc. prof. pathology, 1992-97, prof. pathology, 1997—. Attending staff physician Parkland Meml. Hosp., Dallas, 1986—. Contbr. articles to profl. jours. and chpt. to book. Mem. AMA, AAAS, Am. Soc. Clin. Pathologists, Am. Soc. Human Genetics, Tex. Genetics Soc., Coll. Am. Pathologists, Phi Beta Kappa. Office: Univ Tex Southwestern Med Ctr Dept Pathology 5323 Harry Hines Blvd Dallas TX 75390-7208

SCHNEIDER, PAM HORVITZ, lawyer; b. Cleve., Nov. 29, 1951; m. Milton S. Schneider, June 30, 1973; 1 child, Sarah Anne. BA, U. Pa., 1973; JD, Columbia U., 1976. Bar: N.Y. 1977, Pa. 1979. Assoc. White & Case, N.Y.C., 1976-78, Drinker Biddle & Reath LLP, Phila., 1978-84, ptnr., 1984-2001; founding ptnr. Gadsden Schneider & Woodward LLP, King of Prussia, Pa., 2001—. Contbr. articles to profl. jours. Fellow Am. Coll. Trust and Estate Counsel (past regent); mem. ABA (past chair, real property probate and trust law sect.), Internat. Acad. Estate and Trust Law (academician). Office: Gadsden Schneider & Woodward LLP The Merion Bldg 700 S Henderson Rd Ste 345 King Of Prussia PA 19406 E-mail: pschneider@gsw-llp.com.

SCHNEIDER, PHYLLIS LEAH, writer, editor; b. Seattle, Apr. 19, 1947; d. Edward Lee Booth and Harriet Phyllis (Ebbinghaus) Russell; m. Clifford Donald Schneider, June 14, 1969; 1 child, Pearl Brooke. BA, Pacific Luth. U., 1969; MA, U. Wash., 1972. Fiction, features editor Seventeen Mag., N.Y.C., 1975-80; mng. editor Weight Watchers Mag., N.Y.C., 1980-81; editor YM mag., N.Y.C., 1981-86. Author: Parents Book of Infant Colic, 1990, Kids Who Make a Difference, 1993, Straight Talk on Women's Health: How to Get the Health Care You Deserve, 1993, Hot Health Care Careers, 1993, What Kids Like To Do, 1993; contbr. The Parents Answer Book, 1998; The Prose Reader, 2001, 2004. Recipient Centennial Recognition award Pacific Luth. U., 1990. Democrat. Episcopalian.

SCHNEIDER, RITA JOYCE, property management company executive, real estate broker, mortgage broker; b. Bklyn., June 22, 1932; d. Joseph George and Mary (Cohen) Rothkopf; m. Arthur B. Schneider, Oct. 18, 1953 (dec. Feb. 1995); children: Linda Ellen, Debra Carol. Degree in Comml. Art, Pratt Inst., 1953; BA in Acctg., Bklyn. Coll., 1954. Contr. Central Funding Co., Bklyn., 1973-80; owner, contbr. Riteway Mgmt. Inc., Coral Springs, Fla., 1980-86; realtor Riteway Internat. Realty Corp., Coral Springs, 1985-86, ERA Regal Internat. Realty Inc.; realtor, mortgage broker Regal Fin. Svcs. and LCAM Regal Assn Svcs., Coral Springs, 1986-94, mortgage broker, sr. loan officer contr., 1995—. Cons. in field. Active Cancer Soc., Bklyn., 1954-73, March of Dimes, Bklyn., 1960-70. Recipient 1st art award City of N.Y., 1950. Mem. Nat Bd. Realtors, North Broward Bd. Realtors, Fla. Assn. Mortgage Brokers, Nat. Real Estate Assn., Fla. Assn. Cmty. Mgrs. (lic), Cmty. Assn. Inst. Democrat. Jewish. Avocations: reading, dance, swimming. E-mail: reejay@aol.com.

SCHNEIDER, SHARON M. systems administrator, information technologist; b. Detroit, Mar. 15, 1958; d. Peter and Mary S.; m. Wesley A. Comes, May 23, 1987. BS, Kutztown U., 1990; MS, MSIS, Drexel U., 1998. Reference and info. asst. Bucks County Free Libr., Doylestown, Pa., 1988-94; computer sys. tech. Cedar Crest & Muhlenberg Colls., Allentown, Pa., 1994-95; sys. adminstr., info. technologist Cedar Crest Coll., 1995—. Mem. Assn. Computing Machinery, World Future Soc.

SCHNEIDER, SHERRI, library clerk; b. Bloomington, Ill., Oct. 9, 1954; d. Ronald Deane and Barbara Hinton; m. Kevin Donald Schneider, oct. 29, 1977; 1 child, Rachael. BA magna cum laude, U. Wis., Platteville, 1976; MLS, Drake U., 1982. Intern to editor The Annals of Iowa, Des Moines, 1980-82; spl. collections asst. Bradley U., Peoria, Ill., 1983—. Cons. local history course, divsn. continuing edn. Bradley U., 1986; mem. steering com. Friends of Cullom-Davis Libr., Peoria, 1990; instr. Preservation Workshops at Bradley, 1991, 92. Author law firm history; rschr. Peoria history brochure. Mem., sec. Heart of Ill. Fancy Cats, Peoria, 1983-86; sec. Peoria Hist. Soc., 1986-94; libr. vol. St. Thomas Sch., Peoria Hts., Ill., 1993—; v.p. Jackson Found., Peoria, 1990—. Mem. Ill. State Hist. Soc., Peoria County Old Settlers, Peoria County Lawyers Aux., Bradley Women's Club. Avocations: travel, gardening, reading, needlework, sewing.

SCHNEIDER, SUE R. music educator; b. Rochester, N.Y., Feb. 13, 1955; d. Irving M. and Barbara S. Robinson; m. Steven J. Schneider, Aug. 6, 1977; children: Scott, Jonathan, Jacquelyn. B in Music Edn., Wittenberg U., 1977; MEd, Nazareth Coll., 1983. Music educator vocal and instrumental Springfield (Ohio) Local Schs., 1977—79; music educator instrumental Greece Ctrl. Schs., Rochester, 1979—. Music dir. choir Aldersgate United Meth. Ch., Rochester, 1983—88, music dir. contemporary worship, 1992—. Mem.: Monroe County Music Assn. (exec. bd. dirs. 1999—). Methodist. Home: 8 Wainswright Cir Rochester NY 14626 Office: Greece Ctrl Schs Pine Brook Elem 2300 English Rd Rochester NY 14616

SCHNEIDER, VALERIE LOIS, speech educator; b. Chgo., Feb. 12, 1941; d. Ralph Joseph and Gertrude Blanche (Gaffron) S. BA, Carroll Coll., 1963; MA, U. Wis., 1966; PhD, U. Fla., 1969; CAS, Appalachian State U., 1981. Tchr. English and history, dir. forensics and drama Montello (Wis.) H.S., 1963-64; instr. speech U. Fla., Gainesville, 1966-68, asst. prof. speech, 1969-70, Edinboro (Pa.) State Coll., 1970-71; assoc. prof. speech East Tenn. State U., Johnson City, 1971-76, prof. speech, 1976-97. Instr. newspaper course Johnson City Press Chronicle, 1979, Elizabethton Star, Erwin Record, Mountain City Tomahawk, Jonesboro Herald and Tribune, 1980; mem. investor panel USA Today, 1991-92. Editor East Tenn. State U. evening and off-campus newsletter, 1984-91; assoc. editor Homiletic, 1974-76; columnist Video Visions, Kingsport Times-News, 1984-86; book reviewer Pulpit Digest, 1986-90; contbr. articles to profl. jours. Chmn. AAUW Mass Media Study Group Com., Johnson City, 1973-74. Recipient Creative Writing award Va. Highlands Arts Festival, 1973, award Kingsport Times News, 1984, 85, Tri-Cities Met. Advt. Fedn., 1983, 84, hon. life mem. Tenn. Presbyn. Women, 2000; named Danforth assoc., 1977; finalist Money mag. contest, 1994, Writer's Digest contest, 2000. Mem.: AAUW (v.p. chpt. 1974—75, pres. 1975—76), Tenn. Basic Skills Coun. (pres. 1975—76, exec. bd. 1979—80, v.p. 1980—81), Religious Speech Comm. Assn. (Best Article award 1976), Tenn. Speech Comm. Assn. (exec. bd. 1974—77, publs. bd. 1974—78, pres. 1977—78), So. Speech Comm. Assn., Speech Comm. Assn. (Tenn. rep. to states adv. coun. 1974—75), Mensa, Presbyn. Women (hon.; life mem.), Johnson City Book Club (pres. 2001—03), Bus. and Profl. Women's Club (chpt. exec. bd. 1972—73, v.p. 1976—77), Pi Gamma Mu, Phi Delta Kappa, Tau Kappa Alpha, Delta Sigma Rho. Presbyterian. Home: 3201 Buckingham Rd Johnson City TN 37604-2775 Office: East Tenn State U PO Box 23098 Johnson City TN 37614-1310 E-mail: vlasastre@aol.com.

SCHNEIDER, WILLYS HOPE, lawyer; b. N.Y.C., Sept. 27, 1952; d. Leon and Lillian (Friedman) S.; m. Stephen Andrew Kals, Jan. 21, 1979; children: Peter, Josefine. AB, Princeton U., 1974; JD, Columbia U., 1977. Bar: N.Y. 1978, U.S. Dist. Ct. (ea. and so. dists.) N.Y. 1978, U.S. Tax Ct. 1979. Law clk. to hon. Jack B. Weinstein U.S. Dist. Ct. (ea. dist.) N.Y., Bklyn., 1977-78; assoc. Paul, Weiss, Rifkind, Wharton & Garrison, N.Y.C., 1978-83, Kaye Scholer LLP, N.Y.C., 1983-87, 1987—. Contbr. articles to profl. jours. Mem. ABA, N.Y. State Bar Assn., Assn. of Bar of City of N.Y. Home: 320 W End Ave New York NY 10023-8110 Office: Kaye Scholer LLP 425 Park Ave New York NY 10022-3506 Office Phone: 212-836-8693. E-mail: wschneider@kayescholer.com.

SCHNEIDER-CRIEZIS, SUSAN MARIE, architect; b. St. Louis, Aug. 1, 1953; d. William Alfred and Rosemary Elizabeth (Fischer) Schneider; m. Demetrios Anthony Criezis, Nov. 24, 1978; children: Anthony, John and Andrew. BArch, U. Notre Dame, 1976; MArch, MIT, 1978. Registered architect, Wis. Project designer Eichstaedt Architects, Roselle, Ill., 1978-80, Solomon, Cordwell, Buenz & Assocs., Chgo., 1980-82; project architect Gelick, Foran Assocs., Chgo., 1982-83; asst. prof. Sch. Architecture U. Ill., Chgo., 1980-86; exec. v.p. Criezis Architects, Inc., Northfield, Ill., 1986—. Graham Found. grantee MIT, 1977, MIT scholar, 1976-78; Prestressed Concrete Inst. rsch. grantee, 1981. Mem. AIA, Chgo. Archtl. Club, Chgo. Women in Architecture, Am. Solar Energy Soc., NAFE, Jr. League Evanston, Evanston C. of C. Roman Catholic. Avocations: tennis, swimming. Office: 1775 Winnetka Ave Ste 100 Northfield IL 60093-3386

SCHNEIROV, ALLISON R. lawyer; b. Phila., 1966; BA magna cum laude, U. Pa., 1988; JD cum laude, NYU, 1991. Bar: N.Y. 1992. Atty. Skadden, Arps, Slate, Meagher & Flom LLP, N.Y., 1993—. Office: Skadden Arps Slate Meagher & Flom LLP Four Times Sq New York NY 10036*

SCHNELL, PATRICIA LENORE, military officer; b. Maywood, Ill., Aug. 28, 1975; d. Richard Michael and Jean Marie Cesak. AA Criminology, Fayetteville Tech. C.C., Fayetteville, N.C., 1999; BS Psychology, Campbell U., 2001. Lic. FAA comml. and instrument helicopter and pvt. pilot fixed wing. Aviator US Army, Fort Rucker, Ala., 1997—2002, aviator, commd. warrant officer, 2002—03, 2003—. Tchg. asst., resident asst. Ill. State U., Bloomington, 1994—97. Mem.: Army Aviation Assn. Am. (pres.), Pi Beta Phi. Avocations: working out, travel, flying, scuba diving, sky diving. Home: 1340 Andrus Ave Downers Grove IL 60516 Address: TF 12th AV BDE B/3-158 AV REGT APO AE AE 09302-1393

SCHNIPPER, SYDRA, mathematics educator; b. N.Y.C., Oct. 31, 1944; d. Leo and Deborah Ruth (Deane) S.; children: Merritt, Deborah, Claudia. BA, Queens Coll., 1965; MEd, Cambridge Coll., 1989. Cert. secondary edn., Mass. Tchr. Canarsie H.S., Bklyn., 1965-68, West Haven (Conn.) H.S., 1968-70, Brookline (Mass.) H.S., 1974—, chmn. Dept. Math., 2002—. Sch. com. City of Newton, Mass., 1985-93. Alderman City of Newton, 1994—; ward comm. Newton Dem. City Commn., 1985—; trustee New Philharmonic Orch., 1996-2002. Grantee NSF, 1966-68. Jewish. Avocations: gardening, travel. Home: 273 Ward St Newton MA 02459-1212 Office: Brookline HS 115 Greenough St Brookline MA 02445-6151

SCHNITZER, IRIS TAYMORE, diversified financial services company executive, lawyer, arbitrator, mediator; b. Cambridge, Mass., Aug. 3, 1943; d. Joseph David and Edith (Cooper) Taymore; m. Stephen Mark Schnitzer, Sept. 10, 1966. BA in Econ., Boston U., 1967; JD, Mass. Sch. Law, 1996. CLU; bar: Mass. 1996; lic. real estate broker, registered rep. NASD, CFP, cert. fin. counseling advanced pension planning. Real estate broker Woods Real Estate, Braintree, Mass., 1968; real estate broker, property mgr. Village Gate Realty, Brockton, Mass., 1969; agt. Prudential Ins., Boston, 1970-73, Northwestern Mut. Life, Boston, 1973—78; fin. planning cons. Iris Taymore Schnitzer Assoc., Boston, 1973-79; supr. edn. and advanced underwriting Northwestern Mut. Life, Boston, 1976—78; trainer fin. planners Gerstenblatt Co., Newton, Mass., 1978-79; founder, CEO Fin. Forum, Inc., Boston, 1979-91; CEO TFF, Inc. at Chase Exch., NYC, 1980—83; prin. I&S Assoc., Boston, 1991—; v.p. Fleet Pvt. Clients Group, Boston, 1993-2000; pvt. practice Law Office of Iris Taymore Schnitzer, Boston, 2000—; mediator Mediation Works, Inc., Boston, 2002—. Bd. dirs. Mister Tire, Inc.; arbitrator Nat. Assn. Securities Dealers Regulation, Inc., 1992—. Contbr. articles to profl. jours. Pres. Mass. divsn. Women's Equity Action League, 1977—79; treas., bd. dirs. Festival of Light and Song, 1989—92; bd. dirs. Achievement Rewards Coll. Scientists, Boston, 1991—95; mem. steering com. Fleet Bank Mass. United Way, 1994—95; chair Girls' Bank Patriots' Trail Girl Scout Coun., 1996—98; overseer Boston Lyric Opera, 1999—; bd. dirs. Ledgewood, Brookline, Mass., 1967—70, LWV, Brockton, 1968—70, NOW, Boston, 1972—73; chair credit com., bd. dirs. Mass. Feminist Fed. Credit Union, Cambridge, Mass., 1975—77. Named one of Best Fin. Planners in the U.S., Money Mag., 1987; named to Mut. Funds Panel, Silvia Porter's Personal Fin. Mag., 1988, 1989. Fellow: Am. Assn. Individual Investors (pres. Boston chpt. 1987—89, bd. dirs. 1985—95), Mass. Bar Found.; mem.: ABA, Boston Estate Planning Coun., Boston Bar Assn., Mass. Bar Assn. (probate law sect. coun.), Navy League U.S. (life), Boston Club. Republican. Avocations: horseback riding, sailing, gardening, interior and fashion design, animals, classical music. Office: Law Office of Iris Taymore Schnitzer 65 E India Row Boston MA 02110-3308

SCHOCH, CLARISSA ANTHONY, singer, educator, executive assistant; b. Jan. 17, 1935; d. John Henry and Eleanor (Edwards) Berning; m. Jack Williams Anthony, Jr., June 26, 1960 (dec. 1982); m. Albert E. Schoch, Mar. 22, 1986 (dec. 1993); children: Rebecca Ellen, Julia Kathleen. BA, U. Oreg., 1957, MMus, 1959. Voice instr. William Paterson Coll., Wayne, NJ, 1979—84, Fairleigh Dickinson U., Rutherford, NJ, 1983—89; pvt. practice voice and flute tchr. Upper Montclair, NJ, 1971—. Exec. sec. Nat. Westminster Bancorp, Fleet Bank N.A., 1985—97; owner garden ctr. Jack and the Preacher's, Holmdel, NJ, 1972—83; profl. singer, 1959—; soprano soloist Montclair State Coll., 1981—85, William Paterson Coll., 1981—82, Temple Emanu-EL, N.Y.C., 1962—79, Union Congl. Ch., Montclair, 1973—. Chmn. youth com. Union Congl. Ch., 1983—87, mem. membership com., 1992—97, chmn., 1995—97, 2004—, nominating com., 1997—, mem. parish life, 1985—91, mem. music com., 1983—85, deacon. Recipient Winner voice and oratorio, N.J. Young Artists, Nat. Fedn. Music Clubs, N.J., 1966. Mem.: AAUW, Internat. Bach Soc. (performing fellow 1969), N.Y. Singing Tchrs. Assn. (chairperson young artists auditions 1980—86), Nat. Assn. Tchrs. of Singing (treas. N.J. 1984—92, v.p. 2004—), Rehearsal Club (past program chmn., pres.), Montclair Music Club (Young Artists Audition chairperson 1982—, past pres. and program chmn., pres.), Phi Beta (sec. 2002—04, treas. 2004—, nat. grad. grantee 1964). Home: 8 Waterbury Rd Montclair NJ 07043-1714

SCHOCK, BARBARA JEAN, educational consultant; b. Pitts., Pa., Aug. 21, 1959; d. Arthur Charles and Emily Anderson Schock. BS, Muskingum Coll., 1981; MS in Edn., Duquesne U., 1988. Cert. Instructional II Pa. Dept. Edn., 1981. Tchr. Holy Rosary Sch., Pitts., 1982—87; resident dir. Duquesne U., Pitts., 1987—89; area coord. Villanova (Pa.) U., 1988—90; supr. of prevention programs Family Svcs. We. Pa., New Kensington, 1991—94; support tchr./guidance counselor Highlands Sch. Dist., Natrona Heights, Pa., 1994—97; ednl. cons. Allegheny Intermediate Unit, Pitts., 1997—. Task force on elem. student assistance programs Pa. Dept. Edn., Harrisburg, 2003—. Facilitator/cons. Three Rivers Workforce Investment Bd., Pitts., 2002—03; elder Mt. Hope Cmty. Ch., Penn Hills, Pa., 1993—99; mission com. mem. Pitts. Presbytery - Ptnr. in Mission, Pitts., 2003—03. Mem.: Assn. Sch. Curriculum and Devel. (assoc.), Coun. for Exceptional Children (assoc.). Avocations: musician, travel/mission work, hiking, calligraphy. Office: Allegheny Intermediate Unit 1400 Penn Ave Suite 201 Pittsburgh PA 15222

SCHOCKAERT, BARBARA ANN, marketing professional; b. Queens, N.Y., Dec. 13, 1938; d. Lawrence Henry and Eleanor Veronica (Tollner) Grob; children: Donna Ann, Don. Grad., Ocean County Coll., Toms River, N.J., 1999. Cert. notary pub. V.p. ops. Am. Vitamin Products, Inc., Freehold, N.J., 1977-89, v.p. ops. Foods Plus div., 1990-94, sales coord., 1994—, product devel. mgr., 1996—, pvt. label mgr., DSD mgr., 1998—; assoc. Ocean County Realty, Toms River, N.J., 1987-90, Crossroads Realty, Toms River, 1990—. Contbg. author: Greatest Poems of the Western World, 1989 (Golden Poet award). Past pres. mayor's adv. coun., past pres. of help line Town of Jackson, N.J.; past bd. dirs. Big Bros. of Ocean County; speaker community svc. orgns. Named Woman of Yr., Jaycees, 1974; recipient Capitol award Nat. Leadership Coun., 1991, Silver Bowl award for 1st pl. poetry contest, 1996. Mem. N.J. Realtors Assn., Internat. Platform Assn., Alpha Beta Gamma. Home: 977 Fairview Dr Toms River NJ 08753-3064

SCHOCKET, SANDRA KLAMKIN, career management consultant, writer; b. Amityville, N.Y., May 5, 1936; d. Harry Isaac and Ruth Lillian Klamkin; children: Barry Schocket (dec.), Andrew. BA, Mount Holyoke Coll., South Hadley, Mass., 1958; EdM, Rutgers U., 1966. Nat. cert. counselor Nat. Bd. for Cert. Counselors, career counselor Nat. Bd. for Cert. Counselors. Asst. dir. placement N.J. Inst. Tech., Newark, 1982—90; dir. placement Simmons Grad. Sch. Mgmt., Boston, 1990—91; pvt. practice career mgmt. cons. Mountain Lakes, NJ, 1991—2002. Author: Summer Jobs, 1985 (NJ Author of Year, 1986), My Life Closed Twice: Surviving a Double Loss, 2003; contbr. articles to newspapers. Active Environ. Commn., Mountain Lakes, 1996—2002; vol. N.Y.C. Ballet, N.Y.C., 1995—2002; docent Toledo Mus. Art, 2002—. Mem.: Authors Guild, Ea. Assn. Colls. and Employers (hon.; pres. 1992—93, Disting. Svc. award 1994), Alumnae Assn. Mount Holyoke Coll. (bd. dirs. 1977), Mount Holyoke Coll. Class of 1958 (pres. 1998—2003), Mount Holyoke Club No. N.J. (pres. 1969—71). Personal E mail: sschocket@att.net.

SCHOCKNER, JAN ROSETTA (ROSETTA), sculptor; b. Richmond, Va., May 9, 1945; d. Leo Adolph and Sylvia Jeffers Rosetta; m. Mel W. Schockner, Dec. 27, 1969. BA, U. Del., 1967; postgrad., Art Ctr. Coll. Design, L.A., 1967—69. Graphic designer Sheridan/Solon Assoc., L.A., Calif., 1969—71; advt. designer Weitzman Assoc., Silver Spring, Md., 1972—74; free lance lettering designer Woodacre, Calif., 1974—92; sculptor Loveland, Colo., 1992—. Juror for ann. exhbn. Loveland High Plains Arts Coun., 1993, 94, 95; presenter Brevard Mus. of Art & Sci. Exhibitions include Soc. Animal Artists, 1989—2003, Nat. Acad. Design, N.Y.C., 1992, 1994, 1996, Nat. Sculpture Soc., Palazzo Mediceo, Seravezza, Italy, 1994, N.Y.C., 1994, 2000, 2001, 2002, 2003, Fleischer Mus., Scottsdale, Ariz., 1999, Loveland Mus. and Gallery, Colo., 1995, Nat. Mus. Wildlife Art, Jackson, Wyo., 1995—99, Bennington Ctr. for the Arts, Vt., 1996—2003, Nymeyer Gallery, Chgo., 1996, Nicolaysen Art Mus., Casper, Wyo., 1998, Hiram Blauvelt Art Mus., Oradell, N.J., 2000, Meguro Mus. Art, Tokyo, 2001, Cin. Mus. Ctr., 2002, Southeast Art Mus., Alaska, 2002, Nat. Ctr. for Am. Western Art, San Antonio, 2002, 2003, Nat. Geographic Soc., Washington, D.C., 2003, Brevard Mus. of Art and Sci., Melbourne, Fla., 2003. Recipient Purchase award, Bennington (Vt.) Ctr. for the Arts, 1998, 1999, Bosque Conservatory Arts Coun., 2000, 2001, Steamboat Springs (Colo.) Arts Coun., 2003. Fellow: Nat. Sculpture Soc. (bd. mem. 2003—, Chilmark award 1985, Silver medal 2003); mem.: Am. Women Artists, Soc. Animal Artists (presenter 2001, award of excellence 2000). Office: Rosetta Studio 405 8th St SE #15 Loveland CO 80537

SCHODORF, JEAN, state legislator; b. Cherry Point, N.C., June 11, 1950; m. Richard Schodorf; children: Brian, Kelly, Kristin. BA, U. N.Mex., 1972, MS, 1973; PhD, Wichita State U., 1981. Mem. Kans. State Senate, 2000—. Active USD 259 Bd. Edn., 1989—. Republican. Methodist. Home: 3039 Benjamin Ct Wichita KS 67204 Office: State Capitol Rm 143-N Topeka KS 66612 E-mail: jschodor@swbell.net.

SCHOEN, CAROL BRONSTON, retired English language educator; b. Plainfield, NJ, May 14, 1926; d. Harry E. and Yetta (Cohen) Bronston; m. Andrew J. Schoen, June 26, 1949 (div.); children: Douglas, Sarah. BA, Radcliffe, 1948; MA, Columbia U., 1963, PhD, 1968. Lectr. Lehman Coll. CUNY, N.Y.C., 1968-75, asst. prof., 1975-85, assoc. prof., 1986-91; ret., 1991. Author: The Writing Experience, 1978, Anzia Yezierska, 1982, Sara Teasdale, 1986, Thinking & Writing in College, 1986.

SCHOEN, JILL F. psychologist, educator; b. Aberdeen, S.D., Nov. 28, 1945; d. Fred M. and Ina D. Bruns; m. Rodney Schoen, June 12, 1965; children: Lisa DeJean, Laura Joy, Andrea Jo, Erika Jill. BS in Elem. Edn., No. State U., 1968, MS in Guidance/Counseling, 1977; EdD in Ednl. Psychology/Counseling, U. S.D., 1991. Lic. psychologist, profl. counselor in mental health, cert. tchr. S.D., lic. approved clin. supr. Case mgr. QMRP S.D. Devel. Ctr., Redfield, 1986—88, psychologist, 1990—93; counselor educator S.D. State U., Brookings, 1993—98, Minn. State U., Moorhead, 1998—2000, No. State U., Aberdeen, SD, 2000—03; psychologist cons. S.D. Devel. Ctr., Redfield, 2000—03, psychologist, 2003—. Editor: (jour.) The Dakota Counselor, 2003; reviewer: numerous books in field. Vol. Salvation Army, Aberdeen, 2002; mem. ministry com. St. Johns Luth. Ch., Warner, SD, 2000—. Mem.: S.D. Assn. Adulthood-Aging (pres. 2002—03), S.D. Mental Health Counselors (pres. 2003), S.D. Counseling Assn. (co-chair govt. rels. coun. 2001—03, Mary Lark Humanitarian award 1998), Aberdeen Arts Coun. Democrat. Lutheran. Avocations: reading, travel, playing piano. Home: 38745 146th St Mansfield SD 57460 Office: SD Devel Ctr Redfield SD 57469 Office Phone: 605-472-2400 4376. E-mail: jill.schoen@state.sd.us.

SCHOEN, REGINA NEIMAN, psychotherapist; b. Bronx, N.Y., Feb. 21, 1949; d. Louis and Bertha (Hoffman) Neiman; m. Dennis Leo Schoen, Dec. 2, 1979; 1 child, Leah F. B, Hunter Coll., N.Y.C., 1969; M, Columbia U., N.Y.C., 1971; M (social work), Hunter Coll., N.Y.C., 1977. Cert. Psychoanalytic Psychotherapist, Wash. Square Inst. N.Y.C., 1983, Family Therapist, Postgrad. Ctr. for Mental Health N.Y.C., 1986. Tchr., advisor Brandeis High Sch., N.Y.C., 1972-75; family service counselor N.Y. Assn. for New Am., N.Y.C., 1978-82; psychiatric social worker Lutheran Med. Ctr., Bklyn., 1982-84; mental health practitioner Montefiore Med. Ctr., Riker's Island, N.Y., 1984-86. Moderator, spkr. Nat. Assn. Social Workers Alcoholism Inst. N.Y.C., 1989, 91; presenter YWCA, N.Y.C., 1987—; spkr. Greater N.Y. Hosp. Assn., 1983; commentator WNYC Radio Women and Rape N.Y.C., 1982; mem. faculty Postgrad. Ctr. Mental Health, 1990—; spkr. Empire Blue Cross/Blue Shield, N.Y., 1990-95, Fashion Inst. Employee Assistance Program, 1994—. Mem. Nat. Assn. Social Workers. Office: Regina Schoen CSW 488 7th Ave Apt 9A New York NY 10018-6808

SCHOENBERG, APRIL MINDY, nursing administrator; b. Nassau, N.Y., June 2, 1955; d. Robert and Eleanor (Marks) Christian; m. Gerald Duggan, 1979 (div.); children: Lance, Craig, Danielle; m. Bruce Schoenberg; 1 child, Michael. BSN, Long Island U., 1978. Intravenous cert., 1994, cen. line intravenous cert., 1995; cert. Nassau Fire Commn. Head nurse Sunrise Manor Nursing Home, Bayshore, N.Y., 1982-87; unit coord. East Neck Nursing Ctr., Babylon, N.Y., 1987-89; dir. nursing svcs., asst. dir. nursing svcs. Oceanside (N.Y.) Care Ctr., 1988-91; PRI nurse, medicare nurse, rehab. coord., MDST coord. Ctrl. Island Health Care, Plainview, N.Y., 1993-95; reviewer, monitor restraints and psychoactive medications Quality of Care Mgmt., N.Y.C., 1995—2003; RN discharge planner Northshore Hosp. Plainview (N.Y.), 1995—. Asst. info. Tumor Registry Northshore Hosp., Manhasset, N.Y., 1975. Assoc. mem. Am. Mus. Natural History; sponsor Child Reach, 1984—. Mem. N.Y. State Nurses Assn., Multiple Sclerosis Soc., Nat. Trust Hist. Preservation, The Nature Conservancy Soc. Avocations: puzzles, bowling, racquetball, reading, speed walking. Office Phone: 516-719-2572.

SCHOENBERG, COCO, sculptor; b. Paris, May 3, 1939; arrived in U.S., 1941; d. Heinz Ernst and Kathe (Gassman) Oppenheimer; m. Bernard Schoenberg, Aug. 11, 0963 (dec. Apr. 1979); children: Nara, Jonathan Alexander, Amanda; m. William G. Swartchild III, June 5, 1988. BS in Lit., Sci. and Arts, U. Mich., 1961; MA in Art, Columbia U., 1964. Tchr. handicapped children Steven Sch., N.Y.C., 1962-63; assoc. in pottery for occupational therapy Columbia Tchrs. Coll., N.Y.C., 1963; studio potter, tchr., lectr. various cities, NY, 1965—. Chmn. N.J. Designer Craftsman, New Brunswick, 1983—85; coord. Ctr. Crafts Fair-Old Ch., Demarest, NJ, 1983—84, ACC Craft Fair, Balt., 1985—98, West Springfield, 1985—94; juror Lincoln Ct. Craft Fair, N.Y.C., 1985, Art Rider Craft Fairs, N.Y.C., 1986, Sta. WBAI Craft Fair, N.Y.C., 1989, Am. Craft Exposition, 1992; commd. by Gulick Group, 1988, Harrison, Star Weiner and Beitler Advt., N.Y.C., 1989. Exhibited in group shows at Montclair (N.J.) Mus., Bergen Mus., Paramus, N.J., Morris Mus., Morristown, N.J., Noyes Mus., Oceanville, N.J., Mus. Am. Jewish History, Phila., High Mus., Atlanta, Craft and Folk Mus., L.A., Brockton (Mass.) Mus., Summit (N.J.) Art Ctr., Campbell Mus., Arts Ann. 1996 State Mus. N.Y., Hamburg Mus. 100th Anniversary Celebration, 1996, Represented in permanent collections Art Inst. Chgo., Hamburg (Germany) Mus. Recipient Innovative Sculpture award, Texaco, 1982, Charlotte Simons Glicksman Meml. award, 1983, Mamoroneck Artist Guild award, 1984, Juror's award, Summit Art Ctr., 1985, Purchase award, Noyes Mus., 1986, Highest award for crafts, Craft Concepts, 1986, Merit award in Ceramics, N.Y.C. Artist/Craftsmen N.Y., 1987, Most Innovative Use of Medium award, Toshiko Tokaezu, 1994; grantee N.J. State Coun. Arts, 1983—84. Avocation: horseback riding. Home: 119 Erledon Rd Tenafly NJ 07670-2503

SCHOENE, KATHLEEN SNYDER, lawyer; b. Glen Ridge, N.J., July 24, 1953; d. John Kent and Margaret Ann (Bronder) Snyder. BA, Grinnell Coll., 1974; MS, So. Conn. State Coll., 1976; JD, Washington U., St. Louis, 1982. Bar: Mo. 1982, Ill. 1983. Head libr. Mo. Hist. Soc., St. Louis, 1976-79; assoc. Peper, Martin, Jensen, Maichel & Hetlage, St. Louis, 1982-88, ptnr., 1989-98, Armstrong Teasdale LLP, St. Louis, 1998—, exec. com., 2003—. Bd. dirs. Legal Svcs. of Eastern Mo. Author: (with others) Missouri Corporation Law and Practice, 1985, Missouri Business Organizations, 1998; contbr. articles to profl. jours. Trustee Grinnell (Iowa) Coll., ex officio voting mem., 1991-93, bd. dirs. Jr. League St. Louis, 1995-96, Leadership Ctr. Greater St. Louis, 1995-96, FOCUS St. Louis, 1996-2001, exec. com., 1997-99; active St. Louis Forum, 1997—, Herbert Hoover Boys and Girls Club, St. Louis, 1999—. Mem. ABA, Nat. Conf. Bar Founds. (trustee 1996-2000, pres. elect 1997-98, pres. 1998-99), The Mo. Bar (bd. govs. 1997-99, chair bus. law com. 2000-02), Ill. State Bar Assn., Bar Assn. Met. St. Louis (treas. 1991-92, sec. 1992-93, v.p. 1993-94, pres.-elect 1994-95, pres. 1995-96, chair small bus com. 1987-88, exec. com. 1988-96, chair bus. law sect. 1988-89, mem. exec. com. young lawyers sect. 1988-90), St. Louis Bar Found. (bd. dirs. 1994-2000, v.p. 1995-96, pres. 1996-98). Home: 7824 Cornell Ave Saint Louis MO 63130-3701 Office: Armstrong Teasdale One Metropolitan Sq Saint Louis MO 63102 E-mail: kschoene@armstrongteasdale.com.

SCHOENFELD, DIANA LINDSAY, photographer, educator; b. Knoxville, Tenn., Sept. 3, 1949; d. David Lindsay and Martha Jane (Zigler) S. Student, Fla. Presbyn. Coll., 1967-69, U. Neuchâtel, Switzerland, 1969-70; B in Visual Arts in Art and Art History, Ga. State U., 1972; MA in Studio Art, U. N.Mex., 1974, MFA in History, Practice of Photography, 1984. Instr. Rio Hondo Coll., Whittier, Calif., 1975-76, Coll. of Redwoods, Eureka, Calif., 1976-85; vis. asst. prof. U. Nebr., Lincoln, 1985, U. Mich., Ann Arbor, 1986-87; vis. asst. prof., guest curator U. Hawaii at Manoa, Honolulu, 1987, 88-89; vis. asst. prof. U. Oreg., Eugene, 1994; vis. lectr., artist in residence Ohio State U., Columbus, 1996-97; instr. art studies in Am. West Ohio Wesleyan U., Mont. State U., Bozeman, 1999; instr. mus. and gallery practices Humboldt State U., 2003, instr. photography, 1999—. Diversity cons. Calif. Arts Project, 1995-96, instr./participant summer insts. and visual arts wokshops, 1994—; rep. Calif. Arts Project Leadership Acad., 2002; presenter, exhibitor Northcoast edn. Humboldt State U., Summit, 2003, 2004; exhbn. curator and co-curator Rio Hondo Coll., Clarke Mus., Coll. Redwoods, Ohio State U., U. Hawaii, Maine Photog. Workshops, Rockport, others, 1975—; exhbn. dir., juror Coll. of Redwoods with Eureka C. of C., 1983; presenter on art and rehab., instns. including U.S. HHS, Soc. for Photog. Edn., U. Mich., Nat./Internat. Head Injury Conf., Family Survival Project San Francisco, Sta. KOLN-TV, Lincoln, 1983, others; lectr. U. Hawaii, Claremont Coll., Pomona, Calif., nat. conf. Soc. for Photog. Edn., New Orleans, 1990, Humboldt State U., Arcata, Calif., 1999-2000, 02; juror Humboldt Cultural Ctr., Eureka, Calif., 1999, Humboldt County Fair, Ferndale, Calif., 2002; instr., 2000; cons. Redwood Arts Project, Klamath-Trinity Schs., Calif., 2001-02; actor, Castle Rock Prodns., 2001; photographer Ferndale Repertory Theater, Calif., 2002; lectr., spkr., presenter in field. Author, curator exhbn. and illus. catalog with essay Symbol and Surrogate: The Picture Within, 1989-90; artist, author, Fractures and Severances: Patient as Artist, 1982-84, 84—; artist: Illusory Arrangements, 1978; exhibited photog. Albuquerque Mus. Art., Vietnam Vets' State Memls. West of Miss.; illustrated brochure Diana Schoenfeld: Landscape and Memory sponsored by Humboldt State U. and First St. Gallery, 1999; interviewed by KHSU radio, Arcata, Calif., 2000-01; exhibited in group shows at San Francisco Mus. Modern Art, 1980 (Print awards 1978, 79), 1st St. Gallery, Eureka, 1999, Alinder Gallery, Gualala, Calif., 1992-93, 95, Art Ctr., Eureka, 1992, Ink People Gallery, Eureka, 1992, Solomon-Dubnick Gallery, Sacramento, 1994, Tokyo Inst. Polytechnics, 1995, Ohio State U., 1996, B.C. Space, Laguna Beach, Calif., 1997, Internat. Ctr. Photography, N.Y.C., 1997, Humboldt State U., Arcata, Internat. Photography Hall of Fame and Mus. Okla. City, 1999-2000, Morris Graves Mus. Art, Eureka, 2000; one-woman shows include Humboldt Bay Nat. Wildlife Refuge Welcome Ctr., Loleta, Calif., 2001-02, Travel Advantage, Eureka, 1999, Art Ctr., 1991, Orange Coast Coll., Costa Mesa, Calif., 1991, A.G. Edwards, Eureka, 1992, Ambiance, Eureka, 1993, Iris Inn, Eureka, 1994, Redwood Arts Project, Arcata, 1996, Humboldt State U., 1997-99, Players' Theatre, Ukiah, Calif., 1997, 1st St. Gallery, Eureka, 1999, Morris Graves Mus. Art, 2002, Humboldt Sr. Resource Ctr., Eureka, 2002, others; represented in permanent collections including Houston Mus. Art, Ctr. Creative Photography, Tucson, Ariz., Graham Nash Collection, Barrow Neurol. Inst., Phoenix, Avon Collection, Mus. Contemporary Photography, Chgo., L.A. Ctr. for Photog. Studies, Nat. Mus. Women in Art, Washington, San Francisco Mus. Modern Art, Princeton U., Laguna Beach Mus. Art, Ohio Wesleyan U., Women Photographers Internat. Archive, Yale U., Beinecke Rare Book and Manuscript Libr., Yale U., pvt. collections, others; creator CD-ROM multimedia presentation Schoolhouse Odyssey. Exploring Remote, Rural and Ghost Schools-A Photographer's Notes, 1998. Ctr. for Internat. Media Rsch., Internat. Conf. Visual Sociology,

Bielfield, and others. Vol. Women's Resource Ctr., Eureka, 1996, Lewis Rathburn Wellness Ctr., Asheville, N.C., 1997. Selected for Gov. of Ga. Honors Program in Art, Wesleyan Coll., summer 1966; Marion Crowe scholar Atlanta Press Photographers Assn., 1971; Nat. Endowment for Arts Emerging Artist fellow/grantee, 1980; recipient Reva and David Logan award for New Writing in Photography, Boston U., 1985, Discovery award Art of Calif. jour., 1992. Mem. Soc. for Photog. Edn., Friends of Photography (presenter). Avocations: carpentry and construction, camping, hiking, writing, gardening. Home and Office: PO Box 596 Wildbird Ln Loleta CA 95551-0560

SCHOENFELDER, LASKA, commissioner, farmer; m. Mike Schoenfelder; 5 children. Student, Dakota Wesleyan U. Formerly with Dept. Commerce, Bur. Pers., Office Hwy. Safety; registrar of deeds Davison County, S.D., 1973-82; mem. S.D. Pub. Utilities Commn., Pierre, 1982—. Farmer, nr. Mt. Vernon, S.D.; mem. FCC Fed-State Joint Bd. Mem. Nat. Assn. Regulatory Utility Commrs. (com. oncomm. 1991—). Republican. Office: SD Pub Utilities Commn Capitol Bldg 1st Fl 500 E Capitol Ave Pierre SD 57501-5070 Fax: 605-773-3809.

SCHOENHALS, KATHERINE VIOLA, social worker; b. Detroit, June 3, 1935; d. Anthony Andrew and Claire Elizabeth (Burkhardt) Fodell; m. Donald Eugene Schoenhals; children: Martin, Juliann. BA, U. Mich., 1957, MA, 1963, Oakland U., 1980, PhD, 1991. Cert. tchr. K-12 reading; secondary permanent tchg. cert.; sch. social work approval, Mich. Tchr. h.s. Berkley (Mich.) Schs., 1957-58, Romulus (Mich.) Schs., 1958-60; sch. social worker Bloomfield Hills (Mich.) Schs., 1960-61, 64-69, Walled Lake (Mich.) Schs., 1971-73, Birmingham (Mich.) Schs., 1978-96; tutor, counselor State of Mich. Rehab. Svcs., Pontiac, 1994—. Cons., rschr. Head Start/High Scope, Southfield, Mich., 1997; part-time faculty Schoolcraft C.C., Livonia, Mich., 1997-98; cons. Hamilton (Mich.) Pub. Schs., 1994-95, Bloomfield Hills Assn. for Gifted and Talented, 1978-81; curriculum planning cons. Birmingham Schs., 1984-94; rschr. Southfield (Mich.) Schs./Head Start, 1997; tutor, tchr., trainer, cons. Sarasota Literacy Coun., 1999; asst. artistic dir. Historic Spanish Point, 1999; presenter in field. Editor: (book) Shadows of Blackhawk, 1996. Vol. tutor, reading cons. Baldwin Ctr., Pontiac, 1995; advisor Maple Clinic Adv. Bd., Birmingham, Mich., 1986—; storyteller Birmingham Storytelling Guild, 1994—; pres. PTA, Bloomfield Hills, 1977-78; co-leader Girl Scouts of Am., Bloomfield Hills, 1973-74; mem., vol. Emily's List, Dem. Party, Episcopal Women's Club. Regents Alumni scholar U. Mich., 1953-57. Mem. AAUW (vol.), ACLU (vol.), NEA (Birmingham rep. pers. sect. 1961—), Internat. Reading Assn. (world conf. presenter 1992), Am. Ednl. Rsch. Assn., Sch. Social Workers Assn. of Am., Mich. Sch. Social Worker Presenters (state conf. presenter 1992), Mich. Edn. Assn., Birmingham Edn. Assn. Democrat. Episcopalian. Avocations: reading, needlework/crafts, golf, walking/exercise, gardening. Home: 9397 Midnight Pass Rd Apt 506 Sarasota FL 34242-2950

SCHOENIGER, JANE, music educator; b. Phila., Mar. 25, 1935; d. Robert Morgan and Evelyn (Beckman) Williamson; m. Whitman Cross II, July 13, 1957 (div. Jan. 1978); children: Robert Stevens, Jonathan Whitman, Elizabeth Pendleton, Mary Evelyn; m. Robert Kurt Schoeniger, June 14, 1980. BS in Elem. Edn., U. Pa., 1956; BA in Music, Chestnut Hill Coll., 1991, BA in Art History, 2000; MS in Music Edn., U. Ill., 1994. Tchr. 6th grade Erdenheim (Pa.) Elem. Sch., 1956-57; tchr. piano Phila. Area, 1980—. Active art goes to sch. Jr. League, Phila., 1962-67. Scholar U. Oslo, 1955, U. Pa., Phila., 1956, U. Ill., Champaign-Urbana, 1991-94. Mem. Nat. Guild Piano Tchrs., Music Tchrs. Nat. Assn. Republican. Episcopalian. Avocation: ice skating.

SCHOENING, RUTH IRENE, retired music educator, musician; b. Moline, Ill., Mar. 23, 1922; d. Karl John and Cora Irene (Reynolds) Wilhelmsen; m. Raymond Edward Schoening, Apr. 28, 1945; children: Stephen Ray, Carol Irene Haertel, John Edward. MusB Edn., U. Wis., 1945, MusM, 1979. Cert. music tchr. Pvt. piano instr., Racine, Wis., 1945—; music instr. Racine Christian Sch., 1960-75; workshop presenter Music Educators Nat. Confs., 1975-82; instr. music U. Wis.-Parkside, Racine, 1985-90, 95, 98. Author, editor: From Sound to Symbol, 1969, Can You Do This?, 1984, Shortcuts for the Older Beginner, 1987. Organist Luth. Ch. Resurrection, Racine, 1960—; accompanist Racine Symphonic Chorus, 1987-98; vol. accompanist Racine Pub. Schs., 1983-93, Park High Sch. Concert Choir, 1998—; active vol. Christian Coalition, Chesapeake, Va., 1990—, nat. and state Rep. coms., 1993—. Mem. Am. Guild Organists, Music Tchrs. Nat. Assn. Avocations: reading, walking, computers, entertaining. Home: 923 Illinois St Racine WI 53405-2223 E-mail: ruth_schoening22@juno.com.

SCHOENKE, MARILYN LEILANI, foundation administrator; b. Wahiawa, Hawaii; m. Donald N. Basham; children: Neil, Steven, Leilani. BB, Corpus Christi State U. Exec. dir. Moanalua Gardens Found., Hawaii, 1994—. Exec. dir. Lawyer's Care; vol. Am. Cancer Soc. Mem. Alzheimer's Assn. (support svcs. coord., vol.), Manu O Ke Kai Canoe Club, Native Hawaiian C. of C., U.S. Tennis Assn., Hawaii Pacific Tennis Assn. Office: Moanalua Gardens Found 1352 Pineapple Pl Honolulu HI 96819-1754

SCHOENRICH, EDYTH HULL, internal and preventive medicine physician; b. Cleve., Sept. 9, 1919; d. Edwin John and Maud Mabel (Kelly) Hull; m. Carlos Schoenrich, Aug. 9, 1942; children: Lola, Olaf. AB, Duke U., 1941; MD, U. Chgo., 1947; MPH, John Hopkins U., 1971. Diplomate Am. Bd. Internal Medicine, Am. Bd. Preventive Medicine. Intern John Hopkins Hosp., Balt., 1948-49, asst. resident medicine, 1949-50, fellow medicine, 1950-51, chief resident, pvt. wards, 1951-52; asst. chief, acting chief dept. chronic and cmty. medicine Balt. City Hosp., Balt., 1963-66; dir. svc. to chronically ill and aging Md. State Dept. Health, Balt., 1966-74; dir. divsn. pub. health adminstrn. Sch. Pub. Health, John Hopkins U., Balt., 1974-77, assoc. dean acad. affairs, 1977-86, dir. part time profl. programs and dep. dir. MPH program, 1986—, prof. dept. health policy and mgmt., 1974—, joint appointment medicine, 1978—. Contbr. articles to profl. jours. Trustee Friends Life Care Cmty., 1984—, Kennedy-Krieger Inst., Balt., 1985—, Vis. Nurses Assn., 1990-95, Md. Home and Cmty. Care Found., 1995—. Recipient Stebbins medal John Hopkins U., 1989, Disting. Med. Alumna award, 1997. Fellow ACP, Am. Coll. Preventive Medicine; mem. APHA, Assn. Tchrs. Preventive Medicine, Med. and Chirurg. Soc. Md., Balt. City Med. Soc., Phi Beta Kappa, Alpha Omega Alpha, Delta Omega. Avocations: gardening, music, theater, swimming. Home: 1402 Boyce Ave Baltimore MD 21204-6512 Office: Johns Hopkins Univ Sch Pub Health 615 N Wolfe St Baltimore MD 21205-2103 E-mail: eschoenr@Jhsph.edu.

SCHOETTLE, ENID C.B. government agency administrator; m. Herbert Stuart Okun, Dec. 27, 1990. BA, Radcliffe Coll.; PhD in Polit. Sci., MIT, Cambridge, Mass. Faculty polit. sci. U. Minn., Mpls., Swarthmore Coll.; staff mem. Ford Found., 1976—91, dir. internat. affairs program, 1981—91; sr. fellow Coun. on Fgn. Rels., 1991—93; nat. intelligence officer for global and multilateral issues Nat. Intelligence Coun., 1993—96; chief advocacy and external rels. unit UN Dept. Humanitarian Affairs, 1996—97; spl. advisor Nat. Intelligence Coun., Washington, 1997—. Office: Central Intelligence Agy Nat Intelligence Coun Washington DC 20505*

SCHOETTLER, GAIL SINTON, former ambassador; b. Los Angeles, Oct. 21, 1943; d. James and Norma (McLellan) Sinton; children: Lee, Thomas, James; m. Donald L. Stevens, June 23, 1990. BA in Econs., Stanford U., 1965; MA in History, U. Calif., Santa Barbara, 1969, PhD in History, 1975. Businesswoman, Denver, 1975-83; exec. dir. Colo. Dept. of Personnel, Denver, 1983-86; treas. State of Colo., Denver, 1987—95, lt. gov., 1995—99; former chmn. bd. Fischer Imaging Corp. U.S. amb. World Radio Comm. Conf., Istanbul, 1999-2000; bd. dirs. AspenBio, Inc., CancerVax Corp, Air Gate PCS. Active Douglas County Bd. Edn., Colo., 1979-87, pres., 1983-87; trustee U. No. Colo., Greeley, 1981-87; pres. Denver Children's Mus., 1975-85; bd. dirs. Gunnison Ranchland Conservation Legacy, Colo. Conservation Trust. Decorated Chevalier, French Legion of Honor; recipient Disting. Alumna award U. Calif., Santa Barbara, 1987, Trailblazer award AAUW, 1997, Childrens Advocacy award Colo. Soc. Sch. Psychologists, 1997. Mem. Internat. Women's Forum (mem. bd. dirs. 1981-89, pres. 83-85), Women Execs. in State Govt. (bd. dirs. 1981-87, chmn. 1988), Leadership Denver Assn. (bd. dirs. 1987, named Outstanding Alumna 1985), Nat. Congress Lt. Govs., Stanford Alumni Assn. Democrat.

SCHOFF, MARCIA ANNE, elementary school educator; b. Gloversville, N.Y., Apr. 30, 1951; d. Franklin J. and Gloria I. Wendell; m. Philip H. Schoff, June 9, 1973; children: Wendi, Caryn, Phil. AA, Fulton-Montgomery C. C., Johnstown, N.Y., 1972; BS, Empire State Coll., Saratoga Springs, N.Y., 1981; MEd, SUNY, Cortland, 1988. Cert. tchr. N-6, bus. edn. N.Y., Nat. Bd. Profl. Tchg. Stds. cert., 2003. Computer specialist Knolls Atomic Power Lab, Schenectady, NY, 1970—72, White Mop Wringer Co., Fultonville, NY, 1973—80; tchr. St. Johnsville (N.Y.) Ctrl. Sch., 1982—83, Oppenheim-Ephratah Ctrl. Sch., St. Johnsville, 1983—. Tchr. summer sch., Fonda and Oppenheim; colorguard dir., Oppenheim. Mem.: NEA, Am. Fedn. Tchrs., NY Soc. Univ. Tchrs., Oppenheim-Ephratah Tchrs.' Assn. (pres., v.p.). Roman Catholic. Avocations: running, gardening, reading, movies, music. Office: Oppenheim-Ephratah Ctrl Sch 6486 State Highway 29 Saint Johnsville NY 13452

SCHOFIELD, REGINA BROWN, lobbyist, political consultant; b. Natchez, Miss., Jan. 14, 1962; d. Elvia John and Velma Marie (Cameron) Brown; m. Stephen Gerard Schofield, Nov. 2, 1996. BSBA, Miss. Coll., 1983; MBA, Jackson (Miss.) State U., 1990. Sales rep. Philip Morris, USA, Jackson, 1983-91; spl. asst. U.S. Dept. Edn., Washington, 1991-92, dept. White House liaison, 1992-93; mgr. environ. issues Internat. Coun. Shopping Ctrs., Alexandria, Va., 1993—. Bd. dirs. Nat. Wetlands Coalition, 1997—, Va. Dept. Agrl. and Consumer Svcs., Richmond, 1995—, Va. Fedn. Rep. Women, Richmond, 1996-98; bd. visitors Coll. William and Mary, Williamsburg, Va., 1997—; pres. Commonwealth Rep. Women's Club, Alexandria, 1995. Roman Catholic. Avocation: reading. Office: Internat Coun Shopping Ctrs 1033 N Fairfax St Ste 404 Alexandria VA 22314-1540

SCHOLEFILED, ROBIN MARIE, psychologist; b. Cleve., Aug. 12, 1962; d. Robert Francis Corsiglia and Jeanne Marie Raleigh; m. Daniel B. Scholefield, July 25, 1992; 2 children. BS in Bus., U. So. Calif., 1984; MA in Clin. Psychology, Alliant U., 1997, PhD in Clin. Psychology, 1999. Analyst corp. fin. Dean Witter Reynolds, N.Y.C., 1984—86; tchr. Starehe Boys Ctr., Nairobi, Kenya, 1986—87; agent Jon Douglas Co., Santa Monica, Calif., 1989—92; staff psychologist U. So. Calif., LA, 1999—. Recipient Relay Swimming Bronze medal, Olympics, 1976. Office: USC Student Counseling 857 Downey Way Los Angeles CA 90089-0051 Business E-Mail: rscholef@usc.edu.

SCHOLER, MARGARET D. adult education educator; b. La Habra, Calif., June 14, 1920; d. James Robards Darling and Ula McWhorter; m. Emerson C. Scholar, 1964 (dec.); m. Philip Lynden Evans, 1941 (div. 1960); children: Lynden Anthony Evans, Conrad St. George Evans, Madelon Blythe Evans Mitchell. AB, U. Calif., Berkeley, 1942. Rsch. crew U. Calif., Berkeley, 1942—43; asst. Robert Johnson, Interiors, Oakland, Calif., 1948; libr. asst. Oakland Pub. Libr., 1960—62; asst. mgr. Fairyland Dutchess Caterers, Oakland, 1962—63; mgr. art gallery Bret Harte Board Walk, Oakland, 1962—63; lectr. Am. Antiques Normandale Coll., Mpls., 1969—90, Ohio State U. Continuing Edn., Columbus, 1990—97, Cuesta Coll. Continuing Edn., San Luis Obispo, Calif., 1998—99, Elderhostel, Calif. Poly. U., Cambria Pines, 2000—01. Acquisitions co-chair Godfrey Ho. Mus., Mpls., 1978—90; bd. dirs. decorative arts coun. Mpls. Inst. Arts, 1980—90; lectr., Mpls. and St. Paul, 1970—90. Mem.: AAUW (co-chair programs Morro Bay chpt. 2000—02, garden tour chair 2003). Democrat. Episcopalian. Home: 2751 Ironwood Ave Morro Bay CA 93442

SCHOLER, SUE WYANT, state legislator; b. Topeka, Oct. 20, 1936; d. Zint Elwin and Virginia Louise (Achenbach) Wyant; m. Charles Frey Scholer, Jan. 27, 1957; children: Elizabeth Scholer Truelove, Charles W., Virginia M. Scholer McCal. Student, Kans. State U., 1954-56. Draftsman The Farm Clinic, West Lafayette, Ind., 1978—79; assessor Wabash Twp., West Lafayette, 1979-84; commr. Tippecanoe County, Lafayette, Ind., 1984-90; state rep. Dist. 26 Ind. Statehouse, Indpls., 1990—. Asst. minority whip, 1992-94, Rep. whip, 1994-2000, asst. Rep. leader, 2001—; mem. Tippecanoe County Area Plan Commn., 1984-90; chmn. Midwestern legis. conf. CSG, 1998. Bd. dirs. Crisis Ctr., Lafayette, 1984-89, Tippecanoe Arts Fedn., 1990-99, United Way, Lafayette, 1990-93; mem. Lafayette Conv. and Visitors Bur., 1988-90. Recipient Salute to Women Govt. and Politics award, 1986, United Sr. Action award, Outstanding Legislator award, 1993, Small Bus. Champion award, 1995, Ind. Libr. Fedn. Legislator award, 1995, Disting. Legislator award Nat. Alliance for Mentally Ill, 1997,, 2003, West Ctrl. Ind. Advocate award, 2003, Friend of Cmty. Action award, 1999. Mem. Ind. Assn. County Commrs. (treas. 1990), Assn. Ind. Counties (legis. com. 1988-90), Greater Lafayette C. of C. (ex-officio bd. 1984-90), LWV, P.E.O., Purdue Women's Club (past treas.), Kappa Kappa Kappa (past pres. Epsilon chpt.), Delta Delta Delta (past pres. alumnae, house corp. treas.). Republican. Presbyterian. Avocations: golf, needlework, reading. Home: 807 Essex St West Lafayette IN 47906-1534 Office: Indiana Statehouse 200 W Washington Rm 3-7 Indianapolis IN 46204

SCHOLEY, DIANN PATRICIA, accountant; b. Sacramento, Calif., July 15, 1968; d. Melvn Alvin and connie Mae Ehresman; m. Todd Alan Scholey, Sept. 3, 1994 (div. Aug. 1996); children: Robert, Alexander. AS in Bus., Yuba Coll., Woodland, Calif., 1995; BS in Acctg., U. Phoenix, Sacramento, 1999. Office adminstr. Sutter Med. Found., Woodland, 1992-95; office mgr. Ron Brown PT, Woodland, 1996-97; devel. assoc. WMH Found., Woodland, 1997-98; contr. WECA, Sacramento, 1998-99; staff acct. S.J. Gallina & Co. LLP, CPAs, Sacramento, 1999—. Named Miss Congeniality, County of Yolo, Woodland, 1986. Mem. AICPA. Avocations: exercising and fitness, horseback riding, flying. Office: S J Gallina & Co LLP 8001 Folsom Blvd Ste 211 Sacramento CA 95826-2621 E-mail: SaavyDi@aol.com.

SCHOLIN, MARGO S. lawyer; b. Sioux Center, Iowa, Nov. 16, 1950; BSN with highest distinction, U. Iowa, 1973; MSN, Tex. Woman's U., 1980; JD summa cum laude, U. Houston, 1983. Bar: Tex. 1983; RN, Tex. Ptnr. Baker & Botts, LLP, Houston. Assoc. editor Houston Law Rev., 1982-83. Recipient U. Houston Law Found. Acad. Excellence award, 1983. Fellow Houston Bar Found.; mem. ABA, State Bar of Tex., Houston Bar Assn., Order of the Coif, Order of the Barons, Sigma Theta Tau. Office: Baker & Botts 1 Shell Plz Houston TX 77002

SCHOLL, BELINDA K. librarian; b. Killeen, Tex., Oct. 26, 1957; d. Burton Thomas King and Alice Rose Coghlan-King; m. Timothy J. Scholl, May 31, 1980. MusB in Piano cum laude, Southwestern U., 1979; MusM in Piano Pedagogy, Tex. Christian U., 1987; MSLS, U. North Tex., 1992. Music dir. Rochester (N.Y.) Acad. Performing ARts, 1981-85; tchg. asst. in piano and theory Tex. Christian U., Ft. Worth, 1985-87; organist, accompanist Genesis United Meth. Ch., Ft. Worth, 1987-93; librarian, cataloger Hotho & Co., Ft. Worth, 1994-97; head librarian S.W. Christian Sch., Ft. Worth, 1997—. Mem. regional librarians' forum Ednl. Svc. Ctr., Ft. Worth, 1997—. Contbr. articles to profl. jours. V.p. Southbrook Neighborhood Assn., 1990-92; judge local and state piano contests and festivals, 1993—. Mem. ALA, Tex. Libr. Assn., Am. Coll. Musicians (judge 1997—), Nat. Guild Piano Tchrs. (co-chair Ft. Worth 1993—), Phi Kappa Lambda. Methodist. Avocations: theater, concerts, antiquing, reading, family and friends. Home: 7928 Regency Ln Fort Worth TX 76134-5017 Office: SW Christian Sch 6801 Dan Danciger Rd Fort Worth TX 76133-4903

SCHOLZ, DENISE LIENEMANN, office manager; b. Lincoln, Nebr., Mar. 13, 1964; d. Delmar Arthur and Charlotte Dephayne Lienemann; m. H. Ross Scholz, Mar. 23, 1996; children: Ginger Alison(dec.), Charlotte Amber, Lindsey Victoria. BS, U. Nebr., 1987. Office mgr., asst. Nebr. Scholars Inst., Lincoln, 1985—87; asst. v.p. Affiliated Fin. Svcs., Lincoln, 1987—88; mgr. computer divsn. D.A. Lienemann, CPA, PC, Lincoln, 1988—95; 1st v.p. Ethel S. Abbott Charitable Found., Lincoln, 1993—; office mgr. Harold K. Scholz Co., Omaha, 1996—. Nebr. state rep. United Ostomy Assn., Irvine, Calif., 1990—95; chmn. Ch. Meml. and Gifts Com., Omaha, 1999—; bd. dirs. Am. Cancer Soc., Lincoln, 1991—95; dir. 2 handbell choirs, Lincoln, 1989—98; mem. handbell choir, Lincoln, 1996—. Mem.: Great Plains Porche Club (treas. 2002—, register 2002—), Alpha Xi Delta (sec. membership, 2d v.p., pres. 1991—95, treas. 1998—, fin. advisor 2000—, Nat. trustee 2003). Republican. Presbyterian. Avocations: music, walking, Porsche club racing, golf. Home: 10222 Polk St Omaha NE 68127 E-mail: denise@hkscholz.com.

SCHOLZ, JANE, newspaper publisher; b. St. Louis, July 31, 1948; d. Robert Louis and Mildred Virginia (Hudgins) S.; m. Jay W. Johnson, June 1979 (div. Dec. 1981); m. Douglas C. Balz, Jan. 1, 1983 BA, Mich. State U., 1970; MBA, U. Miami, 1981. Reporter Jour.-Gazette, Fort Wayne, Ind., 1970-73, The Miami Herald, Fla., 1973-77, asst. city editor, 1977-80; advanced mgmt. devel. participant Knight-Ridder Inc., Miami, Fla., 1980-85; pres., pub. Post-Tribune, Gary, Ind., 1985-91; editor Knight-Ridder/Tribune News Svc., Washington. Bd. dirs. United Way of Lake county, Ind., Gary chpt. Urban League, Ind., NW Ind. Forum. Mem. Am. Newspaper Pubs. Assn., Ind. C. of C. (bd. dirs.), Inland Press Assn. (bd. dirs.), Sigma Delta Chi Office: 790 National Press Building Washington DC 20045-1701

SCHOMMER, TRUDY MARIE, pastoral minister, religion education; b. Wayzata, Minn., May 18, 1937; d. Edward and Gertrude (Mergen) S. BA, Coll. St. Catherine, St. Paul, 1966; MA, Manhattanville Coll., 1971, Pacifica Grad. Inst., 1996. Joined Order of Franciscan Sisters of Little Falls, Minn., 1955. Dir. religious edn. St. Pius X, White Bear Lake, Minn., 1971-77; campus min., theology tchr. St. Cloud (Minn.) State Univ., 1977-81; pastoral min. St. Galls, St. Elizabeth, Milw., 1981-85; dir. religious edn. St. Alexander's, Morrisonville, N.Y., 1985-90; pastoral min. of religious edn. St. Mary's, Bryantown, Md., 1990-91; diocesan dir. religious edn. Diocese of New Ulm, Minn., 1991—. Exec. bd. mem. Nat. Assembly Religious Women, Chgo., 1974-78. Author: Easiest Gospel Stories Ever, 1993; book reviewer Sister's Today, 1988-91. Mem. Network, Washington, 1978—. Mem. Nat. Cath. Edn. Assn., Nat. Parish Coords. and Dirs. Democrat. Roman Catholic. Home and Office: 113 Saint Paul St NW Apt 13 Preston MN 55965-8906

SCHOMP, LISA JULIANA, automotive industry executive; b. 1951; d. Ralph and Kay S.; m. Mark Wallace; children: Aaron, Tyler, Logan. From mini-maid to pres. Ralph Schomp Automotive, Littleton, Colo., 1970-88, pres., 1988—. Named 1993 Woman of Yr. Englewood (Colo.) Bus. and Profl. Women. Office: Ralph Schomp Automotive 5700 S Broadway Littleton CO 80121-8007

SCHON, SANDRA DIANE, elementary school educator; b. Oak Park, Ill., May 17, 1961; d. Edwin and Dolores (Donald) Czubakowski; m. Donald Eugene Schon, June 25, 1994. BS in English, Reading, North Tex. State U., 1983. Cert. tchr. English, reading, Tex. Supr. acad. support svcs. So. Ill. U., Carbondale, 1984-87; acct.'s asst. Tex. Woman's U., Denton, 1987-90, memtor trainer, 1995—; tchr. Little Elm (Tex.) Ind. Sch. Dist., 1991-99, site-base team mem., 1994-99, curriculum devel. mem., 1996-99; tchr. grade 5 Lewisville Ind. Sch. Dist., 1999—. Named to Outstanding Young Women in Am., 1988; McMath Music scholar, 1979. Mem. ASCD.

SCHONAUER, KATHLEEN G. jewelry designer, small business owner; b. Chgo., July 8, 1949; d. Bruno Gregory and Virginia Gliva; m. James Russell Schonauer, Apr. 18, 1970; children: Jamie Christine, Erin Kathleen. BS in Edn., Ill. State U., 1971; MA in Edn., Concordia U., 1977. Cert. art specialist grades K-14, tchr. Ill. Art specialist grades K-6 Sch. Dist. 109, Justice, Ill., 1972—79, 1986—90; adj. faculty liberal arts Moraine Valley C.C., Palos Hills, Ill., 1982—; owner, designer Fine Jewelry and Clayworks, Bridgeview, Ill., 1996—. Asst. gallery dir. La Grange (Ill.) Art League, 1991—95; freelance writer Lapidary Jour., 1995—97. Author poems; contbr. articles to profl. jours. Trustee, bd. sec. Bridgeview (Ill.) Pub. Libr., Ill., 1993—96. Named Internat. Visual Artist of Yr., The Internat. Biog. Ctr. Cambridge, England, 2004; recipient 20 Yr. Svc. award, Moraine Valley C.C., 2003; grantee, Mary Packwood Endowment, Ill. State U., 1989, South Suburban Network for Multi-Cultural Edn., 1988. Mem.: Ill. State Mus. Soc., Ill. Artisan Program, Reiki Support Group. Avocations: reading, movies, sculpting, graphic design, pottery. Office: Moraine Valley CC 10900 S 88th Ave Palos Hills IL 60465

SCHONDEL-BOLLINGER, JENNIFER LEIGH, elementary school educator, secondary school educator; b. Medina, Ohio, Mar. 27, 1970; d. Robert Dale Schondel and Marian Sue Destefano; m. Jennifer Leigh Schondel, June 29, 2002. MusB in Edn., Bowling Green State U., Ohio, 1992, MusM in Choral Performance, 2001. Cert. K-12 music tchr. Ohio, 1992. Tchr. Liberty Center Local Sch., Ohio, 1992—95, Pike-Delta-York Local Schs., Delta, Ohio, 1995—. Dir. Jr. Choral Soc., Archbold, Ohio, 1999—. Mem.: Music Edn. Nat. Conf. (assoc.).

SCHONHOLTZ, JOAN SONDRA HIRSCH, banker, civic worker; b. N.Y.C., Sept. 8, 1933; d. Joseph G. and Mildred (Klebanoff) Hirsch; m. George J. Schonholtz, Aug. 21, 1951; children: Margot Beth, Steven Robert, Barbara Ellen. Student, Vassar Coll., 1950-52; BA, Barnard Coll., 1954; postgrad., Am. U., 1963. Chmn. bd. dirs., founding mem. Grand Bank (formerly) 1st Women's Bank of Md., Rockville, 1976-2001. Chmn. FWB Bancorp, Rockville, 1982—98, Grand Bank Inc.; bd. dirs. Century Bank. Pres. Ft. Benning Med. Wives, Ga., 1962—63; sec. Montgomery County Women's Med. Aux., Md., 1968; bd. dirs. Svc. Guild of Washington, 1968—77, sec., 1969—70, pres., 1975—77; bd. dirs. Pilot Sch. for Blind Multiple Handicapped Children, Washington, 1968—77, Strathmore Hall Arts Ctr., North Bethesda, Md.; spl. gifts chmn. Montgomery County Cancer Soc., 1968, 1969; mem. Washington Adv. Coun. on Deaf-Blind Children, 1972—74; chmn. Friends of Washington Adventist Hosp., Takoma Park, Md., 1993—94. Recipient Outstanding Svc. award, Svc. Guild of Washington, 1969. Mem.: Barnard Club, Vassar Club. Republican. Jewish. Home: 32 Beman Woods Ct Potomac MD 20854-5481 E-mail: g.schonholtz@aol.com.

SCHOOLAR, LAUREL ANN, artist, educator; b. Phoenix, Jan. 17, 1950; d. Robert Day and Mary Ellen (Smith) Skelton; m. James Robert Schoolar; children: Tom, Ellen. BFA, Old Dominion U., 1973. Profl. artist, 1973—; drawing and painting instr. enrichment program Millsaps Coll., Jackson, Miss., 1990—; painting instr. cmty. edn. program Rankin County Sch. Dist., Brandon, Miss., 1989-94. Designer cover artwork for enrichment program Millsaps Coll., 1991-96; contbr. art to Unity Canvas, N.Y.C., 2002. Vol. New Stage Theatre, CONTACT Crisis Line, Miss. Symphony, Jackson, 1990—. Mem. Nat. Mus. Women in Arts (assoc.), Miss. Mus. Art (assoc.), Mcpl. Art Gallery (exhibiting mem., bd. dirs.), Miss. Watercolor Soc. (charter mem., signature artist, 2d pl. award Grand Nat. Watercolor Exhbn. 1995), Profl. Artists League of Miss. (rec. sec. 1995—). Home: 175 Summit Ridge Dr Brandon MS 39042-2063

SCHOONMAKER POWELL, THELMA, film editor; b. 1940; m. Michael Powell, 1984 (dec. 1990). Editor: (films) Who's That Knocking at My Door, 1968, Woodstock, 1970 (Academy award nomination best film editing 1970), Raging Bull, 1980 (Academy award best film editing 1980), The King of Comedy, 1983, After Hours, 1985, The Color of Money, 1986, The Last Temptation of Christ, 1988, New York Stories (Life Lessons), 1989, GoodFellas, 1990 (Academy award nomination best film editing 1990), Cape Fear, 1992, The Age of Innocence, 1993, A Personal Journey with Martin Scorsese Through American Movies, 1995, Casino, 1995 (Am. Cinema Editors nomination best film editing 1995), Kundun, 1997, Bringing Out The Dead, 1999, Il Mio Viaggio in Italia, 2000, Gangs of New York, 2002 (Am. Cinema Editors award best dramatic film editing 2003, Acad. Award Nomination best film editing 2003). Office: Cappa Prodns 445 Park Ave Fl 7 New York NY 10022-2606

SCHOONOVER, BRENDA B. ambassador; BA, Morgan State U., Balt.; postgrad., Howard U. Vol. Peace Corps, The Phillipines, 1961, adminstr. Office Talent Search, assoc. dir., dir. sch. partnership program; affirmative action officer Govt of Arlington County, Va.; with Fgn. Svc., U.S. Dept. State, Manila, Colombo, Sri Lanka, Tunis, Tunisia, with Bur. Near East and South Asia, Washington, 1978-88, chief pers. Bur. European and Can. Affairs, 1988-91; adminstrv. officer, dept. dir. Office Joint Adminstrv. Svcs. Am. Embassy, Brussels, 1992-96; mem. Sr. Seminar, U.S. Dept. State, 1996-97; Capstone fellow Nat. Def. U., Washington, 1997; U.S. amb. to Togo, Am. Embassy, Lome, Togo, 1998-2000; amb.-in-residence Chapel Hill, NC, 2000—01; chargé d'affairs, ad interim min. counselor Am. Embassy, Brussels, 2001—. Recipient Order of the Mono award, The Togolese Govt., 2000, Presdl. Meritorious award, US, 2003. Mem.: Zonta Internat. Office: Am Embassy PSC 82 Box 134 APO AE 09710 Office Phone: 011-322 508-2446. E-mail: RCSchoon2@aol.com.

SCHOONOVER, JEAN WAY, public relations consultant; b. Richfield Springs, N.Y. AB, Cornell U., 1941. With D-A-Y Pub. Rels., Ogilvy & Mather Co., N.Y.C., 1949-91, D-A-Y Pub. Rels. Inc. and predecessor, N.Y.C., 1949—; owner, pres. Dudley-Anderson-Yutzy Pub. Rels. Inc. and predecessor, N.Y.C., 1970—, chmn., 1984-88; merger with Ogilvy & Mather, 1983; sr. v.p. Ogilvy & Mather U.S., 1984-91; vice chmn. Ogilvy Pub. Relations Group, 1986-91; ind. cons., 1992—; pres. YWCA of the City of N.Y., 1994-98. Mem., historian, Pub. Rels. Seminar; mem. USDA Agribus. Promotion Coun., 1985-86. Trustee Cornell U., 1975-80; mem. Def. Adv. Com. on Women in Svcs., 1987-89. Named Advt. Woman of Yr. Am. Advt. Fedn., 1972, one of Outstanding Women in Bus. & Labor, Women's Equity Action League, 1985; recipient Matrix award, 1976, Nat. Headliner award, 1984, N.Y. Women in Comm., 1976, Leadership award Internat. Orgn. Women Bus. Owners, 1980, Entrepreneurial Woman award Women Bus. Owners N.Y., 1981, Women of Distinction award Soroptimists Internat. N.Y., 1995, Achievement award LWV of N.Y.C., 1997. Mem. Women Execs. in Pub. Rels. N.Y.C. (pres. 1979-80), Pub. Rels. Soc. Am., Pub. Rels. Soc. N.Y. (pres. 1979), Womens Forum, Women's City Club. Home and Office: 25 Stuyvesant St New York NY 10003-7505

SCHORER, SUKI, ballet teacher; b. Boston; d. Mark and Ruth (Page) S.; 1 child, Nicole. Studied with, George Balanchine. Dancer San Francisco Ballet, 1956-59, N.Y.C. Ballet, 1959-72; prin. dancer N.Y.C. Ballet Co., 1968-72, artistic assoc. lecture demonstration program, 1972-95; mem. faculty Sch. Am. Ballet, 1972—, Brown Found. sr. faculty chair, 1998—. Internat. guest tchr. and lectr. specializing in Balanchine tng. and technique; artist dir., tchr. on Balanchine Essays (videos). Author (monograph) Balanchine Pointework, 1995, Suki Schorer on Balanchine Technique, 1999 (de la Torre Bueno prize 2000); created roles in Balanchine's Harlequinade, Don Quixote, Midsummer Night's Dream, Jewels, La Source, Raymonda Variations; repertory included prin. roles in Apollo, Serenade, Concerto Barocco, Symphony in C, La Somnambula, Stars and Stripes, Tarantella, Valse Fantaisie, The Nutcracker, Brahams Schoenberg, La Valse, Western Symphony, Ivesiana, Divertimento # 15, Ballet Imperial, others. Recipient Disting. Tchr. in Arts award Nat. Found. Advancement in Arts, 1997, award Dance mag., 1998. Office: Sch of Am Ballet 70 Lincoln Center Plz New York NY 10023-6548

SCHORR, LISBETH BAMBERGER, child and family policy analyst, author, educator; b. Munich, Jan. 20, 1931; d. Fred S. and Lotte (Krafft) Bamberger; m. Daniel L. Schorr, Jan. 8, 1967; children: Jonathan, Lisa. BA with highest honors, U. Calif., Berkeley, 1952; LHD (hon.), Wilkes U., 1991, U. Md., 1994, Bank St. Coll. Edn., 1999, Wheelock Coll., 2000, Lewis & Clark Coll., 2001, Whittier Coll., 2003. Med. care cons. U.A.W. and Community Health Assn., Detroit, 1956—58; asst. dir. Dept. Social Security AFL-CIO, Washington, 1958—65; acting chief CAP Health Svcs., OEO, 1965—66; chief program planning Office for Health Affairs, OEO, Washington, 1967. Cons. Children's Def. Fund, Washington, 1973—79; scholar-in-residence Inst. of Medicine NAS, 1979—80; chmn. Select Panel on Promotion Child Health, 1979—80; adj. prof. maternal and child health U. N.C., Chapel Hill, 1981—85; lectr. social medicine Harvard U. Med. Sch., 1984—; dir. project on effective interventions Harvard U., 1988—; nat. coun. Alan Gutmacher Inst., 1974—79, 1982—85; pub. mem. Am. Bd. Pediat., 1978—84; vice chmn. Found. for Child Devel., 1978—84, bd. dirs., 1976—84, 1986—94; mem. coun. Nat. Ctr. for Children in Poverty, 1987—96; mem. children's program adv. com. Edna McConnell Clark Found., 1987—97; bd. dirs. Pub. Edn. Fund Network, 1991—93; co-chair Roundtable on Comprehensive Cmty. Initiatives Aspen Inst., 1992—; mem. bd. on children and families NAS, 1993—95; mem. Nat. Commn. State and Local Pub. Svcs., 1992—94; mem. task force on young children Carnegie Corp., 1992—94; mem. sec.'s adv. com. Head Start quality and expansion, 1993—94; mem. nat. selection com. Ford Found./Kennedy Sch. Awards for Innovations in Am. Govt., 1998—. Author: Within Our Reach: Breaking the Cycle of Disadvantage, 1988, Common Purpose: Strengthening Families and Neighborhoods to Rebuild America, 1997. Co-chmn. Boundaries task force Harvard Children's Initiative, 1998—2000; mem. Brookings Children's Roundtable, 1999—2002; bd. dirs. Nat. Student Partnerships, 2001—03, Eureka Cmtys., 1995—, Civic Ventures, 1997—99. Recipient Dale Richmond Meml. award, Am. Acad. Pediat., 1977, 9th ann. Robert F. Kennedy Book award, 1989, Nelson Cruikshank award, Nat. Coun. Sr. Citizens, 1990, Porter prize, 1993, PASS award, Nat. Coun. on Crime and Delinquency, 1997, Marian F. Langer award, Am. Orthopsychiat. Assn., 1999, Empatheia award, Vols. of Am., 1999. Mem.: Nat. Acad. on Social Ins., Inst. Medicine NAS, Phi Beta Kappa. Home and Office: 3113 Woodley Rd NW Washington DC 20008-3449 E-mail: lisbeth_schorr@hms.harvard.edu.

SCHORR-RIBERA, HILDA KEREN, psychologist; b. N.Y.C., May 2, 1942; d. Leon and Rosa Schorr-Ribera; m. Ira Eli Wessler, Aug. 6, 1971; children: Mike, Daniel. BA, Hunter Coll., 1963; MEd, U. No. Fla., 1982; PhD, U. Pitts., 1988. Lic. psychologist, Pa.; diplomate Am. Bd. Forensic Examiners; diplomate, fellow Am. Bd. Med. Psychotherapists and Psychodiagnosticians; diplomate Am. Bd. Forensic Medicine, Am. Acad. Experts in Traumatic Stress; cert. in clin. hypnosis. Psychotherapist South Hills Interfaith Ministries, Bethel Park, Pa., 1989-92, Profl. Psychol. Assn. of Greater Pitts., 1992; pvt. practice psychologist Pitts., 1993—. Child therapist Forbes Hospice, 1993—; group facilitator of adult wellness group and children's support groups Burger King Cancer Caring Ctr., Pitts., 1989—, Allegheny Hospice, Pitts., 1994—96; psychol. evaluator Washington (Pa.) County Ct., 1993—, Allegheny County Ct., Pitts., 1995—98; cons. psychologist to sch. dists. Allegheny and Washington Counties. Author: (with others) Educating the Child With Cancer, 1993. Keynote spkr. on illness and bereavement to profl. assns., hosps., schs. and agys., Pitts., 1989—. Mem. APA, Internat. Soc. Hypnosis, Am. Soc. Clin. Hypnosis, Am. Acad. Experts in Traumatic Stress, Am. Counseling Assn., Am. Coll. Forensic Examiners, Pa. Psychol. Assn., Greater Pitts. Psychol. Assn. Avocations: music, bilingual activities, reading, walking, traveling. Office: 117 Ridgeway Ct Pittsburgh PA 15228-1729 Office Phone: 412-344-0222. Personal E-mail: schorrribera@yahoo.com.

SCHRADE, ROLANDE MAXWELL YOUNG, composer, pianist, educator; b. Washington, Sept. 13; d. Harry Robert and Isabelle Martha (Maxwell) Young; m. Robert Warren Schrade, Dec. 21, 1949; children: Robelyn, Rhonda Lee, Rolisa, Randolph, Rorianne. Pupil, Harold Bauer, N.Y.C., Vittorio Giannini; student, Manhatten Sch. Music, Juilliard Sch. Music. Debut as concert pianist Town Hall, N.Y.C., 1953, Nat. Gallery, Washington, 1954; concert pianist Constitution Hall, Washington, 1972; founder, dir. ann. performances Sevenars Concerts, Inc., Worthington, Mass., 1968—, music dir., 1975—, also broadcasts, 1984, 85; recitalist Radio Sta. WGMS-FM, Washington; mem. music faculty Allen-Stevenson Sch., N.Y.C., 1968-89; co-founder, v.p., treas. Sevenars Music House, Inc., N.Y.C., 1968—. Concerts include Lincoln Ctr., Alice Tully Hall, 1980, 93, Sevenars Concerts, Inc., 1968—, Lincoln Ctr., 2000; Lifetime T.V. film Tour, N.Z., 1982-84; featured NBC Today Show with Schrade family pianists, 1993; named to Steinway Piano Co. Global Artist List; appearances PM Mag., TV film, 1980-81; composer, pub., recs. of more than 100 songs; albums include America 76, Original and Traditional Songs for Special Days, 1988; editor: songs of Carrie Jacobs Bond, Boston Music Co.; TV feature film with Schrade Family Pianists, 1997; performed in Schrade-James Family Concert Lincoln Ctr., N.Y.C., 2000, Lifetime TV showing. Mem. ASCAP, DAR (Bicentennial award 1972), Mut. Artists Mgmt. Alliance (founder, bd. dirs.). Episcopalian. Home and Office: 30 East End Ave Ste 3A New York NY 10028-7053 Office: Sevenars Concerts Ireland St S at Rte 112 Worthington MA 01098

SCHRAG, ADELE FRISBIE, business education educator; b. Cynthiana, Ky., May 7, 1921; d. Shirley Ledyard and Edna Kate (Ford) S.; m. William Albert Schrag, Apr. 6, 1963; 1 stepchild, Marie Carol. BS, Temple U., 1942; MA, N.Y. U., 1944, PhD, 1961. Tchr. Manor Twp. High Sch., Millersville, Pa., 1942-43, Downingtown (Pa.) Sr. High Sch., 1943-50; instr., asst. prof. Temple U. Sch. Bus. and Pub. Administrn., Phila., 1950-60; prof. bus. edn. and vocat. edn. Coll. Edn., 1960-85, sr. prof. edn., 1985-88, prof. emeritus, 1988—. Vis. lectr. N.Y. U.; cons. Phila. Community Coll., 1967-82 Editor: Business Education for the Automated Office, 1964; author: (with Estelle L. Popham and Wanda Blockhus) A Teaching Learning System for Business Education, 1975, How to Dictate, 1981, Office Procedures Update, 1982, (with Robert Poland) A Teaching System for Business Subjects, 1988; contbr. articles to profl. jours., chpts. to books. Trustee Meth. Hosp., 1981—85, Sun Cities Symphony Assn., 1988—93, Habitat for Humanity of West Valley, 1994—, co-pres., 1999—2001; trustee Habitat for Humanity Ariz., 1999—2003. Recipient Profl. Panhellenic award, 1963; Kensington High Sch. Alumnae award, 1972 Mem. Soc. Automation in Bus. Edn. (pres. 1969-73, dir. 1974), Nat. Assn. Bus. Tchr. Edn. (pres. 1983-84), Bus. Edn. Certification Council, Phi Gamma Nu (nat. treas. 1952-54, nat. sec. 1954-56), Delta Pi Epsilon (policy commn. for bus. and econ. edn. 1975-78, dir. research found. 1978-83, pres. research found. 1983). Home: 14515 W Granite Valley Dr # 644 Sun City West AZ 85375-6021 E-mail: afs107@earthlink.net.

SCHRECK-ROSEN, ELLEN ELIZABETH, special education educator; d. John Joseph Schreck and Eileen Elizabeth Hickey; m. Ira Rosen, Aug. 9, 1980. BA, Caldwell Coll., Caldwell, NJ, 1969—73; MA, Montclair State U., Upper Montclair, NJ, 1975—78. Cert. tchr. elem. edn., reading cons., handicapped, reading, sign lang. NJ. Student intern Caldwell/W. Caldwell Bd. of Edn., Caldwell, 1972—73; classroom tchr. Parsippany/Troy Hills Bd. of Edn., Parsippany, NJ, 1973—83, com. handicapped tchr., 1983—85; spl. edn. tchr. Red Bank Bd. of Edn., NJ, 1985—87; learning disabilities tchr. Bradley Beach Bd. of Edn., NJ, 1987—. Coord. N.J. project fair Rockaway Meadow Sch., Parsippany, NJ, 1977—82; chairperson of the bd. Entertainment On Location, Point Pleasant, NJ, 1989—; faculty liaison Bradley Beach PTA, Bradley Beach, NJ, 1990—92. Author: (children's book) P.S. There's a Spidgit Under My Bed, Penguin Paradise, 2004, (children's poem) A Holiday Alphabet. Cmty. rels. chairperson Bradley Beach Sch., 1992—97; chairperson Cirriculm Cmty., 2003—04; coach Monmouth County Tournament of Champions, Bradley Beach, 1987—91. Grantee Effective Schools grantee, Red Bank Primary Sch., 1985. Mem.: Coun. for Exceptional Children, Bradley Beach Edn. Assn. (corr. sec. 1993—96), N.J. Edn. Assn., NEA, Meridian Life Fitness. Independent. Roman Catholic. Avocations: literature, travel, water sports, arts and crafts, tennis. Office Phone: 732-775-4413.

SCHREIBER, EILEEN SHER, artist; b. Denver, 1925; d. Michael Herschel and Sarah Deborah (Tannenbaum) Sher; m. Jonas Schreiber, Mar. 27, 1945; children: Jeffrey, Barbara, Michael. Student, U. Utah, 1942-45, NYU ext., 1966-68, Montclair (N.J.) State Coll., 1975-79; also pvt. art study. Exhibited Morris Mus. Arts and Scis., Morristown, N.J., 1965-73, N.J. State Mus., 1969, Lever House, N.Y.C., 1971, Paramus (N.J.) Mus., 1973, Newark Mus., 1978, 1991-92, Am. Water Color Soc., Audubon Artists, N.A.D. Gallery, N.Y.C., Pallazzo Vecchio Florence, Italy, Art Expo 1987, 1988, India Mus., 1994, 95, Athens (Greece) Mus., 1996, 97; represented in permanent collections Tex. A&M U., Telesoft Inc., Phoenix, State of N.J., Morris Mus., Seton Hall U., Bloomfield (N.J.) Coll., Barclay Bank of Eng., N.J., Somerset Coll., NYU, Morris County State Coll., Broad Nat. Bank, Newark, Ind. Cmty. Bank, Consulting Actuaries, Internat., IBM, Am. Tel. Co., RCA, Johnson & Johnson, Champion Internat. Paper Co., Sony, Mitsubishi, Celanese Co., Squibb Corp., Nabisco, Nat. Bank Phila., Data Control, Ind. Cmty. Bank, Sperry Univac, Ga. Pacific Co., Pub. Svc. Co. N.J., Diane Levine Gallery, Boston, S.W. Gallery, Long Beach Island, N.J.; others; also pvt. collections. Recipient awards N.J. Watercolor Soc., 1969, 72, 1st award in watercolor Hunterdon Art Ctr., 1972, Best in Show award Short Hills State Show, 1976, Tri-State Purchase award Somerset Coll., 1977, Art Expo, N.Y.C., 1987, 88, numerous others. Mem. Nat. Assn. Women Artists (chmn. watercolor jury, Collage award 1983, Marian Halpren Meml. award 1995), Nat., N.Y. Artists Equity, Printmaker Coun. Visual Artists (1st award in printmaking 1996), Women Visual Artists (Fla.). Home: 22 Powell Dr West Orange NJ 07052-1337 Office: 1011 Atlantic Ave Beach Haven NJ 08008

SCHREIBER, LOLA F. former state legislator; m. Marion Schreiber; 2 children. Student, S.D. State U. Mem. S. D. Ho. Reps., to 1997, vice-chmn. edn. com., mem. state affairs com. Chmn. edn. com., mem. judiciary com., mem. tax com., chmn. legislators exec. bd., 1995, 96, chmn. edn. com. Nat. Conf. State Legislators; commr. Edn. Commn. States; mem. policy and priorities com.; mem. adv. bd. Policymakers Inst., Danforth Found.; mem. Fin. Project. Home: 30045 173rd St Gettysburg SD 57442-5301

SCHREIBMAN, THELMA RABINOWITZ, psychotherapist, educator; b. N.Y.C., July 29, 1945; d. Philip and Gussie (Lubowsky) Rabinowitz; divorced; children: Andrea Rudolph, Jill Schreibman. BA, Coll. of New Rochelle, 1984; MSW, Fordham U., 1989; postgrad., Riverdale Sch. Modern Psychoanalysis. Cert. social worker N.Y. Coord. Albert Einstein Hosp., Bronx, N.Y., 1977-84; adminstr. Goldwater Meml. Hosp., N.Y.C., 1984-96; pvt. practice psychotherapist Bronx and New Rochelle, N.Y., 1984—; adj. prof. Coll. of New Rochelle, N.Y., 1990—. Analyst, tng. supr. Riverdale Sch. Modern Psychotherapy, Bronx, 1985-95. Mem. NASW, N.Y. State Med. Staff Adminstrs. Avocations: photography, swimming. Home: 463 Pelham Rd New Rochelle NY 10805-2240

SCHREIER, KAREN ELIZABETH, judge; U.S. atty. U.S. Dept. Justice, Sioux Falls, S.D., 1993-99; judge U.S. Dist. Ct., Rapid City, SD, 1999—. Office: US Dist Ct 515 9th St Rapid City SD 57701-2626

SCHREMP, FAITH MARYANNE, writer; b. Pickerel, Wis., May 15, 1921; d. Victor W. and E. Elizabeth (Wilkins) Iames; m. Lester V. Schremp, Sept. 19, 1942 (dec. Jan. 2, 2002); children: Mary, Gloria, Tom, Deedee. Student, U. Wis. Author: (as Faythimes) The Last Switcheroo, 1989, Smalltown Wife and Mom, 1989, Gram's Good Grub, 1992; also contbr. poetry, short stories to profl. jour., anthologies. Mem. Internat. Women's Writing Guild, Nat. Writers Club, Wis. Regional Writers, Antigo Writers Club (pres.). Roman Catholic. Avocations: swimming, crafts, reading, sewing, knitting.

SCHRENKO, LINDA C. former state agency administrator; b. July 24, 1949; m. Frank Schrenko; 1 child, Katherine. BA in Elem. Edn., Augusta Coll., 1972, EdS in Adminstrn. and Supervision, 1986; MEd in Counseling, Ga. So. U., 1982. Tchr. 7th grade Richmond County (Ga.) Schs., 1972-74; tchr. 5th grade South Columbia (Ga.) Elem., 1974-76, tchr. Title I grades 1-6, 1976-77, tchr. 2nd grade, 1977-81, asst. prin., 1984-86; tchr. gifted program grades K-3 Columbia County Schs., 1981-82; counselor Evans Middle Sch., Columbia County, 1982-84; prin. South Columbia (Ga.) Elem., 1986-90; tchr. gifted program grades K-3 Columbia County Schs., 1981-82; counselor Evans Middle Sch., Columbia County, 1982-84; nat. and internat. edn. cons., 1990-94; supt. schs. Ga. Dept. Edn., Atlanta, 1994—2003. Bd. dirs. Coun. Sch. Performance, Edn. Commn. of States, Ga. Child Care Coun., Ga. Pub. Telecomm. Commn.; lectr. in field. Author: Teaching in the Learner Centered School. Past pres. Ctrl. Savannah Regional Area Humane Soc.; mem. Columbia County Humane Soc.; past pres. Columbia County Fedn. Republican Women; mem. Ga. Republican Found., Women Who Win.; mem. Kiokee Bapt. Ch., Appling, Ga. Named one of 100 Most Powerful and Influential People in Ga., Ga. Trend Mag., 1995-96. Mem. ASCD, Profl. Assn. Ga. Educators, Ga. Assn. Elem. Sch. Prins., Phi Delta Kappa. Republican.

SCHRIBMAN, SHELLEY IRIS, database engineer, consultant; b. Weehawken, NJ, July 29, 1944; d. George and Mildred (Kamen) Shulman; m. Marshall Melvin Schribman, Aug. 26, 1979. BFA cum laude, Art Inst. Chgo., 1966; MBA, Simmon Coll. Grad. Sch. Mgmt., 1982. Asst. dir. Advanced Inst. Devel. Am. Repertory Theatre, NYC, 1970-71; ptnr. Sir Charles Cleaning Co., Boston, 1982-83; owner SIS Internat., Boston, 1984-87; database developer (freelance) Boston, 1995—; sys. analyst Dept. Pub. Health, Boston, 2000—. Cons. Boston Computer Soc., 1995-96, Catchpole Corp., Wellesley, Mass., 1996-97, Ptnrs. In Home Care Inc., Missoula, Mont., 1996-97; designer, developer Shulman Bankruptcy Program, 1998-99 Pres. Orgn. for Rehab. Through Tng., Boston, 1986-88; mem. LWV, Boston (housing specialist 1989-91, pres. 1990-91, nat. credentials chairperson 1991-92). Mem. Belmont Dramatic Club, Alumni Theatre, Lexington Players. Jewish. Avocations: acting, composing music. Home: 8 Whittier Pl Boston MA 02114-1402 Office: Dept Public Health 250 Washington St Fl 5 Boston MA 02108-4619 Office Phone: 617-642-5595. E-mail: shelleyischribman@rcn.com., Shelley.Schribman@state.ma.us.

SCHRICKER, ETHEL KILLINGSWORTH, retired business management consultant; b. Hagerstown, Md., July 22, 1937; d. Lloyd Granville and Ethel Mull; children: Jeanne, Lori, Jerri. BA in Mgmt., Hood Coll., 1994. Vol. Literacy Coun., Frederick, 1976-84, Dept. Social Svcs., Frederick, 1984; active Frederick County Commn. for Women, 1996, Nat. Presbyn. Ch., Washington. Named Bus. Woman of Yr., 1991, Frederick Bus. and Profl. Women. Mem. Assn. Sch. Bus. Ofcls. (chairperson seminar devel. com. 1990-94, dir. emeritus 1999-2000), Frederick County Assn. Adminstrv. and Supervisory Pers. 1987-94, Frederick County C. of C., Frederick County Advt. Fedn. 1995-97, Rotary Club of Carroll Creek (pres. 1999-2000), Toastmasters Internat. (area gov. 1991-92, pub. rels. 1991-93, v.p. pub. rels. 1995-97). Avocations: photography, bicycling, watercolor. Home: PO Box 15 Frederick MD 21705-0015

SCHROEDER, JOYCE KATHERINE, state agency administrator, research analyst; b. Moline, Ill., Apr. 1, 1951; d. Reinhold J. and Miriam May (Schroeder). BS Math., U. Ill., 1973, MA Ops. rsch., 1978. Underwriter, programmer, Springfield, Ill., 1973-76; ops. rsch. analyst Ill. Dept. Transp., Springfield, 1976-78, data analyst, 1978-80, team leader, fatal accident reporting sys., 1980-83, mgr. safety project evaluation, 1983-92, mgr. accident studies and investigation, 1992—. Sys. engring. del. to China,China Assn. for Sci. and Tech., 1986; mem. staff Driving While Intoxicated Adv. Coun. and Task Force, State of Ill., 1983-86, 89-92, Gov. Task Force on Occupant Protection, 1988-90; Ill. Traffic Safety Info. Sys. Coun., 1993-95. Vol. Animal Protective League, Springfield; leader bd., co-chairperson LPGA Rail Classic, Springfield, 1983-87; amb. of goodwill Lions of Ill. Found., 1993; trustee, 1995-99. Lions Clubs Internat., Melvin Jones fellow, 1993; Lions of Ill. Found. fellow, 1995; Lions of Ill. Found. fellow Laureate, 2002; Disting. Svc. Award, 2003. Mem.: N. Am. Conf. of Lions Found. (ann. conf. steering com. 2001—03), past Dist. Gov. Assn. (sec.-treas. 1993—), Lions of Ill. Endowment Fund (trustee 1998—99, coord. meml. and endowments 1999—), Lions Club (dist. Gov. Ill. 1992—93, state membership coord. 1994—96, Melvin Jones fellow 1993), Springfield Lincoln Land Lions Club (charter pres. 1988—90, news editor 1995—, treas., 1993-95, 2002-), Lions of Ill. Found. (amb. goodwill 1993, trustee 1995—99, treas. found. bd. 1996—97, v.p. found. bd. 1997—98, chmn. long range planning com. 1997—, pres. found. bd. 1998—99, policy ad hoc com. 1999—, chmn. policy ad hoc com. 2002—), Kappa Delta Pi, Phi Kappa Phi. Avocations: travel, music, sports, dogs, humanitarian svc.. Office: Ill Dept Transp 3215 Exec Pk Dr Springfield IL 62703-4514 Office Phone: 217-785-3021. E-mail: jks999@juno.com.

SCHROEDER, LAVERNE, medical/surgical nurse; b. Dover, Colo., Mar. 2, 1925; d. Chester Albert and Thelma May (Warren) Hutchison; m. Herman D. Schroeder, Sept. 5, 1947; children: Gloria, Rodger, Colleen, Darlene. Diploma, St. Anthony Hosp. Sch. Nursing, 1947. RN Colo., Wyo. Head nurse Poudre Valley Hosp., Ft. Collins, Colo., 1948, Longmont (Colo.) Hosp., 1950, Platte County Meml. Hosp., Wheatland, Wyo., 1957—76. Contbr. poetry to anthologies. Pres. PTA; mem. hosp. bd. Platte County, Wheatland; del. State Rep. Party, Wyo. Mem.: Wyo. Nurse Assn. (organizer), Fed. Homemakers of Am.

SCHROEDER, MARY ELLEN, adult education educator; b. Stanley, Wis., Mar. 2, 1952; d. Harry F. and Katherine L. Wald; m. Craig Allen Schroeder, Aug. 23, 1975; children: Michele Catherine, Michael Craig, Cayla Florence. BS in Edn., U. Wis., Eau Claire, 1974; Cert. Electronic Technician, Austin (Minn.) Tech., 1990; MS in Edn., Southwestern State U., Marshall, Minn., 2003. Cert. ESL Hamline U., 2001. Substitute tchr. Medford (Minn.) Pub. Schs., 1976—82, Owatonna (Minn.) Pub. Schs., 1976—82; assembler SPx Corp, Owatonna, Minn., 1982—88, quality technician, 1990—2000; adult and ESL instr. Sch. Dist. 761, Owatonna, Minn., 2000—. Mem. Workforce Adv. Com. to State Taskforce Team, Minn., 2000—01; presenter at pre-conf. summer intensive tng. Dept. Children, Families, and Learning, St. Paul. 4-H parent vol. Steele County, Owatonna, Minn., 1986—2003. Grantee, Literacy Network, 2001. Mem.: Owatonna Art Ctr. Home: 3699 SE 48th Street Owatonna MN 55060 Office: School Dist 761 122 E McKinley Owatonna MN 55060 Personal E-mail: mschroeder@owatonna.k12.mn.

SCHROEDER, MARY MURPHY, federal judge; b. Boulder, Colo., Dec. 4, 1940; d. Richard and Theresa (Kahn) Murphy; m. Milton R. Schroeder, Oct. 15, 1965; children: Caroline Theresa, Katherine Emily. BA, Swarthmore Coll., 1962; JD, U. Chgo., 1965. Bar: Ill. 1966, D.C. 1966, Ariz. 1970. Trial atty. Dept. Justice, Washington, 1965—69; law clk. to Hon. Jesse Udall Ariz. Supreme Ct., 1970; mem. Lewis and Roca, Phoenix, 1971—75; judge Ariz. Ct. Appeals, Phoenix, 1975—79, U.S. Ct. Appeals (9th cir.), Phoenix, 1979—2000, chief judge, 2000—. Vis. instr. Ariz. State U. Coll.

Law, 1976—78. Contbr. articles to profl. jours. Mem.: ABA (Margaret Brent award 2001), Am. Judicature Soc., Am. Law Inst. (coun. mem.), Fed. Bar Assn., Ariz. Bar Assn., Soroptimists. Office: US Ct Appeals 9th Cir US Courthouse Ste 610 401 W Washington St SPC-54 Phoenix AZ 85003-2156 Fax: (602) 322-7329. E-mail: mary_schroeder@ca9.uscourts.gov.

SCHROEDER, PATRICIA SCOTT, trade association administrator, retired congresswoman; b. Portland, Oreg., July 30, 1940; d. Lee Combs and Bernice (Lemoin) Scott; m. James White Schroeder, Aug. 18, 1962; children: Scott William, Jamie Christine. BA magna cum laude, U. Minn., 1961; JD, Harvard U., 1964. Bar: Colo. 1964. Field atty. NLRB, Denver, 1964-66; practiced in Denver, 1966-72; mem. faculty U. Denver, 1969-72, C.C. Denver, 1969-70, Regis Coll., Denver, 1970-72; hearing officer Colo. Dept. Personnel, 1971-72; mem. 93d-104th Congresses from 1st Colo. dist., Washington, 1973-96; co-chmn. Congl. Caucus for Women's Issues, 1976-96; dir. New Solutions for a New Century, Civil Society Inst.; prof. Woodrow Wilson Sch. of Pub. and Internat. Affairs Princeton U., 1997; pres., CEO Assn. Am. Pubs., Washington, 1997—. Mem. Ho. Reps., ranking minority mem. judiciary subcom. on the Constitution, Nat. Security Com.; dean Congl. Women; chair Ho. Select Com. Children, youth and Families, 1991—93. Author: (book) Champion of the Great American Family, 1989, 24 Years of House Work and the Place is Still a Mess: My Life in Politics, 1998. Bd. dirs. Marguerite Casey Found. Named to Nat. Women's Hall of Fame, 1995. Congregationalist. Office: Assn Am Publishers 50 F St NW Fl 4 Washington DC 20001-1530

SCHROEDER, RITA MOLTHEN, retired chiropractor; b. Savanna, Ill., Oct. 25, 1922; d. Frank J. and Ruth J. (McKenzie) Molthen; m. Richard H. Schroeder, Apr. 23, 1948 (div.); children— Richard, Andrew, Barbara, Thomas, Paul, Madeline. Student, Chem. Engring., Immaculate Heart Coll., 1940-41, UCLA, 1941, Palmer Sch. of Chiropractic, 1947-49; D. Chiropractic, Cleve. Coll. of Chiropractic, 1961. Engring.-tooling design data coordinator Douglas Aircraft Co., El Segundo, Santa Monica and Long Beach, Calif., 1941-47; pres. Schroeder Chiropractic, Inc., 1982-93; dir. Pacific States Chiropractic Coll., 1978-80, pres. 1980-81. Recipient Palmer Coll. Ambassador award, 1973. Parker Chiropractic Research Found. Ambassador award, 1976, Coll. Ambassador award Life West Chiropractic Coll. Mem. Internat. Chiropractic Assn., Calif. Chiropractic Assn., Internat. Chiropractic Assn. Calif., Assn. Am. Chiropractic Coll. Presidents, Council Chiropractic Edn. (Pacific State Coll. rep.), Am. Pub. Health Assn., Royal Chiropractic Knights of the Round Table. Home: 8701 N State Highway 41 Spc 18 Fresno CA 93720-1010 Office: Schroeder Chiropractic Inc 2535 N Fresno St Fresno CA 93703-1831

SCHROM, ELIZABETH ANN, retired writer; b. Princeton, Minn, June 7, 1941; d. Raymond Alois and Grace Eleanor (Hayes) S. Student, U. Minn., 1960; BA, St. Scholastica Coll., Duluth, Minn., 1963; postgrad., Princeton U., 1965; MEd, Temple U., 1972; MLS, Drexel U., 1974; postgrad., NYU, 1981, Russian Temple U., 1983. Tchr. Strandquist HS, Minn., 1963-64, Hutchinson HS, Minn., 1964-65, Peace Corps, Ankara, Turkey, 1965-67, Phila. Sch. Dist., 1968-80; children's libr. Laurel Pub. Libr., Del., 1983; writer Ortonville (Minn.) Ind. Newspaper, 1983—. Mem. Jewish Com. on Middle East, Washington, 1988-90, 93, Nat. Coun. Returned Peace Corps. Vol., Washington, 1989-99, Nat. Taxpayers Union, Washington, 1988-92; mem. bd. policy Liberty Lobby, Washington, 1989-2000; mem. Arkadashlar, 2003-04. Populist. Roman Catholic. Avocations: writing, cooking, history, travel, sewing. Home: 1141 US Hwy 12 Lot 8 Ortonville MN 56278

SCHRONK, PATRICIA LYNN, secondary school educator; b. Hubbard, Tex., Apr. 19, 1947; d. Harvey Herman and Bessie Jo (Blackmon) Schronk. Assocs. Degree, Navarro Coll., 1972; BS, Baylor U., 1974, MS, 1979. Cert. tchr. Tex., all-level cert., reading specialist 1979. Jr. high lang. arts/reading tchr. Hubbard Ind. Sch. Dist., 1974—91, family and consumer sci. edn./home econs. tchr., 1991—. Advisor Family Career Cmty. Leaders, Hubbard, 1991—, Future Homemakers Am., 1991—; dist. planning com. Hubbard Ind. Sch. Dist., 2000—. Mem.: Tex. Adult Educators Assn., Tex. Literacy Assn., Assn. Tex. Profl. Educators, Delta Kappa Gamma. Avocations: reading, crafts, farming and cattle ranching. Office: Hubbard Ind Sch Dist PO Box 218 Hubbard TX 76648

SCHROTH, JOYCE ABLE, social worker; b. Bloomington, Ill., Apr. 4, 1948; d. Raymond Daniel Able and Lois Martha Vielhak; m. Thomas H. Schroth, July 22, 1972; children: Bradley, Michael. BA, Ill. Wesleyan U., 1971. Dir. City of Westlake, Ohio, 1998—. Mem. cmty. adv. bd. Lakewood Hosp., Ohio, 1998—, St. John West Shore Hosp., Westlake, 1998—, mem. mission & values com., 1998—; pres. adv. coun. Retired Sr. Vol. Program, Brookpark, 1999—; mem. adv. bd. Brighton Gardens by Marriott, Westlake, 2000—, Westlake Healthcare Ctr., 2002—; pres.-elect Cuyahoga County Mcpl. Offices on Aging Assn. Chmn. citizen's adv. com. Westlake City Schs., 1985—88, chair levy com., 1988. Recipient Cmty. Leadership award, St. John West Shore Hosp., 2002. Mem.: Westlake Lions Club, Sigma Kappa. Republican. Mem. Lds Ch. Avocations: travel, reading, genealogy. Home: 1800 Holdens Arbor Run Westlake OH 44145-2040 Office: City Westlake 29694 Ctr Ridge Rd Westlake OH 44145-5114

SCHUBERT, BARBARA SCHUELE, retired performing company executive; b. Cleve., Feb. 21, 1939; d. William Edward and Mildred Marianne (Matousek) Schuele; m. John Dwan Schubert, June 15, 1963; children: William Edward, Christopher John, David Matthew. BS in Social Scis., John Carroll U, 1962, MA in English, 1967; MEd, 1980. Cert. secondary tchr., elem. remedial reading tchr., Ohio. Tchr. Sch. on Magnolia, Cleve., 1980-82, Ruffing Montessori, Cleve., 1982-83; tchr. English U. Sch., Chagrin Falls, Ohio, 1983-86; gen. mgr. Ohio Ballet, Akron, 1987-90, assoc. dir., 1990-99; ret. Bd. trustees Ohio Ballet, 1974-87, 91-99. Bd. dirs. John Carroll U., 1990—; trustee Boys Hope Girls Hope, 2001. Mem.: Cleve. Skating. Roman Catholic. E-mail: BJSchubert@earthlink.net.

SCHUBERT, HELEN CELIA, public relations executive; b. Washington City, Wis. d. Paul H. and Edna (Schmidt) S. BS, U. Wis., Madison. Dir. pub. rels. United Cerebral Palsy, Chgo., 1961; adminstrv. dir. Nat. Design Ctr., Chgo., 1962-67; owner Schubert Pub. Rels., Chgo., 1967—. Bd. dirs. Fashion Group, Chgo., 1988—95; adj. prof. comm. Roosevelt U., 1992—. Mem. women's bd. Am. Cancer Soc., Chgo., 1988-96, Art Resources in Tchg., Chgo., 1988-92. Recipient Comm. award Am. Soc. Interior Designers, Chgo., 1979, 83, 88, 94; named to Chgo. Women's Hall of Fame City of Chgo., 1990. Fellow Nat. Home Fashion League; mem. Women's Ad Club Chgo. (pres. 1981-83, Woman of Yr. award 1987), Women in Comm. (pres. 1969-70, Matrix award Lifetime Achievement 1996), Am. Advt. Fedn. (lt. gov. 1983-85). Lutheran. E-mail: schube@mail.com.

SCHUBERT, JEANNE, artist; b. Harlan, Ky., June 2, 1932; d. Lewis Marion and Bertha Faye (Paul) Conklin; m. Robert Breckenridge Stroup, Feb. 5, 1953 (dec. May 1954); 1 child, Robert Breckenridge; m. Robert Buxton (div. 1967); 1 child, Beverly Buxton; m. Robert Kenyon Schubert, Apr. 25, 1970. Student, Cumberland Coll., Williamsburg, Ky., 1951, Rollins Coll., Winter Park, Fla., 1974, Art Students' League, N.Y.C., 1984. Mortgage clk. Orlando (Fla.) Fed. Savs., 1962-76; real estate broker Orlando; co-owner, creator Art Works Orlando, 1993-96. Mem./exhibitor Orlando Mus. Art, 1972—, Dayton Beach Mus., 1972—, Arts on Douglas, New Smyrna Beach, Fla., 1995—, Albertson-Peterson Gallery, Winter Park, 1990-99. One woman shows include Lighthouse Gallery, Tequesta, Fla., Orlando Mus Art Assocs., Valencia C.C., Orlando, LeMoyne Ctr. for Visual Arts, Tallahassee, Melvin Gallery, Lakeland, U. Ctrl. Fla., Orlando, Vero Beach (Fla.) Ctr. for the Arts, Osceola Ctr. for Arts, Kissimmee, Fla., Gallery Contemporanea, Hot Springs, Ark., Brevard Art Ctr. and Mus., Melbourne, Fla., Melvin Gallery, Fla. So. Coll., Albertson-Peterson Gallery, First Union Tower, Orlando, Arts on Douglas, New Smyrna Beach; exhibited in group shows at Orlando Mus. Art, 1984, 87, 88, 92, Barbara Gilman Gallery, Miami, Miami-Dade Coll., 1986, North Miami Mus. Art, Salmagundi Club, N.Y., Fla. Gulf Coast Art Ctr., Belleaire, 1986, U. Ctrl. Fla., 1987, Harmon Gallery of Am. Art, Sarasota, Fla., Crealde Art Ctr. Gallery, Winter Park,, Mus. Arts and Sci., Daytona Beach, Daytona Beach Art Ctr., Epcot Ctr., Lake Buena Vista, 1994-2001, Soc. of the Four Arts, West Palm Beach, 1997-2001; works in permanent collections at Maitland Art Ctr., Rollins Coll., Valencia C.C., Mus. Arts and Scis., Walt Disney World, Flagship Banks, Melbourne, Gen. Mills Corp., Orlando, Hyatt Regency Corp., Orlando, City Hall, Orlando, Barnett Bank of Fla., Jacksonville, Orange County Courthouse, Shands Hosp., Gainesville, Mayo Clinic, Jacksonville, Baker & Hostetler, Orlando, Akerman, Senterfitt & Eidson, Orlando, Holland and Knight, Orlando, City Orlando Collections Orange County Collection, Suntrust Collection, Orlando, Fla., others. Bd. dirs. Maitland (Fla.) Art Ctr., 1972—. Art Svcs. Coun. Art grant. Mem. Fla. Watercolor Soc., Fla. Artist Group (area rep. 1985-2001). Home: 318 N Riverside Dr Edgewater FL 32132

SCHUBERT, YVETTE MARIE, music educator; d. Pierce Jonathon and Barbara Ann Schmaus; m. Gerald Schubert, Oct. 2, 1999. AA with honors, Dawson C.C., Glendive, Mont., 1994; BS in Edn. magna cum laude, Dickinson State U., 1997. Music specialist Dickinson (N.D.) Pub. Schs., 1999—. Mem.: N.D. Educators Assn., Music Educators Nat. Conf. Avocations: singing, art, camping, fishing, photography. Office: Roosevelt Elem 230 3rd AVe East Dickinson ND 58601

SCHUCH, BEVERLY, anchor; Bachelor, Muskingum Coll., New Concord, Ohio; grad. student in comm., Simmons Coll., Boston. Anchor, reporter, Portland, Maine, Providence; corr. N.Y. gen. news unit CNN, N.Y.C., reporter Moneyline, host Pinnacle; co-anchor Biz Buzz, CNN Fin. News, N.Y.C., co-anchor Take It Personally. Office: CNN 5 Penn Plz Fl 20 New York NY 10001-1810

SCHUESSLER, ISABELLE SWEENY, school administrator; b. Washington, May 12, 1934; d. Charles Amos and Barbara (Crosser) Sweeny; m. Donald Charles Schuessler, Aug. 8, 1953; children: Donald C. Jr., Janet L., Douglas P., David J. AA, AB, George Washington U., 1962. Dir. St. Patrick's Episcopal Day Sch., Washington, 1962-86; founding head Washington Episcopal Sch., Bethesda, Md., 1986—2001. Cons. St. Andrew's Episcopal Sch., Bethesda, 1976-79, St. James' Children's Ctr., Potomac, 1991-1996, Cadence Episcopal Sch., Washington, 1992-1995; v.p. Nat. Assn. Episcopal Schs., N.Y.C., 1981-84, pres., 1984-86; evaluator Middle States Assn. Colls. and Schs.; cons. to schs. and sch. founding groups, churches for fundraising. Democrat. Episcopal. Avocations: volunteering, crafts. Home and Office: 9 Orchard Way South Potomac MD 20854

SCHUESSLER FIORENZA, ELISABETH, theology educator; b. Tschanad, Romania, Apr. 17, 1938; parents German citizens; d. Peter and Magdalena Schuessler; m. Francis Fiorenza, Dec. 17, 1967; 1 child, Chris. MDiv, U. Wuerzburg, Germany, 1962; Lic. Theol., U. Wuerzburg, 1963; DrTheol, U. Muenster, Germany, 1970. Asst. prof. theology U. Notre Dame, South Bend, Ind., 1970-75, assoc. prof., 1975-80, prof., 1980-84; instr. U. Muenster, 1966-67; Talbot prof. N.T., Episcopal Div. Sch., Cambridge, Mass., 1984-88; Krister Stendahl prof. Divsn. Scripture and Interpretation Harvard U., Cambridge, Mass., 1988—. Harry Emerson Fosdick vis. prof. Union Theol. Sem., N.Y.C., 1974-75; guest prof. U. Tuebingen, Federal Republic of Germany, 1987, Cath. Theol. Faculty Luzern, Switzerland, 1990; Stiftungs prof. Humboldt U., Berlin, 1997; Ernst Troeltsch prof. U. Heidelberg, Germany, 1999. Author: Der Vergessene Partner, 1964, Priester für Gott, 1972, The Apocalypse, 1976, Invitation to the Book of Revelation, 1981, In Memory of Her, 1983, Bread not Stone, 1984, Judgement or Justice, 1985, Revelation: Vision of a Just World, 1991, But She Said - Feminist Practices of Biblical Interpretation, 1992, Discipleship of Equals: A Critical Feminist Ekklesialogy of Liberation, 1993, Jesus: Miriam's Child and Sophia's Prophet, Critical Issues in Feminist Christology, 1994, Sharing Her Word, 1998, Rhetoric and Ethic The Politics of Biblical Studies, 1999, Jesus and the Politics of Interpretation, 2000, Wisdom Ways, 2001, Grenzen uberschreiten, 2004; editor: Searching the Scriptures, 2 vols, 1993, 94, The Power of Naming, 1996; founding co-editor Jour. Feminist Studies in Religion; also editor other works. Mem.: Am. Acad. Arts and Scis., Soc. Bibl. Lit. (past pres.), Am. Acad. Religion. Office: Harvard Div Sch 45 Francis Ave Cambridge MA 02138-1911

SCHUETT, CAROL ANN, travel industry business analyst; b. Columbus, Wis., May 12, 1967; d. Arnold Joseph and Marilyn Delores (Krejcsi) S. BA in Internat. Bus. with honors, Augsburg Coll., 1996; postgrad., U. St. Thomas, 1997—. Travel agt. AAA, Mpls., 1986-88, Am. Express, Mpls., 1988-91, team leader, 1991-97; bus. analyst Northwest Airlines, Mpls., 1997—. Mem. NAFE, AAUW, Delta Mu Delta. Avocations: travel, reading, hiking, writing. Home: 6833 Bloomington Ave Richfield MN 55423-2661

SCHUHART, ANNE DASHLEY (SUSAN SCHUHART ZITO), actress; b. Rochester, N.Y., June 10, 1947; d. Richard Quinabert and Aynn (Miller) Schuhart; m. Frank John Zito, June 23, 1984. B.A. in English and Drama, Nazareth Coll., 1969. Asst. to Robert and Barbara Taylor Bradford, Bradford Enterprises, N.Y.C., 1981; v.p. Bradford Enterprises, 1991; corp sec., dir. Gemmy Prodns., Inc. Asst. to exec. producer miniseries "To Be the Best", CBS, 1992, "Remember", NBC, 1993, Everything to Gain, CBS, 1996, Love in Another Town, CBS, 1997, Her Own Rules, CBS, 1998, A Secret Affair, CBS, 1999. Owner/decorator ASZ Interiors, 2003. Appeared in Hold Me!, Phila., 1978, Vanities, Chgo., 1979. Recipient Comdrs. award Nat. Catholic Theatre Conf., 1965. Mem. AFTRA, N.Y. Celebrity Assts. Democrat. Roman Catholic. Office: Bradford Enterprises 450 Park Ave New York NY 10022-2605

SCHUK, LINDA LEE, legal assistant, business educator; b. Scott Field, Ill., July 19, 1946; d. Frank A. Schuk and Jessie (Bumpass) Stearns; divorced; 1 child, Earl Wade. BBA, U. Tex., El Paso, 1968. Lic. life and health ins. agt., Tex. Acct., traffic mgr. Farah Mfg. Co., El Paso, 1970-71; adminstrv. asst. Horizon Corp., El Paso, 1971-76; adminstrv. asst. in charge office ops. Foster-Scwartz Devel. Corp., El Paso, 1976-78; legal sec. Howell and Fields, El Paso, 1978-80; supr. Southland Corp., San Antonio, Waco, El Paso, 1980-83, sales mgr. San Antonio, 1983-84, dist. mgr., 1984-87; dist. supr. E-Z Mart Convenience Stores, San Antonio, 1987-89; legal asst. Brock & Brock, San Antonio, 1989—. Instr. San Antonio C.C., 1989—. Mem. NAFE. Democrat. Baptist. Avocation: music. Home: 11903 Parliament St Apt 324 San Antonio TX 78216-2451 Office: Brock & Brock 803 E Mistletoe Ave San Antonio TX 78212-3524 E-mail: ischuk@yahoo.com.

SCHULHOFF, KAREN L. information specialist; b. Long Island City, N.Y., Dec. 11, 1959; d. Edward and Eleanor (Gillespie) S. MLS, CUNY, 1993. Tng. program coord. Chem. Bank, N.Y.C., 1983-90; libr. Katharine Gibbs Sch., N.Y.C., 1990-92; cons. Pfizer, N.Y.C., 1993-2001; info. specialist, rschr. Bear, Stearns Investment Banking, N.Y.C., 2001—. Mem. NAFE, Am. Mgmt. Assn. Roman Catholic. Office: Bear Stearns Investment Banking 383 Madison Ave New York NY 10167

SCHULMAN, AMY WEINFELD, lawyer; b. N.Y.C., Oct. 16, 1960; d. Alvin Harold and Ann Schulman; m. David Eli Nachman; children: Ezra, Gideon, Rafael. BA, Wesleyan U., 1982; JD, Yale U., 1989. Law clk. Harold Ackerman, Newark, 1989; assoc. Cleary Gottlieb, N.Y.C., 1990—97; of counsel Piper & Marbury, N.Y.C., 1997; ptnr. Piper Rudnick, N.Y.C., 1998—. Mem. steering com. DI-Drug and Med. Device, 1999—; mem. commn. on jury N.Y. State, 1999—; mem. exec. com. Yale U., 1999—; bd. dirs. N.Y. Lawyers Pub. Interest, N.Y.C.; nat. coord. counsel, trial counsel. Bd. dirs. Bklyn. (N.Y.) Acad. Music, 2002—. Named 45 Under 45, Am. Lawyer, 2003, 1 of 21 rising female litigators, Corp. Counsel Mags. Achievements include design of and implements alternative resolution programs for Fortune 500 companies and has handled nearly 750 mediations. Office: Piper Rudnick 1251 6th Ave New York NY 10020

SCHULMAN, HEIDI, broadcast executive; married; 1 child. BA in Govt., Barnard Coll., 1968. Corr. NBC News, L.A., 1978-90; programming cons. U.S. Info. Agys. Worldnet Television, Washington, 1993-96; dir. Corp. Pub. Broadcasting, Washington, 1996—. Writer, anchor UFWB and KPOL radio, L.A., KCBS Newsradio, San Francisco. Recipient Emmy award, 1994. Office: Corp Pub Broadcasting 901 E St NW Ste 300 Washington DC 20004-2012

SCHULTHEISS, EMILY EKONEN, management consultant, writer; b. Oklahoma City, Feb. 6, 1949; d. Tauno Otto and Dorothy Guhlstorf Ekonen; m. Arthur Howard Schultheiss (dec. Aug. 9, 2000). BBA, U. Okla., 1971; MS, LaRoche Coll., 1985. Human resources generalist Westinghouse Electric Corp., Norman, Okla., 1971—77, human resources supr. Boston, 1977—80, human resources mgr. Norman, 1980—81, mgr. orgn. devel. Pitts., 1981—83, mgr. corp. tng., 1983—95; v.p. Impact Strategy Assocs., Pitts., 1996—97; sole proprietor Thriving Sys., Pitts., 1997—. Chair resource team Evang. Luth. Ch. Am. S.W. Pa. Synod, Pitts., 2003—. Author: (Book) Optimizing the Organization, 1988, Day by Day: A Journey Toward Thriving, 1998. Vice pres. Northland Pub. Libr. Found. Bd., Pitts., 1998—2003. Lutheran. Avocations: music, quilting, reading. Office: Thriving Systems PO Box 97121 Pittsburgh PA 15229 E-mail: thriver@earthlink.net.

SCHULTIS, GAIL ANN, library director; b. Freeport, Ill., May 12, 1951; d. Richard C. and Ida G. Schultis. BA, Cornell Coll., 1973; MLS, U. Mo., 1976; MA, U. Tex., San Antonio, 1989. Reference libr. U. Tex., San Antonio, 1976-79, El Paso, 1979-84, 89, head access svcs., 1984-88; reference libr. Park U., Parkville, Mo., 1989-96, dir. libr. sys., 1996—. Co-author: Best Self-Help & Self-Awareness Books, 1995. Mem. ALA, Am. Hist. Assn., Orgn. Am. Historians. Home: 10307 NW 57th Ter Parkville MO 64152-3396 Office: Park Univ Libr 8700 NW River Park Dr Parkville MO 64152-4358 Office Phone: 816-584-6704. E-mail: ann.schultis@park.edu.

SCHULTZ, AUDREY LYNN, construction executive, consultant; b. Bklyn., Mar. 30, 1962; d. Donald Schultz and Alice Podorson-Schultz. AS in Fashion Mktg., St. Petersburg Jr. Coll., 1982; BA in Interior Design, Marymount U., 1991; MS in Arch., Va. Poly. Inst., 2002. Cert. interior designer Nat. Coun. Interior Design Qualifications. Store mgr. various retail cos., Washington, 1982—93; interior designer The Holland Lessard Group, Washington, 1991—95, EDS, Herndon, Va., 1996—98; sr. interior designer CUH2A, Washington, 1998—99; project asst. Glen Constrn. Co., Gaithersburg, Md., 1999—2000; program cons. CH2M Hill, Herndon, 2000—. Asst. prof. interior design Mt. Vernon Coll./George Washington U., 1998; juror NCIDQ, Arlington, Va., 1999; adj. prof. interior design No. Va. C.C., 1999. Editor: (book) Code Check, A Field Guide to Building a Safe House, 1995; designer (front cover) Koroseal Protective Wall Systems Product Catalog, 1997; co-author: Letters From the Soul Series, 2002, Today's Famous Poems, On the Wings of Pegasus, 2003.

SCHULTZ, BARBARA MARIE, investment advisor representative; b. Chgo., Sept. 9, 1943; d. Edwin and Bernice (Barstis) Legner; m. Ronald J. Schultz Sr., May 1, 1965; 1 child, Ronald J. Student, Prairie State Coll., Chicago Heights, Ill. Fin. planner Metlife Fin. Svcs., N.Y.C., 1981-2001; fin. advisor Morgan Stanley Dean Witter, N.Y.C., 2001—02; agt., investment advisor rep. Country Ins. and Fin. Svcs., Hickory Hills, Ill., 2002—. Qualifier Met. Life Leaders Conf., 1990. Fellow Nat. Assn. Life Underwriters (edn. chmn. 1988-91, nat. quality award Robert L. Rose award 1990), Life Underwriters Tng. Coun. (chmn. 1986-88, citation 1987), South Cook County Assn. Life Underwriters (edn. chmn. 1988-91), Country Club (1st pl. award, 2002). Roman Catholic. Avocations: boating, aerobics, golfing. Office: Country Ins and Fin Svcs 9630 S Roberts Rd Ste B-6B Hickory Hills IL 60457 Office Phone: 708-430-2509.

SCHULTZ, EILEEN HEDY, graphic designer; b. Yonkers, N.Y. d. Harry Arthur and Hedy Evelyn (Morchel) S. BFA, Sch. Visual Arts, 1955. Staff artist C.A. Parshall Studios, N.Y.C., 1955-57; editorial art dir. Paradise of the Pacific, Honolulu, 1957-58; graphic designer Adler Advt. Agy., N.Y.C., 1958-59; art dir. Good Housekeeping Mag., N.Y.C., 1959-82, creative dir. advt. and sales promotion, 1982-86; creative dir. Hearst Promo, 1986-87; pres. Design Internat., N.Y.C., 1987—. Creative dir. The Depository Trust Co., 1987-99. Art dir., editor, designer, 50th Art Directors Club Annual, 1973; columnist: Art Direction, 1969—. Dir. Sch. Visual Arts, N.Y.C., 1978— ; trustee Sch. Art League, 1978—; advisor Fashion Inst. Tech., 1979—; adv. commn. N.Y.C. Cmty. Colls., 1979—. Named Yonkers Ambassador of Good Will to Netherlands, 1955; recipient Outstanding Achievement Sch. Visual Arts Alumni Soc., 1976, Sch. Art League Youth award, 1976. Mem. Art Dirs. Club (pres. 1975-77), Soc. Illustrators (pres. 1991-93), Joint Ethics Com. (chmn. 1978-80), Am. Inst. Graphic Arts, Soc. Publ. Designers, Type Dirs. Club.

SCHULTZ, HELEN WELKLEY, marriage and family therapist, minister; b. Rochester, N.Y., Apr. 29, 1939; d. Russell Edward Sr. and Helen Elizabeth (Mater) Welkley; m. Leroy Benjamin Schultz, June 16, 1963; children: Mary Beth, Leroi George, Helen Susan, Rachel Anne. BA, MacMurray Coll., 1961; MDiv, Asbury Theol. Sem., 1965; MA, Syracuse U., 1974. Min. Cheningo United Meth. Ch., Truxton, N.Y., 1965-80; asst. min. Christ Covenant Ch., Truxton, 1980—; marriage and family therapist Onondaga Pastoral Counseling Ctr., Syracuse, N.Y., 1972-82, St. Andrew's Episcopal Ch., Syracuse, 1982—, Meml. Bapt. Ch., Cortland, N.Y., 1982—. Workshop presenter in field. Troop leader Girl Scouts U.S.A., 1957—, mem. program com. Ctrl. N.Y. coun., mem. wider opportunities com., gold award com.; chaplain Boy Scouts Am., 1997—, unit comdr. Baden Powell coun., 1998—; mem. Gospel Crusade Ministerial Assn. Recipient Appreciation pin Ctrl. N.Y. Girl Scout Coun., Syracuse, 1994. Mem. Am. Assn. for Marriage and Family Therapy (clin.), Gospel Crusade Ministerial Assn. Republican. Avocations: quilting, sewing, backpacking-camping, canoeing, gardening. Home and Office: 5458 Dog Hollow Rd Truxton NY 13158-3163

SCHULTZ, JANET W. intelligence research analyst; b. Balt., Nov. 25, 1957; d. Richard W. and Minna M. (Glaser) S.; m. Jacob L. Williams Jr., Feb. 1, 1992. BA cum laude, U. Md., 1979, BS, 1986; MA, George Washington U., 1982. Crew leader U.S. Bur. of Census, Baltimore County, Md., 1980; mgmt. analyst NASA Hdqrs., Washington, 1981; tech. writer Dynatech Data Sys., Springfield, Va., 1982-85, Catalyst Rsch., Owings Mills, Md., 1985-86; intelligence rsch. analyst U.S. Dept. Def., Ft. Meade, Md., 1986—. Intern U.S. Dept. of State, Washington, 1978. Coach, umpire Arbutus Girls' Athletic Assn., Balt., 1969-80; Sunday sch. tchr. Emmanuel Luth. Ch., Balt., 1972-80; basketball coach Luth. Ch. of St. Andrews, Wheaton, Md., 1984-85; branch v.p. Aid Assn. for Lutherans Holy Nativity Lutheran Ch., Balt., 1996-98. Recipient Merit Scholastic award State of Md., 1975; Wolcott Found. fellow High Twelve Internat., 1980-82. Mem. Phi Beta Kappa, Phi Kappa Phi, Pi Sigma Alpha, Phi Alpha Theta, Alpha Lambda Delta. Democrat. E-mail: jschultz3@hotmail.com.

SCHULTZ, KAREN ROSE, clinical social worker, author, publisher, speaker; b. Huntington, N.Y., June 16, 1958; d. Eugene Alfred and Laura Rose (Palazzolo) Squeri; m. Richard S. Schultz, Apr. 8, 1989; children: Carlos, Sarah Rose. BA with honors, SUNY, Binghamton, 1980; MA, U.

Chgo., 1982. Lic. clin. social worker, Ill. Unit dir., adminstr. Camp Algonquin, Ill., 1981; clin. social worker United Charities Chgo., 1982-86; social worker Hartgrove Hosp., Chgo., 1986-87; pvt. practice, Oak Brook, Ill., 1987—. Owner, founder Inner Space pub. Co., 1993; trainer, speaker various groups, schs. and orgns., 1988-89; group leader Optifast Program, Oak Park and Aurora, Ill., 1989-90; instr. social work Morraine Valley C.C., Palos Hills, Ill., 1989-90; instr. eating disorders Coll. of Dupage, Glen Ellyn, Ill., 1990-92, tchr. intuition and counseling, 1995—; spkr. in field. Author: The River Within, 1993, Shelter in the Forest, 1998, Flashes of Brilliance, 2002; editor, contbg. author: The River Within newsletter, 1989—2000. Mem. NASW (registered, diplomate), Acad. Cert. Social Workers. Avocations: creative writing, aerobics, yoga, personal growth. Office: 900 Jorie Blvd Ste 234 Oak Brook IL 60523-3841

SCHULTZ, NANCY JANSSON, artist; b. Kanas City, Mo., Apr. 15, 1933; d. Carl Albert Jansson and Lora Elizabeth Wilson; m. Everett Hoyle Schultz, June 23, 1955; children: Susan, Frank, Janet, Sally. Student, Pk. Coll., Parkville, Mo., 1951—54. Founder Women on Paper, Augusta, Ga., 1987—. Exhibitions include Genema Gallery, Altanta, Ga., McCormick Arts Ctr., McCormick, S.C. (Purchase award, 2003, 2000), Quinlan Arts Ctr., Gainsville, Ga., Gwinnett Fine Arts Ctr., Duluth, Ga., Univ. S.C., Aiken, S.C., Cotton Exch. Gallery, Augusta, Ga., 1998, Clayton St. Gallery, Athens, Ga., 1998, Emory Univ. Law Sch. Libr., Atlanta, Ga., 2000, Barnes & Noble Bookstore, Augusta, Ga., 2000, State Capitol Gallery, Ga. Arts Day, Atlanta, Ga., 2001, Aiken Ctr. for the Arts, Aiken, S.C., 2001, State Bot. Gardens, Athens, Ga., 2002, Cork Gallery, Avery Fisher Hall, N.Y.C., 2002, 2003, numerous others, Represented in permanent collections Bank of Fla., Deloritte & Touche, Charlotte, N.C., Med. Coll. of Ga., Univ. Hosp., Augusta, Ga., St. Joseph's Hosp., PAC 2000, New Hampshire, Jud. Ctr., Ocala, Fla., numerous others, featured in numerous publ., produced, gift bags, place mats, bookmarks, greeting cards, prin. works include Carptenter's Gallery, Augusta, Ga., Ann Jacob Gallery, Atlanta, Highlands, NC, The Pheasants Eye, Lynchburg, Va., Suzannes Frame Design, St. Petersburg, Fla., represented by, Art on Broad, Augusta, Ga. Named to Archives on Women Artists, The Nat. Mus. of Women in the Arts, Washington, 1995; recipient Hon. Mention, Eyes for the Art, Augusta, Ga., 1992, Merit award, Images in Art, Ocala, Fla., 1992, First Pl., Fine Arts for Watercolor, Blue Crab Festival, N.C., 1989, Merit award, Miss. Watercolor Soc., 1989. Mem.. Gertude Herbert Inst. of Art, Nat. League of Am. Pen Women (first pl.,W.C., Atlanta, Ga. 1994, third pl., spring show 1997, Pres. award. 1997, Marel Brown award, Out of the Ashes 1999, first pl., Mixed Media, spring show 2002, third pl., Overall, spring show 2002), Ga. Watercolor Soc. (newsletter editor 1990—92, signature mem.). Avocations: aerobics, writing, reading, making hand made books. Home and Studio: 608 Aumond Rd Augusta GA 30909

SCHULTZ, NANCY REILLY, artist, b. N.Y.C., July 20, 1930; d. John Francis and Eunice Genevieve (Crowley) Reilly; m. Frederick Henry Schultz, Aug. 11, 1951; children: Catherine, Frederick, Clifford, John Reilly. BA, Smith Coll. for Women, 1951; BFA, U. North Fla., 2000. Pres. The Smash Tennis Shop, Inc., Jacksonville, Fla., 1976-86; chmn. Schultz, Barrett Interiors, Inc. Chmn. Duval County Mothers March, March of Dimes, 1958-59; mem. adv. bd. Women's Bd. Jacksonville Wolfson Children's Hosp. at Bapt. Med. Ctr.; chmn. Docents Cummer Mus. Art, 1968-70; caseworker Family Counseling Ctr., Jacksonville, 1961-62; vol. worker Cmty. Pub. TV, Am. Cancer Soc.; chmn. fund raising Symphony Show House, 1972; met. bd. dirs. YMCA of Fla.'s First Coast, 1989-91; trustee U. North Fla. Found., 1989-2002, mem. exec. com., 1992-96, hon. trustee 2002—; hon. mem. bd. dirs. U. North Fla. Found.. Mem. Jr. League of Jacksonville, Phi Kappa Phi (U. N.Fla. chpt.). Democrat. Roman Catholic. Home: 505 Lancaster St Jacksonville FL 32204-4143 Office: 118 W Adams St Ste 6 Jacksonville FL 32202-3800

SCHULTZ, PATRICIA BOWERS, vocal music educator, performer; b. Gomer, Ohio, Apr. 26, 1941; d. Paul Edward and Blodwen (Watkins) Bowers; m. Charles Albert Schultz; children: Todd Matthew, Vaughn Andrew, Cinnamon Kristine. BS in Edn., French & Music, Miami U., Oxford, Ohio, 1963; MEd in Counseling, U. Ill., 1964; D of Musical Arts in Vocal Performance, U. Mo-Kansas City, 1984. Performer freelance USA and Europe, 1964—; music educator, counselor Northmont Pub. Schs., Dayton, Ohio, 1964-66; French educator Bowling Green (Ohio) H.S., 1967-68; instr. music and French Dickinson (N.D.) State U., 1972-74; instr. voice Ctrl. State U., Wilberforce, Ohio, 1975-76; dir. choral activities Savannah (Mo.) H.S., 1979-80; prof. music N.W. Mo. State U., Maryville, 1981—2002. Dir. music First United Meth. Ch., Maryville, 1977—88; tour mgr. Jenny Lind Ensemble, 1978—; musical dir. N.W. MO. State U., Maryville, 1981—2002; vis. prof. Internat. Enrichment, London, 2000, 02, 04; adjudicator Nat. Assn. Tchrs. of Singing, Mo. H.S. Activities Assn. Accomplishments in music include author, lead role in music drama Encore for Jenny Lind, 1976— (London Premiere 1992); conductor choral music Welsh Gymanfoedd Ganu, 1989— (Nat. Selection 1993); Coloratura soprano recitals and concerts throughout U.S.; soloist European tour Cin. Symphony 1969; presentator Am. Assn. Higher Edn. Teaching Learning & Tech. Conf., 1997. Pres. Univ. Women, Maryville, 1970-79; first judge of vocal competition Nat. Glenn Miller Scholarship Competition, Clarinda, Iowa, 1992, 94, 2001; pres. Faculty Senate N.W. Mo. State U., 1993-95, Centennial Soc. 2002-; organizer, charter mem. Mo. Assn. Faculty Senates, Springfield, Mo., 1993-94. Named Faculty Fellow Mo. Coordinating Bd. for Higher Edn., 1997-98, Outstanding Alumnae Conservatory of Music, U. Mo.-Kansas City, 1990; grantee Mo. State Coun. on Arts, 1991-95. Mem. AAUW, Coll. Music Soc., Nat. Assn. Tchrs. Singing (Teacher of regional state and chpt. winners in Mo., Nebr. and eight state region 1986, 88, 90, 92, 97, 98), Am. Choral Dirs. Assn., (hon.) Mortar Bd. (Outstanding advisor, 2003), Sigma Alpha Iota (patroness and advisor 1995-2002). Avocations: gardening, reading, travel. Home: 1004 W Cooper St Maryville MO 64468-2005 Office: NW Mo State Univ Dept Music 800 University Dr Maryville MO 64468-6015

SCHULTZ, PHYLLIS MAY, financial property manager; b. Knox County, Ill., Dec. 17, 1933; d. Clarence Cleo and Mildred Ruth (Hultberg) Cooper; m. Wayne Willard Mohr, Apr. 23, 1955 (div. Sept. 1965); Jeffery Lee Mohr, Kelly Marie Mohr (dec.); m. Robert William Schultz, Sept. 14, 1968. Student, L.A. Valley Coll., 1979-82. Fire and casualty ins. lic., Calif. Keypunch operator Gale Products Outboard Marine Corp., Galesburg, Ill., 1952-55; office mgr. movie and video distbn. Rainbow Distbrs., Inc., 1965-89; fin. property mgr. and acctg. John Lamb, L.A., 1989—. Co-owner Real Estate Investments, Ill., Calif., 1980-89. Mem. Lutheran Social Svcs., L.A., 1989. Republican. Avocations: bowling, travel, gardening, property investments.

SCHULTZ, VICTORIA L. music educator, entertainer; b. Kansas City, Mo., May 12, 1952; d. Kenneth Leroy and Russie Juanita (McIntosh) S. BMusic, U. Mo., Kansas City, 1975; M Music, Drake U., 1977. Opera coach, accompanist, prof. piano U. Ctrl. Fla., Orlando, 1977-80; prof. voice and piano Valencia C.C., Orlando, 1980-86; music dir. Pine Castle (Fla.) Ctr. of the Arts, 1983-84; pianist, harpist Hyatt Regency Grand Cypress, Orlando, 1984-96; pianist Altamonte Springs (Fla.) Hilton and Towers, 1985-89; pianist, harpist Caruso's Palace, Orlando, 1990-94; harpist Sergio's Restaurant, Orlando, 1994-95. Adj. prof. voice Rollins Coll., Winter Park, Fla., 1991-92; entertainer Walt Disney World, Orlando, 1996—; adj. prof. harp U. Ctrl. Fla., Orlando, 1998—, adj. prof. voice Valencia CC, Orlando, 2002—; pvt. tchr. and freelance entertainer, Fla., 1980—; clinician Harpcon, 2003. Composer: (music for piano and voice) Set of Songs, 1979; composer/arranger : music CD Orange Blossom Tale, 1996, arranger/performer : music CDs Harp Dreams, 1997, Harp Favorites, 1998, Soothing Harp, 1999, composer, harpist: CD Harp Meditation for Chakra Attunement, 2001; author: (textbook) You CAN Play the Harp, 2002. Sponsor, Riverside Musicale Jr. Music Club, Orlando, 1991—; entertainer fund raising events for AHA, Am. Cancer Soc., Muscular Dystrophy, Am. Diabetes Assn.; artist-in-residence Fla. Hosp. Recipient Nat. 1st Place award Encore Prodns. Talent Competition, 1985, 86, State Young Artist 1st prize Fla. Fedn. Music Clubs, 1976, Silver medal Internat. Piano Rec. Competition, Am. Coll. Musicians, 1978. Mem. Ctrl. Fla. Musicians Assn. (local 389), Am. Harp Soc., Fla. Harpers and Friends (1st Place Composition award 2002, People's Choice award 2002), Ctrl. Fla. Music Tchrs. Assn. (recital chmn. 1999-2000), Orlando Music Club (founding mem.), Music Tchrs. Nat. Assn., Scottish Harp Soc. of Am. Democrat. Avocations: reading, movies, going to concerts, shopping. Home: 848 River Cove Ave Orlando FL 32825-8107 Office: Harpspun Prodns PMB 306 425 S Chickasaw Trl Orlando FL 32825-7852

SCHULZ, AMANDA JEAN, real estate consultant, lawyer; b. Dallas, Tex., Sept. 22, 1975; d. Stephen Wayne and Joanna Elizabeth Tenpenny; m. Norbert Jon Schulz, Sept. 4, 1999. BA in Sociology, U. Tex., 1996; JD, St. Mary's U., 1999. Bar: Tex. 1999; lic. real estate salesperson Tex., 2000. Atty. worker's compensation Christian Hill & Assocs., Houston, 1999—2000; real estate sales cons. Keller Williams Realty, Houston, 2000—02, Re/Max, Houston, 2002—. Agt. trainer Keller Williams Realty Greater NW, Houston, 2001—02, mem. leadership coun., 2002. Chmn. com. Longwood Grounds and Maintenance Reforestation Project, Cypress, Tex., 2002. Mem.: Nat. Assn. Realtors, Tex. Assn. Realtors, Houston Assn. Realtors, Delta Gamma Alumnae Assn. (pres. Houston NW chpt. 2003—). Republican. Lutheran. Avocations: home renovation, interior decorating, antiques, writing, poetry. Home: 201 W 16th St Houston TX 77008 Office: Re/Max Professional Group 9234 FM 1960W Houston TX 77070 Office Phone: 281-894-1000.

SCHULZ, DIANA, film company executive; Grad. summa cum laude, Claremont McKenna Coll.; MBA, Stanford U. With Bain and Co., Microsoft Corp., McKinsey and Co. Consulting, L.A., 1991—97; mem. corp. devel. and strategic planning roup Vivendi Universal Entertainment, Universal City, Calif., 1997—99, head of group, 1999—2001, sr. v.p. corp. devel. and strategic planning, 2001—. Office: Vivendi Universal Entertainment 100 Universal City Plaza Universal City CA 91608-1002*

SCHULZ, KAREN ALICE, psychologist, medical psychotherapist, medical and vocational case manager; b. Detroit, Aug. 10, 1952; d. Donald F. and Ethel B. (Johnston) Wallinger. BA, Concordia U., 1974; MA, Wayne State U., 1991. Cert. cognitive behavioral sex therapist; cert. cognitive forensic therapist, cert. med. psychotherapist, disability analyst; lic. psychologist, Mich. Case mgr. Comprehensive Case Mgmt. Svcs., Dearborn, Mich., 1993—; mem. faculty Davenport U., Dearborn, 1993—. Cert. rehab. counselor, addictions counselor, Am. Bd. Disability Analysts, Am. Bd. Med. Psychotherapists; lic. profl. counselor, psychologist. Mem. CMSA, ACA, Mich. Self Insurers Orgn. Office: Comprehensive Case Mgmt Svcs PO Box 871344 Canton MI 48187-6344

SCHULZ, MARIANNE, accountant; b. East Orange, N.J. d. Clifford W. Schulz; m. James A. Willits, Dec. 29, 1991; children: Lukas James, Laura Christine. BA in Bus., U. Wash., 1979. Cert. mgmt. acct. Contr. Farwest Spl. Products, Bellevue, Wash., 1974-88; acct. Lakeside Industries, Issaquah, Wash., 1988—. Mem. Inst. Mgmt. Accts. (bd. dirs. 1990-92, v.p. 1992-93).

SCHULZ, RENATE ADELE, German studies and second language acquisition educator; b. Lohr am Main, Germany, Feb. 24, 1940; came to U.S., 1958; 1 child, Sigrid Diane. BS, Mankato State Coll., 1962; MA, U. Colo., 1967; PhD, Ohio State U., 1974. Edn. officer U.S. Peace Corps, Ife Ezinihitte, Nigeria, 1963-65; asst. prof. Otterbein Coll., Westerville, Ohio, 1974-76, State U. Coll. N.Y., Buffalo, 1976-77, from asst. to assoc. prof. U. Ark., Fayetteville, 1977-81; from assoc. to prof. U. Ariz., Tucson, 1981—, chair dept. German, 1984-90, chair PhD program in second lang. acquisition and teaching, 1994-97. Disting. vis. prof. USAF Acad., Colorado Springs, Colo., 1990-91. Recipient Creative Tchg. award, U. Ariz. Found., Tucson, 1984, Stephen A. Freeman award, N.W. Conf. Tchg. Fgn. Langs., 1984, Bundesverdienstkreuz, Fed. Govt. Germany, 1990, Anthony Papalia award for excellence in tchr. edn., Am. Coun. on the Tchg. of Fgn. Langs./N.Y. State Assn. Fgn. Lang. Tchrs., 2002. Mem.: MLA (del. 1989—91), Nat. Fedn. Modern Lang. Tchrs. Assns. (v.p./pres.-elect 2004—), Am. Assn. Applied Linguistics, Tchrs. of ESL, Am. Assn. Tchrs. German (v.p. 1988—90, pres. 1990—91), Am. Coun. on the Tchg. of Fgn. Langs. (exec. coun. 1979—81, Florence Steiner award 1993). Office: U Ariz Dept German Studies Tucson AZ 85721-0105 Office Phone: 520-621-7388. E-mail: schulzr@u.arizona.edu.

SCHULZ, SANDRA E. art educator; b. Dallas, July 2, 1963; d. Lionel Leigh and Ida Maria Johanna Schulz. BS in Art Edn., Tex. Woman's U., 1985, MFA in Sculpture, 1990. Cert. tchr. art all levels, Tex. Clk. and advt. Bartos Inc., Dallas, 1982—90; art tchr. 7th and 8th grades Harry Stone Mid. Sch., Dallas, 1990—91; art tchr. 9-12th grades Thomas Jefferson H.S., Dallas, 1992—. Art club sponsor, robotics team sponsor Thomas Jefferson H.S., Dallas. Chair publicity and decoration Tex. Cultural Partnership, Dallas, 1994-2001; publicity chair Am. Czech Culture Soc., Dallas, 1992-2001. Named Citizen of the Week, KRLD Radio Sta., 2002; recipient Brookhaven Coll. Pyramid award for tchg., 2001, Tex. Senate Excellence award for outstanding tchrs., Outstanding H.S. Tchr. award, Dallas Rotary Club, 2001—02. Mem. Nat. Art Educators Assn., Tex. Art Educators Assn., Dallas Art Educators Assn. (publicity chair 1996-98), Sculpture Assn. (sec. 1993-95). Lutheran. Avocations: camping, fishing, gardening, music, electric trains. Home: 9218 Clear Dr Sanger TX 76266 Office: Thomas Jefferson HS 4001 Walnut Hill Ln Dallas TX 75229-6239

SCHULZ, SUSAN, magazine editor; b. 1972; Grad., Loyola Coll. Editl. asst. Good Housekeeping; sr. articles writer YM; dep. editor CosmoGIRL, 2000—02, exec. editor, 2002—03, editor-in-chief, 2003—. Contbr. for various publ. including YM, Redbook, Shape. Office: CosmoGIRL 224 W 57th St Lobby New York NY 10019 Office Phone: 212-649-3852.*

SCHULZ, SUZON LOUISE, fine artist; b. Chgo., Sept. 2, 1946; d. Carl George and Ruth Ada (Eberhardt) S. BFA, R.I. Sch. Design, 1968. Studio ptnr. Michael Eaton Smith, El Valle, N.Mex., 1976-79; artist-in-residence Idaho Com. on the Arts, 1980—, Wash. State Arts Com., 1980-82, Mississippi County C.C. Libr., Blytheville, Ark., 1984-85, various art couns., Oreg., 1983—; tchr. elem. art seminar Ea. Oreg. Coll. Bend Br., Bend, 1996. Owner Flying Shoes Studio, Prineville, 1982—; cartoonist, writer, illustrator NOW News, Bend, 1991-94. Painter: (series) In the Home, 1982—, The World Beyond, 1984—, Living With a Man, 1986—, Tipi Now, 1988—, Cats, 1996—, Paintings of Collages, 2002—. Mem. Nat. Mus. Women in Arts, Cen. Oreg. Arts Assn. Avocations: walking, hiking, reading, writing, cross-country skiing. Home: 15887 SE Chippewa Rd Prineville OR 97754-8895

SCHUMACHER, CYNTHIA JO, retired elementary and secondary education educator; b. Sebring, Fla., Sept. 24, 1928; d. Floyd and Espage S. BA, Fla. State U., 1950, MA, 1951; MS, Nova U., 1978; postgrad., Fla. State U., 1968-69. English tchr. Grady County Sch. System, Cairo, Ga., 1951-53; elem. tchr. Brevard County Sch. System, Melbourne, Fla., 1953-55; elem. tchr., curriculum generalist, secondary tchr. Lake County Schs., Tavares, Fla. area, 1955-85; retired, 1985. Mem. Edn. Standards Commn., Fla., 1980-85, Quality Instrn. Incentives Coun., Fla., 1983-84. Author: (poetry) Seeds from Wild Grasses, 1988, Creekstone Crossings, 1993, Soul Candles, 1998, Wellspring Legacies, 2000; (poetry and stories) Butterfly Excursions, 1996; (children's books) Colorful Character, 1998, Searching for S, 1998. Pres. League of Women Voters of Lake County, 1989-91; mem. Lake Conservation Coun., The Nature Conservancy, Habitat for Humanity of Lake County. Named Fla. Tchr. of Yr., Fla. Fedn. Women's Clubs, 1966, Lake County Tchr. of Yr., Lake County Sch. Sys., 1985, East Cen. Fla. Tchr. of Yr. finalist, State of Fla., 1986; recipient Good Egg award, Leesburg Area C. of C., 1991, Lifetime Achievement award, Fla. Edn. Assn. United, 2000. Mem. Lake County Edn. Assn. (pres. 1971-72, cons. 1985—). Democrat. Roman Catholic. Avocations: environ. support activities, gardening, creative writing, macrobiotic cooking,.

SCHUMACHER, DIANE KOSMACH, manufacturing executive, lawyer; b. Chgo., Aug. 13, 1953; BA with high honors, So. Ill. U., 1974; JD magna cum laude, DePaul U., 1977. Bar: Mo. 1977, Ill. 1978, Tex. 1983. Corp. atty. Belden Corp. (acquired by Cooper Industries Inc. 1981), 1980-81; sr. counsel Cooper Industries Inc., Houston, 1981-88, corp. sec., 1988-91, corp. v.p., 1991-93, v.p. adminstrn., corp. sec., 1993-95, sr. v.p., gen. counsel, sec., 1995—2003, sr. v.p., gen. counsel, chief compliance officer, 2003—. Bd. dirs. Gardner Denver, Inc. Mem. ABA, Am. Corp. Counsel Assn., Am. Soc. Corp. Secs. (pres. Houston chpt. 1992-93, bd. dirs. 1995-98), Am. Arbitration Assn. (bd. dirs. 1996—), State Bar Tex. Office: Copper Industries Inc Chase Tower 600 Travis St Ste 5800 Houston TX 77002-2912 E-mail: schumach@cooperindustries.com.

SCHUMACHER, LESLIE, state legislator, artist; b. Oct. 4, 1955; m. Byron Schumacher; 2 children. Freelance artist, Princeton, Minn.; mem. Minn. Ho. of Reps., St. Paul, 1994—. Mem. Dem.-Farmer-Labor Party. Office: Minn Ho of Reps State Capitol Saint Paul MN 55155-0001

SCHUMAN, PATRICIA GLASS, publishing company executive, educator; b. N.Y.C., Mar. 15, 1943; d. Milton and Shirley Rhoda (Goodman) Glass; m. Alan Bruce Schuman, Aug. 30, 1964 (div. 1973); m. Stanley Robert Epstein, June 14, 1997. AB, U. Cin., 1963; MS, Columbia U., 1966. Libr. trainee Bklyn. Pub. Libr., 1963-65; tchr. libr. Brandeis High Sch., N.Y.C., 1966; asst. prof. libr. N.Y. Tech. Coll., Bklyn., 1966-71; assoc. editor Sch. Libr. Jour., N.Y.C., 1970-73; sr. editor R.R. Bowker Co., N.Y.C., 1973-76; pres. Neal-Schuman Pubs., N.Y.C., 1976—. Vis. prof. St. John's U., Queens, N.Y., 1977-79, Columbia U., N.Y.C., 1981-90, Pratt Inst., 1993-2000, Syracuse U., 1997—; cons. N.Y. State Coun. on Arts, 1987, Office Tech. Assessment, U.S. Congress, 1982, 84, Coord. Coun. Lit. Mags., N.Y.C., 1987, NEH, 1980, Temple U., 1978-80; bd. visitors Sch. Libr. and Computer Studies Pratt Inst., 1987-2001; juror Best of Libr. Lit., 1980-88; mem. adv. bd. Sch. Libr. and Info. Studies, Queens Coll., 1989-91. Author: Materials for Occupational Education, 1973, 2d edit., 1983 (Best Edn. Book award 1973), Library Users and Personnel Needs, 1980, Your Right to Know: The Call to Action, 1993; editor: Social Responsibilities and Libraries, 1976; mem. editorial bd. Urban Acad. Libr., 1987-89, Multicultural Review, 1991-95; contbr. articles to profl. jours. Bd. dirs. Women's Studies Abstracts, Albany, N.Y., 1970-74, Pratt Inst. Sch. of Libr. and Info. Studies, 1993—2000, Ctr. for Publ., NYU, 1996—, Am. Libr. in Paris, 2004—; mem. Com. To Elect Major Owens to U.S. Congress, 1983, N.Y.C. Mayor's Com. for N.Y. Pub. Ctr., 1984-85; pres. Met. Reference and Resources Coun./Met. N.Y. Libr. Coun. Recipient Fannie Simon award Spl. Librs. Assn., 1984, Disting. Alumni award Columbia U., 1992; U.S. Office Edn. fellow, 1969. Mem. ALA (councillor 1971-79, 84-88, exec. bd. 1984-88, 90-93, treas. 1984-88, chmn. legis. com. 1989-90, 94-96, chmn. internat. rels. com. 1998, 99, chmn. Libr. Advocacy NOW!, v.p., pres.-elect 1990-91, pres. 1991-92, Disting. Coun. Svc. award 1979, 88, Equality award 1993, hon. mem. Black Caucus, appreciation award 1993, Freedom to Read Found. Honor Roll 1999, Lippincott award for disting. svc. 2001), N.Y. Libr. Assn., Assn. for Libr. and Info. Sci. Edn., Spl. Librs. Assn. Office: Neal-Schuman Pubs Inc 100 William St Ste 2004 New York NY 10038 E-mail: pgs@neal-schuman.com.

SCHUMANN, GAIL L. plant pathologist, educator; BS in Botany, U. Mich., 1972; MS in Plant Pathology, Cornell U., 1976, PhD in Plant Pathology, 1978. From vis. lectr. to prof. U. Mass., Amherst, Mass., 1984—2001, prof. emerita, 2003—; prof. dept. biol. scis. Marquette U., Milw., 2023—. Sr. editor APS Press, 1992; chair APS Press Illustrations of Plant Pathogens and Disease Com.; editor-in-chief The Plant Health Inst., 2000—. Author: Plant Diseases: Their Biology and Social Impact, 1991; co-author: IPM Handbook for Golf Courses, 1998. Recipient APS Excellence in Tchg. award, 1993, Disting. Tchg. award U. Mass., 2994, award of merit MEDAPS, 1996. Mem.: APS (pres. N.E. divsn. 1995). Office: Marquette U Dept Biol Scis 202B Wehr Life Scis 530 N 15th St Milwaukee WI 53233 Business E-Mail: gail.schumann@marquette.edu.

SCHUMANN, LAURA ELAINE, conductor; b. Mpls., Minn., May 13, 1963; d. Aubrey Paul Schumann, Elaine Anne Topka. BMus, U. Colo., 1985; MA, U. Calif.-Santa Barbara, 1988; D in Musical Arts, Tex. Tech. U., 2001. Instr. violin and string methods Wake Forest U., Winston-Salem, NC, 1990—91; instr. upper strings and music theory Winston-Salem State U., 1991—92; asst. condr. orch., instr. strings Murray State U., Murray, Ky., 1992—94; asst. prof. music, dir. orchestral activities, studio strings We. State Coll., Gunnison, Colo., 1994—99; asst. prof. music, music dir., condr. SE Ohio Symphony Muskingum Coll., New Concord, Ohio, 1999—. Instr. violin and string methods Salem Coll., Winston-Salem, 1990—91; asst. condr. orch. Tex. Tech. U., Lubbock, 1997—98; music dir., condr. Ovations Youth Orch. Wheeling (W.Va.) Symphony, 2000—02; freelance violinist; competitor Jordania Internat. Conducting Competition, Kharkov, Ukraine, 2003. Recipient Women of Achievement award, YMCA/YWCA, 2001. Mem.: ASCAP (Adventurous Programming award 2001), Ohio Music Educators Assn., Coll. Music Soc., Music Educators Nat. Conf., Condr.'s Guild, Am. String Tchrs. Assn., Am. Fedn. Musicians, Am. Symphony Orch. League. Office: Music Dept Muskingum Coll New Concord OH 43762 E-mail: schumann@muskingum.edu.

SCHUMANN, PAULA M. L. writer; b. Phila., Pa., Oct. 23, 1938; d. Paschal Francis and Paula Marie Libonati; m. Walter Francis Schumann, June 17, 1967; 2 children. MT, PCMS, Phila. County Med. Soc., 1972. Medical Tech. Phila. Gen. Hosp. Sch. of Med. Tech., Pa., 1971. Author and pub. Renaitre Press, King of Prussia, Pa., 1998—. Author (publisher): A Chapter in the Life of a Poet (a story in verse), 1995, With His Love, Prayers and Poems, 2002; author: (poems in English) Les Saisons de la Vie, 1998. Pres. Legion of Mary, King of Prussia, Pa., 2000—02. Scholar, Franklin Sch. of Sci. and Arts, 1960 to 1961. Mem.: Phila. Writers' Conf., Poetry Soc. of Am., The Acad. of Am. Poets (Disting. mem. of the Internat. Soc. of Poets). Roman Catholic. Avocations: cooking, travel, swimming, piano, dance. Office: Renaitre Press P O Box 61163 King Of Prussia PA 19406-1163

SCHUMM-BURGESS, NANCY LYNN, freelance/self-employed writer; b. Fairview Park, Ohio, July 19, 1963; d. Brooke and Elizabeth Schumm; m. Steven Paul Burgess, Dec. 23, 1988 (div.); children: Amanda Burgess, Patrick Burgess. BA, Ohio State U., 1985. Freelance writer, Chgo., 1995—; freelance lectr., 1997—. Freelance photographer, Chgo.; presenter/lectr. in field. Author: (non-fiction book) The Barns of Lake County, (non-fiction) Hearts Full of Compassion, Gardens and Other Sanctuaries in Long Grove, Illinois; exhibitions include Through the Barn Door, Village Calendar, Oprah Winfrey Show Prairie Sunflower; contbr. articles to jours. and newspapers. Fundraiser Mary Pat Maddex Pl., Gurnee, Ill., 1999—2003; founder/pres. Save-A-Barn, Vernon Hills, Ill., 1998—2003; chmn. Ill. State Hist. Soc./Save Our barns com., Springfield, 2000—02; former bd. mem., cons. McHenry County Barn Preservation Assn., Union, Ill., 2000—03; steward Long Grove (Ill.) Pk. Dist., 1993—2003. Recipient Photography winner, Kodak Corp., 1987, History column pub. on local history website, Ela Area Pub. Libr., 1998—2003. Personal E-mail: nburg719@aol.com.

SCHUNK, MAE GASPARAC, former state official; b. Chgo., May 21, 1934; m. William Schunk; 1 child. BS in Elem. Edn., U. Wis., Eau Claire, 1958; MA in Curriculum and Instrn., Gifted Edn. in Gifted/Talented Edn., U. St. Thomas, St. Paul, 1989, lic. in adminstrv. leadership, 1992. Curriculum specialist, asst. prin., elem. tchr. various pub. schs. in Wis. and St. Paul; lt. gov. State of Minn., St. Paul, 1999—2003; instr. dept. edn. Inver Hills C.C., 2003—. Mem. Minn. Exec. Coun.; chair Capitol Area Archtl. Planning Bd.; co-chair The Minn. Alliance with Youth, the NetDay Minn. Program, Minn. Office of Citizenship and Vol. Svcs. Recipient 1st pl. state award, U. Minn. Coun. on Econ. Edn., 1984, award of commendation, Gov. Perpich, 1986, 1990, award, United Def., 1999, Hmong Am. New Yr., Inc., 1999, St. Paul Fedn. Tchrs., 1999, Mpls. Police Dept., 1999, Minn. Sch. Counselors Assn., 1999, United Vietnamese Mut. Assistance Assn., 1999, Dept. Corrections, 2000, 82d Airborne Divsn. Assn. Am.'s Guard of Honor, 2000, Forward Support Bn., 2000, Outstanding Citizen award, 2000, award, Jobs for Am. Grads., Washington, 2000, Recognition award, Gov. Jesse Ventura, 2002, Minn. State Founders award, Jobs for Minn. Grads. Bd., 2002, proclamation from Gov. Ventura, 2002. Independent. Avocations: flower and vegetable gardening, creative cooking and baking, stained glass, watercolor painting, fishing.

SCHUNKE, HILDEGARD HEIDEL, accountant; b. Indpls., Nov. 24, 1948; d. Edwin Carl and Hildegard Adelheid (Baumbach) S. BA, Ball State U., Muncie, Ind., 1971, MA in German/English, 1973, MA in Acctg., 1975. CPA, Ind., Calif. Exch. tchg. grad. asst. Padagogische Hochschule, Germany, 1971-72; tchg.ing grad. asst. in German and acctg. Ball State U., 1972, 74-75, asst. prof. acctg., 1975-78; investing rschr. Family Partnership, Muncie, 1977-83; staff acct. Am. Lawn Mower Co., Muncie, 1984-88, G&J Seiberlich, CPAs, St. Helena, Calif., 1988-89, R.A. Gullotta, MBA, CPA, Sonoma, Calif., 1989-90; plant acct. Napa (Calif.) Pipe Corp., 1990—2001; sys. engr. Napa Pipe Divsn. Oreg. Steel Mills, Napa, Calif., 2002—03; sys. technician Napa Oreg. Steel Mills, Napa, Calif., 2003—. ESOL instr. Napa County Project Upgrade, 1988-92; ticketing and refreshments com. North Bay Philharm. Orch., Napa, 1988-2003, North Bay Wind Ensemble, Napa, 1988-2003; mem. TC 207 Tag Team. Mem. AICPA, Calif. Soc. CPAs (continuing edn. instr. Redwood City 1990, bd. dirs. East Bay chpt. 1998-2000), Inst. Internal Auditors, Am. Soc. for Quality. Avocations: gardening, building computers, networks and websites, transcribing, translating and reading German. Home: 1117 Devonshire Ct Suisun City CA 94534-7443 Office: HH Schunke MA, CPA 1117 Devonshire Ct Suisun City CA 94534-7443 E-mail: hhschunke@juno.com.

SCHUR KAUFMAN, SUSAN, retired public affairs consultant; b. Feb. 27, 1940; d. Norman and Jeanette (Handelman) Dorfman; m. Clayton Kaufman; children from previous marriage: Diana Elisabeth Schur, Erica M. Rydzewski. BA, Goucher Coll., 1961. Adminstr. fed. housing, fgn. aid, anti-poverty programs, 1961-67; mem. Mass. Housing Appeals Com., 1977-86; mem., v.p. Bd. of Alderman, Newton, Mass., 1974-81; mem. Mass. Ho. of Reps., 1981-94; pvt. pub. affairs cons., 1995—2000. Bd. dirs. Middlesex Bank & Trust Co. Bd. dirs. Newton Cmty. Devel. Found., 1995-99; overseer New Philharmonia Orch., 1997-99; mem. Newton Dem. City Com., 1970-99.

SCHURTZ, ORA SEARS, hypnotist, educator; b. Indpls., July 30, 1919; d. Fred Harrison Sears and Stella; widowed; children: Carl Frederick, Penelope Ann. Student, Ind. Ctrl. Bus. Coll., 1939—40, Ind. U., 1943—44, Rutgers U., 1969—70; BS, Union U., 1978; PhD, Donsbach U., 1980. Ordained minister Alliance of Divine Love, West Palm, Fla., 1994; cert. hypnosis Hyphodyne Found., 1990, instr. Hyphodyne Found., 1996, master hypnotherapists Hyphodyne Found., 1998. Asst. to gen. foreman tool and dye dept. Gen. Motors, Indpls., 1942—43; with Pan Am. Airways, Miami, Fla., 1944—46; mgmt. Macy's, N.Y.C., 1946—47, Mandell Bros., Chgo., 1948—49; co-owner Renor Co., Milw., 1950—53; pub. rels. Bissill Corp., NJ; pres. Food Power Naturally, Inc., 1970—77; owner Survival, Inc., 1976—80; pvt. practice, 1980—. Instr. hypnotist tng., 1996—; workshop leader. Contbr. articles to profl. jours. Mem.: Palm Beach Ctr. Living, Internat. Assn. Counselors and Therapists, Nat. Guild Hypnotists. Avocation: walking. Office: Bldg 3-1D 11811 Ave of PGA Palm Beach Gardens FL 33418

SCHUSSHEIM, JOAN LANA, mathematics educator; b. Montreal, Can., Aug. 4, 1940; d. Irving and Gertrude Yares; m. Arnold Schussheim, June 1, 1963; children: Abigail, Adam. AB in Math. magna cum laude, CUNY, 1961, MS in Edn., 1974. Tchr. math. enrichment lab. Roslyn Pub. Schs., 1974—76; tchr. remedial math. lab. Great Neck (NY) Pub. Schs., 1977—. Adj. prof. Hofstra U., Hempstead, NY, 1998; participant workshops and confs. in field. Contbr. articles to profl. jours. Mem.: Great Neck Tchrs. Assn., Nat. Coun. Tchrs. Math. Avocations: choral singing, reading, travel, piano, golf. Home: 24 Russell Woods Rd Great Neck NY 11021-4633 Office: Lakeville Sch 47-27 Jayson Ave Great Neck NY 11020

SCHUSTER, CARLOTTA LIEF, psychiatrist; b. N.Y.C., Sept. 16, 1936; d. Victor Filler and Nina Lincoln (Rayevsky) Lief; m. David Israel Schuster, Sept. 2, 1962; 1 child, Amanda. BA, Barnard Coll., 1957; MD, NYU, 1964. Cert. Am. Bd. Psychiatry and Neurology; cert. addiction psychiatry. Intern Lenox Hill Hosp., N.Y.C., 1964-65; resident St. Luke's Hosp., N.Y.C., 1965-68; fellow Inst. Sex Edn., U. Pa., Phila., 1968-69; instr. N.Y. Med. Coll., N.Y.C., 1969-72; asst. attending Met. Hosp., N.Y.C., 1969-72; assoc. attending St. Luke's-Roosevelt Hosp. Ctr., N.Y.C., 1972-95; staff psychiatrist Silver Hill Hosp., New Canaan, Conn., 1972-95; clin. assoc. instr. Columbia U., N.Y.C., 1990-95. Chief substance abuse svc. Silver Hill Hosp., New Canaan, 1976-95; dir. Recovery Clinic Bellevue Hosp., N.Y.C., 1993-2003; mem. faculty Dept. Psychiatry Sch. Medicine NYU, 1995—. Author: Alcohol and Sexuality, 1988; co-author: Chapter in Advances in Alcohol and Substance Abuse, 1987; contbr. chpts. to books. Mem. Am. Psychiat. Assn., Am. Med. Soc. on Addictions, Am. Acad. Addiction Psychiatry. Democrat. Jewish. Avocations: cooking, attending concerts, opera, films. Office: 207 E 30th St New York NY 10016-8230 Office Phone: 212-213-2513. E-mail: carlotta_schuster@msn.com.

SCHUSTER, ELAINE, civil rights professional; b. Detroit, Sept. 26, 1947; d. William Alfred and Aimee Isabelle (Cote) LeBlanc; m. James William Schuster, Sept. 6, 1969; 1 child, Cambrian James. BA, Wayne State U., 1972, postgrad., 1974-75, paralegal cert., 1991. Asst. payments Mich. Dept. Social Svcs., Detroit, 1972-73; rights rep. Mich. Dept. Civil Rights, Detroit, 1973-80, 82-87, 90, asst. dir. div., 1987-90, supr., 1993-97, dir. Svc. Ctr., 1997-99, contract coord., 1999—2002, ret., 2003; ct. adminstr. Chippewa-Ottawa Conservation Ct., Bay Mills, Mich., 1980-82; quality assurance coord. State Mental Health Facility, Southgate, Mich., 1991-93; acting interim dir. Mich. Indian Commn., Detroit, 1995; proprietor Good Things to Share, 2003—; trainer HIV/AIDS health support profls., 2004. Author: Beginning a Course of Study of the Anishinaabe Language, 2003, Critique, An Indian Tours Michilimackinac, 1981; contbr. articles and poems to mags. and profl. jours. Bd. dirs. Tri-County Native Ams., Warren, Mich., 1982-89, sec. Native Am. Sesquicentennial subcom., Mich., 1987; mem. Linking Lifetimes, mentor program for Native Am. youth, 1992-93; sec., newsletter editor various civic orgns.; also other polit. and civic activities. Native Am. fellow Mich. State U., 1989. Mem. NAACP (housing com. S. Oakland br. 2000), ACLU (bd. dirs. Union-Oakland county 1987-88). Democrat. Avocations: exploring local historical and natural places of interest, historical re-enactment, research, fitness.

SCHUSTER, INGEBORG IDA, chemistry educator; b. Frankfurt, W. Ger., Oct. 30, 1937; came to U.S. 1947; d. Ludwig Karl and Mariluise (Kautetzky) S. BA, U. Pa., 1960; MS, Carnegie Inst. Tech., Pitts., 1963; PhD, Carnegie Inst. Tech., 1965. Postdoctoral fellow Bryn Mawr (Pa.) Coll., 1965-67; asst. prof. chemistry Pa. State U., Abington, 1967-73, assoc. prof. chemistry, 1973-83, prof. chemistry, 1983—. Contbr. articles to profl. jours. Huff fellow, 1966; E. Gerry fellow, 1982. Mem. Am. Chem. Soc. Republican. Roman Catholic. Avocations: skiing, violin, cartooning. Office: Pa State Univ 1600 Woodland Rd Abington PA 19001-3918

SCHUSTER, SYLVIA M. education educator; b. Germany, July 16, 1949; d. Morris N. and Gena Bergstein; 1 child, Maggie Noah. BA in English Lit., CUNY, 1972, MA in English Lit. and Creative Writing, 1976. Cert. English tchr. NY. Tchr. Brandeis H.S., N.Y.C., 1978—80; homebound English tutor Plainview (NY) H.S., 1984—; asst. dir. RISE program L.I. U., C.W. Post Campus, Brookville, NY, 1992—96, dir. RISE program, 1996—2000; lectr. in English BOCES Cultural Arts Ctr., Syosset, NY, 1999—. Adj. prof. english L.I. U., 1986—, Nassau (NY) C.C., 1994—, SUNY, Farmingdale, 2001—; owner pvt. tutoring bus., L.I., NY, 1984—. Contbr. poetry to anthologies, photographs to mags. Mem. com. L.I. Jr. Soccer League, 1992—; vol. Am. Cancer Assn., 1997, Am. Diabetes Found., 1999. Recipient Pres.' award, Iliad Press, 1996. Mem.: Am. Acad. Poets, Nat. Author's Registry, Nat. Coun. Tchrs. English, Nat. Soc. Poets, Internat. Soc. Poets (Outstanding Achievement award 1997—2002), Nat. Writers Club. Avocations: writing, photography, music, theater, art. Office Phone: 516-299-2391.

SCHUTH, MARY MCDOUGLE, interior designer, educator; b. Kansas City, Mo., Jan. 19, 1942; d. William Darnall and Marie DeArmond (Meiser) McDougle; m. Howard Wayne Schuth, Sept. 4, 1965; 1 child, Andrew Wayne. BS in Interior Design, Comm., Northwestern U., 1964; cert. basic mgmt., U. Mo., 1966. Registered interior designer La. Interior designer Cottington's Interiors, Glen Ellyn, Ill., 1964-65, Robnett-Putman Interiors, Columbia, Mo., 1966-67, Nu-Idea Furniture Co., New Orleans, 1973, Maison Blanche, New Orleans, 1974-75, Mary M. Schuth Interior Design, Metairie, La., 1977—; instr. interior design divsn. continuing edn. U. New Orleans, 1973-97; instr. interior design non credit program Tulane U., 1998. Judge model homes U.S. Homes, Mandeville, La., 1978, Mandeville, 80; bd. dirs. Interior Design Adv. Com., Delgado Coll., New Orleans, 1981—2000; mem. Alpha Chi Omega Frat. housing rev. com., 1991—96; guest lectr. Delta Queen Steamboat Co., 1995—2001; lectr. ASID Super Campus for Longue Vue Home and Garden Tour, New Orleans, 2002. Co-author: cookbook From the Privateers' Galley, 1980; design work featured in profl. jours.; contbr. to Metairie Mag., 1993-94. Recipient 3rd place Batik Design Juried Art Show Columbia (Mo.) Art League, 1969. Mem. AIA (profl. affiliate), Am. Soc. Interior Designers (profl.), New Orleans Old Garden Rose Soc., Alpha Chi Omega Alumnae Club (New Orleans).

SCHUTTE, ANNE JACOBSON, historian, educator; b. Palo Alto, Calif., Apr. 24, 1940; d. David Samuel and Mildred Rose (Ashworth) J.; m. William Metcalf Schutte, Dec. 21, 1967 (div. Jan. 1990). BA in History magna cum laude, Brown U., 1962; AM in History, Stanford U., 1963, PhD in History and Humanities, 1969. Instr. Lawrence U., 1966-69, asst. prof., 1971-77, assoc. prof., 1977-85, prof., 1985-91, U. Va., Charlottesville, 1992—. Bd. dirs. Ctr. for Reformation Rsch., 1980-83; mem. exec. com. Newberry Libr. program Assoc. Colls. Midwest, 1981-83, 86-88, 90-91; mem. steering com. Com. Women's Concerns, 1984-85. Author: Pier Paolo Vergerio: The Making of an Italian Reformer, 1977, Printed Italian Vernacular Religious Books, 1465-1550: A Finding List, 1983, Pier Paolo Vergerio e la Riforma a Venezia, 1489-1549, 1988 (trans. Virginia Cappelletti, Anna Maria Fabbrini), Aspiring Saints: Pretense of Holiness, Inquisition and Gender in the Republic of Venice, 1618-1750, 2001; editor: Cecilia Ferrazzi, Autobiografia di una santa mancata, 1990, English edit., 1996; translator: Heavenly Supper: The Story of Maria Janis (Fulvio Tomizza), 1991, also articles and numerous revs. We. Regional Alumnae scholar Brown U., 1957-59, 60-62, Stanford U., 1963-65, Stanford U./Italian Govt., 1965-66, Newberry Libr., 1978, S.E. Inst. Medieval and Renaissance Studies, 1979, NEH, 1979-80, 88-89, Gladys Krieble Delmas, 1985, 96; scholar Inst. Reformation Rsch., 1965; Grantee Fulbright Found., 1965-66, Pro Helvetia Found., 1966, Am. Philos. Soc., 1971, NEH 1979-80, 88-89, 95. Mem. Am. Hist. Soc., Am. Soc. Ch. History (coun.), Coordinating Com. for Women in History, Renaissance Soc. Am., 16th Century Studies Conf. (editorial bd. jour. 1972—, v.p. 1973-74, 79-80, pres. 1980-81), Soc. Italian Hist. Socs., Soc. Reformation Rsch. (nominating com. 1981-83, exec. coun. 1987-90, program sec. 1992-95, editor your. 1998—). Office: U Va Dept History Charlottesville VA 22903

SCHUTZ, ROBERTA MARIA (BOBBI SCHUTZ), social worker; b. Smithtown, N.Y., July 19, 1962; d. Robert N. S. and Janice (Sharpe) Taylor. BS, U. Utah, 1988, MSW, 1996. Lic. clin. social worker, Divsn. Occupl. and Profl. Licensing, Utah. Intern Salt Lake Rape Crisis Ctr., 1987-88, VA Med. Ctr., 1992, East Valley Mental Health, 1994-95, Obs. & Assessment. Divsn. Youth Corrections, 1995-96; behavior/employment specialist Columbus Cmty. Ctr., Salt Lake City, 1986-88; skills instr. Project TURN/Possibilities, Salt Lake City, 1987-90; indsl. unit supr. South Valley Tng. Co., Sandy, Utah, 1988-90; case mgr. Office Social Svcs./Divsn. Svcs. People with Disabilities, Midvale, Utah, 1990-91; DD/MR home & cmty.-based waiver specialist Dept. Human Svcs./Renevue Mgmt. Unit, Salt Lake City, 1991-93; case mgr. Dept. Human Svcs./Divsn. Svcs. People with Disabilities, Murray, Utah, 1993-96, social worker, 1996-97, Utah State Prison Dept. of Corrections, Draper, 1997—2003, Utah Dept. WorkForce Svc., 2003—. Mem. Nat. Health Svc. Corps Utah State Prison, 2000—02. Author of poems. Vol. Winter Olympics, Salt Lake City, 2002. Mem.: NASW (Utah PACE com. 1995—, Utah bd. dirs. 1995—2000, Salt Lake City rep. 1996—98), Am. Assn. Mental Retardation (Utah bd. dirs. 1996—98). Democrat. Avocations: ice hockey, running, stamp collecting, reading, writing poetry. Office: Dept Workforce Svcs 5735 S Redwood Rd Salt Lake City UT 84123 E-mail: bschutz@utah.gov.

SCHUTZIUS, LUCY JEAN, retired librarian; b. Cin., Dec. 27, 1938; d. Gregory Girard and Harriet Elsa (Wiggers) Wright; m. Paul Robert Wilson, Aug. 25, 1962 (div. 1968); 1 child, Ellen Field ; m. William Carl Schutzius, Dec. 12, 1976; stepchildren: Christopher Matthew, Catharine Alexander, John Benedict, Margaret Elizabeth. BA in French, Middlebury Coll., 1960; MLS, U. Ill., 1963. Tech. libr. Chanute AFB, Rantoul, Ill., 1963-65; libr. Coll. Prep. Sch., Cin., 1969-74; pub. svcs. libr. Raymond Walters Coll., Cin., 1974-79, dir. libr., 1979-92, sr. libr., 1988—2001, sr. libr. emerita, 2001—. Access svcs. libr. U. Cin. Coll. Engring., 1992—2001. Mem.: Friends of Univ. Librarians. Home: 3444 Stettinius Ave Cincinnati OH 45208-1204 E-mail: lucy.wilson@uc.edu.

SCHUTZIUS, MARY JANE, volunteer activist; b. St. Louis, Mar. 12, 1931; d. Francis Xavier and Margaret Mary (Lavin) Krekeler; m. Robert Edward Schutzius, Dec. 11, 1969; children: Mary Jane Schutzius Horvath, Ann Marie Schutzius. AB in English, Fontbonne Coll., St. Louis, 1952; MA in Psychology, So. Ill. U., Edwardsville, 1979. Caseworker Mo. Divsn. Welfare, St. Louis, 1952-55; claims rep. Social Security adminstrn., Clayton, Mo., 1955-61; lay vol. Papal Vols. for L.Am., La Paz, Bolivia, 1961-68; tng. and devel. specialist Dept. of the Army, St. Louis, 1969-70; talk show host WGNU, St. Louis, 1986-95. Translator: (book) On the Holy Mountaintop, 1981; editor Diaspora quar., 1981-84; co-editor St. Louis W.I.L.P.F. Bull., 1995-97. Co-chair Women's Internat. League for Peace and Freedom, St. Louis, 1997—2001, 2003—; mem. Bolivian Soc. St. Louis, treas., 1987—2001; pres. Ch. Women United, St. Louis, 1988—90, Mo. State Ch. Women United, 1992—96, sec., 2001—. Named Valiant Woman, Ch. Women United, 1991; named to Outstanding Young Women of Am., 1965; honoree Mo. Women's Network, 1997. Mem.: Missourians for Single Payer East (chair 1996—97, sec. 1998—99), Missourians for Single Payer (sec. 1997—99, vice-chair 2001—02, treas. 2002—), Mo. Alliance for Campaign Reform (treas. 1996—2001), Fedn. Christian Ministries (pres. 1984—88), Women's Internat. League for Peace & Freedom. Roman Catholic. Home: 3150 Newgate Dr Florissant MO 63033-6218 E-mail: mjschutz@prodigy.net.

SCHUUR, DIANE JOAN, vocalist; b. Tacoma, Dec. 10, 1953; d. David Schuur. Ed. high sch., Vancouver, Wash. Singer: (albums) Pilot of My Destiny, 1983, Deedles, Schuur Thing, 1986, Timeless (Grammy award for female jazz vocal, 1986), Diane Schuur and the Count Basie Orchestra (Grammy award for female jazz vocal, 1987), Talkin' 'Bout You, 1988, Pure Schuur, 1991 (#1 on Billboard contemporary jazz chart, 1991, nominated for Grammy award, 1991), In Tribute, 1992, Love Songs, 1993 (Grammy nomination, Best Traditional Vocal, Grammy nomination for The Christmas Song); singer: (with B.B. King) Heart to Heart, 1994 (No. 1 on Billboard contemporary jazz chart); singer: Love Walked In, 1996, Blues For Schuur, 1997, The Best of Diane Schuur, 1997, Music Is My Life, 1999, Friends for Schuur; singer: (with Maynard Ferguson) 'Swingin' for Schuur, 2001, Midnight, 2003; singer: (performances) White House, Monterey Jazz Festival, Hollywood Bowl, Carnegie Hall, Moscow Symphony, (tours) Japan, Far East, Near East, South Am., Europe, South Africa. Recipient 1st Ella Fitzgerald ann. award Montreal Jazz Festival, 1999, Helen Keller Personal Achievement award Am. Found. for Blind, 2000. Office Phone: 949-240-4400. E-mail: paulcantor@cox.net.

SCHWAB, BARBARA, advertising executive; b. Bklyn., Feb. 21, 1942; d. Samuel Al and Heidi (Weisskirch) Schnitzer; m. Jeffrey Alan Schwab, July 6, 1963; children: Debra Brandt, Michael. BA, Adelphi U., 1963; MS in Edn., Queens Coll., 1965. Tchr. Roosevelt (N.Y.) Jr. Sr. High Sch., 1963-65, Dix Hills, N.Y., 1977-79, Norwalk (Conn.) High Sch., 1980, Weston (Conn.) High Sch., 1980-82; pres. Barbara Schwab & Assoc., Inc., Norwalk, 1982—, UJA Fedn., Conn. Named Top Sales Distributor, Benchmark Products Ohio, 1992-93. Mem. Specialty Advt. Assn. Greater N.Y., Advt. Specialty Inst. Avocations: golf, jogging.

SCHWAB, DENISE MARGARET, speech pathology/audiology services professional; b. Kileen, Tex., June 6, 1963; d. Phillip Francis Chiodo and Catherine Forti; m. Robert Myron Schwab, Nov. 26, 1988. BS, W.Va. U., 1985, MS, 1987. Lic. speech lang. pathologist W.Va., Ohi, cert. Am. Speech Lang. Hearing Assn. Speech lang. pathologist Ea. Ohi Speech Hearing Ctr., Steubenville, Ohio, 1987—2001, Hancock County Schs., New Cumberland, W.Va., 2001—. Home: 3527 Bright Way Weirton WV 26062 Office: Hancock County Schools PO Box 2400 New Cumberland WV 26047 Office Phone: 304-564-3242.

SCHWAB, EILEEN CAULFIELD, lawyer, educator; b. N.Y.C., Feb. 11, 1944; d. James and Mary (Fay) Caulfield; m. Terrance W. Schwab, Jan. 4, 1969; children: Matthew Caulfield, Catherine Grimley Welykoridko, Claire Gillespie. BA, Hunter Coll., 1965; JD, Columbia U., 1971; BA magna cum laude. Bar: N.Y. 1972, U.S. Dist. Ct. (so. and ea. dists.) N.Y. 1975, U.S. Ct. Appeals (2d cir.) 1975, U.S. Tax Ct. 1980, U.S. Ct. Appeals (10th cir.) 1993. Assoc. Poletti Friedin, N.Y.C., 1971-72, Hughes Hubbard & Reed, N.Y.C., 1972-75, Davis Polk & Wardwell, N.Y.C., 1975-81; dep. bur. chief Charities Bur., Atty. Gen. of N.Y., 1981-82; counsel Sidley Austin Brown & Wood LLP, N.Y.C., 1983—, ptnr., 1984. Adj. prof. N.Y. Law Sch. Trustee Cath. Communal Fund; chair planned gifts, bequests and endowment com. Archdiocese of N.Y.; mem. profl. adv. com. Mus. of Modern Art, Met. Mus. Art, Cen. Park Conservancy, Calvary Hosp., Mus. of Arts and Design, N.Y. Pub. Libr., Ascension Sch., Meml. Sloan-Kettering Cancer Ctr.(chair adv. com.); trustee Cooke Ctr. Learning and Devel. Fellow Am. Coll. Trust and Estate Counsel; mem. N.Y. State Bar Assn., Phi Beta Kappa. Democrat. Roman Catholic. E-mail: eschwab@sidley.com.

SCHWAB, GRACE S. state legislator; m. Steven Schwab; 3 children. BS, postgrad., Mankato State U. Mem. Minn. State Senate, 2000—, mem. crime prevention com., edn. com., transp. com., E-12 edn. budget divsn. com., taxes com., income and sales tax budget divsn. com. Home: 1858 Greenwood Dr Albert Lea MN 56007

SCHWAB, SUSAN CARROLL, dean; BA in Polit. Economy, Williams Coll., 1976; MA in Devel. Policy, Stanford U., 1977; PhD in Pub. Adminstrn., George Washington U., 1993. U.S. trade negotiator Office of U.S. Trade Rep., Washington, 1977-79; trade policy officer U.S. Embassy, Tokyo, 1980-81; chief economist, legis. asst. for internat. trade for Senator John C. Danforth, 1981-86, legis. dir., until 1989; asst. sec. commerce, dir. gen. U.S. and Fgn. Comml. Svc. Dept. Commerce, 1989-93; with corp. strategy office Motorola, Inc., Schaumburg, Ill., 1993-95; dean U. Md. Sch. Pub. Affairs, College Park, 1995—. Office: U Md Sch Pub Affairs College Park MD 20742-0001

SCHWABAUER, MARY ANN, secondary school educator, rancher; b. Puebla, Mex., Nov. 3, 1926; arrived in U.S., 1927; d. Paul Joseph and Anne Rose (Oberhelman) Leavens; m. Charles Bedford Schwabauer, Apr. 29, 1958; 1 child, Charles David. BA, Whitworth Coll., 1949; BS, Westminster Choir Coll., Princeton, N.J., 1952; MS, U. So. Calif., 1954. Educator Ventura Unified Sch. Dist., Calif., 1954—61, Moorpark Unified Sch. Dist., Calif., 1966—88; ptnr. Leavens Ranch, Calif., 1954—; v.p., treas., bd. dirs., and pres. First Fin. Credit Union, W. Corina, Calif., 1978—2003. Founder Women's Legacy Fund, Heritage Fund, Disting. Fund; com. chair Ventura County Cmty. Found., 1996—2003; founder and pres. Associated Hist. Soc., 1988—; founder and bd. dirs. New W. Symphony, Thousand Oaks, Calif., 1995. Recipient Lifetime Achievement award, Moorpark C. of C., 2002. Mem.: Moorpark Women's Club (v.p., pres., Lifetime Scholarship award 2002). Avocations: reading, gardening, swimming, concerts, museum. Home: 12681 Broadway Moorpark CA 93021

SCHWAGER, LINDA HELEN, lawyer; b. Bronx, N.Y., Dec. 30, 1948; d. Joseph David and Rose Polonetsky; m. Steven Schwager, Aug. 15, 1971; children: Russell, Mark, Eric. BA, Queens Coll., Flushing, N.Y., 1970; MS, Bklyn. Coll., 1973; JD, CUNY, Flushing, 1995. Bar: N.J. 1996, N.Y. 1997, D.C. 1998, U.S. Supreme Ct. 1999. Tchr. Pub. Sch. 274, Bklyn., 1970-75; retail bus. owner Party Emporium, Oakland, N.J., 1985-92; pvt. practice Oakland, 1996—; councilwoman Borough of Oakland, 1991-99. Co-feature editor Bergen Barrister mag., 1998—. Chairperson Rep. party Borough of Oakland, 1980. Named Oakland Woman of Yr. Woman's Club of Oakland, 1989, Woman of Yr. Oakland C. of C., 1996; Paul Harris fellow Oakland-Franlin Lakes Rotary Club, 1999. Mem. N.J. Bar Assn., N.Y. Bar Assn., D.C. Bar Assn., Bergen County Bar Assn. (membership legal svcs. bd. 1995), Women Lawyer in Bergen County (newsletter editor 1996—). Jewish. Office: 413 Ramapo Valley Rd Oakland NJ 07436-2707 E-mail: lin822@aol.com.

SCHWALB, KLAUDIA, painter, critic; b. N.Y.C., Aug. 25, 1952; d. Lloyd Schwalb and Audrey Hall; 1 child, Heather. BFA, Pratt Inst., 1974. Art critic The Jour. of Art, Cover/Arts N.Y. Solo exhbns. include The Clocktower Gallery, N.Y.C., 1977, New Mus. Contemporary Art, N.Y.C., 1978, Blondies Contemporary Art, N.Y.C., 1992-94, Smithsonian Instn. Archives of Am. Art, 1996, Van Brunt Gallery, Beacon, N.Y., 2003.

SCHWALM, LAURA, school system administrator; BA, U. Calif., Riverside; MA, Calif. State U., Fullerton; PhD, U. So. Calif. Tchr. Garden Grove Unified Sch. Dist., Calif., 1973—79, prin., dir. ednl. svcs., dir. pers. svcs., supt., 1999—. Finalist Broad Prize Urban Edn., 2003. Office: Garden Grove Unified Sch Dist 10331 Stanford Ave Garden Grove CA 92840*

SCHWARTZ, ALLYSON Y. state legislator; b. N.Y.C., Oct. 3, 1948; d. Everett and Renee Perl Young; m. David Schwartz, 1970; children: Daniel, Jordan. BA, Simmons Coll., 1970; MSS, Bryn Mawr Coll., 1972. Founder, exec. dir. Elizabeth Blackwell Health Ctr. for Women, 1975-88; acting commr., 1st dep. commr. Dept. Human Svcs., 1988-90; mem. Pa. Senate, Harrisburg, 1990—, minority chmn. edn. com., 1994. Mem. Aging and Youth Com., Pub. Health and Welfare Com., Policy Commn., Banking and Ins. Commn., Judiciary Commn. Mem. Pa. State Bd. Edn., 1995—, Pa. Coun. on Higher Edn., Pa. 2000, 1990—, Pa. Hist. and Mus. Commn., Edn. Commn. States, Nat. Dem. Leadership Coun.; former vice chair Nat. Conf. State Legislators, 1994; v.p. Women's Network; co-chair Pa. New Dem. Coalition; bd. trustees Arcadia U., Chestnut Hill Healthcare; chair Instl. Review Bd., Phila. Health Mgmt. Corp.; bd. dirs. Nat. Jewish Dem. Coun.; adv. bd. Tuition Assistance (TAP) Office: Pa Senate Senate Box 203004 182 Capitol Bldg Harrisburg PA 17120

SCHWARTZ, ANA STELLA, art dealer, gallery owner; b. San Salvador, El Salvador, July 27, 1957; came to the U.S., 1976; d. José M. (dec.) and Stella Durán de Comas; m. Daniel Marc Schwartz, Apr. 12, 1980; children: Michael, Jessica. BA, Lewis and Clark Coll., 1980; M in Internat. Affairs, Columbia U., 1982. Corr. banking officer Bank of Am., Santiago, Chile, 1982-86; art dealer Schwartz & Martinez, Miami, Fla., 1997—. Com. mem. WIZO, Miami, 1998—. Office: Schwartz & Martinez Art Gallery 2516 Ponce De Leon Blvd Coral Gables FL 33134-6013

SCHWARTZ, ANN SIMMONS, retired publishing executive; b. Midlothian, Tex., Dec. 20, 1916; d. John Thomas Simmons and Katherine Maude Dillard; m. Jerome Stephen Schwartz, Feb. 21, 1943; children: John Benjamin, Katherine. BA, Tex. State Coll. Women, 1938; postgrad., U. Mo., 1938—39. Editl. asst. Inst. Propaganda Analysis Tchrs. Coll. Columbia U., N.Y.C., 1939—41; rsch. dir. and editor newsletter Friends of Democracy, N.Y.C., 1941—50; treas. Key Book Svc., Inc., N.Y.C., 1952—61, Bridgeport, Conn., 1961—79. Founder The Dispute Settlement Ctr., Norwalk, Conn., 1990; Bible tchr. Saugatuck Congl. Ch., Westport, Conn., 1961—78; sec. Norumbega Resident Coun., 2001—03. Address: Norumbega Point 99 Norumbega Rd Weston MA 02493 E-mail: annesimsch@aol.com.

SCHWARTZ, ANNA JACOBSON, economic historian; b. N.Y.C., Nov. 11, 1915; married; four children. BA, Barnard Coll., 1934; MA, Columbia U., 1935, PhD, 1964; LittD (hon.), U. Fla., 1987, Emory U., 2000, ArtsD (hon.), Stonehill Coll., 1989; LLD (hon.), Iona Coll., 1992, Rutgers U., 1998; LHD (hon.), CUNY, 2000; LLD (hon.), Williams Coll., 2002; LHD (hon.), Loyola U., Chicago, 2003. Rschr. USDA, 1936, Columbia U. Social Sci. Rsch. Coun., 1936-41; sr. rsch. staff Nat. Bur. Econ. Rsch. Inc., N.Y.C., 1941—. Instr. Bklyn. Coll., 1952, Baruch Coll., 1959-60; adj. prof. econs. grad. CCNY, 1967-69, grad. sch. CUNY, 1986—, NYU Grad. Sch. Arts and Sci., 1969-70; hon. vis. prof. City U. Bus. Sch., London, 1984—; hon. fellow Inst. of Econ. Affairs, London, 1998. Mem. editorial bd. Am. Econ. Rev., 1972-78, Jour. Money, Credit and Banking, 1974-75, 84—, Jour Monetary Econs., 1975—, Jour. Fin. Svcs. Rsch., 1993—; contbr. articles to profl. jours. Disting. fellow Am. Econ. Assn., 1993; hon fellow Inst. Econ. Affairs, London. Mem. Western Econ. Assn. (pres. 1987-88). Office: Nat Bur Econ Research 365 Fifth Ave 5th Fl New York NY 10016-4309 E-mail: aschwartz@gc.cuny.edu.

SCHWARTZ, ANNA R. music educator, musician; b. Bklyn., Jan. 12, 1946; d. Abraham and Lena (Gross) Schwartz; m. Alan Leonard Schwartz, June 16, 1968. BS, Lebanon Valley Coll., 1968; MS, C.W. Post Coll., L.I. U., 1974. Cert. music tchr. K-12 N.J., elem. tchr. N.J. Music tchr. grades 1-6 Buena Vista Sch. Dist., Buena, NJ, 1968—72; music tchr. grades 1-8 and choral dir. Howell Twp. Sch. Dist., NJ, 1974—2000; freelance accompanist Toms River Sch. Dist., NJ, 2001—03. Mem. N.J. Symphony Orch. Master Tchr. Collaborative, Newark, 1997—98, mem. gov. com., 1999—; accompanist the chorale Georgian Ct. Coll., Lakewood, NJ, 1996—; music dir. Taunton Sch. PTA Drama Club, Howell, 1978—81; mem. faculty N.J. State Star Sch., 1997—98. Founder and cons. cultural arts com. Taunton Sch. PTA, Howell, 1984—2000. Mem.: NEA, Music Educators Nat. Conf. Home: 3 Bay Breeze Dr Toms River NJ 08753

SCHWARTZ, CAROL ANN, investment company executive; m. Michael D. Schwartz, Jun., 1985; children: Matthew, Allison, Elana. B in Bus. Adminstrn., U. Cinn., 1983; M in Bus. Adminstrn., Finance, Xavier U., 1984; graduate, Grad. Real Estate Inst., 1992. Lic. real estate sales agent. Asst. v.p. Fifth Third Bank, 1984-91; exec. v.p. Morris Investment Co., 1991—. Spkr. in field. Group fundraiser United Appeal, 1986—89; group adv. Jr. Achievement, 1984—86; vol. neighborhood coord., solicitor March of Dimes, 1993—; lox box com. Orgn. Rehab. and Tng. Blue Chip chpt., 1993, 1995—96; bd. mem. Yavneh PTA, 1995—97, Sukkot decorating com., Rosh Hashanah Treats co-chair, Tu'Bishvat spkr., 1997, Tu'Bishvat Seder com., 1998; v.p. fundraising Yavneh Day Sch., 2000—, bd. dirs., 1997—, Friends of Yavneh Campaign chair, 1998—2000; young women/young leaders mission to Israel Hadassah Nat., 1997, nat. conv. chat room facilitator, 1998—99, nat. young leaders adv. coun., 1999—2000, conv. attendee, 1996—99; awards dinner com. Nat. Conf. Christians and Jews, 1993; bus. and profl. group program com. Nat. Coun. Jewish Women, 1990—91, bus. and profl. group program com., chpt. legis. com., 1991—92, bus. and profl. group program com., 1992—93, pub. affairs com., computer analysis com., 1992—93, fin. analysis com., 1993—94, life mem., 1993—; mem. United Jewish Cmtys. Nat. Young Leadership Cabinet, 2000—; bd. dirs. Hadassah Cin. chpt., 1993—, donor com. publicity, pre-donor brunch chair, 1992—93, donor com. publicity, 1996—97, chair, 1993—94, donor book, 1994—96, jewels and memorials, 1995—99, budget chair, 1995—97, com., 1997—, leading gifts divsn. co-chair, 1996—97, pres., 1997—99, cons., 1999—2000; fundraising conf. coord. Hadassah Regional, 1993, regional conf. com., 1997—98, bd. dirs., 1995—2000; Nat. Young Leaders adv. coun. rep. Hadassah Regional, 1999—; fundraising conf. attendee Hadassah Midwest Area Coop., 1993, pres. tng. attendee, 1997, young women's co-chair, 1999—2000; bd. dirs. Hillel, 1998—, alumni com., 1998—2000, auction com., 1998—2000; leadership coun. Jewish Fedn. of Cin., 1987—92, solicitor, 1991—92, lect. series com., 1989, kickoff party com., 1990, women's divsn. group, 1992—, campaign co-chair, 1996—97, bus. and profl. women co-chair, 1998—99, Israel programs cabinet, 1998—99, chair, 1999—2000, campaign cabinet program co-chair, 1999—2000, bd. dir., 1999—; hostess liquid assets luncheon Jewish Nat. Fund, 1993, bd. dirs., 1995—, v.p. edn., 1996—99, tchrs. edn. day chair, 1997—99, four star dining com., 1998—2000, trade and industry dinner com., 1997—98, Green Sunday com., 1996—, Walk for Water com., 1998—; life mem. Jewish Women's Auxilliary, 1995—; v.p. Adath Israel Synagogue, 2001—, bd. dirs., 1992—. Recipient State Member of Yr. Fin. Women Internat., 1987, Cin. chpt. Mem. of Yr., 1988, Nat. Leadership award Cin. chpt. Hadassah Ya'al Group, 1994, Clara Geller Young Leadership award Jewish Fedn. Cin.; named among Outstanding Women of Am., 1985, The Cincinnati Business Courier's Who's Who Among Women in Bus. in Cin., 1992, Top 40 Women in Bus., 1993. Mem. AAUW, Cin. Bd. of Realtors (mem. svcs. com. 1992-93), Ohio Assn. Relators (conv. attendee), Nat. Assn. Realtors (conv. attendee), Comm. Indsl. Real Estate Industry (CCIM designate), Cin. Art Mus., Cin., Historical Soc., Cin. Playhouse in the Park, Contemporary Arts Ctr., Nat. Assn. Female Execs., Nat. History Mus., U. Cin. Alumni Assn. (life mem. 1986—), Women's City Club, World Jewish Cong., Xavier U. Alumni Assn. (life).

SCHWARTZ, CAROL LEVITT, government official; b. Greenville, Miss., Jan. 20, 1944; d. Stanley and Hilda (Simmons) Levitt; m. David H. Schwartz (dec.); children: Stephanie, Hilary, Douglas. BS in Spl. and Elem. Edn., U. Tex., 1965. Mem. transiton team Office of Pres. Elect, 1980-81; con. office presdl. personnel The White House, Washington, 1981; cons. U.S. Dept. Edn., Washington, 1982; pres. sec. U.S. Ho. Reps., Washington, 1982-83; mem.-at-large Coun. of D.C., Washington, 1985-89, 97—; candidate for mayor, Washington, 1986, 1994, 1998, 2002. Vice chmn. Nat. Edn. Commn. on Time and Learning, 1992-94, Nat. Adv. Coun. on Disadvantaged Children, 1974-79; lectr. in field; radio commentator, 1990-91; chair transp., vice-chair planning bd. Coun. Govts. Regional columnist Washington Jewish Week, 1995-97. Mem. D.C. Bd. Edn., 1974-82, v.p., 1977-80; bd. dirs. Met. Police Boys and Girls Club, 1st v.p., 1989-93, pres., 1994-96, chmn. membership com., 1984-93; mem. adv. com. Am. Coun. Young Polit. Leaders, 1982-90; mem. Nat. Coun. Friends Kennedy Ctr., 1984-91; bd. dirs. Whitman-Walker Clinic, 1988—, v.p., 1995-96; bd. dirs. St. John's Child Devel. Ctr., 1989-91, Hattie M. Strong Found., 1995—; trustee Kennedy Ctr. Cmty. and Friends Bd., 1991—, chmn. ednl. task force, 1993—; trustee Jewish Coun. on Aging, 1991-93; v.p. adv. bd. Am. Automobile Assn., 1988—; bd. dirs. Washington Hebrew Congregation, 1995-98. Mem. Cosmos Club. Republican. Jewish.

SCHWARTZ, CAROL VIVIAN, lawyer; b. Newark, Apr. 5, 1952; d. A. Harold and Helen (Schwartz) S.; m. Robert L. Sills, June 9, 1985. BA, Tufts U., 1974; JD, Columbia U., 1977. Law clk. to presiding justice U.S. Dist. Ct. N.Y, N.Y.C., 1978-79; assoc. DeLevoise & Plimpton, N.Y.C., 1979-81; assoc. counsel Am. Express Co., N.Y.C., sr. counsel, now group counsel, 1981—. Mem. ABA. Avocation: sailing. Home: 520 E 86th St # 11A New York NY 10028-7534 Office: Am Express Co Am Express Tower 200 Vesey St New York NY 10285-1000

SCHWARTZ, DEBORAH S. airport manager; b. Muncie, Ind., Oct. 4, 1954; d. Martin David and Helen Frances (Berger) Schwartz; m. Paul Hamlen Ledwell III, July 23, 1977; 1 child, Hilary R. BA cum laude, Wheaton Coll., 1975; MA, U. Houston, 1989. Accredited airport exec. Adminstrv. mgr. various cos., 1976-85; asst. airport mgr. William P. Hobby Airport, Houston, 1986-92; airport dir. Worcester (Mass.) Mcpl. Airport, 1992-94; airport mgr. Little Rock Nat. Airport, 1994—. Mem. Ark. Women's Leadership Forum, Little Rock, 1994—. Named among top 100 women in Ark. Ark. Bus., 1996. Mem. Am. Assn. Airport Execs. (vice chair diversity com. 1995—, legis. com. 1995—), Greater Little Rock C. of C. (bd. dirs. 1995—, transportation com. 1996, literacy com. 1995—, literacy com. 1995—), Phi Kappa Phi, Pi Alpha Alpha, Ark. Airport Operators Assn., Little Rock Rotary. Avocations: reading, riding, camping, hiking, parenting. Office: Little Rock Nat Airport One Airport Dr Little Rock AR 72202

SCHWARTZ, ELEANOR BRANTLEY, academic administrator; b. Kite, Ga., Jan. 1, 1937; d. Jesse Melvin and Hazel (Hill) Brantley; children: John, Cynthia. Student, U. Va., 1955, Ga. Southern Coll., 1956-57; BBA, Ga. State U., 1962, MBA, 11963, DBA, 1969. Adminstrv. asst. Fin. Agy., 1954, Fed. Govt., Va., Pa., Ga., 1956-59; asst. dean admissions Ga. State U., Atlanta, 1961-66, asst. prof., 1966-70; assoc. prof. Cleve. State U., 1970-75, prof. and assoc. dean, 1975-80; dean, Harzfeld prof. U. Mo., Kansas City, 1980-87, vice chancellor acad. affairs, 1987-91, interim chancellor, 1991-92, chancellor, 1992-99; prof. mgmt. U. Mo. Block Sch., Kansas City, 1999—2003, prof. emeritus, 2003—. Disting. vis. prof. Berry Coll., Rome, N.Y. State U. Coll., Fredonia, Mons U., Belgium; cons. pvt. industry U.S., Europe, Can.; bd. dirs. Rsch. Med. Ctr., Waddell & Reed Funds, Inc., Toy and Miniature Mus., Menorah Med. Ctr. Found., NCAA, NCCJ, Econ. Devel. Corp. of Kansas City, Silicon Prairie Tech. Assn. Author: Sex Barriers in Business, 1971, Contemporary Readings in Marketing, 1974; (with Muczyk and Smith) Principles of Supervision, 1984. Chmn., Mayor's Task Force in Govt. Efficiency, Kansas City, Mo., 1984; mem. comm. unity planning and rsch. coun. United Way Kansas City, 1983-85; bd. dirs. Jr. Achievement, 1982-86. Named Career Woman of Yr., Kansas City, Mo., 1989; named one of 60 Women of Achievement, Girl Scouts Coun. Mid Continent, 1983; recipient Disting. Faculty award, Cleve. State U., 1974, Disting. Svc. award, Kans. State U., 1992, YWCA Hearts of Gold award, 2002. Mem.: Alpha Iota Delta, Golden Key, Phi Kappa Phi.

SCHWARTZ, ELLEN C. art historian, educator; b. Bklyn., Mar. 19, 1947; d. Sid L. and Sylvia Schwartz; m. Frank Whelon Wayman, Sept. 2, 1979; children: Eric A. Wayman, Bram M. Wayman, Alexander M. Wayman-(dec.). BA magna cum laude with honors in fine arts, Brandeis U., 1969; MFA, NYU Inst. Fine Arts, 1973, PhD, 1978. Prof. art history Ea. Mich. U., Ypsilanti, 1977—; assoc. rsch. scientist, Ctr. Russian and East European Studies U. Mich., Ann Arbor, 1984—. Governing bd. and offices Byzantine Studies Conf., Chgo., 1984—. Contbr. articles to profl. jours. Mem.: Coll. Art Assn. Jewish. Avocations: Wu Style Tai Chi Chuan, Indian cooking, travel. Home: 1805 Ivywood Dr Ann Arbor MI 48103-4525 Office: Eastern Mich U Dept Art Cross St Ypsilanti MI 48197 Personal E-mail: eschwartz@emich.edu.

SCHWARTZ, ESTAR ALMA, lawyer; b. Bklyn., June 29, 1950; d. Henry Israel and Elaine Florence (Scheiner) Sutel; m. Lawrence Gerald Schwartz, June 28, 1976 (div. Dec. 1977); 1 child, Joshua (dec.); m. James Frances Edward Stuart, Sept. 25, 1999 (div. Aug. 2001). JD, NYU, 1980. Mgr., ptnr. Scheiner, Scheiner, DeVito & Wylie, N.Y.C., 1966-81; fed. govt., social security fraud specialist DHHS, OI, OIG, SSFIS, N.Y.C., 1982-83; pensions Todtman, Epstein, et al, N.Y.C., 1983-85; office mgr., sec. Sills, Beck, Cummis, N.Y.C., 1985-86; office mgr., bookkeeper Philip, Birnbaum & Assocs., N.Y.C., 1986-87; office mgr., sec. Stanley Posses, Esq., Queens, N.Y., 1989-90. Owner Estaris Paralegal Svc., Flushing, N.Y., 1992—, Sutel Creative Mgmt. Agy., Flushing, 1999—. Democrat. Jewish. Avocations: needlepoint, horseback riding, tennis, bowling, writing children's and other books. Home and Office: 67-20 Parsons Blvd Apt 2A Flushing NY 11365-2960 E-mail: Sutel@email.com., sutelmmgmt@aol.com.

SCHWARTZ, ILENE, psychotherapist; b. Phila., June 19, 1942; d. Israel Gerson and Jean Schiffman. BS, Temple U., 1970; MEd, Antioch U., 1990. Crisis counselor, Phila., 1972-82; pvt. practice counseling, 1972-84; writer, 1979—. Cons., crisis counselor in field; instr. psychology and edn., 1974-79; designer, writer, crafts coord. for children. Mem. ACA, AAUW, Freud Friends.

SCHWARTZ, JANICE MARIE, dietician; b. Gt. Bend, Kans, Apr. 18, 1957; d. Claud William and Irene Elizabeth (Kuehn) Shapland; m. Lyle Kent Schwartz, Aug. 8, 1975 (div. Apr. 1991); children: Audrey Ann, Shanon Lee; m. Dale E. Hemel, 1998. AAS, Dodge City (Kans.) C.C., 1977; cert. dietary mgr., Barton County C.C., Gt. Bend, 1992. Cert. dietary mgr., cert. food protection profl. Bookkeeper, farm hand, Dighton, Kans., 1979-90; cook helper Lane County Hosp., Dighton, 1973-75, cook, 1977-79, 90-91, dietary mgr., 1991—. Cmty. leader Eager Beavers 4-H Club, Dighton, 1988-90, 96-97; foods leader Lane County 4-H Club, Dighton, 1991—; mem. 4-H Program Devel. Com., Dighton, 1995—; treas. United Meth. Women, Dighton, 1998—. Mem. Nat. Dietary Mgrs. Assn., Kans. Dietary Mgrs. Assn. (edn. com.), West Dist. Dietary Mgrs. Assn. (v.p. 1996—), Wilson Family and Cmty. Edn. Republican. Methodist. Avocations: walking, reading, sewing, knitting, cooking. Home: 94 E Highway 96 Dighton KS 67839-5001 Office: Lane County Hosp 243 S 2d St Dighton KS 67839

SCHWARTZ, JOAN RUTH, writer; b. Newark, June 27, 1938; d. Benjamin S. and Leah Pines Teitel; m. Allen G. Schwartz, Jan. 17, 1965 (dec. Mar. 2003); children: David, Rachel, Deborah. BA, Rutgers U., 1960; MA, U. Chgo., 1961. Editl. positions U. Chgo. Press, 1961, Columbia U. Press, N.Y.C., 1962, Macmillan Pub. Co., N.Y.C., 1962—63, The Free Press, N.Y.C., 1963—66; editor, 1966—73. Author: Macaroni and Cheese, 2001, Meat and Potatoes, 2003; co-author: Mitchel London's Gracie Mansion Cookbook, 1989, David's Delicious Weight-Loss Program, 1990, David's Delicious Weight-Loss Program, reissued in soft cover as David's Lose Weight Permanently, Reduce Your Cholesterol, and Still Eat 97% of the Food You Love Diet, 1991, Memories of a Cuban Kitchen, 1992, Cooking Provence, 1994, Bobby Flay's Bold American Food, 1994, French Food/American Accent, 1996, From My Kitchen to Your Table, 1998, Boy Meets Grill, 1999, The Greenmarket Cookbook, 2000, Matthew Kenney's Big City Cooking, 2003. Jewish.

SCHWARTZ, JUDY ELLEN, cardiothoracic surgeon; b. Mason City, Iowa, Oct. 5, 1946; d. Walter Carl and Alice Nevada (Moore) S. BS, U. Iowa, 1968, MD, 1971; M.P.H., Johns Hopkins U., 1996. Diplomate Am. Bd. Surgery, Am. Bd. Thoracic Surgery, Am. Bd. Med. Mgmt.; cert. physician exec. Cert. Commn. Med. Mgmt. Intern Nat. Naval Med. Ctr., Bethesda, Md., 1971-72, gen. surgery resident, 1972-76, thoracic surgery resident, 1976-78, staff cardiothoracic surgeon, 1979-82, chief cardiothoracic surgeon, 1982-83; chmn. cardiothoracic surg. dept. Naval Hosp., San Diego, 1983-85, quality assurance program dir., 1985-88. Exec. office Rapidly Deployable Med. Facility Four, 1986-88; asst. prof. surgery Uniformed Svcs. U. Health Sci., Bethesda, 1983-99; sr. policy analyst quality assurance Profl. Affairs and Quality Assurance, 1988-90, dep. dir. quality assurance, 1990; dir. clin. policy Health Svcs. Ops., Washington, 1990-94; head performance evaluation and improvement Nat. Naval Med. Ctr., 1994-99; cardiothoracic splty. cons. to naval med. command U.S. Navy, Washington, 1983-84; Dept. Def. rep. to Joint Commn. Accreditation Health Care Orgn. task force on info. mgmt., 1990-93, chmn. 1991-93, task force on IMS Tech., 1993-94; chmn. info mgmt. workshop Fed. Health Care Study Commn.'s Corrd. Fed. Health Care, 1993; corp. med. dir. Medctr. One Health Sys., 1999-2002, ND Dept. Corrections & Rehab., 1999-2002, v.p. med. affairs Medcenter One, 2002; v.p. Surg. Svc. and Electonic Med. Records Informatics, 2003—; bd. dirs. SCCI; trustee Medcenter One Health Sys., 1999-03; adv. com. Blue Cross Blue Shield Care Mgmt., 1999-2002, v.p. med. affairs, 2002. Contbr. articles to various publs. Mem. nat. physician's leadership coun. VHA, 2000—02; trustee St. Vincent's Nursing Home, 2001—. Fellow Am. Coll. Cardiology, Am. Coll. Surgeons (com. allied health pers. 1985 91, exec. com. 1987-91, accreditation review com. edn. physician asst. 1988-94, treas. accreditation review com. 1991-93, sr. mem. com. allied health pers. 1991-94); mem. AMA, Am. Thoracic Soc., Am. Med. Women's Assn., Am. Mgmt. Assn., Am. Coll. Physician Execs. Office: Medcenter One Health Systems PO Box 5525 300 N 7th St Bismarck ND 58506-5525 Business E-Mail: jschwartz@mohs.org.

SCHWARTZ, LILLIAN FELDMAN, artist, filmmaker, art analyst, writer, nurse; b. Cin., July 13, 1927; d. Jacob and Katie (Green) Feldman; m. Jack James Schwartz, Dec. 22, 1946; children: Jeffrey Hugh, Laurens Robert. BSE, U. Cin., 1947; Dr. honoris causa, Kean Coll., 1988. Nurse Cin. Gen. Hosp., 1947; head supr. premature nursery St. Louis Maternity Hosp., 1947-48; cons. AT&T Bell Labs., Murray Hill, N.J., 1968-97; pres. Computer Creations Corp., Watchung, NJ, 1989—2004; cons. Bell Communications Research, Morristown, N.J., 1984-92, Lucent Technologies/Bell Labs. Innovations, 1996—2001. Artist-in-residence Sta. WNET, N.Y.C., 1972-74; cons. T.J. Watson Rsch. Lab. IBM Corp., Yorktown, N.Y., 1975, 82-84; vis. mem. computer sci. dept. U. Md., College Park, 1974-80; adj. prof. fine arts Kean Coll., Union, N.J., 1980-82, Rutgers U., New Brunswick, N.J., 1982-83; adj. prof. dept. psychology NYU, N.Y.C., 1985-86, assoc. prof. computer sci.; guest lectr. Princeton U., Columbia U., Yale U., Rockefeller U.; mem. grad. faculty Sch. Visual Arts, N.Y.C., 1990—; dir. team from Rutgers U. to create world's first computer-generated 3-D model of Leaning Tower of Pisa to test structures, 1999; invited com. mem. info. tech. and creativity NAS, 2000-03; invited juror L'Oreal/Color/Internat., 2000-01; film retrospective Leeds, Eng. Lumen-Evolution, 2002, 2003-04. Author: Information Technology and Creativity, 2001; co-author: The Computer Artist's Handbook; contbd. articles to profl. jours including Scientific Am., 1995; contbr. chpts. to books, also Trans. Am. Philos. Soc., vol. 75, Part 6, 1985; one-woman shows of sculpture and paintings include Columbia U., 1967, 68, Rabin and Krueger Gallery, Newark, 1968; films shown at Met. Mus., N.Y.C., Franklin Inst., Phila., 1972, U. Toronto, 1972, am. Embassy, London, 1972, L.A. County Mus., Corcoran Gallery, Washington, 1972, Whitney Mus., N.Y.C., 1973, Grand Palais, Paris, Musee Nat. d'Art Moderne, Paris, IBM, (digital print show) Bklyn. Mus. Art, 2001, Chelsea Mus. Art, N.Y.C., 2004, others; dir.: Save the Leaning Tower. Recipient numerous art and film awards, Emmy award Mus. Modern Art, 1984, Computer Graphics World Smithsonian awards for virtual reality, art analysis, inventing computer medium for art and animation, 1993; named Outstanding Alumnus, U. Cin., 1987; grantee Nat. Endowment for Arts, 1977, 81, Corp. Pub. Broadcasting, 1979, Nat. Endowment Composers and Librettists, 1981, Arts Coun. Eng., 2003. Fellow World Acad. of Art and Sci.; mem. NATAS, Am. Film Inst., Info. Film Prodrs. Am., Soc. Motion Picture and TV Engrs., Internat. Sculptors Assn., Centro Studi Pierfrancescani (Sansepolcro, Italy, founding mem.). Achievements include pioneer in use of computers as art media; commd. to create computer poster and TV comml. for opening New Mus. Modern Art, 1984; discovered identities of the Mona Lisa, hidden and surface, 1987, and identified steps DaVinci made in transforming Isabella, Duchess of Aragon, into the Mona Lisa using his own features as the model, 1993; discovered perspective used by DaVinci in The Last Supper, 1988; identified time of day and use of thorns in Piero della Francesca's Resurrection; discovered Elizabeth I is model for Martin Droeshout engraving of Shakespeare, 1991; performed first transmission of computer drawing between U.S. and Germany, 1990; used morphing algorithms to determine Leonardo's creative decision-making steps in transforming the Duchess of Aragon into the Mona Lisa using his own features to segue; discovered method Leonardo used to create his Grotesques, 1994; discovered new Renaissance illusion of another figure in a painting of Christ, 1996, rediscovered Renaissance illusion published in visual computer, 1997, Satan-like figure in Leonardo's Munich "Madonna", 1998; created with Professor Madara Ozot and PhD candidate Zheng Zhou, first computer-generated 3D model of the Leaning Tower of Pisa to test the structure, 1999; completed archive/collection acquired by Ohio State U., 2004; discovered why the right hand of Christ in Leonardo's "Last Supper" is in the awkward position it is in., 2004.

SCHWARTZ, NADINE SUSAN, media specialist; b. Austin, Tex., Nov. 27, 1949; d. Jack Eli and Lillian Hodes Schwartz; children: Eric Howard, Melissa Rachelle Brown. BA, Northeastern Ill. U., 1974; MA, Adelphi U., 1975. Cert. tchr. Ill., N.Y., Ariz. Adj. instr. Adelphi U., Garden City, NY, 1974—75, Dowling Coll., Oakdale, NY, 1975—79; English tchr. Paradise Valley H.S., Phoenix, 1979—99, dept. chair, 1995—99; media specialist Shadow Mountain H.S., Phoenix, 1999—. Bd. dirs. Or Adam Congregation for Humanitistic Judaism, Scottsdale/Tempe, Ariz., 1989—2002; bd. mem. Home Owners Assn., Eagle Point Townhomes, Scottsdale, 1996—2003. Mem.: ALA, Ariz. Libr. Assn. Avocations: travel, reading, baseball. Office: Shadow Mountain High Sch 2902 E Shea Blvd Phoenix AZ 85028

SCHWARTZ, NEENA BETTY, endocrinologist, educator; b. Balt., Dec. 10, 1926; d. Paul Howard and Pauline (Shulman) S. AB, Goucher Coll., 1948, DSc (hon.), 1982; MS, Northwestern U., 1950, PhD, 1953. From instr. to prof. U. Ill. Coll. Medicine, Chgo., 1953-72, asst. dean for faculty, 1968-70; prof. physiology Northwestern U. Med. Sch., Chgo., 1973-74; Deering prof. Northwestern U., Evanston, Ill., 1974—99, chmn. dept. biol. scis., 1974-78, acting dean, Coll. Arts and Scis., 1996-97, prof. emeritus, 2000—. Contbr. chpts. to books, articles to profl. jours. NIH rsch. grantee, 1955-. Fellow: AAAS (exec. bd. 1998—2002, Lifetime Mentor award 2003); mem.: Soc. for Neurosci., Am. Physiol. Soc., Soc. for Study of Reproduction (dir. 1975—77, exec. v.p. 1976—77, pres. 1977—78, Carl Hartman award 1992), Endocrine Soc. (v.p. 1970—71, mem. coun. 1979—83, pres. 1982—83, Williams award 1985, Disting. Educator award 1998), Am. Acad. Arts and Scis. Home: 1511 Lincoln St Evanston IL 60201-2338

SCHWARTZ, PAULA MAE, communications company executive; BA in English Lit., Boston U. Formerly with Newsweek; former pub. rels. profl. N.Y.C., Boston; co-founder, CEO Schwartz Comms., Inc., Waltham, Mass., 1990—. Bd. dirs. Gloucester Adventure. Avocations: hiking, theatre, thriller fiction. Office: Schwartz Comms Inc Prospect Pl/230 Third Ave Waltham MA 02451 also: Schwartz Comms Inc 595 Market St Ste 2050 San Francisco CA 94105-2831

SCHWARTZ, PEPPER JUDITH, sociology educator; b. Chgo., May 11, 1945; d. Julius J. and Gertrude (Puris) S.; m. John A. Strait, June 19, 1971; m. Arthur M. Skolnik, Jan. 9, 1982; children— Cooper, Ryder. B.A., Washington U., St. Louis, 1968, M.A., 1970; M. in Philosophy, Yale U., 1972, Ph.D., 1974. Assoc. prof. sociology, adj. assoc. prof. 1972-88, prof. psychiatry and behavioral sci. U. Wash., Seattle, 1988— . Chmn. rev. com. NIMH; bd. dirs. Women's Research Ctr.; frequent guest and host local and network TV shows; apptd. to Pres. Reagan's ad hoc adv. roundtable on the family, 1984; expert appearance in NBC Sacred Sexless, 1987, Some Thoughts on Being Single, 1984, ABC After The Sexual Revolution, 1986. Bd. dirs. Nat. Abortion Rights Action League, Anti-Defamation League; guardian Ad-Litem Program; bd. dirs. Empty Space Theater, Seattle, pres., 1980; past mem. Gov.'s Commn. Venereal Disease; bd. dirs. ACLU; nat. bd. dirs. YWCA, Jewish Family Service; mem. Presdl. Adv. Roundtable on Family, 1984. Named Outstanding Young Woman of the Future, Time-Life mag., 1978; One of Most Powerful People of the 1980s, Next mag., 1981. Mem. Am. Sociol. Assn. (chairperson com. on coms.), Pacific Sociol. Assn. (mem. council), Nat. Conf. Family Relations, Groves Conf. Club: Yale (N.Y.C.). Author: Women at Yale, 1976; (with Judith Laws et al) Sexual Scripts, 1977; (with P. Blumstein) American Couples, 1983; co-author and editor: A Student's Guide to Sex on Campus, 1971; contbr. numerous articles to mags. and jours.; profiles in Savvy, Ladies Home Jour., Playboy, Cosmopolitan, N.Y. Times, Newsweek, others; articles on work in Time, Redbook, New West, others. Office: Dept Sociology Dk 40 U Seattle WA 98195-0001

SCHWARTZ, RENEE GERSTLER, lawyer; b. Bklyn., June 18, 1933; d. Samuel and Lillian (Neulander) Gerstler; m. Alfred L. Schwartz, July 30, 1955; children: Carolyn Susan, Deborah Jane. AB, Bklyn. Coll., 1953; LLB, Columbia U., 1955. Bar: N.Y. 1956, U.S. Dist. Ct. (so. and ea. dists.) N.Y. 1956, U.S. Ct. Appeals (2d cir.) 1956, U.S. Dist. Ct. D.C. 1983, U.S. Supreme Ct. 1986. Assoc. Botein, Hays & Sklar, N.Y.C., 1955-64, ptnr., 1965-89, Kronish, Lieb, Weiner & Hellman, N.Y.C., 1990—. Bd. dirs. New Land Found., N.Y.C., 1965—. Mem. Bar Assn. City of N.Y. Home: 115 Central Park W New York NY 10023-4153 Office: Kronish Lieb Weiner & Hellman 1114 Avenue Of The Americas New York NY 10036-7703 Office Phone: 212-479-6040. E-mail: rschwartz@kronishlieb.com.

SCHWARTZ, SHARON J. state representative; b. Waterville, Kans., Mar. 14, 1940; m. Leo Schwartz; children: Douglas, Cheri. Bus. mgr. Pork Chop Acres, Inc., 1983—; mem. Kans. Ho. of Reps., 1996—. Mem.: Washington Kans. C. of C., Nat. Pork Bd., Kans. Pork Prodrs. Republican. Roman Catholic. Office: 110-S State Capitol 300 SW 10th Ave Topeka KS 66612 Address: 2051 20th Rd Washington KS 66968-2419

SCHWARTZ, SHIRLEY E. chemist, researcher; b. Detroit, Aug. 26, 1935; d. Emil Victor and Jessie Grace (Galbraith) Eckwall; m. Ronald Elmer Schwartz, Aug. 25, 1957; children: Steven Dennis, Bradley Allen, George Byron. BS, U. Mich., 1957, Detroit Inst. Tech., 1978; MS, Wayne State U., 1962, PhD, 1970. Asst. prof. Detroit Inst. Tech., 1973-78, head divsn. math. sci., 1976-78; mem. rsch. staff BASF Wyandotte (Mich.) Corp., 1978-81, head sect. functional fluids, 1981; sr. staff rsch. scientist GM Rsch., Warren, Mich., 1981-99; materials engr. GM Powertrain, 1999—2003. Contbr. articles to profl. jours.; patentee in field. Recipient Gold award Engring. Soc. Detroit, 1989, Life Achievement award Soc. Women Engrs., 1999; inducted U.S. Nat. Acad. of Engring., 2000. Fellow Soc. Automotive Engrs. (Excellence in Oral Presentation award 1986, 91, 94, Arch T. Colwell Merit award 1991, Lloyd L. Withrow Disting. Spkr. award 1995), Soc. Tribologists and Lubrication Engrs. (treas. Detroit sect. 1981, vice chmn. 1982, chmn. 1982-83, chmn. wear tech. com. 1987-88, bd. dirs. 1985-91, assoc. editor 1989-90, contbg. editor 1989—2003, Wilbur Deutsch award 1987, P.M. Ku award 1994), Soc. Automotive Engrs.; mem. Soc. Tribologists and Lubrication Engrs., Am. Chem. Soc., Soc. In Vitro Biology, Mich. Women's Hall of Fame (lifetime achievement award 1996), Women of Wayne (headliners award 2000), U.S. Nat. Acad. Engring., Mensa, Classic Guitar Soc. Mich., U.S. Power Squadrons, Detroit Navigators, Sigma Xi. Lutheran.

SCHWARTZ, SUSAN LYNN HILL, principal; b. Portland, Ind., Aug. 15, 1951; d. Leland Alfred and Marjorie (Halberstadt) Hill; m. William Samuel Schwartz, July 6, 1974; children: Angelica Martinique, Allysia Dominica. BA, DePauw U., 1973; MA, Ball State U., 1976; postgrad., Tri-Coll. U., Fargo, N.D., 1986, Ind. U., 1993—. Cert. tchr. and aminstr., Ind., N.D. 2d and 3d grade tchr. Jay Sch. Corp., Portland, 1973-76; 1st to 3d grade tchr. Minot (N.D.) Pub. Schs., 1976-80; prin. elem. sch. Ward County Schs., Minot, 1980-82, LaPorte (Ind.) Schs., 1988-96; prin. kindergarten to 5th grade Western Wayne Schs., Cambridge City, Ind., 1996-97; prin. pre-K through 6th Cloverdale (Ind.) Elem. Sch., 1997—. Mem. State Sch. Evaluation Team, Bismarck, N.D., 1980-81. Bd. dirs. Am. Cancer Soc., Muncie, Ind., 1985-88, Richmond, Ind., 1992—, Suzuki Music Assn., Muncie, 1986-87; mem./leader Work Area on Edn.-Meth., Muncie, 1985-87; philanthropic chair Delaware County Welcome Wagon, Muncie, 1982-88; treas./fin. sec. Christian Women's Club, Muncie, 1983-86; pres. N.D. State U. Sch. Adminstrs. Assn., Fargo, 1980-81; mem. Wayne County Step Ahead Edn. Com., 1991—; bd. mem. United Way; Putnam County, safe sch. summit rep., 1997—. Named Outstanding Young Educator, Jaycees, 1980, Outstanding Young Career Woman, Bus. and Profl. Women, 1981. Mem. Phi Delta Kappa, Pi Lambda Theta, Delta Kappa Gamma, Psi Iota Xi. Methodist. Avocations: golf, racquetball, bridge. Office: Cloverdale Elem 311 E Logan St Cloverdale IN 46120-8707

SCHWARTZTOL, HOLLY WECHSLER, psychologist; b. Washington, Dec. 20, 1946; d. James Arthur and Nancy (Fraenkel) Wechsler; m. Robert Ira Schwartztol, Nov. 16, 1975; children: Laurence, Andrew. BA, Finch Coll., 1968; MA, C. W. Post Coll., 1971; PhD, U. Miami, 1981. Instr. psychology C. W. Post Coll., Greenvale, N.Y., 1971; tchr. Yorktown High Sch., Yorktown Heights, N.Y., 1971-73; sch. psychologist Dade County Schs., Miami, Fla., 1973-84; pvt. practice holistic psychology Miami, 1983—; Reiki master, trainer radiant heart therapy. Adj. asst. prof. counseling psychology U. Miami, 1984-85; co-founder, co-dir. Miami Inst. Clin. Hypnosis, 1986-93; co-founder, dir. Miami Inst. Expanding Light, 1993-96. Author: (with James A. and Nancy F. Wechsler) In a Darkness, 1972, 2d edit., 1988. Reiki master, trainer and practitioner of radiant heart therapy. Mem. Dade County Psychol. Assn. (pres. 1988), Fla. Psychol. Assn., Am. Psychol. Assn., Am. Soc. Clin. Hypnosis (bd. dirs. 1998-99, pres.-elect 1999-2000, pres. 1999—), South Fla. Soc. for the Study Multiple Personality and Dissociative Disorders (bd. dirs. 1989, pres. 1991). Office: 806 S Douglas Rd Ste 560 Coral Gables FL 33134-3157

SCHWARTZ, BARBARA RUTH BALLOU, elementary school educator; b. East Orange, N.J., Aug. 8, 1930; d. Robert Ingram Ballou and Ruth Edna Sweeney; m. Eugene A. Schwarz, Jr., Dec. 24, 1954 (div. 1977); children: Ruth Ellen, Eugene A. III. BS, Trenton State Coll., 1952. Tchr. West Orange N.J. Schs., 1952-54, Franklin Sch., Ft. Wayne, Ind., 1955-56, Parliament Place Sch., North Babylon, N.Y., 1965-91. Trustee welfare trust fund North Babylon Tchrs. Orgn., N.Y., 1988-91. Vol. Safe Home, Suffolk County Coalition Against Domestic Violence, Bayshore, N.Y., 1979-90; sec. Victims Info. Bur., Suffolk, 1987-88, v.p., 1989-90, pres. bd. dirs., 1990-94, regional bd. dirs., 2002—, rep. to Women's Equal Rights Coalition, Suffolk County Human Rights Commn., 1989-94; mem. adv. bd. Suffolk County Women's Svcs., 1990-96, vice-chair, 1991-93; rep. LD 14 Suffolk County Women's Adv. Commn., 2001—; bd. dirs. Suffolk Abortion Rights Coun., 1992-96; mem. Suffolk-Nassau Abortion Def., 1991-94; pub. affairs com. Planned Parenthood Suffolk County, 1990-92; mem. Long Islanders for Fairness and Equality 1994-97; mem. subcom. Islip Presbyn. Ch. on Legis. Com. of N.Y. State Coalition Against Domestic Violence, 1999—; steering com. Save Our Svcs., Long Island, 1998—; mem. coun. on women, L.I. Presbytery, 2002—. Women's History Month Community Svc. honoree Town of Babylon, 1997. Mem. AAUW (mem. v.p. Islip area br. 1982-84, pres. 1984-88, legis. chair 1988-93, mem. com. promoting individual liberties Nassau-Suffolk dist. VI 1989-91, pro-choice coord. N.Y. state 1990-92, rep. to women on job task force 1986-98, chair dist. VI inter-br. 1991-92, chair N.Y. state pub. policy 1992-96, rep. on L.I. and N.Y. State Pro-Choice Coalitions, chair N.Y. state voter edn. campaign, 1995-98, assoc. pub. policy com. 1996-98, L.I. Achievement award 1996), N.Y. State Ret. Tchrs. Assn., Western Suffolk Ret. Tchrs. Assn., Coalition Ret. Tchrs. L.I., North Babylon Tchrs. Orgn. (retirees chpt.). Republican. Avocations: lobbying, reading, handcrafts, gourmet cooking, volunteer activities. Home: 23 Wyandanch Ave Babylon NY 11702-1920 E-mail: bbschwarz@webtv.net.

SCHWARZ, CHERYL MARITA, special education educator; b. Waukegan, Ill., Aug. 25, 1956; d. Walter George and Catherine Mary Nieds; children: Lindsay, Sarah. BS in Spl. Edn., Western Ill. U., 1978; MA in Learning Disabilities, Northeastern Ill. U., 1992; postgrad. in Ednl. Adminstrn., No. Ill. U., 2002—. Learning disabilities tchr. Golf Jr. HS, Morton Grove, Ill., 1978—81; learning disabilities tchr., coord. Dept. Spl. Edn. Wauconda (Ill.) HS, 1986—. Recipient Citizenship Edn. award, Dept. Ill. VFW, 1999—2000. Avocations: tennis, golf, reading, yoga, walking, running. Home: 1189 Hunters Ln Lake Zurich IL 60047-2249

SCHWARZ, LOUISE A. band director; H.s. band dir. Bethlehem Ctrl. H.S., Delmar, N.Y. Recipient Castleman award for excellence in chamber mus. teaching, 1993. Office: Bethlehem Ctrl High Sch 700 Delaware Ave Delmar NY 12054-2436

SCHWARZ, ROSE OBERMAN, artist; b. Jan. 24, 1910; d. William and Florence Oberman; m. Sidney Schwarz, July 31, 1929 (dec. Mar. 1984); children: Lillian, Elaine. Student, South Fla. Art Inst., 1977—99. Ins. salesperson. Exhibitions include Bacardi Gallery, Miami, Fla., 1979, Miami Beach City Hall, Fla., 1981—82, Viscaya, 1981, Met. Mus., Coral Gables, Fla., 1985, Bay Harbor Gallery, Fla., 1985—. Recipient Rex Art award, Hollywood Cultural Ctr., 1981, hon. mention, Pioneer Mus., 1982, Best in Show award, Hollywood Art Guild, 1983, hon. mention, Pioneer Mus., 1983, Best in show, Hollywood Cultural Ctr., 1984, Best in Show, 1985. Avocations: dress making, piano. Home: 6674 Via Roma Delray Beach FL 33446-3730

SCHWARZKOPF, CONSTANCE GOLDSWORTHY, retired college educator, animal breeder; b. Livingston, N.J., Apr. 5, 1934; d. Edwin Arthur and Leona Ferguson Goldsworthy; m. Daniel B. Schwarzkopf, Oct. 20, 1960. BA, Oberlin Coll., 1956; MA, Middlebury Coll., 1961; student, U. Freiburg im Breisgau U., Germany, 1958—59, Gutenberg U., 1959—60. Organist First Parish Ch., Stow, Mass., 1961—63; lectr. in French & German Mass. Bay C.C., Watertown, Mass., 1964—66; instr. German Curry Coll., Milton, Mass., 1967—73; organic sheep farmer Hampshire Farm, Stow, Mass., 1969—95. Founder Ea. Mass. Shearing Project, Stow, 1973—84; mem. Natural Resources Coun. Maine, 1988—. Editor: BASD Newsletter, 1972—74, Boston Area Spinners & Dyers, 1972—84; contbr. reviews to various newspapers, 1964—99. Chmn. Stow Hist. Commn., Stow, 1977—85; restoration dir. 1825 Brick Schoolhouse, Stow, 1971—75; mus. dir. & curator 1825 Sch. Mus., Stow, 1975—99. Mem.: Natural Resources Def. Coun., Thompson Lake Environ. Assn., Pub. Citizen, Planned Parenthood League, Am. United for Separation, The Thoreau Soc., Stow West Sch. Soc. (treas., sec. 1974—). Baptist. Avocations: sailing, organic gardening, travel, biking, historical preservation.

SCHWARZKOPF, GLORIA A. education educator, psychotherapist; b. Chgo., Apr. 20, 1926; m. Alfred E. Grossenbacher. BE, Chgo. State U., 1949, ME in Libr. Sci., 1956. Cert. nat. recovery specialist, reality therapist; libr. sci. endorsement; cert. hypnotherapist; cert. nat. forensic counselor; nat. cert. domestic violence counselor. Tchr. Chgo. Bd. Edn., 1949-91, inservice trainer in substance abuse, 1990—91; co-therapist ATC outpatient unit Ingalls Meml. Hosp., Chgo., 1981-86; recovery specialist Interaction Inst., Evergreen Park, Ill., 1993-95; ct. watcher Cook County, Chgo., 1994—2003; quality assurance evaluation Ill. State Bd. Edn., 1997-2000; libr. aide Chgo. Bd. Edn., 2001—03. Instr. Govs. State U., University Park, Ill., 1987, University Park, 91, South Suburban Coll., South Holland, Ill., 1991, Prairie State Coll., Chicago Heights, Ill., 1993, Chicago Heights, 96; with CP5 Project Assist Program, 2000—03; presenter in field; co-facilitator CPS Summer Sci. Camp Intervention project, 2000, 03, Ford Grant Camp Invention Summer '01 & '03. Columnist Peoples Choice Weekly, 1991-93. Del. to Russia and Czechoslovakia, Citizens Amb. Program. Recipient Sci. Tchr. of Yr. award, 1976, Svc. Recognition award, 1985, IMSA Recognition award, 1988; grantee Chgo. Pub. Sch., 1981. Mem. NEA, Nat. Assn. Forensic Counselors, Sci. Tchrs. Assn., Ill. Alcoholism Counselors Alliance, Nat. Alcoholism Coun., Am. Assn. Hypnotherapists, Am. Assn. Behavioral Therapists, Soc. of Am. for Recovery (nat. cert. recovery specialist), South Suburban Coun. on Alcoholism, Ill. Alcoholism and Other Drug Abuse Profl. Cert. Assn. Home: 2216 W 91st St Chicago IL 60620-6238

SCHWARZROCK, SHIRLEY PRATT, writer, educator; b. Mpls., Feb. 27, 1914; d. Theodore Ray and Myrtle Pearl (Westphal) Pratt; m. Loren H. Schwarzrock, Oct. 19, 1945 (dec. 1966); children: Kay Linda, Ted Kenneth, Lorraine V. BS, U. Minn., 1935, MA, 1942, PhD, 1974. Sec. to chmn. speech dept. U. Minn., Mpls., 1935, instr. in speech, 1946, team tchr. in creative arts workshops for tchrs., 1955—56, guest lectr. Dental Sch., 1967—72, asst. prof. (part-time) practice adminstrn. Sch. Dentistry, 1972—80; tchr. speech, drama and English Preston H.S., Minn., 1935—37; tchr. speech, drama and English, dir. dramatics Owatonna H.S., Minn., 1937—39; tchr. creative dramatics and English, tchr.-counselor Webster Groves Jr. H.S., Mo., 1939—40; dir. dramatics and tchr.-counselor Webster Groves Sr. H.S., 1940—43; exec. sec. bus. and profl. dept. YWCA, Mpls., 1943—45; tchr. speech and drama Convent of the Visitation, St. Paul, 1958; editor pro-tem Am. Acad. Dental Practice Adminstrn., 1966—68; editor North Country Pages, 2003—. Guest tchr. Coll. St. Catherine, St. Paul, 1969; vol. mgr. Gift Shop, Eitel Hosp., Mpls., 1981-83, Edina Cmty. Resource Pool, 1992-95; cmty. citizen mem. planning, evaluating, reporting com. Edina Pub. Sch. Sys., 1993-96; tutor for reading, writing, and speaking, 1993-96; condr. tutorials in speaking and profl. office mgmt., 1985-96; owner Shirley Schwarzrock's Exec. Support Svc., 1989-99; cons. Ergodyne Corp., St. Paul, 1991-92; freelance editor med. support bus., 1992; cons., lectr. in field. Author: Coping With Personal Identity, Coping With Human Relationships, Coping With Facts and Fantasies, Coping With Teenage Problems, 1984; individual book titles (Coping With series) include: Do I Know the "Me" Others See?, My Life-What Shall I Do With It?, Living With Loneliness, Learning to Make Better Decisions, Grades, What's So Important About Them, Anyway?, Facts and Fantasies About Alcohol, Facts and Fantasies About Smoking, Food as a Crutch, Facts and Fantasies About the Roles of Men and Women, You Always Communicate Something, Appreciating People-Their Likenesses and Differences, Fitting In, To Like and Be Liked, Can You Talk With Someone Else?, Coping With Emotional Pain, Some Common Crutches, Parents Can Be a Problem, Coping With Cliques, Crises Youth Face Today; (with L.H. Schwarzrock) Effective Dental Assisting, 1954, 1st edit., 1967, (with J.R. Jensen) 1973, 3d edit., 1982; (with J.R. Jensen, Kay Schwarzrock, Lorraine Schwarzrock) 1990, 7th edit., 1991, Workbook for Effective Dental Assisting, 1968, 5th edit., 1991; (with Donovan F. Ward) Effective Medical Assisting, 1969, 2d edit., 1976, Manual for Effective Medical Assisting, 1969, 2d edit., 1976; (with C.G. Wrenn) The Coping With Series of Books for High School Students, 1970, The Coping With Manual, 1973, Contemporary Concerns of Youth, 1980, Shirley's Supergoodies: An Old Fashioned Cookbook for the Modern Cook, 2002; cons. editor: North Country Pages, St. Paul, 2003-04; contbr. articles to profl. jours. Pres. Univ. Elem. Sch. PTA, 1955-56; vol. judge Minn. State Hist. Day Program, 1994-98. Fellow Internat. Biog. Assn.; mem. Minn. Acad. Dental Practice Adminstrn. (hon.), Authors Guild, Minn. Hist. Soc., Minn. Geneal. Soc., Zeta Phi Eta (pres. 1948-49), Eta Sigma Upsilon. Home: 7448 W Shore Dr Edina MN 55435-4022

SCHWARZWALD, JULIE NANETTE, elementary school educator; b. Cleve., Nov. 9, 1966; d. Melvin Saul and Susan Herzig Schwarzwald; m. Howard Seth Bochner, Aug. 20, 1989; children: Mark, Joshua. BA in Edn. Policy, Wesleyan U., 1988; MA in Computer Edn., Columbia U., 1994. Tchr. Discovery Ctr. Sch., San Francisco, 1989—90, Willow Grove Elem., Hackettstown, NJ, 1990—92, Mount Horeb Elem., Warren, NJ, 1992—93; tchr. computers Kushner Acad., Caldwell, NJ, 1994; tchr. Solomon Schechter Day Sch. of Essex and Union, Cranford, NJ, 2002—. V.p. Summit (N.J.) Jewish Cmty. Ctr., 1997—. Home: 29 Cinnamon Tree Lane Berkeley Heights NJ 07922

SCHWEBEL, RENATA MANASSE, sculptor; b. Zwickau, Germany, Mar. 6, 1930; came to U.S., 1940, naturalized, 1946; d. George and Anne Marie (Simon) Manasse; m. Jack P. Schwebel, May 10, 1955; children: Judith, Barbara, Diane. BA, Antioch Coll., 1953; MFA, Columbia U., 1961; student, Arts Students League, 1967-69. Cartographer Ecostate Inc., Ridgewood, NJ, 1949; display artist Silvestri Inc., Chgo., 1950-51; asst. Mazzolini Art Foundry, Yellow Springs, Ohio, 1952. One-woman shows include Columbia U., 1961, Greenwich Art Barn, Conn., 1975, Sculpture Ctr., N.Y.C., 1979, Pelham Art Ctr., N.Y., 1981, New Rochelle Libr. Gallery, 1980, Outdoor Installations Katonah Gallery, 1986, 1989, Berman/Dafener Gallery, N.Y.C., 1992—93; artist (group shows) Stamford Mus., Conn., 1967, 1996, Hudson River Mus., Yonkers, N.Y., 1972, 1974, Wadsworth Atheneum, Hartford, 1974, Silvermine Art of the Northwest U.S.A. Anns., 1972, 1976, 1980, 1995, 1998, Silvermine Gallery, 1986, 1991, 2000, 2001, 2002, 2003, New Britain Mus. Am. Art, Conn., 1974, Imprimatur Gallery, St. Paul, 1985, 1986, Bergen County Mus., N.J., 1983, Sculpture Ctr., 1978—88, Katonah Gallery, N.Y., 1986—90, Cast Iron Gallery, N.Y.C., 1991, 1993, Kyoto (Japan) Gallery, 1993; exhibitions include Sculptors Guild Anns., 1974—; artist (traveling show exhibitions) in Am. cultural ctrs. in Egypt and Israel, 1981, 3 Rivers Art Festival, Pitts., 1994, FFS Gallery, N.Y.C., 1994, 1995, Russian Consulate, 1998, Long Beach Island Assn. Arts and Scis., N.J., 1999, Grounds for Sculpture, Hamilton, N.J., 1999, Chesterwood Mus., Stockbridge, Mass., 2000, Troy Arts Ctr., N.Y., 2000—01, Rockland Ctr. for Arts, 2001—02, No. Westchester Arts Coun., 2002, 2003, Westport Arts Ctr., 2003; Represented in permanent collections S.W. Bell, Columbia U., Colt Industries, Am. Airlines, Comcraft Industries, Nairobi, Gruber Haus, Berlin, Mus. Fgn. Art, Sofia, Bulgaria, Housatonic Mus. Bd. dirs. Fine Arts Fedn., N.Y., 1985-87; trustee Sculpture Ctr., 1980-88, chmn. exhbn. com., 1986-88; adv. bd. Pehlham Art Ctr., 1982. Mem.: N.Y. Artists Equity, Silvermine Guild, Conn. N.Y. Soc. Women Artists, Conn. Acad. Fine Arts, Audubon Artists (Chaim Gross award 1980, Medal of Honor 1982, Rennick award 1986, 1990, 1992, 1995), Nat. Assn. Women Artists (Willis Meml. prize 1974, Medal of Honor 1981, Paley Meml. award 1979), Sculptors Guild (bd. dirs. 1975—94, 1995—, pres. 1980—83), Katonah Gallery (artist mem. 1986—90), Ams. for Peace Now (bd. dirs. 1991—2001), Antioch Coll. Assn. (bd. dirs. 1971—77). Home: 10 Dogwood Hills Pound Ridge NY 10576-1508 E-mail: RENATA99M@aol.com.

SCHWEDT, RACHEL ELAINE, librarian; b. Lockport, N.Y., Dec. 2, 1944; d. Richard Thomas and Una May Traver; m. Ronald Anthony Schwedt, Feb. 3, 1967; children: Julie Lynn, Alan Ernest. BA, Roberts Wesleyan Coll., 1967; MLS, SUNY, Geneseo, 1979. Libr. Frewsburg (N.Y.) Ctrl. Sch., 1969-85; adminstrv. asst. Regent U., Virginia Beach, Va., 1986-88; libr. Lynchburg (Va.) Christian Acad., 1989-92, Liberty U., Lynchburg, 1992—. Spkr. various tchr. convs. Author: Core Collection for Small Libraries, 1997, Contemporary Christian Authors, 2000, A Guide to Poetry for Adolescents, 2001; author (newsletter) Libr. News, 1992-97. Tchr. various chs.; singer various choral groups. Mem. Assn. Christian Schs. Internat. (accreditation teams 1994-98). Avocations: reading, antiques, music, interior design, gardening. Home: 4052 Fort Ave Lynchburg VA 24502 Office: Libr Univ 1971 University Blvd Lynchburg VA 24502 E-mail: Spanky519@juno.com.

SCHWEGLER, NANCY ANN, librarian, writer; b. Bklyn., Jan. 22, 1946; d. Richard Donald Newman and Beatrice Ella Stirba; m. Robert Andrew Schwegler, Apr. 6, 1968; children: Brian Alexander, Christopher Robert, Ashley Marie. BA, Hope Coll., Holland, Mich., 1967; MLIS, U. R.I., 1991. Libr. asst. Art Libr., U. of Chgo., Chgo., 1968—71; children's libr. Watertown (Mass.) Pub. Libr., 1971—72; cataloguer Astronomy Libr., U. Cin., 1972—73; children's libr. East Greenwich (R.I.) Free Libr., 1984—89, Bradley Hosp., Riverside, RI, 1988—. Author: (bibliography) Rhode Island Parents' Paper, Writing in Depth, 2004; contbr. articles to newspapers and jours. Mem.: ALA, Delta Phi Delta, Beta Phi Mu, Phi Kappa Phi. Reformed Church Of America. Avocations: lighthouse preservation advocacy, international adoption advocacy, watercolour painting. Home: 83 Darling St Warwick RI 02886 Office: Bradley Hospital 1011 Veterans Meml Pkwy Riverside RI 02915 Personal E-mail: nnschweg@aol.com. E-mail: nschwegler@lifespan.org.

SCHWEGMAN, MONICA JOAN, artist; b. Hamilton, Ohio, Apr. 19, 1958; d. David Michael and LaVerne Henrietta (Mergy) Kiley; m. Craig Alfred Schwegman, Oct. 6, 1978; children: Craig, Sarah. Student, U. Cin., 1976-78; AAS, Brookdale C.C., 1978; postgrad., Kansas City Art Inst., 1990. Mgmt. trainee coll. coop. Marshall Fields, Chgo., 1977-78; decorator, cons. Sears, Toms River, N.J., 1985-88; artist, owner studio and gallery Lampasas, Tex., 1990-94. Chmn. Keystone Art Alliance, Lampasas, 1991-94; art dir. Theatre for Lampasas, 1993-94; bd. dirs. FirstBook Erie. Exhibited in group shows at Gallery One, 1993, Marble Falls, Tex., Found Art, Lampasas, 1992, KBUO TV Set Design, Austin, Tex., 1992, Breckenrdige Fine Arts Ctr., 1992, Pasillo De Artes Gallery, Austin, 1992, Contemporary Art Exhibit, Lampasas, 1991, Gannon U., Erie, Pa., Erie, Barnes & Noble, Erie, Springhill, Erie, Erie Art Mus., 1997, 99, Beacon Gallery, 1999, Kada Gallery, 1999, Erie Art Mus. Spring Show, 1999; solo shows A Woman's Touch, Erie Art Mus. Frame Shop Gallery, 1999, Schuster Gallery, Gannon U., Erie, Pa., 2000. Instr. art City of Lampasas/Sparts, 1993; bd. dirs. First Book Erie, 2003. Mem. Lampasas C. of C. (mem. tourism com. 1993). Republican. Roman Catholic. Avocations: reading, exercise.

SCHWEGMANN, MELINDA, supermarket executive, former state official; b. Austin, Tex., Oct. 25, 1946; m. John F. Schwegmann; 3 children. Student, La. State U.; grad. in Edn., U. New Orleans, 1968. Former pub. sch. tchr.; past pres. La. Soc. for Prevention of Cruelty to Animals; lt. gov. La., 1991-95; now dir. Schwegmann's Giant Supermarkets; now mem. La. Ho. of Reps. Mem. bd. Schwegmann Giant Super Markets; chmn. bd. Goodwill Industries; bd. dirs. Met. Area Com. New Orleans; sec. bd. dir.s Jr. Achievement; former mem. Jefferson Beautification Com. Office: State Representative 104 Sena Srive Metairie LA 70005

SCHWEIKERT, MARY LOU, elementary school educator; b. Bklyn., Aug. 6, 1938; d. Frank Salvatore Como and Angela Licciardi-Como; m. Edgar O. Schweikert, Apr. 7, 1969; 1 child, Marisa. Ba in Journalism, L.I. U., 1962; MSc in Edn., Wagner Coll., 1978. Lic. tchr. N.Y.C., 1965, N.Y., 1965. Tchr. N.Y.C. Bd. Edn., Bklyn., 1962—65, Dept. Def., 1965—72; mgr. dental office Dr. Edgar Schweikert, Bklyn., 1973—. Editor: Multiple Cantilevers in Fixed Prosthesis, 1988, Jour. Prosthetic Dentistry, 1984, Dentistry Today, 1994, 1995, 1999. Mem.: Nat. Assn. Women. Democrat. Roman Catholic. Avocations: tennis, gardening, stock market, travel. Home and Office: Dr Edgar Schweikert Dentistry 429 77th St Brooklyn NY 11209

SCHWEITZER, CAREN S. social worker; b. N.Y.C., Aug. 1, 1931; d. Robert David and Margaret Lane Steefel; m. Ulrich Schweitzer, Jan. 27, 1984; m. Austin K. Haldenstein, Nov. 26, 1953 (div. June 1970); children: Susan Federspiel, Kenneth Haldenstein. BA, Wellesley (Mass.) Coll., 1953; MSW, Hunter Sch. of Social Work, N.Y.C., 1974. LCSW Acad. Cert. Social Workers, N.Y. Job placement for people with disabilities Just One Break, N.Y.C., 1953—56; job placement Cmty. Action Program, Mamaroneck, NY, 1965—70; asst. to psychologist, 1970—72; program dir. West Assn. for Retarded Citizens, White Plains, NY, 1974—80; supr. group homes Westchester Jewish Cmty. Svcs., White Plains, NY, 1980—85; program coord., Tel. support networks Westchester Self-Help Clearinghouse, Hartsdale, NY, 1985—. Author: (column) Westchester Women's News, 1990—99. Campaign mgr. several Dem. party candidates, Westchester, NY, 1960—69. Phi Beta Kappa, Wellesley Coll., Mass., 1953. Democrat. Jewish. Avocations: tennis, bridge, singing. Home: 195 Old Army Rd Scarsdale NY 10583 E-mail: ulcare@aol.com.

SCHWEITZER, MARSHA L. musician, consultant; b. Canton, Ohio, Aug. 26, 1949; d. Paul and Florence Schweitzer; m. Kenji Otani, Mar. 10, 1979 (dec. May 1986). BM, Oberlin Coll., 1971. Assoc. prin. bassoon Honolulu Symphony, 1971—, asst. pers. mgr., 1975-81; bassoon Spring Wind Quintet, Honolulu, 1974—; exec. dir. Chamber Music Hawaii, Honolulu, 1982-87; mgr. Music Projects Honolulu, 1985-94; tchr. Mid Pacific Inst., Honolulu, 1993-94; 2d bassoon Cleve. (Ohio) Ballet and Opera, Cleve., 1994—99. Mgr. Spring Wind Quintet, 1974—; vice chair, treas. Honolulu Symphony Orch. Com., 1987-94; v.p. Hawaii Assn. Music Socs., Hilo, 1988-94; co-founder Hawaii Symphony, Honolulu, 1994. Contbr. articles to profl. jours.; music arranger, 1977—. Dir. ex officio Honolulu Symphony Honolulu Symphony Soc., 1987-89; mem. exec. bd. Hawaii Alliance Art Edn., Honolulu, 1980; lobbyist Hawaii State Legis., Honolulu, 1975-76; mem. grants review panelist Hawaii State Found. Culture & Arts, Honolulu, 1982, 84, Internat. Conf. of Symphony and Opera Musicians, 1996—2002, editor Senza Sordino newsletter, 1996—2002. Mem. ASCAP, Am. Soc. Music Copyists, Am. Fedn. Musicians, Internat. Double Reed Soc., Musicians Assn. Hawaii (sec., treas. 2001—). Home: 905 Spencer St Apt 404 Honolulu HI 96822-3737

SCHWEITZER, N. TINA, fiction writer, photojournalist, television producer, director, international consultant public relations, media relations, government relations; b. Hartford, Conn., Apr. 7, 1941; d. Abraham Aaron Morris and Ruth Blanche (Shifreen) S. BS, Emerson Coll., 1964. Freelance writer, Boston and Washington, 1965-67; mem. press, info. staff Embassy of Republic of Indonesia, Washington, 1967-68; researcher, writer Congl. Quar., Inc., Washington, 1969-70; owner Schweitzer Assocs., Hartford, Conn. and Washington, 1970-78, 79—. Dir. comty. rels., media rels. and govt. rels. Advocacy Svcs. for the Deaf, West Hartford, Conn., 1978-79; del. White House Conf. Small Bus., 1986; mem. faculty Conn. Re-employment Workshop Middlesex Comty. Tech. Coll.; profl. model; ind. TV prodr. Editor, chief prodn. Focus on Indonesia, Washington, 1967-68; corr. The Farmington (Conn.) Valley Herald, 1984; first bus. columnist Hartford Woman newspaper, 1984; contbr. articles to numerous govtl. and comml. publs. including U.S.I.S.; author: Media Kit, 1978, Women's Job Hunting Guide, 1983, You Can Do It! A Practical Guide for Job Hunting and Career-Changing, 1987, Men On the Tor (Violet Hunter), 1990; writer, designer, producer first series of TV videotape pub. svc. announcements on employment deaf or hard-of-hearing in the history of Conn., 1983-84; contbr. editorials to TV Stas. WFSB, 1977, 84, 86, WVIT, 1983; writer, ind. producer, dir., talk-show host Sta. WVIT-TV, 1987; works/fiction included in permanent collection Smith Coll. Lib., Northampton, Mass. Mem. State-wide Health Coordinating Coun., a U.S. Govt./State of Conn. Health Dept. project, 1978-80; adviser Conn. Office Advocacy to Handicapped; mem. legis. task force State of Conn., 1978-79; del. first Conn. Gov.'s Conf. on Libr. and Info. Svcs., 1978; candidate Conn. Ho. of Reps., 1982; aux. police officer Hartford Police Dept., 1976-77; acting chmn. Comm. Com. Unitarian Meeting House, West Hartford; dir. pub. rels. Greater Hartford Com. UNICEF, 1984-86; affiliated Rep. Town Com., Hartford., 1989; apptd. to Nat. Pub. Rels./Advt. Adv. Coun. Am. Mensa Ltd., 1989; press liason Mensa Internat. Offices, press rep. 1st Joint Conf. Am. Coun. Edn. and Conf. European Rectors, 1989. Recipient Presdl. Sports award Pres.'s Coun. on Phys. Fitness and Sports, 1992, 93, 94, 96; hon. fellow John F. Kennedy Presdl. Libr. Mus. Found. Mem. Nat. Writers Union, Nat. Press Photographers Assn., Inter-Am. Press Assn., American Mensa, Ltd., Sherlock Holmes Soc. London, Sigma Delta Chi. Address: Schweitzer Assocs 576C Mountain Rd West Hartford CT 06117-1826 Home: PO Box 974 Hartford CT 06143

SCHWERIN, KATHY ANN, marriage and family therapist; b. Schenectady, NY, July 26, 1949; d. Albert Erwin and Evelyn Mary (Hart) Schwerin. BA, U. Vt., 1971; MA, New Coll. Calif., 1985. Cert. marriage and family therapist Calif., 1988, Nev., 1991. Intern in counseling Unitas, Berkeley, Calif., 1984—86; intern in mediation Family Ct. Svcs., Oakland, Calif., 1985—86; dir. edn. Planned Parenthood, Reno, 1987—90; pvt. practice Carson City, Nev., 1991—. Dharma leader Spirit Rock Meditation Ctr., Woodacre, Calif., 2003—. Mem.: Am. Assn. Marriage Family Counselors. Avocations: meditation, hiking. Office: 116 E 7th St # 204 Carson City NV 89701 Office Phone: 775-882-4980.

SCHWIER, PRISCILLA LAMB GUYTON, television broadcasting company executive; b. Toledo, Ohio, May 8, 1939; d. Edward Oliver and Prudence (Hutchinson) Lamb; m. Robert T. Guyton, June 21, 1963 (dec. Sept. 1976); children: Melissa Guyton, Margaret Guyton, Robert Guyton; m. Frederick W. Schwier, May 11, 1984. BA, Smith Coll., 1961; MA, U. Toledo, 1972. Pres. Gt. Lakes Comm., Inc., 1982—97; vice chmn. Seilon, Inc., Toledo, 1981—83, also dir. Bd. dirs. WGTE-TV, Toledo, Ohio His. Soc., Ft. Meys. Contbr. articles to profl. jours. Trustee Wilberforce U., Ohio, 1983—, Planned Parenthood, Toledo, 1979—83, Maumee Valley Country Day Sch., Toledo; bd. dirs. N.W. Ohio Hospice, 1991—98; trustee Toledo Hosp., Maumee Country Day Sch., 1986—92; pres. Edward Lamb Found., 1987—; bd. dirs. Episcopal Ch., Maumee, Ohio, 1983—. Democrat. Episcopalian. Home and Office: 345 E Front St Perrysburg OH 43551-2131

SCHWIND, AUDREY FRANCES, artist, educator; b. Passaic, N.J., Sept. 19, 1955; d. Ernest Carl and Mary Becker; m. Paul Raymond Schwind, Feb. 7, 1982; children: Mary Beth, Garrett. BA, Kutztown U., 1977; MA, Montclair U., 1979. Art tchr. Ringwood Bd. Edn., NJ, 1977—88, Wayne Twp. Pub. Schs., Wayne, NJ, 1988—. Religious edn. tchr. St. Paul Sch., Prospect Park, NJ, 2000—03. Mem.: Nat. Art Edn. Assn. Roman Catholic. Avocation: painting.

SCHWIND, WANDA RUTH, retail executive; b. Broken Bow, Neb., May 10, 1908; d. Fred Hal and Ethel Winifred (Coleman) Ream; m. Louis William Morgan Schwind, Nov. 26, 1937 (dec. Feb. 1978). Speech and drama student, Northwestern U., 1928-29; bus. adminstrn. student, Ohio State U., 1930-31; law sch. student, U. Ohio, 1932-33. Society editor Dayton Jour. Herald, 1934-37; buyer, mdse. mgr., v.p. Stix Baer and Fuller (now Dillard's), 1940-74; vol. Highcroft Elem. Sch., Chesterfield, Mo., 1979—. Author: Random Thoughts A Nursing Home Jour., Solly Says: A Book of Aphorism. Bd. dirs. St Andrews Episcopal-Presbyn. Found., St. Louis, 1995—; del. Republican. Presdl. Trust, 1992. Recipient Cert. of Award Rep. Presdl. Adv. Commn., 1992; certs. of appreciation Nat. Humane Edn. Soc., 1996, 97, Am. Soc. Prevention of Cruelty to Animals, 1995, Haley Barbour/Chmn. Rep. Nat. Com., 1994, Easter Seal Soc., 1996, Cancer Rsch. Found. Am., 1995. Republican. Avocation: volunteering. Home: 307 S Woods Mill Rd Chesterfield MO 63017-3418

SCHWINN-JORDAN, BARBARA (BARBARA SCHWINN), painter; b. Glen Ridge, N.J. d. Carl Wilhelm Ludwig and Helen Louise (Jordan) Schwinn; m. Frank Bertram Jordan, Jr.; children: Janine Jordan, Frank Bertram III. Grad., N.Y. Sch. Fine and Applied Art, N.Y.C. and Paris; student, Grand Ctrl. Art Sch., Art Students League, N.Y.C., Grand Chaumiere, Acad. Julien, Paris, Columbia U., NAD. Freelance painter, 1970—. Lectr., instr. illustration Parsons Sch., 1952-54; founder adv. coun. Art Instrn Sch., 1956-70. Chmn. art com. UNICEF greeting cards, 1950-61, mem. com. Spence Chapin Sch., Philharm Soc., 1950's-60's. Author: Technique of Barbara Schwinn, 1956, World of Fashion Art, 1968; illustrator mags. including Vogue, 1930's, Ladies Home Jour., Saturday Evening Post, Colliers, Good Housekeeping, Cosmopolitan, McCall's, American, Town and Country, 1940's-60's, Women's Jour., Eng., Hors Zu, Fed. Republic Germany, Marie Claire, France, other fgn. publs., 1950's-60's. Portrait painter, including Queen Sirikit, Princess Margaret, Princess Grace, Mrs. Alfred Lee Loomis, Conrad Hilton, Deborah Kerr; one-woman shows include Soc. of Illustrators, 1940, 50, Barry Stephens Gallery, 1950, Bodley Gallery, N.Y.C., 1971, 80, C.C., West Mifflin, Pa., 1973, Duquesne U., 1973, Mus. Am. Illustration, N.Y.C., 1991, Illustration House, N.Y.C., 1991, Giraffics Gallery, East Hampton, N.Y., 1991-2002 (also rep.), 1999, Seventh Regiment Armory, 1991-2002; exhibited in group shows including NAD, 1955, Royal Acad., London, Guild Hall, N.Y., 1981, Summit N.J. Art Ctr., 1981, Meredith Long Gallery, Houston, 1983, Mus. Soc. Illustrators, N.Y., 1985, The Marcus Gallery, Santa Fe, 1985, 86, The Gerald Peters Gallery, Santa Fe, 1985, 86, Brandywine Mus., Pa., 1986, New Britain (Conn.) Mus. Am. Art, 1986, Armory Show, N.Y.C., 1992-94, The Women's Ctr., Chapel Hill, N.C., 1993-94, Greenville County Mus. Art, S.C., 1995, The Soc. of the Four Arts, Palm Beach, Fla., 1995, The Hyde Collection, Glen Falls, N.Y., 1985, Ga. Mus. Art, 1995, Heckscher Mus., L.I., N.Y., 1995; works represented Holbrook Collection, Ga. Mus. Art, Eureka Coll., Ill., New Britain Mus. Am. Art, Mus. of Soc. of Illustrators, N.Y.C., Brandywine Mus., Pa., Sanford Low Meml. Collection, Del. Art Mus., Wilmington, Mus. Am. Illustration, N.Y.C., Glenbow Mus., Calgary, Alberta, Can.; represented in traveling show Del. Art Mus. 1994-95, The Mus. York County, Rock Hill, S.C., 2002-; various pvt. and gallery collections; work featured in America's Great Women Illustrators 1850-1950, 1985. Winner prizes Art Dirs. Club, 1950, Guild Hall, 1969. Assoc. mem. Guggenheim Mus., mem. Cosmopolitan Club N.Y. Home: 579 Fearrington Post Pittsboro NC 27312 8570

SCHWOY, LAURIE ANNETTE, professional soccer player; b. Balt., Feb. 14, 1978; Mem. U.S. Nat. Women's Soccer Team, 1997—, including U.S. Women's Cup, 1997; mem. Under-20 Women's Nat. Team, 1996—; including bronze medal team at Nordic Cup, 1996; championship team Nordic Cup, Denmark, 1997. Named Soccer Am. Freshman of Yr., 1996, ACC Rookie of Yr., 1996. Avocation: dance. Office: US Soccer Fedn 1801-1811 S Prairie Ave Chicago IL 60616

SCIACCHETANO, GAIL MARY, lawyer; b. Jersey City, N.J., June 10, 1952; d. John Vincent and Anna Veronica (Ciani) Sciacchetano; m. Kevin Casey Dopf, Nov. 2, 1975 (div. Mar. 27, 1998); 1 child, Adrienne Gail. BA cum laude, Seton Hall U., 1974; MA, Villanova U., 1975; JD, U. Louisville, 1982. Bar: Ky. 1989, Kans. 1993, Mo. 2001, diplomate: Am. Coll. Healthcare Execs. Staff counsel Ky. Hosp. Assn., Louisville, 1982—84; dir. cmty. rels. Good Samaritan Hosp., Suffern, NY, 1984—87; dir. quality care mgmt. Phelps County Med. Ctr., Rolla, Mo., 1989—91; risk mgr. Mid-Am. Rehab. Hosp., Overland Pk., Kans., 1992—96; spl. projects dir. Carondelet Health, Kans. City, Mo., 1996—2000; assoc. counsel Cath. Health Initiatives, Seattle, 2000; gen. counsel U. Physician Assocs., Kans. City, 2000—. Pres. Kans. City (Mo.) Health Care Attys., 1999—2000; bd. dirs. St. Joseph Hosp. Aux., Kans. City. Scholar, Villanova U., 1974—75. Mem.: ABA, Greater Kans. City (Mo.) Soc. Hosp. Attys. (past pres.), Mo. Soc. Healthcare Attys., Mo. Bar Assn., Ky. Bar Assn., Kans. City (Mo.) Metro Bar Assn. (chmn. healthcare providers com.), Kans. Bar Assn., Am. Health Lawyers Assn. (mem. in-house counsel), Am. Corp. Counsel Assn., Am. Coll. Healthcare Execs., Delta Theta Phi. Roman Cath. Avocations: music, photography, reading.

SCIALDO, MARY ANN, music educator, musician; b. Westchester, NY, Sept. 21, 1942; d. Camille George Scialdo. MusB, Seton Hill Coll., 1963; MusM, Pius XII Inst. Fine Arts, Florence, Italy, 1964; profl. diploma, Manhattan Sch. Music, 1978; postgrad., Peabody Cons. Cert. tchr. NY, Fla. Supr. music Great Barrington (Mass.) Sch. Sys., 1967—68; music, theater prof. Simons Rock Coll., Great Barrington, 1968—70, Cath. U. PR, Ponce, 1971; performing arts instr. Briarcliff Sch. Dist., 1981, Ossining (NY) Sch. Dist., 1982, Albert Leonard Jr. H.S., 1983, Pleasantville (NY) Sch. Dist., 1984; theater and music tchr. Briarcliff Manor Schs., 1984—98; music tchr. Hillsborough County Schs., Tampa, Fla., 1999—. Dir., prodr., mus. and vocal dir., set and costume numerous student prodns. Debut concert: Merkin Hall, N.Y.C., internat. debut concert: Glinka Mus.; performer: (fund raising concert) Chopin Found. NY, (Giannini retrospective) WQXR, WNCN, (CD) Scriabin 24 Preludes, Opus 11, 1998—99. Recipient Outstanding Drama Tchr. award, Emerson Coll., 1st place award, Young Artist Nat. Competition, Nat. Fedn. Music Clubs competition, Disting. Alumna Leadership award, Seton Hill U. Mem.: Sigma Alpha Iota (life). Democrat. Roman Catholic. Office: Webb Middle Sch 6035 Hanley Rd Tampa FL 33634-4913

SCIAMANDA SZPAK, SYLVIA ANNE, religious studies educator, director; b. Erie, Pa., June 16, 1948; d. Massino Joseph Sciamanda and Angeline Marie Torrelli Sciamanda; m. Michael Walter Szpak, Feb. 2, 1942; children: Angela Elizabeth Szpak, Walter Joseph Szpak, Joseph Joshua Szpak. BS in Edn., Villa Maria Coll., 1970; MEd in Reading Specialist, Wright State U., 1981. Cert. religious edn. Diocese of Columbus, Ohio, 1986; reading specialist Ohio, 1988, ednl. supr. Ohio, 1988, pers. mgmt. and logistical support USAF, 1972. Educator, elem. edn. Holy Rosary Sch., Erie, 1968—71; catechist Wright Patterson AFB Chapel, Dayton, Ohio, 1979—81; office mgr. Scioto Gastroenterology and Internal Medicine Inc., Portsmouth, Ohio, 1981—91; dir. religious edn. St. Mary's Ch., Portsmouth, 1982—86; educator religion, reading, speech Notre Dame Schs., Portsmouth, 1984—89; practice mgr. Digestive Disease Assocs., Albany, Ga., 1991—95; dir. religious edn. St. Teresa's Cath. Ch., Albany, 1993—; practice mgr. Jefferson Underwood Davis, DDS, Md, Albany, 1995—96. Educator devel. studies Darton Coll., Albany, 2001—. Mem. parish staff St. Teresa's Cath. Ch., Albany, 1993—2003. First lt. USAF, 1971—75. Decorated Air Force Commendation award Eglin AFB; recipient St. Ann's award, Girl Scouts Am., 1986. Avocations: digital publishing, public speaking. Home: 5330 Old Dawson Rd Albany GA 31721 Office: St Teresa's Catholic Church 421 Edgewood Ln Albany GA 31707 Personal E-mail: sciamanda@netzero.net. E-mail: sciamanda@netzero.net.

SCILLIA, DIANE GRAYBOWSKI, art historian, researcher; b. Queens, N.Y., Aug. 20, 1945; d. Joseph Francis and Grace Virginia (McNeil) G.; m. Charles Edward Scillia, June 9, 1968 (div. Apr., 1993); 1 child, Matthew Thomas; m. Robert D. Sweeney, Aug. 12, 2000. BA, SUNY, Stony Brook, 1967; PhD, Case Western Reserve U., 1975. Rsch. asst. Cleve. Mus. of Art, 1967-72; vis. lectr. Case Western Reserve U., Cleve, 1971-72, Franklin and Marshall Coll., Lancaster, Pa., 1974; adj. curator, asst. to dir. Chrysler Mus. of Art, Norfolk, Va., 1979-80; adj. asst. prof. Va. Wesleyan Coll., Norfolk, VA., 1980-84, Old Dominion U., Norfolk, 1982-84; asst. prof. art history Kent (Ohio) State U., 1985-91, assoc. prof. art history, 1992—2003, prof. art history, 2003—. Juror travel awards NEH, Washington, 1991, juror grants, 1992. Contbr. articles to profl. jours. and to the Encyclopedia Dutch Art. Mem. Coll. Art Assn., Scholars of Early Modern Europe, Historians of Netherlandish Art (sec.-treas. 1989-91), Mid-West Art Hist. Soc. (bd. dirs. 1992-95). Avocations: making art, reading, gardening. Home: 2941 Somerton Rd Cleveland Hts OH 44118-2044 Office: Kent State U Sch Of Art Kent OH 44242-0001

SCIOLINO, ELAINE, reporter; m. Andrew Plump; children: Alessandra, Gabriela. M of History, NYU, 1971; D (hon.), Syracuse U., Canusius Coll., Dowling Coll. Vaious positions Newsweek, 1970—84, foreign corr., 1978—80, bur. chief Rome, 1980—82, internat. corr. NYC, 1983—84; metropolitan reporter UN Newspapers, 1984, bur. chief, 1985-87; diplomatic corr. The NY Times, 1987-91, covered intelligence beat, 1991-92, chief diplomatic corr., 1992-96, sr. writer, Washington bur.; sr. fellow U.S. Inst. Peace, Washington, 1998. Edward R. Murrow Press Fellow Coun. on Foreign Rels., 1982—83. Author: The Outlaw State: Saddam Hussein's Quest for Power and the Gulf Crisis, 1991, Persian Mirrors: The Elusive Face of Iran, 2000. Recipient Page One Award, 1978, Nat. Headliners Award, 1981, Overseas Press Club citation, 1983, Helen Bernstein Book Award for Excellence in Journalism, NY Public Library, 2001.*

SCIORRA, ANNABELLA, actress; b. Wethersfield, Mar. 24, 1964; Appeared in films, including True Love, 1989, Internal Affairs, 1990, Cadillac Man, 1990, Reversal of Fortune, 1990, The Hard Way, 1991, Jungle Fever, 1991, The Hand That Rocks the Cradle, 1992, Whispers in the Dark, 1992, The Night We Never Met, 1993, Romeo is Bleeding, 1994, The Cure, 1995, The Addiction, 1995, The Funeral, 1996, Underworld, 1996, Copland, 1997, Mr. Jealousy, 1997, Highball, 1997, Underworld, 1997, Destination Anywhere, 1997, What Dreams May Come, 1998, New Rose Hotel, 1998, Little City, 1998, Sam the Man, 1999, King of the Jungle, 1999, American Crime, 2003, Chasing Liberty, 2004; (TV series) The Sopranos, 1999, 2001, 2002, Queens Supreme, 2003; (TV miniseries) Asteroid, 1997

SCITOVSKY, ANNE AICKELIN, economist, researcher; b. Ludwigshafen, Germany, Apr. 17, 1915; arrived in U.S., 1931, naturalized, 1938; d. Hans W. and Gertrude Margarete Aickelin; 1 child, Catherine Margaret. Student, Smith Coll., 1933—35; BA, Barnard Coll., 1937; postgrad., London Sch. Econs., 1937—39; MA in Econs., Columbia U., 1941. Mem. staff legis. reference svc. Libr. of Congress, 1941—44; mem. staff Social Security Bd., 1944—46; with Palo Alto (Calif.) Med. Found./Rsch. Inst., 1963—, chief health econs. div., 1973—94, sr. staff scientist, 1994—. Lectr. Inst. Health Policy Studies, U. Calif., San Francisco, 1975—94; mem. Inst. Medicine of NAS, Nat. Acad. Social Ins., Pres.'s Commn. for Study of Ethical Problems in Medicine and Biomed. and Behavioral Rsch., 1979—82, U.S. Nat. Com. on Vital and Health Stats., 1975—78, Health Resources and Svcs. Adminstrn., AIDS adv. com., 1990—94; cons. HHS, Inst. Medicine Coun. on Health Care Tech. Assessment, 1986—90. Home: 161 Erica Way Portola Valley CA 94028-7439 Office: Palo Alto Med Found Rsch Inst Ames Bldg 795 El Camino Real Palo Alto CA 94301-2302 E-mail: ascitovsky@aol.com.

SCLAFANI, SUSAN K. federal agency administrator; b. Albany, NY, Sept. 22, 1944; AB in German and Math. cum laude, Vassar Coll., 1966; MA in German Lang. and Lit., U. Chgo., 1967; ME in Ednl. Adminstrn., U. Tex., Austin, 1985, PhD, 1987. Cert. Tchr.Math. Ill., N.Y., Lifetime Tchr. Math. and German 6-12 Tex., Adminstr., Supt., Supr., Midmgr. Tex. Tchr. Ctrl. YMCA H.S., Chgo., 1971—72, Woodson Jr. H.S. Houston Ind. Sch. Dist., Tex., 1972—74, H.S. for Engring. Professions, Houston Ind. Sch. Dist., Tex., 1975—78; coord. magnet sch. Washington H.S. Houston Ind. Sch. Dist., 1978—83; ctrl. office coord. instrnl. tech. Houston Ind. Sch. Dist., Tex., 1983—84, exec. dir. curriculum devel., 1987—89, asst. supt. constrn. mgmt. and program planning, 1989—92, assoc. supt. dist. adminstrn., 1992—94, chief of staff, 1994—96, chief of staff ednl. svcs., 1996—2001; counselor to Sec. of Edn. U.S. Dept. Edn., Washington, 2001—04, acting sec., vocational & adult edn., 2003—04, asst. sec., vocational & adult edn., 2004—. V.p. and gen. mgr. Quantum Access, Inc., 1986—87; adj. prof. dept. curriculum and instrn. U. Houston, Tex., 1988—94, adj prof. dept. ednl. leadership, 1999—2001; presenter to numerous ednl. groups. Coauthor (with R. Paige): (Book) Strategies for Reforming Houston's Schools; School Choice or Best Systems, What Improves Education, 2001; contbr. articles to profl. jours. Vol. Star of Hope Women and Family Shelter, Houston, 1988—90; mem. com. Tex. Alliance for Minorities in Engring., Houston, 1975—85; activity vol., conf. spkr. Coun. for Exceptional Children, Houston, 1989—91; com. mem. Tex. Task Force for the Homeless, 1990—92; mem. Hispanic Youth Leadership Forum Steering Com., Houston, 1990—, Pub. Policy, Comty. and Agy. Support, Success by Six Comm., United Way, Houston, 1987—2001; chair Children's Policy Com. United Way, Houston, 1987—2001. Office: US Dept Edn Mary E Switzer Bldg 330 C St SW Rm 4090 Washington DC 20202-7110 E-mail: susan.sclafani@ed.gov.

SCOBEY, MARGARET, ambassador; b. Memphis; d. James and Delores Scobey. B in History, U. Tenn., 1971, M in History, 1973. Consular, Lima, 1981—83; polit. officer Peshawar, 1983—86; chief polit. sect. Jerusalem, 1990—91; polit. counselor U.S. Embassy, Kuwait, 1994—96; dep. chief of mission Sanaa, Yemen, 1996—99; dir. Office of Arabian Peninsula at Dept. of State, 2000—01; dep. chief of mission Am. Embassy, Riyadh, Saudi Arabia, 2001—03; amb. U.S. Embassy, Syria, 2003—. Staff asst. to asst. sec. Near East and South Asian Affairs; watch officer Operation Ctr.; polit. mil. officer Office of Israeli and Arab-Israeli Affairs, dep. dir. of sec. staff. Office: Embassy of USA Abou Roumaneh 2 Al Mansour St PO Box 29 Damascus Syria also: Embassy of USA Damascus Syria Dept State Washington DC 20521-6110*

SCODEL, RUTH, humanities educator; b. Columbus, Ohio, Feb. 29, 1952; d. Alvin and Barbara (Keith) S.; 1 child, Anna Gabrielle. AB, U. Calif., Berkeley, 1973; PhD, Harvard U., 1978. Asst. prof. Harvard Coll., Cambridge, Mass., 1978-83; assoc. prof. classics of Greek and Latin U. Mich., Ann Arbor, 1983-87, prof., 1987—, dir. LSA Honors program, 1991—97. Author: Trojan Trilogy of Euripides, 1980, Sophocles, 1984, Credible Impossibilities, 1999, Listening to Homer, 2002; editor Transactions of Am. Philol. Assn., 1986-91. Office: Univ Mich Dept Classical Studies Ann Arbor MI 48109

SCOGNO, STACIE JOY, financial services company executive; b. Camden, N.J., Dec. 5, 1957; d. Albert Joseph Scogno and Josephine Geovanni Fiorello. AAS, Bay State Coll., Boston, 1978; BS in mgmt., Boston Coll., 1986; cert. of mgmt. and spl. scis., Harvard Ext. Sch., 1994. Software sys. cons., owner North Shore Svcs., Boston, 1984-88; tech. cons. Lotus Devel. Corp., Boston, 1988-90; mgr. MIS Blackwell Sci. Publs., Boston, 1990-93; product design analyst Thomson Fin. Corp., Boston, 1993-95; sr. cons. The Hunters Group, Boston, 1995-96; N.E. regional mgr. nat. fin. systems Coopers & Lybrand, Boston, 1997—, co-dir. Natl. PeopleSoft Ctr. of Excellence, 1996—, dir. east region, 1998-99, dir. global programme office, 1999-2001; v.p. profl. svcs. Paradigm Tech., 2001—. Notary pub. Commonwealth of Mass., 1980—. Trustee Action Dance Theater, treas., 1980-91; bd. dirs. Friends of City Sq., Charlestown, Mass., 1996—. Avocations: triathlons, body building. Office: 30 S 17th St Philadelphia PA 19103-4001

SCOLL, EULALIE ELIZABETH, writer, researcher; b. Vancouver, Wash., Mar. 6, 1920; d. Frederick and Elizabeth (Williamson) Laws; m. James Leslie Hildebrand; children; James, Frederick. BS, Women's U. Tex., 1941; MS, Salve Regina U., 1989, PhD, 1996. Engring. draftsman for Dr. Urey Manhattan Project, N.Y.C.; high fashion designer N.Y.C. Interior decorator. Author: The Role and Abuse of Women as Portrayed in Three Dostoevsky's Major Novels, 1989, Nietzsche Journal of Antichrist Tibetan Buddhism Versus Christianity, 1991, Dostoevsky's Sonya and Martha: Fiction and Reality, 1996. Mem. AAUW, Am. Assn. Advancement Slavic Studies, Nat. Trust for Historic Preservation, Nat. Mus. Women in the Arts, Am. Soc. Phys. Rsch., Inc., The Authors Guild, Inc., Newport Preservation Soc., Newport Hist. Soc., Asian Soc., Naval War Found., Internat. Dostoevsky Soc., Bailey's Beach Oldest Beach Club Am. Home: Cave Cliff 11 Chastellux Ave Newport RI 02840-3811

SCOTCHMER, SUZANNE ANDERSEN, economics educator; b. Seattle, Jan. 23, 1950; d. Toivo Matthias and Margaret (Sangder) Andersen. BA in Econ., U. Wash., 1970; MA in Stats., U. Calif., Berkeley, 1979, PhD in Econ., 1980. From asst. to assoc. prof. econ. Harvard U., Cambridge, Mass., 1981-86; prof. econ. and pub. policy U. Calif., Berkeley, 1986—. Vis. prof. Toronto Sch. Law, 1993, Tel Aviv U., 1994, U. Paris, Sonbonne, 1992, New Sch. of Econ., Moscow, 1993, U. Aukland, 2002; prin. investigator NSF, 1986-2002; lectr. in law. Mem. editl. bd. Am. Econ. Rev., 1991-95, Jour. Pub. Econ., 1986-2001, Jour. Econ. Perspectives, 1994-97, Regional Sci. and Urban Econ., 1991—, Jour. Econ. Lit., 1998—; contbr. articles to profl. jours. Hoover Nat. fellow Stanford U., 1989, Olin fellow Yale Sch. Law, 1991, Sloan fellow, 1979, Phi Beta Kappa fellow, 1978; France/Berkeley Fund grantee, 1994-95. Office: Univ Calif 2607 Hearst Ave Berkeley CA 94720-7320

SCOTLAND, SUSAN JANE, artist, art educator; b. Oakland, Calif., Feb. 01; d. Marie M. Sutton; 1 child, Spencer Joseph. BA, U. Tex., 1992; studied painting with Neal Wilson and Veronica Fernandez, Tex. State U. Cert. tchg. State of Tex. Tchr. Waco (Tex.) Sch. Dist., 1993—; represented by Amsterdam Whitney Gallery, N.Y.C. Author various poetry. Mem.: Art Ctr. Waco, Mus. of Art, Austin Tex., Mexic Arte Mus., Art House at Jones Ctr., Women and Their Works. Independent. Avocations: theater, tennis, travel, painting. Office Phone: 251-715-1326.

SCOTT, ADRIENNE, social worker, psychotherapist; b. N.Y.C. BA, Finch Coll., 1957; postgrad., NYU, 1958-62, MA in English, 1958; MSW, Adelphi U., 1988. Mem. English faculty Fordham U., N.Y.C., 1966-68; editor-in-chief Blueboy Mag., Miami, Fla., 1974; editor "M" Mag., N.Y.C., 1976; mem. English faculty NYU, 1958-65; pres. Googolplex Video, N.Y.C., 1981-86; clin. social worker Mt. Sinai Hosp., N.Y.C., 1988-93, Stuyvesant Polyclinic, N.Y.C., 1993-95. Presenter Nat. Methadone Conf., 1992. Author: Film as Film, 1970; contbg. editor Menstyle Mag., 1995; contbr. articles to numerous mags., including Vogue, Interview, N.Y. mag.; pioneer in fashion video; videographer documentaries; performance artist in Robert Wilson's King of Spain, 1973. Mem. exec. com. Adopt-An-AIDS Rschr. Program Rockefeller U.; nat. co-chairperson Gay Rights Nat. Lobby, 1976. Mem. NASW (cert.), AAUW, Assn. for Psychoanalytic Self Psychology, Am. Psychoanalytic Assn. (assoc.). Home: 165 E 66th St New York NY 10021-6132 Office: 7 Patchin Pl New York NY 10011-8341 E-mail: freudnut@aol.com.

SCOTT, ALICE HOLLY, retired librarian; b. Jefferson, Ga. d. Frank D. and Annie D. (Colbert) Holly; m. Alphonso Scott, Mar. 1, 1959; children—Christopher, Alison AB, Spelman Coll., Atlanta, 1957; M.L.S., Atlanta U., 1958; PhD, U. Chgo., 1983. Librarian Bklyn. Pub. Library, 1958-59; br. librarian Chgo. Pub. Library, 1959-72, dir. Woodson Regional Library, 1974-77, dir. community relations, 1977-82, dep. commr., 1982-87, asst. commr., 1987-98; ret., 1998. Doctoral fellow, 1973 Mem. ALA (councilor 1982-85), Chgo. Spelman Club, DuSable Mus., Chgo. Urban League Democrat. Baptist.

SCOTT, ANNE BYRD FIROR, history educator; b. Montezuma, Ga., Apr. 24, 1921; d. John William and Mary Valentine (Moss) Firor; m. Andrew Mackay Scott, June 2, 1947; children: Rebecca, David MacKay, Donald MacKay. AB, U. Ga., 1941; MA, Northwestern U., 1944; PhD, Radcliffe Coll., 1958; LHD (hon.), Lindenwood Coll., 1968, Queens Coll., 1985, Northwestern U., 1989, Radcliffe Coll., 1990, U. of the South, 1990, Cornell Coll., 1991. Congressional rep., editor LWV of U.S., 1944-53; lectr. history Haverford Coll., 1957-58, U. N.C., Chapel Hill, 1959-60; asst. prof. history Duke U., Durham, N.C., 1961-67, assoc. prof., 1968-70, prof., 1971-80, W.K. Boyd prof., 1980-91, W.K. Boyd prof. emerita, 1992—, chmn. dept., 1981-85; Gastprofessor Universität, Bonn, Germany, 1992-93. Vis. prof. Johns Hopkins U., 1972-73, Stanford U., 1974, Harvard U., 1984, Cornell Coll., 1993, Williams Coll., 1994, U. Miss., 2000; Times-Mirror scholar Huntington Libr., 1995; vice chmn. Nat. Humanities Ctr., 1991-98; mem. adv. com. Schlesinger Libr.; lectr. in field. Author: The Southern Lady, 1970, 25th anniversary edit., 1995, (with Andrew MacKay Scott) One Half the People, 1974, Making the Invisible Woman Visible, 1984, Natural Allies, 1991; editor: Jane Addams, Democracy and Social Ethics, 1964, The American woman, 1970, Women in American Life, 1970, Women and Men in American Life, 1976, Unheard Voices, 1993; mem. editl. bd. Revs. in Am. History, 1976-81, Am. Quar., 1974-78, Jour. So. History, 1978-84; contbr. articles to profl. jours. Chmn. Gov.'s Commn. on Status of Women, 1963-64; mem. Citizens Adv. Council on Status of Women U.S., 1964-68; trustee Carnegie Corp., 1977-85, W.W. Ctr. for Scholars, 1977-84; chmn. bd. dirs. Nat. Cmty. Investment Fund, 1996—2002. AAUW fellow, 1956-57; grantee NEH, 1967-68, 76-77, Nat. Humanities Ctr., 1980-81; grad. medal Radcliffe Coll., 1986, Duke U. medal, 1991, John Caldwell medal N.C. Humanities Coun., 1994; fellow Ctrl. Advanced Study in Behavioral Sci., 1986-87; Fulbright scholar, 1984, 92-93. Mem. Am. Antiquarian Soc., Orgn. Am. Historians (exec. bd. 1973-76, pres. 1983, Disting. Pub. Svc. award 2002), So. Hist. Assn. (exec. bd. 1976-79, pres. 1989), Soc. Am. Historians, Phi Beta Kappa. Democrat. Office: Duke U Dept History Durham NC 27708 E-mail: ascott2@email.unc.edu., ascott@acpub.duke.edu.

SCOTT, BERNICE G. county official; b. Nov. 16, 1944; d. Alexander and Adeline Finch Green; m. Thomas Edward Gilmore, Feb. 25, 1987; children: Valerie La-Mon Scott Washington, Kent Orlando. AA (with honors), Midlands Tech. Coll., 1976. Tax collector Richland County Treasurer's Ofc., Columbia, S.C., 1979-85; asst. clerk of coun. Richland County Council, Columbia, 1984-85; ombudsman Richland County Adminstrn., Columbia, 1985-87; courtroom asst., court adminstrn. Richland County Court Adminstrn., Columbia, 1987-88; paralegal Lewis, Rogers & Lark P.A., Columbia, 1993—. Coun. mem. Richland County, Columbia, S.C., 1988—; mem. Mt. Nebo Bapt. Ch. (sr. choir pres., young adult sch. tchr., usher bd., deacon bd. mem.); appointed mem. transition team Gov.-elect James Hodges, S.C., 1998; chairperson Richland County Devel. and Svcs. com., 1996; mem. Lower Richlarnd Devel. Coun.; chairperson of bd. Lower Richland Cmty. Health Care Assn. Mem. Nat. Assn. of Counties, Nat. Assn. of Black County Officials. Office: Office County Council PO Box 192 Columbia SC 29202-0192

SCOTT, BRENDA D. writer; b. Tampa-Sneads, Fla. d. Alonzie III and Felicia (Lopez) Scott. Diploma in child guidance, Lively Vocat. Tech. Ctr., Tallahassee, 1987; AA in Sci. Edn., Tallahassee CC, 1993; BS in Reading Edn., Fla. State U., 1995; AA in Criminal Justice, Tallahassee CC, 2000. Contbr. poetry to mags., other publs including Internat. Women's Writing Guild; author: (screenplay) Surprise (Guild Membership movie), 1998, Mrs. Jellie Mae's Store, 1999, poetry book, Down-Home-News, 2000. Mem. West Fla. Literary Assn., Am. Black Book Writers Assn., Acad. Am. Poets, Internat. Soc. Poets, Women Ministering Biblically. Democrat. African Meth. Episcopalian. Avocations: reading, writing, movies, church activities, sports. Home and Office: PO Box 171 Sneads FL 32460-0171

SCOTT, CAROL LEE, child care educator; b. Monte Vista, Colo., Jan. 10, 1944; d. Robert A. and Thelma G. (Allen) Jay; m. Bates E. Shaw, June 4, 1966 (dec. Feb. 1976); children: Crystal A., Sharon L.; m. James W. Scott, July 23, 1977. BA in Home Econs., Friends U., 1965; MS, Okla. State U., 1973. Cert. in family and consumer scis., child and parenting specialist; lic. profl. counselor. Receptionist Cen. Assembly of God Ch., Wichita, Kans., summer 1965; office worker Henry's Inc., Wichita, 1965-66; tchr. home econs. Wichita High Sch. South, 1966, Cir. High Sch., Towanda, Kans., 1966-68, Fairfax (Okla.) High Sch., 1968-74; tchr. vocat. home econs. Derby (Kans.) High Sch., 1974-75; child devel. specialist Bi-State Mental Health Found., Ponca City, Okla., 1975-87; instr. child care Pioneer Tech. Ctr., Ponca City, 1987-98, dir., 1987-89, 93-98; training, curriculum splist. Tinker AFB, Ponca City, Okla., 1998—2001; dir. CDC East Tinker AFB, Okla., 2001—. Cons. Phil Fitzgerald Assocs. Archs., Ponca City, 1980, Head Start Okla., 1981-86; trainer, paraprofl. Child Care Careers, 1980—; validator Early Childhood programs, Nat. Assn. Edn. Young Children 1992—; adj. faculty Rose State Coll., Midwest City, Okla., 2002-. Contbg. author Child Abuse Prevention Mini Curriculum. Mem. sch. bd. Ponca City Schs., 1982-85, title IV-A parent com., 1985-89; area chmn. Heart Fund, 1985; chmn. edn. com. Dist. XVII Child Abuse Prevention Task Force, Okla., 1985-98, treas., 1989-98; mem. cultural affairs com. Ponca City Adv. Bd., 1986-89; co-chair Week of the Young Child Com. for Kay County, 1991-98; mem. curriculum adv. com. Ctr. Early Childhood Profl. Devel., Univ. Okla., 1998-. Mem. Am. Assn. Family and Consumer Scis., Okla. Assn. Family and Consumer Scis., Early Childhood Assn. Okla., (sec. 1999, 2000), So. Early Childhood Assn., No. Okla. Early Childhood Assn. (chmn. 1992-93, 93-94, exec. com. at-large 1994-98), Mid Del. Early Childhood Assn. (pres. 2002), Nat. Assn. for Edn. Young Children. Republican. Methodist. Home: 205 Wimbledon Rd Midwest City OK 73130-4917 Office: 72MSGI/SVYE 6120 Arnold St Tinker Afb OK 73145-8106

SCOTT, CATHERINE DOROTHY, librarian, information consultant; b. June 21, 1927; d. Leroy Stearns Scott and Agnes Frances (Meade) Scott Schellenberg. AB in English, Cath. U. Am., 1950, MS in Libr. Sci., 1955. Asst. libr. Export-Import Bank USA, Washington, 1951-55, Nat. Assn. Home Builders, 1955-62, reference libr., 1956-62; founder, chief tech. libr. Bellcomm, Inc., subs. AT&T, 1962-72; chief libr. Nat. Air, Space Mus. Smithsonian Instn., 1972-82, chief libr. Mus. Reference Ctr., 1982-88, sr. reference libr., 1989-95; info. cons., 1995—. Presdl. appointee, mem. Nat. Commn. Librs., Info. Sci., 1971—76; bd. visitors Cath. U. Am. Libr. Sci. Sch., Librs., 1984—93. Editor: International Handbook of Aerospace Awards and Trophies, 1980, 81; guest editor: Aeronautics and Space Flight Collections, 1985, in Spl. Collections, 1984. Vice chmn. DC Rep. Com., Washington, 1960—68; mem. platform com. Rep. Nat. Com., 1964; del. Rep. Nat. Conv., San Francisco, 1964; sec. Rep. Nat. Com., Washington, 1968; del. Rep. Nat. Conv., Miami, Fla., 1968. Named to Hon. Order Ky. Cols., 1968; recipient Sec.'s Disting. Svc. award Smithsonian Instn., 1976, Alumni Achievement award Cath. U. Am., 1977, Century Circle, 1998—, Disting. Fed. Svc. Nat. Commn. Libr. and Info. Sci. medal, 1985. Mem.: Am. Soc. of Info. Sci, League Rep. Women DC (bd. dirs. 1995—97, nominating com. 1996—97, contbg. mem. 1999—), Nat. Fedn. Rep. Women, Cath. U. Am. Devel. Com., Friends of Cath. U. Librs. (founder, pres. 1984—88, exec. coun. 1984—96, sustaining mem. 1998—), Internat. Fedn. Libr. Assns. (del. 1976, 1983, 1985, 1988—89), Nat. Mus. Women in Arts, Am. Soc. Assn. Execs., Spl. Librs. Assn. (assn. pres., Washington chapt. pres. 1973—74, DCSLA, cons. com. 1976—91, award com. 1990—91, pres. elect 1991—92, assn. pres., Washington chapt. pres. 1973—74, pres. 1992—93, aerospace divsn., assn. pres. elect 1992—93, immediate past pres. 1993—94, chair assn. awards and honors 1994—95, chmn. cons. com. 1994—98, anniversary com. aerospace divsn. 1995, convenor ret. causus 1997—99, conf. program facilitator Indpls. 1998, conf. program facilitator Mpls. 1999, conf. program facilitator Phila. 2000, conf. program facilitator San Antonio 2001, conf. program facilitator LA 2002, conf. program facilitator NYC 2003), WW in Am. (hon.), Capital Yacht Club, Cent. Club, Legacy Club. Fax: (202) 483-9223..

SCOTT, CONCETTA CIOTTI, artist, art educator; b. Phila., Jan. 17, 1927; d. Giulio J. Ciotti and Adelina D'Andrea; m. Pierre Brutsche Scott, Apr. 20, 1963; children: Elizabeth Ann, Christopher John. Assocs. Degree, Moore Coll. Art and Design, 1951; student, The Embroiders Guild Am., INc., 1967—78, No. Va. C.C., Woodbridge, Va., 1988. Graphics designer/illustrator, freelance artist various advt. agys. and dept. stores, Phila., 1946—54; art tchr. grades 1-12 Melrose Acad., Melrose Park, Pa., 1951—54; designer ads/direct mail The Hecht Co., Washington, 1954—56; designer, art dir. Woodward and Lothrop Stores, Washington, 1956—63; freelance artist Alexandria, McLean, Va., 1963—66; art tchr. St. Luke's Sch., McLean, 1974—75; art tchr., cons. The Montessori Sch. McLean, 1975—98. McLean rep. Fairfax County Coun. of the Arts, Annandale, Va., 1988—93. Cover-illustrations, Roster of the Nat. League Am. Pen Women, 1982, 1984, rhyme and play book, Move Over Mother Goose, 1987, one-woman shows include Atrium Gallery, Falls Ch., Va., 2003, McLean Art Juried Show, 2003, Arlington Free Clinic, 2003, Brookside Gardens Gallery, Wheaton, Md., 1989, The Charles Sumner Sch. Mus., Washington, 1990, The Manor House Gallery, Green Spring, Alexandria, Va., 1991, Nat. Inst. Health Galleries, Bethesda, Md., 1992, GTE Govt. Sys. Corp., Chantilly, Va., 1993, Barry Gallery, Marymount U., Arlington, Va., 1994, The Asman Gallery, NBC-TV Studios, Washington, 1995, The Clin. Ctr. Galleries, NIH, Bethesda, Md., 1996, La Vignette, Dinan, Brittany, France, 1999, Gallery West, Goodwin House West, Falls Church, Va., 1999, The Asman Gallery, NBC-TV Studios, Washington, 2000, Gallery Walk, Goodwin House, East, Alexandria, Va., 2000, The Manor House Gallery, Green Spring, 2001, Atrium Gallery, Fairfax, 2003, two-persons shows, The XXth Century Gallery, Williamsburg, Va., 1991, The Sporting Club Gallery, McLean, 1992, Georgetown Med. Ctr. Gallery, Washington, 1996, Am. Hort. Soc., River Farm, Alexandria, 1997, U.S. Geol. Survey Gallery, Reston, Va., 2001, internat. exhbn., Miniature Painters, Sculptors and Gravers Washington, 1993, 1997—2003, Miniature Arts Soc. Fla., Dunedin, 2000, 2001, Seaside Gallery Miniature Paintings Show, Nags Head, N.C., 2001, exhibitions include Nat. League Am. Pen Women, Roanoke, Va., 1985, Furman U., S.C., 1987, Fells Point Gallery, Balt., 1994, 1997, 1998, 1999, numerous group shows including, Nat. League Am. Pen Women, George MAson U., 2000, exhibited in group shows at Va. Watercolor Soc., Martinsville, Va., 2000, Phila. Watercolor Soc., Atlantic City, 2000, McLean Art Club, Emerson Gallery, 2000, Arts Coun. Fairfax, Annandale, Va., 2000, Balt. Watercolro Soc., Bethesda, Md., 2001, Va. Watercolor Soc., Richmond, 2001, Washington Water Color Assn., Bethesda, 2001, Ctrl. Va. Watercolor Guild, Charlottesville, 2001, Berryville-Clarke County Coun., Millwood, Va., 2001, Art League/Torpedo Factory, Alexandria, 2001, Phila. Watercolor Soc., The Am. Coll., Bryn Mawr, Pa., 2001, Atlantic City, 2002, Art League, 2002, Internat. Miniature Shows, 2002, Splash 6 Book 4, 2000, Elan Mag., Sept., 2000, exhibited in group shows at Art League, 2003, Intenet Miniature Shows, 2003, Left Bank Cafe, 2003. Vol. art tchr. grades 1-3 Churchill Rd. Sch., McLean, 1972; aide 4H Club, McLean, Great Falls, 1973—75; vol. mail and phones Dem. Party, Washington, 1960. Recipient Distinctive Merit award, Art Dirs. Club Washington, 1961, 1962, 1963, grant, artist residency, Les Amis de La Grande Vigne, 1999; fellow P.P. Morris Grad. fellow, Moore Coll. Art and Design, Phila., 1951. Mem.: Nat. League Am. Pen Women (art editor 1980—82, biennial conv. chmn. 1983—84), Vienna Arts Soc. (lectr. miniature painting 2004), Fairfax Art League (workship instr. miniature painting 2003, group shows 2003), The Art League, Miniature Arts Soc. Fla., Miniature Painters, Sculptors and Gravers Soc. Washington, McLean Art Club (show chmn. 1977, program chair 2003—04), Potomac Valley Watercolorists (publicity/telephone 1996—98), Washington Water Color Assn. (show chmn. 1996—2001, show co-chmn. 2002—), Balt. Watercolor Soc. (signature), Phila. Water Color Soc. (signature), Va. Watercolor Soc. (art bd. 1993, signature, awards com.). Roman Catholic. Avocations: photography, reading, music, opera. Home: 1111 Dead Run Dr Mc Lean VA 22101

SCOTT, DEBORAH EMONT, curator; b. Passaic, N.J. d. Harold and Rhoda (Baumgarten) Emont; m. George Andrew Scott, June 4, 1983; children: Meredith Suzanne, Diana Faith. BA, Rutgers U., Livingston Coll., 1973; MA, Oberlin Coll., 1979. Asst. curator Allen Meml. Art Mus., Oberlin, Ohio, 1977-79; curator collections Memphis Brooks Mus. Art, 1979-83; curator The Nelson-Atkins Mus. Art, Kansas City, 1983—, chief curator, 1998—. Project dir. Kansas City Sculpture Pk., 1986-01. Author: (catalogue) Alan Shields, 1983, (essay) Jonathan Borofsky, 1988, (essay) Judith Shea, 1989, (interview) John Ahearn, 1990, (essay) Gerhard Richter, 1990, (essay) Kathy Muehlemann, 1991, (essay) Nate Fors, 1991, (essay) Julian Schnabel, 1991, (essay) Louise Bourgeois, 1994, (essay) Joel Shapiro, 1995, (essay) Lewis deSoto, 1996, (catalogue) Ursula von Rydingsvard, 1997; contbr.: Celebrating Moore: Works from the Collection of the Henry Moore Foundation, Selected by David Mitchinson, 1998, Modern Sculpture at The Nelson-Atkins Museum of Art: An Anniversary Celebration, 1999, (CD ROM) Masterworks for Learning: A College Collection Catalogue, Allen Memorial Art Museum, Oberlin College, 1998. Office: Nelson-Atkins Mus Art 4525 Oak St Kansas City MO 64111-1873

SCOTT, DEBORAH L. costume designer; Costume designer: (films) E.T. The Extra-Terrestrial, 1982, Twilight Zone-The Movie ("Kick the Can", "Nightmare at 20,000 Feet"), 1983, Back to the Future, 1985, About Last Night..., 1986, Armed and Dangerous, 1986, Who's That Girl?, 1987, Moving, 1988, Coupe de Ville, 1990, Defending Your Life, 1991, Eve of Destruction, 1991, Sliver, 1993, Jack the Bear, 1993, Legends of the Fall, 1994, Indian in the Cupboard, 1995, To Gillian on Her 37th Birthday, 1996, Titanic, 1997 (Acad. award 1998), Wild Wild West, 1999, The Patriot, 2000, Minority Report, 2001. Recipient Academy award, 1998.

SCOTT, DONNA C. human resources specialist; b. Danville, Ky., Dec. 12, 1953; d. Hubert Gladson and Winifred Ann Carpenter; m. Larry David Pike, Mar. 13, 1971 (div. May 1975); m. Gary Leland Scott, Sept. 5, 1981. BA Bus. Adminstrn., Lindsey Wilson Coll., 1993. Material planner Modine, Harrodsburg, Ky., 1984—91; lead material planner Clark Material Handling Co., Danville, Ky., 1991—95; sr. buyer Denyo Mfg. Corp., Danville, 1995—97; logistics specialist Caterpillar, Inc., Danville, 1997—98; scheduling supr., human resources specialist Dana Brake Parts, Inc., Stanford, Ky., 1999—. Home: 10583 Main St Mackville KY 40040

SCOTT, EILEEN ROSE, retail executive; b. Jersey City, Apr. 4, 1953; d. James Anthony and Margaret Rita (D'Errico) S. BSBA, William Paterson Coll., 1976. Asst. store mgr. Supermarket's Gen. Corp. Pathmark Div., Woodbridge, NJ, 1976-79, buyer, 1979-82, buying supr., 1982-85; sales mgr. Pathmark, Carteret, NJ, dir. sales, 1989, exec. v.p. store ops., 2001—01, CEO, 2002—. Mem. Ea. Dairy Deli Assn. Democrat. Roman Catholic. Home: 506 Horizon Way Neshanic Station NJ 08853-4042 Office: Pathmark Stores Inc 200 Milik St Carteret NJ 07008-1102

SCOTT, ELOISE HALE, state legislator; b. Benton County, Miss., Jan. 24, 1932; m. Lex B. Scott; children: Kenny, Kimble. BS, Miss. U. for Women; MA, U. Miss. Mem. Miss. Ho. of Reps. Chmn. edn. com., mem. labor appropriations, banks and banking, and ethics coms. Active Lee County Ext. Svc. Mem. LWV, Dem. Women. Methodist. Democrat. Office: Miss State House State Capitol Jackson MS 39201 Home: 1275 Winwood Cv Tupelo MS 38801-6472

SCOTT, FRANCES FISHER MARKOE, retired secondary school educator; b. Frederick, Md., July 4, 1935; d. Oscar Daniel Fisher, Pearl Edna Burkett; m. Thurbie Keith Markoe, Dec. 29, 1953 (div. Apr. 1973); 1 child, Kevin Thurbie Markoe ; m. Russell Bert Scott, Feb. 7, 1976; stepchildren: Jeffrey R., Clifton W. Student, U. Md., 1957—58; AA, Hartnell Coll., 1969; BA, San Jose State U., 1971, diploma credential program, 1971—72; advanced profl. credential, Prince George's County Profl. Devel., 1976—78. Sub. tchr. Pajard Unified Sch. Dist., Watsonville, Calif., 1971—72; tchr. adult edn. Morgan Hill Sch. Dist., Morgan Hill, Calif., 1972—74; tchr. Santa Cruz City Sch., Santa Cruz, Calif., 1972—75, DuVall Sr. H.S., Prince George's County, Md., 1976—77, Oxon Hill H.S., Oxon Hill, Md., 1977—2003; ret., 2003. Mem.: Md. States Accreditation (chmn. secondary schs. home econs. com. 1981—82). Avocation: Avocations: snow skiing, nutrition, boating. Home: 6806 Berkshire Dr Temple Hills MD 20748-4031 Office: Oxon Hill High Sch 6701 Leyte Dr Oxon Hill MD 20745

SCOTT, GLORIA RANDLE, college president; b. Apr. 14, 1938; d. Freeman and Juanita (Bell) Randle; m. Will Braxton Scott. AB, Ind. U., 1959, MA, 1960, PhD, 1965, LLD, 1977; DHL, Fairleigh Dickinson U., 1978, Westfield State Coll., 1992, Wilson Coll., 1992, Mt. Vernon Coll., Marian Coll., 1999. Rsch. assoc. in genetics Inst. Psychiat. Rsch. Ind. U. Med. Ctr., Indpls., 1961-63; instr. biology Marian Coll., Indpls., 1961-65; dean students Knoxville (Tenn.) Coll., 1965-67; asst. to pres. N.C. Agrl. and Tech. State U., 1967-68, prof., 1967-76, dir. planning Inst. Rsch., 1973-76; prof. Tex. So. U., 1976-78; v.p., prof. Clark Coll., 1978-86; prof. Grambling State U., 1987; pres. Bennett Coll., Greensboro, N.C., 1987-2001, founder Women's Leadership Inst., 1989; owner Scott's Bau Enterprises on Baffin Bay, Riviera, Tex., 1973-98. Sec. bd. dirs., founder Africa U., Mutare, Zimbabwe, 1988-97; bd. dirs. Loew Corp.; vice chair Women's Coll. Coalition, 1990-94. Del. hed UN Decade for Women Internat. Forum, Nairobi, Kenya, 1985; chmn. del. UN Decade for Women Conf., Beijing, 1995; chmn. bd. Nat. Scholarship Fund for Negro Students, 1984-85; 1st v.p. Girl Scouts U.S., 1972-75, pres., 1975-78; bd. dirs. Wilson Coll., 1978-83, Nat. Urban League, 1976-85; mem bd. visitors Ind. U. Sch. Edn., Bloomington, 1988-94; bd. dirs. United Negro Coll. Fund, 1993-95, chair golden anniversary com., 1992-95; chiar edn. adv. com. Delta Sigma Theta, 1989—; mem. adv. bd. James McGregor Leadership Acad., Md. Md., 2000—; mem. divsn. III president's coun. NCAA, 1998-2001; founder Nat. African Am. Women's Leadership Inst., 1999; mentor Leadership Inst., 1997-98; mem. Internat. Women's Forum; chmn. Coun. Presidents Black Coll. Fund, UMC, 1997-99. Recipient Drum Major for Justice award, 1993, N.C. Gov's. award for Outstanding N.C. Women, 1991, Achievement award Delta Sigma Theta, 1994. Mem. Rotary (organizing founder East Greensboro 2000-01). Office: Bennett Coll 900 E Washington St Greensboro NC 27401-3239 E-mail: randle@rivnet.com.

SCOTT, JANE WOOSTER, artist; b. Phila. d. Martin J. Wurster and Irella Jacobs; m. Vernon Scott (div. 1990); children: Vernon IV, Ashley. BA, Harcum Jr. Coll. One person shows include Ankrum Gallery, Beverly Hills, Calif., 1972-75, De Ville Gallery, Beverly Hills, 1976-78, Grand Cen. Gallery, N.Y.C., 1977-79, Petersen Gallery, Beverly Hills, 1980-86, Wentworth Gallery, 1990-95, Gallery Vendome, Beverly Hills, 2002; works featured in (book) An America Jubilee: The Art of Jane Wooster Scott. Recipient Disting. Alumnae award Friends Cen., Pa., 1987; Most Reproduced Artist in Am., Guinness Book of World Records.

SCOTT, JEAN A. university president; B in History, U. Richmond, 1968; M in History, Harvard U., 1969, PhD in History, 1974. Asst. prof. history Duke U., dir. admission; dean undergrad. admission Case We. Res. U., Ohio; assoc. provost acad. adminstrn., dean admissions Coll. William and Mary, Williamsburg, Va., 1989-94; v.p. enrollment and student svcs. SUNY, Potsdam, 1994—. Office: Potsdam Coll Pierrepont Ave Potsdam NY 13676-2294

SCOTT, JENNIFER MARIE, special education educator; b. Royal Oak, Mich., Dec. 10, 1973; d. Bruce Craven and Mary Helen Best Scott. BA in Sci. and Psychology, Purdue U., 1996; MS in Edn., Ind. U., 1998, postgrad., 2003. Cert. tchr. learning disabled/mentally handicapped Ind., dist. adminstr. Ind. Paraprofessional spl. edn. Paoli (Ind.) Jr. Sr. H.S., 1996—97; ADL supr., instr. Orange County Devel. and Rehab. Ctr./First Chance Ctr., Paoli, 1997—98; spl. edn. tchr. K-12 Medora (Ind.) Cmty. Schs., 1999; spl. edn. tchr. K-6 New Albany-Floyd County Schs., Georgetown, Ind., 1999—2002; assoc. instr., field experience supr. Ind. U., Bloomington, 2002—03; spl. edn. tchr. 9-12 Westfield (Ind.) Washington Schs., 2003—. Corp. joint spl. edn. adv. com. New Albany/Floyd County Sch. Corp., 2001—02; mem. leadership team com. Georgetown Elem. Sch., 2001—02, PTA sci. fair chmn., 1999—2001. RCIA sponsor St.Paul's Cath. Ch., Bloomington, 2002—03. Mem.: Ind. U. Sch. Administrs. Assn., Assn. Supervision and Curriculum, Coun. for Exceptional Children (polit. action com. 2003), Nat. Alliance for Mentally Ill, Pi Lambda Theta, Phi Delta Kappa. Democrat. Roman Catholic. Avocations: skiing, running, travel, reading. Home: 3916 Knickerbocker Pl Apt # 2A Indianapolis IN 46240 Office: Westfield Washington Schs Westfield IN Office Phone: 317-513-1678. Personal E-mail: jenstarski7@hotmail.com.

SCOTT, JOYCE, writer; d. Charles William and Emma Reardon; m. Edward Dale Scott, Sept. 13, 1971; 1 child, Tonia Louise. Student, Inst. Children's Lit., 1984, student, 1993, Long Ridge Writers Group, 1994. Mem.: The Internat. Women's Writing Guild, Soc. Children's Book Writers and Illustrators.

SCOTT, JOYCE ALAINE, university official; b. Long Beach, Calif., May 21, 1943; d. Emmett Emery Scott and Grace (Evans) Wedum BA, U. Conn., 1964; MA, U. Va., 1966; PhD, Duke U., 1973. From instr. to assoc. prof. U. Wyo., Laramie, 1971-74, asst. dean, 1974-78, asst. v.p. acad. affairs, 1976-81, assoc. v.p. acad. affairs, 1981-84; provost, v.p. SUNY-Potsdam, 1984-86; exec. v.p. Wichita State U., Kans., 1986-90, v.p. on spl. assignment, 1990-91; sr. cons. Am. Assn. State Colls. and Univs., 1991-92, v.p. acad. and internat. programs, 1992-97; deputy commr. Mont. U. System, Helena, 1998—2003; provost, v.p. acad. and student affairs Texas A&M, 2003—. Mem. Commn. on Ednl. Credit and Credentials of Am. Council on Edn., Washington, 1982-87; cons. faculty Am. Open U., Lincoln, Nebr., 1981-82. Contbr. articles to profl. jours. Trustee Jonus Internat U. Mem, MLA, AAHE, Am. Assn. Tchrs. French, Phi Beta Kappa, Phi Sigma Iota. Republican. Presbyterian. Office: Office of Provost 280 McDowell Adminstrn Bldg 2600 W Neal PO Box 3011 Commerce TX 75429-3011 E-mail: Joyce_Scott@tamu-commerce.edu.

SCOTT, JUSTINE FORD, counselor, educator; b. Newton, N.C., Nov. 3, 1942; d. Laddie Henry, Sr. and Vera Burton Ford; m. Jerry Scott, June 24, 1972; children: David, Alicia. BS, N.C. A&T State U., 1970; MEd, DePaul U., 1999. Cert. tchr., Ill. Customer svc., sales asst. GE, Oak Brook, Ill., 1979-92; tchr.'s aid Sch. Dist. 60, Zion, Ill., 1992-94; 6th grade tchr. Sch. Dist. 187, North Chicago, Ill., 1994-99; SEP counselor Coll. of Lake County, Grayslake, Ill., 1999—. Mentor, Sisters Taking Care, Chgo.; mem. chancel choir, 2d Bapt. Ch., Evanston, Ill. Mem. Am. Counseling Assn., Ill. Counseling Assn., Chgo. Counseling Assn. E-mail: jfordscott@msn.com.

SCOTT, JUTTA R. retired librarian; b. Leipzig, Saxony, Germany, May 5, 1936; arrived in US, 1960; d. Heinz and Hildegard Woltereck; m. Ritchie H. Reed (dec. Oct. 1, 1971); m. Peter R. Scott, Jan. 24, 1981. BS, U. Md., 1966, MLS, 1967. Libr. collections devel. MIT Librs., Cambridge, Mass., 1976—80; dir. collection devel. and bibiographic control Dartmouth Coll. Libr., Hanover, NH, 1980—83; sr. program officer preservation and collection svcs. Assn. Rsch. Librs., Washington, 1983—96, cons. for preservation, 1996—2000. Author, editor: Scholarship Research Libraries and Global Publishing, 1996. Trustee Fairbanks Mus., St. Johnsbury, Vt., 2001—; vol. Boston Lyric Opera, 1996—; asst. with fundraising Peacham (Vt.) Hist. Assn., Peacham Libr. Avocations: hiking, skiing, gardening, opera. Address: PO Box 182 Peacham VT 05862 E-mail: jscott3417@aol.com.

SCOTT, KAMELA KOON, psychologist, educator; b. Carson City, Nev., July 28, 1964; d. Ray Harold and Bert Gardner Koon; m. David Keitt Scott, Feb. 13, 1993; children: Nicolas Keitt, Isaac David. BA, Baylor U., Waco, Tex., 1986; PhD, U. No. Tex., Denton, 1992. Lic. Clin. Psychologist Divsn. Med. Quality Assurance, Fla., 1994. Psychology intern U. Tex. Med. Br. and Shriner's Burns Inst., Galveston, Tex., 1991—92; instr. dept. psychiatry Emory U. Sch. Medicine, Atlanta, 1992—93; asst. prof. dept. of Pediat. U. Fla. Coll. Medicine, Jacksonville, Fla., 1993—96, asst. prof., 1996—2002, assoc. prof. dept. surgery, 2002—. Program dir., psychol. svcs. U. Fla., Dept. Pediat., Dist. Hematology/Sickle Cell Program, Jacksonville, Fla., 1993—96, U. Fla. Regional Trauma Sys., Jacksonville, 2001—; Univ. apptd. investigator U. of Fla. Sexual Harassment Com., Jacksonville, Fla., 1997—; bd. mem. Shands Jacksonville Ethics Com., Jacksonville, Fla., 1997—, Shands Jacksonville Emergency Preparedness Com., Jacksonville, Fla., 1998—; adv. bd. mem. Shands Jacksonville Clin. Pastoral Edn. Adv. Bd., Jacksonville, Fla., 1998—; supervising psychologist Shands Jacksonville Trauma Psychology Post-Doctoral Fellowship, Jacksonville, Fla., 1998—; site reviewer Fla. Brain and Spinal Cord Injury Program, Tallahassee, 1998—; course dir. U. of Fla. Psychiatry Grand Rounds, Jacksonville, Fla., 2000—02; lectr. U. of Fla. Risk Mgmt. Ednl. Series, Gainesville, Fla., 2002—. Author: (book chapter) Surg. Clinics of North Am., (book chapters (2) Behavioral Aspects of Pediatric Burn Injuries, (jour. article) Current Surgery, Jour. of Trauma, Jacksonville Medicine. Adv. bd. mem. Partnerships for Preventing Violence, Jacksonville, Fla., 1998—2003, Serving Child Victims of Traumatic Abuse, Jacksonville, Fla., 2002—03; active mem. Compassionate Families, Inc., Jacksonville, Fla., 1998—2003. Recipient Presdl. Scholar, US, Office of the Pres., 1982; grantee Rsch. Grant, Turning Point: Re-Thinking Violence, City of Jacksonville, Fla., 2001-2003, Rsch. Grant, Mental Health for Youthful Offenders, State of Fla. Byrne Grant, 2001-2002, Rsch. Grant, Turning Point: Re-Thinking Violence, The Blue Found. for a Healthy Fla., 2001-2002, The Jacksonville Jaguars Found., 1999-2001, Rsch. Grant, Correlates of Traumatic Injury in Adolescents Requiring Hospitalization, U. of Fla. Dean's Fund, 1997-1998. Mem.: APA. Republican. Baptist. Avocations: scuba diving, snow skiing, motocross, camping. Office: U Fla Surgery 655 West 8th St Jacksonville FL 32209 E-mail: kamela.scott@jax.ufl.edu.

SCOTT, KAREN BONDURANT, consumer catalog company executive; b. East Orange, N.J., June 4, 1946; d. Walter James and Wanda (French) Schmidt; m. Ian James Anderson, May 12, 1982; children: Steven, Michael. BS, U. Mass., 1968; MBA, Northwestern U., 1977. Bus. analyst Dun & Bradstreet, N.Y.C., 1968-69; asst. mgr. Shay Med. Employment, Chgo., 1970-72; mgr. recruitment Michael Reese Med. Ctr., Chgo., 1972-76; brand mgmt., new bus. devel., dir. mergers & acquisitions Kraft Foods, Inc., Glenview, Ill., 1977-95; pres. Chelsea & Scott dba One Step Ahead, Lake Bluff, Ill., 1987—. Sec.-treas. adv. bd. Lincolnshire (Ill.) Nursery Sch., 1987-89; co-leader Boy Scouts Am., Lincolnshire, 1991. Mem. Juvenile Product Mfrs. Assn. (new product judge 1992-99, speaker nat. catalog conf.), Nat. Assn. Women Bus. Owners (mem. Lake Forest cmty. task force). Office: Chelsea & Scott Ltd 75 Albrecht Dr Lake Bluff IL 60044-2226

SCOTT, LINDA KAY See GRANT, LINDA KAY

SCOTT, LOLITA JEAN, social worker; b. Owensboro, Ky., Apr. 21, 1957; d. James Thomas Jr. and Jewell Dean (Walls) Howard; m. Lindsey Scott, Aug. 15, 1980 (div. 2001); 1 child, Latavia Seneca Scott. AA, Ea. Ky. U., 1980, BSW, 1993; MA in Marriage and Family Therapist, Louisville Theol. Sem., 1999. With child protective svcs. Ky. Dept. Social Svcs., Richmond, 1993, 94-95; social worker sr. placement Richmond Family Resource Ctr., Richmond, 1993; asst. tchg. parent Spring Meadows, Louisville, 1994; sr. case mgr. Seven Counties Svcs., Louisville, 1995—2001; with Family & Children's Counseling Ctrs., Louisville, 2001—. Clin. therapist assoc. Ctr. for Family Ministries, Archdiocese of Louisville, 1996—; mem. adoption-foster care rev. bd., 1998-99. Singer Ea. Ky. Ensemble, 1975-78, Tommy Jones workshop Cmty. Choir, 1995-96; vol. tutor Ky. Dept. Adult Edn. and Literacy, Richmond, 1993; vol. Women's Abuse Ctr., Owensboro, Ky., 1989, Telford Cmty. Ctr., Richmond, 1991. Mem. Am. Assn. Christian Counselors; Am. Assn. Marriage and Family Therapy, Ky. Assn. Marriage and Family Therapy, Omega Psi Phi Pearl. Democrat. Baptist. Avocations: bicycling, volleyball, movies, reading, dance. Home: Apt 18 5508 Delmaria Way Louisville KY 40291-4906 Office: Family & Childrens Counseling Ctrs 731 S 31st St Louisville KY 40211 E-mail: arose4aqueen@aol.com.

SCOTT, LYNN THOMSON, Spanish language and literature educator; b. Mineola, N.Y., Oct. 2, 1942; d. George Campbell and Helen (Gordon) Thomson; m. John Fredrik Scott, July 25, 1964; children: Erik Anderson, Elizabeth Cameron. BA, Vassar Coll., 1964; MA, U. Fla., 1990, PhD, 1999. Editl. asst. McGraw-Hill Pub., N.Y.C., 1964-66; Spanish tchr. St. Thomas More Sch., Houston, 1978-81, Buchholz H.S., Gainesville, Fla., 1983-84; tchg. asst. U. Fla., Gainesville, 1988—. Guest lectr. U. Andes, Bogota, Colombia, 1996. Contbr. articles to profl. jours. Active Christian unity & inter-religious concerns Trinity United Meth. Ch., Gainesville, 1993-95, Project Graduation The Corner Drugstore, Gainesville, 1989. Travel grantee Tinker Found., 1996, rsch. grantee Program Cooperation Spanish Ministry Culture, Madrid, 1996; dissertation fellow U. Fla. Coll. Liberal Arts, 1996; Tybel Spivack award, U. Fla., 1993. Mem. MLA, AAUW, South Atlantic Modern Lang. Assn., PEO, SSSAS, Sigma Delta Pi, Phi Sigma Iota, Phi Kappa Phi. Avocations: cooking, swimming, bird watching, travel. Office: U Fla Dept Romance Langs & Lit Gainesville FL 32611

SCOTT, MARGARET SIMON, retired mortgage broker; b. Boston, May 12, 1934; d. Frank A. and Margaret Alice (Gotham) Simon; m. Walter Neil Scott, Nov. 21, 1959 (div. June 1997); 1 child, Walter David Kimbley; m. Stephen E. Michelman, Feb. 8, 2003. BA in Physics, Wellesley Coll., 1956; MA in Polit. Sci., Boston U., 1965; MS in Human Resources Mgmt., U. Utah, 1974. Rsch. asst. Bell Tel. Labs., Whippany, N.J., 1956-58; rsch. asst. med. sch. U. Louisville, 1959-60, Harvard U., Boston, 1960-64; instr. polit. sci. Trinity U., San Antonio, 1966-67; cons. info. systems U.S. Dept. Labor, Washington, 1968; dir. manpower planning N.Y.C. Human Resources Adminstrn., 1968-71; asst. v.p. First Nat. City Bank, N.Y.C., 1972-77; v.p. Citibank, N.A., N.Y.C., 1978-86, AMEV Asset Mgmt., Inc., N.Y.C., 1986-88; pres. Mortgage Adv. Svcs., Inc., N.Y.C., 1988-99. Vol. Jr. League, Louisville, 1957; bd. mgr. N.Y. Jr. League, N.Y.C., 1970—74; sec. 1095 Park Ave Corp., N.Y.C., 1977—86; bd. mgrs. McBurney YMCA, N.Y.C., 1995—2000, chmn., 1998—2000; trustee United Adult Ministries, 1998—, mem. exec. com., 1999—, chair, fin. com., 1999—; trustee First Presbyn. Ch. in the City N.Y., 1995—98, pres., 1997—98; trustee N.Y. City Presbytery, 1996—98, treas., 1998—2002, chair coun. adminstrn. and support svcs., 2003—; ruling elder First Presbyn. Ch., 2000—03; mem. steering com. Presbyn. Welcome, 1999—, co-moderator, 2001—03; bd. trustees Presbyn. Synod of Northeast, 2002—; bd. dirs. YWCA, N.Y.C., 1980—85. Mem.: Wellesley Club. Democrat. Home: 441 W 24th St New York NY 10011-1253 E-mail: margaretsnyc@mac.com.

SCOTT, MARIAN ALEXIS, journalist; b. Atlanta, Feb. 4, 1949; d. William Alexander and Marian (Willis) Scott; m. Marc Anthony Lewis, Sept. 14, 1968 (div. 1973); m. David Leslie Reeves, Mar. 16, 1974 (div. 1998); children: Cinque Scott, David Leslie Jr. Student, Barnard Coll., 1966-68, Spelman Coll., 1989-90, Regional Leadership Inst., 1992; LHD, Argosy U., 2003. Reporter, asst. city editor, cable TV editor, mgr., video Atlanta Jour. & Constn., 1974-93; dir. diversity Cox Enterprises Inc., 1993-97; pub. Atlanta Daily World, 1997—. Bd. dirs. Atlanta Life Ins. Co.; vis. instr. summer program for minority journalists, Berkeley, Calif., 1980, 81, 84, 85, 87 Grady High Sch., Atlanta, 1982-83; journalist-in-residence Clark Coll., Atlanta, 1983. Rschr., writer: The history of Atlanta NAACP, 1983 (NAACP award 1984). Moderator First Congl. Ch., 1982-92. Named one of 100 Top Black Bus. and Profl. Women, 1986, 20 Women Making a Mark in Atlanta, Atlanta Mag., 1998, Top 25 Women in Bus., The Network Jour., 2004; recipient Disting. Urban Journalism award, Nat. Urban Coalition, 1980, Acad. Achievement award, YWCA, 1989, Media of Yr. award, Ga. Legisl. Black Caucus, 2001, Grimes fellow, Cox Family Enterprise Ctr., Kennesaw State U., Citizen of Yr. award, Southwest Hosp., 2001, Michele Clark fellow, Columbia U. Sch. Journalism, 2004. Mem.: Nat. Assn. Black Journalists, Atlanta Assn. Black Journalists (Commentary Print award 1983, Pioneer Black Journalist award 1998), Nat. Assn. Media Women (pres Atlanta chpt. 1985—87, Media Woman of Yr. award 1983, Media Woman of Yr. nat. award 1993), Atlanta Press Club (pres. 2000), Sigma Delta Chi (bd. dirs. 1980—84, treas. 1985—88). Office: Atlanta Daily World 145 Auburn Ave NE Atlanta GA 30303-2503

SCOTT, MARIANNE FLORENCE, retired librarian, educator; b. Toronto, Dec. 4, 1928; d. Merle Redvers and Florence Ethel (Hutton) S. BA, McGill U., Montreal, Que., Can., 1949, BLS, 1952; LLD (hon.), York U., 1985, Dalhousie U., 1989; DLitt (hon.), Laurentian U., 1990. Asst. librarian Bank of Montreal, 1952-55; law librarian McGill U., 1955-73, law area librarian, 1973-75, dir. libraries, 1975-84, lectr. legal bibliography faculty of law, 1964-75; nat. librarian Nat. Library of Can., Ottawa, Ont., 1984-99, ret., 1999. Co-founder, editor: Index to Can. Legal Periodical Lit, 1963—; contbr. articles to profl. jours. Decorated officer Order of Can., 1995; recipient Queen Elizabeth II Silver Jubilee medal, 1977, IFLA medal, 1996, Queen Elizabeth Golden Jubilee medal, 2002. Mem. Internat. Assn. Law Libraries (dir. 1974-77), Am. Assn. Law Libraries, Can. Assn. Law Libraries (pres. 1963-69, exec. bd. 1973-75, honored mem. 1980—), Can. Library Assn. (council and dir. 1980-82, 1st v.p. 1980-81, pres. 1981-82), Corp. Profl. Librarians of Que. (v.p. 1975-76), Can. Assn. Research Libraries (pres. 1978-79, past pres. 1979-80, exec. com. 1980-81, sec.-treas. 1983-84), Ctr. for Research Libraries (dir. 1980-83), Internat. Fedn. Library Assns. (honor com. for 1982 conf. 1979-82, chair com. on copyright and other legal matters 1998-2003, hon. fellow 2003), Conf. of Dirs. of Nat. Libraries (chmn. 1988-92). Home: 119 Dorothea Dr Ottawa ON Canada K1V 7C6 E-mail: mfscott@rogers.com.

SCOTT, MARTHA G. state legislator; b. Ware Shoals, S.C., Nov. 10, 1935; d. Harold and Pearl (Wardlaw) Smith; children: Marion Jr., Deborah Ann Gilmore. Student, Highland Park Jr. Coll., 1952-54; DHH, Tenn. Sch. Religion, 1990; DHL, Urban Bible Inst., Detroit, 1994. With Mich. Bell Telephone Co., 1960-86; rep. Mich. Ho. of Reps. Mem. Mich. State Dem. Ctrl. Com., 1974-82; commr. Wayne County Bd. Commrs., 1977-80, chairwoman Human Resources Com., 1978-80; vice chairwoman Wayne County Civil Svc. Commn., 1980-82; pres. Highland Park City Council, 1984-87; mayor City of Highland Park, 1988; Dem. precinct del. 1st Congl. Dist.; bd. dirs. Nat. Coun. Alcoholism and Other Dependencies, 1979, Detroit Osteopathic Hosp., 1990; vice chairwoman Mich. Women in Mcpl. Govt.; founding mem. Nat. Polit. Congress Black Women; adv. bd. Met. Region Bus. Alliance; vol. Residential Care Alternatives. Recipient Plaque Highland Park Sch. Bd., 1977, Nat. Polit. Congress of Black Women award, 1981, Resolution, Wayne County Bd. Commrs., 1981, Wayne County Auditors, 1981, Dollars and Sense Mag. award, 1989, Spl. Achievement award Amvets, Golden Heritage award for excellence in svc., 1988, Cmty. Svc. award Knoxville Coll. Alumni, 1988. Mem. Gamma Phi Delta. Office: Michigan House of Reps State Capitol Lansing MI 48909

SCOTT, MELLOUISE JACQUELINE, retired media specialist; b. Sanford, Fla., Mar. 1, 1943; d. Herbert and Mattye (Williams) Cherry; m. Robert Edward Scott, Jr., July 1, 1972; 1 child, Nolan Edward. BA, Talladega Coll., 1965; MLS, Rutgers U., 1974, EdM, 1976, EdS, 1982. Media specialist Seminole County Bd. Edn., Sanford, 1965-72, Edison (N.J.), 1972-98; ret. Edison (N.J.) Bd. Edn., 1999. Mem. ALA, N.J. Ret. Educators Assn., NEA. Baptist. Home: PO Box 1771 Sanford FL 32772-1771

SCOTT, MIMI KOBLENZ, psychotherapist, actress, publicist, journalist, playwright; b. Albany, N.Y., Dec. 15, 1940; d. Edmund Akiba and Tillie (Paul) Koblenz; m. Barry Stuart Scott, Aug. 13, 1961 (dec. Nov. 1991); children: Karen Scott Zantay, Jeffrey B. BA in Speech, English Edn., Russell Sage Coll., 1962; MA in Speech Edn., SUNY, Albany, 1968; M in Social Welfare, SUNY, 1985; PhD in Psychology, Pacific Western U., Encino, Calif., 1985. Cert. tchr., social worker. Tchr. English, speech Albany Pub. Schs., 1961-63; hostess, producer talkshow Sta. WAST-TV 13, Albany, 1973-75; freelance actress N.Y.C., 1975-77; producer, actress Four Seasons Dinner Theater, Albany, 1978-82; instr. of theatre Albany Jr. Coll., 1981-83; pvt. practice psychotherapy Albany, N.Y., 1985-92; exec. producer City of Albany Park Playhouse, 1989-92; actor self-employed N.Y.C., 1992—; actor Off Broadway show Grandma Sylvia's Funeral, 1996-98, Split Ends, 2004. Guest psychotherapist Sally Jessy Raphael Show, 1992, 93, Jane Whitney Show, 1994, A Current Affair, 1995, News Talk TV, 1995; founder Manhattan Playwrights Inc., 2001—, producing artistic dir., 2001—. Scriptwriter, dir., actor (TV films) To Liberty and Justice for All, 1985, featured writer Backstage, 1995—96, featured in ind. film Mr. Vincent, Sundance, 1997, book and lyricist (musical) Dressing Room, Soho Playhouse, N.Y.C., 2000; author: Mind Tricks, 2003; dir.: Mind Tricks, 2003. Event organizer AmFar, 1985; co-chmn. March of Dimes Telethon, 1985-86; fundraiser Leukemia Found., 1987, Aids Benefit, N. Miami Beach, Fla., 1988; elected to SUNY Albany U. Found., 1990. Recipient FDR Nat. Achievement award March of Dimes, 1985, Recognition Cert. Capital Dist. Psychiat. Ctr., 1983, 84, 85; named Woman of Yr. YWCA, 1986, Commr. Albany Tricentennial Celebration, 1986; Mimi Scott Day proclaimed by Mayor of Albany, 1989. Mem.: AFTRA, SAG, AEA, NASW. Jewish. Avocations: horseback riding, boating, golf, tennis. Home and Office: 211 W 71st St Apt 6A New York NY 10023-3767

SCOTT, MISTY ANNE, marketing professional; b. Newark, Ohio, Sept. 9, 1974; d. James Walter and Mary Lou Scott; m. Jonathan Grimm, July 13, 2002. AA in Bus., Ohio State U., 1995, BS in Bus. Adminstrn., 1997; postgrad., Franklin U. Account exec. TMP Worldwide, Chgo., 1998—99; mktg. coord. Argosy Edn. Group, Chgo., 1999—2001; asst. dir. mktg. Franklin U., Columbus, Ohio, 2001—. V.p. Sweet Adelines, pres., choreographer, co-show chmn. Mem.: Am. Mktg. Assn. (co-presenter higher edn. symposium 2002). Avocations: travel, reading, singing. Home: 3991 Berrybush Dr Columbus OH 43230 Office: Franklin U 201 S Grant Ave Columbus OH 43215 E-mail: scottm@franklin.edu.

SCOTT, NANCY L. health facility administrator, consultant; b. Berwyn, Ill., Sept. 11, 1962; d. Kenneth N. and Lolita L. Unger; m. Paul A. Scott, Dec. 29, 1990 (div. Sept. 1995). BS, Univ. of Ill., 1983; MBA with hons., U. of Chgo., 1991. Cert. CHE Am. Coll. of Healthcare Execs., Chgo., 2000. Various positions including implementation specialist to fin. product mgr. Enterprise Systems, Inc., Wheeling, Ill., 1993—96; cytogenetics technologist Univ. of Chgo., 1986—88; supr. Reproductive Genetics Inst., Chgo., 1988—90; dist. agt. The Prudential, Des Plaines, Ill., 1992; mgr., sr. cons. Cap Gemini Ernst & Young U.S., Chgo., 1996—2003; acct. exec. AHA Fin. Solutions, Inc., Chgo., 2003—. Home: 3238 Elm Ave Brookfield IL 60513 Office: AHA Financial Solutions Inc 1 N Franklin 30th Fl Chicago IL 60606-3421 E-mail: NLScott@aol.com.

SCOTT, OMERIA MCDONALD, state legislator; m. Charles Scott. Mem. Miss. Ho. of Reps., 1993—. Mem. Nat. Coun. Negro Women, Federated Women Am., Assn. Excellence in Edn., Eastern Star. Democrat. Baptist. Address: 615 E 19th St Laurel MS 39440-2470 Office: Miss Ho of Reps Rm 400E-NC State Capitol Jackson MS 39205

SCOTT, PAMELA MOYERS, physician assistant; b. Clarksburg, W.Va., Jan. 5, 1961; d. James Edward and Norma Lee (Holbert) Moyers; m. Troy Allen Scott, July 19, 1986. BS summa cum laude, Alderson-Broaddus Coll., 1983; M Physician Asst. Studies, U. Nebr., 1999. Cert. physician asst. Physician asst. Weston (W.Va.) State Hosp., 1983-84, Rainelle (W.Va.) Med. Ctr., 1984-2000, Brierwood Med. Ctr., 2000—01; pvt. practice Williamsburg, W.Va., 2001—. Adj. faculty Mountain State U., Beckley, W.Va., 2003—; support faculty physician asst. program Coll. W.Va., 1994-99, mem. physician asst. adv. coun. 1993-94, physician asst. program admission selection com., 1994-99; keynote spkr. Alderson-Broaddus Coll. Ann. Physician Assn. Banquet, 1992, 2001, 1st Physician Asst. Convocation Ceremony, 1998; spkr., presenter in field; guest Lifetime TV med. program Physician Jour. Update, 1993; adv. coun. W.Va. Rural Health Networking, 1994-95, W.Va. Rural Networking Managed Care Policy Group, 1996, W.Va. Coalition for Managed Care Options, 1997. Mem. editl. bd. Jour. Am. Acad. Physician Assts., 1995-98, dept. editor Procedures in Family Practice Dept., 1996-2004; contbr. articles to profl. jours., chpts. to textbook. Mem. W.Va. State Task Force on Adolescent Pregnancy and Parenting, 1992-2000, sec., 1996-98; mem. W.Va. Rural Networking Managed Care Study Group, 1995, W.Va. Rural Networking Managed Care Policy Group, 1996; mem. adv. com. W.Va. State Bur. Pub. Health Family Planning, 1997-2000, Clin. & Sci. Affairs Coun., 2002—, Profesion Practice Coun., 2002—, Edn. Coun., 2002—; mem. Greenbrier County P.A.T.C.H. Spkr.'s Bur., 1996-2003; mem. Meadow Bridge Cmty. Adv. Group, 1997-2000, Meadow Bridge Domestic Violence Prevention Task Force, 1998-2000; mem. heart profl. edn. adv. panel Nat. Heart, Lung & Blood Inst., 2003—; bd. trustees Physician Asst. Found., 2002-03. Named Young Career Woman of Yr. Rainelle chpt. and Dist. V of W. Va., Citation of Honor at State Level of Competition, Bus. and Profl. Women's Club, 1986, Nominee for W. Va. Women's Commn. Celebrate Women award, 1996, 97, 98; recipient W.Va. Gov.'s award for Outstanding Rural Health Practitioner, 1997, Alderson Broaddus Coll.'s Alumni Achievement award, 1995, Harry Bennington Meml. award, 2001. Fellow: Fellowship of Christian Physicians Assts., Assn. Family Practice physician Assts. (newsletter editor 2001—02, Appreciation award 2002), W.Va. Assn. Physician Assts. (chmn. membership com. 1989—91, nominations and elections com. 1990—91, pres. 1991—94, chair ann. med. Jeopardy tournament 1997—2001, student activities com. 1999—2000, chmn. mentoring program 1999—2000, Outstanding Physician Asst. of Yr. 2003), Am. Acad. Physician Assts. (mem. rural health caucus 1991—98, del. to People's Rep. China 1992, W.Va. chief del. Ho. of Dels. Nat. Conv. 1992, W.Va. del. 1992—98, mem. pub. edn. com. 1992—98, W.Va. chief del. Ho. of Dels. Nat. Conv. 1994—98, chair pub. edn. com. 1996—98, bd. advisor elections com. 1998—99, dir.-at-large 1998—2002, bd. on fin. 1998—, alt. del. 1999—2000, chair bd. commn. on external affairs 1999—2001, bd. advisor pub. rels. com. 2000—01, chair bd. commn. internal affairs 2001—02, bd. advisor clin. affairs coun. 2001—02, chair bd. on appts. 2002—03, chair bd. commn. on external affairs 2002—03, mem. coord com. 2002—03, mem. exec. com. 2002—, bd. advisor to constituent rels. com. 2002—03, co-chair ad hoc work group on governance 2002—03, bd. on budget 2002—03, bd. advisor leadership adv. commn. 2002—, del. leader to Brazil 2003, pres. 2003—, chair 2003—, chair exec. com. 2003—, Outstanding Physician Asst. of Yr. 1991). Republican. Baptist. Avocations: reading, handicrafts, shopping. Home and Office: PO Box 43 Williamsburg WV 24991-0043 E-mail: pamscottpa@citlink.net.

SCOTT, PHYLLIS WRIGHT, coach, music educator; b. Lancaster, Pa., Nov. 9, 1925; d. George Bronson and Edythe Heckroth Wright; m. Edgar Lee Arthur Mixon, Oct. 12, 1946 (div. Nov. 1954); children: Thomas Lee, Raymond Dean, Michael George; m. Gilbert Henry Scott, June 23, 1976 (dec. May 1995). Grad., H.S., 1963; studied music, studied skating. Skating tchr. Health Ctr., Norfolk, Va., 1947, Ringing Rocks Park, Pottstown, Pa., 1945, Gt. Leopard Roller Rink, Chester, Pa., 1946—47, Ringing Rocks Park Roller Rink, Lancaster, Pa., 1948—49, Playland Roller Rink, York, Pa., 1950—51, Skateland Roller Rink, Camden, NJ, 1952—55, Exton (Pa.) Roller Rink, 1956—57; music tchr. Holiday Music, Pennsauken, NJ, 1962—64; pvt. music tchr. Bellmawr, NJ, 1965—98, Keyboard Am., Lewes, Del., 1998—. Prodr.: (skating shows), 1944—62. Den mother Cub Scouts of Am., Bellmawr, NJ, 1950—54. Recipient Silver-Bronze Dance medal, Roller Skating Rinks Operator Assn., 1943, Bronze Figures award, 1944. Mem.: Order of Eastern Star. Republican. Baptist. Avocations: needlepoint, playing keyboard instruments. Home: 29261 White Pine Rd Milton DE 19968 Home Fax: 302-644-3397. Personal E-mail: Pscott1152@aol.com. E-mail: StillTeachingMusic@KeyboardAmerica.com.

SCOTT, PORTIA ADELE, paralegal; b. Port Chester, N.Y., Nov. 1, 1946; d. Frank Thomas, Jr. and Hattie N. Thomas; 1 child, Nicole L. Student, U. Md. Cert. paralegal Md., 2003. Mgr. adminstrn. YMCA of the USA, Washington, 1990—91; office mgr. Thatcher Proffitt & Wood, Washington, 1991—96; paralegal Wilmer Cutler & Pickering, Washington, 1996—. Mem. adv. bd. Legal Studies Dept. U. Md., Adelphi, Md.; bd. dir. Seed, Inc., Riverdale, Md. Author: At Twilight, 2001 (Editor's award, 2003). Mem.: NAFE, Nat. Assn. Legal Assocs. Avocations: writing, singing, poetry. Office: Wilmer Cutler Pickering LLP 2445 M St NW Washington DC 20037 Business E-Mail: portia.scott@wilmer.com.

SCOTT, RITA FAY, art educator; b. Marietta, Okla., July 16, 1954; d. Frank Jimmie and Lavene B. Johnson; m. Larry Charles Scott, Sept. 4, 1976; children: Lesley Jane, David Andrew. BEd, East Ctrl. Okla. State U., 1976, MEd, 1978. Nat. Bd. Cert. in Art for Young Adults/Adolescents 2001. Art/craft tchr. Vanoss Pub. Sch., Ada, Okla., 1976—; Johnson O'Malley summer sch. art tchr. Ada (Okla.) City Schs., 1988—2003; gifted/talented lycium summer art East Ctrl. U., Ada, Okla., 1998—2003. Tchr. upward-bound summer art Chickasaw Nation Murray State Coll, Ada, Okla., 2000. Illustrator: book Lordy Lamb and the Twelve Lisciples, 1989; artwork shown at John F. Kennedy Ctr., Wash., DC, 1980. Recipient Okla. Indian Educator of Yr., Okla. Coun. for Indian Educators, 1998. Mem.: NEA, Okla. Edn. Assn., Okla. Art Edn. Assn., Delta Kappa Gamma Rho. Democrat. Mem. Ch. Of Christ. Avocations: hosting internat. exchange students, collecting baskets, reading, teaching cultural Native American camps. Home: 19623 County Rd 1555 Ada OK 74820 E-mail: larileda@juno.com.

SCOTT, ROSA MAE, art educator, artist; b. East Hampton, N.Y., Apr. 12, 1937; d. James Alexander and Victoria (Square) Nicholson; m. Frank Albert Hanna, Apr. 1, 1957 (div. Mar. 1985); 1 child, Frank Albert Hanna III; m. Warner Bruce Scott, Aug. 3, 1985 (dec. Oct. 2002); children: Bernadine, John, Patricia, Charlene, Lawrence. AA, Dabney Lancaster, 1989; BA, Mary Baldwin, 1992. Cosmetologist Rosa's Beauty Shop, East Hampton, 1962-68; sec. Frank Hanna's Cleaning Co., East Hampton, 1962-77; cashier, clk. Brook's Pharmacy, East Hampton, 1992; lead tchr. East Hampton Day Care, 1992-94, 97-98; substitute tchr. Lexington (Va.) Schs., 1994—, East Hampton Sch. Sys., 1996-97; lead tchr. Suffolk C.C. Child Care Ctr., River Head, N.Y., 1999; substitute tchr. East Hampton Sch., 2000—03; lead tchr. after sch. program Springs Sch., 2000—02, 2004, substitute tchr., 2000—03; receptionist Montauk Artist Assn., 2003—. Receptionist, Montauk (N.Y.) Artist Assn., 2003; sec. Lylburn Downing Cmty. Ctr., Inc., Lexington, 1985-92; arts and crafts tutor, supr. East Hampton Town Youth After Sch. Program, 1996—. Acrylic painter. Pres. Rockbridge Garden Club, Lexington, 1996; co-organizer Va. Co-op. Ex. Garden Clubs, Lexington, 1995; bd. dirs. Rockbridge Area Pres. Homes, 1996, Fine Arts of Rockbridge, 1985-92, Friends of Lime Kiln, Lexington, 1985-92. Mem.: Guild Hall, East End Arts, Montauk Artists Assn. (receptionist 2003), Artist Alliance East Hampton, L.I. Black Artists (v.p. 2000—03), Rockbridge Arts Guild. Avocations: collecting emmett kelly clowns, art, reading, theater, tennis. Home: PO Box 1265 East Hampton NY 11937-0708

SCOTT, SHARON ANN, retired librarian, archivist; b. Wyandotte, Mich., Apr. 15, 1938; d. Jack Leroy Hessler, Anne Margaret (Zellner) Stone; m. Martin Loren Scott, Aug. 20, 1960; children: Laura, Arthur, Sheila Weber. BS, Ea. Mich. U., 1960; MLS, U. Mich., 1985. Cert. media specialist State of Mich. Cataloger reference libr. Toledo Mus. Art, Toledo, 1987—93; bindery clk. law libr. U. Mich., Ann Arbor, Mich., 1993—94; media specialist Dundee Cmty. Schs., Dundee, Mich., 1995—2000. V.p., bookkeeper Scott Equipment and Fabricating, Toledo, 1976—92; archivist Hist. Soc. Clinton, Clinton, Mich., 1974—. Author: School Library Media Annual, 1995, Robinson's 1988-Villages of Lenawee County, 1988, Village of Clinton, Michigan: a History, 1981. Pres. Clinton Township Libr. Bd., Clinton, Mich., 1985—92; sec. Planning Commn. Village of Clinton, 1983—92; chmn. US 12 Heritage Trail Com., Clinton, 1999—; rep. Lenawee County Intergovtl. com. US 12 Heritage Trail, Adrian, Mich., 2001—. Mem.: Mich. Archives Assn., Midwest Archives Assn., Friends of the Archives (sec.-treas. Detroit conf. 1984—), Dexter Cmty. Band. Methodist. Avocation: Avocations: singing, playing tuba, collecting children's books and fine art. Home: 214 E Michigan Ave Clinton MI 49236

SCOTT, SHIRLEY, city council; married; four children. BA, Drew U., 1965; MA Germanic Langs., U. Cin., 1968. Operator Scott Supply Svc. Inc.; city coun. Tucson City Coun., 1995—. Bd. dirs. Tucson Clean and Beautiful. Office: Tucson City Coun 8123 E Poinciana Dr Tucson AZ 85730-4641

SCOTT, SUE A. music educator; b. Brenham, Tex., Oct. 12, 1937; d. Oscar Lee and Ruby Faye Jameson; m. Calvin John Scott, June 16, 1962; children: Cedric John, Kalva Sue. BA, Prairie View A&M U., 1959, MA, 1969. H.S. choir dir. Marlin (Tex.) Ind. Sch. Dist., 1959-64; sch. sec. Garland (Tex.) Ind. Sch. Dist., 1964-65; clk., proof reader White Hall Lab., Dallas, 1965-67; H.S. choir dir. Wilmer Hutchins (Tex.) Ind. Sch. Dist., 1967-72; tchr. instrumental ensemble Dallas Pub. Schs., 1972-99. Music dept. chmn. Wilmer Hutchins H.S., 1967-72; chmn. music dept. Boude Storey Middle Sch., Dallas, 1980-99. Fellow Nat. Assn. Negro Musicians; mem. NEA, Tex. Music Tchrs. Assn., Prairie View A&M U. Music Club (pres. 1958-59, cert. 1959), Mu Alfa Sigma (pres. 1957-59, cert. 1959). Democrat. Baptist.

SCOTT, SUSAN CRAIG, plastic surgeon; b. N.Y.C., 1948; MD, Columbia U., 1974. Diplomate Am. Bd. Plastic Surgery with subspecialty in hand surgery. Intern Roosevelt Hosp., N.Y.C., NY, 1974—75, resident in gen. surgery, 1975—79; resident in plastic surgery NYU Med. Ctr., 1979—81; fellow in hand surgery Roosevelt Hosp., 1981—82; pvt. practice plastic surgery N.Y.C., 1987—. Office: 6 E 78th St New York NY 10021-1922

SCOTT, SYLVIA JANE, small business owner; b. Charleston, Jan. 31, 1945; d. John Mitchell and Christabelle Lillian Johnson; m. Nathanial Myers, 1960 (dec. Mar. 9, 1998); children: Tia Johnson, Nathanial Myers, Norma Griffin, Tralane Mason, Sonia Melton, Troi Mack, Myer Micheal. Student, Trident Tech. Coll., 1975; cosmetology cert., 1987. Owner Shear Beauty, Charleston, SC, 1988—, Rental Units, Charleston, 1997—, Scott Supplies, Charleston, 1999—. Author: The Bookdweller, 2002. Recipient cert., Carolina Monority Supplier Council, Inc. Roman Catholic. Achievements include patents for multi-page doll bookmarks; scheduling board.

SCOTT, TIFFANY, ice skater; b. Weymouth, Mass., May 1, 1977; Student, Del. Tech. U., 1999. Pairs ice skater with Philip Dulebohn. Recipient Bronze medal, U.S. Jr. Championships, 1997. Avocations: sewing, bicycling, camping, collecting skating stamps, postcards. Office: US Figure Skating Headquarters 20 First St Colorado Springs CO 80906*

SCOTT-BATTLE, GLADYS NATALIE, retired social worker; b. Cambridge, Mass., Sept. 16, 1933; d. Dudley Fairfax and Bessie Mae (Mitchell) Scott; m. James Henry Battle, Jr., Oct. 18, 1953 (div. 1975); children: Gregory, James, Jameel. BA, Fordham U., 1975; MSW, Columbia U., 1978. Lic. clin. social worker; cert. social worker, tchr., N.Y. Program dir. Cmty. Svc. Soc., N.Y.C., 1978-79; corp. liaison cities and schs., N.Y.C., 1979-80; psychotherapist Harlem Interfaith Counseling, N.Y.C., 1980-81; psychiat. social worker Met. Hosp., N.Y.C., 1981-83; psychiat. social worker Bronx clin. divsn. N.Y.C. Bd. Edn., 1982—92; ret., 1992. Cons. N.Y. State Disability Determinations, 1982—, N.Y.C. Family Ct., 1987, family and criminal ct.-selected cases. V.p. Women Who Help Other People, N.Y.C., 1985; bd. dirs. Morningside Gardens Coop., N.Y.C., 1986; vol. Met. Mus. Art. Mem. NASW, Nat. Assn. Black Social Workers, United Fedn. Tchrs., Internat. Assn. Social Workers, Bus. and Profl. Women's Club. Democrat. Avocations: visiting museums and art galleries, painting, theatre, travel. Home: 119 Nyack Plz Nyack NY 10960-3851

SCOTT-FINAN, NANCY ISABELLA, government administrator; b. Canton, Ohio, June 13, 1949; d. Milton Kenneth and Gertrude (Baker) Scott; m. Robert James Finan II, Aug. 23, 1986. Student, Malone Coll., 1970-73; BA magna cum laude, postgrad., U. Akron, 1976, Kent State U., 1977; MA in Internat. Transactions, George Mason U., 1995. Legal sec. Krugliak, Wilkins, Griffiths & Dougherty, Canton, 1969, Amerman, Burt & Jones, Canton, 1970-77; legal sec., paralegal Black, McCuskey, Souers & Arbaugh, Canton, Ohio, 1977-81; adminstrv. staff mem. com. on judiciary U.S. Senate, Washington, 1981-86; adminstrv. asst. to counsel to Pres., The White House, Washington, 1986-89; adminstrv. asst. to former counsel to pres. O'Melveny & Myers, Washington, 1989; asst. dir. congl. rels. Office Legis. Affairs U.S. Dept. Justice, Washington, 1989-91; spl. asst. to asst. atty. gen. U.S. Dept. of Justice, Washington, 1991—. Substitute tchr. North Canton City Sch. System, 1979-80; residential tutor Canton City Sch. System, 1980-81, Fairfax (Va.) County Sch. System, 1983; instr. dance and exercise Siffrin Home for Developmentally Disabled, Canton, 1980. East coast regional v.p. for spl. projects Childhelp U.S.A., Washington, 1988-90; mem. Rep. Women of Capitol Hill, Washington, 1984-95; bd. mem. Have a Heart Homes for Abused Children, Washington, 1990-91. Mem. AAUW, Women of Washington, Corcoran Gallery Art, Nat. Mus. Women Arts. Presbyterian. Office: US Dept Justice 950 Pennsylvania Ave NW Washington DC 20530-0001

SCOTT-FLANTON, VERNITA LYNN, consultant; b. Gary, Ind., Oct. 22, 1958; d. Rochelle Ophelia (Williams) Greene; 1 child, Sean Miles Scott. Chief exec. officer Jade 7 Inc., Palmdale, Calif., 2000—. Mem.: Women in Mgmt., Greater L.A. World Trade Ctr. Assn., Andrews U. Alumni Assn., Mizpah Alumni Assn. Democrat. Adventist. Avocations: racquetball, horseback riding, skiing, hiking. Office: PO Box 900012 Palmdale CA 93590-0012 E-mail: jade7inc@yahoo.com.

SCOTTI, RITA ANGELICA, novelist; b. Providence, Dec. 25, 1947; d. Ciro Ottorino and Rita Ward (Dwyer) S.; children: Francesca, Ciro. Student, U. Rome, 1964—65, Loyola U., 1965—67. Author: Kiss of Judas, 1984, The Devil's Own, 1985, The Hammer's Eye, 1987, Cradle Song, 1987, (as Angelica Scott) For Love of Sarah, 1995, Sudden Sea, 2003. Roman Catholic. Home: 224 E 18th St Apt 3A New York NY 10003-3632

SCOTTO, MARY LEE, columnist; b. Hartford, Conn., July 27, 1946; d. Leno J. Rinaldi and Mary Louise (Morgan) Hewitt; m. Frank J. Scotto, Oct. 30, 1975; children: John, Frank Jr. Student pub. schs., Meriden, Conn. Editor IHMSA News, Burlington, Iowa, 1989—99; freelance writer San Diego, 1993-98. Dir. industry IHMSA, Inc., 1990—. Contbr. articles on guns to profl. jours; author numerous poems. Mem. Rep. Nominating Com., Washington, 1996. 1st woman dir. of silhouette com., 1986, outstanding sportsman of yr., 1985, Conn. State Rifle & Pistol Assn., Wallingford; 1st woman dir. of industry rels. Ctrl. Conn. Handgun Silhouette Assn., Wallingford, 1985. Mem. Internat. Handgun Metallic Silhouette Assn. (outstanding support 1986, 87, 88, 89; outstanding family 1988; dir. of internat. championship 1986-89; dir. of industry, editor 1990-99; outstanding mem. 1992, 1st woman dir. of industry, 1990). Republican. Roman Catholic. Avocations: competition shooting, freshwater and deep sea fishing, reading, woodworking.

SCOTTO, RENATA, soprano; b. Savona, Italy, Feb. 24, 1935; m. Lorenzo Anselmi. Studied under, Ghirardini, Merlino and Mercedes Llopart, Accademia Musicale Savonese, Conservatory Giuseppe Verdi, Milan. Opera singer Robert Lombardo Assocs., 1979—. Presenter master classes Juilliard Sch., N.Y.C., Curtis Inst., Phila., Yale U., Russian Opera Ctr., Moscow, Tokyo U., young artist program La Scale, Milan, N.Y. Met. Opera; opened Renata Scotto Opera Acad., Albisola Marina, Italy, 1997—, Music Conservatory of Westchester, White Plains, NY, 2003—; dir. young artist program Verdi Festival, Parma, Italy, 2000 Roles include Feldmarschallin in Der Rosenkavalier (Franco Abiati and Frankfurter Allgemeine awards), 1992, performs Les Nuits d'Ete (Berlioz), Strauss and Mahler songs, Erwartung (Schoenberg), Santa Cecilia Acad. Orch., Rome, 1994, staged Il Parata (Bellini), Festival Belliniano, Catania, Italy, 1993, staged new prodn. La Sonnambula, 1994; dir. new prodn. La Traviata, N.Y.C. Opera, 1995.Kundry in Parsifal, German Schweing Fewtival, 1995, La Voix Humaine, Maggio Musicale Fiorentino, also in Barcelona, Spain, Amsterdam, The Netherlands, Klytemnestra in Elektra, Balt., 2000; dir. Tosca, Grand Opera Miami, 2001; performs with leading orchs. of world, giving concerts and master classes Bd. dirs. Santa Cecilia Acad., Rome Recipient Emmy award for Best Live Mus. Event in TV for Live from Lincoln Ctr., 1995. Office: 5 Stone Hollow Way Armonk NY 10504 Also: care Theatre of La Scala via Filodrammatici 2 Milan Italy*

SCOTTO, ROSANNA, newscaster; b. Brooklyn; BA in Fine Arts, Catholic U. Reporter, assoc. prodr. WTBS, Atlanta; reporter WABC-TV NY, reporter Eyewitness News; corr., anchor FOX 5/WNYW News, N.Y.C., 1986—. Co-owner Fresco by Scotto, 1993—. Co-author: Fresco: Modern Tuscan Cooking for All Seasons, 1997; actor: (films) Miracle on 34th Street, 1994, Ransom, 1996, The Object of My Affection, 1998, Famous, 2000. Nominee Emmy award, 1990, 1995; recipient First Place award for indiv. reporting, NY St. Associated Press Assoc., 1995. Office: WNYW-TV/Fox Broadcasting Co 205 E 67th St New York NY 10021-6050*

SCOTT-WILLIAMS, MILDRED P. food service specialist; b. Americus, Ga., Mar. 21, 1928; d. Bouie Lee and Mary (Jackson) Paschal; m. Mar. 10, 1986 (div.); 1 child, Alan Meadows. BS, Fort Valley State Coll., 1949; MA, Antioch U., 1980. Tchr. elem. schs., Ga., 1949-54; asst. dietitian Met. Hosp., Phila., 1954-57, head dietitian, 1957-67; tchr. home econs. Phila. Bd. Edn., 1967-68, food svc. mgr., 1969-71; dietitian Germantown Hosp., Phila., summer 1968; supr. tng. H.E.A.R.T. (Household Employment Assn. Reevaluation Tng.), Phila., 1968-69; tchr. food svc. Camden (N.J.) Bd. Edn., 1971-73, adminstrv. asst., 1973-81, food svc. supr., 1981-99; ret., 1999. Author: Metropolitan Diet Manual, 1965. Cub mother Boy Scouts Am., Phila., 1970-71; block chairperson 5900 Neighborhood Assn., Phila., 1980-89; Dem. committeewoman 17 Ward 28th Divsn.; mem. Phila. Dist. Atty. Panel for Youth. Recipient award The Chapel of Four Chaplains, Phila., 1977, Disting. Svc. Key award LKM Sorority, 2000, Cert. of Appreciation, USDA, 2000, Recognition of Svc. award Camden City Fedn. Sch. Adminstrs., 2000. Mem. Am. Fedn. Sch. Adminstrs. (merit award 1987), Am. Sch. Food Svc. Assn. (cert., Star Club cert. 1999), N.J. Food Svc. Assn. (sec. 1980-82, appreciation award Elizabeth 1987, President's award New Brunswick 1989), Order Ea. Star (sec. 1979-84). Home: 5956 N 21st St Philadelphia PA 19138-2922 E-mail: mscott9837@aol.com.

SCOTT-WILLIAMS, WENDY LEE, information technology specialist; b. Buffalo, Jan. 22; d. Arthur Raymond and June Amelia Schutt; m. Nigel Simon Scott-Williams, Feb. 29, 1980. BA cum laude, SUNY, Buffalo, 1975; MA with honors, Cambridge U., 1979; MLIS with honors, CUNY-Queens Coll., 1987. Applications rep. Barrister, N.Y.C., 1982-83; coord. computer systems Stroock & Stroock & Lavan, N.Y.C., 1983-87; tech. svcs. mgr. Batten, Barton, Durstein & Osborn (BBDO) Worldwide, N.Y.C., 1987-92; adminstr., mgr. info. resources Fairchild Publs., N.Y.C., 1992-96; info. resource mgr. March of Dimes Birth Defects Found., White Plains, N.Y., 1996—. Active N.Y. Zool. Soc. Mem. Spl. Librs. Assn., Cambridge Union Soc., Oxford-Cambridge Soc., Nature Conservancy, Greenpeace. Presbyterian. Avocations: travel, gardening. Office: March of Dimes Birth Defects Found Nat Hdqs 1275 Mamaroneck Ave White Plains NY 10605-5298

SCOTT-WILSON, SUSAN RICE, vice principal; b. Brownsville, Tenn., Aug. 11, 1942; d. Moreau Estes and E. Estelle (Walker) Rice; m. Charles E. Scott, Feb. 28, 1969 (div. July 1985); children: Tamera W., David W.; m. Lloyd Curlin Wilson, Apr. 7, 1994. BS, U. Tenn., Martin, 1964; EdM, Memphis State U., 1979, EdD, 1989. Cert. master tchr., Tenn. Elem. tchr. Lauderdale County Bd. Edn., Ripley, Tenn., 1964-65; exchange tchr. USIA, Washington, Netherlands, 1986-87; chmn. English dept. Am. Sch. of The Hague, Netherlands, 1987-88; secondary tchr. Haywood County Bd. Edn., Brownsville, Tenn., 1974-86, tchr. vocat. English, 1989-90, dir. adult basic edn., 1990-95; vice prin. Haywood H.S., Brownsville, Tenn., 1995—. Mem. curriculum task force Tenn. Dept. Edn., Nashville, 1985-86, mem. collaborative task force, 1989-92; chair Tenn. Acad. Decathlon Bd., 1998—. Local elector Tenn. Pres.'s Trust, Knoxville, 1989—; mem. Sister Cities Commn., Brownsville, 1990; com. mem. Ptnrs. in Edn., Brownsville, 1992—93; mem. West Star Leadership, 1993, Tenn. Reorgnl. Improvement Mgmt. Sys., 1994—95; mem. steering com. Fayette County-Haywood County Cmty. Enterprise, Brownsville, 1994—2000; bd. dirs. YMCA, Brownsville, 1996—2001. Named Outstanding Tchr. by students U. Chgo., 1989. Mem. NEA, Nat. Coun. Tchrs. English (regional composition judge 1984-86), Tenn. Edn. Assn., Tenn. Tchrs. Study Coun. (state steering com. 1984-86), Tenn. Prins. Study Coun., Sigma Tau Delta, Phi Delta Kappa. Methodist. Avocations: reading, travel. Home: 321 N Washington St Brownsville TN 38012-2063 Office: Haywood HS 1175 E College St Brownsville TN 38012-2208

SCOVEL, MARY ALICE, retired music therapy educator; b. Grand Rapids, Mich., Jan. 28, 1936; d. Carl Edward and Alice Bertha (Bieri) Sennema; m. Ward Norman Scovel, July 7, 1956; children: Marcia, Katherine, Steven (dec.), Carl (dec.). MusB, Western Mich. U., 1969; MusM, Mich. State U., 1975. Registered music therapist; bd. cert. Asst. prof. music Grand Valley State U., Allendale, Mich., 1969-75; instr. U. Dayton (Ohio), 1975-78, Muskegon (Mich.) Community Coll., 1978-80; intern dir. Battle Creek (Mich.) Adventist Hosp., 1980-84; prof. music therapy Western Mich. U., Kalamazoo, 1984-95; ret., 1995; owner, pvt. practice Health Harmonics, Honolulu, 1997-98; ret., 1998. Cons. Pre-sch. Physically Handicapped, Wyo., Mich., 1974, Doris Klausen Devel. Ctr., Battle Creek, 1985-86; music therapist, sound practitioner and trainer, Tahlequah, Okla., 1995-97; pvt. practice health harmonics, 1997—; chmn. Multi-clinic, Kalamazoo, 1988-89. Author: Music Therapy in Treatment of Adults, 1990, Surviving Suicide: My Journey to the Light Within, 2003; co-editor Music Therapy Perspectives; cited in The Mozart Effect by Don Campbell, 1997; contbr. articles to profl. jours. Lay del. United Meth. Ch., Albion, Mich., 1991. Mem. Am. Music Therapy Assn. (del.), Nat. Assn. Mental Illness, Great Lakes Region Music Therapy (past pres.), Mich. Music Therapists, AAUW, Pi Delta Alpha, Pi Kappa Lambda. Avocations: quilting, reading, cross country skiing, singing, swimming. Home: 112 Doncaster Ln Bluffton SC 29909 E-mail: mwscovel@aol.com.

SCOZZAFAVA, DEDE, state representative; b. Buffalo, N.Y. m. Ron McDougall; children: Matt, Molly. BS, Boston U.; MBA, Clarkson Grad. Sch. of Mgmt. Trustee Village of Gouverneur, mayor, 1993—98; N.Y. state rep., 1998—. Investment advisor RBC Dain Rauscher Inc., Watertown, NY; pres. St. Lawrence County Mayors Assn., 1994—95, 1996—97. Assembly standing coms. Econ. Devel., Edn. and Social Svcs., 2001—02; apptd. ranking mem. Assembly's Local Govts. Com.; served on Task Force on Edn. Stds., Nursing Shortage Task Force. Recipient Conf. of Mayor's award, N.Y. State. Mem.: Gouverneur Arts Club (assoc.). Office: 93 E Main St Gouverneur NY 13642 Address: LOB 532 Albany NY 12248 E-mail: scozzad@assembly.state.ny.us.

SCRIBNER, PRINCESS ROSE-MARIE, not-for-profit developer; b. Gardiner, Maine; d. Harvey Clinton and Harriet Gertrude Mason; m. Henry Elden Scribner, Jan. 18, 1958; children: Randall, Dawn, Debra, Shawn, Todd. BS, U. Ea. Conn., 1971; degree (hon.), U. Maine, 2002. Pres., founder White Cloud Indians for Devel., Norwich, Conn., 1970—86; adminstr. Indian Health Clinic, Pequot Nation, Ledyard, Conn., 1977—86. Founder, pres. Indian Women's Non-Profit Orgn., Indian Island, Maine. Active mem. Women's Polit. Caucus, Hartford, Conn., 1970, Nat. Women's Polit. Orgn., Washington, 1971. Recipient Volunteering Recognition award, Pres. Reagan. Democrat. Roman Catholic. Avocations: dance, decorating, puzzle-making, gardening, writing. Home: 65 West St II Old Town ME 04468

SCRIBNER, SHERLIE ANN, language educator; b. Mobile, Ala., Aug. 24, 1945; d. Murl and Eva Coggin Scribner; children: Michael Svestka, Lauren Svestska, Christopher Svestka. BA in English and Philosophy, Baylor U., 1966; MEd, U. Va., 1976; MA, EdD in Ednl. Adminstrn., Columbia U., 1980; diploma, Nat. Def. U., 1984. Classroom tchr. Virginia Beach (Va.) Pub. Schs., 1966-69, Internat. Sch., Bangkok, 1969-70; reading resource tchr. Fairfax (Va.) County Pub. Schs., 1973-76; sr. evaluator U.S. Gen. Acctg. Office, Washington, 1980-97; CEO Children's Fund, Washington, 1997—; devel. officer Washington Episcopal Sch., Bethesda, Md., 1999-2000; program dir., tchr. profl. studies U. Va. Sch. Continuing and Profl. Studies, 2000-2001; ESL and English tchr. Fairfax (Va.) County Pub. Sch., 2001—. Contbr. articles to profl. jours., reports to U.S. Congress. Trustee Episcopal Ctr. for Children; bd. dirs. Tiny Findings Daycare Ctr., Washington; founder Children's Fund, Children's Resource Network, Ctr. for Children's Studies, Child Survival Fund, Children's Hunger Relief Network, Free the Children Fund, Children's Fund Charieies, Children's Edn. and Enrichment Fund, Children's Spl. Needs Fund, Christian Children's Relief Fund, all Washington. Mem. World Orgn. Presch. Edn. Baptist. Address: Children's Fund PO Box 7936 Mc Lean VA 22106-7936 E-mail: SherlieScribner@aol.com.

SCRIMSHAW, SUSAN CROSBY, dean; PhD in Anthropology, Columbia U., 1974. Prof. Sch. Pub. Health UCLA, 1974—94, assoc. dean, 1988—94; dean U. Ill. Sch. Pub. Health, Chgo., 1995—. Recipient Margaret Mead award, 1985. Fellow: AAAS; mem.: Nat. Soc. Med. Anthropology (pres. 1985), Soc. Applied Anthropology, Am. Anthropology Assn., Inst. Medicine NAS. Office: Sch of Pub Health U Ill Chicago 2121 W Taylor St # Mc922 Chicago IL 60612-7260

SCRUGGS, ELAINE M. mayor; m. Larry Scruggs; 1 child, Jennifer. Former mgmt. specialist; elected mem. Glendale (Ariz.) City Coun., 1990-93; mayor City of Glendale, 1994—. Past chmn. Maricopa (Ariz.) Assn. Govts., chair youth policy adv., chmn. Regional Pub. Transp. Authority, chmn. Ariz. Mcpl. Water Users Assn., chair Maricopa Assn.

Govt. Regional Aviation Systems policy com.; chair Ariz. Mcpl. Tax Code Commn. Dir. Glendale Leadership Program, 1984-89; mem. Ariz. Coalition for Tomorrow, Ariz. Women in Mcpl. Govt.; mem. youth adv. commn., Mayor's Alliance Against Drugs and Gangs. Mem. Glendale C. of C. Office: Office Mayor 5850 W Glendale Ave Glendale AZ 85301-2563

SCRUGGS, SANDRA NELL, writer, former school teacher; b. Tupelo, Miss., Mar. 17, 1948; d. Luther Herman and Gladys Lavelle Scruggs; 1 child, Tara Leigh Turner. BS in Edn., Miss. State U., 1970; degree in gifted and talented edn., Delta State U., 1979. Tchr. pub. schs., Miss., 1970-72, 78-89, Bremerhaven (German) Mil. Sch., 1973-75, Anniston (Ala.) Pub. Schs., 1976-77; writer New Orleans, 1989—. Writer Poetry Forum, New Orleans, 1999. Recipient Woman of Yr. award Nat. Club, 1979. Avocations: recording, songwriting, writing children's books, birdwatching, camping. Office: Sissi Angeli Prodns 3216 W Esplanade Ave N # 177 Metairie LA 70002-1667

SCRUGGS, TERRI LAGUARDIA, systems support specialist; b. Kingsport, Tenn., Feb. 7, 1957; d. Thomas Edward LaGuardia, Jr. and Kathryn Huddle LaGuardia; m. Warren Burks Scruggs III, July 10, 1992; children: Matthew, Amanda Healey, Katie LaGuardia, Theresa LaGuardia. Student, Carson Newman Coll., Jefferson City, Tenn., 1975—77. Computer, internet specialist Shop Heaven, Ashburn, Va., Kingsport, Tenn. Internet cons. Shop Heaven, Ashburn, Va.; internet mktg. Shop Now, Seattle, Wild Bird Ctrs., Md. Recipient The Blue Chip Enterprise award, 2000. Mem.: NAFE, Kingsport C. of C. Republican. Roman Catholic. Avocations: computing, gardening, basketball, family, electronics.

SCRUGGS-LEFTWICH, YVONNE, association executive; BA in Polit. Sci. cum laude, N.C. Ctrl. U.; postgrad., Freie U., Berlin, Deutsche Hoch Schule Politics, Johns Hopkins U.; MA in Pub. Adminstrn., U. Minn.; PhD in City and Regional Planning, U. Pa. Housing rsch. technician City Phila. Evaluation Project; coord. rsch. and planning, exec. dir. The Wharton Ctr.-North Phila. Settlement House; cmty. renewal specialist Phila. Cmty. Renewal Program; assoc. dir. Phila. Coun. for Cmty. Advancement Ford Founds. Gray Areas Project, dep. dir. planning, 1962-65; fed. liaison officer U.S. Dept. HUD, 1965-69; coord. field svcs., human resources ctr. U. Pa. Wharton Sch., 1970-75; chairperson, assoc. prof. grad. dept. city/regional planning Howard U., 1974-77; prof. city and regional planning Howard U. Sch. Arch. and Planning, 1979-81; head U.S. del. to OECD and ECE U.S. Dept. HUD, 1977-79, dep. asst. sec. cmty. planning and devel., exec. dir. Pres. Carter's Urban/Regl. Policy Group, 1977-79; regional dir. DHCR, Buffalo, 1981-82; commr. N.Y. State Divsn. Housing and Cmty. Renewal, 1982-85; dep. mayor City Phila., 1985-87; bd. chair, COO Y.E.L. Corp., Bklyn. & Harlem, 1987-91; dir. Urban Pol. Inst., Nat. Pol. Inst., Exec. Leadership Seminar, Joint Ctr. for Pol. and Econ. Studies, 1991—. Lectr. grad. dept. city and regional planning U. Pa., Phila., 1970-76, vis. lectr. urban affairs program, 1978-80, vis. prof. grad. dept. city and regional planning, 1985-87, vis. prof. Fels Ctr. Govt., 1985, vis. prof. grad. program dynamics of orgn., 1987; sr. cons. Jeffalyn Johnson and Assocs., Falls Church, Va., 1980-81; adj. prof. planning SUNY, Buffalo, 1981-82; vis. prof. polit. power and urban diversity Grad. Sch. Polit. Mgmt., George Washington U., 1990-2000; vis. prof. U.S. Info. Agy., Kenya, Ethiopia, South Africa, Nigeria, Ghana; vis. expert West German Office Fgn. Rels. Bd. dirs. Crime Prevention Assn., 1964-69, Mid City YMCA, 1964-71, Gaudenzia House, 1969-72; pres. Phila. Assn. Intergroup Rels. Ofcls., 1967; trustee SUNY, Buffalo, 1982-86; pres. Geneva B. Scruggs Cmty. Health Ctr., 1982-85; bd. dirs. State N.Y. Mortgage Agy., 1983-85, Housing Fin. Agy. N.Y. State, 1983-85, N.Y. State Mortgage Loan Enforcement Corp., 1983-85, N.Y. State Project Fin. Agy.; co-chair Gov.'s Task Force on the Homeless, 1983-85; chair Gov.'s Housing Policy Task Force, 1983-85; exec. com. Women in Govt., 1984, 85; v.p., trustee Milton S. Eisenhower Found., 1991—; bd. mem. Washington Planning Workshop; v.p. Pa. Housing Fin. Agy., 1983-85, Commonwealth Pa.; commr. Mobile Home Stds. Commn., Commonwealth Pa.; bd. dirs. Phila. Coun. for Cmty. Advancement; bd. dirs., membership com. World Affairs Coun.; others. Fulbright fellow, Berlin; study scholar Johns Hopkins U.; Ford Found. grantee, 1979-81. Mem. ASPA, Am. Planning Assn., Nat. Assn. Planners (bd. mem., Diana Donald award), Nat. Coun. Negro Women, Nat. Polit. Congress Black Women, Greater Washington Urban League, Alpha Kappa Alpha (Alpha Chi chpt.), Pi Gamma Nu. Office: Black Leadership Forum Inc Po Box 34506 Washington DC 20043-4506

SCULLION, ANNETTE MURPHY, lawyer, educator; b. Chgo., Apr. 6, 1926; d. Edmund Patrick and Anna (Nugent) Murphy; 1 child, Kevin. BEd, Chgo. Tchrs. Coll., 1960; JD, DePaul U., 1964, MEd, 1966, Loyola U., Chgo., 1970; EdD, No. Ill. U., 1974. Bar: Ill. 1964, U.S. Dist. Ct. (no. dist.) Ill. 1965, U.S. Ct. Appeals (D.C. cir.) 1978. Lectr. Chgo. C.C., 1964-68; pvt. practice Chgo., 1964—; from asst. prof. bus. edn. to prof. Chgo. State U., 1966-98. Founder, adviser Bus. Edn. Students Assn., Chgo. State U., 1976—; sch. law workshop coord. Ill. Divsn. Vocat. and Tech. Edn., 1981, coord. edn. workshops, 1990—. Mem. ABA, Nat. Bus. Edn. Assn., Womens Bar Assn. Ill., Am. Tchr. Edn., Beta Gamma Sigma. Home: 386 Muskegon Ave Calumet City IL 60409-2347

SCULLION, ROSEMARIE, literature educator; Co-editor: Celine and the Politics of Difference, 1995, Studies in Twentieth Century Literature, South Central Rev. Substance; contbr. articles to profl. jours. Mem.: Modern Lang. Assn. Am. (exec. coun. 2000—). Office: Univ Iowa 716 Jefferson Bldg 467 Phillips Hall Iowa City IA 52242 E-mail: rosemarie-scullion@uiowa.edu.

SCULLY, BONNIE DIANE, financial planner; b. Anchorage, June 11, 1948; d. Oakley Walter and Patricia Alberta (Campbell) Baron; m. J. Robert Scully, Aug. 28, 1971; children: Amanda Rose, John Robert Jr. BA in English, Spring Hill Coll., 1970; CFP, Coll. for Fin Planning, Denver, CO, 1986. CFP. Flight attendant Delta Airlines, Atlanta, 1970; bank teller Ctrl. Nat. Bank, Richmond, Va., 1971; educator St. Elizabeth Sch., Richmond, Va., 1972-74; dept. chmn. airline and travel career program Nat. Coll. Bus., Rapid City, S.D., 1976-77; tax preparer H&R Block, Iowa City, 1978-80; bus. mgr. Dr. J. Robert Scully, Asheville, N.C., 1980-83; fin. planner Parsec Fin. Mgmt., Asheville, N.C., 1983-88; fin. counselor Cath. Social Svcs., Asheville, N.C., 1995—. Author: The Scully Files - Organizing Your Finances, 1999, The Scully Files - A Young Couple's Blueprint for Managing Money, 2000. Mem. Leadership Asheville, 1983; bd. dirs. Jr. Achievement, Asheville, 1984-86, Children's Home Soc., Asheville, 1987-89; bd. dirs., allocation com. United Way, Asheville, 1986-88; treas., bd. dirs. St. Joan of ARC Parish Coun., 1986-88; pres. PTA, Asheville Cath. Sch., 1996-97; chmn. spl. event com. St. Joseph Hosp., 1996-97; bd. dirs. Belechere Entertainment Com., bd. dirs. Jesuit House of Prayer, 1995-98; vol. ABCCM (Asheville Buncombe Community Christian Ministry), 1995-98. Mem. ADA, (regional treas. 1997-98), Buncombe County Dental Aux. (treas. 1995-98). Roman Catholic. Avocations: writing, yoga, travel, reading, sewing. Home and Office: 450 N Griffing Blvd Asheville NC 28804-2814

SCURRY, BRIANA COLLETTE, professional soccer player; b. Mpls., Sept. 7, 1971; BS in Polit. Sci., U. Mass., 1995. Goalkeeper U.S. Women's Nat. Soccer Team, Chgo., 1994—99, 2002—; profl. soccer player Atlanta Beat (WUSA), 2001—03. Named Goalkeeper of Yr., Mo. Athletic Club Sports Found., 1993; recipient Gold medal, Atlanta Olympics, 1996, World Cup champion, 1999, Silver medal, Sydney Olympic Games, 2000. Office: US Soccer Fedn US Soccer House 1801 S Prairie Ave Chicago IL 60616-1319

SEABRIGHT, FRANCES, volunteer; b. Laurium, Mich., May 17, 1912; d. Joseph Krausz and Rosa Rosenberg; m. Lawrence H. Seabright (dec.); children: Robert, Carol S. Christensen. BS, Ohio U., 1934; MS, Ohio State U., 1937. Cert. tchr. Ohio. Tchr. Portsmouth Pub. Schs., Ohio, 1934—38; chemist Sears Roebuck, Chgo., 1939—42; asst. prof. Elmhurst Coll., Ill., 1942—44, U. Ill., Chgo., 1953—80. Pk. dist. reporter League Women Voters, Elmhurst, 1988—90; election judge City Elmhurst, 1980—; vol. hist. mus., art gallery. Mem.: AAUW (hon.), Hosp. Guild, Chem. Soc. (com. chmn., pres.), Woman's Club, Travel Club. Democrat. Methodist. Avocations: travel, bridge, flower arranging. Home: 247 Berkley Ave Elmhurst IL 60126

SEABURG, GLEN T. chemistry educator; BA in chemistry, UCLA, 1934, PhD in chemistry, 1937. Recipient Nobel Laurette award, 1951, George C. Pimentel award in Chemical Edn.,1994. Home: Lafayette, Calif. Deceased.

SEACHRIST, DENISE, music educator; b. Youngstown, Ohio, Feb. 2, 1960; d. Glen Wilbert and Eloise Rapp Seachrist. MusB, Heidelberg Coll., 1982; MusM, Youngstown State U., 1985; PhD, Kent State U., 1993. Assoc. prof. Kent State U., Warren, Ohio, 1994—. Dir. Kent Trumbull Choir, Warren, 1996—; bd. mem. Warren Philharm., 1998—; guest dir. Symphony Women's Chorus, Youngstown, 1998; spkr. in field. Author: Musical World of Halim El-Dabh, 2003; contbr. chapters to books, entries to dictionaries. Mem.: Soc. for Ethnomusicology (sec. Niagara chpt. 1997—98), Am. Musicological Soc., Soc. for Am. Music, Coll. Music Soc., Internat. Alliance for Women in Music. Democrat. Mem. United Church of Christ. Avocations: reading, swimming, music, golf, photography. Home: 1443 Stafford Ave NE Warren OH 44483-4339 Office: Kent State Univ 4314 Mahoning Ave NW Warren OH 44483-1998 E-mail: dseachri@kent.edu.

SEAGREN, ALICE, state legislator; b. 1947; m. Fred Seagren; 2 children. BS, SE Mo. State U. Mem. Minn. Ho. of Reps., 1993—, chmn. edn. fin., 1999—. Active Bloomington (Minn.) Sch. Bd., 1989-92. Mem. Bloomington C. of C. (bd. dirs. 1990-92), Phi Gamma Nu, Alpha Chi Omega. Republican. Home: 9730 Palmer Cir Bloomington MN 55437-2017 Office: Minn Ho of Reps State Capital Building Saint Paul MN 55155-0001 E-mail: rep.alice.seagren@house.leg.state.mn.us.

SEALE, N. ALLISON, communications specialist; b. Waco, Tex., May 19, 1965; d. R. Henry Seale and Nanci Myers Bovey. BS in Journalism, Tex. A&M U., 1988. Comm. mgr. Artists Rights Found., L.A., 1996—99; comm. mgr. Hamilton Fish Inst., George Washington U., Washington, 2001—. Advt. sales profl. Ind. Feature Project/West, L.A., 1998—2001. Editor: (booklet) Bullying: Information for Parents, Students and Educators, (newsletter) The Bull., The Artists Rights Report. Grantee, OJJDP, 2001, 2002, 2003. Mem.: IABC (Best Feature 2001). Home: 12000 Moorpark St #10 Studio City CA 91604 Office: Hamilton Fish Inst 2121 K St NW Ste 200 Washington DC 20037-1830 E-mail: aliseal@aol.com

SEALS, LOUISE CRIMRINE, editor; B Journalism, W.Va. U., 1966; M Mass Comms., Va. Commonwealth U. With Dayton (Ohio) Daily News; reporter, editor Rochester (NY) Dem. and Chronicle; with Richmond (Va.) Times Dispatch, 1968—, asst. mng. editor, 1982—92, dep. mng. editor, 1992—94, now mng. editor. Mem. adv. bd. PErly Isaac Reed Sch. Jounalism W.Va. U. Named to Va. Comms. Hall of Fame, 2003; recipient Nat. Communicator Achievement award, Nat. Fedn. Press Women, Outstanding Woman in Comms. award, YWCA of Richmond. Mem.: Soc. Profl. Journalists (bd. dirs. Va. profl. chpt.), Va. Press Assn. (bd. dirs.), AP Mng. Editors (bd. dirs. 1999—). Office: Richmond Times-Dispatch 300 E Franklin St PO Box 85333 Richmond VA 23293

SEALS, MARGARET LOUISE, newspaper editor; b. Buckhannon, W.Va., Oct. 27, 1944; d. James Richard and Helen Margaret (Brown) Crumrine; m. Harry Eugene Seals, Jan. 10, 1975. BS in journalism, W. Va. U., 1966; MS in mass. comm., Va. Commonwealth U., 1983. Reporter, copy editor Democrat & Chronicle, Rochester, NY, 1966-67, Dayton (Ohio) Daily News, 1967-68; copy editor Richmond (Va.) Times-Dispatch, 1968-75, copy desk slot editor, 1975-81, exec. news editor, 1981, asst. mng. editor, 1982-92, dep. mng. editor, 1992-93, mng. editor, 1994—. Mem. Leadership Metro Richmond, 1986, mem. adv. bd. sch. mass. comm. Va. Commonwealth U., 1988-93; mem. vis. com. Sch. Journalism, W.Va. U., 1999—. Named Outstanding Woman in Comms. YWCA Met. Richmond, 1989; recipient Perley Isaac Reed award W.Va. U. Journalism Sch. Alumni Assn., 1996; inducted into Va. Comm. Hall of Fame, 2003. Mem.: Richmond Assn. Black Journalists, Nat. Assn. Black Journalists, Va. Press Assn. (dir. 2001—03, treas. 2003—), AP Mng. Editors (editor APME News 1993—94, dir. 1993—95, treas. 1996—97, dir. 1998—2001, Disting. Svc. award 2002), Va. Press Women (treas. 1986—88, 2d v.p. 1988—90, pres. 1990—92, Press Woman of Yr. 1986, Communicator of Achievement award 1997), Soc. Profl. Journalists (bd. dirs. Va. profl. chpt. 1998—2003, pres. Va. profl. chpt. 2000—02), Nat. Fedn. Press Women (bd. dirs. 1990—92, Communicator of Achievement award 1997), Phi Kappa Phi. Avocations: history, historical fiction, jazz. Office: Richmond-Times Dispatch PO Box 85333 Richmond VA 23293-5333 E-mail: lseals@timesdispatch.com.

SEALS, TERESA MCCRAY, elementary school educator; b. Ft. Lauderdale, Dec. 9, 1945; d. Samuel McCray and Mildred Hill; m. Bobbie Joseph Seals, June 29, 1968; children: Mya, Damon. BS in Sociology, Ky. State U., 1967; M in Early Childhood Edn., Governors State U., 1975. Tchr. Terrell Elem., Chgo., 1967—68, Detroit Pub. Schs., 1968, Bryn Mawr Sch., Chgo., 1969—99, Kozminski Acad., Chgo., 1999—. Mem. Tchr. for Harold Washington, Chgo., 1983, Kennedy-King Cmty. Scholarship Com., 1988—91. Avocations: bowling, jogging, travel. Home: 10515 S Emerald Ave Chicago IL 60628-2303

SEAMAN, JUDITH D. retired adult education educator; b. Merrill, Oreg., Oct. 14, 1940; d. Donald Dungan and Annabelle J. (Stockton) Dod; m. David William Seaman, June 10, 1962 (div. Oct. 1986); children: Amanda Catherine, Natasha Thérèse. BA, Coll. Wooster, 1962; MA, Stanford U., 1967; MS, Marshall U., 1996. Case worker, translator Planned Parenthood, Waukegan, Ill., 1971-72; lectr. in humanities Davis & Elkins Coll., Elkins, W.Va., 1972-75; ESL tchr. Internat. Lang. Inst., Elkins, W.Va., 1975-78; Adult Basic Edn. tchr. Randolph County Schs., Elkins, W.Va., 1980—2004; ret., 2004; freelance grant writer, 2004—. Tutor trainer, program dir. Literacy Vols. Am.-W.Va. Tygart Affiliate, Elkins, 1985—, pres., 1991-95, 2002—; peer trainer W.Va. Adult Basic Edn., Elkins, 1990—; mem. W.Va. adv. com. Inst. for Women's Policy Rsch., 2002-03. Bd. dirs. Women's Aid in Crisis, Elkins, 1991—, pres., 1993-95, treas. 1996-98. Mem. W.Va. Adult Edn. Assn. (pres. 1991-92, legis. chair 1995—), W.Va. Edn. Assn. (W.Va. adult tchr. of yr. award 1990), W.Va. NOW (pres. 1986-88). Mem. Soc. Of Friends. Home: 1316 S Davis Ave Elkins WV 26241-3479 Office: Randolph County Vo-Tech Ctr 200 Kennedy Dr Elkins WV 26241-9527

SEAMAN, MARY, theater educator; d. Donald Joseph Seaman and Mary Constance Menalis. BA in Music Edn., Chestnut Hill Coll., 1985. Cert. tchr. N.J., Pa. Percussionist, arranger, vocal dir. Millstone Players, Freehold, NJ, 1975—95; program dir., prodr., stage mus. dir. Walnut St. Theatre, Phila., 1992—96; fine arts chair, music dir. various schs. Diocese of Trenton, Beverly, Riverside, Maple Shade, NJ, 1993—96; mus. dir., accompanist Haddonfield (N.J.) Plays and Players, 1996; mus./vocal dir. Camden (N.J.) County Coll., 1997; dir. sacred music Corpus Christi Parish, Hasbrouck Heights, NJ, 1997—2001; performing arts educator, fine arts chair Bradley Beach (N.J.) Sch., 2002—. Co-author: (music curriculum/activity book) Shared Music, 1987, composer liturgical music; author, songwriter: children's mus. Mem.: Nat. Pastoral Musicians (sec. pianists profl. concerns 2000—03). Avocations: spending time with nieces and nephews, exercising, reading, volunteering at church.

SEAMANS, BEVERLY BENSON, sculptor; b. Boston, Oct. 30, 1928; d. Philip Benson and Barbara Browne Betts; m. Donald Campbell Seamans, June 24, 1950. Student, Sweet Briar Coll., 1946—48, Mus. Sch. Fine Arts, Boston, 1948—50. Prin. works include Abbott Pub. Libr., Marblehead, Mass., Am. Cathedral, Paris, Babson Inst., Wellesley, Mass., Beverly (Mass.) Hosp., First Nat. Bank, Boston, House Seven Gables, Salem, Mass., Mablehead H.S., Mus. Sci., Boston, MIT, Cambridge, Peabody Essex Mus., Salem, Mass., Salem Hosp. Fellow: Nat. Sculpture Soc.; mem.: New Eng. Sculptor Soc., North Shore Art Assn., Marblehead Art Assn., Copley Soc. Boston, Cambridge Art Assn. Home: 10 Harbor View Ln Marblehead MA 01945

SEAPKER, JANET KAY, museum and architectural history consultant; b. Pitts., Nov. 2, 1947; d. Charles Henry and Kathryn Elizabeth (Dany) S.; m. Edward F. Turberg, May 24, 1975. BA, U. Pitts., 1969; MA, SUNY, Cooperstown, 1975. Park ranger Nat. Park Svc., summers 1967-69; archtl. historian N.C. Archives and History, Raleigh, 1971—76, hist. preservation adminstr., 1976—77, grant-in-aid adminstr., 1977—78; dir. Cape Fear Mus. (formerly New Hanover County Mus.), Wilmington, NC, 1978—2000, ret.; archtl. historian-preservation/mus. cons.; curator U. N.C. Wilmington's Kenan House, 2003—04; bd. dirs. Wrightsville Beach Mus., 2004—. Bd. dirs. Bellamy Mansion Found., Wilmington, 1986-89, 91-97, Lower Cape Fear Hist. Soc., Wilmington, 1985-88; N.C. rep. S.E. Mus. Conf., 1986-90; bd. dirs. Cape Fear Coast Conv. and Vis. Bur., 1997-2001, sec., 2001, Wrightsville Beach Mus., 2004-; field reviewer Inst. Mus. Svcs., 1982-2001 Contbr. articles to profl. jours. Bd. dirs. Downtown Area Revitalization Effort, Wilmington, 1979-81, Thalian Hall Ctr. for Performing Arts, 1996-98; bd. dirs. Hist. Wilmington Found., 1979-84, pres., 1980-81; mem. Cmty. Appearance Commn., Wilmington, 1984-88, 250th Anniversary Commn., Wilmington, 1986-90. Grad. program fellow SUNY, Cooperstown, 1969-70; recipient Profl. Svc. award N.C. Mus. Coun., 1982, Woman of Achievement award YWCA, 1994, William T. Alderson awardN.C. Mus. Coun., 2004. Mem. Am. Assn. Mus. (accreditation vis. com. 1983-2001, reviewer mus. assessment program 1982-2002), Nat. Trust Hist. Preservation, Southeastern Mus. Conf. (N.C. state rep. 1986-90), N.C. Mus. Coun. (sec.-treas. 1978-84, pres. 1984-86; recepient William T. Anderson award, 2004), Hist. Preservation Found N.C. (sec. 1976-78). Presbyterian. Home and Office: 307 N 15th St Wilmington NC 28401-3813 Personal E-mail: jseapker@ec.rr.com.

SEARING, MARJORY ELLEN, government official, economist; b. N.Y.C., Mar. 29, 1945; d. William Edgar Searing and Jean Frances (Smith) Searing Fusaro; 1 child, Stephanie Anne Lane. BA in Econs., SUNY-Binghamton, 1966; MA in Econs., Georgetown U., 1969, PhD in Econs., 1972. Economist Bur. Econs. Analysis U.S. Dept. Commerce, Washington, 1967-73, internat. economist Bur. East-West Trade, 1973-74, dir. Office Internat. Sector Policy, 1980-84, dir. Office Industry Assessment, 1984-86, acting dep. asst. sec. sci. and electronics, 1984-85, dir. Office Multilateral Affairs, 1986-90, dep. asst. sec. for Japan, 1991-97, asst. sec., acting dir. Gen. U.S. and Fgn. Comml. Svc., 1997-98; dep. asst. sec. for Asia and the Pacific, 1998—; sr. internat. economist Office Trade Policy U.S. Dept. Treasury, Washington, 1974-76, dir. Office East-West Econ. Policy, 1976-79. Contbr. numerous articles to profl. publs. N.Y. State Regents scholar, 1962-65; Georgetown U. fellow, 1966-71 Office: US Dept Commerce Constitution Ave NW Washington DC 20230-0001

SEARLE, MICHELLE A. music educator, webmaster; b. Johnstown, Pa., Sept. 2, 1974; d. Larry A. and Carol A. Searle. BS in Music Edn., Clarion U. Pa., 1996. Choral dir. Westlake H.S., Waldorf, Md., 1996—99; instrumental music tchr. Seneca Valley H.S., Germantown, Md., 1999—2001, choral dir., 2001—. Color guard instr. Westlake H.S., Waldorf, 1996—99. Mem.: Am. Choral Dirs. assn., Music Educators Nat. Conf. Avocation: competitive swing dancing. Office: Seneca Valley HS 12700 Middlebrook Rd Germantown MD 20874

SEARLES, EDNA LOWE, artist, illustrator, composer; b. Minden, La., Sept. 10, 1936; m. Thomas D. Searles. AA, Mont. Coll., 1975; BA in Edn., La. Poly., 1958. Tchr. pub. sch., La. & Ga., 1958-65. Guest curator Delaplaine Visual Arts Ctr., Frederick, Md., 1995, East Meets West. Illustrator Soy for the 21st Century, 1984, ABC Coloring Book, 1994, Mind Children, 1995, Mind Travel, 1998, About You, 1998, Choose Life, 2002, Animal Alphabet Book, 2003; one-woman shows include Arnot Art Mus., Elmira, N.Y., 1988, Va. Tech State U., 1989, Gwinnett Coun. of the Arts Gallery, Ga., 1990, VA Honorarium, 1990, Other: Affiliation and Exhibits, Janice Aldridge Gallery, Georgetown, Washington, 1996, Sculpture on the Ground, Md., 1994, 1999, The Artist's Gallery, Frederick, Md., 1997—2002, The Garden Gallery, Carlisle, Pa., 1999—, Nancy Stamm's Galleria, 1999—, Gallery of New Masters, Sandy Spring, Md., 2000—01, Millinneum Exhibit Music for the Eyes, 1999—2000, Musicians and All that Jazz, Frederick, Md., 2000, Gallery of New Masters, Olney, Md., 2000—01, Boarman Art Ctr., Martinsburg, W.Va., 2001. Past pres. Clarksburg (Md.) Cmty. Assn. Recipient Juror's award for painting Montgomery County Art, 1993, Internat. Gold medal for painting Accademia Italia, 1973; named Wilson Wims Citizen of Yr. Clarksburg Comm. Assn., 1974. Mem.: DAR (vice regent Pleasant Plains of Damascus chpt. 2001—02), Nat. League of Am. Pen Women (pres. Chevy Chase br. 1980—82, 2002—04, Md. state pres. 2004—). Methodist. Achievements include invention of music system for the deaf to "see" music as art. Avocations: hammered dulcimer, composing music, folk singer, harp, piano.

SEARLS, EILEEN HAUGHEY, retired lawyer, librarian, educator; b. Madison, Wis., Apr. 27, 1925; d. Edward M. and Anna Mary (Haughey) S. BA, U. Wis., 1948, JD, 1950, MS in LS, 1951. Bar: Wis. 1950. Cataloger Yale U., 1951-52; instr. law St. Louis U., 1952-53, asst. prof., 1953-56, assoc. prof., 1956-64, prof., 1964-2000, law libr., 1952-2000. Chmn. Coun. Law Libr. Consortia, 1984-90; sec. Bd. of Conciliaton and Arbitration, Archdiocese of St. Louis, 1986-98. Named Woman of Yr. Women's Commn., St. Louis U., 1986. Mem. ABA, ALA, Wis. Bar Assn., Bar Assn. Met. St. Louis, Am. Assn. Law Librs. (Marian Gould Gallagher Disting. Svc. award 1999), Mid Am. Assn. Law Librs. (pres. 1984-86), Mid Am. Law Sch. Libr. Consortium (chmn. 1980-84), Southwestern Assn. Law Librs., Altrusa Club. Office: 3700 Lindell Blvd Saint Louis MO 63108-3412

SEARS, DONNA MAE, designer, illustrator; b. St. Paul, Oct. 23, 1951; d. Raymond and Shirley Marie (Dupre) Waldoch; m. Mark D. Sears, Sept. 4, 1993. BA in Art and Edn., Cardinal Stritch Coll., Milw., 1969-73; postgrad., Rock Valley Coll., Rockford, Ill., 1985, 87, 89-90, So. Ill. U., 1983; cert. of tng., Computervision Tech. Ctr., Itasca, Ill., 1986, 88. Electronic assembler Warner Electric Co., Marengo, Ill., 1973-75, machine hand, 1976-78, quality assurance lead insp., 1978-80, draftswoman, 1980-86, CAD-sr. draftswoman, 1986-87; tchr. art Stephen Mack Sch. Dist., Rockford, 1975, Harrison Sch. Dist., Wonder Lake, Ill., 1975-76; CAD specialist Greenlee Textron Inc., Rockford, 1988-89; asst. buyer Ingersoll Milling, Rockford, 1989-90; asst. office mgr. and sign maker Shake-A-Leg Signs, Rockford, 1990-92; tech. writer and illustrator Mathews Co., Crystal Lake, Ill., 1992; engring. CAD illustrator Clinton Electronics, Loves Park, Ill., 1993-2000; engring. adminstrn., mfg. engring. Pacific Bearing Co., Roscoe, Ill., 2000—. Author: (with others) Treasured Poems of America, 1990, Poetic Voices of America, spring 1992, Anthology of American Poetry, fall 1991 (awards of Poetic Excellence 1992), Distinguished Poets of America, spring 1993, The Sound of Poetry, spring 1993. Vol. Boone County Conservation Dist., 1990-92; mem. choir St. James Ch., Belvidere, Ill., 1985-93; assoc.

mem. Spl. Olympics; mem. Macktown Living Hist. Edn. Ctr., 1999-. Recipient Leadership award YWCA, Rockford, 1988. Mem. Am. Bus. Women's Assn., Macktown Living History Edn. Ctr. (bd. dirs., sec. 1999-2002). Roman Catholic. Avocations: bicycling, art, gardening, fishing. Office: Pacific Bearing Co 6402 Rockton Rd Roscoe IL 61073 E-mail: donnase@pacific-bearing.com.

SEARS, JOANN MARIE, school librarian; b. Lafayette, Ind., Aug. 3, 1974; d. Robert E. and Teresa A. Sears. BS, Purdue U., 1996; MLS, Ind. U., 1998. Sci. and tech. reference libr. Auburn U. Libr., Ala., 1998—2002; math. and physics libr. U. Mich., 2002—. Contbr. articles to profl. jours. Mem.: Spl. Libraries Assn., Phi Beta Kappa. Office: 3026-D Shapiro Libr 919 S University Ann Arbor MI 48109-1185 Business E-Mail: josears@umich.edu.

SEARS, LEAH J. state supreme court justice; b. June 13, 1955; d. Thomas E. and Onnye J. Sears; married; children: Addison, Brennan. BA, Cornell U., 1976; JD, Emory U., 1980; M in Apellate Jud. Process, U. Va.; JD (hon.), Morehouse Coll., 1993. Judge City Ct. Atlanta; atty. Alston & Bird, Atlanta; trial judge Superior Ct. Fulton County; justice Supreme Ct. Ga., Atlanta, 1992—. Contbr. articles to profl. jours. Bd. dirs. Sadie G. Mays Nursing Home, Ga. chpt. Nat. Coun. Christians & Jews; mem. adv. bd. United Way Drug Abuse Action Ctr., Outdoor Activity Nature Ctr.; mem. Cornell U. Women's Coun.; mem. steering com. Ga. Women's History Month, Children's Def. Fund Black Cmty. Crusade Children; founder Battered Women's Project, Columbus, Ga. Recipient Outstanding Young Alumna award Emory U., One of 100 Most Influential Georgians Ga. Trend mag., Excellence in Pub. Svc. award Ga. Coalition Black Women, 1992, Outstanding Woman of Achievement YWCA Greater Atlanta, One of Under Forty & On the Fast Track, 1993. Mem. ABA (chair bd. elections), Nat. Assn. Women Judges, Ga. Bar Assn., Women's Forum Ga., Gate City Bar Assn., Atlanta Bar Assn. (past chair jud. sect.), Ga. Assn. Black Women Attys. (founder, pres.), Fourth Tuesday Group, Jack & Jill Am. (Atlanta chpt.), Links Inc. (Atlanta chpt.), Alpha Kappa Alpha. Office: Ga Supreme Ct 244 Washington Street Atlanta GA 30334-9007*

SEARS, MARY HELEN, lawyer; b. Syracuse, N.Y. d. James Louis and Helen Mary (Fitzgerald) Sears. AB, Cornell U., 1950; JD with honors, George Washington U., 1960. Bar: Va. 1960, D.C. 1961, U.S. Supreme Ct. 1963. Chemist Allied Chem. and Dye Corp., Syracuse, 1950-52, Hercules Powder Co., Wilmington, Del., 1952-55; patent examiner U.S. Patent Office, Washington, 1955-60; pvt. practice Washington, 1960-61; assoc. Irons, Birch, Swindler & McKie, Washington, 1961-69; mem. firm Irons and Sears, Washington, 1969-84; chmn. trade regulation practice dept. Memel, Jacobs, Pierno, Gersh & Ellsworth, Washington, 1984-87; ptnr., chmn. intellectual property and unfair competition practice dept. Ginsburg, Feldman & Bress, Washington, 1987-91; ptnr., chmn. intellectual property and telecomm. practice group Reid & Priest, Washington, 1991-94; founder, chmn. M. H. Sears Law Firm, 1994—. Mem. adv. bd. Boardroom Reports, Inc., N.Y.C., 1980-85; mem. Cornell U. Coun., 1981-87, 89-93, life mem., 1995—, mem. adminstrv. bd., 1984-86. Contbr. articles to various publs. Recipient Outstanding Performance award U.S. Dept. Commerce, 1957; named to Guide to the World's Leading Patent Law Experts Euromoney Publs., PLC, 1995, 97. Mem.: ABA (co-chmn. appellate practice com., litigation sect. 1989—92), D.C. Bar Assn., Va. State Bar Assn., Internat. Trademark Assn., Licensing Execs. Soc., Am. Soc. Internat. Law, Am. Intellectual Property Law Assn., George Washington U. Law Alumnae Assn. (bd. dirs. 1995—2001), Order of Coif, Phi Alpha Delta. Republican. Office: MH Sears Law Firm Chartered 910 17th St NW Ste 800 Washington DC 20006-2606 E-mail: Mhsears@mhsears.com.

SEARS, SANDRA LEE, computer consultant; b. Rochester, N.Y., Apr. 25, 1952; AB with distinction, Cornell U., 1974; MA, U. Conn., 1976, postgrad., 1976-81. Cert. in data processing. Tng. cons. Ins. Crime Prevention Inst., Westport, Conn., 1977-78; systems analyst Data Directions, Bloomfield, Conn., 1978-79; prin. S. S. Prindle Consulting, Manchester, Conn., 1979-81; dir. info. svcs. Conn. Attys. Title Ins., Rocky Hill, Conn., 1981-85; mgr., systems, programming Community Health Care Plan, Inc., Wallingford, Conn., 1985-87; assoc. dir. Mass. Mutual Life Ins., Springfield, Mass., 1987-91; cons. mgr. Coopers & Lybrand Cons., East Hartford, Conn., 1991-96; dir. info. architecture and data warehousing CIGNA Healthcare, Bloomfield, Conn., 1996-97; divsn. dir. advanced devel. solutions divsn. Advanced Computing Techniques, Glastonbury, Conn., 1997-98; practice dir. data warehousing and knowledge mgmt. PRT Group, Inc., Windsor, Conn., 1998-99; sr. mgr. KPMG Cons., Hartford, 1999-2001; prin. The Preceptor Group, Manchester, Conn., 2001—. Adj. faculty U. New Haven, West Haven, Conn., 1976-77, Eastern Conn. State U., Willimantic, 1986-2001, Manchester C.C., 1989—; participant Tex. Instruments' Case Satellite Seminar, 1989. Mentor Career Beginnings, Hartford, 1991-95. Presdl. scholar Nat. Merit Program, 1970, William Stout scholar Cornell U., 1973, AAUW fellow U. Conn., 1981. Mem. Cornell Club of Greater Hartford (mem. admissons vol. programs alumni adv. com., exec. bd., book award chair 1987—), Cornell Alumni Admissions Amb. Network (chair 1983-86), Mortar Board, Phi Kappa Phi, Pi Mu Epsilon. Office: The Preceptor Group 10 Gardner St Manchester CT 06040-5625 E-mail: slsears@preceptorgroup.com.

SEARS, VICTORIA CONASON, psychiatrist; 1 child, Andrew John. MD, U. Geneva, Switzerland, 1958. Lic. physician N.Y. Rotating intern St. Johns Episcopal Hosp., Bklyn., 1958—59; resident in pychiatry, sr. psychiatrist Creedmoor State Hosp., Queens Village, NY, 1961—65; staff psychiatrist Nassau County Family Ct. Clinic, Westbury, NY, 1964—66; pvt. pratice Great Neck, NY, 1964—2000; dir. of treatment svcs. Nassau County Dept. of Drug and Alcohol Addiction, Hempstead, NY, 1966—73; dir. of treatment Long Beach (N.Y.) Meml. Hosp. Mental Health Clinic, 1973—77. Cons. dept. of psychiatry North Shore U. Hosp., Manhasset, NY, 1960—75, asst. attending dept. psychiatry, 1964—75, cons. dept. of psyciatry, 1971—75; asst. attending physician Nassau County Med. Ctr., East Meadow, NY, 1960—75; adj. assoc. prof. dept. speech and hearing Hofstra U., Hempstead, NY, 1966—73; clin. asst. prof. of psychiatry Cornell U. Med. Sch., N.Y.C., 1971—75; med. dir. Long Beach Meml. Hosp Mental Health Clinic, 1973—93. Mem.: N.Y. State Med. Soc. (life). Home: 51 Great Neck Rad Great Neck NY 11021 Personal E-mail: viconmax@aol.com. E-mail: viconmax@aol.com.

SEARS, WINSOME EARLE, state representative; b. Kingston, Jamaica, Mar. 11, 1964; m. Terence Owen Sears; children: DeJon L. Williams, Katia E., Janel C. AA cum laude, Tidewater C.C., 1992; BA in English, Old Dominion U., 1992; MA in Orgnl. Leadership, Regent U., 2003—. Mem. Va. Ho. of Dels., 2002—04. With USMC, 1983—86. Republican. Address: PO Box 12912 Norfolk VA 23541 Office Phone: 757-687-8211. E-mail: winsomesearsforcongress@hotmail.com.

SEASE, SUSAN G. social worker; b. Columbia, S.C., Sept. 8, 1955; d. David Lloyd and Betty Lou Gore; m. George Andrew Sease Jr., Apr. 28, 1978; children: Ruth Aurelia, Mary Lebannon. AD, Florence Darlington Tech Coll., Florence, S.C., 1977; BA, Coker Coll., Hartsville, S.C., 1978. Lic. social worker; cert. criminal justice specialist. Rsch. and planning technician Florence Police Dept., 1978-79; juvenile police officer Darlington Police Dept., 1979-80; cmty. specialist Dept. Juvenile Justice, Marion, S.C., 1980-88; social worker, svc. coord. Continuum of Care for Emotionally Disturbed Children, Florence, 1989—2001; tchr. autistic resource Lester Elem. Sch., 2001—. Sec. Pee Dee Criminal Intelligence Coun., Florence, 1978-80; resource person Gov.'s Subcom. on Mentally Retarded Offender, Columbia, S.C., 1981. Bd. dirs. Big Sisters of S.C., Florence, 1984-87; chair St. Jude Bike a Thon, Quinby, S.C., 1983, 84, 88. Mem. N.Am. Assn. Christians in Social Work, Nat. Assn. Forensic Councelors, United Meth. Women (v.p. Florence dist. 1994-98, chair social concerns 1999—), Order Eastern Star. Republican. Methodist. Avocations: directing children and youth choir at church, directing children and youth choir at church, writing poetry, reading. Home: 259 Quinby Cir Quinby SC 29506-7220 Office: Lester Elementary School East Palmetto St Florence SC 29506

SEASHORE, MARGRETTA REED, physician, educator; b. Red Bank, N.J., June 20, 1939; d. Robert Clark and Lillie Ann (Heaviland) Reed; m. John Seashore, Dec. 26, 1964; children: Robert H., Carl J., Carolyn L. BA, Swarthmore Coll., 1961; MD, Yale U., 1965. Diplomate Am. Bd. Pediatrics, Am. Bd. Med. Genetics, Nat. Bd. Med. Examiners. Intern in pediat. Yale U. Sch. Medicine, New Haven, 1965-66, asst. resident in pediat., 1966-68, postdoctoral fellow in genetics and metabolism, depts. pediat. and medicine, 1968-70, asst. clin. prof. human genetics and pediat., 1974-78, from asst. prof. to assoc. prof., 1978-90, prof. genetics and pediatrics, 1990—; clin. asst. prof. pediat. U. Fla. Coll. Medicine, Gainesville, 1970-71, asst. prof., 1971-73; attending physician Duvall Med. Ctr., U. Hosp. Jacksonville, 1970-73, asst. prof., 1970-71; attending physician Hope Haven Children's Hosp., Jacksonville, Fla., 1970-73, Shands Tchg. Hosp., Gainesville, 1971-73, Danbury (Conn.) Hosp., 1977—, Yale-New Haven Hosp., 1974—, dir. Genetic Consultation Svc., 1977-86, 1989—; cons. physician Bridgeport (Conn.) Hosp., 1974—, Lawrence and Meml. Hosp., New London, Conn., 1979—, Norwalk (Conn.) Hosp., 1981—. Contbr. chapters to books. Fellow: Am. Coll. Med. Genetics (founding fellow), Am. Acad. Pediat. (mem. screening com. Conn. chpt. 1977—, mem. genetics com. 1989—94, chair com. genetics 1990—94); mem.: AAAS, AMA, New Eng. Genetics Group (chmn. outreach com. 1979—89, mem. steering com. 1979—98, chmn. screening com. 1989—93, co-dir. 1992—95), Soc. Study Inborn Errors of Metabolism, Am. Bd. Med. Genetics (bd. dirs. 2004—), Soc. Inherited Metabolic Disorders (bd. dirs. 1989—, sec. 1991—96, pres. 1997), Am. Soc. Human Genetics (mem. genetic svcs. com. 1986—91). Avocations: music, gardening, sewing, computers. Office: Yale U Sch Med Dept Genetics 333 Cedar St New Haven CT 06510-3289 E-mail: margretta.seashore@yale.edu.

SEATON, ALBERTA JONES, biologist, educator, consultant; b. Houston, Dec. 31, 1924; d. Charles Alexander and Elizabeth (Polk) Jones; m. Earle Edward Seaton, Dec. 24, 1947 (dec. Aug. 1992); children: Elizabeth Wamboi, Dudley Charles. BS in Zoology and Chemistry, Howard U., 1946, MS in Zoology, 1947; ScD in Zoology, U. Brussels, 1949. Asst. prof. Spelman Coll., Atlanta, 1953-54; assoc. prof. biology Tex. So. U., Houston, 1954-60, prof. biology, 1960-72, 91-95; adminstr. Ministry Edn., Bermuda, 1973-76; lectr. biology Bermuda Coll., Devonshire, 1976-78; prof. anatomy Sch. Allied Health U. Tex. Health Ctr., Houston, 1979-80; cons. sci. sect. Nat. Inst. Pedagogy Ministry of Edn. Sci., Victoria, Seychelles, 1980-89. Head dept. biology Wiley Coll., Marshall, Tex., 1950-51; dir. NSF Summer Sci. Inst. Tex. So. U., 1957-59, gen. studies program, 1970-72, undergrad. and grad. rsch. in biology, 1954-72; mem. Univ. Honors Program Com., Tex. So. U., 1960-70; chair self-study com., Tex. So. U., 1969-71, ednl. policies com., 1968-72; lectr. biology U. Md., USN Air Sta., Bermuda, 1972-78; supr. adminstrn. and budget Office of Ministry Edn., Bermuda, 1973-76; lectr. in field. Author, editor: Conserving the Environment, Part 1, 1984; editor: Reprints of Agrinews, 1982; co-author, co-editor: Conserving the Environment, Part 2, The Seychelles, 1986, Conserving the Environment, Part 3, Focus on Aldabra, 1991; contbr. articles to profl. jours. Evaluator grant proposals NSF, 1957-72; active regional meetings Com. on Undergrad. Edn. in Biol. Sci., 1967-72, AAC-AAUP confs. on curriculum improvement, 1970-72; chair nurses licensing bd., Hamilton, Bermuda, 1973-75; mem. Endangered Species Com., Hamilton, 1974-77. Postdoctoral fellow Calif. Inst. Tech., Pasadena, 1959-60, NSF postdoctoral fellow Roscoe B. Jackson Lab., Bar Harbor, Maine, 1959, U. Brussels, 1965-66. Mem. AAAS, AAUP (apptd. to ad hoc coms. 1968-71, sec.-treas. Tex. State Conf. 1968-70), AAUW, Am. Assn. Zoologists, Assn. des Anatomistes, Assn. Women in Sci., Tex. Acad. Sci., Beta Kappa Chi, Beta Beta Beta. Episcopalian. Home and Office: 3821 Gertin St Houston TX 77004-6503 E-mail: seatonstar@aol.com.

SEATON, JOYAH A. nursing assistant; b. Chgo., Sept. 2, 1968; d. Sherman and Bettye Sue (Payton) Rivers; m. Milton Seaton, Jr., Apr. 8, 1994; 1 child, Christopher Allen Rivers-Collins, Devin Eugene Seaton. Nurse asst., Olive-Harvey, Chgo., 1991, student in phlebotomy, 1996—. Receptionist Braun, Lynch, Strobel & Smith, Chgo., 1995-96; nurse asst. U. Chgo. Hosp., 1995—. Mem. OES/PHA. Baptist. Avocations: remodeling, reading, exercise, praying, helping others.

SEAY-BELL, MARGARETTA, pastoral counselor; b. Bklyn., Jan. 26, 1928; d. William McKinley and Lucy Rose (Puryear) Pankey; adopted children: Ronald K. Bell, Mark David Bell. BS, Longwood Coll., Farmville, Va., 1982; MDiv, Va. Union U., 1992; MA, Presbyn. Grad. Sch. Christian Edn., Richmond, Va., 1993; D in Ministry, Howard U., 1995, Ea. Theol. Sem./Md. Theol. Sem., Lynchburg, Va., 2000. Cert. Ctr. Bibl. Counseling, Forest, Va., 2000. 25 years in positions of increasing scope and responsibility, including 6 yrs. with U.S. State Dept. in Japan and Republic of Korea; with U.S. Dept. Labor, regional office, Phila., 1971—73; ret., 1974. Mem. Amherst County Violence Prevention Team, Amherst County Commn. on Youth Svcs., Amherst County Healthy Beginnings Program; parent rep. Amherst County Family Assessment Program; mem. Amherst County Commn. against Domestic Violence; ct. advocate Women Victims of Domestic Violence; tchr. Parent Nurturing Program, Child Abuse Prevention, Lynchburg, Va.; mem. state governing bd., 1st sect. Va. Organizing Project, Charlottesville, 1997—99; assoc. min. Deliverance Ch. of Christ, Gladstone, Va., 1986—89; elder, adminstr. The Way of the Cross Full Gospel Bapt. Ch., Lynchburg, Va., 1996—98; asst. pastor, pastoral counselor NIA Cmty. Fellowship, Charlotte, NC, 1998—99; guest min. Springfield Bapt. Ch., Appomattox, Va., 2001; vacation bible sch. tchr. Union Hill Bapt. Ch., Buckingham, Va., 2001—02; adminstr., pastoral counselor Spirit and Truth Ministries, Oak Hill, W.Va., 2000—01; vol. tchr. bible study Hidden Valley Nursing Home, Oak Hill, W.Va.; bd. dirs. YMCA, Phila., 1972. Recipient Achievement award, Commonwealth of Va., Welfare Reform Initiative, 1996. Mem.: Am. Assn. Christian Counselors, Assn. Clin. Pastoral Edn., Inc., Zeta Phi Beta (Alpha Phi Zeta chpt.). Democrat. Avocations: golf, writing, travel. Home: Rte 1 Box 1110 Fayetteville WV 25840-9731

SEBALD, JAMA LYNN, academic administrator; b. Dayton, Ohio, Jan. 16, 1949; d. James Arthur and Betty Jean Sebald. BA, Ohio U., 1971; MA, U. Northern Colo., 1973, ednl. specialist cert., 1975. Grad. asst., fin. aid counselor U. Northern Colo., Greeley, 1974—75; asst. dir. fin. aid Med. Coll. Ga., Augusta, 1975—76; student fin. aid advisor U. Idaho, Moscow, 1976—. Mem. affirmative action com. U. Idaho, Moscow, 1987—90, mem. student employee of yr. com., 1996—, mem. parking task force, 2001, mem. parking com., 2001—. Recipient Outstanding Young Woman of Am. award, 1978. Mem.: AAUW (Moscow br. topic chair 1977—79, Moscow br. chair sr. honor awards com. 1979—80, Moscow br. sr. honor awards com. 1979—81, Moscow br. bylaws officer 1980—81, Moscow br. hospitality chair 1981—82, Moscow br. nominations com. chair 1982, Moscow br. treas. 1982—84, Moscow br. corr. sec. 1984—86, Moscow br. pres. elect 1986—87, Moscow br. pres. 1987—88, Idaho divsn. bd. dirs. 1987—88, Moscow br. ednl. found. program officer 1988—89, Moscow br. pres. elect 1991—92, Idaho divsn. bd. dirs. 1992—93, Moscow br. pres. 1992—93, Moscow br. ednl. found. program officer 1993—94, Moscow br. program v.p. 1995—96, Moscow br. co-pres. 1998—99, Idaho Division Board of Directors 1998—99, Moscow br. pres. 1999—2000, Ednl. Found. Name Gift award 1991, 1995), U. Idaho Women's Caucus (chair 1978—80), Idaho Student Fin. Aid Adminstrs. (pres. 1989—90), Idaho Student Fin. Aid Adminstrs. (sec., treas. 1978—79), Western Assn. Student Fin. Aid Adminstrs. (mem. exec. coun. 1989—90), Nat. Assn. Student Fin. Aid Adminstrs., Moscow Pregnancy Counseling Svc. (bd. dirs. 1984—86), Athena. Home: 615 N Washington Moscow ID 83843-2626 Office: U Idaho Student Fin Aid Svcs Moscow ID 83844-4291 Business E-Mail: jama@uidaho.edu.

SEBASTIAN, PHYLIS SUE (INGRAM), real estate broker, antique appraiser; b. Childersburg, Ala., Jan. 24, 1945; d. Albert Freeman and Era Mae (McGowin) Ingram; m. Robert Emmett Martin, March 31, 1965 (div. Sept. 1976); children: Connie, Michael, Toni, Steve; m. Thomas Haskell Sebastian III, June 26, 1985; stepchildren: Shellie, Tabatha, Cherie, Thomas IV. Ordained minister Progressive Universal Life Ch., 2002; lic. real estate broker Mo., real estate appraiser Tenn., Mo., PREA, CIMA. Owner, broker Phylis Sebastian Real Estate, Farmington, Mo., 1989—, U.S. Auto Sales, Park Hills, Mo., 1993—96; owner Bus. Legal Svs., Park Hills, Mo., 1993—; ptnr. La Femme Fine Antique Auction Svc., Ironton, Mo., 1997—. Owner Astrology Cons., 1970—; numerous appearances St. Louis TV; hostess radio show, St. Louis. Contbr. articles to newspapers; author: Marriages in Madison County Missouri for 1848-1868, 1998, 1910 Census for Madison County Missouri, 1998, numerous poems. Co-founder Astrological Assn., St. Louis, 1976-77, Mo. Mental Health Consumer Network, 1989-93, Mineral Area chpt. 1989-93. Mem. Nat. Gardening Club, Libr. Congress, Smithsonian, Nat. Hist. soc., Geneal. Assn. Madison County, Mo. (founder, sec., treas., genealogist). Mem. Lds Ch. Avocations: studying genealogy, astrology, natuapathy, herbal medicine, metaphysics, quatum physics, & parapsychology., reading, walking, gardening, pianist and guitarist. Home: 5231 West 72 Highway Fredericktown MO 63645 Office: Arcadia Valley Auction Company Inc and Real Estate 315A W Russell St Ironton MO 63650-1316 E-mail: phylis@phylissebastian.com.

SEBASTIAN, SUZIE, producer; b. Redding, Calif., Aug. 2, 1962; d. Richard Werner and Hildegard (Goettel) Guenther; m. Ted Sebastian, June 6, 1984 (div. July 1990). AA, Shasta Coll., 1985. Freelance tv prodr., prodn. mgr. commls., 1985-91; freelance underwater model, stunt woman; expedition leader, hostess Adventures on Scuba Dive Travel, Santa Barbara, Calif., 1991—; documentary TV prodr. Discovery Channel, 1998-2000. Asst. instr. Filming Sharks in the Wild, Nassau, Bahamas, 1996—. Prodr.: documentaries, ednl. videos; picture editor, underwater model : Tom Campbell's Film and Video Prodns., 1991—; prodr.: Navy Seals: In Harms Way, How to Survive Hellweek, FBI: Critical Incident Class 234. Mem.: Internat. Documentary Assn., Divers Alert Network, Aquatic Bodyworks. Avocations: snow skiing, triathlon. Home: 919 Veronica Springs Rd Santa Barbara CA 93105-4500 Office: Adventures on Scuba 238 Las Alturas Rd Santa Barbara CA 93103-2170 E-mail: suzies@silcom.com.

SEBEJAIS, MELANIE, federal agency administrator; m. Bob Sabelhaus; 2 children. With IBM; founder Exclusive Interim Properties Ltd. (now Bridgestreet Accomodations), Balt., 1986—97; v.p. global sales Bridgestreet Accomodations (formerly Exvlusive Interim Properties Ltd.), 1997—98; deputy adminstr. Small Bus. Adminstrn., Washington, 2002—. Bd. dirs. United Way, Alzheimer's Assn. Ctrl. Md.; co-chair Nat. Summit Women in Philanthropy. Recipient Outstanding Vol. Fundraiser of Yr. award, Assn. Fundraising Profls., Md., 2002. Office: Small Bus Adminstrn 409 3d St SW Washington DC 20416

SEBELIUS, KATHLEEN GILLIGAN, governor; b. Cin., May 15, 1948; d. John J. and Mary K. (Dixon) Gilligan; m. Keith Gary Sebelius, 1974; children: Edward Keith, John McCall. BA, Trinity Coll., 1970; MA in Pub. Adminstrn., U. Kans., 1977. Cert. ins. agt., Kans. Dir. planning Ctr. for Cmty. Justice, Washington, 1971-74; spl. asst. Kans. Dept. Corrections, Topeka, 1975-78; exec. dir. Kans. Trial Lawyers Assn., 1978—86; mem. Kans. Ho. of Reps., 1987-95; ins. commr. State of Kans., 1995—2002, gov., 2003—. Founder Women's Polit. Caucus; precinct committeewoman, 1980-86; mayor, Potwin, 1985-87; exec. com. Nat. Assn. Ins. Commrs., Kans. Health Care Commn.; appointed Presdl. adv. commn. consumer protection and quality in Health Care Industry, 1997. Mem. Common Cause (state bd., nat. gov. bd. 1975-81), Nat. Assn. Ins. Commrs. (chair). Democrat. Roman Catholic. Office: Office of the Gov State Capitol 2nd Fl Topeka KS 66612-1590 Home: 1 SW Cedar Crest Rd Topeka KS 66606-2275

SEBERT, MICHELLE ANN, school system network administrator; b. Pt. Pleasant, N.J., Feb. 8, 1970; d. Michael Patrick and Lynn Ann McKnight; m. Herman Arthur Sebert Jr., July 24, 1994; 1 child, Herman Arthur III. BA in English, Rutgers U., 1992; MA in Edn., Chapman U., Tucson, Ariz., 1995. Cert. elem., secondary and adult educator, Ariz. Title I reading and phys. edn. tchr. Elgin (Ariz.) Sch., 1994-95, tchr. 3d grade, then 6th grade, 1995-97, tchr. computer skills, 1997—, tech. coord., 1997—, network adminstr., 1998—. Mem. site-based coun., Elgin Sch., also facility planning com. Mem. NEA, Assn. for the Advancement of Computing in Edn., Ariz. Edn. Assn., Sonoita Edn. Assn., Nat. Assn. Elem. Sch. Prins. Republican. Roman Catholic. Avocations: reading, scrapbooking. Home: PO Box 583 Sonoita AZ 85637-0583 Office: Elgin Sch 23 Upper Elgin Rd Elgin AZ 85611 E-mail: michelle@server1.sonoita.k12.az.us.

SEBOLD, ALICE, writer; b. Madison, Wis., 1963; d. Jane and Russell Sebold; m. Glen David Gold, 2001. B.A., Syracuse U., 1984; studied poetry, U. Houston, 1984—85; M.F.A. in fiction, U. Calif., Irvine, 1998. Author: (memoir) Lucky, 1999, The Lovely Bones, 2002. Office: c/o Steven Barclay Agy 12 Western Ave Petaluma CA 94952*

SEBOROVSKI, CAROLE, artist; b. San Diego, June 16, 1960; d. Stanley and Eleanor Ononsko S. BFA, Calif. Coll. Arts and Crafts, 1982; MFA, Hunter Coll., 1987. Artist: solo exhibitions include: Damon Brandt Gallery, N.Y.C., 1986, Hunter Coll. Art Gallery, N.Y.C., 1986, Lorence-Monk Gallery, N.Y.C., 1988, 89, Galerie Karsten Greve, Paris, 1991, 94, 2003, Cologne, 1992, 2004, Milan, 1995, 2001, Angles Gallery, Santa Monica, Calif., 1991, 92, 93, 96, Betsy Senior Contemporary Prints, N.Y.C., 1993, John Weber Gallery, N.Y.C., 1993, 95, John Berggruen Gallery, San Francisco, 1994, Locks Gallery, Phila., 1997, Karsten Greve, Koln, 1997, Galerie Karsten Greve, Milan, Italy, 1997, 2001, John Weber Gallery, N.Y.C., 1998, Cheryl Haines Gallery, San Francisco, 2000, 2002, Mitchell-Innes and Nash Gallery, N.Y.C., Miller Block Gallery, Boston, 2001; group exhbns. at: Willard Gallery, N.Y.C., 1984, Nora Haime Gallery, N.Y.C, 1985, 86, 93, 95, 2002, Manhattan Arts Ctr., N.Y.C., 1985, Hillwood Art Gallery L.I. Univ., Brookville, N.Y., 1985, Damon Brandt Gallery, 1985, 86 (2), 87, Mus. de Arte, La Tertuila, Columbia, 1986, Weatherspoon Gallery, Greensboro, N.C., 1986, Barbara Krakow Gallery, Boston, 1986, 88, 90 (travels to John C. Stoller & Co., Mpls.), Anne Plumb Gallery, N.Y.C., 1987, Am. Acad. and Inst. Arts and Letters, 1987, Bklyn. Mus., 1987, Lorence-Monk Gallery, 1987, 89 (3), 90, 91 (2), Carnegie Mellon U. Art Gallery, Pitts., 1988, Reynolds/ Minor Gallery, Richmond, Va., 1988, John Good Gallery, N.Y.C., 1988, 92, Pamela Auchincloss Gallery, N.Y.C., 1988, Dart Gallery, Chgo., 1988, Angles Gallery, 1989, Persons & Lindell Gallery, Helsinki, Finland, 1989, Anderson Gallery Va. Commonwealth U., Richmond, 1989, Baxter Gallery, Richmond, 1989, Hillwood Art Gallery, Brookville (travels through 1991 to Blum Helman Gallery, N.Y.C., Richard F. Brush Gallery, Canton, N.Y., Contemporary Mus. Art, Caracas, Venezuela), Cheryl Haines Gallery, San Francisco, 1989, 94, 96, 2003, Security Pacific Corp. Gallery, Santa Monica, 1990, Meml. Art Gallery U. Rochester, N.Y., 1990, Hood Mus. Art Dartmouth Coll., Hannover, N.H., 1990, San Francisco Mus. of Art, 1991, Pfizer, Inc. (Mus. Modern Art, N.Y. Collection), 1991, John Berggruen Gallery, 1991, travelling exhbn. to Anthony Ralph Gallery at Earl McGrath, L.A., Mars Gallery, Tokyo, Katonah Mus. Art, N.Y., Ind. U. Fine Arts Gallery, Kerr Gallery, Alberta Coll. of Art, Can., Huntsville Mus. Art, Ala., Worcester Art Mus., Mass., Lamont Gallery N.H., San Diego State U. Gallery, 1992, Barbara Mathes Gallery, N.Y.C., 1993, Transamerica Pyramid Lobby, San Francisco, 1993, travelling exhbn to The Drawing Ctr., N.Y., Corcoran Gallery Art, Washington, Santa Monica Mus., L.A., The Forum, St. Louis, Am. Ctr., Paris, 1993, Addison Gallery, Andover, Mass., 1994, John Weber Gallery, 1994, 96, Huntington Gallery Mass. Coll. Art, Boston, 1995, Rice U. Art Galley, Houston, 1995, The Altered Stages, N.Y., 1995, Brooke Alexander Gallery, N.Y.C., 1995, Thread Waxing Space, N.Y., 1996, Duchess County C.C., N.Y., 1996, Gallery 7, Hong Kong, 1996, Century Club, N.Y.C., 1996, Dutchess Coll., N.Y., 1997, Vassar Coll., Poughkeepsie, N.Y., 1997, Mus. Cantonale d'Arte, Lugano, Switzerland, 1997, Kunst-Mus., Ahlen, Germany, 1998, Kunstmus., Winterhur, Switzerland, 1998, Acad. der Kunste, Berlin, 1999, Mitchell-Innes and Nash, N.Y.C., Nohra Haime Gallery, N.Y.C., 2002, Maragaret Thatcher Projects, N.Y.C., 1999, 2002, San Francisco Mus. Modern Art, Calif., 2000, Block Mus., Chgo., 2000, Contemporary Mus., Honolulu, 2000, Fogg Art Mus., 2000, Neuberger Mus. Art, Purchase, NY, 2000, Lyman Allyn Mus, Conn., 2000, Yale Art Galley, 2002, Bertha and Karl Leubsdorf Art Gallery, N.Y.C., 2002, Charles Cowles Gallery, N.Y.C., 2002, Krannert Art Gallery, Ill., 2002, Anthony Grant, Inc., 2003, Cin. Art Mus., 2003, The Workspace, N.Y.C., 2003, others; represented in permanent collections including Whitney Mus. Art, N.Y., Paine Webber, N.Y., Weatherspoon Art Gallery, Greensboro, N.C., J. Walter Thompson, N.Y., Refco Collection, Chgo., Panza Collection, Italy, San Francisco Mus. Modern Art, Mus. Modern Art, N.Y., Mus. Cantonale d'Arte, Lugano, Switzerland, Met. Mus. Art, N.Y., Merril Lynch Inc., N.Y., MIT Visual Ctr., Hood Mus. Art, Hanover, N.H., Fogg Art Mus., Harvard U., Cambridge, Mass., Cleve. Ctr. Contemporary Art, Chase Manhattan Bank, N.Y., Carnegie Mus. Art, Pitts., Bklyn. Mus., Balt. Mus., Anderson Collection, Calif., Addison Gallery, Phillips Acad., Andover, Mass., Bklyn. Mus., Yale U. Art Gallery, Wadsworth Atheneum, Conn., Tel Aviv Mus., Nat. Gallery Art, Washington. Grantee Pollock-Krausner Found., 1986, NEA, 1991, Art Devel. Com., 1997; named Artist in Residence, Villa Monalvo, Saratoga, Calif., 1989, Djerassi Found., Calif., 1990; Agnes Bourne fellow in visual arts, 1990. Home: 171 E 81st St Apt #3A New York NY 10028

SEBREN, LUCILLE GRIGGS, retired private school educator, public school educator; b. Chesterfield, S.C., May 21, 1922; d. Manley Oscar and Clara Blanche (Rivers) Griggs; m. Herbert Lee Sebren, Dec. 19, 1943; children: Herbert Lee Jr., George Hall, Samuel Robert Franklin. BA, Flora Macdonald Coll., Red Springs, N.C., 1942; MEd, Coll. of William and Mary, 1966. Cert. tchr., Va., N.C., S.C. Tchr. Cheraw (S.C.) Elem. Sch., 1942-44; tchr. kindergarten Larchmont Meth. Ch., Norfolk, Va., 1951-53; tchr. Norfolk Acad., 1953-89, supr., cons., adminstr. primary dept., 1970-89, master tchr., cons. elem. grades, 1970-89, asst. to dir. of admissions, 1987—. Contbr. articles to profl. jours. Mem. Va. Symphony and Symphony Aux., Norfolk, 1946—, Norfolk Soc. Arts, 1970—, Chrysler Mus., Norfolk, 1965—, Va. Opera Assn., Norfolk, 1974—, Norfolk Forum, 1980—, U.S. Capitol Hist. Assn., 1983—, ODU Roundtable, 1990-, Little Theater Norfolk, 1992-, Smithsonian Instn., Met. Opera Guild, Va. Hist. Assn., World Affairs Coun., 2001—, Heritage Found., Nat. Trust Historic Preservation, Hermitage Mus. Found. Aux.; pres. Philanthropic Ednl. Orgn., 1993-96, v.p., 2001—; bicentennial mem. Libr. Congress. Recipient Disting. Svc. award Norfolk Acad., 1991. Mem. AAUW (sec. exec. bd. 1974-76), Joie de Vivre (treas. 1994—), Old Dominion U. Faculty Wives Club (pres. 1958-60), Town-N-Gown (bd. dirs. 1992—, chaplain 1993-96, v.p. 1995-96, pres.-elect 1996-97, pres. 1997-98), Old Dominion U. Town-N-Gown (pres.-elect 1998-99, pres. 1999-2001), bd. dirs. Old Dominion U. Town-N-Gown, 1992—, parliamentarian, 2001-03, Nat. Cathedral Assn., Nat. Trust for Historic Preservation, Nat. M.I. Hummel Club, Hon. Order Ky. Cols., Internat. Assn. Torch Clubs, Inc., Alpha Delta Kappa Internat. (pres., past state, provincial, nat. pres. 1995—, pres. Va. 1978-80, S.E. region 1981-83, internat. grand chaplain 1983-85, internat. grand pres.-elect 1985-87, internat. grand pres. 1987-89, internat. exec. bd. 1985-91, pres.-elect internat. past state pres. 1993-95, pres. 1995—), Kappa Delta Pi. Republican. Baptist. Avocations: reading, travel, collecting antique glassware and Hummels, music. Office: Norfolk Acad 1585 Wesleyan Dr Norfolk VA 23502-5591

SEBRING, MARJORIE MARIE ALLISON, former home furnishings company executive; b. Burnsville, N.C., 1926; d. James William and Mary Will (Ramsey) Allison Shockey; 1 child, Patricia Louise Banner Krohn. Student, Mars Hill Coll., 1943, Home Decorators Sch. Design, N.Y.C., 1948, Wayne State U., 1953; cert. home furnishings rep., U. Va., 1982. Dir. decorating divsn. Robinson Furniture, Detroit, 1949-57; head buyer Tyner Hi-Way House, Ypsilanti, Mich., 1957-63, Town and Country, Dearborn, Mich., 1963-66; instr. Nat. Carpet Inst., 1963-71; owner Adams House, Inc., Plymouth, Mich., 1966-72; exec. v.p. mktg. and sales, regional sales and mktg. mgr. Triangle Industries, L.A., 1972-89; co-owner Markham-Sebring, Inc., St. Petersburg, Fla., 1983-89. Dir. contract divsn. Kane Furniture, 1984-85; co-owner Accessories, Etc., 1985-89; chmn. bd. Heritage Lakes, U.S. Home; co-owner, dir. Talamanca Pipeline Ltd., Costa Rica. Vol. coord. Pasco County Clk. Ct., Suncoast Theatre; adv. bd. Webster Coll.; charter mem. Presdl. Task Force; pres. Presbyn. Ch. Seven Springs; bd. dirs. Fla. Health and Human Svc., Fla. Presbyn. Homes, Gills Trinity YMCA, 2001—; chmn. bd. dirs. Two Westminster Condominium Assn.; mem. Tampa Bay Presbytery Rev. and Evaluation; bd. dirs. James P. Gills Suncoast YMCA, 2001—; citizens adv. com. Pasco County, 2001-. Recipient recognition for work with youth and aged; named to Fla. Finest List, Gov. of Fla., 1994. Mem. Internat. Home Furnishings Assn., Fla. Home Furnishings Rep. Assn. (officer), Am. Security Coun. (coun.), Williamsburg Found., USCG Aux., Nat. Audubon Soc., Internat. Platform Assn., Pasco County Planning Com., Heritage Lake Assn. (bd. dir. 2002-04, chmn.), II Westminster Assn.(pres. 2004), Pasco Rep. Club. Republican. Achievements include contbr. creative display to Better Homes & Gardens, 1957-64. Home: 4902 Cathedral Ct New Port Richey FL 34655-1486 Fax: 727 375-7702.

SEBRING, PENNY BENDER, researcher; b. Nevada City, Calif., Oct. 22, 1942; d. Carl S. and Eunice Goforth Bender; m. Robert Sebring, 1965 (div. 1982); 1 child, Lisa Sebring Carreras ; m. Charles A. Lewis, June 9, 1984; children: Peter C. Lewis, Kathryn Lewis Varella. BA, Grinnell Coll., 1964; MEd, Pa. State U., 1978; PhD, Northwestern U., 1985. Vol. Peace Corps, Venezuela, 1964—66, instr., 1966; social studies tchr. Bellefonte Area H.S., Pa., 1967—71; Upward Bound tchr. Pa. State U., 1969, rsch. asst. Coll. of Edn., 1976—77, staff specialist, 1979—80; survey dir. NORC U. Chgo., 1984—87, sr. survey dir., 1987—90, sr. rsch. assoc., 1990—. Author: School Leadership and the Bottom Line, 2000; co-author: School-Based Management in the United States, 1999, Charting Chicago School Reform, 1998. Co-dir. Consortium of Chgo. Sch. Rsch., 1990—; mem. vis. com. Sch. Edn. and Social Policy, Northwestern U., 1998—; vice chmn. bd. trustees Grinnell Coll., 1993—, McGaw YMCA, Evanston, Ill., 1993—2003; vis. com. divsn. social scis. U. Chgo., 2001—; bd. dirs. Chgo. Pub. Edn. Fund, 2002—. Fellow Univ. fellow, Northwestern U., 1981—83. Mem.: Am. Evaluation Assn., Am. Ednl. Rsch. Assn., Phi Delta Kappa (Rsch. award 1985). Office: Consortium on Chicago Sch Rsch 1313 E 60th St Chicago IL 60637

SEDARIS, AMY, writer, actress; b. NYC, Mar. 19, 1961; d. Lou Sedaris. Performer: (TV series) Exit 57, 1995—96; co-writer (TV series) Exit 57, 1995—96, co-creator, 1995—96; performer: (TV series) Strangers With Candy, 1999—2000; co-writer (TV series) Strangers With Candy, 1999—2000, co-creator, 1999—2000; actor(guest appearances): (TV series) Just Shoot Me, Monk, Sex and the City, Ed, Cracking Up, : (films) Commandments, 1997, Bad Bosses Go to Hell, 1997, Six Days Seven Nights, 1998, Jump Tomorrow, 2001, Maid in Manhattan, 2002, The School of Rock, 2003, Elf, 2003, My Baby's Daddy, 2004; (TV films) Untitled New York Pilot, 2003; (plays) Jamboree, 1993; co-author (with brother David Sedaris): (plays) Jamboree, 1993; actor: (plays) Stump the Host, 1993; co-author (with brother David Sedaris): (plays) Stump the Host, 1993; actor: (plays) One Woman Shoes, 1995; co-author (with brother David Sedaris): (plays) One Woman Shoes, 1995 (Obie award, 1995); actor: (plays) Froggy, The Country Club, 1998—99 (nominated Drama Desk award, 1999), The Most Fabulous Story Ever Told, 1998—99, The Little Freida Mysteries, 1999; co-author (with brother David Sedaris): (plays) The Little Freida Mysteries, 1997; actor: (plays) The Book of Liz; co-author (with brother David Sedaris): (plays) The Book of Liz, 2001; co-author: (book), 2002; actor: (plays) Drama Department, 2001, Wonder of the World, 2001—02 (Lucille Lortel award for outstanding featured actress League of Off-Broadway Theatres and Prodrs., 2002), (short film) Wheels of Fury, 1998; co-writer (short film) Wheels of Fury, 1998; co-author (with brother David Sedaris): (plays) Stitches, Incident at Cobbler's Knob; co-author: (book) Wigfield: The Can-Do Town That Just May Not, 2003. Office: c/o Jonathan Bluman Paradigm 10100 Santa Monica Blvd 25th Fl Los Angeles CA 90067*

SEDDON, JOHANNA MARGARET, ophthalmologist, epidemiologist; b. Pitts. BS, U. Pitts., 1970, MD, 1974; MS in Epidemiology, Harvard U., 1976. Intern Framingham (Mass.) Union Hosp., 1974-75; resident Tufts New Eng. Med. Ctr., Boston, 1976-80; fellow ophthalmic pathology Mass. Eye and Ear Infirmary, Boston, 1980-81, clin. fellow vitreoretinal Retina Svc., 1981-82; instr. clin. ophthalmology Harvard Med. Sch., Boston, 1982-84, asst. prof., asst. surgeon ophthalmolgy, 1984, assoc. prof., 1989—; assoc. surgeon, dir. ultrasound svc. Mass. Eye and Ear Infirmary, Boston, 1989—, orgn. epidemiology rsch. unit, 1984-85, dir. epidemiology unit, 1985—, surgeon in ophthalmology, 1992—; assoc. prof. faculty dept. epidemiology Harvard Sch. Pub. Health, Boston, 1992—. Mem. com. vision Commn. Behavioral and Social Scis. and Edn., NRC, NAS, Washington, 1984; mem. divsn. rsch. grants NIH, 1987-89, 94—; mem. sci. adv. bd. Found for Fighting Blindness, 1994—, Macular Degeneration Internat., 1994—; spkr. in field; lectr. in field. Author books and articles in field, especially in field of ocular tumors and macular degeneration; mem. editl. staff ophthalmic jours. Recipient NIH Nat. Svc. Rsch. awards, 1975, 80-81, Lewis R. Wasserman merit award Rsch. to Prevent Blindness for contbns. to ophthalmic rsch., 1996; grantee, prin. investigator Nat. Eye Inst., 1984—, Nat. Cancer Inst., 1986; med. sch. scholar, 1970-74, Henry H. Clark Med. Edn. Found. scholar, 1973. Mem. AMA (Sr. Honor award 2003), APHA, Am. Acad. Ophthalmology (Honor award 1990, Sr. Honor award 2003), Am. Med. Women's Assn., Assn. Rsch. in Vision and Ophthalmology (elected, chair epidemiology sect. 1990, trustee clin. vision epidemiology sect. 1992-97. v.p. 1996-97), Soc. Epidemiologic Rsch., New Eng. Ophthal. Soc., Am. Coll. Epidemiology, Retina Soc., Macula Soc., Mass. Soc. Eye Physicians and Surgeons (v.p. 2000-2002, Spl. Recognition award 1997), Am. Epidemiol. Soc., Am. Ophthal. Soc. Home: 4 Louisburg Sq Boston MA 02108-1203 E-mail: jseddon@earthlink.net.

SEDEI RODDEN, PAMELA JEAN, therapist; b. Johnstown, Pa., Jan. 31, 1956; d. Joseph and Betty Ruth (Watkins) Sedei; m. William Eugene Rodden, Dec. 4, 1982; 1 child, Gretchen Jean Rodden. BA, Southwestern Coll., Winfield, Kans., 1977; MS, Pittsburg (Kans.) State U., 1979; PhD, Western Colo. U., 1983. Lic. profl. counselor Colo., diplomate in psychotherapy, cert. cognitive behavior therapist, nat. cert. counselor, domestic violence counselor, criminal justice specialist. Staff psychologist Autumn Manors Inc., Florence, Kans., 1982-83; clin. psychologist Richmond (Tex.) State Hosp., 1984-86; unit psychologist Wheat Ridge (Colo.) Regional Ctr., 1986-89, acting unit dir., 1989; dir. behavioral svcs. Colo. State Divsn Devel. Disabilities, Denver, 1989-97; dir. Forensic Mental Health Svcs., Boulder, Colo., 1997—2001, Pamela JS Rodden & Assocs., Fort Collins, Colo., 2001—. Dir. Rodden Consultants, Longmont, Colo., 1986—90, Rodden Assocs., 2001—. Co-author: A Model For Interdisciplinary On Site Evaluation of People Who Have Dual Diagnosis, 1991. Fellow: Am. Coll. Forensic Examiners; mem.: ACA, Assn. Treatment of Sexual Abusers (clin. mem.). Republican. Roman Catholic. also: 315 W Oak St Ste 204 Fort Collins CO 80521-2724 E-mail: Pjsrodden@aol.com.

SEDGWICK, LEVONNE, retired school program administrator; b. Seattle, Feb. 22, 1928; d. Albert Mark and Cecil Irene (Whitley) Nachtwey; m. Robert Ellwood Campbell (div. 1972); children: Caron Candace, Mindy Sue; m. Edward Thomas Sedgwick, Oct. 2, 1976. MS in Edn., Portland State U., 1970. Tchr. Our Lady of Assumption Elem. Sch., Atlanta, 1960-62, Our Lady of Providence Child Ctr., Portland, Oreg., 1963-68, Estacada (Oreg.) Union High Sch., 1969-70, Psychiat. Day Treatment Ctr./U. Oreg. Med. Sch./Portland State U., 1970-73; coord. Coleytown Developmental Ctr., Westport, Conn., 1973-77; dir. spl. programs Yamhill County Intermediate Edn. Dist., McMinnville, Oreg., 1977-78; dir. student svcs. Centennial Sch. Dist., Portland, 1978-93; pvt. practice as mediator, cons. and facilitator, contract spl. edn. investigations, 1993—. Pres. Oreg. Assn. Sch. Suprs., 1980-81, Adminstrv. Consultation and Tng. Bd. dirs. Am. Plaza Condominium Assn., Portland, 1990-96, 99—. Mem. Coun. Adminstrs. Spl. Edn., Coun. Exceptional Children (pres. Oreg. fedn. 1987-88, gov. 1989-92), Phi Delta Kappa. Avocations: travel, photography, cooking. Home: 2309 SW 1st Ave Apt 843 Portland OR 97201-5008

SEDGWICK, SALLY BELLE, publishing company executive; b. Chgo., July 6, 1947; d. William Morton and Dorothy Hyde (Dunlap) Price; m. Roger Stephen Sedgwick, Sept. 7, 1968 (div.); children: Peter, Andrew. BA, Lawrence U., 1968; MFA, U. Alaska, 1974; MA, Gen. Theol. Sem., N.Y.C., 1986; DMin, Grad. Theol. Found., Donaldson, Ind., 1996. Instr. Lake Region Jr. Coll., Devils Lake, N.D., 1974-77; dir. Carousel Creative Arts Program, Oakes, N.D., 1978-80; pricing analyst Orgn. Resources Counselors, N.Y.C., 1981-85; exec. dir. Ch. Periodical Club, N.Y.C., 1985-90; assoc. dir. Forward Movement Publs., Cin., 1990—. Bd. mem. Fountain Sq. Fools, Cin., 1992-95; cons. Episcopal Diocese N.D., 1974-80. Mem. Episcopal Communicators, Nat. Network Lay Profls. Episcopalian. Office: Forward Movement Publs 412 Sycamore St Ste 3 Cincinnati OH 45202-4195

SEDGWICK, SALLY STOWELL, philosophy educator; b. L.A., Sept. 14, 1956; d. Robert Post Sedgwick and Catherine Park (Stowell) Sedgwick Peppard. BA in Philosophy, U. Calif., Santa Cruz, 1978; PhD, U. Chgo., 1985. Asst. prof. philosophy Dartmouth Coll., Hanover, N.H., 1985-91, assoc. prof., 1991—2003; prof. philosophy U. Ill., Chgo., 2003—. Vis. assoc. prof. U. Pa., Phila., 1992, Harvard U., Cambridge, Mass., 1996-97; rev. panelist Applications for Univ. Teaching Fellowships NEH, Washington, 1996. Contbr. articles to profl. jours. Rsch. fellow Alexander von Humboldt Stiftung, 1990, 97; conf. grantee NEH, 1996, summer rsch. grantee DAAD, 1987. Mem. AAUW, Am. Philos. Assn., Hegel Soc. N.Am., N.Am. Kant Soc., Kant Gesellschaft a.v. Bonn. Office: Dept Philosophy Univ Ill 1421 University Hall 601 South Morgan St Chicago IL 60607

SEDIVEC, MARY LYNN, systems development manager; b. Chgo., Apr. 2, 1954; d. Alfred William Rakebrand and Mary Dolores Hail Olander; m. Dale Edward Sedivec, June 13, 1975; 1 child, Dale Alfred. BS in Tchg. Math., U. Ill., Chgo., 1975. Cert. h.s. math. tchr., Ill.; cert. backyard wildlife habitat Nat. Wildlife Fedn. Asst. data processing mgr. West Suburban Bank, Lombard, Ill., 1973-77; sys. analyst Unity Savs., Chgo., 1977; customer svc. mgr. Nat. Sharedata, Oak Park, Ill., 1977-79; instr. Coll. of DuPage, Glen Ellyn, Ill., 1980-82; sys. need analyst Eastman Kodak, Oak Brook, Ill., 1981-82; edn. cons. Wang Labs., Rolling Meadows, Ill., 1982-85, regional support ctr. mgr. Smyrna, Ga., 1985-93, network integration specialist Charlotte, N.C., 1993; asst. v.p. First Union Nat. Bank, Charlotte, 1993-97; dir. product definition First Data Corp./Distributed Sys., Omaha and Charlotte, 1997-98; dir. integration First Consulting Group, Long Beach, Calif., 1998—99, sr. integration mgr. Lansing, Mich., 1999—. Assoc. mem. Pvt. Industry Coun., Atlanta, 1992. Mem. adv. bd. Cmtys. in Shc., Charlotte, 1997; mem. choir, accompanist St. Thomas Aquinas Choir. Roman Catholic. Home: 1163 Asheford Green Ave Concord NC 28027 Office: 2325 Lakeview Pky Ste 425 Alpharetta GA 30004

SEDLAK, VALERIE FRANCES, retired English language educator, retired academic administrator; b. Balt., Mar. 11, 1934; d. Julian Joseph and Eleanor Eva (Pilot) Sedlak; 1 child, Barry. AB in English, Coll. Notre Dame of Md., 1955; MA, U. Hawaii, 1962; PhD, U. Pa., 1992. Grad. teaching fellow East-West Cultural Ctr. U. Hawaii, 1959-60; adminstrv. asst. Korean Consul Gen., 1959-60; tchr. Boyertown (Pa.) Sr. High Sch., 1961-63; asst. prof. English U. Balt., 1963-69; assoc. prof. Morgan State U., Balt., 1970-2000, assoc. prof. English emerita, 2001—, asst. dean Coll. Liberal Arts, 1995-2000, sec. to faculty, 1981-83, faculty rsch. scholar, 1982-83, 92-93, comm. officer, 1989-90, dir. writing for TV program, 1990-97; exec. dir. Renaissance Inst. Coll. of Notre Dame of Md., 2000—03, ret., 2003—. Cons. scholar Md. Humanities Coun., 1992—. Author numerous poems and lit. criticism; editor Liberal Arts Rev., 1996-2000; mem. editl. bd., assoc. editor Md. English Jour., 1994-2000, Morgan Jour. Undergrad. Rsch., 1995-2000, CEA MAGazine, 2002—; assoc. editor, CEA Critic, 2003—; contbr. articles to lit. jours. Coord. Young Reps., Berks County, Pa., 1962-63; chmn. Md. Young Reps., 1964; election judge Baltimore County, Md., 1964-66; regional capt. Am. Cancer Soc., 1978-79; mem. adv. bd. Md. Our Md. Anniversary, 1984, The Living Constitution: Bicentennial of the Fed. Constitution, 1987 Morgan-Penn Faculty fellow, 1977-79, Nat. Endowment Humanities, 1984; named Outstanding Teaching Prof., U. Balt. Coll. Liberal Arts, 1965, Outstanding Teaching Prof. English, Morgan State U., 1987. Mem. MLA, South Atlantic MLA, Coll. Lang. Assn., Coll. English Assn. (Mid-Atlantic Group v.p. 1987-90, pres. 1990-92, exec. bd. 1992—, nat. bd. dirs. 2001—, nat. liaison officer 1993—2004), Women's Caucus for Modern Langs., Md. Coun. Tchrs. English, Md. Poetry and Lit. Soc., Md. Assn. Depts. English (bd. dirs. 1992—), Mid. Atlantic Writers' Assn. (founding 1981, exec. assoc. editor Mid. Atlantic Writers' Assn. Rev. 1989-2000), Delta Epsilon Sigma (v.p. 1992-94, pres. 1994-96), Pi Kappa Delta. Roman Catholic. Home: 17049 Keeney Mill Rd New Freedom PA 17349 Personal E-mail: vfsedlak@aol.com.

SEDLER, ROZANNE FRIEDLANDER, social worker, educator; b. Greensburg, Pa., June 16, 1938; d. Ernest and Belle (Marchel) Friedlander; m. Robert Allen Sedler, Jan. 24, 1960; children: Eric Mark, Beth Ellen. BA, U. Pitts., 1960; MSW, St. Louis U., 1962. Social worker Family & Children's Svc., St. Louis, 1962-63; lectr. Sch. of Social Work Haile Selassie U., Addis Ababa, Ethiopia, 1963-66; social worker U. Ky. Med. Ctr., Lexington, 1966-68, Renaissance Home Health Care, Detroit, 1984-86; geriatric social worker Jewish Family Svc., Southfield, Mich., 1986—. Chair Jewish Family Svc.-Am. Fedn. of State, County, Mcpl. Employees Local 1640; mem. exec. bd. AFSCME Local 1640; chair Oakland County bd. dirs. ACLU. Mem. ACLU (pres. chpt.), Am. Fedn. State, County and Mcpl. Employees (exec. bd. Local 1640, chair Jewish Famil Svc. Bargaining Unit, bd. dirs.). Democrat. Jewish. Home: 18851 Capitol Dr Southfield MI 48075-2680 Office: Jewish Family Svc 24123 Greenfield Rd Southfield MI 48075-3116 Office Phone: 248-559-1500. E-mail: rozsedler@aol.com.

SEDWAY, LYNN MASSEL, real estate economist; b. Washington, Nov. 26, 1941; d. Mark S. and Jean M. (Magnus) Massel; m. Paul H. Sedway, June 12, 1966; children: Mark, Carolyn, Jan. BA in Econs., U. Mich., 1963; MBA, U. Calif., Berkeley, 1976. Economist San Rafael (Calif.) Redevel. Agy., 1976-78; prin. Sedway Group, San Francisco, 1978—99; exec. mng. dir. CB Richard Ellis, San Francisco, 1999—. Instr. Appraisal Bus. Sch. U. Calif., Berkeley; bd. dirs. San Francisco Devel. Fund; corporate bd. mem. Hunting Gate Capital. Mem. Berkeley Bus. Sch. Fund Council, 1984-86, Internat. Coun. of Shopping Ctrs.; chmn San Rafael Downtown Retail Com., 1985; mem. Fisher Center Policy Advisory Bd. of the Haas School; trustee Urban Land Inst., former chmn. retail comml. coun., San Francisco District Council, former chmn., Housing Devel. Fin. Corp., bd. dirs. Marin, Calif. chpt. 1984—. Fellow, Homer Hoyt. Mem. Counselors of Real Estate, San Francisco Chamber of Commerce (former bd. of dirs.), City Club Intl. House, Marin C. of C. (bd. dirs. 1984-87), San Rafael C. of C., Lambda Alpha (past pres., bd. dirs.), Internat. Land Econs. Soc., San Francisco Municipal Fiscal Advisory Com. Avocation: tennis. Home: 765 Market St Apt 26G San Francisco CA 94103-2038

SEDWICK, DEBORAH, state agency administrator; BS, Boston U.; M, U. Alaska. V.p. Jack White Real Estate, Anchorage; commr. Alaska State Dept. Cmty. & Econ. Devel., 1997—. Office: AIDEA 813 W Northern Lights Blvd Anchorage AK 99503

SEE, CAROLYN, English language educator, novelist, book critic; b. Pasadena, Calif., Jan. 13, 1934; d. George Newton Laws and Kate Louise (Sullivan) Daly; m. Richard Edward See, Feb. 18, 1955 (div. June 1959); 1 child, Lisa Lenine; m. Tom Sturak, June 11, 1959; 1 child, Clara Elizabeth Marya. BA, Calif. State U., L.A., 1958; PhD, UCLA, 1963. Prof. English Loyola Marymount Coll., L.A., 1970-85, UCLA, 1985—; book critic L.A. Times, 1981-93, Washington Post, 1993—. Author: Rhine Maidens, 1980, Golden Days, 1986, Making History, 1991, Dreaming: Hard Luck and Good Times In America, 1995, The Handyman, 1999, Making a Literary Life, 2002. Bd. dirs. Calif. Arts Coun., L.A., 1987-91, Day Break, for homeless, Santa Monica, Calif., 1989—, Friends of English, UCLA, 1990—; buddy for life AIDS Project L.A., AIDS relief, L.A., 1990—. Recipient award Sidney Hillman Found., 1972, Robert Kirsch award L.A. Times, 1994; PEN Ctr. USA West Lifetime Achievement award 1998; grantee Nat. Endowment for Arts, 1980, Guggenheim fellow, 1990-91. Mem. Writers Guild Am., Libr. Found. Calif., PEN Ctr. USA West (pres. 1990-91), Nat. Book Critics Cir. (bd. dirs. 1986-90). Democrat. Avocations: gardening, sailing, dance, brush clearing. Home: 17339 Tramonto Dr Pacific Palisades CA 90272-3124 Office: UCLA Dept English 405 Hilgard Ave Los Angeles CA 90095-9000

SEE, SAW-TEEN, structural engineer; b. Georgetown, Penang, Malaysia, Mar. 23, 1954; came to U.S., 1974; d. Hock-Eng and Ewe-See (Lim) S.; m. Leslie Earl Robertson, Aug. 11, 1982; 1 child, Karla Mei. BSCE, Cornell U., 1977, MCE, 1978. Registered profl. engr., N.Y., Calif., Conn., Fla., Mass., Md., N.J., Ohio, Pa., Wash., Ark., Ill., Tex. Design engr. Leslie E. Robertson Assocs., R.L.L.P., N.Y.C., 1978-81, assoc., 1981-85, ptnr., 1986—, mng. ptnr., 1990—. Cons. M of Engring. class Cornell U., 1994-95, mem. adv. coun. Sch. Civil and Environ. Engring., 1999—; project dir., project mgr. Miho Mus., Kyoto, Japan, West Side H.S., N.Y.C., Jr. H.S. 234, Bklyn., Jewelry Trade Ctr., Bangkok, Bilboa (Spain) Emblematic bldgs., Internat. Trade Ctr., Barcelona, Spain, Seattle Art Mus., San Jose (Calif.) Convention Ctr., San Jose Arena; project dir. Hong Kong Sta. South West & North East Tower Structural Audit, Balt. Conv. Ctr., Rock 'N Roll Hall of Fame and Mus., Cleve., Pontiac Marina Hotel and Retail, Singapore, acad. bldgs. and greenhouse, SUNY, Binghamton, N.Y.; project mgr. Coll. of Law bldg. U. Iowa, Iowa City, Neiman-Marcus store, San Francisco, AT&T Exhbn. bldg., N.Y.C., Bank of China Tower, Hong Kong, AIG Tower, Hong Kong, Bellevue Hosp., N.Y.C., W.J. Clinton Presdl. Ctr., Little Rock, Ark., Shanghai World Fin. Ctr., PPG Hdqs., Pitts., AT&T Corp. Hdqs., N.Y.C.; ptnr.-in-charge Nat. Constn. Ctr., Phila. Contbr. articles to profl. jours. Named to Those Who Made Marks in the Constrn. Industry in 1988, Engring. News Record, N.Y.C., 1989, Spl. Recognition award Profl. Women in Constrn., 2002. Fellow ASCE (performance study team World Trade Ctr. with FEMA), Archtl. League, Coun. on Tall Bldgs. and Urban Habitat (past chairperson com. on gravity loads and temperature effects 1982-85), Architects, Designers, Planners for Social Responsiblity, N.Y. Assn. Cons. Engrs. (dir. 1989-93, structural codes com. 1991—). Avocations: sailing, skiing, reading, photography. Home: 45 E 89th St Apt 25C New York NY 10128-1230 Office: Leslie E Robertson Assocs RLLP 30 Broad St Fl 47 New York NY 10004-2304 E-mail: sts@lera.com.

SEEBACH, LYDIA MARIE, physician; b. Red Wing, Minn., Nov. 9, 1920; d. John Henry and Marie (Gleusen) S.; m. Keith Edward Wentz, Oct. 16, 1959; children: Brooke Marie, Scott. BS, U. Minn., 1942, MB, 1943, MD, 1944, MS in Medicine, 1951. Diplomate Am. Bd. Internal Medicine. Intern Kings County Hosp., Bklyn., 1944; fellow Mayo Found., Rochester, Minn., 1945-51; pvt. practice Oakland, Calif., 1952-60, San Francisco, 1961—. Asst. clin. prof. U. Calif., San Francisco, 1981—; mem., vice chmn. Arthritis Clinic, Presbyn. Hosp., San Francisco, 1961-88, pharmacy com., 1963-78; chief St. Mary's Hosp. Arthritis Clinic, San Francisco, 1968-72; exec. bd. Pacific Med. Ctr., San Francisco, 1974-76. Contbr. articles to med. jours. Fellow ACP; mem. AMA, Am. Med. Womens Assn. (pres. Calif. chpt. 1968-70), Am. Rheumatism Assn., Am. Soc. Internal Medicine, Pan Am. Med. Womens Assn. (treas.), Calif. Acad. Medicine, Calif. Soc. Internal Medicine, Calif. Med. Assn., San Francisco Med. Soc., San Francisco Med. Assn., San Francisco Soc. Internal Medicine, No. Calif. Rheumatism Assn., Internat. Med. Women's Assn., Mayo Alumni (bd. dirs. 1983-89), Iota Sigma Pi. Republican. Lutheran. Avocations: music, cooking, gardening, needlepoint. Office: 490 Post St Ste 939 San Francisco CA 94102-1414

SEEBERT, KATHLEEN ANNE, international sales and marketing executive; d. Harold Earl and Marie Anne (Lowery) S. MM, MA, Northwestern U., 1983. Dir. mktg. MidAm. Commodity Exch., 1982-85; internat. trade cons. to Govt. of Ont. Can., 1985-90; dir. mktg. and program devel. Internat. Orientation Resources, 1990-94; v.p. Am. Internat. Group, 1995-97; dir. KPMG Peat Marwick LLP, 1997-98; cons. Watson Wyatt & Co., 1999—. Guest lectr. U. Dayton, U. Notre Dame, Northwestern U., Kellogg Alumni Chgo., French-Am. C. of C., Internat. Employee Relocation Coun., Soc. Intercultural Educators, Trainers and Rschrs., ASTD, Ill. CPA Soc., SBA, KPMG Peat Marwick, Pricewaterhousecoopers, Ernst & Young, Nat. Fgn. Trade Coun., William M. Mercer, Inc. Nat. bd. dirs. U. Dayton. Mem. Futures Industry Assn. Am. (treas.), Notre Dame Club Chgo., Kellogg Mgmt. Club Chgo. Republican. Roman Catholic. Office: 191 N Wacker Dr Ste 2100 Chicago IL 60611

SEEDS, SHARON LYNN, bank processor; d. Don A. and Marguerite Morairty Seeds. BA in Edn. with high distinction, Ariz. State U., 1972. Tchr. gen. and vocal music edn. Paradise Valley Unified Sch. Dist. # 69, Phoenix, 1973—76; advt. coord. Greater Phoenix Jewish News, 1976—83; disbursements/loan rev. processor Merabank, Phoenix, 1984—88; loan processor II Citibank, Scottsdale and Mesa, Ariz., 1989—91; acctg. specialist, ops. processor I and II, store acctg. support, mortgage lending home equity Internet divsn. Wells Fargo & Co., Phoenix, 1992—. Festival adjudicator Ariz. Solo and Ensemble Festival, Phoenix, 1973—99; jr. choir dir. Christ Ch. of the Ascension, Paradise Valley, 1983—87; soloist, sect. leader Congregation Ch., Tempe, Ariz., Presbyn. Ch., Phoenix, Ch. of Divine Sci.; soloist, sect. leader Trinity Episcopal Cathedral St. Barnabas-on-the Desert, 1976—2002. Contr.ghost editor: textbook Arizona Construction Lending and the Law, 1988; actor: (theatrical prodns.) various locations. Vol. libr. catalog area Lillian Vallely Sch., Blackfoot, Idaho, 2002; neighborhood activist on hist. preservation com. Sunview Estates II, Phoenix, 2002—; vol. press release area Episcopal Ch. Gen. Conv., Phoenix, 1991. Mem.: Am. Choral Dirs. Assn., Music Educators Nat. Conf., Phi Kappa Phi, Kappa Delta Pi, Pi Lambda Theta, Sigma Alpha Iota (local chair/co-chair for nat. bazaar at triennial conv. 1987—, nat. elections chair triennial conv. 2003, Sword of Honor 1972, Rose of Honor 1995, Rose of Dedication 2003). Episcopalian. Avocations: music theater/liturgical drama, needlecrafts, reading.

SEEGER, LEINAALA ROBINSON, law librarian, educator; b. Wailuku, Hawaii, July 2, 1944; d. John Adam and Anna Hiilani (Leong) Robinson; 1 child, Maile Lea. BA, U. Wash., 1966; JD, U. Puget Sound, 1977; M in Law Librarianship, U. Wash., 1979. Bar: Wash. 1977. Reference librarian U. Puget Sound Sch. Law., Tacoma, 1977-79, assoc. law librarian, 1981-86; asst. librarian McGeorge Sch. Law, U. of Pacific, Sacramento, 1979-81; assoc. librarian pub. svc. Harvard Law Sch., Cambridge, Mass., 1986-89; dir. law library, assoc. prof. law U. Idaho Coll. Law, Moscow, 1989-97, U. Hawaii Sch. of Law, Honolulu, 1997—. Mem. Assn. Am. Law Schs. (librs. and technol. com. 1997-99, chmn. 1998-99), Wash. state Bar Assn., Am. Assn. Law Librs. (chmn. minority com. 1990-91, v.p., pres.-elect Western Pacific chpt. 1985-86, 90-91, pres. 1991-92, vice chmn. edn. com. 1991-92, chmn. 1992-93). Avocations: scuba, snorkeling, wine education, flying, aerobics.

SEEGER, MELINDA WAYNE, realtor; m. Robert Charles Seeger; 1 child, Jeffrey Wayne. Chief occupl. therapy Rehab. Inst. Oreg., Portland, 1964-66; supr. phys. disabilities and gen. medicine and surgery occupl. therapy Mpls. VA Hosp., 1966-68; supr. phys. disabilities occupl. therapy Nat. Naval Med. Ctr., Bethesda, Md., 1968-71; assoc. chief rehab. svcs., dir. occupl. therapy UCLA Med. Ctr., 1974-85, cons., prin. investigator rheumatology divsn. dept. medicine, 1985-86; realtor Merrill Lynch Realty, L.A., 1987-95, Re/Max Estate Properties, Beverly Hills, Calif., 1995-96, Nelson Shelton & Assocs., Beverly Hills, 1996—. Author, editor articles in field. Mem. utilization rev. com. Vis. Nurse Assn. L.A., 1975-85, mem. profl. adv. com., 1979-80; mem. exec. com. Allied Health Professions sect. Arthritis Found., 1980-85, chmn. edn. com., 1982-85, mem. profl. edn. com.; bd. dirs. Calif. Occupl. Therapy Found., 1984-85, Westwood-Holmby Hills Homeowners Assn.; mem. adv. bd. Save Westwood Village L.A. Recipient Spl. Achievement award Nat. Naval Med. Ctr., 1971, Outstanding Performance award, 1971, Spl. Performance award UCLA, 1980, 84, Addie Thomas Svc. award for outstanding svc. to rheumatology cmty. Arthritis Found., 1986, Cert. of Appreciation award, 1989; mem. Million Dollar Club. Mem. Am. Occupl. Therapy Assn., Occupl. Therapy Assn. Calif., Allied Health Professions Assn. (chmn. edn. com. 1982—), L.A. Bd. Realtors, San Fernando Valley Bd. Realtors, West L.A. C. of C., Million Dollar Club, Blue Diamond Club. Office: 355 N Canon Dr Beverly Hills CA 90210-4704

SEEGER, PEGGY, musician, singer, songwriter; b. N.Y.C., June 17, 1935; d. Charles Louis and Ruth Porter (Crawford) S.; m. Ewan MacColl, Jan. 25, 1977 (dec. Oct. 1989); children: Neill, Calum, Kitty. Attended, Radcliffe Coll., 1953-55. Dir. Ewan MacColl, Ltd., London, 1959—. Co-author: Travellers Songs of England and Scotland, 1977, Till Doomsday in the Afternoon, 1986; author: The Peggy Seeger Songbook, 1997, Essential Ewan MacColl Songbook, 2001; 20 solo albums, 120 shared albums. Avocations: reading, walking, travelling. Home: 3 Woodlawn Ave Asheville NC 28801-2219 Office Phone: 828-258-3466.

SEEGER, VIRGINIA VINCENT, portrait painter; b. San Francisco, May 29, 1923; Student, Cornish Sch. Art, Seattle, U. Wash. Portrait painter, 1948—. Creative works include cartoons for various orgns. Mem. Pacific Art League. Office: 1111 Morse Ave Spc 227 Sunnyvale CA 94089-1630 Home: PO Box 3291 Sunriver OR 97707-0291

SEEGERS, LORI C. lawyer; b. Miami Beach, Fla., June 17, 1955; BA cum laude, U. Pa., 1977; JD, Fordham U., 1982. Bar: N.Y. 1983, Ill. 2002, U.S. Dist. Ct. (so. dist.) N.Y. 1983. Ptnr. Anderson, Kill & Olick, P.C., N.Y.C.; gen. counsel PPM Am., Inc. Contbr. articles to profl. jours. Mem. ABA, N.Y. State Bar Assn. (sect. banking, corp. and bus. law), Assn. of Bar of City of N.Y. Office: PPM Am Inc Ste 1200 225 W Wacker Dr Chicago IL 60606-1276 E-mail: lori.seegers@ppmamerica.com.

SEELBACH, ANNE ELIZABETH, artist; b. Detroit, July 27, 1944; d. William Otto and Elizabeth (Simonds) S. BA, NYU, 1967; MFA, CUNY, 1985. Curator Monhegan (Maine) Mus., 1992—95; art instr. The Victor d'Amico Inst. of Art, Napeague, N.Y., 1994—, Arts Pro Tem, Hancock, NH, 1991—95. One-woman shows include Tower Gallery, Southampton, N.Y., 1981, Newark (N.J.) Mus., 1984, Tower Gallery, N.Y.C., 1985, The Conn. Gallery, Marlborough, 1989, Bunting Inst. of Radcliffe Coll., Cambridge, Mass., 1990, Frick Gallery, Belfast, Maine, 1991, Simmons Coll., Boston, 1991, The Painting Ctr., N.Y.C., 1994, Kouros Gallery, 1996, exhibited in group shows at Kommunale Galerie, Berlin, 1987, Frauenmuseum, Bonn, Germany, 1988, Northeastern U., Boston, 1990, Fed. Res. Bank, 1995, Kouros Gallery, N.Y.C., 1995—, Met. Mus. and Art Ctr., Coral Gables, Fla., —, others, —, Represented in permanent collections Newark Mus., Frauenmuseum, Bonn, Germany, Centrum Frans Masereel, Kasterlee, Belgium, Lyman Allyn Mus., New London, Conn., Bunting Inst. of Radcliffe Coll., Prudential Ins. Co., Newark, Continental Grain Corp., N.Y.C., Phoenix Mut. Life Ins. Co., Hartford, Conn., The Hillier Group, Princeton, N.J. Recipient painting fellowship Bunting Inst., Radcliffe Coll., 1989-90, artist fellowship Triangle Artists' Workshop, Pine Plains, N.Y., 1988, MacDowell Colony, Peterborough, N.H., 1987. Mem.: Soc. Bunting Fellows. Address: 33 Granite St Apt 304 New London CT 06320-5944

SEELER, RUTH ANDREA, pediatrician, educator; b. N.Y.C., June 13, 1936; d. Thomas and Olivia (Patten) S. BA cum laude, U. Vt., 1959, MD, 1962. Diplomate Am. Bd. Pediatrics, Am. Bd. Pediatric Hematology/Oncology. Intern Bronx (N.Y.) Mcpl. Hosp., 1962—65; pediats. hematology/oncology fellow U. Ill., 1965—67; dir. pediatric hematology/oncology Cook County Hosp., 1967—84; prof. pediatrics and pediatric edn. Coll. Medicine U. Ill., Chgo., 1984—; assoc. chief pediatrics Michael Reese Hosp., Chgo., 1990—97, acting chief pediatrics, 1997—99; pediatrician St. Anthony's Hosp./U. Ill. Coll. Medicine, 1999—2001. Course coord. pediatrics Nat. Coll. Advanced Med. Edn., Chgo., 1987-96; mem. subboard Pediatric Hematology/Oncology, Chapel Hill, 1990-95. Mem. editl. bd. Am. Jour. Pediat. Hematology/Oncology, 1985-95. Founder camp for hemophiliacs Hemophilia Found., Ill., 1973—2000, med. dir., pres., 1981—85; jr. and sr. warden, treas. Ch. Our Saviour, Chgo., 1970—92. Mem.: Phi Beta Kappa, Gamma Phi Beta Found. (trustee 1994—2000, 2002—). Avocations: triathalons, biking, swimming. Office: U Ill Coll Medicine Pediats M/C 856 840 S Wood St Chicago IL 60612-7317 Office Phone: 312-355-1021.

SEELIG, JILL, publishing executive; MBA, Fordham U. With fin. svcs. ind., 1984—89; sales rep. NY Mag.; beauty dir. Self Mag., 1994—95; advt. sales rep. Self Mag., 1996—99; advt. dir. Vanity Fair, 1998—99, O, The Oprah Mag., 1999—2000, pub., 2000—. Office: O, The Oprah Magazine 1700 Broadway New York NY 10019

SEELIGER, LISA KAY, social worker, writer; b. Pella, Iowa, July 15, 1972; d. Jon W. Stravers and Sherril Sue Graham; m. Wayne Alan Seeliger, Feb. 19, 1999. BA in Social Work, Calvin Coll., 1994. LCSW Bur. Occupl. Licenses, Idaho. With Peace Corps., Costa Rica, 1994—96; with child abuse prevention divsn. Americorps, Waterloo, Iowa, 1987—98; social worker Infant Toddler Program, Boise, 1998—. Freelance interpreter, Idaho, 1996—, Iowa, 1996—. Author: Color de Mujer the Woman Within, 2001, The Nature of my Spirit, 2003. Mem.: Women of Color Alliance, Escritoras sin Fronteras (co-leader 2001—). Avocations: writing, spiritual study, earth medicine, healing, women's health. Office: Dept Health and Welfare 1720 Westgate Dr Ste B Boise ID 83704

SEELMAN, KATHERINE DOLORES, institute administrator; b. Boston, May 26, 1938; d. Frederick George and Loretta (Tetu) S. BA, Hunter Coll., 1964; MA, NYU, 1970, PhD, 1982. Tchr. N.Y.C. Schs., 1966-73; instr., rschr. N.Y. Inst. Tech., NSF, N.Y.C., 1973-75; project mgr. Nat. Coun. Chs., N.Y.C., 1976-82; cons. Am. Assn. Retired Persons, Washington, 1982-83; rsch. scholar Gallaudet U., Washington, 1984-86; dir. pub. edn. Mass. Comm. for Deaf and Hard of Hearing, Boston, 1986-89; rsch. specialist Nat. Coun. on Disability, Washington, 1989-93; dir. program devel. Adminstrn. on Devel. Disability, Washington, 1993-94; dir. Nat. Inst. on Disability and Rehab. Rsch., Washington, 1994—. Switzer scholar Nat. Rehab. Assn., 1991, Disting. Switzer fellow Dept. Edn. Nat. Inst. Disability and Rehab. Rsch., 1985-86; recipient Scholarships NYU, 1973, Am. Law Inst./ABA, 1977, Fellowships NSF, 1974, Resources for the Future, 1976; named to Hall of Fame Alumni Assn. Hunter Coll., 1995; recipient pub. svc. award Assn. Acad. Physiatrists, 2000. Mem. RESNA, AAAS, Am. Pub. Health Assn. (Disability Achievement award 1999), Assn. for Advancement of Sci., Soc. for Disability Studies, Self-Help for Hard of Hearing. Office: Nat Inst Disability and Rehab Rsch 600 Independence Ave SW Washington DC 20202-0004

SEELY, MARIBETH WALSH, elementary school educator; d. William F. and Agnes C. Walsh; m. Thomas P. Seely; children: Timothy Patrick Francis, Keribeth Francis. BS in Elem. Edn., Lowell U., 1966. Cert. reading specialist Mass. Tchr. Town of Methuen, Mass., 1966—71, City of Lawrence, Mass., Sandyston-Walpack Sch., Layton, NJ. Testified to Ho. Reps. Am. Legion and Citizens Flag Alliance, Washington, 1997; testified for Am. flag Senate Judiciary Com., Washington, 1999. Named Woman of Distinction, Lenni-Lenape Girl Scouts, 1995, Woman of the 90's, N.J. Herald Newspaper, 1995; recipient Gov.'s Tchr. Recognition award, State N.J., 1994. Mem.: Sierra Club (assoc.). Roman Catholic. Avocations: hiking, art museums, travel, baseball. Home: 19 Summit Dr Branchville NJ 07826 Office: Sandyston-Walpack School PO Box 128 Layton NJ 07851

SEEM, EVELYN ASHCRAFT, music educator; b. Sedgwick, Kans., July 10, 1915; d. Frank T. and Esther Hege Ashcraft; m. Herbert A. Seem, June 19, 1938 (dec. Mar. 1994); children: Herbert A. Jr., Quinda Marie Seem-Hatfield. Diploma, Sherwood Music Sch., 1936; B in Piano, Phillips U., 1936, postgrad. Tchr. Phillips U., Enid, Okla., 1960—80; pvt. piano tchr. Enid. Mem. Nat. Music Tchrs. Assn., Okla. Music Tchrs. Assn. Presbyterian. Home: 722 W Illinois Ave Enid OK 73701-7302

SEFTEL, DONNA SELENE, architect; b. N.Y.C., Apr. 26, 1956; d. Lawrence and Roslyn (Kaufman) S.; 1 child, Morgan Luc. Student, 1st Berlin Summer Acad., 1977, Royal Danish Acad. Fine Arts, 1978, Columbia U., 1978; BArch, Cornell U., 1980; postgrad., New Sch. for Social Rsch, N.Y.C., 1997. Registered arch., N.Y., N.J. Arch. Steven Holl Archs., N.Y.C., 1985-86; prin. Donna Selene Seftel Archs., N.Y.C., 1986—; artist-in-residence Mott Hall, N.Y.C., 1987—88; lectr. Archtl. League N.Y., 1987, Acad. Art and Design, Linz, Austria, 1988, Cooper-Hewit Nat. Mus. Design, 1988, CCNY, 1990, 1992, RISD, 1993, Pa. State U., 1994, Columbia U., 1995, Queensland U., RMIT, Australia, 1999; critic Royal Swedish Inst. Tech., Stockholm, 1991, Cornell U., 1991, Columbia U., 1992, 1995, Parsons Sch. Design, 1992—95. Artist-in-residence Mott Hall, N.Y.C., 1987—88; lectr. Archtl. League N.Y., 1987, Acad. Art and Design, Linz, Austria, 1988, Cooper-Hewit Nat. Mus. Design, 1988, CCNY, 1990, 92, Cornell U., 1991, Pa. State U., 1994, Columbia U., 1992, 95. Projects include Rapid Indsl. Plastics, 1985, Vacant Lots, 1987, Calif. Life Guard Tower, 1988, Theatricus Formicus, Gordon Lighting and Lightscreen, 1989, Recycling Industry, 1990, Nara Convention Ctr. Competition, 1991, Lego: Gate of Gates, Culebra House, P.R., 1992, Kulturzeile, Vienna, Austria, 1993, Interactive Playhouse, Greene Loft, N.Y.C., 1996, S-network offices, 1994-97, Wild Pitch Records, Filiberti House, 1994, Tribeca Loft, 1995; prodn. designer ind. feature film Burn, 1997, Holey Landscape: World Trade Ctr. Meml. Competition, 2003; one-woman show Atelier Lorenz Mandl Gasse, Vienna, Austria, 1993; exhibited in group shows, including Urban Ctr., N.Y.C., Archtl. League N.Y., 1987, Kirsten Kiser Gallery for Arch., L.A., 1988, Grand Cen. Sta., 1989, Downtown Whitney Mus., N.Y.C., Gallery 91, N.Y.C., 1989, Storefront for Art & Arch., Nat. Inst. Archtl. Edn., N.Y.C., Cooper-Hewitt Nat. Mus. Design, N.Y.C., 1990, Moderna Museet, Kulturhuset, Stockholm, 1991, Deutsches Architektur Mus., Frankfurt am Main, 1992, Gammel Dok Ctr. for Danish Architecture, Copenhagen, Kasteel d'Erp, Baarlo, Belgium, Kunsthal, Rotterdam, Cornell U., Ithaca, N.Y., 1993, City Art Ctr., Edinburgh, Mus. Finnish Architecture, Helsinki, Mus. fur Gestaltung, Zurich, Katonah Mus. of Art, Haus der Arch., Graz, 1994, Grande Arche in La Defense, Paris, Norton Mus. Art, Palm Beach, 1995, Mus. Decorative Arts, Lausanne, 1996, Gemeente Mus., Helmond, The Netherlands, Mus. de Civilisation, Quebec City, Arch. Ctr., Berlin, 1997; pub. in various publs. including N.Y. Times, DOMUS, Metropolis, Architecture Record, AIA N.Y. Architecture, World Architecture, Shelter & Dreams-Katonah Mus. Catalogue, Unpvt. House-MOMA Catalogue, Mama 27, Gate of The Present-LEGO Catalogue, Ideas for New Social Bldgs., Vacant Lots, New Schs. for N.Y., Showrooms, Front 3, Archtl. Edn. for Children at Mott Hall-Dist. 6, N.Y.C., etc. Recipient award Young Archs. Forum 6, Archtl. League N.Y., 1987, project award N.Y. chpt. AIA, 1989; architecture fellow N.Y. Found. for Arts, 1988; Pritzger fellow Djerassi Resident Artists Program, Woodside, Calif., 1995, in collections of Lego, Denmark and Yamagiwa, Japan. Democrat. Jewish. Address: 95 Drake Ln Manhasset NY 11030-1227 E-mail: dseftel@earthlink.net.

SEGAL, BEATRICE ANN, social worker; b. N.Y.C., Mar. 2, 1962; d. David Isaac and Lore Segal; m. David Barry Segal, Sept. 8, 1986; 1 child, Benjamin Isaac. BA, Kenyon Coll., 1984; MSW, 1988; student in Family Therapy, 98. Social worker Good Shepherd Svcs., N.Y.C., 1988—91, U. Settlement, N.Y.C., 1991—92; psychiatric social worker Woodhill Hosp., Bklyn., 1992—95, Bronx (N.Y.) Lebanon Hosp., 1995—98; social worker N.Y.C. Dept. Edn., Bklyn., 1998—. Mem.: Ackerman Inst. Alumni Assn. Home: 212 Clinton St 4F Brooklyn NY 11201

SEGAL, GERALDINE ROSENBAUM, sociologist; b. Aug. 26, 1908; d. Harry and Mena (Hamburg) Rosenbaum; m. Bernard Gerard Segal, Oct. 22, 1933; children: Loretta Joan Cohen, Richard Murry. BS in Edn., U. Pa., 1930, MA in Human Rels., 1963, PhD in Sociology, 1978; MS in Libr. Sci., Drexel U., 1968; LittD (hon.), Franklin & Marshall Coll., 1990. Social worker County Relief Bd., Phila., 1931-35; sociologist Phila., from 1935. Cons. and lectr. in field. Author: In Any Fight Some Fall, 1975, Blacks in the Law, 1983. Bd. dirs. NCCJ, 1937-47, 82—, sec., 1983-91; bd. overseers U. Pa. Sch. Social Work, 1983-97; bd. dirs. Juvenile Law Ctr., 1984-98; chair Phila. Tutorial Project, 1966-68; 1st v.p. U. Pa. Alumnae Assn., 1967-70. Co-recipient Nat. Neighbors Disting. Leadership in Civil Rights award, 1988; recipient Drum Major award for Human Rights, Phila. Martin Luther King, Jr. Assn. for Nonviolence, 1990, Brotherhood Sisterhood award NCCJ, 1994. Democrat. Jewish. Home: Philadelphia, Pa. Died Jan. 14, 2003.

SEGAL, HELENE ROSE, periodical editor; b. L.A., Jan. 31, 1955; d. Alan and Lila E. Segal. Student, Calif. State U., Fullerton, 1973-75; BA in English, U. Calif., Santa Barbara, 1978. Library asst. ABC-CLIO, Santa Barbara, 1979-80, editorial asst., 1980-81, asst. editor, 1981-83; mng. editor ABC POL SCI, ABC-CLIO, Santa Barbara, 1983-2001; project mgr. ABC-CLIO, Santa Barbara, 2001—. Mem. Am. Polit. Sci. Assn., Current World Leaders (adv. bd. 1989—). Avocations: reading, collecting, swimming. Home: 142 La Vista Grande Santa Barbara CA 93103-2817 Office: ABC CLIO 130 Cremona Dr Ste C Santa Barbara CA 93117-5505 E-mail: hsegal@abc-clio.com.

SEGAL, JANE, newscaster; b. N.Y. BS in Edn., Bernard M. Baruch Coll. Gen. assignment reporter, weekend anchor WLBT, Jackson, Miss.; reporter, anchor WMC-TV, Memphis, 1983; anchor WLBT, Jackson. Avocations: old movies, foreign films. Office: WLBT 715 S Jefferson St Jackson MS 39201

SEGAL, LINDA GALE, retired insurance company executive; b. Panama City, Fla., Dec. 14, 1947; d. Homer Ford Jr. and Mary Virginia (Phillmon) F. m. Howard Arthur Segal, Dec. 29, 1970; 1 child, David Samuel. Student, Orlando (Fla.) Jr. Coll., 1966-69, Rollins Coll., 1972. Sales asst. Sta. WESH-TV, Orlando, Fla., 1973-76; mktg. coordinator Sta. WFBC-TV, Grenneville, S.C., 1976-77; traffic mgr. STa. WRDW-TV, Augusta, Ga., 1978-80; field underwriter Liberty Life Ins. Co., Greenville, 1980-81; agt. benefits dept. J. Rolfe Davis Ins. Agy., Orlando, 1981-84; sr. market sales rep. Humana, Inc., Orlando, 1984-86; dir. mktg. Nat. Med. Mgmt., Orlando, 1986-87; sr. account exec. Physicians Health Plan Fla., Inc., Tampa, 1987-88, N.E. Fin. Services, Orlando, 1988-89; mktg. mgr. Ins. Mgmt. Svcs., Inc., Greenville, S.C., 1989-90; regional mktg. dir. Horizons Internat. Inc., St. Augustine, Fla., 1991-92; dir. bus. devel. ResCare Home Health, Inc., Jacksonville, Fla., 1992—. Pvt. practice ins. cons., Tampa and Orlando, Fla., 1986-89. Mem. Am. Bus. Women's Assn., Nat. Assn. Profl. Saleswomen, Nat. Assn. Health Underwriters, Assn. Life Underwriters, Women Life Underwriters Confedn., Nat. Assn. Securities Dealers (registered rep.). Republican. Office: 4329 Falling Leaf Ct Jacksonville FL 32258-4535 E-mail: lgs@itilink.com.

SEGAL, LORE, writer; b. Vienna, Mar. 8, 1928; came to U.S., 1951, naturalized, 1956; d. Ignatz and Franzi (Stern) Groszmann; m. David I. Segal, Nov. 3, 1960 (dec.); children: Beatrice Ann, Jacob Paul. BA in English, Bedford Coll., U. London, Eng., 1948. Prof. writing div. Sch. Arts, Columbia U., also Princeton U., Sarah Lawrence Coll., Bennington Coll.; prof. English U. Ill., Chgo., 1978-92, Ohio State U., 1992-97. Author: Other People's Houses, 1964; Lucinella, 1976, Her First American, 1985; (children's book) Tell Me A Mitzi, 1970, All the Way Home, 1973, Tell Me a Trudy, 1977; The Story of Mrs. Brubeck and How She Looked for Trouble and Where She Found Him, 1981, The Story of Mrs. Lovewright and Purrless Her Cat, 1985, Morris the Artist, 2003, Why Mole Shouted and Other Stories, 2004; translator: (with W.D. Snodgrass) Gallows Songs, 1968, The Juniper Tree and Other Tales from Grimm, 1973, The Book of Adam to Moses, 1987, The Story of King Saul and King David, 1991; contbr. short stories, articles to N.Y. Times Book Rev., Partisan Rev., New Republic, The New Yorker, others. Guggenheim fellow, 1965-66; Council Arts and Humanities grantee, 1968-69; Artists Public Service grantee, 1970-71; CAPS grantee, 1975; Nat. Endowment Arts grantee, spring 1982, 1987; NEH grantee, 1983; Acad. Arts and Letters award, 1986. Address: 280 Riverside Dr New York NY 10025-9010 E-mail: Lore@usa.net.

SEGAL, MINDY, chef; Grad., Kendall Coll. Pastry asst. Ambria, Chgo.; pastry chef Charlie Trotter's, Chgo., Gordon, Chgo., Marche, Chgo., Spago, Chgo., MK the Restaurant, Chgo. Developed dessert menus Mia Francesca, Harvest on Huron, Thyme. Office: 868 N Franklin Chicago IL 60610

SEGAL, PHYLLIS NICHAMOFF, mediator; b. Apr. 18, 1945; d. Sidney and Theresa Helen (Uroff) Nichamoff; m. Eli J. Segal, June 13, 1965; children: Jonathan, Mora. Student, Brandeis U., 1962-65; BA, U. Mich., 1966; JD, Georgetown U., 1973. Bar: N.Y. 1974, U.S. Dist. Ct. (so. and ea. dists.) N.Y. 1975, Mass. 1983, U.S. Supreme Ct. 1979. Deputy atty. gen. Commonwealth Mass., 1986—88; assoc. Weil, Gotshal and Manges, N.Y.C., 1973—77; legal dir. NOW Legal Def. and Edn. Fund., N.Y.C., 1977-82, gen. counsel, 1986—94; mediator ADR Assoc., L.L.C., Boston, 2001—. Chmn. Fed. Labor Rels. Auth., Washington, 1994-2000; gen. counsel Exec. office Transp. and Constrn., Commonwealth of Mass., 1984-86; adj. asst. prof. law NYU, 1980-82; fellow Bunting Inst. Radcliffe Coll., 1982-83; cons. U.S. Commn. Civil Rights. Contbr. articles to profl. jours. Mem. Commn. on Party Reform Nat. Dem. Party, 1972-73, mem. Compliance Rev. Commn., 1974-76; mem. adv. bd. Mass. Commn. Against Discrimination, 1983—; bd. chmn. Handgun Control Inc./Ctr. to Prevent Handgun Violence; former chairwoman Nat. Labor Rels. Authority. Mem. ABA, Fedn. Women Lawyers Jud. Screening Panel, Mass. Bar Assn. Office: ADR Assoc LLC 85 Newbury Street Ste 3 Boston MA 02116

SEGAL, RENA BETH, artist; b. New Brunswick, N.J., May 27, 1953; d. George and Helen (Steinberg) S. BFA, Montclair State Coll., 1975; MFA, Rutgers U., 1977. One person shows include Ocean County Coll., Toms

River, N.J., 1978, Piscataway (N.J.) Mcpl. Bldg., 1983, Johnson and Johnson, New Brunswick, N.J., 1985, N.J. State Mus., Trenton, 1989, Mystic Knight Gallery, New Brunswick, 1990, Advocate Bldg., Stamford, Conn., 1991, Gratz Gallery, New Hope, Pa., 2001; exhibited in group shows Dumont Landis Gallery, New Brunswick, 1981, Sidney Janis Gallery, N.Y.C., 1984, Laforet Mus. Harajunku, Tokyo, 1986, Morris Mus., Morristown, N.J., 1987, Hunterdon Art Ctr., Clinton, N.J., 1990, Phoenix Group, Metuchen, N.J., 1993, Sound Shore Gallery, Stamford, Conn., 1994, 95, 96, The Gallery at Bristol-Meyer Squibb, Princeton, N.J., 1995, 98, Collectors Edge Summit, N.J., 1999, NJ Ctr. Arts, Summit, 1999, Marsh Ins. Co., Morristown, N.J., 2000, Gratz Gallery, New Hope, Pa., 2001, others; represented in permanent collections Pub. Svc. and Electric, Newark, Pepsico, Purchase, N.Y., Bristol-Meyers Squibb, Lawrenceville, N.J., Johnson & Johnson, New Brunswick, N.J., Chase Manhattan Bank, NY, Marsh Ins. Co., Morristown, N.J., Frederick R. Weisman Found., L.A. N.J. State Coun. on Arts fellow, 1985.

SEGAL, SABRA LEE, artist, graphics designer, illustrator, actress; b. Boston; Student, Elmira Coll., 1955-57; BFA, Boston U., 1963; MA in Art Edn., U. Wis., 1968, MFA, 1969. Author: (poetry) To All Things Alive, 1968, An Artist's Life: Dreams, Letters and Real Things, 2000; one-woman shows include Schenectady (NY) Mus., 1985, Watermark/Cargo Gallery, Kingston, NY, 1991, Woodstock (NY) Artists Assn., Inc., 1992; exhibited in group shows at Smithsonian Inst., 1981, Albany (N.Y.) Inst. History and Art, 1984, Donskoj & Co., Kingston, 1994, Rice Gallery, Albany, 1990, Barnes and Noble, 1997, Syracuse Cultural Workers Women Artist's Calendar, Syracuse, N.Y., 1999, 2000, The Living Rm. Gallery, Kingston, NY, 2003, Woodstock Watercolors Gallery, 2003, The Richard Sena Gallery, Hudson, N.Y., 2003; contbr. Women Artists' Calendar, Syracuse, N.Y., 1999-2000. Lady exercisor, vis. guest Perfo Prodns. N.C., 1993. Home: PO Box 821 Woodstock NY 12498-0821

SEGALE, ALTHEA FRANCES, music educator; b. Huntington, N.Y., May 2, 1951; d. Joseph Thomas and Amalia Mary Hansen; m. Andrew William Segale, Mar. 23, 2002. BA, SUNY, Oneonta, 1973; MA, SUNY, 1986. Tchr. band Farmingdale Pub. Schs., NY, 1983—. Asst. condr. Bay Shore Cmty. Band, NY, 1996—99; v.p. Farmingdale Fed. of Tchrs., 1986—91. 1st basson Northport Cmty. Band, 1969—99; dir. youth choir Northport Presbyn. Ch., NY, 1985—96. Recipient U.S. Congl. Achievement citation, 1998. Mem.: Nassau County Music Educators Assn. (publicity exec. bd. 1987), Music Educators Nat. Conf., Neptune Power Squad. (1st lt. 2001—). Democrat. Avocation: boating. Home: 606 6th St East Northport NY 11731 Office: Farmingdale High Sch 150 Lincoln St Farmingdale NY 11735 Office Phone: 516-752-6761 391. E-mail: reedldy@aol.com.

SEGALL, JOANN BUTTERS, retired school librarian; b. Des Moines, Aug. 26, 1924; d. S. Donald and Aileen Blose (Mutchlar) Butters; m. Edwin Esar Segall, July 17, 1923; children: Jeffrey, Lewis, Becky. MLS, Cath. U., 1983. Asst. children's libr. Des Moines Pub. Libr., 1948; sec., mail clk. Am. Legation, Bucharest, Romania, 1956; USAID libr. Am. Embassy, Bamako, 1977; upper sch. libr. Sidwell Friends Sch., Washington, 1978-85, head libr., 1985-97. Tchr. ESL Lang. Inst., Washington, 1972-74. Vol. libr. Janney Elem. Sch., Washington, 1966; sec. sch. bd. Internat. Sch., Belgrade, 1963-66, chair, sec., Djakarta, Indonesia, 1968-71, girl scout leader, 1967-71, Washington, 1971-75. Recipient Internat. prize Amateur 3-Gaited Horse Show, 1953. Mem. Am. Libr. Assn., Beta Phi Mu (Honor award 1983). Avocations: reading, golf, gardening, cooking, needlecraft. Home: 4333 46th St NW Washington DC 20016-2475

SEGEL, KAREN LYNN JOSEPH, lawyer, taxation specialist; b. Youngstown, Ohio, Jan. 15, 1947; d. Samuel Dennis and Helen Anita Joseph; m. Alvin Gerald Segel, June 9, 1968 (div. Sept. 1976); 1 child, Adam James. BA in Soviet and East European Studies, Boston U., 1968; JD, Southwestern U., 1975. Bar: Calif., 1996, U.S. Tax Ct., 1996, U.S. Dist. Ct. (cen. dist.) Calif., 1996, U.S. Ct. Appeals (9th cir.), 1997. Adminstrv. asst. Olds Brunel & Co., N.Y.C., 1968-69, U.S. Banknote Corp., N.Y.C., 1969-70; tax acct. S.N. Chilkov & Co. CPA's, Beverly Hills, Calif., 1971-74; intern Calif. Corps. Commr., 1975; tax. sr. Oppenheim Appel & Dixon CPA's, L.A., 1978, Fox, Westheimer & Co. CPA's, L.A., 1978, Zebrak, Levine & Mepos CPA's, L.A., 1979; ind. cons. acctg., taxation specialist Beverly Hills, 1980—. Settlement officer L.A. County Superior Ct., 2000; law student mentor Southwestern U., 1996-2002, tax moot ct. judge, 1997. High sch. amb. to Europe People-to-People Orgn., 1963. Mem. Calif. State Bar, Women's Inner Circle of Achievement, Complex Litig. Inns of Ct., L.A. County Bar Assn, Beverly Hills Tinseltown Rose Soc. Avocations: collecting seashells, lhasa apso dog breeding, art, travel, music. E-mail: kjslaw@earthlink.net.

SEGER, LINDA SUE, script consultant, lecturer, writer; b. Peshtigo, Wisc., Aug. 27, 1945; d. Linus Vauld and Agnes Katherine Seger; m. Theodore Newton Youngblood, Jr., Aug. 28, 1968 (div. Jan. 1970); m. Peter Hazen LeVar, April 12, 1987. BA in English, Colo. Coll., Colorado Springs, 1967; MA in theatre arts, Northwestern U., Evanston, 1968; MA in religion and arts, Pacific Sch. of Religion, Berkeley, 1973; ThD in drama and theology, Graduate Theological U., Berkeley, 1976; MA in Feminist Spirituality, Immaculate Heart Coll. Ctr., L.A., 2000. Instr. drama Grand Canyon Coll., Phoenix, 1969-71; instr. drama and theology McPherson (Kans.) Coll., 1976-77; instr. drama and humanities LaVerne (Calif.) U., 1977-79; asst. Provisional Theatre, L.A., 1979-80, Tandem/TAT, L.A., 1980-81; story analyst EMI Films, L.A., 1982-83; pvt. practice script cons. L.A., 1981—; pvt. practice lectr., author, 1984—. Guest prof. The Colo. Coll., 1993—. Author: Making a Good Script Great, 1988, Creating Unforgettable Characters, 1990, The Art of Adaptation, 1992, When Women Call the Shots, 1996, Making a Good Writer Great, 1999, WEBTHINKING: Connecting Not Competing for Success, 2002, Advanced Screenwriting: Raising your Script to the Academy Award Level, 2003; co-author: From Script to Screen, 1994. Mem. NOW, Women in Film. Democrat. Mem. Soc. Of Friends. Avocations: horseback riding, piano, travel. Home and Office: 4705 Hagerman Ave Cascade CO 80809 E-mail: lsseger@aol.com.

SEGERBLOM, SHARON B. social services administrator; b. Miami, Okla., Dec. 19, 1948; d. Charles L. and Doris E. (Randall) Butler; m. Richard Segerblom; children: Eva, Carl. Student, Okla. State U.; degree in nursing, U. Tulsa, 1971; BA in Polit. Sci., U. Nev. Past mgr. Neighborhood Response divsn. City of Las Vegas, past intergovtl. cmty. rels. cood., past chief asst. to the mayor, dir. Neighborhood Svcs., 1997—. Rschr. Focus on Nev.'s Children, 1987, Focus on Nev.'s Women, co-editor, video writer, prodr. Issues chairperson Gov.'s Conf. on Women, 1989-90; 1st v.p. Clark County Area Coun. PTA, 1989-90, Girl Scouts USA Frontier Coun., 1991-93; bd. dirs. WE Can, 1989-90, Martin Luther King Jr. Com., Weed and Seed Steering Com.; bd. dirs., past pres. Clark County Atty.'s Wives, 1988-89; past pres. Women's Dem. Club Clark County; mem. Clark County Dem. Ctrl. Com., 1989-90; past bd. dirs. Jr. League of Las Vegas, 1990; mem. adv. bd. REACH-OUT; fundraiser Boy Scouts Am., Boulder Dam Coun. Recipient Cmty. Svcs. award for excellence Gov.'s Conf. on Women, 1990, Heart of Gold award Focus on Nev.'s Women, Jr. League of Las Vegas, 1989-90. Mem. Assn. for Children for Enforcement of Support (bd. dirs. 1989-90). Office: Dept Neighborhood Svcs City Las Vegas City Hall 400 Stewart Ave Las Vegas NV 89101-2927

SEGIL, LARRAINE DIANE, materials company executive; b. Johannesburg, South Africa, July 15, 1948; came to U.S., 1974; d. Jack and Norma Estelle (Cohen) Wolfowitz; m. Clive Melwyn Segil, Mar. 9, 1969; 1 child, James Harris. BA, U. Witwatersrand, South Africa, 1967, BA with honours, 1969; JD, Southwestern U., L.A., 1979; MBA, Pepperdine U., 1985. Bar: Calif. 1979, U.S. Supreme Ct. 1982. Cons. in internat. transactions, L.A., 1976-79; atty. Long & Levit, L.A., 1979-81; chmn., pres. Marina Credit Corp., L.A., 1981-85; pres., chief exec. officer Electronic Space Products Internat., L.A., 1985-87; mng. ptnr. The Lared Group, L.A., 1987—; pres. Lared Presentations Inc.; keynote spkr. and expert on alliances, globalization, and leadership. Author: (novel) Belonging, 1994, Intelligent Business Alliances, 1996. Bd. govs. Cedars Sinai Med. Ctr., L.A., 1984—; bd. dirs. So. Calif. Tech. Execs. Network, 1984-86, DARE. Mem. ABA (chmn. internat. law com. young lawyers div. 1980-84), Internat. Assn. Young Lawyers (exec. coun. 1979-81, coun. internat. law and practice 1983-84), World Tech. Execs. Network (chmn.). Avocations: piano, horseback riding. Office: The Lared Group 1901 Ave of Stars Los Angeles CA 90067-6001

SEGIL, LAURA CHIPMAN, art dealer, consultant; b. Honolulu, Jan. 6, 1968; d. Gordon Ernest and Mary Ann Dickie; m. William Segil, Apr. 15, 2000. BA in Art History, U. Colo., 1992; fine arts cert., Christie's Edn., London, 1993. Intern Christie's Auction House, San Francisco, 1994—95; interior designer Aspen and Denver, 1995—2000; fine art cons., rep. L.A., 2000—. Bd. mem. Assistance League So. Calif., 2003—; prodn. chair Nine O'Clock Players, 3rd vice chair, 2003—. Mem.: Calif. Ind. Art Rep. Assn. (co-founder 2003). Office Phone: 213-435-6734.

SEGRETO, LINDA MARY JANECZEK, special education educator; b. Troy, N.Y., July 2, 1948; d. Walter John and Margaret Angela (Catallozzi) Janeczek; m. Anthony Joseph Segreto; children: Anthony Walter, Amanda Margaret. AAS, Maria Coll., 1968; BS in Bus. Edn., SUNY, Albany, 1970, M in Libr. Sci., 1976; spl. edn. credentials, Calif. State U., Long Beach, 1999. Tchr. Calif., C.C. tchr. Calif., tchr. N.Y. Bus. tchr. Lansingburgh Ctrl. Sch. Dist., Troy, NY, 1970—78; bus. adminstr. TRW Def. and Space Sys., Redondo Beach, Calif., 1978—87; spl. edn. tchr./transition specialist Manhattan Beach (Calif.) Unified Sch. Dist., 1997—. Bus. instr. Cypress (Calif.) Coll., 1980—82; sch. host, coord., vol. Best Buddies Calif., L.A., 1999—. Active PTA, Palos Verdes, Calif., 1990—, Friends of the Libr., Palos Verdes, 1990—; mem., vol. L.A. Mission, 2000—. Mem.: Calif. Tchrs. Assn., Coun. for Exceptional Children, Pi Lambda Theta. Avocations: travel, music, dramatics, yoga, golf.

SEHRING, HOPE HUTCHINSON, library science educator; b. Akron, Ohio; d. Wesley Harold and Jane (Brown) H.; m. Frederick Albert Sehring, July 15, 1978. BS, Slippery Rock U., 1968; MEd, U. Pitts., 1973; MLS, Seton Hill U., 2002. Cert. instructional media specialist. Reference libr.-intern Carnegie Mellon U., Pitts., 1981; 2003libr. media specialist Gateway Sch. Dist., Monroeville, Pa., 1968—2003; retail sales Wal-Mart, Inc, 2003—. Contbr. articles to profl. jours. Active Pa. Citizens for Better Libraries, Friends of Monroeville Pub. Libr. Recipient Gift of Time Tribute Am. Family Inst., 1992, 96; Henry Clay Frick Found. U. of London scholar, 1969, 73. Sch. Librs. Assn. (treas. 1982-84), Pa. State Edn. Assn., Pa. Citizens for Better Librs., Gateway Edn. Assn., Alpha Xi Delta. Avocation: culinary arts. Home: RR 2 Box 467 New Alexandria PA 15670-9634

SEIBEL, SHARON, music educator; b. Langdon, N.D., Nov. 8, 1944; d. Edwin and Catherine Wiens; m. Marlo D. Seibel, Aug. 19, 1966; children: Trent, Tina. B.Mus.Edn., Tabor Coll., Hillsboro, Kans., 1966; postgrad., N.D. State U., U. N.D. Tchr. K-12 vocal music Hillsboro Pub. Schs., 1966—67, Anamoose Pub. Schs., ND, 1967—69; tchr. 1-5 vocal music Dickinson Pub. Schs., ND, 1969—77; tchr. K-12 music Wyndmere Pub. Schs., ND, 1978—90; tchr. K-1, h.s. choral music Wahpeton Pub. Schs., Wahpeton, ND, 1990—. Keyboard musician, planner Faith Evan. Free Ch., Wahpeton, 1988—; bd. dirs. N.D. H.S. Activities, Valley City, 2000—. Mem.: NEA, Nat. Music Edn. Assn., N.D. Music Edn. Assn., Am. Choral Dirs. Assn., N.D. Edn. Assn. Evangelical Free Ch. Avocations: crafts, music.

SEIBERT, ANN, state legislator, physical therapist; b. Jamestown, N.Y., Jan. 22, 1934; m. Dean J. Seibert; 4 children. BA, Russell Sage Coll., Troy, N.Y., 1956; grad. in phys. therapy, Albany Med. Ctr. Phys. therapist; mem. Vt. Ho. of Reps., Montpelier, 1988—. Bd. dirs. The Family Place, White River Junction, Vt. Bd. dirs. The Family Place, White River Junction, Vt. Mem. LWV, Vt. Lung Assn., Women's Network Upper Valley, Norwich Women's Club. Home: 386 Main St Norwich VT 05055-9453 Office: Vt Ho of Reps Office Of House Mems Montpelier VT 05602

SEIBERT, LESA MARIE, university educator; b. York, Pa., Sept. 4, 1960; d. Lee Allen and Frances Marie Seibert. BS in English Edn., Bob Jones U., 1982, MEd in English Edn., 1988, EdS in Spl. Edn., 2001; postgrad., 2001—. Cert. tchr. English edn. Pa., tchr. English edn. and spl. edn. S.C. H.S. English tchr. Mt. Calvary Christian Sch., Elizabethtown, Pa., 1982—86, Sumter (S.C.) Christian Sch., 1986—87, Mountain View Christian Sch., Hummelstown, Pa., 1989—94, Bob Jones Acad., Greenville, SC, 1994—2001, H.S. spl. edn. tchr. and distance edn. tchr., 2001—04. Prof. spl. edn. Bob Jones U., Greenville, 1998—2001, prof. English education, 2004—; spkr. in field. Contbr. articles to profl. jours. Named Tchr. of Yr., Keystone Christian Tchrs. Assn., 1990—91. Republican. Baptist. Avocations: reading, cross stitch, writing, singing, speaking. Office: Bob Jones Univ 1700 Wade Hampton Blvd Greenville SC 29614

SEIBERT, MARY LEE, college official; b. Evansville, Ind., Jan. 30, 1942; d. Ernest Hensley and Lillian (Schmadel) S. BS, Ind. U., 1963, MS, 1973, EdD, 1979. Cert. med. technologist, med. asst. Lab. supr. Wishard Meml. Hosp., Indpls., 1964-67; chmn. life scis. div. Ind. Tech. Coll., Indpls., 1967-73; assoc. prof., program dir. Ind. U. Sch. Medicine, Indpls., 1973-79; assoc. project coordinator Am. Assn. State Colls. and Univs., Washington, 1979-81; dean coll. allied health professions Temple U., Phila., 1981-90; assoc. provost, dean grad. studies Ithaca (N.Y.) Coll., 1990-99, acting provost, 1996-98; v.p. acad. affairs, dean faculty Utica (N.Y.) Coll. of Syracuse U., 1999—. Vis. prof. U. Tex. Med. Br., Galveston, 1985. Assoc. editor Jour. Med. Tech., 1985-86; mem. edit. bd. Jour. Allied Health. Fellow Am. Soc. Allied Health Profls. (hon., chmn. forum on allied health data, rsch. com. 1983-89, bd. dirs. 1990-92, Outstanding Mem. award 1986); mem. Am. Soc. Clin. Lab. Sci. (profl. affairs com. 1986-89), Am. Assn. Med. Assts. (hon.), Nat. Coun. on Health Professions Edn., Nat. Acad. Scis. (bd. health care svcs. inst. of medicine 1993-99), Phi Delta Kappa, Pi Lambda Theta, Pi Kappa Phi. Republican. Avocations: reading, walking, sailing. Home: 16 Bean Hill Ln Ithaca NY 14850-8537 E-mail: mseibert@utica.edu.

SEIDEL, JOAN BROUDE, securities trader, investment advisor; b. Chgo., Aug. 16, 1933; d. Ned and Betty (Treiger) Broude; m. Arnold Seidel, Aug. 18, 1957; children: David, Craig. BA, UCLA, 1954; postgrad., N.Y. Inst. Fin. Registered prin., investment advisor Morton Seidel & Co. Inc., L.A., 1970-74, v.p., 1974-93; pres., 1993—; also bd. dirs. Morton Seidel & Co. Inc., L.A. Instr. UCLA Extension, 1979-84. Treas. City of Beverly Hills, Calif., 1990-2001, chmn. rent adjustment bd., 1989-90, mem., 1983-89; mem. investment com. YWCA of greater L.A., 1987-2002, treas. 1992-95; bd. dirs. Discovery Fund for Eye Rsch., L.A., 1987—, treas., 1999—; corp. dir. Queen's Care; bd. dirs. L.A. Opera, 2002—; CFO The Maple Couns. Ctr., 2002—04. Named Citizen of Yr. Beverly Hills C. of C., 1993. Fellow Assn. for Investment Mgmt. and Rsch.; mem. Am. Technion Soc. (v.p. 1998-2002, pres. So. Calif. chpt. 2001—, nat. bd. dir. 2002—, internat. bd. 2003—), Nat. Assn. Security Dealers (dist. bus. conduct com. 2S 1993-95, 98-2000, small firm adv. bd. 1998-2000, chair dist. 2 1999-2000), L.A. Soc. Fin. Analysts, Orgn. Women Execs., Rotary, Phi Sigma Alpha. Avocations: reading, travel. Office: Morton Seidel & Co Inc 8730 Wilshire Blvd Ste 530 Beverly Hills CA 90211-2792 E-mail: seidel350@aol.com.

SEIDENBERG, RITA NAGLER, education educator; b. N.Y.C., Mar. 24, 1928; d. Jack and Anna (Weiss) Nagler; m. Irving Seidenberg, Apr. 10, 1949; children: Jack, Melissa Kolodkin. BA, Hunter Coll., 1948; MS, CCNY, 1968; PhD, Fordham U., 1985. Cert. reading tchr., specialist, N.Y. Reading tchr. East Ramapo (N.Y.) Sch. Dist., 1967-68, clinician reading ctr., 1968-83, reading diagnostician, 1983-85, student support specialist, 1985-94. Instr. N.Y. State Dept. Edn., 1978; presenter Northeastern Rsch. Assn., 1978, 85, N.Y. State Reading Assn., 1986-94, 96, 97, Parents and Reading: IRA, 2000; adj. asst. prof. Fordham U. Grad. Sch. Edn., 1986-89, adj. assoc. prof., 1989—. Mem. Internat. Reading Assn., N.Y. State Reading Assn. (presenter 1997, 2000), Phi Delta Kappa, Kappa Delta Pi. Avocations: reading, art mus., opera, travel. Office: Fordham U Grad Sch Edn 113 W 60th St New York NY 10023-7484

SEIDER, PAMELA SUE, business manager; b. Clinton, Mo., May 12, 1953; d. Howard Leon and Winifred Jewell (Garrison) Bauer; m. Larry Gene Seider, June 20, 1997; children: Helen Jewell, Chip, Brian. Diploma in nursing, Barnes Hosp. Sch. Nursing, St. Louis, 1973. Cert. internat. oncology nurse, post anesthesia nurse, Mo. Student, nurse's aide Barnes Hosp., St. Louis, 1972-73; staff nurse Bothwell Meml. Hosp., Sedalia, Mo., 1973-76; charge nurse, staff nurse Ellis Fischel State Cancer Ctr., Columbia, Mo., 1976-86, charge nurse post anesthesia recovery unit, 1986-88; charge nurse psychiat. ICU Laughlin Pavilion, Kirksville, Mo., 1988-89; oncology nurse clinician Kirksville Coll. Osteo. Medicine, Kirksville, Mo., 1989-92; supr. oncology, hematology & neurology Kirksville (Mo.) Osteo. Med. Ctr., 1992-94, supr. oncology, hematology & neuropsychology, 1994-96; farm bus. mgr. B-Seid-er Farms, Rockville, Appleton City, Mo., 1996—. Owner, creator basket weaving bus. Walkersville Holdings Unlimited, 1987—; participant nurses health study Harvard Med. Sch., Mass., 1989—; rsch. participant, co-author underwater rsch. CEDAM Internat., Cozomel, Mex., 1989; facilitator High Hopes Cancer Support Group, Kirksville, Mo., 1989-96; data mgr. Lymphoma study group, U. Nebr., Omaha, 1989-91; governing bd. dirs. Hospice 2000, Kirksville, 1990-96; preceptor nursing divsn. N.E. Mo. State U., 1990-96; mem., participant critical incident debriefing team, 1993-96. Author: (newsletter) Northeast Mo. Medicine News, 1989-91; co-author Oncology Nursing Experience Counts, 1990, The Cancer Information Resource Directory, 1994. Mem., trustee First United Meth. Ch., Rockville, Mo., 1968—; mem. CEDAM Internat., Cozomel, Mex., 1988-90, Am. Cancer Soc., Kirksville, Mo., 1989-96, mem. Mo. nursing edn. subcom. Am. Cancer Soc., Jefferson City, 1989—; TV appearance for breast cancer awareness, Sta. KTVO, Kirksville, 1991, 92, 95; radio prog. for cancer awareness, Sta. KRXL, Kirksville, 1991, 96; com. mem., organizer ann. women's health symposium, Kirksville, 1992-96; publicity com. chmn. Boy Scouts Am., 1995-96. Named Best of Mo.'s Hands State of Mo., Jefferson City, 1987; recipient Nurses Make a Difference award Kirksville Osteo. Med. Ctr., 1994. Mem. Am. Soc. Post Anesthesia Nurses, Oncology Nursing Soc. (nominated for tribute to Mo. nurses 1995). Methodist. Avocations: family, needlework, jewelry making and collecting, basket weaving, gardening.

SEIDLER, DORIS, artist; b. London, Nov. 26, 1912; m. Bernard Seidler, Sept. 5, 1935; 1 son, David. Group exhbns. include Bklyn. Mus. Bi-Ann., Vancouver Internat., Honolulu Acad. Arts, Pa. Acad. Fine Arts, Phila., Soc. Am. Graphic Artists, Assoc. Am. Artists Gallery, Jewish Mus., N.Y.C., Albright-Knox, 1994, Brit. Mus. Recent Acquisitions, 1997, Whitworth Gallery, Manchester, Eng., 2003; represented in permanent collections Libr. of Congress, Smithsonian Instn., Washington, Phila. Mus. Art, Bklyn. Mus., Seattle Mus. Art, Whitney Mus., Nat. Gallery Art, Nassau County (N.Y.) Mus. Fine Arts, Brit. Mus., London, Victoria and Albert Mus. London, Pallant House Coll., Eng., Portland Mus. Art, Oreg., Birmingham Mus., Eng., 1999. Address: 14 Stoner Ave Great Neck NY 11021-2101

SEIDMAN, CHRISTINE E. medical educator; BA, Harvard U.; MD, George Washington U., 1978. Resident in internal medicine Johns Hopkins U., Balt.; resident in cardiology Mass. Gen. Hosp., Boston; staff Brigham and Women's Hosp. Harvard U., Boston, 1987, dir. cardiovasc. genetics svc., prof.; assoc. investigator Howard Hughes Med. Inst. Mem.: Inst. Medicine. Office: Harvard U Siedman Lab Alpert Bldg 5th Fl Boston MA 02115-5701

SEIDMAN, ELLEN SHAPIRO, lawyer, government official; b. N.Y.C., Mar. 12, 1948; d. Benjamin Harry Shapiro and Edna (Eysen) Stern; m. Walter Becker Slocombe, June 14, 1981; 1 child, Benjamin William. AB, Radcliffe Coll., 1969; JD, Georgetown U., 1974; MBA, George Washington U., 1988. Bar: D.C., 1975. Law clk. U.S. Ct. of Claims, Washington, 1974-75; assoc. Caplin & Drysdale, Washington, 1975-78; atty., advisor U.S. Dept. of Transportation, Washington, 1978-79, dep. asst. gen. counsel, 1979-81; assoc. gen. counsel Chrysler Corp Loan Guaranty Bd., Washington, 1981-84; atty., advisor U.S. Dept. of Treasury, Washington, 1981-86, spl. asst. to the Under Sec. Fin., 1986-87; dir. strategic planning Fed. Nat. Mortgage Assn., Washington, 1987-88, v.p., asst. to chmn., 1988-91, sr. v.p. regulation rsch. and econs., 1991-93; spl. asst. to the pres. for econ. policy The White House, Washington, 1993-97; dir. Office Thrift Supervision U.S. Dept. Treasury, Washington, 1997—2001; sr. counsel, Minority Staff, fin. svcs. com. U.S. Ho. of Reps., Washington, 2002, sr. mng. dir. nat. practice Shorebank Adv. Svcs., 2002—. Office Phone: 202-822-9146. Business E-Mail: eseidman@sasbk.com.

SEIFERT, KATHI P. manufacturing executive; b. Appleton, Wis., 1949; m. Steve Seifert; children: Erin, Andrew. BA Valparaiso U., 1971. Various mgmt. positions P&G, Beatruce Foods, Fort Howard Paper Co., 1972—78; from product mgr. to mktg. dir. feminine care products Kimberly-Clark, Inc., Neenah, Wis., 1978—92, pres. feminine care sectory, 1992—94, group pres. N. Am. consumer products, 1994—95, group pres. N. Am. personal care products, 1995—98, group pres. personal care products, 1998—99, exec. v.p., group pres. global personal care products, 1999—. Bd. dirs. Eli Lilly and Co. Bd, dirs. U.S. Fund for UNICEF; bd., dirs. Fox Cities Performing Art Ctr., 1999—, chmn. of bd., 2003—; bd, dirs. Theda Health Care Group, Wis. Commn. in Arts Edn. Office: Kimberly Clark Corp 355 Phelps Dr Irving TX 75038

SEIFERT, KATHRYN ANN HAWKINS, language educator; b. Detroit, Mich., June 7, 1958; d. Harold Leslie and Barbara Joan Hawkins; m. David E. Seifert, Dec. 19, 1994. MEd, Tex. A&M U., 2000; BA in English and History, Houston Bapt. U., 1989; A.A. in Advt. Design, Art Inst. Houston, 1983. Secondary Tchg. cert.: English & History Tex., 1989. Secondary tchr. Brenham Ind. Sch. Dist., Tex., 1990—2000; asst. lectr. Tex. A&M U., College Station, 2002—. Mem. Tex. Classroom Tchrs., 1996—98. Mem.: Aggie Grad. Mentor, Phi Delta Kappa (assoc.). Home: 1111 Apache Brenham TX 77833 Office: Texas A&M Univ TLAC Dept Rm 369 Harrington MS 4232 College Station TX 77843 Office Phone: 979-845-0853. Business E-Mail: kseifert@coe.tamu.edu.

SEIFERT, SHELLEY JANE, bank executive, human resources specialist; b. Aug. 12, 1954; BS in Consumer Econs. and Journalism, U. Mo., 1976; MBA in Fin. with honors, U. Louisville, 1980. Fin. analyst Nat. City Bank, Ky., 1979-81, compensation analyst, 1981-85, mgr. compensation, 1985-86, mgr. compensation, recruiting and tng., 1986-91; mgr. compensation and devel. Nat. City Corp., Cleve., 1988-91, human resource dir., 1991-94, sr. v.p., corp. human resource dir., 1994—2000, exec. v.p., dir. corp. human resources, 2000—. Spkr. in field. Grad. Leadership Cleve.; vice chair bd. dirs. Bus. Vols. Unlimited, Vis. Nurse Assn. Greater Cleve.; bd. dirs. Arthritis Found.; mem. Cleve. Commn. on Econ. Partnership and Inclusion. Recipient Woman of Distinction award YMCA. Mem. Urban League (bd. dirs., chair employment com., Ohio labor adv. com.). Office: Nat City Corp Nat City Ctr 1900 E 9th St Cleveland OH 44114-3401*

SEIFERT-KING, LORI ANN, performing company executive; b. N.Y.C., Oct. 26, 1961; d. Jay J. and Peggy Lillian (Kaufman) S. Student, SUNY, Stony Brook, 1982. Pub. rels. mgr. Grand Circle Travel Internat., N.Y.C., 1982-84; account exec. Marica's Attic Internat., N.Y.C., 1984-87; nat. sales mgr. Judy Nagler & Assocs., N.Y.C., 1987-89; pres. Lori Seifert Publicity Inc., L.A., 1989-92; mktg. mgr. Revlon Inc., 1990-92; v.p. devel. Media Masters, Century City, Calif., 1992—. Ptnr., animation exec., prodr., devel. feature TV, films Dreamworks SK6 TV; pres. Dreamlight TLK Inc. internet-based cons. co., Atlanta, 1998—. Author: Ronald Reagan-The Long Hello, 2000, Chicken Soup for the Abled Soul, 2000. Mem. Press Advance Team/Clinton/Gore Campaign, 1992; comms. adv. Pres. Clinton, 1996. Mem. NAFE, Am. Womens Econ. Devel. Orgn., Acad. TV Arts & Scis., Women in Film, Nat. Captioning Inst. (sr. acct. exec., spokesperson 1993-98). Avocations: writing, travel, politics, sports.

SEIFF, GLORIA LOUISE, volunteer; b. Denver, Apr. 3, 1929; d. Edward Hyatt and Lillian Pearl (Blend) Holtzman; m. Stephen S. Seiff, Apr. 16, 1950; children: Stuart R., Sherri P. Seiff Sloane, Karen E. Seiff Sacks. Student, Washington U., 1947-48. Commr. Pub. Works Commn., Beverly Hills, Calif., 1990-98, bd. pres. 1993, 96; pres. Beverly Vista Elem. Sch. PTA, Beverly Hills, lif.,968-69, PTA Coun., Beverly Hills, 1972-73; bd. dirs. Beverly Hills S.W. Homeowners Assn., 1985—, Braille Inst. Aux., L.A., 1998—; founding mem., bd. dirs., trustee Beverly Hills Edn. Found., 1975-79; v.p. devel. Assistance League So. Calif., L.A., 1994-98, bd. dirs., 1994—; trustee L.A. County Mosquito Abatement Dist., 1984-92, bd. pres. 1988; pres. LWV, Beverly Hills, 1985-87; mem. long range planning com. Assistance League So. Calif., 1997-98, mem. endowment com., 1995—, v.p. pub. rels., 1999—; chmn. Beverly Hills Groundwater Tech. Adv. Com., 1999—; commr. Beverly Hills Traffic and Parking Commn., 2000—, vice chmn., 2002, chair, 2002-2003; mem. City of Beverly Hills Gen. Plan Topics Com./Residential, 2002-- . Recipient Hon. Svc. award PTA, Beverly Hills, 1972, Outstanding Cmty. Svc. award, Beverly Hills City Coun., 1986-87, Resolution Cmty. Svc. award Beverly Bd. Edn., 1986. Mem. Calif. Yacht Club, Beverly Hills Unified Sch. Dist. Citizens Oversight Com. "Measure K". Avocation: sailing.

SEIGLER, ELIZABETH MIDDLETON, retired counselor; b. Athens, Ga., Aug. 18, 1928; d. Robert Meriwether and Marie (Davis) Middleton; m. Charles Judson, Aug. 24, 1955; children: Mary Seigler Peacock, Charles Middleton. BSEd, U. Ga., 1949, MEd, 1955; EdS, Ga. State U., 1976. Tchr., coach Talbot County H.S., Talbotton, Ga., 1949-50; tchr. Atlanta Public Schs., 1950-60, counselor, 1960-85. Mem. S.C. Geneal. Soc. (Old Edgefield dist. archives chpt., Anderson County chpt.), The Meriwether Soc., Inc., Ga. Ret. Educators Assn., Atlanta Ret. Tchrs. Assn., Am. Assn. Ret. Persons, Delta Kappa Gamma, Alpha Lambda Delta, Kappa Delta Pi. Baptist. Avocations: gardening, genealogy.

SEIGLER, RUTH QUEEN, college nursing administrator, educator, consultant, nurse; b. Conway, S.C., July 31, 1942; d. Charles Isaac and Berneta Mae (Weaks) Queen; m. Rallie Marshall Seigler, Sept. 1, 1963; children: Rallie Marshall Jr., Scot Monroe. ADN, Lander Coll., 1962; BSN, U. S.C., 1964, MSN, 1980. Pub. health nurse Richland County Health Dept., Columbia, S.C., 1964-66; dir. nurses Columbia Area Mental Health Ctr., 1966-69; program nurse specialist Midlands Health Dist., 1969-72; discharge planner Richland Meml. Hosp., 1972-73, clin. dir., 1973-75; exec. dir. S.C. State Bd. Nursing, 1976-83; v.p. nursing dept. Self Meml. Hosp., Greenwood, S.C., 1983-86; exec. dir. S.C. Commn. on Aging, Columbia, 1986-95; asst. dean Coll. Nursing U. S.C., Columbia, 1995-96, assoc. clin. prof., 1996—; dir. Cockcroft Leadership Program for Nurse Execs., 2002—. Cons. intergenerational Fam. Studies, 1999—,dir. Cockcraft Leadership Prog. for Nurse Exec.,2003—, bd. dirs. Queen Gas Co., Barnwell, S.C.; nurse cons. Creative Nursing Mgmt., Mpls., 1984—. Advisor: The Role of County Mental Health Nurse, 1971. Recipient Disting. Alumni award Lander Coll., 1978, career Woman recognition award Columbia YWCA, 1980, William S. Hall award S.C. Assn. Residential Care Homes, 1988, U. S.C. Coll. Nursing Disting. Alumni award, 1993, award for excellence S.C. League for Nursing, 1995, Svc. Recognition award S.C. AARP, 1995; named one of Ten Women of Achievement, S.C. March of Dimes, 1987. Mem. ANA, APHA, S.C. Nurses Assn. (sec. 1965-68, bd. dirs. 1986-88, Excellence award 1984, Recognition award 1984), S.C. Hosp. Assn., S.C. Gerontol. Soc., S.C. Nurses Found., S.C. Healthy People 2000 (vice chair), Partnership for Older South Carolinians (founder, chair bd. dirs.), Columbia Luncheon Club (pres. 1997-98), S.C. Fedn. Older Ams., Evening Mission Action Group, Bd. Nursing Home Examiners, Pilot Club, Inc. (pres. 1988-89, 97-98), Vol. of Amer.-Carolinas Bd. of Dirs., chair, 1998-00, elder, 1999-01; christcare equipper, 1999-01, Rotary Internat., Sigma Theta Tau, Beta Sigma Phi-Beta Omega (pres. 1997-98).moderator, Trinity Presbyn., 2003-06 Presbyterian. Avocations: gardening, traveling. Home: 6 Beaver Dam Ct Columbia SC 29223-3100 Office: U SC Coll Nursing Deans Office Columbia SC 29208-0001

SEILER, CHARLOTTE WOODY, retired educator; b. Thorntown, Ind., Jan. 20, 1915; d. Clark and Lois Merle (Long) Woody; m. Wallace Urban Seiler, Oct. 10, 1942 (dec. Aug. 2002); children: Patricia Anne Seiler Bootzin, Janet Alice Seiler Sawyer. AA, Ind. State U., 1933; AB, U. Mich., 1941; MA, Ctrl. Mich. U., 1968. Tchr. elem. schs., Whitestown, Ind., 1933-34, Thorntown, 1934-37, Kokomo, Ind., 1937-40, Ann Arbor, Mich., 1941-44, Willow Run, Mich., 1944-46; instr. English divsn. Delta Coll., University Center, Mich., 1964-69, asst. prof., 1969-77; ret., 1977. Organizer, dir. Delta Coll. Puppeteers, Midland, Mich., 1972—77. Mem. Friends of Grace A. Dow Meml. Libr., 1974—, treas., 1974-75, 77-79, corr. sec., 1975-77; mem. Midland Art Assn.; adv. bd. Salvation Army, 1980-91, sec., 1984-87; leader Sr. Ctr. Humanities program Midland Sr. Ctr., 1977—; vol. Quality Health Care, North Port, Fla., 2001—; leader bridge refresher Harbor Cove, North Port, 2002—. Mem. AAUW (fellow 1979), Mich. Libr. Assn., Midland Symphony League, Tuesday Rev. Club (pres. 1979-80), Seed and Sod Garden Club (v.p. 1986-87, pres. 1987-88), Harbor Cove Civic Assn., Pi Lambda Theta, Chi Omega. Presbyterian. Home: 652 Blackburn Blvd North Port FL 34287

SEILER, KAREN PEAKE, organizational psychologist; b. Seattle, Jan. 31, 1952; d. Louis Joseph and Donna Mae (Waters) Tomaso; m. Arthur J. Seiler; children from previous marriage: Jeremy S. Peake, Anthony K. Peake. BA/BSW magna cum laude, Carroll Coll., 1987; postgrad., MIT, 1994. Cert. strategic planning Pacific Inst.; cert. orgnl. cons. Covey Learning Ctr., 1993. Admissions counselor Shodair Children's Hosp., Helena, Mont., 1984-86; asst. dir., counselor Career Tng. Inst., Helena, 1986-90; pres. Corp. Cons., Helena, 1990—. Apptd. amb. Mont. Ambs., 1990—; active Gov.'s Task Force on Econ. Devel., 1991-94; chairperson Mont. Dist. Export Coun./U.S. Dept. Commerce, 1992-96; exec. com. mem. Mont. World Trade Ctr., Missoula, 1995—, chmn. 1996—; pres. Coun. Carroll Coll., 1997—. Mem. YWCA, 1986-90, pres., 1989; mem. Bus. and Profl. Women's Orgn., 1987-93, sec., 1990; pres. Helena Area Econ. Devel. Coun., 1989-92; exec. com. Leadership Helena, 1990-91; monitoring chair Concentrated Employment Program Pvt. Industry Coun., Mont., 1990—; bd. dirs., exec. com. Mont. Women's Capital Fund, 1990-95; exec. com. Mont. Race for the Cure, 1994—. Mem. NAFE, Partnership for Employment and Tng., Delta Epsilon Sigma (Outstanding Citizen award). Roman Catholic. Avocations: sailing, world travel. Home and Office: 315 N Park Ave Helena MT 59601-5060

SEILING, SHARON LEE, family economics educator; b. Okmulgee, Okla., Aug. 25, 1946; d. Dent and Ruth Burgess; m. John Seiling; 1 child, Clark. BS, Okla. State U., 1968, MS, 1971; PhD, Cornell U., 1980. Tchr. Pauls Valley (Okla.) H.S., 1968-71; grad. asst. Okla. State U., Stillwater, 1971-73; lectr. Calif. Polytechnic State U., San Luis Obispo, 1973-75; grad. asst. Cornell U., Ithaca, N.Y., 1975-78; asst. prof. Fla. State U., Tallahassee, 1978-85, Ohio State U., Columbus, 1985-91, assoc. prof., 1991—. Grad. faculty lectr. Ohio State U., 1995. Assoc. editor Family and Consumer Scis. Rsch. Jour., 1996—2002; contbr. articles to profl. jours. Bd. govs. Ohio Coun. Against Health Fraud, 1989-93; mem. Gov.'s Task Force on Housing and Cmty. Devel., Tallahassee, 1979; mem. housing adv. com. Columbus Urban League, 1994-95; bd. dirs. Creative Play Ctr., 1998-99. Grantee Hewlett Found., 1994, USDA, 1998. Mem. LWV (pres. 1983-84), Am. Assn. Housing Educators (v.p. 1988-89), Am. Assn. Family and Consumer Scis. (sec.-treas. family econs./resource mgmt. divsn. 1996-98), Ohio Assn. Family and Consumer Scis. (chmn. N. Ctrl. Regional Rsch. Team, 2001-). Democrat. Methodist. Office: 265 Campbell Hall 1787 Neil Ave Columbus OH 43210-1295

SEISER, VIRGINIA, librarian; b. Anchorage, Aug. 9, 1948; d. Virgil Owen and Marjorie (Betts) S. BS in Psychology, U. Oreg., 1971; MA in Libr. Sci., U. Chgo., 1974; MS in Psychology, Portland State U., 1982. Libr. I Multhomah County Libr., Portland, Oreg., 1973-74; ednl. psychology libr. Portland State U., 1974-82; readers svcs. dept head, 1982-85; ref. libr. U. N.Mex., Albuquerque, 1985, 2001—, assoc. to dean of Libr. Svcs., 1986-97, dir. budget and pers., 1998—2000. Co-author: Mountaineering and Mountain Club Serials, 1990; column editor: Serials Review (periodical), 1978-80; contbr. articles to profl. jours. Libr. com. Mazamas, Portland, 1981-84 vol. worker Cave Rsch. Found., Carlsbad, N.Mex., 1990-95; rescue team mem. Albuquerque Mountain Rescue, 1987-97. Recipient Sixteen Peaks award Mazamas, Portland, 1987; Watson/Chadwick Meml. Fund grant Am. Alpine Club, Golden, Colo., 1983. Mem. AAUP, Am. Alpine Club, N.Mex. Libr. Assn., Assn. Coll. Rsch. Librs. Avocations: hiking, tai chi. Home: 2132A Central Ave NW # 315 Albuquerque NM 87106 Office: General Library University Of New Mexico Albuquerque NM 87131-0001

SEITER, KATI ELIZABETH, music educator; b. Kane, Pa., Feb. 4, 1979; d. Richard Seiter and Vickie Ball-Seiter(Stepmother). MusB in Edn., U. of Wis., Whitewater, 1997—2002. Cert. instrumental music pre K-12 Wis., 2002, gen. music 6-12 Wis., 2002. Band tchr. Manitowoc (Wis.) Pub. Sch. Dist., 2002—. Oboe specialist U. Wis. Summer Band Camps, Whitewater, Wis., 2001—, counselor, 2001—. Mem.: Wis. Music Educators Assn., Internat. Double Reed Soc., Music Educators Nat. Conf., Delta Omicron.

SEITZ, MARY LEE, mathematics educator; BS in Edn. summa cum laude, SUNY, Buffalo, 1977, MS in Edn., 1982. Cert. secondary tchr., N.Y. Prof. math. Erie C.C.-City Campus, Buffalo, 1982—. Reviewer profl. jours. and coll. textbooks. Reviewer profl. jours. Mem. N.Y. Maths. Assn. Two Yr. Colls., Assn. Maths. Tchrs. N.Y., N.Y. Assn. Two Yr. Colls., Inc., Internat. Platform Assn., Pi Mu Epsilon. Avocations: gardening, photography, bird watching. Office: Erie C C-City Campus 121 Ellicott St Buffalo NY 14203-2601 E-mail: seitzm@ecc.edu.

SEITZ, PATRICIA ANN, federal judge; b. Washington, Sept. 2, 1946; d. Richard J. and Bettie Seitz; m. Alan Graham Greer, Aug. 14, 1981. BA in History cum laude, Kans. State U., 1968; JD, Georgetown U., 1973. Bar: Fla. 1973, D.C. 1975, U.S. Dist. Ct. (no., mid., so. dists., trial bar) Fla., U.S. Ct. Appeals (5th and 11th cirs.), U.S. Supreme Ct. Reporter Dallas Times Herald, Washington, 1970-73; law clk. to Hon. Charles R. Richey U.S. Dist. Ct., Washington, 1973-74; assoc. Steel, Hector & Davis, Miami, Fla., 1974-79, ptnr., 1980-96; dir. office legal counsel Office of Nat. Drug Control Policy, Exec. Office of Pres., Washington, 1996-97; judge U.S. Dist. Ct. (so. dist.) Fla., 1998—. Adj. faculty U. Miami Law Sch., Coral Gables, Fla., 1984-88; faculty Nat. Inst. Trial Advocacy, Boulder, Colo., 1982, 83, 95, Chapel Hill, N.C., 1984, 87. Fla. region, 1989; lectr. in field. Contbr. numerous articles to law jours. Mem. Dade Munroe Mental Health Bd., Miami, 1982-84, United Way of Greater Miami comty. devel. com., 1984-87; chmn. family abuse task force United Way of Greater Miami, 1986; chmn. devel. com. Miami City Ballet, 1986-87, bd. dirs., 1986-90. Fellow Am. Bar Found., Am. Bd. Trial Advocacy, Internat. Soc. Barristers; mem. ABA (chmn. various coms. 1979-85, Ho. Dels. 1992-96), Am. Arbitration Assn. (nat. bd. dirs. 1995-97, complex case panel arbitrator), The Fla. Bar (bd. govs. young lawyer divsn. 1981-82, bd. govs. 1986-92, pres. 1993-94, bd. cert. civil trial), Fla. Assn. Women Lawyers, Dade County Bar Assn. (pub. interest law bank). Roman Catholic. Avocations: travel, art. Office: Fed Courthouse Square 301 N Miami Ave Fl 5 Miami FL 33128-7702

SEITZ, VIRGINIA A. lawyer; BA summa cum laude, Duke U., 1978; MA, Oxford (Eng.) U., 1980; JD, SUNY. Bar: Pa. 1985, D.C. 1986. Jud. law clk. to Hon. Harry T. Edwards, U.S. Ct. Appeals for D.C. Circuit, Washington, 1985-86; jud. law clk. to Hon. William J. Brennan, Jr. U.S. Supreme Ct., Washington, 1986-87; ptnr. Sidley & Austin, Washington. Bd. dirs. Congl. Office Complaince, Washington. Rhodes scholar, 1979-80. Mem. Phi Beta Kappa. Office: Sidley & Austin 1722 E St NW Washington DC 20006 Fax: 202-736-8711. E-mail: vseitz@sidley.com.

SEIVERS, LANA C. commissioner of education; b. Clinton, Tenn, 1951; BEd, Middle Tenn. State U.; MA in Ednl. Adminstrn., D in Ednl. Leadership, U. Tenn. Speech pathologist Spl Edn. Oak Ridge Sch. System, Tenn.; adminstr. early childhood and edn programs Oak Ridge Sch. System, prin. Linden Elem. Sch.; supt. Clinton City Schs., Tenn., 1989—2003; commr. Tenn. Dept. Edn., Nashville, 2003—. Design cons. Inst. Sch. Leaders; mem. adv. coun. Edn of Childen with Disabilities. Mem.: Assn. Ind. and Mcpl. Schs. (bd. dirs.), Tenn. Orgn. Sch. Supts. (treas.), E. Tenn. Supts. Stidy Coun. (chair), So. Assn. Colls. and Schs. (chair). Office: Tenn Dept Edn 6th Fl Andrew Johnson Twr 710 James Robertson Pkwy Nashville TN 37243

SELBEE, MAXINE BUTCHER, county clerk; b. Chapmanville, W.Va., June 1, 1930; d. John Sweet Butcher and Bessie Farley; m. William Arthur Selbee, Feb. 8, 1953 (dec. July 1995). AS, Marshall U., 1951. Ins. agt. C.W. Bennett Ins. Agy., Ashland, Ky., 1954-85; chief dep. clk. County Clk.'s Office, Catlettsburg, Ky., 1986-93, county clk. county elective office, 1994—. Transportation com. mem. County Clerk's Assn., Frankfort, 1996. Mem. Ky. Dem. Women's Club, Ashland, 1986-99. Mem. Order Ea. Star (officer). Democrat. Baptist. Avocations: gardening, sewing, sports, swimming, sunday school teaching. Office: Courthouse PO Box 523 Catlettsburg KY 41129-0523 Home: PO Box 807 Ashland KY 41105-0807 E-mail: maxineselbee@hotmail.com.

SELBY, CECILY CANNAN, dean, educator, scientist; b. London, Feb. 4, 1927; d. Keith and Catherine Anne Cannan; m. Henry M. Selby, Aug. 11, 1951 (div. 1978); children: Norman, William, Russell; m. James Stacy Coles, Feb. 21, 1981. AB cum laude, Radcliffe Coll., 1946; PhD in Phys. Biology, MIT, 1950. Teaching asst. in biology MIT, 1948-49; adminstrv. head virus study sect. Sloan-Kettering Inst., N.Y.C., 1949-50, asst. mem. instr., 1950-55; instr. microscopic anatomy Cornell U. Med. Coll., 1955-57; tchr. sci. Lenox Sch., N.Y.C., 1957-58, headmistress, 1959-72; nat. exec. dir. Girl Scouts U.S.A., N.Y.C., 1972-75; adv. com. Simmons Coll. Grad. Mgmt. Program, 1977-78; mem. Com. Corp. Support of Pvt. Univs., 1977-83; spl. asst. acad. planning N.C. Sch. Sci. and Math., 1979-80, dean acad. affairs, 1980-81, chmn. bd. advisors, 1981-84. Cons. U.S. Dept. Commerce, 1976-77; dir. Avon Products Inc., RCA, NBC, Loehmanns Inc., Nat. Edn. Corp. pres. Am. Energy Ind., 1976; co-chmn. commn. pre-coll. math. and sci. Nat. Sci. Bd., 1982-83; adj. prof. NYU, 1984-86, prof. sci. edn., 1986-94; mem. policy steering com. Gov. Cuomo's Conf. on Sci. and Engring., 1989-90; affil. scholar Radcliffe Pub. Policy Ctr. of Harvard U., 2000-2001. Contbr. articles to profl. jours., chpt. to book. Founder, chmn. N.Y. Ind. Schs. Opportunity Project, 1968-72; mem. invitational workshops Aspen Inst., 1973, 75, 77, 79; trustee MIT, Bklyn. Law Sch., Radcliffe Coll., Woods Hole Oceanographic Instn., Women's Forum N.Y., N.Y. Hall of Sci., 1982—, vice chmn., 1989—, trustee Girls Inc., 1992—, Nat. Coun. Women in Medicine, 1990-94; mem. Yale U. Peabody Mus. Adv. Coun., 1981-89; co-chair program in sci., soc. and gender Radcliffe Inst. of Harvard U., 1999-2001. Named affiliated scholar, Harvard U., 2001; recipient Woman Scientist of Yr. award, N.Y. chpt. Am. Women in Sci., 1992, Alumnae Achievement award, Radcliffe Coll., 2001. Fellow Am. Women Sci., N.Y. Acad Scis.; mem. Century Assn. Club, Woods Hole Golf Club, Cosmopolitan Club, The Explorers Club, Sigma Xi, Phi Delta Kappa. Home and Office: 1 E 66th St New York NY 10021-5854 also: 100 Ransom Rd Falmouth MA 02540-1652 E-mail: selbyc@aol.com.

SELBY, DIANE RAY MILLER, fraternal organization administrator; b. Lorain, Ohio, Oct. 11, 1940; d. Dale Edward and Mildred (Ray) Miller; m. David Baxter Selby, Apr. 14, 1962; children: Elizabeth, Susan, Sarah. BS in Edn., Ohio State U., 1962. Sec. Kappa Kappa Gamma Frat., Columbus, Ohio, 1962-63, editor, 1972-86; tchr. Hilliard (Ohio) High Sch., 1963-65; exec. dir. Mortar Bd., Inc. Nat. Office, Columbus, Ohio, 1986—. Editor The Key of Kappa Kappa Gamma Frat, 1972-86 (Student Life award, 1983, 84, 85). Founding officer Community Coordinating Bd., Worthington, Ohio, 1983; pres. PTA Coun., Worthington, 1984, Worthington Band Boosters, 1985; sec., treas. Sports and Recreation Facilities Bd., Worthington, 1986—; mem. sustaining com. Jr. League Columbus, 1991-93, docent Kelton House, 1979—. Mem. Mortar Bd., Inc., Twig 53 Children's Hosp. (assoc.), Assn. Coll. Honor Soc. (mem. exec. com. 1999-2001, 2003-04, 04—. chmn. bylaws com., trustee 2004—), Ladybugs and Buckeyes, Kappa Kappa Gamma (House Bd. v.p. 1997-2000). Republican. Lutheran. Home: 6750 Merwin Pl Columbus OH 43235-2838 Office: Mortar Bd Inc 1200 Chambers Rd Ste 201 Columbus OH 43212-1754 E-mail: selby.1@osu.edu.

SELDEN, ANNIE, mathematics educator; b. Torrington, Conn., Feb. 1, 1938; d. Adolf Laurer and Annie (Wopperer) Anderson; m. Herbert Lloyd Alexander Jr., Oct. 7, 1961 (div. July 1970); children: Neil Brooks, Kim Anne; m. John Selden, May 24, 1974. BA, Oberlin Coll., 1959; MA, Yale U., 1962; PhD, Clarkson U., 1974. Instr. SUNY, Potsdam, 1969-71; sr. lectr. Bayero U., Kano, Nigeria, 1978-85; asst. prof. Hampden Sydney (Va.) Coll., 1973-74, Bosphorus U., Istanbul, Turkey, 1974-78, Tenn. Technol. U., Cookeville, 1985-90, assoc. prof., 1990—95, prof., 1995—2003, emerita, 2003—. Vis. scholar edn. in math., sci. and tech. U. Calif., Berkeley, 1993; sec.-treas. Math. Edn. Resources Co., 1994—; external examiner Fed. Advanced Tchrs. Coll., Katsina, Nigeria, 1979-82, Gumel, Nigeria, 1981-82; reader advanced placement calculus exams., 1990-92; vis. scholar Ctr. for Rsch. in Math. and Sci. Edn., San Diego State U., 1995-96; vis. prof. Ariz. State U., 1999-2000; adj. prof. N.Mex. State U., 2003—. Dept. editor: UME Trends: News and Reports on Undergrad. Math. Edn., 1989—96, MAA Online's Tchg. and Learning Sect., 1996—; mem. editl. bd. Jour. Computers in Math. and Sci. Teaching, 1992—96, Jour. for Rsch. in Math. Edn., 1997-2000; assoc. editor for tchg. and learning MAA Online, 1997—; assoc. editor Media Highlights sect. Coll. Math. Jour., 1994—contbr. articles to profl. jours. Named Fulbright scholar, 1959-60, Woodrow Wilson fellow, 1960-61, NSF grad. trainee Clarkson U., 1972-73, NSF grantee, 1971, 94-96. Fellow AAAS; mem. AAUP (Tenn. Tech. chpt. sec. 1991-92, v.p. 1992-93, pres. 1994—95), Am. Math. Soc., Math. Assn. Am. (dept. rep. 1986—2000, coord.-elect spl. interest group on rsch. in undergrad. math. edn. 1999-2000, coord. 2000-02, past coord. 2002-03), Assn. Women in Math. (Louise Hay award for contbns. to math. edn. 2002), Nat. Assn. Math., Am. Math. Assn. Two-Yr. Colls., Benjamin Banneker Assn., Nigerian Math. Soc. (organizer 5th ann. conf. 1984), Internat. Group for Psychology Math. Edn., Am. Ednl. Rsch. Assn., Nat. Coun. Tchrs. Math., Rsch. Coun. for Math. Learning, Tenn. Acad. Sci., Women in Higher Edn. Tenn. (Tenn. Tech. chpt. pres. 1990-92, state 1st v.p. 1991-92, state pres. 1992-93), Women Organizing Women (treas. 1992-93), Am. Coun. Edn. (nat. indentification program for women com. 1992-93), Assn. for Sci. Study of Consciousness, Phi Beta Kappa, Sigma Xi, Pi Mu Epsilon, Kappa Mu Epsilon. Office: NMex State U Dept Mathematical Scis PO Box 30001 Las Cruces NM 88003-0001 E-mail: aselden@emmy.nmsa.edu.

SELDES, MARIAN, actress; b. N.Y.C. d. Gilbert and Alice (Hall) S.; m. Julian Claman, Nov. 3, 1953 (div.); 1 child, Katharine; m. Garson Kanin, June 19, 1990 (dec. Mar. 1999). Grad., The Dalton Sch., N.Y.C., 1945, Neighborhood Playhouse, 1947; DHL, Emerson Coll., 1979; DFA (hon.), Julliard Sch., 2003. Faculty drama and dance divsn. Juilliard Sch. Lincoln Center, N.Y.C., 1969-91; faculty drama dept. Fordham U., 2003. Appeared with Cambridge (Mass.) Summer Theatre, 1945, Boston Summer Theatre, 1946, St. Michael's Playhouse, Winooski, Vt., 1947-48, Bermudiana Theatre, Hamilton, Bermuda, 1951, Elitch Gardens Theatre, Denver, 1953, The Cretan Woman, Lysistrata, 1955 (actress/artist-in residence Stanford U.); Broadway appearances include Medea, 1947, Crime and Punishment, 1948, That Lady, 1949, Tower Beyond Tragedy, 1950, The High Ground, 1951, Come of Age, 1952, Ondine, 1954, The Chalk Garden, 1955, The Wall, 1960, A Gift of Time, 1962, The Milk Train Doesn't Stop Here Any More, 1964, Tiny Alice, 1965, A Delicate Balance, 1967 (Tony award for best supporting actress), Before You Go, 1968, Father's Day, 1971 (Drama Desk award, Tony nomination), Mendicants of Evening (Martha Graham Co.), 1973, Equus, 1974-77, The Merchant, 1977, Deathtrap, 1978 (tony nomination), Ivanov (Drama Desk nomination), 1997, Ring Round the Moon, 1999 (Tony nomination), 45 Seconds from Broadway, 2001 Dinner At Eight, 2003 (Tony nomination); off-Broadway appearances include Diff'rent, 1961, The Ginger Man, 1963 (Obie award), All Women Are One, 1964, Juana LaLoca, 1965, Three Sisters, 1969, Am. Shakespeare Festival, Stratford, Conn., Mercy Street at Am. Place Theater, N.Y.C., 1969, Isadora Duncan, 1976 (Obie award), Painting Churches, 1983, 84 (Outer Critics Circle award 1984), Other People, Berkshire Theatre Festival, 1969, The Celebration, Hedgerow Theater, Pa., 1971, Richard III, N.Y. Shakespeare Festival, 1983, Remember Me, Lakewood Theatre, Skowhegan, Maine, Gertrude Stein and a Companion, White Barn Theatre, Westport, Conn., 1985, Lucile Lortel Theatre, N.Y.C., 1986, Richard II, N.Y. Shakespeare Festival, 1987, The Milk Train Doesn't Stop Here Anymore, WPA Theatre, N.Y.C., 1987, Happy Ending, Bristol (Pa.) Riverside Theatre, 1988, Annie 2 John F. Kennedy Ctr., Washington, 1989-90, Goodspeed Opera House, Chester, Conn., 1990, A Bright Room Called Day, N.Y. Shakespeare Festival, 1991, Three Tall Women, River Arts, Woodstock, N.Y., 1994, Another Time, Am. Jewish Theatre, 1993, Breaking the Code, Berkshire Theatre Festival, 1993, Three Tall Women, Vineyard Theatre, N.Y.C., 1994, Promenade Theatre, 1994-95, nat. tour, 1995-96, Boys From Syracuse, City Ctr., N.Y.C., 1997, Dead End: Williamstown, 1997, Dear Liar, Irish Repertory Theater, 1999, The Matchmaker: Williamstown, 1998, Tongue of a Bird, Mark Taper Forum, 1998, Sail Away, Carnegie Hall, 1999, Mad About The Boy, Carnegie Hall, 1999, The Torch-Bearers, 2000, Ancestral Voices, 2000, The Skin of our Teeth, 2000, Williamstown, The Play About the Baby, Alley Theatre, Houston, 2000, The Butterfly Collection, Playwrights Horizon, NY, 2000, The Play About the Baby, Helen, N.Y., 2001, Play Yourself, N.Y. Theater Workshop, 2002, Brekett/Albee, Century Ctr. Theatre, N.Y.C., 2003; nat. tour Three Tall Women, 1995-96; film appearances include The Greatest Story Ever Told, Gertrude Stein and a Companion, 1988, In a Pig's Eye, 1988, The Gun in Betty Lou's Handbag, 1992, Tom and Huck, 1995, Digging to China, 1997, Home Alone 3, 1997, Affliction, 1997, Celebrity, 1998, One Life to Live, 1998, Remember WENN, 1999, The Haunting, 1999, Town and Country, 1999, Duets, 1999, Hollywood Ending, 2002, Mona Lisa Smile, 2003; (TV series) Good and Evil, 1991, Murphy Brown, 1992, Truman, 1995, Cosby, 1996, 98, Trinity, 1998, The Others, 2000, If These Walls Could Talk 2, 2000, Nero Wolfe, 2001 (A&E), The Education of Max Bickford, 2002, American Masters PBS "Juillard Documentary, 2003", Hallmark Hall of Fame,2004; also appeared on radio CBS Mystery Theater, 1976-81, Theatre Guild on The Air; author: The Bright Lights, 1978, Time Together, 1981. Bd. dirs. Neighborhood Playhouse, The Acting Co., Nat. Repertory Theatre, Theatre

Hall of Fame, 1996; bd. trustees Broadway Cares/Equity Fights Aids. Winner Ovation award Theater L.A. for Three Tall Women, 1996, Conn. Critics award for Three Tall Women, 1996; recipient Madge Kennedy/Sidney Kingsley award Dramatists Guild Fund, 2000, Obie award for sustained achievement, Lucille Lortel award for Sustained Achievement, 2003, Edwin Booth award, Players Club, 2003, Lifetime Mem. award Theatre Libr. Assn., 2003, Breukelein Inst. Gaudium award, 2003. Mem. Players Club, Century Assn. Home: 210 Central Park S Apt 19D New York NY 10019-1426

SELDIN, GLORIA, state legislator; b. Bklyn., Apr. 7, 1924; Mem. N.H. Ho. of Reps. (dist. 17), Concord, 1996—; mem. labor, indsl. and rehab. svcs. N.H. Ho. of Reps., Concord, 1996—. Mem. Svc. Coun. Commn., 1983-87, N.H. Women's Lobby, 1989-92, Older Womans League, N.H. Hospice Program; founder Concord Share Program. Jewish. Home: 54 Church St Concord NH 03301-4550

SELDNER, BETTY JANE, environmental engineer, consultant, aerospace transportation executive; b. Balt., Dec. 11, 1923; d. David D. and Miriam M. (Mendes) Miller; m. Warren E. Gray, June 20, 1945 (div. 1965); children: Patricia, Deborah; m. Alvin Seldner, Nov. 15, 1965; children: Jack, Barbara. BA in Journalism, Calif. State U., Northridge, 1975, MA in Communications, 1977. Dir. pub. info. United Way, Van Nuys, Calif., 1958-63, dir. edn. Los Angeles, 1963-68; dir. pub. relations, fin. San Fernando Valley Girl Scout Council, Reseda, Calif., 1968-73; asst. dir. pub. info. Calif. State U., Northridge, 1973-75; dir. environ. mgmt. HR Textron Corp., Valencia, Calif., 1975-87; environ. engr. Northrop Aircraft, Hawthorne, Calif., 1987-88, EMCON Assocs., Burbank, Calif., 1988-92, Atkins Environ., 1992-93, Seldner Environ., Valencia, Calif., 1993—; pres. Seldner Environ. Svcs., 1993—. Author non-fiction. Named Woman of Yr., Santa City C. of C. and vol. orgns., 2000. Mem. Santa Clarita Valley Environ. Mgrs. Soc. (chmn. bd. dirs. 1984), San Fernando Valley Round Table (pres. 1971-72), Hazardous Materials Mgrs.' Assn., Zonta Internat., Valencia Indsl. Assn. (environ. chair). Republican. Jewish. Avocation: sailing. E-mail: Betty13ix@comcast.net.

SELEKMAN, MERIDITH, psychologist; b. New Brunswick, N.J., Dec. 2, 1971; d. Robert Epstein and Paula Meltzer; m. Jeremy Benjamin Selekman, July 8, 2000. PhD in Psychology, Widener U., 1998. Lic. psychologist Pa., cert. sch. psychologist Pa. Neuropsychologist Bancroft Neurohealth, Haddonfield, NJ, 1998—99; sch. psychologist Del. County Intermediate Unit, Media, Pa., 1999—2000; pvt. practice Bala Cynwyd, Pa., 2000—; sch. psychologist Township Cheltenham, Cheltenham, Pa., 2000—. Home: 541 Cedar Hollow Dr Yardley PA 19067 Office: Sch Dist Cheltenham Township 1000 Ashbourne Rd Cheltenham PA 19067

SELES, MONICA, professional tennis player; b. Novi Sad, Yugoslavia, Dec. 2, 1973; came to U.S., 1986; d. Karolj and Esther Seles. Profl. tennis player, 1989—. Mem. U.S. Fed Cup Team, 1996, 99, 2000, WTA Tour Players' Coun., 1998—99. Author: (novels) From Fear to Victory, 1996. Active Spl. Olympics. Winner WTA Singles Championship, 1990-92, Roland Garros, 1990, 91, 92, French Open, 1990, 91, 92, U.S. Open, 1991, 92, Australian Open, 1991, 92, 93, 96, 53 Career Singles Titles and 6 Career Doubles Titles, WTA Tour; named Yugoslavia's sportwoman of yr., 1985, Tennis Mag./Rolex Watch Female Rookie of Yr., 1989, WTA Tour Player of Yr., 1991, Comeback Player of Yr. Tennis mag., 1995, Profl. Female Athlete by Yr., 1995, Most Exciting Player as voted by fans, 1995, 97, Female Pro Athlete of the Yr., Fla. Times-Union, 1998; recipient 1990 Rado Topspin award, Ted Tinling Diamond award Va. Slims, 1990, Inaugural Sanex Hero of the Yr. award, 2002. Achievements include 3rd player in the Open-era to capture the Australian and Roland Garros in same calendar year; World #1 ranked player, 1991, 92, 95; named youngest #1 ranked player in tennis history for women and men at 17 years, 3 months, 9 days. Office: c/o Internat Mgmt Group 1 Erieview Plz Cleveland OH 44114-1715

SELIG, PHYLLIS SIMS, retired architect; b. Topeka, Nov. 16, 1931; d. Willis Nolan and Victoria Clarinda (Oakley) Sims; m. James Richard Selig, Mar. 31, 1957; children: Lin Ann, Susan Nan, Sarah Jo. BS in Architecture, U. Kans., 1956. Realtor Assoc. Realty, Lawrence, Kans., 1965-70; v.p. finance and housing Alpha Phi Internat. Fraternity, Inc., Evanston, Ill., 1968-74, chief exec. officer, internat. pres., 1974-78, trustee, 1978-80; sr. engr. tech. Nebr. Pub. Power, Columbus, 1980-86, staff architect, 1986-89, archtl. supr., 1989-96; retired, 1996. Republican. Lutheran. Avocations: wood working, painting.

SELIGMAN, NICOLE K. broadcast executive, lawyer; BA, Harvard Coll. (Radcliffe), 1978; JD, Harvard Law Sch., 1983. Assoc. editl. page editor The Asian Wall St. Jour., Hong Kong, 1978—80; law clk. to Judge Harry T. Edwards U.S. Ct. of Appeals, Wash., DC, 1983—84; law clk. to Justice Thurgood Marshall U.S. Supreme Ct., 1984—85; ptnr. Williams & Connolly LLP, Wash., DC; exec. v.p., gen. counsel Sony Corp. of Am., 2001—. Office: Sony Corp of Am 550 Madison Ave New York NY 10022

SELIG-PRIEB, WENDY, sports team executive; JD, Marquette U., 1988. With broadcasting dept. Milw. Brewers, from 1982; exec. trainee Office of Baseball Commr.; corp. atty. Foley & Lardner, to 1990; gen. counsel Milw. Brewers, 1990-95, v.p., gen. counsel, 1995-98, now pres., CEO, 1998—. Office: Milw Brewers Baseball % Miller Park 1 Brewers Way Milwaukee WI 53214-3651

SELIGSON, JUDITH, artist; b. Phila., July 8, 1950; d. David and Harriet Tutelman Seligson; m. Allan M. Greenberg, Sept. 7, 1938; 1 child, Hannah Leah. BA cum laude, Harvard U., 1973. One-woman shows include Jane Haslem Gallery, Washington, 1992, Anita Friedman Fine Art, N.Y.C., 1997, Schlesinger Libr., Radcliffe Coll., Cambridge, Mass., 1997, exhibited in group shows at Gary Snyder Fine Art, N.Y.C., 1998, 2002, Signal 66, Washington, 2001, Exit Art, N.Y.C., 2002, Amram Sunday Scholars Series, Washington, 2000; contbr. articles to profl. jours. and pubs.

SELIN, NINA EVVIE, philanthropist; b. N.Y.C., Dec. 16, 1935; d. Louis Harry and Ida Cantor; m. Ivan Selin, June 8, 1957; children: Douglas Scott, Jessica Beth. BS, Boston U., 1957. Cert. elem. tchr., Conn. Tchr. West Haven (Conn.) Sch. Dist., 1957-60; dir. Nat. Consumers League, Washington, 1968-75; propr. Relax-Relocation Cons., Washington, 1975-80; vice chmn. Phoenix Internat. Power Plant Co., Washington, 1995-98; chmn. Nat. Aquarium, Washington, 1986—. Bd. dirs. Am. Cancer Soc., 1972-87, Nat. Geog. Soc., 1995—, Mt. Sinai Hosp. Found., Miami Beach, Fla., 1998—, Rep. Nat. Com., 1991—; chmn. Selin Family Found., Del., 1995; judge Nathan Davis award AMA, Washington, 2001. Recipient Disting. Svc. award Am. Cancer Soc., 1987, Mt. Sinai Found., 1999. Mem. Internat. Club III, Welcome to Washington Internat. Club. Avocations: exotic travel, scuba diving, reading, public service. Home: 1455 Ocean Dr Apt 1602 Miami FL 33139 Office: Phoenix Internat 1050 17th St NW Washington DC 20036 E-mail: nselin@phnx-intl.com.

SELLARS, CHRISTI VON LEHE, music educator; b. Charleston, S.C., July 30, 1954; d. Diedreich Peterman and Fay Johnson von Lehe; m. Robert Marion Sellars, Mar. 21, 1981; children: Katharine Elizabeth, Patrick Grayson. MusB in Edn., Converse Coll., 1976, MusM in Edn., 1986. Choral dir. Spartanburg (S.C.) HS, 1977—82; music instr. Spartanburg (S.C.) Day Sch., 1992—2001; prof. music Wofford Coll., Spartanburg, 1993—. Choir dir. Cannon's Meth. Ch., Spartanburg, 1998—; asst. pianist Spartanburg (S.C.) Little Theatre, 1992—98; founder Spartanburg (S.C.) Day Sch. Singers, 1994, STARTS- Wofford Students in the Arts, 2003. Performer Spartanburg (S.C.) Repertory Co., 1989—92; pres. Spartanburg (S.C.) Little Theatre, 1992—98, Spartanburg (S.C.) Philharm., 1985—87; bd. dir. Spartanburg (S.C.) Little Theatre, 1992—98, Music Found., Spartanburg, 1991—95. Named Spartanburg (S.C.) City Young Career Woman, Bus. and Profl. Women, 1980. Mem.: Am. Choral Dirs. Assn., S.C. Music Educators Assn. Meth. Avocations: reading, composing. Home: 3213 Hwy 56 PO Box 132 Pauline SC 29374 Office: Wofford College Box H 429 N Church St Spartanburg SC 29303

SELLERS, BARBARA JACKSON, federal judge; b. Richmond, Va., Oct. 3, 1940; m. Richard F. Sellers; children: Elizabeth M., Anne W., Catherine A. Attended, Baldwin-Wallace Coll., 1958-60; BA cum laude, Ohio State U., 1962; JD magna cum laude, Capital U. Law Sch., Columbus, Ohio, 1979. Bar: Ohio 1979, U.S. Dist. Ct. (so. dist.) Ohio 1981, U.S. Ct. Appeals (6th cir.), 1986. Jud. law clk. Hon. Robert J. Sidman, U.S. Bankruptcy Judge, Columbus, Ohio, 1979-81; assoc. Lasky & Semons, Columbus, 1981-82; jud. law clk. to Hon. Thomas M. Herbert, U.S. Bankrupcty Ct., Columbus, 1982-84; assoc. Baker & Hostetler, Columbus, 1984-86; U.S. bankruptcy judge So. Dist. Ohio, Columbus, 1986—. Lectr. on bankruptcy univs., insts., assns. Recipient Am. Jurisprudence prize contracts and criminal law, 1975-76, evidence and property, 1976-77, Corpus Juris Secundum awards, 1975-76, 76-77. Mem. Columbus Bar Assn., Am. Bankruptcy Inst., Nat. Conf. Bankruptcy Judges, Order of Curia, Phi Beta Kappa. Office: US Bankruptcy Ct 170 N High St Columbus OH 43215-2403 E-mail: barbara_sellers@ohsb.uscourts.gov.

SELLERS, KATE M. art museum director; From dir. devel. and comm. to acting dir. Walters Art Gallery, Balt., 1987-94; dir. devel. and external affairs Cleve. Mus., 1995-97, dep. dir., 1997-2000; dir. Wadsworth Atheneum, Hartford, Conn., 2000—. Office: Wadsworth Atheneum Museum of Art 600 Main St Hartford CT 06103-2990

SELLERS, LOIS EILEEN WAGNER, art director; b. Darby, Pa., Sept. 8, 1948; d. Raymond Charles and Amy Grace (Briscoe) Wagner; m. Ronnie W. Sellers, Jr., Mar. 15, 1969 (div. June 1976); children: Devin Lee, Dixie Lee, Marissa Mikovna. BFA, U. Arts, Phila., 1988; M in Journalism, Temple U., 1992. Graphic designer Hahnemman U. Hosp., Phila., 1992—98; mktg. mgr. Roberts Filter Group, Darby, 1998—99; art dir. Soc. Indsl. Applied Math., Phila., 1999—. Bd. dirs. Barnstormers Theater, Ridley Park, Pa., 1989—, Phila. Chamber Chorus, 2003. Photographer (exhibitions) Woodmere Art Mus., 1988 (First prize, 1988), Staten Island Children's Mus., 1993. Mem. Swarthmore Friends Meeting, 2002 ; protestor Nonviolent Peace Force, Phila., 2003. Democrat. Mem. Soc. Of Friends. Avocations: gardening, photography, singing, theater. Home: 267 Rambling Way Springfield PA 19064

SELLERS, MARJORIE STEVENSON, retired principal; b. New Orleans, July 10, 1931; d. Samuel Sr. and Lillie Neldare Brown; m. Melvin Stevenson, Feb. 27, 1950 (dec.); children: Melvin Jr. (dec.), Carl F. Anthony (dec.).; m. Lloyd Sellers, Jan. 27, 1974 (dec.). BA in Elem. Edn., Southern U., 1964, MEd in Elem. Edn., 1967; MS in Adminstrn. and Supervision, Alcorn State U., 1982; postgrad., Grambling State U. Dir., tchr. daycare and kindergarten Immaculate Conception Ch., Baton Rouge, 1964-66; tchr. grade 2nd, 6th Carver Elem., De Ridder, La., 1966-68; tchr. math, social studies, reading grades 6,7,8 Walker (La.) Jr. High Sch., 1968-69; acting corr. title I Dept. Corrections, Baton Rouge, 1969-72; instr. reading Alcorn State U., Lorman, Miss., 1972-95; coord. tutor program E.B.R. Recreation/Parks, Baton Rouge, 1995-98; program dir. summer camp, 1995-96; prevention counselor, 1997-98; prin. St. Francis Xavier Sch., Baton Rouge, 1998—; substitute tchr./counselor East Baton Rouge Parish. Adj. faculty U. So. Miss., Natchez, 1975, Sch. Nursing Alcorn State U., Natchez, 1981-82, 90. Stay-In-School challenge grantee Entergy Corp., 1996, Drug Prevention/Edn. program grantee Baton Rouge Found., 1997; Am. coll. scholar U.S. Achieve Acad., 1990. Mem. AARP, AAUW, Nat. Assn. Devel. Edn., Internat. Reading Assn., La. Recreation/Parks, Phi Delta Kappa (sec., pres. 1980). Democrat. Roman Catholic. Avocations: reading, sewing, church activities, ball games, shopping.

SELLICK, KATHLEEN A. hospital administrator; b. Phoenix, Ariz. m. Phil Sellick; 1 child, Grace. BS, Ariz. State U.; MBA, U. Chgo. Grad. Sch. Bus. With Am. Med. Internat., Beverly Hills, Calif., Westgate Med. Ctr., Denton, Tex., Mayo Clinic, Rochester, Minn.; v.p. adminstrn. and dir. outreach devel. Hoag Meml. Hosp. Presbyn., Newport Beach, Calif.; exec. v.p. and COO St. Joseph Hosp., Orange, Calif.; assoc. exec. dir. and COO U. Wash. Med. Ctr., Seattle, 1999—2001, exec. dir., 2001—. Office: U Wash Med Ctr 1959 NE Pacific St Box 356151 Seattle WA 98195-6151

SELMAN, CAROL, retired secondary school educator; b. N.Y.C., Oct. 28, 1946; BA with distinction, Cornell, 1969; MA, SUNY, 1981, postgrad., 1982-83. Cert. secondary sch. social studies tchr., N.J. Tchg. fellow SUNY, Stony Brook, 1982-83; tchr. history Millburn (N.J.) Sr. H.S., 1969—98. Pub. mem. N.J. Hist. Commn., 1992—; adv. organizer Millburn H.S. chpt. Amnesty Internat., 1985-98; mem. Sing-Out Found.; alumni amb. Cornell U., 1992—; mem. West Orange (N.J.) Arts Coun., 1998—. Fellow Nat. Endowment for the Humanities, 1986. Mem. Millburn (N.J.) Edn. Assn. (chmn. legis. action team 1983-86), Orgn. Am. Historians, Cornell Club (no. N.J.), Phi Beta Kappa. Office: The Morristown Beard Sch 70 Whippany Rd Morristown NJ 07960

SELTZER, VICKI LYNN, obstetrician, gynecologist; b. June 2, 1949; d. Herbert Melvin and Marian Elaine (Willinger) Seltzer; m. Richard Stephen Brach, Sept. 2, 1973; children: Jessica Lillian Brach, Eric Robert Brach. BS, Rensselaer Poly. Inst., 1969; MD, NYU, 1973. Diplomate Am. Bd. Ob-Gyn. (examiner 1988-2001). Intern Bellevue Hosp., N.Y.C., 1973-74, resident in ob-gyn., 1974-77; fellow gynecol. cancer Am. Cancer Soc., N.Y.C., 1977-78, Meml. Sloan Kettering Cancer Ctr., N.Y.C., 1978-79; assoc. dir. gynecol. cancer Albert Einstein Coll. Medicine, N.Y.C., 1979-83, prof. ob-gyn., 1989—, Edie and marvin H. Shur prof. ob-gyn. and women's health, 2003—; assoc. prof. ob-gyn. SUNY, Stony Brook, 1983-89. Dir. ob-gyn. Queens Hosp. Ctr., Jamaica, NY, 1983—93, pres. med. bd., 1986—89; chair ob-gyn. L.I. Jewish Med. Ctr., 1993—; v.p. women's health svcs. North Shore-L.I. Jewish Health Sys., 1999—; chair ob-gyn. North Shore U. Hosp., 1999—, chair med. bd., 2001—; mem. N.Y. State Coun. Grad. Med. Edn., 2003—. Author: Every Woman's Guide to Breast Cancer, 1987; editor-in-chief: Primary Care Update for the Ob-Gyn, 1993—; editor: Women's Primary Health Care, 1995, 2d edit., 2000; mem. editl. bd. Women's Life mag., 1980—82, Jour. Jacobs Inst. Women's Health, 1990—95, mem. internat. editl. bd. Jour. Soc. Obstreticians and Gynecologists Can., 2000—; contbr. articles to profl. jours.; host (TV series) Weekly Ob-Gyn. program, Lifetime Med. TV. Mem. Mayor Beame's Task Force on Rape, N.Y.C., 1974—76; chair health com. Nat. Coun. Women, N.Y.C., 1979—84; bd. govs. Nat. Coun. Women's Health, 1985—94; chair Coun. Resident Edn. Ob-Gyn., 1987—93. Recipient citation, Nat. Safety Coun., 1978, Achiever award, L.I. Ctr. Bus. and Profl. Women, 1987; Galloway Fund fellow, 1975. Fellow: ACOG (mem. gynecol. practice com. 1981, v.p. 1993—94, ores.-elect 1996—97, pres. 1997—98), N.Y. Obstet. Soc. (pres. 1999—2000); mem.: Am. Hosp. Assn. (mem. governing coun. maternal and child health 2004—), N.Y. Cancer Soc., Am. Med. Women's Assn. (com. chair 1975—79, mem. editl. bd. jour. 1986—2002, citation 1973), Internat. Fedn. Gynecology and Obstetrics (mem. internat. steering com. to reduce maternal mortality 2000—02), Women's Med. Assn. (v.p. N.Y. 1974—79, mem. resident rev. com. ob-gyn. 1993—98, Lila Wallis Lifetime Achievement award 2002), NYU Sch. Med. Alumni Assn. (bd. govs. 1979—, v.p. 1987—91, pres. 1992—93), Alpha Omega Alpha. Office: LI Jewish Med Ctr New Hyde Park NY 11040

SELTZER, VIVIAN CENTER, psychologist, educator; b. Mpls., May 27, 1931; d. Aaron M. and Hannah (Chazanow) Center; m. William Seltzer; children: Jonathan, Francesca S. Rothseid, Aeryn S. Fenton. BA summa cum laude, U. Minn., 1951; MSW, U. Pa., 1953; PhD, Bryn Mawr Coll., 1976. Lic. psychologist, cert. sch. psychologist, marriage and family therapist; lic. social worker Pa. Family counselor, Phila., Miami, Fla., 1953-60; pvt. practice Phila., 1965—; prof. human devel. and behavior U. Pa., Phila., 1976—. Exch. prof. U. Edinburgh, Scotland, 1979—80; vis. prof. Hebrew U., Jerusalem, 1984—85; chair internat. com. U. Pa., Phila., mem. various coms., chair faculty senate. Author: (book) Adolescent Social Development: Dynamic Functional Interaction, 1982, The Psychosocial Worlds of the Adolescent, 1989; contbr. articles to profl. jours. Mem. bd. regents Gratz Coll., Phila., 1965—, chair acad. affairs com., 1980—, v.p., 1989—97. Mem.: APA, Internat. Coun. Psychologists, Phila. Soc. Clin. Psychologists (bd. dirs. 1975—86, 1999—, program chair 1980—86, 2001—), Pa. Psychol. Assn., Phi Beta Kappa. E-mail: seltzer@ssw.upenn.edu.

SELVIDGE, MARY M. D. psychologist; b. Chelsea, Mass., July 29, 1969; d. William H. E. and Margaret W. Doole; m. Sidney D. D. Selvidge, July 12, 1969; 1 child, Sidney D. PhD, U. Memphis, 2000. Psychology intern U. Akron, Ohio, 1999—2000. Contbr. articles to profl. jours. Mem.: APA. Achievements include research in Factors Related to Psychological Well-being in Lesbian and Bisexual Women; Counselor Training in LGB Issues; Addiction Counselor Competence in Working with LGB Clients. Avocations: travel, dance.

SELVY, BARBARA, dance instructor; b. Little Rock, Jan. 20, 1938; d. James Oliver and Irene Balmat Banks; m. Franklin Delano Selvy, Apr. 15, 1959; children: Lisa Selvy Yeargin, Valerie Selvy Miros, Lauren Kroll, Franklin Michael, Madison Banks Selvy. Student, U. Ctrl. Ark., 1955—57. Founder, dir. Carolina Ballet Theater, Greenville, SC, 1973—; pres. Dance Arts Inc. and Incentives, Inc. Mem. adv. bd. dirs. Met. Arts Coun., and S.C. Govs. Sch., St. Marys Cath. Sch. Appeared in numerous TV commls., on Goodson Toddman game show Play Your Hunch, 1958-59; toured Far East with TV show Hit Parade, 1958; named Miss Ark., 1956, Mrs. S.C., 1981; dir. and staged Mrs. Va., Mrs. N.C., Mrs. S.C. pageants; choreographed Little Theater prodns., Furman U. Opera. Mem. Nat. Rep. Congl. Com., 2003. Mem. So. Assn. Dance Masters (ballet adviser, regional dir.), Dance Educators Am., Dance Masters of Am., Profl. Dance Tchrs. Home: 206 Honey Horn Dr Simpsonville SC 29681-5814

SEMANS, MARY DUKE BIDDLE TRENT, foundation administrator; b. N.Y., Feb. 21, 1920; d. Anthony Joseph Drexel and Mary (Duke) B.; m. Josiah Trent; m. James H. Semans. Attended, Hewitt Sch., N.Y.; AB in History, Duke U.; LLD (hon.), N.C. Cen. U., 1963; HHD (hon.), Elon Coll., 1965; degree (hon.), Davidson Coll., N.C. Wesleyan Coll., 1982, U.N.C. at Chapel Hill, Duke U., 1983; LLD (hon.), Furman U., 1993. Trustee emeritus Duke U., 1961-81; chmn. The Duke Endowment, 1960—; various positions N.C. Sch. Arts, 1981—; former trustee Davidson Coll., N.C. Mus. Art, 1961-83, Shaw U., Converse U., Lincoln Hosp.; vice chmn. The Mary Duke Biddle Found., 1960 ; chmn. Angier B. Duke Meml., Exec. Mansion Fine Arts Com., 1965—, Friends of Duke U. Library; pres. Durham Homes, Inc., 1968; mem. bd. dirs. Goodwill Industries of the Rsch. Triangle Area, 1964—, First Union Corp., 1980-82, N.C. State Library, 1958-61, Durham Pub. Library; numerous other positions. Mem. Durham City Coun., 1951-55; mayor pro-tem City of Durham, 1953-55, commencement speaker Duke U., 1983. Recipient Merit award Duke U. Health and Hosp. Adminstrn. Alumni Assn., 1989, Giannini medal for meritorious svc. to N.C. Sch. of the Arts, 1990, Alan Keith-Lucas Friend of Children award N.C. Childcare Assn., 1991, Elna Spaulding award Women-in-Action, 1993, Outstanding Philanthropist award Triangle Chpt. Nat. Soc. Fund Raising Execs., 1993, Sam Ragan award St. Andrews Coll., 1993. Mem. LWV, Bus. and Profl. Women's Club, Altrusa Club, Half Century Club, Rotary Club. Democrat. Methodist. Home: 1415 Bivins St Durham NC 27707-1519 Office: The Mary Duke Biddle Found 1044 W Forest Hills Blvd Durham NC 27707-1678

SEMAYA, FRANCINE LEVITT, lawyer; b. N.Y.C., Mar. 26, 1951; d. Julie and Ann (Tannenbaum) Levitt; m. Richard Semaya, Aug. 3, 1975; children: Stefanie Rachel, David Steven, Scott Brian. BA magna cum laude, Bklyn. Coll., 1973, MS magna cum laude, 1975; JD cum laude, N.Y. Law Sch., 1982. Bar: N.Y. 1983, U.S. Dist. Ct. (ea. and so. dists.) N.Y. 1983, U.S. Supreme Ct. 2000. Sr. legal analyst, atty. Am. Internat. Group, Inc., N.Y.C., 1977-83; assoc. counsel, asst. v.p. Beneficial Ins. Group, Inc. (formerly Benico, Inc.), Peapack, N.J., 1983-87; v.p., counsel Am. Centennial Ins. Co., Peapack, 1985-87; legal/reins. cons. Peapack, 1987; counsel reins. Integrity Ins. Co. in Liquidation, Paramus, N.J., 1988-91; ptnr. Werner & Kennedy, N.Y.C., 1991-99; sr. mem., chair ins. corp. and regulatory practice group Cozen O'Connor, N.Y.C., 1999—. Spkr. in field. Author: Insurance Insolvency--A New Generation, 2001, Insurance Insolvencies 2002-2003: Is the Industry Prepared?, 2002, Insurance Insolvencies, Has the Cycle Peaked?, 2003; editor: Law and Practice of Insurance Insolvency Revisited, 1999, State of Insurance Regulation: Today and Tomorrow, 1991; contbg. editor: Reference Handbook Ins. Co. Insolvency, 4th edit., 1999; contbr. articles to profl. jours. Mem. ABA (sect. del. to ho. dels. 1998—2004, tort trial and ins. practice sect. coun. 1994-97, chmn. task force on ins. insolvency 1995-2000, chmn. task force on state implementation ins. insolvency report 2003—, chmn. professionalism com. 1997-98, chmn. pub. regulation of ins. law com. 1990-91, chair pub. rels. com. 1993-94, co-editor State Regulation Ins. 1991), Internat. Assn. Ins. Receivers (bd. dirs. 2003—), N.Y. State Bar Assn., Practicing Law Inst. (ins. law adv. com. 1995—), Assn. Bar City N.Y. (ins. law com.), Fedn. Regulatory Counsel, Phi Beta Kappa. Avocations: reading, travel. Office: Cozen O'Connor 16 Fl 45 Broadway Atrium New York NY 10006-3007 E-mail: fsemaya@cozen.com.

SEMMEN, AMBER L. interior designer, graphics designer, web site designer; d. Vern and Lynda Stoffel; m. Michael Dean Semmen. BA in Interior Design, Wash. State U., 1997. Designer Smithgroup, San Francisco, 1997—98; on site interior liason, interior cons. Gen. Motors/Kaplan McLaughlin Diaz, Detroit, 1998—2001; owner, designer design, San Francisco, 1998—. Mem.: Internat. Interior Design Assn. (bd. dirs. No. Calif. chpt. 2001—02). Lutheran. Avocations: travel, running. Office: 1 Bluxome St #201 San Francisco CA 94107-1605 E-mail: a@semmen.com.

SEMMES, SALLY PETERSON, choreographer, educator, performer; b. Rockford, Ill., Nov. 17; d. Edwin Carl and Eva Victoria Peterson; m. David Hamilton Semmes, Jan. 8, 1955; children: Melissa Kay Semmes-Thorne, Laurie Ruth. BS in Edn., U. Wis., 1953, postgrad., 1957-58, 61-62, San Diego State U., London campus, 1976, Northwestern U., 1977. Cert. English, speech/theater tchr., Wis. Tchr. English and speech Oshkosh (Wis.) H.S., 1953-54, Madison (Wis.) East H.S., 1955; instr. Patricia Stevens Finishing Sch., 1956; pvt. tchr. dance Phillips, Wis., 1957-60; project asst. Wis. Idea Theatre U. Wis, Madison, 1963-66; test adminstr. Manitowoc (Wis.) Counseling Ctr., 1967; tchr. English and speech Valders (Wis.) H.S., 1978-81; pub. info. U. Wis., Manitowoc, 1970-72, instr. dance, 1972-78, instr. pub. speaking, 1983—, instr. remedial Coll. English, 1992, freelance instr. dance, 1982-95, tchr. Hatrack Kids classes reading motivation, 1982—; owner Sally Semmes Ednl. Workshops, 1983—; staff Next Act Theatre, 2000. Narrator Green Bay (Wis.) Symphony Childrens Concerts, 1977-81, Manitowoc Symphony Orch., 1992; founder, pres., treas. The Hatrack Storytellers, Inc., 1967—; mem. Readers Theatre Reading Incentive Program for Children, 1967—. Choreographer (musicals) Anything Goes, Mame, Guys and Dolls, The Fantasticks, Broadway Bound, Joseph and the Amazing Technicolor Dreamcoat, (mus. revues including) 7 Showtime Shows, Manitowoc; dir.: (plays) Anything Goes, The Male

Animal, The Boor, The Ugly Duckling, Our Town, The Sandbox, The Staring Match, The Imaginary Invalid; performer: (numerous productions) Daytrips, Trip to Bountiful, Tuck Everlasting, Love Letters, Dancing at Lughnasa, Lovers, Rules of the Game, The Resounding Tinkle, Baby with the Bathwater, The Man Who Came to Dinner, Blithe Spirit, The Glass Managerie, The White House, The Royal Family, See How They Run, Talking With, Marvin's Room, Eleemosynary, (groups) Milw. Repertory Theater, First Stage Milw., Kohler Arts Ctr., Next Act Theatre, Renaissance Theatreworks. Pub. svc. videos City of West Allis, Am. Cancer Soc., assisted living, 1998; lay reader St. James Episcopal Ch., Manitowoc, 1984—97; dir. Miss Manitowoc pageant, 1972—75, Miss Calumet County pageant, New Holstein, Wis., 1974; guest artist Creative Arts Week Minn. Episcopal Cathedral, Mpls., 1997; editor's asst. Wis. Mag. of History of Wis. State Hist. Soc., 1958. Recipient Cultural Achievement award Manitowoc and Two Rivers C. of C., 1984, Cert. of Appreciation Manitowoc Pub. Libr., 1987; named Sec. of Yr. Manitowoc Manpower, 1983; elected to Natl. Museum of Women in the Arts, 2002. Mem.: AAUW, AARP, LWV, Nature Conservancy, Environ. Defense, Arthritis Found., Wis. Alumni Assn., World Wildlife Fedn., PEO Sisterhood, Sierra Club, Phi Beta. Avocations: baking, travel, reading, film. Home and Office: 8501 Old Sauk Rd 305 Middleton WI 53562

SEMPLE, JANE FRANCES, health facility administrator; b. Lakewood, Ohio, Feb. 14, 1951; d. Frank Joseph and Margaret Eleanor (Carpenter) Semple; m. Nick N. Morana, June 24, 1977 (div. Sept. 1981). AAB, Cuyahoga CC, Cleve., 1977; BA, Baldwin-Wallace Coll., 1980; MBA, Case Western Res. U., 1984; ND, Trinity Coll. Natural Health, 1999. Diplomate Am. Bd. Naturopaths. Adminstrv. asst. DeVilbiss Co., Cleve., 1969—77; project dir. Nat. Survey Rsch. Ctr., Cleve., 1977—80; market rsch. mgr. Sherwin-Williams Co., Cleve., 1980—85; instr. Cuyahoga CC, Cleve., 1986—92, Baldwin-Wallace Coll., Berea, Ohio, 1992—93; dir. Alternative Healing Inst., 1993—. Mem. S. B. Anthony Soc. Womenspace, Cleve., 1980—88. Mem.: NOW, Am. Assn. Nutritional Cons. Democrat. Home: 26969 Greenbrooke Dr Olmsted Falls OH 44138

SEN, LAURA J. wholesale distribution executive; Exec. v.p. merchandising BJ's Wholesale Club, Inc., Natick, Mass., 1996—. Office: BJs Wholesale Club Inc 1 Mercer Rd Natick MA 01760-2400 Fax: 508-651-6114.

SENDER, MARYANN, director; b. Fairview, Ohio, Aug. 6, 1956; d. Edward John and Annamay Knecht; m. Emil Robert Syarto, Sept. 9, 1978 (div. Nov. 1991); 1 child, Shannon Syarto ; m. John Peter Sender, July 20, 2001. B in Edn./Therapy, Ohio State U., 1978; M in Counseling/Art Psychology, Ursuline Coll., 1989. Cert. rehab. counselor. HPER and program dir. Lakewood (Ohio) YWCA, 1978—80; activity therapy dir. Northside Hosp., Youngstown, Ohio, 1980—87; instr. art therapy Cleve. State U., 1989—93; acad. counselor Cuyahoga C.C., Cleve., 1989—91, ACCESS dir., 1991—. NOCSD chair No. Ohio Consortium, 1993—; spkr. in field. Chair Nat. Disability Awareness Day, Cleve., 1990—; com. mem., BAC/Global Issues, Cleve. and Atlanta, 1998, 1999, 2001; creator Ed Sparre Scholarship Cuyahoga C.C., 1999—; hon. mem. adv. bd. Cleve. Rapid Transit Authority, 1995—98. Mem.: Advocates for Disabled Ohioans, Assn. for Learning Disabilities, Assn. for Higher Edn., Transition and Comm. Consortium on Learning Disabilities, Dir. of Activities Assn., Profl. Activities Therapy Assn., Assn. Higher Edn. and Disability, Mental Health Assn., Am. Heart Assn., Ams. with Disability Act (coll. chairperson 1991—), Dance Exercise Assn., Am. Dance Assn. Avocations: swimming, dance, art, reading, hiking. Home: 5874 Hickory Trl North Ridgeville OH 44039 Office: Cuyahoga C C 4250 Richmond Rd Highland Hills OH 44122 E-mail: maryann.sender@tri-c.cc.edu.

SENECHAL, ALICE R. federal judge, lawyer; b. Rugby, N.D., June 25, 1955; d. Marvin William and Dora Emma (Erdman) S. BS, N.D. State U., 1977; JD, U. Minn., 1984. Bar: Minn. 1984, U.S. Dist. Ct. Minn. 1984, N.D. 1986, U.S. Ct. Appeals (8th cir.) 1987. Law clk. U.S. Dist. Judge Bruce M. Van Sickle, Bismarck, N.D., 1984-86; with Robert Vogel Law Office, Grand Forks, N.D., 1986—. U.S. magistrate judge, 1990—.

SENERCHIA, DOROTHY SYLVIA, author, urban planner; b. Warwick, R.I. d. Vincenzo Ralph and Theresa Felicia (Petrarca) S. BA, Pembroke Coll., Brown U., 1955; Cert., U. Florence, Italy, 1956. Cert. urban planner, N.Y.C. Tchr. Berlitz Sch. Langs., Florence, 1955-56; adminstrv. asst. Sheraton Corp. Am., N.Y.C., 1956-57, Inter-Am. Coun., N.Y.C., 1958-59, Roger Stevens Devel. Corp., N.Y.C., 1960-61; urban planner N.Y.C. Dept. City Planning, 1962-96. Author: Silent Menace, 1990; co-producer, co-star film The Funeral, 1980; solo concert violinist, 1945-62; co-founder singing group The Chattertocks of Brown U., 1952. One of the pioneers in cmty organization in the urban planning process, N.Y.C., 1962-68; one of the early pioneers in women's movement, N.Y.C., 1969; mem. planning com. 1970 Women's March, N.Y.C., 1970; counselor Big Sisters Orgn., N.Y.C., 1969-82. Mem.: Vet. Feminists Am. (co-founder, adv. bd.), The East River Round Table (founder). Avocations: foreign languages, music, travel, floral design.

SENESE, SUZANNE MARIE, art educator, music educator, performance artist; b. Chgo., Dec. 6, 1950; d. Louis Michael and Angeline Mary Olivo Senese. Student, Quincy Coll., 1968—70; BS in Music Edn. and Vocal, No. Ill. U., 1972; MA in Interdisiplinary Arts, Columbia Coll., 2003. Music educator St. John Vianney Sch., Northlake, Ill., 1973—76, St. Pius X Elem. Sch., Lombard, Ill., 1976—85; choir/orch. dir. Seton H.S., South Holland, Ill., 1985—87; choir, orch., music and theatre educator Regina Dominican H.S., Wilmette, Ill., 1984—99; fine arts and choir educator Fenwick H.S., Oak Park, Ill., 1999—. Vol. St. Leonard's House; music dir., cantor, organist Santa Lucia Ch., Chgo., 1983—91. Recipient Heart of Sch. Arts award, Archdiocese of Chgo., 2001. Mem.: Nat. Assn. Pastoral Musicians, Nat. Cath. Edn. Assn., Ill. Arts Edn. Assn., Am. Choral Dir. Assn., Music Educators Nat. Conf. Roman Catholic. Avocations: theater, reading, crossword puzzles, baseball. Office: Fenwick High Sch 505 Washington Blvd Oak Park IL 60302 Office Phone: 708-386-0217 ext. 198.

SENG, COLEEN JOY, mayor; b. Council Bluffs, Iowa, Feb. 8, 1936; d. Otis A. and Helen V. (Anderson) McElwain; m. Darrel E. Seng, Oct. 22, 1960 (dec. 1993); children: Marcee Lee, Christopher Charles, Phillip Scott. BA, Nebr. Wesleyan U., 1958. Dist. dir. Girl Scouts U.S.A., Saginaw, Mich., 1958-60, Lincoln, Nebr., 1960-62; cmty. ministry 1st United Meth. Ch., Lincoln, 1977-97; mem. Lincoln City Coun., 1987—2003; mayor City of Lincoln, 2003—. Mem. Mayor's first multi-cultural task force, co-chair of Gov. Nelson's urban adv. team, chmn. railroad transp. safety dist. Lincoln/Lancaster county joint budget com., mem. Lincoln/Lancaster county homeless coalition; active U. Place Cmty. Orgn. N.E. Family Resource Ctr.; past chair Lincoln/Lancaster county family resource ctr. bd.; past pres. Lincoln Fellowship of Chs.; mem. Lincoln Interfaith Coun.; mem Lincoln Urban Ministries com.; past pres. Homestead Girl Scouts Coun. Democrat. United Methodist. Avocations: reading, movies, gardening. Home: 6101 Walker Ave Lincoln NE 68507-2467 Office: County City Bldg 555 S 10th St Lincoln NE 68508-2810

SENGERS, JOHANNA M. H. LEVELT, thermophysicist; b. Amsterdam, The Netherlands, Mar. 4, 1929; married, 1963; 4 children. Drs, U. Amsterdam, 1954, PhD in Physics, 1958; PhD (hon.), Delft U. Tech., 1992. Rsch. assoc. U. Amsterdam, Van der Waals Lab, 1954-58, 59-63, U. Wis., Inst. Theoretical Chemistry, Madison, 1958-59; physicist heat divsn. Inst. Basic Stds., Nat. Bur. Stds., Gaithersburg, Md., 1963-78; group leader thermophysics divsn. Nat. Engring. Lab., 1978-87; sr. fellow thermophysics divsn. Nat. Inst. Standards and Tech., 1983-95, fellow emeritus, 1995—. Lectr Cath. U., Louvain, Belgium, 1971; rsch. assoc. Inst. Theoretical Physics, U. Amsterdam, 1974-75; regent's prof. chemistry U. Calif., L.A., 1982. Chair working group A Internat. Assn. Properties Steam, 1985-90; pres. Internat. Assn. Properties Water and Steam, 1991-92. Recipient Silver medal U.S. Dept. Commerce, 1972, Gold medal, 1978, Wise award Interagy. Com. Women in Sci. and Engring., 1985, Alexander von Humboldt Rsch. award Alexander von Humboldt-Stiftung, Bonn, Germany, 1991, L'Oreal-UNESCO Women in Sci. award, 2003. Fellow: AAAS, Am. Phys. Soc., Internat. Assn. Properties Water and Steam (hon.); mem.: ASME, AIChE, Physical Soc., Assn. Women in Sci., Royal Holland Soc. of Scis. and Humanities, Dutch Phys. Soc., Netherlands Royal Acad. Arts and Sci. (corr.), European Phys. Soc., Nat. Acad. Engring., Nat. Acad. Sci., Cosmos Club. Office: Phys & Chem Properties Div Nat Inst Stds & Tech 100 Bureau Dr Stop 8380 Gaithersburg MD 20899-8380 Business E-Mail: johanna.sengers@nist.gov.

SENGSTACKE, ASTRID PRYOR, poet, journalist; b. Chgo., Sept. 4, 1938; d. Whittier A. and Mattie Astrid (Pryor) S.; children: Taasha Lindsey, Syikija Joachim, Seratiel Jones, LaTheena Jones. BA, Goddard Coll., 1995. Circulation mgr. Memphis Tri-State, 1960-62; asst. gen. mgr., journalist Defender, Memphis, 1960-70. Lobbyist Wash. Assoc. Churches, Olympia, 1987-96.

SENKARIK, MIKKI, oil painter; b. Oak Ridge, Tenn., Dec. 2, 1954; d. GEorge and Cleta (VanMarter) S. BFA, U. South Fla., 1976; MS in Med. Illustration, Med. Coll. Ga., 1979. Freelance med. illustrator, San Antonio and Corsicana, Tex., 1979-90. Mem. adv. bd. LOOPS Internat., Odessa, Tex., 1990—; bd. dirs. Flying Horse Ltd., Virginia Beach, Va. Guest Contbr. Equine Images, Ft. Dodge, Iowa, 1990—, Equus, Gaithersburg, Md., 1991—; one-woman shows include Lyon Gallery, Scottsdale, Ariz., Forms Gallery, Del Ray Beach, Fla., Pitzer's of Carmel (Calif.); represented by Alexandra Stevens Gallery. Fundraiser/voter registration Rep. Women's Party, 1976—; fin. contbr. Shelter of Abused Women, Galveston, Tex., 1994—. Recipient award of excellence Assn. Med. Illustrators, 1983, 85, 87, 88, 91. Avocations: travel, writing. Office: 301 E 5th Ave Corsicana TX 75110-5342

SENN, DEBORAH, insurance commissioner; m. Rudi Bertschi. BA, MA, U. Ill.; JD, Loyola U. Rep. cmty. groups, consumers, women & family groups, labor and small bus.; elected Wash. state ins. commr., 1992-96. Avocations: hiking, outdoors. Office: Insurance Bldg PO Box 40255 Olympia WA 98504-0255

SENNETT, PATRICIA M. artist, educator; b. Pitts., May 1, 1934; d. Nikola L. and Mary C. (Stefanac) Knezevich; m. Arthur Hugh Sennett; children: Michael Sean, Susan Hope Sennett Paperno, Peter Hugh. Student, Carnegie-Mellon U.; BS in Art Edn., Edinboro U., 1956; postgrad., SUNY, Potsdam; MFA, Rochester Inst. Tech., 1970. Art tchr. Moorestown (N.J.) Pub. Schs., 1956—57, Hammondsport (N.Y.) C.S., 1958—59, Haverling C.S., Bath, NY, 1959—60, Campus Sch., SUC, Potsdam, NY, 1963—64; faculty art dept. St. Laurence C.S., Brasher Falls, NY, 1964—95; adj. instr. SUC, Potsdam, 1995—96. Represented in permanent collections Carnegie-Mellon U., Pitts., St. Lawrence U., Canton, N.Y., SUNY, Potsdam, Clarkson Coll., Rochester Inst. Tech., St. Lawrence Nat. Bank, Potsdam, Canton, N.Y., Kraft, Inc., North Lawrence, N.Y., one-woman shows include Warren Meml. Libr., Friends Gibson Gallery, 1990, Friends Gibson Gallery, SUNY, 1993, two-person show, Fox-Richmond Gallery, Moulinette Gallery, exhibitions include Massena Artists' Assn., 1990, 1991, 1992, 1992, 1995, North Country Regional, 1990, 1991, 1995, Lake Placid Ctr. for the Arts, exhibited in group shows at Friends Gibson Gallery, 1990, 1991, Massena Artists' Assn., 1994, Canton Gallery, 1994. Mem.: Friends Hist. Jekyll Island, Jekyll Island Arts Assn., Inc., Friends Gibson Gallery (past pres., v.p., bd. dirs.). Home (Summer): 22 Garden St Potsdam NY 13676 Home (Winter): 554 Old Plantation Rd Jekyll Island GA 31527

SENSENICH, ILA JEANNE, federal judge; b. Pitts., Mar. 6, 1939; d. Louis E. and Evelyn Margaret S. BA, Westminster Coll., 1961; JD, Dickinson Sch. Law, 1964, JD (hon.), 1994. Bar: Pa. 1964. Assoc. Stewart, Belden, Sensenich and Harrington, Greensburg, Pa., 1964-70; asst. pub. defender Westmoreland (Pa.) County, 1970-71; U.S. magistrate judge We. Dist. Pa., Pitts., 1971—. Adj. prof. law Duquesne U., 1982-87. Author: Compendium of the Law of Prisinor's Rights, 1979; contbr. articles to profl. jour. Trustee emeritus Dickinson Sch. Law. Vis. fellow Daniel & Florence Guggenheim program in criminal justice Yale Law Sch., 1976-77. Mem. ABA, Fed. Magistrate Judges Assn. (sec. 1979-81, 88-89, treas. 1989-90, 2d v.p. 1990-91, pres.-elect 1992-93, pres. 1993-94), Pa. Bar Assn. (comn. on women in the profession 1998—), Nat. Assn. Women Judges, Westmoreland County Bar Assn., Allegheny County Bar Assn. (fed. ct. sect., com. women in law), Womens Bar Assn. We. Pa., Am. Judicature Soc. Democrat. Presbyterian. Avocations: skiing, sailing, bicycling, classical music, cooking. Office: 518B US PO And Courthouse Pittsburgh PA 15219

SENT, ESTHER-MIRJAM, economics educator; b. Doesburg, Gelderland, Netherlands, Mar. 9, 1967; d. Arno Sent and Alie Mulder-Kerkhof; m. Greg Kucich. PhD, Stanford U., 1994. Asst. prof. U. Notre Dame, Ind., 1994—2001, assoc. prof., 2001—. Author: (book) The Evolving Rationality of Rational Expectations, 1998 (Gunnar Myrdal Book prize, 1999); editor: Science Bought and Sold, 2002. Bd. dirs., webmaster Pet Refuge, Mishawaka, 1999—. Mem.: European Soc. for History of Econ. Thought, Assn. for Evolutionary Econs., Philosophy of Sci. Assn., Soc. for Social Studies of Scis., History of Sci. Soc., European Assn. for Evolutionary Polit. Economy (rsch. area coord. 1998—), Internat. Network for Econ. Methodology (bd. dirs. 2000—), History of Econs. Soc. (elec. comms. 1996—97, exec. com. 2002—), Am. Econ. Assn. Avocations: ballet, piano, reading, dogs, scuba diving. Office: U Notre Dame Dept Econs and Policy Studies Notre Dame IN 46556 Business E-Mail: sent.2@nd.edu.

SENTELL, SUSAN B. telecommunications company executive; married; 2 children. BS in Bus. Adminstrn., Miami U., Oxford, Ohio. In comm. industry, 17 yrs.; market mgr., regional sales dir., various mgmt. positions Sprint, Chgo., from 1987, asst. v.p. mktg. comm., v.p. mktg. and product mgmt.; now pres. mtkg. and ops. Spring Bus. Svcs. Group, Dallas. Office: Sprint Bus Svcs Group 5420 LBJ Fwy Dallas TX 75240-6222

SENTENNE, JUSTINE, corporate ombudsman consultant; b. Montreal, Que., Can. d. Paul Emile and Irene Genevieve (Laliberte) S. MBA, U. Que., Montreal, 1993; postgrad., McGill U., Ecole Nat. d'Adminstrn. Publique, 1989-91. Fin. analyst, assoc. mgr. portfolio Bush Assocs., Montreal, 1970-82; city councillor, mem. exec. com. City of Montreal and Montreal Urban Com., 1978-82; adminstrv. asst. Montreal Conv. Ctr., 1983; dir. sponsorship Ctrl. Com. for Montreal Papal Visit, 1984; dir. pub. rels. Coopers & Lybrand, Montreal, 1985-87; exec. dir. Que. Heart Found., 1987-89; corp. ombudsman Hydro-Que, Montreal, 1991—. Tchr. DSA program Concordia U.; v.p., bd. dirs. Armand Frappier Found., Can., Chateau Dufresne Mus. Decorative Arts, Montreal, 1985-90; chmn. bd. Wilfrid Pelletier Found., Montreal, 1986-91; bd. dirs. St. Joseph's Oratory, 1979-92, Caisse Populaire Desjardins Notre Dame de Grace, Montreal, 1980-96; mem. jury John Labatt Ltd., London, Ont., 1982-86. Notre Dame de Grace v.p. riding assn. Liberal Party of Can., chairperson Women's Commn.; bd. govs. Youth and Music Can., Montreal, 1981-86; chmn. bd. The Women's Ctr., Montreal, 1986-88, Vol. Bur. Montreal, 1986-87; bd. dirs. Palais des Congres de Montreal, 1981-89, Port of Montreal, 1983-84, Can. Ctr. for Ecumenism, Montreal, 1968-85, Villa Notre-Dame de Grace, Montreal, 1979-87, Montreal Diet Dispensary, 1989-2001, treas., 1996, Pathways to Faith, 1990-2000; bd. mgmt. Saidye Bronfman Ctr. for Arts, 1994-99. Named Career Woman of Yr., Sullivan Bus. Coll., 1979; recipient Silver medal ville de Paris, 1981, Women's Kansas City Assn. for Internat. Rels. and Trade medal, 1982. Fellow: Montreal Soc. Investment Analysts, Inst. Fin. Analysts, Fin. Analysts Fedn. N.Y.; mem.: The Ombudsman Assn. (bd. dirs. 1996—99, 2000—03, founding mem. Can. Ombudsmen, bd. dirs. 2001—). Roman Catholic.

SENTER, MERILYN P(ATRICIA), former state legislator and freelance reporter; b. Haverhill, Mass., Mar. 17, 1935, d. Paul Barton and Mary Etta (Herrin) Staples; m. Donald Neil Senter, Apr. 23, 1960; children: Karen Anne Senter, Brian Neil. Grad., McIntosh Bus. Coll., 1955. Sec. F.S. Hamlin Ins. Agy., Haverhill, Mass., 1955-60; free lance reporter Plaistow-Hampstead News, Rockingham county newspapers, Exeter and Stratham, N.H., 1970-89; mem. N.H. Gen. Ct., 1988-96. Mem. Hwy. Safety Com., Plaistow, N.H., 1976—; sec., bd. dirs. Region 10 Commn. Support Svcs. Inc., Atkinson, N.H., 1982-88, 2003—; chmn. Plaistow Area Transit Adv. Com., 1990-93, mem., 1994—; active Devel. Disabilities Coun., 1993-99; mem. Plaistow Bd. Selectmen, 1996—; mem. Rockingham Planning Commn., 1994—; chmn., 2000-2001; bd. dirs. Gr. Salem/Gr. Derry Regional Transp. Coun., 2000—. Named Woman of Yr., N.H. Bus. and Profl. Women, 1983, Nat. Grange Citizen of Yr., 1992. Republican. Avocations: nature, grandchildren, handicapped issues. Home and Office: 11 Maple Ave Plaistow NH 03865-2221 E-mail: mse1056673@aol.com.

SENTURIA, YVONNE DREYFUS, pediatrician, epidemiologist; b. Houston, Jan. 16, 1951; BA in Biology and Sociology, Rice U., 1973; MD, U. Tex., San Antonio, 1977; MSc in Epidemiology, London Sch. Hygiene and Tropical Medicine, 1985. Diplomate Am. Bd. Pediat. resident Shands Tchg. Hosp., Gainesville, Fla., 1977-79, Tex. Children's Hosp., Houston, 1979-80; instr., asst. prof. Coll. Medicine, Baylor U., Houston, 1980-82; sr. clin. med. officer Hammersmith and Fulham Health Authority, London, 1982-83; cons. pediatrician Kingston (Eng.) Hosp., 1983, Northwick Park Hosp., London, 1983; rsch. pediatrician Charing Cross Hosp. Med. Sch., London, 1984-85; clin. lectr. Inst. Child Health, London, 1985-88; attending pediatrician and epidemiologist Children's Meml. Hosp., Chgo., 1989-96; attending pediatrician Jacobi Hosp., Bronx, N.Y., 1996—. Fellow Am. Acad. Pediat.; mem. Ambulatory Pediat. Assn. Office: Albert Einstein Coll Medicine Nurses Residence 7 S 12 1300 Morris Park Ave Bronx NY 10461-1926

SEO, CHRISTINE C. real estate broker; b. Korea, Nov. 6, 1952; d. Lim and Whang; m. Paul Y. Seo, July 3, 1951; children: Clara, Karen, Christine. Diploma in Nursing, Presbyn. Sch. Nursing, Taekoo, Korea, 1975. RN N.Y.; lic. real estate broker N.Y. Nurse Flushing Hosp., N.Y.C., 1979—85; real estate broker Giant Realty, Great Neck, NY, 1985—. Tchr. adult English class, deaconess Korean Presbyn. Ch. of Queens, Flushing, 2003—. Home: 20 Westwoods Rd Great Neck NY 11020 Office: Giant Realty 420 Northern Blvd Great Neck NY 11021-4800

SEPULVEDA, SONJA MARIAN ATKINSON, choral director, accompanist; b. Lancaster, S.C., May 15, 1952; d. Leo Laten and Mary Lou Hatfield Atkinson; m. Juan Pablo Sepulveda, June 10, 1972; children: Dru Adrian, Brys Kristofer. MusB in Edn., Winthrop U., Rock Hill, S.C., 1974; MusM in Choral Conducting, Winthrop U., 1975. Cert. tchr. music edn., choral edn. S.C., 1975. Choral dir. Wilder Fine Arts and Elem. Sch., Sumter, SC, 1975—81, Sumter H.S., SC, 1981—99, Clarendon Sch. Dist. 1, Summerton, SC, 2000—02, DuBose Mid. Sch., Summerville, SC, 2002—. Choral dir. Palmetto Choirs, Sumter, 2000—; choral dir. and organist St. John Meth. Ch., Sumter, 2002—; dance tchr. Freed Spirits Dance Co., Sumter, 1979—89; piano tchr., Sumter, 1975—81; music edn. tchr. U. S.C., Sumter, 1979—83; choral dir. First Presbyn. Ch., Sumter, 1985—2001, Shaw Heights Bapt. Ch., Sumter, SC, 1978—81, Crosswell Bapt. Ch., Sumter, 1965—78. Composer: (musical) Robin Hood. Named SC. Outstanding Educator of the Yr., Jaycees, 1987, Tchr. of the Yr., Wilder Elem. Sch., 1981; recipient Ivey Reuben Edn. award, NAACP, 1990, Paul Harris fellow, Rotary Internat., 1992. Mem.: PTA (life), Music Educators Nat. Conf. (chmn. S.C. all state com. 1994—98), Am. Choral Dirs. Assn. (jazz choir chmn. S.C. 1995—96), Delta Kappa Gamma (music chmn. 1991—2002). R-Consevative. Presbyterian. Achievements include Choral Director for mini seriesNorth and South; Singer in the Robert Shaw Festival Chorus, 1991-1997; Solo performance at the Lincoln Center; Montreat Chamber Singer, 1988-2001; Singer in the National American Choral Directors Multicultural Choir, 2001; Solo performance for the National Television in Mexico. Avocations: travel, bicycling. Home: 618 Antlers Dr Sumter SC 29150 Office: DuBose Middle School 1000 DuBose School Rd Summerville SC 29483 Personal E-mail: sonjasepulveda@hotmail.com.

SERAJI-BOZORGZAD, NASRINE, architecture educator; b. Tehran, Iran, 1957; Bachelor's, Yale U., 1978; diploma, Archtl. Assn. Sch., London, 1983; MArch, Harvard U., 1985. Instr. study abroad program U. Toronto; founder Atelier Seraji; prof. and dir. Meisterschulen fur Architektur Akademie der Bildenden Kunste, Vienna; instr. Archtl. Assn. Sch., London; chair Coll. Arch., Art and Planning Cornell U., 2001—. Prin. works include Temporary Am. Cultural Ctr., Paris, 1991, Pavilion of Caverne du Dragon in Chemin des Dames, Aisne, France, 1996—98. Home: 11 Rue Des Arquebusiers 75003 Paris France Office: Coll Arch Art and Planning Cornell U 129 Sibley Dome Ithaca NY 14853

SERATTI, LORRAINE M. state legislator; b. Oct. 30, 1949; V.p. Wis. Fedn. Taxpayers Orgn.; pres. Florence County Taxpayers Alliance; Wis. state assemblywoman dist. 36, 1992—. Small bus. owner. Mem. Florence Hist. Soc. Mem. NRA. Republican. Address: HC 2 Box 588 Florence WI 54121-9620 Office: Wis Assembly PO Box 8952 Madison WI 53708-8952

SERBUS, PEARL SARAH DIECK, freelance writer, former editor; b. Riverdale, Ill. d. Emil Edwin and Pearl (Kaiser) Dieck; m. Gerald Serbus, Jan. 26, 1946 (dec. Aug. 1969); children: Allan Lester, Bruce Alan, Curt Lyle. Home econs. staff, writer Chgo. Herald Examiner, 1934-39; operator test kitchen Household Sci. Inst., Mdse. Mart, Chgo., 1940-45; free-lance writer grocery chains Chgo., 1945-49; Riv.-Dolton corr. Calumet Index, Chgo., 1953-58, editl. asst., 1958-60, asst. editor, 1960-68, editor, 1968-72; with Suburban Index, Chgo., 1959-72, editor, 1960-72; mng. editor Index Publs., 1972-74; freelance writer, 1974-94; ret., 1994. Vol. pub. rels. New Hope Sch., 1959-67; bd. dirs. United Fund Riverdale, Roseland Mental Health Assn., Thornton chpt. Am. Field Svc.; vol. cmty. rels. Ctrl. Ark. Radiation Therapy Inst., 1984—. Vol. coll. and careers dept. Buffalo Grove H.S., 2000; vol. Omni Youth Svcs., 2001. Recipient Disting. Svc. Meml. scroll PTA, 1959, Sch. Bell award Ill. Edn. Assn., 1965, Outstanding Citizen award Chgo. South C. of C., 1972, Vol. citation Ctrl. Ark. Radiation Therapy Inst., 1994; named Outstanding Civic Leader Am. finalist, State and Nat. Communicator of Achievement award Ark. Press Women and Nat. Fed. of Press Women, 2003 Mem.: Chgo. South C. of C. (v.p., dir. 1970—74), Riverdale C. of C. (v.p. 1966—68), Nat. Fedn. Press Women (past pres., parley of past pres. state, past dir. protocol), Ark. Press Women (Communicator of Achievement award 1991, 2002, honored 55 Yr. Mem. 1999), Ill. Women's Press Assn. (past pres., Woman of Distinction 1968, recipient 46 state awards, 3 nat. awards). Home: 852 Stradford Cir Buffalo Grove IL 60089-3370

SEREBRENNIKOVA, EMILIYA, musician, educator; b. Kharkov, Ukraine, Sept. 27, 1944; came to the U.S., 1992; m. Vladimir Resnikovsky, Oct. 11, 1980 (div. Nov. 1994); m. Boris Zatulovsky, July 27, 1996. MA, St. Petersburg Conservatory, 1968, PhD, 1973. Cert. artist, prof. Concert pianist, piano tchr., San Francisco, 1992—. Mem. Nat. Assn. Profl. Music Tchrs., No. Calif. Fortnightly Music Club, Calif. Music Tchrs. Assn. Home: 255 S Rengstorff Ave Apt 67 Mountain View CA 94040-1738

SERIS, EILEEN JANICE, library information specialist; b. Lyon Station, Pa., Mar. 27, 1937; d. Henry Samuel and Anna Lenora (Schwoyer) Benner; m. Michael Carl Seris, July 21, 1962; children: David, Mark. BS, East Stroudsburg U., 1959; MS, Drexel U., 1960. Cert. tchr., N.Y., Colo. Libr. Ridgewood (N.J.) Sch. Dist., 1960-62, Tioga Ctrl. Schs., Tioga Center, N.Y., 1962-64; libr. info. specialist Weld County Sch. Dist. 6, Greeley, Colo., 1964—. Mem. ALA, NEA, Colo. Edn. Media Assn. (sec.), Colo. Edn. Assn., Greeley Edn. Assn. (rep.). Office: Weld County Sch Dist 6 1025 9th Ave Greeley CO 80631

SEROTA, SUSAN PERLSTADT, lawyer, educator; b. Chgo., Sept. 10, 1945; d. Sidney Morris and Mildred (Penn) Perlstadt; m. James Ian Serota, May 7, 1972; children: Daniel Louis, Jonathan Mark. AB, U. Mich., 1967; JD, NYU, 1971. Bar: Ill. 1971, D.C. 1972, N.Y. 1981, U.S. Dist. Ct. (no. dist.) Ill. 1971, U.S. Dist. Ct. (so. dist.) N.Y. 1981, U.S. Dist. Ct. (ea. dist.) N.Y. 1985, U.S. Ct. Claims 1972, U.S. Tax Ct. 1972, U.S. Ct. Appeals (D.C. cir.) 1972. Ptnr. Pillsbury Winthrop LLP, N.Y.C., 1982—. Adj. prof. Sch. Law, Georgetown U., Washington, 1974-75; mem. faculty Practicing Law Inst., N.Y.C., 1983—. Editor: ERISA Fiduciary Law, 1995, Supplement, 2003; assoc. editor Exec. Compensation Jour., 1973—75, dep. editor Tax Mgmt., Estate and Gift Taxation and Exec. Compensation, 1973—75, mem. editl. adv. bd. Benefits Law Jour., 1973—, Tax Mgmt. Compensation Jour., 1993—, mem. bd. editors ERISA and Benefits Law Jour., 1992—; contbr. articles to profl. jours. Fellow: Am. Coll. of Employee Benefits Counsel (dir., charter fellow), Am. Coll. Tax Counsel (regent); mem.: ABA (chmn. joint com. employee benefits 1987—88, taxation sect. 1991—92, vice-chair taxation sect. 1999—2001, chmn. com. employee benefits), Am. Bar Retirement Assn. (dir. 1994—, pres. 1999—2000), N.Y. State Bar Assn. (exec. com. tax sect. 1988—92), Internat. Pension and Employee Benefit Lawyers Assn. (co-chair 1993—95). Democrat. Office: Pillsbury Winthrop LLP 1540 Broadway New York NY 10036 E-mail: sserota@pillsburywinthrop.com.

SERRA, PATRICIA JANET, social services administrator; b. St. Louis, Mo., Aug. 9, 1933; d. Lewis John and Constance Loyola (Egan) Protheroe; m. Mauricio Tadeo, Sept. 3, 1960; children: Mauricio Antonio, Patricia Suzanne, Mark Lewis. BS, St. Louis U., 1955; MSW, San Jose (Calif.) State U., 1974. Social worker Associated Catholic Charities, New Orleans, 1956-61; med. social worker Charity Hosp., New Orleans, 1961-63; counselor City of New Orleans, 1963-64; child welfare worker City of San Francisco, 1964-66; social worker Cath. Social Svc., San Francisco, 1970-74; counselor Golden Gate Regional Ctr., 1974-76; case mgr. San Andreas Regional Ctr., San Jose, 1976-84; program mgr. United Cerebral Palsy Assn. Santa Clara, Mountain View, Calif., 1984—. Faculty field instr., San Jose State U., San Jose, 1985—. Recipient awards of recognition United Cerebral Palsy Assn. Santa Clara, San Mateo Counties, 1989, Bd. Suprs. County San Mateo, Calif., 1989, Spl. Tech. Ctr., Mountain View, Calif., 1991. Mem. Nat. Assn. Social Workers, Acad. Cert. Social Workers; lic. clin. Soc. Worker (LCSW). Republican. Roman Catholic. Avocations: travel, skiing, theater, reading. Home: 4556 Bald Eagle Way San Jose CA 95118-2019 Office: 480 San Antonio Rd Ste 215 Mountain View CA 94040-1218 E-mail: patlito@ix.netcom.com., pat@ucpscsm.org.

SERSTOCK, DORIS SHAY, retired microbiologist, educator, civic worker; b. Mitchell, SD, June 13, 1926; d. Elmer Howard and Hattie (Christopher) Shay; m. Ellsworth I. Serstock, Aug. 30, 1952; children: Barbara Anne, Robert Ellsworth, Mark Douglas. BA, Augustana Coll., 1947; postgrad., U. Minn., 1966-67, Duke U., summer 1969, Communicable Disease Ctr., Atlanta, 1972. Bacteriologist Civil Svc., S.D., Colo., Mo., 1947-52; rsch. bacteriologist U. Minn., 1952-53; clin. bacteriologist Dr. Lufkin's Lab., 1954-55; chief technologist St. Paul Blood Bank of ARC, 1959-65; microbiologist in charge mycology lab. VA Hosp., Mpls., 1968-93; ret. Instr. Coll. Med. Scis., U. Minn., 1970-79, asst. prof. Coll. Lab. Medicine and Pathology, 1979-93. Contbr. articles to profl. jours. Mem. Richfield Planning Commn., 1965-71, sec., 1968-71; extended ministries commn. Wood Lake Luth. Ch., Richfield, 1993-94; rep. religious coun. Mall Am., Bloomington, Minn., 1993-94; chief nursery caregiver Christ the King Luth. Ch., Bloomington, 1994-99, Hope Presbyn. Ch., Richfield, Minn., 1994-2003; mem. Rep. Presdl. Task Force, Nat. Rep. Senatorial Com., 1997. Fellow Augusta Coll.; named to Exec. and Profl. Hall of Fame; recipient Alumni Achievement award Augustana Coll., 1977, Superior Performance award VA Hosp., 1978, 82, Cert. of Recognition, 1988, Golden Spore awards Mycology Observer, 1985, 87, Congl. Order of Merit Nat. Rep. Congl. Com., 2003; name engraved on founders' wall Ronald Reagan Rep. Ctr., 2000; named Minn. Rep. of Yr. Nat. Rep. Congl. Com., 2003. Mem. Richfield Women's Garden Club (pres. 1959), Wild Flower Garden (chmn. 1961). Republican. Home: 7201 Portland Ave Minneapolis MN 55423-3218 E-mail: dsv9@juno.com.

SERTICH, KELLI ANN, land use planner; b. Riverside, Calif., Nov. 9, 1959; d. Robert Sr. and Lillian Patricia (Hale) S. AAS in Constrn. Drafting, Glendale C.C., 1981; BS in Design Urban Planning, Ariz. State U., 1983; MPA, Western Internat. U., 2002. Draftsman, facilities planner Washington Elem. Sch. Dist., Phoenix, 1980-83; planner various pvt. sector planning & archtl. firms, Phoenix, 1983-88, dir. planning & econ. devel. Town of Buckeye (Ariz.), 1988-93; dir. tourism & econ. devel. City of Williams (Ariz.), 1993-95; dir. cmty. devel., interim city mgr. City of Bisbee (Ariz.), 1995-98; sr. planner Cmty. Scis. Corp., Phoenix, 1998; sr. planner policy analyst Maricopa County Dept. Transp., Phoenix, 1998-2000; regional area planning mgr. Flood Control Dist. Maricopa County, Phoenix, 2000—. Pres. Bisbee Christmas in April, 1997; chmn. Ariz. Cmty. Found. Cochise Project Team, Bisbee, 1997; chmn. Buckeye Clean and Beautiful, 1989-93. Mem. Am. Planning Assn., Ariz. Planning Assn. (dir.-at-large 1993-2001, sec. 1994-99, pres. 2003—). Roman Catholic. Avocations: sewing, horseback riding, travel, gardening. Office: Maricopa County Flood Control 2801 W Durango St Phoenix AZ 85009-6357

SESSIONS, BETTYE JEAN, humanities educator; b. Jacksonville, FL, Jan. 29, 1934; d. John Henry and Willene Porter Hayes; m. Malcolm G.A. Sessions, July 7, 1956; children: Sabrina F., Malcolm G.A. II, Byron Craig. BA, Fla. A&M U., 1956; MAT, Jacksonville U., 1967. Tchr. English, humanities Duval County Pub. Schs., Jacksonville, Fla., 1957—72; prof. humanities Fla. C.C., Jacksonville, Fla., 1972—90; news corr. Fla. Times - Jacksonville Jour., 1981—86; profl. writer, author and poet Jean-Aubrey Ideas, Inc., Jacksonville, 1985—2001.

SESSIONS, JUDITH ANN, librarian, university library dean; b. Lubbock, Tex., Dec. 16, 1947; d. Earl Alva and Anna (Mayer) S. BA cum laude, Cen. Fla. U., 1970; MLS, Fla. State U., 1971; postgrad., Am. U., 1980, George Washington U., 1983. Head libr. U. S.C., Salkehatchie, 1974-77; dir. Libr. and Learing Resources Ctr. Mt. Vernon Coll., Washington, 1977-82; planning and systems libr. George Washington U., Washington, 1981-82, asst. univ. libr. for adminstrn. svcs., acting head tech. svcs., 1982-84; univ. libr. Calif. State U., Chico, 1984-88; univ. libr., dean of libr. Miami U., Oxford, Ohio, 1988—. Cons. Space Planning, SC, 1976, DataPhase Implementation, Bowling Green U., 1982, TV News Study Ctr., George Washington U., 1981; asst. prof. dept. child devel. Mt. Vernon Coll., 1978—81; mem., lectr. U.S.-China Libr. Exch. Del., 1986, 91; lectr., presenter in field; mem. coord. com. OhioLink Adv. Coun., 1995—2003, v.p., 1996—97, chair, 1998—2000; mem. gov. bd. OhioLink, exec. com., 1998—2001; mem. OCLC Users Coun., 1998—2001; convenor Pub. Acad. Libr. Group, 1999—2000; mem. OCLC Preservation Resources Interest Group, 1999—2001, chmn., 2001. Contbr. articles, book revs. to profl. jours. Trustee Christ Hosp., Cin., 1990-94, Deaconness Gamble Rsch. Ctr., Cin., 1990-94, OhioNet, 1990-94, treas. 1993; bd. dirs. Hamilton (Ohio) YWCA, 1994-98, pres., 1995-96, v.p., 1996-97, 97-98; mem. OCLC user's coun., 1998—; mem. steering com. Tri City Reading Initiative, 2002-03. Recipient award for outstanding contbn. D.C. Libr. Assn., 1979; rsch. grantee Mt. Vernon Coll., 1980; recipient Fulbright-Hayes Summer Travel fellowship to Czechoslovakia, 1991. Mem. ALA (Olofson award 1978, councillor-at-large policy making group 1981-94, coun. com. on coms. 1983-84, intellectual freedom com. 1984-88, directions and program rev. com. 1989-91, fin. and audit subcom. 1989-90, mem. exec. bd. 1989-94, mem. del. to Zimbabwe Internat. Book Fair 1997), Assn. Coll. and Rsch. Librs. (editorial bd. Coll. and Rsch. Librs. jour. 1979-84, nominations and appointments com. 1983-85, faculty status com. 1984-86), Libr. and Info. Tech. Assn. (chair legis. and regulation com. 1980-81), Libr. Adminstrn. and Mgmt. Assn. (bd. dirs. libr. orgn. and mgmt. sect. 1985-87), Calif. Inst. Librs. (v.p., pres. elect 1987-88), Mid-Atlantic Regional Libr. Fedn. (mem. exec. bd. 1982-84), Jr. Mems. Round Table (pres. 1981-82), Intellectual Freedom Round Table (sec. 1984-85), Freedom to Read Found. (trustee 1984-88, v.p. 1985-86, treas. 1986-87, pres. 1987-88), Rotary, Beta Phi Mu. Home: 45 Waters Way Hamilton OH 45013-6324 Office: Miami U Edgar W King Oxford OH 45056

SESSIONS, KATHRYN L. state legislator, educator; b. Jackson, Wyo., Feb. 13, 1942; widowed; 3 children. BS, Utah State U., 1970; MS, Leslie Coll., 1990. Educator, Wyo., 1970—; mem. Wyo. Ho. Reps., Cheyenne, 1992-98, Wyo. Senate, Dist. 7, Cheyenne, 1998—; mem. appropriations com. Wyo. Senate, Cheyenne, mem. rules and procedures. com. Mem. NEA, LWV, Wyo. Edn. Assn., Alpha Delta Kappa (edn. com.). Democrat. Mem. Lds Ch. Home: 930 Centennial Dr Cheyenne WY 82001-7407 Office: Wyo Senate State Capitol Cheyenne WY 82002-0001

SESSLER, DONNA JEAN HOTZ, secondary school educator; b. Iowa City, May 3, 1954; d. Raymond Louis and Marie Frances (Klouda) Hotz; m. Allen Henry Sessler, Aug. 8, 1992. BA in Psychology, U. Iowa, 1975; MA in Spl. Edn., U. No. Iowa, 1981. Multicategorial resource tchr. grades 6-12 Beaman-Conrad-Liscomb Community Schs., Conrad, Iowa, 1978-84; multicategorial resource tchr. grades 6-8 Iowa Falls (Iowa) Community Sch., 1984—. Mem. NEA, Iowa Pollettes (sec. 1995-97), Iowa Falls Edn. Assn. (negotiations team 1988-90), Iowa Edn. Assn., Coun. for Exceptional Children. Roman Catholic. Avocations: painting, writing, walking. Office: Riverbend Mid Sch 1124 Union St Iowa Falls IA 50126-1435 Home: 2008 Winston Pl Waterloo IA 50701-9462

SESTANOVICH, MOLLY BROWN, writer; b. Denver, Nov. 30, 1921; d. Ben Miller and Mary (McCord) Brown; m. Stephen Nicholas Sestanovich, July 9, 1949; children: Stephen, Mary, Robert Benjamin. Student, Fairmont Jr. Coll., 1939-41. Radio comml. writer Young & Rubicam Advt., N.Y.C. and Hollywood, Calif., 1941-47; radio scriptwriter Korean Broadcasting Co., Seoul, 1947-48; substitute tchr. County Sch. Bd., Montgomery County, Md., 1956-58; syndicated polit. columnist Lesher Newspapers, various locations, 1971-91; freelance polit. writer Moraga, Calif., 1991—. Active internat. women's orgns., Italy, Thailand, Singapore, Finland, Venezuela, 1949-70. Writer LWV, Diablo Valley, Calif., 1970, 91. Recipient prize for contbn. to cause of peace and justice Mt. Diablo Peace Ctr., 1989. Mem. Am. Fgn. Svc. Assn., Lamorinda Dem. Club (program chmn. 1985). Unitarian Universalist. Avocations: genealogy, gardening. Home: 15 Idlewood Ct Moraga CA 94556-1107 E-mail: mollynsteve@cs.com.

SETLOW, JANE KELLOCK, biophysicist; b. N.Y.C., Dec. 17, 1919; d. Harold A. and Alberta (Thompson) Kellock; m. Richard Setlow, June 6, 1941; children— Peter, Michael, Katherine, Charles. BA, Swarthmore Coll., 1940; PhD in Biophysics, Yale U., 1959. With dept. radiology Yale U., 1959-60; with biology div. Oak Ridge Nat. Lab., 1960-74; biophysicist Brookhaven Nat. Lab., Upton, N.Y., 1974—. Mem. recombinant DNA molecule program adv. com. NIH, chmn., 1978-80 Author articles; mem. editorial bd. jours. Predoctoral fellow USPHS, 1957-59; postdoctoral fellow, 1960-62 Mem. Biophys. Soc. (pres. 1977-78), Am. Soc. Microbiology. Democrat. Home: 57 Valentine Rd Shoreham NY 11786-1243 Office: Biology Dept Brookhaven Nat Lab Upton NY 11973

SETLOW, NEVA DELIHAS, artist, research biologist; b. New Haven, Dec. 29, 1940; d. Nevins Donald and Eve Mary (Kokojan) Cummings; m. Nicholas Delihas, Aug. 21, 1961 (div. 1986); m. Richard Burton Setlow, Mar. 3, 1989; children: Nicholas Delihas, Marcia Hermus, Cynthia DiGiacomo. BA, Empire State Coll., 1975. Rschr. Brookhaven Nat. Lab., Upton, N.Y., 1976-96. Exhibited in group shows at Guild Hall, East Hampton, 1985—98, Ward Nasse Gallery, N.Y.C., 1993, Islip Art Mus., 1993, 1996, Planetary Art Soc., Pasadena, Calif., 1997, Salon des Femmes, Southampton, 1997, The Islip (N.Y.) Mus., 1997, Faber Biren Color Award Show, Stamford, Conn., 1997, Smithtown Arts Coun., 1998, Elaine Benson Gallery, Bridgehampton, N.Y., 1999, Broome St. Gallery, N.Y.C., 1999—2002, Islip Art Mus., 2000, Shelter Rock Art Gallery, Manhasset, N.Y., 2000, Faber Biren Color Award Show, Stamford, Conn., 2001, Gallery at Edison, Piqua, Ohio, 2001, Huntington Arts Coun., Melville, N.Y., 2001, Grounds for Sculpture, N.J., 2001, Binney and Smith Gallery, Bethlehem, Pa., 2002, East End Arts Coun. (Contact!), Riverhead, N.Y., 2003. Recipient Purchase prize, Berkshire Art Assn., Pittsfield, Mass., 1972, 25th Anniversary award, Silvermine Art Guild, New Canaan, Conn., 1972, Sculpture award, Huntington Twp. Art League, 1974, 1976, Painting award, North Shore Art Guild, 1996, Am. Icon - Outer Space award, Nat. Assoc. of Women Artists, 2001, Cleo Hartwig award, 2002. Mem.: Am. Soc. of Contemporary Artists, Nat. Assoc. of Women Artists, Internat. Scupture Coun. Home: 4 Beachland Ave East Quogue NY 11942-4941 Personal E-mail: setlow@optonline.net.

SETLOW, VALERIE PETIT, health science association director; b. New Orleans, Jan. 24, 1950; d. Alvin Joseph and Lorraine Catherine (Kelly) Petit; m. Loren William Setlow, June 26, 1976; children: Daniel Lawrence, Craig Anthony. BS, Xavier U. La., 1970; PhD, Johns Hopkins U., 1976. Dir. policy USPHS, Washington, 1990-92, dept. dir., 1992, asst. dir. nat. aids policy office, 1992-93; dir. health scis. policy Inst. Medicine Nat. Acad. Scis., Washington, 1993-98; dep. dir. Tulane/Xavier Ctr. Bio-Environ. Rsch., New Orleans, 1998—. Cons. NIH, Fairfax County Schs. Contbr. articles to profl. jours. Mem. AAAS, Am. Soc. Biochemists and Molecular Biologists. Avocations: quilting, gardening. Office: Tulane/Xavier Ctr Bio-Environ Rsch 1430 Tulane Ave # Sl3 New Orleans LA 70112-2699

SETO, JUDITH ROBERTS, publishing executive; d. Henry and Becca Alexander Roberts; m. Thomas Akiyoshi Seto, June 13, 1964; children: William, Marc, Daniel, Marianne. BA in English with honors, Cornell U., 1956; MFA, Bklyn. Coll., 1981; MS, Adelphi U., 1986. Tchr., dir. Midwood Drama Workshop, Bklyn., 1971—79; tchr. acting Bklyn. Coll. Prep. Ctr., Bklyn., 1979—83; tchr. NYC Bd. Edn., Bklyn., 1983—95; prodr., actor Mostly Matinees, NYC, 1995—96; tchr., dir. Intergenerational Actors Creative Theatre, NYC, 1996—; prodr., pub. Scheherazade AudioVisions, Bklyn., 1997—. Author: The Young Actors' Workbook, 1979, 1984, (audio play) Forbidden Fruit, 2000; narrator (audio book) The Good Friday Murder, 1997. Mem.: Dramatists Guild (assoc.). Democrat.

SETSER, CAROLE SUE, food science educator; b. Warrenton, Mo., Aug. 26, 1940; d. Wesley August and Mary Elizabeth (Meine) Schulze; m. Donald Wayne Setser, June 2, 1969; children: Bradley Wayne, Kirk Wesley, Brett Donald. BS, U. Mo., 1962; MS, Cornell U., 1964; PhD, Kans. State U., 1971. Grad. asst. Cornell U., Ithaca, N.Y., 1962-64; instr. Kans. State U., Manhattan, 1964-72, asst. prof., 1974-81, assoc. prof., 1981-86, prof., 1986-2001, prof. emeritus, 2001—. Vis. prof. Bogazici U., Istanbul, Turkey, 2000—01. Recipient Rsch. Excellence award Coll. of Human Ecology, Manhattan, 1990. Mem.: Inst. Food Techs. (chmn. sensory evaluation divsn. edn. com. 1989—92, continuing edn. com. 1992—95, sec. product devel. divsn. 1997—99, also other offices), Am. Assn. Cereal Chemists (assoc. editor 1989—93), Kappa Omicron Nu (Excellence for Rsch. award 1987), Sigma Xi, Phi Tau Sigma (Outstanding Food Scientist 1998), Gamma Sigma Delta, Phi Upsilon Omicron, Phi Kappa Phi (Scholar award 1998). E-mail: setser@ksu.edu.

SETSER, PATRICIA A. music educator; b. Kansas City, Mo., June 29, 1951; d. Flo Daulton and George Sterling Waugh; m. Michael W. Setser, Sept. 9, 1972. MusB Edn., Ctrl. Mo. State U., 1973, MA in Music Edn., 1978. Cert. tchr.,Life - Instrumental Music K-12, History K-8 Mo., 1973. Coord. instrumental music North Kansas City Sch. Dist., Mo., 1996—; band dir. Winnetonka H.S., Kansas City, Mo., 1983—. Guest condr., adjudicator Heart of Am. Wind Symphony, Mo., 1978—; musician Kansas City Wind Symphony, Shawnee Mission, Kans., 2002—, Heart of Am. Wind Symphony, Parkville, Mo., 2001—. Condr. (music contest) Nat. Adjudicators Nat. Festival, Va. (Grand Champions, 2002), Chgo. Music Festival (Grand Champions, 2000), St. Louis Music Festival (Grand Champions, 2001), instr. (tchg.) Tchg. (Excellence in Tchg. Award, 1994), condr. (orch. condr.) State Contest (First Pl. Ratings), band condr. (conducting) State Music Contests (First Pl. Ratings - all years); composer: (entry level jazz for young band students) Musical composition. Bd. mem. Warrensburg Cmty. Band, Mo., 2001—. Recipient Sword of Honor, Sigma Alpha Iota, 1974. Mem.: Mo. Music Educators Assn. (assoc.), Music Educators Nat. Conf. (assoc.), Am. Quarter Horse Assn. (assoc.), Epsilon Omega - Sigma Alpha Iota (assoc.; pres, v.p, sec. 1970—73, Sword of Honor - Leadership 1973). Avocations: antique automobiles, gardening, genealogy. Office: North Kansas City Sch Dist 1950 NE 46th St Kansas City MO 64116 E-mail: psetser@nkcsd.k12.mo.us.

SETTERLUND, TINA A.M. music educator; b. Belleville, Ill., Mar. 3, 1955; d. William L. and Elizabeth A. Marietta; m. D. Phillip Setterlund, Dec. 29, 1973 (div.); children: Reid, Lauren; m. Grady A. White, Dec. 21, 1992. AA, Belleville Area Coll., 1987; B in Music Edn., So. Ill. U., 1989. Music dir. St. John U. C.C., Mascoutah, Ill., 1971—; tchr. High Mt. Sch., Swansea, Ill., 1989—95; dir. vocal music Belleville (Ill.) East H.S., 1995—. Dir. Belleville Philharm. Chorale, 1983—91; asst. dir., accompanist Masterworks Children's Chorale, Belleville, 1990—95; dir. Metro-East Cmty. Chorale, Belleville, 1991—94. Mem.: St. Clair County Music Dirs. Assn., Music Educators nat. Conf., Ill. Music Educators Assn., Pi Kappa Lambda (Excellence in Tchg. award 2003). Avocations: interior decorating, reading, gardening, harp. Home: 57 W State Mascoutah IL 62258 Office: Belleville East HS 2555 W Blvd Belleville IL 62221

SETTLES, HOLLY ARLENE (HOLLY WOLOSZYK), microbiologist; b. Chgo., Jan. 19, 1960; d. Leonard Benedict and Dorothy Elaine (Wegehenkel) Woloszyk. BS, U. Ill., 1982. Registered microbiologist. Quality control technician G.D. Searle Pharm., Mount Prospect, Ill., 1982-83, Am. Hosp. Supply, McGaw Park, Ill., 1983-84; sr. technician R & D G.D. Searle, Skokie, Ill., 1984-86, microbiologist R & D, 1986-87, supr. microbiology svcs. R & D, 1987-89; sr. microbiologist Intermedics, Inc., Freeport, Tex., 1989-92; microbiologist Eli Lilly and Co., Indpls., 1992—. Avocations: gourmet cooking, music. Home: 3320 W 42nd St Indianapolis IN 46228 2810 Office: Eli Lilly and Co Lilly Corp Ctr Indianapolis IN 46285-0001

SETZER, ARLENE J. state representative, retired secondary school educator; b. Dayton, Ohio, Mar. 2, 1944; BS in Bus. Adminstrn., U. Dayton, 1966; MEd, Wright State U., 1973. Tchr. Vandalia-Butler HS, 1967—2000; rep. Ohio State Ho. Reps., Columbus, 2000—. Mem. agr. and natural resources com. Ohio State Ho. Reps., chmn. edn. com., mem. energy and environ. com., mem. ins. com., vice chmn. mcpl. and govt. and urban revitilization com. Mem. ins. rev. com. City of Vandalia, 1998—2000, chair Vandalia-Butler Food Pantry Bldg. Fund; pres. Pres.'s Club of Vandalia, 1997—99; precinct capt. Montgomery County Rep. Party, mem. ctrl. com., exec. com.; mem. Vandalia City Coun., vice-mayor, 1986—88, 1995—2000. Named Rep. Woman of Yr., 1997, 2001, 2003; recipient Clara Weisenborn award, 1999, Horace M. Huffman Jr. Svc. to Bicyclists award, Ohio Bicycle Fedn., Appreciation award, S.W. Ohio Hemophilia Found. and W. Ctrl. Ohio Hemophilia Ctr.; scholar Martha Holden Jennings scholar, 1983—84. Mem.: Sister Cities of Vadalia, Montgomery County Farm Bur., Inc., Montgomery County Cattlemen's Assn., Montgomery Agrl. Soc., Miami Valley Mil. Affairs Assn., Vandalia-Butler (Ohio) Hist. Soc. (v.p. 2000), Rotary (hon.; Dist. 6670 dir. 1992—96, pres. 1994—95, Dist. 6670 scholarship com. 1997, Dist. 6670 bd. dirs., asst. dist. gov. 1998—2000, named to Hall of Fame). Republican. Office: Ohio State House of Reps 77 South High Street 13th Floor Columbus OH 43215-6111

SEURKAMP, MARY PAT, college president; b. Pitts., Sept. 6, 1946; d. Frank H. and Loretta (Husic) Reuwer; m. Robert W. Seurkamp, Aug. 6, 1983; children: Kris, Robert, Brooke. BA, Webster U., 1968; MA, Washington U., 1969; PhD, SUNY, Buffalo. Counselor to dir. student living Gannon U., Erie, Pa., 1969-76; assoc. v.p. St. John Fisher Coll., Rochester, N.Y., 1976-92, adj. asst. prof. dept. psychology, 1992—, acting v.p. academic affairs, dean, 1992-98; pres. Coll. of Notre Dame of Md., Balt., 1998—. Mem. planning team Monroe County Ednl. Outcomes Conf.; bd. dirs. Bishop Kennedy High Sch.; cons. Women's Career Ctr., Rochester, N.Y., 1987—. Com. mem. various parish coms., Pittsford, N.Y., 1983—, Diocesan Com. Devel. of Mins. and Employees, Rochester, 1986 89, Internat. Alliance Leadership Conf., 1991; mentor Career Beginnings Program; vol. Career Connections Mentoring Program, 1988-90. Mem. AAUP, Am. Assn. High Edn., Nat. U. Continuing Edn. Assn., Rochester Women's Network. Republican. Roman Catholic. Home: 5502 Lombardy Pl Baltimore MD 21210-1420 Office: Coll Notre Dame Md 4701 N Charles St Baltimore MD 21210-2404

SEVEL, FRANCINE, advocate, researcher; d. Morris and Harriet Sevel; 1 child, Drew. BA, Miami U., Oxford, Ohio, 1976; MA, Ohio State U., 1977, PhD, 1981. Asst. prof. Ohio State U., Columbus, 1984—91; publs. editor Nat. Regulatory Rsch. Inst., Columbus, 1992—96, rsch. assoc., 1996—99, sr. rsch. assoc., 1999—2001, consumer affairs program manager, 2001—. Editor: (journal) NRRI Quar. Bull., author public policy reports: consumer issues. Grad. Leadership Columbus, Columbus, Ohio, 2000—01; bd. mem. Nat. Low-Income Energy Consortium, Washington, 2003—; com. mem. Nat. Assn. of Regulatory Utility Commissioners Staff Subcom. on Consumer Affairs, Washington, 1996—2003; pub. policy panel chair Commn. on Interprofl. Edn. and Practice, Columbus, Ohio, 1988—92. Rsch. grantee, US Dept. HHS, 1988—91, Tandy Corp., 1984. Mem.: Hadassah (co-v.p. membership, Columbus chpt. 2003). Jewish. Achievements include research in consumer affairs issues within the field of public utility regulation; regarding problems of high energy bills and low-income consumers; Regarding Health Promotion And Disease Prevention; Regarding Prevention Of Family Violence. Avocations: crafts, cooking, travel, graphic arts, Judaism. Office: Nat Regulatory Rsch Inst 1080 Carmack Rd Columbus OH 43210 E-mail: sevel.1@osu.edu.

SEVELY, MARIA, architect; b. Ankara, Turkey, Sept. 28, 1957; d. Marvin and Josephine (Lowndes) S. BArch, Tulane U., 1978; student, Harvard U., 1980—82, Wellesley Coll., R.I. Sch. Design. Designer with August Perez & Assocs., New Orleans, 1977, Curtis & Davis/Daniel Mann Johnson & Mendenhall, New Orleans, 1978-80; with Richard Meier & Ptnrs., N.Y.C., 1981-82, Bruner/Cott & Assocs., Cambridge, Mass., 1985; project designer Sasaki Assocs., Boston, 1985—91; project designer, assoc. Akira Yamashita & Assocs., Boston, 1992-95; sr. architect, designer Pei Cobb Freed & Ptnrs., N.Y.C., 1996-98; project architect Philip Johnson/Alan Ritchie Archs., N.Y.C., 1999—. Archtl. projects include Piazza d'Italia, New Orleans, 1977, One Magazine Square (AIA Honor award 1979), New Orleans, La Regie Renault, Paris, 1981, Windsor Place, Boston, 1985, Holyoke (Mass.) C.C., 1985, Sage Labs., Natick, Mass., 1986, Corp. Ctr., Boston, 1986, Resort at Ocean Edge (AIA/Boston Soc. Archs. PRISM Gold award 1987,

Builders' Choice award 1987), Cape Cod, Dartmouth Park housing, Marborough, Mass., 1987, U.S. Holocaust Meml. Mus., Washington, Cathedral of Hope, Dallas. Mem. AIA (assoc., N.Y. chpt. dialogue com. 1996—, vice chair 2000—), The Copley Soc. (fresh paint artists 1993, 94). Home: 5 Tudor City Pl New York NY 10017-6853 Office: Philip Johnson/Alan Ritchie Archs 375 Park Ave New York NY 10152-0002 E-mail: msevely@ureach.com

SEVERANCE, JERI-LYNNE WHITE, elementary school educator; b. El Paso, Tex., Nov. 30, 1965; d. James Claude and Carol Ann (Magee) White; m. Scot Clark Severance, Dec. 30, 1989; children: Jacie, Jared. BA in Music Edn., Eckerd Coll., 1987; M in Music Edn., U. Tex., Austin, 1989. Cert. music K-12 Fla., English spkrs. of other langs.(ESOL) K-12, exceptional student edn. (ESE) K-12. Music tchr. Dunnellon (Fla.) H.S., 1989—90, Gateway H.S., Kissimmee, Fla., 1990—91, Grover C. Fields Middle Sch., New Bern, NC, 1991—92; pres-sch. tchr. 1st Alliance Ch., Orlando, Fla., 1992—93; fine arts tchr. Vanguard Sch., Lake Wales, Fla., 1993—94; music tchr. Midway Elem., Sanford, Fla., 1994—95; instr. Barry U., Orlando, Fla., 1995—97; music tchr. Pleasant Hill Elem., Kissimmee, 1995—98, tchr. exceptional student edn.., 1998—. Co-founder, co-chair Pleasant Hills Elem. Festival of Arts, Kissimmee; sch. rep. Osceola County Edn. in Park, Kissimmee; exceptional student edn. rep. child study com., Kissimmee. Pre-K choir dir. First United Meth. Ch., Kissimmee. Mem.: AAUW (sec., com. chair 1995—2001), Coun. for Exceptional Children (com. chair 2000—02), Phi Delta Kappa (mem. exec. bd. 2003—, com. chair 2003—04), Alpha Delta Kappa (chaplain, pres.-elect 1996—2002, pres. 2003—). Democrat. Methodist. Avocations: reading, sewing, dancing. Office: Pleasant Hill Elem Sch 1253 Pleasant Hill Rd Kissimmee FL 34741

SEVERSON, SALLY, meteorologist; married; 2 children. Student, No. Ill. U., U. Wis., Milw.; BS in Meteorology, Miss. State U. Meteorologist WISN, Milw., 1986—. Vol. Children's Hosp. of Wis. Avocations: hiking, bicycling, astronomy, boating. Office: WISN PO Box 402 Milwaukee WI 53201

SEVILLA-SACASA, FRANCES ALDRICH, bank executive; BA in Langs., U. Miami, 1977; MA in Internat. Mgmt., Am. Grad. Sch. Internat. Mgmt., 1978. Joined Bankers Trust, 1983; mng. dir. L.Am. pvt. banking Bankers Trust Internat. Pvt. Banking Group, Miami, Fla.; sr. v.p. pvt. client svcs. Lehman Bros., Miami, 1997—98; mng. dir. L.Am. pvt. bank divsn. Deutsche Bank; pres. Bankers Trust Internat. Pvt. Banking Corp., 1998—2000; mng. dir., S.E. region head Citibank Pvt. Bank, 2000—01; mng. dir., head L.Am. Citigroup, N.Y.C., 2001—, head Europe Citigroup Pvt. Bank, 2003—. Office: Citigroup Pvt Bank 153 E 53rd St New York NY 10043*

SEWALL, SARAH LEE, foundation administrator; BA, Harvard Coll.; MA, Oxford U. Assoc. dir. Am. Acad. Arts/Scis.; dep. asst. sec. defense Peacekeeping and Humanitarian Assistance, 1993-96; sr. foreign policy advisor Sen. George J. Mitchell, 1987-93. Vis. scholar Harvard Program on Negotiation, lectr. internat. affairs, Stanford U., Washington, D.C.; exec. bd. Women in Internat. Security. Recipient Rhoades scholar, Harvard Coll. and Oxford U. Office: Coun Livable World 110 Maryland Ave NE # 409 Washington DC 20002-5626

SEWARD, GRACE EVANGELINE, retired librarian; b. L.A., Feb. 2, 1914; d. William Henry and Maud Leuty (Elphingstone) Seward. BA, Calif. State, L.A., 1959; MLS, U. So. Calif., L.A., 1961. Cert. tchr. Calif. Page Los Angeles County Pub. Libr., San Gabriel, Calif., 1927-37, asst. branch libr., 1938-40; various clerical positions Zoss Constrn./Consol., San Diego, 1941-42; time keeper Cal Ship Constrn., Wilmington, Calif., 1942-45; turkey ranch mgr. Bagnard Turkey Ranch, Baldwin Park, Calif., 1945-47; filing clk. Union Hardware, L.A., 1947-49; libr. asst. Rosemead (Calif.) HS, 1949-60; libr. Anaheim (Calif.) Union HS, 1960-61; catalog head libr. Pasadena (Calif.) City Coll., 1961-79, libr. classifier, 1979-81; ret., 1981. Author: (bibliographies) Man and Environment, 1970, Black America, 1978, (index) American Rose Mag., 1989—90; editor: Bull. Rose Soc. Rose Parade, 1974—87, Bull. Rancho de Duarte Garden Club, Daisy Chain, 1996—. Mem.: Calif. Libr. Assn., Royal Nat. Rose Soc. (life), Pacific Rose Soc. (life Bronze Honor medal 2000), L.A. Rose Soc. (life Bronze Honor medal 1994), Am. Rose Soc. (life; life judge, cons. 1978—, elected dist. dir. Pacific S.W. 1985—88, Pacific S.W. Dist. Silver Honor medal 1991, Outstanding Dist. Judge award 1995), Calif. Garden Clubs (life; pres. Rancho de Duarte 1991—96), Beta Phi Mu (hon.). Avocations: rosarian, gardening, book collector. Home: 2397 Morslay Rd Altadena CA 91001-2715

SEWARD, JEAN ANN, physical therapist; b. Glumay, Ill., Sept. 5, 1946; d. Charles Virgil Otte Jr. and Elizabeth Jean Otte; m. Rudy Ray Seward, Sept. 6, 1969; children: Rudy Allyn, Erik Russell. B in Phys. Therapy, Quincy U., 1969; cert. in phys. therapy, Mayo Found. Sch. Phys. Theraphy. Staff therapist Dr.'s Meml. Hosp., Carbondale, Ill., 1969—71, Westgate Hosp., Denton, 1971—74; rehab. dir. Denton County Home Health Svc., Denton, Tex., 1974—80; rehab. coord., prenatal edn. coord. Flow Meml. Hosp., Denton, 1980—86; dir. agy. Trinity Home Health/Trinity Care Svcs., Denton, 1987—89; CEO Jean Seward P.T. Contract & Cons. Svcs., Denton, 1989—2001; pres. JSCCS Corp., Denton, 2001—. Pres. Srs. in Motion, Inc., Denton, 2003—. Contbr. articles to profl. jours. Sponsor, pres. Parkinsons and Caregiver's Together Support Group, Denton, 1996—2003; mem. Greater Denton Arts Coun., Denton, 2003. Recipient Phys. Therapist of Yr., Tex. Hospice Assn., 1994. Mem.: Work Friday, Denton C. of C., Am. Parkinsons Disease Assn., Dallas Parkinsons Soc., ex. Phys. Therapy Assn., Am. Phys. Therapy Assn. Democrat. Roman Catholic. Avocations: reading, travel. Office: JSCCS Corp 416 S Elm #104 Denton TX 76201 E-mail: jeanseward@verizon.com.

SEWARD, NANCY H. retired band director, composer; b. Henryetta, Okla., Aug. 9, 1930; d. Albert Louis and Grace Wood Heitmann; m. Raymond Kenneth Seward, Aug. 21, 1952 (dec. Dec. 1980); children: Steven Kenneth, Lynn Annette Seward Fryer. B Music Edn. cum laude, Ctrl. Meth. Coll., 1952; postgrad., U. Mich., 1952, U. Mo., Columbia, 1964, U. Mo., Kansas City, 1973-74. Band dir. Leavenworth (Kans.) pub. schs., 1952-54, Excelsior Springs (Mo.) pub. schs., 1954-58, Ruskin H.S., Hickman Mills, Mo., 1958-64, Ctrl. Meth. Coll., Fayette, Mo., 1964-66, Richmond (Mo.) pub. schs., 1967-81, Stet Pub. Schs., 1967-73, Polo (Mo.) pub. schs., 1982-90; ret., 1990. Dir. band in Tournament of Roses Parade, Pasadena, Calif., 1960, several televised half-time shows for Kansas City Chiefs football games, also Kansas City Royals and St. Louis Cardinals; adjudicator, clinician at festivals and contests in Midwest and Can., 1964—. Composer, arranger numerous works for concert bands. Recipient 2d pl. award Richmond Band, Internat. Youth and Music Festival, Vienna, Austria, 1981, disting. alumni award Ctrl. Meth. Coll., 1978; named to Mo. Bandmasters Hall of Fame, 1993. Mem. World Assn. for Symphonic Bands and Ensembles, Nat. Band Assn., Women Band Dirs. Internat., Mo. Bandmasters' Assn., Tex. Bandmasters' Assn., Music Educators Nat. Conf., Mo. Music Educators Assn., Phi Beta Mu, Avocations: reading, genealogy. Home and Office: 1204 N Ridge Ave Liberty MO 64068-1359

SEWELL, BETH PERRY, gas industry executive; Pres., CEO Perry Gas Cos., Inc., Houston, 1993—. Office: Perry Gas Cos Inc 952 Echo Ln Ste 450 Houston TX 77024-2781 E-mail: energy@perrygas.com.

SEWELL, BEVERLY JEAN, financial executive; b. Oklahoma City, July 10, 1942; d. Benjamin B. Bainbridge and Faith Marie (Mosier) Allision; m. Ralph Byron Sewell, Jan. 23, 1962; children: M. Timothy, Pamela J. Student, U. Okla., 1960-61, Jackson C.C., 1973-77; BA in Bus., Mesa Coll., 1982; cert., Coll. Fin. Planning, 1984, MS in Fin. Planning, 1994. Sole practice fin. planning, Grand Junction, Colo., 1985-87; fin. planner, broker Interpacific Investors Services, Grand Junction, 1987-88; investment broker A.G. Edwards & Sons, Inc., Grand Junction, 1988-92, v.p., 1992—. Mem. ctrl. com. Grand Junction Rep. Orgn., 1988; mem. Grand Junction Planning Commn., 1987-89; bd. dirs. Grand Junction Symphony, 1991-94, Downtown Devel. Authority, St. Mary's Hosp. Mem. Inst. Cert. Fin. Planners, Internat. Assn. Fin. Planning. Avocations: tennis, jogging. Office: A G Edwards & Sons Inc 501 Main St Grand Junction CO 81501-2607 Home: 884 Quail Run Dr Grand Junction CO 81505-8608

SEWELL, GLORIANA, piano teacher; b. Huntington, N.Y., June 6, 1948; d. Reavis Staggs and Evelyn (Vilches) Kurlowich; m. C. Eugene Sewell, Aug. 8, 1969; children: Keren Ligowski, Daniel Sewell. BA in Piano, Bob Jones U., 1970. Piano tchr. in pvt. practice, Santa Barbara, Calif., 1970-71, Sodus, N.Y., 1971-78; Suzuki piano tchr. in pvt. practice Quakertown, Pa., 1979-86, Milford Square, Pa., 1986—; Kindermusik tchr. Milford Square Music Studio, 1996—. Piano accompanist ch. choir Assembly of the Word, Milford Square, 1993—. Recipient Tchr. award for 1st Pl. Winner, Baldwin Jr. Keyboard Competition, 1985, 1992, 2000, Tchr. of Yr. award, 1989, award, Music Tchrs. Nat. Assn. Student Composition Competition, 1993, 1994, 2001, Tchr. award 1st Pl., Yamaha H.S. Keyboard Competition, 2002. Mem.: Dalcroze Soc. Am., Nat. Guild Piano Tchrs., Am. Orff-Schulwerk Assn., Kindermusik Educations Assn., Suzuki Assn. of Ams., Pa. Music Tchrs. Assn. (pres. Lehigh Valley chpt. 1991—92, co-dir. spring music festival 1997, v.p. 1999—2001, pres. 2001—03, immediate past pres. 2003—), Music Tchrs. Nat. Assn. (Disting. Svc. award 2003). Avocation: gardening. Home and Office: Milford Square Music Studio PO Box 199 2244 Milford Square Pike Milford Square PA 18935

SEWELL, LAURA J. POLLOCK, social worker; b. Zolfo Springs, Fla., May 9, 1962; d. Abraham and Catherine Rollins Pollock; m. Clinton James Sewell, May 18, 1991; children: Nkiru Amanda, Imani Katherine. BSW, Tuskegee U., 1987; MSW, Fordham U., 1992. Cert. social worker SUNY, Westbury, 1992; sch. social worker The State Edn. Dept., Westbury, 1995; acad. cert. social workers SUNY, N.Y.C., 1998. Counselor Alliance Counseling Ctr., Hempstead, N.Y., 1987-88; caseworker Harlem Hosp. Ctr., N.Y.C., 1988-90; social worker Louise Wise Svcs., N.Y.C., 1990-94, Queens Hosp. Ctr., Jamaica, N.Y., 1995-96. Rec. sec. Jericho Gardens Civic Assn., Westbury, 1997-99. Democrat. Mem. Church of Christ. Avocations: cooking, reading, gardening, shopping, helping others.

SEWELL, LISA, literature educator; d. George Joseph and Edith Philips Sewell. BA in Biology and Genetics, U. Calif., Berkeley, 1984; MA in English and Creative Writing, NYU, 1988; PhD in English Lit., Tufts U., 1998. Asst. prof. English Villanova (Pa.) U., 1998—. Resident Yaddo, MacDowell Colony, Tyrone Guthrie Ctr. Author: (book of poetry) The Way Out, 1998 (runner-up Beatrice Hawley award, 1997). Recipient Creative Writing award, Nat. Endowment for Arts, 2000, Achievement in Poetry award, The Leeway Found., 2001, Creative Writing award, Pa. Coun. on Arts, 2002; fellow, Fine Arts Work Ctr., Provincetown, 1996—97. Mem.: MLA, Associated Writing Programs, Am. Lit. Assn. Democrat. Jewish. Avocations: whitewater kayaking, bicycling. Office: Villanova Univ Dept English 800 Lancaster Ave Villanova PA 19085

SEWELL, VIOLA L. daycare administrator; b. Harrodsburg, Ky., Jan. 29, 1957; d. Raymond and Dorothy C. Houp; m. Garry Sewell, Feb. 25, 1978 (div. May 17, 1995); children: John Harrison, George. Cert. profl. devel. early childhood, U. Wis., 1997. With Home Day Care, Nicholasville, Ky., 1985—90, Kimberly Child Devel., Nicholasville, 1993—97; tchr. Nat. Acad., Lexington, Ky., 1990—93, Kids Connection Learning Ctr., Nicholasville, 1997—2000, dir., 2000—. Mem. Nat. Campaign Tolerance. Mem.: Nat. Child Care Assn., Nat. Assn. Early Young Child. Avocations: travel, gardening. Home: 209 Keene Crossing Dr Nicholasville KY 40356 Office: Kids Connection Learning Ctr 310 Southview Dr Nicholasville KY 40356

SEXTON, CAROL BURKE, consultant; b. Chgo., Apr. 20, 1939; d. William Patrick and Katharine Marie (Nolan) Burke; m. Thomas W. Sexton Jr., June 30, 1962 (div. June 1976); children: Thomas W., J. Patrick, M. Elizabeth. BA, Barat Coll., 1961; cert. legal, Mallinckrodt Coll., 1974. Tchr. Roosevelt High Sch., Chgo., 1961-63, St. Joseph's Sch., Wilmette, Ill., 1975-80; dir. Jane Byrne Polit. Com., Chgo., 1980-81; mgr. Chgo. Merc. Exch., 1981-84, sr. dir. govt. and civic affairs, 1984-87, v.p. pub. affairs, 1987-94, exec. v.p. corp. rels., 1995-2001. Mem. internat. trade an investment subcom. Chgo. Econ. Devel. Commn., 1989, 90. Bd. dirs. Chgo. Sister Cities, 1992—2000, Ill. Ambs., 1991—98, pres., 1994—98; bd. dirs., sec. Internat. Press Ctr., 1992—97, chmn. bd., 1994. Mem. Execs. Club of Chgo. (bd. dirs. 1992-2001), Chgo. Conv. and Tourism Bur. (sec. 1989-90, exec. com. 1987-2000, chmn.-elect 1990, chmn. 1991-92), Econ. Club of Chgo. Roman Catholic. Avocations: books, gardening, travel.

SEXTON, CHARLINE, secondary school educator; b. Kennett, Mo., Dec. 01; d. Charles Jerome and Dora Myrtle (Wilburn) Lemonds; m. Marcus L. Sexton, Mar. 3, 1939; children: Charolyn Linch, Dan Sexton, Marc Sexton, Elizabeth Morrison. BA with honors, U. Tex Arlington, 1969, MA, 1976. Tchr. English Ft. Worth I.S.D., 1969-83. Author: (mag.) Arlington Review, 1966. Lectr. various churches, Tex., Ark., Tenn., 1963-98. Mem. Ex Libris Book Review Club. Avocation: reading.

SEXTON, DIANA ELIZABETH, communications company executive; b. Hartford, Conn., Jan. 24, 1953; d. Donald E. and Johanna D. Sexton. BA, Smith Coll., 1974. Sales rep. The Archer Group, N.Y.C., 1974-81, sales mgr., 1981-86, v.p. mktg., 1986-92, The Arrow Group, Torrington, Conn., 1992-96, exec. v.p., 1996—. Mem. AAUW, Assn. for Profl. Women (v.p. 1996—), Women in the Arts, Mus. of Contemporary Arts, Wadsworth Atheneum. Avocations: watercolors, dance. Office: PO Box 2137 Torrington CT 06790-8137

SEXTON, JANICE LOUISE, artist; b. Milw., Oct. 23, 1951; d. Harry Kyle Smith and Elsie L. Dietz; m. Joseph J. Sexton, June 10, 2000; children: Troy J. Bortmess, Harmony S. Bortmess; m. James Francis Bortmess, Sept. 9, 1972 (div. June 4, 1982). Degree, John Robert Powers Sch. Modeling, 1970. Cert. nurse, Vis. Nurses Assn. Mass., 1994. Mgr., art instr. The Imagination Sta., Raynham, Mass., 1985—88; mgr. art dept. Ben Franklin Crafts, Reno, 1989—90; mgr., art instr. The Wisteria Vine, Westport, Mass., 1990—94; freelance artist Westport, 1994—. Art tchr. Bridgewater State Coll., West Bridgewater, Mass., 1987—88; staff artist The Folk Art Store, Westport, Mass., 1986—88; guest artist head table Ducks Unlimited Ann. Banquet, 1997, 98, Mass. Waterfowlers, 2000. National art competition, Waterfowl Stamp Competition, Dept. Fisheries and Wildlife (Nat. 2d Pl. award, 2001, Hon. Mention, 2002, 2003). Treas. Mass. State Arts Lottery Coun., Westport, 1988—90. Named to Anthology Of Top 50 Artists In So. Mass., New Bedford Art Forms, 2001; grantee, Mass. State Arts Lottery Coun., 1994, Helen Ellis Trust Fund, 1993, 2001. Mem.: Nat. Soc. Marine Artists (assoc.). Independent. Achievements include designer of Westport, Mass. first state flag since its incorporation in 1787. Avocations: swimming, gardening, walking, camping, running. Office: 193 Forge Rd Westport MA 02790 Personal E-mail: sextonartgallery@aol.com.

SEXTON, JEAN ELIZABETH, librarian; b. Boone, NC, June 24, 1959; d. Warren G. and Carol Jean (Smith) S. AA, Chowan Coll., Murfreesboro, N.C., 1979; AB, U. N.C., 1981, MLS, 1983. Cataloging libr. U. N.C. (formerly Pembroke State U.), 1983—89, coord. tech. svcs., 1989—92, asst. dir., coord. tech. svcs., 1992—2003, assoc. libr., coord. tech. svcs., 2003—. Cons. Whitaker Libr. Chowan Coll., 1989—2001. Editor Libr. Lines, 1992, 1998-; contbr. articles to profl. jours. Order of Silver Feather. Mem. NC Libr. Assn., Southeastern Libr. Assn., Am. Hemerocallis Soc., NC Zool. Soc., NC Aquarium Soc., Nat. Trust for Historic Preservation, Sandhills Daylily Club (sec.). Democrat. Baptist. Avocations: growing/breeding daylilies, collecting estate jewelry, needlework. Home: 8662 NC Highway 211 W Red Springs NC 28377-6036 Office: U NC Pembroke Sampson-Livermore Libr Pembroke NC 28372

SEYBERT, JOANNA, federal judge; b. Bklyn., Sept. 18, 1946; BA, U. Cin., 1967; JD, St. John's U., 1971. Bar: N.Y. 1972, U.S. Dist. Ct. (ea. and so. dists.) N.Y. 1973. Trial staff atty. Legal Aid Soc., N.Y.C., 1971-73, sr. staff atty. Mineola, N.Y., 1976-80; sr. trial atty. Fed. Defender Svc., Bklyn., 1973-75; bur. chief Nassau County Atty's Office, Mineola, 1980-87; judge Nassau County Dist. Ct., Hempstead, N.Y., 1987-92, Nassau County Ct., Mineola, 1992-94, U.S. Dist. Ct. (ea. dist.) N.Y., Uniondale, 1994—. Mem.: Nassau Lawyers Assn. (past pres.), Fed. Judges Assn. (v.p.), Theodore Roosevelt A. Inns of Ct. (past pres.), Suffolk County Bar Assn., Internat. Assn. Judges (del.). Office: 1034 Federal Plz Central Islip NY 11722-4443

SEYDOUX, GERALDINE, molecular biologist; BS, U. Maine, 1986; PhD in Molecular Genetics, Princeton U., 1991. Postdoctoral trainee Carnegie Instn. Washington, Balt., 1991—95; asst. prof. molecular biology and genetics Sch. Medicine Johns Hopkins U., Balt., 1995—. Recipient Jr. Faculty Rsch. award, Am. Cancer Soc., 1996, Searle Scholars award, 1997, Presdl. Early Career award for scientists and engrs., NIH, 1999; fellow, Packard Found., 1996, MacArthur Found., 2001; scholar Basil O'Connor Starter scholar, March of Dimes, 1996. Office: Johns Hopkins U Sch Medicine 725 N Wolfe St 1515 PCTB Baltimore MD 21205

SEYFERTH, VIRGINIA M. public relations executive; b. Detroit; BA, Grand Valley State U., Allendale, Mich. With pub. rels. dept. St. Jude Children's Rsch. Hosp., 1977-79, AMOCO Oil Co., 1979-81, Amway Corp., 1981-84; pres. Seyferth & Assocs., Inc., Grand Rapids, Mich., 1984—. Office: Seyferth & Assocs Inc Ste 202 40 Monroe Ctr NW Grand Rapids MI 49503

SEYFFARTH, LINDA JEAN WILCOX, corporate executive; b. Montour Falls, N.Y., May 10, 1948; d. Maurice Roscoe and Theodora (Van Tassell) Wilcox; m. P. Tomlin Agnew, June 29, 1991; 1 child by previous marriage, Kristin. BA magna cum laude, Syracuse (N.Y.) U., 1970; MBA with honors, NYU, 1977. Programmer Prudential Ins. Co., Newark, 1970-73; with Hoffmann-La Roche Inc., Nutley, N.J., 1973—, corp. controller, 1985-88, v.p., contr., 1989-95, v.p. fin., 1995-99, v.p., treas. U.S., 1999—. Bd. dirs. St. Barnabas Burn Found., West Orange, N.J.; vice chmn. Ind. Coll. Fund, Summit, N.J.; bd. dirs., treas. Glen Ridge (N.J.) Ednl. Found. Mem. Nat. Assn. Accts., Fin. Execs. Inst., Leadership N.J., Phi Beta Kappa, Beta Gamma Sigma. Office: Hoffmann-LaRoche Inc 340 Kingsland St Nutley NJ 07110-1199

SEYMOUR, DAWN YVONNE, manufacturing executive; b. Rochester, July 1, 1917; d. Arthur Julius Rochow and Marguerite Emeline Timme; m. William Edward Balden, May 20, 1944 (dec. Jan. 1946); 1 child, William ; m. A. Morton Seymour, June 23, 1956; children: A. Morton III, Elizabeth, Marguerite, Amie. BS, Cornell U., 1939. Instr. Coll. Home Econ., Cornell U., Ithaca, NY, 1939—41; home demonstration agent N.Y. State Ext. Svc., Ithaca, 1941—43; asst. to CEO Rochow Swirl Mixer Co., Inc., Rochester, 1946—72, CEO, 1972—82, advisor, 1982—2001. Author: (booklet) In Memoriam: Thirty-eight American Women Pilots, 1996. Bd. trustees Nat. Warplane Mus., Geneseo, NY, 1986—92; mem. Women in Flight, Ariz. Aerospace Found., Tucson, 1997—2003; co-chair Women in Flight, Ariz. Aviation Found., 2002; cons. Nat. Women's Hall of Fame, Seneca Falls, NY, 1982—; vol. Genesee Hosp., Rochester Civic Music. With Women Airforce Svc. Pilots USAAF, 1943—44. Named to, Ariz. Aviation Hall of Fame, 1999. Mem.: Order Daedalians, Ninety Nines, Women Airforce Svc. Pilots Inc. (pres., advisor, chair meml. com. 1982—2003). Avocations: flying, sailing, hiking, reading. Office: Rochow Inc 1900 University Ave Rochester NY 14610-0405

SEYMOUR, DOROTHY Z. See MILLS, DOROTHY

SEYMOUR, JANE, actress; b. Hillingdon, Middlesex, Eng., Feb. 15, 1951; came to U.S., 1976; d. John Benjamin and Mieke Frankenberg; m. David Flynn, July 18, 1981 (div. 1991); 2 children; m. James Keach, May 15, 1993; 2 children (twins). Student, Arts Ednl. Sch., London. Appeared in films Oh What A Lovely War, 1968, The Only Way, 1968, Young Winston, 1969, Live and Let Die, 1971, Sinbad and the Eye of the Tiger, 1973, Somewhere in Time, 1979, Oh Heavenly Dog, 1979, Lassiter, 1984, Head Office, Scarlet Pimpernel, Haunting Passion, Dark Mirror, Obsessed with a Married Woman, Killer on Board, The Tunnel, 1988, The French Revolution, Tochiny Wild Horses, 2002; TV films include Frankenstein, The True Story, 1972, Captains and The Kings, 1976 (Emmy nomination), 7th Avenue, 1976, The Awakening Land, 1977, The Four Feathers, 1977, Battlestar Galactica, Dallas Cowboy Cheerleaders, 1979, Our Mutual Friend, PBS, Eng., 1975, Jamaica Inn, 1982, Sun Also Rises, 1984, Crossings, 1986, Keys to Freedom, Angel of Death, 1990, Praying Mantis, 1993; A Passion for Justice: The Hazel Brannon Smith Story, 1994; Broadway appearances include Amadeus, 1980-81, I Remember You, 1992, Matters of the Heart, 1991, Sunstroke, 1992, Praying Mantis, 1993, Heidi, 1993; TV mini-series include East of Eden, 1980, The Richest Man in the World, 1988 (Emmy award), The Woman He Loved, 1988, Jack the Ripper, 1988, War and Remembrance, 1988, 89; host PBS documentary, Japan, 1988; TV series: Dr. Quinn: Medicine Woman, 1993-98 (Emmy nomination, Lead Actress - Drama, 1994, 98, Golden Globe award 1996), A Marriage of Convenience, CBS, 1998, A Memory in My Heart, CBS, 1999, Murder in the Mirror, CBS, 2000, Enslavement: The True Life Story of Fanny Kemble, Showtime, 2000, Blackout, CBS, 2000, Yesterday's Children, CBS, Dr. Quinn Winters Heart, 2001, Heart of a Stranger, 2002; author: Jane Seymour's Guide to Romantic Living, 1986, Two at a Time, 2001; co-author: Yum, Splat, 1998, Boing, 1999. Decorated Order Brit. Empire; recipient OBE award, 2000; named Hon. Citizen of Ill., Gov. Thompson, 1977. Mem. Screen Actors Guild, AFTRA, Actors Equity, Brit. Equity. Office: Guttman Assocs 118 S Beverly Dr Ste 201 Beverly Hills CA 90212-3016

SEYMOUR, LESLEY JANE, magazine editor-in-chief; b. San Juan, P.R. BA, Duke U., 1978. Reporter Women's Wear Daily, 1978, N.Y. Daily News Tonight, 1981—82; writer, sr. editor Vogue Mag., 1982—91; beauty dir. Glamour Mag., 1994—97; editor-in-chief YM/Young & Modern, N.Y.C., 1997—98, Redbook, 1998—2001, Marie Claire mag., N.Y.C., 2001—. Office: Marie Claire 1790 Broadway New York NY 10019*

SEYMOUR, LISA, museum director; b. Oct. 30, 1962; m. E. David Seymour. BA in Mass Comms., U. Denver, 1984; MA in Mass Comms., 1985. Grad. teaching asst. U. Denver, 1985; records clk. typist Kingman (Ariz.) Police Dept., 1985-86; sec. First Presbyn. Ch., Elko, Nev., 1986-87; exec. dir. Elko (Nev.) County Against Domestic Violence, 1987; exec. dir. of found. Elko (Nev.) Gen. Hosp. Found., 1989-90; mgr. cmty. rels. Elko (Nev.) Gen. Hosp., 1987-90; adtg. mgr. Elko (Nev.) Ind., 1990-91, newspaper editor, reporter, photographer, 1991-94; archivist and oral historian Northeastern Nev. Mus., Elko, 1994-95; interim mus. adminstr., 1995; mus. dir., 1996-99. Grantee Newmont Gold Co., E.L. Cord Found., E.L. Wiegard Found., 1996. Office: c/o Northeastern Nev Mus 1515 Idaho St Elko NV 89801-4021

SEYMOUR, STEPHANIE, model; b. San Diego, July 23, 1968; children: Dylan, Peter Jr., Harry. Appeared on the covers of Vogue, Elle, Cosmopolitan, Allure, Marie Claire; featured in comml. Diet Coke, Victoria's Secret,

L'Oreal; worked with Helmut Newton, Herb Ritts, Francesco Scavullo, Irving Penn, Albert Watson, Arthur Elgort, Richard Avedon. Office: IMG Models 304 Park Ave S Ph N New York NY 10010-5339

SEYMOUR, STEPHANIE KULP, federal judge; b. Battle Creek, Mich., Oct. 16, 1940; d. Francis Bruce and Frances Cecelia (Bria) Kulp; m. R. Thomas Seymour, June 10, 1972; children: Bart, Bria, Sara, Anna. BA magna cum laude, Smith Coll., 1962; JD, Harvard U., 1965. Bar: Okla. 1965. Practice, Boston, 1965—66, Tulsa, 1966—67, Houston, 1968—69; assoc. Doerner, Stuart, Saunders, Daniel & Anderson, Tulsa, 1971—75, ptnr., 1975—79; judge U.S. Ct. Appeals (10th cir.) Okla., Tulsa, 1979—94, 2000—, chief judge, 1994—2000. Mem. U.S. Jud. Conf., 1994—, com. defender svcs., 1985—90, chmn., 1987—90, com. to review cir. council conduct and disability, 1996—; joint fed. tribal rels. com. 9th and 10th cirs., 1993—; mem. Okla. State Fed. Tribal Judicial Coun., 1993—94. Task force Tulsa Human Rights Commn., 1972—76; legal adv. panel Tulsa Task Force Battered Women, 1971—77; trustee Tulsa County Law Libr., 1977—78. Mem.: ABA, Am. Inns of Ct. (Council Oak chpt.), Nat. Assn. Women Judges, Fed. Judges Assn., Tulsa County Bar Assn., Okla. Bar Assn. (assoc. bar examiner 1973—79), Phi Beta Kappa. Office: US Courthouse 333 W 4th St Ste 4-562 Tulsa OK 74103-3819*

SGRO, BEVERLY HUSTON, day school administrator, educator, state official; b. Ft. Worth, Jan. 12, 1941; d. James Carl and Dorothy Louise (Foster) Huston; m. Joseph Anthony Sgro, Feb. 1, 1964; children: Anthony, Jennifer. BS, Tex. Woman's U., 1963; MS, Va. Poly. Inst. and State U., 1974, PhD, 1990. Cert. tennis teaching profl. Instr. of deaf Midland (Tex.) Ind. Sch. System, 1963-64; speech pathologist Arlington (Tex.) Pub. Sch. System, 1964; rsch. asst. Tex. Christian U., 1964-65; tennis profl. Blacksburg (Va.) Country Club, 1977-81; from coord. for Greek affairs to exec. asst. to v.p. student affairs Va. Poly. Inst. and State U., Blacksburg, 1981-89, dean of students, 1989-93; sec. of edn. Commonwealth of Va., Richmond, 1994-98; interim head Collegiate Sch., Richmond, 1998-99; head Carolina Day Sch., Asheville, N.C., 1999—. Adj. faculty Coll. Edn., Va. Poly. Inst. and State U.; lectr., presented papers at numerous symposia and convs., 1983—. Trustee Foxcroft Sch., Middleburg, Va., 1989-98, pres. bd. trustees, 1993-96; bd. dirs. Habitat Humanity. Mem. AACD, Nat. Assn. Student Pers. Adminstrs., Am. Coll. Pers. Assn. (sec., com. mem. 1986-88), Omicron Delta Kappa, Phi Kappa Phi, Phi Upsilon Omicron, Pi Lambda Theta, Sigma Alpha Eta, Zeta Phi Eta. Avocations: reading, travel, theatre. Home: 22 Hilltop Rd Asheville NC 28803-3030 Office: Carolina Day Sch 1345 Hendersonville Rd Asheville NC 28803-1923 Office Phone: 828-274-0757.

SHABAZZ, CHERYL ANTOINETTE, legal assistant; b. Kansas City, Mo., Nov. 21, 1964; d. Huey Manning and Juanita Cooper-Rimmer; 1 child, Ku'an Shabazz-Williams. Assoc. in Criminal Justice, Mountain View Coll., 1995; BA in Criminal Justice, U. Tex., Arlington, 1997. Exec. asst. Brian Hulsey Ct. Reporting, Dallas, 1994; adminstrv. asst. Dist. Atty. Frank Crowley, Dallas, 1994—97; legal asst. various law firms, Dallas, Ft. Worth, 1997—. Adv./liaison Social Security Profl. Svcs., Arlington, Tex., 1997—. Vol. spl. svcs. Boys and Girls Club, Arlington, 1997—2002. Named Basketball Mom, City of Arlington, 1999—2002. Mem.: PTA (com. officer 2002—03, Reflections award), NAACP. Avocations: reading, skating, running. Office: Shabazz & Assocs Profl Svcs PO Box 5062 Arlington TX 76005-5062

SHACKELFORD, NANCY KAY, retail executive; b. Wrightsville Beach, N.C., Dec. 28, 1974; d. Rudolph Calder Shackelford, Jr. and Kay (Mathews) Shackelford. BA in Criminal Justice, BA in Psychology, U. N.C., 1997. Mem. exec. team Lead Assets Protection Target Corp., Raleigh, NC, 1998—. Mem.: NAFE. Avocations: reading, gardening, movies, concerts.

SHACKLETON, JEAN L. music educator; b. Clare, Mich., Jan. 18, 1948; d. Paul Estel and Martha Ardeth (Cleveland) Helbling; m. Martin Lynn Shackleton, July 11, 1969; children: Aaron, Jeana, Joann. BA, Azusa Pacific U., 1970; MusM in Piano Performance, U. So. Calif., L.A., 1972. Jr. coll. cert. tchg. credential, Calif. Organist Bixby Knolls Christian Ch., Long Beach, Calif., 1966-67; diet aid Long Beach Hosp., 1966-67; self-employed piano and organ tchr. Calif. and Okla., 1968—; instr. Azusa (Calif.) Pacific U., 1972-73; staff accompanist jr. colls. and univs. Stockton, Calif., 1973-91; instr. Mid. Am. Bible Coll., Oklahoma City, 1991—; profl. accompanist Canterbury Choral Soc., Oklahoma City, 1999. Adj. faculty accompanist Oklahoma City U., 1991—; accompanist Crossings Cmty. Ch., Oklahoma City, 1991—. Arranger: (voice book) Basics of Singing, 1989, 97 Mem. Music Tchrs. Nat. Assn. (bd. dirs. 1973—), Music Tchrs. Assn. Calif. (bd. dirs. 1973—), MTAC (bd. dirs. 1973—, adjudicator 1988-89). Republican. Mem. Ch. of God. Avocation: traveling with musical groups. Home: 12117 S Wentworth Pl Oklahoma City OK 73170-4822 Office: Mid Am Bible Coll 3500 SW 119th St Oklahoma City OK 73170-4500 E-mail: jlshackle@aol.com.

SHADE, LINDA BUNNELL, university chancellor; BA in English and Comm., Baylor U., 1964; MA in English Lang. and Lit., U. Colo., 1967, PhD in English Lit., 1970. Asst. prof. English, acting assoc. dean Coll. Humanities U. Calif., Riverside, 1970-77; dean acad. programs and policy studies Calif. State U. Sys., 1977-87; vice chancellor acad. affairs Minn. State U. Sys., St. Paul, 1987-93; chancellor U. Colo., Colorado Springs, 1993—. Active Minn. Women's Econ. Round Table, 1989-93; mem. exec. com. Nat. Coun. for Accreditation Tchr. Edn., 1996-99. Mem. St. Paul chpt. ARC; mem. cmty. bd. Norwest Bank, Colorado Springs, 1997—, mem. El Pomar awards for Excellence com., 1997—; mem. leadership commn. ACE, 1997—; mem. subcom. ROTC; mem. edn. com. U.S. Army. Recipient Disting. Alumni award Baylor U., 1995; Woodrow Wilson dissertation fellow, Univ. Colo. Avocations: gardening, baseball, cooking, sable burmese cats. Office: U Colo 1420 Austin Bluffs Pkwy Colorado Springs CO 80918-3733

SHADE, MARSHA J. elementary school educator, music educator; b. Clovis, N.Mex., Oct. 1, 1949; d. Maurice T. and Lula Maye Sims; m. Gerald L. Shade, May 24, 1991; m. Brian T. Miller, June 20, 1970 (div. May 28, 1989); children: Chad T. Miller, Alisa R. Miller. BS in Elem. Music Edn., Ea. N.Mex U., 1977, MEd, 1981. Cert. tchr. Dept. of Edn., N.Mex., 1977. From music specialist to reading recovery specialist Clovis (N.Mex.) Mcpl. Schs., 1978—2003, reading recovery specialist Ranchvale Elem. Sch., 2003—. Presenter in field. Lay dir. S.E. secretariat Cursillo-Episcopal Diocese of Rio Grande, Albuquerque, 1998—2000; diocesan youth advisor Episcopal Diocese of Rio Grande, Albuquerque, 1991—94. Mem.: Christian Educators Assn. Internat., Order of the Ea. Star (worthy matron 1983—84, grand organist 1985—86), Daughters of the Nile (pres. 2000—03). Republican. Episc. Avocations: praise music teams, working with the alpha program. Home: 1516 Hickory St Clovis NM 88101-4931 Office: Clovis Municipal Schools P O Box 19000 Clovis NM 88102-9000 Personal E-mail: marshade@3lefties.com. E-mail: mshade@3clovis-schools.org.

SHADEROWFSKY, EVA MARIA, photographer, writer, computer communications specialist; b. Prague, Czechoslovakia, May 20, 1938; came to U.S., 1940; d. Felix Resek and Gertrude (Telatko) Frank; children: Tom, Paul. Student, Oberlin Coll., 1955—56; BA, Barnard Coll., 1960. One-woman shows include Esta Robinson Gallery, 1982, Fairleigh Dickinson U., 1983, Donnell Libr., N.Y.C., 1985, Piermont (N.Y.) Libr., 1987, The Turning Point, Piermont, 1988, Hopper House, Nyack, N.Y., 1989, Puchong Gallery, N.Y., 1991, Rockland Ctr. for Arts, 1992, exhibited in group shows at Soho Photo Gallery, N.Y., 1974, Fashion Inst. Tech., N.Y.C., 1975, Portland (Maine) Mus. Art, 1977, Maine Photog. Workshop, Rockport, 1978, Marcuse Pfeifer, N.Y., 1977, 1978, Foto, 1982, Barnard Coll., N.Y.C., 1983, Rockland Ctr. for Arts, 1978, 1987, 1989, 1996, 1998, Print Club, Phila., 1988, Burd House, Nyack, N.Y., 2003, Represented in permanent collections Bklyn. Mus., Portland Mus. Art, Met. Mus. Art, N.Y.C., Chrysler Mus. Art, Va., Ilford Collection, N.J.; author, photographer: Suburban Portraits, 1977; photographer Women in Transition, 1975, Earth Tones, 1993, The Womansource Catalog and Review: Tools for Connecting the Community of Women, 1996, poetry critic/essayist Contact II, 1980—93, contbr. story to anthology, 1980—93, Moondance Mag., 1999, Touching Fire, 1989, Sexual Harassment: Women Speak Out, 1992, Lovers, 1992, The Time of Our Lives, 1993, photography to Camera 35 mag., Shots mag., Shutterbug. Recipient Photography award Rockland Ctr. for Arts, 1978, Gt. Am. Photo Contest, 1981, Demarais Press, 1982, Harrison Art Coun., SUNY-Purchase, 1982, The Cape Codder, 1976, 79-82. Personal E-mail: evas@aol.com.

SHAEFFER, THELMA JEAN, primary school educator; b. Ft. Collins, Colo., Feb. 1, 1949; d. Harold H. and Gladys June (Ruff) Pfeif; m. Charles F. Shaeffer, June 12, 1971; 1 child, Shannon Emily. BA, Regis U., Denver, 1970; MA, U. No. Colo., 1972. Cert. profl. tchr., type B, Colo. Primary tchr. Adams County Dist 12 Five Star Schs., Northglenn, Colo., 1970-84, Title I lang. arts tchr., 1984—2003, Title I reading tchr., 1992—2001; tchr. McElwain Elem. Sch., Denver, 1999—2004, Title I resource coach for staff, 2003—04. Mem. policy coun. Adams County Dist. # 12 Five Star Schs., Northglenn, 1975-79, dist. sch. improvement team, 1987-89; presenter Nat. Coun. Tchrs. of English, 1990; assessor Nat. Bd. Tchrs., 2000. Vol. 1992 election, Denver, alumni advisor for Career Connections U. No. Colo., 1993-97; mem. supervisory bd. Sch. Dist. 12 Credit Union. Mem. Colo. Tchrs. Assn. (del. 1992), Dist. Tchrs. Edn. Assn. (exec. bd. mem. 1991-93), Internat. Reading Assn. (pres. Colo. coun. 1988), Internat. Order of Job's Daus. (coun.), Order Ea. Star, Delta Omicron. Episcopalian. Home: 2575 Urban St Lakewood CO 80215 Office: McElwain Elem Sch 1020 Dawson Dr Denver CO 80229-4909

SHAFER, ANNE WHALEN, volunteer civic worker; b. Memphis, Tenn., Aug. 22, 1923; m. Robert W. Shafer, June 5, 1948. BLS in Cmty. Devel., Memphis State U. (U. Memphis), 1982. Pres., cons. Colonial Neighborhood Assn., Memphis Ctr. for Neighborhoods, Memphis, 1980—. Sec., past pres., founder, Colonial Acres Neighborhood Assn., Neighborhood Watch, Memphis, 1980—. Pub.: History of the Memphis City Beautiful Commission and Its Impact on Our Lives, 1996. Mem., officer, Ch. Women United, 1960—, Mid South Peace and Justice Ctr., 1970, W. Tenn. Hist. Soc., 1980; del. Tenn. Constnl. Conv., 1965; chair Memphis City Beautiful Commn., 1964-66; project dir. Memphis Panel Am. Women, 1973-75; founder, exec. sec. Yellow Fever Meml., Martyrs Park, Memphis, 1966-73. Recipient Race Rels. award Mid South Peace and Justice Ctr., Memphis, 1996, Alumni Achievement award U. Memphis, 1998, Woman of Achievement award, 2001, Peter Cooper award, 2002; named one of Women Who Made a Difference, Mattie Sengstacke Civil Rights Mus., Memphis, 1994; grantee: Thanks Be to Grandmother Winifred Fedn., Wainscott, N.Y., 1995-96. Mem. LWV (past pres. local chpt. many coms., other offices), Chickasaw Bluffs Conservancy Memphis, Pub. Issues Forum Memphis. Democrat. Avocations: spiritual studies, history, religion, oil painting, gardening. Home: 4963 Essexshire Ave Memphis TN 38117-5628

SHAFER, CAROL LARSEN, retired book reviewer; b. Spencer, Iowa, Sept. 20, 1907; d. John Adolph and Emma Louise (Cook) Larsen; m. Boyd Carlisle Shafer, June 6, 1932 (dec. Feb. 1992); children: Kirstin A. Moritz, Anders C. Shafer. BA, Morningside Coll., 1930; MA, U. Iowa, 1931. Social worker United Charities, Chgo., 1931-32; supr. social work Dunn County, Menomonie, Wis., 1933-35; book reviewer Mpls. Tribune and Mpls. Star, 1964-73, Tucson, 1975-86. Author: Filter of Time, 1996; co-author: Life, Liberty and the Pursuit of Bread, 1940; contbr. articles to profl. jours. Mem. AAUW. Home: 1923 E Joyce Blvd # HC Fayetteville AR 72703-5398

SHAFER, SUSAN WRIGHT, retired elementary school educator; b. Ft. Wayne, Dec. 6, 1941; d. George Wesley and Bernece (Spray) Wright; 1 child, Michael R. BS, St. Francis Coll., Ft. Wayne, 1967, MS in Edn., 1969. Tchr. Ft. Wayne Community Schs., 1967-69, Amphitheatre Pub. Schs., Tucson, 1970-96; ret., 1996. Odyssey of the Mind coord. Prince Elem. Sch., Tucson, 1989-91, Future Problem Solving, 1991-95. Tchr. Green Valley (Ariz.) Cmty. Ch., Vacation Bible Sch., 1987-89, dir. vacation bible sch., 1989-93. Mem.: PEO (pres. chpt. 2001—02), AAUW, NEA (life), Phi Delta Kappa, Alpha Delta Kappa (historian Epsilon chpt. 1990—96, Fidellis chpt. 1996—), Delta Kappa Gamma (pres. Alpha Rho chpt.). Republican. Methodist. Avocations: reading, traveling, walking. Home: 603 W Placita Nueva Green Valley AZ 85614-2827

SHAFER, YVONNE, theater educator, writer; b. LA, Sept. 20, 1936; d. Harvey Jordan and Hazel Bonsall; m. Thomas Shafer, Apr. 4, 1964 (div. 1985). BA Speech and Theatre, U. Calif., Santa Barbara, 1958; MA Speech and Theatre, U. Iowa, 1959, PhD Speech and Theatre, 1965; postgrad., Stanford U., 1961—62. Tchr. Reedley H.S., Calif., 1959—60, San Lorenzo H.S., Calif., 1960—61; asst. prof. Humboldt State Coll., Calif., 1965—67, dir. upward bound theatre program, 1967; asst. prof. Bowling Green State U., 1967—70; with U. Del. Honors Program, 1975—80; assoc. prof. Ohio State U., Columbus, 1980—83, Fla. State U., 1984—87, U. Southern Maine, 1988—89, U. Colo., Boulder, 1989—94; Fulbright prof. U. Libre, Brussels, 1995; with U. Md. Overseas Program, 1995—96; assoc. prof. St. John's U., 1996—. Vis. prof. U. Ga., Athens, 1974—75, U. Calif., Santa Barbara, 1983—84; disting. vis. prof. Nanjing U., China, 1987. Author: (theatre histories) American Women Playwrights, 1995, August Wilson, 1997, Performing O'Neill, 2000; mem. editl. bd. (jours.) Western European Stages, 1995—, Jour. Dramatic Theory and Criticism, 1996—; contbr. articles to profl. jours. Mem.: Eugene O'Neill Soc. (exec. bd.), Ibsen Soc. Am., Am. Soc. Theatre Rsch. Democrat. Avocations: tennis, golf, swimming. Home: 50 Fort Pl B4F Staten Island NY 10301 Office: St Johns U 300 Howard Ave New York NY 10301 Business E-Mail: shafery@stjohns.edu.

SHAFER-KENNEY, JOLIE E. writer, columnist; b. Roswell, N.Mex., Oct. 26, 1953; d. Jack Ernest and Betty Marie (Halstead) Shafer; m. David A. Kenney (div.); children: Matthew Alan, Jack Andrew. Grad., Parks Sch. Bus., 1972; student, Colo. State U., 1971, 74, U. Pitts., 1995-96. Dept. mgr. Joslins Dept. Store, Aurora, Colo., 1972-73; flight attendent United Airlines, 1974-84, publicity rep. com., 1980-84; v.p. Surg. Assocs., Inc., Latrobe, Pa., 1991-98; asst. Women and Talent Gifted Women Forum, Am. Online, 1997-98; ind. contractor AOL, Inc., 1997-99; staff Online Psychol. Svcs., Inc. AOL, 1995-97, seminar host, 1995-97; with prodn. staff AOL's Cmty. Matters, 1997-98, AOL's Alt. Health and Healing, 1997-98. Editl. dir. CelebrityStores.com, 1999—; editor-in-chief Winetree Pub. and The Wine Mag., 1999-2000. Feature/content writer Entertainment Asylum, 1997-99, Electra, 1997-98; editl. dir. Celebritystores.com, 1999—; editor-in-chief Winetree Pub., 1999-2000, www.thewineadvisor.com, www.thewinemagazine.com, www.winetreepublishing.com, 1999-2000; featured columnist ShoutingOut.com; contracted feature writer Gaiam, Inc., 2000—; nat. content writer digitalcity.com, 2000—; author: ASK JES, 1999 (pub. in Chicken Soup for the Soul 1999); contbr. 6th Bowl of Chicken Soup for the Soul, 1999; journalist: AOL's Internat. News, 1997-98, AOL TW's Digital City, Inc. (www.digitalcity.com, cbsswitchboard.com, AOL KW: Pitts.), 1999—; lic. syndicated columnist, ASK JES tm and TEENS ASK JESltm; content provider: iSyndicate.com, 1999—; mng. editor: Feedback-forthought.com, 2001—; contbr. articles to online jours. and newspapers; patent pending in field. Mem. AAUW, Nat. Mus. of Women in Arts, Inst. Noetic Scis., Sea Shepherd Conservation Soc., Ctr. for Marine Conservation, Sierra Club, MADD. Avocations: french language and culture, philosophy, gun control, patient's rights, spirituality. Office: 988 E Pittsburgh Street Ste 13 Greensburg PA 15601 E-mail: jolie@askjes.com.

SHAFF, KAREN E. lawyer, insurance company executive; BA, Northwestern U., Evanston, Ill.; JD, Drake U., Des Moines. Atty. Austin and Gaudineer, Des Moines, 1979—82, Principal Fin. Group, 1982—83, asst. counsel, 1983—86, assoc. counsel, 1986—90, sr. v.p., gen. counsel, 1999—2004, exec. v.p., gen. counsel, 2004—. Bd. mem. Hospice of Ctrl. Iowa Found., Sci. Ctr. of Iowa. Mem.: ABA, Am. Life Ins. Coun., Am. Corp. Counsel Assn., Polk County Bar Assn., Iowa Bar Assn., Am. Coun. Life Ins. Office: Principal Fin Group 711 High St Des Moines IA 50392

SHAFFER, DEBORAH BLAND, adult nurse practitioner; b. Tampa, Fla., Jan. 20, 1954; d. Frank Solomon and Mary Louise (Swann) Shaffer; children: Danny, Dionne. LPN, Suwanee-Hamilton Nursing Sch., Live Oak, Fla., 1984; student, Hillsborough CC, 1992—. LPN, Fla. Author: Skippy Goes to Ybor Square, 1998, Danny's Journey, 2004. Active Ladies Auxillary Post #10208, Vet. of Fgn. Wars of U.S., Salt Springs,Fla.; mem. First Bapt. Ch., Salt Springs; founder of A Journey in Poetry, 2003, Ocala Nat. Forest- Salt Springs newsletter, 2003. Mem.: Brick City Ctr. for the Arts, Fla. State Poets Assn. Avocations: writing, painting, photography, gardening, guitar.

SHAFFER, DOROTHY BROWNE, retired mathematician, educator; b. Feb. 12, 1923; arrived U.S., 1940; d. Hermann and Steffy (Hermann) Browne; m. Lloyd Hamilton Shaffer, July 25, 1943 (dec. 1978); children: Deborah Lee, Diana Louise, Dorothy Leslie. AB, Bryn Mawr Coll., 1943; MA, Harvard U., 1945, PhD, 1962. Mathematician MIT, Cambridge, 1947-48; assoc. mathematician Cornell Aero. Lab., Buffalo, 1952-56; mathematician Dunlap & Assocs., Stamford, Conn., 1958-60; lectr. grad. engrng. U. Conn., Stamford, 1962; prof. math. Fairfield (Conn.) U., 1963-92, prof. emeritus, 1992—. Vis. prof. Imperial Coll. Sci. and Tech., London, fall 1978, U. Md., College Park, spring 1981; vis. prof. U. Calif.-San Diego, summer 1981; vis. scholar, 1986; NSF faculty fellow IBM-T.J. Watson Research Center, Yorktown Heights, N.Y., 1979. Contbr. numerous papers in math. analysis. Mem. Am. Math. Soc., Math. Assn. Am., Assn. Women in Math., London Math. Soc. Achievements include patent in Viscosity Stabilized Solar Pond. Home: 156 Intervale Rd Stamford CT 06905-1311 Office: Fairfield U Dept Math & Computer Sci Fairfield CT 06430 E-mail: dbshaffer@fair1.fairfield.edu.

SHAFFER, JOANNE TYLER, music educator; b. Wabash, Ind., Oct. 13, 1951; d. James W. and O. Faye Tyler; m. Michael L. Shaffer, Nov. 24, 1972; children: Marijke A., Monika L. Bachelor of Music Edn., Wright State U., 1974, Master of Edn., 1989. Tchr. music Tipp City Exempted Village, Ohio, 1974—78, Huber Heights City Schs., Ohio, 1978—, orch. dist. supr., 1996—. String bass player Middletown Symphony Orch., Ohio, 1979—, Lima Symphony Orch., Ohio, 1997—. Orch. musician Salem Ch. of God, Clayton, Ohio, 1980—. Mem.: Music Educator's Nat. Conf. (sec. 1973—74), Sigma Alpha Iota. Republican. Avocation: umpiring college and adult baseball. Home: 7758 Leatherback Ct Dayton OH 45414

SHAFFER, KIMBERLY SAUNDRA, medical technician; b. Seoul, Korea, Aug. 15, 1960; arrived in U.S., 1961; d. Heber and Irma Catherine Shaffer; m. David Bryan Norton (div.); 1 child, Christopher Bryan Norton. Cert. surg. technologist, U.S. Naval Health Scis., Bethesda, Md., 1984. Surg. technologist Surgery Ctr. Okla., Oklahoma City. Pres. Okla. State Assembly, 2000—. With USN, 1983—91. Mem.: Assn. Surg. Technologists. Republican. Home: 231 Barrett Pl Edmond OK 73003 Office: Surgery Ctr Oklahoma 9500 N Broadway Ext Oklahoma City OK 73114

SHAFFER, MARGARET MINOR, retired library director; b. New Orleans, Sept. 20, 1940; d. Milhado Lee and Margaret Minor (Krumbhaar) S. BS, Nicholls State U., Thibodaux, La., 1962; MLS, La. State U., 1965. Asst. dir. Terrebonne Parish Pub. Libr., Houma, La., 1965-72, dir., 1973-95; ret., 1995. Named Woman of Yr., Houma Bus. and Profl. Women's Club, 1981. Mem. ALA, La. Libr. Assn. (chmn. pub. libr. com. 1986-87), Southeastern Libr. Assn. Democrat. Episcopalian. Avocations: crafts, travel. Home: 2678 Highway 311 Schriever LA 70395-3240

SHAFFER, MARY LOUISE, art educator; b. Blufton, Ind., Nov. 23, 1927; d. Gail H. and Mary J. (Graves) S. AB, Northwest Nazerene U., 1950; MA, Ball State U., 1955; EdD, MS, Ind. U., 1964. Art and music tchr. Kuna (Idaho) H.S., 1950-55; asst. prof. art Northwest Nazarene U., Nampa, Idaho, 1955-56, head art dept., 1971-98, dir. Friesen Art Galleries, 1997-2000, faculty emeritus, 1998; asst. prof. art Pasadena (Calif.) U., 1956-61; prof. art Olivet Nazarene U., Kankakee, Ill., 1964-71. Dir. music Kankakee Congl. Ch., 1964-71, Nampa Christian Ch., 1971-76, Nampa Meth. Ch., 1976-81; juror Nampa Art Guild Painting Show, 1994, 2003; head art policy coun. Northwest Nazarene U.; spkr. in field. One-woman show Friesen Art Galleries, 1999; participant European Images Art Show, 1989; cover artist Nazarene Internat. Mag., 1989; painting retrospective, 1999; juror Nampa Art Guild Painting Show, 2003. Dir. music Van Nuys (Calif.) Nazarene Ch., 1957-60. E.I. Lilly grantee, 1961-62; women's singles tennis champion Kankakee, Ill., 1966, 67, 68, Boise (Idaho) Racquet and Swim Club, 1973, Idaho Sr. Tennis champion Sun Valley, 1984; watercolor Sun Valley Mountain selected to go to moon on Endeavour Space Shuttle, 1992. Mem. NAFE, Nat. Art Edn. Assn., Idaho Arts Edn. Assn., Nat. Assn. Univ. Women, Nat. Mus. Women in the Arts, Boise Racquet Swim Club, Boise Art Mus. Avocations: travel, music, renovating buildings, watercolor painting, tennis. Home: Shaffer Studios 4755 E Victory Rd Meridian ID 83642-7011

SHAFFER, SHANNON, special education educator; b. Dallas, Jan. 18, 1967; d. Allen Ardis and Mary Patrica (Freeman) S. BS in Ednl. Curriculum and Instrn., Tex. A&M U., College Station, Tex., 1989, MEd in Ednl. Psychology, 1991. Cert. elem. tchr., generic spl. edn., Tex. Spl. edn. tchr. Williams High Sch. Plano (Tex.) Ind. Sch. Dist., 1990—96, Skaggs Elem. Sch., 1996—2000, Rice Middle Sch., 2000—. Therapeutic recreation vol. Plano Pks. and Recreation, 1984—; mem. decision counselor Prestonwood Bapt. Ch., 1992—, bible study fellowship discussion leader, 1999—. Mem. Coun. for Exceptional Children. Republican. Baptist. Avocations: travel, reading, crafts, photography. Home: 6209 White Pine Mc Kinney TX 75070 Office: Rice Middle Sch Plano ISD 8500 Gifford Dr Plano TX 75025

SHAFFLER, RHONDA, news correspondent; B in broadcast journalism and polit. sci., Penn. State U. Various positions in broadcast and bus. news fields, 1987—95; anchor WPEN-AM, Phila., WMGK-FM, Phila.; broadcast editor AP; news editor, editor Dow Jones Voice Info. Network; freelance reporter News 12, Long Island, NY; reporter, writer bus. and gen. news WPHL-TV Inquirer News Tonight, Phila.; field prodr. CNN Bus. News, 1995—96, corr., 1996; anchor Moneyline Weekend Edit., CNN Bus. News; sr. corr. NY Stock Exchange CNNfn and CNN Bus. News; anchor CNNfn Market Call. Office: CNN 5 Penn Plz Fl 20 New York NY 10001-1810 Office Phone: 212-714-7800.*

SHAFFRON, J. JANET, legislative administrator; b. Welch, W.Va., Mar. 27, 1947; BS, W.Va. U., 1969. Legis. dir. to Rep. Frank R. Wolf U.S. Ho. of Reps., Washington, 1984—. Office: US Ho of Reps 241 Chob Washington DC 20515-0001 E-mail: janet.shaffron@mail.house.gov.

SHAFTMAN, RACHEL ELLEN, music educator, musician; b. Hinsdale, Ill., Dec. 19, 1976; BMus, DePaul U., 2000, MusM, 2003. Performing pianist, 1990—; pvt. piano instr., 1993—; piano instr. Swain Music Studios, Kenilworth, Ill., 1996—2001; faculty DePaul U., Chgo., 2002—. Mem.: Chgo. Dance and Music Alliance, Internat. Assn. Jazz Educators, Music Tchrs. Nat. Assn., Phi Kappa Phi.

SHAHAN, SHERRY JEAN, writer, educator; b. Long Beach, Calif., Aug. 14, 1949; d. Frank Rowe Webb and Sylvia Jean (Brunner) Benedict; m. Edgar Harold Shahan, Oct. 23, 1982; children: Kristina Michelle Beal, Kyle Shannon Beal. BS in Social Scis., Calif. Poly. State U., San Luis Obispo, 1978. Lectr. Saddleback Coll. Writers Conf., Orange County, Calif., 1992, Cuesta Community Coll., San Luis Obispo, 1988—, Calif. Reading Assn., 1998—, Nat. Coun. Tchrs. English, 1999—. Author: Dashing Through the Snow: The Story of the Jr. Iditarod (a photo essay, 1997), (mid. grade novel) Frozen Stiff, 1998, (photoessay) The Little Butterfly, 1998, (photoessays) The Sunflower Family, 1996, Feeding Time at the Zoo, 2000, (picture book) A Jazzy Alphabet, 2002, Working Dogs, 1999; contbr. articles, photographs numerous regional and nat. newspapers and mags. Mem.: Children's Bookwriters and Illustrators, So. Calif. Children's Book Sellers, Am. Travel Writers, Authors Guild, Pi Gamma Mu. Home and Office: 2603 Richard Ave Cayucos CA 93430 E-mail: Kidbooks@thegrid.net.

SHAHAR, ROBIN JOY, lawyer; b. Philadelphia, Pa., Apr. 7, 1963; d. Bunny Doreen Van Adelsberg and Edward Stuart Brown; life ptnr. Fran Greenfield Shahar, July 28, 1991; children: Eli Rafael, Ariel Rose. JD, Emory Law Sch., 1988—91. Attorney: State Bar of Ga. 1991. Sr. asst. city atty. City of Atlanta Dept. of Law, 1996—, assoc., asst. city atty., 1993—96. Recipient Phi Beta Kappa, Tufts U., 1985, Order of the Coif, Emory Law Sch., 1991, Joe Callaway Def. of Right to Privacy award, ACLU, 1994, Plaintiff's award, Stonewall (Ga.) Bar Assn., 1996, Equality award, Human Rights Campaign, NY, 1998; Woodruff fellowship, Emory Law Sch., 1988—91. D-Liberal. Jewish. Achievements include law case asserting the right of gay men's/lesbians' right to freedom of association, freedom of religion, and equal protection under U.S. Constitution. Avocations: hiking, swimming, travel. Office: City of Atlanta Dept of Law 68 Mitchell St Ste 4100 Atlanta GA 30303

SHAHEEN, C. JEANNE, former governor; b. St. Charles, Mo., Jan. 28, 1947; m. William H. Shaheen; 3 children. BA, Shippensburg U., 1969; M of Social Sci. in Polit. Sci., U. Miss., 1973. Mem. N.H. Senate, 1991-96; gov N.H., 1997—2003. Democrat. Protestant.

SHAHEEN ALESI, BARBARA, lawyer; Degree, SUNY; JD, St. John's U. Formerly with Curto, Barton & Alesi, PC; ptnr. Forchelli, Curto, Schwartz, Mineo, Carlino & Cohn LLP, Mineola, NY, 1999—. Adv. bd. North Shore Animal League Am., Port Washington. Mem.: Nat. Assn. Women Bus. Owners (bd. dirs.), Exe. Women's Golf Assn. Office: Forchelli Curto Schwartz Mineo Carlino & Cohn LLP 330 Old Country Rd PO Box 31 Mineola NY 11501

SHAIFER, AUDREY VIRGINIA, director; b. Clifton Forge, Va., Aug. 11, 1955; d. Eugene Edward Simmons and Audrey McKinley Foster; m. James Hulbert Shaifer, Apr. 1, 1977; children: Allison Michelle Williams, Hakeem Kamil, Shaun Emmerick, Jayson Eugene. MEd, Jackson State U., 1994—98. Lic. Tchr. Miss. Dept. of Edn., 1998. Tchr. Ohio Bd. of Edn., 1977—78; mental healthe cons. SW Mental Health Complex, Port Gibson, Miss., 1979—81; sec. Claiborne County Attorney's Office, Port Gibson, Miss., 1979; asst. s-4 U.S. Army Reception Sta., Fort Jackson, SC, 1982—84; property book officer HHD, 1st Tng. Brigade, Fort Jackson, SC, 1984—85; commissary officer U.S. Army Troop Support Agy., Aschaffenburg, Germany, 1986—87; brigade s-4 officer 14th Mil. Police Brigade, Stuttgart, Germany, 1987—90; co. comdr. 16th Corps Support Group, Germany, 1990—92; supply br. chief 98th Tng. Divsn., Rochester, NY, 1992—93; tchr. Hinds County Pub. Schools, Raymond, Miss., 1993—99; customer messaging agent Skytel, Jackson, Miss., 1998—99; program coord. Miss. Dept. of Edn., Jackson, 2000—. Capt. U.S. Army, 1981—93. Decorated Army Commendation medal 3rd Oak Leaf Cluster, Nat. Def. Svc. medal U.S. Army, SW Asia Medal 2 Stars, Kuwait Liberation medal 1 Star U. S. Army, Army Svc. Ribbon U.S. Army, Overseas Svc. Ribbon. Democrat-Npl. Bapt. Home: 347 Old Spanish Trails Jackson MS 39212 Office: Mississippi Dept of Edn 359 North West St Jackson MS 39212 E-mail: ashaifer@mde.k12.ms.us.

SHAIFER, MARGARET S. artist; b. El Paso, Nov. 12, 1922; d. James Lynn and Hazel Bell (Flint) Snell; m. Warren Arthur Minton, Aug. 3, 1940 (div. Aug. 1960); children: Judith Ann, Barbara Jean, Patricia Ruth; m. Edward Fondren Shaifer, Oct. 15, 1965. Student, Coll. of Mines, El Paso, 1939-40, Ariz. State U., Tempe, 1970-71, U. So. Calif., Oxnard, 1980. Lic. realtor. Exhibited paintings/watermedia in 3 internat. shows, also in Tex. Watercolor Soc. shows, N.W. Watercolor Soc. shows. One-woman show Tex. State Capitol Offices Mrs. Laura Bush, 2000. Recipient Best of Show Painting award Guadalupe Watercolor Group, Tex. 1995, 96, 97, 1st Place, 2nd Place, 3rd Place award, Award of Merit Kerrville Art Club 1991-98, award of Excellence Tex. Watercolor Soc. 1997. Mem. Kerrville Art Club (sec. 1993-94), Am. Business Women's Assn. (sec. 1970-71), Oxnard Calif. Women's Club (real estate rep. 1980-82). Republican. Avocations: ballroom dancing, helping young artists to express themselves, cooking mexican food. Home: Hwy 39 1/2 Mile So of Farm Rd 1340 Hunt TX 78024-0619

SHAIN, JO-ANN, editor; b. N.Y., Feb. 7, 1953; d. Arthur and Elinor Shain; life ptnr. M. J. Kennedy; 1 child, Aliya. BA, George Mason U., Fairfax, Va., 1979; MPH, Columbia U., N.Y., 1981. Patien, /health educator Montefiore Med. Ctr., Bronx, NY, 1981—83; practice area editor, med. LexisNexis Matthew Bender, Newark, 1984—. Mem.: APHA, Am. Med. Writer's Assn. Avocations: travel, cooking, bicycling, film. Office: LexisNexis Matthew Bender 744 Broad St Newark NJ 07102 Personal E-mail: jasha7@earthlink.net. E-mail: jshain@bender.com.

SHAINWALD, SYBIL, lawyer; b. N.Y.C., Apr. 27, 1928; d. Samuel and Anne; m. Sidney Shainwald; children: Robert, Louise, Laurie, Marsha. BA, Coll. William and Mary, 1948; MA, Columbia U., 1972; JD, N.Y. Law Sch., 1976, LLD (hon.), 2000. Bar: N.Y. 1976. Legal advisor Am. Found. for Maternal Child and Health; adj. prof. dept. law Baruch Coll., 1981—82. Co-editor: Jour. Women and Health; contbr. articles to profl. jours. Active Abortion Rights Action; co-founder, bd. mem. Trial Lawyers for Pub. Justice, 1982—88; bd. mem. Hysterectomy Edn. Resources and Svcs., 1985—, Dalkon Shield INfo. Network, Nat. Network to Prevent Birth Defects, No. Ariz. Sch. Midwifery, 1989—; bd. advisors Med. Legal Aspects of Breast Implants; bd. dirs. Consumer Interest Rsch. Inst.; fellow Roscoe Pound Inst., Morgan Libr.; trustee Civil Justice Found., 1998—99; bd. dirs. Am. Friends of Tel Aviv Mus., 2000, Friends of Tel Aviv Mus., 2000-; trustee N.Y. Law Sch., 2000—; adv. bd. Southampton The Hamptons Shakespeare Festival, 2000—; co-chair Take Home a Nude N.Y. Acad. Art, 2001; active Sybil Shainwald Charitable Found., N.Y.C. Comptrs. Health Task Force. Recipient Susan B. Anthony award, NOW; grantee, Nat. Endowment for the Humanities, Rockefeller Found., Gov. W. Averell Harriman; scholar Pres. Bryan scholar, Coll. of William and Mary, Edward Coles scholar. Mem.: ATLA (chair environ. and toxic tort sect. 1988—89, co-chair breast implant litigation group 1992—2000, mem. Dalkon shield litigation group 1995, mem. contraceptive implant litigation group 1995, co-chair DES litigation group, environ. law adv. com.), N.Y. State Trial Lawyers (bd. govs.), Assn. of the Bar of the City of N.Y. (judge nat. moot ct. competition 1988—2003), Soc. Med. Jurisprudence, Health Action Internat. U.S. (co-founder, mem. steering com.), Lawyers Com. for Human Rights, Am. Soc. Law, Medicine and Ethics, Nat. Women's Health Alliance (pres.), Nat. Women's Health Network (bd. mem. 1980—86, chair litigation svc. 1980—86, chair health law and regulation 1981—88, chmn. bd. dirs. 1982—86, chair N.Y. state affiliate), Phi Beta Kappa. Avocations: art, music. Home: 25 Sutton Pl New York NY 10022-2445 Office: 950 Third Ave 10th Fl New York NY 10022

SHALALA, DONNA E. university administrator, former federal official, political scientist, educator; b. Cleve., Feb. 14, 1941; d. James Abraham and Edna (Smith) S. AB, Western Coll., 1962; MSSC, Syracuse U., 1968, PhD, 1970; 39 hon. degrees, 1981-91. Vol. Peace Corps, Iran, 1962-64; asst. prof. polit. sci. CUNY, 1970-72; assoc. prof. politics and edn. Tchrs. Coll. Columbia U., 1972-79; asst. sec. for policy devel. and research HUD, Washington, 1977-80; prof. polit. sci., pres. Hunter Coll., CUNY, 1980-87; prof. polit. sci., chancellor U. Wis., Madison, 1987-93; sec. Dept. HHS, Washington, 1993-2001; pres. U. Miami, 2001—. Dir., treas. Mcpl. Assistance Corp. for the City of N.Y., 1975—77. Author: Neighborhood Governance, 1971, The City and the Constitution, 1972, The Property Tax and the Voters, 1973, The Decentralization Approach, 1974. Mem. Trilateral Commn., 1988—92, Knight Commn. on Intercollegiate Sports, 1989—91; bd. govs. Am. Stock Exch., 1981—87; trustee TIAA, 1985—89, Com. Econ. Devel., 1982—92, Brookings Inst., 1989—92; bd. dirs. Children's Def. Fund, 1980—93, Am. Ditchley Found., 1981—93, Spencer Found., 1988—92, M&I Bank of Madison, 1991—92, NCAA Found., 1991, Inst. Internat. Econs., 1981—, Gannett Co., Inc., McLean, Va., United Health Group, Mpls., Lennar Corp., Miami; trustee emeritus Kennedy Ctr. Bd. of Trustees, Washington. Ohio Newspaper Women's scholar, 1958, Western Coll. Trustee scholar, 1958-62; Carnegie fellow, 1966-68; Guggenheim fellow, 1975-76; recipient Disting. Svc. medal Columbia U. Tchrs. Coll., 1989. Mem. ASPA, Am. Polit. Sci. Assn., Nat. Acad. Arts and Scis., Nat. Acad. Pub. Adminstrn., Coun. Fgn. Rels., Nat. Acad. Edn. (Spencer fellow 1972-73). Office: U Miami Office Pres 230 Ashe Bldg Coral Gables FL 33146

SHALLCROSS, DORIS JANE, creative behavioral educator; b. Cranford, N.J., Feb. 28, 1933; d. John William and Ethel Belle (Ruth) S. BA, Montclair State Coll., 1955; MA, Wesleyan U., Middletown, Conn., 1962; EdD, U. Mass., 1973. Tchr. Hunterdon Cen. High Sch., Flemington, N.J., 1955-61, Roosevelt Jr. High Sch., Cleveland Heights, Ohio, 1961-65, Cleveland Heights H.S., 1965-67; adminstr. Cleveland Heights Pub. Schs., 1967-69; dir. humanistic edn. Montague (Mass.) Pub. Schs., 1972-75; program devel. specialist Tchr. Corps., SUNY, Oneonta, N.Y., 1976-78; asst. prof. edn. divsn. home econs. U. Mass., Amherst, 1978-82, prof., dir. grad. studies in creativity, 1982-95; pres. Shallcross Creativity Inst., Haydenville, Mass., 1995—. Pres. bd. trustees Creative Edn. Found., Buffalo, 1989-94; co-dir. Global Odyssey, 1992—; bd. dirs. Ctr. for Critical and Creative Thinking, Hartford, Conn., 1989-92, 95—; prof. internat. grad. program in creativity U. Santiago, Santiage de Compostela, Spain, 1999. Author: Teaching Creative Behavior, 1981; co-author: The Growing Person, 1985, Leadership: Making Things Happen, 1987, Intuition: An Inner Way of Knowing, 1989; cons. editor Jour. Creative Behavior, 1967—; contbr. articles to profl. jours. Mem. Planning Bd., Town of Williamsburg, 1981-89; v.p. bd. dirs. Pioneer Valley Performing Arts H.S., 1995-98, pres., 1998—; chair edn. com. Arts in Edn. Ctr., 1997—, pres. 2002-; bd. dirs. Mass. Charter Schs. Assn., 2001—; mem. Creative Problem Solving Inst. Coun. Recipient Disting. Leader award, Creative Edn. Found., 1986; inductee Creative Problem Solving Inst. Hall of Fame, 2004; grantee, NSF, 1987-89, U. Mass., 1987-89. Mem. NEA, Mass. Soc. of Profs., Inst. for Noetic Scis., Am. Creativity Assn. (bd. dirs. 1990-93). Avocations: music, golf, reading, gardening. Home and Office: 26 S Main St Haydenville MA 01039-9735

SHAMBAN, AVA T. dermatologist; BS, Harvard U., 1977; MD, Case Western Res. U. Pvt. practice dermatology, Santa Monica, Calif.; asst. clin. prof. dermatology UCLA. Cons. ABC's Extreme Makeover; investigator Nat. Acne Rsch. Project; featured regarding cosmetic dermatology Discovery Channel. Bd. dirs. Santa Monica Coll. Found. Fellow: Am. Acad. Dermatology. Office: Laser Inst for Dermatology 2021 Santa Monica Blvd #600E Santa Monica CA 90404

SHAMBAUGH, JOAN DIBBLE, literature educator, writer; b. Hillsdale, Mich., Mar. 14, 1928; d. Edwin Andrew and Helen Melissa (Crum) Dibble; m. Benjamin Shambaugh, Dec. 26, 1950 (div. Apr. 1964); children: Benjamin Dibble, Jeannette Melissa, Nathaniel Capps. AB, Duke U., 1949; MEd, Lesley Coll., 1980. Cert. elem. and secondary tchr., Mich. Fourth grade tchr. Grand Traverse Pub. Schs., Traverse City, Mich., 1949-50; asst. prof. Harvard Extension, Cambridge, Mass., 1966-74; moderator, tchr. creative writing workshop Lincoln Sudbury (Mass.) Adult Edn., 1972-79; tchr. creative writing workshop Concord Carlyle Continuing Edn., 1978-89; tchr. writing workshops Out & About, Morrisville, Vt., 1995; tchr. jour. keeping Trapp Family Lodge, Stowe, Vt., 1995-98. Invited papers to Duke U. Libr. Manuscript Dept. Will Perkins Library, 1982; Directory of American Poets and Fiction Writers, 1980-91. Author: The New Road to China, 1995, sequel China, 1996; editor, pub. Acorn Press, Lincoln, Mass., 1975-98; poet; contbr. articles to literary mags. Mem.: Women's Internat. League for Peace and Freedom. Avocations: walking, swimming, painting, yoga, guitar. Home: 3413 Rte 14 Craftsbury VT 05826

SHAMES, GERMAINE W. journalist, writer; AS summa cum laude, Cornell U., 1976; MS summa cum laude, U. Houston, 1978; cert. in Intercultural Tng., Georgetown U., 1980; MS, Sch. for Internat. Tng., Brattleboro, Vt., 1981—83. Cert. clin. hypnotherapy Wesland Inst., 1995. Corp. spl. projects mgr. Hilton Internat. Hotels, N.Y.C., 1980—90; program dir. Project Self-Sufficiency, Lafayette, NJ, 1990—93. Author: Transcultural Odysseys: The Emerging Global Consciousness, 1997, Between Two Deserts, 2002; co-author: World-Class Service, 1989. Recipient award, Fundacion Valparaiso, 1999; fellow Lit. fellowship in Fiction, Ariz. Commn. on the Arts, 1998; grantee, 1999; scholar Hilton scholarship, U. of Houston, 1978—80, U. of Ariz., 1995. Mem.: Soc. of S.W. Authors, Am. PEN. Achievements include first to being among first group of American journalists invited to Romania by the Romanian government following the fall of Ceausescu. Avocations: ethnology, world issues, environmentalism, ceramic art. Office: Anderson Grinberg Literary Management 266 West 23rd Street Number 3 New York NY 10011 E-mail: kandersongrin@aol.com.

SHAMIM, MAH TALAT, chemist; b. Karachi, Pakistan, Sept. 7, 1952; came to U.S., 1976; d. Syed Hasan and Askaribi (Nuzhat) Akhtar; m. A. Najm Shamim, Dec. 20, 1975. BS in Chemistry, Karachi U., 1972, MS in Chemistry, 1973, Howard U., 1981, PhD in Chemistry, 1983. Postdoctoral fellow NIH, Bethesda, Md., 1983-89, sr. staff fellow, 1989-91; chemist EPA, Washington, 1991-93, sect. chief environ. fate and effects divsn., 1993-97, chief environ. risk br. environ fate and effects divsn., 1997—. Panelist U.S. Merit Sys. Protection Adv. Bd., Washington, 1996—; mem. internat. environ. fate workgroups. Co-author: Rejection Rate Analysis: Environmental Fate Guidelines, 1995; contbr. articles to profl. jours. Mem. Am. Chem. Soc., Assn. Asian-Pacific Ams. Avocations: gardening, sewing, painting, writing. Office: Environ Protection Agy 401 M St SW Washington DC 20024-2610 E-mail: shamim.mah@epa.gov.

SHAMY, JENNIFER ANN, art educator; b. Neenah, Wis., Oct. 19, 1958; d. James Harold Ulmen and Joan Christine Molloy; m. Edward Thomas Shamy, Mar. 21, 1981 (div. Jan. 15, 1993); children: Corinne, Lillian, Alex. BA in Psychology, U. Wis., 1980. Gallery mgr. Humanities Art Gallery U. Wis., Madison, 1979—80; vol. Peace Corps., Paraguay, 1980—83; graphic artist Today's Sunbeam Newspaper, Salem, NJ, 1983—84; graphic designer, illustrator Pocono Outdoor Advt., Bangor, Pa., 1986—89; instr. preschool-12 Studio Programs Art Mus. W.Va., 1992—95; supr. Art Venture: A Children's Ctr., Art Mus. W.Va., 1994—98; coord. children's edn. Art Mus. W.Va., 1998—2000; elem. art tchr. Roanoke City Schs., 2000—; adj. prof. Hollins U., 2002—. Creator and facilitator photography workshop Inner Visions, 1999; coord. devel. and installation tile mural Fishburn Pk. Elem. Sch., 2002. Chair PTA Reflections program Wasena Elem. Sch., 1989—98, chair playground fundraising com, 1991—93; chair designer, fabricator Sweet Charity Fundraiser Arts Coun. of Blue Ridge, 1998. Named Chgo. Citizen of Yr., Cath. Youth Orgn. Rep., 1976; recipient Gov.'s award for Volunteering Excellence, 1994; Grant to establish two schoolrooms, Peace Corps, 1982.

SHANAHAN, EILEEN FRANCES, secondary school educator; b. Bethlehem, Pa., Sept. 10, 1949, d. Edward Vincent and Geraldine Mary (Gilligan) S. BA, Moravian Coll., 1971. Cert. secondary tchr. in Spanish, English, N.J. Tchr. Kingsway Regional High Sch. Dist., Swedesboro, N.J., 1971—. Mem. NEA, N.J. Edn. Assn., Gloucester County Edn. Assn., Fgn. Lang. Educators N.J., Kingsway Edn. Assn. (sec. membership), Archaeol. Soc. N.J., Hellertown Hist. Soc., Gloucester County Hist. Soc. Democrat. Roman Catholic. Avocations: archaeology, historical research, genealogy.

SHANAHAN, ELIZABETH ANNE, art educator; b. High Point, N.C., Apr. 5, 1950; d. Joe Thomas and Nancy Elizabeth (Moran) Gibson; m. Robert James Shanahan, Aug. 31, 1969 (div. Mar. 1987); children: Kimberly Marie Shanahan Conlon, Brigette Susanne Shanahan Foshee. Student, Forsyth Tech. Coll., 1974-83, Tri-County Tech. Coll., 1989, Inst. of Children's Lit., 1989. Owner cleaning bus., Winston-Salem, N.C., 1985-86, 87; instr. Anderson (S.C.) Arts Coun., 1987—, Tri-County Tech. Coll., Pendleton, S.C., 1987-98. Artist Wild Geese, 1985 (Best in Show). Active Libr. of Congress, 1994. Mem. Anderson Art Assn. (con. 1987—), Met. Arts Coun. (Upstate Visual Arts divsn.), Triad Art Assn. (pres. Kernersville, N.C. chpt. 1984-85), Nat. Mus. Women in Arts (charter), Libr. of Congress (charter). Avocations: writing, sewing, traveling, decorating. Home: 2519 Mountain View Church Rd King NC 27021-7645

SHANAHAN, SHEILA ANN, pediatrician, educator; m. Justin Laurence Cashman Jr., Sept. 14, 1968; children: Justin III, Gillis. BA, Trinity Coll., 1963; MD cum laude, Med. Coll. Pa., 1969. Diplomate Nat. Bd. Med. Examiners, Am. Bd. Pediats. Intern Presbyn. Hosp., N.Y.C., 1969-70, resident in pediats., 1970-72, asst. in clin. pediats., 1972-75, assoc. clin. pediats., 1975-78; pvt. practice specializing in pediats. Greenwich, Conn., 1972-78; asst. attending Greenwich Hosp., 1972-73, assoc. attending, 1973-78; from instr. to assoc. Columbia Coll. Physicians and Surgeons, N.Y.C., 1972-78; asst. prof. pediats. George Washington U. Sch. Medicine, Washington, 1980—, Georgetown U. Sch. Medicine, Washington, 1984—; pvt. practice specializing in pediats. Washington, 1984—. Attending dept. ambulatory medicine Children's Hosp. Nat. Med. Ctr., Washington, 1980-84; courtesy staff Georgetown U. Hosp., Washington, 1984—, George Washington U. Hosp., 1984—, Sibley Meml. Hosp., Washington, 1984—, Columbia Hosp. for Women, 1984-2002, Children's Hosp. Nat. Med. Ctr., 1984—. Fellow Am. Acad. Pediats.; mem. Am. Women's Med. Assn. Office: 4900 Massachusetts Ave NW Washington DC 20016-4358

SHANAS, ETHEL, sociology educator; b. Chgo., Sept. 6, 1914; d. Alex and Rebecca (Rich) S.; m. Lester J. Perlman, May 17, 1940; 1 child, Michael Stephen AB, U. Chgo., 1935, AM, 1937, PhD, 1949; LHD (hon.), Hunter Coll., N.Y.C., 1985. Instr. human devel. U. Chgo., 1947-52, rsch. assoc. prof., 1961-65; sr. rsch. analyst City of Chgo., 1952-53; sr. study dir. Nat. Opinion Rsch. Ctr., Chgo., 1956-61; prof. sociology U. Ill., Chgo., 1965-82, prof. emerita, 1982—. Vice chmn. expert com. on aging UN, 1974; mem. com. on aging NRC, Washington, 1978-82, panel on statistics for an aging population, 1984-86; mem. U.S. Com. on Vital and Health Stats., Washington, 1976-79. Author: The Health of Older People, 1962; (with others) Old People in Three Industrial Societies, 1968; editor: (with others) Handbook of Aging and the Social Sciences, 1976, 2d edit., 1985 Bd. govs. Chgo. Heart Assn., 1972-80; mem. adv. council on aging City of Chgo., 1972-78 Keston lectr. U. So. Calif., 1975; recipient Burgess award Nat. Council on Family Relations, 1978; Disting. Chgo. Gerontologist award Assn. for Gerontology in Higher Edn., 1988. Fellow: Am. Sociol. Assn. (chmn. sect. on aging 1985—86, Disting. Scholar award 1987), Gerontol. Soc. Am. (pres. 1974—75, Kleemeier award 1977, Brookdale award 1981); mem.: Inst. Medicine of NAS, Midwest Sociol. Soc. (pres. 1980—81). Home: 222 Main St Evanston IL 60202-2488

SHAND, MARY See RULE, MARY

SHANDS, GAIL MAXINE, environmental scientist; b. Bklyn., Apr. 10, 1952; d. Leon and Mitzi (Edelman) Shands; m. Miles B. Kessler, Dec. 30, 1973; children: Marc Philip, Jeff Eric. BS, Cornell U., 1973; MS, Purdue U., 1975; MPA, NYU, 1985. Soil scientist USDA-NRCS, Colo., 1976, soil conservationist, 1977; project mgr. U.S. AID, Washington, 1978-82; owner/mgr. Coll. Scholarship Network, Colo., 1988-90; dir. urban edn. project Denver Audubon Soc., 1993-97; owner Gail Shands Assocs., Inc., 1998—. Cons. natural resources, environ. scis., NEPA compliance; reservist Fed. Emergency Mgmt. Agy. Reviewer state environ. edn. master plan Colo. Alliance for Environ. Edn.; vol. Denver Russian REsettlement Program, 1992-94, Women's Am. Orgn. for Rehab. and Tng., Denver, 1993—. NYU Acad. scholar, 1982-85. Mem. Am. Soc. Pub. Adminstrn., Am. Soc. Agronomy, Am. Planning Assn. (task force on pub. lands policy 1985). Achievements include participation in initial evaluation of the Senegal River basin development.

SHANE, RITA, opera singer, educator; b. N.Y.C. d. Julius J. and Rebekah (Milner) S.; m. Daniel F. Tritter, June 22, 1958; 1 child, Michael Shane. BA, Barnard Coll., 1958; postgrad., Santa Fe Opera Apprentice Program, 1962-63, Hunter Opera Assn., 1962-64; pvt. study with, Beverly Peck Johnson, Elizabeth Schwartzkopf, Bliss Hebert. Adj. prof. voice Manhattan Sch. of Music, 1993-95. Prof. voice Eastman Sch. Music Rochester U., 1989—, Aspen Music Sch., 1999, Hamamatsu, Japan, 2000—02; pvt. tchr., N.Y.C., 1978—; judge Richard Tucker Music Found., Met. Opera Regional Auditions, Licia Albanese Puccini Found. Performer with numerous opera cos., including profl. debut, Chattanooga Opera, 1964, Met. Opera, San Francisco Opera, N.Y.C. Opera, Chgo. Lyric Opera, San Diego Opera, Santa Fe Opera, Teatro alla Scala, Milan, Italy, Bavarian State Opera, Netherlands Nat. Opera, Geneva Opera, Vienna State Opera, Phila., New Orleans, Balt. Opera, Opera du Rhin, Strasbourg, Scottish Opera, Teatro Reggio, Turin, Opera Metropolitana, Caracas, Portland Opera, Minn. Opera, also others; world premiere Miss Havisham's Fire, Argento; Am. premieres include Reimann-Lear, Schat-Houdini, Henze-Elegy for Young Lovers; participant festivals, including Mozart Festival, Lincoln Center, N.Y.C., Munich Festival, Aspen Festival, Handel Soc., Vienna Festival, Salzburg Festival, Munich Festival, Perugia Festival, Festival Canada, Glyndebourne Festival, performed with orchs. including Santa Cecilia, Rome, Austrian Radio, London Philharmn., Louisville, Cin., Cleve., Phila., RAI, Naples, Denver, Milw., Israel Philharm., rec. artist, RCA, Columbia, Louisville, Turnabout, Myto labels, also radio and TV. Recipient Martha Baird Rockefeller award, William Matheus Sullivan award. Mem. Am. Guild Mus. Artists, Screen Actors Guild, Nat. Assn. Tchrs. Singing. Office: care Daniel F Tritter 330 W 42nd St New York NY 10036-6902 E-mail: rtritter@earthlink.net.

SHANE, SANDRA KULI, postal service administrator; b. Akron, Ohio, Dec. 12, 1939; d. Amiel M. and Margaret E. (Brady) Kuli; m. Fred Shane, May 30, 1962 (div. 1972); 1 child, Mark Richard; m. Byrl William Campbell, Apr. 26, 1981 (dec. 1984). BA, U. Akron, 1987, postgrad., 1988-90. Scheduler motor vehicle bur. Akron Police Dept., 1959-62; flight and ops. control staff Escort Air, Inc., Akron and Cleve., 1972-78; asst. traffic mgr. Keen Transport, Inc., Hudson, Ohio, 1978-83; mem. ops. and mktg. staff Shawnee Airways and Essco, Akron, 1983-86; in distbn. U.S. Postal Svc., Akron, 1986—. Rec. sec. Affirmative Action Coun., Akron, 1988-90. Asst. art tchr. Akron Art Mus., 1979; counselor Support, Inc., Akron, 1983-84; com. chmn. Explorer post Boy Scouts Am., Akron,

1984-85. Mem. Bus. and Profl. Women's Assn. (pres.), Delta Nu Alpha. Democrat. Roman Catholic. Avocations: painting, sculpting, fabric design. Home: 455 E Bath Rd Cuyahoga Falls OH 44223-2511

SHANKLE, KELLI ANN, social worker; b. Yuba City, Calif., Apr. 13, 1970; d. Rodney Eugene and Helen Elizabeth Hughie; m. Roy Daniel Shankle. Assoc. degree, Carl Albert State Coll., 1996; psychology courses, Ark. Tech. U., 1996—97; BSW, Northeastern State U., 1999; postgrad., U. Okla., 2001—. Lic. cert., lic. True Colors. Working with people with mental/phys. disabilities Kibois Supportive Living, Poteau, Okla., 1990—95; case mgr. supportive living Bost Human Svcs., Ft. Smith, Ark., 1995—; intern DHS, Poteau, 2003—. Counselor youth camps, 1988—90; vol. Spl. Olympics, 1990—95, Girl Scouts, 1990—98, Jr. Civic League Ft. Smith, 1999—2003. Mem.: Phi Alpha. Address: 2401 Fordham Ave Fort Smith AR 72908-7854

SHANKLIN, ANNIE THOMAS, retired education educator; b. Crosby, Tex., Oct. 20, 1930; d. James Alexander and M. Pauline (Drenon) Thomas; m. Austin Don Shanklin III, Feb. 11, 1956; children: Penelope Dawn, Wandalyn Ylonde, Miriam Daphne, Donna Lynn, Adrienne Dee, Mia Johnee. BA, Tex. So. U., 1953; MS, U. Houston, 1992. Cert. spl. edn. tchr., Tex. Tchr. Crosby Ind. Sch. Dist., 1954-58, Houston Ind. Sch. Dist., 1959-87; mgmt. positions, 1988-93; adj. prof. S.E. Coll., Houston, 1993-94; ret., 1994. Author: Precious Memories, 1997 (Plaque); participant film Fire Drill-The Life Saving Mission, 1985. Del. Dem. State Conv., San Antonio, 1973; organizer presentation of debutants FLC Pageant-South Park Ch., 1985; block capt. Cloverland Civic Club, Houston, 1986; libr. South Park Bapt. Ch., 1974-82; del. Impact II Conv., Boston, 1987. Recipient Plaque, South Park Bapt. Ch., 1982, Regional Granny Smith award Kroger Stores, 1996; Impact II grantee, 1986. Mem. NAFE, Crosby C. of C., Elias Carson Civic Club (founder, pres. 1993-97), Phi Delta Kappa, Sigma Gamma Rho (chaplain). Avocations: crafts, reading, writing, computer games, walking. Home: 5826 Avenue C Crosby TX 77532-8705

SHANKLIN, ELIZABETH E. secondary school educator; b. Nashville, July 23, 1934; d. J. Gordon and Emily (Shacklett) S. BS, Columbia U., 1956; MA, Sarah Lawrence Coll., 1990. Tchr. N.Y.C. Bd. of Edn., 1968-96. Author: The Answer is Matriarchy, 1978, Toward Matriarchy: The Radical Struggle of Women in the United States to Reconstruct Motherhood 1785-1925, 1990, Authorizing Mothers, 1824-1833, 2004. Mem. AAUW, AFT, Am. Hist. Assn., Orgn. Am. Historians, The Feminists. Green Party. Home: 2600 Netherland Ave Bronx NY 10463-4801

SHANKS, ANN ZANE, filmmaker, producer/director, photographer, writer; b. N.Y.C. d. Louis and Sadye (Rosenthal) Kushner; m. Ira Zane (dec.); children— Jennifer, Anthony; m. Robert Horton Shanks, Sept. 25, 1959; 1 child, John. Student, Carnegie-Mellon U., Columbia U., 1949. Tchr., moderator spl. symposiums Mus. Modern Art, N.Y.C.; tchr. New Sch. U. Photographer, writer: for numerous mags. and newspapers; prodr., dir. (movie shorts) Ctrl. Pk., 1969 (U.S. entry Edinburgh Film Festival, Cine Golden Eagle award, Cambodia Film Festival award), Denmark..A Loving Embrace (Cine Golden Eagle award, 1973), Tivoli, 1972—79 (San Francisco Film Festival award, Am. Film Festival award), (TV series) Am. Life Style (Silver award, 5 Gold medal awards Internat. TV and Film Festival N.Y., 2 Cine Golden Eagle awards), He's Fired, She's Hired; prodr.: (CBS TV Drop-Out Mother), prodr., dir., writer (TV short) Mousie Baby; dir.: (TV movie) Drop-Out Father, CBS; prodr.: (plays, video spl.) The Avante-Garde in Russia 1910-1930, Arts and Entertainment channel, ABC Morning Show, Good Afternoon Detroit (Emmy award nomination); prodr., dir. (TV spl.) A Day in the Country, PBS, (Off Broadway play) S.J. Perelman in Person; prodr.: (Broadway plays) Lillian; exhibited (photographs) Mus. Modern Art, Mus. City N.Y., Transit Mus., Bklyn. Heights, N.Y., Met. Mus. Art, Jewish Mus., Howard Greenberg Gallery, N.Y.C., 1999, photographer (one-woman shows) Ann Shanks one-person exhibition, N.Y. Hist. Soc., N.Y.C., 2003—04, (accompanying catalogue (64 pages) "Ann Zane Shanks Behind the Lens", 2003; prodr.: Discovery channel, U.S.; author: (photographs and text) The Name's the Game, New Jewish ency.; author: (photographer, writer) (book) Old is What You Get, Busted Lives..Dialogues with Kids in Jail, 1983; writer, photographer: book Garbage and Stuff; photography (in collections of) Merv Griffin, N.Y. Pub. Libr., Mus. of City of N.Y., Met. Mus., N.Y., others, represented (permanent collections) N.Y. Pub. Libr. Recipient awards from internat. photography competitions. Mem. Am. Soc. Mag. Photographers (bd. govs.), Women in Film (v.p.), Dirs. Guild Am.; trustee Overseas Press Club.

SHANKS, JUDITH WEIL, editor; b. Montgomery, Ala., Nov. 2, 1941; d. Roman Lee and Charlotte (Alexander) Weil; m. Hershel Shanks, Feb. 20, 1966; children: Elizabeth Shanks Alexander, Julia Emily. BA in Econs., Wellesley Coll., 1963; MBA, Trinity Coll., 1980. Econs. asst. Export-Import Bank, Washington, 1963-68; cons. econs. and social sci., 1968-76; researcher Time-Life Books, Alexandria, Va., 1976-80, prin. researcher, 1980-83, illustrations editor, 1983, adminstrv. editor, 1984-95, dir. editl. adminstrn., 1996; assoc. curator S.C. Jewish Heritage Exhibit, Coll. Charleston, 1998—. Vol. Mentors, Inc. Recipient Sr. Rsch. award Hadassah Brandeis Inst. Democrat. Jewish. Avocations: dance, scuba diving, hiking, gardening, research on women. Home: Box 42456 Washington DC 20015

SHANKS, PATRICIA L. lawyer; b. Salt Lake City, Apr. 3, 1940; BA in Microbiology with honors, Stanford U., 1962; JD, U. Colo., 1978. Bar: Calif. 1978. Mng. ptnr. McCutchen, Doyle, Brown & Enersen, L.A., 1990-94, ptnr., 1985—. Trustee L.A. County Bar Found. Recipient West Publishing award; Stork scholar. Mem. Order of the Coif, Practice in Environ. Law. Office: McCutchen Doyle Brown & Enersen 355 S Grand Ave Ste 4400 Los Angeles CA 90071-3106

SHANNON, BARBARA, dean, nutrition educator; PhD in Nutrition, Purdue U., 1971. Prof. nutrition, dean Coll. Health and Human Devel. Pa. State U., University Park. Achievements include research on application of nutrition principles, behavior change theory and educational methods to the improvement of human dietary habits. Office: Office of Dean Coll Health Pa State Univ 201 Henderson Bldg University Park PA 16802-6501

SHANNON, CAROLYN JEAN, interior designer; b. Vincennes, Ind., Nov. 22, 1943; d. Melvin Eugene and Melita Harriet (Bair) Powell; m. Thomas E. Battle III; children: Timothy Carl, Heather Caroline. BA in Telecomms. and Interior Design, Ind. U., 1985. Interior designer Buchanan & Sons Furniture, also Kitchen and Bath Ctr., Bloomington, Ind., 1975-81; also freelance Bloomington, 1975-81; sales mgr. Kittle's Ethan Allen, Bloomington and Indpls., 1981-82; owner, cons. The Profl. Woman, career enhancement seminars, Bloomington, 1982-84; interior designer Interiors, Bloomington, 1984-87; owner Carolyn Shannon Interiors, Bloomington and Chgo., 1987—. Dir. Atlas Galleries, Chgo., 1991—94; exec. dir. Inner Cir. Edn./Realty U., 2000—; v.p. membership Realty U., 2002—. Rep. Local Coun. of Women, owners Bloomington Hosp., 1985—. Mem.: Am. Soc. Interior Designers, NAFE, Real Estate Educators Consortium, Phi Beta Kappa, Golden Key, Phi Delta Kappa (scholarship 1984), Psi Iota Xi. Methodist. Avocations: bridge, travel, tennis, antique collecting and dealing. Home: 10471 W Grandview Dr Columbus IN 47201-8699 E-mail: cjshannon@insightbb.com.

SHANNON, CHARLOTTE P. music educator; b. Moline, Ill., July 30, 1975; d. Donavin S. and Miriam Gail Calmer; m. Patrick David Shannon. BA in Music, Oral Roberts U., 1997. Cert. music tchr. grades K-12 Okla. Drama, music dir. Lincoln Christian Sch., Tulsa, Okla., 1997—. Mem.: Music Educators Nat. Conf., Am. Choral Dirs. Assn. Avocations: baking, gardening, piano, singing.

SHANNON, DENISE LESLIE, nurse; b. Denver, July 9, 1963; d. Walter Lee and Kathleen Angela (Hyland) S. BSN, U. Colo. Health Sci. Ctr., 1992. RN, Colo. Program dir. Am. Diabetes Assn., Denver, 1986-92; staff nurse Rose Med. Ctr., Denver, 1992-96; admissions dir. Mediplex Rehab. Hosp., Thornton, Colo., 1996-97, program mgr. brain injury rehab., 1997—98; v.p. inpatient svcs. Hospice of Metro Denver, 1998—. Pres. Rose Med. Ctr. Nursing Congress, 1995-96. Newsletter editor Washington Park Cmty. Ctr., Denver, 1994-96. Mem. Colo. Nurses Assn. (co-pres. dist. 19 1994—), Friends of Nursing. Democrat. Avocations: cooking, biking, music, reading. Home: 10186 Flower Ct Broomfield CO 80021-3871 Office Phone: 303-388-7949 5012. E-mail: denise@denverhospice.org.

SHANNON, IRIS REED, health consultant; b. Chgo. d. Ira Paul and Iola Sophia (Williams) Reed; m. Robert Alwood Shannon, Aug. 21, 1953. BS in Nursing, Fisk U.-Meharry Med. Coll., 1948; MA, U. Chgo., 1954; PhD, U. Ill., Chgo., 1987; D in Pub. Svc. (hon.), Elmhurst Coll., 1993. Staff nurse Chgo. Bd. Health, 1948-50; instr. pub. health nursing Meharry Med. Coll., Nashville, 1951-56; tchr.-nurse, health coordinator child devel. Head Start, Chgo. Bd. Edn., 1957-66; dir. community nursing Mile Sq. Neighborhood Health Center, Presbyn.-St. Luke's Hosp., Chgo., 1966-69; co-dir. nurse assoc. programs Rush Presbyn.-St. Luke's Hosp., 1971-76; chairperson community nursing Rush U., Chgo., 1972-77, acting chairperson, 1988-90; asst. prof. pub. health nursing U. Ill., 1971-74; assoc. prof. cmty. nursing Rush U., 1974-97, health sys. mgr., 1988—, health cons., 1974—. Adj. faculty Sch. Pub. Health, U. N.C., 1977—85; mem. profl. adv. bd. Vis. Nurse Assn. Chgo., 1973—75; cons. Video Nursing, Inc.; mem. profl. adv. com. Mile Sq. Home Health Unit, Chgo., 1975—77; mem. nat. adv. coun. on nurse tng. HEW, 1978—81; mem. Nat. Task Force on Credentialing in Nursing, 1979—82; mem. Chgo. regional com. Ill. White House Conf. on Children, 1979—80; v.p. Chgo. Bd. Health, 1989—99. Named Prin. for a Day, Brownell Elem. Sch., Mayor's Office, City of Chgo., 1998—99, Englewood Tech. Prep. Acad., 2000—01; recipient award of merit, Ill. Pub. Health Assn., 1979, 1989—2000, Outstanding Achievement award, YWCA of Met. Chgo., 1988, Disting. Svc. award, Chgo. chpt. Meharry Alumni, 1989, Lowenberg Chair of Excellence in Nursing, Memphis State U., 1993, Bd. Trustees' Svc. medal, Rush-Presby. St. Luke's Med. Ctr., 1996, Lifeline award, Cmty. Mental Health Coun., 2002. Fellow: APHA (chmn. pub. health nursing sect. 1977—79, governing coun. 1980—82, exec. bd. 1985—87, pres. 1988—89, governing coun. 1989—99), Am. Acad. Nursing, Royal Soc. Health (hon. 1989); mem.: ANA (Pearl McIver Pub. Health Nurse award 1998), Inst. of Medicine of NAS, Delta Sigma Theta, Sigma Theta Tau. Home: 3100 S King Dr Chicago IL 60616-3634 E-mail: irisshannon@aol.com.

SHANNON, JACQUELINE, association executive; married; 2 children. MA in Edn., Angelo State U.; postgrad., Villanova U. Formerly tchr. English and reading; pres. nat. bd. dirs. Nat. Alliance for the Mentally Ill, 1998—. A founder Concho Valley (Tex.) affil. chpt. Nat. Alliance for the Mentally Ill, 1980s, pres. Tex. bd. dirs.. Recipient Helen Farabee Wings award Tex. Dept. Mental Health/Mental Retardation, 1995, Friend of Counseling award Three River Counseling Assn., 1995, others. Office: Nat Alliance Mentally Ill 2107 Wilson Blvd Ste 300 Arlington VA 22201-3042

SHANNON, JULIE (JULIE GELLER), musician, music educator, composer, lyricist; b. Springfield, Ohio, Mar. 15, 1941; d. LeRoy Stewart and Marie Arment; m. William Alan Geller, Oct. 1, 1978. MusB, U. Mich., 1963, MusM, 1964. Tchr. vocal music Deerfield (Ill.) Pub. Schs., 1964—83; artist-in-residence Ill. Arts Coun., Chgo., 1985—2000, North Shore Country Day Sch., Winnetka, Ill., 1991—, numerous other pub. & pvt. schs., Ill., 1990—. Composer, lyricist: plays The Christmas Schooner, 1993 (After Dark Outstanding New Work award, Chgo., 1996), Stones, 1989 (Best Musical award, Phoenix, 1994, Black Theatre Alliance award, 2000), Let the Eagle Fly: The Story of Cesar Chavez & the Farm Workers, 2003 (Am. Music Ctr. Copying Assistance Ctr. award, 2003), songs One Breath, 1989 (selected for choral arrangement by Kirby Shaw, 2003), albums Let's Fill Up the House with Stories & Songs, 1999 (Parents Choice Approved award, 2000), We All Have Songs, We All Have Stories, 1995, songs Baby, You're OK, 1983 (Excalibur award for best pub. film from Pub. Rels. Assn., 1984), tv commercial Soxfest, 1989 (Top Mktg. award Baseball Promotion Corp., 1983); composer: (songs) (tv show) Beyond the Magic Door (Emmy award, Chgo., 1983); composer, lyricist: intergenerational church svc. We All Have Stories (Unitarian Churches of Am. award for most outstanding intergenerational worship svc., 1998). Fellow, Ill. Arts Coun., 1984; grantee Chmn.'s Grant, 1986. Mem.: ASCAP (Popular Music award 1986—2003), Am. Fedn. Musicians, Dramatists Guild. Home: 2116 Thornwood Ave Wilmette IL 60091-1452

SHANNON, MARGARET ANNE, lawyer; b. Detroit, July 6, 1945; d. Johannes Jacob and Vera Marie (Spade) Van De Graaf; m. Robert Selby Shannon, Feb. 4, 1967. Student, Brown U., 1963-65; BA in History, Wayne State U., 1966, JD, 1973. Bar: Mich. 1973. Housing aide City of Detroit, 1967-68; employment supr. Sinai Hosp., Detroit, 1968-69; assoc. gen. counsel regulatory affairs Blue Cross Blue Shield Mich., Detroit, 1969-80; ptnr. Honigman Miller Schwartz and Cohn, Detroit, 1980-95, of counsel, 1996—. Nat. Merit scholar, 1963-66. Mem. Mich. State Bar (chmn. health care com. 1991, 92, co-chmn. payor subcom. health law sect.). Home: 111 Orinoco Way Palm Beach Gardens FL 33410 Office: Honigman Miller Schwartz and Cohn 2290 First National Bldg Detroit MI 48226-3583 Office Phone: 313-465-7552. E-mail: mshannon@honigman.com.

SHANNON, MARGARET T. nursing administrator, educator; b. New Haven, June 23, 1939; d. Michael Joseph and Ellen (McNamara) S. MS in Chemistry, St. Louis U., 1967; BSN, Northwestern State U. of La., Nachitoches, 1978; MN, La. State U., New Orleans, 1981; PhD., U. New Orleans, 1987. Staff nurse Touro Infirmary, New Orleans, 1978-80; instr. nursing Touro Infirmary Sch. Nursing, New Orleans, 1980-85; asst. prof. nursing La. State U. Health Sci. Ctr., New Orleans, 1985-88; prof., dean divsn. nursing Our Lady of Holy Cross Coll., New Orleans, 1988—. Author: Giovani & Hayes Drugs and Nursing Implications, 8th edit., 1995, (with B.A. Wilson and C. Stang) Nurses' Drug Guide (Annual), 1993, 94, 95, 96, 97, 98, 99, 00. Mem. ANA, NLN, La. League for Nursing, La. State Nurses Assn., Sigma Theta Tau, Phi Kappa Phi, Phi Delta Kappa.

SHANNON, MARYLIN LINFOOT, state legislator, educator; b. LaGrande, Oreg., Sept. 7, 1941; BA in Edn., Ctrl. Wash. U. Mem. Oreg. Legislature, Salem, 1994—, mem. edn. com., mem. gen. govt. com., mem. health and human svcs. com., chair transp. com., mem. water and land use com. Republican. Home: 7955 Portland Rd NE Brooks OR 97305-9401 Office: S 218 State Capitol Salem OR 97310

SHAO COLLINS, JEANNINE, magazine publisher; married; 1 child. BA in Econs., U. Rochester. Various advt. sales mgmt. positions Woman's Day, N.Y.C., Prevention mag.; N.Y. advt. mgr. Ladies' Home Jour., Meredith Corp., N.Y.C., 1993-95, advt. dir. Better Homes and Gardens, Des Moines, 1995-98, assoc. pub., 1998-99, pub., 1999—2002, v.p., 2000—02, v.p., group pub. N.Y.C., 2002—.*

SHAPERO, ESTHER BAILEY GELLER, artist; b. Boston, Oct. 26, 1921; d. Harry Gregor and Fannie (Geller) Geller; m. Harold Samuel Shapero, Sept. 21, 1945; 1 child, Hannah. Diploma, Sch. Boston Mus. Fine Arts, 1943. Tchr. Boston Mus. Fine Arts, Natick Art Assn., 1945-70. One woman shows include Mus. of Fine Arts Boston, Boris Mirski Art Mus., De Cordova Mus., Am. Acad. Rome, Worcester Art Mus., Decenter Gallery, Denmark, Danforth Mus. Art; exhibited in group shows at Chgo. Art Inst., San Francisco Mus., Smith Coll. Mus., Elders in Arts Show, 1997, Firehouse Studio Artists Show, Natick, Mass., 1998, 31 Main St. Gallery, 1998. Cabot fellow Am. Acad. Rome, 1949, 49-50, 70-71; named Boston's Honored Artists, 1995. Office: Firehouse Studios 5 Summer St Natick MA 01760-4511

SHAPIRO, ABRA BLAIR, real estate company executive; b. Akron, Ohio, Aug. 15, 1956; d. Norman Nathan and Merrill Barron Shapiro; m. Sanford Robert Epstein, Aug. 29, 1982 (div. July 1986). AA, Dekalb C.C., 1976; BA, Ga. State, 1978; CPM, Inst. Real Estate Mgmt., 1987. Lic. realtor Minn. Bd. Realtors, Ga. Bd. Realtors. V.p. Sidney's Mgmt. Co., Chaska, Minn., 1982—2002; ops. dir. Jon Shapiro, Atlanta, 2002—. Adv. bd. Barbers Hairstyling Inc., Mpls., 1986—88; cons. in field. Mem. Designers in Fight for AIDS, Mpls., 1996. Named Restaurator of Yr., Mpls. St. Paul Mag., 1995; recipient Hometown Hero award, WCCO, 2001, honor, Dayton Hudson Found., 1997. Home: 1617 Kinsmon Ln Marietta GA 30062

SHAPIRO, ANGELA, broadcast executive; BA, St. Peter's Coll. Co-owner Brookville Mktg/Greybark Advt.; owner, oper. several businesses; co-founder, pub. Soap Opera Digest, 1975, Soap Opera Update, 1988; co-prodr. Soap Opera Awards; sr. v.p. mkg. and promotion ABC Daytime, 1995, pres., 1998, Buena Vista Prodns., 2000; pres. ABC Family Channel Walt Disney Co., Burbank, Calif., 2002—. Office: 500 S Buena Vista St Burbank CA 91521-9722*

SHAPIRO, ANNA, microbiologist, researcher; b. N.Y.C., Jan. 11, 1910; d. Samuel and Esther (Cohen) Lewis; m. Joseph Shapiro, Feb. 7, 1933 (dec. 1985); children: Joan Elisabeth Brandston (dec.), Joel Elias. BS in Biology and Chemistry, NYU, 1931, MS in Bacteriology, 1934, PhD in Microbiology, 1971. Lab. asst. Bellevue Med. Sch., NYU, 1931-33, instr., 1933-36; lectr. Hofstra U., L.I., 1963, Queensborough U., CUNY, Queens, 1964; rsch. asst. Haskins Lab. of Pace Univ., N.Y.C., 1971-80, rsch. assoc., 1980-83. Author: Methods of Enzymology, 1980, The In Vitro Cultivation of Pathogens of Tropical Diseases, 1980; contbr. articles to profl. jours. Mem. AAAS, N.Y. Acad. Sci. (Disting. Svc. award 1992), Sigma Xi. Achievements include rsch. in the conversion of Nitrobacter agilis from a strict autotroph to a heterotroph by using replica plating techniques which can be considered an adaptive mutation; blockade of respiratory systems of parasites by using iron chelators--this work led to further research in pathogenic African trypanosomes. Home: 143 Cold Spring Point Rd Southampton NY 11968-3517

SHAPIRO, FANIA, computer company executive; CEO Setka Computer Cons., San Ramon, Calif. Office: Setka Computer Cons 3223 Crow Canyon Rd Ste 250 San Ramon CA 94583-1332 Fax: 925-824-0222.

SHAPIRO, FLORENCE, state legislator, advertising, public relations executive; b. N.Y.C., May 2, 1948; d. Martin Nmi and Ann (Spiesman) D.; m. Howard Nmi Shapiro, Dec. 28, 1969; children: Lisa, Todd, Staci. BS, U. Tex., 1970. Tchr. Richardson High Sch., Tex., 1970-72; advt., pub. rels. Shapiro & Co., Plano, Tex., 1982—; formerly mayor and mem. city coun. City of Plano, Tex.; now mem. Tex. Senate, 1992—, chmn. edn. com., mem. fin. com., natural resources com., and infrastructure, devel. and security com. Bd. dirs. Plano C. of C., Presbyn. and Children's Healthcare Ctr., Plano Econ. Devel. Bd., U. Tex. at Dallas Adv. Coun., The North Tex. Commn., The Dallas Regional Mobility Coalition; mem. nat. bd. dirs. Susan B. Komen Breast Cancer Found.; mem. adv. bd. Children's Edn. Fund Dallas, Dallas County Domestic Violence Task Force, Family Violence Prevention Coun. Injury Prevention Ctr. Greater Dallas. Recipient Plano Vol. of Yr. award, 1983, Plano Citizen of Yr. award, 1985, Athena award Plano C. of C. for Businesswoman of Yr., 1990, Child Advocate award Dallas Children's Advocacy Ctr., 1995, Legislator of Yr. award Tex. Mcpl. League, 1995, 97, Nat. Rep. Legislators Assn., 1997, Tex. Ct. Apptd. Spl. Advs., 1997; Outstanding Legislator of Yr. award Tex. Police Chiefs Assn., 1995, Legislator of Yr. award, 1997, Friend of the Taxpayer award Citizens for a Sound Economy, 1999, Centennial Hero award Plano Ind. Sch. Dist., 1999, Voice of Children award, Ct. Apptd. Spl. Advs. of Collin County, 2001, others; Outstanding Legislator award Tex. Assn. Dist. and County Attys., 1997, Leader of Excellence award Free Market Com., 1997, Senate Statesman award Lonestar Found., 1997, Polit. Courage award John Ben Sheppard Pub. Leadership Forum, 1997; named One of 10 Best Legislators family law session State Bar Tex., 1997, One of 3 State Senators on YCT Honor Roll, 1997, Legis. Star, Tex. Classroom Tchrs. Assn., 1997, Guardian of Free Enterprise, Nat. Fedn. Ind. Bus., 1999, Woman of Yr., Les Femmes du Monde, 2002, Woman of Yr., Women's Transp. Seminar Dallas-Ft. Worth, 2002, others; honored by Texans for Lawsuit Reform, 1997, Assn. Ob-Gyn. and Southwestern Med. Sch., 1997. Mem. Rotary (Paul Harris fellow 1990), Alpha Epsilon Phi (Nat. Outstanding Young Alumnae award). Republican. Jewish. Office: Tex Senate PO Box 12068 Austin TX 78711-2068 Home: 1500 Eastwick Ln Plano TX 75093-2443

SHAPIRO, JOAN ISABELLE, lab administrator, medical/surgical nurse; b. Aug. 26, 1943; d. Macy James and Frieda Lockhart; m. Ivan Lee Shapiro, Dec. 28, 1968; children: Audrey, Michael. Diploma, Peoria Meth. Sch. Nursing, 1964. RN. RN Nurse Grant Hosp., Columbus, Ohio, 1975-76, Cardiac Thoracic and Vascular Surgeons Ltd., Geneva, Ill., 1977—; mgr. non-invasive lab., 1979—. Owner operator Shapiro's Mastiff's 1976-82; sec.-treas. Sounds Svcs., 1976—, Mainstream Sounds Inc., 1980-84; co-founder Cardio-Phone Inc., 1982-99, Edgewater Vascular Inst., 1987-89, Associated Profls., 1989-92; v.p., bd. dir. Computer Specialists Inc., 1986-89; founder, pres. Vein Ctr., Edema Ctr. Ltd. Mem. Soc. Non-invasive Technologists, Soc. Peripheral Vascular Nursing (cmty. awareness com. 1984—), Oncology Nursing Soc., Internat. Soc. Lymphology, Kane County Med. Soc. Aux. (pres. 1983-84, adviser, 1984-85). Lutheran. Home: Cardiac Thoracic/Vas Surg PO Box 325 Fort Fairfield ME 04742-0325

SHAPIRO, JUDITH R. academic administrator, anthropology educator; b. N.Y.C., Jan. 24, 1942; Student, Ecole des Haute Etudes Inst. d'Etudes Politiques, Paris, 1961—62; BA, Brandeis U., 1963; PhD, Columbia U., 1972. Asst. prof. U. Chgo., 1970—75; fellow U. Calif., Berkeley, 1974—75; Rosalyn R. Schwartz lectr., asst. prof. anthropology Bryn Mawr Coll., Pa., 1975—78, assoc. prof., 1978—85, prof., 1985—94; pres. Barnard Coll., 1994—. Chmn. dept. Bryn Mawr Coll., 1982—85, acting dean undergrad coll., 1985—86, provost, 1986—94. Contbr. articles to profl. jours. Nat. adv. com. Woodrow Wilson Nat. Fellowship Found.; chair bd. dirs. Consortium on Financing Higher Edn.; bd. dirs. Fund for the City of N.Y.; chair bd. dirs. Women's Coll. Coalition. Fellow, Woodrow Wilson Found., 1963—64, Columbia U., 1964—65, Younger Humanist fellow, NEH, 1974—75, Am. Coun. Learned Socs., 1981—82, Ctr. for Advanced Study in the Behavioral Scis., 1989; grantee Summer Field Tng. grant, NSF, 1965, Ford Found., 1966, NIMH, 1974—75, Social Sci. Rsch. Coun., 1974—75. Mem.: Social Sci. Rsch. Coun. (com. social sci personnel 1977—80), Am. Anthrop. Assn. (ethics com. 1976—79, bd. dirs. 1984—86, exec. com. 1985—86), Am. Ethnol. Soc. (nominations com. 1983—84, pres. elect 1984—85, pres. 1985—86), Phila. Anthrop. Soc. (pres. 1983), Women's Forum, Sigma Xi, Phi Beta Kappa. Office: Barnard Coll Office of the Pres 3009 Broadway New York NY 10027-6501*

SHAPIRO, LUCILLE, molecular biology educator; b. N.Y.C., July 16, 1940; d. Philip and Yetta (Stein) Cohen; m. Roy Shapiro, Jan. 23, 1960 (div. 1977); 1 child, Peter; m. Harley H. McAdams, July 28, 1978; stepchildren: Paul, Heather. BA, Bklyn. Coll., 1962; PhD, Albert Einstein Coll. Medicine, 1966. Asst. prof. Albert Einstein Coll. Medicine, N.Y.C., 1967-72, assoc. prof., 1972-77, Kramer prof., chmn. dept. molecular biology, 1977-86, dir. biol. scis. divsn., 1981-86; Eugene Higgins prof., chmn. dept. microbiology, Coll. Physicians and Surgeons Columbia U., N.Y.C., 1986-89; Joseph D. Grant prof. devel. biology Stanford (Calif.) U. Sch. Medicine, 1989-97, chmn. dept. devel. biology, 1989-97, Virginia and D.K. Ludwig prof. of cancer rsch. dept. devel. biology, 1998—; dir. Beckman Ctr. Molecular & Genetic Medicine Stanford U., 2001—. Mem. bd. sci. counselors NIH, Washington, 1980—84; mem. bd. sci. advisors G.D. Searle Co., Skokie, Ill., 1984—86; mem. sci. adv. bd. SmithKline Beecham, 1993—2000, Glaxo-SmithKline, 2001—, bd. dirs.; mem. sci. adv. bd. PathoGenesis, 1995—2000, Ludwig Found., 2000—, Anacor Pharms., 2001—, bd. dirs.; mem. grants adv. coun. Beckman Found.; trustee Scientists Inst. for Pub Info., 1990—94; lectr. Harvey Soc., 1993; DeWitt Stetten disting. lectr., 89, 2002; John M. Lewis lectr. Rockefeller U., 1998; Marker lectr. Pa. State U., 1999; Lundberg lectr. Gothenburg U., Sweden, 1999; honors lectr. NYU, 1998; disting. scientist lectr. NAS, 1999; Crawford lectr. U. Iowa, 1999; Oshman lectr. Baylor U., 2000; Adam Neville lectr. U. Dundee, Scotland, 2001; Genome lectr. Harvard U., 2001; Jesup lectr. Columbia U., 2002; Hopwood lectr. John Ennes Inst., Norwich, England, 2003; mem. grants adv. coun. Bechman Found., 1999—; Stanier lectr. U. Calif., Berkeley, 2003. Editor: Microbiol. Devel., 1984; mem. editl. bd. Jour. Bacteriology, 1978-86, Trends in Genetics, 1987—, Genes and Development, 1987-91, Cell Regulation, 1990-92, Molecular Biology of the Cell, 1992-98, Molecular Microbiology, 1991-96, Current Opinion on Genetics and Devel., 1991—; contbr. articles to profl. jours. Mem. sci. bd. Helen Hay Witney Found., N.Y.C., 1986-94, Biozentrum, Basel, 1999-2001, Hutchinson Cancer Ctr., Seattle, 1999; mem. grants adv. bd. Beckman Found., 1999—; co-chmn. adv. bd. NSF Biology Directorate, 1988-89; vis. com., bd. overseers Harvard U., Cambridge, Mass., 1987-90, 2003—; mem. sci. bd. Whitehead Inst., MIT, Boston, 1988-93; mem. sci. rev. bd. Howard Hughes Med. Inst., 1990-94, Cancer Ctr. of Mass. Gen. Hosp., Boston, 1994; mem. Presidio Coun. City of San Francisco, 1991-94; mem. pres. coun. U. Calif., 1991-97. Recipient Hirschl Career Scientist award, 1976, Spirit of Achievement award, 1978, Alumna award of honor Bklyn. Coll., 1983, Excellence in Sci. award Fedn. Am. Soc. Exptl. Biology, 1994; Jane Coffin Child fellow, 1966; resident scholar Rockefeller Found., Bellagio, Italy, 1996. Fellow AAAS, Am. Acad. Arts and Scis., Am. Acad. Microbiology, Calif. Coun. on Sci. and Tech.; mem. NAS, Inst. Medicine of NAS, Am. Philos. Soc., Am. Soc. Biochemistry and Molecular Biology (nominating com. 1982, 87, coun. 1990-93), Am. Heart Assn. (sci. adv. bd. 1984-87). Avocation: watercolor painting. Office: Stanford U Sch Medicine Beckman Ctr Dept Devel Biology Stanford CA 94305

SHAPIRO, LUDMILLA NIKOLAEVNA, lecturer, photographer, journalist; b. Moscow, June 11, 1913; came to U.S., 1954; d. Nikolai Pavlovich and Alexandra Vladimirovna (Zhdanovskaya) Nikitin; m. Henry Shapiro Dec. 3, 1933 (dec. Apr. 1991); 1 child, Irina H. Corten. Diploma, Inst. Fgn. Langs., Moscow, 1932, Gorkiy Lit. Inst., 1939. Cert. interpreter in English, French and German, USSR. Translator, lectr., photographer Moscow Bur., UPI and N.Y. Herald Tribune, New York Times, 1935-73; corr. Moscow Bur., Religious News Svc., 1957-59, London Observer, 1960-61; rschr. Russian Rsch. Ctr., Harvard U., Cambridge, Mass., 1957; photographer Moscow Bur. Magnum Photos, 1958-60; Moscow rep. of Sol Hurok, impressario, 1965-68; lectr., cons. on Russia, U. Wis., Madison, 1973—. Author: How Russians Laugh at Themselves, 1975, (booklet) What the Russians Read, 1976; contbg. author: Anthology of 18th Century English and American Writers, 1938. Mem. AAUW, Harvard Dames. Avocation: collecting russian art (donated major collection of russian porcelain to cooper-hewitt museum).

SHAPIRO, MARIAN KAPLUN, psychologist; b. N.Y., July 13, 1939; d. David and Bertha (Pearlman) Kaplun; m. Irwin Ira Shapiro, Dec. 20, 1959; children: Steven, Nancy. BA, Queens Coll., 1959; MA in Tchg., Harvard U., 1961, EdD, 1978. Cert. psychologist. Tchr. North Quincy (Mass.) HS, 1962-64; instr. Carnegie Inst., Boston, 1968-74; staff psychologist South Shore Counselling Assn., Hanover, Mass., 1978-80; pvt. practice Lexington, Mass., 1980—. Adj. instr. Mass. Sch. Profl. Psychology, Dedham, 1985—. Author: (book) 2nd Childhood: Hypnoplay Therapy with Age--Regressed Adults, 1989; contbr. articles to profl. jours., poetry to lit. jours. Fellow: Am. Orthopsychiatric Assn.; mem.: APA, New Eng. Soc. Clin. Hypnosis, Internat. Soc. Study Dissociation, New Eng. Soc. Treatment Trauma and Dissociation, Am. Soc. Clin. Hypnosis (cert. cons.), Am. Soc. Group Psychotherapy (clin.), N.E. Soc. Group Psychotherapy, Mass. Psychol. Assn., Pi Lambda Theta, Sigma Alpha. Avocations: music, singing, piano, violin, writing poetry. Home and Office: 17 Lantern Ln Lexington MA 02421-6029 E-mail: mkshapiro@rcn.com.

SHAPIRO, NELLA IRENE, surgeon; b. NYC, Nov. 13, 1947; d. Eugene and Ethel (Pearl) S.; m. Jack Schwartz, Oct. 16, 1977; children: Max, Molly. BA, Barnard Coll., 1968; MD, Albert Einstein Coll., 1972. Resident in gen. surgery Montefiore Hosp., N.Y.C., 1972-76; mem. staff North Ctrl. Hosp., Bronx, NY, 1976-77, Bronx Mcpl. Hosp., 1977-87; chief gen. surgery Bronx Mcpl. Hosp. Ctr., 1983-87; mem. staff in gen. surgery Albert Einstein Coll. Hosp., Bronx, 1977-93, chief gen. surgery, 1991-93; atty. Lear Surg. Assocs., 1993-94; pvt. solo practice Bronx, 1994—. Asst. prof. surgery Albert Einstein Coll., Bronx, 1980—; assoc. dir. gen. surgery Weller Hosp., Bronx, 1991-93; co-founder Whaecom Breast Ctr., Bronx, 1991—. Fellow: ACS. Avocations: travel, skiing, opera. Office: 2425 Eastchester Rd Bronx NY 10469

SHAPIRO, NORMA SONDRA LEVY, federal judge; b. Phila., July 27, 1928; d. Bert and Jane (Kotkin) Levy; m. Bernard Shapiro, Aug. 21, 1949; children: Finley, Neil, Aaron. BA in Polit. Theory with honors, U. Mich., 1948; JD magna cum laude, U. Pa., 1951. Bar: Pa. 1952, U.S. Supreme Ct. 1978. Law clk. to presiding justice Pa. Supreme Ct., 1951-52; instr. U. Pa. Law Sch., 1951-52, 55-56; assoc. Dechert Price & Rhoads, Phila., 1956-58, 67-73, ptnr., 1973-78; judge U.S. Dist. Ct. (ea. dist.) Pa., 1978—. Assoc. trustee U. Pa. Law Sch., 1978-93; former trustee Women's Law Project, Albert Einstein Med. Ctr.; v.p. Jewish Pub. Soc.; trustee Fedn. Jewish Agys., 1980-83; mem. lawyers adv. panel Pa. Gov.'s Commn. on Status of Women, 1974; legal adv. regional Coun. Child Psychiatry, bd. dirs. Women Judges' Fund for Justice. Guest editor: Shingle, 1972. Mem. Lower Merion County (Pa.) Bd. Sch. Dirs., 1968-77, pres., 1977, v.p., 1976; v.p. Jewish Community Relations Council of Greater Phila., 1975-77; chmn. legal affairs com., 1978; pres. Belmont Hills Home and Sch. Assn., Lower Merion Twp.; legis. chmn. Lower Merion Sch. Dist. Intersch. Council; mem. Task Force on Mental Health of Children and Youth of Pa.; treas., chmn. edn. com. Human Relations Council, Lower Merion; v.p., parliamentarian Nes Ami Penn Valley Congregation, Lower Merion Twp. Named Woman of Yr., Oxford Circle Jewish Community Center, 1979, Woman of Distinction, Golden Slipper Club, 1979; Gowen fellow, 1954-55; recipient Hannah G. Solomon award Nat. Coun. Jewish Women, 1992. Mem. Am. Law Inst., Am. Bar Found., ABA (ho. dels. 1990-96, coun./chmn. conf. fed. judges 1986-87, chmn. jud. divsn. 1996-97), Pa. Bar Assn. (ho. of dels. 1979-81), Phila. Bar Assn. (chmn. com. women's rights 1972, 74-75, chmn. bd. govs. 1977-78, chmn. pub. rels. com. 1978), Fed. Bar Assn. (Bill of Rights award 1991), Nat. Assn. Women Lawyers, Phila. Trial Lawyers Assn., Am. Judicature Soc., Phila., Nat. Assn. Women Judges, Fellowship Commn., Order of Coif (chpt. pres. 1973-75), Tau Epsilon Rho. Office: US Dist Courthouse Independence Mall West 601 Market St Rm 10614 Philadelphia PA 19106-1714

SHAPIRO, ROBYN SUE, lawyer, educator; b. Mpls., July 19, 1952; d. Walter David and Judith Rae (Sweet) S.; m. Charles Howard Barr, June 27, 1976; children: Tania Shapiro-Barr, Jeremy Shapiro-Barr, Michael Shapiro-Barr. BA summa cum laude, U. Mich., 1974; JD, Harvard U., 1977. Bar: D.C., 1977, Wis., 1979, U.S. Supreme Ct., 1990. Assoc. Foley & Lardner, Washington, 1977-79; ptnr. Barr & Shapiro, Menomonee Falls, Wis., 1980-87; assoc. Quarles & Brady, Milw., 1987-92; ptnr. Michael Best & Friedrich, Milw., 1992—, chair, Health Law Practice, 2003—. Adj. asst. prof. law Marquette U., Milw., 1979-83; assoc. dir. bioethics ctr. Med. Coll. Wis., Milw., 1982-85, dir., 1985—; asst. prof. bioethics Med. Coll. Wis., 1984-89, assoc. prof. bioethics, 1989-97, prof. bioethics, 1997—, Ursula Von der Ruhr prof. bioethics, 2000—; dir. Wis. Ethics Com. Network, 1987-98, Midwest Ethics Com. Network, 1998—; bd. dirs. Wis. Health Decisions, 1990-93. Mem. editl. bd. Cambridge Quar., 1991—, HEC Forum, 1988-91, Human Rights, 1998—; contbr. articles to profl. jours. Mem. ethics com. St. Luke's Med. Ctr., Milw., 1983—, Elmbrook Meml. Hosp., Milw., 1983-86, Cmty. Meml. Hosp., Menomonee Falls, 1984—, Aurora Sinai Med.Ctr., Milw., 1986—, Milw. County Mental Health Complex, 1984—, Froedtert Meml. Luth. Hosp., 1985—; mem. subcom. organ transplantation Wis. Health Policy Coun., Madison, 1984, bioethics com., 1986-89; mem. com. study on bioethics Wis. Legis. Coun., Madison, 1984-85; bd. dirs. Jewish Home and Care Ctr., 1994—, chair ethics com., 1994—; chair Bayside Ethics Bd., 1994—; bd. dirs. Milw. area chpt. Girl Scouts U.S., Am. Bioethics Assn., 1995-97, Wis. Perinatal Found., 1996-99, Am. Soc. Bioethics and Humanities, 1997-2000, Manor Park Found., 2002—; mem. sec.'s adv. com. on xenotransplantation U.S. Dept. Health and Human Svcs., 2001—; mem. sci. adv. com. Alzheimer's Assn. Southeastern Wis., 1997—; mem. data and safety monitoring bd. GlaxoWellcome, 1995—2003. James B. Angell scholar, 1971-72. Mem. ABA (health law sec., vice chair clin. ethics group 1998-2001, individual rights and responsibilities sect., health rights com. chair 1994-99, coun. 1999—, coordinating com. on bioethics and law 1993—, chair 1995-99, adv. nat. conf. of commrs. on uniform state laws, misuse of genetic info. study group 2002—, mem. working group on health info. privacy 2000-02, AIDS coordinating com. 2003-), Am. Health Lawyers Assn., Am. Hosp. Assn. (bioethics tech. panel 1991-94, spl. com. HIV practitioners 1991-93), Wis. Bar Assn. (chair Wis. health law sect. 1988-89, individual rights sect. coun. 1987-90), Assn. Women Lawyers, ACLU, Wis. Found. (Atty. of Yr. 1988), Assn. Post-Doctoral Programs in Clin. Neurophysiology (bd. dirs.), Am. Soc. Law, Medicine, and Ethics, Milw. Acad. Medicine (coun. 1992-98, chair bioethics com. 1992-98), Milw. AIDS Coalition (steering com. 1988-91), Am. Soc. Transplant Surgeons (ethics com. 1999—), Internat. Bioethics Assn. (chair task force on ethics coms.), Profl. Dimensions (Golden Compass award 1994), Phi Beta Kappa (Wis. chpt. scholarship com. chair 1990-93), Susan G. Komen Breast Cancer Found., others. Home: 9474 N Broadmoor Rd Milwaukee WI 53217-1309 Office: Med Coll Wis Bioethics Ctr 8701 Watertown Plank Rd Milwaukee WI 53226-3548 E-mail: rshapiro@mcw.edu.

SHAPIRO, SANDRA, lawyer; b. Providence, Oct. 17, 1944; d. Emil and Sarah (Cohen) S. AB magna cum laude, Bryn Mawr Coll., Pa., 1966; LLB magna cum laude, U. Pa., 1969. Bar: Mass. 1970, U.S. Dist. Ct. Mass. 1971, U.S. Ct. Appeals (1st cir.) 1972, U.S. Supreme Ct. 1980. Law clk. U.S. Ct. Appeals (1st cir.), Boston, 1969-70; assoc. Foley, Hoag & Eliot LLP, Boston, 1970-75, ptnr., 1976—. Mem. bd. bar overseers Mass. Supreme Judicial Ct., 1988-92, mem. gender bias study com., 1986-89; dir. Mass. Govt. Land Bank, 1994-96. Contbr. articles to profl. jours. Bd. dirs. Patriots' Trail coun. Girl Scouts U.S., 1994—97; mem. bd. overseers Boston Lyric Opera, 1993—99, New Eng. Conservatory of Music, 1995—2001, Celebrity Series of Boston, 1997—, chair, 2003—. Woodrow Wilson fellow, 1966. Mem.: ABA (ethics, profl. and pub. edn. com. 1994—), U. Pa. Law Sch. Alumni Assn. (bd. mgrs. 1990—94), Boston Bar Assn. (mem. coun.), Mass. Bar Assn. (chmn. real property sect. coun., com. on profl. ethics), Nat. Women's Law Ctr. Network, New Eng. Women in Real Estate, Women's Bar Assn. Mass. (pres. 1985—86), Boston Club, Order of Coif. Office: Foley Hoag LLP 155 Seaport Blvd Boston MA 02210-2600 E-mail: sshapiro@foleyhoag.com.

SHARBEL, JEAN M. editor; b. Lansford, Pa. d. Joseph and Star S. BA in Journalism, Hunter Coll. Editl. dir., v.p. Dauntless Books, N.Y.C., 1962-75; editor romance mags., True Confessions mag. Macfadden Holdings, Inc., N.Y.C., 1976-92; freelance editor fiction and non-fiction books, N.Y.C., 1989—. Home: 165 E 66th St New York NY 10021-6132

SHARBONEAU, LORNA ROSINA, artist, educator, author, poet, illustrator; b. Spokane, Wash., Apr. 5, 1935; d. Stephen Charles Martin and Midgie Montana (Hartzel) Barton; m. Thomas Edward Sharboneau, Jan. 22, 1970; children: Curtis, Carmen, Chet, Cra, Joseph. AA in Arts, Delta Coll., 1986; studies with Steve Lesnick, Las Vegas, Nev.; studies with Bette Myers/Zimmerman, Phoenix and Bonners Ferry, Idaho. Prin. Sharboneau's Art Gallery, Spokane, 1977-80; tchr. art Michell's Art Gallery, Spokane, 1978-79; art therapist Vellencino Sch. Dist., Calif., 1981-83; ind. artist Lind, Wash., 1948—. Dir., producer, stage designer Ch. of Jesus Christ of LDS, San Jose, Sonora, Modesto, Calif., 1978 (1st. place road show San Jose); dir. Sharboneau's Art Show, Spokane, 1979, Hands On-Yr. of the Child; platform spkr., poet, fundraiser, libr., 1984-87; asst., apprentice to Prof. Rowland Cheney, Delta Coll., Stockton, Calif., 1985, 86, 87; demonstrated drip oil technique, Bonners Ferry, Idaho, Spokane, Wash., Stockton, Calif., Delta Coll. Author, illustrator: Through the Eyes of the Turtle Tree, The One-Armed Christmas Tree, The Price of Freedom, 1994, William Will, Bill Can, Song of the Turtle Tree, Chet's Ottle-Bottle: The Unbreakable Bottle, One Drop of Water and a Grain of Sand, The Price of Freedom; poet; prolific artist completed over 4000 paintings and drawings, displayed works in galleries through western states; featured in Magnolia News, Seattle, Delta Coll. Impact, Stockton, Calif., Stockton Record, Union Democrat, Sonora, Calif., Lincoln Center Chronicle, Stockton, Calif., Spokesman Rev., Spokane, Wash., Modesto (Calif) Bee, Angels Camp, Calif., Union Democrat, Sonora, Calif., New-Letter, Ch. of Jesus Christ of L.D.S 1st ward, Sonora; artist mixed media, oil, drip oil works, sculptures, pastel, watercolor; illustrations pen and ink, acrylic; sculptor bronze, lost wax method, ceramic art, soap stone, egg-tempra, original techniques, collage, variation on a theme. Dir., programmer, fundraiser Shelter Their Sorrows, Sonora, Calif., 1989-92, vol. Cmty. Action Agy. and Homeless Shelter; fundraiser for Homeless Flood Victims of No. Calif., 1997. Recipient Golden Rule award J.C. penny, 1991, Recognition award Pres. George Bush, cert. Spl. Congl. Recognition Congressman Richard H. Lehman, 3rd Pl. Best Show East Valley ARtists/Pala Show, 1973, 74, 75, 3d Pl. Artist of Yr., 1974, Valley Fair, Santa Clara, Calif., 1974, 1st and 2d Pl. Spokane County Fair, 1978, 3 honorable mentions, 4 premiums, 1979, 3 1st Pl., 3 2d Pl., 2 3rd Pl., honorable mention Calaveras County Fair/Angels Camp, Calif., 1983, 1st and 3rd Pl. Unitarian Art Festival, Stockton, Calif., 1984, 2d Pl., 1985, 3d Pl., 1986, 1st Pl. Lodi Art Ann., 1985, 3rd Pl., 1986, 1st Pl. 1987, 1st Pl., 1988, honorable mental SJCAC Junque Art Show, Stockton, 1985, 1st Pl Ctrl. Calif. Art League, Modesto, 1986, 88, 2d Pl. 1995; 3d Pl. Camilla Art Show, San Jose, Calif., 1974, and numerous others; 1st, 2d, and 3d Pl., Spokane County Fair, 1978; 4 honorable mentions, Sonora, Calif., 1993, 2nd Pl. Ctrl. Calif. Art Show, 1996. Mem. Ctrl. Sierra Arts Coun., Mother Lode Artists Assn., Sacramento Fine Arts Ctr., Inc., Internat. Platform Assn. (Judges Choice conv. arts competition 1993), The Planetary Soc., The Nat. Mus. of Women of Arts. Mem. Ch. of Jesus Christ of LDS. Achievements include: homeless shelter kitchen named in her honor, Sonora. Office: PO Box 5015 Sonora CA 95370-2015

SHARMA, MARTHA BRIDGES, geography educator; b. Balt., Feb. 2, 1945; d. Gail and S. Evelyn Bridges; m. Narendra P. Sharma, Aug. 16, 1968; 1 child, Stephanie. BA in Geography, Internat. Studies, U. N.C., 1967; postgrad., U. Hawaii, 1967-68, George Washington U., 1986. Geography tchr. Washington Internat. Sch., 1976-80; dir. records/accounts Washington Internat. Sch., 1981-82, adminstrv. dean, 1983-84; geography tchr. Nat. Cathedral Sch., Washington, 1984—. Geography cons.; lectr. in field. Contbr. articles to profl. jours.; joint author: 7-12 Geography: Themes, Key Ideas, and Learning Opportunities, 1989; co-author: The National Council for Geographic Education: The First Seventy-Five Years and Beyond, 1990; contbg. author: Revisiting the Americas: Teaching and Learning the Geography of the Western Hemisphere, 1992. Mem. Nat. Coun. Geographic Edn. (v.p. pubs. and products 1992—, gender/ethnicity project task force 1991—, dir. spl. pub.s 1989-92, Region VIII awards com. 1988-90), Assn. Am. Geographers, Soc. Woman Geographers. Avocations: reading, music, needlework, travel. Office: Nat Cathedral Sch 3609 Woodley Rd NW Washington DC 20016-5096

SHARMA, SANTOSH DEVRAJ, obstetrician/gynecologist, educator; b. Kenya, Feb. 24, 1934; came to U.S., Jan. 1972; d. Devraj Chananram and Lakshmi (Devi) S. BS, MB, B.J. Medical Sch., Pune, India, 1960. House surgeon Sasson Hosp., Poona, India, 1960-61; resident in ob-gyn. various hospitals, England, 1961-67; house officer Maelor Gen. Hosp., Wrexham, U.K., 1961-62; asst. prof. ob-gyn. Howard U. Med. Sch., Washington, 1972-74; assoc. prof. John A. Burns Sch. Med., Honolulu, 1974-78, prof., 1978 --. Fellow Royal Coll. Ob-Gyn., Am. Coll. Ob-Gyn. Avocations: travel, photography, environmental protection. Office: 1319 Punahou St Rm 824 Honolulu HI 96826-1032 E-mail: santosh@hawaii.edu.

SHARMAN, DIANE LEE, secondary school educator; b. Harvey, Ill., May 12, 1948; d. Eric Melvin and Josephine A. (Kut) Van Patten; m. Richard Lee Sharman, Nov. 3, 1973; children: Daria Lee, Deedra Lee. BS, Purdue U., 1970; MBA, U. Chgo., 1973. Cert. secondary sch. math. tchr., Tex. Computers sales rep. GE, Chgo., 1970-73; mgr. sold equipment Xerox Corp., Rochester, N.Y., 1973-81, mgr. fin. ops. analysis worldwide Stamford, N.Y., 1981-84; math. tchr. Conroe (Tex.) Ind. Sch. Dist., 1993—. Mem. DAR, Nat. Coun. Tchrs. of Math., Assn., Tex. Profl. Educators, Purdue Alumni Assn. (life), Nat. Charity League, U. Chgo. Alumni Assn., Chi Omega. Avocations: golf, horseback riding. Home: 26 Fernglen Dr The Woodlands TX 77380-3955 Office: Knox HS 12104 Sawmill Rd The Woodlands TX 77380-2133 E-mail: rshar45854@aol.com., dsharman@conroe.isd.tenet.edu.

SHARON, DEBRA MELINDA, psychologist; b. L.A., Sept. 5, 1954; d. Cy and Harlene Sharon; m. Avedis Panajian, Feb. 14, 1986 (div. June 1997); 1 child, Mitchell Panajian. BA, UCLA, 1975; MA, Calif. State U., Northridge, 1979; PhD, Calif. Grad. Inst., L.A., 1983. Lic. psychologist Calif., marriage and family therapist Calif. Clin. dir. HELP Group, L.A., 1999—. Mem.: APA. Avocations: gardening, swimming. Office: 14425 Riverside Dr Sherman Oaks CA 91423

SHARP, ANNE CATHERINE, artist, educator; b. Red Bank, N.J., Nov. 1, 1943; d. Elmer Eugene and Ethel Violet (Hunter) S. BFA, Pratt Inst., 1965; MFA, Bklyn. Coll., 1973. Tchr. art Sch. Visual Arts, 1978-89, NYU, 1978, SUNY, Purchase, 1983, Pratt Manhattan Ctr., N.Y.C., 1982-84, Parsons Sch. Design, N.Y.C., 1984-90, Visual Arts Ctr. of Alaska, Anchorage, 1991, Anchorage Mus. Hist. and Art, 1991, 93, 94, 95, U. Alaska, Anchorage, 1994-96, Fashion Inst. Tech., SUNY, 1997-98; lectr. AAAS, The 46th Arctic Divsn. Sci. Conf., U. Alaska, Fairbanks, 1995. One-person shows Pace Editions, N.Y.C., Ten/Downtown, N.Y.C., Katonah (N.Y.) Gallery, 1974, Contemporary Gallery, Dallas, 1975, Art in a Public Space, N.Y.C., 1979, Eatontown Hist. Mus., N.J., 1980, N.Y. Pub. Library Epiphany Br., 1988, Books and Co., N.Y., 1989, The Kendall Gallery, N.Y.C., 1990, Alaska Pacific U., Carr-Gottstein Gallery, Anchorage, 1993, Internat. Gallery Contemporary Art, Anchorage, 1993, Art Think Tank Gallery, N.Y.C., 1994, U.S. Geol. Survey, Reston, Va., 1994, Stonington Gallery, Anchorage, 1994, on TV Ltd. Benefit, N.Y.C., 1998-2000; group shows include Arnot Art Mus., Elmira, N.Y., 1975, Bronx Mus., 1975, Mus. Modern Art, N.Y.C., 1975-76, Nat. Arts Club, N.Y.C., 1979, Calif. Mus. Photography, Riverside, 1983-92, Jack Tilton Gallery, N.Y.C., 1983, Lincoln Ctr., N.Y.C., 1983, Cabo Frio Print Biennale, Brazil, 1983, Pratt Graphic Ctr., N.Y.C., 1984, State Mus. N.Y., Albany, 1984, Kenkeleba Gallery, N.Y.C., 1985, Hempstead Harbor Art Assn., Glen Cove, N.Y., 1985, Mus. Mod. Art, Weddel, Fed. Republic of Germany, 1985, Kenkeleba Gallery, N.Y.C., 1985, Paper Art Exhbn. Internat. Mus. Contemporary Art, Bahia, Brazil, 1986, Mus. Salon-de-Provence, France, 1987, Mus. Contemporary Art, Sao Paulo, Brazil, 1985-86, Salon de Provence, France, 1987, Adirondack Lakes Ctr. for Arts, Blue Mountain Lake, N.Y., 1987, Kendall Gallery, N.Y.C., 1988, Exhibition Ctr. Parsons Sch. Design, N.Y.C., 1989, F.M.K. Gallery, Budapest, Hungary, 1989, Galerie des Kulturbundes Schwarzenberg, German Dem. Republic, Q Sen Do Gallery, Kobe, Japan, 1989, Anchorage Mus. History and Art, 1990-91, 94, U. Alaska, Anchorage, 1990, 91, Coos Art Mus., Coos Bay, Oreg., 1990, Spaceship Earth, Mus. Internat. de Neu Art, Vancouver, Can., 1990, Councourse Gallery, Emily Carr Coll. Art and Design, 1990, Nat. Mus. Women in the Arts, Washington, 1991, Visual Arts Ctr. Alaska, 1991, 92, Nomad Mus., Lisbon, Portugal, 1991, Mus. Ostdeutsche Gallery, Regensberg, Germany, 1991, Mcpl. Mus. Cesley Krumlov (So. Bohemia) CSFK, Czechoslovakia, 1991, Böltmiche Dörter Exhbn. Hochstrass 8, Munich, 1992, BBC-TV, Great Britain, U.K., Sta. WXXI-TV, Rochester, N.Y., 1992-93, Site 250 Gallery Contemporary Art., Fairbanks, 1993, Santa Barbara (Calif.) Mus. Art, 1993, The Rochester (N.Y.) Mus. and Sci. Ctr., 1990-94, Space Arc: The Archives of Mankind, Time Capsule in Earth Orbit, Hughes Comm., Divec TV Satellite Launch, 1994, Stonington Gallery, Anchorage, 1994, 95, UAA Art Galley U. Alaska, 1995, Arctic Trading Post, Nome, Alaska, 1995, Allan P. Kikbuarts Ctr. Gallery at the Lawrenceville (N.J.) Sch., 1996, Blue Mountain Gallery, N.Y., 1998, The Book Room, Jersey City, 2000, 01, A.I.R. Gallery, 2002, 03, 04, others; represented in permanent collections Smithsonian Instn., Nat. Air and Space Mus., Washington, Albright Knox Gallery, Buffalo, St. Vincent's Hosp, N.Y.C., N.Y. Pub. Libr., N.Y.C., U.S. Geol. Survey, Reston, Va., White House (Reagan, Bush adminstrns.), Site 250 Gallery Contemporary Art, Fairbanks, Alaska, Anchorage Mus. History and Art, others; Moon Shot series to commemorate moon landing, 1970-76, Cloud Structures of the Universe Painting series, 1980-86, Am. Landscape series, 1987-89, Thoughtlines, fall 1986, Swimming in the Mainstream with Her, U. Va., Charlottesville; author: Artist's Book - Travel Dreams U.S.A., 1989, Artworld-Welt Der Kunst, Synchronicity, 1989—, Art Think Tank: Projects in Art and Ecology, 1990—, The Alaska Series, 1990—, Potraits in the Wilderness, 1990—; columnist: Anchorage Press, 1995. Sponsor Iditorod Trail Com., Libby Riddles. Tchg. fellow Bklyn. Coll., 1972; Artist-in-residence grantee Va. Ctr. for Creative Arts, 1974, Artpark, Lewiston, N.Y., 1980, Vt. Studio Colony, 1989; recipient Pippin award Our Town, N.Y.C., 1984, certificate of Appreciation Art in Embassy program U.S. Dept. State, 1996. Mem. Mus. Women in Arts, Pratt Inst. Alumni Assn., Internat. Assn. Near-Death Studies. Address: Murray Hill Station PO Box 1776 New York NY 10156-1776 also: Decker Morris Gallery 621 W 6th Ave Anchorage AK 99501-2200 also: On Television Ltd 388 Broadway New York NY 10013-3542

SHARP, CHRISTINA KRIEGER, nursing educator, researcher; b. Ft. Montgomery, N.Y., Aug. 4, 1928; d. Joseph Lewis and Mary Agnes Krieger; m. Andrew Asa Sharp, Jr., Feb. 3, 1957 (dec. Jan. 31, 1969); children: Shawn Patrick, Sharon Paula Zegers. RN, cadet nurse, St. Lukes Hosp., Newburgh, N.Y., 1948; BS, Coll. William and Mary, 1955; MA, NYU, 1974. RN N.Y. Staff nurse Vets. Hosp., Richmond, Va., 1948—53, Army Hosp., West Point, NY, 1954—56; instr. nursing Orange County CC, Middletown, NY, 1956—57, Santa Rosa (Calif.) Jr. Coll., 1961—62; supr. nursing Vocat. Edn. and Extension Bd., New City, NY, 1957—60; coord. practical nursing program Newburgh Sch. Dist., 1963—83. Cons. N.Y. State Edn. Dept. Nursing, Albany, 1983—84. Mem.: VFW, AFL-CIO, AAUW (sec. 1999—2001), Fla. Educators Assn., N.Y. State United Tchrs. (Cmty. Svc. award 1998), Orange County Ret. Educators Assn., Fla. Soc. RNs Ret., Inc. (state pres. 1994—97, editor yearbooks 1997—, Orlando dist. pres. 1998—2002, Fla. state coun. 43 pres. 2001—), Tchr. Retirees Fla., Widow and Widowers Soc. Ctrl. Fla. (pres. 1999—2002), Golden Rod Civic Club (bd. dirs. 2001—), Am. Legion Aux. Avocations: travel, opera, ballet, Broadway shows, ice shows. Home: 2735 Mystic Cove Dr Orlando FL 32812-5344 E-mail: tisharp@aol.com.

SHARP, LINDA, professional basketball coach; Profl. basketball coach U. S.C., 1977—89, L.A. Sparks of WBNA, 1997; head coach Concordia U., 2000; profl. basketball coach Phoenix Mercury, 2002—. Color commentator Fox TV. Named WCAA Coach of Yr., Sporting News Coach of Yr. ; named to Women's Hall of Fame, 2001. Office: 201 E Jefferson St Phoenix AZ 85004

SHARP, MARSHA, basketball coach; b. Wash. Bachelor's, Wayland Bapt. U., 1974; Master's, West Tex. State U., 1976. Grad. asst. basketball coach The Flying Queens Wayland Bapt. U., 1974-75; asst. basketball coach Lockney U., 1976-82; head coach Lady Raiders basketball Tex. Tech. U., Lubbock, 1982—. Led Lady Raiders basketball to NCAA Championship, 1993, 5 S.W. Conf. titles, 3 post-season crowns; named Nat. Coach of Yr. Women's Basketball News Svc., Ohio Touchdown Club, 1993, Nat. Coach of Yr. Women's Basketball Coaches Assn., 1994. Office: Tex Tech/United Spirit Arena Jones Stadium North 18th & Indiana Ave Lubbock TX 79409

SHARP, SUSAN F. sociologist, educator; b. Lubock, Tex., Jan. 28, 1951; d. Richard Glover Sharp, Alice Bostick Haas; children: Jared Miles, Rachel Shada, Amy Bowles. B ., Tex. Tech U., 1980, M ., 1982; PhD, U. Tex., 1996. Assoc. prof. U. Okla., Norman, 1996—. Rschr. and site dir. Capital Jury Project. Editor: The Incarcerated Woman, 2002, (newsletter) DivisioNews, 2000—01; contbr. articles to profl. jours. Chair Okla. Coalition to Abolish the Death Penalty, Inc., Oklahoma City, 2001—02. Mem.: Soc. Applied Sociology, Midsouth Sociol. Assn., Acad. Criminal Justice Sci., Am. Soc. Criminology (exec. counselor divsn. women & crime 2001). Office: Univ Okla Dept Sociology 780 Van Vleet Oval KH 331 Norman OK 73019 Office Fax: 405-325-7825. Personal E-mail: ssharp2@cox.net. Business E-Mail: ssharp@ou.edu.

SHARP, VERNA ELLEN, special education educator; b. Pikeville, Ky., July 11, 1959; d. Harold R. and Christine C. Johnson; children: Krista C. Cahall, Phillip. BA in Elem. Edn., BA in Spl. Edn., Morehead State U., 1992, MA, 1995. Emotional/behavioral disorders tchr. Morgan County Mid. Sch., West Liberty, Ky., 1992—95, Greysbranch Elem., Lyod, Ky., 1995—2000, McKell Mid. Sch., South Shore, Ky., 2000—. Mem.: KAPE, CCBD, NEA, Coun. for Behavior Disorder, Coun. for Exceptional Children, Ky. Edn. Assn., Ea. Star. Home: 908 Charles St Flatwoods KY 41139

SHARPE, BOBBIE MAHON, author; b. Fargo, Ark., July 27, 1931; d. Leroy Washington and Caroline Angeline (Hobson) Mahon; m. Johnnie James House, June 10, 1944 (div. July 1945); children: Wilbur Clayton, Wayland LeEverett; m. James Rozelle Sharpe, Dec. 10, 1950 (div. Oct. 1963); children: Maurice, Gwendolyn, Caroline. BS, Philander Smith Coll., Little Rock, 1943; MEd, U. Ark., 1958; Cert. in Media Specialist, Purdue U., 1969; postgrad., U. Calif., Long Beach, 1968, Ball State U., 1969, Washburn U., 1970, U. Mo., 1971, U. Ill., 1977, Fourah Bay Coll., Sierra Leone, West Africa, 1979. Cert. ednl. media specialist, Mo.; cert libr. Fisk U., 1948; cert. elem. sch. tchr., Mo. Tchr. Okla. Pub. Schs., Norman, 1944, Kansas City (Kans.) Pub. Schs., 1944-45, Wynne (Ark.) Pub. Schs., 1947-48, Ark. pvt. schs., Fargo, 1949-51, Little Rock Pub. Schs., 1952-61, Kansas City (Mo.) Pub. Schs., 1961-77, asst. prin., 1978-82, ednl. media specialist, 1982-92. Prof. Avila Coll., Kansas City, Mo., 1979-81; news reporter Kansas City (Kans.) Globe newspaper, 1981-83; tchr. cons. Kansas City (Mo.) Pub. Sch. Sys., dir., 1982-92; condr. workshops in field. Author: African Experience, 1983, African American Folktales, 1984, Apartheid Remedies and Folklore, Recipe Book, 1985, The Black Experience: Musical Instrumens of West Africa, 1986, (poems) My Country 'Tis and Me, 1996, Drug Use and Abuse Activity Study Kit, 1996, The Warm Earth, 1998, (note cards) African Proverbs, 1996; cast mem. film Kansas City, 1989; radio and TV commercials, 1995-96, 1998. Bd. missions United Meth. Ch., Kansas City, Kans., 1989-93, bd. comm., Topeka, 1984—; missionary United Meth. Ch., Port-u-Prince, Haiti, 1986, 90; lay spkr. United Meth. Ch., 1998. Named Outstanding Woman of Yr., YWCA, Kansas City, Kans., 1995, 100 Most Influential Women in Kansas City, 1997; Ford Found. grantee, 1979. Mem. UN Orgn., LWV, Garra Soc. West Africa (drafts person 1979—), Alpha Kappa Alpha, Phi Delta Kappa. Avocations: musician, craft work, art work, storytelling. Home: 3109 Rosewood Ln Oklahoma City OK 73120-5351

SHARPE, DOROTHY JONES, secondary education educator, researcher; b. Suffolk, Va., Feb. 22, 1928; d. James Winton and Helen Rebecca Jones; m. Joseph Lee Sharpe, June 27, 1954 (div. Aug. 1969); 1 child, Alexandra Camille. BS in English and History, Miner Tchrs. Coll., 1950; MA in Edn., The Am. U., 1953; postgrad., U. So. Calif., 1976-82. Tchr. English, dept. chair Randall Jr. H.S., Terrell Jr. H.S., Washington, 1950-66; tchr. trainer English and reading Trinity Coll., D.C. Pub. Schs., Washington, 1966-72; project dir. street acad. Nat. Inst. Edn. and Washington Urban League, Washington, 1972-76; v.p. programs Washington Urban League, 1976-81; proposal developer, writer Match Inst., Washington, 1981; rschr., planner, writer Sterling Tucker Assn., Washington, 1982-84; planning cons. Techworld Trade Assocs., Washington, 1986-88; rsch. analyst Youth Policy Inst., Washington, 1997—. Planning cons., spkr. Nat. 4-H Ctr., D.C. Pub. Schs. Youth Policy Inst., 1981—; conf. chair, planner, writer D.C. U., Mckendree UMC, Washington, 1989-91. Author: Language Arts and Reading, 1960-79, designer urban youth think tank Youth Futures Inst., 1997—. Com. mem. Dixon Commn. Mental Health Law Project, Washington, 1980—; sr. assoc., bd. dirs. Youth Policy Inst., Washington, 1992-96. Recipient San Juan Barnes award Sr. Neighbors and Companions, 1985, others. Avocations: reading, writing poetry, arbouretums, museums, visiting mountains and rivers. Home: 2706 Brentwood Rd NE Washington DC 20018-2608

SHARPE, KATHRYN MOYE, psychologist; b. Barnesville, Ga., Nov. 27, 1922; d. Herbert Johnston and Henri Lucile (Winter) Moye; m. William Herschel Sharpe, Mar. 2, 1946; children: William Herschel Jr., Mark Stephens. AB, Piedmont Coll., Demorest, Ga., 1942; MA, U. N.C., 1947; PhD, U. S.C., 1975. Tchr., guidance counselor Charleston (S.C.) Pub. Schs., 1947-66; prof. sociology, chmn. dept. Bapt. Coll. at Charleston, 1966-88, prof. emeritus, 1988—; pvt. practice psychology, Charleston, 1975—. Named One of Twelve Outstanding Women in Greater Charleston by The Ctr. for Women; Kathryn Moye Sharpe scholarship given in her honor Bapt. Coll. at Charleston, 1988. Fellow Am. Assn. for Marriage and Family Therapy (approved supr., pres. S.C. div. 1975-77, distng. svc. award S.C. chpt. 1999). Congregationalist. Home and Office: 6 Cavalier Ave Charleston SC 29407-7702

SHARPE, PATRICIA LA VONNE, artist; b. Waverly, Tenn., June 19, 1949; d. William Delmas and Maggie Mae McGee; m. Donald Douglas Sharpe, June 25, 1972; 1 child, Margaret Elizabeth. Student, Austin Peay State U. Founder and organizer Clarksville Artist Guild, Tenn., 1999—2002; gallery dir. Montgomery County Hist. Soc., Clarksville, 1999—2002. Sec. Tree Bd., Clarksville, 1997—99. Mem.: Colored Pencil Soc. Am., Tenn. Watercolour Soc., Tenn. Art League, Gamma Beta Phi, Phi Kappa Phi. Democrat. Avocations: gardening, pottery, restoration, stained glass. Home: 607 North Second St Clarksville TN 37040

SHARPE, YOLANDA RUBY, art educator, vocalist; b. Detroit, Jan. 17, 1957; d. Thomas Hugh Sharpe, Rita Cecelia (Nicholson) Sharpe. BA in Art History, BFA in Painting and Printmaking, Mich. State U., 1979; MFA, Wayne State U., 1982. Asst. prof. painting and drawing Mich. State U., East Lansing, 1986—87; chair dept., assoc. prof. painting and drawing SUNY, Coll. Oneonta, Oneonta, NY, 1987—. Master artist, ednl. del. for the arts Krasnoyarsk Sch. of Fine Arts, Siberia, Russia, 2001; gallery dir. SUNY, Coll. Oneonta, NY, 1996—98. Exhibitions include Hale Woodruff Meml. Exhbn., 1994, On Line Exhibit, 2000, 59th Exhbn. Ctrl. N.Y. Artists, 2001; featured in Mid-March Press Publ. Concert organizer and vocalist for fundraiser Red Cross Nat. Disaster Relief Fund, Oneonta, 2001—01, NAACP Scholarship Fund, Oneonta, 2002. Mem.: N.Y. Found. Arts (Board of Governors for Artists Fellowships 1991—96), Temple Beth El (Editor for the Shofar Newsletter 1999—2001), U.S. Colored Troops Inst. (Emancipation Memorial Ball Committee Member 1998—now), Munson Williams Proctor Inst. Mus. (Program Advisory Committee 1995—now). Roman Catholic. Avocations: dance, rollerskating, aerobics, travel. Home: 27 Fair St Oneonta NY 13820 Office: SUNY Oneonta Art Dept Fine Arts Bldg Oneonta NY 13820 Office Fax: 607-436-3715. Business E-Mail: sharpeyr@oneonta.edu.

SHARPLES, RUTH LISSAK, communications executive; b. N.Y.C., Feb. 3, 1952; d. Saul and Nettie (Field) Lissak; m. Winston Sharples, June 26, 1981; stepchildren: Hadley, John, Gillian. BA, CUNY, 1973; MFA, Columbia U., 1975. Rschr. Am. Film Inst./Motion Picture Divsn. of Libr. of Congress, Washington, 1977-79; mgr. audio-visual programs Am. Soc. Microbiology, Washington, 1979-82; mgr. video tech. Am. Gas Assn., Arlington, Va., 1982-96; dir. comm. Am. Gas Cooling Ctr., Arlington, 1996—. V.p., corp. sec. Cantab Motors, Ltd., Purcellville, Va., 1988—; corp. sec. Am. Gas Cooling Ctr., Arlington, 1996—. Editor Cool Times Newsletter, 1996-98. Mem. Nat. Trust Historic Preservation, Nature Conservancy, Mass. Audubon Soc., English Heritage, Nat. Trust, Internat. TV Assn. Avocations: hiking, archaeology. Office: Am Gas Cooling Ctr 420 N Capitol St NW Washington DC 20001-1504

SHARPLESS, MATTIE R. ambassador; b. Hampstead, N.C., July 1943; BA in Bus. Edn., N.C. Coll.; MBA, N.C. Cen. Univ. Former acting adminstr. USDA/Fgn. Agr. Svc.; various positions with Fgn. Agr. Svc., 1965—2001; spl. envoy to emerging economies USDA, 1999—2001; U.S. Amb. to Cen. African Rep., 2001—. Named to USDA's Yearbook of Outstanding Employees, 1990; recipient Presdl. Meritorious Svc. award. Office: DOS Amb 2060 Bangui Pl Washington DC 20521

SHARPNACK, RAYONA, management consultant; b. 1952; 1 child, Chelsea. Grad., U. Nev., Reno. Founder, pres. Inst. Women's Leadership, Redwood City, Calif., 1992—. Faculty Mills Coll., Women in Mgmt. program, 1994; bd. dirs. Profl. Bus. Women Calif. Conf., 1994—99; co-chair State of World Forum, Investing in Women Initiative, 1998—99; pres. Prof. Bus. Women in Calif., 1999; adv. coun. mem. Internat. Mus. Women, 1999—2001; player, mgr. Internat. Women's Profl. Softball League, 1979; shortstop Calif. Express. Office: Inst Women's Leadership PO Box 58 Redwood City CA 94064-0058*

SHARROW, MARILYN JANE, library administrator; b. Oakland, Calif. d. Charles L. and H.Evelyn Sharrow; m. Larry J. Davis. BS in Design, U. Mich., 1967, MALS, 1969. Libr. Detroit Pub. Libr., 1968-70; head fine arts dept. Syracuse (N.Y.) U. Librs., 1970-73; dir. libr. Roseville (Mich.) Pub. Libr., 1973-75; asst. dir. librs. U. Wash., Seattle, 1975-77, assoc. dir. librs., 1978-79; dir. librs. U. Man., Winnipeg, Can., 1979-82; chief libr. U. Toronto, Can., 1982-85; libr. U. Calif., Davis, 1985—. Chair bd. North Regional Libr. Facility, 1999—2001. Recipient Woman of Yr. in Mgmt. award Winnipeg YWCA, 1982; named Woman of Distinction, U. Calif. Faculty Women's Rsch. Group, 1985. Mem. ALA, Assn. Rsch. Librs. (bd. dirs., v.p., pres.-elect 1989-90, pres. 1990-91, chair sci. tech. work group 1994-98, rsch. collections com. 1993-95, 2000-2002, preservation com. 1997-99, 2003—), OCLC-Rsch. Librs. Adv. Com. (vice-chair 1992-93, chair 1993-94), Calif. State Network Resources Libr. Com., Can. Assn. Rsch. Libr. (pres. 1984-85). Office: U Calif Shields Libr 100 NW Quad Davis CA 95616-5292 E-mail: mjsharrow@ucdavis.edu.

SHATIN, JUDITH, music composing educator; b. Boston, Nov. 11, 1949; d. Leo and Harriet Evelyn (Sommer) S.; m. Michael Kubovy, June 28, 1992. AB, Douglass, Coll., 1971; MM, Julliard Sch., 1974; PhD, Princeton U., 1979. Asst. prof. U. Va., Charlottesville, 1979-85, assoc. prof., 1985-92, prof., 1992—, chmn. McIntire dept. music, 1995—, William R. Kenan, Jr. prof., 1999—. Dir. Va. Ctr. Computer Music, 1988—. Composer: (orch.) Aura, 1981, (piano concerto) Passion of St. Cecilia, 1985, (flute concerto) Ruah, 1985, (piano trio) View from Mt. Nebo (commd. by Garth Newel Chamber Players), 1985, (piano trio) Ignoto Numine (commd. Monticello Trio), 1986, (flute, clarinet, violin, cello) Secret Ground (commd. by Roxbury Chamber Players), 1990, (soprano and tape) Three Summers Heat, 1989 (Barlow Found. Commn.), (orch.) Piping the Earth (commd. by Women's Philharm.), 1990, (flute and piano) Gabriel's Wing (commd. by Julia Bogorad and the Upper Midwest Flute Assn.), 1990, (flute and electronics) Kairos (Commd. Va. Commn. for the Arts), 1991, (chorus, brass quintet, tympani) We Hold These Truths (commd. U. Va., for Thomas Jefferson's 250th birthday), 1992, (string orch.) Stringing the Bow (commd. Va. Chamber Orch.), 1992, COAL (commd. as part of 2-yr. retrospective of work, sponsored by Lila Wallace- Readers Digest Arts Ptnrs. Program), 1994, (piano and percussion) 1492 (commd. Arioso Ensemble), 1992, (piano) Chai Variations on Eliahu HaNavi, 1995, (flute and guitar) Dreamtigers (commd. Ekko!), 1996, (chorus) Adonai Roi, 1995, (string quartet) Janus Quartet (commd. for the Arcata Quartet), 1994, (string quartet and electronic playback) Elijah's Chariot (commd. Kronos Quartet), 1995, (amplified clarinet with PVC extensions effects processor, foot pedals and playback sys.) Sea of Reeds (commd. F. Gerard Errante), 1997, (chorus and piano) Songs of War and Peace, 1998, (brass quintet) Fantasia sobre el Flamenco, 1998, (piano, cello, percussion) Houdini: Memories of a Conjurer, 1999 (commd. Core Ensemble), (wind quintet and piano) Ockeghem Variations (commd. Hexagon Ensemble), 2000, Run (piano quartet) (commd. Currents) 2001, Singing the Blue Ridge (commd. Wintergreen Performing Arts through Ams. for the Arts), 2002, Tree Music (coomd. U. Va. Art Mus., interactive electronics), 2003, Penelope's Song (viola and electronics), 2003, Amulet (commd. N.Y. Treble Singers, SSA Chorus), 2003. Nat. Endowment for Arts Composer fellow, 1980, 85, 89, 92; recipient award Va. Commn. for the Arts, 1989, 2002. Mem. Am. Music Ctr., Am. Women Composers (pres. 1989-93), Am. Composers Alliance (bd. dirs. 1993-98), Internat. Alliance for Women in Music (chair nominating com. 1996-98, adv. bd. 1999—). E-mail: shatin@virginia.edu.

SHATTER, SUSAN LOUISE, artist; b. N.Y.C., Jan. 17, 1943; d. Aubrey and Florence (Breines) S.; m. Paul Brown (div. June 1975); 1 child, Scott Brown. Student, Skowhegan Sch. Sculpture, Maine, 1964; BFA, Pratt Inst., 1965; MFA, Boston U., 1972. Artist in residence Skowhegan (Maine) Sch Painting and Sculpture, 1977, 79; art instr. Sch. Visual Arts, N.Y.C., 1980-84, Tyler Sch. of Art, Phila., 1985, San Francisco Art Inst., 1989, Vt. Studio Ctr., Johnson, 1989, Bklyn. Coll., 1991-95. Vis. critic, U. Pa., 1974-85, acting co-chair, 1983-84; bd. govs. Skowhegan Sch. Painting and Sculpture, 1979—, chair, 1988-91. One-woman shows include Catalogue by D. Kuspit, SUNY Fine Arts Ctr., 2003, Fischbach Gallery, N.Y.C., 1973-97, Harcus Gallery, Boston, 1975-87, Mattingly Baker Gallery, Dallas, 1981, John Berggruen Gallery, San Francisco, 1986, Heath Gallery, Atlanta, 1987, SECCA, Winston-Salem, NC, 2001, Lyons Wier Gallery, N.Y.C., 2002, Staller Ctr. Arts, 2003; works reproduced in America '76: A Bicentennial Exhibition, 1976, Boston Watercolor Today, 1976, Realist Drawings and Watercolors: Contemporary Works on Paper, 1980, Contemporary Realism Since 1960, 1981, Perspectives on Contemporary American Realism: Works of Art on Paper from the Collection of Jalane and Richard Davidson, 1983, Eireland, McMullen Mus. of Art, Boston Coll., New Vistas: Contemporary American Landscapes, 1984, American Realism: Twentieth Century Drawings and Watercolors from the Glenn C. Janss Collection, 1984, A Graphic Muse: Prints by American Women, 1987, Spirit of Place: Contemporary Landscape Painting & the American Tradition, 1989, Twentieth Century Watercolors, 1990, American Realism and Figurative Art: 1952-1991, 1991, (catalogue) Meridian Shift, 12 yrs. of paintings by Susan Shatter, U. Tex., San Antonio, 1998; represented in permanent collections Art Inst. Chgo., Mus. Fine Arts, Boston, MIT, Cambridge, Currier Gallery of Art, Manchester, N.H., Hood Art Mus., Dartmouth Coll., Hanover, N.H., Phila. Mus. Art, Utah Mus. Fine Art, Salt Lake City, Farnesworth Mus., Maine, Buffalo Bill Hist. Soc., Cody, Wyo., U. Tex., San Antonio, Nat. Mus. Am. Art, Washington, Yale U. Art Gallery, Boise Mus., Idaho. Recipient grants Mass. Creative Artists Humanities, Radcliff Inst., Ingram-Merrill Found., NEA, N.Y. State Found. for the Arts, Yaddo Corp., Ballinglen Artists Fellowship, Ireland, 1999, Brittany fellow Rochefort-en-Terre, 2002, Childe Hassam Purchase award, Am. Acad. Arts and Letters, 2003; Yaddo resident, Saratoga Springs, NY, 2001, 02. Mem. NAD (W. Paten Prize 2003, treas. 1998-03), The Century Club. Home: 26 W 20th St New York NY 10011-4203

SHATTUCK, CATHIE ANN, lawyer, former government official; b. Salt Lake City, July 18, 1945; d. Robert Ashley S. and Lillian Culp (Shattuck). BA, U. Nebr., 1967, JD, 1970. Bar: Nebr. 1970, U.S. Dist. Ct. Nebr. 1970, Colo. 1971, U.S. Dist. Ct. Colo. 1971, U.S. Supreme Ct. 1974, U.S. Ct. Appeals (10th cir.) 1977, U.S. Dist. Ct. D.C. 1984, U.S. Ct. Appeals (D.C. cir.) 1984. V.p., gen. mgr. Shattuck Farms, Hastings, Nebr., 1967-70; asst. project dir. atty. Colo. Civil Rights Commn., Denver, 1970-72; trial atty. EEOC, Denver, 1973-77, vice chmn. Washington, 1982-84; pvt. practice law Denver, 1977-81; mem. Fgn. Svc. Bd., Washington, 1982-84, Presdl. Pers. Task Force, Washington, 1982-84; ptnr. Epstein, Becker & Green, L.A. and Washington, 1984—. Lectr. Colo. Continuing Legal Edn. Author: Employer's Guide to Controlling Sexual Harrassment, 1992; co-editor Nat. Employment Law Insider, 2004-; mem. editl. bd. The Practical Litigator, 1988-2003. Bd. dirs. KGNU Pub. Radio, Boulder, Colo., 1979, Denver Exch., 1980-81, YWCA Met. Denver, 1979-81. Recipient Nebr. Young Career Woman Bus. and Profl. Women, 1967; recipient Outstanding Nebraskan Daily Nebraskan, Lincoln, 1967. Fellow Am. Coll. of Labor and Employment Lawyers; mem. ABA (mgmt. chair labor and employment law sect. com. on immigration law 1988-90, mgmt. chair com. on legis. devels. 1990-93), Nebr. Bar Assn., Colo. Bar Assn., Colo. Women's Bar Assn., D.C. Bar Assn., Nat. Women's Coalition, Delta Sigma Rho, Tau Kappa Alpha, Pi Sigma Alpha, Alpha Xi Delta, Denver Club. Office Phone: 202-861-1863.

SHATTUCK, THERESA ELENBURG, special education educator; b. Shreveport, La., Sept. 16, 1953; d. Billy D. and Betty N. Elenburg; m. Robert R. Shattuck, May 25, 1996. BA, La. Tech U., 1975; MEd, Tex. Woman's U., 1990, PhD, 2002. Tchr. Bossier Parish Schs., Bossier City, La., 1975—80, Dallas Ind. Sch. Dist., Dallas, 1980—81, first grade tchr., 1984—88; data entry specialist/acctg. Arco Oil & Gas Co., Dallas, 1981—84; tchr. Autistic Treatment Ctr., Dallas, 1988—90, Grapevine-Colleyville Ind. Sch. Dist., Grapevine, Tex., 1990—95; behavior/autism specialist Carrollton-Framers Br. Ind. Sch. Dist., Carrollton, Tex., 1995—98; instrnl. support specialist Plano (Tex.) Ind. Sch. Dist., 1998—99; behavior specialist Collin County Spl. Edn. Coop., Wylie, Tex., 1998—2000; specialist for autism Dallas Ind. Sch. Dist., Dallas, 2000—. Mem.: Dallas Autism Soc. (treas. 1990—97), Assn. for Supervision and Curriculum Devel., Phi Delta Kappa, Coun. for Exceptional Children, Autism Soc. of Am., Zeta Tau Alpha (life). Home: 1524 Eaglepoint Dr Carrollton TX 75007 Office: Dallas Ind Sch Dist 912 S Ervay Dallas TX 75201 Personal E-mail: tshattuk@attbi.com. E-mail: ts5557@dallasisd.org.

SHATZ, CARLA J. biology educator; b. N.Y.C. BA in Chemistry, Radcliffe Coll., 1969, MPhil, Univ. Coll., London, 1971; PhD, Harvard U., 1976, postdoc., 1976—78. Assoc. prof. neurobiology Sch. Medicine Stanford U., Palo Alto, Calif., 1985—89, prof. neurobiology, 1989—92; investigator Howard Hughes Med. Inst., 1994—2000; Class of 1943 prof. neurobiology U. Calif., Berkeley, 1992—2000, prof., chair dept. neurobiology Harvard Med. Sch., Boston, 2000—. Mem. commn. on life scis. NRC, 1990—96; nat. adv. NIH, 1996—99; mem. coun. NAS, 1998—2001. Fellow: Inst. Medicine, Am. Philos. Soc., NAS, AAAS. Office: Harvard Med Sch Dept Neurobiology 220 Longwood Ave Boston MA 02115-5701

SHAUF, JENNIFER ELAINE, music educator; b. Bedford, Ohio, July 17, 1970; d. Jack Edward and Joyce Ann Shauf; m. Douglas Jerome Dressman, June 27, 1998. MusB Edn., Coll. Wooster, 1992; MusM, Kent State U., 1999. Cert. profl. music edn. Ohio, 1999, Orff Level I Orff-Schulwerk Assn., 1994. Shape music tchr. grades K-8 SHAPE Music, Elkhart, Ind., 1992—94; elem. gen. music tchr./beginning band grades 3-5 Bedford City Schs., 1994—2002, band dir. grades 6 - 12, 2002—. Pvt. piano and clarinet tchr., Bedford, 1988—. Mem.: NEA, ASOA, OMEA, Epsilon Kappa Omicron (historian 1986—87). Avocations: travel, reading, sports, music, theater. Home: 144 Woodrow Ave Bedford OH 44146 Office: Bedford City Schools 475 Northfield Rd Bedford OH 44146 Personal E-mail: amadeus17@mac.com. E-mail: jshauf@bedford.k12.oh.us.

SHAUGHNESSY, ELIZABETH ANN, surgeon, researcher; b. Evanston, Ill., Jan. 4, 1959; d. Terrence Joseph and Mary Ann (Nugent) S.; m. James Dennis Stapleton, Oct. 3, 1987. BS in Biology, U. Ill., 1981; MD in Medicine, U. Ill., Chgo., 1985, PhD in Cell Biology, 1990. Cert. Am. Bd. Surgery. Resident in gen. surgery U. Ill. and affiliated hosps. dept. surgery, Chgo., 1985-87, 90-93; fellow in surg. oncology City of Hope Nat. Med. Ctr., Duarte, Calif., 1992-97. Contbr. articles to profl. jours. Mem. bd. dirs. L.A. County chpt. Susan G. Komen Breast Cancer Found., L.A., 1996-97; local grants chmn., LA, Calif., 1996-97, Cin., Ohio, 1997-2002., Fellow ACS (assoc.), Am. Soc. Clin. Oncology (Young Investigator award 1995), Soc. Surg. Oncology, Am. Med. Women's Assn., Am. Assn. for Cancer Rsch., Physicians for Social Responsibility, Sierra Club, Zeta Tau Alpha (Glendale chpt., fedn. rep. 1993-97). Roman Catholic. Avocations: hiking, sewing. Office: Univ Cin Med Ctr Divsn Surg Barrett CtrOncology PO Box 670772 Greenwich KS 67055-0558

SHAUGHNESSY, MARIE KANEKO, artist; b. Detroit, Sept. 14, 1924; d. Eishiro and Kiyo (Yoshida) Kaneko; m. John Thomas Shaughnessy, Sept. 23, 1959. Assocs. in Liberal Arts, Keisen U., Tokyo, 1944. Ops. mgr. Webco Alaska, Inc., Anchorage, 1970-88; ptnr. Webco Partnership, Anchorage, 1983-98, also bd. dirs. Faculty Art League Sch., Alexandria, Va. Paintings, Lilacs, 1984, Blooms, 1985, The Fence, 1986 (Purchase award, 1986). Bd. dirs. Alaska Artists Guild, 1971—87; commr. Mcpl. Anchorage Fine Arts Commn., 1983—87; organizing com. Japanese Soc. Alaska, 1987. Recipient Art Affiliate award, Anchorage C. of C., 1975, 1978, 1984, Univ. Artists award, Alaska Pacific U., 1986, Am. Juror's Choice award, Sumi-E Soc. Am., 1994, Ikebana Internat. award, 1994, Dorothy Klein Meml. award, 1995, Yasutomo Calligraphy award, 1997, 1998, Oriental Calligraphy award, 1997, 1998, Sarasota Chpt Painting award, 1999, Paul Schwartz Meml. award, 2001, Sm. Works Exhibit 1st Pl. award, Wash. Watercolor Assn., 2001, Wang Chi Yuan award, 2000. Mem.: Nat. League Am. Penwomen (Grumbacher Gold medal award excellence 1993), Vienna Art Soc. (bd. dirs. 1995—96), Sumi-E Soc. Am. (past pres. 1992—94, bd. dirs., Nat. Capital Area chpt. past pres. awards 1990, Nat. Capital Area chpt. award 1990—92, 1994, Purchase award 1993), Va. Watercolor Soc. (pres. 1993, co-chmn. 2004 All State Juried Show), Potomac Valley Watercolorists (exhibits chair 1989—93, bd. dirs. 1989—99, newsletter editor 1993—96, v.p., workshop chair 1996—2001, historian 2003, awards 1989, 1991, Spl. award 1995), Alaska Watercolor Soc. (life; charter, Grumbacher Silver medal 1989), McLean Arts Club (1st pl. award 1991). Republican. Roman Catholic. Personal E-mail: markaneko@aol.com.

SHAUGHNESSY, MEGHANN, professional tennis player; b. Richmond, Apr. 13, 1979; d. Bill and Joy. Profl. tennis player, 1996—. Recipient WTA Tour Doubles Title, Quebec City, 2000, German Open, 2001, Gold Coast, 2002, Moscow, 2003, WTA Tour Singles Title, Shanghai, 2000, Quebec City, 2001, Canberra, 2003, Ranked #17, WTA, Ranked #6 Among U.S. Players, Highest Season Ending Single's Ranking #12, 2001, Resident Pro,

Scottsdale Hyatt Gainey Ranch Resort, 6 Internat. Women's Circuit Singles Titles. Mem.: U.S. Fedn. Cup Team. Office: WTA Tour Corporate Headquarters One Progress Plz Ste 1500 Saint Petersburg FL 33701*

SHAVER, JOAN LOUISE FOWLER, adult education educator; BS in Nursing, U. Alberta, Can., 1966; M in Nursing, U. Wash., 1968-70, PhD in Physiology and Biophysics, 1976. Nursing instr. chair med. surgical prog. Holy Cross Hosp. Sch. Nursing, Calgary, Can., 1966-68; staff nurse Virginia Mason Hosp., Seattle, 1970-71; asst. prof. Sch. Nursing U. Ariz., Tucson, 1976-77; assoc. prof. U. Calgary, Can., 1977-80; asst. prof. Dept. Physiological Nursing U. Wash., Seattle, 1980-85, rsch. affil. Regl. Primate Rsch. Ctr., 1983-86, assoc. prof., 1985-89, chair Dept. Physiological Nusring, 1988-95, prof., 1989-95, prof., chair Dept. Biobehavioral Nursing & Health Systems, 1995-96, co-dir. Ctr. Women's Health Rsch., 1989-96; prof., dean Coll. Nursing U. Ill., Chgo., 1996—, co-dir. Rsch. Core Nat. Ctr. Excellence in Women's Health, 1997—. Mem. editl. bd. Health Care for Women Internat., 1984—, Heart and Lung: The Jour. of Critical Care, 1988-90, Jour. of Applied Nursing Rsch., 1988-91, IMAGE: Jour. Nursing Scholarship, editl. adv. bd. Nursing Rsch., 1997—, Biol. Rsch. for Nursing, 1999—, Jour. Nursing Scholarship, 2000—; contbr. artilces to profl. jours. Abe Miller Meml. scholar Alberta Assn. Registered Nurses, 1968-69; Kathryn McLaggen Meml. fellow Can. Nurses Found., fellow Am. Acad. Nursing Am. Nurses Assn., 1988—. Office: U Ill Coll Nursing 845 S Damen Ave # Mc802 Chicago IL 60612-7350

SHAVER, LINDY CAROL, nursing administrator; b. Mayfield, Ky., July 13, 1963; d. Danny W. and Charlotte I. Bruce; m. Stephen B. Shaver, May 23, 1987 (div. Jan. 2003). BS, Murray State U., 1985; ADN, U. Ky., 1995. RN Ky. Nurse EPI - Jefferson Pl., Louisville, 1993—95; dir. nursing EPI - Green Valley Rehab., Carrollton, 1995—2000; adminstr. The Richwood, LaGrange, 2001—. Avocations: boating, swimming, gardening, travel, reading, cooking, golf. Home: 1117 Willow Oak Ln La Grange KY 40031 Office: The Richwood 1012 Richwood Way La Grange KY 40031

SHAVER, MICHELLE M. music educator; b. St. Louis, Mo., Sept. 13, 1963; d. Alfred James and Mary Louise DeManuele; children: Stephen James, Justin Robert, Jonathan Alfred. BA, BS, Maryville U., 1985; student, Webster U., 2001—. Registered music therapist Nat. Assn. Music Therapy, 1985. Pvt. piano tchr., St. Louis, 1984—; music therapist St. Anthony's Med. Ctr., St. Louis, 1986, Luth. Convalescent Home, St. Louis, 1987—89; choir dir. Queen of All Saints, St. Louis, 1990—; music educator St. Raphael Sch., St. Louis, 2001—. Recipient Sr. Patricia Thro award, Maryville U., 1985; scholar Jean M. Sinor scholarship, Webster U., 2003. Mem.: Music Educators Nat. Conf., Nat. Assn. Pastoral Musicians, Pi Gamma Mu.

SHAW, ANNITA LOUISE, art educator; b. Scottsbluff, Nebr., Feb. 13, 1941; d. Harold Kenneth and Velma Loraine Shaw; m. Max Le Roy Shaw, June 29, 1968; 1 child, Justin Owen. BS in Elem. Edn., Chandron State Coll., Chadron, NE, 1963; MA in Art Supervision and Direction, NYU, 1969. Tchr. 2d grade Bridgeport Sch. Dist., Nebr., 1961—64; tchr. 3rd grade Geneva Sch. Dist., Nebr., 1964—66; elem. art specialist Omaha Sch. Dist., 1966—68; tchr. jr. high sci. New London Sch. Dist., Conn., 1968—70; tchr. jr. and sr. high visual arts and visual arts curriculum specialist Ctrl. Kitsap Sch. Dist., Silverdale, Wash., 1974—2003. Mem. adv. com. Wash. State Commn. on Student Learning, Olympia, 1993—95; mem. assessment cert. team Nat. Bd. Profl. Tchg. Stds., San Francisco, 1996; presenter in field. Prodr.: (video) Whistle Wisdom, 1993, Perspective: More than Converging Line, 1999. Mem.: Nat. Art Edn. Assn. (mem. dels. assembly 1994, historian Wash. chpt. 1994, pres. Wash. chpt., treas. Wash. chpt., Pacific Region Elem. Art Educator 1988, Christa McAliffe Excellence in Edn. 1990, Pacific Region Mid. Level Art Educator 2001, Wash. Art Educator of Yr. 2000, Nat. Mid. Level Art Educator of the Yr. 2002), Women in the Arts. Avocations: sculpting, designing pins and medallions. Home: PO Box 737 Silverdale WA 98383-0737

SHAW, BEVERLY C. state official; b. Baton Rouge, Sept. 29, 1955; d. Joseph Louis and Kathryn Cambre; m. James Nelson Shaw, Jan. 26, 1980; children: Amy Rebecca, Ryan Virginia, Jacob Michael. BS in Acctg., La. State U., 1976. Cert. govt. fin. mgr. Acct. La. Dept. Corrections, Baton Rouge, 1976—78, asst. budget officer, 1981—83, budget officer, 1983—98; field auditor La. Office Legis. Auditor, Baton Rouge, 1978—81; fiscal officer La. Dept. Culture, Recreation and Tourism, Baton Rouge, 1998—. Chmn. fin. com. St. Isidore Cath. Ch., Baker, La., mem. sch. adv. bd., mem. parish coun. ministries, mem. baptismal team. Mem.: Nat. Inst. Govtl. Purchasing (bd. dirs.), Women in Mgmt. (treas.), Assn. Govtl. Accts. Roman Catholic. Avocations: sports, reading. Office: La Dept Culture Recreation and Tourism PO Box 94361 Baton Rouge LA 70804-9361 E-mail: bshaw@crt.state.la.us.

SHAW, CAROLE, editor, publisher; b. Bklyn., Jan. 22, 1936; d. Sam and Betty (Neckin) Bergenthal; m. Ray Shaw, Dec. 27, 1957; children: Lori Eve Cohen, Victoria Shaw Locknar. BA, Hunter Coll., 1962. Singer Capitol Records, Hilton Records, Rama Records, Verve Records, 1952-65; TV appearances Ed Sullivan, Steve Allen, Jack Paar, George Gobel Show, 1957; owner The People's Choice, L.A., 1975-79; founder, editor-in-chief Big Beautiful Woman mag., Beverly Hills, Calif., 1979—. Creator Carole Shaw and BBW label clothing line for large-size women. Author: Come Out, Come Out Wherever You Are, 1982. Avocations: piano, painting, swimming, travel. Office: BBW Mag 6666 Brookmont Ter Apt 412 Nashville TN 37205-4622

SHAW, ELEANOR JANE, newspaper editor; b. Columbus, Ohio, Mar. 23, 1949; d. Joseph Cannon and Wanda Jane (Campbell) S. BA, U. Del., 1971. With News-Jour. newspapers, Wilmington, Del., 1970-82, editor HEW desk, asst. met. editor, 1977-80, bus. editor, 1980-82; topics editor USA Today, 1982-83; asst. city editor The Miami Herald, 1983-85; projects editor The Sacramento Bee, 1985-87, news editor, 1987-91, exec. bus. editor, 1991-93, editor capitol bur. news, 1993-95, state editor, 1995-99; mgr. employee comm. The McClatchy Co., Sacramento, 1999—. Bd. dirs. Del. 4-H Found., 1978-83. Mem. Calif. Soc. Newspaper Editors (bd. dirs. 1990-96), No. Calif. Wine Soc. (v.p. 1987-93, pres. 1993-2002). Office: The McClatchy Co PO Box 15779 Sacramento CA 95852-0779 E-mail: eshaw@mcclatchy.com.

SHAW, GLORIA DORIS, art educator; b. Huntington, W.Va., Nov. 10, 1928; d. Charles Bert and Theodosia Doris (Shimer) Haley; m. Arthur Shaw, July 13, 1954 (dec. Aug. 1985); children: Deirdra Elizabeth, Stewart N. Student, SUNY, 1969-70, Art Students League, N.Y.C., 1969-70, 74; BA, SUNY, N.Y.C., 1980; postgrad., U. Tenn., 1982, Nat Kaz, Pietrasanta, Italy, 1992. Sculptor replicator Am. Mus. Natural History, N.Y.C., 1976-77; adj. prof. sculpture Fla. Keys C.C., Key West, 1983—. Prof. TV art history Fla. Keys C.C., 1989—; host moderator Channel 5 TV, Fla. Keys, 1982—; presenter Humanities Studies and Art History Channel 19 TV, 1995—, TV Jour. Channel 16, 1997—. Sculptor (portrait) Jimmy Carter, Carter Meml. Libr., 1976, Tennessee Williams, Tennessee Williams Fine Arts Ctr., 1982, UNICEF, 1978-79, (series) Fla. Panther and Audubon Wall Relief, 1985, (bust) AIDS Meml., 1990; one woman shows include Bank Street Coll., 1979, Hollywood Mus. of Art, 1985, Islander Gallery, 1983, Martello Mus., 1984, Greenpeace, 1987, FKCC Gallery, 2003; exhibited in group shows at Montoya, West Palm Beach, Fla., 1989, N.Y.C. Bd. of Edn. Tour of Schs., 1979, Earthworks East, N.Y., 1987, Man and Sci., 1978, Cuban Club, Key West, Fla., 1991, Leda Bruce Gallery, Big Pine, 1992, Kaz, Pietrasanta, Italy, 1992, Fla. Keys C.C. Gallery, 1993, Tennessee Williams Fine Arts Ctr., Key West, 1993, Internat. Woman's Show, Fla. Keys, 1994, Joy Gallery, 1994, 95, 96, Baron Gallery, Girls of Mauritania to UNICEF, 1996; designer Windows at Greenpeace Bldg., Key West, 1985-88, Pieta at St. Paul's Key West, 1997, Ceramic bird murals, FKCC, 1997; curator Women's Art, Key West, 1999, murals, Tennessee Williams Fine Arts Ctr., 1999, relief nudes Fine Arts Bldg., 1999, St. Francis sculpture and seated figures Garden Club, 2001, FKCC Gallery, 2003; retrospective: Gallery Florida Keys, 2003, Arts of Key West Lazy Lane Gallery, 2004. Recipient Children and Other Endangered Species award Thomas Cultural Ctr., 1980, Purchase award Cuban C. of C., 1982, Sierra Club, 1983, Blue Ribbon, Martello Towers Art and Hist. Soc., 1985, Red Ribbon, South Fla. Sculptors, 1986, Endangered Species award Greenpeace, 1986. Mem. Nat. Sculpture Soc. of N.Y.C., Internat. Sculpture Ctr., Art Students League of N.Y.C. (life), Art and Hist. Soc. Democrat. Avocation: naturalist.

SHAW, GRACE GOODFRIEND (MRS. HERBERT FRANKLIN SHAW), publisher, editor; b. N.Y.C. d. Henry Bernheim and Jane Elizabeth (Stone) Goodfriend; m. Herbert Franklin Shaw (dec. 1992); 1 son, Brandon Hibbs. Student, Bennington Coll.; BA magna cum laude, Fordham U., 1976, MSE, 1991. Reporter Port Chester (N.Y.) Daily Item; editorial coordinator World Scope Ency., N.Y.C.; assoc. editor Clarence L. Barnhart, Inc., Bronxville, N.Y.; freelance-writer for reference books; editing supr. World Pub. Co., mng. editor, sr. editor; mng. editor Peter H. Wyden Co., N.Y.C., 1969-70; assoc. editor Dial Press, N.Y.C., 1971-72, sr. editor, 1972, David McKay Co., N.Y.C., 1972-75, Grosset & Dunlap, 1975-79; chief editor Today Press (Grosset), 1977-79; sr. editor, coll. dept. Bobbs-Merrill, N.Y.C., mng. editor, exec. editor trade div., 1979-80, pub., 1980-84; mng. editor Rawson Assocs. div. Macmillan Pub., 1985-91; pres. Grace Shaw Assocs., Scarsdale, N.Y., 1991-97; profl. respite provider Westchester Jewish Cmty. Svcs., N.Y., 1997—. Home: 85 Lee Rd Scarsdale NY 10583-5212

SHAW, HELEN LESTER ANDERSON, retired dean, nutrition educator, researcher; b. Lexington, Ky., Oct. 18, 1936; d. Walter Southall and Elizabeth (Gyn) Anderson; m. Charles Van Shaw, Mar. 14, 1988. BS, U. Ky., 1958; MS, U. Wis., 1965, PhD, 1969. Registered dietitian. Dietitian Roanoke (Va.) Meml. Hosp., 1959-60, Santa Barbara (Calif.) Cottage Hosp., 1960-61; dietitian, unit mgr. U. Calif., Santa Barbara, 1961-63; rsch. asst., NIH fellow U. Wis., Madison, 1963-68; from asst. prof. to prof. U. Mo., Columbia, 1969-88, assoc. dean, prof., 1977-84; prof., chair dept. food and nutrition U. N.C., Greensboro, 1989-94, dean Sch. Human Environ. Scis., 1994-2000; ret., 2000. Cluster leader Food for 21st Century rsch. program U. Mo., 1985-88. Contbr. articles to rsch. publs. Elder 1st Presbyn. Ch., Columbia, 1974-89, Greensboro, 1992—. Recipient Teaching award Home Econ. Alumni Assn., 1981, Gamma Sigma Delta, 1984; rsch. grantee Nutrition Found., 1971-73, NIH, 1972-75, NSF, 1980-83. Mem. Am. Soc. for Nutrition Scis., Am. Bd. Nutrition, Am. Soc. for Clin. Nutrition, Am. Dietetic Assn., Am. Family and Consumer Sci. Assn., Sigma Xi, Phi Upsilon Omicron, Kappa Omicron Nu. Democrat. Avocations: tennis, choral singing, art, volunteering.

SHAW, KAREN JANE, special education educator; b. Dumas, Tex., Sept. 21, 1955; d. Max E. and Betty L. Nordyke; m. Clarke W. Shaw, Apr. 2, 1983; children: Caitlin E., Molly L., Max W. BS, U. Utah, 1982, MEd, 1987. Cert. secondary tchg. Utah, 2002, spl. edn. tchg. Utah, 2002. Self-contained spl. edn. tchr. Granite Sch. Dist., Holladay, Utah, 1985—89, tchr. leader Salt Lake City, 1989—. Recipient Joanne Gilles Tchr. of the Yr. award, Utah Coun. Exceptional Children, 2003, Outstanding Educator award, Utah Fedn. Coun. for Exceptional Children, Coun. for Children with Behavioral Disorders, 1999. Mem.: Coun. for Exceptional Children (hon.). Avocations: jogging, bicycling, hiking, travel, golf. Office: Hilda B Jones Ctr/Granite Sch Dist 382 E Baird Ave Salt Lake City UT 84115 E-mail: karen.shaw@granite.12.ut.us.

SHAW, LINDA DARE OWENS, county commissioner; b. High Point, N.C., May 30, 1940; d. Elborn James Elijah and Cassandra Myrtle (Hutchens) Owens; m. Roger Bruce Chilton, July 18, 1958 (div. Aug. 1976); children: Joni Lynn Chilton Moffitt, Roger Kyle Chilton; m. Robert Gilbert Shaw, Mar. 27, 1981. Grad. h.s. County commr., Guilford County, N.C., 1999—. Trustee N.C. Mus. Art, Raleigh, 1984-90; bd. dirs. Greensboro Conv. and Visitors Bur., 1990-96; sec. Rep. Nat. Com., 1996—, nat. committeewoman, N.C., 1992-96; sec. Rep. Nat. Conv., Phila., 2000; bd. dirs. ARC, YMCA, 2002—, Guilford County Bd. Health, 1999—; sec. com. on arrangements Rep. Nat. Conv., N.Y.C., 2004, ex-officio, mem. site com., 2004. Office: Bd County Commrs PO Box 3427 Greensboro NC 27402-3427 Home: 5105 Bennington Dr Greensboro NC 27410-3414 E-mail: imlshaw@aol.com.

SHAW, MARY M. computer science educator; b. Washington, Sept. 30, 1943; d. Eldon Earl and Mary Lewis (Holman) Shaw; m. Roy R. Weil, Feb. 15, 1973. BA cum laude, Rice U., 1965; PhD, Carnegie Mellon U., Pitts., 1972. Asst. prof. to prof. computer sci. Carnegie Mellon U., Pitts., 1972—, assoc. dean computer sci. for profl. programs, 1992-99, Alan J. Perlis chair computer sci.; co-dir. Sloan Software Industry Ctr., Pitts., 2001—. Chief scientist Software Engring. Inst., Carnegie Mellon U., Pitts., 1984-88; mem. Computer Sci. and Telecommunications Bd., NRC, Washington, 1986-93. Author: (with W. Wulf, P. Hilfinger, L. Flon) Fundamental Structures of Computer Science, 1981, The Carnegie Mellon Curriculum for Undergraduate Computer Science, 1985, (with David Garlan) Software Architecture: Perspectives on an Emerging Discipline, 1996, (with Roy Weil) Free Wheeling Easy in Western Pennsylvania, 1995, 1996, 1999; contbr. articles to profl. jours. Recipient Warnier prize, 1993, (with Roy Weil) Recreation and Outdoor Stewardship award, 2003; named Woman of Achievement, YWCA of Greater Pitts., 1973. Fellow AAAS, IEEE (disting. lectr.), Assn. for Computing Machinery (SIGPLAN exec. com. 1979-83, Recognition of Svc. award 1985, 90); mem. Sigma Xi. Office: Carnegie Mellon U Dept Computer Sci Pittsburgh PA 15213

SHAW, PATRICIA JILL, retired music educator; b. Thomasville, Ga., Oct. 30, 1951; d. Vernon Thomas and Sarah Evelyn Shaw. BS in Music Edn., Ga. Southwestern U., 1972, M in Elem. Edn., 1976; cert. MusM, Valdosta State U., 1980. Music tchr. Crisp County, Cordele, Ga., 1972—78, Valdosta (Ga.) City, Ga., 1978—85, kindergarten tchr., 1985—86; music tchr. Lowndes County, Valdosta, 1986—, ret., 2003—. Sponsor Clyattville (Ga.) Elem. Fishing Club, 2002—03. Mem.: Music Edn. Nat. Assn. Baptist. Avocations: fishing, camping. Home: 8 Spring Creek Cir Valdosta GA 31602

SHAW, PRISCILLA, music educator, coach; d. Lee and Freddie Shaw. MusB, Tex. Christian U., Ft. Worth, Tex., 1991—94. Cert. National Board Certification Nat. Bd. for Profl. Tchg. Standards, 2002. Dir. of vocal music George Wash. H.S., Denver, 1997—; tennis coach US Profl. Tennis Assn., Denver, 1999—. Tennis coach US Profl. Tennis Assn., Denver, 1999—. Bd. mem. Colo. Fund for Children and Pub. Edn., Denver, Colo., 2001—. Recipient Althea Gibson Vol. Award, Intermountain Tennis Assn., 2002, Tchr. of the Yr., Believe Productions, 2001, Harmony Award, Denver Mountainaires, 2001; grantee Nat. Coaches Conv., Intermountain Tennis Assn., 2000. Mem.: US Profl. Tennis Assn. (multicultural com. chair, lessons for life, chair 2001—03), USTA (assoc.). R-Liberal. Avocations: tennis, travel. Office: George Washington High School 655 S Monaco Parkway Denver CO 80224 Personal E-mail: tennisgalp@hotmail.com.

SHAW, RUTH G. energy company executive; m. Colin Stuart Shaw; 2 children. BA in English magna cum laude, East Carolina U.; PhD, U. Tex. Pres. Central Piedmont Cmty. Coll., 1986—92; v.p. corp. comms. Duke Energy Corp., Charlotte, NC, 1992-94, sr. v.p. corp. resources, 1994-97, exec. v.p., chief adminstrv. officer, 1997—2002, pres., 2003—, El Centro Coll., Dallas. Dir. Wachovia Corp., MedCath Corp.; mem. bd. dirs. Edison Electric Inst., Nuclear Energy Inst., S. E. Electric Exchange; chair Charlotte Rsch. Inst.; mem. Palmetto Bus. Forum. Mem. Order of the Long Leaf Pine; trustee U. N.C., Charlotte; bd. dirs. Rsch. Triangle Found. of N.C.; mem. Conf. Bd. Chief Adminstrv. Officer's Coun.; chmn. Found. for the Carolinas; elder 1st Presbyn. Ch., Charlotte; active United Way, Arts and Scis. Coun., YMCA, Boy Scouts Am. Named Outstanding Alumni, East Carolina U., disting. grad. U. Tex., Charlotte Woman of Yr., 1992, Businesswoman of Yr., 1995; recipient award for comms. excellence, 1997. Office: Duke Energy Corp 526 S Church St Charlotte NC 28202-1802

SHAW, SANDRA, newscaster; Student, U. Miss. Anchor WRKG-TV, Mobile, Ala.; weather anchor, reporter WRBL-TV, Columbus, Ga.; anchor NBC 17, Raleigh, NC. Vol. Duke Children's Hosp. Avocations: running, kickboxing, weightlifting, fishing, reading. Office: NBC 17 Studios 1205 Front St Raleigh NC 27609

SHAW, TESHETESA S. pre-school educator; b. Harricountray, Tex., Dec. 17, 1978; d. Tom Henry and Thelio Maria Shaw. Tchr. Willow H.S., Houston, 1998—99, Acad. Learning Sta., Arcola, Tex., 1999—. Home: Rt 1 Box 444 3605 Kansas Fresno TX 77545

SHAW, THERESA (TERRI) S. federal official; married; 2 children. BS, George Mason U., 1960; Grad. Exec. Devel. Program, George Washington U., 1991. From staff to sr. v.p. and chief info. officer SLM Corp., Reston, Va., 1988—99; exec. v.p., COO eNumerate Solutions, Inc, McLean, Va., 2000—02; COO Fed. Student Aid U. S. Dept. Edn., Washington, 2002—. Office: US Dept Edn 400 Maryland Ave SW Washington DC 20202

SHAW, TIANNA, biomedical engineer; married; 1 child. BS in Biomedical Engring., BSEE, U. So. Calif.; postgrad., Calif. State U., Sacramento. Exptl. facilities engr. NASA Ames Rsch. Ctr. Mem. multicultural leadership coun. NASA Ames Rsch. Ctr., chairperson Native Am. adv. com. Mem.: Am. Indian Sci. and Engring. Soc. (v.p. Calif. profl. chpt.). Office: NASA Ames Rsch Ctr Bldg 239 Rm 213 Moffett Field CA 94035 Business E-Mail: tshaw@mail.arc.nasa.gov.

SHAW, VIRGINIA RUTH, clinical psychologist; b. Salina, Kans., Dec. 10, 1952; d. Lawrence Eugene and Gladys S.; m. Joseph Eugene Scuro Jr., July 14, 1990. BA magna cum laude, Kans. Wesleyan U., 1973; MA, Wichita State U., 1975; PhD, U. Southern Miss., 1984. Diplomate Am. Bd. Med. Psychotherapists (fellow). Rsch. fellow Wichita (Kans.) State U., 1973-75; rsch. fellow, teaching fellow U. So. Miss., 1978-79, 80-81; staff psychologist Big Spring (Tex.) State Hosp., 1976-78; predoctoral clin. psychology intern U. Okla. Health Scis. Ctr., Oklahoma City, 1981-82; postdoctoral fellow in neuropsychology Neuropsychiat. Inst., UCLA, 1982-83; rsch. psychologist, neuropsychologist L.A. VA Med. Ctr. Wadsworth Div., 1983-84; clin. neuropsychologist Patton (Calif.) State Hosp., 1984-85; clin. neuropsychologist Brentwood div. LA VA Med. Ctr., 1985; clinical, neuropsychologist Timberlawn Psychiatric Hosp., Dallas, 1985-87, Dallas Rehab. Inst., 1987-93. Cons. clin. neuropsychology Dallas area hosps., Willowbrook Hosp., Waxahachie, Tex., Cedars Hosp., Waxahachie, 1988-96; br. chief, clin. psychologist Maui child and adolescent mental health team State of Hawaii Dept. Health, 1996—; presenter profl. meetings, 1975—. Contbr. articles to profl. jours. Active 500 Inc., Dallas, 1988—96, Maui Children's Coalition Coun., 1996—, Maui Spl. Edn. Adv. Coun., 1996—2000, Maui Cmty. Children's Coun., 1996—, So. Miss. Football, 1996—; mem. mental health and substance abuse com. Maui Svc. Area Bd., 2003—; active Dallas Mayor's com. Employment of the Disabled, 1987. Remiatte Meml. scholar Kans. Wesleyan U., 1970-73; recipient Nat. Disting. Svc. Registry award in rehab., 1989, Early Career Contbns. to Clin. Neuropsychology award candidate Nat. Acad. Neuropsychology, 1993, 94. Mem. AAUW (v.p. programs Maui chpt. 1996-98), APA Divsn. 35/Psychology of Women (student rsch. prize com. 1996), Internat. Neuropsychol. Soc., Nat. Head Injury Found., Assn. for Women in Psychology, Tex. Head Injury Found., Dallas Head Injury Found. (Vol. award, cert. appreciation 1991), Am. Congress Rehab. Medicine, Nat. Rehab. Assn., Nat. Acad. Neuropsychology (membership com. 1991-94, rsch. consortium 1991-96, co-chair poster program com. 1994-95), Hawaii Psychol.Assn. (Cert. Recognition Hawaiian Spl. Parents Info. Network 2002-03), Maui Youth and Family Svcs. (Cert. of Appreciation 2003), Soroptimist. Avocations: coin collecting, skiing, gourmet cooking, travel, dance. Office: 444 Hana Hwy Ste 202 Kahului HI 96732-2315 E-mail: vrshaw@camhmis.health.state.hi.us.

SHAW-COHEN, LORI EVE, magazine editor; b. Manhattan, N.Y., Apr. 22, 1959; d. Ray and Carole (Bergenthal) Shaw; m. Robert Mark Cohen, Sept. 20, 1981; children: Joshua Samuel, Drew Taylor, Logan Shaw. BA in Journalism, U. So. Calif., 1981. Editl. asst., writer BBW: Big Beautiful Woman Mag., L.A., 1979-80, Intro Mag., L.A., 1980-81; mng. editor 'Teen Mag., L.A., 1981-86. Writer, interviewer Stan Rosenfeld & Assocs. Pub. Rels., L.A., 1980-81; cons. BBW: Big Beautiful Woman Mag., 1981—, Media Rsch. Group, L.A., 1984; condr. seminars Women in Communication, L.A., 1983, Pacific N.W. Writers Conf., Seattle, 1984 Patentee children's toy, 1971; lyricist for songs, 1977—; contbr. articles and poems to profl. jours. and mags. Avocations: travel, reading, photography, horseback riding. Office: BBW: Big Beautiful Woman Mag 6666 Brookmont Ter Apt 412 Nashville TN 37205-4622

SHAWVER, LAURA K. biotechnology company executive; PhD Pharmacology, U. Iowa, 1983. With Triton Bioscis., 1989—92; from dir. preclin. devel. to sr. v.p. preclin. & pharm. devel. Sugen, Inc., San Francisco, 1992—2002. Office: Phenomix Corp Ste 160A 11099 N Torrey Pines Rd La Jolla CA 92037

SHAY, SUSANNE, psychologist; d. Izak and Bella Shay. PhD, Temple U., 1987. Sr. project dir. Arbor, Inc, Media, Pa., 1987—91; survey dir., data mgr. Ctr. for Forensic Econ. Studies, Phila., 1992—2003; sr. cons. LECG, Phila., 2003—. Mem.: APA, Am. Mktg. Assn., Phi Beta Kappa. Avocations: reading, writing, politics. Office: LECG Ste 1200 1608 Walnut St Philadelphia PA 19103-5407

SHAY-BYRNE, OLIVIA, lawyer; b. Trenton, N.J., Aug. 14, 1957; d. Stewart and Elizabeth (Sherrill) B. Student, Vanderbilt U., 1975-76; BA, Bowdoin Coll., 1979; JD, U. Toledo, 1982; LLM in Taxation, Georgetown U., 1987. Bar: Tex. 1982, Ohio 1984, Md. 1985. Assoc. Whiteford, Taylor & Preston, Balt., 1984-87, Linowes & Blocher, Silver Spring, Md., 1987-90; ptnr. Sutherland Asbill & Brenna LLP, Washington, 1996—2000, ReedSmith LLP, Washington, 2000—. Bd. dir. D.C. Mktg. Ctr.; bd. dirs. D.C. Mktg. Ctr., Inc. Author: The At-Risk Rules Under the Tax Reform Act of 1986, The Door Closes on Tax Motivated Investments, IRS Issues New Guidelines for Management Contracts Used for Facilities Financed with Tax Exempt Bonds, 1993, RRA '93 Loosens Real Estate Rules for Exempt Organizations, 1993; editor Nat. Mcpl. Fin. Jour.; contbr. articles to profl. jours. Mem. Tax Coun. for State of Md., Leadership Montgomery, 1996; bd. dirs. Bethesda Acad. Performing Arts, Inc.; chair GULC Nat. Tax Exempt Bond Conf., 1997. Mem. ABA (exempt orgn. com. taxation sect. 1991—), Md. Bar Assn. (coun. taxation sect.), Balt. City Bar Assn. (chmn. speakers bur. young lawyers sect.), Lawyers for Arts Washington, Comml. Real Estate Woman (bd. dirs., pres.), Profls. for Strathmore Hall (co-chmn.), D.C. Bowdoin Coll. Alumni Assn. (pres. 1992—), Howard County C. of C. (legis. com. 1989), Rotary. Home: 1083 Mill Field Ct Great Falls VA 22066 Office: Reed Smith LLP East Tower Fl 11 1301 K St NW Washington DC 20005

SHAYLOR, KAREN ANN, artist, educator; b. East Liverpool, Ohio, Apr. 8, 1952; d. William Howard and Lois May (Andre) Shaylor. EdB, Bowling Green State U., 1976; MFA, Wash. U., St. Louis, 1979. Art tchr. K-6 Fostoria (Ohio) Pub. Schs., 1974—75; art tchr. jr. h.s. South Euclid-Lyndhurst (Ohio) City Sch., 1975—77; tchg. asst. design Wash. U., St. Louis, 1978—79, instr., 1980; adj. instr. U. Wis., Eau Claire, 1979—80; claims rep. Farmers Ins. Group, St. Louis, 1981—85; art dept. chairperson St. Mary Ctrl. Cath. H.S., Sandusky, Ohio, 1985—. Com. mem. Diocese of Toledo (Ohio) Art Curriculum Devel. Com., 1986—99; bd. mem. Cultural Ctr., Sandusky, Ohio, 1995—2003; rev. panel mem. Ohio Arts Coun., Columbus, 1999—2002; instr. Ohio U., Lancaster, 1989, Chillicothe, 1989—91, Chillicothe, 1997; portrait artist Kaman's Art Shops, Sandusky, Ohio, 1999—2002. Exhibitions include Artists Books/Art Books, Midwest Drawing Exhbn., All-Ohio Exhbn. (Best in Show, 1986), one-woman shows include Karen Shaylor, exhibitions include St. Louis Area Women Artists, Women Artists Paperworks, 1979, Wisconsin Artswest, The Number 2 Pencil, An Alternative Valentine, A Circle of Friends, Drawings by 5 Ohio Artists, One on One/ Artists and Mentors, Nevertheless Nine, Three Artists, Metro St. Louis Figurative Invitational, Talismans, 30 Years, 30 Artists, Ohio Women's Caucus for the Arts Annual Juried Exhbn., Concepts and Dimension, All-Ohio Juried Exhbn., The Cooperstown Nat. Named Tchr. of Yr., Walmart, 1997; Arts in Edn. grant, Ohio Arts Coun., 1993—2003, Tchr. Fellowship for Creative Rsch., 1995. Mem.: Nat. Cath. Edn. Assn., Ohio Art Edn. Assn., Nat. Art Edn. Assn., Delta Kappa Gamma. Avocations: artists books, drawing. Office: St Mary Ctrl Cath High Sch 410 W Jefferson Stt Sandusky OH 44870 Personal E-mail: kayshay@hotmail.com. E-mail: ssmc_st_ks@noeca.org.

SHAYWITZ, SALLY E. pediatrics educator; Grad., CUNY; MD, Albert Einstein Coll. Medicine. Resident pediat. Albert Einstein Coll. Medicine, postdoctoral fellow in developmental/behavioral pediat.; faculty mem. Yale U., 1979—, founder, dir. learning disabilities unit dept. pediat., co-dir. Ctr. for the Study of Learning and Attention, prof. pediat. Participant Nat. Summit on Learning Disabilities, spl. advisor U.S. Congress, U.S. Dept. Edn.; cons. Nat. Inst. Child Health and Human Devel., Nat. Inst. Deafness and Other Comm. Disorders; spkr. in field. Active Nat. Reading Panel; mem. com. to prevent reading difficulties in young children Nat. Rsch. Coun. Recipient Disting. Alumnus award Albert Einstein Coll. Medicine, 1995, Clin. Svc. award Soc. for the Advancement of Women's Health Rsch., 1998. Mem. NAS-Inst. Medicine, Dana Alliance for Brain Initiatives, Phi Beta Kappa. Achievements include research on differences between dyslexic and nonimpaired readers in the neural circuitry of the brain for reading; principal investigator of the Connecticut Longitudinal Study a prospective study of reading development based on a representative sample of school children followed since kindergarten. Office: Yale-New Haven Hosp Childrens Hosp 20 York St LMP 3089 New Haven CT 06504 E-mail: sally.shaywitz@yale.edu.

SHEA, CHRISTINA, former mayor; Mayor City of Irvine, Calif., 1996—2000; pres. Christina Shea Consulting. Office: 302 Shadow Oaks Irvine CA 92618 E-mail: christina@christinashea.com.

SHEA, DEBBIE BOWMAN, state legislator; b. Butte, Mont., June 26, 1951; divorced. BS in Elem. Edn., Eastern Mont. Coll., 1974; MA in Edn., U. Mont., 1989. Formerly tchr. 8th grade pub. schs.; mem. Mont. Ho. of Reps., 1994-96, Mont. Senate, Dist. 18, Helena, 1997—; mem. joint appropriations subcom. on corrections/pub. safety Mont. Senate; mem. edn. and cultural resources com. Mont. State Senate, mem. hwys. and transp. com., mem. fin. and claims com. Democrat. Home: 100 Moon Ln Butte MT 59701-3975

SHEA, FRAN, broadcast executive; Sr. v.p. programming E! Entertainment TV, L.A., 1995-98, acting pres. LA, 1998-99, pres., 1999—. Office: E! Entertainment TV 5670 Wilshire Blvd Fl 2D Los Angeles CA 90036-5679 Fax: 213-954-2661.

SHEA, GWYN, secretary of state; 2 children. Student, U. North Tex.; student, Dallas Baptist U.; grad., Dallas Baptist U. Police Acad. Served Tex. Ho. Reps., 1982—92, Ho. Ways and Means Com., Ho. Ins. Com.; pres. Nat. Coun. Ins. Legislators; apptd. Tex. Worker's Compensation Ins. Facility, 1995; Sec. of State State of Tex., 2002—. Constable Dallas County Precint 2 Irving, Coppell, North Dallas, 1994, 96, 2000. Pres. Tex. Healthy Kids Corp., 1997; former dir. Irving C. of C.; past pres. Women's Divsn. of C.; mem. adv. bd. Irving CARES, Profl. Secs. Internat.; mem. 1st Baptist Ch., Irving; mem. adv. bds. Irving Infant Intervention Ctr. Named to legis. commitment to people of Tex., Tex. Mun. League, Tex. Assn. Bus., Tex. Civil Justice League, Tex. Assn. Concerned Tax Payers ; recipient Legislative Leadership award, Tex. C. of C. Republican. Office: PO Box 12887 Austin TX 78711-2887

SHEA, JOAN-EMMA, biophysicist, educator; b. Ottawa, Ont., Canada, July 11, 1972; d. William Rene Joseph and Evelyn Shea; m. Frank Leon Brown, Aug. 14, 2001. BS with 1st class honors, Mc Gill U., Montreal, Que., Can., 1992; PhD, MIT, 1997. Rsch. scientist Scripps Rsch. Inst., La Jolla, Calif., 1997—2000; prof. chemistry U. Chgo., 2000—01; prof. chemistry and biochemistry U. Calif., Santa Barbara, Calif., 2001—. Sci. reviewer Biophysical Jour., Procs. of the NAS, USA, Proteins: Structure, Function and Genetics, Jour. of Chem. Physics, Jour. of Phys. Chemistry, Phys. Rev. E. Contbr. articles to profl. scientific jours. Recipient Career award, NSF, 2000—, Cottage Hosp. Biomed. award, Cottage Hosp. and U. Calif., 2001; fellow Nat. Sci. and Engring. Rsch. Coun. Predoctoral Fellowship, Nat. Sci. and Engring. Rsch. Coun. of Can., 1994-1997, FCAR grad. fellowship, Fonds pour la formation de chercheurs et l'aide à la recherche, 1992-1994; Burroughs Wellcome (LJIS) Postdoctoral fellow, 1998—2000, Nat. Sci. and Engring. Rsch. Coun. Postdoctoral fellow, 1997—99. Mem.: Biophysical Soc., Am. Phys. Soc., Am. Chem. Soc. Achievements include research in field of computational biophysics: theory and simulation of protein folding and protein aggregation; simulations of peptide aggregation with applications to Alzheimer's disease. Office: U Calif Dept Chemistry and Biochemistry Santa Barbara CA 93106 E-mail: shea@chem.ucsb.edu.

SHEA, KATHLEEN E. cultural resources specialist; b. Chgo., June 10, 1946; d. Leonard Edward and Margaret (O'Connor) S.; divorced; 1 child, Laura Lee. BS, NYU, 1971. Dir. conservation Washington U. Tech. Assn. Inc., St. Louis, 1983-88; commr. heritage and urban design City of St. Louis, 1988—. Fellow Leadership St. Louis Inc., 1994—. Office: City of St Louis 1015 Locust St Saint Louis MO 63101-1334

SHEA, STEPHANIE, music educator; b. Pitts., Pa., July 11, 1949; d. Gregory Samuel Squires and Evelyn Margaret Kosko; m. Dennis Raymond Shea, June 11, 1971; children: Jennifer Marie, Markus Gregory. BSc, Ea. Mont. Coll., 1971; MEd, Lesley Coll., 1994. Cert. tchr. Music tchr. Sch. Dist. 1, Butte, Mont., 1973—. Bd. dir. All Am. City, Butte, 1988, Arts Chateau, Butte, 1990—94. Mem.: NEA, Butte (Mont.) Tchrs. Union (negotiation com. 1990—94), Music Educators Nat. Coun. Roman Cath. Avocations: boating, water-skiing, bicycling, crafts, gardening. Home: 2031 Elm St Butte MT 59701 Office: School Dist No 1 111 N Montana St Butte MT 59701

SHEAD, MARY AIRTHRLODIOS, elementary school educator; b. Holly Springs, Miss., Mar. 16, 1948; d. Willie Adolphus and Elerine Walker; widowed; children: Gail, Amy, Anthony, Gennifer. AS, Shelby State Coll., 1984; BS, U. Memphis, 1993. Ednl. asst. Memphis City Schs., 1985-93, tchr., 1993—.

SHEAFFER, KAREN, county official, treasurer; b. Lewistown, Pa., Sept. 8, 1949; d. Clyde William and Betty Beatrice Krepps; m. James G. Sheaffer, Oct. 25, 1969; children: Jeremy James, Jarrod James. Adminstrv. asst. Kyburz Constrn., Edwards, Colo., 1982-86; bookkeeper Eagle (Colo.) County Treas., 1986-89, dep. treas., dep. pub. trustee, 1989-96, county treas., pub. trustee, 1996—. Bd. dirs. Colotrust. Mem.: Internat. Assn. Clks., Recorders, Election Ofcls. and Treas., Colo. County Pub. Trustees Assn., Colo. County Treas. Assn. (cert. county treas., Outstanding Treas. of Yr. 1998, 2000). Republican. Methodist. Office: Eagle County Govt 500 Broadway Eagle CO 81631

SHEAFFER, SUZANNE FRANCES, geriatrics nurse; b. Harrisburg, Pa., Feb. 8, 1963; d. Walter Richard and Catherine Frances (Mourawski) Markham; children: William Chester, Sarah Suzanne, Katye Iona; m. Paul L. Sheaffer Jr. LPN, Harrisburg Stelton Highs, Sch. Practical Nursing, 1984; ADN, Harrisburg (Pa.) Area C.C., 1984; BSN, York (Pa.) Coll., 1997. Lic. nursing home adminstr., Pa. Nurse ICU and critical care unit Meml. Hosp., York, Pa., 1987-88; staff nurse emergency dept. Polyclinic Med. Ctr., Harrisburg, 1988-91; assoc. prof. Nat. Edn. Ctr.-Jr. Coll., Harrisburg, 1991; dir. nursing Camp Hill (Pa.) Care Ctr., 1991-92; resident assessment supr. Susquehanna Ctr., Harrisburg, 1992-94; dir. nursing Susquehanna Luth. Village, Millersburg, Pa., 1994-95; asst. adminstr. Dauphin Manor, Harrisburg, 1995—; mgr. clin. svcs. ea. divsn. HCR Manor Care; med. analyst Medicaid Fraud Control Unit Pa. Atty. Gen. Office, 2003—. ACLS, CPR instr. Am. Heart Assn., Harrisburg, 1989—; BCLS, CPR instr. ARC, Harrisburg, 1992—; RN, paramedic Lebanon (Pa.) County First Aide and Safety Patrol, 1992—. Sec. Little People PTA, Harrisburg, 1991-92; pres. Student Human Resource Mgmt. Club, York (Pa.) Coll., 1992—; v.p. Prince of Peace PTO, 1997-98; cheerleading coach, Midget Footbal Assoc., 2002—; cheerleading coord. Susquehanna Twp. Midget Football Assn., 2003; acad. adviser Eta Sigma Alpha Chi Beta chpt., 2003—. Recipient Nurse of Hope award Am. Cancer Soc., Dauphin County, Harrisburg, 1983-84. Mem. AACN, Pa. Nurses Assn., Pa. Dir. Nursing Assn. for Long Term Care, PANPHA (advocate), York Coll. Alumni Assn. (bd. dirs. Susquehanna Valley), Pa. Homesch. Assn. Roman Catholic. Avocations: ceramics, ballet, flute.

SHEALY, COURTNEY, Olympic athlete; b. Columbia, S.C., Dec. 12, 1977; Student, U. Ga. Team capt. Ga. Bulldogs, 1999—2000. Recipient Gold medal 4 x 100-meter freestyle Sydney Olympics, 2000; named co-NCAA Swimmer of Yr., 2000, 2-time world record holder, 1 olympic record, 2-time NCAA team champion, 3-time NCAA individual champion, 5-time Am. record holder, 26 1st team all-am. awards (most by any Ga. athlete), Ramsey scholar, 1997-2000, NCAA Acad. All-Am., 1997, 1998, 2000, SEC swimmer of the yr., 2000 Office: USA Swimming 1 Olympic Plz Colorado Springs CO 80909-5746

SHEAR, IONE MYLONAS, archaeologist; b. St. Louis, Feb. 19, 1936; d. George Emmanuel and Lella (Papazoglou) Mylonas; m. Theodore Leslie Shear, June 24, 1959; children: Julia Louise, Alexandra. BA, Wellesley Coll., 1958; MA, Bryn Mawr Coll., 1960, PhD, 1968. Rsch. asst. Inst. for Advanced Study, Princeton, N.J., 1963-65; mem. Agora Excavation, Athens, 1967, 72-94; lectr. art and archaeology Princeton U., 1983-84; lectr. Am. Sch. Classical Studies, Athens, summers 1989-98. Also excavator various other sites in Greece and Italy. Author: The Panagia Houses at Mycenae, 1987, Tales of Heroes: The Origins of the Homeric Texts, 2000; contbr. articles to profl. jours. Mem. Archaeol. Inst. Am., Greek Archaeol. Soc. (hon.). Address: 87 Library Pl Princeton NJ 08540-3015 also: Deinokratous 30 Athens 106-76 Greece

SHEAR, NATALIE PICKUS, conference and event management executive; b. N.Y.C., Oct. 18, 1940; d. Sam and Mildred (Shulman) Pickus; m. Daniel H. Shear, Dec. 14, 1968 (dec. Apr. 1989); children: Adam Brian, Tamara Beth; m. Henry D. Lewis, Jan. 10, 1999. BA in Journalism, Fairleigh Dickinson U., 1962. Editorial asst. Show Bus. Newspaper, N.Y.C., 1962-64, The Jewish News, Newark, 1964-66; dir. Manhattan women's div., program asst. Am. Jewish Congress, N.Y.C., 1966-68; mng. editor The Jewish Week, Washington, 1968-71; dir. pub. rels. United Jewish Appeal, Washington, 1973-74; pub. affairs dir. Leadership Conf. on Civil Rights, Washington, 1977-83; pres. Natalie P. Shear Assocs., Inc., Washington, 1983—. Editor (newspaper) Books Alive, 1973-74; editor, pub. (newsletter) Trends, Inc., 1989-94. Vol. nat. bd. Ams. Dem. Action, 2001—; vol., bd. dirs. Nat. Jewish Dem. Coun., Washington, 1996—; bd. dirs. Urban Philharm. Soc., 1998-99; chairperson women's task force Am. Jewish Congress, Washington, 1984-86; v.p. Nat. Child Rsch. Ctr., Washington, 1974-76; pres. Ohr Kodesh Sisterhood, Chevy Chase, Md., 1980-82. Mem. Nat. Press Club. Avocations: needlework, crafts. Home: 4701 Willard Ave Chevy Chase MD 20815-4643 Office: 1730 M St NW Ste 801 Washington DC 20036 Office Phone: 202-833-4456 ext. 101. E-mail: natalie@nataliepshear.com.

SHEARING, MIRIAM, state supreme court justice; b. Waverly, NY, Feb. 24, 1935; BA, Cornell U., 1956; JD, Boston Coll., 1964. Bar: Calif. 1965, Nev. 1969. Justice of peace Las Vegas Justice Ct., 1977-81; judge Nev. Dist. Ct., 1983-92, chief judge, 1986; justice Nevada Supreme Ct., Carson City, 1993-97, chief justice, 1997—. Mem. ABA, Am. Judicature Soc. (chair 2001-), Nev. Judges Assn. (sec. 1978), Nev. Dist. Ct. Judges Assn. (sec. 1984-85, pres. 1986-87), State Bar Nev., State Bar Calif., Clark County Bar Assn. Democrat. E-mail: shearing@nvcourts.state.nv.us.

SHEA-STONUM, MARILYN, federal judge; b. 1947; AB, U. Santa Cruz, 1969; JD, Case Western Res. U., 1975. Law clk. to Hon. Frank J. Battisti, Cleve., 1975-76; ptnr. Jones, Day, Reavis & Pogue, Cleve., 1976-94; bankruptcy judge U.S. Dist. Ct. (no. dist.) Ohio, Akron, 1994—. Mem. Order of Coif. Office: US Bankruptcy Ct No Dist Ohio 240 Fed Bldg 2 S Main St Akron OH 44308-1813 Fax: 330-375-5793.

SHECHTER, LAURA JUDITH, artist; b. Bklyn., Aug. 26, 1944; d. Philip and Jeannette (Newmark) Goldstein; m. Ben-Zion Shechter, Feb. 26, 1969; 1 son, Adam. BA with honors in Art, Bklyn. Coll., 1965. Case worker Dept. Social Service, N.Y.C., 1965-73; artist N.Y.C., 1965—; lectr., 1978—; curator Forum Gallery, N.Y.C., 1978; tchr. Parson Sch. Design, N.Y.C., 1984, Nat. Acad. Design, N.Y.C., 1985-88, 94-98. Exhibited one-woman shows Forum Gallery, N.Y.C., 1976, 80, 83, Greenville County Mus. Art, 1982, Wustum Mus., Racine, Wis., 1982, Schoelkopf Gallery, N.Y.C., 1985, Staempfli Gallery, N.Y.C., 1987, 88, Rahr West Mus., Manitowoc, Wis., U. Richmond, 1991, Perlow Gallery, N.Y.C., 1992, 94, Pucker Gallery, Boston, 1984, 96, 99; group shows include Akron Art Inst., 1974, Minn. Mus. Art, St. Paul, 1981, Pa. Acad. Art, Phila., 1982, Boston Mus., 1982, Bklyn. Mus., 1980, 84, Nat. Mus. Am. Art, Washington, 1985, San Francisco Mus. Modern Art, 1985, Huntsville Mus., Ala., 1987, Butler Inst., Youngstown, Ohio, 1987, 88, Ind. U. Art Mus., Joplin, Mo., 1991, Ark. Art Ctr., 1992; represented in pub. collections including Boston Mus. Fine Art, Bklyn. Mus., Carnegie Inst., Indpls. Mus., Israel Mus., others. Recipient Creative Artist Pub. Service award N.Y. State, 1982 Mem. Artists Equity, Nat. Acad. Design. Home: 429 4th St Brooklyn NY 11215-2901 E-mail: laurart3@aol.com.

SHEEHAN, CAROL SAMA, magazine editor; Editor-in-chief Country Home Mag., Des Moines, 1997—. Office: Country Home Magazine 1716 Locust St Des Moines IA 50309-3038

SHEEHAN, LINDA SUZANNE, education administrator; b. Dayton, Ohio, Aug. 1, 1950; d. Paul J. and Betty L. (Fowler) King; 1 child, Amy Elizabeth. BS in Edn. with honors, Ohio State U., 1971; MEd, U. Tex., 1974; adminstrn. cert., Houston Bapt. U., 1983. Tchr. Upper Arlington Schs., Columbus, Ohio, 1971-72, Brown Sch., San Marcos, Tex., 1972-73, Comal Ind. Schs. Dist., New Braunfels, Tex., 1973-75, Allief Ind. Sch. Dist., Houston, 1975-79; asst. prin. Killough Mid. Sch., Houston, 1979-84; prin. Olle Mid. Sch., Houston, 1984-92, Blue Ribbon Sch., 1991-92, Holub Mid. Sch., 1992—. Named Tchr. of Yr. Olle Mid. Sch., Houston, 1978; recipient Mary Knots Perkins Exemplary Leadership award, 1998, Blue Ribbon Sch. award 1991-92. Mem. Nat. Mid. Sch. Assn., Nat. Assn. Secondary Sch. Prins., Tex. Assn. Secondary Sch. Prins., Tex. Mid. Sch. Assn. (dir. 1979-91, pres. 1991-92, state convention chair 1993-94, 97-98), Houston Coun. Social Studies, Kappa Delta Pi (pres. 1984-85), Phi Delta Kappa. Roman Catholic. Home: 526 Nottingham Oaks Trail Houston TX 77079-6332 Office: Holub Mid Sch 9515 S Dairy Ashford St Houston TX 77099-4909

SHEEHAN, PATTY, professional golfer; b. Middlebury, Vt., Oct. 27, 1956; 4th ranked woman LPGA Tour, 1992; winner U.S. Women's Open, 1992, 94, McDonald's LPGA Championship, 1983-84, 93. Inductee LPGA Hall of Fame, 1993, Sports Illustrated Sportsman of the Yr., 1987. Achievements include being the winner for 31 LPGA Tournaments including Mazda Japan Classic, 1981, 88, Inamori Classic, 1982-83, 86, Orlando Lady Classic, 1982, Safeco Classic, 1982, 90, 95, LPGA Corning Classic, 1983, LPGA Championship, 1983-84, 93, Henredon Classic, 1983-84, Elizabeth Arden Classic, 1984, McDonald's Kids Classic, 1984, 90, Sarasota Classic, 1985-86, 88, J&B Scotch Pro AM, 1985, Konica San Jose Classic, 1986, Rochester Internat., 1989-90, 92, 95, Jamaica Classic, 1990, Ping-Cellular One Championship, 1990, Orix Hawaiian Ladies Open, 1991, Jamie Farr Toledo Classic, 1992, Weetabix Women's Brit. Open, 1992, U.S. Women's Open, 1992, 94, Mazda LPGA Championship, 1993, The Nabisco Championship, 1996; in 17 tournaments earning $179,453, 1997, 16 tounaments earning $342,391, 1996, 35th victory, Nabisco Dinah Shore earning 6th major champ. title, crossed $5 million mark in career earnings, 1996, winner Michelob Light Front Runner Awd. for leading most rounds in season, 1996. Office: LPGA 100 International Golf Dr Daytona Beach FL 32124-1092

SHEEHAN, SAMANTHA, gymnast; b. Cincinnati, OH, May 20, 1986; d. Kevin and Cindy Sheehan. Gymnast Cincinnati Gymnastics/U.S. Natl. Team, 2002—. Achievements include Level 10 National Bar Champion; Level 10 State Champion; Qualified to 2001, 02 U.S. Gymnastics Championships, World Championships, 2002; Bronze Medal Floor Exercise, World Championships, 2002; 1st place All Around, USA-Belgium dual competition, 2003. Office: 3635 Woodbridge Blvd Fairfield OH 45014*

SHEEHAN, SOPHIA ANN, marriage and family therapist, department chairman; b. San Gabriel, Calif., May 13, 1972; d. Mary Angela and Henry C. Gonzalez; m. Joseph Scott Sheehan, Apr. 13, 1996. BA, U. of So. Calif., 1990—94; M, Peperdine U., 1994—96. Lic. Marriage and Family Therapist Bd. of Behavioral Sci., Calif., 2000. Marriage and family therapist trainee Family Assessment Counseling and Ednl. Services, Fullerton, Calif., 1996—97; marriage and family therapist intern Mid Valley Learning Ctr., Baldwin Park, Calif., 1997—99; clin. social worker Canyon Acres Children's Services, Anaheim Hills, Calif., 1999—2002; clin. program supr. Canal St. Elm. Sch. (TEC/Olive Crest), Orange, Calif. Mem.: Am. Assn. of Marriage and Family Therapists. Catholic. Avocations: crocheting, dance, travel.

SHEEHAN, SUSAN, writer, b. Vienna, Aug. 24, 1937; arrived in U.S., 1941, naturalized, 1946; d. Charles and Kitty C. (Herrmann) Sachsel; m. Neil Sheehan, Mar. 30, 1965; children[00bf] Maria Gregory, Catherine Fair. BA, Wellesley Coll., 1958; DHL (hon.), U. Lowell, 1991. Editl. rschr. Esquire-Coronet, N.Y.C., 1959-60; freelance writer N.Y.C., 1960-61, staff writer New Yorker mag., N.Y.C., 1961—; contbg. writer Archtl. Digest, 1997—. Writer-in-residence, lectr. Georgetown U., 1999. Author: Ten Vietnamese, 1967, A Welfare Mother, 1976, A Prison and a Prisoner, 1978, Is There No Place on Earth for Me?, 1982, Kate Quinton's Days, 1984, A Missing Plane, 1986, Life For Me Ain't Been No Crystal Stair, 1993, The Banana Sculptor, the Purple Lady, and the All-Night Swimmer, 2002; contbr. articles to various mags., including N.Y. Times Sunday Mag., Washington Post Sunday Mag., Harper's, Atlantic, New Republic, McCall's, Holiday, Boston Globe Sunday Mag., Life. Judge Robert F. Kennedy Journalism awards, 1980, 84; mem. lit. panel D.C. Commn. on Arts and Humanities, 1979-84; mem. pub. info. and edn. com. Nat. Mental Health Assn., 1982-83; mem. adv. com. on employment and crime Vera Inst. Justice, 1978-86; chair Pulitzer Prize nominating jury in gen. non-fiction for 1988, 1994, mem., 1991. Recipient Sidney Hillman Found. award, 1976, Gavel award ABA, 1978, Individual Reporting award Nat. Mental Health Assn., 1981, Pulitzer prize for gen. non-fiction, 1983, Feature Writing award N.Y. Press Club, 1984, Alumnae Assn. Achievement award Wellesley Coll., 1984, Carroll Kowal Journalism award NASW, 1993, Disting. Grad. award Hunter Coll. H.S., 1995, Pub. Awareness award Nat. Alliance for Mentally Ill, 1995, Casey medal for meritorious journalism, 1997; Durant scholar Wellesley Coll., 1958; fellow Guggenheim Found., 1975-76, Woodrow Wilson Internat. Ctr. for Scholars, 1981, Open Soc. Inst., 1998-99. Mem. Soc. Am. Historians, Phi Beta Kappa, Authors Guild, Lansdowne Club (London). Home: 4505 Klingle St NW Washington DC 20016-3580 Office: New Yorker Mag 4 Times Sq New York NY 10036-7441

SHEEHEY, PATRICIA ANN, secondary school educator; b. Des Moines, Sept. 25, 1946; d. James Michael Sheehey and Elizabeth Ann Markunas; m. William Elwin McConnell, June 24, 1978 (dec. Aug. 1999). BA in English, Marycrest Coll., Davenport, Iowa, 1968; MA in English, We. Ill. U., 1970; postgrad., U. Iowa, 1971—2000, U. London, 1971. Instr. West H.S., Davenport, 1969—, head dept. lang. arts, 1998—. Alumni bd. Marycrest Coll., Davenport, 1980—84. Recipient Golden Apple Outstanding Tchr. award, Scott County, 1980. Mem.: Nat. Coun. Tchrs. English (regional judge), Alpha Delta Kappa, Alpha Delta Kappa (sec., treas., pres. 1978—82, scholarship chair 1983—86). Roman Catholic. Avocations: writing, antiques, reading. Home: 5 Birchwood Dr Blue Grass IA 52726 Office: West High Sch 3505 W Locust Davenport IA 52804 Office Phone: 563-386-5500.

SHEEHY, GAIL HENION, author; b. Mamaroneck, NY, Nov. 27, 1937; d. Harold Merritt and Lillian Rainey (Paquin) Henion; m. Albert F. Sheehy, Aug. 20, 1960 (div. 1967); 1 adopted child, Mohm 1 child, Maura ; m. Clay Felker, Dec. 16, 1984. BS, U. Vt., 1958; fellow, Journalism Sch., Columbia U., 1970. Traveling home economist J.C. Penney & Co., 1958-60; fashion editor Rochester Democrat & Chronicle, 1961-63; feature writer N.Y. Herald Tribune, N.Y.C., 1963-66; contbg. editor New York mag., 1968-77. Contbr. to NY Times Mag., Parade, New Republic, Washington Post; polit. contbg. editor Vanity Fair mag., 1988—; author: Lovesounds, 1970, Panthermania: The Clash of Black Against Black in One American City, 1971, Speed Is of the Essence, 1971, Hustling: Prostitution in Our Wide-Open Society, 1973, Passages: Predictable Crises of Adult Life, 1976, Pathfinders, 1981, Spirit of Survival, 1986, Character: America's Search for Leadership, 1988, Gorbachev: The Man Who Changed the World, 1990, The Silent Passage: Menopause, 1992, New Passages: Mapping Your Life Across Time, 1995, Hillary's Choice, 1999. Middletown, America: One Town's Passage From Trauma to Hope, 2003; (plays) Maggie and Misha, 1991; co-author: Discovering the Power of Self-Hypnosis, 1999. Adv. bd. Women's Health Initiative, NIH; bd. dirs. Girls, Inc., Poets and Writers; eminent citizen's com. UN Internat. Conf. on Population and Devel., 1994. Recipient 5 Front Page awards Newswomen's Club NY, Nat. Mag. award Columbia U., 1973, Penney-Mo. Journalism award U. Mo., 1975, Anisfield-Wolf Book award, 1986, Best Mag. Writer award Wash. Journalism Rev., 1991, NY Pub. Libr. Literary Lion, 1992; Columbia U. fellow, 1970; Alicia Patterson Found. grantee, 1974. Mem. PEN, NOW, Authors Guild. Address: c/o Doug Stumpf Vanity Fair 4 Times Sq New York NY 10036-6522*

SHEEKEY, KATHLEEN D. advocate, director; Legislative dir. Common Cause, 1981-91; dir. congressional relations Fed. Trade Commn.; legislative dir. Consumer Federation of Am.; co-dir. Advocacy Inst., 1992. Office: Advocacy Inst 1707 L St NW Ste 400 Washington DC 20036-4213 Fax: 202-659-8484. E-mail: info@advocacy.org.

SHEELER, HARVA LEE, law librarian; b. Miami, Fla., Feb. 10, 1934; d. Harry Hersh and Rose (Caplan) Young; m. Walter Leon Sheeler, Nov. 9, 1957 (dec. Sept. 1985); children: Charles Harold, Harva Katharine. BA, U. Maine, 1955; MS in LS, Cath. U. Am., 1972. Reference libr. Fairfax County Pub. Libr., Fairfax, Va., 1972-74, Virginiana collection libr., 1974-79; mgr. law libr. Jones Day Reavis & Pogue, Washington, 1979-94, coord. firm librs., 1994—. Contbg. author: Managing the Private Law Library, 1988. Sec., bull. editor Fairfax County Fedn. Citizens Assns., 1966-80. Recipient A. Heath Onthank award for svc. Fairfax County Bd. Suprs., 1978, Nat. Facts on File award ALA, 1980. Mem. Am. Assn. Law Librs. (sec.-treas. pvt. law libr.-spl. interest sect. 1989-91), Spl. Librs. Assn., Law Libr. Soc. Washington (pres. Pvt. law libr.-spl. interest sect. 1982-84), Beta Phi Mu. Home: 2326 Wheystone Ct Vienna VA 22182-5236 Office: Jones Day Reavis & Pogue 51 Lousiana Ave NW Washington DC 20001

SHEEN, PORTIA YUNN-LING, retired physician; b. Republic of China, Jan. 13, 1919; came to U.S., 1988; d. Y. C. and A. Y. (Chow) Sheen; m. Kuo, 1944 (dec. 1970); children: William, Ida, Alexander, David, Mimi. MD, Nat. Med. Coll. Shanghai, 1943. Intern, then resident Cen. Hosp., Chungking, Szechuan, China, 1943; with Hong Kong Govt. Med. and Health Dept., 1948-76; med. supt. Kowloon (Hong Kong) Hosp., 1948-63, Queen Elizabeth Hosp., Kowloon, 1963-73, Med. and Health Hdqrs. and Health Ctr., Kowloon, 1973-76, Yan Chai Hosp., New Territories, Hong Kong, 1976-87; ret., 1987. Fellow Hong Kong Coll. Family Physicians; mem. AAAS, British Med. Assn., Hong Kong Med. Assn., Hong Kong Pediatric Soc., N.Y. Acad. Sci. Methodist. Avocations: reading, music. Home: 1408 Golden Rain Rd Apt 7 Entry 1 Roosmoor Walnut Creek CA 94595-2442

SHEERR, DEIRDRE MCCRYSTAL, architectural firm executive; m. Clinton Jay Sheerr (dec. 1997); m. Martin L. Gross, 2000. BA, Monmouth Coll., 1969; MArch, U. Colo., 1978; MA in Counseling Psychology, Antioch U., 1995. Registered architect, N.H., Colo. Computer systems and program analyst, 1970-75; pres. McCrystal Design & Devel., Inc., Denver, 1976-83; ptnr., head housing divsn. Sheerr & McCrystal, Inc., New London, N.H., 1983-97, pres., 1997-98; owner, pres. Sheerr & White Residential Architecture, 1998—. Instr. passive solar design Denver Free U.; cons. solar and low income housing design Capitol Hill Architects and Planners; solar cons. Bros. Redevelopment, Inc.; bd. dirs. Ledyard Nat. Bank. Prin. works include Lawrence Berkeley (Calif.) Lab., Solar Homestead, Boulder, Colo. (Nat. Passive Solar Design award HUD), 1515 South Pearl St., Curtis Pk. Face Block Renovation Project, Denver (Nat. Honor award AIA), St. Paul's Episcopal Ch. (Archtl. award Gov.'s Commn. Handicapped 1987). Mem. Leadership, N.H., 1998-99; mem. pres.'s adv. coun. Colby Sawyer Coll., 1987-91; mem. fundraising com., chmn. bd., Ausbon Sargent Land Preservation Trust, 1989—, 1998—; chmn. Lands Com., 1993-96, trustee, 1991—; bd. dirs. 1992—, vice-chmn. 1996-98; New London Town Zoning Bd., 1998—, mem. affordable housing task force charrette for City of Laconia, N.H. Housing Authority, 1989; mem. bus. adv. coun. Town of New London, 1990-94; active Nature Conservancy, Wilderness Soc., Sierra Club, Nat. Audubon Soc. Recipient Main St. Comml. Beautification award New London Garden Club, Best Restoration of Yr. award Denver Mag., 1983, Heritage Concord Grand award 1994; Nat. Hist. Preservation grantee Sec. of Interior, 1980. Mem. AIA (bd. dirs. N.H. chpt. 1984-89, sec. 1985, pres.-elect 1986, pres. 1987, immediate past pres. 1988, mem. exec. bd. New Eng. regional coun., 1986-87, spkr. N.W. regional conf., Denver Housing Authority Low Income Housing Design co-winner 1976, Western Regional Merit award 1981, 15 awards for Excellence in Architecture N.H. chpt. 1983, 85, 86, 88, 90, 91, 92, 93, 94, 95, 96, 99, Nat. Honor award 1983), Nat. Trust Hist. Preservation, Homebuilder's Assn. N.H. (SAM Gold award 1999, Silver award 1998, Bronze award 1999), N.H. Hist. Soc., New London Hist. Soc., Appalachian Mountain Club (adv. bd. 2002—). Office: Sheerr & White Architecture PO Box 2445 177 Main St New London NH 03257-2445

SHEESLEY, MARY FRANK, art educator; b. Redwood Falls, Minn., Aug. 1, 1947; d. Wencel and Lois (Dooner) Frank; m. Gary James Sheesley, Apr. 30, 1966 (div. Mar. 25, 1985); children: Jason, John. AA summa cum laude, Chipola Jr. Coll., 1984; BS magna cum laude, Troy State U., 1986; MS, Fla. State U., Panama City, 1991; PhD, Fla. State U., 2000. Child devel. assoc. credential Washington. Co-owner Qurly-Q Pork Farm, Bird Island, Minn., 1969—82; editor Nat. Drillers Buyers Guide, Bonifay, Fla., 1982; art educator Bay Dist. Schs., Panama City, 1986—95, 1996—2003; tchg. asst. Fla. State U., Tallahassee, 1991—92; adj. prof. U. West Fla., Ft. Walton Beach, 1992; art educator Frankfurt Internat. Sch., Oberursel, Germany, 1995—96; adj. prof. Gulf Coast C.C., Panama City, 2002; asst. prof. State U. West Ga., Carrollton, 2003—. Pres. Fla. State Textbook Adoption Com., Tallahassee, 1993—94; mem. adv. bd. Region 6E Head Start, Willmar, Minn., 1975—79; founder Global Art Exch. Program, 1994—. V.p. Minn. Porkettes, 1978—79; mem. ch. coun. Blessed Trinity Cath. Ch., Bonifay, 1982—84; mem. sch. bd. St. John's Cath. Sch., Panama City, 2002—03. Recipient Arrowmont Scholarship, 1987; grantee, Fla. Tobacco Settlement, 1997, Fulbright Meml. Tchr. Scholarship, Tokyo, 1997; scholar, Troy State U., 1984—86; Returning Woman scholar, Marianna Jr. Women's Club, 1981, Art scholar, Chipola Jr. Coll., 1982. Mem.: Bay County Art Tchrs. Assn. (pres. 1996—2001), Ga. Art Edn. Assn., Nat. Art Edn. Assn., Internat. Soc. for Edn. throught Art, Garnet Key Honor Soc., Gamma Beta Phi, Phi Theta Kappa. Republican. Roman Catholic. Avocations: travel, painting, reading, gardening, scuba diving. Office: State U West Ga Art Dept 1600 Maple St Carrollton GA 30118

SHEETS, DOROTHY JANE, school librarian, retired elementary school educator; b. Grant, Ala., Jan. 17, 1933; d. Walker Samuel and Floria Mae (Parks) Campbell; m. Paul Beauford Sheets, Jan. 1, 1958 (div. July 1972); children: Wanda Kay, Jeffrey Lee, Sue Ann Sheets Cagle. AS, Snead Jr. Coll., 1953; BS, U. Ala., Tuscaloosa, 1956; MEd, Auburn U., 1968; grad., Writer's Digest Sch., Cin., 1996, Inst. Children's Lit., 1992; student, Nat. Radio Inst., Washington, 1997. Cert. tchr. and sch. libr., Ala. Children's libr. Cleve. Pub. Libr., 1956-58; tchr. reading Marshall County Bd. Edn., Guntersville, Ala., 1962-76, elem. libr., 1976-91. Pvt. tutor, Albertville, Ala., 1968—. Vol. tax preparer RSVP, Guntersville, 1992—. DAR scholar, 1955. Mem. NEA (life), Ala. Edn. Assn., Ala. Ret. Tchrs. Assn., Marshall County Ret. Tchrs. Assn., Am. Assn. Ret. Persons. Avocations: reading, storytelling, volunteering, gardening. Home: 407 Pecan Ave Albertville AL 35950-2733 E-mail: djsheets3@juno.com.

SHEFFIELD, NANCY, city agency administrator; b. Mpls. BA in Sociology and Psychology, U. Minn., 1969; postgrad., U. Wis., 1992. Participant City of Aurora (Colo.) Supervisory Cert. Series Program, 1988-90. Social worker LeSueur County Human Svcs., Le Centre, Minn., 1969-71; quality control reviewer Minn. Dept. Human Svcs., St. Paul, 1971-74, quality control supr., 1974-75; neighborhood planner City of Aurora, 1987, neighborhood support supr., 1987-94, acting mgr. Original Aurora Renewal, 1994-95, acting mgr. neighborhood support divsn., 1995, dir. neighborhood svcs., 1996—. Mem. PTO, vol. elem. sch. media ctr., 1980-86. Office: City Aurora Dept Neighborhood Svcs 15151 E Alameda Pkwy Aurora CO 80012 Office Phone: 303-739-7280. E-mail: nsheffie@auroragov.org.

SHEFFIELD, STEPHANIE S. portfolio and marketing management consultant; b. Richmond, Va., Aug. 2, 1970; d. Frank Budd Jr. and Carolyn Jean (Parker) Sheffield. BA, Coll. of Charleston, S.C., 1993; MBA, U. Tenn., Knoxville, 1998. Cert. Series 65; cert. intermodal transp. profl. tng. EPA grant videotape prodr. Office of Gov. of S.C., Coll. of Charleston, 1993; analyst State of Tenn., Nashville, 1994-95; portfolio asst. AmeriStar Investment Counsel, Nashville, 1995-96; portfolio mgr. Davidson Ptnrs. Investment Counsel, Nashville, 1998-99; cons. Fin. Perspectives, Nashville, 1999; pres., founder Indextron Inc., 1999—. Pres., portfolio mgr. The Clayton Torch Fund, Knoxville, 1997-98; mktg. cons. Sea Ray Boats, Knoxville, 1997-98; mem. adv. bd. The Tenn. Newspaper A Gannett Co., 2000—. Creator, editor newsletter The Container, 1992-93; asst. editor newsletter/mag. The Gazette, 1999. Mem., coun. rep. Jr. League of Nashvlle, 1998—. Albergotti scholar, 1993. Mem. Nashville Fin. Analyst Soc., Assn. for Investment Mgmt. and Rsch., Tenn. Assn. MBAs, Tri Delta Alumni Assn. (sec. 1995-96). Republican. Episcopalian. Avocations: golf, cooking, U. Tenn. football games, walking, sailing. Home: P O Box 58051 Nashville TN 37205-8051 E-mail: stephsheff@mindspring.com.

SHEFTALL, BEVERLY GUY, women's studies educator; B in English, Spelman Coll.; postgraduate study, Wellesley Coll.; M in English, Atlanta U.; PhD. English instr. Ala. State U., Montgomery; Anna Julia Cooper prof. women's studies Spelman Coll., 1971—; founding dir. Women's Rsch. and Resource Ctr., 1981—. Adj. prof. Emory U. Inst. Women Studies. Founding editor Sage: A Scholarly Journal on Black Women, 1983; co-editor (with Roseann P. Bell and Bettye Parker Smith): Sturdy Black Bridges: Visions of Black Women in Literature, 1979; co-editor: (with Rudolph P. Byrd) Traps: African American Men on Gender and Sexuality, 2001; author: Daughters of Sorrow: Attitudes Toward Black Women, 1880-1920, 1991, Words of Fire: An Anthology of African American Feminist Thought, 1995; co-author (with Johnetta B. Cole): Gender Talk, 2003. Bd. mem. Nat. Coalition 100 Black Women, Nat. Black Women's Health Project, Nat. Coun. Rsch. on Women; bd. trustees Dillard U., New Orleans. Nat. Kellogg Fellowship, Woodrow Wilson Fellowship. Office: Spelman Coll 350 Spelman Ln SW Atlanta GA 30314 Office Phone: 404-681-3643.*

SHEI, JULIANA CHIANG, information technology manager; b. Tokyo, Aug. 27, 1948; d. Wellington J. and Yoshiko (Araki) Chiang; m. Shen-Ann Shei; children: Irene, Ryan. BS, Nat. Cheng Kung U., Taiwan, 1971; MS, U. Mass., 1975; MBA, Rensselaer Poly. Inst., 1987. Tech. interpreter Shionogi Pharm. Co., Taiwan, 1971-73; gen. mgr. Enterpreneurial Pub. Co., Los Alamitos, Calif., 1975-77; asst. chemist Ames Lab. Iowa State U., 1977-81; rsch. scientist Tech. Ctr. U.S. Steel Corp., Monroeville, Pa., 1982-85; group coord. Sterling Drug Inc., Rensselaer, NY, 1986-91; internat. tech. mgr. GE Global Rsch. Ctr., Niskayuna, NY, 1991—. Contbr. to tech. publs.; patentee in field. Bd. mem. U.S. Industry Coalition; chmn. bd. dirs. Chinese Cmty. Ctr. of Capital Dist., 2002—; bd. mem. Japanese Assn. Capital Dist. N.Y. Mem. Am. Chem. Soc. (sec.-treas. Pitts sect. 1983-84), Profl. Women's Network (pres. Capital dist. N.Y. 1986-2002).

SHEINDLIN, JUDITH, television personality, judge; b. Bklyn., Oct. 21, 1942; d. Murray and Ethel Blum; m. Ronald Levy, 1964 (div. 1976); children: Jamie, Adam; m. Gerald Sheindlin, 1977; stepchildren: Greg, Jonathan, Nicole. BA, Am. U., Wash., DC, 1963; law degree, NY Law Sch., 1965; LLD (hon.), Elizabethtown Coll. Supervising judge, Manhattan, NYC, 1986—96; judge Family Ct., Bronx, 1982—86, pros. atty. NYC, 1978—82. Appeared as herself (TV films) ChiPs '99, 1998, (TV series) Judge Judy, 1996— (nominee Daytime Emmy for outstanding special class series, 1999, 2000, 2001, 2002, 2003); author: Don't Pee on My Leg and Tell Me It's Raining: America's Toughest Family Court Judge Speaks Out, 1996, Beauty Fades, Dumb is Forever: The Making of a Happy Woman, 1999, Keep It Simple, Stupid: You're Smarter Than You Look: Uncomplicating Families in Complicated Times, 2000, Judge Judy Sheindlin's Win or Lose by How You Choose, 2000, You're Smarter Than You Look: Uncomplicating Relationships in Complicated Times, 2001, Judge Judy Sheindlin's You Can't Judge a Book By Its Cover: Cool Rules for School, 2001. Office: Judge Judy PO Box 949 Los Angeles CA 90078*

SHEININ, ROSE, biochemist, educator; b. Toronto, Ont., May 18, 1930; d. Harry and Anne (Szyber) Shuber; m. Joseph Sheinin, July 15, 1951; children: David Matthew Khazanov, Lisa Basya Judith, Rachel Sarah Rebecca. BA, U. Toronto, 1951, MA (scholar), 1953, PhD in Biochemistry, 1956, LHD, 1985; DHL (hon.), Mt. St. Vincent U., 1985; DSc (hon.), Acadia U., 1987, U. Guelph, 1991. Demonstrator in biochemistry U. Toronto, Ont., Can., 1951-53, asst. prof. microbiology, 1964-75, asst. prof. med. biophysics, 1967-75, prof. microbiology, 1975-90, assoc. prof. med. biophysics, 1975-78, prof. med. biophysics, 1978-90, chmn. microbiology and parasitology, 1975-82, vice dean Sch. Grad. Studies, 1984-89; vice-rector acad. Concordia U., Montreal, Que., Can., 1989-94, prof. dept. biology, 1989-2000. Mem. Health Scis. Com.; vis. rsch. assoc. chem. microbiology Cambridge U., 1956-57, Nat. Inst. Med. Rsch., London, 1975-58; rsch. assoc. fellow divsn. biol. rsch. Ont. Caner Inst., 1958-67; sci. officer cancer grants panel Med. Rsch. Coun. Can.; mem. Can. Sci. Del. to People's Republic of China, 1973; mem. adv. com. Provincial Lottery Health Rsch. Awards; mem. adv. com. on biotech. NRC Can., 1984-87; mem. Sci. Coun. Can., 1984-87; adv. com. on sci. and tech. CBC, 1980-85; mem. bd. dirs. Can. Bacterial Disease Network, 1989-94; vis. prof. biochemistry U. Alta., 1971. Assoc. editor Can. Jour. Biochemistry, 1968-71, Virology, 1969-72, Intervirology, 1974-85; editl. bd. Microbiol. Revs., 1977-80; author, co-author various publs. Nat. Cancer Inst. Can. fellow, 1953-56, 58-61; Brit. Empire Cancer Campaign fellow, 1956-58; recipient Queen's Silver Jubilee medal, 1978, Woman of Distinction award Health and Edn., YWCA, 1988, Josiah Macy Jr. faculty scholar, 1981-82; fellow Ligue Contre le Cancer, France, 1981-82, Massey Coll., U. Toronto, 1981—, continuing sr. fellow, 1994—; hon. fellow Ryerson Polytech. U., 1993. Fellow Am. Acad. Microbiology, Royal Soc. Can. (chair women in scholarship com. 1990-93); mem. Can. Biochem. Soc. (pres. 1974-75), Can. Soc. Cell Biology (pres. 1975-76), Am. Soc. Virology, Am. Soc. Microbiologists, Can. Assn. Women in Sci., Internat. Assn. Women Bioscientists, Sigma Xi Rsch. Soc., Scitech. Soc. Complex Carbohydrates, Toronto Biochem. and Biophys. Soc. (pres. 1960-70, coun. 1970-74). E-mail: rose.sheinin@utoronto.ca.

SHEIVE, DOREEN LAUREL, fiscal administrator; b. Waterville, Maine, Jan. 30, 1947; d. Albert Sheive and June Marguerite Brown; 1 child, Alexander Richard. Student, Am. U., Washington, 1968-69, Thomas Coll., Waterville, Maine, 1984-86. Spl. asst. to Senator Edmund S. Muskie, Washington, 1969-71; asst. scheduler Edmund S. Muskie for Pres. Com., Washington, 1971-72, Henry "Scoop" Jackson for Pres. Com., Washington, 1973-75; chief scheduler Senator Daniel Patrick Moynihan, Washington, 1976-79; spl. asst. to Gov. Joseph E. Brennan Augusta, Maine, 1980-84; dir. compliance Dept. Fin. and Adminstrn. State of Maine, Augusta, 1984-87, dir. planning and tng. Dept. Audit, 1987-93, fiscal adminstr. unorganized territory, 1993—. Chair Maine Commn. Mcpl. Deorganization, Augusta, 1993—; bd. dirs. Maine State Employees Credit Union, Augusta, 2001—. Author: Sheive Family History, 1999. Mem. Inst. Internal Auditors, Eighteen Year Membership. Democrat. Office: State Maine Dept Audit 66 State House Sta Augusta ME 04333-0066 Fax: 207-624-6273.

SHELBURNE, MERRY CLARE, public information officer, educator; b. L.A., Oct. 29, 1945; d. John Bartholomew and Geneva (Hedges) Delbridge; m. David Michael Shelburne, July 20, 1968. BA, Calif. State U., L.A., 1968; MA, Calif. State U., Northridge, 1993. Editl. asst. pub. affairs Calif. State U., L.A., 1968-71; publs. supr. Papercraft Specialty Co., L.A., 1973-74; creative dir. Family Record Plan, L.A., 1975-76; pub. info. asst. Glendale (Calif.) C.C., 1977-81, pub. info. officer, asst. prof. mass. comms., 1981—. Journalism advisor CourseWise, Atomic Dog, Internet, 1997—. Author: Walking the HighWire: Effective Public Relations, 1998, Effective Public Relations: A Practical Approach, 2001; songwriter Slow Dancin', If It Feels Good, 1990. Publicist Tim Richards Found. Annual Fundraiser Cmty. Faire, La Crescenta, 1980s. Mem. Calif. C.C. Pub. Rels. Orgn. (Radio Advt. 1st pl. award, Sports Publs. 1st pl. award). Avocations: songwriting, gardening, golf, dried flower decorations, golden retrievers. Office: Glendale CC 1500 N Verdugo Rd Glendale CA 91208-2809 E-mail: mshelbur@glendale.cc.ca.us.

SHELBURNE, RENEE D. communications executive; b. Shelbyville, Ky., Jan. 17, 1975; d. Atwell T. and Shirley P. Shelburne; m. Kevin W. Popeck, May 7, 2003. BA, Ballarmine Coll., 1995; MA, U. Louisville, 2002. Team leader Pegasus Satellite, Louisville, 1999—. Mem.: APA, Psi Chi, Alpha Kappa Delta. Democrat. Baptist. Home: PO Box 33332 Louisville KY 40232 Office: Pegasus Satellite 1951 Bishop Ln Louisville KY 40218 E-mail: aletalea@bellsouth.net.

SHELBY, NINA CLAIRE, special education educator; b. Weatherford, Tex., Oct. 23, 1949; d. Bill Hudson and Roselle (Price) S.; m. Richard Dean Powell, May 29, 1971 (div. 1973); 1 child, Stoney Hudson. BA in English, Sul Ross State U., 1974, MEd, 1984; MA in English, U. Tex., 1995. Jr. high lang. arts educator Liberty Hill, Tex., 1974-75; H.S. resource educator Georgetown (Tex.) I. S. D., 1976-77; intermediate resource educator Raymondille (Tex.) I. S. D., 1977-81; educator of severe profound Napper Elem. Pharr (Tex.) San Juan Alamo Ind. Sch. Dist., 1981-90; H.S. life skills educator Pharr (Tex.) San Juan Alamo ISD North H.S., 1990-93; intermediate inclusion educator Carman Elem. Pharr (Tex.) San Juan Alamo Ind. Sch. Dist., 1993—2000, chair dept. spl. edn. Carman Elem., 1998—2000; primary resource/inclusion educator Elgin (Tex.) Elem. Sch., 2000—, chair dept. spl. edn., 2002—. Coach asst. Tex. Spl. Olympics, Pharr, 1981—, sponsor vocat. adj. club, 1990-93, adaptive asst. device team, Edinburg, Tex., 1993-95; spl. edn. rep. to Elgin Primary Campus Performance Adv. Coun., 2000--. Asst. cub scout leader Boy Scouts Am., 1994-95, sec. parental com. bd. rev., 1997—; parent vol. boy's and girl's Club McAllen, 1992-96. Mem. DAR, Assn. of Tex. Profl. Educators, Alpha Delta Kappa. Democrat. Mem. Ch. Of Christ. Avocations: reading, horticulture, piano, opera. Home: PO Box 426 Elgin TX 78621-0426 Office: Elgin Elem Sch Elgin ISD 1001 W 2d St Elgin TX 78621

SHELBY, PEGGY LEE, music educator; d. Robert Charles and Dixie Modean Ross; m. Rick A. Shelby, May 23, 1974; children: Heath A., Steve A., Bill D. B in Music Edn., Okla. Bapt. U., 1978. Tchr. Vian (Okla.) Pub. Schs., 1979—. Chairperson Ea. Dist. Honor Choir, Okla., 1990—. Choir dir. First Bapt. Ch., Webbers Falls, Okla., 1978—. Mem.: Okla. Choral Dirs., Music Educators Nat. Conf., Am. Choral Dirs.

SHELDON, BETTI L. state legislator; b. Aberdeen, Wash. 5 children. Student, Gonzaga U. Mem. Wash. Senate, Dist. 23, Olympia, 1992—; majority flood leader Wash. Senate, Olympia, 1999—; mem. Dem. flood leader Wash. Legislature, Olympia, 1997-98, majority caucus vice chair, 1995, majority whip, 1995-96, majority asst. floor leader, 1993-95, mem. higher edn. com., mem. rules com., mem. ways and means com. Bd. ditrs. Small Bus. Improvement Coun., Commn. on Student Learning's K-123 Accountability Task Force., Nat. Assn. Adminstrv. Rules Rev., YMCA Youth and Govt., Gov.'s Regulatory Reform Task Force, Big Bros. and Big Sisters Kitsap County, Kitsap County Econ. Devel. Coun., Puget Sound Naval Bases Assn., West Sound Arts Coun., Bremerton Olympic Peninsula Coun. Navy League; mem. Wash. Devel. Fin. Authority; mem. adv. bd. for corp. rels. Martha & Mary Luth. Svcs.; mem. delivery plan adv. group Dept. Health Am. Indian Health Care; trustee Keyport Naval Underseas Mus. Found. Recipient Woman of Yr. Bremerton Kitsap YWCA, 1993, Strong Kids, Strong Families, Strong Cmtys. award YMCA, 1999, Dem. Woman of Yr. Wash. State Fedn. Women's Clubs, 1997. Mem. Bremerton Area C. of C. (past exec. dir.), Wash. C. of C. Execs. (v.p.). Democrat. Office: 410A Legislative Bldg Olympia WA 38504-0482

SHELDON, DEENA LYNN, television camera operator; b. Groveland, Mass., Mar. 10, 1962; d. Frederic J. and Penny Margolis. BS, Boston U., 1984. Co. mem. Body Lang. Dancers, 1986; mem. Michael Macchio's Jazz Co., 1980-85, Danny Sloan's Repertory, 1980-82, Celtic's Green Gang, 1980-82, Dean Brittenham's Shiley Elite Athletic Program. Camera operator Redsox and Bruins, Sta. WSBK-TV, Boston, 1985, Am.'s Cup, Major League Baseball and postseason play, Homerun Derby, Boston Marathon, Extreme Games, ESPN, 1986—; NY Mets and NY Islanders, Sportschannel, 1987-92; NY Mets, Sta. WWOR-TV, 1987-92; Monday Night Football, Superbowl XXXIV, Superbowl XXXVII, Academy Awards, NBA Championship., Ky. Derby, Triple Crown, Indy 500, Rose Bowl, Probowl, NFL Hall of Fame game, Superbowl XXIX halftime show, Dem. and Rep. convs., Presdl. inaugurations, 1993, 97, ABC, 1992—, Late Night with David Letterman, NFL, Triple Crown, Olympics, Phil Donahue Show, Macy's Day Parade, NBC, 1986—; Superbowl XXXVIII, NFL and championship games, Daytona 500, Joan Rivers Show, Major League Baseball and postseason play, CBS, 1987—; Superbowl XXXI, World Series, NFL, NHL, Fox Sports, 1994—; robotic camera operator Met. Life and Fuji blimps, NFL championship and playoff games, Daytona 500, Indy 500, 1989—. Youth counselor and instr. athleticism. Recipient Emmy awards for CBS's Postseason Major League Baseball, 1990, CBS's Daytona 500, 1993, ESPN's Extreme Games, 1995-98, NY Emmy for NY Mets, 1992-93, 93-94, Fox's Postseason Maj. League Baseball, 1999; Emmy nominee for ESPN's Am.'s Cup, 1995. Mem. NABET, Internat. Brotherhood Elec. Workers, Internat. Alliance Theatrical Stage Employees. Avocations: trail running, dance, sunshine, instructing in athleticism. Home: 70445 Mottle Cir Rancho Mirage CA 92270 Office Phone: 760-522-1020. E-mail: deena.sheldon@verizon.net.

SHELDON, EDITH LOUISE THACH, writer; b. Walsenburg, CO, Nov. 28, 1941; d. William Mason Thach and Jeannette Violet Faris-Thach; m. John Michael Sheldon, June 27, 1964; children: Michael Mason, William David. Student, Pueblo Jr. Coll., Colo. State Coll., Adam's State Coll., Colo., 1959—74. Assoc. pub. Valley Courier Newspaper, Alamosa, Colo., 1974—81; adminstrv. mgr. Colo. Press Assn., Denver, 1981—83; office mgr. The Villager Newspaper, Englewood, Colo., 1983—85; assoc. pub. The Littleton Times, Littleton, Colo., 1986—87; ad exec. The Denver Parent Newspaper, Denver, 1988—94; editor, pub. Denver Parent News Mag., Denver, 1994—. Pres. Parenting Pub. of Am., San Antonio, 1989—91; mem. Gov.'s Coun. on Edn. of Young Children, 1991—94; pres. Huerfano County Hist. Soc., 1995—97; active numerous orgns. and polit. campaigns; v.p., bd. trustees Huerfano County Hosp. Dist.

SHELDON, ELEANOR HARRIET BERNERT, sociologist, writer; b. Hartford, Conn., Mar. 19, 1920; d. M.G. and Fannie (Myers) Bernert; m. James Sheldon, Mar. 19, 1950 (div. 1960); children: James, John Anthony. AA, Colby Jr. Coll., 1940; AB, U. N.C., 1942; PhD, U. Chgo., 1949. Asst. demographer Office Population Rsch., Washington, 1942-43; social scientist USDA, Washington, 1943-45; assoc. dir. Chgo. Community Inventory, U. Chgo., 1947-50; social scientist Social Sci. Rsch. Coun., N.Y.C., 1950-51, rsch. grantee, 1953-55, pres., 1972-79; rsch. assoc. Bur. Applied Social Rsch. Columbia U., 1950-51, lectr. sociology, 1951-52, vis. prof., 1969-71; social scientist UN, N.Y.C., 1951-52; rsch. assoc., lectr. sociology UCLA, 1955-61; assoc. rsch. sociologist, lectr. Sch. Nursing U. Calif., 1957-61; sociologist, exec. assoc. Russell Sage Found., N.Y.C., 1971—72; vis. prof. U. Calif., Santa Barbara, 1971. Bd. dirs. H.J. Heinz Co., Equitable Life Citicorp, Mobil Corp., NL Industries. Author: (with L. Wirth) Chicago Community Fact Book, 1949, America's Children, 1958, (with R.A. Glazier) Pupils and Schools in N.Y.C., 1965; editor: (with W.E. Moore) Indicators of Social Change, Concepts and Measurements, 1968, Family Economic Behavior, 1973; contbr. articles to profl. jours. Bd. dirs. Colby-Sawyer Coll., 1979-85, UN Rsch. Inst. for Social Devel., 1973-79; trustee Rockefeller Found., 1978-85, Nat. Opinion Rsch. Ctr., 1980-87, Inst. East-West Security Studies, 1984-88, Am. assembly, 1976-95. William Rainey Harper fellow U. Chgo., 1945-47 Fellow AAAS, Am. Acad. Arts and Scis., Am. Sociol. Assn., Am. Statis. Assn.; mem. U. Chgo. Alumni Assn. (Profl. Achievement award), Sociol. Rsch. Assn. (pres. 1971-72), Coun. on Fgn. Rels., Am. Assn. Pub. Opinion Rsch., Ea. Sociol. Soc., Internat. Sociol. Assn., Internat. Union Sci. Study of Population, Population Assn. Am. (2d v.p. 1970-71), Inst. of Medicine (chmn. program com. 1976-77), Cosmopolitan Club. Home and Office: 630 Park Ave New York NY 10021-6544

SHELDON, INGRID KRISTINA, former mayor, bookkeeper; b. Ann Arbor, Mich., Jan. 30, 1945; d. Henry Ragnvald and Virginia Schmidt (Clark) Blom; m. Clifford George Sheldon, June 18, 1966; children: Amy Elizabeth, William David. BS, Eastern Mich. U., 1966; MA, U. Mich., 1970; doctorate (hon.), Cleary U., 2001. Cert. tchr., Mich. Tchr. Livonia (Mich.) Pub. Schs., 1966-67, Ann Arbor Pub. Schs., 1967-68; bookkeeper Huron Valley Tennis Club, Ann Arbor, 1978—; acct. F.A. Black Co., Ann Arbor, 1984-88; coun. mem. Ward II City of Ann Arbor, 1988-92, mayor, 1993-2000. Commr. Housing Bd. Appeals, Ann Arbor, 1988—91; vice chmn. fin. and budget com. S.W. Mich. Coun.Govts.; treas. Huron Valley Child Guidance Clinic, Ann Arbor, 1984—, Ann Arbor Hist. Found., 1985—, Parks Adv. Commn., 1987—92, Ann Arbor Planning Commn., 1988—89; excellence com. Ann Arbor Pub. Schs. reorgn., 1985; treas. SOS Cmty. Crisis Ctr., Ypsilanti, Mich., 1987—93; chair United Meth. Retirement Cmty., Ann Arbor, 2003; trustee Cmty. Found., 2001—; pres. Ann Arbor Summer Festival, 2003; precinct ward city vice chmn. Ann Arbor Rep. City Com., 1978—. Recipient Cmty. Svc. award Ann Arbor Jaycees, 1980, DAR Cmty. Svc. award, 1997; AAUW fellow, 1982. Mem.: Mich. Mcpl. League (del. 1989—97, trustee 1997—, pres. 1999—2000), Rotary (former dir. Ann Arbor chpt.), Ann Arbor Women's City Club (chair endowment com. 1989—90, fin. com. 1987—90, treas. 2003), Alpha Omicron Pi, Kappa Delta Pi. Republican. Methodist. Avocation: musical theatre. Home: 1416 Folkstone Ct Ann Arbor MI 48105-2848 E-mail: aasheldon@aol.com.

SHELDON, Mrs. JOHN See GIBBONS, CELIA

SHELDON, LOUISE ROBERTS, writer; b. Narragansett, R.I., Aug. 30, 1926; d. James Rhodes and Marjorie Starkweather (Chase) Sheldon; m. John Lucien Smith, June 9, 1962 (dec. June 1972); 1 child, Randolph Betts; m. Robert Edward MacDonald, Dec. 23, 1974. BA in German Lit. cum laude, Bryn Mawr Coll., 1948; MA in French Lit., Calif. State U., Northridge, 1972. Accredited fgn. corr. With MD Publs., N.Y., 1949-52; asst. editor LIFE Time Inc., N.Y.C., 1952-64; assoc. editor Smithsonian, Washington, 1972-74; editor Am. C. of C., Casablanca, 1975-80. Sec. Internat. Coun. of Women, Zurich, 1948-49; chmn. lang. dept. Westlake Sch., L.A., 1963-68; fgn. corr. UPI, Paris, 1977-81, Christian Sci. Monitor, Boston, 1977-81, Middle East mag., London, 1977-81; contbg. writer World and I, Washington, 1984-89, Mus. and Arts Washington, 1984-89. Author: (short stories) Casablanca Notebook, 1998, 2002, (novel) Wind in the Sahara, 2002. Docent Balt. Mus. Art., 1990-2003. Mem. Dunes Club, Cross Keys Tennis Club, Alpha Mu Gamma. Democrat. Episcopalian. Avocations: foreign languages, travel, reading, painting. Home: 1004 Malvern Ave Ruxton MD 21204 E-mail: cgbs@connext.net.

SHELDRICK, BARBARA ENGLAND, music educator, consultant; d. James E. and Mary F. England; m. Robert S. Sheldrick, Jr., July 30, 1994; children: Shannon Elaine, Andrew James. B.Mus.Edn., Adrian Coll., Mich., 1979; MusM in Edn., Wayne State U., Detroit, 1995. Cert. music tchr. Music Educators Nat. Conf., 1994. Dir. of elem. bands Lake Orion Cmty. Schs., Lake Orion, 1979—81; music tchr. Kensington Acad., Bloomfield Hills, Mich., 1982—86, Anchor Bay Pub. Schs., New Baltimore, Mich., 1986—. Handbell dir. Lake Orion United Meth. Ch., 1980—84; presenter Mich. Acad. Arts, Sci., and Letters, 1995; youth choral dir. First Congl. Ch., United Ch. Christ, Rochester, Mich., 1999—2003. Mem.: Choristers Guild, Am. Choral Dirs. Assn., Music Educators Nat. Conf. R-Conservative. Christian. Avocations: photography, swimming, ceremony of tea, flute performance, preserving family history. Office: Great Oaks Elem Sch 32900 24 Mile Rd New Baltimore MI 48047 E-mail: bsheldrick@abs.misd.net.

SHELL, MARIA CHRISTINE, writing educator; b. Topeka, Kans., Jan. 15, 1966; d. Noah Noble Shell and Mary Ann McNeal; m. Walt Lipsey Tague, June 17, 1996; children: Fletcher Sequoya, Odysseus Further. Student, Oberlin Coll., 1984—86; BS in Journalism, U. Kans., 1990; MFA, U. Alaska, 2000. Adj. prof. Prince William Jouno C.C., Valdez, Alaska, 2000—. Avocation: quilting. Home: PO Box 2014 Valdez AK 99686

SHELLEY, CAROLE, actress; b. London, Aug. 16, 1939; arrived in U.S., 1964; d. Curtis and Deborah (Bloomstein) Shelley; m. Albert G. Woods, July 26, 1967 (dec.). Student, Arts Ednl. Sch., 1943-56, Prepatory Acad. Royal Acad. Dramatic Art, 1956-57; studied with Iris Warren and Eileen Thorndike. Trustee Am. Shakespeare Theatre, 1974—82. Actor: (plays) The Odd Couple, 1965, Absurd Person Singular, 1973, The Norman Conquests (L.A. Drama Critics Cir. award, 1975), As You Like It, King Lear, She Stoops to Conquer, 1972, The Country Wife, 1973, A Doll's House, Man and Superman, 1977, Misalliance, 1980, Grand Hunt, 1980, The Play's the Thing, 1978, Lion in Winter, 1987, The Elephant Man (Outer Critics Cir. award, 1979, Tony award for Best Actress, 1979), What the Butler Saw, 1989, Broadway Bound, 1987—88, Lettice and Lovage, 1989—90, The Miser, 1990, Cabaret Verboten, 1991, The Destiny of Me, 1992—93, Later Life, 1993 (Outer Critics nominee), Richard II, 1994, London Suite, 1995, Show Boat, 1995—96, 1998, The Film Society, 1997, The Last Night of Ballyhoo, 1997—98, Cabaret, 1999—2002, Wicked, 2002—03; (films) The Boston Strangler, The Odd Couple, The Super, 1990, Devlin, 1991, Quiz Show, 1993, The Road to Wellville, 1993; (TV series) The Odd Couple; (films) others, Robin Phillips Grand Theatre Co., 1983—84, Nat. Co. The Royal Family (L.A. Drama Critics Cir. award, 1977); (Broadway plays) Noises Off, 1985, Stepping Out, 1986 (Tony nominee, 1986), Waltz of the Toreadors, 1986, Oh Coward, 1986—87, Broadway and L.A. Bound, 1987—88; voice actor : (films) Robin Hood; The Aristocats; Hercules. Recipient Obie award for Twelve Dreams, N.Y. Shakespeare Festival, 1982. Jewish. Office: Robert Duva 277 W 10th St New York NY 10014

SHELLHORN, RUTH PATRICIA, landscape architect; b. L.A., Sept. 21, 1909; d. Arthur Lemon and Lodema (Gould) S.; m. Harry Alexander Kueser, Nov. 21, 1940. Student dept. landscape architecture, Oreg. State Coll., 1927—30; landscape architecture program, Cornell U. Coll. Architecture, 1930—33. Pvt. practice landscape architecture, various cities, Calif., 1933—; exec. cons. landscape arch. Bullocks Stores, Calif., 1945-78, Fashion Sqs. Shopping Ctrs., Calif., 1958-78, Marlborough Sch., L.A., 1968-93, El Camino Coll., Torrance, Calif., 1970-78, Harvard Sch., North Hollywood, Calif., 1974-90. Cons. landscape arch., site planner Disneyland, Anaheim, Calif., 1955, U. Calif., Riverside Campus, 1956-64, numerous others, also numerous gardens and estates; landscape arch. Torrance (Calif.) City Goals Com., 1969-70; cons. landscape arch. City of Rolling Hills (Calif.) Cmty. Assn., 1973-93. Contbr. articles to garden and profl. publs.; subject of Oct. 1967 issue Landscape Design & Constrn. mag. Named Woman of Year, L.A. Times, 1955, Woman of Year, South Pasadena-San Marino (Calif.) Bus. Profl. Women, 1955; recipient Charles Goodwin Sands medal, 1930-33, Landscape Architecture award of merit Calif. State Garden Clubs, 1984, 86, Horticulturist of the Yr. award So. Calif. Hort. Inst., numerous nat., state, local awards for excellence. Fellow Am. Soc. Landscape Archs. (past pres. So. Calif. chpt.), Phi Kappa Phi, Kappa Kappa Gamma (Alumni Achievement award 1960). Achievements include oral history and biography published by Pasadena Heritage, 2002. Home and Office: 362 Camino De Las Colinas Redondo Beach CA 90277-6435

SHELLITO, SONIA (SUNNY) TERESE, financial analyst, accountant; b. Cleve., Dec. 4, 1969; d. Vincent Petitti and Carol Heather (Burbank) Moody; m. Christopher John Shellito, May 5, 2001. AA in Bus. Adminstrn., Mont. State U., Billings, 1989, BSBA, 1991; M in Accountancy and Fin. Info. Sys., Cleve. State U., 1995, MBA, 2000. CPA Mont., 1991, Ohio, 1995. Oper. acct. Indian Health Svc., Billings, 1991—93; staff acct. Cath. Charities Svcs. Corp., Cleve., 1995—98; fin. analyst Med. Life Ins. Co., Cleve., 1998—. Mem.: AAUW (web master 1999—, fin. officer 2000—), Am. Soc. Women Accts. (pres. 2002—), Zonta Club (scholarship co-chair 1999—2000, treas. 2003—). Roman Catholic. Avocations: genealogy, society and equality. Office: Med Life Ins Co 20445 Emerald Pkwy Ste 400 Cleveland OH 44135

SHELLMAN-LUCAS, ELIZABETH C. special education educator, researcher; b. Thomas County, Ga., Feb. 5, 1937; d. Herbert and Juanita (Coleman) Smith; m. John Lee Lucas, Jr. (div.); 1 child, Sandie Juanita Lucas Boyce; m. Eddie Joseph Shellman; 1 child, Eddie Joseph Shellman, Jr. MS in Edn., CUNY, 1990. Cert. tchr., N.Y. Pvt. practice cosmetologist, N.Y.C., 1959—; tchr. N.Y.C. Bd. of Edn. High Sch. Dist., 1984—. Vol. various community orgns.; citizen amb. del. People to People Internat., 1994. Mem. Coun. for Exceptional Children. Avocations: reading, music, dance, jogging, languages.

SHELLY, CHRISTINE DEBORAH, foreign service officer; b. Pontiac, Mich., May 1, 1951; d. Chester Price and Margaret Alice (Neafie) S. BA cum laude, Vanderbilt U., 1973; MA, Tufts U., 1974, MA in Diplomacy, 1975. Fgn. affairs analyst Intelligence and Rsch. Bur. Dept. State, Washington, 1975-77, desk officer Near Eastern Affairs, 1977-79; fin. attache Am. Embassy, Cairo, 1979-81; asst. v.p. BankAmerica Internat., N.Y.C., 1981-82; spl. asst. Near Eastern Affairs Dept. State, Washington, 1982-83; econ. and polit. officer Am. Embassy, Lisbon, Portugal, 1983-87; dep. econ. advisor U.S. Mission to NATO, Brussels, 1987-90, dep. cabinet dir. Sec. Gen., 1990-93; dep. spokesman, dep. asst. sec. pub. affairs Dept. State, Washington, 1993-95, mem. Sr. Exec. Seminar, 1995 96; min. counselor polit. affairs Am. Embassy, Ottawa, Ont., Can., 1996-99; polit. adviser to chief of staff Dept. Army, Washington, 1999—. Avocations: equestrian, triathlete. Office: Dept Army DACS-ZK 200 Army Pentagon Rm 3c568 Washington DC 20310-0200

SHELTON, CAROLYN JOHNSON, professional society administrator; d. Ernest Gustav Johnson and Anne Mabel Nemergut; m. Philo Sherwood Johnson, June 27, 1962; children: Philo Sherwood, Anne F. Mele. AS(hon.), U. Bridgeport, 1962. Dir. membership Conn. Audubon Soc., Fairfield, 1984—. V.p. Fairfield Women's Club, Conn., 1980—82. Recipient 10 Yr. Award for Volunteerism on the Four Seasons Ball Com. to raise money for the mentally challenged, The Kenndey Ctr., 10. Mem.: Fairfield Women's Club (v.p. 1980—82). R-Consevative. Catholic. Achievements include design of Designed the pussy willow stencils and applied the stencils for a suite in a National Historic Restoration inn called the Inn at National Hall located in Westport, Conn. Home and Office: Conn Audubon Soc 220 Burr St Fairfield CT 06824 Personal E-mail: chickade88@aol.com. Business E-Mail: cshelton@ctaudubon.org.

SHELTON, MARGARET, counselor; d. Henry and Lucille Dennis; m. Michael Wayne Shelton, May 21, 1988; children: Chelci Arnold, Michael, Christopher. BS Sociology, U. West Ga., Carrollton, Ga.;, 1978; MEd, U. West Ga., Carrollton, Ga., 1985. Lic. Profl. Counselor Tex., 1993, cert. Tex. Sch. Counselor Tex., 1992, Tex. Tchng. Tex., 1992, Mid-Mgmt. Adminstr. Tex., 1999. Unit therapist Murphy-Harpst Home, Cedartown, Ga., 1986—87; tchr. Harris County Dept. of Edn., Houston, 1988—94, sch. counselor, 1991—97, asst. prin., 1997—2001; sch. counselor Windham Sch. Dist., Humble, Tex., 2001—. Counseling,cons. Harris County Juvenile Justice Dept., Houston, 1999—2001. Worthy matron Ea. Stars, Houston, 1993—2001; mem. Phi Delta Kappa, Houston, 1996—2003, Civitan, Carrollton, Ga., 1986—86, Tex. Counseling Assn., Austin, Tex., 1999—2003, Nat. Dem. Party, Washington, 2003. Sgt. U S Army, 1990—91, Fort Hood, Tex. Decorated Nat. Def. Svc. Medal (Operation Desert Storm) U. S. Army; recipient Dean's List, West Ga., 1977, Letter of Commendation, Ga. State Licensure Bd., 1987, Spl. Award, Order of Ea. Star, 2001, . Mem.: Tex. Counseling Assn. Democrat-Npl. Baptist. Avocations: reading, travel, exercising.

SHELTON, NANCY SUE, music educator; b. Greenville, Mich., Aug. 18, 1948; d. James Thomas and Ruth Almira Shelton. B.Mus.Edn., Okla. Bapt. U., Shawnee, 1970; M.Music in Ch. Music, MRE, Southwestern Bapt. Theol. Sem., Ft. Worth, Tex., 1974. Tchg. fellow piano Southwestern Sem., Ft. Worth, 1973—74; pvt. piano tchr. Muskogee, Okla., 1976—; organist First Bapt. Ch., Muskogee, Okla., 1976—, music sec., 1982—; choral/string tchr. Muskogee Pub. Schs., 1970—71. Audition judge Okla. Music Tchrs. Assn./Nat. Guild. Mem.: Music Tchrs. Nat. Assn., Okla. Music Tchrs. Assn. (v.p. for auditions 1998—), Nat. Guild of Piano Tchrs. Democrat. Baptist. Avocations: scrapbooking, ceramics. Home: 2505 Elmira Muskogee OK 74403 Office: First Bapt Ch 111 S 7th St Muskogee OK 74401

SHELTON, PATRICIA A. gas company executive; BBA, MBA, U. Tex., El Paso. CPA; cert. mgmt. acct. With El Paso Natural Gas El Paso Energy Corp., v.p. rates and regulation, 1994-96, v.p. fin., 1996, pres. El Paso Natural Gas Co., 2000—. Mem. AICPA, Tex. Soc. CPAs, Inst. Mgmt. Accts. Office: El Paso Natural Gas Co 100 N Stanton St El Paso TX 79901-1463

SHELTON, STEPHANI, broadcast journalist, consultant; b. Boston; d. Phil and Babette (Belloff) Saltman; m. Frank Herold. BS, Boston U. Corr. CBS News, N.Y.C., 1973-84; news corr. WWOR-TV, N.Y.C., 1984-88; corr., anchor Fin. News Network, N.Y.C., 1989-91. Freelance reporter Sta. WPIX-TV, 1991-95, Sta. WNBC-TV, 1993-96, WWOR-TV, 2003; prodr. CNBC, 2003-; cons. trainer Ctrl. and Eastern Europe broadcast journalists, 1998—; med. health prodr.-reporter PBS, The Learning Channel, 1997—99; co-owner The Fred Group Ltd., video prodn. co., 1998—; freelance radio documentary writer Westinghouse Group W Broadcasting, N.Y.C., 1970-73. Recipient Peabody award, 1972, N.J. Best Spot News award AP, 1987, 88, N.J. Working Press award, 1992-94; Emmy nominee, 1994-95, 98-99. Mem. Soc. Profl. Journalists (award 1999), Radio and TV News Dirs. Assn., N.Y.C. Press Club, Investigative Reporters and Editors, Com. to Protect Journalists. E-mail: backbay38@aol.com., fred@fredgroupltd.com.

SHELTRA, NANCY J. state legislator, legal assistant, auditor; b. Newport, Vt., July 30, 1948; m. Dennis Sheltra; two children. Student, C.C. Vt., Newport. Auditor, Derby, Vt.; legal asst.; mem. Vt. Ho. of Reps., Burlington, 1989—. Mem. fish and wildlife com., 1991-92, mem. transp. com., 1993—. Treas. Derby Rep. Party; v.p. New Eng. Regional Vt. Rep. Assembly. Home: 388 Palin Farm Rd Derby VT 05829-9530 Office: Vt House of Reps Office of House Mems Montpelier VT 05602

SHEMCHUK, MARY ELIZABETH, occupational therapist; b. Meriden, Conn., Dec. 17, 1954; d. Paul John and Rose Virginia (Piccolo) S. AS, Middlesex C.C., Middletown, Conn., 1977; BS, Eastern Mich. U., 1983. Registered occupl. therapist Minn., Conn. Staff occupl. therapist Gaylord Rehab. Hosp., Wallingford, Conn., 1985-89, sr. staff occupl. therapist, 1989-95; clin. supr. occupl. therapy Sundance Rehab. Corp., East Berlin, Conn., 1995; lead therapist in occupl. therapy Symphony Rehab. Svcs., Minnetonka, Minn., 1995—. Guest spkr. Bridgeport (Conn.) Arthritis Support Group, 1992; cons. for hearing impaired Gaylord Hosp., Wallingford, 1992-94. Former church organist Our Lady of Mt. Carmel Ch., Meriden, Conn.; guest spkr. Quota Club of Hamden (Conn.), 1986; vol. St. Vincent DePaul Soc. of Meriden Shelter, Inc., 1988. Mem. Am. Occupl. Therapy Assn. (cons. on hearing impaired 1992—), Minn. Occupl. Therapy Assn., Conn. Occupl. Therapy Assn., Self Help for Hard of Hearing, Inc., Minn. Arthritis Found. Avocations: horseback riding, nature walks, playing piano and organ, handicrafts. Home: 42 Antonio Ave # 3 Meriden CT 06451-2806

SHENK, LOIS ELAINE LANDIS, writer; b. Ephrata, Pa., May 30, 1944; d. Raymond Earle and Esther May (Forry) Landis; m. John Barge Shenk, June 12, 1965; children: Philip Jon, Matthew Alan. BA in English, Eastern Mennonite Coll., 1966; MSc in Edn., Temple U., 1984. English mistress Githumu Secondary Sch., Thika, Kenya, 1966-68; English tchr. Kraybill's Jr. High, Mount Joy, Pa., 1976-77; freelance writer, 1978—; religious news corr. Gospel Herald, Scottdale, Pa., 1978-82. Observer, corr. The U.S. Senate, Washington, 1987—99. Author: Out of Mighty Waters, 1982 (R.I.M. excellence award 1983), The Story of Ephrata Mennonite School, 1996; (one act play) A House for David in (anthology) Swords into Plowshares, 1983; (study guide for Christian edn.) Hebrews, 1988; contbr. poems, stories & features to jours.; editl. work Mennonite Ctrl. Com., Akron, Pa., 1977. Cmty. living advisor Friendship Cmty., Lititz, Pa., 1997-99; Sunday sch. tchr. Ephrata Mennonite Ch., 1997-99. Recipient Rep. Senatorial Medal of Honor, many other honors and awards. Avocations: reading, cooking, music, gardening. Home and Office: 157 E New St Lancaster PA 17602

SHEPARD, COLLEEN, elementary school educator, art educator; b. Chardon, Ohio, Mar. 28, 1966; d. Charles Irvin and Shirley Ann (Weinstein) Hewins; m. Clifford Stephan Shepard, June 31, 1989; 1 child, Christopher. BFA, Fla. Atlantic U., 1989. Art tchr. Logger's Run Mid. Sch., Boca Raton, Fla., 1989-91, Omni Mid. Sch., Boca Raton, Fla., 1991-94, J.C. Mitchell Elem. Sch., Boca Raton, Fla., 1994—, sponsor Art Club, sch. wide art show coord., 1996—. Site coord. Project Leap, West Palm Beach, 1996-98. Artist numerous shows. Nominee William Dwyer award, 1997. Mem. Nat Art Edn. Assn., Fla. Art Edn. Assn., FAU Potter's Guild (pres. 1989-91). Roman Catholic. Avocations: painting, sculpting, gardening, breeding birds, cooking. Office: JC Mitchell Elem 2401 NW 3rd Ave Boca Raton FL 33431-7428

SHEPARD, DEBORAH TRUE, secondary school educator, consultant; b. Eglin Field AFB, Fla., Oct. 17, 1955; d. Marshall Allen and Elizabeth Jewel True; m. David Franklin Shepard, Aug. 14, 1977; 1 child, Sarah Elizabeth. BS in English Edn., Fla. State U., 1977, MS in English Edn., 1991. Cert. tchr. Nat. Bd. for Profl. Tchg. Standards, 1999, profl. educator Fla., 2002. Tchr. Chattanooga Ctrl. HS, Harrison, Tenn., 1977—78, Archbishop Curley HS, Miami, Fla., 1978—79, St. Brendan HS, Miami, Fla., 1979—82, Acad. of the Holy Names, Tampa, Fla., 1982—83, Leto Comprehensive HS, Tampa, Fla., 1983—85, Rickards HS, Tallahassee, 1985—86, Lincoln HS, Tallahassee, 1986—; adj. prof. Tallahassee C.C., Tallahassee, 1991—94. Cons. The Coll. Bd., N.Y.C., NY, 1998—; commr. Edn. Practices Commn., Tallahassee, 2002—; academic assembly rep. So. Region Coun. of The Coll. Bd., Atlanta, 2002—. Editor: Fla. Coun. Tchrs. of English Jour.; cmty. columnist (Tallahassee Democrat (newspaper). Class XI mem. Leadership Tallahassee, Tallahassee, 1992—2003. Mem.: Nat. Coun. Tchrs. of English, Phi Delta Kappa (sec. 2000—03). Office: Lincoln High Sch 3838 Trojan Trail Tallahassee FL 32311 Personal E-mail: shepardd@leon.k12.fl.us.

SHEPARD, JEAN HECK, publishing company consultant, author, agent; b. N.Y.C., Feb. 2, 1930; d. Chester Reed and Anna S. (Charig) Heck; m. Lawrence Vacth Hastings, Mar. 29, 1950 (div. 1953); 1 child, Lance Clifford Hastings; m. Daniel A. Shepard, July 26, 1954 (div. 1981); 1 child, Bradley Reed. BA, Barnard Coll., 1950; postgrad., Columbia U., 1952. Mem. sch. and libr. svc. Viking Press, N.Y.C., 1956-57; asst. dir. sch. and libr. promotion E.P. Dutton, N.Y.C., 1957-58; dir. advt. publicity and promotion Thomas Y. Crowell Co., N.Y.C., 1958-62; dir. advt. and promotion Charles Scribner's Sons, N.Y.C., 1962-67; cons. Stephen Greene Press, Brattleboro, Vt., 1970-73; mktg. mgr. A&W Publishers, N.Y.C., 1979-80, Franklin Watts Publ., N.Y.C., 1980-82; pub. 2 mags., divsn. advt. & promotion mgr. McGraw Hill Book Co., N.Y.C., 1983-85; cons. Monitor Publ. Co., N.Y.C., 1988-2000. Author: Simple Family Favorites, 1971, Herb and Spice Sampler, 1972, Cook With Wine!, 1973, Earth Watch: Notes on a Restless Planet, 1973, Harvest Home Steak Cookbook, 1974, Fresh Fruits and Vegetables, 1974, Yankee Magazine, 1972, Let Them be Sea Captains. Mem. Authors Guild, Pub. Ad Club, Am. Libr. Assn., Women's Nat. Book Assn. Methodist. Avocations: the dance, reading, writing, travel, music. Home: 73 Kingswood Dr Bethel CT 06801-1834 Office Fax: 845-279-3239. E-mail: shepardagcy@mindspring.com.

SHEPARD, JEAN MOYE, nurse; b. Greenville, N.C., Sept. 26, 1936; d. Elbert William and Lossie Belle (Pollard) Moye; m. Glenn Harvey Shepard, Aug. 17, 1958; children: Glenn Harvey Jr., Barclay Moye. BSN, Va. Commonwealth U., 1958; postgrad., U. Va., Coll. William and Mary. RN Va., 1958. Pub. health nurse Joint Health Dept., Charlottesville, Va., 1958-62; instr. Bapt. Hosp. Sch. Nursing, Nashville, 1962-64, 66-69, Med. Coll. Ga., Sch.Nursing, Augusta, 1964 66; acute respiratory care nurse Duke U. Hosp., Durham, N.C., 1969-70; head nurse ambulatory care Duke U. Med. Ctr., Durham, N.C., 1970-72; supr. Peninsula Plastic Surgery Ctr., Newport News, Va., 1972-76, rsch. asst. Riverside Lab. Microvascular Rsch., Newport News, Va., 1976-84; owner, adminstr. Barclay Apts., Newport News, Va., 1983-95; cons. Plastic Surgery Ctr. Hampton Roads, Newport News, Va., 1985—. Contbg. author: Pediatric Nursing, 1967, MCV/VCU School of Nursing: A Proud Heritage, 1992; co-author: Duke University Medical Center Manual, 1972. Bd. trustees Med. Coll. Va. Alumni Assn., Va. Commonwealth U., dir. nursing divsn.; founder, chmn. Com. historic Preservation. Recipient 1st Nurse Alumni award Outstanding Svc., 1989. Mem. AAUW (life), Am. Soc. Plastic & REconstructive Nurses, Newport News Med. Soc. Alliance (v.p., pres., treas.), Raleigh Tavern Soc. Colonial Williamsburg Found. (life), Sigma Theta Tau. Episcopalian. Avocations: reading, herb and flower gardening, bridge, teaching, writing poetry. Home and Office: 36 Barclay Rd Newport News VA 23606-1465

SHEPARD, KATHERINE, science educator, consultant; d. James Shepherd and Jessie Beatrice Wright; m. Franklin Delano McKinney, Apr. 10, 1971 (div. Oct. 1985). BA, Goshen Coll., Ind., 1964; MA, Atlanta U., Ga., 1971; post grad., Case Western Res. U., Cleve., 1971—, Kent State U., Ohio, Hiram Coll., Suffolk U., Boston, Miami U., Oxford, Ohio. Cert. scuba diver. Summer recruiter Goshen Coll., 1967; tchr. HS physical edn. Cleve. Mcpl. Sch. Dist., 1964—65, tchr. HS health, 1993—94, tchr. HS sci., 1964—95, cons. and mentor to entry level tchrs., 1996—. Grant com. mem. Cleve. Pub. Schs. and NSF, 1993; mem. tchr. adv. com. Cleve. Pub. Schs. and Sci. Mus., 1994; mem. sch. governance com. Cleve. Pub. Schs., 1996; founder and dir. George E. Mills Gallery of Excellence, 1994; faculty adv. student coun.; faculty adv. Youth Coun. on Human Rels.; faculty adv. extracurricular clubs. Photographer (talent, fashion shows and Hall of Fame). Vol. Exec. Bd. Alumni Goshen Coll., 1981—84; newsletter publ. Shakerwood Assn., Warrensville Heights, Ohio, 1972—75, 2000—03; trustee Lee Heights Cmty. Ch., Cleve., 1986—89. Named to Gradsnet Found. Hall of Fame, 2001; recipient Inspirational Tchr. award, BP Am., 1996, Lifetime Achievement award, Harvard - Lee Times, 1996; scholar, Martha Holden Jennings Found., 1974—75. Mem.: Com. Political Edn., Assn. Supervision and Curriculum Devel., Cleve. Tchrs. Union. Avocations: photography, gardening, skiing, travel, sports.

SHEPARD, KATHRYN IRENE, public relations executive; b. Tooele, Utah, Jan. 6, 1956; d. James Lewis and Glenda Verleen (Slaughter) Clark; m. Mark L. Shepard, June 5, 1976. BA in History, Boise State U., 1980. On-air writer Sta. KTTV, Channel 11, L.A., 1982-85; publicity dir. Hollywood C. of C., Calif., 1985-87; pres. Kathy Shepard Pub. Rels., Burbank and Portland, 1987-93; dir. pub. rels. Las Vegas Hilton, 1993-94;

dir. comms. Hilton Gaming, 1994-96; dir. corp. comms. Hilton Hotels Corp., 1996—97, v.p. corp. comms., 1997—. Instr. pub. rels. ext. program UCLA, 1991-92. Contbr. articles to profl. publs. Mem.: Pub. Rels. Assn. Am., Pub. Communicators L.A. (pres. 1991—92, bd. dirs. 1987—91). Avocations: genealogy, film, travel. Office: Hilton Hotels Corp PR Dept 9336 Civic Center Dr Beverly Hills CA 90210-3604 E-mail: kathy_shepard@hilton.com.

SHEPARD, LAURA ANN, microbiologist, researcher; b. Ft. Worth, Tex., Dec. 30, 1962; d. Larry and Montie Hopkins; m. Brett David Shepard, May 2, 1998; m. Dale Alan Utt, Jr., May 27, 1984 (div. Apr. 12, 1996); children: Dale Alan Utt, III, Amanda Leigh Utt. Student, Coll. of William and Mary, 1984; BHS summa cum laude, U. Mo., 1986; PhD, U. Okla., Oklahoma City, 1999. Cert. med. technologist Am. Soc. for Clin. Pathology, 1986. Med. technologist Boone Hosp. Ctr., Columbia, Mo., 1986—89; adj. faculty Okla. Bapt. U., Shawnee, Okla., 1991—94; postdoctoral rsch. fellow U. Okla., Oklahoma City and Norman, Okla., 2000—03; rschr. Mayo Clinic, Rochester, Minn., 2004—. Contbr. articles to profl. jours. Grad. fellow, NSF, 1995—98. Mem.: Assn. for Rsch. in Vision and Ophthalmology, Am. Soc. for Microbiology, Am. Soc. for Clin. Pathology, Lambda Tau, Golden Key, Alpha Eta, Alpha Epsilon Lambda, Phi Kappa Phi. Home: 1710 11th Ave NE Rochester MN 55906

SHEPARD, SARAH, public relations company executive; b. N.Y.C., Apr. 24; BFA, C.W. Post Coll., L.I. U., Brookville, N.Y., 1992. Mng. dir. KCSA Pub. Rels. Worldwide, N.Y.C., 1993—. Mem. Nat. Investor Rels. Inst. (profl. devel. com. 1997—). Office: KCSA Pub Rels Worldwide 800 2nd Ave Fl Dave5 New York NY 10017-4709 E-mail: sshepard@kcsa.com.

SHEPARD, SUE ANNETTE, director fund raising; b. Bridgewater, Iowa, Mar. 5, 1943; d. Gerald L. and Sarah Shirley (Sullivan) Campbell; m. Joe Willwerth Shepard, June 10, 1962 (div. May 1984); children: Jonathan Willwerth, Christopher Campbell. BME, Ind. U., 1965; cert. arts adminstrn., U. Wis., 1978; MA in Philanthropic Studies, Ind. U., Indpls., 1995. Cert. fund raising exec. Tchr. St. Dominics Sch., Northfield, Minn., 1970-73; adminstr. Northfield Arts Guild, 1976-85; co-founder Northfield Musical Theater, dir. devel. Waterloo (Iowa) Cmty. Playhouse, 1986-88; officer spl. svcs. devel. U. Minn. Found., Mpls., 1988-89; dir. devel. Inst. Agr., Forestry, Home Econ. U. Minn., St. Paul, 1989-95, dir. devel. Coll. Agr., Food, and Environ. Sci., 1995—. Soprano Dale Warland Singers, 8 recordings; major roles, 2 recordings Opera and Broadway comedy. Mem. Nat. Soc. Fund Raising Execs., Coun. for Advancement and Support of Edn., Nat. Planned Giving Coun., Minn. Planned Giving Coun. Avocations: bicycling, reading, music, gardening. Office: Univ Minn 277 Cofy Hall 1420 Eckles Ave Saint Paul MN 55108-1030

SHEPARD, SUZANNE V. English language educator; b. Montour Falls, N.Y., Mar. 4, 1958; d. William Henry III and A. Louisa (Stenberg) S.; m. Tredwell Burch Jr., May 29, 1982. BA in Music and Lit., Eisenhower Coll., Seneca Falls, N.Y., 1980; MA in English, Binghamton U., 1983, PhD in English, 1995. Tchg. asst. Binghamton U., N.Y., 1981-87, adj. prof., 1987; from adj. prof. to prof. Broome C.C., Binghamton, 1991—2003, prof., 2003—. Author: The Patchwork Quilt: Ideas of Community in Nineteenth Century American Women's Fiction, 2001. Elder Presbyn. Ch., Binghamton, 1988—, lay preacher, 1993—; mem. Multicultural Reading Group, Binghamton, 1995—. Mem. MLA, Nat. Coun. Tchrs. English, Phi Kappa Phi. Presbyterian.

SHEPHERD, CYBILL LYNNE, actress, singer; b. Memphis, Feb. 18, 1950; d. William Jennings and Patty Shobe (Micci) S.; m. David Ford, Nov. 19, 1978 (div., 1982); 1 child, Clementine; m. Bruce Oppenheim, March 1, 1987 (div., 1990); children: Molly Ariel and Cyrus Zachariah (twins) Student, Hunter Coll., 1969, Coll. of New Rochelle, 1970, Washington Sq. Coll., NYU, 1971, U. So. Calif., 1972, NYU, 1973. Appeared in motion pictures Last Picture Show, 1971, The Heartbreak Kid, 1973, Daisy Miller, 1974, At Long Last Love, 1975, Taxi Driver, 1976, Special Delivery, 1976, Silver Bears, 1977, The Lady Vanishes, 1978, Earthright, 1980, The Return, 1986, Chances Are, 1988, Texasville, 1990, Alice, 1990, Once Upon a Crime, 1992, Married to It, 1993; star TV series The Yellow Rose, 1983-84, Moonlighting, 1985-89, Cybill, 1994-98 (also prodr.); TV films include A Guide for the Married Woman, 1978, Secrets of a Married Man, 1984, Seduced, 1985, The Long Hot Summer, 1985, Which Way Home, 1991, Memphis, 1992 (also co-writer, co-exec. prodr.), Stormy Weathers, 1992, Telling Secrets, 1993, There Was a Little Boy, 1993, Journey of the Heart, 1997, Due East, 2002, Martha, Inc.: The Story of Martha Stewart, 2003; record albums include Cybill Does It To Cole Porter, 1974, Cybill and Stan Getz, 1977, Vanilla with Phineas Newborn, Jr, 1978; appeared in stage plays A Shot in the Dark, 1977, Picnic, 1980, Vanities, 1981, The Muse, 1999, Marine Life, 2000; co-author Cybill Disobedience, 2000.*

SHEPHERD, DEBORAH GULICK, elementary school educator; b. Edenton, N.C., Oct. 21, 1953; d. Lyman Mark and Rena (Bakker) Gulick; m. Ronald W. Shepherd. AA, Centenary Coll., Hackettstown, N.J., 1974; BA, Oral Roberts U., 1976; MA, Fairleigh Dickinson U., 1981. Cert. elem. and mid. sch. tchr., K-12 supr. N.J. Tchr. Mt. Olive Twp. Bd. Edn., Budd Lake, NJ, 1976—. Editor: (newsletter) Mountain View News, 1986—97, Light from the Steeple, 1998—. Mem. Chancel Choir, United Presbyn. Ch., Flanders, NJ, 1988—92; mem. sr. choir First Presbyn. Ch., Hackettstown, NJ, 1993—, Sunday sch. treas., 1996—2000; bd. dirs. Heaven Sent Nursery Sch., 1997—99. Recipient Gov.'s Tchr. Recognition award, State of N.J., 1991. Mem.: Edn. Assn. Mt. Olive (rep. 1987—93). Avocations: cross-stitching, sewing, knitting, reading, singing. Home: 663 Rockport Rd Hackettstown NJ 07840-5222 Office: CMS Elem Sch 99 Sunset Dr Budd Lake NJ 07828

SHEPHERD, DONNA LOU, interior designer; b. Uvalde, Tex., Sept. 25, 1948; d. Herbert Quarrels Jr. and Wanna Lou (Ray) Haile; m. Richard Ray Shepherd, June 2003; children from previous marriage: Laura Anne Howell, Christopher J. Huffman. BS, U. Houston, 1969, MEd, 1973. Owner Rainbow Design LLC, Littleton, Colo., 1975—. Spkr. in field. Designer Parade of Homes, 1989, Jr. Symphony Guild Showhome, 1996, designs featured in Colo. Homes and Lifestyles, Denver Post. Founder, pres. Prime Time Today, Littleton. Republican. Baptist. Avocations: water fitness, fly fishing, white-water rafting. Office: PO Box 3285 Littleton CO 80161-3285

SHEPHERD, GAAL, artist; b. Gainesville, Fla., Jan. 25, 1951; d. Charles Claypoole and Ruby Frances (Grogan) S.; m. John Allen Crowl. Student, Stella Adler Theater Studio, 1968-73, U. Tampa, 1974-75, Corcoran Sch. Art, 1985-88. Artist, Atlanta, Tampa, Ga., Fla., 1973-76; graphic designer Art Prodn., Inc., Washington, 1976-79; art dir., illustrations editor Chronicle Higher Edn., Washington, 1979-88; painter, sculptor South Woodstock, Vt., 1988—. Exhbn. agt. The Carving Studio, West Rutland, Vt., 1996—. One-woman shows include Pierre Antoine Gallery, Washington, 1987, 1989, Beside Myself Gallery, Arlington, Vt., 1993, Bromfield Gallery, Boston, 1993, Colby-Sawyer Coll., New London, NH, 1993, Lyndon State Coll., Lyndonville, Ct., 1993, Chaffee Art Ctr., Rutland, Vt., 1994, 1997, 1998, 2002, Vt. Coun. on Arts, Montpelier, 1995, Clarke Galleries, Stowe, Vt., 1995, Between the Muse Gallery, Rockland, Maine, 1996, No B.I.A.S. Gallery, Bennington, Vt., 1997, Steinway Gallery, Chapel Hill,NC, 1998, Red Mill Gallery, Johnson, Vt., AVA Gallery, Lebanon, N.H., 2003, Vt. Supreme Ct., Montpelier, 2003, exhibited in group shows at Middletown (NY) Arts Ctr., 1994, Vt. State Craft Ctr. at Frog Hollow, Middlebury, 1994, Attleboro (Mass.) Mus., 1996, Helen Day Art Ctr., Stowe, 1996, Vt. Coun. on Arts, West Rutland, 1996, AVA Gallery, Lebanon, NH, 1996, Harvard U., Cambridge, Mass., 1996, Ashuah-Irving Gallery, Boston, 1996, Ctr. for Contemporary Arts, Santa Fe, N.Mex., 1997, Guadalupe Fine Arts, Santa Fe, 1997, State Capitol Rotunda, 1997, Vt. Inst. Natural Sci., Woodstock, 1997, Beside Myself Gallery, Arlington, Vt., 1998, Maine Coast Artists, Rockport, 1999, Shelburne Farms, Vt., 2001, N.Mex. State Capitol, Santa Fe, 2002, two-person shows, Colby-Sawyer Coll., New London, NH, 1997, Milton Acad., Mass., 1998, The Munson Gallery, Chatham, Mass., 2001, exhibited in group shows at N.Mex. State Capital, Santa Fe, 2002, Rosewood Gallery, Sunapee, N.H., 2002, Munson Gallery, Chatham, Mass., 2002, Woodstock (Vt.) Folk Art, 2002, Elements Gallery, Rockland, Maine, 2002, Alliance for Visual Arts, Lebanon, N.H., 2003; author: Tranquil Vermont, 2000. Democrat. Avocations: mycology, gardening. Home: Thistle Hill Rd PO Box 307 North Pomfret VT 05053-0307

SHEPHERD, KAREN, retired congresswoman; b. Silver City, N.Mex., July 5, 1940; m. Vincent P. Shepherd. BA, U. Utah, 1962; MA, Brigham Young U., 1963. Former instr. Brigham Young U., Am. U., Cairo; former pres. Webster Pub. Co.; former adminstr. David Eccles Sch. Bus., U. Utah; former dir. Salt Lake County Social Svcs., Utah; former dir. continuing edn. Westminster Coll.; former mem. Utah Senate; mem. 103d Congress from 2d Utah dist., Washington, 1993—94; exec. dir., U.S. rep. European Bank for Reconstruction Devel., London, 1996—2002; mem. exec. com., chair East West Trade and Investment Forum Am. C. of C., England, 1998—2002; dir. EMILY's List, 2002. Mem. Nat. Common Cause Governing Bd., Washington, 1995-96; founder Karen Shepherd Fund; founding mem. Utah Women's Polit. Caucus, Project 2000; mem. Internat. Delegation to Monitor Elections in West Bank and Gaza, Israel; trustee KeyBank Victory Funds; dir. UBS Bank, U.S. Former mem. United Way, Pvt. Industry Coun.; former mem. adv. bd. U.S. West Grad. Sch. Social Work; trustee Westminster Coll.; bd. dirs. ARC, 2002—. Recipient Women in Bus. award U.S. Small Bus. Assn., Woman of Achievement award, Pathfinder award, YWCA Leadership award, 1st place award Nat. Assn. Journalists, Disting. Alumni award U. Utah Coll. Humanities, Eleanor Roosevelt award, 2002, Merit of Honor award U. Utah, 2004. Fellow Inst. Politics Kennedy Sch. Govt., Internat. Women's Forum, Salt Lake Area C. of C. (pub. rels. com.), Coun. on Fgn. Rels. Home: PO Box 1049 Salt Lake City UT 84110-1049 Office: 21 G St Salt Lake City UT 84103-2949

SHEPHERD, KATHLEEN SHEARER MAYNARD, television executive; b. N.Y.C., June 14, 1950; d. Theodore E. and Phyllis (Wildman) Shearer; m. Charles Dix Shepherd; m. Joseph Ashton Maynard (div. June 1977); 1 child, Natasha Candice. Student, Duke U., Durham, N.C., 1972-73, Westchester Community Coll., White Plains, N.Y, 1974-75, NYU, 1975-77. Atty. Tufts U., Medford, Mass., 1968-69; from administrv. asst. to assoc. producer WCBS-TV, N.Y.C., 1973-74, producer, 1975-76; from program devel. supr., exec. producer to dir. pub. affai WPIX TV, N.Y.C., 1977-84, v.p. pub. affairs, prodn., exec. producer, v.p. local prodn. and cmty. affairs. Trustee Coll. Mt. St. Vincent, Nat. Coalitin of 100 Black Women, lower Fairfield chpt., Conn., 1987; bd. dirs. Childrens Village, Dobbs Ferry, N.Y., 1988, Partnership for a Drug Free Am., mem. advt. coun. adv. com. Mem. NATAS. Democrat. Episcopalian. Avocations: jogging, exercise. Office: WPIX Inc 220 E 42nd St New York NY 10017-5806

SHEPHERD, MARY LOU, state representative; b. Spokane, Wash., Apr. 18, 1933; m. James Shepherd; children: Mona, Jerry, Randy, David, Kevin, Glenn, Gaill. Attended, Alan Hancock Coll., 1965—70, North Idaho Coll., 1985—87. State rep. dist. 2A Idaho Ho. of Reps., Boise, 1999—, mem. state afairs and transp. and def. coms. Sec.-treas. Pritchard-Murray Fire Dept.; bd. dirs. Annexation Ad Hoc com., 2000—, Idaho Rural Partnership, 2000—; mem.e-commerce interim com.; bd. dirs. State Hosp. North, 2000—. Democrat. Office: State Capitol Bldg PO Box 83720 Boise ID 83720

SHERBELL, RHODA, artist, sculptor; b. Bklyn. d. Alexander and Syd (Steinberg) S.; m. Mervin Honig, Apr. 28, 1956; 1 child, Susan. Student, Art Students League, 1950—53, Bklyn. Mus. Art Sch., 1959—61; pvt. study art, Italy, France, Eng., 1956. Cons., coun. mem. Emily Lowe Gallery, Hofstra U., Hempstead, N.Y., 1978, pres., 1989-81, instr., 1991—, life mem. bd. friends, pres. bd. trustees; tchr. instr. Mus. Modern Art, N.Y.C., 1959, NAD Art Sch., N.Y.C., 1985—, Art Students League, N.Y.C., 1980—; Nat. Portrait Gallery Mus. rep. to 150th anniversary Smithsonian Instn., Washington, 1996. One-woman shows include Haulington Township Art League,, Embassy of U.S., Prague, 2002-03, Country Art Gallery, Locust Valley, N.Y., Bklyn. Mus. Art Sch., 1961, Adelphi Coll., A.C.A. Galleries, N.Y.C., 1967, Capricorn Galleries, Rehn Gallery, Washington, 1968, Huntington Hartford Mus., N.Y.C., 1969, N.Y. Cultural Ctr., 1970, Nat. Arts Collection, Washington, 1970, Montclair Mus. of Art, 1976, Nat. Art Mus. Sport, 1977, Jewish Mus. N.Y.C., 1980, Morris (N.J.) Mus. Arts and Scis., 1980, Black History Mus., 1981, Queens Mus., 1981-82, Nat. Portrait Gallery, Smithsonian Inst., Washington, 1981-82, Bergen Mus. Arts and Scis., N.J., 1984, William Benton Mus., Conn., 1985, Palace Theatre of the Arts, Stamford, Conn., Bronx Mus. Arts, 1986, Hofstra Mus. Art, L.I., N.Y., 1989-90, 97-98, County Art Gallery, N.Y.C., 1990, Hecksher Mus., 2000, Bronx Mus., N.Y., Bklyn. Mus., Mus. Modern Art, N.Y.C., Country Art Gallery, 1990, Port Washington Libr., Nat. Mus. Am. Art, Smithsonian Instn., 1982, NAD, N.Y.C., 1984, 89, Castle Gallery Mus., N.Y.C., 1987, Emily Lowe Mus., N.Y.C., 1987, Heckshire Mus., N.Y.C., 1989, Islip Art Mus., N.Y.C., 1989, Gallery Emanuel, N.Y.C., 1993, Sundance Gallery, Bridgehampton, N.Y., 1995, Castiron Gallery SoHo Show, 1995, NAD Exhbn., 1995, Main St. Petile Gallery, 2003, Huntington Arts Coun., 2003, 04, Huntington Twp. Art League, 2002-03; 2 person exhbn. Works on Paper, Hofstra Mus., 1997-98; exhibited in group shows at Heckscher Mus., 1989, Islip Mus., 1989, Nassau Dept. Recreation and Parks, 1989, Downtown Gallery, N.Y.C., Maynard Walker Gallery, N.Y.C., F.A.R. Gallery, N.Y.C., Provincetown Art Assn., Detroit Inst. Art, Pa. Acad. Fine Arts, Old Westbury Gardens, Audubon Artists, NAD, Allied Artists, Heckscher Mus., Nat. Art Mus. Sports, Mus. Arts and Scis., L.A., Am. Mus. Natural History, Post of History Mus., 1987-88, Caslte Gallery Mus., N.Y.C., 1987, Emily Lowe Gallery Mus., N.Y., 1987, Bronx Mus. Arts, 1987, Chgo. Hist. Soc., Mus. Modern Art, N.Y.C., 1988, Sands Point Mus., L.I., Hofstra Mus., 1990, Nat. Mus. Sports Art, 1991, Indpls. Art Mus., Phoenix Mus. Art, Corcoran Mus. Art, Washington, IBM, N.Y.C., Fire House Gallery Mus. Nassau Cmty. Coll., L.I., 1992, Nat. Arts Club, 1992, IBM, N.Y.C., 1992, Nat. Sculpture Soc. and The Regina A Quick Ctr. for The Arts Fairfield U. Centennial Anniversary Exbn., 1993, Mus. Modern Art, N.Y.C., Nat. Sculpture Soc. 100 Anniversary Exhbn., 1993, 97, Italy, 1994, 98, Provincetown Assn. and Art Mus., 1993, Kyoto (Japan) Mus. Sculpture Guild, 1993, Nat. Sculpture Soc. Exhbn. in Italy, Lucca, 1994, Sculptures Guild, N.Y.C., 1994-95, Cline Gallery, Santa Fe, 1995, Smithtown Township Art Coun., N.Y.C., 1997, Hofstra Mus. Art, Hempstead, 1997, Hofstra Mus., 1997—, Smithsonian Inst. Nat. Portrait Gallery, 1997, Nat. Sculpture Soc., 1997-99, 2001, Nature Arts Club, 1999, Molloy Coll. Art Gallery, 1999, Nat. Acad. Art, 1999, Nat. Acad. Group Show, 1999, Portrait in bronze of Senator Norman J. Levy for Merrick Train Station, 2000, Aaron Copland's America, Heckscher Mus. Art, 2000, Nat. Art Mus., 2002—, Huntington Arts Coun. Inc., 2003, Petite Gallery; represented permanent collections, Stony Brook Hall of Fame, William Benton Mus. Art, Colby Coll. Mus., Oklahoma City Mus., Montclair (N.J.) Mus., Schonberg Libr. Black Studies, N.Y.C., Albany State Mus., Hofstra U., Bklyn. Mus., Colby Coll. Mus., Nat. Arts Collection, Nat. Portrait Gallery, Smithsonian Instn., Baseball Hall of Fame Cooperstown, N.Y., Nassau C.C., Hofstra U. Emily Lowe Gallery, Art Students League, Jewish Mus., Queens Mus., Black History Mus., Nassau County Mus., Stamford Mus. Art and Nature Ctr., Jericho Pub. Libr., N.Y., African-Am. Mus., Hempstead, N.Y., 1988, Stamford (Conn.) Mus. Art and Scis., Silvermine Artists North East exhbn., 1989, Nassau C.C. Fire House Gallery, 1992, Nat. Portrait Gallery Smithsonian Instn., 1996, Monument Work, Base Ball Club, The Family Grp., TheSea Dogs, 1999, MTA, Pub. Monument for Senator Norman J. Levy Merrik R.R. Sta., N.Y., 1999, Yogi Berra Portrait, Nat. Gallery Smithsonian Inst., 2001, Raphare Soyer Portrait, 2001, others; also pvt. collections, TV shows, ABC, 1968, 81; ednl. TV spl. Rhoda Sherbell-Woman in Bronze, 1977; works include Seated Ballerina, portraits of Aaron Copland (Bruce Stevenson Meml. Best Portrait award Nat. Arts Club 1989), Eleanor Roosevelt, Variations on a Theme (36 works of collaged sculpture), 1982-86; appeared several TV shows; guest various radio programs; contbr. articles to newspapers, popular mags. and art jours.; mem. Conservation Art Group Coun. City of N.Y., 1994-97; group exhbn., The Nat. Acad. Mus., 2003-04. Coun. mem. Nassau County Mus., 1978, trustee, 1st v.p. coun.; assoc. trustee Nat. Art Mus. of Sports, Inc., 1975—; cons., cmty. liaison WNET Channel 13, cultural coord., 1975-83; host radio show Not for Artists Only, 1978-79; trustee Women's Boxing Fedn., 1978; mem. The Art Commn. of The City of New York, 1993. Recipient Gold medal Allied Artists of Am., 1989, Alfred G. B. Steel Meml. award Pa. Acad. Fine Arts, 1963-64; Jersey City Mus. prize for sculpture, 1961, 1st prize sculpture Locust Valley Art Show, 1966, 67, Ann. Sculpture prize Jersey City Mus., Bank for Savs. 1st prize in sculpture, 1950, Ford Found. purchase award, 1964, 2 top sculpture awards Mainstreams 77, Cert. of Merit Salmagundi Club, 1978, prize for sculpture, 1980, 81, award for sculpture Knickerbocker Artists, 1980, 81, top prize for sculpture Hudson Valley Art Assn., 1981, Sawyer award NAD, 1985, Gold medal of honor Audubon Artists, 1985, Silvermine Exhbn. award, Gold medal Allied Artists Am., 1990, Pres.' award Nat Arts Club N.Y.C.; MacDowell Colony fellow, 1976, AAAL and Nat. Arts and Letters grantee, 1960, Louis Comfort Tiffany Found. grantee, 1962, Ford Found. grantee, 1964, 67, also award; named one of top 5 finalist to do Monument of Queen Catherine of England, 1991; named to represent Nat. Portrait Gallery at Smithsonian Mus., 1996, sculpture selected to represent Nat. Portrait Gallery Mus., 1997. Fellow Nat. Sculpture Soc.; mem. Sculpture Guild (dir.), Nat. Assn. Women Artists (Jeffery Childs Willis Meml. prize 1978), Allied Artists Soc. (dir., Gold medal 1990, The Pietro and Alfrieda Montana Meml. award 2000, award 2001), Audubon Artists (dir., Greta Kempton Walker prize 1965, Chaim Gross award, award for disting. contbr. to orgn. 1979, 80, Louis Weskeem award), Woman's Caucus for Art, Coll. Art Assn., Am. Inst. Conservation Hist. and Artistic Works, N.Y. Soc. Women Artists, Artists Equity Assn. N.Y., Nat. Sculpture Soc. (E.N. Richard Meml. prize 1989), Internat. Platform Assn., Profl. Artists Guild L.I., Painters and Sculptors Soc. N.J. (Bertrum R. Hulmes Meml. award), Am. Watercolor Soc. (award for disting. contbn. to orgn.), Catharine Lorillard Wolfe Club (hon. mention 1968), Nat. Arts Club (N.Y.C., Stevenson Meml. award 1989, Pres. award 1992, Robert Sayford award 2000, Bruce Stevenson Meml. award for Portrait 2000, Siegfort award 2000), NAD (Helen F. Barnett prize 1965, Leila Gordon Sawyer prize 1989, The Dessle Green prize 1993, Charlotte Deenevidde award 2003). Home: 64 Jane Ct Westbury NY 11590-1410

SHERBERT, SHARON DEBRA, financial services executive; b. Bklyn., Aug. 18, 1953; d. Joseph George and Leah (Katzman) Goldstein; m. Robert Fisher, Oct. 20, 1973 (div. Nov. 1981); 1 child, Meredith Audra Fisher; m. Michael Sherbert, Apr. 4, 1982; 1 child, Jared Alan. Grad. high sch., Bklyn. Cert. fin. planner; registered fin. cons. Real estate agent Century 21 R.E., Sepulveda, Calif., 1976-80; life ins. agt. Prudential Life Ins., North Hollywood, Calif., 1980-82; sr. v.p. Profl. Planning, Encino, Calif., 1982-90; exec. v.p. Comprehensive Fin. Svcs., Burbank, Calif., 1992—. Columnist on Internet Web site Women in Tech., Inc., Van Nuys, Calif., 1996—. Co-host: (TV show) You and Your Money, 1993—. Mem. NAFE, Nat. Assn. Women Bus. Owners, Internat. Assn. for Fin. Planners, Inst. Cert. Fin. Planners, Zonta Club of Santa Clarita Valley (sunshine sec. 1992-93). Office: Comprehensive Fin Svcs 3811 W Burbank Blvd Burbank CA 91505-2116

SHERBY, KATHLEEN REILLY, lawyer; b. St. Louis, Apr. 5, 1947; d. John Victor and Florian Sylvia (Frederick) Reilly; m. James Wilson Sherby, May 17, 1975; children: Michael R.R., William J.R., David J.R. AB magna cum laude, St. Louis U., 1969, JD magna cum laude, 1976. Bar: Mo. 1976. Assoc. Bryan Cave, St. Louis, 1976-85; ptnr. Bryan Cave LLP, St. Louis, 1985—. Contbr. articles to profl. jours. Bd. dirs Jr. League, St. Louis, 1989-90, St. Louis Forum, 1992-99, pres., 1995-97; chmn. Bequest and Gift Coun. of St. Louis U., 1997-99; jr. warden Ch. of St. Michael and St. George, 1998-2000; bd. dirs. Bistate chpt. ARC, 2000—; bd. trustees St. Louis Sci. Ctr., 2000—. Fellow Am. Coll. Trust and Estate Coun. (regent 1997—), Estate Planning Coun. of St. Louis (pres. 1986-87), Bar Assn. Met. St. Louis (chmn. probate sect. 1986-87), Mo. Bar Assn. (chmn. probate and trust com. 1996-98, chmn. probate law revision subcom. 1988-96). Episcopalian. Home: 47 Crestwood Dr Saint Louis MO 63105-3032 Office: Bryan Cave LLP 1 Metropolitan Sq Ste 3600 Saint Louis MO 63102-2733

SHERIDAN, DIANE FRANCES, public policy facilitator; b. Wilmington, Del., Mar. 12, 1945; d. Robert Kooch and Eileen Elizabeth (Forrest) Bupp; m. Mark MacDonald Sheridan III, Dec. 7, 1968; 1 child, Elizabeth Anne. BA in English, U. Del., 1967. Tchr. English Newark (Del.) Sch. Dist., 1967-68, Lumberton (Tex.) Ind. Sch. Dist., 1969-71, Crown Point (Ind.) Sch. Dist., 1972-75; sr. assoc. The Keystone (Colo.) Ctr., 1986-98; facilitator cmty. adv. panels to chem. plants and refineries Taylor Lake Village, Tex., 1986—. Facilitator cmty. adv. panels to chem. plants and refineries, Tex., Kans.; chair Keystone Siting Process Local Rev. Com.; mem. pub. adv. panel Chem. Mfrs. Assn. Responsible Care, 1989-97. 1st v.p. LWV, Washington, 1992-94, sec. treas. voters edn. fund, sec. treas. Nat. LWV, 1994-96, bd. dirs. 1996-98; pres. LWV of Tex., 1987-91, chair edn. fund, 1987-91, bd. dirs., 1983-87; pres. LWV of the Bay Area, 1981-83, bd. dirs., 2001—; mem. adv. com. Ctr. for Global Studies of Houston Advanced Rsch. Ctr., The Woodlands, Tex., 1991-97, Ctr. for Conflict Analysis and Mgmt., bd. advisors Environ. Inst.; mem. U. Houston-Clear Lake Devel. Adv. Coun., 1989-95; mem. Bay Area Cmty. Awareness and Emergency Response Local Emergency Planning Com., 1988-92; active Tex. House-Senate Select Com. on Urban Affairs Regional Flooding Task Force, 1979-80, Congressman Mike Andrews Environ. Task Force, 1983-85, Gov.'s Task Force on Hazardous Waste Mgmt., 1984-85; dir. local PTAs, 1981-91; coord. Tex. Roundtable on Hazardous Waste, 1982-87; sec., v.p. Tex. Environ. Coalition, 1983-85; co-chair Tex. Risk Commn. Project, 1986-89; mem. Leadership Tex., Class of 1988; mem. cmty. adv. bd. U. Tex. Med. Br. Ctr. Nat. Inst. Environ. Health Studies, 1998—. Mem. LWV (nat. bd. dirs. 1992-98, trustee nat. edn. fund 1992-98), Assn. for Conflict Resolution, Internat. Assn. for Pub. Participation, Mortar Board, East Harris County Mfrs. Assn. (risk mgmt. comm. com. 1994-99, cmty. emergency comm. com., 2003—), Pi Sigma Alpha, Kappa Delta Pi. Office Phone: 281-326-5253. Personal E-mail: DBSheridan@aol.com.

SHERIDAN, RUTH STEWART, business development consultant, playwright; b. Portland, Oreg., Jan. 26, 1937; d. Lynton Norman and Flora Belle (Wright) Stewart; m. Robert Leonard Sheridan, Sept. 21, 1963 (div. Aug. 1966); 1 child, Jessica Lerryn. BA, San Diego State U., 1968, MA, 1974. Sr. scientist Sys., Sci. and Software, La Jolla, Calif., 1970-74; divsn. mgr. Sci. Applications Internat., La Jolla, Calif., 1974-80, sect. mgr., 1982-85; asst. v.p. N.E. Energy, La Jolla, Calif., 1980-82; sr. cons. Arthur Young, N.Y.C., 1986-89; owner, pres. Sheridan Svcs., Astoria, N.Y., 1989—. Dir. Fact Finders, San Diego, 1980-84, Isadora Duncan Internat. Ctr. for Dance, N.Y.C., 1991—; dir., treas. Civic Conservatory Theatre Arts for Youth, San Diego, 1977-85. Editor: Emerging Energy Technologies, 1978. Mem. Grad. Women in Sci., Dramatists Guild, Sigma Pi Sigma. Avocations: reading, theater, music, walking, writing. Home and Office: Sheridan Svcs 33-48 28th St Fl 2 Astoria NY 11106 E-mail: sheridan@panix.com.

SHERIDAN, SONIA LANDY, artist, retired art educator; b. Newark, Ohio, Apr. 10, 1925; d. Avrom Mendel and Goldie Cornelia (Hanon) Landy; m. James Edward Sheridan, Sept. 27, 1947; 1 son, Jamy. AB, Hunter Coll., 1945; postgrad., Columbia U., 1946-48; MFA with high honors, Calif. Coll. Arts and Crafts, 1961. Tchr. art public high schs., Calif., 1951-57; chmn.

dept. art Taipei (Taiwan) Am. Sch., 1957-59; instr. Calif. Coll. Arts and Crafts, 1960-61; asst. prof. art Sch. Art Inst. Chgo., 1961-67, assoc. prof., 1968-75, prof., 1976-80, prof. emeritus, 1980—, founder, head generative sys. program, 1970-80. Artist-in-residence 3M Corp., 1970, 76; cons. French Ministry of Culture, 1986; artist-in-residence Xerox Corp., 1981; lectr., univs., museums, art schs., workshops; lectr. Hungarian Acad. Scis. Symposium Collected Essays & Exhbn., Budapest, 1989, Internat. Soc. of Electronic Arts, Liverpool, UK. One-woman shows include Rosenberg Gallery, Chgo., 1966, Visual Studies Workshop, Rochester, N.Y., 1973, Iowa Mus. Art, Iowa City, 1976, Mus. Sci. Industry, Chgo., 1978; two-person show Mus. Modern Art, N.Y.C., 1974; exhibited in group shows at Print Ann, Boston Mus., 1963, Software, Jewish Mus., N.Y.C., 1969-70, Photography into Art, London, 1972-73, Photokino, Cologne, Germany, 1974, San Francisco Mus. Art, 1975, U. Mich. Mus. Art, 1978, Toledo Mus. Art, 1982-83, Mus. Modern Art, Paris, 1983, Siggraph, U.S., Japan, France, 1982, 83, Reina Sofia Mus., Madrid, Spain, 1986, Smithsonian Instn., 1990, Tokyo Met. Mus. Photography, 1991, Madrid City Cultural Ctr., 1992, Karl Ernst Osthaus Mus., Hagen, Germany, 1992, Circulo des Belles Artes, Madrid, 1992, Yale U. Art Gallery, 1995, Tokyo Intercom. Ctr., 1995, U. Montreal, 1995, Internat. Soc. Electronic Arts, Liverpool, Eng., 1998, Hungarian Art Mus., 1995 Scripton Mus., Netherlands, 1997, Video Gallery, Hungary, 2000-02, Mus. for Kommunikation, Frankfort, Germany, 2001, 2nd biennial, Museo Nacional de Belles Artes, Buenos Aires, 2002; major permanent collection at Hood Mus. Art, Dartmouth; represented in permanent collections Art Inst. Chgo., San Francisco Mus. Art, Mus. Sci. and Industry, Chgo., U. Iowa Mus. Art, Nat. Gallery Art, Ottawa, Can., Visual Studies Workshop, Rochester, Tokyo Met. Mus. Photography, Fundacion Arte y Technologia, Madrid, Tweed Mus., Univ. Minn., 1997, Scryption Mus., Tilburg, Netherlands, 1998; author: Energized Artscience: Sonia Landy Sheridan, 1978; co-editor Leonardo jour., hon. editor, 2000; contbr. articles, essay to profl. jours. Guggenheim fellow, 1973; Nat. Endowment for Arts workshop grantee 1974, pub. media grantee, 1976, artist grantee 1981; Union Ind. Colls. Art grantee 1975. Mem. Coll. Art Assn., Internat. Soc. for Interdisciplinary Study of Symmetry, Internat. Soc. of Electronic Arts. E-mail: sonia.sheridan@valley.net.

SHERIDAN LABARGE, JOAN RUTH, publishing executive; b. Forest Hills, N.Y., July 3, 1956; d. Thomas Patrick and Ruth B. (Stolzer) S.; 1 daughter. BS magna cum laude in Communication Arts, St. John's U., Jamaica, N.Y., 1978. Media planner BBDO, N.Y.C., 1978-81; media supr. Ted Bates & Co., N.Y.C., 1982-84; v.p., assoc. media dir. FCB Leber Katz Ptnrs., N.Y.C., 1985-87; v.p., assoc. pub., Woman's Day Hachette Filipacchi Mags., N.Y.C., 1987—95, v.p., pub. Family Life Mag., 1995—99; exec. v.p., group pub. dir. Weider Pub., 1999—2000; corp. pub., new bus. devel. G + J USA Publishing, 2001—, pub. Rosie, 2001—02, pub. YM Mag., 2003—. Named Top Media Sales Rep, Mediaweek, 1992. Office: G + J USA Publishing 375 Lexington Ave New York NY 10017

SHERLAND, BARBARA C. lawyer; married; 3 children. BA magna cum laude, Hood Coll., 1974; JD, U. Wash., 1984. Bar: Wash., U.S. Dist. Ct. (we. dist.) Wash. Law clk. to Hon. Eugene Wright U.S. Ct. Appeals (9th cir.), 1984; with Stoel River LLP, Seattle. Mem. adv. bd. Stat. KCTS-TV. Vice chmn. bd. dirs. Puget Sound Blood Ctr.; mem. adv. bd. Fred Hutchinson Cancer Rsch. Ctr., Am. Lung Assn.; mem. endowment bd. United Way King County. Named one of Wash.'s Super Lawyers, Wash. Law & Politics, 1999, 2000, 2002, Seattle's Top 100 Lawyers, Seattle Mag., 2001. Fellow: Am. Coll. Trust and Estate Counsel; mem.: Wash. Plannned Giving Coun. (mem. exec. com.), Wash. State Bar Assn. (chair real property, probate and trust sect.). Office: 600 University St Ste 3600 Seattle WA 98101 Business E-Mail: bcsherland@stoel.com.

SHERLOCK, JO ANNE C. librarian; b. Cedar Rapids, Iowa, Jan. 26, 1952; d. Claude Herbert Cypra and Leatrice Anne Meade Cypra; d. Jane Hightower Cypra; m. Stephen L. Sherlock, Sept. 30, 1978 (dec. June 1986); children: Stacey N. Sherlock Farmer, Samantha M. BA in French, Calif. State U., Fresno, 1974; M in Libr. and Info. Studies, U. Calif., Berkeley, 1987. Cert. vol. adminstr. Adminstrv. asst. Chevron Overseas Petroleum, San Francisco, 1974-78; children's libr. Irving (Tex.) Pub. Libr., 1987-94, cmty. rels. libr., 1994—. Bd. mem. Cultural Affairs Coun. V.p. publicity LWV, Irving, 1994-96. Named High Spirited Citizen, City Coun., Irving, 1992. Mem. ALA (various coms.), Assn. Vol. Adminstrs., Pub. Libr. Assn. (various coms.), AAUW (bd. dirs. 1984-86), Greater Irving Las Colinas C. of C. (bd. mem. women's divsn. 1990-2002), YWCA (bd. dir. 2002-). Avocations: needlepoint, travel, reading, cooking, pets. Office: Irving Pub Libr 801 W Irving Blvd Irving TX 75060-2845

SHERMAN, CAROL, poet, educator; b. N.Y.C., N.Y., Oct. 20, 1935; d. Albert and Betty Sherman; m. Eugene M. Cooper, Sept. 5, 1971 (dec. June 1982). BA, Hunter Coll., 1957; AAS, Fashion Inst. Tech., 1962. Cert. tchr. N.Y. Bd. Edn., N.Y.C., N.Y. State . Assoc. prof. fashion design Fashion Inst. Tech., N.Y.C., 1964—68; writer Butterick Fashion Mktg. Co., N.Y.C., 1971—72; fashion designer N.Y.C., 1965—70, 1976—82; poet Bridgehampton, NY, 1976—. Examiner N.Y. Bd. Edn., N.Y.C., 1975; prodr. LTV, E. Hampton, NY, 1997, 2000, dir., 1996, 2000. Author: Bronx Ballads, 2001; contbr. chapters to books. Fellow, Vt. Studio Ctr., 2001. Mem.: Poets & Writers, Southampton Players (best supporting actress award 1999). Democrat. Buddhist. Avocations: community theater, swimming, cooking, dance, travel. E-mail: muffinmama@yahoo.com.

SHERMAN, CINDY, artist; b. Glen Ridge, N.J., 1954; Student, State Univ. Coll. Buffalo, 1972-76. One-woman exhbns. include Hallwalls Gallery, Buffalo, 1976, 77, Contemporary Arts Mus., Houston, 1980, The Kitchen, N.Y., 1980, Metro Pictures, N.Y., 1980, 83, Saman Gallery, Genoa, 1981, Young/Hoffman Gallery, Chgo., 1981, Chantal Crousel Gallery, Paris, 1982, Stedelijk Mus., Amsterdam, 1982, St. Louis Art Mus., 1983, Fine Arts Ctr. Gallery, SUNY-Stony Brook, 1983, Rhona Hoffman Gallery, Chgo., 1983, Douglas Drake Gallery, Kansas City, 1983, 84, Seibu Gallery Contemporary Art, Tokyo, 1984, Akron Art Mus., 1984, Linda Cathcart Gallery, Santa Monica, Calif., 1992, Museo de Monterrey, Mex., 1992; group exhbns. include Albright-Knox Art Gallery, Buffalo, 1975, Artists Space, N.Y., 1978, Max Protetch Gallery, N.Y., 1979, Castelli Graphics, N.Y., 1980, Lisson Gallery, London, 1980, Centre Pompidou, Paris, 1981; NIT, 1981, Renaissance Soc. U. Chgo., 1982, Metro Pictures, N.Y., 1982, La Ciennale de Venezia, Venice, Italy, 1982, Documenta 7, Kassel, West Germany, 1982, Chantall Crousel Gallery, Paris, 1982, San Francisco Mus. Modern Art, 1982, Inst. Contemporary Art, London, 1982, Grey Art Gallery, N.Y., 1982, Inst. Contemporary Art, Phila., 1982, Young Hoffman Gallery, Chgo., 1983, Hirshhorn Gallery, Washington, 1983, 1983, Whitney Mus. Am. Art, N.Y., 1983, 85, 91; represented in permanent collections Mus. Fine Arts, Houston, Albright/Knox Art Gallery, Buffalo, Dallas Mus. Fine Arts, Mus. Boymans-van Beuningen, Rotterdam, Akron Art Mus., Ohio, Mus. Modern Art, N.Y.C., Walker Art Ctr., Mpls., Tate Gallery, London, Rose Art Mus., Brandeis U., Centre Pompidou, Paris, Stedelijk Mus., Amsterdam, Met. Mus. Art, N.Y., St. Louis Art Mus., San Francisco Mus. Modern Art. Address: METRO PICTURES 519 W 24th St New York NY 10011-1104

SHERMAN, DEANE MURRAY, culture organization administrator; b. Beulah, N.D. m. John F. Sherman, Feb. 8, 1944; children: Betsy Deane, Mary Ann. Student, N.D. State U., George Washington U. Emeritus Arts Coun. Montgomery County, Md., 2000—. Bd. trustees Internat. Conservatory of Music, 1981—, sponsor Phia Berghout Harp Series, 1996-97. Decorated chevalier Ordre des Palm Academiques;recipient Hornbook award Montgomery County Tchrs. Assn., 1967, Leadership award Am. Biog. Inst., 1995, Strathmore Hall Found. award, 1998; honored guest Fukui Harp Festival, 1982, Internat. Harp Contest, Israel, 1988-94, U.S., 1991-95, Perugia Classico IV, 1998, Russian Internat. Festival and Harp Competition, 2000. Mem.: Friends of Franklin (founding mem., bd. dirs. 2003—), Help and Resource Porject (chmn. 1989—), World Harp Congress (founder, v.p. 1990—), Women's Com. for Nat. Symphony, Md. Congress PTA (life), Nat. Congress PTA (life), Western Club Glasgow, Elstophos Sci. Club Washington. Home: 11016 Ardwick Dr North Bethesda MD 20852-3204

SHERMAN, MARY ANGUS, public library administrator; b. Lawton, Okla., Jan. 3, 1937; d. Donald Adelbert and Mabel (Felkner) Angus; m. Donald Neil Sherman, Feb. 8, 1958; children: Elizabeth, Donald Neil II. BS in Home Econs., U. Okla., 1958, MLS, 1969. Br. head Pioneer Libr. System, Purcell, Okla., 1966-76, regional libr. Norman, Okla., 1976-78, asst. dir., 1978-80, dir., 1987—. Bd. dirs. McClain Bank, chair audit com., 1997—. Mem. bd. visitors U. Okla. Coll. Arts and Scis., 1998—; bd. dirs. U. Okla. Found., 2004—, Women's Resource Ctr., Norman, 1998—2003, pres., 2002. Named one of Disting. Alumni, Sch. Home Econs. U. Okla., 1980; recipient award of merit, Okla. Sch. Libr. and Info. Sci., 2000. Mem. ALA (councilor 1988-96, planning and budget assembly 1990-91, internat. rels. com. 1992-96, 2001—, internat. rels. round table 1989—, orientation com. 1998-99, mem. com. 1999-2000, chair sister libr. com. 2000-02, exec. bd. 2000-02), Pub. Libr. Assn. (divsn. of ALA, pres. pub. policy for pub. librs. sect. 1995-96, chmn. internat. rels. com., 2002-04), Tech. in Publ. Librs. Com. 2002-04, Internat. Fedn. Libr. Assns. (standing com. on pub. librs. 1999—), AAUW (pres. Okla. chpt. 1975-77, nat. bd. dirs. 1983-87, S.W. ctrl. region dir. 1983-85, v.p. nat. membership 1985-87, Woman of the Yr. Purcell chpt. 1982), Okla. Libr. Assn. (pres. 1982-83, interlibr. cooperation com. 1993-95, chair 1994-95, legis. com. 1998—, Disting. Svc. award 1986), Norman Soc. Internat. Affairs (v.p. 1998-99, pres. 1999-2001), Norman C. of C. (bd. dirs. 1988-96, pres. 1994-95), Rotary (program chair 1991-92, 1999-2001, bd. dirs. 1993-97, pres. 1995-96, Paul Harris fellow, group study exch. leader to Iceland 1998, dist. literacy chair 1998-2000, dist. group study exch. chair 2001—), Norman Assistance League Club (cmty. assoc.), Norman Sister City Com. 1994-98, Delta Gamma Mothers (pres. 1978-79), Kappa Alpha Theta (pres. Alpha Omicron House Corp. 1984-87, nat. dir. house corps. 1987-88), Beta Phi Mu, Phi Beta K Democrat. Methodist. Office: Pioneer Libr System 225 N Webster Ave Norman OK 73069-7133 E-mail: mary@pls.lib.ok.us.

SHERMAN, MILDRED MOZELLE, music educator, vocalist, actress, opera director; b. Mt. Grove, Mo., Nov. 21, 1932; d. William Husley and Jessie Claire (Faulkner) Clark; m. Louis Leroy Sherman, Aug. 14, 1954; children: Clark Michael, Gayla Dawn. MusB, Bethany Coll., Lindsborg, Kans., 1953; MusM, Ind. U., 1955; PhD, U. Wis., 1971; postgrad., U. Wis., Stevens Point, Kans. U., Baylor U. Instr. music Kans. State U., Manhattan, 1962-66; prof. music Howard Payne U., Brownwood, Tex., 1973-80, Grand Canyon U., Phoenix, 1980-84; prof. ch. music, dir. ch. music, drama, theatre So. Bapt. Theol. Sem., Louisville, 1984-2001, founding dir. Ch. Music Drama Theatre, sr. prof. ch. music, 2001—. Instr., rep. Inst. Pan Americano, Panama City, 1955-56; vis. prof. Belem and Rio Bapt. Sems., Brazil; owner Sherman Svcs., 2000—, Ky. Opera Roster, 2001—; vis. lectr. Staley, Cambridge, Union, Furman, Stetson, and Fla. Bapt. univs., 1990-99. Performer, dir. over 1000 operas, musicals, and plays including Women of the Bible, 1986-97; author: The Vocal Technician, 1991, also short stories; translator Mozarts Obligation of the 1st Commandment, 1986, Debussy's Prodigal Son, 1987, Massenet's Herodiade, 1997, Two from Galilee prodn. kit, 1996; also monologues; contbg. author: New Christian Dictionary, 2001. Recipient Orpheus award Phi Mu Alpha Sinfonia, 1978; Lily Found. grantee, 1988-90; Baylor Univ. fellow, 1990-91. Mem. Nat. Opera Assn., Nat. Assn. Tchrs. Singing, Met. Opera Guild, Ch. Music Conf., DAR, Ea. Star, Christian Opera Assn. Bd., Sigma Alpha Iota. Baptist. Avocations: geneology, handwork, animals, travel. Home: 3602 Coronado Dr Louisville KY 40241-2611 Office: So Bapt Theol Sem 2825 Lexington Rd Louisville KY 40280-0001 E-mail: msherman@sbts.edu.

SHERMAN, NANCY, philosophy educator; b. Passaic, N.J., June 20, 1951; d. Seymour and Beatrice (Hoffman) S.; m. Marshall Presser, June 22, 1980; children: Kala, Jonathan. AB in Philosophy magna cum laude, Bryn Mawr Coll., 1973; postgrad., Boston U., 1973; MLitt in Philosophy, U. Edinburgh, Scotland, 1976; PhD, Harvard U., 1982. Tchg. asst. in philosophy Harvard U., Cambridge, Mass., 1980-81; asst. prof. Yale U., New Haven, 1982-88, assoc. prof., 1988-89, Georgetown U., Washington, 1989-94, prof., 1994—, univ prof. Vis. rsch. scholar King's Coll., Cambridge (Eng.) U., spring 1978; vis. prof. Johns Hopkins U., Balt., spring 1995, U. Md., College Park, spring 1995, 96; cons. on ethics to undersec. Dept. Navy, 1994; vis. disting. chair of ethics U.S. Naval Acad., Annapolis, Md., 1997, 98; participant numerous confs., symposia, colloquia; lectr., spkr. in field. Author: The Fabric of Character: Aristotle's Theory of Virtue, 1989, paperback edit., 1991, Making a Necessity of Virtue: Aristotle and Kant on Virtue, 1996; editor: Aristotle's Ethics: Critical Essays, 1999; contbr. articles and revs. to profl. jours. Vans Dunlop scholar U. Edinburgh, 1974-76; Teschemacher fellow Harvard U., 1976-81, Newcombe fellow, 1981-82, fellow NEH, 1984-85, 96, Am. Coun. Learned Socs., 1987, Mellon fellow Yale U., 1988, Whitney Humanities fellow Yale U., 1987-88, fellow Kennedy Inst. Ethics, 1991-96, Mellon summer fellow, 1992, Georgetown U. summer fellow, 1990, 91, 94, 95; Am. Philos. Soc. fellow, 2002. Mem. APA (program com. ea. divsn. 1995-97), Soc. for Ancient Greek Philosophy, N.Am. Kant Soc., Am. Philos. Assn., Washington Psychoanalytic Found. Office: Georgetown U Dept Philosophy 224 New North St NW Washington DC 20057-0001

SHERMAN, PATSY O'CONNELL, technical development administrator, chemist; b. Mpls., Sept. 15, 1930; d. James Patrick and Edna Fern (Stitzel) O'Connell m. Hubert Townsend Sherman, Aug. 15, 1953; children: Sharilyn Kay Sherman Loushin, Wendy Jane Sherman Heil. BA, Gustavus Adolphus Coll., 1952. Chemist 3M, St. Paul, 1952-67, rsch. specialist, 1967-73, tech. mgr., 1973-82, mgr. tech. devel., 1982—. Trustee GMI Engring. and Mgmt. Inst., Flint, Mich., 1986—; bd. dirs. Advanced Optics Inc., Mpls. Contbr. numerous articles to profl. jours.; patentee in field. Trustee Gustavus Adolphus Coll., 1989—. Recipient Disting. Alumni award Gustavus Adolphus Coll., 1975, Spurgeon award Boy Scouts Am., 1980; named to Minn. Inventors Hall of Fame Minn. Inventors Congress, 1989, Nat. Inventors Hall of Fame, 2001. Mem. Am. Chem. Soc., Am. Soc. Tng. and Devel., Am. Soc. Engring. Edn. (dir. continuing profl. devel. div. 1986-89, chair 1989-90). Achievements include invention of Scotchgard (with Samuel Smith) in 1956.*

SHERMAN, RUTH TODD, government advisor, counselor, consultant; b. Memphis, July 3, 1924; d. Robbie M. and Lillie M. (Shreve) Todd. BS, Memphis State U., 1972, MEd, 1975; MA, Western Mich. U., 1986; PhD, Ohio State U., 2001. Cert. tchr., counselor. Youth leader Assembly of God Ch., Memphis, 1962-64, youth dir., 1964-66; counselor Teen Challenge, Memphis, 1973-74; marriage and family therapist Memphis, 1976-77; govt. tng. advisor Def. Logistics Agy., Battle Creek, Mich., 1982-87, advisor Alexandria, Va., 1987-94, ret., 1994; tchr. computer graphics Ohio State U., Columbus, 1998—2001. Agy. to Mil. Svc. cons. Def. Logistics Agy., Oklahoma City, 1990-94. Author: Federal Catalog Training Books/Videos, 1987 (Sustained Superior Performance award 1987). Mem. Internat. Assn. Marriage and Family Counselors, Nat. Employment Counseling Assn., Am. Mental Health Counseling Assn. Avocations: drawing, creating computer animations, photography. Home: 257 Vista Dr Gahanna OH 43230-2986

SHERMAN, SANDRA BROWN, lawyer; b. Galesburg, Ill., May 14, 1953; d. Charles Lewis and Lois Maria (Nelson) Brown; m. Robert Sherman, June 10, 1979; children: Michael Wesley, Stephen Averill, Alexander Joseph. B of Music Edn., Ind. U., 1975; JD, U. Ill., 1979, LLM, 1981. Bar: Ill. 1979, Tex. 1982, N.J. 1984, U.S. Tax Ct. 1988, N.Y. 1997. Instr. law U. Ill., Champaign, 1979-81; assoc. Law Offices of William E. Remy, San Antonio, 1984, Gutkin Miller Shapiro & Selesner, Millburn, N.J., 1985-88, ptnr., 1989-91; counsel Riker Danzig Scherer Hyland & Perretti LLP, Morristown, N.J., 1991-95; ptnr. Riker Danzig Scherer Hyland & Perretti LLP, Morristown, N.J., 1996—. Contbr. articles to profl. jours. Trustee, sec. Found. U. Medicine and Dentistry N.J., 1998—; trustee Jersey Battered Women's Svc., 1999—. Scholar Ind. U., 1971-75, U. Ill., 1977-79. Mem. ABA (probate and trust law divsn.), N.J. Bar Assn., Estate Planning Coun. No. N.J., Estate Planning Coun. N.Y.C., Park Ave. Club. Avocation: music. Home: 15 Hawthorne Dr New Providence NJ 07974-1111 Office: Riker Danzig Scherer Hyland & Perretti LLP Headquarters Plz 1 Speedwell Ave Morristown NJ 07961-1981 E-mail: ssherman@riker.com.

SHERMAN, SIGNE LIDFELDT, portfolio manager, former research chemist; b. Rochester, N.Y., Nov. 11, 1913; d. Carl Leonard Broström and Herta Elvira Maria (Tern) Lidfeldt; m. Joseph V. Sherman, Nov. 18, 1944 (dec. Oct. 1984). BA, U. Rochester, 1935, MS, 1937. Chief chemist Lab. Indsl. Medicine and Toxicology Eastman Kodak Co., Rochester, 1937-43; chief rsch. chemist Chesebrough-Pond's Inc., Clinton, Conn., 1943-44; ptnr. Joseph V. Sherman Cons., N.Y.C., 1944-84; portfolio strategist Sherman Holdings, Troy, Mont., 1984—. Author: The New Fibers, 1946. Fellow Am. Inst. Chemists; mem. AAAS, AAUW (life), Am. Chem. Soc., Am. Econ. Assn., Am. Assn. Ind. Investors (life), Fedn. Am. Scientists (life), Union Concerned Scientists (life), Earthquake Engring. Rsch. Inst., Nat. Ctr. for Earthquake Engring. Rsch., N.Y. Acad. Scis. (life), Cabinet View Country Club. Office: Sherman Holdings Angel Island 648 Halo Dr Troy MT 59935-9415 E-mail: creative@libby.org.

SHERMAN, TRINA ARDEN, elementary school educator; b. Baker, Oreg., Mar. 20, 1974; d. Prudence Tysor and Leonard Frank Sherman; life ptnr. Gary Dolton Willison; children: Kristen Dawn Willison, Tori Nicole-Dolton Willison, Ashley Lillian Willison. BS, Willamette U., 1995; EdM, N.W. Nazarene U., Nampa, Idaho, 2001. Cert. spl. edn. tchr. Oreg. Tchr. Fruitland (Idaho) Elem. Sch., 2000 ; behavior specialist Advocates for Inclusion, Nampa, 2001—03. Devel. disabilities cons., 1997—2003. Amb. Ontario (Oreg.) Ambs., 2000—03; chaplain P.E.O., Ontario, 1996—2003; mem. vestry St. Matthew's Ch., Ontario, 2002—03. Mem.: Coun. Children with Behavior Disorders, Coun. Exceptional Children. Episcopalian. Office: Fruitland Elem Sch PO Box A Fruitland ID 83619 Home: 521 S Minnesota Ave Fruitland ID 83619 2654

SHERN, STEPHANIE MARIE, investment company executive, accountant; b. Taylor, Pa., Jan. 7, 1948; d. Joseph and Stephanie (Malodovitch) Andrews; m. George Emil Shern, Sept. 25, 1971. AA, Keystone Jr. Coll., 1967; BS, Pa. State U., 1969. CPA, N.Y. Staff acct. to ptnr., nat. dir. consumer products industry Ernst & Young, N.Y.C., 1969—, ptnr., vice chmn., global and U.S. dir. R&CP markets. Dir. Met. Retail Fin. Execs., N.Y.C. Contbr. articles to profl. jours. Named Keystonian of Yr., Keystone Jr. Coll., 1984. Mem. AICPA, N.Y. State Soc. CPAs (bd. dirs. 1985—), Women's Econ. Round Table, Panther Valley Golf (Allamuch, N.J.), Beta Alpha Psi (mem. adv. forum 1984—). Republican. Ukrainian Orthodox. Home: 11 Green Briar Ct Little Falls NJ 07424-2307 Office: Ernst & Young 5 Times Sq New York NY 10036-6530

SHERONY, CHERYL ANNE, dietician; b. Lincoln, Nebr., Dec. 5, 1948; d. John Eugene and Hazel Ethel (Stites) Howe; m. Bruce Carl Sherony, Aug. 11, 1973; children: Thomas Carl, Michael Bruce. BS in Dietetics, U. Wis., Stevens Point, 1971, MS, 1979. Registered dietitian. Dietitian Marquette (Mich.) Gen. Hosp., 1979-80, self employed, 1980-85, 89-90, Alger Marquette C.C., Marquette, 1982-87, Upper Peninsula Home Nursing, Marquette, 1989-93; dietitian self employed, Marquette, 1989-93; dietitian, owner Superior Dietetic Svcs. of the Upper Peninsula Inc., Marquette, 1996-99; pvt. practice dietitian dietitian, Marquette, 1999—. Citizen amb. to China, People to People Program, 1995. Sect. reviewer Pediat. Manual of Clin. Dietetics, 1998. Capt. USAF, 1972-90. Mem. Am. Dietetic Assn., Mich. Dietetic Assn., Upper Peninsula Dietetic Assn. Roman Catholic. Avocations: reading, water skiing, cross country skiing. Home and Office: 1781 M-28 East Marquette MI 49855

SHERPA, FRAN MAGRUDER, geography educator, animal scientist, small business owner; b. Midland, Tex., Aug. 20, 1952; d. Edwin Howard Magruder and Barbara June Cowden; m. Ang Kazi Sherpa; children: Sarah, Susie, Sonia, Tsowang. BS Geography, Tex. State U., 1995, M Applied Geography, 1998. Registered massage therapist. Owner, operator Himalayan Excursions, Nepal, 1983—85; investor, mgr. office Nepal Internat. Clinic, Nepal, 1989—91; adj. prof. geography U. Tex. Permian Basin, Odessa, Tex., 2000—; owner Bodywork, 2003—. Mem. Kathmandu Assn. Mothers and Babies Internat., 1989—93; sec. Am. Women of Nepal, Nepal, 1989—93; mem. United Nations Women's Orgn., Nepal, 1989—93; mem. audio visual acom. Road Users Nepal, Nepal, 1992—93. Mem.: Am. Assn. Geographers, U.S. Polo Assn. Avocations: polo, photography, travel. Home: 2201 Neely Midland TX 79705 E-mail: fransherpa@cox.net.

SHERREN, ANNE TERRY, chemistry educator; b. Atlanta, July 1, 1936; d. Edward Allison and Annie Ayres (Lewis) Terry; m. William Samuel Sherren, Aug. 13, 1966. BA, Agnes Scott Coll., 1957; PhD, U. Fla., Gainesville, 1961. Grad. tchg. asst. U. Fla., Gainesville, 1957-61; from instr. to asst. prof. Tex. Womans U., Denton, 1961-66; rsch. participant Argonne Nat. Lab., 1973-80, 93-94; assoc. prof. chemistry North Cen. Coll., Naperville, Ill., 1966-76, prof., 1976-2001, prof. emeritus, 2001—. Contbr. articles to profl. jours. Ruling elder Knox Presbyn. Ch., 1971—, clk. of session, 1976-94. Mem. Am. Chem. Soc., Am. Inst. Chemists, Sigma Xi, Delta Kappa Gamma (chpt. pres. 2002—), Iota Sigma Pi (nat. pres. 1978-81, nat. dir. 1972-78, nat. historian 1989—). Presbyterian. Office: North Ctrl Coll Dept Chemistry Naperville IL 60566 Business E-Mail: atsherren@noctrl.edu.

SHERRICK, REBECCA LOUISE, academic administrator; b. Carthage, Ill., May 28, 1953; d. Otho Downing and Elizabeth (Potter) S. BA, Ill. Wesleyan U., Bloomington, 1975; PhD, Northwestern U., 1980. Asst. prof. Carroll Coll., Waukesha, Wis., 1980-85, assoc. prof., 1987—, dir. women's studies, 1988-89, dir. planning, 1989-90, v.p. planning, 1990-91, v.p. enrollment and planning, 1991-92, v.p. enrollment and student svcs., 1992-93, v.p. adminstrn., 1993—. Cons. Milw. dist. United Meth. Ch., 1990-92. Contbr. articles to profl. jours. Bd. dirs., pres. The Women's Ctr., Waukesha, 1981-89; bd. dirs. Waukesha County Hist. Soc., 1985-88, Gt. Blue Heron coun. Girl Scouts U.S., 1987-90; bd. dirs., v.p. Christoph Meml. YWCA, Waukesha, 1986-89. Recipient Woman of Distinction award Waukesha YWCA, 1991; Lincoln Acad. of Scholars awardee State of Ill., 1975; William Randolph Hearst fellow, 1976, 77. Mem. Alpha Lambda Delta, Phi Alpha Theta, Kappa Delta Pi, Phi Kappa Phi. Methodist. Avocations: swimming, running, gardening.

SHERRILL, KATHERINE CLONTZ, minister; b. Morganton, N.C., Oct. 19, 1953; d. Vance Sprinkle Clontz, Sr. and Katherine Storey Clontz; m. Randy Norris Sherrill, May 17, 1956; children: William Nicholas, Sarah Louise(dec.). AB, Pfeiffer U., 1976; MDiv, Emory U., 1981. Ednl. asst. Ardmore United Meth. Ch., Winston-Salem, NC, 1976—78; assoc. pastor First United Meth. Ch., Newton, NC, 1983—87; pastor Caroleen/Chase (N.C.) United Meth. Churches, 1987—91; co-pastor Grace/Zoar United Meth. Chs., Charlotte, 1991—93; pastor Grace United Meth. Ch., Charlotte, 1993—2000, Burkhead United Meth. Ch., Winston-Salem, 2000—. Bd. dir. Family Guidance Ctr., Hickory, NC, 1983—87. Recipient Nolan Harmon award, Candler Sch. of Theology, Emory U., 1980. United Meth. Avocations: woodcarving, woodturning.

SHERRY, KRYSTAL A. real estate broker; b. Bayonne, N.J., July 26, 1975; d. Joseph James and Elaine M. Sherry. Grad. h.s., West Covina, Calif. Lic. real estate Nev. Realtor, Nev., 1993—2001; broker, owner Realty Success Sys., Ltd., Las Vegas, 2002—. Mem.: Nat. Assn. Realtors. Office: Realty Success Sys Ltd # 100 8064 W Sahara Las Vegas NV 89117 Office Phone: 702-968-6400.

SHERWOOD, GLORIA N. graphic and literary artist, genealogy researcher; b. Winfield, Kans. d. Edwin E. Schroeder and Anna Y. McClure; stepmother Vivian J. Schroeder; children: Christina Knueven, J.E. Jurey, Jeannette Thornhill. B CMT cert., foster parent cert. Pvt. home health care nurse, Eufaula, Okla., 1996—. Author: The Poetic Works of Gloria Sherwood Book 1 vol. 1, 2000, Poetic Work Book 1, vol. 2, 2002, Just Be 2000, Remember Me, 1999, Spiritual Wings, 2001, Awaited Healing, 2001; visual artist: New Trails, 1998, Deep Is the Soul, 2000, Out of Bondage, 2001. Recipient Award of Excellence in Christian Web sites Joyful Mom's Web site. Mem. NAFE, Nat. Home Gardening Club, Nat. Arbor Day Found., Angelwings, Nat. Audubon Soc., Nat. Wildlife Fedn., World Wildlife Fedn. Democrat. Avocations: performing arts, gardening, playing guitar, writing music, crafts.

SHERWOOD, PATRICIA WARING, artist, educator; b. Columbia, SC, Dec. 19, 1933; d. Clark du Val and Florence (Yarbrough) Waring; widowed; children: Cheryl Sherwood Kraft, Jana Sherwood Kern, Marikay Sherwood Taitt. BFA magna cum laude, Calif. State U., Hayward, 1970; MFA, Mills Coll., Oakland, Calif., 1974; postgrad., San Jose State U., 1980-86. Cert. tchr., Calif. Tchr. De Anza Jr. Coll., Cupertino, Calif., 1970-78, Foothill Jr. Coll., Los Altos, Calif., 1972-78, West Valley Jr. Coll., Saratoga, Calif., 1978—. Artist-in-residence Centrum Frans Masereel, Kasterlee, Belgium, 1989. One-woman shows include Triton Mus., Santa Clara, Calif., 1968, 2002, RayChem Corp., Sunnyville, Calif., 1969, Palo Alto (Calif.) Cultural Ctr., 1977, Los Gatos (Calif.) Mus., 1992, Stanford U. faculty club, Palo Alto, 1993, d.p. Fong Gallery, San Jose, Calif., 1995, 97, Heritage Bank, San Jose, 1997, City Jr. Coll., d.p. Fong Gallery, San Jose, 1997, City Coll., San Jose, Calif., 1997, West Valley Coll., Saratoga, Calif., 1998, Mus. West, Palo Alto, 2000-2001, Triton Mus., Santa Clara, 2001; exhibited in group shows at Tressider Union Stanford U., 1969, Oakland (Calif.) Mus. Kaiser Ctr., 1969, Sonoma (Calif.) State Coll., 1969, Bank Am., San Francisco, 1969, Alrich Gallery, San Francisco, U. Calif. Santa Clara, 1967, Charles and Emma Frye Mus., Seattle, 1968, Eufrat Gallery DeAnza Coll., Cupertino, 1975, San Jose Mus. Art, 1976, Lytton Ctr., Palo Alto, 1968 (1st award), Zellerbach Ctr., San Francisco, 1970, Works Gallery, San Jose, 1994, Inst. Contemporary Art, San Jose, 1997, Triton Mus. Art, Santa Clara, Calif., 1997, 98, San Jose Inst. Contemporary Art, 1998, San Jose City Coll. Artists Forum, 1998, West Valley Jr. Coll., Saratoga, Calif., 1998, Calvin Charles Gallery, Scottsdale, Ariz.; represented in permanent collections Mills Coll., Bank Am., San Francisco, Heritage Bank, San Jose, Stanford U., Palo Alto, Calif., San Jose U., Smithsonian Inst. Nat. Mus. Am. Art, Washington, Calrin Charles Gallery, Scottsdale, Ariz. Art judge student show Stanford U., Palo Alto, 1977; mem. d.p. Fong Gallery, San Jose, Calif., 1994, J.J. Brooking Gallery, San Francisco, Mus. West Gallery, Palo Alto, Calif., Gallery Ocean Avenue, Carmel, Calif., 2002, Bryant Street Gallery, Palo Alto, 2003, Calvin Charles Gallery, Scottsdale, Ariz., 1212 Gallery, Burlingame, Calif. Nat. Endowment for Arts/We. States Art Fedn. fellow, 1994. Mem. NEA, Calif. Print Soc., Womens Caucus for Arts, Internat. Platform Assn., Smithsonian Instn., Nat. Mus. Am. Art. Home: 1500 Arriba Ct Los Altos CA 94024-5956

SHERWOOD-FABRE, LIESE ANNE, public health service officer; d. Charles Laverne, Jr. and Nova Anne Sherwood; m. Luis Raul Fabre, May 17, 1981; children: Luis Raul Fabre III, Carlos Roberto Fabre, Fernanda Andrea Fabre. BA, Tex. Christian U., Fort Worth, 1978; MA, Ind. U., 1981, PhD, 1984. Policy rsch. analyst U.S. HHS, Washington, 1983—85, program analyst, 1988—89, pub. health advisor Dallas, 2000—; survey statistician U.S. Bur. of Census, Washington, 1985—88; cons. U.S. AID, Tegucigalpa, Honduras, 1989—90, project mgr. Mexico City, 1990—94, Moscow, 1994—99; cons. Acad. Ednl. Devel., Va., 1999—2000; pub. health advisor U.S. Dept. Health and Human Svcs. Co-author: (book) Performance and Credibility: Developing Excellence in Public and Nonprofit Organizations, 1986, Drug Lessons and Education Programs in Developing Countries, 1995; contbr. articles to profl. jours. Recipient Meritorious Honor award, U.S. Agy. Internat. Devel./Moscow, 1999; grantee, Nat. Inst. Justice, U.S. Dept. of Justice, 1981—82; Fulbright Tchg. fellow, Fulbright Commn., 1990. Mem.: Phi Sigma Iota (life; treas. 1977—78), Phi Beta Kappa (life).

SHETLER, RACHEL KIRSTEN, music educator, director; b. Jackson, Calif., Nov. 1, 1965; d. Ronald K. and Martha Lou Grabke; children: Kirsten Elizabeth, Brianna Ruth. BSc in Music Edn., Ea. Nazarene Coll., 1989, MEd in Elem. Edn., 1999, MEd in Adminstrn., 2000. Music specialist Braintree (Mass.) Pub. Schs., 1989—2000, dir. music, 2000—. Soloist Boylston Congl. Ch., Boston, 1990—, Town of Braintree, 1990—2003; accompanist Quincy (Mass.) Pub. Schs., 1998—2003; condr. Braintree (Mass.) Choral Soc., 2001—02. Singer: Boston (Mass.) Symphony Orch., 1989—; dir.: Quincy (Mass.) Dinner Theater, 1990—93; singer: (albums) The Boston (Mass.) Pops Orch., The Boston (Mass.) Symphony Orch. Republican. Avocations: singing, choreography, piano. Office: Braintree Public Schools 128 Town St Braintree MA 02184

SHICKLEY, MARGARET S. librarian; b. Armstrong County, Pa., Mar. 11, 1938; d. Oscar Henry and Ella Margaret (Titus) Fry; m. Roger Clair Storms, Aug. 24, 1963 (dec. 1980); children: Ethel Charis, Eric Malcolm; m. Nelson W. Shickley Sr., June 23, 1996. BA in Christian Edn., Eastern Coll., 1961; MSLS, Clarion U., 1991. Organist, pianist Lee Bapt. Ch., Maine, 1965-78; tchr. sewing Beth Eden Bapt. Sch., Wheatridge, Colo., 1978-81; organist, pianist Evang. Meth. Ch., Altoona, Pa., 1984-91; libr. Manahath Sch. Theol., Hollidaysburg, Pa., 1984-90; piano tchr. Altoona, Pa., 1986-90; cataloging libr. Lancaster (Pa.) Bible Coll., 1991—. Music libr. Blair Concert Chorale, Altoona, 1987-90; choir dir. Bapt. Ch., New Bethlehem, Pa., 1990-91. Nat. sec. Nat. Temperance and Prohibition Coun., 1983-89, del., sec. Prohibition Nat. Com., Denver, 1979-95; trustee Prohibition Trust Assn., 1992—. Mem. Am. Theol. Libr. Assn., Harmony Club (pres. 1977), Assn. Christian Librs., Lee Lit Club (community project chmn. 1976-77). Avocations: music, needlework, sewing, knitting, reading.

SHIDELER, SHIRLEY ANN WILLIAMS, lawyer; b. Mishawaka, Ind., July 9, 1930; d. William Harmon and Lois Wilma (Koch) Williams; 1 dau., Gail Shideler Frye. LLB, Ind. U., 1964. Bar: Ind. 1964. Legal sec. Barnes, Hickam, Pantzer & Boyd, Indpls., 1953-63; assoc. Barnes & Thornburg, 1964-70, ptnr., 1971-92, of counsel, 1993—. Participant fund drives Indpls. Symphony, 1968-81, Indpls. Mus. Art, 1969-79, Marion County Libr. Restoration, 1985-88, Goodwill Industries, 1988-89; bd. dirs. Bus. Unit Gals Indpls. Mus. Art, 1973-80; bd. dirs. Indpls. Legal Aid Soc., 1982-93, Cmty. Hosp. Found., 1986-94, Ctrl. Newspapers Found., 1979-99. Fellow Am. Coll. Trust and Estate Counsel, 1981-96; mem. Ind. Bar Assn. (sec. 1975-76, chmn. probate, trust and real property sect. 1982), Nat. Conf. Bar. Founds. (trustee 1988-94), Indpls. Bar Assn. (bd. mgrs. 1968-72, v.p. charge affairs 1972), Ind. Bar Found. (bd. mgrs. 1980-92, sec. 1981-82, treas. 1981-86, v.p. 1986-88, pres. 1988-90), Indpls. Bar Found. (bd. mgrs. 1970-82, sec. 1972-77), Women's Rotary (pres. Indpls. club 1969-71, dir. 1968-79). Office: Barnes & Thornburg 11 S Meridian St Ste 1313 Indianapolis IN 46204-3535 Address: PO Box 5031 Indianapolis IN 46255

SHIELD, CAROLYN DOUGLAS, music educator; b. Shreveport, La., Jan. 21, 1963; d. Rufus Roscoe and Beatrice (Lee) Douglas; m. Albert Shield, Jr., July 24, 1999. BS in Acctg., So. U. A&M, Baton Rouge, La., 1985, AA in Music, 1997. Music dir. Interdenominational Faith Assembly, Baton Rouge, 1985—95; choir tchr. Prescott Middle Sch., Baton Rouge, 1998; music dir. Union Antioch Bapt. Ch., Zachary, La., 1995—99, Creative Co. "Jelly's Last Jam", Baton Rouge; music dir. inmate choir E. Baton Rouge Parish Prison, 2001—; music instr. Joyful Sounds Music Studio, Baton Rouge, 1994—; music dir. Oasis Christian Ch., Baton Rouge, 1999— . Author (, composer, producer): (CD featuring Prison choir) When Justice Meets Mercy, 2003. Mem.: Am. Soc. Composers, Authors and Publishers. Avocations: fishing, piano, reading, travel. Home: 13011 Stone Dr Baker LA 70714 Office: Joyful Sounds Music Studio 8932 Plank Rd Baton Rouge LA 70811 E-mail: carolynshield@peoplepc.com.

SHIELD, JULIE MARIE KARST, retired art educator, artist; b. St. Louis, Mar. 28, 1933; d. Lansing Peter and Margaret Mary Shield. A, Briarcliff Jr. Coll., NY, 1953. Oil painting art tchr. Buckingham (Va.) Coun. of Arts, 1995—99; owner, dir. Wooden Boat Art Gallery, River John, Canada, 1997—99; oil and still life art tchr. Julie Shield Workshop, Farmville, Va., 1998—99, oil painting, landscape and still life art tchr., 2000—02; multi-media art tchr. Holly Manor Nursing Home, Farmville, Va., 2001—. Mem. coun. Longwood Ctr. for Visual Arts, Farmville, Va., 2001—03; bd. mem. Ctrl. Va. Arts. Mural pediat. waiting room, Roosevelt Hosp., N.Y., 1966, set design, Ring Around the Moon, 1981, brush and ink drawings on wall panels, ARC, Palm Beach County Chpt., 1982 (Achievement award), 11 oil paintings for movie set design, Illegally Yours, 1987, exhibitions include Va. Patterns, V. Mus. of Fine Arts, Warrenton, Va., 1988 (first prize oil painting, 88), one-woman shows include iol painting and drawing First Nat. Bank of Palm Beach, Palm Beach, Fla., 1984—85, exhibited in group shows at Nena's Choice Art Gallery, 1973, one-woman shows include Drawing Show New Stanley Art Gallery, Nairobi, Kenya, 1969. Recipient Best of the Show Oil Painting, Juried Exhbn. Buckingham Arts Coun., 1999, 1st, 2d and 3d prize sculpting and oil painting, The Women's Club of Buckingham County, 1995, Artistic Achievement award, Am. Red Cross. Mem.: Art Student's League N.Y.C., Buckingham Artists Guild (planning com. 1995—2003), Curdsville Cmty. Ctr., English Speaking Union, Friends of the Libr., Hist. Buckingham Inc., DAR (bd. mem., corr. sec. 1971—75), Audubon Artist's Inc. (assoc.), Buckingham-Dillwyn Garden Club (sec. 1996—2003). Episcopalian. Avocations: museums, gardening, showing miniature horse. Home: Rte 4 Box 700 Farmville VA 23901

SHIELDS, BROOKE CHRISTA CAMILLE, actress, model; ; 1 child. BA, Princeton U., 1987. Model for Ivory Soap commls. starting in 1966, later for Calvin Klein jeans and Colgate toothpaste commls.; actress: (films) Alice, Sweet Alice, 1975, Pretty Baby, 1977, King of the Gypsies, 1978, Wanda Nevada, 1978, Just You and Me Kid, 1978, Blue Lagoon, 1979, Endless Love, 1980, Sahara, 1983, Backstreet Strays, 1989, Brenda Starr, 1992, Seventh Floor, 1993, Running Wild, 1993, Freaked, 1993, Freeway, 1996, The Misadventures of Margaret, 1998, The Weekend, 1999, The Bachelor, 1999, Black & White, 1999. After Sex, 2000, Rent-A-Husband, 2004; (TV movies) The Prince of Central Park, 1977, After the Fall, Wet Gold, I Can Make You Love Me: The Stalking of Laura Black, 1993, Nothing Lasts Forever, 1995, What Makes a Family, 2001, Miss Spider's Sunny Patch Kids, 2003; (TV mini-series) Widows, 2002 (TV shows) The Tonight Show, Bob Hope spls., The Diamond Trap, 1988, Friends, 1996, Suddenly Susan, 1996-99, That 70's Show, 2004; appeared on Broadway in Grease, 1994-95.

SHIELDS, CAROLE, foundation administrator; MBA, U. Miami. Pres. People For the Am. Way Found., Washington, 1996—. Bd. dirs. PFAWF, Fla. State Health and Rehab. Svcs., Dade Childrens Partnership; vice-chair Pub. Health Trust, Dade Co., Fla.; v.p. Hospice Care, Inc.; appearences on PBS NewsHour, CNN Inside Politics, Fox Cables Crier & Co., Hannity & Colms. Bd. dirs. Dade Cmty. Found., Forum Med. Ethics and Philosophy, U. Miami.; mem. Kettering Found., Lilly Endowment Found., Davis Found. Office: People Am Way 2000 M St NW Ste 400 Washington DC 20036-3397 E-mail: pfaw@pfaw.org.

SHIELDS, LISA A. music educator; b. Miles City, Mont., Feb. 5, 1959; d. Don and Rae Hauk; m. James E. Shields; 1 child, A'Lynn. BA in Music Edn., Mont. State U., 1981, MEd, 1998. Tchr. Music Dutton Pub. Schs., Mont., 1981—83; dir. Music Dawson C.C., Glendive, Mont., 1991—. Adjudicator Dist. II Music Festival; dir. adult choir, dir. youth choir Sacred Heart Parish, Glendive; music leader Boy Scout Troop, Glendive. Mem.: Mont. Bandmasters, Mont. Music Educators Assn., Am. Choral Dirs. Assn. Roman Catholic. Home: 43 Seven Mile Dr Glendive MT 59330 Office: Dawson Cmty Coll 300 College Dr Glendive MT 59330

SHIELDS, MARLENE SUE, elementary school educator; b. Denver, Apr. 7, 1939; d. Morris and Rose (Sniderman) Goldberg; m. Charles H. Cohen, Dec. 22, 1957 (dec.); children: Lee, Richard, Monica; m. Harlan Shields. BA magna cum laude, Met. State Coll., 1980; MA, U. No. Colo., 1986. Preschool tchr. Temple Emanuel, Denver, 1970-75; tchr. Kindergarten Temple Sinai, Denver, 1975-80; tchr. pre-Kindergarten St. Mary's Acad., Englewood, Colo., 1980-83; tchr. Beach Court Elem., Denver, 1983-86, Valverde Sch., Denver, 1984-85; tchr. third grade Brown Elem., Denver, 1985-86; tchr. learning disabilities Cowell Elem. Sch., Denver, 1986-87, Sabin Elem. Sch., Denver, 1987-88; tchr. second grade Sabin Elem., Denver, 1988—. Mem. curriculum com. Denver Pub. Sch., 1989—, pers. subcom., 2000-02; citizen amb. Spain joint tchr. conf., 1995. Mem. personal subcom. Sabin Elementary Sch., 2000. Mem. Colo. Coun. Internat. Reading Assn., Nat. Assn. for Young Children, Nat. Tchrs. Colo. Math., Internat. Reading Assn., Carousel of Intervention, Delta Kappa Gamma (sec., v.p., grade level chair), PRIDE (lang. curriculum com., math. curriculum com., impact com., CDM rep. 1994-95), Delta Kappa Gamma (state 1st v.p.). Home: 5800 Big Canon Dr Englewood CO 80111-3516

SHIELDS, MARTHA BUCKLEY, elementary school educator; b. Ridley Park, Pa., Mar. 4, 1942; d. John Edward and Anne Josephine (Hayes) Buckley; m. James F. Shields, Aug. 22, 1964; children: James F., Martha S. Runzer, Katherine Anne Landaiche, John Edward. BA, Wheeling (W.Va) Jesuit U., 1964; postgrad., Widener U., Chester, Pa., 1975-76. Cert.: (paralegal). Exec. asst. Economy Engring. and Machine Works, Chester, 1970-77; tchr. gifted program RoseTree-Media S.D., Media, Pa., 1979-80; tchr. grade 5 St. Kevin Sch., Springfield, Pa., 1980-85; tchr. honors math. grades 4-8 St. Thomas the Apostle Sch., Glen Mills, Pa., 1985-97, tchr. 7th grade, 1997—. Bd. dirs. Chester County Voices Abroad, 1994—2003. Sec. vice-chair adv. com. Children and Youth Svcs. Delaware County, Media, 1979—, chmn. adv. com., 1999—2001; athletic dir. St. Thomas the Apostle, Glen Mills, 1995—; bd. dirs. St. Thomas the Apostle CYO, Glen Mills, 1977—, volleyball and track coach, 1977—; mem. alumni bd. Wheeling Jesuit U., 1996—, pres., 2003—. Named Educator-Vol. of the Yr., Leadership Delaware County Alumni Assn., 1992; named to Harry Watson Track Hall of Fame, KC, 1996; recipient Clifford M. Lewis Alumnus award, Wheeling Jesuit U., 1976, Coaches award for christian leadership, Archdiocese Phila.-Cath. Youth Orgn., 1989, Julia Forst award, Archdiocese Phila., 1999, Father Francis Griffin award, St. Thomas the Apostle Parish, 1999. Roman Catholic. Avocations: travel, sewing, reading. Home: 190 Andrien Rd Glen Mills PA 19342-1168 Office: St Thomas the Apostle Sch 430 Valleybrook Rd Glen Mills PA 19342-9440 E-mail: mopsys@comcast.net.

SHIELDS, PORTIA HOLMES, academic administrator; m. William H. Lewis. BS in Edn., D.C. Tchrs. Coll.; MA in Edn., George Washington U.; PhD in Early Childhood and Elem. Edn., U. Md. Various tchg. positions primary and secondary edn.; dir. med. and biomed. comm. Howard U. Coll. Medicine, Washington, 1989-93, dean Sch. of Edn., 1993-96; pres. Albany (Ga.) State U., 1996—. Presenter and cons. in field. Active Albany Mus. Art, Albany Tomorrow, Inc., Albany/Dougherty Cmty. Partnership for Edn. and Dougherty, 2000; chair steering com. Am. Reads Program; mem. bd. regents U. Sys. Ga., 1997; bd. dirs. Cmtys. in Schs. Mem.: Albany C. of C. (bd. dirs.), Nat. Coun. for Accreditation Tchr. Edn. (bd. dirs.), Am. Coun. on Edn. (bd. dirs., mem. appeals com.), Orgn. Instnl. Affiliates (bd. dirs.), Am. Assn. Colls. for Tchr. Edn. (bd. dirs.), Am. Assn. State Colls. and Univs. (com. on cultural diversity and social change). Office: Albany State U 504 College Dr Albany GA 31705 E-mail: pshields@asurams.edu.

SHIELDS, V. SUE, federal magistrate judge; b. 1939; AB, Ball State U., 1959; LLB, Ind. U., 1961. Atty. Office of the Regional Counsel, IRS, 1961; dept. atty. gen. Office of the Atty. Gen. of Ind., 1962-64; judge Hamilton Superior Ct., 1965-78, Ind. Ct. Appeals, 1978-94; magistrate judge U.S. Dist. Ct. for So. Dist. Ind., Indpls., 1994—. Office: 256 US Courthouse 46 E Ohio St Indianapolis IN 46204-1903

SHIENTAG, FLORENCE PERLOW, lawyer; b. N.Y.C. d. David and Ester (Germane) Perlow; m. Bernard L. Shientag, June 8, 1938. BS, NYU, 1940, LLB, 1933, JD, 1940. Bar: Fla. 1976, N.Y. Law aide Thomas E. Dewey, 1937; law sec. Mayor La Guardia, 1939-42; justice Domestic Relations Ct., 1941-42; mem. Tchrs. Retirement Bd., N.Y.C., 1942-46; asst. U.S. atty. So. dist. N.Y., 1943-53; cir. ct. mediator Fla. Supreme Ct., 1992; pvt. practice N.Y.C., 1960—, Palm Beach, Fla., 1976—. Lectr. on internat. divorce; mem. Nat. Commn. on Wiretapping and Electronic Surveillance, 1973—, Task Force on Women in Cts., 1985-86. Contbr. articles to profl. jours. Candidate N.Y. State Senate, 1954; bd. dirs. UN Devel. Corp., 1972-95, Franklin and Eleanor Roosevelt Inst., 1985—; bd. dirs., assoc. treas. YM and YWHA; hon. commr. commerce, N.Y.C. Mem. ABA, Fed. Bar Assn. (exec. com.), Internat. Bar Assn., N.Y. Women's Bar Assn. (pres., dir., Life Time Achievement award 1994, special award 2002), N.Y. State Bar Assn., N.Y.C. Bar Assn. (chmn. law and art sect.), N.Y. County Lawyers Assn. (dir.), Nat. Assn. Women LAwyers (sec.). Home: 737 Park Ave New York NY 10021-4256 Address: 44 Cocoanut Row Palm Beach FL 33480

SHIER, GLORIA BULAN, mathematics educator; b. The Philippines; came to U.S., 1966. d. Melecio Cauilan and Florentina (Cumagun) Bulan; m. Wayne Thomas Shier; children: John Thomas, Marie Teresita, Anna Christina. BS, U. Santo Tomas, Manila, Philippines; MA, U. Ill., 1968; PhD, U. Minn., 1986. Tchr. Cagayan (Philippines) Valley Coll., St. Paul Coll., Manila, Manila Div. City Schs.; asst. prof. U. of East, Manila; rsch. asst. U. Ill., Urbana, 1968-69; instr. Miramar Community Coll., San Diego, 1974-75, Mesa Community Coll., San Diego, 1975-80, Lakewood Community Coll., St. Paul, 1984, U. Minn., Mpls., 1986-87, North Hennepin Community Coll., Brooklyn Park, Minn., 1987—. Cons. PWS Kent Pub. Co., Boston, 1989—. Chairperson Filipino Am. Edn. Assn., San Diego, 1978-79. Fulbright scholar U.S. State Dept., U. Ill., 1966-70; fellow Nat. Sci. Found., Oberlin Coll., 1967; recipient Excellence in Teaching award UN Ednl. Scientific Cultural Organ., U. Philippines, Cert. Commendation award The Gov. of Minn., 1990, Outstanding Filipino in the Midwest Edn. Cat. award 1992, Cavite Assn., 1998, Gintong Pamana Found.; Outstanding Filipino-Am. in Edn. Mem.: Am. Statis. Assn., Minn. Math. Assn. of Two Yr. Colls., Minn. Coun. Tchrs. Math., Internat. Group for Psychology of Math. Edn., Am. Math. Assn. for Two Yr. Colls., Nat. Coun. Tchrs. Math., Philippine-Am. Acad. Sci. and Engring., Math. Assn. Am., Am. Math. Soc., Fil-Minnesotan Assn. (bd. dirs. 1991—), Cultural Soc. Filipino-Ams. (pres. 2001—), Sigma Xi, Phi Kappa Phi. Roman Catholic. Avocation: piano. E-mail: gloria.shier@nhcc.mnscu.edu.

SHIER, SHELLEY M. production company executive; b. Toronto, Mar. 15, 1957; d. Harry Shier and Rosaline (Cutler) Sonshine; m. Hank O'Neal, May 14, 1985. Student, H.B. Studio, N.Y.C., 1975-76, Stella Adler Conservatory, 1976-80. Company mem., actor Soho Artists Theater, N.Y.C., 1976-81; casting dir. Lawrence Price Prodns., N.Y.C., 1981-82; pres. Hoss, Inc., N.Y.C., 1983—; v.p. Chiaroscuro Records, N.Y.C., 1987—; pres. Broadway Bound, Inc., N.Y.C., 1998—. Cons. Peter Martin Assocs., N.Y.C., 1983, Norwegian Cruise Line, Miami, Fla., 1983-98, Floating Jazz Festival, 1983—, Big Bands At Sea, Rhythm & Blues Cruise, Dixieland At Sea, 1991—, The Blues Cruise, 1991—, Oslo (Norway) Jazz Festival, 1986—, New Sch. for Social Rsch., N.Y.C., 1989—, Beacons In Jazz Awards Ceremony, A Tribute to the Music of Bob Wills and The Texas Playboys, Mardi Gras at Sea. Talent acquisition agt. Save the Children, N.Y.C., 1986, Tomorrow's Children, N.Y.C., 1990, Royal Caribbean Internat., Miami, 1994-96, Ultimate Caribbean Jazz Spectacular, Country Music Festival in the Caribbean, CUNARD N.Y.C., 1994—, Barcelona Olympics, NBC, 1992, Broadway at Sea, 1996, Millennium at Sea, 1999—, Broadway Bound, 1999—, others. Avocations: Karate, photography, riding, fishing, weightlifting. Office: HOSS Inc 830 Broadway New York NY 10003-4827 E-mail: broadwayboundinc@aol.com.

SHIERSHKE, NANCY FAY, artist, educator, property manager; b. St. Helens, Oreg., May 10, 1935; d. David Cline and Matilda Ruth (Pearce) Morrison; m. H. McNeal Kavanagh, Sept. 4. 1955 (dec. Dec. 1978); children: Marjorie L. Wood, David M. Kavanagh, Katherine F. Fiske; m. Richard M. Shiershke, Nov. 29, 1980. AA, Pasadena (Calif.) City Coll., 1956; BA, UCLA, 1965. Substitute elem. sch. tchr., Buena Park, Calif., 1967-69; property mgr. Pky. Cts., Arcadia, Calif., 1977—; libr. Reading Rm., Arcadia, 1979-87; freelance artist Kavanagh-Shiershke Art St., Arcadia, Calif., 1985—; art gallery hostess Descanso Gardens, La Canada, Flintridge, Calif., 1990—; display and sales person Village Fine Arts Gallery, Arcadia, 1991-92; art instr. Tri Cmty. Adult Edn., Covina, Calif., 1994—, Claremont (Calif.) Art Edn., 1998—. Art instr. Claremont (Calif.) Adult Edn. Group shows include Pasadena Presbyn. Ch., 1985—, Hillcrest Ch., 1992—, Descanso Gardens, 1994—, San Gabriel Fine Arts, 1994—. Named Artist of the Yr. Mid Valley art League, 1990; Recipient Best of Show San Gabriel Fine Arts, 1991, Hulsebus award Pasadena Prebyn. Ch., 1996, Best of Show Eagle Rock Rennaisance Plein Air, 2002. Mem. Nat. Watercolor Soc., San Gabriel Fine Arts, Mid Valley Arts League (Artist of Yr. 1998), East Valley Art Assn., Valley Watercolor Soc., Foothill Creative Arts Group, Water Color West, Calif. Art Club.

SHIFFLETT, AUDREY HORTON, academic administrator, researcher; d. Lambert Dewain and Lunette Hammett Horton; m. Andrew Eric Shifflett, May 24, 1997. BA, Wofford Coll., 1988; MA, U. SC, 1991. Cert. Certified Grants Specialist SC, 2003. Tech. writer U. SC, Columbia, SC, 1991—94; biomedical editor U. Miami Sch. Medicine, Miami, Fla., 1994—96; prodn. mgr. SC Ednl. TV, Columbia, SC, 1997—2001; dir. grants Columbia Coll., 2001—. Comm. cons. Bayer Pharm. Divsn., 1996—98. Prodn.mgr. (radio) Marian McPartland's Piano Jazz (NY Internat. Radio Festival, 2000). Citizens police acad. City of Columbia Police Dept., Columbia, SC, 2003. Recipient Phi Beta Kappa, Wofford Coll., 1988. Mem.: Assn. Fundraising Profls., Coun. Advancement Support of Edn. Office: Columbia Coll 1301 Columbia College Dr Columbia SC 29203 Business E-Mail: ashiff@colacoll.edu.

SHIFFMAN, LESLIE BROWN, management executive; b. Fresno, Calif., Dec. 9, 1936; d. Albert Brown and Marion Jean (Riese) Brown-Propp; married, Jan. 20, 1957 (div. 1972); m. Sydney Shiffman, July 4, 1993; children: Susan, Steven, David, Thomas. BS, U. So. Calif., 1958. Office mgr. pvt. practice physician, Long Beach, Calif., 1971-73; cost acct. Panavision, Inc., Tarzana, Calif., 1974-76; exec. sec. Hartman Galleries, Beverly Hills, Calif., 1976-78; adminstrv. exec., corp. treas. Galanos Originals, L.A., 1978-98; adminstrv. asst., rabbinic asst., dir. adult edn. Sinai Temple, L.A., 1998—2002. Alt. del. Nat. Panhellenic Conf., 2003—. Mem. LA Alumnae Panhellenic (v.p.), Woman of Yr. 2000), Alpha Epsilon Phi (nat. pres. 1985-89, 99-2003, trustee 1985-2003, sec. Found. Inc. 1990-91, pres. 1991-95, treas. 1996-98, Woman of Distinction award 1993), Order of Omega, L.A. Alumnae Panhellenic Assn. (v.p. 2003—). Democrat. Jewish. Avocation: designing and hand knitting sweaters. Home: 1745 S Bentley Ave Apt 1 Los Angeles CA 90025-4323 E-mail: lbshiffman@aol.com.

SHIH, PATRICIA ALICE, musician, writer, artist; d. Frank Pao-Hu and Alice Shih; m. Stephen Fricker, June 21, 1997; 1 child, Jennifer Mei Ross. BFA, Lone Mt. Coll. and Acad. of Art Coll., San Francisco, 1975. Adminstrv. asst. to chair, dance dept. U. Md., 1971—72; adminstrv. asst. to chair, art dept. Lone Mt. Coll., San Francisco, 1975—76; prop artist Am. Conservatory Theatre, San Francisco, 1977—78; stained glass instr. Acad. of Art Coll., San Francisco, 1977—79; painting and stained glass instr. Nassau CC, Garden City, NY, 1979—99; mgr., designer Stained Glass Workshop, Syosset, NY, 1979—84; pres. Shih Enterprises, Inc., Huntington, NY, 1984—. Audition judge Huntington Idol/Music For Molly, Huntington, NY, 2003; com. judge pub. art panel Town of Huntington (N.Y.), 2003. CD and Tape recording, Big Ideas!, 1990, Making Fun!, 1996 (Parent's Choice award, 1997), Leap of Faith, 1988, Woman with 1 Closed Eye, 1998; author: (book) Gigging: A Practical Guide for Musicians, 2003. Guest artist Girl Scouts of Am., Washington, 1997, 2002, N.Y. Metro Girl Scouts, N.Y.C., 2002. Named L.I. Woman of Distinction, 2004; recipient Hon. Mention, Am. Song Writing Competition, 1st Pl. Song Writing, Babylon Arts Coun., numerous scholastic and art awards, N.Y. Songwriters Showcase. Mem.: Children's Music Network, Folk Alliance. Avocations: antiques, art, glass, miniatures, travel. Office: Shih Enterprises Inc PO Box 1554 Huntington NY 11743-0658

SHIH-CARDUCCI, JOAN CHIA-MO, cooking educator, biochemist, medical technologist, author, writer; b. Rukuan, Chunghua, Taiwan, Dec. 21, 1933; came to U.S., 1955; d. Luke Chiang-hsi and Lien-chin (Chang) Shih; m. Kenneth M. Carducci, Sept. 30, 1960 (dec. July 1988); children: Suzanne R., Elizabeth M. BS in Chemistry, St. Mary Coll., Xavier, Kans., 1959; intern in med. tech., St. Mary's Hosp., Rochester, N.Y., 1960. Med. rschr. Strong Meml. Hosp. U. Rochester, 1960-61; pharm. chemist quality control Strasenburgh Labs., Rochester, 1961-62; cooking tchr. adult edn. Montgomery County Pub. Schs., Rockville, Md., 1973-79; tchr. The Chinese Cookery Inc., Rockville, 1975-86, Silver Spring, Md., 1986—, pres., bd. dirs., 1975—; chemist NIH, Bethesda, 1987-2000; analytical chemist NIH/WRAIR, Rockville, Md., 1994-96. Author: The Chinese Cookery, 1981, Hunan Cuisine, 1984, Vegetarian Cuisine, 2000, The Art of The Chinese Cookery, 2001. Mem. Am. Chem. Soc., Internat. Assn. Cooking Profls. (Woman of Yr. 1994-2000). Republican. Roman Catholic. Avocations: piano, music, dance, flowers, vegetables. Home and Office: The Chinese Cookery Inc 14209 Sturtevant Rd Silver Spring MD 20905-4448 Office Phone: 301-236-5311.

SHIKASHIO, HIROKO, artist, interpreter, educator; b. Japan; d. Koichi and Kaoru Ogihara; m. Tommy Kiyoshi Shikashio, July 26, 1969; children: Christopher, Michael. BD, Japan Christian Coll., Tokyo, 1965; BFA, Calif. State Coll., L.A., 1969. Coord. internat. art exch. R.I. Watercolor Soc., Pawtucket, 1984—86; coord. internat. art exhibit 19 On Paper, Providence, 1995—97; coord. cultural tour and workshop Japan Cultural Tour and Workshop, 2002—. Mag. cover, Lit. Mag. of Bryant Coll. Surge, 1996, New Art Internat., 2001, R.I. Medicine Health, 2003, book cover, Creation Regained, 1989, one-woman shows include Newport (R.I.) Art Mus., 2002. Recipient Gold prize, New Haven Paints and Clay Club, 1988, award, R.I. Watercolor Soc., 1992, Theilen Meml. award, Watercolor USA, Springfield, Mo., 1995, Jurors award, Wash. & Jefferson Coll., 1996, First Pl. award, Glastonbury (Conn.) Art Show, 1997, Newport Art Mus. award, Newport Artist Guild, 2001, First Pl. in Mixed Media, Narragansett (R.I.) Art Show, 2002, Best in Show, Old Saybrook (Conn.) Art Show, 2002. Mem.: Watercolor USA Honor Soc. (licentiate), 19 On Paper (licentiate), New Haven Paints and Clay Club (licentiate), Pa. Watercolor Soc. (licentiate), R.I. Watercolor Soc. (licentiate).

SHILLING, JENNIFER, state official; b. Oshkosh, Wis., July 4, 1969; married. BA, U. Wis., 1992. State assemblywoman, Wis., 2000—. Mem. fin. instns. com.; mem. health com.; mem. ins. com.; mem. Minn.-Wis. Boundary Area Commn.; mem. personal privacy com. Congl. aide to U.S. Rep. Ron Kind; mem. La Crosse County Dem. Party, La Crosse County LWV. Democrat. Office: State Capitol PO Box 8953 Madison WI 53708-8953

SHILLINGSBURG, MIRIAM JONES, English educator, academic administrator; b. Balt., Oct. 5, 1943; d. W. Elvin and Miriam R. Jones; m. Peter L. Shillingsburg, Nov. 21, 1967; children: Robert, George, John, Alice, Anne Carol. BA, Mars Hill Coll., 1964; MA, U. S.C., 1966, PhD, 1969; BGS, Miss. State U., 1994. Asst. prof. Limestone Coll., Gaffney, S.C., 1969, Miss. State U., 1970-75, assoc. prof., 1975-80, prof. English, 1980-96, assoc. v.p. for acad. affairs, 1988-96, dir. summer sch., 1990-96, dir. undergrad. studies, 1994-96; dean arts and scis. Lamar U., Tex., 1996-99; dean liberal arts and scis. Ind. U., South Bend, 2000—04. Disting. acad. visitor Mark Twain Cir., 1993, 2001; Simms rsch. prof. U. S.C., 1998; vis. fellow Australian Def. Force Acad., 1989; Fulbright lectr. U. New South Wales, Duntroon, Australia, 1984-85. NEH fellow in residence, Columbia U., 1976-77. Author: Mark Twain in Australasia, 1988; editor: Conquest of Granada, 1988, The Cub of the Panther, 1997; mem. editl. bd. Works of W.M. Thackeray, Miss. Quar., So. Quar.; contbr. articles to profl. jours. and mags. Mem. South Ctrl. 18th Century Soc., Am. Lit. Assn., Pop Culture Assn., Sigma Tau Delta, Phi Kappa Phi, Simms Soc. (pres. 1996-97). E-mail: mshillin@iusb.edu.

SHILTS, NANCY S. automotive executive, lawyer; b. Clinton, Mass., Feb. 10, 1942; BA, Smith Coll., 1963; JD, U. Mich., 1980. Bar: Mich. 1980. Assoc. gen. counsel Fed.-Mogul Corp., Southfield, Mich. Mem. ABA, State Bar Mich. Office: Fed Mogul Corp 26555 Northwestern Hwy Southfield MI 48034-2199

SHIMELMAN, SUSAN FROMM, state policy administrator; b. NYC, May 5, 1942; BA, McGill U., Montreal, 1964; MS, Columbia U., 1970. Fellow Harvard U., Cambridge, Mass., 1964-65; Can. coun. fellow McGill U., Montreal, 1965-68; asst. dir. Yale-New Haven Hosp., 1970-80; exec. dir. New Haven Jewish Fedn., 1980-90; undersec. Office Policy and Mgmt., State of Conn., Hartford, 1991-94, sec., 1994—95, dir. presdl. debates, 1995; dir. spl. cts. jud. br. State of Conn., 1995—2001; dir. Office Fiscal Analysis, 2001—. Chair Prison and Jail Overcrowding Commn., Hartford, 1990—, Health Care State Conn., Hartford, 1992—, Exec. Com. Info. and Tech., Hartford, 1994; vice chair Cmty. Econ. Devel. Found., Hartford, 1994. Bd. dirs. Fedn. United Way, New Haven, 1970-94; alt. N.E. Regional Compact, N.J. and Conn., 1991-94; active A Conn. Party, Hartford, 1990-94. Recipient Pres. award New Haven Jewish Fedn., 1990; named Powerful Woman of Vision, YWCA, 1988. Democrat. Home: 4 Kensington Park Bloomfield CT 06002-2146

SHIMMIN, MARGARET ANN, women's health nurse; b. Forbes, N.D., Oct. 26, 1941; d. George and Reba S. Diploma in Nursing, St. Luke's Hosp. Sch. Nursing, Fargo, N.D., 1962; BSW, U. West Fla., 1978; cert. ob-gyn nurse practitioner, U. Ala., Birmingham, 1983, MPH, 1986. Lic. nurse, Fla., N.D., Ala. Head nurse, emergency room St. Luke's Hosps., Fargo, 1962-67; charge nurse, labor and delivery, perinatal nurse educator Sacred Heart Hosp., Pensacola, Fla., 1970-82; ARNP Escambia County Pub. Health Unit, Pensacola, 1983-89; cmty. health nursing cons. Dist. 1 Health and Rehab. Svcs., Pensacola, 1989-96; sr. cmty. health nursing supr. Escambia County Health Dept., Pensacola, 1996—. Capt. nurse corps U.S. Army, 1967-70, Japan. Mem. NAACOG (cert. maternal-gynecol.-neonatal nursing 1978, ob-gyn nurse practitioner 1983), Fla. Nurses' Assn., ANA, N.W. Fla. ARNP (past sec./treas.), Fla. Perinatal Assn., Nat. Perinatal Assn., Healthy Mothers/Healthy Babies Coalition, Fla. Pub. Health Assn., U. West Fla. Alumni Assn., U. Ala. at Birmingham Sch. of Public Health Alumni Assn., Phi Alpha. Republican. Presbyterian. Avocations: cooking, music, travel, photography, reading. Home: 8570 Olympia Rd Pensacola FL 32514-8029 Office: Escambia County Health Dept 1295 W Fairfield Dr Pensacola FL 32501-1107

SHIMOKUBO, JANICE TERUKO, marketing professional; b. Chgo. d. Paul Kazuso and Tsugiye Jane (Fujii) Shimokubo; m. Ronald Theodore Spreigl, Jan. 3, 1982; 1 child, Elizabeth Shimokubo Spreigl. BA, U. Ill., 1973; MBA, Loyola U., Chgo., 1976. Sales rep. 3M Co., Rockford, Ill., 1976-79, mktg. coord. St. Paul, 1979-81, mktg. supr., 1981-83, mktg. mgr., 1983-88, sales and mktg. mgr., 1988-90; mktg. dir. U S WEST Comms., Inc., Phoenix, 1990-95, exec. dir. Denver, 1995—. Advisor Jr. Achievement, St. Paul, 1980-82; mem. 3M Women's Adv. Coun., St. paul, 1984-87. Commr. Colo. Civil Rights commn., Denver, 1997—; bd. dirs. Ariz. Kidney Found., Phoenix, 1994-95, Phoenix Fire Pals, 1990-92, Melpomene Women's Health, St. Paul., 1986, YWCA USA, 1998—. Recipient Unity award KWGN-TV, 1997; Asian Pacific Am. Women's Leadership Inst. fellow, 1996. Fellow Internat. Women's Forum, 1998-99; mem. Am. Mktg. Assn. (nat. bd. dirs. 1999—), Women in Cable and Telecomms., Japanese Am. Citizens League, U. Ill. Alumni Assn., Alpha Omicron Pi. Avocations: golf, yoga, travel, needlework. Home: 440 N Wabash Avenue Apt 2507 Chicago IL 60611

SHIN, I. MIA, real estate broker, interior designer; arrived in U.S., 1968; d. Michael Chang and Tae Uh Shin. BA, San Diego State, Calif., 1982. Pres. Mia Shin Inc., L.A., 1997—2002; mktg. dir. Remington Pvt. Estates, L.A., 2002—03; pres. Global Prop Internat., L.A., 2003—. Recipient top sales, Crescent Heights of Am., Fla., 2002. Mem.: B.H. Bd. Realtors. Republican. Achievements include have sold 30 million dollars in resdental condos in L.A. westside. Avocations: interior decorating, real estate development. Office: Global Properties Internat 10433 Wilshire Bldg Ste 1010 Los Angeles CA 90024

SHINABERY, KIMBERY ANN, minister; b. Lima, Ohio, Dec. 17, 1958; d. E. Ray and Barbara Anne Shinabery. BS, Defiance (Ohio) Coll., 1981; MA, U. Denver, 1990; MDiv, Iliff Sch. Theology, 1994. Ordained to ministry United Ch. of Christ, 1997. Adminstrv. positions U. of Denver, Denver, 1987—2002; chaplain Mt. St. Vincent Home, Denver, 1999—. Dir. Christian edn. Sylvania (Ohio) United Ch. Christ, 1981—87; on-call chaplain The Children's Hosp., Denver, 1999—2001; adj. faculty design for leadership Defiance Coll., Denver, 1997—2001; min. edn. Sixth Ave. United Ch., Denver, 1994—99. Ohio conf. del. United Ch. of Christ Gen. Synod, 1983—85; com. mem. N.W. Ohio Assn. United Ch. Christ Christian Edn., Tiffin, Ohio, 1981—87; dir., tchr., counselor youth camping programs Ohio Conf. United Ch. Christ, Columbus, Ohio, 1981—87; vol. chaplain Dept. Corrections, Denver, 1997—98; vol. Big Sisters/Big Bros. of Greater Toledo, Toledo, 1982—87. Recipient Schauffler award, 1981; Vinnik fellow, U. Denver Ctr. for Judaic Studies & Inst. for Interfaith Studies, 1989—90. Office: Mt St Vincent Home 4144 Lowell Blvd Denver CO 80211 Personal E-mail: chapelkim@onebox.com.

SHINDER, LORRAINE SUSAN, contract administrator, educator; b. Far Rockaway, N.Y., June 10, 1952; d. Cherie Starr Allen and Floyd Shinder; 1 child, Justine Kerner. BA, Calif. State U., Northridge, 1988—90. Sr. contract adminstr. Eaton Aerospance, L.A., 2001—02; contract coord. CKE Restaurants, Carpinteria, Calif., 2002— . Prof. Moorpark Coll., Calif., 1998—. Mem.: Nat. Contract Mgmt. Assn. (assoc.). Liberal. Jewish. Avocations: web design, writing, walking, swimming, travel. Home: 2638 Discovery Cove Port Hueneme CA 93041 Office: CKE Restaurants 6307 Carpinteria Ave Carpinteria CA 93013 Personal E-mail: lshinder@aol.com. E-mail: lshinder@ckr.com.

SHINER, JOSETTE SHEERAN, ambassador; b. Orange, N.J., June 12, 1954; d. James Joseph and Sarah Ann (Gallagher) Sheeran; children: Nicole Munter, Daniel John, Gabrielle. BA, U. Colo., 1976. Nat. desk editor N.Y. News World, 1976-77, Washington bur. chief, 1977-80; corr. The White House, 1980-82; Capital Life and mag. editor Washington Times, 1982-84, asst. mng. editor, 1984-85, dep. mng. editor, 1985-92, mng. editor, 1992-97; pres., CEO Empower Am., 1997-2000; mng. dir. TIS Worldwide, Reston, Va., 2000—01; assoc. U.S. trade repr. for policy & comm Exec. Office of the Pres., Washington, 2001—03, dep. U.S. trade repr., 2003—. Mem. Leadership Washington Alumni Assn., 1987-88, v.p., 1988-89, alumni chmn., 1989-90. Recipient Atrium award U. Ga., 1984, 100 Most Powerful Women in Washington award Washington Mag., 1998. Mem. White House Corrs. Assn., Am. News Womens Club, Nat. Press Club (newsmaker chmn. 1980-82, Meritorious Svc. award 1981, Vivian award 1981), Am. Soc. Newspaper Editors, Coun. Fgn. Rels. (Washington adv. bd. 1999—), Sigma Delta Chi. Office: 600 17th St NW Rm 201 Washington DC 20508

SHINEVAR, KAREN KAY, lawyer; b. Marshall, Mich., Mar. 16, 1956; d. Wayne Alden and Elizabeth Marilyn (Albrecht) Coats; m. Peter O'Neil Shinevar, Aug. 25, 1979; children: Thomas Scott, William Joseph. BA in History and Econs. summa cum laude, Albion Coll., 1978; JD, U. Mich., 1981. Bar: D.C. 1981, Md. 1982, N.Y. 1994. Assoc. Seifman, Semo & Slevin, Washington, 1981-82; atty. MCI Airsignal, Inc., Washington, 1983-86; v.p. McCaw Cellular Comm., Washington, 1986-91; v.p., gen. counsel Cellular Telephone Co. dba AT&T Wireless Svcs., Paramus, NJ, 1992—98, v.p. ops., 1995-98. Mem. Oradell Pub. Sch. Bd. Edn., 1999—2002, pres., 2000—01, Oradel PTA, 2002—04. Avocations: reading, tennis. E-mail: shinevar@optonline.net.

SHINOLT, EILEEN THELMA, artist; b. Washington, May 18, 1919; d. Edward Lee and Blanche Addie (Marsh) Bennett; m. John Francis Shinolt, June 14, 1956 (dec. Aug. 1969). Student, Hans Hoffman Sch Art, 1949, Pa. Acad. Arts, 1950, Corcoran Sch. Art, 1945-51, Am. U., 1973-77. Sect. chief Dept. Army, Washington, 1940-73, retired, 1973. One-woman shows include various locations, 1982, 83, 85, 90, 94, 96; group shows include Perlmutter & Co., 1981, Fitch Fox and Brown, 1986, Foundry Gallery, 1987, Ann. Add Arts, 1986, Westminster Gallery, London, 1995; represented in permanent collections Women's Nat. Mus., Washington, Cameo Gallery, Columbia, S.C., Strathmore Hall Arts Ctr., North Bethesda, Md., 1997, 98, 99, 2000, Internat. Monetary Fund Members Show, Washington, 2000. Mem. Woman's Nat. Dem. Club, Washington, 1980—. Mem. Am. Art League (editor newsletter 1985-86, 1st pl. 1987, 2d pl. 1986), Arts Club Washington (exhbn. com. 1985—, admissions com. 1987-88), Miniature Painters, Sculptors & Gravers Soc. (historian 1989—, editor newsletter 1986-89). Roman Catholic. Avocations: reading, studying art periodicals, art galleries. Home: 4119 Davis Pl NW Apt 203 Washington DC 20007-1254

SHIPP, THETA WANZA, social service organization administrator, educator, consultant, minister; b. Miami, Fla., June 19, 1948; d. James Willie and Fredericka Wanza; m. Robert Glenn Shipp, June 28, 1970 (div. Aug. 1975); children: Tammi LaTrice, Eloria April Michelle. BA, Fisk U., 1970; MS, So. Ill. U., 1977; postgrad., Howard U. Ordained to ministry Christian Faith Ctrs., 1998. Asst. program dir. U. South Fla., Tampa, 1971-72; adminstr. City of Tampa, 1972-74; adminstrv. supr. Juvenile Svcs. Program, St. Petersburg, Fla., 1974-76; staff asst. City of Carbondale, Ill., 1976-77; tchg./rsch. asst., editl. asst. So. Ill. U., Carbondale, 1977-78; staff asst. U.S. Rep. Claude Pepper, Washington, 1978-82; legis./spl. asst. U.S. Rep. Mervyn M. Dymally, Washington, 1982-87; chief of staff U.S. Rep. Major R. Owens, Washington, 1987-88, U.S. Rep. Earl F. Hilliard, Washington, 1993-95; project dir. Nat. Assn. for Equal Opportunity in Higher Edn., Washington, 1998-99; asst. to v.p. for pub. policy Planned Parenthood Fedn. of Am., Washington, 2000—01; instr. D.C. Pub. Schs., 2001—. Ind. cons., 1989-03; part-time instr. dept. sociology Howard U., 1978-82. Campaign worker various congl. campaigns, 1976-2000, campaign fundraiser, 1978-97; mem. ministerial staff Michigan Park Christian Ch., Washington, 2000—; vol. Black Ch. Initiative, Religious Coalition for Reproductive Choice, Washington, 2000; ministerial cons. Soul Saving Sta., Miami, 1990—; campaign coord. Dem. Nat. Com. Office of African Am. Religious Outreach, Washington, 2000. Named one of Outstanding Young Women in Am.; recipient recognition United Negro Coll. Fund, Assn. Urban Univs., Southeastern Coun. on Ednl. Opportunity Assn., Internat. Bus. and Exec. Women, Women's Dept. Ministry of Help. Mem. NAACP, Nat. Urban League, Am. Sociol. Assn., Nat. Black Women's Agenda, Nat. Coalition on Black Civic Participation, Nat. Coalition for Black Voter Participation, Friends of Africa, Delta Sigma Theta, Alpha Kappa Delta, Phi Delta Lambda. Democrat. Avocations: reading, witnessing, movies, swimming, gardening. Home: 1441 N W 168th Terr Miami FL 33169

SHIPPEY, SANDRA LEE, lawyer; b. Casper, Wyo., June 24, 1957; d. Virgil Carr and Doris Louise (Conklin) McClintock; m. Ojars Herberts Ozols, Sept. 2, 1978 (div.); children: Michael Ojars, Sara Ann, Brian Christopher; m. James Robert Shippey, Jan. 13, 1991; 1 child, Matthew James. BA with distinction, U. Colo., 1978; JD magna cum laude, Boston U., 1982. Bar: Colo. 1982, U.S. Dist. Ct. Colo. 1985. Assoc. Cohen, Brame & Smith, Denver, 1983-84, Parcel, Meyer, Schwartz, Ruttum & Mauro, Denver, 1984-85, Mayer, Brown & Platt, Denver, 1985-87; counsel western ops. GE Capital Corp., San Diego, 1987-94; assoc. Page, Polin, Busch & Boatwright, San Diego, 1994-95; v.p., gen. counsel First Comml. Corp., San Diego, 1995-96; legal counsel NextWave Telecom Inc., San Diego, 1996-98; ptnr. Procopio, Cory, Hargreaves and Savitch, LLP, 1998—. Spkr. in field. Contbr. articles to profl. jours. Active Pop Warner football and cheerleading; bd. dirs. Southwestern Christian Schs., Inc., 2002—, San Diego Christian Found., 2001—. Mem. Calif. State Bar (uniform comml. code com.), Phi Beta Kappa, Phi Delta Phi. Republican. Mem. Ch. of Christ. Avocations: tennis, golf, photography. Home: 15839 Big Springs Way San Diego CA 92127-2034 Office: Procopio Cory Et Al 530 B St Ste 2100 San Diego CA 92101-4496 Office Phone: 619-515-3226. E-mail: sls@procopio.com.

SHIRE, LYDIA, food service executive; b. Brookline, Mass. Grad., Cordon Bleu Cooking Sch., London, 1970. Chef Maison Robert, Boston, Harvest, Cambridge, Mass.; restaurant chef Cafe Plaza; chef Parker's, 1981; opened with Jasper White Seasons Restaurant, exec. chef, Four Seasons Hotel on Beverly Hills, Calif., 1986—89; chef, owner Biba, Boston, 1989—, Pignoli, Boston, 1994—. Named Cafe Plaza as Best Dining Rm., Boston mag., One of Am.'s Ten Best Chefs, Food & Wine mag., Pignoli as One of Top Boston Dining Spots, Food & Wine, Biba as One of Top 15 Restaurants in U.S., Money mag., Biba as Best Restaurant in Boston, Boston mag.; recipient Four Stars for Cafe Plaza, Boston Globe, Ivy award. Mem.: Am. Inst. Wine and Food, James Beard Found. (Am.'s Best Chef of N.E., One of Top Chefs in Am.). Office: Biba 272 Boylston St Boston MA 02116

SHIRE, TALIA ROSE, actress; b. Jamaica, N.Y., Apr. 25, 1946; d. Carmine and Italia (Pennino) Coppola; m. David Lee Shire, Mar. 29, 1970 (div.); 1 son, Matthew Orlando; m. Jack Schwartzman, Aug. 23, 1979; children: Jason Francesco, Robert Coppola. Films include The Dunwich Horrors, 1971, The Christian Licorice State, 1971, Godfather, 1972, The Outside Man, 1973, Godfather II, 1974 (Oscar nominee for Best Supporting Actress), Rocky, 1976 (Oscar nominee for best actress, N.Y. Film Critics award for Best Supporting Actress), Old Boyfriends, 1979, Rocky II, 1979, Windows, 1980, Rocky III, 1982, Rocky IV, 1985, Bed and Breakfast, 1990, Gold Heaven, 1990, Godfather Part III, 1990, Rocky V, 1990, Cold Heaven, 1992, Bed & Breakfast, 1992, Deadfall, 1993, (Disney channel movie) Mark Twain, 1990, (HBO movie) getting there, 1991, She's So Lovely, 1997, Lured Innocence, 1998, Divorce: A Contemporary Western, 1998, Can I Play?, 1998, Palmer's Pick Up, 1999, Caminho dos Sonhos, 1999, Lured Innocence, 1999, The Visit, 2000; TV appearances include Foster & Laurie, 1975, Rich Man, Poor Man, 1976, Kill Me If You Can, 1977, Daddy, I Don't Like It Like This, 1978, Blood Vows, 1987, Mark Twain and Me, 1991, For Richer, For Poorer, 1992, Chatilly Lace, 1993, Born into Exile, 1997; prodr. Homo Sapien: People from Another Star, 1986, Lionheart, 1987; assoc. prodr.: The Landlady, 1998.

SHIRIKIAN-HESSELTON, JOAN LEE, safety engineer; b. Schenectady, N.Y.; d. Cecilia Fava Shirikian; m. Clair Russell Hesselton, Mar. 26, 1993. BA in Chemistry, Coll. St. Rose, Albany, N.Y., 1974; MBA, Union Coll., 1986; postgrad., Columbia So. U. Forensic scientist N.Y. State Police, Albany, 1973-86; chair statewide labor mgmt. safety and health com. Pub. Employees Fedn., Albany, 1986-90; agy. safety dir. 2 N.Y. State Office Gen. Svcs., Albany, 1990-96, N.Y. State Workers Compensation Bd., Albany, 1996-99; N.E. regional safety dir. Oldcastle Precast, Inc., S. Bethlehem, N.Y., 1999—. Mem. Am. Soc. Safety Engrs., Am. Indsl. Hygiene Assn., Am. Soc. Pub. Health. Avocations: veterans benefits, fibers, spinning, wild animal care. Home: 428 Settles Hill Rd Altamont NY 12009-5712 Office: Oldcastle Precast Inc 100 County Rte 101 PO Box 155 South Bethlehem NY 12161-0133

SHIRKEY, LINDA SUE, interior designer, film company executive, set designer; b. Denver, June 29, 1948; d. Roger L. and Virginia Ruth (Lee) Williams; m. Larry Wayne, May 2, 1972 (div. Aug. 1982); children Troy Lee, Ian Christopher. BFA, U. Colo., Denver and Boulder, 1970; AAS, Arapahoe C.C., Littleton, 1985. Figure skating coach, Denver, 1972-84; interior design Possibilities For Design, Denver, 1983-85; interior designer For Men Only, Inc., Denver, 1985-95; film prodn. mgr., set styling & interior design Desciose Prodns., Denver, 1991—; pres. Prodn. & Design, Inc., 1996—. Prodn. mgr. (pub. svc. announcement) Going Home-Colo. Christian Home, 1992 (Emmy nomination, 1992), We'll Be There-Heartland chpt. ARC, 2000, Nat. Stroke Assn., 2001. Pres. Sina Care Ctrs., Inc., holistic Healing & Tchg., 1997—; bd. dirs. Front Range Ctr. for Spiritual Growth, Denver, 1993—95, pres., 1995. Mem.: Internat. Interior Design Assn., Fellowship of Yoga, Rotary (US sec. 2001—), Denver Mile High Rotary (chair cmty. svc. 1993—94, fellowship chair 1996—97, joint sec. Rotary Internat. Fellowship of Yoga 2001—03). Avocations: figure skating, coaching figure skating, yoga. Office: Prodn & Design Inc PO Box 100865 Denver CO 80250-0865 Office Phone: 303-946-3196.

SHIRLEY, COURTNEY DYMALLY, nurse; b. Trinidad, July 17; came to U.S., 1960; d. Andrew Hamid Dymally; m. Adolph Shirley, Apr. 8, 1960; children: Ingrid, Robyne, Andrea, Kirk, Sandra. Cert. mgmt./adminstrn. health facilities, UCLA, 1978; BBA, Calif. Coast U., 1980, MBA, 1983. Cert. critical care nurse, advanced critical care nurse, nursing home adminstr., legal nurse cons. Head nurse med. unit Prince of Wales Gen. Hosp., London, 1959-60; asst. head nurse, CCU staff nurse Cedars-Sinai Hosp., L.A., 1962-73; asst. dir. nursing, dir. in-svc. edn., staff nurse Beverly Glen Hosp., 1973-75; supr. ICU/CCU/house Imperial Hosp., 1975-76; house supr. Med. Ctr. of North Hollywood, 1976-77; dir. nursing Crenshaw Ctr. Hosp., 1977-78, Mid-Wilshire Convalescent, 1978-79; supr. ICU/CCU, coord. utilization rev. Temple U., 1979-80; house supr. East L.A. Doctors' Hosp., 1980-81; pvt. nurse various hosps. and homes, 1981-86; utilization rev. coord. Managed Care Resources, L.A., 1986-88; prof. rev. sys. utilization rev. coord., case mgr. Nat. Med. Enterprises, Santa Monica, Calif., 1988—, case mgr., 1993-97; adminstr. Tri-Med Home Care, Inc., Thousand Oaks, Calif., 1997—. Mem. AACN, Internat. Case Mgmt. Assn., Sci. of Mind, Toastmasters (sgt. at arms 1990). Avocations: reading, Scrabble, dominoes, entertaining, blackjack. Office: Tri-Med Home Care Inc 299 W Hillcrest Dr Thousand Oaks CA 91360-4264

SHIRLEY, DONNA, former aerospace engineer, management consultant, speaker; b. Wynnewood, Okla. 1 child, Laura. BS in Aerospace Engring.,

BA in Journalism, U. Okla.; MS in Aerospace Engring., U. So. Calif. With Jet Propulsion Lab., Pasadena, Calif., 1966—, Cassini project engr., mgr. exploration initiative studies, mgr. automation and robotics, mgr. Space Sta. program, mgr. mission design sect., project engr. for Mariner 10, mgr. Mars Pathfinder microrover Flight Experiment team, mgr. Mars exploration program, mgr., 1990, pres. Managing Creativity, Norman, Okla. Leader NASA-wide Sys. Engring. Working Group, 1990-93; leader NASA-wide team on program/project mgmt. NASA, 1991. Author: Managing Martians, 1998. Address: 3911 Bagley Avenue N Seattle WA 98103

SHIRLEY, VIRGINIA LEE, advertising executive; b. Kankakee, Ill., Mar. 24, 1936; d. Glenn Lee and Virginia Helen (Ritter) S. Student, Northwestern U., 1960-61. With prodn. control dept. Armour Pharm., Kankakee, 1954-58; exec. sec. Adolph Richman, Chgo., 1958-61; mgr. media dept. Don Kemper Co., Chgo., 1961-63, 65-69; exec. sec. Playboy mag., Chgo., 1964-65; exec. v.p. SMY Media inc., Chgo., 1969-96, CEO, chmn. bd., 1996-2000, CEO, 2000—. Mem. Tavern Club. Home: 1502-J S Prairie Ave Chicago IL 60605-2856 Office: SMY Media Inc 333 N Michigan Ave Chicago IL 60601-3901

SHIVELY, BONNIE LEE, pastor; b. Dover, Del., Feb. 13, 1961; d. Donald Hudson and Nancy (Durham) Shively. BS, Salisbury (Md.) U., 1984; MDiv, Wesley Theol. Sem., Washington, 1997. Ordained deacon Meth. Ch., 1995, ordained elder Meth. Ch., 2000. Pastor Church Creek (Md.) United Meth. Ch., 1993—97, Bethel United Meth. Ch., Dagsboro, Del., 1997—2003; pastor of caring ministries Kent Island United Meth. Ch., Chester, Md., 2003—. Vol. Cmty. Food Pantry, Selbyville, Del., 1997—2003; mem. Friends of Prince George's Chapel, Dagsboro, 1998—2003, Dover (Del.) Dist. Hispanic Ministries Com., 1999—2002; mem. adv. bd. Interfaith Vol. Caregivers, Frankford, Del., 1999—2002; chaplain Church Creek Vol. Fire Co., 1993—97; bd. dirs. Del. Ecumenical Coun., Wilmington, 2000—03. Mem.: Commn. on Archives and History (sec. 1998—), Dagsboro Century Club. Avocations: genealogy, local history, needlework. Office: Kent Island United Meth Ch 2739 Cox Neck Rd PO Box 308 Chester MD 21619 Office Phone: 410-643-5361.

SHIVELY, JUDITH CAROLYN (JUDY SHIVELY), contract administrator; b. Wilkinsburg, Pa., Jan. 30, 1962; d. John Allen and Edith (Crowell) S. BA in English, U. Nev., Las Vegas, 1984. Circulation aide Charleston Heights Libr., Las Vegas, 1979—86; asst. food editor Las Vegas Sun Newspaper, 1985—88, asst. horse racing editor, 1985—90, features writer, page editor, 1988—89, editor youth activities sect., 1989—90; racebook ticket writer, cashier Palace Sta. Hotel Racebook, Las Vegas, 1989—92; contract adminstr. nat. accts. Loomis, Fargo & Co., Las Vegas, 1992—2000; propr. Creative Computing, Las Vegas, 1996—; content prodn. Preference Techs., Inc., Las Vegas, 2000; data rsch. and processing PurchasePro.com, Las Vegas, 2000; adminstrv. asst. Uinta Bus. Systems, Las Vegas, 2001—02, Law Office of Frank Sorrentino, Las Vegas, 2003—. Horse racing historian, rschr., Las Vegas, 1985—; vol. rsch. asst. Dictionary of Gambling and Gaming, 1982-84; part-time clk. Hometown News, Las Vegas, 1994-96. Staff writer horse race handicaps, columns, articles, feature stories Las Vegas Sun Newspaper, 1985-90; freelance writer for monthly horse racing publ. Inside Track, 1992-94. Mem. Phi Beta Kappa. Republican. Avocations: collecting horse racing books, clippings, materials for personal library of horse racing, computers. Home: PO Box 26426 Las Vegas NV 89126-0426 E-mail: racehors1@aol.com.

SHIVES, PAULA J, lawyer; b. Monongahela, Pa., Sept. 28, 1950; BA, Western Ky. U., 1973; JD, U. Ky., 1979. Bar: Ky. 1979. Assoc. gen. counsel Long John Silver Restaurants, Inc., 1985—95; sr. v.p., gen. counsel, sec. Darden Restaurants, Inc., 1999—. Mem.: ABA, Ky. Bar Assn., Fayette County Bar Assn. Office: 5900 Lake Ellenor Dr Orlando FL 32809

SHOAEE, ROKHSAREH SARAH, marriage and family therapist, counselor; b. Kerman, Iran, Apr. 10, 1945; came to U.S., 1971; d. Jalal Naghibzadeh Shoaee and Iran Nikmorad; m. Mohammad Hassan Faghfoory, June 27, 1970; children: Katie, Amir. BA, U. Tehran, Iran, 1969; MS, U. Wis., 1975, PhD, 1979; MEd, George Mason U., 1993. Lic. profl. counselor, Va.; lic. marriage and family therapist, Va. Asst. prof., chair edn. dept. Open U. Iran, Tehran, 1979-82; rsch. dir. Youth Policy Inst., Washington, 1989-91; designer, coord. holistic health care project ANA, Fairfax County, Va., 1993-96; counselor Mind Brain Behavior Ctrs., McLean, Va., 1996-97; clin. supr. Ctr. Multicultural Human Svcs., Falls Church, Va., 1997-99; faculty assoc. Johns Hopkins U., 1999—. Pvt. practice counseling and marriage and family therapy, Alexandria, Va., 1997—; cons., expert witness, Washington, Va. and Md., 1993—; mem. adv. bd. Breast Cancer Prevention, Fairfax County Health Dept. and Am. Cancer Soc.; mem. women's task force George Mason U., Fairfax, 1993-95; chmn. access to care No. Va. Regional Prenatal Coun., Falls Church, 1994—; co-vice chair, rschr. UCLA; nat. trainer multicultural clin. issues. Assoc. editor Nat. Assn. Alcoholism and Drug Abuse; contbr. articles to profl. publs. Mem. citizens' task force Fairfax County Criminal Justice, 1993; co-vice chair No. Va. Access to Care Consortium, 1997—, mem. legis. com., 1997; contbr. comty. svc., 1997. Recipient cert. of appreciation March of Dimes, 1994, Award of Excellence, Fairfax County Housing Dept.; Open U. Iran scholar Iran-U. Wis., 1976-79. Mem. ACA, Internat. Honor Soc. Avocations: t'ai chi, bird watching, hiking, canoeing, reading. Office: 641 S Washington St Alexandria VA 22314-4109

SHOCKED, MICHELLE, vocalist, songwriter; b. 1963; d. Bill Johnston. Student, U. Tex. Albums include The Texas Campfire Tapes, 1987, Short Sharp Shocked, 1988, Captain Swing, 1989, Arkansas Traveler, 1992, Kind Hearted Woman, 1995, Mercury Poise, 1988-95, 96. Office: care Mercury/Polygram Records Worldwide Plaza 825 8th Ave New York NY 10019-7416 also: Mercury Records 11150 Santa Monica Blvd Los Angeles CA 90025-3380

SHOCKLEY, CAROL FRANCES, psychologist, psychotherapist; b. Atlanta, Nov. 24, 1948; d. Robert Thomas and Frances Lavada (Scrivner) Shockley. BA, Ga. State U., 1974, MEd, 1976; PhD, U. Ga., 1990. Cert. in gerontology, diplomate Am. Bd. Forensic Examiners. Counselor Rape Crisis Ctr., Atlanta, 1979-80; emergency mental health clinician Gwinnett Med. Ctr., Lawrenceville, Ga., 1980-86; psychotherapist Fla. Mental Health Inst., Tampa, 1987-89, Tampa Bay Acad., Riverview, Fla., 1990-91; sr. psychologist State of Fla. Dept. of Corrections, Bushnell, 1991-92; pvt. practice psychologist Brunswick, Ga., 1992—2000, Griffin, Ga., 2002—. Mem. adv. bd. Mental Health/Mental Retardation, 1992—94. Author (with others): (book) Relapse Prevention with Sex Offenders, 1989. Vol. Ga. Mental Health Inst., Atlanta, 1972; leader Alzheimer's Disease Support Group, Athens, Ga., 1984; vol. therapist Reminiscence Group Elderly, Athens, 1984—85. Recipient Meritorious Svc. award, Beta Gamma Sigma, 1975. Mem.: APA, Ga. Psychol. Assn., Psi Chi, Sigma Phi Omega. Avocations: astronomy, archaeology, music, travel. Office: 231B S 10th St Ste B Griffin GA 30223

SHOCKLEY-ZALABAK, PAMELA SUE, academic administrator; b. May 25, 1944; d. James William and Leatha Pearl (Cartwright) Shockley; m. Charles Zalabak, Dec. 30, 1975. BA in Comm., Okla. State U., 1965, MA in Comm., 1972; PHD in Orgnl. Comm., U. Colo., 1980. Instr. comm. Coll. Letters, Arts and Scis. U. Colo., 1976, from asst. to full prof., 1992, prof. comm., 1992—, vice chancellor for student success, interim chancellor, 2001—02, chancellor, 2002—. Cons. in field. Author 4 books; contbr. articles to profl. jours.; prodr.: (6 video documentaries). Recipient Disting. Svc. award, Colo. Speech Comm. Assn.; Lew Wentz Tri Delt scholar, 1961—65. Mem.: INternat. Comm. Assn., Speech Comm. Assn., Phi Kappa Phi. Democrat. Avocations: skiing, hiking, fly fishing. Home: 5905 Ridge Brook Ln Colorado Springs CO 80918-3416 Office: Univ Colorado Dept Communication PO Box 7150 Colorado Springs CO 80933-7150*

SHODEAN, LISA DIANE, military officer; b. Willmar, Minn., Jan. 24, 1964; d. David Allen and Dione Lavonne Shodean. BS in Bus. Fin., Calif. State U., Fresno, 1989; MA in Pub. Adminstrn., Hamline U., 1997. Commd. 2d. lt. U.S. Army, 1988, advanced through grades to maj., 2002—. Mil. affairs. com. C. of C., Starkville, Miss., 1999—2001. Mem.: Adj. Gen. Regimental Assn., Res. Officer Assn. (treas. Minn. 1990—99, Outstanding Jr. Officer award 1999). Lutheran. Avocations: stamp collecting, skiing, bicycling, kayaking, camping. Address: PO Box 32114 Saint Louis MO 63132 Office: Human Resources Command ARADMD-ARO (MAJ SHODEAN) 1 Reserve Way Saint Louis MO 63132 E-mail: shodean@aol.com.

SHOEMAKER, ANNE CUNNINGHAM, retired mathematics educator; b. Milton, Mass., Aug. 26, 1922; d. George Clarendon Cunningham and Anne Bryan Parker; m. Reed Shoemaker, Aug. 25, 1951 (dec. Feb. 1, 2003); children: Edwin Reed (dec.), George Edwin, William Reed. AB in Math., Boston U., 1946; postgrad., Harvard U., U. Mass., Villanova U. Co-dir. Green Mountain Camp for Girls, Brattleboro, Vt., 1941; cartographer Inst. Geog. Exploration Harvard U., Cambridge, Mass., 1942; biometrician R&D divsn. Distiller's Co. Ltd., London, 1946-48; rsch. statistician Smith Kline & French Labs., Phila., 1948-52; math. tchr. Baldwin Sch., Bryn Mawr, Pa., 1962-72, head math. dept., 1964-70, head of sch., 1970-80; ednl. cons. com. for accreditation of elem. schs. Assn. of Ind. Md. Schs., 1980-85. Mem. scholarship selection com. Penwalt Corp., Phila., 1971-86 Bd. trustees, chair Gunston Sch., Centreville, Md., 1973-93, 95-97, sec. bd., 1974-80, v.p., chair oper. com., 1980-85, pres. bd., 1985-90, emeritus, 1999—; bd. trustess Country Sch., Easton, Md., 1981-85; bd. dirs. Coun. for Religion in Ind. Schs., 1976-86, pres., 1983-86; treas., vestryperson, Eucharistic min. St. Luke's Parish, Church Hill, Md., 1989—; judge pub. speaking competition 4-H Pony Club, Centreville, 1991-94; mem. CAPE secretariat screening panel Nat. Elem. Sch. Recogniton Program of US Dept. Edn., 1986-88; chair devel. com. Queen Anne's County Hospice, 2001-02, bd. dirs. 2004-. Elected to Coll. Disting. Alumni, Coll. Liberal Arts, Boston U., 1981. Mem. Nat. Assn. Ind. Schs. (admissions com. 1972-74, staff mem. workshop for new heads of schs. 1976-80, trustee rep., bd. dirs. 1982-86), Nat. Assn. Prins. of Schs. for Girls (chmn. sch. sect. of sch. and jr. coll. com. 1973-74, v.p. Cen. Atlantic area 1976-78), Assn. Headmistresses of the East (sec. to bd. dirs. 1973-75, chmn. nominating com. 1976-77), Pa. Assn. Pvt. Acad. Schs. (exec. com. 1970-79, sec. 1974-76, pres., bd. dirs. 1976-79), Pa. Assn. Ind. Schs. (exec. com. 1972-79, v.p. 1973-74), Mass. Women's Def. Corps of Mass. State Guard (capt. motor transport divsn. 1941-42), Miles River Sail & Power Squadron (comdr. 1992-93), St. Andrews Soc. Ea. Shore. Republican. Episcopalian. Avocations: gardening, music, genealogy. Home: PO Box 328 Centreville MD 21617-0328 E-mail: acshoe@intercom.net.

SHOEMAKER, CAROLYN SPELLMAN, planetary astronomer; b. Gallup, N.Mex., June 24, 1929; d. Leonard Robert and Hazel Adele (Arthur) Spellmann; m. Eugene Merle Shoemaker, Aug. 18, 1951 (dec. July 1997); children: Christine Shoemaker Abanto, Patrick Gene, Linda Shoemaker Salazar. BA cum laude, Chico State Coll., 1949, MA, 1950; ScD, No. Ariz. U., 1990, St. Mary's U., N.S., Can., 2003. Vis. scientist Br. astrogeology U.S. Geol. Survey, Flagstaff, Ariz., 1980—; rsch. asst. Calif. Inst. Tech., Pasadena, 1981-85; rsch. prof. astronomy No. Ariz. U., Flagstaff, 1989—; mem. staff Lowell Obs., Flagstaff, 1993—. Guest observer Palomar Obs., Palomar Mountain, Calif., 1982-94; Ruth Northcott Meml. lectrs. R.A.S.C., 1995; co-McGovern lectr. Cosmos Club Found., 1995. Co-recipient Rittenhouse medal Rittenhouse Astron. Soc., 1988, Scientist of Yr. award ARCS Found., 1995, James C. Watson medal NAS, 1998; recipient Woman of Distinction award Soroptimists, 1994, 20th Anniversary Internat. Women's Yr. award Zonta and 99s, 1995, NASA Exceptional Scientific Achievement medal, 1996, Woman of Distinction award Nat. Assn. Women in Edn., 1996, Shoemaker award Am. Inst. Profl. Geologists, 1997, plaque Internat. Forest Friendship, Atchison, Kans., 1997, Robert Burnham Jr. award Western Regional Astron. League, 2000; named Disting. Alumna of the Calif. State U., Chico, 1996. Fellow AAAS, Am. Acad. Arts and Scis.; mem. Astron. Soc. of Pacific, Am. Geophys. Union, Meteoritical Soc. Achievements include discovery of 32 comets including Periodic Comet Shoemaker-Levy 9 which impacted Jupiter in July 1994, more than 500 asteroids including 44 Earth approachers and approximately 68 Mars crossers, meteorites at Veevers Crater, Australia and impactites at Wolfe Creek Crater, Australia. Home: 5231 Hidden Hollow Rd Flagstaff AZ 86001-3821 Office: Lowell Obs 1400 W Mars Hill Rd Flagstaff AZ 86001-4499

SHOEMAKER, CLARA BRINK, retired chemistry researcher; b. Rolde, Drenthe, The Netherlands, June 20, 1921; came to U.S., 1953; d. Hendrik Gerard and Hendrikje (Smilde) Brink; m. David Powell Shoemaker, Aug. 5. 1955; 1 child, Robert Brink. PhD, Leiden U., The Netherlands, 1950. Instr. in inorganic chemistry Leiden U., 1946-50, 51-53; postdoctoral fellow Oxford (Eng.) U., 1950-51; rsch. assoc. dept. chemistry MIT, Cambridge, 1953-55, 58-70; rsch. assoc. biochemistry Harvard Med. Sch., Boston, 1955-56; project supr. Boston U., 1963-64; rsch. assoc. dept. chemistry Oreg. State U., Corvallis, 1970-75, rsch. assoc. prof. dept. chemistry, 1975-82, sr. rsch. prof. dept. chemistry, 1982-84, prof. emerita, 1984—. Sect. editor: Structure Reports of International Union of Crystallography, 1967, 68, 69; co-author chpts. in books; author numerous sci. papers. Bd. dirs. LWV, Corvallis, 1980-82, bd. dirs., sec., Oreg., 1985-87. Fellow Internat. Fedn. Univ. Women, Oxford U., 1950-51. Mem. Metall. Soc. (com. on alloy phases 1969-79), Internat. Union of Crystallography (commn. on structure reports 1970-90), Am. Crystallographic Assn. (crystallographic data com. 1975-78, Fankuchen award com. 1976), Sigma Xi, Iota Sigma Pi (faculty adv. Oreg. State U. chpt. 1975-84), Phi Lambda Upsilon. Avocation: outdoor activities. Office: Dept Chemistry Oreg State U Corvallis OR 97331

SHOEMAKER, HELEN E. MARTIN ACHOR, civic worker; b. Houston, Mar. 24, 1915; d. Earl L. and Blanche L. (Williams) Martin; m. Harold E. Achor, Oct. 11, 1935; children: Dianne Achor Johnston, Lana Achor Rainville; m. Robert N. Shoemaker, May 19, 1972. AB, Anderson (Ind.) Coll., 1960, LLD, 1978. Resident dir. Anderson Coll., 1967-69, dir. alumni svcs., 1969-72; legis. counsel Ind. Colls. and Univ. Ind., 1970-72; spl. asst. Ctr. Pub. Svc., Anderson, 1973-77, spl. asst. to dean for acad. devel., 1977-78. Sec.-treas. Ind. State Libr. and Hist. Bldg. Expansion Commn., 1973-78; mem. com. region VII, Girl Scouts U.S.A., 1958-66; adv. coun. fin. aid to students Office Edn. HEW, 1976-78; mem. Ind. Ho. of Reps. from Madison County, 1968-70; v.p. Ind. Fedn. Women's Rep. Clubs, 1945-46; treas. Nat. Fedn. Women's Rep. Clubs, 1947-51; Rep. precinct vice chmn. Madison County, 1946-68, vice chmn., Anderson, 1967-68; bd. dirs. Urban League Madison County, 1969-76; adv. com. Georgetown U. Grad. Sch. Acad. in Pub. Svc., 1976-83; mem. adv. com. on sex discrimination Ind. Civil Rights Commn., 1978-83; bd. dirs. Anderson Symphony Orch. Women's Guild, 1987, hon. mem.; trustee Anderson Coll., 1978-85; bd. dirs. Opportunities Industrialization Ctr., Inc., Madison County, 1980-84, Ind. Acad. Pub. Svc., 1981-83, Women's Alternatives Inc., Anderson, 1982-93 (Elizabeth Howard McMahan award 1987); mem. exec. com. devel. bd. St. John's Med. Ctr., Anderson, 1981-92; bd. dirs. life enrichment Park Place Ch. God, 1989-94; bd. dirs. Anderson Symphony Womens Guild. Recipient William B. Harper award Urban League Madison County, 1975; named Sagamore of Wabash, State of Ind., 1979. Mem. LWV (dir. Madison County 1973-76, 78-84, 87), Anderson Coun. Women, Anderson Fine Arts Ctr. (treas.). Mem. Ch. Of God. Home: 5801 W Bethel Ave Muncie IN 47304-9549

SHOEMAKER, INNIS HOWE, art museum curator; b. Reading, Pa. d. William Erety and Jean (Miller) S. AB, Vassar Coll., 1964; MA, Columbia U., 1968, PhD, 1975. Curator Vassar Coll. Art Gallery, Poughkeepsie, N.Y., 1965-68, 73-76; asst. dir. Ackland Art Mus., U. N.C., Chapel Hill, 1976-82, dir., 1983-86; Audrey and William H. Helfand sr. curator prints, drawings and photographs Phila. Mus. Art, 1986—; adj. prof. U. Pa., 2001—. Fellow in art history Am. Acad. in Rome, 1971-73; adj. prof. U. N.C., Chapel Hill, 1983-86. Co-author: The Engravings of Marcantonio Raimondi, 1981, Paul Cézanne: Two Sketchbooks, 1989; author: Mad for Modernism: Earl Horter and His Collection, 1999, Jacques Villon and his Cubist Prints, 2001. Mem. vis. com. Lehman Loeb Art Ctr., Vassar Coll., 1993—; bd. advisors Ctr. for Advanced Studies in the Visual Arts, 2001—. Mem. Coll. Art Assn. Am., Am. Assn. Mus., Print Coun. Am. (bd. dirs. 1986-89). Office: Phila Mus Art PO Box 7646 Philadelphia PA 19101-7646

SHOEMAKER, JENNIFER LYNN, music educator; b. Washington, Mo., Sept. 23, 1967; d. Andrew Peter and Mary Louise Orf; m. Chad Scott Shoemaker; children: Kathryn, Brittany. AA, East Ctrl. C.C., Union, Mo., 1987; B in Music Edn., Truman State U., 1989; M in music edn., U. Mo., 2002. Counselor, cook Forty Legends Children's Summer Camp, Washington, Mo., 1984—88; elem. music educator Ralls County R-II Sch. Dist., Center, Mo., 1989—95, Montgomery County R-II Sch. Dist., Montgomery, Mo., 1995—2001, Mex. Pub. Sch., Mexico, Mo., 2002—. Mem.: Mo. State Tchrs. Assn., Music Educators Nat. Conf. Roman Catholic. Avocation: volleyball.

SHOEMAKER, MARJORIE LYNN, recreational therapist, small business owner; b. Bridgeton, N.J., Apr. 7, 1950; d. Jay Peter and Betty Marie Shoemaker. BS in Animal and Vet. Scis., U. Maine, 1972. Cert. animal-assited activities and therapy, advanced confectionary artist. Rsch. technician Strong Hosp. U. Rochester, NY, 1972—76; owner and confectionary artist Enticing Icing, 1973—; rsch. technician Eastman Kodak, Rochester, 1976—77; animal-assisted therapist for homebound elderly Caring People Alliance, Phila., 1999—. Vol. Pet Pals S. N.J., Bellmawr, NJ; lectr. in field. Grantee, Meth. Hosp. Found., Phila., 1999—, Phila. Corp. Aging, 1999—. Mem.: Am. Hort. Therapy Assn. (bd. dirs. resources 2001—, coord. intergenerational nature programs 1999—, mem. Mid-Atlantic chpt., Program Excellence award 2003). Avocations: quilting, gardening. Home: 9 Wyngate Pl Somerdale NJ 08083-2410 Office: Caring People Alliance Fels S Phila Cmty Ctr 2407 S Broad St Philadelphia PA 19148

SHOGEN, KUSLIMA, pharmaceutical executive; BS, Fairleigh Dickenson U., 1974, MS in Biology, 1976. Founder Alfacell Corp., Bloomfield, NJ, 1981, CFO, 1986—94, pres., 1986—96, CEO, 1986—, chmn., 1996—, acting CFO, 1999—. Cons. Lever Bros. Rsch. Group. Recipient 1st prize, Sigma Xi, 1974, Pinnacle award, Fairleigh Dickenson U., 1998. Mem.: Phi Beta Kappa. Office: Alfacell Corp 225 Belleville Ave Bloomfield NJ 07003

SHOHEN, SAUNDRA ANNE, health care communications and public relations executive; b. Washington, Aug. 22, 1934; d. Aaron Kohn and Malvina (Kleiman) Kohn Blinder; children: Susan, Brian. BS, Columbia Pacific U., 1979, MS in Health Svcs. Adminstrn., 1981. Adminstr. social work dept. Roosevelt Hosp., N.Y.C., 1978-79; adminstr. emergency dept. St. Luke's-Roosevelt Hosp. Ctr., N.Y.C., 1979-83, assoc. dir. pub. rels., 1983-87; pres. Saundra Shohen Assocs., Ltd., N.Y.C., 1987-92; v.p. Prism Internat., N.Y.C., 1988-91; bd. dirs. Tureck Bach Inst., N.Y.C., 1985—. Panelist ann. Emmy awards NATAS, N.Y.C., 1983, 84; tchr. healthcare mktg. Baruch Coll., N.Y.C., 1994. Author: Health Scripts for Radio, 1983, Voice of America, 1983 (Presdl. Recognition award, 1984); author: (with others) AIDS: A Health Care Management Response, 1987; author: EMERGENCY!, 1989. Mem. NATAS, Internat. Hosp. Fedn., Am. Soc. Hosp. Mktg. and Pub. Rels., Vols. in Tech. Assistance. Democrat. Jewish. Home: 240 Central Park S New York NY 10019-1413

SHOOP, LYNN GARISON, real estate executive; b. El Dorado, Ark., Dec. 19, 1954; d. Robert Weaver and Iris Amy (Horton) Lassiter. Student, Randolph-Macon Woman's Coll., 1973-76; BS, Tex. A&M U., 1978. Lic. real estate broker, Tex. From broker assoc. to regional mgr. J. B. Goodwin, Realtors, Residential, Inc., Austin, Tex., 1979-82; comml. broker assoc. Christon Co., Realtors, Inc., Dallas, 1983-87; v.p. Dallas Mkt. Ctr., Dallas, 1987-89; regional v.p. Tenenbaum and Assocs., Inc., Dallas, 1989-92; chmn. bd. Artemis Co., Dallas, 1992—; pres., COO Cons. Svcs. Inc. Bd. dirs. Consumer Credit Counseling Svc. Bd. dirs. Dallas Coun. World Affairs; mem. Mayor's Task Force on Child Abuse, Highland Pk. Presbyn. Ch. Mem. DAR, Daus. of the Republic of Tex., Nat. Assn. Corp. Real Estate, Cert. Comml. Investment Mem., Internat. Merger and Acquisition Profls., Urban Land Inst., Rotary Internat. (bd. dirs. Park Cities club, v.p., pres.). Avocations: fly fishing, collecting antique silver. Home: PO Box 12681 Dallas TX 75225-0681 E-mail: artemis2@concertric.net.

SHORE, ELEANOR GOSSARD, medical school dean; b. Ottawa, Ill., Aug. 11, 1930; d. Arthur Paul and Mary Catherine (Lineberger) Gossard; m. Miles Frederick Shore, July 4, 1953; children: Miles Paul, Rebecca Shore Lewin, Susanna Shore LeBoutillier. BA magna cum laude, Radcliffe Coll., 1951; MD, Harvard U., 1955, MPH, 1970. Diplomate Am. Bd. Preventive Medicine. Med. intern New Eng. Med. Ctr. Hosp., Boston, 1955-56; resident in occup. medicine Harvard U. Health Svcs., Cambridge, Mass., 1966-68; Macy scholar Radcliffe Inst., Radcliffe Coll., Cambridge, 1966-68; resident in preventive medicine Harvard Sch. Pub. Health, Boston, 1970-71; asst. physician Radcliffe Coll., 1959-61, Harvard U. Health Svcs., 1961-73; rsch. assoc. dept. microbiology Harvard U. Sch. Pub. Health, 1971-76; asst. to pres. Harvard U., 1972-81; assoc. dean for faculty affairs Harvard Med. Sch., 1978-89, mem. faculty, 1978—, dean for faculty affairs, 1989—. Mem. editl. bd. Harvard Med. Alumni Bull., 1976—; contbr. numerous articles to profl. jours. Bd. dirs. Mass.-Ukraine Citizens Bridge, Brockton, Mass., 1989-94, pres., 1991-92; bd. dirs. Needham (Mass.) Found. for Pub. Sch. Edn., 1990-94; bd. dirs. Mass. Health Rsch. Inst., Inc., 1990-99, sec., 1995-99; overseer Boston Mus. Sci., 1981—; trustee Schepens Eye Rsch. Inst., Boston, 1993—; mem. acad. coun. Real Colegio Complutense, Harvard U.; dep. dir. Harvard Med. Sch. Ctr. for Excellence in Women's Health. Recipient Pres.'s Recognition award Am. Med. Women's Assn., 1996. Fellow Am. Acad. Preventive Medicine; mem. AAAS, APHA, Mass. Pub. Health Assn., Assn. Am. Med. Colls., Mass. Med. Soc., Aesculapian Club (treas. 1986-89, pres. 1990-91). Home: 62 Meadowbrook Rd Needham MA 02492-1914 Office: Harvard Med Sch 25 Shattuck St Bldg A Boston MA 02115-6027 E-mail: eleanor_shore@hms.harvard.edu.

SHORE, LISA, flight controller, trainer; BS in Aerospace Engring., U. Mich., 1985. With NASA Johnson Space Ctr. Shuttle and Station flight control and tng., Houston. Avocations: golf, softball, billiards, movies, pinball. Office: NASA Johnson Space Ctr Mailcode DX35 Houston TX 77058

SHORENSTEIN, ROSALIND GREENBERG, internist; b. N.Y.C., Jan. 14, 1947; d. Albert Samuel and Natalie Miriam (Sherman) Greenberg; m. Michael Lewis Shorenstein, June 18, 1967; children: Anna Irene, Claire Beth. BA in Chemistry, Wellesley Coll., 1968; MA in Biochemistry and Molecular Biology, Harvard U., 1970, PhD in Biochemistry and Molecular Biology, 1973; MD, Stanford U., 1976. Diplomate Am. Bd. Internal Medicine. Resident in internal medicine UCLA Med. Ctr., 1976-79; pvt. practice internal medicine Santa Cruz, Calif., 1979—. Mem. dept. internal medicine Dominican Hosp., Santa Cruz, 1979—; co-dir. med. svcs. Health Enhancement & Lifestyle Planning Systems, Santa Cruz, 1983—. Contbr. articles to profl. journals. Dir. Santa Cruz Chamber Players, 1993-94, pres., bd. dirs., 1994—. Recipient Charlie Parkhurst award Santa Cruz Women's

Commn., 1989; NSF fellow, 1968-72, Sarah Perry Wood Med. fellow Wellesley Coll., 1972-76. Mem. Am. Soc. Internal Medicine (del. 1994, 95), Calif. Soc. Internal Medicine (trustee 1994—, sec.-treas. 1996-2000), Am. Med. Women's Assn. (Outstanding Svc. award 1987, br. #59 pres. 1986—), Calif. Med. Assn. (com. on women 1987-93), Santa Cruz County Med. Soc. (mem. bd. govs. 1993—, sec. 1997-99, pres. 2000-01, sec. 2002-), Phi Beta Kappa, Sigma Xi. Jewish. Office: 700 Frederick St Ste 103 Santa Cruz CA 95062-2239

SHORT, BETSY ANN, elementary school educator; b. Macon, Ga., Mar. 18, 1958; d. Garland Brooks Jr. and Mary Eleanor (Jordan) Turner; m. Lynn Robin Short, July 21, 1984. BS in Early Childhood Edn., Ga. Coll., Milledgeville, 1981, M in Early Childhood Edn., 1993, EdS in Early Childhood Edn., 1995; EdS in reading, U. West Ga., 2001, cert. specialist in reading, 2001; intech cert., Macon State Coll., 2001; degree in Adminstrn. and Supervision, Ga. Coll. and State U., 2002. Cert. elem. tchr. and tchr. support specialist, Ga., early childhood generalist, Nat. Bd. Early Childhood Generalists, 2003. Tchr. 3d grade Stockbridge (Ga.) Elem. Sch., 1983-84, tchr. kindergarten, 1984-93; tchr. augmented spl. instructional assistance Locust Grove (Ga.) Elem. Sch., 1993-97, kindergarten tchr., 1997-99, first grade tchr., 1999-2000, early intervention reading tchr., 2000—02, 2000—02; student support specialist Unity Grove Elem. and Ola Elem., 2002—03; asst. prin. Morgan County Primary Sch., Madison, Ga., 2003—; v.p. Henry Heritage Reading Coun., 1999—2000. Cons. Saxon Pub. Co.; v.p. Henry Heritage Reading Coun., 1999-2001; specialist in Reading, U. West Ga., Carrollton, 2001. Author: Spinning Yarns, 1995; mem. editl. adv. bd. Ga. Jour. Reading; contbr. articles to profl. jours.; artist oil painting/pen and ink drawing. V.p. Henry Heritage Reading Coun., 1999—2000. Mem. Profl. Assn. of Ga. Educators, Ga. Coun. Tchrs Maths., Ga. Coun. Internat. Reading Assn., Ga. Coun. Social Studies, Ga. Sci. Tchrs. Assn., Henry Heritage Reading Coun. Baptist. Avocations: oil painting, cross-stiching, writing short stories, story telling. Office: Morgan County Primary Sch 993 East Ave Madison GA 30650 Business E-Mail: bshort@morgan.k12.ga.us.

SHORT, ELIZABETH M. internist, educator, retired federal agency administrator; b. Boston, June 2, 1942; d. James Edward and Arlene Elizabeth (Mitchell) Meehan; m. Michael Allen Friedman, June 21, 1976; children: Lia Gabrielle, Hannah Ariel, Eleanor Elana. BA Philosophy magna cum laude, Mt. Holyoke Coll., 1963; MD cum laude, Yale U., 1968. Diplomate Am. Bd. Internal Medicine, Am. Bd. Med. Genetics. Resident internal medicine Yale New Haven Hosp., 1968-70; postdoctoral fellow in human genetics Yale Med. Sch., 1970-72; resident U. Calif., San Francisco, 1972-73; sr. chief resident Stanford (Calif.) Med. Sch., 1973-75; asst. prof. medicine Stanford Med. Sch., 1975-83, assoc. dean student affairs/med. edn., 1978-83; dep. dir. acad. affairs, dir. biomed. rsch. Assn. Am. Med. Colls., Washington, 1983-88; dep. assoc. chief med. dir. for acad. affairs VA, Washington, 1988-92, assoc. chief med. dir. for acad. affairs, 1992-96; health policy cons. HHS, 1996—2001; ret., 2001. Vis. prof. human biology Stanford U., 1983-86; mem. Accreditation Coun. Grad. Med. Edn., 1988-97; mem. White House Task Force on Health Care Reform, 1993. Assoc. editor Clin. Rsch. Jour., 1976-79, editor 1980-84; contbr. articles to profl. jours. Mem. Nat. Child Health Adv. Coun., NIH, 1991-97; mem. com. edn. and tng. Office Sci. and Tech. Policy, White House, Washington, 1991-96. Recipient Maclean Zoology award; Munger scholar, Markle scholar, Sara Williston scholar Mt. Holyoke Coll., 1959-63, Yale Men in Medicine scholar, 1964-68; Bardwell Meml. Med. fellow, 1963. Mem. AAAS, Am. Soc. Human Genetics (pub. policy com. 1984-95, chmn. 1986-94), Am. Fedn. Clin. Rsch. (bd. dirs. 1973-83, co-chmn. com. status women 1975-77, editor Clin. Rsch. Jour., 1978-83, nat. coun., exec. com., pub. policy com. 1977-87), Western Soc. Clin. Investigation, Calif. Acad. Medicine, Phi Beta Kappa, Alpha Omega Alpha. Home and Office: 3535 Ranch Top Rd Pasadena CA 91107 E-mail: elizshort@aol.com.

SHORT, LINDA HUFFSTETLER, state legislator; b. Gastonia, N.C., July 9, 1947; d. Everett Rhyne and Violet Lucille (Kuykendall) Huffstetler; m. Paul E. Short, Jr., June 14, 1968; children: Lindy Lee, Melanie Lynne. BA in Psychology, Winthrop U., 1984. Mem. S.C. Senate, Columbia, 1993—, asst. majority whip, 1993—. Mem. edn. com. So. Legis. Conf., 1997, mem. edn. com., 1997-98; mem. health capacity task force Coun. State Govts., 1997, mem. health capacity task force, 1997-98; mem. bd. Status of Women in State Govt. Task Force, 1997; mem. adv. bd. women's network Nat. Conf. State Legislators, 1997; mem. Legis. Consumer Fin. Study Com., 1997-98. Mem. Chester County Sch. Bd., 1982-92, chmn., 1990-92; bd. dirs. Downtown Devel. Assn., 1989-93, Palmetto Leadership, 1990-91; bd. visitors Presbyn. Coll., 1990-93; mem. Chester County's Fall Affair, 1988-90; former coord. 6th Cir. Guardian Ad Litem Program; former jr. and sr. H.S. Sunday sch. tchr. Purity Presbyn. Ch., former pres. Presbyn. Women; former v.p. Providence Presbytery Presbyn. Women; mem. Children's Case Resolutions Sys. Panel, Joint Legis. com. Children and Families, 1992-95; state mem. nat. edn. policy focus Milken Family Found., 1997; co-chmn. Study Com. on Drug-Impaired Infants, 1997-98. Recipient S.C. Dept. Health and Environ. Control Bur. of Maternal and Child Health Legis.award 1995, Chester County's Econ. Devel. Efforts award 1995, Girl Scouts Women of Achievement award 1996, Ernestine C. Player Friend of Social Work award 1996. Mem. Bench Bar Com., Phi Kappa Phi, Delta Kappa Gamma. Democrat. Address: SC State Senate 502 Gressette Bldg PO Box 142 Columbia SC 29202-0142

SHORT, MARION PRISCILLA, neurogenetics educator; b. Milford, Del., June 12, 1951; d. Raymond Calistus and Barbara Anne (Ferguson) S.; m. Michael Peter Klein; 1 child, Asher Calistus Klein. BA, Bryn Mawr Coll., 1973; diploma, U. Edinburgh (Scotland), 1975; MD, Med. Coll. Pa., 1978. Diplomate Am. Bd. Psychiatry and Neurology, Am. Bd. Internal Medicine. Intern in internal medicine Hahnemann Med. Coll. Hosp., Phila., 1978-79; med. resident in internal medicine St. Lukes-Roosevelt Hosp., N.Y.C., 1979-81; neurology resident U. Pitts. Health Ctr., 1981-84; fellow in med. genetics Mt. Sinai Med. Ctr., N.Y.C., 1984-86; fellow in neurology Mass. Gen. Hosp., Boston, 1986-90, asst. neurologist, 1990-95; asst. prof. dept. neurology Harvard Med. Sch., Boston, 1990-95; asst. prof. dept. neurology, pediat. and pathology U. Chgo., 1995—97; program dir. genetics, transplantation and clin. rsch. AMA, Chgo., 1997—2002; fellow McLean Ctr. for Clin. Med. Ethics U. Chgo., 2002—03, sr. fellow McLean Ctr. for Clin. Med. Ethics, 2003—. Recipient Clin. Investigator Devel. award, NIH, 1988—93; fellow, Inst. Medicine, Chgo., 1999, McLean Ctr. for Clin. Med. Ethics, U. Chgo., 2002—. Mem. AMA, Am. Acad. Neurology, Am. Soc. for Human Genetics, Am. Coll. Med. Genetics. Office: Pediat Neurosurgery U Chgo MC 4066 5481 S Maryland Ave Chicago IL 60637-4325 E-mail: mpshort@surgery.bsd.uchicago.edu.

SHORT, SALLIE LEE, physical plant service worker; b. Knoxville, Tenn., Feb. 17, 1932; d. John J. and Louise Maude (Robertson) Bassett; children: Jacqueline, Carita, Paulette, Shelia, Marilyn, Regina, Panthea, Greta, Michael (dec.). Legal sec. Earl Rossin, Atty., Cleve., 1952-53; nursing technician Meharry Med. Hosp., Nashville, 1958-64; inspector May Hosiery Mill Corp., Nashville, 1964-81; trustee sick leave bank Nashville State Tech. Inst., 1993—. Author poems; guest appearence Cable TV Channel 19 Read Poetry. Campaign worker Dem. Party, Nashville, 1975-80; mem. Com. on Svc. to Persons with Disabilities and Ams. with Disabilities Act. Recipient Poet of Merit award Internat. Soc. Poets, 1997; elected to Internat. Poetry Hall of Fame, 1998. Roman Catholic. Avocations: writing, hiking, reading, traveling. Home: 4113 Meadow Hill Dr Nashville TN 37218-1730 Office: Nashville State Tech Inst 120 White Bridge Rd Nashville TN 37209-4515

SHORT-MAYFIELD, PATRICIA AHLENE, business owner; b. Ft. Benning, Ga., Oct. 12, 1955; d. William Pressley and Ilse Marie (Hofmann) Short; m. Thomas Hicks Fort, June 2, 1973 (div. Jan. 1981); m. Michael Patrick Mayfield, Aug. 11, 1984; 1 child, William Zachary. Grad. high sch., Butler, Ga., 1973. Notary pub., Ga. Staff mem. Fairyland Day Care, Canton, Ga., 1973-74, Small World Child Care, Thomaston, Ga., 1974-77; nurses aide Kenneston Hosp., Marietta, Ga., 1978-80; staff worker Mental Health Ctr., Smyrna, Ga., 1980-81; dir. Kiddie Kollege, Marietta, 1981-85; bus. owner, mgr. Spiffy Clean by Mayfield, Marietta, 1985—95; lead cashier Petsmart, Kennesaw, Ga., 1994—. Choir staff Eastside Bapt. Ch., Marietta, 1988-89; vol. East Valley Elem. Sch., 1989-95, chorus vol., 1994-95; vol. East Cobb Middle Sch., 1995-98; active Nat. Congress Parents and Tchrs., Cobb County Humane Soc., 1991—. Mem. NAFE, Cobb County C. of C., Atlanta High Mus. Art, Dog Lovers Am. Republican. Baptist. Avocations: reading, walking, symphony, art, bicycling. Office: Spiffy Clean By Mayfield 2791 Georgian Ter Marietta GA 30068-3625

SHORTZ, WILMA WILDES, writer, utilities executive; b. Kansas City, Mo., Dec. 16, 1910; d. John Henry Jr. and Viola Alberta (Warner) Wildes; m. Lyle Alton Shortz, Sept. 16, 1939 (dec. Nov. 1994); children: April Irene, Richard Alan, William Frederic. Grad. ct. reporter, Gregg Coll., Chgo., 1931. Freelance ct. reporter, Chgo., 1930-43; freelance ct. reporter, Crawfordsville, Ind., 1951; supr. Montgomery County Soil & Water Conservation Dist., 1970—85, chair, 1981—85, assoc. supr., 1986—. Contbg. author: Montgomery County Legend and Lore, 1988; spkr. weekly program on horses Sta. WCVL, 1980-81; contbr. horse articles, stories and humor to mags. Mem. Presbyn. Ch. Women's Assn., 1955—, pres., 1963—64, Crawfordsville H.S. PTA, 1961—63; mem. organizing com. Montgomery County 4-H Horse and Pony Club, 1960—61, officer, 1961—65; mem. Current Events Club, 1959—, pres., 1966—67, 2000—01. Mem. LWV (pres. Montgomery County 1965-67). Presbyterian. Avocations: writing, contests.

SHOSS, CYNTHIA RENÉE, lawyer; b. Cape Girardeau, Mo., Nov. 29, 1950; d. Milton and Carroll Jane (Duncan) S.; m. David Goodwin Watson, Apr. 13, 1986; 1 child, Lucy J. Watson. BA cum laude, Newcomb Coll., 1971; JD, Tulane U., 1974; LLM in Taxation, NYU, 1980. Bar: La. 1974, Mo. 1977, Ill. 1978, N.Y. 1990. Law clk. to assoc. and chief justices La. Supreme Ct., New Orleans, 1974-76; assoc. Stone, Pigman et al, New Orleans, 1976-77, Lewis & Rice, St. Louis, 1977-79, Curtis, Mallet-Prevost, et al, N.Y.C., 1980-82; ptnr. LeBoeuf, Lamb, Greene & MacRae, L.L.P., N.Y.C., 1982—; mng. ptnr. London office LeBoeuf, Lamb, Leiby & MacRae, 1987-89. Assoc. editor Tulane Law Rev., 1972-74; frequent speaker before profl. orgns. and assns. Contbr. articles to profl. jours. Mem.: ABA, Assn. Life Ins. Counsels, Power of Atty., Inc. (chair bd. dirs.), Am. Mgmt. Assn. (ins. and risk mgmt. coun.). Office: LeBoeuf Lamb Greene Et Al 125 W 55th St New York NY 10019-5369 E-mail: cshoss@llgm.com.

SHOUN, ELLEN LLEWELLYN, retired secondary school educator; b. Germantown, Pa., Sept. 8, 1925; d. William Thomas and Ella (Hall) Llewellyn; m. Glenn Harte Shoun, June 25, 1949; children: Mary Deborah, Paul L., Eleanor C., Peter G., Elizabeth A. AB in Chemistry, Oberlin Coll., 1947; MA in Sci. Edn., Western Mich. U., 1972. Cert. libr. (ltd. profl.) Mich., secondary sch. tchr. Mich. Jr. chemist Am. Cyanamid, Stamford, Conn., 1947-49; Charles M. Hall Chem. instr. Oberlin (Ohio) Coll., 1949-51; br. libr. Bronson (Mich.) Pub. Libr., 1966-67; math. and sci. tchr. Bronson H.S., 1967-79; crew leader 1980 U.S. Census, Branch County, Mich., 1980; bus. mgr. Dr. C.F. Cole's Dental Office, Sturgis, Mich., 1982; reference aide Br. Dist. Libr., Coldwater, Mich., 1982-99; ret., 1999. Founder (with others) Bronson H.S. Cmty. Recycling Group, 1972—79. Trustee Bronson Pub. Libr., 1968—82, Housing Commn., 1975—, Bronson Cmty. Found., 2003—; instr. CPR Cmty. health Ctr., Coldwater, Mich., 1978—80; cmty. chorus Cmty. Found., 1987—; chair refugee family com. Bronson United Meth. Ch., 1974—82, ch. choir, 1967—, sec. adminstrv. bd., 1987—, chair adminstrv. bd., 1984—86; bd. dirs., treas., mgr. Food Pantry, 5 Ch. Coop., Bronson, 1993—. Named Hon. Grand Marshal, Polish Festival Parade, Bronson, 2002; recipient Cmty. Vol. of Yr. award, Gleaner Life Ins. Soc., 2001. Mem.: Phi Beta Kappa. Democrat. Avocations: photography, knitting, Scrabble.

SHOUSHA, ANNETTE GENTRY, retired critical care nurse; b. Nashville, May 25, 1936; d. Thurman and Laura (Pugh) Gentry; m. Alfred Shousha, May 29, 1959; children: Mark André, Anne, Mary, Melanie. Diploma, St. Thomas Hosp., Nashville, 1957; student, Belmont Coll., Nashville, 1958, No. State U., Aberdeen, S.D., 1973; BSN, S.D. State U., 1985. Cert. coronary care. Instr. med. nursing Nashville Gen. Hosp., 1958-59, ob-gyn. nurse, 1959-60; insvc. educator Tri County Hosp., Ft. Oglethorpe, Ga., 1960-61; clin. mgr., office nurse Britton, S.D., 1962-90; med. nursing Nashville VA Hosp., 1990-92, gastrointestinal nurse, 1992-94, critical care nurse ICU, 1994-95; ret., 1995. Contbr. essays to S.D. Jour. Medicine. Del. S.D. Polit. Conv. Recipient Gov.'s Recognition award for outstanding vol. svc. Mem. ANA, AMA Aux. (state pres.), Nat. Hospice Assn., Nurses Orgn. VA, Donelson/Hermitage C. of C. Home: 3632 S Agave Way Chandler AZ 85248-4155

SHOW, RENEE DEANE, music educator; b. UnionTown, Pa., Mar. 2, 1949; d. Wayne and Eleanor Eileen Show. BM magna cum laude, Ohio Wesleyan U., 1971; MA, Ohio State U., 1977. Music tchr. Montgomery County Sch., Rockville, Md., 1971—72; strings music tchr. Zanesville (Ohio) City Sch., 1972—. Concert master S.E. Ohio Symphony, New Concord, 1974—88, first violin sect., 1988—. Supporter Nat. Right To Life, Washington, 1994—. Mem.: Thursday Music Club (secretary 1982—84, v.p. 1984—86, pres. 1986—88), Zanesville Concert Assn. (pres. 1990—93, bd. dirs. 1983—), Delta Kappa Gamma. Church Of Christ. Avocations: gardening, quilting, Irish studies. Home: 1102 S Slope Bay Zanesville OH 43701 Office: Zanesville City Schs 1701 Blve Ave Zanesville OH 43701 Office Phone: 740-453-0335.

SHOWALTER, ELAINE, humanities educator, educator; b. Cambridge, Mass., Jan. 21, 1941; d. Paul and Violet (Rottenberg) Cottler; m. English Showalter, June 8, 1963; children: Vinca, Michael. BA, Bryn Mawr Coll., 1962; MA, Brandeis U., 1964; PhD in English, U. Calif., Davis, 1970. Teaching asst. English U. Calif., 1964-66, from instr. to assoc. prof., 1967-78; prof. English Rutgers U., from 1978, Avalon Found. prof. humanities, Princeton (N.J.) U., 1984—; Avalon Found. prof. humanities Princeton (N.J.) U., 1987—. Vis. prof. English and women's studies U. Del., 1976-77; vis. prof. Sch. Criticism and Theory, Dartmouth Coll., 1986; prof. Salzburg (Austria) Seminars, 1988; Clarendon lectr. Oxford (Eng.) U., 1989; vis. scholar Phi Beta Kappa, 1993-94; numerous radio and TV appearances. Author: A Literature of Their Own, 1977, The Female Malady, 1985, Sexual Anarchy, 1990, Sister's Choice, 1991, Hystories, 1997; co-author: Hysteria Beyond Freud, 1993; editor: These Modern Women, 1978, The New Feminist Criticism, 1985, Alternative Alcott, 1987, Speaking of Gender, 1989, Modern American Women Writers, 1991, Daughters of Decadence, 1993, Scribbling Women, 1997, Hystories, 1997; also articles and revs. Recipient Howard Behrman humanities award Princeton U., 1989; faculty rsch. coun. fellow Ruthers U., 1972-73, Guggenheim fellow, 1977-78, Rockefeller humanities fellow, 1981-82, fellow NEH, 1988-89. Mem. MLA (v.p. 1996-97, pres. 1998). Office: Princeton U Dept Of English Princeton NJ 08544-0001

SHOWALTER, JUDY, state representative; b. Dallas, Aug. 4, 1943; 4 children. BA in Nursing, BS in Nursing, Southwestern Coll. RN. Mem. Kans. Ho. of Reps., 1997—. Mem. Winfield City Commn., 1987—96; past chair Strother Field Indsl. Commn.; mayor Winfield, 1989—96; bd. dirs. Kans. League Mcpls. Named Woman of Yr., Bus. Profl. Women's Assn., 1989. Democrat. Presbyterian. Office: 273-W State Capitol 300 SW 10th Ave Topeka KS 66612 Home: 1917 Simpson Winfield KS 67156

SHOWALTER, MARILYN GRACE, state agency administrator; AB, Harvard U., 1972, JD, 1975. Bar: Wash. 1975. Dep. pros. atty. King County, Wash., 1975—81, counsel to gov., 1981—83; pvt. practice, 1985—89; counsel house appropriations com. State House, Washington, 1989—92, dep. chief clk., house counsel, 1992—93, chief clk., 1994—95, adv. Gov. Gary Locke, 1999, chairwoman, 1999—. Adv. Gov. Gary Locke. Democrat. Office: Washington UTC PO Box 47250 Olympia WA 98504-7250 also: Washington UTC 1300 S Evergreen Park Dr SW Olympia WA 98504-7250 Office Phone: 360-664-1173. E-mail: mshowalter@wutc.wa.gov.

SHOWALTER, SHIRLEY H. academic administrator; b. July 30, 1948; BA cum laude in English, Ea. Mennonite U., Harrisonburg, Va., 1970; MA in Am. civilization, U. Tex., Austin, 1974, PhD in Am. civilization, 1981. Tchr. English Harrisonburg (Va.) H,S, 1970—72; tchg. asst. English and Am. Studies depts. U. Tex., Austin, 1973—75, asst. instr. Am. Studies dept., 1976; dir. continuing edn. Goshen Coll., Ind., 1979—82, project dir. Title II tech. and liberal arts devel. grant, 1982—85, project dir. Consortium Advancemet of Pvt. Higher Edn. grant, 1985—86, asst. to prof. English, 1967—, pres., 1997—. Coord. Humanities program Harrisonburg (Va.) H.S., 1970—72; co-dir. Study-Svc. Term in Haiti Goshen Coll., 1981—82; rsch. asst. Consortium Advancement of Pvt. Higher Edn., Washington, 1986—87, interim v.p., 1987; chair English dept. Goshen Coll., 1990—93; sr. fellow Lilly Fellows program in Humanities and Arts Valparaiso U., Ind., 1993—94; co-dir. Study-Svc. Term in Ivory Coast Goshen Coll., 1993; lectr. and spkr. in humanities. Contbr. chapters to books, articles to profl. jours. Bd. mem. South Bend Symphony Assn.; mem. blue ribbon adv. group Boys and Girls Club; vice chair and mem. Hist. Com. of Mennonite Ch., 1984—88; co-sponsor Kid's Club No. Va. Mennonite Ch., 1987—88; chair curriculum com. Sojourner's Sunday Sch. class Coll. Mennonite Ch., 1987—88, mem. constn. revision com., 1988—92, tchr. H.S. age class, 1988—91, mem. worship commn., 1994—96; bd. mem. Coun. Christian Coll. and U., 2000—, Ind. Colls. of Ind., 1999—, Lantz Ctr. Christian Vocations, Indpls., 1998—; dir. Coun. Ind. Colls., 1999—; bd. dir. Mennonite Mutual Aid Trust, dir. Elkhart County Cmty. Found. Recipient Tchg. Excellence and Campus Leadership award, Sears Roebuck Found., 1990, Faculty Rsch., Goshen Coll., 1990, Knight Presdl. Leadership award, John S. and James L. Knight Found., 1999, 1999; fellow, George H. Gallup Rsch. Inst., 1999—2000, Coolidge Fellow, Yale U., Assn. Religion in Intellectual Life, 1996; grantee Faculty Rsch., Goshen Coll., 1977, 1982, Summer Stipend, Lilly Endowment, 1991. Mem.: AAUW, Am. Studies Assn., Am. Assn. Higher Edn. (Goshen Coll. rep. Forum on Exemplary Tchg. 1992, bd. dir. 1992—96), No. Ind. Partnership for the Arts, Willa Cather Pioneer Mem., Ind. Hist. Soc., Ellen Glasgow Soc., Blue Sky Assoc. Office: Goshen Coll 1700 S Main St Goshen IN 46526*

SHRAUNER, BARBARA WAYNE ABRAHAM, electrical engineer, educator; b. Morristown, N.J., June 21, 1934; d. Leonard Gladstone and Ruth Elizabeth (Thrasher) Abraham; m. James Ely Shrauner, 1965; children: Elizabeth Ann, Jay Arthur. BA cum laude, U. Colo., 1956; AM, Harvard U., 1957, PhD, 1962. Postdoctoral researcher U. Libre de Bruxelles, Brussels, 1962-64; postdoctoral researcher NASA Ames Rsch. Ctr., Moffett Field, Calif., 1964-65; asst. prof. Washington U., St. Louis, 1966-69, assoc. prof., 1969-77, prof., 1977—2003, sr. prof., 2003—. Sabbatical Los Alamos (N.Mex.) Sci. Lab., 1975-76, Lawrence Berkeley Lab., Berkeley, Calif., 1985-86; cons. Los Alamos Nat. Lab., 1979, 84, NASA, Washington, 1980, Naval Surface Weapons Lab., Silver Spring, Md., 1984. Contbr. articles on transport in semiconductors, hidden symmetries of differential equations, plasma physics to profl. jours. Fellow Am. Phys. Soc. (sr. divsn. plasma physics, exec. com. 1980-82, 96-98); mem. IEEE (sr.; sr. exec. com. of standing tech. com. on plasma sci. and applications 1996-98), AAUP (local sec.-treas. 1980-82), Am. Geophys. Union, Univ. Fusion Assn., Phi Beta Kappa, Sigma Xi, Eta Kappa Nu, Sigma Pi Sigma. Home: 7452 Stratford Ave Saint Louis MO 63130-4044 Office: Washington U 1 Brookings Dr Dept Elec Saint Louis MO 63130-4899 E-mail: bas@ee.wustl.edu.

SHREEVE, JEAN'NE MARIE, chemist, educator; b. Deer Lodge, Mont., July 2, 1933; d. Charles William and Maryfrances (Briggerman) Shreeve. BA in Chemistry, U. Mont., 1953, DSc (hon.), 1982; MS in Analytical Chemistry, U. Minn., 1956; PhD in Inorganic Chemistry, U. Wash., 1961. From asst. prof. to assoc. prof. chemistry U. Idaho, Moscow, 1961—67, prof., 1967-73, 2000—, acting chmn. dept. chemistry, 1969-70, 1973, head dept. and prof., 1973-87, v.p. rsch. and grad. studies, prof. chemistry, 1987-99, Jean'ne M. Shreeve chemistry prof., 2004—. Mem. nat. com. Stds. Higher Edn., 1965—67, 1969—73; Lucy W. Pickett lectr. Mt. Holyoke Coll., 1976; George H. Cady lectr. U. Wash., 1993; chmn. Pres.'s Com. Medal Sci., 2003—. Mem. editl. bd. Jour. Fluorine Chemistry, 1970—, Jour. Heteroatom Chemistry, 1988—95, Accounts Chem. Rsch., 1973—75, Inorganic Synthesis, 1976—; contbr. articles to sci. jours. Mem. bd. govs. Argonne (Ill.) Nat. Lab., 1992—98. Named Hon. Alumnus, U. Idaho, 1972; named to Idaho Hall of Fame, 2001; recipient Disting. Alumni award, U. Mont., 1970, Outstanding Achievement award, U. Minn., 1975, Sr. U.S. Scientist award, Alexander Von Humboldt Found., 1978, Excellence in Tchg. award, Chem. Mfrs. Assn., 1980; NSF Postdoctoral fellow, U. Cambridge, Eng., 1967—68, U.S. Hon. Ramsay fellow, 1967—68, Alfred P. Sloan fellow, 1970—72. Mem.: AAUW (officer Moscow chpt. 1962—69), AAAS (bd. dirs. 1991—95), Idaho Acad. Sci. (Disting. Scientist 2001), Am. Chem. Soc. (bd. dirs. 1985—93, chmn. fluorine divsn. 1979—81, mem. adv. bd. Petroleum Rsch. Fund 1975—77, mem. women chemists com. 1972—77, Harry and Carol Mosher award Santa Clara Valley sect. 1992, Shirley B. Radding award Santa Clara Valley sect. 2003, Garvan medal 1972, award for creative work in fluorine chemistry 1978), Göttingen (Germany) Acad. Scis. (corr.), Phi Beta Kappa. Avocations: fishing, gardening. Office: U Idaho Dept Chemistry Moscow ID 83844-2343 Fax: 208-885-9146. Business E-Mail: jshreeve@kidaho.edu.

SHREM, EILEEN MERRY, insurance planner; b. Bklyn., Oct. 17, 1946; d. Joseph Isodor and Beverly Irene (Cohen) Pollak; 1 child, Andrea Joy. MS, Bklyn. Coll. Profl. actress, N.Y.C., 1950-58; tchr. N.Y.C. Sch. Sys., Bklyn., 1968-70; recreation supr. East Brunswick (N.J.) Twp., 1973-80; ins. planner Bradley Beach, N.J., 1980—. Bd. dirs. N.J. Individual Health Coverage Program, chair mktg. com.; instr. Life Underwriter Tng. Coun., N.J., 1993, 94. Sec., chair adv. com. N.J. Com. on Rec for Disabled, Trenton, 1979—. Named Woman of Achievement Mon. Couty Adv. Com. on Status of Women, 1992. Mem. N.J. Assn. of Women Bus. Owners (pres., v.p. 1989-93, state and chpt. bds. 1981-87, Woman of Yr. 1987). Avocations: alpine skiing, bike riding, dance. Home and Office: 215 Mccabe Ave Apt C1 Bradley Beach NJ 07720-1465

SHREVE, PEG, retired state legislator, retired elementary school educator; b. Spencer, Va., July 23, 1927; d. Hubert Smith and Pearl (Looney) Adams; m. Don Franklin Shreve, June 17, 1950 (dec. Sept. 1970); children: Donna, Jennifer, John, Don. BA, Glenville State U., 1948. Reading tchr. Wood County Bd., Parkersburg, W.Va., 1948—50; elem. tchr. Mt. Solon, Va., 1950—52, Bridgewater, 1952—53, Cody, Wyo., 1970—86; mem. Wyo. Ho. of Reps., 1978—98, chmn.. com. travel, recreation and wildlife, 1983—91, majority whip, 1992—94, speaker pro tem, 1995—98; ret., 1998. Mem. Nat. Com. State Legislatures, 1982—; mem. coun. Girl Scouts U.S., White Sulpher Springs, W.Va., 1962—65; co-chair Select Com. Sch. Fin., 1996—99. Named Legislator of the Yr., Wyo. Outfiiters Assn., 1989, Ofcl. of the Yr., Wyo. Wildlife Assn., 1990, Alumna of the Yr., Glenville State Coll., 1994. Mem.: AAUW (exec. bd.), Nat. Women Legislators (Women

Helping Women award 1985), Soroptimists, Beta Sigma Phi (Lady of the Yr. award 1986). Republican. Presbyterian. Avocations: golf, walking, needlepoint, knitting, bridge. Home: PO Box 2257 Cody WY 82414-2257

SHREVE, SUE ANN GARDNER, retired health products company administrator; b. Bklyn., Jan. 26, 1932; d. Homer Frank and Grace Emily (Kohlhagen) Gardner; m. Eugene Sheldon Shreve II, Nov. 20, 1954; children: Pamela Ann, Cynthia Ann Shreve Richard. BBA, Hofstra U., 1955. Co. rep. N.Y. Tel. Co., Bay Shore, 1954-55; engr. Republic Aviation, Farmingdale, N.Y., 1955-58; substitute tchr. East Islip (N.Y.) Sch. Dist., 1966-71; mgr. Patchogue Surg. and Athletic Supplies, Sayville, N.Y., 1971-81, ret., 1981. Invited guest writer Nat. Geneal. Soc. newsletter, 1996, 99; lectr. in genealogy, 1997—; condr. genealogy workshops, 1996—. Author, editor, pub.: The Kohlhagen Family Genealogy, 1994, The Shreve Family Genealogy, an update from 1641, 1997, Hendrickson Genealogy England to Illinois before 1840, 1999, Piscitelli Genealogy Italy to NYC before 1912, 2000; compiler, editor newsletter Gardner/Gardiner Rschrs., 1993—, Amos F.F. Gardner His Maternal Ancestors—Kirkpatrick & Barkley & Descendants, 2001, The Coates Family Genealogy, 2002, The Ridgeway Family Genealogy, 2003, The Mendenhall Family Genealogy, 2003, The Stockton Family Genealogy, 2003; issue reviewer Geneal. Helper Mag., 1995. Life mem. N.Y. State Congress of Parents and Tchrs., 1963—, past pres.; mem. Penataquit Aux. Southside Hosp., 1985—; mem., fund-raiser Hospice of South Shore, 1983—; mem. Bay Shore N.Y. Hist. Soc., 1997—; rec. sec. Bay Shore Beautification Soc., 2000—, Bradish Ln. Homeowners Assn., 1997—2001, treas., 2002—; mem. Sagtikos Manor Hist. Soc., 2003—. Recipient Ofcl. proclamation Village of Frankfort, Ill., 1996; named one of Outstanding Young Women of Am., 1967. Mem.: DAR/Nat. Soc. DAR (vice regent 2001—), AAUW (charter, past pres., past treas. Islip area br., rsch. and project grantee 1989), Bay Shore C. of C., 1st Families of Ohio, Daus. Union Vets. of Civil War (rec. sec. 2004—), German Genealogy Group of L.I., Bay Shore Garden Club (past pres., treas., dir., 2d v.p. 2000—, Woman of Yr. 1997, 2003). Republican. Methodist. Avocations: tennis, gourmet cooking, gardening, needlework, international travel. Home: 5 Anderson Ct Bay Shore NY 11706-7701

SHREVE, SUSAN RICHARDS, writer, educator; b. Toledo, May 2, 1939; d. Robert Kenneth and Helen (Greene) Richards; children— Porter, Elizabeth, Caleb, Kate. BA, U. Pa., 1961; MA, U. Va., 1969. Prof. English lit. George Mason U., Fairfax, Va., 1976—. Vis. prof. Columbia U., N.Y.C., 1982—, Princeton U., 1991, 92, 93. Author: (novels) A Fortunate Madness, 1974, A Woman Like That, 1977, Children of Power, 1979, Miracle Play, 1981, Dreaming of Heroes, 1984, Queen of Hearts, 1986, A Country of Strangers, 1989, Daughters of the New World, 1992, The Train Home, 1993, Skin Deep: Women & Race, 1995, The Visiting Physician, 1995; (pseudonym Annie Waters) Glimmer, 1997, Plum & Jaggers, 2000; (children's books) The Nightmares of Geranium Street, 1977, Family Secrets, 1979, Loveletters, 1979, The Masquerade, 1980, The Bad Dreams of a Good Girl, 1981, The Revolution of Mary Leary, 1982, The Flunking of Joshua T. Bates, 1984, How I Saved the World on Purpose, 1985, Lucy Forever and Miss Rosetree, Shrinks, Inc., 1985, Joshua T. Bates In Charge, 1992, The Gift of the Girl Who Couldn't Hear, 1991, Wait for Me, 1992, Amy Dunn Quits School, 1993, Lucy Forever & the Stolen Baby, 1994, The Formerly Great Alexander Family, 1995, Zoe and Columbo, 1995, Warts, 1996, A Goalie, 1996, Joshua Bates in Trouble Again, 1997, Jonah, The Whale, 1997, Ghost Cats, 1999, The End of Amanda, The Good, 2000; co-editor: How We Want to Live: Narratives on Progress, 1996, (with Porter Shreve) Outside the Law: Narratives on Justice, 1997, How We Want to Live: Narratives on Progress, 1998, Tales Out of School: Narratives on Education, 1999, Blister, 2001, Trout & Me, 2002, Under the Watson's Porch, 2003. Recipient Jenny Moore award George Washington U., 1978; John Simon Guggenheim award in fiction, 1980; Nat. Endowment Arts fiction award, 1982. Mem. PEN/Faulkner Found. (pres.), Phi Beta Kappa. E-mail: srshreve@aol.com.

SHRIER, DIANE KESLER, psychiatrist, educator; b. Mar. 23, 1941; d. Benjamin Arthur and Mollie (Wortman) Kesler; m. Adam Louis Shrier, June 10, 1961; children: Jonathan Laurence, Lydia Anne, Catherine Jane, David Leopold. BS in Chemistry/Biology magna cum laude, Queen's Coll., CUNY, 1961; postgrad., Washington U. Sch. Medicine, St. Louis, 1960-61; MD, Yale U., 1964. Diplomate Am. Bd. Psychiatry and Neurology. Pediat. intern Bellevue Hosp., N.Y.C., 1964-65; psychiat. resident Albert Einstein Coll. Medicine-Bronx Mcpl. Hosp. Ctr., 1966-68, child psychiatry fellow, 1968-70; staff cons. Family Svc. and Child Guidance Ctr. of the Oranges, Maplewood, Milburn-Orange, N.J., 1970-73, cons., 1973-79; pvt. practice Montclair, N.J., 1970-92, Washington, 1994—. Cons. Cmty. Day Nursery, East Orange, NJ, 1970—79, Montclair State Coll., 1976—78; psychiat. cons. Bloomfield (N.J.) pub. schs., 1974—75; clin. instr. Albert Einstein Coll. Medicine, 1970—73; clin. asst. prof. psychiatry U. Medicine and Dentistry N.J., 1978—82, clin. assoc. prof., 1982—89, prof. clin. psychiatry, 1989—92; vice-chmn., dir. clin. psychiat. svcs. dept. psychiatry Children's Nat. Med. Ctr., 1992—94, attending staff, 1994—; prof. psychiatry and pediats. George Washington U. Med. Ctr., 1992—94, clin. prof. psychiatry, behavioral scis. and pediat., 1994—; cons. Walter Reed Med. Ctr., 1994—. Contbr. articles to med. jours. Trustee Montessori Learning Ctr., Montclair, 1973-75. Regents scholar Queen's Coll., 1961. Fellow Am. Psychiat. Assn., Acad. Child Psychiatry; mem. Tri-County Psychiat. Assn. (exec. com., rec. sec. 1977-78, 2d v.p. 1978-79, 1st v.p. 1979-80, pres. 1977-81), N.J. Psychiat. Assn. (councillor 1981-84), Am. Acad. Child and Adolescent Psychiatry (councillor at large 1992-95), Phi Beta Kappa. Home: 4000 Cathedral Ave NW Apt 317B Washington DC 20016-5267 Office: Ste 104 1616 18th St NW Washington DC 20009-2521 Office Phone: 202-667-9005. E-mail: diane.shrier.med.64@aya.yale.edu.

SHRINER, DARLENE KAY, professional athletics coach; b. Coeur d'Alene, Idaho, June 6, 1951; d. Rodney Leroy and Evelyn Mae Shriner. Assoc. in Sci., North Idaho Jr. Coll., 1971; BS, U. Idaho, 1973. Cert. edn.-biol. scis., phys. edn. Tchr., coach Asotin Sch. Dist., Asotin, Wash., 1973—74, Coeur d'Alene Sch. Dist., Coeur d'Alene, Idaho, 1974—2001. DNA vector workshop Cold Spring Harbor, Moscow, 1994—95; cert. track coach Level I and II U.S. Track and Field, Seattle, 1999, coach U.S. Olympic Trials Track and Field qualifier 1992, New Orleans; coach many state champions and placers; coach nat. hs indoor and outdoor high jump champion, 1991—92. Mem.: NEA, Nat. Sci. Tchrs. Assn., Phi Kappa Phi. Avocations: hiking, gardening, bicycling, jogging. Office: Lake City HS 6101 Ramsey Rd Coeur D Alene ID 83815 Office Fax: 208-769-2944. Business E-Mail: dshriner@SD271.K12.ID.US.

SHRINER, JOAN WARD, secondary school educator; b. Bemidji, Minn., Mar. 15, 1938; d. Robert Francis and Ruby Mae (Hagelberg) Ward; m. Larry J. Shriner; 1 child, Natasha. BS, Bemidji State U., 1960; MS, Nova U., 1987. Tchr. Franklin Jr. H.S., Brainerd, Minn., 1960-61, Evanston (Wyo.) H.S., 1963-65, Western H.S., Las Vegas, Nev., 1965-66, Rancho H.S., Las Vegas, 1966-91; chair English dept., 1980-91; tchr. Cheyenne H.S., Las Vegas, 1991—; chair English dept., 1991—. Table leader Proficiency Testing, Nev., 1986-2001, Analytical Trait Assessment, Nev., 1992-2001; head reader Nev. H.S. Proficience Exam, Nev. State Writing Proficiency, 1998—; mem. curriculum com. Clark County, 1980-2001, mem. adv. team N.E. Tchrs., 2001—, Clark County Dist. N.E. Area; mem. Nev. Curriculum Framework Com., 1995, state stds. com., 1999. Mem. NEA, ASCD, Nat. Coun. Tchrs. English, Nev. State Edn. Assn., Nev. English Lang. Arts Network, Clark County Edn. Assn., Clark County English/Lang. Arts Bd. Democrat. Avocations: reading, arts and crafts, aviculture, swimming. Home: 2825 Michael Way Las Vegas NV 89108-4171 E-mail: jmshriner@aol.com.

SHRIVER, EUNICE MARY KENNEDY (MRS. ROBERT SARGENT SHRIVER JR.), civic worker; b. Brookline, Mass. m. Robert Sargent Shriver, Jr., May 23, 1953; children: Robert Sargent III, Maria Owings, Timothy Perry, Mark Kennedy, Anthony Paul Kennedy. BS in Sociology, Stanford U., 1943; student, Manhattanville Coll. of Sacred Heart, LHD (hon.), 1963, D'Youville Coll., 1962, Regis Coll., 1963, Newton Coll., 1973, Brescia Coll., 1974, Holy Cross Coll., 1979, Princeton U., 1979, Boston Coll., 1990; LittD (hon.), U. Santa Clara, 1962; also hon. degrees, U. Vt., Albertus Magnus Coll., St. Mary's Coll. With spl. war problems div. State Dept. Washington, 1943-45; sec. Nat. Conf. on Prevention and Control juvenile Delinquency, Dept. of Justice, Washington, 1947-48; social worker Fed. Penitentiary for Women, Alderson, W.Va., 1950; exec. v.p. Joseph P. Kennedy, Jr. Found., 1956—; founder Spl. Olympics Internat.; social worker House of Good Shepherd, Chgo., also Juvenile Ct., Chgo., 1951-54; regional chmn. women's div. Community Fund-Red Cross Joint Appeal, Chgo., 1958; mem. Chgo. Commn. on Youth Welfare, 1959-62. Cons. to Pres. John F. Kennedy's Panel on Mental Retardation, 1961; founder Community & Caring, Inc., 1986. Editor: A Community of Caring, 1982, 85, Growing Up Caring, 1990. Co-chmn. women's com. Dem. Nat. Conv., Chgo., 1956. Decorated Legion of Honor; recipient Lasker award, Humanitarian award A.A.M.D., 1973, Nat. Vol. Service award, 1973, Phila. Civic Ballet award, 1973, Prix de la Couronne Française, 1974, Presdl. Medal of Freedom, 1984, others.

SHRIVER, MARIA OWINGS, news correspondent; b. Chgo., Nov. 6, 1955; d. Robert Sargent and Eunice Mary (Kennedy) S.; m. Arnold Schwarzenegger, Apr. 26, 1986; children: Katherine, Christina, Patrick & Christopher. BA, Georgetown U. Coll. Am. Studies, Washington, 1977. News producer Sta. KYW-TV, 1977-78; producer Sta. WJZ-TV, 1978-80; nat. reporter PM Mag., 1981-83; news reporter CBS News, Los Angeles, 1983-85; news correspondent, co-anchor CBS Morning News, N.Y.C., 1985-86; co-host Sunday Today, NBC, 1987-90; anchor Main Street, NBC, 1987; co-anchor Yesterday, Today, and Tomorrow, NBC, 1989; anchor NBC Nightly News Weekend Edition, 1989-90, Cutting Edge with Maria Shriver, NBC, 1990, First Person with Maria Shriver, NBC, 1990—2004. Co-anchor summer olympics, Seoul, Korea, 1988; substitute anchor NBC News at Sunrise, Today, NBC Nightly News with Tom Brokaw; contbg. anchor Dateline, NBC, 1995-2004. Appeared in Last Action Hero, 1993; correspondent TV series The American Parade, 1984; author What's Heaven, 1999, Ten Things I Wish I'd Known Before I Went Into the Real World, 2000, What's Wrong With Timmy, 2001. Recipient Christopher award for "Fatal Addictions", 1990, Exceptional Merit Media award Nat. Women's Political Caucus, first-place Commendation award Am. Women in Radio and TV, 1991, Emmy nomination, George Peabody Award, 1998. Democrat. Roman Catholic.*

SHRIVER, PAMELA H. retired professional tennis player, sports analyst; b. Balt., July 4, 1962; m. Joseph Shapiro, 1998. Profl. tennis player, 1979—; winner 21 career singles, 112 career doubles titles 21 career singles, 92 career doubles titles; winner 7 Australian Opens (with Martina Navratilova), 4 French Opens (with Navratilova), 5 Wimbledons (with Navratilova), 6 U.S. Opens, French Open mixed doubles (with Emilio Sanchez); analyst, commentator HBO, NBC, CBS, ABC, BBC, ESPN; part-owner Balt. Orioles baseball team; pres. Women's Sports Legends. Mem. U.S. Fedn. Cup Team, 1986, 87, 89, U.S. Wightman Cup Team, 1978-81, 83, 85, 87; co-winner 1998 Wimbledon 35 and Over Doubles title; mem. President's Coun. on Phys. Fitness and Sports, 1986-92; mem. Md. Fitness Commn.; v.p. Internat. Tennis Hall of Fame. Active ann. charity tennis exhbn. through Balt. Cmty. Found., also trustee; trustee McDonogh Sch.; hon. chmn. Balt. Tennis Patrons. Recipient Gold medal 1988 Olympic Games in doubles (with Zina Garrison), Player Who Makes a Difference award Family Circle mag., 1996. Mem. U.S. Tennis Assn. (bd. dirs. 1997—), Women's Tennis Assn. (pres. 1991-94, Corel Trou David Gray Svc. award 1998), Tour Players Assn. Address: PHS Ltd 401 Washington Ave Ste 902 Towson MD 21204-4835

SHUART, CAREY CHENOWETH, farmer, volunteer; b. Houston, June 1, 1944; d. Robert Carey Chenoweth and Elizabeth Dorothy Smith; m. Willard Warren Shuart, Apr. 17, 1965 (dec. Mar. 1996); children: Nora Wellington Shuart-Faris, Sarah Espy Shuart Szymanski. Student, U. Tex., 1962—66, U. Houston, 1991—93, Glassell Sch. Mus. of Fine Arts, Houston, 1990—2001. Owner, cons. Bien Trouvé Art Gallery, Houston, 1979—85; rice farmer Shuart Farms, Houston. Mem. adv. bd. Blaffer Gallery U. Houston, 2002—. Editor: (newsletter) U Friends, 1992—98. Mem. alumni bd. St. John's Sch., Houston, 1973—75; sustainer Jr. League of Houston, 1975—2001; founder, pres. Pink Ladies-Eagle Lake Cmty. Hosp., 1967—72, Civic Garden Club, Eagle Lake, Tex., 1983—85; chmn. adv. bd. Friends of Women's Studies U. Houston, 2001—03; founder, patron Women's Archive and Rsch. Ctr. U. Houston; mem. photo subcom. Mus. Fine Arts, Houston, 2000—03; bd. dirs. Friends of Women's Studies U. Houston, 1992—2003, Honors Coll., U. Houston, 1992—95. Named Vol. of Yr., U. Houston U. Rels. Divsn., 1992, 1995, U. Houston, 1995, 1996; recipient Nat. CASE award, St. Johns Sch., Houston, 1982, Outstanding Alumni award, 1991. Mem.: Nat. Soc. Colonial Dames in State of Tex. (chmn. 1982—86, 2003—). Episcopalian. Avocations: photography, golf, social work. Office: Shuart Farms 2121 San Felipe #118 Houston TX 77019

SHUBART, DOROTHY LOUISE TEPFER, artist, educator; b. Ft. Collins, Colo, Mar. 1, 1923; d. Adam Christian and Rose Virginia (Ayers) Tepfer; m. Robert Franz Shubart, Apr. 22, 1950; children: Richard, Lorenne. AA, Colo. Women's Coll., 1944; grad., Cleve. Inst. Art, 1946; student, Western Res. U., 1947—48; BA, St. Thomas Aquinas Coll., 1974; MA, Coll. New Rochelle, 1978; student, Santa Fe C.C., 2001—03. Art tchr. Denver Mus., 1944—50; portrait painter, 1947—50; art tchr. adults and children Cleve. Recreation Dept., 1950—60; adult edn. art tchr. Nanuet Pub. Sch., NY, 1950-65, Pearl River Adult Edn., 1960—75. Rec. sec. Van Houten Fields Assn., West Nyack, NY, 1964—66. Exhibited in group shows at Hopper House, Rockland Ctr Arts, CWC, Cleve. Inst. Arts, Coll. New Rochelle, Rockland County Ann. Art Fair, Gonzalez Sr. Ctr.; co-author: (book and brochure) Van Houten Fields 1937-87, 1987; co-author, photographer: Windmills & Dreams, 1997; group show, Watercolor show, Santa Fe Cmty. Coll., 2003, exhibited in group shows at Santa Fe C.C. Leader 4-H Club, Nanuet, 1960—80, Girl Scouts US, 1961—68; mem. scholarship com., gen. com. PTA, 1964—68; rec. sec. Van Houten Fields Assn., West Nyack, NY, 1960—74; com. mem. Environ. Def. Fund, Union Concerned Scientists, Nat. Com. to Preserve Social Security and Medicare; capt., organizer Neighborhood Watch; campaign vol. Jim Baca for Gov., N.Mex., 1996, Gore for Pres., Santa Fe, 2000; bd. mem., mailings Friends of Santa Fe Libr., 2003—; vol. Santa Fe Libr., 1998—; com. mem. Eldorado Cmty. Improvement Assn.-Arterial Rd. Planning Com., 1992—94; campaign vol. Tom Udall for Congress, 1999—2003, 2003; mem. Eldorado Hist. Com., 1995—97; vol. Eldorado's Vista Grande Libr., 2001—03; mem. Eldorado chpt. Security Com., Eldorado Conservation Greenbelt Com., 1996—97, Shakespeare in Santa Fe Guild, 1998, Mil. Hist. Found., 2000—; vol. Cerro Grande Food Bank, 1998—. Gund traveling scholar, Cleve. Inst. Arts, 1946. Mem.: NOW, AAUW, Audubon Soc., Action on Smoking and Health, Union Concerned Scientists, Am. Dem. Action, Environ. Def. Fund, Wilderness Club, Phi Delta Kappa, Delta Tau Kappa. Democrat. Avocations: books, gardening, photography, bicycling, writing. Home: 8 Hidalgo Ct Santa Fe NM 87508-8898

SHUBERT, GABRIELLE S. museum executive director; b. Phila., Apr. 28, 1955; d. Albert H. and Florence (Reiff) S. B in Music, Oberlin Coll., 1977; M in Public Adminstrn., N.Y.U., 1989. Asst. to v.p./dir. of sales Columbia Artist Mgmt., N.Y.C., 1979-80; artist rep. Herbert Barrett Mgmt., N.Y.C., 1980-81; dir. sales Sheldon Soffer Mgmt., N.Y.C., 1981-87; dir. work study program The Parks Coun., N.Y.C., 1987-88; mgr. arts for transit Met. Transp. Authority, N.Y.C., 1988-91; exec. dir. N.Y. Transit Mus., N.Y.C., 1991—. Guest lectr. N.Y.U., 1995, Yale U., New Haven, Conn., 1987; pub. art selection panel Dept. of Cultural Affairs, N.Y.C., 1992. Chmn. Concerned Citizens Upper Broadway, N.Y.C., 1983-85; fellow Coro Found. LEadership N.Y. program. Fellow Mus. Mgmt. Inst. Getty Mus., Berkeley, Calif., 1995, Mayor's Leadership Inst., N.Y.C., 1995. Fellow Mcpl. Art Soc. Office: NY Transit Museum 130 Livingston St Rm 9001 Brooklyn NY 11201-5106

SHUCART, EVELYN ANN, artist, educator; b. Covington, Ky., May 29, 1942; d. Frederick Holroyd and Evelyn Ann (Thomson) Eastabrooks; m. Rexford Lee Hill III, Sept. 12, 1964 (div. 1983); children: Eric Douglas, Rexford Alan, Gerald Alexander, Andrew David; m. James Wood Shucart, Sept. 21, 1991. BS in Design, U. Cin., 1965. Freelance artist, St. Louis, 1960—; office mgr. United Ch. of Christ, St. Louis, 1983-84; program coord. Acme Premium Supply, St. Louis, 1984-86, mgr., 1986-93; v.p. I.B.A. Inc., St. Louis, 1993-97; tchr. fine arts Meramec C.C., St. Louis, 2000—. Illustrator: Life Through Time, 1975. Coord./advisor Guardian Angels N.Y., St. Louis, 1981-82; advisor Pres.'s Commn. on Continuing Edn., Eden Sem., St. Louis, 1982-83; advisor Ecumenical Task Force on Hunger, 1982; cons. Women's Task Force on Employment, 1975-76; cons. Nat. Bd. Homeland Ministries, United Ch. of Christ, 1982, mem. St. Louis Assn. United Ch. of Christ, pres., 1981-82; bd. dirs. Women's Caucus for Art, St. Louis, 2000—, pres. St. Louis chpt. 2003—; bd. dirs. art sect. St. Louis Artist's Guild, 2002. Recipient Best of Show award, Siegfried Reinhardt County Artists, 1976, J.McCall Meml. prize, 1997. Mem. LWV, Amnesty Internat., League Women Voters, Sierra Club. Avocations: gardening, golf, painting, reading, tai chi. Home and Office: 2039 Brookcreek Ln Saint Louis MO 63122-2254 E-mail: evieart@sbcglobal.net.

SHUE, ELISABETH, actress; b. Wilmington, Del., Oct. 6, 1963; m. Davis Guggenheim, 1994; 1 child: Miles. Student, Wellesley Coll.; grad., Harvard U.; studied with Sylvie Leigh, Showcase Theater. Appeared in Broadway plays including Some Americans Abroad, Birth and After Birth; appeared in films including The Karate Kid, 1984 (Young Artist award 1984), Link, 1986, Adventures in Babysitting, 1987, Cocktail, 1988, Body Wars, 1989, Back to the Future Part II, 1989, Back to the Future Part III, 1990, Soapdish, 1991, The Marrying Man, 1991, Twenty Bucks, 1993, Heart and Souls, 1993, Radio Inside, 1994, Blind Justice, 1994, The Underneath, 1995, Leaving Las Vegas, 1995 (Oscar nominee for Best Actress), The Trigger Effect, 1996, The Saint, 1996, Palmetto, 1997, Deconstructing Harry, 1997, Cousin Bette, 1997, Molly, 1998, Hollow Man, 2000, Tuck Everlasting, 2002; appeared in TV movies including Charles and Diana, Double Switch, 1987, Hale the Hero, 1992, Blind Justice; appeared in TV series Call to Glory, 1984, Amy & Isabelle, 2001. Office: Creative Arts Agy 9830 Wilshire Blvd Beverly Hills CA 90212-1804

SHUGART, ANITA CAROL, research and development cosmetologist; b. Memphis, July 2, 1943; d. Thomas Edwin and Lula P. (Shults) Brumbelow; m. Cecil Glen Shugart, Dec. 14, 1985; m. Robert E. Henry (div. Jan. 1985); children: Robert Eugene Henry Jr., Lisa Carol Henry Brown. BA, Memphis State U., 1989, postgrad., 1990-91. Cert. cosmetologist, aesthetician. Cosmetologist, Memphis, 1981-86; aesthetician mgr. Adian Arpel Cosmetics, 1991-92; cosmetologist Maybelline R & D, Memphis, 1992—. Mem. NAFE, Soc. Cosmetic Chemists, Adult Student Assn. (pres. 1987-89), Sigma Tau Delta (sec. 1987-89), Omicron Delta Kappa. Avocations: tennis, dance, reading, traveling, the beach. Home: Unit 112 11483 Front Beach Rd Panama City Beach FL 32407-3617

SHUGART, JILL, retired school system administrator, educational consultant; b. Dallas, July 15, 1940; d. Claude Ernest and Allie Merle (Hamilton) S. BA, Baylor U., 1962; MA, Tex. Woman's U., 1972, PhD, 1980. Middle sch. English tchr. Garland (Tex.) Ind. Sch. Dist., 1962-63, high sch. social studies tchr., 1963-76, high sch. asst. prin., 1976-79, dir. communications, 1979-82, asst. supt., 1982-85, supt., 1985—99, ret., 1999—. Mem. legis. coun. U. Interscholastic League, Tex., 1989-99; chmn. Dist. III music com., Tex., 1989-99; adj. prof. Tex. Women's U., Denton, 1983; chmn. Region X ESC Adv. Coun., rep. to commr.'s supt.'s com., 1993-95; cons. Richardson and Carrollton-Farmers Br. Sch. Dists., 2000-04; coord. Region 10 ESC Supr.'s Acad., 2000-04. Gen. chmn. Boy Scouts Am. Scouting Night, Dallas, 1988-89; chmn. City of Garland Cmty. Action Com., 1995-99; sec. Tex. Sch. Alliance, 1995-96, chmn., 1996-99; life mem. Tex. and nat. PTA; pres. Garland br. Am. Heart Assn., 1990-91; co-chmn. sustaining dr. Garland YMCA, 1995-96; mem. Adv. Com. to Gov. and State Legisture, 1998; mem. steering com. Garland Econ. Devel. Partnership, 1994-99, Tex. Fast Growth Sch. Coalition; chair Tex. Sch. Alliance, 1998—. Recipient Lamar award for excellence Masons, Award of Distinction, Tex. Ret. Tchrs. Assn.; named Top 100 Educators to Watch, Executive Educator mag., 1985, Finalist as Outstanding Tex. Sch. Supt., 1990, Woman of Distinction, Soroptimist Club; Paul Harris fellow. Mem. Quality Tex. Bd. Examiners, Garland Edn. Found. (bd. dirs. 1999-2004), Baylor Med. Ctr. Garland (bd. dirs. 2001-04). Republican. Baptist. Avocations: travel, lake activities.

SHUHLER, PHYLLIS MARIE, physician; b. Sellersville, Pa., Sept. 25, 1947; d. Raymond Harold and Catherine Cecilia (Virus) S.; m. John Howard Schwarz, Sept. 17, 1983; 1 child, Luke Alexander. BS in Chemistry, Chestnut Hill Coll., 1971; MD, Mich. State U., 1976; diploma of Tropical Medicine and Hygiene, U. London, 1980. Diplomate Am. Bd. Family Medicine. With Soc. Cath. Med. Missionaries, Phila., 1966-82; ward clk., nursing asst. Holy Family Hosp., Atlanta, 1971-72; resident in family practice Somerset Family Med. Residency Program, Somerville, N.J., 1976-79; physician East Coast Migrant Health Project, Newton Grove, N.C., 1980; physician, missionary SCMM, Diocese of Sunyani, Berekum, Ghana, West Africa, 1980-81; emergency rm. physician Northeast Emergency Med. Assn., Quakertown, Pa., 1981-82; founder, physician Family Health Care Ctr., Inc., Pennsburg, Pa., 1982-90; physician Lifequest Med. Group, Pennsburg, 1990-93; pvt. practice Pennsburg, 1993-99; physician Tri-Valley Primary Care Group, 1999—. Fellow Royal Soc. Tropical Medicine and Hygiene; mem. Am. Acad. Family Practice, Am. Bd. Family Practice, Am. Med. Women Assn. Pa. Acad. Family Practice, Lehigh Valley Women Med. Assn. Roman Catholic. Avocations: guitar, reading, bicycling, hiking. Office: 101 W 7th St Ste 2C Pennsburg PA 18073-1512

SHULER, SALLY ANN SMITH, retired media consultant; b. Mt. Olive, N.C., June 11, 1934; d. Leon Joseph and Ludia Irene (Montague) Simmons; m. Henry Ralph Smith Jr., Mar. 1, 1957 (div. Jan. 1976); children: Molly Montague, Barbara Ellen, Sara Ann, Mary Kathryn; m. Harold Robert Shuler, Aug. 2, 1987 (div. Mar. 1997). BA in Math., Duke U., 1956; student, U. Liège, Belgium, 1956-57; postgrad., Claremont Grad Sch., 1970-72. Mgr. fed. systems GE Info. Svcs. Co., Washington, 1976-78, mgr. mktg. support Rockville, Md., 1978-81; dir. bus. devel. info. tech. group Electronic Data Sys., Bethesda, Md., 1981-82, v.p. mktg. optimum systems div. Rockville, 1982-83, v.p. planning and comm. Dallas, 1983-84; exec. dir. comml. devel. U.S. West Inc., Englewood, Colo., 1984-90; v.p. mktg. devel. Cin. Bell Info. Sys. Inc., 1990-92; mgmt. cons. in mergers and acquisitions Denver, 1992-93, 1995—2002; v.p. major accounts U.S. Computer Svcs., Denver, 1993-95; ret., 2002. Bd. dirs. Rotary-Denver Tech. Ctr., 1999—2003, Seeking Common Ground, 2001—02. Recipient GE Centennial award, Rockville, 1978. Mem. Women in Telecommunications, Rotary (Found. fellow, prest. Denver Tech. Ctr. 1999-2000, amb. scholar 1956-57), Phi Beta Kappa, Tau Psi Omega, Pi Mu Epsilon, Sigma Kappa. Democrat. Presbyterian. Office Phone: 303-671-5950.

SHULER DONNER, LAUREN, film producer; BS in Film and Broadcasting, Boston U. Assoc. prodr. : (films) Thank God It's Friday, 1978; Mr. Mom, 1983; Ladyhawke, 1985; St. Elmo's Fire, 1985; Pretty in Pink, 1986;

Three Fugitives, 1989; Radio Flyer, 1992; Dave, 1993; Free Willy, 1993; prodr.: (TV films) Amateur Night at the Dixie Bar and Grill, 1979; (films) Free Willy 2: The Adventure Home, 1995, You've Got Mail, 1998, Any Given Sunday, 1999, X-Men, 2000, X2: X-Men United, 2003, Timeline, 2003, Constantine, 2004; exec. prodr. : Assassins, 1995; Free Willy 3, 1997; Volcano, 1997; Out Cold, 2001; Just Married, 2003. Office: The Donners' Co Ste 420 9465 Wilshire Blvd Beverly Hills CA 90212

SHULGASSER-PARKER, BARBARA, writer; b. Manhasset, N.Y., Apr. 10, 1954; d. Lew and Luba (Golante) S.; m. Norman Parker, Sept. 1999; 1 child: Atticus. Student, Sarah Lawrence Coll., 1973-74; BA magna cum laude, CUNY, 1977; MS, Columbia U., 1978. Feature writer Waterbury (Conn.) Rep., 1978-81; reporter, feature writer Chgo. Sun Times, 1981-84; film critic San Francisco Examiner, 1984-98; freelance book critic N.Y. Times Book Rev., N.Y.C., 1983—; film critic Chgo. Tribune, 1999—. Author: Funny Accent, 2001; co-author: (screenplay, with Robert Altman) Ready to Wear, 1994; freelance video columnist N.Y. Times Sunday Arts & Leisure, 1989, features for Vanity Fair, Glamour and Mirabella mags. Home: 3120 S Ocean Blvd Apt 2402 Palm Beach FL 33480-5650

SHULL, CLAIRE, documentary film producer, casting director; b. N.Y.C., Oct. 26, 1925; d. Barnet Joseph and Fannie (Florea) Klar; m. Leo Shull, Aug. 8, 1948; children: Lee Shull Pearlstein, David. Student, Am. Acad. Dramatic Arts, N.Y.C., 1943-44, NYU, 1973-74. Editor, assoc. pub. Show Bus. Publs., N.Y.C., 1957-85; owner, founder Claire/Casting, N.Y.C. and Miami, Fla., 1972—, Claire/Casting Film Prodns., N.Y.C. and Miami, 1978—; cons. dir., prodr., dir. film and TV, The Bass Mus., Miami Beach, Fla., 1992—. Miami corr. film, TV, theatre Show Bus. Weekly, 1999—. Actress in The Front Page, USO European tour, 1945 46, (on Broadway) Tenting Tonight, 1947; prodr., dir. HBO TV series How To Break into Show Business, 1980-81, Cable-TV series, Join Us at the Bass, 1993-97. Recipient gold award and distinctive merit TV award Advt. Club. Hartford, Conn., 1984, Clio award, 1989. Mem.: Drama Desk, Actors Equity Assn., Ind. Casting Dirs. Assn. N.Y., Miami Internat. Press Club.

SHULL, MIKKI, media consultant; b. Cleve. d. Lois Biles; life ptnr. Jerome China. BS, Carnegie-Mellon U., 1983. Bus. transformation cons. PriceWaterhouseCoopers, N.Y.C., 1986-97; media and entertainment cons. IBM Global Svcs., N.Y.C., 1997—. Mem. Advt. Women N.Y. Republican. Office: IBM 590 Madison Ave New York NY 10022 Home: 180 Belmont Ave Jersey City NJ 07304-2002 E-mail: shull@us.ibm.com.

SHULMAN, CAROLE KAREN, professional society administrator; b. Mpls., Nov. 25, 1940; d. Allen Eldon and Beulah Ovidia (Blomsness) Banbury; m. David Arthur Shulman, Mar. 26, 1962; children: Michael, Krista, Tracy, Robbyn. Student, Colo. Coll., 1958-61, California Coast U., 1983-84. Profl. instr. Rochester (Minn.) Figure Skating Club, 1962-84, dir. skating, 1964-79, cons., 1979—; exec. dir. Profl. Skaters Assn., Rochester, 1984—, master rating examiner, 1971—, world profl. judge, 1976, 79, 87-88. Editor Professional Skater mag., 1984—; prodr. U.S. Open Profl. Figure Skating Championships, 1987, 89—. Pres. Rochester Arts Council, 1983. Recipient Achievement award Rochester Arts Coun., 1983, Mayor's Medal of Honor, 1997; named triple gold medalist U.S. Figure Skating Assn., Colorado Springs, Colo., 1959, 63, Master Rated Coach Profl. Skaters Assn., 1970, Sr. Rated Coach in Dance Profl. Skaters Assn., 1970. Mem. Am. Harp Soc., Profl. Skaters Assn. (hon., Lifetime Achievement award 1989). Mem. Covenant ch. Avocations: harp, skiing. Office: Profl Skaters Assn Internat 3006 Allegro Park SW Rochester MN 55902-0886

SHULMAN, MILDRED, artist; b. Perth Amboy, N.J., Aug. 13, 1927; d. Abraham and Estelle (Golub) S.; m. Ben Spina, Feb. 20, 1947 (div. Aug. 1954). Student, Sch. Indsl. Arts, N.Y.C., 1942—45, McDowell Sch. Art, 1946—47, NYU, 1961—62, Art Student's League, 1991—95. Contr. Continental Mdse. Co., Inc., N.Y.C., 1959-65, Famous Fashion Shops, N.Y.C., 1966-69; owner, pres. Luminere Creations, Inc., N.Y.C., 1969-91; self-employed artist N.Y.C., 1991—. Author: Barter*The Silent Giant, 1985. Mem.: New Art Ctr., Midtown West Art Assn., Am. Soc. Portrait Artists, Nat. Mus. Women in the Arts, Art Students League, Salmagundi Club. Achievements include patents for flexible screen partitions; electrical/sculptural lighting design; sculpturing method. Avocations: hiking, swimming. Fax: 212-242-2846.

SHULMAN, PAULA B(AKA PHILLIPS), marriage and family therapist, educator; b. N.Y.C., June 24, 1948; d. Jack and Eugenia Brenner Shulman; m. Ayite Nkromah, Mar. 6, 1971 (div. Apr. 1979); children: Amobiye Nkromah, Toah Nkromah. MEd, Bank St. Coll. Edn., N.Y.C., 1982; MA in Marriage and Family Therapy, Antioch New Eng. Grad. Sch., Keene, NH, 2002. Educator, psychotherapist, trainer, cons., founder, dir. Multiracial Inst., NYC and Leverett/Montague, 1986—; couples, individual, child, and family therapist Leverett/Montague, Mass., 2002—. Founder, dir. Bi-Racial Families Resource Ctr., NYC, 1983—86. Author: The Development of Positive Identity in Bi-Racial Children; founder (organizations) Bi-Racial Families Resource Center, Multi-Racial Family Group of Western Massachusetts. Pilgrim and advance team organizer Interfaith Pilgrimage of the Mid. Passage: Retracing the Journey of Slavery, 1998—99. Mem.: Am. Assn. Marriage Family Therapy. Office: Multiracial Inst PO Box 604 Leverett MA 01054 Office Phone: 413-367-9894. Personal E-mail: paula@crocker.com.

SHULTZ, LEILA MCREYNOLDS, botanist, educator; b. Bartlesville, Okla., Apr. 20, 1946; 1 child, Kirsten. BS, U. Tulsa, 1969; MA, U. Colo., 1975; PhD, Claremont Grad. Sch., 1983. Curator Intermountain Herbarium Utah State U., 1973-92; rschr. Harvard U., Cambridge, Mass., 1994—; rsch. prof. Utah St. U., 1994—. Vis. prof., acting curator dept. botany U. Okla., 1992-93; bibliographer Gray Herbarium Index, Harvard U., Cambridge, 1994-95. Author: Atlas of the Vascular Plants of Utah, 1988; taxon editor, author: Flora of North America (7 vols.), 1993—. Office: Utah State U Logan UT 84322-5230

SHULTZ, LINDA JOYCE, retired library director; b. South Bend, Ind., Aug. 25, 1931; d. Justin Russell and Gladys Ernstine (Miller) Nash; m. Dale Jay Shultz, Apr. 20, 1952; children: Donald Jay, Sally Janine, William Justin, Alan Joel, Kent Jon. AA, Stephens Coll., 1951; BS in Edn., Ind. U., Ft. Wayne, 1971, Cert. I in Libr. Edn., 1975. Sec. John R. Worthman, Inc., Ft. Wayne, 1951-54; farm wife, mother Noble County, Ind., 1954-68; libr. Noble County Pub. Libr., Albion, Ind., 1968-97; ret., 1997; part-time legal sec. Mem. exec. bd. Tri-Alsa Libr. Svc. Authority, Ft. Wayne, 1988-90. Editor: Albion Memories, 1977. Mem. Albion Local Devel. Corp., 1989-92; sec. Cen. Noble Jr. Achievement, 1988-92. Named Albion Citizen of the Yr. Albion Rotary Club, 1977. Mem. DAR, Order Ea. Star, Rotary (pres. Albion club 1993-94, Paul Harris fellow 1999), Toastmasters (pres. U.S. Six Shooters chpt. 1988-89), Gene Stratton Porter Meml. Soc., Ind. Soc. Mayflower Descendants, Geneal. Soc. (sec. 1985-95, pres. 1997—), Noble County Hist. Soc., Noble County Geneal. Soc. (pres.). Republican. Methodist. Avocation: genealogy.

SHULTZ, LOIS FRANCES CASHO, nursing supervisor; b. Phila., Apr. 29, 1936; d. Ellwood Francis Casho and Beatrice Mae Gunther Casho; m. Thomas Eugene Shultz, Aug. 15, 1959 (div. June 1983); children: David T., Patricia Shultz Bichefsky, Jeffrey A. Nursing diploma, Temple U. Hosp., 1957; BSN, U. Pa., 1961. RN Pa., 2003, cert. gerontological nurse, Am. Bd. Gerontological Nursing, 2001, bd. cert. gerontological nursing, ANCC, 2001. Staff nurse Temple U. Hosp., Phila., 1957, pvt. duty nurse, 1958-59; nursing instr. St. Luke's Hosp. Sch. Nursing, Bethlehem, Pa., 1959-61, Reading (Pa.) Area C.C., 1985-88; asst. DON Reading Nursing Ctr., West Reading, 1988-89; night supr. Berks County Home-BerksHeim, Leesport, Pa., 1989—2004; ret., 2004. Mem. Berks County Bd. Assistance, Reading, 1980—, chmn., 1988-2001, chmn. cmty. rels. com., 2001—; pres., dir. Berks County Med. Soc. Aux.; bd. dirs., chmn., mem. children and youth com. Berks County Mental Health Assn.; bd. dirs., past bd. chmn. Berks County Children and Youth Svcs.; organizer, past dir. Reading Is Fundamental for Berks County; past mem., chmn., mem. programs and svcs. sub-com. United Way Home Health Care Study Com. Mem. Nat. Soc. DAR (1st vice-regent br. Berks County chpt.). Republican. Presbyterian. Home: 5 Wendy Rd Reading PA 19601-1031

SHULTZ, MARGARET ANN, retired secondary school educator; b. Jackson, Miss., Oct. 4, 1937; d. Lester Brown and Emily MacMillan Wilson Sylvester; m. Jose Luis Gracia, 1961 (div. 1976); children: Cristina, Angela, Stephanie; m. John Lewis Shultz, Mar. 21, 1980. Student, Millsaps Coll., 1956—58; BA, U. So. Miss., 1960, MS, 1972; adminstrv. cert. edn., Tex. Christian U., 1987. Cert. counselor Miss., Tex., edn. adminstrn. Tex. Tchr. psychology and drama N.E. Jr. Coll., Booneville, Miss., 1961—63; counselor Biloxi and Pascagoula (Miss.) schs., 1963—72, Purvis (Miss.) H.S., 1980—86, Sam Houston H.S., Arlington, Tex., 1980—86; asst. prin. Lamar H.S., Arlington, 1986—89; cons. Amoco Prodn. Co., Houston, 1989—91; counselor Halton H.S., Ft. Worth, 1994—98; dir. testing Birdville H.S., North Richland Hills, Tex., 2002—03; ret. Regional bd. mem. Am. Coll. Test, Atlanta, 1974—76; panelist video Teenage Suicide, 1987. Author: (book) Teens with Single Parents: Why Me?, 1998, (weekly newspaper columnist Parenting) Ft. Worth Star Telegram, 1992—95. Chairperson Ptnrs. in Search of Ednl. Excellence, Arlington, Tex., 1987—89; co-founder CARE Teams Suicide Prevention, Arlington, 1986—89; patron Kimbell Art Mus., Amon Carter Mus. Recipient scholarship, NSF, 1962, Spl. Legis. award, Am. Pers. and Guidance Assn., 1980. Mem.: Am. Pers. and Guidance Assn. (regional dir., govt. liaison 1977—78, Spl. Legis. award 1980), Miss. Sch. Counselor's Assn. (pres. 1979—80), Purveyors of Series Extraordinaire, Ft. Worth Woman's Club (5 writing awards 1993). Democrat. Methodist. Avocations: decorating, travel, reading, handmade books. Home: 8608 Twisted Oaks Way North Richland Hills TX 76180 E-mail: jlshultz1@flash.net.

SHUM, MARGARET, market economy educator; b. Downers Grove, Ill., June 11, 1973; d. Raymond Hing-Yan and Julia (Miao) S. BA, Northwestern U., 1995. Asst. project mgr. Planned Parenthood of Greater No. N.J., Morristown, 1995-97; lectr. in market economy and bus. english Dalian (China) U. Tech., 1997—. Mktg. cons. Williamson Techs. Inc., Livingston, N.J., 1991-92. Editor, author: Dr. Sun Yat-Sen and My Grandfather General Shum Hung-Ying, 1996. Art collection libr. Northwestern U., Evanston, Ill., 1994-95, rsch. asst. Chinese art, dept. art history, 1993-94. NSF fellow, 1992. Mem. Assn. Asian Studies, Chinese History Soc., Chinese Social Scientists in Am. Avocations: reading, jogging, bicycling, travel, photography. Home: 339 Walnut St Livingston NJ 07039-5011 Office: Dalian U Tech Guest-house Apt 310 Dalian China

SHUMADINE, ANNE BALLARD, financial advisor, lawyer; b. Norfolk, Va., Mar. 8, 1943; d. William Pierce Ballard and Helen Caulfield Ballard Hoffman; m. Conrad Moss Shumadine, Sept. 1, 1965; children: John Ballard, James Hunter. AB, Wellesley Coll., 1965; JD, Coll. William and Mary, 1983. Bar: Va. 1983. Assoc. McGuire Woods Battle & Boothe, Norfolk, 1983-88; ptnr. Shumadine & Rose, P.C., 1988-94, McCandlish Kaine & Grant, 1994—; pres. Signature Fin. Mgmt., 1994—. Bd. dirs. CENIT Bancorp, Norfolk; co-chmn. Old Dominion Tax Conf., Norfolk, 1992; mem. adv. coun. William and Mary Tax Conf., 1997—. Trustee William and Mary Law Sch. Found., 1992—; chmn. Tidewater Scholarship Found., Norfolk, 1995—; rector, bd. visitors Old Dominion U., 1996-97. Fellow Va. Law Found., 1999—; named Vol. of Yr., Downtown Norfolk Coun., 1995. Office: Signature Fin Mgmt 999 Waterside Dr Ste 2220 Norfolk VA 23510-3306

SHUMICK, DIANA LYNN, computer executive; b. Canton, Ohio, Feb. 10, 1951; d. Frank A. and Mary J. (Mari) S.; 1 child, Tina Elyse. Student, Walsh Coll., 1969-70, Ohio U., 1970-71, Kent State U., 1971-77. Data entry clk. Ohio Power Co., Canton, 1969-70; clk. City of Canton Police Dept., 1971-73; sys. engr. IBM, Canton, 1973-81, adv. market support rep. Dallas, 1981-89, sys. engr. mgr. Madison, Wis., 1989-93, mktg. customer satisfaction mgr. Research Triangle Park, N.C., 1993; HelpCenter mgr. desktop and consumer sys. support IBM Personal Computer Co., Research Triangle Park, 1993-96, call ctr. brand ops. mgr., 1996-97; solution mgr. product support svcs. IBM Global Svcs., Cary, N.C., 1997-98, tech. solutions mgr. strategic outsourcing Boulder, Colo., 1999—. Author: Technical Coordinator Guidelines, 1984. Mem. Western Stark County Red Cross, Canton, 1980; v.p. Parents Without Ptnrs., Madison, 1991; vol. ARC, 1985—, Paint-A-Thon, Dane County, 1990, Badger State Games Challenge, 1992, Cystic Fibrosis Found. Gt. Strides, 1992—, Cystic Fibrosis Found. Mother's Day Tea, 1991, 1992, 1993, 1994, 1995, 1996, 1998, 2002, N.C. Sr. Olympics, 1998—, The Dorcas Shop, Cary, NC, 1999—, Susan G. Komen Race for the Cure, 2000—, Habitat for Humanity Global Village Project, Jacksonville, Fla., 2003; active Strong Women Organizing Outrageous Projects, 1998—2001; mem. St. Philip Parish Coun., Lewisville, Tex., 1988—89; pres., bd. dirs. Big Bros. and Sisters of Denton (Tex.) County, 1989, v.p., 1988, sec., 1987; founding bd. mem. Single Parents Network, 1991; mem. bd. dirs. Rape Crisis Ctr., Dane County, sec., 1990—91; bd. dirs. Carolina chpt. Cystic Fibrosis, 1996—. Mem. Italian-Am. Women's Club of Cary. Office: IBM Global Svcs 5600 N 63rd St Boulder CO 80314-0001 E-mail: dshumick@nc.rr.com.

SHURBUTT, SYLVIA BAILEY, English language educator; b. Chamblee, Ga., Nov. 15, 1944; AB in English, West Ga. Coll., Carrollton, 1965; MA in English, Ga. So. U., Statesboro, 1974; PhD in English, U. Ga., Athens, 1982. Tchr. Jefferson (Ga.) High, 1965-67; tchr., English dept. chair S.E. Bulloch High, Brooklet, Ga., 1975-78; assoc. prof. Ga. So. U., Statesboro, 1979-87; prof., English dept. chair Shepherd Coll., Shepherdstown, W.Va., 1987—. Project dir. Appalachia Heritage Writer-in-Residence Program, W.Va. Humanities Coun, Phi Kappa Phi. Co-author: (textbook) Reading/Writing Relationships, 1986; contbr. chpts. to books, articles to profl. jours. Editor, herstorian (newsletter) N.O.W., W.Va. Eastern Panhandle, 1993-96. Recipient STAR Tchg. award Ga. C. of C., 1975. Mem. Nat. Coun. Tchrs. of English, Phi Kappa Phi. Democrat. Methodist. Avocation: writing. Home: PO Box 599 Shepherdstown WV 25443-0599 Office: Dept English/Modern Langs Shepherd Coll Shepherdstown WV 25443 E-mail: sshurbut@shepherd.edu.

SHURE, MYRNA BETH, psychologist, educator; b. Chgo., Sept. 11, 1937; d. Sidney Natkin and Frances (Laufman) Shure. Student, U. Colo., 1955; BS, U. Ill., 1959; MS, Cornell U., 1961, PhD, 1966. Lic. psychologist Pa. Asst. prof. U. R.I.; head tchr. Nursery Sch., Kingston, 1961-62; asst. prof. Temple U., Phila., 1966-67, assoc. prof., 1967-68; instr. Hahnemann Med. Coll., Phila., 1968-69, sr. instr. psychology, 1969-70, asst. prof., 1970-73, assoc. prof., 1973-80, prof., 1980—2002, Drexel U., Phila., 2002—. Spl. cons. PBS Children's TV Show The Puzzle Place. Author (with George Spivack): Social Adjustment of Young Children, 1974; author: (with George Spivack and Jerome Platt) The Problem Solving Approach to Adjustment, 1976; author: (with George Spivack) Problem Solving Techniques in Childrearing, 1978; author: (child curricula manual) I Can Problem Solve, 1992; author: (trade book) Raising a Thinking Child, 1994; author: (audiotape, workbook, paperback) Raising a Thinking Preteen, 2000 (Parents' Choice award, 2001, Parent's Guide Classic award, 2001). Recipient Lela Rowland Prevention award, Nat. Mental Health Assn., 1982, Sarah award, Women in Comm. (Phila. chpt., 1998, Psychology in the Media award, Pa. Psychol. Assn., 1999, award, Ctr. for Substance Abuse Prevention, 2001; grantee rsch. grant, NIMH, 1971—75, 1977—79, 1982—85, 1987, 1988—93. Fellow: APA (divsn. clin. psychology, child sect. 1994, Disting. Contbn. award divsn. cmty. psychology 1984, Task Force on Prevention award 1987, Task Force on Model Programs award 1994, U. Utah and Juvenile Justice Dept. of Delinquency Prevention award 1996, U.S. Dept. Edn. award 2001); mem.: Phila. Soc. Clin. Psychologists, Soc. Rsch. in Child Devel., Nat. Assn. Edn. Young Children, Nat. Assn. Sch. Psychologists. Office: Drexel U Dept Psychology 245 N 15th St MS 626 Philadelphia PA 19102 Office Phone: 215-762-7205. E-mail: mshure@drexel.edu.

SHURLEY, ELAINE P. music educator; b. Lancaster, S.C., Oct. 22, 1952; d. Amos Leon and Betty (Williams) Plyler; m. Lynn Edwin Shurley, Jr., Dec. 29, 1973; children: Britton Michael, Justin Plyler. B in Music Edn., Winthrop Coll. (name now Winthrop U.), 1973; M in Music Edn., Murray State U., 1994. Choir dir. E. Side Mid. Sch., Sylacauga, Ala.; choir dir., tchr. Calvert Elem., Benton, Ky., 1990—91, Gilbertsville Elem., Benton, 1991—92, Calvert Elem., Benton, 1992—93, Marshall County HS, Benton, 1990—93, choir dir., 1993—. Co-dir. 2003 Montreat (N.C.) Worship and Music Conf. Presbyn. Assn. Musicians, 2003. Named Gov., Ky. Col., 1994. Mem.: NEA, Music Educators Nat. Conf., Hymn Soc. Am., Am. Guild English Handbell Ringers, Choristers Guild, Ky. Music Educators Assn. (state choral chair 2003—), Am. Choral Dirs. Assn. (pres. Ky. chpt. 2001—03). Office: Marshall County HS 416 High School Rd Benton KY 42025

SHURTLEFF, AKIKO AOYAGI, artist, consultant; b. Tokyo, Jan. 24, 1950; d. Kinjiro and Fumiyo (Sugata) Aoyagi; m. William Roy Shurtleff, Mar. 10, 1977 (div. Jan. 1995); 1 child, Joseph Aoyagi. Grad., Women's Coll. Art, Tokyo, 1971; student, Acad. Art, San Francisco, 1991-92. Fashion designer, illustrator Marimura Co. and Hayakawa Shoji, Inc., Tokyo, 1970-72; co-founder, art dir. Soyfoods Ctr. consulting svcs., Lafayette, Calif., 1976-94; freelance illustrator, graphic designer. Lectr. U.S. Internat. Christian U., Tokyo, 1977, Japanese Tofu Mfrs. Conv., Osaka, 1978; presenter cooking demonstrations; tchr. cooking classes. Avocations: walking, running, dance, designing company logos. Office: PO Box 443 Lafayette CA 94549-0443 E-mail: akiko1717@aol.com.

SHUSS, JANE MARGARET, artist; b. Ost, Kans., Feb. 15, 1936; d. Leo and Mary Catharine Nett; m. Robert Hamilton Shuss, Feb. 19, 1954; children: Patric, Andrea, Matt, Lisa, Robert, Eric. Student, Otis Art Inst., L.A. Sec. Found. for Plein Air Painting, Avalon, Calif., 1995-97. One-woman shows include Challis Galleries, Laguna Beach, Calif., 1981, 1982, 1983, Esther Wells Gallery, 1984, 1985, 1986, 1987, exhibited in group shows at Plein Air Painters of Am., 1985, 1986, 1987, 1988, 1989, 1990, 1991, 1992, 1993, 1994, 1995, 1996, 1997, 1998—99, 2000, 2001, Western Acad. Women Artists, 1996, O'Brien's Gallery, Scottsdale, Ariz., 1996, Desert Caballeros Mus., 1997, 1998. Mem. Am. Acad. Women Artists (signature mem.), Soc. Am. Impressionists, Plein Air Painters Am. (treas. 1996-97, signature mem.), Calif. Art Club. Republican.

SHUSTER, DIANA, former artistic director; Artistic dir. Am. Musical Theatre of San Jose, Calif., 1982—2002. Office: Am Musical Theatre 1717 Technology Dr San Jose CA 95110-1305

SHUSTER, MARGUERITE, minister, educator; b. Oxnard, Calif., Sept. 10, 1947; d. Carroll Lloyd and Grace Margaret (Hornbeck) S. BA with great distinction, Stanford U., 1968; MDiv, Fuller Sem., Pasadena, Calif., 1975; PhD, Fuller Grad. Sch. Psychology, Pasadena, 1977. Ordained to ministry Presbyn. Ch. (U.S.A.), 1980. From asst. to assoc. pastor Arcadia (Calif.) Presbyn. Ch., 1980-86; pastor Knox Presbyn. Ch., Pasadena, Calif., 1987-92; adj. asst. prof. preaching Fuller Sem., Pasadena, 1988-90; assoc. prof. preaching Fuller Theol. Sem., Pasadena, 1992-2001, prof. preaching, 2001. Del. gen. Assembly Mission Consultation Planning Team, 1984—85, Inst. Ecumenical and Cultural Rsch., Collegeville, Minn., 1985, Collegeville, 86; com. chair Gen. Assembly, 1988; Staley lectr. Sterling Coll., 2001; Harp lectr. Anderson Sch. Theology, 2004. Author: Power, Pathology, Paradox, 1987, The Fall and Sin: What We Have Become as Sinners, 2004; mem. editl. bd.: Theology, News and Notes, 1986—; contbr. articles sermons, and revs. in religious jours. and books; editor (contbr.): Perspectives on Christology, 1991, Who We Are: Our Dignity as Human, 1996. Bd. dirs. Sierra Madre Mountain Conservancy, 2002—. Named one of Outstanding Young Women in Am., 1979, 83. Mem. Presbytery of San Gabriel (chair, com. on ministry 1991, moderator, permanent jud. commn. 1993-95, moderator Presbytery 1996), Phi Beta Kappa. Home: 675 Mount Wilson Trl Sierra Madre CA 91024-1232 Office: Fuller Theol Sem 135 N Oakland Ave Pasadena CA 91182-0001 Office Phone: 626-584-5248. E-mail: shuster@fuller.edu.

SHUTE, ROBERTA E. sculptor; b. Saskatoon, Sask., Can. Student, Corcoran Mus. Art Sch., 1949—52, Am. U., 1952—53. Tchr. painting Corcoran Mus. Sch., 1951—52; guest lectr. plastic sculpture Am. U., 1972; tchr. sculpture Glen Echo Creative Adult Edn. Program, 1973; pvt. classes. Represented in permanent collections Alice Denny Collection, Goetz, Paris, Tremaine Collection, N.Y.C., environ. sculpture, Noche Crist, Engrs. and Technicians, Allied Chem., 1970, maj. installation, Wolf Trap, 1971, exhibitions include Balt. Mus., 1953, Corcoran Mus., 1953, 1954, 1956, 1959, 1965, 1967, Pa. Acad., 1954, Madison Sq. Garden, 1958, Happening for Summers in the Park Prog., Nat. Park Svc., Washington, 1972, NAS, 1972, installations, Textile Mus. Garden, 1974, Sculpture on Grounds, Rockville City, 1990, French Embassy, 1995, Japanese Embassy, 1996, Florence and Prato, Italy, Grand Junction, Colo and Livermore Calif., 1999—2001, NIH, Bethesda, Md., 2002, Radnor Mus., Bethesda, 2003, many others. Recipient Nathan Goodman Estate award, 1951, Second prize, Wash. Soc. Artists, 1962, 1st prize, Art and Religion, 1963. Mem.: Internat. Sculpture Ctr., Wash. Sculptors Group. Mailing: 4100 Cathedral Ave NW 604 Washington DC 20016

SHUTLER, MARY ELIZABETH, academic administrator; b. Oakland, Calif., Nov. 14, 1929; d. Hal Wilfred and Elizabeth Frances (Gimbel) Hall; m. Richard Shutler Jr., Sept. 8, 1951 (div. 1975); children: Kathryn Allice (dec.), John Hall, Richard Burnett. BA, U. Calif., Berkeley, 1951; MA, U. Ariz., 1958, PhD, 1967. Asst., assoc., full prof. anthropology, chmn. dept. San Diego State U., 1967-75; prof. anthropology, dept. chmn. Wash. State U., Pullman, 1975-80; dean Coll. Arts and Scis., prof. anthropology U. Alaska, Fairbanks, 1980-84; vice chancellor, dean of faculty, prof. anthropology U. Wis. Parkside, Kenosha, 1984-88; provost, v.p. for acad. affairs, prof. anthropology Calif. State U., L.A., 1988-94; provost West Coast U., L.A., 1994-97; dean Sch. of Arts and Scis. Nat. U., La Jolla, Calif., 1997—. Mem. core staff Lahav Rsch. Project, Miss. State U., 1975-92. Co-author: Oceanic Prehistory, 1975, Deer Creek Cave, 1964, Archaeological Survey of Southern Nevada, 1963, Stuart Rockshelter, 1962; contbr. articles to jours. in field. Mem. coun. Gamble House. Fellow Am. Anthropol. Assn.; mem. Soc. for Am. Archaeology, Am. Schs. for Oriental Rsch., Am. Coun. Edn., Am. Assn. for Higher Edn., Am. Assn. State Colls. and Univs., Delta Zeta. Republican. Roman Catholic. Avocations: travel, gardening, cats. E-mail: eshutler@nu.edu.

SHWAYDER, ELIZABETH YANISH, sculptor; b. St. Louis; d. Sam and Fannie May (Weil) Yaffe; m. Nathan Yanish, July 5, 1944 (dec.); children: Ronald, Marilyn Ginsburg, Mindy; m. M.C. Shwayder, 1988 (dec.). Student, Washington U., 1941, Denver U., 1961; pvt. studies. One-woman shows include Woodstock Gallery, London, 1973, Internat. House, Denver, 1963, Colo. Women's Coll., Denver, 1975, Contemporaries Gallery, Santa Fe, 1963, So. Colo. State Coll. Pueblo, 1967, others; group shows include Salt Lake City Mus., 1964, 71, Denver Art Mus., 1961-75, Oklahoma City Mus., 1969, Joslyn Mus., Omaha, 1964-68, Lucca (Italy) Invitational, 1971, Denver Art Mus., Mus. Natural History, Mizel Mus., Eden Theatrical

Workshop, Rose Hosp. Aux., Nat. Mus. Women in the Arts, Colo. Chpt. 8th Air Force Aux., Women's Art Ctr., others; represented in permanent collections including Colo. State Bank, Bmh Synagogue, Denver., Colo. Women's Coll., Har Ha Shem Congregation, Boulder, Colo., Faith Bible Chapel, Denver, others. Chmn. visual arts Colo. Centennial-Bicentennial, 1974-75; pres. Denver Coun. Arts and Humanities, 1973-75; co-chmn. visual arts spree Denver Pub. Schs., 1975; trustee Denver Ctr. Performing Arts, 1973-75; chmn. Concerned Citizens for the Arts, 1976; pres. Beth Israel Hosp. Aux., 1985-87; organizer Coat Drive for the Needy, Denver, N.Y.C., 1982-87, Common Cents penny drive for homeless, 1991-93; bd. dirs. Mizel Mus., Srs., Inc.; active Mayor's Com. on Cultural Affairs, Denver Art Mus., Mus. Natural History, Freedom Found. at Valley Forge, Hospice of Metro. Denver; bd. dirs. Rainbow Bridge; bd. dirs. Diabetes Found., Asian Arts Assn. Denver Art Mus., also pres.; historian Childrens Diabetes Found., Univ. Colo. Found. Inc. Humanities scholar Auraria Librs.-U. Colo.; recipient McCormick award Ball State U., Muncie, Ind., 1964, purchase award color Women's Coll., Denver, 1963, Tyler (Tex.) Mus., 1963, 1st prize in sculpture 1st Nat. Space Art Show, 1971, humanitarian award Milehi Denver Sertoma, 1994, The Gleitsman Found., 1994, svc. to mankind awards Freedom Found. at Valley Forge, Mile Hi Sertoma Club, Minoruyasui Found., Gleitsman Found. Mem. Denver Art Mus., Asian Arts Assn. (pres.). Home: Unit 503 2400 Cherry Creek South Dr Denver CO 80209-3259

SIBERT, POLLY LOU, conductor, music educator; b. Washington, Pa., Sept. 22, 1962; d. Earl Richard and Virginia Gray Sibert. B in Music Edn., James Madison U., Harrisonburg, Va., 1984, MusM in Orchestral Conducting, 1996; D in Music Edn., Shenandoah Conservatory of Shenandoah U., Winchester, Va., 1999. Orch. dir. Chesterfield (Va.) County Schs., 1985—92; violin maker, restorer self-employed, Chester, Va., 1989—92, Charlottesville, Va., 1992—; orch. dir. Charlottesville (Va.) City Schs., 1992—; first violinist Lynchburg (Va.) Symphony, 2002—. Expert panelist mid. sch. music AECT Project Pa. State U. Edn. Sch., 2002—; cons. music publ. Frank J. Hackinson Music Co., Inc., Ft. Lauderdale, 2003—. Bowing editor (music) Nancy's Waltz, 1997; author: (dissertation) A Study of the Violin Bow: Identification and Application of Criteria and Tchg. Strategies, 1999; contbr. author (book) Strategies for Teaching: Technology, 2001; author: (jour. article) The Am. String Tchr., 2001. Mem.: NEA, Nat. Sch. Orch. Assn., Am. String Tchrs. Assn., Va. Music Educators Assn. Methodist. Achievements include Built two stringed instruments: a violin and a viola. Avocations: golf, antiques, crocheting. Home: 3003 Colonial Dr Charlottesville VA 22911-9109 Office: Charlottesville City Schs 1564 Dairy Rd Charlottesville VA 22903 E-mail: PLSibert@aol.com.

SIBILLA, SUZANNE ROSE, training and organizational development consultant; b. San Jose, Calif., Oct. 15, 1961; d. Susan Pilar Asuzano; m. Michael E. Coutches. BA, Westmont Coll., 1983; MA, Antioch U., 1989. Registered drama therapist Nat. Assn. Drama Therapists, lic. marriage, family, child counselor. Cons. tng. and orgnl. devel. Assn. Psychol. and Ednl. Counselors Asia, Thailand, Malaysia, Singapore; program dir. State of Oreg., Salem, 1988-93; cons. Hewlett Packard, Sun, Raychem, FEMA, CPC Hosps., San Jose, Fremont, Palo Alto, Calif., 1993-95; mgr. tng. and orgnl. devel. Tencor Instruments-KLA and TENCOR, Milpitas, Calif., 1995-97; mng. cons., tng. Sibilla & Assocs., Fremont, Calif., 1997—; orgnl. change specialist NEOPOST, 1998—; corp. tng. mgr. WebMD, 1999—2001; ind. cons. Hewlett Packard, 2001—, Compaq, 2001—, Right Mgmt. Cons., 2001—; cons. Sibilla and Assocs., 2001—. Initiator mentorship program Tencor, Palo Alto, 1997. Guest (film and TV program) People Are Talking, 1993, (TV series) Mornings on Two, 1994. Dir. mentorship program for girls YWCA, Daly City, 1993—95. Mem.: ASTD, NAFE, Women in Tech. Internat., Calif. Assn. Marriage, Family and Child Counselors (cert.), Assn. Psychol. and Ednl. Counselors Asia (cons. tng. and orgnl. devel. 1988—92, Key Presenter award 1992), Toastmasters, Menttium 100 (chairperson steering com. 1996—97). Avocations: acting, waterskiing, sailing, swimming, travel. E-mail: srsibilla@aol.com.

SIBLEY, REBECCA LEIGH CARDWELL, dietician; b. Starkville, Miss., Dec. 29, 1955; d. Joe Thomas and Leota (Patterson) Cardwell; m. Daniel Paul Sibley, May 22, 1976; children: John Paul, Jennifer Leigh. BS, Miss. State U., 1977, MS, 1978. Dietary supr. Oktibbeha County Hosp., Starkville, Miss., 1975-76; nutrition instr. Miss. State Dept. Pub. Welfare, Starkville, 1978-80; univ. food service mgr. Miss. U. for Women, Columbus, 1978, instr. foods, nutrition, 1979; dietary cons. Martha Coker Convalescent Home, Yazoo City, Miss., 1981-86, Yazoo Community Action, 1984-90, King's Daughters Hosp., Yazoo City, 1981-82, 88—, dir. dietary div., 1982-88, Profl. Nutrition Svcs., 1988—; dir. nutrition Regional Med. Ctr., Orangeburg, SC, 1992-93; dietitian Gambro Healthcare, 1993—2001; dietitian cardiac and pulmonary rehab. Regional Med. Ctr., Orangeburg, SC, 1992—. Dietary cons. various civic orgns., lectr. in field. Author: Through It All God Reigns My Battle with Cushing's Disease, 1988, 94. Active Yazoo County Extension Gen. Service Adv. Bd., 1984-90; pres. chmn. Yazoo Extension Home Econs. Adv., 1984-90; food chmn. Miss. State U. Alumni, Yazoo City, 1985-86; mem. Orangeburg-Wilkinson H.S. Athletic Booster Club, Chorus Booster Club. Named One of Outstanding Young Women of Am., 1987, Agriculture and Home Econs. scholar Miss. State U., 1974-77, Miss. Home Econ. Assn. scholar, 1974; recipient Gamma Sigma Delta Alumni award of Merit, 1996. Mem. Am. Dietetic Assn., Phi Kappa Phi, Phi Tau Sigma, Gamma Sigma Delta, Kappa Omicron Phi, Alpha Zeta, Alpha Lambda Delta. Republican. Presbyterian. Avocations: knitting, needlework, cooking, reading, singing. Home and Office: 3387 Hart St NE Orangeburg SC 29118-1938 E-mail: sibley76@oburg.net.

SIBOLSKI, ELIZABETH HAWLEY, higher education administrator; b. Gt. Barrington, Mass., Aug. 18, 1950; d. William Snyder and Frances Harrington (Smith) Gallup; m. John Alfred Sibolski Jr., Aug. 15, 1970. BA, The Am. U., 1973, MPA, 1975, PhD, 1984. Acting dir. acad. adminstrn. Am. U., Washington, 1974, planning analyst, 1974-79, asst. dir. budget and planning, 1980-83, dir. instl. rsch., 1984-85, exec. dir. univ. planning and rsch., 1985-2000; exec. assoc. dir. Middle States Commn. on Higher Edn., Phila., 2000—. Trustee Mortar Bd. Nat. Found., 1989-95. Recipient Comencement award Am. U. Women's Club, 1973. Mem. Soc. Coll. and Univ. Planning (bd. dirs. 1995-2000, pres. 1998-99), Mortar Bd. (sect. coord. 1975-82), Pi Alpha Alpha, Phi Kappa Phi (chpt. officer 1986-92), Pi Sigma Alpha, Omicron Delta Kappa. Avocations: breed, raise and show morgan horses. Home: 565 Wayward Dr Annapolis MD 21401-6747 Office: Middle States Commn on Higher Edn 3624 Market St Philadelphia PA 19104-2614 E-mail: esibolski@msache.org.

SICHERMAN, DARA, art historian, researcher; b. Rochester, Minn., July 8, 1975; d. H. J. Sicherman and S. A. Ferrise; m. Philip L. Graham III, Sept. 20, 2003. BA, Rutgers U. Douglass Coll., 1997; MA, Hunter Coll., 2000; student, The Grad. Ctr., N.Y., 2001—. Instr. of art history Pratt Inst., Bkln, NY, 2002—03; rschr. for the Study of Philanthropy CUNY Ctr., 2003; rschr. Parrish Art Mus., Southampton, NY, 2002—; instr. of art history Fordham U., The Bronx, 2001—02; curator asst. Bklyn Mus. of Art, NY, 1997—2001; adj. instr. of art history Hunter Coll., New York, NY, 2000—01. Author: Interpreting the Silence: Images of Pregnancy in Modernism, 2000, (article) Auguste Rodin's Iris, Messenger of the Gods: An Inquiry into Modern Art and Criticism, 2002. Recipient Sue Rosenberg Zalk Travel and Rsch. Award, The Grad. Ctr., CUNY, 2000—01; fellow Otto Fellowship, Parrish Art Mus., 2002—03, Mall Fellowship, Dept. of Design and Exhibitions, The Grad. Ctr., CUNY, 2001—02, Writing Fellowship, The Grad. Ctr., CUNY, 2003—; scholar Initiatives 2000, Women's Caucus for the Arts, 2001. Mem.: Women's Caucus for the Arts (assoc.), Assn. of Historians of Nineteenth-Century Art (assoc.), Am. Assn. of Mus. (assoc.), Archives of Am. Art (assoc.), Coll. Art Assn. (assoc.; com. chmn. 2001—03). Democrat. Avocation: travel.

SICILIANO, ELIZABETH MARIE, secondary school educator; b. Mansfield, Ohio, Apr. 22, 1934; d. Samuel Sevario and Lucy (Sferro) S. BS in Edn., Ohio State U., 1957; MA in Edn., Ea. Mich. U., 1971; MFA, Bowling Green U., 1975. Cert. tchr., Mich. Instr. adult edn. The Toledo (Ohio) Mus. Art, 1972-81; tchr. art Monroe (Mich.) Pub. Schs., 1975-2001. Workshop facilitator; presenter in field; art tchr. computer graphics. Artist, working in oils, pastels and fabricating jewelry. Judge Monroe Bicentennial, Monroe Arts and Crafts League, other shows. Mem. NEA, Mich. Edn. Assn., Nat. Art Edn. Assn., Mich. Art Edn. Assn., Stratford Festival for the Arts, Toledo Craft Club, Toledo Fedn. Art Socs., Toledo Mus. Art. Avocations: swimming, skiing, classic cars, designing and creating jewelry, portraiture and landscape in oils. Home: 7179 Edinburgh Dr Lambertville MI 48144-9539 Office: Monroe High Sch 901 Herr Rd Monroe MI 48161-9744

SICKLER, JOAN LOUISE, retail store owner; b. Mpls., June 21, 1949; d. George Howard and Evelyn Amelia (Erickson) S.; m. Robert Lee Stableski, June 19, 1971 (div.); 1 child, Nicholas Richard; m. Michael P. Rosow, Oct. 15, 1989. BA cum laude, U. Minn., 1971. Editl. asst. UN Indsl. Devel. Orgn., Vienna, Austria, 1973-74; dir. undergrad. tchg. program Coun. on Learning, New Rochelle, N.Y., 1976-78; freelance writer, editor Putney, Vt., 1978-82, White Plains, N.Y., 1982-85; editor World of Work Report Work in Am. Inst., Scarsdale, N.Y., 1985-86, dir. The Productivity Forum, 1986-89, v.p., 1989-92; owner Purple Sage, Santa Fe, N.Mex., 1994—. Editor: (book) The State of Academic Science, 1978, (newsletter) Ednl. Marketer, 1984-85, also reports in field; contbr. articles to newspapers, chpts. to books. Democrat. Office: Purple Sage 110 Don Gaspar Ave Santa Fe NM 87501-2120

SIDAMON-ERISTOFF, ANNE PHIPPS, community trust executive; b. N.Y.C., Sept. 12, 1932; d. Howard and Harriet Dyer (Price) Phipps; m. Constantine Sidamon-Eristoff, June 29, 1957; children— Simon, Elizabeth, Andrew. BA, Bryn Mawr Coll., 1954. Chmn. emerita Am. Mus. Natural History, N.Y.C.; dir.-at-large Black Rock Forest Consortium; chmn. N.Y. Cmty. Trust. Trustee God Bless Am. Fund, Hudson River Found., Sept. 11th Fund; bd. dirs. Greenacre Found., Highland Falls (N.Y.) Libr.; trustee World Wildlife Fund, Storm King Art Ctr., Mountainville, NY; past bd. dirs. Scenic Hudson, St. Bernard's Sch., N.Y.C., Mus. Modern Art, N.Y.C., Mus. Hudson Highlands. Address: 120 E End Ave New York NY 10028-7552 E-mail: ananouri@aol.com.

SIDDAYAO, CORAZON MORALES, economist, educator, consultant; b. Manila, July 26, 1932; came to U.S., 1968; d. Crispulo S. and Catalina T. (Morales) S. Cert. in elem. teaching, Philippine Normal Coll., 1951; BBA, U. East, Manila, 1962; MA in Econs., George Washington U., 1971, MPhil, PhD, 1975. Cert. Inst. de Francais, France. Tchr. pub. schs., Manila, 1951-53; exec. asst. multinational oil corps., 1953-68; asst. pensions officer IMF, Washington, 1968-71; cons. economist Washington, 1971-75; rsch. assoc. Policy Studies in Sci. and Tech. George Washington U., Washington, 1971-72, teaching fellow dept. econs., 1972-75; natural gas specialist U.S. Fed. Energy Adminstrn., Washington, 1974-75; sr. rsch. economist, assoc. prof. Inst. S.E.A. Studies, Singapore, 1975-78; sr. rsch. fellow energy/economist East-West Ctr., 1978-81, project dir. energy and industrialization, 1981-86; vis. fellow London Sch. Econ., 1984-85; sr. energy economist in charge energy program Econ. Devel. Inst., World Bank, Washington, 1986-94, ret., 1994. Affiliate prof. econs. U. Hawaii, 1979—94; co-dir. UPecon Inst. Resource Studies, 1995—; vis. prof. econs. U. Montpellier, France, 1992, France, 1995—96, France, 1997—; vis. prof. pub. policy Duke U., 1997; lectr. pub. policy George Mason U., 2000; tchr. coord. English for Hispanic program Parish, 2002; cons., spkr. in field. Author or co-author: Increasing the Supply of Medical Personnel, 1973, The Offshore Petroleum Resources of Southeast Asia: Some Potential Conflicts and Related Economic Factors, 1978, Round Table Discussion on Asian and Multinational Corporations, 1978, The Supply of Petroleum Resources in Southeast Asia: Economic Implications of Evolving Property Rights Arrangements, 1980, Critical Energy Issues in Asia and the Pacific: The Next Twenty Years, 1982, Criteria for Energy Pricing Policy, 1985, Energy Demand and Economic Growth, 1986; editor, co-author: Energy Policy and Planning series, 1990-92, Energy Investments and the Environment, 1993; co-editor: Investissements Énergetiques et Environnement, 1993; co-editor: (series) Energy Project Analysis for the CIS Countries (Russian), 1993, Politique d'Efficacité de l'Énergie et Environnement, Expérience pratiques, 1994, Matérial Pedagogique sur la Politique d'Efficacité de l'Energie et Environnement, 1994; contbr. chpts. to books, articles to profl. jours. Grantee in field; recipient Outstanding Alumni award Arellano Pub. H.S., 1998, Philippine Normal U., 2003 Mem.: Alliance Francaise, Internat. Assn. Energy Economists (charter 1986—2003), Am. Econ. Assn., Perpetual Adoration Soc. of St. Agnes (Arlington), John Carroll Soc., World Bank 1818 Soc. (bd. dirs. 1999—2000), Eucharistic Frat. 3d Order of St. P.J. Eymard, Chorale de St. Louis de France, Omicron Delta Epsilon. Roman Catholic. Office: 1201 S Eads St Ste 1712 Arlington VA 22202-2845

SIDDONS, ANNE RIVERS (SYBIL ANNE RIVERS SIDDONS), writer; b. Fairburn, Ga., Jan. 9, 1936; m. Heyward Siddons, 1966; 4 stepchildren. BA Auburn U., student Atlanta Sch. Art., 1958. Mem. advt. dept. bank; sr. editor Atlanta mag., 1960. Author: (novels) John Chancellor Makes Me Cry, 1975, Heartbreak Hotel, 1976, Go Straight on Peachtree, 1977, The House Next Door, 1978, Fox's Earth, 1981, Homeplace, 1987, Peachtree Road, 1988, Kings Oak, 1990, Outer Banks, 1991, Colony, 1992, Hill Towns, 1993, Downtown, 1994, Fault Lines, 1995, Up Island, 1997, Low Country, 1998, Nora, Nora, 2000, Islands, 2003. Home: 60 Church St Charleston SC 29401-2558

SIDDONS, JOY GARBEE, music educator; b. Lynchburg, Va., July 18, 1952; d. Clyde Lewis and Julia Schmitt Garbee; m. James Siddons, July 2, 1977. BS, Liberty U., 1984; MEd, Lynchburg Coll., 1996; MusEdM, Shenandoah U., 1998. Music educator Bedford County Pub. Schools, Bedford, Va., 1989—2003, Fairfax County Pub. Schools, Springfield, Va., 2003—. Dir. of music United Meth. churches, Lynchburg, Va., 1988—2003; founder and dir. Chesterbrook Christian Children's Choir, McLean, Va. Dir.: children's musical theater productions including the Wizard of Oz. Mem.: Music Educators Nat. Conf. United Methodist. Home: 6020 Woodland Ter Mc Lean VA 22101 Office: Fairfax County Pub Sch 6815 Edsall Rd Springfield VA 22151

SIDDONS, SARAH MAE, chemist; b. Conway, S.C., July 20, 1939; d. Willie C. and Lelia (Parker) Crawford; m. John Lathan, June 26, 1958 (div.); m. Ronald Gladstone Siddons, June 26, 1965; 1 child, Ronald George. BA, Coll. New Rochelle, 1980; postgrad., Cornell U., 1975. Lab. technologist DC37-Local 144, Bronx, 1961-65, 65-82; jr. chemist DC37-Local 375, Bronx, 1982-85, assoc. chemist, 1985-90, assoc. chemist, supr., 1990—. Del. DC37-Lcoal 144, 1962-84, DC37-Local 375, 1984—. Mem. Am. Assn. Clin. Chemistry, Dynamic Five Social Club (pres. 1988—, v.p. 1980-88). Home: 3924 Carpenter Ave Bronx NY 10466-3705 Office: Lincoln Med Ctr 234 E 149th St Rm 432 Bronx NY 10451-5504 E-mail: ssiddons@excite.com.

SIDELL, NANCY L. adult education educator; b. Fremont, Ohio, Apr. 11, 1958; d. Robert L. and Mary Margaret Brady; m. Michael J. Sidell, Feb. 9, 1980. BA in Social Work, Kent State U., 1979; M in Rehab. Counseling, Bowling Green State U., 1984; M in Social Work, Case Western Reserve U., 1990; PhD in Social Work, Ohio State U., 1998. Dir. social work svcs. Medical Coll. Ohio, 1985—95; BSW program dir. assoc. prof. Mansfield (Pa.) U., 1998—, chair, dept. social work, anthropology and sociology, 2002—. Office: Mansfield U 211 Pinecrest Mansfield PA 16933 E-mail: nsidell@mnsfld.edu.

SIDEMAN, JILL, engineering executive; MA in Phys. and Inorganic Chemistry, Bryn Mawr (Pa.) Coll., 1963, PhD in Phys. and Inorganic Chemistry, 1965. Postdoctoral rschr. Nat. Bur. Standards; fellow Nat. Inst. Arthritis and Metabolic Diseases; chargee du rsch. Inst. Pasteur, Paris; rschr. U. Wash. Med. Ctr.; co-founder Shapiro and Assocs., Seattle, 1974—84, San Francisco, 1982—84, TRS Cons., San Francisco, 1984—86; from mgr. environ. planning San Francisco (Calif.) Bay Area to dir., v.p. CH2M HILL, 1986, dir. Englewood, Colo., v.p. Mem. Commn. Advancement Women and Minorities in Sci., Engring. and Tech. Fellow, NAS/NRC, NIH. Mem.: Nat. Assn. Women Sci. (bd. dir. 1995—). Office: CH2M HILL 9191 South Jamaica St Englewood CO 80112*

SIDES, I. RUTH S. music educator; d. John Daniel Donald and I. Ruth Schulmeyer; m. Anthony Fred Sides, May 25, 1972 (dec. Sept. 7, 1997); children: Rebecca Ruth Desenti, Connie Susanne Moore. BA, Baldwin Wallace Coll., 1968. Cert. tchg. Ohio, 1968. Dir. band, choruses Ridgemont Local Schs., Ridgeway, Ohio, 1967—71; dir. choral music Groveland H.S., Fla., 1972—93, South Lake H.S., 1993—. Dept. chair fine arts, fgn. lang. South Lake H.S., Groveland, Fla., 2002—. Cert. judge Fla. BBQ Assn., Fla., 2002—. Nominee Disney's Am. Tchr., Walt Disney World, 2001; recipient Tchr. Of The Yr., Hardin County Schools, 1969-1970, Outstanding Young Women Am., 1973, Teacherific - Judge's Choice, Walt Disney World, 2000. Mem.: Fla. Vocal Assn., Fla. Music Educators Assn. Avocations: cooking, sewing, travel. Home: 11844 Lake Minneola Shores Clermont FL 34711 Office: South Lake HS 15600 Silver Eagle Rd Groveland FL 34736

SIDIROPOULOU, ELEFTHERIA ALEXANDROU, minister, family therapist; b. Katerine Macedonia, Greece, Oct. 28, 1940; came to U.S., 1959; d. Alexandros Haralambou Sidiropoulos and Galine A. Kelesides. BA, Gordon Coll., 1964; MRE in Relics, Gordon Corwell Sem., 1966; MDiv in Theology, Andover Newton Theol. Sch., 1981, DMin in Psychology, 1985. Dir. edn. First Bapt. Ch., Norwood, Mass., 1966-69; assoc. min., dir. Boston Christian Counseling Ctr. Tremant Temple Bapt. Ch., Boston, 1969—. Supr. CPE New England Bapt. Hosp., Boston, 1987—. Radio spkr. current issues Trement Temple, 1990—. Maj. USAF, 1982—. Fellow Am. Assn. of Pastoral Counselor, Coll. of Chaplains; mem. Am. Marriage and Family (supr. 1995), Clin. Pastoral Edn. American Baptist. Avocation: feeding the hungary. Home: 149 Winslow Ave Norwood MA 02062-3338 Office: Boston Christian Counseling Ctr 88 Tremont St Norwood MA 02062-4116

SIDRAN, MIRIAM, retired physics educator, researcher; b. Washington, May 25, 1920; d. Morris Samson and Theresa Rena (Gottlieb) S. BA, Bklyn. Coll., 1942; MA, Columbia U., N.Y.C., 1949; PhD, NYU, 1956. Rsch. assoc. dept. physics NYU, N.Y.C., 1950-55, postdoctoral fellow, 1955-57; asst. prof. Staten Island Community Coll., Richmond, N.Y., 1957-59; rsch. scientist Grumman Aerospace Corp., Bethpage, N.Y., 1959-67; prof. N.Y. Inst. Tech., N.Y.C., 1967-72; NSF rsch. fellow Nat. Marine Fisheries Svc., Miami, Fla., 1971-72; assoc. prof. then prof. physics Baruch Coll., N.Y.C., 1972-89, chmn. dept. natural scis., 1983-89, prof. emerita, 1990—. V.p. Baruch chpt. Profl. Staff Congress, 1983-89. Contbr. numerous articles to profl. and govtl. publs., chpts. to books. N.Y. State Regents scholar, 1937-41; NSF summer fellow, Miami, 1970. Mem. N.Y. Acad. Scis., Am. Assn. Physics Tchrs. Avocations: french and hebrew languages, music, bicycling, poetry. Home: 210 W 19th St Apt 5G New York NY 10011-4009

SIEBER, DAWN, food service executive; Student in Psychology, U. Miami; grad., Balt. Internat. Culinary Arts Inst. Owner The Red Star, Balt.; from exec. sous chef to exec. chef Cheeca Lodge, Islamorada, Fla., 1988—. Host Am. Inst. Wine and Food weekend, Celebrity Chefs Eco-Challenge. Featured in Esquire, Food & Wine, Travel & Leisure and The Miami Herald, cooked at Masters of Food and Wine, Carmel, Calif., CBS Morning Show, Julia Child's gala birthday dinner (filmed for PBS). Office: Cheeca Lodge PO Box 527 Islamorada FL 33036

SIEBERT, DEBORAH ANN, public relations and marketing executive; b. Hoisington, Kans., Nov. 12, 1952; d. Kenneth Theodore and Mildred Marie (Steiner) Siebert; m. Donald Raymond McLaughlin, July 17, 1976 (div. Oct. 2001); 1 child, Kalla Dawn. AS, Barton County Coll., Great Bend, Kans., 1972; BS, Kans. State U., 1975. News editor Great Bend Tribune, 1975-76; deposition indexer Turner & Boisseau, Great Bend, 1976-77; feature editor Mid-Kans. Ruralist, Hoisington, 1977-78; copywriter, audio-editor Advt. Assocs., Great Bend, 1978-79; photographer, sales mgr. Clay Ward Color Portraits, Great Bend, 1979-80; news editor, photographer St. John (Kans.) News, 1980-83; freelance writer, photographer Great Bend, 1984-85; pres., owner McLaughlin Pub. Rels. Agy., Great Bend, 1985-87; owner Cen. Kans. Sunrise mag., Great Bend, 1987-88, Creative Mktg. Svcs., Great Bend, 1988—; dir. pub. info. Unified Sch. Dist. 428, Great Bend, 1991-93; editor Ellinwood Leader, 1995-97; acct. exec. Multimedia Cable Ad Sales, 1998-99, Cox Comms., 2000—03; mktg. cons. Wailt Media, 2004—. Contbr. articles and photographs to various publs. Mem. Coalition for Prevention Child Abuse, Great Bend, 1986-87; mem. 75th anniversary com. Kansas State U. Coll. Journalism and Mass Communications, Manhattan, 1986. Mem. Kans. State U. Alumni Assn. Roman Catholic. Avocations: gardening, gourmet cooking, interior decorating, swimming. Home: 381 Grove Ter Great Bend KS 67530-9710

SIEBERT, DIANE DOLORES, author, poet; b. Chgo., Ill., Mar. 18, 1948; m. Robert William Siebert, Sept. 21, 1969. RN. Author: Truck Song, 1984 (Notable Childrens Book award ALA 1984, Sch. Libr. Jour. one of Best Books 1984, Outstanding Childrens Book award NY Times Book Rev. 1984, Reading Rainbow Selection book 1991), Mojave, 1988 (Childrens Editors Choice 1988, Internat. Reading Assn. Tchr. Choice award 1989, others), Heartland, 1989 (award Nat. Coun. for Social Studies/Childrens Book Coun. 1989, on John Burroughs List Nature Book for Young Readers 1989, Ohio Farm Bur. Women award 1991), Train Song, 1990 (Notable Childrens Book award ALA, 1990, Redbook Mag. one of Top Ten Picture Books 1990, one of Best Books award Sch. Libr. Jour. 1990, others), Sierra, 1991 (Outstanding Sci. Trade Book for Children award NSTA 1991, Notable Childrens Trade Book in Field Social Studies award Nat. Coun. Social Studies 1991, Beatty award Calif. Libr. Assn. 1992), Plane Song, 1993 (Outstanding Sci. Trade Book for Children 1994, Reading Rainbow Selection book, Platinum award Oppenheim Toy Portfolio, Tchrs. Choice award Internat. Reading Assn. 1994), Cave, 2000 (Notable children's Book in the english Language Arts, 2001, Nat. Coun. of English Tchr., named to John Burroughs List of Nature Books for Young Readers 2000), Mississippi (named to John Burroughs List 2001), 2001, Motorcycle Song, 2002, Rhyolite, 2003. Avocations: environmental affairs, running, classical guitar, motorcycle, animals. Home: 9676 SW Jordan Rd Culver OR 97734-9567

SIEBERT, MURIEL (MICKIE), brokerage house executive, former state banking official; b. Cleve., 1932; d. Irwin J. and Margaret Eunice (Roseman) Siebert. Student, Western Res. U., 1949-52; DCS (hon.), St. John's U., St. Bonaventure U., Molloy Coll., Adelphi U., St. Francis Coll., Mercy Coll., Coll. New Rochelle, St. Lawrence U., Manhattan Coll., Seton Hall Coll., Case Western Res. U., Marymount Manhattan Coll., Hofstra U. Security analyst Bache & Co., 1954-57; analyst Utilities & Industries Mgmt. Corp., 1958, Shields & Co., 1959-60; ptnr. Stearns & Co., 1961,

Finkle & Co., 1962-65, Brimberg & Co., N.Y.C., 1965-67; individual mem. (first woman mem.) N.Y. Stock Exch., 1967; chmn., pres. Muriel Siebert & Co., Inc., 1969-77; trustee Manhattan Savs. Bank, 1975-77; supt. banks, dept. banking State of N.Y., 1977-82; dir. Urban Devel. Corp., N.Y.C., 1977-82, Job Devel. Authority, N.Y.C., 1977-82, State of N.Y. Mortgage Agy., 1977-82; chmn., pres. Muriel Siebert & Co., Inc., N.Y.C., 1983—. Assoc. in mgmt. Simmons Coll.; mem. adv. com. Fin. Acctg. Stds. Bd., 1981-84; adv. bd. Minority & Women-Owned Bus. Enterprise; guest lectr. numerous colls. Ran for Rep. nomination, U.S.Senate, 1982; former mem. women's adv. com. Econ. Devel. Adminstrn., N.Y.C.; former trustee Manhattan Coll.; v.p., former mem. exec. com. Greater N.Y. Area coun. Boy Scouts Am.; mem. N.Y. State Econ. Devel. Bd., N.Y. Coun. Economy; bd. overseers NYU Sch. Bus., 1984-88; former bd. dirs. United Way of N.Y.C.; trustee Citizens Budget Commn., L.I. U.; mem. bus. com. Met. Mus., bus. com. of N.Y. State Bus. Coun.; advive Women's Campaign Fund.; bd. dirs. N.Y. Women's Agenda; bd. trustees Guild Hall Mus. EH; current appointee Commn. Jud. Nomination; founding mem. The Mus. Women-The Leadership Coun; founder, bd.dirs. The WISH List; Tokyo adv. com. Sister City Program N.Y.C. Recipient Spirit of Achievement award Albert Einstein Coll. Medicine, 1977, Women's Equity Action League award, 1978, Outstanding Contbns. to Equal Oppty. for Women award Bus. Coun. UN Decade for Women, 1979, Silver Beaver award Boy Scouts Am., 1981, Elizabeth Cutter Morrow award YWCA, 1983, Emily Roebling award Nat. Women's Hall of Fame, 1984, Entrepreneurial Excellence award White House Conf. on Small Bus., 1986, NOW Legal Def. and Edn. Fund award, 1981, Brotherhood award NCCJ. 1989, Women on the Move award Anti-Defamation League, 1990, Bus. Philanthropist of Yr. award So. Calif. Conf. for Women Bus. Owner's, 1990, award Borough of Manhattan, 1991, Benjamin Botwinick prize Columbia Bus. Sch., 1992, Women in Bus. Making History award Women's Bus. Coun. N.Y. C. of C., 1993, Disting. Woman of Yr. award Greater N.Y. Boy Scouts of Am., 1993, Corning Excellence award N.Y.C. Bus. Coun., 1993, Star award, N.Y. Women's Agenda, 1993, Woman of Yr. award Fin. Women's Assn. N.Y., 1994, Medal of Honor award Ellis Island, 1994, Star award N.Y. Women's Agenda, 1994, N.Y. Urban Coalition's Achievement award, 1994, Women of Distinction award Crohn's and Colitis Found., 1994, Entrepreneurial Leadership award Nat. Found. Tchg. Entrepreneurship, 1994, Athena award, 1997, USO Women of Yr. award, 1998, Sara Lee Frontrunner award, 1998, Mattel/Barbie Ambassador of Dreams award, 1999; inductee Nat. Woman's Hall of Fame, Seneca Falls, N.Y., 1994, Internat. Women's Forum Hall of Fame, 1994, Ohio Women's Hall Fame, 1994; N.Y. Univ.'s Stern Sch. Bus. 1st Woman Stovall fellow, 1992; Established Siebert Entrepreneurial Philanthropic Program, 1990. Mem. Women's Forum (founding mem., pres.), Com. 200, Fin. Women's Assn. (Cmty. Svc. award 1993), River Club, Doubles Club, Westchester Club, West Palm Beach Polo and Country Club, Nat. Assn. Women Bus. Owners (NAWBO's Veuve Clicquot Bus. Women of Yr. award 1992, Mayor's Lifetime Achievement award for Women Bus. Owners 1993), Econ. Club (exec. com.), Southampton Bath and Tennis Club (founding mem., bd. dirs.), Women's Campaign Fund, Fashion Group Internat., River Club, Doubles Club, Westchester County Club, West Palm Beach Polo and Country Club (former mem.); adv. coun. Women's Econ. Roundtable. Office: Muriel Siebert & Co Inc 885 3rd Ave Ste 1720 New York NY 10022-4834*

SIEFERT-KAZANJIAN, DONNA, corporate librarian; b. N.Y.C. d. Merrill Emil and Esther (Levins) S.; m. George John Kazanjian, June 15, 1974; 1 child, Merrill George. BA, NYU, 1969; MSLS, Columbia U., 1973; MBA, Fordham U., 1977. Asst. librarian Dun & Bradstreet, N.Y.C., 1969-73; research assoc. William E. Hill & Co., N.Y.C., 1973-76; sr. info. analyst Info. for Bus., N.Y.C., 1976-77; librarian Handy Assocs., N.Y.C., 1979-90; mgr. Infoserve Fuchs Cuthrell & Co., Inc., N.Y.C., 1991-94; info. specialist Heidrick & Struggles, Inc., N.Y.C., 1994-2001; learning media specialist St. Mary's Elem. Sch., Manhasset, NY, 2002—03; libr. I Manhasset Pub. Libr., 2003—. Mem. Am. Mensa Ltd. Roman Catholic.

SIEFKER, JUDITH MARIE, writer; b. St. Louis, Nov. 12, 1946; d. Joseph Alphonse and Mary Gertrude Siefker; m. Darrell R. Dobson, Mar. 16, 1984. BA in Psychology, Quincy Coll., 1967; MA in Clin. Psychology, Bradley U., 1971. Registered counselor Wash., 1988, cert. rehab. counselor 1981, profl. guardian 2002. Intern Peoria State Hosp., Ill., 1971—72; psychologist Divsn. Vocat. Rehab., 1973—74; vocat. evaluator Seattle Hearing & Speech Ctr., 1977—80; br. mgr. Intracorp, 1980—86, Crawford & Co., 1987—89; counselor, cons. pvt. practice, 1989—. Author: Vocational Evaluation in Private Sector Rehabilitation, 1992, Tests and Test Use in Vocational Evaluation and Assessment, 1996, Fundamentals of Case Measurement, 1997; mem. editl. bd.: Vocat. Evaluation and Work Adjustment Bulletin, 1988—96. Vol. Idaho Pk. Found., Boise, 1977, Farmers India, Hyderabad, 1994; del. UN Fourth World Conf. Women, Beijing, 1995. Mem.: Wash. Assn. Profl. Guardians. Democrat. Avocations: travel, needlecrafts, sailing, skiing. Office Phone: 206-772-6497.

SIEG, SANDRA NISHKIAN, entrepreneur, dental hygienist; b. Long Beach, Calif., Oct. 16, 1938; d. Martin Aris and Rose (Boyd) Nishkian; m. Thomas Lyon Hall, Nov. 13, 1960 (div. 1965); 1 child, Gina; m. James Wallace Sieg Jr., Dec. 28, 1967; children: Christine, Stephanie, Gina, Summer. BA in Dental Hygiene, U. So. Calif., 1960; postgrad., Loma Linda U., 1983; M in Liberal Studies, NYU, 1996. Dental hygienist David Brandon, DDS, Dana Point, Calif., 1985—2003; artistic dir. Cosimo & Co., Laguna Beach, Calif., 1990—2003; pres. Harbour Trading Children's Arts Games, Laguna Beach, 1989—. Vol. fund raiser Laguna Beach Volleyball Assn., 1989—, Laguna Beach Fire Victims, 1994—. Home: 454 Palmer Pl Laguna Beach CA 92651-3316

SIEGAL, PEGGY, public relations executive; Owner Smith & Siegal Public Relations, The Peggy Siegal Co., Lizzie Grubman / Peggy Siegal Public Relations, 2000—01, Harriet Weintraub / Peggy Siegal Public Relations, 2001—. Co-prodr.(with Barbara Koppel): (films) The Hamptons, 2002. Office: Harriet Weintraub/Peggy Siegal PR 140 W 57th St New York NY 10019*

SIEGAL, RITA GORAN, engineering company executive; b. Chgo., July 16, 1934; d. Leonard and Anabelle (Soloway) Goran; m. Burton L. Siegal, Apr. 11, 1954; children: Norman, Laurence Scott. Student, U. Ill., 1951-53; BA, DePaul U., 1956. Cert. elem. tchr., Ill. Tchr. Chgo. Public Schs., 1956-58; founder, chief exec. officer Budd Engring. Corp., Skokie, Ill., 1959—; founder, pres. Easy Living Products Co., Skokie, 1960—; pvt. practice in interior design, Chgo., 1968-73; dist. sales mgr. Super Girls, Skokie, 1976. Lectr. Northwestern U., 1983; guest speaker nat. radio and TV, 1979—. Contbr. to profl. jours. Mem. adv. bd. Skokie High Schs., 1975-79; advisor Cub Scouts Skokie coun. Boy Scouts Am., 1975; bus. mgr. Nutrition for Optimal Health Assn., Winnetka, Ill., 1980-82, pres., 1982-84, v.p. med./profl., 1985-93; leader Great Books Found., 1972; founder Profit Plus Investment, 1970; bd. dirs. Noha, Internat. Named Prominent Alumni, Sullivan H.S., 2001; recipient Cub Scout awards, Boy Scouts Am., 1971—72, Nat. Charlotte Danstrom award, Nat. Women of Achievement, 1988, Corp. Achievement award, 1988. Mem. North Shore Women in Mgmt. (pres, 1987-88), Presidents Assn. Ill. (bd. dirs 1990-94, membership chair 1991-93), Inventors Coun., Oriental Art Soc. Chgo. (publicity chair). Office: Skokie IL

SIEGAL, SUSAN E. biotechnology company executive; With Bio Red Lab., Bio Image/Kodak, E.I. DuPont, Amersham Pharmacia Biotech; sr. v.p. mktg. & sales Affymetrix, Inc., Santa Clara, Calif., 1998—99, pres., 1999—. Office: Affymetrix Inc 3380 Central Expwy Santa Clara CA 95051

SIEGEL, BETTY LENTZ, university president; b. Cumberland, Ky., Jan. 24, 1931; d. Carl N. and Vera (Hogg) Lentz; m. Joel H. Siegel, June 6; children: David Jonathan, Michael Jeremy. BA, Wake Forest U., 1952; M.Ed., U. N.C., 1953; PhD, Fla. State U., 1961; postgrad., Ind. U., 1964-66; hon. doctorate, Miami U., 1985, Cumberland Coll., 1985, Ea. Ky. U., 1992, Morehead State U., 2002. Asst. prof. Lenoir Rhyne Coll., Hickory, N.C., 1956-59; assoc. prof., 1961-64; asst. prof. U. Fla., Gainesville, 1967-70, assoc. prof., 1970-72, prof., 1973-76, dean acad. affairs for continuing edn., 1972-76; dean Sch. Edn. and Psychology Western Carolina U., Cullowhee, N.C., 1976-81; pres. Kennesaw State U., Marietta, Ga., 1981—. Bd. dirs. Nat. Services Industries; cons. numerous sch. systems. Author: Problem Situations in Teaching, 1971, Becoming An Invitational Leader, 2002; contbr. articles to profl. jours. Bd. dirs. United Way Atlanta, Ga. Partnership for Excellence in Edn., Ga. Coun. Econ. Edn., Northside Hosp. Found., Atlanta Ballet; Ga. rep. so. growth policy bd. Commn. on Future of South, 1998. Recipient Outstanding Tchr. award U. Fla., 1969; Mortar Bd. Woman of Yr. award U. Fla., 1973, Mortar Bd. Educator of Yr., Ga. State U., 1983, CASE award, 1986, Alumna of Yr. award Wake Forest U., 1987, "Grad Made Good" award Fla. State U. Alumni Assn, Omicron Delta Kappa, 1991, Spirit of Life award City of Hope, 1992, Woman of Achievement award Cobb Chamber YWCA, 1992; named One of 100 Most Influential People in State of Ga., Ga. Trend Mag., Outstanding Alumni, Fla. State U. Coll. Edn. Alumni Assn., 1992, Cobb Citizen of the Yr. award, 1996, Ga. Woman of Yr. Ga. Commn. Women, 1997. Mem. Am. Psychol. Assn., Am. Assn. State Colls. and Univs. (bd. dirs., chmn. 1990), Am. Coun. Edn. (bd. dirs., bd. advisors), Am. Inst. Mng. Diversity (bd. dis.), Soc. Internat. Bus. Fellows, Internat. Alliance for Invitational Edn. (co-founder, co-dir.), Bus./Higher Edn. Forum, mem. exec. com.), Cobb C. of C. (chair 1996), Kiwanis (Atlanta chpt.), Phi Alpha Theta, Pi Kappa Delta, Alpha Psi Omega, Kappa Delta Pi, Pi Lambda Theta, Phi Delta Kappa, Delta Kappa Gamma. Baptist. Office: Kennesaw State Univ Office of the President 1000 Chastain Rd NW Kennesaw GA 30144-5591

SIEGEL, CAROLE ETHEL, mathematician; b. N.Y., Sept. 29, 1936; d. David and Helen (Mayer) Schore; m. Bertram Siegel, Aug. 18, 1957; children: Sharon, David. BA in Math., NYU, 1957, MS in Math., 1959, PhD in Math., 1963. With computer dept. Atomic Energy Commn., 1957-59; rsch. asst. Courant Inst. of Math. Sci., 1959-63; rsch. scientist dept. of engring NYU, N.Y.C., 1963-64; rsch. math. Info. Scis. Div. Rockland Rsch. Inst., Orangeburg, N.Y., 1963-74, head Epidemiology and Health Svcs. Rsch. Lab Stat. Scis., Epidemiology divsn. Nathan S. Kline Inst. Psychiat. Rsch., Orangeburg, NY, 1974—2003, dir. stats. and rsch. div., 2003—. Adj. assoc. prof. Wagner Grad. Sch. Pub. Svc., NYU; rsch. prof. dept. psychiatry NYU, 1987—; dep. dir. WHO Collaborating Ctr., Nathan S. Kline Inst., 1987—; grant reviewer NIHM, 1988—; prin. investigator Ctr. for Study of Issues in Public Mental Health, NIMH, 1993--, prin. investigator, dir., 1995—. Editor: (with S. Fischer) Psychiatric Records in Mental Health Care, 1981; contbr. articles to profl. jours. Recipient Carl Taube award, mental health sect. APHA, 2001; grantee SAMHSA, CMHS, 1997—, NIMH, 1993—, 1988—91, Nat. Ctr. for Health Svcs. Rsch., 1979—82, Nat. Inst. Alcohol Abuse, 1978—82. Mem. Assn. for Health Svcs. Rsch., Am. Soc. Clin. Pharmacology and Therapeutics, Assn. Women in Math., Am. Statis. Assn. Avocations: pottery, gardening, cooking. Office: Nathan S Kline Inst Orangeburg NY 10962

SIEGEL, CAROLYN AUGUSTA, social worker, lawyer; b. Buffalo, Dec. 29, 1943; d. Joseph Frederick and Louise Augusta (Knecht) S.; m. Roger John Fenlon, Feb. 15, 1969 (div. Nov. 1, 1989); children: Kristin M. Fenlon, Jocelyn N. Fenlon. BA, St. Bonaventure U., 1965; MS, SUNY, Buffalo, 1973, MSW, JD, SUNY, Buffalo, 1999. Lic.: N.Y. (atty.), bar: N.Y. 2000; cert. elem. and exceptional tchr. Indsl. investigator N.Y. Dept. Labor, Buffalo, 1966-67; tchr. St. Bonaventure Grammar Sch., Buffalo, 1967; adminstrv. analyst N.Y. State Dept. Law, Albany, 1967-68; caseworker N.Y. State Dept. Social Svcs., Buffalo, 1968-72; resource agent N.Y. State Dept. Mental Hygiene, Buffalo, 1972-73; resource and reimbursement agt. N.Y. State Office Mental Retardation and Developmental Disabilities, Buffalo, 1982—2001; coord. policy svcs. Erie 1 BOCES, West Seneca, NY, 2001—; town justice Town of Colden, 2004—. Mem. surrogate decision-making panel N.Y. State Commn. on Quality of Care. Contbr. articles to profl. jours. Pres. Bd. Edn. Springville (N.Y.)-Griffith Inst. Ctrl. Sch. Dist., 1980-95; bd. visitors Buffalo Psychiat. Ctr., 1994—, pres., 1998—; bd. dirs. Erie County Mental Health Assn., Buffalo; 4H Group Leader Erie County Coop. Extension, East Aurora, N.Y., 1974-92; town chmn. Am. Cancer Soc., Buffalo. Mem. AAUW, Delta Epsilon Sigma. Home: PO Box 360 West Falls NY 14170-9624 Office: Erie 1 BOCES 355 Harlem Rd West Seneca NY 14224 Office Phone: 716-821-7448. E-mail: csiegel@e1b.org.

SIEGEL, KIM ANNETTE, speech pathology/audiology services professional; b. Smithville, Mo., May 10, 1960; d. Billie Simeon and Florence Ann Stevens; m. Danny Dewayne Siegel, May 21, 1982; 1 child, Andrew Christopher. BS in Edn., summa cum laude, Ctrl. Mo. State Univ., Warrensburg, Mo., 1982, MS in Speech Pathology, 1986. Cert. clin. competence Mo., lic. speech-lang. pathologist Mo. Speech-lang. pathologist Raytown C-II Sch. Dist., Mo., 1987—. Mem.; Nat. Edn. Assn., Mo. Speech-Lang.-Hearing Assn., Am. Speech-Lang.-Hearing Assn. Avocations: reading, travel. Home: 1925 Larkspur Dr Liberty MO 64068 Office: Raytown C-II Sch Dist Personnel Office 10500 E 60 Terr Raytown MO 64133

SIEGEL, LUCY BOSWELL, public relations executive; b. N.Y.C., July 5, 1950; d. Werner Leiser and Carol (Fleischer) Boswell; m. Henry Winter Siegel, Nov. 11, 1979 (div.); children: David Alan Siegel, Joshua Adam Siegel. BA, Conn. Coll., 1972. Assoc. editor Conn. Western, Litchfield, Conn., 1972-73; assoc. editor, editor United Bus. Publ., N.Y.C., 1974—78; mgr. external communications Equitable Life Assurance Soc., N.Y.C., 1978—86; mgr. internat. affairs Cosmo Pub. Relations Corp., Tokyo, 1986-87, dir. internat. affairs, 1987-88; pres. Cosmo Pub. Rels. Corp., N.Y.C., 1988—90, Siegel Assocs. Internat., N.Y.C., 1990—; sr. v.p. Lobsenz Stevens, N.Y.C., 1997—99; sr. prin., mng. dir. Publicis Dialog, N.Y.C., 1999—2000, exec. v.p., group mng. dir., 2000—. Contbr. articles to jours. and mags. Bd. dirs., sec. N.Y.C. chpt. Am. Jewish Com., 1993—. Mem. Pub. Rels. Soc. Am. (bd. dirs. N.Y.C. chpt. 2001-), Women Execs. in Pub. Rels. (bd. dirs. 1997-99), Japan Soc. Democrat. Jewish. Home: 41 W 96th St Apt 12B New York NY 10025-6519 Office: 4 Herald Sq 950 Ave of the Ams New York NY 10001

SIEGEL, MARY ANN GARVIN, writer; b. Louisville, Apr. 3, 1944; d. Samuel Hughes and Ann Wendell (Smith) Garvin; m. Charles Holladay Siegel, Sept. 2, 1967 (div.); children: Emily Hughes, Charles Holladay, Jr., Margaret Shafer. BA, Conn. Coll., 1966. Photog. rschr. Time Inc., NYC, 1966—67, Nat. Geog. Soc., Washington, 1967—68; content author and editor FundraisingINFO.com, 2000—01. Leadership Atlanta, 1993-94, exec. com., 1995-96. Trustee Conn. Coll., New London, 1985-90; chair Friends of Spelman Coll., Atlanta, 1990-92; active Atlanta/Fulton County adv. bd. United Way Met. Atlanta, 1994-96; Olympic Envoy to Republic of Nauru, Atlanta Com. Olympic Games, 1994-96; formerly active adv. bd. N.C. Outward Bound Sch., Asheville. Recipient Agnes Berkeley Leahy award Conn. Coll. Alumni Assn., 1991.

SIEGEL, WILMA BULKIN, oncologist, educator, artist; b. Phila., Dec. 2, 1936; d. Morris and Minnie (Staffin) Bulkin; m. Jesse Sanders Siegel, Nov. 11, 1976 (div. 1975); children: Hillary Siegel Levin, Nancy Siegel Jaffee. BA, U. Pa., 1958; MD, Women's Med. Coll. Pa., 1962; student, Nat. Acad. Design, N.Y., 1989-93, New Sch., 1974-84; studied with Rowena Smith, Ft. Lauderdale, 1991-94. Lic. physician, Pa., N.Y. Rotating intern Mt. Sinai Hosp., N.Y.C., 1963; resident in internal medicine Temple U. Hosp., 1964-65; fellow in hematology Mt. Sinai Hosp., N.Y.C., 1966; fellow in cancer chemotherapy Meml. Sloan Kettering Hosp., 1967; asst. attending physician divsn. neoplastic medicine Montefiore Med. Ctr., N.Y.C., 1967-74; clin. asst. physician Mt. Sinai Hosp., N.Y.C., 1974-75; pvt. practice Extra Greenspan, M.D. and Assocs., 1974-75; attending physician Trafalgar Hosp., N.Y.C., 1975; asst. attending physician Montefiore Med. Ctr., N.Y.C., 1976-81, attending physician, 1981—; med. dir. Beth Abraham Hosp., Ritter-Scheuer Hosp., N.Y.C., 1983-87; dir. hospice edn. and rsch. Beth Abraham Hosp., N.Y.C., 1988—. Asst. prof. medicine dept. oncology Albert Einstein Coll. of Medicine, Bronx, 1979-90, asst. prof. medicine dept. epidemiology and social medicine, 1988—, emeritus prof., 1990—; mem. cancer com. Montefiore Med. Ctr., mem. adv. com. home care dept.; mem. adv. com. Bronx Comty. Home Care, Hospice Visiting Nurse Svc. of the Bronx. One-person shows include AIDS Resource Ctr. of Wis., Hotel Pfister, Milw., 1997; exhibited in group shows Bailey Hall Exhibits, Ft. Lauderdale, 1992-97, Ft. Lauderdale City Hall, 1992, Lauderhill Libr., Ft. Lauderdale, 1993, LeGrange (Ga.) Mus., 1995, Marcella Geltman Gallery, No. N.J., 1995, Women for the Visual Arts, Boca Raton, Fla., 1995, Northwood U. Art Gallery, West Palm Beach, Fla., 1995-97, Gwinnett Fine Arts Ctr., Duluth, Ga., 1996, San Diego Watercolor Soc. Internat. Exhbn., 1996, North Valley Art League Nat. Show, Redding, Calif., 1997, San Bernardino (Calif.) Art Assn. Nat. Show, 1997, Hollywood (Fla.) Art and Culture Ctr., 1997, Ky. Watercolor Soc., Elizabethtown, 1997; represented in pvt. collections; contbr. articles to med. jours. Mem. AMA, Am. Soc. Clin. Oncology, Ea. Pain Assn., Acad. Hospice Physicians, Found. Thanatology, Found. for Rsch. on Sexually Transmitted Diseases, N.Y. Cancer Soc., N.Y. County Med. Soc., Ea. Clin. Oncology Group, Bronx PSRO, Nat. Assn. Women Artists Inc. (juried, 1st Place award 1999, Moore Greenblatt Meml. award 1995), 2+3 Artist Group Inc. (juried), Fla. Artist Group Inc. (juried), Gold Coast Watercolor Soc. (Dick Blick award 1994), Ga. Watercolor Soc., Fla. Watercolor Soc., Catherine Lorillard Wolfe Assn. (assoc.), Internat. Arts-Medicine Assn., Am. Physicians Art Assn. Home: 2504 Lajune Terr Fort Lauderdale FL 33316

SIEGMUND, MARY KAY, priest, counselor, marriage and family therapist; b. Kans. City, Mo., Aug. 18, 1953; d. John Riley Thompson and Agnes Ann Purcell; m. Mark Steven Siegmund, Dec. 27, 1979; children: Melissa, Michael. BA, Park Coll., 1977; MA, U. Mo., 1988; MDiv, Midwestern Bapt. Theol. Sem., 1995. Lic. profl. counselor. Chaplain Independence (Mo.) Regional Hosp., 1985—88, therapist, 1985—88; chaplain Marillac Ctr., Kansas City, 1995—98, therapist, 1995—98; vicar St. John's Northland, Kansas City, 1997—2001; asst. rector Ch. of Good Shepherd, Nashua, NH, 2001—. Episc.

SIEMER, DEANNE CLEMENCE, lawyer; b. Buffalo, Dec. 25, 1940; d. Edward D. and Dorothy J. (Helsdon) S.; m. Howard P. Willens; 1 child, Jason L. BA, George Washington U., 1962; LLB, Harvard U., 1968. Bar: N.Y. 1968, D.C. 1969, Md. 1972. Economist Office of Mgmt. and Budget, Washington, 1964-67; assoc., then ptnr. Wilmer, Cutler & Pickering, Washington, 1968-77, 80-90; ptnr. Pillsbury, Madison & Sutro, Washington, 1990-95; mng. dir. Wilsie Co., Washington and Saipan, 1995—. Gen. counsel U.S. Dept. of Def., Washington, 1977—79; spl. asst. to sec. U.S. Dept. of Energy, Washington, 1979—80. Author: Tangible Evidence, 3d edit., 1996, National Security and Self-Determination: United States Policy in Micronesia, 1999, Corel Presentations for Litigators, 2000, PowerPoint for Litigators, 2000, Effective Use of Courtroom Technology: A Judge's Guide to Pretrial and Trial, 2001, An Honorable Accord: The Covenant Between the Northern Mariana Islands and the United States, 2001, Effective Use of Courtroom Technology: A Lawyer's Guide to Pretrial and Trial, 2002, Easy Tech: Cases and Materials on Courtroom Technology, 2002, The Patronus Technique: A Practical Proposal In Asbestos-Driven Bankruptcies, 2002, Power Point 2002 for Litigators, 2002, Basic Power Point Slides, 2003, Argument Slides, 2003, The Evidence Camera, 2004. Mem. Lawyers Com. for Civil Rights, Washington, 1973—; mediator D.C. Superior Ct., Washington, 1986—, U.S. Ct. Appeals, Washington, 1988—; trustee Nat. Inst. Trial Advocacy, 1989—, Am. Law Inst., 1990—; arbitrator Atty. Client Arbitration Bd., NASD; mem roundtable on sci. and security NAS. Recipient citation Air Force Assn., 1977, Dist. Pub. Svc. medal Sec. of Def., 1979, Commendation Pres. of U.S. 1981. Mem. ABA, D.C. Bar Assn., No. Marianas Bar Assn. Episcopalian.

SIEMSEN, SUSAN ANNE, physician assistant; b. Monnett, Mo., Nov. 26, 1963; d. Norman Lee Snook and E. Avis Foster; m. Wayne Fredrick Siemsen, May 28, 1982; 1 child, Natalie Marie. B of Health Sci., Wichita State U., 1987. Nat. certified and state registered phys. asst. Phys. asst. to William Henderson, MD, Albuquerque, N.Y., 1988-89; subspecialty in pediatric GI/hematology/oncology KUMC Pediatrics, Kansas City, Kans., 1989-92; phys. asst. South Federal FP, Denver, 1992-97, Lawrence (Kans.) Family Practice Ctr., 1997—. Proctor for phys. asst. students, Colorado/Denver program, 1992-97, KUMC NP program, Lawrence, 1997—. Presbyterian. Avocations: golf, skiing, family. Home: 2820 Meadow Dr Lawrence KS 66047-3240 Office: Lawrence Fam Practice Ct 3510 Clinton Pkwy Ste 320 Lawrence KS 66047-2145

SIERENS, GAYLE, newscaster; married; 3 children. BS in Mass Comm., Fla. State U. Reporter WFSU-TV, Tallahassee; weekend sports anchor, reporter WFLA-TV, Tampa, Fla., 1977—83, weekday sports anchor, 1983—85, sportscaster, news anchor, 1985—. Mem. adv. bd. Fla. Poison Info. Ctr. Found.; bd. dirs. Judeo-Christian Health Clinic. Appeared (weekly) NFL Live, NBC. Chairperson ann. Bowl for Kids' Sake fundraiser Boys and Girls Clubs of Greater Tampa, bd. dirs. Achievements include first woman to do play-by-play for an NFL game. Office: WFLA-TV PO Box 1410 Tampa FL 33601

SIERRA-AMOR, ROSA ISABEL, health facility administrator; b. Tampico, Mex., Apr. 28, 1954; Licensure Degree in Clin. Biochemistry, Nat. Autonomous U. Mexico, 1979, MS, 1992, PhD, 1995; postgrad., U. Reading, Eng., 1986. Fellow dept. endocrinology and metabolism Jewish Hosp. and Washington U. Sch. Medicine, St. Louis, 1982; mem. staff dept. nephrology and mineral metabolism, assoc. investigator Nat. Inst. Nutrition Salvador Zubiran, Mexico City, 1978-90; dir. Mineral Metabolism Rsch. Lab., divsn. neonatology Children's Hosp.-U. Cin. Med. Ctr., 1990-96; lab. mgr. Pediat. Bone Rsch. Ctr. Children's Hosp. Med. Ctr., 1996—. Lectr. in field. Contbr. articles to profl. jours. Recipient Ames/Bayer L.Am. award, 1993, award Mexican Coll. Profls. in Chemistry, 1994. Mem.: Spanish Soc. Clin. Chemistry and Molecular Pathology, Iberoamerican Soc. for Rsch. on Bone Metabolism, Nat. Acad. Pharm. Scis. (Mexico), Mexican Assn. Clin. Biochemistry, Am. Assn. for Bone and Mineral Rsch., Am. Assn. for Clin. Chemistry (mem. internat. rels. com. 1992—94, chair OVS membership com. 1994, mem. internat. adv. panel 1994—96, chair exch. program in clin. chemistry OVS 1994—, chair Ohio Valley sect. awards com. 1997—, treas. pediat. materno-fetal divsn. 2002—, Internat. Fellowship award 1996, Bernard Katchman ann. award 2001), Mex. Assn. Clin. Biochemistry (chair continuing edn. com., chmn. sci. proc. 8th internat. congress on lab. automation, mem. sci. program), Internat. Fedn. Clin. Chemistry (alt. rep. to Mexican Assn. Clin. Biochemistry 1992—96, newsletter corr. and reviewer jour. 1992—, mem. sci. program XVII Internat. Congress in Clin. Chemistry 1996—, assoc. mem. com. in metabolic bone disease and bone markers sci. divsn 1996—, mem. at large 1997—99, mem. EB 2000—02, co-chmn. sci. com. XIX ICCC 2005). Office: Childrens Hosp Med Ctr B Rm 4315 ML 11011 3333 Burnet Ave Cincinnati OH 45229-3039 E-mail: rsierramor@hotmail.com.

SIEVERT, MARY ELIZABETH, small business owner, retired secondary school educator; b. Sioux City, Iowa, Sept. 28, 1939; d. Arthur Harry and Bertha Busboom Sievert. BS, Morningside Coll., 1960; MA, U. Nebr., 1962; postgrad., U. Iowa, Hope Coll., U. Calif., Irvine. Instr. chemistry lab. Morningside Coll., Sioux City, Iowa, 1959—60; tchr. chemistry Davenport Schs., Iowa, 1962—86, Blackhawk Coll., Moline, Ill.; admissions officer St. Luke's Hosp., Davenport; SSTP counselor U. Iowa, Iowa City; computer instr. Grinnell Coll., Iowa, 1983; P/K-12/A sci. coord. Davenport Schs., 1986—96, AGATE dept. chair, 1995—99; pres., CEO Memorabilia ExtraOrdinaire, Davenport, 1996—. Exchange tchr. Rowley Regis Coll., Birmingham, England, 1975; pres., CEO Quad Cities Sci. and Engring. Fair, Davenport, 1962—99; adv. evaluation coun. Antique Am., Davenport, 2000—01; antiques and collectibles lectr. Ea. Iowa C.C., Davenport, 2001—, Blackhawk Coll., Moline, Ill., 2002—. Contbr. articles to profl. jours. Fundraising v.p. Miss Iowa Bd., Davenport, 1999—2001; mem. plan and zone commn. City of Davenport, 1988—94; WelcomeAires mem. QC vol. bur. QC Internat. Airport, 2000—; charter mem. 1st in the Nation in Edn. Rschr. Found., 1986—97; 63 com. woman Scott County Rep. Party; handbell ringer, former dir. vacation Bible sch. Holy Cross Luth. Ch., Davenport; mem. bd. Christ Lutheran Ch., 2002—. Named Outstanding H.S. Chemistry Tchr. of Yr. in Iowa, Iowa Acad. Scis., 1969, Outstanding Young Educator, Davenport Jaycees, Centennial Tchr. of Yr. in Iowa, NIH, 1987; named to Iowa Sci. Tchrs. Hall of Fame, 2002; recipient Regional Catalyst award for outstanding chemistry tchr., Chem. Mfg. Assn., 1985, Golden Apple award for top educator, Scott County Edn. Orgn., 1998; fellow Woodrow Wilson fellow for outstanding H.S. chemistry tchrs., Princeton U., 1982; scholar NSF. Mem.: AAUW (past pres. local br. and Iowa State), NEA (life), U. Nebr. Alumni Assn. (life), Morningside Alumni Assn. (life), Delta Kappa Gamma (former local and state parliamentarian, mem. Hapke scholarship com.), Pi Lambda Theta (life; mem. charter alumni chpt.), Sigma Kappa (life). Avocations: bridge, gardening, travel, theater, symphony. Office: Memorabilia ExtraOrdinaire Inc 2707 East Hayes St Davenport IA 52803

SIFF, MARLENE IDA, artist, designer; b. N.Y.C. d. Irving Louis and Dorothy Gertrude (Lahn) Marmer; m. Elliott Justin Siff, July 11, 1959; children: Bradford Evan, Brian Douglas. BA, Hunter Coll., 1957. Cert. tchr. elem. edn., N.Y., N.J. Tchr. Stewart Manor (N.Y.) Sch. Sys., 1957-59, Teaneck (N.J.) Sch. Sys., 1959-60; freelance interior designer Westport, Conn., 1966-70; designer Varo Inertial Products, Trumbull, Conn., 1970; designer signature collections J.P. Stevens & Co. Inc., N.Y., 1974-78, J.C. Penney Co., N.Y., 1978, C.R. Gibson Co., Norwalk, Conn., 1980. Corp. sec., treas., bd. dirs. Belmar Corp., Westport, 1972—; chmn. bd. Marlene Designs Inc., Westport, 1973-77; owner Marlene Siff Design Studio, Westport, 1978—; aesthetic cons. Alcide Corp., Norwalk, 1980-88. One-person shows include David Segal Gallery, N.Y.C., 1987, Conn. Pub. TV Gallery, Hartford, 1987, Paul Mellon Art Ctr., Choate Rosemary Hall, Wallingford, Conn., 1989, Conn. Nat. Bank Hdqs., Norwalk, 1990, Michael Stone Collection, Washington, 1992, Bergdorf Goodman Men, N.Y.C., 1993, Joel Kessler Fine Art, Miami Beach, Fla., 1994, Park Pl., Stamford, Conn., 1995, Westport Arts Ctr., 1995, Mitchells, Westport, 1998, NIH, Bethesda, Md., 1999, Durst Lobby Gallery, N.Y.C., 1999; represented in permanent collections B'nai Brith Klutznick Nat. Jewish Mus., Washington, 1997. Decorator Easter Seal Home Svc. Charity Ball, 1976; bd. dirs. United Jewish Appeal, Westport, 1982-86; com. mem. Levitt Pavillion of the Performing Arts, Westport, 1982-89. Recipient award for creating the most beautiful working environment in an indsl. facility in lower Conn., Lower Conn. Mfrs. Assn., 1970. Mem.: LVW, Anti Defamation League, Nat. Coun. Jewish Women, Kappa Pi. Jewish. Avocations: tennis, swimming, race walking, gardening. Home: 15 Broadview Rd Westport CT 06880-2303 Office Phone: 203-226-8557. Business E-Mail: marlene@marlenesiff.com.

SIFTON, ELISABETH, book publisher; b. N.Y.C., Jan. 13, 1939; d. Reinhold and Ursula (Keppel-Compton) Niebuhr; m. Charles P. Sifton, 1962 (div. 1984); children: Peter Samuel, Charles Tobias, John Paul Gustav; m. Fritz R. Stern, 1996. BA magna cum laude, Radcliffe Coll., Cambridge, Mass., 1960; postgrad., U. Paris, 1960-61. Asst. to dep. asst. sec. of state U.S. Dept. of State, Washington, 1961-62; editorial asst., assoc. editor, editor, sr. editor Frederick A. Praeger Pubs., N.Y.C., 1962-68; editor, sr. editor, editor-in-chief The Viking Press, N.Y.C., 1969-83; v.p., pub. Elisabeth Sifton Books, Viking Penguin, N.Y.C., 1984-87; exec. v.p. Alfred A. Knopf, Inc., N.Y.C., 1987-92; sr. v.p. Farrar, Straus & Giroux, 1993—; pub. Hill & Wang, 1993—. Fulbright fellow, 1960-61 Democrat. Episcopalian. Home: 15 Claremont Ave New York NY 10027-6802 Office: Farrar Straus & Giroux 19 Union Sq W Fl 4 New York NY 10003-3304

SIGAL-IBSEN, ROSE, artist; b. Bucharest, Romania, Aug. 22; arrived in U.S., 1957; d. Joseph and Tilly (Eckstein) Cohen; m. Albert D. Sigal, Dec. 25, 1941 (dec. May 1970); 1 child, Daniel M.; m. Joseph Ibsen, Oct. 1973 Diploma, Fashion Inst. Technology, N.Y.C., 1978; Parson, Sch. of Design, N.Y.C., 1985-86; student, Koho Sch. of Sumi-E, N.Y.C., 1979-90, Zhejiang Acad. Fine Arts, China, 1990. Curator Metro N.Y. Chpt. of Sumi-E Soc., 1990—, v.p., 1990—. One-woman shows include China-Gallery Weizhi Schubert, Hanover, Germany, 1991, Manhattan Savs. Bank, N.Y.C., 1993—94, Chem. Bank, 1993—95, N.Y. Pub. Libr., 1996, Bankers Fed., N.Y.C., 1996, Rep. Bank for Savs., 1996, Roumanian Cultural Found., Bucharest, 1998, World Fine Art Gallery, N.Y.C., 1998, Romanian Embassy, Washington, 2000, others, exhibited in group shows at China Nat. Acad. of Fine Arts, Hangzhou, 1994, Fourth World Conf. on Women, Beijing, 1995, Steinhardt Conservatory, Bklyn. Bot. Garden, 1996, Nat. Mus. of Women in the Arts, Washington, 1996, 80 Washington Square East Galleries, N.Y.C., 1996, Seton Hall U., South Orange, N.J., 1996, Golden West Coll. Fine Arts Gallery, Huntington Beach, Calif., 1995, Seton Hall Gallery, South Orange, N.J., 1996, Wesleyan U., Middletown, Conn., 1998, Taipei Gallery Chinese Info. and Culture Ctr. and the Chinese-Am. Arts Coun., 1998, Cork Gallery/Lincoln Ctr., N.Y.C., 1998, Pen and Brush, (All-sections award), Sumi-e Soc. Am., Inc., 1999, Japanese Am. Cultural & Cmty. Ctr. at Doizaki Gallery, 1999, Broome St. Gallery, N.Y.C., 1999, 2001—02, Nat. Mus. of Women in Arts, 1999, Asia Soc. Store, 1999, ASCA, 1999—2000, Japanese Cultural Ctr., L.A., 1999, Pen and Brush All Media Millennium Celebration, 2000, Pen and Brush Ann. Watercolor, 2000, Broome St. Gallery Invitational, 2000, Contemporary Artists Guild, 2000, Newark Mus. and Taiwan Art Edn. Inst., 2000, Sumi-e Soc. Am. Inc. at Courthouse Galleries of Portsmouth Va., 2001 (Hallie Hazen Meml. award, 2001), Pen and Brush Ann. Mixed Media, 2002, Korean Cultural Ctr., L.A., 2002, Japanese Artists Assn. N.Y., 2002, others; artwork Courage Card design, 1998. Recipient Manhattan Arts award Cover Art Competition, N.Y.C., 1992, 94, 95, 97, King Point award, Fla., 1991, Tenth Japanese Internat. Calligraphy Exhbn. award, N.Y.C., 1996, Manhattan Arts Internat. Showcase award, Emily N. Hatch Meml. award Pen and Brush, Inc., Spring Watercolor Exhbn., 1998, Hallie Hazen Meml. award Sumi-e Soc. Am., Inc., 2001. Mem. Nat. Mus. of Women in the Arts, Artist Equity of N.Y., Am. Soc. Contemporary Artists, Art of Ink in Am., The Oriental Brushwork Soc. of Am., Sumi-e Soc. (hon.). Avocations: sculptor in clay, dance. Home: One Irving Pl #222B New York NY 10003-9741

SIGLER, HOLLIS, artist, educator, author; b. Gary, Ind., Mar. 2, 1948; Studied in Florence, Italy, 1968-69; BFA, Moore Coll. Art, 1970, DFA (hon.), 1994; MFA, Sch. Art Inst. Chgo., 1973. Mem. faculty Columbia Coll., Chgo., 1978—, instr. painting and drawing, 1984—. One-woman shows include Akron (Ohio) Art Mus., 1986, S.W. Craft Ctr., San Antonio, 1989, Nat. Mus. Women Arts, Washington, 1991, 93, Printworks Gallery, Chgo., 1991, 93, Priebe Art Gallery, U. Wis., Oshkosh, 1992, Susan Cummins Gallery, Mill Valley, Calif., 1992, 94, Steven Scott Gallery, Balt., 1993, 94, Hartman Ctr. Gallery, Bradley U., Peoria, Ill., 1994, Mus. Contemporary Art, Chgo., 1994, Suburban Fine Arts Ctr., Highland Park, Ill., 1994, Lakeview Mus. Arts and Sci., Peoria, 1994, Decordova Mus. and Sculpture Park, Lincoln, Mass., 1994, Leedy-Voulkos Art Ctr. Gallery, Kansas City, Mo., 1995, Ark. Art Ctr., Little Rock, 1996, Elvehjem Mus. Art., U. Wis., Madison, 1997, Palo Alto Cultural Ctr., Calif., 1998, Carl Hammer Gallery, Chgo., 1998, Printworks Gallery, Chgo., 1999; exhibited in group shows Whitney Mus. Art, N.Y.C., 1981, Walker Art Mus., Mpls., 1982, Mus. Modern Art, N.Y.C., 1984, Corcoran Gallery Art, Washington, 1985, Chgo. Cultural Ctr., 1992, The Drawing Ctr., N.Y.C., 1993, The Contemporary Mus., Honolulu, 1994, Butler Inst. Am. Art, Youngstown, Ohio, 1995, Nat. Mus. Am. Art, Smithsonian, Washington, 1996, Corcoran Sch. of Art and U.S. Senate, Russell Rotunda Gallery, Washington, 1998; represented in permanent collections Mus. Contemporary Art, Chgo., Indpls. Mus. Art, Seattle Art Mus., Madison Art Ctr., High Mus. Art, Atlanta, Nat. Mus. Am. Art, Smithsonian, Nat. Mus. Women in the Arts, Washington, John D. and Catherine T. MacArthur Found., Johns Hopkins Hosp. Oncology Ctr., Balt.; pub.: Hollis Sigler's Breast Cancer Journal, 1999; also others. Recipient cash award Southwestern Ctr. for Contemporary Art, Winston-Salem, N.C., 1987, Childe Hassam purchase award AAAL, 1988; grantee Ill. Arts Coun., 1986, Nat. Endowment for Arts, 1987. Office: Columbia Coll 600 S Michigan Ave Chicago IL 60605-1900 Home: 2040 Berkeley Rd Highland Park IL 60035-2743

SIGLER, RHONDA LEA, special education educator; b. Georgetown, Ill., Oct. 22, 1968; d. David L. and Deana M. Black; m. A.B. Chris Sigler; 1 child. BA in Art and Advt. Design, Western Ill. U., 1989; MEd in Curriculum and Instrn. Elem. Edn., U. Ill., 1995; MA in Spl. Edn., Adams State Coll., 2001. Cert. elem. tchr. K-8, instrnl. leader grades K-12. Tchr. grade 6 Newcomb (N.Mex.) Elem., 1996—97; tchr. grade 5 Eva B. Stokely Elem., Shiprock, N.Mex., 1997—2000; tchr. spl. edn. classroom Nizhoni Elem., Shiprock, 2000—02, Ruth N. Band Elem. Sch., 2002—. Scholar, ACCESS/ Adams State Coll., Alamosa, Colo., 1999—2001. Mem.: ASCD, Coun. Exceptional Children, N.Mex. Fedn. Student Coun. Exceptional Children (v.p. 2001—02).

SIGMOND, CAROL ANN, lawyer; b. Phila., Jan. 9, 1951; d. Irwin and Mary Florence (Vollmer) S. BA, Grinnell Coll., 1972; JD, Cath. U., 1975. Bar: Va. 1975, D.C. 1980, Md. 1988, N.Y. 1990, U.S. Dist. Ct. (ea. dist.) Va. 1975, U.S. Dist. Ct. (so. and ea. dist.) N.Y. 1991, U.S. Ct. Appeals (4th cir.) 1976, U.S. Ct. Appeals (fed. cir.) 1987, U.S. Ct. Appeals (2d cir.) 2000. Asst. gen. counsel Washington Met. Area Transit Authority, 1978-85; acting assoc. gen. counsel for appeals and gen. law, 1985-86; assoc. Patterson, Belknap, Webb & Tyler, Washington, 1986-89, Berman, Paley, Goldstein & Kannry, N.Y.C., 1991-93; prin. Law Offices of Carol A. Sigmond, N.Y.C., 1993-97; of counsel Pollack & Greene, LLP, N.Y.C., 1998-2000; pvt. practice N.Y.C., 2000—03; prin. Kehl, Kilzun, & Sigmond, 2004—. Mem. Women's Nat. Dem. Club. Active Womens Nat. Dem. Club. Mem. ABA, D.C. Bar Assn., Arlington County Bar Assn., Va. State Bar Assn., Md. State Bar Assn., Assn. of Bar of City of N.Y. Democrat. Mem. Lds Ch. Avocations: piano, bridge. Office: 317 Madison Av 21st Fl New York NY 10017-5208 E-mail: CASigmond@KKSLegal.net.

SIGMUND, DIANE WEISS, judge; b. N.Y.C., Mar. 1, 1943; BS, Pa. State U., 1963; JD magna cum laude, Temple U., 1977. Bar: Pa. 1977. Atty. Blank, Rome, Cominsky & McCauley, Phila.; judge U.S. Bankruptcy Ct. (Pa. ea. dist.), 3rd circuit, Phila., 1993—. Mem. steering com. Ea. Dist. Pa. Bankruptcy Conf., 1995—, 3d Cir. Task Force Equal Treatment in Cts., Gender Commn., 1995-97; chmn. endowment edn. Nat. Conf. Bankruptcy Judges., 1996—, bd. govs., 1998—; mem. com. on automation and tech. Jud. Conf. U.S., 1997—. Fellow Am. Coll. Bankruptcy. Office: Robert NC Nix Courthouse 900 Market St Rm 203 Philadelphia PA 19107-4237

SIKANDER, SHAHZIA, artist; b. Lahore, Pakistan, 1969; BFA, Nat. Coll. Arts, Lahore, 1992; MFA, RISD, Providence, 1995. One-woman shows include Barbara Davis Gallery, Houston, 1996, Hosfelt Gallery, San Francisco, 1997, Deitch Project, N.Y.C., 1997, Renaissance Soc. U. Chgo., 1998, Kemper Mus. Contemporary Art and Design, Kansas City, Mo., 1998—88, Hirshhorn Mus., Washington, 1999, exhibited in group shows at Rhotas Gallery, Islamabad, Pakistan, 1992, Pacific Asia Mus., Pasadena, Calif., 1994—95, Bradford (Eng.) City Mus., 1996, Glassell Sch. Art Mus. Fine Arts, 1996, 1997, Laing Gallery, Newcastle, Eng., 1997, Whitney Mus. Am. Art, 1997, Queens Mus. Art, Flushing Meadows, N.Y., 1997, Yerba Buena Gardens Ctr. Arts, San Francisco, Forum for Contemporary Art, St. Louis, 1998, Bard Coll., Annandale-on-Hudson, N.Y., 1998, Ludwig (Austria) Mus., 1998, Aldrich Mus. Contemporary Art, Conn., 1998, also exhbns. in Portugal, Johannesburg, South Africa, Mexico City, work represented in numerous newspapers and mags. Recipient Haji Sharif award for miniature painting, Shakik Ali award and Kipling award, Nat. Coll. Art, Lahore, 1993; grad. fellow, RISD, 1993—95, core fellow, Glassel Sch. Art Mus. Fine Arts, 1995—97, grantee, Louis Comfort Tiffany Found., 1997, Joan Mitchell grantee, 1998—99. Address: care Deitch Projects 76 Grand St New York NY 10013-2220

SIKES, CYNTHIA LEE, actress, children's advocate, singer; b. Coffeyville, Kans., Jan. 2, 1954; d. Neil and Pat (Scott) S.; m. Alan Bud Yorkin, June 24, 1989. Student, Am. Conservatory Theater, San Francisco, 1977-79. Actor: (TV series) St. Elsewhere, 1981—83, L.A. Law, 1989, JAG, 2000—01, (TV movies) Oceans of Fire, 1986, His Mistress, 1990; prodr., actor : Sins of Silence, 1996; actor: (films) Man Who Loved Women, That's Life, Arthur on the Rocks, Love Hurts, 1988, Possums, 1998, Going Shopping, 2004, (Broadway musical) Into the Woods, 1988—89. Active Hollywood Women's Polit. Com.; apptd. Pres. Clinton's Adv. Com. on Arts John F. Kennedy Ctr. for Performing Arts, 1999. Recipient Gov.'s Medal of Merit, Kans., 1986. Democrat. Avocations: hiking, writing, reading.

SIKORA, BARBARA JEAN, library director; b. Passaic, N.J., Apr. 12, 1943; d. Stanley Francis and Jean (Sobczyk) S. BA in Edn., English, William Paterson Coll., 1969, MEd in Learning Disabilities, 1978; MLS, Rutgers U., 1978; Cert. in Fundraising Mgmt., Fairleigh Dickinson U., 1990. Profl. libr. N.J. Tchr. Clifton (N.J.) Pub. Schs., 1969-73; office mgr. Singer/TRW, Fairfield, N.J., 1974-76; prin. libr. Passaic Pub. Libr., 1978-88; asst. libr. dir. Pub. Libr. Livingston, N.J., 1989-90, libr. dir., 1991—. Adj. faculty William Paterson Coll., 1977-90; trustee Wayne Pub. Libr., 1986-88; bd. dirs. Polish and Slavic Fed. Credit Union, 1999—. Mem. Polish Heritage Festival Com., Holmdel, N.J., 1987—, gen. chmn., 1999; trustee, bd. dirs. Livingston Area C. of C., 1998—; pres. Libr. Pub. Rels. Coun., 1997; West Essex br. YMCA of the Oranges, 1997—; mem. Polish Children's Heartline, Inc. Grantee U.S. Dept. Edn. libr. literacy program, 1987, N.J. State Libr. Leadership Inst., 1988, Christopher Leadership Inst., 1997; Paul Harris fellow Rotary Internat., 1999. Mem. ALA (ethics com. 1995-99), AAUW, N.J. Libr. Assn., Nat. Spkrs.' Assn., Rotary (pres. Livingston chpt. 1994-96, 2000), Rutgers Sch. Comm. and Info. Libr. Studies Alumni Assn. (pres. 1991-94), Beta Phi Mu. Avocations: writing, speaking, adult education, psychology, leadership skills training. Home: The Mill 300 Main St Apt 314 Little Falls NJ 07424-1359 Office: Pub Libr Livingston 10 Robert Harp Dr Livingston NJ 07039 E-mail: sikora@bcols.org.

SIKORA, ROSANNA DAWN, emergency physician, educator; b. Weirton, W.Va., Nov. 16, 1955; d. Edward and Dorothy Ann (Wade) S.; m. Odus E. Brown, Nov. 25, 1994; stepchildren: Aza, Katherine, Hannah. AB in Biology, W.Va. U., 1978, MD, 1982. Cert. in emergency medicine; cert. in pediats., specialty in pediat. emergency medicine; cert. in internal medicine. Resident in pediat. internal medicine W.Va. U. Hosps. Inc., Morgantown, 1982-86, with. Assoc. prof. emergency medicine, pediats., internal medicine W.Va. U. Sch. Medicine, 1996—; mem. pediat. advanced life support subcom. Am. Heart Assn., Charleston, 1987-97, mem. pediat. advanced life support affiliate faculty, 1987-97. Physician men's/women's varsity swim/diving team W.Va. U., Morgantown, 1994—. Fellow Am. Coll. Emergency Physicians (bd. dirs. 1990—, sec.-treas. 1995-96, v.p. 1996-97, pres.-elect 1997-98); mem. AMA, ACP, Am. Acad. Pediats., Alpha Omega Alpha. Democrat. Roman Catholic. Office: W Va U Dept Emergency Medicine PO Box 9149 Morgantown WV 26506-9149

SIKYTA, JAYNE A. insurance agent; b. Columbus, Ohio, Sept. 10, 1954; d. Robert Lee and Lucille Neal Wrights; m. Lawrence R. Sikyta, May 18, 1985; children: Ruth Ann, Rebekah Elizabeth. BS in Bus., Purdue U., West Lafayette, Ind., 1982. Cert. sr. advisor Soc. Sr. Advisors. Divisional v.p. human rels. L.S. Ayres, Indpls., 1987—91, Famous-Barr, St. Louis, 1991—96; v.p. human rels. The May Dept. Stores Co., St. Louis, 1996—99; divisional v.p. human rels. Famous-Barr, St. Louis, 1999—2000; v.p. human resources House of Lloyd, Grandview, Mo., 2000—03; ins. sales Banker's Life, Overland Park, Kans., 2002—. Mem. adv. bd. DECA, Ft. Wayne, Ind., 1981—84, Indpls., 1983—84; mem. budget review com. United Way, Ft. Wayne, Ind., 1982—84; fundraiser The Leukemia and Lymphoma Soc., Kansas City/St. Louis, Mo., 1999—; mem. congl. coun., Sunday sch. tchr., worhip leader The Shepherd's Ctr., Raytown, Mo. Avocations: reading, music, bicycling, running. Home: 2829 SW Saddlewood Dr Lees Summit MO 64081 Office: Bankers Life and Casualty Co 10800 Farley Ste 230 Overland Park KS 66210

SILAGI, BARBARA WEIBLER, corporate administrator; b. Chgo., June 26, 1930; d. Carleton Thomas and Catherine Josephine (Wolph) Weibler; m. Joseph Edward Sturgulewski (Sturgus), Feb. 12, 1953 (div. Aug. 1954); 1 child, Mariann Catherine; m. John Louis Silagi, Jr., July 2, 1960 (div. July 1968). BM in Edn., Northwestern U., 1958; MS in Edn., No. Ill. U., 1965. Cert. K-14 supervisory teaching, spl. edn. tchr., airline transport pilot, FAA dispatcher. Elem. sch. tchr. St. Mary's Sch., Chgo., 1947-49, Kingman, Ariz., 1949-52; legal sec. Judge Edward J. Mahoney, Quincy, Ill., 1954-55; elem. sch. tchr. C.M. Bardwell Sch., Aurora, Ill., 1955-76; flight instr. flight schs. Chgo., Aurora and Frankfort, Ill., Clinton, Iowa, 1970-77; aircraft dispatcher Transcontinental Airlines, Zantop Internat. Airlines, Ypsilanti, Mich., 1977-81; airline pilot Mannion Air Charter, Ypsilanti, 1977-80; head night auditor Howard Johnson, Quality Inn, Travelodge, BestWestern, others, Ocala, Fla., Silver Springs, Fla., 1983-87; sec.-treas. Diamond Design Svcs., Inc., Ocklawaha, Fla., 1985—. Pub. Forest Shopper, Springs Shopper, Belle Shopper. Author: Dispatch Training, 1989; editor tng. manuals, 1977-85. Violist Chgo. Suburban Symphony, Naperville, Ill., 1956-60; contralto Palestrina A capella Choir, Aurora, Ill., 1956-60; life mem. Ill. PTA, Aurora, 1974—; apptd. vice chmn. adv. bd. Dunellon Airport and Indsl. Park, 1992-96. Recipient 1st place Suburban Aviation Assn., Chgo., 1975, 5th place Illi-Nines Air Derby, Chgo., Moline, Ill., 1973, 2d place Leg prize Powder Puff Derby, McLean to Lincoln, Nebr., 1971; Eckstein scholar Northwestern U., 1952. Mem. AAUW (life), NEA (life), Ill. Edn. Assn., Ninety Nines Internat. (life), Illi-Nines Air Derby (handicap chmn. 1972-76, air marking chmn. 99's Chgo. chpt. 1972-76, corr. sec. Chgo. chpt. 1976-77, 1st pl. achievement awards 1972-78), Pi Lambda Theta (charter, life, rsch. chmn. Beta Delta chpt. 1962-63). Roman Catholic. Avocations: needlework, gardening, reading, music. Home: 6305 SE 158th Ct Ocklawaha FL 32179-2988 Office: Diamond Design Svcs Inc PO Box 186 Ocklawaha FL 32183-0186

SILAK, CATHY R. lawyer, former state supreme court justice; b. Astoria, N.Y., May 25, 1950; d. Michael John and Rose Marie (Janor) S.; m. Nicholas G. Miller, Aug. 9, 1980; 3 children. BA, NYU, 1971; M in City Planning, Harvard U., 1973; JD, U. Calif., 1976. Bar: Calif. 1977, U.S. Dist. Ct. (no. dist.) Calif. 1977, D.C. 1979, U.S. Ct. Appeals (D.C. cir.) 1979, U.S. Dist. Ct. (so. dist.) N.Y. 1980, Idaho 1983, U.S. Dist. Ct. Idaho 1983, U.S. Ct. Appeals (2nd cir.) 1983, U.S. Ct. Appeals (9th cir.) 1985. Law clk. to Hon. William W. Schwarzer U.S. Dist. Ct. (no dist.), Calif., 1976-77; pvt. practice San Francisco, 1977-79, Washington, 1979-80; asst. U.S. atty. So. Dist. of N.Y., 1980-83; spl. asst. U.S. atty. Dist. of Idaho, 1983-84; pvt. practice Boise, Idaho, 1984-90; judge Idaho Ct. Appeals, 1990-93; justice Idaho Supreme Ct., Boise, 1993—2000; ptnr. Hawley, Troxell, Ennis, and Hawley, 2001—. Assoc. gen. counsel Morrison Knudsen Corp., 1989-90; mem. fairness com. Idaho Supreme Ct. and Gov.'s Task Force on Alternative Dispute Resolution; instr. and lectr. in field. Assoc. note and comment editor Calif. Law Rev., 1975-76. Land use planner Mass. Dept. Natural Resources, 1973; founder Idaho Coalition for Adult Literacy; bd. dirs. Literacy Lab., Inc.; mem. adv. bd. Boise State U. Legal Asst. Program. Recipient Jouce Stein award Boise YWCA, 1992, Women Helping Women award Soroptimist, Boise, 1993. Fellow Idaho Law Found (ann., lectr.); mem. ABA (nat. conf. state trial judges jud. adminstrn. divsn.), Nat. Assn. Women Judges, Idaho State Bar (corp./securities sect., instr.), Am. Law Inst., Fellows of the Am. Bar Found, Am. Judicature Soc. (bd. dirs.). Office: Hawley Troxell Ennis & Hawley PO Box 1617 Boise ID 83702-1617*

SILBER, JOAN KAREN, writer, educator; b. Newark, June 14, 1945; d. Samuel Sanford and Dorothy (Arlein) S. BA, Sarah Lawrence Coll., 1967; MA, NYU, 1979. Mem. writing faculty 92d St. Y, N.Y.C., Sarah Lawrence Coll., Bronxville, NY, 1985—, Warren Wilson Coll., Asheville, NC, 1986—. Author: Household Words, 1980 (Hemingway award), In the City, 1987, In My Other Life, 2000, Lucky Us, 2001, Ideas of Heaven, 2004; also stories. Grantee N.Y. Found. Arts, 1986; Guggenheim fellow, 1984-85, NEA fellow, 1986. Home: 43 Bond St New York NY 10012-2463 Office: Sarah Lawrence Coll 1 Meadway Bronxville NY 10708-5931 E-mail: jksilber@earthlink.net.

SILBER, JUDY G. dermatologist; b. Newark, July 26, 1953; MD, SUNY, Bklyn., 1978. Intern Brookdale Med. Ctr., Bklyn., 1978-79; resident in dermatology Kings County Hosp., Bklyn., 1979-82; pvt. practice dermatology. Affiliated with Meadowlands Med. Ctr., Secaucus, N.J. Fellow Am. Acad. Dermatology; mem. AMA, N.J. Med. Soc. Office: 992 Clifton Ave Clifton NJ 07013-3502

SILBERBERG, INGA, dermatologist; b. Kassel, Germany, Sept. 16, 1934; came to U.S., 1938; d. Willi and Erna (Rosenbaum) S.; m. Herbert M. Sinakin, Feb. 16, 1969; 1 child, William Elias. BA, Hunter Coll., 1955; MD, SUNY, 1959; MS in Dermatology, NYU, 1965. Diplomate Am. Bd. Dermatologists, 1964. Instr., clin. dermatology NYU Med. Ctr., N.Y.C., 1963-65, clin. asst. prof., 1965-66, asst. prof. dermatology, 1966-71, clin. assoc. prof. dermatology, 1971-76; cons., dermatology Newcomb Hosp., Vineland, N.J., 1975-98. Recipient Henry Silver award Dermatologic Soc. Greater N.Y., 1962, 65, Dermatology Found. Discovery award, 1993, Dr. Rose Hirschler award Women's Dermatologic Soc., 1999; Jonas Salk scholar, City of N.Y., 1955-59. Fellow Am. Acad. Dermatology; mem. AMA. E-mail: hmsina@pol.net.

SILBERGELD, ELLEN KOVNER, environmental epidemiologist, researcher, toxicologist; b. Washington, July 29, 1945; d. Joseph and Mary (Gion) Kovner; m. Alan Mark Silbergeld, 1969; children: Sophia, Nicholas. AB, Vassar Coll., 1967; PhD, Johns Hopkins U., 1972. Kennedy fellow Johns Hopkins Med. Sch., Balt., 1974—75; scientist NIH, Bethesda, Md., 1975—81; chief toxics scientist Environ. Def. Fund, Washington, 1982—90; prof. epidemiology, toxicology and pharmacology U.Md., Balt., 1990—2001, affil. prof. environ. law, 1990—2001, dir. program in human health and environ., 1996—2000, prof. dept. pathology toxicology, 1995—2000, adj. prof. dept. pharmacology and exptl. therapeutics, 1995—2000; Prof. Environ. Health Scis. epidemiology, and health policy and mgmt. Bloomberg School of Public Health, Johns Hopkins U., Balt., 2001—. Mem. sci. adv. bd. EPA, 1983—89, 1993—99, Dept. Energy, 1994—95; mem. bd. on environ. sci. and toxicology NAS-NRC, 1983—89; mem. Com. Geosci. Environ. and Resources, 1994—98; mem. bd. biotech. and agr., 1999—; mem. bd. sci. counselors Nat. Inst. Health Scis., 1987—93; cons. Oil and Chem. Atomic Workers, 1970, NSF, 1974—75, OECD, 1987—90. Mem. editl. bd.: Neurobehavioral Toxicology, 1979—87, Am. Jour. Medicine, 1980—, Neurotoxicology, 1981—86, Environ. Rsch., 1983—, editor-in-chief:, 1994—. Mem. Homewood Friends Meeting. Recipient Wolman award, Md. Pub. Health Assn., 1991, Barsky award, APHA, 1992, Md. Gov. Excellence citation, 1990, 1993; scholar Baldwin scholar, Coll. Notre Dame; Fulbright fellow, London,

1967, Woodrow Wilson and Danforth fellow, 1967, NAS Exch. fellow, Yugoslavia, 1976, MacArthur Found. fellow, 1993—98. Mem.: APHA, AAAS, Soc. for Neurosci., Soc. for Occupl. and Environ. Health (sec.-treas. 1983—85, pres. 1987—89), Am. Soc. Tropical Med. Hygiene, Am. Soc. Pharmacology and Exptl. Therapeutics, Collegium Ramazzini (councillor), Phi Beta Kappa. Office: Bloomberg Sch Pub Health 615 N Wolfe St Baltimore MD 21205

SILBERMAN, DEBORAH F. general counsel; b. Washington, Feb. 27, 1952; m. May 30, 1974. BA (hons.), Clark U., 1974; JD, Cath. U. Am., 1981. Bar: D.C. 1981. Editor Urban Land Inst., Washington, 1974-75; law clerk, office mgr. Leo Resnick, Washington, 1975-82, atty. adv., 1982-86; special coun. Securities and Exchange Commn., Washington, 1986; dep. dir. corp. and securities divsn. Fed. Home Loan Bank Bd., Washington, 1986-89; asst. chief counsel bus. transactions divsn. Office of Thrift Supervision, Washington, 1990-94; from dep. gen. counsel to gen. counsel Fed. Housing Finance Bd., Washington, 1994-98, gen. counsel, 1998—. Recipient Special Act award Dept. Treasury, 1992, 94. Mem. ABA, FBA, Women in Housing and Finance, Conf. on Consumer Finance Law. Avocations: travel, singing, writing, reading. Office: Office of Gen Counsel Fed Housing Finance Bd 1777 F St NW Washington DC 20006-5210

SILBERSTANG, JOYCE ESTHER, psychologist, consultant; BA in Psychology, N.Y.U., 1983; PhD in Indsl./Orgnl. Psychology, George Washington U., 1999. Pvt. sch. dirs. lic. N.Y. State Dept. Edn. Dir. Berk Trade and Bus. Sch., Bklyn., 1982—86; fellow George Washington U., Washington, 1986—90; rsch. intern-disaster ops. ARC Hdqrs., Washington, 1987—88; orgnl. cons. Laventhol & Horvath, Washington, 1988—89; pers./rsch. psychologist Office of the Under Sec. of the Navy, Washington, 1989—96; dir. orgnl. devel. svcs. Burgess Levin & Co., Sterling, Va., 1998—99; pres. Orgnl. Consulting Svcs., Arlington, Va., 1999—. Presenter in field. Contbr. articles to profl. jours. Mem. govt. affairs com. Nat. Assn. Trade and Tech. Schs., Washington, 1995—97, key mem. for N.Y. state, 1993—97. Mem.: APA, Pers. Testing Coun., Soc. for Indsl. and Orgnl. Psychologists (program com. reviewer ann. conf. 2000—03). Office: Organizational Consulting Services 1601 North Garfield St Arlington VA 22201 Office Phone: 703-528-0112. E-mail: jsilberstang@aol.com.

SILCOX, FRANCES ELEANOR, museum and exhibits planning consultant; b. Orange, Calif., Sept. 26, 1956; d. William Henry and M. Eleanor (Saulpaugh) S.; m. David William Smith, June 21, 1986; children: Lena Celeste, Reid Whitney. BA in English, U. San Francisco, 1979; MA in Mus. Studies, George Washington U., 1984. Intern divsn. performing arts Smithsonian Instn., Washington, 1978, adminstrv. asst. exhibits dept. Calif. Acad. Scis., San Francisco, 1979-81; gallery coord. The George Washington U., Washington, 1981-83; intern art dept. aide Smithsonian Instn., Washington, 1983-84; asst. dir. Torpedo Factory Arts Ctr., Alexandria, Va., 1983-84; accreditation coord. Am. Assn. Mus., Washington, 1984-86; interpretive planner Design and Prodn. Inc., Lorton, Va., 1986-88; mus. planner West Office Exhbn. Design, San Francisco, 1988-91; ind. mus. and exhibits planner, owner Dallas, 1991—99; prin., owner ExhibiTree, Moraga, Calif., 2000—. Bd. mem. St. Gerard Circle, St. Rita Cath. Cmty., Dallas, 1995-98; contbr. numerous natural and cultural resources orgns. Scholar Nat. Endowment for the Arts-Am. Law Inst.-ABA, Washington, 1982. Mem. Am. Assn. for State and Local History, Am. Assn. Mus., Archaeol. Inst. Am., Internat. Coun. Mus., Nat. Assn. for Mus. Exhbn., Western Mus. Assn., Cultural Connections, Calif. Assn. Mus., World Monuments Fund. Democrat. Avocations: travel, correspondence, photography, reading, walking. Home and Office: 463 Fernwood Dr Moraga CA 94556-2119

SILER, SUSAN REEDER, communications educator; b. Knoxville, Tenn., May 31, 1940; d. Claude S. Jr. and Mary Frances (Cook) Reeder; m. Theodore Paul Siler Jr., Sept. 3, 1960; children: Mary Siler Walker, Theodore Paul III. BS in Communications and Journalism, U. Tenn., Knoxville, 1988, MS in Mass Comms., 1994, postgrad. 2d grade tchr. Lawton (Okla.) Pub. Schs., 1961-62, substitute tchr., 1963-64; with By Design, 1987-88; English tutor, 1991-95; adj. instr. comm. U. Tenn., 1994—, U. Tenn., Pellissippi State Tech. C.C., Knoxville, Tenn. Bd. dirs. Hlen Ross McNabb Mental Health Ctr., Knoxville. Tutor Episc. Ch. Ascension, Knoxville, 1990—; instr. United Meth. Ch., Knoxville, 1985-92; chmn. Dogwood Arts Festival, Knoxville, 1980-85; chmn. Bd. Govs . of East Tenn. Presentation Soc., 1988-96, Dogwood Trails; chmn., sec. bd. dirs. YWCA, Knoxville, 1982-88, editor newsletter, membership chmn., placement adv., sec.; Knoxville Jr. League, 1979-95; bd. dirs. Knoxville Women's Ctr., 1993-94; spl. events chmn. St. Mary's Med. Ctr. Found., 1986-89; Pres. Knoxville area Literacy Assn., 1989-92, tutor Episcopal Ch. Literacy program, Knoxville, 1990-95. Mem. Internat. Mass Comm. Assn., Soc. Profl. Journalists, Am. Journalism Historians Assn., Assn. for Edn. in Journalism and Mass Comms., Kappa Tau Alpha, Golden Key. Home: 717 Kenesaw Ave Knoxville TN 37919-6662

SILL, MELANIE, editor; m. Bennett Groshong. Grad. in journalism, U. N.C., 1981. Mng. editor, 1998; asst. metro editor, 1988; with The Transylvania Times, Brevard, NC, United Press Internat., Raleigh; project editor Boss Hog; exec. editor, sr. v.p. The News & Observer, Raleigh, NC, 2002—. Recipient Pulitzer prize, Boss Hog, 1996; fellow Nieman, Harvard U., 1993—94. Office: 215 S McDowell St Raleigh NC 27601

SILLIMAN, NANCY PRISCILLA, artist, writer; b. Manchester, N.H., Mar. 7, 1948; d. Theodore J. and Lillian Doucette; m. Robert Silliman, Oct. 18, 1986; children from previous marriage: Danielle Carbonneau, Keith Carbonneau. BA, Dartmouth Coll., Hanover, N.H., 1994; MA in Liberal Studies, Dartmouth Coll., 1996. Asst. to dir. Jaffe Friede & Strauss Galleries, Dartmouth Coll., Hanover, NH, 1998—. Author: (plays) A Different Destiny, 1996. Mem.: ASGAAD (sec. 2000—), MALS (v.p. alumni coun. bd. 1999—). Home: 2505 County Rd Windsor VT Office: Dartmouth Coll 129 Hopkins Ctr Hanover NH 03755

SILLS, BEVERLY (MRS. PETER B. GREENOUGH), performing arts organization executive, coloratura soprano; b. Bklyn., May 25, 1929; d. Morris and Sonia (Bahn) Silverman; m. Peter B. Greenough, 1956; children: Meredith, Peter B.; stepchildren: Lindley, Nancy, Diana. Student voice, Estelle Leibling; student piano, Paolo Gallico; student stagecraft, Desire Defrere; hon. doctorates, Harvard U., NYU, New Eng. Conservatory, Temple U.; degree (hon.), Harvard U., N.Y.U., Calif. Inst. Arts. Gen. dir. N.Y.C. Opera, 1979-1989; pres. N.Y.C. Opera Bd., 1989-90; mng. dir. Met. Opera, N.Y.C., 1991-94; chairwoman Lincoln Ctr. for Performing Arts, Inc., N.Y.C., 1994—2002; vice chairwoman Lincoln Ctr. for Performing Arts, N.Y.C., 2002—; chairwoman Met. Opera, N.Y.C., 2002—. Bd. dirs. Met. Opera, 1991-; cons. Nat. Coun. on Arts. Radio debut as Bubbles Silverman on Uncle Bob's Rainbow House, 1932; appeared on Major Bowes Capitol Family Hour, 1934-41, on Our Gal Sunday; toured with Shubert Tours, Charles Wagner Opera Co., 1950, 51; operatic debut Phila. Civic Opera, 1947; debut, N.Y.C. Opera Co. as Rosalinda in Die Fledermaus, 1955; debut San Francisco Opera, 1953; debut La Scala, Milan as Pamira in Siege of Corinth, 1969, Royal Opera, Covent Garden in Lucia di Lammermoor, London, 1971, Met. Opera, N.Y.C., 1975, Vienna State Opera, 1967, Teatro Fenice in La Traviata, Venice; appeared Teatro Colon, Buenos Aires; recital debut Paris, 1971, London Symphony Orch., 1971; appeared throughout U.S., Europe, S. Am. including Boston Symphony, Tanglewood Festival, 1968, 69, Robin Hood Dell, Phila., 1969; title roles in: Don Pasquale, Norma, Ballad of Baby Doe, Thais, La Traviata, Anna Bolena, Maria Stuarda, Lucia de Lammermoor, Barber of Seville, Manon, Louise, Tales of Hoffmann, Daughter of the Regiment, The Magic Flute, Elizabeth in Roberto Devereaux, I Puritana, Julius Caesar, Suor Angelica, Il Tabarro, Gianni Schicchi, Faust, La Loca, Merry Widow, Turk in Italy, Rigoletto, I Capuleti e I Montecchi, Lucrezia Borgia, Ariodante, Le Coq D'Or, others; recordings include The Art of Beverly Sills, Welcome to Vienna, Great Scores (with Placido Domingo); ret. from opera and concert stage, 1980; numerous TV spls; author: Bubbles:A Self-Portrait, 1976, Bubbles: An Encore, Beverly: An Autobiography. Active with March of Dimes, 1971- (Past chmn. bd., past nat. chmn. Mothers' March on Birth Defects); bd. dirs. Apollo Theatre Found., 1999-2001. Recipient Handel medallion, 1973, Pearl S. Buck Women's award, 1979, Emmy award for Profiles in Music, 1976, Emmy award for Lifestyles with Beverly Sills, 1978, Presdl. Medal of Freedom, 1980, Kennedy Ctr. Honors award, 1980, Heinz award in Arts and Humanities, 1995, Grammy award for Best Classical Vocal Soloist Performance, 1976, Best Opera Recording, 1978, Bess Wallace Truman award, March of Dimes, 1994, Juanita Kreps award, JC Penny Co., 1996, MS Hope award, Nat. Multiple Sclerosis Soc., 1998, Medal of the Order of Arts and Letters, Min. French Culture, 2000. Office: Met Opera Lincoln Ctr Performing Arts 140 W 65th St New York NY 10023*

SILSBY, PAULA, prosecutor; U.S. atty. U.S. Dept. Justice, Maine, 2001—. Office: PO Box 9718 Portland ME 04104

SILVA, ALBERTINA, computer company executive; b. Providence, Feb. 23, 1964; d. Manuel R. and Mary P. Silva. BS in Bus. Adminstrn., Bryant Coll., 1986, MBA, 1992. Cert. PMP. Programmer Gen. Dynamics, Norwich, Conn., 1986-87; cons. Orbis, East Providence, R.I., 1987-88; mgr., cons. Early Cloud & Co., Middletown, R.I., 1988-96; project mgr. IBM, Middletown, 1996—. Ptnr. R.I. Sports Exch., Warwick. Mem. PMI.

SILVA, JOANNE RIZZO, family nurse practitioner; b. Boston, Feb. 20, 1950; d. Anthony M. and Barbara A. Rizzo. BS, Northeastern U., 1972; MS, U. Colo., Denver, 1976. ACLS; cert. family nurse practitioner. RN pediat. Mass. Gen. Hosp., Boston, 1972—75, family nurse practitioner Frontier Nursing Svc., Hyden, Ky., 1976—78; nurse practitioner migrant health program U. Colo., Alamosa, 1978—79; family nurse practitioner, clinic mgr. Plan de Salud del Valle, Ft. Lupton, Colo., 1979—82; family nurse practitioner Family Health Svc., Worcester, Mass., 1982—89; fgn. svc. nurse practitioner State Dept., Washington, 1989—, Am. Embassy, Bucharest, Romania, 1989—91, Lima, Peru, 1991—96, fgn. svc. Kathmandu, Nepal, 1996—98, Am. Embassy Quito, Ecuador, 1998—2001, family nurse practitioner, Fla. Regional Ctr. Dept. of State, Ft. Lauderdale, 2002—. Nurse practitioner preceptor Robert Wood Johnson plan de salud del valle, Platteville, Colo., 1980-81, U. Lowell, Worcester, 1984-88, U. Wash., 1995. Recipient Cert. of Appreciation, Agy. Internat. Devel., Romania, 1990, Meritorious Honor award & Group Valor award, Romania, 1990, Dept. of State Health Practitioner of Yr. award, 1995. Mem. Sigma Theta Tau. Avocations: reading, scuba diving, traveling, photography. Address: 4511 S Ocean Blvd # 701 Highland Beach FL 33487 Office: Fla Regional Ctr Dept State 4000 N Andrews Ave Fort Lauderdale FL 33309

SILVA, MONICA, gifted education educator; b. Miami, May 13, 1927; d. Arthur E. and Laura E. (Fernandez) S.; m. Alfred Bethel, Apr. 30, 1955 (annulled 1959); 1 child, Leonard James. BA in Edn., Fordham U., 1970, MS in Adminstrn. Supervision, 1976. Cert. tchr. elem. edn., N.Y.; cert. math. tchr. K-8, Va.; cert. social studies tchr. 7-12, N.Y.; cert. adminstr., N.Y. Tchr., adminstrv. asst. Intermediate Sch. 10 Bd. of Edn., N.Y.C., 1970-73, St. Peter's U.F.S.D., Peekskill, N.Y., 1973-76; assoc. dir. Harlem Hosp. Med. Ctr., N.Y.C., 1976-78; tchr. math., K-8 Bd. Edn., N.Y.C., 1980-83; tchr. math. Middle. Sch., Newport News, Va., 1983-86; tchr. talented and gifted Pub. Sch. 31 Bd. Edn., N.Y.C., 1986-91. Dir. summer ednl. program Episcopal Diocese, N.Y., 1970-89; dir. Arista Honor Soc., Intermediate Sch. 10, N.Y. Pub. Schs., 1971-73. Co-editor: (handbook) Frederick Douglass Teacher's Handbook, 1971. Counselor/tutor N.Y.C. Pub. Schs., 1970-73, mem. PTA, 1970-76, 80-83; mem. Cancer Support Group, Newport News, Va., 1994; vol. tchr. Queen Street Bapt. Ch., Hampton, Va., 1993-94. Grantee Chase Bank, N.Y.C., 1972. Mem. Libr. Congress, AAUW, Smithsonian Inst. Democrat. Episcopalian. Avocations: reading, playing piano, gardening, sewing and numismatics. Home: 3423 Shell Rd Hampton VA 23661-1441

SILVA, OMEGA LOGAN, physician; b. Washington, Dec. 14, 1936; d. Louis Jasper and Ruth (Dickerson) Logan; m. C. Francis A. Silva, Oct. 25, 1958 (div. 1981); 1 child, Frances Cecile; m. Harold Bryant Webb, Nov. 28, 1982. BS cum laude with honors in chemistry, Howard U., Washington, 1958, MD, 1967. Bio-chemist NIH, Bethesda, Md., 1958-63; resident in medicine Vets. Affairs Med. Ctr., Washington, 1967—70, fellow in endocrinology, 1970—71, asst. chief endocrinology, 1977-96, dir. diabetes clin., 1977—96; assoc. prof. medicine George Washington U., Washington, 1975-91; physician Mitchell-Trotman Med. Group, P.C., Washington, 1996-97; prof. George Washington U., Washington, 1991-98, prof. emeritus, 1999—; prof. Howard U., Washington, 1977-96. Mem. exec. com. Health Care Coun. Nat. Capital Area, 1995—, bd. dirs.; med. rev. officer Employee Health Programs, Bethesda, 1998—. Author: (with others) Endocrinology, 1990; featured Nat. Libr. Medicine's Changing the Face of Medicine, an Exhibition on America's Women Physicians, 2003; contbr. articles to profl. jours. Charter mem. Nat. Mus. of Women in the Arts, Washington, 1986; trustee Howard U., 1991-97. Recipient Disting. Alumni award Howard U. Coll. Medicine, 1997. Master ACP (Best Sci. Presentation award 1974); mem. Am. Chem. Soc., Am. Med. Women's Assn. (br. I v.p. 1986-87, pres. 1987-88, anti-smoking task force 1989-92, chair govtl. affairs, 1992-96, mem. nominations com. 1992, gov. region III 1996-97, v.p. program 1997-99, chmn. leadership com. 1996-97, pres. elect 1999-2000, pres. 2000-2002), Howard U. Med. Alumni (pres. 1983-88, bd. dirs. 1983—), Alpha Omega Alpha. Avocations: dress and hat design, furniture design, home construction.

SILVA, PAT A. artist; b. Pitts., Aug. 6, 1939; d. Andrew J. and Ann Loiselle; m. Thomas R. Silva, Nov. 12, 1995. Student, Art Inst. Pitts., 1954—59. Owner, graphic artist, typesetter Type II, Pitts., 1971—90; typesetting apprentice Loftin's Bus. Forms Co., Phoenix, 1968—71. Instr. Intergenerational Arts and Edn. Program, U. Pitts.; mem., chairperson Comty. Exhbn. Space, North Hills Art Ctr., 1990. Exhibitions include North Hills Art Ctr., 1989, 1990, Westmoreland Arts and Heritage and Westmoreland Art Nats., 1992, Cranberry Arts Festival, 1993, 1994, Pitts. Progressive Artists, 1994 (Best Sculpture award, 1993, Outstanding Artistic Achievement award, 1994), People's Art Show, 1995, one-woman shows include LaRoche Coll., 1996, exhibitions include Generations Together, Harrisburg, Pa., 1998, one-woman shows include Vahalla Restaurant, Pitts., 1999, TAG Gallery, Mt. Jackson, Va., 2002, Studio Z Gallery, Pitts., 2002, exhibitions include Butler Inst. Am. Art, 2002. Recipient Golden Sable award for watercolor, Arts and Crafts Showcase, 1994, 1st prize for painting, 1994, Judges award for painting, 1994, Grumbacher Gold Medallion, Gatehouse at North Park, 1997, Arttrain Juror's award, Murray Home, 1999, Best in Divsn. for mixed media, Corn Hill Art Festival, 2001, 1st pl. for mixed media, Allentown Arts Festival, 2001. Mem.: Pitts. Progressive Artists (pres. 1993—2000, sec., awards chairperson, exhbn./installation chairperson 1991—93). Home: 1604 Pauloski Ln Sewickley PA 15143 E-mail: patsilva@att.net.

SILVER, JOAN MICKLIN, film director, screenwriter; b. Omaha, May 24, 1935; d. Maurice David and Doris (Shoshone) Micklin; m. Raphael D. Silver, June 28, 1956; children: Dina, Marisa, Claudia. BA, Sarah Lawrence Coll., 1956. Writer, dir. (movies) Hester Street, 1975 (Writers Guild best screenplay nomination), Chilly Scenes of Winter, 1981, (TV film PBS) Bernice Bobs Her Hair starring Shelly Du Vall, 1975; dir. (TV films HBO) Finnegan, Begin Again with Robert Preston and Mary Tyler Moore, Parole Board, A Private Matter with Sissy Spacek and Aidan Quinn, (TV film Showtime) In The Presence of Mine Enemies, 1997, (films) Between the Lines, 1976, Crossing Delancey with Amy Irving, 1988, Loverboy, 1989, Stepkids, 1991; dir. stage plays and musicals including Album, Maybe I'm Doing It Wrong, Off-Broaday prodn. A...My Name is Alice; prod. On The Yard, (radio) Great Jewish Stories from Eastern Europe and Beyond, 1995; dir. (feature film) A Fish in the Bathtub, 1998, (TV film Lifetime) Invisible Child, 1999, (TV film Showtime) Charms for the Easy Life, 2001, TV film LifeTime) Hunger Point, 2003. Office: Silverfilm Prodns Inc 510 Park Ave New York NY 10022-1105 Office Phone: 646-282-0312.

SILVER, KYLA MARIE, music educator; b. Denver, Oct. 3, 1968; d. Oneil Joseph and Beverly Ann Fontenot; children: David, Emma. Student, Loretto Heights Coll., Englewood, Colo., 1985—87; BA, Oral Robert U., Tulsa, 1995. Cert. tchr. vocal performance Va. Exec. asst. Denver Ctr. for Performing Arts Complex, 1986—90; sales cons. Franchise Distbn., Inc., Denver, 1990—92; founder, CEO Children's Charities, Denver, 1992—; promotions coord., model Maximum Talent Agy., Denver, 1992—97; v.p. ops., multi media mgmt. B.A.M. Cos., Denver, 1994—98; field mgr. Innova Mktg., L.A., 1997—98; choral tchr. Lunenbura City Schs., Victoria, Va., 2001—. Owner, entrepreneur DHT Mgmt., Keysville, Va., 2003—; soprano soloist Denver Opera Co., 1993; guest artist Colo. Concert Chorale, Denver, 1992; founder Voices of Essence Choir, Victoria, 2001—; prin. vocal artist Gethsemane Presbyn. Ch., 2001—; music minister Holy Manor Nursing Home, Farmville, Va., 2001—, Brookview Retirement Home, Farmville, 2001—; actress numerous roles film and TV including Bedazzled, Monkey Bone, Nothing is Easy, Reverend Do Wrong, Days of Our Lives, Asteroid, Dying to be Perfect, Perry Mason, The Price is Right; actress TV commls. including Allstate, Plastic Surgeon, Inc., Saturn Dearlership, Billy Blues Restaurant; exec. dir. Miss So. Va. Pageant Miss Am. Orgn. Inc., 2004. Composer (CD) Straight From the Heart, 1997, songwriter various sheet music pieces, 1987—2002; actor: (plays) Oru Theatre Co., 1987—90, Oru Dinner Theatre, 1987—88. Named Runner up, Mrs. Photogenic, Mrs. Congeniality, Mrs. Colo. Am. Pageant, 1994; scholar, Bayview Conservatory scholar, 1994, acad. scholar, Sachs Found., Colorado Springs, Colo., 1990—93. Mem.: Sigma Gamma Rho, Alpha Kappa Alpha. Republican. Christian Ch. Avocations: travel, music, gardening. Home and Office: PO Box 211 Keysville VA 23947

SILVER, LYNNE MILLER, garden designer; d. Sidney and Phyllis Miller; m. Ron Silver, Dec. 25, 1975 (div. July 1, 1997); children: Adam, Alexandra. B.A. cum laude, SUNY, Buffalo, 1967; postgrad., NYU Inst. Of Fine Arts, 1970; Diploma in Ornamental Horticulture, N.Y. Bot. Garden Sch. Of Profl. Horticulture, 1999. Cert. comml. horticulture N.Y. Bot. Garden, 1999. Asst. Friends of Mario Cuomo, N.Y.C., 1994—95; pres. Outer Spaces Garden Design, Ltd, N.Y.C., 1999—. Com. mem. Wave Hill Friends of Horticulture, N.Y.C., 1999—. Benefit com. mem. Children's Def. Fund, N.Y.C., 1995—98. Mem.: Metro Horticulture. Democrat-Npl. Avocations: stock trading, reading, cooking Personal E-mail: outerspaces@nyc.rr.com.

SILVER, MARY WILCOX, oceanography educator; b. San Francisco, July 13, 1941; d. Philip E. and Mary C. (Kartes) Wilcox; children: Monica, Joel. BA in Zoology, U. Calif., Berkeley, 1963; PhD in Oceanography, U. Calif., La Jolla, 1971. Asst. prof. biology San Francisco State U., 1971-72; prof. marine sci. U. Calif., Santa Cruz, 1972—, chmn. dept., 1992-95. Contbr. numerous articles on biol. oceanography to profl. jours. Grantee NSF, 1979—; recipient Bigelow medal, 1992. Mem. Am. Soc. Limnology and Oceanography, Am. Phycological Soc. Office: U Calif Dept Ocean Sci Santa Cruz CA 95064 E-mail: msilver@cats.ucsc.edu.

SILVER, ROSLYN O. federal judge; b. Phoenix, Feb. 28, 1946; m. Steven J. Silver. BA, U. Calif. Santa Barbara, 1968; JD, Ariz. State U., 1971. Law clk. Hon. Lorna E. Lockwood Ariz. Supreme Ct., Phoenix, 1971-72; advisor, litigator Navajo Nation Native Am. Rights Fund, Phoenix, 1974-76; legal counsel Dial Corp., Phoenix, 1976-78; ptnr. Logan and Aguirre, Phoenix, 1978-79; legal counsel EEOC, Phoenix, 1979-80; asst. U.S. Atty. Dist. Ariz., Phoenix, 1980-84; asst. atty. gen. Ariz. Atty. Gen.'s Office, Phoenix, 1984-86; acting 1st asst., chief criminal divsn. dist. Ariz. U.S. Atty. Office, Phoenix, 1986-94; judge Dist. Ariz. U.S. Dist. Ct., Phoenix, 1994—. Chair 9th Cir. Article III judges edn. com.; mem. regional sect. panel Harry S Truman Scholarship Found. Contbg. editor: Rutter Group Practice Guide. Mem. bd. visitors U. Ariz. Law Sch.; mem. adv. panel Lodestar Mediation Clinic, Ariz. State U. Law Sch. Named one of 100 Significant Women and Minorities in Ariz.'s Legal History, 2000. Mem. ABA, Fed. Bar Assn., Nat. Assn. Women Judges, Ariz. Bar Assn. (Pub. Lawyer of Yr.), Ariz. Women Lawyers Assn. (outstanding legal practitioner award 1999), Ariz. State U. Alumni Assn. (outstanding alumnus award 1996). Office: US Dist Ct 401 W Washington SPC 59 Phoenix AZ 85003

SILVER, THELMA, social worker; b. Nfld., Can., Nov. 17, 1948; d. Mike and Monya Silver. BA, McGill U., 1969, MSW, 1971; PhD in Social Welfare, Case Western Res. U., 1995. Clin. supr. Neighboring: Supporting Svcs. for Mental Health, Mentor, Ohio, 1983-94; lectr. Case Western Res. U. Sch. Applied Social Sci., Cleve., 1990; asst. prof. social work D'Youville Coll., Buffalo, 1994-99; asst. prof. Youngstown State U., 1999—. Mem. Lake County Cmty. Crisis Intervention Team, Painesville, 1985-94; bd. dirs. Solomon Schechter Day Sch., Cleve., 1980-85. Mem. citizen's adv. bd. Northcoast Behavioral Healthcare Ctr., 2000—. Mem. NASW, Coun. on Social Work Edn., Am. Assn. for Advancement of Social Work with Groups. Avocations: walking, reading, gardening. Home: 24525 Penshurst Dr Cleveland OH 44122-1386 Office: Humanistic Counseling Ctr 4979 Mayfield Rd Lyndhurst OH 44124-2601 E-mail: doovil@aol.com.

SILVERMAN, CHARLOTTE, epidemiologist, educator; b. N.Y.C., May 21, 1913; d. Harry and Gussie (Goldman) S. BA, Bklyn. Coll., 1933; MD, Woman's Med. Coll. Pa., 1938; MPH, Johns Hopkins U., 1942, DrPH, 1948. Diplomate Am. Bd. Preventive Medicine. Intern Beekman Hosp., N.Y.C., 1939-40; resident Sea View Hosp., Staten Island, N.Y., 1940-41; asst. dir., dir. Bur. Tuberculosis Balt. City Health Dept., 1946-56; chief epidemiology, planning and rsch. Md. State Dept. Health, Balt., 1956-62; med. officer in various programs NIMH, Bethesda, Md., 1962-68; dep. dir. div. biol. effects and other positions Bur. Radiol. Health USPHS, Rockville, Md., 1968-83; assoc. dir. for human studies FDA, Rockville, 1983-92. Mem. faculty dept. epidemiology Johns Hopkins U. Sch. Hygiene and Pub. Health, Balt., 1950—. Author: Epidemiology of Depression, 1968; contbr. articles to profl. jours. Sr. Surg. USPHS, 1944-45. Recipient Mary Pemberton Nourse Meml. award AAUW, 1941-42, Merit award FDA, 1974, Alumni Life Achievement award Bklyn. Coll., 1994. Fellow APHA, Am. Coll. Preventive Medicine, Am. Orthopsychiat. Assn., Am. Coll. Epidemiology; mem. Delta Omega. Home: 501 Lincoln Ave Takoma Park MD 20912-5823

SILVERMAN, ELLEN-MARIE, speech and language pathologist; b. Milw., Oct. 12, 1942; d. Roy and Bettie (Schlaeger) Loebel; m. Feb. 5, 1967 (div.); 1 child, Catherine Bette. BS, U. Wis., Milw., 1964; MA, U. Iowa, 1967, PhD, 1970. Rsch. assoc. U. Ill., Urbana, 1969-71; asst. prof. speech pathology Marquette U., Milw., 1973-79; assoc. clin. prof. otolaryngology Med. Coll. Wis., 1980—83; assoc. prof. speech pathology Marquette U., 1979-85; pvt. practice speech and lang. pathology, Milw., 1985—. Founder, CEO TSS-The Speech Source, Inc., 1995—. Author, illustrator: Jason's Secret; contbr. articles to profl. jours., chpts. to books. Marquette U. grantee, 1982. Fellow Am. Speech, Hearing, Lang. Assn.; mem. Wis. Speech, Hearing, Lang. Assn., Sigma Xi, Delta Kappa Gamma. Avocations: photography, painting, gardening, writing. E-mail: tsss920499@aol.com.

SILVERMAN, FRANCINE TERRY, writer; b. N.Y.C., Apr. 24, 1943; d. Michael and Jeanne (Friedman) Scherr; m. Ronald Silverman, May 26, 1968; 1 child, Amy. BA, Coll. Mt. St. Vincent, 1980. Freelance writer,

1980—; with Gannett Newspapers, Yonkers, N.Y., 1985-90; staff reporter News Communications, Bronx, 1993—98. Author: Catskills Alive, 2000, 2003, Long Island Alive, 2003; editor: Promotion Newsletter. Mem.: Guidebookwriters.com. Avocations: reading, fitness, movies. Home and Office: 4455 Douglas Ave Bronx NY 10471-3519

SILVERMAN, LESLIE E. federal agency administrator; b. Needham, Mass. Grad., U. Vt.; JD, Am. U.; M with distinction, Georgetown U. Bar: D.C., Mass. Law clk. U.S. Atty.'s Office; assoc. Keller and Heckman, 1990—97; labor counsel Senate Healtn, Edn., Labor and Pensions Com.; commr. Equal Opportunity Commn., Washington, 2002—. Office: EEOC 1801 L St NW Washington DC 20507

SILVERMAN, MARCIA, public relations executive; b. Lexington, Ky., Dec. 4, 1943; d. Harry and Rebecca (Green) S.; m. Stephen Regenstreif, Mar. 13, 1977; 1 child, Jacob Anthony. AB in Polit. Sci., U. Pa., 1965, MA in Econs., 1966. Reporter Nat. Jour., Washington, 1969-72; pub. rels. exec. J. Walter Thompson, N.Y.C., 1979-80, Ogilvy, Adams & Rinehart, Washington, 1981-95, pres., 1992-98, Ogilvy Pub. Rels. Worldwide, 1992—, pub. rels. exec., 1998—. Bd. dirs. Washington Internat Sch., 1994-95, Mex. Am. Legal Def. & Edn. Fund, L.A., 1994-98, vice chair, 1997, Women's Campaign Fund, Washington, 1993-94. Recipient Pub. Rels. Star award Inside PR mag. Office: Ogilvy Pub Rels Worldwide 1901 L St NW Ste 300 Washington DC 20036-3506

SILVERMAN, MARYLIN A. advertising agency executive; b. N.Y.C., Mar. 15, 1941; d. Morris George and Sophie (Betesh) Adler; m. Joseph Elias Silverman, May 30, 1965; children: Lisa, Jennifer. BA, Ind. U., 1962; postgrad., CUNY, 1963-65. Rsch. analyst Compton Advt., N.Y.C., 1962-63; account rsch. supr. Foote, Cone & Belding, N.Y.C., 1963-68; self-employed market rsch. cons. N.Y.C., 1968-78; rsch. group head Ogilvy & Mather, Inc., N.Y.C., 1978-82; sr. v.p., assoc. rsch. dir. Backer Spielvogel Bates, Inc., N.Y.C., 1982-88, exec. dir. strategic planning and internat. rsch., 1989-91; exec. v.p. strategic planning Bates Worldwide, N.Y.C., 1991-97; exec. dir. strategic planning and rsch. Bates USA, N.Y.C., 1997-99, exec. v.p. strategic planning, chief knowledge mgmt. officer, 1999—. Cons. Am. Assn. Advt. Agys., Boys Clubs Am., N.Y.C.; bd. dirs. Women at Risk; mem. conf. bd. Learning and Knowledge Mgmt. Coun. Co-author: Marketing Review, 1980, American Demographics, 1990, Marketing Review, 1997; mem. editl. adv. bd. Jour. Advt. Rsch. Mem. exec. coun. Washington Sq. Pk. Coun., 1969-74; mem. exec. bd. Friends Sem. PTA, N.Y.C., 1980-82, Advt. Rsch. Found., Children's Rsch. Coun. Devel. Com. Mem. Am. Mktg. Assn. (chair Effie awards), Women in Comm., Am. Assn. Advt. Agys. (rsch. com.), Grenwich Ho. Potters and Sculptors Assn. Office: Bates Worldwide 498 7th Ave New York NY 10018-6798 E-mail: msilverman@batesww.com.

SILVERMAN, VICTORIA LILLIAN, consultant, fundraiser, cultural organization administrator; b. St. Louis, July 2, 1961; d. Thomas and Eva Alice (Hasko) Schiff; m. Lloyd Alan Silverman, Dec. 31, 1995; children: Anyu Isabella, Emmanuelle Snow. BA, Washington U., 1983; postgrad., St. Louis U., 1985-86. Assoc. dir. devel. Jewish Cmty. Ctr., St. Louis, 1983-85; assoc. dir. devel. engring. Washington U., 1986-89; dir. engring. fund Stanford (Calif.) U., 1989-92; dir. major gifts and planned giving U. Calif., Santa Barbara, 1992-95; v.p. devel., exec. dir. found. St. Francis Med. Ctr., Santa Barbara, 1995; dir. devel. Am. Film Inst., L.A., 1995—2001; v.p. external affairs St. Louis Symphony Orch., 2001—03; prin. VLS Strategies, Inc., 2003—; v.p. Internat. Mus. of Women, 2004—. Cons. Stanford Engring. Sch., 1992, COCA, St. Louis, 2002—03, various orgns. Bd. dirs. Santa Barbara Ballet, 1990-92; vol. fundraiser Walter Capps for Congress, Santa Barbara, 1991. Mem. Coun. Advancement Support Edn. (presentor 1992—, conf. dir. 1995). Democrat. Jewish. Avocations: percussionist, dance and film enthusiaist. Office: Ste 460 101 Howard St San Francisco CA 94119 Home: 775 E Blithedale Ave #410 Mill Valley CA 94941-1554 Office Phone: 415-543-4669.

SILVERS, ANN, peri-operative nurse, educator; b. Omaha, Mar. 1, 1943; d. John Stephen and M. Georgina Marie Mary McNeil; m. Ralph L. Silvers, Oct. 30, 1993. Diploma, St. Joseph Hosp. Sch. Nursing, Phoenix, 1966; BS in Health Care Scis., Chapman Coll., Travis AFB, Calif., 1979. RN Ariz. Pvt. scrub nurse Drs. Nelson, Brown, Cornell, Phoenix, 1969; staff nurse operating room St. Joseph Hosp., Phoenix, 1966-69, 70, Tucson, 1970—71, Washoe Med. Ctr., Reno, 1976—77; staff nurse U. Ariz. Med. Ctr., Tucson, 1971—75, asst. oper. rm. supr., 1975—76; oper. rm. staff nurse David Grant Med. Ctr., Travis AFB, Calif., 1977—81; coord. oper. rm. edn. Seton Med. Ctr., Daly City, Calif., 1981—85; staff nurse operating room Yavapai Regional Med. Ctr., Prescott, Ariz., 1985—88, John C. Lincoln Hosp., Phoenix, 1988—2000. Instr. surg. technician program and perioperative nurse program Gateway C.C., Phoenix, 1989-91, also extern preceptor. Capt. USAF, 1977-81. Mem. Assn. Operating Room Nurses (cert.), Sigma Theta Tau.

SILVERS, SALLY, choreographer, performing company executive; b. Greeneville, Tenn., June 19, 1952; d. Herbert Ralston and Sara Elizabeth (Buchanan) S.; life ptnr. Bruce Erroll Andrews. BA in Dance and Polit. Sci., Antioch Coll., 1975. Artistic dir. Sally Silvers & Dancers, N.Y.C., 1980—. Mem. faculty Leicester Poly., 1986, 87, 89, summer choreography project Bennington Coll., 1988-92, Chisenhale Dance Space, London, 1989, 91, Am. Dance Festival, Durham, N.C., 1990, 92; guest tchr. European Dance Devel. Ctr., Arnhem, The Netherlands, 1992—. Choreographer (performances) Politics of the Body Microscope of Conduct, 1980, Social Movement, 1981, Connective Tissue, 1981, Less Time You Know Praxis, 1981, Don't No Do And This, 1981, Lack of Entrepreneurial Thrift, 1982, Celluoid Sally and Mr. E, 1982, Mutate, 1982, Being Red Enough, 1982, Disgusting, 1982, Bedtime at the Reformatory, 1982, Eat the Rich, 1982, They Can't Get It in the Shopping Cart, 1982, Blazing Forceps, 1982, And Find Out Why, 1983, Choose Your Weapons, 1984, Extend the Wish for Entire, 1985, No Best Better Way, 1985, Every All Which is Not Us, 1986, Swaps Ego Say So, 1986, Be Careful Now, You Know Sugar Melts in Water, 1987, Fact Confected, 1987, Both, Both, 1987, Tizzy boost, 1988, Moebius, 1988, Whatever Ever, 1989, Get Tough, Sports and Divertissement, 1989, Flap, 1989, Swan's Crayon, 1989, Fanfare Tripwire, 1990, Harry Meets Sally, 1990, Along the Skid Mark of Recorded History, 1990, Matinee Double-You, 1991, Grand Guignol, 1991, Dash Dash Slang Plural Plus, 1992, The Bubble Cut, 1992, Vigilant Corsage, 1992, Oops Fact, 1992, Small Room, 1993, Exwhyzee, 1993, Elegy, 1993, Now That It Is Now, 1994, Give Em Enough Rope, Swoon Noir, 1994, Radio Rouge, 1995, Braceletizing, 1995, Hush Comet, 1995, Bite the Pillow, 1995, Pandora's Cake Stain, 1996, Secrets Of, 1997, HUSHHUSH, Sugar Raised, 1998 Capture, Teddy Growl, 1999, Storming Heaven, 2000, Swaphot Trouble, 2001, Strike Me Lightning, 2002, Spaced Out, 2003; video and performance filmmaker : (films) Little Lieutenant, 1993 (Silver); N.Y. Dance on Camera Festival, Mechanics of the Brain, 1997; co-author: (book) Resurgant New Writings By Women, 1992; contbr. articles to profl. jours. Grantee Nat. Endowment Arts, 1987, 89, 90, 91, 98, Jerome Found., 1993, 1996, Meet the Composer N.Y. Found. for the Arts, 1995; Guggenheim Found. fellow, 1988; Found. Contemporary Performance Arts, 2001. Mem. Segue Found. (bd. dirs. Segue Performance Space 1992-2002). Avocations: reading, writing, art events, costume design. Home: 303 E 8th St Apt 4F New York NY 10009-5212

SILVERSTEIN, BARBARA ANN, conductor, artistic director; b. Phila., July 24, 1947; d. Charles and Selma (Brenner) S.; m. Bernard J. Taylor II, Aug. 19, 1978. Student, Bennington Coll., 1965-67; BMus, Phila. Coll. Performing Arts, 1970; MA, U. Del., 1997. Assoc. music dir. Suburban Opera Co., Chester, Pa., 1967-75; asst. condr. Toledo Opera Assn., 1975-76; asst. condr., coach Curtis Inst. Music, Phila., 1973-77; asst. condr. Phila. Lyric Opera, 1971-74, Des Moines Opera Festival, Indianola, Iowa, 1974-78; music dir., condr. Savoy Co., Phila., 1977-80, Miss. Opera, Jackson, 1979-82; artistic dir., condr. Pa. Opera Theater, Phila., 1976-93; guest condr. Anchorage Opera, 1982, Opera Del., Wilmington, 1981, 83, Utah Festival Opera Co., 1993-96, Lyric Opera Kansas City, 1995—, Opera Roanoke, Va., 1995, 98, Hollins U., 1999; mng. editor Epotec Inc., 1999-2000, dir. comm., 2000—; prof. English U. Del., Ursinus, 1996—. Recipient alumni award U. of Arts. Mem. Am. Fedn. Musicians, Jusic Fund Soc., Pa. Coun. on the Arts (adv. panel 1987-90, OPERA Am. (bd. dirs. 1987-93, exec. com. 1988-93). Jewish. Avocations: scuba diving, reading.

SILVERSTONE, ALICIA, actress; b. San Francisco, Oct. 4, 1976; d. Monty and Didi Silverstone. Stage debut in Carol's Eve at Met Theater, L.A.; starred in three Aerosmith videos, including Cryin', Amazing, Crazy; actress (films): The Crush, 1993, True Crime, 1995, Le Nouveau Monde, 1995, Hideaway, 1995, Clueless, 1995, The Babysitter, 1995, Batman & Robin, 1997, Blast from the Past, 1999, Love's Labour Lost, 2000, Scorched, 2002, Global Heresy, 2002, Scooby-Doo 2: Monsters Unleashed, 2004; actress, prodr.(film) Excess Baggage, 1997; exec. prodr. (TV Series) Braceface, 2001; appeared in TV programs including Torch Song, 1993, Scattered Dreams, 1993, The Cool and the Crazy, 1994; appeared in TV series: The Wonder Years, 1992, Braceface (voice only), 2001, Miss Match, 2003-. Office: c/o Innovative Artists 1999 Ave of the Stars #2850 Los Angeles CA 90067

SILVERTHORNE, HOLLY APPEL, sculptor, educator; b. N.Y.C., Dec. 25, 1922; d. John Wilberforce and Ethel Smith Appel; m. Spencer Victor Silverthorne, Oct. 18, 1947; children: Spencer V. III, John Roberts, Daniel Appel. BA, Bennington Coll., 1980; sculpture cert., Pa. Acad. Fine Art, 1980; MFA, U. Pa., 1985. Part-time sculpture tchr. Baldwin Sch., Bryn Mawr, Pa., 1975—80, Shipley Sch., Bryn Mawr, 1975—80; tchr. sculpture Wayne (Pa.) Art Ctr., 1985—89; Maine art tchr. Maine Line Sch. Night, Wayne, 1985—89, Main Line Art Ctr., Haverford, Pa., 1989—97; sculpture tchr. Kimberton (Pa.) Waldorf Sch., 1989—2002, Chester County Art Ctr., West Chester, Pa., 1989—, Chester County Art Assn., West Chester, 1989—2003. Recipient 1st prize for sculpture, Harrisburg (Pa.) Art Assn., 2003. Mem.: Artists of Penn Women. Home: 400 N Walnut St West Chester PA 19380 Office: Chester County Art Assn 100 N Bradford West Chester PA 19380

SILVERTON, NANCY, food service executive; b. June 20, 1954; m. Mark Peel; three children. Student, Calif. State U., Cordon Bleu, London, Ecole Le Notre, France. Pastry chef Michael's Restaurant, Santa Monica, Calif.; 1st exec. pastry chef Spago, West Hollywood, Calif.; founder LaBrea Bakery, L.A., 1989, v.p. product devel., exec. v.p. Recipient Chef of Yr. award James Beard Found., Top 10 Chefs award Food and Wine Mag. Office: Campanile Restaurant 624 S LaBrea Ave Los Angeles CA 90036

SILVESTRI, HEATHER L. psychologist; b. Passaic, NJ, Mar. 3, 1972; d. Philip J and Dorothy J Silvestri; m. Christopher M Ferguson, Sept. 23, 2000. PhD, LI U., 1997—2002. Lic. Psychologist NY, 2003, cert. Hospice Vol. Hospice of NJ., Bergen County Agy., 1994. Postdoctoral fellow Beth Israel Med. Ctr., NYC, 2002—03, NY U., NYC, 2002—. Psychology instr. Coll. of New Rochelle, Bronx, 1999—2000; pvt. practice psychologist Self-employed, NYC, 2003—; asst. adj. prof. John Jay Coll., 2003—. Mem. Greenpeace, 2001, Amnesty Internat., New Yorkers Against the Death Penalty, The Nature Conservancy, Habitat for Humanity, Nat. Resources Def. Coun., World Wildlife Fedn. Tchg. Fellowship, LI U., 2000, Garden State Disting. scholar, State of NJ., 1994, Rotary Scholarship, Rotary Club of Nutley, NJ., 1990—94, Italian-American Scholarship for Proficiency in the Italian Lang., Italian-American Club of Nutley, NJ., 1990, PTA scholarship, PTA of Nutley, NJ, 1990. Mem.: APA (assoc.), Internat. Soc. for Theoretical Psychology, Phi Beta Kappa, Phi Eta Sigma, Alpha Lambda Delta, Psi Chi, Pi Beta Phi. D-Liberal. Avocations: travel, rollerblading, jogging. Home: 290 Third Avenue 9B New York NY 10010 Office: 103 St Mark's Pl Ste A New York NY 10009

SILVEY, ANITA LYNNE, editor; b. Bridgeport, Conn., Sept. 3, 1947; d. John Oscar and Juanita Lucille (McKitrick) Silvey. BS in Edn., Ind. U., 1965-69; MA in Comm. Arts, U. Wis., 1970. Editorial asst. children's book dept. Little Brown and Co., Boston, 1970-71; asst. editor Horn Book Mag., Boston, 1971-75; mng. editor, founder New Boston Rev., 1975-76; mktg. mgr. children's books, libr. svcs. mgr. trade divsn. Houghton Mifflin, Boston, 1976-84; editor-in-chief Horn Book Mag., Boston, 1985-95; v.p., pub. Children's Books Houghton Mifflin Co., Boston, 1995—2001. Editor: Children's Books and Their Creators, 1995, Help Wanted: Stories About Young People and Work, 1997, Essential Guide to Children's Books and their Creators, 2002, 100 Best Books for Children, 2004. Named one of 70 Women Who Have Made a Difference, Women's Nat. Book Assn., 1987. Mem.: ALA (chmn. children's librs., Laura Ingalls Wilder award 1987—89), Assn. Am. Pubs. (mem. libr. com.), Internat. Reading Assn. (mem. IRA Book award com. 1985—87), New Eng. Round Table (chmn. 1978—79). Personal E-mail: anitasilvey@aol.com.

SILVIA, LORI A. speech pathology/audiology services professional; b. Fall River, Massachusetts, June 19, 1973; d. Manuel N. and Patricia M. Sousa; m. Michael D. Silvia, June 1, 2002. BA in Comm. disorder, Bridgewater State Coll., Bridgewater, Mass., 1991—95; MA in Speech lang. pathology, Kent State U., Kent, oh., 1995—97. Lic. speech lang. pathologist Mass., 1995, cert. ASHA Bd. Edn, Mass. Speech lang. pathologist Sundance Rehab. Corp., RI, 1997—98, New Bedford Pub. Schools, Mass., 1998—. Mem.: Mass. Teachers Assn. Democrat. Roman Catholic. Avocations: running, bicycling, weightlifting, tennis, reading. Office: JB DeValles Sch New Bedford MA

SIMECKA, BETTY JEAN, marketing executive; b. Topeka, Apr. 15, 1935; d. William Bryan and Regina Marie (Rezac) S.; m. Alex Pappas, Jan. 15, 1956 (div. Apr. 1983); 1 child, Alex William. Student, Butler County C.C., 1983—85. Freelance writer and photographer, L.A., also St. Marys, Kans., 1969-77; co-owner Creative Enterprises, El Dorado, Kans., 1977-83; coord. excursions into history Butler County C.C., El Dorado, 1983-84; dir. Hutchinson (Kans.) Conv. & Visitors Bur., 1984-85; dir. mktg. divsn. Exec. Mgmt., Inc., Wichita, 1985-87; exec. dir. Topeka Conv. and Visitors Bur., 1987-91, pres., CEO, 1991-96; pres. Internat. Connections, Inc., 1996-97, Simecka and Assoc., 1996-99, Pinnacle Prodns., L.L.C., 1997-99; pres., CEO Cultural Exhbns. and Events, L.L.C., 1999—2003; organizer Czars: 400 Years of Imperial Grandeur exhbn., 2002—; v.p. mktg. Sunflower Exhbns., L.L.C., 2003—; mktg. cons., 2003—. Dir. promotion El Dorado Thunderboat Races, 1977-78. Contbr. articles to jours. and mags.; columnist St. Marys Star, 1973-79. Pres. El Dorado Art Assn., 1984; chair Santa Fe Trail Bike Assn., Kans., 1988-90; co-dir. St. Marys Summer Track Festival, 1973-81; chair spl. events Mulvane Art Mus., 1990, sec., 1991-92; membership chair, 1993-94, bd. dirs., 1995-96; bd. dirs. Topeka Civic Theater, 1991-96, co-chair spl. events, 1992; Kans. chair Russian Festival Com., 1992-93; vice-chair Kans. Film Commn., 1993-94, chair, 1994; bd. dirs. Kans. Expoctr. Adv. Bd., 1990-96, Brain Injury Assn. Greater Kansas City, Concerned Citizens Topeka, 1998-2000; pres. Kans. Internat. Mus., 1994-96. Recipient Kans. Gov.'s Tourism award Kans. Broadcaster's Assn., 1993, Disting. Svc award City of Topeka, 1995, Hist. Ward Meade Disting. award Topeka Parks & Recreation Dept., 1995; named Kansan of Yr., Topeka Capitol-Jour., 1995, Sales and Mktg. Exec. of Yr., 1995, Internat. Soroptomists, Topeka chpt., Woman of Distinction, 1996. Mem. Nat. Tour Assn., Sales and Mktg. execs. (bd. dirs. 1991-92), Internat. Assn. Conv. and Visitors Burs. (co-chair rural tourism com. 1994), Am. Soc. Assn. Execs., Travel Industry Assn. Kans. (membership chair 1988-89, sec. 1990, pres. 1991-92, Outstanding Merit award 1994), St. Marys C. of C. (pres. 1975), I-70 Assn. (v.p. 1989, pres. 1990), Optimists (social sec. Topeka chpt. 1988-89). Republican. Methodist. Avocations: writing, painting, photography, masters track. Holder Nat. AAU record for 100-yard dash, 1074. E-mail: bettyj5@sbcglobal.net.

SIMEONE, CHERYL, artist; b. Providence, June 4, 1952; d. Nicholas and Angela Simeone. BS in Art Edn., BA in Art/Painting, R.I. Coll., 1975; MA in Art, R.I. Sch. Design, 1998. Graphic designer Simeone Design, Berkeley, 1977—2003; artist Berkeley, Calif., 1978—. One-woman shows include AnyArt Gallery Contemporary Art, Providence, 1979, San Francisco Mus. Modern Art Artists Gallery, 1981, Fobo Gallery, San Francisco, 1990, Kidder Smith Gallery, Boston, 2003, exhibited in group shows at Attleboro (Mass.) Mus. Exhbn., 1976, R.I. State Coun. on Arts, Providence, 1978, Berkeley Art Ctr., 1991, Andrew Shire Gallery, L.A., 1994, Van Straten Gallery, Chgo., 1996, Terrace Gallery, San Francisco, 1998, 2002, Kidder Smith Gallery, 2002, Provincetown (Mass.) Fine Arts Workshop Ctr., 2002—03. E-mail: cheryl@cherylsimeone.com.

SIMMONDS, RAE NICHOLS, musician, composer, educator; b. Lynn, Mass., Feb. 25, 1919; d. Raymond Edward and Abbie Iola (Spinney) Nichols; m. Carter Fillebrown, Jr., June 27, 1941 (div. May 15, 1971); children: Douglas C. (dec.), Richard A., Mary L., Donald E.; m. Ronald John Simmonds, Oct. 9, 1971 (dec. Nov. 1995). AA, Westbrook Coll., Portland, Maine, 1981; B in Music Performance summa cum laude, U. Maine, 1984; MS in Edn., U. So. Maine, 1989; PhD, Walden U., 1994. Founder, dir. Studio of Music/Children's Studio of Drama, Portsmouth, N.H., 1964-71, Studio of Music, Bromley, Eng., 1971-73, Bromley Children's Theatre, 1971-73, Oughterard Children's Theatre, County Galway, Ireland, 1973-74, Studio of Music, Portland, Maine, 1977-96, West Baldwin, Maine, 1997—; resident playwright Children's Theatre of Maine, Portland, 1979-81; organist, choir dir. Stevens Ave. Congl. Ch., Portland, 1987-95; field faculty advisor Norwich U., Montpelier, Vt., 1995. Field advisor grad. program Vt. Coll., Norwich U., 1995; cons./educator mus. tng. for disabled vets. VA, Portsmouth, N.H., 1966-69; show pianist and organist, mainland U.S.A., 1939-59, Hawaii, 1959-62, Rae Nichols Trio, 1962—; mus. dir. Theatre By the Sea, Portsmouth, N.H., 1969-70. Author/composer children's musical: Shamrock Road, 1980 (Blue Stocking award 1980), Glooscap, 1980; author/composer original scripts and music: Cinderella, If I Were a Princess, Beauty and the Beast, Baba Yaga - A Russian Folk Tale, The Journey - Musical Bible Story, The Perfect Gift - A Christmas Legend; original stories set to music include: Heidi, A Little Princess, Tom Sawyer, Jungle Book, Treasure Island; compositions include: London Jazz Suite, Bitter Suite, Jazz Suite for Trio, Sea Dream, Easter (chorale), Rae Simmonds Jazz Trio Songbook Series, (CD) Fascinatin' Gershwin Rae Simmonds Jazz Trio, 2000; contbr. Maine Women Writers Collection. Recipient Am. Theatre Wing Svc. award, 1944, Pease AFB Svc. Club award, 1967, Bumpus award Westbrook Coll., 1980; Nat. Endowment for Arts grantee, 1969-70; Women's Lit. scholar, 1980, Westbrook scholar, 1980-81, Nason scholar, 1983; Kelaniya U. (Colombo, Sri Lanka) rsch. fellow, 1985-86. Mem. ASCAP, Internat. Soc. Poets, Internat. League Women Composers, Music Tchrs. of Maine, Am. Guild of Organists, Music Tchrs. Nat. Assn., Internat. Alliance for Women in Music, Doctorate Assn. N.Y. Educators, Inc., Delta Omicron, Phi Kappa Phi. Democrat. Episcopalian. Avocations: travel, stamp collecting/philately. Home: 230 Douglas Hill Rd West Baldwin ME 04091-9715

SIMMONS, ANNE L. federal official; b. Spencer, Iowa, Jan. 4, 1964; d. Donald Lewis and Lois Amber (Blass) S. B in Spl. Studies, Cornell Coll., 1986. Intern for Congressman Berkley Bedell, Washington, 1986; field staff Iowans for Clayton Hodgson, Sioux City, Iowa, 1986; exec. sec. Atomic Indsl. Forum, Bethesda, Md., 1986-87; staff asst. House Armed Svcs. Com., Washington, 1987; legis. asst. to Congressman Tim Johnson Washington, 1988-93; staff dir. gen. farms commodities subcom. House Agriculture Com., Washington, 1993, staff dir. environ., credit and rural devel. subcom., 1994, minority resource conservation rsch. and forestry subcom., 1995-96. Profl. Staff Ho. Com. on Agrl., 1997—. Music scholar Cornell Coll., 1982-86. Mem. Delta Phi Alpha. Democrat. Office: House Agriculture Com 1301 Longworth House Ofc Bldg Washington DC 20515-0001 E-mail: anne.simmons@mail.house.gov.

SIMMONS, BARBARA ANN, music educator; b. Bellefonte, Pa., Feb. 21, 1965; d. Edward Alfred Miller and Cathy Nan Hoffman; m. William Clark Simmons, June 17, 2000; 1 child, Reid William. BS in Music Edn., West Chester U., 1987, MusM in Music Edn., 1993. Cert. tchr. Pa. Elem. music specialist Coatesville (Pa.) Area Sch. Dist., 1987—. Coop. tchr. West Chester (Pa.) U., 1991—99; presenter workshops in field. Recipient Outstanding Svc. award, Coatesville Area Parent Coun., 1990, 1999, Gift of Time Tribute, Am. Family Inst., 1992. Mem.: Pa. Music Educators Assn. (citation of excellence 2000), Am. Orff Schulwerk Assn., Music Educators Edn. Assn., NEA. Democrat. Lutheran. Avocations: boating, skiing, travel, cooking. Home: 160 Park St Honey Brook PA 19344 Office: Coatesville Area Sch Dist 1515 Lincoln Hwy Coatesville PA 19320

SIMMONS, BETTY JO, civil engineer, draftsman; b. Caddo, Okla., Dec. 13, 1936; d. Robert Lee and Beatrice (Alexander) S.; m. Donald Sherrill Stauffer, Jan. 3, 1959 (div. 1963); m. Daniel Oliver Amos, Oct. 20, 1972 (div. 1975). BA, City Coll.; student, U. Calif. Drafting clk. PacBell, 1956-59, jr. civil engr. draftsperson, 1959—62, sr. civil engr. draftsperson, 1961-62, civil engr. draftsperson, 1962-82, EEO counselor, 1973-77, supr., civil engr. draftsperson, 1982-83, liaison cons. civil rights, 1983-87; project adminstr. pre-apprenticeship tng. program Caltrans, Compton, Calif., 1987-89; coord. govtl. affairs Caltran, L.A., 1989, chief facilities ops., 1989-93, dist. claims officer, 1993-94, dist. materiel mgr., 1994—97, customer svcs. coord., 1997—2000; ret., 2000. Facilitator Govs. Commn. on the Status of Women, Fresno, Calif., 1980. Producer: Building a Future, 1988 (bronze Cindy award Assn. Visual Communicators). Bd. dirs. Morgan Canyon Inst. of Higher Learning, Fresno, 1978-82; fund raiser Hunger Project, L.A., Fresno, 1980—, Youth at Risk, L.A., 1986—. Recipient Excellence in Transp. Facilities award, 1993. Avocations: flying, scuba diving, travel, whitewater rafting, studying metaphysics. Office: Caltrans 120 S Spring St Los Angeles CA 90012-3602

SIMMONS, BETTYE H. career officer; BSc in Nursing, Incarnate Word Coll.; MSc in Nursing, U. Tex. Commd. 2d. lt. U.S. Army, 1971, advanced through grades to brigadier gen.; instr., clin. staff nurse Brooke Army Med. Ctr.; army nurse corps. coun. U.S. Army Recruiting Command; head nurse Walter Reed Army Med. Ctr.; dep. chief Acad. Helath Scis.; chief nurse Bayne-Jones U.S. Army Cmty. Hosp.; cons. to surgeon gen. Nursing Adminstrn.; various assignments U.S. Army Med. Command; dep. comdr. U.S. Army Med. Dept. Ctr. and Sch.; dep. installation comdr. Fort Sam Houston, Tex.; chief Army Nurse Corps., 1995—; command surgeon U.S. Army Forces Command, 1997—. Decorated Legion of Merit with one oak leaf cluster, Meritorious Svc. medal with four oak leaf clusters. Mem. Order of Military Med. Merit.

SIMMONS, CAROLINE JENNERMANN, biomedical researcher, writer; d. Donald L. and M. Ann Jennermann; m. Kirt E. Simmons, Nov. 29, 1996. BS, Purdue U., 1989; MS, Ind. U., 1993. Cert. editor life scis. Bd. Editors in Life Scis. Sr. rsch. technician Ind. U., Indpls., 1989—93; scientist Glaxo Wellcome, Inc., Rsch. Triangle Pk., NC, 1993—97; program adminstr. Ark. Cancer Rsch. Ctr., Little Rock, 1998—2000; biomedical rsch. editor Ark. Ctr for Birth Defects Rsch., Little Rock, 2000—. Grant reviewer Mar. of Dimes, Little Rock, 2001—; rsch. mentor NIH: Minority Rsch. Apprenticeship Prgm., Indpls., 1992; tchg. asst. dept. biol. sci. Purdue U., West Lafayette, Ind., 1989. Contbr. articles to profl. jours. (Best of Conf. in Category: Surveillance award, 2002); reviewer: Jour. Young Investigators, 2001—. Vol. Ark. Children's Hosp., Little Rock, 1999—2000. Mem.: Nat. Orgn. for Rare Disorders, The ARC of Ark., The Magic Found., Coun. of

Sci. Editors, Bd. of Editors in the Life Sciences, Am. Med. Writers Assn. (regional dir. Ark. chpt. 2001—), Nat. Birth Defects Prevention Network. Avocations: miniatures, antiques, cooking. Office: Ark Ctr for Birth Defects Research 11219 Financial Centre Parkway Ste 250 Little Rock AR 72211 E-mail: simmonscarolinej@uams.edu.

SIMMONS, CAROLINE THOMPSON, civic worker; b. Denver, Aug. 22, 1910; d. Huston and Caroline Margaret (Cordes) Thompson; m. John Farr Simmons, Nov. 11, 1936; children: John Farr (dec.), Huston T., Malcolm M. (dec.). AB, Bryn Mawr Coll., 1931; MA with honors, Amherst Coll. Chmn. women's com. Corcoran Gallery Art, 1965-66; vice chmn. women's com. Smithsonian Assocs., 1969-71; pres. Decatur House Coun., 1963-71; mem. bd. Nat. Theatre, 1979-80; trustee Washington Opera, 1955-65; bd. dirs. Fgn. Student Svc. Coun., 1956-79; mem. Washington Home Bd., 1955-60; bd. dirs. Smithsonian Friends of Music, 1977-79; commr. Nat. Mus. Am. Art, 1979-89; mem. Folger com. Folger Shakespeare Libr., 1979-86, trustee emeritus, 1986—; mem. Washington bd. Am. Mus. in Britain, 1970-93; bd. dirs. Found. Preservation Historic Georgetown, 1975-89; trustee Marpat Found., 1987—, Amherst Coll., 1979-81, Dacor-Bacon House Found., Phillips Collection, 1990—, Georgetown Presbyn. Ch., 1989-91; v.p. internat. coun. Mus. Modern Art, N.Y.C., 1964-90, emeritus trustee. Recipient award for eminent svc. Folger Shakespeare Libr., 1986. Mem. Soc. Women Geographers, Sulgrave Club, Chevy Chase Club. Address: 1508 Dumbarton Rock Ct NW Washington DC 20007-3048

SIMMONS, DEBRA ADAMS, editor; m. Jonathan Simmons; children: Jacob, Jonathan. BA, Syracuse (N.Y.) U.; diploma in Advanced Exec. Program, Northwestern U. Reporter Syracuse (N.Y.) Herald-Jour., The Hartford (Conn.) Courant; metro editor The Virginian Post; asst. metro editor and reporter Detroit (Mich.) Free Press; dep. mng. editor The Virginian-Pilot, Norfolk, Va., 2000—03; mng. editor Akron (Ohio) Beacon Jour., 2003, editor, 2003—, v.p., 2003—. Office: Akron Beacon Journal 44 E Exchange St PO Box 640 Akron OH 44309-0640

SIMMONS, DEIDRE WARNER, retired performing company executive, arts consultant; b. Easton, Pa., May 11, 1955; d. Francis Joseph and Irene Carol (Burd) Mooney; m. Robert D. Jacobson, June 27, 1981 (div. Mar. 1989); m. William Richard Simmons, Aug. 18, 1990; children: Caitlin Dawn, Abigail Patricia, Samantha Irene. BA in Music, Montclair State Coll., 1978. Music tchr. Warren Hills Regional Sch., Washington, NJ, 1978-80; devel. dir. N.J. Shakespeare Festival, Madison, 1981-83; dir. contbns. Parent Found., Lancaster, Pa., 1983-86; exec. dir. Fulton Opera House, Lancaster, 1986—2003, capital campaign counsel, 1990-95, dir. theatre advancement, 2000—03; arts cons., 2003—. Bd. dirs. WITF, 2000—. Vice chmn. bd. dirs. Ind. Eye, Lancaster, 1986—89; bd. dirs. Pa. Dutch Conv. and Visitors Bur., Lancaster Campaign; chair Destination Downtown. Recipient Exemplar award, Lancaster C. of C. and Industry, 2003. Mem.: League Hist. Theatres, Theatre Comm. Group. Avocations: piano, singing. E-mail: dwsimmons@comcast.net.

SIMMONS, EMMY B, federal agency administrator; b. Suring, Ws. m. Roger Simmons. B, U. Wis., Milw.; M Agrl. Econs., Cornell U. Vol. Peace Corps, agrl. rschr.; agrl. economist USAID, 1978—91, supv. program economist regional office East and So. Africa, 1991—94, sr. program officer mission in Moscow, 1994—97, deputy asst. adminstr., 1997—2002, asst. adminstr. bus. econ. growth, agrl. and trade, 2002—. Office: USAID RRB 1300 Pannsylvanis AVe NW Washington DC 20523-3900

SIMMONS, ENID BROWN, retired state agency administrator; b. Washington, June 6, 1947; d. Charles Mathews Brown and Susie (Nickens) Ludlow; m. Warren Simmons, Nov. 30, 1985; children: Stacey Arlene Herndon, Robert Eric Herndon, Nicholas Maxville Simmons. BA cum laude, Howard U., 1970, MA, 1973. With D.C. Pub. Schs., 1970-73; sr. evaluation cons. CTB/McGraw-Hill, Washington, 1973-79; sr. policy fellow Nat. Inst. Edn., Washington, 1979-80, sr. rsch. assoc.; rsch. area team leader Office Edn. Rsch. U.S. Dept. Edn., Washington, 1980-87; dep. assoc. dir. Office of Policy and Program Evaluation, Exec. Office Mayor, Washington, 1987-90; dir. office of policy and program evaluation Office of the Mayor, 1991—. Cons. Mid-Atlantic Equity Ctr., Am. U., Washington, 1988—. Author: Your Child and Testing, 1980, 89; exec. producer TV series Who's Keeping Score?, 1981. Bd. dirs. Lowell Sch., Community Prevention Partnership and Consortium and Univs. of Washington. Mem. Jack and Jill. Avocation: aerobics. Office: Govt of DC 441 4th St NW Washington DC 20001-2714

SIMMONS, JANET BRYANT, writer, publisher; b. Oakland, Calif., Apr. 22, 1925; d. Howard Pelton and Janet Horn (McNab) Bryant; m. William Ellis Simmons, May 17, 1944 (div. 1979); children: William Howard, Janet Margaret Simmons McAlpine. BA, San Jose State U., 1965; MA, U. San Francisco, 1979. Social worker Santa Clara County Social Svcs., San Jose, Calif., 1965-91; editor, pub. Enlightenment Press, Santa Clara, 1994—. Author: The Mystical Child, 1996. Mem. AAUW, Am. Booksellers Assn., Pubs. Mktg. Assn., Bay Area Ind. Pubs. Assn., Audubon Soc., Jacques Cousteau Soc. Avocations: playing piano, swimming, tai chi, travel, gardening. Office: Enlightenment Press PO Box 3314 Santa Clara CA 95055-3314 Personal E-mail: Janet-Simmons@aol.com.

SIMMONS, MARGUERITE SAFFOLD, pharmaceutical sales professional; b. Montgomery, Ala., Oct. 21, 1954; d. Arthur Edward and Gwendolyn Jane (Saffold) S. BS in Communications, U. Tenn., 1976. Press sec. Met. Mayor's Office, Nashville, 1977-78; advt. copywriter United Meth. Pub. House, Nashville, 1976-77; sales rep. No Nonsense Pantyhose, Houston, 1978-81, Breon Labs., Houston, 1981-82; profl. sales rep. Janssen Pharmaceutica, Inc., Houston, 1982-88, sr. sales rep., 1988-97; territory sales mgr. Bristol-Myers Squibb Co., Atlanta, 1997-2001, sr. territory bus. mgr., 2001—02, long-term care specialty rep., 2002—. Vol. Dem. Nat. Conv., Atlanta, 1988. Named to Outstanding Young Women in Am., 1981, 87. Mem. NAFE, U. Tenn. Alumni Assn. (bd. dirs. Atlanta chpt. 1989-90, v.p. 2000—), U. Tenn. Black Alumni Assn. (bd. dirs. Atlanta chpt. 1989—, pres. Atlanta chpt. 1995-96, bd. govs. dist. 5 rep. 1995-2000), Ga. Trust Hist. Soc., Ala. Geneal. Soc., Ga. Geneal. Soc., Nat. Trust Hist. Preservation, Delta Sigma Theta. Baptist. Avocations: reading, genealogical research, personal computing.

SIMMONS, MARSHA THRIFT, science and reading educator, musician; b. Brunswick, Ga., Jan. 18, 1953; d. James Russell II and Ouida (Tyre) Thrift; m. Samuel Leland Simmons, Aug. 2, 1975; 1 child, Natalie Renee. BA, Agnes Scott Coll., 1975; MEd, Coll. of Charleston, 1980; MA, Regent U., 2001. Cert. tchr., Tenn., postgrad. profl. lic., Va. Organist Epworth United Meth. Ch., Atlanta, 1975-76; tchr. 3d grade Hanahan (S.C.) Acad., 1976-77; grad. asst. Coll. of Charleston, S.C., 1977-78, sub. tchr. Early Childhood Devel. Ctr., 1978-79; owner, tchr. Marsha's Music (Studio and Store), S.C., Ga., Tex., Tenn., Va., 1979—; tchr. presch. Sykes Daycare, Lawrenceville, Ga., 1994; sub. tchr. Glynn County Schs., Brunswick, Ga., 1994; tchr. 6th grade sci. and reading Jackson (Tenn.)-Madison County Schs., 1995-97; sub. tchr. Virginia Beach (Va.) City Pub. Schs., 1997—. Treas. Kingwood (Tex.) Music Tchrs. Assn., 1985-87; mem. local sch. adv. com. Gwinnett County Bd. Edn., Lawrenceville, Ga., 1993-94; Odyssey of the Mind coord., coach N.E. Mid. Sch., Jackson, 1995-97; lead tchr. sci. stds. implementation Jackson-Madison County Schs., 1996-97; subst. tchr. Va. Beach City Schs., 1997-99; tchr. asst. Regent U., 2002-03; adminstrv. asst. U. Psychol. Svcs. Ctr., 2003—. Leader Girl Scouts Am., St. Simons Island, Ga., 1988-89; PTA v.p. and cultural arts chmn. Benefield Elem. Sch., Lawrenceville, 1991-93; chmn. cmty. outreach West Tenn. Music Tchr.'s Assn., Jackson, 1996-97. Recipient Spl. Svc. award Girl Scouts Am., 1989, Outstanding Woman in Bus. and Edn. award Parker Chapel Christian Meth. Episcopal Ch., Tenn., 1996, Lockheed Martin fellow Lockheed Martin Corp., 1997. Mem. ACA, Am. Guild Organists, Music Tchrs. Nat. Assn., Am. Assn. of Christian Counselors, Am. Psychol. Assn. Avocations: reading, cooking, sewing, crafts, drawing, painting. Home: 313 Chase Arbor Ct Virginia Beach VA 23462-7407

SIMMONS, MARY JANE, state legislator; b. Leominster, Mass., May 14, 1953; Mem. Mass. Ho. of Reps., Boston, 1993—. Office: Mass Ho of Reps State House Rm 146 Boston MA 02133 E-mail: rep.maryjanesimmons@hou.state.ma.us.

SIMMONS, PATRICIA ANN, pharmacist, consultant; b. Monroe, Wis., Apr. 17, 1964; d. Wendell Louis and Gladys Lemae (Casey) S. Student, Mercer U., Macon, Ga., 1982-84; PharmD, Mercer So. Sch. Pharmacy, Atlanta, 1990. Registered pharmacist, Ga., Fla.; cons. pharmacist, Fla.; cert. geriat. pharmacist. Intern in pharmacy Joel N Jerry's Pharmacy, Clearwater, Fla., 1987-90, staff pharmacist, 1990-96, mgr., 1991-92; resident in pharmacy VA Med. Ctr., Gainesville, Fla., 1990-91; cons., staff pharmacist Sun Pharmacy, Largo, Fla., 1991—2002; pharmacist Lesco and Pharmacistance, Tampa and Largo, Fla., 1993—2001, Medicine Shop in Kash-n-Karry, 2001—. Vol. pharmacist Pasco County Free Clinic, Hudson, Fla., 1994-99, mgr., 1996-97. Author: Drugs of Abuse for Non-Medical Professional, 1993. Sec. Choice Single Friends in Faith, Tampa, 1994-95, svc. coord., 1995-97, asst. coord., 1996-97, coord., 1997-99; eucharist minister St. Luke Ch., Palm Harbor, Fla., 1995-99, youth ministry asst., 1995-98; mem. Young Reps., 1982-85; instr. CPR ARC, 1982-91, mem. local disaster team, 1986-90; spkr. poison prevention elem. schs., Pinellas County, Fla., 1993-97; svc. coord. Mercer U. Circle-K, 1983-84. Named Disting. Young Pharmacist, Hoechst-Marion Roussel, Inc., Fla., 1996. Mem. Am. Pharm. Assn., Pinellas Pharmacy Assn. (chair poison prevention 1993-97, sec. 1994-95, pres. 1996-97, Pharmacist of Yr. 1994). Roman Catholic. Avocations: dog walking, activities with friends. Office: Simmons Realty 1780 Main St Dunedin FL 34698-6427

SIMMONS, PATRICIA T. marketing analyst, researcher; b. Louisville, Ky., Aug. 21, 1974; d. Vic P. and Lee B. Thacker, Patricia R. Thacker (Stepmother); m. Bradford R. Simmons, Aug. 2, 1997; 1 child, Samuel Bradford. BS, Ga. So. U., 1996; MA, Vanderbilt U., 1999, postgrad., 1999—2003. Adj. prof. Volunteer State C.C., Gallatin, Tenn., 1999; sr. rsch. analyst AAA Auto Club South, Tampa, Fla., 2000—. Editor: (employee newsletter) On Target. Nursery vol. St. Andrew Presbyn. Ch., Tampa, 2003. Advanced Grad. Student grantee, Am. Polit. Sci. Assn., 1999. Mem.: ARC (life), Am. Humane Soc. (life), Pi Sigma Alpha (Outstanding Student in Polit. Sci. award 1996), Order of Omega (life), Kappa Kappa Gamma (life; pres. Tampa Bay alumnae assn., scholarship chair 2001—02, grad. scholar 2000). Presbyterian. Avocations: cooking, reading, gardening, arts, crafting. Office: AAA Auto Club South 1515 N Westshore Blvd Tampa FL 33607 Personal E-mail: patti_t_simmons@yahoo.com. E-mail: psimmons@aaasouth.com.

SIMMONS, ROBERTA JOHNSON, public relations firm executive; b. St. Louis, June 28, 1947; d. Robert Andrew and Thelma Josephine (Bunch) J.; m. Clifford Michael Simmons, Aug. 10, 1968; children: Andrew Park, Matthew Clay, Jordan Michael. BA, Ind. U., South Bend, 1972. Lic. real estate broker, Ind.; accredited pub. rels. practitioner; mem. Inst. Residential Mktg. Account exec., supr. Juhl Advt., Inc., Mishawaka, Ind., 1971-74, pub. rels. dir., 1974-79, v.p., 1979, v.p., pub. rels. dir. Mishawaka and Indpls., 1984-89; v.p. E.L. Yoder & Assocs., Inc., Granger, Ind., 1979-80; pres. Simmons Communications, Inc., Mishawaka, 1981-82; v.p., gen. mgr. Juhl Bldg. Communications, Inc., South Bend, 1983-84; sr. v.p. Wyse Advt., Inc., Indpls., 1989-90; v.p., pub. rels. dir. Caldwell VanRiper, Inc., Indpls., 1990-94; v.p. Pub. Rels. Network, Indpls., 1995—. Contbr. articles to profl. publs. Mem. pub. rels. com. Ind. Adult Literacy Coalition, Indpls., 1989; chairperson pub. rels. com. Crossroads of Am. coun. Boy Scouts Am., Indpls., 1990-91; dep. community info. com. Indpls. C. of C. Infrastructure Study, 1990-91. Mem. PRSA (accredited, mem. counsellors acad., Hoosier chpt. job bank com. 1993—, Nat. Assembly Del., 1996—, v.p. programs, 1997), Nat. Sales Mktg. Coun. (trustee 1991-92), Inst. Residential Mktg. Elder Christian Ch. (Disciples of Christ). Avocations: travel, reading. Office: Pub Rels Network 111 Monument Cir Ste 882 Indianapolis IN 46204-5173

SIMMONS, RUTH DORIS, retired women's health nurse, educator; b. Bklyn., July 30, 1942; d. Stanley George and Doris Louise (Beckert) S. LPN, Glen Cove (N.Y.) Community, 1964; AD, SUNY, Farmingdale, 1976; BS in Profl. Arts in Edn., St. Joseph's Coll., 1994. Nurse labor/delivery unit Syosset (N.Y.) Hosp., 1964-66; staff nurse ob./gyn. and pediatrics unit Glen Cove Community Hosp., 1966-76; staff nurse labor, delivery, postpartum units Mercy Hosp., Scranton, Pa., 1976-99, ret., disabled, 1999. Asst. childbirth edn. classes Mercy Hosp., Scranton, 1976-99. Home: 2083 Hickory Ridge Rd Factoryville PA 18419-9658

SIMMONS, RUTH J. academic administrator; b. Grapeland, Tex., July 3, 1945; d. Isaac and Fannie Stubblefield; m. Norbert Simmons, 1968 (div. 1989); children: Khari, Maya. Student, Universidad Internacional, Saltillo, Mex., 1965, Wellesley Coll., 1965—66; BA, Dillard U., 1967; postgrad., Universite de Lyon, 1967—68, George Washington U., 1968—69; AM, Harvard U., 1970, PhD in Romance Langs., 1973; LLD (hon.), Amherst Coll., 1995; LHD (hon.), Howard U., 1996, Dillard U., 1996; LLD (hon.), Princeton U., 1996, Lake Forest Coll., 1997; LHD (hon.), U. Mass., 1997; LLD (hon.), Dartmouth Coll., 1997, Mt. Holyoke Coll., 2001, U. Pa., 2001, Harvard U., 2002, George Washington U., 2002, Columbia U., 2002, Washington U., 2002, U. So. Calif., 2003, Boston U., Rensselaer Polytechnic Inst., N.Y. U., Northeastern. Interpreter lang. svcs. divsn. U.S. Dept. State, Washington, 1968—69; instr. French George Washington U., 1968—69; admissions officer Radcliffe Coll., 1970—72; asst. prof. French U. New Orleans, 1973—75, asst. dean coll. liberal arts, asst. prof. French, 1975—76; adminstrv. coord. NEH liberal studies project Calif. State U., Northridge, 1977—78, acting dir. internat. programs, vis. assoc. prof. Pan-African studies, 1978—79; asst. dean grad. sch. U. So. Calif., 1979—82, assoc. dean grad. sch., 1982—83; dir. studies Butler Coll. Princeton U., NJ, 1983—85, acting dir. Afro-Am. studies, 1985—87, asst. dean faculty, 1986—87, assoc. dean faculty, 1986—90, vice provost, 1992—95; provost Spelman Coll., 1990—91; pres. Smith Coll., Northampton, Mass., 1995—2001; pres Brown Univ., Providence, 2001—. Peer reviewer higher edn. divsn. NEH, 1980—83, bd. cons., 1981; mem. grad. adv. bd. Calif. Student Aid Commn., 1981—83; chair com. to visit dept. African-Am. studies Harvard U., 1991; mem. strategic planning task force N.J. Dept. Higher Edn., 1992—93; mem. nat. adv. commn. EQUITY 2000 Coll. Bd., 1992—95; mem. adv. bd. ctrl. N.J. NAACP Legal Def. Fund, 1992—95; mem. Mid. States Assn. Accreditation Team, Johns Hopkins U., 1993; chmn. accreditation team Bryn Mawr Coll., 1999; chair rev. panel for model instns. planning grants NSF, 1993; mem. Conf. Bd., 1995; bd. dirs. MetLife, JSTOR, Pfizer Inc., 1997—, COFHE, Com. Econ. Devel., Goldman Sachs, 1999—, Tex. Instruments, 1999—; mem. adv. coun. dept. Romance Langs. and Lit. Princeton U., 1996; trustee Carnegie Corp., 1999—; presenter, spkr. and panelist in field. Mem. editl. bd.: World Edn. series Am. Assn. Collegiate Registrars and Admissions Officers, 1984—86; contbr. articles to profl. jours. Named mem. Women's Progress Commemoration Commn. by Pres. Bill Clinton, 1999; mem. adv. coun. Bill and Melinda Gates Millennium Scholars Found.; mem. adv. bd. N.J. Master Faculty Program Woodrow Wilson Nat. Fellowship Found., 1987—90, bd. trustees, 1991—96; trustee Inst. Advances Study, 1995—98, The Clarke Sch. for Deaf, 1995—; chmn. bd. trustees Acad. Music, 1995—98; mem. adv. com. Healthy Steps for Young Children Program, 1996—98; mem. bd. advisors 1st Internat. Conf. on AIDS, Ethiopia, 1998. Named Women of Yr., CBS, 1996, Glamour Mag., 1996, Disting. Fulbright Alumna, Inst. Internat. Edn., 1997, Woman of World, NASA, 1998, Am. Best Coll. Pres., Time mag., 2001, Woman Yr., Ms. mag., 2002; named one of Newsweek Person to Watch, 2002; recipient Disting. Svc. award, Assn. Black Princeton Alumni, 1989, Dillard U., 1992, Pres.'s Recognition award, Bloomfield Coll., 1993, TWIN award, Princeton Area YWCA, 1993, Women's orgn. Tribute award, Princeton U., 1994, Leadership award, Third World Ctr. Princeton U., 1995, Tex. Excellence award, Leap Program, 1995, Benjamin E. Mays award, A Better Chance, 1995, Centennial medal, HArvard U. Grad. Sch. Arts & Scis., 1997, Achievement award, Nat. Urban League, 1998, Tchr. Coll. Medal for Disting. Svc., Columbia U., 1999, Pres. award, United Negro Coll. Fund, 2001, "Drum Major for Justice" Edn. award, So. Christian Leadership Conf./W.O.M.E.N., 2002, Fulbright Lifetime Achievement Medal, 2002, fellowship, DAAD; fellow, Danforth Found., 1967—73, Sr. Fulbright fellow, 1981; scholar, KYOK, 1963, Worthing Found., 1963—67, Fulbright scholar, U. de Lyon, 1967—68. Fellow: Am. Acad. Arts & Scis.; mem.: AAAS, Coun. Foreign Rels., Am. Philos. Soc. Office: Office of the President Brown University 1 Prospect Street, Campus Box 1860 Providence RI 02912 Mailing: Brown University President's Office Box 1860 Providence RI 02912-1860*

SIMMONS, SARAH R. lawyer; b. Ducktown, Tenn., Jan. 23, 1948; BA magna cum laude, U. Ariz., 1970, postgrad.; JD magna cum laude, U. Denver, 1973. Bar: Colo. 1974, Ariz. 1975. Mem. Molloy, Jones & Donahue, Tucson, Brown & Bain, P.A., Tucson, Lewis & Roca LLP. Trustee Tohono Club Park, 1995—, sec., 1997-99, v.p. 1999-2001, pres., 2001—03; trustee Tucson Airport Authority, 1996—; mem. Law Coll. Assn. Bd., 1996—, sec. 1998—99, pres. 2000-01; 4th R bd. Tucson Unified Sch., 1996—; bd. dirs. United Way of Tucson, 1995-2000, Family Advocacy Resource and Wellness Ctrs., Resources for Women, 1995-2000; bd. dirs. Ariz. Town Hall, 1998—; mem. adv. bd. Ariz. for a Drug Free Workplace, 1991—, So. Ariz. Sports Devel. Corp., U. Ariz. Social and Behavioral Scis., 1994-96; sec. So. Ariz. Minutemen, 1996-98. Recipient Tucson Woman of Yr. C. of C., 1994, Women on the Move award YWCA, 1995, Outstanding Alumni award U. Ariz. Coll. of Law, 1993; named one of 100 Women and Minorities in the Law, 2000. Fellow ABA, Ariz. Bar Assn.; mem. Nat. Assn. Bond Lawyers, State Bar Ariz. (bd. govs. 1987-95, sec.-treas. 1989-90, 2d v.p. 1990-91, 1st v.p. 1991-92, pres.-elect 1992-93, pres. 1993-94, employment law sect., profl. conduct com., fee arbitration com.), Ariz. Women Lawyers Assn. (charter), Colo. Bar Assn., Pima County Bar Assn. (bd. dirs. 1985-94), Am. Judicature Soc., So. Ariz. Legal Aid (bd. dirs. 1990-93), Lawyers Against Hunger (bd. dirs., v.p. D-M 50 1996-98, pres. 1998-2000), Order St. Ives, Phi Beta Kappa, Phi Kappa Phi, Phi Alpha Theta, Kappa Beta Pi. Office: Lewis and Roca LLP 1 S Church Ave Ste 700 Tucson AZ 85701-1612 E-mail: sally_simmons@lrlaw.com.

SIMMONS, SUE, newscaster; d. John Simmons. Corr. WTNH-TV, New Haven, 1973-74, WBAL-TV, Balt., 1974, anchor, host Balt. at One, 1975—76; corr./anchor. WRC-TV, Washington, 1976—80; co-anchor Live at Five & News Channel 4 at 11/WNBC News Channel 4, N.Y.C., 1980—; host Images: A Year in Review, WNBC, 2002—. Recipient four Emmy awards, award for Outstanding Performance by a News Commentator, Barnabus McHenry, Vice-Chmn. Pres.'s Task Force on Arts and Humanities, 1981. Office: WNBC-TV 30 Rockefeller Plz New York NY 10112-0002*

SIMMONS, SYLVIA (SYLVIA SIMMONS NEUMANN), advertising executive, writer; b. N.Y.C. m. Hans H. Neumann, 1962. BA, Bklyn. Coll.; MA in English Lit., Columbia U. Dir. sales promotion and direct mail divsn. McCann Erickson, Inc., N.Y.C., 1958-62; v.p., asst. to pres. Young & Rubicam, Inc., N.Y.C., 1962-73; sr. v.p., dir. spl. projects Kenyon & Eckhardt, Inc., N.Y.C., 1975-86; sr. v.p., dir. corp. comms. Bozell, Jacobs, Kenyon & Eckhardt, 1985-86, cons., 1986-88; free-lance speech writer and coach advt. cons., 1987—. Author: New Speakers Handbook, 1972, The Great Garage Sale Book, 1982, new edit. 2000, (with Hans H. Neumann) The Straight Story on VD, 1974, new edit., 2000; Dr. Neumann's Guide to the New Sexually Transmitted Diseases, 1983; co-author: (with Thomas D. Rees) More Than Just a Pretty Face, 1987, How to be the Life of the Podium, 1991, also articles. Recipient Medal of Freedom, 1946, award for best radio comml. N.Y. Radio Broadcasters Assn., 1976-77, award for contbns. in direct mail promotions Sales Promotion Execs. Assn. Mem. Nat. League Am. Pen Women, Authors Guild, Propylaea, Sigma Tau Delta.

SIMMONS, SYLVIA JEANNE QUARLES (MRS. HERBERT G. SIMMONS JR.), university administrator, educator, executive; b. Boston, May 8, 1935; d. Lorenzo Christopher and Margaret Mary (Thomas) Quarles; m. Herbert G. Simmons, Jr., Oct. 26, 1957; children: Stephen, Alison, Lisa. BA, Manhattanville Coll., 1957; MEd, Boston Coll., 1962, PhD, 1990; DHL (hon.), St. Joseph's Coll., 1994; EdD (hon.), Merrimack Coll., 1999. Montessori tchr. Charles River Park Nursery Sch., Boston, 1970-76; registrar Boston Coll. Sch. Mgmt., Chestnut Hill, 1966-70; dir. fin. aid Radcliffe Coll., Cambridge, Mass., 1970-75, assoc. dean admissions and fin. aid, 1972-75, assoc. dean admissions, fin. aid and women's edn., 1975; assoc. dean admissions and fin. aid Harvard and Radcliffe, from 1975; assoc. v.p. for acad. affairs ctrl. adminstrn. U. Mass., Boston, 1976-79, spl. asst. to chancellor, 1979; v.p. field svcs. Am. Student Assistance, 1982-84, sr. v.p., 1984-93, exec. v.p., 1983-95, pres., 1996; mem. faculty Harvard U., 1970-77, pres. faculty, 1995-96; lectr. Boston U., 1991—. Cons. Mass. Bd. Higher Edn., 1973-77. Past bd. dirs. Rivers Country Day Sch., Weston, Mass., Simons's Rock Coll., Great Barrington, Mass., Wayland (Mass.) Fair Housing, Cambridge Mental Health Assn., Family Svcs. Greater Boston, Concerts in Black and White, Mass., Higher Edn. Assistance Corp.; chmn. bd. dirs. North Shore Cmty. Coll., 1986-88, mem. bd. dirs., 1985—; trustee and alumnae bd. dirs. Manhattanville Coll., 1986—; mem. adv. com. Upward Bound, Chestnut Hill Boston Coll., 1972-74, Women in Politics John McCormick Inst., 1994—; Camp Chimney Corners, Becket, Mass., 1971-77; bd. dirs. Am. Cancer Soc. Mass., 1987-89, Boston Coll., 1990—, Merrimack Coll., 1992—, Mass. Found. for Humanities, 1990-92, Mass. Bay United Way, 1990-94, Grimes King Found., 1992—, St. Elizabeta's Hosp., 1991—, Anna Stearns Found., 1996—, Regis Coll., 1997—; overseer Mt. Ida Coll., 1990—, Exec. Svc. Corp., 1997—; chair Coll. Club Scholarship com., 1997. Recipient Educator of Yr. award Boston and Vicinity Club, 1989, Bicentennial meda; Boston Coll., 1976, Achievement award Greater Boston YMCA, 1977, Human Rights awsard Mass. Tchrs. Assn., 1988, Pres'. award Mass. Ednl. Opportunity Assn., 1988, ARchbishop Timothy Healy award, 1997; named One of Ten Outstanding Yung Leaders, Boston Jr. C. of C., 1971, Sojourner's Daus.: 25 African women who have made a difference, 1991. Mem. Eastern Assns. Fin. Aid Officers (2st v.p. 1973), Coll. Scholarship Svc. Coun., Links (pres. local chpt. 1967-69), Nat. Inst. Fin. Aid Adminstrs. (dir. 1975-77), Jack and Jill Am. (pres. Newton chpt. 1972-74), Manhattanville Club (pres. Boston 1966-68), Delta Sigma Theta, Delta Kappa Gamma (pres. 1988-90). Home: 19 Clifford St Roxbury MA 02119-2120 Office: 330 Stuart St Boston MA 02116-5237

SIMMS, JACQUELINE KAMP, secondary school educator; Tchr. sci. Recipient Tandy Tech. Scholars prize Tandy Corp., 1994, Regional Catalyst award for Excellence in Chemistry Tchg. Chem. Mfrs. Assn., 1994, Presdl. award for Excellence in Sci. and Math. Tchg., 1994, Educator award Continental Cablevision, 1997. Office: Sandalwood High Sch 2750 John Prom Blvd Jacksonville FL 32246-3921

SIMMS, LOIS AVERETTA, retired secondary school educator; b. Charleston, SC, May 27, 1919; d. Jasper Simeon and Anna Inez (Ferguson) S. BA, Johnson C. Smith U., 1941; MA, Howard U., 1954. Cert. English and social studies educator, S.C. Directive tchr. Avery Normal Inst., Charleston, 1941-42; tchr. English and French Laing H.S., Mt. Pleasant, S.C., 1942-44; tchr. English and math. Henry P. Archer Sch., Charleston,

1944-45; tchr. social studies and English Burke H.S., Charleston, 1945-52; tchr. English Avery H.S., Charleston, 1952-54, Burke H.S., Charleston, 1954-73; tchr. English and history Charleston H.S., 1973-76; ret., 1976. Co-adviser Dramatic Club, Burke H.S., 1945-46, trainer section of chorus, 1945-47, chief advisor 1961 Bulldog Yearbook, 1960-61; advisor Crochet Club, Avery H.S., 1952-54, Charleston H.S., 1973-76. Author: Growing Up Presbyterian: Life in Presbyterian Colleges and Churches, 1991, Profiles of African American Females in Low Country of South Carolina, 1992, A Chalk and Chalkboard Career in Carolina, 1995, A History of Zion, Olivet, and Zion-Olivet Churches 1850-1985, 1989; editor The Scroll newsletter, 1984-94. Sec. exec. bd. YWCA of Greater Charleston, 1950s; active YWCA, SC Hist. Soc., SC ETV Endowment. Recipient plaque Zion-Olivet Presbyn. Ch., 1987, C.L. Campbell award Presbyn. Ch., 1988, plaque Staff of The Scroll, 1990. Mem. NAACP (Silver life, Trailblazer award 2002), Charleston County Ret. Educators Assn. Unit 2, Pres.'s Club (plaque 1991), Avery Inst. Afro-Am. History and Culture (editor The Bull. 1990-2000, Cert.), SC Soc., Assn. for Study of African-Am. Life and History, Johnson C. Smith U. Alumni Assn., Presbytn. Womens Assn. (chair com. qtrly. birthday celebration and grad. ceremony 1999-2003). Avocations: reading, playing music, playing scrabble, planting flowers, writing prose. Home: 28 Jasper St Charleston SC 29403-6006

SIMON, BERNECE KERN, retired social work educator; b. Denver, Nov. 27, 1914; d. Maurice Meyer and Jennie (Bloch) Kern; m. Marvin L. Simon, Feb. 26, 1939; 1 dau., Anne Elizabeth. BA, U. Chgo., 1936, MA, 1942. Social worker Jewish Children's Bur. Chgo., 1938-40, U. Chgo. Hosps. and Clinics, 1940-44; mem. faculty U. Chgo., 1944-81, instr., 1944-48, asst. prof., 1948-60, prof. social casework, 1960—, Samuel Deutsch prof. Sch. Social Service Adminstrn., 1960-81, emeritus, 1981—. Mem. bd. editors 17th Edit. Ency. Social Work, 1975-77, Social Svc. Rev., 1975-99; bd. editors: Social Work, 1978-82, book rev. editor, 1982-87; cons. editor Journal of Social Work Education, 1991-94; contbr. articles to profl. jours., book chpts., monographs. Mem. NASW, Coun. Social Work Edn. (mem. nat. bd., sec. 1972-74), Acad. Cert. Social Workers, Nat. Acads. Practice: Social Work Office: U Chgo Sch of Social Svc Adminstrn 969 E 60th St Chicago IL 60637-2677

SIMON, DIANE ROSE, music educator, writer, poet; b. Appleton, Wis., Oct. 19, 1945; d. Raymond George and Violet Beatrice (Behnke) Rippl; m. Ronald Philip Simon, Sept. 18, 1938; children: David Clarence, Mary Anne. Saxophone student, Stevens Point State Tchrs. Coll., Wis., 1966; BMus, Ariz. State U., 1969, postgrad., 1971—94; saxophone student, Paris (France) Am. Acad., 1970, Union Coll., Schenectady, N.Y., 1970; student, Westminster Choir Coll., Princeton, N.J., 1979, Grand Canyon Coll., Phoenix, 1992, Inst. of Children's Lit., West Redding, Conn., 1998—2003, Poetry Laureate Program, Owings Mills, Md., 2002—04. Band dir., chorus, gen. music Wellton Elem. Sch. Dist., Ariz., 1969—70; saxophone instr. Ariz. Western Coll., Yuma, 1969—70; woodwind specialist Yuma Sch. Dist., 1970—72; band dir. Balsz Sch. Dist., Phoenix, 1972—76, Paradise Valley Sch. Dist., Phoenix, 1976—77; band dir., chorus, gen. music Mesa Pub. Schs., Ariz., 1978—94; ret., 1994. Saxophone clinician, adjudicator Ariz. Music Educators Assn., 1972—76, 2002—; dir. saxophone ensembles Yuma Sch. Dist. #1, 1970—72. Author: Expressions of the Heart, 1997, Family Treasures, 1998, With a Giggle and a Tear, 1998, Butterflies in the Meadow, 1999, Into the Millennium, 2000; pub. Beneath the Mesquite, 1999, Sunrise Over the Desert, 1999, poet (poetry) The Stain, 2003, Arm of Doom, 2003, poet pub. numerous anthologies (Editors Choice Award cert., 1996, 1997, 1998, 99, 2000, 2001, 2002, 2003); contbr. articles to profl. publs. Named one of Best Poets of 2002, Internat. Libr. Poetry, 2002; recipient The Muse of Fire trophy, medallion, The Famous Poets Soc., 2000. Mem.: Internat. Libr. of Poetry (Internat. Poetry Hall of Fame 1996), Internat. Soc. Poets (Disting. Membership 1996, Internat. Poet of Merit award Medallion and Commemorative Plaque 1996, 1998, Poet of Merit award medallion 2002, Silver award bowl trophy 2002, Poet of Merit award medallion 2004, Outstanding Achievement in Poetry Silver award cup 2004). Republican. Roman Catholic. Avocations: hiking, bicycling, tennis, cross stitch, embroidery. Home: 732 W Curry St Chandler AZ 85225

SIMON, DOLORES DALY, copy editor; b. San Francisco, Nov. 18, 1928; d. Francis Edward and Jeannette (Cooke) Daly; m. Sidney Blair Simon, Aug. 24, 1952 (div. Nov. 1955); children: John Roderick, Douglas Brian. BA in Journalism, Pa. State U., 1950. County editor Centre Daily Times, State College, Pa., 1950-51; sec. editor Bradford (Pa.) Era, 1951-52; copy editor Harper & Bros., Pubs., N.Y.C., 1955-60; copy chief Harper & Row, Pubs., N.Y.C., 1960-88; freelance editor, copy editor Warwick, N.Y., 1988—. Co-author: Recipes into Type, 1993 (Best Food Reference 1994). Mem. James Beard Found., Phi Mu. Democrat. Avocation: book collecting. Office: Editl Svcs 63 Blooms Corners Rd Warwick NY 10990-2403

SIMON, ERICA CECELIA, research scientist, consultant; b. Montego Bay, Jamaica, Nov. 27, 1972; d. Pamela Ann and Rolla Paul McCrary(Stepfather); 1 child, Briana Arielle. BA in English, U. Tex., 1997, EdM, postgrad., U. Tex., 2001—. Cert. secondary tchr. Tex., 1997. Tchr. Austin (Tex.) Ind. Sch. Dist., 1997—2000; rsch. assoc. U. Tex., Austin, 2000—. Cons. in field. Contbr. articles to profl. jours. Bd. dirs. Dancer's Edge, Austin, 2003. Mem.: ASCD, Nat. Assn. Black Sch. Educators, Coun. for Learning Disabilities, Tex. Coun. for Learning Disabilities (assoc.; sec. 2000—03), Tex. Coun. for Learning Disabilities (assoc.), Kappa Delta Pi. Democrat. Baptist. Avocations: reading, writing, travel. Home: 909 Thackeray Ln Pflugerville TX 07860 Office: Texas Center for Reading and Language 1 University Station D4900 Austin TX 78712-0365 Personal E-mail: serica@hotmail.com. E-mail: erica_simon@texasreading.org.

SIMON, EVELYN, lawyer; b. N.Y.C., May 13, 1943; d. Joseph and Adele (Holzschlag) Berkman; m. Fredrick Simon, Aug. 18, 1963; children: Amy Jocelyn, Marcie Ann. AB in Physics, Barnard Coll., 1963; MS in Physics, U. Pitts., 1964; JD, Wayne State U., 1978; LLB, Monash U., Melbourne, Australia, 1980. Bar: Mich. 1980, Victoria (Australia) 1981. Supr. engring. Chrysler Corp., Detroit, 1964-72; edn. and profl. mgr. Engring. Soc. Detroit, 1972-78; solicitor Arthur Robinson & Co., Melbourne, 1980-81; sr. atty. Ford Motor Co., Detroit, 1981-89; assoc. gen. counsel Sheller-Globe Corp., Detroit, 1989-90; v.p. planning, gen. counsel United Techs. Automotive Inc., Dearborn, Mich., 1991-94, v.p. bus. devel. and legal affairs, 1995-96, v.p. Asian bus. devel., 1997-98; pvt. practice, 1999—. Cons. internat. bus. devel., 1998-99. Mem. Mich. Bar Assn. Office: 1787 Alexander Dr Bloomfield Hills MI 48302-1204 E-mail: evelynsimon@prodigy.net.

SIMON, JACQUELINE ALBERT, political scientist, journalist; d. Louis and Rose (Axelroad) Albert; m. Pierre Simon; children: Lisette, Orville. BA cum laude, NYU, MA, 1972, PhD, 1977. Adj. assoc. prof. Southampton Coll., 1977-79; mng. editor Point of Contact, NYC, 1975-76; assoc. editor, US bur. chief Politique Internationale, Paris, 1979—. Sr. fellow, Inst. French Studies, NYU, 1980—, assoc. prof. govt., 1982-83; frequent appearances French TV and radio. Contbg. editor Harper's mag., 1984-92; contbr. numerous articles to French mag., revs., books on internat. affairs. Bd. dir. Fresh Air Fund, 1984—. Mem. Women's Fgn. Policy Group, Overseas Press Club of Am. (bd. dirs., treas. 2000--), Phi Beta Kappa. Home: 988 5th Ave New York NY 10021-0143 E-mail: jasimon@ix.netcom.com.

SIMON, JAMI LEA, actress; b. Ames, Iowa, Apr. 19, 1958; d. James Marvin and Letha Jane (Spillers) S. BA in Theater, BS in Dance, Iowa State U., 1981; MS in Dance, Ill. State U., 1983. Basketball pub. address announcer, Ames, 1976-81; TV and radio spokesperson for the arts, 1976-81. Grad. teaching asst. Ill. State U., Normal, 1981-82; children's dance tchr., Ames, 1981, N.Y.C., 1992; co-founder Footfalls Dance Concert, Ames, 1979; choreographer various dance concerts, Ames, Normal, 1976-82. Actress (TV shows) Saturday Night Live, Law and Order, Guiding Light, Reading Rainbow, Late Night with Conan O'Brien, All My Children, As The World Turns, 1983-; (films) Teen TV Terrorist, The Oracle, Eyes of a Blue Dog, 1983—; (off-Broadway) That Time of Year, What About Love, Cinderella, 1983—; also music videos, commls., indsl. films, 1983—; actress, writer, prodr. Fred the Caterpillar, Baby Vaudeville, Grandma's Poems, The Reading Rap, Rocking Chair, 1999-; author: Episodes and Other Works, 1982, (play) Like a Poet's Dream, 1993. Mem. com., co-chair Muscular Dystrophy Assn. Dance-a-thon, Ames, 1976-81. Recipient Achievement award in Writing Nat. Coun. Tchrs. English, 1975, Citizenship award Soroptimists Soc., 1976, Honorary Stars and Bars Internat. Thespian Soc., 1976, Bronze Medal in Social Dance Brigham Young U., 1981, Writers Digest Honorable mention for playwriting, 1995; grantee Manhattan (N.Y.) Cmty. Arts Fund, 1999-2001, Puffin Found. grant, 2004. Mem. SAG, Actors Equity Assn., AFTRA, Episc. Actors Guild, 12th Night Club (asst. treas.), Phi Eta Sigma.

SIMON, KAREN MICHELE, clinical psychologist, educator; b. L.A., Nov. 18, 1953; d. Herbert and Miriam Simon. BA with honors, UCLA, 1975; PhD, Stanford U., 1979. Asst. prof. psychology U. Notre Dame, South Bend, Ind., 1979-81; postdoctoral fellow U. Pa., Phila., 1981-82; clin. asst. prof. Hahnemann U., Phila., 1984-87; clin. assoc. U. Pa., Phila., 1985-88, clin. asst. prof., 1988-92; dir. cognitive therapy CPC Santa Ana (Calif.) Hosp., 1992-93; dir. clin. ops. Ctr. for Cognitive Therapy, Newport Beach, Calif., 1993-97. Vis. asst. prof. Stanford U., 1980; cons. in field. Co-author: Clinical Applications of Cognitive Therapy, 1990, Cognitive Therapy of Personality Disorders, 1990, 2d edit., 2003; co-editor: Depression in the Family, 1986, Comprehensive Handbook of Cognitive Therapy, 1989; contbr. articles to sci. and profl. jours. Mem. Am. Psychol. Assn., Assn. for Advancement of Behavior Therapy, Internat. Assn. Cognitive Psychotherapy, Calif. Psychol. Assn., Cognitive Behavior Therapy Newport Beach. Avocations: reading, theater, rollerblading, snow skiing. Office: 1101 Dove St Ste 260 Newport Beach CA 92660-2803

SIMON, LATEEFAH, foundation administrator, director; Counselor Ctr. for Young Women's Devel., San Francisco, 1993—97, exec. dir., 1997—. Organizer and spokesperson Rock the Vote; adv. mem. San Francisco Youth Commn.; adv. panelist Juvenile Justice Commn. Recipient Leadership for a changing world award, Ford Found., 2001, Women who make a difference Honoree, The Nat. Coun. for Rsch. on Women, 2000; fellow MacArthur Found., 2003. Office: 1550 Bryant St Ste 700 San Francisco CA 94103-4876

SIMON, LOIS PREM, interior designer, artist; b. N.Y.C., Apr. 27, 1933; d. Frank Herbert and Sybil Gertrude (Nichols) Prem; m. William Patterson Simon, Mar. 24, 1956; children: William Patterson, Beth Hanson, Stuart Prem. BA, Wells Coll., 1955; postgrad., Parsons Sch. Design, N.Y.C., 1955. Self-employed portrait painter, Pitts., 1954-72; self-employed guitar tchr., 1972-76; designer Lois Simon Interior Designs, Pitts., 1976—. Self-employed writer, illustrator, 1972—; freelance designer, Pitts., 1972—78; curator Cultural Ctr. of Ponte Vedra, 2000—. Author, artist: (children's book) Moo Moo, 1971, Lefty and Righty, 1975; landscape artist. Mem. Pitts. Opera Guild, 1968-72; coach Spl. Olympics, Pitts., 1985—; chair various coms., mem. exec. bd. Jr. League Pitts., 1958—; bd. dirs., program designer South Hills Performing Arts, Upper St. Clair, 1966-70; mem. exec. bd., program and pub. relations chair Three Rivers Art Festival, Pitts., 1967-77; bd. dirs. Pitts. Plan for Arts, 1968-70; Sunday Sch. tchr., Pitts., 1972—; mem. Younglife Adult Com., 1973-83; mem. session, elder, Southminster ch., 1982-84. Named Vol. of Yr., Jr. League Pitts., 1962, Jr. League Show House Designer, 1985. Mem.: Am. Soc. Interior Designers, Associated Artists, Sawgrass Country (Ponte Vedra Beach, Fla.), Ponte Vedra Club (founder, pres. 1999—). Republican. Presbyterian. Avocations: running, tennis, hiking, golf, painting. Home and Office: 201 Settlers Row N Ponte Vedra Beach FL 32082-3941

SIMON, LOU ANNA KIMSEY, academic administrator; V.p. acad. affairs, provost Coll. Human Medicine Mich. State U., 1993—. Office: Mich State U 438 Administration Bldg East Lansing MI 48824-1046

SIMON, MARGARET B(ALLIF), elementary school educator, writer; b. Washington, Sept. 12, 1942; d. Paul Shirvington and Lucy White (Grasty) Ballif; m. Roger Tillison, 1964 (div. 1965); 1 child, Melle Broaderick ; m. Bruce Boston, Apr. 7, 2001. BA, U. No. Colo., 1969, MA, 1970. Art tchr. Marion County Sch. Sys., Ocala, Fla., 1973—. Author: Eonian Variations, 1995, Night Smoke, 2002, Artist of Anthithesis, 2003; illustrator: CD-ROM Extremes 2, 2001 (Bram Stoker award, 2002); illustrator Consumed, Reduced to Beautiful Gray Ashes, 2001 (Bram Stoker award, 02); illustrator: Thy Kingdom Come, 2002, illustrator, editor: Mystic Hoofbeats, 1988; editor: Poets of the Fantastic, 1992; art/poetry editor: Small Press Writers/Artists Orgn. Internat. Showcase, 1987—92. V.p. Marion Art Educators Assn., Ocala, 1987. Mem.: Horror Writers Assn. (membership chmn. 1999—), Sci. Fiction Poetry Assn. Internat. (editor Star*Line 1993—96, pres. 1996—2000, Rhysling Best Long Poem award 1995), Small Press Writers/Artists Orgn. Internat. (pres. 1988—90, Best Artist award 1991, Dale Donaldson award 1991). Home: 1412 NE 35th St Ocala FL 34479

SIMON, NORMA PLAVNICK, psychologist; b. Washington, Sept. 20, 1930; d. Mark and Mary Plavnick; m. Robert G. Simon, Dec. 18, 1949; children: Mark Allan, Susan. BA, NYU, 1952, cert. in psychoanalysis, 1977; MA, Columbia U., 1953, EdD, 1968. Diplomate Am. Bd. Profl. Psychology, 1988, Counseling Psychology, Psychoanalysis, 1997. Psychologist Queens Coll. Counseling Ctr., Flushing, N.Y., 1968-70, asst. dir., 1970-76, dir., 1976; gen. practice psychology N.Y.C., 1970—. Faculty, supr. New Hope Guild, Bklyn., 1976—, dir. child and adolescent tng. prog., 1988-98; adj. prof. clin. psychology Columbia U., N.Y.C., 1986—; supr. NYU Postdoctoral Prog. in Psychoanalysis, 1988—. Author: (with Robert G. Simon): Choosing a College Major: Social Science, 1981; co-author 3 book chpts. on licensure and ethics in psychology; mem. editl. bd. The Counseling Psychologist jour., 1986-89, Profl. Practice and Rsch. in Psychology, 1994-99, Jour. Infant, Child and Adolescent Psych Therapy, 1999—, Vice chairperson N.Y. State Bd. for Psychology State Edn. Dept., Albany, 1978-82, chairperson, 1982-88; bd. dirs. Pelham (N.Y.) Guidance Coun., 1980-83; pres.-elect Assn. State and Provincial Psychology Bds., 1990, pres., 1991. Recipient Karl Heiser award, 1993, Morton Berger award Assn. State and Provincial Psychology Bds., 1998. Fellow: APA (mem. bd. profl. affairs 1987—89, chair bd. profl. affairs 1989—90, policy and planning bd. 1991—93, mem. ethics com. 1995—98, vice chair ethics com. 1996—97, chair ethics com. 1997, workgroup on telehealth 1998—2000, mem. accreditation com. 2004—, John Black award 1994), Am. Bd. Counseling Psychology (bd. dirs. 1992—2000, pres.-elect 1999, pres. 2001—), Nat. Acads. of Practice (elected disting. practitioner), Am. Bd. Profl. Psychology (trustee 1998—2001, pres.-elect 2001—, pres. 2004—). E-mail: normasimon@aol.com.

SIMON, ROSALYN MCCORD, public relations executive; BS in special edn., MA in edn. adminstrn.; PhD, U. Md. Sr. dir. customer advocacy/communications Amtrak, Washington. Mgmt. cons. Mass Transit Adminstrn., Baltimore; exec. dir. Project Accessible Transportation In Our Nation; Md. adv. com. Individuals with Disabilities. Recipient Chester Troy award for Outstanding Pub. Svc. to Persons with Disabilities, Md. Govs. Com. Employment People with Disabilities, Transportation Special Recognition award, Fed. Dept. Transportation. Office: Amtrak 60 Massachusetts Ave NE Washington DC 20002-4285

SIMON, SANDRA RUTH WALDMAN, state agency administrator; b. N.Y.C., May 11, 1943; d. Jacob S. and Ann Waldman; m. Sanford R. Simon, Aug. 23, 1964 (div.); m. E. Jerry Lucia, Apr. 30, 1989; children: Hilary G., Taylor M., Pamela Lucia, David Lucia. BA, Barnard Coll., 1965; PhD, Rockefeller U., 1972; MSW, SUNY, Stony Brook, 1985. Postdoctoral rsch. assoc. Brookhaven (N.Y.) Nat. Lab., 1972; rsch. assoc. SUNY, Stony Brook, 1972; cons. Developed and Directed Health Edn. Programs, Islip Town, N.Y., 1977-81; coord. Suffolk County creative learning program L.I. Regional Adv. Coun. Higher Edn., 1979-80; mng. dir. Pandion Stony Brook Assocs., 1984-87; evaluation and planning specialist Tex. Dept. Human Svcs., Austin, 1987-91, supr. planning and evaluation, 1991-93, dir. policy analysis and program evaluation, 1993—. Lectr., conf. coord. Women's Health Alliance L.I., St. James, N.Y., 1975-77; cons., 1998—; field instr. U. Tex. Sch. Social Work, 1989, 2000-01. Welfare Reform Evaluation grantee, 1997—. Mem. Nat. Coun. Jewish Women. Avocations: walking, opera. Office: Tex Dept Human Svcs 701 W 51st St # MC W-340 Austin TX 78751-2312 Fax: 512-438-4675.

SIMON-BOYD, GAIL DEBORAH, psychotherapist; b. Bethpage, N.Y., July 26, 1972; d. Warren Douglas Simon and Christine Mary Adolphus; m. Aaron John Boyd, Sept. 2, 2001. BA in Psychology cum laude, Binghamton (N.Y.) U., 1994; MEd in Counseling Psychology, Rutgers U., 1996; PhD in Counseling Psychology, Pa. State U., 2002. Grad. extern counselor Livingston Coll. Counseling Svc., Piscataway, NJ, 1994—95; residence counselor Residential Experience in Adult Living, Plainview, NY, 1996—96; academic advisor, Rehab. Svcs. Program Pa. State U., University Park, Pa., 1996—98, career practicum counselor, Career Svcs., 1997—97, intake supr., Coll. Edn. Counseling Ctr., 1998—99, practicum counselor, Ctr. Counseling and Psychol. Svcs., 1997—99; psychology intern counselor Counseling Ctr. for Human Devel., U. South Fla., Tampa, Fla., 1999—2000; psychotherapist Stoney Brook Counseling Ctr., Chelmsford, Mass., 2002—. Child assoc. Primary Mental Health Project, MacArthur Elem. Sch., Binghamton, NY, 1993—94; outreach program facilitator, Minority Internship Program Pa. State U., 1997, co-instr. edn., Dept. Counselor Edn., Counseling Psychology and Rehab. Svcs., 98; outreach cons. Counseling Ctr. for Human Devel., U. South Fla., Tampa, Fla., 1999—2000. Workshop vol. Upward Bound Program, Pa. State U., University Park, Pa., 1998; guest spkr./instr. Gt. Am. Teach-In, C. Leon King Sr. HS, Fla., 1999. Mem.: APA (divsn. 17, sect. advancement of women), Mass. Psychol. Assn., Assn. for Women in Psychology, Pi Lambda Theta, Kappa Delta Pi. Avocations: travel, skiing, reading, enjoying the creative arts (music concerts, museums, theater), cooking.

SIMONDS, MARIE CELESTE, architect; b. Miami, Fla., Mar. 30, 1947; d. Hinton Joseph and Frances Olivia (Burnett) Baker; m. Albert Rhett Simonds, Jr., Oct. 9, 1974; children: Caroline Lamar, Frances Rhett. BA, U. Pa., 1968; BArch, U. Md., 1973. Registered architect, Va. Architect Harry Weese & Assocs., Washington, 1973-75; pvt. practice Alexandria, Va., 1976—. Mem. Jr. League Washington, 1978—. NSF grantee, 1972; recipient Design award No. Va. Chpt. AIA, 1990. Mem. AIA (scholar 1971, Design award No. Va. 1990), Va. Soc. AIA, Severn Sailing Assn. (Annapolis, Md.). Episcopalian. Avocations: sailboat racing, horseback riding. Home and Office: 624 S Lee St Alexandria VA 22314-3820

SIMONDS, THERESA M. TROEGNER, accountant; b. Flemington, N.J., Apr. 15, 1958; d. William and Theresa E. Troegner; m. Raymond E. Simonds, Oct. 25, 1980; children: Ben, Jason, Gregory. BS in Acctg., U. Vt., 1980; MBA in Fin., Rider Coll., 1990. CPA, N.J. Staff level I Amper, Politzine & Mattia, Flemington, 1980, sr. through to supr., 1982-88, mgr., 1988-93, ptnr., 1993—. Spkr. N.J. Bar Assn., ATLA. Contbg. author: Income Reconstruction: A Guide to Discovering Unreported Income, 1999. Bd. trustees Mid Jersey chpt. Nat. M.S. Soc., 1998—; founding mem. Carpe Diem, Flemington, 1985; mem. planned giving com. Hunterdon Med. Ctr., Flemington, 1998. Named One of 1st Ladies of Hunterdon, Flemington C. of C., 1999. Mem. Am. Inst. CPAs, Am. Soc. Appraisers, N.J. Soc. CPAs, Inst. Bus. Appraisers. Roman Catholic. Avocations: tennis, bike riding, swimming. Office: Amper Politzinger & Mattia PO Box 415 Flemington NJ 08822-0415

SIMONE, ALBERTINA, accountant; b. Briey, France, Nov. 30, 1962; came to U.S., 1994; d. Americo and Maria Antonia (Santavicca) S. B in Commerce with honors, U. Windsor, Ont., Can., 1985. Chartered acct., Can. Acct. Clarkson Gordon-Ernst & Young, Windsor, 1985-88; mgr. internal audit Allied Domecq, Windsor, 1988-90; mgr. sales svcs. Hiram Walker & Sons, Inc. (subs. of Allied Domecq), Southfield, Mich., 1990-92, asst. contr., 1992-93, contr., 1993-96, dir. fin. and adminstrn., 1996-97, v.p. comml. fin., 1998—. Office: Hiram Walker & Sons Inc 355 Riverside Ave Westport CT 06880-4810

SIMONE, GAIL ELISABETH, manufacturing executive; b. Boston, Dec. 3, 1944; d. Hugh Nelson and Louise Amelia (Shedrick) Saunders; m. Edburne R. Hare, Sept. 7, 1968 (div. 1974); m. Joseph R. Simone, June 27, 1987. BA, The King's Coll., 1966; postgrad., Harvard U., 1976-77, N.H. Coll., 1991—92. Placement dir. Boston Bar Assn., 1966-67; pub. relations Emerson Coll., Boston, 1967-69; asst. to v.p. Vance, Sanders, Inc., Boston, 1969-70; office mgr. Trans. Displays, Inc., Boston, 1970-71; seminar coordinator Assn. Trial Lawyers Am., Cambridge, Mass., 1971-74; writer, researcher Ednl. Expeditions Internat., Belmont, Mass., 1975-76; analyst United Brands Co., N.Y.C., 1976-80, Mil. Sealift Commd., USN, Washington, 1980-84, legis. affairs officer, 1984-88; rsch. analyst Bath (Maine) Iron Works Corp., 1988—. Freelance writer, editor, Boston, 1970—73. Active New Missions, Haiti, 2000—; mem. Amnesty Internat., N.Y.C., 1987—; bd. dirs. Coastal Transp.; various other orgns. Mem.: NAFE, AAUW, People for Ethical Treatment Animals. Avocations: ballet, writing, gardening. Office: Bath Iron Works 700 Washington St Stop 1 Bath ME 04530-2556

SIMONE, HEATHER ANN, management consultant; b. Hollywood, Fla., July 25, 1967; d. Paul John and Cathie Ann Simone. A in Mgmt., Clayton State Coll., 1991; B in Mgmt., Ga. Tech., 1993. Software support tech. Peachtree Software, Norcross, Ga., 1992-93; tng. specialist XcelleNet, Atlanta, 1993; LAN adminstr. J.O. Patterson & Co., Atlanta, 1993-95; Americas field program mgr. Hewlett Packard, Atlanta, 1995—98, Equifax mgr. internet consumer products, 1998—99; sr. ebusiness cons. IBM, 1999—2000, sr. bus. devel. mgr., 2000—. Vol. Nat. Wildlife Fedn., 1992-93; Olympic vol., 1996. Mem. Am. Mktg. Assn. Republican. Lutheran. Avocations: 5k racing, flower arranging/crafts, interior decorating, gardening.

SIMONE, SHARON ELIZABETH, education educator, filmmaker, writer; b. Teaneck, N.J., Aug. 17, 1944; d. Edward James Rodgers and Dorothy Irene Von Ruden; m. Patrick Joseph Simone, June 12, 1967; children: Patrick Edward, Dorothy Ann, Timothy Francis, Molly Eileen, Mark Joseph, Mary Sharon. BS, Marygrove Coll., 1967; EdM, Harvard U., 1985, postgrad., 1986—93. Cert. sci. tchr. gradesK-12 Dept. Edn., 1978. Chemist Henry Ford Hosp., Detroit, 1966—68; med. technologist Ctrl. Vt. Hosp., Berlin, 1977—82; faculty Vt. C.C., Barre, 1979—83, Vt. Tech. Coll., Randolph, 1982—83; asst. prof. Lesley Grad. Sch., Cambridge, Mass., 1985—88; tchg. fellow Harvard Grad. Sch. Edn., Cambridge, Mass., 1986—92; activist child abuse prevention Boston, 1990—; pres./founder The Hunter Inst., Jamaica Plain, Mass., 1998—2001; pres. Headwaters Prodns., Redlands, Calif., 2002—. Dir. weekend learning cmty. Lesley Grad. Sch., Cambridge, 1987—88; cons. violence prevention, Boston, 1990—; nat./internat. pub. spkr. on generational transmission of violence, Boston, 1990—. Quilt (domestic violence escape), The House of Women exhibited De Cordova Museum Lincoln, Massachusetts;, author poetry. Initiator and won passage of the child abuse accountability act. Congresswoman Pat Schroeder sponsored legislation at my request, Washington,

1994—94; features guest Profiles of Hope TV Program, Kingston, Jamaica, 1998—98; subject of documentary segment: incest: a crime never forgotten 20/20 ABC News, Ny, NY, 1991—91; subject of cbs tv film ultimate betrayal CBS TV, Hollywood, Calif., 1994—94; spokeswoman Dan Rather Live: Town Hall Meeting: Children and Violence, Phoenix, Ariz., 1998—98. Recipient Rose Fund Recognition award for leadership and commitment to ending violence against women and children., The Rose Fund, 1995, Leadership award, Atty. Gen. Commonwealth Mass., 1997. Democrat. Achievements include first to Won prescendent-setting case against father for child abuse (1990) in Denver District Court. Opened doors legally for women to sue perpetrators of abuse occurring decades earlier; Worked with Congresswoman Pat Schroeder to write and win passage of The Child Abuse Accountability Act 1994. Now federal pensions can be garnished for child abuse judgments. Avocations: photography, travel. Office: Headwaters Productions 1010 College Ave Redlands CA 92374 Office Fax: 909-335-9225. Personal E-mail: sharon@headwatersproductions.com. E-mail: sharon@headwatersproductions.com.

SIMONEAU, CYNTHIA LAMBERT, newspaper editor, journalism educator; b. Central Falls, R.I., May 18, 1958; d. Roland and L. Jean Simoneau; m. Paul E. Lambert, Oct. 24, 1981; children: Thomas S. Lambert, Marc S. Lambert. BA, U. R.I., 1980. Asst. news editor Newtown (Conn.) Bee, 1980-82; reporter Bridgeport (Conn.) Post & Telegram, 1982-83, bur. chief, 1983-91; editor Woman Wise Conn. Post, Bridgeport, 1991-97, asst. mng. editor, 1997—. Adj. prof. So. Conn. State U., New Haven, 1993—, Fairfield (Conn.) 2003—, Sacred Heart U., Fairfield, Conn., 2004. Eucharistic min., mem. parish adv. coun., former religious edn. tchr., St. Thomas Aquinas Ch., Fairfield, Conn. Mem. Soc. Profl. Journalists (bd. dirs. Conn. chpt. 1983-2003, treas. Conn. chpt. 1985-95, 2003—, pres. Conn. chpt. 1995-97, Journalism Excellence awards for news stories and columns, 2 Pres.'s award Conn. chpt., Women of Dist. award girl Scout Coun.). Avocation: reading. Office: Conn Post 410 State St Bridgeport CT 06604 E-mail: csimoneau@ctpost.com.

SIMON-GILLO, JEHANNE E. physicist, science administrator; b. Liege, Belgium, Mar. 27, 1963; came to U.S., 1967; d. Nicolas Victor and Noelle Marie (Van Den Peereboom) Simon; m. Andrew James Gillo, June 9, 1990; children: Nicole Cecelia, Joshua Andrew Gillo. BS, Juniata Coll., 1985; PhD, Tex. A&M U., 1991. Postdoctoral work Los Alamos (N.Mex.) Nat. Lab., 1991-94, staff mem., physicist, 1994-1999; nat. program mgr. facilities and instrumentation in nuclear physics U.S. Dept. Energy, Germantown, Md., 2000—; nat. program mgr. facilitation and instrumentation Dept. Energy, Germantown, Md. Project mgr PHENIX Multiplicity Vertex Detector; adj. asst. prof. U. N.Mex. Mem. Am. Chem. Soc., Am. Phys. Soc. Republican. Roman Catholic. Achievements include work on E814, NA44, PHENIX experiments; exptl. physicist studying relativistic heavy-ion collisions, specifically low PT phenomena and deuteron formation; subsystem mgr. and detector coun. mem. for PHENIX multiplicity vertex detector. Office: Dept Energy Office of Science 1000 Independence Ave Washington DC 20585-1290

SIMONS, AUDREY KAY, music educator; b. Allentown, Pa., Feb. 9, 1967; d. Edward Wilson and Claire Christine Buss; m. Anthony Russell Simons; 1 child, Luke Edward. MusM, Temple U., Philadelphia, Pa., 1989—92; MusB, Susquehanna U., Selinsgrove, Pa., 1985—89. Cello & piano Instr. Susquehanna U. Cmity Music Program, Selinsgrove, Pa., 1986—89; instr. music history Temple U. Tchg. Assistantship, Philadelphia, Pa., 1989—91, Montgomery County Cmty. Coll., Blue Bell, Pa., 1993—98; artist/lectr. Moravian Coll., Bethlehem, Pa., 1993—; asst. music dir. Pocono Youth Orchestra, Stroudsburg, Pa., 1993—. Cellist Allentown Symphony Orchestra, Allentown, 1992—, Classical Attitude String Quartet, Bethlehem, 1993—, Chestnut Hill Chamber Players, Center Valley, 2003—. Recipient Presser Found. music scholarship, Susquehanna U., 1988, Elizabeth G. Eyster award music, 1987, music scholarship, 1985—89; scholar dean's list, 1985—89. Mem.: Internet Cello Soc., Violoncello Soc., Music Tchrs. Nat. Assn., Am. String Tchrs. Assn., Sigma Alpha Iota. Home: 4955 Chestnut Hill Rd Center Valley PA 18034 Office: Moravian Coll 1200 Main St Bethlehem PA 18018

SIMONS, CAROL LENORE, magazine editor; b. Bklyn., Feb. 2, 1942; d. Paul and Grace (Rotwein) Seiderman; m. Lewis M. Simons, Feb. 7, 1965; children: Justine, Rebecca, Adam. BA, Tufts U., 1963; MS, Columbia U., 1964. Rschr. Newsweek mag., N.Y.C., 1964-65, CBS News, N.Y.C. and Saigon, Vietnam, 1967-68; reporter Denver Post, 1965-67; editor Pres. Commn. on Marijuana and Drug Abuse, Washington, 1971-72; assoc. editor Smithsonian mag., Washington, 1978-82; dir. publs. Am. C. of C. in Japan, Tokyo, 1991-96; exec. editor AARP The Mag., Washington, 2003—. Office: AARP The Magazine 601 E St NW Washington DC 20049-0001

SIMONS, ELIZABETH R(EIMAN), biochemist, educator; b. Vienna, Sept. 1, 1929; came to U.S., 1941, naturalized, 1948; d. William and Erna Engle (Weisselberg) Reiman; m. Harold Lee Simons, Aug. 12, 1951; children: Leslie Ann Mulert, Robert David. BChemE, Cooper Union, N.Y.C., 1950; MS, Yale U., 1951, PhD, 1954. Rsch. chemist Tech. Ops., Arlington, Mass., 1953-54; instr. chemistry Wellesley (Mass.) Coll., 1954-57; rsch. asst. children's Hosp. Med. Ctr. and Cancer Rsch. Found., Boston, 1957-59, rsch. assoc. pathology, 1959-62; rsch. assoc. Harvard Med. Sch., 1962-66, lectr. biol. chemistry, 1966-72; tutor biochem. scis. Harvard Coll., 1971-94; assoc. prof. biochemistry Boston (Mass.) U., 1972-78, prof., 1978—, asst. dir. Office Med. Edn., 2000—. Contbr. articles to profl. jours. Grantee in field. Mem.: AAAS, Soc. for Neurosci., Biophys. Soc., Am. Soc. Hematology, Am. Soc. Cell Biology, Am. Soc. Biol. Chemists, Am. Chem. Soc. Office: Boston U Sch Medicine 80 E Concord St Roxbury MA 02118-2307 Office Phone: 617-638-4332. E-mail: esimons@bu.edu.

SIMONS, GAIL S. artist, educator, librarian; b. Elgin, Ill., Aug. 13, 1963; d. James Philip and Vivian Faith (Ewalt) S. Cert. Christian edn., Lincoln Christian Coll., 1986; BFA, Judson Coll., 1991. Tchg. asst. Pub. Sch. Dist. 300, Dundee, Ill., 1986-89; illustrator computer clip art Media Mktg. Svcs., St. Charles, Ill., 1989; computer data plant ops. Judson Coll., Elgin, Ill., 1990-91, watercolor painting instr., 1991—; libr. Dundee Twp. Pub. Libr., East Dundee, Ill., 1994—, staff artist, 1997—. Youth/adult choral dir. First Congl. Ch., Carpentersville, Ill., 1986-96; stop motion animator, Chgo., 1991. Exhibited works at Ruth M. Wendt Gallery, East Dundee, 1997-99, Agora Gallery, N.Y.C., 1999—, Incognito Gallery, Fox Lake, Ill., 2001, art-exchange.com, 2003; actress, asst. dir., set/prop designer various musicals and plays. Deaconess/Sunday sch. dir. Congl. Ch., Carpentersville, 1986-96; watercolor/craft tchr. Pub. Libr, East Dundee, 1997—; wildlife adv.; youth leader. Mem. Christians in the Visual Arts, N.W. Area Arts Coun., Dundee Twp. Fine Arts Coun., Alpha Chi Soc. Avocations: collecting, gardening, writing, entomology, old movies. Office: Dundee Twp Pub Libr Dist 555 Barrington Ave East Dundee IL 60118-1422

SIMONS, LYNN OSBORN, educational consultant; b. Havre, Mont., June 1, 1934; d. Robert Blair and Dorothy (Briggs) Osborn; m. John Powell Simons, Jan. 19, 1957; children: Clayton Osborn, William Blair. Tchr. Midvale (Utah) Jr. H.S., 1956-57, Sweetwater county Sch. Dist. 1, Rock Springs, Wyo., 1957-58, U. Wyo., 1959-61, Natrona County Sch. Dist. 1, Casper, Wyo., 1963-64; credit mgr. Gallery 323, Casper, 1972-77; Wyo. state supt. pub. instrn. Cheyenne, 1979-91; sec.'s regional rep. region VIII U.S. Dept. Edn., Denver, 1993—2001; mem. Denver Fed. Exec. Bd., 1995-2001; mem. exec. bd. combined Fed. campaign, 1994—2001; ednl. cons., 2001—03; state planning coord. Capitol Bldg., Cheyenne, Wyo., 2003—. Mem. State Bds. Charities and Reform, Land Commrs., Farm Loan, 1979-91; mem. State Commns. Capitol Bldg., Liquor, 1979-91; Ex-officio mem. bd. trustees U. Wyo., 1979-91; ex-officio mem. Wyo. Community Coll. Commn., 1979-91; mem. steering com. Edn. Commn. of the States, 1988-90, 2003; mem. State Bd. Edn., 1971-77, chmn., 1976-77; advisor Nat. Trust for Hist. Preservation, 1980-86. Mem. LWV (pres. 1970-71). Democrat. Episcopalian. Office: Capitol Building Cheyenne WY 82003 E-mail: isimon@state.wy.us.

SIMONS, NANCY, naturopathic physician, hypnotherapist; b. Phila., June 7, 1947; d. Michael Gerard Kalman and Irene Ann Ivaska; m. James Pickering Simons, Nov. 4, 1967 (dec. Feb. 24, 1982); children: James Michael, Matthew Alexander. BA, Neumann Coll., Pa., 1978; MA, West Chester U., Pa., 1981; PhD, Walden U., Mpls., 1995; Naturopathic Dr., Clayton Coll., Birmingham, Ala., 1997. Diplomate Am. Coll. Forensic Medicine, cert. Am. Naturopathic Med. Assn.; Ericksonian Hypontherapist, Hypnobirthing Practitioner. Naturopath Main Line Health, Phila., 1995—97; naturopath, hypnotherapist Riddle Healthcare Assn., Media, Pa., 1997—. Bd. drug and alcohol awareness Pa. State U. Mem.: Am. Psychol. Assn., Del. County Press Club (founding mem., bd. mem. 1977—81). Avocations: gardening, needlecrafts, crossword puzzles, kayaking, collecting cat whiskers. Home: 1673 Valley Rd Newtown Square PA 19073 Office: Westtown Med Ctr 1601 McDaniel Dr West Chester PA 19380 E-mail: Ai9000@aol.com.

SIMONS, SHEILA R. healthcare educator; d. Ronald P. and N. Jean Simons; m. L. M. Berra, July 17, 2002. BS, Ea. Ill. U., 1991, MS, 1992; PhD, So. Ill. U., 2002. Instr. Ea. Ill. U., Charleston, 1992—2002, asst. prof., 2002—. Cons. Prevention Resource Ctr., Springfield, Ill., 1994—97. Fire fighter Lincoln Fire Protection Dist., Charleston, 1997—2002; vol. Emergency Svcs. & Disaster Agy., Coles County, Ill., 1997—. Mem.: Ill. Assn. Pub. Health (com. chair 2003—), Am. Allinace Health, Phys. Edn., Recreation & Dance, Am. Sch. Health Assn. Avocation: gardening.

SIMONSON, DONNA JEANNE, accountant; b. Malden, Mass., Sept. 6, 1947; d. George Francis and Dorothy Josephine (Bridges) Yost; m. Scott N. Simonson, June 30, 1967 (div. Feb. 1989); children: Stephanie Louise Burke, Kelly Lynn Pratt. AA Bus. Adminstrn., Corning Community Coll., 1979; BS in Mgmt., Keuka Coll., 1981. Bus. office supr. Steuben Allegany B.O.C.E.S., Bath, N.Y., 1969-75; staff acct. David L. Snyderwine & Co. CPA's, Bath, 1979-82; fin. dir. Steuben Assoc. for Retarded Children, Inc., Bath, 1982-98; owner Donna J. Simonson, Taxes, & Acctg., Bath, 1982--. Pres. Pulteney Vol. Firemen's Auxiliary, 1973. Mem. Am. Assn. Univ. Women, Bath Area Humane Soc., Pulteney Free Library Assn., Fiscal Mgrs. Assn. Democrat. Presbyterian. Home and Office: 1 Ellis Ave Bath NY 14810-1107

SIMPERS, MARY PALMER, state legislator; b. East Middlebury, Vt., Mar. 17, 1934; m. Harold J. Simpers Sr.; 2 children. BS, U. Vt., 1957. Mem. edn. com. Vt. Ho. of Reps., 1983-84, mem. health and welfare com., 1985-86, mem. mcpl. corp. com., 1987-88, mem. instnl. com., 1989-92, 95-98, mem., 1983-92, 95—; co-owner Poeseidon Breathing Air System, Colchester. Bd. dirs. Vt. Retail Assoc. Ins. Co-author: Looking Around Colchester and Milton. Mem. Colchester Civil Bd. of Authority and J.P., 1970—; mem. Colchester Sch. Bd., 1978-85; bd. dirs. Lake Champlain Access TV. Mem. Zonta Club of Burlington (past pres.), Vt. Hist. Soc., Colchester & Chittenden County Hist. Soc.

SIMPSON, AGNES MONIKA, financial advisor; b. Vienna, Nov. 30, 1956; came to U.S., 1957; d. Jozsef and Katalin (Havasi) Toth; m. Michael E. Simpson, Nov. 29, 1986; 1 child, Kathryn. BS in Indsl. Econs., Union Coll., 1977, MBA, 1982. CFP. Oil and gas analyst The Ayco Co., LP, Albany, N.Y., 1980-83; pres. Rexco Energy Securities, Shreveport, La., 1984-87, v.p. mktg., 1983-87; dir. mktg. The Ayco Co., LP, Albany, 1987-88, dir. oil and gas adv. svc., 1988-92, assoc. account mgr., 1992-94, account mgr., ptnr., 1995—. Trustee Albany Acad. for Girls, 1992-95. Recipient Disting. Alumna award Albany Acad. for Girls, 1995. Mem. Albany Acad. for Girls Alumnae Assn. (treas. 1987-95). Avocations: reading, cooking. Office: The Ayco Co LP 2839 Paces Ferry Rd SE Ste 210 Atlanta GA 30339-5769

SIMPSON, ALLYSON BILICH, lawyer; b. Pasadena, Calif., Feb. 5, 1951; d. John Joseph and Barbaran Rita (Bessolo) Bilich; m. Roland Gilbert Simpson, Aug. 11, 1979; children: Megan Elise, Erin Marie, Brian Patrick. BS, U. So. Calif., L.A., 1973, JD, 1976. Bar: Calif. 1976. Staff atty. Gen. Telephone Co., Thousand Oaks, Calif., 1978-79; group staff atty., dir. legis. compliance Pacific Mut. Life Ins. Co., Newport Beach, Calif., 1980-86; corp. counsel and sec. Amicare Ins. Co., Beverly Hills, Calif., 1986; assoc. Leboeuf, Lamb, Leiby & MacRae, L.A., 1986-87; from assoc. to ptnr. Musick, Peeler & Garrett, L.A., 1988-94; ptnr. Sonnenschein Nath & Rosenthal, L.A., 1994-95; sr. v.p., sec., gen. counsel Fremont Compensation Ins. Group, Glendale, Calif., 1995—. Vis. pro. bus. law U. So. Calif., L.A., 1981. Trustee St. Anne's Maternity Home Found., L.A., 1991-97; bd. dirs. St. Anne's Maternity Home, L.A., 1993-97. Mem. Western Pension and Benefits Conf., Conf. Ins. Counsel, Am. Corp. Counsel Assn. Republican. Roman Catholic. Avocations: music, reading, family. Office: Fremont Compensation Ins Group 500 N Brand Blvd Ste 1100 Glendale CA 91203-3392

SIMPSON, ANDREA LYNN, communications executive; b. Altadena, Calif., Feb. 10, 1948; d. Kenneth and Barbara Simpson; 1 child, Christopher Ryan Myrdal. BA, U. So. Calif., 1969, MS, 1983; postgrad., U. Colo., Boulder Sch. Bank Mktg., 1977. Mktg. officer United Calif. Bank, L.A., 1969-73; asst. v.p. mktg. 1st Hawaiian Bank, Honolulu, 1973-78; v.p. corp. comms. Pacific Resources Inc., Honolulu, 1978-89, BHP Hawaii, Inc., 1989-98; v.p. corp. rels. Tesoro Petroleum Corp., San Antonio, 1998-2000; v.p. corp. comms. Edison Internat., Rosemead, Calif., 2000—01; pres. Simpson Comm., 2001—. Bd. dirs. Arts Coun., Hawaii, 1977-81, Hawaii Heart Assn., 1978-83, Coun. Pacific Girls Scouts USA, 1982-85, Child and Family Svcs., 1984-86, Honolulu Symphony Soc., 1985-91, Sta. KHPR Hawaii Pub. Radio, 1988-92, Kapiolani Found., 1990-95, Hanahauoli Sch., 1991-98, Hawaii Strategic Devel. Corp., 1991-98, Children's Discovery Ctr., 1994-98, Pacific Asian Affairs Coun., 1994-96, adv. dir. Hawaii Kids at Work, 1991-98, Hawaii MADD, 1992-96; bd. dirs., 2d v.p. Girl Scout Coun. Hawaii, 1994-96, mem. adv. bd., 1996-98; trustee Hawaii Loa Coll., 1984-86, Kapiolani Women's and Children's Hosp., 1988-97, Hawaii Sch. for Girls at LaPietra, 1989-91, Kapiolani Med. Ctr. at Pali Momi, 1994-98; bd. dirs. Aloha coun. Boy Scouts Am., 1998-2000, Alamo coun., Hawaii Pub. TV, 1998, bd. dirs., San Pedro Playhouse, 1999-2000; bd. dirs. Red Cross of San Antonio, 1999-2000; commr. Hawaii State Commn. on Status of Women, 1985-87, State Sesquecentennial of Pub. Schs. Commn., 1990-91. Named Advt. Woman of Yr., Honolulu Advt. Fedn., 1982, Pub. Rels. Profl. of Yr., Honolulu Pub. Rels. Soc., 1993, Communicator of Yr., Utilities Communicators Internat., 1983; recipient Silver Anvil award Pub. Rels. Soc. Am., 1983, 97. Mem. Internat. Pub. Rels. Assn. (Golden World award 1997), Am. Mktg. Assn., Pub. Rels. Soc. Am. (bd. dirs. Honolulu chpt. 1984-86, Silver Anvil award 1984, Pub. Rels. Profl. Yr. 1991), U. So. Calif. Alumni Assn. (bd. dirs. Hawaii 1981-83), Outrigger Canoe Club, Pacific Club, Rotary (pub. rels. chmn. 1988-97, Honolulu chpt., bd. dirs. 1998), Rotary Club of San Antonio, Alpha Phi (past pres., dir. Hawaii), Hawaii Jaycees (Outstanding Young Person of Hawaii 1978).

SIMPSON, BERYL BRINTNALL, botany educator; b. Dallas, Apr. 28, 1942; d. Edward Everett and Barbara Frances (Brintnall) S.; children: Jonathan, Meghan. AB, Radcliffe Coll., 1964; MA, PhD, Harvard U., 1968. Rsch. fellow Arnold Arboretum/Gray Herbarium, Cambridge, Mass., 1969-71; curator Smithsonian Instn., Washington, 1971-78; prof. U. Tex., Austin, 1978—. Chmn. U.S. Com. to IUBS, 1985-88; co-pres. Internat. Congress Systematic and Evolutionary Biology, 1980-85. Author: Economic Botany, 1994; editor: Mesquite, 1977; contbr. over 100 articles and notes to profl. jours. Recipient Greenman award Mo. Bot. Garden, 1970. Fellow AAAS, Am. Acad. Arts and Sci.; mem. Soc. for Study Evolution (coun. 1975-80, pres. 1985-86), Bot. Soc. Am. (pres. 1990-91, Merit award 1992), Bot. Soc. Washington (v.p. 1975), Am. Soc. Plant Taxonomists (pres. 1994, Cooley award), Am. Inst. Biol. Scis. (bd. dirs. 1993-95), U.S.-Mex. Found. for Sci. (bd. govs.), Soc. Econ. Botany (pres. 1999). Office: U Tex Sect Integrative Biology Austin TX 78713

SIMPSON, CAROL, elementary school educator; b. Galesburg, Ill., Nov. 7, 1945; d. William Lawrence Bailey and Ruby Elaine Peterson; m. Robert Carter Simpson, Aug. 28, 1965; 1 child, Bradley William. BS in Elem. Edn., Western Ill. U., 1971, MS in Edn. Adminstrn., 1974. Tchr. 1st grade Cooke Sch., Galesburg, 1971-75, Silas Willard Sch., Galesburg, 1975-76, 79-82, tchr. 2d grade, 1976-79; tchr. 1st grade Gale Sch., Galesburg, 1982-94; tchr. Title 1 reading Steele Accelerated Sch., Galesburg, 1994—. Spkr. in field. Author: Daily Journals, 1993, Daily Poetry, 1995, Daily Guided Writing, 1998, Daily Writing Prompts, 1999. Sec., precinct committeeman Knox County (Ill.) Rep. Ctrl. Com., 1998—; bd. Knox County, 2000—. Mem. Australian Literacy Educators Assn., Ill. Title 1 Assn. (sec. 1997-2000), Western Ill. Reading Coun. (pres. 1997-98), Internat. Reading Assn., Alpha Delta Kappa (newsletter editor 1998-2003). Republican. Avocations: travel, writing poetry and childrens stories. Office: 1480 W Main St Galesburg IL 61401-3318

SIMPSON, CAROL LOUISE, investment company executive; b. Phila., Jan. 30, 1937; d. William Huffington and Hilda Agnes (Johnston) S. Student, Community Coll., 1985, 86, 87, U. Minn., 1986, 87, 88. Cert. Nat. Assn. Securities Dealers, Inc., Washington; registered options, mcpl. securities, gen. securities, fin. and ops. prin.; lic. life, accident, health ins. Exec. asst. Germantown Fed. Savs., Phila., 1954-67; asst. sec. Am. Med. Investment Co., Inc. (formerly Cannon and Co., Inc.), Blue Bell, Pa., 1967-91; also bd. dirs. Cannon & Co., Inc., 1986; v.p., sec. AMA Investment Advisers, Inc. (formerly Pro Svcs., Inc.), Blue Bell, Pa., 1967-91; also bd. dirs. AMA Investment Advisers, Inc. (formerly PRO Svcs., Inc.), Blue Bell, Pa., 1984-86; fin. svcs. compliance cons., 1991; exec. v.p., sec. Rutherford Fin. Corp., Phila., 1991-2000, Rutherford, Brown & Catherwood Inc., Phila., 1991-2000, Walnut Asset Mgmt. Inc., Phila., 1991-98. Mem. Investment Co. Inst. (fed. legis. com. 1984-91, investment advisers com. 1988-2000, compliance com. 1990-2000), VNA Cmty. Svcs. Found. (bd. dirs. 1995-2001), Vis. Nurse Assn. Cmty. Svcs. (bd. dirs. 1997-2000), Whitemarsh Valley Country Club. Republican. Home: 7701 Lawnton St Philadelphia PA 19128-3105

SIMPSON, DEBRA BRASHEAR, artist; b. Tulsa, Dec. 4, 1938; d. Chapman Claude Brashear and Ruby Maxine (Muck Brashear) Speed; m. Robert Thomas Oedamer, Aug. 27, 1957 (div. May 1969); 1 child, Demetra Suzanne Oedamer Haymes ; m. John Garlington III Simpson, Aug. 9, 1976; 1 child, Zachary Claude Taliaferro. Student, U. Ala., 1961—77, Broward C.C., Melboourne, Fla., 1970—71, Tyler Sch. Fine Art, Phila., Temple U., Art Students League, N.Y.C., 1998. Writer/editor Chrysler Corp., Huntsville, Ala., 1958—61, NASA, Huntsville, Ala., 1961—62, personal sec., 1962—67; adminstrv. asst. Life Support, Melbourne, Fla., 1970—71; sec., editor U.S. Army, Huntsville, 1972—78; fashion designer Betty Grisham Inc., Huntsville, 1981—83. Art instr. Huntsville Mus. Art, 1995—97; art instr., color cons. Simpson Assocs., Huntsville, 1997—; dir. adv. bd. Monte Sano Art Assn., Huntsville, 1999—; pvt. tchr. art. Exhibitions include Huntsville Art League and Mus. Assn., 1973—76, Birmingham Art Guild Exhbn., 1979, Birmingham Bot. Gardens, 1980, Woodlawn Plantation Show, Washington, 1982 (award), Decatur Art Guild, 1985, Huntsville Mus. of Art Partnership Gallery, 1985—86, Panoply of the Arts, Huntsville, 1985—89 (merit, purchase and monetary awards), Huntsville Mus. Art, 1986 (award), Acad. of Arts and Acad., Huntsville, 1990, Marilyn Wilson Gallery, Birmingham, 1990, Connie Ulrich Gallery, Huntsville, 1991, Salon France-America, Paris, 1991 (Kabeltechnik Dietz award for portraiture), Oklahoma City, 1991, Huntsville Art League, 1995, one-woman shows include Kennedy Douglas Ctr., Florence, Ala., 1996, 1998, exhibitions include Tenn. Valley Art Ctr., 1998, Cornell Grisham Art Gallery, Decatur, 1998, numerous other shows. Fellow mem. Monte Sano Civic Assn., Huntsville, 1979—. Fellow: Internat. Assn. Exptl. Artists; mem.: Am. Soc. Portrait Artists. Avocations: hiking, gardening, swimming, jewelry designing. Home: 3415 Highland Plz SE Huntsville AL 35801

SIMPSON, DIANE JEANNETTE, school social worker, counselor, adoption home study worker; b. Denver, Sept. 20, 1952; d. Arthur Henry and Irma Virginia (Jordan) S.; 1 child, Shantē N. BS, Nebr. Wesleyan U., 1974; MSW, U. Denver, 1977. Asst. Mile Hi coun. Girl Scouts U.S.A., Denver, 1971-77; social worker asst. Denver Pub. Schs., 1974-75, social worker, 1977—. Field instr. Grad. Sch. Social Work, U. Denver, 1984-2000. Tour leader Kenyan Safari to Kenya, East Africa, 1988. V.p. United Meth. Women, Christ United Meth. Ch., Denver, 1989-91; chmn. Christian action com., 1985-88, active Girl Scouts U.S.A., 1959—; mem. collaborative decision making com. Denver Pub. Schs., 1993-95; Denver Pub. Schs. rep. to Denver Child Fatality Rev. Bd., 1998—; mem. Shorter A.M.E. Ch., sr. usher bd. and edn. and scholarship com., 1996—. Mem. NASW, A.M.E. Ch. Breast Cancer Support/Awareness Ministry. Democrat. Avocations: reading, health and fitness, travel, genealogy. Home: 6865 E Arizona Ave # D Denver CO 80224-1829 Office: Denver Pub Schs 900 Grant St Denver CO 80203-2907 E-mail: d_32191@msn.com.

SIMPSON, DOROTHY AUDREY, retired speech educator; b. Las Vegas, N.Mex., Feb. 29, 1944; d. Clyde Joseph and Audrey Shirley (Clements) Simpson; m. Gary Alan Beimer, May 13, 1972 (div. Apr. 1986); children: Laura Lea Beimer Nelson, Rose Anne Colleen Beimer; m. Ian B. Croxton, Dec. 27, 1992 (div. Oct. 1993); m. Doyle W. Hauschulz, Feb. 23, 2001 (div. June 2003). BA, N.Mex. Highlands U., 1965; MS, U. Utah, 1968; EdD, U. N.Mex., 1989. Cert. secondary edn., N.Mex. Tchr. West Las Vegas (N.Mex.) H.S., 1966-67, Santa Rosa (N.Mex.) H.S., 1968-71, Questa (N.Mex.) Consol. Schs., 1972-73; prof. speech comm., assoc. dean coll. arts and scis. N.Mex. Highlands U., Las Vegas, 1975—2003, prof. emeritus, 2003—. Ednl. cons. Rancho Valmora, 2003—. Author: Hovels, Haciendas, and House Calls: The Life of Carl H. Gellenthien, M.D., 1986, Speaking for Life: A Speech Communication Guide for Adults, 1990, Wreck of the Destiny Train, 1993; From Pajarito to Lun gchow, 2003. Active Calvary Bapt. Ch., Las Vegas, 1959—. Recipient Educator of Yr. award Pub. Svc. Co. of N.Mex., Albuquerque, 1990. Mem. P.E.O. Republican. Avocation: writing. Home: PO Box 778 Las Vegas NM 87701-0778

SIMPSON, ELIZABETH, archaeologist, educator; b. San Francisco, June 16, 1947; d. William Tracy Simpson and Ann Bruck. Student, Smith Coll., 1965—68; BA in Math., U. Oreg., 1969, MA in Art History, 1973; PhD in Classical Archaeology, U. Pa., 1985. Rsch. assoc. U. Pa. Mus. Archaeology and Anthropology, Phila., 1983—; assoc. prof. Bard Grad. Ctr., N.Y.C., 1993—. Asst. curator Met. Mus. Art, N.Y.C., 1986—89, rsch. assoc., 1989—90; vis. prof. Sarah Lawrence Coll., Bronxville, NY, 1990—92, Duke U., Durham, NC, 1992—93; dir. Gordion Furniture Project U. Pa. Mus., Phila. and Ankara, Turkey, 1983—; pres. Cultural Property Rsch. Found., 1998—; mem. adv. panel Presdl. Adv. Commn. on Holocaust and Assets in the U.S., 1999—2001. Author: Gordion Wooden Furniture, 1999; editor: The Spoils of War, 1997. Chmn. Project for the Documentation of Wartime Cultural Losses, 1998—. Recipient Spl. award, Ministry Culture, Turkey, 1998; grantee, Nat. Endowment for the Humanities, Samuel H. Kress Found., Nat. Geog. Soc., CASVA, Nat. Gallery, Am. Coun. Learned Socs., Getty Grant Program, Brit. Acad. Mem.: Brit. Inst. Archaeology, Am. Rsch. Inst. in Turkey, Archaeol. Inst. Am. (mem. profl. responsibilities com. 2000—, mem. cultural properties legis. and policy com. 1999—). Achievements include conservation and reconstruction of the wooden furniture and small objects excavated at the site of Gordion, Turkey. Avocation: archaeological illustration. Office: The Bard Grad Ctr 18 W 86th St New York NY 10024

SIMPSON, INDIA.ARIE, musician; b. Denver, Oct. 3, 1976; d. Ralph and Joyce Simpson, Gary Harris (Stepfather). Student, Savannah Coll. Art and Design. With Motown Records, 1999—. Musician: (recordings) Acoustic Soul, 1999 (Cert. Gold), (songs) Peaceful World (with John Mellencamp), Just Another Parade, Just Another Parade (with Cassandra Wilson), Good Man for film We Were Soldiers, (tour) Women in Hip-Hop and Soul, 2001, (recordings) Voyage to India (Gest R&B Album Grammy, 03); contbg. musician (compilation) Conceptions: Musical Tribute to Stevie Wonder, 2003. Nominee 7 Grammy awards, 2002; named Best New Artist, Vibe Mag., 2001, MTV2, 2001, Billboard Video Awards, 2001, Best R&B Female Artist, BET, 2002, Best Female R&B Artist, 2003; named one of Top 100 It Entertainers, Entertainment Weekly mag., 2001; recipient Essence award, 2002, Best Urban/Alternative Performance for Little Things, Grammy Awards, 2003. Office: Universal Music Enterprises Motown Records 2220 Colorado Ave Santa Monica CA 90404*

SIMPSON, JENNIFER A. director; BA in Psychology, Boston Coll., 1998. Asst. dir. of admissions Boston U., Boston, 1998—.

SIMPSON, JESSICA ANN, vocalist; b. Dallas, July 10, 1980; d. Joe and Tina Simpson; m. Nick Lachey, Oct. 26, 2002. Singer: (albums) Sweet Kisses, 1999, Irresistable, 2001, In This Skin, 2003; actor: (TV series) That '70s Show, 2003, Newlyweds: Nick and Jessica, 2003—; co-author: I Do: Achieving Your Dream Wedding, 2003; host : Saturday Night Live, 2004. Office: Top 40 Entertainment 156 West 56th St 5th Floor New York NY 10019*

SIMPSON, JOANNE MALKUS, meteorologist; b. Boston, Mar. 23, 1923; d. Russell and Virginia (Vaughan) Gerould; m. Robert H. Simpson, Jan. 6, 1965; children by previous marriage: David Starr Malkus, Steven Willem Malkus, Karen Elizabeth Malkus. BS, U. Chgo., 1943, MS, 1945, PhD, 1949; DSc (hon.), SUNY, Albany, 1991. Instr. physics and meteorology Ill. Inst. Tech., 1946-49, asst. prof., 1949-51; meteorologist Woods Hole Oceanographic Instn., 1951-61; prof. meteorology UCLA, 1961-65; dir. exptl. meteorology lab. NOAA, Dept. Commerce, Washington, 1965-74; prof. environ. scis. U. Va., Charlottesville, 1974-76, W.W. Corcoran prof. environ. scis., 1976-81; head Severe Storms br. Goddard Lab. Atmospheres, NASA, Greenbelt, Md., 1981-88, chief scientist for meteorology, 1988—; Goddard sr. fellow, earth scis. dir. Goddard Space Flight Ctr., NASA, 1988—; project scientist tropical rainfall measuring mission, 1986-98. Mem. Bd. on Atmospheric Scis. and Climate, NRC/NAS, 1990-93, 97-2000, Bd. on Geophys. and Environ. Data, 1993-96, com. on climate, ecosystems, infectious diseases and human health, 1998-2000; mem. sr. adv. bd. NOAA, 1998-2003. Author: (with Herbert Riehl) Cloud Structure and Distributions Over the Tropical Pacific Ocean; assoc. editor: Revs. Geophysics and Space Physics, 1964-72, 75-77; contbr. articles to profl. jours. Mem. Fla. Gov.'s Environ. Coordinating Coun., 1971-74. Recipient Disting. Authorship award NOAA, 1969, Silver medal Dept. Commerce, 1967, Gold medal, 1972, Vincent J. Schaefer award Weather Modification Assn., 1979, Cmty. Headliner award Women in Comm., 1973, Profl. Achievement award U. Chgo. Alumni Assn., 1975, 92, Lifetime Achievement award Women in Sci. Engring., 1990, Exceptional Sci. Achievement award NASA, 1982, William Nordberg award NASA, 1994, NASA Medal Outstanding Leadership, 1998, I.M.O. prize World Meteorol. Orgn., 2002; named Woman of Yr. L.A. Times, 1963; Guggenheim fellow, 1954-55, Goddard Sr. fellow, 1988—. Fellow Am. Geophys. Union, Am. Meterol. Soc. (mem. coun. 1975-77, 79-81, mem. exec. com. 1977, 79-81, commr. sci. and tech. activities 1982-88, pres.-elect 1988, pres. 1989, publs. commr. 1992-98, hon. mem. 1995, Meisinger award 1962, Rossby Rsch. medal 1983, Charles Franklin Brooks award 1992, Charles E. Anderson award 2001), World Meterol. Orgn. (IMO prize 2002, Presdl. Rank award 2003), Explorers Club, Nat. Acad. Engring.; mem. Royal Meteorol. Soc. (hon.), Cosmos Club, Phi Beta Kappa, Sigma Xi. Home: 540 N St SW Washington DC 20024-4557 Office: NASA Goddard Space Flight Ctr Earth Scis Greenbelt MD 20771-0001 E-mail: nasajoanne@earthlink.net., simpson@agnes.gsfc.nasa.gov.

SIMPSON, LINDA SUE, elementary school educator; b. Rogers, Ark., Oct. 13, 1947; d. Richard Eugene and Shirley Joan (Kilpatrick) S. BS in Edn., Ohio State U., 1969, postgrad., 1989-91; MA in Edn., Ea. Ky. U., 1978. Cert. elem. tchr. Tchr. Conrad Sch., Newark, Ohio, 1969-71; tchr. 1-6 North Elem. Sch., Newark, 1971-89; tchr. K-3 Cherry Valley Elem., Newark, 1989—; primary literacy coordinator Cherry Valley Sch., 1999—. Adv. bd. Ohio Coun. of Social Studies, Columbus, 1994—; planning team Ctrl. Ohio Regional Profl. Devel., Columbus, 1994-95. Elder 1st Presbyn. Ch., Newark, 1990-93; tutor Licking County Children's Home, Newark, 1969-73. Jenning scholar Martha H. Found., 1987; named Newark Tchr. of the Yr., 1981; recipient Ashland Oil Tchg. award Ashland Oil Co., 1995. Mem. DAR (history and scholarship chair 1982—), Delta Kappa Gamma. Presbyterian. Avocations: genealogy, golf, bowling. Home: 579 Manor Dr Newark OH 43055-2119 Office: Cherry Valley Sch 1040 W Main St Newark OH 43055-2556

SIMPSON, LISA ANN, physician, educator; b. Lagos, Nigeria, Feb. 9, 1958; (parents Am. citizens); d. Howard Russell and Mary Alice (Turner) Simpson; m. Richard L. Wittenberg; children: Ethan Simpson Wittenberg, Sydney Simpson Wittenberg. MB, B of Surgery, Trinity Coll., Dublin, Ireland, 1981; MPH, U. Hawaii, 1986. Diplomate Am. Bd. Pediat. Resident in pediat. U. Hawaii, Honolulu, 1982-85; resident in preventive medicine U. NC, Chapel Hill, 1987-88; dir. Maternal and Child Health Bur. State Dept. Health, Honolulu, 1988-90, acting dir. family health svcs. divsn., 1990; policy advisor Office of Asst. Sec. for Health HHS, Washington, 1993-94, sr. advisor Agy. for Health Care Policy and Rsch. Rockville, Md., 1994-95, acting dep. adminstr. Agy. for Health Care Policy and Rsch., 1995-96, dep. adminstr. Agy. for Health Care Policy and Rsch., 1996-99, dep. dir. Agy. Healthcare Rsch. and Quality, 1999—2002; prof., All Children's Hosp. Guild endowed chair child health policy dept. pediat. U. South Fla., St. Petersburg, 2003—. Mid-career fellow Inst. Health Policy Studies, San Francisco, 1991-93; adj. faculty dept. health policy and mgmt. Johns Hopkins U., Balt., 1995—; vis. prof. U. Wash., 2000, U. Mich., 2000. Mem. editl. bd. Future Children, Maternal and Child Health Jour., 1996-2003; contbr. articles to profl. jours. Recipient Preventive Medicine traineeship Pub. Health Svc., 1986, Sec. Disting. Svcs. award Dept. HHS, 2000, Dir. Disting. Svc. award AHRQ, 2001, Meritorious Rank SES Presdl. award, 2002. Fellow: Am. Acad. Pediat. (Excellence in Pub. Svc. award 2002); mem.: APHA (governing coun. 1994—96), Nat. Acad. for Social Ins., Ambulatory Pediat. Assn., Acad. Health. Avocations: hiking, cuisine, gardening. Office: Acad Health 601 4th St S CRI 1008 Saint Petersburg FL 33701 E-mail: lsimpso1@hsc.usf.edu.

SIMPSON, MARY MICHAEL, priest, psychotherapist; b. Evansville, Ind., 1925; d. Link Wilson and Mary Garrett (Price) S. BA, BS, Tex. Women's U., 1946; grad., N.Y. Tng. Sch. Deaconesses, 1949, Westchester Inst. Tng. in Psychoanalysis and Psychotherapy, 1976; S.T.M., Gen. Theol. Seminary, 1982. ordained priest Episcopal Ch., 1977. Missionary Holy Cross Mission, Bolahun, Liberia, 1950-52; mem. Order of St. Helena, 1952—; acad. head Margaret Hall Sch., Versailles, Ky., 1958-61; sister in charge Convent of St. Helena, Bolahan, 1962-67, dir. novices, 1968-74; pastoral counselor on staff St. John the Divine, N.Y.C., 1974-87, canon residentiary, canon counselor, 1977-87, hon. canon, 1988—. Pvt. practice psychoanalyst, 1974—; dir. Cathedral Counseling Svc., 1975-87; cons. psychotherapist Union Theol. Seminary, 1980-83; bd. dirs. Westchester Inst. Tng. in Psychoanalysis and Psychotherapy, 1982-84; priest-in-charge St. John's Ch., Wilmot, New Rochelle, N.Y., 1987-88; trustee Coun. Internat. and Pub. Affairs, 1983-87;interim pastor St. Michael's Ch., Manhattan, 1992-94; cons. Diocese of N.Y., 1990—. Author: The Ordination of Women in the American Episcopal Church: The Present Situation, 1981; contbg. author: Yes to Women Priests, 1978. Mem. Nat. Assn. Advancement of Psychoanalysis, N.Y. State Assn. Practicing Psychotherapists, N.Y. Soc. Clin. Psychologists. Home and Office: 151 E 31st St Apt 8H New York NY 10016-9502 Office Phone: 212-951-4316.

SIMPSON, PAMELA HEMENWAY, art historian, educator; b. Omaha, Sept. 8, 1946; d. Myrle E. and Leone K. (Cook) Hemenway; m. Henry H. Simpson III, Apr. 4, 1970; 1 child, Peter Stuart Hay. BA, Gettysburg Coll., 1968; MA, U. Mo., 1970; PhD, U. Del., 1974. Instr. art history Pa. State Extension Campus, Media, 1973, Washington and Lee U., Lexington, Va., 1973-74, asst. prof., 1974-79, assoc. prof., 1979-85, prof. art history, 1985—, Ernest Williams prof., 1993, chair art dept., 1987—, assoc. dean of coll., 1981-86. Chair co-edn. steering com. Washington and Lee Univ., Lexington, 1984-86; cons., head county survey Va. Hist. Landmarks Commn., Richmond, 1977-81. Author: Architecture of Historic Lexington, 1977 (Am. Assn. for State and Local History award 1977), The Sculptor's Clay: Charles Gafly, 1862-1929, 1996 (SECAC award), Cheap, Quick and Easy: Imitative Architectural Materials, 1870-1930, 1999; book reviewer Women's Art Jour., columnist, 1990—; contbr. articles to profl. jours. Officer Rockbridge Hist. Soc., Lexington, 1980—, Rockbridge Valley Nat. Orgn. for Women, Rockbridge County, Va., 1984—, Historic Lexington (Va.) Found., 1987—; founder, officer Rockbridge Area Coalition Against Sexual Assault, Lexington, 1990—; bd. dirs. Project Horizon, domestic violence, sexual assault, 1998—. Recipient Outstanding Faculty award State Coun. of Higher Edn., State of Va., 1995; grantee Nat. Endowment for Arts, 1974, NEH, 1975, 77, Glenn, Washington and Lee U., 1980-81, 91; NEH Summer Inst. scholar, 1989; Hagley-Winterthur Mus. fellow, 1991, 96. Fellow Nat. Humanities Ctr.; mem. Southeastern Soc. Archtl. Historians (bd. dirs. 1990-94, v.p. 1993-94, pres. 1994-95, editor Arris 1998—), Soc. Archtl. Historians (book rev. editor Am. section Jour. 1999—), Coll. Art Assn., Vernacular Architecture Forum (bd. dirs. 1982-84, 2d v.p. 1988-91, pres. 1997-99), Southeastern Coll. Art Conf. (pres. 1986-90, 2d v.p. 1994—, editor rev. 1979-82). Democrat. Episcopalian. Avocations: painting, reading mysteries. Office: Washington and Lee U Dupont Hall Lexington VA 24450

SIMPSON, SANDRA KAY, logistics management specialist; b. Rutland, Vt., Feb. 26, 1949; d. Freeman Edward and Ruth Gail (Smith) Campbell. BA, U. Vt., 1971; M of Pub. Adminstrn., Troy State U., Europe, 1988, MSc in Internat. Rels., 1991. Isntr., trainer U.S. Govt., Ft. McClellan, Ala., 1975-79, asst. logistics officer Kitzingen, Germany, 1979-82, property acctg. officer Ft. Hood, Tex., 1982-86, Wiesbaden, Germany, 1986-93; exec. mgmt. asst. Sport and Sound, Mainz Kastel, Germany, 1993-94; maintenance mgmt. coord. U.S. Govt., Wiesbaden, 1994—, dep. dir. internal logistics, 1999—2002, theater level logistics mgr., 2002—03, def. logistics agy., 2003—. Cons. U.S. Govt., Heidelberg, Germany, 1994—. Served with U.S. Army, 1973—93. Mem. Women in Mil. Svc. to Am. Found. (charter mem.), USAREUR Retiree Coun., Wiesbaden/Mainz Retiree Coun. (sec. 1994—), Oxford Club. Avocations: photography, ultra-marathons. Home: Cmr 467 Box 1505 APO AE 09096-1505

SIMPSON, VERONICA ANN, photographer, lab technician; b. Bethlehem, Pa., Feb. 21, 1955; d. Peter H. and Shirley A. (DeWalt) Ricci; m. Richard James Simpson, Sept. 29, 1984; children: Jesse, Jenna. Cert. photography, Northampton C.C., Bethlehem, Pa., 1980, cert. in fine and performing arts, 1981; attended, Baum Sch. Art, Allentown, Pa. Lab. technician Ronn Studio, Bethlehem, 1978-82; lab. technician, photographer Sam Smith Studio, Allentown, 1980-85; pvt. photographer Nazareth, Pa., 1980—; owner pvt. shop, 1995—. Sch. dir. Nazareth Area Sch. Bd., 1995—. Mem. Nazareth Area C. of C. Roman Catholic. Avocations: painting, stained glass, organic gardening, cheerleading coach nazareths wrestling program. Office: Unique Images by Ronnie 1 N Main St Nazareth PA 18064-1437

SIMPSON, VI, state senator; b. L.A., Mar. 18, 1946; d. Lloyd M. and Helen (Chacon) Sentman; m. William D. McCarty; children: Jason, Kristina. Student, Ind. U., Indpls. Asst. to chmn. Com. on Status of Women, Calif., 1974-75; dir. pub. affairs Calif. Parks and Recreation Soc., Sacramento, 1975-77; county auditor Monroe County, Ind., 1980-84; mem. Ind. Senate, Indpls., 1984—; exec. dir. Heritage Edn. Found., Indpls., 1989—. Editor Equal Rights Monitor mag., 1974-76; syndicated newspaper columnist Know You Rights, 1975-76. Named Fresman Dem. Senator of Yr., Ind. Broadcasters Assn., 1985, Legislator of Yr., Ind. State Employees Assn., 1985, various legis. awards Sierra Club, Ind. Wildlife Fedn., Isaac Walton League, Ind. Parks and Recreation Assn. Mem. NAACP, AAUW. Methodist. Office: Heritage Edn Found 7821 W Morris St Indianapolis IN 46231-1364 also: Ind Senate Dist 40 200 W Washington St Indianapolis IN 46204-2728

SIMPSON-JEFF, WILMA, social worker; b. Chapel Hill, Tex., Oct. 19, 1939; d. Robert Dell and Pearline (Collins) Simpson. BA, Wiley Coll., 1960; MSW, Atlanta U., 1962; postgrad., NYU, 1970-73, Hunter Coll., 1984. Cert. social work adminstrn. Asst. teen supr. Bronx (N.Y.) River Neighborhood Ctr., 1962-64; asst. dir. program Claremont Neighborhood Ctr., Bronx, 1964-66; program planning and rev. specialist N.Y.C. Youth Svc. Agy./Youth Bd., 1966-69; social worker, counselor NYU, N.Y.C., 1969-73; instr., counselor N.Y. Tech. Coll., Bklyn., 1973-75; parent coord. regional Deaf-Blind Ctr., Bronx, 1975-84; program social worker N.Y. Inst. for Spl. Edn., 1984-87, coord. parent edn., 1987—. Instr. Lehman Coll., Bronx, 1984-86, Boro Manhattan C.C., N.Y.C., 1986-91. Bd. dirs. Parenting Coalition Internat., 1999. Mem. Clark Atlanta U. Nat. Alumni Assn. (v.p. 1995—, fin. sec. 1990-95, v.p. Sch. Social Work 1975-79, 85-87), CAUA of Greater N.Y. (pres. 1992—), Alpha Kappa Alpha. Avocations: reading, bowling, planning, writing. Home: 3001 Henry Hudson Pky Bronx NY 10463-4717 Office: NY Inst for Spl Edn 999 Pelham Pky N Bronx NY 10469-4905

SIMS, BETTY, state legislator; b. St. Louis, Mo., Dec. 15, 1935; Mem. Mo. Senate from 24th dist., Jefferson City, 1994—. Active United Way, Girl Scout Coun., Jr. League Girls, Inc., 1972—. Office: Mo State Mems Rm 226 State Capitol Bldg Jefferson City MO 65101

SIMS, DEBORAH LYDE, counselor; b. Brunswick, Ga., May 25, 1944; d. Nelson Lucius and Marion Geneva (Thompson) Lyde; m. Ronald Wendell Sims, May 11, 1968 (dec. Jan. 1996); children: Ronald W. II, Reginald Wendell. BS, Morris Brown Coll., 1966; MS, Atlanta U., 1971; MEd, Ga. State U., 1974. Tchr. Atlanta Pub. Schs., 1978-83, counselor, 1983—. CEO, owner Ronald W Wims Philanthropic Found., Atlanta, 1996—, LSGB, Inc., Atlanta, 1996—, DLY Sims, Inc., Atlanta, 1996—. Author: (musical drama) Martin Luther King, Jr. - Drum Major for Justice, 1989, Lest We Forget - Black History, 1990. Vol. Carrie Steele Pitts Orphanage, Atlanta, Dept. Family & Children's Svcs., Atlanta; deputy registrar Fulton County, Atlanta; mem. United Way, Atlanta, 1984-86. Mem. Am. Sch. Counselors Assn., Am. Counseling Assn., Ga. Sch. Counselors Assn., Atlanta Sch. Counselors Assn., Assn. Multicultural Counseling, Alpha Kappa Alpha. Democrat. Baptist. Avocations: reading, piano, musical writing, singing, philanthropy. Office: Ronald W Sims Philanthropic Meml Found 5105 Greentree Trl College Park GA 30349-1737

SIMS, KAREN SUE, small business owner; d. Loren and Reola Imogene McNeill; life ptnr. David Raymond Devine; children: Keith David, Craig Daniel. AS with hons. in Travel and Tourism, John A. Logan Jr. Coll., 1991. Cert. tchrs. aide Ill., 1983. Asst. dir. ops. Travelmax, Inc., Ft. Lauderdale, Fla., 1996—99; internet sales cons. Trader Pub. Co./Traderonline.com, Va. Beach, Va., 1999—2002; bus. devel. exec. Xperts, Inc., Glen Allen, Va., 2002—03; ind. contractor Flashpoint Mktg., Richmond, Va., 2003—, HamptonRoadsSaves.com, 2003—. Mem., vol. Parrothead Club of Tidewater, Norfolk, 1999—2003, Chesapeake Bay Found., Norfolk, 2002—03, Project: Schooner Va., Norfolk, 2002—03. Mem.: So. Bay Sailing Club, Alpha Beta Gamma.

SIMS, MARTHA J. library director; b. Portsmouth, Va., Oct. 29, 1946; m. Hunter Sims; children: Hunter, Clara. BA in English, Mary Baldwin Coll., 1968; MS in Libr. Sci., U. N.C., 1969; MBA in Pub. Adminstrn., Old Dominion U., 1979. Reference asst. U. N.C., Chapel Hill, 1968-69; libr. art and music dept. Richmond Pub. Libr., 1969-71; br. libr. Virginia Beach Pub. Libr., 1971-74, asst. dir., 1974-76, dir., 1976—. Mem. adv. bd. New Va. Review, 1976-80. Contbr. articles to profl. jours. Bd. dirs. Va. Beach Arts Ctr., 1971-82, treas., 1974-75; mem. Va. Beach Bicentennial Commn., 1975-76, Jr. League Norfolk, Virginia Beach, 1976-82; sec. Tidewater Area Libr. Dir.'s Coun., 1984-85; bd. dirs. Boys Club Norfolk/Virginia Beach, 1986-90, Literacy Action South Hampton Roads, 1988—, Va. Ctr. for the Book, 1987—, pres. 1995—, Va. Literacy Found., 1989—; mem. steering com. Virginia Beach Roundtable, 1988-92; census chairperson Mayor's Complete Count Com. 1990, 1989-90; lead agt. region 12 literacy coord. com. State Office Adult Literacy, 1989-92; trustee, sec. Va. Beach Pub. Libr. Endowment Found., 1982—; mem. adv. bd. Tidewater Literacy Coun., 1984-90; tchr. Sunday sch. 1st Presbyn. Ch., 1988—; mem. steering com. Adult Literacy Lab, Adult Lng. Ctr. Va. Beach Pub. Schs., 1989—; keel divsn. leader United Way, 1991-92; bd. trustees Norfolk Acad., 1991—; keel club chairperson United Way, Virginia Beach, 1992-93; city chmn. United Way, Virginia Beach, 1995. Mem. ALA, Am. Soc. Pub. Adminstrs., Southeastern Libr. Assn., Va. Libr. Assn. (sec. 1976-78, legis. com. 1979-85, local arrangements 1982 conv. 1981-82, chmn. pub. libr. sect. 1982-84, state libr. bd. liaison com. 1984-88). Home: 1160 Cedar Point Dr Virginia Beach VA 23451-3864 Office: Virginia Beach Dept of Public Libraries Municipal Ctr Bldg 192nd Virginia Beach VA 23456-9115

SIMS, PAM, writer, minister; Attended Tulane Univ., Sch. Law seminars. Past pres. Ikebana Internat., Le Gals Inc.; pres. Titanic Bead Co. Taught legal secretarial classes. Prin. works include Ikebana design articles; contbr. articles to mags. Mem. Pensacola Camellia Club; former bd. mem. Women for Responsible Legis.; charter mem. Bush/Cheney 2004, Inc. re-election campaign, Arlington, Va.; mem. Pensacola Christian Women's Club. Recipient Cert. of Recognition, Rep. Nat. Com., signed by Pres. George Bush, 2002, Congl. Award of Merit, 2004. Mem.: Nat. Notary Public Assn., Ikebana Internat. (past pres.), Fla. Notary Pub. Commn. Office: 4051 G Barrancas Ave PMB #286 Pensacola FL 32507

SIMS, RITA LOUISE, minister; b. LaMarque, Tex., Aug. 31, 1961; d. Jimmie Olda and Margaret Louise (Irvine) Sims; m. John Crawford Wills, II, May 25, 1985 (div. Jan. 1995); 1 child, Tabitha Mae Sims Wills. AA, Lon Morris Coll., 1981; BA, Tex. Wesleyan U., 1983; MDiv, So. Meth. U., 1987. Co-pastor Rehobeth/St. Andrew's/Murvaul, Carthage, Tex., 1986—89; pastor Faith United Meth. Ch., Fannett, Tex., 1989—95, Trinity United Meth. Ch., Longview, Tex., 1995—96; sr. assoc. pastor Marvin United Meth. Ch., Tyler, Tex., 1996—2000; pastor Perritte Meml. United Meth. Ch., Nacogdoches, Tex., 2000—. Chairperson Conf. Commn. on Religion and Race Tex. Conf. United Meth. Ch., 1992—96, mentor pastor Developing Connectional Ministry, 2000—03; mentor pastor Perkins Sch. Theology, Dallas, 1999—2000; mem. Dist. Com. on Ordained Ministry, 2000—03; v.p., mem. Dist. Trustees, 2000—03; dist. rep. Conf. Com. on Hispanic Ministry, 2000—03. Recipient Bishop's award for excellence in Evangelism, Tex. Conf. United Meth. Ch., 1991, Torchbearer award, Black Meth. for Ch. Renewal, 1995, Cmty. Svc. award, Ministerial Alliance, 1995. Avocations: aerobics, crossword puzzles, playing card and board games, travel. Office: Perritte Meml United Meth Ch 1025 Durst St Nacogdoches TX 75964

SIMS, TERRE LYNN, insurance company executive; b. Madison, Wis., Dec. 26, 1951; d. Roy Charles and Ruth Marie (McCloskey) Pierstorff; m. Gary Peter Laufenberg, Feb. 15, 1969 (div.); children: Amie, Monte, Tawna; m. Perry Allen Sims, May 3, 1994 (dec. Aug. 2000). Sales agt. Bankers Life and Casualty, Madison, 1977-80, asst. mgr., 1981-84, br. mgr. Peoria, 1984-91; co-owner Complete Ins. Svcs., Inc., Madison, Wis., 1991—; owner, operator Ohio Tavern, Madison, 1993—; co-owner Nu Brick Inn Bar and Grill, Madison, 2000—01. Office: 4521 Stein Ave Madison WI 53714-1731

SIMS-CURRY, KRISTY, women's college basketball coach; b. Olla, La., 1967; m. Kelly Curry. BS in Health and Phys. Edn., N.E. La. U., 1988; MS in Kinesiology, Stephen F. Austin U., 1992. Coach Weston H.S., Mansfield H.S., La.; women's asst. basketball coach Tulane U., 1991-93, Stephen F. Austin U., 1993-94, Tex. A&M U., 1994-96; asst. coach La. Tech. U., 1996-99; head coach Purdue U., West Lafayette, 1999—. Office: care Women's Basketball 1790 Mackey Arena Rm 44 West Lafayette IN 47907-1790

SIMSON, BEVLYN, artist; b. Columbus, Ohio, Sept. 9, 1917; d. Amon and Fannie Florence (Gilbert) Thall; m. Theodore Richard Simson, Mar. 25, 1938; children: Sherran Blair, Douglas A. BFA, Ohio State U., 1969, MFA, 1972. Author, artist Prints and Poetry, 1969. One woman shows include J.B. Speed Art Mus., Louisville, 1970, Huntington Gallery, Columbus, Ohio, 1970, 73, United Christian Ctr., Columbus, 1970, Bodley Gallery, N.Y., 1971, 74, Gilman Galleries, Chgo., 1971, Gallery 200, Columbus, 1972, Hopkins Hall Gallery, Ohio State U., Columbus, 1972, Meth. Theol Sch., Deleware, Ohio, 1973, Columbus Public Lib., 1973, Garfinkels, Washington, 1973, City Hall, Mayor's Office, Columbus, 1974, 82, Capital U., Bexley, Ohio, 1977, Hillel Found., Ohio State U., 1978, Columbus Tech. Inst., 1979, Springfield (Ohio) Art Mus., 1980, Peace Luth. Ch., Gahanna, Ohio, 1981, Franklin U. Gallery, Columbus, 1981, Columbus Mus. Art Collectors Gallery, 1983; exhibited in juried and invitational shows at Columbus Mus. Art-Ohio Art League, 1968, 70, 71, 73, 74, 75, 77, 78, 79, 80, 86, Ohio Statehouse and State Office Tower, Columbus, 1968-78, Battelle Meml. Inst., Columbus, 1969-73, 75, 78, 81-82, Schumacher Gallery, Capital U., Columbus, 1969-85, 87, 88, Salles d'Exposition, Paris, 1969, Am. Cultural Ctr., Kyoto, Japan, J.B. Speed Art Mus. Collector's Gallery, Louisville, 1970-85, Studio San Guiseppe, Mt. St. Joseph Coll., Cin., 1971, Silver Anniversary Coll. Arts, 2nd Biennial Alumni Exhbn., Hopkins Hall Gallery, 1972, 2nd Internat. Art Exhbn., Paramaribo, Serinam, 1974, Mansfield (Ohio) Art Ctr., 1971, Collector's Showroom, Chgo., 1971-82, Gov.'s MansionState of Ohio, 1972, 74, Western Ill. U., 1972, Albatross Gallery, Rome, 1972, Palazzo Dell Exprizioni, Rome, 1972, Place-Allrich Gallery, San Francisco, 1973-75, Chautauqua Assn., N.Y., 1973, Butler Inst. Am. Art, Youngtown, Ohio, 1973, 76, Huntington Gallery, Columbus, 1973, 74, Gallery 200, Columbus, 1972-76, Columbus C. of C., 1974, 75, Zanesville (Ohio) Art Ctr., 1976, Columbus Inst. Contemporary Art, 1978, Nationwide Plaza Gallery, Columbus, 1980, Franklin U., Columbus, 1980, Ohio State U., 1993, Ohio Art League, 1987, Jeffrey Mansion, Bexley, Ohio, 1996, 10th Ann. Women Artists Expo Seal of Ohio Girl Scout Coun., Inc. Columbus, 1996, Financial Group Gallery, Worthington, Ohio, 1997, Ohio Art League, 1997, 4th Hall Gallery, Ohio State U., 1997, Concourse Gallery, Upper Arlington, Ohio, 1998, 13th Ann. Women Artists Expo Art in The Nation Wide Atrium, Columbus, Ohio, 1999, Bexley (Ohio) Art League, Jeffrey Mansion, 2000;(Ohio) Art League Mem. Curated Exhbn., Structure/Consequences, 1997, Fourth Biennial Alumni Exhbn.:ReSiDivist, Hopkins Hall Gallery, Ohio State U., 1997, Concourse Gallery, Arlington Ohio, 1998, Bexley Art League, Precision Concepts, Dublin, Ohio, 1999, Art in the Atrium, Columbus, Ohio, 1999, Art on Main

Street, Schumacher Gallery, 2002, others; represented in permanent collections Columbus Mus. Arts, J.B. Speed Art Mus., Louisville, Capital U., Bexley, Fordham U., N.Y.C., Kyoto City U. Fine Arts, Springfield (Ohio) Art Mus., Tyler (Tex.) Mus. Art, Wichita (Kans.) Mus. Art, Zanesville (Ohio) Art Ctr., Ohio State U., Columbus, Meth. Theol. Sch., Delaware, Ohio, Yerke Mortgage Co., Columbus, Marcorp, N.Y., Kresge Co., Detroit, IBM, Columbus, Chase Manhattan Bank, N.Y.C., Chase Bank Ohio, Am. Bancorp., Columbus, Ohio Nat. Bank Plaza, Columbus, Pan Western Life Ins. Co., Columbus, First Investment Co., Columbus, Children's Hosp., Phila., Franklin County Crippled Children's Ctr., Columbus, Zenith East, N.Y.C., First Cmty. Bank, Columbus, First City Bank, Columbus, Ohio, Ronald McDonald House, Columbus, Columbia Gas of Ohio, Columbus, Midland Title Security Co., Columbus, Huntington Nat. Bank Ctr., Columbus, Lehman Bros., N.Y.C., Columbus Sch. for Girls, Grand Prix Assocs., Inc., Columbus, Grant Hosp. Med Ctr., Columbus, Libr. and Rsch. Ctr. Nat. Mus. Women in Arts, Washington, D.C., Ohio State U. Libr. Rare Books Room Collection, Laredo (Tex.) Pub. Libr.; represented in private collections. Mem. Nat. League Am. Pen Women, Nat. Artists Equity Assn., Bexley Art League, Columbus Mus. Art, Ohio Art League (bd. dirs. 1965-96, treas., sec., pres. 1977), Ohio State U. Alumni Assn., Pres.'s Club (Ohio State U.), Winding Hollow Country Club, Phi Sigma Sigma. Avocations: golf, theater, symphony, travel. Studio: Bevlyn Simson Studio 4300 E Broad St 1st Cmty Bank Bldg Columbus OH 43213-1243 E-mail: trsimson@netwalk.com.

SINCLAIR, CAROLE, publisher, editor, author; b. Haddonfield, N.J., May 13, 1942; d. Earl Walter and Ruth (Sinclair) Dunham; 1 child, Wendy. Student, U. Florence, Italy, 1963; BA in Polit. Sci., Bucknell U, 1964. Advt. copywriter BBD&O Advertising, N.Y.C., 1966-67; sales promotion mgr. Macmillan Pub. Co., N.Y.C., 1967-71; mktg. mgr. Doubleday & Co., Inc., N.Y.C., 1972-74, promotion dir., 1974-76, advt. mgr., sales and promotion, chmn. mktg. com., 1976-80; v.p. mktg., editorial dir. Davis Pubs., N.Y.C., 1980-83; founder, pub., editorial dir., sr. v.p. Sylvia Porter's Personal Fin. Mag., N.Y.C., 1983-90; pres. The Sylvia Porter Orgn., Inc., N.Y.C., 1980-91; founder, pres. Sinclair Media Inc., N.Y.C., 1990—. Mktg. dir. Denver Pub. Inst., summers 1975-78; lectr. Columbia U. Bus. Sch. and Sch. of Journalism, 1976; host nationally syndicated TV show, Sylvia Porter's Money Tips, syndicated daily radio show, Sylvia Porter's Personal Fin. Report, audio cassette series on fin. topics. Author: Keys for Women Starting and Owning a Business, 1991, Keys to Women's Basic Professional Needs, 1991, When Women Retire, 1992; contbg. editor Pushcart Prize, 1977; contbr. The Business of Publishing, 1980. Renaissance Art Program fellow, Florence, Italy, 1963; White House intern, 1962. Mem. Women's Forum, Intercorp. Communications Group, Mag. Pubs.' Assn., Advt. Women in N.Y., Spence Sch. Parent's League. Clubs: Pubs. Lunch. Presbyterian. Avocation: boating.

SINCLAIR, DAISY, casting executive; b. Perth Amboy, N.J., Mar. 22, 1941; d. James Patrick and Margaret Mary (McAniff) Nieland; m. James Pratt Sinclair, May 25, 1978; children: Duncan, Gibbons. BA, Caldwell Coll., 1962. Jr. copywriter Young & Rubican, N.Y.C., 1962-64; various positions in casting dept. Ogilvy & Mather, N.Y.C., 1964-90, sr. v.p., dir. casting, 1990—. Mem.: Drama League N.Y. (3d v.p. 1982—), Am. Assn. Advt. (talent agt. com. 1972—), N.Y. Yacht Club, Union Club, Tuxedo Club, Chapaquoit Yacht Club, Edgartown Yacht Club, Knickerbocker Greys (pres.). Republican. Episcopalian. Avocations: opera, theater, sailing, skiing. Home: 4 E 95th St New York NY 10128-0705

SINCLAIR, LINDA DRUMWRIGHT, educational consultant; b. Norfolk, Va., Aug. 4, 1942; d. Raymond Edward and Evelyn Elizabeth (Edwards) Drumwright; m. Charles Armstrong Sinclair, Oct. 5, 1962; children: William, Dianne, Sandy. BS, U. S.C., 1974, MA, 1976, postgrad. Cert. tchr. in biology, chemistry, physics. Sci. tchr. Keenan H.S., Columbia, S.C., 1976-77; chemistry/physics tchr. Lexington (S.C.) H.S., 1977-93; talented/gifted tchr. U. S.C., Columbia, 1988; tchr. rsch. program Oak Ridge (Tenn.) Nat. Lab., 1989; rschr. Savannah River Ecology Lab., Aiken, S.C., 1991-92; state sci. edn. cons. S.C. Dept. Edn., Columbia, 1993—. Cons. Prentice Hall Pub., Princeton, N.J., 1992-93. Author: Operation Radon, 1993. Adv. bd. S.C. Forestry Commn., Columbia, 1993—, S.C. Environ. Coalition, Columbia, 1993—, S.C. Sci. Coun., Columbia, 1989—; mem., com. chair Lexington Woman's Club, 1986—; v.p. Lexington Garden Club, 1983—. Named S.C. Sci. Tchr. of the Yr., S.C. Acad. Sci., 1986, Sigma Xi, 1986, S.C. Chemistry Tchr. of the Yr., S.C. Chem. Soc., 1992; recipient Presdl. Award for Excellence in Sci. Teaching, NSF, 1993. Mem. S.C. Sci. Coun. (v.p., pres.), S.C. Chemistry Tchrs. Assn. (bd. dirs. 1987—), S.C. Acad. Sci. (bd. dirs. 1982—), S.C. Jr. Acad. Sci. (bd. dirs. 1980—), S.C. Environ. Edn. Assn. (bd. dirs. 1990—), Nat. Sci. Tchrs. Assn. (bd. dirs. 1992-94). Lutheran. Avocatins: horseback riding, gardening, swimming, water sports. Home: 107 Hermitage Rd Lexington SC 29072-2221 Office: SC Dept Edn 801-H Rutledge Bldg 1429 Senate St Columbia SC 29201-3730 Office Phone: 803-734-0887. E-mail: lsinclair@sde.state.sc.us

SINCLAIR, RUTH SPEARS SMITH, piano teacher; b. Rowland, N.C., Apr. 21, 1931; d. Charles McDuffie and Frances Paul Smith; m. Joe N. Sinclair Jr., Dec. 30, 1954; children: Frances T. Sinclair-Galland, David Neal Sinclair. MusB, Flora MacDonald Coll., 1953. Pvt. piano tchr., NC, 1953—; chmn. So. Pines chpt. Nat. Guild Auditions, Southern Pines, NC, 1975—. Pres. music dept. Fayetteville Presbytery, 1968-70; mem. Weymouth Festival for Young Musicians, Southern Pines, 1988-92; deacon Bethesda Presbyn. Ch., Aberdeen, 1996-98; bd. dirs. Moore County N.C. Symphony, 1997—. Mem. N.C. Music Tchrs. Assn. (state contest dir. 1997-99, coll. audition chair 2000—2002), Nat. Guild Piano Tchrs. (chmn. Fairmont chpt. 1955-56, Maxton chpt. 1962-67), Moore Music Soc. (chmn. and performer young musicians concert), Cardinal Book Club. Republican. Presbyterian. Avocations: bridge, water aerobics, reading, gardening, walking. Home: 604 Mcqueen Rd Aberdeen NC 28315-2106

SINCLAIR, SARA VORIS, health facility administrator, nurse; b. Kansas City, Mo., Apr. 13, 1942; d. Franklin Defenbaugh and Inez Estelle (Figenbaum) Voris; m. James W. Sinclair, June 13, 1964; children: Thomas James, Elizabeth Kathleen, Joan Sara. BSN, UCLA, 1965. RN, Utah; lic. health care facility adminstr.; cert. health care adminstr. Staff nurse UCLA Med. Ctr. Hosp., 1964-65; charge nurse Boulder (Colo.) Meml. Hosp., 1966, Boulder (Colo.) Manor Nursing Home, 1974-75, Four Seasons Nursing Home, Joliet, Ill., 1975-76; dir. nursing Home Health Agy of Olympia Fields, Joliet, Ill., 1977-79, Sunshine Terr. Found., Inc., Logan, Utah, 1980, asst. adminstr., 1980-81, adminstr., 1981-93; dir. divsn. health systems improvement Utah Dept. Health, Salt Lake City, 1993-97; CEO Sunshine Terr. Found., 1997—. Long term care profl. and tech. adv. com. Joint Commn. on Accreditation Healthcare Orgns., Chgo., 1987—91, chmn., 1990—91; adj. lectr. Utah State U., 1991—93, search com. for dir. major gifts, 2001; adj. clin. faculty Weber State U., Ogden, Utah; moderator radio program Healthwise Sta. KUSU-FM, 1985—93; del. White House Conf. on Aging, 1995; chmn. Utah Dept. of Health's Ethics, Instl. Rev. Bd. Com., 1995—97, Utah Dept. Health Rist Mgmt. Com., 1995—97; exec. com. Utah Long Term Care Coalition, 1995, chmn., 1997—2001; oversight com. and long term care tech. adv. group Utah Health Policy Commn., 1996—2000, Health Insight Utah State Coun., 1996—2001; adj. vol. faculty U. Utah Gerontology Ctr., 1997—; moderator Living Well Longer Utah Pub. Radio weekly program, 1998—; bd. dirs. Bridgerland Area Tech. Coll., Logan, Logan Regional Hosp., chair quality assurance, 2001—; mem. regional adv. bd. Zions Bank, 2001—; chair quality subcom. Am. Health Care Assn., 2003—; spkr., presenter in field. Contbg. author: Associate Degree Nursing and The Nursing Home, 1988; contbr. articles to profl. jours. Deans adv. coun. Coll. Bus. Utah State U., Logan, 1989—91, mem. presdl. search com., 1991—92; chmn., co-founder Cache Cmty. Health Coun., 1985, co-chair, 2000; bd. dirs. Bridgerland Area Tech. Coll., 2001—, Utah Assistive Tech. Found., 2001, vice chair; chmn. bd. Hospice of Cache Valley, Logan, 1986; apptd. chmn. Utah Health Facilities Com., 1989—91; chmn. health and human svcs. subcom. Cache 2010, 1992—93; mem. long term care tech. adv. group oversight com. Utah Health Policy Commn., 1997; dir. Health Insight, 1996; trustee Utah State U., 1997—2001; chmn. Utah State U. Trustee's Acad. Affairs Com., 1999—2001; co-chair Living Well Longer Coun., 1997—, Cache Cmty. Health Coun., 2000—; apptd. Utah State Bd. Regents, 2001; apptd. mem. Utah State Bd. Edn., 2002; bd. dir. Utah Higher Edn. Assistance Authority, 2002—03. Named Rotarian of Yr., Logan Rotary Club, 2002; recipient Disting. Svc. award, Utah State U., 1989, Total Citizen award, Cache C. of C., 2002, Pioneer award, Utah Area Health Edn. Ctr., 2003. Fellow: Am. Coll. Health Care Adminstrs. (presenter 1992—93, convocation and edn. coms. 1992—93, v.p. Utah chpt. 1992—94, region IX vice gov. 1994—96, presenter 1995, 1996, bylaws com. 1996—2000, region IX vice gov. 1998—2000, presenter ACHCA Winter Marketplace 1999, chmn. bylaws com. 1999—2000, chair edn. com. 2000, nominating com. 2000, presenter 2001, 2002, bd. dirs. 2002—, ann. convocations); mem.: Logan Bus. and Profl. Women's Club (pres. 1989, Woman of Achievement award 1982, Woman of Yr. 1982), Utah Gerontol. Soc. (bd. dirs. 1992—93, chmn. nominating com. 1993—94, bd. dirs. 1995—97, chmn. ann. conf. 1996, pres. 1997), Utah Health Care Assn. (pres. 1983—85, treas. 1991—93, pres. 2000—01, Disting. Svc. award 1991, Sv. award for long term care 1996), Am. Health Care Assn. (non-proprietary v.p. 1986—87, region v.p. 1987—89, presenter various confs. and convs., exec. com. 1993, chmn. quality subcom. 2003, cert. facilitator 2002), Cache C. of C. (pres. 1991, named Total Citizen of Yr. 2002), Rotary (Logan chpt. chair cmty. svc. com. 1989—90, pres. Logan club 1999—2000, Rotarian of Yr. 2002), Golden Key Nat. Honor Soc. (hon.). Avocations: walking, reading. Office Phone: 435-754-0216. E-mail: sarasinclair@sunshineterrace.com.

SINCLAIRE, ESTELLE FOSTER, appraiser, writer, former educator; b. Trenton, N.J. d. Douglas Cumming and Lydia (Foster) Sinclaire; m. Frederic Breakspear Farrar, March 14, 1942 (div.); 1 child: Frederic Douglas. BA, Douglas Coll., Rutgers U.; MA, Hofstra U. Cert. Grant Writing. Libr., tchr. Waldorf Sch., Adelphi Coll.; adjunt assoc. prof. Art Dept. Hofstra U. Tchr., lectr. glass courses Hofstra, Cooper-Hewitt, Rider Coll., Internat. Assn. History Glass Spain. Writer for N.J. Art Princeton Packet "Time Off", 1986-90; author H.P. Sinclaire Jr. Glassmaker Vol. 1, Vol. 11, 1975; co-author (with Jane Spillman) The Cut and Engraved Glass of Corning, 1868-1940, (1st and 2d edition), 1997; author: American Fine Glass: The Birmingham Connection, A Century of Misconceptions European Fine Glass Sold as American. Appraiser, fundraiser On Air Hofstra Annual Art History Dept. Auction, Princeton Packet. Mem. Appraisers Assn. Am. (cert.), Nat. Am. Glass Club (founder empire branch). Home: 524 Spencer Ln Jamesburg NJ 08831-1818

SINERIUS-RUPP-BLOOR, SHARON KAY, sculptor; b. Deer-Lodge, Mont., Feb. 15, 1955; d. Ben and Larada Sinerius; children: Amity, Jason, Aaron, Matthew, Brian. BA, U. Great Falls, 1995. Mem.: Wash. State Arts Alliance (bd. legis. affairs 2000—02), Artist Trust (grant 1998), N.W. Women's Caucus for Art (v.p. N.W. chpt.). Avocations: painting, sculpting, photography, drawing, cats. Home: 603 Muriel St Richland WA 99352

SINGER, BARBARA HELEN, photographer; b. NYC, Jan. 29, 1927; d. Robert and Rose (Kaplowitz) S.; m. Nat Herz, Jan. 15, 1956 (dec. Nov. 1964); m. Melvin C. Zalkan, Sept. 7, 1983 (dec. Nov. 1993). BA in Biology, NYU, 1947; studied with Eli Siegel, 1944-76. Radiographer, 1951-90; instr. Meth. Hosp. Sch. Radiologic Tech., Bklyn., 1968-72; asst. to Benedict J. Fernandez N.Y.C., N.Y., 1985-91; asst. to Lucien Clergue New Sch./Parsons, N.Y.C., 1989; photographer N.Y.C., 1983—. Lectr. NY Film Acad., NYC, 2000; panel mem. Phoenix Gallery, NYC, 1999, St. Francis Coll., NYC, 2001. Represented by John Stevenson Gallery, Bridgeman Art Library Internat. Ltd., photonica, workbookstock.com, Steelpetal, Inc.; exhibited in numerous group shows including most recently John Stevenson Gallery, N.Y.C., 1999, 2003, Pietra di Luna Gallery, Fla., 1999, 2000, Park Ave. Armory, N.Y.C., 1999, AIPAD, N.Y.C., 1999, George A. Spiva Ctr. for the Arts, Mo., 2000, Hist. Yellow Springs, Chester, Pa., 2000, Nat. League Am. Pen Women Art Exhbn., N.Y.C., 2000, AIR Gallery, NYC, 2000, Pietra di Luna Gall., Hollywood FL., 2000, St. Francis Coll., NYC, 2001, Modernage, N.Y.C., 2001, Ashforth-Warburg Downtown, N.Y.C., 2002, The Gallery in Stamford, Conn., 2003, WBENC Conf. and Bus. Fair, N.Y.C., 2003, Photo-Plus Expo, N.Y.C., 2003, APA, N.Y.C., 2003; CD-ROM Urbane Photography, 1996; photography published in The Murray Hill News, 1983, Profl. Women Photographers Newsletter, 1985, 95, Light and Shade, 1985, Best of Photography Annual 1990, Women of Vision, 1990, Tear Sheet, 1995, Wildlife Conservation Soc. Annual Report, Photonica 21, 1996, In Shape, 1996, Summer of Betrayal, Farrar Straus Giroux, 1997, Wildlife Conservation Mag., 1997, Worldcare Annual Report, 1997, Svenska Missions, 1997, Photonica 25, 1997, Fotophile, 1997, Photonica 34, 1998, Photonica 38, 44, 1999, 49, 2000, Shots, vol. 63, 1999, Photo Dist. News Online, 2003, lit. published in PWP Newsletter, 2001, Tear Sheet, vol. 3, 1995, Today's Great Poems, 1994, Evangelism in America, 1988, Radiologic Tech., 1969, 71; editor, pub. The Impossible Landscapes of Nat Herz and Kurt Seligmann, 1999; appeared in website video, 2003. Photographers' Forum Finalist, 1990; recipient Photography award Beaux Arts Soc., 1994, fiscal sponsorship N.Y. Found. for the Arts, 2000, 2d pl. winner for poetry E.F.S. 1999 Ann. Writing Competition, 2000. Cert. by Women Pres. Ednl. Orgn., 2002. Mem.: Poetry Soc. Am., Women Presidents Ednl. Orgn., Am. Soc. Media Photographers, Profl. Women Photographers, Am. Soc. Picture Profls., Women's Bus. Enterprise Nat. Coun. Avocation: ballroom dancing. Office: Madison Sq Sta PO Box 1150 New York NY 10159-1150 Fax: (212) 684-1051. Office Phone: 212-689-0395. E-mail: barbara@barbarasinger.com.

SINGER, CAROL ANN, librarian, researcher; b. Tarentum, Pa., Mar. 13, 1953; d. Richard Meade and Eleanor (Weir) S. BA, Bowling Green State U., 1975; MLS, Ind. U., 1979. Instr. info. svc. Wayne (Nebr.) State Coll., 1979-84; govt. documents libr. U. Nebr., Omaha, 1984-85, Kenyon Coll., Gambier, Ohio, 1985-91; sr. ref. libr. U.S. Dept. Energy, Washington, 1991-92; ref. libr. USDA, Washington, 1992-97; asst. libr. U.S. Dept. Justice, Washington, 1997-98; ref. libr. Bowling Green (Ohio) State U., 1998—. Temp. instr. Kent State U., Bowling Green, Ohio, 1999; researcher. Contbr. articles to profl. jours. Mem. ALA, Acad. Libr. Assn. Ohio, Ohio Govt. Documents Roundtable. Office: Bowling Green State U Jerome Libr Rm 152 Bowling Green OH 43403 Office Phone: 419-372-9412. E-mail: singerc@bgnet.bgsu.edu.

SINGER, CECILE DORIS, bank executive, former state legislator; BA, Queens Coll.; DHL (hon.), Pace U., 1997. Past rep. Spl. Svcs. for Children, N.Y.C.; past exec. dir. N.Y. State Assembly Social Svcs. and Judiciary Coms., Joint Legis. Com. on Corps., Authorities and Commns.; past pub. rep. Yonkers (N.Y.) Emergency Control Bd.; past dep. leader Westchester County Assembly Dels.; past chief of staff for dep. minority leader; mem. N.Y. State Assembly, Albany, 1988—94, leadership sec. Rep. Conf., mem. assembly children & families com., mem. various other coms.; bd. dirs. Hudson Valley Bank; prin. Cecile D. Singer Cons. Past rep. Temp. Commn. to Revise Social Svcs. Law; mem. Presdl. Commn. on Privacy Conf., N.Y. State Senate Transp. Conf.; task force on substance abuse Am. Legis. Exch. Coun., task force on econ. devel., crime victims' rights, hosp. crisis, women's issues, com. on mass transit; sec. Rep. Conf. Nat. Adv. Panel Child Care Action Campaign; chmn. Westchester County Commn. on Pub. Financing of Campaigns; chmn. Lower Hudson Valley Adv. Com. N.Y. State Divsn. for Women; past dir. commn. on poverty and pregnancy, Yonkers IDA, N.Y.; treas. Riverside Corp.; chair, N.Y. State Hudson Valley Coun.; pres. Women's Enterprise Devel. Ctr.; bd. dirs. Hudson Valley Bank, N.Y.; prin. Cecile D. Singer Cons. Chair adv. com. Westchester C.C. Found., Westchester 2000 Rsch., Womens Adv. Bd. Westchester County; task force on certiorari Westchester County Sch. Bds. Assn.; sch. and cmty. chmn. Yonkers PTA; bd. dirs. Yonkers chpt. United Jewish Appeal; v.p. Westchester Sr. Housing; chair Women's Networking, Women in Bus. and the Professions; v.p. Westchester Srs. Housing; trustee, treas. St. John Hosp. Recipient Jenkins Meml. award, Nat. PTA award, Bus. and Profl. award Yonkers C. of C.; inducted Women's Hall of Fame, 1996, Sr. Citizens Hall of Fame, 1996. Mem. Mental Health Assn. (bd. dirs., v.p., nominating and pub. affairs coms. Westchester County chpt., Steering award), Rotary. Office: 21 Scarsdale Rd Yonkers NY 10707-3204 Home: 1 Scarsdale Rd Tuckahoe NY 10707-3215

SINGER, DAVIDA, poet, journalist, educator; b. Burlington, Vt., Oct. 31, 1957; d. Benjamin Singerman and Lilyan (Ostrow) Fishman. BA in Writing, Columbia U., 1983; MA in Journalism, NYU, 1991. Arts journalist The Villager newspaper, 1994—, Gay City News, 2002—; instr. Sch. Visual Arts CUNY, 2000—. Freelance mag. writer, 1992—. Author: shelter island poems, 1995; creator, prodr. (performance art piece) khupe, 1996. Mem. Nat. Writers Union, Transp. Alternative. Jewish. Avocations: swimming, biking, astrology, tarot, yoga. Home and Office: 223 W 105th St Apt 3FW New York NY 10025-3968

SINGER, DINAH, federal agency administrator, immunologist, researcher; MPhil, PhD, Columbia U. Dir. divsn. cancer biology Nat. Cancer Inst., 1999—. Mem.: Am. Assn. Immunologists. Office: Nat Cancer Inst Divsn Cancer Biology Executive Plaza North Ste 5000 Bethesda MD 20892

SINGER, DONNA LEA, writer, editor, educator; b. Wilmington, Del., Oct. 6, 1944; d. Marshall Richard and Sara Emma (Eppihimer) S. BA in English cum laude, Gettysburg Coll., 1966; postgrad., Montclair State Coll., 1972-73, U. Birmingham, Eng., 1977; M of Letters, Drew U., 1985. Asst. to dir. student activities Fairleigh Dickinson U., Madison, crw., 1966-68; tchr., drama coach Morris Hills High Sch., Rockaway, N.J., 1968-84; free-lance editor Basic Books, Inc., N.Y.C., 1983-86; adj. instr. Fairleigh Dickinson U., Madison, 1986-87; free-lance writer, editor Visual Edn. Corp., Princeton, N.J., 1988—, Fact's on File, Bantam, Random House, Fodor's Travel Books, N.Y.C., 1990—, John Wiley & Sons, N.Y.C., 1990—; tchr. Sylvan Learning and Tech. Ctr., Sarasota, Fla., 1999—. Co-founder, co-dir. Traveling Hist. Troupe, Rockaway, 1976-78; tour leader Am. Leadership Study Groups, 1976, 78, 82; theatre studies participant Royal Shakespeare Co., Stratford, Eng., 1978, 79, 81; docent, lectr. acting co. Hist. Spanish Point, Osprey, Fla., 1989-2001. Contbg. author (poetry) Chasing Rainbows, 1987, An American Heritage, 1994, The Nitty Gritty, 1997, Doorways, 1997, The Best Poems of 1998, The Lasting Joy, 1998, Everlasting Dreams, 1998, America at the Millennium, 2000, The Sound of Poetry, 2001, (biography) Past and Promise: Lives of New Jersey Women, 1990, World Explorers and Discoverers, 1992, American Cultural Leaders, 1993, Structures That Changed the World, 1997, (fiction) Thema, 2000, Tapestry, 2002; contbr. articles to profl. jours. Big sister Big Bros./Big Sisters, Sarasota, Fla., 1990-98. Mem. Internat. Women's Writing Guild, West Coast Writers, Met. Mus. Art, Royal Shakespeare Company Assocs., Emerald Coast Writers, Travel Writers Internat. Network. Avocations: dance, theatre, travel, antiquing. E-mail: shakesds@aol.com.

SINGER, ELEANOR, sociologist, editor; b. Vienna, Mar. 4, 1930; arrived in U.S., 1938; d. Alfons and Anna (Troedl) Schwarzbart; m. Alan Gerard Singer, Sept. 8, 1949; children: Emily Ann, Lawrence Alexander. BA, Queens Coll., 1951; PhD, Columbia U., 1966. Asst. editor Am. Scholar, Williamsburg, Va., 1951-52; editor Tchrs. Coll. Press, N.Y.C., 1952-56, Dryden-Holt, N.Y.C., 1956-57; rsch. assoc., sr. rsch. assoc., sr. rsch. scholar Columbia U., N.Y.C., 1966-94; sr. rsch. scientist Inst. for Social Rsch. U. Mich., Ann Arbor, 1994—2003, acting assoc. dir., 1998-99, assoc. dir., 1999—2002, rsch. prof., 2004—; editor Pub. Opinion Quar., N.Y.C., 1975-86. Author: (with Carol Weiss) The Reporting of Social Science in the Mass Media, 1988, (with Phyllis Endreny) Reporting On Risk, 1993; editor: (with Herbert H. Hyman) Readings in Reference Group Theory and Research, 1968, (with Stanley Presser) Survey Research Methods: A Reader, 1989; contbr. articles to profl. jours. Mem. Am. Assn. Pub. Opinion Rsch. (pres. N.Y.C. chpt. 1983-84, pres. 1987-88, Exceptionally Disting. Achievement award 1996), Am. Sociol. Assn., Am. Statis. Assn. Office: U Mich Inst Social Rsch PO Box 1248 Ann Arbor MI 48106-1248 Office Phone: 734-647-4599.

SINGER, ELLA NORRIS, writer, artist; b. Midnight, Miss., Sept. 16, 1949; d. Sadie Mae Norris; m. David Lowell Singer, Jan. 7, 1978. BFA, Wayne State U., 1998, civic literacy counselor, 1999. Arts mentor Arts League of Mich. Project coord. Wayne State U., Detroit, 1998—2002; dir. Plantation Studio Cultural Arts, Hamtramck, Mich., 2002—3. Contbr. poetry to anthologies (Artists & Poets Among Us, 2002). Project coord. Wayne State U. Youth Urban Agenda Civic Literacy Project, Detroit, 1998—2002. With USN, 1968—70. Recipient Pushcart Prize nomination, 2002. Mem.: PSI Inc. (assoc.; performance coach 1998—2003, Best Team Performance 2002). Avocations: travel, collecting. E-mail: ella_singer@yahoo.com.

SINGER, EMEL, staffing industry executive; b. Gaziantep, Turkey, Apr. 7, 1944; came to U.S., 1960; d. Mehmet Resit and Nesrin (Kescioglu) Tuzun; m. James Michael Singer, Apr. 28, 1968 (dec. 1987); children: Justin Michael, Jodi Michelle. BBA, Bradley U., 1968. Adminstrv. asst. U. Ky. Med. Ctr., Lexington, 1968; exec. sec. Hoffman Products/Cortron Industries, Chgo., 1968-70; co-founder, adminstr. Banner Pers. Svc., Inc., Chgo., 1970-87, chmn., CEO, 1988—; co-founder Banner Temp. Svc., 1982—; founder Banner Tng. Ctrs., 1996—, Banner Acctg. and Fin., 1999—. Guest spkr. Chgo. Entrepreneurship Program, U. Ill., Chgo., 1993—; fund-raising co-chair U. Chgo., Divsn. Mid. Ea. Studies, 1993-95. Mem. parents bd. Bradley U., Peoria, Ill., 1989-90, assoc. trustee, 1992-93, alumni master, 1993, mem. Bradley coun., 1993-95, bd. trustees, 1995—. Listed in Crains Chgo. Bus. as a Top Woman-Owned Firm, 1989, 90, 91, Today's Chgo. Woman as one of 100 Women Making a Difference, 1997; named to Entrepreneurship Hall of Fame, 1993. Mem. ASTD, Chgo. Orgn. Data Processing Educators, Nat. Assn. Pers. Svcs., Nat. Assn. Temp. Svcs., Ill. Assn. Pers. Svcs., Ill. Assn. Temporary Svcs. Avocations: skiing, scuba diving, traveling, sailing. Home: 3750 N Lake Shore Dr Chicago IL 60613-4238 Office: Banner Personnel Service Inc 125 S Wacker Dr #1250 Chicago IL 60606-4424

SINGER, JAYNE MARIE, psychologist; b. N.Y., N.Y., Mar. 3, 1960; d. Joseph Paul Singer and Joan Marie Rosembaum Singer; m. Jonathan Jesse Small, May 30, 1987; children: David, Jesse, Danielle, Siara. BA with hons., SUNY, 1982; PhD, St. Johns U., 1990. Lic. psychologist Mass., 1991. With Bd. Coop. Edn. Svcs., Westchester, NY, 1982—84; staff psychologist Children's Hosp., Boston, 1989—. Clin. co-dir. Judge Baker Children's Ctr. Manville Sch., 1997—99; lead faculty early care and edn. initiative Brazelton Touchpoints Ctr., Boston, 1999; instr. psychology Children's Hosp. Harvard Med. Sch., Boston, 1999; clin. dir. Parent-Infant Mental Health Program Children's Hosp., 2000—; lectr. in field. Contbr. articles to profl. jours. Fellow, St. John's U., 1984—88; scholar Regents scholarship, N.Y., 1978—82. Mem.: Mass. Psychol. Assn., Am. Psychol. Assn. Home: 151 Davis Ave Brookline MA 02445

SINGER, MAXINE FRANK, retired biochemist, scientific institute executive; b. N.Y.C., Feb. 15, 1931; d. Hyman S. and Henrietta (Perlowitz) Frank; m. Daniel Morris Singer, June 15, 1952; children: Amy Elizabeth, Ellen Ruth, David Byrd, Stephanie Frank. AB, Swarthmore Coll., 1952, DSc (hon.), 1978; PhD, Yale U., 1957, DSc (hon.), 1994, Wesleyan U., 1977, U. Md.-Baltimore County, 1985, Cedar Crest Coll., 1986, CUNY,

1988, Brandeis U., 1988, Radcliffe Coll., 2000, Williams Coll., 1990, Franklin and Marshall Coll., 1991, George Washington U., 1991, NYU, 1992, Lehigh U., 1992, Dartmouth Coll., 1993, Harvard U., 1994, Yale U., 1994; PhD honoris causa (hon.), Weizmann Inst. Sci., 1995. USPHS postdoctoral fellow NIH, Bethesda, Md., 1956—58, rsch. chemist biochemistry, 1958—74, head sect. on nucleic acid enzymology Nat. Cancer Inst., 1974—79; chief Lab. of Biochemistry, Nat. Cancer Inst., 1979—87, rsch. chemist, 1987—88; pres. Carnegie Inst. Washington, 1988—2002. Regents vis. lectr. U. Calif., Berkeley, 1981; bd. dirs. Johnson & Johnson, Perlegen Sci., Inc. Mem. editl. bd.: Jour. Biol. Chemistry, 1968—74, Sci. mag, 1972—82, chmn. editl. bd.: Procs. of NAS, 1985—88; co-author (with Paul Berg): 3 books on molecular biology and a sci. biog.; contbr. Chmn. Smithsonian Coun., 1992—93; trustee Wesleyan U., Middletown, Colo., 1972—75, Yale Corp., New Haven, 1975—90; bd. govs. Weizmann Inst. Sci., Rehovot, Israel, 1978—; bd. dirs. Whitehead Inst., 1985—94, chmn. bd., 2003—. Named to Washington D.C. Hall of Fame, 2000; recipient award for achievement in biol. scis., Washington Acad. Scis., 1969, award for rsch. in biol. scis., Yale Sci. and Engring. Assn., 1974, Superior Svc. Honor award, HEW, 1975, Dirs. award, NIH, 1977, Disting. Svc. medal, HHS, 1983, Presdl. Disting. Exec. Rank award, 1987, U.S. Disting. Exec. Rank award, 1987, Mory's Cup, Bd. Govs. Mory's Assn., 1991, Wilbur Lucius Cross Medal for Honor, Yale Grad. Sch. Assn., 1991, Nat. Medal Sci., NSF, 1992, Pub. Svc. award, NIH Alumni Assn., 1995, Vannevar Bush award, Nat. Sci. Bd., 1999. Fellow: Am. Acad. Arts and Scis.; mem.: AAAS (Sci. Freedom and Responsibility award 1982), NAS (coun. 1982—85, sci., engring. and pub. policy 1989—91, chmn. 1999—, com. sci., engring. and pub. policy), N.Y. Acad. Scis., Human Genome Orgn., Pontifical Acad. of Scis., Inst. Medicine of NAS, Am. Philos. Soc., Am. Chem. Soc., Am. Soc. Microbiologists, Am. Soc. Biol. Chemists. Home: 5410 39th St NW Washington DC 20015-2902 Office: Carnegie Inst Washington 1530 P St NW Washington DC 20005-1933

SINGER, NIKI, media consultant; b. Rochester, NY, Sept. 10, 1937; d. Goodman A. and Evelyn (Simon) Sarachan; m. Michael J. Sheets, 1973; children: Romaine Kitty, Nicholas Simon Feramorz. BA cum laude, U. Mich., 1959. Mgr. advt. sales promotion Fairchild Publ., NYC, 1959-67; acct. exec., acct. supr. Vernon Pope Co., NYC, 1967-69, v.p., 1969-71; pres. Niki Singer, Inc., NYC, 1971-93; sr. v.p. M. Shanken Comm., Cigar Aficionado, Wine Spectator, 1994—2002; founder Niki Singer, LLC, 2003—. Mem.: Les Dames d'Escoffier (bd. dirs.), Am. Inst. Wine and Food (bd. dirs.). Office: 1035 5th Ave New York NY 10028-0135 E-mail: sheets@nyc.rr.com.

SINGER, SUZANNE FRIED, editor; b. N.Y.C., July 9, 1935; d. Maurice Aaron and Augusta G. (Ginsberg) Fried; m. Max Singer, Feb. 12, 1959; children: Saul, Alexander (dec.), Daniel, Benjamin. BA with honors, Swarthmore Coll., 1956; MA, Columbia U., 1958. Program asst. NSF, Washington, 1958-60; assoc. editor Bibl. Archaeology Rev., Washington, 1979-84, mng. editor, 1984-96, exec. editor, 1996-99, contbg. editor, 1999—; mng. editor Bibl. Rev., Washington, 1984-96, exec. editor, 1994-99, contbg. editor, 1999—; mng. editor Moment, Washington, 1990-99, exec. editor, 1999—, Archaeology Odyssey, 1998-99, contbg. editor, 1999—. Jewish. Office: Bibl Archaeology Soc 4710 41st St NW Washington DC 20016-1706 also: 1 Barak Jerusalem Israel 93502

SINGER-CHANG, GAIL LESLIE, social sciences educator, assistant dean for student affairs; d. Frank Max (Stepfather) and Rona Jane Singer; m. Anthony Chang. BA in Journalism, San Diego State U., 1988; MS in Counseling, Calif. State U., Fullerton, 1992; MA in Clin. Psychology, Calif. Sch. Profl. Psychology, 1994, D of Psychology in Clin. Psychology, 1996. Pupil pers. svcs. credential Calif. Asst. prof. family medicine, social and behavioral scis., asst. dean student affairs Western U. of Health Scis., Pomona, Calif., 1999—. Orgnl. cons., Irvine, Calif., 1998—99; program dir., doctor-patient communication program Western U. of Health Sciences, Pomona, Calif., 1999—; post-doctoral psychology intern El Toro Marine Base Family Services Ctr., El Toro, Calif., 1997—99; psychology intern Kaiser Permanente, Tustin, Calif., 1995—96, Orange Coast Coll. Student Health Ctr., Costa Mesa, Calif., 1994—95; counseling intern Teen-Age Pregnancy and Parenting Program, Fullerton, Calif., 1991—91; adj. prof. Concordia U., Irvine, Calif., 1998—99, Calif. State U., Fullerton, 1999; presenter in field. Presenter (profl. presentation) Enabling Disability Education: The Value of Using Disabled Persons as Standardized Patients, 10th Internat. Ottawa Conf. Med. Edn., 2002 (Greatest Profl. Promise, 1992), Creative Use of Assessment and Feedback: Increasing Deep Learning and Professionalism, Western Assn. Schs. and Colls., 2002, Psychosocial Aspects of the Physician-Patient Intervention, Soc. Psychol. Anthropology, 2003. Mem.: Assn. Profl. Cons., Am. Anthropol. Assn., Assn. for the Behavioral Scis. and Med. Edn., Soc. of Teachers of Family Medicine. Office: Western U Health Scis 309 East 2d St Pomona CA 91766 E-mail: gsingerchang@westernu.edu.

SINGH, DEANN COATES, small business owner, artist, educator; d. Nathan Devere Coates and Maxcine Nelson; m. Rajendra Singh, July 30, 1977; children: Jonathan Ray, Donavan Ray, Hailey Rae. Student, Weber State Coll., Santa Monica Coll., Cerritos College. Master calligrapher Apprenticeship to Master Calligraphers, 1988. Art and calligraphy tchr., 1981—; calligrapher for county suprs. County L.A., 1987—91; owner Designing Letters Studio, L.A., 1988—. Calligraphy and lettering arts, Calligraph Mag. Cub scout den leader Boy Scouts Am., L.A. Mem.: Soc. for Calligraphy (pres. 2000—). Democrat. Mem. Lds Ch. Avocations: art history, paleography, art, painting, poetry. Personal E-mail: designingletters.com. E-mail: societyforcalligraphy.org.

SINGLEHURST, DONA GEISENHEYNER, horse farm owner; b. Tacoma, June 19, 1928; d. Herbert Russell and Rose Evelyn (Rubish) Geisenheyner; m. Thomas G. Singlehurst, May 16, 1959 (dec.); 1 child, Suanna Singlehurst. BA in Psychology, Whitman Coll., 1950. With pub. rels. and advt. staff Lane Wells, L.A., 1950-52; staff mem. in charge new bus. Bishop Trust Co., Honolulu, 1953-58; mgr. Town & Country Stables, Honolulu, 1958-62; co-owner, v.p. pub. rels. Carol & Mary, Ltd., Honolulu, 1964-84; owner Stanhope Farms, Waialua, Hawaii, 1969—. Internat. dressage judge, sport horse breeding judge US Equestrian; sr. judge Can. Dressage Fedn. Chmn. ways and means com. The Outdoor Cir., Hawaii, 1958-64, life mem.; pres. emeritus Morris Animal Found., Englewood, Colo., 1988—, pres., 1984-88; bd. dirs., pres. Delta Soc., Renton, Wash., 1994-97, chmn. emeritus 1998—, N.Y.C.; mem. Jr. League of Honolulu; mem. devel. com. Honolulu Symphony. Recipient Best Friends award Honolulu Vet. Soc., 1986, Spl. Recognition award Am. Animal Hosp. Assn., 1988, Recognition award Am. Vet. Med. Assn. Mem. NAFE, AAUW, Hawaii Horse Show Assn. (Harry Hutaff award 1985, past pres., bd. dirs.), Hawaii Combined Tng. Assn. (past pres. bd. dirs.), Calif. Dressage Soc., U.S. Dressage Fedn., U.S. Equestrian Team (area chmn. 1981-85), Hawaiian Humane Soc. (life), U.S. Pony Clubs (dist. commr. 1970-75, nat. examiner 1970-75), Pacific Club, Outrigger Canoe Club. Republican. Episcopalian. Avocations: music, travel. Home and Office: Stanhope Farms PO Box 546 Waialua HI 96791 Office Phone: 808-637-5625.

SINGLETON, STELLA WOOD, nurse; b. Moore County, N.C., Nov. 3, 1948; d. Jay and Thelma A. Wood; children: Jennifer, Mike. Diploma, Hamlet Hosp. Sch. Nursing, Hamlet, N.C., 1975; postgrad., Appalachian State U., Boone, N.C., 1990—. RN, N.C. Dir. Hospice of Boone (N.C.) Area, 1982-83; Hospice dir. Hospice of Avery County, Newland, N.C., 1983-85; DON Toe River Health Dist., Newland, N.C., 1983-84; mental health nurse II New River Mental Health, Newland, N.C., 1977-82, 85-95; beauty cons. Mary Kay Cosmetics, 1986—; habilitation asst. Devl. Disabilities Svcs., Boone, N.C., 1995-98; personal care supr. HomeCare Mgmt. Corp., Boone, N.C., 1996-98; co-assoc., program mgr. Avery Citizens Against Domestic Abuse, 1998-2000; nurse Broughton Hosp., Morganton, N.C., 2000—. Instr. Mayland C.C., Spruce Pine, N.C., 1996-99. Co-facilitator Avery County Alzheimer's Support Group; group facilitator Cancer Support Group Svc., 1985-98; rehab. chmn. Am. Cancer Soc., 1977-99, cmty. amb. Celebration on the Hill, 2002; HIV counselor. Recipient Gov's. award for administrv. vol. Home: PO Box 483 Crossnore NC 28616-0483 Office: Broughton Hosp Morganton NC 28655 Office Phone: 828-433-2135. E-mail: sane2b@yahoo.com.

SINICKI, CHRISTINE, state official; b. Mar. 28, 1960; married; 2 children. Mgr. small bus.; state assemblywoman, 1998—; del. U.S. Presdl. Electoral Coll., 2000. Mem. children and families com.; mem. edn. com.; mem. edn. reform com.; mem. personal privacy com.; mem. Wis. Housing and Econ. Devel. Authority. Mem. Milw. Sch. Bd., 1991—98. Democrat. Office: State Capitol Rm 321F W PO Box 8953 Madison WI 53708-8953

SINKFIELD, GEORGANNA T. state legislator; m. Richard H. Sinkfield; 2 children. BS, Tenn. State U.; student law sch., Emory U. Mem. Ga. Ho. of Reps., Atlanta, 1982—. Chairperson children and youth com.; mem. appropriations com., edn. com. Mem. adv. bd. Spl. Audiences Inc., Martin Luther King Day Care, Applecorp. Recipient Friend of Children award Coun. on Children, Disting. Svc. award Atlanta. Democrat. Office: State Capitol Rm 416 Atlanta GA 30334

SINKFORD, JEANNE CRAIG, dental association administrator, retired dentist, retired dean, educator; b. Washington, Jan. 30, 1933; d. Richard E. and Geneva (Jefferson) Craig; m. Stanley M. Sinkford, Dec. 8, 1951; children: Dianne Sylvia, Janet Lynn, Stanley M. III. BS, Howard U., 1953, MS, 1962, DDS, 1958, PhD, 1963; DSc (hon.), Georgetown U., 1978, U. Med. and Dentistry of N.J., 1992, Detroit Mercy U., 1996. Instr. prosthodontics Sch. Dentistry Howard U., Washington, 1958—60, faculty dentistry, 1964—, rsch. coord., co-chmn. dept. restorative dentistry, assoc. dean, 1968—75, dean, 1975—91, prof. Prosthodontics Grad. Sch., 1977—91, dean emeritus, prof., 1991—; spl. asst. Am. Assn. Dental Schs., 1991—93, dir. office women and minority affairs, 1993—97, assoc. exec. dir., 1998—. Instr. rsch. and crown and bridge Northwestern U. Sch. Dentistry, 1963—64; cons. prosthodontics and rsch. VA Hosp., Washington, 1965—; resident Children's Hosp. Nat. Med. Ctr., 1974—75; cons. St. Elizabeth's Hosp.; mem. attending staff Freedman's Hosp., Washington, 1964—; adv. bd. D.C. Gen. Hosp., 1975—; mem. nat. adv. dental rsch. coun. Nat. Bd. Dental Examiners; mem. ad hoc adv. panel Tuskegee Syphilis Study for HEW; sponsor D.C. Pub. Health Apprentice Program; mem. adv. coun. to dir. NIH; adv. com. NIH/NIDR/NIA Aging Rsch. Coun.; mem. dental devices classification panel FDA; mem. select panel for promotion child health, 1979—80; mem. spl. med. adv. group VA; bd. overseers U. Pa. Dental Sch., Boston U. Dental Sch.; bd. advisors U. Pitts. Dental Sch.; mem. bd. visitors Temple U. Sch. Dentistry; mem. anat. rev. bd. D.C. NRC Governing Bd.; cons. FDA; mem. Nat. Adv. Dental Rsch. Coun., 1993—96; active NRC Governing Bd. Mem. editl. bd. Jour. Am. Coll. Dentists, 1988—. Mem. Mayor's Block Grant Adv. Com., 1982; mem. parents' coun. Sidwell Friends, 1983; adv. bd. United Negro Coll. Fund, Robert Wood Johnson Health Policy Fellowships; mem. women's health task force NIH; bd. dirs. Girl Scouts U.S.A., 1993—95; bd. visitors Temple U. Sch. Dentistry. Fellow Louise C. Ball fellow grad. tng., 1960—63. Fellow: Internat. Coll. Dentists (Merit award), Am. Coll. Dentists (sec.-treas. Wash. met. sect.); mem.: ADA (chmn. appeal bd. coun. on dental edn. 1975—82), Links Inc., Dean's Coun. (chair), Smithsonian Assocs., N.Y. Acad. Scis., Am. Soc. Dentistry for Children, Inst. Medicine of NAS (coun.), Nat. Dental Assn., Fed. Prosthodontic Orgn., Am. Prosthodontic Soc., Am. Pedodontic Soc., Leadership in Acad. Medicine (adv. bd.), Health Professions Partnership Initiative (adv. bd.), Assn. Am. Women Dentists, Wash. Coun. Adminstrv. Women, So. Conf. Dental Deans (chmn.), Inst. Grad. Dentists (trustee), Am. Inst. Oral Biology, Dist. Dental Soc., Internat. Assn. Dental Rsch., Am. Soc. for Geriatric Dentistry (bd. dirs.), North Portal Civic League, Golden Key, Beta Kappa Chi, Psi Chi, Omicron Kappa Upsilon, Phi Beta Kappa, Sigma Xi (pres.). Achievements include first female dental dean at Howard University.

SINKIN, FAY MARIE, environmentalist; b. N.Y.C., Mar. 24, 1918; d. Joseph E. and Amelia (Kronish) Bloom; m. William R. Sinkin, May 31, 1942; children: Richard, Lanny. BA, Syracuse U., 1938. Pres. LWV, San Antonio, 1947-51; pres., organizer Vis. Nurse Assn., San Antonio, 1952-54; pres. Brandeis U. Women's Com., San Antonio, 1954-56; recruiter, cons. U.S. State Dept. (A.I.D.), Washington, 1963-67; pres. Aquifer Protection Assn., San Antonio, 1974-80, Portrait of Am. Women, San Antonio, 1976-82; chair Bexar County/Edwards Underground Water Dist., San Antonio, 1983-89; chairwoman Edwards Aquifer Preservation Trust, San Antonio, 1990. Editor (pamphlet) Is Applewhite Necessary?, 1978. Named Woman of Yr. Express New Publ., 1964, Sunday Woman San Antonio Light, 1965, Mother of Yr. Avance, 1988; recipient WICI award Women in Comm., 1989, Spirit of Giving award J.C. Penney, 1993, Best and Brightest award U. Round Table, 1998; elected to Women's Hall of Fame, San Antonio, 1985. Mem. San Antonio 100, Tex. Internat. Woman's Forum, Bexar Audobon Soc. (Oustanding Cmty. Svc. award 2003), San Antonio Conservation Soc. (award for preservation of the environment 2002). Democrat. Jewish. Avocations: folk art museum, needlepoint, swimming, reading. Home: 7887 Broadway St Apt 706 San Antonio TX 78209-2537 E-mail: fay2646@aol.com.

SINNARD, ELAINE JANICE, painter, sculptor; b. Fort Collins, Colo., Feb. 14, 1926; d. Elven Orestes and Catherine (Bennet) S. Student, Art Students League, 1948, NYU, 1953, Sculpture Ctr., N.Y.C., 1954, Academie Grande Chaumiere, Paris, 1956. Painter, sculptor. Works exhibited Riverside Mus., N.Y.C., 1955, City Ctr., N.Y.C., 1954-56, Nat. Arts Club, N.Y.C., 1959-90, Lord & Taylor, N.Y.C., 1963-78, Bergdorf Goodman, N.Y.C., 1980-90, Zantman Art Galleries, Carmel-by-the-Sea, Calif., 1970-73, Chevy Chase Gallery, Washington, 1981-88; one woman shows and group exhbns. include: Bergdorf Goodman Nena's Choice Gallery, Sinnard Art Studios; tchr. open workshop for artists. Mem. Nat. Arts Club N.Y.C. Home: PO Box 304 New Hampton NY 10958-0304 Personal E-mail: sinnard@warwick.net.

SIPE, DORIS ELAINE, college dean; b. Hickory, N.C., Aug. 20, 1942; d. Elmer Eugene and Beaulah Viola (Herman) Sipe. BS, Concordia Coll., 1964; MA, Appalachian State U., 1970; EdD, N.C. State U., 1988. Secondary sch. tchr. U.S. Peace Corps, Bentong, Pahang, Malaysia, 1964-66; elem. sch. tchr. Concordia Christian Sch., Conover, N.C., 1967-69; asst. prpof. Sacred Heart Coll., Belmont, N.C., 1970-81, dean adult edn., 1982-87; dir. adult degree program Belmont (N.C.) Abbey Coll., 1987-90; dean coll. continuing edn. Concordia U., River Forest, Ill., 1990—. Faculty adv. com. Ill. Bd. for Higher Edn., Springfield, 1995—; cons., evaluator North Ctrl. Assn., Chgo., 1996—. Named Tchr./Adminstr. of the Yr., Sacred Heart Coll., 1986. Mem. LWV (chpt. pres. 1984), Am. Assn. Higher Edn., Assn. for Continuing Higher Edn., Ill. Coun. for Continuing Higher Edn. (program com. 1990—), Oak Park (Ill.) Rotary Club (bd. dirs. 1995—). Democrat. Lutheran. Home: 209 Augusta St Maywood IL 60153-1028 Office: Concordia Univ 7400 Augusta St River Forest IL 60305-1402

SIPES, CONNIE W. state legislator, educator; b. New Albany, Ind., Aug. 6, 1949; m. Stephen Sipes; children: Cassie, Zachary. BS, Ind. U.-S.E., 1971, MS in Edn., 1975, MS in Adminstrn., 1991. Prin. Fairmont Elem. Sch., New Albany, Ind., 1991—; mem. Ind. Senate from 46th dist., Indpls., 1997—; mem. edn. com., mem. pension and labor com.; ranking minority elections com.; mem. transp. and interstate coop. com. Mem. Dem. Women's Club. Recipient Woman of Achievement award BPW, 1986. Mem. LWV, Ind. State Prins. Assn., Nat. Assn. Elem. Prins. Avocation: running. Office: 200 W Washington St Indianapolis IN 46204-2728

SIPES, KAREN KAY, communications executive; b. Higginsville, Mo., Jan. 8, 1947; d. Walter John and Katherine Marie (McLelland) Heins; m. Joel Rodney Sipes, Sept. 24, 1971; 1 child, Lesley Katherine. BS in Edn., Ctrl. Mo. State U., 1970. Reporter/news editor Newton Kansan, 1973—76; sports writer Capital-Jour., Topeka, 1976—83, spl. sects. editor, 1983—85, editl. page editor, 1985—92, mng. editor/features, 1992—2002, asst. editl. page editor, 2002—03; dir. commn. Kans. Dept. Aging, Topeka, 2003—. Co-chair Mayor's Commn. on Literacy, Topeka, 1995-96; mem. Act Against Violence Com., Topeka, 1995-96, Mayor's Task Force on Race Rels., 1998; mem. planning com. Leadership Greater Topeka, 1997; Great Am. Cleanup, 1999-2001, ERC/Resource and Referral, 2001—; mem. Martin Luther King Living the Dream Bus. Ptnrs. Com., 2001—; mem. Centennial planning com. Family Svc. and Guidance Ctr., 2003-04; mem. Project Topeka Com., 2004—, Arthritis Walk Com., 2004, Faith in Action-No Place Like Home Coalition, 2003—; bd. dirs. Western Swing Music Soc. Kans., 2003--. Mem. Ctrl. Mo. State U. Alumni Assn. (bd. dirs. 1996-2002, v.p. 1999, pres. 2000). Avocations: music, gardening, art. Office: Kans Dept Aging New England Bldg 503 S Kans Ave Topeka KS 66603-3404 Office Phone: 785-296-6154. E-mail: critterkaren@aol.com., karen.sipes@aging.state.ks.us.

SIPOTZ, NAOMI C. music educator; b. Fountainhill, Pa., Feb. 24, 1977; d. Michael and Darlene Sipotz. BS in Edn., Millersville U., 1999. Cert. tchr. Md., Pa. Vocal/gen. music tchr. Kutztown (Pa.) Elem. Sch., 1999—2000, Allenwood Elem. Sch., Temple Hills, Md., 2000—02, Birdsboro Elem. Sch., 2002—. Marching band music staff Gov. Mifflin H.S., Shillington, 1999—2000; pit orch. mem. Ephrata Playhouse in the Park, Ephrata, Pa., 1999; presenter in field. Dir.(musical): Millersville U. Spring Prodn., 1998. Recipient Music award, Pa. Bandmaster's Assn., 2000; scholar All-Am. Collegiate scholar, Millersville U., 1999. Mem.: NEA, Md. Music Edn. Assn., Md. State Edn. Assn., Music Educators Nat. Conf. (pub. dir. collegiate level 1996—97). Republican. Roman Catholic. Avocations: music, singing. Home: 261 Friedensburg Rd Mount Penn PA 19606 Office: 400 West 2nd St Birdsboro PA 19508 Personal E-mail: naomi.sipotz@verizon.net.

SIPSKI, MARY LEONIDE, physician, healthcare administrator; b. Somerville, N.J., July 6, 1950; d. Joseph John and Sophia Barbara (Marcewicz) Sipski; m. Thomas Edward Lammertse, June 16, 1979; children: Meredith, Matthew, Evan. AB, Douglass Coll./Rutgers U., 1972; PhD in Phys. Biochemistry, Ohio U., 1976; MD, Ohio State U., 1979; M in Med. Mgmt., U. So. Calif., 2003. Diplomate Am. Bd. Phys. Medicine and Rehab., Am. Bd. Managed Care Medicine, cert. in med. mgmt. Am. Coll. Physician Execs. and U. So. Calif., 2001. Intern, resident in phys. medicine and rehab. Ohio State U. Hosps., 1979-83; dir. phys. medicine and rehab. Gaylord Hosp., Wallingford, Conn., 1983-90; dir. brain injury program, dir. outpatient svcs. Kessler Inst. Rehab., Chester, NJ, 1990-97; chief med. officer Consumer Health Network Solutions, South Plainfield, NJ, 1997—. Selective Ins. Managed Care Solutions, Hamilton, NJ, 2002—. Med. dir. Gaylord/Yale-New haven Ctr. at Long Wharf, 1989-90; asst. clin. prof. dept. orthopedics and rehab. Yale U., New Haven, 1989-90; cons. Bur. Disability Determination, Columbus, Ohio, 1982-83; pvt. practice cons. in brain injury, disability, and expert medico-legal testimony, Far Hills, 1991—. Fellow Am. Acad. Phys. Medicine and Rehab. (sec. Conn. soc.); mem. AMA, Am. Coll. Physician Execs., Am. Coll. Managed Care Medicine, Consumer Health Network Solutions. Office: Consumer Health Network Solutions 3525 Quakerbridge Rd Hamilton NJ 08619 E-mail: dr.sipski@chn.com.

SIRIGNANO, MONICA ANN, performing company executive, playwright; b. Princeton, N.J., May 18, 1971; d. William Alfonso and Molly Wilhelmina Sirignano. BA in English, Stetson U., 1993; postgrad., CUNY. Mng. editor Encore Mag., Miami, Fla., 1993—95; asst. mng. editor PC Mag., N.Y.C., 1995—2000; performer, playwright N.Y.C., 1995—; artistic dir., pres. Screaming Venus Prodns., N.Y.C., 1999—, also bd. dirs. Adjudicator Fringe NYC, 2000, 01; mem. adv. bd. Blue Allied Theatre Co., N.Y.C., 2002—. Contbr. articles to mags. Mem. membership com., mem. creative black tie invitation com. Am. Cancer Soc., Miami, 1993—94; mem. Habitat for Humanity, Ft. Lauderdale, Fla., 1994. Recipient award, Off-Off Broadway Rev., 2001; grantee, Harburg Found., 2000. Mem.: Theatre Comm. Group, Dramatists Guild. Avocations: photography, painting, graphic design. Office: Screaming Venus Prodns 29-22 Hoyt Ave S # 21 Astoria NY 11102

SIRLIN, DEANNA LOUISE, artist; b. Bklyn., Mar. 7, 1958; d. Robert and Sylvia (Goldsmith) S.; m. Philip Auslander, Aug. 29, 1990. BA, SUNY at Albany, 1978; MFA, CUNY, 1980. Bd. dirs. Contemporary Art Soc., High Mus. Art, Atlanta, Nexus Contemporary Art Ctr., Atlanta. One-woman shows include Fay Gold Gallery, 1993, 95, Cheekwood Fine Arts Ctr., 1995, Nexus Contemporary Arts Ctr., 1996, Solomon Projects, 1998, High Mus. Art, Atlanta, 1999, Ca Foscari Venezia, Venice, 2001, Saltworks Gallery, Atlanta, 2003; represented in permanent collections High Mus. Art, Ca Foscari Venezia, Kunsthaus, Nurnberg, Germany, Macon (Ga.) Mus. of Arts and Scis., Ga. Pacific, United Airlines, CSX Corp., Egleston Hosp., Shenzhen (China) Inst. Fine Arts; commd. pub. art N.E. Regional Libr. Fulton County, 1998. Recipient Yaddo fellowship, 1983, Artist grant Artist's Space, 1987, Artist award Fulton County Arts Coun., 1994, Ga. Coun. for the Arts, 1994. Home and Office: 120 N Christophers Run Alpharetta GA 30004-3100

SIROLA, LINDA F. interior designer; b. Detroit, Dec. 9, 1940; d. Elmer Louis and Hazel C. (Stuteville) Chall; divorced; children: Carrie L., Craig A., Jennifer L. Roban. AA, MacLean Coll., 1961; degree in design, Wayne State C.C., 1964. Owner, designer Designs and Interiors, Livonia, Mich., 1963-76, Sirola Designs Ltd., Birmingham, Mich., 1994—; designer Carpeting Retailer, Bloomfield Hills, Mich., 1983-88; mgr., designer retail drapery shop Rochester, Mich., 1988-90; interior designer McGowen Assoc., Rochester, 1990-94. Staff instr. design John Robert Powers, Southfield, Mich.; staff designer Detroit Jr. League Showcase House, Grosse Pointe, Mich., 1992, Homearama Showcase House, Milford, Mich., 1990; interior designer Greenmead Hist. Christmas Tour, 1994. Interior design photographs appeared in Detroit Monthly, Oakland Life Mag., Showcase of Interior Photographs Design, Midwest Edit. III, 1996-97. Mem. selections bd. Am. Field Svc., Livonia, 1970-75; fgn. exch. student to Germany, AFS Program, 1959. Mem. Nat. Trust for Hist. Preservation (design assoc.). Avocations: antiques, photography, jewelry making, art.

SISCHY, INGRID BARBARA, editor, art critic; b. Johannesburg, Republic of South Africa, Mar. 2, 1952; came to U.S., 1967; d. Benjamin and Claire S. BS, Sarah Lawrence Coll., 1973; PhD (hon.), Moore Coll. Art, 1987. Assoc. editor Print Collector's Newsletter, N.Y.C., 1974-77; dir. Printed Matter, N.Y.C., 1977-78; curatorial intern Mus. Modern Art, N.Y.C., 1978-79; editor ArtForum Mag., N.Y.C., 1979-88; editor-in-chief Interview, N.Y.C., 1989—. Office: Interview Magazine 575 Broadway Fl 5 New York NY 10012-3230

SISCO, CAROL, broadcast executive, educator; b. Bristol, Conn. m. Stuart Jay Sisco, Sept. 27, 1986; children: Kayley Jean, Kyle Jay, Kevin Robert. B in Comm. TV and Film Prodn., U. Mass., 1981; M in Bus. and Orgnl. Comm., Emerson Coll., 1987; EdM, U. Hartford, 2002. Assoc. news prodr. Sta. WVIT-TV, Hartford, Conn., 1984—86; advt. promotion mgr. Record-Jour. Pub. Co., Meriden, Conn., 1986—91; pub. rels. mgr. Life Ins.

Mktg. and Rsch. Assn., Windsor, Conn., 1991—94; dir. corp. comm. and cmty. affairs Bristol (Conn.) Hosp., 1994—98; v.p. corp. and mktg. comm. Conn. Pub. Broadcasting, Inc., Hartford, 1998—. Adj. prof. Teikyo Post U., Waterbury, Conn., 1986—, U. Conn., Waterbury, 1988—94. Mktg. cons. Main St. Cmty. Found., Bristol, 1997—2003; bd. dirs. SINA, Hartford, Conn., 2001—02. Mem.: Am. Mktg. Assn. (assoc.), Jr. Women's Club Bristol (sec. 1998—), Kappa Delta Pi (life). Office: Connt Pub Broadcasting Inc 240 New Britain Ave Hartford CT 06106 Personal E-mail: soundview@snet.net. E-mail: csisco@cptv.org.

SISCO, MARY ANN, director; b. South Williamson, Ky., Oct. 3, 1963; d. George Michael and Sara Ann (Coleman) Stanley; m. Eugene Sisco, Jr., Apr. 20, 1985; children: Eugene III, Alexandria Michaelle, Sara Elizabeth, Anna Gabrielle. AS in Office Adminstrn., Pikeville Coll., 1989, BS in Psychology, BBA in Bus., Pikeville Coll., 1996. Sect. 8 coord. Pike County Housing Authority, Pikeville, 1987—94; computer tchr. vol. St. Francis Assisi Sch., Pikeville, 1996—2001; student devel. specialist Pikeville Coll. ACE Program, Pikeville, 2001—. Contbr. story to textbook Appalachian Education, 1984. Vol. Ky. Organ Donor Affiliate, Pikeville, St. Francis of Assisi Sch., Pikeville, 1991—; parent vol. Boy Scouts of Am. and Girl Scouts of Am., Pikeville, 1995—. Mem.: SAEOPP, KAEOPP (scholarship com. 2003). Roman Catholic. Home: 2596 Island Creek Rd Pikeville KY 41501 Office: Pikeville Coll ACE Program 147 Sycamore St Pikeville KY 41501 E-mail: msisco@pc.edu.

SISEMORE, CLAUDIA, educational films and videos producer, director; b. Salt Lake City, Sept. 16, 1937; d. Darrell Daniel and Alice Larril (Barton) S. BS in English, Brigham Young U., 1959; MFA in Filmmaking, U. Utah, 1976. Cert. secondary tchr., Utah. Tchr. English, drama and writing Salt Lake Sch. Dist., Salt Lake City, 1959-66; tchr. English Davis Sch. Dist., Bountiful, Utah, 1966-68; ind. filmmaker Salt Lake City, 1972—. Filmmaker-in-residence Wyo. Coun. for Arts and Nat. Endowment for Arts, Dubois, Wyo., 1977-78; prodr., dir. ednl. films Utah Office Edn., Salt Lake City, 1979-93, Canyon Video, 1993—. Prodr., dir. Beginning of Winning, 1984 (film festival award 1984), Dancing through the Magic Eye, 1986, Se Hable Espanol, 1986-87, Alvin Clffine, Realist, 1980, Maestro Maruice Abravanel, 1982; writer, dir., editor (film) Building on a Legacy, 1988, (videos) Energy Conservation, 1990, Alternative Energy Sources, 1990, Restructuring Learning, 1991, Kidsercise, 1991, Traditional Energy Sources, 1992, Canyon Video, 1993—; videos Western Mountains and Basins, 1994, Ramps and Rails, 1994, Fitness After 50, 1995, Timescape, 1996, A Winter's Hush: Understanding Depression, 1996, Your Guide to the Internet, 1997, Desert Southwest, 1998, Utah Landscape and the Arts, 2001, Repertory Dance Theater, 2003, Rirle Woodbury Dance, 2003; exhibited in group show Phillips Gallery; represented in pvt. and pub. collections. Juror Park City (Utah) Arts Festival, 1982, Utah Arts Festival, Salt Lake City, 1982, Am. Film Festival, 1985-86, Best of West Film Festival, 1985-86; bd. dirs. Utah Media Ctr., Salt Lake City, 1981-87; mem. multi-disciplinary program Utah Arts Coun., Salt Lake City, 1983-87. Recipient award Utah Media Ctr., 1984, 85; Nat. Endowment for Arts grantee, 1978, Utah Arts Coun. grantee, 1980. Mem. Lds Ch. Avocations: writing, reading, music.

SISK, JANE ELIZABETH, economist, educator; b. West Reading, Pa., Sept. 23, 1942; 2 children. BA with honors, Brown U., 1963; MA, George Washington U., 1965; PhD, McGill U., Montreal, Que., Can., 1976. Cons. Nat. Planning Assn., Washington, 1976; scholar VA, Washington, 1978-81; rsch. dir. Office Tech. Assessment, U.S. Congress, Washington, 1976-78, sr. analyst, 1981-84, sr. assoc., 1984-91. Vis. prof. Columbia U. Sch. Pub. Health, N.Y.C., 1990-91, prof., 1992—99; prof. Mt. Sinai Sch. Medicine, N.Y.C., 1999—. Co-author: Toward Rational Technology in Medicine, 1981; mem. editl. bd. Internat. Jour. Tech. Assessment in Health Care, 1987—, vol. editor, 1990, 98; asst. editor Am. Jour. Pub. Health, 1990-91; mem. editl. bd. Health Svcs. Rsch., 1994—; contbr. articles to profl. jours. Pres. Internat Soc. Tech. Assessment in Health Care, 1991-93, bd. dirs., 1987-95; mem. N.Y. State Task Force on Clin. Guidelines & Med. Tech. Assessment, 1994-96; mem. study sect. on health care quality and effectiveness rsch. U.S. Agy. for Health Care Policy and Rsch., 1997-2001. Elisah Benjamin Andrews scholar Brown U., 1961, 63; Bronfman fellow McGill U., 1971. Fellow Assn. for Health Svcs. Rsch.; mem. Inst. of Medicine, NAS (mem. cancer policy bd. 1997-2000, inst. medicine, 2001—), Phi Beta Kappa.

SISKE, REGINA, artist; b. Varen Muritz, Germany, Oct. 11, 1944; d. Peter Paul and Olga Vanda Markunas; m. Roger Charles Siske, May 31, 1969; children: Kelly, Jennifer, Kimberly. BSN, U. Ill., 1966; postgrad. in MSN program, U. Mich., 1968—69; ind. fine art studies, North Shore Art League, Winnetka, Ill., 1970s, Alain Gavin, Art Inst. Chgo., 1980s, Tom James, Wilmette, Ill., 2000—; Asian brush painting and Chinese calligraphy studies Prof. Lampo Leong, U. Mo., Columbia, 1998—; Asian brush painting and Chinese calligraphy studies, Kay Thomas, Highland Pk., Ill., 1997—; Asian brush painting and Chinese calligraphy studies Madeleine Jossem and Qi-Gi Jiang, Art Inst., Chgo., 1999—2002; Asian brush painting and Chinese calligraphy studies Moon Yan Huen, City Coll., San Francisco, 1999—2002; Asian brush painting and Chinese calligraphy studies, Charles Liu, Westmont, Ill., 1999—, numerous workshops, N.Y.C. and Chgo. RN Ill., 1966. Staff med.-surg. nurse Presbyn.-St. Luke's Hosp., Chgo., 1966—67, Mass. Gen. Hosp., Boston, 1967—68; nursing staff devel. VA Rsch. Hosp., Chgo., 1969—70, Evanston/Northwestern Hosp., Evanston, Ill., 1971, St. Francis Hosp., Evanston, Ill., 1971—73; nursing cons. Evanston Hosp., 1971; rsch. and quality control studies VA Hosp., Chgo., 1969—70; cmty. outreach and edn. Evanston and St. Francis Hosps., 1971—73. Exhibitions include Mobile (Ala.) Mus. Art, 1998, Bayard Cutting Arboretum, Long Island, N.Y., 1999, Strathmore Hall of Arts, Bethesda, Md., 2000 (award, 2000), 2003 (award, 2003), Courthouse Gallery, Norfolk, Va., 2001, Virtual Exhbn., Internet, 2002, Suburban Fine Arts Ctr., Highland Pk., Ill., 1999—2004 (award, 2001), Chinese Fine Arts Soc., Westmont, Ill., 2001, Alliance Gallery, Indpls. Mus. Art, 2000—01, Represented in permanent collections Chgo. Bot. Gardens, pub. collections, numerous pvt. collections, local exhibits. Vol. Kellogg Cancer Rsch. Ctr., Evanston Hosp., 1988—89; bd. dir. St. Elizabeth Nursery Sch., Glencoe, Ill., 1981—82, Josselyn Ctr. for Mental Health, Northfield, Ill., 1989—93, devel. chmn., 1992—93. Named hon. lifetime trustee, Josselyn Ctr. Mental Health, 1993—. Mem.: Nat. Sumi-e Soc. Am., Midwest Sumi-e Soc. (program dir. 2000—04). Avocations: piano, jewelry design, skiing, swimming. Home and Studio: 248 Hawthorn Ave Glencoe IL 60022 E-mail: sisker@aol.com.*

SISKIN, SHARON VALERIE, art educator; b. Elkins Park, Pa., Feb. 22, 1955; d. Jack and Lora (Wexler) S.; m. John Christopher Lavine, Sept. 29, 1991. BFA, Tyler Sch. Art, 1976; MFA, U. Calif., Berkeley, 1981; MA, U. N.Mex., 1979. Artist-in-residence Calif. Arts Coun., Bay Area, 1988—; instr. Chabot Coll., Hayward, Calif., 1988—, Contra Costa Coll., San Pablo, Calif., 1992—, Calif. Coll. Arts and Crafts, 2003; asst. prof. U. San Francisco, 2003. Adj. prof. John F. Kennedy U., Orinda, Calif., 1991—; lectr. in field. One-woman shows include Tyler Sch. Art, Elkins Park, Pa., 1976, U. Calif., berkeley, 1981, Pro Arts Gallery, Oakland, Calif., 1984, Gregory Ghent Gallery, San Francisco, 1987, Richard Reynolds Gallery, Stockton, Calif., 1991, Arts and Consciousness Gallery, Orinda, 1991, Addison St. Windows Installation Space, Berkeley, 1992, 93, Falkirk Cultural Ctr., San Rafael, Calif., 1994, Kennedy Art Ctr. Gallery, Oakland, 1995, Palo Alto (Calif.) Cultural Ctr., 1995-96, Gallery Rt. One, 2003, others; group shows include Teh Galleria, Albuquerque, 1978, Downtown Ctr. Arts, Albuquerque, 1979, 80, Univ. Art Mus., Berkeley, 1981, Univ. Gallery, Hayward, 1982, Richmond (Calif.) Art Ctr., 1983, Napa (Calif.) Valley Coll. Art Gallery, 1984, Irvine (Calif.) Art Ctr., 1985, Chabot Coll., Hayward, 1986, Mission Cultural Ctr., San Francisco, 1987, Berkeley Art Ctr., 1988, Sun Gallery, Hayward, 1990, Eddie Rhodes Gallery, San Pablo, Calif., 1991, Prieto Gallery, Oakland, 1992, The Drawing Ctr., N.Y.C., 1993, M.H. de Young Meml. Mus., San Francisco, 1994, Alternative Mus., N.Y.C., 1995, Bedford Gallery, Walnut Creek, Calif., 1996, Kans. City Artist Coalition, Works Gallery, San Jose, Oakland Mus., S.F. Jewish Mus., San Diego Ctr. Jewish Culture, others. Grantee Ford Found., 1978, 79, Calif. Arts Coun., Sacramento, 1988-91, 92-95, 96-97, John F. Kennedy U., Orinda, Calif., 1995, 96, Reva and David Logan Found., Chgo., 1991—, LEF Found., 1995, 96, Inst. Noetic Scis., 2000, Berkeley Civic, 2000 Arts Commn., 2000, San Francisco Arts Commn., 2001, Potvevo Nuevo Prize, 2001; Artist fellow Calif. Arts Coun., 2003. Mem. Coll. Art Assn., Women's Caucus Art, Pro Art. Green Party. Jewish. Home: 2434 9th St Berkeley CA 94710-2505 Studio: Nexus Inst 2701 8th St Berkeley CA 94710-2603 E-mail: sharonsiskin@earthlink.net.

SISLEY, BECKY LYNN, physical education educator; b. Seattle, May 10, 1939; d. Leslie James and Blanche (Howe) S.; m. Jerry Newcomb, 1994. BA, U. Wash., 1961; MSPE, U. N.C., Greensboro, 1964, EdD, 1973. Tchr. Lake Washington H.S., Kirkland, Wash., 1961-62; instr. U. Wis., Madison, 1963-65, U. Oreg., Eugene, 1965-68, prof. phys. edn., 1968—2004, women's athletic dir., 1973-79, head undergrad. studies in phys. edn., 1985-92. Co-author: Softball for Girls, 1971; contbr. articles to profl. jours. Mem. athletic adv. bd. Women's Sports Found., 1993-96. Named to Hall of Fame, U. Oreg. Athletics, 1998, N.W. Women's Sports Found., Seattle, 1981, Nat. Masters Track and Field Hall of Fame, 2001; recipient Honor award, N.W. Dist. AAHPERD, 1988, Nat. Assn. for Girls and Women in Sports, 1995, Disting. Alumni award, Sch. Health and Human Performance, U. N.C., Greensboro, 1996. Mem. AAHPERD, Oreg. Alliance Health, Phys. Edn., Recreation and Dance (hon. life mem.), Western Soc. for Phys. Edn. of Coll. Women (hon. mem., exec. bd. 1982-85), Oreg. High Sch. Coaches Assn., N.W. Coll. Women's Sports Assn. (pres. 1977-78), Oreg. Women's Sports Leadership Network (dir. 1987-97), Phi Epsilon Kappa, others. Office: U Oreg Phys Activity & Recreation Svcs Eugene OR 97403

SISLEY, NINA MAE, physician, public health service officer; b. Jacksonville, Fla., Aug. 19, 1924; d. Leonard Percy and Verna (Martin) S.; m. George W. Fischer, May 16, 1962 (dec. 1990). BA, Tex. State Coll. for Women, 1944; MD, U. Tex., Galveston, 1950; MPH, U. Mich., 1963. Intern City of Detroit Receiving Hosp., 1950-51, resident in gen. practice St. Mary's Infirmary, Galveston, Tex., 1951-52; sch. physician Galveston Ind. Sch. Dist., 1953-56; dir. med. svcs. San Antonio Health Dept., 1960-63, acting dir., 1963-64; resident in pub. health Tex. Dept. Pub. Health, San Antonio, 1963-65; dir. cmty. health svcs. Corpus Christi-Nueces County Dept. Health, Tex., 1964-67; dir. Tb control region 5 Tex. Dept. Health, Corpus Christi, 1967-73; chief chronic illness control City of Houston Health Dept., Rosenberg, 1973-78; dir. pub. health region 11 Tex. Dept. Health, Rosenberg, 1978-87; dir. Corpus Christi-Nueces County Dept. Pub. Health, 1987—2002. Lectr. Incarnate Word Coll., San Antonio, 1963-64; adj. prof. U. Tex. Sch. Pub. Health, Houston, 1980—; adj. prof. Tex. A&M U., Corpus Christi, 1997—; pvt. practice Galveston, Stockdale, Hereford and Borger, Tex., 1952-59; mem. adv. bd. Cmty. Adv. Coun.; clin. instr. U. Tex. Health Sci. Ctr., San Antonio, 1997—. Bd. dirs. Coastal Bend chpt. ARC, Corpus Christi, 1990-94, 2003—, pres., 1990-91; bd. dirs. United Way-Coastal Bend, Coastal Bend Coalition on AIDS, 1988-94; mem. Nueces County Child Fatality Rev. Com.; mem. adv. com. Nueces County Hosp. Dist.; mem. adv. bd. Alzheimers Assn.; mem. health adv. bd. Corpus Christi Ind. Sch. Dist.; bd. dirs. Charlie's Place Alcohol and Drug Rehab. Ctr. Fellow Am. Coll. Preventive Medicine; mem. Tex. Med. Assn., Nueces County Med. Soc. (pres. 1997-98), Tex. Assn. Pub. Health Physicians, Tex. Pub. Health Assn. (pres. 1991-92), Local Emergency Planning Assn., Long Term Health Assn. Episcopalian. Avocations: fishing, crossword puzzles, raising african violets. Home: 62 Rock Creek Dr Corpus Christi TX 78412-4214 Office: Corpus Christi-Nueces County Dept Health 1702 Horne Rd Corpus Christi TX 78416-1902 E-mail: nms@ci.corpus.christi.tx.us.

SISSON, JEAN CRALLE, retired primary school educator; b. Village, Va., Nov. 16, 1941; d. Willard Andrew and Carolyn (Headley) Cralle; m. James B. Sisson, June 20, 1964 (div. Oct. 1994); 1 child, Kimberly Carol; m. donald Wimer (div. 1998). BS in Elem. Edn., Longwood Coll., 1964; MA in Adminstrn. and Supervision, Va. Commonwealth U., 1979. Tchr. 2nd grade Tappahannock (Va.) Elem. Sch., 1964-67; tchr. 2nd and 4th grades Farnham (Va.) Elem. Sch., 1967-71; tchr. 6th grade Callao (Va.) Elem. Sch., 1971-81; tchr. 6th and 7th grades Northumberland Mid. Sch., Heathsville, Va., 1981—2003; ret., 2003. Sr. mem. Supt. Adv. Com., Heathsville, 1986-93. Author: My Survival, 1994; author of children's books, short stories and poetry. Lifetime mem. Gibeon Bapt. Ch., Village, Va., 1942—. Mem.: IDEA, ASCD, NEA, Nat. Wildlife Fedn., Nat. Coun. English Tchrs., Exercise Safety Assn., Va. Mid. Sch. Assn., Aerobics and Fitness Assn., PETA, Alpha Delta Kappa. Republican. Avocations: aerobics, dance, music, art, travel. Home: 1068 Lodge Rd Callao VA 22435-2105 Office: Northumberland Mid Sch PO Box 100 Heathsville VA 22473-0100 E-mail: jsisson@nucps.com.

SITARZ, ANNELIESE LOTTE, pediatrics educator, physician; b. Medellin, Colombia, Aug. 31, 1928; came to U.S., 1935; d. Hans and Elisabeth (Noll) S. BA cum laude, Bryn Mawr (Pa.) Coll., 1950; MD, Columbia U., 1954. Diplomate Nat. Bd. Med. Examiners, Am. Bd. Pediatrics., Am. Bd. Pediatric Hematology and Oncology. Intern Children's Med. Ctr., Boston, 1954-55; resident in pediat. Babies Hosp.-Columbia-Presbyn. Med. Ctr., N.Y.C., 1955-57; mem. faculty Columbia U., N.Y.C., 1957—, assoc. prof. clin. pediat., 1974-83, prof. clin. pediat., 1983-2000, prof. emerita clin. pediat., spl. lectr. in pediat., 2000—; attending in pediat. Babies and Children's Hosp., N.Y.C., 1983—. Cons. pediatrics, hematology and oncology Harlem Hosp., N.Y.C., 1967—72, Overlook Hosp., Summit, NJ, 1975—2001. Contbr. numerous articles to profl. jours. Pres. Mt. Prospect Assn., Summit, 1987—. Fellow Am. Acad. Pediatrics; mem. Am. Assn. Cancer Rsch., Am. Soc. Clin. Oncology, Am. Soc. Hematology, Internat. Soc. Hematology, Harvey Soc. Republican. Episcopalian. Avocations: gardening, sewing, skiing, hiking, stamp collecting. Office: Childrens Hosp of NY Presbyn Irving Pavilion 161 Ft Washington Ave New York NY 10032-3710

SITOMER, SHEILA MARIE, television producer, director; b. Hartford, Conn., Aug. 25, 1951; d. George W. and Mary E. (Chaponis) Bowe; m. Daniel J. Sitomer, Aug. 25, 1985. BA, Smith Coll., 1973. Field producer, dir. Good Morning Am., ABC-TV, N.Y.C., 1981-86; field producer Evening Magazine, WWOR-TV, KDKA-TV, Pitts. and Secaucus, N.J., 1978-79, 88; supervising producer The Reporters, Fox Broadcasting, N.Y.C., 1988; producer Inside Edition, King World Prodns., N.Y.C., 1988-95; co-exec. prodr. Inside Edition and Am. Jour., 1995-98; exec. prodr. Extra, 1998-2000; exec. prodr. program devel. ABC News, N.Y.C., 2000—. Recipient Peabody award, Columbia Dupont award, AWRT award, 3 Emmys, New England chpt. TV Acad. Arts & Scis., 1975-78, 2 Emmys, N.Y. chpt. TV Acad. Arts & Scis., 1979, 89, recipient first prize Internat. Film & TV Festival N.Y., 1988, No. N.J. Press Club award, 1988, George Polk award, Sigma Delta Chi award, IRE award Nat. Headliners, Columbus Film Festival. Mem. Dirs. Guild Am., Actors Equity Assn. Office: ABC News 47 W 66th St New York NY 10023 E-mail: sheila.sitomer@abc.com.

SITTON, WINDY, mayor; m. Frank Sitton, 1965; 1 child, John. BEd in History and English, N. Tex. U.; MA in Counseling, Tex. Women's U. Tchr. English, secondary schs. Dallas Bd. Edn., counselor; owner, mgr. Sitton Selections Co., Lubbock, 1992—; mayor Lubbock, Tex. Owner, mgr. Employee Imaging Co., Dallas, 1980-87. Chair major gifts Capital Campaign for Women's Protective Svcs. and YWCA; mem. Chancellor's Coun., Red Raider Club, Tex. Tech. U., Jr. League Comty. Adv. Com., Lubbock Symphony Guild; mem. Leadership Am., 2001—. Nominated Woman Entrepreneur of Yr., 1996; inducted Tex. Leaderhip Hall of Fame, 1996; recipient Disting. Alumni award Tex. Women's U., 1998. Mem. South Plains Assn. Govts. (bd. dirs.), Greater Lubbock C. of C., Lubbock C. of C., West Tex. Home Builders' Assn. Baptist. Avocations: volunteering, antiquing, golf, reading, collecting. Office: PO Box 2000 Lubbock TX 79457-0001 E-mail: wsitton@mail.ci.lubbock.tx.us.

SIVAK, MADELINE ANN, not-for-profit developer; b. Erie, Pa., Aug. 30, 1957; d. Michael Valerian and Madeline Mary (Mentz) S. BA, John Carroll U., 1980; RN diploma, Huron Rd. Hosp. Sch. Nursing, 1986; grad. cert. nonprofit mgmt., Case Western Res. U., 1992. RN, Ohio. CEO Michael's House, Inc., Cleve., 1993—. Cons. Great Lakes Theater, Cleve., 1991-92, Michael's House, Cleve., 1992-93. Trustee Alzheimer's Assn., Cleve., 1988-93, Am. Liver Found., Cleve., 1991-94; mem. United Way Leadership Assn., Cleve., 1991. Mem. Am. Psychiat. Nurses Assn., Nat. Coun. on Family Rels., Assn. Death Edn./Counseling, Ohio Coun. Fundraising Execs., Jr. League Cleve., Pi Gamma Mu. Republican. Roman Catholic.

SIVCO, DEBORAH LEE, research materials scientist; b. Somerville, N.J., Dec. 21, 1957; d. Lawrence M. Skurkay and Elizabeth J. McCulla; m. Gregory Charles Sivco, July 11, 1981; children: Scott Gregory, Michelle Elizabeth, Carolyn Suzanne, David Charles. BA in chem. edn., Rutgers Univ., 1980; MS in material sci., Stevens Inst., 1988. III-V processing tech. Laser Diode Labs, New Brunswick, N.J., 1980-81; materials scientist Bell Labs. Lucent Technologies, Murray Hill, N.J., 1981—. Contbr. articles to profl. jours.; 22 patents in field. Recipient Newcomb Cleveland prize AAAS, 1993-94, Electronics Letters premium Instn. Elec. Engrs. U.K., 1995, Group Achievement award NASA, 2000. Office: Bell Labs Lucent Technologies 600 Mountain Ave New Providence NJ 07974-2008 E-mail: dls@lucent.com.

SIVERTSEN, LINDA JOYCE, writer, publishing consultant, editor; b. Stanford, Calif., Aug. 31, 1964; d. Alfred Eugene and Joanne Rose Tisch; m. Mark Duanne Sivertsen, Sept. 10, 1988; 1 child, Tosh. Student, U. So. Calif., 1984—87. Life coach, L.A., 1987—89; owner pet sitting bus. Beverly Hills, 1989—94; cons. writing, nat. and internat., 1995—; author Health Comms., Deerfield Beach, Fla., 1998—; West Coast editor Balance Mag., Ft. Lauderdale, Fla., 2002—. Book proposal writer Illiani Co., L.A., 1999—; ghostwriter, co-author Jodere Pub. Group, San Diego, 2001, San Diego, 03, individuals, 2001—; spkr. in field; tchr. Learning Annex, L.A., 2001—03. Author: Lives Charmed: Intimate Conversations with Extraordinary People, 1998 (Earth Island Jour. award, 2000); co-author: Will to Survive: A Mental and Emotional Survival Guide for Law Enforcement Professionals, 2003; contbr. columns in newspapers. Mem.: Nat. Assn. Women Bus. Owners, Delta Gamma (life). Avocations: tennis, gardening, hiking, painting, reading. Office: ILLIANI Co PO Box 41 1893 Los Angeles CA 90041

SIVINSKI, TINA M. human resources specialist, Grad. magna cum laude, Springfield Coll. V.p. Data Gen. Corp.; corp. v.p. mktg. and innovation Sci. Applications Internat. Corp.; v.p. strategic mktg., sales and bus. devel. GrandBasin; pres. Energy Global Industry Solutions, 2001—02; exec. v.p. human resources Elec. Data Systems, Plano, Tex., 2002—. Office: Elec Data Systems 5400 Legacy Dr Plano TX 75024-3199

SIVOLI-KRAMER, DIANNE, management analyst, social worker; b. Kenosha, Wis., Dec. 28, 1958; d. Frank Phillip and Dusanka Rita (Hirsch) Sivoli; m. Thomas Matthew Kramer, May 23, 1996. BA in Sociology, U. Nev., Las Vegas, 1992, B of Social Work, 1994, MSW, 1998. Cashier supr. Tropicana Hotel, Las Vegas, Nev., 1986-90; cons. Clark County Dept. Family & Youth Svcs., Las Vegas, Nev., 1992—, mgmt. analyst, 1995—. Com. mem. family advocates for cmty. empowerment, Las Vegas, 1996. Exemplery prog. award Ctr. for Substance Abuse, Nat. Assn. Substance Abuse & Drug Abuse, Washington, 1997. Mem. NASW. Democrat. Avocations: reading, gardening, swimming, yoga, needlepoint. Office: Clark County Family & Youth Svcs 601 N Pecos Rd Las Vegas NV 89101-2408

SIZEMORE, BARBARA ANN, Black studies educator; b. Chgo., Dec. 17, 1927; d. Sylvester Walter Laffoon and Delila Mae (Alexander) Stewart; m. Furman E. Sizemore, June 28, 1947 (div. Oct. 1964); children: Kymara, Furman G.; m. Jake Milliones, Sept. 29, 1979 (div. Feb. 1992). BA, Northwestern U., 1947, MA, 1954; PhD, U. Chgo., 1979; LLD (hon.), Del. State Coll., 1974; LittD (hon.), Cen. State U., 1974; DHL (hon.), Bal. Coll. of Bible, 1975; D of Pedagogy (hon.), Niagara U., 1994. Tchr., prin., dir. Chgo. Pub. Schs., 1947-72; assoc. sec. Am. Assn. Sch. Adminstrs., Arlington, Va., 1972-73; supt. schs. D.C. Pub. Schs., Washington, 1973-75; ednl. cons. Washington and Pitts., 1975—; prof. Black studies U. Pitts., 1977-92; dean Sch. of Edn. DePaul U., Chgo., 1992-98, prof. emeritus Sch. Edn., 1998—. Author: The Ruptured Diamond, 1981; bd. mem. Jour. Negro Edn., 1974-83, Rev. Edn., 1977-85. Candidate city coun. Washington, 1977; mem. NAACP. Recipient Merit award Northwestern U. Alumni Assn., 1974, Excellence award Nat. Alliance Black Sch. Educators, 1984, Human Rights award UN Assn., 1985, Racial Justice award YMCA, 1995, Harold Delaney Ednl. award, Am. Assn. for Higher Edn. Black Caucas, 1999, Disting. Scholarship award Am. Ednl. Rsch. Assn., 2001, Pres. award Nat. Alliance of Black Sch. Educators, 2002; named to U.S. Nat. Com., UNESCO, 1974-77. Mem. Nat. Coun. for Black Studies, African Heritage Studies Assn. (bd. mem. 1972—), Nat. Alliance Black Sch. Educators, Delta Sigma Theta. Democrat. Baptist. Avocations: reading, writing. Personal E-mail: bas_60657@yahoo.com. Business E-Mail: bsizemor@depaul.edu.

SJOGREN, JAIME LYNN, dancer, choreographer; b. Arlington Heights, Ill., Mar. 31, 1978; d. Dan Alan and Helen Adele Deithloff. Dance instr., coord. Addison Pk. Dist., Addison, Ill., 1993—; dance instr. Wheaton Pk. Dist., Wheaton, Ill., 1998—99. Choreographer Legacy Theatre, Addison, 2000; half time performer Citrus Bowl, Orlando, Fla., 2002, Capital One Bowl, Orlando, 2003; supernumerary Chgo. Joffrey Ballets Prodn. of Romeo and Juliet. Avocations: cooking, camping, photography, muscle cars, drawing. Home: 1125 Ash St Saint Charles IL 60174

SJURSEN, HOPE BIANCHI, marketing professional; b. Arcadia, Calif., Mar. 8, 1959; d. John Ernest and Donna Shirlene (Gill) Bianchi; m. John Norman Sjursen V, Oct. 1, 1988; children: Lauren Michelle, John Norman VI. BS, Pepperdine U. Asst. dept. mgr. Bullock's Dept. Store, Century City, Calif., 1980, asst. buyer L.A., 1980-81; factory sales rep. Bianchi Internat., Temecula, Calif., 1981-85, sales mgr. western region, 1986-88, mktg. mgr., 1989-91, dir. mktg., svcs. and corporate support, 1991—; co-owner Mesa Heights Growers, Fallbrook, Calif., 1997—, Mesa & Co., 2003—. Mem. NRA (life, instr. women's personal protection 1993-95), NAFE, Am. Defense Preparedness Assn., Rally for Children, Nat. Charity League. Republican. Roman Catholic. Avocations: cooking, crafts, bicycling. Home: 3318 Via Zara Fallbrook CA 92028-3800 Office: Bianchi Internat 27969 Jefferson Ave Temecula CA 92590-2604

SKADDEN, NANCY LEE MACKEY, information technology manager; b. River Falls, WI, May 18, 1939; d. Harold Elbert Mackey and Dorothy E. (Newville) Brand; m. William Stewart Skadden, July 11, 1958; children: Anita Joanne S. Pandolfe, William Harold Skadden. BA, U Wis., Green Bay, 1973. Cert. lang. arts tchr., secondary. Tchr. So. Door Middle Sch., Brussels, Wis., 1973-96; project mgr. Cmty. Agr., 2003—. Negotiator Wis. Edn. Assn., Madison, 1984-88; mediator farm mediation program Wis. Dept. Agr., Madison, 1992—. Dem. candidate for Wis. senate dist. 1, 1982; del. Dem. Nat. Conv., 1984, 88; mem. Lake Mich. Comml. Fishing Bd., 1985-89, Fed. Merit Selection Commn. Ea. Dist., Wis., 1986-88; mem.

Door County Bd. Adjustment, Sturgeon Bay, 1990-2000, chair, 1993-2000; moderator United Ch. of Christ, 2002—. Mem. Wis. Edn. Assn. (bd. dirs. 1974-78, 80-83). Mem. United Ch. of Christ. Home: 9240 Lime Kiln Rd Sturgeon Bay WI 54235 8661

SKADDEN, VANDA SUE, retired music educator; b. Salida, Colo., Jan. 10, 1942; d. Clarence Walter and Lulu Corinne (Van Fossen) Sydenham; m. James Timothy Skadden, June 8, 1964; children: Javan Marie Skadden Carson, Gayla Sue. B.Music Edn., U. Denver, 1964; Music Cert., Internat. Culture Symposium, Neuberg, Austria, 1977. Cert. tchr. Ill., 1964, Colo., 1967. Tchr. instrumental music Rantoul City Schs., Ill., 1964—67; tchr., strings specialist Widefield Sch. Dist. #3, Colorado Springs, Colo., 1967—69, orch. dir., 1975—99; ret., 1999. Bd. dirs. Colo. All State Orch., Colorado Springs, 1996—98; judge various music contests; clinician Pueblo Pub. Schs. All City Orch. Music editor (newspaper) Clarion, U. Denver, 1962—64; editor: (newsletter) String Vibrations, 1991—94 (cert., 1994). Choir dir. Good Shepherd United Meth. Ch., 1983—92; violinist Colorado Springs Symphony, 1967—77; concert master Cmty. Orch./Pikes Peak Civic, Colorado Springs, 1979—85; violinist Chamber Orch. of Springs, Colorado Springs, 1979—, bd. sec., 2000—. Recipient Outstanding Tchr. awards, Colo. Music Educators, 1986, 1987, 1989, 1996; scholar, U. Denver, 1960—64. Mem.: Am. String Tchrs. Assn. (state bd. 1985—90, state bd. pres., editor 1991—94, Lifetime Achievement award 1999), Mu Phi Epsilon. Republican. Methodist. Avocations: painting, sewing, travel, genealogy, history. Home: 7025 Defoe Ave Colorado Springs CO 80911

SKADEN, ANNE MARIE, library director; b. Emmetsburg, Iowa, Feb. 19, 1955; d. Dixon Wayne and Ruth Marie Parish; m. David M. Skaden, June 14, 1980; children: Erik, Mark, Mary. MLS, U. Wis., 1981. Reference/young adult libr. Frank L. Weyenberg Libr., Mequon, Wis., 1982-85; media specialist St. James Sch., Washington, 1993-95; dir. Kalona (Iowa) Pub. Libr., 1994—. Trustee Kalona Pub. Libr., 1986—94, pres. bd. trustees, 1990—92. Mem.: ALA, Libr. Adminstrn. and Mgmt. Assn. (sec., treas.), Iowa Libr. Assn., Washington County Libr. Assn. (pres., v.p., sec., treas.), Iowa Small Libr. Assn. (sec.), Iowa Libr. Assn. Office: Kalona Pub Libr PO Box 1212 Kalona IA 52247-1212

SKAGGS, BEBE REBECCA PATTEN, college dean, clergywoman; b. Berkeley, Calif., Jan. 30, 1950; d. Carl Thomas and Bebe (Harrison) P. BS in Bible, Patten Coll., 1969; BA in Philosophy, Holy Names Coll., 1970; MA in Bibl. Studies New Testament, Wheaton Coll., 1972; PhD in Bibl. Studies New Testament, Drew U., 1976; MA in Philosophy, Dominican Sch. Philosophy & Theology, 1990; postgrad., U. Calif., Berkeley, 1991-92. Ordained to ministry Christian Evang. Ch., 1963. Co-pastor Christian Cathedral, Christian Evang. Chs. Am., Inc., 1964—; assoc. prof. Patten Coll., Oakland, Calif., 1975-82, dean, 1977—, prof. N.T., 1982—. Presenter in field. Author: Before the Times, 1980, The World of the Early Church, 1990; contbg. author: Internat. Standard Bibl. Ency., rev. edit., 1983, Women's Study Bible, Pneuma Faculty Dialogue. Active Wheaton Coll. Symphony, 1971-72, Drew U. Ensemble, 1971-75, Young Artists Symphony, N.J., 1972-75, Somerset Hill Symphony, N.J., 1973-74, Peninsula Symphony, 1977, 80-81, Madison Chamber Trio, N.J., 1973-75. Named one of Outstanding Young Women of Am., 1976, 77, 80-81, 82; St. Olaf's Coll. fellow, 1990. Mem. AAUP, Am. Acad. Religion, Soc. Bibl. Lit., Internat. Biographical Assn., Christian Evang. Chs. of Am., Inc. (bd. dirs. 1964—), Inst. for Bibl. Rsch., Soc. for Pentecostal Studies (pres. 1998-99), Phi Delta Kappa.

SKALKA, ANNA MARIE, molecular biologist, virologist; b. N.Y.C., July 2, 1938; AB, Adelphi U., 1959; PhD in Microbiology, NYU, 1964. Am. Cancer Soc. fellow molecular biology genetics rsch. unit Carnegie Inst., 1964-66, fellow, 1966-69; asst. mem. dept. cell biology lab. molecular and biochemical genetics Roche Inst. Molecular Biology, 1969-71, assoc. mem., 1971-76, mem., 1976-80, head, 1980-87; now dir. Inst. Cancer Rsch., Phila., 1987—; sr. v.p. basic sci. Fox Chase Cancer Ctr., Phila., 1987—. Adj. prof. microbiology, Sch. Medicine, U. Pa., 1973—, Rockefeller U., 1975. Mem. AAAS, Am. Soc. Microbiology, Am. Soc. Biol. Chem., Assn. Women Sci., Sigma Xi. Achievements include research in the structure and function of DNA, host and viral functions in the synthesis of viral DNA and RNA, phage DNA as a vehicle for the amplification and study of eukaryotic genes, molecular biology of avian retroviruses. Office: Inst for Cancer Rsch Fox Chase Cancer Ctr 7701 Burholme Ave Philadelphia PA 19111-2412

SKANDERA-TROMBLEY, LAURA ELISE, language professional, English; b. L.A., Nov. 1, 1960; d. John and Mary Ruth (Chaney) S.; m. Nelson Edmund Trombley, July 13, 1991. BA, Pepperdine U., 1981, MA, 1983; PhD, U. So. Calif., 1989. Asst. lectr. U. So. Calif., L.A., 1983-87; vis. prof. U. Eichstatt, Bavaria, Germany, 1985-87, Pepperdine U., Malibu, Calif., 1988-90; asst. prof. Potsdam Coll., SUNY, 1990—. Author: Mark Twain's Literary Marriage, 1992; editor: Poetry and Epistemology, 1986. Named Quarry Farm fellow Ctr. for Mark Twain Studies, 1988, Finklestein fellow U. Soc. Calif., 1988. Office: Potsdam Coll Dept Of English Potsdam NY 13676

SKARDA, PATRICIA LYN, English language educator; b. Clovis, N.Mex., Mar. 31, 1946; d. Lynell Griffith and Kathryn Rose (Burns) S. Student, Sweet Briar Coll., 1964-67; BA, Tex. Tech. U., 1969; PhD, U. Tex., 1973. Prof. English Smith Coll., Northampton, Mass., 1973—. Edn. dir. Girls Nation, Washington, 1973-75, A.P. Inst. Leader, U. No. Colo., Greeley, 1988-91, 94-2003; cons. USCCB Bishop's Com. on Vocations, 1998—. Editor: The Evil Image, 1981, Smith Voices, 1990, 99, Textured Lives: Celebrating Ada Comstock Scholars at Smith College, 2000, Instrumentum Laboris for the Third Continental Congress of Vocations, 2001; contbr. articles to profl. jours. Dir. Girls State, N.Mex., 1973. Fellow in Acad. Adminstrn., Am. Coun. on Edn., 1978-79, NDEA grad. fellowship, Disting. Vis. prof. USAF Acad., 1992-93. Mem. MLA, N.Am. Soc. Study Romanticism, Phi Beta Kappa, Sigma Tau Delta, Phi Kappa Phi. Democrat. Roman Catholic. Avocations: reading, swimming, playing piano, traveling, praying. Office: Smith Coll Dept English Northampton MA 01063-0001 E-mail: pskarda@smith.edu.

SKAVLEM, MELISSA KLINE, publisher; Pres. Hanser Gardner Pub., Cin. Office: Hanser Gardner Pub 6600 Clough Pike Cincinnati OH 45244-4028

SKEETE, HELEN WATKINS, minister, counselor; b. Wallace, N.C., Mar. 2, 1938; d. James Edward Newkirk, Edith Newkirk; m. Paul Louis, Sr. Watkins, Aug. 31, 1958; children: Paul Jr. Watkins, Stella Ross Finch, Trina Joy Gatlin. BTh, Calvary Grace Inst., Columbus, Ohio, 1977. Cert. crisis counselor. Internat. evangelist Soul Saving Sta. Every Nation, N.Y.C., 1959—84; asst. adminstr., assoc. min. Grace Ch. All Nations, Boston, 1983—88; founder, CEO Love Unlimited Drug Rehab. Outreach Programs, Inc., Boston, 1988—; founder, dir. Love U God's Gang, Brookline, Mass., 1991—; founder, CEO, pastor Love Unlimited Outreach Ministries, Inc., Boston, 1991—; overseer Men & Women of Crossroads Ministries, Dorchester, Mass., 1996—, Gospel Truth Ministries. Mem. adv. bd. New Eng. Med. Ctr. Hosp., Boston, 1981—83, Boston Against Drugs, 1991—96, Living After Murder Program, Inc., Roxbury, Mass., 1993—95. Author: (plays) Life on the Streets in a World of Drugs, 1990 (Proclamation from Mayor Flynn of Boston, 1990), Matriac of Ministry, 2002, Official Resolution - Boston City Council, 2002; co-author: Boston Area Violence Prevention Resource Directory, 1993 (Hon. Cmty. Svc. award, 1993). Facilitator Healthy Boston, 1997—99; mem. AIDS Action Com., Boston, 1995—2001; counselor Boston Safe Neighborhood, 1990—97; mem. evaluation team Boston Against Drugs, 1993—97; dir. March Against Violence, 1991. Recipient Recognition of Achievement, Gov. Paul Cellucci of Mass., 1997, Ofcl. Resolution, Boston City Coun., Recognition of Achievement, Commonwealth of Mass. Ho. Reps., 1997, Letter of Recognition, U.S. Pres. George Bush, 1990, Letter of Appreciation, U.S. Pres. Bill Clinton, 1997, cert. of Appreciation, Boston Police Dept., 1997, Proclamation, City of Boston Mayor Menino, 1997, Letter of Recognition, U.S. Pres. Ronald Regan, 1983; grantee, Boston Safe Neighborhood, 1991. Mem.: Grandparents Raising Their Grandchildren (facilitator 1996—99, cert. of Appreciation 1997). Democrat. Avocations: travel, reading, sewing, singing, writing. Home: 99 Kent St Ste 7-317 Brookline MA 02445-7955 Office: Love Unlimited Drug Rehabilitation Out Brookline MA 02445-7955 Personal E-mail: revhelenwatkinsskeete@yahoo.com. Business E-Mail: revhelenwatkinsskeete@yahoo.com.

SKELLEY, BILLIE HOLLADAY, clinical nurse specialist; b. Atlanta, July 16, 1952; d. Howard Kelly Holladay and Ida Frances Adams; m. Mark Joseph Skelley, June 16, 1979; children: Allison, James, Nathan, Logan. BS, U. Wis., 1974, MS, 1978. Registered nurse ACCN. RN Univ. Hosps., Madison, Wis., 1974—79; tchr. nursing U. Wis. Sch. of Nursing, Madison, 1979; tchr., curriculum dept. Clarke Coll., Dubuque, Iowa, 1980.

SKELTON, WINIFRED KARGER (FREDDIE SKELTON), advertising agency executive, painter; b. McKees Rocks, Penn., Jan. 10, 1930; d. Robert Frank and Elfrieda Rose (Allert) Karger; m. Howard C. Skelton, May 19, 1962; 1 child, Susan. BA, Am. Acad. Art, Chgo., 1949; student, Corcoran Sch. Art, Washington, 1950-52. Asst. art dir. Rich's, Inc., Atlanta, 1949-50; art dir. Hecht Co., Washington, 1950-54, Mandel's, Chgo., 1954-55, Loveman's, Birmingham, Ala., 1955-60, Rich's, Inc., Atlanta, 1960-62, Wm. Buckley Design, N.Y.C., 1966-72; creative dir. Howard Skelton Assocs., Atlanta, Sarasota, Fla., 1973-94, pres. Sarasota, Fla., 1994—. Recipient 196 Addy awards from 1976-96. Mem. Gainesville Fine Arts Assn., St. Augustine Art Assn., The Centre Club (Tampa), Tampa Bay Soc., Bradenton C. of C., The Atlanta Ad Club, The Tampa Ad Club, Suncoast Ad Club. Republican. Presbyterian. Achievements include paintings hanging in numerous galleries. Home: 2512 Birnam Woods Way Gainesville FL 32605-1663

SKERL, DIANA M. stockbroker; b. Zagreb, Croatia, Aug. 17, 1959; d. Damir Steven and Zdenka (Klaric) S.; m. Michael Karakasians, June 14, 1986. BBA, Texas Christian, 1981; MBA, Columbia U., 1999. Dept. mngr. Lord & Taylor, N.Y.C., 1981-1985; buyer Bloomingdales, N.Y.C., 1985-1987; stockbroker Gruntal & Co., N.Y.C., 1987-1989, Donaldson, Lufkin & Jenrette, N.Y.C., 1989—. Dir. Marquis Studios. Treas. Children in Crisis. Mem. Women's Nat. Rep. Club, N.Y. Jr. League (Mentoring Ptnrs. 1998—, Children in Crisis 1995-98, Heartsong 1992-95). Rupublican. Roman Catholic. Avocations: music, diving, literature, traveling. Home: 120 E 87th St New York NY 10128-1116 E-mail: dskerl@dlj.com.

SKIDMORE, DOROTHY L. music educator; b. Champaign, Ill., Oct. 30, 1940; d. Robert Koehn and Ella Faye Hubbard; m. William R. Skidmore, Sept. 12, 1964; children: Robert William, Daniel James. MusB, U. Ill., 1962, MusM, 1969; MA in Eng., W.Va. U., 1992; study, Hochschule fur Musik, Germany. Pvt. flute tchr., 1960—; flute prof. Fairmont (W.Va.) State Coll., 1990—. Flute tchr. Cath. U. Am., Washington, 1965—71; adj. prof. Montgomery Coll., Rockville, Md., 1965—74; flute tchr. & coach No. Va. Music Ctr., Reston, Va., 1967—70, W.Va. Wesleyan Coll., Buckhannon, W.Va., 1997—98. Performer (flutist): John. F. Kennedy Ctr. Orch., 1974—77; performer: (flutist/piccolist) Nat. Gallery of Art Orch., 1967—72; performer: (flutist) Monongahela Trio, 1990—, (record) The Book of Imaginary Beings, 1974— (Recording of Spl. Merit award Stereo Rev., 1975), (video) Musical Masterpieces, 1988. Grantee, Fulbright, 1962—63. Mem.: Nat. Flute Assn., Am. Fedn. Musicians. Home: 1266 Baker's Ridge Rd Morgantown WV 26505 Office: Fairmont State Coll 1201 Locust Ave Fairmont WV 26554

SKIDMORE, MARGARET COOKE, fundraiser; b. N.Y.C., Sept. 10, 1938; d. M. Bernard and Mary Frances (Adams) Cooke; m. Louis Skidmore Jr., Sept. 10, 1960; children: Christopher, Elizabeth, Heather. BA, Chatham Coll., 1960; cert. Mgmt. Program, Rice U., 1986. Devel. asst. Yale U., New Haven, 1960-62, sec. French dept., 1963; devel. asst. Chgo. Symphony, 1976; dir. devel. Children's Meml. Hosp., Chgo., 1976-77, Mus. Fine Arts, Houston, 1978—. Adv. bd. mem. Cultural Arts Coun., Houston, 1990-96. Named Outstanding Women Am., 1971. Fellow Am. Leadership Forum (Class XV 1998); mem. Assn. of Fundraising Profls. (nat. bd. dirs. 1981-85, chpt. pres. 1982-83, bd. dirs. 1979-85, 88-91, cert., Outstanding Fundraising award 1980, 81, 82, Outstanding Fundraising Exec. award 1985), Art Mus. Devel. Assn. (pres. 1983, 98). Episcopalian. Avocations: tennis, needlepoint. Home: 302 Litchfield Ln Houston TX 77024-6039 Office: Museum Fine Arts PO Box 6826 Houston TX 77265-6826 Office Phone: 713-639-7522. E-mail: mskidmore@mfah.org.

SKIGEN, PATRICIA SUE, lawyer; b. Springfield, Mass., June 16, 1942; d. David P. and Gertrude H. (Hirschhaut) Skigen; m. Irwin J. Sugarman, May 1973 (div. Nov. 1994); 1 child, Alexander David Sugarman ; m. Gary W. Guttman, May 2001. BA with distinction, Cornell U., 1964; LLB, Yale U., 1968. Bar: N.Y. 1968, U.S. Dist. Ct. (so. dist.) N.Y. 1969. Law clk. Anderson, Mori & Rabinowitz, Tokyo, 1966-67; assoc. Rosenman Colin Kaye Petschek Freund & Emil, N.Y.C., 1968-70, Willkie Farr & Gallagher, N.Y.C., 1970-75, ptnr., 1977-95; v.p., corp. fin. group legal dept. J.P. Morgan Chase & Co., N.Y.C., 1995—2002, mng. dir., assoc. gen. counsel, 2002—. Dep. supt., gen. counsel N.Y. State Banking Dept., N.Y.C., 1975-77, first dep. supt. banks, 1977; adj. prof. Benjamin Cardozo Law Sch. Yeshiva U., 1979. Contbr. articles to profl. jours. Cornell U. Dean's scholar, 1960-64, Regent's scholar, 1960-64, Yale Law Sch. scholar, 1964-68. Mem.: ABA (corp. banking and bus. law sect.), Assn. of Bar of City of N.Y. (chmn. com. banking 1991—94, long range planning com. 1994—96, audit com. 1994—2001), Phi Kappa Phi, Phi Beta Kappa. Office: JP Morgan Chase and Co 270 Park Ave Fl 40 New York NY 10017-2014

SKILLING, MARIE L. music educator; b. Alma, Mich., Aug. 26, 1931; d. Dan Ernest and Florence Marie (Tolles) Harper; m. Darroll Dean Skilling, June 10, 1951; children: Ann Marie, James Dean, Stephen Richard. BS cum laude, U. Minn., 1974. Piano tchr., St. Paul. Scout leader Girl Scouts USA, St. Paul, 1958-64; ch. nursery dir. Presbyn. Ch., Wausau, Wis., 1956-60, ch. youth evening dir. weekly program, 1963-68. Mem. Nat. Music Tchrs. Assn., Minn. Music Tchrs. Assn. (test ctr. chmn., treas., constn. chair 1993-99, Disting. Svc. award 1998), St. Paul Piano Tchrs. Assn. (treas. 1975-78, pres. 1984-86, 1st v.p. 1982-84, 3d v.p. 1978-82). Avocations: sewing, needlework, sailing, camping, backpacking.

SKILLMAN, BECKY SUE, state legislator; b. Bedford, Ind., Sept. 26, 1950; d. Jack Delmar and Catherine Louise (Flinn) Foddrill; m. Stephen E. Skillman, 1969. Dep. recorder Lawrence County, 1971-76, county recorder, 1977-84; clerk Lawrence County crct. ct., 1985—; mem. Ind. Senate from 44th dist., 1992—. Co-dir. Lawrence County Young Reps., 1973-78; co-chmn. State Young Reps. Conv., 1975, 77; vice chmn. Lawrence County Rep. Ctrl. Com. Office: Ind Senate Dist 44 200 W Washington St Indianapolis IN 46204-2728

SKILLMAN, JUDITH ANNE, humanities educator; b. Syracuse, N.Y., May 4, 1954; d. Sidney Oscar and Bernice Broom Kastner; m. Thomas L. Skillman, Dec. 31, 1976; children: Alissa R., Andrew L., Jocelyn A. BA in English, MA in English Lit., U. Md.; student, U. Wash., Cath. Sch. Law, 1978—79. Tchg. asst. U. Md., College Park, 1977—78; instr. poetry Bellevue (Wash.) C.C., 1983—85, adj. faculty in humanities City U., Bellevue, 1985—. Co-editor: Fine Madness, 2000—03; author: Worship of the Visible Spectron, 1988, Beethoven and the Birds, 1986, Storm, 1988, Red Town, 2001, Circe's Island, 2003, Latticework, 2004. Recipient Eric Mathias King Fund award, Acad. Am. Poets, 1998; grantee, King County Arts Commn., 1987, Wash. State Arts Commn., 1994, The Centrum Found. Mem.: MLA, Am. Lit. Translators Assn., Nature Conservancy. Democrat. Lutheran. Office: City Univ 11900 NE 1st St Bellevue WA 98005

SKINNER, HELEN CATHERINE WILD, biomineralogist; b. Bklyn., Jan. 25, 1931; d. Edward Herman and Minnie (Bertsch) Wild; m. Brian John Skinner, Oct. 9, 1954; children: Adrienne, Stephanie, Thalassa. BA, Mt. Holyoke Coll., 1952; MA, Radcliffe/Harvard, 1954; PhD, Adelaide (Australia) U., 1959. Mineralogist sect. molecular structure Nat. Inst. Arthritis and Metabolic Diseases, NIH, 1961-65; with sect. crystal chemistry Lab. Histology and Pathology Nat. Inst. Dental Rsch., NIH, 1965-66; lectr. dept. geology and geophysics Yale U., 1967-69, rsch. assoc. dept. surgery, 1967-72, sr. rsch. assoc. dept. surgery Medical Sch., 1972-75; Alexander Agassiz vis. lectr. dept. biology Harvard U., 1976-77; lectr. dept. biology Yale U., 1977-83, assoc. prof. biochemistry in surgery, Medical Sch., 1978-84, lectr. dept. orthopaedic surgery, 1972—, lectr., rsch. affiliate in geology and geophysics, 1987—. Pres. Conn. Acad. Arts and Scis., 1986—94, publs. chair, 1994—2001; faculty affiliate in mineralogy Yale U. Peabody Mus., 2001—; mineralogist AEC, summer, 1953; master Jonathan Edwards Coll., Yale U., 1977—82; Alexander Agassiz vis. lectr. dept. biology Harvard U., 1976—77; vis. prof. sect. ecology and systematics dept. biology Cornell U., 1980—83; disting. prof. geology Adelaide U., 1990—91, disting .lectr., 1993; disting. prof. geology U. Wyo., 1996; Alan Cox vis. prof. Stanford U., 2003; mem. dental adv. com. Yale-New Haven Hosp., 1973—80, Yale-New Haven Tchrs. Inst., 1983—99; chmn. site visit team Nat. Inst. Dental Rsch., 1974—75; mem. publs. com. Yale U. Press., 1979—84, Am. Geol. Inst., 1993—96, 2000—; MSA del. Internat. Mineral. Commn. Applied Mineralogy, 1992—. Author: Asbestos and Other Fibrous Materials, 1988, Biomineralization: Iron and Manganese, 1992, Dana's New Mineralogy, 8th edit., 1997, Geology and Health, 2003; contbr. articles to profl. jours. and mags., chpts. to 4 books. Mem. bd. edn. com. Conn. Fund for Environ., 1983-89, mem. sci. adv. com., 1989-92; founder, pres. Investor's Strategy Inst., New Haven, 1983-85; trustee Miss Porter's Sch., Farmington, Conn., 1984-91, mem. edn. com., 1986-88, mem. salaries and benefits com., 1988-91; treas. YWCA, New Haven, 1983-84; trustee Geol. Soc. Am. Found., 1998—. Fellow: AAAS, Geol. Soc. Am., Mineralogical Soc. Am.; mem.: Conn. Acad. Arts and Sci. (dir.). Home: 39 Temple Ct New Haven CT 06511-6820 Office: Yale U Dept Geology Geophysics PO Box 208109 New Haven CT 06520-8109 Office Phone: 203-432-3787. E-mail: catherine.skinner@yale.edu.

SKINNER, JILL SUZANNE, special education educator; b. Indpls., Ind., Feb. 4, 1973; d. Edward John and JoAnn Nancy Conover; m. Ian Chistiaan Skinner, Oct. 4, 1997. BS in Spl. Edn., Ea. Ky. U., 1996, Rank 2 of Spl. Edn., 1998—2002. Aquatic dir./program dir. YMCA Camp Ernst, Burlington, Ky., 1992—95; aquatic dir. Telford YMCA, Richmond, Ky., 1995—96; spl. educator Garrard County Pub. Schs., Lancaster, Ky., 1997—98; swim instr. Winchester YMCA, Winchester, Ky., 1997—2002; spl. educator Clark County Schs., Winchester, Ky., 1998—. Vol. for bldg. blitz Habitat for Humanity, Winchester, Ky., 2002; adult mem. Youth Com. Transylvana Presbytery; youth sponser/Sunday sch. tchr. First Christian Ch., Richmond, Ky., 1997—2001; camp dir. Christian Ch. of Ky., Lexington, Ky., 1995—2003, mem. of outdoor ministry, 2001—03; Christian educator, youth leader First Presbyn. Ch., Winchester, Ky., 2001—. Mem.: Partners of Am. (assoc.; chair of path committe 2002—03), Coun. of Exceptional Children (assoc.), Light in the Attic of Transylvana Presbytery (assoc.). Presbyterian. Achievements include designed and implemented a hydrotherapy program for a special needs school in Quito, Ecuador; created and implemented a children/youth program that was non-existant for First Presbyterian Church in Winchester, KY; Implemented A Swim Program For Special Needs Children And Adults at YMCA; design of implemented, and directed high school high adventure camp Christian Church of Kentucky; created and implemented Presbyterian Animals with Seniors (PAWS) in the First Presbyterian Church in Winchester, KY. Avocations: hiking, swimming, Karate, reading, walking. Home: 423 Colby Ridge Blvd Winchester KY 40391 Office: Strode Station Elem Sch 2 Educational Plz Winchester KY 40391 Personal E-mail: buyskinart@aol.com. E-mail: jskinner@clark.ky.k12.us.

SKINNER, LYNN STRICKLAND, secondary school mathematics educator; b. Newnan, Ga., July 30, 1959; d. Elonza Floyd and Irene (Smith) S.; m. Walter Winston Skinner, Jr., Sept. 8, 1979; children: Sara Irene (Sallie), Jane Golden. Student, Clayton State Coll., 1977-78, Ga. Southwestern Coll., 1981; BBA, U. Ga., 1981; MEd, West Ga. Coll., 1990; EdS, State U. West Ga., 1998. Bus. mgr. Lee County Ledger, Leesburg, Ga., 1980-82; ins. rep. West Ga. Med. Ctr., La Grange, Ga., 1982-83; advt. rep. Newnan Times-Herald, 1983-85; chmn. dept. math. Greenville (Ga.) H.S., 1985-92; project success math. tchr. E. Coweta H.S., Sharpsburg, Ga., 1992—. Greenville H.S. STAR tchr., 1988-89. Founding mem. Lee County Women's Club, Leesburg, 1982; local fund drive chmn. Nat. Kidney Found., Luthersville, Ga., 1985, Am. Heart Assn., Luthersville, 1992; Sunday sch. tchr., program chmn. Women's Missionary Union, Mt. Zion Bapt. Ch., Alvaton, Ga., 1986—; neighborhood chmn. March of Dimes, 1998. Mem. Nat. Coun. Tchrs. Math., Ga. Coun. Tchrs. Math. (life), Ga. Assn. Educators, Coweta Assn. Educators (publicity chmn.), Delta Kappa Gamma (treas. 1990—). Democrat. Baptist. Avocations: oil painting, gardening, reading. Home: 60 Temple Ave Newnan GA 30263-2023 Office: East Coweta HS 400 Sharpsburg Mccollum Rd Sharpsburg GA 30277-2317

SKINNER, MARY "HONEY" JACOBS, lawyer; b. 1957; m. Sam Skinner, Aug. 17, 1989; stepchildren: Thomas, Steven, Jane. BA cum laude, Harvard U., 1978; JD, Northwestern U., 1981. Bar: Ill. 1981, D.C. 1990, U.S. Supreme Ct. 1990. With Sidley Austin Brown & Wood, Chgo., 1981—, ptnr., 1989—; counsel to spkr. Ill. Ho. of Reps., Springfield, Ill., 1983—85. Intern White House, 1979. Former trustee RAdcliffe Coll.; participant leadership coun. Greater Chgo. Fellowship Program, 1984. Named One of Forty under 40 Most Outstanding Leaders in Chco., Crain's Chgo. Bus. Mem.. Harvard Alumni Assn. (bd. dirs.), Radcliffe Coll. Alumni Assn. (past pres.). Office: Sidley Austin Brown and Wood Bank One Plz 10 S Dearborn St Chicago IL 60603*

SKINNER, PATRICIA MORAG, state legislator; b. Glasgow, Scotland, Dec. 3, 1932; d. John Stuart and Frances Charlotte (Swann) Robertson; m. Robert A. Skinner, Dec. 28, 1957; children: Robin Ann, Pamela. BA, NYU, 1953. Mdse. trainee Lord & Taylor, N.Y.C.; adminstrv. asst. Atlantic Products, N.Y.C.; newspaper corr. Salem Observer, N.H., 1964-84; mem. N.H. Ho. of Reps., 1972-94, chmn. labor, human resources, and rehab. com., 1975-86, mem. House edn. com., 1987, chmn., 1989-94, exec. com. Nat. Conf. State Legislatures, 1987-90; chmn. N.H. Adv. Coun. Unemployment Compensation, 1984-94. Mem. State Libr. Adv. Coun., 2001—. Bd. dirs. Castle Jr. Coll., 1975, chmn. bd., 1988-96; v.p. bd. Swift Water coun. Girl Scouts U.S., v.p., 1987-92; N.H. Voc-Tech. Coll., Nashua, 1978-83; trustee Nesmith Libr., Windham, N.H., 1982—, chmn. bd. trustees, 1994-99; pres. N.H. Fedn. Rep. Women's Clubs, parliamentarian, legis. chmn., 1984-86, 94-96. Mem. Windham Woman's Club (pres. 1981-83), Order Ea. Star. Christian Scientist.

SKINNER, SHARI L. dermatologist; b. Paducah, Ky., Nov. 11, 1964; d. William G. and Carolyn Ann (Englert) Skinner. BS, Samford U., 1987; MD, U. Louisville, 1994. Pharmacist Bapt. Hosp., Paducah, 1987-88, Super X Pharmacy, Louisville, 1988-94; intern U. Louisville Med. Ctr., 1994-95, resident in dermatology Pa. State Geissinger Health Sys., Hershey, Pa., 1995-98; dermatologist Assocs. Dermatology, Ft. Myers, Fla., 1998—. Primary investigator pharm. clin. trials SFBC, Ft. Myers, 2001—; mem. adv. bd. The Medwell Group Inc., 2003—. Contbr. articles to profl. jours.

Trustee S.W. Fla. Symphony, 2003—; mem. small bus. adv. coun. Nat. Rep. Congl. Com., hon. co-chmn. physicians adv. bd., 2002. Recipient Nat. Leadership award, Nat. Rep. Congl. Com., 2002. Mem.: NRA, AMA, Am. Contact Dermatitis Soc. (grantee 1997), Women's Dermatol. Soc., Lee County Med. Soc., Fla. Soc. Dermatology and Dermatologic Surgery, Fla. Med. Assn., Am. Acad. Dermatology.

SKINNER, TILLIAN ESTHER, daycare administrator; b. Orland Park, Ill., June 15, 1960; d. Aaron James and Hermione Porter; m. Joel Timothy Skinner, Aug. 15, 1986; children: Mark Andrew, Nathan James, Julia Rose. BA, Georgetown U., 1982; MA, Villanova U., 1986. Tchr. James Madison Elem. Sch., Flossmoor, Ill., 1987—95; adminstr. Meriks Daycare Ctr., Blue Island, Ill., 1995—. Protestant. Avocations: camping, puzzles, demitasse spoon collecting. Office: Meriks Daycare Ctr 2757 John St Blue Island IL 60406-2856

SKIRBOLL, LANA R. federal health policy director; b. Balt., Dec. 7, 1948; m. Leonard Taylor, Feb. 19, 1986; 2 children. BA, NYU, 1970; MS in Zoology and Physiology, Miami U., 1972; PhD in Pharmacology, Georgetown U., 1977. Postdoctoral tng. in psychiatry and pharmacology Yale U. Sch. Medicine, New Haven, 1977-79; vis. scientist dept. histology and neurobiology Karolinska Inst., Stockholm, 1979-81; chief electrophysiology unit NIMH, 1981—86; dep. sci. advisor Alcohol Drug Abuse and Mental Health Adminstrn., 1986—88, exec. asst. to adminstr., 1989-91, assoc. adminstr. for sci., 1990—92; dir. office of sci. policy and program planning NIMH, 1992-95, 95—. Cons. Ctr. Environ. Health and Human Toxicology, 1985-87. Author: Pharmacology of Biochemical Behavior, 1988, Neuroanatomical Tract-Tracing Methods II: 1981-86, 1990, (with T. Hokfelt, G. Foster, O. Johannsson et alCentral Phenylethanolamine N-Methyltransferase Immunoreactive Neurons: Distribution Projections, Fine Structure, Ontogeny and Co-Existing Peptides, 1988, (with G.Stoner, S. Werkman, D. Hommer) Effects of Caffeine on the Substania Nigra, Biological Psychiatry, 1988, (with J.A. Stivers, R. Long, J. Crawley) Anatomical Analysis of Frontal Cortex Sites at Which Carbachol Induces Moteor Seizures in the Rat, (with T. Hokfelt, B. Robertson) Retrograde Flourescent Tracers with Immunohistochemistry, (with M. Palkovits, E. Mezey, T. Hokfelt) Adrenergic Projections from the Lower Brainstem to the Hypothalamic Paraventricular Nucleus, the Lateral Hypothalamic Area and the Central Nucleus of the Amygdala in Rats, vol. 1020, 1992. Biol. Scis. fellow in in psychiatry NIMH, 1977-79, Fogarty fellow, Internat. fellow Swedish Med. Rsch. Coun., 1979-81. Mem. AAAS, Am. Coll. Neuropsychopharmacology (Mead Johnson award), N.Y. Acad. Scis., Nat. Com. Edn. (Potomac chpt. pres. 1988-89), European Neurosci. Soc., Soc. Neurosci. Office: HHS NIH 9000 Rockville Pike Bldg 1 Bethesda MD 20892-0001

SKLADAL, ELIZABETH LEE, retired elementary school educator; b. NYC, May 23, 1937; d. Angier Joseph and Julia May (Roberts) Gallo; m. George Wayne Skladal, Dec. 26, 1956; children: George Wayne Jr., Joseph Lee. BA, Sweet Briar Coll., 1958; postgrad., U. Kans., 1966-67; EdM, U. Alaska, 1976. Choir dir. Main Chapel, Camp Zama, Japan, 1958-59, Ft. Lee, Va., 1963-65, Main Chapel and Snowhawk, Ft. Richardson, Alaska, 1968-70; tchr. Anchorage (Alaska) Sch. Dist., 1970-98; ret. Active Citizen's Adv. Com. for Gifted and Talented, Anchorage, 1981-83; mem. music com. Anchorage Sch. Dist., 1983-86; soloist Anchorage Opera Chorus, 1969-80, Cmty. Chorus, Anchorage, 1968-80; mem. choir First Presbyn. Ch., Anchorage, 1971—, deacon, 1988—, elder, 1996—, mission com. chair, 1996-99, mem. pastoral nominating com., 2001-03; participant 1st cultural exch. from Anchorage to Magadan, Russia with Alaska Chamber Singers, 1992; participant mission trip to Swaziland, Africa with First Presbyn. Ch., Anchorage, summer 1995. Named Am. Coll. Theater Festival winner Amoco Oil Co., 1974; recipient Cmty. Svc. award Anchorage U. Alaska Alumni Assn., 1994-95. Mem. AAUW, Anchorage Concert Assn. Patron Soc. (assocs. coun. of dirs.), Alaska Chamber Singers, Anchoragae Women's Club, Am. Guild Organists (former dean, former treas., mem.-at-large), Local Delta Kappa Gamma (1st v.p.). Republican. Presbyterian. Avocations: camping, travel, cycling, fishing, cross-country skiing, gardening. Home: 1841 S Salem Dr Anchorage AK 99508-5156

SKLAR, GAIL JANICE, secondary special education educator; b. Phila., Nov. 10, 1949; d. Harold and Irma (Lusky) S.; m. David William Tucker, May 30, 1976 (div. May 1984); 1 child, Benjamin; m. Howard Rod Cohen, Jan. 2, 1997. BS in Edn., Temple U., 1971, MEd, 1974. Tchr. Simon Gratz High Sch., Phila., 1971—; ednl. diagnostician Phila./Ardmore, Pa., 1980—. Prin., owner Native Am. Arts, Etc. Recipient Dr. Ruth Hayre Svc. award. Mem. Phila. Writing Project, Greater Phila. Orchid Soc., Southeastern Pa. Orchid Soc. Avocations: reading, researching women in history, orchid growing. Home: 402 Marple Rd Broomall PA 19008-2044 Office: Simon Gratz High Sch 18th & Hunting Park Ave Philadelphia PA 19140 Office Phone: 610-325-3108. E-mail: gailjsklar@erol.com.

SKLAR, HOLLY L. nonfiction writer; b. N.Y.C., May 6, 1955; BA Oberlin Coll., 1977; MA in Polit. Sci., Columbia U., 1980. Rschr. UN Ctr. Transnat. Corps., N.Y., 1978; writer, rschr. N. Am. Congress Latin Am., N.Y., 1981-82; exec. dir. Inst. New Communications, N.Y., 1982-84; writer, lectr. N.Y., Boston. Review panelist NEH, Washington, 1989; del. Soviet-Am. Women's Summit, N.Y., Washington, 1990; dir. MediaVision, Boston, 1997—. Author, co-author (books) Trilateralism, 1980, Poverty in the American Dream: Women and Children First, 1983, Washington's War on Nicaragua, 1988, Streets of Hope: The Fall and Rise of an Urban Neighborhood, 1994, Chaos or Community? Seeking Solutions, Not Scapegoats for Bad Economics, 1995, Shifting Fortunes: The Perils of the Growing American Wealth Gap, 1999, Raise the Floor: Wages and Policies that Work for All of Us, 2001. Mem. adv. bd. The Progressive Media Project, Polit. Rsch. Assocs.; bd. dirs. United for a Fair Economy, 1996-2000; mem. steering com. Caribbean Basin Info. Project, 1982-85; mem. working group on global econs. Am. Friends Svc. Com., 2002—. Recipient Outstanding Book award Gustavus Myers Ctr. for Study Human Rights in U.S., 1988, Assocs. award Polit. Rsch. Assocs., Cambridge, 1991-97; fellow Columbia U. Grad. Sch. Arts and Scis., 1978-80. Mem. Nat. Writers Union, Acad. Polit. Sci. Office: 52 Parley Ave Boston MA 02130-1857 E-mail: Mediavi@aol.com.

SKLAR, KATHRYN KISH, historian, educator; b. Columbus, Ohio, Dec. 26, 1939; d. William Edward and Elizabeth Sue (Rhodes) Kish; m. Robert A. Sklar, 1958 (div. 1978); children: Leonard Scott, Susan Rebecca Sklar Friedman; m. Thomas L. Dublin, Apr. 30, 1988. BA magna cum laude, Radcliffe Coll., 1965; PhD, U. Mich., 1969. Asst. prof., lectr. U. Mich., Ann Arbor, 1969-74; assoc. prof. history UCLA, 1974-81, chmn. com. to administer program in women's studies Coll. Letters and Sci., 1974-81, prof., 1981-88; Disting. Prof. history SUNY, Binghamton, 1988—, co-dir., Ctr. Hist. Study of Women and Gender, 1998—. Pulitzer juror in history, 1976; fellow Newberry Libr. Family and Community History Seminar, 1973; active Calif. Coun. for Humanities, 1981-85, N.Y. Coun. for Humanities, 1992—. Author: Catharine Beecher: A Study in American Domesticity, 1973 (Berkshire pri e 1974); editor: Catharine Beecher: A Treatise on Domestic Economy, 1977, Harriet Beecher Stowe: Uncle Tom's Cabin, or Life Among the Lowly: The Minister's Wooing, Oldtown Folks, 1981, Notes of Sixty Years: The Autobiography of Florence Kelley, 1849-1926, 1984, (with Thomas Dublin) Women and Power in American History: A Reader (2 vols.), 1991, (with Linda Kerber and Alice Kessler-Harris) U.S. History as Women's History: New Feminist Essays, 1995, Women's Rights Emerges within the Antislavery Movement: A Short History with Documents, 1830-1870, 2000; co-editor: The Social Survey Movement in Historical Perspective, 1992, Florence Kelley and the Nation's Work: The Rise of Women's Political Culture, 1830-1900, 1995 (Berkshire prize 1996). Social Justice Feminists in the United States and Germany: A Dialogue in Documents, 1885-1933, 1998; mem. editl. bd. Jour. Women's History, 1987—, Women's History Rev., 1990—, Jour. Am. History, 1978-81; contbr. chpts. to books. Fellow Woodrow Wilson Found., 1965-67, Danforth Found., 1967-69, Radcliffe Inst., 1973-74, Nat. Humanities Inst., 1975-76, Rockefeller Found. Humanities, 1981-82, Woodrow Wilson Internat. Ctr. for Scholars, 1982, 1992-93, Guggenheim Found., 1984, Ctr. Advanced Study Behavioral and Social Scis., Stanford U., 1987-88, AAUW, 1990-91; Daniels fellow Am. Antiquarian Soc., 1976, NEH fellow Newberry Library, 1982-83; Ford Found. faculty rsch. grantee, 1973-74; grantee NEH, 1976-78, UCLA Coun. for Internat. and Comparative Studies, 1983. Mem. Am. Hist. Assn. (chmn. com. on women historians 1980-83, v.p. Pacific Coast br. 1986-87, pres. 1987-88), Orgn. Am. Historians (exec. bd. 1983-86, Merle Curti award com. 1978-79, lectr. 1982—), Am. Studies Assn. (coun. mem.-at-large 1978-80), Berkshire Conf. Women Historians, Am. Antiquarian Soc., Phi Beta Kappa. Avocation: photography. Office: SUNY Dept History Binghamton NY 13902

SKLAR, LOUISE MARGARET, computer company executive; b. L.A., Aug. 12, 1934; d. Samuel Baldwin Smith and Judith LeRoy (Boughton) Nelson; m. Edwynn Edgar Schroeder, Mar. 20, 1955 (div. July 1975); children: Neil Nelson Schroeder, Leslie Louise Schroeder Grandclaudon, Samuel George Schroeder; m. Martin Sklar, Oct. 17, 1983. Student, U. So. Calif., 1952-54, UCLA, 1977-79. Acct. Valentine Assocs., Northridge, Calif., 1976-78, programmer, 1978-79; contr. Western Monetary, Encino, Calif., 1979-81; pres. Automatic Computer Composition, Reno, 1984—. Mem.: DAR, New England Hist. Genealogical Soc., So. Calif. Assistance League, Conn. Soc. Genealogists, Greater L.A. Zoo. Assn., Am. Contract Bridge League (bd. govs. 1993—99, mem. nat. charity com. 1982—, mem. nat. goodwill com. 1994—), Assn. Los Angeles County Bridge Units (bd. dirs. 1990—2000, sec. 1984—86), Ky. Hist. Soc., Safari Club Internat., Zeta Tau Alpha. Republican. Avocations: tournament bridge, travel. Office: Automatic Computer Composition Inc Reno NV 89511

SKLARIN, ANN H. artist; b. N.Y.C., May 21, 1933; d. Sidney and Revera (Myers) Hirsch; m. Burton S. Sklarin, June 29, 1960; children: Laurie Sklarin Ember, Richard, Peter. BA in Art History, Wellesley Coll., 1955; MA in Secondary Art Edn., Columbia U., 1956. Art tchr. jr. high sch. N.Y.C. Sch. System, 1956-61, chmn. art. dept. jr. high sch., 1957-61. One-woman shows include Long Beach (N.Y.) Libr., 1973, Silvermine Guild Galleries, New Canaan, Conn., 1986, 98, Long Beach Mus. Art, 1986, Discovery Art Gallery, Glen Cove, N.Y., 1987, 92, 93, 94, Freeport (N.Y.) Libr., 1997; exhibited in juried shows at Nassau C.C., Garden City, N.Y., 1970, Nassau County (N.Y.) John F. Kennedy Ctr. Performing Arts, 1970 (1st Pl. award 1970), Long Beach Art Assn., 1970 (1st Pl. award 1970), Gregory Mus., 1973-74, L.I. Arts 76, Hempstead, N.Y., 1976, 5 Towns Music and Art Found., Woodmere, N.Y., 1980 (1st Pl. award 1981, Honorable Mention 1981, 3d Pl. award 1983), 85, Long Beach Art Assn. and Long Beach Mus. Art, 1982 (1st Pl. award), 84, 85 (3d Pl. award), Silvermine Guild Arts, 1984 (Richardson-Vicks Inc. award 1985, 87, Pepperidge Farm Inc. award 1987), Long Beach Mus. Art, 1985 (Best in Show-Grumbacher award 1985), Heckscher Mus., Huntington, N.Y., 1985, Fine Arts Mus. L.I., Hempstead, 1985, 91, Long Beach Art League and Long Beach Mus. Art, 1986 (2d Pl. award 1986), Wunsch Arts Ctr., Glen Cove, 1986, 87, Smithtown Twp. Arts Coun., St. James, 1989 (Honorable Mention award 1989), Chelsesa Ctr., Muttontown, NY, 2000; exhibited in group shows at Hewlett-Woodmere Libr., 1969, B.J. Spoke Gallery, Port Washington, N.Y., 1985, Shirley Scott Gallery, Southampton, N.Y., 1986, Smithtown Twp. Arts Coun., St. James, N.Y., 1988, 90, N.Y. Inst. Tech., Old Westbury, N.Y., 1989, Dowling Coll., Oakdale, N.Y., 1990, Discovery Art Gallery, 1992, 93, 94, 95, 96, Silvermine Guild Arts Ctr., 1984, 1992, 95, 97, 2000, Sound Shore Gallery, Stamford, Conn., 1993, Krasdale Foods Gallery, N.Y.C., 1993. Mem. exec. bd. 5 Towns Music and Art Found., 1960-2002, pres., 1971-74. Avocations: tennis, jogging, hiking, traveling, reading.

SKOCHELAK, SUSAN E. college dean; BS, Mich. Tech. U., 1975, MS in Biol. Sci., 1977; MD, U. Mich., 1981; MPH, U. N.C., 1986. Diplomae Am. Bd. Family Medicine. Intern, resident family medicine U. N.C.-N.C. Meml. Hosp., Chapel Hill, 1977-81; assoc. dean Academic Affairs U. Wis., Madison, 1993—. Cons. in field; assoc. prof. U. Wis. Author: (with others) Preceptor Education Project, Handbook for Clerkship Directors. Mem. Wis. Rural Health Dev. Council, Consortium Primary Care in Wis.; co-dir. Wis. Area Health Edn. Sys. Recipient National award Patient Care mag., 1997. Mem. AMA, Soc. Tchrs. Family Medicine, Assn. Am. Med. Colls., Am. Med. Women's ssn., ACPHE. Office: Univ Wisconsin Med School 1300 University Ave Madison WI 53706-1510

SKOGLUND, MARILYN, state supreme court justice; b. Chgo., Aug. 28, 1946; BA, So. Ill. U., 1971; clerkship, 1977-81. Bar: Vt. 1981, U.S. Dist. Ct. Vt. 1981, U.S. Ct. Appeals (2d cir.) 1983. Asst. atty. gen. Civil Law Divsn., 1981—89, chief, 1988—93, Pub. Protection Divsn., 1993-94; judge Vt. Dist. Ct., 1994-97; assoc. justice Vt. Supreme Ct., 1997—. Office: Vt Supreme Ct 109 State St Montpelier VT 05609-0001

SKOLER, CELIA REBECCA, retired art gallery director; b. Sioux City, Iowa, Apr. 7, 1931; d. Jacob and Flora (Gorchow) Stern; m. Louis Skoler, Aug. 24, 1952; children: Elisa Anne, Harry Jay. BFA in Art and Music magna cum laude, Syracuse U., 1976. Fin. planner Architects' Partnership, Syracuse, NY, 1969-71; bus. mgr. Skoler & Lee Architects P.C., Syracuse, 1971-89; owner, dir. New Acquisitions Gallery, Syracuse, 1981-95, 1995—2003; ptnr. Gallery Metro, Syracuse, 1991-93, mng. ptnr., 1992-93; contbg. writer Syracuse Herald and Syracuse Newtimes, Syracuse, 1989-91; ret., 2003. Art cons. Costello, Cooney & Fearon, Syracuse, 1981—83, IBM Hdqs., Syracuse, NY, 1983, Rochester, NY, 84, Albany, NY, 86, Menter, Rudin & Trivelpiece, Syracuse, 1987—88, Blue Cross/Blue Shield, Ctrl. N.Y., Syracuse, 1990, Syracuse Newspapers, 1992—94, GTE Svcs. Corp., Syracuse, 1995; gallery supr. of sudent interns Syracuse U., 1981—93; dir. mayoral portrait City of Syracuse, 1983; dir. Gelling Meml. portrait U. Coll., 1984; dir. Levine Meml. Commn. Temple Concord, 1984; TV producer Syracuse U. Friends of Art, 1979—80; panelist for art critique Everson Mus. Art, Syracuse, 1989; lectr. on gallery mgmt. Syracuse U. Sch. of Art, 1989; juror fine art N.Y. State Fair, 1982, 89; panelist Cultural Resources Coun., Onondaga County, NY, 2001—. One-man shows include Camillus Plaza, 1972, The Associated Artists Gallery, Syracuse, 1973, Libr. Fayetteville, N.Y., 1974; exhibited in group shows at N.Y. State Fair (1st prize 1974), U. Coll, 1967, 69, 71, Rochester Meml. Gallery, 1969-72, 74, The Associated Artists, 1971-72, Cen. N.Y. Art Open, 1970, 71, (Purchase prize 1970, 71), Munson Williams Protor Inst, Utica, N.Y., 1971, 72, Cayuga Mus., Auburn, N.Y., 1972, Oneida (N.Y.) Art Festival, 1969, (1st prize), Jewish Community Ctr., Syracuse, 1968 (1st prize 1969), St. David's Invitational, Dewitt, N.Y., 1970-75, Cooperstown Art Inst., Nat. Show, 1973, 74, Arena Nat. Show, Binghamton, N.Y., 1975 (Purchase prize 1975); prodr.: (autobiographical CD-ROM) In Rehearsal, 1997; represented in permanent collection at Savannah (Ga.) Coll. Art and Design & Syracuse U. Peer counselor Univ. Coll., Syracuse, 1980-85; Tel-auc auctioneer Sta. WCNY-TV, Liverpool, N.Y., 1982; mem. steering and implementation com. Gelling Meml. Lounge U. Coll., 1984-85; exec. bd. Syracuse U. Friends of Art, 1977-80; fine art juror Downtown Com., Syracuse, 1982, Oswego (N.Y.) Art Guild, 1984. Recipient Purchase prize Marine Midland Bank, 1974, Crouse-Irving Hosp., 1971, 1974; named to Sioux City Ctrl. High Roster Hall of Fame, 1998. Mem. Everson Mus. Art (corp.) mem. Phi Kappa Phi, Alpha Sigma Lambda (pres. 1980-81). Home and Office: 213 Scottholm Ter Syracuse NY 13224-1737

SKOLFIELD, MELISSA T. public relations executive, government official; b. New Orleans, June 25, 1958; m. Frank W. Curtis. BA in Econ. and Behavioral Sci., Rice U., 1980; MA in Pub. Affairs, George Washington U., 1986. Account exec. McDaniel & Tate Pub. Rels., Houston, 1981-84; press sec. Rep. Michael Andrews of Tex., 1985-87; press. sec. Senator Dale Bumpers of Ark., 1987-93; dep. asst. sec. for pub. affairs for policy and strategy Dept. Health and Human Svcs., Washington, 1993-95, asst. sec. pub. affairs, 1995—2001; sr. v.p., dir. healthcare practice group Golin/Harris Internat., Washington, 2001—03; comm. counsel Dem. Leader Nancy Pelosi U.S. House of Reps., Washington, 2003—. Press asst. Dem. Nat. Com., Dem. Nat. Conv., 1988, Clinton Pres. Campaign, Dem. Nat. Com., 1992. Mem. Senate Press Secs. Assn. (pres.), Assn. Dem. Press Assts., Pub. Rels. Soc. Am. Office: US Ho of Reps Office Dem Leader Washington DC 20515

SKOLL, PEARL A. retired mathematics and special education educator; b. N.Y.C., Apr. 15, 1927; d. Samuel and Lillian Ruth Adler; m. Ralph Lewis Skoll (dec. 1959); children: Jeffrey A., Steve, Lyle. BA, Hunter Coll., 1950; MA in Adminstrn./Supervision, Calif. State U., Northridge, 1974. Math. tchr. various schs., L.A. and N.Y.C., 1954-71; program coord. The Mobilecomputer Math Lab L.A. Unified Sch. Dist., L.A., 1971-77, leader tchr. tng., 1967-83, mainstream tchr., 1977-83, spl. edn. vocat. assessment counselor, 1983-86; retired, 1986. Mem. task force State Dept. of Edn., Sacramento, Calif., 1976; instr. Calif. State U., Northridge, 1975-76, Pepperdine U., Malibu, Calif., 1975-76. Author (book) Coping with the Calculator, 1975; editor (book) The Calculator Book, 1975; contbr. articles to profl. jours. Reader tapes for literacy program U. Nev., Las Vegas, 1986-87; hon. mem. adv. coun. IBC, Cambridge, Eng. 3d Internat. Congress of Math. Edn. grantee U.S. Office of Edn., 1976, Internat. Biog. Ctr. (Cambridge, Eng.) 20th Century award for Meritorious Achievement, 1994, IB Citation of Meritorious Achievement in Math. Svcs., various miscellaneous honors from IBC, 1995; named Woman of Yr., Am. Biog. Inst., 1994. Mem. Calif. Math. Coun., Nat. Coun. of Tchrs. of Math., Calif. State U. Alumni Assn. Democrat. Jewish. Avocations: volunteer work, cooking, baking, jigsaw & crossword puzzles, gardening. Home: 7684 Keating Cir Las Vegas NV 89147-4908 E-mail: angel415@prodigy.net.

SKOLNICK, MARILYN, civic worker; b. N.Y.C., Jan. 17, 1925; d. Max and Annie Ruth (Stern) Kassel; n. Herbert Skolnick, Aug. 2, 1948; 1 child, Tamara. BA, Bklyn. Coll., 1946; MA, U. Okla., 1948; postgrad., State U. Iowa, 1948-52. Host, prodr. cable TV program Focus on Issues, 1983—; chair citizen participation com. Transp. Rsch. Bd., Nat. Acad. Sci., 1987-94; sec. local transp. fin. com., 1987—. Bd. dirs. Port Authority of Allegheny County, 1982-95, pres. Allegheny County Transp. Coun., 1997-99, v.p., 1999—; mem. Pa. Small Bus. Compliance Adv. Com., 1992—. Chair Monroeville Planning Commn., 1983-85; bd. dirs. Pa. Planning Assn., 1983-85; mem. Allegheny County Hazardous Waste Task Force, 1983-85; bd. dirs. Group Against Smog and Pllution; mem. Pa. Transp. Adv. Com., 1983-86; mem. air pollution ctrl. adv. com. Allegheny County Health Dept., 1985—; mem. Allegheny County Local Emergency Planning Com., 1987—. Mem. LWV (former bd. dirs.), N.Y. Acad. Scis., Pa. Acad. Scis., Sierra Club (bd. dirs. Pa. chpt. 1986—, chair Allegheny Group 1988-91), Sigma Xi. Home: 109 Southridge Dr Monroeville PA 15146-4739

SKONEY, SOPHIE ESSA, educational administrator; b. Detroit, Jan. 29, 1929; d. George Essa and Helena (Dihmes) Cokalay; m. Daniel J. Skoney, Dec. 28, 1957; children: Joseph Anthony, James Francis, Carol Anne. PhB, U. Detroit, 1951; MEd, Wayne State U., 1960, EdD, 1975; postgrad., Ednl. Inst. Harvard Grad. Sch., 1986—. Tchr. elem. sch. Detroit Bd. Edn., 1952-69, remedial reading specialist, 1969-70, curriculum coord., 1970-71, region 6 article 3 title 1 coord., 1971-83, area achievement specialist, 1984-88, adminstrv. asst. Office Grant Procurement and Compliance, 1988-2000. Mem. dean's adv. coun. Coll. Edn. Wayne State U., 1995—; cons. in field. Editor newsletter Alliance to the Mich. Dental Assn., 1993-2000. Recipient Disting. Alumni award Wayne State U., 1993. Mem. ASCD, Wayne State U. Edn. Alumni Assn. (pres. bd. govs. 1979-80, newsletter editor 1975-77, 80—), Macomb Dental Aux. (pres. 1969-70), Mich. Dental Aux. (pres. 1980-81), Alliance Mich. Dental Assn. (pres. 1998-2000), Am. Assn. Sch. Adminstrs., Wayne State U. Alumni Assn. (dir., v.p. 1985-86), Internat. Reading Assn., Mich. Reading Assn., Mich. Assn. State and Fed. Program Specialists, Profl. Women's Network (newsletter editor 1981-83, pres. 1985-87, Anthony Wayne award for leadership 1981), Retirees Orgn. Sch. Adminstrs. and Suprs. (pres. 2003—), Anthony Wayne Soc., Delta Kappa Gamma, Beta Sigma Phi, Phi Delta Kappa (v.p. 1988-90, pres. 1990-91, Educator of Yr. 1985, 91, 96, 2000). Roman Catholic. Home: 20813 Lakeland St Saint Clair Shores MI 48081-2104 Personal E-mail: skoneys@aol.com.

SKRIP, LINDA JEAN, nurse; b. Neenah, Wis., Apr. 16, 1963; d. Donald Charles and Kathryn Amelia Patrikus; m. Stephen Michael, May 21, 1988. BSN, U. Wis., 1986. RN Va. Staff nurse U. Hosp. Ill., Chgo., 1986-87; asst. clin. nurse mgr. Northwestern Meml. Hosp., Chgo., 1987-88; nursing coord. Pitt County Meml. Hosp., Greenville, N.C., 1988-91; nursing supr. Chesapeake (Va.) Gen. Hosp., 1991-92, case mgmt. coord., 1992—2000, cert. case mgr., 1993-2000, dir. care mgmt., 2000—02. Roman Catholic. Avocations: tennis, travel. Home: 1253 Smokey Mountain Trail Chesapeake VA 23320-8187 E-mail: ljsccm@msn.com.

SKURDENIS, JULIANN VERONICA, librarian, educator, writer, editor; b. July 13, 1942; d. Julius J. and Anna M. (Zilys) S.; m. Lawrence J. Smircich, Aug. 21, 1965 (div. July 1978); m. Paul J. Lalli, Oct. 1, 1978; 1 adopted child, Kathryn Leila Skurdenis-Lalli. AB with honors, Coll. New Rochelle, 1964; MS, Columbia U., 1966; MA, Hunter Coll., 1974. Young adult libr. Bklyn. Pub. Libr., 1964-66; periodicals libr., instr. Kingsborough C.C., Bklyn., 1966-67; acquisitions libr. Pratt Inst., Bklyn., 1967-68; acquisitions libr., asst. prof. Bronx (N.Y.) C.C., 1968-75, head tech. svcs., assoc. prof., 1975-97, prof., 1998—. Acting dir. Libr. Resource Learning Ctr., 1994-97. Author: Walk Straight Through the Square, 1976, More Walk Straight Through the Square, 1977; contbg. editor Internat. Travel News, 1989—, Travel Your Way/N.Y. Times, 1996-98; travel editor Archaeology mag., 1986-89; contbr. over 400 travel, hist., and archaeol. pieces. N.Y. State fellow, 1960-66, Columbia U. fellow, 1964-66, Pratt Inst. fellow, 1965. Mem. AAUP, Libr. Assn. CUNY (chairwoman numerous coms.), Archaeol. Inst. Am. Avocations: archaeology, travel, travel writing. Office: CUNY Bronx CC University Ave Bronx NY 10453-6994 Office Phone: 718-289-5436. E-mail: julie13@optonline.net.

SKURNIK, JOAN IRIS, educational consultant; b. Bklyn., Apr. 14, 1935; d. Benjamin and Dorothy (Blum) Hessel; m. Maurice Skurnik, Sept. 1, 1955 (div. Jan. 1982); children: Jennifer, Jonathan. BA magna cum laude, CCNY, 1973; MA, Columbia U., 1975. Cert. tchr. nursery to 6th grade, N.Y. Pvt. practice remedial therapist, diagnostician, N.Y.C., 1974—; ednl. cons. in learning disabilities The Calhoun Sch., N.Y.C., 1977-85, The Collegiate Sch., N.Y.C., 1984-87, Riverdale (N.Y.) Country Sch., 1989-90, Abraham Joshua Heschel Sch., N.Y.C., 1991—. Cons. Holy Rosary Sch., Pitts., 1976; mem. planning com. Ethical Culture Schs., N.Y.C., 1980-82; presenter, conf. and workshop coord. in field. Mem. NOW, Internat. Reading Assn., Internat. Dyslexia Soc. (N.Y. br. bd. mem. 1985-88), Profl. Colleagues Group, Phi Beta Kappa, Planned Parenthood (N.Y.C.), Appalachian Mountain Club (N.Y.C.). Avocations: archaeology, hiking, traveling, reading, theatre.

SKURZYNSKI, GLORIA JOAN, writer; b. Duquesne, Pa., July 6, 1930; d. Aylmer Kearney and Serena Elizabeth (Decker) Flister; m. Edward Joseph Skurzynski, Dec. 1, 1951; children: Serena Nolan, Janine Skurzynski-Mahoney, Joan Alm, Alane Ferguson, Lauren Thliveris. Student, Carlow Coll., 1948-50. Author: The Magic Pumpkin, 1971, The Remarkable Journey of Gustavus Bell, 1973, The Poltergeist of Jason Morey, 1975, In a Bottle with a Cork on Top, 1976, Two Fools and a Faker, 1977, Bionic Parts for People, 1978 (Golden Kite Honor Bk. award Soc. Children's Bk. Writers), Martin by Himself, 1979, What Happened in Hamelin, 1979 (telecast on Storybreak, CBS, 1987, Christopher award,

Reviewer's Choice award, Horn Bk. Honor List, ALA Booklist), Honest Andrew, 1981, Safeguarding the Land, 1981, Three Folktales, 1981, Manwolf, 1981 (Best Bks. for Young Adults award ALA, Reviewer's Choice award ALA Booklist, Bks. of Yr. award Child Study Assn., Notable Children's Trade Bk. in Field of Social Studies), Lost In the Devil's Desert, 1982 (Utah Children's Bk. award), The Tempering, 1983 (Golden Kite award Soc. Children's Bk. Writers, Best Bks. for Young Adults award ALA, Best Bks. of Yr. award Sch. Libr. Jour., Children's Bks. of Yr. award Libr. Congress, Bks. of Yr. award Child Study Assn.), Trapped in the Slickrock Canyon, 1984 (Golden Spur award Western Writers Am., Am. Booksellers Pick of the List, Jr. Lit. Guild Selection), Caught in the Moving Mountains, 1984, Swept in the Wave of Terror, 1985, The Minstrel in the Tower, 1988, Dangerous Ground, 1989, Robots, 1990 (100 Children's Bks. award N.Y. Pub. Libr. 1990, Outstanding Science Trade Bk. for Children award NSTA/CBC 1991), Almost the Real Thing, 1991 (Children's Sci. Bk. award Am. Inst. Physics 1992), Here Comes the Mail, 1992, Good-Bye, Billy Radish, 1992 (Best Bks. of Yr. award Sch. Libr. Jour., Jefferson Cup Hon. award Va. Libr. Assn., Judy Lopez Meml. Hon. Bk., Women's Nat. Bk. Assn.), Get the Message, 1993 (Outstanding Sci. Trade Bks. for Children award NSTA/CBC 1994, Bks. for the Teen Age award N.Y. Pub. Libr. 1994), Know the Score, 1994 (Bks. for the Teen Age award N.Y. Pub. Libr. 1995), Zero Gravity, 1994 (Outstanding Sci. Trade Bks. for Children award NSTA/CBC 1995, Children's Bk. of Yr., Bank Street Coll. Child Study Com.), Cyberstorm, 1995, Caitlin's Big Idea, 1995, Waves, the Electromagnetic Universe, 1996, Virtual War, 1997, (with Alane Ferguson) The Mystery of the Spooky Shadow, 1996, The Mystery of the Vanishing Creatures, 1996, Wolf Stalker, 1997, Rage of Fire, 1998, Discover Mars, 1998, Cliff-Hanger, 1999, Spider's Voice, 1999, Deadly Waters, 1999. Mem. Soc. of Children's Book Writers and Illustrators, Utah Women's Forum, Internat. Women's Forum. Home and Office: 5898 W Riverbend Ln Boise ID 83703-6249

SKYLAR, ALAYNE, television producer, writer, talent scout, talent agent, educator; b. N.Y.C., July 12, 1957; BA, Hunter Coll., 1979. Talent agent Funny Face, N.Y.C., 1984-85; owner, pres. Skylar Talent, N.Y.C., 1985-91; freelance TV prodr. various mag. and talk shows, N.Y.C., 1991—; owner, pres. Skylar Prodn., 1997—; owner Automat Cafe, 2003. Spkr. in field.

SLACK, VICKIE, human services administrator; b. Monroe, La., Mar. 27; d. Rufus J. and Minnie (Starr) S. BS, Sacramento State U., 1988; MPA, Golden Gate U., 1989. Phys. therapy asst. Easter Seals, Sacramento, 1983-84; intern aide to Congresswoman Barbara Boxer, Vallejo, Calif., 1986-87; phys. therapist asst. U. Calif.-Davis Med. Ctr., Sacramento, 1984-85; adminstrv. asst. St. Luke Hosp., San Francisco, 1987-88; ins. rep. Am. Nat. Ins. Co., Vallejo, 1988-89; health info. specialist Solano County Health Dept., Vallejo, Calif., 1990-93; supr., health educator, dir. tobacco edn. programs Bay Area Urban League, Oakland, Calif., 1993-95, health and human svc. dir., 1995—. Mem. Housing and Redevel. Commn., Cultural Commn., Commn. on Aging and Sister City Assn., City of Vallejo. Mem. NAFE, NAACP, Nat. Assn. Pub. Adminstrs., Nat. Council Negro Women, Delta Sigma Theta. Democrat. Baptist. Home: 161 Gary Cir Vallejo CA 94591-8228 Office: Bay Area Urban League 2201 Broadway Ste 100A Oakland CA 94612-3039

SLADE, BARBARA ANN, art educator; b. Bklyn., N.Y., May 15, 1941; d. Steve Licata, Margie Licata; m. George Drakos, Sept. 16, 1961 (div.); 1 child, Matthew Drakos ; m. Fred Slade, Aug. 18, 1996. Student, Sch. Art and Design, N.Y., 1955—59; AAS, Fash Inst. Tech., N.Y., 1961; student, Art Student League, N.Y., 1975—83. Instr. art U. Nev., Las Vegas, 1992—93, Las Vegas Art Mus., Las Vegas, 1993—97, Sun City Summelin Art Club, Las Vegas, 1995—. Lectr., demo in pastel Sun City DelWeb Art Club, 2001. Mem.: Nev. Pastel Soc. (pres., co-founder 1998—2001). Avocation: birdwatching. Home: 1775 Montessouri St Las Vegas NV 89117-1623

SLADE, BARBIE EVETTE DELK, special education educator; b. Orlando, Fla., Sept. 5, 1961; d. Jack Everett and Barbara Nell (Corley) Delk; m. Mark Anthony Slade, Sept. 22, 1984; children: Nicholas Mark, Wesley Evan. BS with honors, U. So. Miss., 1992, MS, 2000, postgrad. in spl. edn., 2001—. Specific learning disability (SLD) tchr. K-12 North Forrest H.S., Hattiesburg, Miss., 1992—. Mem. various coms. and couns. North Forrest H.S., 1996—. Vol. Spl. Olympics, cmty. elderly. Mem.: Am. Fedn. Tchrs., Coun. Exceptional Children. Baptist. Avocation: reading. Office: North Forrest High Sch 693 Eatonville Rd Hattiesburg MS 39401 Home: 45 Ben Thompson Rd Moselle MS 39459-9654 Office Phone: 601-545-9304. E-mail: sladebl@bellsouth.net.

SLADE, PRISCILLA DEAN, academic administrator; d. Percy and Louise Dean; children: Alzo, Maurice. MPA, Jackson State U.; BS in Bus., Miss. State U.; PhD, U. Tex., Austin. Dept. chair acctg. and bus. sch. Tex. So. U., Houston, 1991—93, dean bus. sch., 1993—99, acting pres., 1999, pres., 1999—. Bd. dirs. Houston 2012 Found., BioHouston, INROADS, Houston, Inc., Greater Houston Partnership, Houston Mus. Natural Sci., Houston Tech. Ctr., Tex. Internat. Consortium, Houston, Tex. State Bd. Pub. Accountancy, Houston, The Houston Forum, The Houston Internat. Festival, The Telecom Opportunity Inst., Houston, YMCA of Greater Houston, Fed. Res. Bank, Houston, Jr. Achievement, Houston; exec. adv. bd. KPMG Cons. Higher Edn., Houston; gov. bd. Super Bowl XXXVIII 2004, Houston. Mem. Alpha Kappa Alpha Sorority, Inc., Houston, Tex., Gov. Perry's Transition Team, Austin, Tex., Gov. Perry's Commn. for Women, Austin, Tex., Windsor Village United Meth. Ch., Houston, Tex., 1991. Recipient Achiever's award, Houston Bus. and Profl. Men's Club, 2001, Appreciation award, Kay On-Going Edn. Ctr., 2001, Gutenberg Award, Houston Mus. Printing History, 2001, Zenith Honoree, Houston League of Bus. & Profl. Women, 2001, Outstanding Woman of Achievement, YWCA, Houston, 2001, Award of Distinction, Orch. X, 2002, Shattered Glass award, Harris County Women's Polit. Caucus, 2002, Leadership Honoree, JP Morgan Chase & Ctr. for Houston's Future, 2002, Barrier Breakers Award, Career & Recovery Resrouces, 2003, Outstanding Texan award in Edn., Tex. Legis. Black Caucus, 2003. Mem.: AAUW, Internat. Assn. Univ. Pres., HBCU/MI Consortium, Coun. Pub. Univ. Pres. and Chancellors, Am. Soc. Women Accountants, Am. Mgmt. Assn., Am. Coun. Edn., Profl. Black Women's Enterprise, Am. Acctg. Assn., Beta Alpha Psi, Alpha Kappa Alpha. Office: Tex Southern Univ 3100 Cleburne St Houston TX 77004

SLADEK, CELIA DAVIS, neuroscientist, educator; b. Denver, Mar. 25, 1944; d. Charles Willard Davis and Mildred (Bozarth) Davis TeSelle; m. John R. Sladek, May 23, 1970; children: Jonathan A., Stefan Z., Jessica A. BA, Hastings Coll., 1966; MS, Northwestern U., 1969, PhD, 1971. Asst. prof. physiology U. Ill. Sch. Medicine, Chgo., 1970-73; asst. prof. biology SUNY, Brockport, 1973-74; research assoc. in neurology U. Rochester (N.Y.) Sch. Medicine, 1974-76, asst. prof. neurology, 1976-80, assoc. prof. neurology and neurobiology, 1980-88, prof. neurology and neurobiology, 1988-91; prof. physiology Chgo. Med. Sch., North Chicago, Ill., 1991—. Cons. Am. Heart Assn., Dallas, 1986-89, 96—, NIH, 1997—; dir. interdepartmental neurosci. grad. program U. Rochester, 1989-91. Grantee NINDS, 1977-82, 91—, NIDKD, 1977-91, NIHLBI, 1982-88, Nat. Inst. Aging, 1978-81, 90-91, 94-97 Mem. Soc. for Neurosci., Endocrine Soc., N.Y. Acad. Sci., Am. Physiol. Soc. (councillor). Office: Chgo Med Sch Dept Physiology North Chicago IL 60064

SLADE-MARTIN, PHYLLIS E. director; b. Newport News, Va., Dec. 4, 1956; d. John W. and Ruth (Brown) Slade; m. Charles Martin; children: Christina Martin, Charles Martin, Christopher Martin. BS in Comm. Disorders, Radford Coll., 1979; MA, Bowling Green State U., 1980; MA in History, George Mason U., 2003. Asst. dean, dir. housing Kurtztown (Pa.) U.; assoc. dir. resident life U. Mo., College Park, George Mason U., Fairfax, Va., assoc. dir. African Am. studies, dir. African Am. Studies Rsch. and Rsch. Ctr. Trainer, cons. Mem.: Assn. Black Faculty Staff & Adminstrs. (v.p.), African Studies Assn., Toni Morrison Soc., Phi Alpha Theta, Phi Beta Delta. Democrat. Baptist. Avocations: antiques, hiking, reading, travel. Office: George Mason U 4400 University Dr Fairfax VA 22030 Business E-Mail: pslade@gmu.edu.

SLAPER, RACHAEL MAREE, landscape company executive, poet; b. Tucson, Dec. 20, 1958; d. Roger Patrick Slaper, Marie Stella and Donold Burton Damon(Stepfather). Co-owner Bonsai Babes Landscaping, Tucson, 1998—. Author poetry. Exec. dir. Pathfinder Critters Inc., Tucson, 2003—. Recipient Marston award, Bay Players, 1976. Office: Bonsai Babes Landscaping 6260 Desert Foothills Dr Tucson AZ 85743 Personal E-mail: sarasixpence@hotmail.com. E-mail: bonsaibabes@hotmail.com.

SLATER, EVE, federal agency administrator; 2 children. Grad., Vassar Coll. Cert. internal medicine and cardiology. Intern and resident Mass. Gen. Hosp., chief resident medicine; chief hypertension unit, asst. prof. medicine Harvard Med. Sch., 1977—82; sr. dir. biochem. endocrinology Merck Rsch. Labs., 1983—88, sr. v.p. external policy, v.p. corp. pub. affairs; asst. sec. for health Dept. HHS, Washington, 2002—. Chmn. Internat. Conf. on Harmonization Com. on the Structure and Content of Clin. Studies Reports; chmn. regulations adv. bd. Ctr. for Medicine Rsch.; mem. Keystone Nat. Policy Dialogue on HIV; founder Forum for HIV Rsch. Mem.: Phi Beta Kappa. Avocation: flute. Office: Dept HHS Pub Health and Sci 200 Independence Ave SW Washington DC 20201

SLATER, KRISTIE, small business owner; b. Rock Springs, Wyo., Nov. 14, 1957; d. Fredrick Earl and Shirley Joan (McWilliams) Alexander; m. C. James Slater, May 11, 1992. A in Bus. Adminstrn., Salt Lake City Coll., 1978. EMT, Wyo. Cost engr., material coord. Project Constrn. Corp., LaBarge, Wyo., 1985; cost engr., scheduler Flour Daniel Constrn. Co., Salt Lake City, 1985-86, Bibby Edible Oils, Liverpool, Eng., 1986-87; cost engr., safety technician Sunvic, Inc./I.S.T.S., Inc., Augusta, Ga., 1987-88; cost engr. Brown & Root, Inc., Ashdown, Ark., 1988-89, Wickliffe, Ky., 1989, sr. cost engr. Pasadena, Tex., 1989-90, LaPorte, Tex., 1990-91; project controls mgr. Yeargin Inc., Thousand Oaks, Calif., 1991-92; corp. controls mgr. Suitt Constrn. Co., Greenville, S.C., 1993-95; assoc. fin. analyst Fluor Daniel Constrn. Co., Seaford, Del., 1996-2000; freelancer, 2000—03; fin. cost analyst Fluor Global Constrn. Co., Seaford, Del., 2003—. Pres. 4-H State Coun., Laramie, Wyo., 1976; mem. Houston Livestock Show and Rodeo. Avocations: horseback riding, reading. E-mail: kristie82941@earthlink.net.

SLATER, LORI ANNETTE, project manager; b. Houston, Aug. 8, 1964; d. Ted Gerald Patterson, JoAnn Patterson. AAS in Bus., Blinn Coll., 1984; BA in Applied Behavioral Sci., Nat. Louis U., 2000. Cert. profl. project mgr. Sec. Century Coating, Houston, 1984—85; asst. Ted's Pool Svc., Houston, 1985—88; sec. Freestone County Attorney's Office, Fairfield, Tex., 1989—90; dispatcher Tex. Instruments, Inc., Houston, 1990—93, Hewlett Packard Co., Atlanta, 1993—95; global accounts tech. adminstr. Hewlett Packard Co., Atlanta, 1995—98; bus. process analyst Hewlett Packard Co., Atlanta, 1998—2000, project/program mgr., 2000—. Mem. Friends of the Ctr. So. Poverty Law Ctr., Montgomery, 2001—, founding mem. Nat. Campaign for Tolerance, 2001—. Mem.: Project Mgmt. Inst. Avocations: reading, tennis, watching old movies. Business E-Mail: lori_slater@hp.com.

SLATER, NANCY LYNNE, special education educator, marketing professional, consultant; b. Bklyn., Feb. 1, 1957; d. Herbert Jerome and Rhoda Jean Slater; m. Steven Andrew Saslow, Aug. 28, 1980 (div. Aug. 1987); 1 child, Adam Grant Saslow ; m. Barry David Erenburg, Nov. 22, 1992; 1 child, Danny Erenburg. BA in Comm. Arts, L.I. U., 1978; MS in Spl. Edn., Hofstra U., 1981. Cert. tchr. spl. edn. K-12 N.Y. Spl. edn. tchr. Nathan Hale Mid. Sch., Bklyn., 1980—81, Tamanend Mid. Sch., Warrington, Pa., 1981—82; account exec. Harold Katz Advt., Great Neck, NY, 1985—87; spl. edn. tchr. Garden City (N.Y.) H.S., 1992—. Dir. of girls West Hills Day Camp, Huntington, NY, 1989—99, mktg., advt. cons., 2000—03. Mem.: N.Y. State Tchrs. Assn. Avocations: stenciling, interior design, curriculum development. Office: Garden City H S 170 Rockaway Ave Garden City NY 11530

SLATER, VALERIE A. lawyer; b. Passaic, N.J., Oct. 13, 1952; BA magna cum laude, Allegheny Coll., 1974; JD, Cath. U. Am., 1977. Bar: D.C. 1977, U.S. Ct. Appeals (D.C. cir.) 1978, U.S. Dist. Ct. (D.C. dist.) 1982, U.S. Ct. Internat. Trade 1984, U.S. Ct. Appeals (fed. cir.) 1984. With Akin, Gump, Strauss et al., Washington. Mem. Phi Beta Kappa. Office: Akin Gump Strauss Hauer & Feld Ste 400 1333 New Hampshire Ave NW Washington DC 20036-1564 Business E-Mail: vslater@akingump.com.

SLATER, VALERIE PERIOLAT, volunteer; b. Michigan City, Ind., May 6, 1949; d. Emmett Gerard and Alma Rosalee (Keys) Wozniak; m. John Grey Periolat, Jan. 24, 1970 (div. Aug. 1975); 1 child, Jason; m. Donald Joseph Slater, Mar. 30, 1976; stepchildren: Meredith M., Julie. Cert. in French, L'Inst. De'Catholique, Paris, 1968; student, Western Mich. U., 1968-69, U. South Fla., 1973-75. Registrar Tampa (Fla.) Bus. Coll., 1971-75; adminstrv. asst. Crown Ins., Tampa, 1975-77; key employee S&A Restaurant Corp., Atlanta and Miami, Fla., 1977-82; realtor Century 21, Atlanta, 1982-84; owner Horizon Concepts, Plano, Tex., 1988-89. Co-owner Horizon Properties, Plano, 1979-89. Vol. HCA Med. Ctr., Plano, 1986-95; bd. dirs. Cystic Fibrosis Found., Dallas, 1988, 89, 2000. Republican. Roman Catholic. Home: 5785 Stony Point Rd Barboursville VA 22923-1804

SLATER, WANDA MARIE WORTH, property manager; b. Thurston, Ohio, Feb. 18, 1927; d. Daniel Harrison and Grace Marie (Neel) Worth; m. Charles Edwin Slater; children: Margaret Grace(dec.), Daniel Worthington-(dec.), Donald Edwin. Student, Denison U., 1941-45, Bethany Coll., 1945-46. Recipient certs. Ohio Ho. Reps. and Senate, 116th Ohio Assembly, Creative Living, Columbus. Sub. tchr. Licking County Schs., Union Twp., Ohio, 1946; clerical typist Farm Bur. Ins. Co., Columbus, Ohio, 1947-49; salesperson Avon Co., Clyde, Ohio, 1954-63; dep. registrar Sandusky County, Ohio, 1960-64; notary pub. State of Ohio, Clyde, 1965-78, Hebron-Buckeye Lake, Ohio, 1978-98. Owner, mgr. rental property. Editor OFWC Buckeye mag., 1970-74, 88-98. Pres. Welcome Wagon, Clyde, 1957, Clyde Jr. League of Women, 1966, Leads-Licking County Cmty. Action Com., 1988, 94, 2000-01. Recipient Disting. Leadership award 1992, certificate of appreciation CARE. Mem.: Twentieth Century Club (pres. 1976—77), Order Eastern Star (worthy matron Clyde chpt. 1965, 1978, Hebron Eagon chpt. 1989, 1994, 2001), Mut. and Civic Improvement Club (pres. 1994—), Ohio Fedn. Women's Clubs (pres. 1986—88), Gen. Fedn. Women's Clubs Marionettes (pres. 1988—). Republican. Avocations: monologues, flower arranging, travel, crafts. Home and Office: 36 Worth Dr Hebron OH 43025-9760

SLATON, DANIELLE VICTORIA, professional soccer player; b. San Jose, Calif., June 10, 1980; Majored in psychology, Santa Clara U., Calif., 1998—2001. Capt. U.S. Under-16 Nat. Team, 1996—97; mem. U.S. Under-21 Nat. Team, 1999, starter, Nordic Cup championship team, 1999; soccer player, defender U.S. Women's Nat. Team, 1999—; mem. U.S. soccer team Summer Olympics, Sydney, Australia, 2000; team mem. Carolina Courage, WUSA. Finalist Mo. Athletic Club award, 2000, 2001, Hermann trophy, 2001; named third team All-Am., NSCAA, 1998, first team All-Am., 1999, 2001, 2002. Office: US Soccer Fedn 1801 S Prairie Ave Chicago IL 60616*

SLAUGHTER, LOUISE MCINTOSH, congresswoman; b. Harlan County, Ky., Aug. 14, 1929; d. Oscar Lewis and Grace (Byers) McIntosh; m. Robert Slaughter, 1956; children: Megan Rae, Amy Louise, Emily Robin. BS, U. Ky., 1951, MS, 1953. Bacteriologist Ky. Dept. Health, Louisville, 1951-52, U. Ky., 1952-53; market researcher Procter & Gamble, Cin., 1953-56; mem. staff Office of the Lt. Gov. N.Y., Albany, 1978-82; state rep. N.Y. Gen. Assembly, Albany, 1983-86; mem. U.S. Congress from 28th N.Y. dist., Washington, 1987—; mem. Ho. rules com. Del. Dem. Nat. Conv., 1972, 76, 80, 88, 92, 96; mem. Commn. on Security and Coop. in Europe, Nat. Ctr. for Policy Alternatives Adv. Bd., League of Women Voters, Nat. Women's Polit. Caucus. Office: US Ho of Reps Office of House Mems 2469 Rayburn Bldg Washington DC 20515-3228*

SLAUGHTER ANDREW, ANNE, lawyer; b. Evansville, Ind., Sept. 23, 1955; d. Owen L. and Marjorie (Specht) Slaughter; m. Joseph J. Andrew, Sept. 9, 1989. BA, Georgetown U., 1977; JD cum laude, Ind. U., 1983. Bar: Ind. 1983, U.S. Dist. Ct. (so. dist.) Ind. Ptnr. Baker & Daniels, Indpls. Adj. prof. environ. law Ind. U. Sch. Law, Indpls. Editor-in-chief Ind. U. Law Rev., 1982-83; contbr. articles to profl. jours. Bd. dirs. Nature Conservancy, 1997—, Ind. Natural Resources Found., 1994—; mem. Indpls. Pub. Sch. Found. Com., 1997—; mem. Brownfield Remediation Adv. Com., 1997—. Mem. ABA (chair state and regional environ. coop. com. 1996-98), Ind. Bar Assn. (chair environ. law sect. 1992-93), Ind. C. of C. (govt. affairs commn.). Office: Baker & Daniels 300 N Meridian St Ste 2700 Indianapolis IN 46204-1782

SLAUGHTER-DEFOE, DIANA TRESA, education educator; b. Chgo., Oct. 28, 1941; d. John Ison and Gwendolyn Malva (Armstead) S.; m. Michael Defoe (div.). BA, U. Chgo., 1962, MA, 1964, PhD, 1968. Instr. dept. psychiatry Howard U., Washington, 1967-68; rsch. assoc., asst. prof. Yale U. Child Study Ctr., New Haven, 1968-70; asst. prof. dept. behavioral scis. and edn. U. Chgo., 1970-77; asst. to assoc. prof. edn. and African Am. studies and Ctr. for Urban Affairs and Policy Rsch. (now Inst. for Policy Rsch.) Northwestern U., Evanston, Ill., 1977-90, prof., 1990-97; Constance E. Clayton prof. urban edn. Grad. Sch. Edn. U. Pa., 1998—. Mem. nat. adv. bd. Fed. Ctr. for Child Abuse & Neglect, 1979-82, coord. Human Devel. and Social Policy Program, 1994-97; mem. nat. adv. bd. Learning Rsch. and Devel. Ctr. U. Pitts., Ednl. Rsch. & Devel. Ctr., U. Tex., Austin; formerly chmn., dir. public policy program com. Chgo. Black Child Devel. Inst., 1982-84; dir. Ill. Infant Mental Health Com., 1982-83; mem. res. adv. bd. Chgo. Urban League, 1986-97. Contbr. articles to profl. jours. Fellow APA (mem. divsn. ethnic and minority affairs, com. on children, youth and families, devel. psychology, sch. psychology, bd. sci. affairs 1995-97, bd. advancement psychology pub. interest 2003-, assoc. editor, mem. editl. bd. Child Devel. 1995-98, Disting. Contbn. to Rsch. in Pub. Policy award 1993, mem. bd. for advancement of psychol. in the pub. intrest 2003—); mem. Soc. for Rsch. in Child Devel. (governing coun. 1981-87), Am. Ednl. Rsch. Assn. (editl. bd. Rev. Ednl. Rsch.), Nat. Assn. Edn. Young Children, Assn. Study African Ams. and History, Nat. Head Start (past mem. R & E adv. bd.), Nat. Acad. Scis. (com. on child devel. and publ. policy 1987-93), Delta Sigma Theta. Office: U Pa Grad Sch Edn 3700 Walnut St Philadelphia PA 19104-6216 Business E-Mail: dianasd@gse.upenn.edu.

SLAVICK, ANN LILLIAN, retired art educator; b. Chgo., Sept. 29, 1933; d. Irving and Goldie (Bernstein) Friedman; m. Lester Irwin Slavick, Nov. 21, 1954 (div. Mar. 1987); children: Jack, Rachel. BFA, Sch. of Art Inst. of Chgo., 1973, MA in Art History, Theory, Criticism, 1991. Dir. art gallery South Shore Commn., Chgo., 1963-67; tchr. painting, drawing, crafts Halfway House, Chgo., 1972-73; tchr. studio art Conant H.S., Hoffman Estates, Ill., 1973-74; tchr. art history and studio arts New Trier H.S., Winnetka and Northfield, Ill., 1974-80; tchr. 20th century art history New Trier Adult Edn. Program, Winnetka, 1980-81; tchr. art adult edn. program H.S. Dist. 113, Highland Park, Ill., 1980-81; rschr., writer Art History Notes McDougall-Littel Pub., Evanston, Ill., 1984-85; tchr. art and art history Highland Park and Deerfield (Ill.) H.S., 1980-2000; tchr. art history Coll. of Lake County, Grayslake, Ill., 1986-88; ret., 2000. Faculty chair for visual arts Focus on the Arts, Highland Park H.S., 1981-85, faculty coord. Focus on the Arts, 1987—; panelist Ill. Arts Coun. Arts Tour, 1999, Evanston Arts Coun., 2000-02, Ill. Arts Coun. Multidisciplinary Grant Awards, 2001-03; reader advanced placement art history exams, 2003. One woman show Bernal Gallery, 1979, U. Ill., Chgo., 1983, Ann Brierly Gallery, Winnetka, 1984; exhibited paintings, drawings, prints and constrns. throughout Chgo. area; work represented by Art Rental and Sales Gallery, Art Inst. Chgo., 1960-87, Bernal Gallery, 1978-82; group shows at Bernal Gallery; work in pvt. collections in Ill., N.Y., Calif., Ariz., Ohio. Recipient Outstanding Svc. in Art Edn. award Ea. Ill. U., 1992, Mayors award for contbn. to the arts, Highland Park, 1995. Mem.: Ill. Art Edn. Assn., Nat. Art Edn. Assn. Avocations: cooking, reading, theatre. Home: 5057 N Sheridan Rd Chicago IL 60640-3127 Office: Highland Park High Sch 433 Vine Ave Highland Park IL 60035-2099

SLAVIN, ALEXANDRA NADAL, artistic director, educator; b. Port-au-Prince, Haiti, Oct. 26, 1943; came to U.S., 1946; d. Pierre E. and Marie Therese (Clerié) Nadal; m. Eugene Slavin, Dec. 24, 1967; 1 child, Nicholas V. Grad. high sch., Chgo. Dancer Ballet Russe de Monte Carlo, N.Y.C., 1960-61, Chgo. Opera Ballet and N.Y.C. Opera Ballet, 1961-64, Am. Ballet Theatre, N.Y.C., 1965-66, Ballet de Monte Carlo, 1966-67, The Royal Winnipeg (Can.) Ballet, 1967-72; artistic dir. Ballet Austin, Tex., 1972-89; owner, dir. The Slavin Nadal Sch. Ballet, Austin, 1989—. Recipient Achievement in the Arts award Austin chpt. YWCA, 1987. Roman Catholic. Avocation: gardening. Office: Slavin-Nadal Sch Ballet 5521 Burnet Rd Austin TX 78756-1603

SLAVIN, ARLENE, artist; b. N.Y.C., Oct. 26, 1942; d. Louis and Sally (Bryck) Eisenberg; m. Neal Slavin, May 24, 1964 (div. 1979); m. Eric Bregman, Sept. 21, 1980; 1 child, Ethan. BFA, Cooper Union for the Advancement of Sci. and Art, 1964; MFA, Pratt Inst., 1967. One-woman shows include Fischbach Gallery, N.Y., 1973, 1974, 2003, Brooke Alexander Gallery, 1976, Alexander Milliken Gallery, N.Y.C., 1979, 1980, 1981, 1983, U. Colo., 1981, Pratt Inst., N.Y.C., 1981, Am. Embassy, Belgrad, Yugoslavia, 1984, Heckscher Mus., Huntington, N.Y., 1987, Katherine Rich Perlow Gallery, 1988, Chauncey Gallery, Princeton, N.J., 1990, The Gallery Benjamin N. Cardoza Sch. Law, 1991, Norton Ctr. for Arts, Danville, Ky., 1992, Kavesh Gallery, Ketchum, Idaho, 1993, exhibited in group shows at Bass Mus. Art, Fla., Whitney Museum of Art, 1973, The Contempory Arts Center, Cin., 1974, Indpls. Mus. Art, 1974, Madison (Wis.) Art Ctr., Santa Barbara (Calif.) Mus., Winnipeg (Can.) Art Gallery, Gensler Assocs., San Francisco, 1986, Eliane Benson Gallery, Bridgehampton, N.Y., 1987, 1989, 1991, 1993, City of N.Y. Parks and Recreation Central Park, N.Y.C., 1989, Benton Gallery, Southampton, N.Y., 1991, Parish Mus., Southampton, 1991, Michele Miller Fine Art, 1993, Dillon Gallery, N.Y.C., 1998, Hebrew Union Coll., 2000—01, Fischbach Gallery, 2003, Am. Inst. Archs., 2003, Represented in permanent collections Met. Mus. of Art, N.Y.C., Fogg Art Mus., Cambridge, Mass., Hudson River Mus., Yonkers, N.Y., Heckscher Mus., Huntington, N.Y., Cin. Art Mus., Readers' Digest, Pleasantville, N.Y., pub. commns., N.C. Zoo, 1999, N.Y.C. Parks and Recreation, 1999, NJ Transit, Hoboken Terminal and Middletown Station, NJ, 1999—2002, Forest City Ratner, Ct. St Devel., 2000, Assunpink (N.Y.) Wildlife Ctr., 2004; subject: bibliography Arlene Slavin: Mediating Public Space, 2001; pub. commns., Town of Chapel Hill, N.C., 2002, PS 89, NYC, 2003, Assunpink Wildlife Preserve, N.J., 2004, one-woman shows include Fischbach Gallery, N.Y., 2003, artist mem. design team Hillsborough Area Regional Transit, Tampa, Fla., 2003—05. Grantee Nat. Endowment for Arts, 1977-78, Threshold Found., 1991. Home: 119 E 18th St New York NY 10003-2107 E-mail: slavin@arleneslavin.com.

SLAVIN, ROSANNE SINGER, textile converter; b. N.Y.C., Mar. 24, 1930; d. Lee H. and Rose (Winkler) Singer; divorced; children: Laurie Jo, Sharon Lee. Student, U. Ill. Prodn. converter Doucet Fabrics, silk prints, N.Y.C., 1953-57; sales mgr., mdse. mgr. print divsn. Crown Fabrics, N.Y.C., 1957-65; owner Matisse Fabrics, Inc. printed fabrics (now Hottmomma Inc.), N.Y.C., 1965—. Recipient Tommy award Am. Printed Fabrics Coun., 1978, 93; designated ofcl. printed fabric supplier for U.S. Olympic swimteam, 1984. Office: 1071 Avenue Of The Americas New York NY 10018-3704

SLAWSKY, DONNA SUSAN, librarian, singer; b. N.Y.C., Jan. 18, 1956; d. Samuel Slawsky and Lillian (Freizer) Alexander. BA, City Coll. N.Y., 1977; M of Infor. Libr. Sci., Pratt Inst., 1998. Coord. NYNEX Market Info. Ctr., White Plains, NY, 1985—87; dir. Info. Ctr./Archives, exhbns. curator HarperCollins Pubs., N.Y.C., 1988-99; singer N.Y.C., 1987—; dir. content devel. BuyerWeb, Inc., N.Y.C., 1999-2000; founder Info Diva, N.Y.C., 2001—02; mgr. indexing for digital archive Scholastic, Inc., N.Y.C., 2002—. Contbr. articles to profl. jours.; co-founder (quartet women's voices) Rose Ensemble debut Weill Recital Hall, Carnegie Hall, 1997. Pres. Assn. HarperCollins Employees, N.Y.C., 1990-94; dir. Tenants Assn., N.Y.C., 1994. Recipient Schubertiade Lieder Competition award 92d St. Y, N.Y.C., 1990. Mem.: Am. Soc. Info. Sci. and Tech., Assn. Ind. Info. Profls., Profl. Women Singers Assn. (treas. 1992—96, mem.-at-large 1997—, webmaster 2001—), Spl. Librs. Assn., Beta Phi Mu. Avocations: bicycling, theater, crafts. Office: Scholastic Inc 568 Broadway Rm 1045 New York NY 10012 Office Phone: 212-343-7716. E-mail: dslawsky@scholastic.com.

SLAYMAN, CAROLYN WALCH, geneticist, educator; b. Portland, Maine, Mar. 11, 1937; d. John Weston and Ruth Dyer (Sanborn) Walch; m. Clifford L. Slayman; children: Andrew, Rachel BA with highest honors, Swarthmore Coll., 1958; PhD, Rockefeller U., 1963; DSc (hon.), Bowdoin Coll., 1985. Instr., then asst. prof. Case Western Res. U., Cleve., 1967; from asst. prof. to prof. genetics Yale U. Sch. Medicine, New Haven, 1967—, Sterling prof. genetics, 1991—, chmn. dept. genetics, 1984-95, dep. dean acad. and sci. affairs, 1995—. Chmn. genetic basis of disease rev. commn. NIH, 1981—85, nat. adv. gen. med. scis. coun., 1989—93; bd. dirs. J. Weston Walch Pub., Portland, Maine, Applera Corp.; mem. sci. rev. bd. Howard Hughes Med. Inst., 1992—97. Mem. editl. bd. Jour. Biol. Chemistry, 1989-94; contbr. articles to sci. jours. Trustee Foote Sch., New Haven, 1983—89, Hopkins Sch., New Haven, 1988—93; bd. overseers Dartmouth Med. Sch., 1997—, Woods Hole Oceanographic Instn., 1997—, Bowdoin Coll., Brunswick, Maine, 1976—88, trustee, 1988—2001. Recipient Deborah Morton award Westbrook Coll., 1986. Mem. Am. Soc. Biol. Chemists, Genetics Soc. Am., Soc. Gen. Physiologists, Am. Soc. Microbiology, Inst. Medicine, Phi Beta Kappa Office: Yale U Sch Medicine Dept Genetics 333 Cedar St New Haven CT 06510-3289

SLEDZINSKI, JESSICA K. elementary school educator; b. Berwick, Pa., Nov. 2, 1975; d. John A. and Linda C. Thomas(Stepmother); m. Daniel D. Sledzinski, June 17, 2000. BA, Waynesburg (Pa.) Coll., 1998. Ednl. tech. asst. NE Elem. Sch., Farmington, N.Mex., 2000—01; educator Mesa Alta Jr. HS, Bloomfield, N.Mex., 2001—. Educator San Juan Coll. Cmty. Learning Ctr., Farmington, N.Mex., 2000—02. Cover art, The Green Fuse. Mem. Middletown Grange, Wrightstown, Pa., 1998—2000. Environ. grantee, Wal Mart, 2001. Mem.: NEA. Republican. Presbyterian. Avocations: painting, reading, hiking, poetry, computer gaming. Office: Mesa Alta Jr High Sch 329 North Bergin Ln Bloomfield NM 87413 Home: 47 Road 2581 Aztec NM 87410-1019 Personal E-mail: arsgratisars@yahoo.com.

SLEEMAN, MARY (MRS. JOHN PAUL SLEEMAN), retired librarian; b. Cleve., June 28, 1928; d. John and Mary Lillian (Jakub) Gerba; m. John Paul Sleeman, Apr. 27, 1946; children: Sandra (Sleeman) Swyrydenko, Robert, Gary, Linda. BS, Kent State U., 1965, MLS. Children's libr. Twinsburg Pub. Libr., Twinsburg, Ohio, 1965—66; supr. libr. mid. sch. Nordonia Hills Bd. Edn., Northfield, Ohio, 1965—93, ret., 1993. Mem.: No. Eastern Ohio Tchr. Assn., Storytellers Assn., Summit County Librarians Assn., ALA. Meth. Home: 18171 Logan Dr Cleveland OH 44146-5236 Office: 72 Leonard Ave Northfield OH 44067-1945

SLEIGH, SYLVIA, artist, educator; b. Llandudno, North Wales; came to U.S., 1961; d. John Harold and Katherine Amy (Miller) S.; m. Lawrence Alloway, June 28, 1954. Student, Sch. Art, Brighton, Sussex, Eng., 1932-36; diploma, U. London Extra-Mural Dept., 1947. Vis. asst. prof. SUNY-Stony Brook, 1978; instr. New Sch. Social Research, N.Y.C., 1974-77, 78-80; Edith Kreeger Wolf disting. prof. Northwestern U., Evanston, Ill., 1977; vis. artist Baldwin Seminar Oberlin Coll., Ohio, 1982, New Sch. Social Rsch., N.Y.C. One person shows include Bennington (Vt.) Coll., 1963, Soho 20 Art Gallery, N.Y.C., 1974, 76, 80, 82, A.I.R. Gallery, N.Y.C., 1974, 76, 78, Ohio State U., Columbus, 1976, Matrix, Wadsworth Atheneum, Hartford, Conn., 1976, Marianne Deson Gallery, Chgo., 1990, G.W. Einstein, Inc., N.Y.C., 1980, 83, 85, U. Mo., Saint Louis, 1981, Zaks Gallery, Chgo., 1985, 95, Milw. Art Mus., Butler Inst., Youngstown, Ohio, 1990, Stiebel Modern, N.Y.C., 1992, 94, Gallery 609, Denver, Canton (Ohio) Art Inst., Soho 20 Gallery, 1999, Deven Golden Fine Arts, N.Y., 1999, The Art of Sylvia Sleigh and Lawrence Allway Phila. Art Alliance, Phila., 2001; exhibited in group shows Newhouse Gallery, S.I., N.Y., Stamford (Conn.) Mus., 1985, Albany (N.Y.) Inst. Art, Cin. Art Mus., New Orleans Mus. Art, Denver Art Mus., Pa. Acad. Fine Arts, 1989, Carlsten Art Gallery, Stevens Point, Wis., 1993, Stiebel Modern, N.Y.C., 1994, Soho 20, N.Y.C., 1993, 96, Katzen Brown Gallery, N.Y.C., 1989, Zaks Gallery, Chgo., 1986, Steinbaum Krauss Gallery, 1997, Deven Golden Fine Arts, Ltd., N.Y.C., 1997, Rutgers U., New Brunswick, N.J., 1984, 86, RioArriba Gallery, Abiquiu, N.Mex., 1996, Milw. Art Mus., 1996, Steinbaum Krauss Gallery, 1997, N.Y. Mus. exhbn. traveling until 2001, David and Alfred Smart Mus., Chgo., Broome St. Gallery, N.Y.C., Deven Golden Fine Arts, N.Y.C., A.I.R. Gallery, N.Y.C., Apex Art Co., N.Y.C., 1998, McKee Gallery, N.Y.C., 1998, Royal Coll. Art, London, 1998, Heckscher Mus. Art, Huntington, N.Y., 1999, Printworks Gallery, 2000, others. Panelist Creative Artists Pub. Service Program, N.Y.C., 1976. Nat. Endowment for Arts grantee, 1982, Pollock-Krasner Found. grantee, 1985. Home: 330 W 20th St New York NY 10011-3302 Fax: 212-691-3312. E-mail: ssleigh@mindspring.com.

SLIKER, SHIRLEY J. BROCKER, bookseller; b. Irwin, Pa., Sept. 5, 1929; d. Robert John and Hannah Alberta (McGrew) Brocker; m. Alan Sliker, June 23, 1956; children: Mark Alan (dec.), William James, Barbara Louise Sliker-Seewer. BS, Syracuse U., 1951, MS, 1954. Owner Shirley's Book Svcs., Okemos, Mich., 1987—; tchr. evening coll. Mich. State U., East Lansing, 1988—2000. Mgr. Book Burrow, Friends of Lansing (Mich.) Pub. Libr., 1985-86. Commr. Lansing Charter Commn., 1976-78. Mem. Mid-Mich. Antiquarian Bookdealers Assn., Zonta (chmn. various coms. 1992—), Lansing Woman's Club. Avocations: collector of glass artistry, paperweights. Office: Shirleys Book Services 4330 Hulett Rd Okemos MI 48864-2434

SLINGERLAND, MARY JO, literature educator; b. Lansing, Mich., Oct. 19, 1958; d. Thomas James and Maxine Margaret Slingerland; 1 child, Nicole Charisse Ballesteros. BA in English/Journalism, Mich. State U., 1983; MA in Tchg., Wayne State U., 2004. Owner, writer, editor Vision Decisions, SCS, Mich., 1982—; substitute tchr. k-12 Lansing (Mich.) Sch. Dist., 1982—84; proposal writer Mich. State U., 1989—90; writer, editor Daimler-Chrysler Corp., Auburn Hills, Mich., 1995—98; substitute tchr. k-12 St. Clair Shores (Mich.) Sch. Dist., 1996—97; writer, editor for CDI Ford Motor Co., Livonia, Mich., 1999—2001; substitute tchr. k-5 Brownstown/Woodbury (Mich.) Sch. Dist., 2000—01; instr. English lit./composition, tech. writing/speaking Wayne County Coll., Detroit, 2002—. Editor: Arthroscopic Surgery, 1986; contbr. articles to profl. jours. Scholar, Wayne State U., 2004—; Wheaton Tutor scholar, Mich. State U., 1980. Mem.: Nat. Orgn. for Women Bus. Owners. Avocations: golf, tennis, swimming, fishing. Home: 17771 Feather Ln Brownstown MI 48192

SLIPKO, NATALIE M. actress, choreographer, dancer, writer; d. Gerald and Elaine Claire Slipko. BFA in Theater summa cum laude, Niagara U., 1993; MA in Theater summa cum laude, Bowling Green State U., 1994. Dance tchr., dance asst. Beverly Fletcher Sch. of Dance, Niagara Falls, 1983—90; actress in mus. theater, TV and films, 1983—; box office mgr. 3 theaters Bowling Green (Ohio) State U., 1993—94; lectr. dance Niagara U., Niagara Falls, 1994; exec. sec. Hard Rock Cafe, N.Y.C., 1997; legal sec. Edward P. Kallen, N.Y.C., 1997; makeup artist, cons. Clinique, N.Y.C., 1997—; vocalist, dancer Chezzam Entertainment, N.Y.C., 1999—; choreographer Chess in Concert, Niagara U., Niagara Falls, 2000, Pfeifer Theatre, Buffalo, 1994; Product Specialist Infiniti Luxury Car Co., 2003—. Singer, dancer Niagara U. Alumni, N.Y.C., 1995, N.Y.C., 97; dance capt. prodn. of High Society, Westchester Broadway Dinner Theater, Elmsford, NY, 2001; asst. dir., stage mgr. Artpark Repertory Theatre and Performing Ednl. Artists of Niagara U., Niagara Falls, 1999; writer, performer, choreographer, dir. & prodr. of one-woman cabaret show Makeup Your Mind! Tales of a Beauty Consultant, N.Y.C., 2004. Mem. Niagara U. Friends, Niagara Falls, 1993—; singer with chapel choir Niagara U. Chapel, Niagara Falls, 1989—93; treas. Niagara U. Players, Niagara U., Niagara Falls, 1991—92, pres., 1992—93; dance participant Can. Kiwanis Club Festival, Niagara Falls, Canada, 1979—87. Named Peach Queen, Lewiston Kiwanis Club, 1988—89; recipient voice scholarship, Niagara U., 1989—93, grad. assistantship, Bowling Green State U., 1993—94, numerous dance competition awards, Summer Dance Festival, Rochester Dance Invitational, Kiwanis Music Festival. Mem.: SAG, Am. Fedn. Radio and TV Artists, Actors Equity Assn., Delta Epsilon Sigma. Russian Orthodox. Avocations: bowling, tennis, music lyricist, comedic writing, dance.

SLITKIN, BARBARA ANN, artist; b. Newark, N.J., Oct. 15, 1948; d. Lewis Leonard Small and Charlotte Deborah Rothgessor Small; m. Kenneth Bernard Slitkin, Sept. 23, 1967 (div. July 12, 1991); 1 child, Tiffany Simone. Mem. faculty The Art Sch. Ednl. Alliance, N.Y., 1999—. Actor: (plays) Dolly Pardon Me, 1999; one-woman shows include Ortho Diagnostics, Raritan, N.J., 1986, exhibited in group shows at Paterson (N.J.) Mus., 1987, Krasdale Gallery Bronx (N.Y.) Mus., 89, Represented in permanent collections Franklin Furnace Archive Mus. Modern Art, N.Y.C., N.Y., Mid Hudson Arts Ctr., Poughkeepsie, N.Y., New Eng. Ctr. Contemporary Art, Conn., Das Deutsche Gartenzwerg Mus., Germany, exhibitions include Avanian Awards Gallery, N.Y., N.Y., 1988—90, 2004, Bass Mus. Broward C.C., 1996, Bonnie Clearwater, 1997; juror Mus. Contemporary Art, Broward Cmty. Coll., 1997. Scholar, Internat. Fine Arts, 1966—67. Mem.: The Nat. Mural Soc. Office: 175 Est 96 St 12-0 New York NY 10128

SLOAN, DEBRA LYNNE, interior designer; b. Bloomfield, Iowa, Sept. 24, 1965; d. William Leon Sloan and Sandra Kay Garrett Sloan. BS, Mankato State U., 1988. Cert. interior designer, NCIDQ, IIDA. Sales, interior designer Woodstock/Sofas by Design, West Des Moines, Iowa, 1988—90; interior designer Ethan Allen, Mendota Heights, Minn., 1990—91; interior designer, project mgr. CNK, Inc., Mendota Heights; sr. designer Facility Sys., Inc., Plymouth, Minn., 1998—2000; interior designer Archtl. Alliance, Mpls., 2000—. Mem.: Nat. Trust Hist. Preservation, Internat. Interior Design Assn. (co-chair programs 2000—01, v.p. membership 2001—02, pres.-elect 2002—03, pres. 2003—04). Avocations: travel, music, movies. Office: Archtl Alliance 400 Clifton Ave Minneapolis MN 55403 Business E-Mail: dsloan@archalliance.com.

SLOAN, JEANETTE PASIN, artist; b. Chgo., Mar. 18, 1946; d. Antonio and Anna (Baggio) Pasin; children: Eugene Blakely, Anna Jeanette. BFA, Marymount Coll., Tarrytown, N.Y., 1967; MFA, U. Chgo., 1969. Exhibited in one-woman shows G.W. Einstein Gallery, N.Y.C., 1977-85, Landfall Press Gallery, Chgo., N.Y.C., 1978, 87, Roger Ramsay Gallery, Chgo., 1987, 89, 92, Tatischeff Gallery, Santa Monica, Calif., 1989, Steven Scott Gallery, Balt., 1989, Butters Gallery, Portland, Oreg., 1989, 91, 94, 96, 99, Tatistcheff & Co. Inc., 1995, 97, 99, Ouartet Editions, N.Y.C., 1995, Elliot Smith Gallery, St. Louis, 1994, Peltz Gallery, Milw., 1994-95, 99, Gerhard Wurzer Gallery, Houston, 1997, 2001, Cline Fine Arts Gallery, Santa Fe, 1998, 2001, J. Cacciola Gallery, N.Y.C., 2004; represented in permanent collections Art Mus. Chgo., Cleve. Mus. Art, Ill. State Mus., Indpls. Mus. Art, Canton (Ohio) Art Inst., Ball State Bus., Mpls., Inst. Art, Fogg Mus. Harvard U., Yale U. Art Gallery, Snite Mus. U. Notre Dame, Met. Mus. Art, N.Y.C., Herbert F. Johnson Mus. Cornell U., Ithaca, N.Y., Valpariaso (Ind.) Mus. Art, Nat. Gallery Art, Washington; exhibited in group shows; subject of book by Gerritt Henry, Jeanette Pasin Sloan, 2000; subject of book, The Prints of Jeanette Pasin Sloan, by James Yood, 2003. Studio: 301 Loma Arisco Santa Fe NM 87501 Address: 100 Forest Pl Apt P10 Oak Park IL 60301 E-mail: jeanettepasin@aol.com.

SLOAN, JUDI C. former physical education educator; b. Kansas City, Mo., July 17, 1944; d. Oscar H. Wilde and Florance (Janes) Wilde Graupner; m. Richard J. Sloan; children: Blake, Tracy. BS in Phys. Edn., No. Ill. U., 1966, postgrad.; MS in Phys. Edn., Ind. U., 1970; postgrad., U. Ill., DePaul U., Loyola U., Nat. Louis U. Tchr. phys. edn., coach Niles West High Sch., Skokie, Ill., 1966-99. Former coach gymnastics, tennis; coach cross-country; coop. tchr.; creator, dir. Galibo Gymnastics Show, 1968-75; founder, co-chair staff wellness com., Niles Township Sch. Dist., 1988—, curriculum coun., 1988-91; creator phys. mgmt. course, sophomore health and fitness program, evening children's, summer girls' gymnastics programs; co-dir. Indian Cross Country Invitational, Niles West Gymnastics Invitational; adv. com. cross country Ill. High Sch. Assn. Recipient All-Am. High Sch. Gymnastics Coach award U.S. Gymnastics Fedn., 1981, award of Honor Nat. Sch. Pub. Rels. Assn., 1990, Ill. Disting. Educator award, 1992; Named Ill. Tchr. Yr., 1992-93. Mem. AAHPERD, Am. Fedn. Tchrs., Nat. Assn. Secondary Physical Edn., Nat. Coaches Fedn., Ill. Fedn. Tchrs., Ill. Assn. Health, Phys. Edn., Recreation, Dance (Outstanding Phys. Edn. award 1986), Nat. Assn. Girls' and Women's Sports, Ill. Track and Cross Country Coaches Assn., Ill. Girls' Coaches Assn. Office: Niles West High Sch 5701 Oakton St Skokie IL 60077-2681

SLOAN, MARY JEAN, retired media specialist; b. Lakeland, Fla., Nov. 29, 1927; d. Marion Wilder and Elba (Jinks) Sloan. BS, Peabody Coll., Nashville, 1949; MLS, Atlanta U., 1978, SLS, 1980. Cert. libr. media specialist. Music dir. Pinecrest Sch., Tampa, Fla., 1949-50, Polk County Schs., Bartow, Fla., 1950-54; pvt. music tchr. Lakeland, 1954-58; tchr. Clayton County Schs., Jonesboro, Ga., 1958-59; media specialist Eastualley Sch., Marietta, Ga., 1959-89; ret., 1988. Coord. conf. Ga. Libr. Media Dept., Jekyll Island, 1982-83, sec., Atlanta, 1982-83, com. chmn. ethnic conf., Atlanta, 1978, pres., 1984-85, state pres., 1985-86; program chmn. Ga. Media Orgns. Conf, Jekyll Island, 1988. Contbr. to bibliographies. Recipient Walter Bell award Ga. Assn. Instrnl. Tech., 1988, Disting. Svc. award, 1991. Mem. ALA (del. 1984, 85, 90), NEA, Southeastern Libr. Assn., Am. Assn. Sch. Librs., Soc. for Sch. Librs., Internat., Ga. Assn. Educators (polit. action com. 1983), Beta Phi Mu, Phi Delta Kappa. Republican. Methodist. Home: 797 Yorkshire Rd NE Atlanta GA 30306-3264

SLOANE, BEVERLY LEBOV, writer, consultant; b. N.Y.C., May 26, 1936; d. Benjamin S. and Anne (Weinberg) LeBov; m. Robert Malcolm Sloane, Sept. 27, 1959 (dec. May 16, 2002); 1 child, Alison Lori Sloane Gaylin. AB, Vassar Coll., 1958; MA, Claremont Grad. U., 1975, postgrad., 1975-76; cert. in exec. mgmt., grad. exec. mgmt. program, UCLA Grad. Sch. Mgmt., 1982; grad. intensive bioethics course Kennedy Inst. Ethics, Georgetown U., 1987, advanced bioethics course, 1988; grad. sem. in Health Care Ethics, U. Wash. Sch. Medicine, Seattle, summer 1988-90, 94; grad. Summer Bioethics Inst., Loyola Marymount U., summer 1990; grad. Annual Summer Inst. on Teaching of Writing, Columbia U. Tchrs. Coll., summer 1990; grad. Annual Summer Inst. on Advanced Teaching of Writing, Columbia Tchrs. Coll., summer 1993; grad. Annual Inst. Pub. Health and Human Rights, Harvard U. Sch. Pub. Health, 1994; grad. pub. course profl. pub., Stanford U., 1982; Ethics Fellow, cert. clin. intensive biomedical ethics, Loma Linda U. Med. Ctr., 1989; grad. exec. refresher course profl. pub., Stanford U., 1994; cert Exec. Mgmt. Inst. in Health Care, U. So. Calif., 1995; cert. in ethics corps tng. program, Josephson Inst. of Ethics, 1991; cert. advanced exec. program Grad. Sch. Mgmt., UCLA, 1995; grad. Women's Campaign Sch., Yale U., 1998. Circulation libr. Harvard Med. Libr., Boston, 1958-59; social worker Conn. State Welfare, New Haven, 1960-61; tchr. English Hebrew Day Sch., New Haven, 1961-64; instr. creative writing and English lit. Monmouth Coll., West Long Branch, NJ, 1967-69; writer, cons., 1970—. V.p. council grad. students, Claremont Grad. U., 1971-72, adj. dir. Writing Ctr. Speaker Series, 1993-2000, spkr., 1996-98, Claremont Grad. U.; mem. Star. Planning Task Force Com. Campaign Pre-eminence. 1986-87, Alumni Coun., bd. dirs. Alumni Assn., 1993-96; mem. Vol. Devel. Com., 1994-96, Alumni Awards Com., 1993-96; visitors Claremont Grad. U. Ctrs. for Arts and Humanities, 2001—; adv. coun. tech. and profl. writing Dept. English, Calif. State U., Long Beach, 1980-82; adv. bd. Calif. Health Rev., 1982-83; mem. Foothill Health Dist. Adv. Coun. L.A. County Dept. Health Svcs., 1987-93, pres., 1989-91; vis. scholar Hastings Ctr., 1996; spkr. N.Y. State Task Force on Life and the Law, 1996; panel spkr. Annual Conf. Am. Assn. Suicidology, 1998. Author: From Vassar to Kitchen, 1967, A Guide to Health Facilities: Personnel and Management, 1971, 2nd edit., 1977, 3d edit., 1992, Introduction to Healthcare Delivery Organization: Functions and Management, 4th edit., 1999. Co-chmn. Vassar Christmas Showcase Vassar Club, New Haven, 1965—66; pub. rels. bd. Monmouth County Mental Health Assn., 1968—69; co-chmn. Vassar Club So. Calif. award Vassar Coll., 1970—71; chmn. creative writing group Calif. Inst. Tech. Woman's Club, 1975—79; mem. task force edn. and cultural activities City of Duarte, 1987—88; class rep. Alumnae Assn., 1989; chmn. creative writing group Yale U. Newcomers, 1965—66; dir. creative writing group Yale U. Women's Orgn., 1966—67; mem. Exec. Program Network UCLA Grad. Sch. Mgmt., 1987—2000; trustee Ctr. Improvement Child Caring, 1981—83; mem. League Crippled Children, 1982—, treas. for gen. meetings, 1990—91, chmn. hostesses com., 1988—89, pub. rels. com., 1990—91; del. Task Force on Minorities in Newspaper Bus., 1987—89; rep. cmty. County Health Network Tobacco Control Program, 1991; mem. NY Citizens Com. Health Care Decisions, Gift Com., 1998; chmn. 1st ann. Rabbi Camillus Angel Interfaith Svc. Temple Beth David, 1978, v.p., 1983—86; cmty. rels. com. Jewish Fedn. Coun. Greater L.A., 1985—87; bd. dirs. League Crippled Children, 1988—91; ethics com., human subjects protection com. Jewish Home for Aging, Reseda, Calif., 1994—97; various positions and coms. Claremont Grad. U., 1986—; bd. visitors Claremont Grad. U. Ctr. Arts and Humanities, 2001—; bd. dirs. L.A. Commn. Assaults Against Women, 1983—84; class corr. Vassar Coll. Quar. Alumnae Mag., 1993—98; class of 1958 coms. Vassar Coll., class v.p., 1998—2000, class co-pres., 2000—01, class pres., 2001—03, program chmn. 40th reunion, 1998. Recipient cert. of appreciation City of Duarte, 1988, County of L.A., 1988, Ann. Key Mem. award L.A. Dept. Health Svcs., 1990, cert. of appreciation Alumni Coun. Claremont Grad Sch., 1996; Coro Found. fellow, 1979, Ethics fellow Loma Linda U. Med. Ctr., 1989; named Calif. Communicator of Achievement, Woman of Yr. Calif. Press Women, 1992. Fellow: Am. Med. Writers Asn. (Pacific S.W. del. to nat. bd. 1980—87, dir. 1980—93, chmn. nat. book awards trade category 1982—83, chmn. Nat. Networking Luncheon 1983—84, nat. chmn. freelance sect. 1984—85, workshop leader, Nat. Ann. Conf. 1984—89, gen. chmn. Asilomar Western Regional Conf. 1985, workshop leader, Asilomar Western Regional Conf. 1985, nat. exec. bd. dirs. 1985—86, nat. adminr. sects. 1985—86, pres.-elect Pacific Southwest chpt. 1985—87, chmn. gen. session nat. conf. 1986—87, chmn. Walter C. Alvarez Mem. Found award 1986—87, program co-chmn. 1987, program chmn. nat. conf. 1987, moderator gen. session. nat. conf. 1987, pres. Pacific S.W. chap. 1987—89, workshop leader, Asilomar Western Nat. Conf. 1988, spkr. Pacific S.W. chpt. 1988—89, program co-chmn. 1989, workshop leader, Asilomar Western Nat. Conf. 1989, Pacific Southwest deleg. to nat. bd. 1989—91, immediate past pres. 1989—91, workshop leader, Nat. Ann. Conf. 1990—92, bd. dirs. 1991—93, workshop leader, Nat. Ann. Conf. 1995, chmn. conv. coms., Appreciation award for outstanding leadership 1989, named to Workshop Leaders Honor Roll 1991); mem.: AAUP, APHA, AAUW (creative writing chmn. 1969—70, books and plays chmn. Arcadia Br. 1973—74, 1st v.p. program dir. 1975—76, legis. chmn. Arcadia Br. 1976—77, networking chmn. 1981—82, spkr. 1987, chmn. task force promoting individual liberties 1987—88, pres.-elect 1998—99, educ. equity chmn. 1998—99, chmn. deleg. to national conv. 1999, chmn. Technical Trek Sci. Camp Scholarship for Girls 1999, Career Day 1999, pres. Arcadia br. 1999—2000, writer in res Calif. State Comm. Com. 1999—2000, diversity chmn. Arcadia br. 2000—01, Interbr. Coun. Arcadia br. repr. 2000—02, program vice chmn. LA County Interbr. Coun. 2000—02, Calif. State diversity com. 2000—02, Woman of Achievement Arcadia br. 1986, cert. of appreciation 1987), AAUW Calif. State Diversity Comt. (program co-v.p. 2002), Town Hall Calif. (vice chmn. cmty. affairs sect. 1982—87, faculty-instr. Exec. Breakfast Inst. 1985—86, Exec. Breakfast Inst. spkr. 1986), Pasadena Athletic, Claremont Cols. Faculty House, Women's City (Pasadena), Nat. Writer's Union, Authors Guild, Assn. Writing Programs, NY Acad. Medicine (met. NY Ethics Network), Soc. Health and Human Values, Kennedy Inst. Ethics, Soc. Technical Comt., Nat. Fedn. Press Women (chmn. state women of achievement comt. 1986—87, nat. co-chmn. task force recruitment minorities 1987—89, del. 1987—89, bd. dirs. 1987—93, nat. dir. spkrs. bur. 1989—93, Plenary past pres. state 1989—, workshop leader, spkr. annual nat. conf. 1990, editor spkrs. bur. directory 1991—92, editor spkrs. bur. addendum dir. 1992, cert. of appreciation 1991, 1st runner up, Nat. Communicator of Achievement 1992, cert. of appreciation 1993), Hastings Cent. (vis. scholar 1996), Ind. Writers So. Calif. (bd. dirs. corp. 1988—89, bd. dirs. 1989—90, dir. specialized groups 1989—90, dir. at large 1989—90, dir. speech writing group 1991—92), NY Acad. Scis., Calif. Press Women (v.p. programs L.A. chpt. 1982—85, pres. 1985—87, state pres. 1987—89, immediate past state pres. 1989—91, chmn. state speakers bur. 1989—95, deleg. nat. bd. 1989—95, dir. family literacy day Calif. 1990, moderator, ann. spring conv. 1990, chmn. nominating comt. 1990—91, Calif. literacy dir. 1990—92, dir. state literacy com. 1990—92, moderator, ann. spring conv. 1992, Cert. of Appreciation 1991, Calif. Communicator of Achievement 1992), Am. Soc. Law, Medicine, Ethics, AAUW Calif. State Comns. Comt. (writer in residence 1999—2000), Coro Nat. Alumni Assn. (bd. dirs. 1999—, continuing edn. com. 2003—), Am. Assn. Higher Edn., Women in Comm. Inc. (N.E. area rep. 1980—81, bd. dirs. 1980—82, v.p. cmty. affairs 1981—82, chmn. awards banquet 1982, chmn. LA chpt. Agnes Underwood Freedom Info. Awards banquet 1982, nominating com. 1982—83, seminar leader, spkr., ann. nat. profl. conf. 1985, program adv. com. L.A. chpt. 1987, com. Women of the Press awards luncheon 1988, bd. dirs. 1989—90, v.p. activities 1989—90, Recognition award 1983), Duarte Rotary Club. Home and Office: 1301 N Santa Anita Ave Arcadia CA 91006-2419 Office Phone: 626-355-8915.

SLOAT, BARBARA FURIN, cell biologist, educator; b. Youngstown, Ohio, Jan. 20, 1942; d. Walter and Mary Helen (Maceyko) Furin; m. John Barry Sloat, Nov. 2, 1968; children: John Andrew, Eric Furin. BS, Denison U., 1963; MS, U. Mich., 1966, PhD, 1968. Lic. and cert. emergency med. technician, paramedic. Lab. asst. U. Ghent, Belgium, 1964; tchg. fellow, lectr. U. Mich., Ann Arbor, 1964-66, 68-70, asst. rsch. biologist Mental Health Rsch. Inst., 1972-74, vis. asst. prof., lectr. Ann Arbor and Dearborn, 1974-76, dir. women in sci. Ann Arbor, 1980-84, assoc. dir. honors, 1986-87, rsch. scientist, 1976—, lectr. Residential Coll., 1984—, assoc. Inst. Humanities, 1991—. Author: Laboratory Guide for Zoology, 1979, Summer Internships in the Sciences for High School Women (CASE Silver medal, 1985, Excellence in Edn. award, U. Mich., 1993). Recipient Acad.

Women's Caucus award, U. Mich., 1984, Grace Lyon Alumnae Award, Denison U., 1988; grantee NSF, U.S. Dept. Edn., Warner Lambert Found., others. Mem. AAAS, Am. Soc. Cell Biology, N.Y. Acad. Scis., Nat. Assn. Women Deans, Adminstrs. and Counselors, Assn. for Women in Sci. (councilor 1988-90, pres. elect 1990, mentor of yr. award Detroit area chpt 1994), Phi Beta Kappa, Sigma Xi. Avocations: hiking, yoga, tibetology, Tibetan medicine. Home: 240 Indian River Pl Ann Arbor MI 48104-1825 Office: U Mich Residential Coll 216 Tyler East Quad Ann Arbor MI 48109-1245 E-mail: bsloat@umich.edu.

SLOBIN, KATHLEEN OVERIN, sociology educator, researcher, consultant; b. Santa Ana, Calif., July 18, 1942; d. Courtenay Stuyvesant Overin and Janet Kathleen (Raitt) Church; m. Dan Isaac Slobin, May 21, 1969 (div. Sept. 1983); children: Heida Slobin Shoemaker, Shem. BA, Pomona Coll., 1964; MFA, Calif. Coll. Arts and Crafts, 1980; MPA, Calif. State U., Hayward, 1984; PhD, U. Calif., San Francisco, 1991. Instr. fine arts Indian Valley CC, Novato, Calif., 1981-82; coord. edn. Nat. Energy Found., San Francisco, 1982; assoc. dir. continuing edn. dept. psychiatry U. Calif., 1983-86, rsch. asst., 1986-90, staff rsch. assoc., 1990; asst. prof. sociology ND State U., Fargo, 1991-96, assoc. prof., 1997—2004, prof., 2004—, dir. women's studies, 1997—2001, chair dept. sociology-anthropology, 2003—. Rschr., cons. West River Regional Med. Ctr., Hettinger, N.D., 1994—, African women refugee agus., Fargo, 1993-95, 2002. Contbr. articles to profl. jours., chpt. to book. Anthony fellow U. Calif., 1988, 89, grad. rsch. grantee, 1989. Mem. Am. Sociol. Assn., African Studies Assn., Soc. for Symbolic Interaction, Soc. for Women Sociologists (editor SWS Network News 1997-2000—). Democrat. Unitarian Universalists. Avocations: painting, music. Office: ND State U Dept Sociology-Anthropology PO Box 5075 Fargo ND 58105-5075 Office Phone: 701-231-8939. E-mail: kathleen.slobin@ndsu.nodak.edu.

SLOCUM, ROSEMARIE, physician services consultant, recruiter; b. Port Arthur, Tex., Dec. 19, 1948; d. Edly and Ella (McNeely) Raccard; m. James Rubenstein; 1 child from previous marriage, Blair Ashton. BS, La. State U., Baton Rouge, 1971; MA in Bus. Comm., Jones Internat. U., Englewood, Colo., 1999. Cert. tchr. La. Edn. specialist La. Dept. Occupl. Stds., Baton Rouge, 1971-74; account exec. Uarco, Inc., Baton Rouge, 1974-77; owner, broker Rosemarie Slocum Real Estate, Baton Rouge, 1977—85; physician recruiter MSI, New Orleans, 1985-86; assoc. dir. physician recruitment Physician Svcs. Cons., Fairfax, Va., 1986-88; spl. cons. Caswell/Winters Physician Search Cons., Milw., 1988-89; v.p. U.S. Med. Search, Inc. subs. of Caswell/Winters, Milw., 1988-89; dir. physician recruitment/mktg. East Range Clinics, Ltd., Virginia, Minn., 1989-91; pres. RSI Physician Svcs. Cons., Mpls., 1991—. Office: RSI Physician Svcs Cons 3622 W 44th St Minneapolis MN 55410-1366 E-mail: rsi@scc.net.

SLOCUM, SUSANNE TUNNO, medical/surgical nurse; b. Atlanta, Aug. 28, 1962; d. Dean Dunwody and Patricia Murphey Tunno; m. Everett Ward Hogsed, May 14, 1988 (div. Feb. 1991); m. Robert Daniell Slocum, May 11, 1996. BSN, Emory U., 1987. Staff nurse St. Joseph's Hosp. Atlanta, 1987—98, mgr. neurovas. unit, 1998—2000, coord. CV screening & prevention, 2000—. Spkr. in field. Mem. St. Joseph's Edn. Coun., Atlanta, 1992—98, St. Joseph's Practice Coun., Atlanta, 1992—93; nurse Camp Breathe Easy, Atlanta Lung Assn., 1990—2001, Atlanta Olympics, 1996. Recipient Key Vol. award, Am. Stroke Assn., 2001—03. Mem.: Preventative Cardiology Nurses Assn., Acad. Med.-Surg. Nurses (immediate past pres. immediate past pres. 2002—03). Methodist. Avocations: boating, reading, four-wheeling. Home: 540 Old Preston Tr Alpharetta GA 30022 Office: St Joseph's Hosp Atlanta 5665 Peachtree Dunwoody Rd Atlanta GA 30342

SLONAKER, MARY JOANNA KING, columnist; b. Richmond, Ind., July 18, 1930; d. Claiborn F. and Carlyle (Diffendenfer) King; divorced; children: Mary Sue Hosey, Steven, Allis Ann Fox. Student, Earlham Coll., 1948-49; BS, Ball State U., 1969; MA in Teaching, Ind. U., 1974. Cert. residential child care worker. Home econs. tchr. Lewisville (Ind.) Sch., 1978-79, Morton Meml. Sch., Knightstown, Ind., 1970-83; town coun. mem. Cambridge City, Ind., 1991-2001. Mem. Ind. U. Chancellor's Medallion Dinner Com., 2001. Recipient Kiwanis Cmty. award, 1983-84, 95, Appreciation award Am. Bus. Women, 1985, Appreciation award Waseda U. Japanese Exch. Program, 1986-88. Mem. AAUW, Soc. Profl. Journalists, Ind. U. Alumni Club, Ind. U. Varsity Club, The Woman's Club, Psi Iota Xi, Alpha Delta Kappa, Pi Beta Phi. Democrat. Presbyterian. Avocations: basketball, football, harness racing, walking, gardening. Home: 36 W Church St Cambridge City IN 47327-1615 Office: 127 N Foote St Cambridge City IN 47327-1144

SLONE, CHARLOTTE M. telecommunications executive; b. Cleve., Jan. 12, 1970; d. John J. and Elsie M. (Estep) S. Student, John Carroll U., 1988-89, Virginia Marti Coll. Art, 1989-90. Loan officer Nat. Auto Credit, Cleve., 1991-92; entrepreneur Page One Comms., Cleve., 1992-97; pres. Telemaxx Comms., Cleve., 1997—. Cons. Ameritech Paging, N.Y.c., 1996—. Vol. Am. Heart Assn., Cleve., 1996. Mem. NAFE. Democrat. Avocations: photography, travel, ballet. Home: 17209 Valleyview Ave Cleveland OH 44135-4355 Office: Telemaxx 1401 Lakeside Ave Cleveland OH 44114-1136

SLONE, RICCA C, state representative; b. Ottawa, Ontario, Feb. 19, 1947; m. William Berkman; children: Zachary Berkman, Sydney Berkman, Seth Berkman. BA, Wash. Univ., St. Louis, 1968; MA, Univ. of Calif., Los Angeles, Calif., 1970, Ohio State Univ., Ohio, 1978; JD, Univ. of Ill, Coll. of Law, Ill., 1990. Atty. self employed, 1991—96; free lance writer/cons., 1981—86; sr. rsch. assoc. US Dept. of Housing and Urban Develop., 1979—81, Ohio Legis. Svc. Comm., 1975—79; assoc. US Office of Mgmt. and Budget; Rep., Dist. 92 US State Rep., Ill., 1996—. Ill. State House of Rep., 1996—; mem. Peoria City-County Landfill Comm., 1994—96. Mem.: Growth Task Force, 1998-1999, Ill. House Smart (chair), Ill. Growth Task Force (Vice chair 2001—02), Bd. of Visitors, Univ. of Ill. Coll. of Law, Regional Conference, Law and the Great Lakes: Into the Twenty-First Century (planning chair), Ill. State Bar Assoc., Environ. Law Sect. Coun. (former chair 1994—95), Ill. State Bar Assoc., 1990-pres., Am. Bar Assoc., Sect. on Natural Resources, Energy and Environ. Law. Democrat. Jewish. Office: 256-W Stratton Office Bldg Springfield IL 62706 Mailing: 456 Fulton Suite 150 Peoria IL 61602 Home: 1904 Grandview Terr Peoria IL 61614

SLONE, SANDI, artist; b. Boston, Oct. 1, 1939; d. Louis and Ida (Spind) Sudikoff; children: Erric Solomon, Jon Solomon. Student, Boston Mus. Fine Arts Sch., 1970-73; BA magna cum laude, Wellesley Coll., 1974. Sr., grad. painting faculty Boston Mus. Fine Arts Sch./Tufts U., 1975—; instr. grad. program Sch. Visual Art, N.Y.C., 1989-90; lectr. painting Harvard U., Cambridge, Mass., 1982. Vis. artist Triangle Artists Workshop, N.Y., 1982, 87, 90; co-founder, dir. Art/Omi Internat. Artists Found., N.Y.C., 1992—. One-woman shows include ICA, Boston, 1977, Harcus Krakow Gallery, Boston, 1978, 79, 80, 82, 84, 86, Acquavella Contemporary Art, N.Y., 1977, 79, 80, 82, 84, Stephen Rosenberg Gallery, N.Y., 1988, Levinson Kane Gallery, Boston, 1989, Smith Jariwala Gallery, London, 1990, Jersey City Mus., 1996, The Artists Mus., Lodz, Poland, 1997, Cristinerose Gallery, N.Y.C., 1999, Savage Gallery, Portland, Oreg., 2001; exhibited in group shows at Mus. Fine Arts, Boston, 1977, Corcoran Gallery of Art 35th Biennial, Washington, 1977, Edmonton Art Mus., 1977, 85, Hayden Gallery MIT, Cambridge, Mass., 1978, New Generation Andre Emmerich Gallery, N.Y., 1980-81, Am. Ctr., Paris, 1980-81, Amerika Haus, Berlin, 1980-81, Carpenter Ctr., Harvard U., Ctr. de la Cultura Contemporania, Barcelona, 1987, Federated Union of Black Artists, Johannesburg, South Africa, 1989, Jan Weiss Gallery, N.Y., 1990, Olympia Internat. Art Fairs, London, 1991, Gallery Korea, N.Y., 1992, Klarfeld Perry Gallery, N.Y., 1994, Out of the Blue Gallery, Edinburgh, Scotland, 1994, Gallery One, Toronto, 1996, Fine Arts Ctr., U. R.I., Kingston, 1996, Crieger Dane Gallery, Boston, 1996, Visual Arts Gallery, N.Y., 1997, TransHudson Gallery, N.Y., 1997, Butler Inst. of Am. Art, Youngstown, Ohio, 1998, 45th Biennial Corcoran Mus. Art, Washington, 1998, Lombard-Freid Fine Arts, N.Y., 1999, 2000, Cristinerose Gallery, N.Y., 2001, Savage Gallery, Portland, Oreg., 2004, others; represented in permanent collections Mus. Modern Art, N.Y.C., Mus. Contemporary Art, Barcelona, Mus. Fine Arts, Boston, Hirshhorn Mus., Washington, Corcoran Gallery & Mus. Art, Washington; artist-in-residence City Hall, Barcelona, 1987, 89. Mus. Fine Arts Boston fellow, 1977, 81; Ford Found. grantee, 1979; internat. artists residency East-South Project, Poland, 1997. Studio: 13 Worth St New York NY 10013-2922

SLOSBURG-ACKERMAN, JILL ROSE, artist, educator; b. Omaha, Aug. 28, 1948; d. Harold Walter and Marion (Gill) Slosburg; m. James Sloss Ackerman, Aug. 8, 1987; 1 child, Jesse August. Diploma, Boston Mus. Sch., 1971; BFA, Tufts U., 1971, MFA, 1983. Prof. art Mass. Coll. of Art, Boston, 1973—; vis. artist Cranbrook Acad. of Art, Bloomfield, Mich., Spring 1993. One-person shows include Harcus-Krakow Gallery, Boston, 1978, 80, Helen Shlien Gallery, Boston, 1980, 82, Cohen Arts Ctr., Tufts U., Medford, Mass., 1982, Van Buren/Brazelton/Cutting Gallery, Cambridge, Mass., 1985, Genovese Gallery, Boston, 1995, Manwaring Gallery Cummings Art Ctr., Conn. Coll., New London, 1995, Rose Art Mus., Brandeis U., Waltham, Mass., 1996, Atrium Gallery/U. Mass., Dartmouth, 1999, Judy Ann Goldman Fine Art, Boston, 1999; exhibited in group shows including Naga Gallery, Boston, Boston, 1980, DeCordova Mus., Lincoln, Mass., 1980, Jewett Art Ctr., Wellesley, Mass., 1982, Helen Shlien Gallery, Boston, 1982, Cherry Stone Gallery, Wellfleet, Mass., 1984, Quadrum Gallery, Chestnut Hill, Mass., 1985, Fed. Res. Gallery, Boston, 1986, Danforth Mus., 1986, Conseil de la Sculpture, Montreal, 1986, North Hall Gallery, Boston, 1987, Artists Found. Gallery, Boston, 1990, Mus. Decorative Arts, Prague, 1991, Nancy Margolis Gallery, N.Y.C., 1991, Bellevue (Wash.) Art Mus., 1992, Artwear, N.Y., 1992, Genovese Gallery, Albany, N.Y., 1992, Judy Ann Goldman Fine Art, Boston, 1997, Mills Gallery, Boston, 1997, 98, Traveling Scholars/Boston Mus. Fine Arts, 1999, DeCordova Mus. Ann. Exhbn., Lincoln, Mass., 2000, Judy Ann Goldman Fine Art, Boston, 2002, Forest Hills Cemetary, Boston, 2002; represented in permanent collections J.L. Brandeis & Sons, Omaha, Mass. Coll. Art, Boston, Boston Pub. Libr., also pvt. collections; contbr. articles to profl. jours. Founder, mem. Boston Women's Action Coalition; bd. dirs. Cambridge (Mass.) Multi-Cultural Ctr., Gallery at Green St., 1993. Recipient Patricia Jellinek Hallowell prize for jewelry, 1984, Disting. Svc. award Mass. Coll. of Art, 1980, 4th prize sterling silver design competition Nat. Guild of Sterling Silversmiths, 1970; fellow Haystack Mountain Sch. Crafts, Deer Isle, Maine, 1972, 76, Nat. Endowment Arts, 1974, 86, The Artists Found., Boston, 1984, Mary Ingraham Bunting Inst., 1985-86; Mass. Coll. Art profl. devel. grantee, 1987, Polaroid Corp. photography grantee, 1988, Sch. Boston Mus. Fine Arts traveling scholar, 1998, New Eng. Found. for the Arts fellow, 1998; Mass. Cultural Coun. Artist's grantee, 1999, grantee Artist's Resource Trust, 2001. Jewish. Home: 12 Coolidge Hill Rd Cambridge MA 02138-5510 Studio: One Fitchburg St Apt C415 Somerville MA 02143-2128 E-mail: jackerman86@comcast.net.

SLOSEK, THERESA J. media specialist, school librarian; b. Oswego, N.Y., July 20, 1949; d. Anthony M. Slosek and Margaret M. Even Slosek. BA, LeMoyne Coll., Syracuse, NY, 1971; MLS, SUNY, Geneseo, 1972; CAS, SUNY, Oswego, 1990. Cert. sch. libr. media specialist N.Y., 1975, sch. dist. adminstr. N.Y., 1990. Sch. libr. media specialist Overlook Elem. Sch., Arlington Sch. Dist., Poughkeepsie, NY, 1972—74, Ctrl. Sq. Sch. Dist., 1974—76, Fulton City Sch. Dist., 1976—92; staff devel. program specialist Oneida Herkimer Madison BOCES, Utica, 1992—93; asst. prin. Transit Mid. Sch., Williamsville, 1993—94, Honeoye Falls - Lima H.S., Honeoye Falls, 1994—96; sch. libr. media specialist Pulaski Jr. and Sr. HS, 1996—99; libr. media specialist Somers HS, 1999—2001; sch. libr. media specialist H. C. Crittenden Mid. Sch., Byram Hills Sch. Dist., Armonk, 2001—. Recipient Excellence in Sch. Libr., N.Y. Libr. Assn., 1991. Mem.: ALA, N.Y. Libr. Assn., Am. Assn. of Sch. Librs., Phi Delta Kappa. Avocations: travel, decorating, gardening. Office: H C Crittenden Mid Sch 10 MacDonald Ave Armonk NY 10504

SLOSS, MERLE, shoe company executive; b. Atlantic City, N.J., Feb. 26, 1948; d. Ralph and Annette (Nemirosky) S.; m. Matthew Barry Smith, June 10, 1973. BA in Chemistry, U. Pa., 1970; MBA, Boston U., 1972. Asst. product mgr. Gen. Foods Corp., White Plains, N.Y., 1972-73, assoc. product mgr., 1974-75, product mgr., 1976-78, group product mgr., 1979-82; dir. mktg. Bally of Switzerland, New Rochelle, N.Y., 1982-83, v.p. mktg., 1984, exec. v.p., gen. mgr., 1985-92, also bd. dirs., pres. and CEO, 1992-93; pres. of licensing Anne Klein, New York, NY, 1995-96; pres. Ralph Lauren Footware; pres. of licensing Anne Klein, 2000—. Mem. Women in Mgmt., Phi Lamda Upsilon, Beta Gamma Sigma. Democrat. Jewish. Avocations: photography, art history, travel. Office: Anne Klein 11 W 42nd St New York NY 10036-8002

SLOVITER, DOLORES KORMAN, federal judge; b. Phila., Sept. 5, 1932; d. David and Tillie Korman; m. Henry A. Sloviter, Apr. 3, 1969 (dec. May 2003); 1 child, Vikki Amanda. AB in Econs. with distinction, Temple U., 1953, LHD (hon.), 1986; LLB magna cum laude, U. Pa., 1956; LLD (hon.), Dickinson Sch. Law, 1984, U. Richmond, 1992, Widener U., 1994. Bar: Pa. 1957. From assoc. to ptnr. Dilworth, Paxson, Kalish, Kohn & Levy, Phila., 1956—69; mem. Harold E. Kohn PA, Phila., 1969—72; from assoc. prof. to prof. Temple U. Law Sch., Phila., 1972—79; judge U.S. Ct. Appeals (3rd cir.), Phila., 1979—, chief judge, 1991—98. Bd. overseers U. Pa. Law Sch., 1993—99; bd. trustees Nat. Constitution Ctr., 1998—; mem. Jud. Conf. of U.S., 1991—98; chmn. selection com. Rhodes Scholarship Found., 2003—. Chair Pa. Rhodes Scholarship Selection Com., 2003—; mem. S.E. region Pa. Gov.'s Conf. on Aging, 1976—79, Com. of 70, 1976—79; U.S. com. Bicentennial Constn., 1987—90; com. on Rules of Practice and Procedure, 1990—93; trustee Jewish Publ. Soc. Am., 1983—89. Recipient Juliette Low medal, Girl Scouts Greater Phila., Inc., 1990, Honor award, Girls High Alumnae Assn., 1991, Jud. award, Pa. Bar Assn., 1994, James Wilson award, U. Pa., 1996, Cert. of Honor award, Temple U., 1996; Disting. Fulbright scholar, Chile, 1990. Mem.: ABA, Phila. Bar Assn. (gov. 1976—78, Sandra Day O'Connor award 1997), Am. Judicature Soc. (bd. dirs. 1990—95), Nat. Assn. Women Judges, Am. Law Inst., Fed. Judges Assn., Fed. Bar Assn., Order of Coif (pres. U. Pa. chpt. 1975—77), Phi Beta Kappa. Office: US Ct Appeals 18614 US Courthouse 601 Market St Philadelphia PA 19106-1713

SLOWIK, SHARON A. real estate agent; b. Rochester, N.Y., Apr. 23, 1944; d. Edward and Evelyn (McGillis) Schreiner; m. William G. Slowik, Sept. 12, 1970; children: Heather, Elizabeth, Michael, Matthew. Assoc., Lab. Inst. Mdse., 1964. Agent Long & Foster Real Estate Inc., Vienna, Va., 1990—. Mem. Nat. Realtors Assn., Graduate Realtor Inst. (cert.), Cert. Residential Specialist (cert.), No. Va. Bd. Realtors (Million Dollar Sales Club 1993-2003, polit. action com. 1991—, Top Prodr. 2002-2003). Home: 10901 Treeview Ct Great Falls VA 22066-1639 Office: Long & Foster Real Estate Inc 8227 Old Courthouse Rd Ste 100 Vienna VA 22182-3815 Office Phone: 703-556-8600 142. E-mail: slowik@erols.com.

SLUGA, YVONNE MARIE, radio producer, announcer; b. Cudahy, Wis., Dec. 30, 1966; d. Anthony Anton Sluga and Margaret Ann Honkala. AA in Aplied Arts/Bus., Milw. Area Tech. Coll., Milw., Wis., 1988; BA in Comms., Marquette U., Milw., 1999. Prodr., announcer WYMS Pub. Radio 88.9 FM, Milw., 1994—2001; voice-over talent Arlene Wilson Talent Mgr., Milw., 2000—. Author: poems. Founding mem. Nat. Campaign of Tolerance, 2000—. Mem.: Internat. Soc. Poets (disting. mem.), Nat. Mus. Women Artists. Avocations: collecting books, photography, collecting movies. E-mail: DeMereVoice@yahoo.com.

SLUSHER, KIMBERLY GOODE, researcher; b. Benham, Ky., Oct. 4, 1960; d. Herschel James and Nevelyn Faye (Hayes) Goode; m. Joe Allan Slusher, May 1, 1985; children: Tarah Rena, Preston Cole. BS in Agr., Ea. Ky. U., 1982; MS in Agr., U. Tenn., 1989. Rsch. asst. U. Tenn., Knoxville, 1983-89; info. analyst Oak Ridge (Tenn.) Nat. Lab., 1989—, tchr., cons. sci. honors program, 1993. Author: (army study) Drinking Water Contamination Study, 1995; contbr. chpt.: Teratogens: Chemicals Which Cause Birth Defects, 1993. Methodist. Avocations: gardening, piano. Office: Human Gene Info Analysis Sect 1060 Commerce Park Dr # Ms6480 Oak Ridge TN 37830-8043 E-mail: Kfg@ornl.gov.

SLUTSKY, LORIE A.(ANN), foundation executive; b. N.Y.C., Jan. 5, 1953; d. Edward and Adele (Moskowitz) S. BA, Colgate U, 1975; MA in Urban Policy and Analysis, New Sch. for Social Rsch., N.Y.C., 1977. Program officer N.Y. Cmty. Trust, N.Y.C., 1977-83, v.p., 1983-87, exec. v.p., 1987-89, pres., CEO, 1990—. Former mem. and chmn. bd. Coun. on Founds., Inc., Washington, 1986-95. Trustee emerita, former chmn. budget com. Colgate U., Hamilton, N.Y., 1989-98; former mem. bd. dirs. Found. Ctr., Inc., N.Y.C., L.A. Wallace Fund for Met. Mus. Art, N.Y.C., D. Wallace Fund for Meml. Sloan Kettering, United Way of N.Y.C.; bd. dirs. Board-Source, Alliance Capital; trustee New Sch. U. Office: NY Community Trust 2 Park Ave Fl 24 New York NY 10016-9301

SLUTZ, PAMELA JO HOWELL, ambassador; b. Chgo., 1949; d. Robert and Rose Slutz; m. Ronald Deutch; 2 children. B in politics, Hollins Coll., 1970; M in Asian Studies and Polit. Sci., U. Hawaii, 1972. Office of Korean affairs Bur. of East Asian and Pacific Affairs, 1981—82, office of China and Mongolia affairs, 1995—97, office of East Asian and Pacific regional security and policy planning, 1997—99; amb. U.S. Dept. of State, 1981—84, fgn. svc. officer, 1984, amb., 1982—84, Jakarta, Indonesia, 1984—87, 1999—2001, Shanghai, 1991—94, Am. Inst. in Taiwan, 2001—03. Mem. U.S. Del. to Nuc. and Space Talks with Russia, Geneva, 1987—89. Fellow, East West Ctr. Office: US Embassy in Mongolia PO Box 1021 Ulaanbaatar Mongolia Fax: 976-11-320776.*

SMAHA, DONNA ALVEY, adult nurse practitioner, consultant, acute care nurse practitioner; b. Mobile, Ala., Mar. 23, 1953; m. Richard Joseph Smaha; children: Jennifer Smaha Wolfe, Joseph Richard Smaha II. BSN, U. Ala., Birmingham, 1975, MSN, 1997; diploma in asthma care, Nat. Asthma and Respiratory Tng. Ctr., Eng., 1998. RN Ala., cert. acute care nurse practitioner, AANP, adult primary care nurse practitioner, ANA. Resident Mass. Gen. Hosp., Boston, Rush Presbyn. St. Lukes Hosp., Chgo.; pub. health nurse, team leader Jefferson County Dept. Health, Birmingham, 1975—76; from critical care nurse to outcomes mgr. Brookwood Med. Ctr., Birmingham, 1979—2000; nurse practitioner Brookwood Srs. Health Ctr., Birmingham, 2000—03; clin. dir. Brookwood Vascular Ctr. Excellence, Birmingham, 2003—. Cons. Asthma Ctr. Excellence, Birmingham, Ala., 1997—2002. Contbr. Asthma Management Program Overview of The Asthma Center of Excellence, 1999, articles to profl. jours. Pres. Birmingham Children's Theatre Women's Com., 1985—86; exec. bd. mem. Birmingham Children's Theatre, 1985—86; bd. mem. Cahaba Heights Cmty. Sch. Bd., Birmingham, 1987—90; vol. nurse ARC, Birmingham, 1980—83; vol. Med. Svcs., 1996 Summer Olympics, Soccer Venue, Birmingham, 1996. Recipient Best Practice in Pharm. Care award, Am. Soc.Health Syst. Pharmacists, 1999. Mem.: ANA, Am. Lung Assn. Ala. (co-chair Asthma summit 1999—2001), Brookwood Homes Svcs. Profl. Adv. Com., Ala. State Nurses Assn. Dist. 3 (v.p. 1997—99, bd. dirs. 2000—02), Respiratory Nursing Soc. (dir. 2000—), Sigma Theta Tau. Roman Catholic. Avocations: travel, skiing, music. Office: Brookwood Vascular Ctr Ste 202 200 Montgomery Hwy Birmingham AL 35216 Business E-Mail: donna.smaha@tenethealth.com.

SMALE, ANN-LAURA, public relations company executive, writer, researcher; b. Toledo, Nov. 11, 1955; d. Leonard F. and Theresa M. (Geraldo) Monahan; m. Terrence L. Monahan Smale, June 30, 1972; children: Terrence II, Michelle, Seth, Nina. Student, U. Toledo, 1986. Internat. journalist, freelance writer various mags., Toledo, 1978-97; profl. model, 1981-85; pub. rels. cons. Sethco Inc., Toledo, 1992-93; owner Ann-Laura & Assocs., Toledo, 1994—; pub. rels. instr. Stautzenburger Coll., Toledo, 1996. Project launcher cons. Ann-Laura & Assocs., Toledo, 1995—; tech. computer support cons., Sethco, Toledo, 1992-94. Author: (novel) Fabia, 1989 (Fictional Romance award 1990); med. writer, rschr. online mags., 1994; screenwriter, 1986. Environmentalist, Toledo, 1986—. Recipient Internat. Fiction award Am. Girl Mag., 1967. Fellow Internat. Platform Assn., Authors' Guild. Roman Catholic. Office: Ann-Laura & Assocs PO Box 140574 Toledo OH 43614

SMALL, BERTRICE W. writer; b. N.Y.C., Dec. 9, 1937; d. David Roger Williams, Doris Melissa (Maud) Steen; m. George Sumner Small, Oct. 5, 1963; 1 child, Thomas David. Student, Western Coll. for Women, Oxford, Ohio, Katherine Gibbs Sectl. Sch., N.Y.C., 1959. With Young & Rubicon, N.Y.C., 1959—60, Weed Radio & TV, N.Y.C., 1960—61, Edward Petry & Co., N.Y.C., 1961—63. Author: The Kadin, 1978, Sky O'Malley, 1980, All The Sweet Tomorrows, 1984, Amount In Time, 1991, Betrayal, 1998, The Innocent, 1999, Rosamund, 2002, 25 others. Vestrywoman Redeemer Episc. Ch., Mattituck, NY, 1998—2001. Recipient Career Achievement Reviewers Choice award, Romantic Times Mag., 1983, 1988, 1995, 2001. Mem.: L.I. Romance Writers (bd. dirs. 1999—2001), Romance Writers of Am., Authors Guild. Episcopalian. Avocation: gardening. Mailing: PO Box 765 Southold NY 11971

SMALL, ELISABETH CHAN, psychiatrist, educator; b. Beijing, July 11, 1934; came to U.S., 1937; d. Stanley Hong and Lily Luella (Lum) Chan; m. Donald M. Small, July 8, 1957 (div. 1980); children Geoffrey Brooks, Philip Willard Stanley; m. H. Sidney Robinson, Jan. 12, 1991 (div. 2001). Student, Immaculate Heart Coll., L.A., 1951-52; BA in Polit. Sci., UCLA, 1955, MD, 1960. Intern Newton-Wellesley Hosp., Mass., 1960-61; asst. dir. for venereal diseases Mass. Dept. Pub. Health, 1961-63; resident in psychiatry Boston State Hosp., Mattapan, Mass., 1965-66, Tufts New Eng. Med. Ctr. Hosps., 1966-69, psychiat. cons. dept. gynecology, 1973-75; asst. clin. prof. psychiatry Sch. Medicine Tufts U., 1973-75, assoc. clin. prof., 1975-82, asst. clin. prof. ob-gyn, 1977-80, assoc. clin. prof. ob-gyn, 1980-82; from assoc. prof. to prof. psychiatry U. Nev. Sch. Med., Reno, 1982-95; practice psychiatry specializing in psychological effects of bodily changes on women, 1969—; emeritus prof. psychiatry and behavioral scis. U. Nev. Sch. Medicine, Reno, 1995—, from assoc. prof. to clin. assoc. prof. ob-gyn, 1982-88; mem. staff Tufts New Eng. Med. Ctr. Hosps., 1977-82, St. Margaret's Hosps., Boston, 1977-82, Washoe Med. Ctr., Reno, Sparks (Nev.) Family Hosp., Truckee Meadows Hosp., Reno, St. Mary's Hosp., Reno; chief psychiatry svc. Reno VA Med. Ctr., 1989-94. Lectr., cons. in field; mem. psychiatry adv. panel Hosp. Satellite Network; mem. office external peer rev. NIMH, HEW; psychiat. cons. to Boston Redevelopment Authority on Relocation of Chinese Families of South Cove Area, 1968-70; mem. New Eng. Med. Ctr. Hosps. Cancer Ctr. Com., 1979-80, Pain Control Com., 1981-82; reproductive sys. curriculum com. Tufts Univ. Sch. Medicine, 1975-82. Mem. editorial bd. Psychiat. Update Am. (Psychiat. Assn. ann. rev.), 1983-85; reviewer Psychosomatics and Hosp. Community Psychiatry, New Eng. Jour. of Medicine, Am. Jour. of Psychiatry Psychosomatic Medicine; contbr. articles to profl. jours. Immaculate Heart Coll. scholar, 1951-52, Mira Hershey scholar UCLA, 1955; fellow Radcliffe Inst., 1967-70. Fellow Am. Coll. Psychiatrists (sci. program com. 1989-98); mem. AMA, Am. Psychiat. Assn. (rep. to sect. com. AAAS, chmn. ad hoc com. Asian-Am. Psychiatrists 1975, task force 1975-77, task force cost effectiveness in consultation 1984—, caucus chmn. 1981-82, sci. program com. 1982-88, courses subcom. chmn. sci. program com. 1986-88), Nev. Psychiat. Assn. (life), Assn. for Acad. Psychiatry (fellowship com. 1982), Washoe County Med. Assn., Nev. Med. Soc. Avocations: snow skiing, culinary arts. Home and Office: 825 Caughlin Crossing Reno NV 89509-0647

SMALL, JOYCE GRAHAM, psychiatrist, educator; b. Edmonton, Alta., Can., June 12, 1931; came to U.S., 1956; d. John Earl and Rachel C. (Redmond) Graham; m. Iver Francis Small, May 26, 1954; children: Michael, Jeffrey. BA, U. Sask., Saskatoon, Can., 1951; MD, U. Man., Alta., Can., 1956; MS, U. Mich., 1959. Diplomat Am. Bd. Psychiatry and Neurology, Am. Bd. Electroencephalography. Instr. in psychiatry Neuropsychiat. Inst. U. Mich., Ann Arbor, 1959-60; instr. in psychiatry med. sch. U. Oreg., Portland, 1960-61, asst. prof. in psychiatry med. sch., 1961-62; asst. prof. in psychiatry sch. of medicine Washington U., St. Louis, 1962-65; assoc. prof. in psychiatry sch. of medicine Ind. U., Indpls., 1965-69, prof. psychiatry sch. of medicine, 1969—. Mem. initial rev. groups NIMH, Washington, 1972-76, 79-82, 87-91; assoc. mem. Inst. Psychiat. Rsch., Indpls., 1974—. Mem. editl. bd. Quar. Jour. Convulsive Therapy, 1984, Clin. EEG, 1990, and more than 150 publs. in field; contbr. articles to profl. jours. Rsch. grantee NIMH, Portland, Oreg., 1961-62, St. Louis, 1962-64, Indpls., 1967—, Epilepsy Found., Dreyfus Found., Indpls., 1965; recipient Merit award NIMH, Indpls., 1990, Career award EEG and Clin. Neurosci. Soc., 2003. Fellow Am. Psychiat. Assn., Am. EEG Soc. (councillor 1972-75, 1982); mem. Soc. Biol. Psychiatry, Cen. Assn. Electroencephalographers (sec., treas. 1967-68, pres. 1970, councillor 1971-72), Sigma Xi. Office: Larue D Carter Meml Hosp 2601 Cold Spring Rd Indianapolis IN 46222-2202

SMALL, MARY E. state legislator; b. Bath, Maine, Sept. 12, 1954; d. Donald Nichols and Marguerite (Brown) S. Grad., Green Mountain Coll., 1973; MA, U. So. Maine, 1976. Mem. Maine Ho. of Reps., Augusta, 1979-94, mem. edn. com.; mem. dist. 19 Maine Senate, Augusta, 1995—. Campaign coord. Re-election U.S. Rep. David Emery, 1976. Mem. Delta Zeta. Home: 175 Oak St Bath ME 04530-2431 Office: Maine State Senate 3 State House Sta Augusta ME 04333-0003

SMALL, NATALIE SETTIMELLI, pediatric mental health counselor; b. Quincy, Mass., June 2, 1933; d. Joseph Peter and Edmea Natalie (Bagnaschi) Settimelli; m. Parker Adams Small, Jr., Aug. 26, 1956; children: Parker Adams III, Peter McMichael, Carla Edmea. BA, Tufts U., 1955; MA, EdS, U. Fla., 1976, PhD, 1987. Cert. child life specialist. Pediatric counselor U. Fla. Coll. Medicine, Gainesville, 1976-80, Shands Hosp.-U. Fla., Gainesville, 1980-87, supr. child life dept. patient and family resources, 1987—2003; pres. Small Group Cons.com, 2003—. Adminstrv. liaison for self-dir. work teams, mem. faculty Ctr. for Coop. Learning for Health and Sci. Edn., Gainesville, 1988-2003, assoc. dir., 1996, supr. pastoral svcs., 1998-2003; cons. and lectr. in field. Author: Parents Know Best, 1991; co-author team packs series for teaching at risk adolescent health edn. Building Strong Families, 1998. Bd. dirs. Ronald McDonald House, Gainesville, 1980—, mem. exec. com., 1991—; bd. dirs. Gainesville Assn. Creative Arts, 1994—; mem. health profl. adv. com. March of Dimes, Gainesville, 1986-96, HIV prevention planning partnership, 1995-96; mem. Teen Pregnancy Prevention Action Com., 1998-2000, exec. com. Children's Hosp., 1998-2003. Boston Stewart Club scholar, Florence, Italy, 1955; grantee Jessie Ball Du Pont Fund, 1978, Children's Miracle Network, 1990, 92-95, 97, 2000, 2001-2003; recipient Caring and Sharing award Ronald McDonald House, 1995, Appreciation award March of Dimes, 1996. Mem. ACA, Nat. Bd. Cert. Counselors. Roman Catholic. Avocations: travel, reading, swimming. Home: 3454 NW 12th Ave Gainesville FL 32605-4811 E-mail: smallgroup2@aol.com.

SMALL, PATRICIA ANN, minister; b. Jacksonville, Fla., Mar. 31, 1961; d. Enoch and Laura Lucille Small. BS, Edward Waters Coll., 1962. Receptionist, adminstrv. clk., intake clk. FBI Adminstrv. Office-U.S. Cts., Jacksonville, 1965—96; local ch. pastor United Meth. Ch., Jacksonville, 1989—2000; chaplain resident Bapt. Med. Ctr., Jacksonville, 2000—. Trustee Girls, Inc., Jacksonville, 1999—. Democrat. Avocations: reading, hiking, mountain climbing, travel. Home: 1545 Steele St Jacksonville FL 32209

SMALLEY, DONNA WESSON, lawyer, educator; b. Ft. Sill, Okla., Oct. 8, 1955; d. Robert Eugene and Frances Marie (Yates) Wesson; m. Jack Smalley Jr., July 31, 1978 (div. Jan. 1987); 1 child, Jack Smalley III. BA in Journalism, U. Ala., 1975, JD, 1978; cert. instr. Nat. Inst. Trial Advocacy, U. Calif. Berkeley, San Francisco, 1994. Bar: Ala. 1978. State lobbyist U. Ala., Tuscaloosa, 1974-75; personal injury claims adjuster State Farm Mutual Auto Ins., Birmingham, 1978-82; assoc. Williams & Pradat, Tuscaloosa, 1982-83; legal clk., adminstrv. asst. Tuscaloosa County Dist. Ct., 1983-84; assoc. atty., ptnr. Gibson & Smalley, P.C., Tuscaloosa, 1984-88; pvt. practice Tuscaloosa, 1988-95; ptnr., gen. practitioner Smalley & Carr, L.L.C., Tuscaloosa, 1996—. Adj. English instr. U. Ala., Tuscaloosa, 1988-91, adj. trial advocacy instr., 1991—; bd. mem. Ala. Lawyers for Children, Montgomery, 1993-96, Ala. Children's Trust Fund Bd., Montgomery, 1994—; cir. judge pro-tem Ala. Adminstrv. Office of Cts., Tuscaloosa, 1995; chair citizen's edn. Ala. State Bar Assn., Montgomery, 1995-96; spkr. in field. Paintings exhibited Jr. League, 1990 (3d place), Lawyers for Children Charitable Auction, 1996. Chair mediation com. Tuscaloosa County Bar, 1989-91; task force mem. Lt. Gov.'s Task Force-Juvenile Crime, Montgomery, 1993-96; exec. com. Ala. State Dem. Party, Birmingham, 1994—; parent-bd. liason Tuscaloosa Acad., 1994-95. Named Outstanding Young Businesswoman, Jaycees, Tuscaloosa, 1984, Outstanding Young Careerist, Bus. and Profl. Women, Tuscaloosa, 1985; recipient Outstanding Achievement-CLE award Ala. State Bar, Montgomery, 1994, 95, Pro Bono award Ala. State Bar, 1997. Fellow Am. Acad. Matrimonial Lawyers; mem. Ala. Trial Lawyers (exec. bd. 1994—). Methodist. Avocations: reading, walking, computers. Office: Smalley & Carr LLC Attys 601 Greensboro Ave Tuscaloosa AL 35401-1730

SMALLEY, PENNY JUDITH, healthcare technology consultant; b. Chgo., Feb. 20, 1947; d. Ernest Rich and Muriel L. (Touff) Brown; m. Ivan H. Smalley, Jan. 11, 1972; children: Cherie Ann, Michael John, Geoffry Paul. Grad., Evanston Hosp. Sch. Nursing, Ill., 1980. Cert. Am. Bd. Laser Surgery, 1989. Staff nurse Evanston Hosp., 1979-81, laser coord., 1981-83; office mgr. Women's Health Group, 1981; laser nurse specialist Cooper Lasersonics, various, 1983-86; pres., CEO Technology Concepts Internat., Inc., Chgo., 1986—. Lectr., writer Sino Fgn. Laser Conf., People's Republic of China, 1987; bd. dirs. Laser Inst. Am.; rep. Assn. Perioperative RN's. Contbg. author: Nursing Clinics of North America, 1990; editorial bd. Clin. Laser Monthly, Laser Nursing mag., 1989—, Minimally Invasive Surg. Nursing; contbr. articles to profl. jours. Mem. Am. Soc. Laser Medicine and Surgery (chmn. edn. com. 1987-90, standards of practice com. 1990, quality assurance com., nursing sect. chmn. 1992-94, chair safety com.), award for Excellence in Laser Nursing 1993), Laser Inst. Am. (bd. dirs.), Am. Nat. Standards Com., Inst. Com. Lasers in Health Care, Brit. Med. Laser Assn. (course dir. first laser nursing conf. in U.K., 1990), Assn. Oper. Rm. Nurses (tchr. nat. seminars, spl. com. on internat. issues, liaison to ANSI Z136, Australian/N.Z. 4173 laser safety stds.), Internat. Soc. Laser Surgery and Medicine (chmn. nursing 1988—, chmn. safety com. 2002), Internat. Electrotech. Commn. (Am. delegation tech. com. 76 for internat. stds. regarding lasers and electromed. equipment). Democrat. Avocations: music, community theater, travel, photography. Home and Office: 1444 W Farwell Ave Chicago IL 60626-3410 Office Phone: 773-262-2810. Personal E-mail: pennyjs@aol.com.

SMALLEY, RHONDA E. music educator; b. Portsmouth, Ohio, July 14, 1949; d. Lloyd H. and Florine S. Smith; m. Jerry L. Smalley, Feb. 25, 1978; children: Jason, Jerod. BA, Marshall U., 1971, MA, 1973. Band dir. West Jr. H.S., Huntington, W.Va., 1971—86, Beverly Hills Jr. High, Huntington, 1986—93, Barboursville (W.Va.) H.S., 1993—94, Cabell Midland H.S., Ona, W.Va., 1994—. Region III band festival chmn. W.Va. Secondary Sch. Activities Commn., Parkersburg, 1999—2003; W.Va. region III rep. W.Va. Bandmasters Exec. Bd., Parkersburg, 1999—2003; chmn. W.Va. Band Festival Parade, Huntington, 1999—2003. Named to Hall of Fame, W.Va. Music Educators Assn., 2003; recipient Senate Resolution, W.Va. State Legis., 2000. Mem.: NEA, W.Va. Bandmasters Assn. (state band com.), Music Educators Nat. Conf. Democrat. Avocations: travel, sports. Home: 221 Forest View Dr Huntington WV 25705 Office: Cabell Midland HS 2300 Route 60 East Ona WV 25545

SMALLEY, TERRI BARNES, social worker; b. Jacksonville, Fla., July 19, 1966; d. Wayne F. and Virginia M. Barnes. BA, U. North Fla., 1988; MSW, Fla. State U., 1993. LCSW. Crisis counselor Youth Crisis Ctr., Jacksonville, 1989—92, family link counselor, 1992—94, family link counselor/supr., 1994—98, prevention/intervention coord., 1998—2000, clin. mgr., 2000—. V.p. Tutor and Learn, Inc., 1999—2000; mem. Jacksonville United Against Turancy, 1998—, Quality Improvement Com., 1995—2003. Named Counselor of the Yr., Fla. Network of Youth and Families, 1995. Mem.: NASW. Avocations: gardening, Bible study, flute, photography. Home: 1925 Clemson Rd Jacksonville FL 32217-2308

SMALLIN, MICHELLE DEANNE, marketing professional; b. Oneonta, N.Y., May 19, 1978; d. Terry Smallin and Debra Hunsberger. BA in Mgmt., Hartwick Coll., 2000. Mktg. coord. F. Cappiello Dairy Products, Inc., Schenectady, NY, 2000—. Mem.: Am. Cheese Soc., Internat. Dairy Deli Bake Assn., Am. Mktg. Assn. Office: F Cappiello Dairy Products Inc 115 Van Guysling Ave Schenectady NY 12305 Home: 37 Fairview Ave #1 Albany NY 12208-2405

SMALLS, PEGGY ANN, educational consultant, retired elementary school educator; b. Atlanta, Feb. 25, 1943; d. Calton D. and Alberta (Wardlaw) Lamar. BA, Clark Coll. (Clark Atlanta Univ.), 1965; MEd, U. Ga., 1975; EDS, Brenau U., 1995. Cert. elem. grades, 7-12 social studies, middle grades, gifted and instructional supervision. Tchr. Atlanta Pub. Schs.; self employed ednl. cons. Founder River Run Civic Assn., Dekalb County, Ga.; campaign worker AFL-CIO/AFT, Atlanta; mem. Greenforest Community. Baptist Ch. Reading grantee Apple Corps; named Technology Tchr. of Yr. IBM. Mem. AFT (zone coord., editor, 2d v.p., work shop presenter, editor, writer newsletter, service award Local 1564, 1991), ASCD, Internat. Reading Assn., Alpha Kappa Alpha (philactor, sec., v.p., pres.), Phi Delta Kappa, Alpha Kappa Alpha (Lambda Epsilon Omega chpt. officer of the year, soror of yr.), . Avocations: writing, mentoring high school students.

SMALLWOOD, CAROL, librarian, writer; b. Cheboygan, Mich., May 3, 1939; d. Lloyd Gouine and Lucille Drozdowska; m. T.M. Smallwood, 1963 (div. 1976); 2 children. BS, Ea. Mich. U., 1961, M in History, 1963; MLS, We. Mich. U., 1976. Tchr. Redford Union High Sch., Livonia, Mich., 1961-62, Flat Rock (Mich.) Jr. High Sch., 1963-64; grad. asst. Western Mich. U., Kalamazoo, 1975-76; Title I libr. cons. Northland (Mich.), Grand Traverse (Mich.) Library Systems, 1976-77; head media dir. Pellston (Mich.) Pub. Schs., 1977—97; writer, libr. cons. Mt. Pleasant, 1998—. Asst. dir. Northland Libr. System, Alpena, Mich., 1977; developer, operator ednl. materials clearinghouse, 1981-83; adult edn. tchr. Cheboygan Area Schs., 1985-86. Author: Free Michigan Materials for Educators, 1980, 2nd edit., 1986, Free Materials Resource Disk, 1983, Exceptional Free Library Resource Materials, 1984, Free Resource Builder, 1985, 2d edit., 1992, A Guide to Selected Federal Agency Programs and Publications for Librarians and Teachers, 1986, Health Resource Builder, 1988, An Educational Guide to the National Park System, 1989, Current Issues Builder, 1989, Library Puzzles and Word Games, for Grades 7-12, 1990, Reference Puzzles and Word Games for Grades 7-12, 1991, Michigan Authors, 1993, Helpful Hints for the School Library, 1993, Recycling Tips for Teachers and Librarians, 1995, An Insider's Guide to Libraries, 1997, Free or Low-Cost Health Information, 1998, (with S. McElmeel) WWW Almanac, 1999; columnist Detroit News, 1983-85, Morning Sun, 2003—, Catch: The Entertainment News, 1988-89, Essential Resources for Schools and Libraries, 1997—2003, lit., poetry and fiction mags. Charter bd. mem., publicity chmn. Cheboygan Area Arts Coun.; founder, pres. Cheboygan County Humane Soc.; co-founder Humanr Animal Treatment Soc. Mem.: Mich. Fedn. Humane Socs. Home: 543 S Whiteville Rd Mount Pleasant MI 48858-9761 E-mail: csmallwo@edcen.ehhs.cmich.edu.

SMART, ANN CATHERINE, dean; b. Anderson, Ind., Nov. 27, 1946; d. Edward Vernon and Virginia Ruth (Hersberger) Dillie; m. Houston Wynnlee Crisp, Aug. 17, 1968 (div. 1980); m. William H. Smart, Aug. 16, 1987. BS in Edn., Ball State U., 1969; postgrad., U. Alaska, 1971—73; M in Home Econs., Oreg. State U., 1975, PhD, 1991. Youth nutrition specialist U. Alaska, Fairbanks, 1970—73, extension mgmt. info. coord., 1972—73; specialist nutrition edn. Oreg. State U., Corvallis, Oreg., 1975; parent edn. and home econs. coord. Linn-Benton C.C., Albany, NY, 1975—77, Albany (N.Y.) Ctr. dir., 1977—79, Benton Ctr. dir., 1979—85, cmty. edn. divsn. dir., 1985—89, spl. asst. to v.p. bus. affairs, 1987, interim v.p. instrn., 1989—90, dean student svcs. and extended learning, 1991—94, dean extended learning and info. svcs., 1994—; ret. Rsch. assoc. Western Oreg. State Coll., Monmouth, Oreg., 1983; chmn. task force Cmty. Edn. Dirs., Oreg., 1983. Author: Anotated Bibliography Nutrition Education Resources, 1975, Program Planning Activities Nutrition for Elderly, 1975; co-prodr.: (films) Alaskan Food Choices, 1973; contbr. articles to bulls. Founding pres. Oreg. Coast C.C. Svc. Dist., Newport, Oreg., 1987—88; chmn. task force Charting the Future of Corvallis, 1988—89; mem. UN Forum 85, Nairobi, Kenya, 1985; sec. Benton County United Way, 1984—87, pres., 1991—92, Zonta Svc. Found. Corvallis, 1991—92, treas., 1994—. Named Leader of the 80s, League Innovation in Cmty. Colls., 1982. Mem.: LWV, Oreg. Cmty. Edn., Am. Assn. Women in C.C., Oreg. C.C. Assn., Nat. Coun. Cmty. Svcs. and Continuing Edn. (Oreg. rep. 1994—, Regional Person of Yr. award 1993), Am. Assn. Adult and Continuing Edn. (v.p. region VIII 1987—89), Oreg. Home Econs. Assn. (sec. 1979—81, mem. joint bds. articulation commn. 1992—95, named Disting. Leader 1984), N.W. Adult Edn. Assn. (pres. 1984—85, named Adult Educator of Yr. 1987), Corvallis C. of C. (bd. dirs.), Rotary, Albany (N.Y.) Club, Zonta Club (pres. Corvallis club 1982—83, internat. del. 1982, alt. 1984, African study tour 1985, named Zontian of Yr. 1994), Phi Kappa Phi, Phi Theta Kappa, Sigma Zeta. Democrat. Office: Linn-Benton Community Coll 6500 Pacific Blvd SW Albany OR 97321-3755

SMART, EDITH MERRILL, civic worker; b. Sept. 10, 1929; d. Edwin Katte and Helen Phelps (Stokes) Merrill; m. S. Bruce Smart, Jr., Sept. 10, 1949; children: Edith Minturn Smart Moore, William Candler, Charlotte Merrill Smart Rogan, Priscilla Smart Schwarzenbach. Student, Smith Coll., 1947—49, Barnard Coll., 1949—50. Tchr. elem. schs., Gibson Island, Md., 1959—60; guide, instr. Mill River Wetlands Com., Fairfield, Conn., 1967—85; treas. Near and Far Aid Assn., Fairfield, 1970—75, v.p., 1975—77, pres., 1977—79, Nature Ctr. of Environ. Activities, Westport, Conn., chmn., 1981—85; trustee Fairfield U., 1987—93; leader No. Cook county coun. Girl Scouts Am., Kenilworth, Ill., 1962—64; chmn. Southport-Westport Antiques Show, 1974—76; trustee Conn. chpt. Nature Conservancy, 1981—91, Va. chpt. Nature Conservancy, 1992—. Guide Nat. Aquarium, 1985—90; dir. Piedmont Child Devel. Ctr., 1991—97, Land Trust of Va., 2002—. Vestryman St. Timothy's Ch., Fairfield, 1976—79. Mem.: MFH The Fairfax Hunt Club, Upperville Garden Club. Republican. Episcopalian. Home: 20561 Trappe Rd Upperville VA 20184-3021

SMART, ELLA JO, special education educator; b. Morrilton, Ark., Sept. 24, 1952; d. Roy Junior and Willard Frances (Bryant) Prince; m. Jacky Lynn Smart, June 8, 1973; children: Lora Sue Rixham, Jody Lynn. BS in Edn., East Ctrl. U., 1990; cert. in spl. edn., U. Mo., St. Louis, 2000. Cert. tchr. elem. grades 1-8, endorsements for mid. sch. sci. and social studies, pre-K - 12 spl. edn. Elem. tchr. Stuart (Okla.) Elem. Sch., 1991—98; spl. edn. tchr. Dixon (Mo.) Mid. Sch., 1998—2001, Marshall (Tex.) Jr. High, 2001—02, Earlsboro (Okla.) High and Jr. High, 2002—. Pres. Stuart Classroom Tchrs. Assn., 1995—96; dir. Afterschool Day Care Stuart Schs., 1996—97; mentor tchr. Marshall Jr. High, 2001—02. Edzoocation grantee, Oklahoma City Zoo, 1997, 1998. Mem.: Tex. Classroom Tchrs. Assn., Coun. Exceptional Children. Democrat. Mem. Ch. Of Christ. Avocations: gardening, camping, sewing, cake decorating, reading. Home: PO Box 1161 Henryetta OK 74437 Office: Earlsboro Pub Schs PO Box 10 Earlsboro OK 74840

SMART, MARY-LEIGH CALL (MRS. J. SCOTT SMART), civic worker; b. Springfield, Ill., Feb. 27, 1917; d. S(amuel) Leigh and Mary (Bradish) Call; m. J. Scott Smart, Sept. 11, 1951 (dec. 1960). Diploma, Monticello Coll., 1934; student, Oxford U., 1935; BA, Wellesley Coll., 1937; MA, Columbia U., 1939, postgrad., 1940-41, NYU, 1940-41; painting student, with Bernard Karfiol, 1937-38. Dir. mgmt. Cen. Ill. Grain Farms, Logan County, 1939—; owner Lowtrek Kennel, Ogunquit, Maine, 1957-73, Cove Studio Art Gallery, Ogunquit, 1961-68; art collector, patron, publicist, 1954—. Cons. in field. Editor: Hamilton Easter Field Art Found. Collection Catalog, 1966; originator, dir. show, compiler of catalog Art: Ogunquit, 1967; Peggy Bacon-A Celebration, Barn Gallery, Ogunquit, 1979. Program dir., sec. bd. Barn Gallery Assoc., Inc., 1958-69, pres., 1969-70, 82 87, asst. treas., 1987-92, hon. dir., 1970-78, adv. trustee, 1992-94, v.p., 1994-2003; curator Hamilton Easter Field Art Found. Collection, 1978-79, curator exhbn., 1979-86, chair exhbn. com., 1987-94; acquisition com. DeCordova Mus., Lincoln, Mass., 1966-78; chancellor's coun. U. Tex., 1972—; pres. coun. U. NH, 1978—; bd. dir. Ogunquit C. of C., 1966, treas., 1966-67, hon. life mem., 1968—; bd. overseers Strawbery Banke, Inc., Portsmouth, NH, 1972-75, 3d vice chmn., 1973, 2d vice-chmn., 1974; bd. advisors U. Art Galleries, U. NH, 1973-89; pres., 1981-89; bd. dir. Old York Hist. and Improvement Soc., York, Maine, 1979-81, v.p., 1981-82; adv. com. Bowdoin Coll. Mus. Art Invitational exhibit, 1975, '76 Maine Artists Invitational Exhbn., Maine State Mus., Maine Coast Artists, Rockport, 1975-78, All Maine Biennial '79, Bowdoin Coll. Mus. Art juried exhbn.; mem. jury for scholarship awards Maine com. Skowhegan Sch. Painting & Sculpture, 1982-84; nat. com. Wellesley Coll. Friends of Art, 1983—; adv. trustee Portland Mus. Art, 1983-85, fellow, 1985—; mus. panel Maine State Commn. on Arts and Humanities, 1983-86; adv. com. Maine Biennial, Colby Coll. Mus. Art, 1983; coun. advisors Farnsworth Art Mus., Rockland, Maine, 1986-98; collections com. Payson Gallery, Westbrook Coll., Portland, 1987-91; dir. Greater Piscataqua Cmty. Found., NH Charitable Fund, 1991 97; com. to establish artist's advancement grant, 2001; mem. corp. Ogunquit Mus. Am. Art, 1988-90, 95-2000; active Maine Women's Forum, 1993—; mem. art com. York Pub. Libr., 2002—; pres. Class of 1937, Wellesley Coll., 2001—. Lt. (j.g.) WAVES, 1942-45. Recipient Deborah Morton award Westbrook Coll., 1988, Friend of the Arts award Maine Art Dealers Assn., 1993. Mem. Springfield Art Assn., Jr. League Springfield Ill., Western Maine Wellesley Club. Episcopalian. Address: 30 Surf Point Rd York ME 03909-5053

SMEAL, ELEANOR CUTRI, civil rights executive; b. Ashtabula, Ohio, July 30, 1939; d. Peter Anthony and Josephine E. (Agresti) Cutri; m. Charles R. Smeal, Apr. 27, 1963; children: Tod, Lori. BA, Duke U., 1961, LLD (hon.), 1991; MA, U. Fla., 1963. Mem. bd. Upper St. Clair (Pa.) chpt. LWV, 1968-72, sec.-treas. Allegheny County Council, 1971-72; mem. NOW, 1971—; convenor, 1st pres. S. Hills (Pa.) chpt. NOW, 1971-73, 1st pres., state coordinator, 1972-75; nat. bd. dirs. NOW, 1973-75, chairwoman bd., 1975-77, pres., 1977-82, 85-87, mem. bd. Legal Def. and Edn. Fund, 1975—, chairwoman ERA Strike Force, 1977—; pres. Fund for Feminist Majority, Arlington, Va., 1987—. Mem. 1st nominating com., founding conf. Nat. Women's Polit. Caucus, 1971; bd. dirs. Allegheny County Women's Polit. Caucus, 1971-72; co-founder, bd. dirs. S. Hills NOW Day Nursery Sch., 1972— ; mem. Nat. Commn., Observance of Internat. Women's Year, 1977; mem. exec. com. Leadership Conf. on Civil Rights, 1979— ; mem. Nat. Adv. Com. on Women, 1978 Named One of 25 Most Influential Women in U.S. World Almanac, 1978 Office: The Feminist Majority 1600 Wilson Blvd Ste 801 Arlington VA 22209-2513

SMEAL, JANIS LEA, osteopath; b. Johnstown, Pa., Aug. 31, 1953; d. Charles Truman S. and Clara Belle (Smeal) Satterlee. RN, Mercy Hosp. Sch. Nursing, 1974; BS summa cum laude, U. Houston, 1996; DO, U. North Tex., 2001. RN, Tex.; cert. oper. rm. nurse; cert. ACLS. Staff, relief charge nurse emergency room Mercy Hosp., Altoona, Pa., 1974-85; staff nurse operating room McAllen (Tex.) Med. Ctr., 1985-87, Rio Grande Regional Hosp., McAllen, Tex., 1987-88; co-owner Associated Hypnotherapy and Pain Mgmt. Svcs. Tex., Bellaire, 1991-97; staff nurse operating room Meml. City Hosp., Houston, 1992-97; psychiatry resident U. Tex., Houston, 2001—. Co-owner, cons. J.L. Med. Svcs., McAllen, Tex., 1988-94. Recognition Golden Key Nat. Honor Soc., 1993, Phi Kappa Phi, 1994, Natural Sci. and Math. Scholars and Fellows, 1995. Mem.: AOA, AMA, Tex. Osteo. Med. Assn., Am. Psychiat. Assn., Golden Key, Phi Kappa Phi. Avocations: travel, dog training, interior design. Office: Assoc Hypnotherapy/Pain Svc 6300 West Loop S Ste 333 Bellaire TX 77401-2900

SMEDLEY, KEYUE MA, engineering educator, researcher; m. Greg Smedley, June 19, 1989; children: Aurora, Orion. BSEE, Zhejiang U., Hangzhou, China, 1982; MSEE, Zhejiang U., 1985, Calif. Inst. Tech., Pasadena, 1987; PhD in Elec. Engring., Calif. Inst. Tech., 1991. Engr. III Superconducting Super Collider, Dallas, 1990—92; asst. prof. dept. elec. and computer engring. U. Calif., Irvine, 1992—98, assoc. prof., 1998—2003, prof., 2003—. Contbr. numerous articles to profl. jours. Recipient Golden Lectureship, Tel Aviv U., 1996; Powell fellow, Calif. Inst. Tech., 1988. Mem.: IEEE (sr.; assoc. editor Power Electronics 1995—, ad com. mem. 1997—, Supreme Presentation award Nuclear Sci. Symposium 1991), IEEE Power Electronics Soc., Power Sources Mfrs. Assn., Eta Kappa Nu. Achievements include patents for one cycle control of amplifiers, power factor correction, active power filter, inverters. Avocations: travel, snorkeling. Mailing: Univ of Calif Dept Elec and Computer Engring Irvine CA 92697

SMELSER, RUTH MALONE, volunteer; b. Tescott, Kans., Dec. 20, 1917; d. Dial Pete and Mamie Evelyn (Donbarger) Moss; m. Raymond U. Schoonover, 1939 (div. 1950); children: Marion, Karen, Linda; m. Charles Fay Stiles, Nov. 15, 1951 (dec. June 1960); children: Vicki, Rhonda, Bonnie; m. Everett Frey, 1962 (div. 1963); m. Stanley Malone, 1964 (div. 1981); m. Hershel Smelser, 1982. Grad., Custer County Jr. Coll., Miles City, Mont., 1936; student, Mont. U., 1977, 78. Tchr., Campbell County, Wyo., 1936-37; rancher Johnson County, Wyo., 1939-51; owner Cattle and Irrigated Farm, Custer County, Mont., 1951-70; mgr. House of Fabrics, Tempo Store, Miles City, Mont., 1970-77; owner Ruth's Draperies, Miles City, 1978-80; builder Passive Solar-Earth Sheltered Home, Buffalo, Wyo., 1982-85; organizer recycling program Buffalo, 1990-95. Leader 4-H Club Willing Workers, Miles City, 1965-75; pres. Buffalo/Johnson County Recycling Bd., 1990-97. Recipient Cert. of award as Wyo. Recycler of Yr., 1997. Democrat. Methodist. Avocations: sewing, fine arts painting. Home: 515 W Hogerson St Buffalo WY 82834-1537

SMICK, SUSAN SCHNEE, manufacturing executive, tile designer, marketing professional; b. Bklyn., July 12, 1947; d. Henry and Rhoda (Noskin) Schnee; m. Edward Lewis Smick, Feb. 5, 1972 (separated 1994); 1 child, Joshua Henry. BA with honors, C.W. Post Coll., 1970; postgrad., NYU, 1970-71. Cert. tchr., N.Y. Customer svc. and campus rep. Trans World

Airlines, N.Y.C., 1966-71, strategic airline mktg. planner, 1971-72, fleet planning analyst, 1972-73; propr. Sailor's Valentine, Chatham, Mass., 1974-76; ednl. and corp. tour developer Crimson Travel, Cambridge, Mass., 1977-80; propr., tile designer, mfr. Cape Cod Tile Co., 1986-97; founding ptnr. TileGraphics, Weston, Mass., 1994-97; founding ptnr., tile designer, mfr. Great Am. Tile Works, Weston, Mass., 1997—. Cons. U.S. Dept. Transp., 1975. Author (ednl. tours) The Flying Classroom, 1977-80; ceramic artist; author mktg. software. Friends of McLean, McLean Hosp., Belmont, Mass., 1997; mem. Mass. Horticulture Soc., 1995—; bd. dirs. Women's Cmty. League of Weston, 1999, chmn. ways and means com., 2000; chmn. of events Pub. Action for the Arts, 1999, adv. bd. mem., 2000. Recipient Howard Gold Polit. Sci. scholarship Howard Gold Meml. Fund, 1965, acad. scholarship C.W. Post Coll., 1967-70, Nat. Profl. Devel. Act fellowship NYU Grad. Sch. Edn. and History, 1970. Mem. Soc. Glass and Ceramic Decorators, Pi Gamma Mu, Phi Beta Kappa. Avocations: fund-raising, Am. folk art, interior design, fashion design, horticulture. Home: 89 Ash St Weston MA 02493-1940 Office: Great Am Tile Works PO Box 363 Weston MA 02493-0002 E-mail: ssmick@mediaone.net.

SMILEY, CAROL ANNE, home health administrator, sculptor; b. Cedar Rapids, Iowa, Sept. 11, 1937; d. Ralph Derold and Mary C. Miller; m. Donald Victor Smiley, June 29, 1956 (div. Aug. 1970); children: Donald Victor Jr., Julie Ann, Joseph Charles, Thomas Wayne; m. Douglas Brewster Reed, Aug. 6, 1976 (div. Jan. 1988); 1 child, Brook (dec.). Co-founder, v.p., sec., treas. Anvic Enterprise, Cedar Rapids, Iowa, 1963-70; co-founder, dir. Yankee Horse Trader, Bennington, Vt., 1984-86; organic farmer Solon, Iowa, Argyle, N.Y., 1970-86; fiber sculptor, 1970-86; tchr. Solon (Iowa) H.S., 1973-74; caregiver, coord. Home Health Care and Hospice, Brattleboro, Vt., 1986—. Sculpture shows include Green Mt. Collaborative, Bennington, 1974-78, Woman Art Gallery, N.Y.C., 1977-78, Lincoln Ctr. Group Show, N.Y.C., 1978; exhbns. various group shows. Mem. GOP cen. com. for Johnson County, Iowa, 1971-72. Mem.: ACLU. Office: Home Health Care Hospice 142 Green St Brattleboro VT 05301

SMILEY, JANE GRAVES, author, educator; b. L.A., Sept. 26, 1949; d. James La Verne and Frances Nuelle (Graves) S.; m. John Whiston, Sept. 4, 1970 (div.); m. William Silag, May 1, 1978 (div.); children: Phoebe Silag, Lucy Silag; m. Stephen Mark Mortensen, July 25, 1987; 1 child, Axel James Mortensen. BA, Vassar Coll., 1971; MFA, U. Iowa, 1976, MA, PhD, U. Iowa, 1978. Asst. prof. Iowa State U., Ames, 1981-84, assoc. prof., 1984-89, prof., 1989-90, Disting. prof., 1992-96. Vis. asst. prof. U. Iowa, Iowa City, 1981, 87. Author: (fiction) Barn Blind, 1980, At Paradise Gate, 1981 (Friends of American Writers prize 1981), Duplicate Keys, 1984, The Age of Grief, 1987 (Nat. Book Critics Cirle award nomination 1987), The Greenlanders, 1988, Ordinary Love and Goodwill, 1989, A Thousand Acres, 1991 (Pulitzer Prize for fiction 1992, Nat. Book Critics Cirle award 1992, Midland Authors award 1992, Amb. award 1992, Heartland prize 1992), Moo: A Novel, 1995; (non-fiction) Catskill Crafts: Artisans of the Catskill Mountains, 1987, The All-True Travels and Adventures of Lidie Newton, 1998, Horse Heaven, 2001, Good Faith, 2003. Grantee Fulbright U.S. Govt., Iceland, 1976-77, NEA, 1978, 87; recipient O. Henry award, 1982, 85, 88. Mem. Author's Guild, Screenwriters Guild. Avocations: cooking, swimming, playing piano, quilting. Office: c/o Molly Friedrich Dept English 708 3rd Ave Fl 23 New York NY 10017-4201

SMILEY, MARILYNN JEAN, musicologist; b. Columbia City, Ind., June 5, 1932; d. Orla Raymond and Mary Jane (Bailey) S. BS (State scholar), Ball State U., 1954; MusM, Northwestern U., 1958; cert., Ecoles d'Art Americaines, Fontainebleau, France, 1959; PhD (Grad. scholar, Delta Kampa Gamma scholar), U. Ill., 1970. Public sch. music tchr., Logansport, Ind., 1954-61; faculty music dept. SUNY-Oswego, 1961—, Disting. Teaching prof., 1974—, chmn. dept., 1976-81. Presenter papers at confs. Contbr. articles to profl. jours. Bd. dirs. Oswego Opera Theatre, 1978—, Oswego Orch. Soc., 1978—, Penfield Libr. Assocs., 1985—. Recipient Chancellor's award for Excellence in Tchg., 1973; fellow SUNY Rsch. Found. fellow, summers, 1971, 1972, 1974; grantee NEH grantee, 1990—91. Mem.: AAUW (grantee 1984, pres. Oswego br. 1984—86, br. coun. rep. dist. III, N.Y. State divsn. 1986—88, br. coun. coord. N.Y. State divsn. 1988—90, N.Y. divsn. area intererst rep. cultural interests 1990—92, N.Y. divsn. diversity dir. 1993—96, Oswego br. diversity chair 1995—, N.Y. divsn. historian, archivist 2000—), NOW, Oswego County Hist. Soc., Early Music Am., Am. Recorder Soc., Soc. Am. Music (membership chair 1998—2003), Renaissance Soc. Am., Coll. Music Soc., Music Libr. Assn., Medieval Acad. Am., Am. Musicol. Soc. (chmn. N.Y. chpt. 1975—77, chpt. rep. to AMS coun. 1993—96, bd. dirs. N.Y. State-St. Lawrence chpt. 1993—96, mem. status of women com. 1997—2000), Oswego Recorder Consort, Ontario Singers, Heritage Found. of Oswego, Phi Kappa Phi, Kappa Delta Pi, Sigma Tau Delta, Sigma Alpha Iota, Pi Kappa Lambda, Delta Phi Alpha, Phi Delta Kappa, Delta Kappa Gamma (music chair State of Ind. 1961, music chair State of N.Y. 1968). Methodist. Office: SUNY Dept Music Oswego NY 13126 E-mail: smiley@oswego.edu.

SMITH, ABBIE OLIVER, college administrator, educator; b. Augusta, Ga., Jan. 31, 1931; d. Rowland Sheppard and Abigail Seabrook (Hanahan) Oliver; m. William Parkhurst Smith, Jr., July 2, 1953; children: William Parkhurst Smith, III, Oliver Hamilton. BS, George Washington U., 1953, MEd, 1958, EdDin Higher Edn., 1986. Tchr. St. Mary's Acad., Monroe, Mich., 1954-55; tchr., coach Washington-Lee H.S., Arlington, Va., 1955-58; homemaker, cmty. vol. Bethesda, Md., 1959-64; asst. professorial lectr. George Washington U., Washington, 1965-69, adminstr. continuing edn., 1969-80, asst. dean, dir., 1981-89, acting dean divsn. continuing edn., 1989-93, asst. v.p., asst. to dean institutional advancement, 1993—. Panelist TV series WETA, Washington; mem. exec. bd., newsletter editor Tng. Officers Conf., 1989—, chair charter expansion 1992—. Co-author: (workbook) Developing New Horizons for Women, 1975, Manual for Counselors for Developing New Horizons for Women, 1975. Mem. adv. bd. Washington Bd. Trade, 1975-77, women's branch adv. bd. State Nat. Bank, Bethesda, Md., 1978-81; collegiate adv. bd. Episcopal Diocese of Washington, 1977-79. Recipient Leadership in Adult Edn. award, 1976, GW award for outstanding contbn. to univ. life Office of GW Pres., 1991, Washington Women of Achievement, Washington Edn. TV Assn., 1980. Mem. Nat. U. Continuing Edn. Assn. (awards chair divsn. women's edn. 1977-78, nat. chair 1977-78, chair-elect divsn. part-time students program 1984-86, nat. chair 1984-86, chair coun. human resources 1985-86, nat. spl. com. on couns. and divsn. 1984-86, nat. exec. bd. 1984-86, nat. bd. dirs. 1984-98, nat. charters and bylaws coms. 1987-89, sec.-elect divsn. cert. and nontraditional degree programs 1987-89, chair-elect 1989-90, nat. chair 1990-91, nat. ann. planning coms. 1987, 92, sec. region II 1989-90, chair-elect, ann. conf. chair, single host instn. ann. conf. region II 1990-91, chair region II 1991-92, awards com. chair 1992, Walton S. Bittner Svc. Citation 1994, hon. mention for program catalog nat. divsn. mktg. 1988, Floyd B. Fisher Leadership award 1996), Phi Delta Kappa Internat. (G.W. chpt., v.p. for programs 1995-96, pres. 1996-97, newsletter editor 1977—, Newsletter Award Merit 1998-99, Outstanding Newsletter award 1999-2000, 2000-01). Democrat. Episcopalian. Avocations: writing, painting, swimming, dance, traveling. Home: 3751 Jocelyn St NW Washington DC 20015-1836 Office: George Washington U 2134 G St NW Washington DC 20037-2797 E-mail: asmith@gwu.edu.

SMITH, ADA L. state legislator; b. Amherst County, Va. d. Thomas and Lillian Smith. Grad., CUNY. Dep. clk. N.Y.C.; state senator N.Y. Legislature, Albany, 1988—, mem. various coms., ranking corp. commn. and authorities, 1994, minority whip, 1994—2003, senate chair dem. conf., 2003—. Mem. Senate Minority Puerto Rican and Hispanic Task Force; chair Senate Minority Task Force on Privatization of Kennedy and Laguardia Airports. Trustee, life dir. Coll. Fund Baruch Coll. Recipient Outstanding Alumni award Baruch Coll. Mem. African Am. Clergy and Elected Ofcls., Inc., N.Y. Assn. of State Black and Puerto Rican Legislators, Baruch Coll. Alumni Assn. (pres., Disting. Svc. award, Outstanding Achievement award). Office: NY State Senate Rm 808 Legis Office Bldg Albany NY 12247 also: Queens Dist Office 11643 Sutphin Blvd Jamaica NY 11434-1526

SMITH, AGNES MONROE, history educator; b. Hiram, Ohio, Aug. 8, 1920; d. Bernie Alfred and Joyce (Messenger) Monroe; m. Stanley Blair Smith; children: David, Doris, Darl, Diane. BA, Hiram Coll., 1940; MA, W.Va. U., 1945; PhD, Western Res. U., 1966. Social sci. tchr. Freedom (Ohio) High Sch., 1940-44; instr. of history W.Va. U., Morgantown, 1945; instr. of social sci. Hiram Coll., 1946; inst. history and social sci. Youngstown (Ohio) State U., 1964-66, asst. prof. to prof. of history, 1966-84, prof. history emeritus, 1984—; vis. prof. history Hiram Coll., 1988-90. Co-editor: Bourgeois, Sans Culottes and other Frenchmen, 1981; contbr. articles to profl. jours. Mem. Ohio Acad. History, Delta Kappa Gamma, Phi Alpha Theta, Pi Gamma Mu. Mem. Christian Ch. (Disciples Of Christ). Home: 16759 Main Market Rd West Farmington OH 44491-9608

SMITH, ALISON LEIGH, lawyer; b. Brownsville, Tex., Sept. 24, 1952; d. Arthur Lee and June (Allen) Smith; m. Dean A. Burkhardt, Apr. 24, 1981. B in Journalism summa cum laude, U. Tex., 1974, JD cum laude, 1977. Bar: Tex. 1977, U.S. Dist. Ct. (so. dist.) Tex. (1978), U.S. Ct. Appeals (5th cir.) 1981, U.S. Dist. Ct. (no. dist.) Tex. 1987, U.S. Ct. Appeals (D.C. cir.) 1989. Assoc. Vinson & Elkins LLP, Houston, 1977-84, ptnr., 1984-89, 91—; dep. asst. atty. gen. antitrust divsn. U.S. Dept. Justice, Washington, 1989-91. Adj. prof. law U. Tex., Austin, 1992-93. Alternate del. Rep. Nat. Conv., New Orleans, 1988; mem. ethics com. City of Houston, 1988-89. Mem. ABA (antitrust law sect., chair transp. industry com., 1992-95, co-chmn. pvt. antitrust litig. com. 2001-), Am. Law Inst., Tex. Bar Found., Houston Bar Assn. Home: 2125 Bolsover St Houston TX 77005-1617 Office: Vinson & Elkins 3300 First City Tower 1001 Fannin St Ste 3300 Houston TX 77002-6706 Office Phone: 713-758-2250. E-mail: asmith@velaw.com.

SMITH, ALMA WHEELER, state legislator; b. Aug. 6, 1941; BA, U. Mich. Legis. coord. Senator Lane Pollack; mem. Mich. Senate from 18th dist., Lansing, 1995—; mem. appropriations com. Mem. South Lyon (Mich.) Bd. Edn.

SMITH, ANDREA DAWN, financial planner; b. St Andrew, Jamaica, Mar. 10, 1958; d. Lloyd Maxwell Sr. and Phyllis Leonie Maxwell; m. Mark Davidson Smith, Sept. 1, 1979; children: Kagan Neal, Kerke Davidson, Shari Monique, Marc Maxwell. Degree in fin., Simon Bolivar U., Venezuela, 1978. Cert. fin. mgr., Donald T. Reagan Sch. Bus., 1998. Internat. banking specialist Ctrl. Nat. Bank, Miami, 1978—79, Fla. Nat. Bank, Miami, 1979—80; credit negotiator Bank of Boston, Miami, 1980—84; credit supr. NCNB Bank, Miami, 1984—86; off. mgr. Citicorp NA, Miami, 1986—95; asst. pvt. banker Citibank Internat., Houston, 1995—97; wealth mgmt. adv. Merrill Lynch, Houston, 1997—. Pres., founder Kleidev Group, Spring, Tex., 2002—03. Adv. bd. mem. Houston Ebony Opera Guild, 2003—. Mem.: Nat. Assoc. Female Exe. Avocations: photography, reading, travel, theatre arts, bird watching. Office: Merrill Lynch 1221 McKinney Ste 3900 Houston TX 77010

SMITH, ANGELA LANTZ, psychiatrist, researcher; b. Christiansburg, Va., Mar. 20, 1955; d. Joseph David Lantz Jr. and Elaine Muntzing Lantz; m. Lance Christopher Smith, Nov. 24, 1979; children: Courtney, Natalie, Allison, Madeline. BA summa cum laude, Duke U., 1978; MD, Columbia U., 1990. Diplomate Am. Bd. Psychiatry. Resident St. Luke's Hosp., N.Y.C., 1990—92, Roosevelt Hosp, N.Y.C., 1996—98; fellow N.Y. U., Bellevue Hosp., N.Y.C., 1998—2000; attending psychiatrist, rsch. assoc. N.Y. U. Child Study Ctr., N.Y.C., 2000—; attending psychiatrist Harlem Hosp., N.Y.C., 2002—. Faculty Columbia U., 2002—; cons. psychiatrist Broadway Cmty. Inc., N.Y.C., 1993—, bd. dirs., 1999—; family therapy, cons. Bklyn. Children's. Contbr. articles to profl. jours., chapters to books Handbook of Affective Disorders, 1991. Bd. dirs. Kids Meeting Kids Can Make a Difference, N.Y.C., 1995—; pres. Manhattan Sch. for Children PTA, N.Y.C., 1995—97; co-founder Physicians for Social Responsibility, 1986; charter founder The Family Annex, N.Y.C., 1982. Grantee, Woodwond Found., 2000—. Mem.: Soc. Cmty. Psychiatry, Am. Psychiat. Assn., Am. Acad. Child & Adolescent Psychiatry. Avocations: running, skiing, piano, theater, travel. Home: 603 W 111th St #4E New York NY 10025 Office: NY Univ Child Study Ctr 550 1st Ave New York NY 10016 also: Harlem Hosp Med Ctr Dept Child Psychiatry K Bldg 5th Flr Lennox Ave & 135th St New York NY 10016 E-mail: Angela.Smith@med.nyu.edu.

SMITH, ANN DELORISE, municipal official; b. Union, S.C., June 26, 1941; 1 child. BS in Social Svc., Ea. Mich. U., 1962, postgrad., 1992-93. Planner III demonstration agy. City of L.A., 1970-75, sr. grants mgmt. specialist cmty. devel. dept., 1975-83, sr. mgmt. analyst I dept. aging, 1983-94, gen. mgr. dept. aging, 1994—. Del. White House Conf. on Aging, 1995; tchr. h.s. social studies, Flint and Ecors, Mich., 1962-63, grant cons., 1964-69, L.A./Detroit. Mem. adv. bd. Roybal Inst., Drew/RAND Ctr. on Health and Aging, KCET; mem. L.A. Urban League; mem. bd. dirs. Delta Sigma Theta HeadStart/State Presch.; involved in fed. grant programs including War on Poverty, 1960's. Mem. Am. Soc. on Aging, Nat. Ctr. and Caucus on Black Aging, Nat. Assn. of Area Agencies on Aging, Calif. Assn. of Area Agencies on Aging, Nat. Coun. on Aging, Gerontol. Soc. Am., Delta Sigma Theta. Home: 3803 S Dunsmuir Ave Los Angeles CA 90008-1016 Office: City of LA Dept Aging 2404 Wilshire Blvd Los Angeles CA 90057-3310

SMITH, ANN WHEELER, exercise specialist; b. Hinsdale, Ill., Sept. 18, 1927; d. Bradner Dundy Wheeler and Mary Isabel Trigg; m. L. Roger Smith, Nov. 4, 1950; children: Eric William, Rebecca Ann Smith Koladis, Susan Marie Smith Briggs. Student, Miami U., Oxford, Ohio, 1945—47, Jacob's Pillow Dance, Lee, Mass., 1950; master's cert., Am. U., 1998. Modern dance tchr. Rockland Country Day Sch., Congers, NY, 1962—69; dance exercise teacher Clarkstown Adult Edn., New City, NY, 1962—70; mktg./sales dr. Cornerstone Libr., N.Y.C., 1969—74; freelance writer/artist, stretch exercise specialist. Video prodr., performer Stretch Exercise with Ann Smith, 1997, Stretching for Seniors, 1997, Moving to Mozart, 1999, Moving with Grace and Pride, 2000, Rise and Shine, 2001; author: 5 books on stretch exercise, 1969—84. Mem.: Internat. Assn. Phys. Activity and Aging (cons., bd. mem. 1999—), Fifty+ Fitness Orgn. (amb. 1998—). Episc. Avocations: opera, art. Home and Office: 107 S West St # 326 Alexandria VA 22314

SMITH, ANNA DEAVERE, actress, educator, playwright; b. Balt., Sept. 18, 1950; d. Deavere Young and Anna (Young) S. BA, Beaver Coll., Pa., 1971, D hon., 1973; MFA, Am. Conservatory Theatre, 1977; D hon., U. N.C., 1995; hon. degree, Wheelock Coll., 1995, Colgate U., 1997, Sch. Visual Arts, 1997, Wesleyan U., 1997, Northwestern U., 1997, Coll. of the Holy Cross, 1997. Ann O'Day Maples prof. arts and drama Stanford U. Artist-in-residence Ford Found., 1997. Playwright, performer one-woman shows On the Road: A Search for American Character, 1983, Aye, Aye, Aye, I'm Integrated, 1984, Piano, 1991 (Drama-Logue award), Fires in the Mirror, 1989 (Obie award 1992, Drama Desk award 1992, N.Y. Drama Critics spl. citation 1993-94), Twilight: Los Angeles 1992 (Obie award, 2 Tony award nominations, Drama Critics Cir. spl. citation, Outer Critics Cir. award, Drama Desk award, Audelco award, Beverly Hills, Hollywood NAACP theatre awards), House Arrest, 1997; writer libretto for Judith Jamison, performer Hymn, 1993; appeared in (films) Dave, 1993, Philadelphia, 1993, The American President, 1995, Twilight: Los Angeles, 2000. Founding dir. The Inst. on Arts and Civic Dialogue Harvard U., 1998. Named One of Women of Yr., Glamour mag., 1993; fellow Bunting Inst., Radcliffe Coll.; genius fellow The MacArthur Found., 1996. Office: 1460 4th St Ste 212 Santa Monica CA 90401-3414 also: Stanford U Dept Drama Memorial Hall Stanford CA 94305

SMITH, ANNA NICOLE (VICKIE LYNN HOGAN), television personality, model; b. Mexia, Tex., Nov. 28, 1967; m. Billy Smith, 1985 (div. 1987); 1 child, Daniel; m. J. Howard Marshall II, Jun. 27, 1994 (dec.). Model for Guess? jeans. Spokesperson Trim Spa, 2003—. Appeared in films Naked Gun 33 1/3: The Final Insult, 1994, The Hudsucker Proxy, 1994; (TV series) The Anna Nicole Smith Show, 2002-; guest TV appearance, Ally McBeal; cover model Playboy, 1992 (Playmate of the Yr. 1993). Office: Alein Souliers 121 Madison Ave New York NY 10016-7033*

SMITH, ANNICK, writer; b. Paris, May 11, 1936; came to U.S., 1937; d. Stephen and Helene Deutch; m. David James Smith (dec. 1974); children: Eric, Stephen, Alex, Andrew. Student, Cornell Univ., 1954-55, U. Chgo., 1955-57; BA, U. Wash., 1961. Editor U. Wash. Press, Seattle, 1961-64, Montana Bus. Quarterly, U. Montana, Missoula, 1971-72; founding bd. mem. Sundance Film Inst., Sundance, Utah, 1981-85; founding mem. Ind. Film Project, N.Y.C., 1981-84; acting dir. Montana Com. for the Humanities, Missoula, 1983-84; devel. dir. Hellgate Writers, Inc., Missoula, 1986-96; creative dir. Yellow Bay Writers Workshop, U. Montana Continuing Edn. Dept, Missoula, 1987-98. Freelance filmmaker, producer, arts administrator, writer, Mont., 1974—; past H.S. tchr., cmty. organizer, environ. worker. Exec. prodr. Heartland, 1981; co-prodr. A River Runs Through It, 1992; co-editor: (with William Kittredge) The Last Best Place; author: Homestead, 1994, Big BlueStem A Journey into the Tall Grass, 1996, In This We Are Native, 2001; contbr. to anthologies including Best Am. Short Stories, 1992. Recipient Western Heritage award Cowboy Hall of Fame, 1981; Mont. Humanites award Mont. Com. for Humanities, 1988, Okla. Book award, 1997, Bancroft Prize Denver Pub. Libr., 1998. Mem. Trout Unlimited, Blackfoot Challenge. Democrat. Office: HC70 Box 173 Bonner MT 59823

SMITH, AUDREY LEE, psychologist, consultant; b. Columbus, Ohio, Aug. 14, 1970; d. Alphonse Lehman and Betty Carolyn Smith. BS in Psychology, Ohio State U., Columbus, 1992; PhD in Psychology, Wright State U., Dayton, Ohio, 1997. Lic. Psychologist Mo. Resident and day treatment therapist Niles Home for Children, Kansas City, Mo., 1997—2000; rsch. analyst Cmty. Movement for Urban Progress, Kansas City, 2000—01; cons. psychologist Samuel Roogus Home for Children, 2001—, Midtown Psychol. Svcs., Kansas City, Mo., 2000—. Advocate for alternative life-style rights; treas. Kansas City Pride Dem. Club, 2002. Mem.: Assn. Black Psychologists, Am. Psychol. Assn., Sisters Circle (founder, facilitator). Democrat. Avocations: reading, tennis, volleyball. Office: Midtown Psychol Svcs 3914 Washington Kansas City MO 64111

SMITH, BABS G. music educator; b. Welch, W.Va., Oct. 21, 1952; d. Richard David and Myra Phyllis (Wickham) Hamden; m. Chris Alan Ashcraft, Aug. 3, 1974 (div. Sept. 1983); 1 child, Rachel Ann ; m. Howard Lane Smith, June 8, 1985; children: Ricky, Joy 1 stepchild, Christina Dyane. AA in Secretarial Studies, Fairmont State Coll., 1972, BA in Music Edn., 1975; postgrad., W.Va. U., 1979—92. Sec. Consol. Gas Co., Clarksburg, W.Va., 1977—78; music tchr. Harrison County Bd. Edn., Clarksburg, 1978—, Bridgeport H.S., Clarksburg, 1978—86, South Harrison H.S. and Mid. Sch., Clarksburg, 1987—88, Shinnston Mid. Sch., Clarksburg, 1988—89, Gore Mid. Sch., Clarksburg, 1989—93, South Harrison H.S. and Mid. Sch., Clarksburg, 1993—. Choral dir. Stealey Assembly of God, Clarksburg, 1980—82, Faith Fellowship, Clarksburg, 1986—88, All-County Choirs, Clarksburg, 1994—, Trinity Assembly of God, Fairmont, W.Va., 1999—2001; vocal soloist various orgns., W.Va., 1977—; vocal soloist Wheeling (W.Va.) Symphony Orch., 1978, W.Va. U. Orch., 1978. Vol. in 5 prisons, W.Va. Recipient 1st Pl. award for South Harrison H.S. Show Choir, Kennywood Competition, 2001, Cedar Point Competition, 2003; Bridgeport H.S. choral group named State Honor Choir, 1986. Mem.: Am. Choral Dirs. Assn., Music Educators Nat. Conf. Republican. Avocation: boating. Office: South Harrison High Sch Rte 1 Box 58 Lost Creek WV 26385 Office Phone: 304-745-3315.

SMITH, BARBARA, food service executive, model; Owner B. Smith Restaurant Group; former model. Trustee Culinary Inst. Am. Host (TV series) B. Smith With Style, 2000—, appeared on Today Show, —, Good Morning America, —, CBS Morning, —, Oprah Winfrey, —, Extra, —; author: (novels) B. Smith's Entertaining and Cooking for Friends, 1995—, B. Smith's Rituals and Celebrations, 1999— (Best of the Best Book award, Food and Wine Mag., 1999). Mem.: Screen Actors Guild, Feminist Press (founding bd. mem.), NY Women's Found. (founding bd. mem.), Times Sq. Bus. Improvement Dist. (founding bd. mem.). Achievements include appeared in over 100 radio, print, and TV ads; First African Am. woman elected to bd. trustees Culinary Inst. Am. Mailing: 320 W 46th St New York NY 10036*

SMITH, BARBARA ANNE, health facility administrator, consultant; b. N.Y.C., Oct. 10, 1946; d. John Allen and Lelia Maria (De Silva) Santoro; m. Joseph Newton Smith, Feb. 5, 1966 (div. Sept. 1984); children: J. Michael, Robert Lawrence. Student, Oceanside/Carlsbad Coll. Real estate agt. Routh Robbins, Inc., Washington, 1973-75; gen. mgr. Mall Shops, Inc., Kansas City, Kans., 1975-80; regional mgr. FAO Schwarz, N.Y.C., 1980-84; clin. adminstr. North Denver Med. Ctr., Thornton, Colo., 1984-88; adminstrv. dir. Country Side Ambulatory Surgery Ctr., Leesburg, Va., 1989-91; pres. SCS Healthcare Mgmt. Inc., Washington, 1991—. Bd. dirs. Franz Carl Weber Internat., Geneva, 1982-84; mng. dir. Nat. Healthcare Consortium, 1997—; mng. assoc. Monarch Assocs. in Healthcare. Pres. Am. Women Chile, 1968; v.p. Oak Park Assn., Kansas City, 1977-78, pres., 1978-79; vol. Visitor Info. and Assn. Reception Ctr. program Smithsonian Instn., Washington. Mem. NAFE, Network Colo., Profl. Bus. Women Assn., Med. Group Mgmt. Assn., Federated Ambulatory Surgery Assn.

SMITH, BARBARA JEAN, lawyer; b. Washington, Jan. 9, 1947; d. Harry Wallace and Jean (Fraser) S.; m. Philip R. Chall, July 13, 1991; children: Brian C.S. Brown, Craig F.S. Brown, Amy E. Spiers, Carrie A. Chall. BA, Old Dominion Coll., 1968; MBA, Pepperdine U., 1974; JD, Case Western Res. U., 1977. Bar: Ohio 1977. Assoc. Squire, Sanders & Dempsey, Cleve., 1977-88, ptnr., 1988-93; shareholder McDonald, Hopkins, Burke & Haber Co., L.P.A., Cleve., 1993—. Bd. editors Health Law Jour. of Ohio, 1989-95; contbr. articles to health jours. and periodicals. Trustee Urban Community Sch., Cleve., 1984-86, Alzheimer's Assn. Greater Cleve., 2000—. Mem. Ohio Women's Bar Assn. (pres. 1994-95), Cleve. Bar Assn. (pres. 1998-99, trustee 1992-95, chair health law sect. 1991-92), Am. Health Lawyers Assn., Ohio State Bar Assn. (health law com. 1991—), Soc. Ohio Hosp. Attys. Democrat. Mem. United Ch. of Christ. Avocations: reading, hiking. Home: 416 Fairway Vw Chagrin Falls OH 44023-6718 Office: McDonald Hopkins Burke & Haber 2100 Bank One Ctr 600 Superior Ave E Cleveland OH 44114-2653 E-mail: bsmith@mhbh.com.

SMITH, BARBARA JEANNE, retired librarian; b. Jersey Shore, Pa., Apr. 14, 1939; d. Moyer Emmerson and Mary Kathryn (Ebner) S. BS in Edn. (Biology), Pa. State U., 1961, DEd in Higher Edn., 1981; MS in Edn. (English), SUNY, Oswego, N.Y., 1967; MLS, U. Pitts., 1970. Reference libr. Pa. State U. Librs., University Park, 1970-75, commonwealth campus coord., 1975-82, asst. dean librs., head commonwealth campus librs. divsn., 1982-89; dir. Smithsonian Instn. Librs., Washington, 1989-98. Gen. sci. tchr., Binghampton (N.Y.) City Schs., 1961-62; English tchr., North Syracuse (N.Y.) Ctrl. Schs., 1970-75; mem. Smithsonian Instn. Rsch. Info. Svc. (chair 1993-95), Planning Adv. Group, 1989-93; chair Internet Implementation Com., Smithsonian Instn. Libraries User Adv. Com., 1989-97; founding dir. Chesapeake Info. and Rsch. Libr. Alliance, 1996-98. Contbr. articles to profl. jours.; speaker in field. UCLA Grad. Sch. of Libr. and Info. Sci. Sr. fellow, 1982. Mem. AAUW, ALA (mem. coun. 1987-91), Cosmos Club (Washington), Centre County (Pa.) Hist. Soc. (life), U. Pitts. Alumni Assn. (bd. dirs. 1991-94), Ctr. Hills Country Club, Beta Phi Mu. E-mail: bsmith5598@pennswoods.net.

SMITH, BARBARA RUTHJENA DRUCKER, writer, educator; b. Newport News, Va., June 5, 1936; d. Abraham Louis and Loraine Blechman Drucker; children: Lisa Lorraine, Eric Drucker. BA in English, Speech and Journalism, Coll. William and Mary, 1964. Cert. hypnotherapist Ea. Va. Hypnotherapy Inst., 1999, Nat. Assn. Transpersonal Hypnotherapists, 2003. Freelance writer, Newport News, 1960—; pvt. practice hypnotherapy, 1999—; hypnotist Positive Changes Hypnosis Neurolinguistic Programming, Newport News, 2000—. Workshop leader various pub. schs., Newport News, 1976—; tchr. in English and remedial reading various schs., Newport News, 1966—; mem. adv. bd. Christopher Newport Writer's Conf., Newport News, 1989—2003. Author: Darling Loraine The Story of A. Louis Drucker A Grateful Jewish Immigrant, 2000 (Nominated Best Non-Fiction Book of 2000 award Libr. Va., 2001); contbr. Poet's Domain 4 Others, 1987—2000. Crisis teleph. worker Contact Peninsula, Newport News, 1981—; docent Mariner's Mus., Newport News, 1982—. Mem.: Nat. Assn. Transpersonal Hypnotherapists, Poetry Soc. Va., Tidewater Writers Assn., Va. Writers Club. Avocations: bicycling, taking care of woods, swimming, tai chi, piano. Home and Office: 120 Selden Road Newport News VA 23606

SMITH, BERT KRUGER, retired mental health services professional; b. Wichita Falls, Tex., Nov. 18, 1915; d. Sam and Fania (Feldman) Kruger; m. Sidney Stewart Smith, Jan. 19, 1936; children: Sheldon Stuart, Jared Burt (dec.), Randy Smith Huke. BJ, U. Mo., 1936; MA, U. Tex., 1949; DHL (hon.), U. Mo., 1985. Soc. and entertainment editor Wichita Falls Post, 1936-37; freelance writer Juneau, Alaska, 1937; assoc. pub. Coleman Daily Dem. Voice, 1950-51; assoc. editor Jr. Coll. Jour., Austin, Tex., 1952-55; spl. cons., exec. Hogg Found. for Mental Health, Austin, Tex., 1952—2001, ret. 2001. Founder, chmn. Austin Groups for the Elderly, 1985—; mem. ethics com. St. David's Hosp.; panelist Nat. Assn. Southwest Conf. Mental Health and Aging; instr. mental health info., special edn., gerontology U. Tex., Austin; mem. com.. Geriatric Rsch., Edn. Clin. Ctr. and Aging Rsch. and Edn. Ctr., U. Tex. Health Sci. Ctr., San Antonio. Author: No Language But A Cry, 1964, Your Non-Learning Child, 1968, A Teaspoon of Honey, 1970, Insights for Uptights, 1973, Aging in America, 1973, The Pursuit of Dignity, 1977, Looking Forward, 1983; contbr. numerous articles to profl. jours. Bert Kruger Smith professorship Sch. Social Work U. Tex., 1982; recipient Disting. Svc. award City of Austin, 1988, Cert. of Appreciation, Tex. Dept. Human Svcs., 1989, Ann Bert Smith award Sr.'s Respite Svc., 1989, S.W. Found. Founders' Spirit award, 1990, Tex. Leadership award Ann. Tex. Joint Conf. on Aging, 1992, Tex. Leadership award Tex. Dept. on Aging, 1992, Tex. Long-Term Care Vol. award, Women in Comm. Lifetime Achievement award, Mental Health Assn. Cmty. Svc. award, Internat. Tng. in Comm. Founder's Day Woman of Yr. award, Most Worthy Citizen award, Golden Rule award Memento, J.C. Penney, Inc., Disting. Svc. award City of Austin, Amazing Aging award Jewish Family Svcs., U. Tex. Sch. Social Work Founder's award Holt House, 1998; named Woman of Distinction, Girl Scouts U.S., 2002, named to Tex. Women's Hall of Fame, 1988. Mem. Conf. Southwest Founds. (founder's spirit award, archives, film, & video com.), Adult Svcs. Coun. and Family Eldercare (bd. dirs.), Found. Religious Studies Tex. (bd. trustees), Timely Solutions (adv. bd.). Jewish. Avocations: walking, reading. Home: 5818 Westslope Dr Austin TX 78731-3633 Fax: 512-453-8400.

SMITH, BETHANY RAE, accountant; b. Middletown, N.Y., Jan. 4, 1972; d. Walter Vincent Poharski and Linda Joy Diffendale Ovitt. BS in Acctg., SUNY, Plattsburgh, 1993. Svc. ctr. assoc. Hannaford Bros., Amsterdam, NY, 1988-90, bookkeeper Plattsburgh, NY, 1990-93, bookkeeper, asst. office mgr. Troy, NY, 1994—; bus. assurance assoc. Coopers & Lybrand L.L.P., Albany, 1994—97, Price Waterhouse Coopers, LLP, Albany, 1997—. Recipient N.Y. State Soc. CPAs award, 1993. Democrat. Episcopalian. Avocations: skiing, reading, boating, movies, physical fitness. Home: 1718 Crawford Rd Schenectady NY 12306-7317 Office: Price Waterhouse Coopers LLP 80 State St Albany NY 12207-2544

SMITH, BETTY, writer, nonprofit foundation executive; b. Bonham, Tex., Sept. 16; d. Sim and Gertrude (Dearing) S. Student, Stephens Coll.; BJ, U. Tex. Women's editor Daily Texan; pres. Hope Assocs. Corp., N.Y.C.; pres., owner Betty Smith Assocs., N.Y.C. Author: A Matter of Heart, 1969. Bd. dirs. Melchior Heldentenor Found., N.Y.C., 1968—, pres., 1987-97; pres., CEO Gerda Lissner Found., 1994—; v.p. Herman Lissner Found., 1990—. Mem. Author's Guild. Home: 322 E 55th St New York NY 10022-4157 Office: care Lissner Found 135 E 55th St 8th Fl New York NY 10022-4049 Office Phone: 212-826-6100.

SMITH, BETTY DENNY, county official, administrator, fashion executive; b. Centralia, Ill., Nov. 12, 1932; d. Otto and Ferne Elizabeth (Beier) Hasenfuss; m. Peter S. Smith, Dec. 5, 1964; children: Carla Kip, Bruce Kimball. Student, U. Ill., 1950-52; student, L.A. City Coll., 1953-57, UCLA, 1965, U. San Francisco, 1982-84. Freelance fashion coordinator, L.A., N.Y.C., 1953-58; tchr. fashion Rita LeRoy Internat. Studios, 1959-60; mgr. Mo Nadler Fashion, L.A., 1961-64; showroom dir. Jean of Calif. Fashions, L.A., 1965—. Freelance polit. book reviewer for community newspapers, 1961-62; staff writer Valley Citizen News, 1963. Bd. dirs. Pet Assistance Found., 1969-76; founder, pres., dir. Vol. Services to Animals L.A., 1972-76; mem. County Com. To Discuss Animals in Rsch., 1973-74; mem. blue ribbon com. on animal control L.A. County, 1973-74; dir. L.A. County Animal Care and Control, 1976-82; mem. Calif. Animal Health Technician Exam. Com., 1975-82, chmn., 1979; bd. dirs. L.A. Soc. for Prevention Cruelty to Animals, 1984-94, Calif. Coun. Companion Animal Advocates, 1993-97; dir. West Coast Regional Office, Am. Humane Assn., 1988-97; CFO Coalition for Pet Population Control, 1987-92; trustee Gladys W. Sargent Found., 1997—, Coalition to End Pet Overpopulation, 1998—; cons. Jungle Book II, Disney Studios, 1997; mem. Coalition to Protect Calif. Wildlife, 1996-97, Spl. Commn. Spay/Neuter City L.A., 1998-99; adv. com. La. Dept. of Animal Reg. 2000; mem. Calif. Rep. Cen. Com., 1964-72, mem. exec. com., 1971-73; mem. L.A. County Rep. Cen. Com., 1964-70, mem. exec. com., 1966-70; chmn. 29th Congl. Cen. Com., 1969-70; sec. 28th Senatorial Cen. Com., 1967-68, Dept. Animal Reg., 2000-, Calif. Dept. Fish & Games Animal Care Advisory Com., 2003-; mem. speakers bur. George Murphy for U.S. Senate, 1970; campaign mgr. Los Angeles County for Spencer Williams for Atty. Gen., 1966; mem. adv. com. Moorpark Coll., 1988-97; mem. adv. bd. Wishbone Prodn., 1995-97, Dept. of animal Reg., 2003; mem. L.A. County Art Mus., Calif. Dept. of Fish & Games Animal Care Adv. Com., Calif. Rep Ctr., L.A. Libr. Assn. Mem. Internat. Platform Assn., Mannequins Assn. (bd. dirs. 1967-68), Motion Picture and TV Industry Assn. (govt. rels. and pub. affairs com. 1992-97), Lawyer's Wives San Gabriel Valley (bd. dirs. 1971-74, pres. 1972-73), L.A. Athletic Club, Town Hall. Home: 1766 Bluffhill Dr Monterey Park CA 91754-4533

SMITH, BETTY GENE, physical education educator; b. Pitts., Tex., July 17, 1947; d. Billy Gene and Betty Louise (Blakestead) S. BS, Okla. State U., 1969. Camp counselor, program dir. YWCA camp, Va. Beach; instr. physical edn. Tulsa Pub. Schs., 1969—. Bldg. coord. Tulsa Run, Tulsa Pub. Schs., Am. Heart Assn.; chair Sports Days in track and field, volleyball, gymnastics, synchronized swimming, cross country and fitness pentathlon Tulsa Pub. Schs., also coach; mem. Save our Schs. com. Tulsa Pub. Schs.; workshop presenter Tulsa Pub. Schs. Co-author handbooks, ednl. guides; photographer, editor videos. Coach basketball, track, volleyball Okla. Spl. Olympics; summer camp Tulsa Assn. Retarded; physical edn. coord. Autistic summer camp; swim instr. ARC; presentor Tulsa Great Expectations summer camp; worker Doenges Bros. Triathlon; coach in-sch. bowling program Am. Bowling Alliance; league and divsn. coord. Tulsa Women's Amateur Softball Assn. Recipient Cert. of Excellence Tulsa Bd. Edn., 1992, 93, Middle Sch. Physical Edn. Tchr. of the Yr. Nat. Assn. for Sport and Physical Edn., 1993. Mem. NEA, Okla. Edn. Assn. (Instrnl. Excellence in Edn. award 1993), PTA, Am. Alliance for Health, Physical Edn., Recreation and Dance, Okla. Alliance Health, Physical Edn., Recreation and Dance (Educator of Yr. 1992, legis. fitness day, conv. arrangements com., program presenter), So. Dist. Am. Alliance Health, Recreation and Dance (Middle Sch. Educator of Yr. 1992, Middle Sch. Physical Educator of Yr. 1993, gen. arrangements com.), Tulsa Classroom Tchrs. Assn. (bldg. del./alternate, re-write com. drug policy, chair middle sch. com.), Nat. Assn. Sport and Physical Edn., N.Am. Fisherman's Assn. Avocations: fly fishing, wood working, creative writing. Home: 9061 E 33rd St Tulsa OK 74145-1617 Office: Whitney Middle Sch 2177 S 67th East Ave Tulsa OK 74129-2007

SMITH, BETTY MALLETT, philosopher, educator; b. Tulsa, Dec. 4, 1924; d. James L. and Eula (Gravitt) Mallett; m. Myron Chawner Smith, Aug. 28, 1948; children: Marston, Shelley, Shonti. BA, William Jewell Coll., 1947; MA, Brown U., 1949. Instr. philosophy Baylor U., Waco, Tex., 1950-51, Santa Monica (Calif) Coll., 1968-69; lectr. philosophy Mt. St. Mary's Coll., L.A., 1963-64, 66-67, Calif. Luth. U., Thousand Oaks, 1969-73; instr. C.G. Jung Inst., L.A., 1974—. Founder, dir. Poiesis, Malibu, Calif., 1966-; lectr.-dir. mythology tours to Greece, 1973-1996; lectr. in field. Author: (book on audio casette) Loved by a God, 1997. Mem. LWV. Marston scholar Brown U., 1947-48. Mem. AAUW, assoc. mem. C.G. Jung Inst. L.A. Democrat. Mem. Soc. Of Friends. Avocation: poetry and story writing.

SMITH, BETTY PAULINE, television producer; b. Benton, Ill., Nov. 27, 1926; d. Roy Herman and Goldie Ada (Rodgers) Keen; m. Richard Caldwell Smith, Jan. 11, 1946; children: Constance Raelene, Elana Gayle, Jill Christina. AA in Mgmt., U. Nev., 1982; cert., Ikenbo Sch. Floral Art, 1985; student, Hawaii Pacific U., 1994. Lic. real estate broker, Nev.; cert. real estate salesperson, Hawaii. TV producer Old Plantation Prodns., Inc. Active Coalition of Women-Legis., Domestic Violence Divsn., State of Hawaii, 1994-96; pres. NaKupuna U. Hawaii, 1999. Exec. prodr. Hawaiin Music, 1985; prodr. (TV) The Open Door, 1992, 95, 96, Health Issues: Issues for Women over 55 Years Old, 1992, Honolulu Police Dept., 1995, There's No Excuse for Abuse, 1995, Gang Violence in the Schools, 1995, Women Against Violence, 1996; poem carried by 2002 Olympic Torchbearers who were firefighters at World Trade Center, Sept. 11, 2001; contbr. poetry to lit. books, also on Poetry.com. Recipient Comm. Svc. award Aloha State Assn. of the Deaf, 1993, scholarship Americorps, 1996, cert. Hope Domestic Violence Counselor, 1996, Oahu Unsung Angel award, 1998, Internat. Poet merit Internat. Soc. Poets, 1999, Mayor's Proclomation award City of Honolulu, 1999, seal City and County Honolulu, 1999, Pres. award Nat. Authors Registry, 1999, Powers of Expression Through Poetry commendation Gov. of Hawaii, 2000 Prometheus Trophy award The Famous Soc. Poets, 2000; named Poet of Merit The Famous Soc. Poets, 2000, Muse of Fire, 2000, Internat. Poet of Merit Internat. Soc. Poets, 2002, Poet Laureate, 2003. Mem. Ind. TV Producers Assn., Hometown Media Alliance TV Producers, Elks, LWV, OES, Mason/White Shrine of Jerusalem, Toastmasters (Hall of Fame), others. Avocations: swimming, bicycling, walking, kayaking, hawaiian music.

SMITH, BETTY W. librarian; b. Lincoln, Nebr., June 29, 1919; d. Clem and Edith Margaret (Stanley) Wilder; m. Dulaney Dale Smith, Mar. 20, 1946; children: Douglas D., Diane E., Richard W. BA, Wayne U., 1940; BS, U. Minn., 1941; MA, Mich. State U., 1955. Cert. libr. Br. libr. Pub. Libr., Park Ridge, Ill., 1941-42, reference libr. Dearborn, Mich., 1942-44; U.S.C.G. SPAR, libr. asst. U.S.C.G. Acad., New London, Conn., 1945-46; reference libr. Libr. Hawaii, Honolulu, 1946-47; libr. Hawaiian Econ. Found., Honolulu, 1947-49; reference libr. Lansing Pub. Libr., Mich., 1967-86, substitute libr., 1986-98. Mem. Citizens for Actions in Mental Health, 1980—86; steering com. Long-Range Planning Mich. Dept. Mental Health, 1986—90; bd. dirs. Tri-Co. Cmty. Mental Health, Lansing, 1992—98; founding and exec. com. mem. Alliance for Mentally Ill, Mich., 1985—2003, now v.p.; adv. coun. Mich. Forensic Ctr., 1988—, Lafayette Clinic, Detroit, 1986—92. Mem. LWV, Mental Health Assn., Mich. Assn. Emotionally Disturbed Children (bd. dirs. 1963-68), Mich. Mental Health (adv. coun. 1986-90), Phi Alpha Theta. Home: 1782 Eifert Rd Holt MI 48842-1976

SMITH, BEULAH MAE, music educator; b. Okmulgee, Okla., Aug. 14, 1920; d. Willie Arthur Geller and Pearl Oretha Miears; m. Jodie C. Smith, May 16, 1943; 1 child, Joni Smith Levinson. BA in Music Edn., Ctrl. State U., 1942; MA in Music Edn., Okla. U., 1948. Cert. piano specialist. H.S. music tchr., Lindsay, Okla., Newkirk, Okla.; jr. high music tchr. Guthrie, Okla.; H.S. music tchr. Purcell, Okla.; elem. music tchr. Norman, Okla.; tchr. North Ea. U., Tahlequah, Okla.; jr. high music tchr. Hobbs, N.Mex.; piano specialist Norman. Piano cons. Warner (Okla.) State Coll., 1980. Recipient Cert. of Achievement, Howell-Aretta Conservatory Music, 1955; Beulah Mae Smith Day named in honor Town of Hobbs, 1978. Democrat. Methodist. Avocations: traveling, fishing, musicals, interior decorating. Home: 2007 Creighton Dr Norman OK 73071-7338

SMITH, BEVERLY HARRIETT, elementary school educator; b. Cleve. d. William Nathaniel and Tommie Lee (Hooks) Stovall; m. Levi Smith, July 3, 1970; children: Kimberly Varese, Tommy Levi. BA in Edn., Ky. State U., 1970; MA in Curriculum and Instrn., Cleve. State U., 1975. Guidance liaison Almira Elem. Sch., Cleve., 1986—2002, drug liaison, 1988—2002, sci. lead tchr., 1993—2002; bldg. chairperson Cleve. Tchr. Union, 1990—2002, exec. bd. dirs., 1996—2002, chair salary and benefits, 1996—2002. Supt. tchr. for practicum tchrs., 1989-2000, supt tchr. for student tchrs., 1990-2001. Fin. sec. Shiloh Bapt. Ch. Ednl. Bd., Cleve., 1984-86. Recipient career edn. grant, 1989-90, Sunshine Energy award East Ohio Gas Co., 1984-85, 1988-89; named Educator of Yr., 1995; Martha Holden Jennings scholar, 1997. Mem. ASCD. Avocations: reading, arts and crafts, travel. Office: Almira Elem Sch 3380 W 98th St Cleveland OH 44102-4639

SMITH, CANDA BANKS, educational consultant; b. Suffolk, Va., Oct. 17, 1929; d. John Thomas Banks and Edla Ruth Eure; m. Robert Luther Smith, Aug. 18, 1951; children: Kimberley Smith Kidd, Valerie Smith Eudy, Alexandra Eure. AA, Anderson (S.C.) Coll., 1946; BA, Coll. Notre Dame, Balt., 1991, MA, 1995. Tchr. presch., 1980-95; treas. Interface Resources, Ltd., Alexandria, Va., 1985—. Ednl. cons., 1995—. Active vol. profl. and community orgns; mem. exec. bd. dirs. Alexandria Early Childhood Commn., 1996-2000; pub. chmn. Inova Alexandria Hosp. Aux., 1997, 98, pres., 1998, 99, mem. Inova Alexandria Found. bd. trustees, 1999-, sect., 2002, bd. lady mgrs., 2001-, recording sect. 2002-, 1872 hosp. bd.; area chmn. Am. Heart Assn., 1975-2000; vol. Ptnrs. in Edn., 1998-2002. Mem. DAR (state judge essay contest 1997-2002), Alexandria Kiwanianne Club (v.p. 1998). Home: 1102 Bayliss Dr Alexandria VA 22302-3506

SMITH, CARLA ANNE, music educator; b. Albany, N.Y., Feb. 1, 1955; d. William Anthony and Florence Emma Africano; m. Gil Raymond Smith, Aug. 18, 1974; children: Alycia Erin(dec.), Turner Anthony. Student Ithaca (N.Y.) Coll., 1973—74; student, Potsdam (N.Y.) State U., 1974—75; BS magna cum laude, Pa. State U., 1977, MEd, 1983; postgrad., Ea. Ky. U., 2001—. Music tchr. Park Forest Jr. H.S., State College, Pa., 1978; chorus and music tchr. Bellefonte Mid. Sch., Pa., 1978—82; piano tchr. Muncie, Ind., 1985—95; choir dir. United Meth. Ch., Cammack, Ind., 1986—95; elem. music tchr. Model Lab Sch., Richmond, Ky., 1997—98; piano/oboe tchr. Richmond, Ky., 1985—; band dir., music tchr. Madison Bd. of Edn., Richmond, Ky., 1998—. Accompanist Madison Bd. Edn., Richmond, 1996—; keyboardist St. Mark's Ch., Richmond, 1995—. Mem. Friend of the Fine Arts, Richmond, 1996—; sch. counselor 4H Talent Show Club, Richmond, 2000—; founding mem. Wall of Tolerance, 2003. Recipient Arts in Edn. award, Richmond Area Arts Coun., 1999, Achievement award, Muncie Matinee Musicals, 1995, Vivian Conley award, AAUW, 1994, Madison County Internat. Artist Exch. Japan, 2003; grantee Fine Arts Mini grantee, Madison Bd. Edn., 1998—2001. Mem.: NEA, Ky. Edn. Assn., Ky. Fedn. of Music Clubs (jr. counselor 1996—), Ky. Music Educators Assn., Madison Music Makers Club (founder, counselor 1996—), Cecilian Music Club (jr. counselor 1996—), Mortar Bd., Phi Kappa Phi. Avocations: attending art galleries, reading. Home: 1104 Valley Run Dr Richmond KY 40475 Office: Clark-Moores Middle Sch 1143 Berea Rd Richmond KY 40475

SMITH, CAROL ANN, academic administrator; b. Waterbury, Conn., Dec. 22, 1941; d. Prosper Mark and Emma Edna (Dumschott) Zailskas; m. Gordon B. Jobe; children from previous marriage: Amy, Christian, Meghan. BSN, Boston Coll., 1965; MSN, Boston U., 1971, PhD in Adminstrn., 1977. Chmn. grad. nursing dept. Boston Coll. Sch. Nursing, 1973—78; coord. Harvard Med. Sch. program Boston Coll., 1975—78; dir. baccalaureate nursing program Coll. of Our Lady of Elms, 1978—80; dean sch. nursing Duquesne U., 1980—83, acting acad. v.p., 1983—85; vis. v.p. for acad. affairs Carnegie-Mellon U., 1985—86; acad. v.p. Marshall U., Huntington, W.Va., 1985—89; pres. Mater Dei Coll., Ogdensburg, NY, 1989—. Field reader US Dept. Edn., 1990—91. Exec. com. Sisters of St. Joseph Consortium, 1990—; bd. dirs. Commn. Ind. Colls. and Univs., 1990—, Boys and Girls Club, A. Barton Hepburn Hosp. Found. Mem.: LWV, St. Lawrence C. of C. (bd. dirs.), Boston Coll. Club, Rotary, Delta Gamma Kappa, Phi Delta Kappa, Sigma Theta Tau, Delta Kappa Gamma. Roman Catholic. Office: Mater Dei Coll Riverside Dr Ogdensburg NY 13669

SMITH, CAROL E. judge; b. Balt., July 30, 1946; 1 child, Ellen Elizabeth. BA, Coll. Notre Dame Md., 1970; JD, Cath. U. Am., 1975. Staff atty. domestic law unit, staff atty. and chief atty. housing law unit, chief atty. mental health law project Legal Aid Bur. Inc., 1975—80; with Matricciani & Smith, 1980—83; pvt. practice., 1983—85; assoc. judge Dist. Ct. Md., 1984—93, Cir. Ct. Balt. City, 1993—. Trustee Bryn Mawr Sch., 1997—; mem. adv. bd. Mercy Med. Ctr., Women's Ctr. for Health and Medicine, 1993—96, Girl Scouts Beyond Bars, 1993—97; coach Balt. City Dept. of Recreation and Parks, North Harford Recreation Ctr. Basketball Program, 1992—93. Recipient Bd. Dirs. award, Girl Scouts of Cen. Md., 1994. Mem.: Nat. Assn. Women Judges (pres. Md. chpt. 1993—95, chair women in prison task force 1995—97). Office: 111 N Calvert St Baltimore MD 21202

SMITH, CAROL ESTES, retired councilman; b. Phoenix, Nov. 13, 1934; d. John William and Kathleen (Poynter) Estes; m. David Liles Smith, Jan. 8, 1954 (div. Oct. 1981); children: Kelly Liles, Kevin Estes, Kathleen Marie. BS in Edn., Tex. Christian U., 1957. Ptnr. Waste Control Ariz., N.Mex., Tex., various, 1964-81; mem. city coun. City of Tempe, Ariz., 1986-98; ret., 1998. Bd. dirs., pres. S.W. Ctr. Edn. and Environment, Tempe, 1988—, Papago/Salado Assocs., Tempe, 1990—. Bd. dirs., chmn. Ariz. Recycling Bd., Phoenix, 1991—96; Tempe Gov.'s past pres. Named Jr. Advisor of the Yr., 1984, Woman of Distinction, Tempe St. Lukes Aux., 1985, Carol Estes Smith Grove in her honor, 1999; recipient Silver medallion, Boys and Girls Clubs Am., 1991, Spirit of Tempe award, 2002. Mem.: Rotary, Zonta East Valley (pres. 1998—2000, Don Carlos Humanitarian award 1999). Republican. Presbyterian. Avocations: reading, theater. Home: 2169 E Alameda Dr Tempe AZ 85282

SMITH, CAROLE DIANNE, retired lawyer, editor, writer, product developer; b. Seattle, June 12, 1945; d. Glaude Francis and Elaine Claire (Finkenstein) S.; m. Stephen Bruce Presser, June 18, 1968 (div. June 1987); children: David Carter, Elisabeth Catherine. AB cum laude, Harvard U., Radcliffe Coll., 1968; JD, Georgetown U., 1974. Bar: Pa. 1974. Law clk. Hon. Judith Jamison, Phila., 1974—75; assoc. Gratz, Tate, Spiegel, Ervin & Ruthrouff, Phila., 1975—76; freelance editor, writer Evanston, Ill., 1983—87; editor Ill. Inst. Tech., Chgo., 1987—88; mng. editor LawLetters, Inc., Chgo., 1988—89; editor ABA, Chgo., 1989—95; product devel. dir. Gt. Lakes divsn. Lawyers Coop. Pub., Deerfield, Ill., 1995—96; product devel. mgr. Midwest Market Ctr. West Group, Deerfield, Ill., 1996—97; mgr acquisitions, bus. and fin. group CCH, Inc., Riverwoods, Ill., 1997—2002; ret. Author Jour. of Legal Medicine, 1975, Selling and the Law: Advertising and Promotion, 1987; (under pseudonym Sarah Toast) 79 children's books and stories, 1994-2002; editor The Brief, 1990-95, Criminal Justice, 1989-90, 92-95 (Gen. Excellence award Soc. Nat. Assn. Pubs. 1990, Feature Article award-bronze Soc. Nat. Assn. Pubs. 1994), Franchise Law Jour., 1995; mem. editl. bd. The Brief, 1995-2000. Dir. Radcliffe Club of Chgo., 1990-93; mem. parents coun. Latin Sch. Chgo., 1995-96; trustee Winnetka-Northfield Libr., 2003 , mem. Winnetka Plan Commn.2003—. Mem. ABA (editl. bd., tort trial and ins. practice sect. 1995-2000, mem. publs. editl. bd., 2002—).

SMITH, CECE, venture capitalist; b. Washington, Nov. 16, 1944; d. Linn Charles and Grace Inez (Walker) S.; m. John Ford Lacy, Apr. 22, 1978. BBA, U. Mich., 1966; MA, So. Meth. U., 1974. CPA, Tex. Staff acct. Arthur Young & Co. (CPAs), Boston, 1966-68; staff acct., then asst. to contr. Wyly Corp., Dallas, 1969-72; contr., treas. subs. Univ. Computing Co., Dallas, 1972-74; contr. Steak and Ale Restaurants Am., Inc., Dallas, 1974-76, v.p. fin., 1976-80, exec. v.p., 1980-81, Pearle Health Services, Inc., 1981-84, pres. Primacare divsn., 1984-86; gen. ptnr. Phillips-Smith-Machens Venture Ptnrs., 1986—; pres. Le Sportsac Dallas, Inc., 1981-87. Bd. dirs. Brinker Internat. Inc., Michaels Stores, Inc., Beautyco, Inc.; chmn. Fed. Res. Bank Dallas, 1994—96; past v.p., dir. IWF-Dallas. Former co-chmn. pres.'s rsch. coun. U. Tex. S.W. Med. Ctr. Dallas; former mem. vis. com. U. Mich. Bus. Sch.; exec. bd. So. Meth. U. Cox Sch. Bus.; former v.p., bd. dirs. Jr. Achievement Dallas; past pres. Charter 100; past treas. Dallas Assembly. Mem.: Com. of 200. Home: 3710 Shenandoah St Dallas TX 75205-2121 Office: 5080 Spectrum Dr Ste 805 W Addison TX 75001-4648 Business E-Mail: cece@phillips-smith.com.

SMITH, CECILIA MAY, hospital official; b. Oakland, Calif., Feb. 18, 1933; d. Frederick Arthur and Inez Calista Small; m. Harold Joseph Smith, June 17, 1957 (dec. June 18, 1966); children: Harold Frederick, Estelle Marie. BS, Holy Name Coll., 1956; MS, U. Calif., San Francisco, 1966; postgrad., U. Calif., Berkeley, 1972. RN Calif. Asst. prof. U. Nev., Reno, 1966-69; instr. U. Wash., Seattle, 1972-74; dir. continuing edn. Wash. State Nurses Assn., Seattle, 1974-78; pres., ptnr. World of Continuing Edn., Seattle, 1975-85; continuing edn. specialist U. Calif., San Francisco, 1979-82; asst. adminstr. Cordilleras Mental Health Ctr., Redwood City, Calif., 1984-86, adminstr., 1986-90; dir. psychiat. svcs. St. Luke's Hosp., San Francisco, 1990—. Mem. ANA Nat. Accreditation Bd., Kansas City, 1974-7; sec., workshop leader Nat. Staffing Systems, San Francisco, 1981-82; cons. WHO, New Delhi, 1985. Editor ind. study courses for nurses and nursing home adminstrs., 1975-85; author AIDS ind. study courses, 1984; contbr. articles to Jour. of Continuing Edn. Recipient Marie Durocher scholarship Coll. of Holy Name, 1952, NIMH traineeship U. Calif. San Francisco, 1963, Nursing Rsch. fellowship U. Calif. Berkeley, 1969-71. Mem.: Sigma Theta Tau. Office: St Luke's Hosp 3555 Cesar Chavez San Francisco CA 94110-4403 E-mail: ceciliams33@hotmail.com.

SMITH, CHARLOTTE REED, retired music educator; b. Eubank, Ky., Sept. 15, 1921; d. Joseph Lumpkin and Cornelia Elizabeth (Spenser) Reed;

m. Walter Lindsay Smith, Aug. 24, 1949; children— Walter Lindsay IV, Elizabeth Reed. B.A. in Music, Tift Coll., 1941; M.A. in Mus. Theory, Eastman Sch. of Music, 1946; postgrad. Juilliard Sch., 1949. Asst. prof. theory Okla. Bapt. U., 1944-45, Washburn U., 1946-48; prof. music Furman U., Greenville, S.C., 1948-92, chmn. dept. music 1987-92. Editor: Seven Penitential Psalms with Two Laudate Psalms, 1983; author: Manual of Sixteenth-Century Contrapuntal Style, 1989. Mem. Internat. Musicological Soc., Am. Musicological Soc., Soc. for Music Theory, AAUP (sec.-treas. Furman chpt. 1984-85), Nat. Fedn. Music Clubs, Pi Kappa Lambda. Republican. Baptist.

SMITH, CHERYL DIANE, music educator; b. Princeton, Ind., Jan. 17, 1952; d. Ralph Eugene and Beulah J. Smith. BA, Oakland City U., 1974; MS, Ind. State U., 1980. Substitute tchr. North Gibson Sch. Corp., Princeton, Ind., 1974—77, South Gibson Sch. Corp., Ft. Branch, 1974—77; tchr. choral, gen. music South Knox Sch. Corp., Vincennes, 1977, North Knox Sch. Corp., Birknell, 1977—. Co-author: Introduction to Theater, 1999. Mem. exec. com. North Knox Social Mins., 1997—. Mem.: Choral Dirs. Nat. Assn., Nat. Music Educators Assn. Avocations: cross stitch, piano, reading.

SMITH, CHERYL T. pharmaceutical executive, public relations executive; BA, MA, Pa. State U. Systems analyst U.S. Ho. of Reps., Washington, 1975—78; various positions Ernst & Young, Honeywell, Verizon, 1978—85; chief info. officer Keyspan Techs., N.Y.C., 1985—2002; sr. v.p., chief info. officer McKesson Corp., San Francisco, 2002—. Office: McKesson Corp Hdqtrs One Post St San Francisco CA 94104

SMITH, CLAIRE, chef; Grad., Calif. Culinary Acad., San Francisco; grad. in art and art history, Rice U. Chef Green, Oliveto, San Francisco Bay area, The Daily Review Cafe, Houston, 1994—. Office: 3412 W Lamar Houston TX 77019

SMITH, CLAIRE LAREMONT, language educator; b. Panama City, Panama, Dec. 30, 1939; came to U.S., 1965; d. Sebastian Hamlet and Ambrozine Beatriz (Simon) Laremont; m. Stephen E. Greaves, Nov. 29, 1961 (div. 1968); children: Liza N. Greaves Smith, Katia T. Laremont Smith; m. James Elliott Smith, Dec. 20, 1969; 1 child, Raquel J. Student, U. Panama, Panama City, 1959-62; BA, SUNY, Fredonia, 1968, MS, 1970; postgrad., SUNY, Buffalo, 1983-93. Cert. tchr. secondary social studies, elem. bilingual edn., secondary Spanish and ESL, N.Y. Bilingual stenographer, bookkeeper, cashier Foto Internat., Panama City, 1960-65; tchr. secondary social studies and Spanish Forestville (N.Y.) Cen. Schs., 1968-69; grad. asst. dept. history SUNY, Fredonia, 1969-70; substitute tchr. Am. Overseas Schs. of Army Dependents, Camp Livorno, Italy, 1983-95; tchr. early childhood bilingual Dunkirk (N.Y.) Migrant Daycare Ctr., 1972-73; tchr., home instr. Head Start program Durkirk Schs., 1973-74; tchr. adult basic edn. N.Y. State Migrant Workers Opportunities, Dunkirk, 1977-80; tchr. social studies, bilingual, Spanish and ESL Dunkirk Mid. Sch., 1973-98; adj. instr. ESL SUNY, Fredonia, 1992, 93. Mem. affirmative action com. on cultural ethnic rels. SUNY, Fredonia, 1989-98; mem. com. on discipline Dunkirk Sch. Dist., 1991-98, compact learning com., 1993-98, Youth Empowerment System, wellness com.; mem. sch. improvement team Dunkirk Med. Sch., 1991-92; presenter profl. confs., U.S., Mex.; guest speaker Hispanic Heritage Week Celebration, N.Y. State Migrant Daycare, Fredonia, 1991. Bd. dirs. North County Counseling Svc., Dunkirk, 1992-96, People's Action Coaliton, Dunkirk, 1992-95, v.p., 1993-94, 95—; chairperson cultural awareness task force Dunkirk Cmty. Challenge, 1993-95; bd. dirs. Chautauqua County Connections, 1993-96, First Night Internat. Alliance, Boston, 1994-99; chair First Night Dunkirk, 1994-96, exec. dir., 1996-97; harborfest com. City of Dunkirk, 1992-96; vol. ARC fundraiser, 1995; founder, advisor Dunkirk H.S. ASPIRA Leadership Club, 1994-98, Dunkirk Schs. Step and Drill Team, 1994-97; N.Y. State advisor, trainer Hispanic Youth Leadership Inst. Conf., Albany, 1994-98. Named Person of Yr., Dunkirk Kiwanis, 1995; recipient Cmty. Svc. award N.Y. State Senator Jess Present, 1997. Mem. AAUW, NAAPC (edn. com. 1976), N.Y. State Assn. Bilingual Educators, Tchrs. of English to Speakers of Other Langs., Nat. Assn. Bilingual Edn., Dunkirk Tchrs. Assn. (bilingual scholarship fund, annual dinner awards program, 1979-92, active voter registration drive 1992), N.Y. State United Tchrs., SUNY Buffalo Grad. Student Assn. (senator 1990-92, co-pres. dept. learning and instrn. 1991-92), Phi Delta Kappa (SUNY Buffalo chpt.). Democrat. Roman Catholic. Avocations: jogging, reading, travel. Office: SUNY Coll Fredonia Dept Edn Fredonia NY 14048-1328 Home: 53 Berkley Pl Buffalo NY 14209-1001

SMITH, D(AISY) MULLETT, publisher; b. Washington, Aug. 17, 1948; d. Gordon Hunt and Suzanne Myrick (Mullett) Smith. BA, Am. U., 1970; cert. computer programming, U. So. Calif., Arlington, Va., 1986; cert. in records mgmt., Assn. Records Mgrs. Am., Prairie Village, Kans., 1987. Christian Sci. practitioner The First Ch. of Christ, Scientist, Boston, 1970-86; clk. Fifth Ch. of Christ, Scientist, Washington, 1971-74; Christian Sci. campus counsellor The Am. U., Washington, 1976-81; editor, computer specialist, desktop pub. Mullett-Smith Press, Washington, 1984-89, owner, pub., author, 1989—, music copyist, pub. on computer, 1990—, web weaver, 1996—. Computer cons. and pub. spkr. in field; guest participant divsn. children in trouble White House Conf. on Children, 1970. Author, editor, pub.: AB Mullett, His Relevance in American Architecture, 1990 (Printers award 1990); editor: AB Mullett, Architect Engineer 1862-90, 1985; contbr. articles to profl. jours.; desktop pub. musical scores by Richard Henry Lee, 1991—; art pamphlets by Suzanne M. Smith, 1999—. Participant White House Conf. on Children, 1970; active Save Pioneer Post Office, Portland, Oreg., 1996—; fund raiser com. U.S. Treasury Bill Restoration Fund, 1998-2000; libr. Christian Sci. Reading Rm., 1999-2002; renovator TH-7, 2003; spkr. JCPASH, 2003, Charlestown, Va., 2003, commrs. Jefferson County, W.Va., 2003; interviewer PBS radio, saving Jefferson County Jail . Recipient Key to the City, Mayor Lincoln, Nebr., 1989. Mem. Nat. Soc. Arts and Letters (editor/pub. directory 1971-88, 89-91, 92—, treas. 1988-90, web weaver 1996—), Nat. Trust for Hist. Preservation, Assn. Records Mgrs. and Adminstrs., Assn. for Info. and Image Mgmt. Internat., U.S. Treasury Hist. Assn. (spkr. 1992-96), U.S. Capitol Hist. Soc. Avocations: art, design, teaching and playing classical guitar, windsurfing, computers. E-mail: mspress@mullett-smithpress.com.

SMITH, DEBBIE ILEE RANDALL, elementary school educator; b. Pampa, Tex., Oct. 8, 1955; d. Lester R. and Launa I. (Elmner) Randall; m. Jimmie E. Smith, July 20, 1974; children: Christi I., James R., Stacy L. AA, Seward County Community Coll., Liberal, Kans.; student, Panhandle State U., Goodwell, Okla. Paraprofl. High Plains Edn. Coop., Garden City, Kans.; tchr. USD 480, Liberal; TESOL DISD, Dumas, Tex. Mem. Phi Theta Kappa.

SMITH, DEBORAH K. human resources executive; b. New York, July 28, 1947; BA, U. Rochester, 1968; MA, Cornell U., 1971. V.p., dir. corp. employee resources Xerox Corp., 1994-95; sr. v.p. human resouces Bausch & Lomb Inc., 1995-96; sr. v.p. human resources Merck & Co., Inc., Whitehouse Station, 1996-99; exec. v.p. human resources, mem. exec. com. Coty, Inc., N.Y.C., 1999. Advisor, investor HireDesk. Office: HireDesk 150 - 10271 Shellbridge Way Richmond BC V6X 2W8 c Canada

SMITH, DEBORAH L. music educator, secondary school educator; b. Santurce, P.R., Aug. 28, 1964; d. Richard M. Smith and Carmen M. Cruz. Student, U. Surrey, Guildford, Eng., 1985—86; MusB cum laude, U. Mass., 1987; MusM in Choral Conducting, U. Conn., 1992. Cert. tchr. grades 5-12 Mass. Choral music dir. Granby (Mass.) Jr.-Sr. H.S., 1987—88, Claremont (N H) Pub. Schs., 1988 90; grad. tchg. asst. in theory U. Conn., Storrs, 1990—92; dir. choral music Lincoln-Sudbury (Mass.) Regional H.S., 1992—. Founder, condr. Chamber Singers U. Surrey, Guildford, England, 1985—86; conductor Reading (Mass.) Cmty. Singers, 1995—2002, Braintree Choral Soc., 2002. Mem.: Mass. Tchrs. Assn., Mass. Music Educators Assn. (adjudicator dist. festivals 1987, 1996, 1999, asst. mgr. Mass. All State Chorus 2000—01, mgr. Mass. All-State Chorus 2001—02), Music Educators Nat. Conf., Am. Choral Dirs. Assn. (clinician workshop at state conf. 2000), Pi Kappa Lambda. Avocations: theatre, dance, traveling.

SMITH, DEBRA L. humanities educator; b. Fort Benning, Ga., Feb. 8, 1969; d. Jack H. and Pauline Leveillee Smith. BS in Music Edn., Troy State U., 1992, MS in Music Edn., 1994. Cert. tchr. grades N-12 Ala., 1992. Band dir. Pacelli H.S., Columbus, Ga., 1992—93; educator humanities and band Escambia County Mid. Sch., Atmore, Ala., 1995—. Clinician various music programs, 1990—; student/cmty. liason and tchr. Learn and Serve, Atmore, 2000—; after-school tutor Smart-Links, Atmore, 2001—. Mem. Relay for Life, Atmore, 2000—02; bd. mem. Atmore Arts Coun., 1999—2003. Mem.: NEA (assoc.), Music Educator's Nat. Conf. (assoc.), Ala. Bandmaster's Assn. (assoc.), Ala. Educator's Assn. (assoc.), Omicron Delta Kappa (life), Gamma Beta Phi (life), Pi Kappa Phi (life), Sigma Alpha Iota (life), Tau Beta Sigma (life). Avocations: travel, reading, politics, music, theater. Office: Escambia County Middle School PO Drawer 1236 Atmore AL 36504 Personal E-mail: educ8or@frontiernet.net.

SMITH, DENISE GROLEAU, data processing professional; b. Worcester, Mass., Feb. 7, 1951; d. Edmond Laurence and Audrey Mildred (Paquin) Groleau; m. Wayne Marshall Smith, Apr. 17, 1976; 1 child, Andrew. BSBA, Fitchburg State U., 1983. Bindery worker Atlantic Bus. Forms, Hudson, Mass., 1969-73; proofreader New Eng. Bus., Townsend, Mass., 1974-75, computer operator Groton, Mass., 1975-80, adminstrv. asst. bus. systems, 1980-82, adminstrv. asst. info. ctr., 1982-85; info. ctr. analyst Wright Line Inc., Worcester, 1985-88; personal computer coord. Thom McAn Shoe Co., Worcester, 1988-91. Cons. personal computer Buckingham Transp., Groton, 1987-2001, Software Mgr. Moppet Sch., 1993—; Maple Dene Elem. Sch., 1993—, software mgr. Avocations: reading, sewing, quilting. Home: 14 Cedar Cir Townsend MA 01469-1336

SMITH, DONNA DALE, music educator; b. Russellville, Ark., Oct. 31, 1952; d. William Clint and Mattie Wait Dale; m. David Lee Smith, Jan. 11, 1974; children: Matthew David, Mark Allen. BA, Harding U., 1974. Cert. music educator K - 12 Mo. State Bd. Edn., 1975. Educator music Beebe Pub. Schs., Ark., 1974—75, Senath-Hornersville Pub. Schs., Mo., 1978—82, Clay County Ctrl. Schs., Rector, 1983—85, Paragould Pub. Schs., 1985—96, Kennett Pub. Schs. Asst. dir. Gifted and Talented Summer Program, Paragould, 1989—91. Tchr. Sunday sch. Slicer St. Ch. Christ, Kennett, 1975—2003. Mem.: Mo. State Tchrs. Assn. Independent. Church Of Christ. Avocations: bicycling, painting, drawing, crafts, knitting, crocheting, travel, reading. Office: Kennett Mid Sch 501 College Kennett MO 63857

SMITH, DORIS IRENE, music educator; b. Cleve., Sept. 22, 1950; d. Erwin John and Irene Janet Sladewski; m. Jerrold J. Smith, May 19, 1973 (div. Mar. 2002); children: Laura Diane, Carolyn Joy, Michael Everett, Rebecca Ann, Matthew William. Student, Otterbein Coll., 1968—69; B in Music Edn., Baldwin-Wallace Coll., 1972; MFA in Music Edn., U. Akron, 2002. Pvt. flute tchr., Lyndhurst, Ohio, 1968—; music tchr. Garfield Heights (Ohio) Schs., Garfield Heights, 1973—75; flute tchr. Cleve. Music Settlement, 1992—96; music tchr., band dir. Kenston Schs., Bainbridge, Ohio, 1996—. Flutist Cleve. Women's Orch., 1971—72. Mem.: NEA, No. Ohio Flute Assn., Ohio Music Educator Assn. Republican. Evangelical. Avocations: calligraphy, crafts, stained glass.

SMITH, DOROTHY OTTINGER, jewelry designer, civic worker; b. Indpls., 1922; d. Albert Ellsworth and Leona Aurelia (Waller) Ottinger; m. James Emory Smith, June 25, 1943 (div. 1984); children: Michael Ottinger, Sarah Anne, Theodore Arnold, Lisa Marie. Student, Herron Art Sch. of Purdue U. and Ind. U., 1941-42. Comml. artist William H. Block Co., Indpls., 1942-43, H.P. Wasson Co., 1943-44; dir. Riverside (Calif.) Art Ctr., 1963-64; jewelry designer Riverside, 1970—; numerous design commns. Adviser Riverside chpt. Freedom's Found. of Valley Forge; co-chmn. fund raising com. Riverside Art Ctr. and Mus., 1966-67, bd. dirs. Art Alliance, 1980-81; mem. Riverside City Hall sculpture selection panel Nat. Endowment for the Arts, 1974-75; chmn. fundraising benefit Riverside Art Ctr. and Mus., 1973-74, trustee, 1980-84, chmn. permanent collection, 1981-84, co-chmn. fund drive, 1982-84, trustee, 1998—; chmn. Riverside Mcpl. Arts Commn., 1974-76, Silver Anniversary Gala, 1992; juror Riverside Civic Ctr. Purchase Prize Art Show, 1975; mem. pub. bldgs. and grounds subcom., gen. plan citizens com. City of Riverside, 1965-66; mem. Mayor's Commn. on Civic Beauty, Mayor's Commn. on Sister City Sendai, 1965-66; bd. dirs., chmn. spl. events Children's League of Riverside Community Hosp., 1952-53; bd. dirs. Crippled Children's Soc. of Riverside, spl. events. chmn., 1952-53; bd. dirs. Nat. Charity League, pres. Riverside chpt., 1965-66; mem. exec. com. bd. trustees Riverside Arts Found., 1977-91, fund drive chmn., 1978-79, project rev. chmn., 1978-79, advisor Eveing for the Arts, 1998, juror Gemco Charitable and Scholarship Found., 1977-85; mem. bd. women deacons Calvary Presbyn. Ch., 1978-80, elder, 1989-92; mem. incorporating bd. Inland Empire United Fund for the Arts, 1980-81; bd dirs. Hospice Orgn. Riverside County, 1982-84; trustee Riverside Art Mus., 1998—; mem. Calif. Coun. Humanities, 1982-86. Recipient cert. Riverside City Coun., 1977, plaque Mayor of Riverside, 1977, Spl. Recognition Riverside Cultural Arts Coun., 1981, Disting. Svc. plaque Riverside Art Ctr. and Mus., Jr. League Silver Raincross Community Svc. award, 1989, Cert Appreciation Outstanding Svc. to the Arts Community Riverside Arts Found., 1990, Top Dog award Riverside Art Mus., 1999. Mem. Riverside Art Assn. (pres. 1961-63, 1st. v.p. 1964-65, 67-68, trustee 1959-70, 80-84, 87-92), Art Alliance of Riverside Art Ctr. and Museum (founder 1964, pres. 1969-70). Address: 3979 Chapman Pl Riverside CA 92506-1150

SMITH, ELAINE DIANA, foreign service officer; b. Glencoe, Ill., Sept. 15, 1924; d. John Raymond and Elsie (Gelbard) S. BA, Grinnell Coll., 1946; MA, Johns Hopkins U., 1947; PhD, Am. U., 1959. Commd. fgn. svc. officer U.S. Dept. State, 1947; assigned to Brussels, 1947-50, Tehran, Iran, 1951-53, Wellington, New Zealand, 1954-56, Dept. State, Washington, 1956-60, Ankara, Turkey, 1960-69, Istanbul, Turkey, 1969-72, Dept. Commerce Exch., 1972-73; dep. examiner Fgn. Svc. Bd. Examiners, 1974-75; Turkish desk officer Dept. State, Washington, 1975-78. Consul gen., Izmir, Turkey, 1978-. Author: Origins of the Kemalist Movement, 1919-1923, 1959. Recipient Alumni award Grinnell Coll., 1957. Mem. U.S. Fgn. Svc. Assn., Phi Beta Kappa. Home: The Plaza 800 25th St NW Apt 306 Washington DC 20037-2207

SMITH, ELAINE E. school system administrator; b. Gooding, Idaho; m. Rich L. Smith, June 8, 1968; children: Camille, Kirk, Brenda. BA in Secondary Edn., Idaho State U. Cert. secondary tchr. Coord. vol. svcs.-bus. and edn. partnerships Sch. Dist. # 25, Pocatello, Idaho, 1985—. Coord. Expanding Your Horizons Conf., S.E. Idaho, 1986—. Past pres. Community Svcs. Coun., Pocatello; active Bannock County Youth at Risk, Pocatello, 1988—; mem. Pocatello Area Foster Grandparents Adv., Pocatello, 1989—; bd. dirs. YWCA of Ea. Idaho, 1990—; mem. Idaho West Point Parents Club, 1990-95; active United Way of S.E. Idaho; mem., coord. Portneuf Cropwalk. Recipient Friend of Edn. award Pocatello Edn. Assn., 1990, Disting. Young Woman of Yr. Jaycees, 1980. Mem. AAUW (past state pres.), Nat. Assn. Ptnrs. Edn., Nat. Coalition for Sex Equity Edn., Assn. Vol. Adminstrs., Greater Pocatello C. of C. (K-12 edn. com 1985—, state issues com. 1985—), Soroptimists (Women Helping award 1993 Pocatello chpt.), Alpha Omicron Pi, Delta Kappa Gamma. Office: Sch Dist # 25 3115 Poleline Rd Pocatello ID 83201-6119

SMITH, ELEANOR JANE, university chancellor, retired, consultant; b. Circleville, Ohio, Jan. 10, 1933; d. John Allen and Eleanor Jane (Dade) Lewis; m. James L. Banner, Aug. 10, 1957 (div. 1972); 1 child, Teresa M. Banner Watters; m. Paul M. Smith Jr. BS, Capital U., 1955; PhD, The Union Inst., Cin., 1972. Tchr. Columbus (Ohio) Pub. Schs., 1956-64, Worthington (Ohio) Pub. Schs., 1964-72; from faculty to administrator U. Cin., 1972-88; dean Smith Coll., Northampton, Mass., 1988-90; v.p. acad. affairs, provost William Paterson Coll., Wayne, N.J., 1990-94; chancellor U. Wis.-Parkside, Kenosha, 1994-97, ret., 1997; ind. cons. in higher edn. Dir. Afrikan Am. Inst., Cin., 1977-84; adv. bd. Edwina Bookwalter Gantz Undergrad. Studies Ctr., Cin.; mem. Gov.'s Tobacco Tax adv. coun. Performances include (concert) Black Heritage: History, Music and Dance, 1972—. Spl. Arts Night Com., Northampton, 1988-89; bd. dirs. Planned Parenthood No. and Ctrl. Ariz., Am. Lung Assn. Ariz./N.Mex. Named career woman of achievement YWCA, Cin., 1983. Mem. AAUW, Nat. Assn. Women in Higher Edn., Am. Assn. for Higher Edn., Leadership Am. (bd. dirs., treas. 1993-95), Nat. Assn. Black Women Historians (co-founder, co-dir. 1979-82), Am. Coun. on Edn. (mem. com. on internat. edn. 1994-97, bd. dirs. 1995-97), Am. Assn. State Colls. and Univs. (mem. com. on policies and purposes 1994-97). Avocations: music, pen and ink drawing, travel, reading. Home: 24823 S Lakestar Dr Sun Lakes AZ 85248-7465

SMITH, ELEANOR VAN LAW, paralegal; b. Richmond, Va., Aug. 11, 1964; d. William Preston Jr. and Priscilla Norris Smith. AS, U. S.C., Columbia, 1985, BA in Interdisciplinary Studies, 1986; Paralegal Cert., Nat. Ctr. Paralegal Tng., Atlanta, 1987. Sales assoc. Ship n' Shore, Columbia, 1984-85, The Ltd., Columbia, 1985-86; office asst. Universal Printing, Charleston, S.C., 1986-87; sales assoc. Evelyn Rubin, Charleston, 1987; paralegal First Union Nat. Bank, Atlanta, 1988-89, L.J. Hooker Devel., Atlanta, 1989-90; sr. paralegal James Lang La Salle Americas, Inc., Atlanta, 1990—. Participant Habitat for Humanity, Atlanta, 1993-95, Multiple Sclerosis Soc., Atlanta, 1994-95, Osteoporosis Soc., Atlanta, 1997, Ptnr. for Spl. Olympics, 1999. Mem. Internat. Collectors Soc., Carolina Merchandising Club (sec. 1985-86), Delta Delta Delta. Republican. Episcopalian. Avocations: travel, tennis, cooking, knitting, exercise. Office: Jones Lang La Salle 3500 Piedmont Rd NE Ste 600 Atlanta GA 30305-1507 Home: 3136 Saint Ives Country Club P Duluth GA 30097-5993

SMITH, ELISE FIBER, international non-profit development agency administrator; b. Detroit, June 14, 1932; d. Guy and Mildred Geneva (Johnson) Fiber; m. James Frederick Smith, Aug. 11, 1956 (div. 1983); children: Gregory Douglas, Guy Charles; life ptnr. Jac Smit, 1990. BA, U. Mich., 1954; postgrad., U. Strasbourg, France, 1954-55; MA, Case Western Res. U., 1956. Tchr. U.S. Binat. Ctr., Caracas, Venezuela, 1964-66; instr. English Am. U., 1966-68; prof. lang. faculty Catholic U., Lima, Peru, 1968-70; coord. English lang. and culture program, lang. faculty El Rosario U., Bogota, Colombia, 1971-73; lang. specialist, mem. faculty Am. U., English Lang. Inst., 1975-78; exec. dir. OEF Internat. (name formerly Overseas Edn. Fund), Washington, 1978-89, bd. dirs.; dir. Global Women's Leadership Program Winrock Internat., 1989-98, sr. policy advisor on gender, 1998—. Founder, pres. Women's EDGE, 1997—; v.p. Pvt. Agys. Collaborating Together, NYC, 1983-89; trustee Internat. Devel. Conf., Washington, 1983-2001, exec. com., 1985-90; hon. com. for Global Crossroads Nat. Assembly, Global Perspectives in Edn., Inc., NYC, 1984, Washington, 1984-92, gen. assembly, 1992; nat. com. Focus on Hunger '84, LA; ofcl. observer UN Conf. on Status Women, 1980, UN 3rd World Conf. on Women, 1985, del. NGO Forum, UN 4th World Conf. on Women, del. NGO Forum, 1995; mental health adv. com. Dept. State, 1974-76; U.S. del. planning seminar integration women in devel. OAS, 1978; participant Women, Law and Devel. Forum; exec. com., chair commn. advancement women Interaction (Am. Coun. for Vol. Internat. Action), 1994-97, co-founder, 1985-88, chmn. bd.; bd. dirs. Sudan-Am. Found.; adv. bd. Global Links Devel. Edn., Washington, 1985-86; adv. coun. Global Fund for Women, 1988-93; U.S. del. Vital Voices Conf. Women and Democracy, Iceland, 1999; U.S. del. Women in Democracy Conf., Lithuania, 2000; U.S del Baltic Women in Democracy Conf., Estonia, 2003. Co-editor: Toward Internationalism: Readings in Cross-cultural Communication, 1979, 2d edit. 1986. Bd. dirs. Internat. Ctr. Rsch. on Women, 1992-2001; adv. com. on vol. fgn. aid US AID, 1994—; women and conservation adv. com. World Wildlife Fund, 1998-2002; mem. State Dept. Adv. Com. US Internat. Econ. Policy, 2000—. Rotary Internat. ambassadorial scholar Strasbourg, France, 1954-55; grantee Dept. State, 1975. Mem. Assn. Women in Devel., UNIFEM, Coalition Women in Internat. Devel. (co-founder 1979, chair 1993-96),pvt. Agys. in Internat. Devel. (co-chmn. 1980-82, pres. 1982-85), Nat. Assn. Fgn. Student Affairs (grantee 1975), U. Mich. Alumni Assn., Women's Fgn. Policy Group, Rotary Internat. (mem. global com. Women in Future Soc. 1996). Unitarian Universalist. Home: 4701 Connecticut Ave NW Apt 304 Washington DC 20008-5617

SMITH, ELIZABETH, artist; b. New Britain, Conn., Aug. 13, 1943; BS, Cen. Conn. State U., 1969, MS, 1974; student, U. Vt., U. Hartford. Exhibited in group shows at Nat. Acad. Design, N.Y.C., 1988, Mus. Fine Arts, Springfield, Mass., 1988, 90, 92, Bergen Mus. Art and Sci., Paramus, N.J., 1990, Allied Artists Am., N.Y.C., 1988-89, 91, 99, Pastel Soc. Am., N.Y.C., 1990, 91, 92, Silvermine Guild Arts Ctr., Wash. and Lee U., 1991, New Canaan, Conn., 1992, Butler Inst. Am. Art, 2001. Included in book The Best of Pastel II--Collected by the Pastel Soc. of Am.; finalist Artists Mag. Painting Competition, 1991-92. Mem. Am. Artists Profl. League (Coun. Am. Artists Socs. award 1988), Audubon Artists, Acad. Artists Assn. (award 1991), Nat. Assn. Women Artists (Nydia Preede award 1987, C.L. Mason and A.V. Mason Meml. award 1989), Conn. Acad. Fine Arts (bd. dirs. 1991-92, pres. 1992-93), Knickerbocker Artists N.Y. (Silver medal of Honor 1986, 91), Katharine Lorillard Wolfe Art Club (medal of honor 1986, IBM award 1987, Ida Becker Meml. award 1989). Home: PO Box 493 Mendham NJ 07945-0493

SMITH, ELIZABETH MACKEY, financial consultant; b. Phila., Mar. 23, 1941; d. William Norman and Celeste (Parvin) Mackey; m. George Van Riper Smith, Aug. 15, 1964; children: Douglas George, Todd Mackey. BA, Gettysburg Coll., 1963; MAT in French, Ga. State U., 1978. ChFC. Tchr. fgn. lang. Haverford (Pa.) H.S., 1963-65; registered rep. Am. Express Fin. Advisors, Inc., Macon and Savannah, Ga., 1979-2000, br. mgr. Tybee Island, Ga., 2000—. Reader Atlanta Serv for the Blind, 1968; hostess Atlanta Coun Int Visitors, 1972—74; foreign exchange student coord Loisirs Culturels a l'Etranger, 1990; staff protocol vol sailing venue Olympic Games, Savannah, 1996. Mem.: Delta Gamma, Delta Phi Alpha, Phi Sigma Iota. Avocations: tennis, swimming. Home: 59 Fiddlers Ct Savannah GA 31419 Office: Am Express 303 3d St PO Box 2926 Tybee Island GA 31328-2926

SMITH, ERLINDA FAY, occupational therapist; b. Kansas City, Mo., July 4, 1963; d. Neathy Woods and Lillie Mae (Morgan) Woods-Beatty; m. Tommy Lee Smith, Sept. 19, 1992 (div. Sept. 95). BS in Occupl. Therapy, U. Kans., 1989; grad., Kansas City Coll. of Med. and Dental Assts., 1982; student, Fla. State U., 2001—. Clin. occupl. therapist Truman Med. Ctr., Kansas City, Mo., 1989-92; indsl. rehab. specialist St. Mary's Hosp., Blue Springs, Mo., 1992-96, occupl. therapist, 1996-98, Bay Med. Ctr., Panama City, Fla., 1998-2000, Ctr. for Ind. Living, Tallahassee, 2002—. Registered Occupl. Therapist. Mem. Am. Occupl. Therapy Assn., Am. Soc. Hand Therapists, Nat. Black Occupl. Therapy Caucus, Met. Kansas City Black Occupl. Therapy Caucus (v.p. 1995—), Mo. Occupl. Therapy Assn., Fla. Occupl. Therapy Assn., Kansas City Hand Study Group. Bapt. Avocations: sewing, travelling, crafts. Home: 2315 Jackson Bluff Rd Apt 302A Tallahassee FL 32304-4570 Office: Center for Independent Living 1823 Buford Court Tallahassee FL 32308

SMITH, ESTHER MARIAN GREENWELL, education educator; b. Portland, Oreg. d. George Richard Greenwell and Adah Evelyn Long; m. Elton E. Smith, Oct. 17, 1942; children: Elton G., Esther R. Shaw, Stephen L. BA, Linfield Coll., 1937, MEd, 1955; student, Andover Theol. Sch., Newton Centre, Mass., 1940—42; PhD, U. Fla., 1972. Cert. tchr. Oreg., Mass., Fla. Tchr. Dallas H.S., Oreg., 1937—40; min. of edn. First Bapt. Ch., Medford, Mass., 1941—42; tchr. Portland State, 1954—57, North H.S., Syracuse, NY, 1957—58, Camillus H.S., NY, 1958—61; instr. Fla. So. Coll., Lakeland, 1961—64, Polk C.C., Winter Haven, Fla., 1964—80. Author: Mrs. Humphry Ward, 1980, The Cascade Empire, 1989, Jairus's Daughter, John Beaumont of Rockfort, 2000, Conversations with Truth, 2003; co-author: The Last Eight Days, 1985; contbr. chapters to books;, author poems.

SMITH, ESTHER THOMAS, communications executive; b. Jesup, Ga., Mar. 13, 1939; d. Joseph H. and Leslie (McCarthy) Thomas; m. James D. Smith, June 2, 1962; children: Leslie, Amy, James Thomas. BA, Agnes Scott Coll., 1962. Staff writer Sunday women's editor Atlanta Jour.-Constn., 1961-62; mng. editor Bull. of U. Miami Sch. Medicine, 1965-66; corr. Atlanta Jour.-Constn. and Fla. Times-Union, 1964, 67-68; founding editor Bus. Rev. of Washington, 1978-81; founding editor, gen. mgr. Washington Bus. Jour., 1982; pres., bd. dirs. TechNews, Inc., 1986-96, CEO, 1995-96; founder, editor-at-large Washington Tech., 1986-97, Tech. Transfer Bus. Mag., 1992-95; co-chair editl. bd. TechCapital Mag., 1997-99; prin. Poretz Group Investor Rels., McLean, Va., 1998—2000; ptnr. Qorvis Comm. LLC (successor to Poretz Group), McLean, 2000—. Bd. dirs. Provant Inc., Women Connect.com, telezoo inc., World Affairs Coun. Washington, The Atlantic Coun.; mem. adv. Netpreneur Program Morino Inst., 1996—2002; mem. internat. adv. bd. Kilby Awards Found.; mem. MIT Enterprise Forum of Washington/Balt., 1981—82, Internat. Women's Forum, 1981—, No. Va. Bus. Round Table, exec. com., 1993—98; mem. adv. bd. Va. Math Coalition, 1991—94; commr. NACD Blue Ribbon Commn., 2001; trustee Ctr. for Excellence in Edn., 1993—96; bd. dirs., trustee Capital Region Technology Investors Conf.; bd. advisors George Washington U., Va., 1996—99. Named to, Washington Bus. Hall of Fame, 2002; recipient Lifetime Achievement award, Women in Tech., 2000. Mem.: Md. High Tech. Coun., No. Va. Tech. Coun. (sr. adv. bd. 1998—2000, exec. com., bd. dirs., Earle C. Williams Leadership award 1999), Assn. Tech. Bus. Couns. (chmn. bd. advisors 1989—94). Office: Qorvis Comm LLC 8484 Westpark Dr 8th Fl Mc Lean VA 22102 E-mail: esmith@qorvis.com.

SMITH, EUGENIA SEWELL, funeral home executive; b. Albany, Ky., Oct. 24, 1922; d. Leo Matheny and Marjorie (Warinner) Sewell; m. James Frederick Smith, June 25, 1948; 1 child, Bryson Sewell (dec.). Student Berea Coll., 1937-41, Bowling Green Coll. Commerce, 1944-45. Owner, operator Sewell Funeral Home, Albany, 1977—; bd. dir. Citizens Bank of Albany, Ky., 1989—. Sec. Albany Woman's Club, 1950-54; den mother Cub Scouts, Boy Scouts Am., 1958-62; pres. Clinton County Homemakers, Albany, 1968-70, Modern Homemakers, 1992-98; mission action chmn. Missionary Baptist Ch., 1965-91; v.p. Modern Homemakers Club of Albany, 1990-92, pres., 1994-98. Democrat. Lodge: Demolay Mother's (pres. Albany club 1966-67), Order Eastern Star (former assoc. conductress, former Martha and Esther). Home: RR 5 Box 104 Burkesville Rd Albany KY 42602-9310 Office: Sewell Funeral Home 115 Cross St Albany KY 42602

SMITH, EVELYN ELAINE, language educator; b. Waco, Tex., July 25, 1952; d. Walstein Bennett and Evelyn Dougherty (Box) S. BA, Baylor U., 1974, MA, 1979; PhD, Tex. Christian U., 1995. Cert. secondary tchr., Tex. Grad. asst. Baylor U., Waco, Tex., 1975, proofreader, 1980, rsch. assoc., 1981-86; reporter Killeen (Tex.) Daily Herald, 1981; writing tchr. Waco (Tex.) Ind. Sch. Dist., 1989-90; grad. asst. Tex. Christian U., Ft. Worth, 1992-93; adj. prof. English McLennan C.C., Waco, Tex., 1993-94; adj. instr. English Tex. State Tech. Coll., Waco, 1993-94, 97; instr. English Hill Coll., Hillsboro, Tex., 1997, Ctrl. Tex. Coll., Killeen, 1997, So. Meth. U., Dallas, 1997, El Centro Coll., Dallas, 1998, North Ctrl. Tex. Coll., Lewisville, 1998. Adj. lectr. Ctrl. Tex. Coll., Killeen, 1997, So. Meth. U., Dallas, 1997; adj. instr. El Centro Coll., Dallas, 1998, North Ctrl. Tex. Coll., Lewisville, 1998; vis. asst. prof. Idaho State U., Pocatello, 1998—. Contbr. articles to profl. jours. Bd. dirs., newsletter editor Historic Waco Found., 1981-85, sec., exec., mem. nominating coms., 1994-96. Mem. MLA, South Ctrl. MLA, S.W./Tex. PGA/ACA, Nat. Conf. Tchrs. English, Conf. Coll. Composition and Comm. Democrat. Mem. So. Bapt. Ch. Avocation: historical preservation. Office: Idaho State U Dept English & Philosophy PO Box 8056 Pocatello ID 83209-0001

SMITH, F. LOUISE, elementary school educator; b. Balt., Nov. 4, 1946; d. Joseph L. and Catherine L. Lilley; m. Wayne F. Smith, Aug. 7, 1976; 1 child, Ryan. BA, Mt. St. Agnes Coll., 1968; MEd, Loyola Coll. Elem. tchr. St. Clement Sch. Diocese Balt., 1966—68, elem. tchr. St. Mark Sch., 1968—71; elem. tchr. Longfellow Elem. Howard County, Columbia, Md., 1971—72, elem. tchr. Hammond Elem. Laurel, Md., 1972—2002. Tutor, Catonsville, Md. Named Tchr. of Yr., Am. Legion, 1997, Sunpapers All-Star Reading Tchr., Balt. Sun, 2001. Mem.: State Md. Reading Assn., Md. Congress Parents and Tchrs. (life), State Md. Internat. Reading Coun. Home and Office: 312 Locust Dr Catonsville MD 21228

SMITH, FAYE, state legislator; b. Greenville, S.C. m. Tommy Smith; 4 children. Grad., Truett McConnell Coll., 1966; Bachelor's, U. Ga., 1968; MEd, Ga. Coll., 1975. Ret. tchr.; mem. 25th dist. Ga. State Senate, 1999—, sec. retirement com. Democrat. Office: 18 Capitol Sq SW Atlanta GA 30334-9003

SMITH, FERN M. judge; b. San Francisco; children: Susan, Julue. AA, Foothill Coll., 1970; BA, Stanford U., 1972, JD, 1975. Bar: Calif. 1975. Assoc. Bronson, Bronson & McKlinnon, San Francisco, 1975-81, ptnr., 1982-86; judge San Francisco County Superior Ct., 1986-88, U.S. Dist. Ct. (no. dist.) Calif., 1988—. Dir. Fed. Jud. Ctr., Wash., 1999—; mem. adv. com. on Jud. Conf. U.S., Rules of Evidence, 1993-96, chair, 1996-99; rep. standing com. Jud. Conf. Com. Rules of Practice and Procedure, 1996-99; mem. exec. com. Ninth Cir. Jud. Conf., 1994-96, Ninth Cir. State-Fed. Jud. Coun., 1990-93, Calif. Jud.Coun. 1987-88, 92— (mem. adv. Task Force on Gender Bias, 1988-90), hiring, mgmt. and pers. coms., active recruiting various law schs.; faculty Inst. Study and Devel. Legal Sys., 1992, Egypt & Bolivia, 1994, Mexico and Tunisia, 1995, Israel, Jordan, Greece and Egypt, 1996, India, 1998, Jordan and Italy, 1998, ISDLS Rule of Law Conf., Berkeley, Calif.; bd. vis. Law Sch. Stanford U., 1990-92, 99—. Contbr. articles to legal publ. Mem. ABA, Queen's Br. Nat. Assn. Women Judges, Calif. Women Lawyers Assn., Bar Assn. San Francisco, Fed. Judges Assn., 9th Cir. Dist. Judges Assn., Am. Judicature Soc., Calif. State Fed. Jud. Coun., Phi Beta Kappa.

SMITH, FREDRICA EMRICH, rheumatologist, internist; b. Princeton, N.J., Apr. 28, 1945; d. Raymond Jay and Carolyn Sarah (Schleicher) Emrich; m. Paul David Smith, June 10, 1967. AB, Bryn Mawr Coll., 1967; MD, Duke U., 1971. Intern, resident U. N.Mex. Affiliated Hosps., 1971-73; fellow U. Va. Hosp., Charlottesville, 1974-75; pvt. practice, Los Alamos, N.Mex., 1975—. Chmn. credentials com. Los Alamos Med. Ctr., 1983—, chief staff, 1990, 2003; bd. dirs. N.Mex. Physicians Mut. Liability Ins. Co., Albuquerque. Contbr. articles to med. jours. Mem. bass sect. Los Alamos Symphony, 1975—; mem. Los Alamos County Parks and Recreation Bd., 1984-88, 92-96, Los Alamos County Med. Indigent Health Care Task Force, 1989—; mem. ops. subcom. Aquatic Ctr., Los Alamos County, 1988—. Fellow ACP, Am. Coll. Rheumatology; mem. N.Mex. Soc. Internal Medicine (pres. 1993-96), Friends of Bandelier. Democrat. Avocations: swimming, music, reading, hiking. Office: Los Alamos Med Ctr 3917 West Rd Los Alamos NM 87544-2275 Office Phone: 505-662-9400.

SMITH, GAIL MARIE, special education educator, educational consultant; b. Buffalo, June 7, 1947; d. Daniel James and Geraldine Francis (Whalen) Healy; children: Christopher Alan Southworth, Jennifer Morgan Elizabeth. Student, Trinity Coll., Dublin, Ireland, 1968; BA in English and Edn. with hons., St. John's U., N.Y., 1969; postgrad., U. Md., Okinawa, Japan, 1970; MS in Spl. Edn. with honors, So. Conn. State U., 1982; postgrad., Wesleyan U., 1985, Mattatuck C.C., 1989, Conn. Adult Devel. Program, 1993. Cert. ESL, Conn., comprehensive spl. edn., Conn., nursery, kindergarten, grades 1-8, Conn., English grades 7-12, Conn., h.s. credit diploma program, Conn., external diploma program/non-credit mandated programs, Conn., CAPP facilitator, Conn., program leader WERACE, psychol. mgmt. tng., crisis mgmt. tng., CPR, 1st aid, respite, CTH, Conn.; pub. svc. lic. Tchr. Machinato Elem. Sch. Dept. of Def. Overseas Dependent Schs., Okinawa, 1969-70, tchr., chair dept. English Port Wheel Nine Sch., 1970-71; tchr. grades 5 and 6 regular and spl. edn. Woodbridge (Conn.) Pub. Schs., 1971-81, tchr. spl. edn., 1981-82; tchr. adjusted curriculum program Trumbull (Conn.) H.S., 1982-83, tchr. elem. self-contained resource room programs, cons., 1983-88, tchr. spl. edn., 1994; tchr. spl. edn. and regular edn. grades 9-12 Trumbull Alt. Sch., 1988-94; tchr. spl. edn., vocat. liaison Trumbull Pub. Schs., 1994; tchr. grades 9-12 at-risk adolescents (regular/spl. edn.) Regional Alt. Sch., Trumbull, 1995—. Ednl., behavioral cons.; active Conn. Ind. Living Adult Residential Program, 1988-89, medically fragile program Trumbull Pub. Schs., 1989, Datahr Rehab. Inst., Conn., 1994-96, Western Regional Adult Continuing Edn. Program, 1989-96; enl. specialist State of Conn. Dept. Edn., summers 1987, 88, 90; mgr. semi-supervised apt. program, 1989-93. Advocate Lyme disease, 1991—, spl. edn., 1989—; mem. edn. com. Fed. Correctional Instn., Danbury, Conn., 1994; alt. schs. rep. Trumbull Ednl. Assn., 1989-99, mem. exec. bd., 1986-94, rep. coun., 1985; mem. coun. Fairfield County, State of Conn. Edn. Assn. Fairfield County, 1988-89; mem. adv. bd., 1988-89; Trumbull Edn. Assn. rep. supt.'s adv. com. Trumbull Pub. Schs., 1988-89, spl. edn. rep. tchr. evaluation com., 1988—, Middlebrook Elem. Sch. rep. tchr. evaluation com., 1986-88, mem. lang. arts com., 1984-85, Middlebrook Elem. Sch. PTA liaison, 1983-84, v.p. Trumbull H.S. PTSA Coun. and Exec. Bd., 1982-83; mem. bd. mgrs. State of Conn. PTA, 1983-86, advisor Key Club, 1982-83; mem. coun. Newtown (Conn.) PTA, 1984-85, v.p., legis. rep., bd. edn. liaison, 1982-86; co-sponsor spl. edn. svc. club Nonnewaug H.S., Woodbury, Conn., 1976-80; bd. dirs. Children's Adventure Ctr., Inc., Newtown, Conn., 1982-89; evaluator State of Conn. Spl. Edn. Network for Software, 1985-95; co-chairperson child abuse com. St. of Ct., 1984-85, Bd. of mgrs. PTA, 1984-86. Mem. AAUW, NEA, Conn. Edn. Assn., Conn. Assn. Learning Disabilities, Trumbull Edn. Assn. (v.p. 1988-89, alt. sch. rep. 1985—), Conn. Adult Profl. Program (cert.), Western Edn. Regional Acad. and Adult Continuing Edn., Cmty. Tng. Home (lic.). Avocations: skiing, swimming, hiking, antiques, camping. Office: Trumbull Alternate Sch Madison Mid Sch Madison Ave Trumbull CT 06611 Home: Apt 134 920 Mohawk St Lewiston NY 14092-1406

SMITH, GAYLE SUE SWARTZ, theater director, choreographer; b. Greenville, Ohio, Sept. 19, 1947; d. Ralph Leonard and Eleanor Elizabeth Swartz; m. Lani Kamiki Smith, Sept. 22, 1972 (div. Jan. 1978). BFA in Dance, Wright State U., 1980; MFA in Dance, So. Meth. U., 1981; MA in Theatre, U. Cin., 1983, MFA in Theatre, 1984. Asst. prof. theatre/dance Ea. N.Mex. U., Portales, 1984—91; asst. dir. Cleve. Play House, 1990—91; asst. artistic dir. Players Theatre, Columbus, Ohio, 1991—92; artistic dir. ROM Factory, Mexico City, 1993—95; dir., choreographer Springboro (Ohio) H.S., 1995—.

SMITH, GERALDINE, historic site administrator; Supt. Jean Lafitte Nat. Hist. Park and Preserve, New Orleans. Office: Jean Lafitte Nat Hist Park and Preserve 365 Canal St Ste 2400 New Orleans LA 70130-1142

SMITH, GERALDINE MAY, nutritionist; b. Arkansaw, Wis. d. Clive E. and Delight (McMahon) Metcalf; m. Roy M. Smith (dec. Dec. 1990); children: Randal M., Pamela J., Richard A., Patricia A. AA, Graceland Coll., Lamoni, Iowa, 1948; BS, U. Minn., 1978. Nutrition educator U. Minn. Coutny Ext., Mpls., 1971-84; program dir. Child Care Food Program, Kansas City, Kans., 1984-86; nutritionist Women, Infants & Children, Kansas City, Mo., 1988-96; program coord., co-founder Nutra-Net, Inc., Independence, Mo., 1986—. Mem. home econ. adv. bd. Mpls. Pub. Sch. Sys., 1980-84. Author: (sr. nutrition program) Recipes and Reminiscence, 1999. Mem. AAUW, Am. Assn. Family and Consumer Sci. (cert.). Avocations: watercolor painting, writing. Home: 402 NE Velie Rd Lees Summit MO 64064-1205

SMITH, GLORIA RICHARDSON, nursing educator; b. Chgo., Sept. 29, 1934; BSN, Wayne State U., 1955; MPH, U. Mich., 1959; cert., UCLA, 1971; MA in Anthropology, U. Okla., 1977; PhD, Union for Experimenting Colls. and Univs., 1979; D Honoris Causa (hon.), U. Cin., 1992. Pub. health nurse Detroit Vis. Nurse Assn., 1955-56, sr. pub. health nurse, 1957-58, asst. dist. office supr., 1959-63; asst. prof. nursing Tuskegee Inst. Sch. Nursing, Ala., 1963-66, Albany (Ga.) State Coll., 1966-68, cons. nurse home health care Okla. State Health Dept., 1968-70, medicare nurse cons., 1970-71; asst. prof. U. Okla. Coll. Nursing, Oklahoma City, 1971-73, assoc. prof. and interim dean, 1973-75; state health dir. Mich. Dept. Pub. Health, 1983-88; prof., dean Coll. Nursing Wayne State U., 1988-91; coord., program dir. in health WK Kellogg Found., 1991-95, v.p. programs in health, 1995—. Chair Mich. Task Force on Nursing Issues, 1989-90, Nat. Commn. on Nursing Shortage, 1990-91; cons. on nursing Colo. Commn. Higher Edn., 1990, U. N.C., 1990; mem. adv. com. nursing Okla. State Regents for Higher Edn., 1973-83; cons. VA Hosp., 1975-77, HEW, 1977-78, U. Mich. External Rev. Sch. Nursing, 1980. Contbr. articles on health care and nursing edn. to profl. publs. Mem. Mayor's Com. to Study In-Migrants, Detroit, 1963; bd. dirs. St. Peter Claver Cmty. Credit Union, 1961-63, YMCA, Oklahoma City, 1972-76, Better Homes Found. for Homeless, 1986—; mem. steering com. Kellogg Fellowship Internat. Program in Health, 1985-89; mem. study com. health care for homeless Inst. Medicine, 1987-88. Recipient Outstanding Svc. award Franklin Settlement, 1963, Disting. Alumni award Wayne State U., 1984, Disting. Scholar award Am. Nurses Found., 1987—. Mem. Nat. League Nursing (dir. from 1979), Am. Nurses Assn. (mem. commn. on nursing edn. 1978-82), Okla. League Nursing, Midwest Alliance in Nursing (dir. 1977-80), Black Pers. (exec. com. 1974-76), Am. Assn. Colls. Nursing (exec. com. from 1976), Nat. Black Nurses Assn. (dir. 1972-78), Okla. State Nurses Assn. (Nurse of Yr. 1972), Am. Assn. for Higher Edn., Okla. State Assn. for Black Pers. in Higher Edn. (rec. sec. 1976-78), Am. Acad. Nursing (governing coun. 1983-85), Assn. State and Territorial Health Officers, Am. Pub. Health Assn., Okla. Pub. Health Assn., Sigma Gamma Rho (Outstanding Sigma of Yr. 1963), Sigma Theta Tau.

SMITH, GLORIA S. local commissioner, educator; b. Midland, SD, July 25, 1924; d. John and Hattie Leora Saucerman; m. Albert Francis Smith, July 21, 1945; children: Gregory, Bradley, Karen. Grad., Dakota Wesleyan U., 1942, U. Minn., 1945. Cert. elem. edn. Elem. tchr. Sansarc (S.D.) Sch. Dist., 1943-44; ins. underwriter Firemans Fund Ins. Co., San Francisco, 1945-46; supr. disability ins. General Electric Co., Schenectady, NY, 1947-49; v.p., then pres. bd. edn. Upper St. Clair (Pa.) Sch. Dist., 1964-77; from bd. dir. to v.p. elect South Hills Area Coun. of Govs., Pitts., 1994—2003, pres. elect, 2003; commr., v.p. Upper St. Clair (Pa.) Twp., 1994—. Mem. Upper St. Clair Bd. Commrs., Pa., 1994—; bd. dir. special edn. Allegheny County Intermediate Unit, Pitts., 1974-77; bd. dir. Outreach Teen and Family Svcs., Mt. Lebanon, Pa., 1979—, treas. 1990—. Americans Abroad selection com. Am. Field Svc. Upper St. Clair, Pa., 1970-77; ch. sch. tchr. United Methodist Ch., Bethel Park, Pa., 1960—; mem. Advisory Com. to Establish Home Rule Charter dists., Allegheny Cty., Pa., 1998. Recipient Outstanding Citizen award Upper St. Clair Repub. Com., Pa., 1967. Republican. Methodist. Avocations: family, travel, home decorating, community block parties. Home: 529 Long Dr Upper Saint Clair PA 15241 Office: Twp Bd of Commissioners 1820 Mclaughlin Run Rd Upper Saint Clair PA 15241

SMITH, GLORIA YOUNG, retired graphic artist, art educator; b. N.Y.C., Jan. 15, 1926; d. Frederick William and Anastasia Margaret (Regan) Young; m. Henry George Smith, Oct. 1, 1949; children: Stephanie, Kevin, Brian, Robert, Sean. Student, Art Students League, N.Y.C., 1944, 45, Nat. Acad. Design, 1946, 47, 48, Nassau C.C., Uniondale, N.Y., 1971, 72. Artist Lynn Mfg. Co., Astoria, N.Y., 1947-50; forms designer, graphic artist Mercy Hosp., Rockville Centre, N.Y., 1972-81; art tchr. Art Inst. & Gallery, Salisbury, Md., 1992-98, Art League of Ocean City, Md., 1995—. Mem. com. Nat. Juried Art Show, Salisbury, 1996-2000. Artist numerous paintings. Pres. Artists Co-op, Salisbury, 1998—; bd. dirs. Art League of Ocean City, Md., 1997--; sec., bd. dirs. Art Inst. & Gallery, Salisbury, 1991-95; hdqrs. mgr. congl. campaign Rep. Orgn., Baldwin, N.Y., 1968; treas. Conservative Women, L.I., 1971; judge Nat. Seashore Poster Art Contest, Assateague Island, Md., 1992. Recipient Best in Category award Ann. Arts and Crafts Show, Indian Harbour Beach, Fla., 1987, 2d pl. award Arts Atlantica-Worcester County Heritage, 1996, 1st pl. award Art League Ocean City, 1992, Mem.'s award Fells Point Art Gallery, 1993. Mem. Nat. League Am. Pen Women, Portrait Soc. Am., Inc., Art Students League N.Y. (life), Miniature Art Soc. Fla. Republican. Roman Catholic. Avocations: reading, music, foreign travel, walking. Home: 260 Ocean Pkwy Berlin MD 21811-1525

SMITH, GWENDOLYN, elementary school educator; b. Chgo., Dec. 17, 1954; d. Levi and Juanita Alexander; m. L. T. Smith, June 28, 1972; children: LaSean, Stacy, Serena. BS in Early Childhood Edn., Old Dominion U., 1983; postgrad., Concordia U. Cert. tchr. Ariz. Dept. Edn. Educator Roosevelt Sch. Dist., Phoenix, 1983—. Dir. Jambo Spl. People, Phoenix, 1999—. Sunday sch. tchr. Pilgrim Rest Bapt. Ch., Phoenix, 1998—, youth ministry leader, 1998—2000. Named Target Tchr. of the Yr., Hudson/Daytona, Phoenix, 1999; recipient award Tchr. Space Program, NASA, 1998. Mem.: Competent Toastmaster, Cocoa Quilters, Toastmaster Internat. (v.p. edn., CTM 2002). Avocation: quilting.

SMITH, HARRI ANNE, state legislator; b. Houston County, Ala., Jan. 20, 1962; m. Charlie Smith. BS, Troy State U. Mem. Ala. State Senate, Montgomery, 1999—, chmn. small bus. and econ. devel. com., vice chmn. agr. and forestry com., banking and ins. com., indsl. devel. and recruitment com., commerce, transp. and utilities com. V.p. Slocomb Nat. Bank. Bd. dirs. Geneva County United Way; previously mayor pro-tem, Slocomb; mem. city coun., Slocomb, 1989—. Mem. So. Ala. Reg. Coun. Aging (bd. dirs.), State of Ala. Agribus. Coun., Dothan Area C. of C., Cmty. Bankers Assn., Ala. Bankers Assn. Republican. Baptist. Office: Ala State House 11 S Unio St Montgomery AL 36130-0001

SMITH, HEATHER LYNN, psychotherapist, recreational therapist; b. Modesto, Calif., May 31, 1956; d. Gary Fremont and Marilyn Rae (Brown) S. BS, Calif. State U., Fresno, 1979; MA, U. San Francisco, 1989. Lic. marriage, family and child counselor, Calif. Recreational therapist Casa Colina Rehab. Hops., Pomona, Calif., 1979-82; evaluator developmentally delayed, coord. family edn. Cath. Charities, Modesto, 1982-87; bereavement counselor Hospice, Modesto, 1983-87; high risk youth counselor Ctr. Human Svcs., Modesto, 1987—; pvt. practice, family therapist Modesto, 1988—. Program dir. chemically dependent treatment program Stanislaus County Juvenile Hall, 1990—; program adminstr. First Step, 1999—. Named Outstanding Young Woman of Stanislaus County, 1986, Citizen of Yr., Civitan, 1986, Outstanding Individual award Stanislaus County, 1992. Mem. Calif. Assn. Marriage and Family Therapists, Kappa Kappa Gamma. Republican. Episcopalian. Avocations: skiing, running, backpacking, tennis. Home: 806 Claratina Ave Modesto CA 95356-9610 Office: PO Box 577456 Modesto CA 95357-7456 Office Phone: 209-521-7254. E-mail: serenity.mft@aol.com.

SMITH, HEIDI, political organization administrator; Political worker Goldwater for Pres. Campaign; pres. Oreg. Fedn. Rep. Women, Reno Club Fedn. Rep. Women; 2nd v.p. Nev. Fedn. Rep. Women; chairwoman Oreg. Women Reagan Campaign; treas., dir. region 9 Nat. Fedn. Rep. Women, Alexandria, Va., mem. exec. com. Mgr. Smith Ins. Agy.; tchr. genealogy. Planning commr., parks commr., fair bd. dirs., ct. apptd. spl. advocate, candidate mem. for Nat. State Assembly; events chmn. Truckee Meadows Habitat for Humanity; active The Gift of Life. Mem. No. Nev. Assn. Life Underwriters (exec. dir.). Office: Nat Fedn Rep Women 124 N Alfred St Alexandria VA 22314-3011 Fax: 703-548-9836. E-mail: ssmith@aci.net.

SMITH, HELEN ELIZABETH, retired career officer; b. San Rafael, Calif., Aug. 11, 1946; d. Jack Dillard and Marian Elizabeth (Miller) S. BA in Geography, Calif. State U., Northridge, 1968; MA in Internat. Rels., Salve Regina, Newport, R.I., 1983; MS in Tech. Comm., Rensselaer Poly. Inst., 1988; postgrad., Naval War Coll., 1982-83. Commd. ensign USN, 1968, advanced through grades to capt., 1989; adminstrv. asst. USN Fighter Squadron 101, Key West, Fla., 1969-70; adminstrv. officer Fleet Operational Tng. Group, Mountain View, Calif., 1970-72; leader human resource team Human Resource Ctr., Rota, Spain, 1977-79; adminstrv. officer Pearl Harbor (Hawaii) Naval Sta., 1979-80; dir. Family Svc. Ctr., Pearl Harbor, 1980-82; officer-in-charge R&D lab. Naval Ocean Systems Ctr., Kaneohe, Hawaii, 1983-85; exec. officer Naval ROTC, assoc. prof. Rensselaer Poly. Inst., Troy, N.Y., 1985-88; comdg. officer Navy Alcohol Rehab. Ctr., Norfolk, Va., 1988-90; faculty mem., commanding officer Naval Adminstrv. Command, dean adminstrv. support, comptr. Armed Forces Staff Coll., Norfolk, Va., 1990-93; ret., 1993; exec. dir. Calif. for Drug-Free Youth, 1995-96. Author: (walking tour) Albany's Historic Pastures, 1987; composer (cantata) Night of Wonder, 1983. Chair Hawaii State Childcare Com., Honolulu, 1981-82; coun. mem. Hist. Pastures Neighborhood Assn., Albany, N.Y., 1985-88; mem. working group Mayors Task Force on Drugs, Norfolk, 1989-90; chair, bd. dirs. Va. Coun. on Alcoholism, 1989-92, Calif. for Drug Free Youth, 1995-96; singer North County Baroque Ensemble; assoc. Westar Inst. Avocation: writing. Home: 952 Frederico Blvd Belen NM 87002-7027 E-mail: capthelen@webeworld.com.

SMITH, IRENE HELEN-NORDINE, music educator; d. John J. and Dorothy J. Horzepa; m. Thomas Carlyle Smith, Dec. 19, 1982; children: Julie Ann Nordine, Ryan Carlyle. AA in Music Edn. K-12, Broward C.C., Fort Lauderdale, Fla., 1973; BA in Music Edn. K-12, Fla. Atlantic U., 1975; BA in Elem. Edn., Kennesaw State U., 1991. Cert. tchr. Ga. Profl. Stds. Commn., 2003. Elem. music tchr. Tedder Elem. Broward County Sch. Sys., Pompano, Fla., 1976—77, elem. music tchr. Harbordale Elem. Fort Lauderdale, 1979—83, elem. music tchr. Meadowbrook Elem., 1979—83, elem. music tchr. Banyan Elem., 1979—83; pvt. piano and voice tchr. Roswell, Ga., 1983—; tchr. Mabry Mid. Sch. Cobb County Bd. Edn., Marietta, Ga., 1993—. Organist, choir dir. Coral Springs (Fla.) United Meth. Ch., 1976—83; organist / choir dir. Birmingham United Meth. Ch., Alpharetta, Ga., 1994—99; accompanist Ga. Music Educators Assn. Dist. 12 Mid. Sch. Honor Chorus, Marietta, 1999—. Composer: (Rocky Mount Elem. spirit song) Rocky Mountain Warriors, (Shallowford Falls Elem. spirit song) The Foxy Foxes, (Tritt Elem. Sch. spirit song) I Am A Tritt Tiger, (music high school alma mater) Alan Pope High School Alma Mater. Dir., accompanist Roswell United Meth. Ch., 1983—90. Scholar, Broward C.C., 1971—73, Fla. Atlantic U., 1973—75. Mem.: Music Educators Nat. Conf., Ga. Music Educators Assn., Phi Theta Kappa. Republican. Methodist. Avocations: travel, piano, attend football games, art, reading. Office: Mabry Middle School 2700 Jims Rd Marietta GA 30066 Personal E-mail: irenesmith@bellsouth.net.

SMITH, JACLYN, actress; b. Houston, Oct. 26, 1947; d. Jack and Margaret Ellen S.; m. Dennis Cole (div. 1981); m. Tony Richmond, Aug. 4, 1981; 1 dau., Spencer Margaret. Student, Trinity U., San Antonio. Worked as model. Motion picture appearances include The Adventurers, 1970, Bootleggers, Deja Vu; TV film appearances include Bogen County, 1977, The Users, 1978, Rage of Angels, 1980, Nightkill, 1980, Jacqueline Bouvier Kennedy, 1981, Sentimental Journey, 1984, George Washington (miniseries), 1984, Florence Nightingale, 1985, The Night They Saved Christmas, 1986, Wind Mills of the Gods (miniseries), 1988, The Bourne Identity, 1988, Settle the Score, 1989, Danielle Steele's Kaleidoscope, 1990, Lies Before Kisses, 1991, The Rape of Dr. Willis, 1991, In The Arms Of A Killer, 1992, Love Can Be Murder, 1992, Family Album, 1994, Cries Unheard: The Donna Yaklich Story, 1994, My Very Best Friend, 1996, Married to a Stranger, 1997, Before He Wakes, 1998, Three Secrets, 1999, Freefall, 1999; one of prin. roles TV series Charlie's Angels, 1976-80, (ABC Saturday Night Movie) Christine Cromwell, 1989-90; other TV appearances include Get Christy Love, McCloud, The Rookies, Love Boat, Switch, Navigating the Heart, 2000, The District, 2000; appeared in numerous TV comml. Mem. AFTRA. Office: ICM 8942 Wilshire Blvd Beverly Hills CA 90211-1934

SMITH, JAMESETTA DELORISE, author; b. Chgo., Jan. 26, 1942; d. James Gilbert and Ora Mae (Roberts) Howell; m. Leroy Smith, June 2, 1962; children: Leroy, Darryll Keith. Student, Oxford Bus. Coll., Chgo., 1961-62. Office clerk Justice of the Peace, Gary, Ind., 1966-69; bookkeeper, office mgr. Jones Electric, Gary, Ind., 1971-85. Author: How Strong is Strong, 1988; contbr. articles to profl. jours., newspapers. Treas., bd. dirs. N.W. Ind. Lupus Found., Gary, 1988-92; co-founder, pres. Ark. chpt. Lupus Found., 1993—, mem., race organizer, 1995; facilitator Gary Meth. Hosp. for Lupus Found., 1991-92; pastor's aide Bible study leader Greater St. Paul Bapt. Ch., 1995, sec. ch. food com., 1994-2000, ch. trustee, 1994, hostess and announcing clk., 1997—, spl. recognition trustee, 1998, Sunday sch. tchr., 1998; Bible enrichment instr., 1996—; pastor's aide sec. Clark Rd. M.B. Ch., 1990-92; mem. nomination com. Nat. Lupus Found. Am. Named Vol. of Yr., Ark. chpt. Lupus Found., 1995; recipient Legacy award pin AARP, 1998, Growth award, Lupus Found. Am., 1995-96, 98-99, 2002-2003, Nat. Fleur-De-Lis award for outstanding svc., 2001, award for fin. support Ark. chpt., 2001, award for Dedicated work with Ark. chpt. Lupus Found. Am. Dreams of Heartland; nominated while pres. as Outstanding Organ. of the Yr., Lupus Found. Am., 2002; recipient African Am. Trail Blazers award 2002. Mem. Jones Electric Gary Ind. (Sec. 1986). Democratic. Baptist. Avocations: writing, cooking, numbers, crafts. E-mail: lupusarkhs@cs.com.

SMITH, JANET HUGIE, lawyer; b. Logan, Utah, Aug. 1, 1945; BA magna cum laude, Utah State U., 1967; MA cum laude, Stanford U., 1969; JD, U. Utah, 1976. Bar: Utah 1976, U.S. Supreme Ct. 1992, U.S. Ct. Appeals (10th cir.) 1977. Shareholder, exec. com. Ray, Quinney & Nebeker, Salt Lake City, 1983—. Mem. ABA (labor and employment law sect.), Utah State Bar (labor and employment law sect.), CUE (labor lawyers adv. coun.), Am. Law Coun., Am. Coll. Trial Lawyers, Aldon J. Anderson Am. Inns of Ct. Office: Ray Quinney & Nebeker 36 S State St Ste 1400 Salt Lake City UT 84111-1431 E-mail: jhsmith@rqn.com.

SMITH, JANET L. BASS, musician, educator; b. Cheyenne, Wyo., Jan. 11, 1936; d. Ellwood Aven and Clara Anna (Hahn) Bass; m. Charles Warren Smith, Aug. 24, 1957; children: Randal Allan, Bradley Taylor, Bryan Keith, Roger Andrew. BMus, U. Wyoming, 1957; advanced study, Eastman Sch. of Music, Rochester, N.Y., 1967-68; MMus in Piano Performance, U. N.C., 1972; D in Musical Arts (Piano Performance), U. Mo. Conservatory, Kansas City, 1987. Piano instr. Salem Coll. (prep. dept.), Winston Salem, N.C., 1969-70; instr. in music U. N.C., Greensboro, 1970-72; asst. prof. of music Livingstone Coll., Salisbury, N.C., 1972-75; piano instr. (part time) S.E. Mo. State U., Cape Girardeau, Mo., 1975-89, dir. music prep. program, 1985-89; co-dir. of music and organist St. Andrew LUth. Ch., Cape Girardeau, 1980-89. Prin. keyboardist, bd. dirs. Bowling Green (Ky.) Chamber Orch.; pres. bd. dirs. Bowling Green Chamber Orch., 2001—02, mktg. dir., 2002—; adminstrv. dir. String Acad., 2002—; pianist, tchr., instr., Bowling Green, 1951—; pk. ranger, docent Mammoth Cave, Ky., 1993—. Author: The Golden Protion of the Published Solo Piano Music of Vincent Persichetti, 1987, Cave Research Foundation Songs, 1999; musician (piano soloist): St. Petersburg (Russia) Orch. Popular Classical Music. Theodore Pressor Found. scholar, U. Wyo., 1954, Cashman and Stubbs Charitable Trust grantee, Women's Coun. U. Mo., 1986. Mem.: Beethoven Soc. for Pianists, S.E. Mo. Music Tchrs. Assn. (organizer, pres. 1980—89), Ind. Music Tchrs. Assn. (pres. 1991—93, sec. 1995—97), Ky. Music Tchrs. Assn. (sec. 1990—92, v.p. 1992—94, pres. 1994—96), Music Tchrs. Nat. Assn. (cert. master tchr.). Avocations: caving, oil painting, reading, camping, hiking. Home: 2737 Utah Dr Bowling Green KY 42104-4305 E-mail: jlbsmithpiano@insightBB.com.

SMITH, JANET MARIE, sports and entertainment executive; b. Jackson, Miss., Dec. 13, 1957; d. Thomas Henry and Nellie Brown (Smith) S. BArch, Miss. State U., 1981; MA in Urban Planning, CCNY, 1984. Draftsman Thomas H. Smith and Assocs. Architects, Jackson, 1979; mktg. coord. The Eggers Group, P.C. Architects and Planners, N.Y.C., 1980; program assoc. Ptnrs. for Livable Places, Washington, 1980-82; coord. asst. Lance Jay Brown, Architect and Urban Planner, N.Y.C., 1983-84; coord. architecture and design Battery Park City Authority, N.Y.C., 1982-84; pres., chief exec. officer Pershing Sq. Mgmt. Assn., L.A., 1985-89; v.p. stadium planning and devel. Balt. Orioles Oriole Park at Camden Yard, 1989-94; v.p. sports facilities Turner Properties, Atlanta, 1994-97; v.p. planning and devel. Atlanta Braves, Braves, 1994—; pres. TBS Sports Devel., Inc., 1997-2000; with Struever Brothers, Eccles & Rouse, Inc., Balt., 2000—. Bd. dirs. Assn. Collegiate Schs. Architecture, Washington, 1979-82, Assn. Student Chpts. AIA, Washington, 1979-82. Guest editor: Urban Design Internat., 1985; assoc. editor: Crit, 1979-82; contbr. articles to profl. jours. Named Disting. Grad., Nat. Assn. State Univs. and Land Grant Colls., 1988, One of Outstanding Young Women of Am., 1982; recipient Spirit of Miss. award, Sta. WLBT, Jackson, 1987, Disting. Grad. award Nat. Assn. State Univs., 1988, Outstanding Alumni award Miss. State U., 1994, Andrew White medal Loyola Coll., 1997, Ptnrs. Livable Cmtys. award, 1998, City Coll. N.Y. award, 1998. Mem. AIA (assoc.), Urban Land Inst. Democrat. Episcopalian. Office: Struever Brothers Eccles & Rouse Inc 519 N Charles St Baltimore MD 21201-5099

SMITH, JANET SUE, systems specialist; b. Chgo., Jan. 15, 1945; d. Curtis Edwin and Margaret Louise (Yost) Smith. BA, Ind. U., 1967. Sales mgr. Marshall Field & Co., Chgo., 1968-70, programmer, 1970-72; sr. programmer, analyst Trailer Train Co., Chgo., 1972-75; mgr. data base and systems devel. Railinc-Assn. Am. R.R., Washington, 1975-85, asst. v.p. corp. sec., 1985-93, asst. v.p. strategic systems, 1994-98; exec. dir. Interline Svc., 1998-99, asst. v.p. bus. svc., 1999—2001; self-employed JSSmith Consulting LLC, 2002—. Nat. student v.p. YWCA, 1966-67; bd. dir., v.p. planning and fin. Guide Internat.; advisor Jr. Achievement; pres. Homeowner's Assn.; mem. alumni bd. dir. Ind. U. Coll. Arts and Scis., co-chair Ind. U. Colloquium for Women. Mem.: Woodburn Guild, Am. Coun. R.R. Women, Ind. U. Alumni Assn. (life). Home and Office: JSSmith Cons LLC 903 N Columbia St Chapel Hill NC 27516-1824

SMITH, JEAN, interior design firm executive; b. Oklahoma City; d. A. H. and Goldy K. (Engle) Hearn; m. W. D. Smith; children: Kaye Smith Hunt, Sidney P. Student Chgo. Sch. Interior Design, 1970. v.p. Billco-Aladdin Wholesale, Albuquerque, 1950-92, v.p. Billco Carpet One of Am, 1970. Pres. Opera Southwest, 1979-83, advisor to bd. dirs.; active Civic Chorus, 1st Meth. Ch.; pres. Inez PTA, 1954-55, life mem., hon. life mem. Albuquerque Little Theater, bd. dirs. Republican. Clubs: Albuquerque County, Four Hills Country, Daus. of the Nile (soloist Yucca Temple). Home: 1417 Wagon Train Dr SE Albuquerque NM 87123-4295 Office: 1417 Wagon Train Dr SE Albuquerque NM 87123-4295

SMITH, JEAN KATHERINE MARTIN, English language educator; b. Richmond, Va., Apr. 5, 1946; d. William Patrick and Doris Ruth (Garf) Martin; m. Colin Frank Smith, Apr. 15, 1972 (div. Oct. 1981); 1 child, Andrea Megan Smith. BA in English, Averett Coll., Danville, Va., 1978; MA in Humanities, Hollins Coll., Roanoke, Va., 1993. Cert. tchr., Va. Tchr. English Martinsville (Va.) H.S., 1978-87; tchr. English, journalism, dept. chair Carlisle Sch., Martinsville, 1987—98; tchr. English Bassett HS, 1998—99; tchr. AP English Martinsville H.S., 1999—, coord. internat. baccalaureate diploma sch., 1999—. Adj. instr. English Patrick Henry C.C., Martinsville, 1993-96. Contbr. poems to anthologies, chpt. to book. Recipient Shakespeare Workshop grantee U. Va., 1990, Ind. Study fellow, 1992. Mem. ACLU, Nat. Coun. Tchrs. English, Va. Assn. Tchrs. English, Amnesty Internat., So. Poverty Law Ctr. Democrat. Avocations: photography, writing fiction, poetry, travel. Home: 1016 Jefferson Cir Martinsville VA 24112-3944 Office: Martinsville High School Martinsville VA 24112 Business E-Mail: jsmith@martinsville.k12.va.us.

SMITH, JEAN KENNEDY, former ambassador; b. Brookline, Mass., Feb. 20, 1928; d. Joseph P. and Rose Kennedy; m. Stephen E. Smith (dec.); 4 children. BA, Manhattanville Coll. Founder, dir., chair Very Spl. Arts, 1974—; amb. to Ireland Dublin, 1993-98. Author: (with George Plimpton) Chronicles of Courage, 1993; contbr. articles on the disabled to profl. jours. Trustee Joseph P. Kennedy, Jr. Found., 1964—, John F. Kennedy Ctr. Performing Arts. Recipient Sec.'s award Dept. Vets. Affairs, Vol. of Yr. award People-to-People Com. Handicapped, Margaret Mead Humanitarian award Coun. Cerebral Palsy Auxs., Jefferson award Am. Inst. Pub. Svc., Spirit of Achievement award Yeshiva U., Humanitarian award Capital Children's Mus.

SMITH, JEAN WEBB (MRS. WILLIAM FRENCH SMITH), civic worker; b. L.A.; d. James Ellwood and Violet (Hughes) Webb; B.A. summa cum laude, Stanford U., 1940; m. George William Vaughan, Mar. 14, 1942 (dec. Sept. 1963); children: George William, Merry; m. William French Smith, Nov. 6, 1964. Mem. Nat. Vol. Svc. Adv. Coun. (ACTION), 1973-76, vice chmn., 1974-76; dir. Beneficial Standard Corp., 1976-85. bd. dirs. Cmty. TV So. Calif., 1979-93; mem. Calif. Arts Commn., 1971-74, vice chmn., 1973-74; bd. dirs. The Founders, Music Ctr., L.A., 1971-74; bd. dirs. costume coun. L.A. County Mus. Art, 1971-73; bd. dirs. United Way, Inc., 1973-80, Hosp. Good Samaritan, 1973-80, L.A. chpt. NCCJ, 1977-80, Nat. Symphony Orch., 1980-85, L.A. World Affairs Coun., 1990, L.A. chpt. ARC, 1994-95; bd. fellows Claremont Univ. Ctr. and Grad. Sch., 1987—; bd. dirs. Hosp. Good Samaritan, 1973-80; mem. exec. com., 1975-80; mem. nat. bd. dirs. Boys' Clubs Am., 1977-80; mem. adv. bd. Salvation Army, 1979—; bd. overseers The Hoover Instn. on War, Revolution and Peace, 1989-94; mem. President's Commn. on White House Fellowships, 1980-90, Nat. Coun. on the Humanities, 1987-90; bd. govs. Calif. Cmty. Found., 1990—; bd. regents Children's Hosp. L.A., 1993—. Named Woman of Yr. for cmty. svc. L.A. Times, 1958; recipient Citizens of Yr. award Boys Clubs Greater L.A., 1982, Life Achievement award Boy Scouts Am., L.A. coun., 1985. Mem. Jr. League of L.A. (pres. 1954-55, Spirit of Volunteerism award 1996), Assn. Jr. Leagues of Am. (dir. Region XII, 1956-58, pres. 1958-60), Phi Beta Kappa, Kappa Kappa Gamma. Home: 11718 Wetherby Ln Los Angeles CA 90077-1348

SMITH, JESSIE P. DOWLING, retired social services administrator; b. Sturgills, NC, June 15, 1918; d. Rohe V. and Stella Pennington (Eller) Smith; m. F. P. Smith, July 22, 1983. AB, Berea Coll., 1939; MSW, Columbia U., 1945. Social work assignments WPA, Ky., 1939—43; social worker ARC, New Orleans, 1943—45, Bklyn., 1943—45, Huntington, W.Va., 1946—56, Washington, 1946—56; instr., sch. social work W.Va. U., Morgantown, 1953—54; cons. W.Va. Dept. Mental Health, Charleston, 1954—55; program supr. USPHS Clin. Ctr., Bethesda, Md., 1956—62; cons., social work NIMH, Chgo., 1962—66, NYC, 1962—66; assoc. regional health dir. Mental Health Programs, NYC, 1966—81; ret., 1981; v.p. adv. bd., Mental Retardation Substance Abuse Programs Davidson County Mental Health, NC, 1987—89, pres., 1988—89. Mem.: Columbia U. Alumni Fedn. Bd., Columbia U. Sch. Social Work Alumni Assn. (pres. 1979—81), Nat. Assn. Social Workers (exec. bd. 1968—70, pres. Washington Met. Area chpt.), Columbia U. Sch. Social Work (adv. coun.), Social Casework (editl. adv. bd. 1968—70), NC Coun. of Cmty. Mental Health Programs (adv. bd. 1987—). Home: Apt 703 1330 Massachusetts Ave NW Washington DC 20005-4154

SMITH, JO ANNE, writer, retired educator; b. Mpls., Mar. 18, 1930; d. Robert Bradburn and Virginia Mae S. BA, U. Minn., 1951, MA, 1957. Wire and script editor Rhinelander (Wis.) Daily News, 1951-52; staff corr., night mgr. UPI, Mpls., 1952-56; interim instr. U. N.C., Chapel Hill, 1957-58; instr. U. Fla., Gainesville, 1959-65, asst. prof. journalism, communications, 1965-68, assoc. prof., 1968-76, prof., 1976-88, disting. lectr., 1977, prof. emeritus. Author: JM409 Casebook and Study Guide, 1976, Mass Communications Law Casebook, 1979, 3d edit., 1985. Active, Friends of Libr., Alachua County Humane Soc. Recipient outstanding Prof. award Fla. Blue Key, 1976; Danforth assoc., 1976-85. Mem. Women in Communications, Assn. Edn. in Journalism, Phi Beta Kappa, Kappa Tau Alpha. Democrat. Unitarian Universalist. Home: 208 NW 21st Ter Gainesville FL 32603-1732

SMITH, JOAN H. retired women's health nurse, educator; b. Akron, Ohio; d. Joseph A. and Troynette M. (Lower) McDonald; m. William G. Smith; children: Sue Ann, Priscilla, Timothy. Diploma, Akron City Hosp., 1948; BSN in Edn., U. Akron, 1972, MA in Family Devel., 1980. Cert. in inpatient obstetric nursing. Mem. faculty Akron Gen. Med. Ctr. Sch. Nursing, 1964; former dir. obstet. spl. procedures Speakers Bur., Women's Health Ctrs. Akron Gen. Med. Ctr., 1988; ret., 1990. Cons., speaker women's health care. Mem. Assn. Women's Health, Obstet. and Neonatal Nursing (charter, past sec.-treas., past vice chmn. Ohio sect., chmn. program various confs.). Home: 873 Kirkwall Dr Copley OH 44321-1751

SMITH, JOAN LOWELL, syndicated columnist, feature writer; b. Orange, N.J., June 20, 1933; d. William Jr. and Katherine Margaret (Macpherson) Lowell; m. John A. Nave, Dec. 14, 1957 (div. May 1961); children: Deborah Lowell Kelly, Nancy Nave Ferguson; m. Warren W. Smith, July 19, 1969. Student, Lasell Coll., 1951-52, Drake Bus. Sch., N.Y.C., 1952-53. Exec. sec. Amb. Ernest A. Gross, N.Y.C., 1954-57; adminstrv. asst./v.p. J.B. Williams Co. (Geritol), Clark, N.J., 1966-74; pub. rels. dir. N.J. State Opera, Newark, 1974-78; weekly talk show host-radio WJDM (AM) WFME (AM-FM), Elizabeth and West Orange, N.J., 1974-82; weekly talk show host Sta. WCTV, Wometco, 1975-79; exec. dir. Chamber of Commerce, Westfield, N.J., 1976-79; legis. aide Assemblyman C. Hardwick, N.J., 1980-82; exec. dir. Alzheimer's Disease Fund, Westfield, N.J., 1986-87; pub. rels. dir. Children's Specialized Hosp., Mountainside, N.J., 1993-94; pres./owner Media Mgmt., Westfield, 1974-95; feature writer, weekly columnist on animals The Star-Ledger, Newark, N.J., 1996—. Named one of 40 Women of Achievement, N.J. State Assembly, 2001; recipient 46 awards, N.J. Press Woman, 1991—, Humane Edn. award, Jersey Animal Coalition, 2001, Hero to Animals award, Animal Welfare Fedn. of N.J., 2003, Dedication to Animals award, Humane Soc. US NE Region, 2003. Mem.: DAR (regent 1987—89), Westfield Day Care Ctr. (bd. dirs.), Nat. Fedn. Press Women (2d pl. award 1997, 1st pl. columnist award 1998), Assn. Children with Learning Disabilities (chmn. bd. dirs. 1980—82), Cat Writers Assn. Am. (2d pl. columnist 1999), Dog Writers Assn. Am. (top features writer 1999, top columnist award 2001, top features writer 2003), Daus. of Cin., Geneal. Soc. of West Fields (bd. dirs. 1984—88). Republican. Presbyterian. Avocations: bible studies, swimming, bridge, geneology. Office: PO Box 302 Garwood NJ 07027-0302

SMITH, JOAN TRIMBLE, artist; b. N.Y.C., Oct. 6, 1924; d. Rufus James and Verna Lee (Rooney) Trimble; m. Robinson Vohr Smith, Dec. 17, 1949; children: Melissa, Rufus Vohr, Jared Robinson. BA, Vassar Coll., 1945; student, Art Students League, 1945-50. Art tchr., lectr. various orgns.; gallery dir. Bentley Coll., Waltham, Mass., 1977-84, artist in residence, from 1984. Works include oil portrait in Supreme Ct., Washington, 1969; represented in pvt. collections. Mem. N.H. Art Assn., Concord (Mass.) Art Assn. (Disting. Artist), Copley Soc., Nat. Arts Club N.Y.C. Democrat. Unitarian Universalist. Avocations: cooking, travel. Home: Wayland, Mass. Died Sept. 7, 2003.

SMITH, JULIA AMELIA, retired English language educator; b. San Antonio, Tex., Dec. 25, 1935; d. George Leon and Julia E. (Garcia) S. BA, Our Lady of the Lake, San Antonio, Tex., 1956; MA, U. Tex., 1958; postgrad., Harvard U., 1961; PhD, U. Tex, 1969. Elem. tchr. San Antonio (Tex.) Sch. Dist., 1956-57; instr. Laredo (Tex.) Jr. Coll., 1959-68; asst. prof. English, Tex. A&M U., Kingsville, 1969-72; assoc. prof. Tex. A&I U., Kingsville, 1972-78, prof., 1978—98, chmn. dept., 1977-83, prof. emeritus, 2000, ret. Contbr. articles to profl. jours. Organist St. Martin's Ch., Kingsville, Tex. Mem. Modern Language Assn., Music Club Kingsville, Audubon Soc., Delta Kappa Gamma, Kappa Nu. Democrat. Roman Catholic. Avocations: birding, gardening. Office: Tex A&M PO Box 162 Kingsville TX 78364-0162

SMITH, JULIA LADD, medical oncologist, hospice physician; b. Rochester, N.Y., July 26, 1951; d. John Herbert and Isabel (Walcott) Ladd; m. Stephen Slade Smith; 1 child. BA, Smith Coll., 1973; MD, N.Y. Med. Coll., 1976. Diplomate Am. Bd. Internal Medicine, Am. Bd. Med. Oncology, Am. Bd. Hospice and Palliative Medicine. Intern in medicine N.Y. Med. Coll., N.Y.C., 1976-77; resident in medicine Rochester Gen. Hosp., 1977-79; internist Genesee Valley Group Health, Rochester, 1979-80; oncology fellow U. Rochester, 1980-82, asst. prof. oncology in medicine sch. medicine and dentistry, 1986—; oncologist Med. Ctr. Clinic, Ltd., Pitts., 1982-83; oncologist, internist Rutgers Community Health Plan, New Brunswick, N.J., 1983-86; med. dir. Genesee Region Home Care Assn./Hospice, Rochester, 1988—; med. oncologist Genesee Hosp., Rochester, 1996—2001, chief hematology/oncology, 1996—2001; med. oncologist Rochester Gen. Hosp., 2001—. Bd. dirs. Am. Cancer Soc., Monroe County, 1988-92. Nat. Cancer Inst. rsch. grantee, 1993-95. Fellow Acad. Hospice Physicians; mem. ACP, Am. Soc. Clin. Oncology. Unitarian-Universalist. Avocations: sailing, reading, movies, bridge. Address: Lipson Blood and Cancer Ctr 1425 Portland Ave Rochester NY 14621

SMITH, JULIE SHELTON, artist; b. Amarillo, Tex., Apr. 1, 1946; d. Earl Talmadge Smith and Betty Lou Shelton McBride; m. Francis McCaffrey (dec. June 1981); 1 child, Ann Elise McCaffrey ; m. Julia Lorillard Wampage Pell, Jan. 21, 1983 (div. Mar. 12, 2002). BFA, U. Tex., 1969; MFA, R.I. Sch. Design, 1993. One-woman shows include Newport Art Mus., 2001, Sinclair C.C., 2002, Configurations, Fraser Gallery, Washington, D.C., 2004, exhibited in group shows at Santa Fe C.C., 2003. Pres. bd. dirs. Cmty. Musicworks, Providence, 2002—; bd. adv. Equity Action Fund R.I. Found., Providence; bd. adv. Started Glance, Newport County, RI, 2002—. Recipient Best in Show award, Newport Art Mus., 2000; grantee, R.I. Coun. Humanities, 2001. E-mail: julie.smith@earthlink.net.

SMITH, JUNE SYLVIA KOLBE, artist, educator; b. Chgo., June 8, 1926; d. Clarence William and Marie Wilma Colby; m. Harold Eugene Reed, Sept. 23, 1947 (div. June 1948); m. Joseph Patric Smith, June 7, 1951; children: Donna Kaye, Craig Douglas. AA, UCLA, 1948; student, Occidental Coll., 1961, Am. Inst. Fine Arts, 1962. Artist Biltmore Hotel, L.A., 1966-78; docent, instr. pub. rels. San Gabriel (Calif.) Fine Arts Assn., 1997—; instr. Michael's Arts & Crafts, Pasadena, Glendale, Monrovia, Calif., 1998—99, 2001—02. Represented in permanent collections Millard Sheets Gallery, one-woman shows include San Gabriel Fine Arts, 1991; contbr. New Voices in American Poetry, 1979. Public rels. St. James Ch., S. Pasadena, 1991-99. Recipient 2d pl. Santa Paula Art C.C., 1963, 2d pl. Highland Park Art Assn., 1968. Mem. Calif. Art Club. Democrat. Episcopalian. Avocations: rollerskating, gardening. Office: San Gabriel Fine Arts Assn Mission and Santa Anita San Gabriel CA 90032 Home: 3409 Camero Ave La Verne CA 91750-3412

SMITH, KAREN ANN, visual artist; b. Trenton, NJ, May 25, 1964; d. James Roy and Clara Patricia (Walton) S. A in Comml. Art, Art Inst. Phila., 1984; BFA in Graphic Design and Art Therapy, U. Arts, Phila., 1989; grad. in graphic design, Basel Sch. for Design, 1991; MA in Expressive Therapies, Lesley Coll., 1993. Graphic designer Mercer County C.C., Trenton, 1984-86; mural painter, supr. Anti-Graffiti Network, Phila., 1988; tchr. drawing and set design Chestnut Hill (Mass.) Sch., 1995, 96; freelance graphic designer Swiss Fed. Rys., Bern, 1993-95; tchr. drawing Wentworth Inst. Tech., Boston, 1996, 97; tchr. design Northeastern U., Boston, 1997. Fireworks crew Pyrotech. Inc., Boston, 1997; apprentice Johnson Atelier Tech. Inst. of Sculpture, Trenton, 1997-99; artist Airtex Interiors, Fallsington, 2000-03, Midnight Kiwi Design, Newtown, Pa., 2003—; artist, activities asst. Pennswood Village, Newtown, 2003—; visual artist, activities asst. Pennswood Village, Newtown, Pa., 2003-. One-woman shows include Contempo Galerie, Bern, Switzerland, 1994, Boston Archtl. Ctr. Atelier, 1997, George Sch., Newtown, Pa., 1997, exhibited in group shows at Howard Yezerski Gallery, Boston, 1994, Kingston Gallery, 1995, Phillips' Mill, New Hope, Pa., 1997, Woodmere Art Mus., Chestnut Hill, Pa., 1998, Princeton (NJ) Day Sch., 1999, Trenton City Mus., 1999, Vorpal Gallery, N.Y.C., 2000—02, Artsbridge, Prallsville Mills, N.J., 2000, Riverbank Arts, Stockton, N.J., 2000—, iTheo.com, San Francisco, 2000—01, Nat. Bottle Mus., Ballston Spa, N.Y., 2001, Artsbridge Photography Exhbn., Lamberville, NJ, 2003, Artists at the Farm, Langhorne, Pa., 2003—;, author numerous poems. Scholar Women in Graphic Arts, 1987-89; grantee Mystic Studios Trust, 1994-97, Artists at the Farm, Langhorne, Pa., 2003—. Mem. Coll. Art Assn., Boston Athenaeum, Origami USA, Artsbridge.

SMITH, KAREN LYNN, principal; b. San Francisco, Calif., Aug. 10, 1950; d. Joseph P. and Madelyn E. Smith; m. Charles J. Gegen, Apr. 2, 1981. BA, Marymount Coll., New York, NY, 1972; MA, UCLA, Los Angeles, CA, 1975. Founder / owner Hart Ho. Tutors, Santa Monica, Calif., 1977—89; prin. / owner Smith Sch., New York, NY, 1990—. Recipient Disting. Svc. in Field of Edn., Marymount Coll., 1986. Home: 317 East 78th Street New York NY 10021 Office: Smith School 1393 York Avenue New York NY 10021 Personal E-mail: gegen@aol.com.

SMITH, KATHERINE TERESA, history educator; b. New Orleans, Apr. 30, 1946; d. Gerald Alfred and Margaret Mary (Murphy) S. BA in History, Nazareth Coll., 1967, BS in Elem. Edn., 1970; MA in History, SUNY, Genesco, 1975. Cert. Elem. Educator. Tchr. Rochester (N.Y.) Cath. Schs., 1969-70, Rush-Henrietta (N.Y.) Schs., 1970—. Mem. Henrietta Planning bd., 1975-82; membership com. Rochester Orchestra, 1982-85; treas., sec. Henrietta Dem. com., 1969-2000; bd. dirs. Riverton, sec., treas., 1973-74, 82-85; sec., treas. PTA R-H, 1970-2000. Recipient Citizenship award Henrietta Planning bd., 1982, Svc. award Riverton Cmty. Assn., Henrietta, 1985. Mem. Rush-Henrietta Educators Assn. (v.p. 1974-84, gold apple award 1984, delegate NEX, AFT, NYSUT). Democrat. Roman Cath. Home: 292 Countess Dr West Henrietta NY 14586-9416 Office: Rush Henrietta Schs 5509 E Henrietta Rd Rush NY 14543-9755

SMITH, KATHERYN JEANETTE, music educator; b. Siloam Springs, Ark., July 6, 1944; d. Charlie H. and Victoria Virginia (Jameson) Porter; m. Curtis Barth Smith, Jan. 10, 1975; 1 child, Melody Jeanette. B in Music Edn., So. Nazarene U., 1966; M in Music Edn., Kent (Ohio) State U., 1970. Gen. music tchr. Duncan (Okla.) Jr. H.S., 1966-68; elem. music tchr. Akron (Ohio) Pub. Schs., 1971-72; music prof. MidAm. Nazarene U., Olathe, Kans., 1972—. Clinician Lillenas Music Confs., Olathe, Kans., 1994, 96, 97. Keyboard accompanist Coll. Ch. of the Nazarene, 1973—. Mem. Music Educators Nat. Conf., Music Tchrs. Nat. Assn., MidAm. Nazarene Univ. Women's Aux. (chairperson 1973-74, 94-98). Avocation: whale collection. Office: MidAm Nazarene Univ 2030 E College Way Olathe KS 66062-1831 E-mail: ksmith@mnu.edu.

SMITH, KATHRYN ANN, art educator; BA cum laude, Yale U., 1982; MA, NYU, 1989, PhD, 1996. Asst. prof. art history Tyler Sch. Art, Temple U., Phila., 1995—98; asst. prof. fine arts dept. fine arts NYU, N.Y.C., 1998—. Cons. Leaves of Gold exhbn. Phila. Mus. Art, 1998—2001. Author: Art, Identity and Devotion in Fourteenth Century England: Three Women and Their Books of Hours, 2003; contbr. essay Leaves of Gold, articles to art jours. Recipient dissertation grant, Fulbright Commn., 1992—93, Mary Davis fellowship, Ctr. Advanced Study Visual Arts, 1993—95; fellow, NEH, 2001. Mem.: Coll. Art Assn., Internat. Ctr. for Medieval Art (nominating com. 1996—98), Medieval Acad. Am. (program com. 2000—02). Office: NYU Dept Fine Arts 303 Silver Center 100 Washington Sq E New York NY 10003-6688

SMITH, KATIE, professional basketball player; b. June 4, 1974; Grad., Ohio State U., 1996. Player Minn. Lynx WNBA, Mpls., 1999—. Recipient Gold medal Jones Cup, 1996; Jr. World Championship, 1993, Kodak All-American, 1993, 96, Gold medal U.S. World Championship Team, 1998; named to All-WNBA Team, 2000-03, WNBA All-Star Team, 2000-03. Achievements include mem. Gold medal U.S. Women's Basketball Team, Sydney Olympics, 2000. Avocations: music, being outside, being with friends. Office: Minn Lynx 600 First Ave North Minneapolis MN 55403

SMITH, KATRINA DIANE, writer; b. Oakland, Calif., Dec. 23, 1957; d. Mack Edward and Mary Jean Smith; children: Rose, Jason Larenzo. Student, Alameda Coll., Calif., Laney Coll., Oakland, Calif., Careercom Bus. Coll., Oakland, 1998. Author: The Founders Guide of Girl Scouting, 1994, The Floral Factor of the Cotton Mill, 1998, The History of the War in Theatrical Genology, 1997. Vol. So. Poverty Law Ctr., Montgomery, Ala., 1996, Sr. Citizens League, Washington, 1996, Notch Reform Campaign, Washington, 1996; adv. bd. Missing Persons, Oakland, Calif., 1999, Consular Search Statistics, Dept. State, 2001; mem. U.S. Olympic Com., 1996. Named to Internet Poetry Hall of Fame; recipient Colgate Youth for Am. award, Colgate Palmolive Co., 1993—94, Editor's Choice award, Internet Libr. Poetry. Mem.: AARP (bd. dirs. 2001—02), Nat. Geog. Soc. (bd. dirs. 1989), TWA Club (SFO bd. 1991). Avocation: reading. Home: 1699 70th Ave Oakland CA 94621 Office: Internet Library of Poetry 1 Poetry Plz Owings Mills MD 21117

SMITH, KAY FRANCES, social worker; b. Monroe, Wis., Nov. 22, 1949; d. Bernard Joseph and Frances Geneva Smith. BS, U. Ariz., 1977; MSW, Ariz. State U., 1980. Med. social worker Carondelet St. Mary's Hosp., Tucson, 1980-91; renal social worker Desert Dialysis, Tucson, 1991-95; home health social worker Samaritan Home Health, Tucson, 1993-95; renal social worker Gambro Healthcare, Tucson, 1995—. Editl. bd. Nat. Kidney Found., 1996-98; exhibited wood carvings in various shows, including Arts Alive, Phoenix, Ariz., Ariz. Kidney Found. Ann. Arts Show. Sec. Ariz. Kidney Found., Tucson, 1990-95, v.p. 1995—, chairperson black gospel music concert, 1995-97, chairperson theatre event, 1995; pres. Coun. of Nephology Social Work, Tucson, 1990—. Mem. NASW, Old Pueblo Australian Shepherd Club, Coun. of Nephrology Social Workers. Avocations: artist, dog obedience training, gardening. Office: Gambro Health Care 3662 S 16th Ave Tucson AZ 85713-6001

SMITH, KAYE TRAIN, artist; b. Camden, N.J., July 15, 1927; d. William Matthew Biddle and Jennie May Leibensperger; m. Robert L. Smith, Aug. 18, 1995; m. John Martin Train, June 3, 1945 (dec. Jan. 2, 1993); children: Jeanne Carole Train, Suzanne Kathryn Train, Kurt Robert Train. Airbrush artist Norcross Greetings Corp., N.Y.C., 1945—46; profl. in-house model Jo Collins Sportswear Corp., St. Louis, 1947—48; freelance artist Fremont, Roseville, Calif., 1967—2003. Exhibit coord. Placerville Art Assn., 1971—72. Recipient Nat. Design award, Am. Greetings Corp., 1966. Mem.: Roseville Arts Ctr., Sun City Roseville Art Club (pres. 1996—97, various coms., signature painting, 8th ann. show 2003). Home: 7260 Timberrose Way Roseville CA 95747

SMITH, KELLY MCCOIG, secondary school educator; b. Hampton, Va., Nov. 5, 1977; d. Forrest Daniel and Janet Ward McCoig; m. Chris Steven Smith, July 26, 2003. BA, Coll. William and Mary, 2000; Ednl. Leadership/Adminstrn., Old Dominion U., 2002. English tchr./yearbook advisor Denbigh H.S., Newport News, Va., 2000—. New tchr. mentor Denbigh H.S., Newport News, 2003. Mem./sec. UDC, Hampton, Va., 2000—03. Mem.: ASCD, NEA, Va. Educator's Assn., Nat. Coun. Tchrs. English, Phi Kappa Phi, Phi Delta Kappa. Baptist. Avocations: health and fitness, music, dance. Office: Denbigh High School 259 Denbigh Blvd Newport News VA 23608 Personal E-mail: kelly.smith@nn.k12.va.us. E-mail: kelly.mccoig@nn.k12.va.us.

SMITH, KESTRA JAN, prosecutor; b. Erie, Pa., July 17, 1951; d. LeRoy Benjamin and Beatrice Shelby Smith. BA, Oberlin Coll., 1985; MusB in Piano Performance, Oberlin Conservatory, 1985; JD, U. of Cin., 1989; courses in bus. mgmt., U. Md., Kaiserslautern, Germany; courses in secondary education in French, Edinboro State Coll.; studied piano with Florence Wagner, Robert Shannon, Sanford Margolis, Julian Martin, Jack Radunsky, studied organ with Garth Peacock. Bar: Ohio 1990. Libr. technician Dept. of the Army, Kaiserslautern, Germany, 1978—79; pers. supr. Army and Air Force Exch. Services (AAFES), Kaiserslautern, Germany, 1981—82; pvt. complaint officer City of Cin., 1987—90; law clerk Pinales, Schwartz, Mezibov and Howard, 1988; extern, Hon. Nathaniel Jones 6th Circuit Ct. of Appeals, 1989; law clk., Hon. Ann Marie Tracey Hamilton County Ct. of Common Pleas, Cin., 1990—92; asst. pros. atty. Cuyahoga County, Cleve., 1992—, with maj. trial divsn., child victim sect., 2000—01, asst. pros. atty., supr., Juvenile Justice Unit, 2002, asst. pros. atty., supr., Gen. Felony Unit, 2002—. Career day presenter Cleve. Bd. of Edn., Cleve., 1995—2003; dir. early intevention program, 2002—; instr. Cleve. Police Acad., 2003. Musician (piano tchr.) recitals, performances, accompaniments. Spkrs. panel Lead Diversity, Cleve., 2002; pianist and asst. organist First Ch. of God, Cambridge Springs, Pa., 1956—67; asst. organist/musician United Presbyn. Ch., Edinboro, Pa., 1967—75; musician/musical dir. Bethel United Pentecostal Ch., Kaiserslautern, Germany, 1977—82; min. of music Mt. Zion Bapt. Ch., Oberlin, Ohio, 1984—86, Olivet Bapt. Ch., Cin., 1990—92; dir. children's choir Mega Ch., Cleveland, Ohio, 1993—94; min. music East Glenville United Meth. Ch., Cleve., 1996—98, The Master's United Meth. Ch., Euclid, Ohio, 1999—2001; mem. bd. dirs. In the Spirit Ministries, Cleveland, Ohio, 1996—97. Mem.: Cleve. Bar Assn. (assoc.; exec. com. - rep., prosecutor Cuyahoga County 2003). Born Again Christian. Avocations: travel, reading. Office: Cuyahoga County Prosecutor's Office 1200 Ontario St Cleveland OH 44113

SMITH, KIKI, artist; b. Nuremberg, Germany, 1954; One-woman shows include The Kitchen, N.Y.C., 1982, Fawbush Gallery, 1988, 1992, 1993, Galerie René Blouin, Montreal, 1989, 1991—92, 1994, Dallas Mus. Art, 1989, Ezra and Cecile Zilkha Gallery Ctr. for the Arts Wesleyan U., Middletown, Conn., 1989, Tyler Gallery Tyler Sch. Art Temple U., Phila., 1990, Ctr. d'Arte Contemporaine, Geneva, 1990, Inst. Art and Urban Resources The Clocktower, Long Island, N.Y., 1990, Inst. Contemporary Art, Amsterdam, 1990, Mus. Modern Art, N.Y.C., 1990—91, Shoshana Wayne Gallery, Santa Monica, Calif., 1991, 1992, 1992—93, MAK Galerie, Vienna, 1991, U. Art Mus., Berkeley, Calif., 1991, Art Awareness, Inc., Lexington, N.Y., 1991, Corcoran Gallery Art, Washington, 1991, Greg Kucera Gallery, Seattle, 1991, Rose Art Mus. Brandeis U., Waltham, Mass., 1992, Österreichisches Mus. angewandte Kunst, Vienna, 1992, Moderna Mus., Stockholm, 1992, Bonner Kunstverein, Bonn, 1992, Galerie M & R Fricke, Düsseldorf, Germany, 1992—93, Williams Coll. Mus. Art, Williamstown, Mass., 1992—93, Ohio State U., Columbus, 1992—93, Anthony d'Offay Gallery, London, 1993, 1995, Phoenix Art Mus., 1993, U. Art Mus., Santa Barbara, Calif., 1994, La. Mus. Modern Art, Humlebaek, Denmark, 1994, The Israel Mus., Jerusalem, 1994, Barbara Gross Galerie, Munich, 1994, Laura Carpenter Fine Art, Santa Fe, 1994, Pace Wildenstein, N.Y., 1994, Royal LePage Gallery, Toronto, 1994—95, Barbara Krakow Gallery, Boston, 1994—96, Whitechapel Art Gallery, London, 1995, numerous others, exhibited in group shows at Brooke Alexander Gallery, N.Y., 1980, 1991, White Columns, N.Y., 1981, 1983, 1990, Artists Space, 1981, 1990, Barbara Gladstone Gallery, 1982, Hallwalls, Buffalo, N.Y., 1983, Susan Caldwell Gallery, N.Y., 1984, 1987, Galerie Engstrom, Stockholm, 1984, Art City, N.Y., 1985, Moderna Mus., Stockholm, 1985, Cin. Art Mus., 1985, Bklyn. Mus., 1986, 1989, Curt Marcus Gallery, N.Y., 1986, Fawbush Gallery, 1987, 1989, 1990, Mus. Modern Art, N.Y.C., 1988, 1992, IBM Gallery, N.Y., 1988, Arch Gallery, Amsterdam, 1988, Tom Cugliani Gallery, 1989, Simon Watson Gallery, N.Y., 0190, Mus. Fine Arts, Boston, 1990, Hunter Coll. Art Gallery, 1991, Milw. Art Mus., 1992, Paula Cooper Gallery, 1993, Serpentine Gallery, London, 1994, PaceWildenstein, N.Y., 1995, 1997, 1998, Ace Gallery, Mex., 1997, Yale U. Art Gallery, New Haven, Conn., 1998, numerous others. Office: c/o Pace Wildenstein 32 E 57th St New York NY 10022-2513

SMITH, LEILA HENTZEN, artist; b. Milw., May 20, 1932; d. Erwin Albert and Marian Leila (Austin) Hentzen; m. Richard Howard Smith, Sept. 12, 1959; 1 child, Jennie. BFA, Miami U., 1955; cert., Famous Artists Schs., 1959. Quilting tchr. Milw. Pub. Schs., 1975-79. One-woman shows include Boerner Bot. Gardens, Whitnall Park, Wis., 1993, 2 person show, Firefly Gallery, Wauwatosa, Wis., 2003, exhibited in group shows at Milw. Art Ctr., 1961, West Bend (Wis.) Gallery Fine Arts, 1963, Wustum Mus. Art, Racine, Wis., 1966, Mapledale Sch. Gallery, Bayside, Wis., 1977, 1981, Mount Mary Coll., Milw., 1969—77, Artist's World Gallery, Cedarburg, Wis., 1975, Mount Mary Coll., Milw., 1979—2001, Ozaukee Art Ctr, Cedarburg, Wis., 1982—86, John Michael Kohler Arts Ctr., Sheboygan, Wis., 1984, 1987, 1989, 2002, Cedarburg Cultural Ctr., 1988—2001, West Bend Gallery Fine Arts, 1993, Ozaukee Art Ctr, Cedarburg, Wis., 1993, Rahr-West Art Mus., Manitowoc, Wis., 1994, West Bend Gallery Fine Arts, 1996, Gallery 110 North, Plymouth, Wis., 1996, Rahr-West Art Mus., Manitowoc, Wis., 1997, Cardinal Stritch U., 1998—2003, West Bend Gallery Fine Arts, 1999, 2002, Represented in permanent collections Milw. County Art Commn. Women's aux. vol. Salvation Army, Milw.; mem. dean's adv. coun. U. Wis. Milw. Sch. Arts. Recipient Honorable Mention for painting Bayshore Merchants Assn, 1969, Delta Gamma Art Fair, 1981, Best of Show for painting John Michael Kohler Arts Ctr., 1988. Mem. AAUW, Cedarburg Artists Guild, Wis. Watercolor Soc., Seven Arts Soc. Milw. (pres. 1967-68, painters group chmn. 1962-63), DAR (Milw. chpt. Holiday Folk Fair chmn. 1965-76, libr. historian 1974-77, corr. sec. 1977-80, dir. 1983-86, rec. sec. 1992-95, regent 1995-98, Outstanding Jr. Mem. 1966), Wis. Soc. Daus. of Founders and Patriots of Am. (pres. 1964-66, 2d v.p. 1966-68, 70-73, corr. sec. 1976-79), Wis. Ct. Assts., Nat. Soc. Women Descendants Ancient and Hon. Arty. Co. Boston, Wis. Soc. Mayflower Descendants (sec. 1999-02), Delta Zeta. Congregationalist. Avocations: quilting, needlework, swimming.

SMITH, LEONORE RAE, artist; b. Chgo. d. Leon and Rose (Hershfield) Goodman; m. Paul Carl Smith, Apr. 17, 1943; children: Jill Henderson, Laurie Christman. Student, Chgo. Art Inst., 1935-40, U. Chgo., 1939—. Performer in many Broadway shows, with Met. Opera Quartet, Carnegie Hall, nat. concerts; portrait, landscape painter; signature artist Oil Painters of Am., Chgo., 1992-2000, Am. Acad. of Women Artists, 1997-98; ofcl. artist U.S. Coast Guard, Washington, 1989-2000; cert. artist Am. Portrait Soc., Huntington Harbor, Calif., 1985; nat. adv. bd. The Portrait Club, N.Y.C., 1983. Pres. Pacific Palisades Rep. Women, Calif. Named one of Master Artists of the World, Internat. Artist Mag., 1996; recipient Best of Show awards, Salamagundi U.S. Coast Guard, 1989, Pacific Palisades Art Assn., 1987, 1st prize in oils, Greater L.A. Art Competition, Santa Monica, Calif., 1995, prize, The Artist's Mag., 1995, Internat. Soc. Artists, 1977, 1st pl. award, Dream Studio competition, 1996, 1st pl. in portrait, O.P.A. Nat. Show, 2001, award, Northlight Art Mag., 2002, Internat. Artist Mag., 2002, several awards, Calif. Art Club, shown at Nat. Mus. Naval Aviation, Carnegie Mus., Frederick Weisman Mus., Malibu, Calif. Mem. Am. Acad. Women Artists (signature), Salmagundi Club, Pacific Palisades Art Assn. (past pres.), Calif. Art Club, Oil Painters of Am. (signature, 1st Pl. 2001), Am. Portrait Soc. (cert.). Avocations: singing, acting, poetry.

SMITH, LINDA A. retired congresswoman; m. Vern Smith; children: Sheri, Robi. Office mgr.; former mem. Wash. State Ho. of Reps.; mem. Wash. State Senate; congresswoman, Wash. 3rd Dist. U.S. House Reps., Washington, 1995-98; mem. resources com., small bus. com.; founder, dir. Shared Hope Internat., Vancouver, Wash., 1998—. Republican. Home: 10009 NW Ridgecrest Ave Vancouver WA 98685-5159 Office: Shared Hope Internat PO Box 65337 Vancouver WA 98665

SMITH, LINDA ANN GLIDEWELL, accountant; b. Birmingham, Ala., Aug. 11, 1944; d. Emmett O'Neal and Iola Florence (Harris) Glidewell; m. Lindsey Stribling Smith, Nov. 5, 1966 (div. Dec. 1990); 1 child, Lindsey Nelson; m. Charles G. Espey, Sept. 11, 1997 (div. Sept. 2001); 1 stepchild, Heidi Espey Holladay. BA cum laude, Birmingham-So. Coll., 1984. Stenographer Cook's Pest Control, Decatur, Ala., 1962, Nelson-Weaver Cos., Birmingham, Ala., 1963-69; resident mgr. Twin Homes of Mt. Brook, Ala., 1966-69; bookkeeper, sect. to v.p. Molton, Allen & Williams, 1969-72; sec. quality assurance dept. So. Co. Svc., Birmingham, 1972-74, sec. sys. constrn. budget, 1974-82, sr. sec. treasury dept., 1982-83; jr. acct. major projects-acctg. Ala. Power Co., Birmingham, 1983-87, sr. acct. fuel dept., 1987-90, sr. acct. stats. dept., 1990-92; fin. adminstr., comptr. Ala. Bapt., Inc., Birmingham, 1992-99; bus. revenue tax compliance officer Shelby County, 1999—2002. Dep. clk. Bay County, Panama City, Fla., 2002—. Asst. treas. So. Co. Svcs. State and Fed. PAC., Ala. PowerCo. State and Fed. PAC. Mem. Am. Soc. Women Accts., The Club, Inc., Alpha Lambda Delta, Birmingham So. Alumni Assn. (coun. mem.). Baptist. Avocations: travel, culinary art, walking, fishing.

SMITH, LINDA GENE, legislative staff member; BA, Brigham Young U., 1964, MA, 1966; postgrad., Denver U., U. Nat. Mexico, Mexico City. TV script writer, prodr., on-camera tchr. WETA, 1974; press sec., legis. asst. Rep. Allan Howe, 1975-76; spl. asst. Rep. Teno Roncalio, Wyo., 1977-78; press sec. Rep. Gillis Long, La., 1978-85, Ho. Dem. Caucus, 1981-85; chief of staff U.S. Rep. Tim Wirth, Colo., 1985-86, U.S. Rep. Howard L. Berman, Washington, 1986—. Office: 2330 Rayburn Ho Office Bldg Washington DC 20515-0001

SMITH, LINDA S. music educator, musician; b. Topeka, Kans., Oct. 8, 1955; d. Wilbur Porter and Esther Nadine (Faith) Smith. MusB, Oklahoma City U., 1977; MusM, Eastman Sch. Music, 1979; postgrad., EAstman Sch. Music, 1979—81; degree preparatoire superieur, Conservatoire Nat. de Region, Paris, 1982. Organist Calvary Bapt. Ch., Topeka, 1965—73, Ctrl. Presbyn. Ch., Oklahoma City, 1973—77, 1st Reformed Ch., Rochester, NY, 1977—81, St. Michael's Ch., Paris, 1981—83, West Side Christian Ch., Topeka, 1983—; dir. music Accent Acad., Topeka, 1997—99. CEO, pres., founder Genesis Music Found., Inc., 1999—. Editor: Kids Music Jour., 1999—, composer more than 400 songs. Piano tchr. Salvation Army, Topeka, 1999. Mem.: Music Tchrs. Nat. Assn., N.E. Kans. Music Tchrs. Assn., Topeka Music Tchrs. Assn. (v.p. 2000—, publicist 1998—99, sec. 1999—2000, pres. 2001—). Home: 2416 SE Monroe Topeka KS 66605 E-mail: Smithlinmu@aol.com.

SMITH, LIZ (MARY ELIZABETH SMITH), newspaper columnist, broadcast journalist; b. Ft. Worth, Feb. 2, 1923; d. Sloan and Sarah Elizabeth (McCall) S. B.J., U. Tex., 1948. Editor Dell Publns., N.Y.C., 1950-53; assoc. producer CBS Radio, 1953-55, NBC-TV, 1955-59; assoc. Cholly Knickerbocker newspaper column, N.Y.C., 1959-64; film critic Cosmpolitan mag., 1966; columnist Chgo. Tribune-N.Y. Daily News Syndicate (now Tribune Media Services), 1976-91; TV commentator WNBC-TV, N.Y.C., 1978-91; commentator Fox-TV, N.Y.C., 1991—; columnist Newsday, L.A. Times Syndicate, 1991—, Family Circle mag., 1993—; freelance mag. writer; commentator Gossip Show E! Entertainment, 1993—; columnist N.Y. Post, N.Y.C., 1995—, 1995—. Author: The Mother Book, 1978. Home and Office: 160 E 38th St New York NY 10016-2651

SMITH, LOIS ADKINS, science educator; b. Union, Miss., Jan. 11, 1947; d. Davie A. Adkins and Mavis V. Chisholm; m. James Keith Smith, Dec. 23, 1967; children: Stephen, Michael, Maria, Philip. BS in Microbiology, U. Ala., 1969; M in Christian Edn., New Orleans Bapt. Theol. Sem., 1986; M in Secondary Edn., William Carey Coll., 2002. Technologist Miss. State Bd. Health, Jackson, 1969—74; environ. chemist First Chem. Corp., Pascagoala, Miss., 1987—89; med. technologist/toxicology Med. Pathology Lab., Meridian, Miss., 1990—2000; tchr. sci. Lauderdale County Schs., Meridian, 2000—. Grantee, Miss. Power, 2002—03; Michael Jordan grantee, Michael Jordan Found., 2002—03. Republican. Baptist. Avocations: gardening, sewing, reading, walking. Office: Southeast Lauderdale HS 2362 Long Creek Rd Meridian MS 39307*

SMITH, LOIS ANN, real estate executive; b. Chgo., Jan. 1, 1941; d. Alburn M. and Ruth A. (Beaver) Beaudoin; m. Dickson K. Smith, Mar. 24, 1962 (div. May 1982); children: Michelle D., Jeffrey D. BA, U. Utah, 1962; MBA, Marquette U., 1972. Asst. mgr. prodn. Northwestern Mut. Life Ins. Co., Milw., 1979-83, asst. mgr., asset mgr., 1983-88; assoc. dir., asset mgmt. Asset Mgmt., 1988-89; dir. asset mgmt. Northwestern Mut. Life Ins. Co., Milw., 1990-95, dir. real estate equities, 1995—. Cons. Girl Scouts Am., Milw., 1986, YWCA, Milw., 1986, bd. dirs. YWCA, 1981-87; bd. dirs. YWCA, 1999—, Planned Parenthood of Wis., 1998—, Present Music, 1999—. Mem. Internat. Council Shopping Ctrs., Profl. Dimensions, Beta Gamma Sigma. Unitarian Universalist. Home: 808 E Kilbourn Ave Milwaukee WI 53202-3462 Office: Northwestern Mut Life Ins Co 720 E Wisconsin Ave Milwaukee WI 53202-4703 E-mail: loissmith@northwesternmutual.com.

SMITH, LOIS ARLENE, actress, writer; b. Topeka, Nov. 3, 1930; d. William Oren and Carrie D. (Gottshalk) Humbert; m. Wesley Dale Smith, Nov. 5, 1948 (div. 1973); 1 child, Moon Elizabeth. Student, U. Wash., 1948-50; studied with Lee Strasberg, Actor's Studio, N.Y.C., 1955—. Guest dir. Juilliard Sch., 1987; Clarence Ross fellow Am. Theater Wing at Eugene O'Neill Theater Ctr., 1983; mem. adv. panel program fund Pub. Broadcasting Service, 1981-82; hon. founder Harold Clurman Theatre Artists Fund, Ctr. for Arts, SUNY-Purchase, 1981 Author: play All There Is, 1982; debut in Time Out for Ginger, 1952; actress Broadway and off-Broadway prodns., 1952—; stage appearances include Theater of the Living Arts, Mark Taper Forum, Long Wharf Theater, Balt. Centerstage and Steppenwolf Theater Co.; appears on network and pub. TV programs; stage appearances include, The Young and the Beautiful, 1955, The Glass Menagerie, 1956, Blues for Mr. Charlie, 1964, Orpheus Descending, 1957, Miss Julie, 1966, Uncle Vanya, 1965, 69, The Iceman Cometh, 1973, Harry Outside, 1975, Hillbilly Women, 1979, 81, the Vienna Notes, 1985, The Stick Wife, April Snow, 1987, The Grapes of Wrath, 1988-89, 90, Measure for Measure, Beside Herself, 1989, Escape from Happiness, 1993, Buried Child, 1995-96, Defying Gravity, 1997, Impossible Marriage, 1998, Mrs. Warren's Profession, 1999, Give Me Your Answer, Do, 1999, Mother Courage, 2001; films include East of Eden, 1955, Five Easy Pieces, 1970, Next Stop Greenwich Village, 1975, Resurrection, 1980, Green Card, 1990, Fried Green Tomatoes, 1991, Falling Down, 1993, How to Make an American Quilt, 1995, Dead Man Walking, 1995, Larger than Life, 1996, Twister, 1996, Tumbleweeds, 1998, Minority Report, 2002, The Laramie Project, 2002, Iron-Jawed Angels, 2004, Best Thief in the World, 2004, P.S., 2004. Named Best Supporting Actress for Five Easy Pieces, Nat. Soc. Film Critics, 1971; recipient Tony nominations for Grapes of Wrath, 1990, Buried Child, 1996; named to Filmdom's Famous Fives for East of Eden, Failm Daily mag., 1955, Steppenwolf Ensemble Nat. Medal of Arts, 1990. Mem. SAG, AFTRA, Actors Equity Assn., Dramatists Guild, Actors Studio, Ensemble Studio Theater, Steppenwolf Theatre Co. Ensemble, Acad. Motion Picture Arts and Scis.

SMITH, LUCY, intercultural communication specialist; b. Krakow, Poland, June 15, 1933; came to U.S., 1968; d. Henryk Kreisler and Mina Grunhut; divorced; 1 child, Daniel. MFA equivalent, Acad. Fine Arts, Warsaw, Poland, 1959; postgrad., Sorbonne, Paris, 1961-65, l'Acad. Grande Chaumiere, 1963. Cert. ESL trainer Minn. Literacy Coun. Rschr. Spanish art Doubleday, Spain, 1963; comty. faculty mem. Met. State U., St. Paul, 1970-79; media coord. St. Paul Open Sch., 1979; costume designer Penumbra Theater, St. Paul, 1979; interculturalist, 1980—. Spkr. on Holocaust, Nat. Conf., The Jewish Hist. Soc., Omaha, 1989, Jewish Cmty. Rels. Coun. of Minn. and the Dakotas, 1989—; intercultural presenter Nat. Tchrs. ESL Conf., St. Paul, 1990; spkr. on status of women in Poland, Internat. Women's Rights Watch, The Humphrey Inst., U. Minn., 1990; intercultural workshop leader Internat. Soc. for Intercultural Edn., Tng. and Rsch., Internat. Congress, Banff, Can., 1991, Internat. Congress, Montego Bay, Jamaica, 1992; intercultural presenter Minn. Assn. of Continuing Adult Edn., St. Paul, 1992, 93, 94; intercultural workshop leader Nat. Laubach Literacy Confs., Raleigh, N.C., 1992, Little Rock, 1994; trainer Minn. Alts. to Violence Program, 1991—; spkr., leader workshop U. Tenn., Clarksville, 1997. Pub. art: Une Experience d'Orientation/Esprit mag., Paris, 1966, (textbook) Every Woman Has a Story, 1982; editor: (newsletters) The Citizen, 1980-82, AVP Matters, 1995—; apppeared in The Holocaust Remembrance, 1997; contbr. to profl. publs. Chair The Ethiopian Jewry Com., The Jewish Comty. Rels. Coun. of Minn. and the Dakotas, 1988-90; conceived program for mut. exch. of Spanish and Am. cultures, St. Paul YWCA. Recipient 2d prize for story St. Paul Jewish Comty. Ctr., 1985. Mem. NOW (bd. dirs. Minn. chpt. 1994—), Jewish Storytellers Guild, Jewish Women Choir. Avocations: playing piano, listening to classical music, storytelling. Home: 1747 Randolph Ave Saint Paul MN 55105-2154

SMITH, MABEL HARGIS, retired secondary school educator, musician; b. Ruby, La., Sept. 29, 1917; d. Ildephonso Albinos Hargis and Stella Gertrude Baker; m. Thomas Leonard Smith, Jr., Dec. 29, 1950; 1 child, Susan Claire Smith McLaughlin. BA, La. Coll., 1938; Master of Music, Northwestern U., 1952. Tchr. Tioga H.S., La., 1938—75; pianist-organist children's choir Tioga First Bapt. Ch., La., 1941—2002. Named Sr. Adult of Yr., First Bapt. Ch., 1989, Disting. Alumna, La. Coll., 1977; named one of Women of the Century, Daily Town Talk, Alexandria, La., 1999; recipient Cmty. Svc. award, Matinee Music Club, 1953—54, Recognition for musical contbns., Curtis T. Hines Masonic Lodge, 1997. Mem.: La. Music Educators (Hall of Fame 1999), Music Educator's Nat. Conf., Delta Omicron Internat., Delta Kappa Gamma. Baptist. Avocations: sewing, cooking, reading, gardening. Home: 27 Purser Pineville LA 71360

SMITH, MAGGIE CARROLL See SMITH, MARGARET A.

SMITH, MARCIA J. pastor; b. Columbus, Ohio, Apr. 7, 1958; d. William Wilson and Mary Anna Gibbs, Bill and Anna Lee Sutton; m. George E. Smith, Sept. 27, 1975 (div. May 1985); children: Eugenia Marie, Todd Jefferson; m. George E. Smith, June 16, 2003. Degree in bus. mgmt., Ohio Dept. Transportation, 1988; degree in law, Scott Inst., 1989. Ministerial ordination Higher Ground Always Abounding Assemblies, 1994. Evangelist Higher Ground Always Abounding Assemblies, Columbus, Ohio, 1991—94; pastor Living Water Chosen Generation, Circleville, Ohio, 1994—. Dean of students Prophecy Ctr., Columbus, 2001—, bd. of adjustors, 2000—. Profl. football player Cleve. Fusion, 2002. Achievements include first to only woman pastor in Columbus Ohio to also be a profl. football player. Avocations: computer games, fishing, photography, musician. Home: PO Box 1432 Westerville OH 43086 Office: Living Water Bible Fellow Worldwide Chosen Gen Ch 5393 Sinclair Rd Columbus OH 43229 E-mail: chozngenpastor@aol.com.

SMITH, MARGARET, state legislator; b. Chgo. m. Fred J. Smith; 2 sons, (dec.). Student, Tenn. State U. Mem. Ill. Ho. of Reps., 1981-83, Ill. Senate dist. 12, 1983—. Trustee Chgo. Bapt. Inst. Democrat. Office: State Senate State Capital Rm 103A Springfield IL 62706-0001 Address: 4949 N Melvina Ave Chicago IL 60630-2907

SMITH, MARGARET (PEGGY) JANE, psychologist; b. Salt Lake City, 1972; d. Philip and Margaret Clayton; m. Ted Smith, Feb. 1999; children: Isabelle, T.J. BS in Psychology, U. Utah, 1994, MS in Ednl. Psychology, 1998—2003; PhD in Psychology, U. Minn., 2003. Cert. sch. psychologist Utah. Presch. specialist Behavioral and Ednl. Strategies for Tchrs., Utah Dept. Edn., Salt Lake City, 1997—99; psychologist Mounds ViewPub. Sch., Mpls., 1999, Rochester (Minn.) Pub. Sch., 2000, Carmen B. Pingree Sch. for Autism/Valley Mental Health, Salt Lake City, 2000—. Grantee Fellowship Dissertation grant, U. Minn., 2001. Avocations: teaching piano, basketball.

SMITH, MARGARET A. (MAGGIE CARROLL SMITH), community volunteer; b. Akron, Ohio, Nov. 2, 1928; d. John Raymond Seiler and Helen Joseph Roach; m. Richard C. Carroll, Feb. 1, 1958 (div.); children: Stephan, Christopher, Daniel, John, Michael; m. Wiley Smith, Jr., May 3, 1985. Grad., St. Vincent H.S., Akron, Ohio, 1947. Interviewer Ohio Bur. of Employees Svcs., Akron, 1949-53; sales agt. Boebinger Realtors, 1979-86; lectr. on mental health, Akron U., Kent State U., Summit County Paramedics, Akron Police Dept., others; developer spl. mental health crisis intervention tng. program for Akron Police and Fire Dept., Ohio, 2000. Editor: (newsletter) National Alliance for the Mentally Ill of Summit County, 1987-99. Founding pres. Nat. Alliance/Mentally Ill of Summit County, Akron, 1986; pres. Nat. Alliance/Mentally Ill of Ohio, Columbus, 1988; steering com. for redesigning cmty. mental health system, 1986. Recipient Heart of Gold award Mental Health Assn. of Summit County, 1989, Recognition for Advocacy, Alcohol, Drug, and Mental Health, Summit County, 1996, Vol. of Yr. award We. Res. Psychiat. Hosp., Summit County, 1988, Solid Gold Mem. award Alliance for the Monthly Ill of Ohio, Columbus, 1991; Maggie C Smith House Residential Facility named in her honor, Ohio, 2000. Avocation: gardening. Office: Nat Alliance/Mentally Ill PO Box 462 Cuyahoga Falls OH 44222-0462

SMITH, MARGARET TAYLOR, volunteer; b. Roanoke Rapids, N.C., May 31, 1925; d. George Napoleon and Sarah Luella (Waller) T.; m. Sidney William Smith Jr., Aug. 15, 1947; children: Sarah Smith, Sidney William Smith III, Susan Smith, Amy Smith. BA in Sociology, Duke U., 1947. Chair emeritus bd. trustees Kresge Found., Troy, Mich., 1985—; chmn. Nat. Coun. for Women's Studies Duke U., N.C., 1986—, chmn. Trinity Bd. Visitors, 1988-98; chair emeritus. Chmn. bd. visitors Wayne State U. Med. Sch., 1993; bd. dirs., mem. exec. com. Detroit Med. Ctr.; mem. bd. govs. Detroit Med. Ctr. Recipient the Merrill-Palmer award Wayne State U., Detroit, 1987, Zimmerman award Gtr. Detroit Health Coun., Athena award C. of C., 1998, Women of Achievement award Mich. Women's Fedn., 1999, disting. svc. award Wayne State U., 1999; named disting. alumna award Duke U. Mem. The Village Club, Internat. Women's Forum, Pi Beta Phi, Phi Beta Kappa. Methodist. E-mail: sidmyth@aol.com.

SMITH, MARGHERITA, writer, editor; b. Chgo., May 24, 1922; d. Henry Christian and Alicia (Koke) Steinhoff; m. Rufus Zartman Smith, June 26, 1943; children: Matthew Benjamin, Timothy Rufus. AB, Ill. Coll., 1943. Proofreader Editorial Experts, Inc., Alexandria, Va., 1974, mgr. proofreading div., 1978-79, mgr. publs. div., 1979-81, asst. to pres., 1980-81; freelance editor, cons. Annandale, Va., 1981-97. Instr. proofreading and copy editing, George Washington U., Washington, 1978-82; presenter workshops on proofreading for various profl. orgns., 1981-95. Author: (as Peggy Smith) Simplified Proofreading, 1980, Proofreading Manual and Reference Guide, 1981, Proofreading Workbook, 1981, The Proof Is In the Reading: A Comprehensive Guide to Staffing and Management of Typographic Proofreading, 1986, Mark My Words: Instructions and Practice in Proofreading, 1987, rev. edit., 1993, 98, 2003, Letter Perfect: A Guide to Practical Proofreading, 1995; contbr. articles to revs. to various publs. Recipient Best Instrnl. Reporting award Newsletter Assn. Am., 1980, Disting. Achievement award for excellence in ednl. journalism Ednl. Press Assn. Am., 1981, Disting. Citizen award Ill. Coll., 1992. Avocation: writing verse. Home and Office: 9120 Belvoir Woods Pkwy Apt 110 Fort Belvoir VA 22060-2722 E-mail: mssmss@pobox.com.

SMITH, MARGUERITE IRENE, gifted and talented educator; b. Duryea, Pa., Aug. 10, 1950; d. John Sylvester and Irene Anne Morris; m. James Michael Smith, June 9, 1973; children: Jennifer Lynn Smith Ruth, Kimberly Ann Smith Ikeler. BS in Secondary Edn., Bloomsburg U., 1972, EdM in Reading, 1995. Tchr. head start, home visitor CSIU #16, Montandon, Pa., 1987—91; tchr. high sch. Spanish Lewisburg Area Sch. Dist., 1991—92, TELLS aide, spl. ed. aide, TRAC aide, 1992—94; intervention specialist CSIU #16, Montandon, 1993; tchr. reading Lewisburg Area Sch. Dist., Donald H. Eichhorn Mid. Sch., 1994—98, Title I reading specialist and gifted coord., 1998—. Mem. Am. Legion Post #841 Marching Band, Montandon; sec., treas. No. Deanery Coun. of Cath. Women, Sacred Heart Coun. of Cath. Women, Lewisburg, 1984—88; pres. Parish Coun. Sacred Heart, 1988—89; eucharistic min. Sacred Heart Jesus Ch., 1989—2003; asst. to Cath. chaplain Geisinger Med. Ctr., Danville, 1988—91. Mem.: AAUW (v.p. membership 1988—89), ASCD, Keystone State Reading Assn., Susquehanna Valley Reading Coun., Internat. Reading Assn., Buffalo Valley Singers (pres. 2001—02), Mifflinburg Buggy Mus. Roman Catholic. Avocations: French horn, singing, reading, needlecrafts, gardening. Office: Donald H Eichhorn Mid Sch 2057 Washington Ave Lewisburg PA 17837

SMITH, MARIA LYNN, school system administrator; b. Salisbury, Md., July 20, 1952; d. Benhamin Jones Sr. and Beulah Jones; children: Eric Wood, Brian. BS, U. Md., 1974; MEd, Bowie State U., 1990, ABD in Ednl. Leadership, 2003. Tchr. Prince George's County Pub. Schs., counselor, staff developer, regional instructional supr. Chair instructional chair Nicolas Orem Mid. Sch., Hyattsville, Md., 1992—94; curriculum writer Prince George's County Pub. Schs., Upper Marlboro, 1976—80. Sec. campaign Friends of Ken Johnson, Largo, Md., 1990—2000. Mem.: ASCD. Democrat. Baptist. Avocations: movies, reading, singing, cooking. Office: Prince George's County Pub Schs 10001 Ardwick/Archmore Rd Harwood MD 20776 E-mail: msmith1@pgcps.org.

SMITH, MARIE B. college president; BA, San Francisco State U.; MA in Biology, Sonoma State U.; DEdn, U. San Francisco. Biology instr. to acting pres. Indian Valley Coll., Novato, Calif., 1974; dean Coll. at Life Chiropractic Coll.-West San Lorenzo, 1985; staff to dean instrn. Coll. of Alameda, 1990, pres., 1991-94, Am. River Coll., 1995—. Chair planning team McClennan AFB Privatization and Reuse adv. com.; co-chair strategic planning teams Los Rio C.C. Dist. Mem. Grant Joint Union H.S. Dist. Vol. Integration Cmty. adv. coun.; mem. Golden Gate U. Women's Leadership Inst., Calif. Ctr. for Health Improvement, Life College West, San Lorenzo, Calif.; pres. ARC. Mem. Biol. Field Svc. Assn. Office: Am River Coll 4700 College Oak Dr Sacramento CA 95841-4217

SMITH, MARIE BURNLEY, music educator; d. Samuel William and Janette Sackett Burnley; m. Charles Joseph Smith, July 15, 1972; children: Charles Denman, Rachel Kathleen. BME, Ctrl. Mich. U., Mt. Pleasant, 1972; MA, Ohio State U., Columbus, 1977. Music tchr. Reynoldsburg (Ohio) City Schs., 1972—80, string music and orch. dir., 1974—2002; ret., 2002. Sec. - treas. Ohio Music Edn. Assn. South Ctrl. region, 1980—84, chair, 1990—96. Ward rep. Saratoga Civic Assn., Gahanna, Ohio, 1975—76. Named Ohio Tchr. of Yr., Ohio Orch. and String Tchrs. Assn., 2001; recipient Golden Apple award, Ashland, 1990. Mem.: NEA, Ohio Edn. Assn., Am. String Tchrs. Assn., Ohio Music Edn. Assn. Achievements include founder, Reynoldsburg City Schs. Orch. program.

SMITH, MARIE EDMONDS, real estate agent, property manager; b. Quapaw, Okla., Oct. 5, 1927; d. Thomas Joseph and Maud Ethel Edmonds; m. Robert Lee Smith, Aug. 14, 1966 (dec. 1983). Grad. vocat. nurse, Hoag Hosp., Costa Mesa, Calif., 1953; BA, Vanguard U., 1955; MS, U. Alaska, 1963. Lic. vocat. nurse, Calif.; cert. sci. tchr., Alaska. Nurse Calif. Dept. Nurses, Costa Mesa, 1952-60; tchr. Alaska Dept. Edn., Aniak and Anchorage, 1955-60; tchr. sci. Garden Grove (Calif.) Sch. Dist., 1960-87; property mgr. Huntington Beach, Calif., 1970—; agent Sterling Realtors, Huntington Beach, 1988—. Author: Ocean Biology, 1969. Bd. dirs., tchr. Newport Mesa Christian Ctr., Costa Mesa, 1983-2001; com. chmn. Garden Grove Unified Sch. Dist. PTA, 1977. NSF grantee, 1960-62. Mem. AAUW, Vangaurd U. Alumnae Assn. Republican. Avocations: skin diving, travel. Home: 83ll Reilly Dr Huntington Beach CA 92646 Office: L8153 Brookhurst St Fountain Valley CA 92708

SMITH, MARIE F. small business owner, writer; b. Kahakuloa, Hawaii; Dir. manpower mgmt. and orgn. planning Social Security Adminstrn.; realtor assoc., 1987—; small bus. owner, 1987—; freelance writer, 1987—; commr. State of Women Gov. Hawaii; chair Nat. Legis. Coun. AARP, Washington, spokesperson Women's Initiative Program, mem. audit and fin. com., 2000—02, mem. exec. dir. search com., 2000—02, treas. found. bd. dirs., 2000—02, pres., 2004—. Active Interfaith Vol. Caregivers; sec. bd. dirs. Maui Adult Day Care Ctr.; pres. bd. dirs. Maui Vol. Ctr. Recipient Woman of Excellence award, Commn. on the Status of Women, Circle of Women award, County Commn. on the Status of Women. Mem.: Nat. Assn. Ret. Fed. Employees (pres.), African Am. Heritage Found. Maui (pres.). Office: AARP 601 E St W Washington DC 20049*

SMITH, MARIE FORD, small business owner; d. David and Christina Ford; m. Richard Stanley Smith, Dec. 13, 1986; stepchildren: Jeffrey, Reginald, Laurie Debrotz. BA, Fisk U., 1961. Mgr. Social Security Adminstrn., San Francisco, Wailuku, Hawaii; realtor assoc. Wailuku; owner Tropical Garden, Kahakuloa, Hawaii, 1992—. Commr. Hawaii Commn. on Women, Honolulu; interim commr. Martin Luther King Commn., Honolulu, 1988—90; pres. AARP, Washington, 2004—. Named to Cir. of Women, Com. on the Status of Women, Maui, Hawaii, 1991. Mem.: Zonta Internat. (pres. 1990—91). Avocations: writing, travel, golf. Office: AARP 601 E St NW Washington DC 20049 E-mail: mfsmith@aarp.org.

SMITH, MARILYN NOELTNER, retired science educator; b. LA, Feb. 14, 1933; d. Clarence Frederick and Gertrude Bertha (Smith) Noeltner; m. Edward Christopher Smith, Sept. 11, 1971 (dec. Oct. 1999). BA, Marymount Coll., 1957; MA, U. Notre Dame, 1966; MS, Boston Coll., 1969. Cert. tchr.; cert. community coll. tchr., Calif.; cert. adminstr., Calif. Tchr., chmn. sci. dept. Marymount High Sch., Santa Barbara, Calif., 1954-57, LA, 1957-58, 69-79, tchr., chmn. sci. and math. depts. Palos Verdes, Calif., 1959-69; tchr., chmn. math. dept. Corvallis High Sch., Studio City, Calif., 1958-59; instr. tchr. tng. Marymount-Loyola U., LA, 1965-71, instr. freshman interdisciplinary program, 1970-71; tchr. math. Santa Monica (Calif.) HS, 1971-72; instr. math., chemistry, physics Santa Monica Coll., 1971—79; tchr. sci. Beverly Vista Sch., Beverly Hills, Calif., 1972—2002; ret., 2002. Cons. Calif. State Sci. Framework Revision Com., LA, 1975; chmn. NASA Youth Sci. Congress, Pasadena, Calif., 1968-69, Hawaii, 1969-70; participant NASA Educators Conf. Jupiter Mission, Ames Research, San Francisco, 1973, NASA Educators Conf. Viking-Mars Ames Project, San Francisco, 1976-77, NASA Landsat Conf., Edward's AFB, Calif., 1978, NASA Uranus Mission, Pasadena, Calif., 1986, NASA Uranus-Voyager Mission, Pasadena, 1989, NASA Neptune-Voyager Mission, Pasadena, 1989; test scoring com. Calif. Learning Assessment System, U. Santa Barbara, 1993, writing com. Trainers Manual, 1993. Author books and computer progs. including NASA Voyager-Uranus Sci. Symposium for Educators, 1989, NASA Voyager 2 Neptune Encounter Conf., 1989, others; contbr. articles to profl. jours. Sponsor Social Svc. Club, Palos Verdes, 1959-69, moderator, sponsor ARC Youth Svc. Chmn., Beverly Hills, 1974-77, judge L.A. County Sci. Fair, 1969—, blue ribbon com. NATAS, 1971—; bd. dirs. Children First, Beverly Hills, 1990-91; vol. sch. initiative, Beverly Hills, 1989-90; steering com. on tech. Beverly Vista Sch., 1994-95; del. Congress of Am. Women Scientists to Cuba, People to People Amb. Program, 2001; active U. Notre Dame Badin Guild, 1989—. Recipient Commendation in Teaching cert. Am. Soc. Microbiology, 1962, Salute to Edn. award So. Calif. Industry Edn. Council, 1962, Outstanding Teaching citation Cons. Engrs. Assn. Calif., 1967, Cert. Honor, Silver Plaque Westinghouse Sci. Talent Search, 1963-68, Tchr. award Ford-Future Scientists of Am., 1968, Biomed. award Com. Advance Sci. Tng., 1971, Outstanding Tchr. award LA County Sci. Fair Com., 1975-76, Contbns. to Youth Service citation ARC, 1976-77, Outstanding Tchr. award Kiwanis, Beverly Hills, 1987, NAST Pres'. award, 1990, Woman of Yr. award, 1990, cert. appreciation Profl. Leadership and Support for Advancing Sci. Edn. Calif. Dept. Edn., 1992-93, Outstanding Tchr. Gifted Students award Johns Hopkins U., 1999-2000. Mem. We. Assn. Schs. and Colls. (vis. com. 1968, writing com. 1969—), Assn. Advancement Biomed. Edn. (pres. 1970-71), 1st Internat. Sci. Tchrs. Conf. (presider, evaluator 1977), Nat. Sci. Tchrs. Assn. (presider, evaluator 1976, chmn. contributed papers com. 1977-78, presenter 1990), Beverly Hills Edn. Assn.(pres. faculty coun. 1980-81, 85-86, sch. rep. 1990—, Ann. WHO award 1995, 96), Chemist's Club, Calif. Statewide Math. Adv. Com., So. Calif. Industry Edn. Council, Calif. Assn. Chemistry Tchrs. (program chmn. 1960), Calif. Sci. Tchrs. Assn., Am. Chem. Soc., AAAS, South Bay Math. League (sec. 1967-68, pres. 1968-69, 72, 1969-70), Calif. Math. Council, Nat. Assn. Biology Tchrs., U. Notre Dame Sorin Soc. Republican. Roman Catholic. Avocations: stone age architecture, Gaelic, Irish fisheries population samplings and contributions to data bank. Home: 3934 Sapphire Dr Encino CA 91436-3635 Office: Beverly Vista Sch 200 S Elm Dr Beverly Hills CA 90212-4011

SMITH, MARILYN PAULETTE, guidance counselor; b. Okla. City, Okla., Feb. 18, 1950; d. Paul Eugene Hoffman and Ramona Jean (Satterlee) Davidson; m. Douglas Alan Smith, Dec. 12, 1977; children: Zachary, Matthew. Cert. libr. sci., Northeastern Okla. State U., 1975; BA in Sociology, Northeastern State Coll., 1973; MS in Counseling Psych., Northeastern State U., 1994. Shelter mgr. Help in Crisis, Tahlequah, Okla., 1990-93, rape responder, 1990—, counselor, 1994-95; psych asst. Wagoner (Okla.) County Guidance Ctr., 1995—. Crisis line vol. Help in Crisis, 1986-93. Bd. mem. Opportunity House Bill Willis Mental Health, 1994-96. Democrat. Avocations: cooking, gardening.

SMITH, MARJI L. artist; b. Bellevue, Ohio, Feb. 1, 1944; d. Albert John and Elizabeth Laub; m. Ernest Jackson Smith, July 17, 1976; children: Scott Alan, Christine Deborah, Gregory Jackson. Owner, artist, tchr. Marji Smith Studio, Knoxville, Tenn., 1970—; owner Proof of Purchase Apparel, 2000—; creator featured cartoon Donna Quixote Nat. Mus. Women in Arts Mag., 1996—2003. Bd. dirs. Sarasota Bay Estuary Program, 1996—97. Recipient Best of Show, Dogwood Arts Fest., 1998, Purchase award, Tenn. Valley Authority, 2001; grantee Guideposts Mag., 1986. Mem.: Am. Soc. Portrait Artists, Nat. Mus. Women in Arts, Fla. Watercolor Soc. Avocations: writing, kayaking, snorkeling, gardening, travel. E-mail: marjsmithart@aol.com.

SMITH, MARJORIE AILEEN MATTHEWS, museum director; b. Richmond, Va., Aug. 19, 1918; d. Harry Anderson and Adelia Charlotte (Howland) Matthews; m. Robert Woodrow Smith, July 23, 1945 (dec. Mar. 1992). Pilot lic., Taneytown (Md.) Aviation Svc., 1944, cert. CAA navigation ground sch. instr., 1945. Founder, editor, pub. Spinning Wheel, Taneytown, 1945-63; v.p. Antiques Publs., Inc., Taneytown, 1960-68; pres. Prism Inc., Taneytown, 1968-78; mus. dir. Trapshooting Hall of Fame, Vandalia, Ohio, 1976-2000, mus. dir. emeritus, 2001—, sec., 1993-99. Co-author: Handbook of Tomorrow's Antiques, 1954; contbr. articles to profl. publs. Sec. Balt. area coun. Girl Scouts USA, 1950. Named to All-Am. Trapshooting team Sports Afield mag., 1960, 61; inductee Trapshooting Hall of Fame, 1998. Mem. Nat. League Am. Pen Women, Amateur Trapshooting Assn. (life), Internat. Assn. Sports Mus. and Halls of Fame (bd. dirs. 1993-94, W.R. Schroeder Disting. Svc. award 1999). Lutheran. Avocations: duplicate bridge, trapshooting, antiques collecting.

SMITH, MARJORIE K. state legislator; b. Feb. 22, 1944; d. Harold E. and Rose (Rothstein) Kester; m. Peter Sheridan Smith, 1966; children: Abigail, Douglas. BA, Beaver Coll., 1961, MPA, 1962. Mem. N.H. Ho. of Reps. (dist. 8), Concord, 1996—. Trustee Dunham Pub. Libr., 1997—. Office: NH State Legis State House Concord NH 03301

SMITH, MARSHA H. state agency administrator, lawyer; b. Boise, Idaho, Mar. 24, 1950; d. Eugene F. and Joyce (Ross) Hatch; m. Terrell F. Smith, Aug. 29, 1970; 2 children. BS in Biology/Edn., Idaho State U., 1973; MLS, Brigham Young U., 1975; JD, U. Wash., 1980. Bar: Idaho, U.S. Dist. Ct. Idaho, U.S. Ct. Appeals (9th cir.), U.S. Ct. Appeals (D.C. cir.). Dep. atty. gen. Bus./Consumer Protection Divsn., Boise, 1980-81, Idaho Pub. Utilities Commn., Boise, 1981-89, dir. policy and external rels., 1989-91, commr., 1991—, pres., 1991-95. Mem. Harvard Electricity Policy Group, Nat. Coun. on Competition and The Electric Industry; chair com. for regional electric power coop. Western Interstate Energy Bd. Legis. dist. chair Ada County Democrats, Idaho, 1986-89. Mem. Nat. Assn. Regulatory Utility Commrs. (chair electricity com.). Office: Idaho Pub Utilities Commn PO Box 83720 Boise ID 83720-0074

SMITH, MARTHA A. academic administrator; b. Bradford, Pa., Aug. 31, 1948; BA, Slippery Rock State U., Pa., 1970; EdM, U. Hawaii, 1972; EdD, U. No. Colo., 1974. Dir. Hawaii Open program U. Hawaii, 1975—77; v.p. student affairs Coll. of St. Theresa, 1977—81; dean of students Dundalk CC, 1982—87, acting pres., 1987, pres., 1988—94, Anne Arundel CC, Arnold, Md., 1994—. Mem. pres.'s adv. coun. St. John's Coll.; mem. Gov.'s Workforce Investment Bd.; mem. commn. on higher edn. Mid. States Assn. of Coll. and Sch.; bd. dir. Inst. CC Devel. at Cornell U.; commr. Am. Assn. of CC Workforce Devel.; mem. Md. Partnership Tchg. and Learning K-16; co-chair K-16 Std. Competency Assessment Team. Campaign chair Anne Arundel County United Way, 1999, mem. partnership bd., 1999; bd. dir. Anne Arundel Med. Ctr., Anne Arundel County Trade Coun., Harundale Youth Ctr. Named Bus. Leader of Yr., Anne Arundel Trade Coun., 1998; named one of Md.'s Top 100 Women, Daily Record, 1998, 2000; recipient First Women award, YECA of Annapolis and Anne Arundel County, 1995, Tribute to Women in Industry award, YMCA, 1995, Cmty Trustee award, 2001, Leadership Anne Arundel, 2001, Inside the Field Nat. Leadership award, Nat. Coun. Continuing Edn., 2001, CC of Yr. award, Nat. Alliance of Bus., 2001. Mem.: Md. Coun. of CC Pres., Rotary Club of Annapolis. Office: Anne Arundel CC 101 College Pkwy Arnold MD 21012-2222*

SMITH, MARTHA VIRGINIA BARNES, retired elementary school educator; b. Camden, Ark., Oct. 12, 1940; d. William Victor and Lillian Louise (Givens) Barnes; m. Basil Loren Smith, Oct. 11, 1975; children: Jennifer Frost, Sean Barnes. BS in Edn., Ouachita Bapt. U., 1963; postgrad., Auburn U., 1974, Henderson State U., 1975. Cert. tchr., Mo. 2d and 1st grade tchr. Brevard County Schs., Titusville and Cocoa, Fla., 1963-65, 69-70; 1st grade tchr. Lakeside Sch. Dist., Hot Springs, Ark., 1965-66, Harmony Grove Sch., Camden, 1972-76; 1st and 5th grade tchr. Cumberland County Schs., Fayetteville, N.C., 1966-69; kindergarten tchr. Pulaski County Schs., Ft. Leonard Wood, Mo., 1970-72; 3d grade tchr. Mountain Grove (Mo.) Schs., 1976-99; ret., 1999. Chmn. career ladder com. Mountain Grove Dist., 1991-99. Children's pastor 1st Bapt. Ch., Vanzant, Mo., 1984-88. Mem. NEA (pres.-elect Mountain Grove chpt. 1995-97, pres. Mountain Grove chpt. 1997-99), Kappa Kappa Iota. Avocation: antique and classic cars.

SMITH, MARTHE ELISABETH, retired pathologist; b. N.Y.C., Apr. 17, 1928; d. Glenn Waldo and Frankie Ernestine (Faul) S. BA, U. Oreg., 1948; MS, MD, U. Oreg. Med. Sch., 1951. Diplomate Am. Bd. Nuclear Medicine, Am. Bd. Anatomic and Clin. Pathology. Dir. cytology lab. U. Calif. Med. Sch., San Francisco, 1956-58; assoc. pathologist St. Luke's Hosp., San Francisco, 1957-87; ret., 1987. Asst. clin. prof. U. Calif. Med. Sch., 1958—. Mem. Medicare utilization rev. com. for extended care facility San Francisco Med. Soc., 1970-75. Mem. Marin Ski Club (corr. sec. 1970—, historian, trophy 1960, Gold medal Triway race 1987, Blue Ribbon 1986), 4th Thursday Salmon Fishing Club. Avocations: skiing, ocean fishing, painting, knitting, growing orchids.

SMITH, MARY HILL, volunteer; b. Dallas, Jan. 14, 1943; d. Wendell Tennyson and Laura Leta (Massey) Hill; m. Andrew Jeptha Kincannon Smith, July 10, 1965; children: Emily Catherine Smith McGrath, Andrew III, Bradley Tennyson. BA with Volunteer Adminstrn. Cert., Metro. State U., 1987. Pres., mem. Raggedy Ann chpt. Children's Health Ctr. Assn., Mpls., 1972-83; pres. exec. com. Jr. League Mpls., 1973-84; dir. 75th Anniversary bd. Minn. Orchestral Assn., Mpls., 1977-78; dir. Guthrie Theater Bd., Mpls., 1979-83; bd. dirs. YWCA, 1981-82; pres. Wayzata (Minn.) Cmty. Edn. Bd., 1981-83; mem. adv. bd. N. Hennepin C. C., Brooklyn Center, Minn., 1982-84; chair, sec. Wayzata Sch. Bd., 1984-92; chair Minn. Women's Polit. Caucus, St. Paul, 1984-92; bd. dirs. Hennepin Tech. Coll., Plymouth, Minn., 1985-92; chair, bd. dirs. Art Ctr. Minn., Orono, 1985-92; mem. Metro. Coun., St. Paul, 1993—. Active Hennepin County Libr. Found., 1996—99, Sheltering Arms Found., 1996—2002, pres., 1999—2000; del. Orono (Minn.) Rep. Party, 1992; chmn. transp. com. West Chamber Leadership com., Minnetonka, Minn., 1992, vice chair, 1996—2002, sec., 2003—; mem. Twin State Ethical Practice Bd., St. Paul, 1986—91, Gov. Carlson's Re-election com., 1994—95, State Adv. Coun. on Metro Airports, St. Paul, 1995; bd. dirs. Minn. Women's Campaign Fund, 1996—2003, pres., 2000—02; mem. exec. com. U. Minn. Ctr. for Transp. Studies, 1995—2001, 2003—; bd. dirs. Met. State U. Found., St. Paul, 2000—; chair Met. Airports Commn. Joint Zoning Bd., 2001—. Named Woman of the Yr., Women's Transp. Seminar, Minn., 2001; recipient Disting. Pub. Leadership award, U. Minn. Ctr. Transp. Studies,

2002. Republican. Episcopalian. Avocations: reading, gardening, cooking. Home: 515 Ferndale Rd N Wayzata MN 55391-1008 Office: Metro Coun 230 5th St E Saint Paul MN 55101-1672 E-mail: maryhillsmith@aol.com., mary.smith@metc.state.mn.us.

SMITH, MARY LOUISE, real estate broker; b. Eldorado, Ill., May 29, 1935; d. Joseph Henry Smith and Opal Marie (Smith) Hungerford; m. David Lee Smith, June 18, 1961; children: Ricky Eugene, Brenda Sue Smith Millsap. Student, So. Ill. U., 1954-56, 57-58. Cert. substitute tchr., Mo.; cert. real estate broker, Mo. With acctg. dept. Cen. Hardware Co., St. Louis, 1958-61; mgr. income tax office Tax Teller Inc., St. Louis, 1967-69; substitute tchr. Mo., 1967—; mgr. income tax office H&R Block Co., St. Louis, 1970—76, tax preparer, 1992—2001; with acctg. dept. Weis Neumann Co., St. Louis, 1976-79; broker/salesperson Century 21 Neubauer Realty Inc., St. Louis, 1980-83, 88-90; sales assoc. John R. Green Realtor, Inc., St. Louis, 1983-85, Century 21 Action Properties, St. Louis, 1985-88, real estate broker/salesperson, 1986-88, Century 21 Neubauer Realty, Inc., St. Louis, 1988-90, L.K. Wood Realtors, 1992-96; security officer Reliance Security, 1995-97; tax preparer H&R Block Co., St. Louis, 1983, 1992—2001. Younger children's dir. Lafayette Park Bapt. Ch., St. Louis, 1981-95; children dir. Kingshwy. Bapt. Ch., 1999-01; vol. tax preparer for UAW Local 136 retirees, 2000-04. Mem. Am. Fedn. Tchrs., St. Louis Real Estate Bd. (equal rights com. 1986-88). Baptist. Avocation: writing children's stories.

SMITH, MARY SCOTT, elementary school educator, education educator; b. Fordyce, Ark., Sept. 16, 1926; d. Arthur and Jo Anna Scott; m. Joe Cephas Smith, Apr. 13, 1952; children: Marylyn Joe Anna Washington, Reginald Joseá. BS, Ark. Bapt. Coll., Little Rock, 1949; MA, U. Wis., Madison, 1952; postgrad., U. Ark., Fayetteville, 1966—70. Tchr. Childs' Sch. Dist., Banks, Ark., 1944—48; registrar Ark. Bapt. Coll., 1950—52, bus. mgr., 1952—54; tchr. Dallas County Tng. Sch., Fordyce, Ark., 1954—66, Little Rock Sch. Dist., 1966—86; asst. prof. edn. Ark. Bapt. Coll., 1986—93. Bd. dirs. Ark Tchrs. Credit Union, Little Rock, 1985—90. Mem.: Ark. Edn. Assn., Nat. Edn. Assn., Classroom Tchrs. Assn. (bldg. rep. 1974—80), Am. Retired Educator Assn. (chairperson 1997—), AAUW, Order of Eastern Star (state treas. 1979—, worthy matron), Fed. Womans' Club (pres. 1995—), Pi Lambda Theta, Zeta Phi Beta (Ouststanding Educator 1996). Democrat. Baptist. Avocations: reading, traveling, singing, crossword puzzles. Home: 2400 Howard St Little Rock AR 72206

SMITH, MARYA JEAN, writer; b. Youngstown, Ohio, Nov. 12, 1945; d. Cameron Reynolds and Jean Rose (Sause) Argetsinger; m. Arthur Beverly Smith Jr., Dec. 30, 1968 (div. 1996); children: Arthur Cameron, Sarah Reynolds. BA, Cornell U., 1967. Editorial asst. Seventeen Mag., N.Y.C., 1967-68; promotion writer U. Chgo. Press, 1968-70; asst. account exec. Drucilla Handy Co., Chgo., 1970-72; feature writer various mags. Chgo., 1972-74; freelance writer Cornell U., Ithaca, N.Y., 1975-76, lectr., 1976-77; playwright Playwrights' Ctr. Prodn., Chgo., 1978; humor columnist various jours. Chgo., 1979-81; freelance writer, 1982—. Author: Across the Creek, 1989, Winter-Broken, 1990, Danish edit., 1991, (play) Hire Power, 1998; contbr. poetry Primavera, Ariel VI and VIII, 1974, 87, 89; contbr. articles and essays to mags. and papers, 1984—. Vol. reading tutor Literacy Vols. Western Cook County, Oak Park, Ill., 1988-89, Oak Park Pub. Libr. Reading Program, 1990-94. Recipient 1st place for news writing Assoc. Ch. Press, 1986, poetry award Poets and Patrons, 1986, Triton Coll. Salute to Arts, 1987, 89, 2d Grand prize Mississippi Valley Poetry Contest, 2003. Mem. Nat. Writers Union, Authors Guild, Soc. Midland Authors. Roman Catholic.

SMITH, MAURA ABELN, lawyer; b. Reading, Pa., Oct. 3, 1955; d. Henry Joseph and Lynn (Blashe) Abeln; children: Gwendolyn Casebeer, Karl Casebeer; m. Steven A. Smith, Dec. 18, 1999. AB, Vassar Coll., 1977; M Philosophy, Oxford U., 1979; JD, U. Miami, 1982. Bar: Fla. 1982, Ohio 1999. Assoc. Steel, Hector & Davis, Miami, 1982—87; ptnr. Baker & McKenzie, Miami, 1987-91; v.p., gen. counsel GE Co./Plastics, Pittsfield, Mass., 1991-98; sr. v.p., gen. counsel, sec. Owens Corning, Toledo, 1998-2000, chief restructuring officer, sr. v.p., gen. counsel, sec., 2000—03, bd. dirs.; sr. v.p., gen. counsel, sec. Internat. Paper, Stamford, Conn., 2003—. Rhodes scholar, Oxford, Eng., 1977-79; John M. Olin fellow in law and econs., Olin Found., 1979-82. Mem.: Phi Beta Kappa. Avocations: skiing, horseback riding, tennis, golf.

SMITH, MERILYN ROBERTA, art educator; b. Tolley, N.D., July 24, 1933; d. Robert Coleman and Mathilda Marie (Staael) S. BA, Concordia Coll., Minn., 1953; MA, State U. of Iowa, Iowa City, 1956, MFA, 1966. Tchr. Badger (Minn.) High Sch., 1954; instr. in art Valley City (N.D.) State Tchrs. Coll., 1957, 58, U. Wis., Oshkosh, 1967, asst. prof. art, 1969, assoc. prof., 1977-91, prof., 1991-93, prof. emeritus, 1993—; represented by Miriam Perlman Gallery, Chgo. Counselor Luth. Student Ctr. U. Iowa, 1959-65, rsch. asst. in printmaking, 1960-65; owner, dir. James House Gallery, Oshkosh, 1972-77; dir. Allen Priebe Gallery, U. Wis., Oshkosh, 1975. Exhibited in group shows at N.W. Printmakers Internat., Seattle and Portland, Oreg., 1964, Ultimate Concerns 6th Nat. Exhbn., Athens, Ohio, 1965, 55th Nat. Exhbn., Springfield, Mass., 1974, 11th An. So. Tier Arts and Crafts, Corning, N.Y., 1974, Soc. of the Four Arts, Palm Beach, Fla., 1974, Appalachian Nat. Drawing Competition, Boone, N.C., 1975, Rutgers Nat. Drawing Exhbn., Camden, N.J., 1975, 8th and 9th Biennial Nat. Art Exhibit, Valley City, N.D., 1973, 75, Clary-Miner Gallery, Buffalo, 1988, Nat. Art Show, Redding, Calif., 1989, Internat. Printmaker, Buffalo, 1990, Westmoreland Nat. Juried Competition, Youngwood, Pa., 1990, Ariel Gallery, Soho, N.Y., 1990, Grand Prix de Paris Internat., Chapelle De La Sorbonne, Paris, 1990, Nat. Juried Exhbn., Rockford, Ill., 1991, Nat. Invitational Exhbn., Buffalo, 1991, East Coast Artists Nat. Invitational Art Exhbn., Havre de Grace, Md., 1991, Ariel Gallery, Soho, N.Y., 1991, N.Y. Art Expo, 1991, Milw. Art for AIDS Auction, 1991, 92, 94. Mem. Winnebago Hist. Soc., Oshkosh, 1987—. Lutheran. Avocation: gardening. Home: 226 High Ave Oshkosh WI 54901-4734

SMITH, MICHELE KATHLEEN, marriage and family therapist; b. Waterbury, Conn., Mar. 7, 1973; d. Theodore W. and Rosemary (Luca) S. BS cum laude, U. Conn., 1995; MS, So. Conn. State U., 1997. Cert. gestalt therapist. Counselor heart program U. Conn., Storrs, 1994-95; therapist Head Start Program, New Haven, Conn., 1996, SCSU's Family Clinic, New Haven, 1996-97, Adult Probation, New Haven, 1996-97, Naugatuck (Conn.) Youth Svcs., 1996-98; Gestalt therapy tng. supr. family therapy masters program So. Conn. State U., New Haven, 1997; dir. Liberation & Meridian: Ptnrs. in Prevention & Recovery, Inc., Stamford, Conn., 1997—. Group facilitator Naugatnuck Youth Svcs., 1996-98; coord., trainer Adult Probation, New Haven, 1997. Vol. christmas party Head Start Children, N.Y., 1996. All Am. Collegiate scholar U. Conn., 1995, Nutmeg scholar, 1995. Mem. Am. Assn. Marriage and Family Therapy (assoc., conf. vol. 1997), Golden Key Nat. Honor Soc.

SMITH, MICHELE LINDSAY, music educator; b. Anderson, Ind., June 12, 1954; d. John Robert and Janice Irene Smith. BS, Ball State U., 1976, MA, 1982. Permanent tchg. cert. Ohio. Elem. music tchr. Greenville (Ohio) City Schs., 1976—78, HS vocal music dir., 1978—80, HS vocal music dir., fine arts dept. chair, music coord., 1982—; HS vocal music dir. Marion (Ind.) Cmty. Schs., 1980—81; mid./high sch. vocal music dir. Maconaquah Schools, Bunker Hill, Ind., 1981—82. Recipient Tchr. of Yr. award, Darke County Kiwanis, 2002. Mem.: Am. Choral Dirs. Assn. (assoc.), Music Edn. Nat. Conf. (assoc.; vocal affairs chair Ohio 2003), Phi Delta Kappa (assoc.), Sigma Alpha Iota (assoc.; v.p. 1975—76, Sword of Honor 1976), Pi Kappa Lambda (assoc.).

SMITH, MIGNON C. publishing executive; AA, Briarcliff Jr. Coll., Briarcliff Manor, N.Y., 1952. Bur. chief Washington/Ala. News Reports, Washington, 1980—. Office: Washington/Ala News Reports PO Box 58058 Washington DC 20037-8058

SMITH, MIRANDA CONSTANCE, writer, educator; b. Denver, June 19, 1944; d. Duncan Campbell and Mabel Elsie (Roller) Clark; m. Charles Ellsworth Smith, May 3, 1963 (div. 1967); m. Armand Cecil Lepage, July 9, 1979 (div. 1982); children: Tagore Duncan Smith, Simone Michelle Lepage. BA in Writing and Lit., Burlington (Vt.) Coll., 1992. Employment counselor San Jose (Calif.) Employment Agy., 1966-68; adminstrv. asst. to pres. Rochdale Coll., Toronto, Ont., Can., 1968-70; tchr. Mylora Farms, Richmond, B.C., Can., 1972; asst. dir. campaign save whales Greenpeace East, Montreal, Can., 1973-74; tchr., grower Rooftop Gardens, Montreal, 1974-76; dir. urban agrl. Inst. Local Self Reliance, Washington, 1976-78; group leader agrl., waste and recycling Nat. Ctr. Appropriate Tech., Butte, Mont., 1978-79; horticultural dir. Coolidge Farms, Topsfield, Mass., 1981-82; farmer, tchr. Hardwick (Vt.) Organic, 1985-86; cons. Memphremagog Group, Newport, Vt., and Can., 1979-88; writer, tchr. Vt., Mass., 1989-97; tchr. horticulturalist Sullivan Diagnostic Treatment, Harris, N.Y., 1997-99; sr. editor, gardening Creative Home Press, Upper Saddle River, N.J., 1999—. Author: Advanced Home Gardening, 2001, Your Backyard Herb Garden, 1996, 200 Tips for Growing Vegetables in the Northeast, 1995, 200 Tips for Growing Flowers in the Northeast, 1995, Rodale's Pest and Disease Problem Solver, 1995, Backyard Fruits and Berries, 1994, The Real Dirt, Farmers Tell about Organic and Low-Input Farming in the Northeast, 1994, The Expert's Book of Garden Hints, 1993, Rodale's All-New Encyclopedia of Organic Gardening, 1992, The Chemical Free Yard and Garden, 1991, Rodale's Garden Insect, Disease and Weed Identification Guide, 1988, Greenhouse Gardening, 1985. Organizer Lampson Brook Food Group, Belchertown, 1996-97. Mem. New Eng. Small Farm Inst. (bd. dirs. 1976-97, 2001—). Office: 24 Park Way Upper Saddle River NJ 07458

SMITH, MOLLY D. theater director; b. Yakima, Wash. d. Kay. BA, Cath. U.; MA in Theatre, Am. U., PhD (hon.), 2001. Founder Perserverance Theatre, Juneau, Alaska, 1979—98; artistic dir. Arena Stage, Washington, 1998—. Creative advisor Sundance Inst. New Plays; lit. advisor Banff Playwright's Colony, Canada; bd. dir. Theatre Comms. Group; panelist Ctr. Internat. Theatre Devel.; spkr. in field; prof. Arts, Music and Theatre Dept. Georgetown U.; judge Susan B. Blackburn Prize. Dir.: (plays). Named Artist of Yr., Alaska State Coun. Arts; named one of 100 Most Powerful Women, Washingtonian Mag., 2001; recipient Cmty. Leader award, U. Alaska Southeast. Office: Arena Stage 1101 6th St SW Washington DC 20024*

SMITH, MONA RILEY, psychotherapist; b. Sioux City, Iowa, Nov. 17, 1943; d. John Collins and Mary Mc Hugh Riley; m. Scot Edward Smith II, June 17, 1967 (div. Dec. 1975). BA, U. Iowa, 1965; degree, Sorbonne U., Paris, 1964; MS, Calif. State U., Hayward, 1981. Lic. marriage, family, child psychotherapist Calif., cert. hypnotherapist. Founder and pres. Incest Help, Inc., Albany, Calif., 1976—; psychotherapist Psychol. Svcs. Dublin, Calif., 1985—. Lectr. and trainer Parents United Internat., San Jose and San Leandro, Calif., 1977—81, co-head of staff, San Leandro, 1980; life skills trainer, San Francisco, 1994—; grief counselor and post trauma stress trainer, San Francisco, 2001; lectr. in field. Co-founder A.I.M., San Francisco, 1980. Recipient reception and luncheon honor, Commonwealth Club, 1987, Women Helping Women awards, Soroptimist Internat. Ams., Inc., 1989. Mem.: St. Laurence Inst. Hypnotherapy (co-trainer), Calif. Assn. Family Therapists (Cert. of Appreciation 1983), Nat. Exch. Club (Spl. Svc. award 1987), Delta Gamma. Avocations: films, literature, visiting eldercare homes. Address: 2635 Mt Pleasant St Unit 103 Burlington IA 52601-2194

SMITH, NANCY ANGELYNN, federal agency administrator; b. Nashville, Mar. 28, 1950; d. Russell Monroe and Louise (Stephenson) Smith; m. Richard Christian Egan, Jan. 1, 1999. Student, Blair Acad. Music, 1966, Am. Internat. Acad. Europe, 1970; BA in Psychology with distinction, Rhodes Coll., 1972; MS with honors, U. Tenn., 1974; cert. in acctg., U. New Orleans, 1985, U. SC, 1987. Contract adminstr. State of Tex. Dept. Health and Human Svcs., Houston, 1976-78; dept. Head Coop. Edn. Program No. Va. C.C., Annandale, 1978-81; revenue agt. IRS Dept. of Treasury, Nashville, 1988-99, mgr., adminstr. IRS, 1999—. Faculty rep. Faculty Senate No. Va. C.C., Annandale, 1979—81. Contbr. articles to profl. jours. Vol. Voter Registration program, Denver, 1981—84, Adopt-a-Sch., Nashville, 1993—97, Tenn. State Guard; disaster relief coord. Ky. and Tenn., 1998—99, Red Cross Inst., 1976—78, VITA, 1990—95; vol. Congresswoman Pat Shroeder, Denver, 1981—84, Al Gore for Senate, Nashville, 1987—88, Federica Pena for Mayor, Denver, 1981—; bd. dirs. No. Va. C.C., Annandale, 1978—81; vol. DAR. Mem.: Advancement Individual Minorities (commissions rep. 2002—), Profl. Mgrs. Assn., Cert. Fraud Examiners Assn., Gamma Beta Phi, Alpha Omicron Pi (chmn. bd. dirs. Colo. chpt.), Omicron Nu (hon.), Phi Kappa Pi (hon.). Avocations: painting, skeet shooting, camping, historical battlefields.

SMITH, NANCY HOHENDORF, retired sales and marketing executive; b. Detroit, Jan. 30, 1943; d. Donald Gerald and Lucille Marie (Kopp) Hohendorf; m. Richard Harold Smith, Aug. 21, 1978 (div. Jan. 1984). BA, U. Detroit, 1965; MA, Wayne State U., 1969. Customer rep. Xerox Corp., Detroit, 1965-67, mktg. rep. Univ. Microfilms subs. Ann Arbor, Mich., 1967-73, mktg. coord., 1973-74, mgr. dir. mktg., 1975-76, mgr. mktg., 1976-77, major account mktg. exec., 1978-79, New Haven, 1979-80, account exec. State of N.Y. N.Y.C., 1981, N.Y. region mgr. customer support Greenwich, Conn., 1982, N.Y. region sales ops. mgr., 1982, State of Ohio account exec. Columbus, 1983, new bus. sales mgr. Dayton, Ohio, 1983, major accounts sales mgr., 1984, info. systems sales and support mgr., quality specialist Detroit, 1985-87, new product launch mgr., ops. quality mgr., 1988, dist. mktg. mgr., 1989-92, major accounts sales mgr., 1992—; graphics arts industry sales mgr., 1998—; ret. Reg. graphic arts industry cons. mgr., 1999. Named to Outstanding Young Women of Am., 1968, Outstanding Bus. Woman, Dayton C. of C., 1984, Women's Inner Circle of Achievement, 1990. Mem. NAFE, Am. Mgmt. Assn., Women's Econ. Club Detroit, Detroit Inst. Arts Founders' Soc., Detroit Hist. Soc., Detroit Hist. Soc. Republican. Roman Catholic. Avocations: interior decorating, reading, music, art. Home: 6462 West Oaks Dr West Bloomfield MI 48324-3269

SMITH, NANCY IRENE, director; d. Rudolph Strong and Helen Louise Falk; m. Dean Richard Smith, June 17, 1966; children: Kimberley Ann Baker, Leslie Marie Miller, Theodore Brooke. BS, Geneva Coll., 1962—66; MEd, Slippery Rock U., 1997—99. Dir. acad. counseling ctr. and ednl. support svcs. (ACCESS) Geneva Coll., Beaver Falls, Pa., 1996—, adminstrv. asst., 1990—96. Singer: (performance) Mrs. Beaton's Book of Household Management. Tchr. Coll. Hill Ref. Presbyn. Ch., Beaver Falls, Pa., 2000. Mem.: Nat. Assn. of Develop. Educators, Pa. Assn. of Devel. Educators. Reformed Presbyterian Church Of North America. Avocations: piano teacher, travel. Home: 3600 36th Street Place Beaver Falls PA 15010 Office: Geneva Coll 3200 Coll Ave Beaver Falls PA 15010 Office Phone: 724-847-5566.

SMITH, NANCY L. information technology executive; BS in Mgmt. and Orgnl. Behavior, U. San Francisco. Western regional sales mgr., nat. sales mgr. Electronic Arts, Redwood City, Calif., 1984, v.p. sales, 1988—93, sr. v.p. N.Am. sales and distbn., 1993—96, exec. v.p. N.Am. sales, 1996—98, exec. v.p., gen. mgr. N.AM. pub., 1998—. Office: Electronic Arts Inc 209 Redwood Shores Pkwy Redwood City CA 94065-1175

SMITH, NANCY LEE, communications official; b. Junction City, Kans., May 10, 1953; d. James Emerson and Donna Lee (Cousins) Smith. BA with hons., Stephens Coll., Columbia, Mo., 1975; MPA with hons., Am. U., 1990. Appt. sec. to chief of staff The White House, Washington, 1975; appt. sec. to sec. of def. Dept. Def., Washington, 1975-77; sec., office mgr. to various congressmen U.S. Ho. of Reps., Washington, 1977-83; Congl. specialist U.S. Geol. Survey, Washington, 1983-84; staff asst. to sec. of land and mineral mgmt. U.S. Dept. Interior, Washington, 1984-85; Congl. liaison officer Office of Surface Mining, Reclamation and Enforcement, Washington, 1985-95, comms. officer, 1995-2000; group mgr. legis. affairs Bur. of Land Mgmt., Washington, 2000—. Mem.: Pi Alpha Alpha, Alpha Lambda Delta. Avocations: white-water rafting, photography, reading, origami, fitness. Office: Bur of Land Mgmt 1849 C St NW 401L5 Washington DC 20240-0001

SMITH, NANCY WOOLVERTON, journalist, real estate agent; b. San Antonio, July 31, 1947; d. Tillman Louis and Enid Maxine (Woolverton) Brown; 1 dau., Christina Elizabeth Woolverton Jones; m. William F. Pry II, Mar. 7, 1998 (div. July 31, 2003). Student, Ecole Nouvelle de la Suisse, Romande, Lausanne, Switzerland, 1962, Vandervilt U., 1964; BA, So. Meth. U., 1968, postgrad., 1969-70. Cert. S.E. Paralegal Inst. Tchr. spl. edn. Hot Springs Sch. Dist. (Ark.), 1970-72; reporter, soc. editor Dallas Morning News, 1974-82; soc./celebrity columnist Dallas Times Herald, 1982-91; owner, pub. High Society, Society Fax; bus .editor DFW Cmty. Newspapers divsn. Lionheart Newspapers Inc., Plano, Tex., 1999—. Realtor, Ebby Halliday Realtors; stringer Washington Post, 1978; owner Nancy Smith Pub. Rels. Contbg. editor Ultra mag., Houston, 1981-82, Tex. Woman mag., Dallas, 1979-80, Profl. Woman mag., Dallas, 1979-80; mem. bd. advisors Ultra Mag., 1985—; columnist North Dallas People; writer D Homes; appeared on TV series Jocelyn's Weekend, Sta. KDFI-TV, 1985. Bd. dirs. TACA arts support orgn., Dallas, 1980—, asst. chmn. custom auction, 1978-83; judge Miss Tex. USA Contest, 1984; bd. dirs. Am. Parkinson Disease Assn. (Dallas chpt.), mem. adv. bd. Cattle Baron's Ball Com., Dallas Symphony Debutante presentations; mem. bd. dirs. Dallas Opera Women's Bd., Northwood Inst. Women's Bd., Dallas Symphony Leauge; mem. Friends of Winston Churchill Meml. and libr., Dallas Theatre Ctr. Women's Guild, Childrens' Med. Ctr. Aux.; mem. women's com. Dallas Theatre Ctr.; hon. mem. Crystal Charity Ball Com.; mem. Cmty. Coun. Greater Dallas Cmty. Awareness Goals Com. Impact '88, 1985—; com. mem. Dallas Arboretum, Preservation Dallas; co-chmn. Multiple Sclerosis San Simeon Gala, 1988; celebrity co-chmn. Greer Garson Gala of Hope 1990-91; gala chmn. Greer Garson Gala of Hope for Am. Parkinson's Disease Assn., 1991-93; chmn. gala benefit Northwood U., 1994; co-chmn. star-studded stomp Mar. Dimes, 1994; mem. Femmes du Monde spl. activities com., 1999 luncheon com., com. Dallas Coun. World Affairs; bd. dirs. Dallas Ballet's Lone Star Adagio. Mem. Soc. Profl. Journalists (v.p. coms. 1978-79), Nat. Press Club, Dallas Press Club, DAR, Daus. of Republic of Tex. (registrar 1972), Dallas So. Meml. Assn., Dallas County Heritage Soc. (bd. dirs.), Dallas Mus. Art League, Dallas Opera Guild, Tower Club, Trippers Club, Plano Rotary Club, Pub. Affairs Luncheon Club, Argyle Club (sec. 1983-84), The 500 Club (Dallas), Lancaster Hist. Soc., City of Plano Sister Cities Com., French Heritage Soc, Flagler Mus., Argyle Club, Rondo/Carrousel Club, Thalia Club, Caterie Club, Kermis Club, S'Amuser. Home: 5727 Covehaven Dr Dallas TX 75252-4934 Office Phone: 214-625-1162. E-mail: nancywoolvertonsmith@comcast.net.

SMITH, NINA J. music educator; b. Laurel, Miss., Aug. 19, 1953; d. Thomas H. and Ruth Jennings Jones; m. Norman L. Smith; children: Jennifer Smith Mills, Joel. B in Music Edn., Miss. U. Women, 1974; MEd, William Carey Coll., 1997. Music tchr. Jones County Schs., Ellisville, Miss., 1978—. Recipient Excellence in Edn. award, Assn. Excellence in Edn., 1992; grantee, 1993, Bell South, 1994, 1995, AEE, 2002, Miss. Power, 2002, Howard Industries, 2002. Mem.: Am. Fedn. Tchrs. Baptist. Office: Ellisville Elem Deason St Ellisville MS 39437

SMITH, NONA COATES, academic administrator; b. West Grove, Pa., Apr. 1, 1942; d. John Truman and Elizabeth Zane (Trumbo) Coates; m. David Smith, Oct. 12, 1968 (div. May 1986); children: Kirth Ayrl, Del Kerry, Michael Sargent, Sherri Lee. BA, West Chester (Pa.) U., 1988; PhD, Temple U., 1998. Legal sec. Gawthrop & Greenwood, West Chester, 1968-73, MacElree, Gallagher, O'Donnell, West Chester, 1981-84; social sec. Mrs. John B. Hannum, Unionville, Pa., 1975-81; rsch. asst. West Chester U., 1984-88, cons., 1988; dir. sponsored rsch. Bryn Mawr (Pa.) Coll., 1989—, chair rsch./tchg. evaluation, 1993-95. Treas. Kennett Vol. Fire Co., Kennett Square, Pa., 1984-86; founding mem. Colls. of Liberal Arts-Sponsored Programs. Recipient Scholastic All-Am. award U.S. Achievement Acad., 1988, Rsch. award Truman Libr., 1992, Goldsmith Rsch. award Harvard U., 1993; fellow Truman Dissertation, 1997—. Fellow Phi Alpha Theta; mem. AAUW, Am. Hist. Assn., Soc. Historians of Am. Fgn. Rels., Nat. Coun. Univ. Rsch. Adminstrs. (mem. nat. conf. com. 1995-96). Republican. Presbyterian. Avocations: reading, gardening, travel, cultural events. Home: PO Box 239 Unionville PA 19375-0239 Office: Bryn Mawr Coll 101 N Merion Ave Bryn Mawr PA 19010-2859

SMITH, PAMELA HYDE, ambassador; b. Tacoma, July 1945; m. Sidney G. Smith (dec.); 2 children. BA in Art History, Wellesley Coll., 1967. Joined US Info. Agy., 1975; asst. & cultural attaché US Embassy, Bucharest, 1976—77; special asst. to USIA Dir., 1977—81; cultural asst. US Embassy, Belgrade, 1982—86; dep. chief Acad. Exch. Program USIA, 1986—91; press attaché US Embassy, Jakarta, 1991—95; dir. Office Geog. Liaison U.S. Info. Agy., 1995—97; pub. affairs officer US Embassy, London, 1997—2001; U.S. amb. to Moldova Dept. State, 2001—. Office: Dept of State Amb 7080 Chisinau Pl Washington DC 20521

SMITH, PAMELA LATRICE, psychologist; b. Monroe, La., Jan. 11, 1975; d. Tommy Lee Smith and Lovely Marie Bams. BA, N.E. La. Univ., Monroe, La., 1997, MS, M, N.E. La. Univ., Monroe, La., 1999. Specialist in sch. psychology Univ. La., 2000. Sch. psychologist Westside Alternative Sch., Tallulah, La., 1999—2000, Monroe City Schs., Office of Spl. Edn., Monroe, La., 2000—. Instr. psychology Univ. La., Monroe, La., 2002—; instr. Crisis Prevention Inst., Monroe, La., 2001; contract psychologist Delhi Charter Sch., La., 2001—. Founding mem. Wall of Tolerance, Montgomery, Ala., 2002. Recipient Outstanding Academic Achievement, 1992—93; scholar Scholarship award, 1993. Mem.: La. Sch. Psychol. Assn., Phi Kappa Phi, Psi Chi Nat. Honor Soc., Delta Sigma Theta Sorority Inc. Non-Demon. Avocations: travel, reading, music, shopping. Home: 507 Auburn Ave Monroe LA 71201 Office: Office Spl Ednl Svcs PO Box 4180 Monroe LA 71211

SMITH, PAMELA ROSEVEAR, air transportation executive; b. Corvallis, Oreg., Nov. 26, 1953; BS, U. Oreg., Eugene, 1977; MBA, C.W. Post Coll., L.I. U, 2003. V.p. inflight customer svc. Air America, L.A., 1984—90, MGM Grand Air, L.A., 1990—95; dir. sales Ogden Aviation, New York, 1995—98; v.p. sales, the americas Pourshins P/C, New York, 1998—. Recipient Dean's Award for acad. Excellence, L.I. U., 2003. Mem.: Inflight Food Svc. Assn. (bd. dirs. 1999—), Greater L.I. Running Club, Kappa Alpha Theta (N.Y. Alumni chpt.) (v.p. 1998—99). Avocation: sports, travel, education, cooking, Japanese language.. Office: 63 Tooker Ave Oyster Bay NY 11771

SMITH, PATRICIA, state representative; b. Bklyn., June 14, 1943; two children. AS, U. S. Fla., 1974; BS, Norwich U., 1991. Former town clk. and treas. Sudbury; rep. Vt. Ho. of Reps., 1996—. Mem. Vt. Munic Clkrs. and Treas. assn. (v.p.), N.E. Assn. Town Clks., Internat. Inst. Munic Clks. Roman Catholic.

SMITH, PATRICIA ANNE, special education educator; b. West Chester, Pa., Aug. 19, 1967; d. William Richard and Carol Anne (Benn) S. BS in Spl. Edn. cum laude, West Chester U., 1989; postgrad., Immaculata Coll., 1993-98. Cert. mentally and physically handicapped tchr., Pa. Learning support tchr. Chester County Intermediate Unit, Downingtown, Pa., 1989-90, early intervention tchr., 1990-92, autistic support tchr. Coatesville (Pa.) Area Sch. Dist., 1992—, event coord. WOYC workshops, 1993-2000, event coord. WOYC ext. workshops, 1999-2000, event coord. WOYC childrens workshops, 1999-2000. Presenter ann. conf. Pa. Assn. of Resources for People with Mental Retardation, Hershey, 1994, Pa. Fedn. Coun. for Exceptional Children 2003 Conv., 44th Ann. conv. No Child Left Behind in Pa., Pa. Fedn. Coun. for Exceptional Children Ann. Conf., Grantville, 2003; co-presenter ARC, 1996, Paoli Meml. Hosp., 1997; presenter info. sessions ann. conf. Del. Valley Assn. for Edn. of Young Children, Phila., 1994, Lions, Downingtown, Pa., 1992, early childhood conf. Capital Area Assn. for Edn. of Young Children, Harrisburg, Pa., 1995, vols. Caln Athletic Assn. Challenger League, 1995-96, Chester County MH/MR Consultation and Edn. Adv. Bd. Com., 1997-2000; mentor West Chester U., 1995-98. Mem. recreation adv. bd. dirs. Assn. for Retarded Citizens, Exton, Pa., 1993-98, Daisy Girl Scout Leader, 1995-96; vol. tutor Chester County Libr. Adult Literacy Program, 1995-98, vol. monitor, Residential Living Options Home, 2001—; respite provider ARC, Kencrest, 1998—. Recipient Outstanding Svc. award Coatesville Area Parent Coun., 1994, 96, Vol. award Friendship PTA, 1993, 96, 99, Pa. Early Childhood Edn. Assn. Workshop presenter award, 1993; grantee Pa.Dept. Edn., 1993, Coatesville Area Sch. Dist., 1990, Pa. Bur. Spl. Edn., 2001, 02. Mem.: ASCD, Coun. for Exceptional Children, Autism Soc. Am., Nat. Assn. for Edn. of Young Children, Kappa Delta Pi. Republican. Roman Catholic. Home: 501 Clover Mill Rd Exton PA 19341-2505 Office: Friendship Elem Sch 296 Reeceville Rd Coatesville PA 19320-1520 Office Phone: 610-383-3770.

SMITH, PATRICIA GRACE, government official; b. Nov. 10, 1947; d. Douglas and Wilhelmina (Griffin) Jones; m. J. Clay Smith, Jr., June 25, 1983; children: Eugene Douglas, Stager Clay, Michelle L., Michael L. BA in English, Tuskegee Inst., 1968; postgrad., Auburn U., 1969-71, Harvard U., 1974, George Washington U., 1983, Fed. Exec. Inst., 1997. Cert. exec. mgmt. tng. devel. assignments Dept. Def., 1986, U.S. Senate Commerce Com., 1987. Instr. Tuskegee Inst., Ala., 1969-71; program mgr. Curber Assocs., Washington, 1971-73; dir. placement Nat. Assn. Broadcasters, Washington, 1973-74, dir. pub. affairs, 1974-77; assoc. prodr. Group W Broadcasting, Balt., 1977, prodr., 1977-78; dir. affiliate rels. and programming Sheridan Broadcasting Network, Crystal City, Va., 1978-80; dep. dir. policy, assoc. mng. dir. pub. info./reference svc. FCC, Washington, 1992-94, acting assoc. mng. dir., pub. info. and reference svcs., 1994—. Chief of staff office assoc. adminstr. for comml. space transp. FAA, U.S. Dept. Transp., 1994-96, dep. assoc. adminstr. for comml. space transp., 1996-97, acting assoc. adminstr., 1997, assoc. adminstr., 1998—. Vice-chmn. Nat. Conf. Black Lawyers Task Force on Comms., Washington, 1975-87; trustee, mem. exec. com., nominating com., youth adv. com. Nat. Urban League, 1976-81; mem. comms. com. Cancer Coordinating Coun., 1977-84; mem. Braintrust Subcom. on Children's Programming, Congl. Black Caucus, 1976—; mem. adv. bd. Black Arts Celebration, 1978-83; mem. NAACP; mem. journalism and comms. adv. coun. Auburn U., 1976-78; mem. Washington Urban League, 1985—; bd. dirs. Black Film Rev., 1989-91; mem. D.C. Commn. on Human Rights, 1986-88, chmn., 1988-91; mem. adv. coun. NIH, 1992-96; mem. bd. advisors The Salvation Army, 1993-2000.. Named Outstanding Young Woman of Yr., Washington, 1975, 78; recipient Sustained Superior Performance award FCC, Washington, 1982-95, Disting. Alumnus award Tuskegee U., 1996, C. Alfred Anderson award, 2002. Mem. Women in Comms., Inc. (mem. nat. adv. com.), Broadcasters Club (bd. dirs. 1976-77), Lambda Iota Tau. Democrat. Baptist. Avocations: writing, swimming. Home: 4010 16th St NW Washington DC 20011-7002 Office: DOT/AST 800 Independence Ave SW Rm 331 Washington DC 20591-0001 Office Phone: 202-267-7793.

SMITH, PATRICIA LYNNE, visual artist; b. Camden, N.J., Nov. 3, 1955; d. Thomas Patrick Connelly and Elizabeth Jean (Swope) Shober; m. William Clarence Smith, Nov. 30, 1973 (div. June 1980); children: Travis Smith, Taryn Smith. BA, Rutgers U., Camden, N.J., 1980; MFA, Rutgers U., New Brunswick, N.J., 1984. Adj. instr. Rutgers U., New Brunswick, N.J., 1983-84, Trenton State Coll., 1989-90. Solo exhbns. of numerous shows including most recently: Art Exch. Fair, N.Y.C., 1996, Bklyn. Mus. Art, 1997, Cornerhouse, Manchester, England, 1997, Gas Works, London, 1997, Art Exch. Fair, 1997, Gramercy Art Fair, 1997, The Rotunda Gallery, 1997, Kunstlerhause, Vienna, 1998, Vassar Coll., Poughkeepsie, N.Y., 1998, Bard Coll., Rheinbeck, N.Y., 1998, Eyewash Gallery, Bklyn., 1994, 99, 2000, Project Space, Toronto, Can., 2001, Sideshow Gallery, Bklyn., N.Y., 2001, The Rotunda Gallery, Bklyn., N.Y., 2002, Exit Art, N.Y.C., N.Y., 2002, Voorkamer, Lien, Belgium, 2002, Art Ctr. Coll. Design, Pasadena, Calif., 2002, U. Md., Coll. Pk., Md., 2003, Solway Jones Gallery, LA, Calif., 2003. Recipient Stedman Purchase prize Rutgers U., 1980, Garden State fellow, 1982-84, Exhbn. grantee Artist's Space, 1988, 90. Home: 7 Dutch St Rm 1 New York NY 10038-3713

SMITH, PATTI, state representative; m. Leroy Smith; 5 children. Attended, Mt. Hood C.C. State rep., dist. 52 Oreg. House Rep., Salem, 2003—; owner Family Farm. Chair Trade and Econ. Devel. Com.; mem. Agr. and Natural Resources Com.; support enforcement officer Baker County Dist. Atty.; adminstrv. sec. Woodland Park Hosp.; staff asst. Multnomah County Charter Rev. Com. Mem.: Farm Bur., East Multnomah County Pioneer Assn., Crown Point Hist. Soc., Troutdale Hist. Soc. Republican. Office: 900 Court St NE H-487 Salem OR 97301

SMITH, PAULA MARIE, medical technologist; b. Meadville, Pa., July 22, 1964; d. William Paul and Mary Frances (Siegel) S. BS in Applied Sci., Youngstown State U., 1988. Cert. specialist in blood banking ARC Blood Svcs., No. Ohio Region, 1992-93, med. technologist with specialization in blood bank certification. Med. technologist St. Joseph Health Ctr., Warren, Ohio, 1988-92, blood bank supr., 1993—96; med. technologist specializing in blood bank certification, 1996—. Active Rainforest Action Internat. Network, Cleve. Metroparks Zoo, 1993. Youngstown Found. scholar Youngstown State U., 1984, 85. Mem.ASPCA, AAUW, NOW, Am. Soc. Clin. Pathologists, Am. Assn. Blood Banks, Ohio Assn. Blood Banks. Home: 331 Hazelwood Ave SE Warren OH 44483-6137 Office: St Joseph Health Ctr Lab 667 Eastland Ave SE Warren OH 44484-4503

SMITH, PEG L. foundation administrator; b. Ind. Tchr. Head Start, 1974—77, dir. child adult resource svcs., 1977—89, dir. child adult resource svcs. children's div., 1989—91; dir. step ahead initiative Office of Gov., 1991—95; exec. dir. Ind. Youth Inst., Indpls., 1995—98, Am. Camping Assn., Matrinsville, Ind., 1998—. Spkr. in field. Office: Am Camping Assn 5000 State Rd 67 North Martinsville IN 46151-7902

SMITH, PEGGY O'DONIEL, physicist, researcher; b. Lakeland, Fla., Nov. 27, 1920; d. John Arthur and Carrie Mattie (Jackson) O'Doniel; m. Fenton Frederick Smith, Oct. 11, 1943; children: James Scott, Stephen Arthur, Melody Ann, Candy Lou. Aviation Pilot Lic., Stetson U., Deland, Fla., 1941; BS in Sci. and Math., Fla. So. Coll., 1942; MA in Edn., U.S. Internat. U., San Diego, 1968. Physicist degausser U.S. Navy, Key West, Fla., 1942, physicist compass compensator Charleston, S.C., 1943, physicist magnetic signature analyst Washington, 1944; tchr. Chula Vista (Calif.) Sch. Dist., 1963-73, math specialist, 1974-77; owner Mineral Store, Chula Vista, 1977-82; ret. Leader math. workshops for girls, 1992-96. Author: Laz Goes to New Zealand; contbr. articles to profl. jours. Del. White House Conf. on Edn., 1956; sec. Chula Vista Rep. Women, 1995-97; chmn. Orphans of Italy, 1957-58. Recipient Kazanjian award, Joint Coun. Econ. Edn., Chula Vista, 1972, Fla. So. Coll. Alumni Achievement citation, 1999; Chula Vista Sch. Dist. math grantee, 1975. Mem. AAUW (v.p. 1989, 2001-03, 04—), Inner Circle, Calif. Ret. Tchrs. Assn. (v.p. 1998-2000), San Diego Gem and Mineral Soc. Avocations: golf, mineral collecting, coin collecting, bridge, travel. Home: 87 K St Chula Vista CA 91911-1409

SMITH, PHYLLIS MAE, healthcare consultant, educator; b. Coeur d'Alene, Idaho, May 2, 1935; d. Elmer Lee Smith and Kathryn Alice (Newell) Wilson. Diploma, Luth. Bible Inst., Seattle, 1956, Emanuel Hosp. Sch. Nursing, Portland, Oreg., 1959, Coll. San Mateo, Calif., 1971. Staff nurse in surgery Emanuel Hosp., Portland, 1962-63; head nurse ctrl. svc. Sacred Heart Hosp., Eugene, Oreg., 1964-69; dir. ctrl. svcs. Peninsula Hosp., Burlingame, Calif., 1969-74; pres. Phyllis Smith Assocs., Inc., Lewiston, Idaho, 1975-88; sr. tech. advisor, dir. ednl. programs Parkside Material Mgmt. Svcs., Park Ridge, Ill., 1988-90; AIDS coord. Asotin County Health Dist., 1989-2000. Lectr., cons. in field in over 14 countries. Contbr. to manuals and profl. jours. Mem. NAFE, Internat. Assn. Hosp. Ctrl. Svc. Mgmt. (dir. edn. 1973-88, chmn. technician edn. and affairs com. 1978-88, John Perkins award 1977, Cheshire award 1977, Lifetime Achievement award 2003), Assn. for Advancement Med. Instrumentation. Lutheran. Avocations: fishing, walking, photography, chess, reading. Home and Office: 1415 Chestnut St Clarkston WA 99403-2429

SMITH, PRISCILLA R. social sciences educator; b. Pasadena, CA, Oct. 27, 1949; d. Aldric Joseph and Ruth Chenoweth Smith; m. H. Russell Searight, Sept. 10, 1977 (div. Nov. 1988). AB, Indiana U., 1972; MSW, Wash. U., 1980; PhD, Saint Louis U., 1988. A.C.S.W., L.C.S.W., L.S.W. Social worker Special Svcs. Co-op., Imperial, MO, 1984-86; adj. prof. St. Louis (Mo.) U., 1990-91; asst. prof. Southern Ill. U., Edwardsville, 1987-94; adj. prof. U. Kans., 1994-95; sch. social worker Wichita (Kans.) Pub. Schs., 1994-95; therapist Lakepoint Psychiatry, Wichita, KS, 1994-95; asst. prof. U. Akron, OH, 1995—. Family therapist Children's Ctr. Behavioral Devel., E. St. Louis, Ill., 1982-84; therapist Logos Sch. St. Louis, Mo., 1980-82; social worker Consol. Neighborhood Svcs., Inc., St. Louis, Mo, 1980, therapist MADD Belleville, Ill., 1991-93. Contbr. articles, chpts. to profl. publs. Adv. bd. mem. Salvation Army St. Louis, Mo., 1990-94; petitioner Dollars & Democracy Akron, Ohio, 1998-99, Akron Clean Money, 2000; bd. mem. Coop. Market, Akron, 1997-99; Econ. Justice and Empowerment bd. mem. Am. Friends Svc. Com. Akron, 1999-2003. Mem. Nat. Assn. Social Workers, Acad. Cert. Social Workers. Avocations: the arts, acting, volunteering. Office: Univ Akron Polsky Bldg Akron OH 44325-8001 E-mail: psmith@uakron.edu.

SMITH, REBECCA BEACH, federal judge; b. 1949; BA, Coll. William and Mary, 1971; postgrad., U. Va., 1971-73; JD, Coll. William and Mary, 1979. Assoc. Wilcox & Savage, 1980-85; U.S. magistrate Ea. Dist. Va., 1985-89; dist. judge U.S. Dist. Ct. (ea. dist.) Va., Norfolk, 1989—. Exec. editor Law Review, 1978-79. Active Chrysler Mus. Norfolk, Jean Outland Chrysler Libr. Assocs., Va. Opera Assn., Friends of the Zoo, Friends of Norfolk Pub. Libr., Ch. of the Good Shepherd. John Marshall Soc. fellow; recipient Acad. Achievement and Leadership award St. George Tucker Soc.; named one of Outstanding Women of Am., 1979. Mem. ABA, Va. State Bar Assn., Fed. Bar Assn. Supreme Ct. Hist. Soc., Fourth Cir. Judicial Conf., The Harbor Club, Order of Coif., Phi Beta Kappa. Office: US Dist Ct US Courthouse 600 Granby St Ste 358 Norfolk VA 23510-1915

SMITH, REBECCA MCCULLOCH, human relations educator; b. Greensboro, N.C., Feb. 29, 1928; d. David Martin and Virginia Pearl (Woodburn) McCulloch; m. George Clarence Smith Jr., Mar. 30, 1945; 1 child, John Randolph. BS, Woman's Coll., U. N.C., 1947, MS, 1952; PhD, U. N.C., Greensboro, 1967; postgrad., Harvard U., 1989. Tchr. pub. schs., N.C., S.C.; instr. U. N.C., Greensboro, 1958—91, asst. prof. to prof. emeritus human devel./family studies. Dir. grad. program, 1975-82; ednl. cons. depts. edn. N.C., S.C., Ind., Ont., Man.; vis. prof. N.W. La. State U., 1965, 67, U. Wash., 1970, Hood Coll., 1976, 86. Author: Teaching About Family Relationships, 1975, Klemer's Marriage and Family Relationships, 2d edit., 1975, Resources for Teaching About Family Life Education, 1976, Family Matters: Concepts in Marriage and Personal Relationships, 1982; co-author: History of the School of Human Environmental Sciences: 1892-1992, 1992, assoc. editor Jour. Applied Family and Child Studies, 1980-90; ednl. cons. Current Life Studies, 1977-84. Bd. dirs. Sch. HES Alumni, 1997-99. Named Outstanding Alumna Sch. Home Econs., 1976; recipient Sperry award for service to families N.C. Family Life Coun., 1979. Mem. Nat. Coun. Family Rels. (exec. com. 1974-76, treas. 1987-89, Osborne award 1973), U. N.C. at Greensboro Alumni Assn. (chair membership recruitment com. 1994-96). Home: 1212 Ritters Lake Rd Greensboro NC 27406-7816 Office: U NC Dept Human Devel Sch Human Environ Scis Greensboro NC 27412-0001

SMITH, RENAE COLLEEN, music educator; d. James Alvin and Eleanore Lillian Adrian; m. Miles Cameron Smith, Aug. 28, 1993. BA in Music Edn., U. of Wis., 1991; MA in Human Svcs. Counseling, Regent U., 2003. Music tchr. Wash. Episcopal Sch., Bethesda, Md., 1998—; lay counselor Grace Luth. Ch., Falls Church, Va., 2003—. Tchr. Grace Luth. Ch., Falls Church, Va., 1999—2003. Scholar, Regent U., 2002—03. Mem.: APA, Am. Assn. of Christian Counselors. Republican. Luth. Home: 4004 Justine Drive Annandale VA 22003 Office: Washington Episcopal School 5600 Little Falls Parkway Bethesda MD 20816 Personal E-mail: peshtigo7@aol.com. E-mail: rsmith@w-e-s.org.

SMITH, ROBIN L. municipal official; b. Buffalo, July 22, 1955; d. Vernon Myron and Lois Alice (Kerr) Dean; m. Rickie J. Chilson, Nov. 24, 1973 (div. Dec. 1980); m. Garry Edward Smith, Apr. 17, 1982; children: Kevin Michael, Steven Garry. Grad., Belmont (N.Y.) H.S., 1973. Asst. dir. civil def. Allegany County, Belmont, 1980; exec. sec. pers. CVC Products, Rochester, NY, 1980—81; inside sales Atlas Alloys, Rochester, NY, 1981—82; office mgr. Nasco Carpets & Rugs, Waverly, NY, 1992—99; twp. supr. Athens Twp., Pa., 1998—2003, twp. sec., 1999—, asst. permit officer, 2004—. Asst. emergency coord. Athens (Pa.) Township, 2004—. Mem., pres. Belmont Fireman's Aux., 1976—80; treas. Cmty. Chest, Belmont, 1977; EMT Amity Rescue Squad, Belmont, 1979—80; mem. mitigation com. Valley Project Impact, 1999—; sec. Athens Twp. Authority, 1999—2002, Satterlee Creek Watershed Assn., 2000—. Mem.: Pa. State Assn. Twp. Suprs. Democrat. Baptist. Avocations: knitting, crafts, family. Home: RD #1 Box 12-A Sayre PA 18840 Office: Athens Twp 184 Herrick Ave Sayre PA 18840

SMITH, ROBLYN CAROL, speech pathology/audiology services professional; b. Jonesboro, Ark., July 6, 1957; d. Joe T. and Doris (Merritt) Thompson; m. Phillip Eugene Smith, Oct. 3, 1985; children: Ashlin Elaine, Phillip Ethan. BS in Edn., Ark. State U., 1977; M in Speech Pathology, U. Miss., 1979. Cert. tchr. speech pathology, spl. edn., other health impaired, lic. speech pathologist Ark. Speech lang. pathologist Yellville Summit Schs., Ark., 1979—81, Manila Pub. Schs., Ark., 1981—83, Bryan County Child Guidance, Durant, Okla., 1983—85, Mayes County Child Guidance, Pryor, Okla., 1985—90, Tulsa County Health Dept., 1990—98; spl. edn. team mem. Verdigris Pub. Schs., Claremore, Okla., 1998—2000; speech lang. pathologist Kids First U. Ark. Med. Scis., Springdale, 2000—. Mem.: Am. Speech-Lang.-Hearing Assn. (cert. clin. competence), Phi Mu. Avocations: skiing, antiques, travel, singing. Home: 1600 Rosewood Ln Siloam Springs AR 72761 Office: Kids First Univ Ark Med Scis 417 W Maple Springdale AR 72764 Office Phone: 479-750-0130.*

SMITH, ROSEMARY, artist, educator; b. Bklyn., May 6, 1941; d. John Joseph Smith and Katherine Olivia Francis; m. James Barron Swick, May 6, 1970; 1 child, Barron Francis Smith Swick ; 1 child from previous marriage, George Maximillian Smith Egermann. BA, Case Western Res. U.; MA, U. Iowa; MFA, U. Minn., Mpls.-St. Paul. Mem. art faculty Minn. State Colls. and Univs., U. Iowa, Cleve. Mus. Art, Nottingham (Eng.) Poly.; lectr., guest artist, multiple workshops various univs. Book, Herstory in Lace, 1989—92, series of image scrolls, Scrolling Time, 1999—, Lead in the City, 1990—93, series of paintings and drawings, Color as Form, 1980—86, series of paintings, Field Paintings, 1970—78, exhibitions include Minn. Statewide Art Exhibit, 1993, Westminster Ch. Gallery, 1993, Fisea Exhbn., MCAD Gallery, Minn., 1993, Rochester (Minn.) Inst. Tech., 1993—94, St. Catherine's Coll., St. Paul, 1993, Internat. Traveling Art Show, 1998—, traveling exhbn., Mus. Sch. Chgo. Art Inst., Phila. U. Arts, Rochester Inst. Tech., 1994—, exhibitions include numerous exhbns., Beijing, St. Paul, Austria, Eng., Mpls., Cleve., Represented in permanent collections Minn. Ctr. Book Arts, Cleve. Art Inst., Sackler Archives, Miami, Georgetown U., U. Iowa, Marist Coll., Vassar Coll., numerous others. Recipient numerous other grants and awards; McKnight fellow in Photography, 1990, Jerome Found. fellow, Minn. Ctr. Book Arts, 1989—91, NEH fellow in Film Theory. Mem.: U. Minn. Alumni Assn., U. Iowa Alumni Assn., Univ. Club St. Paul. Avocations: swimming, flute and piano, architectural design. Home: 703 Laurel Ave 1W St Paul MN 55104

SMITH, RUBY LUCILLE, retired librarian; b. Nobob, Ky., Sept. 19, 1917; d. James Ira and Myrtie Olive (Crabtree) Jones; m. Kenneth Cornelius Smith, Dec. 25, 1946; children: Kenneth Cornelius, Corma Ann. AB, Western Ky. State Tchrs. Coll., 1943, MA, 1966. Tchr. rural schs., Barren County, Ky., 1941-42; tchr. secondary sch. English, libr. Temple Hill Consol. Sch., Glasgow, Ky., 1943-47, 49-51, 53-56, sch. libr., 1956-83. Sec. Barren County Cancer Soc., 1968—70, Barren County Fair Bd., 1969—70; leader 4-H Club, 1957—72; coord. tax-aide program AARP, 1985—88, dist. dir., 1988—2000, local chpt. v.p., 1996—98, pres., 1999—2000, instr. 55 Alive Mature Driving, 1993—; sec. Oak Grove Bapt. Ch., 1979—; coun. mem. Barren County; bd. dirs. Barren County Hist. Found., Inc., 1997—; trustee Mary Wood Weldon Meml. Libr., 1964—, Barren County Pub. Libr. Bd., 1969—2001; sec. Barren County Pub. Libr., 1969—2001; trustee Barren County Hist. Found., 1996—. Mem. NEA (life), Ky. Edn. Assn., Ky. Sch. Media Assn. (sec. 1970-71), 3d Dist. Libr. Assn. (pres. 1944, 66), Barren County Edn. Assn. (pres. 1960-62, treas. 1979-80), 3d Dist. Ret. Tchrs. Assn. (pres. 1991-92), Ky. Ret. Tchrs. Assn. (v.p. 1992-93, pres.-elect 1993-94, pres. 1994-95), Glasgow-Barren County Ret. Tchrs. Assn. (pres. 1984-86, 96-98, sec. 1989, treas. 1990), Ky. Libr. Trustee Assn. (bd. dirs. 1985-98, pres. 1986-88, 93-95, dir. Barren River region 1985-97), Barren County Rep. Women's Club, Monroe Assn. Woman's Missionary Union (dir. 1968-72, 79-83, sec. 1985-98), Monroe Assn. Bapts. (libr. dir. 1972-88), Ky. Libr. Assn., South Ctrl. Hist. Soc. (v.p. 1997-98, pres. 1998-2000), DAR (chaplain Edmund Rogers chpt. 1998—), Delta Kappa Gamma (pres. Delta chpt. 1996-98). Home: 54 E Nobob Rd Summer Shade KY 42166-8405

SMITH, SALIESH ANNE, comptroller, payroll administrator; b. Salmon, Idaho, June 27, 1974; d. Annette Marie (Schmidt) Lewis. Degree in fin. (Cum Laude), Boise State U., 1996. Sales assoc. Sears Roebuck & Co., Boise, 1992; nanny Mary Rockrohr, Boise, 1992; receptionist IFECO, Boise, 1992-93; asst. office mgr. Tupper Constrn., Inc., Challis, Idaho, 1992, 94, asst. fin. mgr., 1995; secretarial asst. Boise State U., 1993-96; comptroller PCS Edn. Sys., Inc., Boise, 1996—. Attendee ABRA Payroll Yr. End, San Francisco, 1997, Wage & Hour Law Update, Boise, 1997. Bd. mem. Hugh O'Brian Youth Leadership (co-dir. recruitment), 1997—. Scholar Boise State U.. Mem. Fin. Mgmt. Assn. (v.p. 1995-96, chairperson 1996). Avocations: reading, walking, skiing, going to movies. Home: 1298 N Carissa Ave Boise ID 83704-0636 Office: PCS Education Systems Inc 1655 W Fairview Ave Ste 100 Boise ID 83702-5173 Fax: 208-343-1321. E-mail: ssmith@pcsedu.com.

SMITH, SALLYE WRYE, librarian; b. Birmingham, Ala., Nov. 11, 1923; d. William Florin and Margaret (Howard) Wrye; m. Stuart Werner Smith, Sept. 20, 1947 (dec. June 1981); children: Carol Ann, Susan Patricia, Michael Christopher, Julie Lynn, Lori Kathleen. BA, U. Ala., 1945; MA, U. Denver, 1969. Psychometrician U.S. Army, Deshon Gen. Hosp., Butler, Pa., 1945-46, U.S. Vet. Adminstrn. Vocat. Guidance, U. Ala., Tuscaloosa, 1946; clin. psychologist U.S. Army, Walter Reed Gen. Hosp., Washington, 1946-47, U.S. Army, Fitzsimons Gen. Hosp., Denver, 1948, U.S. Vets. Adminstrn., Ft. Logan, Colo., 1948-50; head sci.-engring. libr. U. Denver, Colo., 1969-72; instr., reference libr. Penrose Libr., U. Denver, 1972-80, asst. prof., reference libr., 1980-90, interim dir., 1990-92, asst. prof. emerita, 1992—. Vis. prof. U. Denver Grad. Sch. Libr. Info. Mgmt., 1975-77, 83; info. broker Colo. Rschrs., Denver, 1979—; cons., presenter The Indsl. Info. Workshop Inst. de Investigaciones Tecnologicas, Bogota, Colombia, 1979, LIPI-DRI-PDIN workshop on R&D mgmt., Jakarta, Indonesia, 1982; mem. BRS User Adv. Bd., Latham, N.Y., 1983-86. Indexer: Statistical Abstract of Colorado 1976-77, 1977. Recipient Cert. of Recognition, Sigma Xi, U. Denver chpt., 1983. Mem. ALA, Am. Soc. Indexers, Spl. Libr. Assn., Colo. Assn. Librs., Phi Beta Kappa, Beta Phi Mu. Office: Colo Researchers PO Box 22779 Denver CO 80222-0779

SMITH, SARA D. minister, lawyer; b. Hodgenville, Ky., July 17, 1963; d. Robert Sydnor and Dorothy Deane (Doyle) Smith; m. Lee A. Bryce, Nov. 21, 1998. BS, Tex. Christian U., 1985; JD, U. Houston, 1988; MDiv, Tex. Christian U., 1995. Bar: Tex. 1989; ordained minister United Ch. of Christ, 1996. Trial atty. U.S. Dept. Labor, Dallas, 1988—91; minister, exec. dir. United Ministries Higher Edn., Colo. U., Boulder, 1996—2003; pastor Kenilworth United Ch. of Christ, Buffalo, 2003—. Avocations: gardening, woodworking, writing. Home: 24 Kettering Dr Buffalo NY 14223 E-mail: kuccrevsara@verizon.net.

SMITH, SARAH BAGWELL, sculptor, artist, printmaker; b. Onancock, Va., Aug. 7, 1918; d. Isaiah William Bagwell II and Mary Eugenia Taylor; m. Harry LeCato Smith Jr., Mar. 7, 1942 (dec.); children: Harry LeCato Smith III, Douglass Bagwell, Susan Smith Haberly. AB, Randolph-Macon Woman's Coll., 1939. Biology lab asst. Richmond (Va.) Prof. Inst. (now Va. Commonwealth U.), 1939—41; biology & chem. tchr. St. Anne's Sch., Charlottesville, Va., 1943—44; history of art tchr. Va. Art Inst., Charlottesville, Va., 1965—73; instr. U. Va, School Continuing Edn., Charlottesville, Va., 1974—76; sculptor McGuffey Arts Ctr., Charlottesville, 1976—84, 2003. Represented in permanent collections City of Charlottesville, Fed. Res. Bank, Richmond, U. Va. Med. Ctr., numerous other pub. and pvt. collections; patent of elevated toilet seat. Chair com. art enhancement Welfare Offices, Charlottesville, 1960; garden designer St. Anne's Sch., Charlottesville, Va., 1955. Mem.: Abingdon Sq. Painters Inc., Tri-State Sculptor's Guild, McGuffey Arts Ctr. (studio). Avocation: gardening. Home: 2030 Spottswood Rd Charlottesville VA 22903-1245 Studio: McGuffey Art Ctr 201 2d St NW Charlottesville VA 22901

SMITH, SARAH JANE (SALLY SMITH), mayor; b. Pekin, Ill., Jan. 23, 1945; d. Claude P. and Jane (Prettyman) S.; B.S. in Music Edn., U. Ill.; postgrad. U. Alaska. Tchr. jr. high sch. Los Angels City Schs., 1968-69; adminstrv. asst. Office of Gov. of Alaska, 1971-74; project field rep Alaska Dept. Community and Regional Affairs, 1974-76; expeditor H.W. Blackstock, Inc., 1979-82; mem. Alaska Ho. of Reps. from 20th Dist., 1977-83, majority whip, 1977-79, mem. fin. com., 1979-81, chmn. rules chmn., 1981; exec. dir. Fairbanks Pvt. Industry Council, 1983-84; dir. div. pub. services Alaska Dept. Revenue, 1984— ; mayor City and Borough of Juneau, 2000—. Dir. choir Juneau Meth. and Presbyn. chs., 1972-74, 86—, Fairbanks Presbyn. Ch., 1974-75; historian Fairbanks Drama Assn., 1974-76; adv. bd. Assn. Children with Learning Disabilities, 1978-80; commr. Fairbanks Historic Preservation Commn., 1982-84; bd. dirs. Friends of U. Alaska Mus., 1983-84. Named Outstanding Freshman Legislator, 1976. Mem. Fairbanks Assn. Arts. Democrat. Club: PEO.

SMITH, SAREBA G. special education educator; b. High Point, N.C., Nov. 28, 1930; d. Shannon and Mahaley (Blackwell) Gripper; m. Harold F. Smith, June 21, 1958; children: Sabrina Denise, Etta Marie, Sheri Ann, Harold F. Jr. BA, Clark Coll., Atlanta, 1954; MEd, Boston U., 1973; postgrad., R.I. Coll., 1986, U. R.I., Kingston, 1987. Tchr., dir. music Thomaston (Ga.) Sch., So. Pines (N.C.) Schs.; supr. edn., tchr. Hayden Sch. for Boys, Boston; spl. edn. tchr. S. Kingstown Pub. Schs., Wakefield, R.I. Mem. Human Svc. Adv. Bd. Recipient Cert. of Merit in recognition and appreciation of active interest and concern in the ednl. community, Citation for dedicated svc. to youth of Mass., others. Mem. Nat. Tchrs. Assn., Coun. for Exceptional Children. Home: PO Box 198 Kingston RI 02881-0198

SMITH, SELMA MOIDEL, lawyer, composer; b. Warren, Ohio, Apr. 3, 1919; d. Louis and Mary (Oyer) Moidel; 1 child, Mark Lee. Student, UCLA, 1936-39, U. So. Calif. Law School, 1939-41; JD, Pacific Coast U., 1942. Bar: Calif. 1943, U.S. Dist. Ct. 1943, U.S. Supreme Ct. 1958. Gen. practice law; mem. firm Moidel, Moidel, Moidel & Smith, 1943—. Field dir. civilian adv. com. WAC, 1943—45; charter mem. nat. bd. Med. Coll. Pa. (formerly Woman's Med. Coll. Pa.), 1953—, mem. exec. bd., 1976—80, pres., 1980—82, chmn, past pres. com., 1990—92, spkr., honoree 50th anniversary gala, 2003. Author: A Century of Achievement: The National Association of Women Lawyers, 1998, The First Women Members of the ABA, 1999; composer: Espressivo-Four Piano Pieces (orchestral premiere, 1987, performance Nat. Mus. Women in the Arts, 1989), numerous works. Decorated La Orden del Merito Juan Pablo Duarte (Dominican Republic), 1956. Fellow: Am. Bar Found. (life); mem.: ASCAP, ABA (jr. bar conf. 1946—52, activities com. 1948—49), Calif. Supreme Ct. Hist. Soc. (bd. dirs. 2001—), ABA Sr. Lawyers Divsn. (vice-chair editl. bd. Experience mag. 1997—99, chair arts com. 1998—99, chair editl. bd. Experience mag. 1999—2001, exec. coun. 1999—, Experience mag. adv. bd. 2001—, nominating com. 2003—, co-chair newsletter 2003-, dist. service award 2003-), Assn. Learning in Retirement Orgns. in West (pres. 1993—94, exec. com. 1994—95, Disting. Svc. award 1995), Plato Soc. UCLA (discussion leader UCLA Constitution Bicentennial Project 1985—87, moderator UCLA extension lecture series 1990, Toga editor 1990—93, sec. 1991—92, chmn. colloquium com. 1992—93, Exceptional Leadership award 1994), Euterpe Opera Club (chair auditions 1972, chair awards 1973—75, v.p. 1974—75), Docents LA Philharm. (press and pub. rels. 1972—75, cons. coord. 1973—75, v.p. 1973—83, chair Latin Am. cmty. rels.), Calif. Fedn. Music Clubs (chair Am. music 1971—75, conv. chair 1972), Nat. Fedn. Music Clubs (vice-chair Western region 1973—78), Nat. Assn. Composers USA (dir. 1974—79, luncheon chair 1975), Calif. Pres. Coun. (1st v.p.), LA Bus. Women's Coun. (pres. 1952), Calif. Bus. Women's Coun. (dir. 1951), Coun. Bar Assns. LA County (charter sec. 1950), So. Calif. Women Lawyers Assn. (pres. 1947, 1948), Inter-Am. Bar Assn., League of Ams. (dir.), Nat. Assn. Women Lawyers (regional dir. western states, Hawaii 1949—51, jud. adminstrn. com. 1960, nat. chair world peace through law com. 1966—67, liaison to ABA Sr. Lawyers Divsn. 1996—, chair bd. elections 1997—98, centennial com. 1997—99, chair com. unauthorized practice of law, social commn. UN, Lifetime Svc. award 1999), LA Lawyers Club (pub. defenders com. 1951), LA Bar Assn. (servicemen's legal aid com. 1944—45, psychopathic ct. com. 1948—53, Outstanding Svc. award 1993), State Bar Calif. (conf. com. on unauthorized practice of medicine 1964, Disting. Svc. award 1993), Women Lawyers Assn. LA (hon life; chair Law Day com. 1966, subject of oral hist. project 1986, 2001), Iota Tau Tau Legal Scholastic Soc. (dean LA 1947, supreme treas. 1959—62, 1st prize 1942). Home: 5272 Lindley Ave Encino CA 91316-3518

SMITH, SHARMAN BRIDGES, former state librarian; b. Lambert, Miss. BS, Miss. U. for Women, Columbus, 1972; MLS, George Peabody Coll., Nashville, 1975. Head libr. Clinton (Miss.) Pub. Libr., 1972-74; asst. dir. Lincoln-Lawrence-Franklin Regional Libr., Brookhaven, Miss., 1975-77, dir., 1977-78; info. svcs. mgr. Miss. Libr. Commn., Jackson, 1978-87, asst. dir. libr. ops., 1987-89, dir. libr. svcs. div., 1989-92; state libr. State Libr. Iowa, Des Moines, 1992—2001; exec. dir. Miss. Libr. Commn., Jackson, Miss., 2001—. Recipient Iowa Computer Using Educators Friend of Edn. award, 1995, Iowa Libr. Assn. Mem. of Yr. award, 1996. Office: Miss Libr Commn 1221 Ellis Ave Jackson MS 39209

SMITH, SHARON ELAINE, music educator; b. West Islip, N.Y., Jan. 24, 1972; d. Kenneth Richard and Sally Ann Knop; m. David Allen Smith, Aug. 4, 1995; 1 child, Bryan Thomas. MusB in Music Edn., SUNY, Fredonia, 1994; MA in Liberal Studies, SUNY, Stonybrook, 1998. Mid. sch. chorus tchr. West Islip Pub. Schs., 1994—96; elem. music tchr. East Islip Pub. Schs., 1996—98; mid. sch. chorus/string tchr. South Huntington Union Free Schs., Huntington Station, NY, 1998—, summer music theater dir. Mem.: L.I. String Festival Assn., Music Educators Nat. Conf., Suffolk County Music Educators Assn. Democrat. Methodist. Avocations: reading, theater, writing, decorating. Office: Silas Wood 6th Grade Ctr 23 Harding Pl Huntington Station NY 11746

SMITH, SHARON MARIE, music educator; b. Spokane, Wash., July 26, 1949; d. John Piper and Marie Minda (Larson) Rodkey; m. Dennis Gene Smith, Aug. 16, 1969; children: Minda Johanna, Erik Eugene, Matthew Dennis. BA, MusB, Pacific Luth. U., 1971; MusM, U. Ariz., 1974. Elem. music tchr. Tacoma Pub. Schs., 1971—78; music educator Omaha Pub. Schs., 1979—. Choir dir. Little Ch. on the Prairie, Tacoma, 1972—78; choral dir. First United Meth., Omaha, 1978—92, First Ctrl. Congl., Omaha, 1999—; dir. Nebr. Children's Choruses, Omaha, 1993—; voice tchr. Pacific Luth. U., Tacoma, 1977—78. Mem.: Nebr. Choral Dirs. Assn. (pres. 1999—2001, repertoire and stds. chair children's choirs 1990—98), Nebr. Music Educators Nat. Conf., Am. Choral Dirs. Assn. (pres. 1999—2001, repertoire and stds. chair child choirs 2002—). Office: Omaha Ctrl High Omaha NE

SMITH, SHARRON WILLIAMS, chemistry educator; b. Ashland, Ky., Apr. 3, 1941; d. James Archie and May (Waggoner) Williams; m. William Owen Smith, Jr., Aug. 16, 1964; children: Leslie Dyan, Kevin Andrew. BA, Transylvania U., 1963; PhD, U. Ky., 1975. Chemist Proctor & Gamble, Cin., 1963-64, NIH, Bethesda, Md., 1974-75; tchr. sci. Lexington (Ky.) Pub. Schs., Bethesda, Md., 1964-67; asst. prof. chemistry Hood Coll., Frederick, Md., 1975-81, assoc. prof., 1981-87, prof., 1987—, chair dept. chemistry and physics, 1982-86, 95-99, acting dean grad. sch., 1989-91, Whitaker prof. chemistry, 1993—. NDEA fellow, 1967-70, Beneficial-Hodson faculty fellow Hood Coll., 1984, 92; grantee Hood Coll. Bd. Assocs., 1981, 85, 91, NSF, 1986, 2001. Mem. AAAS, Am. Chem. Soc. (E. Emmet Reid award 2001), Mid.-Atlantic Assn. Liberal Arts and Chemistry Tchrs. (pres. 1984-85). Democrat. Office: Hood Coll Dept Chemistry Frederick MD 21701 E-mail: ssmith@hood.edu.

SMITH, SHEILA ROBERTSON, laboratory technician; b. Washington, Jan. 4, 1945; d. Philip Franklin and Emelyn Fiske Smith. AS, Penn Hall Coll., 1965. Hematology technician Duke U. Med. Ctr., Durham, NC, 1966—72, North Arundel Hosp., Glen Burnie, Md., 1972—73, Anne Arundel Med. Ctr., Annapolis, Md., 1973—93. Rep. on employees coun. Duke U. Med. Ctr., Durham, 1968—72. Bd. dirs. Smallwood Found., LaPlata, Md., 1997—. Mem.: Soc. for Restoration Port Tobacco (bd. dirs. 1997—), Charles County Hist. Soc., Charles County Garden Club. Republican. Episcopalian. Avocations: gardening, needlepoint, travel. Home: PO Box 365 Port Tobacco MD 20677-0365

SMITH, SHELAGH ALISON, public health educator; b. Oak Ridge, Tenn., June 3, 1949; d. Nicholas Monroe and Elizabeth (Kimbrough) Smith; m. Milton John Axley, 1991; 1 child, Elizabeth Claire Axley. BS in Edn., U. Tenn., 1971, AS in Dental Hygiene, 1974; MPH in Health Svcs. Adminstrn., Johns Hopkins, 1979. Lic. cert. health edn. specialist 1989. Social sci. rsch. analyst Dept. Health and Human Svcs., Health Care Fin. Adminstrn., Balt., 1980-85; pub. health educator, evaluator Nat. Cancer Inst.-NIH, Bethesda, Md., 1985-90; sr. policy analyst NIMH, Rockville, Md., 1990-92; pub. health advisor, ctr. mental health svcs. Substance Abuse & Mental Health Svcs. Adminstrn., Rockville, Md., 1992—96, sr. pub. health advisor, ctr. mental health svcs., 1997—. Elected mem. profl. devel. bd. Nat. Commn. for Health Edn. Credentialing, Inc., 2003—. Nominee C. Shepard Sci. Award for Outstanding Contbn. to Pub. Health, CDC, 2003; recipient Adminstr.'s Citation, Health Care Fin. Adminstrn., 1981, Dir.'s award, Nat. Cancer Inst., 1989, Spl. Act Svc. award, 1997, 1999, 2000, 2001, 2002, 2003, Quality Step Increase, 2001. Mem.: APHA (chmn. fin. and reimbursement for prevention svcs. com. 1987—89, 1996, governing coun. 1996—98, resolutions chair 1999, del. coalition nat. health edn. orgn. 1999—2004, advocacy chair 2001, pub. health edn. sect.), Washington Ethical Soc., Soc. Pub. Health Edn. (legis. co-chmn. 1990—91, governing bd. and ho. of dels. 1993—95, profl. devel. chair 1996, chpt. pres. 1997, treas. 1998—2000, nat. capital area exec. bd., mem. local D.C. chpt. and nat., Honor award 1999), Phi Kappa Phi. Democrat. Avocations: swimming, cooking, animal activism, sailing. Home: 14106 Heathfield Ct Rockville MD 20853-2760 Office: SAMHSA Ctr Mental Health Svc Office of Orgn and Financing 5600 Fishers Ln Rockville MD 20857-0001 E-mail: ssmith@samhsa.gov.

SMITH, SHERRI LEE, law educator; b. Dec. 30, 1964; PhD, Fla. State U. Adj. prof. Fla. Agrl. and Mech. U., Tallahassee, 1992-94; asst. prof. U. South Fla., Ft. Myers, 1995-97; asst. prof., vis. faculty cons. for instrnl. tech. Fla. Gulf Coast U., Ft. Myers, 1995—. Assoc. editor: Encyclopedia of Women and Crime, 1997-99. Mem. edn. com. Lee County Domestic Violence Coun., Ft. Myers, 1995—; bd. dirs. girls initiative workgroup dist. 8 State of Fla., Ft. Myers, 1997—. Mem. U.S. Distance Learning Assn., Am. Acad. Criminal Justice, Am. Soc. Criminology, Fla. Coun. on Crime and Delinquincy. Home and Office: 275 Forest St Huntington WV 25705-3706

SMITH, SHIRLEY, artist; b. Wichita, Kans., Apr. 17, 1929; d. Harold Marvin and Blanche Carrie (Alexander) S. BFA, Kans. State U., 1951; postgrad., Provincetown (Mass.) Workshop, 1962-66. One-woman shows include 55 Mercer St. Gallery, N.Y.C., 1973, Wichita Art Mus., Kanas, 1978, Stamford Mus. and Nature Ctr., Conn., 1987, Aaron Gallery, Washington, 1987, 1988, Joan Hodgell Gallery, Sarasota, Fla., 1987, Marianna Kistler Beach Mus. 38 Yr. Retrospective, Kans. State U., 1999—2000, John Jay Gallery, N.Y.C., 2000, Represented in permanent collections Whitney Mus. Am. Art, Phoenix Art Mus., The Aldrich Mus. Contemporary Art, Ridgefield, Conn., Ulrich Mus., Wichita State U., Everson Mus., Syracuse, N.Y., U. Calif. Berkeley Art Mus., Marianna Kistler Beach Mus., Manhattan, Kans., Telfair Mus. of Art, Savannah, Ga. Recipient Grumbacher Cash award for mixed media New Eng. Exhibition, Silvermine, Conn., 1967, Acad. Inst. award Am. Acad. Arts and Letters, N.Y.C., 1991, Richard Florsheim Art Funds grantee, 1998, Retrospective Opening grantee, 1999. Mem. Artist Equity. Democrat. Presbyterian. Home: 141 Wooster St New York NY 10012-3163

SMITH, SHIRLEY A. state legislator, state representative; b. 1950; 2 children. AA, Cuyahoga C.C.; BA, Cleve. (Ohio) State U. Rep. Ohio State Ho. Reps., Columbus, 1998—. Mem. banking, pensions and securities com. Ohio State Ho. Reps., mem. criminal justice com., mem. health com., mem. childrens healthcare and family svcs. subcom., mem. juvenile and family law com. Mem.: NOW, Ohio Legis. Women's Caucus, Nat. Black Caucus of State Legis., Women in Govt., Emily's List. Democrat. Office: Ohio State House Reps 77 South High Street 10th Floor Columbus OH 43215-6111

SMITH, STEPHANIE S. middle school educator, councilwoman; b. Evanston, Ill., June 22, 1957; d. Harold A. and Eva C. Smith; m. Jeffery T. Engelhart, Nov. 28, 1992. BA in Music, Brigham Young U., Provo, Ut., 1983. Tchr. Wash. County Sch. Dist., St. George, Utah, 1982—84, Davis County Sch. Dist., Farmington, Utah, 1984—87, Clark County Sch. Dist., Las Vegas, Nev., 1987—. Assemblywoman Nev. Legislature, Las Vegas, 1992—94; councilwoman City of N. Las Vegas, 1997—; mem. adv. bd. KNPR Radio, N. Las Vegas, Nev. Bd. dirs. Clark County Health Dist., N. Las Vegas; chmn. bd. trustees N. Las Vegas Libr. Dist.; bd. dirs. Nev. Arts Advocates.; mem. bd. N. Las Vegas Housing Authority; 2d v.p. Nev. League of Cities and Municipalities; mem. bd. So. Nev. Regional Planning Coalition; former mem. Gov.'s Maternal Child Health Bd. Democrat. Mem. Lds Ch. Avocation: music. Office: City North Las Vegas 2200 Civic Ctr Dr North Las Vegas NV 89084

SMITH, STUART LEWIS, volunteer; b. Richmond, Va., Mar. 28, 1936; d. John Minor Botts Lewis Jr. and Elise Davis Deyerle; m. Isaac Noyes Smith IV, Apr. 30, 1960; children: Isaac Noyes V, Minor Botts, Lyle Davis, Lisa Lewis. BA in Sociology, Hollins Coll., 1958. Home svc. caseworker ARC, Richmond, 1958—60; kindergarten tchr. First Presbyn. Ch. Sch., Charleston, W.Va., 1960—61; W.Va. sales assoc. Stanmar Homes, Sudbury, Mass., 1974—81; sales assoc., clothes cons. The Worth Collection, Charleston, 1992—2002. Mem. devel. com. Hollins Coll., Roanoke, Va., 1985—88; mem. legis. adv. com. Charleston Meml. Hosp., 1975—76; mem. budget and adv. coms. United Way, Charleston, 1965—77, resdl. chair, trustee, 1977—92; mem. legis. adv. com. Cmty. Coun.-Children's Svcs., Charleston, 1985—92; master gardener vol. pks. and hosp. planting Wonderful W.Va. Mag.; chairperson cmty. opportunity for study book and author series U. Charleston; contbr., local documentor Smithsonian Archive Am. Gardens; pks. commr., chair long range planning com. Kanawha County Pks. Sys., 1986—; elder Kanawha United Presbyn. Ch., Charleston, 1968; past pres., bd. dirs. U. Charleston Builders, 1973, Kanawha Garden Club, Charleston, 1973, Briar Hills Garden Club, Charleston, 1969. Recipient award, W.Va. State Garden Club, 1985, 20 Yrs. of Bd. Svc. award, Ronald McDonald Ho., 2002. Mem.: Robert E. Lee Meml. Assn. (W.Va. dir., sec. to the bd. 1975), Garden Club Am. (nat. vice chair, scholarship com. 1990, Outstanding Cmty. Leadership award 2000). Avocations: tennis, travel, gardening, fishing, reading. Home: 153 Abney Cir Charleston WV 25314

SMITH, SUE FRANCES, newspaper editor; b. Lockhart, Tex., July 4, 1940; d. Monroe John Baylor and Myrtle (Krause) Mueck; m. Michael Vogtel Smith, Apr. 20, 1963 (div. July 1977); 1 child, Jordan Meredith; m. Kirkland Gideon Smith, Apr. 17, 1999. B of Journalism, U. Tex., 1962. Feature writer, photographer Corpus Christi Caller Times, 1962-64; feature writer, editor Chgo. Tribune, 1964-76; features editor Dallas Times Herald, 1976-82; sales assoc. Bumpas Assocs., Dallas, 1982-83; asst. mng. editor for features Denver Post, 1983-84, assoc. editor, 1984-91; asst. mng. editor in charge of Sunday paper Dallas Morning News, 1991-94, asst. mng. editor Lifestyles, 1994-96, dep. mng. editor Lifestyles, 1996—2001, dep. mng. editor recruiting/devel., 2001—. Active Coun. Pres., 1993; juror Pulitzer Prize, 2002-03. Mem. Am. Assn. Sunday and Feature Editors (pres. 1993), Newspaper Features Coun. (pres. 2002), Tex. Associated Press Mng. Editors (pres. 1999-2000), Delta Gamma. Home: 6241 Park Meadow Ln Plano TX 75093-8863 Office: 508 Young St Dallas TX 75202-4893 E-mail: ssmith@dallasnews.com.

SMITH, SUSAN ELIZABETH, guidance director; b. Phila., Mar. 24, 1950; d. E. Burke Hogue and Janet Coffin Hogue Ebert; m. J. Russell Smith, June 17, 1972 (div. June 1989); 1 child, Drew Russell. BS in Elem. Edn., E. Stroudsburg Coll., 1972; MEd in Counseling, U. Okla., 1974, postgrad., 1976-77, Trenton State Coll., 1989-90; EdM in Devel. Disabilities, Rutgers U., 1992, postgrad., 1994—. Cert. elem. tchr., N.C.; cert. elem. tchr., early childhood edn. tchr., guidance and counseling, Okla.; cert. elem. tchr., guidance and counseling, tchr. of handicapped, psychology tchr., supr. instrn., dir. student pers. svcs., N.J. Elem. tchr. Morton Elem. Sch. Onslow County Schs., Jacksonville, N.C., 1971-72; instr. U. Isfahan, Iran, 1974-76; guidance counselor Moore (Okla.) Pub. Schs., 1976-77; counselor Johnstone Tng. Ctr. N.J. Divsn. Devel. Disabilities, Bordentown, 1988-90; spl. edn. tchr. Willingboro (N.J.) Schs., 1990-91; guidance counselor Haledon (N.J.) Pub. Schs., 1991-92; spl. edn. adj. tchr. Gateway Sch., Carteret, N.J., 1991-93; guidance counselor Bloomfield (N.J.) Pub. Schs., 1992-94; dir. guidance Somerville (N.J.) Pub. Schs., 1994-95. Adj. prof. in spl. edn. Essex County (N.J.) Coll., 1994; guidance Ft. Lee (N.J.) Schs., 1995-2001; guidance dir. Bogota Schs., N.J., 2001-02, Closter Schs., Closter, N.J., 2002—; cons., seminar and workshop presenter on behavior mgmt., parenting skills, and behavior modification techniques; cons. N.J. Fragile X Assn. Author: Motivational Awards for ESL Students, 1993, Parent Contracts to Improve School Behaviors, 1996; contbr. articles to profl. jours. Leader Boy Scouts Am., Oklahoma City, 1983-87, com. chmn., Redmond, Wash., 1987-88. Recipient Rsch. award ERIC/CAPS, 1992, Svc. award N.J. Fragile X Assn., 1993. Mem. ACA, Am. Sch. Counselor Assn. (grantee 1992), N.J. Counseling Assn., N.J. Sch. Counseling Assn., Assn. for Multicultural Counseling and Devel., AAUW, Assn. for Counselor Edn. and Supervision, N.J. Assn. for Counselor Edn. and Supervision, N.J. Prins. and Suprs. Assn., Nat. Assn. Coll. Admissions Counselors (grantee 1995), Alpha Omicron Pi. Episcopalian. Home: 916 Lincoln Pl Teaneck NJ 07666-2572

SMITH, SUSAN J, music educator, flutist; b. Mpls., Minn., Jan. 5, 1952; d. Frank William and Florence E Johnson; m. Patrick Warren Smith, Sept. 8, 1973. MusB, Ind. U., Bloomington, 1975; MusM, Temple U., Phila., 1989, tchg. cert., 1991. Cert. k-12 tchr. Pa. Flutist Orchesta Sinfonica De Xalapa, 1974—79, South Fla. Symphony, Boca Raton, 1983—86, Miami Beach (Fla.) Symphony, 1980—82; elem. music tchr. Walther Sch., Lumberton, NJ, 1991—94; music tchr. Haddonfield (NJ) Mid. Sch., 1995—97; tchr. instrumental music Collingswood (NJ) Schs., 1997—; flutist Freelance Musician, Phila., 2002—, Bach Festival Orch., Bethlehem, Pa., 1988—91, Haddonfield Symphony, 1993—94. Pvt. flute studio Perkins Ctr. Arts, Moorestown, NJ, 1995—97, Settlement Music Sch., Philadelphia, Pa., 1988—91. Recipient Tchg. Assistantship, Temple U., 1988-1990, Winner, Minn. Orch. Young Artist Competition, Wamso, 1970. Mem.: NJ Music Educators Assn., Music Educators Nat. Conf., Am. Fedn. Musicians.

SMITH, SUSIE IRENE, histotechnologist, cytometrist; b. Oct. 10, 1942; d. Taft and Evelyn (Samuels) Woodford; m. Eugene Smith, Dec. 2, 1960; children: Regina Marie, Kimberly Denise, Teresa Yvette, Stacia Ann. Student, Boston State coll., 1975—80. Med. worker Boston City Hosp., 1970, lab asst., 1970—75; lab. tech. hematopathology lab Mallory Inst. Pathology, 1975—80, chief med. technologist, 1982—90; owner, pres. Easy Travel Internat., Inc., 2000—. Lectr. and cons. in field; rsch. assoc., health & safety officer CytoLogix Corp., 1998—. Contbr. articles to sci. jours. Treas. Whittier St. Tenants Assn., 1985—86, pres., 1987—88, Tenants United for Pub. Housing Progress, 1985—87, Com. Boston Pub. Housing, 1987—88; sec. Com. to Elect Jesse L. Corbin for State Rep., 1981—82. Mem.: Am. Soc. Clin. Pathologists (notary pub. 1988—). Office: 99 Erie St Cambridge MA 02139 Home: 54 Annunciation Rd AptL Roxbury Crossing MA 02120-1871

SMITH, SUZANNE NAOMI, lobbyist; b. Dallas, Tex., Aug. 31, 1976; d. Ernest Edward and Marie Dudley Smith. BA, U. of Tex., 1994—97, Tex. Acad. of Math & Sci., 1992—94. Dir. of planning Phoenix Ho., Dallas, 1998—2001; advocacy cons. Am. Heart Assn., Dallas, 2001—. Bd. of adjustment City of Dallas, 2003; bd. mem. YMCA Tex. Youth & Govt., 1995. Power Pipeline Participant, Leadership Tex., 2003. R-Liberal. Catholic. Avocations: reading, movies, leadership studies, river rafting. Home: 5640 Ellsworth Ave Dallas TX 75206 Office: Am Heart Assn 7272 Greenville Ave Dallas TX 75231 Personal E-mail: snstexas@yahoo.com. E-mail: suzanne.smith@heart.org.

SMITH, TANYA GAY, editor; b. Waukegan, Ill., Apr. 28, 1953; d. Ralph Joseph and Evelyn Elaine Smith; m. Jack Richard Gerson, Nov. 27, 2002. BA, U. Calif., Berkeley, 1978. Publs. coord. Ctrs. for South and SE Asia Studies/UC Berkeley, Berkeley, Calif., 1987—91; editor Archaeol. Rsch. Facility, U. Calif., Berkeley, Calif., 1991—. Co-chair U. Calif. Berkeley Labor Coalition, 2003—. Founding mem. North Oakland Neighbors for Peace, Oakland, Calif., 2003—04. Socialist. Avocations: dogwalking/hiking, union organizing, reading, gardening. Office: Archaeological Rsch Facility UC Berkeley - 1076 Berkeley CA 94720-1076 Office Phone: 510-643-3538.

SMITH, THELMA TINA HARRIETTE, gallery owner, artist; b. Folkston, Ga., May 5, 1938; d. Harry Charles and Malinda Estelle (Kennison) Causey; m. Billy Wayne Smith, July 23, 1955; children: Sherry Yvonne, Susan Marie, Dennis Wayne, Chris Michael. Student, U. Tex., Arlington, 1968-70; studies with various art instrs. Gen. office worker Superior Ins. Corp., Dallas, 1956-57, Zanes-Ewalt Warehouse, Dallas, 1957-67; bookkeeper Atlas Match Co., Arlington, 1967-68; sr. acct. Automated Refrigerated Air Conditioner Mfg. Corp., Arlington, 1968-70; acct. Conn. Gen. Life Ins. Corp., Dallas, 1972-74; freelance artist Denton, Tex., 1974—; gallery owner, custom framer Tina Smith Studio-Gallery, Mabank, Tex., 1983—. Painting in pub. and pvt. collections in numerous states including N.Y., Fla., Ga. and N.D.; editor Cedar Creek Art Soc. Yearbook, 1983—. Treas. Cedar Creek Art Soc., 1987-88, 89—; mem. com. to establish state endorsed Arts Coun. for Cedar Creek Lake Area, Gun Barrel City, Tex. Recipient numerous watercolor and pastel awards Henderson County Art League, Cedar Creek Art Soc., Cmty. Svc. award Mayor Wilson Tippit, Gun Barrel City, Tex., 1986. Mem. Southwestern Watercolor Soc. (Dallas), Soc. Outdoor Painters, Pastel Soc. of the S.W. (Dallas), Cedar Creek Art Soc. (Gun Barrel City)(v.p. 1983-86, treas.), Profl. Picture Framers Assn. Baptist. Avocations: water activities, gardening. Studio: Tina Smith Studio-Gallery 251 Shady Shores Dr Mabank TX 75156-

SMITH, TOOTIE, state representative; m. Nate Smith; 1 child. AS, Mt. Hood C.C.; BS cum laude, Concordia Coll. State rep., dist. 28 Oreg. House Rep., Salem, 2001—03, state rep., dist. 18, 2003—; mng. ptnr. Rural Resources, Inc., Meadowbrook Hill Farm; libr. asst. Molalla Elem. Sch. Mem. com. Agr. and Forestry; vice chair Student Achievement and Sch. Accountability; mem. sub com. Ways and Means Edn. Office: 900 Court St NE H-290 Salem OR 97301

SMITH, TRICIA E. artist; d. George Gregory and G. Jean Smith; m. Richard Rene Kuntz, Nov. 26, 1966; 1 child, Rene Kuntz Heidt. BA, U. S.C., 1965; postgrad., Columbia U., 1968; MA, Ga. State U., 1970, postgrad., 1972, Cornell U., 1973. Media specialist Ga. Retardation Ctr., Atlanta, 1973—76; tchr., coord. Bd. Coop. Ednl. Svcs., Elmira, NY, 1976—86; v.p. internat. affairs Savannah Coll. Art And Design, Ga., 1986—93; free-lance artist Tybee Island. V.p.-at large Internat. Union Mail-Artists, Tilburg, Netherlands, 2000—; artist in residence Buchakian Found., East Hampton, NY. Exhibitions include Pilgrimage:Journey Towards The Sacred. Charter mem., bd. mem. Internat. Breakfast Club, Tybee Island, 1986—2003. Barksdale fellow, Ga. State U., 1970. Avocations: travel, mail-art, sailing. Home: Pelican House 142 Pelican Dr Tybee Island GA 31328 Personal E-mail: visions888@yahoo.com.

SMITH, TRINA, academic administrator; b. Rogersville, Ala., Sept. 18, 1971; d. Will Buford and Margaret Cannon Smith. BS, Athens State U., 1993; MS, U. Ala., Huntsville, 2000; M of Accountancy, U. Ala., 2001. Cert. Notary Pub. Br. ops. supr. Union Planters Bank, Athens, Ala., 1994—2000; acct. Calhoun Coll., Decatur, Ala., 2000—. Dir. Habitat for Humanity, Athens, 1994—2000; mem. adv. bd. Dogwood Festival Com., Athens, 1999. Vol. Jr. Achievement, Decatur, Ala., 1997—2000, Care Assurance Sys. for Aging and Homebound, Athens, 1995—99, Found. of

Aging, Athens, 1999—2002. Recipient Outstanding Support award, Habitat for Humanity, 1996. Mem.: NAFE, NAACP, Am. Inst. of Cert. Pub. Accts., Nat. Assn. Black Accts., Am. Acctg. Assn., Am. Soc. Women Accts., Nat. Notary Assn., Inst. Mgmt. Accts. Baptist. Avocations: gardening, photography, collecting antiques, investments, outdoor activities. Home: 13708 Dort Cir Athens AL 35611 Office: Calhoun Cmty Coll Hwy 31 S Decatur AL 35609

SMITH, VALENE, anthropologist, educator; b. Spokane, Wash., Feb. 14, 1926; d. Ernest Frank and Lucy (Blachly) S.; m. Edwin Chesteen Golay, June 7, 1970 (dec. June 1980); m. Stanley George McIntyre, Nov. 26, 1983 (dec. Oct. 2000). BA in Geography, U. Calif., 1946, MA in Geography, 1950; PhD in Anthropology, U. Utah, 1966. Prof. earth sci. L.A. City Coll., 1947-67; prof. anthropology Calif. State U., Chico, 1967—. Cons. World Tourism Orgn., Madrid, 1987. Editor: Hosts and Guests: The Anthrop, 1989, Tourism Alternatives: Potentials and Problems in the Development of Tourism, 1992, Hosts and Guests Revisited, 2001. Mem. Internat. Acad. for Study Tourism, Cert. Travel Counselors, Am. Anthrop. Assn., AAUW, Canyon Oaks Country Club, Soroptimists. Republican. Avocations: traveling, aviation, photography. Office: U Calif Dept Anthropology Chico CA 95929-0004

SMITH, VALERIE CHRISTINE, registered nurse, writer; b. Beatrice, Ala., Oct. 1, 1951; d. Eugene and Elmira (Smith) Payne; divorced; children: Patrice Namon Smith, Aleta Wileen Smith. AA in Nursing, Wayne County C.C., 1978; BSN, U. Detroit, 1991. RN Mich. Staff nurse, med.-surg. DMC Grace Hosp., Detroit, 1979-82, staff nurse, orthopedic nursing, 1982-85; staff nurse, gen. surgery DMC Hutzel Hosp., Detroit, 1985-87, staff nurse, preceptor, 1987-98; staff nurse ICU stepdown St. John Detroit Riverview Hosp., 1998—. Pres., founder Coalition of Citizens, Detroit, 1997—. Democrat. Avocations: aerobic exercise, walking, tennis, softball. Home: 16800 Greenview Ave Detroit MI 48219-4154

SMITH, VANGY EDITH, accountant, consultant, writer, artist; b. Saskatoon, Sask., Can., Dec. 17, 1937; d. Wilhelm and Anne Ellen (Hartshorne) Gogel: m. Clifford Wilson, May 12, 1958 (de. Dec. 1978); children: Kenneth, Koral, Kevin, Korey, Kyle; m. Terrence Raymond Smith, Dec. 14, 1979. Student, Saskatoon Tech. Collegiate Inst., 1956, BBA, 1958, MBA, 1987, PhD in English with honors, 1988. Prin. Vangy Enterprises, Springfield, Oreg., 1960—; accounts payable clk. Maxwell Labs., Inc., San Diego, 1978; invoice clk. Davies Electric, Saskatoon, 1980-81; office mgr. Ladee Bug Ceramics, Saskatoon, 1981-87, Lazars Investments Corp., Eugene, Oreg., 1987; bookkeeper accounts payable Pop Geer, Eugene, Oreg., 1987; office mgr., bookkeeper Willamette Sports Ctr., Inc., Eugene, Oreg., 1985-89; clk. I Lane C.C., Springfield, Oreg., 1992-96. Self-employed Vangy Enterprises, 1992—; circulation mgr. Nat. WCTU, 1990-92, UN rep. for World WCTUm 1989-91; appointed mem. Parliament for the U. for Peace, Holland, 1991; adv. chair Lane C.C. Ctr. for Leisure and Learning, 1999-2001. Contbr. articles to scholarly jours. (recipient doctoral award 1987). Counselor Drug and Rehab. Ctr., Eugene, 1970—88; trustee Children's Farm Home, Corvallis, Oreg., 1989—91, 3d v.p., 1989—90; co-pres. Lane County UN Assn., 1989—90; mem. artist Nat. Bd. Edn., 1989, 1990; mem. adv. com. Dept. Pub. Safety for City of Eugene, 1989—90; exec. dir. H.E.L.P., 1993—; pres. Lane County Coun. of Orgns., 1994—96; treas. Cascade/Coast chpt. Alzheimers Assn., 1994; mem. UN Devel. Fund for Women, mem. exec. com., 1999; chair adv. com. Ctr. for Leisure and Learning, Lane C.C., 1999—2001; state pres. Rebekah Assembly Oreg., 2004—05; mem. Found. Christian Living; pres. Oreg. State Christian Temperance Union, 1989—90. Recipient 3d and 4th place artists' awards Lane County Fair, 1987, 1st and 2d place awards Nat. Writing Contest, 1987, 88, 89, 90, 91, Oasis Vol. Model award, 1998; named City of Eugene Hometown Hero, 1998, named Woman of Yr., Am. Bus. Women's Assn., 1999-00. Mem. WCTU (life, pres., state bd. dirs. projection methods circulation 1987-90, Appreciation award 1982, Presdl. award 1985, Lane County Eugene Woman of Yr. 1990), UNIFEM (chpt. pres. 1997—, exec. bd. 1999—, Women in Leadership award 1997), Am. Soc. Writers, Alzheimers Assn. (treas. Cascade/Coast chpt. 1994), Rebekah Lodge (Noble Grand 1995-99), Lions (sec. 1994), Oasis (adv. coun. chair 1993-98), Am. Bus. Women's Assn. (pres. 2000—). Democrat. Avocations: needlework, rug hooking, reading, writing, oil painting. Home and Office: 5728 Ridge Ct Springfield OR 97478 E-mail: vsmith3237@aol.com.

SMITH, VICKY LYNN, geriatrics nurse; b. Millington, Tenn., June 27, 1951; d. Bobbie T. Smith and Bobbie OKeesling; stepdau. Corbit O. Keesling Jr.; m. Reagan Smith, Mar. 13, 1973 (div. Nov. 1975); children: Christopher Reagan, Justin Heath. ASN, Walters State C.C., Morristown and Knoxville, Tenn., 1977. RN; cert. CPR instr., ARC. RN II, clin. mgr. Lakeshore Mental Health, Knoxville, 1977-83; br. mgr. PRN, Profl. Inc. Home Health, Knoxville, 1983-84; state adminstr., mem. adv. bd. Healthmaster Home Health, Knoxville, 1984-85; clin. supr., mem. adv. bd. Cmty. Home Health, Knoxville, 1985-90; dir. nursing, mem. adv. bd. Superior Home Health, Knoxville, 1990-91; asst. unit mgr. Oakwood Med. Ctr., Knoxville, 1991-94; nurse, clin. skilled coord. Knoxville Health Care Ctr., 1994-95; adminstrv. asst., mem. adv. bd. First Choice Home Health, 1995—. Cons. Behavior Modification Programming, Knoxville, 1977-83. Recipient scholarship Walters State C.C., 1975-77. Mem. Tenn. Nurses Assn., Knoxville Jayces, Phi Beta Kappa. Baptist. Avocations: arts and crafts, writing, camping, playing piano and dulcimer. Home: 1324 Wellington West Dr Knoxville TN 37932-3613

SMITH, VIRGINIA, real estate broker; b. N.y.C., Oct. 24, 1928; d. John Harvey Woodhull and Sally Horton Hurd Warren; m. Ward William Smith III, June 28, 1952 (div. Aug. 1977); children: Ward William IV, Sally Hurd, Carluie Farnsworth, George M., Judy McCourbrey. AA, Green Mt. Coll., 1948. Asst. to buyer Gourmets Bazaar, N.Y.C., 1948-49, rschr. food articles, 1949-50; asst. editor Table Topics, N.Y.C., 1950-51; asst. mktg. editor House & Garden, N.Y.C., 1951-52; real estate broker DeVre Realty, Kent, Conn., 1973-95, asst. mgr. Cornwall, Conn., 1976-77; broker, owner Virginia Smith Real Estate, New Milford, Conn., 1997—. Theatre critic Sharon Playhouse, 1977-78. Active Christmas Bazaar, St. Andrews Ch., Kent, 1977-97, Bd. Assessment Appeals, New Milford, 1992—, Dem. Town Com., New Milford, 1992—. Episcopalian. Avocations: reading, swimming, gardening, cooking, antiques. Home: 55 Curtiss Rd New Preston Marble Dale CT 06777-1003 Office: 52 Squire Hill Rd New Milford CT 06776-5013

SMITH, VME EDOM (VERNA MAE EDOM SMITH), sociology educator, freelance writer, photographer; b. Marshfield, Wis., June 19, 1929; d. Clifton Cedric and Vilia Clarissa (Patefield) Edom; children: Teri Smith Freas, Anthony Thomas. AB in Sociology, U. Mo., 1951; MA in Sociology, George Washington, 1965; PhD in Human Devel., U. Md., 1981. Tchr. Alcohol Safety Action Program Fairfax County, Va., 1973-75; instr. sociology No. Va. C.C., Manassas, 1975-77, asst. prof., 1977-81, assoc. prof., 1981-84, prof., 1984-94, prof. emerita, 1995, coord. coop. edn., 1983-89, Chancellor's Commonwealth prof., 1991-93; adj. faculty Tidewater C.C., 1996—; freelance writer, editor and photographer, 1965—; dir. Clifton C. Edom Truth With a Camera (photography workshops), 1994—. Asst. prodr. history of photography program Sta. WETA-TV, Washington, 1965; rsch. and prodn. asst., photographer, publs. editor No. Va. Ednl. TV, Sta. WNVT, 1970—71; cons. migrant divsn. Md. Dept. Edn., Balt., 1977; rschr. photographer Roundabout presch. high sch. series Am. Values Sta. WNVT, 1970—71; documentary photographer Portsmouth (Va.) Redevel. and Housing Authority, 1998—2000. Author, photographer: Middleburg and Nearby, 1986; co-author: Small Town America, 1993; contbr. photography to various works including Visual Impact in Print (Hurley and McDougall), 1971, Looking Forward to a Career in Education (Moses), 1976, Child Growth and Development (Terry, Sorrentino and Flatter), 1979, Photojournalism (Edom), 1976, 80, Migrant Child Welfare, 1977, (Cavenaugh), Caring for Children, 1973 (5 publs. by L.B. Murphy), Dept. Health, Edn. and Welfare, Nat. Geog., 1961, Head Start Newsletter, 1973-74, Women in Photojournalism, Nat. Press Photographers Assn., Nat. Fedn. Press Women, Photographic Soc. Am., Va. Found. for Humanities and Pub. Policy exhibits. Mem. ednl. adv. com. Head Start, Warrenton, Va. Recipient Emmy, Ohio State Children's Programming award; Fulbright-Hays rsch. grantee, 1993, Va. Found. for Humanities and Pub. Policy grantee, 1997-99. Mem. Va. Assn. Coop. Edn. (com. mem.). Democrat. E-mail: vme@macs.net.

SMITH, WENDY CAROL, music educator; d. Hubert and Verna Smith. B in Music Edn., Troy State U., 1995. Band dir. Beverlye Mid. Sch., Dothan, Ala., 1995—97, Staley Mid. Sch., Americus, Ga., 1997—. Named Outstanding Young Woman of Am., 1995, Outstanding Young Am., 1997. Mem.: Ga. Assn. Educators, Women Band Dirs. Internat., Ga. Music Educators Assn. Avocations: golf, fishing, travel, reading.

SMITH, WENDY HAIMES, federal agency administrator; b. Tex. m. Jay L. Smith. BA in Econs., U. Mich.; postgrad., Ohio State U., Am. U., Washington Studio Sch., Aspen Inst., Wye, Md., 1997. Cert. real estate agt. Office mgr. Haimes Travel Agy., Ohio, 1972-73; mgmt. intern US Dept. Commerce, 1973-75, country specialist for Korea, 1973, spl. asst. to dep. asst. sec. for internat. commerce, 1973-74, project officer, maj. projects divsn., 1974-75, project mgr. indsl. sys., maj. projects divsn., 1975-77, country specialist for Brazil, 1978, project mgr., hydrocarbons and chem. process plants, maj. export projects divsn., 1977-79, exec. asst. to dep. asst. sec. of commerce for export devel. and staff dir. Pres. Export Coun., 1979-81, dir. Pres. Export Coun., 1981-92, acting dir. Office Planning and Coordination, 1988-89, dir. adv. coms. and pvt. sector programs Internat. Trade Adminstrn., 1992-97; dir. Trade Info. Ctr., Wash., DC, 1997—, acting dir. office of export promotion, 1999, 2000-01. Author, editor US Trade in Transition: Maintaining the Gains, 1988, co-author, editor The Export Imperative, 1980, Coping with the Dynamics of World Trade in the 1980s, 1984; Exhibited in group shows at Courtyard Gallery, Brian Logan Artspace, Artists Mus., Washington, Designer's Art Gallery, Bethesda, Md., one-woman shows include Courtyard Gallery, Washington, 2001. Active Art League, Smithsonian Instn., Washington Opera Guild; bd. dir. Washington Studio Sch; one man show Courtyard Gallery, 2001.

SMITH, WENDY L. foundation executive; b. Chgo., Sept. 12, 1950; d. John Arthur and Dolores Mae (Webb) Rothenberger; m. Alan Richard Smith; children: Angela Fuhs, Erica Smith. Ed., Oakton C.C., Des Plaines, Ill., 1986, Mundelein Coll., 1990. Purchasing clk. AIT Industries, Skokie, Ill., 1975-76; purchasing agt. MCC Powers, Skokie, 1976-78; office mgr. Spartan Engring., Skokie, 1978-80, Brunswick Corp., Skokie, 1980—; successively sr. sec., coord. indsl. rels., dir. Brunswick Found., Lake Forest, Ill., 1982-89, pres., 1989—. Asst. sec. Brunswick Pub. Charitable Found., Lake Forest, 1989—; mem. adv. com. Found. for Ind. Higher Edn., Stamford, Conn., 1989—, Coun. Better Bus. Burs., Arlington, Va., 1988-90; bd. dirs. Associated Colls. of Ill., 1991—; bd. dirs., mem. trustees com., mem. compensation and benefits com. Donors Forum of Chgo., 1988-93. Bd. dirs. INROADS/Chgo., Inc., 1994—; mem. steering com. Dist. 57 Edn. Found., Mt. Prospect, Ill., 1996—. Recipient Pvt. Sector Initiative Commendation, U.S. Pres., 1987-89. Mem. Donors Forum Chgo. (treas. 1988-91, bd. dirs., mem. exec. com., chairperson audit and fin. com., mem. trustees com. 1992—), Coun. on Founds., Ind. Sector Suburban Contbns. Network (chairperson 1987-89), Women in Philanthropy Corp. Founds. (mem. cmty. rels. com. 1985-87), Chgo. Women in Philanthropy. Avocations: antique restoration, pleasure reading, bowling, golf. Home: 2606 N Brighton Pl Arlington Heights IL 60004-2717

SMITH, YVONNE SMART, advertising executive; b. Asheville, N.C. BFA, Auburn U. Asst. art dir. Mademoiselle mag., N.Y.C.; art dir. Cargill, Wilson & Acree Advt. divsn. Doyle Dane Bernbach; v.p., assoc. creative dir., exec. art dir. Chiat/Day Advt., L.A., sr. v.p., assoc. creative dir. Venice, Calif., Venice, N.Y.C., London, mng. ptnr., creative dir. L.A.; prin. Yvonne Smith, Inc. Guest lectr. UCLA, Art Ctr. Coll. Design, L.A., U. So. Calif., L.A., Art Dirs. Club, Paris; co-chair Internat. Clio Awards, 1999. Subject profl. articles. Recipient One Show awards, N.Y. Art Dirs. Club, Andy awards, Belding awards, award, Art Dirs. Club, Steven Kelly awards, Clio awards, Emmy award, 1998, Silver and Bronze Lions, Cannes Film Festival, 1998. Office: 21344 Rambla Vista Malibu CA 90265-5348

SMITH BRINTON, MARCIA, psychologist, consultant; b. Miami, Fla., Feb. 19, 1945; d. Clarence Hall and Felicia (Trombetta) Smith; m. James Conrad Hilderbrand, Aug. 3, 1964 (div. Mar. 1978); children: Mark Gregory, James Christopher; m. George Albert Brinton, Aug. 31, 1986. BA, U. Miami, 1970; MA, Montclair State U., 1982; PhD, NYU, 1996. Rsch. assoc. Metro Ctr., NYU, 1983-85; sch. psychologist Frankford Twp. (N.J.) Pub. Sch. Sys., 1985, Green Twp. (N.J.) Pub. Schs., 1985-86; mental health clinician emergency svcs. Newton (N.J.) Meml. Hosp. Ctr. for Mental Health, 1989-92; intern in psychology Queens Childrens Psychiat. Ctr., Bellerose, N.Y., 1992-93; psychologist St. Christopher Ottilie Residential Treatment Facility, Briarwood, N.J., 1996-98; clin. specialist Inhealth Assocs., Sparta, N.J., 1998—. Cons. Gifted/Talented parent Counseling program, Green Twp. Elem. Sch., 1985-86, Sussex County Assn. for Retarded Citizens, 1998—. Co-author: Finding, Loving and Marrying Your Lifetime Partner, 1988; contbr. articles to profl. jours. Vol. summer program dir. Sunray, Bristol, Vt., 1994, 95, 96, advisor to bd. trustees, 1995-96. Mem. APA, NYU Alumni Assn. Democrat. Unitarian Universalist. Avocations: gardening, hiking, canoeing, horseback ridng, flute.

SMITH-BUCKINGHAM, MINNIE M. surgery technologist; b. Lexington, Miss., Feb. 23, 1947; m. John Lester Buckingham; children: Jacqueline Hamilton, Jerrick Smith. Cert., St.Francis Hosp., 1966; student, Worsham Coll. Mortuary Sci. Cert. surg. technologist. Surg. technologist instr. St.Louis Coll., St. Louis, 1996—2001; surg. technologist St. Lukes Hosp., Chesterfield, Mo., 1995—. Mem.: Assn. Surg. Technologist. Roman Catholic. Avocations: gardening, travel.

SMITH-CAMPBELL, CHARMAINE, secondary school educator; b. Kingston, Jamaica, West Indies, Jan. 6, 1956; d. Orville Clifford and Mabel Rebecca Smith; m. Carnel Charles Campbell, Apr. 20, 1978; children: Damali, Jelani, Pschopelia. BA in history, U. West Indies, 1982; MA in history, Queens Coll., 1989. Cert. tchr. social studies, N.Y. Instr. high sch. John Bowne H.S., Flushing, N.Y., 1979-83, high sch. tchr., 1981-87, special edn. tchr., 1984-91, social studies tchr., 1991—, grade advisor, 1997—. Advisor and coord. Caribbean Club, John Bowne H.S., Queens, N.Y., 1985-95, Am. History Month Activities, 1996—. Mem. Jamaica Progessive Club, Brooklyn, 1984-91, bd. dirs. Rosedale Condominium, 1998—. Democrat. Methodist. Avocations: sewing, gardening, reading, travel. Office: 6325 Main St Flushing NY 11367-1303 E-mail: charmsoup@aol.com.

SMITH-EPSTEIN, MARY KATHLEEN, dancer; b. Austin, Tex., Sept. 12, 1940; d. Walter Bentley Jr. and Kathleen Beatrice (Lancaster) Smith; m. Witaly Osins, June 6, 1967 (div. 1975); m. Howard Irwin Epstein, June 20, 1987. Grad. high sch., Dallas. Demi soloist Am. Festival Ballet, European Tour, 1961; prin. dancer HET Nat. Ballet, Amsterdam, Holland, 1962-67; guest artist Berliner Ballet, Berlin, 1964, Ballet De L'Atlantique, Nantes, France, 1967-68, Cologne, Fed. Republic Germany, 1968-70, Ballet Spectacular, Miami, Fla., 1973-74; prin. dancer Opernhaus, Hannover, Fed. Republic Germany, 1968-70, Musiktheater, Gelsenkirchen, Fed. Republic Germany, 1968-71, Ballet Van Vlaanderen, Antwerp, Belgium, 1971-73, Ballet De Wallonie, Charleroi, Belgium, 1973-74, Irish Nat. Ballet, Cork, Ireland, 1975-85, Chgo. Ballet, 1977-78, Ballet Met., Columbus, Ohio, 1978-79; founder, co-dir. Conservatory Classical Dance, Eugene, Oreg., 1989—. Founder N.W. Chamber Ballet, 1988—; artistic dir. 8 Dance Ensemble; guest tchr. Imperial Eleven Ballet, 2000-01, Internat. Ballet Sch., 2000. Choreographer: (ballet) Opus 1, 1978, For Him From Her, 1982, The Catalyst, 1983 (Bursary Irish Arts Council award 1985), Pas De Deux, 1985 (Bursary Irish Arts Council 1985), Logic of the Heart, 1988, Masquerade Suite, 1988, Tango, 1999, Nocturne, 1998, Pro-Fun-Ditties, 1997, No One Knew, 1997; choreographer Ballet N.W., Performing Ensemble Conservatory Classical Dance, 1989—. Treas. Neighborhood Watch, Vida, Oreg., 1988-89, bd. mem. (sec. to pres.) of Lane Arts Coun., 1993-96; dir. bldg. fund, pres. bd. dirs. Kaygu Dakshang Chuling, 1995—. Alexandra Danilova scholar, Dallas, 1958. Buddhist. E-mail: hepsteinor@earthlink.net.

SMITHERAM, MARGARET ETHERIDGE, health facility administrator, director; b. Atlanta, Jan. 5, 1938; d. Philip Fitzgerald and Mary Catharine (Dwyer) E.; m. Roy Charles McCracken, May 5, 1975; m. William Bertram Smitheram, Aug. 17, 1985. BA, Emory U., 1960; M in Health Adminstrn., Washington U., St. Louis, 1973. Registered record adminstr., 1960-71; spl. asst. to dir. VA Med. Ctr., Roseburg, Oreg., 1973-74; hosp. adminstrn. specialist VA Central Office, Washington, 1974-75; asst. dir. trainee VA Med. Ctr., Phila., 1976, assoc. dir. Hampton, Va., 1976--80, Buffalo, N.Y., 1980-81; presdl. exchange exec. Kimberly Clark Corp., Neenah, Wis., 1981-82, Roswell, Ga., 1981-82; dir. VA Med. Ctr., Grand Island, Nebr., 1982-94; interim dir. Grand Island-Hall County Health Dept., 1996-97; instr. Cerritos Coll., 1969-70. Bd. dirs. Project 2M Coordinating Coun., Inc., Grand Island, 1985-87, Hall County Leadership Unlimited, Inc., 1990. Bd. dirs. Grand Island Area United Way, 1987-90 (pres. 1989), Grand Island Concert Assn, 1987-92, Ctrl. Nebr. Goodwill Industries, Inc., 1987-93 (pres. 1991-92). Fellow Am. Coll. Healthcare Execs. (life); mem. rev. bd. State of Nebr. Foster Care, Am. Hosp. Assn., Fed. Exec. Assn. (pres. Grand Island chpt. 1987), Nebr. Hosp. Assn., Grand Island C. of C. (bd. dirs. 1988-92, legis. affairs com 1984-85, priorities com. 1984-85, govtl. affairs com. 1984-88, nominating com. 1991-92, 94-95, audit com. 1992-93, pres. club 1993-94), Rotary Internat. Club #1485 (v.p. 1998-2000, pres. 2000-2001, District 5630 Group Study Exchange Team Leader to South Korea District 3710, 1999, Paul Harris fellow), Riverside Golf Club. Roman Catholic. Home: 221 Trail of the Flowers Georgetown TX 78628 E-mail: montuma@juno.com.

SMITHERS, RUTH ANNE HALL, special education educator, consultant; b. Phoenix, Nov. 17, 1928; d. Frank Ernest and Anne Marie (Diechelbohrer) Hall; m. Charles F. Smithers Jr., May 21, 1955 (div. Apr. 1993); children: Charles F. III, Claire Hall, Bonnie Louisa Smithers de Falla. BA, Tex. Woman's U., 1949; MAT, Manhattanville Coll., 1977; postgrad., Hertford Coll., Oxford, Eng., 1985. Loan closer So. Abst. & Title Co., Houston, 1949-55; pvt. tutor learning disabled, pvt. practice ednl. cons. New Canaan, Conn., 1977—; pvt. tutor learning disabled Harvey Sch., Katonah, N.Y., 1978-80. Active various polit. campaigns Dem. Party, New Canaan, 1965—; vice chmn. Dem. Town Com., New Canaan, 1982-84, chmn., 1990-92; candidate 1st selectman Town of New Canaan, 1995; mem. town coun. New Canaan, Conn., 1999-2003, incumbant, 2003—; bd. mgrs. East Side House, N.Y.C., N.Y., 1963-2003; bd. trustees Weir Farm Trust, 1989-2003. Mem. Orton Soc., Elem. Sch. Bldg. Com. Roman Catholic. Avocations: politics, reading, travel, art history, collecting works from american painters. Home and Office: 25 Kimberly Pl New Canaan CT 06840-4512

SMITHEY, SUSAN WILLETT, music educator; d. Henry A. and Glenda F. Willett; m. Walt A. Smithey, July 17, 1999. BA, U. South Fla., 1985. Band dir. Harllee Mid. Sch., Bradenton, Fla., 1985—87; elem. music tchr. Escambia County Sch., Pensacola, Fla., 1987—90; band dir. Gulf Breeze (Fla.) Mid. Sch., 1990—. Bd. dirs. Dixie Band Camp, Conway, Ark., 1990—; mid. sch. band rep. Santa Rosa County Band Program, Gulf Breeze, Fla., 2002—. Mem.: Fla. Sch. Music Educators Assn., Fla. Music Educators Assn., Fla. Bandmasters Assn. Office: Gulf Breeze Mid Sch 649 Gulf Breeze Pkwy Gulf Breeze FL 32561 E-mail: smitheys@mail.santarosa.k12.fl.us.

SMITH HEINZ, AMY, publishing executive; b. Tullahoma, Tenn., Dec. 12, 1966; d. Robert Pierson and Martha Parsons Smith. Bachelor Degree, Belmont U., 1991. Creative dir. Harlan Howard Songs, Nashville, Waylon Jennings Music, Nashville, W&R Music Group, N.Y.C.; owner Wilderness Music, Nashville. Ind. song plugger Rick Giles Music, Nashville, Jason Blume Music, Nashville, Tommy Polk Music, Nashville. Eucharistic min. Cathedral of the Incarnation, Nashville, 2001—. Mem.: NARAS. Avocations: hiking, kickboxing, basketball, triathelon competitions. Office: Wilderness Music 1808 Division Nashville TN 37203

SMITH-LEINS, TERRI L. mathematics educator; b. Salina, Kans., Sept. 19, 1950; d. John W. and Myldred M. (Hays) Smith; m. Larry L. Leins, May 26, 1984. BS, Ft. Hays (Kans.) U., 1973, MS, 1976; AA, Stephen Coll., Columbia, Mo., 1970. Math tchr. Scott City (Kans.) Jr. H.S., Howard (Kans.) Schs.; instr. math. U. Ark., Ft. Smith. Contbr. articles to profl. jours., chpts. to books. Mem. AADE, ASCD, Nat. Assn. Devel. Edn. (state sec. 1986-88, computer access com. 1980-85), Phi Delta Kappa (Kappan of Yr. 1985), Delta Kappa Gamma (state chairperson women in art 1993-95, area one leader 1999-2001, Kappa state corr. sec., 2003—). Home: PO Box 3446 Fort Smith AR 72913-3446 E-mail: tleins@uafortsmith.edu.

SMITH-LOEB, MARGARET, marketing educator; b. Columbus, Ohio, Apr. 17, 1932; d. Frederick James Church and Margaret MacWhannell; m. Dennis Patrick Delaney, Aug. 7, 1954 (div. Apr. 1959); m. Curtis Malchman Smith, Oct. 15, 1959 (div. Jan. 1967); 1 child, Jean Delaney Smith; m. John Meltzer Loeb, July 9, 1976 (dec. Jan. 1995). BA, Hood Coll., 1953; postgrad., St. Johns, Santa Fe, N.Mex, 1969. Buyer, asst. buyer Malchman's, Falmouth, Mass., 1960-63; tchr. Sandia Middle Sch., Albuquerque, 1963-67; dean Kent Middle Sch., Englewood, Colo., 1967-69; buyer intimate apparel May D&F, Denver, 1969-73; buyer young jr. dept. Gertz, Jamaica, N.Y., 1973-74; buyer, product developer Belk Store Svcs., N.Y.C., 1974-76; divsnl. mdse. mgr. Kirby Block/Irene Johns, N.Y.C., 1976-79; buyer, dept. mgr. Bloomingdale's, N.Y.C., 1979-81; asst. prof. fashion buying and mdsg. dept. Fashion Inst. Tech., N.Y.C., 1981-88, asst. prof., chairperson cosmetics and fragrance mkgt. dept., 1988—. Chairperson cert. bd. Fragrance Found., N.Y.C., 1993—; participant confs. Inst. Supervision Harvard Sch. Edn., 1969, workshop Am. Mgmt. Assn., 1974, Excellence in Coll. Tchg. Lilly Conf., Oxford, Ohio, 1990. Mem. Cosmetic Exec. Women. Avocations: reading, music, travel, theater. Office: Fashion Inst Tech 7th Ave at 27th St New York NY 10001-5992

SMITH-LOMBARDINI, MARYELIZABETH ANNE, opera singer, artistic director; b. Norfolk, Va., Sept. 1, 1957; d. John George and Alma Mary (Ross) Smith; m. Danilo Piero Luigi Lombardini, Oct. 30, 1987. MusB, U. Mich., 1979, MusM, 1980; student, Conservatory G. Verdi, Milan, Italy, 1980-83; diploma, La Scala Opera Studio, Milan, Italy, 1982-84. Apprentice Vienna (Austria) State Opera Studio, 1984—86; artistic dir. Laboratorio Lirico-Chamber Music Soc., Palermo, Italy, 1994—96; prof. State Music Conservatory A. Scontrino, Trapani, Italy, 1995—96; artistic dir. Operalaboratorio-City of Palermo Opera, 1997—. Tchr. Ars Nova Schola Cantorum, Palermo, 1991-97, The Brass Group, Palermo, 1995-98; dir. Palermo-Detroit Cultural Exch., City of Palermo, 1998-2002, artistic dir. I Solisti di Operalaboratorio Music Soc., Palermo, 2002—. Singing debut Turin Opera Theatere, 1984, Vienna State Opera, 1985, La Scala Theater, Milan, 1991; recordings include La Griselda (Vivaldi), Stabat Mater (Boccherini). Participant Med. Rsch. Benefits, M.D. Cancer Rsch. Benefits for UNICEF, Palermo, 1994—. Winner internat. singing competition, Turin Opera Theater, 1984; scholar Kosciuszko

Found., N.Y., 1978; postgrad. fellow Rotary Internat., Detroit, 1980. Mem. Sicilian Chamber Music Soc., Friends of the Teatro Massimo, Coll. Music Soc., Accademia Siculo-Normanna, Mu Phi Epsilon, Pi Kappa Lambda. Roman Catholic. Avocations: house plants, reading, cats, embroidery, horseback riding. Office: Cortile Farina 8 I-90133 Palermo Italy

SMITH-MEYER, LINDA HELENE (LINDA SMITH), artist; b. Manhattan, Nov. 18, 1947; d. Murray and Beatrice Victory (Waters) Smith; m. Charles Emil Meyer, Oct. 28, 1995. BFA, SUNY, 1969; MFA, NYU, 1973. One-woman shows include Sushi Gallery, West Hollywood, Calif., 1983, The Ivey Gallery, L.A., 1987, Schwartz Cierlak Gallery, Santa Monica, Calif., 1990; group shows include Cicchinelli Gallery, N.Y.C., 1981, Proteus Gallery, Beverly Hills, Calif., 1981, Elizalde Gallery Internat., Laguna Beach, Calif., 1981, 82, Gallery Helene, West Hollywood, 1982, Factory Place Gallery, L.A., 1983, 84, The Ivey Gallery, 1986, Ratliff-Williams Gallery, Sedona, Ariz., 1990-91, Spago Restaurant, Hollywood, Calif., 1985-2001, Orlando Gallery, Tarzana, Calif., others; represented in permanent collections at Peter Selz, Berkeley, Calif., Cedars-Sinai Med. Ctr., L.A., Martin Blinder/Barry Levine-Martin Lawrence Galleries, L.A., Ms. Found. for Women, N.Y.C., also pvt. collections; contbr. articles to profl. jours. Home: 1261 S Highland Ave Los Angeles CA 90019-1731

SMITH-MOONEY, MARILYN PATRICIA, city government official, management consultant and facilitator; b. Jamaica, NY, July 5, 1942; d. Raymond Lionel and Katherine Marie (Doepp) Cowan; m."Jack" (John) J. Mooney, Sept. 1, 2002; 1 child, Paul William Hibner. Student various aviation schs., St. Joseph's Coll., N.Y. cert. in Leadership and Human Resources Devel., Goldratt Inst., Conn., JONAH cert. Inst. Elected Ofcls., Advanced Inst. for Elected Ofcls., Leadership Charlotte Class of 97-98, Local Govt. Leadership Fla., Class IV-99. Exec. sec. to chief design Wiedersum Assoc., Arch. and Engr., Valley Stream, NY, 1960-61; office mgr., arch. apprentice, interior designer Keith I. Hibner, Arch., Hicksville, Garden City, NY, 1961-73; owner, pres. Hibner Atelier, Ltd., Garden City, 1968-75; interior design and gen. constrn. Garden City, 1968-76; office mgr., tech. planning, manual writer for county dept. structure & operation Ward Assoc./Planning Assoc., Arch. and Engr., Bohemia, NY, 1975-76; chief pilot, flight/ground aviation instr. Islip Aviation Ltd., NY, 1974-77; exec. asst. to pres. Arkay Packaging Corp., Hauppauge, NY, 1977-80; in-house constrn. mgr., 1980-82; adminstrn. and human resources mgr. Arkay Packaging Corp., Hauppauge, NY, 1986-89, dir. corp. devel., 1989, dir. materials mgmt., 1989-90. Cert. assoc. Goldratt Inst. for LI/Metro NY area, 1990-92; owner Concepts for Constructive Change, Educators and Facilitators for Continuous Improvement, Lake Grove, NY, 1990-92; ind. aviation flight/ground instr. airplane and instrument, 1977—; safety counselor FAA, 1974 92, FAA Ea. region counselors coord., 1985-86; mem. city charter rev. com. City Punta Gorda, Fla., 1996; mem. city coun. City of Punta Gorda, Fla., 1996—, vice mayor, 1998-99, 2000-01, first woman mayor, 2001-02, 2002-03; selected "top 100" west influential in Charlotte County by "Charlotte SUN", 2002, 2003; past bd. dir., officer Aviation Coun. LI; founder Seminar on Air Travel for Everyone (S.A.F.E.), 1975, Fly-C-Cure/We Air Condition People, 1979; city coun. appointee to S.W. Fla. Regional Planning Coun., 1999—, Charlotte County tourist devel. coun., 1998—, Charlotte County Assembly, 1998, 2001, Punta Gorda Historic Mural Soc., past mem. bd. dir.; county appointee Enterprise Charlotte Econ. Devel. team. Author articles, seminar syllabus. Past mem. nat. panel Consumer Arbitrators, Nat. Consumer Arbitration Program, Better Bus. Bur.; lic. comml. pilot, flight and ground instr.; chmn. bd. Charlotte Skatepark, Inc.; past Bd. mem., past officer Punta Gorda Elks Lodge 2606. Past chmn. ninety-nines L.I. chpt., founding internat. chmn. safety edn., Amelia Earhart Bronze medal 1975, Old Punta Gorda, Inc.; mem. various cmty. non-profit org., (past mem. bd. dir.). Home: 654 Andros Ct Punta Gorda FL 33950-5809

SMITH-ROMER, HELENE BONNIE, artist, educator; b. Chgo., July 6, 1948; d. Julius and Annie (Kaminsky) Smith; m. Eric R. Romer. BFA, Columbia Coll., 1984; MFA, U. Ill., 1990. Gallery asst. Edwyn Houk Gallery, Chgo., 1983-84; inst. art and photography Jewish Cmty. Ctr.-Summer of the Arts, Skokie, Ill., 1984-85; instr. photography Truman Coll., Chgo., 1984-90; instr. computer graphics, exptl. images, multi-media Columbia Coll., Chgo., 1991—; curator, coord./curator vis. artist program I Due Art 4 You Mus., Chgo., 1993, 95—. Curator Ukranian Inst. Modern Art, 1986, U. Ill., 1988, Art Inst. Chgo., 1990, I Due Art 4 You Mus., 1998; with vis. artist program Columbia Coll., 1992-96; dir. Chgo. Women Artist Program, 1992-97. Author: Conversations with Elmer, 1983, 4 Women Scrapbook, 1990, Confession of A Space Rider, 1993, Letters From Home, 1996-98; photo editor Nit and Wit mag. Recipient scholarship Albert P. Weisman, 1981, 82, 83; Ragdale Artist residency; grant Chgo. Coun. on Fine Arts, 1990-91, Photography grant Ill. Arts Coun., 1992. Mem. Women Caucus for Arts (vis. artist/curator 1994—), Soc. for Photog. Educators. Avocations: reading, films, collecting. Home: 7348 N Ridge Blvd Chicago IL 60645-6905

SMITH TARCHALSKI, HELEN MARIE, piano educator; b. Washington, Dec. 24, 1957; d. Albert John and Marie Ethel (Wellens) Smith; m. Stanislaw Edward Tarchalski, Sept. 26, 1981. MusB in Applied Piano, Peabody Conservatory Md., 1979. Master cert. music tchr. Ind. piano instr., accompanist, various cities, 1978—; edn. rep., clinician Baldwin Piano and Organ Co., various cities, 1982-94. Clinician various univs., 1984—; com. mem., seminar leader Nat. Conf. on Piano Pedagogy, Chgo., 1990-94; mem. adv. bd. Pacific Music Alliance, Pasadena, Calif., 1994-97; mem. organizing com. World Piano Pedagogy Conf., 1996—. Editor (periodical) Soundboard, 1989-94, (textbook) Teaching Toward Tomorrow, 1994; contbg. author Encyclopedia of Keyboard Instruments, 1994, various jours.; author (computer software) Symbol Simon, 1995. Mem. Am. Liszt Soc. (bd. dirs. 1996—), Music Tchrs. Nat. Assn., Md. State Music Tchrs. Assn. (tech. chair 1996—), Montgomery County Music Tchrs. Assn. (pres. 1999—), Anapolis Sch. Music, 1998—. Avocations: scuba diving, water skiing, sailing, biking, rollerblading. Home: 1802 River Watch Ln Annapolis MD 21401-2009

SMITH-THOMPSON, PATRICIA ANN, public relations consultant, educator; b. Chgo., June 7, 1933; d. Clarence Richard and Ruth Margaret (Jacobson) Nowack; m. Tyler Thompson, Aug. 2, 1992; children from previous marriage: Deborah, Kurt, Nancy, Janna, Gail, Lori. Student, Cornell U., 1951—52; BA, Centenary Coll., Hackettstown, N.J., 1983. Prodn. asst. Your Hit Parade Batten, Barton, Durstine & Osborne, 1953-54; pvt. practice polit. cons., 1954-66; legal sec., asst. Atty. John C. Cushman, 1966-68; field dep. L.A. County Assessor Office, 1968-69; pub. info. officer L.A. County Probation Dept., 1969-73; dir. consumer rels. Fireman's Fund, San Francisco, 1973-76; spl. projects officer L.A. County Transp. Commn., 1977-78; tchr. Calif. State U., Dominguez Hills, 1979-86. Editor, writer Jet Propulsion Lab., 1979—80; pub. info. dir. L.A. Bd. Pub. Works, 1980—82; pub. info. cons. City of Pasadena, Calif., 1982—84, pub. rels. cons., 1983—90; cmty. affairs cons. Worldport L.A., 1990—92; tchr. Kern County Schs., 2002—. Contbr. articles to profl. jours. Active First United Meth. Ch. Commn. Missions and Social Concerns, 1983—89; bd. dirs. Depot, 1983—87; mem. devel. com. Pasadena Guidance Clinics, 1984—85; pres. Cultural Arts Assn., Bear Valley Springs, 1999—2000, Calif. Press Women, Bay Area, 1975. Recipient Pro award, L.A. Publicity Club, 1978, Outstanding Achievement award, Soc. Consumer Affairs Profls. Bus., 1976, Disting. Alumni award, Centenary Coll., 1992. Mem.: Nat. Assn. Mental Health Info. Officers (3 regional awards 1986), Calif. Press Women (pres. Bay area 1975—76, award 1974, 1978, 1983, 1984, 1985, Cmty. Rels. 1st pl. winner 1986, 1987, 1988, 1989), Nat. Press Women (Calif. chpt. pres. 1975—76, Pub. Rels. award 1986), Pub. Rels. Soc. Am. (accredited mem., consumer program award 1977, 2 awards 1984, Joseph Roos Cmty. Svc. award 1985). Republican. Home and Office: 24145 Jacaranda Dr Tehachapi CA 93561-8309

SMITS, HELEN LIDA, physician, medical administrator, educator; b. Long Beach, Calif., Dec. 3, 1936; d. Theodore Richard Smits and Anna Mary Wells; m. Roger LeCompte, Aug. 28, 1976; 1 child, Theodore. BA with honors, Swarthmore Coll., 1958; MA, Yale U., 1961, MD cum laude, 1967. Intern, asst. resident Hosp. U. Pa., 1967-68; fellow Beth Israel Hosp., Boston, 1969-70; chief resident Hosp. U. Pa., 1970-71; chief med. clinic U. Pa., 1971-75; assoc. adminstr. for patient care svcs. U. Pa. Hosp., 1975-77; v.p. med. affairs Community Health Plan Georgetown U., Washington, 1977; dir. health standards and quality bur. Health Care Financing Adminstrn., HHS, Washington, 1977-80; sr. rsch. assoc. The Urban Inst., Washington, 1980-81; assoc. prof. Yale U. Med. Sch., New Haven, 1981-85; assoc. v.p. for health affairs U. Conn. Health Ctr., Farmington, 1985-87; prof. community medicine U. Conn. Sch. Medicine, Farmington, 1985-93; hosp. dir. John Dempsey Hosp., Farmington, 1987-93; dep. adminstr. Health Care Financing Adminstrn., Washington, 1993-96; pres., chmn. Health Right, Inc., Meriden, Conn., 1996-99; vis. prof. Robert F. Wagner Grad. Sch. Pub. Svc., NYU, 1999—2001. Commr. Joint Com. on Accreditation Hosps., Chgo., 1989-93, chair, 1991-92; mem., co-chair strategic framework bd. Nat. Forum on Health Care Quality Measurement and Reporting, 2000—01; Fulbright lectr. faculty medicine Eduardo Mondlane U., Maputo, Mozambique, 2003-. Contbr. numerous articles to profl. jours. Bd. dirs. The Ivoryton Playhouse Fedn., Inc., 1990-92, The Connecticut River Mus., 1990-93, Hartford Stage, 1990-93; mem. Dem. Town Com., Essex, Conn., 1982-89. Recipient Superior Svc. award HHS, Washington, 1982; Royal Soc. Medicine Found. fellow, London, 1973; Fulbright scholar, 1959-60. Mem. ACP (master, regent 1984-90), Inst. Medicine, Nat. Acad. Scis., Phi Beta Kappa, Alpha Omega Alpha. Episcopalian. Avocations: sailing, cooking, gardening. Office: 4 Washington Sq N Rm 23 New York NY 10003-6671

SMOKVINA, GLORIA JACQUELINE, nursing educator; b. East Chicago, Ind., July 29, 1937; Diploma in nursing, St. Margaret Hosp. Sch. Nursing, 1959; BSN, DePaul U., 1964; MSN, Ind. U., 1966; PhD in Nursing, Wayne State U., 1977. RN, Ind. Staff and charge nurse surgical units St. Catherine Hosp., East Chgo., Ind., 1959-61, charge nurse surgical units, 1962-64; asst. head nurse ICU El Camino Hosp., Mountain View, Calif., 1961-62; instr. nursing South Chgo. Community Hosp., Chgo., 1964-65; asst. prof. med.-surgical nursing U. Evansville, Ind., 1966-70, assoc. prof. nursing Purdue U. Calumet, Hammond, Ind., 1970-80, prof. nursing, 1980—, acting head dept. nursing, 1986-87, head dept. nursing, 1987—, head sch. nursing, 1996—, dean schs. of profl. programs, 1996—2002, dean Sch. of Nursing, 2002—. Bd. dir. Health East Chgo. Cmty. Bd., St. Catherine Hosp.; cons. ICU St. Catherine Hosp., 1971, 74, 77, 79, 81, staff nurse, 71, 74, 77, 79, 81; cons. Vis. Nurses Assn., 1979, 80, Klapper, Issac & Parish Law Firm, Indpls., 1995; mem. adv. com. Vis. Nurse Assn. of NW Ind., 1977—; mem. Statewide Task Force on Nursing in Ind., 1987—; mem. Health E. Chgo. Task Force, 1996—; peer reviewer Coll. Nursing Valparaiso U., Ind., 1989; mem. gov. bd. St. Margaret Mercy Healthcare Ctrs. Inc., 1992—, chair quality svcs. com., 1992—, v.p., 1998—2001; mem. gov. bd. Sisters of St. Francis Regional Bd.; expert witness in several cases. Contbr. chpt. to Normal Aging: Dimensions of Wellness, 1986, Medical-Surgical Nursing, 1981; contbr. articles to profl. jours.; numerous rsch. projects. Mem. planning com. Lake County Health Fair, 1975, 77, nursing chair, 1978-80; chmn. nominations com. Ind. League for Nursing, 1995—; mem. adv. bd. Horizon Career Coll., Merriville, Ind., 1994—; mem. adv. com. Community Ctr. Devel. Corp., Hammond, 1993—, Three City Empowerment Zone E. Chgo., Gary and Hammond, 1994-95, grad. edn. Ind. U. Purdue U., 1981-85, Westhaysen Med. Edn. Trust Com. Calumet Nat. Bank, Hammond, 1987—; mem. panel Healthy E. Chgo., 1994-96; mem. Community Health Assn., 1979-84; v.p. Am. Heart Assn. N.W. Ind. affiliate, 1984-87, mem. edn. com. 1982-87; bd. dirs. Our Lady of Mercy Hosp., Dyer, Ind., 1989-92, Health Adv., 1979-82; bd. dirs. Am. Heart Assn. Ind. affiliate, 1981-87, chair community programs, 1982-87; bd. dirs. Lakeshore Health Care System, 1988-89, quality assurance com. Grantee HHS, 1983-85, 84, 85-88, 90—, Helene Fuld Health Trust, 1989, 92, 93-94, Pub. Health Svc., 1989-90, 1990-91, Meth. Hosp., 1993-98; recipient Meritorious Svc. award Am. Cancer Soc. of N.W. Ind., 1979, Lake Area United Way, 1979, Cert. of Recognition Am. Heart Assn., 1983-84, Med. and Sci. Disting. Program award, 1985, Franciscan Award, Svc. Recogn. St. Margaret Mercy Healthcare Ctr., 2002. Mem. AACN, N.W. Ind. Orgn. Nurse Execs., Nurse Exec. Resource Group (U. Chgo.), Nat. League for Nursing, Ind. Deans and Dirs. of AD, BS and Higher Degree Programs, Nurse Exec. Forum, Wayne State Alumni Assn., St. Margaret Alumni Assn. (v.p. program com., chmn. scholarship com.), Ind. U. Alumni Assn., Mu Omega (chpt. commitment award 1994, chair fin. com. 1991—), Sigma Theta Tau (hon.). Office: Purdue U Calumet 2200 169th St Hammond IN 46323-2068 E-mail: smokvina@calumet.purdue.edu.

SMOLEK, ROCHELLE THÉRÈSE, interior designer; b. Stamford, Conn., Jan. 31, 1948; d. Joseph Peter and Gladys Therese Bruno; m. Howard Thomas Uhal, Oct. 19, 1972 (div. July 1995); 1 child, Geoffrey Thomas; m. Frank D. Smolek, Jr., Aug. 30, 1995; stepchildren: Jason David, Kevin Kent. Designer Celange, Inc., N.Y.C., 1976-79, Len Coleman Designs, Charleston, S.C., 1980-83; cons. Rochelle T. Uhal Interiors, Cleve., 1983-86; owner Heritage Interiors, Ledyard, Conn., 1988-94; designer Jane Mabry Interior Design, Alpharetta, Ga., 1994-95; owner Fine Room Design, Inc., Roswell, Ga., 1995—. Chair 1999 Magnolia Ball, Bullock Hall, Roswell, 1999; chair Encore ASA Atlanta Symphony Assoc., 1996, asst. membership chair, 1998-99, showhouse opening night party, 1996, 97, chmn. Ensemble unit, 2001-, designer for decoration show house, 2000, 01. Mem. Am. Soc. Interior Design, Interior Design Soc. Republican. Roman Catholic. Avocation: travel.

SMOLENSKI, LISABETH ANN, family practice physician; b. Pitts., Oct. 1, 1950; d. Anthony Edward and Betty Jean (Gross) S.; m. William Ward Daniels, May 24, 1980; 1 child, Kathryn Elizabeth. BA, Carlow Coll., 1972; MD, Hahnemann U., 1982. Diplomate Am. Bd. Family Practice. Resident in family practice West Jersey Health Sys., Voorhees, N.J., 1982-85; pvt. practice, Somerville, Tenn., 1985-90, Memphis, 1990—2003; with Spectrum Pain Clinics, Franklin-Nashville, Tenn., 2003—. Sec. exec. com. med. staff Meth. Hosp. Somerville, 1988-90. Fellow Am. Acad. Family Physicians. Republican. Avocation: reading. Office: Spectrum Pain Clinics 324 Cool Springs Blvd Franklin TN 37067 Office Phone: 615-794-5009.

SMOLLER, IRENE MILDRED, artist, educator; b. Chgo., July 28, 1919; d. Frank and Martha (Rothwell) Volkert; m. Louis Ben Smoller (dec.); 1 child, William. Student, N.Y. Acad., 1937-40, Art Inst. Chgo., 1950-51. One-man shows include Chgo. Pub. Libr., Merchants and Mfrs. Club, Chgo., Bernheim and Jeune Galerie, Paris, O'Hanna Gallery, London, Broadway Galleries, Ltd., Milw., LeBow Gallery, Evanston, Ill., Thor Gallery, Louisville, Palm Beach (Fla.) Gallery, Price Gallery, Chgo.; exhibited in groups shows including St. Paul Gallery and Sch. Arts, Russell Gallery, Bloomington, Ill., Adele Rosenberg Gallery, Chgo., Harper Gallery, Chgo., Butler Inst., Youngstown, Ohio, N.Y. Acad., Evanston (Ill.) Art Ctr., Denver Mus., Art Inst. Chgo., Krannert Mus., Springfield, Ill., McKerrie Galleries, Pitts., Biennale Internationale France, Paris, Rual Askew Gallery, Dallas, Ft. Wayne (Ind.) Mus., Societe des Artistes Independants Annuelle, Paris, Berheim-Jeune Gallery, Paris, Memmel Gallery, Milw., Downtown Gallery, New Orleans, Thor Gallery, Louisville, Internat. Exhbn., Lucca, Italy, Palm Beach (Fla.) Gallery, others; represented in permanent collections Galerie Bernheim and Jeune, Paris, Vincent Price collection, Cedar Rapids (Mich.) Mus. Art; pvt. instr., Chgo., 1960—. Midwest regional dir. Nat. Arts Coun. Recipient Maxwell Pearl purchase award, London, 1960, 2d prize Solomon Art purchase award, Phila., 1960, 2d prize Lincolnwood (Ill.) Art Festival, 1967, 1st prize Suburban Art Ctr. Ann., Highland Park, Ill., 1965, 1st prize Midwest Regional Representational, Chgo., 1964, Silver medal Internat. Italian Exbn., Rome; diplome d'honneur Laureate la France, 1964. Mem. Artist Equity Am., Renaissance Soc. U. Chgo., Royal Acad. (London). Home: 33 N La Salle St Ste 2131 Chicago IL 60602-622

SMOLYANSKY, JULIE, consumer products company executive; d. Michael and Ludmila Smolyansky. BA, U. Ill., 1996. Dir. sales and mktg. Lifeway Foods Inc., Morton Grove, Ill., 1997—2002, pres., 2002—, CEO, 2002—, CFO, 2002—, treas., 2002—, dir. Office: Lifeway Foods Inc 6431 West Oakton Ave Morton Grove IL 60053

SMOOT, DONNA JEAN, music educator; b. Mt. Pleasant, Iowa, Jan. 27, 1944; d. Carl Jay and Mae Lucille (Simkin) Register; m. Robert Earl Smoot, Dec. 30, 1962; children: Kristen Kay, Tina Renee Ballard. MusB in music edn., Iowa Wesleyan Coll., 1962—66; M in music edn., Wichita State U., 1980—86. Cert. Teacher State Dept of Edn. of Kans., 1992. Music tchr. West Burlington Sch. Dist., Iowa, 1966—68, Poudre R #1 Sch. Dist., Ft. Collins, Colo., 1968—71; instrumental tchr. Laramie Co. Sch. Dist., Cheyenne, Wyo., 1971—74; instrumental music tchr. USD #443 Sch. Dist., Dodge City, Kans., 1980—90; instrumental & vocal tchr. Mex. Sch. Dist., Mo., 1990—92; instrumental music tchr. USD #443 Sch. Dist., Dodge City, 1993—2002; dir. of bands USD #442 Sch. Dist., Dodge City, Kans., 2002—. Recipient Blue Key, Iowa Wesleyan Coll., 1962. Mem.: NEA (life), Music Edn. Nat. Conf., Kans. Bandmaster Assn. (assoc.), Phi Beta Mu (assoc.). Bapt. Avocations: knitting, cross stitch. Home: 1510 8th Ave Dodge City KS 67801 Office: Dodge City High School 2201 Ross Blvd Dodge City KS 67801

SMOOT, SKIPI LUNDQUIST, psychologist; b. Aberdeen, Wash., Apr. 10, 1934; d. Warren Duncan and Miriam Stephen (Bishop) Dobbins; m. Harold Richard Lundquist, June 2, 1951 (div. Mar. 1973); children: Kurt Richard, Mark David, Ted Douglas, Blake Donald; m. Edward Lee Smoot, June 14, 1975. BA in Psychology, Coll. of William and Mary, 1978; MA, Pepperdine U., 1980; PhD, Calif. Sch. of Profl., Psychology, San Diego, 1985. Lic. clin. psychologist, Calif.; lic. marriage and family therapist, Calif. Owner, operator McDonald's Restaurants, San Pedro and Torrance, Calif., 1965-76, Williamsburg, Va., 1965-76; psychotherapist Coll. Hosp., Cerritos, Calif., 1979-81, Orange County Child Guidance, Laguna Hills, Calif., 1981-82, Calif. State Police, Costa Mesa, 1982-83, Anaheim, 1983-84; psychologist Orange County Mental Health, Santa Ana, Calif., 1984-85, Psychol. Ctr., Orange and El Toro, Calif., 1985-91; clin. dir. Career Ambitions, Lake Forest, Calif., 1991-98, Psychol. Decisions, Irvine-Laguna Hills, Calif., 1991-94. Psychol. cons. seminars and workshops for bus., Irvine and Laguna Hills, 1991-98. Mem. APA, Calif. Psychol. Assn. Democrat. Avocations: music, travel, rsch. Office: Psychol Decisions Career Ambitions Unltd 23832 Rockfield Blue # 165 Lake Forest CA 92630-6822 Office Phone: 949-770-2675. Personal E-mail: skipilsmootphd@cox.net.

SMOTHERS, ANN ELIZABETH, museum director; b. Chgo., Dec. 20, 1946; With adminstn. Mercy Hosp., Iowa City, 1982-85; asst. dir. Old Capital Mus., Iowa City, 1985-95, dir., 1995—. Recipient Hon. Achievement for Women award YWCA, 1996. Mem. Altrusa. Office: Old Capitol Mus Univ Iowa 24 Old Capitol Iowa City IA 52242 E-mail: ann.smothers@niowa.edu.

SMULKSTYS, INGA, operations and management executive; b. Ind., July 1961; BA in Pub. Policy, U. Chgo.; MPA, Ind. U. Neighborhood specialist Cmty. Devel. and Planning, City of Ft. Wayne, Ind., 1986, housing program mgr., 1987-88; adminstr. asst. to Rep. Jill Long, Ind., 1989-95; exec. asst. to under sec. for rural devel., Jill Long Thompson Dept. Agr., Washington, 1995-96, dep. under sec. for ops. and mgmt. rural devel., 1996—. Office: Dept Agr Rural Devel Ops and Mgmgt 1400 Independence Ave SW Washington DC 20250-0003

SMULLENS, SARAKAY COHEN, psychotherapist, writer; b. Balt. m. Stanton N. Smullens; children: Elizabeth R. Smullens, Douglas R. Smullens, Elisabeth J. Cohen, Kathyanne S. Cohen. Student, Skidmore Coll., 1958-60, Goucher Coll., 1960-62, Cath. U., 1963-64, U. pa., 1964-65. Cert. social worker, group therapist, family life educator; diplomate Am. Bd. Examiners in Clin. Social Work. Regional coord. for Young Dems. Dem. Nat. Com., Washington, 1962-63; protective svc. counselor Soc. to Protect Children from Cruelty, Phila., 1965-66; family therapist Phila. Psychiat. Hosp., 1966-68; marriage and family counselor Jewish Family Svc. of Phila., 1968-73, dir. family life edn., 1971-73; pvt. practice marital, couple, family, group psychotherapy Phila., 1973—. Instr. mental health tech. Hahnemann Med. U., 1974-78, sr. instr., 1978-90, clin. asst. prof., 1990-97; presenter, lectr. in field; appearances on local and nat. TV and radio programs. Author: Whoever Said Life is Fair?, 1982, 2d edit., 1988, Japanese edit., 1985, Setting Yourself Free: Breaking the Cycles of Emotional Abuse in Family, Friendship, Love and Work, 2002; columnist Phila. Inquirer, 1976-81, Phila. Bull., 1981-82. Mem. Goucher Com. for Towson Integration, 1960-62; 8th ward committeewoman Dem. Party, 1967-71; co-founder Women's Way, 1971; mem. cmty. edn. and pub. rels. com. Jewish Family and Children's Agy., 1977-86, bd. dirs. Family Svc. Phila., 1987-92; mem. women's bd. Thomas Jefferson U. Hosp., 1984—, sec., 1989-95; bd. overseers Sch. Social Work, originator of Crystal Stair award U. Pa., 1990—; bd. dirs. Center City Resident's Assn., 1990-94, Phila. chpt. Am. Jewish Congress, 1994—; vice chair Child Welfare Adv. Bd. Phila., 1994, chair, 1994-97; mem. Interdisciplinary Task Force of Child Welfare Sys., 1997; founding co-chair Sabbath of Domestic Peace, 1995. Recipient Peace medal Women's Internat. League for Peace and Freedom, 1962, Louise Waterman Wise award Am. Jewish Congress, 1996. Mem. NASW, Acad. Cert. Social Workers, Am. Assn. Marriage and Family Therapy, Nat. Coun. Family Rels., Am. Group Therapy Assn., Pa. Assn. marriage and Family Therapy, Authors' Guild. Home and Office: 1710 Pine St Philadelphia PA 19103-6702 Fax: 215-732-4603.

SMUNT, MARSHA LYNN HAEFLINGER, financial executive; b. Chgo., July 9, 1955; m. Timothy Lawrence Smunt, Aug. 17, 1974. BS in Acctg., Purdue U., 1976; MBA in Finance and Investments, Ind. U., 1980. CPA, cert. mgmt. acct., fin. mgmt.; CFA level I. Auditor Deloitte & Touche, St. Louis, 1977-78; analyst corp. diversification McDonnell Douglas Corp., St. Louis, 1979; sr. fin. analyst Cummins Engine Co., Columbus, Ind., 1980-81, capital investments mgr., 1981-82; corp. capital analysis mgr. Gen. Dynamics Corp., St. Louis, 1982-84, corp. mgr. fin. planning, 1984-87; sr. capital investments Anheuser-Busch Cos., Inc., St. Louis, 1987-88, mgr. treasury ops., 1988-91, exec. asst. to treas., 1991-92, mgr. investor rels., 1992-94; dir. fin. planning and forecasting R.J. Reynolds Internat. Inc., Winston-Salem, N.C., 1995-96; sr. v.p. corp. analysis Wachovia Corp., Winston-Salem, 1997-99, sr. v.p. investor rels., 1999—. Mentor, career symposium spkr. MBA program Wake Forest U., 1995-96; bd. dirs. Sawtooth Ctr. for Visual Art; with Jr. League, Habitat for Humanity. Mem. AICPA, Inst. Mgmt. Accts. (treas., bd. dirs. Piedmont-Winston-Salem chpt.), Profl. Women of Winston-Salem (pres. 1999-2000, bd. dirs.), Nat. Investor Rels. Inst. (pres. St. Louis chpt. 1993-94), Beta Gamma Sigma. Home: 1061 W Kent Rd Winston Salem NC 27104-1131

SNAPP, ELIZABETH, librarian, educator; b. Lubbock, Tex., Mar. 31, 1937; d. William James and Louise (Lanham) Mitchell; m. Henry Franklin Snapp, June 1, 1956 (div. Dec. 2001). BA magna cum laude, North Tex. State U., Denton, 1968, MLS, 1969, MA, 1977. Asst. to archivist Archive of New Orleans Jazz Tulane U., 1960-63; catalog libr. Tex. Woman's U., Denton, 1969-71, head acquisitions dept., 1971-74, coord. readers svcs., 1974-77, asst. to dean Grad. Sch., 1977-79, instr. libr. sci., 1977-88, acting Univ. libr., 1979-82, dir. librs., 1982—2002, dir. librs. emeritus, 2002—, univ. historian, 1995—2002; adj. prof. dept. history and govt. Tex. Woman's U., Denton, 2002—; rsch. assoc. Tex. Woman's U. Libr., Denton,

2002—. Chair-elect Tex. Coun. State U. Librs., 1988—90, chmn., 1990—92; adv. com. on libr. formula Coord. Bd. Tex. Coll. and Univ. Sys., 1981—92; Libr. Sys. Act adv. bd. Tex. State Libr. and Archives Commn., 1999—2002; del. OCLC Nat. Users Coun., 1985—87, by-laws com., 1985—86, com. on less-than-full-svcs. networks, 1986—87; trustee AMI-GOS Libr. Svcs., 1994—2000, sec. bd. trustees, 1996—97, vice-chmn. bd. trustees, 1997—99, chair bd. trustees, 1999—2000; project dir. NEH consultancy grant on devel. core curriculum for women's studies, 1981—82; chmn. Blue Ribbon com. 1986 Gov.'s Commn. for Women to select 150 outstanding women in Tex. History; project dir. math./sci. anthology project Tex. Found. Women's Resources; co-sponsor Irish Lecture Series, Denton, 1968, 70, 73, 78. Co-editor: Read All About Her! Texas Women's History: A Working Bibliography, 1995; contbr. articles to profl. jours. Trustee, treas. Adult Day Care of North Tex., 2002—04, v.p., 2004—; sec. Denton County Dem. Caucus, 1970. Recipient Ann. Pioneer award, Tex. Woman's U., 1986, Women's Studies Vision award, 1998. Mem.: AAUW (legis. br. chmn. 1973—74, br. v.p. 1975—76, br. pres. 1979—80, state historian 1986—88, treas. 1998—99), ALA (stds. com. 1983—85), AAUP, Tex. Assn. Coll. Tchrs. (pres. Tex. Woman's U. chpt. 1976—77), So. Conf. Brit. Studies, Women's Collecting Group (chmn. ad hoc com. 1984—86), Tex. Hist. Commn. (judge for Farenbach History prize 1990—93), Tex. Libr. Assn. (program com. 1978, Dist. VII chmn. 1985—86, archives and oral history com. 1990—92, co-chair conf. program com. 1994, Tall Texan selection com. 1995—96, treas. exec. bd. 1996—99, Centennial com. 2000—02), AAUW Ednl. Found. (rsch. and awards panel 1990—94), Alliance Higher Edn. (chair coun. libr. dirs. 1993—95), Rotary Internat. (sec. local chpt. 1999—2002), Soroptimist Internat. (pres. Denton chpt. 1986—88), Women's Shakespeare Club (pres. 1967—69), Pi Delta Phi, Alpha Lambda Sigma (pres. 1970—71), Alpha Chi, Beta Phi Mu (pres. chpt. 1976 1978, sec. nat. adv. assembly 1978—79, pres. 1979—80, nat. dir. 1981—83). Methodist. Home: 2513 Coffey Dr Denton TX 76207-0002 Office: TWU Sta PO Box 424093 Denton TX 76204-4093 E-mail: Snappe@charter.net.

SNEDAKER, CATHERINE RAUPAGH (KIT SNEDAKER), editor; d. Paul and Charity (Primmer) Raupagh; m. William Brooks; children: Eleanor, Peter William; m. 2d Weldon Snedaker. BA, Duke U. Promotion mgr. Sta. WINR-TV and WNBF-TV, Binghamton, N.Y.; TV editor, feature writer Binghamton Sun, 1960-68; mem. staff, food editor, restaurant critic L.A. Herald Examiner, 1978-80, food and travel editor. Author: The Great Convertibles; editor: The Food Package; guest editor: Mademoiselle mag., 1942; contbr. numerous articles on food and travel to nat. mags. and newspapers. Recipient 3 awards L.A. Press Club, VISTA award, 1979. Mem. Nat. Writers Union-UAW Local. Democrat. Home: 140 San Vicente Blvd Apt A Santa Monica CA 90402-1533

SNEED, MARIE ELEANOR WILKEY, retired secondary school educator; b. Dahlgren, Ill., June 12, 1915; d. Charles N. and Hazel (Miller) Wilkey; m. John Sneed, Jr., Sept. 18, 1937; children: Suzanne (Mrs. Geoffrey B. Newton), John Corwin. Student, U. Ill., 1933-35; BS, Northwestern U., 1937; postgrad., Wayne State U., 1954-60, U. Mich., 1967. Tchr. English, drama, creative writing Berkley (Mich.) Sch. Dist., 1952-76. Mem. Mich. Statewide Tchr. Edn. Preparation, 1968-72, regional sec., 1969-70; mem. Pleasant Ridge Arts Coun., 1982—; mem. Pleasant Ridge Parks and Recreation Commn., 1982-88, sr. citizen cons., 1989—; chmn. Student Tchr. Planning Com. Berkley, 1971-72. Mem. NEA, Mich. Edn. Assn., Berkley Edn. Assn. (pres. 1961-62, 82-87), Oakland Tchr. Edn. Coun. (exec. bd. 1973-76), Farm Bur. Ill., Founder's Soc., Phi Alpha Chi, Pi Lambda Theta, Alpha Delta Kappa, Alpha Omicron Pi. Clubs: Pleasant Ridge Woman's (pres. 1980-83), Royal Oak Rep. Woman's, Nomad's. Home: 21 Norwich Rd Pleasant Ridge MI 48069-1027 also: Miller Heritage Farm LLC Dahlgren IL 62828

SNEED, MICHAEL (MICHELE SNEED), columnist; b. Mandan, N.D., Nov. 16, 1943; d. Richard Edward and June Marie (Ritchey) S.; m. William J. Griffin, Sept. 16, 1978; 1 child, Patrick BS, Wayne State U., 1965. Tchr. Barrington High Sch., Ill., 1965-66; legis. asst. Congressman Ray Clevenger, 1966-67; reporter City News Bur., Chgo., 1967-69, Chgo. Tribune, 1969-86, columnist, 1981-86; pres. sec. Mayor Jane Byrne, Chgo., 1979; gossip columnist Chgo. Sun-Times, 1986—. Co-editor Chgo. Journalism Rev., 1971-72 Vice pres. No. Mich. U. chpt. Young Democrats, 1962 Mem.: Women's Athletic. Roman Catholic. Avocation: gardening. Office: Chgo Sun-Times Inc 401 N Wabash Ave Chicago IL 60611-5642

SNEED, PAULA ANN, food products executive; b. Everett, Mass., Nov. 10, 1947; d. Thomas Edwin and F. Mary (Turner) S.; m. Lawrence Paul Bass, Sept. 2, 1978; children: Courtney Jameson. BA, Simmons Coll., 1969; MBA, Harvard U., 1977; D Bus. Adminstrn. (hon.), Johnson & Wales U., 1991. Ednl. supr., femal coord. Outreach Program for Problem Drinkers, 1969-71; dir. plans, program devel. and evaluations Ecumenical Ctr. in Roxbury, Mass., 1971-72; program coord. Boston Sickle Cell Ctr., 1972-75; asst. product mgr. Gen. Food Corp., White Plains, N.Y., 1977-79, assoc. product mgr., 1979-80; product mgr. Gen. Foods Corp., White Plains, N.Y., 1980-82, sr. product mgr., 1982-83, product group mgr., 1983-86, category mgr., 1986-87, v.p. consumer affairs, 1986-90, pres. food svc. div., sr. v.p., 1990-95; sr. v.p. mktg. svcs. Kraft Foods N.Am., 1995—. Mem. bd. dirs. Hercules Inc.. Bd. dirs. Crispus Attucks Scholarship Fund, Ridgewood, N.J., 1982—, bd. dirs. Westchester/Fairfield Inroads. Recipient Benevolent Heart award Graham-Windham, 1987, Black Achiever award Harlem YWCA, 1982, MBA of Yr. Harvard Bus. Sch., 1987, Benevolent Heart award Graham Windham Soc., 1987; named MBA of Yr. Harvard Bus. Sch. Black Alumni Orgn., 1987; named one of 100 Top Black Women in Corp. Am. Ebony Mag., 1990, 91, 21 Most Influential African Ams. in Corp. Am., 1991, 97 (ONe of 40 Most Influential, 1993), Breakthrough 50 Exec. Female Mag., 50 Most Powerful Women Mgrs., 1994, 25 Most Influential Mothers Working Mother Mag., 1998; inducted Acad. Women Achievers N.Y. YWCA, 1990. Mem. AAUW, Exec. Leadership Coun., adv. coun. to dean Howard U. Bus. Sch., Nat. Assn. Negro Bus. and Profl. Women, Coalition of 100 Black Women, Soc. Consumer Affairs Profls., Women's Forum. Office: Kraft Foods Inc Three Lakes Dr Northfield IL 60093-2753 Home: 1755 Paddock Ln Lake Forest IL 60045-3675

SNELL, MARILYN NELSON, psychologist, researcher, director; b. American Fork, Utah, Feb. 11, 1951; d. Ray C. and Affra M. Nelson; m. Paul Decker Snell, Aug. 13, 1969; children: Ben, Matt, Scott, Nelson, Jeff, Robby. BS in Psychology, Brigham Young U., 1972; MS in Counseling Psychology, U. Utah, 1996, PhD in Counseling Psychology, 1999. Postdoc. fellow, resident U. Counseling Ctr. and Dept. Family Preventive Medicine, U. Utah, Salt Lake City, 1999—2000; vis. asst. prof. U. Utah, Salt Lake City, 2000—02; pvt. practice Sandy (Utah) Counseling Ctrs., 2001—, dir. rsch., 2001—; clin. dir. Journey at Willow Creek, Utah, 2003—. Presenter in field; rev. manuscripts Covenant Pub., American Fork, 2002—. Co-author: Quality Assurance in Residential Care: Organizational Assessment, 2001. Acad. scholar, Brigham Young U., 1969—72. Mem.: Assn. Women Psychologists, Utah Psychol. Assn., Am. Psychol. Assn. Mem. Lds Ch. Avocations: gardening, sports, travel, reading. Office: Sandy Counseling Ctr 8184 S Highland Dr C-8 Sandy UT 84093 Office Phone: 801-944-1666.

SNELL, PATRICIA POLDERVAART, librarian, consultant; b. Santa Fe, Apr. 11, 1943; d. Arie and Edna Beryl (Kerchmar) Poldervaart; m. Charles Eliot Snell, June 7, 1966. BA in Edn., U. N.M., 1965; MSLS, U. So. Calif., 1966. Asst. edn. libr. U. So. Calif., L.A., 1966—68; med. libr. Bedford (Mass.) VA Hosp., 1968—69; asst. law libr. U. Miami, Coral Gables, Fla., 1970—71; acquistions libr. U. N.Mex. Law Sch. Libr., Albuquerque, 1971—72; order libr. Los Angeles County Law Libr., 1972—76, cataloguer, 1976—90; libr. Parks Coll., Albuquerque, 1990—92; records technician Technadyne Engring. Cons. to Sandia Nat. Labs., 1992—93; libr. Tireman Learning Materials Ctr. U. N.Mex., Albuquerque, 1993—96, instr. libr. sci. program Coll. Edn., 1991—; rsch. technician City of Albuquerque, 1996—. Ch. libr.. Beverly Hills Presbyn. Ch., 1974-90, ch. choir libr., 1976-90. Southwestern Library Assn. scholar 1965. Mem.: ALA, N.Mex. Libr. Assn., Pi Lambda Theta. Avocations: travel, reading. Office: Law Libr BCMDC 5800 Shelly Rd SW Albuquerque NM 87151

SNELLING, BARBARA W. retired state legislator; b. Fall River, Mass., Mar. 22, 1928; d. Frank Taylor and Hazel (Mitchell) Weil; m. Richard Arkwright Snelling, June 14, 1947 (dec. Aug. 1991); children: Jacqueline, Mark, Diane, Andrew. AB magna cum laude, Radcliffe Coll., 1950; D of Pub. Svc. (hon.), Norwich U., 1981; LLD (hon.), Middlebury Coll., 1997; LLD (hon.), St. Michaels Coll., 2002. Pres. Snelling and Kolb, Inc., 1982-95; lt. gov. State of Vt., 1993-97; mem. Vt. Senate, Montpelier, Vt., 1997—99, 2001 —02, ret., 2002. Bd. dir. U.S. Inst. Peace; mem. adv. bd. Westaff Inc. of Vt., 1997—. Trustee Radcliffe Coll., 1990-95; bd. dirs. Vt. Cmty. Found., 1986-94, Shelburne Mus., 1988-98; mem. Vt. Ednl. Partnerships, 1992—2000; v.p. for devel. and external affairs U. Vt., 1974-82; mem. Vt. State Bd. Edn., 1971-77; trustee Champlain Coll., 1971-74; mem. Vt. Alcohol and Drug Rehab. Commn., 1970-73, Shelburne Sch. Bd., 1958-73, chmn. 1965-73; mem. Vt. Edn. Adv. Coun., 1968-71, New Eng. Tchr. Edn. Adv. Com., 1968-70, Bd. of Sch. Dirs., Champlain Valley Union H.S., 1962-69, chmn. 1962-68, others; mem. New Eng. Bd. Dollars for Scholars, 1997-2002; bd. dirs. Vt. Program for Quality, 1997—2002; mem. Champlain Valley Area Health Edn. Coun., 1997—2002. Recipient Fanny G. Shaw award for Disting. Cmty. Svc., Burlington Cmty. Coun., 1972, Laymen's award Vt. Edn. Assn., 1965, Hope award MS Cmty. Champion, 1996, Philanthropy Day award Nat. Soc. Fundraising Execs., 1997, Susan B. Anthony award YWCA of Vt., 2001; named Vt. Citizen of Yr. Vt. State C. of C., 2002, Robert Skiff Cmty. Svc. award Lake Champlain C. of C., 2002, Vt. Children's Trust Found. award, 2002, Patricia S. Walton award Vt. Soc. for Pub. Adminstrn., 2002, AHEC Bi State Primary Care Assn. award, 2002, Vt. Alzheimer's Assn. award, 2002, Gold Heart, Am. Heart Assn., 2002. E-mail: ulfkiel@aol.com.

SNELLING, DIANE, state senator, artist; b. Phila., Mar. 18, 1952; BA, Radcliffe Coll., 1974; MA in Art, N.Y. U., 1994. Artist; senator State of Vt., 2002—. Lectr. arts and comm. Trinity Coll., Vt., 1994—97; bd. advisor Friends of U. Vt. Horticulture Farm, 2001—02. Mem. Hinesburg Planning Commn., 1984, Hinesburg Selectboard, 1985—91, Chittenden Affordable Housing Com., 1989—90; bd. trustees King St. Youth Ctr., 1992—95; adv. bd. Robert Hull Fleming Mus., 1994—2001. Republican. Office: 304 Piette Rd Hinesburg VT 05461

SNIDER, KAREN, human services administrator; b. Reading, Pa., Jan. 4, 1940; d. Howard Calvin and Margaret (Davis) Goeringer; m. Jack F. Snider, Sep. 2, 1961; children: Todd Jefferey, Kipp David. BA, Susquehanna U., Selinsgrove, Pa., 1961. Civil rights program dir. Office of Mental Health, Harrisburg, Pa., 1974-75; acting dep. sec., dir. field ops., spl. asst. to dep. Office of Mental REtardation, Harrisburg, 1975-82; exec. asst. to exec. dep. sec. Pa. Dept. Pub. Welfare, Harrisburg, 1982-83, area mgr. income maintenance, 1983-85, spl. asst. to sec., 1985-89, dep. sec. for mental health, 1989-91, sec., 1991-95; pvt. cons. Human Svcs. Innovations, Mechanicsburg, Pa., 1995-97; chief oper. officer Northwestern Human Svcs., Lafayette Hill, Pa., 1997—. Chair fin. campaign Pa. Alliance for Mentally Ill, Harrisburg, 1995-99. Recipient Human Svcs. award The Northwesetern Corp., 1990, Pres.'s award Pa. Assn. County Human Svcs. Adminstrs., 1993, Pres.'s award Domestic Rels. Assn. Pa., 1993, Outstanding Pub. Svc. award Assn. for Retarded Citizens Pa., 1994, Leadership award Shippensburg State U., 1994, Outstanding Leadership award Pa. Assn. Residences for People with Mental Retardation, 1994, others. Avocations: gardening, interior design. Home: 20 Manor Dr Mechanicsburg PA 17055-6133

SNIDER, MARIE ANNA, syndicated columnist; b. Croghan, N.Y., Aug. 9, 1927; d. Nicholas and Dorothy (Moser) Gingerich; m. Howard Mervin, Nov. 27, 1954; children: Vada Marie, Conrad Howard. BS, Goshen Coll., 1949; M in Religious Edn., Mennonite Bibl. Sem., 1957; MS, Kans. State U., 1980. High sch. tchr. Rockway Collegiate, Kitchener, Ont., Can., 1949-53; free-lance writer, 1953-54; pub. rels. Goshen Coll., Ind., 1955-57; free-lance writer, homemaker, 1957-67; info. editor Prairie View, Inc., Newton, Kans., 1967-76, dir., pub. info. & edn., 1976-85, dir. communications, 1985-91; freelance writer, columnist North Newton, 1991—; syndicated columnist "This Side of 60", 1992—. Bd. dirs. Health Systems Agy. of S.E. Kans., 1981-86, v.p., 1986-87; workshop presenter Nat. Coun. of Community Mental Health Ctrs., Atlanta, 1980, N.Y., 1982, 89, Miami, 1987. Editor: Media and Terrorism--The Psychological Impact, 1976; columnist: This Side of 60. Pres. City Council, N Newton, 1977-79, pres. 1980. Recipient 1st Pl. MacEachern award Assn. of Hosp. Pub. Rels., 1981, 1st Pl. Media award Nat. Coun. Community Mental Health Ctrs., 1977, 84, runner-up Pub. Rels. award Nat. Assn. Pvt. Psychiat. Hosps., 1980. Mem. Nat. Soc. Newspaper Columnists. Democrat. Avocations: research on role of women in american comics (speaker and media interviews on this topic), empowerment in aging. Home and Office: PO Box 332 North Newton KS 67117-0332 E-mail: thisside60@aol.com.

SNIDER, PATRICIA STAPLETON, assistant principal; b. Yonkers, N.Y., Apr. 7, 1951; d. Herbert William and Ruth Thomson Stapleton; m. Craig Stephen Snider, Mar. 12, 1977; 1 child, Ian McAfee. MusB in Music Edn., Converse Coll., Spartanburg, S.C., 1973; MEd in Adminstrn. and Supervision, Clemson U., 1978. Cert. secondary music tchr. S.C., 2003, secondary sch. prin. S.C., 2003. Choral dir. Easley (S.C.) HS, 1973—2000; asst. prin. Gettys Mid. Sch., Easley, SC, 2000—. Dir. music Easley First United Meth. Ch., 1977—2002; sch. dist. of Pickens County lead tchr. in music, Easley, SC, 1989—90; tchr. cadet tchr. Easley HS, 1989—2000, musical dir. play prodns., 1990—2000. Recipient Pickens County Young Careerist award, 1980, Golden Apple award, WYFF TV, 1994, Cadet Tchr. award, SC. Ctr. for Tchr. Recruitment, 1990. Mem.: ASCD, S.C. Music Educator's Assn. (choral divsn. pres. 1997—99), S.C. Mid. Sch. Assn., Nat. Assn. of Secondary Sch. Prins., Phi Delta Kappa. Methodist. Avocations: walking, lighthouse enthusiast, travel, singing. Office: Gettys Middle Sch 105 Stewart Dr Easley SC 29640

SNIDER, STACEY, film company executive; b. Phila., Penn., Apr. 29, 1961; m. Gary Jones; children: Katie, Natalie. BA, U. of Penn., 1982; JD, U. of Calif. at Los Angeles, Sch. of Law, 1985. Dir. of development Guber-Peters Entertainment Co., 1986—90, exec. v.p., 1990—92; pres. prodn. TriStar Pictures, 1992-96; co-pres. prodn. Universal Pictures, Universal City, Calif., 1996-98, head prodn., 1998, pres. prodn., 1998—99, co-chmn., 1999, chmn., 1999—. Bd. dirs. Am. Film Inst. Bd. dirs. Spl. Olympics of So. Calif.; bd. trustees Art Ctr. Coll. of Design, Pasadena, Calif. Recipient Dorothy and Sherrill C. Corwin Human Rels. Award, Am. Jewish Com., 2003. Office: Universal Pictures 100 Universal City Plz Universal City CA 91608-1002

SNIDER, VIRGINIA L. antitrust consultant; b. Chgo., July 17, 1946; d. Edwin Gaines and Sue (Kemmer) Lansford; m. L. Britt Snider, Aug. 24, 1974; 1 child, Britt Arnold. BA, Wash. State U., Pullman, 1971. Merger analyst U.S. Fed. Trade Commn., Washington, 1973-89, spl. projects dir., 1989-94; antitrust cons. Clifford Chance US LLP, N.Y.C. and Washington, 1994—2003; antitrust conts. Weil, Gotshal & Manges LLP, NYCand Washington, 2003—. Co-author of U.S. merger guidelines for U.S. Govt., 1992; contbr. articles to profl. jours. Mem. bd. visitors Washington Episcopal Sch., 1988—, founding trustee, 1986. Recipient Disting. Svc. award U.S. Govt., 1994. Episcopalian. Office: Weil Gotshal & Manges 1501 K St NW Washington DC 20006

SNIFFEN, FRANCES P. artist; d. Esther Wade; m. Richard Sniffen; children: William, Kevin, Jeffrey, John, Caroline. BFA, Corcoran Coll. Art and Design, 1996. Resident artist Arlington Arts Ctr., Arlington, Va., 2001—, tchr. art summer workshop; studio Millennium Art Co., Washington, 2003. Mem. women's com. Nat. Mus. Women in Arts, Washington, 2001—. Author (with Caroline Sniffen): Coloring Shadows, 1994 (Dorothy Tabak Meml. award NAWA, 2002); exhibitions include Artscape 97, Balt., Md., 1997, WPA Space, Washington, 1998, Bristol (RI) Art Mus., 2001, The DCCA, Wilmington, Del., 2002, Russian Embassy Cultural Ctr., Washington, 2002, Attleboro (Mass.) Mus., 2002, IASG, 2002, Tsinghua U., Bejing, China, Gallery K, Washington, 2002, Biennale Internazionale Dell'Arte Contemporanea Citta di Firenze, 2003, one-woman shows include Gallery K, Wash., 2003, mentioned in critical review by John Blee, Art Critics Rev., Georgetowner Newspaper, 2003. Mem. gala com. Imperial Collections, State Hermitage Mus. for Nat. Mus. Women in the Arts, Washington, 2003; vol. White House, Washington, 1992—93; mem. art com., event chmn. Hospitality Info. Svc. Meridian House Internat., Washington, 1986—; mem. women's com., event chair Nat. Symphony Orch. Kennedy Ctr., Washington, 1986—; women's bd. exec. vol. Georgetown U. Hosp., Washington, 1988—2002. Mem.: Nat. Assn. Women Artists, Inc. (juried membership, N.Y.C.). Avocations: creative writing, music, sports, politics, nutrition.

SNIPES, MIGNONNE ELVIRA, academic administrator; b. NYC, Nov. 23, 1968; d. Johnny and Gloria Morris Snipes. BS in Polit. Sci., Tuskegee U., Ala., 1991; MDiv, Hood Theol. Sem., Salisbury, N.C., 1997. Grad. asst. Livingstone Coll., Salisbury, 1994—97, coll. skills instr., 1995—97, dir. female hons. hall, 1994—97, dir. programs, 1995—97, acting dir. residence life, 1997—99, dir. residence life, 1999—2001, assoc. v.p. for student affairs, 2001—. Grad. advisor Alpha Kappa Alpha, Salisbury, 2001—; founder, coord. Livingstone Coll. Student Leadership Program, 1996—; student affairs subcom. mem. Livingstone Coll., 1994—. Participant Leadership Rowan, Salisbury, 2000—01, Bridges, Chapel Hill, NC, 2001—02, Summer Inst. for Women, Bryn Mawr, Pa., 2003; bd. dirs. Adolescent Family and Enrichment Coun., 2001—. Mem.: Nat. Assn. Student Affairs Profls., Alpha Kappa Alpha. African Methodist Episcopal. Avocations: reading, travel, public speaking. Home: PO Box 181 Salisbury NC 28145 Office: Livingstone Coll 701 W Monroe St Salisbury NC 28144 Office Phone: 704-216-6163. Business E-Mail: msnipes@livingstone.edu.

SNIVELY, CAROL A. social worker, educator; b. Bellaire, Ohio, Dec. 12, 1962; d. William Alexander and Teresa Marie Snively. BA, Capital U., Columbus, Ohio, 1985; MA, Norwich U., Montpelier, Vt, 1986; MSW, Ohio State U., 1996, PhD, 2002. LCSW Ohio, 2000. Art therapist Ctrl. Ohio Psychiatric Hosp., Columbus, Ohio, 1986—89, Wesley Health Ctr., Riverside Meth. Hosps., Columbus, 1986—90; treatment specialist Riverside Recovery Ctr. for Youth Choices, Columbus, 1990—94; family life specialist Buckeye Ranch, Inc., Grove City, Ohio, 1994—99; adj. faculty Columbus (Ohio) State C.C., 1994—98; asst. prof. U. Mo. Sch. Social Work, Columbia, Mo., 2000—. Adv. bd. mem. Prism, Columbia, Mo., 2000—03; steering com. Mid-Missouri/Columbia Lesbian-Gay-Bisexual-Transgender Coalition, Columbia, Mo., 2003—; adv. bd. mem. The McCambridge Ctr. for Women, Columbia, Mo. Recipient Catalyst award, 2003. Fellow: U. of Mo.-Columbia's Ctr. for Family Policy & Rsch.; mem.: NASW, Mo. Art Therapy Assn., Am. Art Therapy Assn., Assn. for Cmty. Orgn. and Social Adminstrn., Inter-University Consortium for Internat. Social Devel., Soc. for Social Work Rsch., Coun. on Social Work Edn. Unitarian Universalist. Avocations: photography, travel. Office: U Mo-Columbia Sch Social Work 702 Clark Hall Columbia MO 65211-4470 E-mail: snivelyc@missouri.edu.

SNODDERLY, LOUISE DAVIS, librarian; b. Polk County, Oreg., Feb. 1, 1925; d. Charles Benjamin Franklin and Grace L. (Cassady) Davis; m. Charles Hugh Snodderly, May 19, 1949; 1 son, Lynn Jerome. B.S., E. Tenn. State U., 1946; M.S., U. Tenn., 1962, postgrad., 1979, 82. Tchr., girls' coach Rush Strong High Sch., Strawberry Plains, Tenn., 1946-49, librarian, 1954-62; tchr., girls' coach Cosby High Sch., Tenn., 1949-50; tchr., librarian Maury High Sch., Dandridge, Tenn., 1951-54; cataloger City of Knoxville, Tenn., 1962-67; periodicals librarian Carson-Newman Coll., Jefferson City, Tenn., 1967-90; cons. Jefferson County Librarians, Tenn., 1976— . Sch. commr. Jefferson County, 1976— ; com. woman Nat. Fedn. Republican Women, Jefferson County, 1976— . Mem. ALA, Southeastern Library Assn., Tenn. Library Assn., Am. Sch. Bd. Assn., Tenn. Sch. Bd. Assn., PTA, Women's Faculty Club, Les Aimes Club, Order Ea. Star, Pi Lambda Theta. Baptist. Home: 2131 W Highway 11E Strawberry Plains TN 37871-3556

SNODGRASS, LYNN, small business owner, former state legislator; married; children: Jenne, Megan. BS in Elem. Edn., Oreg. State U., 1973; degree, Portland State U., 1975. Owner Drake's 7 Dees Nursery & Landscape Co., Oreg.; mem. Oreg. Ho. of Reps., 1995—2000; dep. majority leader, 1995-97; majority leader, 1997—2000; speaker of the house Oregon House of Reps, Salem, 1998—2000. Mem. Damascus (Oreg.) Sch. Dist. Budget Com., 1985-88, Damascus Sch. Bd., 1991-94; mem. Oreg. Ho. of Reps. Human Resources and Edn. Com. (Edn. sub-com.), 1995-97, Labor Com., 1995-97, Commerce Com. (Bus. sub-com.), 1995-97, Children and Families Com., 1995-97, Emergency Bd. Com. (Edn. sub-com.), 1995-97, Interim Edn. Com., 1995-97, Legis. Adminstrn. Com., 1995—, Rules and Election Com., 1997—. Mem., past pres. Mt. Hood Med. Ctr. Found.; bd. dirs. Specialized Housing, Inc., Metro Home Builder; mem. Good Shepherd Cmty. Ch.; tchr. Jr. Achievement; classroom vol. Avocations: racquetball, reading, singing, camping, cooking. Fax: 503-986-1347.

SNOW, KIMBERLEY, editor, writer; b. Greenwood, S.C., Nov. 10, 1939; d. Kimberly and Louise (Hodges) Hartzog; m. Barry Spacks, Feb. 25, 1987; children: Kimberley Harrison, Simms Teramoto. PhD, U. Ky., 1979. Tchr. U. Calif., Santa Barbara, 1980—; editor Chagdud Gonpa Found., Junction City, Calif., 1990—. Author: Writing Yourself Home, 1990, Keys to the Open Gate, 1994, In Buddha's Kitchen, 2003, (play) Multiple, 1986 (Jacksonville U. Ann. Playwrights award 1987). Vol. Dawn Hospice, Weaverville, Conn., 1995—. Buddhist. Avocation: setting up web sites for nonprofit organizations. Home: 1111 Bath St Santa Barbara CA 93101-3609

SNOW, LINDA SUE, family educator, consumer sciences educator, secondary school educator; b. Everett, Ala., Nov. 15, 1958; d. Loren Dean and Helen V. Cooper; m. James Robert Snow; children: Kevin, Bradley. BS in Home Econs. Edn., Messiah Coll., Grantham, Pa., 1980; MEd in Curriculum and Instrn., Gannon U., Erie, Pa., 2002. Tchr./Dept. chair Everett (Pa.) Area HS, 1982—2002. Mem. Everett Area Renaissance Found., Everett, Pa.; Relay for Life. Mem.: NEA, Pa. State Edn. Assn., Everett Area Alumni Assn. Avocation: travel. Home: 1210 French Creek Rd Everett PA 15537 Office: Everett Area High Sch One Renaissance Cir Everett PA 15537 Personal E-mail: jlsnow@nb.net. Business E-Mail: lsnow@everett.k12.pa.us.

SNOW, MARINA SEXTON, writer; b. Boston, Apr. 9, 1937; d. Charles Ernest Snow and Katherine Alice Townsend; m. Richard DeVere Horton, 1958 (div. 1968); children: Heather Kertchem, James Horton; m. Charles A. Washburn, 1978 (div. 1979). BA, U. Iowa, 1958; MA in Speech Pathology, N.Mex. State U., 1967; MA in Librarianship, San Jose State U., 1976; MA in Theatre Arts, Calif. State U., Sacramento, 1979. Cert. clin. competence Am. Speech and Hearing Assn. Tchr. ESL Inst. Colombo-Americano, Cali, Colombia, 1958-59; tchr. Las Cruces (N.Mex.) Pub. Schs., 1964-66; speech therapist Sutter County Schs., Yuba City, Calif., 1967-72; reference libr. Calif. State U., Sacramento, 1976-95. Author: (novels) The Walking Wounded, 2001 (Best First Novel of 2001-2002 award Bay Area Ind. Pub. Assn., 2001), Look No Further, 2004, (plays) Apricot Coffee, Alkali Flat, (short stories) The Black Iris, 1999; contbr. articles to profl. jours. Pres. Alkali Flat Neighborhood Assn., Sacramento, 1987—94. Mem.: Calif. Writer's Club, Sacramento Old City Assn. Avocations: theater, historic preservation, gardening.

SNOW, REBECCA, lawyer; b. Boulder City, Nev., Dec. 7, 1960; BA summa cum laude, Brigham Young U., 1983; JD cum laude, Harvard U., 1986. Bar: Nev. 1986, D.C. 1987. Legis. aide U.S. Dept. Interior Office Legis. Counsel, Washington, 1982, 83; ptnr. Covington & Burling, Washington, 1994—. Co-author: Superfund Law and Procedure, 1992. Office: Covington & Burling PO Box 7566 1201 Pennsylvania Ave NW Washington DC 20044-7566

SNOW, SANDRA INEZ, mortgage company executive; b. Detroit, Aug. 8, 1960; d. Teddy and Phyllis B. (Marlowe) Rowland; children: Jason P., Shannon B. Comml. lending diploma, Am. Inst. of Banking, 1987; AS cum laude, Oakland Cmty. Coll., 1990. Credit analyst Huntington Banks of Mich., Troy, 1984-93; loan officer The Huntington Mortgage Co., Troy, 1992-93; v.p. Suburban Mortgage Corp., Rochester Hills, Mich., 1993-94; pres., CEO The Mortgage Store, Inc., Clarkston, Mich., 1994—. Fund raiser Easter Seals, Clinton Twp., 1994. Named among Top 10 Women Owned Businesses, Dun & Bradstreet and Entrepreneur Mag., 1998. Mem. NAFE, Womens Coun. of Realtors (assoc. mem., mem. state chpt.), Profl. Assn. Svcs. (South Oakland bd. realtors), Davisburg Rotary. Republican. Avocations: boating, exercise, camping. Office: Mortgage Store Inc 5896 Dixie Hwy Clarkston MI 48346-3358

SNOW, SUE, principal; Math. tchr. Carrollton (Ga.) Jr. High Sch.; curriculum dir. Rockdale County Pub. Schs., Conyers, Ga.; prin. Conyers Mid. Sch. Named Ga. State Math. Tchr. of Yr., 1992.

SNOWDEN, BERNICE RIVES, former construction company executive; b. Houston, Mar. 21, 1923; d. Charles Samuel and Annie Pearl (Rorex) Rives; m. Walter G. Snowden; 1 child. Grad., Smalley Comml. Coll., 1941; student, U. Houston, 1965. With Houston Pipe Line Co., 1944-45; clk.-typist Charles G. Heyne & Co., Inc., Houston, 1951-53, payroll asst., 1953-56, sec. to pres., also office mgr., 1956-62, sec. to pres., also controller, 1962-70, sec.-treas., 1970-77, CFO, also dir. Mem. Women in Constrn., Nat. Assn. Women in Constrn. (past pres.), San Leon C. of C., Lord and Ladies Dance Club. Methodist. Home: 6611 Kury Ln Houston TX 77008-5101

SNOWDEN, RUTH, artist, educator, executive secretary; b. Quincy, Ill., Apr. 29, 1939; d. Emil G. and Edith M. Pfaffe; m. Howard L. Snowden; children: Jim, David, Sam, Amy. BS, Quincy U., 1964, BFA, 1989; MFA, U. So. Ill., 1991. Math. tchr. Notre Dame H.S., Quincy, 1964-67; math. lectr. Quincy U., 1974-83; legal sec. Snowden & Snowden Attys., Quincy, 1983—. Curator Significant Arch. in Quincy, Bell Tel., Chgo., 1986; mem. multi-arts panel Ill. Arts Coun., Chgo., 1986-89; art lectr. Quincy U., 1994—. Artist, editor: Visualizing Revelation, 1993; artist: Artists of Illinois, 1995, Quincy Women, 1838-1996, 1996; exhbns. include Biblical Arts Ctr., Dallas, The Michael Stone Collection Gallery, Washington, Art and The Law at Kennedy Galleries, N.Y.C., Loyola Law Sch., L.A., Minn. Mus. Am. Art, St. Paul, State of Ill. Ctr., Chgo., Oak Knoll, St. Louis, Overland Park, Kans. Bd. dirs. YMCA and YWCA, Quincy, 1978-96, Quincy Mus., 1984; Adams County campaign coord. U.S. Senator Dick Durbin, Quincy, 1980. Mem. Quincy Art Ctr. (pres. 1984-86, chair exhbn. com. 1995-96, adv. bd.). Democrat. Lutheran. Avocations: international travel, bible study.

SNOWDEN, RUTH O'DELL GILLESPIE, artist; b. Gary, W.Va., Apr. 16, 1926; d. Haynes Thornton and Blanche Beaula (Boling) Gillespie; m. Eugene Louis Snowden, Dec. 21, 1946; children: Wanda Snowden Ballard, Eugene III, Ronald, Marian Snowden Warren, Jeffry. RN, Natharith Coll., 1946; student Sch. Art, Transylvania U., 1983-84, U. Ky., 1985-89. RN. Painter, publicity chmn. Artists's Attic Inc., Lexington, Ky., 1988-89. Exhibited in group shows at U. Ky. Art Mus., Lexington, 1988, 5th Internat. Juried Exhibition Pastels, Nyack, N.Y., 1988, Small Paintings Nat., Ky. Highlands Mus., Ashland, 1988, The Appalachian Cen., U. Ky., 1988, Ft. Wayne (Ind.) Mus. Art, 1986, John Howard Sanden Nat. Artists Seminar, Washington, Nat. Artists' Seminar, Chgo., Huntington (W.Va.) Galleries, Nat. Nursing Art Exhibit, Meth. Med. Cen., Peoria, Ill., Chautauqua Art Assn. Galleries, N.Y., 1990, Central Bank gallery, Chataugua, 1990, Pastel & Chisel Acad. Fine Arts, 1990, Opera House Gallery, 1990, Sacramento Fine Arts Ctr., 1990, Ariel Gallery, Soho, N.Y., 1990, 91, Sumi-e Soc. Am., Inc., 1993, Watercolor Soc. Ala., 1994; represented in the Director of American Portrait Artists, Am. Portrait Soc., Huntington Harbour, Calif.; numerous local and nat. shows; in pvt. collections. Recipient Assn. Alliance award Am. Frame Co., 1993, Elizabeth Morris Genious award, 2002, Winsor Newton Merchandising award Summie Soc. Am., 2002. Mem. Oil Pastel Assn., Winchester Art Guild, Lexington Art League, Ky. Watercolor Assn. (Bluegrass regional dir. 1988, 89, 90, 91, 92), Ky. Guild Artists and Craftsmen, Inc., Northwest Pastel Soc., Degas Pastel Soc., Pen & Brush Soc. (Perfect Proportion award). Avocations: golfing, bowling. Home: 2800 Old Boonesboro Rd Winchester KY 40391-8805 Office: Artists Attic Inc Victorian Square 401 W Main St Lexington KY 40507-1640

SNOWE, OLYMPIA J. senator; b. Augusta, Maine, Feb. 21, 1947; d. George John and Georgia G. Bouchles; m. John McKernan. BA, U. Maine, 1969; LLD (hon.), U. Maine, Machias, 1982, U. Maine, Orono, 1981, Nasson Coll., 1981, Bowdoin Coll., 1982, Colby Coll., 1985; LHD (hon.), Thomas Coll., 1987; LLD (hon.), Suffolk U., 1994; DSc (hon.), Maine Maritime Acad., 1995; LLD (hon.), Colby Coll., 1996, U. New England, 1996; hon. degree, John F. Kennedy Sch. Govt. Harvard U., 1997; LLD (hon.), Bates Coll., 1998. Businesswoman; mem. Maine Ho. of Reps., 1973-76, Maine Senate, 1976-78, 96th-103d Congresses from 2d Maine Dist., 1979-94, mem. budget com., foreign affairs com., com. on aging, 1979-94; co-chair Congl. Caucus for Women's Issues, 1983-94; U.S. senator from Maine, 1995—. Mem. Senate com. armed svcs., 1997-2001, chair, seapower subcom., Senate com. on commerce, sci. and transp., 1995—, chair, oceans and fisheries subcom., Senate Budget com., 1995—, Senate com. small business, 1995—, Senate com. Fgn. Rels., 1995-97; counsel to asst. majority leader, 1997—, House Budget com., 1991-95, House Fgn. Affairs com., 1979-95, House Aging com. 1979-95, Congl. Caucus on Women's Issues 1979-84, co-chair 1983-95; dep. Repub. Whip, 1984-95; dep. Whip, 1996-97; corporator Mechanics Savs. Bank. Recipient Homeric award for adv. of human rights Chian Fedn., 1999, award for "Excelling in Standing up for Choice" Women's Campaign Fund, 1999, Spirit of Enterprise award U.S. Chamber of Commerce, 1997, 99, Woman of Yr. award Glamour Mag., 1998, David and Sherry Huber award for leadership on family planning, women's health issues, Family Planning Assn. of ME, 1998, Golden Bulldog award Watchdogs of the Treasury, Inc., Wash., 1994, 96, 98, Guardian of Small Business award Nat. Fedn. Indep. Bus., Wash., 1994, 96, 98, Responsible Choices award Planned Parenthood of Am., 1998, Spl. honor Nat. Assn. Devel. Orgns., 1998, Disting. Pub. Svc. award Am. Legion, Wash., 1998, Neil W. Allen award Greater Portland Chamber of Commerce, 1997, Legis. award for outstanding svc. to schs. and pub. librs., White Ho. Conf. on Libr. and Info. Svcs. Task Force, Wash., 1997, Pub. Leadership award, Nat. Breast Cancer Coalition, 1997, Magnificent Seven award Bus. & Profl. Women/USA, Wash., 1997, Deborah Morton award Westbrook Coll., Portland, ME, 1997, Golden Gavel award U.S. Senate Leadership, Wash., 1996, Nat. Osteoporosis Assn. award for leadership, Wash., 1996, award for leadership U.S. Distance Learning Assn., Crystal City, Va., 1996, award for leadership United Hellenic Am. Cong., 1995, William H. Natcher Disting. Svc. award Com. for Edn. Funding, 1995, Pub. Svc. award Am. Coll. Obstetricians and Gynecologists, 1995, Nat. Security Leadership award Am. Security Coun., Wash., 1994, Thomas Jefferson award Nat. Am. Wholesale Grocers Assn./Internat. Foodsvc. Distbrs. Assn., 1994, Grace Caucus award Citizens Against Govt. Waste, 1994, Sound Dollar award Free Cong. Found., 1994, Appreciation award Agrl. Stblzn. and Conservation Com. Somerset County chpt., Lifetime Achievement award Am. Hellenic Inst., 1994, Golden Heart award Assn. for Children for Enforcement of Support, ME chpt., 1993, Am. Social Health Assn. award on behalf of women's health issues, 1993, Medal of St. Andrew presented by His All Holiness Dimitrios Ecumenical Patriarch of Constantinople, Wash., 1990, Congl. Waste Watchers award Coalition to Reform the Davis-Bacon Act, 1990; named to "CQ 50" Congl. Quarterly Mag., Wash., 1999, Maine Women's Hall of Fame, 1999, Washingtonian Mag. 100 Most Powerful Women, 1997, All Maine Women Honor Soc. U. Maine, 1996, Deficit Reduction Honor Roll Concord Coalition, 1994, Honor Roll for dairy farmer support Associated Milk Prodrs., 1993; named Taxpayer's Hero for preventing govt. waste Citizens Against Govt. Waste, 1997, No Nonsense Am. Women, No Nonsense Coun. on Women's Issues, 1995, Congresswoman of Yr. Nat. Assn. for Transp. Alternatives, 1986; honored by Nat. Coalition for Osteoporosis and Related Bone Diseases, 1999, Edn. and Libr. Networks Coalition, 1997, Am. Assn. Univ. Pres., 1996, Pub. Policy Com. for Hellenic-Am. Women, 1995, Nat. Vietnam Vet. Coalition, 1994. Mem.: Philoptochos Soc. Republican. Greek Orthodox. Office: US Senate 154 Russell Senate Bldg Washington DC 20510-1903 E-mail: olympia@snowe.senate.gov.*

SNOW-SMITH, JOANNE INLOES, art history educator; b. Balt. d. Henry Williams and Elsie Orrick (Bagley) Snow; m. Robert Porter Smith (dec.); children: Joanne Tyndale Darby, Henry Webster Smith, III (dec.), Constance Elizabeth Bagley, Cynthia Porter Bloom, Robert Porter Smith, Jr.; m. Robert Edward Willstadter. BA, Goucher Coll.; MA, U. Ariz., 1968; PhD, UCLA, 1976. Prof. Italian Renaissance art history U. Wash., Seattle, 1981—. Program dir. of art history U. Wash. Rome Ctr. in Palazzo Pio, Rome, 1998, 2000, 2002. Author: (book) The Salvator Mundi of Leonardo da Vinci, 1982 (Internat. award 1983), The Primavera of Sandro Botticelli: A Neoplatonic Interpretaion, 1993; contbr. numerous articles to profl. jours. Recipient Rsch. Professorship to study in Oxford and London, U. Wash. Grad. Sch., 1986. Mem. Nat. Soc. Colonial Dames of Am., Renaissance Soc. of Am., Leonardo Soc./U. London, Coll. Art Assn., Seattle Art Mus., Met. Mus. Art, Ashmolean Mus. (Oxford, Eng.). Home: 1414 Shenandoah Dr E Seattle WA 98112-3730 Office: Univ Wash PO Box 353440 Seattle WA 98195-3440 E-mail: jsnowsmi@u.washington.edu.

SNYDER, ALLEGRA FULLER, dance educator; b. Chgo., Aug. 28, 1927; d. R. Buckminster and Anne (Hewlett) Fuller; m. Robert Snyder, June 30, 1951 (div. Apr. 1975, remarried Sept. 1980); children: Alexandra, Jaime. BA in Dance, Bennington Coll., 1951; MA in Dance, UCLA, 1967. Asst. to curator, dance archives Mus. Modern Art, N.Y.C., 1945-47; dancer Ballet Soc. of N.Y.C. Ballet Co., 1945-47; mem. office and prodn. staff Internat. Film Found., N.Y.C., 1950-52; editor, dance films Film News mag., N.Y.C., 1966-72; lectr. dance and film adv., dept. dance UCLA, 1967-73, chmn. dept. dance, 1974-80, 90-91, acting chair, spring 1985, chair of faculty Sch. of the Arts, 1989-91, prof. dance and dance ethnology, 1973-91, prof. emeritus, 1991—; pres. Buckminster Fuller Inst., Santa Barbara, Calif., chairwoman bd. dirs., 1984—. Vis. lectr. Calif. Inst. Arts, Valencia, 1972; co-dir. dance and TV workshop Am. Dance Festival, Conn. Coll., New London, 1973; dir. NEH summer seminar for coll. tchrs. Asian Performing Arts, 1978, 81; coord. Ethnic Arts Intercoll. Interdisciplinary Program, 1974-73, acting chmn., 1986; vis. prof. performance studies NYU, 1982-83; hon. vis. prof. U. Surrey, Guildford, Eng., 1983-84; cons. Thyodia Found., Salt Lake City, 1973-74; mem. dance adv. panel Nat. Endowment Arts, 1968-72, Calif. Arts Commn., 1974-91; mem. adv. screening com. Coun. Internat. Exch. of Scholars, 1979-82; mem. various panels NEH, 1979-85; core cons. for Dancing, Sta. WNET-TV, 1988—. Dir. film Baroque Dance 1625-1725, in 1977; co-dir. film Gods of Bali, 1952; dir. and wrote film Bayanihan, 1962 (named Best Folkloric Documentary at Bilboa Film Festival, winner Golden Eagle award); asst. dir. and asst. editor film The Bennington Story, 1952; created films Gestures of Sand, 1968, Reflections on Choreography, 1973, When the Fire Dances Between Two Poles, 1982; created film, video loop and text Celebration: A World of Art and Ritual, 1982-83; supr. post-prodn. film Erick Hawkins, 1964, in 1973. Also contbr. articles to profl. jours. and mags. Adv. com. Pacific Asia Mus., 1980-84, Festival of the Mask, Craft and Folk Art Mus., 1979-84; adv. panel Los Angeles Dance Currents II, Mus. Ctr. Dance Assn., 1974-75; bd. dirs. Council Grove Sch. III, Compton, Calif., 1976-81; apptd. mem. Adv. Dance Com., Pasadena (Calif.) Art Mus., 1970-71, Los Angeles Festival of Performing Arts com., Studio Watts, 1970; mem. Technology and Cultural Transformation com., UNESCO, 1977. Fulbright research fellow, 1983-84; grantee Nat. Endowment Arts, 1981, Nat. Endowment Humanities, 1977, 79, 81, UCLA, 1968, 77, 80, 82, 85; recipient Amer. Dance Guild Award for Outstanding Achievement in Dance, 1992. Mem. Am. Dance Therapy Assn., Congress on Rsch. in Dance (bd. dirs. 1970-76, chmn. 1975-77, nat. conf. chmn. 1972), Coun. Dance Adminstrs., Am. Dance Guild (chmn. com. awards 1972), Soc. for Ethnomusicology, Am. Anthrop. Assn., Am. Folklore Soc., Soc. Anthropology of Visual Comm., Soc. Humanistic Anthropology, Calif. Dance Educators Assn. (conf. chmn. 1972), L.A. Area Dance Alliance (adv. bd. 1978-84, selection com. Dance Kaleidoscope project 1979-81), Fulbright Alumni Assn. Home: 15313 Whitfield Ave Pacific Palisades CA 90272-2548 Office: Buckminster Fuller Inst 111 N Main St Sebastopol CA 95472-3448

SNYDER, ANDREA, performing arts association administrator; BS, The Am. U.; MA in Arts Mgmt., NYU. Asst. to dir. Dance Notation Bureau; assoc. adminstr. Cunningham Dance Found.; adminstr. of arts dance dept. NYU Tisch Sch.; booking agent Sheldon Soffer Mgmt.; exec. dir. Laura Dean Dancers & Musicians; asst. dir. Nat. Endowment for Arts Dance Program, 1987—93; dir. Nat. Initiative to Preserve Am.'s Dance, 1993—2000; pres., exec. dir. Dance/USA, Washington, 2000—. Adj. prof. The Am. U. Office: Dance USA 1156 15th St NW Washington DC 20005

SNYDER, BARBARA K. pediatrician, educator; MD, George Washington Univ., Washington, D.C., 1979. Diplomate Pediatrics Am. Bd. Pediat., 1985, Adolescent Medicine Am. Bd. Pediat., 1994, Am. Bd. Pediat., 2001. Intern Chidlren's Nat. Med. Ctr., Washington, 1979—80, resident in Pediatrics, 1980—82; fellow in Adolescent Medicine U. Rochester (N.Y.) Sch. of Medicine, 1986—88; chief divsn. Adolescent Medicine, dept. Pediatrics Robert Wood Johnson Med. Sch., New Brunswick, NJ, 1990—. Assoc. prof. Pediatrics Robert Wood Johnson Med. Sch., New Brunswick, NJ, 1994—, dir. Eating Disorders Program, Adolescent Medicine Program, 1990—. Office: U Medicine and Dentistry NJ-Robert Wood Johnson Med Sch Dept Pediats New Brunswick NJ 08903-0019

SNYDER, BARBARA ROYALTY, pharmaceutical executive; b. Kokomo, Ind., May 20, 1958; d. Donald Edgar and Alma Frances Snyder; life ptnr. Yvon Lauren. BA in Brit. Lit. & Composition magna cum laude, U. Evansville, 1980; MA in Am. Lit., Conn. State U., 1986. Med. writer Bristol-Myers Co., Evansville, Ind., 1980—88; mgr., med. writing Lorex Pharms., Skokie, Ill., 1988—94; dir. med. writing Proctor & Gamble Pharms., Mason, Ohio, 1994—. Treas. Tri-State Alliance, Evansville, 1984—86. Mem.: Drug Info. Assn., Am. Med. Writers Assn. (bd. of directors 2001—, pres. Ohio Valley chpt. 2001—02). Democrat. Avocations: fishing, gardening, painting. Office: Procter & Gamble Pharms 8700 Mason Montgomery Rd Mason OH 45040-9462 E-mail: snyder.br@pg.com.

SNYDER, CAROLYN ANN, education educator, librarian; b. Elgin, Nebr., Nov. 5, 1942; d. Ralph and Florence Wagner. Student, Nebr. Wesleyan U., 1960-61; BS cum laude, Kearney State Coll., 1964; MS in Librarianship, U. Denver, 1965. Asst. libr. sci. and tech. U. Nebr., Lincoln, 1965-67, asst. pub. svc. libr., 1967-68, 70-73; pers. libr. Ind. U. Librs., Bloomington, 1973-76, acting dean of univ. librs., 1980, 88-89, assoc. dean for pub. svcs., 1977-88, 89-91, interim devel. officer, 1989-91; adminstrv. army libr. Spl. Svcs. Agy., Europe, 1968-70; dean libr. affairs So. Ill. U., Carbondale, 1991-2000, prof., dir. found. rels., 2000—. Team leader Midwest Univs. Consortium for Internat. Activities-World Bank IX project to develop libr. system and implement automation U. Indonesia, Jakarta, 1984-86; libr. devel. cons. Inst. Tech. MARA/Midwest Univs. Consortium for Internat. Activities Program in Malaysia, 1985; ofcl. rep. EDUCAUSE, 1996-2000; mem. working group on scholarly comm. Nat. Commn. on Librs. and Info. Sci., 1998-2000. Editor Library and Other Academic Support Services for Distance Learning, 1997; contbr. chpt. to book and articles to profl. jours. Active Humane Assn. Jackson County, 1991—, Carbondale Pub. Libr. Friends, 1991—, Morris Libr. Friends, 1991—. Cooperative Rsch. grant Coun. on Libr. Resources, Washington, 1984. Mem. ALA (councilor 1985-89, Bogle Internat. Travel award 1988, H.W. Wilson Libr. Staff devel. grant 1981), Libr. Adminstrn./Mgmt. Assn. (pres. 1981-82), Com. on Instnl. Coop./Resource Sharing (chair 1987-91), Coalition for Networked Info. (So. Ill. U. at Carbondale rep. 1991-2000), Coun. Dirs. State Univ. Librs. in Ill. (chair 1992-93, 99-2000), Coun. on Libr. and Info. Resources Digital Leadership Inst. Steering Com. (Assn. Rsch. Librs. rep. 1998-2000), Ill. Assn. Coll. and Rsch. Librs. (chair Ill. Bd. Higher Edn. liaison com. 1993-94), Ill. Network (bd. dirs.), Ind. Libr. Assn. (chair coll./univ. divsn. 1982-83), U.S. Grant Assn. (bd. dirs. 1992—), Ill. Libr. Computer Sys. Orgn. (policy coun. 1992-95, 96-2000), Nat. Assn. State Univs. and Land-Grant Colls. (commn. on info. tech. and its distance learning and libr. bds. 1994-96), NetIllinois (bd. dirs. 1994-96), OCLC Users Coun. (elected rep. 1995-98), Big 12 Plus Libr. Consortium (chair 1997-98), Nat. Commn. on Librs. and Info. Sci. Working Group on Scholarly Comms., Assn. Rsch. Libr. (vis. program officer 2000—01). Avocations: antiques, theater, movies, reading. Office: So Ill U Ctrl Devel Carbondale IL 62901-6632 Office Phone: 618-453-1447.

SNYDER, CAROLYN L. SMITH, medical writing director; m. Mike Snyder; children: S, N. PhD, U. Pa, Phila., 1986. Sr. dir., med. writing Johnson & Johnson Pharm. R&D, Raritan, NJ, 1992—.

SNYDER, CLAIR A. state legislator; b. Boston, Oct. 6, 1924; divorced; 2 children. BS, N.H. Coll., Portsmouth, 1978; postgrad., U. N.H., Durham. Formerly acct. and bus. mgr.; now mem. N.H. Ho. of Reps. Bd. dirs. N.H. Sch. Bd. Assn., 1987—; trustee various trust funds; chmn. N.H. Sch. Bd. Ins. Trust, 1993-94. Mem. Bus. and Profl. Women. Office: NH House of Reps State Capitol Concord NH 03301

SNYDER, COLLEEN M. music educator; b. Sanger, Calif., Apr. 24, 1946; d. Tarance Smith and Loramae Hockett Magee; m. C. Ray Slape, Apr. 19, 1980; children: K. C. Simba-Torres, Isaac Slape; m. Arthur M. Snyder, Aug. 27, 1966 (div. 1970). BA, Stanford U., 1968, MA, MusD, 1975, D in Mus. Arts. Instr. Lower Columbia Coll., Longview, Wash., 1978—81, Kelso (Wash.) Unified Sch. Dist., 1981—89; dir. instrumental music Reedley (Calif.) Coll., 1989—. Conductor Kings Symphony Orch., Hanford, Calif., 1991—; asst. conductor Tulare County Symphony Orch., Visalia, Calif., 1992—; guest condr. Fresno-Madera County Honor Orch., San Luis Obispo County Honor Band, Tulare County Honor Band. Mem.: Calif. Orch. Dirs. Assn. (bd. dirs. 2000—, pres. 2004—).

SNYDER, DEBORAH SHUSMAN, literature educator, columnist, poet; b. Springfield, Mass., Jan. 11, 1949; d. Tevis and Mildred Shusman; m. Jeffrey Stuart Snyder; 1 child, Rachel Ma'ayon. BA cum laude, Univ. Hartford, W. Hartford, Conn., 1974; MFA, George Mason Univ., Fairfax, Va., 1989. Logistics analyst Raytheon Svc. Co., Arlington, Va., 1980—90; libr. asst. Mary Wash. Hosp., Fredricksburg, Va., 1990—98; tutor Germanna C.C., Fredricksburg, Va., 2000—01, inst. English, 2001—. Columnist (poet) Fredricksburg Ctr. for the Arts, Va., 2002—; columnist Stafford Sun News, Va., 2003—. Author: (poetry) to profl. jour. and anthologies, 1986—97 (1st place for poem); contbr. columns in newspapers. Avocations: reading, swimming, woodworking finishing/refinishing, family activities. Home: 8 Biscoe Ct Stafford VA 22556

SNYDER, ESTHER, food service executive; m. Harry (dec.); children: Guy, Rich. Founder, pres. In-N-Out Burger, Baldwin Park, Calif., 1948—. Office: In-N-Out Burger 13502 Hamburger Ln Baldwin Park CA 91706-5885

SNYDER, FRANCINE, psychotherapist, registered nurse, writer; b. Balt., Mar. 13, 1947; d. Jack and Naomi (Rapoport) S. AA, C.C. Balt., 1968; BA in Psychology, Antioch Coll. W, 1973; MA in MFCC, Azusa Pacific Coll., 1975; PhD in Clin. and Ednl. Psychology, Internat. Coll., 1981. RN, Hawaii; lic. marriage, family, and child counselor diplomate in psychotherapy counselor, Calif.; instr., Calif.; counselor, Calif.; credentialed cmty. coll. counselor, Calif., cmty. coll. instr. health, phys. care svcs., related techs., nursing and psychology; doctoral addictions counselor, cert. addiction specialist, cognitive behavioral therapist; endorsed domestic violence counselor 1, 2 & 3 Nat. Bd. Cognitive Behavioral Therapists. Staff and relief nurse Midway Hosp., L.A., 1972-77; counselor So. Calif. Counseling Ctr., L.A., 1972-77; counselor, exec. bd. mem., steering com. mem. Healing Ctr. for the Whole Person, Northridge, Calif., 1974-75; counselor The Family Home, North Hollywood, Calif., 1976; pvt. practice Beverly Hills, Calif., 1975-86; asst. had nurse St. Johns Mental Health Ctr., Santa Monica, Calif., 1977-79; counselor Calif. Family Study Ctr., Burbank, 1979-80; pvt. practice Kauai, Hawaii, 1986—; clin. dir., therapist Kauai YWCA Sex Abuse Treatment Program, Hawaii, 1989-90; clin. cons. Iniki Ohana Project, Kapaa, Hawaii, 1993. Student nurse Johns Hopkins Hosp., Balt., 1965-68; head and relief nurse, team leader, 1966-70; nurse Nix Meml. Hosp., San Antonio, Tex., 1970; staff nurse, team leader Cmty. Hosp, Chandler, Ariz.; cons. Slim Bionics Med. Group, L.A., 1974-75; instr. Pierce Coll., Woodland Hills, Calif., 1977, Saint Johns Med. Ctr., Santa Monica, Calif., 1977-79, Maple Ctr., Beverly Hills, Calif., 1979-80. Speaker in field. Mem. Am. Anorexia Nervosa/Bulimia Assn., Inc., Am. Mental Affiliates for Israel (exec. bd., head of allocations com.), Am. Assn. Marriage and Family Therapists (clin.), Internat. Platform Assn., Calif. Assn. Marriage and Family Therapists (clin.), Assn. for Humanistic Psychology, Children's Coalition for TV, Ctr. for the Healing Arts, Alliance for Survival, UCLA Alumni Assn.; cons. Help Anorexia, Inc., Performance Design Syss. Office: InnerVisions Change Tech PO Box 1303 Hanalei HI 96714-1303

SNYDER, HEATHER, social sciences educator; d. Arlene and Steven Snyder. BA, La Salle U., 1994; MA, John Jay Coll. Criminal Justice, CUNY, 1996; PhD, Fordham U., 2002. Adj. asst. prof., lectr. Lehman Coll., CUNY, Bronx, NY, 1997—2002; item writer Regents Coll., NY, 1999; adj. lectr., tchg. fellow Fordham U., Bronx, NY, 1999—2001; cons. Forward Face, N.Y.C., 2001—02; asst. prof. Edinboro U. Pa., 2002—. Presenter in field. Psychology team vol. Cleft Palate Clinic, Northwestern, Pa., 2003—. Scholar, John Jay Coll. Criminal Justice, 1994, Presdl. scholar, Fordham U., 1996—99; Pathways Partial scholar, Met. Life Ins., 1992—94. Mem.: APA, Soc. Rsch. Adolescence, Am. Psychol. Soc. Office: Edinboro U Pa Dept Psychology Edinboro PA 16444 E-mail: hsnyder@edinboro.edu.

SNYDER, HELEN DIANE, state senator; Project/event mgr.; Rep. senator dist. 15 N.Mex. State Senate. Mem. corps. and transp., Indian and cultural affairs coms. N.Mex. State Senate. Office: NMex State Senate State Capitol Mail Rm Dept Santa Fe NM 87503 Home: 7006 Elna Ct NE Albuquerque NM 87110-1408 E-mail: senate@state.nm.us.

SNYDER, JAN LOUISE, administrative aide; b. Warrington Twp., Pa., Sept. 15, 1935; d. Wilbert Adam and Alice (Myers) March; divorced; children: Steven Michael Krone, David Sylvan Snyder. Grad. H.S., Dover, Pa. Employment sec. personnel dept. stores divsn. McCrory Corp., York, 1966—94, receptionist exec. buying divsn., 1994—97; receptionist, switchboard operator human resources Healthsouth Rehab. Hosp., York, Pa., 1997-99; gen. office specialist, shared svcs. Dentsply Internat., 2002—. Active Northwestern region York Hosp. Aux., 1979—, mem. membership com. and administer II, 2002; active York Symphony Assn., 1990—, membership com., 1992—; active York chpt. Am. Cancer Soc. Am., 1990—, York Chorus, 1988-90; Dover Twp. Fire Co. Aux. for Women, 1975—, Harrisburg Jr. League Lectr. Series, 1980-95, York Jr. League Lectr. series, 1989-96, Messiah United Meth. Ch., 2003—.; womens aux. Johns Hopkins Hosp., 1999—; mem. Md. House and Garden Pilgrimage House Tours, 1968—. Mem. Am. Bus. Women's Assn. (pres. Colonial York charter chpt. 1980, mem. adv. bd. 1980-89), nat. Trust for Historic Preservation. Democrat. Avocations: traveling, music, educational lecturing series, flower and vegetable gardening. Home: 2823 Grandview Ave York PA 17404-3905

SNYDER, JEAN MACLEAN, lawyer; b. Chgo., Jan. 26, 1942; d. Norman Fitzroy and Jessie (Burns) Maclean; m. Joel Martin Snyder, Sept. 4, 1964; children: Jacob Samuel, Noah Scot. BA, U. Chgo., 1963, JD, 1979. Bar: Ill. 1979, U.S. Dist. Ct. (no. dist.) Ill. 1979, U.S. Ct. Appeals (7th cir.) 1981. Ptnr. D'Ancona & Pflaum, Chgo., 1979-92; prin. Law Office of Jean Maclean Snyder, Chgo., 1993-97, 2004—; trial counsel The MacArthur Justice Ctr. U. Chgo. Law Sch., 1997—2004; of counsel, 2004—. Contbr. articles to profl. jours. Mem.: Lawyers for the Creative Arts (bd. dirs. 1995—97), ACLU of Ill. (bd. dirs. 1996—99), ABA (mem. coun. on litigation sect. 1989—92, editor-in-chief Litigation mag. 1987—88, co-chair First Amendment and media litigation com. 1995—96, co-chair sect. litigation task force on gender, racial and ethnic bias 1998—2001, standing com. on strategic comms. 1996—2001). Office: The MacArthur Justice Ctr Univ of Chgo Law Sch 1111 E 60th St Chicago IL 60637-2776 Business E-Mail: jsnyder@law.uchicago.edu.

SNYDER, JUDITH LYNN, fund development consultant; b. Louisville, Apr. 8, 1950; d. William P. Snyder and Jean Gahlert (Schmidt) Stallings; m. Ivo Ronald Ware, Sr., May 20, 1978 (div. Sept. 1989); m. John Joseph Mason III, Dec. 22, 1991 (div. Aug. 1999). BA, Ind. U., 1972; M in Pub. Svc., Western Ky. U., 1974; postgrad., U. Louisville, 1978, 90-91. Cert. fund raising exec. Dir. fund raising & vol. rels. Big Brothers/Big Sisters of Kentuckiana, Louisville, 1983-85; from alumni rels. adminstrv. officer to dir. res. curriculum U. Louisville, 1985-92; dir. corp./found. rels. Defiance (Ohio) Coll., 1992-94, U. Toledo, 1994-96; cons. JSM Consulting Group, Inc., Canton, Ohio, 1996—. Cons. in field. Bd. dirs. David's House Compassion, Inc., 1995-96, bd. dirs. Women's Network, Ohio Assn. of Nonprofit Orgns. Mem. Nat. Soc. Fund Raising Execs. (bd. dirs., chair program greater Toledo chpt. 1994, treas. 1995-96, sec. bd. dirs. North Ctrl. Ohio chpg. 1996, membership chair, 1999), Ohio Coun. Fund Raising Execs., No. Ohio Planning Giving. Avocations: cross-stitch, flower gardening, basket weaving, photography, beach walking. Home and Office: 4130 Belden Ave SE Canton OH 44707-1663

SNYDER, KATHARINE A. social sciences educator, researcher; b. Balt, Mar. 11, 1970; d. Ray L. and Betty Ann Snyder. BA magna cum laude in psychology, W. Va. Wesleyan Coll., 1992; MS in applied exptl. psychology, Va. Poly. Inst. and State U., 1993, PhD in behavioral and exptl. neuropsychology, 1996. Instr. Va. Poly. Inst. and State U., 1992—96; vis. asst. prof. Southwestern Coll., Winfield, Kans., 1996—97; vis. assist. prof. Shenandoah U., 1997—98; asst. prof. Shepherd Coll., Martinsburg, Va., 1998—. Faculty rsch. supr. NSF grant; reviewer, mini-grant proposals Office of Assessment and Learning, 2001; rsch. cons. Buros Inst., 2002; vis. instr. Musselman HS, 2001; mem. assessment com. Shepherd Coll., mem. assessment task force, mem. curriculum and instr. com., faculty advisor, psychology club; stats. and rsch. cons. Contbr. articles to profl. jours., chapters to books; presenter (papers to profl. confs.). Recipient Undergraduate Rsch. award, W. Va. Psychological Assn., 1992; grantee Dalton Alliances, Inc., 2003—. Mem.: AAUW, W. Va. Acad. of Sci., Faculty for Undergraduate Neurosci. Soc., Cognitive Neuroscience Soc., Ea. Psychological Assn., Am. Psychological Assn., Consortium Computing in Small Colls., Alpha Lambda Delta, Omicron Delta Kappa, Phi Kappa Phi, Mortar Bd., Sigma Alpha Iota, Beta Beta Beta, Psi Chi. Methodist. Avocations: music, sewing, reading, sports.

SNYDER, KATHLEEN THERESA, state agency administrator; b. Balt., Oct. 8, 1951; children: Jay, Matt, Carrie. BS, U. Md., 1973; MS, Am. U., 1978. Info. specialist Prince George's Pub. Sch., 1981—84, exec. v.p. adv. coun., 1984—87; exec. v.p. Prince George's Md. Chamber, 1987—92; pres., CEO Alexandria (Va.) Chamber, 1992—99, Md. C. of C., 1999—. V.p. Va. Assn. C. of C., 1996—99; bd. mem. Am. C. of C. Execs., 2000—01; pres. Mo. Assn. Ch. Execs., 2003. Mem. Scholarship Fund Alexandria, 1994—99; founding bd. First Night Alexandria, 1994—99; chair employers adv. com. Alexandria Works, 1996—99. Named Chamber Exec. of Yr., Va. Assn. Chamber Execs., 1996, Bus. Woman of Yr., Alexandria Commn. on Women, 1996, Cert. Chamber Exec., Am. C. of C. Execs., 2000, Md. Top 100 Women, 2001, 2003; recipient Brotherhood/Sisterhood award, Nat. Conf. Christians and Jews Prince George's chpt., 1992. Office: Md C of C Ste 100 60 West St Annapolis MD 21401

SNYDER, LINDA ANN, editor; b. Pitts., Feb. 24, 1957; d. Arthur Anthony and Patricia Ann (Balzer) Krysinski; m. Christopher Lee Snyder, June 1, 1996. BFA, Carnegie Mellon U., 1979. Systems adminstr. Duncan, Lagnese & Assocs. (now known as Killam Assocs.), Pitts., 1979-86; editorial office supr. Materials Rsch. Soc., Pitts., 1986-94; monographs editor Air & Waste Mgmt. Assn., Pitts., 1994-95; mktg. specialist Killam Assocs., Warrendale, Pa., 1995-96; mng. editor Soc. of Automotive Engrs., Warrendale, Pa., 1996—. Freelance corr. Pitts. Post-Gazette, 1990-93. Named Jaycee of Quar., North Hills Jaycees, 1990. Republican. Roman Catholic. Avocations: photography, gardening, hiking, writing. Home: 210 Hillendale Rd Pittsburgh PA 15237-1804 Office: Soc of Automotive Engrs 400 Commonwealth Dr Warrendale PA 15096-0001 Office Phone: 724-772-4018. E-mail: lsnyder@sae.org.

SNYDER, LIZA, actress; b. Northampton, Mass., Mar. 20, 1968; Appeared in T.V. movie Race Against Time: The Search for Sarah, 1996; T.V. series Sirens, 1993, Jesse, 1998-2000, Yes, Dear, 2000-; T.V. guest appearance Chgo. Hope, 1996; Film appearance in Pay it Forward, 2001. Office: William Morris Agency One William Morris Pl Beverly Hills CA 90212

SNYDER, LUCY KARLA, lawyer, finance company executive; d. Maurice F. and Miriam E. Snyder. BS, Boston Coll., 1991; MBA, U. Mass., 1993; JD, Suffolk U., 2000, Wayne State U., 2002. Bar: Mich. Asst. investment analyst Liberty Mut. Ins. Co, Boston, 1993—94; fiscal analyst Exec. Office for Adminstrn. and Fin., Boston, 1994—94, pub. fin. mgr., 1994—96; dir. fin. Mich. Supreme Ct. - State Appellate Defenders Office, Detroit, 1997—99; jud. clk. Hon. Judge Conlin, Mich. Dist. Ct., Ann Arbor, 2002—02. Criminal appellate intern Mich. Supreme Ct. - State Appellate Defenders Office, Detroit, 2002—02. Author: (book) Govenor's Budget Recommendation, 1997, International Anethesiology Clinics, 2000. Exec. com. for state membership Mass. Med. Soc., Waltham, 2000—01, v.p. Suffolk County, Boston, 2000—01; pres. Mass. Med. Soc. - Alliance, Suffolk County, Boston, 2001—02. Recipient State Rep. for Mass., Nat. Conv. for the AMA (AMA) Alliance, Chgo., Ilinois, Mass. Med. Soc. - Alliance, 2001. Mem.: NAFE, AMA Alliance, Detroit Met. Bar Assn. Avocations: scuba diving, snorkeling. Home: 3977 S Michael Rd Ann Arbor MI 48103 Personal E-mail: Lucy.K.Snyder@bc.edu.

SNYDER, NADINE ELDORA, music educator; d. Clair Ernest and Eldora Irene Snyder. BA in Music, Moravian Coll., 1982; MS in Edn., Temple U., 1987. Cert. music tchr. N.J. Dept. Edn., 1982, music tchr. instrnl. I Pa. Dept. Edn., 1982, music tchr. instrn. II Pa. Dept. Edn., 1989. Music tchr. Voorhees H.S., Glen Gardner, NJ, 1982—83, Palisades Jr./Sr. H.S., Ottsville, Pa., 1983—84, Lehighton (Pa.) Area Schs., 1984—85; supr. Wee Care Nursery Sch., Palmerton, Pa., 1985—88; music tchr. Pleasant Valley Schs., Brodheadsville, Pa., 1988—, music dept. chair, 1992—. Mem. curriculum coun. Pleasant Valley Sch. Dist., Brodheadsville, 1992—, mem. prin. adv. coun., 2000—; pvt. music instr., Pa., 1980—; organist, choir dir. various chs., Allentown, Pa., 1983—93. Recipient Lioness award, Lehigh Twp. Lioness Club, 1994; Thursby scholar, Moravian Coll., 1979, 1980, 1981. Mem.: ASCD, Kimmel Ctr. for the Performing Arts, Am. Choral Dirs. Assn., State Theater Easton, Moravian Coll. Music Alliance, Monroe County Arts Coun., Monroe County Arts Coun., Pa. State Edn. Assn., Pa. Music Educators Assn., Music Educators Nat. Conf., Moravian Coll. Alumni Assn., Order Ea. Star (Gnaden Huetten chpt.), Phi Delta Kappa (Recognition award 2001). Democrat. Avocations: walking, reading, swimming, travel, drama/musicals. Office: Pleasant Valley Sch Dist School Ln Brodheadsville PA 18322 Office Phone: 570-402-1000 x3152.

SNYDER, PATRICIA, volunteer; b. Fox, Ark., Nov. 3, 1948; d. Burton Joseph and Mary Mottinger May; m. Neil N. Snyder III, May 4, 1968; 1 child, Neil N. IV. BS, U. Ark., 1971. Chmn. tours Officers' Wives Club, Heidelberg, Germany, 1981-82, pres., Frankfurt, 1982-83, Ft. Jackson, S.C., 1987-88, second v.p., Heidelberg, 1993-94, hon. v.p., Ft. Jackson, 1994-96; dental vol. ARC, Ft. Jackson, 1987-88, chpt. advisor, 1994-96, chmn. vols., Ft. Monroe, Va., 1996; publicity chmn. PTA, Frankfurt, 1990-91; Am. liaison Steuben-Schurz Damengruppe, Frankfurt, 1990-91; mem. bazaar com. Am. Women's Club, Frankfurt, 1990-92, pres., 1991-92; spl. events com. Heidelberg Bazaar, 1992-94; mem. Sch. Adv. Com., Heidelberg, 1992-94; chmn. Sr. Parents, Heidelberg, 1993-94; pres. Heidelberg 2000, 1993-94; chmn. family support group Soldier Support Inst., Ft. Jackson, 1994-96. Recipient Caroline Scott Harrison award Ft. Benjamin Harrison, Indpls., 1975, Scroll of Appreciation, 1st Pers. Command, Heidelberg, 1982, Scroll of Appreciation, U.S. Army V Corps, Frankfurt, 1992, Heidelberg Star, Heidelberg Cmty., 1994, Scroll of Appreciation, 411th Base Support Bn., Heidelberg, 1994, Cert. Appreciation, Heidelberg H.S., 1994, Soaring Eagle award U.S. Army Europe, Heidelberg, 1994, Outstanding Civilian Svc. medal U.S. Dept. Army, Ft. Monroe, 1996, Commdrs. award for pub. svc. U.S. Dept. Army, Ft. Jackson, 1996, Cert. Appreciation, U.S. Dept. Army, Washington, 1996. Republican. Episcopalian. Avocations: writing, reading, dogs.

SNYDER, PATRICIA DI BENEDETTO, theater director and administrator; BA in English and Speech Edn., SUNY, Albany, 1967; MA in Theater Arts, Syracuse U., 1967; PhD in Arts and Humanities, NYU, 1991. Tchr. English, speech and drama West Genesee Sr. High Sch., Camillus, N.Y., 1962-64; tchr. English and drama, chair humanities teaching team Chestnut Hill Mid. Sch., Liverpool, N.Y., 1964-66; grad. asst. Syracuse (N.Y.) U., 1966-67; instr. dept. theatre SUNY, Albany, 1967-74, spl. asst. to chancellor, adj. assoc. prof. dept. theatre, 1974-75, founder, producing dir. Empire State Youth Theatre Inst., 1975-92; exec. dir. Gov. Nelson A. Rockefeller Empire State Plz. Performing Arts Ctr. Corp., 1982-89; producing dir., CEO N.Y. State Theatre Inst. Corp., 1992—. Cons. Spanish and Portuguese Mins., Madrid and Lisbon, 1968, U.S. Office Edn. 1979, Spanish Min. Culture, 1982, Time Warner, Inc., 1991; mem. edn. bd. Saratoga Performing Arts Ctr., 1973; apptd. arts and humanities planning com. N.Y. State Edn. Dept., 1975; mem. arts task force on arts in edn. NEH, 1977; apptd. N.Y. State Edn. Commr.'s Adv. Coun., 1978; panelist U.S. Children;s Lit. Assn., 1978; del. UNESCO Conf., Sibenek, Yugoslavia, 1979; lectr. Syracuse U., 1988; mem. acad. coun. Richard Porter Leach Fund for Arts, 1989; adj. prof. theatre Russell Sage Coll., 1992.; lectr. and presenter in field. Prodr. (stage prodns.) The Wizard of Oz, 1977, Lancashire Lad, 1980, Sleeping Beauty, 1981, 83, 90, Handy Dandy, 1985, Rag Dolly, 1986, Aladdin, 1987, Hizzoner!, 1988, 89, Beauty and the Beast, 1991, Slow Dance on the Killing Ground, 1993 (Best dir. theatre N.E. Metroland for '94); exec. prodr. (CD) Atlantic Theatre, A Tale of Cinderella, 1995; stage and video dir. A Tale of Cinderella, 1995; contbr. articles to profl. jours. Guest fellow Hungaiarn Theatre Inst., 1970, USSR Min. Culture, 1970, 84; recipient Mayor's medal City of Milan, Italy, 1977, Spl. Recognition award John F. Kennedy Ctr. for Performing Arts, 1978, 81, Recognition award NATAS, 1986, Albany League Arts award, 1986, Spl. Recognition award N.Y. State Theatre Edn Assn., 1993, silver award Worldfest, 1996, cert. merit Chgo. Internat. Film Festival, 1996. Mem. Am. Theatre Assn. (commn. on theatre devel. 1976, Spl. Recognition citation 1973, 74, Jennie Heiden award 1985), Children's Theatre Assn. Am. (Zeta Phi Eta award 1972), League Am. Theatres and Prodrs., Soc. State Dirs. and Choreographers, Assn. Internat. du Theatre pour l'Enfants et al Jeunesse (del. 1968, 70, 74, 78, 79 congresses, exec. com. 1969, fundraiser 1972 conf., editor ofcl. report 1973, chair U.S. ctr. 1977), N.Y. Women in Film and TV, N.Y. League Profl. Theatre Women, U. Albany Alumni Assn. (Disting. Alumni award 1987), Cosmopolitan Club, Phi Delta Kappa. Home: 722 N Broadway Saratoga Springs NY 12866-1621 Office: NY State Theatre Inst PO Box 28 Troy NY 12181-0028

SNYDER, SUSAN LEACH, science educator, writer; b. Columbus, Ohio, Nov. 25, 1946; d. Russell and Helen Marie (Sharpe) Leach; m. James Floyd Snyder, June 18, 1988. BS in comprehensive sci. edn., Miami U., 1968; MS in entomology, U. Hawaii, 1970. Gen. and health sci. tchr. Columbus Pub. Schs., 1971-73; life, earth & physical sci. tchr. Upper Arlington (Ohio) Schs., 1975—2000. Author: The Ocean Environment, 1992, 96; co-author: Focus on Earth Science, 1987, 89, Merrill Earth Science, 1993, 95. Glencoe Earth Science, 1997, 99, 2002, The Air Around Us, 2002, The Changing Surface of Earth, 2002, The Water Planet, 2002; mem. author team: Science Interactions, 1993, 95, 98, Science Voyages, 2000, 2001, Glencoe Science, 2002, 2003, Integrated Science, 2003; contbr. articles to profl. jours. Trustee N.Am. Astrophys. Obs., Delaware, Ohio, 1983-97; pres. Consortium of Aquatic and Marine Educators Ohio, 1983-84; sec. Ohio chpt. Nat. Tchrs. of Yr., 1993-95; docent, vol. Conservancy of S.W. Fla. Mus. Natural History, 2000—. Named Outstanding Earth Sci. Tchr. of State of Ohio and East Cen Sect. Nat. Assn. Geology Tchrs., 1983, Ohio Tchr. of Yr. Ohio State Dept. Edn., 1987, Finalist Nat. Tchr. of Yr. Coun. of Chief State Sch. Officers, 1987; Pres. award for Excellence in Sci. and Math Teaching Nat. Sci. Tchrs. Assn., 1992, Outstanding Tchr. award Geological Soc. Am., 1992. Mem. Nat. Sci. Tchrs. Assn. (Exemplary Earth Sci. Teaching Team 1983, 84, 85, conf. workshop presenter 1985), Nat. Marine Educators Assn. (Nat. Outstanding Marine Sci. Tchr. 1984-85, bd. mem. 1984, hist. com. chair, 2000—, conf. workshop presenter 1983, 84, 86, 92), Great Lakes Educators of Aquatic and Marine Scis. Avocation: photography. Home: 1361 Marlyn Dr Columbus OH 43220-3973

SNYDER, VIRGINIA ANNE, gifted and talented educator; b. Dayton, Ohio, Jan. 27, 1948; d. Edwin Paul and Bernadette Helen Good; 1 child, Christiane Elizabeth Jenkins. BS in Elem. Edn., Kent State U., 1975, MA in English Lit., 2000; MS in Spl. Edn., U. Akron, 1986. Cert. profl. std. tchr. grades 1-8 Ohio, 1995, gifted edn. Ohio, 1986. First grade tchr. Springfield Local Schs., Akron, Ohio, 1975—86; fourth grade tchr. Hudson (Ohio) City Schs., 1986—90, tchr. gifted edn., 1990—94, dist. coord. gifted edn., 1994—. Author poetry. Recipient Hon. Mention, Local Poetry Contest, 1995; Jennings scholar, Jennings Granting Org., 1977. Mem.: ASCD, NAGC, Phi Delta Kappa. Democrat. Roman Catholic. Avocations: writing, reading. Home: 115 Ravenna St Hudson OH 44236 Office: Hudson High School 2500 Hudson-Aurora Rd Hudson OH 44236 Personal E-mail: snyderv@hudson.edu. E-mail: snyderv@hudson.edu.

SNYDER-HAUG, DIANE LESLIE, writer; b. La Crosse, Wis., Nov. 1, 1960; d. Leslie Edward and Carol Helen Snyder; m. Loren Michael Yunk, Aug. 5, 1978 (div. Feb. 1989); m. Robert Layton Haug Jr., Sept. 16, 1994. Typist Equifax Svcs., La Crosse, 1977—78; bookkeeper Midwestern Nat. Ins. Corp., La Crosse, 1978—80; sec. We. Wis. Tech. Coll., La Crosse, 1980—95; owner Grand Designs, Savannah, Ga., 1995—96; mgr. Molinaro Manor, St. Petersburg, Fla., 2000—03; antique dealer St. Petersburg, 1996—; author, 1989—. Author: Our Lady of Seven Sorrows and Other Stories, 2002, Antique and Vintage Clothing, 1997, Shiftings, 1993; contbr. articles to profl. jours. Recipient Preservationist of Yr., Preservation Alliance of La Crosse, 1991, Hometown Pride award, Midwest Living Mag., 1990, Disting. Activist award, NOW, 1989. Mem.: 4000 Found. (life; com. chair). Democrat. Avocations: gardening, antiques, reading, historic preservation. Home: 344 7th St N #2 Saint Petersburg FL 33701-2747*

SNYDERMAN, NANCY, surgeon, medical journalist; m. Doug Snyderman; 3 children. PhD in medicine, U. Nebr. Med. Sch. Cert. otolaryngology U. Pitts., UMDA. Resident in pediatrics and ear, nose, and throat surgery U. Pitts.; dir. head and neck surgery U. Ark. Med. Scis., 1983—87; surgical practice Calif. Pacific Med. Ctr., San Francisco, 1988—; med. corr. Good Morning Am., 1987—2003, 20/20, 1987—2003, ABC News, 1987—2003; v.p. med. affairs corp. staff Johnson & Johnson, 2003—. Contbr. to med. jour.; author: Dr. Nancy Snyderman's Guide to Good Health for Women Over Forty, Necessary Journeys, Girl in the Mirror: Raising Adolescent Daughters. Mem.: Am. Acad. of Otolaryngology Head and Neck Surgery (bd. dirs.). Achievements include reporting on med. topics affecting both men and women; traveled and reported extensively from Eastern and Western Europe, Saudi Arabia during Persian Gulf War, Russia, Somalia, Kosovo, Pakistan, and Afghanistan. Office: Calif Pacific Med Ctr 2100 Webster St #320 San Francisco CA 94115 Office Phone: 415-923-3319. Office Fax: 415-600-7890.*

SNYDERMAN, SELMA ELEANORE, pediatrician, educator; b. Phila., July 22, 1916; d. Harry Samuel and Rose (Koss) S.; m. Joseph Schein, Aug. 4, 1939; children: Roland M. H., Oliver Douglas. AB, U. Pa., 1937, MD, 1940. Diplomate Am. Bd. of Physican Nutrition Specialists, Am. Bd. Pediatrics. Intern Einstein Med. Ctr., Phila., 1940-42; resident Bellevue Hosp., N.Y.C., 1944-45; fellow NYU Med. Ctr., N.Y.C., 1945-46; from instr. to prof. pediat. NYU Sch. Medicine, N.Y.C., 1946—95; prof. emerita pediat., 1995—; assoc. prof. U. Tex. Med. Br., Galveston, 1952-53; attending physician Bellevue Hosp., 1947—; dir. Pediatric Metabolic Disease Ctr. Bellevue Med. Ctr., 1965-95; attending physician Tisch Hosp., N.Y.C., 1947-95; prof. human genetics and pediat., attending physician Mt. Sinai Med. Ctr., N.Y.C., 1995—, dir. Metabolic Disease Ctr., 1995—. Mem. nutrition study sect. NIH, Bethesda, Md., 1973-77. Contbr. numerous med. articles to profl. jours. Named career scientist Health Rsch. Coun., 1961-75. Fellow Am. Acad. Pediatrics (Borden award 1975); mem. Am. Inst. Nutrition, Am. Pediatric Soc., Soc. for Pediatric Rsch., Am. Soc. Clin. Nutrition, Soc. Inherited Metabolic Disorders (v.p. 1978, pres. 1979, bd. dirs. 1980-83), Soc. Parenteral and Enteral Nutrition, Soc. for Study of Inborn Errors of Metabolism, Phi Beta Kappa. Jewish. Avocations: gardening, orchid growing, reading. Office: Mount Sinai Med Ctr Dept Human Genetics Fifth Ave & 100th St New York NY 10029 E-mail: selma_snyderman@mssm.edu.

SO, CONNIE CHING, ethnic studies educator; b. Kowloon, Hong Kong, June 12, 1964; d. Ka Chick and Big Yin (Woo) So.; m. Brett Edward Eckelberg, Aug. 31, 1991; children: Han, Wen. BA, U. Wash., 1987; MPA, Princeton U., 1989; PhD, U. Calif., Berkeley, 2000. Reader U. Wash., Seattle, 1986-87; minority affairs advisor Princeton (N.J.) U., 1988-89; instr. U. Calif., Davis, 1991-92, Berkeley, 1989-93; lectr. U. Wash., Seattle, 1990—, dir. Am. ethnic studies internships, 1993-96, 97—. Cons. Wing Luke Asian Mus., Seattle, 1993—, Asian Am. Commn., Seattle, 1995-96, Wash. State Hist. Sites, Seattle, 1991-92, Nat. Com. on U.S. China Rels., N.Y.C., 1988; spkr. in field. Contbr. articles, essays to profl. publs. Advisor, asst. treas. Campaign Connections, Seattle, 1989; cons., panelist Asian Pacific Am. Leadership Conf., Seattle, 1995—; trustee N.W. Asian Am. Theater, Seattle, 1986-87; del. Wash. Dem. Com., Seattle, 1984. Fellow Alfred P. Sloan Found., 1985, U.S. Info. Agy., 1988, U. Calif.-Berkeley, 1989-95. Mem. Am. Studies Assn., Nat. Assn. Asian Am. Studies (co-chair conf. Seattle 1997), Orgn. Chinese Ams. (bd. dirs. 1998—, v.p. 1999, 2003). Democrat. Avocations: drawing, gourmet cooking, reading. Home: 3611 S Cloverdale St Seattle WA 98118-4529 Office: U Wash Am Ethnic Studies Seattle WA 98195 Office Phone: 206-543-3424. E-mail: ccso@u.washington.edu.

SOAVE, ROSEMARY, internist; b. N.Y.C., Jan. 23, 1949; BS, Fordham U., 1970; MD, Cornell Med. Coll., 1976. Diplomate Am. Bd. Internal Medicine, Subspecialty Bd. in Infectious Diseases. Intern, resident N.Y. Hosp., N.Y.C., 1976-79; chief med. resident Meml.-Sloan Kettering Cancer Ctr., N.Y.C., 1979-80; fellow infectious diseases N.Y. Hosp., N.Y.C., 1980-82, asst. prof. medicine, 1982-89, assoc. prof. medicine and pub. health, 1989—. Spkr. in field; mem. Nat. Insts. Allergy and Infectious Diseases-AIDS and Related Diseases Study Sect. Contbr. numerous articles to profl. jours., chpts. to books, reviews and abstracts to profl. jours. Recipient Mary Putnam Jacobi fellowship for rsch., 1981-82, Leopold Schepp Rsch. fellowship, 1983-84, Nat. Found. for Infectious Diseases Young Investigator Matching Grant award, 1984-85; NIH grantee, 1986-89, 83-86, 87-90, 99-00. Fellow ACP, Infectious Diseases Soc. Am.; mem. AAAS, Am. Fedn. Med. Rsch., N.Y. Acad. Scis., Am. Soc. for Microbiology, Harvey Soc., Sigma Xi. Office: NY Presbyn Hosp Weill Cornell Med Ctr Box 125 1300 York Ave New York NY 10021-4805

SOBEL, FAYE WALTON, elementary school educator; d. Richard Lee and Margaret Walton; m. Bryant Blain Goodloe, July 9, 1966 (div.); children: Jason Cameron, Elizabeth Blaine; m. Ronald Sobel, June 25, 1994. BS, Radford Coll., 1966; MS, Madison Coll., 1971. Cert. reading specialist, elem. sch. adminstr. Tchr. Nelson County Sch. Bd., Lovington, Va., 1966—68, Augusta County Sch. Bd., Fishersville, Va., 1968—71; reading specialist, asst. prin., parent rels. coord. Suffolk Pub. Sch. Bd., Va., 1972—. Mem.: Internat. Dyslexic Assn., Internat. Reading Assn., AAUW, Va. Ed. Assn., Nat. Ed. Assn., Am. Assn. of Univ. of Women, DAR, Phi Delta Kappa. Democrat. Presbyterian. Avocations: bridge, bowling, quilting, genealogy.

SOBER, DEBRA EVONNE, environmental services administrator; b. Oklahoma City, May 20, 1953; d. Donald E. and Zona E. (Taylor) Tillman; m. Gary L. Sober, May 24, 1980; children: Kara, Jeffrey, Kimberly, Riley Nicole. BS, Columbia Pacific U. Lic. water and wastewater operator; registered X-ray lab. technician; notary pub. Chmn. bd. PACE Corp., Austin, 1986—; gen. mgr. Envir-O-Spec, Inc., Austin, 1972-95; owner, pres. Environ. Tng., Inc., 1980—. Cons. B40-Gon PX-109, 1990—. Author numerous textbooks on water and wastewater treatment and operation. Founder ann. Just Fishin Show, Austin, 1989; bd. dirs. Austin Women's Soccer League, 1991-93; bd. dirs., founder Austin Amateur Soccer Assn., 1991; women's commr. Tex. State Soccer Assn. South, 1994-99, v.p., 1999— (Mem. Soccer Hall of Fame 1999); nat. cup commr. United States Soccer Fedn./U.S. Amateur Soccer Assn., Region III, 1996—. Mem. Nat. Environ. Tng. Assn., Tex. Water Utilities Assn. (chmn. pub. rels. 1981-85, safety chmn. 1987-88), Okla. Water and Pollution Control Assn., Am. Water Works Assn., Water Pollution Control Fedn., Am. Bus. Women's Assn., N.W. Adult Athletic Assn. (founder and dir. 1986), N.W. Austin Women's Basketball Assn. (founder and pres. 1986), N.W. Austin Women's Soccer

Assn. (founder and pres. 1986), Beta Sigma Phi. Baptist. Office: PO Box 200815 Austin TX 78720-0815 Home: 3080 S Lakeshore Drive Saint Joseph MI 49085

SOBERON, PRESENTACION ZABLAN, state bar administrator; b. Cabambangan, Bacolor, Pampanga, Philippines, Feb. 23, 1935; came to U.S., 1977; naturalized, 1984; d. Pioquinto Yalung and Lourdes (David) Zablan; m. Damaso Reyes Soberon, Apr. 2, 1961; children: Shirley, Sherman, Sidney, Sedwin. Office mgmt., stenography, typing cert., East Cen. Colls., Philippies, 1953; profl. sec. diploma, Internat. Corr. Schs., 1971; A in Mgmt. Supervision, Skyline and Diablo Coll., 1979, LaSalle Ext. U., 1980-82; AA, cert. in Mgmt. and Supervision, Diablo Valley Coll. With U.S. Fed. Svc. Naval Base, Subic Bay, Philippines, 22 yrs, clerical, stenography and secretarial positions, 1955-73, adminstrv. asst., 1973-77; secretarial positions Mt. Zion Hosp. and Med. Ctr., San Francisco, 1977, City Hall, Oakland, Calif., 1978; with State Bar Calif., San Francisco, 1978-79; secretarial positions gen. counsel divsn. and state bar ct. divsn., adminstrv. asst. fin. and ops. divsn., 1979-81; office mgr. sects. and coms. dept., profl. and pub. svcs., 1981-83; appointment adminstr. office of bar rels., 1983-86; adminstr. state bar sects. bus. law sect., estate planning, trust and probate law sect., labor and employment law sect., office of bar rels., 1986-89; adminstr. antitrust and trade regulation law sect., labor and employment law sect., workers' compensation sect., edn. and meeting svcs., 1989-96; adminstr. criminal law sect., 1996—; labor and law employment law sect., 1996—; internat. law sect., 1996—; workers' compensation sect., 1996—; edn. and meeting svcs., 1996-98; ret., 1998. Disc jockey, announcer Radio Sta. DZYZ, DZOR and DWHL, Philippines, 1966-77. Organizer Neighborhood Alert Program, South Catamaran Circle, Pittsburg, Calif., 1979-80. Recipient 13 commendation certs. and outstanding pers. monetary awards U.S. Fed. Svc., 1964-77, 20 Yr. U.S. Fed. Svc. cert., 1975, Nat. 1st prize award Nat. Inner Wheel Clubs Philippines, 1975, Kaiser Vol. Svc. Mem. NAFE, Am. Soc. Assn. Execs., N.Y.C. Ulongapo-Subic Bay Assn. Am. (Pitts. rep. 1982-87, bus. mgr. 1988-89, 1997-, bus. mgr., Ulongapo Assn. Am. 2003-2004, pub. rels. officer 1993-94), ULO NG APO Assn. in Am., Castillejos Assn. No. Calif., SRF Tigers No. Calif., lector, min. Our Lady Queen of the World Ch. Filipino Assn. (lector min.). Roman Catholic. Home: 207 South Catamaran Circle Pittsburg CA 94565-3613 Office: State Bar of Calif 180 Howard St San Francisco CA 94105-1639

SOBKOWICZ, HANNA MARIA, neurology researcher; b. Warsaw, Jan. 1, 1931; came to U.S., 1963; d. Stanislaw and Jadwiga (Ignaczak) S.; m. Jerzy E. Rose, Mar. 12, 1972. BA, Girls State Lyceum, Gilwice, Poland, 1949; M.D, Med. Acad., Warsaw, 1954, PhD, 1962. Intern. 1st Internal Med. Clinic Med. Acad., Warsaw, 1954-55; resident 1st Internal Med. Clinic, Med. Acad., Warsaw, 1955-59, Neurol. Clinic, Med. Acad., 1959, jr. asst., 1959-61, sr. asst., 1961-63; research fellow neurology Mt. Sinai Hosp., N.Y.C., 1963-65; Nat. Multiple Sclerosis Soc. fellow Columbia U., N.Y.C., 1965-66; asst. prof. neurology U. Wis., Madison, 1966-72, assoc. prof., 1972-79, prof., 1979—. Contbr. articles to profl. jours. NIH research grantee, 1968— Mem. Internat. Brain Rsch. Orgn., Assn. Rsch. in Otolaryngology, Soc. Neurosci., Internat. Soc. Devel. Neurosci. (editorial bd. 1984—), Electron Microscopy Soc. Am. Office: U Wis Dept Neurology 1300 University Ave Madison WI 53706-1510 Office Phone: 608-262-7332.

SOBOL, ELISE SCHWARCZ, music educator; b. Chgo., June 12, 1951; d. Morton and Harriet Jacobsohn Schwarcz; m. Lawrence Paul Sobol, Aug. 21, 1977 (div. Sept. 1989); children: Marlon I., Aaron L. AA, Simon's Rock of Bard Coll., 1971; student, Mannes Coll. Music, 1971—73, Juillard Sch. Music, 1973—74; BA, New Sch. for Social Rsch., 1985; MA, Columbia U., 1987. Staff auditorium events, concerts, lectures Met. Mus. Art, 1972-73; sec. to pres. Harry Beall Mgmt. Inc., N.Y.C., 1973-76; sales rep. M.L. Falcone Pub. Rels., N.Y.C., 1976-77; asst. to pres. Jacques Leiser Artist Mgmt., N.Y.C., 1977-78; artist rep. Elise Sobol Mgmt. Inc., South Huntington, N.Y., 1978-82; tchr. music Nassau Boces Elem., 1988—; dir. L.I. Music Workshop, 1992—. Adj. prof. NYU Steinhardt Sch. Edn., 2000—; advisor arts and humanities Internat. Biog. Ctr., Cambridge, England; guest lectr. NYU, 1999, Hofstra, 2000; adj. faculty C.W. Post Coll. L.I. U., 2000; instr. SUNY, Farmingdale, 1993—98; music tchr. The Roslyn Middle Sch., 1987—88; dir. Early Musical Devel. Program for Children at Calling All Kids, South Huntington, 1981—86; tchr. young and adult piano students, 1968; piano adj. educator N.Y. State, 1993—. Musician: (piano concerts) Chamber Music series at U.S. Mil. Acad., N.Y./N.J. met. area concerts, Disting. Artists series, 2002—03, Met. Area Concerts, 2003, Am. Assn. Univ. Women Commentary and Concerts, 2003; author: An Attitude and Approach for Teaching Music to Special Learners, 2001; musician: (commentary and concert) A Gentlewoman's Pursuit, AAUW, 2003. Active Nassau Boces Elem. Program PTA, cultural arts coord., 1988—. Recipient Award of Honor, L.I. Very Spl. Arts Festival, 1993, Spl. Citation N.Y. State Assembly Ames Elem. Program, 1998, Spl. Recognition Nassau Music Educators Assn., 1999, 1st prize Dr. Martin Luther King Jr. Performing Arts Competition for Exceptional Students Nassau County, 1999, 2000, 01, Internat. Peace Prize, United Cultural Convention, May 2002, Town of Oyster Bay citation, 2002; nominated N.Y. Senate Women of Distinction Program, 2003; named Internat. Musician of Yr., 2004. Mem. NAFE, ASCD, AAUW, N.Y. State Sch. Music Assn. (chair music for spl. learners 1993—), Amnesty Internat., Music Educators Nat. Conf., Music Tchrs. Nat. Assn., Nassau Music Educators Assn., Nat. Mus. for Women, Met. Mus. of Art. Home: 21 Saxon St Melville NY 11747

SOBRERO, KATE (KATHRYN MICHELE SOBRERO), professional soccer player; b. Pontiac, Mich., Aug. 23, 1976; BA in Bus., U. Notre Dame, 1997. Mem. U.S. Nat. Women's Soccer Team, 1995—2001; profl. soccer player Boston Breakers (WUSA), 2001—03. Mem. U.S. Under-20 Nat. Team, 1993—. Named Defensive Most Valuable Player, NCAA Final Four, 1995. Achievements include on cover of Soccer Am. mag., 1995; member Notre Dame NCAA National Championship Team, 1995; member U.S. World Cup Championship Team, 1999; member U.S. Olympic Silver Medal Team, 2000. Office: US Soccer Fedn 1801-1811 S Prairie Ave Chicago IL 60616

SOBUS, KERSTIN MARYLOUISE, physician, physical therapist; b. Washington, June 16, 1960; d. Earl Francis and Dolores Jane (Gill) G.; m. Paul John Jr., March 10, 1990; children: Darlene Marie, Julieann Marie. BS in Phys. Therapy summa cum laude, U. N.D., 1981, MD, 1987. Clinic instr. pediatric physical therapy U.N.D. Sch. Medicine, Grand Forks, 1981-83; pediat. phys. theraist child evaluation-treatment program Med. Rehab. Ctr., Grand Forks, 1981-83, med. dir. program, 1997—; asst. prof. dept. pediatrics, asst. prof. dept. physical medicine and rehab. U. Ark. for Med. Scis., Little Rock, 1992-96; resident in internal medicine Sinai Hosp. Balt., 1987-88; resident in phys. medicine and rehab. Johns Hopkins program Sinai Hosp., Balt., 1988-91; pediatric rehab. clin. and rsch. fellow Alfred I. DuPont Inst., Wilmington, Del., 1991-92; pediatric pysiatrist Altru Health System, Grand Forks, 1997—. Contbr. articles to med. jours. Mem. Am. Acad. Cerebral Palsy and Devel. Medicine, Alpha Omega Alpha Honor Soc. Office: Altru Health Sys PO Box 6002 1300 S Columbia Rd Grand Forks ND 58201-4012 Home: 7451 S 25th St Grand Forks ND 58201

SOCHEN, JUNE, history educator; b. Chgo., Nov. 26, 1937; d. Sam and Ruth (Finkelstein) S. BA, U. Chgo., 1958; MA, Northwestern U., 1960, PhD, 1967. Project editor Chgo. Superior and Talented Student Project, 1959-60; high sch. tchr. English and history North Shore Country Day Sch., Winnetka, Ill., 1961-64; instr. history Northeastern Ill. U., 1964-67, asst. prof., 1967-69, assoc. prof., 1969-72, prof., 1972—. Author: The New Woman, 1971, Movers and Shakers, 1973, Herstory: A Woman's View of American History, 1975, 2d edit., 1981, Consecrate Every Day: The Public Lives of Jewish American Women, 1981, Enduring Values: Women in Popular Culture, 1987, Cafeteria America: New Identities in Contemporary Life, 1988, Mae West: She Who Laughs Lasts, 1992, From Mae to Madonna: Women Entertainers in 20th Century America, 1999; editor: The New Feminism in 20th Century America, 1972, Women's Comic Visions, 1991; contbr. articles to profl. jours. Nat. Endowment for Humanities grantee, 1971-72 Office: Northeastern Ill U 5500 N Saint Louis Ave Chicago IL 60625-4679 Office Phone: 773-442-5607. E-mail: j-sochen@neiu.edu.

SODEN, RUTH M. geriatrics nurse, educator; b. Tipton, Iowa, Nov. 29, 1940; d. Tony and Clarissa Arlene (Beall) Koreman; m. James D. Soden; children: Shannon, Scott, Suzan, Staci. AA, Highline Community Coll., Midway, Wash. Cert. in intravenous therapy. Charge nurse Wildwood Health Care Ctr., Puyallup, Wash.; admissions coord. Forestglen Nursing Ctr., Seattle, staff devel. dir.; charge nurse Green River Terrace Nursing Ctr., Auburn, Wash., Discovery Care Ctr., Hamilton, Mont.; nurse mgr. Tacoma Luth. Home; charge nurse and minimum data set coord. Discovery Care Ctr., Hamilton. Mem. Clover Park Tech. Coll., Tacoma. Mem. Nat. Gerontol. Nursing Assn. (practical nurse program adv. com.), Wash. State Nurses Assn., Assn. for Practitioners in Infection Control, Nat. Coun. on Family Rels., Phi Theta Kappa. Home: 157 West Hills Way Hamilton MT 59840-9316

SODETZ, CAROL JEAN, aquatic fitness educator; b. Chgo., Aug. 24, 1943; d. Frank John Shamel and Stella Mary Wozniak; m. Frank Jack Sodetz Jr., Aug. 24, 1963; children: Lynn, Frank, Diane. Student, Fenger Jr. Coll., 1962—63, Montgomery Coll., 1999—. Typist Fed. Sign & Signal, Blue Island, Ill., 1961; sec. Verson All Steel, Chgo., 1962; office mgr. Tri-State Elec., 1963; fitness instr. Silver Spring YMCA, Silver Spring, Md., 1975—84, aquatic dir., 1980—84; owner, CEO Swimming Sch., Bangkok, 1984—94; lesson coord. Montgomery County OSC, Olney, Md., 1998—; fitness expert Wellness Network, 2000—. Sec. Tomorrow Group Assocs., Silver Spring, Md., 1998—; mem. Niams, Washington, 2000—; chair Internat. Women's Club, Bangkok, 1987—94. Pres. Am. Women's Club, Bangkok, 1992—93; sec. Reps. Abroad, 1986—94; pres. Scleroderma Found. of Greater Washington, 2002. Republican. Roman Catholic. Avocations: reading, gardening, travel. Office: Olney Swim Ctr 16601 Georgia Ave Olney MD 20832 E-mail: carolsod@att.net.

SODORA, ROSALYN HARPOLD, elementary education educator, school librarian; b. Parke County, Ind., May 19, 1935; d. Bradford Warren and Marjorie Eloise (Smiley) Van Hook; m. Jackie Gene Harpold, Feb. 11, 1955 (dec. Aug. 1967); children: Jill Harpold Savage, Joni Harpold Callahan, Judy Beth Harpold Hoke; m. Gabriel Sodora, Apr. 14, 1972 (dec. Dec. 2002). BS, Ind. State U., Terre Haute, 1973, MS, 1977, postgrad., 1989. Cert. in lang. arts, sch. libr. and audiovisual svcs., gen. edn., Ind. Tchr. 5th grade Mecca (Ind.) Sch., 1974-75, tchr. 4th grade, 1975-79, tchr. 8th grade, 1979-86; sch. libr. Southwest Parke Sch. Corp., Montezuma, Ind., 1986-92; tchr. 4th grade Rosedale (Ind.) Sch., 1992-97; dir. Montezuma (Ind.) Pub. Libr., 1997—2000. Author: Van Hook Genealogy from Holland to Samuel and Martha Elizabeth Ashley Van Hook's Descendants in Indiana, 1993. Mem. Delta Kappa Gamma, Phi Delta Kappa, Pi Lambda Theta, Kappa Delta Pi. Avocations: genealogy, walking, sewing, writing poetry. Home: 588 Cardinal Rd Rockville IN 47872-9206

SOETAERT, PAMELA JOYCE, journalist, editor; b. Victorville, Calif., May 25, 1953; d. Theodore John and Ruby Ester (Spitzenberger) Ogrodnik; m. Gerald Robert Soetaert, Sept. 15, 1974. Degree in graphic design, NEAK Tech. Sch., Aichison, Kans., 1973; fellow, U. Md., College Park, 1995. Layout, graphic artist Neff Printing, Mission, Kans., 1973-74, Clester Comms., Belle Plaine, Kans., 1979-81, 83-85; editor Southern View Mag., Haysville, Kans., 1985-88; staff writer Winfield (Kans.) Daily Courier, 1988-91; editor Table Rock Gazette, Kimberling City, Mo., 1991-97; owner, editor Stone County Gazette, West Branson, Mo., 1997—2002; asst. pub. Russell (Kans.) County News, 2003—. Editor Lifelines Mo. Press Women, 1994-95, mktg. dir., 1994-95, outside mktg. dir., 1995-96, mktg. dir., 1997—; mem. Harbor Lights Women's Crisis, Kimberling City, 1995-97. V.p. Kimberlig Area Merchants Assn., 1993-97. Recipient numerous awards in field including Emma McKinney award Nat. Newspaper Assn., 2000. Mem. Kimberling City Rotary Club (pub. rels. chair 1994, 95, internat. chair 1996, v.p. 1997, pres. 1998). Office: Russell County News PO Box 513 Russell KS 67665

SOETEBER, ELLEN, journalist, editor; b. East St. Louis, Ill., June 14, 1950; d. Lyle Potter and Norma Elizabeth (Osborn) S.; m. Richard M. Martins, Mar. 16, 1974. BJ, Northwestern U., 1972. Edn. writer, copy editor Chgo. Today, 1972-74; reporter Chgo. Tribune, 1974-76, asst. met. editor, 1976-84, assoc. met. editor, 1984-86, TV and media editor, 1986, met. editor, 1987-89, assoc. mng. editor for met. news, 1989-91, dep. editor editorial page, 1991-94; mng. editor South Fla. Sun-Sentinel, Ft. Lauderdale, 1994-2001; editor St. Louis Post-Dispatch, 2001—. Fellow journalism U. Mich., Ann Arbor, 1986-87. Named to Hall of Achievement, Medill Sch. of Journalism, 2003. Office: The St Louis Post-Dispatch 900 N Tucker Blvd Saint Louis MO 63101 E-mail: esoeteber@post-dispatch.com.

SOFFER, GRACE FLOREY, retired elementary school educator, artist; b. Jeannette, Pa. d. James Paul Florey and Mary Ann Wlnewski; m. Rubin Soffer, Mar. 16, 1946; 1 child, Jerry Paul. BA, Ohio State U., 1944; MA, Adelphi U., 1975. Tchr. common br. N.Y.C. Bd. of Edn., 1966-85. One women shows include N.Y. Poly. U., Farmingdale, 1995, South Nassau Unitarian Ch., 1989, Parlor Gallery Cmty. Ch., 1989, Malverne Pub. Lib., 1985; exhibited in group shows at Fine Arts Mus. of L.I., Art Circa 2100, 1995, Inter-Media Art Ctr., Huntington, Art Circa 2100, 1995, 97, South Nassau Cmty. Hosp., 1990, TriCounty Arts Invitational Small Group Fine Arts exhibit, N.Y., 1999, N.Y. Tech. U., Wisser Libr., Old Westbury, 1990, Shelter Rock Gallery, Manhasset, 1994, Adelphi Art and Art History Alumni Assn., N.Y.C., 1990, Five Towns Music and Art Found., Woodmere, 1990, others, Village Art Club, 1988-91 (prizes), Lee Scarfone Gallery, 1998, Guild Hall East Hampton, 1992, Fine Arts Mus. of L.I., 1997 (3d pl. winner 1998), Nassau County Mus. of Fine Art, 1992, Long Beach Art League, 1999, 2002 (prize), South Nassau Unitarian Ch., 1989, 92 (prizes), Village Art Club at Chelsea Ctr., 1991, others. Mem. Nat. Assn. Women Artists, Long Beach Art League, Nat. League Am. Pen Women (exhibits chair 1995-2001), Nat. Mus. Women in the Arts (charter), Village Art Club, Tri County Artists of L.I. (newsletter 1980-95, prizes), Art Circa 2100, Adelphi Art Hist. Alumni Assn., Mensa. Home: 56 Dickson St Inwood NY 11096-1004 E-mail: depainter@aol.com.

SOFTIC, TANJA, artist; BFA, U. Sarajevo, Bosnia and Herzegovina, 1988; MFA, Old Dominion U./Norfolk State, 1992; student bookbinding, letterpress, Ctr. Book Arts, N.Y.C., 1993; student hand papermaking, Dieu Donne Paper Mill, N.Y.C., 1993. Printer Kathy Caraccio Printmaking Workshop, N.Y.C., 1991; adj. instr. Norfolk (Va.) State U., 1991—92; asst. prof. art Rollins Coll., 1992—2000; assoc. prof. art Richmond (Va.) U., 2000—. Asst. to gallery dir. Old Dominion U. Gallery, Norfolk, 1991—92; juror various exhbns., 1993—94; instr. workshops on printmaking history and techniques for docents Ctr. Fla. Art Mus., 1992—95; presenter in field. One-woman shows include various mus., Dubrovnik, Yugoslavia, 1989, Stanley Gallery, Norfolk, 1990, Collegium Artisticum, Sarajevo, 1991, Peninsula Fine Arts Ctr., Newport News, Va., 1992, Cornell Fine Arts Mus., Rollins Coll., Winter Park, Fla., 1994, Wyndy Moorehead Fine Arts, New Orleans, 1994, Coker Coll. Art Gallery, Hartsville, S.C., 1995, Kendall Gallery of Miami-Dade C.C., Miami, Fla., 1996, Allen R. Hite Art Inst., U. Louisville, 1996, Catherine J. Smith Gallery, Appalachian State U., Boone, N.C., 1997, exhibited in group shows at City Hall Gallery, Orlando, Fla., 1994 (Purchase award), Jacksonville (Fla.) C.C. Gallery, 1995 (hon. mention), U. Wis. at Parkside Gallery, Kenosha, 1995, Niagara C.C. Art Gallery, Buffalo, 1995, Catherine D. Smith Gallery, Appalachian State U., Boone, 1995, Kanagawa Prefectural Gallery, Japan, 1995, Paul Mesaros Gallery, W.Va. U., Morgantown, 1996, Hokkaido Mus. Modern Art, Sapporo, Japan, 1996, others, Represented in permanent collections. Recipient Best Debut prize, XV Biennial of Watercolor of Yugoslavia, 1989, Purchase award, Valencia Small Works, 1994, Orlando Biennial, 1994; fellow Grad. fellow, Old Dominion U. Coll. Arts and Letters, 1989; grantee Visual Artist grantee, Southeastern Coll. Art Conf., 1994; scholar Charles Sibley Grad. scholar, 1990—91, Artist scholar, Acad. Arts and Scis. of Bosnia and Herzegovina, 1990—91. E-mail: tsoftic@richmond.edu.

SOHAILI, MONIRA, special education educator, writer; b. Pune, India, Nov. 4, 1933; d. Ispandiar and Keshvar Yaganegi; m. Shahpur Sohaili, Oct. 15, 1953 (dec. Dec. 2000). BA in Edn., Northeastern Ill. U., 1981, MA, 1982. Cert. behavioral therapy Behavioral Therapy Tng. Ctr., L.A., 1996. Tchr. Parramalta Marist H.S., Australia, 1970—71; guide Bahai House of Worship, Chgo., 1973—83; ESL instr. Cuban/Hatian Refugee Program, Chgo., 1983—84, Chgo. Bd. Edn., 1984—87; ESL and Eng. instr. Santa Monica (Calif.) City Coll., 1987—89; ESL, Eng. and reading tchr. Le Conte Mid. Sch., L.A., 1989—96; head dept. Ctr. Mid. Sch., 1994—96, spl. edn. tchr., 1996—, dept. head, 1996—2000; tchr. spl. edn. J. Burroughs Mid. Sch., L.A., 2000—. Storyteller in field, 2002—. Author: (children's book) Monira's Fables, 2000, From Earth and Beyond, 2003. Coord. childproof medicine vials donation, Papua New Guinea, 1995—97. Recipient Cert. of Achievement, L.A. USD Lang. Acquisition, 1993, I Made a Difference award, L.A. Dept. Edn., 1995. Mem.: NEA (reading and writing program 1990—), Calif. Tchrs. Assn. (assisted in program 1990—). Avocations: reading, writing, traveling, swimming. Office: John Burroughs HS 600 McCadden Pl Los Angeles CA 90005 Address: PO Box 95 Santa Monica CA 90406-0095

SOHL, JOYCE DARLENE, religious organization administrator; b. Aurora, Ill., Dec. 15, 1935; m. Lowell Sohl (dec.); children: John, Stephen. BA, Westmar Coll., 1957; MA, U. Nebr., 1959; MBA, Fordham U., 1984. Math. tchr. Irving Jr. H.S., Lincoln, Nebr., 1959-61, Lincoln H.S., 1961-64; assoc. treas. gen. bd. global ministries women's divsn. United Meth. Ch., 1976-90, dep. gen. sec. gen. bd. global ministries women's divsn., 1991—. Author: (book) Managing Our Money, Workbook on Women and Finance; (videos) Giving: A Gift of God's Grace, 1988, Called to Mission, 1994, Managing Our Money, 1990, Count Me In, 1994; columnist: monthly column Responsively Yours, in Response, 1991—; also articles in ch. publs. and program materials for program book of Women's Soc. of World Svc. and United Meth. Women. Past mem. bd. trustees, treas. Meml. United Meth. Ch., White Plains, current lay del. to ann. conf., mem. pastor/parish rels. com., adminstrv. bd., substitute organist; bd. dirs. Scarritt-Bennett Ctr.; trustee Bennett Coll., Greensboro, N.C. Mem. NAFE, Am. Mgmt. Assn. Office: Gen Bd Global Ministries United Meth Ch 475 Riverside Dr Rm 1504 New York NY 10115-0122

SOHN, CATHERINE ANGELL, pharmaceutical executive, pharmacist; b. San Francisco, Mar. 21, 1953; d. Vincent Herbert and Margaret Ann Ware Angell; m. John Edwin Sohn, Aug. 10, 1974; children: Karen Elizabeth, Jennifer Michele. Ed., U. Calif., Davis; PharmD, U. Calif., San Francisco, 1977. Registered pharmacist, Calif., Pa. Pharmacist Kaiser Permanente, San Francisco, 1977-78; asst. prof. pharmacy Phila. Coll. Pharmacy and Sci., 1978-82; mgr. med. affairs Smith Kline & French, Phila., 1982-86; assoc. dir. bus. devel. pharm. divsn. Smith Kline Beecham, Phila., 1986-88, product dir., 1988-93, v.p. worldwide strategic product devel., 1994-97; v.p. worldwide bus. devel. Glaxo Smith Kline Consumer Healthcare, Phila., 1998—. Lectr. St. Andrew the Apostle, Gibbsboro, NJ, 1989—; adv. bd. Healthcare Bus. Women's Assn., N.Y.C., NY, 1996—; bd. overseers U. Calif. Sch. Pharmacy, San Francisco, 1997—; health adv. bd. Johns Hopkins U. Sch. Pub. Health, Balt., 1998—. Author: (with others) Applied Clinical Therapeutics, 1980, Handbook of Non-Prescription Drugs, 1980, rev. edit., 1982; contbr. chpts. to profl. pubs. Mem. Am. Pharm. Assn., Calif. Pharmacists Assn., Consumer Healthcare Products Assn. (chmn. internat. affairs com. 1998—, bd. dirs. 1999—), Licensing Exec. Soc., Rho Chi. Roman Catholic. Avocations: family activities, swimming, bicycling. Office: GlaxoSmithKline FP1370 200 N 16th St Philadelphia PA 19102-1282

SOHN, JEANNE, librarian; b. Milton, Pa. d. Robert Wilson and Juliette Lightner (Hedenberg) Gift; m. Steven Neil Sohn, Nov. 23, 1962. BA, Temple U., 1966; MSLS, Drexel U., 1971. Lit. bibliographer Temple U., Phila., 1971-75, chief of collection devel., 1975-81; asst. dean for collection devel. U. N.Mex., Albuquerque, 1981-86, assoc. dean for libr. svcs., 1986-89; dir. libr. svcs. Cen. Conn. State U., New Britain, 1989—. Cons. New Eng. Assn. Schs. and Colls., Winchester, Mass., 1991—. Mem. editorial bd. Collection Mgmt., 1984—; contbr. articles to profl. jours. Mem. Gov.'s Blue Ribbon Commn. on the Future of Libraries, 1994-96. Mem. ALA, New Eng. Libr. Assn., Conn. Libr. Assn., Assn. Coll. and Rsch. Librs., Beta Phi Mu. Home: 1820 Boulevard West Hartford CT 06107-2815 Office: Cen Conn State Univ Elihu Burritt Libr New Britain CT 06050

SOHNEN-MOE, CHERIE MARILYN, business consultant; b. Tucson, Jan. 2, 1956; d. D. Ralph and Angelina Helen (Spiro) Sohnen; m. James Madison Moe, Jr., May 23, 1981. BA, UCLA, 1977. Rsch. asst. UCLA, 1975-77; ind. cons. L.A., 1978-83; cons. Sohnen-Moe Assocs., Inc., Tucson, 1984—. Author: Business Mastery, 1988, 2d edit., 1991, 3d edit., 1998; co author: The Ethics of Touch, 2003; contbr. to Compendium mag., 1987-90, Massage Mag., 1992-94, 96-97, Am. Massage Therapy Assn. Jour., 1989—2003; bus. editor Massage Therapy Jour., 1998-2002. Vol. Am. Cancer Soc., Tucson, 1984—; mem. Ariz. Sonora Desert Mus., Tucson; pres. Women in Tucson, 1989. Recipient Outstanding Instr. award Desert Inst. of Healing Arts, 1992. Mem. NOW, ASTD (dir. mem. svcs. 1988, dir. mktg., Disting. Svc. award 1988, Profl. Achievement award 1997), Nat. Fed. Independent Bus., Nat. Assn. Women Bus. Owners, Small Pubs. Assn. N.Am., Pubs. Mktg. Assn. Avocations: reading, swimming, crossword puzzles, board games, singing. Office: Sohnen-Moe Assocs Inc 3906 W Ina Rd #200-367 Tucson AZ 85741-2295 E-mail: info@sohnen-moe.com.

SOKOL, JAN D. lawyer; b. N.Y., May 27, 1952; BS magna cum laude, Rutgers U., 1974; JD Northwestern Sch. of Law, Lewis and Clark Coll., 1977. Bar: Oreg. 1978, U.S. Dist. Ct. (dist. Oreg.), U.S. Ct. Appeals (9th cir.) 1981, U.S. Claims Ct. 1982, U.S. Supreme Ct. 1982. Law clerk to Hon. George A. Juba U.S. Dist. Ct. (dist. Oreg.), 1978-79, law clerk to Hon. Gus J. Solomon, 1979-80, law clerk to Hon. James A. Redden, 1980; mng. mem. Stewart, Sokol & Gray, 1994. Case note and comment editor Environmental Law, 1976-77. Mem. ABA (mem. forum com. on the construction industry, fidelity and surety, forest resources com.), Multnomah County. Office: Stewart Sokol & Gray 1500 Benjamin Franklin Plz One SW Columbia Portland OR 97258

SOKOLOFF, AUDREY L. lawyer; b. Providence, R.I., 1966; AB, Dartmouth Coll., 1987; JD, U. Calif., LA, 1990. Bar: Calif. 1990, N.Y. 1999. Atty. Skadden, Arps, Slate, Meagher & Flom LLP, New York, 1999—. Office: Skadden Arps Slate Meagher & Flom LLP Four Times Sq New York NY 10036*

SOKOLOW, ISOBEL FOLB, sculptor; b. Bklyn. d. Henry Folb and Betty Forshaw; m. Gilbert Sokolow; children: Helene, Cheryl. Student, Silvermine Coll. Art, 1965-68, Art Students League, Nat. Acad. Design, Westchester C.C., N.Y., Ednl. Alliance Art Sch. Tchr., art therapist Jewish Guild for the Blind, Yonkers, N.Y., 1974-76; dir. Westchester Art & Culture Assn., Ardsley, NY, 1984—86; coord. sculpture workshops Pietrasanta, Italy, 1984-86; coord. summer workshop Pratt U., Venice, Italy, 1987. Artist in residence Nat. Woman's Com., Brandeis U., 1995; prodr., host cable TV show Art Scene Thru An Artist's Eye, 1995—. One-woman shows include

Bell Gallery, Greenwich, Conn., 1977, River View Gallery, Dobbs Ferry, N.Y., 1978, North Shore Sculpture Ctr., Great Neck, N.Y., 1980, Harkness House, N.Y.C., 1981, Musavi Art Ctr., N.Y.C., 1984, Atlantic Gallery, N.Y.C., 1988, 90, 92, 94, 96, 98, 2000, 2002, Sara Lawrence Coll., 1995-96, 2002, Shelter Rock Art Gallery, 1997, La Lac Gallery, Lake Lugano, Switzerland, 2002; exhibited in group shows at Monmouth Mus. Art, Red Bank, N.J., 1990, Westbeth Gallery, N.Y.C., 1991, Capital Bldg. Gallery, Tallahassee, 1991, Atlantic Gallery, N.Y.C., 1991, N.Y. Acad. Sci., N.Y.C., 1991, Broome St. Gallery, N.Y.C., 1991, Gallery Stendahl, N.Y.C., 1991, 97, 2002, Raleigh Gallery, Dania, Fla., 1993, Casa d'arte Gadiva Gallery, Forte dei Marmi, Italy, 1993, Bigi Art Gallery, Florence, Italy, 1993, Living Arts Gallery, Milan, Italy, 1994, Steiner Gallery, Bal Harbor, Fla., 1995, 97, Atlantic Gallery, 2002, Galleria Faustini, Florence, Italy, 2000, Gallery Art, Aventura, Fla., 2003; permanent collections include Mus. Vitomele, S. Maria de Finibus Terrae, Italy, Mus. dei Bozzetti, Pietrasonta, Italy; selected exhibits include Yonkers Art Assn., 1978, Audubon Artists Guild, 1978-80, N.J. Painters and Sculptors, 1980, Sculptors Alliance, 1982, Nat. Assn. Women Artists, 1984, N.Y. Soc. Women Artists, 1986, Am. Soc. Contemporary Artists, 1992; spl. exhibits include Dancer, GM Bldg., N.Y.C., 1978-79, Torso, Schulman Realty Group, N.Y.C., 1983-85, Dancer I, Westchester C.C., Valhalla, N.Y., 1982-92, Dancer Reborn, Roosevelt H.S., Yonkers, N.Y., 1992-98. Recipient Silver medal Audubon Artists, 1978, Sculpture award Mamaroneck (N.Y.) Artists Guild; Tres Jolle des Arts award Nat. Assn. Women Artists, 1984, Best in Show award, 1993, David Perce Meml. prize, 2001. Mem.: Art Students League, Artists Equity (past bd. dirs., past v.p.), Am. Soc. Contemporary Artists (v.p., Meml. award 2001). Avocations: music, literature, travel. Home: 498 Winding Rd N Ardsley NY 10502-2702 E-mail: isart24184@aol.com.

SOKOLOWSKI, ELIZABETH CATHERINE, music educator; b. Somerset, N.J., June 19, 1972; d. Marcel William and Greta Ann Wagner; m. Robert Joseph Sokolowski, Jan. 2, 1999; 1 child, Ana Clare. BA in Music, Temple U., Phila., 1994. Cert. tchr. Pa, 1994. Music tchr. North Penn Sch. Dist., Lansdale, Pa., 1994—. Field hockey coach Penndale Mid. Sch., Lansdale, 1994—2000, softball coach, 1994—2000, wind ensemble condr., small ensembles condr., 1994—, concert band condr., 1994—, student coun. advisor, 1998—2000, basketball asst. coach, 1998—99. Mem.: Pa, State Edn. Assn., North Penn Edn. Assn., Music Educators Nat. Conf., Pa, Music Educators Assn. Home: 4104 Dara Cir Collegeville PA 19426 Office: North Penn School District 400 Penn St Lansdale PA 19446

SOLA, JANET ELAINE, secondary school educator; b. New Britain, Conn., Oct. 23, 1935; d. Walter Andrew and Helen (Mandl) Sinkiewicz; m. Raymond Albert Sola BS, Ctrl. Conn. State U., 1957; MS, So. Conn. State U., 1962; postgrad., U. Conn, 1969. Tchr. bus. Amity Regional High Sch., Woodbridge, Conn., 1957-60; bus. instr. Stone Coll., New Haven, 1962; instr. Manpower Devel. and Tng. Act, New Britain, 1970-74, So. Ctrl. C.C., New Haven, 1977, lectr., 1987; mgmt. lectr. II, Quinnipiac Coll., Hamden, Conn., 1981-87; mayor's aide Town of Hamden, 1987-89, recycling coord., 1989-92; tchr. bus. edn. Hamden High Sch., 1992—, coord. coop. work experience and diversified occupations, 1992—. Assessor credit for life Quinn Coll., Hamden, 1986-89; advisor Hamden Hub Student Interns, 2000. Author: (poetry) Flights of Fancy, 1991, Recycled Thoughts, 1992; contbr. poetry to Contemporary, The Hamden Chronicle, Treasured Poems of Am., Nat. Arts Soc. Campaigner Sola for Town Clk. Com., Hamden, 1981; community liaison Carusone for Mayor Com., Hamden, 1981-87; v.p., Am. Legion Aux. Unit 88, Hamden, 1985-95; treas. Green Dragon Enterprises, Inc., 2002—; chmn. unit 88 Laurel Girl States. Named Tchr. Yr., Hamden H.S., 2000—01. Mem.: AAUW, NAFE, ASCD, Conn. Bus. Educators Assn. (bd. dirs. 2003), Nat. Bus. Educators, Internat. Platform Assn., Nat. Assn. Italian Women, Internat. Soc. Poetry (disting. mem.), Lions Internat. Hamden chpt., Ctrl. Conn. U. State Alumni Assn. (bd. dirs., Disting. Alumni Svc. award 2003), Delta Pi Epsilon Nat. Bus. Educators Hon. Soc. Avocations: bowling, swimming. Home: 50 Vernon St Hamden CT 06518-2825 Office: Hamden HS 2040 Dixwell Ave Hamden CT 06514-2404 E-mail: jsola@hamdenschools.org.

SOLBERG, ELIZABETH TRANSOU, public relations executive; b. Dallas, Aug. 10, 1939; d. Ross W. and Josephine V. (Perkins) Transou; m. Frederick M. Solberg Jr., Mar. 8, 1969; 1 son, Frederick W. BJ, U. Mo., 1961. Reporter Kansas City (Mo.) Star, 1963-70, asst. city editor, 1970-73; reporter spl. events, documentaries Sta. WDAF-TV, Kansas City, Mo., 1973-74; prof. dept. journalism Park Coll., Kansas City, Mo., 1975-76, advisor, 1976-79; mng. ptnr. Fleishman-Hillard Inc., Kansas City, Mo., then exec. v.p., sr. ptnr., gen. mgr. Kansas City br., now regional pres., sr. ptnr., gen. mgr.; also pres. Fleishman-Hillard/Can. Mem. Kansas City Commn. Planned Indsl. Expansion Authority, 1974-91; bd. dirs. Kansas City Life Ins. Co., Ferrellgas, Midwest Airlines. Mem. long range planning com. Heart of Am. coun. Boy Scouts Am., 1980-82, bd. dirs., 1986-89; mem. Clay County (Mo.) Devel. Commn., 1979-88; bd. govs. Citizens Assn., 1975—; mem. exec. com. bd. Kansas City Area Devel. Coun., 1989-96, co-chair, 1991-93; trustee Pembroke Hill Sch., 1987-93, U. Kansas City, 1990—, exec. com., 1992—, Midwest Rsch. Inst., 1995—; bd. dirs. Greater Kansas City Cmty. Found. and Affiliated Trusts, 1996—, Starlight Theatre, 1996—; regent Rockhurst Coll., 1984-96; active Bus. Coun., Nelson Gallery Found., Nelson-Atkins Mus. Art, 1990—; bd. dirs. Civic Coun. Greater Kansas City, 1992—; mem. Jr. League Kansas City. Recipient award for contbn. to mental health Mo. Psychiat. Assn., 1973, Arthur E. Lowell award for excellence in orgn. comm. Kansas City/IABC, 1985, Kansas City Spirit award Gillis Ctr., 1994. Mem. Pub. Rels. Soc. Am. (nat. honors and awards com., co-chmn. SilverAnvil com. 1983, Silver Anvil award 1979-82, chair nat. membership com. 1989-91, assembly del.-at-large 1995-96), Counselor's Acad. (exec. com. 1991-92), Mo. C. of C. Pub. Rels. Coun., Greater Kans. City C. of C. (chair 1994-95, bd. exec. com.), River Club, Carriage Club, Ctrl. Exch. Club. Office: Fleishman Hillard Inc 2405 Grand Blvd Ste 700 Kansas City MO 64108-2522

SOLBERG, MARY ANN, federal agency administrator; Grad., Western Mich. U. Dep. dir. Office Nat. Drug Control Policy Exec. Office of Pres., Washington, 2001—; exec. dir. Coalition of Health Comtys., Troy (Mich.) Cmty. Coalition for Prevention of Drug and Alcohol Abuse; various positions Troy Adult and Cmty. Edn., 1977—91. Mem. adv. com. to develop a nat. prevention sys. Nat. Ctr. for Substance Abuse Prevention; mem. adv. com. Nat. Ad Coun.'s Cmty. Anti-Drug Campaign; mem. Pres.'s Commn. on Drug-Free Cmtys., 1998, co-chairperson. Office: Exec Office of Pres Office Nat Drug Control Policy 750 17th St NW Washington DC 20503

SOLBRIG, INGEBORG HILDEGARD, literature educator, writer; b. Weissenfels, Germany, July 31, 1923; arrived in U.S., 1961, naturalized, 1966; d. Reinhold J. and Hildegard M. A. (Ferchland) Solbrig. Grad. in chemistry, U. Halle, Germany, 1948; BA summa cum laude, San Francisco State U., 1964; postgrad., U. Calif., Berkeley, 1964-65; MA, Stanford U., 1966, PhD in Humanities and German, 1969. Asst. prof. U. R.I., 1969-70, U. Tenn., Chattanooga, 1970-72, U. Ky., Lexington, 1972-75; assoc. prof. German U. Iowa, 1975-81, prof., 1981-93, prof. emerita, 1993—. Domestic and abroad lectr.; lectr. Conv. on Culture, Al-Sharja, United Arab Emirates, 2003. Author: Hammer-Purgstall und Goethe, 1973, Modulationen von Gold und Licht in Goethes Kunstmärchen, 1997, Momentaufnahmem, 2000, J.G. Herder: Echo of the Cultural Philospher's Ideas in Early African-American Intellectual Writing, 2000, Maria Sibylla Merian..., 2001; main editor: Rilke Heute, Beziehungen und Wirkungen, 1975; editor (and translator): Reinhard Goering: Seeschlacht/Seabattle, 1977; editor: Orient-Rezeption, 1996, Orient-Rezeption, Fischer Lexikon Literatur, 1996; mem. editl. bd.: Kairoer Germanistische Studien, vol. 9 & 10, 1998; contbr. articles to profl. jours., chpts. to books; editor: Orient-Rezeption, Fischer Lexikon Literatur, 2000. Mem. Iowa Gov.'s Com. 300th Anniversey German-Am. Rels. 1683-1983, 1983. Named Ky. Col., 1975; recipient Hammer-Purgstall Gold medal, Austria, 1974; fellow, Standford U., 1965—66, 1968—69, Austrian Ministry Edn., 1968—69; Old Gold fellow, Iowa, 1977, Am. Coun. Learned Socs. grantee, German Acad. Exch. Svc. grantee, 1980, Sr. Faculty Rsch. fellow in humanities, 1983, NEH grantee, 1985, May Brodbeck fellow in humanities, 1989, numerous summer faculty rsch. grants. Mem.: MLA (life), Soc. for History Alchemy and Chemistry, Internat. Herder Soc. (founding mem.), Goethe Soc. N.Am., Inc., Can. Soc. 18th Century Studies, Am. Soc. 18th Century Studies, Deutsche Schiller Gesellschaft, Goethe Gesellschaft, Internat. Vereinigung fur Germanische Sprach und Lit. Wiss., Egyptian Soc. Lit. Criticism (hon.). Avocations: horseback riding, photography, writing, travel. Home: 1126 Pine St Iowa City IA 52240-5711 E-mail: isolbrig@blue.weeg.uiowa.edu.

SOLDAN, ANGELIKA, philosopher, political scientist, educator; b. Hennigsdorf, Germany, Feb. 10, 1953; d. Hans and Erika Potempa; m. Wolfgang Karl Soldan, May 8, 1987; 1 child, Anja Soldan. MA in Philosophy, Humboldt U., 1975, PhD, 1990, Martin Luther U., Halle-Wittenberg, Germany, 1982. Assoc. prof. philosophy, polit. ethics Humboldt U., Berlin, 1989-91; adj. prof. philosophy, ethics, govt. U. Tex., Brownsville, 1991-98, lectr. social issues and philosophy, 1999—2000, asst. prof., 2000—. Sr. lectr. U. Wis. Eau Claire, 1998-99. Contbr. articles to profl. jours. Supporter Sch. Tchr. Exch. Program USA-Germany, 1991—; co-founder Gesellschaft für Solidarische Entwicklungszusammenarbeit, 1990. Scholarship Max Planck Gesellschaft, 1990. Mem. Am. Philos. Assn., Internat. Fromm Soc. Office: U Tex Brownsville 80 Fort Brown St Brownsville TX 78520-4956 E-mail: asoldan@utb.edu.

SOLDAY, ALIDRA (LINDA BROWN), psychotherapist, psychoanalyst, filmmaker; b. Mineola, N.Y., Feb. 18, 1941; d. Charles Harold and Helen (Golbach) Brown. Student, Smith Coll., Northampton, Mass., 1958—60; BA, Barnard Coll., N.Y.C., 1962; MPS in Art Therapy, Pratt Inst., Bklyn., 1973; MSW, Hunter Coll., N.Y.C., 1976. Cert. social worker, psychoanalyst, N.Y.; lic. clin. social worker, Calif.; diplomate clin. social work Am. Bd. Examiners in Clin. Social Work. Singer, actress Broadway theatres, N.Y.C., 1962-65, pub. rels./community rels. specialist, real estate, publicist/editor, pub., edn. cons., 1965-71; art therapist Bronx (N.Y.) Psychiat. Ctr., 1972-74; clin. social worker North Richmond Community Mental Health Ctr., S.I., N.Y., 1977-79; staff therapist Lincoln Inst. Psychotherapy, N.Y.C., 1978-80; sr. staff therapist Ctr. for Study Anorexia and Bulimia, N.Y.C., 1983-85; staff therapist Inst. Contemporary Psychotherapy, N.Y.C., 1988-95; pvt. practice psychotherapy N.Y.C., 1978—. Mem. human svc. faculty Tristate Inst. Traditional Chinese Acupuncture, N.Y.C., 1986—89; mem. faculty N.Y. Open Ctr., N.Y.C., 1987—98; adj. faculty Health Choices Ctr. for Healing Arts, Princeton, NJ, 1987—90; clin. cons. Personal Performance Cons., EAP, 1988; human resources cons. industry, N.Y.C., 1988—; workshop leader seminars on stress mgmt., assertiveness tng., comm. and counseling skills, creative expression; prodr., dir. video documentaries for TV on elderly in Am., 2001—. Mem. NASW. Office: 3195 California St San Francisco CA 94115 E-mail: asolday@aol.com.

SOLER, ESTA, foundation administrator; Founder, pres. Family Violence Prevention Fund, 1980—. Cons. and adv. Dept. Justice, U.S. Dept. Health and Human Svcs., CDC, others; bd. dirs. The Ctr. on Fathers, Families and Pub. Policy. Co-author: Ending Domestic Violence: Changing Public Perceptions/Halting the Epidemic, 1997. Bd. dirs. Blue Shield Calif. Found., Bay Area United Way Safe Cmtys. Cabinet. Recipient Koret Israel Prize, 1989, Public Health Heroes award, U. Calif., 1998; fellow, Kellogg Found. Nat. Leadership, 1990. Office: 383 Rhode Island St Ste 304 San Francisco CA 94103-5133*

SOLES, ADA LEIGH, former state legislator, government advisor; b. Jacksonville, Fla., May 19, 1937; d. Albert Thomas and Dorothy (Winter) Wall; m. James Ralph Soles, 1959; children: Nancy Beth, Catherine. BA, Fla. State U., 1959. Mem. New Castle County Libr. Adv. Bd., 1975-80, 95—, chmn., 1975-77; chmn. Del. State Libr. Adv. Bd., 1975-78; mem. Del. State Ho. Reps., 1980-92; sr. advisor Gov. of Del., 1993-94; mem. U. Del. Libr. Assocs. Bd., 1995—; adminstrv. asst. U. Del. Commn. on Status of Women, 1976-77; acad. advisor U. Del. Coll. Arts and Scis., 1977-92. Mem. LWV (state pres. 1978-80), Phi Beta Kappa, Phi Kappa Phi, Mortar Bd., Alpha Chi Omega. Episcopalian.

SOLEYMANI, NANCY, psychologist, researcher; b. N.Y.C., May 20, 1972; d. Yosef and Louise Soleymani. BA in Psychology magna cum laude, Columbia U., 1994; MA in Psychology with distinction, Hofstra U., 1995, PhD in Combined Clin. & Sch. Psychology, 1999. Cert. of qualification in sch. psychology, N.Y. Rsch. asst. Barnard Toddler Ctr., N.Y.C., 1993-94, Columbia Presbyn. Med. Ctr., N.Y.C., 1994; tchrs. asst. Little Village Sch., Garden City, N.Y., 1994; sch. psychology intern JLM Great Neck (N.Y.) North High Sch., 1996-97; sch. psychologist Port Washington Sch. Dist., 1997; counselor S.E. Nassau Guidance Ctr., Seaford, N.Y., 1997-99; asst. psychologist, rschr. Inst. for Bio-Behavioral Therapy & Rsch., Great Neck, 1999—. Invited guest lectr. Hofstra U., Hempstead, N.Y., 1998-99, Hunter Coll., Grad. Sch. Social Work, N.Y.C., 1998, Adelphi U., Garden City, 1999. Mem. fund raising com. Juvenile Diabetes Found., N.Y.C., 1994—. Mem. APA, Assn. for Advancement of Behavior Therapy. Jewish. Avocations: volleyball, painting, pottery, ice-skating. Office: Inst for Bio-Behavioral Therapy & Rsch 935 Northern Blvd Great Neck NY 11021-5309 E-mail: nsoleymani@aol.com.

SOLIS, HILDA LUCIA, congresswoman, educational administrator; b. Los Angeles, Oct. 20, 1957; d. Raul and Juana (Sequiera) S.; m. Sam H. Sayyad, June 26, 1982. BA in Polit. Sci., Calif. State Poly U., 1979; MA in Pub. Adminstrn., U. So. Calif., 1981. Interpreter Immigration and Naturalization Service, Los Angeles, 1977-79; editor in chief Office Hispanic Affairs, The White House, Washington, 1980-81; mgmt. analyst Office Mgmt. and Budget, Washington, 1981-82; field rep. Office Assemblyman Art Torres, L.A., 1982; dir. Calif. Student Opportunity and Access, Whittier, 1982—; rep. 57th assembly dist. Calif. State Assembly, Sacramento, 1992-94; mem. Calif. Senate from 24th dist., 1994-2000, U.S. Congress from Calif. 32nd dist., Washington, 2001—; mem. resources com., energy & commerce com., former mem. edn. and workforce com. Cons. South Coast Consortium, L.A., 1986—; mem. South Coast Ednl. Opportunity Pers. Consortium. Bd. dirs. Calif. Commn. on Status of Women, 1993—; corr. pres. Friendly El Monte (Calif.) Dem. Club, 1986—; mem. credentials com. Calif. Dem. Com., 1987-88; trustee Rio Hondo C.C., 1985-92. Recipient Meritorious Svc. award Dept. Def., 1981, Young Careerist award El Monte Bus. and Profl. Women, 1987; fellow Nat. Edn. Inst., Kellogg Found., 1984-85. Mem. Western Assn. Ednl. Opportunity Pers. (sec. bd. dirs. 1986—), Comision Feminil de Los Angeles (bd. dirs. 1983-84, edn. chmn.), Women of Moose. Democrat. Roman Catholic. Home: 5250 La Madera Ave El Monte CA 91732-1236 Office: 1725 Longworth House Office Bldg Washington DC 20515*

SOLNIT, REBECCA, writer, art critic; Author: Secret Exhibition: Six California Artists of the Cold War Era, 1994, Savage Dreams: A Journey into the Landscape Wars of the American West, 1995, A Book of Migrations: Some Passages in Ireland, 1998, Wanderlust: A History of Walking, 2001, As Eve Said to the Serpent: On Landscape, Gender and Art, 2001, Hollow City: The Siege of San Francisco and the Crisis of American Urbanism, 2002, Motion Studies: Time, Space and Eadweard Muybridge, 2003, River of Shadows, 2003 (Nat. Book Critics Circle award, 2004). Grantee Guggenheim Fellowship, NEA Fellowship. Office: c/o Bloomsbury USA 175 5th Ave New York NY 10010*

SOLOD, LISA, writer; b. Knoxville, Tenn., Jan. 3, 1956; d. Jay Lawrence and Fredlyn Kovitch Solod; m. John Addison Lambeth, June 23, 1985; children: Philip Stanhope Lambeth, Grace Amelia Lambeth. AB in Semiotics with honors, Brown U., 1978. Pub. info. officer Mus. Fine Arts, Boston, 1978-79; asst. editor Boston Mag., 1979-80; editor Moviegoer Mag. Whittle Comms., 1980-83; chief advt. copywriter Parsons, Friedman and Cen. Advt. Agy., Boston, 1984-85; pub. rels. dir. So. Va. Coll. for Women, Buena Vista, Va., 1985-86; pub. info. dir. The George C. Marshall Found., Lexington, Va., 1986-88. Instr. expository writing U. R.I., 1984; editl. cons. TeenAge Mag., Cambridge Free Press, The Illustrated, 1983-85; bd. dirs. Project Horizon, 1988-90. Bd. dirs. Montessori Ctr. for Children, Lexington, 1995-99, sec., 1996-98; bd. dirs. Lexington City Sch. Bd., 1997—2001, v.p., 1998—2001; bd. dirs. Temple House of Israel; sec. Valley region Va. Sch. Bd. Assn., 1997-98, v.p. Valley region, 1998-99, chmn. Valley region, 1999-2001. Recipient 11 fellowships/residencies Va. Ctr. for Creative Arts, Mt. San Angelo, 1989-2000. Democrat. Jewish. Home: 310 Enfield Rd Lexington VA 24450-1756 E-mail: lisa@rockbridge.net.

SOLOMON, CAREN GROSSBARD, internist; b. N.Y.C., Feb. 20, 1963; MD, Harvard U., 1988. Resident Brigham and Women's Hosp., Boston, 1988-90, fellow in endocrinology, 1990-93, assoc. physician, 1993—. Asst. prof. medicine Harvard Med. Sch., 1998—. Mem.: AMA, Endocrine Soc., Mass. Med. Soc., Am. Diabetes Assn. Office: Brigham Womens Hosp Div Womens Health 45 Francis St # St5 Boston MA 02115-6105

SOLOMON, DOROTHY JEANNE ALLRED, writer, communications executive; b. Salt Lake City, June 24, 1949; d. Rulon Clark and Mabel (Finlayson) Allred; m. Bruce Craig Solomon, Jan. 8, 1968; children: Denise, Layla, Jeffrey, Laurie. BA in Lit., Theater and Speech, U. Utah, 1971, MA in Lit. and Creative Writing, 1981. Cert. secondary edn. educator, Utah. Storyteller, libr. Salt Lake City Libr., 1971; tchr. Salt Lake Sch. Dist., 1971-74; instr. U. Utah/Columbia Coll., Salt Lake City, 1974-80; writer-in-residence Utah Arts Coun., Salt Lake City, 1980-93; human devel. trainer Lifespring, San Rafael, Calif., 1983-87; media specialist Rivendell Psychiat. Hosps., West Jordan, Utah, 1987-90; curriculum writer Positive Action Pub., Twin Falls, Idaho, 1990-96; co-founder, v.p. Rising Star Comm. and Team Resource Assocs., Salt Lake City, 1994—. Bd. dirs. Rising Star Comm. Author: In My Father's House, 1984 (1st prize Biography, 1981, Pub. prize 1982), Inside Out: Creative Writing, 1989, Of Predators, Prey and Other Kin, 1996 (1st prize Non-fiction 1996); contbr. stories to anthologies Stories That Shape Us, What There Is, The Best of Writers at Work, A New Genesis, Great and Peculiar Beauty, In Our Lovely Deseret, Mormon Fictions, 1998, Predators, Prey, and Other Kinfolk: Growing Up in Polygamy, 2003; screenwriter: In My Father's House, 1986-87. Bd. dirs. The Children's Ctr., Salt Lake City, 1982-85, Writers at Work, Park City, Utah, 1986-89, Lifespring Found., San Rafael, Calif., 1985-89; mem. curriculum com. Salt Lake Sch. Dist., 1971-74; coord. (with Bruce Solomon) lit. arts Utah Arts Festival "Performing Word", Salt Lake City, 1982; vol. Big Sisters, Salt Lake City, 1970-71; coord. cmty. edn. Rivendell Conf., West Jordan, Utah, 1987-89. Recipient Disting. Journalism 1st prize Am. Acad. Pediat., San Francisco, 1979, 1st prize feature writing Sigma Delta Chi, Salt Lake City, 1979, 1st prize essay Utah Original Writing Contest, Salt Lake City, 1995, 1st prize Biography, 1981, 96, award of excellence Gov.'s Media Awards, Utah, 1990, Utah State Pub. prize, 1982. Mem. Associated Writing Programs, Acad. Am. Poets, Sierra Club, Amnesty Internat. Mem. Lds Ch. Avocations: golf, reading, movies, environmental protection, child/family advocacy projects. Home: 6521 Snowview Dr Park City UT 84098-6167 Office Phone: 801-975-1000.

SOLOMON, ELINOR HARRIS, economics educator; b. Boston, Feb. 26, 1923; d. Ralph and Linna Harris; m. Richard A. Solomon, Mar. 30, 1957; children: Joan S. Griffin, Robert H., Thomas H. AB, Mt. Holyoke Coll., 1944; MA, Radcliffe U., 1945; PhD, Harvard U., 1948. Jr. economist Fed. Res. Bank Boston, 1945-48; economist Fed. Res. Bd. Govs., Washington, 1949-56; internat. economist U.S. State Dept., Washington, 1957-58; professorial lectr. Am. U., Washington, 1964-66; sr. economist antitrust div. U.S. Dept. Justice, Washington, 1966-82; prof. econs. George Washington U., Washington, 1982—. Econ. cons., Washington, 1982—; expert witness antitrust, fin. networks, electronic funds transfer cases, Washington, 1988—. Author: Virtual Money, 1997; author, editor: Electronic Funds Transfers and Payments, 1987, Electronic Money Flows, 1991; contbr. articles on econs., banking and law to profl. jours. Mem. Am. Econs. Assn., Nat. Economists Club (bd. govs. 1997-2000), The Cosmos Club (chair Digital Age series 1999-2001, chair Frontiers of Sci. 2001-2004. Home: 6805 Delaware St Chevy Chase MD 20815-4164 Office: George Washington U Dept Econs Washington DC 20052-0001

SOLOMON, GAIL ELLEN, physician; b. Bklyn., May 26, 1938; d. Samuel and Estelle (Suffin) S.; m. Harvey Hecht, Oct. 28, 1962; children: Daniel, Jonathan, Elizabeth. AB, Smith Coll., 1958; MD, Albert Einstein Coll. Medicine, 1962. Diplomate Am. Bd. Pediats., Am. Bd. Psychiatry and Neurology (assoc. examiner), Am. Bd. Electroencephalography, Am. Bd. Electroencephalography and Neurophysiology, Am. Bd. Clin. Neurophysiology. Intern in pediat. Bronx Mcpl. Hosp. Ctr., 1962-63, resident in pediat., 1963-64, N.Y. Hosp.-Cornell U. Med. Coll., N.Y.C., 1964-65; NIH vis. fellow in neurology and child neurology Columbia-Presbyn. Med. Ctr., N.Y.C., 1965-68, NIH vis. fellow in clin. neurophysiology and electroenceph.; instr. neurology Columbia U. Coll. of Physicians and Surgeons, N.Y.C., 1968-69; instr. in neurology and pediat. Cornell U. Med. Coll., 1969-70, asst. prof. neurology and pediat., 1970-76; asst. attending in neurology and pediat. N.Y. Hosp., N.Y.C., 1969-76, dir. electroencephalography, 1969—; assoc. prof. clin. neurology and pediat. Cornell U. Med. Coll., 1976—, assoc. prof. clin. neurology in psychiatry, 1983; assoc. attending in neurology and pediat. N.Y. Hosp., 1976—, assoc. attending neurologist in psychiatry, 1983—. Mem. joint com. for stroke facilities NIH; mem. FDA Peripheral and CNS Adv. Com., 1979-83, chmn., 1983, cons., 1983-84; mem. med. audit com. N.Y. Hosp., mem. utilization rev. com.; mem. profl. adv. bd. N.Y. State Epilepsy Assn.; adj. attending physician in neurology Meml.-Sloan Kettering Cancer Ctr., 1982-93; assoc. attending pediatrician Hosp. Spl. Surgery, 1987—; neurology cons. Blythedale Children's Hosp., Valhalla, N.Y., 1991—, Meml.-Sloan Kettering Cancer Ctr., 1993—. Author: (with F. Plum) Clinical Management of Seizures: A Guide for the Physician, 1976, (with Plum and Kutt) 2d edit., 1983; editor: (with Kaufman and Pfeffer) Child and Adolescent Neurology for Psychiatrists, 1992, Neurologic Disorders: Developmental and Behavioral Sequelae, 1999; contbr. articles to profl. jours., chpts. to med. books. Fellow Am. Acad. Neurology, Am. Acad. Pediats., Am. Electroencephalographic Soc. mem. AMA (Physician's Recognition award in Continuing Med. Edn.), N.Y. State Med. Soc., N.Y. County Med. Soc., Am. Med. Women's Assn., Am. Epilepsy Soc., Am. Acad. Clin. Neurophysiology, Eastern EEG Soc., Am. Med. EEG Assn., Child Neurology Soc., Internat. Child Neurology Assn., Tristate Child Neurology Soc., Assn. for Rsch. in Nervous and Mental Diseases, N.Y. Acad. Sci. Avocations: art museums, reading literature, french language, travel. Office: NY Presbyn Hosp Cornell U Med Coll 525 E 68th St New York NY 10021-4870 Office Phone: 212-746-3280.

SOLOMON, HILDA PEARL, wholesale executive; b. Conway, S.C., Dec. 15, 1948; d. Ezel and Dorothy (Gottlieb) S. BFA, U. S.C., 1968. Buyer Solomon Bros. Dept. Store, Conway, 1969-73; coutourier sales Julius Lewis, Memphis, 1973-75; buyer Helen of Memphis, 1975-78, George M. Muse Clothing Co., Atlanta, 1978-83; sales rep. Whiting & Davis Co. Inc., Plainville, Mass., 1983-84, exec. sales mgr. southeast dist., 1984-92; owner Solomon, Atlanta, 1992—. Sec. bd. dirs. Bur. Wholesale Accessory Reps., Atlanta, 1983-87, Accessories On 6 Atlanta Apparel Mart, 1986-87; dir. trade shows, key accounts, export mgr., 1994-98; nat. key account mgr.

Westminster, Inc., 1999-2000; dir. sales Decorative Expressions, Inc., Atlanta, 2000—. Prin. works include Posh Petals, Atlanta, 1986—. Mem. Atlanta Hist. Soc., Young Careers High Mus. Art. Jewish. Avocations: design, travel, writing. Home: 2917 Hamilton Sq Decatur GA 30033-1140

SOLOMON, MARSHA HARRIS, draftsman, artist; b. Tulsa, Oct. 21, 1940; d. Ruel Sutton and Anna May (Fellows) Harris; m. Robert E. Collier, Aug. 13, 1960 (div. Dec. 1968); 1 child, Craig Robert Collier; m. Louis G. Solomon, Sept. 5, 1984. Student, U. Tex., 1958-61; BFA, U. Houston, 1966. Chief draftsman Internat. Paper, Petroleum and Minerals Divsn., Houston, 1985—2003; artist, ptnr. Archway Gallery, Houston, 1994. Mem. Nat. Mus. Women in Art (charter). Mem. Watercolor Art Soc. Houston (bd. dirs. 1984-91, treas. 1987-89, pres. 1990-91), Tex. Watercolor Soc. (signature mem.), N.Mex. Watercolor Soc. (signature mem.), Okla. Watercolor Soc. (signature mem.), Ariz. Watercolor Soc. (Royal Scorpion mem.). Home: 5832 Valley Forge Dr Houston TX 77057-2248

SOLOMON, PHYLLIS LINDA, social work educator, researcher; b. Hartford, Conn., Dec. 6, 1945; d. Louis Calvin and Annabell Lee (Nitzberg) S. BA in Sociology, Russell Sage Coll., 1968; MA in Sociology, Case Western Res. U., 1970, PhD in Social Welfare, 1978. Lic. social worker, Pa. Rsch. assoc. Inst. Urban Studies Cleve. State U., 1970-71; program evaluator Cleve. State Hosp., 1971-74; project dir. Ohio Mental Health and Mental Retardation Rsch. Ctr., Cleve., 1974-75; rsch. assoc. Psychiat. Rsch. Found. of Cleve., 1975; project dir. Ohio Mental Health and Mental Retardation Rsch. Ctr., 1977-78; rsch. assoc. dirs. rsch. and mental health planning Fedn. for Cmty. Planning, 1978-88; prof. dept. mental health scis., dir. sect. mental health svcs. and systems rsch. Hahnemann U., Phila., 1988-94; prof. Sch. Social Work U. Pa., Phila., 1994—. Secondary appointment Prof. Social Work in Psychiatry U. Pa. Sch. Medicine, 1994—; adj. prof. dept. psychiatry Allegheny U., 1994-97. Author: (with others) Community Services to Discharged Psychiatric Patients, 1984; co-editor: New Developments in Psychiatric Rehabilitation, 1990, Psychiatric Rehabilitation in Practice, 1993; editl. adv. bd. Community Mental Health Jour., 1988—; editl. bd. Jour. Rsch. in Social Work, 1997-2000, Social Work Forum, 1997—, Health and Social Work, 1998-2000, Psychiat. Rehab. Jour., 1999—, Mental Health Svcs. Rsch. Jour., 2001—, Brief Treatment and Crisis Intervention, 2001—, Social Work, 2003—; contbr. articles to profl. jours. Trustee Cleve. Rape Crisis Ctr., 1981-84, CIT Mental Health Svcs., Cleve., 1985-88; mem. citizen's adv. bd. Sagamore Hills (Ohio) Children's Psychiat. Hosp., 1984-88; bd. dirs. Plan of Pa., 2004—, pres., 2004—. Named Evaluator of the Yr., Ohio Program Evaluators Group, 1987; recipient Ann. award Cuyahoga County Cmty. Mental Health Bd., 1988, Armin Loeb award Internat. Assn. Psychosocial Rehab. Svcs., 1999, Outstanding Non-Psychiatrist award Am. Assn. Cmty. Psychiatrists, 2002. Mem. NASW, Internat. Assn. Psychosocial Rehab. Svcs., Soc. for Social Work and Rsch. (1st place award for pub. article 1997). Jewish. Home: 104 Woodside Rd Apt A108 Haverford PA 19041-1831 Office: U Pa Sch Social Work 3701 Locust Walk Philadelphia PA 19104-6214

SOLOMON, RUTH, state legislator, teacher; b. Phila., Apr. 16, 1941; d. David and Bella (Azeff) Epstein; m. Arthur Solomon; 1 child, Barry. BA, U. Ariz., 1971. Tchr. Tucson (Ariz.) Unified Sch. Dist., 1971—; mem. Ariz. Ho. of Reps., Phoenix, 1988-94, Ariz. Senate, Dist. 14, Phoenix, 1994-. Pres. Tucson Edn. Assn., 1983-85; dir. Ariz. Edn. Assn., Phoenix, 1986—. Bd. dirs. Pima County Community Action Agy., Tucson, 1986—. Mayor's Coun. Youth Initiatives, Tucson, 1987—. Mem. Bus. and Profl. Women's Coun., Alpha Delta Kappa, Phi Kappa Phi. Avocation: swimming. Office: Ariz Senate 1700 W Washington St Rm 313 Phoenix AZ 85007-2812

SOLOMON, SUSAN, chemist, scientist; b. Chicago, Ill., Jan. 19, 1956; d. Leonard Marvin and Alice (Rutman) Solomon; m. Barry Lane Sidwell, Sept. 20, 1988. BS in Chemistry, Ill. Inst. Tech., 1977; MS in Chemistry, U. Calif., Berkeley, 1979, PhD in Chemistry, 1981. Rsch. chemist aeronomy lab. NOAA, Boulder, Colo., 1981—88, program leader middle atmosphere group aeronomy lab., 1988—. Adj. faculty U. Colo., 1982—; head project sci. Nat. Ozone Expdn., McMurdo Station, Antarctica, 1986, McMurdo Station, Antarctica, 87. Co-author: Aeronomy of the Middle Atmosphere, 1984; contbr. articles to sci. jours. Recipient Gold medal, U.S. Dept. Commerce, 1989, Scientist of the Yr. award, 1992, Nat. Medal of Sci., R&D Mag., 1999. Fellow: Am. Geophys. Union (J.B. McElwane award 1985), Am. Meteorol. Soc., Royal Meteorol. Soc.; mem.: Am. Acad. Arts and Scis., NAS. Avocations: creative writing, crafts, scuba diving.

SOLOMON, SUSANNE NINA, podiatrist, surgeon; b. Buffalo, Aug. 1, 1956; d. Joseph Michael and Olga (Kyzmir) S.; m. Jack M. Thompson, July 8, 1989; 1 child, Katherine Olga. AB cum laude, Cornell U., 1978; D of Podiatric Medicine, Pa. Coll., 1984. Diplomate Am. Bd. Podiatric Orthopedics, Am. Bd. Acad. of Wound Mgmt.; cert. wound specialist. Chief resident dept. podiatry Cambridge Hosp./Harvard Med. Sch., 1984-85; chief podiatric medicine and surgery Lemuel Shattuck Hosp., Jamaica Plain, Mass., 1986-89; podiatrist Deaconess Hosp., Cin., 1989—, Jewish Hosp., Cin., Bethesda Hosp., Cin., Miami Valley Hosp., Dayton, Ohio, 1999—; pediatric dir. Wound Care Ctr. Wright State Sch. of Medicine, Ohio, 1999—. Chief podiatric medicine and surgery Deaconess Hosp., Cin., 1996—, lectr. diabetes and athletes tchg. team, 1990—; dance medicine dir. Am. Acad. Podiatric Sports Medicine, 1993-94; dance medicine physician Met. Classical Ballet Co., Cin., 1991-93; supr. in podiatry Boston Marathon, 1985—; spokesperson women's health issues; U.S. Olympic com., Jacobs Inst. of Women's Health; com. mem. Impact of Tng. on Early Menarchal Athletes; pres., CEO Baby Greek, Inc. Co-author: (one act play) Courting Falia, 1997. Spokesperson Health Care Reform, Washington, 1994-95; health care task force Pres. Coun. of Cornell Women, 1995—. Fellow Am. Coll. Foot and Ankle Orthop. and Medicine, Am. Acad. Podiatric Sports Medicine; mem. Internat. Marathon Med. Dirs. Assn., Am. Med. Womens Assn. (Cin. chpt.), Am. Coll. Sports Medicine, Am. Podiatric Med. Assn., Cornell U. Club S.W. Ohio (pres. 1994-97), Alpha Phi (pres. Cin. chpt. 1992-95, trustee Cornell chpt. 1995—). Democrat. Russian Orthodox. Avocations: gardening, art, theatre, gourmet cooking, music. Home: 5241 Wandering Way Mason OH 45040-9184 Office: 71 E Hollister St Cincinnati OH 45219-1703

SOLON, DEBORAH EPSTEIN, curator; b. N.Y.C., Apr. 5, 1961; d. Gerson and Lila Epstein; married; children: Alexandra, Gabrielle. BA, Vassar Coll., 1982; MPhil, CUNY, 1990, PhD, 2003. Adminstr. Sotheby's, N.Y.C., 1982—86; lectr. SUNY, Purchase, 1988—90; dir. rsch. Karges Fine Art, L.A., 1991—96; guest curator Laguna Art Mus., Laguna Beach, Calif., 1998—99, adj. curator, 1999—. Acquisitions com., collections com Laguna Art Mus., Laguna Beach, 1999—, hist. collections coun., 2001—; adj. curator Pasadena Mus. Calif. Art. Author: Birds, Boughs and Blossoms, 1995, Cornelis Botke, 1996, Colonies of American Impressionism, 1999, In and Out of California: Travels of American Impressionists, 2002. Avocation: music. Home and Office: 30801 Palmetto Pl Laguna Niguel CA 92677 E-mail: deborahsolon@aol.com.

SOLOTAR, ANNE PAULA, real estate agent; b. Washington, Aug. 6, 1945; d. Edward Marc Solotar, Sophie Solotar; m. Michael Eric Siegel; 1 child, Sophie Siegel. BA, U. Md., 1969. Cert. Realtor 1981. Graphic artist Sears, Bethesda, Md., 1969—77, Rockvile, Md., 1977; dept. mgr., head cashier Bloomingdales, Kensington, Md., 1977—80; dir. tenant rels. Am. Invesco, Chgo., 1980—82; realtor Century 21, Bethesda, 1981—92, Long and Foster, Bethesda, 1992—. Builder Habitat for Humanity, 2002; active McGovern for Pres. Campaign, 1972, Udal for Pres. Campaign, 1976; precinct chairperson Dem. Ctrl. Com., Kensington, 1975—; dist. coord. Ventoulis for Gov., Balt., 1975—76; mem. Alliance for Dem. Reform, 1976, Young Dems., 1976; mem. forum steering com. Montgomery County Democratic Issues, 1977; founder Kol Shalom Synagogue, 2001; pres. Grosvenor Park Tenants Assn., Rockville, 1978—79. Named Top Prodr., Greater Capital Area Assn. Realtors, 1998, 1999, 2000; recipient Million Dollar Club, Montgomery County Assn. Realtors, 1984 to 1987, Outstanding Young Women of Am., 1979; grantee Young Leadership Conf., U.S. Dept. State, 1976. Avocations: swimming, photography, gardening. Business E-Mail: anne@annesolotar.com.

SOLOW, JAMIE ELISE, psychologist, vocalist; b. New Rochelle, N.Y., May 12, 1960; d. Herbert Franklin and Maxine Debora Solow; m. Kenneth Ohashi, Oct. 10, 1998; 1 child, Elijah. BA cum laude in Psychology, U. Calif., Santa Cruz, Calif., 1981; MA in Human Devel., U. Pacific Oaks, 1989; PhD in Clin. Psychology, The Fielding Inst., 2000. Play therapist Cedars Sinai Med. Ctr., 1987—92; pvt. practice LA, 2000—. Cons. Wright Inst., LA. Composer: (films) Healing the Wounds, Incest, 1989, (albums) Riddles, 2000. Mem.: Am. Psychol. Assn., Am. Soc. Composers and Pubs.

SOLOWAY, ROSE ANN GOULD, clinical toxicologist; b. Plainfield, N.J., Apr. 19, 1949; d. George Spencer Jr. and Rose Emma (Frank) Gould; m. Irving H. Soloway, Dec. 13, 1979. BSN, Villanova U., 1971; MS in Edn., U. Pa., 1976. Diplomate Am. Bd. Applied Toxicology. Staff nurse Hosp. of U. Pa., Phila., 1971-73; asst. clin. instr. Hosp. of U. Pa. Sch. Nursing, Phila., 1973-77; staff devel. instr. Hosp. of Med. Coll. Pa., Phila., 1977-78; dir. emergency nurse tng. program Ctr. for Study of Emergency Health Svcs., U. Pa., Phila., 1979-80; edn./comms. coord. Nat. Capital Poison Ctr. Georgetown U. Hosp., Washington, 1980-94; clin. toxicologist Nat. Capital Poison Ctr. George Washington U. Med. Ctr., Washington, 1994—; adminstr. Am. Assn. Poison Control Ctrs., Washington, 1994-99, assoc. dir., 1999—. Mem. clin. toxicology and substance abuse adv. panel U.S. Pharmacopeial Conv., Inc., Washington, 1990—2000, mem. expert panel clin. toxicology and substance abuse, 2000—. Contbr. articles to profl. jours. Mem.: APHA, Poison Prevention Week Coun. (vice-chair 1988—91, 2001—03, chair 1991—93, 2003—), Am. Acad. Clin. Toxicology (edn. com. 2000—), Am. Assn. Poison Control Ctrs. (co-chmn. pub. edn. com. 1985—90). Avocations: reading, cooking, knitting, jewelry making. Office: Am Assn Poison Control Ctrs Ste 330 3201 New Mexico Ave NW Washington DC 20016-2756

SOLTERO, MICHELLE DOLORES, director; b. San Diego, Calif., Mar. 25, 1960; d. Albert Lloyd and Dolores Luque Cardenas; m. Richard Soltero, Dec. 31, 1985; children: Cecilio Miguel, Patrick Anthony. BS in child develop., San Diego State U., 1978—83; M in human develop., Pacific Oaks Coll., 1990—95. Regular Children's Ctr. Supervision Permit State of Calif. Commn. on Tchr. Credentialing, 1996. Site dir. Child Devel. Associates, Inc., Chula Vista, Calif., 1985—89; program dir. YMCA of San Diego County, 1989—90; resource specialist YMCA of San Diego County Childcare Resource Svc., 1990—93, edn. and profl. devel. coord. Ednl. Enrichment Systems, Inc, San Diego, 1993—98; hsqic infant toddler specialist Devel. Associates, Inc, Walnut Creek, Calif., 1998—99; regional trainer/coord. WestED, Sausalito, Calif., 1999—. Pres. San Diego Assn. for the Edn. of Young Children, 1996—98; coun. mem. San Diego County Child Care and Devel. Planning Coun., 1997—; state pres. Calif. Assn. for the Edn. of Young Children, 2001—03. Marcia Fochler Grad./Post Grad. award, Calif. Assn. for the Edn. of Young Children, 1994. Mem.: Chicano Fedn. San Diego County, Nat. Assn. Edn. Young Children (gov. bd. 2004—). Avocations: hinge box collector, memory books. Home: 10157 Tres Lagos Court Spring Valley CA 91977 Office Phone: 619-644-7717. E-mail: msolter@wested.org.

SOLTES, JOANN MARGARET, retired music educator, realtor; b. Sewickley, Pa., Nov. 11, 1942; d. Mary Ann Soltes. BS in Music Edn., Duquesne U., 1964; MA, Mich. State U., 1977; student, Goethe Institut, Germany, 1992, Big Bend Coll., 1992. Music tchr. grades K-12 Ctr. Twp. Schs., Monaca, Pa., 1964—69; facilitator of masters program Nat.-Louis U., Heidelberg, Germany, 1995—99; music tchr., classroom tchr. Dept. Def. Dependent Schools Overseas, Okinawa, Turkey, Germany, Japan, 1969—99; realtor Coldwell Banker, Monaca, Pa., 1999—; substitute tchr. Facilitator The Study of Teaching Study Groups, Schweinufirt, Germany, 1992—95; presenter in field, Germany and Japan, 1992, Germany and Japan, 85. Mem. sch. advisory coun. Schweinfurt Am. Sch., Germany, 1995—96, mem. fine arts com., 1987—, chair grade level com., 1990—91, mem. sch. improvement com., 1989—90; vol. Adult Literacy Action, Beaver, Pa., 1999—2002; Ch. organist. Mem.: AAUW, Assn. for Supervision and Curriculum Devel., Beaver Falls Bus. and Career Women's Club (program chmn.), Beaver County Assn. Realtors, Nat. Assn. Realtors, Pa. Assn. Realtors, Community Concert Patron Board, Outlook Club, Phi Delta Kappa. Roman Catholic. Avocations: reading, cooking, bridge, singing, theatrical performance, church organist. Office: Coldwell Banker 3468 Brodhead Rd Monaca PA 15061

SOLTIS, KATHERINE, editor; b. Pitts., Apr. 15, 1950; d. John Andrew and Katherine (Hnidec) Goidich; m. Patrick T. Soltis, July 27, 1973 (div. 1998). BA, Mich. State U., 1972; MA in English/Linguistics, Case Western Res. U., 1982. Part time clk. Case Western Res. U., Cleve., 1974-03, lexicographer Webster's New World Dictionaries Macmillan/Simon & Schuster, Cleve., 1983—. Free-lance copy editor. Editor: Webster's New World Vest Pocket Dictionary, 2nd edit., 1994; style guide editor, Webster's New World Desk Dictionary and Style Guide. Trustee Cleve.- Volgograd Ptnr. Cities, 1990—; pres. Women Speak Out for Peace & Justice/Women's Internat. League for Peace & Freedom, 1993-95, chair program com., 1995-2001; orgn. rep., chair Cleve. Coalition Against the Death Penalty, 2002—; supporter/advocate Ariz. death row inmate, 1981—; mem. Cleve. Pro-Choice Action League, 1996—, Windsong Cleve. Feminist Chorus. Mellon fellow Case Western Res. U. Phi Beta Kappa. Mem. Soc. Of Friends. Avocations: classical music, gardening, composting/recycling, foreign travel, reading. Home: 896 Englewood Rd Cleveland Heights OH 44121-2042

SOLTZ, JUDITH E. insurance company executive, lawyer; BA, Barnard Coll., 1968; JD cum laude, Boston Coll., 1971; LLM in Taxation, NYU, 1978. Tax atty. Conn. Gen. Corp., 1973—85; asst. gen. counsel Cigna Corp., 1985—90, v.p. taxes, 1990—98, exec. v.p., gen. counsel, 1998—2001, 2001—. Mem. exec. com. CPR Inst. Dispute Resolution; past mem. adv. coun. Hartford Inst. Ins. Taxation; past chair tax com. Am. Ins. Assn. Trustee Acad. Natural Scis. Phila. Mem.: ABA (tax and bus. law sects.). Office: Cigna Corp 1 Liberty Pl Philadelphia PA 19192-1552

SOLUM, PAMELA BYARD, psychotherapist, educator; b. L.A., Nov. 02; d. Robert Frank Byard and Eleanor Mary Bremer Shephard; m. Clayton Lawrence Solum, June 5, 1980 (div. July 2000); 1 child, Alexandra Lawrence Sloan. MA, Pacific Oaks Coll., Pasadena, Calif., 1982. Lic. marriage and family therapist Calif., cert. tchr. Calif. Vis. faculty Pacific Oaks Coll., Pasadena, 1979—80; tchr. Montebello Adult Edn., Calif., 1972—, North Orange County C.C., Orange County, Calif., 1980—90, East L.A. Coll., 1980—83; pvt. practice psychotherapy Cerritos, Calif. Cons., facilitator Beverly Hosp., Montebello; psychol. advisor various parent groups; corr. sec. UN, Whittier, Calif. Contbr. articles to profl. jours. Hon. mem. City of Hope for Mental Health. Recipient Self Esteem award, L.A. County Commn. on Women, 1987, 1990, Family Svc. Honor award, L.A., 1994. Mem.: Fine Arts Club of Pasadena (corr. sec.). Home: 5262 Javalambre Dr Whittier CA 90601 Office: 11010 Artesia Ste 202 Cerritos CA 90703

SOLYMOSY, HATTIE MAY, writer, publisher, storyteller, educator; b. Kew Gardens, N.Y., Apr. 1, 1945; d. Julius and Sylvia Becky (Glantz) Fuld (dec.); m. Abraham Edward Solymosy, Apr. 21, 1974 (div., Sept. 2000). BA, Queens Coll., 1966, MS in Edn., 1973. Cert. tchr., N.Y.C. and N.Y. Actress, model, 1950-60; elem. tchr. N.Y.C. Bd. of Edn., 1966—; owner Ultimate Jewelry, N.Y.C., 1976-80; tutor N.Y.C., 1983-91; children's writer, 1991—; romance writer, 1993—; owner Hatties' Tales, Cedarhurst, N.Y., 1993—, Cigar Box Factory, Cedarhurst, N.Y., 1993—. Bd. dirs. Hamajama Gifts; co-owner Cigar Box Factory, 1996—, Spouse-For-Hire, 1999—, Pen Pal psychic advisor, 1999, Psychic Line, 1999—, ATM Mktg., 1999—, Credit Card Machines, 2000—, Ads-in Motion, Hot Nuts, Teaching Kids to Cook!, 2003, Ally-for-Hire, 2003, Cool Kids Cook!, 2003. Author: (sound recs.) Delancy Dolphin, 1993, Thaddius Thoroughbred, 1993, Willie's War, 1993, Noodles-An Autobiography, 1993, (with Jared Marc Milk) Trapped With The Past, 1993, Thick Slick Tangled Webs, 1993, Cinderella Cockroach, 1993, A Christmas Tale, 1993, Chanukah Tale, 1993, Doc Simon, 1995, Mr. Music, 1996, Women on Film, 1996, Buying a Dream, 1996, Rock and Roll, 1996, The Psycho Line, 1999, Legally Raped, 1999; author: Myster of the Old Fishing Shack, 1999, Hot Nuts, 2000, Cool Kids Cook!, 2003. Social sec., fundraiser Children's Med. Ctr., N.Y.C., 1969-79; aux. mem. St. John's Hosp., N.Y., 1987—; storyteller children's stories Oklahoma City Fed. Bldg. bombing victims, Mo. flood victims, children's hosps.; assoc. mem. Mus. Natural History; fundraiser Lung Assn., 1997—, Am. Heart Assn., 1998—. Mem. Romance Writers of Am., Soc. of Children's Writers and Illustrators, Simon Wiesenthal Ctr., World Jewish Congress, del. People to People Internat. Missions in Understanding. Democrat. Jewish. Avocations: music, tennis, movies, gardening, dance. Home: Chatham Sq 326 A Peninsula Blvd Cedarhurst NY 11516 Office: Hatties Tales Cigar Box Factory and Spouse-for-Hire Psychic Line Pen Pal Psych PO Box 24 Cedarhurst NY 11516-0024

SOMEKAWA, MINA C. pianist, educator; b. Dec. 25, 1958; d. Akira and Nobuko Somekawa. BA in English, Sophia U., 1981; postgrad., U. Mo., 1990—92; MusB in Piano Performance, U. Ill., 1993, MusM in Piano Performance, postgrad., U. Ill., 1995—. Piano tchg. asst. U. Ill., Urbana-Champaign, 1994—96; keyboardist Civic Orch. of Chgo., 1995—96; prin. keyboardist Sinfonia da Camera, Urbana, 1995—2001, Champaign-Urbana Symphony, 1996—, Ill. Symphony Orch., Springfield, Ill., 1997—, Fresno Philharmonic, Calif., 1998—, Miss. Sympony Orch., Jackson, 2002—03. Pvt. piano instr., various cities, Ill., 1996—2001, various cities, Miss., 2002—; piano faculty mem. Blue Lake Fine Arts Camp, Twin Lake, Mich., 1998; audition judge Nat. Fedn. Music Clubs, 1998, Miss. Music Tchrs. Assn., 2003—, vis. asst. prof. music Millsaps Coll., Jackson, Miss., 2002. Musician: St. Louis Artist Presentation Soc., 1993, Brahms First Piano Concerto, 1994, Dame Myra Hess Meml. Concert, 1998; musician: (piano/harpsichord solo) Ill. Chamber Orch., 2000; author: The Snowman: Easy Piano Picture Book Series, 1989, (recorded music) Ballet Class I Played by Mina Somekawa, 1989, The Snowman, 1987. Recipient Phi Beta Kappa Jr. honor, U. Mo., Columbia, 1991, Ruth Melcher Allen Meml. award, Sigma Alpha Iota, 1991, Artist Presentation Soc. award, The St. Louis Artist Presentation Soc., 1992, Simone Belsky Music award, Litchfield, Conn., 1993, Bartók-Kabalevsky Internat. Piano Competition, Radford, Va., 1993, Beethoven Piano Sonata Competition, Memphis, Tenn., 1995; Music fellow, U. Ill., 1993—94. Mem.: Coll. Music Soc., Am. Fedn. Musicians, Pi Kappa Lambda, Golden Key Nat. Honor Soc. Home: Apt 214 1315 N Jefferson St Jackson MS 39202-1764 E-mail: msomekaw@msn.com.

SOMER-GREIF, PENNY LYNN, lawyer; b. New Hyde Park, N.Y., Mar. 30, 1970; d. Stanley Jerome and Janice Somer; m. Brian Scott Greif. BS, SUNY, Binghamton, 1992; JD, Am. U., 1995. Bar: N.J. 1996, N.Y. 1996, D.C. 2000. Atty.-advisor U.S. SEC, Washington, 1995-2000; assoc. Arnold & Porter, Washington, 2000—. Avocations: reading, exercise. Office: 555 Twelfth NW Washington DC 20004-1206 Office Phone: 202-942-6402.

SOMERMAN, MARTHA J. academic administrator; DDS, NYU, 1975; PhD, U. Rochester, 1980. Asst. prof., periodontics and pharmacology Balt. Coll. Dental Surgery, 1984—87, assoc. prof., pharmacology, 1987—91, U. Mich., 1991—95, chair, dept. periodontics, prevention and geriatrics, 1991—2001, prof., pharmacology, 1995—2000, assoc. dean rsch., Sch. Dentistry, 2001—02; dean, Sch. Dentistry U. Wash., 2002—. Contbr. articles to profl. jours. Office: RMD 322 Box 356365 Seattle WA 98195

SOMERS, ANNE RAMSAY, retired medical educator; b. Memphis, Sept. 9, 1913; d. Henry Ashton and Amanda Vick (Woolfolk) Somers; m. Herman Miles Somers, Aug. 31, 1946; children: Sara Ramsay, Margaret Ramsay. BA, Vassar Coll., 1935; postgrad., U. N.C., 1939—40; DSc (hon.), Med. Coll. Wis., 1975. Edn1. dir. Internat. Ladies Garment Workers Union, 1937—42; labor economist U.S. Dept. Labor, 1943—46; rsch. assoc. Haverford Coll., 1957—63; rsch. assoc. indsl. rels. sect. Princeton U., 1964—84; prof. U. Medicine and Dentistry of N.J.-R. Wood Johnson Med. Sch. (formerly Rutgers Med. Sch.), 1971—84, adj. prof., 1984—2002. Adj. prof. geriat. medicine U. Pa. Sch. Medicine, 1990—2002; mem. Nat. Bd. Med. Examiners, 1983—86; cons. in health econs., health edn., geriats., gerontology, realted areas. Author: Hospital Regulation: The Dilemma of Public Policy, 1969, Health Care in Transition: Directions for the Future, 1971, author: (with H.M. Somers) Workmen's Compensation: The Prevention, Rehabilitation and Financing of Occupational Disability, 1954; author: Medicare and the Hospitals, 1967, Doctors, Patients and Health Insurance, 1961, Health and Health Care: Policies in Perspective, 1971; author: (with N.L. Spears) The Continuing Care Retirement Community: A Significant Option for Long Care?, 1992; editor (with D.R. Fabian): he Geriatric Imperative: An Introduction to Gerontology and Clinical Geriatrics, 1981. Mem. bd. visitors Duke U. Med. Ctr., 1972—77, U. Tex. Health Scis. Ctr., Houston, 1982—86. Named to Health Care Hall of Fame, 1993; recipient Elizur Wright award, Am. Risk and Ins. Assn., 1962. Fellow: Coll. Physicians Phila. (hon.), Am. Coll. Hosp. Adminstrs. (hon.); mem.: Nat. Acad. Social Ins., Inst. Medicine of NAS, Soc. Tchrs. of Family Medicine (hon.). Home: Pennswood Village # C-202 Newtown PA 18940-2401

SOMERS, MARION, gerontologist, family counselor; children: Lynne, Randy, Cortney, Jessica, Craig, Matthew. M in Neuro Linguistic Programming, PhD, The Fielding Inst. Lic. nursing home adminstr. N.Y. Dir. profl. geriatric care mgrs. Brookdale Ctr. on Aging Hunter Coll. Grant reader HHS, Washington; observer White House Conf. on Aging. Author: The Home: A Brief Moment in Time. Office: 601 7th St Brooklyn NY 11215-3708

SOMERS, SUZANNE MARIE, actress, writer, singer; b. San Bruno, Calif., Oct. 16, 1946; d. Frank and Marion Mahoney; m. Greg Somers (div.); 1 child ; m. Alan Hamel, 1977. Student, Lone Mountain Sch., San Francisco Coll. for Women; studies with Charles Conrad. Owner, founder Suzanne Somers Collection. Actress: (films) American Graffiti, 1973, Billy Jack Goes to Washington, 1977, Yesterday's Hero, 1979, Nothing Personal, 1980, Rusty: A Dog's Tale, 1997; (TV films) Sky Heist, 1975, It Happened at Lakewood Manor, 1977, Happily Ever After, 1978, Zuma Beach, 1978, Goodbye Charlie, 1985, Totally Minnie, 1988, Rich Men, Single Women, 1990, Seduced by Evil, 1994, Devil's Food, 1996, Love-Struck, 1997, No Laughing Matter, 1998, The Darklings, 1999; (TV series) Anniversary Game, 1969, High Rollers, 1974, Three's Company, 1977-81, She's the Sheriff, 1987-89, Step by Step, 1991—98; (TV mini-series) Hollywood Wives, 1985; actress, co-exec. prodr.: (films) Exclusive, 1992; host: (TV series) The Suzanne Somers Show, 1994, VH1's 8-Track Flashback, 1995, Candid Camera (co-host), 1997-2000; performer Las Vegas (Nev.) Hilton, MGM Grand, Las Vegas, Sands Hotel, Atlantic City, USO, various TV comms.; author: Touch Me Again, 1973, Keeping Secrets (autobiography), 1988, Suzanne Somers' Eat Great, Lose Weight, 1997, After the Fall: How I Picked Myself Up, Dusted Myself Off and Started All Over Again (autobiography), 1998, Suzanne Somers' Get Skinny on Fabulous Food, 1999, Suzanne Somers 365 Ways to Change Your Life, 1999, Eat, Cheat, and Melt the Fat Away, 2001, The Sexy Years: Discover the Hormone Connection, 2004. Recipient Humanitarian award, Nat. Council on Alcoholism, 1992, President's award, Nat. Assoc. of American Drug Counselors.*

SOMERSTEIN-CAMPBELL, JASMINE AURORA ABRERA, preschool administrator, educator; b. Manila, Feb. 17, 1943; d. Bernardo Paez and Rosalia (Sityar) Abrera; m. Jules Leon Somerstein, Dec. 10, 1967 (div. July 1995); children: Joseph, Sandra, Marc (dec. Mar. 2001); m. James Walter Campbell, Jan. 13, 2001. BA in English, U. Philippines, Manila, 1964; MA in English Edn., NYU, 1978, MA in Elem. Edn., 1987; postgrad., U. Pitts., Oxford (Eng.) U., 1964-66, 86. Cert. tchr., N.Y. Instr. U. Pitts., 1965-66, U. of the East, Manila, 1968-69; tchr. Am. Internat. Sch., Manila, 1966, Domenec High Sch., Pitts., 1967-68; substitute tchr. Lakeland and Peekskill Sch. Dist., NY, 1975-77; exec. dir. Internat. Pre-Sch. Ctr., Inc., NY, 1977—; instr. Bd. Coop. Ednl. Svcs., N.Y.C., 1989-97; exec. dir. Horas Alegres Bilingual Presch., Dallas, 1997—2003, Internat. Tots, Inc., 2003; early childhood coord. Good Shepherd Cath. Ch., Colleyville, 2000—; dir. Good Shepherd Little Lambs Program, 2002—. Exec. sec. Ctr. Ednl. TV, Manila, 1964; sec. NYU, 1973—74, UN, N.Y.C., 1975; prodr., interviewer Continental Cablevision, N.Y.C., 1984—97; child devel. advisor Westchester County, N.Y.C., 1989—; cons. Hudson Valley Export-Import, Inc., N.Y.C., 1988—92; adj. instr. Tarrant County Coll., Hurst, 2001—. Vol. Philippine Band of Mercy, Manila, 1963-93. Mem. Nat. Child Care Assn., Nat. Assn. Edn. Young Children, Nat. Coun. Tchrs. English, N.Y. Child Care Assn., Assn. Childhood Edn. Internat., Child Care Coun. Westchester, Manitoga, Peekskill/Cortlandt C. of C. (bd. dirs. 1989-92), Greater Dallas Hispanic C. of C., Hispanic Bus. Alliance. Democrat. Avocations: reading, photography, music, travel, piano. Office: PO Box 93056 Southlake TX 76092-1056 E-mail: Jasminvale@aol.com.

SOMERVILL, BARBARA ANN, small business owner, writer; b. New Rochelle, N.Y., July 28, 1948; d. Harold Phillip and Hope Agatha (Hayden) Klesius; m. Michael O. McWilliams, June 10, 1972 (div. June 1986); children: Scott, Matthew; m. Charles Forrest Somervill, June 30, 1990; children: Seth, Taylor. BA, St. Lawrence U., 1970. Chmn. dept. writing techniques Pinewood Pvt. Sch., Los Altos, Calif., 1980-86; mgr. corp. comm. Karastan Bigelow, Greenville, S.C., 1986-88; editor Monarch Edge, food mag., Greenville, 1988-94; pres. Somervill Inc., Simpsonville, S.C., 1994—. Mem. adv. bd. Local advt. rev. bd. Better Bus. Bur., Greenville, 1989-93; mem. adv. bd. Pearce Young Angel/Monarch Health Care, Greenville, 1990-93. Author: The Best Guide to Success in Your Career, 1998, Ida M. Tarbell: Pioneer Investigative Journalist, 2002, Striking a Blow for Women: Carrie Chapman Catt., 2002, Franklin Pierce, 2002, Sea to Shining Sea: Fla., 2001, Sea to Shining Sea: Alaska, 2002, Sea to Shining Sea: Maryland, 2003, Sea to Shining Sea: Pennsylvania, 2003, Sea to Shining Sea: West Virginia, 2003, Sea to Shining Sea: Mississippi, 2003, Enchantment of the World: Iceland, 2003, Andrew Jackson, 2003, James K. Polk, 2003. Bd. dirs. Christmas Is For Kids, Greenville, 1989-94, Greenville Soup Kitchen, 1994-96. Mem. NAFE, Internat. Documentary Assn., N.C. Writers' Network, Assn. Women in Comm., Greenville Duplicate Bridge Club (bd. dirs. 1994—). Episcopalian. Avocations: duplicate bridge, golf, reading, theater. Home and Office: 103 Rainwood Dr Simpsonville SC 29681-3440

SOMERVILLE, DAPHINE HOLMES, retired elementary education educator; b. Clinton, N.C., Jan. 19, 1940; d. George Henry and Mamie Estelle (Streeter) Holmes; m. Kalford Burton Somerville, Dec. 26, 1970 (div. Sept. 1992); 1 child, Daria Lynn. AA, Blackburn Coll., 1959, BA, 1961; MS in Edn., Hofstra U., 1967; postgrad., Columbia U., 1971, SUNY, Farmingdale, 1999-2000. Permanent teaching cert. common br. subjects grades 1-8. Tchr. East Islip (N.Y.) Sch. Dist., 1961-99, ret., 1999; tchr. computer/writing Opportunities Industrialization Ctr., 1998—2003, cert. webmaster, 2000—. Mem., instr. Outcome Based/Mastery Learning/Excellence in Learning Com., East Islip, 1984—89; mentor East Islip Sch. Dist., 1987—88, mem. sch. improvement team, 1989—91, staff devel. com., 1992—96; chair Ptnrs. in Edn., 1991—2001; instr. AARP's Driver Safety, 2001—03; election inspector, 2001—04. Author: Beaman Family Reunion Journal, 2001, Baptist Training Union Study Guide; founder, co-author: tutoring program Adopt-A-School Child/Family, 1990. Mem. Bay Shore (N.Y.) Civic Assn. and Bay Shore Pub. Schs. Task Force for the Advancement of Equality of Ednl. Opportunity, 1967—69; sec. Islip Town NAACP, Bay Shore, 1965—90; dir. Bapt. Tng. Union, 1974—81; trustee First Bapt. Ch., Bay Shore, 1972—90. Recipient Cmty. Svc. award Town Bd.-Town of Islip, Suffolk County, 1982, Recognition award Islip Town NAACP, 1987, Disting. Svc. award L.I. Region NAACP, 1993, Dedicated Svc. award Ptnrs. in Edn. First Bapt. Ch. of Bayshore, 1995, 98, Proclamation for genuine concern edn. residents Suffolk County Exec. Robert Gaffney, 1997, Cert. Spl. Congl. Recognition, Congressman Rick Lazio, 1997, African-Am. Educators award Martin L. King Commn. of Suffolk County, 1997, Editors Choice award The Nat. Libr. of Poetry, 1999, Citation, Town of Islip, 1999; L.I. Sch. to Career Partnership for Proposed Sch./Bus. Govt. Project grantee, 1998. Mem. Nat. Coun. Negro Women (life, ednl. involvement award 1993), East Islip Tchrs. Assn. (past bldg. rep.), N.Y. State United Tchrs., Huntington Christian Women's Club (fin. coord. 2003-04) . Democrat. Avocations: theater, writing, tennis, reading, working with children, travel. Home: 130 Carman Rd Dix Hills NY 11746-5648

SOMERVILLE, DIANA ELIZABETH, author; b. Lincoln, Nebr., June 12, 1942; d. Edward John and Eunice Louise (Johnson) Wagner; m. Dale Springer Johnson, Aug. 7, 1961 (div. 1971); children: Carlyle Johnson Lee, Kelmie Blake. BA in English Lit., Centenary Coll., 1967. Dir. info. office Nat. Ctr. Atmospheric Rsch., Boulder, Colo., 1969-81; mgr. info. svcs. RDD Cons., Boulder, 1981-82; sci. writer U. Colo., Boulder, 1983-87; mgr. comm. Optoelectronic Computing Sys. Ctr., Boulder, 1987-88; columnist Daily Camera, Boulder, 1992—99; lectr. Peninsula Coll., 2001—. Lectr. U. Colo., 1996-99; founder Colo. Mag. Writers Inst. Editor: Optimum Utilization of Human Knowledge, 1983, Artful Meditation, 1995; contbr. numerous articles to mags. including New Scientist, Earth mag. and in World Book Ency. Mem. women's caucus AAAS, 1969-75; mem. com. on pub. info. Am. Geophys. Union, 1977-78; mem. ednl. programs com. Am. Meteorol. Soc., 1978-80; mem. Turning the Wheel Dance/Theatre Co.; bd. dirs. Womanfest. Recipient Exceptional Achievement award Coun. for the Advancement and Support of Edn., Gold medal, 1986, Gold Pick award Pub. Rels. Soc. Am., 1985, Gold Quill award Internat. Assn. Bus. Comms., 1985. Mem. Nat. Assn. Sci. Writers, Am. Soc. Journalists and Authors, Boulder Media Women. Avocations: theatre, dance, jungian dreamwork, healing rituals, women's issues.

SOMMER, ANNEMARIE, pediatrician; b. Königsberg, Prussia, Federal Republic Germany, Jan. 1, 1932; came to U.S., 1955; d. Heinrich Otto and Maria Magdalena (Kruppa) S. BA, Wittenberg U., Springfield, Ohio, 1960; MD, Ohio State U., 1964. Diplomate Am. Bd. Pediat., Am. Bd. Med. Genetics. Intern Grant Hosp., Columbus, Ohio, 1964-65; resident in pediat. Children's Hosp., Columbus, 1965-67; NIH fellow in med. genetics, 1968-70; from asst. prof. pediatrics to assoc. prof. Coll. Medicine Ohio State U., Columbus, 1975-97, prof., 1997-99, chief genetics div., 1984-98. Mem. adv. bd. Heinzerling Found., Columbus, 1980—; bd. dirs. Regional Genetics Ctr., Columbus. Contbr. articles to profl. jours. Com. mem. Ohio Prevention MR/DD Coalition, Columbus, 1987; bd. dirs. Franklin County Bd. Health, Columbus, 1985—. Fellow Am. Acad. Pediatrics, Am. Bd. Med. Genetics, Am. Coll. Med. Genetics (founder); mem. Ctrl. Ohio Pediatric Soc., Midwest Soc. for Pediatric Research, Dublin (Ohio) Hist. Soc. Lutheran. Home: 4700 Brand Rd Dublin OH 43017-9530 Office: Ohio State Coll Medicine Sect Human and Molecular Genetics 700 Childrens Dr Columbus OH 43205 2664

SOMMER, DEBORAH KELLY, language educator; b. Great Lakes, Ill., Apr. 19, 1952; d. Gerald Joseph Kelly and Mary Ann Koch; m. Douglas Eliot Sommer, June 18, 1978 (div. Sept. 1989); 1 child, Lauren Michelle Summer. BA, Madison Coll., 1974. Sales clk. W7 Grants, Alexandria, Va., 1968—70; sales clk., make-up artist Merle Norman Cosmetics, Springfield, 1971—73; sales clk. Montgomery Wards, 1973—74; tchr. Spanish Jefferson Davis Jr. High Sch., Hampton, 1974—85, Bethel High Sch., 1985—2003; adminstr. ESL/fgn. lang. Hampton City Schs., 2003—. Fulbright Hays fellow, 1993. Mem.: Fgn. Lang. Assn. Va. (nominations chair 2001—03), Hampton Edn. Assn. (v.p. 1981—83, pres. 1983—85), Va. Edn. Assn. (mem. resolutions com. 1983—). Avocations: reading, exercise, travel, music, stamp collecting. Home: 89 Charles Paresh Dr Poquoson VA 23662 E-mail: cruela89@erols.com.

SOMMERFELD, MARIANNA, retired social worker, writer; b. Frankfurt, Germany, Jan. 25, 1920; d. Martin and Helene (Schott) S. BA, Smith Coll., 1940; MA, Radcliffe Coll., 1946; MSW, Simmons Coll., 1957. Lic. ind. social worker. Tchr. Latin, German, English Burnham Sch. Girls, Northampton, Mass., 1940-43; German translator Yale Inst. Human Rels., New Haven, 1943-44; tchr. Northfield (Mass.) Sch. Girls, 1944-45; psychiat. social worker McLean Hosp., Belmont, Mass., 1957-59, Gaebler Children's Unit/Met. State Hosp., Waltham, Mass., 1959-62, Boston U./Boston City Hosp., 1962-67, New Eng. Med. Ctr., Boston, 1967-71; pvt. practice Cambridge, Mass., 1962-68; supr. clin. social work Erich Lindemann Mental Health Ctr., Boston, 1971-90; writer, 1976—. Author: Marianna Sommerfeld: Diary of a Single Woman, 1991. Vol. Cambridge Sch., 1993. Mem. NOW, AFL-CIO, Planned Parenthood, Nat. Writers Union, Women's Nat. Book Assn., PEN New Eng. (assoc.).

SOMOGYI, JENNIE, dancer; b. Easton, Pa. Studied with Madame Nina Youshkevitch; student, Sch. Am. Ballet. Apprentice N.Y.C. Ballet, 1993—94, mem. corps de ballet, 1994—98, soloist, 1998—2000, prin., 2000—. Dancer (ballets) The Nutcracker, Allegro Brillante, Apollo, Tschaikovskys Pas De Deux, Glass Pieces, The Sleeping Beauty, Swan Lake, Quartet for Strings, Appalachia Waltz, Urban Dances, Swerve Poems, Polyphonia. Recipient Mae L. Wien award, The Princess Grace Found. award, Martin E. Segal award. Office: NYC Ballet NY State Theatre 20 Lincoln Ctr Plz New York NY 10023-6913

SOMOVA, MARLA JO, counseling administrator, psychologist; b. Hudson, NY, Sept. 25, 1970; d. Charles W. and Jo-Ed Woodward; m. Pavel G. Somov, Dec. 8, 1991. PhD, SUNY, 1996—2000; MS, U. of Ctrl. Ark., Conway, Arkansas, 1993—95, BA, 1988—92. Lic. Licensed Clinical Psychologist Pa, 2002. Asst. dir. / tng. coord. Duquesne U. Counseling Ctr., Pitts., 2001—; postdoctoral resident U. of Wyo. Counseling Ctr., Laramie, Wyo., 2000—01. Psychologist pvt. practice Vista Behavioral Health, Pitts., 2003—. Author: (journal articles) Am. Jour. of Hospice and Palliative Care. Mem.: APA. Avocations: travel, running, knitting, writing screenplays. Office: Duquesne University Counseling Center 308 Administration Building Pittsburgh PA 15282

SONBUCHNER, GAIL MURPHY, secondary special education educator; b. St. Paul, Aug. 26, 1942; d. Harold Alvin and Marian Rose (Erickson) Anderson; (div.); children: Marla Estelle, Sean Steven, Jason James Francis; m. Hugo Frank Sonbuchner, July 18, 1983; children: Gregory, Jon, Viktoria. BS in Elem. Edn., U. Minn., 1964; MS in Elem. Edn., Bemidji State U., 1980. Cert. elem. edn., elem. remedial reading, secondary remedial reading, secondary developmental reading, learning disabilities. Elem. classroom tchr. S.W. Elem. Sch., Grand Rapids, Minn., 1964-67; middle/H.S. spl. edn. tchr. Deer River (Minn.) H.S., 1979-80; spl. edn. tchr. Monticello (Minn.) H.S., 1980—. Spkr. Laubach Literacy Conv., Raleigh, N.C., 1992; mem. adv. bd. Hamline U. Collaborating for Learning and Studying Strategies, St. Paul, 1995, State Minn. Spl. Edn. Licensure Stds. Team, Bd. Tchg., 1996. Author: Help Yourself: How to Take Advantage of Your Learning Styles, 1991. Mem. Minn. Fedn. Tchrs. Roman Catholic. Avocations: quilting, writing. Home: 1504 W River St Monticello MN 55362-8957 Office: Monticello HS PO Box 897 Monticello MN 55362-0897

SONDERBY, SUSAN PIERSON, federal judge; b. Chicago, May 15, 1947; d. George W. and Shirley L. (Eckstrom) Pierson; m. James A. De Witt, June 14, 1975 (dec. 1978); m. Peter R. Sonderby, Apr. 7, 1990. AA, Joliet Jr. Coll., Joliet, Ill., 1967; BA, U. Ill., 1969; JD, John Marshall Law Sch., 1973. Bar: Ill., 1973; U.S. Dist. Ct. (cen. and so. dists.) Ill., 1978,; U.S. Dist. Ct. (no. dist.) Ill., 1984; U.S. Ct. Appeals (7th Cir.), 1984. Assoc. O'Brien, Garrison, Berard, Kusta, and De Witt, Joliet, Ill., 1973-75, ptnr., 1975-77; asst. atty. gen. consumer protection div., litig. sect. Office of the Atty. Gen., Chgo., 1977-78, asst. atty. gen., chief consumer protection divsn. Springfield, Ill., 1978-83; U.S. trustee (no. dist.) Ill. Chgo., 1983-86; judge U.S. Bankruptcy Ct. (no. dist.) Ill., Chgo., 1986—, chief fed. bankruptcy judge, 1998—2002. Mem. law faculty Fed. Jud. Tng. Ctr., Ill., Practicing Law Inst., Ill., U.S. Dept. Justice, Ill., Nat. Bankruptcy Inst., Ill., Ill. Continuing Edn.; spl. asst. atty. gen., Ill., 1972—78; adj. faculty De Paul U. Coll. Law, Chgo., 1986; past mem. U.S. Trustee adv. com., Ill.; consumer adv. coun. Fed. Res. Bd., Ill.; past sec. of State Fraudulent I.D. com. Dept. of Ins. Task Force on Improper Claims Practices, Ill.; former chair pers. rev. bd., mem. task force race and gender bias, U.S. Dist. Ct.; jud. conf. planning com. 7th Cir. Jud. Conf.; former mem. Civil Justice Reform Act Adv. Com.; mem. Adminstrv. Office of the U.S. Cts. Bankruptcy Judges Adv. Group; former mem. Ct. Security com.; mem. Adminstrv. Office of the U.S. Cts. Budget and Fin. Coun. Contbr. articles to profl. jour. Mem. Fourth Presbyn. Ch., Art Inst. Chgo.; past mem. Westminster Presbyn. Ch., Chgo. Coun. of Fgn. Rels.; past bd. dirs. Land of Lincoln Coun. Girl Scouts U.S.; past mem. individual guarantors com. Goodman Theatre, Chgo.; past chair clubs and orgns. Sangamon County United Way Capital campaign; past bd. dirs., chair house rules com. and legal subcom. Lake Point Tower; past mem. Family Svc. Ctr., Aid to Retarded Citizens, Henson Robinson Zoo. Named Young Career Woman, Bus. and Profl. Women, One of Ten Outstanding Bankruptcy Judges, Turnarounds and Workouts, 2002; recipient Spl. Achievement Award, Dept. Justice, 1984, Disting. Svc. Alumni Award, Joliet Jr. Coll., 1987, Disting. Alumni Award, John Marshall Law Sch., 1988, Dir. Award, Exec. Office U.S. Trustee, Leadership Award, Internat. Orgn. Women Exec., Outstanding Svc. to Bench, Am. Bankruptcy Inst., 1990. Master: Abraham Lincoln Marovitz Inn of Ct. (former pres., membership com.); fellow: Am. Coll. Bankruptcy (circuit admissions com.); mem.: ATLA, Comml. Law League Am. (former exec. coun. mem., bankruptcy and insolvency sect., coord. with nat. conf. bankruptcy judges com.), Nat. Conf. Bankruptcy Judges (co-chair ednl. program com. conf. 2001, liaison with bankruptcy rev. commn. com.), Bar Assn. (7th cir.) (former treas., judicial conf. planning com.), Am. Bankruptcy Inst. (bd. dirs. Chgo. chpt.), Fed. Bar Assn., Chgo. Archtl. Found., John Marshall Law Sch. Alumni Assn. (bd. dirs.), Nordic Law Club (past legis. com.), Lawyers Club Chgo. (hon.). Avocations: travel, flying, interior decorating. Office: US Bankruptcy Ct 219 S Dearborn St Ste 638 Chicago IL 60604-1702

SONDEREGGER, THEO BROWN, psychology educator; b. Birmingham, Ala., May 31, 1925; d. Ernest T. and Vera M. (Sillox) Brown; children: Richard Paul, Diane Carol, Douglas Robert. BS, Fla. State U., 1946; MA in Chemistry, U. Nebr., 1948, MA in Exptl. Psychology, 1960; PhD in Clin. Psychology, U. Nebr., 1965. Lic. psychologist, Nebr., Calif; clin. lic., cert. Nebr. Asst. prof. U. Nebr. Med. Ctr., Omaha, 1965-71, Nebr. Wesleyan U., Lincoln, 1965-68, U. Nebr., Lincoln, 1968-71, assoc. prof., 1971-76, prof., 1976-94; ret., 1994; prof. emeritus, 1995—. Vol. assoc. prof. U. Nebr. Med. Ctr., 1972-77, courtesy prof. med. psychology, 1977-95. Editor: Nebr. Symposium on Motivation, 1974, 84, 91, Problems of Perinatal Drug Dependence: Research and Clinical Implications, 1986, Neurobehavioral Toxicology and Teratology vol. 8, 1988-89, Problems of Perinatal Drug Dependence, 1979, 82, 84, Feminist Therapy Interchange, 1988-89, 91, Perinatal Substance Abuse: Research and Clinical Implications, 1992, Agendas for Aging, 1994-97. Mem. grant rev. coms. Nat. Inst. Drug Abuse, 1983-84, 85, 91-94. Tribute to Women award Lincoln YMCA, 1985, named Outstanding Rsch. Scientist Nebr. Chpt. Sigma Xi, 1991, Outstanding Contbn. to Status of Women, U N-L Chancellors Commn. on Status of Women, 1994, Pound Howard Disting. Career Achievement award, 1996. Fellow: AAAS, Am. Psychol. Soc., Am. Psychol. Assn.; mem.: Region V Adv. Coun. on Drugs, Fetal Alcohol (bd. dir. child guidance ctr. 1997—2002, bd. dir. UN-L emeriti assoc. 1999—2001), Soc. Neurosci., Nebr. Psychol. Assn. (pres. 1972), Internat. Soc. Psychoneuroendocrinology, Internat. Soc. Devel. Psychobiology, Midwestern Psychol. Assn., Advanced Feminist Therapy Inst., Altrusa YWCA, Sigma Xi (pres. 1986), Phi Beta Kappa (sec. Nebr. chpt. 1974). Avocations: painting, photography.

SONDOCK, RUBY KLESS, retired judge; b. Apr. 26, 1926; d. Herman Lewis and Celia (Juran) Kless; m. Melvin Adolph Sondock, Apr. 22, 1944; children: Marcia Cohen, Sandra Marcus. AA, Cottey Coll., Nevada, Mo., 1944; BS, U. Houston, 1959, LLB, 1961. Bar: Tex. 1961, U.S. Supreme Ct. 1977. Pvt. practice, Houston, 1961-73, 89—; judge Harris County Ct. Domestic Rels. (312th Dist.), 1973-77, 234th Jud. Dist. Ct., Houston, 1977-82, 83-89; justice Tex. Supreme Ct., Austin, 1982; of counsel Weil Gotshal and Manges, 1989-93, Houston Ctr., 1993—. Mem. ABA, Tex. Bar Assn., Houston Bar Assn., Houston Assn. Women Lawyers, Order of Barons, Phi Theta Phi, Kappa Beta Pi, Phi Kappa Phi, Alpha Epsilon Pi. Address: 550 Westcott #220 Houston TX 77007

SONIAT, KATHERINE THOMPSON, English educator, poet; b. Washington, D.C., Jan. 11, 1942; d. Raymond Webb Thompson and Katherine Lenox (Hayward) Claiborne; children: Shelton, Ashton. BA n History, Newcomb Coll., New Orleans, 1964; MA in English, Tulane U., 1983. Asst. prof. English Hollins Coll., Roanoke, Va., 1989-91; assoc. prof. English Va. Poly. Inst. and State U., Blacksburg, 1991—. Poet: Notes of Departure, 1984 (Camden Poetry prize), Winter Toys, 1990, Cracking Eggs, 1991, A Shared Life, 1993 (Iowa prize), The Fire Setters, 2003. Mem. steering com. Second Harvest Foodbank, Roanoke, 1994-95; local organizer Share Our Strength, Washington, 1995. Recipient Camden (N.J.) Poetry award Walt Whitman Ctr. for Arts, 1984, fellowship, scholarship Breadloaf Writers Conf., Middlebury Coll., Vt., 1985, 89, Va. Prize for poetry Va. Coun. for Arts, Richmond, 1989, Edwin Ford Piper award U. Iowa Press, Iowa City, 1993, Ann Stanford prizes U. Soc. Calif., L.A., 1993, 95; Va. Commn. for the Arts fellow in poetry, 1998; McDowell Colony fellow, 1994, 95, 96, Yaddo fellow, 1994, 95, 96. Mem. Associated Writing Programs. Avocation: outreach programs of creative writing in local schs. Office: Va Tech English Dept Williams Hall Blacksburg VA 24061-0112 E-mail: ksoniat@vt.edu.

SONNEMAN, EVE, artist; b. Chgo., 1946; d. Eric O. and Edith S. BFA, U. Ill., 1967; MFA, U. N.Mex., 1969. One-woman shows include Castelli Gallery, N.Y.C., 1976, 78, 80, 82, 84-86, Tex. Gallery, Houston, 1976, 78, 80, 82, 85, Galerie Farideh Cadot, Paris, 1978, 80, 83, François Lambert Gallery, Milan,Italy, 1980, 87, Mpls. Inst. Arts, 1980, La Noveau Musèe, Lyon, France, 1980, Musèe de Toulon (France), 1983, Centre Georges Pompidou, Paris, 1984, Circus Gallery, L.A., 1989, 97, Jones Troyer Fitzpatrick, Washington, 1989, Zabriskie Gallery, N.Y., 1990, Gloria Luria Gallery, Miami, 1990, Grand Central Terminal, N.Y.C., 1991, Charles Cowles Gallery, 1992, Sidney Janis Gallery, N.Y.C., 1996, La Geode Mus., Paris, 1996, Cirrus Gallery, 1997, Bruce Silverstein Gallery, N.Y., 2002, Jadite Gallery, N.Y., 2002, 03, 04, Galeria Turchi, Sienna, Italy, 2002; author: America's Cottage Gardens, 1990, Where Birds Live, 1992; co-author: How To Touch What, 2000; photographs subject of book Real Time, 1976. Grantee Nat. Endowment Arts, 1971, 78, Polaroid Corp., 1978; Cartier fellowship, France, 1989. Address: 446 W 47th St Apt 5C New York NY 10036-2381

SONNHALTER, CAROLYN THERESE, physical therapist, consultant; b. Bedford, Ohio, Apr. 26, 1942; d. Gabriel Edward Jr. and Josephine Irene (Kubera) Farkas; m. Donald Joseph Lippert, June 11, 1966 (div. June 1981); 1 child, Kevin Michael; m. Robert Louis Sonnhalter, Aug. 31, 1985. BS, Ohio State U., 1964. Lic. phys. therapist, Ohio. Staff and sr. phys. therapist Akron (Ohio) City Hosp., 1964-69; asst. dir. phys. therapy Akron Gen. Med. Ctr., 1975-82; dir. phys. therapy Litchfield Rehab. Ctr., Akron, 1983-87; phys. therapist HMO Health Ohio, Akron, 1987-97, Phoenix-Hudson Corp., Middleburg Heights, Ohio, 1993-98; dir. phys. therapy Tri-County Home Nursing, Mogadore, Ohio, 1997-99; phys. therapist VNS, Kent, Ohio, 1999—. Revel. phys. therapy first outpatient Chronic Pain Mgmt. Program, Ohio, 1983; cons. video animation on mechanism of whiplash for use by med. and legal profls., Ohio, 1996. Mem. Am. Phys. Therapy Assn., Alpha Gamma Delta. Avocations: traveling ohio and nearby states in search of antiques, gardening. Home: 3631 Oak Rd Stow OH 44224-3934 Office: VNS 234 S Water St Kent OH 44240-3526

SONNIER, PATRICIA BENNETT, business management educator; b. Park River, N.D., Mar. 25, 1935; d. Benjamin Beekman Bennett and Alice Catherine (Peerboom) Bennett Brenckinridge; m. William McGregor Castellini (dec.); m. Cecil Sherwood Sonnier; children: Bruce Bennett Wells (Nabil Subhani), Barbara Lea Ragland.. AA, Allan Handcock Coll., Santa Maria, Calif., 1964; BS magna cum laude, U. Great Falls, 1966; MS, U. N.D., 1967, PhD, 1971. Fiscal acct. USIA, Washington, 1954-56; pub. acct. Bremerton, Wash., 1956; statistician USN, Bremerton, Wash., 1957-59; med. svcs. accounts officer USAF, Vandenberg AFB, Calif., 1962-64; instr. bus. adminstrn. Western New Eng. Coll., 1967-69; vis. prof. econs. Chapman Coll., 1970; vis. prof. U. So. Calif. Sys., Griffith AFB, N.Y., 1971-72; assoc. prof., dir. adminstrv. mgmt. program Va. State U., 1973-74; assoc. prof. bus. adminstrn. Oreg. State U., Corvallis, 1974-81, prof. mgmt., 1982-90, emeritus prof. mgmt., 1990—, univ. curriculum coord., 1984-86, dir. adminstrv. mgmt. program, 1974-81, pres. Faculty Senate, 1981. Mem. Interinstl. Faculty Senate, 1986-90, pres.; 1989-90; exec. dir. Bus. Enterprise Ctr., 1990-92, Enterprise Ctr. L.A., Inc., 1992-95; commr. Lafayette Econ. Devel. Authority, 1994-2000, treas., 1995-96, vice chmn., 1996-97, chmn., 1997-98, past chmn., 1998-99, sec., 1999-00, chmn. bldg. com., 1999-00; cons. process tech. devel. Digital Equipment Corp., 1982. Pres., chmn. bd. dirs. Adminstrv. Orgnl. Svcs., Inc., Corvallis, 1976-83, Dynamic Achievement, Inc., 1983-92; bd. dirs. Oreg. State U. Bookstores, Inc., 1987-90, Internat. Trade Devel. Group, 1992-97; cons. Oregonians in Action, 1990-91, sec., 1999, 2000; cert. adminstrv. mng. pres. TYEE Mobil Home Park, Inc., 1987-92; del. N.Mex. State Rep. Conv., 2002. Fellow Assn. Bus. Comm. (internat. bd. 1980-86, v.p. Northwest 1981, 2nd v.p. 1982-83, 1st v.p. 1983-84, pres. 1984-85); mem. Am. Bus. Women's Assn. (chpt. v.p. 1979, pres. 1980, named Top Businesswoman in Nation 1980, Bus. Assoc. Yr. 1986), Assn. Info. Sys. Profls. (chpt. v.p. 1977, chpt. pres. 1978-81), Adminstrv. Mgmt. Soc., AAUP (chpt. sec. 1973, chpt. bd. dirs. 1982, 84-89, pres. Oreg. conf. 1983-85, pres. chpt. 1985-86), Am. Vocat. Assn. (nominating com. 1976), Associated Oreg. Faculties, Nat. Bus. Edn. Assn., Better Bus. Bur. (sec. 1994, 99, treas. 1995, vice-chair 1996, chmn. 1997, past chair 1998, chmn. nominating com. 1999, blue ribbon edn. com. 1999-2000, chmn. pub. rels.), Nat. Assn. Tchr. Edn. for Bus. Office Edn. (pres. 1976-77, chmn. pub. rels. com. 1978-81), La. Bus. Incubation Assn. (sec.-treas. 1993-95), Corvallis Area C. of C. (v.p. chamber devel. 1987-88, pres. 1988-89, chmn. bd. 1989-90, Pres.' award 1986), Boys and Girls Club of Corvallis (pres. 1991-92), Sigma Kappa, Rotary Corvallis (bd. dirs. 1990-92, dir. voc. svcs. 1991-92, pres.-elect 1992), Rotary Lafayette (bd. dirs. 1993—, cmty. svc. dir. 1993-94, treas. 1995-96, sec. 1996-97, v.p. 1997-98, pres. 1998-99, Dist. 6200 award 2000), Alherns for Gov. Com., Acadiana Rep. Women (first v.p. 1997, 98, pres. 1998-2000, asst. state CAP chmn. 1999-2000, gen. chmn. La. Fedn. Rep. Women's Clubs State Conv. 1997, Leadership La. 1998), Albuquerque Federated Rep. Women (hospitality chmn. 2003), Rotary of Albuquerque del Norte (silent auction chmn.

2001-02, dep. dir. internat. svc. com. 2002, dep. dir. permanent fund dist. 5520, asst. gov. 2003-04, dist. 5520 Rotary Found. chmn. 2003—, chmn. Rotary Local Yellow Pages 2002). E-mail: PatriciaSonnier@aol.com.

SONS, LINDA RUTH, mathematician, educator; b. Chicago Heights, Ill., Oct. 31, 1939; d. Robert and Ruth (Diekelman) Sons. AB in Math., Ind. U., 1961; MS in Math., Cornell U., 1963, PhD in Math., 1966. Tchg. asst. Cornell U., Ithaca, NY, 1961-63, instr. math., summer 1963, rsch. asst., 1963-65; from asst. prof. to assoc. prof. math. No. Ill. U., De Kalb, 1965—78, prof., 1978—, presdl. tchg. prof., 1994-98, disting. tchg. prof., 1998—, dir. undergrad. studies math. dept., 1971—77, exec. sec. univ. coun., 1978—79, chair faculty fund, 1982—. Author (with others): A Study Guide for Introduction to Mathematics, 1976, Mathematical Thinking in a Quantitative World, 1990, 2003; contbr. articles to profl. jours. Bd. dirs., treas. DeKalb County Migrant Ministry, 1967—78; pres. Luth. Women's Missionary League, 1974—87; mem. campus ministry com. No. Ill. Dist. Luth. Ch./Mo. Synod, Hillside, 1977—2001; mem. ch. coun. Immanuel Luth. Ch., DeKalb, 1978—85, 1987—89. Recipient Excellence in Coll. Tchg. award, Ill. Coun. Tchrs. Math., 1991; NSF Rsch. grantee, 1970—72, 1974—75. Mem.: London Math. Soc., Ill. Sect. Math. Assn. Am. (v.p. sect., pres.-elect, pres., past pres. 1982—87, bd. dirs. 1989—92, Disting. Svc. award 1988), Math. Assn. Am. (mem. nat. bd. govs. 1989—92, mem. com. undergrad. program math. 1990—96, chmn. coun. awards 1997—2003, Disting. Coll. or Univ. Tchg. Math. Sect. award 1995, Cert. Meritorious Svc. Nat. award 1998), Assn. Women in Math., Am. Math. Soc., Sigma Xi (past chpt. pres.), Phi Beta Kappa (pres. No. Ill. assn. 1981—85). Achievements include research in classical complex analysis, especially value distribution for meromorphic functions with unbounded characteristics in the unit disc. Office: No Ill U Dept Math Scis Dekalb IL 60115

SONSTEBY, KRISTI LEE, healthcare consultant; b. Anoka, Minn., Nov. 16, 1958; d. Glenn and Rosella (Rebischke) S. Charge nurse Baylor U. Med. Ctr., Dallas, 1980-81; clin. nurse specialist ARA Living Ctrs., Houston, 1981-86; pres., owner KristiCare Inc., Dallas, 1986-89; healthcare cons. SDG Ent., Inc., Austin, Tex., 1989-90; pres., owner NursePlus Inc. (now dba Internat. Healthcare Edn. Inst.), Mpls., 1991—. Judge Provider Mag., Washington, 1988; cons. in field; lectr. in field; conductor workshops in field. Several patents in field; author: Handbooks for Nurses, Vols. I-X, 1991; contbr. articles to profl. jours. Vol. to elderly various civic orgns. Avocations: violinist, chamber music.

SONTAG, SUSAN, writer; b. N.Y.C., Jan. 16, 1933; m. Philip Rieff, 1950 (div. 1958); 1 son, David. BA, U. Chgo., 1951; MA in English, Harvard U., 1954, MA in Philosophy, 1955. Instr. English U. Conn., Storrs, 1953-54; editor Commentary, N.Y.C., 1959; lectr. philosophy City Coll., N.Y.C., 1959-60, Sarah Lawrence Coll., Bronxville, 1959-60; instr. dept. religion Columbia U., N.Y.C., 1960-64. Writer in residence Rutgers U., 1964-65. Author: (novels) The Benefactor, 1963, Death Kit, 1967, The Volcano Lover: A Romance, 1992, In America (Nat. Book award 2000), Where the Stress Falls, 2001, Regarding the Pain of Others, 2003; (plays) Alice in Bed: A Play in Eight Scenes, 1993; (stories) I, Etcetera, 1978, The Way We Live Now, 1991; (essays) Against Interpretation, 1966 (Nat. Book award nomination 1966), Styles of Radical Will, 1969, Trip to Hanoi, 1969, On Photography, 1977 (Nat. Book Critics Circle award for criticism 1978), Illness as Metaphor, 1978, Under the Sign of Saturn, 1980, AIDS and Its Metaphors, 1989; (anthology) A Susan Sontag Reader, 1982; screenwriter, dir.: (films) Duet for Cannibals, 1969, Brother Carl, 1971; dir.: (films) Promised Lands, 1974, Unguided Tour, 1983; editor, author of introduction: Antonin Artaud: Selected Writings, 1976, A Roland Barthes Reader, 1982, Danilo Kis's Homo Poeticus: Essays & Interviews, 1995. Guggenheim fellow, 1966, 75, Rockefeller Found. fellow, 1965, 74, MacArthur fellow, 1990-95; recipient George Polk Meml. award, 1966, 2002, Ingram Merrill Found. award in lit. in field of Am. Letters, 1976, Creative Arts award Brandeis U., 1976, Malaparte prize, 1992, Peace Prize, German Bookseller Assoc., 2003; named Officier de l'Ordre des Arts et des Lettres, France, 1984. Mem. Am. Acad. Arts and Scis. (elected 1993), Am. Acad. Arts and Letters (Arts and Letters award 1976), PEN (pres. Am. Ctr. 1987-89). Office: Farrar, Straus & Giroux 19 Union Square West New York NY 10003*

SOOKIK, BONNIE W. air transportation executive; b. NJ; B in psychology, George Wash. U.; MS in admin., Calif. State U.; grad., Advanced Mgmt. Inst. Claremont Grad. Sch. Mgmt. Douglas Aircraft; oper. McDonnell Douglas Space Sys.; quality assurance and leadership Boeing Space and Comm.; v.p. of people Boeing Space and Comm. Unit, 2001; pres. Shared Svcs. Group, Bellevue, Wash., 2002; sr. v.p. Boeing Co., Office Internal Governance, Chgo., 2003—. Office: Boeing Co 100 N Riverside Chicago IL 60606

SOPHER, VICKI ELAINE, museum curator; b. Streator, Ill., May 22, 1943; d. Donald Bird and Thelma Elsie (Saxton) Watson; m. Terry Ray Sr., Jan. 20, 1962 (div. Aug. 1982); 1 child, Terry Ray Jr. AA, No. Va. Community Coll., 1973; BA, Am. U., 1976; MS, Bank State Coll. Edn., 1986. Adminstrv. asst. Decatur & Wilson House, Washington, 1977-81; asst. dir. Decatur House/Nat. Trust for Hist. Preservation, Washington, 1981-84, dir., 1984-95; exec. dir. Hammond-Harwood House Assn., Annapolis, Md., 1996-98, Getty Mus. Mgmt. Inst., 1998—; curator Nat. Am. Red Cross, Washington, 1999—. Cons.; founder, pres. Historic House Mus. Met. Washington. Mem. Am. Assn. Museums, Mid-Atlantic Assn. Museums, Am. Assn. for State and Local History, Victorian Soc. Am. (bd. dirs.). Home: 2621 12th St S Arlington VA 22204-4819 Office: Am Red Cross 1730 E St NW Washington DC 20006-5300 E-mail: sopherv@juno.com.

SOPKIN, CAROLE A. realtor; b. Chgo., Feb. 26, 1934; d. Earle E. and Pauline M. Zahn; children: Dawn Glaser, Terry, April, Rob, Greg. Realtor, Harper, 1978. Cert. realtor. Importer Tamp Internat., Schaumburg, Ill., 1973—84, Leidecker, Elk Grove, Ill., 1984—85; realtor Century 21 Cambridge, Schaumburg, 1986—97, Century 21 1st Class, Schaumburg, 1998—2000, Coldwell Banker, Schaumburg, 2000—03. Election judge Republican Hoff, Ill., 1980—90. Mem.: Million Dollar Club. Avocations: aerobics, dance.

SORELLE, RUTH DOYLE, medical writer, journalist; b. Port Arthur, Tex., Oct. 9, 1948; d. Richard Thomas and Ruth Elaine (Droddy) D.; m. Paul Charles SoRelle, Apr. 10, 1970; children: Danielle Amanda, Richard Paul. BJ, U. Tex., 1971; MPH, U. Tex., Houston, 1988. Reporter Port Arthur News, summer 1968, 69, Univ. and Info. Svc., Austin, Tex., 1970-71; med. editor U. Tex. MD Anderson Hosp., Houston, 1973-74; editor Resources Devel. Corp., Houston, 1974-76; med. editor Baylor Coll. Medicine, Houston, 1977-78; copy editor Houston Chronicle, Houston, 1978-79, med. writer, 1979-99; sr. dir. for spl. projects Baylor Coll., 1999—, editor 2 online newsletters. Instr. U. Houston, 1986, 87, 89; editor websites. Leader Presbyn. Youth Fellowship, Houston, 1989. Recipient John P. McGovern award Am. Med. Writers Assn., Community Svc. award Tex. Assoc. Press, 1993, Katie award Dallas Press Club, 1992, 93, Anson Jones award Tex. Med. Assn., 1981, 83, 85, 86, 88, 90, 92, 95, 96, 98, Francis C. Moore award Harris County Med. Assn., 1984-98, Silver Star Tex. award Tex. Hosp. Assn., 1984, 86, 89, 92, Tex. Pub. Health Assn. award, 1981, 89, 90, 91, 94, Houston Area Health Care Coalition's Health Policy Leadership award, 1990, Paul Ellis award Am. Heart Assn., 1988, 95, Nat. Multiple Sclerosis Soc. award for med. writing, 1998, Inernat. Health Reporting award Pan Am Health Orgn., 1998, others. Mem. Am. Med. Writer's Assn. (bd. dirs. southwest chpt. 1994-95), Press Club of Houston (Deadline Coverage award 1984, Investigative Series award 1990, Mag. Feature award 1994). E-mail: dsorelle@bcm.tmc.edu.

SORENSEN, ELIZABETH JULIA, retired cultural administrator; b. Kenora, Ont., Can., Nov. 24, 1934; d. John Frederick and Irene Margaret (Dowd) MacKellar; m. O. Leo P. Sorensen, July 7, 1956 (div. 1963); children: Lianne Kim Sorensen Kruger. BA, Lakehead U., 1970; MA, Brigham Young U., 1972; Assoc. Royal Conservatory, U. Toronto, 1978; Assoc., Mt. Royal Coll., Calgary, AB, 1978. Sec. Canadian Med. Assn. Manitoba, Winnipeg, 1956-59; legal sec. Filmore, Riley & Co., Winnipeg, 1961-63; tchr. Fort Frances (Ont.) High Sch., 1963-70; instr. drama, speech, English Lethbridge (Alta.) C.C., 1972-77; tchr. bus. edn. Henderson Coll. Bus., Lethbridge, 1978-80; supt. cultural svcs. City Medicine Hat, Alta., 1980-99; ret., 1999. Mem. Stirling Hist. Soc. (sec.). Mem. Lds Ch. Avocations: directing plays, writing, genealogy, storytelling, scrapbooking.

SORENSEN, GILLIAN MARTIN, United Nations official; b. Columbus, Ohio, Mar. 4, 1941; d. John Butlin and Helen (Hickam) Martin; m. Theodore C. Sorensen, June 28, 1969; 1 child, Juliet. BA, Smith Coll., 1963. Commr. N.Y.C. Commn. for UN and Consular Corps, 1978-90; pres. Nat. Conf., 1990-93; undersec gen., spl. advisor for pub. policy UN, N.Y.C., 1993-97, UN asst. sec. gen. for external rels., 1997—2003; sr. advisor UN Found., N.Y.C., 2003—. Del. Dem. Nat. Conv., 1976, 84, 88. Mem.: Acad. Coun. on the UN, Women's Forum, Coun. on Fgn. Rels. Democrat. Office: UN Found 801 Second Ave Ste 404 New York NY 10017 Office Phone: 212-697-3315.

SORENSEN, JACKI FAYE, choreographer, aerobic dance company executive; b. Oakland, Calif., Dec. 10, 1942; d. Roy C. and Juanita F. (Bullon) Mills; m. Neil A. Sorensen, Jan. 3, 1965. BA, U. Calif., 1964. Cert. tchr., Calif. Ptnr., Big Spring Sch. Dance, 1965; tchr. Pasadena Ave. Sch., Sacramento, 1968; founder, pres., choreographer Jacki's Inc., DeLand, Fla., 1990—; cons., lectr. on phys. fitness. Author: Aerobic Dancing, 1979, Jacki Sorensen's Aerobic Lifestyle Book, 1983; choreographer numerous dance exercises for records and videocassettes. Trustee Women's Sports Found. Recipient Diamond Pin award Am. Heart Assn., 1979, Individual Contbn. award Am. Assn. Fitness Dirs. in Bus. and Industry, 1981, Spl. Olympics Contbn. award, 1982, Contbn. to Women's Fitness award Pres.'s Coun. Phys. Fitness and Sports, 1982, Healthy Am. Fitness Leader award U.S. Jaycees, 1984, Lifetime Achievement award Internat. Dance Exercise Assn., 1985, New Horizons award Caldwell (N.J.) Coll., 1985, Legend of Aerobics award City Sports mag., 1985; Pres. Coun. award Calif. Womens' Leadership Conf., 1986, Hall of Fame award Club Industry mag., 1986, IDEA, 1992. Mem. AAHPERD, AFTRA, Am. Coll. Sports Medicine, Nat. Intramural and Recreation Assn. Office: care Jacki's Inc 129 1/2 N Woodland Blvd Ste 5 Deland FL 32720-4269

SORENSEN, LINDA, lawyer; b. Eureka, Calif., Mar. 3, 1945; BS, U. Wis., 1967; JD, U. Calif., 1976. Bar: Calif. 1976, U.S. Dist. Ct. (no. dist.) Calif. 1976, U.S. Ct. Appeals (9th cir.) 1976, U.S. Dist. Ct. (ea. dist.) Calif. 1977. Assoc., ptnr. Rothschild, Phelan & Mortali, San Francisco, 1976-88; dir. Howard, Rice, Nemerovski, Canady, Falk & Rabkin, San Francisco, 1988-95; shareholder Feldman, Waldman & Kline, P.C., San Francisco, 1997-99; pvt. practice Berkeley, Calif., 1999—; of counsel Stromsheim & Assoc., 2001—. Mem. ABA (mem. subcom. on avoiding powers, bus. bankruptcy com. 1983-95), Bar Assn. of San Francisco (chmn. comml. law and bankruptcy sect. 1984, editor fed. cts. com., no. dist. Calif. digest 1979-82). Office: PO Box 7997 Berkeley CA 94707-7997 Fax: 510 845 1785. E-mail: lindasorensen@earthlink.net.

SORENSEN, SHEILA, state legislator; b. Chgo., Sept. 20, 1947; d. Martin Thomas Moloney and Elizabeth (Koehr) Paulus; m. Wayne B. Slaughter, May, 1969 (div. 1976); 1 child, Wayne Benjamin III; m. Dean E. Sorensen, Feb. 14, 1977; (stepchildren) Michael, Debbie, Kevin, Dean C. BS, Loretto Heights Coll., Denver, 1965; postgrad. pediatric nurse practicioner, U. Colo., Denver, 1969-70. Pediatric nurse practicioner Pub. Health Dept., Denver, 1970-71, Boise, Idaho, 1971-72, Boise (Idaho) Pediatric Group, 1972-74, Pediatric Assocs., Boise, 1974-77; mem. Idaho Ho. Reps., 1987-92, Idaho Senate, Dist. 13, Boise, 1992—; chair senate health and welfare com. Idaho Senate, 1992-94, chair senate majority caucus, 1994-96, vice chair state affairs com., 1996-98, chair state affairs, 1998—. State chair Am. Legis. Exchange Coun. Precinct committeeman Ada County Rep. Ctrl. Com., Boise, 1982-86, dist. vice chair, 1985-88; polit. chair Idaho Med. Assn. Aux., 1984-87, Ada County Med. Assocs., 1986-87; bd. dirs. Family Practice Residency Program, 1992-94, Univ./Cmty. Health Sci. Assn., Bishop Kelly Found., 1993—99; chair Senate Majority Caucus, 1995-96, chair state affairs com., 1999—; mem. adv. com. on health care edn. and workforce devel. State Bd. Edn., mem. adv. bd. Drug Free Idaho., Boise State U. Master of Health Sci. Recipient AMA Nathan Davis award for Outstanding State Legislator, 1994. Mem. Nat. Conf. State Legislators, Nat. Orgn. Women Legislators (state chair), Am. Legis. Exch. Coun. (Legis of Yr. award 1999). Roman Catholic.

SORENSON, GEORGIA LYNN JONES, political scientist, educator; b. Abilene, Tex., Aug. 23, 1947; d. Wyly King and Olive M. (Sorenson) Jones; 1 child, Suzanna Simmonds Strasburg. BA, Am. U., 1974; MA, Hood Coll., 1976; PhD, U. Md., 1992. Social scientist Nat. Inst. Edn., Washington, 1978-79, U.S. Commn. Civil Rights, Washington, 1976-79; sr. policy analyst The White House, Washington, 1979-80; founder, sr. scholar James MacGregor Burns Acad. Leadership U. Md., College Park, 1980—. Adv. mem. W.K. Kellogg Found. Nat Fellows, Battle Creek, Mich., 1996-99. Co-author: (with James MacGregor Burns) Dead-Center: Clinton-Gore Leadership and the Perils of Moderation, 1999; editor: (with George Goethals and James MacGregor Burns) Encyclopeida of Leadership, 2004; contbr. articles to profl. jours. Chair Md. Women's Polit. Caucus, 1991-94; mem. White House Productivity Coun., Washington, 1979; mem. V.P. Youth Employment Task Force, 1979-80. Mem. Am. Polit. Sci. Assn., Internat. Soc. Polit. Psychologists, A.K. Rice Inst. Office: James MacGregor Burns Acad Leadership Univ Md College Park MD 20742-0001 E-mail: gsorenson@academy.umd.edu.

SORENSON, KATHERINE ANN, elementary school educator; b. Hastings, Minn., Aug. 30, 1947; d. Fredrick William Nearing and Marguerite Lucille Keene-Nearing; m. Michael Alfred Sorenson; children: Brock, Scott. BS in Edn., Black Hills State Coll., 1972; MA in Early Childhood Edn., U. Colo., Denver, 1995. Profl. tchr. lic. Colo., cert. reading recover tchr. Tchr. Maternity Mary Cath. Sch., St. Paul, 1967—68, St. Andrew's Cath. Sch., St. Paul, 1968—70, Hill City Pub. Sch., 1972—73, Groton Pub. Sch., 1973—75; substitute tchr. Billings Pub. Sch., 1975—76; tchr. Livingston Pub. Sch., 1977—85; asst. dir. childcare Children's Creative Encounters, Littleton, Colo., 1986—87; tchr. Cherry Creek Sch. Dist., Eastridge Elem., Aurora, Colo., 1987—96, 1996—, creator immerson program for mobile at risk students. Co-author: Blue Ribbon Application, 1998 (Blue Ribbon School, 1999), Reading Recovery Longitudinal Analysis, National Association for Year Round Education Application. Pack leader Boy Scouts Am., Parker, 1988—94, bd. dirs., 1988—94; mem. Cherry Creek Schs. North Area Task Force, Aurora, 2001—; Sunday sch. tchr. St. Mary's Cath. Ch., Livingston, 1978—84, religious edn. coord., 1981—82; Sunday sch. tchr. Ave Maria Cath. Ch., Parker, 1992—94; mem. team fundraising Parker Baseball, 1989—92; sec. Moorhead Foster Parent Assn., 1976—77. Recipient Dewitt Wallace Libr. Power award, Dewitt Wallace Found., 1997, Exemplary Reading Program award, Colo. Coun. Internat. Reading, 1998-1999, Tchr. of the Yr. award, Cherry Creek Sch.-Eastridge Elem., 2003. Mem.: Cherry Creek Edn. Assn., Reading Recovery Assn., Colo. Coun. Internat. Reading Assn. Avocations: reading, sewing, travel, south west history, baseball. Home: 11182 Cambridge Ct Parker CO 80138 Office: Eastridge Elem Sch 11777 E Wesley Ave Aurora CO 80014

SORENSON, KATY, county commissioner; married; 2 children. BS, U. Wis., 1977, MSW, 1980. Exec. dir. Calif. Women Lawyers Bar Assn.; legis. aide Ill. State Senator Dawn Clark Netsch; commr. dist. 8 Metro Dade County Commn., Fla., 1994—. Apptd. mem. Gov.'s Commn. to Study Bldg. Codes; apptd. chair Fla. Assn. Counties' Select Com. on Telecomms. Chair Citizens' Coalition for Pub. Schs.; pres. Women's Emergency Network, Palmetto Elem. Sch. PTA; legis. chairperson Dade County Coun. PTA; fundraiser EMILY's List; active F.C. Martin Elem. Sch. PTA, Palmetto Mid. Sch. PTA. Mem. AAUW, Nat. PTA (life). Office: Office County Commr 111 NW 1st St Fl 2 Miami FL 33128-1902

SORENSON, LIANE BETH MCDOWELL, women's affairs director, state legislator; b. Chgo., Aug. 13, 1947; d. Harold Davidson McDowell and Frances Elanor (Williams) Daisey Van Kleeck; m. Boyd Wayne Sorenson, June 30, 1973; children: Nathan, Matthew, Dana. BS in Edn., U. Del., 1969, M in Counseling with honors, 1986. Tchr. Avon Grove Sch. Dist., West Grove, Pa., 1969-70, Alexis I. duPont Sch. Dist., Wilmington, Del., 1970-73, Barrington (Ill.) Sch. Dist., 1973-75; counseling intern Medill Intensive Learning Ctr.-Christina Sch. Dist., Newark, Del., 1985; counselor Family Violence Shelter CHILD, Inc., Wilmington, 1985, 86-87, dir. parent edn. programs, 1987-88; dir. Office Women's Affairs, exec. dir. Commn. on Status of Women U. Del., Newark, 1988—; mem. Dist. 6 Del. Senate, Dover, 1992—, minority whip. Chair Del. Ho. Edn. Com., 1992—, Adv. Bd. Del. Breast Cancer Coalition, 1998—; commr. Edn. Commn. State Del.; mem. tng. com. Nat. Conf. State Legislatures; mem. Bd. Women's Network Nat. Conf. State Legislatures; mem. joint sunset com. Del. Legislature, Del. House of Reps., 1992-94, Del. Senate, 1994—, Del. Legis. Joint Fin. Com. Del. Legis., 1994—, Coun. State Govts. Toll Fellowship. Presenter papers various meetings & confs. Pres. bd. dirs. Nursing Mothers, Inc., 1980-81; trustee Hockessin Montessori Sch., 1982-84, enrollment chair, 1982-83; trustee Hockessin Pub. Libr., 1982-84, pres. bd., 1982-84; bd. dirs. Del. Coalition for Children, 1986-88; bd. dirs. Children's Bur. Del., 1984-87, sec., 1985-87; pres. Jr. League Wilmington, 1986-87, rsch. coun. v.p., 1985-86; bd. dirs. YWCA New Castle County, 1989-91; pres. Del. Women's Agenda, 1986-88; vice-chair Women's Leadership Ctr., 1992—; mem. Del. Work Family Coalition; bd. dirs. Del. divsn. Am. Cancer Soc., 1993—. Grantee Del. Dept. Svcs. to Children, Youth and Their Families, 1987-88, 1988, State of Del. Gen. Assembly, 1992; recipient Disting. Legis. Svc. award Del. State Bar Assn., 1997, Del Tufo award Delaware Humanities Forum, 1999. Mem.: Hockessin Hist. Soc. (bd. mem. 2000—), Del. Family Law Commn., Del. Alliance for Arts in Edn., Del. Greenway and Trails Coun., Am. Assn. for Higher Edn. (chair women's caucus 1991—92, program chair women's caucus 1990—91, pre-conf. workshop coord. women's caucus 1990 Ann. Conf.), Rotary (charter mem. Hackessin Pike Creek club 1994—). Republican. Methodist. Avocations: camping, hiking. Office: State of Delaware Legislative Hall Rm 210 PO Box 1401 Dover DE 19903-1401

SORENSON, SANDRA LOUISE, merchandising manager; b. Santa Monica, Calif., Nov. 30, 1948; d. Edward John and Gordon Dudley (Pollock) S. BA in Telecommunications, BS in Mktg., U. So. Calif., 1970. Merchandiser Montgomery Ward Inc., Los Angeles, 1970-82; sr. fin. planner Plums Co., Los Angeles, 1982-84; mgr. merchandising systems devel. and tng. Millers Outpost, Ontario, Calif., 1984-89; merchandising systems specialist Oshmans Sporting Goods, Santa Ana, Calif., 1989-90; sr. dir. planning and allocations Clothestime, Anaheim, Calif., 1990-96; dir. planning and allocation Pacific Sunwear, Anaheim, 1996-97; sr. dir. planning and allocation Clothestime Anaheim, 1997—2003; ret., 2003. Recipient Achievement award Bicentennial Com. Norwalk, Calif., 1976. Mem. Commerce Assocs., Assn. Retail Technologies, Internat. Platform Soc., Casitas San Jose, Players of Orange Club, Chi Omega, Phi Chi Theta, Alpha Epsilon Rho. Republican. Mem. Reformed Ch. Am. Home: 14913 Little Bend Rd Chino Hills CA 91709-3494 Office: Clothestime 5325 E Hunter Ave Anaheim CA 92807-2090 E-mail: ssorenso@aol.com.

SORENSTAM, ANNIKA, professional golfer; b. Stockholm, Oct. 9, 1970; m. David Esch. Student, U. Ariz. With Women's Profl. Golf European Tour, 1992—, LPGA, 1993—, Swedish Nat. Team, 1987-92, Solheim Cup Team, 1994, 96, 98. Recipient Vare Trophy award, 1998; named Rolex Player of Yr., 1995, 97, 98. Achievements in Tournaments won include: Australian Ladies Open, 1994, U.S. Women's Open, 1995, 96, Australian Ladies Masters, 1995, GHP Heartland Classic, 1995, Betsy King LPGA Classic, 1996, Samsung World Championship of Women's Golf, 1995, 96, Michelob Light Classic, 1997, 98, Chrysler-Plymouth Tournament of Champions, 1997, Shop Rite LPGA Classic, 1998, JAL Big Apple Classic, 1998, SAFECO Classic, 1998, Michelob Light Classic, 1999, Welch's/Circle K Championships, 2000, Firstar LPGA Classic, 2000. Office: LPGA 100 International Golf Dr Daytona Beach FL 32124-1092

SORGE, KAREN LEE, commercial printing company executive, consultant; b. Warwick, N.Y., May 27, 1958; d. Wesley Thomas and Margaret Anne (Storms) Kervatt; m. David W. Farquhar, July 16, 1982 (div. Feb. 1990); 1 child: Lauren Nicole; m. Thomas E. Sorge, May 16, 1997; children: Natalie MaKalen Sorge, Ryan Thomas. AS, Roger Williams Coll., 1978, BS cum laude, 1980. Office mgr. Price-Rite Printing Co., Dover, N.J., summer 1975-76; cons. SBA, Bristol, R.I., 1978-80; account exec. P.M. Press Inc., Dallas, 1980-90, sales trainer, 1984-85; v.p. KDF Bus. Forms Inc., Dallas, 1984-90; account exec. Jarvis Press, Dallas, 1990—; pres. Print Trends, Dallas, 1990—. Printer Tex. Aux. Charity Auction Orgn., Dallas, 1985, Cystic Fibrosis, Dallas, 1989—93, Life Enhancement Assn. Programs Found., 1992—, Dallas Soc. Visual Comm., 1992, AIDS Resources Com., Dallas chpt. Cerebral Palsy, 1994, Lloyd-Paxton AIDS Benefit, 1994, Feast for the Eyes Gala-Benefit to Prevent Blindness, 2001, Genesis Women's Chelter, 2002, others. Recipient various awards Clampitt Paper Co., Dallas., 1982, P.M. Press Inc., 1983-89, Mead Paper Co., 1985-89, award Feast for the Eyes Gala, 2001. Mem. Printing Industry in Am. (recipient Judges Favorite award 1992, Best of Show Hon. Mention award 1994, gold award Best of Tex. 1996), Internat. Assn. Bus. Communicators, Nat. Bus. Forms Assn. Republican. Baptist. Avocation: piano. Home: 2600 Raintree Dr Southlake TX 76092-5536

SORGEN, ELIZABETH ANN, retired educator; b. Ft. Wayne, Ind., Aug. 21, 1931; d. Lee E. and Miriam N. (Bixler) Waller; m. Don DuWayne Sorgen, Mar. 8, 1952; children: Kevin D., Karen Lee Sorgen Hoeppner, Keith Alan. BS in Edn., Ind. U., 1953; MS in Edn., St. Francis Coll., Ft. Wayne, 1967. Tchr., bldg. rep. and math. book adoption rep. East Allen County Schs., Monroeville, Ind., 1953-94, ret., 1994. Founder nursery sch., choir mem. St. Marks Luth. Ch., Monroeville, 1960—; vol. Sci. Ctrl.; pres. Heritage Homemakers, 1990-2000; substitute tchr. Recipient Golden Apple award East Allen County Schs., 1976, Monroeville Tchr. of Yr. award, 1993. Mem.: AAUW, Ft. Wayne Ret. Tchrs. Assn. Avocations: square and line dancing, camping, gardening. Home: 25214 Lincoln Hwy E Monroeville IN 46773-9710

SORGI, MERCEDES PRIETO, psychologist; b. Havana, Cuba, Sept. 8, 1953; came to the U.S., 1961; d. Roberto Isaac and Dora Natalia (Fernandez) Prieto; m. John David Sorgi, Sept. 2, 1978; children: James, John, Roberto. BA in Psychology, Vanderbilt U., 1974; MA in Spl. Edn., George Peabody Coll., 1976; EdS in Spl. Edn., U. Miami, 1978; PhD in Sch. Psychology, Kent State U., 1994—. Cert. sch. psychologist, Ohio. Lead tchr. Mailman Ctr. for Child Devel., Miami, Fla., 1976, parent tng. coord., 1976-78; owner, buyer, salesperson The Land of Make Believe Shop, Hudson, Ohio, 1979-87; pre-sch. owner Mother's Day Out, Hudson, 1984-87; Open Doors program dir. Hattie Larlham Found., Mantau, Ohio, 1986-91, dir. cmty. alternatives, 1988-92; pvt. cons. N.E. Ohio Agys., 1992-93; sch. psychology intern Orange (Ohio) Sch. Dist., 1996-97; sch. psychologist Seton Elem. Sch., Hudson, 1997-98; tchg. fellow Kent State U., 1997-99; bilingual sch. psychologist Cleve. City Schs., 1998—. Bd. mem., chair various coms. Summit County Assn. for Retarded Citizens,

Akron, Ohio, 1980—; mem. adv. bd. Pre-Sch. Parents Assn., Hudson, 1982-85, Chem. Abuse Reduction Through Edn., Hudson, 1983-85; founding mem., chair Hattie Larlham League Hudson, 1985—. Mem. Rep. Women's League, Hudson, 1983-94; coun. mem. St. Mary Parish Coun., Hudson, 1985-88. Mem. APA, Nat. Assn. Sch. Psychologists, Ohio Assn. Sch. Psychologists, Cleve. Assn. for Sch. Psychologists, Support Spl. Edn. in Hudson (founder), Grad. Orgn. Sch. Pscyhology Studies (founder, chair). Roman Catholic. Avocations: gardening, horses, antiques. Home: 333 Aurora St Hudson OH 44236-2917

SORIANO, CRISTINA, dietician; b. Manila, Feb. 27, 1944; d. Teofilo and Zoila (Valino) S. BS in Foods and Nutrition cum laude, U. Santo Tomas, Manila, The Philippines, 1965; M in Dietetics, U. Louisville, 1984. Registered, lic. dietitian, Ky. Therapeutic dietitian Mt. Sinai Med. Ctr., Milw., 1969-76; dietetic adminstr. Ctrl. State Hosp., Louisville, Ky., 1976—. Mem. Am. Dietetic Assn., Filipino-Am. Heritage Assn., Inc. (pro 1990-97, pres. 1997-98), Louisville (Ky.) Dist. Dietetic Assn. (chairperson publs. 1994, policies and procedures 1996). Roman Catholic. Avocations: quilting, sewing, gardening. Office: Ctrl State Hosp 10510 Lagrange Rd Louisville KY 40223-1228

SORIANO, NANCY MERNIT, editor-in-chief; married; 1 child. Degree in Art History, Bard Coll. Former editor Good Food; former contbg. editor Cosmopolitan, Food & Wine, Brides; joined Country Living, 1982, assoc. decorating editor, home bldg. and arch. editor, exec. editor, 1995—97, editor, 1997—98, editor-in-chief, 1998—. Founder Country Living Restoration Mag., 1996. Design editor (book series) American Country Design, Time Life Books, editor spl. interest publ. Country Living Dream Homes. Office: Heart Mags 224 W 57th St Fl 7 New York NY 10019-3212

SORINI, SUSAN SANTINA, chemist; d. Bernardo Batista and Faye A. Sorini; m. Gregory Kelly Wong, Aug. 29, 1998. AS in Biology, BS in Chemistry, Mont. Coll. Mineral Sci. and Tech., 1983. Lead scientist Western Rsch. Inst., Laramie, Wyo., 1983—. Apptd. mem. ASTM Com. on Standards, West Conshohocken, Pa., 2003—. Participant leadership program Laramie (Wyo.) C. of C., 2003—. Recipient Alumni Recognition award, Mont. Coll. Mineral Sci. and Tech., 1997. Mem.: ASTM (com. D 34 vice chair, co-chair subcom. D 34.01, task group chair D 34.01.04 on waste leaching techs., chair of task group D 34.01.06 on analytical methods ASTM standards, Devel. award 1992, Appreciation award 2000), Am. Chem. Soc. (Regional Indsl. Innovation award 2001). Achievements include invention of diesel dog soil test kit. Avocations: travel, gardening, crafts, sewing, fishing. Office: Western Rsch Inst 365 N 9th St Laramie WY 82072

SOROS, SUSAN WEBER, educational administrator; b. Bklyn., Apr. 15, 1955; d. Murray and Iris (Horowitz) Weber; m. George Soros, June 19, 1983; children: Alexander George, Gregory James. BA, Barnard Coll., N.Y.C., 1977; MA, Parsons Sch. Design, N.Y.C., 1990; PhD, Royal Coll. Art, London, 1998. Asst. dir. New York: The State of Art Exhbn., Albany, 1977; assoc. prodr. The Big Picture (film), 1978, In Search of Rothko (film), 1979; dir. Philip Colleck of London, Ltd., N.Y.C., 1988-91; exec. dir. The Open Soc. Fund, Inc., N.Y.C., 1985-91; pub. Source: Notes in the History of Art, N.Y.C., 1980—; founder, dir. The Bard Grad. Ctr. for Studies in Decorative Arts, N.Y.C., 1991—. Author: The Secular Furniture of E.W. Godwin, 1999, Rediscovering H.W. Batley (1846-1932), British Aesthetic Movement Artist and Designer, 1999, (exhbn. catalog) E.W. Godwin: Aesthetic Movement Architect and Designer, 1999, Trustee Am. Fedn. of the Arts, N.Y.C., 1995-98, the Bklyn. Mus., 1992—, Bard Coll., Annandale, N.Y., 1991—; mem. vis. com. European sculpture and decorative arts Mus. of Fine Art, 1994—, Watson Libr., 1995—, Met. Mus. Art, Thomas J. Watson Libr. Recipient Woman of Achievement award Women in Fin. Devel., 1996, Bard medal for outstanding svc. Bard Coll., 1995, Award for Achievements in Art Edn., AWED, 1993, Gold Medal award Nat. Arts Club, 1997, Spirit of the City award Cathedral Ch. of St. John the Divine, 1999, George Wittenborn Meml. Book award, 2000, Henry-Russel Hitchcock award N.Y. Met. chpt. Victoria Soc. in Am., 2000, Philip C. Johnson award Soc. Archtl. Historians, 2000; named Woman of Achievement, Barnard Coll. Mem. Am. Assn. Mus. (applied art com. 1992—), Furniture History Soc., Internat. Coun. Mus. Office: The Bard Grad Ctr for Studies in Decorative Arts 18 W 86th St New York NY 10024-3602

SOROSKY, JERI RUTH, academic administrator; b. Chgo. d. Hans S. and Florence J. (Hurwitz) Pakula; m. Gene E. Sorosky; children: Cindi, Dana, Lesli. BA, Roosevelt U., Chgo., 1952; MEd, Fla. Atlantic U., Boca Raton, 1967; EdS, Nova Southeastern U., Ft. Lauderdale, Fla., 1972; EdD, MS, Nova Southeastern U., 1981. Cert. adminstr., supr., media specialist, gifted and elem. educator, Fla. Chairperson Elem. Highland Oaks, North Miami Beach, Fla., 1967-75; mem. faculty gifted program Highland Oaks Gifted Ctr., North Miami Beach, 1975-85; chairperson gifted program Miami (Fla.) Dade C.C., 1985-2000; site adminstr. grad. tchr. edn. program Nova. Southeastern U., Ft. Lauderdale, 1992—. Adj. prof. Nova Southeastern U., Ft. Lauderdale, 1979-87, adv. doctoral practicums, 1985-2000, cluster coord., 1987—, admissions com. doctoral programs Tech. & Distance Edn. and Child & Youth Studies, 1996—; chairperson gifted edn. Dade County Schs., Miami, 1990-93; mem. com. State Gifted Task Force, Tallahassee, 1992; presenter in field. Author: GEM Major Module in Gifted Education, 1981, Ideas Unlimited, 1985, Guide for Elementary Educators, 1995, Technology in the Curriculum, 1998; editor: Readings: Gifted Education, 1991, Early Childhood Education, 1982. Project chairperson Kids in Distress, Ft. Lauderdale, 1989. Named Woman of Yr. Bus. Profl. Women, 1985. Mem. Fla. Assn. Gifted (charter, v.p. 1975-97), Nova Southeastern U. Alumni (bd. dirs. 1981-97), AAUW, Phi Delta Kappa (chairperson newsletter 1985-97). Avocations: dance, technology. Office: Nova Southeastern U 1750 NE 167th St North Miami Beach FL 33162-3017

SORRELS, CARRIE L. federal agency administrator; BA in Polit. Sci., Tex. Tech U., 1983; MPA, Tex. Tech. U., 1985. Presdl. mgmt. intern Office Space Sci. and Applications NASA, Washington, 1985, program analyst, 1989—93, dir. policy and bus. mgmt. divsn. Office Space Scis., 1993—. Pub. svc. fellow, 1983. Office: NASA Hdqrs Mail Code S 300 E St SW Washington DC 20546

SORRENTINO, CHARLENE H. federal judge; b. 1942; BA, U. Fla., 1963; JD cum laude, U. Miami, 1967. Law clk. to Judge Charles Fulton U.s. Dist. Ct., 1967-71; asst. fed. pub. defender Miami, 1971-75; magistrate judge U.S. Dist. Ct. (so. dist.) Fla., Miami, 1975—. Mem. Fla. Bar Assn. Office: 132 US Courthouse 300 NE 1st Ave Miami FL 33132-2126

SORRENTINO, RENATE MARIA, illustrator; b. Mallnitz, Carinthia, Austria, June 21, 1942; came to the U.S., 1962; d. Johann and Theresia (Kritzer) Weinberger; m. Philip Rosenberg, Nov. 22, 1968 (dec. 1982); m. Francis J. Sorrentino, Sept. 4, 1988. Grad. gold and silversmith artist, Höhere Technische Lehranstalt, Austria, 1961. Draftswoman Elecon Inc., N.Y.C., 1962-65; jr. designer Automatics Metal Prod. Corp., N.Y.C., 1965-70; designer, art dir. Autosplice, Inc., Woodside, N.Y., 1970-90; freelance artist Jupiter, Fla., 1990—. Patentee Quick Disconnect from Continuous Wire, 1977. Home: 2301 Marina Isle Way Apt 404 Jupiter FL 33477-9423 Office: Autosplice Inc 10121 Barnes Canyon Rd San Diego CA 92121-5797 E-mail: sorrenate@adelphia.net.

SORSTOKKE, ELLEN KATHLEEN, marketing executive, educator; b. Seattle, Mar. 31, 1954; d. Harold William and Carrol Jean (Russ) Sorstokke. MusB with distinction, U. Ariz., 1976; postgrad., UCLA Extension, 1979-83, L.A. Valley Coll., 1984-85, Juilliard Extension, fall 1987, U. Calif. Berkeley Extension, 1992-93. Pvt. practice music tchr., Tucson, 1975—77, Whiteriver, Ariz., 1977—78, L.A., 1980—85, S.I., N.Y.C., 1986—89; music tchr. Eloy (Ariz.) Elem. Schs., 1976-77, Whiteriver (Ariz.) Pub. Schs., 1977-78; svc. writer, asst. svc. mgr. Alfa of Santa Monica, Calif., 1978-79; purchasing agt. Advance Machine Corp., L.A., 1979-80; asst. mgr. Atlantic Nuclear Svcs., Gardena, Calif., 1980-81; mgr. Blue Lady's World Music Ctr., L.A., 1981-83; instrument specialist Baxter-Northup Music Co., Sherman Oaks, Calif., 1983-85; dir. mktg. Mandolin Bros., Ltd., S.I., N.Y., 1985-89; product mgr. Gibson Guitar Corp., Nashville, 1989; sales mgr. Saga Musical Instruments, South San Francisco, Calif., 1990-91, mktg. dir., 1991-95, mktg. analyst, 2002—. Freelance mktg. cons., S.I., Foster City, Atlanta, 1986—; freelance cons. www.fussycats.com, 2002; music cons. 20th Century Fox, L.A., 1984; freelance music copyist and orchestrator, Tucson, L.A., N.Y.C., 1972-89; freelance graphic designer and advt., N.Y.C., S.I., Foster City, Atlanta, 1986—. Contbr. articles to profl. jours. Campaign worker Richard Jones for Supr., Tucson, 1972; mem., program book designer Marina Del Rey-Westchester Symphony Orch., L.A., 1981-83. Scholar U. Ariz., 1973-76, ASCAP scholar UCLA, 1980-81. Mem. Tucson Flute Club (publicity chmn. 1974-75, v.p. 1975-76). Republican. Office Phone: 770-932-5281. Personal E-mail: esorstok@bellsouth.net.

SORSTOKKE, SUSAN EILEEN, systems engineer; b. Seattle, May 2, 1955; d. Harold William and Carrol Jean (Russ) Sorstokke. BS in Systems Engring., U. Ariz., 1976; MBA, U. Wash., Richland, 1983. Warehouse team mgr. Procter and Gamble Paper Products, Modesto, Calif., 1976-78; quality assurance engr. Westinghouse Hanford Co., Richland, Wash., 1978-80, supr. engring. document ctr., 1980-81; mgr. data control and adminstrn. Westinghouse Electric Corp., Madison, Pa., 1981-82, mgr. data control and records mgmt., 1982-84; prin. engr. Westinghouse Elevator Co., Morristown, N.J., 1984-87, region adminstrn. mgr. Arleta, Calif., 1987-90; ops. rsch. analyst Am. Honda Motor Co. Inc., Torrance, Calif., 1990-95; project leader parts sys. Am. Honda Motor Co., Inc., Torrance, Calif., 1995-96, mgr. parts systems and part number adminstrn., 1996-97, mgr. parts systems, 1997-2000, mgr. supply chain mgmt., 2000—02, mgr. process control and regulatory issues, 2002—. Adj. prof. U. LaVerne, Calif., 1991—92; pres. Fussy Cuts Inc., Torrance, Calif., 2000—. Advisor Jr. Achievement, 1982—83; literacy tutor Westmoreland Literacy Coun., 1983—84; host parent EF Found., Saugus, Calif., 1987—88, Am. Edn. Connection, Saugus, 1988—89, 1991; instr. Excell, L.A., 1991—92; mem. Calif. Acad. Math. and Sci., 1996—97. Mem.: Am. Inst. Indsl. Engrs., Soc. Women Engrs., Optomists Charities Inc. (bd. dirs. Acton, Calif. 1991—94). Republican. Methodist. Home: 2567 Plaza Del Amo Unit 205 Torrance CA 90503-8962 Office: Am Honda Motor Co Inc Dept Parts 100 5C 3B 1919 Torrance Blvd Torrance CA 90501-2722

SORTUN, ANA, food service executive; b. Seattle; Fluency degree, L'Ecole Francais; grand diplome, La Varenne Ecole de Cuisine, Paris; diploma in Wine Studies, L'Academie du Vin. Pastry asst. and rounds cook with chef Tom Douglas Café Sport, Seattle; exec. chef Aigo Bistro, Concord, Mass., 1990; co-opener with Moncef Medeb 8 Holyoke, Cambridge, Mass.; exec. chef Casablanca, Cambridge; chef, owner Oleana, Cambridge, 2001—. Nominee Best New Restaurant, James Beard, 2002, Best Chef, Northeast, 2003, 2004; named Best New Chef, Boston Mag., Rising Star in the city's restaurant cmty., Esquire Mag. Avocation: travel. Office: Oleana 134 Hampshire St Cambridge MA 02139

SORUM, CHRISTINA ELLIOTT, academic administrator; BA in Greek, Wellesley Coll., 1967; PhD, Brown U., 1975. Asst. prof. dept. fgn. langs. and lits. N.C. State U., 1975—82; assoc. prof. dept. classics Union Coll., Schenectady, NY, 1982—86, chmn. dept. classics, 1982—92, Frank Bailey assoc. prof., 1986—92, Frank Bailey prof. classics, 1992—, dean arts and scis., 1994—, dean of faculty, v.p. for acad. affairs, 2000—. Mem. nat. drafting com. Strong Founds. in Gen. Edn. Am. Assn. Colls., 1991; presenter in field; participant confs. in field. Contbr. articles to profl. jours.; reviewer, referee: jours. in field. Grantee, Pew Meml. Trust, 1983, Pew Charitable Trusts, 1992. Mem.: AAUW, Assn. Gen. and Liberal Studies, Assn. Am. Colls. and Univs., Classical Assn. of Empire State, Classical Assn. of Mid. West and South, Classical Assn. of Atlantic States, Am. Philol. Assn. Office: Union Coll VP Acad Affairs/Dean of Faculty Schenectady NY 12308-3107

SORVINO, MIRA, actress; b. Tenafly, N.J., Sept. 28, 1967; d. Paul S. AB, Harvard U., 1990. Appeared in films including Amongst Friends, 1993, The Second Greatest Story Ever Told, 1994, Quiz Show, 1994, Barcelona, 1994, Tarantella, 1996, Sweet Nothing, 1996, Mighty Aphrodite, 1995 (Oscar for Best Supporting Actress), The Dutch Master, 1994, Blue in the Face, 1995, Beautiful Girls, 1996, (TV) Parallel Lives, 1994, The Buccaneers, 1995, Norma Jean and Marilyn, 1996, Jake's Women, 1996, Romy and Michele's High School Reunion, 1997, The Replacement Killers, 1998, Mimic, 1997, Free Money, 1998, Summer of Sam, 1999, At First Sight, 1999, Joan of Arc: The Virgin Warrior, 2000, The Great Gatsby, 2000, prodr. Famous, 2000, Triumph of Love, 2001, The Grey Zone, 2001, Wise Girls, 2002, Semana Santa, 2002, Between Strangers, 2002, Gods and Generals, 2003 (TV); assoc. prodr. Amongst Friends, 1993. Office: The William Morris Agy 151 El Camino Dr Beverly Hills CA 90212

SOSMAN, MARTHA B. state supreme court justice; b. Boston, Mass., Oct. 20, 1950; BA Middlebury Coll, JD U. Mich. Assoc. Foley, Hoag & Eliot, Boston, 1979—84; with U.S. Atty.'s Office, Boston, 1984—89; founding ptnr. Kern, Sosman, Hagerty, Roach & Carpenter, Boston, 1989—93; apptd. judge Superior Ct., Concord, Mass., 1993; assoc. justice Mass. Supreme Jud. Ct., 2000—. Office: Mass Supreme Jud Ct 1300 New Ct Hse Pemberton Sq Boston MA 02108

SOSNOWSKI, V. SUSAN, state legislator; b. Warwick, R.I., Dec. 20, 1955; m. Michael Sosnowski; children: Ronald, Deborah, Stephen, Michael Jr. Grad., Ocean State Bus. Inst. Co-owner Sosnowski Farm, West Kingston, R.I., 1986—; mem. R.I. Senate, Dist. 6, Providence, 1996—. Vice chair fin. com. R.I. State Senate, spl. legis. com., joint environ. and energy com., dep. majority leader, chair conservation com.; lobbyist R.I. Nurserymen's Assn., 1995, 96; mem. Gov.'s Adv. Coun. On Environ., 1997. Mem. bd. dirs. Farm Family Ins. Co., 1993-95; mem. R.I. Audubon Soc., Richmond Grange, Save the Bay; mem. Clean Water Fin. Agy.; mem. South Kingstown Planning Bd., 1993-96, South Kingstown Dem. Town Com., 1997-99. Mem. R.I. Nursery and Landscape Assn., N.E. Organic Farming Assn., South Kingstown Farmer's Market Assn., Rotary. Office: RI State Senate Ste House Providence RI 02903 E-mail: sen-sosnowski@rilin.state.ri.us.

SOSSAMON, NANCY H. city official; b. Concord, N.C. m. D.H. Sossamon, Jr., 1980; 4 children: David, Kathy, Jill, Kelly. student, cert. govt. purchase officer, U. N.C., Chapel Hill. Life cert. local govt. purchasing officer. Collections clk. City of Concord, N.C., 1967-68, customer svc. rep., 1968-69, accounts payable, inventory and payroll clk., 1970-74, purchasing and records agt., 1975-86, purchasing agt., 1986-92, buyer, 1992-98, purchasing officer, 1998—. Mem. Nat. Assn. Purchasing Mgmt., Am. Purchasing Soc., Nat. Notary Assn., Carolina Assn. Govtl. Purchasing. Avocations: computer applications and new technology, cooking, spending time with her grandchildren. Office: City of Concord PO Box 308 26 Union St S Concord NC 28025-5010 Fax: 704-786-7818.

SOTIR, JUDITH SOPHIA, educational technology consultant, researcher; b. Chgo., Nov. 18, 1951; 1 child, Heather Genevieve. BA, Elmhurst (Ill.) Coll., 1974. Sales mgr. Unicorn, Ltd., Chgo., 1982-86; lab. coord. Waubonsee Coll., Aurora, Ill., 1987-90; promotions mgr. MidAm. Savings Bank, Clarendon Hills, Ill., 1988-90; assessment coord. Waubonsee Coll., 1990-92, ESL coord., 1992-95, dir. Innovative Tech. Design Ctr., 1992—; pres. Ednl. Tech. Concepts, 1997—. Mem. editl. rev. bd. Nat. Ctr. on Adult Literacy, U. Pa., Phila., 1995—; mem. peer evaluation team No. Ill. U., Dekalb, 1995; presenter various workshops. Contbr. articles to profl. jours. Dir. bd. edn. Indian Prarie Dist. 204, Naperville, Ill., 1983—; gov. bd. mem. Ill. Assn. Sch. Bds., Glen Ellyn, 1986-90; dir. Indian Prarie Ednl. Found., Naperville, 1988—; mem. ad-hoc com. edn. State Rep. Mary Lou Cowlishaw, Springfield, Ill., 1986—; bd. dirs. Fox Metro Water Dist., 1997—. Mem. Am. Assn. for Adult and Continuing Edn., Ill. Assn. for Adult and Continuing Edn., Ill. Computing Educators, Internat. Soc. Tech. Educators, Assn. for Curriculum and Devel. Republican. Roman Catholic. Avocations: tennis, swimming. Home: 933 Parkhill Cir Aurora IL 60504-9092 Office: Waubonsee Coll Innovative Tech Design Ctr 5 E Galena Blvd Aurora IL 60506-4128

SOTIRIOU-LEVENTIS, CHARIKLIA, chemist, educator, researcher; b. Nicosia, Cyprus, Jan. 20, 1960; came to U.S., 1982; d. Sotiris and Eleni (Papakyriacou) S.; m. Nicholas Leventis, Nov. 12, 1988; children: Theodora, Helen, Julia. BS in Chemistry summa cum laude, U. Athens, Greece, 1982; PhD in Organic Chemistry, Mich. State U., 1987. Grad. asst. Mich. State U., East Lansing, 1982-87; rsch. assoc. Northeastern U., Boston, 1987-89, Harvard U., Cambridge, Mass., 1989-92; rsch. scientist Ciba Corning Diagnostics, East Walpole, Mass., 1992-93, sr. rsch. scientist, 1993; adj. asst. prof. U. Mo., Rolla, 1994-95, asst. prof., 1995-2001, assoc. prof., 2001—. Contbr. articles to profl. jours. including Jour. Am. Chem. Soc., Jour. Organic Chemistry, Tetrahedron; patentee hydrophilic Acridinium Esters. Fellow SOHIO, 1986; recipient Greek Inst. State scholarship awards, 1978-82, Gustel Giessen Advanced Rsch. award Barnett Inst. Chem. Analysis and Materials Sci., 1988, Outstanding Tchg. award U. Mo., Rolla, 1996-97, 99-2000, 01-02. Mem. AAAS, Am. Chem. Soc. Office: U Mo-Rolla Dept Chemistry Rolla MO 65409-0001

SOTO, NELL, state senator; b. Pomona, Calif., June 18, 1926; children: Philip, Robert, Michael, Patrick, Anna, Tom. Grad., Pomona High Sch., 1944; student, Mt. San Antonio Jr. Coll., 1946—49, UCLA. Govt. affairs rep. Equal Opportunity Agy., 1971—73; commr. status of women L.A. County, 1972—74; pers. dir. Rest Haven Hosp., 1973—76; govt. affairs rep. Health Sys. Agy., 1976—80; commr. cmty. life commn. City of Pomona, 1979—83, mem. city coun., 1987—98; govt. affairs rep. Rapid Transit Dist., 1984—93; mem., dist. 61 Calif. State Assembly, 1998—2000; mem., dist. 32 Calif. State Senate, 2000—. Mem. Air Quality Mgmt. Dist., 1993—99, Vets. Affairs Com., Transp. Com., Local Govt. Com., Ins. Com., Govtl. Orgn. Com.; chair Pub. Employment and Retirement Com. Mem. PTA St. Joseph Sch. and Giano Sch., Nogales, Calif., 1955—78. Democrat. Roman Catholic. Mailing: State Capitol Rm 4074 Sacramento CA 95814 Office: 822 N Euclid Ave Ontario CA 91762 Office Phone: 916-445-6868.

SOTO, PATRICIA MCFARLANE, elementary school educator; b. Oak Park, Ill., Aug. 21, 1948; m. Alex Soto. BA, Fla. State U., 1970; MSc in Edn., Fla. Internat. U., 1991. Nat. bd. cert. tchr. 1996. Tchr., sci. dept. chair George Washington Carver Middle Sch., Coconut Grove, Fla., 1984—. Named Outstanding Health Educator, Ednl. Devel. Corp. Mem.: Nat. Sci. Tchrs. Assn. (Optical Data Corps. Videodisc Tech. award 1992), Nat. Bd. for Profl. Tchg. Stds. (bd. mem.). Office: Carver Middle Sch 4901 Lincoln Dr Coconut Grove FL 33133-5699

SOTO, VERONICA MARIA, school librarian; b. Yahualica, Mex., Sept. 2, 1970; d. Guadalupe Jose and Maria Soto; m. Jose Manuel Perez; 1 child, Maria Veronica Perez-Soto. BS in Elem. Edn., No. Ariz. U., 1994, M in Ednl. Leadership, 1999. Cert. elem. edn. K-8 Ariz., prin. Ariz., bilingual edn. endorsement Ariz. 4th grade elem. tchr. Gadsden Sch. Dist., San Luis, Ariz., 1994—96, 4th grade tchr., 1998—2002, libr., 2003—; 5th grade elem. tchr. Pecan Grove Elem. Sch., Yuma, Ariz., 1996—97. Asst. prin. Rio Colorado Elem. Sch., San Luis, 1999—2002, site coun. mem., 1999—2001; summer sch. prin. Gadsden Elem. Sch., 2000. Named Yuma County Intermediate Tchr. of Yr., Rotary Club, 2001; scholar, Nat. Hispanic Scholarship Fund, 1993. Avocations: reading, motorcycling, physical fitness, cake decorating, writing. Home: P O Box 1416 San Luis AZ 85349 Office: Rio Colorado Elem Sch Hwy 95 and Rio Colorado San Luis AZ 85349 Personal E-mail: mvsoto31@hotmail.com.

SOTO BALTRUSITIS, ARLEANE, financial analyst/benefits compensation analyst; b. N.Y.C., May 30, 1951; d. Carmelo Soto and Iris Ramirez; m. Bruce J. Baltrusitis, May 14, 1978. AAS, Kings Borough Cmty. Coll., N.Y.C., 1971; BBA, Baruch Coll., 1979. Adminstrv. asst. James Talcott, Inc., N.Y.C., 1971-1973; mgr. benefits adminstrn. Warner Communication, N.Y.C., 1973-1984; benefits mgr. M. Fortunoff of Westbury, Westbury, N.Y., 1984-1987; mgr. corporate benefits Avon Products, N.Y.C., 1987-1993, mgr. global benefits design, 1993-1996; mgr. benefits planning design Cushman & Wakefield, N.Y.C., 1996-1997; dir. benefits planning Revlon, N.Y.C., 1997-1999, vice president benefits world-wide, 1999-2000; v.p. benefits Am. Express, N.Y.C., 2000—. Mem. Web/Network of Benefit Professionals (treas./nat. bd.), Internat. Soc. Human Resources Profls., Soc. Human Resources Profls., Am. Compensation Assn., Internat. Foundation Employee Benefits Plans, Network Hispanic Profls. (treas./bd. mem.). Home: 49-53 Utopia Pky Fresh Meadows NY 11365

SOTOMAYOR, SONIA, federal judge; b. N.Y.C., June 25, 1954; d. Sonia and Celina (Baez) Sotomayor; m. Kevin Edward Noonan, Aug. 14, 1976 (div. 1983). AB, Princeton U., 1976; JD, Yale U., 1979; LLD honoris causa (hon.), 1999, JD (hon.) honoris causa, 2001. Bar: N.Y. 1980, U.S. Dist. Ct. (ea. and so. dists.) N.Y. 1984. Asst. dist. atty. Office of Dist. Atty. County of N.Y., N.Y.C., 1979—84; assoc., ptnr. Pavia & Harcourt, N.Y.C., 1984—92; fed. judge U.S. Dist. Ct. (so. dist.) N.Y., N.Y.C., 1992—98; cir. judge U.S. Ct. Appeals (2d Cir.), N.Y.C., 1998—. Adj. prof. NYU Sch. Law, 1998; lectr. law Columbia Law Sch., 1999. Editor: Yale U. Law Rev., 1979. Mem. State Adv. Panel on Inter-Group Rels., N.Y.C., 1990—92, 1990—91; bd. dirs. P.R. Legal Def. and Edn. Fund, N.Y.C., 1980—92, State of N.Y. Mortgage Agy., N.Y.C., 1987—92, N.Y.C. Campaign Fin. Bd., 1988—92. Mem.: ABA, Am. Philos. Soc., N.Y. Women's Bar Assn., P.R. Bar Assn., Hispanic Bar Assn., Phi Beta Kappa. Office: US Courthouse 410 US Corthouse 40 Centre St New York NY 10007-1502*

SOTTILE, KATHY WATSON, publisher, writer; b. Selma, Ala., Dec. 16, 1951; d. Edward A. and Nell K. (Keeton) Watson. BS with honors, Auburn U., 1974; MA, N.Mex. State U., 1978. Tchr. spl. edn. Montgomery (Ala.) Pub. Schs., 1974-75, Alamogordo (N.Mex.) Pub. Schs., 1975-83, Waxahatchie (Tex.) Pub. Schs., 1983-86; founder, pres. Fedn. Internat. Canines, Bridgewater, N.J., 1986-90, v.p. Montgomery, Ala., 1990—; v.p. ops. Ala. Emergency Svcs. and Securities, Montgomery, Ala., 1994—; asst. sec. L.C.P. Trust Co., Birmingham, Ala., 1996—. Sec. N.M.C.A., 1987-93; v.p. F.I.C.A., 1993—. Author: My Other Side, 1995; author (brochure) Masterpiece Guide to the Cane Corso, 1993; editor (newsletter) Neonews, 1986-93, (newsletter) C.C.C.A., 1988-96; contbr. articles to profl. jours. Mem. NAFE, AAUW, Nat. Pks. and Conservation Assn., Nat. Mus. Women in Arts, Nat. Trust Historic Preservation, Libr. Congress Assocs., Ala. Preservation Alliance, North Shore Animal League Gold Club, Friends Pintlala Branch Libr., Cane Corso Club Am (pres. 1988-96). Avocations: swimming, horseback riding, internet surfing, movies, collecting rare books. Office: Fedn Internat Canines PO Box 250307 Montgomery AL 36125-0307

SOUD, GINGER, city councilwoman; m. A.C. Soud Jr.; children: Jeff, John, Adrian. City councilwoman-at-large Jacksonville (Fla.) City Coun., 1994—, chmn. Pub. Health and Safety Com., mem. Land Use and Zoning

Com., mem. Telecomm. Com., v.p., 1998-99, pres., 1999—. Real estate broker Mem. Nat. Assn. Realtors, Fla. Assn. Realtors, Jacksonville Assn. Realtors, Jacksonville Women's Network. Republican. Office: 117 W Duval St Ste 425 Jacksonville FL 32202-5712

SOUDERS, JEAN SWEDELL, artist, educator; b. Braham, Minn., July 13, 1922; d. John Almond and Frances Johanna (Alm) Swedell; m. Robert Livingston Souders, Sep. 22, 1945 (dec. 1985). BA, Duluth (Minn.) State Coll., 1944; postgrad., Minn. Sch. of Art, 1944, Walker Sch. of Art, 1948; MA, U. Iowa, 1955, MFA, 1956. Instr. art St. Olaf Coll., Northfield, Minn., 1947-50; instr. craft U. Minn., 1951; prof. art history painting Calif. State U., Chico, Calif., 1957-74, prof. art history, 1959-60, faculty gen. studies, 1971-73. Exhbn. Creative Art Ctr., 1975, Des Moines Art Ctr., Crocker Mus. of Art, Chico State U. and Chico Art Gallery, 1994, and various others; paintings in over 200 collections. Mem.: Women Artists Assn. San Francisco, Mus. of Women in the Arts, Nat. Archives (work and exhibit records). Lutheran. Avocations: photography, hiking, backpacking, classical music.

SOUKUP, BETTY A. state legislator; b. Clarksburg, W.Va. m. Robert Soukup; 3 children. AS in Bus. Mgmt., BA in Comms. Arts. Mem. Iowa Senate from 15th dist., Des Moines, 1998—; mem. agr. com., mem. appropriations com.; mem. small bus., econs. devel. and tourism com. Iowa Senate, Des Moines, mem. ways and means com. Democrat. Office: State Capitol 9th And Grand Ave Des Moines IA 50319-0001 E-mail: betty_soukup@legis.state.ia.us.

SOULE, LUCILE SNYDER, pianist, music educator; b. Fargo, N.D., Sept. 21, 1922; d. Roy Henry and Gene (McGhee) Snyder; m. Leon Cyprian Soule Jr., Sept. 1, 1954 (dec. Dec. 1994); children: Robert Leon, Anne Lucile. MusB, MusB in Edn., MacPhail Coll. Music, 1943; MA, Smith Coll., Northampton, Mass., 1945; postgrad. diploma, Juilliard Sch. Music, 1948. Organist various chs., Mont., La., and Ohio, 1935-68; instr. Smith Coll., Northampton, 1945-46; freelance pianist, accompanist Juilliard Sch. Music, also pvt. groups and individuals, N.Y.C., 1946-49; from instr. to assoc. prof. Newcomb Coll., Tulane U., New Orleans, 1949-61; staff pianist, soloist New Orleans Symphony, 1954-61; guest artist Contemporary Music Festival La. State U., Baton Rouge, 1953-61; lectr. Lakewood br. Ohio State U., 1964-66; music tchr. East Cleveland (Ohio) Pub. Schs., 1969-85; music dir. East Cleveland Theater, 1985—2001; cons. and mgr. of spl. programs East Cleve. (Ohio) Theater, 2001—03; pianist Zhao Rong Chun, Cleve., 1995—; pianist for William Dempsey, Cleve., 1997—. Pres. New Orleans Music Tchrs. Assn., 1958-59; publicity chair Rocky River (Ohio) Chamber Music Soc., 1963-67; v.p. Cleve. chpt. Am. Orff Schluwerk Assn., 1974-75, presenter in field; mem. The Trio, 1998—. Pianist (compact disc with Zhao) Master of the Erhu, 1996; debut recital with Zhao at Weill Recital Hall, Carnegie Hall, 1999; composer Serenity Prayer, 1998, The Crown of Life, 1999. Mem. Citizens Adv. Group, East Cleveland, 1967-69; vocal coach, 1946—. Woolley Found. fellow, 1950-51, Tchg. fellow Case Western Res. U., 1967-68, Smith Coll., 1943-45; Juilliard Sch. Music scholar, 1946-48. Mem. Darius Millhaud Soc. (bd. dirs. 1984—), Fortnightly Mus. Club (corr. sec. 1996-2000), Lecture Recital Club (bd. dirs. 1993-95), Mu Phi Epsilon. Democrat. Christian Scientist. Avocations: church work, gourmet cooking, travel, art. Home and Office: 15617 Hazel Rd East Cleveland OH 44112-2904

SOULTOUKIS, DONNA ZOCCOLA, library director; b. Princeton, N.J., July 28, 1949; d. Peter Joseph and Josephine (Taraschi) Zoccola; m. Dimitrios Athanasios Soultoukis, July 26, 1980. AB, Georgian Ct. Coll., Lakewood, N.J., 1971; MS, Drexel U., 1976; Cert., Italian U. for Foreigners, Perugia, 1974. Libr. asst. Geology Libr. Princeton U., 1971-73; libr. Friends Hosp., Phila., 1976-86, dir. libr. svcs., 1986-98; head libr. Temple U., Sch. Podiatric, 1998-99; ref. libr. MCP/Hahnemann U., Phila., 1999-2000; sr. info. scientist Bristol-Myers Squibb Pharm. Rsch. Inst., Hopewell, N.J., N.J., 2000; libr. Our Lady of Lourdes Sch. Nursing, Camden, NJ, 2001—. Cons. Lower Bucks Hosp., Bristol, Pa., 1991-95. Vol. outreach program Old St. Joseph's Ch., Phila., 1992-95, sanctuary min., 1993—, mem. pastoral coun., 1995-98, 2001--, bd. ministers 1999-2001, mem. outreach program, bd. dirs., 1997—2002. Mem. Med. Libr. Assn. (chair mental librs. divsn. 1991-93, chair rsch. com. 1996—), Spl. Librs. Assn. (Phila. chpt. bd. dirs. 1985-88, pres. 1982-84, chmn. long-range planning 1993, mem. adv. bd. 1995-2001, sec. solo divsn. 2000-01, devel. com. 2003[00bf]). Avocations: travel, cooking. Home: 290 Cinnabar Ln Yardley PA 19067-5717

SOUSA, MARILYN FELSKE, medical educator, consultant; d. William Albert Felske and Helen Ruth Morgan; m. Gordon Wallace Sousa, June 22, 1946; children: Gordon Jr., Guy Morgan, Gary Edward. BS, U. Conn., 1948, MS in Biol. Scis.; EdM, So. Conn. U. Asst. instr. Peabody mus. Yale U., 1945—47; instr. gen scis., animal diseases U. Conn., 1947—48, asst. prof. gen scis., animal diseases, 1948—50; resource tchr. Cheshire Sch. Sys., 1956-67, West Hartford Sch. Sys., 1968—79; admin. asst. West Hartford, Conn., 1979—82; patient/instr. clin. skills assessment program U. Conn. Sch. of Med., 1987—. Chair Internat. Assocs., 2003—; mem. patient adv. for rheumatology divsn. U. Conn., 1975—, mem. multipurpose arthritis ctr. adv. coun., 1976—97; site trainer Nat. Bd. Med. Examiners. Contbr. articles to jours. and periodicals; spokesperson (in print and media). Founder Nat. Lupus Found., Washington, 1975, Conn. Lupus Found., 1973—. Recipient Hall of Fame award, Lupus Soc. Am., 1992, Heroes Among Us award, Conn. Forum, 1997, Women Who Dare to Make a Difference award, Coun. of Jewish Women, 1998, YWCA Leadership award, 1999, Heroes Among Us award, Hartford Courant, 2000, Sumna award, 2002, Jefferson award, 2003, 1998, Achievement award, Pres. Gerald Ford, A. C. Perry award. Mem.: AANC, Lupus Foundn. of Am. (1st v.p., exec. coun. 1966—, chair med. adv. bd. 1989—, chair ednl. svcs. 1996—, editl. bd. Lupus News 1996—, chair ann. awards com. 1998—, nominating com. 1998—, adv. to support groups 1996—, co-leader Hartford area support group 1998—, mem. credentials, chapter svcs. and rels. com. 1999—, Vol. Appreciation award 1999, Outstanding Svc. and Continuing Efforts award 1998). Avocations: sports, reading, movies, computers, exercise. Home: 27 Woodbridge Cir West Hartford CT 06107 E-mail: mfsousa@aol.com.

SOUTH, SHERI COBB, writer, publishing executive; b. Huntsville, Ala., July 23, 1959; d. William Elbert and Jayne Braswell Cobb; m. Michael Steven South, Sept. 5, 1980; children: Jessamy Lynn, Trevor Blake. AA magna cum laude, Wallace State C.C., Hanceville, Ala., 1980; BA summa cum laude, U. South Ala., 1992. Founder PrinnyWorld Press, Saraland, 1998—. Spkr. Silken Sands Conf., Gulf Shores, Ala., 1991—. Editor: (book) Georgette Heyer: A Critical Retrospective, 2001; author: (novel) Wrong-Way Romance, 1991, That Certain Feeling, 1991, The Cinderella Game, 1992, Don't Bet on Love, 1994, Blame It on Love, 1995, The Cobra and the Lily, 1999, The Weaver Takes a Wife, 1999, Brighton Honeymoon, 2000, Restless Hearts, 2000, Miss Darby's Duenna, 2000 (Royal Ascot award, 1996, Hon. Mention Writer's Digest Self-Published Book Awards, 2000), French Leave, 2001. Spkr. various sch. groups, Mobile, 1991—2003; judge Ala. Penman Creative Writing Competition, Mobile. Mem.: Sisters in Crime, The Beau Monde (pres. 1998), Romance Writers Am.-Gulf Coast Chpt. (pres. 1993—95), Romance Writers Am., Publishers Mktg. Assn. Avocations: reading, singing, golf, travel. Office: PrinnyWorld Press PO Box 248 Saraland AL 36571 E-mail: prinnywrld@aol.com.

SOUTHALL, VIRGINIA LAWRENCE, retired artist; b. Portsmouth, Va., Aug. 25, 1927; d. Malachi Ashley Lewis and Bessie (Oliver) Lawrence; m. Junius Nathan Southall, Apr. 18, 1959; children: Lawrence Nathan. Student Norfolk divsn., Va. State Coll., 1945-46; student, Prince George's C.C., Largo, Md., 1988—. Sec. to dean sch. engring. Tuskegee (Ala.) Inst., 1949-51; passport clk., ID clk. dept. army The Pentagon, Washington, 1951-62; pers. clk. AID, Dept. State, Washington, 1963-67. Exhibited in group shows including U. Md. Coll. Arts Program Gallery, College Park, 1993, Prince Georges C.C., Marlboro Gallery, Largo, Md., 1993-94, Montpelier Cultural Art Ctr., Laurel, Md., 1996, Md. State Ho., Annapolis, 1998, Children's Nat. Med. Ctr. Atrium Gallery 1, Washington, 1999, Mary McCleod Bethune Coun. Ho., Washington, 1999; one-woman shows include Outreach and Devel. Ctr. Ebenezer United Meth. Ch., Lanham, Md., Art Atrium II Gallery, Portsmouth, Va., 1998. Concert choir mem. Prince Georges C.C.; Chancel Choir mem. Ebenezer United Meth. Ch., vol. art tchr. for youth programs. Mem. Nat. Mus. Women in the Arts, Md. Choral Soc. Avocations: arts and crafts, music, singing. Home: 9015 Wallace Rd Lanham Seabrook MD 20706-4211

SOUTHARD, RUTH AUDREY, medical/surgical nurse; b. Kearny, N.J., Aug. 17, 1923; d. Robert James and Edna Leola Zerbe; m. Carl B. Southard, Dec. 17, 1983 (dec. Mar. 1989). Diploma, Muhlenberg Hosp. Sch. Nursing, Plainfield, N.J., 1944; BSN, Seton U., 1953; MA in Pub. Health Nursing, N.Y. U., 1968. Dir. svc. MCOSS Family Health and Nursing Svc., Red Bank, NJ, 1945—72; asst. prof., sr. coord. Mankato State U., Minn., 1972—74; coord. sr. level cmty. health nursing, asst. prof. U. R.I., 1974—75; coord. ambulatory care svcs. Jersey City Med. Ctr., 1977—78; adminstrv./supr. nurse Jewish Child Care Assn. N.Y., 1978—79; primary nurse Loeb Ctr. Nursing and Rehab., Montefiore Hosp., Bronx, NY, 1980; with employee health dept. J.P. Morgan Trust Co., NY, 1980; nurse crisis intervention unit Hahneman U. Hosp., Phila., 1982—83; nurse psychiat. unit John F. Kennedy Hosp., Cherry Hill, NJ, 1983—84. Contbr. articles to profl. jours. Mem. N.J. Libr.for Blind and Disabled, Defenders of Wildlife. Capt. U.S. Army Nuse Corps, 1945—58. Mem.: ANA, Am. Nurses Found., N.J. Sate Nurses Assn., Gloucester County Stamp Club, AARP, Sierra Club, Century Club. Protestant. Home: 5105 N Park Dr S1418 Pennsauken NJ 08109

SOUTHER, LISA, music educator; b. Syracuse, N.Y., Apr. 24, 1967; d. William Arthur Ours, Jr. and Jeannette Pauline Ours; m. Brian Keith Souther, May 20, 1989; children: Ashley, Deanna, Keri, Jared. BS in Acctg., Liberty U., Lynchburg, Va., 1989. Accounts payable clk. Kewani Plant, Statesville, NC, 1989—90; pvt. music tchr Melody Studio, Statesville, NC, 1992—; fine arts dir. Southview Christian Sch., Statesville, 1995—2003; music tchr. Fairview Fine Arts Acad., Statesville, 1999—. Substitute tchr. Southview Christian Sch., Statesville, 1995—. Composer, arranger many band and orch. pieces. Vol. Right to Life, 1990—, WRA, 1990—. Mem.: Nat. Fedn. Music Clubs, McDowell Music Club (counselor 1995—). Republican. Baptist. Avocations: scrapbooks, skiing, reading, painting, rock climbing.

SOUTHERLAND, DEBORAH LEE, psychologist; b. Abilene, Tex., Dec. 2, 1965; d. Walter Lee and Emilia Alcaire Baker; m. Kevin Lee Southerland, Sept. 5, 1993; 1 child, Calder James. BA in English, U. NC, 1987; MA in Marriage, Family, and Child Counseling, U. So. Calif., 1993, PhD, 1999. Lic. marriage and family therapist Calif., psychologist Calif. Counselor Project Cope Women's Program, Lynn, Mass., 1989—90; drug counselor Kazi Ho., Inc., Compton, Calif., 1990—91; clin. coord. Substance Abuse Found., Long Beach, Calif., 1992—94; marriage, family, and child counselor intern Brentwood, Calif., 1994—98, psychology intern Emory U. Counseling Ctr., Atlanta, 1998—99; psychologist counseling and psychol. svcs. Mt. St. Mary's Coll., L.A., 1999—2001; coord., drug and alcohol abuse prevention program Calif. Inst. Tech., Pasadena, 1996—98, coord. drug and alcohol abuse prevention program, 1999—2001, inst. psychologist student counseling ctr., 2001—; pvt. practice psychology Beverly Hills, Calif., 2001—. Choices grantee, NCAA, 1998, Town and Gown scholar, U. So. Calif., 1992—93. Mem.: APA, Calif. Assn. Marriage and Family Therapists. Office: Deborah L Southerland PhD 315 S Beverly Drive Suite 409 Beverly Hills CA 90212 Personal E-mail: dlsoutherland@sbcglobal.net.

SOUTHERN, ANN GAYLE, medical/surgical nurse, educator; b. Radford, Va., Oct. 1, 1950; d. William Gale and Harless (Rogers) Farmer. Degree in nursing cum laude, Wytheville (Va.) C.C., 1985; BS, Radford (Va.) U., 1988, MS, 1995. RN. Nurse Pulaski (Va.) Cmty. Hosp., 1985-88, St. Alban's Psychiat. Hosp., Radford, 1988-98; clin. instr. Wytheville RN Program, 1996-98; nurse Sunbridge of New River Valley, Dublin, 1999—2003, Columbia Pulaski Cmty. Hosp., Pulaski, Va., 1999—2003. Counselor AIDS/hepatitis disease process cmty. support groups, Radford, 1992-2003; lectr. breast cancer and self-exam., Radford, 1995. Mem. ANA, Sigma Theta Tau. Methodist. Avocations: old movies, gardening. Home: 6746 Dudley Ferry Rd Radford VA 24141-8876

SOUTHERN, NANCY C. utilities executive; Co-chmn., CEO ATCO Ltd. and Can. Utilities, Calgary, Canada, 2000—02, pres., CEO, 2003—, also bd. dirs. Exec. v.p. Spruce Meadows; bd. dirs. Shell Can. Ltd., Akita Drilling Ltd., Sentgraf Enterprises Ltd. Former mem. Can. Equestrian Team. Office: ATCO Ltd 1500/1600 909 11th Ave SW Calgary AB Canada T2R 1N6

SOUTHGATE, MARIE THERESE, physician, editor; b. Detroit, Apr. 27, 1928; d. Clair and Josephine Marie (Hoefeyzers) S. BS, Coll. St. Francis, 1948, LLD (hon.), 1974; MD, Marquette U., 1960. Duplomate Nat. Bd. Med. Examiners. Rsch. editor Ill. Inst. Tech. Rsch. Inst., Chgo., 1951-55; intern St. Mary's Hosp., San Francisco, 1960-61; sr. editor Jour. of AMA, Chgo., 1962-75, dep. editor, 1975-88, sr. contbg. editor, 1988—. Mem. editorial bd. Forum, from 1978; mem. ad hoc com. on biol. scis. Ill. Bd. Huigher Edn., 1969-70; mem. ad hoc com. on lay deacons Archdiocese Chgo., 1973; trustee Coll. St. Francis, from 1978. Editor-in-chief Marquette Med. Rev., 1959-60. Mem. AMA, AAAS, Am. Med. Women's Assn. (v.p Chgo. chpt. 1967-68, mem. continuing med. edn. com. from 1978), Coun. Biology Editors. Office: JAMA 515 N State St Chicago IL 60610-4325

SOUTHWARD, PATRICIA C. volunteer; b. Alexandria, La., Mar. 9, 1942; d. George Emerson and Mary Alice (Boland) Cilley; m. Arnold Lester Greenfield, May 18, 1963 (div. June 1968); m. Ernest Merritt Southward, Mar. 1970 (dec. 2002); 1 daughter. BA, U. Fla., Gainesville, 1963; MS, Fla. State U., Tallahassee, 1966; postgrad., U. Ctrl. Fla. Office mgr. Southward Gardens, Lake Mary, Fla., 1977-84, Southward Investment and Realty, Lake Mary, Fla., 1970—2001. Adj. instr. Caldwell C.C., Boone, NC, 1999—, Seminole C.C., Lake Mary, Fla., 2001—; city commr. Lake Mary, 1977-79, 82. Com. mem. Fla. Govs. Coun. on Housing Goals, 1980; sponsor, vol. and social worker Refugee Resettlement Office, Cath., 1980—; bd. dirs., sec. Ctrl. Fla. Migrant and Community Health Clinic, Sanford, 1981-89. Mem.: LWV (bd. dirs. Seminole County, Fla. 1982—92, 1st v.p. Seminole County 1990—94, voters svc. chair, bd. dirs. Fla. 1989—90). Republican. Avocation: anthropology. Home: 316 Oak Leaf Cir Lake Mary FL 32746-3059 Office: PO Box 950730 Lake Mary FL 32795-0730 also: 161 Meadow Avenue Loop Rd Banner Elk NC 28604-9659 E-mail: psouthward@hotmail.com.

SOUTHWORTH, JAMIE MACINTYRE, retired education educator; b. Ironton, Ohio, Oct. 16, 1931; d. Gaylord and Lydia Marcum (Adkins) MacIntyre; m. Horton C. Southworth; children: Jaye, Brad, Alexandra, Sueann, Janet, Jim. BS, Ball State U., 1952, MA, 1961; EdD, U. Pitts., 1981; attended, Oxford (Eng.) U., 1997. Cert. adminstr. and tchr., reading specialist, Pa. Instr. Mich. State U., East Lansing, 1964-67; instr., coord. U. Minn., Mpls., 1967-71; rsch. assoc. Pitts. Pub. Schs., 1971-80; assoc. prof. California U., Pitts., 1988, prof. edn., 1993—, state grants educator, 1990-95, dir. leadership tng. proposal, 1996-00; ret., 2000. Chancellor state adv. com., California U. rep., 1994—, faculty profl. devel. com. state rep., 1991-99; invited participant Oxford (Eng.) U. Leadership Studies, 1995, 97; cons. TITL project Duquesne U.; CEO Learning Tree Corp., 1975-2000; presenter, rsch. conf. 2000, Waikato U., New Zealand, rsch. young childrens conf. 2000-02, San Diego; chair-IRA, internat. conf. nat. Fulbright scholars, San Francisco, 2002. Contbr. articles to profl. jours. Recipient Seal of St. Peter's Coll., Oxford, 1997; U.S. Office of Edn. title III & IVC grantee; grantee Pa. Vocat. Tech. State, 1990-91, 93, Bibliotherapy Project California Univ. Pa., 1992, Pa. State, 1993, Pa. Campus Compac, 1993. Mem. Am. Assn. Colls. Tchr. Edn., NEA Young Children, Kappa Delta Pi (counselor), Phi Delta Kappa. Home: 619 S Linden Ave Pittsburgh PA 15208-2812

SOUTHWORTH, LINDA JEAN, artist, critic, educator, poet; b. Milw., May 11, 1951; d. William Dixon and Violet Elsie (Kuehn) S.; m. David Joseph Roger, Nov. 16, 1985 (div. July 1989). BFA, St. John's U., Queens, N.Y., 1974; MFA, Pratt Inst., Bklyn., 1978. Pvt. practice self-employed, N.Y.C., 1974—; art critic Resident Publs., N.Y.C., 1993-95. Adj. prof. art history St. Francis Coll., Bklyn., 1985-94; artist-in-residence Our Saviour's Atonement Luth. Ch., N.Y.C., 1993-95. One-woman shows include Galimaufry, Croton-on-Hudson, N.Y., 1977, Kristen Richard Gallery, N.Y.C., 1982, Gallery 84, 1990, The Bernhardt Collection, Washington, 1991, Netherland Club, N.Y.C., 1992, Chuck Levitan Gallery, Soho, 1996, Seventh and Second Photo Gallery, 1998, Pen & Brush Solo Award Show, 2001, N.Y.C. Pub. Libr., 2002, exhibited in group shows at Union St. Graphics, San Francisco, 1974, Nuance Gallery, Tampa, 1987, 1988, Illustrators Ann. Drawing Show, N.Y.C., 1989—90, Salmagundi Club, 1991, 1992, Henry Howells Gallery, 1992—93, Mus. Gallery, 1994, Cavalier Gallery, Greenwich, Conn., 1995, CaribGallery, N.Y.C., 1996, N.Y. State Mus., 1997, Knickerbocker Gallery, 1999, Maison Royale, New Orleans, La., 2002, Christmas Card/UNICEF, 1992, Represented in permanent collections Peltz,Walker & Dubinsky, Valois of Am., one-woman shows include New York City Pub. Libr., 2002. Recipient first prize award annual watercolor exhibit, Pen and Brush, 2000. Mem. Pen and Brush, Poetry Soc. Am. Mem. Collegiate Ch. Avocations: ballroom dancing, old inns and architecture. Home: 106 Cabrini Blvd Apt 5D New York NY 10033-3422 E-mail: linda@lindasouthworth.com.

SOUZA, BLASE CAMACHO, librarian, educator; b. Kohala, Hawaii, Feb. 3, 1918; d. Lawrence Lorenzo Ramos and Mary Maria (Caravalho) Camacho; m. Alfred Patrick Souza, Nov. 26, 1949; children: Michelle Louise, Patricia Ann. EdB, U. Hawaii, Honolulu, 1939; PD, U. Hawaii, 1940; MLS with honors, Pratt Inst., 1947. Cert. tchr., Hawaii. Tchr. Honolulu Dept. Pub. Instruction, 1940-42, Lahaina (Maui, Hawaii) Dept. Pub. Instruction, 1941-42, Waialua (Oahu, Hawaii) Dept. Pub. Instruction, 1943-46, libr., 1947-66; rsch. libr. dept. of edn. U. Hawaii, Honolulu, 1967-68, adminstr., rsch. libr. dept. of edn., 1968-70; edn. officer, program specialist media svcs. Hawaii Dept. of Edn., Honolulu, 1970-75; local historian P.R. Heritage Soc. of Hawaii, Honolulu, 1976—. Cons. Hawaii Multi Cultural Ctr., Honolulu, 1976-80, Hawaii Heritage Ctr., Honolulu, 1981—; lectr., cons. P.R. Heritage Soc. of Hawaii, Honolulu, 1984—. Author: Boricua Hawaiiana: Puerto Ricans of Hawaii, Reflections of the Past and Mirror of the Future, 1983, De Borinquen a Hawaii, 1985, A Puerto Rican Poet On The Sugar Plantations of Hawaii, 2000; co-author: Legacy of Diversity, 1975, MONTAGE-An Ethnic History of Women in Hawaii, 1977, A Puerto Rican Poet on the Super Plantations of Hawaii, 2000; contbr. articles to profl. jours. Bd. dirs. Friends of Waipahu Cultural Garden Park, 1983-92; active Hist. Hawaii Found., Honolulu, 1984, Bishop Mus., Honolulu, 1985—. Hawaii Com. for the Humanities grantee, 1980, 91. Mem. Hawaii Assn. Sch. Librs. (pres. 1965), Hawaii Libr. Assn. (pres. 1975), Hawaii Mus. Assn., P.R. Heritage Soc. Hawaii (founder, pres. 1980-84, 93-99), AAUW. Roman Catholic. Avocations: collect sculpture, music, reading. Office: 4220 Lafayette Pl Culver City CA 90232-2820

SOUZA, DIANE D, corporate financial executive; BS in acctg. with high honors, U. Mass.; AS in dental hygiene, Forsyth Sch. at Northeastern U. CPA. Dir. northeast ins. Price Waterhouse; sr. mgr. Deloitte Haskins & Sells; asst. v.p. Aetna Inc., 1994—96; v.p., CFO Large Case Pensions divsn. of Aetna Inc., 1996—98; v.p., dir. of internal audit Aetna Inc., 1998—2001, v.p., nat. customer ops., 2001—. Mem.: Conn. Soc. of CPA's (mem. ins. com.), Am. Inst. Cert. Pub. Accountants. Office: Aetna Inc 151 Farmington Ave Hartford CT 06156

SOWDER, KATHLEEN ADAMS, marketing executive; b. Person county, N.C., Feb. 9, 1951; d. George W. and Mary W. (Woody) Adams; m. Angelo R. LoMascolo, Apr. 11, 1980 (div.); 1 child, Mary Jennifer. BS, Radford Coll., 1976; MBA, Va. Poly. Inst., 1978. Bd. cert. in security mgmt. Cert. Protection Profl. Asst. product mgr. GTE Sylvania, Waltham, Mass., 1978—79, product mgr. video products, 1979—80; comml. mktg. mgr. Am. Dist. Telegraph, N.Y.C., 1980—87; v.p. mktg. ESL, Hingham, Mass., 1987—91; exec. v.p. Falcon Detection Techs., Inc., Plymouth, Mass., 1991—94; gen. mgr. Westec Bus. Security, Irvine, Calif., 1995—2002; CEO Nova Security Sys., Fullerton, Calif., 2002—. Mem.: Am. Soc. Indsl. Security (past chair standing com. on phys. security), Am. Mktg. Assn. Republican. Office: Nova Security Systems 819 Pueblo Fullerton CA 92835 Home: 10473 La Sombra Ave Fountain Valley CA 92708-5210 E-mail: ksowder@novasecuritysystems.com.

SOWERS, AMELIA BARNET, speech and language pathologist; b. Houston, Mar. 13, 1952; d. Albert Glenn and Helen June (Meador) Barnet; m. George Vernon Sowers Jr., Aug. 23, 1975; children: George Vernon III, Adam Glenn. BA, U. Houston, 1975, MA, 1993. Lic. and cert. speech-lang. pathologist, Tex. Speech-lang. pathologist Aldine Ind. Sch. Dist., Houston, 1976-78, Tomball (Tex.) Ind. Sch. Dist., 1978-83, Conroe (Tex.) Ind. Sch. Dist., 1984-96; pvt. practice, 1996—. Mem. Crighton Players; organizer Crighton Kids, Crighton Players Performing Arts Sch. for Youth; apptd. to City of Conroe Commn. on Arts & Culture; pres. Crighton Theatre Found. 1999-2001; clin. supr. Grad. Sch., Tex. Women's U. 1997-98. Mem. NEA, Am. Speech, Lang. and Hearing Assn., Tex. Speech and Hearing Assn., Tex. Tchrs. Assn., Houston Assn. Comm. Disorders, Montgomery County Performing Arts Soc. (com.), Conroe Svc. League. Methodist. Avocations: reading, crafts, dance, community theatre. Home and Office: 25 Village Hill Dr Conroe TX 77304-3525

SOWLES, BETH A. secretary; b. Battle Creek, Mich., June 11, 1960; AS, Ferris State U., Big Rapids, Mich., 1981. Legal sec. Kidston-Peterson, P.C., Kalamazoo, Mich., 1981-82, Christovich & Kearney, New Orleans, 1982-84; sec. Cath. Family Svcs., Kalamazoo, 1984-87; sec. bldgs. dept. City of Kalamazoo, 1987-88, sr. sec. dept. transp. metro transit div., 1988—. Contbg. author Resource Ctr. Newsletter; editor monthly newsletter Women's Therapist Network. Organizing mem. Take Back the Night, Kalamazoo, 1990, Victories Over Violence, Kalamazoo, 1991; mem. Kalamazoo Area Legal Secs. Assn., 1981-83. Avocations: piano tchr., community activities. Home: 133 Candlewyck Dr Apt 110 Kalamazoo MI 49001-5496 Office: City of Kalamazoo 530 N Rose St Kalamazoo MI 49007-3638

SOYSTER, MARGARET BLAIR, lawyer; b. Washington, Aug. 5, 1951; d. Peter and Eliza (Shumaker) S. AB magna cum laude, Smith Coll., 1973; JD, U. Va., 1976. Bar: N.Y. 1977, U.S. Dist. Ct. (so. and ea. dists.) N.Y. 1977, U.S. Ct. Appeals (2nd cir.) 1979, U.S. Supreme Ct. 1981, U.S. Ct. Appeals (4th cir.) 1982, U.S. ct. Appeals (11th cir.) 1987, U.S. Ct. Appeals (7th cir.) 1991, U.S. Ct. Appeals (3d cir.) 1992. Assoc. Rogers & Wells, N.Y.C., 1976-84, ptnr., 1984-99, Clifford Chance U.S. LLP, N.Y.C., 2000—. Mem. ABA, Assn. of Bar of City of N.Y., Nat. Assn. Coll. and Univ. Attys., Phi Beta Kappa. Office: Clifford Chance US LLP 200 Park Ave Ste 5200 New York NY 10166-0005

SPACEK, SISSY (MARY ELIZABETH SPACEK), actress; b. Quitman, Tex., Dec. 25, 1949; d. Edwin S. and Virginia S.; m. Jack Fisk, 1974; children: Schuyler Elizabeth, Virginia Madison. Student, Lee Strasberg Theatrical Inst. Motion picture appearances include Prime Cut, 1972, Badlands, 1974, Carrie, 1976 (Acad. award nomination for best actress 1976), Three Women, 1977 (Best Supporting Actress 1977), Welcome to L.A., 1977, Heartbeat, 1980, Coal Miner's Daughter, 1980 (Acad. award best actress 1980, Golden Globe best actress 1980, Brit. Acad. award nomination best actress 1980, L.A. Film Critics for best actress 1980, Nat. Soc. Film Critics best actress 1980), Raggedy Man (Golden Globe nomination best actress 1981), 1981, Missing, 1982 (Acad. award nomination best actress, Golden Globe nomination best actress 1982, Brit. Acad. award nomination best actress 1982), The River, 1984 (Acad. award nomination best actress), Marie, 1985, 'Night Mother, 1986, Crimes of the Heart, 1986 (Acad. award nomination best actress, Golden Globe best actress 1986), Violets Are Blue, 1986, JFK, 1991, The Long Walk Home, 1990, Hard Promises, 1992, Trading Mom, 1994, The Grass Harp, 1995, Affliction, 1997, Blast From the Past, 1998, Songs in Ordinary Time, 2000, In the Bedroom, 2001 (Best Actress in Drama Golden Globe 2001, Am. Film Inst. award, Ind. Spirit award, Broadcast Critics award, Chgo. Film Critics award, Fla. Film Critics award, Golden Satellite award, Sundance Film Festival award, Southeastern Film award, N.Y. Film Critics award, L.A. Film Critics award 2001), Midwives, 2001, (TV movie) Last Call, 2002 (nominee Outstanding Supporting Actress in Miniseries or Movie Emmy award) Tuck Everlasting, 2002, Home at the End of the World, 2004; TV movie appearances include Straight Story, 1999, In the Bedroom, 2001 (Acad. award nomination best actress 2001, Brit. Acad. award nomination best actress 2001, Brit. Film Critics Choice award best actress 2001, Sundance Film Festival Spl. prize 2001, Golden Globe best actress 2001, Ind. Spirit award best felmale lead 2001, AFI, Actress of Yr. 2001, L.A. Film Critics best actress 2001, N.Y. Film Critics best actress 2001, SAG nomination best actress 2001, nominee Best Actress Acad. award 2001), The Migrants, 1973, Katherine, 1975, Verna: USO Girl, 1978, A Private Matter, 1992, A Place for Annie, 1994, The Good Old Boys, 1995, Streets of Laredo, 1995, If These Walls Could Talk, 1996, Midwives (SAG nomination best actress 2001), 2001, Beyond the Call (Emmy nomination best actress 2002), 2002; guest host TV show Saturday Night Live, 1977; appeared in episode TV show The Waltons. Office: care Creative Artists Agy LLC c/o Steve Tellez 9830 Wilshire Blvd Beverly Hills CA 90212-1804*

SPACKS, PATRICIA MEYER, English educator; b. San Francisco, Nov. 17, 1929; d. Norman B. and Lillian (Talcott) Meyer; 1 child, Judith Elizabeth Spacks. BA, Rollins Coll., Winter Park, Fla., 1949, DHL, 1976; MA, Yale U., 1950; PhD, U. Calif., Berkeley, 1955. Instr. English Ind. U., Bloomington, 1954-56; instr. humanities U. Fla., Gainesville, 1958-59; from instr. to prof. Wellesley Coll., Mass., 1959-79; prof. English Yale U., New Haven, 1979-89, chmn. dept., 1985-88; Edgar F. Shannon prof. English U. Va., 1989—, chmn. dept., 1991-97. Author: The Poetry of Vision, 1967, The Female Imagination, 1975, Imagining a Self, 1976, The Adolescent Idea, 1982, Gossip, 1985, Desire and Truth, 1990, Boredom: The Literary History of a State of Mind, 1995. Fellow Guggenheim Found., 1969-70, NEH, 1974, Am. Council Learned Socs., 1978-79, Nat. Humanities Ctr., 1982-83, 89. Mem. MLA (2nd v.p. 1992, 1st v.p. 1993, pres. 1994, mem. adv. com. 1976-80, mem. exec. coun. 1986-89), Am. Acad. Arts and Scis., Am. Coun. Learned Socs. (mem. bd. trustees 1992—, vice chair 1994-97, chair 1997—), Am. Philos. Soc. Office: U Va Dept English PO Box 400121 219 Bryan Hall Charlottesville VA 22904-4121 Home: 502 Pebble Hill Ct Charlottesville VA 22903-7873

SPADE, KATE (KATHERINE NOEL SPADE), apparel designer; b. Kansas City, Mo., 1962; m. Andy Spade, 1994. BA in journalism and broadcasting, Arizona State U., 1985. From asst. to accessories editor Mademoiselle mag., 1985—92; co-founder, designer Kate Spade Inc., N.Y.C., 1993—; designer Kate Spade paper and social stationary, 1998—, Kate Spade shoe collection, 1999—, Kate Spade glasses, 2001, Kate Spade beauty, 2002—; co-founder Jack Spade, 1999—, Kate Spade Home, 2002—. Designer (uniforms) Song Airlines (subs. Delta Airlines), 2004. Recipient Perry Ellis award, New Fashion Talent, Coun. Fashion Designers of Am., 1996, Accessory Designer of the Year, 1998, FiFi award for Bath & Body Star of the Year, U.S. Fragrance Found., 2003, FiFi award for Best Fragrance in Ltd. Distribution, U.K. Fragrance Found., 2003. Achievements include stores opening in N.Y.C. in 1996, Boston and LA in 1998, and Chicago and San Francisco in 2000. Office: Kate Spade Inc 48 W 25th St New York NY 10010*

SPADORA, HOPE GEORGEANNE, real estate company executive; b. Long Branch, N.J., May 13, 1965; d. Joseph Vincent and Gladys Beatrice (Clayton) S.; life ptnr. Rebecca Elise DeAnda; 1 child, Clayton Vincent Spadora. Cert. in Mktg. Comm., San Jose State U., 1988; AA in Biology with hons., Cabrillo Coll., Aptos, Calif., 1991; BA in Sociology with hons., U. Calif., Santa Cruz, 1993; M in Corp. Real Estate, Inst. Corp. Real Estate, 1998. Lic. real estate broker, Calif. Fin. analyst Lam Rsch., Fremont, Calif., 1993-94, portfolio mgr., 1994-96; v.p. internat. svcs. Cawley Internat., San Jose, Calif., 1996-97; v.p. real estate facilities Sybase Corp., Emeryville, Calif., 1997—. Bd. dirs. Emeryville (Calif.) Industries Assn., 1997-98. Mem. editl. bd. Jour. of Corporate Real Estate. Mem. Human Rights Campaign, San Francisco, 1997, The Commonwealth Club of Calif., San Francisco, 1998, Calif. Elected Womens Assn. for Edn. and Rsch., Sacramento, 1998; bd. dirs. Emeryville Cmty. Action Program. Mem. Internat. Assn. Corp. Real Estate Executives, Nat. Assn. Corp. Real Estate Execs., Bldg. Owners and Mgrs. Assn. Democrat. Avocations: golf, fishing, sailing, boating. Office: Sybase 6475 Christie Ave Emeryville CA 94608-1010

SPADY, JOANNE SMITH, secondary school educator; b. Phila., Jan. 17, 1935; d. Houston Thomas and Odeas Frances (Ewell) Savage; m. Sydney thomas Smith, June 1, 1963 (dec. July 1989); children: Deborah, Gregory; m. Lester Herbert Spady Sr., Apr. 3, 1994. AS, Norfolk State U., 1954; BA, U. Md., 1956. Choral, band tchr. Worcester County H.S., Snow Hill, Md., 1956-57; tchr. choral, history Acomac County, Mary N. Smith H.S., Accomac, Va., 1957-73; part-time tchr. Montgomerycounty Dept. Edn., Rockville, Md., 1973-76; asst. mgr. csh office Bradlees Inc., Rockville, 1976-86; tchr. fine arts Northampton County Dept. Edn., Eastville, Va., 1987-97. Vice chmn. planning commn. City of Cape Charles; sec. Arts Coun.; me. AFS BlackCoalition; bd. dirs. Eastern Shore C.C., Melfa, Va., 1989—. Mem. NEA, NAACP, Northampton County Edn. Ass., Edn.Assn. Va., Assn. Am. Choral Dirs., Va. Music Educators Assn., Nat. Music Educators Assn., Nat. Assn. Female Execs. Democrat. Methodist-Episcopalian. Avocations: music teaching, creative needle work. Home: PO Box 170 Capeville VA 23313-0170

SPAETH, BARBETTE STANLEY, classics educator; b. Chgo., Mar. 26, 1956; d. Harold Opie and Barbara Adeline (Yunker) Stanley; m. Robert Thomas Spaeth, June 24, 1978 (div. June 1990). BA summa cum laude, MA, Northwestern U., 1977; PhD, Johns Hopkins U., 1987. Lectr. European divsn. U. Md., Heidelberg, Germany, 1983-84, U. Md. Baltimore County, Catonsville, 1984; asst. prof. dept. classical studies Tulane U., New Orleans, 1987-94, assoc. prof., 1994—2001; assoc. prof. classical studies Coll. William and Mary, 2001—. Excavator Sanctuary of Apollo, Kourion, Cyprus, summers 1982-83; trenchmaster Kommos (Crete, Greece) Excavations, summers 1984-85. Author: The Roman Goddess Ceres, 1996; contbr. articles to profl. jours. Jacob Hirsch fellow Am. Sch. Classical Studies, Athens, 1986-87, Oscar Broneer fellow Am. Acad. in Rome, 1990-91. Mem. Am. Philol. Assn., Archaeol. Inst. Am., Classical Assn. Mid. West and South, Am. Acad. Religion. Democrat. Avocation: folk dancing. Office: Coll William and Mary Dept Classical Studies Williamsburg VA 23187

SPAHR, ELIZABETH, environmental services administrator; b. Warren, Ohio, Nov. 12, 1930; d. Sullivan and Elizabeth (St. Clair) Spahr; children: Gretchen, Carolyn. BS, Case Western Res. U., 1952, MS, 1954, PhD, 1957, MBA, 1973. Sr. rsch. scientist Nat. Aeronautics & Space Adminstrn., Clevel., 1956-71; mgr. internat. ops., mgr spl projects The Standard Oil Co., Clevel., 1973-86; v.p. strategic planning Ameritrust Corp., Clevel., 1987-92; dir. fin. & adminstrn. AAUW, Washington, 1993-98; CEO Technol. Exec. Inst., 1998—2002; pres. AcromaTech Group, Inc., 1999—2002; asst. dir. U. Md. Ctr. for Environ. Scis. Horn Point Lab., Cambridge, 2002—. Dir. supply emergency team Internat. Energy Agy., Paris, 1984-86; chair fed. women's program Fed. Exec. Bd., Cleve., 1969-71. Trustee Case Western Res. U., Cleve., 1988-92, chair ann. fund, 1989-93; pres. bd. dirs. Cuyahoga City Hosp. Found., Cleve., 1983-85. Grantee USPHS, 1952-56. Mem. Women in Tech., Arlington C. of C., Strategic Alliance Va. Employers, Strategic Alliance Md. Employer. Office: Univ Md Ctr Environ Sci Horn Point Lab PO Box 775 Cambridge MD 21613-0775 Home: PO Box 352 Trappe MD 21673-0352 E-mail: espahr@hpl.umces.edu.

SPAKE, KLUANE, minister, writer; b. Sarasota, Fla., Jan. 24; d. H. Austin and M. June Simonds; m. Rodell A Spake; children: Shawn Miller, Rod, David; 1 child, Dyanna. PhD, N.D., Vision Christian U., Romana, Calif., 1991. Pastor Jubilee, Dededo, 1984—99, traveling spkr. and author Atlanta, 1999—. Lectr. in field; internat. dir. Vision Internat. U. Author: From Enmity to Equality, 1999, Understanding Headship, 1999, (children's book) "Angel's Friends", 2001, Finding Wisdom, 2000, Whole & Holy, 1999. Mem. governing bd. sr. citizens Govt.of Guam, Agana, 1995—97. Mem.: Internat. Coalition Apostles, Nat. Christian Coun. Assoc., Internat. Convent of Faith Ministers, Faith Christian Fellowship. Personal E-mail: spake@mindspring.com.

SPAKE, MARY BARBARA, music educator; b. Mpls., Apr. 7, 1919; d. Donald Nivison and Arline Calista (Folsom) F.; m. Virgil F. Spake, July 2, 1978. BS, U. Minn., 1942, M. Music Edn., 1949. Tchr. Grand Marais (Minn.) Pub. Schs., 1942-43, Litchfield (Minn.) Pub. Schs., 1943-45, Mpls. Pub. Schs., 1945-79, Mpls. Coll. Music, 1949-55, Macalestar Coll., St. Paul, 1950-56; pvt. music tchr. Golden Valley, Minn., 1949—. Asst. choir dir. Cen. Luth. Ch., Mpls., 1946-56; choir dir. Grace U. Luth. Ch., Mpls., 1950-55. Mem. Retired Tchrs. Mpls., Music Educators Nat. Conf., Nat. Assn. Tchrs. of Singing, Sigma Alpha Iota. Avocation: dress making. Home and Office: Apt C227 5800 Saint Croix Ave N Minneapolis MN 55422-4763

SPAKOSKI, MARCIA, insurance agent; b. Bklyn., Oct. 8, 1936; d. Matthew Dabrowski and Helen Tomaszewski; m. Francis L. Spakoski, Apr. 16, 1955 (div. Feb. 1969); children: Francis L. Jr., Evelyn M., Louise A. A in Bus., Mohegan Coll., 1977. CLU; ChFC; comml. pilot; cert. flight instr. Cert. flight instr. Coastal Airways, Groton, Conn., 1967—76; real estate sales staff Century 21, Groton, 1977-80; tax preparer H&R Block, 1977-78; ins. sales staff Allstate Ins., Groton, 1980-99; ret., 1999. Dist. leader Rep. Town Com., Groton, 1973—74; majority leader Rep. Town Meeting, Groton, 1974—75; mem. City Planning and Zoning Commn., Groton, 1979—87; support group leader Multiple Sclerosis Soc., 1983—91; mem. mystic River Chorale, 1991—99; vol. Spl. Olympics, Groton Food Bank, Mary Elizabeth Nursing Home, Child and Family Agy., Nutmeg Pavilion, Meals on Wheels; bd. dirs. Habitat for Humanity, 1993—96, site selection chmn., 1993—96; chmn. Conn. Chpt. 99s, 1978—80, 1980 New Eng. Air Race, 1980. Shirley Mann Aviation scholar New Eng. Sect. 99s, 1977. Mem. Mensa (area cood. 1980-82). Republican. Congregationalist. Avocations: flying, sailing, volunteering, travel. Home (Summer): 16 Whitehall Pond Mystic CT 06355-1954 Home (Winter): 2960 59th St South #515 Gulfport FL 33707 E-mail: marciactfla@aol.com.

SPALDING, HELEN H. library director; BA in English, U. Iowa, 1972, MA in Libr. Sci., 1974; MPA, U. Mo., Kansas City, 1985. Serials records libr. Iowa State U. Librs., Iowa, 1974—76, serials cataloger, 1976—79; head tech. svcs. U. Mo. Kansas City Librs., 1979—85; assoc. dir. librs. U. Mo., Kansas City, 1985—. Coun. Libr. Resources Acad. Libr. mgmt. intern Northwestern U., 1983—84; spkr. in field. Mem.: Assn. Coll. and Rsch. Librs. (pres. 2002—03). Office: Univ Mo Kansas City 5100 Rockhill Rd Kansas City MO 64110-2499

SPANDORFER, MERLE SUE, artist, educator, author; b. Balt., Sept. 4, 1934; d. Simon Louis and Bernice P. (Jacobson) S.; m. Lester M. Spandorfer, June 17, 1956; children: Cathy, John. Student, Syracuse U., 1952-54; BS, U. Md., 1956. Mem. faculty Cheltenham (Pa.) Sch. Fine Arts, 1969—; instr. printmaking Tyler Sch. Art Temple U., Phila., 1980-84; faculty Pratt Graphics Ctr., N.Y.C., 1985-86. One woman shows include Richard Feigen Gallery, N.Y.C., 1970, U. Pa., 1974, Phila. Coll. Textiles and Sci., 1977, Ericson Gallery, N.Y.C., 1978, 79, R.I. Sch. Design, 1980, Syracuse U., 1981, Marian Locks Gallery, Phila., 1973, 78, 82, Temple U., 1984, Tyler Sch. Art, 1985, University City Sci. Ctr., 1987, Gov.'s Residence, 1988, Wenninger Graphics Gallery, Provinceton, Mass., 1989, Widener U. Art Mus., 1995, Gloucester County Coll., 1996, Mangel Gallery, 1992, 97, 2000, 03, Cabrini Coll., 1999; group shows Bklyn. Mus. Art, 1973, San Francisco Mus. Art, 1973, Balt. Mus. Art, 1970, 71, 74, Phila. Mus. Art, 1972, 77, Fundacio Joan Miro. Barcelona, Spain, 1977, Del. Mus. Art, Wilmington, 1978, Carlsberg Glyptotek Mus., Copenhagen, 1980, Moore Coll. Art, Phila., 1982, Tyler Sch. Art, 1983, William Penn Meml. Mus., Harrisburg, Pa., 1984, Ariz. State U., 1985, Tiajin Fine Arts Coll., China, 1986, Beaver Coll., Phila., 1988, The Port of History Mus., Phils., 1987, Sichuan Fine Arts Inst., Chong Qing, China, 1988, Glynn Vivian Mus., Swansea, Wales, 1989, Phila. Mus. Art, 1990, Fgn. Mus., Riga, Latvia, 1995, Woodmere Art Mus., Phila., 1996, Am. Coll., 1997, Cheltenham Ctr. for the Arts, Phila., 1997, Rowan Coll., 1997, Villanova U., 1998, U. Pa., 1999, U. of the Arts, 2001, others; represented in permanent collections Met. Mus. Art, N.Y.C., Whitney Mus. Am. Art, N.Y.C., Mus. Modern Art, N.Y.C., The Israel Mus., Balt. Mus. (gov.'s prize and purchase award 1970), Phila. Mus. Art (purchase award 1977), Toyoh Bijutsu Gakko, Tokyo, Library of Congress, Temple U.; commd. works represented in U. Pa. Inst. Comtemporary Art, 1991; co-author: Making Art Safely, 1993. Recipient award Balt. Mus. Art/Md. Inst. Art, 1971, Govs. prize and Purchase award Balt. Mus. Art, 1970, Outstanding Art Educators award Pa. Art Edn. Assn., 1982, Purchase award Berman Mus., 1995, Artist Equity award, 1996; grantee Pa. Coun. Arts, 1989. Mem. Am. Color Print Soc., Pa. Art Edn. Assn. Jewish. Office: 307 E Gowen Ave Philadelphia PA 19119-1023 E-mail: lesspand@home.com.

SPANEL, HARRIET, state legislator; b. Audubon, Iowa, Jan. 15, 1939; 3 children. BS in Math., Iowa State U., 1961. Mem. Wash. Ho. of Reps., 1987-93, Wash. Senate, Dist. 40, Olympia, 1993—. Office: Wash Senate PO Box 40440 Olympia WA 98504-0440

SPANGENBERG, RUTH BEAHRS, psychologist, educator; b. Eufaula, Ala., Nov. 17, 1918; m. Karl R. Spangenberg, Mar. 21, 1943 (dec. Sept. 1964); children: Kristin, Eric Karl, Karen, Karla, Kathy, Rudy. BA, Pomona Coll., 1940; MA, Stanford U., 1965. Cert. marriage, family and child counselor Calif. Math. and history tchr. Chaffey HS, Ontario, Calif., 1941-43; psychology prof. San Mateo (Calif.) Coll., 1965-69; pscyhologist, counselor Canada Coll., Woodside, Calif., 1969-85; pvt. practice Palo Alto, Calif., 1965—. Founder, pres. bd. dirs. Samaritan Counseling Ctr., Palo Alto, 1989—97; adv. bd. Foothill Coll., Los Altos Hills, Calif., 1996—; regent John F. Kennedy U., Orinda, Calif., 1985—2003, regent emeritus, 2003. Contbr. articles to profl. jours. Vol. DeBakey U.S. Brigade The Uniformed Svcs. U. of Health Sci., Bethedsa, Md., 2001; mem. DeBakey Brigade, 2001—; dedicated David Packard Hall Uniformed Svcs. U. Health Scis., 1998; pres. bd. dirs., trustee Meth. Ch. Conf., Calif.-Nev., 1980—93; founding bd. dirs. Am. Musical, Bay Area, 1986—; founder Com. Green Foothills, Bay Area, San Mateo, 1964—; bd. dirs., capital fund chair YWCA Palo Alto, Stanford, 1962—68. Named Ruth Beahrs Spangenberg Plz. in Concord in her honor, JFK U., 2003; recipient Samaritan award, Samaritan Counseling Ctr., 1996, WAVE award, GirlSource, 2003, Kennedy citation, JFK U., 1997, Jacqueline Kennedy award, 1999, Lifetime Achievement award, Sr. Coord. Ctr., 1997. Mem.: Am. Assn. Family Therapists. Republican. Methodist. Avocations: music, gardening, reading, travel, creative crafts. Home and Office: 2100 Old Page Mill Rd Palo Alto CA 94304-1326

SPANGLER, EDRA MILDRED, clinical psychologist; b. Webbville, Ky., Sept. 6, 1941; d. Chester A. and Laura B. (Webb) Sawyer; m. Robert Noel Spangler, Sept. 6, 1959; children: Robert Mark Spangler, Kendra Lynn Lovett. AS in Bus. Adminstrn., Franklin U., 1975; BA in Social Psychology, Park Coll., 1979; MA in Mgmt. and Supervision, Ctrl. Mich. U., 1980; D in Psychology, Wright State U., 1989. Lic. psychologist Ohio, Fla.; diplomate clin. hypnotherapy; diplomate Am. Bd. Psychol. Specialties in Med. Psychology, Forensic Clin. Psychology and Neuropsychology. With adminstrn., mgmt., fin. and computer sys. design various pvt. and govt. orgns., 1958-85; psychology assoc. Stonegate Psychol. Assocs., Columbus, Ohio, 1989-91; dir. pain & stress program The Rehab. Ctr., Columbus, 1991-94; pvt. practice, 1991—; mem. med. staff Riverside Meth. Hosps., Columbus, 1992—, health psychologist, 1993-95, Mind/Body Med. Inst., 1993-95; mem. med. staff Grady Meml. Hosp., Delaware, Ohio, 1997—. Fellow Biofeedback Cert. Inst. of Am.; mem. Am. Pain Soc., Am. Coll. Forensic Examiners, Ohio Psychol. Assn., Fla. Psychol. Assn., Assn. Applied Psychophysiology and Biofeedback. Avocations: reading, travel, hiking, family, research in mind/body. Office: Wedgewood Behavioral Health 4141 N Hampton Dr Powell OH 43065-7550

SPANGLER, MARY, college president; BA, Chestnut Hill Coll.; MA in English, UCLA, DEdn, 1994. Prof. English L.A. Valley Coll., assoc. dean of admissions, dean of student svcs., v.p. acad. affairs, pres., 1997—. Adj. faculty Sch. of Edn. Nat. U.; presenter in field. Co-author four textbooks; contbr. articles to profl. jours. Mem. exec. edn. coun. U. Phoenix; adv. com. edn. svcs. C.C. League of Calif.; state chancellor Calif. C.C.; adv. com. Calif. Acad. Partnership Program. Mem. Hollywood C. of C. (bd. dirs.), Am. Assn. for Higher Edn., Nat. Coun. for Rsch. and Planning, Assn. for Rsch. on Nonprofit Orgns. and Vol. Action, Assn. of Calif. C.C. Adminstrs., Pi Lambda Theta. Office: Los Angeles City Coll 855 N Vermont Ave Los Angeles CA 90029-3516

SPANGLER, NITA REIFSCHNEIDER, volunteer; b. Ukiah, Calif., Apr. 17, 1923; d. John Charles and Olga Augusta (Wuertz) Reifschneider; m. Raymond Luper Spangler, Sept. 22, 1946 (dec.); children: Jon Martin, Mary Raymond, Thor Raymond. BA, Univ. Nev., 1944. News reporter Redwood (Calif.) City Tribune, 1944-46, Country Almanac, Woodside, Calif., 1969-77. Mem. bd. dirs. San Mateo (Calif.) County Hist. Assn., 1961-68, pres., 1964-66; founder, 1st pres. Portolá Expedition Bicentennial Found., 1966-70; chmn. San Mateo County Scenic Rds. Com., 1967-76; mem. San Mateo County Hist. Resource Adv.; mem. commn. San Mateo County Parks and Recreation, 1983-97, past chmn.; cons. hwy. aesthetics Cal Trans., 1981-83; mem. sch. coms. Recipient Commendation, County Bd. Suprs., 1968, 1977, 92. Mem. Sierra Club, Western History Assn., Mormon History Assn., Nev. State Hist. Soc. (life), San Mateo County Hist. Assn. (life, Resolution of Thanks 1968, 76, 94), Friends Redwood City, Kappa Alpha Theta. Democrat. Episcopalian. Avocation: historic preservation. Home: 970 Edgewood Rd Redwood City CA 94062-1818

SPANNINGER, BETH ANNE, lawyer; b. Bucks County, Pa., July 3, 1950; d. Feryl Louis and Nancy Elizabeth (Hendricks) S. AB magna cum laude, Muhlenberg Coll., 1972; MA, MEd, Lehigh U., 1975; JD, Temple U., 1979. Bar: Pa. 1979. Asst. dist. atty. Phila. Dist. Atty.'s Office, 1979-81; assoc. Bolger, Picker, Hankin & Tannenbaum, Phila., 1981-86, ptnr., 1986-88; sr. counsel SmithKline Beecham Corp., Phila., 1988-96; v.p., assoc. gen. counsel Glaxosmithkline, Phila., 1996—. Mem. ABA, Pa. Bar Assn., Phila. Bar Assn. (law com. 1992—), Phi Beta Kappa. Avocations: literature, jogging, theater, piano. E-mail: beth.a.spanninger@gsk.com.

SPARACINO, JOANN, lawyer, consultant; b. Passaic, N.J., Feb. 25, 1956; d. Carlo and Lillian Ida (Thinschmidt) S.; 1 child, Jason Alexander Leshner. BA cum laude, NYU, 1978; JD, U. Miami, 1989. Bar: Fla. 1989. Contract atty. pvt. firms, Miami and Washington, 1989-94; pres., gen. counsel Alexis Internat., Inc., Washington, 1994—. Cons., spkr. SADC Ambs. Workshop on Trade and Investment, Washington, 1998; participant meetings on the devel. of the African Growth and Opportunity Act, Washington, 1994-99; del. U.S. Presdl. Mission to the African-African Am. Summit, Harare, Zimbabwe, 1997; cons. White House Roundtables on Trade and Investment in Africa, Washington, 1998. Contbr. articles to profl. jours. Recipient scholarship NYU, 1977. Mem. ABA (co-chair subcom. on African trade and investment 1994-98), Fla. Bar. Avocations: world cultures, international travel, raising awareness about African issues and U.S.-Africa interests. Home: 5415 Connecticut Ave NW Apt 406 Washington DC 20015-2743 Office: Alexis Internat Inc 1730 K St NW Ste 304 Washington DC 20006-3839 E-mail: jsparacino@alexisint.com.

SPARKS, JEANNE, columnist, photographer, educator; b. Melbourne, Fla., Aug. 26, 1960; d. William Frank and Armintha Viola Sparks. BA, U. So. Calif., 1982. Reporter City News Svc., L.A., 1984-85; reporter, announcer WNMB Radio Sta., North Myrtle Beach, S.C., 1985-86; reporter, photographer Santa Maria (Calif.) Times, 1987-90; county supr.'s exec. asst. County of Santa Barbara, Fifth Dist. Office, Santa Maria, 1991—2003; newspaper columnist Santa Maria Times, 1999—. Founder, bd. dirs. No. Santa Barbara County Habitat for Humanity, Santa Maria, 1994, Santa Maria Valley Sustainable Garden, 1994—, No. Santa Barbara County Women's Polit. Com., 1997—; grad. Leadership Santa Maria Valley, 1997; a founder, coord, Livable Cmtys. Group, Santa Maria, 1999-2002; bd. dirs. Natural History Mus., Santa Maria, 1999-2000, Santa Maria Valley YMCA, 1992-99, People for Nonviolence, Santa Maria, 1997-2000, Santa Maria Valley Water Conservation Dist., 2002—, Santa Maria Valley Beautiful, v.p., pres., mem., 1996—; founder, pres. Winners of Off-leash Freedom, 2001—. Recipient Pres.'s Cup, U.S. Jaycees, 1991, Presdl. medallion Calif. Jaycees, 1991, Women of Excellence/Women of Spirit award Santa Maria Women's Network, 1998. Avocations: theater sports, photography, art, hiking, soccer. Home: PO Box 6437 Santa Maria CA 93456-6437 E-mail: sparkie@sparkie.us.

SPARKS, MILDRED THOMAS, state agency administrator, educator; b. Montgomery, Ala., Oct. 2, 1942; d. Leon and Annie Lee (Johnson) Thomas; m. John H. Sparks, Aug. 29, 1964; children: Melanie J. Bosak, Jennifer L. David-Gerhartz, Regina F. BS, Ala. State U., 1964; MS, Pepperdine U., 1978; postgrad., Claremont Coll., Calif. State U., Boston Coll. Cert. reading specialist, contract mgmt., U. Phoenix, U. Wyo. Tchr. Dayton (Ohio) Schs., 1964-66, Oxon Hill (Md.) Schs., 1966-70; technician Reading Lab. Grambling (La.) State U., 1972; reading lab. aide Calif. City (Calif.) Schs., 1975; reading instr. Cerro Coso So. Outreach, Edwards AFB, Calif., 1976-78; substitute tchr. San Bernardino City Schs., 1979, Aquinas H.S., San Bernardino, 1978-79; reading lab. tchr. San Bernardino H.S., 1979; instr. reading lab. San Bernardino Valley Coll., 1980-81, assoc. prof. reading, dept. head, 1981-86; contract adminstr. Hercules Missile Ordinance and Space Group, Magna, Utah, 1986, Alliant Techsys. (formerly Hercules Missile Ordnance and Space Group), 1987-97; dir. Office of Black Affairs State of Utah, 1997—. Mem. Black Adv. Coun., Office of Black Affairs; presenter workshops, cmty. events; troop vol. Girl Scouts U.S.; vol. The March of Dimes, Am. Heart Assn., Visitation of the Elderly Homebound, Am. Cancer Soc. and Marriage and Family Workshop for Teens, Cath. Cmty. Svcs.; civil rights movement participant Ala. Bus Boycott; mem.

minority health adv. bd. Utah Health Dept.; mem. Cath. Women League, Black Caths. Utah, Salt Lake City, African Am. Task Force, Gov.'s Initiative on Family Today, Anti-Discrimination Com.; planning com. United Way Greater Salt Lake, vol.; past pres. Salt Lake Diocesan Pastoral Coun., vol. Mem. Calif Tchrs. Assn., Nat. Coun. Tchrs. English, Assn. Supervision and Curriculum Devel., Western Coll. Reading Assn., Bus. and Profl. Women's Club, Link's, Jack and Jill of Am. Inc., Delta Kappa Gamma, Alpha Kappa Alpha. Roman Catholic (Norton lav lector). Avocations: reading, writing, gardening, cross-country skiing. Home: 3790 Becky Cir Salt Lake City UT 84109-3302 Office: Office Black Affairs 324 S State St Ste 500 Salt Lake City UT 84111 Fax: (801) 538-8678. E-mail: msparks@dced.state.ut.us.

SPARLING, MARY LEE, biology educator; b. Ft. Wayne, Ind., May 20, 1934; d. George Hewson and Velmah Evelyn (McClain) S.; m. Albert Alcide Barber, Sept. 1, 1956 (div. Jan. 1975); children: Bonnie Lee Barber, Bradley Paul Barber. BS, U. Miami, Coral Gables, Fla., 1955; MA, Duke U., 1958; PhD, UCLA, 1962. Lectr. UCLA, 1962-63; asst. prof. Calif. State U., Northridge, 1966-72, assoc. prof., 1972-76, prof., 1976—. Statewide acad. senator Calif. State U., 1996-98. Contbr. articles to profl. jours. NSF grantee Calif. State U., Northridge, 1971-72, 81-83, 89, NIH grantee Calif. State U., Northridge, 1987-89. Mem. AAUP (pres. 1981-82), Am. Soc. Cell Biology, Soc. for Devel. Biology, Am. Soc. Zoologists, Sigma Xi (bd. dirs. Research Triangle, N.C. 1974-91). Avocations: tennis, gardening, travel. Home: 3662 Stoner Ave Los Angeles CA 90066-2839 Office: Calif State U Biology Dept Northridge CA 91330-0001

SPARROW, ALISON KIDDER, painter, sculptor; b. Grosse Pointe, Mich., Feb. 13, 1974; d. Herbert George and Nancy Woodruff Sparrow. BFA, RISD, 1994—97. Fellow Byrdcliffe Art Colony, Woodstock Guild, Woodstock, NY, 2002—03, Va. Ctr. for the Creative Arts, Lynchburg, 2002, 2004; artist grant Vt. Studio Ctr., Woodstock, Vt., 2002, 2004; artist in residence Mary Anderson Ctr. for the Arts, Mt. St Francis, Ind., 2003; Hambidge fellow, 2003. Exhibitions include Internat. Salon Exhbn. of Small Works, 2002—03, Inst. for Unpopular Culture of San Francisco, Detroit Artists Market, Scarab Club of Detroit, Moore Art Gallery of St. Clair, Nat. Scholastic Hallmark award (Best of Show (Mich. region). Tchr. Literacy Volunteers of Am., Detroit, 2000—03; vol. Inst. for Unpopular Culture, San Francisco, 1999—2002, Providence Pub. Schools, 2001, Detroit Inst. of Arts. Recipient Advanced Standing, RISD, 1996. Fellow: Scarab Club (assoc.); mem.: Nat. Mus. of Women in the Arts (assoc.; work, records stored in archives). Green Party. Protestant. Avocation: sculpture.

SPARROW, LAURA, secondary educator; b. Boston, June 15, 1947; d. John Henry Jr. and Laura Josephine (Thickens) Halford; m. William Talbot Sparrow, July 11, 1970. BA, U. Mich.; MAT, Johns Hopkins U., 1970. Cert. secondary tchr. Instr. social sci. C.C. of Balt., 1970; English tchr. North Farmington H.S., Farmington Hills, Mich., 1970-71; tchr. English and humanities Harrison H.S., Farmington Hills, 1971-95, tchr. English, chair dept., 1995—. Author: The White Wave, 1983, Hostages to Fortune, 1984, Firesigns, 1986, Seaswept, 1990. Named Oakland County Secondary Tchr. of Yr., Newsweek/WDIV-TV, 1998; Shakespeare study grantee NEH, 1992, Galileo leader Kellogg Found., 1999. Mem. ASCD, Nat. Coun. Tchrs. English, Detroit Working Writers, Authors Guild. Avocations: travel, music, kayaking, writing. Office: Harrison HS 29995 W 12 Mile Rd Farmington Hills MI 48334-3901 Office Phone: 248-489-3502.

SPARROW, RUTH S. lawyer; b. Boston; d. Marvin and Dorothy Jane (Goldman) S. BA in Politics with honors, U. Calif., Santa Cruz, 1980; JD, NYU, 1987. Bar: Pa., 1987. Assoc. tax dept. Wolf Block Schorr and Solis-Cohen LLP, Phila., 1987-95, ptnr. tax dept., 1995—, vice chmn. Wolf Block Govt. Asst. & Affordable Housing Group. Articles editor NYU Rev. of Law and Social Change, 1986-87; contbg. editor Jour. Affordable Housing and Cmty. Devel. Law. Mem. adv. bd. LIHC (Low Income Housing Credit) Monthly Report. Mem. ABA (mem. tax sect. 1987—), Pa. Bar Assn. (mem. tax sect. 1987—), Phila. Bar Assn. (mem. tax sect. 1987—), U.S. Amateur Ballroom Dance Assn. (mem. non-profit legal coun. 1996—). Office: PO Box 187 Olympia WA 98507-0187

SPARTZ, ALICE ANNE LENORE, retired retail executive; b. NYC, May 14, 1925; d. John Francis and Alice Philomena (Murray) Rattenbury; m. George Eugene Spartz, Oct. 29, 1949; children: Mary Elizabeth, James, Barbara, Anne, Thomas, William, Michael, John, Matthew, Clare, Robert, Richard. Student, Wright Coll., 1945-47, No. Ill. U., 1950; AA, Triton Coll., 1987. Svc. rep. Ill. Bell Tel., Chgo., 1945-46; stewardess United Airlines, Denver, 1947-49; ret. mgr. Family Life League Resale Shop, Oak Park, Ill., 1987-95; retired, 1995. Mem. Cicero Cmty. Coun., Ill., 1967—69, Pk. Dist. Oak Pk. Com., 1973—74; active Ill. Right to Life Com., Chgo., 1971—2002, Com. Pro-Life Cath., Chgo., 1992—; pres., bd. trustees Trailwood Village Bd., Kingwood, Tex., 2003; bd. dirs. Direct Energy Techs., A Solar Co., Locaterin, Tex.; mem. St. Martha's Roman Cath.. Ch.; former bd. dir. Ill. Pro-Life Coalition, Family Life League; vol. canteen worker ARC, Chgo., 1942—45. Mem.: Trailwood Village Cmty. Assn. (trustee 2004). Republican. Roman Catholic. Avocations: travel, sewing, reading, swimming, pro-life activist. Office: 2026 Seven Oaks Dr Kingwood TX 77339

SPATARO, SANDRA ELIZABETH, business educator, consultant; b. Sacramento, July 27, 1966; d. Sam and Susan Spataro. PhD, U. Calif., Berkeley, 2000. Program mgr. Oracle Corp., Redwood Shores, Calif., 1988—95; asst. prof. of organizational behavior Yale Sch. Mgmt., New Haven, 2000—; cons., individual contractor New Haven, 2001—. Cons. as individual contractor, Berkeley, 1994—2000. Author: (book chpt.) Research on Groups and Teams, 2001, Organizational Behavior: The State of the Science, 2002. Bd. dirs. New Haven Chorale, 2001—. Mem.: APA, Acad. Mgmt. Avocations: music, travel. Office: Yale Sch Mgmt Box 208200 135 Prospect St New Haven CT 06520

SPAULDING, LILA BERNICE, marriage and family counselor; b. Lake Waccamaw, N.C., Mar. 3, 1931; d. Samuel Leslie and Mary Elease (Graham) Mitchell; m. Lloyd Leslie Spaulding, June 24, 1972 (dec. July 1982). BA in Psychology, Molloy Coll., 1985; MA, Hofstra U., 1987. LPN, N.Y., N.C., N.J. Nurse, oper. tech. Burdette Tomlin Hosp., Cape May, N.J., 1963-80; oper. rm. tech. Lydia E. Hall Hosp., Freeport, N.Y., 1980-87; marriage and family counselor North Shore Mental Health, Wantaugh, N.Y., 1987-89; marriage and family counselor in pvt. practice Lake Waccamaw, 1989—; owner, operator Live Christmas Farm, Lake Waccamaw, 1994—, Wacca Country Gift Shop, Lake Waccamaw, 1995—. Mem. health and human svcs. bd. N.C. Comm., Raleigh, 1993—; mem. adv. bd. Columbus County Med. Ctr., Whiteville, N.C.; mem. Columbus County Med. Clinic. Author: Waccamaw Siouan Cooking, 1994, (postcards) Native Am. Scenes, 1994. Bd. dirs., sec., treas., mem. econ. devel. N.C. Cmty. Affairs, Raleigh, 1993—; vol. State of N.C., 1996, pres. of the Concerned Citizens, Inc. of Lake Waccamaw, chmn., Homemade Handmade Festival, 1997. Mem. N.Y. State Psychol. Assn., N.C. Ind. Bus. Assn. (treas. 1994—), Waccamaw Siquan Devel. Assn. (chair fin. com. 1993—). Democrat. Baptist. Avocations: yoga, church activities, organist, crafts, doll collecting. Home and Office: PO Box 170 #555 Carver Moore Rd Lake Waccamaw NC 28450

SPAULDING, MAR, retired special education educator, therapist; b. Bellevue, Ky., Oct. 16, 1933; d. Mickey and Blanche Harris; m. Stan Lee Spaulding; children: Karla, Julie Underwood, Lisa Williams, Gregory. MA, Ea. Mich. U., 1978; BS, George Mason U., 1973. Cert. educator Emotionally/Neurologically Impaired, Pre-primary Impaired 1978. Head tchr. in nursery sch., Ann Arbor, Mich., 1973—75; intern Ypsilanti State Mental Instn., Mich., 1975—76; tchr. emotionally impaired and pre-primary impaired Monroe County Intermediate Dist., Monroe, Mich., 1978—93. Leader of groups of parents of handicapped children Monroe County Intermediate Sch. Dist., Monroe, Mich., 1978—93, mem. of grant com., 1980—96, tester on child find com., 1979—85. Author: (children's educational book) Kate Lynn's Fantastic Dream, 1999 (Spl. Edn. Tchr. of the Yr. in Monroe County, Mich., 1995), (companion book) Activities to use with Kate Lynn's Fantastic Dream. Includes cognitive, speech and language, fine motor, gross motor and behavioral, emotional skill areas for teachers and parents., 1999. Story lady Head Start, Baker Devel. Ctr., Punta Gorda, Fla., 1996—2002; tutor Continuing Edn. Ctr. and Even Start, Port Charlotte and Punta Gorda, 1996—2003; membership involvement chairperson Peace River Power Squadron, Punta Gorda, 1996—2003; pub. spkr. topics concerning early childhood edn. Early Childhood Edn. Assn. of SW Fla., Punta Gorda, 1999—2003. Recipient Writer's Award, US Power Squadrons, 2001. Mem.: AAUW (Ft. Myers, Fla. chpt.), U.S. Sail and Power Squadrons, Thomas Paine Nat. Hist. Soc., Nat. Honor Soc., Phi Kappa Phi. Liberal. Avocation: travel, sailing (lived on 41 foot sailboat from 1993 to 1996),writing children's stories, swimming, biking, reading, playing the piano, attending concerts and plays, hiking.. Home: 1536 Islamorada Blvd Punta Gorda FL 33955 Personal E-mail: marstan@nut-n-but.net.

SPEAR, LAURINDA HOPE, architect; BFA, Brown U., 1972; MArch, Columbia U., 1975. Registered architect, Fla., N.Y.; cert. Nat. Coun. Archtl. Registration. Founding prin. Arquitectonica (ARQ), Miami, Fla. Lectr. in field. Prin. works include Pink Ho., Miami, Fla., 1978, The Palace, Miami, 1982 (Honor award Miami chpt. AIA 1982), The Atlantis, Miami, 1982 (Miami chpt. AIA award 1983), The Imperial, Miami, 1983, Casa los Andes (Record Hos. award Archtl. Record 1986), North Dade Justice Ctr., Miami, 1987 (Honor award Miami chpt. AIA 1989), Rio, Atlanta, 1988 (Honor award Miami chpt. AIA 1989), Banco de Credito del Peru, Lima, 1988 (Honor award Miami chpt. AIA 1989), The Ctr. Innovative Tech., Herndon, Va., 1988 (Honor award Va. chpt. AIA 1989, Honor award Miami chpt. 1990, Merit award Fairfax, Va., County Exceptional Design Awards Program 1990), Sawgrass Mills (Merit award Miami chpt. AIA 1990, Honor award Fla. chpt. 1991), Miracle Ctr. (Honor award Miami chpt. AIA 1989), Internat. Swimming Hall of Fame, Ft. Lauderdale, Fla., 1991, Banque de Luxembourg, 1993, Disney All-Star Resorts, Orlando, Fla., 1994, U.S. Embassy, Lima, 1994, USCG Family Housing, Bayamon, P.R., 1994, Altamira Ctr., Caracas, Venezuela, 1994, Festival Walk, Hong Kong, 1998, Miami Fed. Courthouse, Am. Airlines Arena, Miami, 1999, Philips Arena, Atlanta, 1999, Miami Internat. Airport D-E-F Wrap. Mem. beaux arts support group Lowe Art Mus., Miami; bd. dirs. Miami Youth Mus. Recipient Design Awards citation Progressive Architecture, 1975, 80, Rome Prize in Architecture, 1978, Award of Excellence, Atlanta Urban Design Commn., 1989; inductee Interior Design Hall of Fame, 1999. Fellow AIA (Silver medal for design 1998); mem. Internat. Womens Forum. Office: Arquitectonica 550 Brickell Ave Ste 200 Miami FL 33131-2517

SPEAR, SARAH G. county administrator; b. Montgomery, Ala., Apr. 23, 1939; d. Penson Raybon and Dora Nell (McLauchin) Graham; m. James Rufus Spear, Nov. 8, 1996; children: Deborah, Connie, Beth. Cert. in tax adminstrn., Auburn U. From clk. to chief clk. Montgomery County Office of Tax Collections, Montgomery, 1958-91, tax collector, 1991-97, revenue commr., 1997—. Active Easter Seals, Mothers March of Dimes, Am. Heart Assn.; bd. dirs. Montgomery Area United Way, mem. budget and allocation com.; bd. dirs. Leadership Montgomery, co-chmn. program com., past pres., exec. bd. dirs. Montgomery Coun. on Aging; numerous officers Frazer United Meth. Ch., Montgomery, past bd. dirs. Ala. Credit Union Adminstrn., past bd. dirs., vice-chmn., sec. Ala. Credit Union League. Mem. Nat. Assn. Female Execs., Nat. Assn. County Officers, LWV, Internat. Assn. Assessing Officers, Tax Assessors and Tax Collectors of Ala. (pres., mem. exec. bd.), Ala. Assn. Assessing Ofcls., Fellowship of Christian Athletics, Kiwanis, Montgomery Auburn Club. Democrat. Avocations: family, friends, college football, bridge, fishing. Home: 648 Pimblico Rd Montgomery AL 36109-4646 Office: Montgomery Cty Office Revenue Commr 1005 S Lawrence St Montgomery AL 36104-5035

SPEARING, KAREN MARIE, physical education educator, coach; b. Chgo., Apr. 17, 1949; d. John Richard and Naomi (Allen) Miller; m. Edward B. Spearing III, Apr. 28, 1973. BS in Phys. Edn., U. Wis., Whitewater, 1972; MS in Outdoor Edn., No. Ill. U., 1978. Cert. phys. edn. tchr., Ill.; cert. CPR instr., master hunter safety instr., boating safety instr., master snowmobile instr., Ill. Tchr., coach Glenside Mid. Sch., Glendale Heights, Ill., 1973—, athletic dir., 1981—92, 1995—98, chair dept., 1992-93. Hunter safety instr. State of Ill., 1988—, water safety instr., 1989—, snowmobile instr., 1990-2000, master snowmobile instr., 1995, CPR instr., 1996—. Amb. People to People Citizen Amb. Program, Russia and Belarus, 1993; awards chairperson U.S. Power Squadron, Chgo., 1987—93; mem. exec. com. DuPage Power Squadron., 1993—96, comdr., 2000—01, edn. officer, 1996—98, Adminst. Officer, 1998; mem. com. Ill. Hunting and Fishing Days, Silver Springs State Pk., 1993; mem. Outdoor Wilderness Leadership Class, 1997; pres. Allied Ill. Markswomen, 2001—02. Mem. AAHPERD, Ill. Assn. Health, Phys. Edn., Recreation and Dance, Ill. H.S. Assn. (volleyball referee). Avocations: clock collecting, hunting, fishing, boating. Office: Glenside Mid Sch 1560 Bloomingdale Rd Glendale Heights IL 60139-2734

SPEARMAN, MAXIE ANN, financial analyst, administrator; b. Piedmont, S.C., Sept. 14, 1942; d. J. Mac and Margaret Cecille S. BS, U. S.C., 1965; postgrad., Ga. State U., 1985; student, U. Ga. Acct. Shell Oil Co., Atlanta, 1965-66; internal auditor Sears, Roebuck & Co., Atlanta, 1966-67; acct. Econ. Opportunity Atlanta, Atlanta, 1967-68, City of Atlanta, 1968-78, fin. analyst, 1978-89, sr. fin. analyst planner, 1989—. Investment cons., Atlanta, Conyers, Ga., 1980—. Mem. Rep. Presdl. Task Force, 1985—, U.S. Senatorial Club, Rep. Nat. Com., 1988—, Ga. Rep. Party, 1990—, Atlanta Safety Com., 1985—, Mayor's Spl. Events Task Force, 1990; charter founder Ronald Reagan Rep. Ctr., 1988; del.-at-large Rep. Platform Planning Com., 1992, 94. Recipient safety award Atlanta City Govt., 1990, Presdl. Commn. Exec. Com. of Republican Party award, 1992; Order of Merit award Nat. Rep. Senatorial Com., 1996. Mem. AAUW, NAFE, Am. Mgmt. Assn., Ga. Assn. Med. Victims, Inc. (sec., treas. 1985—), Nat. Trust for Historic Preservation. Methodist. Avocations: writing, tennis, decorating, investing. Home: 1280 Vineyard Dr SE Conyers GA 30013-2466

SPEARS, BRITNEY, vocalist, actress; b. McComb, Miss., Dec. 2, 1981; d. Jamie and Lynne Spears. Singer: (albums) ...Baby One More Time, 1999, Oops! I Did It Again, 2000 (Billboard Album artist of the Year, 2000), Britney, 2001, In the Zone, 2003; actor(voice): (TV films) Hooves of Fire, 1999, Legends of the Lost Tribe, 2002, : (films) Longshot, 2000, Crossroads, 2002; composer: (songs) (for film Drive Me Crazy) You Drive Me Crazy, 1999, (for film Pokémon the First Movie: Mewtwo Strikes Back) Soda Pop, 1999, (for film On The Line) Let Me Be, 2001, (for film Jimmy Neutron: Boy Genius) Intimidated, 2001, (for film Austin Powers in Goldmember) Boys, 2002. Britney Spears Found. Recipient Female Artist of the Year, Billboard, 1999, New Artist of the Year, 1999, Best New Artist, Am. Music Awards, 2000. Mailing: Jive Records 137 W 25th St New York NY 10001-7216

SPEARS, DIANE SHIELDS, artist, retired art academy administrator; b. Seattle, May 21, 1942; d. Richard Keene McKinney and Dorothy Jean (Shields) Thacker; m. Howard Truman Spears, Sept. 3, 1977; 1 child, Truman Eugene. BA in Art, English, Edn., Trinity U., 1964; MA in Christian Counseling, San Antonio Theol. Sem., 1986, D of Christian Edn., 1988. Cert. tchr. secondary edn., elem. edn., ednl. supervision, Tex. Instr. ESL Dliel-Geb (Def. Lang. Inst.), San Antonio, 1973-74, Ceta/Ace Bexar County Sch. Bd., San Antonio, 1975-78; tchr. elem. edn., art, music New Covenant Faith Acad., San Antonio, 1983-89; instr. ESL Jewish Family Svc., San Antonio, 1991; tchr. elem. art Edgewood Ind. Sch. Dist., San Antonio, 1992-93, dist. art specialist, 1993-95, fine arts coord., 1995-98, dir. visual arts, 1998—; tchr. 4th-7th grade reading, lang. arts, art tchr. Pipe Creek Christian Sch., Tex. Owner, operator Art for Kings, San Antonio, 1985—. Illustrator teacher-created materials-lit. activities for young children, 1989-90; author: (art curriculum) Art for Kings, 1987; editor: (art curriculum) Edgewood Ind. Sch. Dist. Elem. Art Curriculum, 1993; exhibited in group shows at Charles and Emma Frye Mus., Seattle, 1966, 68, Centro Cultural Aztlan Galerie Expression, 1998 (Best of Show 1998). Dir. intercessory prayer New Covenant Fellowship, San Antonio, 1980-90. Recipient awards for painting and graphics, San Antonio, 1996-98. Mem.: San Antonio Art Edn. Assn. (1st pl. 1995), Tex. Art Edn. Assn. (1st pl. graphics divsn. 1995), Nat. Mus. for Women in Arts (charter). Republican. Avocations: water skiing, motorcycle riding, sewing, writing. Home: 264 Mountain Dr Lakehills TX 78063-6725 E-mail: shieldsandspears@earthlink.net.

SPEARS, DORIS ANN HACHMUTH, entrepreneur, writer, publisher, real estate and management consultant; b. Jersey City, July 6, 1951; d. Arthur Charles Hachmuth and Diana Sofia Moroz; m. Richard Alan Spears, May 13, 1969; children: Andrew, Mark, Daniel. B, Barry U., 1993, MS, 1997. Broker, owner Doris Spears Realty, Inc., Port Jervis, 1981-86, Spears & Spears, INc., Stuart, Fla., 1987-97; owner, pub. Arrow Pub., Inc., Palm City, Fla., 1988—2001; editor, pub. Today's Fla. Woman, Inc., Palm City, 1994-96; owner, broker, sr. cons. Suncastle Realty, Inc., Palm City, 1997—. Adj. instr. Indian River C.C., Ft. Pierce, Fla., 1994—; founder-owner Sunny Lifestyles TM, 1996. Author: Living Better for Less, 2000; (annual seminar) Building Wealth/Buying Property. Bd. dirs. Hibiscus Children's Ctr., Jensen Beach, Fla., 1993-96; sec. bd. dirs. Hibiscus Children's Found., Jensen Beach, 1996-99; mem. bus. adv. bd. Indian River C.C. Mem. Internat. Assn. Female Execs., Women's Coun. of Realtors, Real Estate Brokerage Mgrs. Coun., Martin County Bd. Realtors (bd. dirs. 1988-90), Realtor Assn. of Martin County, Nat. Spkrs. Assn., Sierra Club, Martin County C. of C., Nature Conservancy, Fla. Spkrs. Assn. Avocations: tennis, reading, travel. Office: 828 SW Palm City Rd Stuart FL 34994

SPEARS, JAE, state legislator; b. Latonia, Ky. d. James and Sylvia (Fox) Marshall; m. Lawrence E. Spears; children: Katherine Spears Cooper, Martha Spears-Duncan, Lawrence M., James W. Student, U. Ky. Reporter Cin. Post, Cin. Enquirer newspapers; rschr. Stas. WLW-WSAI, Cin.; tchr. Jiya Gakuen Sch., Japan; lectr. U.S. Mil. installations East Anglia, Eng.; del. State of W.Va., Charleston, 1974-80; mem. W.Va. Senate, Charleston, 1980-1993. Mem. vis. com. W.Va. Extension and Continuing Edn., Morgantown, 1993-2000, W.Va. U. Sch. Medicine, 1992—; with state sen., 1980-93; apptd. to Jud. Hearing Bd., 1993-2000. Chmn. adv bd. Sta. WNPB, 1992-94; congl. liaison Am. Pub. TV Stas. and Sta. WNPB-TV, 1992-97, mem. coun. W.Va. Autism Task Force, Huntington, 1981-90; mem. W.Va. exec. bd. Literacy Vols. Am., 1986-90, 94—, pres., 1990-92; mem. Gov.'s State Literacy Coun., 1991-97; bd. dirs. Found. Ind. Colls. W.Va., 1986—; mem. regional adv. com. W.Va. Gov.'s Task Force for Children, Youth and Family, 1989; mem. USS W.Va. Commn., 1989; mem. exec. com. W.Va. Employer Support Group for Guard and Res., 1989, mem. steering com., 1990-92. Decorated Purple Heart (hon.); recipient Susan B. Anthony award NOW, 1982, edn. award Profl. Educators Assn. W.Va., 1986, ann. award W.Va. Assn. Ret. Sch. Employees, 1985, Meritorious Svc. award W.Va. State Vets. Commn., 1984, Vets. Employment and Tng. Svc. award U.S. Dept. Labor, 1984, award W.Va. Vets. Coun., 1984; named Admiral in N.C. Navy, Gov. of N.C., 1982, hon. Brigadier Gen. W.Va. N.G., 1984, One of 11 Women Pioneers of W.Va. Legislature, W.Va. U. Inst. for Pub. Affairs, 1997. Mem. DAR, VFW (aux.), Bus. and Profl. Women (Woman of Yr. award 1978), Nat. League Am. Pen Women (Pen Woman of Yr. 1984), Nat. Order Women Legislators, Am. Legion (aux.), Delta Kappa Gamma, Alpha Xi Delta. Democrat. Home and Office: PO Box 98 Shinnston WV 26431

SPEARS, LOUISE ELIZABETH, minister, secondary school educator; b. Liberty, Miss., Feb. 2, 1945; d. Willie and Alice Gray Spears; 1 child, Guy Alice. BSc, Alcorn State U., 1966; MSc, Ind. U., 1969; PhD, U. N. Colo., 1975; MDiv, Garrett-Evang. Theol. Sem., 1983. Cert. African Meth. Episcopal Ch., 90; Tchr. Ga. Tchr. Hazlehurst H.S., Hazlehurst, Miss., 1967—68; tchg. asst. Ind. U., Bloomington, Ind., 1968—70; tchr. Ala. State U., Montgomery, Ala., 1970—72, Ky. State U., Frankfort, Ky., 1972—73, Jackson State U., Jackson, Miss., 1975—81; pastor United Meth. Ch., Keosauqua, Iowa, 1983—85, Detroit, 1985—88; tchr. Clarke County Sch. Dist., Athens, Ga., 1998—; pastor African Meth. Episcopal Ch., various, Ga., 2000—. Realtor Ga. Real Estate, Atlanta, 1989—92; academic adminstr. Emmanuel Bible Coll., Macon, Ga., 1992—93; substitute tchr. Atlanta Pub. Sch., Atlanta, 1994—98; co-chmn. Augusta Ga. Conf., Augusta, Ga., 2001, mem. stewardship commn.; fin. coord. Reach Out and Touch Club, Inc., 2002—03; mem. Athens-Clarke County Commn. on Disability, 2003; mem. career and tech. edn. exec. adv. bd. Athens-Clarke County Commn. on Disability; mem. career and tech. edn. adv. bd. Tech. Prep Awareness, 2003, mem. sub-com., 03. Co-author: National Poetry Book, 1995; featured cover story: Zebra Mag., 2001. Bd. dir. Reach Out & Touch Club, Inc., Athens, 2001—. Recipient Cmty. Svc. award, Reach Out & Touch Club, Inc., 2000. Mem.: NEA, Nat. Assn. Social Studies, Reach Out and Touch Club (fin. coord.). Democrat. African Meth. Episcopal. Avocations: reading, travel, writing, listening, helping. Home: 200 Crane Drive 18 Bogart GA 30622 Office: Alternative Education Program 440 Dearing Extension Athens GA 30606

SPEARS, MARIAN CADDY, dietetics and institutional management educator; b. East Liverpool, Ohio, Jan. 12, 1921; d. Frederick Louis and Marie Caddy Spears-Ralston; m. Sholto M. Spears, May 29, 1959; m. Joseph D. Ralston, May 29, 1998. BS, Case Western Res. U., 1942, MS, 1947; PhD, U. Mo., 1971. Chief dietitian Bellefaire Children's Home, Cleve., 1942-53; head dietitian Drs. Hosp., Cleve., 1953-57; assoc. dir. dietetics Barnes Hosp., St. Louis, 1957-59; asst. prof. U. Ark., Fayetteville, 1959-68; assoc. prof. U. Mo., Columbia, 1971-75; prof., head dept. hotel, restaurant, instn. mgmt. and dietetics Kans. State U., Manhattan, 1975-89. Cons. dietitian small hosps. and nursing homes; cons. dietetic edn. Author: Foodservice Organizations Textbook, 4th edit., 2000, Foodservice Procurement Textbook, 1st edit., 1998, 99; contbr. articles to profl. jours. Recipient Kans. State U. Advancement award, 1997. Mem. Am. Dietetic Assn. (Copher award 1989), Am. Sch. Foodsvc. Assn., Food Systems Mgmt. Edn. Coun., Soc. Advancement of Foodsvc. Rsch., Nat. Restaurant Assn., Coun. Hotel, Restaurant, Inst. Mgmt. Edn., Manhattan C. of C., Sigma Xi, Gamma Sigma Delta, Omicron Nu, Phi Kappa Phi. Office: Kans State U 105 Justin Hall Manhattan KS 66506-1400 Home: 2025 Meadowlark Rd Manhattan KS 66502-4558

SPEARS, REBECCA ANN, writer, educator; b. Waco, Tex., Feb. 27, 1954; d. George Harrison and Jane Thompson Spears; m. David Paul Schwartz, Oct. 20, 1975 (div. June 2002); children: Paul Schwartz, Claire Schwartz, Andrea Schwartz. BA, U. Tex., 1976; MA, So. Ill. U., 1986; MFA, Bennington Coll., 2002. Editor Perfection Learning Co., Des Moines, 1987—90; writer, editor Fine Lines, 1990—; instr. Honors Coll., U. Houston, 2000—02; writer in residence HS for the Performing and Visual Arts, Houston, 2001—02; faculty North Lake Coll., Dallas, 2003. Lectr. various writing workshops for educators, 1987—. Author various poetry; contbr. articles various publications, 1984—98; author: Jackdaw Study Guides, 1993—, Texas: A Lone Star History, 1996, Story of the Constitution, 1997, Story of the Declaration of Independence, 1999, The Stock Market Crash of 1929, 2003, The Watergate Break-In, 2003, Portals to Literature, 1993, Northern European Myths, 1993, African Myths, 1992, Greek & Roman Myths, vol 3, 1992, World Myths, 1992, English Words from Latin Origins, 1989, English Words from Greek Origins, 1989. D.H.

Lawrence fellowship, U. N. Mex., 1997, fellowship, Vt. Studio Ctr., 2004. Mem.: Associated Writing Programs, Acad. Am. Poets, Baylor U. Med. Ctr. Healing Environ. Com., Sierra Club, Phi Kappa Phi, Phi Beta Kappa. Democrat. Avocations: reading, hiking, travel. E-mail: rssfineline@netzero.net.

SPEARS, SALLY, lawyer; b. San Antonio, Aug. 29, 1938; d. Adrian Anthony and Elizabeth (Wylie) S.; m. Tor Hultgreen, July 15, 1961 (div. Jan. 1983); children: Dagny Elizabeth, Sara Kirsten, Kara Spears. BA, U. Tex., 1960, LLB, 1965. Bar: Tex. 1961, Ill. 1971. Practice law, Stamford, Conn., 1966-67, Chgo., 1970-71, Northbrook, Ill., 1972-73, Toronto, Ont., Can., 1973-81; assoc. firm Cummings & Lockwood, Stamford, 1966-67, Kirkland & Ellis, Chgo., 1970-71; sr. atty. Allstate Ins. Co., Northbrook, Ill., 1971-73; gen. counsel, sec. Reed Paper Ltd., Reed Ltd., Toronto, 1973-78, Denison Mines Ltd., Toronto, 1978-81; pvt. practice law San Antonio, 1981—. Apptd. by Sec. of Def. to serve on Def. Adv. Com., Women in the Svcs., 1997-99. Author: Call Sign Revlon: The Life and Death of Navy Fighter Pilot Kara Hultgreen, 1998. Mem. Tex. Bar Assn., San Antonio Bar Assn., Bankruptcy Bar Assn., Bexar County Women's Bar Assn., San Antonio Country Club, The Club at Sonterra. Home: 433 Evans Ave San Antonio TX 78209-3725 Office: Ste 106 8151 Broadway San Antonio TX 78209-1938 Office Phone: 210-826-7020. Personal E-mail: sespears@swbell.net.

SPECHT, ALICE WILSON, university libraries dean; b. Caracus, Venezuela, Apr. 3, 1948; (parents Am. citizens); d. Ned and Helen (Lockwood) Wilson; m. Joe W. Specht, Dec. 30, 1972; 1 child, Mary Helen. BA, U. Pacific, 1969; MLS, Emory U., 1970; MBA, Hardin-Simmons U., 1983. Libr. social scis. North Tex. State U., Denton, 1971-73; reference libr. Lubbock (Tex.) City and County Libr., 1974-75; system coord. Big Country Libr. System, Abilene, Tex., 1975-79; assoc. dir. Hardin-Simmons U., Abilene, 1981-88, dir. univ. librs., 1988—. Apptd. Mayor's Task Force Libr. Svcs., 1995-96. Author bibliog. instrn. aids, 1981-90; editor; The College Man, For Pilots Eyes Only. Mem. mayor's task force Abilene Pub. Libr., 1995—96; mem. Libr. Sci. Art. Bd. for Tx. Recipient Boss of Yr., Am. Bus. Women's Assn., 1994. Mem.: ALA, Abilene Libr. Consortium (chair adminstrv. coun. 1990, coord. nat. conf. 1991, chair adminstrv. coun. 1993, coord. nat. conf. 1993, chair adminstrv. coun. 1998, 2002, coord. nat. conf. 2002), Tex. Libr. Assn. (chair com. 1978—84, sec.-treas. coll. and univ. librs. divsn. 1993—94, legis. com. 1994—), Texshare Ednl. Working Group (chair 1999, 2002, libr. systems act adv. bd. mem. 2001—), Rotary (chair com. 1989—90). Home: 918 Grand Ave Abilene TX 79605-3233 Office: Hardin-Simmons U PO Box 16195 2200 Hickory St Abilene TX 79698-6195

SPECTOR, ELEANOR RUTH, corporation executive; b. N.Y.C., Dec. 2, 1943; d. Sidney and Helen Lebost; m. Mel Alan Spector, Dec. 10, 1966; children: Nancy, Kenneth. BA, Barnard Coll., 1964; postgrad. sch. pub. adminstrn., George Washington U., 1965-67; postgrad sch. edn., Nazareth Coll., 1974. Indsl. investigator N.Y. State Dept. Labor, White Plains, 1964-65; mgmt. intern Navy Dept., Washington, 1965, contract negotiator, 1965-68, contract specialist, 1975-78, contracting officer/br. head, 1978-82, dir. div. cost estimating, 1982-84; dep. asst. sec. def. for procurement Washington, 1984-91; dir. Def. Procurement, Washington, 1991-2000; v.p. contracts Lockheed Martin Corp., Bethesda, Md., 2000—. Advisor Nat. Contract Mgmt. Assn., 1984— Recipient Def. Meritoroius Civilian Svc. medal, 1986, 93, 96, Meritorious Svc. Presdl. award, 1989, 94, Disting. Civilian Svc. Presdl. award, 1990, 97, Def. Disting. Civilian Svc. medal, 1991, 94, 2000, Nat. Pub. Svc. award, 1998, Sec. Def. award for Excellence, 1997. Office: Lockheed Martin Corp MP 110 6801 Rockledge Dr Bethesda MD 20817-1877

SPECTOR, JOHANNA LICHTENBERG, ethnomusicologist, former educator; b. Libau, Latvia; came to U.S., 1947, naturalized, 1954; d. Jacob C. and Anna (Meyer) Lichtenberg; m. Robert Spector, Nov. 20, 1939 (dec. Dec. 1941). DHS, Hebrew Union Coll., 1950; MA, Columbia U., 1960. Rsch. fellow Hebrew U., Jerusalem, 1951-53; faculty Jewish Theol. Sem. Am., N.Y.C., 1954—, dir., founder dept. ethnomusicology, 1962-85, assoc. prof. musicology, 1966-70, Sem. prof., 1970-85, prof. emeritus, 1985—. Author: Ghetto-und Kzlieder, 1947, Samaritan Chant, 1965, Musical Tradition and Innovation in Central Asia, 1966, Bridal Songs from Sana Yemen, 1960, Jewish Music in a Changing World Vol. 1, 2001; documentary films The Samaritans, 1971, Chicago International, 1973, Middle Eastern Music, 1973, About the Jews of India: Cochin, 1976 (Cine Golden Eagle 1979), The Shanwar Telis or Bene Israel of India, 1978 (Cine Golden Eagle 1979), About the Jews of Yemen, A Vanishing Culture, 1986 (Cine Golden Eagle 1986, Blue Ribbon, Am. Film Festival 1986), 2000 Years of Freedom and Honor: The Cochin Jews of India, 1992, Margaret Mead, 1992, Columbus International, 1993; religious and folk recs. number over 10,000; contbr. articles to encys., various jours.; editorial bd. Asian Music. Fellow Am. Anthrop. Assn.; mem. Am. Ethnol. Soc., Am. Musicol. Soc., Internat. Folks Music Coun., World Assn. Jewish Studies, Yivo, Asian Mus. Soc. (v.p. 1964—, pres. 1974-78), Soc. Ethnomusicology (sec.-treas. N.Y.C. chpt. 1960-64). Home: 400 W 119th St New York NY 10027-7125

SPECTOR, ROSE, state supreme court justice; BA, Columbia U.; JD, St. Mary's Sch. Law, 1965. Judge County Ct. at Law 5, 1975-80, 131st Dist. Ct., 1981-92; justice Tex. Supreme Ct., 1993-98; atty. Bickerstaff, Heath, Pollan, Kever & McDaniel, L.L.P., Austin, Tex., 1998—. Office: Bickerstaff Heath et al 1700 Frost Bank Plz 816 Congress Ave Ste 1700 Austin TX 78701-2643

SPECTOR, SHELLY, company executive; MS, Syracuse U. Pres., creative dir. Spector & Assocs., 1991—. Recipient Creative All Star Nat. award, 1998. Office: 636 Morris Tpke Short Hills NJ 07078-2608

SPEED, CHRISTA A. WITT, music educator; b. North Platte, Nebr., Sept. 28, 1955; d. Randall J. and Helen G. Witt; m. Terry S. Speed, June 18, 1977; 1 child, Anna L. BA in Edn., U. Nebr., Kearney, 1978; MusM in Music Performance, U. Nebr., Omaha, 1998. Tchr. Grand Island (Nebr.) Pub. Schs., 1978—. Dir. Tri-City Jr. Youth Symphony, Hastings, Nebr., 2002—; mem. Hastings Symphony and String Quartet, 1977—2003. Co-author: Teaching Musicianship Through Music Performance, 2000. Named Arts Educator of Yr., Moonshell Arts Orgn., 2003. Mem.: Nebr. Music Educators Assn. (orch. chair 1995—96), Am. String Tchrs. Assn. (pres. Nebr. chpt. 1993—94, nat. sec. 1997—98, chair mem. Nebr. chpt. 2000—03, Tchr. of Yr. 1995). Democrat. Lutheran. Avocations: reading, swimming, sewing.

SPEERSTRA, KAREN M. former publishing executive; b. Toledo, Ohio, July 25, 1940; BA, U. Wis., 1962. Dir. music & art acquisition William C. Brown Pub., Debuke, Ill., 1981-87; tech. pub. dir. Focal Press Digitals Press Newnes & Butterworth Heinemann, Woburn, Mass., 1991-00, ret., 2000—. Office: Focal Press Digitals Press Newnes & Butterworth-Heinemann 225 Wildwood Ave Woburn MA 01801-2025

SPEIER, JACKIE, state senator; b. San Francisco; widowed; 2 children. BA, U. Calif., Davis; JD, U. Calif., San Francisco, 1976. Legal counsel Congressman Leo J. Ryan; mem. San Mateo County Bd. Suprs., chair, 1985-86; mem. Calif. State Assembly, 1986-96, chair consumer protection com.; mem. Calif. State Senate, 1998—, chair select com. on govt. oversight, chair select com. on spl. edn., mem. transp. com., appropriations com., mem. edn. com., others, chair ins. com., mem. joint legis. audit com. V.p. govt. and cmty. affairs Electronic Arts. Democrat. Office: State Capitol Rm 2032 Sacramento CA 95814 also: 400 S El Camino Ste 630 San Mateo CA 94402 also: Hiram W Johnson State Office Bldg 455 Golden Gate Ave Ste 14200 San Francisco CA 94102-7007

SPEIER, KAREN RINARDO, psychologist; b. New Orleans, Aug. 19, 1947; d. William Joseph Rinardo and Shirley Eva (Spreen) Christensen; m. Joe Max Sobotka, Nov. 27, 1970 (div. 1972); m. Anthony Herman Speier, May 29, 1982; children: Anthony Herman III, Austin Clay. Student, Vanderbilt U., 1965-67; BA, La. State U., New Orleans, 1969; MS, U. New Orleans, 1974; PhD, La. State U., 1985. Lic. psychologist, La. Tchr. spl. edn. Huntsville (Ala.) Achievement Sch., 1970-72; instr. neurology La. State U. Med. Ctr., New Orleans, 1972-78; clin. assoc. Dawson Psychol. Assocs., Baton Rouge, 1979-81; tchr. asst. dept. psychology La. State U., Baton Rouge, 1979-81; psychol. examiner La. Sch. for Deaf, Baton Rouge, 1979-80; psychology intern VA Med. Ctr., Martinez, Calif., 1981-82; psychology extern East La. State Hosp., Jackson, 1982-83; clin. assoc. Baton Rouge Psychol. Assocs., 1983-86, pvt. practice clin. psychology, 1986—; psychologist Rehab. Hosp. of Baton Rouge, 1990-93, 94, neuropsychologist, 1995-96; clin. neuropsychologist Baton Rouge Gen. Med. Ctr., 1996-99. Sec. bd. dirs. Baton Rouge Employment Devel. Svcs., 1987-89; mem. psychology cons. com. Meadow Wood Hosp., Baton Rouge, 1987-89; mem. psychology adv. com. Parkland Hosp., Baton Rouge, 1989-92; med. cons. Social Security Disability Determinations Svc., 1999—. Contbr. articles to profl. publs. Mem. steering com. Baton Rouge Stepfamily Support Group, 1983-90; tchr. Sunday sch. St. James Episcopal, Baton Rouge, 1984-86, 90-91, 92-99. Mem.: APA, Mental Health Assn. La., Nat. Acad. Neuropsychology, La. Psychol. Assn., Baton Rouge Area Soc. Psychologists (pres. 2001—02), Internat. Dyslexia Assn. (bd. dirs. 1988—98, pres. La. br. 1995—96). Office: Ctr Psychol Resources 650 Steele Blvd Baton Rouge LA 70806-5742

SPEIRS, PEG, art educator, artist, researcher; b. Youngstown, Ohio, Jan. 30, 1959; d. Stephen and Margaret Mary (Guilinger) Evanson; m. Glen Speirs, Dec. 22, 1990. BA, Hiram Coll., 1981; MA, Miami U., Oxford, Ohio, 1991; PhD, Pa. State U., 1998. Cert. permanent tchg. cert. K-12 art Ohio, tchr. level I cert. K-12 art Pa. Supr. Lark Enterprises, New Castle, Pa., 1981—82; freelance artist Peg's Photography, Struthers, Ohio, 1982—85; art tchr. So. Local Sch. Dist., Salineville, Ohio, 1985—95; grad. asst. Pa. State U., University Park, 1995—98; assoc. prof. Kutztown (Pa.) U., 1998—. Exhibiting artist, 1981—; co-owner Gallery 908, Reading, Pa., 2003—. Co-editor: (book) Contemporary Issues in Art Education, 2002; contbr. articles to profl. jours. Mem. edn. com. Reading (Pa.) Pub. Mus., 2000—. Recipient rsch. grant, Kutztown U., 2002, Binney & Smith, 2002, U. Ark. Fulbright Rsch. Com., 2002. Mem.: Berks Art Alliance, Nat. Art Edn. Assn. Women's Caucus (editor The Report 1999—2002), Pa. Art Edn. Assn., Nat. Art Edn. Assn. Avocations: backpacking, hiking, travel. Home: 906 N 8th St Reading PA 19604 Office: Kutztown U Dept Art Edn and Crafts PO Box 730 Kutztown PA 19530 Office Phone: 610-683-4513. Business E-Mail: speirs@kutztown.edu.

SPELLERBERG, ELINOR M. riding instructor; b. Seymour, Ind., Feb. 27, 1927; d. Ellis Leroy and Edna (Linke) Hawk; m. Thomas Richard Spellerberg, May 10, 1947; children: Eric (dec.), Scott, Janet, Jeffrey, Lance. Student, Ohio State U., 1945-47. Horse breeder and trainer, Tiffin, Ohio, 1960-99; dressage instr., 1980-2001; judge dressage horses Am. Horse Show Assn., Lexington, Ky., 1982-2001; ret, 2002—. Head instr. Riding for Handicapped, Tiffin, 1975-2001; mem. U.S. Equestrian Team, 1990-2001. Author, illustrator: The Test, 1995, (workbook) 4-H Dressage, 1990. Mem. exec. com. Elder Coll. Terra C.C., Fremont, Ohio, 1995-2001; mem. sch. bd. Mohawk H.S., Sycamore, Ohio, 1962-71; leader Seneca County 4-H, Tiffin, 1969-90; established Hope on Horseback, Tiffin, 1975-90, 1st 4-H Handicapped Riding Club and Program, Ohio, State 4-H Horse com.; sec. 4-H English divsn. Ohio State Fair; bd. dirs. Freedom Trails Therapeutic Riding Program, 2002-03. Named Woman of Yr., VFW, Tiffin, 1991, hon. chpt. farmer Future Farmers Am.; recipient Svc. award Kiwanis Club, Tiffin, 1990. Republican. Avocation: painting. Home: 1379 W Township Rd 58 Tiffin OH 44883

SPELLINGS, MARGARET LAMONTAGNE, assistant to US President on domestic policy; b. Houston, 1958; married. BA, U. Houston. Worked for Tex. Gov. William P. Clements, mem. of Tex. House Rep.; assoc. exec. dir. Tex. Assn. Sch. Bds.; polit. dir. Gov. George W. Bush gubernatorial campaign, Tex., 1994; sr. adv. to Gov. George W. Bush, Tex., 1994—2000; asst. to Pres. George W. Bush for domestic policy, 2001—. Host online interactive forum Ask the White House. Named one of 100 Most Powerful Women in Wash., Washingtonian mag., 2001. Office: Asst to Pres for Domestic Policy Exec Office Bldg Rm 464 Washington DC 20502*

SPELMAN, LUCY H. zoological park administrator; b. Bridgeport, Conn. BS in Biology, Brown U., 1985; DVM, U. Calif., Davis, 1990. Intern in small animal medicine and cardiology Dr. S. Ettinger and Assocs., L.A., 1990—91; resident in zool. medicine NC State Coll. Vet. Medicine/NC State Zool. Park, Asheboro, 1991—94; assoc. vet. med. officer Nat. Zool. Pk., Washington, 1995—99, sr. vet. med. officer, 1999—2000, dir., 2000—. Vet. advisor giant panda species survival plan Am. Zoo and Aquarium Assn., 1998—. Editor: Jour. Zoo and Wildlife Medicine, 1994—. Mem.: Am. Coll. Zool. Medicine (mem. exam. com. 1995—). Office: Nat Zool Park 3001 Connecticut Ave NW Washington DC 20008*

SPELMAN, NANCY LATTING, developmental psychologist; b. Oklahoma City, Sept. 13, 1945; d. Trimble Baggett and Patience Francelia (Sewell) Latting; m. Douglas Gordon Spelman, June 21, 1970; children: Brooke Patience, Erin Latting. BA in Polit. Sci., Boston U., 1967; MA in Psychology, Bucknell U., 1972; PhD in Psychology, U. Hong Kong, 1987. Tour guide UN, N.Y.C., summer 1966; tchr. emotionally disturbed and retarded pre-sch. children Mass. Dept. Mental Health, Boston, 1968-70; coord. vols. campaign for mayor Patience Latting, Oklahoma City, 1971; lectr. psychology Petaling Jaya Community Coll., Kuala Lumpur, Malaysia, 1987-88, George Mason U., Fairfax, Va., 1989; interactive skills observer, facilitator mgmt. programs Xerox Corp. Edn. and Tng., Leesburg, Va., 1989-91; pers. officer Am. Inst. in Taiwan, Taipei, 1993-95; tchr. psychology U. Hong Kong, 1996-99; adj. fellow psychology Nat. U. Singapore, 2000—01. Bd. dirs. Internat. Sch. Kuala Lumpur, 1986-87, sec., 1987-88, Golf Course Square Cluster, Reston, Va., 1991, Shanghai Am. Schs., 2002-; com. mem. Hong Kong Soc. for Disabled, 1976-77. Democrat. Avocations: hiking, tennis. E-mail: spelman@pacific.net.sg.

SPENCE, JANET BLAKE CONLEY (MRS. ALEXANDER PYOTT SPENCE), civic worker; b. Upper Montclair, N.J., Aug. 17, 1915; d. Walter Abbott and Ethel Maud (Blake) Conley; m. Alexander Pyott Spence, June 10, 1939; children: Janet Spence Kerr, Robert Moray, Richard Taylor. Student, Vassar Coll., 1933-35; cert., Katharine Gibbs Sch., 1936. Active various community drives; chmn. Darien (Conn.) Assembly, 1955-56; sec., chmn. Wilton Jr. Assembly, 1961-63; subscription chmn. Candlelight Concerts Wilton, Conn., 1963-65; rec. sec. Pub. Health Nursing Assn. Wilton Bd., 1964-67; corr., rec. sec. Royle Sch. Bd., Darien, 1952-55; fund raiser Vassar Class of 1937; mem. Washington Valley Community Assn.; mem. N.J. Symphony Orch. League, treas. Morris County br. 1978-83, corr. sec. 1982-83, pres. 1985-89, acting pres. 1989—, state coun. mem. 1985-89, acting pres. Morris br. 1989-90; docent Macculloch Hall Historica Mus., Morristown, N.J., 1992—. Mem. Vassar Alumni Assn., Dobbs Alumni Assn., Jersey Hills Vassar Club Morristown (ann. fund raiser), Woman's Club (sec. 2003—), Wilton Garden Club (life), Washington Valley Cmty. Assn. (life corr. sec. 1977-82, pres. 1982-84, v.p. 1984-85, co-pres. 1985-86, chmn. membership com. 1987-89, archives com. 1988—, treas. 1990—), Washington Valley Home Econs. Club, Del. Ref. Club (charter mem.). Mem. United Ch. Of Christ. Home: Apt 5D 1212 Foulk Rd Wilmington DE 19803-2752 Address: 8 Evergreen Ave Kennebunk ME 04043

SPENCE, MARY LEE, historian, educator; b. Kyle, Tex., Aug. 4, 1927; d. Jeremiah Milton and Mary Louise (Hutchison) Nance; m. Clark Christian Spence, Sept. 12, 1953; children: Thomas Christian, Ann Leslie. BA, U. Tex., 1947, MA, 1948; PhD, U. Minn., 1957. Instr., asst. prof. S.W. Tex. State U., San Marcos, 1948-53; lectr. Pa. State U., State College, 1955-58; mem. faculty U. Ill., Urbana-Champaign, 1973—, asst. prof., assoc. prof., 1973-81, 81-89, prof. history, 1989-90, prof. emerita, 1990—. Editor (with Donald Jackson) The Expeditions of John Charles Fremont, 3 vols., 1970-84, (with Clark Spence) Fanny Kelly's Narrative of Her Captivity Among the Sioux Indians, 1990, (with Pamela Herr) The Letters of Jessie Benton Fremont, 1993, The Arizona Diary of Lily Fremont, 1878-1881, 1997; contbr. articles to profl. jours. Mem. Children's Theater Bd., Urbana-Champaign, 1965-73. Grantee Nat. Hist. Pub. and Records Commn., Washington, 1977-78, 87-90, Huntington Libr., 1992; recipient Excellent Advisor award Liberal Arts and Sci. Coll./U. Ill., 1986. Mem. Western History Assn. (pres. 1981-82), Phi Beta Kappa (exec. sect. Gamma chpt. 1985-89, pres. 1991-92), Phi Alpha Theta. Episcopalian. Home: 1107 Foley Ave Champaign IL 61820-6326 Office: U Ill Dept History 810 S Wright St Urbana IL 61801-3644

SPENCE, NANCY JOAN, state representative; b. Denver, Dec. 12, 1936; m. Peter Spence; 4 children. Attended, Colo. State U. State rep. dist. 39 Colo. Ho. of Reps., Denver, 1998—, mem. joint com. on edn., joint com. on legis. ethics, and transp. and energy com. Mem. Interstate Migrant Edn. Coun., Cherry Creek Schs. Bd. Edn., Colo., 1980—93. Named Woman of Yr., Villager Newspapers, 1991, Legislator of Yr., Colo. Assn. Cmty. Centered Bds., 2001, Bus. Legislator of Yr., Colo. Assn. Commerce and Industry, 2000, Legislator of Yr., Am. Heart Assn., 1999; recipient Guardian of Small Bus. award, Nat. Fedn. Ind. Bus., 2002, Pres.'s award, U. Colo. Sch. Dentistry, Alumni Legis. Recognition award, U. Colo., 2001. Republican. Roman Catholic. Office: State Capitol Denver CO 80203

SPENCE, SANDRA, retired professional society administrator; b. McKeesport, Pa., Mar. 25, 1941; d. Cedric Leroy and Suzanne (Haudenshield) S. BA, Allegheny Coll., 1963; MA, Rutgers U., 1964. With Pa. State Govt., Harrisburg, 1964-68, Appalachian Regional Commn., Washington, 1968-75; legis. rep. Nat. Assn. Counties, Washington, 1975-77; fed. rep. Calif. Dept. Transp., Washington, 1977-78; dir. congl. affairs Amtrak, Washington, 1978-81, corp. sec., 1981-83; dir. computer svcs. Nat. R.R. Passenger Corp., Washington, 1983-84; co-owner Parkhurst-Spence Inc., 1985; owner The Spence Group, 1986-90; v.p. Bostrom Corp., Washington, 1990-92; exec. dir. Soc. Glass and Ceramic Decorators, 1992-2000. Chmn. legis. com. Womens Transp. Seminar, 1977-79, dir., 1982-83, v.p., 1983-84, chmn. edn. com., 1982-83; com. on edn. and tng. Transp. Rsch. Bd., 1982-85; mng. ptnr. Cambio Capital Club, 1996. Contbr. articles to profl. jours. Commnr. DC Commn. for Women, 1983—88, sec., 1983—88; pres. Found. for Work of Laity, 2001—; del. Ward III Dem. Com., 1982—90, 1st vice chmn., 1987—88; bd. dir. DC Habitat for Humanity, 1998—2002, chmn. devel. com., 1998—2000, sec., 2000—01; corr. sec. Sussex County (Del.) Habitat for Humanity, 2003—. Fellow Eagleton Inst. Politics, 1963-64; recipient Achievement award Transp. Seminar, 1982, 83 Mem. Greater Washington Soc. Assn. Execs. (vice-chair law and legis. com. 1989-90, chmn. 1990-91, chmn. scholarship com. 1992-93, bd. dirs. 1993-96, Rising Star award 1989, Chmn.'s award for Excel. Rels. 1991), Am. Soc. Assn. Execs. (mgmt. cert. 1987), Phi Beta Kappa. Home: 18471 Seashell Blvd Lewes DE 19958 E-mail: sandy_s@juno.com.

SPENCE, SIQUE (MARY STEWART SPENCE), art dealer; b. Balt., Aug. 16, 1946; d. Joseph Adolphus and Nell Orum (Jones) Stoll; m. Ronald A. Kuchta, Nov. 2, 1969 (div. 1975); m. Andrew R. Spence, June 24, 1977. Dir. Galeria del Sol/Fairtree Fine Crafts Inst., Santa Barbara, Calif., 1970-75; asst. to dir. Arco Ctr. for the Visual Arts, L.A., 1975-77; registrar Droll/Kolbert Gallery, N.Y.C., 1977-78; gallery asst. Nancy Hoffman Gallery, N.Y.C., 1978-81, dir., 1981—. Office: Nancy Hoffman Gallery 429 W Broadway New York NY 10012-3799 Fax: 212-334-5078.

SPENCER, BEVERLY ANN, medical administrator, health services consultant; b. Niagara Falls, N.Y., Nov. 20, 1948; d. Leon and Hattie Virginia (Reddick) S.; m. Robert Lee Palmer II, Feb. 8, 1982; children: Monifa, Reginald, Robert III. Cert. x-ray technician, Franklin Sch. Sci. & Arts, Phila., 1968; BA, U. Buffalo, 1979, MA, 1981, postgrad., 1983—. X-ray technician Children's Hosp., Phila., 1968-71; office mgr. Ob-Gyn. Bariatrics Practice, Buffalo, 1977-81; from asst. to assoc. v.p. for acad. affairs SUNY, Buffalo, 1981-84; dir. spl. svcs. project. U. Buffalo, 1984-87, adminstr. Sch. Medicine, 1987-94, 1st asst. dean for cmty. affairs Sch. Dental Medicine, 1994—, cons., founder Minority Engrs. Soc., 1984. Cons. acad. devel. program Rutgers U., 1994; spkr. structure urban pub. health World Health Orgn. conf., Buffalo, 1992, managed care program N.Y. State Dept. Social Svcs., Springville, 1994; presenter Am. Assn. Dental Schs. 72nd Ann. Session, San Antonio, 1995. Author: Women's Herbal Cures, 1996. Campaign mgr. Dem. Orgn.; 1st chair, co-founder Western N.Y. Legis. Task Force on Lead Poisoning Prevention, Buffalo, 1992-95; 1st chair N.Y. State Sch. Health Coun., Buffalo, 1992-96; founder, dir. Buffalo Sch. for Pregnant Teens, 1994-96. Recipient Outstanding Pub. Health Svc. award N.Y. Upstate Med. Alliance Buffalo, 1994. Mem. Western N.Y. Dental Assn. (CEO, founder 1996—), Am. Assn. Dental Schs., Assn. Health Care Execs., Links, Inc. Avocations: gourmet cooking, writing poetry, horseback riding, sailing. Office: So Calif Coll Optometry 2572 Yorba Linda Blvd Fullerton CA 92831 Home: PO Box 1363 Chino Hills CA 91709-0046

SPENCER, CAROL BROWN, association executive; b. Normal, Ill., Aug. 26, 1936; d. Fred William and Sorado (Gross) B.; m. James Calvin Spencer, Dec. 18, 1965 (div. July 1978); children: James Calvin Jr., Anne Elizabeth. BA in English, Calif. State U., Los Angeles, 1964, MA in Pub. Adminstrn., 1986. Cert. secondary edn. tchr., Calif. Tchr. English Seneca Vocat. High Sch., Buffalo, 1966-70; pub. info. officer City of Pasadena, Calif., 1979-90, City of Mountain View, Calif., 1990-93; exec. dir. Calif. Assn. for the Gifted, 1993-98. Owner PR to Go, 1994—. Sec., bd. dirs. Calif. Music Theatre, 1987-90; bd. dirs. Pasadena Beautiful Found., 1984-90, Pasadena Cultural Festival Found., 1983-86, Palo Alto-Stanford Heritage, 1990-93, Mountain View Libr. Found., 1997-98, Las Vegas Art Mus.; mayoral appointee Strategic Planning Adv. Com., Pasadena, 1985-86; active Mountain View Lib. Found., 1997-98; trainer Clark County Election Dept.; mem. Nev. Arts Advocates. Mem. NOW, Pub. Rels. Soc. Am., Calif. Assn. Pub. Info. Ofcls. (Paul Clark Achievment award 1986, award for mktg. 1990), City/County Comms. and Mktg. Assn. (bd. dirs. 1988-90, Savvy award for mktg. 1990), Las Vegas Art Mus., Las Vegas Opera Guild. Democrat. Episcopalian. Home: 7915 Laurena Ave Las Vegas NV 89147-5064

SPENCER, CAROLE A. medical association administrator, medical educator; BSc in Applied Biochemistry, Bath U. Tech., Bath, Somerset, Eng., 1969; PhD, Glasgow U., Scotland, 1972. Lic. clin. chemist med. technologist Calif., 1985. Lectr. in biochemistry Glasgow U., Scotland, 1972—73; asst. prof. rsch. medicine U. So. Calif., L.A., 1980—88, assoc. prof. rsch. medicine, 1988—94, prof. rsch. medicine, 1995—, dir. Endocrine Svcs. Lab., 1980—, GCRC Core Lab. dir. Clin. Rsch. Ctr., 1977—, GCRC Core Low Level Ligand Detection lab. dir., 1993—. Biochemist dept. pathol. biochemistry Glasgow Royal Infirmary, 1973—77; lectr. in field; cons. in field. Editl. bd. Jour. Clin. endocrinology and Metabolism, 1984—88, Am. Assn. Clin. Chemistry Jours., 1996—, Hormone and Metabolic Rsch., 1996—, reviewer Annals of Internal Medicine, —, Clin. Chemistry, —, Gerontology, —, Hormone and Metabolic Rsch., —, Jour. of Clin. Endocrinology and Metabolism, —, Jour. of Clin. Investigation, —, Jour. of Endocrinol. Investigation, —; contbr. articles to profl. jours. Mem.: European Thyroid Assn., Assn. Clin. Biochemists U.K., Endocrine Soc.,

Clin. Ligand Assay Soc. (Disting. Scientist award 1998), Am. Thyroid Assn. (pub. health com. 1991—, pres., exec. coun. 1995—), Am. Fedn. Clin. Rsch., Am. Assn. Clin. endocrinologists, Am. Assn. Clin. Chemists (Outstanding Spkr. award 1992, 1997), Cross-Town Endocrine Club. Achievements include research in includes thyroid physiology and pathology; thyroglobulin and thyroid cancer; thyroid hormone metabolism; immunoassay techniques. Office: U Southern Calif EDM111 9560 Los Angeles CA 90089

SPENCER, CAROLINE, retired library director; BA, AMLS, U. Mich. Past pres. Hawaii Libr. Assn. Office: HI State Public Lib 478 S King St Honolulu HI 96813-2901

SPENCER, ELIZABETH, author; b. Carrollton, Miss., 1921; d. James Luther and Mary James (McCain) S.; m. John Arthur Blackwood Rusher, Sept. 29, 1956. BA, Belhaven Coll., 1942; MA, Vanderbilt U., 1943; LittD (hon.), Southwestern U. at Memphis, 1968; LLD (hon.), Concordia U. at Montreal, 1988; LittD (hon.), U. of the South, 1992; DLitt (hon.), U. N.C., Chapel Hill, 1998, Belhaven Coll., 1999. Instr. N.W. Miss. Jr. Coll., 1943-44, Ward-Belmont, Nashville, 1944-45; reporter The Nashville Tennessean, 1945-46; instr. U. Miss., Oxford, 1948-51, 52-53. Vis. prof. Concordia U., Montreal, Que., Can., 1976-81, adj. prof., 1981-86; vis. prof. U. N.C., Chapel Hill, 1986-92. Author: Fire in the Morning, 1948, This Crooked Way, 1952, The Voice at the Back Door, 1956, The Light in the Piazza, 1960, Knights and Dragons, 1965, No Place for an Angel, 1967, Ship Island and Other Stories, 1968, The Snare, 1972, The Stories of Elizabeth Spencer, 1981, Marilee, 1981, The Salt Line, 1984, Jack of Diamonds and Other Stories, 1988, (play) For Lease or Sale, 1989, On the Gulf, 1991, The Night Travellers, 1991, (memoir) Landscapes of the Heart, 1998, The Southern Woman, 2001; contbr. short stories to mags. and anthologies. Named to N.C. Hall of Fame, 2002; recipient Women's Dem. Com. award, 1949, recognition award, Nat. Inst. Arts and Letters, 1952, Richard and Hinda Rosenthal Found. award, Am. Acad. Arts and Letters, 1957, Fortner award for lit., 1998, Award of Merit medal for the short story, 1983, 1st McGraw-Hill Fiction award, 1960, Henry Bellamann award for creative writing, 1968, Salem award for lit., 1992, Dos Passos award for fiction, 1992, N.C. Gov.'s award for lit., 1994, Corrington award for lit., 1997, Richard Wright award for lit., 1997, award for non-fiction, Miss. Libr. Assn., 1999, Brooks medal, Fellowship of So. Writers, 2001, Thomas Wolfe award for lit., 2002, William Faulkner award for lit. excellence, 2002; fellow, Guggenheim Found., 1953; Kenyon Rev. fellow in fiction, 1957, Bryn Mawr Coll. Donnelly fellow, 1962, Nat. Endowment for Arts grantee in lit., 1983, Sr. Arts Award grantee, Nat. Endowment for the Arts, 1988. Mem. Am. Acad. Arts and Letters, Fellowship of So. Writers (charter; vice chancellor 1993-97). Home: 402 Longleaf Dr Chapel Hill NC 27517-3042 E-mail: elizabeth0222@earthlink.net.

SPENCER, HEIDI HONNOLD, psychotherapist, writer, educator; b. Washington, June 30, 1943; d. John Otis and Annamarie (Kunz) Honnold; m. Charles David Spencer, Dec. 28, 1962; children: Hans Steven, Jason John, Tanya Anna. BA, U. Pa., 1965; MA, Columbia U., 1966; MSW, Cath. U., 1982; PhD in Adult and Family Psychology, Union Inst., Cin., 1990. Cert. clin. social worker, cert. nat. bd. addictions examiners; lic. social worker, D.C., Md., W.Va. Tchr. h.s. Peace Corps, Yap Island, 1966-68; faculty instr. Ctrl. Wash. State Coll., Ellensburg, 1972-75; parent group facilitator Individual Psychology Assocs., Chevy Chase, Md., 1975-79; group facilitator Georgetown U. Med. Sch., Washington, 1977-80; staff clinician D.C. Inst. Mental Health, 1980-86; pvt. practice in adult psychotherapy Bethesda, Md., 1985—; faculty Cath. U. Wa. Psychoanalytic Found., 1989-91; bd. dirs., cons., faculty, supr. Clin. Social Work Inst. Mem. bd. doctoral program for clin. social workers; counselor, tchr. The Spl. Sch. for Pregnant Teenagers, Seattle, 1969-71; crisis intervention counselor Montgomery County (Md.) Hotline, 1975-79; mental health intern No. Va. Mental Health Inst., Falls Ch., 1979-80; mem. part-time faculty Cath. U., Washington, 1991; cons., counselor Christ Child Soc., Rockville, Md., 1985-86; cons. Jewish Cmty. Ctr., Rockville, 1992, Brooklane Psychiat. Ctr., Hagerstown, Md., 1992, AmeriCorps, Washington, 1996, Affiliated Cmty. Counselors, Inc., Rockville, 1996—; insvc. instr. psychol. and learning ctr. Am. U., Washington, 1990—; chair, Conf. Washington Psychoanalytic Found., 1989-90; cons. The Bilingual Project/Project BUILD, Yakima, Wash., 1973-75; mem. curriculum com. Clin. Social Work Inst., 1991-94; spkr. and presenter in field. Author: (2 vols. book and record) Our Valley-Our Song, 1974, (book) Did I Do Something Wrong: A Supportive Guide for Parents and Loved Ones or People in Psychotherapy, 1995; columnist Family Therapy Acad., 1996-97. Trainer, cons. cmty.-based overflow shelters for homeless, Bethesda, 1989-94; vice chair bd. social concerns Cedar Ln. Unitarian Ch., 1986-87; active dr.-lawyer anti-drug program Fairfax Bar Assn., 1997. Mem. Greater Washington Soc. Clin. Social Work (v.p. for edn. 1992-94, at-large 1994-96, membership task force 1995-96). Baha'I. Avocations: violin, piano, accordion, gardening, writing. Office: 5204 Chandler St Bethesda MD 20814-2865

SPENCER, JEAN, food products executive; b. Bklyn., Oct. 26, 1946; d. Frederic R. and Lucy Anne Spencer. BBA cum laude, Adelphi U., 1973, MBA, 1989; MS in Human Nutrition, U. Bridgeport, 1998. Notary public, 1986—. Exec. adminstrv. mgmt. Underwriters Labs., Inc., Melville, NY, 1966—2003, ret., 2003; pres., CEO All Natural Health Corp., Seaford, NY, 1990—. Vol., life mem. Nat. Ski Patrol, Colo. Recipient NASTAR, Bronze medal, Silver medal. Mem. Am. Coll. Nutrition, Am. Soc. Quality Control, Nat. Nutritional Foods Assn., Nat. Ctr. for Homeopathy. Avocations: snow skiing, bicycle riding, physical fitness, opera, theater. Office: All Natural Health Inc 3830 Sunrise Hwy Seaford NY 11783-2634

SPENCER, KATHELEN V. insurance company executive; m. Tracy Spencer; 3 children. BA in Polit. Sci., Emory U.; JD, U. Ga., 1982. Bar: Tex., Ga. Lawyer pvt. practice, Columbus, Ga., 1983-85; assoc. counsel AFLAC, Columbus, Ga., 1985-87, dep. counsel, 1987-89, v.p., dir. pub. rels., 1989-92, sr. v.p., dep. counsel, dir. corp. comm., 1992—. Bd. dirs. Columbus Bank and Trust Co.; mem. AFLAC Donations Com., dir. shareholder svcs. dept. Trustee Brookstone Sch., Columbus Coll. Found., Pastoral Inst., Columbus Mus; mem. adv. bd. Emory U. Sch. of Pub. Health; past pres. Jr. League Columbus; alumna Leadership Ga. Office: AFLAC Inc 1932 Wynnton Rd Columbus GA 31999-0002

SPENCER, MARGARET GILLIAM, lawyer; b. Spokane, Wash., Aug. 30, 1951; d. Jackson Earl and Margaret Kathleen (Hindley) Gilliam; m. John Bernard Spencer, Feb. 21, 1993. BA in Sociology, U. Mont., 1974, MA in Sociology, 1978, JD, 1982. Bar: Mont. 1982, Colo. 1982. Assoc. Holland & Hart, Denver, 1982-84, Roath & Brega, P.C., Denver, 1984-88, shareholder, dir., 1988-89; spl. counsel Brega & Winters, P.C., Denver, 1989; corp. counsel CH2M Hill, Inc., Denver, 1989—. Democrat. Episcopalian. Avocations: skiing, scuba diving. Office: CH2M Hill Inc 9191 S Jamaica St Englewood CO 80112

SPENCER, MARIAN ALEXANDER, volunteer; b. Gallipolis, Ohio, June 28, 1920; d. Harry McDonal and Rosanna (Carter) Alexander; m. Donald Andrew Spencer, Aug. 1940; children: Donald Andrew Jr., Edward Alexander. BA, U. Cin., 1942. Pres. Fellowship House, Cin., 1942-46, Cin. Chpt. Links, Inc., Cin., 1968-72, Woman's City Club, Cin., 1972-73, NAACP, Cin., 1980-82; trustee U. Cin., 1975-79; chairperson Ohio Adv. Com. on Civil Rights, Cin., 1980-86; vice-mayor City of Cin., 1983-85; mem. task force to monitor de-segregation of Cin. pub. schs., 1984-96. Recipient Recognition cert. Nat. Conf. of Christians and Jews, Cin., 1968, Black Excellence award Operation PUSH (People United to Save Humanity), Cin., 1972, Pres.'s award NAACP, Cin., 1980, Disting. Alumna award for outstanding leadership U. Cin., 1982, award NASW, Cin., 1986, A Life Dedicated to the Fulfillment of the Dream of Dr. Martin Luther King award Bapt. Mins. Conf., Cin., 1987, $10,000 Jacob E. Davis Vol. Leadership award Greater Cin. Found., 1993, Champion for Democracy award Ctr. for Voting and Democracy, Washington, 1994, Civil Rights Efforts award Urban League, Am. Jewish Com., Cin. Hist. Soc., 1995; named Woman of Yr., Cin. Enquirer, 1972; inductee Ohio Women's Hall of Fame, State of Ohio, 1984. Democrat. Methodist. Avocations: travel, swimming, drawing, reading, playing cards. Home: 940 Lexington Ave Cincinnati OH 45229-2726

SPENCER, MARY ELIZABETH, minister; d. Russell Dan Tripplehorn and Marjorie Leah Kocek; m. Michael John Kulhanek; children: Michael, Mark, Matthew. Diploma, Garrett Seminary, Ill., 2001. Bus. mgr. Chippewa Redi Mix, Owosso, Mich., 1972—92; pastor Eastwood Meth. Ch., Flint, Mich., 1997—. Human rights city coun. City of Flint, Mich., 2001—03. Home: 2101 Stark Weather Flint MI 48506

SPENCER, MARY HELEN, interior designer; b. Paris, Tex., Oct. 21, 1950; d. Otha Cleo and Billie Ermine (Abernathy) S. Student, East Tex. State U., 1969-72. Interior designer William Hammon & Assoc., Dallas, 1973-75; sales rep. Seymour Mirrow Co., Dallas, 1975-76; prin. Mary Spencer Co., Dallas, 1976—. Cons. design dept. East Tex. State U., Commerce. Fund raiser Am. Paralysis Assn., Dallas, 1979, Wadley Whoppee, Dallas, 1986, Easter Seals Soc., Dallas, 1987. Mem. Inst. Bus. Designers, Assn. Women Entreprenuers. Republican. Methodist. Avocations: sailing, reading, planning. Home: 6943 Wildgrove Ave Dallas TX 75214-3837 Office: The Spencer Co 2713 Mckinney Ave Dallas TX 75204-2563

SPENCER, MARY MILLER, civic worker; b. Comanche, Tex., May 25, 1924; d. Aaron Gaynor and Alma (Grissom) Miller; 1 child, Mara Lynn. BS, U. North Tex., 1943. Cafeteria dir. Mercedes (Tex.) Pub. Schs., 1943-46; home economist coord. All-Orange Dessert Contest Fla. Citrus Commn., Lakeland, 1959-62, 64; tchr. purchasing sch. lunch dept. Fla. Dept. Edn., 1960. Clothing judge Polk County (Fla.) Youth Fair, 1951-68, Polk County Federated Women's Clubs, 1964-66; pres. Dixieland Elem. Sch. PTA, 1955-57, Polk County Coun. PTA's, 1958-60; chmn. pub. edn. com. Polk County unit Am. Cancer Soc., 1959-60, bd. dirs., 1962-70; charter mem., bd. dirs. Lakeland YMCA, 1962-72; sec. Greater Lakeland Cmty. Nursing Coun., 1965-72; trustee, vice-chmn. Polk County Eye Clinic, Inc., 1962-64, pres., 1964-82; bd. dirs. Polk County Scholarship and Loan Fund, 1962-70; mem. exec. com. West Polk County (Fla.) Cmty. Welfare Coun., 1960-62, 65-68; mem. budget and audit com. Greater Lakeland United Fund, 1960-62, bd. dirs., 1967-70, residential chmn. fund drive, 1968; mem. adv. bd. Polk County Juvenile and Domestic Rels. Ct., 1960-69; sec. bd. dirs. Fla. West Coast Ednl. TV, 1960-81; mem. Polk County Home Econs. Adv. Com., 1965-71; mem. exec. com. Suncoast Health Coun., 1968-71; worker children's svcs. divsn. family svcs. Dept. Health and Rehab. Svcs., State of Fla., 1969-70, social worker, 1970-72, 74-82, social worker Overpayment Fraud Recoupment unit, 1977-81, with other pers. svcs., 1981-82, supr. Overpayment Fraud Recoupment unit, 1982-83, pub. assistance specialist IV, 1984-89; bd. dirs. Lake Region United Way, Winter Haven, 1976-81; mem. Polk County Cmty. Svcs. Coun., 1978-88; with other pers. svcs. Emergency Fin. Assistance Housing Program, 1990-96. Mem. AAUW (pres. Lakeland br. 1960-61), Nat. Welfare Fraud Assn., Fla. Congress Parents and Tchrs. (hon. life, pres. dist. 7 1961-63, chmn. pub. rels. 1962-66), Fla. Health and Welfare Coun., Fla. Health and Social Svc. Coun., Polk County Mental Health Assn., U. North Tex. Alumni Assn., Order Ea. Star. Democrat. Methodist. Home and Office: PO Box 2161 Lakeland FL 33806-2161

SPENCER-JACOBS, JAMELLE ELIZABETH, minister, performing company executive; d. James Earl Spencer and Joyce Elaine Walker Spencer; m. Reginald Eugene Jacobs Sr., Apr. 16, 1994 (div. June 2001); 1 child, Reginald Eugene Jacobs Jr. BA in Sociology, U. Va., 1985, MEd, 1986; MDiv, Interdenominational Theol. Ctr./Morehouse Sch., Atlanta, 1994; D of Ministry, Va. Sem., Lynchburg, 2003. Cert. tchr. Ga. Sales mgr. RH Macy's, N.Y.C., 1986—87, asst. buyer, 1987—89, Atlanta, 1987—89; tchr. Atlanta Pub. Schs., 1990—95; owner and dir. Jacobs Ctr. Performing Arts, Atlanta, 1996—; pastor and sr. min. Knights Monumental AME Ch., Stockbridge, Ga., 1998—. Com. chair Henry County Ministerial Alliance, 2001—; chmn. bd. dirs. Knights-Densley Cmty. Devel. Corp., Stockbridge, 2003—. Vol. Henry County Meals on Wheels, 2002—. Recipient Sons and Daughters award, Bethel Bapt. Ch., 1995. Democrat. Avocations: walking, cooking, reading. Office: Knights Monumental AME Church 224 Red Oak Rd Stockbridge GA 30281 E-mail: jjacobs5@bellsouth.net.

SPERANSKY, HELEN I. psychotherapist, consultant; b. Lenigrad, Russia, Dec. 9, 1959; arrived in U.S., 1987; d. Moysey I. and Nina V. Iskin; m. Jeffrey P. Horowitz, Aug. 1, 1993; 1 child, Jake ; m. Andrew Speransky, Apr. 1982 (div. Jan. 1987); 1 child, Lisa. BA, Leningrad U., Russia, 1980, MA, 1982; MSW, Yeshiva U., N.Y.C., 1994; postgrad., Weiter Sch. Ackerman Inst. for Families, N.Y.C., 1995. Cert. social worker N.Y. Pres., owner Family Psychotherapy PC, NY, 1995—; mgr., psychotherapist FEGS, Bronx, NY, 1996—99; dir. children in crisis program FBFCS, NY, 1999—2000; child and family psychotherapist Col. Presbyn. Hosp. Child Psychology, NY, 2000—03. Asst. prof. English LT Coll., Leningrad, Russia, 1980—82; supr., family therapist NYANA, N.Y.C., 1988—96. Co-author: (book) Business Guide to Moscow, 1990, History of Russia, 1991. Recipient Cert. of Appreciation, White House Com. Group, 1988, Cert. of Honor, UJA, 1992. Mem.: Nat. Assn. Social Work, APA. Democrat. Jewish. Avocations: theater, reading, travel, art, exploring nature. Office: Family Psychotherapy PC 235 W 71st St #2 New York NY 10023

SPERIN, AMELIA HARRISON, medical/surgical nurse, obstetrics/gynecological nurse; b. Eatonton, Ga., Apr. 5, 1961; d. Patrick Wesley and Mary Lee (Covert) Harrison; m. Phillip M. Sperin (div. Dec. 1987); children: Phillip Wesley, Lauren Heicha. LPN, Pickens Vocat. Tech. Sch., 1980; BSN, Med. Coll. Ga., 1984. RN, Ga. Med.-surg. nurse Cobb Gen. Hosp., Austell, Ga., 1983-85; nurse case mgr. N.W. Home Health, Jasper, Ga., 1991-93; nurse Northside Hosp.-Cherokee at R.T. Jones Campus, Canton, Ga., 1987—. Active mem. Jasper First Bapt. Ch. Office: Northside Hosp-Cherokee 201 Hospital Rd Canton GA 30114-2408

SPERLING, IRENE R. publishing executive; Asst. mktg. coord. seminars and trade shows Security World Publ., 1979—80; asst. show mgr. Cahners Expn. Group Kitchen and Bath and Office Product Shows, 1980—83, co-pub., 1983—86, v.p. sales and mktg., 1986—2000, publ., 2000—; publisher Tradeshow Week, LA, 2000—02; v.p. spl. projects and internat. sales Trade Show Exec. Mag., 2003—. Office: Trade Show Exec 21250 Hawthorne Blvd Ste 500 Torrance CA 90503 E-mail: isperling@tsweek.com.

SPERO, JOAN EDELMAN, foundation president; b. Davenport, Iowa, Oct. 2, 1944; d. Samuel and Sylvia (Halpern) Edelman; m. C. Michael Spero, Nov. 9, 1969; children: Jason, Benjamin. Student, L'Inst. d'Etudes Politiques, Paris, 1964-65; BA in Internat. Rels. with honors, U. Wis., 1966; MA, Columbia U., 1968, PhD, 1973; LLD (hon.), Amherst Coll., 1997. Asst. prof. Columbia U., N.Y.C., 1973-79; amb. of U.S. to UN Econ. and Social Coun., N.Y.C., 1980-81; v.p. Am. Express Co., N.Y.C., 1981-83, sr. v.p. internat. corp. affairs, 1983-89; treas., sr. v.p., 1989-91; exec. v.p. corp. affairs and communications Am. Express Co., 1991-93; under sec. for econ., bus. and agrl. affairs Dept. of State, Washington, 1993-97; pres. Doris Duke Charitable Found., N.Y.C., 1997—. Vis. scholar Fed. Res. Bank N.Y., 1976—77; dir. IBM, bd. dirs., 1st Data Corp., Delta Air Lines Inc. Author: The Politics of International Economic Relations, 6th edit., 2003, The Failure of the Franklin National Bank, 1980; contbr. articles to profl. jours. Trustee Wis. Alumni Rsch. Found., 1997—, Columbia U., 1998; trustee emeritus Amherst Coll.; mem. Coun. Am. Ambs. Named to Acad. Women Achievers, YWCA, 1983; named Fin. Woman of Yr., Fin. Women's Assn., 1990; recipient George Washington U. Disting. Statesperson award, 1994; Woodrow Wilson fellow. Mem. Am. Acad. Diplomacy, Coun. on Fgn. Rels. (bd. dirs.), Am. Philos. Soc., Phi Beta Kappa. Democrat. Jewish. Avocations: writing, swimming. Office: Doris Duke Charitable Found 650 5th Ave 19th Fl New York NY 10019-6108

SPETH, CAMILLE, engineer; b. Midvale, Utah, Aug. 24, 1956; d. Gerald L. and Dora (Goff) S. Grad. high sch., Indpls. Systems coord. Allied Fidelity, Indpls., 1984-85; bus. analyst EDS/MIC, Detroit, 1985-91; local area network adminstr. EDS/GMAC, Detroit, 1991-97; network engr. Elec. Data Systems, Corydon, Ind., 1997—. Author: (manuals) V4 Users Guide, 1985, Genealogy Training Manual, 1990, Network Users Guide, 1992, Site Administration Manual, 1997. Leader Ch. Young Women Camp, 1975-85, coach sports program, 1975-85. Mem. NAFE, Ind. High Sch. Athletic Assn. (high sch. sports referee 1976—), Netware Users Internat. Avocations: music, golf, woodworking. Home and Office: 1970 Lears Ln NE Corydon IN 47112-7657 E-mail: camispeth@earthlink.net.

SPETSIERIS, PHOEBE GEORGE, physicist, application developer, researcher; b. Athens, Greece, Apr. 26, 1944; came to U.S., 1947; d. Elis P. and Helen Elis George; m. Spyridon Spetsieris, June 30, 1972; 1 child, Zoe. BS in Physics, U. Athens, 1968; MA in Physics, CCNY, 1970; MPhil in Physics, CUNY, 1979, PhD in Physics, 1980. Adj. lectr. in physics and math. CCNY, N.Y.C., 1968—77; rsch. asst. in physics CUNY, N.Y.C., 1972—79; engr., sys. analyst Am. Electric Power Svc. Corp., N.Y.C., 1979—83; sr. sci. programmer analyst Meml. Sloan-Kettering Cancer Ctr., N.Y.C., 1984—89; sys. analyst, assoc. investigator Ctr. Neuroscis. Functional Brain Imaging Lab. North Shore L.I. Jewish Rsch. Inst., Manhasset, NY, 1990—; rsch. assoc. prof. neurology NYU Sch. Medicine, 2001—. Presenter, cons. in field; adj. asst. prof. bioengring. Sch. Health Scis., Touro Coll., Dix Hills, NY, 1994—95. Contbr. articles to profl. publs. N.Y. State Regents scholar, 1962, CUNY scholar, 1971; CUNY rsch. fellow, 1976. Mem. IEEE Engring. in Medicine and Biology. Democrat. Greek Orthodox. Avocations: art, computer graphics, scientific visualization. Office: North Shore U Hosp Dept Neurology 350 Community Dr Manhasset NY 11030-3849

SPICER, BEVERLY WHITE, writer, photojournalist, artist; m. Christopher Hanes Spicer, 1969 (div. 1976). BA in Physiol. Psychology, Converse Coll., 1969; MS in Arch., U. Tex., 2000. Rschr. U. Va., Charlotteville, Va., 1969—71; asst. to pub. Tex. Monthly Mag., Austin, Tex., 1976—77; freelance photojournalist, 1978—. Author: The Ka'Bah: Rhythms of Culture, Faith and Physiology, 2004; co-author: Open Ceilings: Women of Power Outside The Paradigm, 1994; various jours. Vol. Seton Hosp., Austin, 1990—94. Grantee, NIH, 1982, Mike Hogg grant, U. Tex., 1999. Mem.: Am. Inst. Archs. (assoc.). Avocations: swimming, walking, movies, music, instr. kondalin yoga. Home: 4705 Eilers Ave Austin TX 78751

SPICER, SUSAN, food service executive; Apprentice to Chef Daniel Bonnot Louis XVI Restaurant, New Orleans, 1979; chef under Chef Ronald Durand Hotel Sofitel, Paris, 1982; owner, chef de cuisine Savoir Faire bistro, New Orleans, 1982; cons. chef to Marc Haeberlin of l'Auberge de l'Ill Meridien Hotel, New Orleans, 1985—86; owner, chef Bistro at Maison deVille, New Orleans, 1986—90; ptnr., chef Bayona, New Orleans, 1990—. Guest chef James Beard Ho., Cunard's Sea Goddess, Oriental Hotel, Bangkok. Recipient James Beard award, Best Chef, Southeast Region, 1993, Mondavi Culinary Excellence award, 1995, Ivy award, Restaurant and Instn. mag., 1996, 5 Beans award, New Orleans Times Picayune, 1996. Office: Bayona 430 Dauphine St New Orleans LA 70112

SPICKNALL, JOAN, music educator; b. Arlington, Va., Feb. 13, 1942; d. Joseph Richard and Rhoda Louise (Beran) Singer; m. Marvin Herbert Spitz, Dec. 12, 1992; children from previous marriage: Lisa Sharon Spicknall Fruth, Richard Mark Spicknall. B of Mus, Peabody Conservatory, 1962, MusM, 1963; D of Musical Arts, U.Md., 1974. Grad. asst. U. Md., College Park, 1966-69; asst. prof. St. Mary of the Woods (Ind.) Coll., 1971-83; instr. piano pvt. practice, Columbia, Md., 1983-88; instr. Essex C.C., Balt., 1983-84, Loyola Coll., Balt., 1983-84, Howard C.C., Columbia, 1983-86; pres., dir. Suzuki Music Sch. Md., Inc., Columbia, 1988—. Adj. prof. Rose-Hulman Inst. Tech., Terre Haute, Ind., 1973-83; piano tchr. Howard County Schs., 1986—; guest faculty, lectr. nat. and internat. music convs., 1991-. Pianist (new 2 CD album): The Piano Music of Aaron Copland, 2004; contbr. articles to profl. articles, newspapers, jours., and mags. Mem. MTNA, SAA, Inc., ISA, AAUW, SAGWA, MENC, CMS, People to People Amb. Programs, Music Educator's Dels., Mu Phi Epsilon, Delta Kappa Gamma. Home: 10659 Green Mt Cir Columbia MD 21044 Office: Suzuki Music Sch Md Inc PO Box 1284 Columbia MD 21044-0284 E-mail: director@suzukimusicschool.com.

SPIEGEL, EDNA Z. lawyer; b. N.Y.C., Oct. 27; m. Rubin E. Spiegel; children: Linda F. Spiegel Duboff, Joyce I., Bennett L. BS, NYU, 1948, MA, 1949; JD, Seton Hall U., 1986. Bar: N.J. 1988, U.S. Dist. Ct. N.J. 1988, U.S. Supreme Ct. 1993; lic. asst. prin., lic. prin. N.Y.C. Bd. Edn. Substitute tchr. music N.Y.C. Bd. Edn., 1950-52, tchr. music, 1952-81; pvt. legal practice River Edge, N.J., 1990—. Atty. River Edge Environ. Protection Commn., 1987—96; with cmty. outreach on advance directives Holy Name Hosp., Teaneck, NJ, 1994—97; trustee Bergen County Legal Svcs., Hackensack, 1999—2002; lawyer law day Divsn. Human Svcs. Bergen County, Hackensack, 1988—2004. Mem. Nat. Acad. Elder Law Attys. (charter mem. N.J. chpt.), N.J. Women Lawyers' Assn., N.J. State Bar Assn. (charter, elder law sect.), Bergen County Bar Assn. (charter, elder law com.), Women Lawyers in Bergen County, Hadassah/The Womens Zionist Orgn. of Am. (River Dell chpt., v.p. programs 1978-80, 96—, chmn. Am. affairs 1979—, Woman of the Yr. 1996, Nat. Leadership award 1997). Avocations: gardening, painting, cooking, swimming, collectibles. Office: 1106 Roosevelt Ave New Milford NJ 07646 Office Phone: 201-836-9330. E-mail: ezsesq@aol.com.

SPIEGEL, EVELYN SCLUFER, biology educator, researcher; b. Phila., Mar. 20, 1924; d. George and Helen (Laurantos) Sclufer; m. Melvin Spiegel, Apr. 16, 1955; children: Judith Ellen, Rebecca Ann. BA, Temple U., 1947; MA, Bryn Mawr Coll., 1951; PhD, U. Pa., 1954. Asst. program dir. for regulatory biology NSF, Washington, 1954-55; instr. in biology Colby Coll., Waterville, Maine, 1955-59; rsch. assoc. Dartmouth Coll., Hanover, N.H., 1961-74, rsch. assoc. prof. biology, 1974-78, rsch. prof. biology, 1978-91; rsch. prof. biology emerita, 1991—. Vis. scholar Calif. Inst. Tech., Pasadena, 1964-65, U. Calif.-San Diego, La Jolla, 1970, Nat. Inst. for Med. Rsch., Mill Hill, Eng., 1971, NIH, Washington, 1975-76, U. Basel (Switzerland) Biocenter, 1979, 80, 81, 82, 85. Contbr. numerous articles to profl. jours., chpts. to books and book reviews. Mem. Soc. for Devel. Biology, Marine Biol. Lab. Corp. (trustee 1981-86, 88-92). Office: Dartmouth Coll Dept Biol Scis Hanover NH 03755

SPIEGEL, MARILYN HARRIET, real estate executive; b. Bklyn., Apr. 3, 1935; d. Harry and Sadie (Oscher) Unger; m. Murray Spiegel, June 12, 1954; children: Eric Lawrence, Dana Cheryl Mann, Jay Barry. Grad. high sch., Bklyn. Exec. sec. S & W Paper Co., N.Y.C., 1954-58; salesperson Red Carpet Realtors, Los Alamitos, Calif., 1974-75, Coll. Park Realtors, Garden Grove, Calif., 1975-79; owner, broker S & S Properties, Los Alamitos, 1979—. Named Realtor of Yr., 1989. Mem. Calif. Assn. Realtors (bd. dirs. 1984—), West Orange County Bd. Realtors (bd. dirs. 1984—, 1st v.p. 1987, pres. 1988), Million Dollar Sales Club, Long Beach C. of C., Seal Beach C.

of C., Orange County C. of C., Summit Orgn., Toastmasters (pres. founders group Garden Grove, 1990). Home: 1371 Oakmont Rd Apt 150D Seal Beach CA 90740-3732 Office: S & S Properties 3502 Katella Ave Ste 208 Los Alamitos CA 90720-3130

SPIEGEL, PHYLLIS, public relations consultant, journalist; b. Bronx, N.Y. d. Bernard and Lillian (Horowitz) Finkelberg; m. Stanley Spiegel, Sept. 20, 1959 (div. 1981); children: Mark, Adam. BA, NYU. Feature writer various newspapers, pubs., 1960's-70's; dir. pub. rels. Mort Barish Assocs., Princeton, N.J., 1975-80; account exec. pub. rels. Keyes Martin, Springfield, N.J., 1980-84; pres. Phyllis Spiegel Assocs., Plainsboro, N.J., 1984—. Pub. rels. dir., founder Red Oak Coop. Nursery Sch., Middletown, N.J., 1960's, Matawan (N.J.) Student Enrichment Program, 1960s-70s; pub. rels. cons., event organizer New Philharm. of N.J., Morristown, 1991-93; mem. Child Placement Rev. Bd. of Family Ct., Mercer County, N.J., 1994-98. Recipient Commendation from Gov. N.J. for U. Med. and Dentistry of N.J. campaign, 1983, Commendation for N.J. Pharm. Assn. campaign Pub. Rels. News Assn., 1979. Mem. Soc. for Humanistic Judaism (bd. dirs. 1983-85). Avocations: film and theatre, classical music, reading, travel, walks. Office: Phyllis Spiegel Assocs PO Box 243 Plainsboro NJ 08536-0243

SPIEGELBERG, EMMA JO, business education educator, academic administrator; b. Mt. View, Wyo., Nov. 22, 1936; d. Joseph Clyde and Dorcas (Reese) Hatch; m. James Walter Spiegelberg, June 22, 1957; children: William L., Emory Walter, Joseph John. BA with honors, U. Wyo., 1958, MEd, 1985; EdD, Boston U., 1990. Tchr. bus. edn. Laramie (Wyo.) H.S., 1960-61, 65-93, adminstr., 1993-97; prin. McCormick Jr. H.S., Cheyenne, Wyo., 1997—2002; exec. dir. Wyo. Assn. Secondary Sch. Prins., 2001—. Author: Branigan's Accounting Simulation, 1986, London & Co. II, 1993; co-author: Glencoe Computerized Accounting, 1993, 2d edit., 1995, Microcomputer Accounting: Daceasy, 1994, Microcomputer Accounting: Peachtree, 1994, 3d edit., 2000, Microcomputer Accounting: Accpac, 1994, Computerized Accounting with Peachtree, 1995, 2000, 02. Mem. United Ch. of Christ; bd. dirs. Cathedral Home for Children, Laramie, 1967-70, 72—, pres., 1985-88, Laramie Plains Mus., 1970-79. Named Wyo. Bus. Tchr. of Yr., 1982, Wyo. Asst. Prin. of Yr., 1997. Mem.: NASSP, NEA, Wyo. Assn. Secondary Sch. Prins. (sec., treas. 1997—2001), Albany County Edn. Assn. (sec. 1970—71), Wyo. Edn. Assn., Wyo. Bus. Edn. Assn. (pres. 1979—80), Internat. Soc. Bus. Edn., Mt. Plains Bus. Edn. Assn. (Wyo. rep. to bd. dirs. 1982—85, pres. 1987—88, Sec. Tchr. of Yr. 1991, Leadership award 1992), Nat. Bus. Edn. Assn. (bd. dirs. 1987—88, 1991—96, Sec. Tchr. of Yr. 1991), Wyo. Vocat. Assn. (exec. bd. 1978—80, pres. 1981—82, exec. sec. 1986—89, Outstanding Contbns. to Vocat. Edn. award 1983, Tchr. of Yr. 1985), Am. Vocat. Assn. (policy com. region V 1984—87, region V Tchr. of Yr. 1986), U. Wyo. Alumni Assn. (bd. dirs. 1985—90, pres. 1988—89), Laramie C. of C. (bd. dirs. 1985—88), Zonta Internat. (Laramie) (v.p. 2002—03, pres. 2003—), Delta Pi Epsilon, Pi Lambda Theta, Chi Omega, Alpha Delta Kappa (state pres. 1978—82), Phi Delta Kappa, Kappa Delta Pi. Home: 3301 Grays Gable Rd Laramie WY 82072-5031 Office Phone: 307-745-5468.

SPIELMAN, BARBARA HELEN NEW, editor, consultant; b. Canton, Ohio, June 28, 1929; d. Arthur Daniel and Helen Barbara (Rickenmann) New; m. David Vernon Spielman, Nov. 24, 1956; children: Daniel Bruce, Linda Barbara. BS in English and History Edn. cum laude, Miami U., Oxford, Ohio, 1951. Cert. tchr., Ohio, Tex. Tchr. Canton Pub. Schs., 1951-53; vets. aide U. Tex., Austin, 1954-57; copy editor, mng. editor U. Tex. Press, Austin, 1964-91; ret., 1991. Editorial cons. Chicago Manual of Style, 13th edit., 1975, Amon Carter Mus., Ft. Worth, 1970—, Ctr. for Mex. Am. Studies, Austin, 1980, Jack S. Blanton Mus. Art (formerly Archer M. Huntington Art Gallery), Austin, 1975—, 64 Beds Project for Homeless and Hungry, Austin, 1989—; mem. search com. for dir., U. Tex. Press, 1991. Troop leader Girl Scouts Am., Austin, 1970-73; officer PTA, Austin, 1964-73. Mem.: Seton Med. Ctr. Aux., Althenoi, Smithsonian Instn., Nat. Geog. Soc., Phi Beta Kappa, Sigma Sigma Sigma, Kappa Delta Pi. Democrat. Presbyterian. Avocations: reading, gardening, piano, painting, drawing. Home: 3301 Perry Ln Austin TX 78731-5330

SPIER, PAULA, retired dean; BA, Antioch Coll., 1945; MA, Ohio State U., 1968; LLD, Antioch U. Assoc. Antioch Edn. Abroad, 1957—77; dir. student programs Antioch Internat., 1977—79, dean, 1979—81, acad. dean, 1981—85, dean emerita, 1985—. Presenter, spkr. in field; mem. Fulbright screening com., German Exch. Project Coun. on Internat. Exch. of Scholars, 1982—83, chair, 1983; bd. dirs. Coun. on Internat. Ednl. Exch., 1975—79, 1981—85, profl. affairs com., 1983—85, jr. coll. com., 1983—84, exec. coord., 1987—88, mem. editl. bd., 1986—94; mem. Pres.' a cabinet Antioch U., 1979—81, univ. coun., 1978—79; bd. dirs. Alumni Assn., Antioch Coll., 1995—, scholarship com., 1995—, strategic planning task force, 1996—98, coop. edn. task force, 1997—98, edn. abroad task force, 1986—88, 1998—. Contbr. articles to profl. jours. Recipient Award for Svc. to Profession of Internat. Edn., Coun. on Internat. Ednl. Exch., 1985; scholar Fulbright, 1981. Mem.: Gt. Lakes Colls. Assn. (urban studies, Japan, India, Scotland, Yugoslavia adv. coms. 1977—85, chair Japan adv. com. 1978—82), Assn. Internat. Educators (life; region VI Sect. on U.S. Students Abroad (SECUSSA) rep. 1977—78, nat. team SECUSSA 1979—81, commn. on profl. devel. 1979—81, task force on women in internat. devel. 1982, personnel com. 1985—88, field svc. cons. 1981—, bd. dirs. 1982—85, task force on info. sharing 1984—86, liaison com. 1983—85, chair commn. on info. svcs. 1982—85, Leo Dowling award of Excellence 1990).

SPIES, PHYLLIS BOVA, information services company executive; b. Syracuse, N.Y., Nov. 10, 1949; d. Ralph Anthony and Elizabeth Margaret (Caputo) Bova; m. John William Spies, June 28, 1980; children: Fletcher, Logan. BA in Art History, SUNY, Cortland, 1971; MLS in Libr. and Info. Sci., Syracuse U., 1972. Libr. systems analyst Ohio Coll. Library Ctr., Columbus, 1973-78; mgr. libr. systems analysis OCLC Online Computer Libr. Ctr., Dublin, Ohio, 1978-83, div. v.p., 1983-89, v.p. internat., 1989-92, v.p. mem. svcs., sales and internat., 1992—, OCLC Online Computer LIbr. Ctr., Dublin, Ohio, 1994-98, v.p. worldwide sales, 1998—. Trustee Maps Micrographic Preservation Svc., Bethlehem, Pa., 1990—. Contbr. articles to profl. jours. Mem. Columbus Coun. World Affairs. Fellow The Gaylord Co., 1971. Mem. ALA, Internat. Fedn. Libr. Assns., Dublin Women in Bus. Avocations: gardening, cooking. Office: Online Computer Libr Ctr 6565 Frantz Rd Dublin OH 43017-5308

SPIGLER, KAREN JENSEN, lawyer, accountant; d. Earl E. and Kathy Jensen; m. Harvey N. Spigler, Aug. 14, 1989; children: Paul Michael Jensen, Kris Kelly. BS, U. Tex., 1984, MA in Internat. Mgmt., 1986, MBA, 1990; JD, U. Miami, 1999, LLM, 2000. CPA Tex., 1986, S.C., 1989, Fla., 1991; bar: Fla. 1999. Pvt. practice CPA, Plantation, Fla., 1986—; pvt. practice law, 1999—. Mng. editor: U. Miami Entertainment and Sports Law Rev. Office: Law Firm Karen Spigler LLC 499 NW 70th Ave #105 Plantation FL 33317 E-mail: kspigler@justice.com.

SPILIOTIS, JOYCE A. state legislator; State rep. Mass. House, 2003—. Mem. Mass. Dem. State Com., N. Shore Labor Coun.; counilor-at-large City of Peabody; trustee City of Peabody Libr., 1986—88. Democrat. Office: State House Rm 540 Boston MA 02133

SPILKA, KAREN, state legislator, lawyer; BS in Social Work, Cornell U.; JD, Northeastern U. Sch. Law. State rep. Mass. House, 2001—. Bd. dirs. Metro West Econ. Rsch. Ctr., Metro West YMCA; Ashland Sch. Com.; Ashland Fiscal Affaris Com.; bd. dirs. So. Middlesex Assn. for Retarded Citizens. Mem.: Indsl. Relations Rsch. Assn., Mass. Bar Assn., Boston Bar Assn. Democrat. Office: Rm 443 State House Boston MA 02133 Office Phone: 617-722-2460.

SPILKER, LINDA JOYCE, aerospace scientist; b. Mpls., Apr. 26, 1955; d. Arthur Elzear and Bonnie Joy (Jansen) Bies; m. John Leonard Horn, Jr., July 31, 1976 (div.); children: Jennifer, Jessica; m. Thomas Richard Spilker, 1997. BA in Physics, Calif. State U., Fullerton, 1977; MS in Physics, Calif. State U., L.A., 1983; PhD in Geophysics and Space Physics, UCLA, 1992. Rep. Voyager Infrared Radiometer and Spectrometer expt. Jet Propulsion Lab., Pasadena, Calif., 1977-90, sci. assoc. Voyager Photopolarimeter, 1984-90, sc. assoc. Voyager Infrared Radiometer and Spectrometer, 1988-90, study scientist Cassini asst., 1988-90, co-investigator Cassini Composite Infrared Spectrometer, 1990—, dep. project scientist Cassini mission, 1990—, prin. investigator planetary geology and geophysics, 1993—. Mem. planetary sci. data steering group NASA, Washington, 1991-95, adv. coun. for planetary data sys. ring node, Moffett Field, Calif., 1990—. Contbr. chpt. Van Nostrand Encyclopedia of Planetary Science, 1994; contbr. jour. articles Icarus. Pres. North San Gabriel Valley Dem. Club, Monrovia, Calif., 1992-94. Named to Hall of Fame, Placentia-Yorba Linda Unified Sch. Dist., 1998—99; recipient Exceptional Service medal, NASA, 1990, Sci. Achievement award, 1992, Disting. Alumna award, Calif. State U., 1996. Mem. AAAS, Divsn. of Planetary Sci. Democrat. Presbyterian. Avocations: hiking, astronomical observing, piano, jogging. Home: 457 Granite Ave Monrovia CA 91016-2324 Office: Jet Propulsion Lab MS 230-205 4800 Oak Grove Dr Pasadena CA 91109-8001 E-mail: Linda.J.Spilker@jpl.nasa.gov.

SPILLETT, ROXANNE, social services administrator; 1 son, Keith. BA in Edn., SUNY; postgrad., St. Lawrence U., Hunter Coll., N.Y. Tchr., curriculum writer N.Y. State Schs., 1971-73; program specialist Girl Scouts U.S.A., 1973; dir. nat. health project Boys & Girls Clubs Am., Atlanta, 1978-79, dir. program svcs., 1979-91, asst. nat. dir. program svcs., 1991-1995, v.p. N.E. regional office, 1995, acting pres., 1995-96, pres., 1996—. Vice chair bd. dirs. Nat. Assembly of Health and Human Svc. Orgns. Office: Boys & Girls Clubs Am 1230 W Peachtree St NW Atlanta GA 30309-3404*

SPILLMAN, JANE SHADEL, curator, researcher, writer; b. Huntsville, Ala., Apr. 30, 1942; d. Marvin and Elizabeth (Russell) Shadel; m. Don Lewis Spillman, Feb. 18, 1973 (dec. Jan. 1999); children: K. Elizabeth, Samuel Shadel. AB, Vassar Coll., 1964; MA, SUNY, 1965. Rsch. asst. Corning (N.Y.) Mus. Glass, 1965-70, asst. curator, 1971-73, assoc. curator Am. glass, 1974-77, curator, 1978—, head of curatorial dept., 1994-99, dep. dir. collections, 1999—. Cons. The White House Curator's Office, Washington, 1987-90, other museums. Author: Complete Cut and Engraved Glass of Corning, 1979, rev. edit., 1997, Knopf Collectors Guide to Glass, Vol. 1, 1982, Vol. 2, 1983, White House Glassware, 1989, Masterpieces of American Glass, 1990, The American Cut Glass Industry: T.G. Hawkes and His Competitors, 1996, also 6 other books, numerous articles; editor The Glass Club Bull., 1999—. Mem. Am. Assn. Mus. (chairperson curators com. 1989-93), Nat. Early Am. Glass Club (bd. dirs. 1989-95), Glass Circle of London. Office: Corning Mus Glass 1 Museum Way Corning NY 14830-2253

SPILLMAN, MARJORIE ROSE, producer, dancer; b. Norfolk, Va., Jan. 5, 1958; d. William Bert and Rose Marjorie (Naperski) S.; m. David E. Marks, Apr. 4, 1985 (dec. July 1997); children: F. Oscar Marks, Miranda Rose. AS, Mt. Ida Jr. Coll., 1974; CT, Northeastern U., 1975; BS in Nursing, U. Mass., 1977. RN, Mass. Charge nurse VA Med. Ctr., Northampton, Mass., 1977-82; dancer N.E. Am. Ballet, Northampton, 1982, Ballet Theater Sch., Springfield, Mass., 1982-84, Smith Coll., Northampton, 1984-96; sales rep. Winthrop Pharm., N.Y.C., 1982-94, Nycomed, N.Y.C., 1994-96; dir. mktg. and devel. The Northampton Ctr. for the Arts, 1997. Prin. dancer Project Opera, Northampton, 1984—86; dancer Polobulus East St. Dance, Hadley, Mass., 1985; dance and theatre reviewer Holyoke T. Telegram, 1991—92; theater critic Daily Hampshire Gazette, 1993—96; dance panelist Mass. Cultural Coun., 1998; curator The Refrigerator Door art exhibit Smith Coll., 1999—2001; prodr. Pioneer Valley Performing Arts H.S., 1998; founder Open Door Prodns., 1999; cons. Organic Trade Assn., 1999, New Eng. Artist Trust, 1999—; organizer Congl. Edn. Day in Washington, D.C.; tchr. Easthampton HS, 2000—. Dancer, creator part of Carmen in Carmen, 1985, Ruth St. Denis in the House of Ruth Ted and Martha, 1994; dancer, choreographer A Victorian Evening, 1986; dancer Nutcracker Ballet, Pioneer Valley Ballet, 1988; creator, prodr. The Halloween House at Sunnyside, 1990, producing dir., 1991-92; actor, author play Mary P. Wells Smith Narrates, 1987; founder, prodr., dir. Northampton Children's Theater, 1993—; prodr. Northampton's First Night Children's Parade, 1996, dir. First Night Northampton, 1997-98, Saturday As a Work of Art—Summer Series, 1997; contbg. writer Healthy & Natural Mag. Theater panelist Mass. Cultural Coun., 1997, 2000; devel. com. Cooley Dickerson Hosp., 1999; religious tchr. St. Mary of the Assumption, 2001-04. Democrat. Roman Catholic.

SPILMAN, PATRICIA, artist, educator; b. Charlottesville, Va., Oct. 3, 1930; d. Harry Franklin and Katherine Elizabeth (Alexander) Black; m. William Bruce Spilman, Feb. 3, 1951 (dec. May 1987); children: Rebecca, Elizabeth, Barbara, William. BA, Madison Coll., 1969, MEd, 1971. Art tchr. Stuarts Draft (Va.) H.S., 1969-86; artist in residence Augusta County Schs., Fishersville, Va., 1987—. Pvt. tchr. art, Waynesboro, Va., 1986—; docent Shenandoah Valley Art Ctr., Waynesboro, 1986—. Mem. Main St. U. Meth. Ch., Waynesboro; troop leader Girl Scouts U.S., 1958-66. Mem. Nat. Assn. Women Artists, Am. Inst. Fgn. Study (travel tchr. 1977-83), Va. Watercolor Soc., Shenandoah Valley Art Ctr., Shenandoah Valley Watercolor Soc., Delta Kappa Gamma. Avocations: gardening, travel. Home: 1837 Cherokee Rd Waynesboro VA 22980-2228

SPIRA, PATRICIA GOODSITT, association executive; b. Milw. d. Lawrence Manfred and Ruth Pauline (Miller) Goodsitt; m. Marvin Alfred Spira, July 12, 1952; children: David, James, Ann, Ellen. BA in History, U. Wis., Milw., 1967. Dir. group sales Swan Theatre and Supper Club, Milw., 1962-63; mgr. box office Performing Arts Ctr., Milw., 1969-80; dir. devel. St. Louis Conservatory and Schs., 1980-81; pres. The Internat. Ticketing Assn., N.Y.C., 1981—2002; ret., 2002. Tchr. Creative Dramatics, Milw., 1962-66; adv. coun. Town Hall, N.Y.C., 1989—; bd. dirs. Theatre and Dance Co., N.Y.C., 1986-89. Bd. dirs. Milw. Chamber Music Soc., 1974-80, Soc. Preservation of Profl. Touring Entertainment History; chair bd. dirs. Great Am. Children's Theatre, 1977-80, bd. dirs. Sledgehammer Theatre, 2003—. Mem. Am. Soc. Assn. Execs. (cert.). Avocations: reading, travel, theater. Home: 645 Front St unit 607 San Diego CA 92101 E-mail: pspira@cox.net.

SPIRES, ROBERTA LYNN, small business owner; b. Gary, Ind., Sept. 4, 1952; d. Merle Russell and Kathryn Dias (Felts) Harris; m. Richard John Badovinich, Aug. 16, 1975 (div. 1989); m. Patrick Robert Spires, Mar. 14, 1992; 1 child, Zachary Robert. Grad. h.s., Griffith, Ind. Dep. clk. U.S. Bankruptcy Ct., Gary, 1970-80, chief dep. clk., 1980-97; owner, mgr. Spl. Touch, personal shopping svc., Griffith, 1997—; owner Specialized Secretarial Svcs., Highland, Ind., 1997-99, Special Touch Typing Svc., Griffith, 1999—. Mem. Fed. Ct. Clks. Assn., FBA (cert., lectr.). Democrat. Roman Catholic. Avocations: water skiing, boating, sewing, handcrafts, reading. Home and Office: 719 N Rueth Dr Griffith IN 46319-3817 Office Phone: 219-922-2877. Personal E-mail: RSpires799@aol.com.

SPIRN, MICHELE SOBEL, communications professional, writer; b. Newark, Jan. 26, 1943; d. Jack and Sylvia (Cohen) Sobel; m. Steven Frederick Spirn, Jan. 27, 1968; 1 child, Joshua. BA, Syracuse U., 1965; MFA, The New Sch., 1999. Creative dir. Planned Communications Svcs., N.Y.C., 1966-72, EDL Prodns., N.Y.C., 1972-73; free-lance writer Bklyn., 1973-83; dir. pub. rels. Nat. Coun. Jewish Women, N.Y.C., 1983-90, dir. communications, 1990-95; freelance writer Bklyn., 1995—. Adj. lectr. CUNY, Bklyn., 1977—81; instr. The New Sch., N.Y.C., 1999—, NYU, 2002—. Author: The Fast Shoes, 1985, The Boy Who Liked Green, 1985, The Know-Nothings, 1995; co-author: A Man Can Be..., 1981, A Know-Nothing Birthday, 1997, Birth Celebrations, 1998, New Year Celebrations, 1998; co-author: The Nutcracker, 1998, A Know-Nothing Halloween, 2000, The Know-Nothings Talk Turkey, 2000, The Bridges in London, 2000, All Washed Up, 2000, Racing To The Light, 2000, Wait Til The Midnight Hour, 2000, Jackie Joyner-Kersee, 2000, The Bridges in Paris, 2000, Race to the Sea, 2001, A Twist in Time, 2001, I Am the Turkey, 2004, The Bridges in Edinburgh, 2004, Cold-Blooded Creatures, 2004, Arachnids, 2004; editor, columnist Children's Entertainment Rev. mag., N.Y.C., 1982; columnist The Phoenix newspaper, Bklyn., 1983. Pres. Tenth St. Block Assn., Bklyn., 1989-91; vol. Model Media Program, Bklyn., 1985—. Recipient Silver medal for pub. svc. film N.Y. Internat. Film and TV Festival, 1972. Mem.: Authors Guild, Soc. Children's Book Writers and Illustrators, Mystery Writers Am. Avocations: reading, gardening.

SPIRO, ROSANN LEE, marketing professional, educator; b. Fort Wayne, Ind., Oct. 13, 1945; d. Samuel G. and Vivian Marie Spiro; m. Rockney G. Walters, June 10, 1990; children: Samantha G., Jennifer Lauren Walters, Christi Marie Walters. AB, Ind. U., 1967, MBA, 1969; PhD, U. of Ga., 1976. Prof. and chairperson Dept. of Mktg., Kelley Sch. of Bus., Ind. U., Bloomington, Ind., 1992—; vis. prof. Insitute of Mgmt., U. of Aarhus, Aarhus, Denmark, 1991—92, I.E.S.E., Barcelona, 2000. Author: (textbook) Management of a Salesforce, 11th edition; contbr. articles to profl. jours. Recipient Outstanding Article award, Pi Sigma Epsilon, 1981, 1996. Mem.: Am. Mktg. Assn. (chairperson of the bd. 1994—95, Ann. Excellence in Rsch. award 2002). Office: Kelley Sch of Business Indiana University Bloomington IN 47405

SPIRTOS, MARIA, magazine publisher; BS, U. So. Calif., 1988; postgrad., UCLA, 1997. CPA, Calif. Mem. audit staff Ernst & Young, LLP, 1988-93; dir. fin. and adminstrn. Winsford Corp., 1993-96, v.p., CFO, 1996—; pres. Am. Collegiate Network, Inc., pub. U, The Nat. Coll. Mag., 1997—. Office: 1800 Century Park E Ste 820 Los Angeles CA 90067-1511

SPITZ, BARBARA SALOMON, artist; b. Chgo., Jan. 8, 1926; d. Fred B. and Sadie (Lorch) Salomon; m. Lawrence S. Spitz, Mar. 19, 1949; children— Thomas R., Linda J., Joanne L. AB, Brown U., 1947; student, Art Inst. Chgo., 1942-43, R.I. Sch. Design, 1945. One-woman exhbns. include Benjamin Galleries, Chgo., 1971, 73, Kunsthaus Buhler, Stuttgart, Germany, 1973, Van Straaten Gallery, Chgo., 1976, 80, Elca London Studio, Montreal, Que., Can., 1977, Loyola U. Chgo., 1988, Schneider, Bluhm, Loeb gallery, Chgo., 1993, Newport Beach Pub. Lib., 2002, The Ctr. Gallery, 1994; group exhibitions include Am. Acad. Arts and Letters, Library of Congress traveling print exhbn., Tokyo Cen. Mus. Arts, Nat. Acad. Design, NYC, Pratt Graphic Ctr., Honolulu Acad. Arts, Wadsworth Atheneum, Nat. Aperture, 1986—, Laguna Art Mus., others; represented in permanent collections, Phila. Mus. Art, DeCordova Mus., Okla. Art Ctr., Milw. Art Ctr., Los Angeles County Mus. Art, Art Inst. Chgo., Portland Mus. Art, med. arts program UCLA, Block Mus./Northwestern U., Smart Mus./U. Chgo. Vice-chmn. Chgo. area Brown U. Bicentennial Drive; treas. Hearing and Speech Rehab. Ctr., Michael Reese Hosp., 1960; fine arts patron bd. Newport Harbor Art Mus. Mem. Print Club Phila., Boston Printmakers, Arts Club of Chgo., Soc. Am. Graphic Artists. Address: 1106 Somerset Ln Newport Beach CA 92660-5629 E-mail: bsslss@aol.com.

SPITZE, GLENYS SMITH, retired educator; b. Rozel, Kans., May 20, 1919; d. Harry H. and Mary Louisa (Mishler) Smith; m. LeRoy A. Spitze, Dec. 31, 1942 (dec. Nov. 1995); children: Randall LeRoy, Kevin Lance, Kimett Alvin, Terril Christian, Shawn Smith; 1 fosterchild, Theo Ritz-Spitze. Cert. tchg., U. Kans., 1939; AA, San Jose (Calif.) City Coll., 1963; BA in Psychology, San Jose State U., 1965, MA in Child Devel., 1968. Cert. tchr., counselor, Calif. Elem. sch. tchr. Topeka County Schs., Richland, Kans., 1939-40, Kinsley (Kans.) Pub. Schs., 1940-42; presch. substitute tchr. AAUW Kindergarten, Newark, Ohio, 1945—46; presch. tchr. Meth. Ch. Facility, Campbell, Calif., 1956-58; guest lectr. Govt. Sch. Social Work, Colombo, Sri Lanka, 1965-66; instr. man-woman relationship San Jose State Free U., 1966-67; child devel. lab. psychol. examiner Child Labs San Jose State U., 1967-68; pvt. informal practice tchr., counselor, cons. San Jose, Kailua, Hawaii. Vocal music dir. grades 1-3 Southside Sch., 1940-41; 6th dist. Calif. Congress Parent-Tchrs. Social Welfare dir., officer 6th dist. com. Calif. Coun. on Crime and Delinquency, San Jose, 1956-62; mem. kindergarten com. AAUW, Newark, Ohio, 1945-46; coord. Sangha Symposium, Asian Philosophy Club, San Jose State U., 1964-65; lectr. in field. Contbr. articles, poems to profl. publs. Hon. del. Gov. Brown's Conf. on Prevention of Juvenile Delinquency, Sacramento, 1963; co-organizer Post Polio Support Group, Kailua-Kona, HI, 2000. Mem. Psi Chi. Avocations: writing, reading, swimming, snorkeling, anthropology and archeology travel. Home: 78-6800 Alii Dr KKSRC 5-103 Kailua Kona HI 96740-4421 Home (Summer): 311 E Bowman Woodland Park CO 80863 also: PO Gen Delivery Woodland Park CO 80863 E-mail: GMGlenys@webtv.net.

SPIVAK, CAROL, investment manager, philanthropist; b. L.A., Dec. 27, 1934; d. Ralph and Muriel Dorothy (Wexler) DeSure; m. Roy Andrew Moss, Feb. 14, 1954 (dec. Dec. 1982); 1 child, Steven Moss; m. Julius Spivak, Mar. 28, 1987. AA, Santa Monica Coll., 1983; BA, UCLA, 1998. Established trust fund Guide Dogs for the Blind, Inc., San Rafael, Calif., 1989—; major. contbr. Guide Dogs of the Desert, Palm Springs, Calif., 1995—; established Carol Moss Spivak Cell Imaging Facility, Brain Rsch. Inst. of UCLA, 1998—. Established cancer care unit at Stanford U. Hosp., Palo Alto, Calif., 1991. Author: Cathy's Sandy, 1947. Trustee UCLA Found., 1992; bd. dirs. United Hostesses' Charities; rec. sec. cardiology rsch. support group at Cedars Sinai Hosp. Avocation: raising orchids.

SPIVAK, JACQUE R. bank executive; b. San Francisco, Nov. 5, 1929; d. Robert Morris and Sadonia Clardine Breistein; m. Herbert Spivak, Aug. 26, 1960; children: Susan, Donald, Joel, Sheri. BS, U. So. Calif., 1949, MS, 1950, MBA, 1959. Mgr. Internat. Escrow, Inc., L.A., 1960-65, Greater L.A. Investment Co., 1965-75; mgr. escrow Transam. Title Ins. Co., L.A., 1975-78; mgr. escrow, asst. v.p. Wells Fargo Bank, Beverly Hills, Calif., 1979-80; adminstr. escrow, v.p. 1st Pacific Bank, Beverly Hills, 1980-85; escrow adminstr. Century City Savs. & Loan Assn., L.A., 1986-87; pres. Prodrs. Escrow Corp., Beverly Hills, 1987—. Recipient award, PTA, Girl Scouts U.S., Jewish Fedn. L.A. Mem.: Inst. Trustees Sales Officers, Calif. Escrow Assn., Nat. Assn. Bank Women, Hadassah (nat. bd. dirs., pres. L.A. chpt., mem. Nat. Young Yudea Scholarship bur., mem. audit com., award). Republican. Jewish. Office: Producers Escrow Corp PO Box 5771 Beverly Hills CA 90209-5771

SPIVAK, JOAN CAROL, healthcare communications specialist; b. Phila., May 12, 1950; d. Jack and Evelyn Lee (Copelman) S.; m. John D. Goldman, May 17, 1980; children: Jesse, Marcus. AB, Barnard Coll., 1972; M of Health Scis., Johns Hopkins U., 1980. Freelance writer, N.Y.C., 1980-84; project dir. Impact Med. Communication, N.Y.C., 1984-87; exec. v.p., gen. mgr. health and sci. strategies Edelman Worldwide, N.Y.C., 1987—2002; pres. Prime Medica, Inc., 2002—. Co-author: (pamphlet) Lead: New Perspectives on an Old Problem, 1978; contbr. The Book of Health, 1981, articles to profl. jours. Bd. dirs. May O'Donnell Dance Co., N.Y.C., 1983-85, Chamber Ballet U.S.A., N.Y.C., 1985-87, Nat. Child Labor Commn., 1991—, Cases, 1995—. Mem. N.Y. Acad. Sci. Democrat. Jewish. Avocations: pottery, sailing. Office Phone: 212-921-1250. E-mail: joan.spivak@prime-medica.com.

SPIVEY, (DOLORES) JOANNE, retired music educator; b. Ames, Iowa, Aug. 14, 1930; d. James Potter Smith and Pruedence Beatrice Welty Smith; m. Willard Henry Spivey, Aug. 13, 1955; children: Deborah Ann, James

Calvin. B in Music Edn., U. Nebr., 1952; M in Secondary Edn., No. Ill. U., 1980. Sales mgr. warehousing Beauty Counselor Cosmetic Co., Grosse Point, Mich., 1952; music tchr. choral and gen. Scottsbluff (Nebr.) Sch. Dist., 1952—53; music tchr., dept. head jr. high Pueblo (Colo.) Sch. Dist., 1953—55; music tchr. jr. high Glen Ellyn (Ill.) Sch. Dist., 1955—56; music tchr. Elmwood Park (Ill.) Sch. Dist., Elgin (Ill.) Acad., 1978—83, Schaumburg (Ill.) Elem., 1984—92. Bd. mem. jr. high music Ill. State Music Educators, 1983—92. Bd. dir. Tenn. State PEO, 1997—, pres. bd., 2003—. Mem.: Music Educators Nat. Conf., Am. Choral Dirs. Assn. Republican. Presbyterian. Avocations: track and field, needlecrafts, reading, gardening, cooking. Home: 696 Laurel Cir Crossville TN 38555

SPLICHAL, CHRISTINE, restaurant owner; m. Joachim Splichal. BBA, Ecole Superieure de Commerce, Poitiers, France, 1982; MBA, Am. Grad. Sch. Internat. Mgmt., Phoenix, 1983. Formerly with Pershing Sq. Mgmt. Assn., L.A.; co-owner Patina Restaurant, L.A., 1989—, Pinot Bistro, Cafe Pinot, Pinot Hollywood. Recipient Hollywood Woman of Distinction award, L.A. Coun. Mem. Jackie Goldberg and U.S. Senator Barbara Boxer, 1996. Office: Patina Restaurant 5955 Melrose Ave Los Angeles CA 90038

SPOFFORD, SALLY (SALLY HYSLOP), artist; b. N.Y.C., Aug. 20, 1929; d. George Hall and Esther (McNaull) Hyslop; m. Gavin Spofford, Mar. 11, 1950 (dec. Jan. 1976); children: Lizabeth Spofford Smith, Leslie Spofford Russell. Student, The China Inst., N.Y.C., 1949, The Art Students League, 1950; BA with high honors, Swarthmore Coll., 1952. Instr. Somerset Art Assn., Peapack, N.J., 1978-95, Hunterdon Mus. Art, Clinton, N.J., 1985—; adv. bd., lectr. Apollo Muses, Inc., Gladstone, N.J.; trustee Artshowcase, Inc. One-woman shows include Riverside Studio, Pottersville, N.J., 1985, Morris Mus., Morristown, N.J. 1989, Schering-Plough Gallery, Madison, N.J., 1989, Phoenix Gallery, N.Y.C., 1990, Robin Hutchins Gallery, Maplewood, N.J., 1992, Berlex Labs. Corp. Office, Wayne, N.J., 1992, Hunterdon Mus. Art, Clinton, 1993, 2003, Newark Acad., Livingston, N.J., 1997, Simon Gallery, Morristown, 2004; exhibited in group shows at Hickory (N.C.) Mus., 1983, Purdue U., 1983, Monmouth (N.J.), 1984, Nabisco Brands Gallery, East Hanover, N.J., 1985, 89, Hunterdon Mus. Art, 1988, 93, 99, Schering-Plough Gallery, Madison, 1988, Morris Mus., Morristown, 1989, Montclair (N.J.) State U., 1995, Williams Gallery, Princeton, N.J., 1997, Monmouth Mus., Lincroft, N.J., 1998, Newark Acad., Livingston, 2000; represented in permanent collections N.J. State Mus., Trenton, Newark Mus., Morris Mus., Morristown. Painting residency fellow Vt. Studio Ctr., 1992. Mem. Assoc. Artists N.J. (pres. 1985-87), N.J. Watercolor Soc., Federated Art Assns. of N.J. (panel mem. 1985, demonstrator 1991). Home: PO Box 443 Bernardsville NJ 07924-0443

SPRACHER, NANCY A. psychotherapist; b. Seattle, Wash., July 4, 1940; d. Walter Joseph and Anita Kathleen Brown; m. Larry Frazier, Aug 24, 1962 (div. Nov. 1979); children: Larry K., Jay W., Susannah J.; m. Thomas Peter Utterback, July 24, 1999. RN, Sacred Heart Sch. Nursing, 1961; BA in Commn., Marylhurst Coll., 1979; MA in Counseling Psychology, Vt. Coll./Norwich U., 1992. RN; cert. mental health counselor. RN various hosps. and clinics, 1961-85; coll. instr. Portland State U., 1979-81; psychiat. nurse Yakima (Wash.) Valley Meml. Hosp., 1990—; psychiatric nurse Ctrl. Wash. Comprehensive Mental Health, Yakima, 1987-92; psychotherapist pvt. practice, Yakima, 1993—. Cons. Womens Health Ctr., Yakima, 1994—; instr. Yakima Valley Cmty. Coll., 1988-94; pub. spkr. women's issues. Co-author: (workbook) Structured Experiences in Human Communications, 1979; author: (manual) How to Teach the Adult Learner, 1983. Adv. bd. Womens Program, Yakima Valley Cmty. Coll., 1999; founder Women Together, Yakima, Wash., 1994—. Recipient tchg. asst. Portland State U., 1979-80. Avocations: drawing, painting, reading, theater. Office: 37 House Profl Ctr 4002 Englewood Ave Ste 202 Yakima WA 98908-4320

SPRADLEY, LOLA, state representative; b. Colo., June 28, 1946; married; 1 child. BA, BS, Regis Coll. Republican. Methodist. Office: State Capitol # 246 200 E Colfax Ave Denver CO 30386

SPRAGUE, AMARIS JEANNE, real estate broker; b. Jackson, Mich., Feb. 18, 1935; d. Leslie Markham and Blanche Lorraine (Basnaw) Reed; m. John M. Vetterling, Oct. 1985; children by previous marriage, Anthony John, James Stuart. Student, Mich. State U., 1952-53; BS, Colo. State U., 1965. Cert. real estate broker. Real estate sales Seibel and Benedict Realty, Ft. Collins, Colo., 1968-69; salesman Realty Brokers Exch., Ft. Collins, 1969-72; broker, pres. Sprague and Assocs., Inc., Realtors, Ft. Collins, 1972-80; broker assoc. Van Schaack & Co., Ft. Collins, 1980-86; broker, ptnr. The Group, Inc., 1986—. Dir. Univ. Nat. Bank. Mem. bus. adv. council Colo. State U., 1976-84, chmn. 1979-80, mem. adv. council Coll. of Engring., 1981. Named Honor Alumni, Colo. State U., 1983. Mem. Nat. Assn. Realtors, Colo. Assn. Realtors, Ft. Collins Bd. Realtors, Ft. Collins C. of C. (bd. dirs. 1978-84, pres. 1982-83). Republican. Epsicopalian. Home: PO Box 475 Fort Collins CO 80522-0475 Office: 401 W Mulberry St Fort Collins CO 80521-2839

SPRAGUE, ANN LOUISE, space scientist; b. Bellfonte, Pa., Feb. 25, 1946; d. David Carpenter and Opal (Wheat) S.; m. Donald M. Hunten, 1995. BA in Geology, Syracuse U., 1969; MA, Boston U., 1980; PhD, U. Ariz., 1990. Sci. tchr. Selinsgrove Mid. Sch., 1970-79; space scientist Lunar and Planetary Lab. U. Ariz., Tucson, 1990—. Mem. Com. Lunar and Planetary Exploration (COMPLEX) NRC, 2000—. Contbg. author: Caloris Basin: An Enhanced Source for Potassium in Mercury's Atmosphere, 1990, Sulfur at Mercury, Elemental at the Poles and Sulfides in the Regolith, 1995, Water Brought In to Jupiter's Atmosphere by Fragments R and W of Comet SL-9, 1996, Distribution and Abundance of Sodium in Mercury's Atmosphere, 1985-1988, 1997, Exploring Mercury: The Iron Planet, 2003; editl. bd. ICARUS. Mem. AAAS, Internat. Astron. Union, Am. Astron. Soc. (com. divsn. planetary scis.), Am. Geophys. Union. Office: U Ariz Lunar & Planetary Lab Tucson AZ 85721-0001 Office Phone: 520-621-2282. E-mail: sprague@lpl.arizona.edn.

SPRAGUE, JO ANN, state legislator; b. Nashville, Nov. 3, 1931; m. Warren G. Sprague; 6 children. BA, U. Mass., 1980. Mem. Mass. Ho. of Reps., Boston, 1992-98, mem. capital budget com., 1990-92; mem. Mass. Senate, 1998—. Mem. Walpole Prison Adv. Com., 1970-92, Rep. Town Meeting, 1979—. Bd. trustees Walpole Scholar Found., 1990-92; bd. advisors NE Sinai Hosp., 1999—. 2d lt. U.S. Army, 1950-53. Mem. Walpole Vis. Nurses Assn. (bd. dirs. 1989-92), Walpole LVW, Norfolk Am. Legion (Post No. 335). Republican. Home: 305 Elm St Walpole MA 02081-1903 Office: Room 206 State House Boston MA 02133 E-mail: jsprague@senate.state.ma.us.

SPRAGUE, MARCIA SCOVEL, small business owner; b. Rockford, Ill., Aug. 4, 1957; d. Mary Alice and Ward Norman Scovel; m. Tom K Sprague, Nov. 2, 1991; children: Kayla Rachon, Devi Mackenzie. BS in sociology, Ctrl. Mich. U., 1975—79. Teaching K-12 Music State of NH., 2003, lic. Massage Therapist Conn., 1993, Neuro-Linguistic Programming Mass., 1988, Touch for Health Practitioner Touch for Health, Internat., Switzerland, 1996, lic. Massage Therapist NH., 1995, Reike I John Harvey Gray, Mass., 1992, Foot Reflexology Inst. of Foot Reflexology, Fla., 1981, Bach Flower Practitioner Ellon, USA, 1983, Reike 2 NH., 1996. Tchr. Peace Corps, Sierra Leone, 1979—80; psychiat. counselor Battle Creek Sanitarium, Battle Creek, Mich., 1981—82; educator - developed and taught assertiveness classes at mt. holyoke coll., amherst coll., belchertown state sch., and cmty. edn. Self-employed, Hadley, Mass., 1985—86; program dir. Gardner Social Services, Gardner, Mass., 1986—88; counselor Conn. Halfway Ho., Hartford, Conn., 1989—90, Beech Hill Hosp., Dublin, NH, 1990—91; lic. massage therapist self-employed, New Haven, 1993—94, Self-employed, Concord, NH, 1995—99; music tchr. Pembroke Sch. Dist., Pembroke, NH, 1999—2003; educator/cons. Self-employed, Concord, NH, 2002—. Educator - touch for health self-employed, Concord, NH, 1996—98; educator - pregnancy massage Yale-New Haven Hosp., New Haven, 1992—93; family mediator Northampton Social Services, Mass., 1985—87; educator - profl. tng. for mental health agencies United Way Goodwill, Grand Rapids, Mich., 1984—85. Dir. (kids are authors - book writing contest for second and fourth graders) Scholastic, Concord, NH, 2001—02; editor and writer of cmty. newsletter Lamplighters, Concord, NH, 1995—97; mentor to a six week speechcrafters class Toastmasters Internat., Concord, NH, 2003—03; educator - commn. and pub. speaking classes Cinderella Modeling, Manchester, NH, 2003—03; girl scout leader Girl Scouts, Concord, NH, 2000—02; bell choir dir. for adult and youth handbell choirs Wesley United Meth. Ch., Concord, NH, 1995—2001; bell choir dir. Branford United Meth. Ch., Conn., 1993—94; lay spkr. First United Meth. Ch., Concord, NH, 1998—, youth leader, 2000—01; camp program dir. Wanakee Meth. Camp, Meredith, NH, 2000—03. Recipient Advanced Toastmaster, Silver level, Competent Leader, Toastmasters Internat. Mem.: Toastmasters Internat. (sec.club #2112 2002—03, v.p. of membership, club #6954 2003—, recipient first place Eval. and Humorous Speech contests Area Level 2003). Avocations: biking, writing, storytelling. Home: 157 Mountain Rd Concord NH 03301 Personal E-mail: mtkdo@aol.com.

SPRAGUE, MARY GABRIELLE, lawyer; b. Phila., Oct. 7, 1957; AB summa cum laude, Harvard U., 1979; JD, Yale U., 1983. Bar: Colo. 1984, D.C. 1992. Law clk. to Hon. Jim R. Carrigan U.S. Dist. Ct. Colo., 1984-85; law clk. to Hon. Byron R. White U.S. Supreme Ct., Washington, 1986-87; ptnr. Arnold & Porter, Washington. Mem. Phi Beta Kappa. Office: Arnold & Porter 555 12th St NW Washington DC 20004-1206

SPRANZA, MAUREEN, music educator, elementary school educator; d. Donald Thomas and Carol Wojciechowski Spranza; m. Jesse Edward Doron, Feb. 12, 1995 (div. Apr. 2003); children: Natasha Jade Doron, Haley Sage Doron. MusB, Berklee Coll. Music, 1987; MFA, Mills Coll., 1991. Single subject music tchg. credential Calif., 1999. Profl. freelance musician, Boston, 1984—95, San Leandro, Calif., 1984—95; ind. music tchr., 1990—97; music tchr. San Lorenzo (Calif.) Unified Sch. Dist., 1997—. Vol. Girls Scouts Am., 1999—, St. Leander Cath. Ch., San Leandro, 2003. Mem.: Tech. Inst. Music Educators, Music Educators Nat. Conf. Home: 990 Alice Ave San Leandro CA 94577 Office: Lorenzo Manor Elem 18250 Bengal Ave Hayward CA 94541

SPRAYBERRY, ROSLYN RAYE, retired secondary school educator; b. Newnan, Ga., June 29, 1942; d. Henry Ray and Grace (Bernhard) S. BA, Valdosta State Coll., 1964; MA in Teaching, Ga. State U., 1976, EdS in Spanish, 1988; EdD, Nova U., 1993. Cert. tchr., Ga. Tchr. history Griffin (Ga.) High Sch., 1964-65; tchr. 6th grade Beaverbrook Elem. Sch., Griffin, 1965-66; tchr. Spanish, chair fgn. lang. dept. Forest Park (Ga.) High Sch., 1969-77, Riverdale (Ga.) High Sch., 1977-99; ret., 1999. Correlator Harcourt, Brace, Jovanovich, 1989; adv. bd. So. Conf. Lang. Teaching, 1992-99; lectr. and speaker in field. Contbr. articles to The Edn. Resource Info. Ctr. Clearinghouse on Langs. and Linguistics, Ctr. for Applied Linguistics, Washington; designed courses for the Gifted, Ga. Dept. of Edn. Convener Acad. Alliances Atlanta II, Clayton County, Ga., 1982-99; advisor, workshop leader Ga. Fgn. Lang. Camp, Atlanta, 1983; dir. Clayton County Fgn. Lang. Festival, 1990-91. Recipient STAR Tchr. award Ga. C. of C., 1982; Fulbright-Hays scholar, 1978; NEH grantee, 1977, 84. Mem. NEA, Am. Coun. Tchrs. Fgn. Langs., Am. Assn. Tchrs. Spanish and Portuguese, Ga. Assn. Educators, Fgn. Lang. Assn. Ga. (treas. 1977-85, assoc. editor jour. 1981-86, Tchr. of Yr. award 1976), Clayton County Edn. Assn., So. Conf. Lang. Teaching, KPS Leadership Specialists (co-founder 1993). Methodist. Avocations: guitar playing, traveling, reading, writing. Home: 104 Hickory Trail Stockbridge GA 30281-7361

SPRIESER, JUDITH A. food products company executive; BA in Linguistics, MBA in Fin., Northwestern U. CPA, Ill., 1982. Comml. banker Harris Bank, Chgo., 1974-81; dir. treasury ops. Esmark, 1981-84; asst. treas. internat. Nalco Chem. Co., 1984-87; asst. treas. corp. fin. Sara Lee Corp., 1987-90; sr. v.p., CFO Sara Lee Bakery N.Am., 1990-93, pres., CEO, 1993-94; sr. v.p., CFO Sara Lee Corp., 1994-99, CEO, Foods and Food Svc., 2000-2001; CEO Transora, Chgo., 2001—. Bd. dirs. USG Corp. Bd. dirs. Hinsdale Hosp. Found.; trustee Northwestern U. Mem. AICPA, Chgo. Network, Young Pres. Orgn., Chgo. coun. Fgn. Rels., Econ. Club, Conf. Bd. Coun. Fin. Execs. Office: 547 W Jackson Blvd Ste 900 Chicago IL 60661-5717

SPRINCE, LEILA JOY, librarian; b. Toronto, Ont., Can., July 10, 1936; came to U.S., 1981; d. Harry and Anna Helen Caller; children: Alan Rosenthal, Joel Rosenthal; m. Arnold Joel Sprince, Feb. 16, 1982 BA, U. Toronto, 1957, B of Edn., 1962; MA, U. South Fla., 1987. Cert. tchr., Ont. Ballet dancer Volkoff Can. Ballet, Toronto, 1953-54; tchr. h.s. North York Bd. Edn., Toronto, 1958-60; libr. Broward County Libr. Sys., Plantation, Fla., 1987-88, 91-93, Margate, Fla., 1988-91, head youth svcs. Coconut Creek, Fla., 1996—2001; ret., 2001. Advisor Omnigraphics Pub., Detroit, 1993—; cons. Gale/U*X*L* Pubs., N.Y.C., 1996—; state facilitator summer programs State Libr. Fla., 1993. Contbr. articles to profl. jours. Mem. nat. children and youth membership orgns. outreach com. ALA/ALSC, 2001—. Mem. ALA (Best Books for Young Adult Cmty. spkr. 1989, 90), Fla. Libr. Assn. (spkr.), B'nai B'rith Women (fin. sec. 1983, pres. 1984, 85), Phi Kappa Phi, Beta Phi Mu. Democrat. Jewish. Avocations: music/dance, computers, traveling, history. Personal E-mail: ajsprince@aol.com.

SPRING, BARBARA ETHEL, sculptor; b. Theydon Bois, Essex, Eng., Feb. 16, 1917; came to U.S., 1946; d. Edward Alexander and Iris Maud (Roberts) Jackson; m. William Whelan Spring, Oct. 9, 1942; children: Cynthia, Frances. Student, Gads Hill Pl., Gravesend Sch. Art, Ctrl. Sch. Art London. Tchr. art Hillwood Sch., San Francisco. One man shows include Oakland (Calif.) Mus. Sculpture Ct., 1997, Hawthorne Gallery, Big Sur, Calif., 1996, John Natsoulas Gallery, Davis, Calif., 1995, Fine Arts Bldg., L.A., 1994, William Sawyer Gallery, San Francisco, 1992, 90, 87, 85, 82, 79, 76, 69, Charleston Heights Art Ctr., Las Vegas, Nev., 1990-91; exhibited in group shows at Berkeley Art Ctr., 1997, San Francisco Internat. Airport, 1995, 87, 86, 82, Garth Clark Gallery, L.A., 1995, Pacific Rim Sculpture Exhbn., Honolulu, 1994, Transamerica Pyramid, San Francisco, 1992, 89, Braunstein Quay Gallery, San Francisco, 1980; numerous pvt. collections. With WAAF, 1939-42. Home: Burns Creek Hwy One Big Sur CA 93920

SPRING, TERRI, political organization executive; BA, U. Wis., 1975. 2d vice chair Dem. Party—Wis., Madison, 1994-97, state chair, 1997; legis. asst. State Senate, Madison, 1996-00; state chair Dem. Party-Wis., Madison, 2000—. Mem. Assn. State Dem. Chairs. Office: 222 State St Ste 400 Madison WI 53703-2273

SPRINGER, LINDA, portfolio manager, controller; BS, Ursinus. Staff assoc. Coopers and Lybrand, 1977—79; exec. asst. to pres. Penn Mutual Life Ins. Co., Phila., 1986—87; asst. v.p. and prod. mgr. Penn Mut. Life Ins. Co., Phila., 1987—90, v.p. and prod. mgr., 1990—92; actuary Provident Mut. Life Ins. Co., Berwyn, Pa., 1992—95, asst. v.p. and actuary, 1995—96, v.p. and contr., 1996—2000, sr. v.p. and contr., 2001—02, counselor to the dep. dir. for mgmt., office mgmt. and budget, 2002—03. Achievements include The Senatge has confirmed Linda M. Springer as Controller of the fOffice of Fed. Fin. Mgmt. in the Office of Mgmt. and Budget. Office: New Exec Office Build 725 - 17th St NW, Rm 9013 Washington DC 20503

SPRINGER, MARLENE, university administrator, educator; b. Murfreesboro, Tenn., Nov. 16, 1937; d. Foster V. and Josephine Jones; children: Ann Springer, Rebecca Springer. BA in English and Bus. Adminstrn., Centre Coll., 1959; MA in Am. Lit., Ind. U., 1963, PhD in English Lit., 1969. Chair English dept. U. Mo., Kansas City, 1980-81, acting assoc. dean grad. sch., 1982; Am. Coun. of Edn. Adminstrn. fellow U. Kans., Lawrence, 1982-83; dean of grad. sch. U. Mo., Kansas City, 1983-84, assoc. vice chancellor for acad. affairs and grad. studies, 1985-89; vice chancellor for acad. affairs East Carolina U., Greenville, N.C., 1989-94; pres. CUNY Coll., Staten Island, 1994—. Author: Edith Wharton and Kate Chopin: A Reference Guide, 1976; What Manner of Woman: Essays, 1977, Thomas Hardy's Use of Allusion, 1983, Plains Woman: The Diary of Martha Farnsworth, 1986 (Choice award 1986), Ethan Frome: A Nightmare of Need, 1993. Huntington Libr. fellow, 1988. Mem.: Coun. Grad. Schs. (chair 1986—88), Assn. Tchr. Educators (chair 1992), Acad. Leadership Acad. (exec. com. 1992—94), Am. Assn. State Colls. and Univs., Am. Coun. on Edn. (profl. devel. com. 1991—, invited participant Nat. Forum 1984, bd. dirs. 2001—). Office: Coll Staten Island 2800 Victory Blvd Rm 1a-404 Staten Island NY 10314-6609

SPRINGER, RUTH WIREN, music educator; b. Bronx, N.Y., July 17, 1956; d. Bror Stanley Wiren and Ingrid Katerina Walderman; life ptnr. Dominick Frank Lettera. BS in Music Edn., Taylor U., 1978; MA in Music Edn., Ball State U., 1981. Cert. tchr. Am. Orff Schulwerk Assn., 1980. Music educator Maconaquah Sch. Corp., Bunker Hill, Ind., 1978—2001, Darien (Conn.) Pub. Schs., 2001—. Pvt. piano tchr., Kokomo, Ind., 1978—94; area coord. Cir. State With Song, Ind. Children's Choral Festival, Muncie, 1996—97; pianist Svea Lodge 253, Vasa Order Am., Indpls., 1996—2001. Actress, singer, rehearsal accompanist and vocal music dir. Kokomo Civic Theatre, 1983—2001; dir., actress, singer, accompanist and stage crew mem. Curtain Call Children's Theatre, Kokomo, 1988—91; singer Kokomo Symphonic Chorus. Named Outstanding Ind. Elem. Music Educator of Yr., Ind. Music Educators Assn., 2000—01; recipient 25 Years of Service in Music Education award, CT Music Educators Assn., 2004; grantee, Sydnor and Miriam Reiss Tchr's. Fund for Further Study, 2003. Mem.: NEA, Am. Guild Organists, Am. Choral Dirs. Assn., Darien Edn. Assn., Conn. State Tchrs. Assn., Conn. Music Educators Assn., Music Educators Nat. Conf., Theatre 308 (rehearsal and performance pianist 2002—). Conservative-R. Protestant. Achievements include being selected as one of four educators from across the United States to participate in the Singers On Stage Broadway Workshop and performed in the chorus of On Broadway 1998, NYC; Randall School Choir performed, under my direction, for First Lady, Barbara Bush in 1991; Randall School Choir and Holmes School Choir performed on television in The World's Largest Concert in 1990 and 2004; Randall School Choir, under my direction, were featured performers at the Indiana Children's Choral Festival, 1989; Pipe Creek School Choir, under my direction, performed twice for Youth Art Month at the Indiana State Capitol building. Avocations: theater, dance, gardening, travel, tennis. Office: Holmes Sch 18 Hoyt St Darien CT 06820

SPRINKLE, MARTHA CLARE, elementary school educator; b. Tehachapi, Calif., Oct. 17, 1944; d. William Foote and Mildred Sprinkle; BA, U. Calif., Santa Barbara, 1966; MA in Orgn. Mgmt., U. Phoenix, 2000. Cert. tchr. Calif., water aerobics instr. 1986. Tchr. Muroc Unified Sch. Dist., Edwards, Calif., 1966—71, Elk Hills Sch., Tipman, Calif., 1971—79, Tehachopi Valley Recreation and Pks., 1979—, So. Kern Unified Sch., Rosamond, Calif., 1985—2003. Planning commr. City of Tehachapi, Calif., 1984—. Home: PO Box 852 Tehachapi CA 93581

SPROAT, KEZIA VANMETER, communications executive, writer; b. Chillicothe, Ohio, Nov. 8, 1937; d. Joseph Vause and Helen Rose (Janes) Vanmeter; children: Cornelia Sisson Vanmeter, Eliza Bradford Delano. AB, Vassar Coll., 1959; MA, Ohio State U., 1963, PhD, 1975. Field dir. Miami Valley Campfire Girls, Dayton, Ohio, 1959-60; tchr. English Kingswood Sch. Cranbrook, Bloomfield Hills, Mich., 1960-61; grad. asst. Dept. English Ohio State U., Columbus, 1961-68, lectr. comparative lit., 1968-73, editor ctr. human resource rsch., 1979-85; dir. food for thought Univ. Ctr. Ministries, Columbus, 1978-79; pres. Sproat Comm., Inc., Columbus, 1985—. Editor, writer Ross Labs., Columbus, 1987-91; dir. Vanmeter Farm, Inc., Piketon, Ohio, 1993-2002; pres., founder Highbank Farm Peace Edn. Ctr., Chillicothe, 1994. Author, editor: National Longitudinal Surveys: Bibliography, 1985; editor: Malnutrition: A Hidden Cost, 1993 (2 Addy awards 1994); editor 7 books; editor Peace Grows Bull., 1996—. Founder, co-chair Community Film Assn., Columbus, 1979—; publicist Peace Grows, Inc., Columbus and Akron, Ohio, 1990—; coord. South Ctrl. Ohio Preservation Soc., 1992—; pres. Vassar Coll. Class of 1959, 1999-; mem. Martin Luther King, Jr. bd. sponsors Morehouse Coll., 2002-. Recipient Florence Howe award MLA, 1975, Mayor's award for vol. svcs Mayor of Columbus, 1980, Pres. award Abbott Labs., 1988; grantee Ohio Humanities Coun., 1977, 78. Mem. Lucy Webb Hayes Heritage Ctr., Women's Poetry Workshop. Avocations: collecting art, poetry. E-mail: keziav@aol.com.

SPROUL, ROBIN, television news bureau chief; Joined ABC, 1981—, mgr. radio news; bureau chief Wash., DC ABC Radio; dep. bureau chief ABC TV Wash., 1992—93; v.p. news coverage ABC Wash., 1993—; Wash. bureau chief ABC TV News, 1993—. Named one of 100 Most Powerful Women in Wash., Washingtonian mag., 2001. Office: ABC News 1717 DeSales St NW Washington DC 20036 Office Phone: 202-222-7200. Office Fax: 202-222-7684. Business E-Mail: robin.sproul@abc.com., robin.v.sproul@abc.com.*

SPROULE, BETTY ANN, computer industry strategic consultant; b. Evanston, Ill., Dec. 30, 1948; d. Harold Fletcher and Lois (Reno) Mathis; m. J. Michael Sproule, Mar. 3, 1973; children: John Harold, Kevin William. BS, Ohio State U., 1969, MS, 1970, PhD, 1972. Mem. tech. staff Bell Telephone Labs., Columbus, Ohio, 1973-74; asst. prof. U. Tex., Odessa, 1974-77; analyst bus. systems Maj. Appliance Bus. div. GE, Louisville, 1977-78; dir. forecasting and analysis Brown and Williamson Tobacco, Louisville, 1978-86; strategic planning mgr. Hewlett-Packard Co., Palo Alto, Calif., 1986—2002; sr. cons. Everest Adv. Group, Palo Alto, 2003—. Contbr. articles to profl. jours.; patentee in field. Sr. mem. IEEE, Soc. Women Engrs. Home: 1501 Muirfield Dr Bowling Green OH 43402-5214 Office: Everest Advisory Group 555 Bryant Street Ste 360 Palo Alto CA 94301 Office Phone: 650-599-2740. E-mail: sproule101@yahoo.com., sproule@everestag.com.

SPROULE, DEBORAH W. art educator, artist; b. Inglewood, Calif., Sept. 1, 1957; d. Joseph Fredrick and Martha Ann (Gross) Wagner; m. Dale Fenton Sproule, May 1, 1955; 1 child, Andrew Martin. BS Fine Art, U. Oreg., 1982; BS Art Edn., U. Minn., 1985; MA, U. Wis., 2000, MFA, 2001. Cert. art tchr. Wis., 1986. One-woman shows include, Oreg., Minn., Wis., 1980—2003, exhibited in group shows, 2000—03, Represented in permanent collections Soloman Kamm, Chgo. Refugee vol. Calvary Episcopal Ch., Rochester, Minn., 1991—98, channel 1 food shelf vol., 1991—98, youth min. vol., 1991—98; vol. Cmty. Svc., Refugee Resettlement. Mem.: Coll. Arts Assn., Am. Crafts Coun., U. Wis. Alumni Assn. Avocation: cmty. advocacy visual art. Home: 1617 Tarragon Dr Madison WI 53716

SPROUSE, EARLENE PENTECOST, special education educator; b. Hopewell, Va., Apr. 23, 1939; d. Earl Paige and Sophia Marlene (Chairky) Pentecost; m. David Andrew Koren, July 3, 1957 (div. Jan. 1963); children: David Andrew Jr., Elysia Marlene, Merri Paige; m. Wayne Alexander Sprouse, Sept. 2, 1964; 1 child, Michael Wayne. AS, Paul D. Camp C.C., Franklin, Va., 1973; BS in Comm. Disorders, Old Dominion U., 1975, MEd in Spl. Edn., 1977. Tchg. cert. with endorsement in speech lang. pathology, learning disabilities and emotional disturbance, Va. Speech lang. pathologist

Southampton County Schs., Va., 1975-76; learning disabled tchr. itinerant Franklin (Va.) City Pub. Schs., 1976-78, emotionally disturbed/learning disabled tchr., 1978-85, speech lang. pathologist, 1986-91, ednl. diagnostician, 1992—2003, lead tchr. spl. edn., 2000—03; resource specialist TideWater Acad., 1999—; speech lang. pathologist South Hampton Co. Pub. Sch., 2003—. Project leader curriculum guide Listening and Lang. Processing Skills, 1990-91; speech/lang. pathologist Southampton County, 2003—. Mem. Career Edn. Adv. Com., Va. Dept. Edn., 1995—; mem. field-based cons. network Old Dominion U., Coll. of William and Mary, 1997—. Recipient Excellence in Edn. award C. of C., Hampton Roads, Va., 1988-89; grantee Va. Edn. Assn., Richmond, 1994—, Project UNITE Dept. Edn., Richmond, 1994—, Project Payroll, 1999-2000, DOE/VBEP Project Second Chance, 2000-01. Mem. Franklin City Edn. Assn. (pres. 1980, 91), Internat. Dyslexia Assn., Coun. for Learning Disabilities. Methodist. Avocations: fishing, music. Home: 272 Colonia Dr Surry VA 23883 E-mail: esprouse39@hotmail.com.

SPRUCE, SIMONE RENEE, art educator; b. Toledo, Ohio, May 8, 1960; d. George and Helen Spruce. Student, Ohio State U., 1978—79; BA, Findlay U., 1982; postgrad., Howard U., 1987; MFA, Pratt Inst., 1990. Instr. art Boys and Girls Club, Toledo, 1999, Meadows Choice Cmty. Sch., Oregon, Ohio, 1999—2001; exhbn. staff Toledo Mus. Art, 2001—02; counselor Child Care Cath. Club, Toledo, 2002—. Tchg. artist Common Space Ctr. for Creativity, Toledo, 2000; instr. art YMCA, Toledo, 2000; program instr. Girls Scouts Maumee Valley, Toledo, 2002—03. Cpl. USMC, 1985—89. New Works Grant, Arts Commn. Greater Toledo, 1994, 2003. Mem.: Spectrum Friends of Fine Art (Award of Distinction 2003). Avocations: bowling, swimming, exercising. Home: 2534 Key St Apt 20 Toledo OH 43614*

SPRUDE, MARGARET, credit services company executive; b. 1946; BS in Bus., MS of Accountancy, Western Ill. U. CPA. Various fin.-exec.-level positions card divsn. including CFO Bank of Am., 1986—2000, mng. dir., CFO Household Internat. Credit Card Svcs. divsn., 2000—. Office: Household Internat Inc 1441 Schilling Pl Salinas CA 93901-4543 E-mail: masprude@household.com.

SPRUNGER, LESLIE KAREN, physiologist, educator; b. Palo Alto, Calif., Aug. 29, 1961; d. Richard Marmion and Patricia Joann (Sprunger) Oldacre; 1 child, Katherine Elyse Traynor. BS, U. Alaska, 1983; DVM, Wash. State U., 1987; PhD, U. Minn., 1995. Vet. Alder Trail Animal Hosp., Bremerton, Wash., 1987-88; vet. med. assoc. U. Minn. Dept. Vet. Pathobiology, St. Paul, 1988-94; rsch. assoc. U. Minn. Dept. Physiology, Mpls., 1994-95; rsch. investigator human genetics U. Mich., Ann Arbor, 1995—2000; asst. prof. Wash. State U., 2000—. Howard Huges Med. Inst. cons., 2003—. Contbr. articles to profl. jours. including Neuron, Jour. Neurosci., Human Molecular Genetics. Tutor ESL Project Literacy, Mpls., 1988-89. Grantee NIH, 1994—; Howard Hughes Med. Inst. fellow, 1989-94. Mem. Am. Physiol. Soc., Soc. Gen. Physiologists, Soc.for Neuroscience, Internat. Mouse Genome Soc., Sigma Xi, Phi Zeta. Democrat. Avocations: reading, music, fitness. Office: Dept of Veterinary and Comparative Anatomy Pharmacology and Physiology Wash State U 205 Wegner Hall Pullman WA 99164-6520 Business E-Mail: lsprunger@wsu.edu.

SPUHLER, JACILYN ERICKSON, librarian; b. Oct. 1, 1949; BA, U. Calif., Riverside, 1971; MLS, U. Hawaii, 1973; Cert. in Preservation Mgmt., Rutgers U., 2003. Dir. Garfield County Pub. Libr. Sys., New Castle, Colo., 1997—. Office: PO Box 320 New Castle CO 81647-0320 E-mail: jspuhler@marmot.org.

SPURLOCK, EVELYN HARVEY, retired elementary school educator, minister; b. June 25, 1914; d. Forrest and Maude Hunter Harvey; m. Junius White; 1 child, Matona ; m. Richard Spurlock; 1 child, Maxella. Grad., Storer Coll., 1934, Miner Tchrs. Coll., Hampton Inst.; postgrad., NYU. Ordained min. Cross Bapt. Ch., 1994. Tchr. Carver H.S., Mt. Olive, NC, Watson H.S., Covington; ret., 1979. Home: 332 S Marion Ave Covington VA 24426-1717

SPURRIER, MARY EILEEN, investment advisor, financial planner; b. Mpls., Sept. 16, 1943; d. Charles Joseph and Ruth Eileen (Rowles) Dickman; m. Joseph Leo Spurrier, Jan. 16, 1965 (div. Aug. 1976); 1 child, Christopher Jude; m. Gary Albert Gutfrucht, July 8, 1988. BS, U. Minn., 1965. CFP; CDP; registered prin., registered investment adviser. Rsch. fellow, libr. Sch. Bus. Adminstrn. U. Minn., Mpls., 1965-68; exec. dir. Zero Population Growth, N.Y., 1972-76; fin. cons. Merrill Lynch, Rochester, N.Y., 1977-84, Shearson/Smith Barney, 1984-89; investment cons. Citi-Corp, Rochester, 1989-91; assoc. v.p. Essex Investment, Rochester, 1991-95; pres. M. Spurrier Fin. Svcs., Rochester, 1995—. Bd. dirs. Micro Bus. Alliance, Rochester; cons. Fund Devel. Rochester Women's Network, 1995-97, Women's Coun. C. of C., Rochester, 1992-97; spkr. in field. Advisor Blue Jean Mag.; contbr. articles to newspapers. Chmn. endowment campaign YWCA, Rochester, 1994-98, bd. dirs., mem. fin. com. 1997—; mentor Wilson Commencement Park, Rochester, 1993—; v.p., bd. dirs. N.Y. State Environ. Planning Lobby, 1973-75; bd. dirs. N.Y. State Family Planning Coalition, 1973-75; fin. dir. LWV, Rochester, 1989-90; capital campaign com. Susan B. Anthony House, 1997-99. Recipient Eminent Rochester Women award Upstate Mag., 1974. Mem. NAFE (spkr. 1990-95), Rochester Women's Network (bd. dirs. 1997—, v.p. 1999—), Women's Coun. C. of C. (chair W award 2000, nominee W award 1999), Nat. Assn. Women Bus. Owners (bd. dirs. Greater Rochester chpt. 1997-2000, chair Top Women's Bus. Owners Awards 1997-2000). Avocations: gardening, reading, walking. Office: 315 Westminster Rd Rochester NY 14607-3230

SPURRIER-BRIGHT, PATRICIA ANN, professional society administrator; b. El Paso, Tex., Feb. 27, 1943; d. James Ray and Lucile Gray (Lafferty) Spurrier; m. Martin Oliver Bright, Sept. 18, 1964 (div. 1967); 1 child, James R. Student, Frederick Coll., 1962-64. Planning technician Reston Va, Inc./Gulf Reston, Inc., 1966-75; adminstrv. asst. Gulf Oil, Tulsa, 1975-79; planner Conde Engring., El Paso, Tex., 1979-82; adjutant U.S. Horse Cavalry Assn., Ft. Bliss, Tex., 1983-91; exec. dir. U.S. Cavalry Assn., Ft. Riley, Kans., 1991—, sec., 1991—. Sec. U.S. Cavalry Meml. Found., Fort Riley, 1994—; trustee Spurrier Trust, El Paso, 1990—; mem. Bigheart Cemetery Found., Barnsdale, Okla., 1989—; bd. dirs. 1st Kans. Territorial Capital. Editor The Cavalry Jour., 1990—. Mem. U.S. Army Daus. Republican. Avocations: research, painting, genealogy. Home: 1517 Leavenworth St Manhattan KS 66502-4154 Office: US Cavalry Assn PO Box 2325 Fort Riley KS 66442-0325 E-mail: cavalry@flinthills.com.

SQUIER, RITA ANN HOLMBERG, graphic designer; b. Norwalk, Conn., Jan. 4, 1967; d. Stig H. and Julia Mildred Tjader Holmberg; m. Michael Craig Squier, May 19, 1990. BS in Visual Arts, U. Bridgeport, 1988. Art dir., web designer Squier Design, Chatham, N.Y., 1995—; graphic designer, owner Studio 46, Chatham, 1990-99. Mem. Mooresville Artist Guild, Columbia County Coun. on the Arts. Republican. Avocations: watercolor, pen and ink, gardening, acrylics, photography. Office: Squier Design 46 Payn Ave Chatham NY 12037-1427

SQUIRE, ANNE MARGUERITE, religious leader; b. Amherstburg, Ont., Can., Oct. 17, 1920; d. Alexander Samuel and Coral Marguerite Park; m. William Robert Squire, June 24, 1943; children: Frances, Laura, Margaret. BA, Carleton U., Ottawa, 1972, BA with honors, 1974, MA, 1975; LLD (hon.), Carleton U., 1988; DD (hon.), United Theol. Coll., 1979, Queen's U., 1985. Cert. tchr., Ont. Adj. prof. Carleton U., 1975-82; sec. div. ministry personnel and edn. United Ch. Can., Toronto, 1982-85, moderator, 1986-88. Author curriculum materials, 1959—; contbr. articles to profl. jours. Mem. bd. mgmt. St. Andrew's Coll., Saskatoon, Sask., 1982, Queens Theol. Coll., Kingston, Ont., 1999-2003; founding mem. Muslim-Christian Dialogue Group. Recipient Senate medal Carleton U., 1972. Mem. Can. Research Inst. for Advancement Women, Delta Kappa Gamma (pres. 1978-79). Mem. United Ch. Can. Office: 731 Weston Dr Ottawa ON Canada K1G 1W1 E-mail: asquire@netrover.com

SQUIRE, BEVERLY, business owner, entrepreneur; b. San Antonio, Sept. 11, 1947; d. Orville Herbert and Theda Lenora Atkinson; m. Roger W. Squire, Apr. 10, 1970; children: Ryan Christopher, Suzanne Louise. Grad. H.S., Escondido, Calif. Owner, entrepreneur, pres. Inventory Control Sys., Arcadia, Calif., 1971—. Active L.A. County Mus. Art, 1992, L.A. World Affairs Coun., 1993, Nat. Fedn. Ind. Bus., Washington, 1995; donor U. Calif. Riverside Found., 1997; co-chmn. bus. adv. coun. Rep. Congl. Com., 1999. Recipient Medal of Merit, Rep. Congl. Com., 1999; named Bus. Woman of the Yr., Rep. Congl. Com., 1998. Mem. Nat. Watercolor Soc. (assoc.), Nat. Mus. Women in the Arts, Am. Watercolor Soc. (assoc.), U.S. Lighthouse Soc. Roman Catholic. Avocations: visual arts, playing piano, lighthouse history.

SQUIRE, GILDA N. brand manager, publicist, writer; b. Balt., July 11, 1969; d. Gilbert Squire. BA in Comms., George Mason U., 1995. Adminstrv. sec. FBI, Washington, 1987—90; adminstrv. asst. Office Tech. Assessment U.S. Congress, Washington, 1990—95; mktg. mgr. Goldman Sachs, N.Y.C., 1996—2001; publicist Penguin Putnam, Inc., N.Y.C., 2001—. Freelance writer Sister 2 Sister Mag., Washington, 1992—93, Black Elegance and Belle Mags., N.Y.C., 1995—2000, Upscale Mag., N.Y.C., 1999—. Author: Dark Eros: Black Erotic Writings, 1998. Mem.: Dance Theatre of Harlem Jr. Coun. (treas. 2000—01). Home: 422 W 160th St #3 New York NY 10032 Personal E-mail: gnsquire@aol.com.

SQUIRE, LAURIE RUBIN, media consultant; b. N.Y.C., Jan. 30, 1953; d. Daniel and Ruth Thelma (Deutsch) Rubin; m. Herbert E. Squire Jr., Aug. 6, 1975; children: Amy Ruth, Julie Wynn. BA cum laude (scholar), Finch Coll., 1974; MA, NYU, 1976; postgrad., Columbia U., 1977—. Actress TV commls., 1960-65; arts editor Finch/Metro newspaper, N.Y.C., 1970-74; co-editor Finch Alumnae mag., 1971-72; intern producer Sta. WBAI-FM, N.Y.C., 1973; music prodn. coord. Ballet Theatre spl. Sta. WNET-TV, 1973; coll. bd. writer Mademoiselle mag., 1973; intern asst. pub. affairs dir. N.Y. Cultural Ctr., 1974; mdse. coord. Sta. WOR-AM, N.Y.C., 1974-76, contbg. writer Bob and Ray's Mary Backstage serial, contbr. nostalgia features Joe Franklin Show, producer Jean Shepherd Show and sydicated markets, 1975-77, producer Bernard Meltzer What's Your Problem, 1977-80; broadcast stage mgr. Texaco Met. Opera, 1976—. Dance critic Show Bus., theatre newspaper; bd. dirs. publicity and advt. L.I. Playhouse, 1982-84; press rep. Great Neck Pla. Contbg. writer Newsday, Can. Publs. Publicity cons. Nassau County Mus. Fine Art; v.p. pub. rels. United Community Fund. Recipient commendations for Leukemia Radiothons Peabody Broadcasting citation, 1983. Home and Office: 25 Loft Dr Martinsville NJ 08876-1400

SQUIRE, MOLLY ANN, organizational psychologist; b. Highland Park, Mich., Aug. 18; d. George Edward and Dorothy Laura (Molteni) Squirrell; m. Arthur Bruce Hanson, June 23, 1990; 1 child, Mark Arthur Hanson. AA, NYU, 1978; BS cum laude, U. LaVerne, 1980; MA, Claremont (Calif.) Grad. Univ., 1982; PhD, Pacific-Western U., 1991. Cert. cons. to mgmt. Health svcs. adminstr. health care delivery orgns., 1978-82; nat. dir. Huntington's Disease Rsch. Project, Calif., 1981-82; CEO Claremont Mgmt. Cons. (now Squire Trainers), L.A., Calif., 1982—. Past statis. analyst to pres. L.A. City Coll.; past part-time instr. L.A. Trade Tech.; part-time instr. Glendale C.C., 1994—96. Editor: BEACON newsletter, 1989—96; contbr. articles to profl. jours. Lt. 78th Fraser Highland Regiment San Juan Capistrano Bn. Decorated Knight Templar of Jerusalem, Internat. br. Netherlands; named a Krauthamer & Squire 'Thelma & Louise' Women's Scholarship, L.A. City Coll., 1993—; named Woman of Magic scholarship, 1997—; recipient Cert. Appreciation, City of Ukiah, Calif., 1984, We. Square Dance Assn., 1986, Am. Heart Assn., 1990, So. Calif. Skeptics, 1987, Pacific Bell, 1990, Achievement award, No. Am. Women's Inner Circle, 1991, Cert. Appreciation, L.A. City Coll., 1995, Clan MacKenzie Soc. So. Calif., 1996; fellow, Claremont Grad. Sch., 1980—82. Mem.: ASTD, Soc. Indsl. and Orgnl. Psychologists, Nat. Bur. Cert. Cons., Assn. Psychol. Type, Pacific Coast Assn. Magicians (golden cir.), Soc. Am. Magicians (life Zinger award, Cert. Appreciation, Merit award 1991, 1994, Best Character Act 1994, Peller Meml. trophy 1994), Internat. Brotherhood Magicians (past pres. #254, sec., Best Mentalist trophy 1987, Cert. Appreciation, Blackstone Floating Ring), Arthurian Soc. Arthuret U.K. (life), Mensa (past proctor). Achievements include patents for bus. and health care products. Office: PO Box 41633 Los Angeles CA 90041-0633 E-mail: hansons@worldnet.att.net.

SQUIRES, CONNIE JO, special education educator; b. Omaha, Nebr., July 14, 1933; d. Paul Sydney Hilt, Lillian Elvera (Holstrom) Hilt; m. Daryl Jessup Squires, Sept. 2, 1955; children: Stephen, Chadwick, Scott. BEd, Whitworth Coll., 1955; MEd, Seattle Pacific U., 1978; postgrad., U. Wash., Ea. Wash. U. Cert. tchr. spl. edn. and reading Wash., sch. psychologist Wash., drug and alcohol counselor Wash. Tchr. elem. Mead Sch. Dist., Spokane, Wash., 1955—59; tchr. spl. edn. Cle Elum Sch. Dist., 1959—60; tchr. elem. Goleta Sch., Santa Barbara, Calif., 1960—62, Anacortes Sch. Dist., Anacorte, Wash., 1962—63, Bellevue Sch. Dist., Bellevue, Wash., 1963—77; sch. psychologist/ednl. specialist Spokane Sch. Dist., 1977—88; sch. psychologist West Valley Sch. Dist., Spokane, 1990—98; ret., 1998. Counselor drug and alcohol, cons. Assocs. in Counseling, Spokane, 1984—99. Bd. dirs. Friends of Little Spokane River Valley. Named Sch. Psychologist of Yr., Washington State, 1995. Mem.: Spokane Ret. Tchrs. (bd. dirs.), Nat. Assn. Sch. Psychologists, Whitworth Women's Aux. Republican. Presbyterian. Avocations: writing, gardening, computers.

SRERE, LINDA JEAN, former advertising executive; b. N.Y.C., Aug. 14, 1955; d. Rudolph Joseph and Muriel Evelyn (Weigand) Forquignon. m. Jeremy Earle Brown, Nov. 28, 1998. BA, SUNY, Oswego, 1975. Asst. account exec. to acct. exec. BBDO, Inc., N.Y.C., 1975-79; v.p., account supr. Ogilvy and Mather, Inc., N.Y.C., 1979-82, McCaffrey and McCall, Inc., N.Y.C., 1982; with Rosenfeld, Sirowitz, Humphrey, & Strauss, Inc., N.Y.C., 1983-94, exec. v.p., 1986-90, pres., 1990-94; chmn. Earle, Palmer, Brown/N.Y., N.Y.C., 1992-94; exec. v.p., dir. bus. devel. Young & Rubicam N.Y., N.Y.C., 1994-95, head global new bus., 1995-96, group mng. dir., 1996-97, pres., CEO, 1997—2001, vice chmn., 1998—2001; mktg. and advt. cons. Bd. dirs. Electronic Arts Inc., 2001—. Mem. Am. Mgmt. Assn., Young Pres.'s Orgn., Advt. Women of N.Y.*

SRINATH, LATHA, physician; b. Bangalore, India, Jan. 1, 1958; came to U.S., 1985; d. Krishna and Shamanthaka (Ananthachar) Iyengar; m. Sampath Holevanahalli Srinath, Jan. 22, 1984; children: Shilpa, Preetha. BS, Bangalore U., 1978; MB, BChir, Bangalore Med. Coll., 1984; MD, Georgetown U., 1990. Diplomate Am. Bd. Internal Medicine. Fellow in infectious diseases U. Louisville, 1992-94; pvt. practice Boynton Beach, Fla., 1994—. Staff Bethesda Meml. Hosp., Boynton Beach, 1994—, JFK Med. Ctr., Boynton Beach, 1994—; cons. HIV Adv. Bd., Fla., 1997—. Contbr. articles to profl. jours. Nat. Merit scholar, India, 1975. Mem. Am. Assn. Physicians from India, Fla. Med. Assn., Palm Beach Med. Soc. Hindu. Avocations: travel, yoga, tennis, oil painting, athletics. Home: 473 N Country Club Dr Lake Worth FL 33462-1003 Office: ID Cons Inc 2623 S Seacrest Blvd Boynton Beach FL 33435-7501 E-mail: lsrinath@idconsults.net.

SRINIVASAN, JAYASREE M. research scientist; b. Madras, India, Apr. 24, 1971; arrived in U.S., 1997; d. M. R. and Vijaya Srinivasan; m. S. Iyengar Srinivasan, May 2, 1997. BS, U. Madras, 1991, MS, 1994, U. Houston, 1999. Rsch. assoc. I Synaptic Pharm. Corp., Paramus, NJ, 2000—01; rsch. assoc. II Myriad Pharm. Inc., Salt Lake City, 2001—. Mem.: Am. Chem. Soc. Achievements include research in discovery of drug to cure cancer patent pending. Home: 2631 E 2nd St Apt 8 Bloomington IN 47401-7855*

SRINIVASAN, SEETHA, publishing company executive; b. Bangalore, Mysore, India, Dec. 27, 1943; came to U.S., 1967; d. R. and S. (Sethuraman) Ananthakrishnan; m. Asoka Srinivasan, July 14, 1967; children: Arjun, Gautam. BA, Ferguson Coll., Poona, India, 1963; MA, U. Poona, 1965, Mills Coll., Oakland, Calif., 1969; M in Journalism and Comm., U. Fla., 1979. Instr. English Tougaloo (Miss.) Coll., 1969-72, asst. prof., 1972-77; editor Univ. Press of Miss., Jackson, 1979-82, asst. dir., exec. editor, 1982-87, assoc. dir., editor-in-chief, 1987-98; dir., 1998—. Bd. dirs. Assn. Am. Univ. Presses, N.Y.C., 1989-92. Pres. Jackson Symphony Youth Orch., 1986-88, Millsoups Arts and Lectures Series; sec. Jackson Friends of Libr., 1985-89. Office: Univ Press of Miss 3825 Ridgewood Rd Jackson MS 39211-6497

STAAB, MARGARET E. social services administrator; b. Rock Springs, Wyo., Apr. 18, 1962; d. George A. Pat and Margaret J. (Fox) Brown; m. Steven A. Staab, Dec. 20, 1984; children: Shane, Brenden. BS, U. Wyo., 1983. With Washakie Sch. Dist., Worland, Wyo., 1996—2001; exec. dir. Big Bros./Big Sisters, 2001—. Coun. mem. Youth Alternatives Coun., Worland, 2001—; pres. Human Resources Coun., 2001—02; mem. South Side PTA, 1994—2003, pres., 1998—2000. Mem.: Nat. Profl. Orgns. Episcopalian. Avocations: skiing, swimming, piano, reading, writing. Home: 500 S 16th St Worland WY 82401 Office: Big Bros/Big Sisters 1313 Big Horn Ave Worland WY 82401 Office Phone: 307-347-8875. E-mail: sastaabe@bresnan.net.

STABENOW, DEBORAH ANN, senator, former congresswoman; b. Gladwin, Mich., Apr. 29, 1950; d. Robert Lee and Anna Merle (Hallmark) Greer; children: Todd Dennis, Michelle Deborah. BS magna cum laude, Mich. State U., 1972, MSW magna cum laude, 1975. With spl. svcs. Lansing (Mich.) Sch. Dist., 1972-73; county commr. Ingham County, Mason, Mich., 1975-78; state rep. State of Mich., Lansing, 1979—, state senator, 1990—94; mem. 103rd-106th Congress from Mich. 8th dist. U.S. Ho. Reps.; senator State of Mich., 2000—. Founder Ingham County Women's Commn.; co-founder Council Against Domestic Assault. Recipient Service to Children award Council for Prevention of Child Abuse and Neglect, 1983, Disting. Service to Mich. Families award Mich. Council Family Relations, 1983, Outstanding Leadership award Nat. Council Community Mental Health Ctrs., 1983, Snyder-Kok award Mental Health Assn. Mich., Awareness Leader of Yr. award Awareness Communications Team Developmentally Disabled, 1984, Communicator of Yr. award Woman in Communications, 1984, Lawmaker of Yr. award Nat. Child Support Enforcement Assn., 1985, Disting. Service award Lansing Jaycees, 1985, Disting. Service in Govt. award Retarded Citizens of Mich., 1986, Boxing Glove award Nat. Com. to Preserve Social Security and Medicare, 1999, Home Health Hero Nat. Assn. for Home Care, 1999, Friend of Farm Bur. Mich. Farm Bur., 1999, Leadership award Nat. Coun. of Space Grant Dirs., 1998, Outstanding Achievement Nat. Farmers Union, 1998, Legislator of Yr. award Nat. Multiple Sclerosis Soc., 1992, Assn. for Children's Mental Health, 1991, Mich. Assn. of Vol. Adminstrs., 1989, Citizens Alliace to Uphold Spl. Edn., 1989, Recognition award State 4-H Alumni, 1991, Cmty. award Mich. Mental Health, 1988; named One of Ten Outstanding Young Ams. Jaycees, 1986. Mem. NAACP, Lansing Regional C. of C., Delta Kappa Gamma. Democrat. Office: US Senate 702 Hart Senate Office Bldg Washington DC 20510 E-mail: senator@stabenow.senate.gov.*

STACK, MAY ELIZABETH, library director; b. Jackson, Miss., Nov. 10, 1940; d. James William and Irene Thelma (Baldwin) Garrett; m. Richard Gardiner, Apr. 15, 1962; children: Elinor, Harley David. BS, Miss. State Coll. for Women, 1962; MBA, Western New Eng. Coll., 1981; MLS, So. Conn. State U., 1989. Clk. Western New Eng. Coll., Springfield, Mass., 1965-66, acquisitions staff, 1966-72, cataloger, 1972-84, asst. dir., 1984-89, acting dir., 1989-90, dir., 1990—. Chair Ctrl./Western Mass. Automated Resource Sharing Collection Devel. Com., Paxton, Mass., 1993-95, exec. bd., 1993-96. Mem. East Longmeadow (Mass.) Hist. Soc., 1989-92. Mem. ALA, Mass. Libr. Assn., Assn. Coll. and Rsch. Librs., Libr. and Mgmt. Assn., Libr. Info. and Technology Assn. Methodist. Avocations: horseback riding, show dogs. Office: Western New Eng Coll D'Amour Libr 1215 Wilbraham Rd Springfield MA 01119-2612 Office Phone: 413-782-1531. E-mail: mstack@wnec.edu.

STACK, TERESA MARIE, publishing executive; b. Barberton, Ohio, June 12, 1962; d. Roy Edward and Dorothy Ann (Faix) S. BA, Pa. State U., 1984. Asst. fulfillment mgr. Fairchild Publs., N.Y.C., 1985-86; asst. promotion mgr. Faichild Publs., N.Y.C., 1986-87, circulation mgr., 1987-90, corp. circulation dir., 1990-93; v.p. The Nation, L.P., N.Y.C., 1993-96, assoc. publisher, 1996—98, pres., 1998—. Bd. dirs. Ind. Press Assn., 2003-, mem. social venture network, 2003-; vol. vis. neighbors Box Project and S.P.C.A. Office: The Nation Company LP 33 Irving Place New York NY 10003 Office Phone: 212-209-5401. E-mail: totack@thenation.com.

STACOM, DARCY A. real estate company executive; d. Matthew and Claire Stacom; m. Chris Kraus. Degree in mktg., Lehigh U., 1980. Lic. comml. real estate agent. Capital markets intermediary Cushman & Wakefield, Inc., N.Y.C., 1980; exec v.p. Cushman Wakefield, Inc., N.Y.C., 2000—02; exec v.p. and ptnr. investment properties institutional group CB Richard Ellis, 2002—. Bd. dirs. Comml. Real Estate Women N.Y., mem. adv. com. Mem. adv. coun. Acad. Woman Achievers of YWCA; fundraiser United Way; mem. women's bd. Madison Sq. Boys & Girls Clubs, 1999—. Named one of Top 100 Women in Bus. in N.Y.C., Crain's N.Y. Bus. Mag. Mem.: Real Estate Bd. of N.Y. (bd. govs. 2001—). Office: CB Richard Ellis Group Inc 200 Park Ave New York NY 10166*

STACY, FRANCES H. federal judge; b. 1955; BA, Baylor Univ., 1977; JD, Baylor Law Sch., 1979. With U.S. Atty.'s Office (Tex. so. dist.) Criminal Divsn., 1980, Civil Rights Divsn., 1980-81, Land and Resources Divsn., 1981-87, Civil Divsn., 1987-88, Appelate Divsn., 1988-90; magistrate judge U.S. Dist. Ct. (Tex. so. dist.), 5th circuit, Houston, 1990—. Author: Federal Civil Procedure Before Trial, Lawyers Cooperative Practice Guide. Mem. Tex. Bar Found. Office: Fed Bldg 515 Rusk St Ste 7727 Houston TX 77002-2600

STACY, TRUDY L. elementary school educator; b. Malone, N.Y., Apr. 3, 1953; d. John P. Keefe and Rita B. Bushey; m. Ronald W. Stacy, July 1, 1978; children: Nicole L., Steven J. BS, SUNY, Potsdam, 1975. Tchr. grade 6 East Side Elem. Sch., Gouverneur, NY. Mem.: AAUW (sec., treas. 1997—2001). Avocations: travel, reading. Home: 2106 County Route 35 Norwood NY 13668 Office: East Side Elem Sch 111 Gleason St Gouverneur NY 13642

STADLER, KATHERINE LOY, advertising sales executive; b. N.Y.C., Mar. 26, 1930; d. William L. and Catherine Stadler. Student, St. John's U., 1948-49, Hunter Coll., 1957-59, NYU Mgmt. Inst., 1963-69. Br. mgr. Hull Travel Service, Inc., N.Y.C., 1959-63; with Loire Imports, Inc., N.Y.C., 1963-69; dist. mgr. Sweet's divsn. McGraw-Hill Info. Sys. Co., N.Y.C., 1969-74; nat. sales mgr. Floor Covering Weekly, N.Y.C., 1974-76; account exec. Ziff-Davis Pub. Co., Hotel and Travel Index, L.A., 1976-81; founder Katherine Stadler & Assocs., 1981—83; regional mgr. Modern Salon, 1984-94; founder, CEO Bone Cancer Internat., Inc., 1999—. Mem. Nat. Cancer Inst./Consumer Advocates in Rsch. and Related Activities. Mem. Med. Mission Sisters, Roman Catholic. Ch., 1949-57; mem. Early Music

Ensemble L.A., 1985-87; mem. Thousand Oaks Coun. on Aging, 2003—. Named Sweet's Eastern Region Salesman of Yr., 1972, Salesman of Yr., Vance Pub., 1992. Mem. Nat. Assn. Profl. Saleswomen, L.A. Ad Club, Toastmasters. Home: 22 Robertson Way Newbury Park CA 91320-3939

STADLER, SELISE MCNEIL, laboratory and x-ray technician; b. Portsmouth, Va., Dec. 27, 1960; d. William M. and Jorja Lee (Rigg) Gaidos; m. Stephen Michael McNeill, Feb. 29, 1988 (div. July 1993); 1 child, Stephen Michael Jr.; m. David Robert Stadler, June 15, 1996. Cert. chiropractic asst., Practice Mgmt. Assn., 1983; student, Tarrant County Coll., 2000—01. Cert. radiologic technologist, instr. cert. World Modeling Assn., artificial external defibrilator, cardiopulmonary resuscitation and breath alcohol technician, bone scan technician, lab. technician. Chiropractic asst. Dr. Brad Hayes, D.C., Tulsa, Okla., 1982-84; adminstrv. asst. Dr. Wallace Gauntner, M.D., Pitts., 1984, sec., 1985-87; traffic mgr., office mgr. WVBS-AM/FM, Wilmington, NC, 1985-87; med. asst. Dr. J. Bailey Bland, D.C., Wilmington, 1988-90; therapy/radiology supr. Dr. Roy L. Creasy Jr., D.C., Wilmington, 1990-91; sec. TRC Staffing Svcs., Ft. Worth, 1991; med. asst., radiologist Westside Clinic, Dallas, 1991-94; model, exec. instr. Aleksaundra's Prodns., Ft. Worth, 1994-96; med. asst., radiologist Dr. Wayne R. English Jr., D.O., Ft. Worth, 1994-2000; lab/x-ray technician, med. asst. Care Now, Ft. Worth, 2001—02; x-ray/bone scan technician Kaner Med. Group, Bedford, Tex., 2001—02; med. asst./x-ray tech. Premier Orthopedics, Dr. Craig Saunders, 2002—. Author published poetry. Vol. Holy Family Cath. Ch., Ft. Worth, 1997-99. Mem. Tex. Soc. Radiologic Technologists (cert. in CPR and automated external defibrillation program). Episcopalian. Avocations: scuba diving, horseback riding, tennis, rollerblading. Office Phone: 817-267-4492.

STADTMAN, THRESSA CAMPBELL, biochemist; b. Sterling, N.Y., Feb. 12, 1920; d. Earl and Bessie (Waldron) Campbell; m. Earl Reece Stadtman, Oct. 19, 1943 BS, Cornell U., 1940, MS, 1942; PhD, U. Calif., Berkeley, 1949. Rsch. assoc. U. Calif., Berkeley, 1942-47, Harvard U. Med. Sch., Boston, 1949-50; biochemist Nat. Heart, Lung and Blood Inst. NIH, USPHS, HHS, Bethesda, Md., 1950—. Mem. Burroughs-Wellcome Fund Toxicology Adv. Commn., 1994-97; pres. Internat. Soc. Vitamins and Related BioFactors, 1998—. Editor Jour. Biol. Chemistry, Archives Biochemistry and Biophysics, Molecular and Cellular Biochemistry; editor-in-chief Bio Factors, 1991-95; contbr. articles on amino acid metabolism, methane biosynthesis, vitamin B12 biochemistry, selenium biochemistry to profl. jours. Helen Haye Whitney fellow Oxford U., Eng., 1954-55; Rockefeller Found. grantee U. Munich, 1959-60; recipient Rose award, 1987, Klaus Schwarz medal, 1988, Life Achievement Women in Sci. award L'Oreal-UNESCO, 2000, Bertrand medal and prize Assn. European Trace Elements and Metals in Biology and Medicine, Venice, 2001. Mem. NAS, Am. Soc. Microbiology, Biochem. Soc., Soc. Am. Biochemists, Am. Chem. Soc., Am. Acad. Arts and Scis., Sigma Delta Epsilon (hon.). Home: 16907 Redland Rd Derwood MD 20855-1954 Office Phone: 301 496 3002. E-mail: tcstadtman@nih.gov.

STAFFEL, MEGAN, writer, educator; d. Rudolf Harry Staffel and Doris Lucy Staffel Malarkey; m. Graham Marks, May 16, 1976; children: Arley, Annabeth. BFA in Creative Writing, Emerson Coll., 1974; MFA in Fiction, U. Iowa, 1980. Tchg. asst. Kans. State U., Manhattan, 1976—78, U. Iowa, Iowa City, 1978—80; adj. Rochester (N.Y.) Inst. Tech., 1981—86, Alfred (N.Y.) U., 1993, Vt. Coll., Montpelier, 1993—. Author: (story collection) A Length of Wire and Other Stories, 1983, (novels) She Wanted Something Else, 1987, The Notebook of Lost Things, 1999; contbr. book collection Letters to a Fiction Writer, 1999, stories to quars. including Ploughshares. E-mail: mstaffel@eznet.net.

STAFFIER, PAMELA MOORMAN, psychologist; b. Passaic, N.J., Dec. 7, 1942; d. Wynant Clair and Jeannette Frances (Rentzsch) Moorman; m. John Staffier, Jr., Apr. 5, 1975; children: M. Anthony, C. Matthew. BA, Bucknell U., 1964; MA in Psychology, Assumption Coll., Worcester, Mass., 1970, CAGS, 1977; PhD, Union Inst., 1978. Psychologist Westboro (Mass.) State Hosp., 1965; prin. psychologist, also asst. to supt., 1973-76; psychologist Moriarty Mental Health Clinic; psychiat. cons. local gen. hosp. Rsch. psychologist Wrentham (Mass.) State Sch., 1966, Cushing Hosp., Framingham, Mass., 1967; prin. psychologist, also asst. to supt. Grafton (Mass.) State Hosp., 1967-72; dir. Staffier Clinic, 1978—. Mem. Am. Psychol. Assn. (assoc.), Am. Psychol. Practitioners Assn. (founding mem.), Mass. Psychol. Assn., Nat. Register Health Svc. Providers in Psychology. Achievements include research on state hosp. closings, biochem. basis of Schizophrenia. Home: 68 Adams St Westborough MA 01581 Office: 57 E Main St Westborough MA 01581-1464 Office Phone: 508-366-0406.

STAFFORD, DEBBIE, state senator; widowed; 3 children ; 2 stepchildren. Attended, Pikes Peak Inst. Med. Tech., Nazarene Bible Coll., World Wide Coll. Auctioneering. Ordained min.; approved domestic violence counselor Colo. State rep. Colo. Ho. of Reps., Denver; state sen. dist. 40 Colo. State Senate, Denver, 2002—, vice chair, health, environment, welfare and instns. com., mem. transp. and energy com. Republican. Office: State Capitol # 320 200 E Colfax Ave Denver CO 80203

STAFFORD, LORI, reporter; b. Birmingham, Ala. m. Jeff Stafford. Student, Auburn U., U. Ala.; MA, Northwestern U. Mem. staff TV sta., Reno, Cin., Chattanooga, Evansville, Ind.; reporter WISN, Milw. Office: WISN PO Box 402 Milwaukee WI 53201-0402

STAFFORD, REBECCA, retired academic administrator, sociologist, education consultant; b. Topeka, July 9, 1936; d. Frank C. and Anne Elizabeth (Larrick) S.; m. Willard Van Hazel. AB magna cum laude, Radcliffe Coll., 1958, MA, 1961; PhD, Harvard U., 1964. Sociology lectr., dept. social rels. Sch. Edn., Harvard U., Cambridge, Mass., 1964-70, mem. vis. com. bd. overseers, 1973-79; assoc. prof. sociology U. Nev., Reno, 1970-74, prof., 1973-80, chmn. dept. sociology, 1974-77, dean Coll. Arts and Scis., 1977-80; pres. Bemidji (Minn.) State U., 1980-82; exec. v.p., prof. sociology Colo. State U., Ft. Collins, 1982-83; pres. Chatham Coll., Pitts., 1983-91, prof. sociology, 1992-93; pres. Monmouth U., West Long Branch, NJ, 1993—2003. Cons. higher edn., 1992—, U.S. Internat. U. on Acad. Planning, 1992-94, USDA, 1992-93, Integra Bank, 1992-93, Millsaps Coll, Jackson, Miss., 1991, U. Pitts. Med. Sch., 1992-93; co-dir. acad. leadership inst. Carnegie Mellon U., 1991-93, U. Tenn., Knoxville, 1992-93; vis. scholar dept. sociology Harvard U., 1991; mem. faculty coll. mgmt. program. Carnegie Mellon U., Pitts., 1984-93; cons. adult devel. grant Harvard U. Health Svcs., Cambridge, 1979, rsch. sociologist, 1964-69; dir. ednl. enrichment project Harvard Sch. Edn., 1966-67, 69-70. Mem. editl. bd. Sociometry, 1974-77, Sociol. Focus., 1974-77; contbr. articles to profl. jours.; presenter papers at profl. confs. Trustee Monmouth Med. Ctr., 1993—, Winchester-Thurston Sch., Pitts., 1986-91, Montefiore Hosp., Pitts., 1990-93; trustee Presbyn.-Univ. Hosp., Pitts., 1984-93, exec. planning com., 1986-89, fin. com., 1989-93; pres. Pitts. Coun. Higher Edn., 1990; mem. Found. Ind. Colls. Inc. Pa., 1984-91, sec., 1986; mem. Colo. Commn. Higher Edn. Task Force on Quality, 1981; mem. adv. bd. Animal Rescue League, Pitts., 1989-93; founder Bemidji Area Women's Network, Minn., 1980-82; mem. intergovtl. planning steering com. Bemidji, 1980-82; mem. cmty. rels. com. Girl Scouts Southwestern Pa., 1983-86; mem. brotherhood dinner coun. Nat. Conf. Christians and Jews, 1985; mem. hon. centennial com. Pa. Sch. Blind Children, Pitts., 1986; mem. citizens sponsoring com. Allegheny Conf. Cmty. Devel., Pitts., 1983-91; mem. five state regional bd. First Union Nat. Bank, 1996—; bd. dirs. Pitts. Symphony, 1984-93, First Fidelity Bank, N.A., N.J., 1993-95, Integra Bank, Pitts., 1987-97, Urban League, Pitts., 1984-87, Women's Ctr., Ft. Collins, Colo., 1982-83, Coun. Colls. Arts and Scis., 1978-81; chmn. Harvard U. Grad. Soc. Coun., 1987-93. Recipient McCurdy-Rinkle prize for rsch. Eastern Psychiat. Assn., 1970; named Woman of Yr. in Edn., City of Pitts., 1986, Vectors/Pitts., 1987, Woman of Yr. in Edn., YWCA Tribute to Women, 1989, Women of Distinction award Muscular Dystrophy Assn., 1999, Women of Leadership award Monmouth County Girl Scouts Am., 1995, Woman of Achievement in Edn. award Monmouth County Adv. Commn. on Status of Women, 1994, Salute to Policymakers award Exec. Women in N.J., 1994; grantee Am. Coun. Edn. Inst. Acad. Deans, 1979, Inst. Ednl. Mgmt., Harvard U., 1984. Mem. Assn. Ind. Colls. and Univs. of N.J. (v.p. 1999—, sec. 1998-99, treas. 1994-98, pres. northeastern conf. 1995-99, bd. dirs. 1993—), Am. Coun. on Edn., Assn. Am. Colls., Soc. for Coll. and Univ. Planning (mem. instl. decision making and resource planning acad. 1994—), Ind. Coll. Fund (treas. 1995-96, bd. dirs. 1993—), Nat. Coun. Family Rels., Harvard U. Alumni Assn. (bd. dirs. 1985-87), Phi Beta Kappa, Phi Kappa Phi. E-mail: Becky@monmouth.edu.

STAFFORD HUMBERS, LINDA LOGAN, family practice nurse practitioner; b. Aberdeen, Miss., Oct. 6, 1949; d. Stephen Andrew and Katie Lou Logan; m. Fredrick Humbers; children from previous marriage: Tessa Deanne Stafford Holloway, Thomas Dale Stafford II. AD Nursing, ICC, 1985; BSN, MUW, 1993; MSN, NMMC, 1995. Nurse Evergreen Clinic, Nettleton, Miss., 1998—99, Hamilton Family Clinic, 1999, J.B. Noble Clinic, Beattyville, Ky., 1999—2000, 3 Forks Med. Clinic, Beattyville, 2000—01; family nurse practitioner Crisis Interventional Ctr., Corinth, Miss., 2001—. Bd. dirs. NMSH Pharmacy & Therapeutics Com. Democrat. Baptist. Avocations: cross stitch, computer programming, camping, fishing. Office: North Miss State Hosp CIC 1000 State St Corinth MS 38834

STAGE, GINGER ROOKS, psychologist; b. Allentown, Pa., Sept. 23, 1946; d. John Myers Rooks and Catherine Estelle (Graser) Rooks Bistritz; m. Robert Roy Stage, Aug. 23, 1969; 1 child, Stephen. BA in Psychology magna cum laude, Moravian Coll., 1968; MA in Psychology, Temple U., 1969. Lic. psychologist, Pa.; cert. clin. hypnotherapist Nat. Bd. Clin. Hypnotherapists. Instr. Beaver campus Pa. State U., Monaca, 1969-74; staff psychologist St. Francis Cmty. Mental Health Ctr., Pitts., 1974-83; pvt. practice family therapy Coraopolis, Pa., 1977—. Mem. Greenstein Family Therapy Consultation Group, Pitts., 1981-2000; mem., spkr. Human Sexuality Alliance, Pitts., 1989-91; spkr. in field. Mem. APA, Greater Pitts. Psychol. Assn., Western Pa. Family Ctr. Episcopalian. Avocations: needlework, guitar, exercise, walking. Home: 112 Wessex Hills Dr Coraopolis PA 15108-1021 Office: 409 Mill St Coraopolis PA 15108-1607 Office Phone: 412-262-5260.

STAGEN, MARY-PATRICIA HEALY, marketing executive; b. Ridgewood, N.J. BA in History, lic. in secondary edn.-libr. sci., Elms Coll., Chicopee, Mass., 1977; MBA in Mktg. and Info. Svcs., Rutgers U., 1994. Adminstrv. asst. to meeting dir. Am. Inst. Chem. Engrs., N.Y.C., 1980-81, meetings coord., 1981-84, mgr. spl. projects to exec. dir., 1984-89; v.p. mktg. Wall St. Rsch. Svcs., Inc., Clifton, N.J., 1990—; with Equifax Svcs., East Rutherford, N.J., 1992-96; bus. devel. Allied Signal, Inc., 1997-99, with Internat. Mktg.-Honeywell, Inc., 2000—01, NICE Systems, Inc., 2002—. Meeting planner Am. Assn. Engring. Socs., Washington, 1984-85. Mem. NAFE, Am. Mktg. Assn. Republican. Roman Catholic.

STAGGERS, MARY E. minister; b. Rocky Mount, N.C., Sept. 28, 1923; d. John and Emma Jane White; m. Calvin Staggers, Jr., May 18, 1938; children: Luther, Gervis, Earlie Mae, Curtis, Herbert, Betty Joann, Yvonne. BA, Coll. New Rochelle, 1983; M Profl. Studies, N.Y. Theol. Sem., 1985; M in Humanities, Ctr. Humanities N.Y., 1985; D of Theology of Bible, Internat. Sem. Fla., 1990; DD, Balt. Coll. Bible, 1988. Pastor Holy Redeemer Bapt. Ch., Bklyn., 1961—. Family therapist Beth Israel Hosp., N.Y.C., 1980—98. Author: It's Seed Time, 1999, The Spirit Supercedes Nature, 2003. Liaison N.Y.C. Cmty. Bd. Dist. 16; v.p. Women's Nat. Evang. and Missionary Conf., 1996—2001; pres. World Conf. Gospel Explosion, 1994—, United Ladies Ministers Counsel, 1978—99; pres. Ea. N.Y. br. Women's Nat. Evang. and Missionary Conf., 1997—2001; pres. Mother's Bd. Cedar Grove Bapt. Ch., 1940—51. Mem.: N.Y.C. Clergy Conf., Ea. Bapt. Conf., So. Bapt. Conf., Nat. Bapt. Conf. Democrat. K. Avocations: cooking, reading, writing. Home: 133 Westervelt Ave Staten Island NY 10301 Office: Holy Redeemer Bapt Ch 855 Saratoga Ave Brooklyn NY 11212 Office Phone: 718-816-5181.*

STAGGS, BARBARA, state representative; b. Hulbert, Okla., July 18, 1940; d. Truman and Veleria (Trapp) Masterson; m. Ross Staggs; children: Rick, Matt. BA in Edn., Northeastern U., 1963; MA, U. Tulsa, 1968, EdD, 1987. Tchr., adminstr.; mem. Okla. Ho. of Reps., 1995—, chair common edn. com. Named Outstanding Adminstr., Okla. Schs. Adv. Coun., 1993, Woman of Distinction, Muskogee Soroptimist's, 1996. Democrat. Office: State Capitol 2300 N Lincoln Blvd Rm 302 Oklahoma City OK 73105

STAGGS, BARBARA J. vice mayor; b. Trotwood, Ohio, Aug. 25, 1944; d. Campbell Cester and Zelma Ann (Barlow) Phillips; m. Edward Lowell Staggs, June 10, 1961; children: Terrence Lee, Deann Lorraine Staggs Roediger, Eric Justin. Lic. real estate salesperson, Ohio. In retail sales, Dayton; secretarial aide, tchrs. aide Trotwood (Ohio) Sch. Sys.; real estate agt. Hussman Realty, Dayton, 1988-90, Dever-Schenk Realty, Trotwood, 1990-93; mem. city coun. City of Trotwood, 1994—; exec. dir. Trotwood C. of C., 1990—2001. Advisor Civil Svc. Commn., Trotwood; bd. dirs. Miami Valley Career Tech. Ctr., Job Adv. Bd., Clayton, Choices in Cmty. Living, Dayton. Pres. Cmty. Investment, Trotwood; bd. dirs. Northwest Devel. Assn., Trotwood, Resolution Commn., Nat. League of Cities, human devel. policy com., info. tech. and comm. policy com., coun. re. zoning appeals bd., program planning com. Mem.: Women in Govt., Trotwood Rotary. Avocations: doll collecting, building doll houses, sewing and crafts. Home: 19 W Sunrise Ave Trotwood OH 45426-3525 Office: City of Trotwood 35 Olive Rd Ste 2 Trotwood OH 45426-2698

STAHELI, LINDA ANNE, social science executive; b. Salt Lake City, Dec. 9, 1959; m. David Samuel Abramowitz, May 17, 1992. BA, U. Wash., 1983; M in Pub. Mgmt., U. Md., 1988. Consumer rels. intern Atty. Gen.'s Office, Seattle, 1981; project coord. Metrocenter YMCA, Seattle, 1983; lobbyist Coun. for a Livable World, Washington, 1984-86; MacArthur fellow Ctr. for Internat. Security Studies U. Md., College Park, 1986—88; coord. for constituency outreach Dem. Nat. Com., Washington, 1988; rsch. analyst Pacific Sierra Rsch. Corp., Arlington, Va., 1989; fgn. affairs officer Bur. of Oceans, Environment and Sci. Affairs, Dept. of State, Washington, 1990-93; sr. policy advisor for internat. affairs White House Office of Sci. and Tech. Policy, Washington, 1993-95; acting dir. divsn. internat. rels. Fogarty Internat. Ctr., NIH, Washington, 1995-98; pres. Staheli and Assocs. Consulting, Washington, 1998—2002; sr. staff assoc. U.S. Civilian R&D Found., 2001—. Mem. adv. bd. Yosemite Nat. Insts., San Francisco, 1996-99, Global HELP; bd. dirs. Internat. Network for Cancer Treatment and Rsch., 1999-2002.

STAHL, ALICE SLATER, retired psychiatrist; b. Vienna, Jan. 28, 1913; came to U.S., 1938; d. Sam and Helen (Bluman) Slater; widowed; children: Kenneth Lee, June Audrey. Baccalaureate, Gymnasium, Vienna, 1932; Med. Dr., U. Vienna Med. Sch., 1938. Intern Williamsport (Pa.) Gen. Hosp., 1939-40; resident in psychiatry Gallinger Mcpl. Hosp., Washington, 1940-41, Independence State Hosp., 1941-42, Bellevue Hosp., N.Y.C., 1942-43, attending psychiatrist, 1945-48; staff psychiatrist Jewish Bd. of Guardians, N.Y.C., 1943-45; attending psychiatrist Jamaica Hosp., Queens, NY, 1948-52; dir. adolescent pavilion Hillside Hosp., Glen Oaks, NY, 1954-96, staff psychiatrist, 1982—95; supervising psychiatrist Bergen Regional Hosp., Paramus, NJ, 1987—2002. Asst. prof. clin. psychiatry Yeshiva U. Med. Sch., 1978-96. Fellow AMA (life), Am. Psychiat. Assn. (life); mem. Am. Psychoanalytic Assn. (life), Am. Soc. for Adolescent Psychiatry (life) Avocations: swimming, hiking, gardening, grandmotherhood. Home and Office: 305 Joan Pl Wyckoff NJ 07481-2818

STAHL, ARLEEN MARIE, nursing educator; b. Joliet, Ill., Mar. 19, 1947; d. Joseph Ralph and Mary Margaret (Stariha) Dusa; m. Robert John Stahl, Aug. 23, 1969; children: Jennifer, Erika, Alicia, Raymond. Diploma in nursing, Little Co. of Mary Hosp., 1968; BS in Profl. Arts, Coll. St. Francis, 1973; BSN, No. Ill. U., 1980, MSN in Clin. Nurse Specialist, 1984, PhD, 1996. RN, Ill. Staff/charge nurse critical care units St. Joseph Med. Ctr., Joliet, 1968-73, 77-80, instr. nursing Sch. Nursing, 1973-76, 80-88; tchg. asst. No. Ill. U., Dekalb, 1992-93, rsch. asst., 1994-95; prof. nursing St. Joseph Coll. Nursing/U. St. Francis, Joliet, 1989—, coord. MSN program, 1989—. Textbook cons. J.B. Lippincott Co., Phila., 1991-92; com. mem. Joliet Area Cmty. Hospice Edn. Com., Joliet, 1991-92. Rsch. grantee NIH, 1995, 96. Mem. ANA, Ill. Nurses Assn., Sigma Theta Tau (Beta Omega chpt.), Phi Sigma Soc. (Beta Epsilon chpt.). Home: 1013 Windsor Dr Shorewood IL 60431-9162 Office: Univ St Francis Coll Nursing and Allied Health 290 Springfield Ave Joliet IL 60435-6510

STAHL, LESLEY R. news correspondent; b. Lynn, Mass., Dec. 16, 1941; d. Louis and Dorothy J. (Tishler) Stahl; m. Aaron Latham; 1 child. BA cum laude, Wheaton Coll., Norton, Mass., 1963. Asst. to speechwriter Mayor Lindsay's Office, N.Y.C., 1966—67; rschr. N.Y. Election unit CBS News, 1967—68; rschr. London-Huntley Brinkley Report, NBC News, 1969; prodr., reporter WHDH-TV, Boston, 1970—72; news corr. CBS News, Washington, 1972—, White House corr., 1979-91; moderator Face the Nation, 1983-91; co-editor, corr. CBS News, 60 Minutes, 1991—. Trustee Wheaton Coll. Named Best White House Corr., Washington Journalism Rev., 1991; named to Broadcasting Mag. Hall of Fame, 1992; recipient Tex. Headliners award, 1973, Dennis Kauff award for lifetime achievement in journalism, Fifth Estate award, Fred Friendly First Amendment award, 1996. Office: CBS News 60 Minutes 524 W 57th St New York NY 10019-2924*

STAHLECKER, BARBARA JEAN, marketing professional, consultant; b. Stamford, Conn., Jan. 22, 1958; d. Roger Francis and Lillian Ann Beauleau; m. Richard Walter Stahlecker; children: Shannon Lee Banks, Brande Lauren Beach; children: Cori, Cara. Grad., Brien McMahon H.S., Norwalk, Conn., 1975. New bus. adminstr. Mutual of Omaha Ins. Co., L.A., 1983—85; ind. ins. agt. L.A., 1985—88; mktg. coord. LifeCare Assurance Corp., Canoga Park, Calif., 1988—96; v.p., nat. mktg. dir. Centrelink Ins. & Fin. Svcs., Woodland, Calif., 1996—. Author: (Continuing Education Courses) Everything You've Always Wanted to Know about LTC - and Then Some, 1998, (Continuing Education Course) The Nuts and Bolts of Long Term Care Insurance, 2000, TQ vs. NTQ LTCI, 2001; contbr. articles to profl. jours., 2001. Recipient Million Dollar Prodr. award, UNUM/Provident, 2001. Mem.: Soc. Cert. Sr. Advisors (cert. sr. advisor), Long-Term Care Profl., Am. Assn. Long-Term Care Ins. (Top Prodr. award 2000, 2001, BRAMCO Million Dollar Club award 2002), Nat. Assn. Health Underwriters (cons. 1999—). Office: Centrelink Ins & Fin Svc 20750 Ventura Blvd #300 Woodland Hills CA 91364 Business E-Mail: barbara@centrelink.com.

STAHLMAN, MILDRED THORNTON, pediatrics and pathology educator, researcher; b. Nashville, July 31, 1922; d. James Geddes and Mildred (Thornton) Stahlman. AB, Vanderbilt U., 1943, MD, 1946, MD (hon.), U. Goteborg, Sweden, 1973, U. Nancy, France, 1982. Diplomate Am. Bd. Pediat., Am. Bd. Neonatology. Intern Boston Children's Hosp., 1947—48; resident Vanderbilt Univ. Hosp., 1948—49; fellow Royal Caroline Inst. Medicine, Sweden, 1949—50; cardiac resident La Rabida Sanitarium, Chgo., 1951; instr. pediat. Vanderbilt U., Nashville, 1951—58, instr. physiology, 1954—60, asst. prof. pediat., 1959—64, asst. prof. physiology, 1960—62, assoc. prof. pediat., 1964—70, prof., 1970—, prof. pathology, 1982—, Harvie Branscomb Disting. prof., 1984, dir. divsn. neonatology, 1961—89, now prof. pediat. and pathology. Editor: Respiratory Distress Syndromes, 1989; contbr. over 175 articles to profl. publs., chpts. to books. Recipient Apgar award, Am. Acad. Pediat., 1987; grantee NIH, 1954—. Mem.: AAAS, Inst. Medicine NAS, Royal Swedish Acad. Scis., So. Soc. Pediatric Rsch. (pres. 1961—62), Am. Physiology Soc., Soc. Pediatric Rsch., Am. Pediatric Soc. (pres. 1984, John Howland award 1996). Episcopalian. Home: 538 Beech Creek Rd S Brentwood TN 37027-3421 Office: Vanderbilt U Med Ctr A-0109 Med Ctr N 21st Ave S Nashville TN 37232-2370 E-mail: mildred.stahlman@vanderbilt.edu.

STAHMER, ANN MIKLOFSKY, choral music director, producer; b. Washington, Jan. 30, 1951; d. Haaren Albert Miklofsky and Rita Barbara Nelson; m. Timothy Ralph Stahmer, July 23, 1972. B.Choral Music Edn., U. of Ariz., 1975, M.Reading, 1979; postgrad., Rider U., Princeton, N.J., 1993. Cert. tchr. Va., 1993. Chair, interdisciplinary studies dept. WMST PCHS, Washington, 1999—; interview writer JazzReview.com, 2002; artistic dir. Noble Voices, Washington, 1995—. Prodr. Choral Arts Soc. of Washington, Washington, 1995—99; pres. WMST Faculty Senate, 2002—03. Composer: (choral music) Pray for the Child, You Are My God, My Heart, We Are One, You Are My God, My Heart; condr. (CD) Birth and Rebirth, 1995. Mem. Cultural Alliance of Greater Washington; mem. steering com. MLK Choral Tribute, Washington, 1996—2003. Recipient Chimes, U. of Ariz., 1972; scholar Haldeman Music scholar, 1974. Mem.: Va. Music Educators Assn. (all-state chorus mgr. 1988—94), Music Educators Nat. Conf., Am. Choral Dirs. Assn., Mortar Bd., Alpha Lambda Delta, Phi Lambda Theta. Independent. Jewish. Avocation: travel. Home: 7451 Digby Green Kingstowne VA 22315-5219 Office: WMST PCHS 770 M St SE Washington DC 20003 Personal E-mail: ann@assortedstuff.com. E-mail: ann.stahmer@wmstpchs.net.

STAHR, BETH A. school librarian; b. Elmhurst, Ill, June 13, 1951; d. John H. Pohlmann and Mary Anne Price; m. Charles Ward Stahr, Aug. 25, 1973; children: Margaret L., Andrew J. BS Engring., Purdue U., 1973; MLS, Syracuse U., 1999. Environ. specialist Owens Corning Fiberglas, Toledo, 1973—78; genealogical rschr. pvt. practice, Wausau, Wis., 1988—98; libr. Southeastern La. U., Hammond, La., 1999—; asst. prof. Southeastern La. Univ., Hammond, La., 2000—. V.p., trustee Wis. Genealogical Coun., 1992—98; treas., trustee Assn. Profl. Genealogists, Washington, 1994—95, Bd. Cert. Genealogists, 1998—; v.p. Louisiana Genealogical and Hist. Soc., 2001—. Vol. Birch Trails coun. Girl Scouts Am., Tomahawk, Wis., 1980—91; v.p., trustee La. Genealogical and Hist. Soc., La., 2001—. Mem.: ALA, ACRL. Episcopalian. Home: 55 Dogwood Ln Covington LA 70435

STAINBROOK, MARGARET COLLINS, retired school system administrator; b. Zanesville, Ohio, Mar. 24, 1927; d. Cecil Nicholas Collins and Mary Jane Roberts; m. Alfred Richard Stainbrook (dec. July 27, 2000); children: Ginger Margaret, Jeffrey Richard. BEd, Ohio U., 1966, MA in Edn. Adminstrn., 1970. Elem. tchr. Zanesville (Ohio) City Schs., 1960—71, elem. prin., 1971—92; ret., 1992. Docent Pioneer Hist. Assn., Zanesville, Ohio, 1992—2003; vol. Genesis Hosp., Zanesville, Ohio, 1993—2003. Grantee Jennings Scholar, Jennings Found., Ohio U., 1970. Mem.: Soroptimist Internat. (pres. 1975—76), DAR, Ohio Assn. Elem. Prins., Nat. Assn. Elem. Prins., Phi Delta Kappa. Avocation: genealogy. Home: 709 Brighton Blvd Zanesville OH 43701

STALEY, DAWN, professional basketball player; b. Phila., May 4, 1970; Grad., U. Va., 1992. Basketball player, guard Charlotte Sting, SC, 1997—. Mem. U.S. Nat. Women's Basketball Gold Medal Olympic Team, 1996, 2000, U.S. Nat. Women's Basketball Olympic Team, 1999. Named USA Basketball Female Athlete of Yr., 1994; named to Ea. Conf. All-Star team,

2001; scholar, U. Va. Achievements include first women in professional basketball history to record 1,000 career assists. Avocation: playing professional basketball in Italy, Brazil, Spain and France. Office: 100 Hive Dr Charlotte NC 28208-7707

STALEY, LYNN, English educator; b. Madisonville, Ky., Dec. 24, 1947; d. James Mulford and Florine (Hurt) Staley. AB, U. Ky., 1969; MA, PhD, Princeton U., 1973. Grad. asst. Princeton (N.J.) U., 1971-73; instr. English Colgate U., Hamilton, N.Y., 1974-75, from asst. to assoc. prof., 1975-86, prof., 1986—. Author: The Voice of the Gawain-Poet, 1984, The Shepheardes Calendar: An Introduction, 1990, Margery Kempe's Dissenting Fictions, 1994, (with David Aers) The Powers of the Holy: Religion, Politics and Gender in Late Medieval English Culture, 1996; editor: The Book of Margery Kempe, 1996; translator: The Book of Margery Kempe, 2001; contbr. articles to profl. jours. NEH fellow, 2003—04, Guggenheim fellow, 2003—04. Mem. MLA, Medieval Acad. Am., Renaissance Soc. Am., New Chaucer Soc., Spenser Soc. Office: Colgate U Dept English 13 Oak Dr Dept English Hamilton NY 13346-1383

STALKER, JACQUELINE D'AOUST, academic administrator, educator; b. Penetang, Ont., Can., Oct. 16, 1933; d. Phillip and Rose (Eaton) D'Aoust; m. Robert Stalker; children: Patricia, Lynn, Roberta. Teaching cert., U. Ottawa, 1952; tchr. music, Royal Toronto Conservatory Music, 1952; teaching cert., Lakeshore Tchrs. Coll., 1958; BEd with honors, U. Manitoba, 1977, MEd, 1979; EdD, Nova U., 1985. Cert. tchr. Ont., Man., Can. Adminstr., tchr., prin. various schs., Ont. and Que., 1952-65; area commr. Girl Guides of Can., throughout Europe, 1965-69; administr., tchr. Algonquin Community Coll., Ottawa, Ont., 1970-74; tchr., program devel. Frontenac County Bd. Edn., Kingston, Ont., 1974-75; lectr., faculty advisor dept. curriculum, edn. U. Man., Can., 1977-79; lectr. U. Winnipeg, Man., Can., 1977-79; cons. colls. div. Man. Dept. Edn., 1980-81, sr. cons. programming br., 1981-84, sr. cons. post secondary, adult and continuing edn. div., 1985-88, dir. post secondary career devel. br. and adult and continuing edn. br., 1989; asst. prof. higher edn., coord. grad. program in higher edn. U. Man., 1989-92, assoc. prof., coord. grad. program in higher edn., 1992-95. Cons. lectures, seminars, workshops throughout Can. Contbr. articles to profl. jours.; mng. editor Can. Jour. of Higher Edn., 1989-93. Mem. U. Man. Senate, 1976-81, 86-89, bd. govs., 1979-82; Can. rep. Internat. Youth Conf., Garmisch, Fed. Republic of Germany, 1968; vol. Can. Cancer Soc.; mem. Assn. RN Accreditation Coun., 1980-85; chair Child Care Accreditation Com., Man., 1983-90; chair Task Force Post-Secondary Accessibility, Man., 1983; vol. United Way Planning and Allocations; provincial dir., mem. nat. bd. Can. Congress for Learning Opportunities for Women. Recipient award for enhancing the Outreach activities of the univ. U. Man., 1994. Mem. Can. Soc. Study Higher Edn., Man. Tchrs. Soc., U. Man. Alumni Assn., Women's Legal Edn. and Action Fund. Home: 3844 Northwest 9Lth Way Sunrise FL 33351

STALKER, LINDA J. retired secondary school educator; d. Joe Ray and Ruth Bound Montgomery; m. Bob D. Stalker, Sept. 1, 1964 (div. Mar. 1992); children: David, Brian. BA, Ind. State U., 1966, MS, 1975. Tchr. Montezuma (Ind.) HS, 1966—69, North Putnam Jr.-Sr. H.S., Bainbridge, Ind., 1969—71, Rockville (Ind.) Jr.-Sr. H.S., 1973—96, speech, media specialist, 1997—2002; tech. prep. coord. Parke-Vermillion edn. and Training Interlocal, Hillsdale, Ind., 2002—03; ret., 2003. Clk. Election Polls, Rockville, 2002. Avocations: travel, painting, acting, interior decorating, crafts.

STALLING, JANET KITTS, music educator; b. Waycross, Ga., Apr. 6, 1960; d. Kenneth Kermit and Nancy Buckner Kitts; m. James Reed Bethel, Dec. 20, 1986 (div. Dec. 1998); children: Rachel Allison, Stuart Reed, Mary Susan, Victoria Elizabeth; m. Jeffrey Bryant Stalling, Apr. 16, 2004. B in Music Edn., U. N.C., 1982; MusM, Notre Dame U., 1984. Cert. tchr. N.C., Ga., nat. bd. cert. music Nat. Bd. Profl. Tchg. Stds. Educator State Bridge Crossing Elem., Alpharetta. Mem. leadership team State Bridge Crossing Elem., Alpharetta, 2002—; prin. Johns Creek Bapt. Ch. Orch., Alpharetta, 2003—. Mem.: Ga. Music Assn., Music Educators Nat. Conf. Baptist. Home: 3790 Crescent Walk Ln Suwanee GA 30024 Office: State Bridge Crossing Elem 5530 State Bridge Rd Alpharetta GA 30022

STALLINGS, VALERIE A. physician, state agency administrator; b. N.Y.C., Nov. 27, 1943; BS in Zoology, Duke U., 1964; MD, U. N.C., 1968, MPH, 1988. Intern, resident Pediat. Med. Coll. Va., 1968-71; physician Va. Dept. Health Bur. Crippled Children, Norfolk, 1972—75, Portsmouth (Va.) Health Dept., 1972—75; dir. Tidewater Child Devel. Clin., Norfolk, 1977-82; dep. dir. Norfolk Dept. Pub. Health, 1982-89, dir., 1989—. Office: Norfolk Dept Pub Health 830 Southampton Ave Norfolk VA 23510-1001

STALLINGS, VALERIE AILEEN, retired councilwoman, consultant; b. Chgo., Dec. 23, 1939; d. Jay Sims and Mary Elizabeth (Batson) Spire; adoptive dau. Willian Mundo Spire; m. John R. Stallings, July 14, 1961 (div. 1970); children: Dana Elizabeth, Marshall Brigg. AA, Palomar (Calif.) Coll., 1978; BA, U. Calif., San Diego, 1980. Rschr., lab. mgr. Salk Inst., La Jolla, Calif., 1970-91; mem. coun. City of San Diego, 1991-2001, ret., 2001. Sabbatical rschr. Netherlands Cancer Inst., 1981; city rep. Jack Murphy Stadium Authority, San Diego, 1991-2000; chmn. pub. facilities and recreation City of San Diego, 1992-95; chmn. fiscal policy San Diego Wastewater, 1993-94; dir. San Diego Area Wastewater Mgmt. Dist., 1993—. Contbr. articles to sci. jours. Pres. Pacific Beach Dem. Club, San Diego; mem. Pacific Beach Planning Commn., San Diego. Named Legislator of Yr., SEIU Svc. Coun., 1992. Mem. Nat. Women's Polit. Caucus, Calif. Elected Women's Assn. for Edn. and Rsch., U. Calif. Alumni Assn. (bd. dirs.). Democrat. Avocations: triathlons, jogging, leading safaris in east africa, photography. Office: Dist 6 1536 Frankfort St San Diego CA 92110

STALLINGS, VIOLA PATRICIA ELIZABETH, systems engineer, educational systems specialist, retired information technology manager; b. Norfolk, Va., Nov. 6, 1946; d. Harold Albert and Marie Blanche (Welch) S.; m. (div. Oct. 1984); 1 child, Patricia N.P. Stallings. BS in Psychology, Va. State U., 1968; MBA with distinction, U. Pa., 1975; postgrad., Temple U., 1972-74, Calif. State U., San Francisco, 1973; EdD with specialization in tech., Nova Southeastern U., Ft. Lauderdale, Fla., 1996. Cert. exec. project mgr., project mgmt. profl. Project Mgmt. Inst. Tchr., supr. Peace Corps, Liberia, West Africa, 1968-71; tchr. Day Care Ctr., disruptive h.s. students Tioga Comm. Youth Ctr., 1972-73; tchr. Phila. Sch. Dist., 1972-76; bus. cons. Phila., 1976; sr. sys. engr./sr. industry svcs. specialist, retiring project mgr. IBM/K-12 Edn. and IBM Global Industry, Mt. Laurel; retiring cert. exec. project mgr. IBM Global Svcs. Task force leader IBM Corp., 1990—91. Com. mem. AFNA, 1977—83; bd. dirs. Woodrock, 1976—83, 1987—92, Unity Ch. of Christ, 1993—95, 2000—03, v.p., 1994—95, sec., 2000—01. Recipient Outstanding Svc. awards IBM Black Workers Alliance, Washington, 1984, Recipient IBM Black Workers Svc. award, 1984. Recipient Outstanding Svcs. and Achievement, 1977-2001. Mem. AAUW, World Affairs Coun., Project Mgmt. Inst., St. Joseph's Carpenter Soc. (bd. dirs. 1999—), Women of Arts, Beta Gamma Sigma. Baptist. Avocations: reading, writing, drawing, gardening, cooking, dance, sewing.

STALLWORTH, ALMA GRACE, former state legislator; Grad., Highland Park Community Coll., 1956; student, Wayne State U., 1956. Mem. Mich. Ho. of Reps., Lansing, 1970-74, 81-96; dep. dir. Hist. Dept. City of Detroit, 1975-78, job developer, 1978-79. Mem. exec. com. Nat. Conf. State Legislatures, 1986-89. Commr. Wayne County Charter, Detroit, 1978-79, Martin Luther King Commn., Detroit, 1987; chairperson bd. dirs. task force on infant mortality Mich. Legislature, 1987; pres. Nat. Black Child Devel. Inst., Detroit; vol. United Negro Coll. Fund, 1987—; founder, adminstr. Black Caucus Found. of Mich., 1987—. Recipient cert. of appreciation Mich. Dept. Edn., 1986, Advs. award Mich. Health Mothers, Health Babies Coalition, 1987; named Woman Leader in Pub. Health, Mi ch. Assn. Local Pub. Health, 1987, Woman of Yr., Minority Women's Network, 1988. Mem. NAACP, Nat. Conf. State Legislators (exec. commr. 1986), Nat. Black Caucus State Legislators, (sec. women's caucus) Mich. Legis. Black Causus (chair 1987), Alpha Kappa Alpha. Clubs: Cameo, Top Ladies of Distinction. Democrat. Home: 19793 Sorrento St Detroit MI 48235-1149

STALLWORTH-BARRON, DORIS A. CARTER, librarian, educator; b. Ala., June 12, 1931; d. Henry Lee Carter and Hattie Belle Stallworth; m. George Stallworth, 1950 (dec.); children: Annette LaVerne, Vanzette Yvonne; m. Walter L. Barron, 1989. BS, Ala. State U., 1955; MLS, CUNY, 1968; postgrad., Columbia U., St. John's U., NYU. Cert. supr. and tchr. sch. libr. media, N.Y. Libr. media specialist N.Y.C. Bd. Edn.; head libr. Calhoun County High Sch., Hobson City, Ala. Cons. Libr. Unit, N.Y.C. Bd. Edn.; cons. evaluator So. Assn. Secondary Schs., Ala.; supr., adminstr., liason rep. Community Sch. Dist. #24 N.Y.C. Sch. System; previewer libr. media Preview Mag., 1971-73; mem. ednl. svcs. adv. coun. Sta. WNET, 1987-89; mem. coun. N.Y.C. Schs. Libr. System, 1987-90, mem. N.Y.C. bd. examiners for tchr. librs., 1972-89; turn-key tchr. trainer N.Y. State Dept. Edn., 1988; spl. guest speaker and lectr. Queens Coll., City U., Community Sch. Dist. #24, PTA, N.Y. City Sch. System, Libr. unit, 1980-90; curriculum writer libr. unit N.Y.C. Bd. Edn., 1985-86. Contbr. articles to ednl. publs. Mem. State of Ala. Dem. Exec. Com., 1994—; active A+ for Kids. Mem. NAFE, ALA, Am. Assn. Sch. Librs. (spl. guest speaker and lectr. for conv. 1987), Am. Sch. Libr.'s Assn., Nat. Assn. Black Pub. Adminstrs., N.Y. State Libr. Assn., N.Y.C. Sch. Librs. Assn., Nat. Forum for Black Pub. Adminstrs., N.Y. Coalition 100 Black Women, Lambda Kappa Mu Sorority, Inc., Alpha Kappa Alpha Sorority Inc.

STAMATAKIS, CAROL MARIE, lawyer, former state legislator; b. Canton, Ohio, Apr. 27, 1960; d. Emmanuel and Catherine Lucille Stamatakis; m. Michael Shklar, Mar. 23, 1985. BA in Criminology and Criminal Justice, Ohio State U., 1982; JD, Case Western Res., 1985. Bar: N.H. 1985, U.S. Dist. Ct. N.H. 1985. Atty. Elliott, Jasper & Stamatakis, Newport, N.H., 1990-93; state rep. N.H. State Legislature, 1988-94; atty. N.H. Dept. Health and Human Svcs., Concord, 1994—. Instr. Am. Inst. Banking, Claremont, 1987-88, 91-92, 95. Asst. editor: (jours.) Health Matrix: The Jour. of Health Services Mangement, 1983-85. Treas., mem. Town of Lempster N.H. Conservation Commn., 1987—; bd. dirs. Orion House, Inc., Newport, N.H., 1987-91; town chair N.H. Dem. Party, 1987—; mem. Town of Lempster Recycling Com., 1988—, Community Task Force on Drug and alcohol Abuse, 1988. Mem. N.H. Bar Assn., Sierra Club, Upper Valley Group (former vice chair and solid waste chair). Avocations: drawing, painting. Home: PO Box 807 Newport NH 03773-0807

STAMBERG, SUSAN LEVITT, radio broadcaster; b. Newark, Sept. 7, 1938; d. Robert I. and Anne (Rosenberg) Levitt; m. Louis Collins Stamberg, Apr. 14, 1962; 1 child, Joshua Collins BA, Barnard Coll, 1959; DHL (hon.), Gettysburg Coll., 1982, Dartmouth Coll., 1984, Knox Coll., U. N.H., SUNY, Brockport. Editorial asst. Daedalus, Cambridge, Mass., 1960-62; editorial asst. The New Republic, Washington, 1962-63; host, producer, mgr., program dir. Sta. WAMU-FM, Washington, 1963-69; host All Things Considered Washington, 1971-86; host Weekend Edition Nat Pub. Radio, Washington, 1987-89; spl. corr. Nat. Pub. Radio, 1990—. Bd. dirs. AIA, Washington, 1983-85, PEN/Faulkner Fiction Award Found., 1985—. Author: Every Night at Five, 1982, The Wedding Cake in the Middle of the Road, 1992, Talk: NPR's Susan Stamberg Considers All Things, 1993. Recipient Honor award Ohio U., 1977, Edward R. Murrow award Corp. for Pub. Broadcasting, 1980; named Woman of Yr., Barnard Coll., 1984; fellow Silliman Coll. Yale U., 1984—; inducted Broadcasting Hall of Fame, 1994, Radio Hall of Fame, 1996. Avocations: sketching; piano; knitting. Office: Nat Pub Radio 635 Massachusetts Ave NW Washington DC 20001-3753

STAMILE, JENNIFER, materials engineer; b. Denver; d. Stephen and Patricia Stamile. BA in Anthropology magna cum laude, U. of Colo., Denver, 1996; M. Basic Sci., U. of Colo., Denver, Colorado, 2000; M.Engring. in Metall. and Materials Engring., Colo. Sch. of Mines, 2003. Rsch. asst. U. of Colo., Denver, 1999—2000; r & d technician Tetrad, Inc., Englewood, Colo., 2000—01; rsch. asst. Colo. Sch. of Mines, Golden, 2000—. Mem.: NAFE, Soc. of Women Engrs., Pi Tau Sigma, Golden Key. Home: 9390 W Chatfield Pl Unit 208 Littleton CO 80126-9262 E-mail: fea_engr@yahoo.com.

STAMM, CAROL ANN, obstetrician, gynecologist; b. Denver, Aug. 8, 1959; d. Robert L. and Mary Ellen Stamm. BA in Biology cum laude, U. Colo., 1981, cert. in elem. tchg., 1985; MD with honors, U. Colo., Denver, 1991. Diplomate Am. Bd. Ob-Gyn. Bilingual elem. tchr. Denver Pub. Schs., 1986—87; intern in ob-gyn U. Colo. Sch. Medicine, Denver, 1991—92, resident in ob-gyn, 1992—95, asst. prof., 1997—2003; staff ob-gyn, asst. prof. Denver Health Med. Ctr., 1995—2003; dir. of women's health rotation High St. Primary Care Clinic, Denver, 2003—, asst. prof. of clin. medicine, 2003—. Mem. Patient and Family Edn. Work Group, 1996—97; mem. edn. com. U. Colo. Health Scis. Ctr., 1997—2003; dir. ob-gyn Grand Rounds, 1997—2001; provider design team Lifetime Clin. Record Project, 1998—2001; alt. mem. Colo. Multiple Instl. Rev. Bd., 1998—2003; presenter in field. Co-author: (book) Management of High-Risk Pregnancy, 4th edit., 1999, Medical Care of the Pregnant Patient, 2000, The Female Athlete, 2002, Contemporary Therapy in Obstetrics and Gynecology, 2002; contbr. articles to profl. jours.; peer reviewer Jour. Obstetrics and Gynecology, 1999—, Am. Jour. Obstetrics and Gynecology, 1999—. Recipient Richard Whitehead award, Phi Rho Sigma, 1989; grantee, March of Dimes, 2000—01; Trust fellow, Am. Cancer Soc. Brooks, 1988, Acad. Enrichment grantee, U. Colo. Health Scis. Ctr., 1993—95, NIH grantee, U. Pitts., 2000—03, IBBEX, 2002. Fellow: ACOG; mem.: Am. Med. Women's Assn., Golden Key, Phi Beta Kappa (mem. mortar bd.). Avocations: reading, running, pilates, symphony, opera. Home: 155 S Jackson St Unit C Denver CO 80209 Office: Health One Alliance/High St Primary Care Clinic 1801 High St Denver CO 80218 Business E-Mail: cstamm@health1.org.

STAMMERJOHAN, ELIZABETH CLAIRE ALLISON, finance educator; d. Arthur Vernon and Beverly Jean Berndt Allison; m. William W. Stammerjohan, May 22, 1970; children: Will, Kathy. BFA, Miss. State U., 1998, PhD, 2002. Owner Bill's Custom Machine, Sacramento, 1975—91; mgr. Tognottis Printing, Sacramento, 1991—95; vis. asst. prof. Wash. State U., Pullman, 2003. Mem. Ctrl. Bus. Devel. Com.; tutor Alexander Sch., 1998. Mem.: Pullman C. of C., Beta Gamma Sigma, Phi Kappa Phi. Office: Wash State U PO Box 644730 Pullman WA 99164

STAMP, MELVA ELAINE, special education educator; b. Elmira, N.Y., Aug. 20, 1951; d. Edward J. and Cleoral Alberta Lovell; m. Howard William Stamp, Jan. 16, 1970; children: Robert Anthony, Sherry Ann. AA in Liberal Arts, Corning C.C., Corning, NY, 1980; BA in Psychology, Elmira Coll., 1982; MS in Varying Exceptionalities, U. Ctrl. Fla., 1999. Profl. educator's cert. Fla. Adj. prof. humanities Corning C.C., 1985—87; substitute tchr. Exceptional Student Edn. Osceola City Sch. Dist., Kissimmee, Fla., 1989—95, varying exceptionalities tchr., 1995—. Avocations: gardening, writing. Office: Osceola City Sch Narcoossee Cmty Sch 2700 N Narcoossee Rd Saint Cloud FL 34771

STAMPER, EWA SZUMOTALSKA, psychologist; b. Warsaw, Sept. 8, 1954; came to U.S., 1984; d. Tadeusz and Regina S.; m. Ryszard Zwierowicz, Dec. 30, 1980 (div. Jan. 13, 1986); m. Allen Malcolm Stamper, Oct. 23, 1992. MA in Clin. Psychology, U. Warsaw, Poland, 1978; PhD in Psychology, New Sch. U., N.Y.C., 1992. Staff therapist Marital Therapy Counseling Ctr., Warsaw, 1978—79, Ctr. for Psychotherapy and Personality Growth, Warsaw, 1978—80; sr. staff therapist Lab. for Psychoedn. Polish Psychol. Assn., Warsaw, 1981—85; postgrad. affiliate Washington Sq. Inst. for Psychotherapy, N.Y.C., 1990—92; police psychologist Honolulu Police Dept., 1993—98; pvt. practice, Honolulu, 1994—. With Tng. Ctr. for Family Therapy, Warsaw, 1970—78, Stuyvesant Poly., N.Y.C., 1988—89, North Ctrl. Bronx (N.Y.) Hosp., 1988—89, Yale Psychiat. Inst., 1989—90, Castle Med. Ctr., Kailua, Hawaii, 1993—94; co-chmn. Crystal Methampetamine Forum, Honolulu, 1996—99. Mem. APA, Am. Acad. Experts in Traumatic Stress, Hawaii Psychol. Assn. (clin. divsn. rep. 1998-99). Avocations: horseback riding, raising German shorthaired pointers and Siamese cats, gardening, fiction and poetry writing, running. Office: 1188 Bishop St Ste 1108 Honolulu HI 96813-3313 Office Phone: 808-531-1991.

STAMPS, LAURA ANNE, writer, poet; b. Indpls., Apr. 2, 1957; d. James Oliver and Isabelle Anne (Holland) Smith; m. Carl Thomas Stamps, Jr., June 30, 1979. Student, Dalton (Ga.) Jr. Coll., 1977, Coll. of Charleston, S.C., 1979. Owner Kittyfeather Press, Columbia, SC, 1985—. Author: Art Marketing Manual, 1988, How to Create the Life You Desire, 1995, How to Become a Prosperous Woman, 1995, Songs of Power, 1996, (fiction) Earth Lessons, 1995, Tuning Out, 1996, The Way of Love, 1998, I Can Do Anything, vol. 1, 2000, vol. 2, 2000, Restore my Soul, 2002, In the Company of Cats, 2002, Joy Unspeakable, 2003, Evergreen, 2003; editor The Artist's Forum, 1989-94, Laura's Letter for Women, 1996-97. Avocations: gardening, cats. Office: Kittyfeather Press PO Box 212534 Columbia SC 29221-2534

STAMSTA, JEAN F. artist; b. Sheboygan, Wis., Nov. 2, 1936; d. Herbert R. and Lucile Caroline (Malwitz) Nagel; m. Duane R. Stamsta, Aug. 18, 1956; children: Marc, David. BS, BA, U. Wis., 1958. Guest curator Milw. Art Mus., 1986; resident artist Leighton Artist Colony, Banff, Alta., Can., 1987. One-woman shows include Am. Craft Mus., N.Y.C., 1971, Winona (Minn.) State U., 1986, Lawrence U., Appleton, Wis., 1990, Walkers Point Ctr. Arts, Milw., 1990, U. Wis. Ctr., Sheboygan, 1998, Wis. Luth. Coll., Milw., 1999, exhibited in group shows at Cleve. Mus. Art, 1977, Milw. Art Mus., 1986, 1988, Nat. Air and Space Mus., Smithsonian Instn., Washington, 1986, Madison (Wis.) Art Ctr., 1987, 1990, Paper Press Gallery, Chgo., 1988, North Arts Ctr., Atlanta, 1990, Dairy Barn Cultural Arts Ctr., Athens, Ohio, 1991, Paper Arts Festival, Appleton, 1992, Fine Arts Mus., Budapest, Hungary, 1992, Tilburg Textile Mus., Netherlands, 1993, U. Wis. Union Gallery, 1994, Holland Area Arts Coun. Gallery, U. Mich., Ann Arbor, 1996, Charles Allis Art Mus., Milw., 1996, Bergstrom-Mahler Mus., Neenah, Wis., 1998, West Bend Mus. Art, Wis., 2000, Three Rivers Arts Festival, Pitts., 2001, U. Wis. Alumni Assn., Milw., 2002, Racine (Wis.) Art Mus., 2003. NEA craftsman fellow, 1974. Avocations: swimming, travel. Home: 9313 Center Oak Rd Hartland WI 53029 E-mail: jstamsta@aol.com.

STANBERRY, D(OSI) ELAINE, English literature educator, writer; b. Elk Park, N.C. m. Earl Stanberry; 1 child, Anita St. Lawrence. Student in Bus. Edn., Steed Coll. Tech., 1956; BS in Bus. and English, East Tenn. State U., 1961, MA in Shakespearean Lit., 1962; PhD, Tex. A&M U., 1975; postgrad., North Tex. State U., U. South Fla., NYU, Duke U., U. N.C. Prof. Manatee Jr. Coll., Bradenton, Fla., 1964-67; Disting. prof. English Dickinson State U., N.D., 1967-81; retired, 1981. Author: Poetic Heartstrings, Mountain Echoes, Love's Perplexing Obsession Experienced by Heinrich Heine and Percy Bysshe Shelley, Poetry from the Ancients to Moderns: A Critical Anthology, Finley Forest, Chapel Hill's Tree-lined Tuck, (plays) The Big Toe, The Funeral Factory; contbr. articles, poetry to jours., mags. Recipient Editor's Choice award Nat. Libr. Poetry, 1988, 95, Distinguished Professor of English Award, Dickinson State U., 1981; included in Best Poems of 1995. Mem. Acad. Am. Poets, N.C. Writers Network, N.C. Poetry Soc. (Carl Sandburg Poetry award 1988), Poetic Page, Writers Jour., Poets and Writers, Friday-Noon Poets, Delta Kappa Gamma. Home: 1840 Crawford Rd Graham NC 27253-9204

STANCIL, IRENE MACK, family counselor; b. St. Helena Island, Sept. 29, 1938; d. Rufus and Irene (Wilson) Mack; m. Nesby Stancil, Dec. 29, 1968; 1 child, Steve Lamar. BA, Benedict Coll., 1960, CUNY, 1983; MA, New World Bible Coll., 1984; SSD, United Christian Coll., 1985; cert., Mercy Coll., 1993. Supr. City of New York; tchr. local bd. edn., S.C.; supr, case worker, counselor City of New York. Mem. Am. Ctr. for Law & Justice.

STANDFAST, SUSAN J(ANE), retired state official, educator, researcher; b. Callicoon, NY, July 2, 1935; m. Theodore P. Wright Jr., 1967; children: Henry S., Margaret S., Catherine B. AB in Biology and Chemistry, Wells Coll., 1957; MD, Columbia U., 1961; MPH in Epidemiology, U. Calif., Berkeley, 1965. Diplomate Am. Bd. Preventive Medicine. Intern King County Hosp., Swedish Hosp, Seattle, 1961-62; pediatric resident U. Wash., Seattle, 1963; sr. resident in epidemiology N.Y. State Health Dept., 1965-67; instr. dept. cmty. health Albany (N.Y.) Med. Coll., 1965-67, asst. prof. dept. preventive and cmty. medicine, 1968-72, cons. in epidemiology, 1968-72, adj. asst. prof. preventive and cmty. medicine, 1975-80, adj. assoc. prof., 1980-91, cons. preventive medicine dept. family practice, 1983-91; rsch. physician bur. cancer control divsn. epidemiology N.Y. State Dept. Health, Albany, 1975-83, dir. cancer surveillance unit cancer control sect. bur. chronic disease prevention, 1983-85, asst. to dir. divsn. epidemiology, 1985-86, dir. injury control program divsn. epidemiology, 1986-90; physician pub. health Albany, 1983-95; ret., 1995; dir. disability prevention program, 1988-91; cons. epidemiologist div. family health N.Y. State Dept. Health, Albany, 1991-95. Vis. lectr. G.S. Med. Coll., Bombay, 1969-70, London Sch. Hygiene, 1974-75, Coll. Cmty. Medicine, Lahore, Pakistan, 1991; cons. in epidemiology Bombay Cancer Registry Tata Meml. Hosp., Bombay, 1969-70; cons. infectious diseas sect. VA Med. Ctr., Albany, 1979; mem. ad hoc task force on data resource devel. for dir. epidemiology and biometry rsch. program Nat. Inst. Child Health and Human Devel., Bethesda, Md., 1979-80; assoc. prof. epidemiology Sch. Pub. Health, SUNY, 1987-97, adj. prof. epidemiology, 1997-99, co-dir. master's pub. health program, 1991-97; instr. AARP 55 Alive, 1996-99; human svcs. coord. Colonic Sr. Svc. Ctrs., 1999-2000; lectr. in field. Contbr. articles to profl. jours. Mem. med. adv. bd. Hudson-Mohawk chpt. Nat. Found. SIDS, 1976-84; mem. med. adv. bd coun. on human sexuality Planned Parenthood, Albany, 1971-88; mem. Physicians for Social Responsibility, 1984—, also numerous pub. health task forces and coms.; bd. dirs. Eddy Cmty. Care, Troy, N.Y., Albany-Tula Alliance, 2000--; vol. Colonie Sr. Svcs. Ctr., Newtonville, N.Y., 1996-2002; vol. Glen Eddy Retirement Cmty., 2002--. Recipient Disting. Alumnae award Wells Coll., 1994, Vol. Svc. fro Health award, Ret. Sr. Vol. Program, 2002. Fellow Am. Coll. Preventive Medicine, Am. Coll. Epidemiology; mem. APHA. Home: 17 Wellington Way Niskayuna NY 12309

STANDIFORD, NATALIE ANNE, writer; b. Balt., Nov. 20, 1961; d. John Willard Eagleston and Natalie Elizabeth Standiford; m. Robert Craig Tracy, Apr. 29, 1989. BA, Brown Univ., 1983. Clerk Shakespeare and Co. Bookstore, N.Y.C., 1983; editl. asst. Random House, N.Y.C., 1984-85, asst. editor books for young readers divsn., 1985-87; freelance writer N.Y.C., 1987—. Author: The Best Little Monkeys in the World, 1987, The Bravest Dog Ever: The True Story of Balto, 1989 (Puffin award Alaska Assn. Sch. Libr. 1992), The Headless Horseman, 1992, Brave Maddie Egg, 1995, Space Dog and Roy, 1990, Space Dog and the Pet Show, 1990, Space Dog in Trouble, 1991, Space Dog the Hero, 1991 (Fifty Books of Yr. citation Fedn. Children's Book Groups 1992), The Power #2: The Witness, 1992, The Power #4: The Diary, 1992, The Power #7: Vampire's Kiss, 1992, (picture book) Dollhouse Mouse, 1989, (as Emily James) Fifteen: Hillside Live!, 1993, Jafar's Curse, 1993, (picture book) Santa's Surprise, 1992, The Mixed-Up Witch, 1993, Astronauts are Sleeping, 1996, The Stone Giant,

2000. Reader, N.Y.C. Author Read-Aloud Program, 1992—. Mem. Soc. Children's Book Writers and Illustrators, Author's Guild, Authors League Am. Avocations: travel, movies, music, the beach.

STANDING, KIMBERLY ANNA, educational researcher; b. Hagerstown, Md., Mar. 24, 1965; d. Thomas Townsend and Ruth Annadeane (Powell) Stone; m. Christopher G. Standing, May 20, 1989; children: Iain Christopher, Leah Elizabeth. BA in Math., St. Mary's Coll., 1988; MA in Higher Edn. Adminstrn., George Washington U., 1996, postgrad. Sr. analyst Westat, Inc., Rockville, Md., 1988—. Mem. Am. Ednl. Rsch. Assn., Assn. Study Higher Edn. Home: 11545 Brundidge Ter Germantown MD 20876-5500 Office: Westat Inc RW2564 1650 Research Blvd Rockville MD 20850-3195 E-mail: KimStanding@westat.com.

STANDRIDGE, DIANE H. secondary school educator; b. Anderson, S.C., Dec. 12, 1955; d. Harold Edward and Wilma Ulara Hamby; m. Bobby Joe Standridge, Jan. 31, 1992; children: Stacey McGuffin Gibson, Jenna Claire McGuffin. B, Erskine Coll., 1990; M, Lander U., 1996; postgrad., Furman U., 2000—01. Cert. elem. edn. S.C., learning disabilities S.C., adminstrn. State Dept. Edn. Tchr. Anderson Sch. Dist. 5, 1990—97, Crescent H.S., Iva, SC, 1997—. IDEA grantee, S.C. Dept. Edn., 2002. Mem.: ASCD (assoc.), NEA (assoc.), Coun. Exceptional Children (assoc.). Baptist. Avocations: reading, jigsaw puzzles, crossword puzzles. Home: 112 Beaver Creek Rd Anderson SC 29624 Office: Crescent HS 9104 Hwy 81 S Iva SC 29655 Office Phone: 864-352-6175. Personal E-mail: bobbydian@hotmail.com. E-mail: standridged@anderson3.k12.sc.us.

STANDRIDGE, JEAN, real estate executive, real estate broker; b. Danville, Ala., July 14, 1931; d. Elbert Eugene and Pearl May Rogers Brown; m. Arch Standridge, Jr., June 21, 1952; 1 child, Terry Brian. Grad., Burroughs Bus. Sch., Birmingham, 1951, Am. Real Estate Inst., 1975; student, Jefferson State Coll., Birmingham, 1980. Cert. real estate broker. Bookkeeper Mac Wates Coal Co., Birmingham, Ala., 1952-57; music tchr. County Schs., Blount County, Ala., 1957-75; real estate broker, owner Standridge Realty, Hayden, Ala., 1977—. Organist Meth. Ch., Hayden, 1957-77; sponsor Young Boys Soft Ball, Hayden, 1985-86; city coun. mem. Town of Hayden, 1988-92. Mem. Nat. Assn. Realtors, Ala. Assn. Realtors, Birmingham Assn. Realtors. Avocations: photography, indoor gardening, reading, music. Home: 177 Main St Hayden AL 35079-6452 Office: Standridge Realty Inc 177 Main St Hayden AL 35079-6452 also: 177 Main St Hayden AL 35079-6452

STANFEL, JANE ELLEN, artist, adult education educator; b. Chgo., Mar. 7, 1941; d. Raymond Roy and Lucille Pauline Yetter; m. Larry Eugene Stanfel, Sept. 1, 1962; children: Kenneth, Larry, Christine, Rebecca. Student, Dominican U., 1959—61, Loyola U., 1961, U. Fla., 1968—70, Colo. State U., 1970, U. Tex., Arlington, 1978—80. Grade sch. tchr. St. William's Sch., Oak Park, Ill., 1961—62; H.S. tchr. East Baton Rouge Parish, Greenwell Springs, La., 1985—88; office mgr. Def. Comm. Agy., Arlington, Va., 1989—90; adult basic edn. specialist Tuscaloosa (Ala.) County Sch. Bd., 1990—94; contractor Kelly Svcs., Reston, Va., 1996, Tuscaloosa, 1996; workplace edn. specialist Tuscaloosa County Sch. Bd., 1997—2002; artist Tuscaloosa, 1995—, Roundup, Mont., 1995—. One-woman shows include Downtown Gallery, Tuscaloosa, 1997—98, Christina's Art Gallery, 1998, Nordic Heritage Mus., Seattle, 2000—02, Royal Norwegian Embassy, Washington, 2001, 2001—02, exhibitions include Montmartre, Brussels, 2002, Represented in permanent collections Royal Norwegian Embassy, Washington; contbr. articles to profl. jours. and newspapers. Tutor literacy program Tuscaloosa Country Sch. Bd., 1988—89; designer, head vol. literacy program Def. Comm. Agy., Arlington, 1989—90. Recipient First prize internat. logo competition, Def. Comm. Agy., 1989, Presdl. Points of Light award, Office of the U.S. Pres., 1991. Mem.: Archives on Women Artists, Nat. Mus. Women in the Arts. Avocations: cross country skiing, ballet, mineralogy, lapidary arts, hiking. Home: PO Box 348 Roundup MT 59072

STANFIELD, REBECCA, radio personality; b. Newport Beach, Calif. Grad. Broadcast Journalism and History, U. Southern Calif. Assignment editor, sr. reporter Sta. KRCR-TV, Redding, Calif.; gen. assignment reporter Cable 12 News, Brooklyn Park; freelance writer Fox TV, Mpls.; news anchor Sta. WCCO Radio. Navigator Great Am. Race. Office: WCCO 625 2nd Ave S Minneapolis MN 55402

STANFORD, DIANA L. librarian; b. East St. Louis, Ill., Feb. 22, 1952; d. Richard Leland and Helen Jeanette (Hoy) Ninness; children: James Kent LeBlanc Jr., Jonathan Brice LeBlanc; m. John C. Stanford, June 1999. Grad. high sch., Collinsville, Ill. Dir. & head libr. Caseyville (Ill.) Pub. Libr. Sec. 1st Bapt. Ch. Caseyville, 1986-95, treas., 1974-89. Recipient Hardees Home Town Award for Public Service, 1999. Republican. Avocations: painting, cross stitch, gardening, sewing, crafts, baking. Office: 419 S 2nd St Caseyville IL 62232-1525

STANFORD, ELAINE P. secondary school educator; b. Anderson, S.C., Dec. 20, 1955; B in Music Edn., Baylor U., 1978. CPA; cert. Music K-12 Va., Early Edn. K-4 Va., Middle Edn. 4-8 Va., Choral Music K-12 Tex., Elem. Edn. Tex. Elem. music tchr. Eagle Mtn., Saginaw, Tex., 1982—83; 4th gr. tchr. Era Elem., Tex., 1984—85; elem. music tchr. Dublin Elem., 1986—88; choral. dir. Oakton H.S., Vienna, Va., 1988—. Chair performing arts dept. Oakton H.S., 1990—. Mem.: Am. Choral Dir. Assn., Va. Music Educators Assn., Music Educators Nat. Conf., Mu Alpha Theta, Kappa Delta Pi. Home: PO Box 6412 Falls Church VA 22040 Office Phone: 703-319-2747. E-mail: elaine.stanford@fcps.edu.

STANFORD, JANE HERRING, management consultant and educator, author; b. Lockhart, Tex., Dec. 17, 1939; d. John William and Frances Argyra (Cheatham) H. Jr.; m. Rube Valton Stanford, Sept. 17, 1966; children: (Steven) Scott, Lisa Ann. BS, Texas A&M U., Kingsville; MS in Counseling, Texas A&M U., Corpus Christi; MBA, Texas A&M U., Kingsville; PhD in Orgn. Theory and Strategic Mgmt., U. North Tex. Instr. cmty. coll., Corpus Christi, 1981—88; tchg. fellow U. North Tex., Denton, 1988-90; assoc. prof. bus. policy and internat. mgmt., pres. faculty senate Texas A&M U., Kingsville, 1990—99, full mem. grad. faculty, 1992-99, grad. rsch. advisor, MBA program, Coll. Bus., 1992-98, head, asst. v.p. acad. affairs, 1998-99, ret., 1999; mgmt. cons. Strategic Mgmt. Solutions, Inc., 1999—, pres., primary cons., 2000—; vis. assoc. prof. mgmt. Coll. of Bus., Texas A&M U., Chorpus Christi, Tex., 2003—. Chair univ. assessment, budgeting and planning com. Tex. A&M U., 1997—98; internat. lectr. strategic mgmt. within internat. context, Columbia, Argentina; workshop leader and participant in acad. issues; paper presenter internat. conf. Soc. for the Advancement Mgmt., 1998—2003; initiator corp. learning cons. Key to Success guidebooks and workshops; vis. assoc. prof. mgmt. Tex. A&M U., Corpus Christi, 2003—. Author: Building Competitiveness: U.S. Expatriate Management Strategies in Mexico, 1995; contbr. articles to profl. jours. and conf. procs. Apptd. to water resources adv. com. City of Corpus Christi, 2003—. Named Leadership Corpus Christi Class of XXX, 2001—02; fellow Sys. Chancellor's fellow in leadership in higher edn. program, Tex. A&M U., 1997. Mem.: Univ. Grad. Faculty, Soc. Advancement Mgmt., Acad. Mgmt., Inst. Mgmt. Cons., Strategic Mgmt. Soc., Delta Signa Pi, Kappa Delta Pi (life). Presbyterian. Avocations: book collecting, photography, travel. Home: 13526 Carlos Fifth Ct Corpus Christi TX 78418-6913 Office: Strategic Mgmt Solutions Inc 13526 Carlos Fifth Ct Corpus Christi TX 78418-6913 E-mail: planyourbiz@aol.com.

STANFORD, JANET LEE, physician, epidemiologist; RN, Grady Meml Hosp., Atlanta, 1974; BS, Ga. State U., 1980; MPH, Emory U., 1982; PhD, John Hopkins U., 1985. Various to asst. prof. dept. epidemiology Sch. of Pub. Health and Cmty. Medicine/U. Wash., Seattle, 1986-92; assoc. prof. Sch. Pub. Health and Cmty. Medicine U. Wash., Seattle, 1992-98, prof. epidemiology Sch. Pub. Health and Cmty. Medicine, 1999—; assoc. mem. program in epidemiology Divsn. Pub. Health Scis. Fred Hutchinson Cancer Rsch. Ctr., Seattle, 1991-96, co-investigator Cancer Surveillance System, 1993-96, co-prin. investigator Tracking Resource Ctr., 1995-96; dir. Utah State Cancer Registry/U. Utah, Salt Lake City, 1996-97; prof. Divn. Pub. Health Scis./Huntsman Cancer Inst. U. Utah, Salt Lake City, 1996-97; mem. program in epidemiology/Divsn. Pub. Health Scis. Fred Hutchinson Cancer Rsch. Ctr., Seattle, 1996—, head program in prostate cancer rsch., 1997—, affil. mem. cancer prevention rsch. program, 1999—. Rschr. and investigator in field of hormonal and environ. exposures that may alter cancer risk, and how such risks may be modified by genetic predisposition. Editor: Am. Jour. Epidemiology, 1999—, assoc. editor 1991-96; editl. bd.: Human Genome Epidemiology Network, 1999—; editl. positions: Am. Jour. Pub. Health, Annals of Epidemiology, Cancer, Cancer Causes and Control, Cancer Epidemiology, Biomarkers and Prevention, Human Molecular Genetics, others; contbr. numerous articles to profl. jours. and publs. Grantee HHS, 1982-83, NIH, 1983-85; fellowships Nat. Cancer Inst., NIH, HHS, 1985-86; recipient Preventive Oncology Acad. awards Nat. Cancer Inst., NIH, HHS, 1988-93. Mem. AHA, Soc. Epidemiologic Rsch., APHA, Assn. of Wash. State Epidemiologists, Sigma Theta Tau, others. Office: Fred Hutchinson Cancer Rsch Ctr PO Box 19024 1100 Fairview Ave N MW 814 Seattle WA 98109-1024

STANFORD, JENNIFER LAURA, nurse, educator; b. St. Catherine, Jamaica, West Indies; came to U.S., 1978; d. Armon F. and Doris M. Stanford. BSN, George Mason U., 1980; MS in Nursing Edn., U. Md., 1997. Staff nurse, technician Holy Cross Hosp., Silver Spring, Md., 1974-85; asst. head nurse King Faisal Specialist Hosp., Riyadh, Saudi Arabia, 1986-89; clin. coord. Montgomery Surgery Ctr., Rockville, Md., 1990-93; clin. resource nurse Montgomery Gen. Hosp., Olney, Md., 1993-96, liaison nurse, 1996—. Treas. United Meth. Women, Rockville, 1996—; chairperson singles ministry Jerusalem Mt. Pleasant United Meth. Ch., Rockville, 1994-96; mentor Beale Elem. Sch., Rockville, 1993—. Mem. Am. Soc. Post Anesthesia Care Nurses, Chesepeak Bay Post Anesthesia Nurses (treas. 1995-97). Avocations: needlepoint, reading, walking. Home: 3405 Kilkenny St Silver Spring MD 20904-1738

STANFORD, KATHLEEN THERESA, secondary school educator; b. Belize City, Belize, Sept. 28, 1933; d. Frederick Gill and Ila Mae (Cherrington) Hyde; m. Herman Emanuel Stanford., Oct. 3, 1970 (dec. Feb., 1989). Student (summer), S. We. La. U., Lafayette, 1958; BA, Seton Hill Coll., 1962; student (summer), Xavier U., New Orleans, 1956, 68; postgrad., Southern U. and A&M Coll., 1962, 67, Adelphi U., 1988, C.W. Post, N.Y., 1988. Cert. sci. tchr., La. (life). Tchr. Mem. Sisters of Holy Family Order, various cities, U.S. & Belize, 1953-69; sci. tchr., moderator Sisters of Holy Family, Grand Coteau, La., 1967-68, Lafayette, La., 1968-70; laicized, 1970; sci. tchr., sponsor of sci. fair N.Y.C. Bd. of Edn., Bklyn., 1981—. Sci. coord. La. Sci. Acad., Lafayette, 1968-70; mem. U.F.T. /IHS sci. com., N.Y.C., 1984-85. Contbr. poetry to Poetry Mags., 1974—. Hon. mem. Pres. Clinton's 2d Term Com., Washington, 1997; sci. sponsor Ford Future Scientists of Am., 1968, Dist. Sci. Fair, Bklyn., 1984; sec. Belize Parkfest of N.Y., Inc., 1990-92 Recipient Commendation for pupils 20th Internat. Sci. Fair, 1969, poetry awards Am. Poetry Assn., 1989, 90, cert. for leadership, Dem. Nat. Com., Washington, 1997. Mem. Belize Cosmopolitan Benevolent Assn. (v.p.). Democrat. Avocations: writing poetry, photography, bird watching, swimming, walking, singing.

STANGER, ILA, writer, editor; b. N.Y.C. d. Jack Simon and Shirley Ruth (Nadelson) S. BA, Bklyn. Coll., 1961. Feature and travel editor Harpers Bazaar, N.Y.C., 1969-75; exec. editor Travel and Leisure mag., N.Y.C., 1975-85; editor in chief Food and Wine Mag., N.Y.C., 1985-89, Travel and Leisure mag., N.Y.C., 1990-93; mng. editor More mag., N.Y.C., 1993—. Writer on arts, features and travel. Mem. Am. Soc. Mag. Editors Office: More Magazine 125 Park Ave New York NY 10017-5529 Personal E-mail: ila.stanger@meredith.com.

STANLEY, CAROL LYNN, psychologist; b. NYC, Mar. 21, 1950; d. George Edward and Caroline L. (Blanke) Eales; m. Russell Rice Taylor, Sept. 27, 1968 (div. Dec. 1972); m. William B. Stanley, Dec. 8, 1972; children: Kenyon George, Brandon Chandler. BA in Speech Comm., Whittier Coll., 1974; MA, City U., Bellevue, Wash., 1992; PhD in Psychology, Seattle Pacific U., 2001. Tchr., Calif., 1969—72; eligibility worker Social Svcs., Riverside, Calif., 1972—77; claims adjuster State Farm, Calif., 1972—91; pvt. practice Redmond, Wash., 1991—92, Renton, Wash., 1992—; clin. dir. Valley Counseling, Renton, Wash., 1993—. Sys. cons. Leadership Inst. Seattle, 1993—94; cons. Crosby Kerr & Minno, Issaquah, 1998—2002; chair ethics tng. Wash. Marriage Family Therapy, Renton, Wash., 2001—; adj. prof. St. Martins Coll., Lacey, Wash., 2001—02. Ch. and min. com. United Ch. of Christ. Mem.: Am. Psychol. Assn., Am. Assn. Marital Family Therapy (approved supr.). Democrat. Avocations: reading, travel, camping. Office: Valley Counseling Assocs 9806 S Carr Rd Renton WA 98055

STANLEY, ELLEN MAY, historian, consultant; b. Dighton, Kans., Feb. 3, 1921; d. Delmar Orange and Lena May (Bobb) Durr; m. Max Neal Stanley, Nov. 5, 1939; children: Ann Y. Stanley Epps, Janet M. Stanley Horsky, Gail L. Stanley Peck, Kenneth D., Neal M., Mary E. Stanley McEniry. BA in English and Journalism, Ft. Hays (Kans.) State U., 1972, MA in History, 1984. Pvt. practice local/state historian, cons., writer local history, Dighton, 1973—; cons. genealogy, 1980—. Vice chmn. State Preservation Bd. Rev., Kans., 1980-87; area rep. Kans. State Mus. Assn., 1978-84. Author: Early Lane County History: 12,000 B.C.--A.D. 1884, 1993 (Cert. of Commendation, Am. Assn. for State and Local History, 1994), Cowboy Josh: Adventures of a Real Cowboy, 1996, Early Lane County Development, 1993, Golden Age, Great Depression and Dust Bowl, 2001 (Ferguson Kans. History Book award Kans. Author Club, 2002); contbr. articles to profl. jours. Precinct woman com. Alamota Township, Kans., 1962-86; mem. Dem. State Affirmative Action Com., 1975. Recipient hon. mention for photography Ann. Christian Arts Festival, 1974, Artist of Month award Dane G. Hansen Mus., 1975. Mem. Kans. State Hist. Soc. (pres. 1990-91), Lane County Hist. Soc. (sec. 1970-78). Methodist. Avocations: fossil hunting, walking, photography, antiques. Home: 100 N 4th Dighton KS 67839 Office: 110 E Pearl St Dighton KS 67839

STANLEY, FRANCES LUCILLE, human resources manager, fire commissioner; b. Bklyn. d. Vito C. and Rose Lamia; m. Gilbert James Stanley, Oct. 28, 1962 (dec. Aug. 1984). Student, CCNY, 1967; hon., Drake Bus. Sch., N.Y.C., 1980. Adminstrv. asst. N.Y. Hosp./Cornell Med. Ctr., N.Y.C., 1957-59; personnel asst. Inst. Muscle Disease, MDA, N.Y.C., 1959-62; sr. personnel asst., human resources Meml. Sloan-Kettering Cancer Ctr., N.Y.C., 1962-88; owner My Mother's Cookies, Hartsdale, N.Y., 1990—. Composer, singer Off-Broadway musical Collateral, 1995; USO soloist, N.Y.C., 1960's; poetry pub. (anthology) The Voice Within, 1996, Thoughts by Candlelight, 1998; singer Carnegie Hall, N.Y. Fire Commr. (elected) Hartsdale Fire Dist., 1984—; fundraiser N.Y. Heart Assn., United Cerebral Palsy, N.Y. Assn. for the Blind, MDA; mem. Am. Appeal com. Soc. Meml. Sloan-Kettering Cancer Ctr., including orgn. and dir. of choral group to sing for patients, 1963-73, also entertaining N.Y. Hosp. Cornell Med. Ctr. and The Hosp. for Special Surgery, N.Y.C., 1972, dir., v.p. Mem. Antique Automobile Club of Am., Assn. Fire Dists. Westchester (N.Y.) County (v.p.), Westchester County Assn. Fire Chiefs. Roman Catholic. Avocations: writing music and lyrics, poetry, antiques, art, antique automobiles. Office Phone: 914-949-0861.

STANLEY, HARRIETT LARI, state legislator; b. Arlington County, Va., Mar. 30, 1950; d. E. L. and Mariana T. Stanley. AB, Coll. William and Mary, 1972; MS with honors, Boston U., 1974; MBA, Harvard U., 1982. NASD registered. Asst. to dir. Close-up Found., Washington, 1974-76; spokesman Boston Edison Co., 1976-79; asst. dir. Mass. Energy Office, Boston, 1979-80, Smith Barney, Harris Upham & Co., N.Y.C., 1983-87; v.p. Prudential-Bache Capital Funding, N.Y.C., 1987-90; mng. prin. The Hadley Group, Boston, 1990-94; mem. Mass. Ho. of Reps., Boston, 1995—, vice chmn. ways & means com., 1997-2001, chair health care com., 2001—. Mem. Town Dem. Com., Merrimac, Mass., 1989—; mem. Town Fin. Com., Merrimac, 1990, vice chmn., 1990-92, town treas., 1992-95; mem. William and Mary Soc. of Alumni, 1984-90, treas., 1986-88, exec. com., 1988—, v.p., 1989. Mem. Publicity Club Boston (bd. dirs., pres. 1979-80, Bellringer award 1978). Avocation: competitive equestrian activities. Office: Ho of Reps Beacon St Rm 130 State House Boston MA 02133

STANLEY, HELEN CAMILLE, composer, musician; b. Tampa, Fla. d. Edward and Lucy Gage (Crehore) S.; widowed; 1 child, Helen Marjorie. MusB, Cin. Conservatory Music, 1951; MusM, Fla. State U., 1954; BS, Muskingum Coll., 1961. Instr. music and fine arts Jacksonville (Fla.) U., 1962-67; instr. music in communications Jones Coll., Jacksonville, 1965-66; composer, condr. St. Paul's by-the-Sea, Jacksonville Beach, Fla., 1976; composer-in-residence, pianist Fla. Contemporary Ensemble, Jacksonville, 1986; ind. composer, lectr., pianist, 1963—. Cons. Beaches Fine Arts Series, Neptune Beach, Fla., 1973—. Composer Rhapsody for Electronic Tape and Orchestra, 1972 (Composition Commn. award), Allegro, Passacaglia, Sonata for trombone and piano, various instrumental and vocal works, Evocation I for piano; orchestral works on CD include: Fanfare for Orchestra (Warsaw Nat. Philharmonic Orch. and Owensboro Symphony), 1994, Passacaglia (St. Petersburg Philharmonic), Concerto Romantico, Prague, 1997, Fanfare for Orchestra (All American Celebration by Owensboro Symphony), 1999; composer website theme music The Living Music Found., composer Dorian Diversion in Functional Chromaticism, 2003. Mem. Nat. Soc. Arts and Letters, Soc. Mayflower Descs., 1987—. Recipient Pogner Music Composition award, Cin., 1950, C. Hugo Ensemble Composition award, Cin., 1951, Anthem Descant award St. Paul's by-the-Sea, 1980, Art Ventures Fund award, 1992, Jacksonville Comty. Found. award, 1994; named Outstanding Achievements Classical Music, Jacksonville, 1997. Mem. ASCAP, Am. Music Ctr., Am. Keyboard Artists, Performing Arts Directory, Pi Kappa Lambda. Avocations: art, walking, dance. Home: 1768 Emory Cir S Jacksonville FL 32207-7707 Studio: Aladdin Farm 12047 Aladdin Rd Jacksonville FL 32223-3201

STANLEY, KAREN GWENEITH, vocational nurse; b. Malvern, Ark., Oct. 4, 1943; d. Raybon and Gwendolyn (Smith) Kindrick; m. Lewis Frank Stanley, Aug. 31, 1962; children: Mark Steven, Catherine Leigh, James Lawson. Cert. vocat. nurse, Med. Arts Clnic Hosp., 1964; student, Jefferson County C.C., Louisville, 1973. Surg. scrub tech. Louisville Gen. Hosp.; vocat. nurse Med. Arts Clinic Hosp., Big Spring, Tex., 1965, So. Clinic, Texarkana, Tex., 1965-66, Rome (N.Y.) City Hosp., 1966-67, Geriat. Hosp., Louisville, 1969, St.'s Mary and Elizabeth Hosp., Louisville, 1971-76, Louisville Gen. Hosp., 1976-78, Quality Care Nursing Svc., Louisville, 1978-79, Wesley Manor Nursing Home, Louisville, 1979-84, Collom and Carney Clinic, Texarkana, 1984—. Mem. NOW. Democrat. Humanist. Avocations: artist, writer, history and genealogy enthusiast.

STANLEY, LANETT LORRAINE, state legislator; b. Atlanta, Nov. 5, 1962; d. Archie and Ethel Francis (Dixon) S. BS, U. Tenn., 1985; postgrad., Carver Bible Coll., Atlanta, 1991—. Children's reporter Sta. WXIA-TV, Atlanta, 1979-80; model, sales clk. Rich's Dept. Store, Atlanta, 1979-83; copy clk. Knoxville (Tenn.) Jour., 1984-85; reporter Atlanta Daily World, 1986; intern Sta. WTBS-TV, Atlanta, 1986; adminstrv. aide Bd. Commrs. Fulton County, Atlanta, 1986-87; mem., sec to the caucus Ga. Ho. of Reps., Atlanta, 1987—; ind. mktg. cons., 1991—. Mem. Nat. and Ga. Legis. Black Caucus, 1987. Bd. dirs. West End Med. Ctrs., Inc., 1988—, Southside Youth Athletic Acad. Assn., 1991—. Democrat. Baptist. Avocations: public speaking, swimming, bible study, travel, modeling. Office: Ga Gen Assembly Ga State Capitol Atlanta GA 30318

STANLEY, LILA GAIL, political scientist, antique appraiser; b. Marietta, Ga., Mar. 23, 1941; d. James Miller and Louise (Land) S. AB cum laude, Randolph-Macon Woman's Coll., 1963; MA in Polit. Sci., Emory U., 1964; cert. appraisal studies decorative arts, George Washington U., 1997. Polit. sci. instr. U. West Ga., Carrollton, 1964-66; Am. history tcrh. Foxcroft Sch., Middleburg, Va., 1966-67; staff asst. Rep. John J. Flynt U.S. Ho. Reps., Washington, 1967-74; legis. asst. Sen. Robert C. Byrd U.S. Senate, Washington, 1974-80; asst. to arch. Arch. of the Capitol, Washington, 1980-97; appraiser Gail Stanley Appraisers, Washington, 1997—. Participation Winter Inst., Winterthur (Del.) Mus., 2000. Vol. worker various nat. polit. campaigns Dem. Orgn., Washington, 1968-80; bd. dirs., 1st v.p., treas. Watergate East Inc., Washington, 1986-96; vol. rsch. asst. Nat. Mus. Am. History, Smithsonian Instn., Washington, 1999—; docent, curatorial vol. Tudor Pl., Washington, 1999—. Mem. DAR, Am. Soc. Appraisers, Appraisers Assn. Am., Washington Decorative Arts Forum, Zeta Tau Alpha. Democrat. Methodist. Home and Office: Ste 814 19375 Cypress Ridge Terr Lansdowne VA 20176

STANLEY, MARGARET KING, performing arts administrator; b. San Antonio, Dec. 11, 1929; d. Creston Alexander and Margaret (Haymore) King; children: Torrey Margaret, Jean Cullen. Student, Mary Baldwin Coll., 1948-50; BA, U. Tex., Austin, 1952; MA, U. Incarnate Word, 1959. Cert. elem. tchr. Tex. Elem. tchr. San Antonio Ind. Sch. Dist., 1953-54, 55-56, Arlington County Schs., Va., 1954-55, Ft. Sam Houston Schs., San Antonio, 1955-57; art and art history tchr. St. Pius X Sch., San Antonio, 1959-60; English tchr. Trinity U., 1963-65; designer-mfr., owner CrisStan Clothes, Inc., San Antonio, 1967-73; founder, exec. dir. San Antonio Performing Arts Assn., 1976-92; founder Arts Coun. of San Antonio, 1962; founding chmn. Joffrey Workshop, San Antonio, 1979; originator, founding chairwoman Student Music Fair, San Antonio, 1963; host On Stage with Margaret Stanley Sta. KTRU-FM, San Antonio, 1983-98. Orginator (ballets) Jamboree, 1984. Mem. Met. Opera Nat. Coun., 1969—80; pres. San Antonio Symphony League, 1971—74; v.p., founder San Antonio Opera Guild, 1974—76, pres., 2002—; v.p. Arts Coun. San Antonio, 1975; bd. govs. Artists Alliance San Antonio, 1982; founder Early Music Festival, San Antonio, 1990—92; artistic advisor, dir. presentation San Antonio Symphony, 1992—94; founding organizer Musica San Antonio, 1997—98; v.p. Instnl. Devel. Carver Cultural Ctr., 1998—2000; adv. bd. Hertzberg Circus Collection, San Antonio Dance Umbrella, Houston Early Music, Morgan-Scott Ballet. Named to Women's Hall of Fame, San Antonio, 1984, Disting. Alumnae, St. Mary's Hall, 1990; recipient Outstanding Tchr. award, Arlington County Sch. Dist., 1954, Emily Smith award for outstanding alumni, Mary Baldwin Coll., 1973, Today's Woman award, San Antonio Light Newspaper, 1980, Woman of the Yr. in Arts award, San Antonio Express News, 1983, Erasmus medal, Dutch Consulate, 1992, Mary Baldwin Sesquicentennial medallion, 1992, Opera Guild award, 2000; Tchg. fellow, Trinity U., San Antonio, 1964—66. Mem.: S.W. Performing Arts Presenters (chmn. 1988—92), Battle Flowers Assn., Jr. League San Antonio (Vol. Extraodinaire 2001), Women in Comm. (Headliner award 1982), Assn. Performing Arts Presenters (award for creation of Jamboree 1984), Internat. Soc. for Performing Arts (regional rep. 1982—85, bd. dirs. 1991—97). Avocations: traveling, reading, cooking, music, dance.

STANLEY, MARIANNE, professional athletics coach; 1 child, Michelle. BS in Sociology, Immaculata Coll., 1976. Asst. coach women's basketball Old Dominion U., Norfolk, Va., 1976—77, head coach, 1977—87; coach women's basketball U. Pa., 1987—89, U. So. Calif., 1989—93, Stanford U., Calif., 1995—96, U. Calif., Berkeley, 1996—2000; asst. L.A. Sparks,

2000—01; asst. coach Washington Mystics, Washington, 2001—02, head coach, 2002—. Mem. coaching staff US Nat. Team, 1981—93. Named Conf. Coach of the Yr., Nat. Coach of the Yr.; named to Women's Basketball Hall of Fame, 2002. Office: Washington Mystics MCI Ctr 601 F St NW Washington DC 20004*

STANLEY, MARLYSE REED, horse breeder; b. Fairmont, Minn., Sept. 19, 1934; d. Glenn Orson and Lura Mabel (Ross) Reed; m. James Arthur Stapleton, 1956 (div. 1976); 1 child, Elisabeth Katharene; m. John David Stanley, Oct. 22, 1982. BA, U. Minn., 1957. Registered breeder Arabian horses in Spain, 1976-94. Chmn. bd. dirs. Sitting Rock Spanish Arabians, Inc., Greensboro, N.C., 1978-81, pres. Hollister, Calif., 1981-91, Stanley Ranch, Yerington, Nev., 1991—. Bd. dirs. Glenn Reed Tire Co., Fairmont, Minn. Author Arabian hunter/jumper rules Am. Horse Shows Assn.; contbr. articles to horse jours. Named Palomino Queen of Minn., 1951, Miss Fairmont, 1954, Miss Minn., 1955. Mem.: AAUW, World Arabian Horse Assn., Assn. Española de Criadores de Caballos Arabes (Spain), Am. Paint Horse Assn. (nat. bd. dirs. 1967—70), Minn. Arabian Assn. (bd. dirs. 1972—75), Internat. Arabian Assn. (Minn. and Wis. 1973—76, nat. chmn. hunter-jumper com. 1976—81, chair IAHA sport horse rules com. 1998—2001, bd. dirs. region 10), Arabian Horse Registry Am., U.S. Nat. Arabian Sport Horse Finals--Show Commn., Alpha Xi Delta. Republican. Episcopalian. Avocations: fox hunting, fishing, breeding and importing Arabian horses.

STANLEY, MARTHA BARBEE, music educator; b. Ft. Clayton, Panama Canal Zone, Nov. 22, 1950; d. Henry Quinton and Kathleen A. Barbee; m. Ray H Stanley. MusB in Edn., Fla. State U., 1971, MusM in Edn., 1978. Cert. Orff-Schulwerk III Am. Orff-Schulwerk Assn., 1985, tchr. 2002. Elem. music tchr. Leon Dist. Schs., Tallahassee, 1972—, tchr. of gifted students, 1989—99. Ednl. cons., clinician Tallahassee Symphony Orch., 1999—; co-author of district's first music scope and sequence Leon County Schs., Tallahassee, 1981; clinician Very Spl. Arts Festival, Tallahassee, 1983—85; chair, instrnl. and profl. devel. Leon Classroom Teachers Assn., Tallahassee, 1981—83; facilitator, sch. improvement team Hartsfield Elem. Sch., Tallahassee, 1983—85; facilitating coun., tchr. edn. ctr. Leon Dist. Schs., Tallahassee, 1978—83; clinician Tallahassee Area Orff Chpt., 2000—01, pres., 1986—87, v.p., 1995—2001; elem. rep. to tchr. competency com. Fla. Music Educators Assn., Tallahassee; pres. Tallahassee Area Orff Chpt., Tallahassee, 2001—02; presenter Fla. Elem. Music Educators Assn., Tampa, Fla., 2002. Author (co-author with Margaret Van Every): (jazz curriculum) Open Ears Curriculum; creator and webmaster (ednl. website) Tallahassee Symphony Orch, Ednl. Site; contbr. articles to profl. jours. Musician, asst. music dir., accompanist Tallahassee Little Theater; dir. of reps. and pubs./website author VOICES, Inc., Tallahassee, 2001—03; min. Cir. of Light/Tallahassee Light Ctr., Tallahassee, 1996—2000. Grantee Tech. and Classroom grantee, Leon County Schools, Leon Schools Found., 1986, 1992, 1997, 2000, 2002. Mem.: Fla. Music Educators Assn., Am. Fedn. Of Tchrs., Am. Orff-Shulwerk Assn., Music Educators Nat. Conf. Avocations: reading, mandolin.

STANLEY, MARY ELIZABETH, judge; AB, Mt. Holyoke Coll., 1970; JD, Univ. of Va., 1973. Bar: W.Va., U.S. Dist. Ct. (so. dist.) W.Va., U.S. Ct. Appeals (4th cir.). Atty. Columbia Gas Transmission Corp., 1973-76; law clk. to Judge Dennis R. Knapp, 1976-77; asst. U.S. atty., 1977-92; magistrate judge U.S. Dist. Ct. (so. dist.) W. Va., Bluefield, W. Va., 1992-01, Charleston, W. Va., 2001—. Office: Robert C Byrd US Courthouse Rm 5408 300 Virginia St E Charleston WV 25301

STANLEY, MYRTLE BROOKS, minister, educational and religious consultant; b. Balt., May 13, 1929; d. Benjamin Franklin and Ora Estell (Robinson) Brooks; m. Theodore Freeland Stanley, June 4, 1949; children: Theodora Stanley Snyder, Benjamin Brooks, Jonathan Stephen. BS, Morgan State Coll., 1951, MS, 1972; MA in Theology, St. Mary Sem. and U., Balt., 1987; postgrad., Fordham U., 1989-91; PhD, Am. U., 2001. Tchr., curriculum coord. Balt. City Pub. Schs., 1958-83; dir. propagation of faith Archdiocese of Balt., Roman Cath. Ch., Balt., 1984-95; coord. rite of Christian initiation for adults St. Matthew Roman Cath. Ch., Balt., 1996—; instr. Ch. Leadership Inst., Archdiocese of Balt., 1999—. Author, prodr. play It's Your Own Funeral, 1980, Miracle on 22d Street, 1980. Bd. dirs. Balt. Clergy and Laity Concerned, 1984-94, Towson (Md.) Cath. H.S., 1993-95, Good Samaritan Hosp., Balt., 1994-96; coord. Internat. Sisters in Struggle, 1991—. Mem. AAUW, Religious Sisters of Mercy of the Ams. (assoc.), Phi Delta Kappa.

STANLEY, PAMELA AURELIA, state legislator; b. Mar. 13, 1956; 2 children. Student, Ga. Tech., Ga. State, Morris Brown Coll. Former clk. U.S. Postal Svc.; mem. Ga. Ho. of Reps., 1992—. Mem. game, fish & parks, ins. and state planning and cmty. affairs coms. Democrat. Baptist. Home: 706 Foundry St NW Atlanta GA 30314-4004 Office: Ga Ho of Reps 512 Legislative Office Bldg Atlanta GA 30334

STANLEY, SHERRY A. lawyer; b. Buffalo, N.Y., Oct. 17, 1955; d. Arthur A. and Irene S. Stanley. BA, U. West Fla., 1975; JD, U. Fla., 1978. Bar: Fla. 1978. Assoc. Mahoney, Hadlow & Adams, Miami, Fla., 1978-80; ptnr. Steel, Hector & Davis, Miami, 1980-87, Weil, Gotshal & Manges, Miami, 1987-92; sr. counsel Barnett Banks, Inc., Miami, 1992-94; ptnr. Coll, Davidson, Carter, Smith, Salter & Barkett, P.A., Miami, Fla., 1994—. Dir. investments and legal affairs Greenstreet Ptnrs. Mem. Fla. Bar, Order of Coif, Phi Theta Kappa. Republican. Roman Catholic. Office: 201 S Biscayne Blvd Ste 320 Miami FL 33131-4324

STANLEY, SHIRLEY DAVIS, artist; b. Mt. Vernon, N.Y., Dec. 5, 1929; d. Walter Thompson and Elsie Viola (Lumpp) Davis; m. Charles B. Coble Jr., June 11, 1951 (div. 1968); children: Jennifer Susan Farmer, Charles B. Coble III; m. Marvin M. Stanley, Dec. 18, 1983 (dec.). BA in Home Econs. and Gen. Sci., Greensboro Coll., 1951; grad., Real Estate Inst., 1962. Tchr. Dryher H.S., Columbia, SC, 1951-52, Haw River (N.C.) Sch., 1954-56, Alexander Wilson Sch., Graham, NC, 1957-58; guest essayist for news Mebane (N.C.) Enterprise, 1955-56; pres. Shirley, Inc., Burlington, NC, 1962-94; artist, 1956—. One woman show Art Gallery Originals, Winston-Salem, 1976, Olive Garden Gallery, 21st Century Gallery, Williamsburg, Va., numerous galleries in Fla., N.C. Bd. dirs. Girl Scouts Am. Kings Daus., Burlington, 1961, Williamsburg Libr. Found., 1997—; life mem. Rep. Inner Cir., Washington, 1990—; active Salvation Army; com. mem. York County Rep. Party, 1995; vol. disaster & blood banks ARC, 1990—; founding mem. Am. Air Force Mus.; bd. dirs. William Burg Libr. Found., 1997—. Recipient Rep. Medal of Freedom, 1994, 2002, 2003. Mem. AAUW, Am. Watercolor Soc. (assoc.), Va. Watercolor Soc., Sierra Club, Williamsburg Bibliophiles, Raleigh Tavern Soc. Colonial Williamsburg, Christopher Wren Soc., Williamsburg C. of C., Williamsburg Photography Soc., Mil. Officers Assn. (life), Army-Navy Country Club. Episcopalian. Avocations: travel, gardening, writing, dance, reading. Home: 103 Little John Rd Williamsburg VA 23185-4907 also: 1953 Shirley Dr Burlington NC 27215-4831

STANO, SISTER DIANA, academic administrator; AB, Ursuline Coll.; PhD, Ohio State U. Prof. edn. Ursuline Coll., Pepper Pike, Ohio, chair edn. dept., dir. grad. program in non-pub. sch. adminstrn., dir. master's degree program, dean of grad. studies, dir. of instl. rsch., pres., 1996—. Bd. trustees Coll. of New Rochelle; sec. bd. trustees Ohio Found. Ind. Coll.; cons. in field. Recipient YWCA Women of Profl. Excellence award, No. Ohio Live Rainmaker in Edn. award. Mem.: In Counsel With Women, Exec. Women's Leadership Forum. Office: Ursuline Coll 2550 Lander Rd Pepper Pike OH 44124-4398*

STANSFIELD, CLAIRE, apparel designer; b. London, Eng., Aug. 27, 1964; Co-founder C&C California, 2003—. Actor: (films) The Doors, 1991, Nervous Ticks, 1992, Best of the Best II, 1993, The Swordsman, 1993, The Favor, 1994, Drop Zone, 1994, Gladiator Cop, 1994, Sensation, 1995, Red Shoe Diaries 5: Weekend Pass, 1995, The Outpost, 1995, Darkdrive, 1996, Steel, 1997, Sweepers, 1999; (TV series) Xena The Warrior Princess, Frasier, Twin Peaks. Office: c/o Lela Tillem #705 127 E 9th St Los Angeles CA 90015*

STANSIL, SHERYL, medical/surgical nurse; b. Birmingham, Ala., May 17, 1963; d. Willie Caesar and Irene (Fisher) Stansil; 1 child, Tyler Christina. BSN, Dillard U., 1987; MSN in Trauma Nursing, U. Ala. in Birmingham, 1992. Cert. nurse case mgr. Asst. prof. nursing BSN program Coppin State Coll., Balt., 1997-99; staff nurse Progressive Care Ctr., Colorado Springs, Colo., 1995-96; clin. instr. nursing Beth-El Coll. Nursing, Colorado Springs, Colo., 1995; staff nurse VA Med. Ctr., Balt., 1996—, Nursefinders of Balt., 1996—; staff nurse surgery Johns Hopkins Hosp., Balt., 1997-99; nurse care mgr. VA Med. Ctr., Balt., 1999—. Past instr. clin. nursing Beth-El Coll. Nursing; past asst. prof. and clin. instr. BSN program Coppin State Coll. Mem.: AACN, ANA, Case Mgmt. Soc. Am., State Nurses Assn., Am. Assn. Managed Care Nurses, Sigma Theta Tau Internat.

STANTON, JEANNE FRANCES, retired lawyer; b. Vicksburg, Miss., Jan. 22, 1920; d. John Francis and Hazel (Mitchell) S. Student, George Washington U., 1938-39; BA, U. Cin., 1940; JD, Salmon P. Chase Coll. Law, 1954. Bar: Ohio 1954. Chief clk. Selective Svc. Bd., Cin., 1940-43; instr. USAAF Tech. Schs., Biloxi, Miss., 1943-44; with Procter & Gamble, Cin., 1945-84, legal asst., 1952-54, head advt. svcs. sect. legal divsn., trade practice dept., 1954-73, mgr. advt. svcs., legal divsn., 1973-84, ret., 1984. Team capt. Cmty. Chest Cin., 1983; mem. ann. meeting com. Archaeol. Inst. Am., 1983; trustee, asst. corr. sec., statutory agt. Friends of Bronze Age Archaeology in the Aegean area, 1987—. Mem. ABA (chmn. subcom. D of com. 307 copyright sect. 1987-88, 89, 90), Ohio Bar Assn. (chmn. uniform state laws com. 1968-70), Cin. Bar Assn. (sec. law day com. 1965-66, chmn. com. on preservation hist. documents 1968-71), Vicksburg and Warren County Hist. Soc., Cin. Hist. Soc., Intercontinental Biog. Assn., Lawyers Club Cin. (exec. com., pres. 1983). Home: 3580 Shaw Ave Apt 323 Cincinnati OH 45208-1454

STANTON, KATHRYN, retail bookstores/educ products and services executive; b. Nov. 29, 1954; BS in Acctg., U. Ill., 1976; MBA, U. Chgo., 1996. CPA, Ill. From auditor to mgr. Arthur Anderson, Chgo., 1976-81, mgr., 1981-86; from controller to v.p. finance, CFO Follett Corp., Chgo., River Grove, Ill., 1986-97, v.p. finance, CFO River Grove, Ill., 1997—. Bd. dirs. Mus. Sci. and Industry, Chgo. Mem. Am. Inst. CPAs, Financial Exec. Inst., Ill. CPA Soc., Chgo. Council Foreign Rels. Office: Follett Corp 2233 N West St River Grove IL 60171-1895 Fax: 708-452-9347.

STANTON, PAMELA FREEMAN, interior designer, writer; b. Jacksonville, Tex., July 18, 1941; d. William Thomas and Ruth Ethel (Branton) Freeman; m. Karl F. Edmonds, Jr., Jan. 28, 1961 (div. 1966); m. Charles Calvin Stanton, Sept. 1, 1973; 1 child, Julie Anne. AA in Bus., Kilgore Coll., 1961. Design cons., Denver, Boston and Salem, Oreg., 1963-69; exec. sec. Alexander: Alexander of Tex. Inc., Dallas, 1967-69; interior designer Milmac Furniture, Dallas, 1969-73, Homestead House, Denver, 1973-76; case aide counselor Eliot Cmty. Mental Health Ctr., Concord, Mass., 1980-82; pres., owner Stancom Designs, Virginia Beach, Va., 1990-2000; interior designer Willis Furniture Co., 2000—. Author: I Am That I Am, 1994 (Best Book of Yr. N.Am. Bookdealers Exch., 1995). Recipient Cert. of Appreciation for vol. work Emerson Hosp., Concord, 1981; named Internat. Writer of Yr., 2003. Republican. Avocations: collecting art, travel, gardening, theatre-plays, entertaining. Home and Office: 4401 Leatherwood Dr Virginia Beach VA 23462-5704

STANTON, VIVIAN BRENNAN (MRS. ERNEST STANTON), retired guidance counselor; b. Waterbury, Conn.; d. Francis P. and Josephine (Ryan) Brennan; B.A., Albertus Magnus Coll.; M.S., So. Conn. State Coll., 1962, 6th yr. degree, 1965; postgrad. Columbia U.; m. Ernest Stanton, May 31, 1947; children— Pamela L., Bonita F., Kim Ernest. Tchr. English, history, govt. Milford (Conn.) High Sch., 1940-48; tchr. English, history, fgn. Born Night Sch., New Haven, 1948-54, Simon Lake Sch., Milford, 1960-62; guidance counselor, psychol. examiner Jonathan Law High Sch., Milford, 1962-73, Nat. Honor Soc. adv., 1966-73, mem. Curriculum Councils, Graduation Requirement Council, Gifted Child Com., others, 1940-48, 60-73; guidance dir. Foran High Sch., Milford, 1973-79, career center coordinator, 1976-79, ret., 1979. Active various community drives; mem. exec. bd. Ridge Rd PTA, 1956-59; mem. Parent-Tchr. council Hopkins Grammer Sch., New Haven; mem. Human Relations Council, North Haven, 1967-69; vol., patient rep. surg. waiting rm. Fawcett Meml. Hosp., P.C., Sun City Ctr. Emergency Squad, Good Samaritans. Mem. Nat. Assn. Secondary Schs. and Colls. (evaluation com.; chmn. testing com.), AAUW, LWV, Conn. Personnel and Guidance Assn., Conn. Sch. Counselors Assn., Conn. Assn. Sch. Psychol. Personnel, Conn., Milford (pres. 1945-47) edn. assns. Clubs: Univ., Charlotte Harbor Yacht, Sun City Ctr. Golf and Racquet. Home: 237 Courtyard Blvd Apt 202 Sun City Center FL 33573-5779

STAPLES, ALICE MARIE, elementary school educator; b. Onsted, Mich., Aug. 26, 1935; d. Faye Walter and Bernice Belle (Matthews) Barrows; m. Charles Albert Staples, Jr., Mar. 8, 1952; children: Linda Joan Staples Bird, Patricia Suzanne Staples Buwalda. BS in Edn., Siena Heights Coll., Adrian, Mich., 1971, MA in Edn., 1975; student in spl. edn., U. Toledo, 1988. Cert. tchr., Mich. Elem. sch. tchr. Tecumseh (Mich.) Pub. Schs., 1971—97. Chair, diaconate First Bapt. Ch., Tecumseh, 1994-99, adult Sunday Sch. instr., 1990—, chair C.E., 2000—. Mem. Tecumseh Edn. Assn. (nom. com. 1980-95), Lenawee Reading Assn. (pres., v.p., sec. 1972-80), Phi Delta Kappa (nom. com. 1989). American Baptist. Avocations: travel, hiking, walking, reading, nurturing. Home: 1202 Shady Ln Tecumseh MI 49286-1741

STAPLES, ELIZABETH ANN, counselor; b. San Francisco, Calif., Dec. 10, 1942; d. Wayne Grady Gordon and Virginia Rose Choate; m. James Lilley Staples III, Sept. 28, 1969; children: James Michael, Roxanne Michelle children: Serenity Elizabeth Stanfield. Grad., Westport HS, Kansas City, Mo., 1959. Ordained min. Fla., 1994. Owner operator Agape' Ceramics, Belleview, Fla., 1984—96; pastor Breath of Fire Ministries, Belleview, Fla., 1989—96; family svc. counselor Forest Lawn Memory Gardens, Ocala, Fla., 1997—2003, Good Shepherd Meml. Gardens, Ocala, 2003—. Guardian ad litem Dept. Children and Families, Ocala, Fla., 1997—99. Marcher Choose Life, Ocala, Fla., 1994—95. R-Conservative. Full Gospel. Avocations: fishing, painting, ceramics, roses, crossword puzzles. Office: Good Shepherd Meml Gardens 5050 SW 20th St Ocala FL 34474 Office Phone: 352-812-7942.

STAPLES, LYNNE LIVINGSTON MILLS, retired psychologist, educator, consultant; b. Detroit, Sept. 18, 1934; d. Robert Livingston Mills Staples and Lyda Charlotte (Diehr) Staples; m. Lee Edward Burmeister, July 16, 1955 (div. 1982); children: Benjamin Lee, Lynne Ann. BS, Ctrl. Mich. U., 1957; MA, U. Mich., 1965; student, Marygrove Coll., Cen. Mich. U., 1971-74. Ltd. lic. psychologist, sch. psychologist; cert. social worker, elem. permanent cons. and tchr. for mentally handicapped. First grade tchr. Shepherd (Mich) Schs., 1957-59; tchr. Kingston (Mich.) Schs., 1959-65; tchr. educationally handicapped Rialto (Calif.) Unified Sch. Dist., 1965-66; tchr., cons. Tuscola Int. Sch. Dist., Caro, Mich., 1966-71; sch. psychologist Huron Int. Sch. Dist., Bad Axe, Mich., 1971-74, Tuscola Int. Sch. Dist., Caro, 1974-89; instr. Delta Coll., University Center, Mich., 1976-88; tchr. spl. day classes Victorville (Calif.) High Sch., 1989; sch. psychologist Bedford (Ind.) Schs., 1990-91; clin. psychologist ACT team and outpatient therapy Sanilac County Mental Health Svcs., Sandusky, Mich., 1991-99; ret., 1999. Cons. sch. psychologist Marlette (Mich.) Schs., 1982-86, Bartholomew Pub. Schs., Columbus, Ind., 1989, Johnson County Schs., Franklin, Ind., 1990; clin. psychologist Thumb Family Counseling, Caro, 1985-88; personnel com. Team One Credit Union, 1993; instr. St. Clair C.C., 1993. Conf. presenter in field. Del. NEA-Mich. Edn. Assn. Rep. Assemblies, 1970—89; pres., auction chmn. Altrusa Club, Marlette, 1982—88; style show chmn. Marlette Band Boosters, 1983; mem. exec. bd. Lawrence County Tchrs. Assn., Bedford, 1991; mem. Meth. Choir, 2000—03; mem. pit orch. prodn. Bye Bye Birdie, Sandusky, 2001; dist. dir. social action United Meth. Women, 2000—02; tour guide Gagetown Octagon Barn, 2003; precinct del. Dem. Party, 2000—04; v.p. Port Huron dist. United Meth. Women, 2002—04; mem. Marlette First United Meth. Praise Band, 1999—2003; bd. dirs. Team One Credit Union, 1994—, bd. dirs., exec. bd. sec., 2004; bd. dirs. Vassar City Band, 1998—2003, Flint Concert Band, 2000—04, Bay City Concert Band, 2000—02, Unionville-Sebewaing Cmty. Band, 2001—02, Vassar Orch., 2001—03, Honsinger Wind Ensemble, 2001—04, Mott Cmty. Coll. Band, 2004; mem. Sanilac Three-Minute Band, 2001—03, Sanilac Symphonic Band, 1993—2000. Fed. govt. grantee Wayne State U., 1968. Mem.: Ind. Assn. Sch. Psychologists (pub. rels. bd. 1990—91), Ind. State Tchrs. Assn. (rep. assembly del. 1991), Am. Federated State and Mcpl. Employees (chairperson #15 chpt. 1993—96), Mich. Edn. Assn-Ret. Thumb Area (sec. 1996—2002, exec. bd. 2002—03), Emmaus Reunion Group, Lions (bd. dirs. 1996—99, 2d v.p. 1999). Democrat. Avocations: antiques, swimming, gardening, pets, traveling. Home: 6726 Clothier Rd Clifford MI 48727-9501

STAPLES, THORI YVETTE, former soccer player; b. Balt., Apr. 17, 1974; Student in sports mgmt., N.C. State U. Asst. women's soccer coach Va. Poly. Inst. and State U. Mem. silver medal U.S. squad1993 World Univ. Games, Buffalo; mem. 3d-place U.S. team FIFA Women's World Cup, Sweden, 1995; alt. U.S. Olympic Team, 1996; 1994 NSCAA All-Am.; 3-time All-Atlantic Coast Conf. and All-South Region selection for N.C. State U. Wolfpack. Nominee Mo. Athletic Club Nat. Player of Yr., 1994, 1995; named winner N.C. state championships in long jump, 400-meter dash, 800-meter run, ACC Rookie of Yr., 1994, 5-yr. player, Columbia (Md.) Crusaders; recipient Gold medal heptathlon, Nat. Amateur Athletic Union Jr. Olympics, 1991, 1992. Office: US Soccer Fedn 1801-1811 S Prairie Ave Chicago IL 60616

STAPLETON, CLAUDIA ANN, school director; b. Memphis, July 14, 1947; m. Mark Phillip Stapleton, Sept. 18, 1985. AS, Amarillo Coll., 1995; BS, Wayland Bapt. U., 1997, postgrad., 1997-98. Sch. dir. Acad. Profl. Careers, Amarillo, Tex., 2002—. Republican. Methodist. Home: 3321 Lenwood Dr Amarillo TX 79109-3345 Office: Acad Profl Careers 2201 S Western Ste 102-3 Amarillo TX 79109

STAPLETON, JEAN, journalism educator; b. Albuquerque, June 24, 1942; d. James L. and Mary (Behrman) S.; m. John Clegg, Apr. 15, 1965 (dec. Sept. 1972); m. Richard Bright, Jan. 13, 1973 (div. 1985); children: Lynn, Paul Bright; m. William Walter Farran, Nov. 9, 1996. BA, U. N.Mex., 1964; MS in Journalism, Northwestern U., 1968. Reporter Glenview (Ill.) Announcements, 1967-68, Angeles Mesa News Advertiser, L.A., 1968-69, City News Svc., Radio News West, L.A., 1969-71; press sec. polit. campaign, 1972; instr. journalism East L.A. Coll., 1973-75, prof., dept. chair, 1975—. Author: Equal Marriage, 1975, Equal Dating, 1979. Mem. NOW (pres. L.A. chpt. 1973-74), Assn. Women in Comm., Soc. Profl. Journalists, Ninety Nines, L.A. Poets Writers Collective. Democrat. Methodist. Home: 3232 Philo St Los Angeles CA 90064-4719 Office: East LA Coll 1301 Avenida Cesar Chavez Monterey Park CA 91754-6001

STAPLETON, KATHARINE HALL (KATIE STAPLETON), food broadcaster, writer; m. Benjamin Franklin Stapleton; children: Benjamin Franklin III, Craig Roberts, Katharine Hall. BA, Vassar Coll., 1941. Prodr., writer, host Cooking with Katie Sta. KOA, 1979—89. Author: Denver Delicious, 1980, 3d edit., 1983, High Notes, 1985-. Chmn. women's divsn. United Fund, 1955-56; founder, chmn. Denver Debutante Ball, 1956, 57; hon. chmn. Nat. Travelers Aid Assn., 1952-56, 93-96; commr. Denver Centennial Authority, 1958-60; trustee Washington Cathedral, regional v.p., 1967-73; trustee Colo. Women's Coll., 1975-80; sole trustee Harmes C. Fishback Found.; hon. chmn. Le Bal à Versailles, 2000, 02, 2004. Decorated Chevalier de L'Etoile Noire, France; recipient People-to-People citations, 1960, 66, Beautiful Activist award, Colo.-Wyo. Restaurant Assn. award, 1981, Humanitarian of Yr. award Arthritis Found., 1995, Arts award Colo. Symphony, 1998; named Chevalier de Tastevin, 1989, Outstanding Vol. Fundraiser, Nat. Philanthropy Day, 1995, Outstanding Alumna, Barstow Sch., 2003, Comdr., 2004. Mem. Denver Country Club. Republican. Episcopalian. Home: 8 Village Rd Cherry Hills Village CO 80113-4908

STAPLETON, MARYLYN ALECIA, diplomat; b. St. Thomas, V.I., Sept. 25, 1936; d. Lambert George and Aletha C. (Callendar) John; m. Frank Stapleton, Oct. 22, 1967 (div. Apr. 1983); 1 child, Linda E. Student, Washington Bus. Inst., 1959. Reservations agt. Caribair Airlines, St. Thomas, 1954-56; sales clk. Macy's Dept. Store, N.Y.C., 1956-57, Gift Shop, N.Y.C., 1957-63; supr. Ea. Airlines, Inc., N.Y.C. and St. Thomas, 1964-86; travel cons. Caribbean Travel Agy., St. Thomas, 1986-87; asst. commr. Dept. Licensing and Consumer Affairs, Govt. of V.I., St. Thomas, 1987-95, dep. of planning and natural resources, 1995—, small bus. tech. assistance program coord., 1995—; state exec. dir. Internat. Assn. Plumbing Mech. Officials, 1999—. Owner, pres. Stapleton Enterprises, St. Thomas, 1989—. Pub. rels. officer Nevis Benevolent Soc., St. Thomas, 1966-85; state chair Dem. party V.I., 1986—, dist. chair, 1984-86; small bus. ombudsman Clean Air Act of 1990, 1998—. Recipient Legis. Resolution V.I. Legislature, St. Thomas, 1986. Mem. Internat. Assn. Plumbing and Mech. Ofcls., Nat. Assn. of Plumbing, Heating and Cooling Contrs., St. Thomas/St. John Plumbing Assn. (pres. 1995—), St. Thomas Lioness Club (treas. 1985-86, pagent chair 1986-87, pres. 1987-88, mem. chair 1988-89, Melvin Jones fellow 1989), Lions Club of Charlotte Amalie. Democrat. Anglican. Home: 148-87 Est Annas Retreat PO Box 303739 Saint Thomas VI 00803-3739 Office: Democratic Party of Virgin Islns PO Box 3739 Saint Thomas Charlotte Amalie VI 00801

STAPLETON, SHERYL WILLIAMS, state representative; b. July 30, 1957; m. Edreade Stapleton; children: David, Veronica. BEd, N.Mex. State U., 1978; MA, U. N.Mex., 1987, edn. specialist, edn. adminstr., 1990. Sch.-to-careers coord. Albuquerque Pub. Schs.; state rep. dist. 19 N.Mex. Ho. of Reps., Santa Fe, 1995—, chair, labor and human resources com., mem. N.Mex. fin. authority oversight interim com., mem. legis. edn. study interim com., edn. com., and legis. health and human svcs. interim com. Vice chair, state chair N.Mex. Dem. Party. Democrat. Office: State Capitol Room 312A Santa Fe NM 87503

STAR, GLORIA GAY, astrologer, writer, educator, consultant; b. Abilene, Tex., Sept. 6, 1948; d. Jess Jerl and Frances Louise (Watts) Franklin; m. Richard Gordon Brownd, July 1967 (div. 1974); 1 child, Taletha Brownd; m. Jack Miller, Aug. 1980 (div. Mar. 1983); 1 child, Christopher Miller; m. Richard H. Roess, Jan. 25, 1991. Student, N.W. Tex. Hosp. Sch. Nursing, 1968-69, West Tex. State U., 1967-70, U. Okla., 1975-80. Rsch. assoc. dept. family practice Okla. U. Heath Sci. Ctr., Oklahoma City, 1971-76, ednl. liaison dept. family practice, 1976-78; owner/mgr. The Earth Natural Foods, Norman, Okla., 1979-82. Astrological counselor, Norman, San Diego, Clinton, Conn., 1974—; faculty United Astrology Congress, Inc., L.A., 1986—; mgr. Astrology Channel ThirdAge.com, 2000. Author: Optimum Child, 1987, Astrology and Your Child, 2000, Sun Sign Book (annually), 1990—2002, Llewellyn's Moon Sign Book Personal Forecasts, 1995-2003, (software) Woman to Woman, 1997, Optimum Child, 2002, Inner Child, 2002; contbg. author: How to Measure and Manage Crisis, 1993; feature writer The Mountain Astrologer mag., 1995—; editor Assn. for Astrological Networking newsletter, 1990-97; editor and contbg. author: Astrology for Women, 1997; editor, contbr. Astrology for Women, 1995. Bd. dirs. United Astrology Conf., 1999—2002. Mem. Assn. for Astrological Networking (advisor, sec. 1990-92, newsletter comm. dir. 1992-95), Nat. Coun. for Geocosmic Rsch. (adv. bd. 1989—), Internat. Soc. for Astrol. Rsch. Democrat. Avocations: singing, community theatre, gardening.

STARCHER-DELL'AQUILA, JUDY LYNN, special education educator; b. Cuyahoga Falls, Ohio, Sept. 20, 1956; d. James Calvin and Jane Yvonne (Hart) Starcher; m. Richard Paul Dell'Aquila, July 16, 1983; 1 child, Jessica Lynn Dell'Aquila. BS in Hearing & Speech Scis., Ohio U., 1978; MEd in Deaf Edn., U. Cin., 1980; PhD in Spl. Edn., Kent State U., 1996. Cert. supr. and tchr., Ohio. Tchr. deaf Parma (Ohio) City Schs., 1978-79, Mayfield (Ohio) City Schs., 1980-81; tchr. deaf, low incidence work study coord. Trumbull County Ednl. Svc. Ctr., Warren, Ohio, 1981-84; work study coord. Cuyahoga Ednl. Svc. Ctr., Valley View, Ohio, 1984-88; instr., student tchg. supr. Kent (Ohio) State U., 1993-95; project dir. Children's Hosp. Med. Ctr./Family Child Learning Ctr., Tallmadge, Ohio, 1995-2000; coord. spl. edn. Cleveland Heights/University Heights (Ohio) City Sch. System, 2000—. Am. Sign Lang. instr. Cuyahoga C.C., Cleve., 1993-2000; dir. adv. bd. Hearing Impaired Toddler Infant & Families Program, Tallmadge, 1995-2000; mem. County Collaborative Group, Medina, Summit counties, Ohio, 1995-2000; state trainer SKI—HI, Logan, Utah, 1997—. Mem. Coun. Exceptional Children. Grantee Job Tng. & Partnership Act, Cleve., 1982, 86-88; Univ. fellow Kent State U., 1991. Democrat. Avocations: antique collector, exercise, reading. Home: 151 E Pleasant Valley Rd Seven Hills OH 44131-5601 Office: Cleveland Hgts/Univ Hgts Bd Edn 2155 Miramar Blvd University Heights OH 44118

STARFIELD, BARBARA HELEN, pediatrician, educator; b. Bklyn., Dec. 18, 1932; d. Martin and Eva (Illions) Starfield; m. Neil A. Holtzman, June 12, 1955; children: Robert, Jon, Steven. AB, Swarthmore Coll., 1954; MD, SUNY, 1959; MPH, Johns Hopkins U., 1963. Teaching asst. in anatomy Downstate Med. Ctr., N.Y.C., 1955—57, intern in pediat. Johns Hopkins U., 1959—60, resident, 1960—62, dir. pediatric med. care clinic, 1963—66, dir. cmty. staff comprehensive child care project, 1966—67, dir. pediatric clin. scholars program, 1971—76, prof. health policy, joint appointment in pediatrics, 1975—, disting. univ. prof., 1994—. Mem. Nat. Com. Vital Stats., 1994—2002; cons. DHHS; mem. nat. adv. coun. Agy. for Health Care Policy and Rsch., 1990—94; adv. subcom. on Health Systems and Svcs. RSch. Pan Am. Health Orgn., 1988—92, 1995—; cons. Health Care Fin. Adminstrn., 1980—. Editl. bd. Med. Care, 1977—79, Pediat., 1977—82, Internat. Jour. Health Svcs., 1978—, Med. Care Rev., 1980—84, Health Svc. Rsch., 1996—, assoc. editor Ann. Rev. Pub. Health, 1996—2001; contbr. articles to profl. jours. Recipient Dave Luckman Meml. award, 1958, HEW Career Devel. award, 1970—75, APHA Martha May Eliot award, 1995, Disting. Investigator award, Assn. Health Svcs. Rsch., 1995, 1st Primary Care Achievement award, Pew Charitable Trust Fund, 1994, 1st Ann. Rsch. award, Ambulatory Pediatric Assn., 1990. Fellow: Am. Acad. Pediat.; mem.: APHA (Martha May Eliot award 1995), Internat. Soc. for Equity in Health (pres. 2000—02), Ambulatory Pediatric Assn. (pres. 1980), Internat. Epidemiologic Assn., Soc. Pediatric Rsch., NAS Inst. Medicine (governing coun. 1981—83), Alpha Omega Alpha, Sigma Xi. Office: Johns Hopkins Sch Hygiene 624 N Broadway Baltimore MD 21205-1900

STARGER, VICTORIA GONDEK, artist; Diploma in art cum laude-(hon.), du Cret Sch. of the Arts, Plainfield, NJ, 1976. Instr. drawing and painting Joe Kubert Sch. of Cartoon and Graphic Art, Dover, NJ, Morris County Art Assn., Morristown and Boonton, NJ, Somerset Art Assn., Bedminster, NJ. Exhibitions include numerous, including Galerie Le Carre d'Or, Eloge du petit Format dans l'art d'aujourd'hui, Paris, 2000, exhibitions include The Art of the Portrait, Cerulean Gallery, 2000, 12th Internat. Book and Press Fair, Geneva, Switzerland, 1998, Artworks, The Visual Art Sch. of Princeton and Trenton, 1997, Lever House, Park Ave., N.Y.C., 1991, Salon d'Automne 1988, Paris, Morris Mus., Morristown, N.J., 2003, Ctr. Culturel Christiane Peugeot, Paris, 2003—04. Office: Victoria Starger Art Studio 6 Vale Dr Mountain Lakes NJ 07046

STARK, ANDREA MARIE, theater educator; d. Andrew Paul Stark and Cynthia Anne Carlberg-Minton, Irwin Joseph Atkins (Stepfather) and Barbara Stark(Stepmother), Doe Viola (Stepmother); m. Christopher James Tickner, Sept. 9, 1995. BA in Theatre and Acting, BA in in English Lit., Fairleigh Dickinson U., 1986; MFA in Acting, No. Ill. U., 1991; student, Uta Hagen Heartland Theater Workshops, 1997—, Actors Online / NOW workshops, Burbank, Calif., 2000—. Theatre prof. / dir. acting and voice, dialect coach Coll. of DuPage /Buffalo Theatre Ensemble, Glen Ellyn, Ill., 1992—98; comml. actress SAG, Chgo., Ill., 1995—98; columnist PerformInk, Chgo., 1995—2000; adv. / lit. asst. Cale Kenney, Howlings Publs., Tell Tale Pub., Denver, 1998—2002; actress Arvada (Colo.) Ctr. for the Arts, Arvada, Colo., 1998—2000, theatre tchr. / theatre camp dir., 1998—2000; artistan, jewelry maker The Arvada Ctr. for the Arts Gift Shop, 1998—2000; artisan, jewelry maker Woman Wild Gallery, The Gifted Hand Gallery, Holiday Art Tea Assn., Chgo., 1991—98; pvt. acting coach Chgo., 1991—98; speech and communication prof. The Met. State Coll. of Denver, Denver, 1998—2000; comml. actress SAG, L.A., Calif., 2000—; speech and communication prof. Coll. of Dupage, Glen Ellyn, Ill., 1993—98; profl. stage actress Actors Equity Assn., L.A., Calif., 2000—; speech and communication prof. Glendale (Calif.) C.C., 2000—; adj. prof. theater Calif. State U., Northridge, 2001—; dir. of fun ReMed Recovery Care Ctrs., Phila., 1986—89; profl. actress/acting tchr. Walnut St. Theatre, Phila., 1986—89; tchr./creative cons. Colo. Ednl. Theatre, Denver, 1998—2000; theatre tchr./ dir. Aurora (Colo.) Fox Theatre, 1998—2000; acting tchr. Francis Parker Sch., Chgo., 1997—98, Actor's Ctr. of DuPage, Villa Park, Ill., 1992—94, Children's Theatre of Western Springs, Ill., 1992—94; profl. actress Buffalo Theatre Ensemble, Glen Ellyn, Ill., 1994—98; acting tchr. Metuchen (N.J.) Bd. Edn., 1987—88; dir. / acting tchr. Chgo. Studio for Dance and Musical Theatre, 1991—95, The Sycamores, Altadena, Calif., 1999—; freelance casting sessions/cons. Sag Talent Agencies, Chgo., 1994—98; grad. asst. tchr. No. Ill. U., DeKalb, Ill., 1988—91; studio acting tchr., dir. Armory Ctr. for the Arts, Pasadena, Calif., 1999—; writer The Sycamores Theatre Day Treatment, Altadena and Pasadena, Calif., 2000—03, Youth Ensemble Theatre, Chgo., 1994—98; writer / playwright Aurora Fox Theatre, 1998—2002; freelance writer L.A., Calif., 2000—03; dir. and dialect coach Coll. of Dupage Buffalo Theatre Ensemble, Glen Ellyn, Ill., 1994—98; freelance writer Chgo., 1989—98; artisian, jewelry maker The Printed Page, Boulder, Colo., 1998—2000; artistic dir. Youth Ensemble Theatre/ The Studio at Tracey Kaplan Casting Inc., Chgo., 1993—98; casting dir. Tracey Kaplan Casting Inc., Chgo., 1993—97; ind. casting dir. Chgo., 1997—98, Denver, 1998—2001; profl. actress Shoestring Players, New Brunswick, NJ, 1983—84. Actor: (stage) Into the Woods (Jeff nominated Prodn.), Wrens (Joseph Jefferson Acting Award, 1996); author: (play) After the Ball, (a series of plays for youth theatre) Multiple Titles, (children's book) The Magic Sleeping Bag. Vol. Cabrini Connections, Chicago, Ill., 1991—94, St. Anthony's Rescue, Lomita, Calif., 2000—03; bd. mem. Niños del Lago Guatemalan Relief Project; activist SAG, Los Angeles, Calif., 1999—2000. Recipient Prize for Poetry, Jour. of N.J. Poets, 1983, acting award, Joseph Jefferson Com., 1996. Mem.: Nat. Assn. for the Edn. of Young Children, N.Y. Mask Theatre (assoc.), SAG (life), Actors Equity Assn. (life). Green Party. Avocations: hiking, camping, gardening, beach activities, volunteerism.

STARK, DIANA, public relations executive; b. N.Y.C., July 01; d. Benjamin and Sara (Zelasny) S. BA, Hunter Coll. Promotion mgr. TV Guide mag., N.Y.C., 1950-61, Show Bus. Illustrated, N.Y.C., 1961-62; broadcast specialist Young & Rubicam, N.Y.C., 1962-69; pres. Stark Comms. Inc., N.Y.C., 1969-76; pub. svc. publicity account exec. Y & R E, N.Y.C., 1976-77; pres. Stark Comms. Internat., N.Y.C., 1978—. Pub. rels. workshop leader Chgo. Econ. Devel. Corp., 1973-76; cons. to Asahi Shimbun for English Language Newsletter. 1991-92, columnist Host mag., 1960-65; writer, producer programs for women's TV shows, 1962—. Book developer Ellis Island: The First Experience With Liberty, 1991. Coord. We Have Arrived, Portraits at Ellis Island, Augustus Sherman Photographs, 1902-24. Mem. NATAS (trustee 1974-78, publicity com., chmn., chpt. gov. 1972-76, 82-86, 87-91, editor N.Y. TV Directory 1987-90). Office Fax: 212-765-3670.

STARK, JOAN SCISM, education educator; b. Hudson, N.Y., Jan. 6, 1937; d. Ormonde F. and Myrtle Margaret (Kirkey) S.; m. William L. Stark, June 28, 1958 (dec.); children: Eugene William, Susan Elizabeth, Linda Anne, Ellen Scism; m. Malcolm A. Lowther, Jan. 31, 1981. BS, Syracuse U., 1957; MA (Hoadly fellow), Columbia U., 1960; Ed.D., SUNY, Albany, 1971. Tchr. Ossining (N.Y.) High Sch., 1957-59; free-lance editor Holt, Rinehart & Winston, Harcourt, Brace & World, 1960-70; lectr. Ulster County Community Coll., Stone Ridge, N.Y., 1968-70; asst. dean Goucher Coll., Balt., 1970-73, asso. dean, 1973-74; assoc. prof., chmn. dept. higher postsecondary edn. Syracuse (N.Y.) U., 1974-78; dean Sch. Edn. U. Mich., Ann Arbor, 1978-83, prof., 1983-2001, prof. and dean emeritus, 2001—; dir. Nat. Ctr. for Improving Postsecondary Teaching and Learning, 1986—91. Editor: Rev. of Higher Edn., 1991-96; contbr. articles to various publs. Leader Girl Scouts U.S.A., Cub Scouts Am.; coach girls Little League; dist. officer PTA, intermittently, 1968-80; mem. adv. com. Gerald R. Ford Library, U. Mich., 1980-83; trustee Kalamazoo Coll., 1979-85; mem. exec. com. Inst. Social Research, U. Mich., 1979-81; bd. dirs. Mich. Assn. Colls. Tchr. Edn., 1979-81. Mem. Am. Assn. for Higher Edn., Am. Ednl. Rsch. Assn. (Div. J. Rsch. award 1998), Assn. Study Higher Edn. (dir. 1977-79, v.p. 1983, pres. 1984, Rsch. Achievement award 1992, svc. award 1998, Disting. Career award 1999), Assn. Innovation Higher Edn. (nat. chmn. 1974-75), Assn. Instl. Rsch. (disting. mem., Sidney Suslow award 1999), Assn. Colls. and Schs. Edn. State Univs. and Land Grant Colls. (dir. 1981-83), Acctg. Edn. Change Commn., Phi Beta Kappa, Phi Kappa Phi, Sigma Pi Sigma, Eta Pi Upsilon, Lambda Sigma Sigma, Phi Delta Kappa, Pi Lambda Theta.

STARK, NELLIE MAY, forester, ecologist, educator; b. Norwich, Conn., Nov. 20, 1933; d. Theodore Benjamin and Dorothy Josephine (Pendleton) Beetham; m. Oscar Elder Stark, Oct. 1962 (dec.). BA, Conn. Coll., 1956; AM, Duke U., 1958, PhD, 1962. Botanist Exptl. Sta., U.S. Forest Svc., Old Strawberry, Calif., 1958-66; botanist, ecologist Desert Rsch. Inst., Reno, 1966-72; prof. forest ecology Sch. Forestry, U. Mont., Missoula, 1972-92; pvt. cons. Philomath, Oreg. Pres. Camas Analytical Lab., Inc., Missoula, 1987-92. Author: Will Your Family Survive the 21st Century, 1997, Memories of Wren, Oregon, 1998, So You Want to Build a Little Log Cabin in the Woods, 2002; contbr. articles to profl. jours. Named Disting. Dau. Norwich, Conn., 1985; recipient Conn. award Conn. Coll., 1986, 54 grants. Mem. Ecol. Soc. Am. (chair ethics com. 1974, 76), Soc. Am. Foresters (taskforce 1987-88).

STARK, PATRICIA ANN, psychologist; b. Ames, Iowa, Apr. 21, 1937; d. Keith C. and Mary L. (Johnston) Moore. BS, So. Ill. U., Edwardsville, 1970, MS, 1972; PhD, St. Louis U., 1976. Counselor to alcoholics Bapt. Rescue Mission, East St. Louis, Ill., 1969; rschr. alcoholics Gateway Rehab. Ctr., East St. Louis, 1972; psychologist intern Henry-Stark Counties Spl. Edn. Dist. and Galesburg State Rsch. Hosp., Ill., 1972-73; instr. Lewis and Clark C.C., Godfrey, Ill., 1973-76, asst. prof., 1976-84, assoc. prof., 1984, coord. child care svcs., 1974-84; mem. staff dept. psychiatry Meml. Hosp., St. Elizabeth's Hosp., 1979-2001; supr. various workshops in field, 1974-84. Dir. child and family svc. Collinsville Counseling Ctr., 1977-82; clin. dir., owner Empas-Complete Family Psychol. and Hypnosis Svcs., Collinsville, 1982—; cons. cmty. agys., 1974—; mem. adv. bd. Madison County Coun. on Alcoholism and Drug Dependency, 1977-80. Mem. APA, Ill. Psychol. Assn., Midwestern Psychol. Assn., Nat. Assn. Sch. Psychologists, Am. Soc. Clin. Hypnosis, Internat. Soc. Hypnosis. Office: 2802 Maryville Rd Maryville IL 62062 Office Phone: 618-345-6632.

STARK, ROBIN CARYL, psychotherapist, consultant; b. Yonkers, N.Y., Apr. 16, 1953; d. Louis and Bernice (Cooper) S. BA in Psychology cum laude with honors, Hunter Coll., 1979; MSW, NYU, 1982. Diplomate Am. Bd. Clin. Social Work; lic. social worker, N.Y.; cert. psychoanalytic psychotherapy, psychotherapy of eating disorders, trauma tng. for mental health profls., ARC. Pvt. practice psychotherapy, N.Y.C., 1983—. Mem. adj. field faculty Grad. Sch. Social Svc. Fordham U., N.Y.C., 1986—87, Grad. Sch. Social Work, Hunter Coll., N.Y.C., 1987—88; coord. patient care svcs. Achievement and Guidance Ctrs. Am., Inc., N.Y.C., 1988—89; staff psychotherapist Ctr. for Study of Anorexia and Bulimia, 1990—94, facilitator wellness support chronic & life-challenging illness, 1993—; bd. dirs. N.Y. Met. Cmty. of Mindfulness, 1999—2000; pro bono svc. provider Project Liberty's post Sept. 11 trauma counseling program, N.Y.C., 2001—. Recipient service award Young Adult Inst., 1987; N.Y.C. Youth Bur. grantee, 1983-85. Mem. NASW, Acad. Cert. Social Workers. Office: 410 E 57th St Ste 1A New York NY 10022-3059

STARK, SUSAN R. film critic; b. N.Y.C., July 9, 1940; d. Albert A. and Lillian H. (Landau) Rothenberg; m. Allan F. Stark, June 26, 1968 (div. 1983); children: Allana Fredericka, Paula-Rose. BA, Smith Coll., 1962; MAT., Harvard U., 1963. Film critic Detroit Free Press, 1968-79, Detroit News, 1979—. Mem. Phi Beta Kappa Office: Detroit News 615 W Lafayette Blvd Detroit MI 48226-3197

STARKEY, ALETA RAE, music educator; b. Canonsburg, Pa., June 6, 1946; d. David Frederick Weaver and Dorothy Aleta Knupp; m. Tedd Lee Starkey, Dec. 21, 1968 (div. Oct. 30, 1982); children: Tiffany Rae, Crissy Lynn. BS in Edn., Ind. U. Pa., 1968. Profl. Cert. Pa, Dept. Edn., 1978. Tchr. Washington Sch. Dist., Pa., 1968—72; tchr. vocal music Canon-McMillan Sch. Dist., Canonsburg, Pa., 1972—. Choir dir., organist Venice Presbyn. Ch., McDonald, Pa., 1983—. Dir.: (music condr.) Cmty. Grange Chorus (First Pl. in State Competition); musician: (mem. female quartet) Sang for local orgns. (first Pl. in state competition and second Pl. in Nat. Competion, 1967). Dir. heart telethon for local cable sta. Heart Assn., Cannonsburg, Pa., 1980—81; mem. Washington Cmty. Fine Arts Chorus, Pa., 2003—. Mem.: Cannon-McMillan Edn. Assn. (assoc.; union rep. 1997—2001), Pa. Music Educators Conf. (assoc.), Music Educators Nat. Conf. (assoc.), Internat. Order Ea. Star (adah 2002—03), Order of Patrons of Husbandry (lectr. 1985—89), Internat. Order Rainbow Girls (life). R-Liberal. Presbyterian. Avocations: knitting, crocheting, sewing. Home: 20 Plum Run Rd Mc Donald PA 15057 Personal E-mail: arstarkey@hotmail.com.

STARKMAN, BETTY PROVIZER, genealogist, writer, educator; b. Detroit, July 18, 1929; d. Jack and Rose (Bodenstein) Provizer; m. Morris Starkman, Dec. 25, 1952; children: Susan Lynn Starkman Rott, Robert David Starkman. AB, Wayne State U., 1951; postgrad., U. Wis., 1949; MA, Wayne U., 1954. Cert. social worker, Mich. Social worker Wayne County Social Aid, Detroit, 1951-54, B'nai B'rith Youth Orgn., Detroit, 1951-54; genealogist, historian Birmingham, Mich., 1979—. Tchr. Midrasha Coll., Southfield, Mich., 1986-88, Coll. Jewish Studies, Birmingham, 1986-88; lectr. Jewish Cmty. Ctr., West Bloomfield, Mich., 1986-89. Editor jour. Generations, 1986; contbr. articles to Jwish News, Generations, Search, others. Bd. dirs. Anti Defamation League,Detroit, 1980—, Jewish Cmty. Coun., Southfield, 1980—, Tribute Fund, Detroit, 1979-85; v.p. Maimonides, Detroit, 1966-67; bd. dirs. Am. Mogen David for Israel, Mich. br.; del. 1st conf. Jews of Old China, Harvard U., 1992; mem. archives com. Jewish Welfare Fedn. Mich., 1993—. Recipient Humanitarian award State of Israel Bonds, 1980; Helping Hand award Israel Red Cross, 1980, Humanitarian award, 1991; honored by Mich. region Am. Red Mogen Dovid for Israel, 1997, Jewish Geneal. Soc. Mich., 1997. Mem. Jewish Genealogy Soc. Mich. (founder, pres. 1982-84, bd. dirs. 1995—), Jewish Genealogy Soc. Ill., Jewish Genealogy Soc. Inc., Jewish Hist. Soc. (Mich. bd. dirs. 1986-88), Jewish Genealogy Soc. L.A., Jewish Genealogy Soc. Phila., Jewish Genealogy Soc. Washington, Jewish Genealogy Soc. Toronto, Polish Genealogy Soc. Mich. Avocations: travel, reading, collecting art, music, archaeology. Home and Office: 1260 Stuyvessant Rd Bloomfield Hills MI 48301-2141

STARKS, CAROL ELIZABETH, retired principal; b. Elizabeth, NJ, Oct. 16, 1941; d. Arthur E. and Argetha P. (Henderson) Starks. AA, Graceland Coll., Lamoni, Iowa, 1961; BA in Elem. Edn., Mich. State U., 1963; MA in Elem. Adminstrn., San Jose State U., 1972. Cert. elem. sch. tchr. Calif., life diploma for elem. edn. Calif., specialist tchr. in reading Calif., std. svc. credential in supervision Calif., elem. sch. tchr. N.J. Tchr. grade 3 Hayes Sch., Monterey, Calif., 1963—65; tchr. grade 2 Woodruff Sch., Berkeley Heights, NJ, 1965—67; tchr. remedial reading and educationally handicapped Ord Terrace Sch., Monterey, 1967—68, asst. prin., 1975—77, prin., 1984—88; tchr. grade 3 Manzanita Sch., Monterey, 1968—73; asst. prin. La Mesa Sch., Monterey, 1973—74, tchr. grade 6, 1974—75; prin. Foothill Sch., Monterey, 1977—80, Olson Sch., Monterey, 1980—84, Highland Sch., Monterey, 1988—95, Bay View Sch., Monterey, 1995—99. Interviewed as representative of elementary principals Calif. Commn. on the Tchg. Profession, 1984—85. Mem. world ch. pubs. com. Remnant Ch. Jesus Christ of Latter Day Saints, 2001—, music dir. Blue Springs congregation, 2001—, mem. world ch. hymnbook com., 2003—. Recipient Calif. Disting. Sch. Prin.'s award, 1989, 1993, Proclamation for profl. accomplishments and 19 yrs. of svc., City of Seaside (Calif.), 1995. Mem.: AAUW (sec. independence br. 2003—), Kansas City Coun. (scholarship com. 2000—01, treas. 2002—), Monterey Bay Sch. Adminstr. Assn. (pres. 1997—98), Assn. Calif. Sch. Adminstr. (sec./treas. Monterey Peninsula charter 1977—78, v.p. 1978—79, pres. 1979—80, treas. region X 1979—81, pres. region X 1981—82, mem. elem. adminstrn. com. 1982—86, del. to Nat. Assn. Elem. Sch.Prins. Convention 1983—84, state facilitator Elem. Adminstrn. Acad. North 1984—85, state dir. Elem. Adminstrn. Acad. North 1985—86, invited writer for case studies for Calif. sch. leadership acad. 1985—86, state del. to rep. assembly 1986—91, Region X Blanche Montague award for Outstanding Sch. Adminstr. 1987), Delta Kappa Gamma (1st v.p. Delta Lambda chpt. Calif. 1986—88, 2nd v.p. Delta Lambda chpt.Calif. 1988—90, pres. Delta Lambda chpt.Calif. 1990—92, Calif.membership task force 1991—93, Calif.personal growth and svcs. com. 1993—95, dir. area V Calif. 1995—97, state chairperson comms. com. 1997—99, mem. scholarship com. Kansas City coun. 2000—01, pres. Phi chpt. Mo. 2000—02, state comm. com. 2001—03, chair state comm. com. 2003 , chmn. state comm. com. 2003—). Republican. Remnant Ch. Of Jesus Christ Of Latter Day Saints. Avocations: travel, reading, music, computer. Home: 3341 S Cochise Ave Independence MO 64057

STARKS, FLORENCE ELIZABETH, retired special education educator; b. Summit, N.J., Dec. 6, 1932; d. Edward and Winnie (Morris) S. BA, Morgan State U., 1956; MS in Edn., CUNY, 1962; postgrad., Fairleigh Dickinson U., 1962-63, Seton Hall U., 1963, Newark State Coll. Cert. blind and visually handicapped and social studies tchr., N.J. Tchr. adult edn. Newark Bd. of Edn.; ret., 1995; tchr. N.Y. Inst. for Edn. of the Blind. Developer first class for multiple handicapped blind children in pub. sch. system, Newark, 1960; ptnr. World Vision Internat. Mem. ASCD, AFL-CIO, AAUW, Coun. Exceptional Children, Am. Assn. U. Women, Nat. Assn. Negro Bus. and Profl. Women's Club Inc., N.J. Edn. Assn., Newark Tchrs. Assn., Newark Tchrs. Union-Am. Fedn. Tchrs., World Vision Internat. (ptnr.). Home: 4 Park Ave Summit NJ 07901-3942

STARLING, ELIZABETH ANNE, strategic planner; b. Bellefonte, Pa., Oct. 17, 1970; d. James L. and Martha Lewis Starling; m. Kevin Gerald Dutcher, May 18, 2002. BA, English Lit., Swarthmore Coll., Swarthmore, Pennsylvania, 1988—92; M.Planning in Pub. Affairs, Humphrey Inst., U. of Minn., Minneapolis, MN, 1994—96. Dir. of policy, planning and measures Minn. Dept of Employment and Economic Devel., St. Paul, 2000—; rsch. dir. (acting) Minn. Dept of Econ. Security, St. Paul, 1999—2000, sr rsch. analysis specialist and team leader, 1997—99, rsch. analysis specialist, 1996—97. Bd. of directors Civics, Incorporateed, St. Paul, 1999—; chair, bd. of trustees First Unitarian Soc. of Mpls., Minneapolis, Minn., 2001—, bd. of trustees, 1998—. Unitarian Universalist. Home: 1109 Idaho Avenue West Saint Paul MN 55108 Office: Minnesota Dept of Employment and Economic Development 390 North Robert Street Saint Paul MN 55101 Personal E-mail: estarling@visi.com. E-mail: elizabeth.starling@state.mn.us.

STARLING, VIRGINIA R. music educator, consultant; b. Loraine, TX, Apr. 26, 1929; d. Lawrence Livingston and Ruth Cleo (Martin) Trott; widowed; children: Catherine, Caroline, Randall. B of Music Edn., Mary Hardin Baylor U., 1950; MusM, 1976; MS in Psychology, Coll. of Southwest, 1989. Choir dir. Methodist Ch., Belton, TX, 1949-50; music instr. Monahans (Tex.) Pub. Schs., 1950-52, Lovington (N.Mex.) Pub. Schs., 1952-54, N.M. Jr. Coll., Hobbs, 1976-79; pvt. sch. music tchr. Hobbs, N.M., 1987-93; ch. organist, pvt. tchr. Lovington, Hobbs, N.M., 1952-99; ch. organist, cons. Cloudcroft, N.M., 1999—. Soloist: (CD) Enduring Devotion; composer piano solos for children, Just For You, 2000; concert performances in Hobbs, N. Mex., Carnegie Hall. Bd. dirs. Southwest Symphony. Mem. Music Tchrs. Nat. Assn., Profl. Music Tchrs. of N.Mex. (bd. dirs.), Lee County Music Forum, Sigma Alpha Iota. Baptist. Avocations: gardening, travel, history, music. Home: PO Box 1003 Cloudcroft NM 88317-1003 E-mail: skyhigh@zianet.com.

STARNER, BARBARA KAZMARK, marketing, advertising and export sales executive; b. Detroit, Sept. 2, 1940; d. Eugene Anthony and Lucille Ann Kazmark; m. G. Frederick Starner, June 30, 1962; 1 child, Natasha Lucienne. BA with honors, U. Mich., 1962; BS, Ohio State U., 1965. Tchr. art Columbus (Ohio) Pub. Schs., 1965-68, Mt. Olive Pub. Schs., Budd Lake, N.J., 1968-71; stained glass designer Barbara Designs, LaCrosse, Wis., 1975-87; from trade show mgr. to v.p. advt., mktg., export sales Kart-A-Bag divsn. Remin, Joliet, Ill., 1978—. Advt. and mktg. cons. Starner Mktg., L.A., 1987-95; ptnr. PreciousGem, L.A., 1999—. Mem., pres. East Bank Artists, LaCrosse, 1979-86; co-founder, dir. crafts Great River Traditional Music & Crafts Festival, LaCrosse, 1975-87; chmn. Spiritual Frontiers Fellowship, Mpls., 1979-85, 85-87; co-chmn. Spiritual Sci. Fellowship, 1985-87; fund raiser, mem./cook 1st crew Sloop Clearwater Restoration, Maine-N.Y., 1969 (Hudson River pollution clean-up). Democrat. Mem. Universalist Ch. Avocation: landscape and portrait painting. Office: Kart-A-Bag 510 Manhattan Rd Joliet IL 60433-3099

STARNES, SUSAN SMITH, elementary school educator; b. Grinnell, Iowa, Oct. 8, 1942; d. Edwin Fay Smith Jr. and Miriam Jane (Spaulding) Smith Simms; m. Wayman J. Starnes, Apr. 25, 1964; children: Michele Ann Starnes Hoffman, Mary Shannon Starnes Zornes. BS in Edn. summa cum laude, Mo. Bapt. U., 1991. Cert. early childhood tchr., elem. tchr. 1-8. Adminstr. Presbyn. Ch. in Am. Hist. Ctr., St. Louis, 1985-90; tchr. 3rd grade Ctrl. Christian Sch., St. Louis, 1991-98; subst. tchr. Ctrl. Christian Sch., Kirk Day Sch., Twin Oaks Christian Sch., St. Louis, 1998—. Mem. chapel com. Ctrl. Christian Sch., St. Louis, 1991-98. Children's dir. Canaan Bapt. Ch., St. Louis, 1991—96, Bible Study Fellowship children's leader, 1986—89, mission trip vol., 1992, 1993, 1999—2004; camp counselor

Youth for Christ, Kansas City, 1992, 1993, Awana leader, 1996—; mem. Mo. Bapt. Conv. Disaster Relief Childcare Unit, 1997—. Mem. Kappa Delta Pi. Avocations: biking, swimming, hiking.

STAROBIN, CHRISTINA F. artist, educator; b. N.Y.; d. Herman Starobin and Carol Fljan. BA cum laude, Harvard U., 1972; MA in English and Comparitive Lit., Columbia U., 1979; PhD in English, NYU, 1992. Sec. various firms, 1971—91; adj. prof. Coll. New Rochelle, N.Y., 1993, Queensboro C.C., Bayside, NY, 1993—94; asst. prof. lit. Ramapo Coll., Mahwah, NJ, 1994—96; asst. adj. prof. La Guardia C. C., Long Island, NY, 1998—99, Ulster County C.C., Stone Ridge, NY, 1999—2001; adj. prof. Bard Coll., Annandale-on-Hudson, NY, 2001, Culinary Inst. Am., Hyde Park, NY, 2001—. Asst. adj. prof. in English St. John's U., Jamaica, NY, 1992—94, St. Vincent's Coll., Jamaica, 1992—94; contest judge Browning Soc. Poetry, 1992—93; workship leader in field; spkr. in field. Author: Souvenirs from the Bog and Other Poems, 1995, Who Can Come to America?, 1996, No Room at the Inn: Home and Homeless in December, 1996; co-author: The Orchard Book of Poems, 1993 (Duncan Lawrie award, 82), Directing Puppet Theatre, 1989; contbr. articles to profl. jours. Vol. Beth Israel Med. Ctr., N.Y., 1985. Recipient First prize in poetry, Nat. Sr. Scholastic Mag., 1967. Home: 7 Old Patch Rd Saugerties NY 12477

STAROBIN, NANCY RUTH, photographer; b. Washington, Feb. 14, 1955; d. Sam David Starobin and Rita Sternberg. Diploma, Howard H.S., Ellicot City, Md., 1973; student in Photography, Howard Vocat., Columbia, Md., 1974; student in photography, Hamilton Sch. Photography, 1980—81. Photographer Howard County Times, Ellicot City, Md., 1974—75, Columbia Flier, Md., 1975—76; ofcl. photographer United Way, Balt., 1976—78; stringer AP, UPI, L.A. Daily News, L.A., 1983—90; ofcl. photographer NOW, L.A., 1982—84; freelance photographer Nancy Starobin Photography, Columbia, Md., 1974—; ofcl. photographer Outward Bound Sch. Wayzata, Minn., 1971, United Way, Md., 1976—78. N.Y. Times, L.A. Times, Horse Illustrated, Capitol Records, Wilhelmina West, Car Craft, Petersen's Photographic, Photographer's Market, and others. Vol. George McGovern Campaign, Washington, 1972. Recipient Photography award, Women in Photography Orgn., 1985, Am. Soc. Mag. Photographers, 1995. Mem.: Am. Soc. Mag. Photographers, San Fernando Valley Arts Coun. (Women in Photography award 1985). Avocation: nostalgia collector. Home: PO Box 1893 Glendora CA 91740

STAROST, DIANE JOAN, music educator; b. Huntington, N.Y., June 27, 1963; d. Frank Basil and Therese Basile Castrogivanni; m. Alan Francis Starost, May 20, 1990; children: Nicholas Francis, Arianna Marie. MusB in Music Edn., SUNY, 1985; MusM in Music Performance, Manhattan Sch. Music, 1988. Cert. tchr. N.Y. Pvt. practice, Greenlawn, NY, 1980—; vocal music tchr. Manetuck & Oquenock Elem. Schs., West Islip, NY, 1985—92, Udall Mid. Sch., West Islip, NY, 1992—97; dir. youth music Old First Presbyn. Ch., Huntington, NY, 1997—. String tchr. Northport (N.Y.)-East Northport Schs., 1987—91, summer music coord., 1991; colorguard dir., choreographer West Islip (N.Y.) Schs., 1987—91, all dist. chorus dir., 1991—94; musical theater dir., adv. Udall Middle Sch., West Islip, 1992—97, West Side Elem., Syosset, NY, 2000—01, Cold Spring Harbor Schs. Soloist Old First Ch., Huntington, NY, 1984—. Recipient Crane Performers cert., Crane Student Tchg. award; Crane Merit scholar, SUNY, 1985. Mem.: Music Educators Nat. Conf., N.Y. State Sch. Music Assn., Suffolk County Music Educators Assn. Roman Catholic. Avocations: music, art, cooking, gardening. Home: 16 Geneva Pl Greenlawn NY 11740 E-mail: dialstar@yahoo.com.

STARR, ANN ELIZABETH, obstetrician, gynecologist, educator; b. Latrobe, Pa., Sept. 30, 1969; d. Robert James and Letitia Hindman Starr. BS in Biomedical Engring., Tulane U., 1991; MD, Washington U., 1995. Diplomate Am. Bd. Ob-gyn. Resident in ob-gyn Northwestern Meml. Hosp., Chgo., 1995—99; ob-gyn Northwestern Meml. Physician's Group, Chgo., 1999—. Adminstrv. chief resident dept. ob-gyn Feinberg Sch. Medicine Northwestern U., Chgo., 1998—99, instr. ob-gyn Feinberg Sch. Medicine, 1999—. Home: 2300 W Armitage Ave Apt 4 Chicago IL 60647-4478

STARR, DARLENE R. special education educator, education educator; b. Bucyrus, Ohio, Aug. 25, 1943; d. Dale H. and Helen J. (Rettig) Laipply; m. Douglas K. Rudy, Sept. 12, 1987; children: Kris, Kim, Kirk, Shane, Aubry. BS in Elem. Edn., St. Cloud State U., 1976; reading specialist, Avila Coll., 1981; MS in Spl. Edn., Kans. U., 1987. Cert. grades K-9 elem. reading/learning disabilities. Tchr. Wright Devel. Ctr., Monticello, Minn., 1977-78; tchr., dir. chpt. 1 Maple Lake (Minn.) Dist. Schs., 1978-80; chpt. 1 tchr. Olate (Kans.) Dist. Schs., 1980-82; first grade tchr. Spring Hill (Kans.) Dist. Schs., 1982-85; kindergarten tchr. Marietta (Ga.) City Schs., 1985-86; learning disabilites tchr. Louisburg (Kans.) Dist. Schs., 1987-90, tchr. grade 2, 1990-91; learning disabilities tchr. Olathe (Kans.) Dist. Schs., 1991—. Adj. prof. Ottawa U., Overland Park, Kans., 1993—; learning disabilities cons., Olathe, 1992—. Mem. Nat. Coun. for Tchrs. Math., Coun. for Learning Disabilities, Internat. Reading Assn., Kans. Reading Assn. (chair parents and reading com.), Delta Kappa Gamma. Lutheran. Avocations: golf, tennis, antiquing, reading. Home: RR 1 Box 51A Pleasanton KS 66075-9793

STARR, MONICA, company executive; b. Chgo., Oct. 8, 1958; d. Myrtis (Saville) Harrold; 1 child, Kristopher. BS, U. Ill., 1980; PhD, St. Regis U. News dir., announcer, prodn. dir., program dir. Sta. KXOK, St. Louis, 1989-93; music rsch. dir. promotions, sales coord., announcer Sta. KMJM, St. Louis, 1989-91; announcer, programming asst. Sta. WPEG, Charlotte, N.C., 1993-94; program dir. Sta. WEJM, Chgo., 1994-96, Sta. WMXD, Detroit, 1996—2002; pres., CEO Starr Innovative Concepts, Inc., West Bloomfield, Mich., 1998—. Conf. chairperson Midwest Radio and Records Assn., 1995; cons. Multiverse Networks, L.A., 1996. Spkr. Minority Spkrs. Bur., 1997. Recipient GRIOT award Midwest Radio and Records Assn., 1996, Music Pioneer award Columbia's Music Assn., 1996; named Outstanding Young Woman of Yr., 1982, 85, 97. Mem. Nat. Black Programmers Coalition (treas., v.p., pres., nat. chpt. Spirit award 1994, FM Personality of Yr. nat. chpt. 1994, Carolina's chpt. 1994), Women in Radio, Nat. Assn. Black Female Execs. in Music and Entertainment Industry. Avocations: computers, bike riding, writing, photography. Office: Starr Innovative Concepts Inc 5123 Rock Run West Bloomfield MI 48322

STARR, SANDRA SCHJELDAHL, music educator; b. Torrance, Calif., Oct. 19, 1941; d. Norris Goodwin Schjeldahl and Zora Ellen Shearer; m. Kenneth Ray Starr, Aug. 18, 1974; 1 child, Rebecca Ellen. BA, St. Olaf Coll., 1963; M of Music Edn., U. N.D., 1966. Cert. tchr. N.D. Vocal music tchr. Lake Mills (Iowa) Cmty. Schs., 1963—67; music edn. prof. Minot (N.D.) State U., 1967—. Dir. of music 1st Luth. Ch., Minot, 1972—; founder, dir. Western Plains Children's Choir, Western Plains Opera Co., Minot, 1991—. Contbr. articles. Adjudicator various music festivals, N.D. and Mont., 1972—; clinician N.D. Music Educators Assn. Confs. Mem.: Music Educators Nat. Conf. (bd. dirs. 1970—74, 1982—86), Am. Choral Dirs. Assn. (life), Delta Kappa Gamma. Lutheran. Avocations: travel, sewing, music, computer, games. Home: 1118 Valley View Dr Minot ND 58703 Office: Minot State Univ 500 W University Ave Minot ND 58707

STARRATT, PATRICIA ELIZABETH, writer, actress, composer, pianist; b. Boston, Nov. 7, 1943; d. Alfred Byron and Anna (Mazur) S. AB, Smith Coll., 1965; grad. prep. dept., Peabody Conservatory Music, 1961; postgrad., Saybrook Grad. Sch./Rsch. Ctr., San Francisco, 1999. Tchg. asst. Harvard U. Grad. Sch. Bus. Adminstrn., 1965-67; mng. dir. INS Assocs., Washington, 1967-68; adminstrv. asst. George Washington U. Hosp., 1970-71; legal asst. Morgan, Lewis & Bockius, Washington, 1971-72; profl. staff energy analyst Nat. Fuels & Energy Policy Study U.S. Senate Interior Com., 1972-74; cons., exec. asst. energy resource devel. Fed. Energy Adminstrn., Washington, 1974-75; sr. cons. energy policy Atlantic Richfield Co., 1975-76; energy cons. Alaska, 1977-78; govt. affairs assoc. Sohio Alaska Petroleum Co., Anchorage, 1978-85; legal asst. Hughes, Thorsness, Gantz, Powell and Brudin, Anchorage, 1989-90; writer, media specialist corp. affairs Alyeska Pipeline Svc. Co., 1990-95; legal asst. Hughes Thorsness Powell Huddleston & Bauman LLC, 1996-97; sr. paralegal Brit. Petroleum, 1997-98; writer, editor Inst. Circumpolar Health Studies U. Alaska, Anchorage, 1998—; exec. dir. Anchorage Cmty. Theatre, 1999—2002. Mem. econ. devel. commn. Municipality of Anchorage, 1981. Actress, asst. dir. Brattle St. Players, Boston, 1966-67, Washington Theater Club, 1967-68, Gene Frankel, Broadway, 1968-69; actress Aspen Resident Theater, Colo., 1985-86, Ranyevskya (The Cherry Orchard), Anchorage, 1994, Bonfila (SLAVS!), Frau Schmidt (The Sound of Music), Anchorage, 1995, Maria (Moonlight), Anchorage, 1997, Olga (Three Sisters), Eccentric Theatre Co., Anchorage, 1998, Mrs. Barker (The American Dream), 7th Ann. Edward Albee Theatre Conf., Valdez, Alaska, 1999, Ethel (Moon Over Buffalo), Eccentric Theatre Co., Anchorage, 1999; writer, assoc. prodr.: Then One Night I Hit Her, 1983, Stephanie (Yardsale) 9th Ann. Edward Albee Theatre Conf., Valdez, Alaska, 2001, Prudence (Landfall) Loblolly Theatre Co., Pensacola, Fla., 2002; screenwriter, prodr., actress, composer, pianist: A Call to Live, 1995, Marmee (Little Women), 1997; appeared off-Broadway in to Be Young, Gifted and Black; performed as Mary in Tennessee, Blanche in A Streetcar Named Desire, Stephanie Dickinson in Cactus Flower, Angela in Papa's Wine, Elizabeth Procter in The Crucible, Candida in Candida, Zeuss in J.B., Martha in Who's Afraid of Virginia Woolf, Amy in Dinny and the Witches, as Columbina in Servant of Two Masters, as Singer in Death of Morris Biederman, as Joan in Joan of Lorraine, as Mado in Amadee, as Mrs. Rowlands in Before Breakfast, as the girl in Hello Out There, as Angela in Bedtime Story, as Hannah in Night of the Iguana, as Lavinia in Androcles and the Lion, as Catherine in Great Catherine, as Julie in Lilliom, as First Nurse in Death of Bessie Smith, as Laura in Tea and Sympathy, as Amelia Earhart in Chamber Music; appeared at Detroit Summer Theatre in Oklahoma, Guys and Dolls, Carousel, Brigadoon, Kiss Me Kate, Finnian's Rainbow; asst. to dir. Broadway plays A Cry of Players, A Way of Life, Off-Broadway play To Be Young, Gifted and Black; screenwriter Challenge in Alaska, 1986, Martin Poll Films; asst. dir. Dustin Hoffman, 1974; contbr. articles on natural gas and Alaskan econ. and environ. to profl. jours. Bd. dirs. Anchorage Comty. Theatre, Alaska Assn. Legal Assts., 1996-98; industry rep. Alaska Eskimo Whaling Commn.; mem. Alaska New Music Forum. Mem. Actors' Equity. Episcopalian. Avocations: skiing, horseback riding, biking, hiking. Home: 6920 Sea Turtle Cir Navarre FL 32566 E-mail: starward1@yahoo.com.

STARRETT, LUCINDA, lawyer; b. Washington, June 21, 1957; BA magna cum laude, Princeton U., 1979; student, U. Nigeria, Nsukka, 1980-84; JU cum laude, U. Pa., 1984. Bar: Calif. 1986. Law clerk to Hon. Dorothy W. Nelson U.S. Ct. Appeals (9th cir), 1984-85; ptnr. Latham & Watkins, L.A., 1991—. Chief comment editor Jour. Capital Markets and Securities Regulation, 1983. Mem. bd. alternative dispute resolution Western Justice Ctr. Mem. ABA, L.A. County Bar Assn. Office: Latham & Watkins 633 W 5th St Ste 4000 Los Angeles CA 90071-2005*

STARR-WILSON, CAROL ANN, small business owner, genealogist, researcher; b. Camp Mackall, N.C., Dec. 22, 1943; d. Hinkle Melvin Starr and Katie Ruth Holcombe-Starr; m. Neil Elmo Rizzotto, Jan. 12, 1967 (div. Mar. 1972); children: Tab Anthoney, Tammy Ann, Scotti Ivan, Kimberly Kay Johnson-Rizzotto-Grace; m. James Edward Wilson, May 14, 1988. Student, Long Beach City Coll., Calif., 1983, Marrinellos Beauty Coll., 1983, Herald Bus. Coll., Walnut Creek, Calif., 1984—85. Sec. Peavy Automotive, Hayward, Calif., 1980—81, Clinic for Adults and Children, San Leandro, Calif., 1981, Baca & Sons Painting, San Francisco, 1981—85; sec. to dir. Naval Supply Ctr., Oakland, Calif., 1985—86; sec. Mil-Spec Industries, Brisbane, Calif., 1986; genealogist, rschr. Amonsoquath Tribe of Cherokee, 1996—2000; owner, genealogist, rschr. Rsch. Desk of Tat-su-hwa (The Redbird), 2000—. Genealogist, rschr. Amonsoquath Tribe of Cherokee, 1996—2000; owner, genealogist, rschr. Rsch. Desk of Tat-su-hwa. Mem.: Little Rock Hist. Soc., Pope/Faulkner Counties Hist. Soc., Beta Sigma Chi. Democrat. Seventh Day Adventist. Home: 233 Bright Ave Bessemer City NC 28016-8513 E-mail: carolann@carolina.rr.com.

STASH, SUSAN MICHELE, critical care nurse; b. Inglewood, Calif., Mar. 28, 1965; d. Michael Paul and JoAnn Patricia (Margan) S. BSN, Westminster Coll., Salt Lake City, 1987. RN, Calif.; cert. med.-surg. nurse ANCC. Staff nurse gen. surg. unit St. Joseph Hosp., Orange, Calif., 1987-91; staff nurse gen. med. surg. unit Castle Med. Ctr., Kailua, Hawaii, 1992-94; staff nurse renal/pulmonary/telemetry unit Mary Washington Hosp., Fredericksburg, Va., 1994-95; intermediate med. care unit staff nurse Onslow Meml. Hosp., Jacksonville, N.C., 1995-97; staff nurse progressive care unit Swedish Med. Ctr., Englewood, Colo., 1998—; staff nurse subacute ICU Hoag Meml. Hosp. Presbyn., Newport Beach, Calif., 1999—. Mem. ANA, AACN, Am. Assn. Cert. Nurses, Sigma Theta Tau.

STATEN, DONNA KAY, elementary school educator; b. Temple, Tex., Apr. 17, 1958; d. Paul James and Doris Mary (Kleypas) Hoelscher; 1 child, Ryan. BS in Edn., U. Mary Hardin-Baylor, Belton, Tex., 1980. Cert. tchr. in art, elem. edn., health, phys. edn., recreation, gifted and talented edn., Tex. Art tchr. Meridith Magnet Sch., Temple, 1980-84, 1991—2000; bank officer mktg. Tex. Am. Bank, Houston, 1985-88; pvt. practice art tchr., designer Houston, 1989; tchr. ESL Aldine Ind. Sch. Dist., Houston, 1990; art tchr. Kennedy-Powell Acad., Temple, 2000—. Exec. dir. Visual Arts Friends of the Cultural Activities Ctr., Temple, 1993-95, Temple Sister Cities Corp., Temple, 1994-97; chmn. fine arts team Meridith Campus, 1993-96; state rev. panelist Tex. Edn. Agy., 1997; curator Artsonia.com student art gallery, 2002--; dir. Binney & Smith Camp Crayola, 2003. Curator Internat. Children's Art Exhbn., 1996, 2003, 04, art exhibit From Russia with Love, 1992-95. Mem. Contemporaries, Temple, 1994—2001; treas. Oaks Homeowners Assn., Temple, 1994—95, sec. bd. dirs., 1997—99; mem. Temple Mayor's Panel; bd. sec. Keep Temple Beautiful, 1997—99; Tchr.'s Honor Scroll Internat. Project, 2001—02; pres. Assn. Tex. Profl. Educators; singer St. Luke's Ch. Choir, Temple, 1991—; mem. St. Luke's Women's Soc., 1993—. Recipient honorable mention in Christmas Decorating Contest Women's Day mag., 1989, cert. of recognition Crayola/Binney & Smith, 1993-94, 95-96, 97-2001, 03-04, Golden Apple Tchr. award Sta. KWTX-TV, 2002; Focus on Edn. grantee, Wal-Mart, 2001. Mem. ASCD, AAUW, Fine Arts Network, Internat. Soc. for Edn. Through Art, Nat. Art Edn. Assn., Tex. Classrm. Tchrs. Assn., Am. Craft Coun., Soc. Craft Designers, Tex. Computer Edn. Assn., Tex. Fine Arts Assn., Tex. Art Edn. Assn., Nat. Mus. of Women in the Arts, Cultural Activities Ctr., Temple Assn. for the Gifted, Electronic Media Interest Group, Tex. Alliance Edn. and the Arts., Friends of the Temple Libr., Tex. Assn. Gifted and Talented. Roman Catholic. Avocations: gardening, painting and drawing, singing. Office: Kennedy-Powell Acad 3707 W Nugent Ave Temple TX 76504 Address: 2420 Holly Ln Temple TX 76502-2669 Office Phone: 254-791-6670. E-mail: donna.staten@tisd.org.

STATOM, LAURENA EDITH, retired special education educator; b. Winter Haven, Fla., Jan. 10, 1927; d. James Alphonso and Rodella Berry Thompson; m. William Lee Statom, Feb. 3, 1944; children: William, Therman, Deborah, Maria. BS, Coppin State Coll., 1984. Cert. spl. edn. tchr. Tchr./coord. The Nursery-Nannie Helen Burroughs Sch., 1984-96; tchr. People to People Exch. Programs: U.S. China. Conf. on Edn., 1992, People to People Exch. Programs: U.S./Russia/Poland Conf., 1992. Mem. Young Women's League, Inc. (pres. 1984-92), Washing and Vicinity Fedn. of Women's Clubs (chmn. exec. bd. 1992-94, pres. 1994-96), Irene McCoy Gaines Community Club (pres. 1987-96). Avocations: sewing, designing/decorating, dance, travel, cooking. Home; 7828 Orchid St NW Washington DC 20012-1132

STAUBER, MARILYN JEAN, retired secondary school educator, retired elementary school educator; b. Duluth, Minn., Feb. 5, 1938; d. Harold Milton and Dorothy Florence (Thompson) Froehlich; children: Kenneth D. and James H. Atkinson; m. Lawrence B. Stauber Sr., Jan. 11, 1991. BS in Edn., U. Minn., Duluth, 1969, MEd in Math., 1977. Cert. elem. and secondary reading tchr., remedial reading specialist, devel. reading tchr., reading cons. Sec. div. vocat. rehab. State Minn., Duluth, 1956-59; sec. Travelers Ins. Co., Duluth, 1962-66; lead tchr. Title 1 reading and math. Proctor, Minn., 1969-98; ret. Mem. choirs and Choral Soc. John Duss Music, chairperson Outreach, Forbes Meth. Ch., proctor. Mem. NEA, VFW, Internat. Reading Assn., Nat. Reading Assn., Minn. Arrowhead Reading Coun., Elem. Coun. (pres. 1983-84, 86-87), Proctor Fedn. Tchrs. (recert. com. 1980—, treas. 1981-86), Proctor Edn. Assn. (chairperson recert. com.), Am. Legion, Euclid Ea. Star, Phi Delta Kappa. Home: 6713 Grand Lake Rd Saginaw MN 55779-9782

STAUFFER, JOANNE ROGAN, steel company official; b. Coatesville, Pa., Oct. 15, 1956; d. Joseph Chester and Anne Mary (Kauffman) Rogan; m. Robert Lee Marvin Stauffer, Oct. 15, 1988. AS in Bus. Adminstrn., Harrisburg Area C.C., 1979, student, 1986-88; BS in Leadership, Duquesne U ., 2000. Store acct. Giant Foods, Harrisburg, Pa., 1977—79; payroll clk. Bethlehem Steel (name changed to Pa. Steel Techs.), Steelton, Pa., 1980—83, material and cost acct., 1983—86, cost analyst, 1986—96, bus. mgr. for gen. mech. dept., 1996—2002, coord. steelmaking dept., 2002—. Treas. Pot of Gold Investors, 1997—. Mem. Internat. Platform Assn., Am. Bus. Women's Assn. (corr. sec. Rainbow Valley charter chpt. 1991-92, v.p. 1992-93, pres. 1993-94), Steelton Plant Engrs. Club (sec. 1982-85, v.p. 1985-86, pres. 1986-87). Republican. Avocations: outdoor activities, swimming, horses, reading, crafts. Home: 401 Sheetz Rd Halifax PA 17032-9695

STAUFFER, VALERIE VILAS, civic volunteer; b. N.Y.C., Aug. 29, 1935; d. Frank Jay and Kathleen Vilas Brown; m. John Eugene Stauffer, June 5, 1956; children: Jill Stauffer Cobbs, Karen Stauffer Murphy, John Christian, Peter Eugene. BA, Wellesley Coll., 1956. V.p. Stauffer Tech., Greenwich, Conn., 1985—. Editor: (nonfiction) Quality Assurance of Food, 1988, (newsletter) Round Hill Association Newsletter, 1991-92; contbr. Greenwich Rev. mag., 1971-73. Chmn. dist. 7 Rep. Town Meeting, Greenwich, Conn., 1984—, chmn. social svcs. com., 1997; chmn. Friends of Greenwich Libr., 1997—99; trustee, exec. com., sec. bd. trustees Greenwich Libr., 1999—. Mem. Greenwich Garden Club (pres. 1999-2001). Home: 6 Pecksland Rd Greenwich CT 06831-3738 Office: Stauffer Tech 6 Pecksland Rd Greenwich CT 06831-3738 Fax: (203) 618-0479. E-mail: stauftek@aol.com.

STAVES, SUSAN, English educator; b. N.Y.C., Oct. 5, 1942; d. Henry Tracy and Margaret (McClemon) Staves. AB, U. Chgo., 1963; MA, U. Va., 1964, PhD, 1967. Woodrow Wilson intern Bennett Coll., Greensboro, NC, 1965-66; from asst. prof. to prof. Brandeis U., Waltham, Mass., 1967-93, Paul Proswimmer prof. of Humanities, 1993—2001, dept. chair, 1986-89, 95-98, prof. emerita, 2001—. Clark prof. UCLA, 1989—90. Author: Players' Scepters: Fictions of Authority in the Restoration, 1979, Married Women's Separate Property in England, 1660-1833, 1990, Articles in Eighteenth Century: Theory and Interpretation, Studies on Voltaire and the 18th Century, (essays) Fetter'd or Free?: Collected Essays on 18th Century Women Novelists, 1986, History, Gender, and 18th Century Literature, 1994, Woman and Political Writing, 1998; co-author (with John Brewer): Early Modern Conceptions of Property, 1994; co-editor (with Cynthia Ricciardi): Elizabeth Griffith's Delicate Distress, 1997; contbr. articles to profl. jours. Mem. ACLU, 1967—; assoc. mem. Belmont Dem. Town Com., Belmont, Mass. Woodrow Wilson fellow, 1963—64, Woodrow Wilson Dissertation fellow, 1966—67, Harvard Liberal Arts fellow, 1980—81, John Simon Guggenheim fellow, 1981—82. Mem.: AAUP, MLA (exec. com. divsn. on late 18th century English lit. 1984—86), English Inst., Am. Soc. for 18th Century Studies (exec. bd. 1987—90). Episcopalian. Avocations: hiking, squash. Office: Brandeis U Dept English MS 023 Waltham MA 02454 Office Phone: 781-736-2161.

STAVISKY, TOBY ANN, state legislator; b. N.Y.C. m. Leonard Stavisky; 1 child, Evan. BA, Syracuse U.; Grad. Degree, Hunter Coll., Queens Coll. Social studies tchr. N.Y.C. Pub. High Schs.; dist. mgr. N.E. Queens 1980 Census; mem. N.Y. Senate from 16th Dist., Albany, 1999—, mem. aging, civil svc. and pensions, edn., ranking minority higher edn., consumer protection, transp., investigations, taxation and govt. ops. coms., 2001—. Co-chair Minority Task Force on Sch. Aid Equity; mem. legis. commn. on sci. and tech.; mem. legis. commn. skills devel. and vocat. edn. Founder North Flushing Sr. Ctr., bd. dirs.; hon. trustee Whitestone Hebrew Ctr. Democrat. Office: Rm 504 Legislative Office Bldg Albany NY 12247 also: 14436 Willets Point Blvd Flushing NY 11357-3411 E-mail: stavisky@senate.state.ny.us.

STAVROPOULOS, ROSE MARY GRANT, community activist, volunteer; b. Decatur, Ill. d. Walter Edwin and Ora Lenore (Kepler) Grant; m. Stan Stavropoulos; children: Becky Ann Stavropoulos Betian, Stephanie Diane. BS, Ea. Ill. U. Cert. elem. edn. Tchr. 2nd grade Garfield Sch., Decatur, 1666; bd. dirs. Wilmot Sch. Bd. PTA, Deerfield, Moraine Girl Scout Coun., Deerfield, also bd. dirs.; chmn. Human Rels. Commn., Deerfield; mem. sr. citizen adv. com. Deerfield Park Dist.; pres. Lake County (Ill.) LWV; chmn. Deerfield Village Caucus; pres. Caring For Others, Inc., Deerfield, Deerfield Area LWV; bd. mem., pres. Deerfield Area United Way, pres. Mem. Deerfield Village Caucus Adv. Coun. Recipient Deerfield Human Rels. Humanitarian award, 1984, Lerner Life's Citizen of Month, 1987. Mem. Deerfield Area Hist. Soc., Highland Park Hosp. Aux, Legacy at Bryant Ranch Home Assn. (bd. dirs., treas., sec.), Delta Zeta. Home: 23959 Sanctuary Pkwy Yorba Linda CA 92887

STAY, BARBARA, zoologist, educator; b. Cleve., Aug. 31, 1926; d. Theron David and Florence (Finley) S. AB, Vassar Coll., 1947; MA, Radcliffe Coll., 1949, PhD, 1953. Entomologist Army Research Center, Natick, Mass., 1954-60; vis. asst. prof. Pomona Coll., 1960; asst. prof. biology U. Pa., 1961-67; asso. prof. zoology U. Iowa, Iowa City, 1967-77, prof., 1977—. Fulbright fellow to Australia, 1953; Lalor fellow Harvard U., 1960 Fellow AAAS, Entomol. Soc. Am.; mem. Soc. Comparative and Integrative Biology, Am. Inst. Biol. Scis., Am. Soc. Cell Biology, Iowa Acad. Scis., Sigma Xi. Office: U Iowa Dept Biological Scis Iowa City IA 52242

STEAD LEE, POLLY JAE See LEE, PALI

STEADMAN, LYDIA DUFF, symphony violinist, retired elementary school educator; b. Hollywood, Calif., Dec. 31, 1934; d. Lewis Marshall and Margaret Scville (Williams) Duff; m. John Gilford Steadman, Apr. 14, 1961 (dec.). Student, Pepperdine U., 1952-55; BA in Music Edn., U. So. Calif., 1957. Cert. spl. secondary music, edn. tchr., Calif. Instrumental music tchr. Lancaster (Calif.) Sch. Dist., 1957-62, Simi Sch. Dist., Simi Valley, Calif., 1962-70, elem. tchr., 1970—2001. Tchr. Polynesian culture, dances, games, 1970—; hist. play wright for elem. grades, organizer elem. sch. dance festivals; dir. All Dist. Orch., Lancaster, Simi Valley Schs., 1957-70; compile Japanese Culture Study Unit for elem. grades Ventura County. 1st violinist San Fernando Valley Symphony, Sherman Oaks, Calif., 1962-75, Valley Symphony, Van Nuys, 2001--, Simi Valley's Santa Susana Symphony, Conejo Valley Symphony, Thousand Oaks, 1975-81, tour concert mistress, 1980; 2d violinist Ventura County Symphony, Santa Susana Symphony, 1981-95, L.A. Drs. Symphony, 2001-; prin. 2d violinist Calif. Luth. U. Orch. Pres. San Fernando Cmty. Concerts, Van Nuys, Calif., 1982-94; free lancing with pit orch. Cabrillo Music Theatre, Conejo Players Theater, Moorpark Coll. Theatre, Newbury Park H.S. Theater Orch., 2001—; 2d violinist L.A. Doctors Symphony, 2001—, Young Artists Ensemble, Civic Arts Plaza, Camarillo H.S. Theatre Orch., 2003, Loyola Marymount Orch., 2003; organizer ann. sch. Jump Rope-a-Thon for Am. Heart Assn., Nat. Geog. Geography Bee; bd. dirs. East Ventura County Cmty. Concert Assn. Mem. AAUW, NAFE, L.A. World Affairs Coun., Bus. and Profl. Women of Conejo Valley (pres. Golden Triangle chpg. 1988-90, 95-96, issues and mgmt. chair 1990, ways and means chair Coast chpt. 1990, editor Golden Triangle newsletter 1988-90, treas. 1992-93, sec. 1993-94, v.p. 1994—), Pacific Asia Mus., Armand Hammer Mus., Sigma Xi. Republican. Lutheran. Avocations: hula dancing, walking, collecting world coins, world traveling, violin. Home: 32016 Allenby Ct Westlake Village CA 91361-4001

STEARNS, CHERYL ANN, commercial airline pilot; b. Albuquerque, July 14, 1955; d. William Paul and Joan Reid (Meyers) S. AA, Scottsdale (Ariz.) C.C., 1975; BS Aviation Adminstrn. magna cum laude, Embry-Riddle Aero. U., 1978, MS of Aero. Sci., 1985. Pilot Raeford (N.C.) Aviation, 1975-77; instr. aerobatics Duane Cole Sch. Aerobatics, Burleson, Tex., 1980-81; pilot Fla. Med. AirEvac, Orlando, 1981-82, Henson Airlines, Salisbury, Md., 1985-86, Piedmont Airlines, Winston-Salem, N.C., 1986-88, US Air, Charlotte, N.C., 1988—. Sgt. U.S. Army, 1977-80, 82-85, master sgt. USAR. Recipient Diplome Leonardo da Vinci Fedn. Aeronautique Internat., 1990; recipient numerous nat. and internat. championship awards in skydiving. Mem. Internat. Soc. Women Airline Pilots, U.S. Parachute Assn. (Double Ruby Expert Parachutist Wings, Penta Diamond Freefall Badge). Avocations: championship parachuting/skydiving, bicycling, hiking. Office: US Air Charlotte Douglas Airport PO Box 19004 Charlotte NC 28219-9004

STEARNS, MARILYN TARPY, music educator; b. Peoria, Ill., Aug. 3, 1936; d. Roger Maynard Tarpy and Nellie Mae Livingston; m. Gordon Woodburn Stearns, June 13, 1958; children from previous marriage: Gordon Schuyler Livingston, Jennifer Maye Livingston, William Livingston. Student, Ohio Wesleyan U., 1954—56, BA, Mt. Holyoke Coll., 1958; MA, Goddard Coll., 1988; MDiv. Instr. piano, vocal pvt. practice, 1959—98; substitute tchr. Portslade Schs. C.C., England, 1973—75; owner Grain Weaving, Inc., Springfield, Vt., 1976—85; tchr. Head Start, 1977—78; instr. spl. edn., 1980—81; adminstrv. asst. Epilepsy Found. Greater Chgo., 1991; tchr., adminstr., devel. officer Stechman Studio Music, Chgo., 1991—95, Oak Park, 1991—95; tutor voice, piano, music literacy pvt. practice, Chgo., 1995—98, Oak Park, 1995—98; ret. Author: Sunday's Child, 1978, (workbook) The Art of Grain Weaving, 1978, A HAndbook on Our Churches, 1990; editor: Don't Throw it Away, Through A Glass Darkly, Children's Sermons for Young Stewards, Reflections on Tithing, Simply Christmas - Good Stewardship, Stewards of History, Stewardship Lenten Devotions, A Church Treasurer's Handbook. Trustee Vt. Hist. Soc., Montpelier, 1983—90; bd. dirs. Epilepsy Found. Vt., Rutland, 1979—83; mission, stewardship, cons. Vt. Conf. United Ch. Christ, 1982—90. Independent. Avocations: archaeology, poetry, travel, art, reading.

STEBBINS, VRINA GRIMES, retired elementary school educator, counselor; b. Columbus, Ohio, Aug. 24, 1939; d. Marion Edward and Vrina Elizabeth (Davis) Grimes; m. Gary Frank Stebbins, Dec. 23, 1959; 1 child, Gregory Gary. Student, Ohio U., 1957—59; BS in Edn., Miami U., Oxford, Ohio, 1965; MS in Edn., St. Francis Coll., 1971; Counseling Endorsement, Ind.-Purdue U., Ft. Wayne, 1988. Cert. elem. classroom educator K-6, sch. counselor, social worker, Ind. 1st grade tchr. Greenville (Ohio) Pub. Schs., 1963—68; elem. educator East Allen County Schs., New Haven, Ind., 1969—84, elem. sch. counselor, 1984—98; ret., 1998. Presenter at Ind. profl. orgns., 1985-92, 1st Presbyn. Ch., Ft. Wayne, 1984—, Project 2000, Ft. Wayne, 1992—; participant Bus.-Edn. Exch., Ft. Wayne C. of C., 1993. Mem. ACA, Ind. Counseling Assn. (com. mem. 1992-93, Ind. Elem. Counselor of Yr. 1991), East Allen Educators' Assn. (chair com. 1989-98, East Allen County Schs. Elem. Educator of Yr. 1989, 95), Arts United, Phi Delta Kappa, Delta Kappa Gamma (1st v.p. Ind. state 1993-95, Ind. state pres. 1995-97). Democrat. Presbyterian. Avocations: travel, collecting antiques and angels. Home: 1416 Shingle Oak Pointe Fort Wayne IN 46814 Personal E-mail: vstebbinsg@aol.com.

STEBLETON, MICHELLE MARIE, music educator, musician; b. Midland, Mich., Apr. 10, 1966; d. Leo Frederick and Sally Joanne (Brosman) Stebleton. MusB in Horn Performance, U. Mich., 1988, MusM in Horn Performance, 1989; diploma, European Mozart Found., Prague, Czech Republic, 1993. Third horn Ann Arbor (Mich.) Symphony, 1986-89, Saginaw (Mich.) Symphony, 1988-89; hornist Lone Star Brass Quintet, Midland, Tex., 1989-90; prin. horn Midland (Tex.)/Odessa Symphony, 1989-90; adj. prof. horn Odessa (Tex.) Coll., 1990; assoc. prof. horn Fla. State U., Tallahassee, 1990—. Clinician First Internat. Swiss Horn Workshop, 1994, Nove Straseci Internat. Interpreters Course, 1996, 2001; bd. dirs., co. pres. RM Williams Pub., Tallahassee, 1997—; chair faculty senate profl. devel. and welfare com. Fla. State U., Tallahassee, 1999—; lectr. in field. Performer Internat. Mozart Festival, 1991, Orquesta Filarmonica de la UNAM, Mexico City, 1992, Vienna Philharm. Chamber Players, Sapporo, Japan, 1994, 95, Pacific Music Festival, Sapporo, Tokyo, 1994, Sapporo, Hiroshima, Tokyo, 1995, Vienna Chamber Players, Santo Domingo, Dominican Republic, 1997, Internat. Orch. Festival Santo Domingo, 1997, 99, others; soloist (concert tour Vietnam) Fla. State U. Singers, 1999. Fin. advisor Sigma Alpha Iota, Fla. State U., Tallahassee, 1994—; performer Peace Concert, Pacific Music Festival, Hiroshima, Japan, 1995; coord. dept. fundraising United Way Big Bend, Tallahassee, 1998. Recipient second prize Am. Horn Competition-Natural Horn Divsn., 1989, second prize Am. Horn Competition-Profl. Divsn., 1994, 99, Tchg. Incentive Program award State of Fla., Fla. State U., 1996; com. on faculty rsch. support grantee Fla. State U., 1992, 97. Mem. Internat. Horn Soc. (life, co-host, lectr., bd. mem. S.E. region conf. adv. bd. 1991—, first prize solo competition 1987), Nat. Assn. Coll. Wind and Percussion Instrs., Music Educators Nat. Conf., Music Tchrs. Nat. Assn., Pi Kappa Lambda. Avocations: travel, photography, T'ai Chi teaching. Home: 2519 Prest Ct Tallahassee FL 32301-3386 Office: Fla State Univ HMU 127 Tallahassee FL 32306-1180

STECHER, ESTA E. lawyer, investment company executive; b. Mpls., Apr. 3, 1957; BA summa cum laude, U. Minn., 1979; JD, Columbia U., 1982. Bar: N.Y. 1983. Ptnr. Sullivan & Cromwell, 1982—94; gen. counsel, mng. dir. Goldman, Sachs & Co., N.Y.C., 1994—. Mem.: ABA, Assn. Bar City of New York, N.Y. Bar Assn. Office: Goldman Sachs and Co Legal Dept 1 New York Plz 37th Fl New York NY 10004

STECK, JODI, photojournalist; Sr. nat. photo editor Assoc. Press, NY, NY, 1999—; dir. of photography The Orange County Register; asst. chief of bur. Assoc. Press, Los Angeles, Calif.; photo editor San Francisco; dir. of photography Santa Rosa Press Dem., Calif., 1989—92; photo editor NY Times, NY, NY, 1985—86, Assoc. Press, Los Angeles, Calif.; tchr. UCLA, Calif.; news editor Mesa Tribune, Ariz.; copy editor San Francisco Chronicle, Calif. While employed at the Orange County Register, the paper was honored for best use of photos in NPPA/POY competition. Office: The Assoc Press 50 Rockefeller Plz New York NY 10020

STECK, LINDA MARIE, elementary school educator; b. Omaha, Oct. 19, 1948; d. Frances Clyde and Barbara Ann Baines; m. Gary Matthew Steck, Nov. 25, 1970 (div. Apr. 25, 1979); children: Bret, Nicholas. BA in Elem. Edn., U. No. Colo., 1970. Cert. Tchg. Colo., 1987. Tchr. 2nd grade St. Louis Cath. Sch., Englewood, Colo., 1970—74; mgr. Michael Handler Carpets Draperies, Denver, 1978—83; tchr. kindergarten St. Louis Cath. Sch., 1983—87, Littleton Pub. Schs., 1987—. Dir. extended day program Franklin Elem. L.P.S., Colo., 1996—2001, task force leader, 1990—94. Mem. Littleton Edn. Assn., Colo., 1987—; sec. St. Louis Ch. Parish Coun., 1972—74, 1996—98. Mem.: Colo. Reading Assn., Colo. Edn. Assn. Roman Catholic. Avocations: sewing, reading, walking, interior decorating, calligraphy. E-mail: lsteck@lps.kiz.co.us.

STECKLER, PHYLLIS BETTY, publishing company executive; b. N.Y.C. d. Irwin H. and Bertha (Fellner) Schwartzbard; m. Stuart J. Steckler; children: Randall, Sharon Steckler-Slotky. BA, Hunter Coll.; MA, NYU. Editorial dir. R.R. Bowker Co., N.Y.C., Crowell Collier Macmillan Info. Pub. Co., N.Y.C., Holt Rinehart & Winston Info. Systems, N.Y.C.; pres., CEO Oryx Press, Scottsdale, Ariz., 1973-76, Phoenix, 1976—2000, Zephyr Info., Phoenix, 2001—; pub. cons., 2001—. Adj. prof. mktg. scholarly publs. Grad. History dept., Ariz. State U., Tempe; mem. dean's coun. Coll. of Extended Edn., Ariz. State U., Phoenix. Past chmn. Info. Industry Assn.; past chair Ariz. Ctr. for the Book; past pres. Contemporary Forum of Phoenix Art Mus.; founding mem. Nat. Edn. Network, U.S. Dept. Edn.; past pres. Friends of the Libr., U.S.A.; mem. Ariz. Women's Forum; bd. dirs. Ariz. region com. for the Weizmann Inst. Sci. Recipient Women Who Make a Difference award The Internat. Women's Forum, 1995, Excellence in Pub. award Ariz. Book Pub. Assn., 1997, The Pub. History Program Ariz. State U. Founding Friend award, 2000; elected to Hunter Coll. Hall of Fame. Mem.: Univ. Club of Phoenix, Ariz. Libr. Assn., ALA. Home and Office: 6446 N 28th St Phoenix AZ 85016-8946 E-mail: pbs.zephyr@cox.net.

STEDMAN, MOLLY RENEE, special education educator, researcher; b. Peoria, Ill., Aug. 29, 1972; d. Gary Paul and Kathryn Ann Stedman. BS in Edn., Ill. State U., 1996; MS in Edn., U. Nebr., 1999, postgrad., 2000—. Tchr. Cert. Ill., 1996, Iowa, 1996, Nebr., 2000. Asst. prof., project dir. - deaf and hard of hearing program Marshall U. Grad. Coll., South Charleston, W.Va., 2003—; doctoral grad. tchg. asst. U. Nebr., Lincoln, 2000—03; resource tchr. Nebr. Dept. Edn., Lincoln, 2001—03; tchr. Iowa Sch. for Deaf, Council Bluffs, 1996—2000. Cons. tech. support W.Va. Dept. Edn., Charleston, 2003—. Mem.: W. Va. Deaf-blind Project Adv. Com., Commn. on Multiculturalism Com. (Disabled Student Com.), W. Va. Speech-Language-Hearing Assn., W. Va. Commn. Deaf and Hard of Hearing, W.Va. Assn. of the Deaf, Newborn Hearing Adv. Com., Early Childhood Focus Com., Assn. Coll. Educators-Deaf and Hard of Hearing, Coun. on Edn. of Deaf, Coun. for Exceptional Children. Roman Catholic. Achievements include researching the literacy practices in the homes and preschools of young deaf and hard of hearing children. Office: Marshall University Graduate School 100 Angus E Peyton Drive South Charleston WV 25303-1600 Office Phone: 304-746-1957. E-mail: stedman@marshall.edu.

STEDMAN, MYRTLE LILLIAN, artist; b. Charleston, Ill., Feb. 5, 1908; d. Edward Bullard and Myrtie (Harrell) Kelly; m. Wilfred Henry Stedman, Nov. 15, 1928 (dec. 1950); children: Thomas Wilfred, Wilfred Donald. Student, Mus. Fine Arts, Houston, 1927-34, Art Student's League, N.Y.C., 1979-80. Fine artist, illustrator Stedman Studio, Houston, 1927—34. Designer, builder Tesuque Home Builder, 1952-87. Prin. works include preservation of historic homes Adobe Morada, Taos, N.Mex., 1954, redesign of Tesuque Elem. Playground and Parking Lot, 1974; author, illustrator: The Way Things Are Or Could Be: A New Consciousness, 1996, Ongoing Life, 1993, Artists in Adobe, 1993, A House Not Made With Hands, 1993, Rural Architecture of Southern Colorado and Northern New Mexico, Featuring Barns, Fences, and Corrals, 1990, Of One Mind, 1974, Adobe Architecture, 1936-73, 86, Adobe Remodeling and Fireplaces, 1973, 86, Of Things to Come, 1998, The Ups and Downs of Living Alone in Later Life, 2000. Mem. bd. Las Tres Villas, Tesuque, 1973-83, Santa Fe (N.Mex.) Water Basin, 1970-80, Pojoaque (N.Mex.) Water Bd., 1960's; mem. County Recreational Adv. Com., Santa Fe, 1960's. Recipient Visual and Lit. Arts award N.Mex. Arts Commn., Mayor's award City of Santa Fe, 1994, Old Santa Fe Assn. award, 1993, Watercolor awards Houston Fine Arts Mus., 1933, N.Mex. Gov.'s award for Excellence in the Arts Art/Arch., 1997; named Living Treasure Santa Fe Networks, 1985. Mem. PEN/USA/West, Mus. N.Mex. Found. (life), Inst. Noetic Scis. (charter), Women in the Arts Nat. Mus. (charter), Santa Fe Hist. Found., Old Santa Fe Assn. Avocations: keeping scrapbooks, photography, walking, reading. Home: 4043 Shell Rd Sarasota FL 34242-113

STEDMAN, SUSAN GOODWILLIE, writer, consultant; b. N.Y., Dec. 16, 1941; d. John Morley and Mary Louise Rhodes Goodwillie; m. R. Bruce Stedman, Dec. 18, 1993; m. Wesley C. Umphrey, Feb. 14, 1971 (div. Nov. 18, 1988). BA, Stanford U., Palo Alto, Calif., 1963; MA, Fletcher Sch. of Law and Diplomacy, Medford, Mass., 1966; MPA, Kennedy Sch., Harvard U., Cambridge, Mass., 1979. Dir. of spl. projects Nat. Coun. of Negro Women, Washington, 1963—65; press officer UN, N.Y., 1966—66; area officer UN Devel. Program, N.Y., 1968—70; asst. rep. The Ford Found., Lagos, Nigeria, 1971—73, Abidjan, 1973—75, program officer New York, NY, 1975—78, acting rep. Lagos, Nigeria, 1977—77; pres. The Goodwillie Group, Inc., Washington, 1979—93; exec. dir. Refugees Internat., Washington, 1984—88; writer Inst. for Edn. and the Arts, Washington, 2003. Founding mem. Women's Fgn. Policy Coun., Washington, 1985—90; v.p. Internat. Devel. Conf., Washington, 1988—91; mem., exec. com. INTERACTION, N.Y., 1987—88; mem. Govs. Internat. Trade Coun., Boston, 1983—85; fgn. policy advisor Dukakis for Pres. Campaign, Washington, 1988. Editor: Voices From the Future: Children Speak Out About Violence in America, 1993; author: Now Hear This: The Life of Hugh S. Knowles, Acoustical Engineer and Entrepreneur, 1999; contbg. author: Open Wide the Freedom Gates, 2003. Pres. The Morris Farm Trust, Wiscasset, Maine, 1998—2000; mem. and faculty mem. Midcoast Sr. Coll., Bath, Maine, 2002—03; bd. dirs. Heartwood REgional Theater Co., 2003—. Recipient For Outstanding Svc. on Behalf of Refugees, Refugees Internat., 1988; fellow Lucius N. Littauer Fellowship, Harvard U., 1978, Full Fellowship for Grad. Study, The Ford Found., 1978. D-Liberal. Avocations: cooking, gardening, theater, singing, needlepoint. Home: 167 Fowles Point Rd Westport Island ME 04578

STEED, CONNIE MANTLE, nurse; b. Ft. Riley, Kans., Oct. 6, 1956; d. Ronald James Jr. and Ivey Coene (Jenkins) Mantle; m. Thomas Joseph Steed, Jr., Aug. 27, 1979; children: Christopher Michael, Robert James. ADN, Columbus Coll., 1976; postgrad. RN, S.C.; cert. in infection control. Nurse aide Bradley Ctr. Psychiatric Hosp., Columbus, Ga., 1975-76; staff nurse West Ga. Med. CTr., LaGrange, 1976-78, nurse epidemiologist, 1978-87, nurse edn. coord., 1987-88; employee health coord. Spartanburg Regional Med. Ctr., S.C., 1988-89; nurse epidemiologist Greenville Meml. Hosp., S.C., 1989—. Nat. infection control adv. bd. mem. SmithKline and Beecham, Inc., 1991-92; nat. adv. com. mem. Standard Textiles, Inc., Cin., 1993-94; cons. Kimberly Clark Healthcare Divsn., Roswell, Ga., 1992, B. Braun, Inc., Bethlehem, Pa., 1992-93; mem. regulatory affairs com. S.C. Hosp. Assn., 1995, 96; chmn. S.C. TB Task Force, 1993-98. Co-author: Home Health Infection Control Manual, 1988; contbr. articles to profl. jours. Recipient scholarship for abstract devel. Palmetto Hosp. Trust, Inc., 1995. Mem. Am. Heart Assn. (dist. 4 chmn. 1984-87, Ray Johnson award for edn. achievement Ga. affiliate 1987), Assn. for Profls. in Infection Control and Epidemiology, Inc (Horizon award Palmetto chpt. 1995, nat. govt. affairs com. mem. 1994, 95), Nat. Assn. for Profls. in Infection Control and Epidemiology, Ga. Infection Control Network (mem. of yr. award 1988), Inc (chmn. bd. 1982-91, award 1988). Republican. Avocations: reading, softball. Office: Greenville Meml Hosp 701 Grove Rd Greenville SC 29605-4295

STEED, MICHELLE ELNORA, special education educator, counselor; b. Raleigh, N.C., Sept. 23, 1967; d. Johnnie Wilbert and Ednell (Thornton) S. BA, N.C. State U., 1989, MEd, 1990. Cert. spl. edn. Tchr. Franklin County Schs., Youngsville, N.C., 1999—. N.C. State U. fellow, 1989-90, All Am. scholar N.C. State U. Democrat. Baptist. Avocations: pianist, organist. Home: 5512 Thornton Rd Raleigh NC 27616-5728

STEED, THERESA JEAN, manufacturing executive; b. Grapeland, Tex., Mar. 10, 1932; d. Robert Tresband and Alma Inez (Denson) Bobbitt; m. Jarvis Lacy Steed, July 8, 1950; children: Judy Karen, Pamela Kay, Kim Lacy. Grad., Elliott Bus. Sch., Houston, 1949; BMus. Edn., So. Coll. Fine Arts, Houston, 1956; postgrad., U. Tex., 1961, Sul Ross U., Alpine, Tex., 1962; M. of Rhymes (hon.), Duke U., 1961. Exec. sec. various cos., Houston, 1950-57; elem. sch. tchr. Rosenburg (Tex.) Ind. Sch. Dist., 1957-58; kindergarten/music edn. tchr. Sonora (Tex.) Ind. Sch. Dist., 1959-65; elem. sch. tchr. Houston Ind. Sch. Dist., 1965-67, Conroe (Tex.) Ind. Sch. Dist., 1968-70; co-founder, co-owner Steed Tile & Mfg. Co., Conroe, 1965—. Author: Audio-Visual Curriculums for Music Education: Kindergarten Through Eighth Grade, 1962. Mem. Dem. Nat. Com., Washington, 1993—, Dem. Senatorial Campaign Com., Washington, 1996, Dem. Nat. Com., 2003-04. Fellow: Internat. Biographical Ctr. (life); mem.: Am.'s Nat. World War II Mus. (charter), Nat. Women's History Mus. (charter), Order Eastern Star (assoc. matron 1963), Nat. Trust for Hist. Preservation, Women in Constrn. (charter, reporter 1970—75), Pilot Club, Delta Kappa Gamma (publicity chmn. 1962—65). Methodist. Avocations: cooking, gardening, grandparenting, politicking. Home: 17595 W FM1097 Montgomery TX 77356-8471

STEEDMAN, DORIA LYNNE SILBERBERG, organization executive; b. L.A. d. Mendel B. and Dorothy H. (Howell) Silberberg; m. Richard Cantey Steedman, Feb. 19, 1966; 1 child, Alexandra Loren. BA summa cum laude, UCLA. Producer EUE/Screen Gems, N.Y.C., 1963-66, Jack Tinker & Ptnrs., N.Y.C., 1966-68, Telpac Mgmt., N.Y.C., 1968-72; v.p. broadcast prodn. Geer DuBois Advt., N.Y.C., 1973-78, account mgr., dir. ops., 1979-92; exec. v.p., pro bono dir. creative devel. Partnership for a Drug Free America, N.Y.C., 1992—. Bd. dirs. Friends of the Earth. Recipient Andy award Art Dirs. Club, 1968, 71; named one of 100 Best and Brightest Women in Advt., Advt. Age mag.; named Advt. Woman of Yr., 1996. Mem. Advt. Women N.Y. (pres. 1993-95), Advt. Women N.Y. Found. (pres. 1995-97), Phi Beta Kappa. Office: Partnership for a Drug-Free Am 405 Lexington Ave New York NY 10174-0002 E-mail: doria_steedman@drugfree.org.

STEEL, DANIELLE FERNANDE, author; b. N.Y.C., Aug. 14, 1947; d. John and Norma (Stone) Schuelein-Steel. Student, Parsons Sch. Design, 1963, NYU, 1963-67. Vice pres. pub. relations and new bus. Supergirls Ltd., N.Y.C., 1968-71; copywriter Grey Advt., San Francisco, 1973-74. Author novels Going Home, 1973, Passion's Promise, 1977, Now and Forever, 1978, The Promise, 1978, Season of Passion, 1979, Summers End, 1979, To Love Again, 1980, The Ring, 1981, Loving, 1980, Love, 1981, Remembrance, 1981, Palomino, 1981, Once in a Lifetime, 1982, Crossings, 1982, A Perfect Stranger, 1982, Thurston House, 1983, Changes, 1983, Full Circle, 1984, (non-fiction) Having A Baby, 1984, Family Album, 1985, Secrets, 1985, Wanderlust, 1986, Fine Things, 1987, Kaleidoscope, 1987, Zoya, 1988, Star, 1988, Daddy, 1989, Message from Nam, 1990, Heartbeat, 1991, No Greater Love, 1991, Jewels, 1992, Mixed Blessings, 1992, Vanished, 1993, Accident, 1994, The Gift, 1994, Wings, 1994, Lightning, 1995, Five Days in Paris, 1995, Malice, 1996, The Ghost, 1997, The Ranch, 1998, The Long Road Home, 1998, The Klone & I, 1998, Silent Honor, 1997, His Bright Light, 1998, Mirror Image, 1998, Bittersweet, 1999, Granny Dan, 1999, Irresistible Forces, 1999, The Wedding, 2000, The House on Hope Street, 2000, Journey, 2000, Lone Eagle, 2001, Leap of Faith, 2001, The Kiss, 2001, The Cottage, 2002, Sunset in St. Tropez, 2002, Answered Prayers, 2002, Dating Game, 2003, Johnny Angel, 2003, Safe Harbour, 2003, Ransom, 2004, (children's) Martha's Best Friend, Martha's New School, Martha's New Daddy, Max's New Daddy, Max and The Babysitter, Max's Daddy Goes To The Hospital; contbr. poetry to mags., including Cosmopolitan, McCall's, Ladies Home Jour., Good Housekeeping. Chevalier of the distinguished Order of Arts and Letters, France. Home: PO Box 1637 New York NY 10156-1637 Office: care Dell Publishing 1540 Broadway New York NY 10036-4039*

STEELE, ANA MERCEDES, former government official; b. Jan. 18, 1939; d. Sydney and Mercedes (Hernandez) S.; m. John Hunter Clark, June 2, 1979. AB magna cum laude, Marywood Coll., 1958. Actress, 1959-64; sec. Nat. Endowment for Arts, Washington, 1965-67, dir. budget and rsch., 1968-75, dir. planning, 1976-78, dir. program coordination, sr. exec. svc., 1979-81, assoc. dep. chmn. programs, dir. program coordination, 1982-93, acting chmn., acting sr. dep. chmn., 1993, sr. dep. chmn., sr. exec. svc., 1993-96, dep. chmn. mgmt. and budget, sr. exec. svc., 1996-98; ret., 1998. Guest lectr. George Washington U., 1987; trustee Marywood Coll., 1989-96, Marywood U., 1997-98. Author, editor report: History of the National Council on the Arts and National Endowment for the Arts During the Johnson Administration, 1968; editor: Museums USA (Fed. Design Coun. award of Excellence 1975), 1974, National Endowment Arts, 1965-85: A Brief Chronology of Federal Involvement in the Arts, 1985. Former reader Rec. for the Blind, N.Y.C.; former tutor Future for Jimmy, Washington; judge Helen Hayes Awards, 2003—. Named Disting. Grad. in Field of Arts, Marywood Coll., 1976; recipient Sustained Superior Performance award Nat. Endowment for Arts, 1980, Disting. Svc. award, 1983, 84, 85, 89, 92, 96, presdl. medal Marywood U., 2000; named to Disting. Alumnae Hall of Fame, Ursuline Acad., 2001. Mem. Actors' Equity Assn., Screen Actors Guild, Delta Epsilon Sigma, Kappa Gamma Pi. Home: 2475 Virginia Ave NW Apt 604 Washington DC 20037-2639

STEELE, BETTE HULSE, medical/surgical nurse; d. David Carlisle and Lavina Mae Hulse; m. Mark Allen Steele, Oct. 5, 1990. ADN cum laude, Wallace State Coll., Hanceville, Ala., 1997. RN Ala., 1997. Labor and delivery nurse Decatur (Ala.) Gen. Hosp., 1997—2001; care coord., maternity care program Decatur Gen. Hosp./HealthGroup of Ala., 2002—. Spl. friend FACES, Decatur, Ala., 2000—03. Mem.: Phi Theta Kappa. Home: 2211 Almon Way SW Decatur AL 35603-1109 Office: Decatur Gen Hosp Decatur AL

STEELE, BEVERLY J. elementary school educator; b. Gary, Ind., June 16, 1948; d. Earl Robert S. and Mandy Pearl Hearon; stepfather: James T. Hearon. BS in Edn., Lincoln U., 1970; MEd, Ind. U., 1974. Cert. elem. sch. tchr. Tchr. grades 2, 4, 6 Norton Sch. Gary (Ind.) Cmty. Sch. Corp., 1970-72, tchr. grades 3-5 Vohr Sch., 1972-83; tchr. grade 1 Vohr Sch., 1983-95; tchr. grade 4, 1995—. Tchr. challenge gratn program Gary Cmty. Sch. Corp., 1997, 98. Asst. min. music United Male Chorus Gary-Calumet Region, Gary, 1989—; mem. The Sounds of Peace Singing Ensemble, Gary and Calumet, 1974—; tchr. Voices of Praise Children's Choir; min. music Carter Meml. Christian Meth. Episcopal Ch., 1997, past bd. dirs. Recipient numerous plaques Carter Meml. CME Ch., Gary, 1993, 99. Mem. Delta Sigma Theta, Phi Delta Kappa. Democrat. Avocations: computers, piano and organ, teaching. Office: Vohr Elem Sch 1900 W 7th Ave Gary IN 46404-1408 E-mail: bjsteele51@hotmail.com.

STEELE, CYNTHIA, literary critic, translator, educator; b. Colusa, Calif., Aug. 7, 1951; d. Ned and Lorraine (Heard) S. BA in English and Spanish, Calif. State U., Chico, 1973; MA in Spanish Lit., U. Calif., San Diego, 1979, PhD in Spanish Lit., 1980. Asst. prof. Spanish Ohio State U., Columbus, 1980-85, Columbia U., N.Y.C., 1985-86; from asst. prof. to assoc. prof. Spanish U. Wash., Seattle, 1986-96, prof. Spanish, Comparative Lit. and Internat. Studies, 1996—. Mem. joint com. Latin Am. studies Social Sci. Rsch. Coun.-Am. Coun. Learned Socs., N.Y.C., 1994-96; del. West Coast MLA, N.Y.C., 1996—; bd. dirs. Inst. de Lit. Iberoamericana, Pitts., 1996—. Translator: Underground River and Other Stories by Inés Arredondo, 1996; (with David Laur) City of Memory (José Emilio

Pacheco), 1997. Advanced grantee Social Sci. Rsch. Coun., 1990-91; Royalty Rsch. grantee U. Wash. Grad. Sch., 1997—. Mem. Latin Am. Studies Assn. Democrat. Avocations: movies, travel in latin america. Office: U Wash Dept Spanish & Portuguese Seattle WA 98195-0001

STEELE, DALE [illegible] women's healthcare company executive; Co-founder, CFO, M.W. Steele Group, 1983-89, corp. sec., treas., 1994-96; owner, mgr. Dale Fitzmorris, 1989-94; co-founder, co-CEO, As We Change, LLC, 1995-98; v.p. catalog ops. Women First HealthCare, Inc., San Diego, 1998—. Office: Women First HealthCare Inc 12220 El Camino Real Ste 400 San Diego CA 92130-2091 Fax: 619-509-1353.

STEELE, KAREN DORN, journalist; b. Portland, Oreg., Oct. 27, 1943; d. Ronald Gottche and Margaret Elizabeth (Cates) Moxness; m. Charles Stuart Dorn, Oct. 30, 1965 (div. Oct. 1982); children: Trilby Constance Elizabeth Dorn, Blythe Estella Dorn; m. Richard Donald Steele, July 4, 1983. BA, Stanford U., 1965; MA, U. Calif., Berkeley, 1967. Prodr. Sta. KSPS-TV, Spokane, Wash., 1970-72, dir. news and pub. affairs, 1972-82; reporter Spokesman-Rev., Spokane, 1982-87, environ./spl. projects reporter, 1987—. Contbr. articles to sci. publs. (Olive Br. award NYU Ctr. War, Peace & The Media 1989). Bd. dirs. Women Helping Women, Spokane, 1994; trustee St. George's Sch., Spokane, 1988-92. Mid-career fellow Stanford Knight Fellowship Program, 1986-87, Arms Control fellow Ctr. for Internat. Security and Arms Control, Stanford U., 1986-87; Japan Travel grantee Japan Press Found., Tokyo, 1987, rsch. grantee John D. and Catherine T. MacArthur Found., 1992; recipient Gerald Loeb award Anderson Sch. Mgmt. UCLA, 1995, George Polk award L.I. U., 1995, William Stokes award U. Mo., 1988, Nat. Headliner award, Excellence in Legal Journalism award, Wash. State Bar Assn., 2000; inductee State Hall of Journalistic Achievement, Wash. State U., Pullman, 1995. Unitarian Universalist. Office: Spokesman Rev PO Box 2160 999 W Riverside Ave Spokane WA 99201-1098 Office Phone: 509-459-5462. E-mail: karend@spokesman.com.

STEELE, KAREN KIARSIS, retired state legislator; b. Haverhill, Mass., Sept. 26, 1942; d. Victor and Barbara (McFee) Kiarsis; m. Edward E. Steele, Apr. 16, 1966; children: Shawn Robert, Gretchen Garvey. BA, U. Vt., 1964. Tchr. Waterbury Sch. System, 1964-65, Burlington (Vt.) Sch. System, 1965-67; legislator State of Vt., Montpelier, 1982-2000; ret., 2000. Trustee Ctrl. Vt. Hosp., Berlin, Woodridge Nursing Home, Berlin. Mem. Am. Legis. Exch. Coun. (mem. exec. com. health and human svcs. task force). Republican. Avocations: golf, swimming, reading. Home: 1553 Perry Hill Rd Waterbury VT 05676-9633 E-mail: kksteele@aol.com.

STEELE, RAMONA GRACE JESSE, physical therapist; d. Franklin Culver and Ethel Helen (Bubolz) Jesse; m. Thomas Hartman Steele, Sept. 10, 1958; children: Karen Ann, Todd Hartman, Heidi Jeanne, Alyson Elizabeth. BS, Columbia U., 1961. Physical Therapy NY, 1961. Owner Mona Steele & Assocs., Madison, Wis., 2000—. Docent Elevhjem Mus. of Art, Madison, Wis., 1978—84; vice chair Friends of Pub. Edn., Wis., 1995—97; chair State Pub. Affairs Com., Jr. Leagues of Wis., Wis., 1995—97; co-chair Wis. Supreme Ct. Selection Com., Wis., 2000—02; pres. Wis. Women's Network Edn. Fund, Wis., 1997—2001; mem. Wis. Women's Network Exec. Com., Wis., 1998—2001; chair Wis. Women's Network - Various task forces, Wis., 1980—95; task force chair Wis. Women's Network - Marital Property Reform, Madison, Wis., 1980—90; chair Wis. Women's Network, Wis., 2002—; mem. - steering com. Ctr. for Disease Control - Vaccine Pub. Engagemenet Project, 2002—; invitee Ctr. for Policy Alternatives Grassroots Leadership Retreat, Wis., 2002—; mem. - steering com. Ctr. for Policy Alternative Grassroots Leadership Retreat, 2002—; owner Mona Steele & Assocs., Madison, Wis., 2001—; pub. mem. Wis. Legislative Coun. Tech. Adv. Com. on Marital Property/Divorce Reform, Madison, Wis., 1988, Wis. Legislative Coun. Com. on Lobby Law Reform, Madison, Wis., 1986—87, Wis. Assembly Natural Resources Committee's Subcommittee on, Wis., 1987—88; Wis. women's network del. Nat. Women's Conf., 1989—97; exec. com. Nat. Women's Confrence, Wis., 1989—90; lectr. U. of Wis. Ext., Madison, Wis., 1986—93. Dir.: (performance) Women's Equality Day. Chair Wis. Women's Network, Wis., 2001—03; sec./ treas. LWV of the US, 1998—2000; et cetera; sec./treas. LWV of the US Edn. Fund, 1998—2000; chair - ednl. and advocacy Wis. Women's Network Edn. Fund, Wis., 1997—2001. Mem.: LWV (legis. coord. 1986—89, chair Wis. edn. fund 1989—90, pres. 1989—93, nom. com. 1994—96), NOW (task force on rights of women in marriage 1987—90), Attic Angels Assn., Jr. League Madison (corr. sec. 1996—97, pres. 1984—86, bd. dirs. 1997—98). Home: 306 Yosemite Trail Madison WI 53705-2438 Office: Wisconsin Women's Network 122 State St Madison WI 53703 Personal E-mail: steele@danenet.wicip.org. E-mail: wiwomen@execpc.com.

STEELE, SHARI, think-tank executive; Grad., Widener U.; LLM in Advocacy, Georgetown U.; MS in Instrnl. Media, West Chester U. Legal dir. Electronic Frontier Found., San Francisco, 1992—2000, exec. dir., pres., 2000—. Spkr. in field; tchg. fellow Georgetown U. Law Ctr. Office: Electronic Frontier Found 454 Shotwell St San Francisco CA 94110-1914

STEELE, SHIRLEY SUE, retired special resource educator; b. Shelbyville, Tenn., Apr. 10, 1939; d. Clarence Sr. and Laura Ocie (Marr) McCullough; m. James Harold Levi Steele, June 23, 1957; children: Tonya Sue, Michaele Ann. BS magna cum laude, U. Tenn., 1973. Cert. spl. edn. tchr., Tenn. Spl. resource tchr. Chattanooga City Schs., ret.; tchr. spl. edn. Orange Grove Ctr., Chattanooga. Bd. dirs. Scouting for Spl. Citizens; leader Explorers Club for the Retarded. Mem. Alpha Soc. (tchr. Sunday sch. autistic children), Kappa Delta Pi. Home: 5720 Laurel Ridge Rd Chattanooga TN 37416-1050 Office Phone: 423-326-1921.

STEELEY, DOLORES ANN, music educator; b. Middletown, N.Y., Sept. 14, 1956; d. Richard and Martha Steeley. AAS in Music, Orange County C.C., Middletown, N.Y., 1977; BA in Music, West Chester U., Pa., 1980; MS in Music Edn., Coll. St. Rose, Albany, N.Y., 1991. Cert. tchr. music edn., nat. bd. cert. tchr. Pvt. music tchr., Albany, NY, 1986—; music tchr. Town of Colonie, Latham, NY, 1986—93, Coxsackie-Athens Sch. Dist., NY, 1986—93, Niskayuna Sch. Dist., NY, 1993—. Mem.: N.Y. State Sch. Music Assn., Music Educators Nat. Conf. Home: 95 Southbury Rd Clifton Park NY 12065 Office: Iroquois Mid Sch 2495 Rosendale Rd Niskayuna NY 12309

STEELMAN, DEBORAH MACON, pharmaceutical consultant; b. Sale, Mo., Feb. 4, 1955; BA, U. Mo., 1976, JD, 1978. Asst. pub. defender, Kansas City, Mo.; campaign mgr. for re-election effort Atty. Gen. John Ashcroft; dep. dir. Mo. Dept. Natural Resources; legis. dir. to Senator John Heinza, Pa.; dir. intergovernmental affairs Environ. Protection Agy., 1983—85; dep. asst. to pres. and dir. Office Intergovernmental Affairs, 1985—; pres. Steelman Health Strategies; v.p. corp. affairs Eli Lilly and Co., 2001—03, con. govtl. affairs and health policy issues, 2003—. Apptd. by Senate Majority Leader Trent Lott, healthcare advisor to George W. Bush's 2000 campaign to Medicare Commn. Named one of 100 Most Powerful Women in Wash., Washingtonian mag., 2001.*

STEELMAN, SARA GERLING, art association administrator; b. Wichita, Kans., Apr. 24, 1946; d. Paul Henry and Amy (Gessner) Gerling; m. John Henry Steelman; 1 child, Amy. BS in Zoology, U. Chgo., 1967; PhD in Behavior Genetics, Stanford U., 1976. Instr. dept. psychology No. Ill. U., DeKalb, 1974-75; instr. Fullerton (Calif.) Jr. Coll., 1976-80; postdoctoral fellow dept. psychobiology U. Calif., Irvine, 1976-80; asst. prof. dept. biology Skidmore Coll., Saratoga Springs, N.Y., 1980-83; staff writer Saratogian, Saratoga Springs, 1983-86; contbg. writer Indiana Gazette, 1987-93; elected mem. Pa. Ho. of Reps., Harrisburg, 1990—2002; adminstr. Indiana Arts Coun., Indiana, Pa., 2002—. Contbr. articles to sci. publs. Co-chair com. on women in politics Pitts. Inst. Politics, 1993—. Rsch. fellow, Nat. Inst. Aging, 1979—80. Mem.: LWV, AAUW (Notable Woman 1991), Ind. Symphony Soc. (bd. dirs.), Common Cause (state bd. dirs.). Democrat. Avocations: gardening, music, horseback riding. Office: Indiana Arts Council 637 Philadelphia Indiana PA 15701 E-mail: iacinet@upia.net.

STEELMAN, SARAH, state legislator; Mem. Mo. State Senate, 1998—, mem. civil and criminal jurisprudence com., chair commerce and environment com., mem. edn. com., vice chair judiciary com., vice chair pub. health and welfare com. Republican. Home: 11820 Springhouse Ln Rolla MO 65401 Office: 900 Pine St Rolla MO 65401 also: State Capitol Bldg Rm 433 Jefferson City MO 65101 Fax: 573-751-2745.

STEEN, NANCY G. volunteer, retired rare books librarian; b. Mar. 4, 1939; BA, Bowling Green State U., 1961, MA in History, 1963; AMLS, U. Mich., 1966. Rare books libr. Bowling Green State U., Ohio, 1982-90; discography editor newsletter José Carreras Soc. Am., Elkins Pk., Pa., 1996—. Vol. José Carreras Internat. Leukemia Found., Barcelona and Seattle, 1995—; mem. Met. Opera Guild, NYC, 2002--, patron Met. Opera, 1998-2002; mem. Playwright's Circle, Stratford Festival of Can. Mem. Friends of Libr. at Bowling Green State U., Order Eastern Star.

STEEN-HINDERLIE, DIANE EVELYN, social worker, musician; b. Duluth, Minn., June 13, 1947; d. Julian Sem and Evelyn Synnove (Helgaas) Steen; m. John Peter Hinderlie, June 27, 1971 (div. Sept. 1987); children: Peder Donald, Erik Steen; m. John Richard Olson, July 21, 1989. BA in Asian Studies/Social Psychology cum laude, St. Olaf Coll., 1969; MusB equivalency, U. Minn. and other instns., 1970-91; postgrad., Hamline U., 1989-91. Lic. social worker, Minn.; cert. music tchr. Music Tchrs. Nat. Assn. Social worker child care licensing Hennepin County Welfare Dept., Mpls., 1970-73; mem. clergy team exch. program Luth. World Fedn., Göppingen, Germany, 1973-77; mem. clergy team, music dir. Jubilation Singers Bethel Luth. Ch., Rochester, Minn., 1978-83; mem. clergy team, music dir. youth choir First Luth. Ch., St. Louis Park, Minn., 1983-86; adminstr. Family Child Care facility, St. Louis Park, 1986-90; faculty, tchr. Stenson Suzuki Studios and Home Studio, St. Louis Park, 1988-92; small group leader, tchr. vol. Mt. Olive Ch., Children's Hosp., Mpls., 1993, 96-98; workshop and children's ministry Augsburg Coll. Youth and Family Inst., Trinity Congregation and U. Luth. Ch. of Hope, 1998—; founding dir. Fair Pay Inst., Mpls., 1995—; trainer United for a Fair Economy, 1997—. Founder orgn. and curriculum Early Childhood Orgn. for Edn. with Singing, 1993—, co-leader German-Am. youth group exch., 1979-82; co-founder Family DayCare Cert. Program and Babygarten (B-12 edn.) classes, 1970-73; bd. dirs. Midwest Coun., Nat. Peace Inst. Found., Grinnell, Iowa, 1991; presenter in field.; mem. root causes of violence action team Initiative for Violence-Free Families, 4th Jud. Dist. Minn., 1997—. Author: (tng. manual) Mother Tongue Singing/Voice Method, 1988, (study packet) School Start Time/Teen Sleep Deprivation, 1996-97, A+=Baby Church School, 2002; rec. artist, mem. ensemble record/cassettes Nowell Sing We, 1986; performer Nordic Am. Psalmodikon Forbundet, 1997—. Vol. People of Faith Peacemakers, Feminists in Faith/ReImagining and Jewish Cmty. Rels. Coun., 1992-2003, Muslim-Christian Rels. Coun., Joint Religious Legis. Coalition, Bread for the World; founder People for Reforming Early Start Time for Teens Orgn., Mpls., 1993—; mem. steering com. Progressive Cmty. and FairVote, Minn., 1994-99; local host youth com. NAACP Conv., Mpls., 1995; vol. Common Cause, St. Paul and Washington; charter mem. U.S. Holocaust Mus., 1993. Recipient appreciation plaque Christian Boy/Girl Scouts Germany; Svc. pin Am. Luth. Ch. Women; listed in Minn. Profiles, Minn. Hist. Soc. A Tribute to Outstanding Minn. Women by Marilyn Chelstrom, 2001; named Asset Builder of Month, St. Louis Park Children First Initiative, 1997; named to Honor Roll, Mendota Mdewakanton Dakota Cmty., 1999. Mem.: MADD, Minn. Music Tchrs. Assn. (first early childhood music chair 2001—03), Assn. Pre- and Perinatal Psychology and Health, Wash. Nat. Cathedral, Early Childhood Music and Movement Assn. Minn., Soc. for Psychol. Studies of Social Issues, Interfaith Alliance Minn., Nat. Luth. Choir Acad., Suzuki Assn. Americas (study area co-organizer, editl. adviser), Internat. Suzuki Assn., Nat. Assn. Tchrs. Singing and VoiceCare Network, UN Assn., Sojourner Project, Inc., World Wildlife Fund, Ctr. for Victims of Torture, Minn. Parenting Assn., Amnesty Internat., Nat. Peace Found., Germanic-Am. Inst., Am.'s Jr. Miss. Coun., Sons of Norway (lodge trustee 1991—), Phi Beta Kappa, Am. Mensa. Green. Lutheran. Avocations: reading, political activism, concerts, travel, memory albums. Office: Fair Pay Inst PO Box 16031 Minneapolis MN 55416-0031

STEFANI, GWEN RENEE, musician; b. Orange County, Calif., Oct. 3, 1969; Student, Calif. State U., Fullerton. Musician band No Doubt. Singer: (albums) No Doubt, 1992, Tragic Kingdom, 1995, Beacon Street Collection, 1995, Collector's Orange Crate, 1997, Return of Saturn, 2000, Rock Steady, 2001 (Grammy awards: Best Pop Performance By A Duo Or Group With Vocal for song "Hey Baby", 2002, Best Pop Performance By A Duo Or Group With Vocal for song "Underneath it All", 2003), (songs) "Let Me Blow Your Mind" (with Eve), 2001 (Grammy award, Best Rap/Song Collaboration, 2001).*

STEFANICS, CHARLOTTE LOUISE, retired mental health nurse; b. Leechburg, Pa., Dec. 30, 1927; d. George J. and Mary Magadelene (Boronyak) S. Diploma Sch. Nursing, St. Elizabeth Hosp., 1948; BSN, Seton Hall U., 1968; MS, Ohio State U., 1971; EdD, U. Sarasota, 1982. Diplomate Logotherapy. Various nursing positions, 1952-69; staff nurse Med. Ctr. NYU, N.Y.C., 1969-70; pvt. practice, 1971-73; instr. Sch. Nursing Duke U., Durham, N.C., 1974-77; clin. nurse specialist VA Med. Ctr., Bay Pines, Fla., 1977-93; ret., 1993. Instr., pvt. practice Community Hosp. Springfield, Ohio; cons. in field; part-time chaplain Miami Valley Hosp., Dayton, Ohio; lectr. U. South Fla. Coll. Nursing, 1978-92. Co-author (with G. Niklas): Ministry to the Sick, 1982; co-author: (with R. Peck) Learning to Say Good-bye, 1987. Vol. community classes and workshops; vol. Habitat for Humanity Internat. Hungary, nursing exchange with Chinese Nurses Assn. Mem. Assn. Death Educators and Counselors (cert.), Assn. Christian Therapists, Nurses Orgn. Vet. Affairs. Home: 1342 Rosehaven Cir Dayton OH 45429-5744

STEFANSSON, WANDA GAE, language educator, literature educator; b. Tucson, Ariz., Dec. 3, 1936; d. Alva Harold and Beryl Eaks Roberson; m. Joseph Robert Henry, Dec. 28, 1963 (div. Dec. 1997); 1 child, Michael Joseph Henry ; m. Rafn Stefansson, Apr. 25, 1998. AA, Stephens Coll., 1956; BA, U. Oreg., 1958; MA, U. Wash., 1961. Instr. German lang. and lit. Pomona (Calif.) Coll., 1961—66; acad. studies counselor Art Ctr. Coll. Design, Pasadena, Calif., 1980—87; registrar Art Ctr. Europe, La Tour-de-Peilz, Switzerland, 1987—90; develop. officer Huntington Libr., San Marino, Calif., 1995—98. Mem., officer PEO, 2001—03; leader creative christian cmty San Marino Cmty. Ch., 1975—77, chair adult edn., 1977—80, chair pastor search com., 1981—82; tchr. disciple bible study 1st United Meth. Ch., Pasadena, 1993—94, 1996—99, chair adminstrv. coun., 1998—2001, founder ongoing journey, 1999—2001, tchr. spiritual growth, 2001—03, chair info. program chapel restoration campaign, 2002. Home: 1825 Alpine Dr San Marino CA 91108

STEFFEE, NINA DEAN, publisher; b. Mahopac, N.Y., Apr. 11, 1917; d. Henry Jackson and Eliza May (Willson) Dean; m. Clay Runels Steffee, June 21, 1942; children: Eliza May Steffee Karpook, Clay Jackson, Henry Morgan. Student, Cornell U., 1934-36. Sec., asst. editor Fla. Audubon Soc., Maitland, 1965-71; owner/mgr. Flying Carpet Tours, Orlando, Fla., 1971-80, Russ's Natural History Tours, Kissimmee, Fla., 1980-83, Lake Helen, Fla., 1983-94; pub., compiler Nina Steffee Pub., Lake Helen, 1994—. Compiler bird checklists; contbr. articles to profl. jours. Mem.: West Volusia Audubon (pres.), Kissimmee Valley Audibon (pres.). Avocation: birding. Home: 3839 NW 48th PL Gainesville FL 32606-4426

STEFFEN, ELIZABETH DUCAS, political organization worker; b. N.Y.C., June 9, 1942; d. Ernest Bloch and Natalie Ducas Steffen. BS, NYU, 1964, MA, 1965. 7-12 premanent tchg. lic. N.Y. Tchr. Bd. Edn., Yonkers, NY, 1964—83; owner, operator Le Cochon Vert, Old Sybrook, Conn., 1983—91; chief rschr. Friends of Saybrook, Old Saybrook, 1994—97; registrar voters Dems., Old Saybrook, 2001—. Alt. Zoning Commn., 1997—2003; sec. Old Saybrook Dem. Com., 1996—. Fellow Regents, N.Y. State Dept. Edn., 1968. Jewish. Avocations: cooking, reading, travel, golf, swimming. Home: 16 Crowley Dr Old Saybrook CT 06475 Office: Registrar Voters 302 Main St Old Saybrook CT 06475 Personal E-mail: steffen@snet.net.

STEFFEN, PENNY DAWN, interior designer, consultant, writer; d. Kenneth Joseph Michael Ptaszek and Star Lynn Kathy Monica Norini; m. Donald Douglas Steffen, Jr., Sept. 26, 1998; children: Samantha Mary, Madelaine Josephine. BA, No. Ill. U., DeKalb, IL, 1996. Designer and sec. Distinctive Kitchen Designs, Wauconda, Ill., 1991—2000; pres., designer Penny Layne Designs, Grayslake, Ill., 2000—. Co-designer showcase ho. kitchen Am. Soc. of Interior Design, 1999. Photographer (prin. works) The Road Unforseen; author: (novel) The Crimson Door; contbr. articles to trade periodicals. Guest spkr. Frederick Mid. Sch., Grayslake, 2001—03. Mem.: Acad. of Am. Poets (assoc.). Roman Catholic. Avocations: tap and ballet dance, sculpture, photography, writing, travel.

STEFFENS, ANNIE LAURIE, sign language educator, interpreter; b. N.Y.C. d. Robert William and Irene Marie (Hoecker) S. Cert., U. Ariz., Tucson, NYU, Gallaudet U., Washington D.C. Cert. sign lang. interpreter, sign lang. educator. Sign language interpreter high sch., Brattleboro, Vt., Longmeadow, Mass.; tchr. sign language pvt. sch., Putney, Vt., Main Street Arts, Saxtons River, Vt., Cmty. Coll., Greenfield, Mass., Cheshire Hosp., Keene, N.H., YMCA, Keene, Brattleboro Sr. Ctr., Brattleboro Recreation Ctr.; pvt. practice. Developer new program using Am. sign lang., 1995—; mem. sign lang. choir Gallaudet U., NYU; poetry educator Main Street Arts; mem. new Am. Sign Lang. program Grace Cottage Hosp., Townsend, Vt., 1996; developer, designer Am. Sign Lang. Mentorship, 1997—, Am. Sign Lang. Linguistics program, 1998—. Author: (poem) Down Peaceful Paths. Advocate Women's Shelter, Brattleboro; counselor Vt. respite care project Mental Health of Southeastern Vt., Brattleboro. Named Am. Sign Language Tchr. of Excellence, 1998; recipient Bronze medal for excellence in Am. sign lang., 1999, Angel award, 2000. Mem. Nat. Assn. Deaf, Sign Instrs. Guidance Network. Avocations: signing to music, dance, singing, poetry, painting abstract designs. Home: 14 Spruce St Brattleboro VT 05301-2716

STEFFEY, A KAY, accountant; b. Decatur, Ind., Sept. 26, 1959; d. Marvin Chester and Barbara Ellen (Merkle) DeBolt; m. Richard Lee Steffey II, Jan. 1, 1986; children: Brittaney Nicole, Luke Vaughn. AAS with acctg. certs., U. Alaska, 2000. Customer svc. agent Northwest Airlines, Traverse City, Mich., 1989-93; supr. ERA Aviation, Kodiak, Alaska, 1993-95; staff acct. Shaffer & Harrington CPAs, Sitka, Alaska, 1995-97, Sheldon Jackson Coll., Sitka, 1997-99; acct. tech. Altman, Rogers & Co. CPA, Anchorage, 1999-2000, USCG ISC Kodiak, Kodiak, 2000—. Editor ROTORWASH Coast Guard Family Newsletter, 1988 (Alex Haley award excellence in info. 1988). Treas. Girl Scouts Tongass Coun. Sitka Cmty., 1997-98. Lutheran. Avocations: fishing, wilderness camping, hiking, swimming. Office: ISC Kodiak Comptr Divsn Kodiak AK 99615-7300 Fax: 907-486-5696. E-mail: steffey@gci.net.

STEFFY, MARION NANCY, state agency administrator; b. Fairport Harbor, Ohio, Sept. 23, 1937; d. Felix and Anna (Kosaber) Jackopin; 1 child, Christopher C. BA, Ohio State U., 1959; postgrad., Butler U., 1962-65, Ind. U., 1983. Exec. sec. Franklin County Mental Health Assn., Columbus, Ohio, 1959-61; caseworker Marion County Dept. Pub. Welfare, Indpls., 1961-63, supr., 1963-66, asst. chief supr., 1966-73; dir. divsn. pub. assistance Ind. Dept. Pub. Welfare, Indpls., 1973-77, asst. adminstr., 1977-85; regional adminstr. Adminstrn. Children and Families Ill. Dept. Health and Human Svcs., Chgo., 1985-98; nat. dir. Performance Intitiative, 1998—. Lectr. Ball State U., Lockyear Coll., Ind. U. Grad. Sch. Social Work; mem. Ind. Devel. Disabilities Coun., 1979-81, Ind. Cmty. Svc.s Adv. Coun., 1978-81; Ind. Child Support Adv. Coun., 1976-82, Welfare Svc. League, 1968—; chmn. rules com. Ind. Health Facilities Coun., 1974-81. Chmn. Lawrence Twp. Roundtable, 1983—. Mem. Nat. Assn. State Pub. Welfare Adminstrs., Am. Pub. Welfare Assn., Network of Women in Bus. Roman Catholic.

STEHN, LORRAINE STRELNICK, physician; b. Richmond, Ind., Aug. 27, 1950; d. Daniel H. and Eleanor Gayle (Robertson) Strelnick; m. Thomas Veasey Stehn, June 16, 1973; children: Alexander Veasey, Andrew Thomas. BA, Carleton Coll., 1972; DO, Coll. Osteo. Medicine & Surg., 1976. Diplomate Am. Bd. Family Practice. Intern Pontiac (Mich.) Osteo. Hosp., 1976-77; vol. med. officer U.S. Peace Corps, Swaziland, 1977-79; resident family practice St. Mary's Hosp., Port Arthur, Tex., 1980-82; family practice osteo. medicine Aransas Pass, Tex., 1982—; med. adv. Christian Svc. Ctr., Aransas Pass, Tex., 1983—. Chief staff Coastal Bend Hosp., Aransas Pass, 1985, 90, 95, North Bay Hosp., 2003. Pres. bd. dirs. Corpus Christi (Tex.) Chorale, 1995-96; pres. Aransas Pass H.S. Band Booster, 1998-2000. Recipient Svc. award Aransas Pass Jr. High, 1984. Fellow Am. Acad. Family Practice (pres. bd. dirs. profl. counseling svcs.); mem. Tex. Med. Assn., SPAR County Med. Soc. (pres. 2001-2002). Democrat. Home: 1613 S Saunders St Aransas Pass TX 78336-3107 E-mail: stehn@cableone.net.

STEICHEN, JOANNA T(AUB), psychotherapist, writer; b. N.Y.C., Feb. 22, 1933; d. William James and Edna (Notice) Taub; m. Edward Steichen, Mar. 19, 1960 (dec. 1973). BA, Smith Coll., 1954; MS, Columbia U., 1973. Diplomate Am. Bd. Social Work. Copywriter Young & Rubicam, Inc., N.Y.C., 1955-60; asst. social worker Mount Sinai Hosp., N.Y.C., 1970-71; pvt. practice N.Y.C., 1975—2001; cons. supr. Baltic St. Svc., South Beach Psychiat. Ctr., Bklyn., 1976-77; supr. psychotherapy New Hope Guild Ctrs., Bklyn., 1977—88, dir. group therapy tng., 1980-88; dir. acad. tng. Ctr. for Advancement of Group Studies, N.Y.C., 1989-90, faculty, supr., 1989—99. Author: Marrying Up: An American Dream-and Reality, 1983, Steichen's Legacy, 2000; contbr. articles to mags. Task force schs. self-study Columbia U. Sch. Social Work, N.Y.C., 1972-75; trustee Internat. Mus. Photography, Rochester, N.Y., 1980-1996, trustee emeritus, 1996—; active Creative Arts Awards Commn., Brandeis U., 1985-91, Long House Res. Arts Com., 1996—; bd. dirs. Edward F. Albee Found., 1980—, Hampton Day Sch., 1994-97. Mem. NASW (diplomate), Am. Group Psychotherapy Assn. (Meritorious Contbn. award 1984), N.Y. State Soc. Clin. Social Work Psychotherapists, Am. Acad. Psychotherapists (edtl. bd. Voices 1979-82), Authors Guild, Ea. Group Psychotherapy Soc. (tng. com. 1988-91), Coffee Ho. Club (N.Y.C.). Democrat. Episcopalian. Avocations: architectural renovation, theater, opera, piano. Office: Apt 14F 252 7th Ave New York NY 10001-7347

STEIDER, DORIS, artist; b. Decatur, Ill., Apr. 10, 1924; d. Rudy C. and Helen (Regan) Sleeter; m. Robert E. Steider, Nov. 16, 1944 (div.); children: Kristen (Mrs. Gerald Latham), Robert S., Tim D; m. Carroll B. McCampbell, May 19, 1972. BS, Purdue U.; MA, U. N.Mex. Exhibited in more than 190 maj. juried shows including Smithsonian Instn., Washington, Gilcrease Inst., Tulsa, Army Traveling Print Shows, 1963, 64, Witte Mus. Western Art, San Antonio, Mont. State Hist. Soc. Mus., Helena, Mus. N.Mex. Biennials,

N.Mex. State Fair Profl. Show, Nat. Art Shows, La Junta, Colo., 1978, 81, 83, Nebraskaland Days Invitational Art Exhbn., 1976—; exhibited in over 100 one-woman shows; represented in permanent collections Holt Rinehart and Winston, Purdue U. Galleries, Time Inc., Loewen Group British Columbia, West Tex. Mus., U. N.Mex. Art Mus., N.Mex. State Fair Collection, Albuquerque Pub. Libr., over 2600 in pvt. collections; Book (by Mary Carroll Nelson) A Vision of Silence: The Egg Tempera Landscapes of Doris Steider, 1997. Mem. Albuquerque Fine Arts Adv. Bd., 1966-72; chmn. standards com. N.Mex. Arts and Crafts Bd., 1964-70; chmn. invitational rev. bd. SW Arts and Crafts Fair, 1977-78. Doris Steider St. named in her honor Albuquerque, 1989; recipient over 85 local, regional, nat. and internat. awards, Disting. Alumni honor Purdue U., 2000. Mem.: Soc. of Layerists in Multi-Media. Home: 12905 Sunrise Trail Pl NE Albuquerque NM 87111-8194 Office Phone: 505-797-1979. E-mail: steiderart@cs.com.

STEIDL, MARY CATHERINE, food service executive; b. Saratoga, N.Y., Dec. 13, 1961; d. Peter Anthony Fabbozzi and Catherine Mary Moody; m. Scott Vincent Steidl Sr., July 7, 1986 (div. Dec. 1995); children: Scott Jr., Martin C. Student, Seton Hall U., 1980—81. Dir. ops. McDonalds Corp., Oakbrook, Ill., 1980—; trustee Ronald McDonald House, Long Branch, NJ, 2000—; bd. dirs. Queens (NY) Cmty. Cadet Corp. Pres. emeritus Sacred Heart Grammar Sch. PTA, Clifton, NJ, 2000. Roman Catholic. Avocations: backgammon, gardening. Office: McDonalds NY Region 105 Eisenhower Pkwy Roseland NJ 07068

STEIGERWALD-CLAUSEN, BEVERLY, sculptor, educator; b. Akron, Ohio, Nov. 15, 1934; d. Benjamin Wilford and Marion Eleanor (Ion) Betz; m. James Carl Steigerwald, June 21, 1958 (dec. 1988); children: Mary Jo, Michael, James, Denise, Michelle, Suzanne, Beth; m. Kenneth E. Clausen, Feb. 14, 1997. Attended, Cleve. Inst. Art, 1952-54. Sculpture tchr. Art Students League, Denver, 1995—. Chmn. organizing com. Foothills Art Ctr., N.Am. Sculpture Exhbn., Golden, Colo., 1985-92; presenter Interfaith Forum on Religion, Art and Architecture, Brno, Czechoslovakia, 1992; presenter Exposition des Artistes Americains, Auvillar, France, 1996; lectr. Cath. City Women's Club, Akron, Ohio, 1995; presenter Lancaster Theological Sem., Lancaster, Pa., 2000; juror, Internat. Snow Sculpture Championships, Breckenridge, Colo., 2003, Art Students League, Denver, 2004. Prin. works include life-size bronze figures St. Michael the Archangel Ch., Aurora, Colo., 1990, 15 relief bronze plaques St. Patrick Ch., Colorado Springs, Colo., 1991, bronze relief figure and wall Mercy Hosp. Chapel, Denver, 1992, outdoor life-size bronze Queen of Peace Ch., Aurora, Colo., 1993, lobby bronze Queen of Peace Ch., Aurora, 1999, outdoor bronze Lancaster (Pa.) Theol. Sem., 2000, lobby life-size bronze Northside Hosp., Atlanta, 2001, outdoor life-size bronze Lakewood, Colo., 2004. Vol. Foothills Art Ctr., 1976-92. Recipient Excaliber Bronze award Catherine Lorillard Wolfe Art Club, 1986, Roman Bronze award Pen and Brush, 1987, Internat. Visual Arts Citation award Interfaith Forum on Religion, Art and Architecture, 1991, Colo. Best of Show Colo. Art Exhbn., 1999, Calif. Best of Show, Ministry & Liturgy Mag., 2002, 2nd pl., 2004. Mem.: No. Colo. Artist Assn. Avocation: studying life through the arts. Home and Office: 782 S Emporia St Denver CO 80247-1908 Office Phone: 303-364-8498.

STEIL, JANICE M. social psychology educator; b. Fall River, Mass., Mar. 1, 1941; d. Alfred Edward Ingham and Rita Hindle; m. M. Peter Steil Jr., June 28, 1970; children: Justin Peter, Alexis Ingham. BA, U. Mass., 1962; EdM, Boston U., 1965; PhD, Columbia U., 1979. Lectr. Boston U., 1966, Brandeis Coll., Waltham, Mass., 1967, 69; project dir. Nat. Commn. on Resources for Youth, N.Y.C., 1971-73; rsch. scientist State of N.Y., N.Y.C., 1978-79; prof. social psychology Adelphi U., Garden City, N.Y., 1979—, dir. rsch. tng., 1997—, chair univ.-wide self-study for re-accreditation, 1997-99. Presenter in field.; scholar in-residence Catalyst, N.Y.C., 1997-98; mem. steering com. Feminist Conf. Series, 1993-94. Assoc. editor Psychology of Women Quar., 1993-98; author: Marital Equality: Its relationship to the well-being of husbands and wives, 1997; contbr. numerous articles to profl. jours., chpts. to books; ad hoc reviewer numerous jours. in field. Fellow APA; mem. Am. Psychol. Soc., Internat. Soc. for Study of Personal Relationships, Internat. Network on Personal Relationships, Ea. Psychol. Assn. (program com. 1988-91). Office: Adelphi U Derner Inst Garden City NY 11530

STEIN, CHERYL DENISE, lawyer; b. N.Y.C., Nov. 3, 1953; d. Arthur Earl and Joyce (Weitzman) S. BA magna cum laude, Yale U., 1974; postgrad., U. Chgo., 1974-75; JD, Yale U., 1977. Bar: D.C. 1978, U.S. Dist. Ct. D.C. 1983, U.S. Dist. Ct. Md. 1995, U.S. Ct. Appeals (D.C. cir.) 1988. Atty. advisor CAB, Washington, 1978-79; assoc. Cohn & Marks, Washington, 1979-82; pvt. practice Washington, 1982—. Vol. reader radio reading svc. for the blind Washington Ear, Silver Spring, Md., 1982-91; vol. tutor Friends of Tyler Sch., 1992-95, Habitat for Humanity, Washington, 1997-99; pvt. vol. tutor, 1995-97. Mem. Nat. Assn. Criminal Def. Lawyers, D.C. Assn. Criminal Def. Lawyers. Democrat. Jewish. Avocations: horseback riding, gardening. Office: 705 8th St SE Ste 100 Washington DC 20003-2856

STEIN, ELEANOR BENSON (ELLIE STEIN), playwright, writer; b. New Haven, Conn., Feb. 18, 1922; d. Harry Lorin and Bertha Adeline (Schwolow) Benson; m. Louis Stein; children: Eleanor Smith, Patrice King, Mary Kelly, Paul Stein. Student, Rockland C.C., Suffern, N.Y., 1966-67, S.D. State U., 1969-70, Mesa Coll., 1975, S.D. City Coll., 1976. Office mgr. Thatcher & Hurst Attys., San Diego, Calif., 1968-73. Author: (plays) Squeeze, 1989, Emily Dickinson, 1996; prodr. (plays) Epitaph, Edgar Allan Poe: The Man, The Legend, Paul Revere: An American Rebel, 60 and Holding, Always, Harriet Tubman: A Woman Called Moses, Sacagawea: Indian Guide to Lewis and Clark Expedition, Hans Christian Andersen: An Ugly Duckling, Frederick Douglass: An American Slave, Visions and Images, 2001 (award San Diego Pub. Libr.). Bd. dirs., v.p. NewWorks Theatre. Recipient Roll of Honored Women Unitarian Universalist Women's Fedn., 1978, Aurelia Reinhardt Roll of Honored Women, 1983, Unitarian Universalist award for cmty. svc. First Unitarian-Universalist Ch., 1990, Woman of Yr. So. Regional Conf. Women, 1991. Mem. Nat. League Am. Pen Women, Older Women's League, Actors' Alliance San Diego, Dramatists Guild, U.U. Women's Fedn., Scripteasers, Poets in Profile, Looking Glass Mobile Theatre. Home and Office: 4870 1/2 Old Cliffs Rd San Diego CA 92120-1144

STEIN, ELLEN GAIL, executive manager; b. N.Y.C., May 19, 1951; d. Manuel W. and Bella (Skutel) Stein. BA, SUNY, Stony Brook, 1972; M of Urban Planning, Hunter Coll., 1976; cert. program execs. state/local govt., Harvard U., 1985. Sr. rsch. assoc. Nassau Suffolk (N.Y.) Regional Med. Program, 1976-77; sr. planner N.Y.C. Dept. Correction, 1977-79; group leader criminal justice Mayor's Office, Dept. Ops., N.Y.C., 1979-81, dep. asst. dir. citywide spl. projects, 1981, dir. citywide audit implementation, 1981-84; adminstr. Bur. Supplied N.Y.C. Bd. Edn., 1984-90; mgmt. cons. Project Provide Hope, Russia, Citizen's Budget Commn., 1990-94; pres., CEO FEDVentures Inc., 1994-99; assoc. commnr. Office of CIO N.Y.C. Dept. Tech. and Telecomm., 1999—. Mem. Nat. Assn. Purchasing Mgmt., Am. Women Econ. Devel., Ctrl. Women's Focus, Gov.'s Procurement Coun. (N.Y.), Human Svcs. Coun. (contracting com.). Home: 67 Park Ter E New York NY 10034-1445 Office: 75 Park Pl Fl 9 New York NY 10007-2146 Personal E-mail: egstein@hotmail.com. Business E-mail: estein@doitt.nyc.gov.

STEIN, EMILY JO, psychologist; b. N.Y., Aug. 26, 1950; d. Alvin and Frances Stein. BA, Skidmore Coll., 1972; MEd, Boston (Mass.) Coll., 1973, PhD, 1975. From cons. psychologist to mgr. internal comms. Polaroid Corp., 1973—81; pvt. practice N.Y., 1977—; mgr. internal comms. Polaroid Corp., 1981—87; from trainer to dir. human resources Mt. Sinai Med. Ctr., 1987—91, dir. human resources, 1991—2001. Adj. prof. Boston (Mass.) U., 1974—85, Boston (Mass.) Coll., 1974—85, Boston (Mass.) State Coll., 1974—85; rsch. assoc. Bus. Sch. Harvard U., Cambridge, Mass., 1977—79; adj. prof. Cornell U., N.Y., 1988—; instr. Med. Sch. Mount Sinai U., N.Y., 1988—92, asst. prof., 1993—; presenter in field. Contbr. articles to profl. jours. Mem.: Am. Group Psychotherapy Assn. Home and Office: 60 West 57 4C New York NY 10019

STEIN, KATHY W. state representative; b. Birmingham, Ala., Jan. 31, 1955; m. Alan M. Stein; children: Hadley, Scooter, Wade. JD, Univ. of KY Coll. of Law, 1983; Grad., Va. Polytechnic and State Univ.; BA, Clinch Valley Coll. of the Univ. of Va., 1974. State Rep. House of Rep., Dist. 75, 1996—; owner Kathey W. Stein, Atty. at Law, 1997—; dir. of Domestic Violence, Violence Prosecution Fayette County Atty., 1993—97; prosecutor Fayette County Atty. Office, 1993—97; Pub. Defender Fayette County Legal Aid, Inc., 1988—93; Assoc. Atty. Marshall and Gullette, 1984—86; tchr., faculty, adv. chair, county delegate Pound HS, wise County Sch. Bd., 1976—80; instr. Clinch Valley Coll. of the Univ. of Va., 1977—80; bookkeeper Appalachian Film Workshop, "Appalshop", 1974—75. Mem. Judiciary, Criminal Justice Coun.; trustee Cmty. Action Coun., 1999—; mem. Gov. Coun. on Dom. Violence, 1997—; Vice-chair Fayette County Domes. Violence Bd., 1993—; elector-at-large Va. Electoral Coll., 1980; treas., clk. Town of Wise, 1974—75; mem. Gov. Contract Rev., Gov. Task Force on the econ. Status of Women, appropriations and Revenue, Ed., Post-Secondary and subcomm., Classified Employee compensation subcomm.; vice-chair Health & Welfare; Long-term Care (Subcommittee); mem. Families and Children (subcommittee), Gardian ad Litem Comm. of the admin. Office of the Courts, Legis. Rsch. Comm. Sr. Citizens Adv. Group, Paul Mason Hiv/AIDS Task Force Rules. mem. of: Am. Civil Liberties Union, Nat. Bd.; Am. United for the Seperation of Ch. and State; Appalachian Sch. of Law, Advisory Committee; mem, Ctrl. Ky. Coun. for Peace and Justec, 1998-present; Criminal Justice Council for the Gov. Coun. on Dom. Violence fand Sexual Abuse; Vice-chmn, Fayette County Dom. Violence Prevention Bd.;Life mem., Hadassah, 1990; mem. Kentuckians for the Commonwealth, 1998-present; mem., Ky. Fairness Alliance, 1996-present; Ky. Fairness campaignh; Kentuckians for the Commonwealth, Ky. Women's Political Causus; Chair, Mental Health Comm. of the Fayette County Dom. Violence Prevention Bd.; Milbank Memorial Fund, Reforming State Group, Steering Committee Nat. conference of State Legislators; Nat. Hon. Roll of State Legislators, Ctr. for Women's studies;Nat. Org. for Woman; Nat. Org. of Woman Legislators; chmn. emeritus, Ohavay Zion Synagogue, Social Acton comm.; Southern Conference of State Legislators. Democrat. Jewish. Office: Capitol Capitol Annex Rm 429 Frankfort KY 40601 also: Dist 364 Transylvania Pk Lexington KY 40508

STEIN, MARY KATHERINE, writer, editor, photographer, communications executive; b. Denver, Sept. 7, 1944; d. Robert Addison and Minta Mary (MacDonald) Dunlap; m. Lawrence Bronstein, June 29, 1970 (div. 1974); m. Donald L. Stein, Aug. 16, 1982. BS in Journalism, U. Kans., 1966. Sr. editor Am Family Physician mag., Kansas City, Mo., 1967-78; editor-in-chief Current Prescribing mag., Oradell, N.J., 1978-79; sr. editor Diagnosis mag., Oradell, 1979-83; mng. editor Advances in Reproductive Medicine, Bolton, Conn., 1983-85; pres. MD Comm., Tucson, 1983—; pres. Desert Light Photography, Tucson. Author: Child Abuse, 1987, Caring for the AIDS Patient, 1987, Lifetime Weight Control, 1988, Substance Abuse, 1988, An Overview of HIV Infections and AIDS, 1989, Cardiovascular Disease: Evaluation and Prevention, 1989, Substance Abuse: A Guide for Healthcare Professionals, 1997; mng. editor: Eating Disorders Rev., 1990—; editor Nutrition and the M.D., 1992-95; contbr. articles to mags. Mem. Women in Comm. (pres. Greater Kansas City chpt. 1977-78, pres. Orange County chpt. 1990-92), Am. Med. Writers Assn., Profl. Photographers Am. Democrat. Lutheran. Avocation: photography. Office: MD Comm Inc 302 S Pinto Pl Tucson AZ 85748-6902 E-mail: marykaystein1@aol.com.

STEIN, MARY MARGARET, actor; b. Marquette, Mich., Nov. 07; d. Paul and Ann Stein. BA in Theatre/Dramatic Lit., Marquette U., 1980; diploma in acting, The Juilliard Sch., 1982. Pvt. acting coach Whimsical World Inc., L.A., 2000—. Actor: (films) Dead Man on Campus, Monkeybone, Man of the Year, Men in Black 2, Babe: Pig in the City, The Grinch, others; (TV series) Beyond Belief, The Cosby Show, Deadly Games, Murphy Brown, Married with Children, Star Trek: Next Generation, MD's, Push, Nevada, Providence, others. Big sister Westside Kids, Westchester, Calif., 1991—92; participant Free Arts for Abused Kids, L.A., 1995—2002; tchr. Inside Out Program L.A. Ctrl. Juvenile Hall, 1999. Mem.: SAG, TV Acad., Women in Film. Democrat. Buddhist. Avocations: yoga, skiing, kayaking, bicycling, horseback riding. Home and Office: Whimsical World Inc PO Box 461366 Los Angeles CA 90046

STEIN, PAULA JEAN ANNE BARTON, hotel real estate executive, broker; b. Chgo., July 29, 1929; m. Marshall L. Stein; children: Guy G., George L.; guardian of Bradley Stein, Gregory Stein. BA, Lake Forest (Ill.) U., 1951; postgrad., Roosevelt U., Chgo., 1955-77, UCLA, 1978-79. Adminstrv. asst. publicity Kefauver for Pres., Chgo., 1951; adminstrv. asst. Wells Orgns., Chgo., 1952; rschr., writer Employers Assn. Am., Chgo., 1951-52; writer Woodworking Jobbers Assn., Chgo., 1953; cons. L.A., 1978-80; pres., broker Steinvest, Inc., Chgo., 1980—; freelance writer, 1996—. Cons., hotels Nat. Diversified Svcs., Inc., Chgo., 1990—, Beach Hotel, Inc., Monterey, Calif., IBA Women's Adv. Bd., 1999; advicate for learning disorder causes. Script for first TV bus. prog. on WGN-TV, 1951-52. Mem. Ragdale Found., Lake Forest, Ill. IBA fellow, 1990. Mem. World Future Soc. (profl.), Sisters in Crime, Mystery Writers, So. Poverty Law Ctr., others. Avocations: oil painting, grandparenting, social services causes, citizen-diplomacy, mystery writing. Home and Office: Steinvest Inc 2291 Hybernia Dr Highland Park IL 60035-5509 E-mail: steinvest@msn.com.

STEIN, RUTH ELIZABETH KLEIN, physician; b. N.Y.C., Nov. 2, 1941; d. Theodore and Mimi (Foges) Klein; m. H. David Stein, June 9, 1963; children: Lynn Andrea Stein Melnick, Sharon Lisa, Deborah Michelle. AB, Barnard Coll., 1962; MD, Albert Einstein Coll. Medicine, 1966. Diplomate Am. Bd. Pediat. Intern, then resident Bronx Mcpl. Hosp. Ctr., 1966-68; sr. resident, fellow; instr. dept. pediats. George Washington U., Washington, 1968-70; with Albert Einstein Coll. of Medicine, Bronx, 1970-77, assoc. prof. pediats., 1977-83, prof., 1983—; vice-chmn. dept. pediats. Albert Einstein Coll., 1992—2002, dir. office of acad. affairs, dept. pediats., 1997—2002; pediatrician-in-chief, dir. pediats. Jacobi Med. Ctr. (formerly Bronx Mcpl. Hosp. Ctr.), 1992-97. Vis. prof. pub. health dept. epidemiology Yale U. Sch. of Medicine, New Haven, 1986-87; scholar-in-residence United Hosp. Fund, N.Y., 1995-97; dir., prin. investigator Preventive Intervention Rsch. Ctr. for Child Health, N.Y., 1983-94, Nat. Child Health Assessment Planning Project, N.Y., Behavioral Pediatric Tng. Program, N.Y.; dir. gen. pediatrics Pediat. Divsn., N.Y., 1992-97; apptd. to Montefiore Med. Ctr., North Ctrl. Bronx Hosp., Jacobi Med. Ctr.; bd. dirs. Ctr. for Child Health Rsch. of Am. Acad. Pediatrics, mem. exec. com., 1999—; bd. Children, Youth and Families, NRC/Inst. Medicine, 1999—; co-chmn. com. on evaluation of child health Bd. Children, Youth and Families, 2002—. Editor: Caring for Children with Chronic Illness: Issues and Strategies, 1989, Health Care for Children: What's Right, What's Wrong, What's Next, 1997; mem. editorial bd. Jour. Behavioral and Devel. Pediatrics; contbr. articles to profl. jours. Fellow Am. Acad. Pediats.; mem. APHA, Am. Pediatric Soc., Soc. for Pediat. Rsch., Ambulatory Pediat. Assn. (bd. dirs. 1982-89, pres. 1987-88, rsch. award 1995, Ray Helfer award 1999), N.Y. Acad. Medicine (chmn. N.Y. forum on child health 2001--), Soc. for Devel. and Behavioral Pediats., Alpha Omega Alpha. Jewish. Home: 91 Larchmont Ave Larchmont NY 10538-3748 Office: Albert Einstein Coll Med Montefiore Med Ctr 111 E 210 St Bronx NY 10467-2804 E-mail: rstein@aecom.yu.edu.

STEIN, SANDRA LOU, educational psychologist, educator; b. Freeport, Ill., Oct. 6, 1942; d. William Kenneth and Marien Elizabeth Stein. BS, U. Wis., Madison, 1964; MS in Edn., No. Ill. U., 1967, EdD, 1969. Tchr. English Rockford (Ill.) Sch. Dist., 1964-65; tchr. Russian Jefferson County Sch. Dist., Lakewood, Colo., 1965-66; asst. prof. edn. U. S.C., Columbia, 1969-71, No. Ill. U., DeKalb, 1971-72, Rider U., Lawrenceville, N.J., 1972-75, assoc. prof. edn., 1975-81; prof. edn. Rider Coll., Lawrenceville, N.J., 1981—, dept. chair, 1983-91. Cons. on measurement and evaluation, women's edn., 1973—. Contbr. articles to ednl. publs. Deacon Presbyn. Ch. Lawrenceville, 1984-87. Recipient Disting. Teaching award Rider Coll. and Lindback Found., 1981. Mem. AAUP (Outstanding Achievement award Rider Coll. chpt. 1988), Am. Ednl. Rsch. Assn., Am. Psychol. Assn., Phi Delta Kappa (chpt. pres. 1986-87, Svc. Key award 1991, faculty advisor 1994—). Office: Rider U 2083 Lawrenceville Rd Trenton NJ 08648-3099 E-mail: stein@rider.edu.

STEIN, ZENA A. health facility administrator, psychiatry educator; BA in History, U. Capetown, South Africa, 1941, MA in History, 1942; MB, BChir, U. Witwatersand, Johannesburg, South Africa, 1950. Dir. epidemiology of brain disorders rsch. dept. N.Y. State Psychiat. Inst., N.Y.C., 1968—; prof. pub. health Columbia U. Sch. Pub. Health, N.Y.C., 1973—, prof. pub. health Gertrude H. Sergievsky Ctr., 1977—, assoc. dir. rsch. and acad. affairs, 1986—; co-dir. HIV Ctr. for Clin. and Behavioral Studies N.Y. State Psychiat. Inst. and Columbia U., N.Y.C., 1987—; prof. psychiatry dept. psychiatry Columbia U., N.Y.C., 1991—. Cons. WHO, UNICEF; mem. study sects. NIMH, NIEHS, NIOSH, NICHD; com. mem. NAS. Co-editor: (with M. Wright, J. Scandlyn) Women's Health and Apartheid: The Health of Women and Children and the Future of Progressive Health Care in Southern Africa, 1988, (with A. Zwi) Action on AIDS in Southern Africa: Maputo Conference on Health in Transition in Southern Africa, 1990; contbr. chpts. to books and articles to profl. jours. Grantee Fogarty Ctr., NIMH. Office: HIV Ctr NY State Psychiat Inst 722 W 168th St New York NY 10032-2603

STEINBACH, ALICE, journalist; b. Balt. Student, U. London. Feature writer Balt. Sun, 1981—; formerly dir. pub. info. Balt. Mus. Art. Recip. Pulitzer Prize for feature writing, 1985. Office: Balt Sun 501 N Calvert St Baltimore MD 21278-0001

STEINBERG, JANET ECKSTEIN, journalist; d. Charles and Adele (Ehrenfeld) Eckstein; m. Irvin S. Silverstein, Oct. 22, 1988; children: Susan Carole Steinberg Somerstein, Jody Lynn Steinberg Lazarow. BS, U. Cin., 1964. Travel cons., 1994—; pub. Paine Webber Vantage Living website, 2000—02; guest lectr. Tri State Travel Sch., 1999—2001. Freelance writer: ; guest appearance Braun & Co., Sta. WLW-TV, Sta. WMK-TV, travel editor Am. Israelite, 1996—, Jewish News, 1996—, N.J. Jewish News, 1997—; travel editor Miami Herald Jewish Star Times, 2002—03; travel editor S. Fla. Single Living, 1988—92, Cin. Post, 1978—86, Ky. Post, 1978—86, Cin. Enquirer, 1986—94, MetroWest Jewish News, N.J., 1996—, Jewish News-New Orleans, 1996—, L.A. Jewish Jour., 1997—; contbg. editor: Travel Agt., 1986—88, Birnbaum Travel Guides, 1988—98, The Writer, 1988, 1992, 1998, Entree, 1986—97; travel columnist Northeast Mag., 1986—88, South Fla. Single Living, 1984—92, Eastside Weekend Mag., 1994—96; contbr. articles to newspapers, mags., and books. Recipient Lowell Thomas Travel Journalism award, 1984, 1985, 1990, Henry E. Bradshaw travel journalism award, 1st pl., best of show, 1988, Buckeye Travel award, Ohio Divsn. Travl & Tourism, 1992, Cipriani Best Overall WRiter award, 1981, 13 awards, Soc. Am. Travel Writers, 1981—96, 15 awards, Midwest Travel Writers, 1981—2002. Home: 900 Adams Xing Ste 9200 Cincinnati OH 45202-1677 E-mail: jxs4travel@aol.com.

STEINBERG, JOAN EMILY, retired secondary school educator; b. San Francisco, Dec. 9, 1932; d. John Emil and Kathleen Helen (Montgomery) S. BA, U. Calif., Berkeley, 1954; EdD, U. San Francisco, 1981. Tchr. Vallejo (Calif.) Unified Sch. Dist., 1959-61, San Francisco Unified Sch. Dist., 1961-93, elem. tchr., 1961-78, tchr. life and phys. sci. jr. high sch., 1978-85, 87-93, sci. cons., 1985-87; lectr. elem. edn. San Francisco State U., 1993-94. Ind. sci. edn. cons., 1993-2002. Contbr. articles to zool. and edn. books and profl. jours. Recipient Calif. Educator award, 1988, Outstanding Educator in Tchg. award U. San Francisco Alumni Soc., 1989; Fulbright scholar U. Sydney, Australia, 1955-56. Mem. San Francisco Zool. Soc., Exploratorium, Am. Fedn. Tchrs., Calif. Acad. Scis., Calif. Malacozool. Soc., Nat. Sci. Tchrs. Assn., Elem. Sch. Sci. Assn. (sec. 1984-85, pres. 1986-87, newsletter editor 1994-99), Sigma Xi. Democrat.

STEINBERG, LAURA, lawyer; b. Phila., Feb. 3, 1948; d. Leonard and Pearl (Zeid) S.; children: Seth, Adam, Bree. BA magna cum laude with honors, Bryn Mawr Coll., 1968; JD cum laude, Harvard U., 1972. Bar: Mass. 1972, U.S. Dist. Ct. Mass. 1972, U.S. Dist. Ct. R.I. 1974, U.S. Ct. Appeals (1st cir.) 1973, U.S. Ct. Appeals (10th and D.C. cirs.) 1986, U.S. Ct. Appeals (4th cir.) 1988, U.S. Claims Ct. 1979, U.S. Supreme Ct. 1988. Assoc. Sullivan & Worcester, Boston, 1972-79, ptnr., 1979—, mem. mgmt. com., 1988-2000, head litigation dept., 1988-99. Dir. Greater Boston Legal Svcs., 1987-90. Bd. dirs. Law Firm Resources Project, Boston, 1980-86, Lawyers Com. for Civil Rights Under Law, 1998—; pres. Peirce Extended Day Program, Inc., West Newton, Mass., 1983-86. Spl. career fellow U. Calif., Berkeley, 1968-69; Fulbright scholar, 1968. Mem. Boston Bar Assn. (vice-chmn. litigation sect. 1992-94, chmn. 1994-95). Avocations: reading, tennis. Office: Sullivan & Worcester LLP One Post Office Sq Ste 2100 Boston MA 02109-2129 Office Phone: 617-338-2800. E-mail: lsteinberg@sandw.com.

STEINBERG, MARILYN MARIE, psychotherapist; b. Hammond, Ind., July 13, 1965; d. Willard and Lorraine Cassity; m. Brian David Steinberg, Apr. 13, 1985 (div. Aug. 2002). BA, Purdue U., West Lafayette, Ind., 1993; MS, Purdue U., 1999. Psychology intern Southlake Ctr. for Mental Health, Schererville, Ind., 1992, St. Margaret Mercy, Dyer, Ind., 1993; mental health counselor Charter Behavioral Health Systems, Hobart, Ind., 1994—95; and family therapy intern Purdue U. MFT Ctr., Hammond, 1996; psychology instr. Purdue U., 1995—96; and family therapy intern Thornton Twp. Youth Com., South Holland, Ill., 1997; psychotherapist Willowglen Acad., Gary, Ind., 1999—. Lectr. in field. Contbr. articles to profl. jours., chpt. to book. Pres. Golden Harvest Condominium Assn., Crown Point, Ind., 2002—. Mem.: Internat. Family Therapy Assn., Ind. Assn. Marriage and Family therapy, Am. Assn. Marriage and Family therapy, Alpha Chi. Republican. Roman Catholic. Avocations: travel, cooking, scrapbooking, Chicago White Sox, Purdue football. Office: Willowglen Acad 308 E 21st Ave Gary IN 46407

STEINBERG, NANCY, healthcare public relations executive; m. Jonathan Steinberg; 1 child. Grad., U. Mich. Account assoc. corp. divsn. Tiffany's; assoc. pub. info. officer AMA, 1992—96; dir. pub. rels. Cabrini Med. Ctr., NYC, 1996—2002; sr. media rels. specialist, NY region City of Hope Nat. Med. Ctr., NYC. Mem.: Publicity Club NY (treas.), Healthcare Pub. Rels. and Mktg. Soc. Greater NY (pres. 2002—), NY Women in Comm. Office: City of Hope NY Regional Office 30 W 26th St Ste 301 New York NY 10010 Office Phone: 212-645-3800. Business E-Mail: nsteinberg@coh.org.*

STEINBERG, SALME ELIZABETH HARJU, academic administrator, historian; b. N.Y.C. d. Johan Edward and Jenny Lydia (Peltonen) Harju; m. Michael Stephen Steinberg, Sept. 15, 1963; children: William, Katharine Lovisa. BA, Hunter Coll., 1960; MA, CCNY, 1962; PhD, Johns Hopkins U., 1971. Lectr. history Goucher Coll., Towson, Md., 1971—72; asst. prof. history Northwestern U., Evanston, Ill., 1972—75; prof. Northeastern Ill. U., Chgo., 1975—83, chmn. dept., 1983—87, assoc. provost then acting provost, 1987—92, provost, v.p. for acad. affairs, 1992—95, pres., 1995—. Author: Reformer in the Marketplace: Edward W. Bok and The Ladies' Home Journal, 1979; contbr. articles to profl. jours. Named to, Hunter Coll. Hall of Fame, 1997; recipient 14th Ann. award Appreciation, Asian Am. Coalition Chgo., 1997; grantee, Danforth Found., 1967—68. Episcopalian. Avocations: opera, theater. Office: Northeastern Ill U Office of President 5500 N Saint Louis Ave Chicago IL 60625-4679

STEINBERG-EPSTEIN, ROBIN BETH, pediatrician, educator; d. Merrill E. and Cecile Steinberg; m. Roger J. Epstein; children: Izak, Sam. BA, U. Calif., Berkeley, 1988; MD, U. Calif., Irvine, 1993. Lic. pediatrician, behavioral devel. pediatrician. Resident in pediats. Harbor-UCLA, Torrance, Calif., 1993—96; fellow in child psychiatry Harbor UCLA, Torrance, Calif., 1997—99; physician Kaiser Bellflower, Bellflower, Calif., 1996—98; asst. clin. prof. pediats. U. Calif., Irvine, 1999—; asst. med. dir. Child Devel. Ctr., Irvine, 1999—. Cons. McNeil Pharms., 2000—, Shire Pharms., 2000—; co-investigator studies for treatment of ADHD and genetics of ADHD and autism. Mem. curriculum devel. interagy. autism com. Jewish Comty. Ctr. Presch., Calif., 1999—2001. Fellow: Am. Acad. Pediats.; mem.: Devel. Behavioral Pediats. Assn.

STEINEGER, MARGARET LEISY, non-profit organization officer; b. Newton, Kans., Feb. 8, 1926; d. Ernest Erwin and Elva Agnes (Krehbiel) L.; m. John Francis Steineger, Dec. 2, 1949; children: John Steineger III, Cindy Blair, Melissa, Chris. B., So. Meth. U., 1947; M. in Social Work, U. Kans., 1949. County vice-chair United Way, Kansas City, Kans., 1960-61; bd., sec., treas. Wyandotte County Bar Aux., Kans., 1960-63; bd. Jr. League of Kansas City, 1962-66, County Coun. PTA, Wyandotte County, 1963-66, KCK Friends of the Arts, Kansas City, 1974-77; pres. Grinter Place Mus. Friends, Kans., 1977-78; bd. Kaw Valley Arts Coun., Kansas City, 1982-86; commr. Landmarks Commn., Kansas City, 1985-87; bd. Arts with the Handicapped, Wyandotte County, 1986—. Bd. dirs. Kans. Arts Adv. Bd., Grinter Place Friends, Kans., Tri-County Tourism Coun., Kans. V.p. Kans. Legis. Wives, Topeka, 1975-76; bd. dirs. KCK Friends of the Libr., Kansas City, 1984-94, Shepherd's Ctr., 1996-2002; founder Wyandotte County Libr., 1963-64, Creative Experiences, Kansas City, 1967; commr. Kans. Arts Commn., 1965-85; mem. Kaw Valley Arts and Humanities Bd., 1988-92; mem. adv. bd. Parents as Tchrs., 1992-99; mem. Kansas City Ballet Guild. Recipient Humanities award Kans. Com. for the Humanities, 1989; named Citizen of Yr. Kansas City, Kans., 1978. Mem. Kappa Kappa Gamma (C.C. Endowment Bd. 1989—). Democrat. Methodist. Avocations: skiing, sailing, inventing. Home: 6400 Valleyview Ave Kansas City KS 66111-2013

STEINEM, GLORIA, writer, editor, lecturer, activist; b. Toledo, Mar. 25, 1934; d. Leo and Ruth (Nuneviller) S.; m. David Bale, Sept. 3, 2000. BA, Smith Coll., 1956; postgrad. (Chester Bowles Asian fellow), India, 1957-58; D. Human Justice, Simmons Coll., 1973, PhD (hon.). Co-dir., dir. ednl. found. Ind. Rsch. Svc., Cambridge, Mass. and N.Y.C., 1959-60; contbg. editor Glamour Mag., N.Y.C., 1962-69; co-founder, contbg. editor New York Mag., 1968-72; feminist lectr., 1969—; co-founder, editor Ms. Mag., 1971-87, columnist, 1980-87, cons. editor, 1987—. Active various civil rights and peace campaigns including United Farmworkers, Vietnam War Tax Protest, Com. for the Legal Def. of Angela Davis (treas., 1971-72); active polit. campaigns of Adlai Stevenson, Robert Kennedy, Eugene McCarthy, Shirley Chisholm, George McGovern; Co-founder, bd. dirs. Women's Action Alliance, 1970—; co-founder, convenor, mem. nat. adv. com. Nat. Women's Polit. Caucus, 1971—; co-founder, pres. bd. dirs. Ms. Found. for Women, 1972-1990; founding mem. Coalition of Labor Union Women, 1974, Pres. Voters for Choice, 1979-; mem. Internat. Women's Year Commn., 1977, pres. Choice USA, co-founder, chmn. Liberty Media for Women, 1998- ; editorial cons., Conde Nast Publications, 1962-69, Curtis Publishing, 1964-65, Random House Publishing, 1988—, McCall Publishing. Author: The Thousand Indias, 1957, The Beach Book, 1963, Wonder Woman, 1972, Outrageous Acts and Everyday Rebellions, 1983, Marilyn: Norma Jeane, 1986, Revolution from Within: A Book of Self-Esteem, 1992, Moving Beyond Words, 1994; contgb. corr. NBC Today Show, 1987-88; contbr. to various anthologies. Recipient Penney-Missouri Journalism award, 1970, Ohio Gov.'s award for Journalism, 1972, Bill of Rights award ACLU of So. Calif., 1975; named Woman of the Yr. McCall's mag., 1972; Woodrow Wilson Internat. Ctr. for Scholars fellow, 1977; inducted into Nat. Women's Hall of Fame, 1993. Mem. NOW, AFTRA, Nat. Press Club, Soc. Mag. Writers, Authors' Guild, Phi Beta Kappa. Office: Choice USA 1010 Wisconsin Ave NW Ste 410 Washington DC 20007 also: MS Magazine 433 S Beverly Dr Beverly Hills CA 90212-4401*

STEINER, BARBARA ANNE, secondary school educator; b. Lebanon, Oreg., June 17, 1944; d. Balf Wellington and Doris Ardell (Philpott) Bond; m. Ernest David Steiner, June 29, 1971; children; Julie Lanee, Jaime Michele. BA, Columbia Union Coll., 1967; MA, Andrews U., 1975. Tchr. piano, organ Ga.-Cumberland Acad., Calhoun, 1968-71; tchr. music Battle Creek (Mich.) Acad., 1975-76; ind. tchr. music, 1965—; tchr. music Emerald Jr. Acad., Pleasant Hill, Oreg., 1990-92, Reno (Nev.) Jr. Acad., 1995-98. Pres. aux. group Battle Creek Sanatorium/Hosp., 1978-79; v.p. Mich. Assn. Hosp. Aux., Lansing, 1979-81. Mem. Nat. Music Tchr. Assn., Nat. Guild Organists. Republican. Seventh-Day Aventist. Avocations: music composition and arrangements, photography, yard work. Home: 13794 Palomino Creek Dr Corona CA 92883-8965

STEINER, CAROL SEATON, social worker, educator; d. Richard Lewis Steiner and Jane Seaton Rodman; m. Michael David Beckman, Aug. 5, 1972 (div. June 1990); children: Benjamin Woods Beckman, Jake Seaton Beckman. BA, Wheaton Coll., 1968; MSW, U. Mich., 1971. Lic. ind. social worker. Mentorship developer displaced homemakers Cuyahoga C.C., Cleve., 1986—87, counselor, 1989—95; hotline mgr. Bellflower Ctr. Prevention of Child Abuse, Cleve., 1988—89; social worker Vis. Nurse Svc. Geauga County, Akron, Ohio, 1992—95; pvt. practice Cleve., 1993—95; social worker and preceptor U. Hosps. Cleve./Case We. Res. U., Cleve., 1995—2002; bereavement coord. VNA Hospice, Cleve., 2002—. Vol. Revolutionary Communist Party, Cleve., 1976—92, Not in Our Name, Cleve., 2002—03. Avocations: gardening, reading, kayaking, rollerskating, films.

STEINER, DONNA FORBES, minister, executive consultant; b. Pierson, Iowa, Sept. 8, 1937; d. Dewey Wainwright and Veda Mae (Vannorsdel) Forbes; m. Paul David Steiner, Sept. 21, 1974; children: David Paul, Jonathan L., Ethan Greg. BA in Music Edn., Drake U., 1959; MA in Religious Edn., Bethany Theol. Seminary, Ill., 1964. Ordained to ministry, 1974. Tchr. English and music Brethren Vol. Svc. Ch. of the Brethren, Jos, Nigeria, 1960-62, min. of edn. Palmyra, Pa., 1964-68, adminstrv. asst. Mid-Atlantic Ellicott City, Md., 1968-69, mgr. theol. bookstore Bethany Sem. Oak Brook, Ill., 1969-70, assoc. min. York Ctr. Lombard, Ill., 1969-74, co-pastor Union Bridge, Md., 1976-82, congregation cons. Mid-Atlantic Ellicott City, 1982-85, ministry cons., 1985-96; assoc. exec. Atlantic N.W. dist., 1997—2002; min. Christian edn. St. Paul's United Ch. of Christ, Westminster, Md., 1987—95; summer pastor Reading Ch. of the Brethren, 2003. Spkr. Ch. of the Brethren Conf., Dayton, Ohio, 1975, 98, retreat leader, Ohio, Pa., Va., Md., 1996; theol. tchr. Ch. of the Brethren Mid-Atlantic Dist., Frederick, Md., moderator Mid-Atlantic dist., 1994; co-chmn. Nat. Coun. Chs. Comm. Ch./Ministries in Edn., Cin., 1984-2002; mem. devel. coun. Jubilee Anabapt. Curriculum, 1986-92. Author: (study resource) Partners in Learning, 1991. Mem. AAUW (v.p. membership, ednl. found. chair 1985—), Ch. of the Brethren assn. of Christian Educators (charter, pres. 1978—). Democrat. Avocations: music, walking, needlework, reading, boating. Home: 201 S Homestead Dr Landisville PA 17538-1378

STEINER, GLORIA LITWIN, psychologist; b. Newark, Oct. 21, 1922; d. David Milton and Minna (Krasner) Litwin; m. Charles Steiner, Aug. 29, 1942; children: Charles Jr., Susan Steiner Sher, Jeanne. BA, U. Pa., 1944; MS, CCNY, 1956; EdD, Columbia U., 1965. Psychologist St. Michael's Hosp. and Mt. Carmel, Newark, 1956-62; chief psychologist Children's Hosp., Newark, 1965-78; prof. psychology, dir. psychol. svc. Child Study Ctr., Kean Coll., Union, N.J., 1971-78; vis. assoc. prof. grad. sch. applied and profl. psychology Rutgers U., Piscataway, N.J., 1976-94; clin. assoc. prof., former dir. psychology tng. U. Medicine and Dentistry N.J.-N.J. Med. Sch., Newark, 1978—. Psychology cons. Nat. Pediatric HIV Resource Ctr., 1991-94; trustee Sister Rose Thering endowment dept. Jewish Christian studies Seton Hall U., 1992—. Co-author: Traumatic Abuse/Children, 1980; co-editor: Children, Families and HIV/AIDS: Psychosocial and Psychotherapeutic Issues, 1995; contbr. articles to profl. jours.; mem. editl. bd. Jour. Psychotherapy, 1981-96. Mem. N.J. State Task Force on AIDS, 1986-89, N.J. State Bd. Psychol. Exam., 1978-84, Regional Health Planning Coun., N.J., 1984-85, child adv. com. Mental Health Assn., N.J., 1974-80; trustee, founder N.J. Acad. Psychology, 1978-83, bd. trustees, 1994-97; bd. govs. Metro N.J. chpt. Am. Jewish. Com., 1996—. Grantee tng. health care workers Regional AIDS Edn. and Tng. Ctr. U. Medicine and Dentistry N.J., Newark, 1990, Nat. Pediat. HIV Resource Ctr., Newark, 1991-94. Fellow Am. Orthopsychiat. Assn.; mem. N.Y. Acad. Scis., N.J. Assn. for the Advancement Family Therapy (vice-chmn. 1979-81), Am. Psychol. Assn. Avocation: grandchildren. Home and Office: 321 N Wyoming Ave Apt 4D South Orange NJ 07079-1671 E-mail: charglorsteiner@verizon.net.

STEINER, HOPE ELIZABETH, school counselor; b. St. Louis, Feb. 24, 1952; d. William Frank and Antonette (Liolios) Speros; m. Jeffrey Jay Steiner, July 23, 1977; children: Sarah Elizabeth, Laura Antonette. BS, U. Mo., 1973, MEd, 1974. Lic. profl. counselor, Mo.; nat. cert. counselor. Counselor, dir. counseling Cowley County C.C., Arkansas City, Kans., 1974-82; dir. counseling svcs. St. Louis C.C.- Meramec, 1982-93, counselor, assoc. prof., dept. chair, 1993-96, counselor, prof., 1996—, mem. profl. growth/sabbatical com., 1997—. Mem. campus coms. Wellness, AIDS Awareness, Instrnl. Coun., St. Louis C.C.- Meramec, 1982—; clin. dir. screening depression and eating disorders, 1995, 96, 97; pvt. practice counselor St. Louis Ctr. Healing Arts, 1993-95; presenter in field; spkr. in field. Co-chair cookie sales Girl Scouts, 1988-90; vol. counselor to Flood '93 victims ARC, 1993; active citizen's adv. com. Parkway Sch. Dist., St. Louis, 1994-96, exec. com. PTO Southwest Middle Sch., St. Louis, 1995-96, adv. coun. Valley Park Sch. Dist.- A-Plus Sch. Grant, St. Louis, 1995—; fund raiser Parkway Sch. Dist.; with Handbook of Community Resources for Counselors; coll. liaison Mo. Tech./Prep. Program, 1990—; team capt. United Way, 1982-2000; mem. organizing com. Domestic Violence Awareness Day, 1999. Recipient cert. Leadership, YWCA, St. Louis, 1984; named for Outstanding Merit in the Area of Continuing Edn., Nat. Bd. Certified Counselors, 1990-94, scholastic judge Jr. Miss, South St. Louis County, 1994. Mem. Assn. for Adult Devel. and Aging, Am. Coll. Counseling Assn., Mo. Coll. Counseling Assn., Kans. Coll. Counseling Assn. (pres. 1976), Mo. C.C. Assn., St. Louis Counseling Assn. (pres.-elect 1995-96, pres. 1996-97, past pres. 1997-98), St. Louis Psychol. Assn., Nat. Mo. and Local Edn. Assns. Avocations: reading, playing piano, travel. Office: St Louis CC-Meramec 11333 Big Bend Rd Saint Louis MO 63122-5720 Office Phone: 314-984-7577. E-mail: hsteiner@stlcc.edu.

STEINER, JANET, educational association administrator; Bachelors Degree, Blackburn Coll.; Masters Degree, D in Ednl. Leadership, So. Ill. U. Instr. Blackburn Coll.; ret.; mem. Ill. State Bd. Edn., 1999—, chairperson, 2003—. Office: Ill State Bd Edn 100 N 1st St Springfield IL 62777

STEINER, SALLY ANN, psychiatric nurse practitioner; b. Bayshore, NY, Oct. 21, 1968; d. Richard and Carol Julia (Rotter) Hendershot; m. Michael Francis Steiner, July 6, 2002. BSN, USNY; MSN in pediatric nurse practitioner, U. So. Fla., 2001; post master's cert. family nurse practitioner, U. South Fla., 2002, post master's cert. psychiat. and mental health nurse practitioner, 2003. RN NY State, Fla. State, Advanced Reg. Nurse Practitioner, Fla. State. Grad. tchg. asst. U. So. Fla., Coll. of Nursing, Tampa, 2000—02; parttime prof. U. So. Fla., Coll. of Medicine, Tampa, 2003; psychiat. advanced registered nurse practitioner Hillsborough County Dept. of Children's Svcs., Tampa, 2003—. Social skills counselor Tampa Children's Devel. Ctr., Tampa, 2002—; cons. U. So. Fla., 2003—. Vol. nurse Boggy Creek Camp, Eustis, Fla., 2000—; vol. activities related to med. care underpriviledged. Mem.: Nat. Assn. Pediat. Nurses and Advanced Practitioners, Am. Acad. of Nurse Practitioners, Am. Psychiat. Nurses Assn., Tampa Bay Advance Practice Nurses Coun. Avocations: swimming, reading, travel, writing poetry and short stories, rollerblading. Office: Hillsborough County Dept of Childrens Svcs 3110 Clay Mangum Ln Tampa FL 33618 E-mail: sallyrn@tampabay.rr.com.

STEINER, SHARI YVONNE, publisher, editor, journalist; b. Colorado Springs, Colo., Mar. 3, 1941; d. Evan Keith and Blanche Marie (Ketzner) Montgomery; m. Clyde Lionel Steiner, June 16, 1962; children: Vienna Kay, Marco Romano. BA, Adams State Coll., 1962; cert. in sociology, London Sch. Econs., 1978; postgrad., U. Calif., Berkeley, 1988—. Lic. real estate broker, Calif. Freelance journalist various publs., 1964—; owner, mgr. SREI Group, San Francisco, 1985—; tng. design developer 1st Nationwide Bank, San Francisco, 1987-90; pub., editor Ind. Info. Publs., San Francisco, 1990—; pres. The SREI Group, San Francisco. Feature writer Internat. Herald Tribune, Rome, 1964-79; acct. exec. Allen, Ingersol & Weber, Rome, 1970-72; gen. ptnr. Greenhaven Park, Sacramento, 1990-2003, Port Chicago Indsl., Concord, Calif., 1991-98, Star/Steiner, 1997—. Author: The Female Factor: A Report on Women in Europe, 1972, 2d edit., 1996, Steiners' Complete How to Move Handbook, 1997, 2d edit., 1999, Steiners' Complete How to Talk Mortgage Talk, 1998, 3d edit., 1999, Relocation Guru, 2000; editor The Bottom Line newsletter, 1985-92; assoc. editor The Semaphore, 1990-92; columnist Country's Best Log Homes and Vacation Homes, 1999—. Coord. urban reforestation Friends of Urban Forest, San Francisco, 1989; co-founder New Sch. for Internat. Elem. Students, Rome, 1970. Recipient internat. journalism award Guida Monaci, 1970, award of merit Lotus Club, N.Y.C., 1975; corr. in archives Am. Heritage Ctr., U. Wyo. Mem. Nat. Assn. Realtors (multiple listing svc. selection com. 1986, 91, investment real estate group 1991), Comml. Real Estate Women (editor, bd. dirs. 1985-2001), Am. Soc. Journalists and Authors (exec. bd. dirs. 1998—), PEN Internat., Employee Relocation Coun. Avocation: gardening.

STEINER-HOUCK, SANDRA LYNN, interior designer; b. Columbia, Pa., May 29, 1962; d. Howard Jr. and Mary Louise Steiner; children: Brandon Paul, Brittany Leigh. AA in Interior Design, Bauder Fashion Coll., 1981. Cert. kitchen designer. Designer Bob Harry's Kitchen Ctr., Inc., York, Pa., 1982-87, Leggett, Inc., Camp Hill, Pa., 1987-90, Mother Hubbard's Kitchen Ctr., Mechanicsburg, Pa., 1990-93; owner ind. design svc., 1994—. Designer: Bath Industry Technical Manuals Vol.3, 1993; contbr. designs to profl. jours. Recipient 1st pl. award and Best of Show Resdl. Bath Design, 1986, Showroom Design, 1989, 3d pl. award Resdl. Kitchen, 1992, Resdl. Bath Design, 1992, Heritage Custom Kitchens Mfr.'s Design award, 1986, 94, 3 Nat. Design. awards Resdl. Kitchen, 1994, Kasmar Kitchen Design award 1994, 95, 96, 2d pl. Nat. Design award Kitchen Design, 1997, 1st pl. Nat. Design award Bath Design, 1997, 2000. Mem. Am. Soc. Interior Design, Soc. Cert. Kitchen Designers. Home: 515 Mockingbird Dr Columbia PA 17512-8438 Office: Steiner & Houck Inc 515 Mockingbird Dr Columbia PA 17512-8438 Fax: 717-591-0563.

STEINGASS, SUSAN R. lawyer; b. Cambridge, Mass., Dec. 18, 1941; BA in English Lit., Denison U., 1963; MA in English Lit. with honors, Northwestern U., 1965; JD with honors, U. Wis., 1976. Bar: Wis. 1976, U.S. Dist. Ct. Wis. 1976. Instr. dept. English La. State U., 1965-66, Calif. State Coll., L.A., 1966-68, U. Wis., Stevens Point, 1968-72; law clk. Hon. Nathan S. Heffernan Wis. Supreme Ct., 1976-77; ptnr. Stafford, Rosenbaum, Reiser and Hansen, 1977-85; judge Dane County Cir. Ct., Wis., 1985-93; ptnr. Habush, Habush & Rottier, S.C., Madison, Wis., 1993—. Lectr. civil procedure, environ. law, evidence, trial advocacy Law Sch., U. Wis., 1981—, dir. advocacy and comm., 2003—; instr. Nat. Inst. for Trial Advocacy, 1987—, trustee, 2002—; instr. Nat. Jud. Coll., 1993—. Note and comment editor Wis. Law Rev., 1974-76; co-editor: Wisconsin Civil Procedure Before Trial, 1994, The Wisconsin Rules of Evidence: A Courtroom Handbook, 1998—. Chair Wis. Equal Justice Task Force, 1989-91. Recipient Disting. Svc. award Am. Assn. Mediators, 1991, Presdl. award of excellence State Bar Wis., 2000; named Wis. Trial Judge of Yr. Am. Bd. Trial Advocates, 1992. Fellow Wis. Bar Found.; mem. ATLA, ABA (ho. dels. 2000—), Am. Bar Found., Am. Law Inst., Wis. Bar Assn. (pres. 1998-99), Wis. Law Alumni Assn. (bd. dirs., pres.), Wis. Acad. Trial Lawyers, Wis. Equal Justice Fund (pres.), Dane County Bar Assn., Wis. Trust Account Found. (bd. dirs. 1999—), Order of the Coif (Marygold Melli Achievement award 2001). Office: Habush Habush Davis & Rottier SC 150 E Gilman St Ste 2000 Madison WI 53703-1481 E-mail: ssteinga@habush.com.

STEINHAUER, SHERRI, professional golfer; b. Madison, Wis., Dec. 27, 1962; Student, U. Tex. Golfer LPGA, 1986—; winner du Maurier Classic, 1992, Sprint Championship, 1994, Weetabix Women's British Open Championship, 1998, 99; mem. U.S. Solheim Cup Team, 1994, 98, 2000, Japan Airlines Big Apple Classic, 1999. Achievements include 3 LPGA career hole-in-ones. Office: c/o LPGA 100 International Golf Dr Daytona Beach FL 32124-1082

STEINHAUSER, JANICE MAUREEN, arts administrator, educator, artist; b. Oklahoma City, Okla., Apr. 3, 1935; d. Max Charles and Charlotte (Gold) Glass; m. Stuart Z. Hirschman, Dec. 30, 1954 (div. 1965); children: Shayle, David, Susan; m. Sheldon Steinhauser, May 2, 1965; children: Karen, Lisa Steinhauser Hackel. BFA, U. Colo., Denver, 1972; student, U. Mich., 1953-55. Community affairs adminstr. United Bank Denver, 1973-76; dir. visual arts program Western States Arts Found., Denver, 1976-79; exec. dir. Artreach, Inc., Denver, 1980-82; v.p. mktg. Mammoth Gardens, Denver, 1982-83; dir. pub. rels. Denver Ctr. for Performing Arts, 1983-86; founder, pres. Resource Co., Denver, 1986-88; dir. liberal studies div. Univ. Coll. U. Denver, 1992-97; sculptor, 1997—. Bd. dirs. Met. Denver Arts Alliance, 1982-85, Denver Internat. Film Festival, 1983-86, Colo. Nat. Abortion Rights Action League, 1991-95, Mizel Mus. Judaica, 1995-2000; mem. Women's Forum of Colo., 1981-2002. Mem. Nat. Assn. Women Artists, Colo. New Music Assn. (bd. dirs. 1987-91), Asian Performing Arts Colo. (bd. dirs.), Phi Beta Kappa, Kappa Delta Phi. Democrat. Jewish. Avocations: travel, reading, films. E-mail: jansart3@aol.com.

STEINMAN, LISA MALINOWSKI, English literature educator, writer; b. Willimantic, Conn., Apr. 8, 1950; d. Zenon Stanislaus and Shirley Belle Malinowski; m. James A. Steinman, Apr. 1968 (div. 1980); m. James L. Shugrue, July 23, 1984. BA, Cornell U., 1971, MFA, 1973, PhD, 1976. Asst. prof. English Reed Coll., Portland, Oreg., 1976-82, assoc. prof., 1982-90, prof., 1990—, Kenan prof. English lit. and humanities, 1993—. Cons. NEH, Washington, 1984-85. Author: Lost Poems, 1976, Made in America, 1987, All That Comes to Light, 1989, A Book of Other Days, 1992, Ordinary Songs, 1996, Masters of Repetition, 1998, Carslaw's Sequences, 2003; editor: Hubbub Mag., 1983—; mem. editl. bd. Williams Rev., 1991—, Stevens Jour., 1994—; contbr. articles to profl. jours. Fellow Danforth Found., 1971-75, NEH, 1983, 96, Oreg. Arts Commn., 1983, Nat. Endowment for Arts, 1984; Rockefeller Found. scholar, 1987-88; recipient Pablo Neruda award, 1987, Oreg. Inst. Lit. Arts award, 1993. Mem. MLA, Poets and Writers, PEN (N.W. chpt., co-founder, officer 1989-93). Home: 5344 SE 38th Ave Portland OR 97202-4208 Office: Reed Coll Dept English 3203 SE Woodstock Blvd Portland OR 97202-8138 E-mail: lisa.steinman@reed.edu.

STEITZ, JOAN ARGETSINGER, biochemistry educator; b. Mpls., Jan. 26, 1941; d. Glenn D. and Elaine (Magnusson) Argetsinger; m. Thomas A. Steitz, Aug. 20, 1966. BS, Antioch Coll., 1963; PhD, Harvard U., 1967; D.Sc. (hon.), Lawrence U., Appleton, Wis., 1982, Rochester U. Sch. Medicine, 1984, Mt. Sinai Sch. Medicine, 1989, Bates Coll., 1990; DSc (hon.), Trinity Coll., 1992, Harvard U., 1992. Postdoctoral fellow MRC Lab. Molecular Biology, Cambridge, Eng., 1967-70; asst. prof. molecular biophysics and biochemistry Yale U., New Haven, 1970-74, assoc. prof., 1974-78, prof. molecular biophysics and biochemistry, 1978—, Sterling prof. molecular biophysics and biochemistry, 1978—, chair dept. molecular biophysics and biochemistry, 1996—. Investigator Howard Hughes Med. Inst, 1986—. Recipient Young Scientist award, Passano Found., 1975, Eli Lilly award in biol. chemistry, 1976, U.S. Steel Found. award in molecular biology, 1982, Lee Hawley, Sr. award for arthritis rsch., 1984, Nat. Medal of Sci., 1986, Dickson prize for Sci., Carnegie-Mellon U., 1988, Warren Triennial prize, Mass. Gen. Hosp., 1989, Christopher Columbus Disc. award in biomed. rsch., 1992, Weizmann Women and Sci. award, 1994, City of Medicine award, 1996. Fellow: AAAS; mem.: NY Acad. of Scis. (Weizmann Women & Sci. award 1994), Am. Phil. Soc., Nat. Acad. Arts and Sci., Am. Acad. Arts and Sci. Home: 45 Prospect Hill Rd Branford CT 06405-5711 Office: HHMI at Yale Univ BCMM 136 E 295 Congress Ave New Haven CT 06519-1418

STELCK, MICKIE JOANN, technologist; b. Des Moines, Nov. 12, 1959; d. Richard Findley and Betty Marie Woolsey; m. Michael Lowell Stelck, July 29, 1978. Cert. in surg. tech., Des Moines Area C.C., 1980. Cert. surg. technologist Mayo Clinic, Rochester, Minn., 1980—. Mem. surg. tech. adv. bd. Rochester C.C., 1995—. Co-author: (book) Bronchoscopy, 1994; contbr. articles to profl. jours. Mentor Family Y, Rochester, 1997—. Mem.: Assn. Surg. Technologists (cert.), Lambda Beta. Office: Mayo Clinic Saint Marys Hosp 1216 2d St SW Rochester MN 55902

STELZER, PATRICIA JACOBS, retired secondary school educator; b. Springfield, Ohio, Sept. 7, 1936; d. George Kenneth and Beatrice Snook Jacobs; m. James Glea Stelzer, May 12, 1956; children: Michael G., Samantha S. Moehn, James Todd. BS in Edn., Wright State U., 1973, MA in History, 1997. Reporter, features writer, columnist Springfield News-Sun, 1962—65; social studies tchr. Schaefer Jr. H.S., Springfield, 1975—77, 1978—81, South H.S., Springfield, 1977—78, 1981—2000; ret., 2000; chmn. social studies dept. South H.S., Springfield, 1991—2000. Adj. prof. history Clark State C.C., Springfield, 2001—; cons. Ohio test scholastic achievement State of Ohio Dept. Edn., Columbus, 1985—87; participant cert. assessment pilot program social studies program Nat. Bd. Profl. Tchg. Stds., 1998. Author (book): Dangerous Research, By George!, Deadly Research By George!. Pres. Springfield Civic Theater, 1984—85; performer, mem. pub. rels. com. Music-Stage Theater, Springfield, 1964—68, 1975; dir., choreographer Northwestern H.S. and South H.S., Springfield, 1977—91. Lutheran. Avocations: golf, travel, theater, writing. Home: 6541 Troy Rd Springfield OH 45502 Office: Clark State CC 570 E Leffel Ln Springfield OH 45501

STEMMONS, RANDEE SMITH, lawyer; b. Springfield, Mo., July 15, 1958; d. Robert Lee and Connie (Smith) S. BA, William Woods Coll., 1980; JD, U. Mo., 1983. Bar: Mo. 1983, U.S. Dist. Ct. (we. dist.) Mo., 1983. Ptnr. Stemmons & Stemmons, Mt. Vernon, Mo., 1983—. V.p. Democratic Alliance, Springfield, 1984—; mem. adv. bd. Hospice. Recipient Profl. Responsibility award Am. Jurisprudence, 1983. Mem. ABA, Assn. Trial Lawyers Am., Mo. Assn. Trial Lawyers, 39th Judicial Cir. Bar Assn. (pres. 1984—), Student Bar Assn. (v.p. 1982-83), Mt. Vernon C. of C. (bd. dirs., v.p. 1984-87, pres. 1987), Order of the Coif, Phi Delta Phi. Democrat. Presbyterian. Home: 520 E Center St Mount Vernon MO 65712-1208 Office: 101 E Dallas St Mount Vernon MO 65712-1401

STENDAHL, BRITA KRISTINA, humanities educator, social studies educator; b. Stockholm, Jan. 10, 1925; came to U.S., 1954; d. Johan Victor and Ingeborg (Normann) Johnsson; m. Krister Stendahl, Sept. 7, 1946; children: Johan, Anna, Dan. Cand. Theology, Uppsala (Sweden) U., 1949, can. Philosophy, 1954, PhD (hon.), 1981. Hist. and lit. tchr. Gymnasium, Uppsala, Sweden, 1949-54; hist. and lit. tchr. extension program Harvard U., Cambridge, Mass., 1956-59, hist. and lit. tchr. freshman program, 1964-74; hist. and lit. tchr. seminar program Radcliffe Coll., Cambridge, 1976-84; cultural sec. Ch. of Sweden, Stockholm, 1984-88. Mem. Govt. Coun. for Coord. and Planning of Rsch., Stockholm, 1985-88. Author: (monographs) Søren Kierkegaard, 1976, The Force of Tradition, 1984, The Education of a Self-Made Woman, Fredrika Bremer, 1801-1865, 1994, (autobiography) Sabbatical Reflections, 1978; contbr. Multicultural Writers from Antiquity to 1945, 2002; book reviewer:. Co-chair Fellowship in Israel for Arab-Jewish Youth, Boston, 1972-84, 88-95; bd. dirs. The Abraham Fund, N.Y.C., 1996— Bunting fellow, Radcliffe Coll., Cambridge, Mass., 1961-63; assoc. fellow Henry A. Murray Ctr. at Radcliffe, 1981-82; recipient Myron B. Bloy award The Assn. for Religion and Intellectual Life, 1993. Mem. Arstasallskapet for Fredika Bremer-Studier (chmn. 1985—89). Democrat. Lutheran. Avocations: walking, Tai Chi.

STENGE, LYNDA ANN, music marketing executive; b. Newport Beach, Calif., Nov. 16, 1967; d. Ronald David Stenge and Diane Margaret (Chapman) Swarts. Club coord. JFK Prodn., Hollywood, 1985-90; music mgr. Smash Pop, Studio City, Calif., 1990-94, Q Mgmt., L.A., 1994-95; ind. tour coord. L.A., 1995—96; dir. music mktg. freelance, L.A., Calif., 1996—. Prodr.: Rockin Little Runaways, 1993, Rock Against Rape, 1994, Faces of rock; co-prodr.: Benefit for Children, L.A., 1992 Mem. Planned Parenthood, Rock for Choice.; exec. com. City of Hope, Music and Entertainment. Mem. ASPCA. Democrat. Avocations: skiing, traveling, music. Home: 425 N Alta Vista Blvd Los Angeles CA 90036-2540

STENGER, SARAH, chef; Grad., Dumas Pere Cooking Sch.; studied with chef Pierre Orsi, Pierre Orsi restaurant, Lyons, France. From apprentice to chef The Dining Room, Ritz-Carlton hotel, Chgo., 1984—. Founder Women Chefs of Chgo. Named U.S. winner, Prix Culinaire Internat. Pierre Taittinger competition, Paris, 1991, Rising Star Chef of the Yr. in Am., James Beard Found., 1994, Best Chef of the Midwest, 1998. Office: Ritz-Carlton 106 E Pearson St Chicago IL 60611

STENMARK, JEAN KERR, mathematics educator; b. Davis, Calif., Aug. 25, 1922; d. Norman and Rachel Kerr; m. Roy M., Aug. 24, 1952, (div. July 1975); children: Ruthann, John, Jane. BA, U. Calif., Berkeley, 1942; MS, Calif. State U., Hayward, 1978. Cert. elem. tchr., Calif. With civil svc. U.S. Navy-Aviation Supply, Oakland, Calif., 1942-45; acct. various acctg. firms, San Francisco, 1945-56; tchr. Oakland Unified Sch. Dist., 1969-80; maths. specialist EQUALS and Family Math. Programs U. Calif., Berkeley, 1980-95. Cons. Calif. Assessment Program, Sacramento, 1975-92, New Standards Assessment Project, Oakland, Calif., 1991-2004. Editor: 101 Short Problems, 1995, Mathematics Assessment: Myths, Models, Good Questions and Practical Suggestions, 1991; author: Assessment Alternatives in Mathematics, 1989; co-author: Family Math, 1986, Math for Girls and Other Problem Solvers, 1981, Family Math for Young Children: Comparing, 1997; co-editor: Mathematics Assessment: a practical handbook for grades 3-5, 2001; co-writer, core advisor: Mathematics Assessment: A Video Library, K-12 Guide, 1998. Mem. Calif. Math. Coun., PTA (hon. life). Democrat. Protestant. Avocations: walking, reading. Home and Office: 242 Ashbury Ave El Cerrito CA 94530-4104 E-mail: jkstenmark@aol.com.

STEPHANI, NANCY JEAN, social worker, journalist; b. Garden City, Mich., Feb. 19, 1955; d. Ernest Helmut Schulz and Margaret Mary Fowler Thompson; m. Edward Jeffrey Stephani, Aug. 29, 1975; children: Edward J., Margaret J., James E. AA, Northwood Inst., Midland, Mich., 1975; student in theology, Boston Coll., 1991; BS summa cum laude, Lourdes Coll., Sylvania, Ohio, 1992; MSW, Ohio State U., 1995. Lic. ind. social worker; cert. cognitive behavioral therapist, master addictions counselor. Profl. facilitator Parents United, Findlay, Ohio, 1989-94; contbg. writer Cath. Chronicle, Toledo, 1988-95; mem. ministry formation faculty Cath. Diocese of Toledo, 1992-96; crisis intervention specialist John C. Hutson Ctr., 1994-98; contbg. writer Sunset Gazette, Findlay, Ohio, 1996-98; mgr. Century Health Svcs., Findlay, Ohio, 1998, dir. emergency mental health svcs., 1998—, co-chair strategic planning action team, 1999-00; prof., field coord. MSW program Ohio State U., Lima, 2000—. Social work clinician Family Svc. Hancock County, coord. clin. svcs. Family Svc., 1997—98, Blanchard Valley Home Health Social Svc.; trustee, bd. dirs. Hope House for Homeless, Findlay, 1990—99, v.p., 1996—97, pres., 1997—99; mem. Hancock County Cluster on Elderly; v.p., pres. parish coun. St. Michael Parish, Findlay, 1985—89, adult edn . coord., 1986—93, mem. strategic plan core com., 1989—91; program planning com. Family Life Conf., Cath. Diocese, 1994—95, mem. accreditation com. ministry formation dept.; profl. facilitator Hope Plus Program through Hancock County Common Pleas Ct., 1996—; coord. critical incident stress mgmt. team Hancock County, 1997—; profl. facilitator Hancock County Survivors of Suicide group, 1997—2000; coord. Hancock County Survivors of Suicide Group, 1997—; field instr. dept. social work U. Findlay, Ohio, 1996—, mem. social work adv. coun., 1998—; adj. faculty U. Findley, Ohio; field instr. Capital U., Bowling Green State U., Heidelberg U., 1997—98; mem. adj. faculty Owens Tech. Coll., Findlay; trustee City Mission, 2000—04; co-program coord., field edn. coord. MSW program Ohio State U., Lima, 2001—. Founder Food Coop., MPBA, Findlay, 1981; founding mem. Chopin Hall, Findlay, 1983; mem. Hancock County AIDS Task Force, 1994-98; strategic planning com. mem., co-chair goal setting com. Findlay Pub. Schs., 1994, steering com., Call to Action Northwest Ohio, 1997—; trustee City Mission, 1999—. Nat. Inst. Food Svcs. grantee, 1974; Diocese of Toledo grantee, 1991; Ohio State U. Coll. Social Work grantee, 1994. Mem. NOW, NASW (ethics com. Ohio 1997—, v.p. bd. trustees 2000-02, nat. com. on nominations and leadership 2001—, region VII rep. nat. leadership identification com. 2001-04, treas.-elect 2003—, program planning com., Social Worker of Yr. Region 1, 2000), AAUW (legis. chair Findlay chpt.), Internat. Critical Incident Stress Found., Am. Assn. on Child Abuse, Transpsychol. Assn., Friends of Creation Spirituality, Cognitive/Behavioral Profl. Soc., Call to Action, Pax Christi, Women in Ch. Leadership. Avocations: jogging, hiking, cooking, travel. Home: 2615 Goldenrod Ln Findlay OH 45840-1025 E-mail: NancyStephani@hotmail.com.

STEPHANICK, CAROL ANN, dentist, consultant; b. South Amboy, N.J., Feb. 5, 1952; d. Edward Eugene and Gladys (Pionkowski) S. BS, Rutgers U., 1974; MS, Med. Coll. Pa., 1980; DMD, Temple U., 1984. Lic. dentist, Pa., N.J., Vt. Med. technologist Jersey Shore Med. Ctr., Neptune, N.J., 1975-76, South Amboy Meml. Hosp., 1976-78, Smith-Kline Clin. Labs., King of Prussia, Pa., 1981; instr. dept. biology St. Peter's Coll., Jersey City, 1976-78; instr., edn. coord. Coll. Allied Health, Hahnemann U., Phila., 1978-80; instr. dept. oral radiology Sch. Dentistry, Temple U., Phila., 1984-87; assoc. dentist Personal Choice Dental Assocs., South Amboy, 1985-86, Marcucci and Marcucci, P.C., Phila., 1986-90, Gwynedd Dental Assocs., Springhouse, Pa., 1990-92. Spl. events coord. Liberty Dental Conf., Phila., 1990—. Neighbor patrol Sprague St. Neighbors Town Watch, Phila., 1986-93. Named to Legion of Honor, Chapel of Four Chaplains, 1987. Mem. ADA, Pa. Dental Assn., Philadelphia County Dental Soc. (publicity coord. 1990—, pub. info. coord. 1991, semi-finalist judge sr. smile contest 1990—, com. on concerns of women dentists, select com. 1988—), Delaware Valley Assn. Women Dentists, Am. Assn. for Functional Orthodontics, Am. Soc. Clin. Pathologists (med. technologist), Kiwanis Club (pres. 2002—), Delta Sigma Delta. Roman Catholic. Avocations: reading, weight training, walking, sailing, dog training. Home: PO Box 386 Haddonfield NJ 08033-0310 Office: 777 White Horse Pike S Hammonton NJ 08037-2029

STEPHEN, ANNE DIIORIO, music educator; b. Trenton, N.J., July 30, 1952; d. Roland Joseph DiIorio and Mary Clementina Angelini; m. C. R. Stephen, Aug. 6, 1982; stepchildren: Daniel, Tim Stephen. BA, U. Nev., 1974, M of Music Edn., 1987. Music specialist Mabel Hoggard 6th Grade Ctr., Clark County Sch. Dist., Las Vegas, Nev., 1982—84; dir. choral studies Las Vegas H.S., Clark County Sch. Dist., 1984—. Part-time instr. music dept. U. Nev., Las Vegas, 2002; chair, co-chair honor choir Clark County Sch. Dist., Las Vegas, 1991—95, mem. curriculum com. for madrigals, 2000—01, choral clinician, adjudicator. Named Educator of Yr., Kiwanis Club, 1993, N.W. Chpt. Optimists, 2001, Disting. Tchr., White House Commn. on Presdl. Scholars, 1993. Mem.: Nev. Music Educators Assn. (chair, co-chair all-state choir 1998—2001, Nev. Music Educator of Yr. 2003), Am. Choral Dirs. Assn (chair for show and jazz choirs Nev. R&D 2001—, Nev. state treas. 1991—95), Las Vegas Philharmonic Chorus, Lamplight Carolers. Democrat. Roman Catholic. Avocations: golf, sailing, reading, singing, dance. Home: 10769 Hawes End Ct Las Vegas NV 89123 Office: Las Vegas HS 6500 E Sahara Ave Las Vegas NV 89142 Office Phone: 702-799-0180. E-mail: missanan@aol.com.

STEPHEN, DORIS MOYER, music educator; b. Buffalo, N.Y., Nov. 27, 1928; d. Arthur Burness and Helen May Moyer; m. Robert Mill Stephen Jr., Aug. 30, 1952 (dec. June 1999); children: Robert Mill III, Elizabeth Lynn Stephen Benck. Student, Bethany Coll., 1946-48, NYU, 1948-49. Piano tchr., Naperville, Ill., 1958-70, 91—. Editor (newspaper) Lake Wildwood Sunbeam, 1971-76; newswriter, reporter Naperville Sun, 1971-74; author of stories and poetry. Various positions ending with pres. LWV, Naperville, 1958-68. Mem. Music Tchrs. Assn. Republican. Methodist. Avocations: writing, painting, bridge, church, playing the piano. Home: 545 Juniper Dr Naperville IL 60540-7228

STEPHEN, ELIZABETH HERVEY, sociologist, educator; b. Fort Collins, Colo., Jan. 19, 1953; d. Donald Franklin Hervey and Bettie Culbertson Wilcox; m. Todd I. Malkoff, Nov. 24, 1990; 1 child, Anne Malkoff. BA, Colo. Women's Coll., 1975; MA, Georgetown U., 1982; PhD, U. Tex., Austin, 1985. Asst. prof. Georgetown U., Washington, 1987—93, assoc. prof., 1993—. Contbr. articles to profl. jours., 2000. Mem.: Population Assn. of Am. (sec.-treas. 1996—99). Democrat-Npl. Unitarian Universalist. Avocations: bicycling, quilting. Home: 10015 Leafy Ave Silver Spring MD 20910 Office: Georgetown Univ Sch of Fgn Svc ICC 301 Washington DC 20057 Business E-Mail: stepheel@georgetown.edu.

STEPHENS, ALICE ELIZABETH (ALICE WANKE STEPHENS), artist; b. Portland, Oreg., Feb. 2, 1926; d. A.E. and Elfrieda I. (Strauch) Wanke; m. Farrold Franklin Stephens, Feb. 2, 1950; children: Scott, Lynn, Todd. Student, Oreg. State U., 1944-46; BA, Stanford U., Palo Alto, Calif., 1948. Bd. dirs., cons. Wanke Cascade, Portland. Exhibited in numerous one-woman shows including Thor Gallery, Louisville, 1971, Unitarian Ch., Portland, 1976, George Fox Coll., Newberg, Oreg., 1987, Beaverton (Oreg.) Arts Commn., 1988, Clackamas C.C., Oreg. City, 1988, World Forestry Ctr., 1989, 94, 98, 99, World Forestry Ctr., 1998, 2002, West Hills Unitarian Fellowship, Portland, 1991, First United Meth. Ch., Portland, 1991, 2000, Japanese Garden Pavilion, Portland, 1991, Auditor's Office Portland City Hall, 1990, 95, Belinki DuPrey Art Gallery, 2002; represented at Rental Sales Gallery, Portland Art Mus., Belinki DuPrey Art Gallery. Mem. Oreg. Soc. Artists, Cap and Gown of Stanford U., City Club Portland, Pi Beta Phi. Democrat. Mem. Christian Ch. (Disciples Of Christ). Avocations: swimming, photography, choral singing, hiking. Home: 2323 SW Park Pl Apt 805 Portland OR 97205-1039

STEPHENS, B. CONSUELA, minister, consultant; b. Bklyn., May 12, 1947; d. Bernadine Whitley and Montiphus DeReyes Mortimer King. PhD in Religion, Clayton Theological Inst., 1983. Pastor Chenaniah Missionary Ch., Hollis, NY, 1986—. Cons. Chenaniah Missionary Ch., Hollis, United States, 1986—. Author: (book) Behold, I Shew You A Mystery, 1998. Dir. CASE Group, Inc., 2003—. Avocation: gardening. Home: 18625 Henderson Ave Hollis NY 11423-3132 Office: Chenaniah Missionary Ch 18625 Henderson Ave Hollis NY Office Phone: 212-412-7097. Business E-Mail: Consuela.Stephens@cwt.com. E-mail: earthling512@msn.com.

STEPHENS, BESS, computer company executive; Grad., Tuskegee Inst. Govt. and pub. affairs mgr. Hewlett Packard Co., human resources mgr., v.p. and global dir. philanthropy and edn., 2002—. Pres., exec. dir. Hewlett Packard Co. Found. Trustee Western Govs. U., Salt Lake City, Bay Area Sch. Reform Collaborative; mem. bd. fellows Santa Clara U., 1991—. Mem.: Nat. Bd. for Profl. Tchg. Stds. (bd. mem.), Gifts in Kind Internat. (bd. dirs.). Office: Hewlett Packard Co MS 1029 3000 Hanover St Palo Alto CA 94304

STEPHENS, BRENDA WILSON, librarian; b. Durham, N.C., Oct. 22, 1952; d. Leroy Thomas and Lucy Mae (Umstead) Wilson; m. Gregory Frederick Stephens, Mar. 6, 1977; children: Seth, Sara. Student, Vincennes U., 1970-71; BA, Winston-Salem State U., 1974; MLS, N.C. Cen. U., 1981. Cert. pub. libr., N.C. From bookmobile coord. to county libr. Orange County Pub. Libr., Hillsborough, N.C., 1976-92, regional libr. dir., 1992—. Sec. United Way of Greater Orange County, 1991—93; elected mem. Orange County Sch. Bd., 1998—, chair, 2001—03, vice chair, 2003—; sec. Lipscomb Bapt. Ch., 1998—2002. With U.S. Army, 1974—76. Mem.: ALA, N.C. Pub. Libr. Dirs. Assn. (officer, pres. 2001), N.C. Libr. Assn. (chair adult sect. 1987—93, co-chair 1985—87, lit. com. 1983—85), A.L. Stanback Mid. Sch. PTO (pres. 1991—92), Kiwanis Club (pres. 1992—93). Democrat. Baptist. Avocation: quilting. Home: 5807 Craig Rd Durham NC 27712-1008 Office: Orange County Pub Libr 300 W Tryon St Hillsborough NC 27278-2438

STEPHENS, CECILE HIGDON, artist; b. Linden, Ala., July 12, 1925; d. Cecil Rudolph and Mildred (Thomas) Hinson; m. William Travis Higdon, Jr., June 28, 1947 (div. Dec. 1971); children: William Travis III, Kent Thomas, Dean Gregory; m. John Pearson Stephens, June 29, 1973. BFA, Auburn U., 1968; MA, U. South Ala., 1971; 2d MA, U. Miss., 1976; postgrad., Nova U., 1973-80. Head art program, art instr. Miss. Gulf Coast C.C., Gautier, 1968-80; art instr. William Carey Coll., Gulfport, Miss., 1982-83. Art instr. U. So. Miss., Hattiesburg, 1968-73; juror and judge various art shows, 1975-85. Exhibited in solo shows at Birmingham So. U., 1960, Auburn U., 1968, La Font Gallery, Pascagoula, Miss., 1991, U. Miss., Oxford, 1994, Singing River Depot Gallery, Pascagoula, 1995, Eastern Shore Art Ctr., Fairhope Ala., 1995, Space 504 Gallery, N.Y.C., 1996, others; group shows include U. Ala., Tuscaloosa, Birmingham So. U., Biloxi (Miss.) Art Mus., Montgomery (Ala.) Mus. Art, Mobile (Ala.) Coll., Palais des Congres, Paris, Auburn U., U. So. Miss., Hattiesburg, James Russell Gallery, Gautier, Miss., Nat. Mus. of Women in the Arts, Washington. Mem. Rep. Women, Pascagoula, 1984-97; past state chmn., pres. gen.'s project DAR, Pascagoula, 1988-92, past regent, Pascagoula, 1988-92; v.p., bd. mem. cmty. concerts, Gautier, Pascagoua and Moss Point, Miss., 1986-90; ship christening com. mem. Ingalls Ship Bldg., Pascagoula, 1997; mem. adv. bd. Melange Dance Co., Pascagoula, 1995-97. Recipient Exemplary Achievement Alumna award Auburn U. Centennial of the Admission of Women, 1992, Unsung Hero's award Moss Point Miss. C. of C., 1996. Mem. Am. Soc. Portrait Painters, Washington Soc. Portrait Artists (charter), Nat. Mus. Women in the Arts (charter), Jackson County Arts Coun. (bd. mem.), Mobile Mus. Art, Ea. Shore Miss. Mus. Art, Walter Anderson Mus. Art (mem. adv. bd.). Episcopalian. Avocations: gardening, antique collecting, traveling. Home: 3855 River Rd Moss Point MS 39563-3711

STEPHENS, ELISA, college president; Pres. Acad. of Art Coll., San Francisco, 1992—. Office: 79 New Montgomery St 6th Fl San Francisco CA 94105-3410*

STEPHENS, GAY, human services executive; b. Aurora, Ill., Sept. 29, 1951; d. Benjamin Mark Jr. and Joyce Audrey (Sinclair) S. BA magna cum laude, George Williams Coll., 1973, MS summa cum laude, 1975. Clin. dir. Village of Downers Grove (Ill.) Dept. Health and Human Svcs., 1975—78; exec. dir. Villages of Bloomingdale (Ill.) Police Program, Bloomingdale, 1978—81, Family Support Ctr., Aurora, 1981—83; devel. dir. Family Svc. and Mental Health Ctr. of Oak Park, Ill., 1983—88; mgmt. cons. United Way Chgo., 1988—89; exec. Office Insp. Gen., Ill. Dept. Mental Health and Devel. Disabilities, Chgo., 1989—96, Ill. Dept. Pub. Aid, Chgo., 1996—98; dir. Little City Found., Palatine, Ill., 1998—2000; exec. dir. Rich Port YMCA, LaGrange, Ill., 2001—02, Stephens and Assocs., Geneva, Ill., 2002—. Mem. Unity Temple, 1998—; vol. Girl Scouts U.S. of DuPage County, Naperville, 1973-77; bd. dirs. Horizons, 1991-92. Mem. Women in Mgmt., Chgo. Area Runners Assn., Kappa Delta Phi. Democrat. Avocations: writing, cycling, running. Home: 740 Fox Run Dr Geneva IL 60134-2866

STEPHENS, HELEN JANSSENS, principal; b. Chgo., July 7, 1947; d. Albert Joseph and Lucille Catherine (Gietel) Janssens; m. James Richard Stephens, May 18, 1968; children: James Albert, Andrea Renée. Student, No. Ill. U., 1965-67; BA in Math., Northeastern Ill. U., Chgo., 1981; MEd, Loyola U., Chgo., 1991. Sec. ALD, Inc., Chgo., 1967-68; spl. typist Bankers Life & Casualty, Chgo., 1971-73; tchr. St. Edward Sch., Chgo., 1982-99; prin. St. Tarcissus Sch., Chgo., 1999—. Moderator St. Edward Student Coun., Chgo., 1989-99, handbook com., 1987; mem. Math. Curriculum Improvement Project, Chgo, 1986-89. Found. for Excellence in Teaching grant, 1988. Mem.: ASCD, Archdiocesan Prin.'s Assn., Am. Legion Aux., Nat. Cath. Edn. Assn., Nat. Coun. Tchrs. Math., Ill. Coun. Tchrs. Math., Phi Delta Kappa. Roman Catholic. Avocations: reading, collecting bells. Home: 3100 N Kilbourn Ave Chicago IL 60641-5364 Office: St Tarcissus Sch 6040 W Ardmore Ave Chicago IL 60646-5320

STEPHENS, MARTHA, retired psychiatrist; b. Phila., Feb. 21, 1927; d. Elmer Martin and Mary (Corwin) S. BA, Wells Coll.; MD, N.Y. Med. Coll.; MSc, Columbia U. Diplomate Am. Bd. Psychiatry and Neurology; diplomate Am. Bd. Pediat. Mem. Am. Psychiat. Assn., N.Y. State Med. Soc. Avocations: gardening, wood working, drawing.

STEPHENS, PATRICIA ANN, marketing professional; b. Gulfport, Miss., Feb. 1, 1945; d. James Marshall and Edna Mathilda (Hogan) Stephens. BA, St. Louis U., 1967; MA, Memphis State U., 1971. Lic. secondary educator speech, theatre, English, religion. Exec. v.p. Prodns. Unltd., Memphis, 1971-73; chairperson speech dept. Southaven (Miss.) HS, 1973-77; instr. speech N.W. Jr. Coll., Southaven, 1974-76; pub. rels. dir., instr. St. Agnes Acad., Memphis, 1977-78; religion and English instr. Memphis Cath. HS, 1978-82; resource tchr. comm. Mobile (Ala.) City Schs., 1982-84; mktg. devel. specialist/mktg. mgr. Prime Health Ala., Mobile, 1984-85; mktg. mgr. Blue Cross Blue Shield Fla./Health Options, Lakeland and Orlando, Fla., 1986-92; ind. agt., 1992-94; nat. mktg. and svc. coord. Delta Care, PMI, Tampa, Fla., 1994—2002, dir. account svcs. eastern region, 2002—. Speech instr. Keiser Coll., Lakeland, Orlando. Bd. dirs. Red Balloon Players, Memphis, 1971—73, Cir. Playhouse/Playhouse on the Sq., Memphis, 1980—82, WIFS Ctrl. Fla., 2002—. Recipient Pres.'s Club BCBSF/Health Options Sales Mgr. award, Health Options Polk County, 1987; Wall St. Jour. Newspaper Fund fellow, U. Oreg., 1968, Writing fellow, Memphis State U., 1980, Part-Time Masters fellow, 1981—82. Democrat. Roman Catholic. Home: 4128 Sunny Land Dr Lakeland FL 33813-3946 Office: Delta Dental Ins Co Ste 350 258 Southhall Ln Maitland FL 32751-7427

STEPHENS, SALLIE L. retired assistant principal, commissioner; b. Crawfordville, Ga., May 23, 1931; d. Columbus and Bertha (Swain) Stephens; 1 child, Marilyn E. BA in Elem. Edn., Clark Coll., 1954; MS, Nova Southeastern U., 1975, EdD, 1998. Tchr. elem. sch. Broward County Sch. Dist., Ft. Lauderdale, Fla., 1954—78, asst. prin., 1978—2001. City commr. City of Miramar, Fla., 1999—, vice mayor, 1999—; vol., mentor Broward County Sch. Dist., 2002—. Mem.: Miramar Pembroke C. of C. (bd. dirs. 1982—), Phi Delta Kappa (bd. dirs. 1995—). Democrat. Baptist. Avocations: golf, dance. Home: 2740 Huron Way Miramar FL 33025 Office: City of Miramar 6700 Miramar Pkwy Miramar FL 33023

STEPHENS, SARA CECILE, music educator; b. Cleve., Ohio, Sept. 13, 1974; d. Norman Roland and Lillian Dean Selinas; m. Corey Jamal Stephens, June 12, 1999; children: Brandon Jamal, Jordan Emmanuel. BS in Music Edn., Tenn. State U., 1997; MME, Ind. State U., 1999. Dir. bands Head Magnet Sch., Nashville, 1999—2000, Kendrick Mid. Sch., Jonesboro, Ga., 2000—, chmn. Dept. Fine Arts, 2001—. Leadership team mem. Kendrick Mid. Sch., 2001—. Mem.: MENC, Ga. Music Educators Assn., Ga. Educators Assn. Avocation: flute. Home: 1589 Bonanza Church Rd Jonesboro GA 30238

STEPHENS, WANDA BREWER, social services administrator, investor; b. Bolckow, Mo., Nov. 6, 1932; d. Perry Clark and Mary Carolyn (Fisher) Brewer; m. Lloyd Wesley Stephens, June 19, 1954; children: Ruth Ann, Susie Jo, John Allen, Donna Lynn. BS in home econs., U. Ark., 1954, MS, 1958. Cert. secondary edn. Home economics tchr. West Fork (Ark.) High Sch., 1954-58; pres. Devel. Child Care Assn., Fayetteville, Ark., 1971-74; pres., founding bd. Infant Devel. Ctr., Fayetteville, Ark., 1972-75, treas., 1975-81; edn. chmn., fin. com., admin. bd. Cen. United Meth. Ch., Fayetteville, Ark., 1976-79; pres. League of Women Voters, Fayetteville, Ark., 1979-83, Nat. Orgn. Women, Fayetteville, Ark., 1983-89; state legis. v.p. NOW, Fayetteville, 1985-90, 93-98; state pres. Nat. Orgn. Women Ark., Fayetteville, 1991-93, 98—. Bd. sec., headstart, Econ. Opportunity Agy., Fayetteville, 1969-70; treas. Mama's Mink Investment Club, 1970-72. Co-author: Bylaws for Economic Opportunity Agy., 1969; co-editor: Washington County, Ark., 1982. Fundraiser United Fund, 1972-75; polit. organizer NOW, 1986; treas. Washington County Dem. Women, 1990-92; organizer/staff/fund Women's Libr., 1982-91, 99-2000; cons./organizer Ctrl. Child Care Ctr., 1977-78. Recipient Internat. 4-H Youth Exch., 1953-54, Infant Devel. Ctr. Founders Plaque Univ. Ark., 1987; Fayetteville Women's History honoree, 2001; named Lay Person of Yr., Ctrl. United Meth. Ch., 1977. Mem. Mental Health Assn. (Cmty. Svc. award 1972), AAUW (pres. Fayetteville 1975-77, state treas. 1996-2000, Edn. Found. fellow 1984), ACLU (Susan B. Anthony award 1985, Disting. Svc. award 1999), Ark. Women's Polit. Caucus (Uppity Woman award 1987, 92). Democrat. Methodist. Avocations: genealogy, reading, investing. Home: 1177 E Ridgeway Dr Fayetteville AR 72701-2612 Personal E-mail: wandasteph@aol.com.

STEPHENSON, DOROTHY GRIFFITH See GRIFFITH, DOTTY

STEPHENSON, HELENE RUTH, painter, consultant; b. Phila., Aug. 6, 1926; d. Eugene Frank and Ida Gertrude (Loeffert) Schweitzer; m. Robert Louis Stephenson, June 12, 1948; children: John, Wayne, Cynthia. Diploma, Phila. Coll. Art, 1948. One-woman shows include Woodmere Art Mus., Phila., 1976, Gallery 500, Elkins Park, Pa., 1983, 91, Toro Gallery, Huntingdon Valley, Pa., 1998; exhibited in group shows Woodmere Art Mus., 1966, 81, Allentown (Pa.) Mus., 1977, Tel-Aviv Mus., 1978, Pa. State Mus., Harrisburg, 1992, others; represented in permanent collections Wills Eye Hosp., Anheuser-Busch, Bryn Mawr Coll., American Design, Ltd., others. Pres., dir. Old York Rd. Art Guild, Alverthorpe, Abington, Pa.; bd. dirs. Woodmere Art Mus.; recording sec. Artists' Equity, Phila. Mem. James Michener Art Mus., Woodmere Art Mus. Avocations: gardening, needlepoint. Home: 1501 County Line Rd Huntingdon Valley PA 19006-1406

STEPHENSON, IRENE HAMLEN, biorhythm analyst, consultant, editor, educator; b. Chgo., Oct. 7, 1923; d. Charles Martin and Carolyn Hilda (Hilgers) Hamlin; m. Edgar B. Stephenson, Sr., Aug. 16, 1941 (div. 1946); 1 child, Edgar B. Author biorhythm compatibilities column Nat. Singles Register, Norwalk, Calif., 1979-81; instr. biorhythm Learning Tree Open U., Canoga Park, Calif., 1982-83, instr. biorhythm personality analysis, 1980—, instr. biorhythm compatibility, 1982—; owner, pres. matchmaking svc. Pen Pals Using Biorhythm, Chatsworth, Calif., 1979—. Editor newsletter The Truth, 1979-85, Mini Examiner, Chatsworth, 1985—; rschr. biorhythm personality and compatibility, 1974—, biorhythm columnist Psyhic Astrology Horoscope, 1989-94, True Astrology Forecast, 1989-94, Psychic Astrology Predictions, 1990-94, Con Artist Types, 1995, Pedophile (child molester) Types, 1995-2000, Personality Types, 1996, Trouble-Addict (Suicide) Types, 1997, Domineering/Nag Types, 1998, Con Artists, Sweetheart Swindlers, Super Con Artist Types, 1998, Bully types, 2000, Deadly Compatibility Combination, 2000, Fatal Attraction Types, 2000, Sadism, Sadistic, Sadistic Predators, 2000, Salesperson, Practical Joker Types, 2000, Doormat Types, 2000, Famous/Queen Bee/Rescuer Types, 2000, Prostitution, 2000. Author: Learn Biorhythm Personality Analysis, 1980, Do-It-Yourself Biorhythm Compatibilities, 1982; contbr. numerous articles to mags. Office: PO Box 3893 Chatsworth CA 91313-3893

STEPHENSON, JANE CONNELL, artist, educator; b. Ruston, La., Feb. 23, 1932; m. Alvis Doyle Stephenson, June 28, 1957; children: John Thomas, Deborah Lynn, Mary Elizabeth, Ann Lidell. BA, La. Tech. U., 1953; degree in art edn., U. Colo., 1955. Art instr. Clarksdale (Miss.) Ind. Sch. Dist., Clarksdale; art tchr. Dallas Ind. Sch. Dist., 1955—58; designer Atelier Stephenson, Dallas, 1977—85; artist Artisan Studio, Dallas, 1989—99; asst. masterclass figure La. Tech. U., Ruston, 1989—95; faculty art North Lake Coll. Continuing Edn., Dallas, 1983—93; faculty art dept. Creative Art Ctr., Dallas, 2001—. Leader drawing tours, The Netherlands, Belgium, France, 1992, 93, 94, 95, 96, 98, 99, Italy, 99. Exhibitions include Am. Artist Mag., 1999, Tex. Watercolor Commemorative, 1997, Watercolor without Boundaries, Tex. and Italy, 2001, exhibitions include (donations) Dallas Shelter for Battered Women, 2002, exhibitions include Dallas Garden Ctr. Calendar, 1996—98, Found. Fighting Blindness, 1990, 1991, 1992, 1994, Truing Art Ctr., 1992, Goodrich Gallery, 2001, one-woman shows include, Dallas area, Represented in permanent collections Jackson Art Mus. Named one of Nation's Top 50 Experimental Artists, Artist Mag., 1991; recipient Exxon Mobile Award of Excellence, Tex. Neighbors Exhibit, 2002. Mem.: Irving Art Assn. (recipient over 150 awards in 200 nat. exhbns.), Nat. Women's Mus. Washington, Nat. Watercolor Soc. Calif. (signature mem.), Watercolor Soc. Miss. (signature mem.), Watercolor Soc. La. (signature mem.), Watercolor Soc. Tex. (signature mem.), Okla. Watercolor Soc., Western Fedn. Watercolor Socs., Southwestern Art Soc. (signature mem., bd. dirs.), Tex. Visual Art Assn. (signature mem., bd. dirs., show chmn.). Avocations: travel, music, anthropology, gardening, reading. Home: 3524 Northaven Rd Dallas TX 75229

STEPHENSON, JANE ELLEN, educational association administrator; b. Banner Elk, N.C., Apr. 2, 1938; d. Braxton Leo and Mary Helen (Barlow) Baucom; m. John Bell Stephenson (dec. 1994); children: Jennifer Stephenson McLamb, Rebecca, David. AA, Lees McRae Coll., 1957; BS in Secretarial Adminstrn./Edn., U. N.C., Greensboro, 1959; MA in Bus. Edn., Appalachian State U., 1962; MS in Higher Edn. Adminstrn., U. Ky., 1976; Doctorate (hon.), Berea Coll., 1995. Acad. intern continuing edn. U. Ky., Lexington, 1977, coord. student svcs., 1978-80, dir. acad. support svcs., 1980-83, dir. human rels. ctr., 1983-84; exec. dir. Berea (Ky.) C. of C., 1988-89; found., dir. New Opportunity Sch. for Women, Berea, 1987—. Asst. prof. bus. and econs. Berea Coll., fall 1987. Author: (book) Courageous Paths: Stories of Nine Appalachian Women, 1995. Bd. dirs. Berea Hosp., 1985—, Mountain Assn. for Comty. Econ. Devel., 1995-96, Ky. Nat. Identification Program for Advancement of Women in Higher Edn. Adminstrn., 1984-86; mem. adv. bd. Ency. of Appalachia, 1996—; vol. coord. Berea Forum, 1985-95; mem. adv. bd. Ea. Ky. Women's Leadership, 1996—; mem. Leadership Madison County, Richmond, Ky., 1988; mem., bd. dirs. Ky. Women's Leadership Network, Lexington, 1993; chairperson state adv. bd. Elderhostel, 1987-94; mem. Foster Care Rev. Bd., 1990-91; commr. Ky. Commn. on Women, 1993-97, Ky. Appalachian Commn., 1995—; Appalachian dir. Steele-Reese Found., 1997—. Recipient Woman Advocate for Women award Women Mean Bus. Conf., 1996, Anderson medal Commonwealth of Ky., 1991, Women of Achievement State and Local award Bus. and Profl. Women Ky., 1988; named Citizen of Yr., Berea Lions Club, 1989. Mem. AAUW (Women as Agts. of Change award 1990), LWV. Presbyterian. Avocations: reading, piano. Home: 3121 Grantham Way Lexington KY 40509-2373 Office: New Opportunity Sch for Women 204 Chestnut St Berea KY 40403-1538

STEPHENSON, NANCY LOUISE, medical products company professional; b. Bemidji, Minn., Nov. 7, 1945; d. Raymond Julian and Dorothy Marion Stephenson. BSN, Pacific Luth. U., 1972. RN, Wash., Minn. ICU/CCU nurse various hosps., Tacoma and Mpls., 1967-72; instr. med. nursing Luth. Deaconess Hosp., Mpls., 1972-73; clin. rsch. assoc. Medtronic, Mpls., 1973-76, clin. evaluation mgr., 1976-82, sr. clin. evaluation mgr., 1982-86, mgr. physicians rels., 1986-98, dir. physician rels., 1998—. Vol. Big Bros./Big Sisters Am., St. Paul, 1978-82; bd. dirs. Sight and Hearing Assn., Mpls., 1998—, Heartbeat Internat., Tampa, 2000—. Mem. N.Am. Soc. Pacing and Electrophysiology, Am. Heart Assn. Coun. Cardiovasc. Nursing, Am. Coll. Cardiology (corp. liaison bd. mem. 1996-2002, 50th Anniv. com. 1998-99), Order of Eastern Star. Democrat. Methodist. Avocations: travel, reading, writing, poetry. Home: 4895 Kent Dr Saint Paul MN 55126-2073 Office: Medtronic USA Inc 7000 Central Ave NE Minneapolis MN 55432-3576

STEPHENSON, VIVIAN M. former retail executive; B Math., NYU; MBA, U. Havana. Mgmt. positions Rand Info. Sys., Occidental Petroleum Corp., Assoc. Credit Burs. Svcs., Inc.; dir. info. sys. devel. Mervyn's, 1989-90, v.p. MIS, 1990-94, sr. v.p., 1994-95; sr. v.p., chief info. officer Dayton Hudson Corp., Mpls., 1995-2000; exec. v.p., chief info. officer Target Corp., Mpls., —2000; ret., 2000. Bd. dirs. MobiNetrix Sys. Inc.; mem. info. sys. customer adv. coun. IBM; mem. Tandem Americas Customer Coun. Chair bd. dirs. San Francisco AIDS Found.; mem. Nat. Retail Fedn. Info. Sys. Bd. Mem. Calif. C. of C. Office: Target Corp 1000 Nicollet Mall Minneapolis MN 55403-2467

STEPP, CATHY, state senator; b. Aug. 17, 1963; married. Supr., New Home Consultants First Stepp Builders, Inc., Racine, Wis.; state sen. Wis. State Senate, Madison, 2002—. 3-time judge Met. Milw. Area Parade of Homes; chair Parade of Homes, 1998—99; apptd. dept. natural resources bd. former Gov. Tommy Thompson, 2000—; bd. dirs. Girl Scouts of Racine County. Mem.: Wis. Builders Assn. (bd. dirs. 1996—), Racine-Kenosha Builders Assn. (pres. 1998—99, past sec.), Nat. Assn. Home Builders (bd. dirs. 1999—). Office: State Capitol Rm 7 S PO Box 7882 Madison WI 53u70-7882

STEPP, LAURA SESSIONS, journalist; b. Ft. Smith, Ark., July 27, 1951; d. Robert Paul Sessions and M. Rae Barnes; m. Carl Sessions Stepp; children: Ashli, Amber, Jeffrey. BA, Earlham Coll., 1973; MA, Columnia U., 1974. Reporter Palm Beach Times, West Palm Beach, Fla., 1974; MA Columbia U., Phila., 1975; projects editor The Charlotte (N.C.) Observer, 1979-81, asst. editorial page editor, 1981-82; Md. editor The Washington Post, 1982-86, religion editor, 1987-92, writer Style sect., 1992—. Bd. advisors U. Md. Casey Journalism Ctr. Children and Families, College Park. Recipient Nat. Reporting award Religion Writers Am., Feature Writing award AAUW, 1994. Mem. Investigative Reporters and Editors (bd. dirs. 1986-90). Office: Washington Post Co 1150 15th St NW Washington DC 20071-0002

STEPS, BARBARA JILL, lawyer; b. Springfield, Mo., June 19, 1945; d. Louis Edward and Margaret Pearl (Stiver) Bredeman; m. Robert William Steps, Dec. 21, 1968; children: Rebecca Harper, Aaron Andrew, Jessica Anne. BA in Psychology, St. Louis U., 1966; JD, U. Mo., 1969; MBA, U. Conn., 1983. Atty. Ralston Purina Co., St. Louis, 1969; law clerk U.S. Dist. Ct., St. Louis, 1969-72; assoc. Stone, Keck & Staser, Evansville, Ind., 1973-75, Cline & Callahan, Indpls., 1975-77, Law Office, Herbert V. Camp, Ridgefield, Conn., 1978-81; from comml. counsel to corp. counsel, sec. Framatome Connectors USA, Inc. (now FCI USA, Inc.), Fairfield, Conn., 1981-93; v.p., counsel, sec. FCI USA, Inc. (formerly Framatome Connectors USA, Inc.), Etters, Pa., 1993—2002, sr. v.p. adminstrn., counsel, sec., 2002—. Mem.: ABA, Am. Corp. Counsel Assn. Home: 23 Emlyn Ln Mechanicsburg PA 17055-8017 Office: FCI USA Inc 825 Old Trail Rd Etters PA 17319-9392

STEPTOE, MARY LOU, lawyer; b. Washington, July 15, 1949; d. Philip Pendleton and Irene (Hellen) S.; m. Peter E. Carson, Sept. 1986; children: Elizabeth Maud, Julia Grace. BA, Occidental Coll., 1971; JD, U. Va., 1974. Bar: Va., 1974, Supreme Ct., 1987, D.C. 1996. Staff atty., Bur. of Competition FTC, Washington, 1974-79, atty. advisor to commr., 1979-86, exec. asst. to chmn., 1988-89, assoc. dir., Bur. of Competition, 1989-90, dep. dir., 1990-92, acting dir., 1992-95, dep. dir., 1995-96; ptnr. Skadden Arps Slate Meagher & Flom LLP, Washington.

STERKOVSKY, JULIA ELLEN, activist, organizer; b. Toledo, Ohio, Aug. 30, 1960; D. William Thomas and Jacquelyn Agnes (Swick) Lester; m. Brian Keith Culkowski Sterkovsky, Feb. 11, 1984. BA in Psychology, U. Toledo, 1982; MA in Social Scis., U. Chgo., 1986. Patient advocate, trainer Ctr. for Choice II, Toledo, 1986-88; dir. Collingwood Springs Redevel. Corp., Toledo, 1986-88, Coalition for People, New Haven, Conn., 1988-89; vol. coord. Anawim Homeless Shelter for Men, New Haven, Conn., 1990; organizational facilitator Domestic Violence Tng. Project, New Haven, 1990-91; dir. New Haven Women's Liberation Ctr., 1989-91, Women's Ctr. Miami U., Oxford, Ohio, 1991-96. Student cons. Dwight Hall at Yale U., New Haven, 1990; faculty cons., Winona (Minn.) State U. Women Studies, 1994; cons. Fla. Internat. U., 1994-95, Wright State U. Women's Ctr., Dayton, Ohio, 1995-96; instr. U. Wash. Associated Student's Exptl. Coll., 1997—; propr. Woven Gloaming, 1997—; founding mem. tryptos studio collective; instr. fusion beads Loom Weaving of Beads: Design and Practice, 1998-99; presenter confs. on women's issues and social change, 1992—. Dir. Seattle Human Svcs. Coalition, 1998—; founding mem. King County Alliance for Human Svcs; mem. Ind. Sector's Nat. Working Group on Human Svcs. and Social Change, 2004; mem. Steering Com., Human Svcs. and Housing, 2003. Named Hon. Woman of Color, Creative Women's Collective, New Haven, Conn., 1991; recipient Lila Wallace Internat. Artist's award, Lila Wallace Reader's Digest, N.Y.C., 1994, Disting. Svc. award, Miami U. Ctr. for Black Culture, Oxford, Ohio, 1995, Alumna Achievement award U. Toledo, 1995. Mem. AAUW, NOW, Nat. Assn. Women in Edn., Juno Network (founding mem.), Butler County Alliance for Women (founding mem., steering com.), Nat. Assn. Women's Ctrs. (internal coord. 1992-94, officer). Avocations: reading, gardening. Studio: 5227 Leary Ave NW Apt 405 Seattle WA 98107-4829 E-mail: sterkovsky@yahoo.com.

STERLING, CHARLOTTE B. hotel executive; b. San Francisco, June 2, 1946; d. Robert and Lee Butler; m. James Campbell Sharf; children: Elizabeth, Stephanie. AA, BA, Stephens Coll., Columbia, Mo.; MA in Journalism, U. Mo. Journalist Bolivar (Mo.) Herald Free Press, 1967-73; v.p. mktg. svcs. Hill & Knowlton, Washington, 1973-83; v.p. pub. affairs Fannie Mae, Washington, 1984-96; exec. v.p. comms. Marriott Internat., Washington, 1996—. Bd. dirs. Fed. City Coun., Washington, 1998—, Studio Theatre, Washington, 1995. Mem. Press Club (bd. dirs. Washington chpt. 1985), Econs. Club (bd. dirs. Washington chpt. 1998—). Avocation: painting. Office: Marriott Internat Marriott Dr Washington DC 20058-0001

STERLING, JENNIFER ELIZABETH, application developer, educator; b. Portsmouth, Va., May 16, 1975; d. Richard Allen Sterling, Linda Crowe Sterling. MusB, Meredith Coll., 1997; M in Music Tech., U. Tenn., 1999; PhD, U. Md., 2002. Tchg. asst. Meredith Coll., Raleigh, NC, 1995—97; grad. tchg. asst. U. Tenn., Knoxville, 1997—99; instr. U. Md., College Park, 1999—2002; lectr. Ind. U., Purdue U., Indpls., 2002—. Mentor Ctr. Tchg. Excellence, College Park, 2000—01. Author: (software) Voice Leading, 1999, Inform, 2001; singer: Nat. Chamber Singers, 2000, Md. Chamber Singers, 2001, Indpls. Symphonic Choir, 2002—. Campus min. REACH, Raleigh, 1995—97; tchr. Laurel (Md.) Ch. of Christ, 1999—2001, South Ctrl. Ch. of Christ, 2003—. Recipient Silver Shield Leadership award, Meredith Coll., 1996, Tchg. Excellence award, IUPUI, 2003; grantee Sariff Rsch., U. Tenn., 1998, SBC Ameritech, 2003—; scholar Theodore Presser, Meredith Coll., 1996. Mem.: Assn. Tech. Music Instrn., Soc. Music Theory, Coll. Music Soc., Phi Kappa Lambda, Sigma Alpha Iota (v.p. 1996—99, Sword of Honor, Leadership 1996, 1999). Avocations: singing, travel, tennis, hiking. Office: IUPUI Sch Music 525 N Blackford St Indianapolis IN 46202 Office Phone: 317-278-4138. Business E-Mail: jensterl@iupui.edu.

STERLING, LORRAINE, volunteer; b. So. Norwalk, Conn., Apr. 22, 1923; d. Edward and Irene Terris; m. Alvin Sterling, Nov. 11, 1946 (dec. Jan. 1981); children: Richard, Kenneth, Glenn. BA, Bklyn. Coll., 1945. From bd. adv. to v.p. trustees Nassau County Mus., Roslyn, NY, 1986—90, v.p. trustees, 1990—91. Artists expn. Fashion Inst. Tech., N.Y.C., 1994—96; design cons. Lisette Lingerie, N.Y.C., 1970—80, Sterling Sophisticates, N.Y.C., 1982—87. Bd. dir. L.I. Opera Co., L.I., NY, 1991—93; mem. fin. bd. Nassau C.C., N.Y.C., 1993—94. Mem.: Lake Success Club, Boca West Club. Home: 4 Lakeview Drive Great Neck NY 11020 also: 20031 Waters Edge Cir Boca Raton FL 33434

STERLING, SARAH L. archaeologist, educator; b. Portland, Oreg., Apr. 12, 1964; d. Donald J. and Julie C. Sterling. BA, Barnard Coll., N.Y., 1987; MA, U. Wash., Seattle, Wash., 1995; PhD, U. Wash., Seattle, 2004—. Lectr. Portland State U., Portland, Oreg., 2000—. Editor: (book) Posing Questions for a Scientific Archaeology; contbr. articles to profl. jour. Niles Fellowship, U. Wash., 1997-1998. Mem.: Am. Rsch. Ctr. in Egypt, Soc. of Am. Archaeology. Democrat-Npl.

STERLING, SHIRLEY FRAMPTON, artist, educator; b. L.A., Oct. 9, 1920; d. James Alexander and Elizabeth Mary (Herman) F.; m. Edwin Leigh Sterling, Mar. 26, 1942; children: Michael Leigh, Marianne. BA, Occidental Coll., 1942; postgrad., La. Tech. U., 1979-89. Cert. tchr. Tchr., Glendale, Calif., 1942-45; artist, tchr. Watercolor Art Soc., Houston, Pasadena, Kemah, Tex., 1973—. Lectr., demonstrator various art socs. Active as Gray Lady Internat. Red Cross, Wiesbaden, Fed. Republic Germany, 1960-61, Honolulu, 1968-69. Mem. Nat. Watercolor Soc.(elected signature mem.), Knickerbocker Artists, Southwestern Watercolor Soc., Tex. Watercolor Soc. (Patron of Arts award), So. Watercolor Soc., Watercolor Art Soc.-Houston, Western Fedn. Watercolor Soc., Phi Beta Kappa. Republican. Home: 4011 Manorfield Dr Seabrook TX 77586-4209

STERN, ARLENE HELEN, human resources specialist; b. Bklyn., Nov. 7, 1950; d. Irving and Shirley Judith (Koretz) Stern. BS in Labor Rels., U. Bridgeport, 1971; postgrad., Pace U., 1972—75. From Pers. asst. to dir. human resource planning Pathmark, Woodbridge, NJ, 1971—77, dir. pers. and labor rels. Phila., 1977—81; v.p. human resources Howland-Steinbach-Hochschild's, White Plains, NY, 1981—85; sr. v.p. human resources and distbn. P.A. Bergner & Co., Milw., 1985—89, exec. v.p. human resources and distbn., 1989—. Mem. Frederick Atkins Pers. Adv. Bd., NYC, 1981—86, chmn., 1984. Women's divsn. Wis. State of Israel Bonds, 1988, Milw. Jewish Fedn., 1987—, Milw. Jewish Coun., 1987—; bd. dirs. Clavis Theatre, 1986—. Mem.: ASTD, Am. Soc. Pers. Adminstrs. Home: 628 West Rd New Canaan CT 06840-2513 Office: Gantos Inc Soundview Plz 1266 E Main St 5th Fl Stamford CT 06902

STERN, EDITH LOIS, counselor, hypno-therapist; b. Paterson, N.J., Apr. 20, 1928; d. Meyer Zenack and Helen Rebecca (Jarvis) Zenack-Kollin; m. Eugene Stern, June 23, 1949 (div. Dec. 1978); children: Michael, Jonathan, Andrew. BA in Edn., Bklyn. Coll., 1949; MS in Counseling, C.W. Post U., 1971. Cert. counselor, N.Y. Tchr. Pub. Sch. 70, Bklyn., 1949-53; counselor Jericho (N.Y.) H.S., 1972, Farmingdale (N.Y.) H.S., 1973, 75, Uniondale (N.Y.) H.S., 1974; dir. New Directions, Massapequa, N.Y., 1971-91. Mem. adv. bd. Mid-Queens Cmty. Coun., Jamaica, N.Y., 1957-64, Peacesmith's, Inc., Massapequa, 1972-75, Nassau Women's Polit. Caucus, Mineola, 1973-80; dir. Kaplan Meml. Libr., Mineola, N.Y., 1968-80; counselor Nassau County CETA, Hempstead, N.Y., 1977-81; tax agt. N.Y. State Dept. Taxation, Hempstead, 1982-92. Editor (editl.) Temple Judea Newsletter, 1967. Pres. PTA Pub. Sch. 165, Flushing, N.Y., 1962-64; committeewoman Nassau County Dem., Massapequa, 1965-85; campaign mgr. Krupsak for Lt. Gov., Nassau County, 1974. Mem. NOW, Am. Pers. and Guidance Assn., Am. Assn. Ret. Persons, N.Y. State Ret. Pub. Employees Assn., Hawaiian Gardens Women's Club (v.p. 1995-97, pres. 1997-99), Ilana Hadassah (corr. sec. 1995-97, pres. 1997—). Jewish. Avocations: reading, attending the theatre, writing. Home: Apt D210 5041 W Oakland Park Blvd Fort Lauderdale FL 33313-1517

STERN, GAIL FRIEDA, historical association director; b. Atlantic City, May 18, 1950; d. Herbert and Faith (Beldegreen) Stern; m. Irwin Allen Popowsky (div.); m. Shawn Paul Aubitz (div.); 1 child, Jonathan. Student, Brown U., 1972; postgrad., U. Pa., 1973. Asst. in decorative arts Phila. Mus. Art, 1972-75; asst. curator Wheaton Mus. Glass, Millville, N.J., 1973-74; assoc. dir. Pa. Humanities Coun., Phila., 1976-79; mus. curator The Balch Inst. for Ethnic Studies, Phila., 1979-83, mus. dir., 1984-93; dir. Hist. Soc. Princeton, N.J., 1993—. Chair Pa. Task Force on Folk Arts and Culture, 1981-82; vice chmn. crafts panel Pa. Coun. on the Arts, Harrisburg, 1988-89; chair cultural conservation com., Pa. Heritage Affairs Commn., Harrisburg, 1990-92; participant Internat. Partnership in Mus., Singapore, 1991. Recipient pub. programming award, NJ Coun. Humanities, 1996, award for outstanding contbns. to NJ history, NJ Hist. Commn., 1999. Mem. Mus. Coun. Phila. (v.p. 1982-83), Am. Assn. Mus./Internat. Coun. Mus. (bd. dirs. 1991-97), N.J. Mus. Assn. (bd. dirs., sec. 1993-98, John Cotton Dana award 2000), Am. Assn. for State and Local History Awards (N.J. chair 1994-95, 2002-03), Mid-Atlantic Assn. Mus. (bd. dirs. 1997-98). Home: 41 Lafayette Street Hopewell NJ 08525 Office: Hist Soc Princeton 158 Nassau St Princeton NJ 08542-7006 E-mail: gailfstern@aol.com.

STERN, GRACE MARY, former state legislator; b. Holyoke, Mass., July 10, 1925; d. Frank McLellan and Marguerite M. (Nason) Dain; m. Charles H. Suber, June 21, 1947 (div. 1959); children: Ann, Peter, Thomas, John; m. Herbert L. Stern, May 13, 1962; stepchildren: Gwen, Herbert III, Robert. Student, Wellesley Coll., 1942-45; LLD (hon.), Shimer Coll., 1984. Asst. supr. Deerfield Twp., Lake County, Ill., 1967-70; county clk. Lake County, Ill., 1970-82; mem. Ill. Ho. of Reps., Springfield, 1984-92, Ill. State Senate, 1993-95. Author: With a Stern Eye, 1967, Still Stern, 1969. Candidate lt. gov. State of Ill., 1982. Democrat. Presbyterian. Home: 140 S Dearborn St Ste 1400 Chicago IL 60603-5208

STERN, JOAN NAOMI, lawyer; b. Phila., Mar. 7, 1944; d. Clarence J. and Diana D. (Goldberg) S. BA, U. Pa., 1965; JD, Temple U., 1977. Bar: Pa. 1977. Assoc. Blank, Rome LLP, Phila., 1977—83, ptnr., 1983—, co-chair pub. fin. group, 1983-92, chair pub. fin. group, 1993, chair pub. fin. dept., 1994—. Cons. counsel Phila. Charter Commn., 1993-94. Contbr. articles to profl. jours. Mem. Sch. Dist. Task Force on Regulatory Reform, Phila., 1987, Tax Policy and Budget Com., Phila., 1989, Phila. Mayor's Fiscal Adv. Com., 1990; chair Sch. Dist. of Phila. Task Force on Alternate Financing Strategies, 1995; bd. mgrs. Moore Coll. Art and Design, Phila., 1993—, vice chair bd. trustees, bd. mgrs., 1995—; bd. dirs. Police Athletic League, Phila., 1994—, Jewish Fedn. of Greater Phila., 2000—, Am. Jewish Congress, 1995—, Urban Tree Connection, 2000—, Mother Bethel Found., 2002—; bd. trustees The Franklin Inst., 2004—. Fellow Am. Bar Found. (life); mem. ABA, Nat. Assn. Bond Lawyers, Phila. Bar Assn., Phila. Bar Assn. (chmn. mcpl. govt. com. 1983-97), Pa. Assn. Bond Lawyers. Office: Blank Rome LLP One Logan Square Philadelphia PA 19103-6998 E-mail: stern@blankrome.com.

STERN, JUDITH SCHNEIDER, nutritionist, researcher, educator; b. Bklyn. d. Sidney and Lillian (Rosen) Schneider; m. Richard C. Stern; 1 child, Daniel Arthur. BS, Cornell U., 1964; MS, Harvard U. Sch. Pub. Health, 1966, ScD, 1970. Rsch. asst., dept. food sci. and nutrition MIT, Cambridge, 1964-65; rsch. assoc. dept. human behavior and metabolism The Rockefeller U., N.Y.C., 1969-72, asst. prof. dept. human behavior and metabolism, 1972-74; contbg. editor Vogue Mag., Conde Nast Publs., N.Y.C., 1974; asst. prof. nutrition U. Calif., Davis, 1975-77, assoc. prof. dept. nutrition, 1977-82, dir. food intake lab. group, 1980—2001, prof. dept. nutrition, 1982—, prof. divsn. endocrinology, clin. nutrition and vascular biology, 1988—, disting. prof., 2003—. Mem. editl. bd. Internat. Jour. Obesity, 1976-85, Appetite, 1990, Obesity Rsch., 1993—, Nutrition Today, 1999—. Bd. sci. advisors Am. Coun. Sci. and Health, 1980—; mem. U.S. Dept. Agr. Dietary Guidelines Adv. Com., 1983—85; mem. obesity task force NIDDK, 1996—2002, AAAS; mem. expert com. U.S. Pharmacopeia Bioavailability and Nutrient Absorption, 2000—; mem. adv. bd. USDA Nat. Agrl. Rsch. Ext., Edn. and Econs., 2000—03. NIH tng. grant, 1979—. Fellow Am. Heart Assn.; mem. Am. Soc. Clin. Nutrition (pres. 1995-96), Am. Dietetic Assn., Am. Diabetic Assn., Am. Obesity Assn. (v.p. 1995), N.Am. Assn. for Study of Obesity (pres. 1992-93), Inst. Medicine NAS, Inst. Food Technologists, Am. Soc. Nutrition Sci. (chair pub. info. com. 1992-94), Sigma Xi, Delta Omega. Office: U Calif Dept Nutrition 1 Shields Ave Davis CA 95616-5271 Office Phone: 530-752-6575. E-mail: jsstern@ucdavis.edu., sternhome@aol.com.

STERN, LYNN SOLINGER, photographer; b. N.Y.C., Mar. 31, 1942; d. David Morris and Hope Alva (Gimbel) Solinger; m. Robert A. M. Stern, May 22, 1966 (div. 1977); 1 child, Nicholas; m. Jeremy Pollard Lang, Dec. 3, 1980. BA cum laude, Smith Coll., 1964. Apprentice editor Ross-Gaffney Films, N.Y.C., 1965-66; photographic archivist Stern & Hagmann Archs., N.Y.C., 1968-77; photographer N.Y.C., 1978—. Author, photographer: Unveilings, 1989, Dispossession, 1995 (Ernst Haas award 1995), Animus, 2000. Mem. nat. coun. Environ. Def. Fund, N.Y.C., 1991—; dir. Bernard F. and Alva B. Gimbel Found., 1988—; bd. advisors Nat. Abortion and

Reproductive Rights Action League, N.Y.C., 1997—. Democrat. Home and Office: 101 Central Park W New York NY 10023-4204

STERN, MADELEINE BETTINA, rare books dealer, author; b. N.Y.C., July 1, 1912; d. Moses Roland and Lillie (Mack) S. BA, Barnard Coll., 1932; MA, Columbia U., 1934. Tchr. English N.Y.C. High Schs., 1934-43; ptnr. Leona Rostenberg Rare Books, N.Y.C., 1945—, Leona Rostenberg and Madeleine B. Stern Rare Books, N.Y.C., 1980—. Lectr. history of book, feminism, pub. history, lt. Author: We Are Taken, 1935, The Life of Margaret Fuller, 1942, Louisa May Alcott, 1950, new edit., 1996, Purple Passage: The Life of Mrs. Frank Leslie, 1953, Imprints on History: Book Publishers and American Frontiers, 1956, We the Women: Career Firsts of Nineteenth Century America, 1962, new edit., 1994, So Much in a Lifetime: The Story of Dr. Isabel Barrows, 1965, Queen of Publishers' Row: Mrs. Frank Leslie, 1966, The Pantarch: A Biography of Stephen Pearl Andrews, 1968, Heads and Headlines: The Phrenological Fowlers, 1971, Books and Book People in 19th-Century America, 1978, Antiquarian Bookselling in the United States: A History from the Origins to the 1940s, 1985, Nicholas Gouin Dufief of Philadelphia Franco-American Bookseller, 1776-1834, 1988, The Life of Margaret Fuller: A Revised Second Edition, 1991, Louisa May Alcott: From Blood & Thunder to Hearth & Home, 1998; (with Leona Rostenberg) Old and Rare: Forty Years in the Book Business, 1974, rev. edit. 1988, Between Boards: New Thoughts on Old Books, 1978, Bookman's Quintet: Five Catalogues about Books, 1980, Quest Book-Guest Book: A Biblio-Folly, 1993, Connections: Our Selves-Our Books, 1994, Old Books in the Old World: Reminiscences of Book Buying Abroad, 1996, Old Books, Rare Friends: Two Literary Sleuths and Their Shared Passion, 1997, New Worlds in Old Books, 1999, Books Have Their Fates, 2001, Bookends: Two Women, One Enduring Friendship, 2001, From Revolution to Revolution: Perspectives on Publishing and Bookselling, 2002; editor: Women on the Move, 4 vols., 1972, Victoria Woodhull Reader, 1974, Louisa's Wonder Book-An Unknown Alcott Juvenile, 1975, Behind a Mask: The Unknown Thrillers of Louisa May Alcott, 1975, new edit., 1995, Plots and Counterplots: More Unknown Thrillers of Louisa May Alcott, 1976, Publishers for Mass Entertainment in 19th-Century America, 1980, A Phrenological Dictionary of 19th-Century Americans, 1982, Critical Essays on Louisa May Alcott, 1984, A Modern Mephistopheles and Taming a Tartar by Louisa May Alcott, 1987, Louisa May Alcott Unmasked: Collected Thrillers, 1995, Modern Magic by Louisa May Alcott, 1995, The Feminist Alcott: Stories of a Woman's Power, 1996, Louisa May Alcott: Signature of Reform, 2002; co-editor: Selected Letters of Louisa May Alcott, 1987, A Double Life: Newly Discovered Thrillers of Louisa May Alcott, 1988, The Journals of Louisa May Alcott, 1989, Louisa May Alcott: Selected Fiction, 1990, (co-editor) Freaks of Genius: Unknown Thrillers of Louisa May Alcott, 1991, From Jo March's Attic: Stories of Intrigue and Suspense, 1993 (Victorian Soc. award), The Lost Stories of Louisa May Alcott, 1995. Guggenheim fellow, 1943-45; recipient Medalie award Barnard Coll., 1982, Victorian Soc. award, Disting. Alumna award Barnard Coll., 1997. Mem. Antiquarian Booksellers Assn. Am. (gov. 1966-68, 78-80), Internat. League Antiquarian Booksellers, MLA, Am. Printing History Assn. (co-recipient award 1983), Authors League, Manuscript Soc. (former trustee), Phi Beta Kappa. Jewish. Home: 40 E 88th St New York NY 10128-1176

STERN, MARCI ANN, English educator; b. Plainview, N.Y., May 27, 1968; d. Jeffrey Ellner and Janet (Zeichner) Stark; m. David Emanuel Stern, Aug. 13, 1995; children: Mitchell Ethan, Nina Simone. BA in English Lit., SUNY, New Paltz, 1990; MS in English Edn., L.I. U., 1996. Retail asst. mgr. Merry Go Round Enterprises, Woodbridge, N.J., 1990; graphic artist Getting To Know You, Westbury, N.Y., 1991-92; adminstrv. asst. data mgmt. FI Serv, Melville, N.Y., 1992; photographer, studio mgr. Moto Photo, Inc., New Hyde Park, N.Y., 1992; pub. rels. asst. Sumner Rider & Assoc. Inc., N.Y.C., 1992-93; pub. rels. mgr. adminstrv. asst. Greenville Baker Boys and Girls Club, Locust Valley, N.Y., 1993; English educator Commack (N.Y.) Mid. Sch., 1995, Dawnwood Mid. Sch., Centereach, NY, 1995—2001, dir. musical theatre, 1995—2001, John H. Glenn HS, Elwood, NY, 2003—; ind. beauty cons. Mary Kay Cosmetics, 2002—. Cons. computers in edn., 1995-96, coord. spelling bee, 1995-96; soprano Northport (N.Y.) Chorale, 2001—; music libr., bd. dir., 2001—. Letter writing campaign organizer Commack Mid. Sch., 1995; actor, singer Glen Players, Glen Cove, N.Y., 1993. Mem. Nat. Coun. of Tchrs. of English (local pub. rels. rep. 1995—), Internat. Reading Assn., Libr. of Congress, Internat. Soc. of Poets. Democrat. Jewish. Avocations: singing, computers, movies, cats, writing. Office: Dawnwood Middle Sch 10 43rd St Centereach NY 11720-2325

STERN, MARGARET BASSETT, retired special education educator, author; b. Bklyn., June 6, 1920; d. Preston Rogers and Jeanne (Mordorf) Bassett; m. Fritz R. Stern Oct. 11, 1947 (div. Dec. 1992); children: Frederick Preston, Katherine Stern Brennan. BA, Wellesley Coll., 1942; MEd, Bank Street Coll. Edn., N.Y.C., 1943, MEd, 1974. Propr. Castle Sch., N.Y.C., 1944-51; dir. Mothers' Coop. Nursery Sch., Ithaca, N.Y., 1952-54; tchr. sci. and math. The Brearley Sch., N.Y.C, 1956-57. Cons., lectr. Head Start, Tuskegee, Ala., 1964; cons. in math. The Gateway Sch., N.Y.C., 1967-90; spl. lectr. Columbia U. Tchrs. Coll., N.Y.C., 1990-94; condr. workshops in Eng., 1960-88. Author: (with Catherine Stern and Toni Gould) Structural Reading Program, Workbooks and Teachers Guides A through E, 1963, 3d edit., 1978, Structural Arithmetic Workbooks and Teachers Guides Grades 1-3, 1965, 2d edit., 1966, (with Stern) Children Discover Arithmetic, 1971, (with Gould) Spotlight on Phonics, Four Workbooks and Teachers Guides, 1980, Sound/Symbol Activities and Decoding Activities, 1980, 2d edit., 1994; Experimenting with Numbers, 1988, Structural Arithmetic, 1-3, 1992. Recipient award, Orton Dyslexia Soc. N.Y., 1989, Bank St. Coll. Edn., 1998. Mem.: Nat. Coun. Tchrs. Math., Internat. Dyslexia Assn. Home: 3204 River Crescent Dr Annapolis MD 21401

STERN, MARILYN, photographer, writer, picture editor; b. Detroit, Nov. 8, 1953; d. Julian and Phyllis Stern. BA, Brown U., 1976. Photographer's asst., N.Y.C., 1976-82; freelance photographer, 1976—; freelance writer, 1985—; picture editor Across the Board mag., N.Y.C., 1990-96; tchr. Internat. Ctr. of Photography, 2001. Photographer, organizer: (book) Masked Culture: The Greenwich Village Halloween Parade, 1994; author, photographer: Kval! Die Walfänger der Lofoten, 1990; solo exhbns. Profil Gallery, Bratislava, 2001, Scandinavia House, N.Y.C., 2003; several group exhbns., 1976--; represented in permanent collection Detroit Inst. Arts, also numerous pvt. collections. Travel Study grantee Royal Norwegian Consulate to Norway in the U.S., 1987, Am.-Scandinavian Found., 1986.

STERN, PAULA, international trade advisor; b. Chgo., Mar. 31, 1945; d. Lloyd and Fan (Wener) Stern; m. Paul A. London; children: Gabriel Stern London, Genevieve Stern London. BA, Goucher Coll., 1967; MA in Middle Eastern Studies, Harvard U., 1969; MA in Internat. Affairs, MA in Law and Diplomacy, Fletcher Sch. of Law and Diplomacy, 1970, PhD, 1976; D Comml. Sci. (hon.), Babson Coll., 1985; LLD (hon.), Goucher Coll., 1985. Legis. asst., sr. legis. asst. to U.S. Sen. Gaylord Nelson U.S. Senate, Washington, 1972—74, 1976; guest scholar Brookings Inst., Washington, 1975-76; policy analyst Pres. Carter-V.P. Mondale Transition Team, Washington, 1977-78; internat. affairs fellow Council on Fgn. Relations, Washington, 1977-78; commr. U.S. Internat. Trade Commn., Washington, 1978-87; chairwoman Internat. Trade Commn., Washington, 1984-86; sr. assoc. Carnegie Endowment for Internat. Peace, Washington, 1986-88. Howard W. Alkire chair internat. bus. and econs. Hamline U., 1994—2000; chairwoman Stern Group, Inc., 1988—; bd. dirs. Avaya, Inc., Avon Products, Inc., Hasbro, Inc., Neiman Marcus Group; mem., sr. advisor U.S. Trade Policy Coun. Competition Policy Inst., 1991—93; sr. fellow Progressive Policy Inst., 1994—95; pub. vice chairwoman Atlantic Coun. U.S.; trustee Com. Econ. Devel.; mem. Inter-Am. Dialogue, Coun. Fgn. Rels.; past co-chair Internat. Competition Adv. Com.; past chair antitrust div. U.S. Dept. Justice; past chair U.S. Exp. Bank; past mem. U.S. Pres. Adv. Com. on Trade Policy and Negotiation; bd. dirs. Carnegie Coun. Ethics and Internat. Affairs. Author: Water's Edge--Domestic Politics and the Making of American Foreign Policy, 1979; contbg. author newspapers; contbr. articles to profl. jours. Democrat. Jewish. Avocations: sculpting, tennis, dance. Office: 3314 Ross Pl NW Washington DC 20008-3332 Office Phone: 202-966-7894. E-mail: pstern@sterngroup.biz.

STERN, ROSLYNE PAIGE, magazine publisher; b. Chgo., May 26, 1926; d. Benjamin Gross and Clara (Sniderman) Roer; m. William E. Weber, May 3, 1944 (div. Mar. 1956); m. Richard S. Paige, June 28, 1958 (div. Apr. 1978); children: Sandra Weber Porr, Barbara Paige Kaplan, Elizabeth Paige (dec.); m. Robert D. Stern, June 5, 1978. Cert., U. Chgo., 1945. Profl. model, singer, 1947-53; account exec. Interstate United, Chgo., 1955-58; sales mgr. Getting To Know You Internat., Great Neck, N.Y., 1963-71, exec. v.p., 1971-78; pub. After Dark Mag., N.Y.C., 1978-82; assoc. pub. Dance Mag., N.Y.C., 1978-85, pres., pub., 1985—2001, pres. emeritus, 2001—. Bd. dirs. Rudor Consol. Industries, Inc., N.Y.C., AGC/Sedgwick, Inc., Princeton, N.J. Founding pres. Dance Mag. Found., N.Y.C., 1984-86 chmn. Dance Mag. awards, 1986-; life mem. nat. women's com. Brandeis U., Waltham, Mass., 1958—; bd. dirs. Westport Arts Ctr.; The Internation Com. for Dance Libr. of Israel. Recipient Disting. Svc. award Dance Notation Bur., 1996, Am. Coll. Dance Festival award, 1998, Pres.'s award Dance Masters of Am., Inc., 1998, Documents of Dance award Dance Library of Israel, 1999. Mem. Pub. Relations Soc. Am., LWV, Am. Theatre Wing, Nat. Arts Club. Democrat. Jewish. Avocations: dance, theater, opera, visual arts, travel. Home: 2 Imperial Lndg Westport CT 06880-4934 Office: 60 W 66th St Ste 26A New York NY 10023

STERN, RUTH SZOLD, business executive, artist; b. Bronx, N.Y., Oct. 14, 1929; d. Albert and Margaret (Karl) Nussbacher; m. Martin Szold, Apr. 10, 1949 (div. Sept. 1978); children: Lauren, Terry; m. James C. Stern, Aug. 22, 1982. Student, Hunter Coll., N.Y.C., 1947; cert. in writing, UCLA, 1988; BFA, Calif. Inst. Arts, 1994, MFA, 1996. Exec. legal sec. to sr. ptnr. Paul, Weiss, Rifkind, Wharton & Garrison, N.Y.C., 1958-62; asst. to pres. M.E. Green & Co. brokerage, N.Y.C., 1962-65; demonstrator, cons. various cosmetic cos., 1965-85; founder, pres. Ruth Szold Promotional Models, 1968-84, Cosmetic Art, Inc., 1979-85, founder, pres., designer, promoter cosmetic line, 1979-85; columnist Fire Island News, Ocean Beach, N.Y., 1985-89; asst. to pres., CEO Gladden Entertainment, L.A., 1989-90; exec. adminstr. C&O Cogent Light and Techs., 1990-91. Demonstrator-lectr. for TV, also videotapes; condr. cosmetic workshops for N.Y. Salute to Fashion Industries, 1981; chmn. earthquake com. Fountainview Assn., 1989-98, bd. dirs., 1997-98; cons. in field; tchr. art to homeless Found. House, West Hollywood, Calif., 2000. One-woman shows include Fire Island Transmission, 1997; group exhbns. include SPLICE Side St. Projects, Santa Monica, Calif., 1997-98, 5th Ann. Miracle on 18th St. Side St. Projects, Santa Monica, 1997, (videos) Mel and Alice's Wedding 1950, 2000, Santa Barbara Contemporary Arts Forum, 2002, others, (edible books) Occidental Coll., 2002, (armory N.W. installation) "24 Hours", Pasadena, Calif., 2004; N.Y.C. Internat. Film & Video Fest. "Mel & Alice's Wedding", W. Hollywood, 2004. Mem. coun. Girl Scouts U.S.A., 1964-69; bd. dirs. Bleecker Tower Tenants Corp., N.Y.C., 1979-80, chmn. architecture and design com., 1979-80, chmn. maintenance, 1980-85, pres., 1981-82; mem. Hunger Project, Fin. Family; lectr., panelist Am. Women's Econ. Devel. Corp., 1981; nom. bd. dir. alumni assn., Calif. Inst. of the Arts, 2002. Recipient gold medal Deborah Fund Raising Dinner, 1955, others. Mem. Foragers of Am., Nat. Retail Mchts. Assn., Fragrance Found., Cosmetic Exec. Women, Brandeis U. Club, Hadassah Club. Home: 1414 N Harper Ave Ste 3 West Hollywood CA 90046

STERNBERG, ESTHER MAY, neuroendocrinologist, immunologist, rheumatologist; b. Montreal, May 9, 1951; came to U.S., 1980, naturalized, 1991; d. Joseph and Ghitta (Wexler) Sternberg; 1 child, Penny Rebecca Herscovitch. BSc with great distinction, McGill U., 1972, MD, 1974. Diplomate Nat. Bd. Med. Examiners; lic. physician, Can., Mo. Intern Royal Victoria Hosp./McGill U., Montreal, 1974-75, resident II in medicine, 1977-78, clin. fellow rheumatology, 1978-79, clin. and rsch. fellow rheumatology, 1979-80; gen. practice medicine Mount Royal, Que., 1975-77; rsch. assoc. divsn. allergy/clin. immunology Washington U., St. Louis, 1981-83, rsch. assoc. Howard Hughes Med. Inst., 1983-84, assoc. Howard Hughes Med. Inst., 1984-86, instr. divs. rheumatology, 1984-86; attending physician Barnes Hosp., St. Louis, 1984-86; tenured sr. scientist NIMH/NIH, Bethesda, 1991—, med. officer, chief unit on neuroendocrine immunology, 1991-95, assoc. br. chief clin. neuroendocrinology br., 1994-2000, med. officer, chief sect. neuroendocrine immunology, 1995—, dir. integrative neural-immune program, 1999—. Vis. scientist Nat. Inst. Arthritis Musculoskeletal and Skin Disease, NIH and head Inter-Inst. Unit on Neuroendocrine Immunology and Behavior, NIMH and Nat. Inst. Arthritis, Musculoskeletal and Skin Diseases, Bethesda, 1989-90; rsch. full prof. Am. U., Washington, 1995—; temporary advisor WHO, 1991; ad hoc mem. NIH/NIMH/Libr. Congress Human Genome Project liaison com., 1990-91; invited expert CDC, Atlanta, 1989-93; spl. cons. Inst. Health (Hygienic) Scis., Min. of Health, Japan, 1992-94; med. adv. bd. Scleroderma Fedn., 1993-95; cons. John D. and Catherine T. MacArthur Found. Network on Mind-Body Interactions, 1994—; participant WHO/Pan Am. Health Orgn. Collaborating Ctr. for Health of the Elderly Work Group meeting, 1995; mem. com. on military nutrition rsch. Inst. of Medicine of NAS, 1998—; advisor Nat. Libr. of Medicine Planning Com., Breath of Life: An Exhbn. on Asthma, 1997-98, NIMH/NIH Ctr. for Sci. Rev., 1998; reviewer FDA's Office of Women's Health, 1998; co-dir. Exhibition on Emotions and Disease Nat. Libr. Medicine, 1996-97, others; dir. NIMH Program on Integrative Neural-Immune, 1999—; co-chair/chair/organizer numerous confs. Author: The Balance Within. The Science Connecting Health and Emotions; edtl. bd. Brain, Behavior and Immunity, Jour. Neuroimmunology, Neuroimmunomodulation, Molecular Psychiatry, Immunologic Rsch.; invited guest series editor Jour. Clin. Investigation, 1997; reviewer Jour. Clin. Investigation, New Eng. Jour. Medicine, Jour. Immunology, Endocrinology, Jour. Clin. Endocrinology and Metabolism, Arthritis and Rheumatism, Am. Jour. Physiology, Jour. Neuroimmunology, Brain, Behavior and Immunity; editor: Stress: Mechanisms and Clinical Implications, 1995, Neuroimmune Interactions: Molecular, Integrative Systems and Clinical Implications, 1998; assoc. editor Brain, Behavior and Immunity, Neuroimmunomodulation; contbr. chpts. to books and articles to profl. jours.; patentee in field. Recipient Arthritis Found. Met. Washington William R. Felts award for excellence in rheumatology rsch. pubs., 1991, FDA's Commr.'s Spl. Citation, 1991, USPHS Surgeon Svc. award, 1994; McGill U. scholar, 1967-68, 68-71; Am. Acad. Allergy/Schering Travel grantee, 1982, United Scleroderma Found. grantee, 1985-86, 86-87, Scleroderma Found. Greater Washington, 1987, 88; NIH New Investigator awardee, 1985-88, others. Fellow Am. Coll. Rheumatology; mem. AAAS, Soc. Neurosci., Am. Soc. Clin. Investigation, Am. Assn. Immunologists, N.Y. Acad. Scis., Can. Med. Assn., Internat. Soc. Neuroimmunology (mem. internat. adv. com. 1995), PsychoNeuroImmunology Rsch. Soc. (councillor 1997—), Soc. for Neuroimmunomodulation (sec. 1997-99, pres. 1999—). Office: NIMH/NIH Bldg 10 10 Center Dr MSC-1284 Bethesda MD 20892-1284 Fax: 301-496-6095. E-mail: ems@codon.nih.gov.

STERNHAGEN, FRANCES, actress; b. Washington, DC, Jan. 13, 1930; Student, Vassar Coll., Perry-Mansfield Sch. Theatre; studied with Sanford Meisner, NY. Tchr. Milton Acad., Cath. U. Ams., Mass.; actress Arena Stage, Washington, DC, 1953-54. Debut Thieves Carnival, NY, 1955; plays include The Carefree Tree, The Admirable Bashville (Clarence Derwent award, Obie award), Ulysses in Night Town, Red Eye of Love, Misalliance, The Return of Herbert Bracewell, Laughing Stock, The Displaced Person, The Pinter Plays (Obie award); Broadway shows include The Skin of Our Teeth, Viva Madison Avenue, Great Day in the Morning, The Right Honorable Gentleman, The Cocktail Party, Cock-a-Doodle Dandy, Playboy of the Western World, The Sign in Sidney Brustein's Window, The Good Doctor (Tony award 1973), Equus (Drama Desk award), Angel, On Golden Pond (Drama League award), The Father, Grownups, Summer, You Can't Take It With You, Home Front, Driving Miss Daisy, Remembrance, A Perfect Ganesh, The Heiress (Tony award 1995), Long Day's Journey into Night, 1998, The Exact Center of the Universe, 1999, Morning's at Seven, 2003; actress (films) Up The Down Staircase, 1967, Starting Over, 1979, Outland, 1981, Independence Day, 1983, Romantic Comedy, 1983, Bright Lights, Big City, 1988, See You in the Morning, 1989, Communion, 1989, Misery, 1990, Doc Hollywood, 1991, Raising Cain, 1992, Curtain Call, Land Fall, 1997, The Rising Place, 1998; (TV series) Love of Life, The Doctors, Secret Storm, Cheers, Golden Years, Under One Roof, The Road Home, E.R., Sex and the City; (TV movies) Who Will Save Our Children?, 1978, Prototype, 1982, Resting Place, 1986, Follow Your Heart, 1990, She Woke Up, 1992, Labor of Love: The Arlette Schweitzer Story, 1993, Reunion, 1994, Tales from the Crypt, Outer Limits, Law and Order, 1990, 96, The Con, 1997, To Live Again, 1997, New York: A Documentary Film, 1999, The Laramie Project, 2001.*

STERN-LAROSA, CARYL M. advocate, educational association administrator; BA in Studio Art, SUNY, Oneonta; MD in Student Personnel Adminstrn., We. Ill. U.; postgrad., Loyola U. Dean students Polytecn. U.; former sr. mgmt. World of Difference Inst., 1991, former dir. spl. tng. program, dir.; dir. edn. divsn. Anti-Defamation League. Nat. chairperson Nat. Assn. Campus Activites; former chairperson Boroughof Bklyn. Unity Task Forcce. Co-author: Future Perfect: A Model for Professional Development. Recipient Founder's award, Nat. Assn. Campus Activities, 1992, Borough of Bklyn. Unity award, Borough of Queen's Citation for Contbn. to Racial and Religious Harmony, Oneonta Alumni Recognition award, SUNY, Alumni Achievement award, We. Ill. U., Senn award for profl. excellence. Office: Anti-Defamation League 823 United Nations Plz New York NY 10017

STETTER, AIMEE RAE, finance company executive; b. Huntingburg, Ind., Aug. 24, 1976; d. William Oscar and Marcia Kaye Stetter. BS, Ind. State U., Terre Haute, 1998. CLU Am. Coll., 2003. Fin. bus. analyst State Farm Ins. Co., Bloomington, Ill., 1998—2001. Mem.: Soc. of Fin. Svc. Professionals (assoc.), Ind. State U. Alumni Assn., Alpha Kappa Psi, Gamma Iota Sigma. Home: 3251 Chelmsford Dr Lafayette IN 47909 Office: State Farm Ins 2550 Northwestern Av West Lafayette IN 47906

STEVENS, ANNE BICKETT PARKER, architectural designer; b. Marshville, N.C., Dec. 25, 1921; d. Benjiman Carl and Rosa Mae (Blakeney) Parker; m. Jack Elmer Stevens, Mar. 31, 1945 (dec.); children: Susan, Barbara, Martha. Student, U. N.C., Greensboro, 1938—40, Syracuse U., 1940—42; BArch, Columbia U., 1945; postgrad., U. N.C., 1971—75. Archtl. draftsman J.N. Pease & Co., Charlotte, NC, 1942, draftsman, 1944, So. Mapping and Engr., Greensboro, NC, 1943, Charles and Edward Stotz, Pitts., 1945—51; ptnr. Jack E. Stevens Builder, Pitts., 1951—68, Chapel Hill, 1969—74, Charlotte, NC, 1975—77, Pinehurst, NC, 1978—82; pvt. practice Parker Stevens Builder, Pinehurst, 1983—84, Anne P. Stevens Builder, Surf City, NC, 1984—2001; ret. Avocations: art, painting. Home: Apt 2 14482 Tramore Dr Chesterfield MO 63017

STEVENS, BARBARA HELEN, economist; b. Ft. Knox, Ky., Mar. 24, 1952; d. Edgar C. and Marguerite Florence (Nordberg) S.; m. Michael Kent Robertson, June 16, 1973. BA, So. Ill. U., 1974; MA, No. Ill. U., 1977. Coord. natural resources Ill. Dept. Transp., Springfield, 1985-88, socio-economic analyst, 1989-92, socio-economic specialist, 1993—. Adj. faculty St. Mary of the Woods (Ind.) Coll., 1982-84; rsch. panel mem. Transp. Rsch. Bd., Washington, 1992, 95; peer review com. Fed. Hwy. Adminstrn., Washington, 1993, mem. cmty. impacts rsch. steering com., 1998. Co-author: Community Impact Assessment, 1996. Mem. AAUW, Am. Econ. Assn., Midwest Econs. Assn. Home: 2250 N 400 East Rd Rochester IL 62563-8102 Office: Ill Dept Transp 2300 S Dirksen Pkwy Springfield IL 62764-0001

STEVENS, CHERITA WYMAN, social sciences educator, writer; b. Erick, Okla., Jan. 12, 1938; d. Forrest Clarence and Wilma Peter Wyman; m. Paul Donald Stevens, May 30, 1958 (div. Nov. 10, 1978); children: Paul McDonald, Mark Liu. BA in Social Sci., Phillips U., 1961; MA in Sch. Law and Fin., Calif. State U., LA, 1976; cert. in ESL, U. Calif., LA. Adminstrv. credential K-12 and adult; LA, Calif. Cashmere Sch. tchr. grades 7-9 South Pasadena (Calif.) Unified, 1966—74; assoc. regional pastor Disciples of Christ, Pacific Southwest, 1976—82; computer store owner Claremont (Calif.) Computer, 1982—87; tchr., prinl. Cabrillo Unified Sch. Dist., Half Moon Bay, Calif., 1987—97; ESL computer lab. media instr. Chapman Edn. Ctr., Garden Grove, Calif., 1997—2004. Legis. intern Calif. State Assembly, Sacramento, 1978—80; fin. analyst Primerica Life/Citigroup, Orange, Calif., 2000—04; grant reviewer U.S. Dept. Edn., Washington, 2002. Editor: Direction Newspaper, 1976—82; author: (software) Apartment Maintenance, 1988, Grants Tracking, 1989, Financial Management, 1991 (articles) to newspapers, mags., (book lab curriculum, 500 pages) Curriculum and Lesson Plans for the Independent Learning Lab, 1995; designer: lesson plan OTAN Website, 2003; contributor KOCE (PBS) Schoolhouse Video Project, 2004. Mem. Ams. for Dem. Action, Pasadena, 1963—80; civil rights activist, 1960—69; organizer first Martin Luther King Jr. celebration in U.S., 1972; active First Christian Ch., Orange, 1963—2002, Pasadena, Calif. Grantee Consortium grant adult edn., Calif. Dept. Edn./Joint Partnership Training Act, Half Moon Bay, 1996. Mem.: Assn. Calif. Sch. Adminstrs. (site rep. 1993—97). Avocations: golf, photography, genealogy. Home: 401 W La Veta Ave #220 Orange CA 92866

STEVENS, CHRISTINE TREML, music educator; b. Akron, Ohio, Apr. 9, 1952; d. Joseph Stephen Treml and Patricia Ann Blazey; m. William T. Stevens, May 24, 1975; 1 child, Anne Kathleen. BS in Music Edn., U. Akron, 1974. Vocal music tchr. Barberton Pub. Schs., Ohio, 1975—78, Columbus Southwestern City Schs., 1980—87; vocal, instrumental music tchr. Shaler Area Schs., Glenshaw, Pa., 1988—. Founding mem., co-dir. Young String Players Club, Pitts., 2001—; sch. rep. Meet the Composer, Pitts., 2001—04; dir. sch. musicals Shaler Area Schs., Glenshaw, 1996—; dir. All-Star Band Shaler Mid. Sch., 1995—. Grantee, Shaler Area Sch. Dist., 2002—04. Avocations: musical programs, movies. Home: 117 Windgate Dr Wexford PA 15090 Office: Shaler Area Middle Sch 700 Scott Ave Glenshaw PA 15116

STEVENS, CONNIE, actress, singer; b. Bklyn., Aug. 8, 1938; d. Peter and Eleanore (McGinley) Ingolia; m. Maurice Elias; m. Edwin Jack Fisher (div.); children: Joely, Tricia Leigh. Pres. Forever Spring Cosmetics; founder Windfeather Foundation. Show bus. debut as vocalist with, The Three Debs, Hollywood, at age 16; appeared in: Finians Rainbow for Hollywood Repertory Co.; numerous motion pictures, including Way, Way Out, Scorchy, Eighteen and Animals, Young and Dangerous, Drag Strip Riot, Rock-a-bye Baby, Parish, Susan Slade, Palm Springs Weekend, The Grissom Gang, Never Too Late, Grease II, 1983, Back to the Beach, 1987, Bring Me the Head of Dobie Gillis, 1988, Love Is All There Is, 1996; starred in TV series Wendy and Me and TV series Hawaiian Eye, 1959-62, Head Over Heals, 1997, Titus, 2000-02, TV films for ABC-TV Movie-of-the-Week; Call Her Mom, 1972, Playmates, Mister Jericho, Cole Porter in Paris, The Sex Symbol, 1974, Starting From Scratch, 1988, James Dean: Live Fast, Die Young, 1997; guest star on TV with, Bob Hope, Red Skelton, Englebert Humperdinck, Tom Jones, Perry Como and Laugh-In; TV appearance comedy spl. Harry's Battles; headliner at Flamingo Hotel, Las Vegas, also, Hilton Internat., Sands Hotel, Desert Inn, Aladdin, MGM, Sahara, 1969-76; stage appearances include The Wizard of Oz at Carousel

Theatre in So. Calif., Any Wednesday at Melodyland, Anaheim, Calif.; made Broadway debut in Star Spangled Girl, 1967; accompanied Bob Hope around world on his Christmas tour, 1969, Persian Gulf Christmas tour, 1987; dir., prodr., writer, editor, cinematographer: A Healing, 1997 (Santa Clarita Internat. Film Festival Award, 1998); created line of cosmetics called Forever Spring and opened the Garden Sanctuary day spa in Los Angeles Bd. dirs. Ctr. for Plastic and Reconstructive Surgery, South Vietnam. Recipient Lady of Humanities Award, Shriners Hospital, 1991, Humanitarian of the Year, Sons of Italy, 2001, Distinguished Civilian Service Medal, 2002.

STEVENS, DIANA LYNN, elementary school educator; b. Waterloo, Iowa, Dec. 12, 1950; d. Marcus Henry and Clarissa Ann (Funk) Carr; m. Paul John Stevens; 1 child, Drew Spencer. BS, Mid Am. Nazarene Coll., 1973; M in Liberal Arts, Baker U., 1989. Elem. tchr. Olathe (Kans.) Sch. Dist. #233, 1975—. Artwork appeared in traveling exhibit ARC/Nat. Art Edn. Assn., 1968, Delta Kappa Gamma Bull., 2001. Pres. Artists' League, Olathe, 1990—. Olathe Sch. Dist. Action grantee, 1996-97. Mem. NEA, Kans. Edn. Assn., Olathe Edn. Assn. (social com.), Nat. Art Edn. Assn., Delta Kappa Gamma (profl. affairs com. mem.), Coll. Ch. of the Nazarene. Avocations: portrait art, reading biographies, power walking, exhibiting artwork. Home: 217 S Montclaire Dr Olathe KS 66061-3828

STEVENS, DOROTHY FROST, retired television producer; b. Rockville Centre, N.Y., June 18, 1924; d. George Sanford Frost and Theodora Barbara Emmanuel; m. Kenneth Hayes Stevens, Aug. 14, 1949 (dec. Apr. 1967). BA, Stanford U., 1945. Tchr. adult edn., San Jose, 1946—49; tchr. Los Gatos H.S. Dist., Calif., 1946—51; various positions Calif. State. E.D.D., 1956—82; host, prodr., exec. prodr. Cupertino (Calif) Sr. TV Prodns., 1983—2001, ret., 2001. Prodr.: The Better Part, 1983—2001. Named Vol. of Yr., Retired Sr. Vol. Program Santa Clara County, 1994; recipient Civic Svc. award, City of Cupertino, 1984, Vol. award, Calif. Parks & Recreation Soc., 1988, Golden Rule award, J.C. Penney, 1993, Outstanding Prodr. award, City of Cupertino, 1997, Ripp King Meml. award, Bay Area Cable Excellence, 1998. Presbyterian. Avocations: travel, reading, sewing, gardening. Home: 15243 Clydelle Ave San Jose CA 95124

STEVENS, ELISABETH GOSS (MRS. ROBERT SCHLEUSSNER JR.), writer, journalist, graphic artist; b. Rome, N.Y., Aug. 11, 1929; d. George May and Elisabeth (Stryker) Stevens; m. Robert Schleussner, Jr., Mar. 12, 1966 (dec. 1977); 1 child, Laura Stevens BA, Wellesley Coll., 1951; MA with high honors, Columbia U., 1956. Editl. assoc. Art News Mag., 1964-65; art critic and reporter Washington Post, Washington, 1965-66; freelance art critic and reporter Balt., 1966—; contbg. art critic Wall Street Jour., N.Y.C., 1969-72; art critic Trenton (NJ) Times, 1974-77; art and architecture critic The Balt. Sun, 1978-86; critic-at-large Madyradio.com, 2004—. Author: Elisabeth Stevens' Guide to Baltimore's Inner Harbor, 1981, Fire and Water: Six Short Stories, 1982, Children of Dust: Portraits and Preludes, 1985, Horse and Cart: Stories from the Country, 1990, The Night Lover: Art & Poetry, 1995, In Foreign Parts, 1997, Household Words, 1999, 2000, Eranos, 2000, Cherry Pie & Other Stories, 2001; one-woman shows include Coll. Notre Dame of Md., 1997, Galerie Francoise, Lutherville, Md., 2000, exhibited in group shows at The Corcoran Gallery of Art, Washington, Towson State U., Balt., Atelier A/E, N.Y.C., Stephen Gang Gallery, Govt. Ho., Annapolis, U. Minn., Morris, Cooperstown (N.Y.) Art Assn., Armory Art Ctr., West Palm Beach, Fla., Venice (Fla.) Art Ctr., Ft. Meyers (Fla.) Alliance for the Art; contbr. articles, poetry and short stories to jours., nat. newspapers and popular mags. Recipient A.D. Emmart award for journalism, 1980, Critical Writing citation Balt.-Washington Newspaper Guild, 1980, fiction awards Md. Poetry Rev., 1992, 93, 94, 2d prize Lite Circle, 1994, 1st prize in fiction Lite Circle, 1995, 96, Balt. Writers Alliance Play Writing Contest award, 1994; art critics' fellow NEA, 1973-74, fellow MacDowell Colony, 1981, Va. Ctr. for Creative Arts, 1982-85, 88-90, 92, 93, 95, 97, 2000, Ragdale Found., 1984, 89, Yaddo, 1991, Villa Montalvo, 1995; Work-in-Progress grantee for poetry Md. Art Coun., 1986, Creative Devel. grantee for short fiction collection Balt. Mayor's Com. on Art and Culture, 1986. Mem. Coll. Art Assn., Authors Guild, Fla. Printmakers Assn., Poetry Soc. Am., Am. Soc. Graphic Artists, Nat. Book Critics Circle, Women Contemporary Artists Sarasota. Home: Bards Castle 5353 Creekside Trail Sarasota FL 34243

STEVENS, HELEN JEAN, music educator; b. Nevada, Iowa, July 11, 1934; d. Paul Ellison and Helen Margaret (Ives) Stevens. MusB, U. So. Calif., 1956. Cert. secondary music tchr. Calif. Tchr. San Francisco Sch. Dist., 1956-58; prin. oboist Marin Symphony Orch., San Rafael, Calif., 1956-94, Santa Rosa (Calif.) Symphony, 1956-86; tchr. Santa Venetia Mid. Sch., San Rafael, 1958-83; asst. prof. music Sonoma State Coll., Rohnert Park, Calif., 1963-76; tchr. Davidson Mid. Sch., San Rafael, 1984-89; pvt. tchr. oboe. Oboist Eveings on the Roof Series, L.A., 1953—56, Debut TV Show, L.A., 1954—56, Carmel (Calif.) Bach Festival, 1954—82; prin. oboist Light Opera Curren Theatre, San Francisco, 1966—67, Marin Opera Co., San Rafael, 1980—84. Leader Sonoma County 4-H Guide Dog Project Guide Dogs for Blind, Inc., 1974—87; organist, choir dir. Korean Meth. Ch., L.A., 1953—56, United Meth. Ch., St. James, Mo., 2002—. Named Outstanding Tchr., Marin Edn. Found., 1986; recipient Svc. award, PTA, 1974, Golden Bell award, Marin County Office Edn., 1984, Continuing Svc. award, Calif. Congress Parents, Tchrs. and Students, Inc., 1989. Mem.: German Shepherd Dog Club Am. Avocations: computers, animals. Home: 14713 State Rt BB Saint James MO 65559 E-mail: stevfam@fidnet.com.

STEVENS, JANE, advertising executive; Exec. v.p., exec. media dir. Bernstein-Rein Advertising Inc, Kansas City, Mo., 1990—. Office: Bernstein-Rein Advertising Inc 4600 Madison Ave Ste 1500 Kansas City MO 64112-3016

STEVENS, JOCELYN ALEXIS, music educator; b. Tucson, Oct. 24, 1978; d. Mark Barry Stevens and C. Lynn Kiaer. MusB in Music Edn., Butler U., 2000. Music tchr. U. H.S., Carmel, Ind., 2000—. Performer Ind. Wind Symphony, Indpls., 2000—, bd. sec., 2002—; performer, mem. Indpls. Brass Choir, 2000—; condr. Cen. Ind. Trombone Ensemble, Indpls., 2002—; collegiate rep. Ind. Music Educators Assn., 1997—99. Columnist: jour. Indiana Musicator. Named Outstanding Future Music Educator, Ind. Music Educators Assn., 2000; recipient Collegiate Profl. Achievement award, Music Educators Nat. Conf., 2000. Mem.: Am. String Tchrs. Assn., Am. Choral Dirs. Assn., Music Educators Nat. Conf. Avocations: soccer coach, theatrical director. Office: University H S 2825 W 116th St Carmel IN 46032 Personal E-mail: jocelynstevens88@hotmail.com. E-mail: jstevens@universityhighschool.org.

STEVENS, KENDRA ANN, speech-language pathologist; b. Sholo, Ariz., Sept. 4, 1973; d. George A. and Caroline A. Phillips; m. Curtis R. Stevens, Aug. 15, 1995; 1 child, Cole R. BS, U. Wyo., 1995, MS, 1997. Lic. speech-lang. pathology Oreg. Clin. speech-lang. pathologist Merle West Med. Ctr., Klamath Falls, Oreg., 1998—2001; sch. speech-lang. pathologist Klamath Falls City Schs., 2001—. Clin. speech-lang. cons. Cmty. Connections Network, Klamath Falls, 1999—. Ch. bell ringer Canterbury Bells, Klamath Falls, 1999. Mem.: PEO (life; new mem.), Am. Speech Hearing Assn. (life; none, cert. clin. competence). Presbyterian. Achievements include research in swallowing changes as normal aging occurs. Avocations: quilting, gardening, swimming, reading. Office: Klamath Falls City Schs 1336 Avalon Klamath Falls OR 97603 Personal E-mail: ckcstevens@charter.net. E-mail: stevensk@kfalls.k12.or.us.

STEVENS, LEOTA MAE, retired elementary education educator; b. Waverly, Kans., Mar. 27, 1921; d. Clinton Ralph and Velma Mae (Kukuk) Chapman; m. James Oliver Stevens, Nov. 7, 1944 (dec.); children: James Harold, Mary Ann Hooker Tibbits. BA, McPherson Coll., 1954; MS, Emporia U., 1964, postgrad., 1969-77, Wichita U., 1977. Educator Pleasant Mound Sch., Waverly, 1940-41; prin. educator Halls Summit Sch., Waverly, 1941-42; educator Waverly Grade Sch., 1942-43, Ellinwood (Kans.) Jr. H.S., 1943-45, Hutchinson (Kans.) Grade Sch., 1945-48, Lincoln Sch., Darlow, Kans., 1948-49; educator prin. Mitchell-Yaggy Consol. Sch., Hutchinson, 1949-57; educator elem. Hutchinson Sch. Dist. 308, 1957-85, ret., 1985. V.p. Reno County Tchrs. Assn. Hutchinson, 1956-57, pres. Assn. Childhood Edn. Internat., 1978-79. Author of numerous poems; compiler The Alexander-Kukuk Descendants: 1754 to 1998. Mem. Worker ARC Blood Mobile, 1986—2000, Hutchinson Cmty. Concerts, 1970—; historian Women's Civic Ctr., 1988—92, art com. chmn, 1992—96; den mother Cub Scouts, 1963—66; leader Girl Scouts Ellinwood, 1944—45; bell ringer ARC Blood Mobile, 1986—2000; ch. sch. tchr. Trinity United Meth. Ch., 1959—71, attendance chair, 1994. Mem. AAUW (news reporter 1984-87, legis. chmn. program com. 1991-94, 2d v.p., 1994-95), Ret. Nation State and Local Edn. Assn., Reno County Tchrs. Assn. (v.p. 1956-57), Assn. Childhood Edn. Internat. (pres. 1978-79), Reno County Extension Homemaker Coun. (rep. 1987—), Rainbow Extension Club (pres. 1986-92), Hutchinson Area Ret. Tchrs. Assn. (historian 1996-99), Am. Legion Aux., Friends of Preservation, Delta Kappa Gamma (sec., v.p. 1972-80, grant chmn. 1980-88, publicity com. 1990-93, legis. chmn. 1994-2000). Republican. Avocations: art, music, traveling, gardening, camping, genealogy. Home: 426 S Tulip St Mcpherson KS 67460-4935

STEVENS, LYDIA HASTINGS, community volunteer; b. Highland Park, Ill., Aug. 2, 1918; d. Rolland T.R. and Ruth Shotwell (Beebe) Hastings; m. George Cooke Stevens, Nov. 2, 1940; children: Lydia Stevens Gustin, Priscilla Stevens Goldfarb, Frederick S., Elizabeth Stevens MacLeod, George H., Ruth Stevens Stellard. BA, Vassar Coll., 1939. State rep. 151st Dist. of Conn., Greenwich, 1988-92. Cons. Nat. Exec. Svc. Corps, N.Y.C., 1985. Pres. Greenwich YWCA, 1971-74, Greenwich Housing Coalition, 1982-86; v.p. planning Greenwich United Way, 1973-76; sr. warden Greenwich Christ Episcopal Ch., 1981-86; chmn. rev. commn. Episcopal Diocese of Conn., 1985-87; bd. dirs. Greenwich Libr., 1985-93; chmn. Greenwich Commn. Aging, 1986-88; pres., bd. dirs. Greenwich Broadcasting Corp., 1977-79; bd. dirs. Fairfield County Cmty. Found., 1992, United Way of Greenwich, Save the Sound, 1996—, League Conservation Voters Conn., 1999. Recipient Golden Rule award J.C. Penney, 1987, President's award Greenwich YWCA, 1992, Braua award, 1994, Conn. Assn. for Human Svc. Dirs. award, 1992; named Layperson of Yr., Coun. Chs. and Synagogues, 1995. Republican. Episcopalian. Avocations: sailing, organic gardening. Home: 125 West Ln Guilford CT 06437-3230

STEVENS, MARILYN RUTH, editor; b. Wooster, Ohio, May 30, 1943; d. Glenn Willard and Gretchen Elizabeth (Ihrig) Amstutz; m. Bryan J. Stevens, Oct. 11, 1969; children: Jennifer Marie, Gretchen Anna. BA, Coll. Wooster, 1965; MAT, Harvard U., 1966; JD, Suffolk U., 1975. Bar: Mass. 1975. Tchr. Lexington (Mass.) Pub. Schs., 1966-69; with Houghton Mifflin Co., Boston, 1969—, editl. dir. sch. depts., 1978-81, editl. dir. math. scies. sch. divsn., 1981-84, mng. editor sch. pub., 1984—. Mem. Mass. Bar Assn. Office: Houghton Mifflin 222 Berkeley St Fl 7 Boston MA 02116-3764

STEVENS, MARY ANN, state legislator; b. West, Miss. m. A.J. Stevesn, III; 1 child, Elizabeth Ann. Grad., West H.S. Mem. Miss. Ho. of Reps., 1981—, chmn. ins. com., mem. appropriations com., jud. com., juvenile justice com.; former banker; landowner; project dir. West Primary Health Care Clinic. Former mayor, former alderman Town of West. Mem. West Garden Club (past pres.), Miss. Women's Club. Democrat. Methodist. Office: Miss State Senate State Capitol PO Box 1018 Jackson MS 39215-1018

STEVENS, MAY, artist; b. Boston, June 9, 1924; d. Ralph Stanley and Alice Margaret (Dick) S.; m. Rudolf Baranik, June 5, 1948; 1 child, Steven. BFA, Mass. Coll. Art, 1946; postgrad., Academie Julian, Paris, 1948-49, Art Students League, 1948. Mem. faculty Sch. Visual Arts, N.Y.C., 1964-96, Skowhegan Sch. Painting and Sculpture, 1992, Vt. Studio Ctr., 1997, Santa Fe Art Inst., 2000, 2003. Lectr. Royal Coll. Art, London, 1981, U. Wis.-Racine, 1973, Coll. Art Assn., Washington, 1975; sole juror Am. Drawing Biennial, Coll. William and Mary, Williamsburg, Va., 2000; lectr. Coll. Santa Fe, 1998, Santa Fe Art Inst., 2003. One-woman shows: Terry Dintenfass Gallery, N.Y.C., 1971, Cornell U., 1973, Douglass Coll., Rutgers U., 1974, Lerner-Heller Gallery, N.Y.C., 1975, 76, 78, 81, Clark U., 1982, Boston U. Art Gallery, 1984, Frederick S. Wight Gallery, UCLA, 1985, U. Md., College Park, 1985, Real Art Ways, Hartford, Conn., 1988, New Mus. Contemporary Art, 1988, Orchard Gallery, Derry, No. Ireland, 1988, Kenyon Coll., Gambier, Ohio, 1988, Greenville County (S.C.) Art Mus., 1991, Herter Gallery, U. Mass., Amherst, 1991, U. Colo., Boulder, 1993, U. N.Mex., Albuquerque, 1996, Mary Ryan Gallery, N.Y.C., 1996, 97, 99, 2001, 03, Mus. Fine Arts, Boston, 1999, Lew Allen Contemporary, Santa Fe, 1998; exhibited in group shows: Inst. Contemporary Arts, London, 1980, Gemeente Mus., The Hague, 1979, Whitney Mus., 1970, Gedok, Kunsthaus, Hamburg, Germany, 1972, Everson Mus., Syracuse, N.Y., 1976, Clocktower, N.Y.C., 1986, Guerrilla Girls Exbn. at Palladium, N.Y.C., 1985, One Penn Pla., 1985, Pentonville Gallery, London, 1986, Heckscher Mus., N.Y., 1987, Univ. Art Mus., Berkeley, Calif., 1987, Mus. Modern Art, 1988, Exit Art, N.Y.C., 1988, Sao Paulo (Brazil) Mus. Modern Art, 1989, Blum Helman Gallery, N.Y.C., 1989, Univ. Art Mus., Long Beach, Calif., 1990, Angels Gate, San Pedro, Calif., 1990, Newark Mus., 1990, Städtliche Kunsthalle, Düsseldorf, Germany, 1990, DeCordova Mus., Lincoln, Mass., 1991, Exit Art, N.Y.C., 1994, Mary Delahoyd Gallery, N.Y.C., 1995, Mary Ryan Gallery, N.Y.C., 1995, Gwenda Jay Gallery, Chgo., 1995, Lizardi Harp Gallery, L.A., 1995, ACA Galleries, N.Y.C., 1996, Nassau County Mus., Roslyn, N.Y., 1997, Santa Fe Art Inst., 2002, Mus. Fine Art, Sante Fe, 2002, Guild Hall, East Hampton, N.Y., 2002, Hobart & William Smith Colls., 2002, We. Wash. U. Bellingham, 2002, UBS Paine Webber Art Gallery, N.Y.C., 2002, Deutsche Bank, N.Y.C., 2002, Bass Mus. Art, Miami Beach, Fla., 2002, Bklyn. Mus., 2003, Nat. Mus. Women in the Arts, Washington, 2003, Danese Gallery, N.Y.C., 2004, CCA Gallery, Santa Fe, 2004, others; represented in permanent collections: Met. Mus. Art, N.Y.C., Mus. Modern Art, N.Y.C., Moca, L.A., San Francisco Mus. Art, New Mus. Contemporary Art, Whitney Mus., Bklyn. Mus., Herbert F. Johnson Mus., Cornell U., Mus. Fine Arts Boston, De Cordova Mus., Lincoln, Mass., Harwood Mus., Taos, N.Mex., Joslyn Art Mus., Omaha; contbr. articles to various mags. Recipient Childe Hassam Purchase awards Nat. Inst. Arts and Letters, 1968, 69, 75, N.Y. State Coun. on Arts award, 1974, Disting. Alumna award Mass. Coll. Art, 1997, Disting. Artist award Coll. Art Assn., 2001, Andy Warhol Found. grant for project space Headlands Ctr. for Arts, Sausalito, Calif., 2001; MacDowell Colony fellow, 1971, 72, 74, 75, 81, 82, 84, Bunting Inst. fellow Radcliffe Coll., 1988-89; Line Assn. grantee for artists books, 1978; grantee NEA, 1983, Guggenheim, 1986; honoree Women's Caucus for Art, 1990. Mem. Coll. Art Assn.

STEVENS, PAULETTE, daycare administrator; b. Cleve., Jan. 26, 1947; d. Joseph George and Mildred Margie Henderson; m. David Leon Stevens, Jan. 28; children: Dewayne, Fred, Derrick, Lisa, Shaun Knox. Degree, Pitts. C.C., 1976, Calif. State U., 1977, Allegheny C.C., 1976. Dir., owner, asst. tchr. Sewickley (Pa.) Care and Devel. Ctr., 1973-81, Family Day Care, Coraopolis, Pa., 1982-91; dir., owner Mt. Olive Day Care, Coraopolis, Pa., 1991—. Mem. Kiwanis, Women in Christian Ministries (bd. dirs. 1992—). Baptist. Avocations: reading, sewing. Home: 1413 5th Ave Coraopolis PA 15108-2025

STEVENS, PHYLLIS A. conceptual artist; b. Wash., DC, June 14, 1931; d. Carle Wright Stevens and Maybelle Bayley Whiting; 1 child, Karen. Attended, Antioch Coll., 1953, Art Students League, Acad. of Realist Art. Self employed free lance artist, 1956—; set designer Eccentric Circles Theater, N.Y.C.; stage sets dir. Theater Genesis, N.Y.C.; designer CBS Network, Shadow Puppet Productions, N.Y.C., Am. Opera Soc., Shadow Puppet Production, N.Y.C. Exhibitions include The Salmagundi Club, N.Y.C., Philmont Ranch, N. Mex., Art Expo, N.Y.C., Artist and Artisans, NJ, Hunter Crafts Show, N.Y.C., Living Handcrafts, Mus. of Contemporary Crafts, Mus. of Fine Arts, Del., Bonwit-Teller, N.Y.C., Bratta Gallery, Antioch Coll., Ohio, prin. works include Mural in Lobby, Internat. Longshoreman's Union, Anthony Anastasia Med. Ctr., NY, Four built-in panels, Private home, NY; contbr. articles various profl. jours. Mem.: Writers Guild of Am. East, NY Artists Equity Assn., Graphic Artists Guild, Salmagundi Club. Home: 214 Weaver Mine Trail Chapel Hill NC 27517 Personal E-mail: phyllisstevens@earthlink.net.

STEVENS, RHEA CHRISTINA, lawyer; b. Chgo., Dec. 25, 1964; d. Samuel Nowell and Rhea Mae (Lipham) S.; m. Peter Linzer, June 20, 1992; 1 child, Grayson Nowell. BS in Psychology, U. Houston, 1989; MEd, Cambridge Coll., 1987; JD, U. Houston, 1992. Bar: Tex. 1992. Instr., client liaison Hippocrates Health Inst., Boston, 1985-86; reorganization cons. Psychotechnics, Inc., Cary, Glenview, Ill., 1987-88; pvt. practice law Houston, 1992—. Founder, owner Aristic Enterprises I and II, 1995, breeder Great Danes, Anatolian Shepherds, Papillons and Dobermans for svc. orgns. and show-August Kennels, 1988—; canine behaviorist; founder DemiSance Ctr., 1999. Rep. mid-Am. chpt. ARC to Nat. Conv., 1980; bd. dirs., treas. Clark Rd. Found., Houston, 1990-92, Houston ACLU, 1990-92; counsellor Boston Area Rape Crisis Ctr., 1986-87. Recipient cert. commendation ARC, 1979-80. Mem. State Bar Tex. (disability issues com. 1996—, Pro Bono Coll. 1995—). Avocations: training and exhibiting dogs, locksmithing, computer consulting. Office: 6655 Arabia Ln Ste 100 Sealy TX 77474

STEVENS, RISË, performing arts company administrator; b. N.Y.C. m. Walter Surovy; 1 child, Nicolas. Student, Juilliard Sch.; Hon. Degree Smith Coll., Coll. of Senecas, Russell Sage Coll., Rider Coll., U. Pa., Baylor U., Rice U., Mercy Coll., Mannes Coll Music, Hobart Coll., Cleve. Inst. Music, Va. Commonwealth U. Co-gen. mgr. Met. Opera Nat. Co., N.Y.C., 1980-88; pres. The Mannes Coll. Music, N.Y.C., 1975-78; mng. dir. Met. Opera Bd. Performer Prague Opera, Vienna State Opera, Royal Opera, NY Met. Opera, 1938-61; starred in films, concerts, TV, and radio. Mem. Nat. Endowment for Arts (co-chair music panel 1981-83), N.Y. State Coun. on Arts (chmn. music panel), Met. Opera Guild (bd. dirs.), Wagnerian Soc. Buenos Aires, Sigma Alpha Iota. Office: Met Opera Assn Lincoln Ctr New York NY 10023

STEVENS, ROSEMARY A. medicine and public health historian; b. Bourne, Eng. came to U.S., 1961, naturalized, 1968; d. William Edward and Mary Agnes (Tricks) Wallace; m. Robert B. Stevens, Jan. 28, 1961 (div. 1983); children: Carey, Richard; m. Jack D. Barchas, Aug. 9, 1994. BA, Oxford (Eng.) U., 1957; Diploma in Social Adminstrn., Manchester (Eng.) U., 1959; MPH, Yale U., 1963, PhD, 1968; LHD (hon.), Hahnemann U., 1988; DSc (hon.), Northeastern Ohio U. Coll. Medicine, 1995. Various hosp. adminstrv. positions, Eng., 1959-61; rsch. assoc. Med. Sch. Yale U., 1962-68, asst. prof. Med. Sch., 1968-71, assoc. prof. Med. Sch., 1971-74, prof. pub. health Med. Sch., 1974-76; master Jonathan Edwards Coll., 1974-75; prof. dept. health systems mgmt. and polit. sci. Tulane U., New Orleans, 1976-78, chmn. dept. health systems mgmt., 1977-78; prof. history and sociology of sci. U. Pa., Phila., 1979—2002, chmn. dept., 1980-83, 86-91, UPS Found. prof., 1990-91, dean Sch. Arts and Scis., Thomas S. Gates prof., 1991-96, Stanley I. Sheerr prof., 1997—2001, prof. emeritus, 2002—. Prof. emeritus U. Pa., Phila., 2002-; vis. lectr. Johns Hopkins U., 1967-68; guest scholar Brookings Instn., Washington, 1967-68; acad. visitor London Sch. Econs., 1962-64, 1973-74. Author: Medical Practice in Modern England: The Impact of Specialization and State Medicine, 1966, new edit., 2003, American Medicine and the Public Interest, 1971, rev. edit., 1998, In Sickness and in Wealth: American Hospitals in the Twentieth Century, 1989, rev. edit., 1999, (with others) Foreign Trained Physicians and American Medicine, 1972, Welfare Medicine in America, 1974, new edit., 2003, Alien-Doctors: Foreign Medical Graduates in American Hospitals, 1978. Bd. dirs. Milbank Meml. Fund. Rockefeller Humanities fellow, 1982-83, Guggenheim fellow, 1984-85; Bellagio Study and Conf. scholar, 1984; recipient Frohlich medal Royal Soc. Medicine, London, 1986, Baxter Found. prize distinction in health svcs. rsch., 1990, James A. Hamilton Book award Am. Coll. Healthcare Execs. best book, 1990, Welch medal distinction in history of medicine Am. Assn. History Medicine, 1990, Arthur Viseltear award history pub. health Am. Pub. Health Assn., 1990, Nicholas E. Davies award Piedmont Hosp., Atlanta, 1997, Investigator award in health policy rsch. Robert Wood Johnson Found., 1998-, Carlson award for extraordinary contbns. to history of medicine Cornell U., Weill Med. Coll., 2000., Lifetime Achievement award Am. Assn. History Medicine, 2002. Fellow Am. Acad. Arts and Scis.; mem. AAAS (chmn. sect. history and philosophy of sci., 2002-03), Inst. Medicine of Nat. Acad. Sci., Am. Sociol. Assn., Am. Assn. for History of Medicine, Coll. Physicians of Phila.Am. Bd. Med. Specialties (pub. mem., exec. com.), Cosmopolitan Club. Home: 1900 Rittenhouse Sq # 18 A Philadelphia PA 19103-5767 Office: U Pa 303 Logan Hall 249 South 36th St Philadelphia PA 19104-6304 E-mail: rstevens@sas.upenn.edu.

STEVENS, VAL, state legislator; m. Keith Stevens; 2 children. Mem. Wash. Senate, Dist. 39, Olympia, 1996—; mem. senate agr. and rural econ. devel. com. Wash. Legislature, Olympia, Wash. state chair Am. Legis. Exch. Coun., mem. agr. and rural econ. devel. com., mem. human svcs. and corrections com., mem. natural resources, parks and recreation com., mem. child abuse investigation work group, mem. joint selection com. on DNA, mem. family policy coun., mem. civil justice task force subcom. on Y2K, mem. Gov.'s coun. on substance abuse. Mem. Northshore Christian Ch.; bd. dirs. 1991 Concerned Women for Am.; past mem. Gov.'s Task Force for Natural Death Act; charter mem. Better Govt. Bur.; mem. ad hoc bd. dirs. Naval Aux. Air Sta. Mus. Recipient 100 Percent Voting Record award Wash. State Farm Bur., gold medal Ind. Bus. Assn., Sentinel award Wash. State Law Enforcement Assn., 1996, Outstanding Support Vocat. Tech. Edn. award WAVA, 1996, Cornerstone award Assn. Wash. Bus., Outstanding Support award Wash. Retail Assn., 1996, Guardian of Small Bus. award Nat. Fedn. Ind. Bus., Pub. Safety award Snohomish County Law Enforcement, 1993. Mem. Christian Armed Svcs. Assn. Republican. Office: 105 Irving Newhouse Ofc Olympia WA 98504-0001

STEVENSON, ALEXANDRA, professional tennis player; b. San Diego, Calif., Dec. 15, 1980; d. Samantha. Student, U. Colo. Mem. U.S. Fed Cup Team, 2003. Winner ITF/Midland, Mich., 1998, 13 of 15 grass court matches, 1999; semifinalist Wimbledon, 1999, U.S. Open, 1999; mem. U.S. Pan Am Games Team, 1999; jr. competition winner U.S. Open Jr., 1997, USTA Nat. Girls' 18s, 1997; jr. competition singles finalist USTA Nat. Girls' 18 Clay Courts, 1996; named Roles Rookie of the Yr., Tennis Mag., 1999. Avocations: singing, ballet, swimming, dance. Office: WTA 1266 E Main St Ste 4 Stamford CT 06902-3546

STEVENSON, AMANDA (SANDY STEVENS), librettist, composer, document examiner; b. Bklyn., Oct. 24, 1943; d. Haakon and Grace Svendsen. Grad., Bay Ridge H.S., Bklyn., 1961. Cert. Nat. Bur. Document Examiners. Composer, librettist, Nellie Bly, Victorine, (screenplay) The Last Assignment Mem. Actors Equity Assn., GMI, Songwriters Guild. Democrat. Unitarian Universalist. Avocations: chess, art history, pen pals. Home and Office: 3543 84th St Apt 327 Jackson Heights NY 11372

STEVENSON, FRANCES KELLOGG, museum program director; b. Boston; d. Charles Summers and Alice deGueldry (Stevens) S.; m. James Richard Wein, 1971 (div. 1989). BA, Wells Coll., Aurora, N.Y., 1967; MA, Oxford U., 1972; MBA, U. Pa., 1992. Publs. officer Nat. Portrait Gallery Smithsonian Instn., Washington, 1974—2001, strategic planning officer, 2001—. Mem. St. John's Episcopal Ch., Lafayette Sq. James E. Webb fellow Smithsonian Instn., 1988-89. Mem. Sulgrave Club. Home: 2724 Ordway St NW Apt 4 Washington DC 20008-5047 Office: Smithsonian Instn Nat Portrait Gallery PO Box 37012 Victor Bldg MRC 973 Washington DC 20013-7012

STEVENSON, JO ANN C. federal bankruptcy judge; b. 1942; AB, Rutgers U., 1965; JD cum laude, Detroit Coll. Law, 1979. Bar: Mich. 1979. Law clk. to Vincent J. Brennan, Mich. Ct. Appeals, Detroit, 1979; law clk. to Cornelia G. Kenendy, U.S. Ct. Appeals for 6th Cir., Detroit, 1980; assoc. Hertzberg, Jacob & Weingarten, P.C., Detroit, 1980-87; judge U.S. Bankruptcy Ct., Grand Rapids, Mich., 1987—. Office: US Bankruptcy Ct PO Box 3310 Grand Rapids MI 49501-3310

STEVENSON, JUDY G. instrument manufacturing executive; Bookeeper Magnetrol, Naperville, Ill., 1964-65, accounting supr./mgr., 1965-76, treas./admin. v.p., 1967-75, pres., 1975-78, owner, 1978—. Bd. trustees N. Ctrl. Coll.; established Harold E. Meiley, Judy G. Stevenson, African Scholarship Funds; supports Naperville Heritage Soc., Edward Hosp., the Riverwalk, Millennium Carillon Found., Good Samaritan Hosp., DuPage Intergenerational Village. Recipient YWCA Businesswoman Yr. DuPage Co., 1985, YWCA Outstanding Woman Leader DuPage Co., 1997, Top 500 Woman-Owned Businesses, Working Woman Mag., 1998. Mem. Chief Exec. Officers Club, Nat. Assn. Women Bus. Owners, Nat. Assn. Female Execs., Eastern Star. Avocations: gardening, gourmet cooking, music, ballet, horses. Office: Magnetrol Internat 5300 Belmont Rd Downers Grove IL 60515-4499

STEVENSON, KAREN, lawyer; b. Bay Shore, N.Y., Oct. 02; BA summa cum laude, UCLA, 1971; JD, U. Calif., 1970. Bar: Calif. 1980, U.S. Dist. Ct. (no. dist.) Calif. Law clk. Judge William W. Schwarzer U.S. Dist. Ct. (no. dist.) Calif., 1980-81, v.p., assoc. gen. counsel Transam Corp., 1987-88, v.p. law, sec., 1989-90; v.p., gen. counsel Knight-Ridder, Inc., San Jose, Calif. Mem. jury instrns. com. U.S. Ct. Appeals (9th cir.), 1983-84. Assoc. editor Calif. Law Rev., 1978-79, articles editor, 1979-80. Regents fellow, 1978-79. Mem. State Bar Calif. (mem. corps. com. 1991-94, legis. liaison 1991-92, vice-chair 1992-93, chair 1993-94), Phi Beta Kappa, Pi Gamma Mu. Office: 50 W San Fernando St Ste 1500 San Jose CA 95113-2434

STEVENSON, KAREN LEE (RIZZO), psychologist, consultant; d. Raymond Salvatore and Carolyn Amelia Rizzo; married, Sept. 20, 1985; children: Kelsey Rae, Kristian Wesley. BS in Psychology magna cum laude, St. Joseph's U., Phila., 1983; MEd, Temple U., Phila., 1987; post grad., West Chester (Pa.) U., 1994, Immaculata Coll., Rosemont, Pa., 1994. Lic. psychologist Pa., 1995, cert. biofeedback 1984, primary rational and emotive therapy 1983, intermediate rational and emotive therapy 1986, hypnotherapy 1990. Mental health worker Satinsky Inst., Phila., 1982—83; adminstr., coord. and biofeedback technician Michael I. Broder, PhD., Phila., 1983—86, Inst. Rational - Emotive Therapy, Phila., 1983—86; psychotherapist and psychologist Robert Zibelman, M.D., Jenkintown, Pa., 1986—98; psychol. evaluator Pa. Hosp. Hall Mercer Cmty. Mental Health Ctr., Phila., 1996—, behavioral specialist, 1996, mobile therapist, 1996—, clin. supr., 1996—; psychol. evaluator Child Guidance Resource Ctr., Media, Pa., 1996—97, behavioral specialist, 1996—97, mobile therapist, 1996—97, clin. supr., 1996—97; psychol. evaluator Elwyn, Inc., Media, 2002—, clin. supr., 2002—; outpatient psychologist and clin. supr. PA Sharpe Svcs., Inc., Secane, 2002—; pvt. practice Media, 1990—. Workshop presenter and leader, 1984—. Developer and author: professional audiotape Stress Mgmt. and Relaxation, 1990. Mem.: Nat. Inst. of Sports Psychology, Internat. Assn. of Counselors and Therapists, Pa. Psychol. Assn., Am. Psychol. Assn., Psi Chi. Home and Office: 210 Meadowcroft Ln Media PA 19063

STEVENSON, KATHERINE HOLLER, federal agency administrator; b. Jan. 20, 1948; d. Jacob W. and Sheila Holler; m. Donald Stevenson, aug. 14, 1982; 2 children. BA, Skidmore Coll., 1969; MA, U. Del., 1971. Researcher Nat. portrait Gallery, Smithsonian Inst., Washington, 1971; with Nat. Park Svc., Washington, 1972-80, Denver, 1980-87, Phila., 1987-95, assoc. dir. Washington, 1995—. Co-author: Houses by Mail, 1983. Recipient Meritorious Svc. award Dept. Interior, 1994. Office: Nat Park Svc Cultural Resource 1849 C St NW Washington DC 20240-0001 E-mail: Kate_Stevenson@nps.gov.

STEVENSON, MARSHA JOAN, librarian; b. Moline, Ill., July 10, 1953; d. Theodore Thomas Stevenson, Laverne Joan Stevenson; m. George King Rugg; 1 child, Gwendolyn Rugg. MA in Libr. Sci., U. Wis., 1976. Ref. libr. Ohio State U., Newark, Ohio, 1976—79; catalog/ref. libr. U. Pitts., 1979—83; head access svc. divsn. U. Mo., Columbia, Mo., 1984—89; head ref. dept. U. Notre Dame, Ind., 1990—. Contbr. chapters to books What is Written Remains: Historical Essays on the Libraries of Notre Dame, 1994, Technical Services Today and Tomorrow, 1990, articles to profl. jours. Bd. dirs. Holy Cross Athletic Assn., South Bend, Ind., 1997—2002. Mem.: ALA (vice chair/chair LAMA bldg. and equipment sect. 2001—03), Beta Phi Mu. Home: 127 E North Shore Dr South Bend IN 46617 Office: Univ Notre Dame 243 Hesburgh Libr Notre Dame IN 46556 Business E-Mail: stevenson.2@nd.edu.

STEVENSON, NANCY NELSON, museum executive; b. Annapolis, Md., Oct. 23, 1950; d. Perry Waldemar and Grace Anne Nelson; m. Roger Stevenson Jr., Nov. 18, 1972; children: Jennifer Loren, Matthew Austin. BA, Sarah Lawrence Coll., 1972. Tchr. Montgomery County (Md.) Pub. Schs., 1972—76; bd. dirs. Jr. League of Washington, 1988—89, 1990—92; trustee Nat. Mus. Women in the Arts, Washington, 1996—, sec. bd. of trustees, 1997—98, treas. bd. of trustees, 1998—2002, v.p. bd. trustees, 2002—04, pres. bd. trustees, 2004—. Co-author French immersion curriculum, 1974. Pres. Country Pl. Citizens Assn., Potomac, Md., 1983-84. Office: Nat Mus Women in the Arts 1250 New York Ave NW Washington DC 20005-3970

STEVENSON, SUSAN MARIE, music educator; d. Raymond Earl and Nancy Lee Cook; m. Gerald Lewis Stevenson, July 11, 1987; children: Deborah Elisabeth, David John. BS in Music Edn., Pensacola Christian Coll., 1985, MS in Secondary Edn., 1986; EdM, Converse Coll., 1995. Tchr. Pensacola (Fla.) Christian Sch., 1985—86, Pensacola Christian Sch., 1987—89, Bethel Bapt. Ch. Sch., Santa Ana, Calif., 1986—87; bank teller Carolina First Bank, Greenville, SC, 1989—90; tchr. Shannon Forest Christian Sch., Greenville, 1990—2000, Sch. Dist. Greenville County, 2000—. Awana sec. Calvary Bapt. Ch., Simpsonville, SC, 1999—. Mem.: SC Music Educators Assn., Am. Orff Shulwerk Assn. (sec. Foothills chpt. 2000—), Music Educators Nat. Conf. Avocations: bicycling, reading, walking. Office: Bells Crossing Elem Sch 804 Scuffletown Rd Simpsonville SC 29681

STEVES, GALE C. marketing professional, writer, editor-in-chief, publishing executive; b. Mineola, N.Y., Dec. 20, 1942; d. William Harry and Ruth (May) S.; m. David B. Stocker, Mar. 31, 1972 (div. Apr. 1978); m. Philip L. Perrone, Aug. 14, 1983. BS, Cornell U., 1964; MA, NYU, 1966. Editorial asst. Ladies Home Jour., N.Y.C., 1966-69; seafood consumer specialist U.S. Dept. Commerce, N.Y.C., 1969-73; editor food Homelife mag., N.Y.C., 1973-74; editor food and equipment Co-Ed mag., N.Y.C., 1974-76, Am. Home mag., N.Y.C., 1976-78; editor kitchen design and equipment Woman's Day mag., N.Y.C., 1979-83; editor-in-chief Woman's Day Spls., N.Y.C., 1983-91; v.p., editor-in-chief Home Mag. Group, N.Y.C., 1991—2001; pres. Open House Prodns., N.Y.C., 2001—03; v.p., editl. dir., pub. AMI Mini Mags. Group, N.Y.C., 2003—. Bd. dirs. Les Dames d'Escoffier, N.Y.C., Coun. Sr. Ctrs. and Svcs. of N.Y.C., 1982-98, The Catskill Ctr. for Cons. and Econ. Devel.; mem. editl. bd. Sr. Summary, N.Y.C., 1982-88; co-chmn. Alder Lake Restoration Soc. Author: Game Cookery, 1974, The International Cook, 1980, Creative Microwave Cookery, 1981, (with Lee M. Elman) Country Weekend Cooking, Home Magazine's Best Little Houses, 1998. Chmn. alumni adv. bd. Coll. Human Ecology, Cornell U., 1993-97, mem. univ. coun., 1996-2000, mem. Pres.'s Coun. for Cornell Women, 1992-2001; mem. adv. bd. Cornell Plantations. Mem. Internat. Furnishings and Design Assn., Am. Soc. Mag. Editors, Garden Writers Assn. Am., Acad. of Women Achievers at YWCA of N.Y.C. Address: 185 West End Ave Ste 26C New York NY 10023-5551

STEWARD, JENNIFER A. academic administrator; d. Georgia A. and Christopher J. Sadler(Stepfather); m. Mathew Steward. BA in French, SUNY, Binghamton, 1992; MS in Edn., U. Rochester, 1998, MS in Edn., 2003. Asst. de langue vivante Faculte de Rennes, France, 1992—93; program asst. U. Rochester, 1995—99; program mgr. U. Rochester Anthony Ctr. for Women's Leadership, 1999—2002; admissions counselor U. Rochester Warner Sch. Edn., 2002; dir. mktg. and recruitment divsn. tchr. edn. Roberts Wesleyan Coll., 2002—, adj. prof., 2003—. Mem.: AAUW (publicity chair, web site coord. greater Rochester area br. 2001—). Roman Catholic. Office: Roberts Wesleyan College Divsn Tchr Edn 2301 Westside Drive Rochester NY 14624

STEWART, ANN TEFERTILLER, interior designer, secondary school educator; b. Wynnewood, Okla., May 31, 1951; d. Charles Lester and La Vera Robberson Tefertiller; m. Robert George Stewart, Sept. 20, 1948; 1 child, Megan Ann. MLA, So. Meth. U., Dallas, TX, 1982; BA, U. of Okla., Norman, OK, 1972. Cert. secondary edn.tchr. Okla. and Tex. Adult bilingual educator / coord. Migrant Program, Altus, Okla., 1973—73; h.s. educator Richardson Ind. Sch. Dist., Richardson, Tex., 1973—80; substitute tchr. Dept. of Def., Zaragoza, Spain, 1980—82, home bound tchr., 1980—82; substitute tchr. Trinity Valley Upper Sch., Fort Worth, Tex., 1983—83; tchr. St. Elizabeth Ann Seton Sch., Edmond, Okla., 1996; mid. sch. educator Ctrl. Mid. Sch., Edmond, Okla., 1996—2000; h.s. educator North H.S., Edmond, Okla., 2000—; interior designer Ann Stewart Designs, Edmond, Okla., 1986—. Com. mem. Profl. Devel., Edmond, Okla., 1997; dept. head Spanish Richardson (Tex.) Ind. Sch. Dist., 1975—80. Career day participant Will Rogers Elem., Edmond, Okla., vol. Parent Tchr. Assn., Edmond, Okla.; chmn. United Meth. Women, Edmond, Okla. Recipient Del. to Mid. Sch. Conf., Faculty of Ctrl. Mid. Sch., 1999. Mem.: Okla. Ednl. Assn., NEA. Home: 1413 Woodbury Circle Edmond OK 73003

STEWART, ANNE WILLIAMS, historian, writer, researcher; b. New Haven, Oct. 13, 1933; d. Howard Dudley and Minnie Victoria (Rattelsdorfer) Williams; m. Kenneth Neal Stewart (div. Oct. 1985); children: Elizabeth Anne Stewart-Marshall, Kenneth Neal Jr. BA, Allegheny Coll., Meadville, Pa., 1955. Coord. hist. sites survey Crawford County Planning, Meadville, 1976-80; chmn. hist. sites survey Meadville Redevel. Authority, 1980-83; program coord. Crawford County Hist. Soc., Meadville, 1981-88; bd. dirs. Meadville Bicentennial, 1986-88; dir. Academy Theater restoration Meadville Redevel. Authority, 1988-90; gen. reporter Meadville Tribune, 1990-92, grantsman Meadville Redevel. Authority, 1991—; adminstr. The Col. Inc., Drake Well Mus., Titusville, Pa., 1992-95. Historian, advisor Meadville Main St., 1986—90; historian Meadville Comprehensive Plan, 1992—93. Author: John A. Mather: Legacy of Pennsylvania's Oil Region Photographer, 1995, A Concise History of Meadville, 1995, 4th edit., 2002; author: (with Jonathan Miller Design) Meadville: Heart of the French Creek Valley, 1997; author: (with William B. Moore) Images of America, Meadville, 2001; editor: A Guide to City and County, 1972, Meadville: Yesterday and Today, 1976, Gentle Giants: Stories of Ballooning, 1992, George Washington's French Creek Trip, 1999, The Oilfield Barker, 1993—96, Market Square Messenger, 1996—99, Crawford County History, 2001—; contbr. articles to mags.; editor: John Brown: From the Record, 1999, Erie: Jour. of Erie Studies, 2002. Planning commr. Crawford County, Meadville, 1971—95, City of Meadville, 2000—; bd. dirs. Meadville Area Meml., 1983—95; chmn. bd. dirs. Health Svcs. Inc. Crawford County, 1976—81; coord. Meadville Area Coalition; chair The Founders Forum, 1997—. Mem.: Pa. Planning Assn. (bd. dirs. 1974—80), Crawford County Hist. Soc. (bd. dirs. 2003—), Woman's Lit. Club (lectr.). Avocations: travel, research, textile crafts. Office: 443 Byllesby Ave Meadville PA 16335-1411 E-mail: byllesby@alltel.net.

STEWART, ARDEN RUTH, automotive aftermarket manufacturing executive; b. Wheeling, W.Va., Sept. 29, 1930; d. Oliver Shaw and Helen (Neitzel) Stewart; children: Mark, Todd. BA, Baldwin Wallace Coll., 1952. Trainee GM, Cleve., 1952-57; tchr. Elyria (Ohio) City Bd. Edn., 1967-85; pres., CEO AAR, Inc., Cleve., 1984—, also chmn. bd. dirs. Pres. Elyria Schs. PTA, 1967; treas. Homeowners Assn., North Ridgeville, Ohio, 1988-89; mem. adv. com. bus. and tech. Cuyahoga C.C. Recipient Weatherhead 100 award Case Western Res. U., 1990, 91, 92, 93, 94, 95. Republican. Episcopalian. Avocations: music, scuba diving, dance. Home: 32889 Brownstone Ln PO Box 39359 North Ridgeville OH 44039-0359 Office: AAR Inc 34999 Mills Rd North Ridgeville OH 44039-1366 Personal E-mail: arden9201@aol.com.

STEWART, ARLENE JEAN GOLDEN, designer, stylist; b. Chgo., Nov. 26, 1943; d. Alexander Emerald and Nettie (Rosen) Golden; m. Randall Edward Stewart, Nov. 6, 1970; 1 child, Alexis Anne. BFA, Sch. of Art Inst. Chgo., 1966; postgrad., Ox Bow Summer Sch. Painting, Saugatuck, Mich., 1966. Designer, stylist Formica Corp., Cin., 1966-68; with Armstrong World Industries, Inc., Lancaster, Pa., 1968-96, interior furnishings analyst, 1974-76, internat. staff project stylist, 1976-78, sr. stylist Corlon flooring, 1979-80, sr. exptl. project stylist, 1980-89, sr. project stylist residential DIY flooring floor divsn., 1989-96, master stylist DIY residential tile, 1992-96; creative dir. Stewart Graphics, Lancaster, Pa., 1996—. Mem. Exhibited textiles Art Inst. Chgo., 1966, Ox-Bow Gallery, Saugatuck, Mich., 1966. Home and Office: 114 E Vine St Lancaster PA 17602-3550 E-mail: stewartgraphics@redrose.net.

STEWART, BARBARA LYNN, church secretary, bookkeeper; b. Billings, Mont., May 13, 1954; d. Joseph Isacc and Ima Evelyn (Daugherty) Gates; m. Forrest Y. Stewart, Nov. 15, 1997. BS in Elem. Edn., Eastern Mont. Coll., 1976. Cert. tchr., Mont. Tchr. Union Sch., Lindsay, Mont., 1976-79, Greycliff Sch., Mont., 1979-80; supr. Alliance Christian Sch., Lewistown, Mont., 1981-83, prin., supr., 1983-86, Paradise Christian Acad., Lewistown, 1986-91; driver, dispatcher, contracts and svcs. coord. Spl. Transp. Inc., Billings, Mont., 1991-94; in-home caregiver Billings, 1994-97; tax preparer H&R Block, Carbondale, Ill., 1999, Herrin, Ill., 1999—2000; ch. sec., bookkeeper First Presbyn. Ch., Carbondale, 2000—.

STEWART, BARBARA LYNNE, geriatrics nursing educator; b. Youngstown, Ohio, May 10, 1953; d. Carl Arvid and Margaret Swanson; m. James G. Stewart, Mar. 17, 1973; children: Trevor J., Troy C. AAS, Youngstown State U., 1973, BS, 1982. Cert. gerontol. nurse, ANCC. Supr., dir. nursing svcs. Peaceful Acres Nursing Home, North Lima, Ohio; nurse repondent Health Sci. Ctr. U. Colo., Denver; charge nurse Westwood Rehab. Med. Ctr., Inc., Boardman, Ohio, Park Vista Health Care Ctr., Youngstown, Ohio; dir. nursing Rolling Acres Care Ctr., North Lima, Ohio; primary instr. Alliance (Ohio) Tng. Ctr., Inc.; asst. supr. Akron (Ohio) Dist. Office Divsn. Quality Assurance Bur. Long Term Care Quality, 2003—; supr. div. of quality assurance, bur. of Long Term Care Quality Ohio Dept. of Health. Former instr. CPR, ARC; mem. Western Res. Joint Fire Dept. Emergency Med. Svcs., 1st responder, Poland, Ohio. Mem. Tri County Dir. Nurses Assn., Nat. Gerontol. Nursing Assn. (nomination com.), Youngstown State U. Alumni Assn.

STEWART, CHRISTINE MARIE, church music director; b. Akron, Ohio, Nov. 9, 1973; d. William Harold and Mary Jo (Kuchenbrod) Stewart. MusB magna cum laude, U. Akron, Ohio, 1996; MusM, U. Akron, 2003—. Cert. tchr. Ohio, 1999. Vocal music dir. Aurora (Ohio) Schs., 1997—2001; vocal music tchr. Cuyahoga Falls (Ohio) City Schs., 2001—. Dir. music First Christian Ch., Cuyahoga Falls, Ohio, 2001—; vocalist, pianist, various weddings, funerals, private clubs, Ohio, 1993—; musical dir. comty. theatre groups, Ohio, 1996—. Grantee Ednl grant for Cleve. Opera Residency, Aurora (Ohio) PTO, 1999. Mem.: Music Educators Nat. Conf., Golden Key, Omicron Delta Kappa. Achievements include Her middle-sch. students participated in Cleve. Opera Co. mini-residency project in 1999,2001, performed with profls. in Carmen, The Barber of Seville. Avocations: crafts, rubber stamping. Office: Roberts Middle Sch 3333 Charles Ave Cuyahoga Falls OH 44221

STEWART, DEBBIE ELAINE, artist, librarian, artist; b. Bad Kreuznach, Germany, Sept. 24, 1962; d. Jesse Arthur and Rebecca Stewart; 1 child, Jesse. BA, Kent (Ohio) State U., 1984; MS in Libr. Sci., Drexel U., Phila., 1991. Cert. profl. librarian, Mich. Youth svcs. librarian Grand Rapids (Mich.) Pub. Library, 1994-99, youth svcs. specialist, 1999—. Lectr. Mich. Assn. of Educators of Young Children Conf., 2002—, Calcin Coll. Young Writers Conf., 2002, 03. Reviewer: Sch. Library Jour., 2000—; Remembering Summer, 1999, one-woman shows include Franciscan Life Process Ctr., 2001, exhibitions include First United Meth. Ch., 2002. Active church choir Blessed Sacrament Ch., Grand Rapids, Mich., 1998—. Recipient juried art award Festival Regional Arts Exhbn., 2000, Franciscan Life Process Ctr., 1999, 2001, 2003, First United Meth. Ch., 2000, 2002. Mem. Soc. Children's Book Writers & Illustrators (assoc., adv, com. Mich. 1998—, Mich. illustrator coord. 1999-2001), Am. Library Assn. (life). Roman Catholic. Avocations: music, gardening, balloon animals. Office: Debbie's Home Studio 1218 Ridgeway St NE Grand Rapids MI 49505 E-mail: dstewart@grpl.org

STEWART, DEBORAH CLAIRE, dean; b. Freeport, Ill., Sept. 14, 1951; Student, Monterey Peninsula Coll., 1969-71; BS in Zoology, U. Calif., Davis, 1973; MD, U. Calif., San Francisco, 1977. Diplomate Am. Bd. Peds. Intern Children's Hosp. L.A., 1977-78, resident in peds., 1978-79, fellow in adolescent medicine, 1979-81, attending physician emergency med. svcs., 1980-81; med. dir. comprehensive adolescent program dept. ob-gyn. Charles R. Drew Postgrad. Med. Sch., L.A., 1981-83; asst. prof. dept. ob-gyn. UCLA/Charles R. Drew Postgrad. Med. Sch., 1982-83; mem. ped. staff Children's Hosp. of Orange County, Orange, Calif., 1983-86, U. Calif. Irvine Med. Ctr., Orange, 1983-99; assoc. prof. ob-gyn., assoc. prof. medicine U. Calif., Irvine, 1983-99, dir. child sexual abuse program, 1983-99, assoc. prof. clin. peds., chief divsn. gen. peds., dir. adol, 1988-95, assoc. dean for med. student and resident affairs, 1992-99; med. dir. child protection ctr. Meml. Miller Children's Hosp., Long Beach, Calif., 1995-99; assoc. dean med. edn. program U. Calif.-San Francisco, Fresno, 1999—. Project dir. South Ctrl. L.A. Sexual Trauma Program, 1983; med. cons. L.A. Commn. on Assaults Against Women, 1982-84, Calif. Children's Svcs., 1980-85, Sexual Assault Protocol Office of Criminal Justice Planning, 1984-86, Sexual Assault Protocol L.A. County, 1984-86; med. dir. Child Abuse Svcs. Team County of Orange, 1987—; physician mem. Calif. State Atty. Gen.'s Investigative Pilot Projects Rsch. and Evaluation Adv. Panel; cons. County of Orange Coroner's Office, 1994-99. Contbr. articles to profl. jours.; presenter in field; reviewer: Ped. and Adolescent Gyn., 1988—, Jour. Adolescent Health Care, 1986—, Peds., 1988—, Am. Jour. Obs. and Gyn., 1991— Mem. med. adv. bd. Planned Parenthood, 1983-94. Fellow Am. Acad. Pediatrics (pres. Dist. IX Chpt. 4, 1995-97, sec. chpt. IV, chair chpt. IV com. on child abuse 1983—); mem. N.Am. Soc. Pediatric And Adolescent Gynecology (co-chair collaborative rsch. com. 1988—), Orange County Ped. Assn. Office: U Calif San Francisco-Fresno Med Edn Program 2615 E Clinton Ave Fresno CA 93703-2223 E-mail: deborah.stewart@ucsfresno.edu.

STEWART, DEBRA WEHRLE, academic administrator; b. Petersburg, Va., May 22, 1943; BA in Philosophy and Polit. Sci., Marquette U., 1965; MA in Govt., U. Md., 1967; PhD in Polit. Sci., U. N.C., 1975. Instr. polit. sci. European divsn. U. Md., Nuremberg, Germany, 1967-69; instr. polit. sci. and pub. adminstrn. N.C. State U., Raleigh, 1974-75, asst. prof., 1975-78, assoc. prof., 1979-83, prof., 1984—, acting dir. MPA program, 1978, assoc. dean Grad. Sch., 1983-86, interim vice provost and dean Grad. Sch., 1986-88, dean Grad. Sch., 1988-2000, vice provost, 1995-98, vice chancellor, dean Grad. Sch., 1998-2000; pres. Coun. Grad. Schs., Washington, 2000—. Interim chancellor U. N.C., Greensboro, 1994; mem. com. on assessment of rsch. doctorate NRC, 1992-95; mem. Grad. Record Exam. Bd., 1992-96, chmn.-elect, 1994-95, chmn., 1995-96; bd. dirs. Coun. Grad. Schs., 1990—, chmn.-elect, 1992-93, chmn., 1993-94; mem. Test English as Fgn. Lang. Bd., 1992-95; councilor Oak Ridge Assoc. Univs., 1988-92, bd. dirs., 1993—, chair-elect 1997—; bd. dirs. Nat. Phys. Scis. Consortium, 1998—; mem. exec. com. Coun. So. Grad. Schs., 1989-91; trustee Triangle U. Ctr. for Advanced Studies, 1989—; mem. Commn. on Peer Rev. and Accreditation, Nat. Assn. of Schs. of Pub. Affairs and Adminstrn., 1997-99. Author: The Women's Movement in Community Politics: The Role of Local Commissions on the Status of Women, 1980, (with G. David Garson) Organizational Behavior and Public Management, 1983, 3d edit. (with Vasu and Garson), 1998; editor: Women in Local Politics, 1980; mem. editl. bd. Rev. Pub. Pres. Adminstrn., 1981-89, Annals Pub. Adminstrn., 1982-84, Women and Politics, 1980-88, Politics and Policy, 1983-86; contbr. articles to profl. jours., chpts. to books. Recipient edn. award YWCA Acad. Women, 1988 Mem. Nat. Assn. State Univs. and Land-Grant Colls. (bd. dirs. 1992-94, exec. com. coun. on rsch. policy and grad. edn. 1989-92, chmn. 1990-91), Am. Soc. for Pub. Adminstrn. (com. on status of women in pub. adminstrn. 1976-78, com. on profl. stds. and ethics 1980-89, chmn. com. on whistle blowing and dissent channels of profl. stds. and ethics com. 1985-86, Burchfield award 1976), So. Polit. Sci. Assn. (nominating com. 1978, coord. pub. adminstrn. sect. 1979), Women's Forum N.C., Phi Kappa Phi, Pi Sigma Alpha, Pi Alpha Alpha. Office: Coun Grad Schs Grad Sch 1 Dupont Cir NW Ste 430 Washington DC 20036-1136

STEWART, DORIS MAE, biology educator; b. Sandsprings, Mont., Dec. 12, 1927; d. Virgil E. and Violet M. (Weaver) S.; m. Felix Loren Powell, Oct. 8, 1956; children: Leslie, Loren. BS, Coll. Puget Sound, 1948, MS, 1949; PhD, U. Wash., 1953. Instr. U. Mont., Missoula, 1954-56, asst. prof., 1956-57, U. Puget Sound, Tacoma, 1957-58; head sci. dept. Am. Kiz Lisesi, Istanbul, Turkey, 1958-62; rsch. asst. prof. U. Wash., Seattle, 1963-67, rsch. assoc. prof., 1967-68; assoc. prof. Cen. Mich. U., Mt. Pleasant, 1970-72, U. Balt., 1973-81, prof., 1981-95, prof. emeritus, 1995—. Contbr. numerous articles to profl. jours. Mem. Am. Physiol. Soc., Sigma Xi. Home: 1103 Frederick Rd Baltimore MD 21228-5032

STEWART, DOROTHY K. librarian; b. Bristol, Conn., Sept. 28, 1928; d. Robert and Anna Esther (Schwitz) Konopask; m. David Benjamin Stewart, Sept. 27, 1952 (div. Nov. 1979); children: Douglas Neil, Diane Alison. BA in Romance Langs. and Lit. cum laude, Boston U., 1950; MSLS, Cath. U. Am., 1959. Children's libr. Brookline (Mass.) Pub. Libr., 1953-55, Takoma Park (Md.) Libr., 1955-57; reference libr. U.S. Geol. Survey, 1961; libr. Washington Internat. Sch., 1979-80, Office Sea Grant NOAA, Rockville, Md., 1980-82; info. specialist Life Ring, Inc., Silver Spring, Md., 1983-84; pub. svc. libr. Urban Inst., Washington, 1984-85; user svcs. coord. ERIC Clearinghouse on Tchg. and Tchr. Edn., Washington, 1985-97; ret., 1997. Active, past pres. PTA, Rockville, Md., 1973-78; chmn., mem. com. Potomac (Md.) Libr. Adv. Com., 1975-85. Mem. Capital PC User Group, French lang. clubs, Phi Beta Kappa, Beta Phi Mu. Democrat. Avocations: travel, hiking, birding, microcomputers. E-mail: dkstewart1@netzero.net.

STEWART, FELECIA MARCIA, purchasing agent; b. Sparta, Ga., Aug. 22, 1960; d. Clarence and Lillie Pearl Stewart; 1 child, Rameiz Ezell Lewis. AD, Ctrl. Piedmont C.C., 1980; student, Dallas Bapt. U., 1999—. Acting systems site mgr. Northrop Grumman, Stuart, Fla., 1994—96; buyer, purchasing and materials dept. Vought Aircraft Industries, Inc., Milledgeville, Ga., 1997— Computer ops. Grumman Aircraft Industries, Milledgeville, 1982—92. Bd. mem. Hancock County Sch. Sys., 2003—; dir. outrech ministry New Beginnings & Enhancement Agy., Inc, 2000—03; founder, dir. Youth Success In Christ, Sparta, Ga., 1998—2003. Home: 2 Church St Sparta GA 31087 Office: Vought Aircraft Industries Inc Hwy 22 West Milledgeville GA 31061 Personal E-mail: fstewart@hancock.k12.ga.us. E-mail: felecia_stewart@voughtaircraft.com.

STEWART, GEORGIANA LICCIONE, writer; b. Mount Vernon, N.Y., May 18, 1943; d. Arthur Alfred and Grace Marie (Zuzzolo) Liccione; m. William Lawrence Stewart, July 18, 1975. BA, Columbia U., 1971; MA, Columbia Tchr.'s Coll., N.Y.C., 1973; MAT, Manhattanville Coll., 1973. Author, cons. Kimbo Ednl., Long Branch, N.J., 1970—; spl. edn. tchr. Bronxville (N.Y.) H.S., 1989—. Cons. NAEYC, SACUS, 1975-89, Pres.'s Coun. on Physical Fitness, 1979-81. Author: (69 children's musical activity records and books including) Adaptive Motor Learning, 1982, Bean Bag Activities, 1983, Preschool Aerobic Fun, 1989, Children of the World, 1991, ulticultural Rhythm Stick Fun, 1992, Toddlerific, 1993, World of Parachute Play, 1997, Children's Folk Dances, 1998, Moving with Mozart, 1999 (Early Childhood Dir.'s Choice award NAEYC), Nursery Rhyme Time, 2000, Cool Aerobics for Kids, 2001, Musical Scarves, 2002, Circle Time, 2004. Recipient Student Advocacy Overcoming the Odds award, 1997. Mem. AAHPERD, Nat. Assn. for Edn. of Young Children, So. Assn. for Children Under Six, Faculty Dance Educators Am., Assn. for Retarded Citizens, Columbia Club, Women's Nat. Rep. Club. Avocations: Heatsong music and art therapy program, organizing local benefit programs. Home: 81 Pondfield Rd # 328 Bronxville NY 10708-3818 Office: Kimbo Ednl PO Box 477 Long Branch NJ 07740-0477

STEWART, GWENDOLYN JOHNS, music educator; b. Winston-Salem, N.C., Feb. 11, 1926; d. Island Lemuel Johns and Vandelia Trumilla Perry-Johns; m. Jason Hawkins, Sr. (dec.); 1 child, Jason Hawkins Jr.; m. George Sturgis (dec.); 1 child, Daryl Sturgis ; m. Robert H. Stewart, Jan. 20, 1979 (dec.). Student, Spelman Coll., 1943—46, Juilliard Sch. Music, 1947; BS in Edn., Winston-Salem Tchrs. Coll., 1950; postgrad., A & T State U., Greensboro, N.C., 1955. Tchr. Pub. Sch. Sys., Gastonia, NC, 1951—57, Mooresville, NC, 1957—61, Forsyth County Pub. Sch. Sys., Winston-Salem, 1961—65; owner-oper. Jack & Jill Kindergarten #2, Winston-Salem, 1965—68; dir. chancel choir Friendship Bapt. Ch., Winston-Salem, 1961—79; pianist, organist, dir. Grace Presbyn. Ch. USA, Winston-Salem, 1997—; pianist, organist Gen. Bapt. State Conv. N.C., Winston-Salem, 1982—86, dir. music, 1986—90. Chmn. music dept. Shiloh Bapt. Ch., Winston-Salem, 1997—2002. Author: The Gwen Johns Basic Music Guide, 2000, Bells Alive Book One, 2003, composer song collection; contbr. poetry to anthologies. Avocations: sewing, cooking. Home: 2795 Bethabara Rd Winston Salem NC 27106 E-mail: gjstewart12@triad.rr.com.

STEWART, IDALEE ADEL, educational administrator, consultant; b. Chicago, Ill., Aug. 11, 1941; d. Jack and Rose Adel; m. David Henry Stewart, Mar. 16, 2002; children: Stacey Elyn Garrison, Douglas Joel Lusky, Zoe Claire Alvarez. BA, UCLA, 1959—78; MA, Calif. State U., Dominguez Hills, 2001—02. Administrative Credential Calif. State U., Dominguez Hills, 2002, Language Development Specialist Credential LA Unified Sch. Dist.-Commn. on Tchr. Credentialing, 1985, Multiple Subjects Teacher Credential Commn. on Tchr. Credentialing, Calif., 1979. U. supr. NOVA Southeastern U., North Miami Beach, 2002—; tchr. LA Unified Sch. Dist., 1979—98; cons. Los Angeles Unified Sch. Dist., 1998—; publishers rep. Gt. Source Edn. Group(HoughtonMifflin), Los Angeles, 2001—02; profl. expert LA Unified Sch. Dist., 1999—2001, mentor, 1984—98, tchr., 1979—98; reviewer(textbook) Ballard & Tighe, Brea, Calif., 1996—98; publishers rep. Gt. Source Edn. Group(HoughtonMifflin), Los Angeles, 2000—02; univ. supr. Loyola Marymount U., 2003—. Cons./event coord. LA Unified Sch. Dist., 1998—2002; profl. test devel. Dept. of Edn. Calif., 1986—91; textbook reviewer Ballard & Tighe Publishers, Brea, Calif., 1996—98; spl. edn. adviser East LA Coll., Monterey Pk., Calif., 1976—80; test devel. UCLA-CREEST/Los Angeles Unified Sch. Dist., 1989—91. Vol. Camp Ronald McDonald for GoodTimes, Los Angeles, 2000—03. Integrated Hist., Art Tchg. Unit grant, LA Ednl. Partnership, 1987, 1988. Mem.: Women in Ednl. Leadership (assoc.), Assn. for Profl. and Curriculum Devel. (assoc.). Avocations: travel, reading, fashion development, outdoors. Personal E-mail: iastewart2@hotmail.com.

STEWART, JANET, artist; b. Des Moines, July 5, 1931; d. Joseph Kenneth Siberz and Bertha Schiltz; m. Clifford Charles Russell, Oct. 3, 1950 (div. 1967); children: Lynn Marie, Wayne Kenneth; m. Donald Roy Stewart (dec. May 1996). Represented by Wyland Gallery of Las Vegas, 1996—2002, Island Art Galleries, Honolulu, 1999—, Wyland Galleries of Hawaii, 1988-98, Wyland Galleries of Fla., 1997—, Dreams of Paradise, Hilo, Hawaii, 1999—, Rift Zone, Kona, Hawaii, 2001—, Aloha Fine Arts, Kauai, Hawaii, 1999—. Author: Ohana O Janet Stewart, 1997. Mem. San Gabriel Fine Arts Assn, Calif. Art Club. Avocations: reading, dance, singing.

STEWART, JANICE MAE, federal judge; b. Medford, Oreg., Feb. 13, 1951; d. Glenn Logan and Eathel Mae (Jones) S.; m. F. Gordon Allen III, Aug. 10, 1975; children: Benjamin Stewart, Rebecca Mae. AB in Econs., Stanford U., 1972; JD, U. Chgo., 1975. Bar: Ill. 1976, Oreg. 1977, U.S. Dist. Ct. Oreg. 1977, U.S. Ct. Appeals (9th cir.) 1978. Assoc. Winston & Strawn, Chgo., 1975-76, McEwen, Gisvold, Rankin & Stewart, Portland, Oreg., 1976-81, ptnr., 1981-93; U.S. Magistrate Judge Portland, 1993—. Mem. Multonomah County Profl. Responsbility Com., Portland, 1979-82, Oreg. Profl. Responsibility Bd., 1982-85, Oreg. State Bar Practice and Procedure Com., 1985-88, Profl. Liability Fund Def. Panel, Portland, 1985-93, Multnomah County Jud. Selection Com., 1985-88, Oreg. State Bar Professionalism Com., 1989-91, Oreg. State Bar Fed. Practice and Procedure Com., 1996-99, 2004-, Coun. Ct. Procedures, 1991-93, lawyer rep. 9th Cir. Jud. Conf., 1990-93, Multnomah County Professionalism Com., 1997-2000. Mem. ABA, Am. Arbitration Assn. (arbitrator 1990-93), Oreg. Bar Assn., Multnomah County Bar Assn. (dir. 1990-93), Phi Beta Kappa. Democrat. Office: 1027 US Courthouse 1000 SW 3rd Ave Portland OR 97204-2930 Office Phone: 503-326-8260.

STEWART, JOAN HINDE, academic administrator; b. N.Y.C., Aug. 11, 1944; d. Wade and Dorothy (Ronning) H.; m. Philip Robert Stewart, Jan. 31, 1970; children: Anna Faye, Justin. Student, Université Laval Summer Sch, Quebec, 1963, Middlebury Coll. Summer Sch., 1964-65; BA summa cum laude, St. Joseph's Coll., 1965; student, Salzburg Summer Sch., Austria, 1966; MPhil, Yale U., 1969, PhD, 1970. Tchg. assoc. French Yale U., New Haven, 1967—69, acting instr. French, 1969—70; instr. French Wellesley (Mass.) Coll., 1970—71, asst. prof. French, 1971—72, N.C. State U., Raleigh, 1973—77, assoc. prof. French, 1977—81, prof. French, 1981—99, asst. head dept. fgn. langs. and lits., 1978—82, asst. dean rsch. and grad. programs, 1983—85, acting head dept. fgn. langs. and lits., 1984—85, head dept. fgn. langs. and lit., 1985—97; prof., dean liberal arts U. S.C., 1999—2003; pres., prof. French Hamilton Coll., Clinton, NY, 2003—. Author: The Novels of Mme Riccoboni, 1976, Colette, 1983, 1996, Gynographs: French Novels by Women of the Late Eighteenth Century, 1993; editor: Mme Riccoboni's Lettres de Mistriss Fanni Butlerd, 1979; co-editor: Isabelle de Charrière's Lettres de Mistriss Henley, 1993, Marie Riccoboni's Histoire d'Ernestine, 1998. Chmn. N.C. Humanities Coun., 1988-89. Fellow Camargo Found., Cassis, France, 1979, Nat. Humanities Ctr., 1982-83, (sr.) ctr. for humanities Wesleyan U., 1990; NEH summer seminar fellowship, Princeton U., 1980; NEH fellowship Coll. Tchrs. and Ind. Scholars, 1990-91, 1994-95; fellow Ctr. d'Etude du XVIII Siecle, U. Paul Valery, Montpellier, France, 1995, Liguria Study Ctr. for the Arts and Scis., Bogliasco, Italy, 1997, Beinecke Rare Book and Manuscript Libr., Yale U., 1997; stipend younger humanists NEH, 1973; travel grantee ACLS, 1983; travel to collections grantee NEH, 1984; vis. scholar European Humanities Rsch. Ctr., Oxford U., 1995. Mem. AAUP, MLA, Am. Assn. Tchrs. French.

STEWART, JOANNE, director; b. Vancouver, Wash., Mar. 10, 1944; d. Edward Charles and Claudine Marie Spencer; m. William Lemley Stewart, Sept. 2, 1966 (dec. June 1983); children: Amy Diane Stemple, Nicholas William. BS, Wash. State U., 1966, MA, 1973. Cert. tchr., Mont., Idaho, Wash., Calif. Tchr. foods Seaside High Sch., Monterey, Calif., 1966-67; tchr. home econs. Marysville (Wash.) High Sch., 1967 68, Palouse (Wash.) High Sch., 1968-73, Ennis (Mont.) High Sch., 1973-76, Genesee (Idaho) High Sch., 1976-77; instr. young family Missoula (Mont.) County High Sch., 1983-84; tchr. home econs. Woodman Sch., Lolo, Mont., 1985-86; travel cons. Travel Masters, Missoula, 1984-87; ticketing mgr. Blue Caboose Travel, Missoula, 1987-91; tchr. family and consumer scis. Victor (Mont.) High Sch., 1991-2001; dir. Victor 21st Century Learning Ctr., 2001—, After Sch. Learning Ctr. Project dir. sch.-to-work implementation Victor Sch. Reaching Out for Positive Ednl. Success (ROPES), 1996—2002, project dir. Op. Green Thumb, gender equity Carl Perkins grant, 1997—98. Co-pres. Lolo PTO, 1980-81; v.p. Lolo Community Ctr., 1981; sec. Lolo Mosquito Control Bd., 1988—; mem. telecommunications com. Conrad Burns & Gov. Racicot; sec. state supt. edn. task force on vocat. edn., 1995-96; coord. Health Rocks!, Nat. 4-H Program, 2000-01. Marysville Edn. Assn. scholar, 1962, Future Homemakers Am. scholar, 1962. Mem. AAUW (sec. 1986, program chmn. 1987), Forestry Triangle (pres. 1981, editor cookbook 1982), Washington State Future Homemakers Am. (hon. mem.), Am. Family and Consumer Scis. Assn., Mont. Family and Consumer Scis. Assn. (bylaws chair 1994, pres. elect 1995-96, pres. 1996-97, Profl. of Yr. 1997), Mont. Vocat. Tchrs. Assn. (returning Rookie of Yr. 1992, Am. Federated Tchrs., Mont. Vocat. Family and Consumer Scis. Tchrs. (v.p. 1993-94, pres. 1994-95, Tchr. of Yr. 1998). Republican. Methodist. Avocations: homemaking, swimming. Home: 1200 Lakeside Dr Lolo MT 59847-9705 Office: Victor High Sch ROPES 425 4th Ave Victor MT 59875-9468

STEWART, KAREN ELIZABETH VICTORIA, research scientist, artist; M, U. of Ctrl. Fla., 1999—2002; MA in social sci. sociology and anthropology, U. of Costa Rica Empresarial U., 1998—2000. Rschr., social scientist Elizabeth Stewart, New Orleans, 1992—2002, social scientist, rschr., under cover as one of the homeless South Tex., Tex., 1992—, social scientist, rschr. Designer (clothing) Created The Blousson Sweater. Grant, U. of Ctrl. Fla., 2001, Scholarship, U. of Costa Rica Empresarial U., 1998. Achievements include research in solutions to homelessness in the USA; more than 50 inventions. E-mail: estewart7@lycos.com.

STEWART, KAY BOONE, writer, retired educator and administrator; b. Amarillo, Tex., Feb. 2, 1934; d. Howard Taft and Olive Eugenia (Greer) Boone; m. Robert N. Alkire, July 22, 1952 (div. Aug. 1971); children: Shelley Kay Alkire, Kristin Lynne Alkire Porter; m. Elmer Donald Stewart, July 16, 1978. Student, Phoenix Coll., 1957-64, Glendale (Ariz.) C.C., 1967; BA in Elem. Edn. with distinction, Ariz. State U., 1969; postgrad., Seattle Pacific U., 1988-90. Cert. tchr. elem. edn., Ariz. Tchr. Glendale (Ariz.) Meth. Day Sch., 1960-63, Trinity Meth. Day Sch., Glendale, 1966-67, Ctrl. Meth. Day Sch., Phoenix, 1967-68, Catalina Elem. Sch., Phoenix, 1969-70, Valencia Elem. Sch., Phoenix, 1970-71, Palo Alto Pre-Sch., Tempe, Ariz., 1971-73; sales rep., ednl. program Western Pub., southwestern states, 1972-75; dist. mgr. Brittanica Films Divsn., 1975—78; adminstr., program developer, thcr. Palo Alto and Glendale Meth. Day Sch. Adminstr. Skytech Cons., Inc., Elk Grove, Calif., 1999; prin., owner Kay's Kards, 2001—, Glass Painting, 2002—; watercolor artist, glass painting Kay's Kards: Giftware, 2003. Author: (novel) Chariots of Dawn, 1992, (poetry) Sunrise Over Galilee, 1993, Here's Help, A Management System for Chronic Fatigue Syndrome, 1996. (poetry) The Color Red, 1994; editor Writers Info. Network, 1986-99; composer and lyricist children's and adults' choir music. Mem. Am. Penwomen (pres. 1990-92), Writers Info. Network, Kappa Delta Phi. Republican. Presbyterian. Avocations: storytelling, singing, harp, directing children's choir. Home: 202 Rainbow Dr # 10261 Livingston TX 77399-2002 Office: Writers Info Network PO Box 11337 Bainbridge Island WA 98110 E-mail: kstew2234@aol.com., ksb@mymailstation.com.

STEWART, LEORA KLAYMER, textile artist, educator; b. Jerusalem, June 5, 1943; came to the U.S., 1952; d. Errol and Reva (Svirsky) Klaymer. BFA, Art Inst. Chgo., 1962, MFA, 1968. Asst. prof. Tyler Sch. Art, Phila., 1970-72, New Sch. Parsons, N.Y.C., 1974-77; prof. art Baruch Coll., N.Y.C., 1977-96, Fashion Inst. Tech., N.Y.C., 1987—. Textile designer LLAMA Studios, Bklyn., 1990—; lectr. Textile Conservation Group, fall 1988; guest artist Textile Study Group N.Y., 1992, Textile Arts Conf., Chgo., 1993, Textile Conservation Group, 1990; juror/curator of numerous exhbns. One-woman exhibits include Hadler/Rodriguez Galleries, N.Y.C., 1976, 79, 2/20 Gallery, NYC, 2001, Gayle Willson Gallery, Sothampton, NY, Helsinki Mus. Art & Design, Helen Drutt Gallery, Phila.; two-person shows include Gayle Wilson Gallery, Southampton, L.I., N.Y., 1988; group exhibits include Gayle Wilson Gallery, Southampton, 1993-94, Pres.'s Office-FIT, N.Y., 1993-94, Colonial House Gallery, N.Y., 1994, Faculty Exhbn.-FIT Galleries, N.Y., 1994-95, Acad. of the Arts, Easton, Md., 1996, many others; archtl. commn. Knoll Internat. Showrooms, World Trade Ctr., Dallas, Gotaas-Larsen Shipping Corp., N.Y.C., Bank of Hong Kong, World Trade Ctr., N.Y.C., Bullock's Corp., Chistown Mall, Phoenix; represented in permanent collections Prudential Life Ins., Chase Manhattan Bank, Continental Wheat and Grain Corp., S.E. Banking Corp., Becton-Dickson Pharm. Corp. Travel grantee Art Inst. Chgo., 1968-69; craftsman fellow Nat. Endowment for the Arts, Washington, 1972-73, 76-77. Avocations: traveling, hiking, bicycling, swimming. Office: Fashion Inst Tech 27th St & 7th Ave New York NY 10001 Address: 3605 S Ocean Blvd Palm Beach FL 33480 Office Phone: 212-217-7037. E-mail: klaymer1@aol.com.

STEWART, LOIS, humanities educator, curriculum coordinator; b. Quessua, Malange, Angola, Feb. 28, 1938; d. Ralph Edward and Eunice Elvira Dodge; m. John McIntyre Stewart, Aug. 15, 1964; children: Jeannie McIntyre Eisenhart, Alison Carroll. BA, Carleton Coll., 1955—59; MA, Yale U., 1959—60; PCE, U. of Rhodesia and Nyasaland, 1961. Cert. Teaching; English and French Mo. Dept. of Elem. and Secondary Edn., 1974, Secondary Teaching in English NY State Dept. of Edn., 1965. Tchr. English and French Hartzell Secondary Sch., Old Umtali Mission, Zimbabwe, 1962—65; tchr. English Pittsford (N.Y.) Ctrl. HS, 1965—66; tchr. English, chmn.English dept. Internat. Sch. of Brussels, 1966—70, Am. Sch. of Switzerland, 1970—73; tchr.English Ash Grove (Mo.) Jr. HS, 1974—83; tchr. English and French Springfield Pub. Schs., 1983—. Dist. curriculum chmn. for fgn. languages Springfield Pub. Schools, Mo., 1995—. Editor: (family history) The Ancestors and Descendants of James Montaney (1799-1857); editor: (publisher) (newsletter) Newsletter of the Society of Descendants of Johannes de la Montagne. Chmn. Glendale Site Coun., Springfield, Mo., 1994—95; del. Dem. Party, Springfield, Mo. Recipient Outstanding Tchr., 417 Mag., 1998; Full coll. scholarship, Inland Steel, 1956—59. Mem.: Nat. Geneal. Soc., NY Biog. and Geneal. Soc., Am. Coun. on the Tchg. of Fgn. Languages, Fgn. Lang. Assn. of Mo., Ozarks Fgn. Lang. Assn., Phi Beta Kappa. Democrat-Npl. Meth. Avocation: travel. Home: 3657 West Nichols Springfield MO 65803-5670 Office: Glendale HS 2727 Ingram Mill Rd Springfield MO 65804 Personal E-mail: loissdjm2@aol.com. E-mail: lstewart@sps.org.

STEWART, LUCILLE MARIE, retired special education educator; b. Pitts., Feb. 24; d. William H. and Edna (Hoffman) S. BEd, Duquesne U.; MEd, U. Pitts.; postgrad., Columbia U., U. Calif., Calif. State U. Cert. elem. and secondary tchr., spl. edn. tchr., supr., adminstr. Tchr., group leader mentally retarded Ednl. Alliance, N.Y.C., 1950—53; tchr. Lincoln (Ill.) State Sch., 1953; tchr., program leader, sec. Edn. Alliance, N.Y.C., 1954-58; tchr. mentally retarded Ramapo Ctrl. Sch. Dist., Spring Valley, N.Y., 1958-60, tchr. seriously emotionally disturbed, 1960-64, supr. presch. program for educationally disadvantaged, 1965-67; program dir. Pomona (N.Y.) Camp for Retarded, summers 1960-63; tchr. mentally retarded Stockton Sch., San Diego, 1964-65; tchr. mentally retarded sch. Cathedral City Sch., 1967-78; program specialist spl. edn. Palm Springs (Calif.) Unified Sch. Dist., 1978-95; prin. elem. summer schs. Palm Springs (Calif.) Unified Sch. Dist., 1971-72; tchr. elem. mentally retarded sch. Palm Springs (Calif.) Unified; prin.-tchr. Summer Extended Sch. for Spl. Students, summer 1979-99. Exec. com. U. Calif. Extension, area adv. com.; spl. edn. surrogate parent Palm Springs Unified Sch. Dist. Mem. NEA, AAUW, ASCD, Calif. Adminstrs. Spl. Edn. (desert cmty. mental health childrens com.), Coun. Exceptional Children (adminstrn. divsn., early childhood-learning handicap divsns.), Am. Assn. Childhood Edn., Autism Soc., Coachella Valley, Learning Disabilities Assn., Creative Desert, Desert Theater League, Alpha Kappa Alpha, Phi Delta Kappa, Delta Kappa Gamma.

STEWART, MARGARET MCBRIDE, biology educator, researcher; b. Guilford County, N.C., Feb. 6, 1927; d. David Henry and Mary Ellen (Morrow) S.; m. Paul C. Lemon, June 1962 (div. 1968); m. George Edward Martin, Dec. 19, 1969. AB, U. N.C.-Greensboro, 1948; MA, U. N.C.-Chapel Hill, 1951; PhD, Cornell U., 1956; DSc (hon.), U. P.R., Mayaquez, 1996. Instr. biology Greensboro Evening Coll. U. N.C., Greensboro, 1950-51; instr. biology Catawba Coll., Salisbury, N.C., 1951-53; extension botanist Cornell U., Ithaca, N.Y., 1954-56; asst. prof. biology SUNY, Albany, 1956-59, assoc. prof., 1959-65, prof. vertebrate biology, 1965-97, disting. tchg. prof., 1977—, disting. tchg. prof. emerita, 1997; dir. Program in Biodiversity Conservation and Policy, 1997-2000. Faculty rsch. participant Oak Ridge Assoc. Univs., 1983. Author: (with A.H. Benton) Keys to the Vertebrates of the Northeastern States, 1964, Amphibians of Malawi, 1967; contbr. numerous articles and revs. to profl. jours. Bd. dirs. E.N. Huyck Nature Preserve, Rensselaerville, N.Y., 1976-86; bd. dirs. Ea. N.Y. chpt. Nature Conservancy, 1983-88, 90-96, 97-, N.Y. State chpt., 1987-90; mem. Albany Pine Bush Commn., 1993—. Recipient Citizen Laureate award SUNY Found., 1987, Oak Leaf award Nature Conservancy, 1997; Am. Philos. Soc. rsch. grantee, 1975, 81, NSF grantee, 1978-80, Oak Ridge Assocs. Univs. grantee, 1983-97. Fellow Herpetologists League (bd. dirs. 1978-80); mem. Soc. for Study of Amphibians and Reptiles (pres. 1979), Am. Soc. Ichthyologists and Herpetologists (bd. govs. 1975-80, 87-90, 96—, herpetology editor 1983-85, pres. 1996, historian 1999—), Ecol. Soc. Am., Assn. for Tropical Biologists, Soc. Study of Evolution, III World Congress of Herpetology (mem. exec. com. 1995-01), Sigma Xi, Sigma Delta Epsilon, Phi Kappa Phi. Democrat. Presbyterian. Avocations: photography, gardening, reading, travel. Office: SUNY Dept Biol Scis 1400 Washington Ave Albany NY 12222-1000

STEWART, MARTHA KOSTYRA, entrepreneur, lecturer, author; b. Jersey City, Aug. 3, 1941; d. Edward and Martha (Ruszkowski) Kostyra; m. Andy Stewart, July 1, 1961 (div. 1990); 1 child, Alexis. BA European History and Archtl. History, Barnard Coll. Former model; former stockbroker; former profl. caterer; mag. owner, editor-in-chief Martha Stewart Living, 1990—97; CEO Martha Stewart Living Omnimedia, 1997—2003, chief creative officer, 2003—04, chmn., 1997—2004, founding editorial dir., 2004—. Lifestyle cons. for K-Mart Corp., 1987; bd. dirs., NYSE, 2002. Host (TV show) Martha Stewart Living, 1993-2004; Author: (with Elizabeth Hawes) Entertaining, 1982, Weddings, 1987; Martha Stewart Hors d'Oeurvres: The Creation and Presentation of Fabulous Finger Food, 1984, Martha Stewart's Pies and Tarts, 1985, Martha Stewart's Quick Cook Menus: Fifty-two Meals You Can Make in Under an Hour, 1988, The Wedding Planner, 1988, Martha Stewart's Gardening: Month by Month, 1991, Martha Stewart's New Old House: Restoration, Renovation, Decoration, 1992, Martha Stewart's Christmas, 1993, Martha Stewart's Menus for Entertaining, 1994, Holidays, 1994, Good Things: The Best of Martha Stewart Living, 1997, Four Seasons of Great Menus to Make Every Day, 1997, Hors D'Oeuves Handbook, 1999, The Best of Martha Stewart Living: Weddings, 1999, The Barefoot Contessa Cookbook: Secrets from the East Hampton Specialty Food Store for Simple Food and Party Platters You Can Make at Home, 1999, (with Ina Garten) Favorite Comfort Food, 1999, The Martha Stewart Living Cookbook, 2000, Halloween: The Best of Martha Stewart Living, 2001, Classic Crafts and Recipes Inspired by the Songs of Christmas, 2002, Martha Stewart Living 2003 Recipes, 2002; appears in semi-monthly cooking segment on Today Show. Office: 10 Saugatuck Ave Westport CT 06880-5720 also: care Susan Magrino Agy 40 W 57th St Fl 31 New York NY 10019-4001

STEWART, MARY R, education educator, artist; b. Santa Cruz, Calif., Sept. 16, 1952; BFA, U. New Mex., 1975; MFA, Ind. U., 1980. Asst. prof. U. of Ark., 1980—81; instr. Santa Rosa Jr. Coll., Calif., 1981—82; asst. prof. Dickinson Coll., Carlisle, Pa., 1982—85; assoc. prof. Syracuse U., 1985—2001, No. Ill. U., 2001—. Cons. SUNY, Oswego, NY, 2000, U. Tenn., Knoxville, 2000; scholarly artist in residence Colo. Coll., 2000; artists fellowship Va. Ctr. for the Creative Arts, 1994, 95, 98, 99, 2003, Ore. Coll. of Art and Craft, 1993; v.p. conf. program Found. in Art Theory and Edn., 1995—97, v.p. for regional programming, 2001—03. Exhibitions include St. BonAventure U., 2001, Everson Mus. of Art, 1993, U. of Richmond, 2003; author: (books) Launching the Imagination: A Comprehensive Guide to Basic Design, Launching the Imagination: 2D Design, Launching the Imagination: 3D Design. Office: Sch of Art No Ill U 314D Ahrends Hall Dekalb IL 60115 E-mail: mstewart@niu.edu.

STEWART, MIMI (MIRIAM) (KAY) (MIMI STEWART), state legislator, educator; b. Sarasota, Fla., Jan. 27, 1947; d. Wilbur H. Stewart and Alice Miriam Beck; children: Boris Nathan Margolin, Hannah Beck Margolin. BA cum laude, Boston U., 1971; MS, Wheelock Coll., 1977. Spl. educator, 1977—2004; mem. N.Mex. Ho. of Reps., Albuquerque, 1994—. Democrat. Address: 313 Moon St NE Albuquerque NM 87123-1151

STEWART, NANCY SUE SPURLOCK, education educator; b. Phoenix, Dec. 31, 1933; d. Ernest Neal and Ethel Ora (Boothe) Spurlock; m. Biven Stewart, Dec. 31, 1953 (div. 1962); 1 child, Sally K. BA in Edn., Ariz. State U., 1961, MA in Edn., 1968, Reading Specialist Cert., 1970. Cert. tchr. 1-12, Ariz. Elem. tchr., reading specialist Chandler (Ariz.) Pub. Schs. Dist. 80, 1961-92; instr. Greater Phoenix Area Writing Project Ariz. State U. and Chandler Unified Sch. Dist. 80, 1983—. Mem. AAUW, NEA, Chandler Edn. Assn., Ariz. Edn. Assn., Delta Kappa Gamma Soc. Internat., Kappa Delta. Mem. Ch. of Christ. Avocations: crafts, reading. Home: 4308 E Ahwatukee Dr Phoenix AZ 85044-2702

STEWART, PAMELA L. lawyer; b. Bogalusa, La., Mar. 13, 1953; d. James Adrian and Patricia Lynn (Wood) Lloyd; m. Steven Bernard Stewart, Aug. 31, 1974 (div. July 1980); 1 child, Christopher. BA, U. New Orleans, 1986; JD, U. Houston, 1990. Intern La. Supreme Ct., New Orleans, 1984, Councilman Bryan Wagner, New Orleans, 1984-85; legal asst. Clann, Bell & Murphy, Houston, 1988-89, Tejas Gas Corp., Houston, 1989-90; atty. Law Offices of Pamela L. Stewart, Houston, 1991—. Bd. dirs. Alliance for Good Govt., New Orleans, 1983-84, Attention Deficit Hyperactivity Disorder Assn. Tex., 1989-90; vol. Houston Vol. Lawyers Program, Houston, 1992—; mem. Planned Giving Coun.; bd. dirs. West Lane Place Civic Assn., sec., 2001-2003, v.p., 2003—; mem. com. Lawyers Against Waste, Habitat for Humanity; apptd. Harris County Appraisal Rev. Bd. Innsbruck scholar, U. New Orleans, 1985. Fellow Inst. Politics; mem. ABA, Tax Freedom Inst., Nat. Assn. Consumer Bankruptcy Attys., Nat. Assn. Elder Law Attys., Am. Networking Trust Planning Attys., Houston Bar Assn., Nat. Assn. of Chpt. 13 Trustees (assoc.), Katy Bar Assn. (3d v.p. 1997-98), Houston Assn. Debtors Attys. (pres. 1996-98), Upper Kirby Dist. Optimist Club (v.p. 2000-01, pres. 2001-02), Planned Giving Coun., Feng Shui Guild, Feng Shui Basics (pres.), Nat. Assn. Consumer Advs. Methodist. Avocations: music, cooking, swimming, politics. Home: 24503 Alexander Crossing Ln Katy TX 77494 Office: 4265 San Felipe St Ste 1100 Houston TX 77027-2998 E-mail: plsatty@swbell.net.

STEWART, PATRICIA ANN, banker; b. Phoenix, Nov. 3, 1953; d. Travis Delano and Ann Helen (Lopez) Hill. BS, Ariz. State U., 1975. Programmer, analyst Victor Comptometer Corp., Phoenix, 1975-77, Lewis & Roca, Attys., Phoenix, 1977-79; data processing mgr. Central Mgmt. Corp., Phoenix, 1979-80; corp. systems cons. S.W. Forest Industries, Phoenix, 1981-87; human resources system mgr. Western Savs. and Loan, Phoenix, 1987-90; asst. v.p., loan and deposit systems mgr. Bank of Am., Ariz., 1990-91, v.p., 1993-97, 1997—; application mgr. Data Line S.W. div., 1991-93; ptnr. Mnt2be Enterprises, 1997—2003. Mem. Data Processing Mgmt. Assn. (pres. Phoenix chpt. 1982), Ariz. HP Users Group (mem. dir. 1987). Office: Bank of Am Ill 2727 W Bell Rd Phoenix AZ 85053 Home: 7410 W Piute Ave Glendale AZ 85308-5639 Office Phone: 623-869-8231. E-mail: patricia.a.stewart@bankofamerica.com.

STEWART, PATRICIA CARRY, foundation administrator; b. Bklyn., May 19, 1928; d. William J. and Eleanor (Murphy) Carry; m. Charles Thorp Stewart, May 30, 1976. Student, U. Paris, 1948—49; BA, Cornell U., 1950. Fgn. corr. Irving Trust Co., N.Y.C., 1950-51; with Janeway Rsch. Co., N.Y.C., 1951-60, sec., treas., 1955-60; with Buckner & Co. and successor firms, N.Y.C., 1961-73, ptnr., 1962-70, v.p., treas., 1970-71, pres., treas., 1971-73, Knight, Carry, Bliss & Co., Inc., N.Y.C., 1971-73, G. Tsai & Co., Inc., 1973; v.p. Edna McConnell Clark Found. Inc., 1974-92. Dir. Cmty. Found. Palm Beach and Martin Counties, 1993-2001, chair, 1998, 2000; allied mem. N.Y. Stock Exch., 1962-73; past mem. nominating com. Am. Stock Exch., N.Y. Stock Exch., N.Y.C. Fin. Svcs. Corp.; dir. emeritus, past chmn. Investor Responsibility Rsch. Ctr. Trustee emerita, vice chair Cornell U., mem. bd. life overseers Cornell Med. Coll.; mem. vis. com. Grad. Sch Bus., Harvard U., 1974-80; bd. dirs. NOW Legal Def. and Edn. Fund, 1984-92, Women in Founds./Corp. Philanthropy, 1980-86; v.p. fin. com. Women's Forum, 1982-90; vice chmn. CUNY, 1976-80; bd. dirs. United Way of Tri-State, 1977-81, Inst. for Edn. and Rsch. on Women and Work; voting mem. Blue Cross and Blue Shield Greater N.Y., 1975-82; trustee N.Y. State 4-H Found., 1970-76, Internt. Inst. Rural Reconstrn., 1974-79; mem. N.Y.C. panel White House Fellows, 1976-78; mem. bus. adv. coun. The Hosp. Chaplaincy. Recipient Elizabeth Cutter Morrow award YWCA, 1977, Catalyst award Women Dirs. in Corps., 1978, Trustee medal CUNY, 1983, Acomplishment award Wings Club N.Y. 1984, Women's Funding Coalition Innovators for Women$hare award, 1986, Banking Industry Achievement award Nat. Assn. Bank Women, 1987, Cert. Disting. Accomplishments Barnard Coll., 1989; named to YWCA Acad. Women Achievers. Mem. Fin. Women's Assn. N.Y., Country Club of Fla. (bd. dirs.), Univ. Club (N.Y.C), Gullane Golf Club (Scotland), North Berwick Golf Club (Scotland), Dunbar Golf Club (Scotland), St. Andrews Club (Delray Beach, Fla.), Phi Beta Phi. Home and Office: 2613 N Ocean Blvd Delray Beach FL 33483-7367 also: Halfland Barns North Berwick EH395PW Scotland E-mail: stewartpc@aol.com.

STEWART, RITA JOAN, academic administrator; b. Muncie, Ind., June 6, 1945; d. John Marion and Crystalee Masterson; children: Jon Lewis, Robert Forrest. BS, Ball State U., 1967, MA, 1974. Tchr. Blue River H.S., Mt. Summit, Ind., 1968-69, Sunnyside Elem. Sch., New Castle, Ind., 1967-68; copywriter, announcer Sta. WTIM, Taylorville, Ill., 1974-75; dir. Kitselman Conf. Ctr. Ball State U., Muncie, Ind., 1978-2000, dir. conf. and spl. events, 2000—. Contbr. articles to profl. jours. Precinct committee-woman Henry County Dem. Party, New Castle, Ind., 1969-70; precinct chmn. March of Dimes, New Castle, Ind., 1974-75; chmn. edn. com. West Viwe Sch. Coun., Muncie, 1987-88; sec., bd. dirs. PAL Club, Muncie, 1988-93; pres., bd. dirs. Altrusa Club Found., Muncie, 1997-98, v.p., 2001-01, pres., 2002. Mem.: AAUW (v.p. 1984—85), Ind. Conf. Dirs. Assn., Assn. Collegiate Conf. and Event Dirs. Internat. (dir. region 8 1999—2000, internat. bd. dirs., Mentor Yr. award 2004), Altrusa Club of Muncie (pres. 2002—03), Kappa Delta Pi (Disting. Svc. award 1995). Methodist. Office: Ball State U Confs and Spl Events Muncie IN 47306 Home: # 1-203 4501 N Wheeling Ave Muncie IN 47304-1277 Fax: (765) 285-5457. E-mail: rstewart@bsu.edu.

STEWART, RUTH ANN, public policy educator; b. Chgo., Apr. 4, 1942; d. Elmer Ashton and Ann (Mitchell) Stewart; m. David Levering Lewis; children: Allegra, Jason Lewis, Allison Lewis, Eric Lewis. Student, U. Chgo., 1960-61, Simmons Coll., 1963; BA, Wheaton Coll., Norton, Mass., 1963; MS, Columbia U., 1965; postgrad., Fisk U., 1970, Harvard U., 1976, postgrad., 1987. Mktg. mgr. Macmillan Co., N.Y.C., 1968-70; asst. chief Schomburg Ctr. Rsch. Black Culture, N.Y.C., 1970-80; assoc. dir. external svcs. N.Y. Pub. Libr., 1980-86; asst. Libr. Congress Nat. Programs, Washington, 1986-89; assoc. Dir. Resource Devel., Washington, 1989-95; sr. policy analyst arts, humanities & social legis. Congl. Rsch. Svc., Washington, 1989-97; rsch. prof. cultural policy Ctr. Urban Policy Rsch. Bloustein Sch. Planning and Pub. Policy, Rutgers U., New Brunswick, NJ, 1997—2003; clin. prof. Wagner Sch. Pub. Svc., NYU, N.Y.C., 2003—. Trustee, sec. Wheaton Coll., Norton, 1980—99; mem. libr. vis. com. Harvard U., 1975—88, MIT, 1986—90. Cons. editor: Jour. Arts Mgmt. Law and Soc., 1998—, founding co-editor: book series Public Life of the Arts, 1998—. Bd. dirs. Nat. Pk. Found., Washington, 1978—84, Fund Folk Culture, Santa Fe, 1991—2003, Lab. Sch. Washington, 1992—94, Women's Fgn. Policy Group, 1999—2003, Bklyn. Bot. Garden, 2000—, Studio in Sch., 2000—, Cooper-Hewitt Nat. Design Mus., Smithsonian Instn., 2003—; mem. rsch. adv. coun. Ctr. Arts and Culture, Washington, 1997—; sch. com. Alvin Ailey Sch., 1998—. Fellow, NY State Coun. Arts. Mem.: Coun. Fgn. Rels., ArtTable (nat. bd. dirs. 2002—), Mus. Modern Art. Office: NYU Wagner Sch 4 Washington Sq N New York NY 10003

STEWART, SANDRA KAY, music educator; b. New Albany, Ind., Dec. 24, 1947; d. Dale F. and June V. (Martin) Byrne; m. William Lee Stewart, June 25, 1971. B Music Edn., Ind. U., 1969; MusM, Norfolk State U., 1992; D Mus. Arts, U. S.C., 1995. Cert. vocal music tchr., N.Y., Mo.; nat. cert., state cert. piano tchr. Vocal music tchr., choral dir. Ritenour Sch. Dist., St. Louis, 1969-75, Sch. Dist. # 54, Chgo., 1975-76, Waverly (N.Y.) Jr./Sr. H.S., 1977-78, Clarence (N.Y.) H.S., 1978-82; piano instr., show choir dir. Inst. Fine Arts, Reading, Pa., 1982-85; piano accompanist Berks Grand Opera Co., Reading, Pa., 1982-85, Va. Opera Co., Norfolk, 1986, U. S.C., Columbia, 1992-95, Jacksonville Masterworks Sr. Chorale, 1996-99, Bolles Sr. H.S., 1996-98, Pinewood Presbyn. Ch., 1996-98; piano and music theory instr. Acad. of Music, Virginia Beach, Va., 1986-91, 2002—03; piano instr., choral dir., vocal jazz dir., accompanist Jacksonville (Fla.) U., 1995—2000; chair vocal music dept. Douglas Anderson Sch. of Arts, 1998—2000; prof. music U. North Fla., Jacksonville, 2000—. Editor: Florida Music Teacher, 1999-2000; contbr. articles to profl. publs. Mem. Virginia Beach Pops Orch., 1989-91. Recipient Fla. First Lady's Art Scholar award, 2000. Mem. AAUW (numerous offices 1975—), Am. Choral Dirs. Assn., Coll. Music Soc., Nat. Piano Found., Music Educators Nat. Conf., Nat. Guild Piano Tchrs., Music Tchrs. Nat. Assn., Delius Assn. Fla. (bd. dirs. 1997-99), Phi Kappa Lambda, Mu Phi Epsilon, Delta Kappa Gamma Soc. Internat., TRI-M Music Honor Soc. Home: 4782 Harpers Ferry Ln Jacksonville FL 32257-4544

STEWART, SARAH, elementary school educator; BS in Edn., Ohio State U., 1963; MS, U. N.C., 1978. Reading recovery/reading resource tchr. McDougle Elem. Sch., Chapel Hill, NC, 1998—. Recipient N.C. Gov.'s Long Leaf Pine award, 1992. Mem.: Am. Fedn. Tchrs. in N.C. (past pres.), Nat. Bd. for Profl. Tchg. Stds. (bd. mem.). Office: Chapel Hill-Carrboro City Schs-McDougle 900 Old Fayetteville Rd Chapel Hill NC 27516

STEWART, SUE S. lawyer; b. Oct. 9, 1942; d. Fraizer McVale and Carolyn Eliabeth (Hunt) S.; m. Arthur L. Stern, III, July 31, 1965 (div.); m. children: Anne, Mark Alan; m. John A. Ciampa, Sept. 1, 1985 (div.); m. Stephen L. Raymond (dec.). BA, Wellesley Coll., 1964; postgrad., Harvard U. Law Sch., 1964-65; JD, Georgetown U., 1967. Bar: N.Y. 1968. Clk. to judges Juvenile Ct., Washington, 1967-68; mem. Nixon, Hargrave, Devans & Doyle (now Nixon Peabody LLP), Rochester, N.Y., 1968-74, ptnr., 1975—2001, mng. ptnr., 1998—2001, ret., 2001; v.p., gen. counsel U. Rochester, 2003—. Lectr. in field; trustee Found. of Monroe County (N.Y.) Bar, 1976-78; v.p. & Gen. Counsel Univ. Rochester, NY, 2003-. Author: Charitable Giving and Solicitation. Sec., dir. United Cmty. Chest of Greater Rochester, 1973-87, 1992-; trustee, sec. Internat. Mus. Photography at George Eastman House, Rochester, 1974-97, 2000-03, Genesee Country Mus., Mumford, N.Y., 1976-2002; bd. dirs. Ctr. for Govtl. Rsch., 1990-97; trustee, chmn. United Neighborhood Ctr. of Greater Rochester Found., 1991-2003; trustee, chmn. exec. com. Nat. Ctr. Edn. and Economy, 1997-; dir. Canandaigua (N.H.) Nat. Bank, 2000-. Mem. ABA (chmn. task force on charitable giving, exempt orgns. com. tax sect. 1981-2003), N.Y. State Bar (exec. com. tax sect. 1974-76, chmn. com. exempt orgns. 1975-76), Monroe County Bar Assn. (trustee 1974-75), BNA Portfolio, Pvt. Found. Distbns. (Athena award 2000, de Tocqueville award 2003). Office: Office of Counsel 266 Wallis Hall PO Box 270040 Rochester NY 14627-0040

STEWART, SUSAN, writer; b. 1952; BA, Dickinson Coll., 1973; MA, Johns Hopkins U., 1975; PhD, U. Pa., 1978. Asst. prof. dept. English Temple U., Phila., 1978—81, assoc. prof., 1981—85, prof., 1986—87, Regan prof. English U. Pa., Phila., 1997—. Vis. scholar Getty Ctr. for the History of Art and the Humanities, Santa Monica, Calif., 1995. Author: Nonsense: Aspects of Intertextuality in Folklore and Literature, 1979, On Longing: Narratives of the Miniature, the Gigantic, the Souvenir, the Collection, 1984, Crimes of Writing: Problems in the Containment of Representation, 1991, poetry. Recipient Individual Writer's award, Lila Wallace-Reader's Digest Found., 1996; fellow, Nat. Endowment for the Arts, 1982, 1990, Pa. Coun. on the Arts, 1984, 1988, John Simon Guggenheim Meml. Found., 1987; MacArthur fellow, 1997. Office: Univ Pa Dept English 119 Bennett Hall 3340 Walnut St Philadelphia PA 19104-6273

STEWART, VERLINDSEY LAQUETTA, accounting educator; b. Birmingham, Ala., Dec. 27, 1965; d. Nathan Jr. and Shirley Ruth Brown; m. Kelvin Lorenzo Stewart I, June 22, 1991 (div. Feb. 1999), 1 child, Kelvin Lorenzo II. BS in Acctg., Ala. A&M U., 1988, MS in Bus. Edn., 1995, AA Cert. in Bus. Edn., 1997. Cert. tchr. bus. grades 7-12, Ala. Jr. acct. Childress Acctg., Huntsville, Ala., 1990-93; acctg. clk. Appeal Beauty Salon, Huntsville, 1988-94; receptionist Coop. Ext., Normal, Ala., 1992-94; grad. asst. Ala. A&M U., Normal, 1995; student tchr. J.O. Johnson H.S., Huntsville, Ala., 1995; acctg. instr. J.F. Drake State Tech., Huntsville, 1996—. Cons. Jr. Achievement, Huntsville, 1995—96. Post-reviewer: (book) College Accounting 9th, 1999 (Honorarium 1999). Vol. Habitat for Humanity, Huntsville, 1995-97; vol. asst. leader Girl Scouts North Ala., Huntsville, 1995-96. Recipient Adminstrv. Acad. award Rust Coll., 1999, Emerging Leaders Sch. award Ala. Edn. Assn., 1994, Ala. Master Tchr. Seminar, 2001. Mem. Nat. Bus. Edn., Ea. Star Mitzpah Ctr., Phi Beta Lambda (adviser 1998—), Delta Sigma Theta. Democrat. Baptist. Avocations: aerobics, weights, reading, listening to jazz music. Office: JF Drake State Tech Coll 3421 Meridian St N Huntsville AL 35811-1544 Personal E-mail: vbdst28@aol.com.

STEWART NELSON, PAMELA, home health administrator, consultant; b. Chgo., June 27, 1948; d. Donald and Lena (Brevard) Paquet; m. William Frank Nelson, June 16, 2000. Diploma, St. Elizabeth Hosp. Sch. Nursing, Chgo., 1969; B. Nursing, Governor State U., 1978. Staff nurse emergency rm. St. Elizabeth's Hosp., Chgo., 1969-72, charge nurse emergency rm., 1973-76; staff nurse trauma Christ Hosp., Oaklawn, Ill., 1972-73; staff nurse SO Suburban Home Health, North Riverside, Ill., 1976-79, supr., 1979, dir., 1979-81; cons. home health HQR, North Riverside, 1981-82; exec. dir. Superior Care, Great Neck, N.Y., 1982—; pres. Health Care Design, Plainfield, Ill., 1984—. Cons. Steuben County Pub. Health, BAth, N.Y., 1986-88, Evang. Hosp. Systems, Oakbrook, Ill., 1989-90, Midwest Home Care, Chgo., 1991-92; adv. bd. chmn. Primary Care Svcs., Chgo., 1989—. Author: Nurse, Therapists Notes and Summaries, 1981, Modual Approach, 1984, 87, Computers in Health Care and Home Care Economics, Documentation for Home Care, 1992. Mem. APHA, Ill. Home Care Coun. (reimbursement com. 1986-88, bd. dirs. and edn. chmn. 1989-91). Avocations: reading, writing, decorating, debating issues. Office: Health Care Design 1400 N Penny Ln Plainfield IL 60544-9468 E-mail: stewpan@aol.com.

STEWART-PÉREZ, RENICE ANN, technology writer, internal systems professional; b. Milw., Jan. 2, 1947; d. Fredrick and Lucia (Stewart) Fregin; children: Jennifer Jean, Whitney Susan; m. Robert Anthony Pérez, Dec. 21, 1995. BA, U. San Diego, 1989, MA, 1991. Pres. Chubby Bumpkins, Inc., Houston, 1980-82; contracts adminstr. Gulf States Computer Svcs., Houston, 1980-82; pres. RAM Prodns., Houston, 1981-82, Pizza Internat., Inc., Houston, 1982-84; contracts adminstr. First Alliance Corp., Houston, 1982-85; freelance pub. rels. cons. San Diego, 1985-97, Nortel Networks, Plano, Tex., 1997-98; mgr. mktg. comms. FirstWorld Comms., San Diego, Tex., 1998; web mgr. GERS Retail Sys., San Diego, 1998-2000, Zama Networks, Seattle, 2000—01, Microsoft Corp., Redmond, 2001—02, Hardy Instruments, San Diego, 2002—. Tutor U. San Diego Writing Ctr., 1987-89; founder, dir. pub. rels.-tng. Montgomery County (Tex.) Crisis Action Line, Houston, 1979-84; founder, v.p., bd. dirs. Montgomery County Rape Crisis Coalition, 1982-84, speaker, 1982-84; speaker Rape Trauma Coalition, 1982-84; mem. prodn. com. Community Women Together, Montgomery County, 1980-82; pres. Living Arts Coun., Houston, 1980-81. Named Woman of Yr. YWCA, 1981, 82. Mem. Internat. Assn. Bus. Communicators, Am. Assn. Bus. Women (dir. activities Houston chpt. 1983-84), Bus. Women's Forum (bd. dir. community awareness Houston chpt. 1982-83), Assn. Women Bus. Owners, Lions (hon.), Phi Alpha Delta.

STEWART TYLER, VIVIAN DELOIS, primary school educator; b. Birmingham, Ala., June 30, 1940; d. Hessie Stewart and Johnnie Lee Bell Stewart; children: Evelyn, Elizabeth, Felicia. BA, Shaw U., Raleigh, N.C., 1976; MA, Governor's State U., Park Forest South, Ill., 1985. Tchr. St. Mary's Alternative HS, Chgo., 1976—81; commr. State Ill. Human Rights Commn., Ill., 1993—99; tchr., k-9th grades Chgo. Bd. Edn., Chgo., 1976—. Cons. Midwest Cmty. Coun.; mem. Midwest Cmty. Coun. Women Aux.; sec. Introspect Youth Services; unit chairperson & co-chairperson Chgo. LWV, Unit 11, Chgo. Recipient Westside Jewel award, Midwest Cmty. Coun., 1970, Svc. in Leadership award, 1997, Legacy award, Martin Luther King Jr. Boys and Girls Clubs of Chgo., 1995, Everyday Hero award, Lt. Gov., 2000. Mem.: The Excellentia (v.p., polit. affairs, Mem. of the Yr. 1997, 1998).

STEYTLER, C. ANNE WEBSTER, clinical social worker; b. Milw., Jan. 10, 1921; d. Royden Erastus and Jessie Emily (Beebe) Webster; m. Walter David Stimple, Dec. 31, 1941 (dec. May 1951); children: Jeanne Elizabeth Pitz, Alan Lee Steytler, Margaret Anne Rosenfield; m. Edmund John Steytler, Dec. 25, 1951 (dec. May 1998); 1 child, Carolyn Sue. BS, U. Wis., 1943, MA, 1945; MSSA, Western Res. U., Cleve., 1967. LSW, Pa. Instr. U. Wis., Madison, Wis., 1946-47; pediatric aide Wis. Gen. Hosp., Madison, 1947-49; tchr. Blacksburg (Va.) High Sch., 1951-52; order clerk med. libr. U. N.C., Chapel Hill, 1953-55; caseworker children's svcs. Lake County Welfare Dept., Painesville, Ohio, 1964-65; psychiatric social worker Lake County MH-MR Ctr., Mentor, Ohio, 1967-69; psychiatric unit dir. Southeastern MH-MR Ctr., Pitts., 1969-77; pvt. practice Pitts., 1974-95; staff therapist Persad Ctr., Inc., Pitts., 1983-95; sex educator Family Health Coun., Pitts., 1991—. In house therapist Dr. John Morocca, Sewickley, Pa., 1981-83; cons. Project Headstart, Pitts., 1980-83; cons., educator Parent and Child Guidance Ctr., Pitts., 1984-86; sex educator, Women's Health Svcs., Pitts., 1978-90. Co-founder Pub. Library, ad hoc com., Murray, Ky., 1962, Family Planning Svcs., Lake and Geauga Counties, Ohio, 1968, Women's Ctr. and Shelter, Pitts., 1974; lay leader Unitarian Universalist Ch. South Hills, Pitts., 1975-77; bd. dir., troop leader, day camp dir., Girl Scouts U.S., Murray, 1957; bd. dirs. Thomas Merton Ctr., Alliance for Progressive Action, 1995—. Mem. NASW (diplomate), Internat. Transactional Analysis Assn., Am. Assn. Marriage and Family Therapists. Democrat. Avocations: reading, theatre, camping, gardening. Home: 1001 Allegheny Ave # 2 Pittsburgh PA 15233

STIASSNY, MELANIE L.J. curator; BSc in Zoology with honors, U. London, 1976, PhD in Zoology, 1980. Fellow Rijksuniversiteit and Rijksmuseum, Leiden, Netherlands, 1980—83; asst. prof. dept organismic and evolutionary biology Harvard U., 1983—87; asst. curator dept. herpetology and ichthyology Am. Mus. Natural History, N.Y.C., 1987—92, assoc. curator dept. herpetology and ichthyology, 1992—97, Herbert R. and evelyn Axelrod rsch. curator, curator-in-charge dept. ichthyology, 1997—. Adj. prof. CUNY, 1992—, Ctr. for Environ. Rsch. and Conservation, NY, 1999—; sci. adv. World Wildlife Fund for Nature, Conservation Internat., World Resources Inst., Internat. Found. for Sci. Contbr. articles to profl. jours. Grantee, NSF, 1993—2001, Nat. Geog. Soc., 1997—98, Am. Mus. Natural History, 1997—99. Office: Am Mus Natural History Dept Ichthyology Central Park West at 79th St New York NY 10024

STIBBENS, BEVERLY, marketing professional, director; b. Decature, Ill., Aug. 11, 1955; d. Joseh C. and Mildred M. Ambrose; m. Neil J. Stibbens, Jan. 22, 1977; 1 child, Tennille K. Sr. buyer Zaks Stores, Dallas, 1988—93, Amberly Stores Inc., Dallas, 1993—95; dir. mktg. Cicwa Corp., Dallas, 1995—97; sr. dir. Dallas (Tex.) Market Ctr., 1997—. Mem. adv. bd. Annri-Christmas, San Diego, 1993—95. Mem. coun. City Coun., McHendon-Chisholm, Tex., 1985—2003; bd. dirs. Vol. Ctr. North Tex., Dallas, 2003—, Quall Creek Hentaences Assn., Rockwall, Tex., 2003—. Named Citizen of Yr., City of McLenden-Chisholm, 2002. Mem.: Gift Assn. Am., Nat. Assn. Ltd. Edition Dealers, Am. Mktg. Assn., Am. Specialty Toy Retialing Assn., Am. Inst. Floral Designers, Licensing Industry Manufacturers Assn., Soc. Florists, Hobby Industry Assn., Wholesale Florists and Floral Supply Assn., Mus. Store Assn. Office: Dallas Market Ctr 2100 Stemmons Fray US Hwy 120 Dallas TX 75207 Home: 279 Partridge Dr Rockwall TX 75032-7401

STICK, ALYCE CUSHING, systems administrator, consultant; b. N.J., July 13, 1944; d. George William and Adele Margaret (Wilderotter) Cushing; m. James McAlpin Easter, July 1970 (div. Aug. 1986); m. T. Howard F. Stick, June 1989. AA, Colby-Sawyer Coll., 1964; student, Boston U., 1964-65, Johns Hopkins U., 1972-74; cert., Control Data Inst. and Life Office Mgmt. Assn., 1976. Claims investigator Continental Casualty Co., Phila., 1967-69; data processing coord. Chesapeake Life Ins. Co., Balt., 1970-72; sr. systems analyst Comml. Credit Computer Corp., Balt., 1972-80; v.p. Shawmut Computer Systems, Inc., Owings Mills, Md., 1980-85; pres. Computer Relevance, Inc., Gladwyne, Pa., 1985—. Cons. Sinai Hosp., Balt., 1982—85, AT&T, Reading, Pa., 1987—88, Dun and Bradstreet, Allentown, Pa., 1988, Arco Chem. Co., Newtown Square, Pa., 1990—91, Rohm and Haas Co., Phila., 1992—. Designer, author (computer software systems) Claim-Track, 1977, Property-Profiles, 1979, Stat-Model, 1989, co-designer, author Patient-Profiles, 1983. Treas. Sales and Rental Gallery Balt. Mus. Art, 1984. Mem.: Ind. Computer Cons. Assn., Data Processing Mgmt. Assn., Assn. Sys. Mgmt., Merion Cricket Club (Haverford, Pa.). Republican. Avocations: American antiques, Chinese export porcelain dealer. Office: Computer Relevance Inc 1501 Monticello Dr Gladwyne PA 19035-1206

STICKELER, CARL ANN LOUISE, professional parliamentarian; b. Plant City, Fla., Dec. 26, 1930; d. Carl Ulysses and Marian Lucille (Churchill) Sangster; m. Nickolas Joseph Stickeler, May 14, 1949; children: Nickolas J., Juliann E., Carl A., John C., Katherine M. Profl. registered parliamentarian. Bus. mgr. Kendall Automobile Sales, Inc., Miami, 1967-82; parliamentarian Stickeler & Assocs., P.A., Miami, 1982-88, Ocala, Fla., 1988—. Editor: The Answer, 1983-89, 97-2002, The Florida Parliamentarian, 1983-87. Recipient Internat. Woman of Distinction Beta Sigma Phi Internat., 1980, Order of the Rose award Beta Sigma Phi Internat., 1969. Mem. Nat. Assn. Parliamentarians (bd. dirs. 1979-83, 91-93, 95-97, 99-2002, v.p. 1983-89, pres. 1989-91, parliamentarian 1997-99), Acad. Parliamentary Procedure and Law (bd. dirs. 1979—, pres. 1985-87), Gen. Fedn. Women's Clubs, Fla. Fedn. of Women's Clubs (parliamentarian 1992-98, 2000--), DAR (parliamentarian Fla. state soc. 1997-98), Beta Sigma Phi. Republican. Roman Catholic. Avocation: parliamentary research. Office: Stickeler & Assocs 102 Almond Rd Ocala FL 34472-8634 E-mail: CAStickeler@earthlink.net.

STICKLES, BONNIE JEAN, nurse; b. Waukesha, Wis., Nov. 24, 1944; d. Donald William and Betty Jane S. BSN, U. Wis., 1967; MSN in Midwifery, Columbia U., 1974. Mem. nursing staff Grace Hosp., Detroit, 1970-73; mem. faculty and staff U. Minn. Sch. Nursing and Nurse-Midwifery Svc., Mpls., 1974-76; chief nurse-midwife, clin. instr. St. Paul-Ramsey Med. Ctr., 1976-84; midwifery supr. IHS/PHS Chinle Hosp., 1984-85; program mgr. maternal health sect. N.Mex. Dept. Health and Environ., 1985-90, Lovelance Med. Ctr., 1990-91, St. Vincent's Hosp., 1991-94, NMC Dialysis Divsn., 1994-95; blackjack dealer, 1995-97; nurse CMS Penitentiary, N.Mex., 1997—2002. Author articles in field; patentee tchg. model. Mem. FDA Anesthetics, Life Support Adv. com.; adv. bd. Childbirth Edn. Assn., 1980-85. Served with USNR, 1965-70. Mem. Am. Coll. Nurse-Midwives (chmn. profl. affairs com. 1975-80), Nurses Assn. Am. Coll. Obstetricians and Gynecologists (charter), Aircraft Owners and Pilot Assn., Gt. Plains Perinatal Orgn., Alpha Tau Delta.

STICKNEY, JESSICA, former state legislator; b. Duluth, Minn., May 16, 1929; d. Ralph Emerson and Claudia Alice (Cox) Page; m. Edwin Levi Stickney, June 17, 1951; children: Claudia, Laura, Jeffrey. BA, Macalester Coll., St. Paul, Minn., 1951; PhD (hon), Rocky Mtn. Coll., Billings, Mont., 1986. Rep. State of Mont., 1989-92. Mem. Gov.'s Commn. on Post-Sec. Edn., Mont., 1973-75. Mem. Sch. Bd. Trustees, Miles City, Mont., 1968-74; mem., chmn. zoning bd., Miles City, 1975-89; mem. Govt. Study Commn., Miles City, 1974-76, United Ch. Christ Bd. Homeland Ministries, 1975-81; chmn., conf. moderator United Ch. Christ Bd. Mont.-Northern Wyo. Conf., 1980-82; chmn. Town Meeting on the Arts, Mont., 1980; mem., chmn. Miles Community Coll. Bd., 1975-89, chmn. 1978-80. Mem. Mont. Arts Coun. (chmn. 1982-85), Western States Arts Found. (vice chmn. 1984), Nat. Assembly State Arts Agys. (bd. dirs. 1982-88), AAUW (pres. 1964-66). Democrat. Avocations: writing, sewing, painting, reading.

STICKNEY, NANCY CARVER, state legislator; b. Bethel, Maine, July 20, 1936; d. Irving L. and Ruth W. (Homsted) Carver; m. Wallace E. Stickney, 1957; children: Peter, Christopher J., Daniel C., Adam K. BS, U. NH, 1960. Mem. NH Ho. of Reps. (dist. 26), Concord, Maine, 1997—2000. Methodist. Home: PO Box 177 North Salem NH 03073-0177 Office: NH State Legis State House Concord NH 03301

STIDMAN, EDITH (JANET) SCALES, parliamentarian; b. Balt., Sept. 19; d. Joseph Edward and Edith Morris (Caulk) Scales; m. Herbert Jean Silcox, May 18, 1944 (dec. Mar. 1945); m. John Charles Stidman, Sept. 27, 1947; children: Janet Stidman Eveleth, John Scales Stidman. BS in Instn. Mgmt., U. Md., 1944. With Cen. Club for Nurses, N.Y.C., 1944-45; asst. dietitian, trouble shooter Studio Club YWCA, N.Y.C., 1944-45; food svc. supr. AT&T, N.Y.C., 1945-47. Parliamentarian, tchr., lectr., spk., opinion writer and cons. in field. Editor (newsletter) Govans Guidepost, 1959-62, Md. Parent Tchr., 1960's,Md. Assn. Capsule Epistle, 1991-93, editor-in-chief, 1995-97; editor, parliamentarian, contbr. The Pen Woman, 1992-96; editor-in-chief Nat. Parliamentation, 1987-89; contbr. articles to profl. jours. Vice-chmn., chmn. Grace United Meth. Ch., adminstrn. bd., fin., nominating, edn., pastor/parish rels., worship com., lay mem. to conf.; tchr., jr. dept. supt., counseling tchr., pres. Grace United Meth. Women, 1984-88, 89-90; recording sec. Md. Congress of Parents & Tchrs., Inc., 1965-68, dist. v.p., 1962-65, bd. dirs., 1960-68; trustee William Lemmel Scholarship Fund and Screening Com., 1960's, The Boy's Latin Sch. Md., 1969-70; charter mem. jr. bd. and sec. Florence Crittenden Home Inc., 1948-50; coord. Cub Scout pack Boy Scouts Am.; bd. dirs. Safety Coun. of Md., 1968—; v.p. 3 divsns. Balt. Safety Coun., 1969-75; parliamentarian Roland Park Civic League; pres. Legisl. Clearing House of Md., 1971-75; corr. sec. Balt. City PTA Coun. pres., 1959-61; pres. Govans PTA, 1959-62, Northern H.S. PTA, 1965-67; hon. life mem. Md. PTA, Nat. PTA; past pres. Md. Coun. on Edn.; parliamentarian Woman's Club Roland Park, Balt., 1976-98, 2d v.p., 1992-94 1st v.p., 1994-96, pres. elect, 1996-98, pres. 1998-2000, hospitality chmn., 2000-02, chmn. cmty. projects com., 2002--, gov. bd. dirs., 2002-04; judge parliamentary performance contests H.S. teams statewide for State Dept. Edn., Md., 1973—, national contests 1984, 88, 92, 96; bylaws chmn. Union Meml. Hosp. Aux., 1990-92, parliamentarian, 1973—. Recipient Vol. Svc. cert. Balt. City Health Dept. 1957, Generous Svc. and Committment to Bus. Edn. cert. Balt. County Bd. Edn., 1983, Recognition of Svc. to Blue Ridge Region cert. Internat. Toastmistress Orgn., 1983, Appreciation cert. Howard Vocat. Tech. Sch., 1983, Towson State U., Profl. Secs. Internat., Future Bus. Leaders Am., Spl. Mission Recognition award United Meth. Women, 1981. Mem. AAUW (parliamentarian Md. chpt. 1973-75), Nat. Assn. Parliamentarians (pres. 1987-89), Md. Assn. Parliamentarians (pres. 1973-75, 95-97), Am. Inst. Parliamentarians, Am. Home Econs. Assn., Internat. Platform Assn., Nat. League Am. Pen Women (parliamentarian 1992-96, 5th v.p. 1994, 4th v.p. 1994-96), U. Md. Alumni Assn. (life, reunion com. 1995, awarded 50 year medal), Md. Assn. Hosp. Aux. (parliamentarian 1973—), Edith S. Stidman Parliamentary Unit (pres. 1984-87, 2002—, parliamentarian 1984-2002, pres. parliamentary edn. unit 1971-73, pres. M.W. Wheelock unit 1976-79), Md. Registered Parliamentarians (pres. unit 1993-94), Maine Assn. Parliamentarians (founder), Morgan State Univ. Unit (founded Edith S. Stidman unit, 1981), Nat. Wildlife Assn., Nat. Parks and Conservation Assn., Gold Star Wives, Women's Civic League (officer, parliamentarian 2002—), The Star Spangled Banner Flag House, Hopkins Rep. Women's Club, John Hopkins Club, Cross & Key (hon.), Ky. Col. (hon.). Republican. Methodist. Avocations: working crossword puzzles, reading, water skiing, dance, sports. Home and Office: 606 Cedarcroft Rd Baltimore MD 21212-2703

STIEBER, TAMAR, journalist; b. Bklyn., Sept. 15, 1955; d. Alfred and Florence (Spector) Stieber. Student, Rockland C.C., 1972—75, West London (Eng.) Coll., 1973—74; BA in Film cum laude, U. Calif., Berkeley, 1985, postgrad. in comparative lit., 1985—86; grad. police res. acad. cum laude, Napa Valley Coll., 1988. Office mgr., confidential sec. AP, San Francisco, 1981—83; stringer Daily Californian, Berkeley, Calif., 1983—84; film rsch. tchg. asst. U. Calif., Berkeley, 1984—86; libr. and rsch. asst. Pacific Film Archive, Berkeley, 1984—86; intern San Francisco Examiner, 1984; reporter Sonoma (Calif.) Index-Tribune, 1987—88, Vallejo (Calif.) Times-Herald, 1988—89, Albuquerque Journal, 1989—94, freelancer, 1994—. Recipient Pulitzer Prize for specialized reporting, 1990, 1st pl. pub. svc. divsn., N.Mex. Press Assn., 1990, Pub. Svc. award, Albuquerque Press Club, 1990, 1st pl. newswriting, N.Mex. Press Assn., 1991, Hon. Mention, AP Mng. Editors, 1994. Mem.: AAUW, Phi Beta Kappa. Home: PO Box 9835 Santa Fe NM 87504-9835

STIEFEL, LINDA SHIELDS, lawyer; b. Syracuse, N.Y., Nov. 14, 1948; d. Harold F. and Ellen (Brown) Shields; m. John L. Stiefel, Sept. 20, 1969; 1 child, John L. BS, Tusculum Coll., 1988; JD, Akron Sch. Law, 1991. Bar: Ohio 1992, D.C. 1993, N.Y. 1998, U.S. Dist. Ct. (no. dist.) Ohio 1993, U.S. Supreme Ct. 1997. Judicial law clk. Stark County Common Pleas, Canton, Ohio, 1991-94; pvt. practice Louisville, Ohio, 1992-97, Cape Vincent, N.Y., 1998—. Trustee, mem. exec. com. Am. Handweaving Mus., 1997-2001. Mem. ABA, NOW, N.Y. State Bar Assn., Jefferson County Bar Assn. Methodist. Home and Office: 596 West Broadway Cape Vincent NY 13618

STIEHL, RUTH RASCO, nursing educator; b. Miami, Fla., Oct. 31, 1939; d. Russell Austin and Beatrice (Tanner) Rasco; m. Paul A. Stiehl, June 5, 1959; children: Mark Russell, Kristin Stiehl Murray, Eric Paul. BS, U. Miami, 1961; MA, U. South Fla., 1972, PhD, 1977; MN, U. Fla., 1989. RN, Fla. Staff nurse ob/gyn. Bapt. Hosp., Miami, 1961-62; staff nurse pediatrics Broward Gen. Hosp., Ft. Lauderdale, Fla., 1963-65; staff nurse dialysis Tampa (Fla.) Gen. Hosp., 1967-70; faculty Coll. Nursing, U. South Fla., Tampa, 1973-76; nursing edn. dir. Fla. Bd. Nursing, Jacksonville, 1977-82; dir. Sch. Nursing, Jacksonville (Fla.) U., 1982—; exec. dir. Florida Board of Nursing, Jacksonville, 1997-. Mem. examination com. Nat. Coun. State Bds. of Nursing, Chgo., 1978-82. Bd. dirs. Cypress Village Retirement Community, Jacksonville, 1990—, Mayor's Commn. on Status of Women, Jacksonville, 1985-92, Gateway Coun. Girl Scouts U.S.A., 1989—, S.E. Heart Assn., Jacksonville, 1986-88, N.E. Fla. Easter Seals, Jacksonville, 1982-86; mem. task force Women and AIDS, Jacksonville, 1991—; treas. Fla. Commn. on Future of Nursing, 1987-91. Mem. ANA, Fla. Nurses Assn., Nat. League for Nursing, Sigma Theta Tau. Avocations: reading, jogging, cross-stitch, singing. Office: Jacksonville Univ 2800 University Blvd N Jacksonville FL 32211-3394 Address: Florida Bd of Nursing 4080 Woodcock Dr Ste 202 Jacksonville FL 32207-2723

STIEHM, JUDITH HICKS, university official, political science educator; b. Madison, Wis., Oct. 9, 1935; d. Stratton Elson and Eleanor Spencer (Kilbourn) Hicks; m. E. Richard Stiehm, July 12, 1958; children: Jamie Elizabeth, Carrie Eleanor, Meredith Ellen. Student, Oberlin Coll., 1953; BA in E. Asian Studies, U. Wis., 1957; MA in Am. History, Temple U., 1961; PhD in Polit. Theory, Columbia U., 1969. Dir. resident hons. program U. So. Calif., Los Angeles, 1970-73, asst. prof., 1970-74, assoc. prof., 1974-83, dir. program for study of women and men in soc., 1975-81, prof. polit. sci., 1983, vice provost, 1984-87; provost Fla. Internat. U., Miami, 1987-91, prof. polit. sci., 1987—. Vis. prof. U. Wis., 1994, U.S. Army Peacekeeping Inst., U.S. Army War Coll., 1995-96, U.S. Army Strategic Studies Inst., U.S. Army War Coll., 1996, U. So. Calif., 2002-; lectr. U. Wis., Madison, 1966-69, UCLA, 1969-70; vis. lectr. San Francisco State U., 1965-66; affiliate NAS Project, 1981-82; cons. UN Div. for the Advancement of Women, Calif. Elected Women, Dept. HEW, AAUW, LWV L.A., UN Lessons Learned Unit, Dept. Peacekeeping Ops. Author: Nonviolent Power: Active and Passive Resistance in America, 1972, Bring Me Men and Women..., 1981, Arms and the Enlisted Woman, 1989, The U.S. Army War College: Military Education in a Democracy, 2002; editor: The Frontiers of Knowledge, 1976, Women and Men's Wars, 1983, Women's Views of the Political World of Men, 1984, It's Our Military, Too!, 1996, The U.S. Army War College: Military Education in a Democracy, 2002; mem. editorial bd. Western Polit. Quar., 1972-75, Signs, 1981-84, Women and Politics, 1986-88, 2000-. Mem. Calif. Postsecondary Edn. Commn., 1978, Calif. Adv. Coun. on Vocat. Edn., 1978-82, Def. Adv. Com. on Women in Svcs., 1979-82; bd. dirs. So. Calif. and Miami chpts. ACLU. Named Woman of Yr., Santa Monica YWCA, 1981; recipient Outstanding Civilian Svc. medal U.S. Army, 1996. Mem. Am. Polit. Sci. Assn. (exec. coun. 1989, sec. 2000), Western Polit. Sci. Assn. (pres. 1986), Women's Caucus Polit. Sci. (pres. 1996-97), Nat. Council for Research on Women (exec. council 1982), Council on Fgn. Relations, Phi Beta Kappa, Phi Kappa Phi (Victoria Schuck Book award 1990). Avocations: tennis, skiing, stained glass. Home: 434 24th St Santa Monica CA 90402-3102 Office: Fla Internat U Dept Polit Sci Tamiami Trl Miami FL 33199-0001 E-mail: stiehmj@fiu.edu.

STIEHR, LIZETTE ESTELLE, special education educator, director; b. Chgo., Sept. 23, 1946; d. Benton Hoooper and Georgialou Fleager Burns; children: Jesse Hopper, Auguste Micah, Magayr Alexia. MA, Ind. U., 1970. Cert. tchr. Dept. of Edn., Alaska, 1974. Spl. edn. instr. Brown County (Ind.) Sch. Dist., 1971—74; dir. profl. svcs. Hope Cmty. Resources, Anchorage, 1974—77; mental health clinician South Ctrl. Counseling, Anchorage, 1978—81; project coord. Communicative Disorders Prog., Anchorage, 1983—85; health program mgr. Sect. of Maternal Child Health, Anchorage, 1988—99; exec. dir. Family Outreach Ctr. for Understanding Spl. Needs, Chugiak, Alaska, 1999—. Officer Divsn. Early Childhood, Anchorage, 1994—2000. Pres. bd. dirs. Child Care Connection, Anchorage, 1995—2000. Recipient Early Intervention Appreciation award, Alaska Assn. Infant Learning Programs, 1997, Plaque of Appreciation award, Hope Cmty. Resources, 1978, Plaque of Recognition award, Alaska Speech Lang. Hearing Assn., 1990; fellow, Ind. U., 1970. Mem.: Anchorage (Alaska) Assn. Edn. Young Children, Eagle River C. of C. (assoc.). Independent. Avocations: travel, astrology, camping, hiking, bicycling. Home: PO Box 671902 Chugiak AK 99567 Office: Focus PO Box 671750 Chugiak AK 99567 Office Fax: N/A. Personal E-mail: lizette-stiehr@gci.net. E-mail: lizette-stiehr@gci.net.

STIENMIER, SAUNDRA KAY YOUNG, aviation educator; b. Abilene, Kans., Apr. 27, 1938; d. Bruce Waring and Helen E. (Rutz) Young; m. Richard H. Stienmier, Dec. 20, 1958; children: Richard, Susan, Julia, Laura. AA, Colo. Women's Coll., 1957; postgrad., U. Colo., 1959, 69; BS, Temple Buell Coll., 1969; ed., Embre Riddle Aviation U., Ramstein, Germany. Cert. FAA pilot. Dir. Beaumont Gallery, El Paso, Tex., 1972-77; mem. grad. studies faculty Embre Riddle Aviation U., 1979-80; mgr. Ramstein Aero Club, USAF, 1977-80, Peterson Flight Tng. Ctr., Peterson AFB, Colo., 1980-97, Flight Tng. Ctr., Rocky Mtn. AFB, Colo., 1997—. Named Outstanding S.W. Artist. Mem.: AAUW, Assn. Profl. Flight Tng. Ctrs., Soc. Arts and Letters, Women in Aviation, Colo. Pilots Assn., Nat. Pilot Assn., Aircraft Owners and Pilots Assn., Nat. Air Transp. Assn. (flight tng. com.), Interant. Women Pilots Assn., Scots Heritage Soc., Scottish Soc. Pikes' Peak, 99's Club, Order Eastern Star, Delta Psi Omega, Beta Sigma Phi. Office: PO Box 14123 Colorado Springs CO 80914-0123 E-mail: saundra@viawest.net.

STIENON, ELAINE BURR, writer, music educator; b. Detroit, Oct. 9, 1935; d. Henry Leonard and Verna Ruth (Buyer) Burr; m. Francis M. Stienon, Jan. 23, 1958; children: Christopher, Ruth. BA, U. Mich., 1957. Pvt. music tchr., Glendale, Calif., 1978—2003; mng. editor Ensign Pub. House, Glendale, 1988—. Author: (novels) Lightning in the Fog, 1977, Utah Spring, 1979, The Light of the Morning, 1988, short stories. Mem.: Nat. Writers Assn. Democrat. Home: 1241 Irving Ave Glendale CA 91201

STIENSTRA, STEPHANI ANN, editor, writer; b. Baytown, Tex., Aug. 6, 1955; d. Herbert Howard and Janice Faye (Stowe) Cruickshank; m. George Keyston III, Oct. 8, 1983 (div. Mar. 1997); children: Jeremy George, Kristopher Samuel; m. Thomas Frank Stienstra, Dec. 4, 1998. AA with honors, Merced (Calif.) Coll., 1975; BA in Journalism with distinction, San Jose State U., 1976. Reporter Fresno (Calif.) Bee, 1974-75; reporter, photographer Merced (Calif.) Sun-Star, 1974-77; pub. info. officer Fresno City Coll., 1977—80; dir. comms. Aerojet Tactical Sys. Co., Sacramento, 1980—83; co-owner, v.p. Keyco Landscape Contractor Inc., Loomis, Calif., 1984—96; co-owner Stienstra Outdoor Books, Inc., 2003—. Co-author (with Tom Stienstra): (book) Northern California Cabins and Cottages, 2002 (Hon. Mention Book award Outdoor Writers Assn. Calif., 2002), Washington Camping, 2002. Co-coord. Aeroject United Way Campaign, 1981; Aeroject Tactical Sys. Co. coord. West Coast Nat. Derby Rallies, 1981-83; co-founder, pres. Calif. Lion Awareness. Mem. Internat. Assn. Bus. Communicators (dir. Sacramento chpt. 1983), Citrus Heights C. of C. (v.p. 1983). Office: PO Box 151 Mount Shasta CA 96067-0151 E-mail: stienstra@jps.net.

STIER, MARY P. publishing executive; b. Memphis, Tennessee, Nov. 9, 1956; m. Jeff Stier; 2 children. Grad. in comm., broadcasting, U. Iowa. With Gannett Co., 1982—; retail advt. mgr. Iowa City Press-Citizen, 1982—84, advt. dir., 1984—87, pres., pub., 1987—91; v.p. Ctrl. Region Newspaper Divsn., 1990—93; pres., pub. Rockford (Ill.) Register Star, 1991—2000; pres. Midwest Newspaper Group, 1993—2000; pres., pub. The Des Moines Register, 2000—; sr. group pres. Midwest Newspaper Group, 2000—. Bd. trustees Drake U. Mem.: The Greater Des Moines Partnership, Am. Press Inst., Iowa Newspaper Assn., Newspaper Assn. Am., Phi Beta Kappa. Office: Des Moines Register PO Box 957 Des Moines IA 50304-0957*

STIERLE, LINDA J. military officer; BSN magna cum laude, Incarnate Word Coll., 1978; grad., Air Command and Staff Coll., 1980; MSN with honors, U. Calif., San Francisco, 1983; grad., Air War Coll., 1986; grad. Interagy. Inst. Healthcare Execs., George Washington U., 1993; grad. CAPSTONE, Nat. Def. U., 1996. Commd. 2d. lt. USAF, 1970, advanced through grades to brigadier gen., 1995; staff nurse med. unit Wiesbaden (West Germany) USAF Med. Ctr., 1974-76, asst. charge nurse surg. unit, 1976; charge nurse female med. unit David Grant USAF Med. Ctr., Travis AFB, Calif., 1978-81, edn. coord. dept. nursing, 1981; divsn. chief, sr. mgmt. cons. mgmt. strategies/edn. dir. Leadership and Mgmt. Devel. Ctr., Maxwell AFB, Ala., 1984-86; asst. chmn. dept. nursing David Grant USAF Med. Ctr., Travis AFB, 1986-88; chief nurse 48th Tactical Fighter Wing Hosp., RAF, Lakenheath, England, 1988-90; dep. chief divsn. nursing Wilford Hall USAF Med. Ctr., Lackland AFB, Tex., 1991-93; command nurse Office of Command Surgeon Air Mobility Command, Scott AFB, Ill., 1993-95; dir. nursing svds. Office of Air Force Surgeon Gen., Bolling AFB, DC, 1995, dir. Med. Readiness Doctrine and Planning and Nursing Svcs., 1995—99; CEO ANA, Washington, 2000—. Decorated Legion of Merit with oak leaf cluster, Meritorious Svc. medal with 3 oak leaf clusters, D.S.M. USAF. Mem. Am. Soc. Assn. Execs., Soc. Air Force Nurses, Am. Orgn. of Nurse Execs., Md. Nurses Assn., Sigma Theta Tau. Office: ANA Ste 100W 600 Maryn Ave SW Washington DC 20024

STIGALL, PHYLLIS GRAHAM, retired librarian; b. Ft. Wayne, Ind., Oct. 3, 1917; d. Edwin James and Mary Josephine (Palmer) Graham; m. Richard Patten Pooley, Apr. 4, 1943 (dec. Dec. 1950); 1 child, Samuel Graham Pooley ; m. William Jasper Stigall Jr., Aug. 11, 1956 (dec. Sept. 2001). AA, Stephens Coll., 1937; AB, Northwestern U., 1939; MALS, U. Mich., 1952. Asst. counselor Stephens Coll., Columbia, Mo., 1939-42; asst. to dir. USO-YWCA Clubs, various locations, 1942-46; co-dir. U. Mich. Cmty. Ctr., Ann Arbor and Willow Run, 1946-47; libr., dean, instr. Lincoln (Ill.) Coll., 1952-66; mgr. publs. and librs. IBM Rsch. Ctr., Yorktown Heights, N.Y., 1966-88; ret. Author: Notes on 46 Women Writers, 1991, Journeys of the Brave, 1992, Ireland: Reader's Guide. Women, 1995; co-editor: I Couldn't be Better, 2002. Mem. AAUW, LWV (chpt. bd. dirs., pres. 1947-66). Democrat. Episcopalian. Avocations: photography, research, biography, history, genealogy. Home: PO Box 211 Scarborough NY 10510

STILES, JULIA, actress; b. N.Y.C., Mar. 28, 1981; Student, Columbia U., 2000—. Actor: (TV films) Before Women Had Wings, 1997, The '60s, 1999; (films) I Love You, I Love You Not, 1996, The Devil's Own, 1997, Wicked, 1998, Wide Awake, 1998, 10 Things I Hate About You, 1999, Down to You, 2000, Hamlet, 2000, State and Main, 2000, Save the Last Dance, 2001, The Business of Strangers, 2001, O, 2001, The Bourne Identity, 2002, A Guy Thing, 2003, Carolina, 2003, Mona Lisa Smile, 2003; TV guest appearances include Ghostwriter, 1992, Promised Land, 1996, Chicago Hope, 1994. Voted one of, People Mag.'s 50 Most Beautiful People, 2001. Office: Clare Ryu c/o United Talent Agy 9560 Wilshire Blvd Beverly Hills CA 90212*

STILES, MARY ANN, lawyer, author, lobbyist; b. Tampa, Fla., Nov. 16, 1944; d. Ralph A. and Bonnie (Smith) S.; m. Barry Smith. AA, Hills Community Coll., 1973; BS, Fla. State U., 1975; JD, Antioch Sch. Law, 1978. Bar: Fla. 1978. Legis. analyst Fla. Ho. of Reps., Tallahassee, 1973-74, 74-75; intern U.S. Senate, Washington, 1977; v.p., gen. counsel Associated Industries Fla., Tallahassee, 1978-81, gen. counsel, 1981-84, spl. counsel, 1986-97; assoc. Deschler, Reed & Crichfield, Boca Raton, Fla., 1980-81; founding ptnr. Stiles, Taylor, & Grace, P.A., Boca Raton, Tampa, Orlando, Jacksonville, Talahassee, and Miami, Fla., 1982—, shareholder, dir. Tampa; gen. counsel Associated Industries Ins. Co., Inc., 1996—, Associated Industries Fla., Inc., 1997—, Associated Industries Ins. Svcs., Inc., 1997—. Shareholder, dir. Six Stars Devel. Co. of Fla., Inc. Platnum Bank; dr. Eclipse, Inc.; owner, pres. Styles by Stiles; shareholder, pres. 42nd St., The Bistro; mem. Workers' Compensation Task Force, 2000-01. Author: Workers' Compensation Law Handbook, 1980-94 edit. Bd. dirs., sec. Hillsborough C.C. Found., Tampa, 1985-87, 94-96; bd. dirs. Hillsborough Area Regional Transit Authority, Tampa, 1986-89, Boys and Girls Club of Tampa, 1986—; The Spring, 1992-93, What's My Chance, 1992-94; mem. Gov.'s Oversite Bd. on Workers' Compensation, 1989-90, Workers' Compensation Rules Com., Fla. Bar, 1990-95, 2000—, Workers' Compensation Exec. Counsel Fla. Bar, 1990-95, Jud. Nominating Commn. for Workers' Compensation Cts., 1990-93, trustee Hillsborough Cmty. Coll., 1994-99, vice-chair, 1996-97, chair, 1996-97; bd. dirs. Seminole Boosters, Inc., Fla. State U., 1996—. Mem. ABA, Fla. Bar Assn., Hillsborough County Bar Assn., Hillsborough Assn. Women Lawyers, Fla. Assn. Women Lawyers, Fla. Women's Alliance, Hillsborough County Seminole Boosters (past pres.), Tiger Bay Club (Tampa, past. pres., sec.). Republican. Baptist. Avocations: boating, reading. Office: 315 S Plant Ave Tampa FL 33606-2325 also: 317 N Calhoun St Tallahassee FL 32301-7605 also: PO Box 310397 Miami FL 33231-0397 Address: PO Box 294349 Boca Raton FL 33429 also: PO Box 48190 Jacksonville FL 32247

STILL, CANDACE TYSON, music educator; b. Huntsville, Ala., Aug. 4, 1954; d. John Donald Tyson, Sr. and Kathleen Kennamer Tyson; m. G. Leslie Still, Aug. 1, 1976; children: Leslie Anne Still Oubre, Jennifer Lynne. EdB in music, Jacksonville State U., 1972—76, MEd, 1986—90; Edn. specialist in instrumental music, U. of Ga., 2001—02. T-6 Profl. Educator State of Ga. Profl. Standards Commn., 2002, Tchr. Support Specialist State of Ga. Profl. Standards Commn., 2002. Dir. of bands Pine Mountain Mid. Sch., Kennesaw, Ga., 2002—; assoc. dir. of bands Awtrey Mid. Sch., Kennesaw, Ga., 1994—2002. Participating rschr. Music Educators Nat. Conf., So. Divsn., Savannah, Ga., 2003. Performer Still Swinging, The Les Still Big Band, Atlanta, Ga., 1996—2003; del. Ga. Edn. Summit, Perry, Ga., 2003—03; dir. of instrumental music Midway Presbyn. Ch. PCA, Powder Springs, Ga., 1998—2003. Ednl. grant, The Jr. League of Marietta/Cobb, 1998. Mem.: PA of Ga. Educators (pres. Cobb county 1999—2002, Mem. of the Yr. 2001), Women Band Directors Nat. Assn., Ga. Music Educators Assn. (festival coord. 2000—03), The Nat. Band Assn., Music Educators Nat. Conf. R-Consevative. Presbyn.Ch. Achievements include research in the affect of instrumental music education on the reading achievement of learning disabled and emotionally disabled students. Avocations: gardening, water-skiing. Office: Cobb Cty Sch Dist 2720 Pine Mountain Circle Kennesaw GA 30152 E-mail: candace.still@cobbk12.org.

STILLER, JENNIFER ANNE, lawyer; b. Washington, May 4, 1948; d. Ralph Sophian and Joy (Dancis) S. AB in Econs. and History, U. Mich., 1970; JD, NYU, 1973. Bar: Pa. 1973, U.S. Dist. Ct. (mid. dist.) Pa. 1977, U.S. Supreme Ct. 1978, Ill. 1979, U.S. Dist. Ct. (no. dist.) Ill. 1979, U.S. Dist. Ct. (ea. dist.) Pa. 1983, U.S. Ct. Appeals (3rd cir.) 1983, U.S. Ct. Appeals (D.C. cir.), 1996. Dep. atty. gen. Pa. Dept. Justice, Harrisburg, 1973-75, Pa. Dept. Health, Harrisburg, 1975-78; sr. staff atty. Am. Hosp. Assn., Chgo., 1978-80, mgr., dept. fed. law, 1980-81; gen. counsel Ill. Health Fin. Authority, 1981-82; sr. assoc. Berriman & Schwartz, King of Prussia, Pa., 1983-85, Wolf, Block, Schorr & Solis-Cohen, Phila., 1985-88, Montgomery, McCracken, Walker & Rhoads, LLP, Phila., 1988-90; ptnr. Montgomery, McCracken, Walker & Rhoads, Phila., 1990-2000, chair health law group, 1991-2000; sr. counsel Tenet Healthcare Corp., Phila., 2000-2001; pvt. practice Haverford, Pa., 2001—. Contbr. health law articles to profl. jours. Mem. ABA (gov. com. Health Law Forum 1994-95), Am. Health Lawyers Assn. (bd. dirs. 1997-2003, exec. com. 2002-03), Pa. Soc. Healthcare Attys. (pres. 1995). Avocations: gardening, bicycling, hiking, music. Office: Law Office Jennifer A Stiller 625 Haydock Ln Haverford PA 19041-1207 Office Phone: 610-642-3366. E-mail: stiller@healthregs.com.

STILLINGS, IRENE ELLA GRACE CORDINER, ret.foundation executive; b. Boston, Aug. 17, 1918; d. Matthew Wilson and Susan F. (Mason) Cordiner; m. Gordon A. Stillings, May 13, 1945; children: David Gordon, Susan Irene. Student, Radcliffe Coll., 1936-39; diploma, Burdett Coll., 1941. Sec., bookkeeper Boston Refrigerator Co., 1941-42; sec., tchr. Burdett Coll., 1942-44; sec., bookkeeper Gertrude Rittenburg, Boston, 1944-46. Town chmn. Heart Fund, Woodland, Maine, 1953-61; Brownie leader Girl Scouts U.S., 1954-58; pres. Woodland Woman's Club 1961-63; sec. PTA, 1961-62; chmn. Baileyville Superintending Sch. Com., 1962-64; chmn. women's activities Nat. Found., East Washington County, 1959-61; pres. Hosp. Aid, 1961-63; chmn. Newcomers Coll. group YWCA, 1965-66, chmn. theatre group, 1968-70, pres. Suburbanites, 1970-71; Stamford (Conn.) chmn. Expt. in Internat. Living, 1965-68; bd. dirs. YWCA of Stamford, 1969-78, chmn. antique show, 1960-77, chmn. devotion, 1970-92, ann. Antique Show benefit, 1970-77; pres. New Suburbanites, Stamford, 1994-95, ret. 1996. Mem. Mass. Hort. Soc., St. Luke's Guild (treas. 1954-63), Radcliffe Club, Stamford Woman's Club (treas. 1975-79, program com., co-chmn. Am. home dept. 1974, 75, pres. 1981-83, bd. dirs. 1981—, 2d v.p. fin. 1979-81, 83-85, 87-89, chmn. bldg. investment 1979-81, parliamentarian 1990—, pres., newcomers/suburbanites, 1994-95), Theta Alpha Chi. Episcopalian. Home: 277 W Hill Rd Stamford CT 06902-1708

STILLMAN, ANDREA L. state legislator; b. N.Y.C. BA, Calif. State U., Northridge. Mem. Conn. Ho. of Reps., Hartford, 1993—. Rep. town meeting, 1980-83; memb. Bd. Fin., 1984-92; bd. dirs. Conn. Resource Recovery Authority, 1988-92, Conn. Low Level Radioactive Waste Adv. Coun., 1992; mem. Waterford Dem. Town Com., Waterford Hist. Soc., Citizen's Task Force on Substance Abuse, 1996. Mem. AAUW, LWV, Nat. Women's Political Caucus, Nat. Assn. Women, Lions Club. Democrat. Jewish. Address: 5 Coolidge Ct Waterford CT 06385-3309 Office: Conn Ho of Reps State Capitol Hartford CT 06106

STILLMAN, ELINOR HADLEY, retired lawyer; b. Kansas City, Mo., Oct. 12, 1938; d. Hugh Gordon and Freda (Brooks) Hadley; m. Richard C. Stillman, June 25, 1965 (div. Apr. 1975). BA, U. Kans., 1960; MA, Yale U., 1961; JD, George Washington U., 1972. Bar: D.C. 1973, U.S. Ct. Appeals (10th cir.) 1975, U.S. Ct. Appeals (9th cir.) 1976, U.S. Ct. Appeals (2d cir.) 1976, U.S. Ct. Appeals (5th cir.) 1983, U.S. Ct. Appeals (4th cir.) 1985, U.S. Supreme Ct. 1976. Lectr. in English CUNY, 1963-65; asst. editor Stanford (Calif.) U. Press., 1967-69; law clk. to judge U.S. Dist. Ct. D.C., Washington, 1972-73; appellate atty. NLRB, Washington, 1973-78; asst. to solicitor gen. U.S. Dept. Justice, Washington, 1978-82; supr appellate atty.

NLRB, Washington, 1982-86, chief counsel to mem. bd., 1986-88, 94-00, chief counsel to chmn. bd., 1988-94; ret., 2000. Mem.: D.C. Bar Assn., Order of Coif, Phi Beta Kappa. Democrat.

STILLMAN, JEANNE BETSOCK, public health administrator, consultant; b. Bethlehem, Pa., Dec. 15, 1942; d. Paul Thomas and Juliana Habera Betsock; m. David George Stillman, 1965; children: J. Alexander, Gregory D., Juliana E. C. BA, Am. U., 1964; MSPH, U. N.C., 1971; postgrad., Columbia U. Sch. Pub. Health, 1979-81. Assoc. dir. Quaker Svc./AFSC, Lome, Togo, 1969-70; from instr. to lectr. health adminstrn. Sch. Pub. Health U. N.C., Chapel Hill, 1971-74, rsch. assoc. Population Ctr., 1971-74; staff assoc., Tunisia project mgr. The Population Coun., N.Y.C., 1982-83; dir. N.Y. office Inst. for Devel. Tng., N.Y.C., 1989-93; Nigeria project mgr. The Africa-Am. Inst., N.Y.C., 1993-96; prin. Strategies for Devel., Inc., Hastings-on-Hudson, N.Y., 1998—. Dep. dir. devel. The Children's Village, Dobbs Ferry, 2002; mem. adv. com. UN Population Fund, N.Y.C., 1998; cons. in field. Assoc. editor, contbr. International Encyclopedia of Population, 2 vols., 1982; editor: (tng. manuals) Training Course in Women's Health, 2nd edit., 11 vols., 1993; editor, writer: UNHCR Manual for Health Services in Afghan Refugee Camps, 1985; project dir.: (video) Population and People of Faith, 1991 (N.Y. Internat. Film Festival Bronze medal 1992). Ch. coord. Habitat for Humanity, Hastings-on-Hudson, 1997—2000; vol. Internat. Microcredit Summit Meeting of Couns., N.Y.C., 1998; bd. sec. Greater Westchester Youth Orch. Assn., Valhalla, N.Y., 1997-99; parent fund vol. Phillips Exeter Acad., 1998-; mem. Ch. Vestry, 2001—; vol. Bus. Coun. of Westchester, 2002—; vol. emergency preparedness ARC, 2002—. Mem. APHA, Assn. Devel. Officers (bd. dirs. 2003—), UN Assn. USA (Westchester chpt., bd. dirs. 2002—), Am. Freedom Assn. (hon. bd. dirs. 2003-). Democrat. Episcopalian. Avocations: reading, theater, music. Office: Strategies for Development Inc 166 Edgars Ln Hastings On Hudson NY 10706-1108 Office Fax: 914-478-7859. Business E-Mail: jbs@stratdev.com.

STILLMAN, MARGARET D. library director; m. Peter R. Stillman; children: Lindsay H. and Walker H. Forehand. BA in Edn., U. Richmond, 1973; MA in Edn., Va. Commonwealth U., 1974; MLS, U. Ky., 1977. Mem. staff to dir. Chesapeake (Va.) Pub. Libr. Sys., 1975-85, dir., 1985—. Chmn. State Adult Literacy Initiative, 1989-95; mem. Govs. Rural Econ. Devel. Task Force, 1990-92, U. Va. Continuing Edn. Ctr. Council, 1990-94, bd. dirs. United Way Hampton Rds., 1995—, Vol. Hampton Rds., 1996-98, Va. Stage Co., 1979-85 (v.p. 1981-82), Colonial Girl Scouts, 1993-95, Cultural Alliance, 1985-91, Tidewater Red Cross, 1980-83. Recipient Outstanding Young Career Woman of Va. award, 1978, Outstanding Profl. Woman, 1993. Mem. Pub. Libr. Assn. (bd. dirs. 1997-98, chmn. leadership dev. com. 1997), Libr. Va. Found. (bd. dirs. 1996—), WHRO Found. (bd. dirs. 1997—). Office: Chesapeake Public Library 298 Cedar Rd Chesapeake VA 23322-5598 Home: 3924 Oak Dr E Chesapeake VA 23321-5905

STILLMAN, NINA GIDDEN, lawyer; b. NYC, Apr. 3, 1948; d. Melvin and Joyce Audrey (Gidden) S. AB with distinction, Smith Coll., 1970; JD cum laude, Northwestern U., 1973. Bar: Ill. 1973, U.S. Dist. Ct. (no. dist.) Ill. 1973, U.S. Dist. Ct. (ea. dist.) Wis. 1979, U.S. Dist. Ct. (no. dist. trial bar) Ill. 1983, U.S. Ct. Appeals (7th cir.) 1974, U.S. Supreme Ct. 1981, U.S. Dist. Ct. (ctrl. dist.) Ill. 1994, U.S. Dist. Ct. (ea. dist.) Tex., 1996, U.S. Dist. Ct. (Colo.), 1999, U.S. Dist. Ct. (ND) 2002. Assoc. Vedder, Price, Kaufman & Kammholz, Chgo., 1973-79, ptnr., 1980—. Adv. bd. occupational health and safety tng. program U. Mich., Ann Arbor, 1980-83; adj. faculty Inst. Human Resources and Indsl. Rels., Loyola U., Chgo., 1983-86, bd. advisors, 1986—. Author: (with others) Women, Work, and Health: Challenge to Corporate Policy, 1979, Occupational Health Law: A Guide for Industry, 1981, Employment Discrimination, 1981, Personnel Management: Labor Relations, 1981, Occupational Safety and Health Law, 1988; contbg. author: Occupational Medicine: State of the Art Reviews, 1996; contbr. articles to profl. jours. Legal advisor, v.p. Planned Parenthood Assn. Chgo., 1979—81; sec. jr. governing bd. Chgo. Symphony Orch., 1983; trustee Merit Sch. Music, 2000—, vice chmn. bd. trustees, 2001—. Recipient Svc. award Northwestern U., 1994. Mem.: ABA (occupl. safety and health law com. 1978—), Human Resources Mgmt. Assn. Chgo. (bd. dirs. 1986—88, officer), Am. Inns of Ct. (v.p. Wigmore chpt. 1988—89), Chgo. Bar Assn. (chmn. labor and employment law com. 1986—87), Northwestern U. Sch. Law Alumni Assn. (pres. 1991—92), Univ. Club Chgo. (bd. dirs. 1988—2001, sec. 1999—2000, v.p. 2000—01), The Chgo. Com., Econ. Club Chgo., Lawyers Club, Smith Coll. Club Chgo. (pres. 1972). Avocations: travel, reading, the arts, collecting art. Office: Vedder Price Kaufman & Kammholz 222 N La Salle St Ste 2600 Chicago IL 60601-1100

STILLMAN, SHARON J. real estate broker; b. Milw., May 17, 1949; Mktg. and sales cons. Haddonstone, Brighton Ridge Subdivsns., 1988-92; dir. career devel. Overlake Condominium, Greendale, Wis. Contbr. articles to The Christian Courier. Dir., bd. co-founder Whitefish Bay 4th July Parade and Festivities, 1976-79; develpoer short term mission project Eastbrook Ch., Miw., 1980's; vol. Discipleship Unltd. Taycheetah Prison, 1990-98. Mem. Met. Bd. Realtors, Urban Day Sch., Alliance Francaise, AIWF Republican. Avocations: watercolors, interior design, reading, travel. Office: Realty Execs 705 E Silver Spring Dr Whitefish Bay WI 53217-5231

STILLMAN-MYERS, JOYCE L. artist, educator, writer, illustrator, consultant; b. N.Y.C., Jan. 19, 1943; d. Murray W. and Evelyn (Berger) Stillman. BA, NYU, 1964; student, Art Students League, 1965, Pratt Inst., 1972; MFA, L.I. U., 1975; postgrad., Calif. Inst. Integral Studies, 1994—. Tchr. N.Y.C. Pub. Schs., 1964-71; artist, 1974-76, Louis K. Meisel Gallery, N.Y.C., 1975-84, Tolarno Gallery, Melbourne, Australia, 1976—, Allan Stone Gallery, N.Y.C., 1990—; founder CoCreative Inst. Art, Fingerlakes Region, N.Y. Vis. assoc. prof. Towson State U., 1982; tchr. Tompkins Cortland C.C., 1988; lectr. Cornell U., 1990; founder Ithaca Women Artists Salon, Artistic Applications Decorative Arts Ctr. One-woman shows include Ctrl. Hall Gallery, Port Washington, 1975, Tolarno Gallery, Melbourne, 1976, Louis K. Meisel Gallery, N.Y.C., 1977, 1980—82, Heckscher Mus., Huntington, N.Y., 1980, Holtzman Gallery, Towson (Md.) State U., 1982, Roslyn Oxley Gallery, Sydney, 1976, 1982, Tomasulo Gallery, Union Coll., N.J., 1983, Stages Keuka Coll., Keuka Park, N.Y., 1985, New Visions, Ithaca, N.Y., 1989, Her-Chambliss, Hot Springs, Ark., 1990, Artist on the Lake, Hector, N.Y., 1992, Arnot Mus., Elmira, N.Y., Mus. Modern Art Christmas Card Collection, 1994, Arnot Mus., Elmira, N.Y., 2002, over 75 group shows, designer, Mus. Modern Art Christmas Card Collection, 1978—81, 1994, Time-Life Poster, 1978, Doing Dionysos, Arts of the So. Trees, 2000—02. Mem. Literacy Vols. Am. Recipient Flower Painting award, Artist's Mag., 1986, Distinctive Merit award, Art Dir.'s Club 58th Ann., 1979; grantee Pub. Svc., N.Y. State Creative Artist's, 1979. Mem.: AAUW, Nat. Assn. Women Artists. Home: 112 Brooklyn Ter Odessa NY 14869-9786 Office Phone: 607-594-2200. E-mail: jstillman1@stny.rr.com.

STIMMELL, ANNE KRUEGER, special education educator; b. Stuart, Fla., Mar. 7, 1959; d. Karl John Krueger, Jr. and Geraldine Koestner Krueger; m. William Andrew Stimmell, May 29, 1977; children: Melissa Anne, William Andrew Stimmell, Jr. AA in Pre-Med, Indian River C.C., Ft. Pierce, Fla., 1978; BS in Spl. Edn., Fla. Atlantic U., 1998. Cert. tchr. K-12, varying exceptionalities Fla., 1998. Mgr. Krueger's Florist, Inc., Stuart, Fla., 1978—86; office mgr. Britt-Britt Constructors, Inc., Stuart, Fla., 1986—95; teacher's aide Martin Co. Sch. Dist., Stuart, Fla., 1995—96; tchr., spl. edn. Martin County Sch. Dist., Stuart, Fla., 1998—. Mem.: Coun. for Exceptional Children, Kappa Delta Pi. Republican. Avocations: antiques, genealogy, gardening, camping, fishing. Home: 1170 SE Ocean Blvd Stuart FL 34996

STIMMELL, TAMARA, special education educator; b. Charleroi, Pa., Apr. 4, 1958; d. John R. and Patricia (Strenske) Stimmell. BA in Edn., Westminster Coll., 1980; MEd, Calif. U. of Pa., 1982; PhD, U. Pitts., 1990. Cert. elem. tchr., reading specialist, curriculum and supervision; supt. letter of eligibility. Reading specialist Somerset Area Sch. Dist., Pa., 1982-92, gifted and talented edn. educator, 1982-92, dir. spl. edn., 1992—. Mem. student assistance core team Somerset Area Sch. Dist., 1986-94, active drug adv. commn., 1989-92; dir. drug and alcohol edn. program Twin Lakes, 1992—; peer monitor Dept. of Edn., Pa., 1992—. Active drug and alcohol exec. commn. Somerset County, chair edn. rep. 1987—, chair planned courses and instructional practice com. Recipient award for Outstanding Contbn. Twin Lakes Rehab. Ctr., Red Ribbon Campaign for Drug Prevention, 1990, 94, 97. Mem. Coun. Exceptional Children, Phi Delta Kappa, Kappa Delta Pi. Home: 515 Rostraver Rd Belle Vernon PA 15012-1926

STIMPSON, CATHARINE ROSLYN, English language educator, writer; b. Bellingham, Wash., June 4, 1936; d. Edward Keown and Catharine (Watts) Stimpson. AB, Bryn Mawr Coll., 1958; BA, MA, Cambridge U., Eng., 1960; PhD, Columbia U., 1967. Mem. faculty Barnard Coll., N.Y.C., 1963—80; prof. English, dean of grad. sch., vice provost grad. edn. Rutgers U., New Brunswick, NJ, 1980—92, univ. prof., 1991—; chmn. bd. scholars Ms. Mag., N.Y.C., 1981—92; dir. fellows program MacArthur Found., 1994—97; univ. prof., dean Grad. Sch. Arts and Sci. NYU, N.Y.C., 1998—. Author: Class Notes, 1979, Where the Meanings Are, 1988; editor: Signs: Jour. Women in Culture and Soc., 1974—81, Women in Culture and Society book series, 1981; contbr. Change Mag., 1992—93. Chmn. N.Y. Coun. Humanites, 1984—87, Nat. Coun. Rsch. on Women, 1984—89; trustee Bates Coll., 1990—; pres. Assn. Grad. Schs., 2000—01; bd. dir. Stephens Coll., Columbia, Mo., 1982—85, Legal Def. and Edn. Fund, 1991—96. Fellow, Woodrow Wilson Found., 1958, Fulbright fellow, 1958—60, Nat. Humanities Inst., 1975—76, Rockefeller Humanities fellow, 1983—84. Mem.: PBS (bd. dirs. 1994—2000), NOW, AAUP, PEN, MLA (exec. coun., chmn. acad. freedom com., 1st v.p., pres. 1990). Democrat. Home: 29 Washington Sq W Apt 15C New York NY 10011-9199 Office: NYU 6 Washington Sq N New York NY 10003-6668 E mail: catharine.stimpson@nyu.edu.

STIMPSON, PATRICIA, software company executive; BA in Math. and Physics cum laude, Wheaton Coll.; MA in Math., U. Mich.; grad. exec. edn. program, Babson Coll. Various mgmt., cons. and engring. positions Camex, Inc., Data Resources, Inc., Nixdorf Computer, Wang Labs, Inc.; sr. devel. positions, dir. Lotus Devel. Corp., until 1995; v.p. R & D, Silknet Software, Inc., Manchester, N.H., 1995—. Office: Silknet Software Inc Gateway Bldg 50 Phillippe Cote St Ste 301 Manchester NH 03101-1186 Fax: 603-625-0428.

STINE, CATHERINE MORRIS, artist; b. Roanoke, Va., Jan. 12, 1953; d. Richard Dengler and Dorothy Geraldine (Cornog) S.; m. Norris Jewett Chumley, Oct. 22, 1983; children: Jack H.M., Nathaniel B. BFA, Mus. Sch. Fine Arts, Boston, 1975; MFA in Creative Writing, New Sch., NYC, 2002. Art dir. Ear Mag., N.Y.C., 1980-83; asst. art dir. Jacmel Jewelry, N.Y.C., 1984-88; textile designer Style Coun., N.Y.C., 1989-90, Ruvetta Designs, N.Y.C., 1990—; represented by Margaret Bodell Gallery, N.Y.C., 1999—, Red Piano Gallery, Saint Helena, S.C. Curator Bratton Gallery, NYC, 1989. One-woman shows include Plant Factory, Boston, 1974, Sixth Sense Gallery, N.Y.C., 1986, Pinnacle Awards/Am. Women in Radio and TV, N.Y.C., 1987, Limelight Club, N.Y.C., 1987, Parker-Bratton Gallery, N.Y.C., 1987, Bratton Gallery, N.Y.C., 1988, Carol Getz Gallery, Miami, Fla., 1990, Sunnen Gallery, N.Y.C., 1993-94, Galley B.A.I., N.Y.C., 1996, Margaret Bodell Gallery, N.Y.C., 2000; group shows include Mus. Fine Arts Gallery, Boston, 1974, Williamsburg, Bklyn., 1982, ABC No Rio, N.Y.C., 1983, 85, City Without Walls Gallery, Newark, 1984-85, Parsons Gallery, N.Y.C., 1985, author, illustrator: The Halcyon, 1984, Hudson Valley Exhbn., Poughkeepsie, 1985, Parker-Bratton Gallery, N.Y.C., 1986, Bratton Gallery, 1989, Neo Persona, N.Y.C., 1990, Tribeca 148, N.Y.C., 1991, Helio Gallery, N.Y.C., 1991, S. Bitter Larkin, N.Y.C., 1992, Sarah Rentschler Gallery, N.Y.C., 1992, Dooley-Le Cappellaine, N.Y.C., 1993, NYU Law Sch., 1994, Margaret Bodell Gallery, N.Y.C., 2001; reviewed by Art in Am., 2001; represented in permanent collections Art Mus. Western Va., Paramount Pictures, others; represented by Margaret Bodell Gall., N.Y.C.; author: Wild at Heart/End of the Race, 2002. Mem. Fifteenth St. Quaker Meeting, N.Y.C. Curatorial grantee Artist Space, N.Y.C., 1989. Mem. Soc. Childrens' Book Writers and Illustrators. Avocation: writing for young readers. Home: 214 E 17th St Apt 2 New York NY 10003-3647

STINE, KATIE KRATZ, state legislator; b. Dec. 6, 1956; BS, U. Cin.; JD, No. Ky. U. Atty.; mem. Ky. Ho. of Reps., Frankfort, 1995-98, Ky. Senate, Frankfort, 1999—, mem. econ. devel. & tourism, health & welfare, judiciary com. Active Jr. League Cin., Episcopal Ch. Women, No. Ky. Right to Life, Johnson Elem. Sch. PTA; former vice chair Ft. Thomas Bd. Adjustments. Mem. DAR, Ky. Bar Assn., Ft. Thomas Garden Club. Republican. Office: Ky Senate 24th Dist 702 Capitol Ave Rm 225 Frankfort KY 40601-3448 Home: 15 Cliffview Ave Fort Thomas KY 41075-1102

STINES, BETTY IRENE, artist; b. Stinesville, Ind., May 3, 1918; d. Claude Everett Parham and Helen Bryan Acuff Parham; m. Willard Russell Elliott, Oct. 11, 1936 (dec. Aug. 1969); children: Jerry Lee Elliott, Gillespie-Kathy Lyn Elliott Holtsclaw, Willard Keith Elliott; m. Edmond Glen Stines, Feb. 19, 1972. Grad. high sch., Bloomington, Ind. Organizer, mem. Hoosier Hills Art Guild, Bloomington, Ind., 1963—80; organizer Hoosier Hills Art Guild Ann. Student Art Exhibit, 1963—73; floral designer Unique Florist Shoppe, Ellettsville, Ind., 1963—69. Oil and water color paintings, 1950—2001, exhibited in group shows at Ind. U., Manchester Coll., Swope Art Gallery, Terre Haute, Ind., Hoosier Hills Art Gallery, Bloomington, Ind., Owen County Art Gallery, Spencer, Ind., Represented in permanent collections, exhibited in group shows at Ind. State House Art Salon. Chmn., co-chair art exhibits Monroe County Festival, Ellettsville, Ind., 1950—60; Sunday sch. tchr. Gave Chalk Talks Bapt. Ch., 1950; leader Brownie Scouts, 1943—47. Recipient numerous First, Best in Show and Champion Exhibitor awards. Mem.: Ind. Women in Arts, Nat. Mus. Women in Arts. Baptist. Avocations: genealogy, antiques. Home: 7935 W Ratliff Rd Bloomington IN 47404-9685

STINGER, FANCHON, newscaster; d. Edward and Zelma Stinger; m. Tony Camilleri. BA in English and Comm., U. Mich., 1993. Reporter WJBK-TV, Detroit, 1997—, editor and co-anchor 5:30pm news, 2000—. Recipient 5 Emmy awards, NATAS, 1998—, Best Reporter award, AP-Mich., 2000, Insp. Gen.'s Integrity award, U.S. Dept. HHS, 2002. Office: WJBK-TV Fox 2 PO Box 2000 Southfield MI 48037-2000

STINSMUEHLEN-AMEND, SUSAN, artist; b. Balt., Nov. 5, 1948; d. William I. and Geraldine S. (Dodds) Hamilton; m. Richard E. Amend, Nov. 27, 1987; children: Jason Stinsmuehlen, Wyatt Amend. Student, Hood Coll., U. Tex. Designer, owner Renaissance Glass Co., Austin, 1973-87; artist dba. Impresa, Inc., L.A. and Ojai, Calif., 1987—. Mem. Art in Pub. Places Panel, Austin, 1986-87; cons. Nat. Endowment for the Arts, Washington, 1986, 87, Cmty. Redevel. Agy., L.A., 1990-92; artist trustee Am. Craft Coun., 1988-92; lectr., lead artist Hollywood Blvd. Streetscape Team, Hollywood, Calif., 1991-94; mem. Arts Commn., Ojai, Calif., 2000—; mem. Hollywood Art and Design Adv. Panel, 1994-2003; educator in field. One-woman shows include Mattingly Baker Gallery, Dallas, 1984, Kurland Summers Gallery, L.A., 1985, 88, 90, 92, Traver Sutton Gallery, Seattle, 1986, Habatat Galleries, Detroit, 1991, The Nest Gallery, Ojai, Calif., 1997, The Glass Gallery, Bethesda, Md., 2000, Carnegie Mus. Art, Oxnard, Calif., 2004; exhibited in group shows at Whatcom Mus., Bellingham, Wash., 1992-94, Finegood Art Gallery, West Hills, Calif., 1993-94, Miller Gallery, N.Y.C., 1994, The Wignall Mus., Chaffey Coll., Rancho Cucamonga, Calif., 1995, Traver Gallery, Seattle, 1995, Smithsonian Inst. Travelling Exhbn., 1999, Muckenthaler Cultural Arts Ctr., Calif., 1999, Loveland (Colo.) Mus. Gallery, 1998, 99, Fresno Art Mus., 1998, SOFA Chgo., 1998, Santa Cruz Mus. Art and History, 1999, Smithsonian Inst., 1998-2000, L.A. County Mus. Art, 1999, Orange County Mus. Art, 1999, L.A. Mcpl. Art Gallery, 2003, Reynolds Gallery, Richmond, Va., 2003, others; represented in permanent collection Am. Airlines, Dallas, Renwick Gallery Nat. Mus. Art, Washington, The Jewish Mus., N.Y.C., The Corning (N.Y.) Mus. Glass, Detroit Inst. Arts, Leigh Yawkey Woodson Mus., Wausau, Wis., Oakland (Calif.) Mus., Wagga Wagga City Art Gallery, NSW, Australia, Nishida Mus., Toyoma, Japan, Pilchuck Glass Ctr., Stanwood, Wash., Am. Craft Mus., N.Y.C., L.A. (Calif.) County Mus. Art, Radisson Hotel, Austin, AT&T, Dallas, AT&T, N.Y.C., Marshall Fields Corp. Collection, Chgo., City of L.A., Mus. Am. Art/Smithsonian Instn., others plus numerous pvt. collections. Nat. Endowment for the Arts grantee, Washington, 1982, 88; Hauberg fellow Pilchuck Glass Sch., 2001. Mem. Glass Art Soc. (hon. life; bd. dirs. 1982-86, pres. 1984-86), Mus. Contemporary Art (L.A.), L.A. County Mus. Avocations: gardening, swimming, walking, hiking, golf.

STINSON, ANDREA MARIA, professional basketball player; b. Mooresville, N.C., Nov. 25, 1967; BA, N.C. State U., 1991. Guard Charlotte Sting, 1997—. Named Kodak All-Am., 1990, 1991, MVP, ACC Tournament, ACC Player of Yr., 1991, lead scorer, Charlotte Sting, 1997—2001; named to All-ACC Tournament Team, Italian League All-Star Team, Ea. Conf. All-Star Team, 2001; recipient Gold medal, 1992 Jones Cup Team, Bronze medal, 1991 Pan Am. Team playing overseas for Thiene in Italy, 1996—97. Office: Charlotte Sting 100 Hive Dr Charlotte NC 28208-7707*

STINSON, MARY FLORENCE, retired nursing educator; b. Wheeling, W.Va., Feb. 11, 1931; d. Rolland Francis and Mary Angela (Voellinger) Kellogg; m. Charles Walter Stinson, Feb. 12, 1955; children: Kenneth Charles, Karen Marie, Kathryn Anne. BSN, Coll. Mt. St. Joseph, 1953, postgrad., 1983; MEd, Xavier U., Cin., 1967; postgrad., U. Cin., 1981. Staff nurse contagious disease ward Cin. Gen. Hosp., 1953-54, asst. head nurse med. and polio wards, 1955, acting head nurse, clin. instr., 1955-56; instr. St. Francis Hosp. Sch. Practical Nursing, Cin., 1956-57, Good Samaritan Hosp. Sch. Nursing, Cin., 1957—66; instr. refresher courses for nurses Cin. Bd.. Edn. and Ohio State Nurses Assn. Dist. 8, 1967-70; coord. sch. health office Coll. Mt. St. Joseph, Ohio, 1969-72, instr. dept. nursing, 1974-79, asst. prof., 1979-89; RN assessor Passport program Coun. on Aging Southwestern Ohio, 1989-90, quality assurance coord. Passport program, 1990-93; quality assurance supr. Passport and Elderly Svcs. Program, 1993-94; quality assurance mgr. Coun. Aging Southwestern Ohio, 1995-2000; ret., 2000. Staff nurse St. Francis/St. George Hosp., Cin., 1988-89. Charter mem. Adoptive Parents Assn. St. Joseph Infant and Maternity Home; women's com. for performing arts series Coll. Mt. St. Joseph; chmn. by-law com. Mt. St. Joseph Nursing Honor Soc., 1996—98; active St. Antoninus Rosary Altar and St. Sch. Soc., St. Antoninus Athletic Club, com. chmn., 1969—70; bd. dirs. Coll. Mt. St. Joseph Alumni Assn., 1982—84, sec., 1968—69, v.p., 1969—70, pres., 1970—71, chmn. revision of constn., 1976—77; homecoming chmn. Coll. Mt. St. Joseph, 1970, co-chmn., 1977, co-chair com. to celebrate 75 years of nursing edn., 2001—02; mem. com. to plan 50th ann. of graduation Coll. Mt. St. Joseph Alumni Assn. Democrat. Roman Catholic. Mem. River Squares Club (v.p. 1967), Sigma Theta Tau (charter Omicron Omicron chpt. 1998—). Home: 5549 Cleander Dr Cincinnati OH 45238-4266 E-mail: flostinson@fuse.net.

STINSON, SUSAN ELIZABETH, director, writer; b. Amarillo, Tex., Oct. 17, 1960; d. Billy Ray and Mollie Elizabeth (Jordan) S. BA, U. Colo., Boulder, 1983. Dir. devel. Ctr. for Popular Econs., Amherst, Mass., 1990—99. Editor Orogeny Press, Northampton, 1992-97. Author: Belly Songs, 1993, Fat Girl Dances with Rocks, 1994, Martha Moody, 1995 (Benjamin Franklin award 1996), Gracious Flab/Gracious Bone (video), 1995, Venus of Chalk, 2003. Fiction fellow The Millay Colony, Austerlitz, N.Y., 1991, Helene Wurlitzer Found., Taos, N.M., 1991, Blue Mountain Ctr., Blue Mountain Lake, N.Y., 1994; fiction grantee Ludwig Vogelstein Found., N.Y.C., 1992, Mass. Arts lottery grantee, 1993, 97. Home: PO Box 1272 Northampton MA 01061-0433

STIPEK, DEBORAH, education educator, dean; BS in Psychology, U. Wash., 1972; PhD in Devel. Psychology, Yale U., 1977. Prof. Grad. Sch. Edn. UCLA, 1977—2000; co-dir. NIMH Tng. Program in Applied Human Devel.; dir. Corinne Seeds U. Elme. Sch., Urban Edn. Studies Ctr.; I. James Quillen dean, prof. edn. Stanford (Calif.) U., 2001—. Mem. bd. on children, youth and families NRC; dir. MacArthur Found. Network on Tchg. and Learning. Author: Motivation to Learn: From Theory to Practice, 2002; author: (with A. Bohart) Constructive and Destructive Behavior: Implications for Family, School, and Society, 2001; author: (with K. Seal) Motivated Minds: Raising Children to Love Learning, 2001. Congl. Sci. fellow, Soc. for Rsch. in Child Devel., Office Senator Bill Bradley, 1983—84. Office: Stanford Univ Sch Edn 485 Lasuen Mall Stanford CA 94305-3096

STIPEK, KATHLEEN, reference librarian; b. Oakland, Calif., Nov. 14, 1946; d. William Antone and Geraldine Catherine (Cullen) S. BA, Fla. Atlantic U., 1967; MLS, Fla. State U., 1982. Clerical/secretarial positions U. Fla., Gainesville, 1968-81; dir. Haines City (Fla.) Pub. Libr., 1982-86; adult svcs. coord. Ctrl. Fla. Regional Libr., Ocala, 1986-89; reference libr. Hernando County Libr. Sys., Brooksville, Fla., 1989; freelance writer and editor, 1989-91; reference libr. Alachua County Libr. Dist., Gainesville, 1991—. Contbr. chpt. to book, articles to profl. jours. Higher Edn. Act Title IIB fellow, 1981-82. Mem. ALA, Fla. Libr. Assn., Fla. Pub. Libr. Assn., Am. Mensa. Avocations: reading, cookery, embroidery. Office: Alachua County Libr Dist 401 E University Ave Gainesville FL 32601-5453

STIRLING, CHRISTINE ANNE, music educator; MusB, SUNY, Potsdam, 1975, MS, 1979. Cert. tchr. levels I, II and III Am. Orff-Shulwerk Assn., 1994. Elem. music tchr. Thousand Islands Ctrl. Sch. Dist., Clayton, NY, 1975—76, Indian River Ctrl. Sch. Dist., Philadelphia, NY, 1976—80, Thousand Islands Ctrl. Sch. Dist., Clayton, NY, 1980—. Dist. music dept. dir. Thousand Islands Ctrl. Sch. Dist., Clayton, NY, 2002—03; ch. organist First Bapt. Ch. of the 1000 Islands, Clayton, NY, 1990—2003. Contbr. material and ideas: Resource Guide for the New York State Standards of the Arts in Music (materials pub. in document). Team mem. Am. Cancer Relay for Life, Clayton, NY, 1999—. Mem.: Greater Rochester Chpt. of the Am. Orff-Schulwerk Assn., N.Y. State Sch. Music Assn., Music Educators Nat. Conf., Am. Orff-Schulwerk Assn., Delta Kappa Gamma. Avocations: reading, travel, kayaking.

STIRLING, ELLEN ADAIR, retail executive; b. Chgo., June 21, 1949; d. Volney W. and Ellen Adair (Orr) Foster; m. James P. Stirling, June 6, 1970; children: Elizabeth Ginevra, Diana Leslie, Alexandra Curtiss. Student, U. Chgo., 1970-71; BA, Wheaton Coll., Norton, Mass., 1971; postgrad., U. London, 1974. Pres., CEO, The Lake Forest Shop, 1986—. Bd. dirs. Lake Forest Bank and Trust. Founder, v.p. aux. bd. Art Inst. Chgo., 1972-91; dir. Friends of Ryerson Woods, 1992—; mem. women's bd. Lyric Opera, Chgo., 1992—, Lake Forest Coll., 1989—; mem. adv. bd. Hope C. McCormick Costume Ctr., Chgo. Hist. Soc.; trustee Nat. Louis U., 1999—. Mem. Onwentsia Club, Racquet Club, Chgo. Club. Office: The Lake Forest Shop 165 E Market Sq Lake Forest IL 60045

STIRM, DORIS ELIZABETH, artist; b. Bingharton, N.Y., U.S.A., July 25, 1919; d. Williamh and Amanda Maria (Hall) Wusthof. B.A., Stanford U., 1941; Grad. Work (hon.), Coll. San Mateo, Calif., 1951. Passenger agent TWA Airlines, SanFrancisco, Calif., 1942—46; art dir. Recreation Dept., Calif., 1970—99; dir. Redwood City Art Gallery, Redwood, Calif., 1998—2003. Pres. Soc. of Xioestern, San Francisco, 1990—91. Water colors, Redwood City Art Ctr. Chmn. Cancer Soc. Drive, Calif., 1951;

co-chmn. Art in Pub. Places, Calif., 1990—95. Recipient Artist of The Yr., Burcwcame Art Soc., 1979. Mem.: Pastel Soc. Democrat. Protestant. Avocations: painting, aerobics, tennis, gardening. Home: 442 Cumberland Dr Burlingame CA 94010 Office: Redwood City Art Gallery 2625 Broadway Redwood City CA 94063

STITCH, ROBERTA LYNN, not-for-profit fundraiser, social worker; b. N.Y.C., N.Y., May 23, 1948; d. Melvin Harold Stitch and Shirley Pearl Kaplan-Stitch. Student, U. Rochester, 1965—67; BA, Bklyn. Coll., 1970; MSW, Hunter Coll., 1972; postgrad., Stanford Law Sch., 1980—85. Cert. social worker N.Y. Legal asst. Howard Deutsch Atty. at Law, N.Y.C., 1977—80, Donald Lindover Atty. at Law, N.Y.C., 1982; rsch. asst. sociology dept. Stanford (Calif.) U., 1986—87; rsch. asst. Merit Co., Jerusalem, 1989—91; fundraiser Nat. Symphony Orch. Assn., Washington, 1991—95, Nat. Rep. Senatorial Com., Washington, 1995—97, Nat. Capital Teleservices, LLC, Washington, 1998—. Telephone solicitor Nat. Children's Ctr. Value Village Project Inc., Adelphi, Md., 1992—. Mem. Smithsonian Instn., Washington, 1996—, U.S. Holocaust Mus., Washington, 2000—, D.C. Rep. Com., Washington, 2000—. Mem.: Nat. Trust Historic Preservation, Stanford Alumni Assn. (life). Republican. Jewish. Avocations: surfing the Internet, cassettes and videos, casino gambling, travel, fashion. Home: Apt 208 1255 New Hampshire Ave NW Washington DC 20036 Office: CAPTEL 300 5th St NE Washington DC 20002 E-mail: robersti@aol.com.

STITES, M(ARY) ELIZABETH, architecture educator; b. N.Y.C., July 28, 1915; d. Otto and Olivia (Stites) Gaertner; m. Raymond S. Stites, Jul. 29, 1938; 1 child: Mary Elizabeth. BArch, NYU, 1940; postgrad., U. Vienna, 1961. Instr. U. Md. Coll. Arts & Scis., College Park, 1949-67, adminstrv. asst., 1959-76, assoc. prof., 1967-76; cons. Md. Coll. Art and Design, Silver Spring, 1976-89; asst. organist St. Luke's Ch., Bethesda, Md., 1976—95. Lectr. religious architecture, history architecture, archtl. studies of Leonardo da Vinci. Contbr. articles to Book of Knowledge Grolier Soc., 1952, New Cath. Ency., 1965. Past mem. Yellow Springs Town Planning Commn.; mem. Montgomery County com. Md. Hist. Trust for Archtl. Preservation. Mem. Coll. Art Assn., Soc. Archtl. Historians, Archaeol. Inst. Am., AIA. Episcopalian. Home: PO Box 98 Garrett Park MD 20896-0098

STITES, SUSAN KAY, writer, human resources consultant; b. Colorado Springs, Colo., Sept. 20, 1952; d. William Wallace and Betty Jane (Kosley) Stites; m. Gerald Frederick Simon, Aug. 14, 1988. BA, Wichita State U., 1974; MA, Northwestern U., 1979. Benefits authorizer Social Security Adminstrn., Chgo., 1974-77; trainer Chgo. Urban Skills Inst., 1977-79; human resources mgr. Montgomery Ward, Chgo., 1979-83; mgr. tng. Lands' End, Dodgeville, Wis., 1983-87; dir. human resources Cen. Life Assurance, Madison, Wis., 1988-90; owner Mgmt. Allegories, Madison, Wis., 1987—. Author: Delegating for Results, 1992, Business Communications, 1992, Managing with a Quality Focus, 1994, Training and Orientation for the Small Business, 1994, Powerful Performance Management, 1994, Safety Management Techniques, 1995, Teaching First Aid and CPR, 1995, Alive at 25, 1995, Strategic Thinking and Planning, 1995, Teaching Alice at 25, 1996, Fundamentals of Industrial Hygiene, 1996, Recruiting, Developing and Retaining Volunteers, 1996, Creating a Credit Union University: An Administrator's Guide, 1997, 2d edit., 2001, Creating a Corporate University, 1997, Strategic Thinking for the Automotive Industry, 1997, Managing Sales and Service, 1997, Sales and Service Management in Credit Unions, 1997, Provide Training Without Straining Your Budget, 1997, Car America Sales Training manual, 1998, Introduction to Community Organizing, 1998, Car America Leader's Guide, 1998, Effective Loan Interviewing, 1999, Driven to Extremes, 2000, Safety Inspections, 2001, Job Safety Analysis, 2001, Incident Investigations, 2001, Ergonomics for the Small Business, 2003, Creating a Safety Culture; Strategies for Small Business, 2004, The Nine Elements of Safety Managment System, 2004; editor: Backstay, 1999-2001. Vol. tutor Japanese students in English, Evanston, Ill., 1977-80; reader to the blind Chgo. Coun. for the Blind, 1974-76. Named Outstanding Woman of the Yr. Wichita State U., 1974. Mem. ASTD (chpt. pres. 1988, v.p. membership 1986, region V awards chair 1992), Soc. Applied Learning Tech., Madison Area Quality Improvement Network, Assn. for Quality and Participation, Rotary (vol. fundraiser), Mendota Yacht Club (treas. 1990-94). Avocations: sailing, boardsailing, gardening, cooking, travel. Office: Mgmt Allegories 3788 Highridge Rd Madison WI 53718-6206

STITH, LAURA DENVIR, state supreme court justice; b. St. Louis, Oct. 30, 1953; BA magna cum laude, Tufts U., 1975; JD magna cum laude, Georgetown U., 1978. Law clk. to Hon. Robert E. Seiler, Mo. Supreme Ct., 1978—79; assoc. Shook, Hardy & Bacon, Kansas City, Mo., 1979—84, ptnr., 1984—94; judge. Mo. Ct. Appeals (we. dist.), 1994—2001; judge Supreme Ct. Mo., 2001—. Office: Supreme Ct Mo PO Box 150 Jefferson City MO 65102

STITT, DOROTHY JEWETT, journalist; b. Houston, Sept. 4, 1914; d. Harry Berkey and Gladys (Norfleet) Jewett; m. James Wilson Stitt, Feb. 14, 1939; children: James Harry (dec. 1999), Thomas Paul. AB, Rice U., 1937; MS, Columbia U., 1938. Reporter Houston Post, 1936-38, asst. city editor, 1938; editor of publs. Jewett Family of Am., 1971-94, editor emeritus, 1994—. Spl. asst. to pub. Jewett Genealogy Vols. III and IV, 1995-97; Jewett family Dir.-for-Life, 1995—; gen. chair Jewett Family Reunion, 1996; exec. com. Jewett 2000 Millennium Reunion. Author, editor: The 100th Anniversary Yearbook and History of the George Taylor Chapter, DAR, 1895-1995, 1994, Easton Red Cross Fiftieth Anniversary Booklet and History—Fifty Years of Service, 1967. Adv. bd. Easton Salvation Army, pub. chmn., 1956—, chmn. bd. dirs., 1964, bd. treas., 1981; bd. dirs., pub. chmn. Easton chpt. ARC, 1952-67, vol. Lehigh Valley chpt., 1995-96, 98; founding chmn., pres. Easton JC Wives, 1950-53; mem. fin. com. Little Stone House Mus. Assn., 1974-76, 80, organizing bd. dirs. sec. and pub. chmn., 1974-91; bd. dirs. Easton United Comty. Chest/United Way, 1957-60, publicity chmn. for 1st campaign, 1960; active Easton Civil Def. Comms., 1956-60; charter mem. bd. Montgomery County Pa. Girl Scouts USA, 1946-48, publicity chmn., initiator and editor county newsletter; den mother cub scouts Easton Boy Scouts Am., 1948-55; capt. renovation campaign area YWCA, 1956; mem. March Sch., Easton PTA, 1948-57, sec., 1952-54, v.p., 1954-56, bylaws chmn., 1953, Easton H.S., 1954-61, membership chmn., 1955-57, 59-60; bd. dirs. Easton Young Woman's Christian Assn., 1965-68, publicity chmn. Y-Teen com., 1953-68; sponsoring dir. Easton area H.S. Students weekly TV 30-minute news program, 1955-56; class agent 60th reunion Pulitzer Grad. Sch. Journalism Class of 1938 Columbia U., 1998. Recipient plaques Salvation Army, 1982, 91, Jewett Family of Am., 1993, cited for Outstanding Svcs., Easton chpt. ARC, 1967, cert. for Outstanding Svc. and Support, 1997, citation Hist. and Geneal. Soc. Northampton County for outstanding svc. in restoration and pub. of Little Stone House Mus., 1993, citation United Way of Easton, 1960, Molly Pitcher gold medal of appreciation SAR, 1980. Mem. AAUW (treas. Easton br. 1950-52, newsletter initiator and editor 1951-60, rep. of br. to UN N.Y.C. conf. 1961-68, internat. rels. chair 1960-68; Pa. achievement award 2000), UDC (Jefferson Davis chpt./Houston), DAR (George Taylor chpt. regent 1974-80, 89-95, vice regent 1980-83, historian 1971-74, 95—, pub. chair 1969—, Pa. state chair vol. svcs. 1995-98, DAR chmn. Kressler Meml. Garden, Easton, 1999—), DAR, PEO (chpt. AF Houston), Easton Tavern House Soc., World Affairs Coun. Phila., Woman's Club of Easton (pres. 1961-64, bd. dirs. 1957—, pub. chair 1952-68, 70-82, 92-96, parliamentarian 1984-92, 2000—, spl. fin. chair 1969-78, legis. chair 1982-84, internat. affairs chair 1996-2000, history update chair 1997—. Outstanding Woman of Yr. 1992, Gold Medal of Honor 1992), Pa. Northeastern Dist. Regents Club (pres. 1980-83, treas. 1997—), Northampton Country Club (Niners' Golf chair 1957-91), Women's Golf Assn. (constn. and bylaws chair, publicity chmn. 1957-92, parliamentarian 1960-92), Libr. of Congress Assn. (founding nat. mem., charter assoc.). Republican. Episcopalian. Avocations: antiques, historical research, golf, swimming, grandmothering. Home: 110 Upper Shawnee Ave Easton PA 18042-1356

STITT, THERESA MARY, special education educator; b. New Kensington, Pa., July 21, 1951; d. Bruno Bosco and Dorina Agnes (Brunelli) Ciciarelli; m. Michael Eugene Stitt, June 14, 1975. BE, Slippery Rock State Coll., 1973, MEd, 1975. Cert. instrnl. II mentally retarded elem. edn. Pa. Iteneran sped tchr. Burrell Sch. Dist., Lower Burrell, Pa., 1973—74; part-time elem. learning support tchr. Westmoreland-Intermediate Unit, Greensburg, Pa., 1974—. Homebound instr. New Kensington-Arnold Sch. Dist., 1977—95; weekend supr. Valley Spl. Sch. Dist. Needs, Springdale, Pa., 1980; transition aide Allegheny Valley Mental Health, Tarentum, Pa., 1990; cooperating tchr. Ind. U. Pa., Duquense, Pa. State U., 1978—2002, Clarion U., 2003—. Sec. Tri-City Jaycettes, New Kensington, 1980; rep. of tchrs. H.D. Berkey Sch. to New Kensington-Arnold Sch. Bd., 1995; rep. IU # 7 Tchr.'s Union bd., 1998—; with Sunshine Grandparent program New Kensington-Arnold Sch. Dist.; mem. PTA; vol. club civil functions. Mem.: Ea. Star (Ruth), Delta Kappa Gamma (chmn. projects on yearbook and hist. records, com. head Chinese auction, sec. 2000—). Democrat. Roman Catholic. Avocations: reading, walking, wreath making. Home: 1126 Dime Road Vandergrift PA 15690 E-mail: sttlab4@kiski.net.

STOCK, ANN, federal official; m. Stuart C. Stock; 1 child. Grad., Purdue U. Dep. press sec. to V.p. Walter F. Mondale, 1980, 84; regional dir. pub. rels. Bloomingdales Dept. Stores, 1982-88, dir. br. stores, 1988-92, v.p. pub. rels., 1988-93; dep. asst. to Pres. and Social Sec. The White House, Washington, 1993-97; v.p. institutional affairs The Kennedy Ctr., Washington, 1997—. Asst. sec. Kennedy Ctr. Bd. Trustees; bd. dirs. Young Concert Artists, Cultural Alliance Greater Washington, United Artists. Mem. Capital Children's Mus. (co-founder), The Women's Forum, N.Y. Fashion Group (former program chmn.), Washington Woman Roundtable (founder), "Race for the Cure" (co-founder). Office: Institutional Affairs The Kennedy Ctr Washington DC 20566-0001

STOCK, PEGGY A(NN), college president, educator; b. Jan. 30, 1936; married; 5 children. BS in Psychology, St. Lawrence U., 1957; MA in Counseling, U. Ky., 1963, EdD, 1970. Lic. psychologist, Ohio. Instr., rsch. asst. dept. psychology and spl. edn. U. Ky., Lexington, 1958-59, 63-67, staff psychologist Med. Ctr., 1964-66; dir. edn. United Cerebral Palsy of the Bluegrass, Lexington, 1962-64; exec. dir. Community Council for Physically Handicapped and Mentally Retarded, Lexington, 1964-66; dir. clin. program No. Ky. Regional Cmty. Mental Health Ctr., Covington, 1969-71; pres. Midwest Inst. Tng. and Edn., Cin., 1971-75; assoc. prof., counseling psychologist Mont. State U., Bozeman, 1975-79, asst. dean Office of Student Affairs and Service, 1977-79; spl. asst. to pres. U. Hartford, Conn., 1979-80, assoc. prof. Coll. Edn., 1980-85, v.p. adminstrn., 1981-86; prof., pres. Colby-Sawyer Coll., New London, N.H., 1986-95; pres. Westminster Coll., Salt Lake City, 1995—. Mem. wild horse and burro adv. bd. Bur. Land Mgmt./Dept. Interior, 1997—2000; bd. dirs. BMW Bank of N.Am., Pacificorp, Fed. Res. Bank, Salt Lake City; trustee St. Mark's Hosp., 2000—. Contbr. chpts. to books, articles to profl. jours. Mem. adv. com. Rowland Hall-St. Mark's Sch., 1999—; chair Utah selection com. Rhodes Scholarships, 1995—; mem. program com. Coun. Ind. Coll., 1996—2000; bd. dirs. Utah Partnership for Edn. and Econ. Devel., 1996—; hon. bd. dirs. Big Bros./Big Sisters, 1999—. Recipient Disting. Alumna award, St. Lawrence U., 1989, Athena Pathfinder award, 2001; fellow, U. Ky., 1966—68, Am. Coun. Edn., 1979—80, United Jewish Com., 1981; grantee, George I. Alden Trust, Helene Fuld Health Trust, Surdna, Cogswell, U.S. Dept. Edn., numerous others. Mem. Am. Coun. on Edn., Am. Assn. for Higher Edn., Advancement Women in Higher Edn., Nat. Assn. Ind. Colls. and Univs. (bd. dirs. 1998—), Am. Assn. Pres.'s Ind. Colls. and Univs. (bd. dirs. 1996—), Salt Lake Area C. of C. (bd. govs. 1996-99), Utah Info. Techs. Assn. (trustee 1998-99). Avocations: breeding arabian horses, reading, fishing. Office: Westminster Coll 1840 S 1300 E Salt Lake City UT 84105-3617

STOCKAR, HELENA MARIE MAGDALENA, artist; b. Bratislava, Czechoslovakia, Mar. 22, 1933; came to the U.S., 1968; d. Arnost J. and Helen R. (Strakova) Kubasek; m. Ivo J. Stockar, Oct. 31, 1959; children: David, Laura Bates. Diploma, Graficka Skola, Prague, 1952, Music Conservatory, 1954. Piano tchr. Music Sch., Prague, 1954-68; company pianist State Ballet/Breacrest Sch., R.I., 1968-74; piano tchr. Music Tchr. Assn., R.I., 1968-86. One-woman shows include Warwick (R.I.) Mus., 1986, Brown U., Providence, 1987, Westerly (R.I.) Art Gallery, 1987, Westerly Art Gallery/Morin-Miller, 1988, 1989, Galerie Horizon, Paris, 1989, Barnes & Noble, Warwick, 1999, 2000, Bohemian Gallery, N.Y.C., 1999, Hoxie Gallery, Westerly, 2000, Happy White Gallery, Barrington, R.I., 2000, C.C. R.I., Lincoln, 2000, Pittenween Art Festival, Scotland, 2001, Pawtucket Congl. Ch., 2002, Bell St. Chapel, Providence, 2002, Courthouse Ctr. Arts, West Kingston, R.I., 2003, two-person shows at: R.I. State Com. Nat. Mus. Women in the Arts, Triboro Studio, R.I., 1995, Bush Gallery, Bryce Studio, Providence, 1995, Monserat Gallery, Soho, 2002, Courthouse Ctr. for the Arts, West Kingston, R.I., 2002, De Blois Gallery, Newport, 2002, Stonington Vineyards Gallery, Conn., 2002, Teichman Gallery, Cape Cod, Mass., 2003, Gallery Z, Providence, 2003, exhibited in group shows at World Congress Czechoslovak Soc. Art and Sci., Washington, 1988, Prague, 1992, Morin-Miller Internat., N.Y.C., 1989, Ariel Gallery, Soho, N.Y.C., 1989, Art Expo N.Y.C., 1989, New Eng. Internat. Art Expo, 1993, R.I. State Com. Nat. Mus. Women Arts, 1995, Providence Art Club, 1996—97, Sarah Doyle Galery, Brown U., Providence, 1997, Visions, Newport, 2001, 2002, Gallery Z, Providence, 2003, 2004, Krause Gallery, 2003, Breslin Fine Arts, Inc., Warwick, RI, 2003, exhibited in group shows, Warwick Mus., 2003, Represented in permanent collections; featured on TV shows. Participant Art in Public Places: Convention Ctr., Providence, 1994. Recipient Second prize Nat. Competition of Children's Book Illustration, Prague, 1965; named finalist Internat. Art Competition, L.A., 1984. Mem.: Czechoslovak Soc. Art and Sci. Avocations: traveling, gardening.

STOCKARD, SUSAN See **CHANNING, STOCKARD**

STOCKBURGER, JEAN DAWSON, lawyer; b. Scottsboro, Ala., Feb. 4, 1936; d. Joseph Mathis Scott and Mary Frances (Alley) Dawson; m. John Calvin Stockburger, Mar. 23, 1963; children: John Scott, Mary Staci, Christopher Sean. Student, Gulf Park Coll., 1954-55; BA, Auburn U., 1958; M in Social Work, Tulane U., 1962; JD, U. Ark., Little Rock, 1979. Bar: Ark. 1979, U.S. Dist. Ct. (ea. dist.) Ark. 1980. Assoc. Mitchell, Williams, Selig, Gates & Woodyard and predecessor, Little Rock, 1979-85, ptnr., 1985-94, of counsel, 1994—. Bd. dirs., sec. Cen. Ark. Estate Coun., Little Rock, 1984-85, 2d v.p., 1985-86, pres. 1987-88. Assoc. editor U. Ark. Law Rev., 1978-79. Bd. dirs. Little Rock Cmty. Mental Health Ctr., 1994—, v.p., 1996—99, pres., 1999—2001; bd. dirs. Sr. Citizens Activities Today, Little Rock, 1983—88, treas., 1986—88; bd. dirs. Vol. Orgn. for Ctrl. Ark. Legal Svcs., 1986—91, sec., 1987—88, chmn., 1989—91, H.I.R.E. Inc., 1994—2001. Mem. ABA, Ark. Bar Assn. (chmn. probate and trust law sect. 1986-88), Pulaski County Bar Assn. (bd. dirs. 1994-97), Ark. Bar Found., Am. Coll. Trust and Estate Counsel. Democrat. Methodist. Office: Mitchell Williams Selig Gates & Woodyard 425 W Capitol Ave Ste 1800 Little Rock AR 72201-3525

STOCKDALE, KAY LITTLE, librarian; b. Ft. Jackson, S.C., Nov. 3, 1942; d. Edward Earl and Hazel Appie (Price) Little; m. Dennis LeRoy Stockdale, June 27, 1965; 1 child, Lee. BA, Barton Coll., 1965; MLS, U. Ala. Tuscaloosa, 1972; EdD, U. N.C. Greensboro. Tchr. English North Johnston H.S., Kenly, N.C., 1965-66, Greene Ctrl. H.S., Snow Hill, N.C., 1966-68, Druid H.S., Tuscaloosa, Ala., 1968-69; dir. Ridgecrest area program U. Ala. Tuscaloosa, 1969-71; tchr. English Stillman Coll., Tuscaloosa, Ala., 1971-72; libr. Hist. Found. Presbyn. Ch. U.S., Montreat, N.C., 1972-88; libr. C.D. Owen H.S., Swannanoa, N.C., 1988-91, Accelerated Learning Ctr., Asheville, N.C., 1994—. Contbr. articles to profl. jours. Mem. AAUW (pres. Tuscaloosa chpt. 1970-72, v.p. Ala. divsn. 1972, bd. dirs. N.C. divsn. 1975-80), NEA, N.C. Assn. Educators, N.C. Libr. Assn., Sierra Club. Avocations: reading, writing, gardening, hiking. Home: 33 Rainbow Ridge Rd Swannanoa NC 28778-3412 Office: Accelerated Learning Ctr 441 Haywood St Asheville NC 28801-3150

STOCKLIN, ALMA KATHERINE, retired public relations executive; b. New London, Conn., May 9, 1926; d. Stephen Sullivan and Theresa Catherine (Flynn) Sheehan; m. Philip L. Stocklin, Jan. 28, 1950 (div. 1984); children: Brian, Christopher, Virginia Katherine, Walter, Stephen. Student, U. Conn., 1945-46, Conn. Coll., 1946; cert., Sch. Modern Photography, N.Y.C., 1948; AA, Charter Oak Coll., 1979; BA cum laude, Eastern Conn. State U., 1981. Advt. photographer GE, Bridgeport, Conn., 1948-49; chmn. Conn. PTA State Juvenile Protection, 1959; pub. rels. cons. Norwich and Groton, Conn., 1983-86; asst. to dean Ea. Conn. State U., Willimantic, 1984-91, ret., 1991, adminstr. br. office U.S. Submarine Base Groton, 1984-91; pub. rels. cons., 1994—. Coord. videotape courses for submarines, New London, 1984-91. Founder, chmn. bd. dirs. Newport (R.I.) Holiday for Sr. Citizens, 1972, Uncas on Thames Conn. State Hosp. Aux., 1978; mem. Norwich Harbor Day Com., 1982-83, Catchment Area coun. 11 S.E. Coun. Mental Health Bd., 1989-90, Norwich Regional Mental Health Adv. Bd., 1987-90, Norwich State Hosp. Adv. Bd., 1987-89; vice chair Ea. Conn. Regional Mental Health Bd., 1988-89; founder, chmn. Norwich Nuclear Freeze Com., 1982; bd. dirs. Ea. Conn. Symphony Orch., New London, 1984-87, Friend of the Symphony, 1987-90, Laurel Glen, Groton, 1984-91; co-founder, bd. dirs. Newport Ch. Cmty. Housing Corp., 1969-72; founder, chmn. Holiday for Sr. Citizens, Newport R.I., 1972; chair Conn. State PTA Juvenile Protection, 1957; founder, pres. Cath. Mother's Cir., Dorset, Eng., 1962; exec. sec. Overnight Shelter, Loughborough, Eng., 1973-74; founder, chair Bicycle Paths for Schoolchildren, Loughborough, 1974; bd. dirs. Friends of the Fairfield County Dist. Libr., Lancaster, Ohio, 1994-99, Fairfield Affordable Housing Bd.; mem. Fairfield County Literacy Coun., 1996—; bd. dirs. Fairfield Affordable Housing, 1999—; vol. ARC, 1991-; co-founder No. Lights Prescription Referral Svc., 2001. Recipient award for outstanding svc. in founding the Newport Holiday for Sr. Citizens, City Coun. of Newport, 1972, Outstanding Svc. award, Pres. of Conn. PTAs, 1967. Mem. Fairfield County (Conn.) Respiratory Disease and TB Assn. (bd. dirs. 1991-95), Friends of Libr. Assn. Fairfield County Dist. (bd. dirs. 1994-99), Nat. Alliance for the Mentally Ill, Sierra Club, Phi Beta Phi, Conn. Alpha Pi Beta Phi. Democrat. Roman Catholic.

STOCKWELL, MARY DIAMOND, information technology manager; b. Baton Rouge, La., Mar. 7, 1957; d. Jack Lamar and Frances Eaton Diamond; m. Julius Reginald Stockwell, Aug. 16, 1952; 1 child, Katherine Rachel. Catering asst. Prince Murat Inn, Baton Rouge, 1976; key punch operator 1 La. Dept. Health & Human Resources, 1976—77, keypunch operator 2, 1977; data entry operator 2 La. Dept. Social Services, 1977—79, info. systems data entry operator 3, 1979—84, info. systems prodn. control technician 2, 1984—93, info. systems prodn. control technician 3, 1993—96, La. Dept. Transp. & Devel., 1996—98, info. systems prodn. control supr. 1, 1998—99, info. tech. prodn. control supr., 1999—. Troop leader, co-leader, asst. leader, religious emblems counselor Girl Scouts Am., 1997—2003. Named Green Angel, Girl Scouts Am., 2000. Mem.: Cath. Dau. of Am. (parlimentarian 1989—91), Baton Rouge Village Krewe (New Eng. village dir., publicity chmn., v.p. 1992—2003), Bengal Belles, Beta Sigma Phi (life; pres., v.p, sec., city coun. rep. 1976, Perfect Attendance award 1976—2000, Woman of Yr. award 1977, 1985, Order of the Rose award 1995, Woman of Yr. award 1999, 2001, Silver Cir. award 2001). Roman Catholic. Avocations: travel, photography, community service, volunteer work, football. Office: La Dept Transp & Devel 1201 Capitol Access Rd Baton Rouge LA 70802 Personal E-mail: marydsto@eatel.net.

STODDARD, ALEXANDRA, designer, writer, lecturer; b. Weston, Mass., Nov. 8, 1941; d. Robert Powell and Barbara Rutledge (Green) Johns; m. Brandon Stoddard (div.); children: Alexandra Brandon, Brooke Goodwin; m. Peter Megargee Brown, May 18, 1974. Diploma in design, N.Y. Sch. Interior Design, 1961. Designer McMillen, Inc., N.Y.C., 1963-77; pres., CEO Alexandra Stoddard Inc., N.Y.C., 1977—. Founder, pres. Design & Art Soc., Ltd., N.Y., 1987—. Author: Style for Living: How to Make Where You Live You, A Child's Place: How to Create a Living Environment for Your Child From Birth through Adolescence, Reflections on Beauty: Lectures and Notes on Interior Design, The Postcard as Art: Bring the Museum Home (Cert. of Merit award 1986), Living a Beautiful Life: 500 Ways to Add Elegance, Order, Beauty and Joy To Every Day of Your Life, Alexandra Stoddard's Living Beautifully Together, Alexandra Stoddard's Book of Color, Gift of a Letter, Daring to be Yourself, Creating a Beautiful Home, Grace Notes, Making Choices, Alexandra Stoddard's Tea Celebrations, The Art of the Possible, Mothers: A Celebration, Gracious Living in a New World, The Decoration of Houses, Open Your Eyes - 1000 Simple Ways to Bring Beauty into Your Home and Life Each Day, Feeling at Home - Defining Who You are and How You Want to Live, Choosing Happiness: Keys to a Joyful Life; contbg. editor Country Antiques and Collectibles, Decorating with Americana; back page columnist Design Times - The Art of Interiors; columnist McCall's mag.; contbr. articles to profl mags. and jours. Founding mem., chmn. spiritual direction com. Ch. of Heavenly Rest, 1975-77; former mem. bd. regents Cathedral St. John the Divine; dame Am. Soc. of Order of St. John Hosp. of Jerusalem. Recipient Burlington prize, 1975, award for design Greenwich Arts Coun., 1985, Interior Design award Brandeis U., 1986, cert. of spl. merit Graphic Art Inst., Designer of Yr. award Kips Bay Boys and Girls Club, 1997, Disting. Womans' award Northwood U., 1999, Lit. Lion, 100th Anniversary prize 2000 Stonington (Conn.) Libr. Mem. English Speaking Union, Decorators Club, Coral Beach and Tennis Club (Paget, Bermuda), New Eng. Soc. Republican. Episcopalian. Home: 1125 Park Ave New York NY 10128-1243 Office: John Rathbone House 87 Water St Stonington CT 06378-1432 also: 1125 Park Ave Ste 6A New York NY 10128-1243 Fax: 212-996.4625. Office Phone: 212-289-5509.

STODDARD, ELIZABETH (LOLLY), artist, writer; b. Balt., Aug. 21, 1947; d. Donald Garcelon and Madeline Blanche Fales; m. Duncan C. Stoddard, July 4, 1946; children: Christina Ross, Andrew, John. AA, Mitchell Coll., 1967; BA, Armstrong Atlantic U., 1971. Artist, author self employed, Mystic, Conn., 2002—. Author (also illustration): (childrens books) Town Small, 2002, Nora, The Fifty Cent Dog, 2003. Named Best Local Artist, Mystic Outdoor Art Festival, 1993, 1996, 2002. Mem.: Mystic Art Assoc. Office: PO Box 9162 Groton CT 06340

STODDARD, ERIN, actress, artist; d. Carl and Lynne Stoddard. BA, NYU, 1989—92. Performer Evita (European Tour), Italy, 1992—93, Joseph and the Amazing Technicolor Dreamcoat (U.S. Nat. Tour), 1996—96, Showboat (U.S. Nat. Tour), 1997—98, A Christmas Carol, NYC, 1999—2000, Beauty and the Beast, NYC, 2000—01, 42 St, NYC, 2001—. Guest spkr. Broadway Classroom, NYC, 2001—. Singer: K2 The Band; prodr.: (industrial performance) Coca-Cola Employee Choice Awards; singer: (new musical recording) One Way Ticket to Hell. Recipient White Sweater award, David Prouty H.S., 1989, Miss Dance of Conn., Dance Masters of Am., 1989; scholarship, Joffrey Ballet - NYC, 1983, Edward Villella - Cape Cod Conservatory, Overall scholarship, Dance Masters of Am., 1988. Mem.: Actor's Fed. TV and Radio Assn., Actor's Equity Assn., Conversations with Millionaires Group. Avocations: sculpting, writing, painting. Personal E-mail: erinstoddard@nyc.rr.com.

STODDARD, PATRICIA FLORENCE COULTER, retired psychologist; b. Detroit, Oct. 13, 1923; d. Glenn Monroe and Doris Carlyle (McDonald) Coulter; m. Charles Hatch Stoddard, June 30, 1956 (div. 1991); children: Glenn, Jeffrey. BA, U. Mich., 1945; MA, George Washington U., 1953; MA in Gerontology, Coll. of Scholastica, Duluth, Minn., 1987. Asst. to dir. personnel Dewey & Almy Chem. Co., Cambridge, Mass., 1946-48; asst. dir. mgmt. tng. program Radcliffe Coll., Cambridge, 1948-49; tng. rep. Woodward Lothrop, Washington, 1949; personnel assoc. Hot Shoppes, Inc., Washington, 1950-53; placement officer George Washington U., Washington, 1953-58; placement asst. U. Minn., Duluth, 1967; psychiat. social worker Northwood Children's Home, Duluth, 1968-80; coord. adult day svcs. Benedictine Health Ctr., Duluth, 1980-98; ret. Adv. com. on aging Regional Area Redevel. Agy., Duluth, 1992—; apptd. State Commn. on Aging, Minn., 1997. Author: Wolf Springs 100 Years: A Century of Life on One Piece of Land, 1991; contbr. articles to profl. jours. Pres. Maple Crest Village Homeowners Assn., Duluth, 1997; vol. recruiter Am. Reads Project. Mem. LWV, Area Aging Network, Algonquin Club. Avocations: tennis, elderhostels, reading, aerobics. Home: 320 Wildwood Dr Duluth MN 55811-5203

STODDARD, SANDOL, freelance/self-employed writer; b. Birmingham, Ala., Dec. 16, 1927; d. Carlos French and Caroline (Harris) S.; m. Felix M. Warburg (div. 1966); children: Anthony, Peter, Gerald, Jason; m. Peter R. Goethals, May 1, 1984. BA magna cum laude, Bryn Mawr Coll., 1959. Author 26 books including: Growing Time, 1971, The Doubleday Children's Bible, 1983 (Lewis citation 1983), The Hospice Movement: Updated and Expanded Edition, 1992, Prayers, Praises and Thanksgivings, 1992. Bd. dirs., co-founder Hospice of Kona, Kailua-Kona, Hawaii, 1985; co-founder Kona Theol. Inst., 1990; bd. dirs. Choice in Dying, N.Y.C. Recipient Humanitarian Svc. award Forbes Health System, 1979, Notable Book award Am. Libr. Assn., 1964. Mem. AAUW, Nat. Writer's Guild, Cosmpolitan Club. Democrat. Episcopalian. Home and Office: 78-6646 Mamalahoa Hwy Holualoa HI 96725-9734

STODDARD-HAYES, MARLANA KAY, artist, educator; b. Ottumwa, Iowa, Nov. 5, 1957; d. Roy Keables Stoddard, Jr. and Joyce Ellen McNeight; m. Robert Lee Hayes, Sept. 25, 1993. BFA in Painting, Colo. State U., 1980; MFA in Painting, Wichita State U., 1983; MA in Interdisciplinary Studies, Maryhurst U., 2002. Artist-in-residence Kans. Arts Commn., 1983—95, Neskowin Coast Found., Cascade Head, Oreg., 1990—91; prof. art Dodge City (Kans.) CC, 1995—2000; adj. prof. drawing Clark Coll., Vancouver, W.Va., 2000—; adj. prof. art Portland (Oreg.) CC, 2001—. Exhibited in group shows at St. John's Coll., 2002, one-woman shows include Trish Higgins Gallery, 2003, exhibitions include Mid-Four Biennial, Nelson-Atkins Mus., 1987, Newman U., Kans., 1987, Lawrence Lithography Workshop, 1987, exhibitions include solo Reuben Saunders Gallery, 1983, 1987, 1991. Mem.: PEO, Coll. Art Assn. Democrat. Episcopalian. Avocations: gardening, reading, walking. Home: 4424 Cedar Oak Dr West Linn OR 97068 Personal E-mail: marlana.stoddard@comcast.net.

STOELTING, FREDA ANN, special education educator; b. Danville, Ill., Sept. 10, 1957; d. Frederick Lee and Rebeccah Josephine Brock; m. Andy Linden Stoelting, June 4, 1983; children: Aaron Lee, Ryan Christopher, Corey Joseph. AA, Danville Area C.C., 1980; BS, Ind. State U., 1982; MA, Ball State U., 2001. Lic. tchr. spl. edn. State of Ind., 1983. Spl. ed. MOMD/SMD tchr. Vigo County Sch. Corp., Terre Haute, Ind., 1999—. Pvt. tutor, Terre Haute, 1985—; homebound tchr. Vigo County Sch. Corp., Terre Haute, 2000—02; disability awareness edn., Terre Haute, 1993—. Contbr. manual Papaprofessional Protocol for the Functional Curriculum, manual Transition Manual for Vigo County, manual Professional Based Assessment for Farrington Grove Elementary School. Chair First Steps, Terre Haute, 1992—2002; facilitator Parent to Parent Support Group, Brazil, Ind., 1998—99. Recipient Everyday Hero Award, ARC, 2003; grantee Grant for Parent To Parent Support Group, Clay County Step Ahead, 1998—99. Mem.: Coun. Exceptional Children, Ind. State Tchr's. Assn. (assoc.), NEA (assoc.). Jehovah'S Witnesses. Avocations: raising dairy goats, gardening, sewing, reading. Home: 7243 Jones Rd Terre Haute IN 47805 Personal E-mail: lindenandlee@msn.com.

STOENNER, JESSAMINE, music educator; b. Dalton, Ga., Aug. 12, 1908; d. John Fletcher and Johnnie Jessamine (Richardson) Tarver; m. Walter George Stoenner, June 22, 1930 (dec. July 1987); children: Jessamine Marie, June Louise, Willa Jean, James Tarver. B in Music, Mo. Valley Coll., 1928, BA, 1930; cert. piano tchr., Music Tchrs. Nat. Assn., Warrensburg, Mo., 1977. Music tchr.; ch. oganist Presbyn. Ch., Richmond, Mo., 1945-95; dir. Girls Glee Club, Mo. Valley Coll., Marshall, Mo., 1929, tchr. asst. music dept., 1929-30. Pres. PTA, Richmond Schs., 1942; leader Girl Scouts Am., Richmond, 1942-51; literacy tchr., Richmond, 1994-97; contbr., adoptee Children's Internat., 1996-99; mem. Ray County Meml. Hosp. Aux., Richmond, 1989-99, Ray County Cmty. Arts Assn., Richmond, 1993-99, Ray County Hist. Soc. Recipient Christian Family award Richmond Presbyn. Ch., 1976, Dedicated Svc. award, 1999. Mem. AAUW, PEO, DAR (regent 1949-50, Am. Heritage Music award 1998), Music Tchrs. Nat. Assn., Mo. Music Tchrs. Assn., Warrensburg Area Music Tchrs. Assn. Republican. Presbyterian. Avocations: reading, flowers, travel, writing poetry, bridge. Home: 804 Wollard Blvd #531 Richmond MO 64085-2227

STOFFEL, CANDACE JO, secondary school educator; b. Findlay, Ohio, Aug. 2, 1949; d. Raymond Charles and Betty Janice Rike; children: Erica Jo(dec.), Andrea Rae(dec.). BME, Heidelberg Coll., Tiffin, Ohio, 1971; MA, Ohio State U., 1976; EdS, U. Ga., 1996. Tchr. Ctrl. Local Sch. Dist., Sherwood, Ohio, 1971—73; sec. Ohio State U., Columbus, 1973—76; tchr. Emmanuel Jr. Coll., Franklin Springs, Ga., 1979—85, Clarke County Sch. Dist., Athens, Ga., 1985—2000, Barrow County Sch. Dist., Winder, Ga., 2000. Choreographer Heidelberg Coll., Tiffin, 1971—79; accompanist Ohio U., Athens, 1976—79; musical accompanist Clarke Ctrl. H.S., Athens, 1997—; dir., choreographer U. Ga., 1983—86. Named Tchr. of the Yr., Clarke County Sch. Dist., 1991, Class Act Tchr., NBC-Channel 11 News, 1998; recipient Found. of Tchg. Excellence award, Clarke County Sch. Dist., 1990. Mem.: Ga. Music Educators Assn. (dist. choral chair 2002—, All-state coord. chair 2003—), Am. Choral Drs. Assn., Pi Kappa Lambda, Kappa Delta Pi. Presbyterian. Avocations: sewing, reading. Home: 400 Birchfield Dr Statham GA 30666 Office: Apalachee High Sch 940 Haymon Morris Rd Winder GA 30680

STOFFEL, PEGGI SMITH, music educator; BA, UCLA, 1992, MEd, 1994. Cert. tchr. Ill., 1996, Calif., 1994. Band dir., tchr. Granger Mid. Sch., Aurora, Ill., 1998—99, Still Mid. Sch., Aurora, Ill., 1999—. Pvt. bassoon instr., Ill., 1996—; music contest adjudicator, Ill.; double reed clinician, Ill. Contbr. articles to profl. jours. Recipient Most Influential Educator award, Indian Prairie Ednl. Found., 2003; Grantee, 2001. Mem.: Ill. Music Educators Assn., Am. String Teachers Assn., Music Educators Nat. Conf., Golden Key.

STOFFLE, CARLA JOY, university library dean; b. Pueblo, Colo., June 19, 1943; d. Samuel Bernard and Virginia Irene (Berry) Hayden; m. Richard William Stoffle, June 12, 1964; children: Brent William, Kami Ann. AA, So. Colo. State Coll., Pueblo, 1963; BA, U. Colo., 1965; MLS, U. Ky., 1969; postgrad., U. Wis., 1980. Head govt. publ. dept. John G. Crabbe Library, Eastern Ky. U., Richmond, 1969-72; from head pub. svcs. to asst. chancellor edn. svcs. U. Wis. Parkside Libr., Kenosha, 1972—85; dep. dir. U. Mich. Libr., Ann Arbor, 1986—91; prof. libr. sci. U. Ariz., Tucson, 1991—, dean librs. and ctr. for creative photography, 1991—, acting dir. Sch. Info. Resources and Libr. Sci., 1999—2001. Adv. bd. Bowker Librs., NY, 1985—90; bd. dirs. Trejo Foster Found., 2000—; state adv. com. Ariz. State Dept. of Libr. Archives and Pub. Records, 2000—; adv. com. U. Mich. Sch. Libr. Sci., 1986—92, OCLC Rsch. Librs., 1995—2000. Co-author: Administration of Government Documents Collection, 1974, Materials and Method for History Research, 1979, Materials and Methods for Political Science Research, 1979; mem. editl. bd. The Collection Bldg., 1978—95, The Bottom Line, 1989—95, Internet and Higher Edn., 1998—99, The Univ. Ariz. Press, 1992—. Vol. Peace Corps, Barbados, West Indies, 1965—67. Named Outstanding Alumnus, Coll. Libr. and Info. Sci., U. Ky., 1989; recipient Pres.'s award, Ariz. Ednl. Media Assn., 1993, YWCA Tucson Outstanding Women of 1992: A Women on the Move award, 1992, Ariz. Libr. of Yr. award, 2000. Mem.: ALA (Councilor 1983—93, exec. bd. dirs. 1985—93, treas. 1988—93, endowment trustee 1988—93, Endowment Campaign Com. 1989—93, Pres. Adv. Com. 1993—96, Legis. Com. 1994—96, Nominations Com. 1997, Lippincott Award Com. 1997, Libr. and Outreach Svcs. Adv. Com., (chair, 1997-98) 1997—99, Spectrum Scholarship Com. 1998—2002, endowment trustee 2001—, chair com. accreditation 2002—03, ALA Elizabeth Futas Catalyst for Change award 2002, ALA Equality award 2003, Loleta Fyan award Jury 2003—04), Center for Rsch. Libraries (Budget and Finance Com. 1994—95, exec. com., bd. dirs. 1998—, tres. 1999—2000, vice chair, bd. dirs. 2001—03, chair, bd. dirs. 2003), Ariz. State Libr. Assn., Assn. Coll. Rsch. Librs. (bd. dirs. 1978—84, mem. exec. com. 1981—84, pres. 1982—83, Planning Com. 1993—95, chair, Nat. Conference Planning Com. 1995—97, Miriam Dudley Bibliographic Instruction Librarian of the Year award 1991, Academic Rsch. Librarian of the Year 1992, ACRL Excellence in Academic Libraries award 2001), Assn. Rsch. Librs. (chair com. on stats and measurement 1994—2003, bd. dirs. 1997—2001, mem. steering com. Scholarly Pub. and Acad. Resource Coalition 1998—2001, Govt. Documents Digitization Project Work Group 2004—, Information Policies Com. 2004—). Office: U Arizona Main Libr 1510 E University Blvd Tucson AZ 85721-0055

STOHLMAN, CONNIE SUZANNE, obstetrical gynecological nurse; b. Tucson, Sept. 27, 1960; d. Irvin Wendell and Betty Jo (Stewart) Holmes; m. Bruce R. Stohlman, Sept. 14, 1991. BSN, Bishop Clarkson Coll. Nursing, 1987; BA, U. Nebr., 1982; cert. med. asst., Omaha Coll. Health Careers, 1983. Primary nurse I U. Md. Med. System, Balt., 1987-90; staff nurse St. Joseph Hosp., Omaha, 1990—. Mem. quality assurance task force U. Md. Med. System, 1987-90; mem. quality assurance com. St. Joseph Hosp., 1992-96. Named to Outstanding Young Women of Am., 1986.

STOIAN, CRISTINA, sales professional, real estate agent, real estate broker; b. Resita, Romania, Dec. 7, 1963; came to the U.S., 1993; d. Ion and Gina Nicu; m. Costin A. Stoian, Feb. 28, 1987; children: Andreea P., Raoul S. Mech. engr., Engring. Inst. Resita, 1987; quality contr., Constrn. Machinery Corp., Resita, 1989. Lic. real estate broker; registered investor svc. rep.; registered, lic. NASD. Engr. QQ bearings ICM, Resita, 1988-93; real estate broker Frontier Real Estate, Denver, 1994—; convenience store owner Lakewood, Colo., 1996-98; rental sales agt. Avis, Denver, 1998-00; registered rep. Janus, 2000—. Tax preparer Jackson Hewitt, 1999. Tennis coach Tennis Drs. Assn. Resita, 1980-83. 2nd Place winner Nat. Tennis Championship Costinesti-Romania, 1976-77. Mem. SEC, Assn. Realtors Jefferson. Avocations: painting, crafting, hiking, tennis, rock climbing. Home: 1434 W 103rd Pl Northglenn CO 80260-7116

STOIBER, SUSANNE A. health science organization administrator; Degree in econs. and mgmt., U. Colo., London Sch. Econs. Dir. divsn. soc. and econ. studies NRC HHS, 1990-94, past adminstr. Clin. Rsch. Ctr. NIH, 1998, past sr. advisor to dep. dir. sci. NIH, past dir. health care reform Pub. Health Svc., past dep. asst. sec. health, dep. asst. sec. planning and evaluation/program sys., acting dep. asst. sec. health/disease prevention and health promotion; exec. dir. Inst. Medicine, 1998—. Contbr. articles to profl. jours. Recipient NIH Directors Award, 1985, Presidential Rank Award for lifetime achievement in Senior Exec. Service. Office: Inst Medicine 500 5th St NW Washington DC 20418-0007 Fax: 908-771-8618.

STOICA, SUSANA, computer/electrical engineer, scientist, author, healer; b. Tirgu Muresh, Romania, Apr. 26, 1946; came to U.S., 1985; d. Andrei and Clara (Heisikovitsch) Gerson; m. Vladimir Stoica, Sept. 5, 1970; 1 child, Andrei. MS, Polytech. Inst., Bucharest, Romania, 1969, PhD, 1991. Reg. profl. engr., Ont., Can.; cert. healing touch practitioner, hypnotherapist. Jr. rsch. engr. Inst. Computer Rsch., Bucharest, 1969-72, sr. rsch. engr., 1972-77; engr. Ramzorei Siemens Industry Ltd., Tel Aviv, 1977-78; sr. elec. engr. Control Data Can. Ltd., Toronto, Ont., 1979-85, Control Data Corp., Mpls., 1985-86, cons., 1986-87, mgr. support, 1987-88; cons. very large scale integration/electronic computer aided design tech., 1988-90; chief scientist, mgr. advanced rsch. Delphax Systems, Toronto, 1990-92; sr. tech. specialist Advanced Vehicle Tech. Divsn. Ford Motor Co., Dearborn, Mich., 1993—; sr. tech. specialist hardware and software test strategies Rsch. and Vehicle Tech. divsn. Ford Motor Co., Dearborn, Mich., 1996—. Contbr. articles to profl. jours.and confs.; inventor. Mem. IEEE, Internat. Med. and Dental Hypnotherapy Assn., Profl. Engrs. Ont., Healing Touch Internat. E-mail: DoctorStoica@aol.com., sstorica@ford.com.

STOKAN, LANA J. LADD, state legislator; b. El Dorado, Ark., Sept. 5, 1958; children: Garrett, Adair. BA, MA in Secondary Edn. and History, So. Ill. U. Rep. dist. 76 State of Mo. Office: 625 Wilshire Dr Florissant MO 63033-3824 also: State Capital Rm 305A Jefferson City MO 65101

STOKES, CONNIE, state legislator; m. James Stokes; children: Bernard, Jason, Marcus. AA, Art Inst. Atlanta; BBA, Ga. State U. Owner, pres. First Choice Travel Agy.; co-owner Remax Pacesetters Real Estate; mem. Ga. Senate, Atlanta; vice chmn. consumer affairs com.; mem. banking and fin. instn., health and human svcs. coms.; also ins. and labor, judiciary, appropriations coms.; mem. state commn. on family violence. Mem. bd. dirs. Regional Leadership Found.; mem. women's coun. NAREB; active St. Phillip's AME Ch., DeKalb. Recipient Hall of Fame award for Cmty. Svc. Mem. Coalition 100 Black Women, Women's Polit. Caucus, Nat. Polit. Congress Black Women (devel. coord.), Leadership DeKalb, Leadership Atlanta. Democrat. Office: Rm 319 Legis Office Bldg Atlanta GA 30334 also: PO Box 360350 Decatur GA 30036-0350

STOKES, JEANETT BARRETT, editor; Mng. editor Gannett News Svc., Arlington, Va., 2000—. Office: Gannett News Svcs 1000 Wilson Blvd Fl 10 Arlington VA 22209-3901

STOKES, KATHLEEN SARAH, dermatologist, educator; b. Springfield, Mass., Oct. 18, 1954; d. John Francis and Margaret Cecelia (MacDonnell) Stokes; m. William Walter Greaves; children: Ian R., Spencer W., Malcolm W. BS, U. Utah, 1978, MS, 1980; MD, Med. Coll. Wis., 1987. Diplomate Am. Bd. Dermatology. Intern in internal medicine Med. Coll. Wis., Milw., 1987-88, resident in dermatology, 1988-90, chief resident, 1990-91, asst. clin. prof. dermatology, 1991—; pvt. practice, Milw., 1991—. Contbr. articles to med. jours., including Critical Care Medicine, Jour. Pediatric Dermatology. Named A Top Physician, Milw. mag., 1996, 2000 & 2004 Fellow Am. Acad. Dermatology, Milw. Acad. Medicine; mem. AMA, Wis. Dermatol. Soc. (sec.-treas. 2003—), Women's Dermatologic Soc., Tempo, Alpha Omega Alpha. Office: Affiliated Dermatologists 2300 N Mayfair Rd Milwaukee WI 53226-1505

STOKES, LORI, newscaster; Attended, Ohio State U.; grad., Howard U. Weekend anchor, med. reporter CBS affiliate WCIA-TV, Champaign-Urbana, Ill.; weekend anchor CBS affiliate WBTC, Charlotte, NC, 1988—90; reporter Fox station WBFF, Balt., 1991—92; anchor evening news for 6pm and 11pm broadcasts WJLA-TV, Wash., DC, 1992—96. Achievements include credited with breaking the Gianni Versace's murder story. Office: 7 Lincoln Sq New York NY 10023*

STOKES, MELANIE MILLER, art educator; b. Macon, Ga., Mar. 22, 1956; d. William Starr and Sarah (Fallin) Miller; m. Stephen Wayne Stokes, June 3, 1978; children: Benjamin Luke, Mark Ezra. BA in Comm., Shorter Coll., 1978; MEd in Art Edn., Ga. So. U., 2000. Cert. educator Ga. Writer Ocilla Star Newspaper, Ga., 1987—88; tchr. Pine St. Sch., Norris Elem. Sch., Thomson, Ga., 1990—94; tchr. reading, art Long County Sch., Ludowici, Ga., 1994—2000; tchr. art Smiley Elem. Sch., Ludowici, 2000—. Mem. Grassroots Adv. Bd. Golden Isles Arts and Humanities, Brunswick, Ga., 1998—; trustee Brewton Parker Coll., Mt. Vernon, Ga., 2001—. Represented in permanent collections Mural of Jones Creek Cmty., Long County Hist. Mural, A Look Outside Mural. Ga. Challenge Art Grant, Ga. Coun. for Arts, 1996, 1997. Mem.: Ga. Art Educators Assn. (Youth Art Mth. Outstanding Art Educator 2003), Profl. Assn. Ga. Educators, Nat. Art Educators Assn.9. Baptist. Avocations: painting, writing, singing, illustrating. Home: Rte 2 Box 36 Ludowici GA 31316 Office: Smiley Elem Sch PO Box 729 Ludowici GA 31316*

STOKES, SUSAN, political science educator; MA in Anthropology, Stanford U., 1985, MA in Polit. Sci., 1986, PhD, 1988. Assoc. prof. polit. sci. U. Chgo. Contbr. articles to profl. jours.; author: Social Movements and the State in Peru, 1995, Neoliberalism by Surprise in Latin America; editor: Political Support for Market Reforms in New Democracies, 2001; co-editor: Democracy, Accountability, and Representation. Recipient Guggenheim fellowship, 2003. Office: U Chgo Dept Polit Sci Pick Hall 414 5828 S University Ave Barkhamsted CT 06063

STOKSTAD, MARILYN JANE, art history educator, curator; b. Lansing, Mich., Feb. 16, 1929; d. Olaf Lawrence and Edythe Marian (Gardiner) S. BA, Carleton Coll., 1950; MA, Mich. State U., 1953; PhD, U. Mich., 1957; postgrad., U. Oslo, 1951-52; LHD (hon.), Carleton Coll., 1997. Instr. U. Mich., Ann Arbor, 1956-58; mem. faculty U. Kans., Lawrence, 1958—, assoc. prof., 1961-66, prof., 1966-80, Univ. Disting. prof. art history, 1980-94, Judith Harris Murphy disting. prof. art, 1994—, dir. mus. art, 1961-67, research assoc., summers 1965-66, 67, 71, 72; assoc. dean Coll. Liberal Arts and Scis., U. Kans., 1972-76; research curator Nelson-Atkins Mus. Art, Kansas City, Mo., 1969-80, consultative curator medieval art, 1980—. Bd. dirs. Internat. Ctr. Medieval Art, 1972-75, 81-84, 88-96, v.p., 1990-93, pres., 1993-96, sr. advisor, 1996-97; cons., evaluator North Ctrl. Assn. Colls. and Univs., 1972—, commr.-at-large, 1984-89. Author: Santiago de Compostela, 1978, The Scottish World, 1981, Medieval Art, 1986, Art History, 1995, rev. edit., 1999, Art: A Brief History, 2000. Recipient Disting. Service award Alumni Assn. Carleton Coll., 1983, Kans. Gov.'s Arts award, 1997; Fulbright fellow, 1951-52; NEH grantee, 1967-68 Fellow AAUW; mem. AAUP (nat. coun. 1972-75), Archeol. Inst. Am. (pres. Kans. chpt. 1960-61), Midwest Coll. Art Conf. (pres. 1964-65), Coll. Art Assn. (bd. dirs. 1970-80, pres. 1978-80), Soc. Archtl. Historians (chpt. bd. dirs. 1971-73). E-mail: stokstad@ku.edu.

STOLER, DOROTHY ANNE, engineer; b. LaPorte, Ind., July 13, 1948; d. Otto Edward and Cleda Irene Giese; 1 child, Kimberly. A, Purdue U., 1982, B, 1998, MBA, 2001. Engr. NIPSCO, LaPorte, Ind., 1975—95, supr., 1995—2002, engr. Gary, 2002—. Mem.: AAUW (treas. 2002—, coord. reading is fundamental com. 2001—). Home: 2107 W 250 S La Porte IN 46350

STOLLER, PATRICIA SYPHER, structural engineer, engineering executive; b. Jackson Heights, N.Y., Dec. 16, 1947; d. Carleton Roy and Mildred Vivian (Ferron) Sypher; m. David A. Stoller, Sr.; children: Stephanie Jean, Sheri Lynn. BSCE, Washington U., St. Louis, 1975; M in Mgmt., Northwestern U., 1989. R & D engr. Amcar divsn. ACF Industries, St. Charles, Mo., 1972-79; project engr. Truck Axle divsn. Rockwell Internat., Troy, Mich., 1979-81; sr. engr. ABB Impell, Norcross, Ga., 1981-83, supervising mgr., client mgr., divsn. mgr. Lincolnshire, Ill., 1983—; dir. bus. devel., v.p. VECTRA (formerly ABB Impell), Lincolnshire, 1991-94; pres., CEO ASC Svcs. Co., LLC, Chgo., 1994-97; CEO, pres. Beaumont Svcs. Co., LLC, Royal Oak, Mich., 1997—, ReSourcing Svcs. Co., LLC, Chgo., 2003—; v.p. Greenville Operations Jacobs Engring. Inc., 1997—. Author: (computer program) Quickpipe, 1983. Mem.: NAFE, ASCE, World Pres. Orgn., Chgo. Real Estate Women, Am. Nuc. Soc. (mem. exec. bd. Chgo. sect. 1991—93), Soc. Women Engrs. Achievements include patents in field. Avocations: golf, music. Office: Jacobs Engring Inc 1041 E Butler Rd Greenville SC 29607

STOLLER, ROSE, think-tank executive; With N.D. Dept. Human Svcs.; exec. dir. Mental Health Assn., ND, The Consensus Coun., Bismarck, ND, 2002—. Chairperson Bismarck Human Rels. Com.; vol. Mo. Slope United Way; grad. leadership program Bismarck C. of C. Recipient Mental Health Svcs. award, N.D. Psychiat. Soc. Welcome Back award, Eli Lilly Co. Office: The Consensus Coun Inc Ste 7 1003 E Interstate Ave Bismarck ND 58503-0500

STOLZ, CLAUDIA GRACE, humanities educator, consultant; b. Port Jefferson, N.Y., Oct. 26, 1945; d. Claude Clendenon and Grace Eleanor Matherly; m. William Stolz, Aug. 15, 1966; children: William Timothy, Ryan Matherly, Casey Caleb, Caitlin Matherly. RN, Kings Park (N.Y.) Hosp. Sch. Nursing, 1966; BS, U. Tex., El Paso, 1971; MA, U. of Dayton, Ohio, 1983; PhD, Miami U. Oxford, Ohio, 1996. Instr. pediatric nursing Miami Valley Hosp. Sch. of Nursing, Dayton, Ohio, 1980—81; prof. humanities. Instr. U. of Dayton, Dayton, Ohio, 1983—84; cons. Hallinan Consulting, Venice, Calif., 1997—, Edn. Testing Svc., Princeton, NJ, 1996—98; vis. instr. Miami U., Oxford, Ohio, 1987—96, vis. asst. prof., 1997—98, Ind. U. East, Richmond, Ind., 1998—99; quality editor, sr. recruiting assoc., trainer LexisNexis (Case Law Summaries), Miamisburg, Ohio, 1999—2001; asst. prof. Urbana U., Urbana, Ohio, 2001—. Editor (introduction): (children's book) Candle in the Window; author (director): (play) Each for the Other, Both for God; contbr. articles to profl. jours.; cons.: Mobil Masterpiece Theater American Collection, New York Life's The Rise and Fall of Jim Crow. Discussion leader for classic conversation (reading group) Dayton-Montgomery County Pub. Libr., West Carrollton, Ohio, 2000—03; serve meals to homeless The Other Pl., Dayton, Ohio, 2002—03; bd. of Christian edn./adult edn. David's United Ch. of Christ, Kettering, Ohio, 1998—2001. Mem.: MLA (del. 2001—03), Nat. Coun. Tchrs. English, Kappa Delta Pi, Phi Alpha Theta, Phi Kappa Phi. Democrat. United Church Of Christ. Avocation: gardening. Home: 274 Orchard Hill Drive West Carrollton OH 45449-2260 Office: Urbana University 579 College Way Urbana OH 43078 Personal E-mail: cgmstolz@aol.com. E-mail: cstolz@urbana.edu.

STOMFAY-STITZ, ALINE MARIA, education educator; b. Newark, N.J. d. Adolph and Irene (Badowska) Wegrocki; m. Emery Stomfay-Stitz (dec.); children: Peter, John, Robert. BA, Barnard Coll.; MA, Case Western Reserve U.; EdD, No. Ill. U., 1984. Asst. prof. Coll. St Scholastica, Duluth, Minn., 1984-85, St. Leo (Fla.) Coll., 1985-87, Nicholls State U., Thibodaux, La., 1989-91; assoc. prof. edn. Christopher Newport U., Newport News, Va., 1991-96. Vis. prof., assoc. prof. edn. U. No. Fla., Jacksonville, 1996-2003; assoc. editor Joun. Early Childhood Tchr. Edn. Author: Peace Education in America 1828-1990, 1993; author (book chpt.): Toward Education That is Multicultural, 1992, Multicultural Education for the 21st Century, 1993; contbr. articles to profl. jours. Mem.: Internat. Peace Rsch. Assn., Nat. Assn. for Early Childhood Tchrs. Educators, Am. Ednl. Rsch. Assn. (SIG exec. com.). E-mail: stitza@bellsouth.net.

STONE, AMY, reporter; b. Brunswick, Maine; m. Paul Stone. B in Comm. and Film, U. Mich., 1989. Prodr. Sta. WDIV-TV, Detroit; reporter New Eng. Sports Network, Boston, 1991—94; anchor SportsChannel, 1994—97; reporter Sta. WMAQ-TV, Chgo., 1997—2000, Sta. WCBS-TV, N.Y.C., 2000—. Recipient Emmy, 1999, 2000. Office: CBS 524 W 57th St New York NY 10019

STONE, ANN E.W. direct marketing company executive; BA in History and Comms., George Washington U.; postgrad., U. Pa. Founder, pres. The Stone Group, Inc., 1982—; chmn. Capstone Lists Inc. Spkr. in field. Bd. dirs. Nat. Women's History Mus., Assn. Direct Mktg. Agys., Washington Ctr., Rep. Liberty Caucus, Campagna Ctr., Make Women Count, others; past chmn. Alexandria br. Am. Heart Assn., Alexandria Seaport Found.; founder, chmn. Republicans for Choice, Alexandria, Va; internat. chair Empowered Women Internat.; trustee Va. Historic Preservation Found.; exec. global adv. bd. European/Am. Women's Coun. Mem.: Non-Profit Mailers Fedn., Direct Mktg. Club Washington, Nat. Women's Hall of Fame, Am. Assn. Polit. Consultants (bd. dirs.), Nat. Assn. Women Bus. Owners, Alexandria C. of C. (bd. dirs.), Animal Welfare League, Soc. for Preservation of Black Heritage, Va. Trust for Hist. Preservation. Office: The Stone Group 2760 Eisenhower Ave Ste 250 Alexandria VA 22314-4553 E-mail: tsgrp@aol.com.

STONE, BETTY FRANCES, music educator; MusB, Queen's Coll., 1973; M in Music Edn., U. Ga., 1974. Music tchr. Charleston (S.C.) County Schs., 1974—83; choreographer Young Charleston Theatre Co., 1979—83; arts supr. City of Mississauga, Canada, 1983—93; music tchr., arts coord. Florence Sch. Dist. #3, Lake City, SC, 1993—; dance tchr. Dancin On Main, Lake City, 2002—. Dir. Lake City Concert Series, 1996—; grants mgr., arts coord. Florence Dist. #3, Lake City, 1999—. Vol. Lake City C. of C., 1996—2003; master of cermonies Miss Lake City Beauty Pagent, 2001—03; performer Lake City Cmty. Theater, 1993—2003. Recipient Champion for Pub. Edn. award, S.C. Sch. Bds. Assn., 1999, Contbr. of Yr. award, SC C. of C., 2003; grantee, S.C. Arts Commn., 1999—2003. Mem.: Music Educators Nat. Conf., Delta Kappa Gamma. Office: Florence School District #3 125 SBlanding St Lake City SC 29560

STONE, CAROLINE FLEMING, artist; b. N.Y.C., Mar. 26, 1936; d. Ralph Emerson and Elizabeth (Fleming) Stone; m. Oakleigh B. Thorne, June 1956 (div. 1969); children: Oakleigh, Henry; m. John Roderick Keating, July 2002. Student, Art Students' League, 1954-57, 71-72, Pratt Graphics, 1973-74. One-woman shows include Washington Art Assn., Conn., Ella Sharp Mus., Mich., 1980, San Diego Pub. Library, 1981, Trustman Gallery Simmons Coll., Boston, 1985, Mary Ryan Gallery, N.Y.C., 1989, Boston Pub. Libr., 1994, Messiah Coll., 1995; two-person shows include Mary Ryan Gallery, 1985, Katonah Gallery, N.Y., 1986, Davidson Gallery, Seattle, 1990, The Millbrook (N.Y.) Gallery, 1993; juried shows include Silvermine Nat. Printmaking, Conn., 1978, Print Club, Phila., 1981, Trenton State (Nat. Print Exhibn. Purchase award), 1982, Minot State Coll., N.D., 1985, Boston Printmakers (Jurors Commendation), 1986; group shows include Mus. N.Mex., 1984, De Cordova and Dana Mus., Nat. Acad. Art, N.Y.C., Boston Pub. Library, Mus. Contemporary Hispanic Art, N.Y.C., 1987, World Print Exhbn., San Francisco, Smith Coll. Gallery, Northampton, Mass., Mary Ryan Gallery, 1988, Virginia Lynch Gallery, R.I., 1989, 91, Accent on Paper, Lintas, N.Y., 1991, Women Printmaker's Nat. Touring Show, Boston Pub. Libr. 1991, The Tenth Anniversary Show Virginia Lynch Gallery, 1993; represented in permanent collections Art Inst. Chgo., Mid-West Mus. Am. Art, Ind., Mus. N.Mex., Nat. Mus. Am. Art, Boston Pub. Library, U. Chgo., U. Mich., The Portland Art Mus. Mem.: The Kitchen (bd. dirs.). Home and Office: C Stone Press 80 Wooster St New York NY 10012-4347

STONE, CATHY JEAN, elementary school educator; b. Dowagiac, Mich., Jan. 28, 1963; d. Gorden Jerry and Elizabeth Lemke Gwilt; m. Ronald Keith Stone, Aug. 23, 1986; children: Erica Elizabeth, Chase Edward, Ethan Matthew. AA, BA, Anderson U., 1985. Elem. tchr. Penn-Harris-Madison Sch. Corp., Mishawaka, Ind., 1987—2002, primary reading coach, 2002—. Worship team mem. Michiana Cmty. Ch. of God, Granger, Ind. Protestant. Avocations: singing, reading, counted cross stitch. Home: 66746 Conrad Rd Edwardsburg MI 49112 Office: Penn-Harris-Madison Sch Corp 55900 Bittersweet Rd Mishawaka IN 46545 E-mail: cstone@phm.k12.in.us.

STONE, CYNTHIA S. director; b. Oak Park, Ill., Nov. 18, 1949; d. Gordon E. and Shirlee K. Stone; m. David I. Kronberg, Jan. 1, 1985; 1 child, Julian Stone-Kronberg. BA, St. Olaf Coll., 1971; MA, U. Mass., 1974. Boston Pub. Schs. coord. edn. dept. Mus. Fine Arts, 1974—77, head sch. program edn. dept., 1977—78, head workshop program edn. dept., 1979—81; curator edn. Inst. Contemporary Art, 1981—82; dir. Old South Meeting House, Boston, 1983—92; exec. dir. North Bennet St. Sch., Boston, 1992—. Bd. mem. Plymouth (Mass.) Plantation. Mem. vis. com. Boston Archtl. Ctr., 1993—96; bd. mem. New Eng. Mus. Assn., Boston, 1985—92, Freedom Trail Found., Boston, 1988—92, Mass. Assn. Pvt. Career Schs., 1993—97, Winchester (Mass.) Tomorrow, 2001—. Mem.: AFP, Friday Forum.

STONE, DEE WALLACE, actress; b. Kansas City, Mo., Dec. 14, 1948; d. Robert Stanley and Maxine (Nichols) Bowers; m. Christopher Stone, June 28, 1980 (dec.); m. Skip Belyea. BA, U. Kans., 1971. Actress feature films The Christmas Visitor, Secret Admirer, Cujo, E.T., Jimmy the Kid, The Howling, 10; actress ABC movies of the week Eminent Domain, Hostage Flight, A Whale for a Killing; actress CBS movies of the week An Enemy Among Us, Sin of Innocence, The Sky is No Limit, Happy, Surprise, Surprise, The Five of Me, Young Love, First Love; actress NBC movies of the week Wait Til Your Mother Gets Home, Child Bride of Short Creek, Skeezer; actress CBS After School Special Dad's Out of a Job; actress ABC After School Special Run Don't Walk; actress CBS series Police Story, Together We Stand/Nothing is Easy, Lou Grant; actress stage prodns. including Annie Get Your Gun, Oklahoma, My Fair Lady, Applause, Butterflies are Free, Middle of the Night. Spkr. in field; mgr. DWS Acting Studio, Burbank, Calif. Appeared in films including Nevada, 1997, Mutual Needs, 1997, Black Circle Boys, 1997, Bad As I Wanna Be: The Dennis Rodman Story, 1998, Flamingo Dreams, 1998, To Love, Honor and Betray, 1999, Invisible Mom II, 1999, Pirates of the Plain, 1999, Out of the Black, A Month of Sundays, Dead Canaries, others. Fundraiser Actors and Others for Animals, L.A., 1980—, Amanda Found., L.A., 1986, 87; co-host, fundraiser Children's Hospital Telethon, Sta. KCET, L.A., 1985—; spokesperson Nat. Assn. of Children of Alcoholics, 1987—. Mem. Screen Actors Guild, Actors Equity, AFTRA. Methodist. Avocations: dance, singing.

STONE, ELAINE MURRAY, author, composer, television producer; b. NYC, Jan. 22, 1922; d. H. and Catherine Fairbanks Murray-Jacoby; m. F. Courtney Stone, May 30, 1944; children: Catherine Gustavson, Pamela Webb, Victoria Mattson. Student, Juilliard Sch., 1939-41; BA, N.Y. Coll. Music, 1943; licentiate in organ, Trinity Coll. Music, London, 1947; student, U. Miami, 1952, Fla. Inst. Tech., 1963; PhD (hon.), World U., 1985, Oxford (Eng.) U., 1998. Organist, choir dir. St. Ignatius Episc. Ch., 1940-44; accompanist Strawbridge Ballet on Tour, N.Y.C., 1944; organist All Saints Episc. Ch., Ft. Lauderdale, 1951-54, St. John's Episc. Ch., Melbourne, Fla., 1956-59, First Christian Ch., Melbourne, 1962-63, United Ch. Christ, Melbourne, 1963-65, piano studio, Melbourne, 1955-70; editor-in-chief Cass Inc., 1970-71; dir. continuity radio Sta. WTAI, AM-FM, Melbourne, 1971-74; mem. sales staff Engle Realty Inc., Indialantic, Fla., 1975-78; v.p. pub. relations Consol. Cybertronics Inc., Cocoa Beach, Fla., 1969-70; writer, producer Countdown News, Sta. KXTX-TV, Dallas, 1978-80; assoc. producer Focus News, Dallas, 1980. Host producer TV show, Focus on History, 1982-94, Episc. Digest, 1984-90; judge Writer's Contest sponsored Brevard Cmty. Coll., 1987; v.p. Judges Fla. Space Coast Writer's Conf., 1985—, chmn., 1987. Author: The Taming of the Tongue, 1954, Love One Another, 1957, Menéndez de Avilés, 1968, Bedtime Bible Stories, Travel Fun, Sleepytime Tales, Improve Your Spelling for Better Grades, Improve Your Business Spelling, Tranquility Tapes, 1970, The Melbourne Bi-Centennial Book, 1976, Uganda: Fire and Blood, 1977, Tekla and the Lion, 1981 (1st pl. Nat. League Am. Pen Women), Brevard County: From Cape of the Canes to Space Coast, 1988, Kizito, Boy Saint of Uganda, 1989 (2d pl. Nat. League Am. Pen Women 1990), Christopher Columbus: His World, His Faith., His Adventures, 1991 (1st pl. Nat. League Am. Pen Women 1992), Elizabeth Bayley Seton: An American Saint, 1993 (3d pl. Nat. League Am. Pen Women 1994), Dimples The Dolphin, 1994 (1st pl. Fla. Space Coast Writer's Guild, 1994), Brevard at The Edge of Sea and Space, 1995, The Widow's Might, 1996 (1st pl. Space Coast Writer's Contest), Carter G. Woodson Father of Black History, 1997 (1st pl. Am. Heritage Contest Nat. Soc. Daus. of Am. Revolution 1997), Maximilian Kolbe: Saint of Auschwitz, 1997 (Cath. Bestseller list 1997), Albert's Jungle Piano, 1997 (1st pl. Nat. League Am. Pen Women 1997, 2d pl., Nat. League of Am. Pen Women, 1999), Mother Teresa: A Life of Love, 1999, The Taming of the Tongue, 1999, C.S. Lewis: Creator of Narnia, 2001 (3d place Nat. League Am. Pen Women 2001), Mary and the Apparitions of Guadalupe, Lourdes and Fatima, 2003, A Saint and His Lion The Story of Tekla of Ethiopia, 2003, A New Life (1st place Fla. Assn. Univ. Women 2003), Saints of the Americas, 2004, Dorothy Day: Champion of the Poor, 2004; composer: Christopher Columbus Suite, 1992 (1st pl. Pen Women Music Awards 1992, 2d pl. 1993), Florida Suite for cello and piano, 1993, Two Crowns of St. Maximilian, 1998 (1st pl. in music Nat. League Am. Pen Women 1997), Pastorale, 2000 (1st pl. Nat. League Am. Pen Women, Washington, 2000), Anima Christi, 2000 (hon. mention Nat. League Am. Pen Women, Washington, 2000); contbr. articles to mags., newspapers including N.Y. Herald Tribune, Living Church, Christian Life, Episcopal Life; space corr. Religious News Service, Kennedy Space Ctr., 1962-78. Exec. bd. Women's Assn., Brevard Symphony, 1967—; heritage com. Melbourne Bicentennial Commn.; mem. Evangelism Commn. Episc. Diocese Cen. Fla., 1985-94; v.p. churchwomen group Holy Trinity Episcopal Ch., Melbourne, 1988-89, Stephen minister, 1988—, pres. churchwomen group, 1989—; bd. dirs. Fla. Space Coast Council Internat. Visitors, Fla. Space Coast Philharm., 1989—, Aid for the Arts, 1994; appointee Hist. Preservation Com., Melbourne, Fla., 2003. Recipient 1st place for piano Ashley Hall, 1935-39, S.C. State Music Contest, 1939, 1st place for piano composition Colonial Suite, Constitution Hall, Washington 1987, 88, 89, 3d place for vocal composition, 1989, honorable mention for article, 1989, 2nd place for piano composition, 1989, award lit. contest Fla. AAUW, 1989, 1st place award Fla. State PEN Women, 1990, 1st Place award Nat. Black History Essay Contest, 1990, 2d place Nat. League Am. Pen Women, 1999, 2d place for music composition, 1999, named Woman of Achievement, 1999, Disting. Author of Yr. plaque Fla. Space Coast Writers Guild, 1992, 96, Woman of Achievement plaque AAUW, 1997; honoree Nat. Polish Alliance, 3d place award for essay "Remembering C.S. Lewis" Mount Dora Festival of Music and Literature, 2001. Mem. ASCAP, Nat. League Am. PEN Women (1st place awards Tex. 1979, 1st place award for duet, Washington, 2000, pres. Dallas br. 1978-80, organizing pres. Cape Canaveral br. 1969, pres. 1988-90, 96—), Women in Comms., DAR (Fla. state chmn. music 1962-63), Colonial Dames Am. (organizing pres. Melbourne chpt. 1994), Nat. Soc. DAR (organizing regent Rufus Fairbanks chpt. 1981-85, vice regent 1987—, historian 1989—, Fla. state chmn. Am. Heritage), Children Am. Revolution (past N.Y. state chaplain), Am. Guild Organists (organizing warden Ft. Lauderdale), Space Pioneers, Fla. Press, Aid for the Arts, Space Coast Writers Guild (past v.p.). Home: 1945 Pineapple Ave Melbourne FL 32935-7656

STONE, ELIZABETH CECILIA, anthropology educator; b. Oxford, Eng., Feb. 4, 1949; d. Lawrence and Jeanne Cecilia (Fawtier) S.; m. Paul Edmund Zimansky, Nov. 5, 1976. BA, U. Pa., 1971; MA, Harvard U., 1973; PhD, U. Chgo., 1979. Lectr. anthropology SUNY, Stony Brook, 1977-78, asst. prof., 1978-85, assoc. prof., 1985-95, prof., 1995—2002. Participated archaeol. in Eng., Iran, Iraq, Afghanistan; dir. archaeol. projects Ain Dara, Syria,, Tell Abu Duwari, Iraq, Ayanis Survey, Turkey. Author: Nippur Neighborhoods, 1987; co-author: (monograph) Old Babylonian Contracts from Nippur 1, 1976, Adoption in Old Babylonian Nippur and the Archive of Mannum-meshu-lissur, 1991, The Iron Age Settlement at Ain Dara, Syria, 1999; co-editor: The Cradle of Civilization Recent Archaeology in Iraq-Biblical Archaeologist, 1992, Velles Paraules: Ancient Near Eastern Studies in Honor of Miguel Civil on the Occasion of His 65th Birthday, 1991; mem. editl. bd. Bull. Am. Schs. Oriental Rsch., 1993-95, 99—; contbr. articles to profl. jours. Assoc. trustee Am. Schs. of Oriental Rsch., 1983-90. Fulbright fellow, 1986-87; rsch. grantee Ford Found., 1974, Nat. Geog. Soc., 1983, 84, 88, 90, 97-99, 2002, 03, Am. Schs. of Oriental Rsch., 1987, 88, NSF, 1989-92, 2000-02, NEH, 1989-93. Office: SUNY Dept Anthropology Stony Brook NY 11794-0001 E-mail: estone@notes.cc.sunysb.edu.

STONE, ELIZABETH WALKER, English educator; b. Washington, Aug. 17, 1921; d. Micajah Theodore and Isabelle Morris (Grinnage) Walker; m. Frank Daniel Reeves (div.); children: Deborah E., Daniel R.; m. French Franklin Stone. BA in English, Howard U., 1940, MA in Am. Lit., 1942; MFA in Drama, Cath. U. Am., 1948; EdD in Speech and Drama, Columbia U., 1956. From instr. to asst. prof. liberal arts Howard U., Washington, 1944-55; supr. speech therapists D.C. Pub. Schs., Washington, 1955-58; assoc. prof. speech and drama D.C. Tchrs. Coll., Washington, 1958-62; edn. specialist ISIA, Washington, 1965-67; dep. dir. Internat. Agy. Com. on Mexican-Am. Affairs, Washington, 1967-69; dir. univs. and founds. divsn. U.S. Dept. of Commerce, Washington, 1969-71; dir. stds. for edn. instns. Social and Rehab./HEW, Washington, 1971-73, dir. tng., 1973-75; dir. comm. skills Howard U. Sch. Law, Washington, 1975-90; writer, 1990—. Editor: Higher Education Aid for Minority Business, 1970; author, dir. (TV documentary) High Expectations, 1988 (Gannett award 1989); contbr. articles to profl. jours. Writer seconding nomination speech J.F. Kennedy Campaign, L.A. Conv., 1960; spl. asst. White House Conf. on Civil Rights, Washington, 1966; writer, dir. TV campaign commls. Doug Wilder, State of Va., 1985; writer, cons. Project Vote, Washington, 1987; mem. bd. visitors Mount Vernon, Va., 1988-95. Recipient First Outstanding Alumna award Howard U. Sch. Comm., Washington. Mem. Federally Employed Women (adv. bd., bd. mem. 1978—), Black Women's Agenda (founding nat. pres., 1st pres. 1978—, Outstanding Svc. award 1990), Nat. Smart Set (nat. pres., Spl. Svc. award 1991), Nat. Gallery Art (vice chair widening horizons program), Woman's Nat. Dem. Club (co-chair art in overseas embassies). Episcopalian. Avocation: creative writing. Home: 2795 Windham Ct Delray Beach FL 33445-7110

STONE, FLORENCE SMITH, film festival executive, consultant; b. Balt., June 15, 1938; d. Howard Chandler and Mary (Burnam) Smith; m. Roger David Stone; 1 child, Leslie Burnam. BA, Vassar Coll., 1960; cert. Inst. Arts Adminstrn., Harvard U., 1978. Asst. to v.p. for pub. rels. Transam. Corp., San Francisco, 1962-64; newsletter editor U.S. Embassy, Rio de Janeiro, 1964-66; coord. cmty. rels. Am. Mus. Natural History, N.Y.C., 1970-79, coord. spl. progrm, 1977-84; dir. Washington Office Earthwatch, Washington, 1985-90; ind. cons. to mus. and ednl. orgns. Washington, 1990—; coord., founder Environ. Film Festival, Washington, 1993—. Co-chmn. Margaret Mead Film Festival, 1977-84. Trustee The Textile Mus., Washington, 1994—, Laura Boulton Found., N.Y.C., 1980-99, Mus. of the Hudson Highlands, Cornwall-on-Hudson, N.Y., 1974-96; mem. adv. com. Margaret Mead Film Festival, N.Y.C., 1992—; chmn. Trees for Georgetown Com., Washington, 1996-2004. Mem.: Textile Soc., Women in Film and Video, Ind. Film and Video Assn., Internat. Documentary Assn., Am. Assn. Mus., Cosmos Club, Cosmopolitan Club, Georgetown Garden Club. Democrat. Avocations: textiles, film, trees, performing arts, outdoor activities. Office: Environ Film Festival 1228 1/2 31st St NW Washington DC 20007-3402 Office Phone: 202-342-2564. E-mail: flostonc@igc.org.

STONE, HAZEL ANNE DECKER, artist; b. Salt Lake City, Oct. 30, 1934; d. Carl Marcellus and Hazel Sheets (Van Cott) Decker; m. William Samuel Stone, July 20, 1956; children: Cynthia Anne Stone Barkanic, Lisa Marie. BS, RN, U. Utah, 1956; postgrad. in arts and humanities, Ariz. State U., 1979-81; studied with various artists, Ariz., N.Mex., 1985—. Nurse out-patient dept. Salt Lake County Hosp., 1956-57; instr. med.-surg. nursing U. Utah Coll. Nursing, 1957-59; watercolor fine artist. One-woman show Sun Cities Mus. of Art, Sun City, Ariz., 1997; exhibited in group show Chandler (Ariz.) Ctr. for the Arts, 1997; nat. juried exhbns. include:Pitts. Watercolor Soc. Aqueous Open, 2003, John Stobart's Three rivers gallery, Pitts., 2003, Beverly Arts Ctr., Chgo., 2003, Depot Rd. Aberdare, Wales, 2004, Pikes Peak Watercolor Soc. exhbn., 2001,2003, Tubac, Ariz., Ctr. Arts, 2003, Az. Watercolor Assn. exhbn., 2000, Pa. Watercolor Soc., exhbn., 2000, 17th Annual Gallery '76, Wenatchee, 2000, Woodmere Art Gallery, 2000, Chandler Ctr. Arts, 1999, Watercolors Gallery, Pitts., 2000, Farmington Mus. at Gateway Park, Farmington, N.Mex., 1999 (regional exhbn.), Wenatchee (Wash.) Valley Coll., 1999, 2000, Tubac (Ariz.) Ctr. for Arts, 1999, Sangre de Cristo Arts Ctr., Pueblo, Colo., 1999, Watercolors Gallery, Pitts., 1999, 16th Annual Gallery '76, Wenatchee, Wash., 1999, West Valley Art Mus. (Ariz. juried exhbns.), Surprise, Ariz., 1999, Van Vechten-Lineberry Taos (N.Mex.) Art Mus., 1997, Wenatchee (Wash.) Valley Coll., 1997, Stables Gallery, Taos, 1996, Walton Arts Ctr., Fayetteville, Ark., 1995, Bareiss Gallery, Taos, 1995, Foothills Art Ctr., 1994, Golden, Colo., Tucson Mus. Art regional exhbn., 1988, Vision Gallery (2d Place award Chandler Ostrich Festival Fine Arts Print Contest 1998), others; one person exhbn. include Phoenix (Ariz.) 17 paintings, Sun Cities (Ariz.) Mus. Art, 1997; two person exhbns. include Gallery Nineteen, Phoenix, 1996, Ch. of the Beatitudes, Phoenix, 1995; Ariz. juried exhbn. include Vistas, 1989, 91, 93; commd. Chandler Ctr. Arts, 1999; TV interview includes Open My Album: A Collection of Watercolor Paintings and Stories Connecting Generations Channel 20 Ednl. TV Chandler Unified Sch. Dist., Ariz., 1997. Docent Phoenix Art Mus., 1979-80, master docent, 1989-96; mem. Ariz. Women's Caucus Art, 1988-91. Finalist annual art competition exptl. art category Artists Magazine, 1996. Mem. Ariz. Artists Guild (juried 1986—), Ariz. Watercolor Assn. (Coatimundi Honor Soc.,Royal Scorpion, juried 1988—, Award of Merit, 97 Merchant award 1994, 2003, bd. dirs. 1994-2001, co-chair nat. watercolor exhbn. 1999, chmn. nat. watercolor exhbn. 2002, gen.chmn., 2002, 2003), Contemporary Watercolorists Ariz. (signature mem., Merit award 1998, Award of Excellence 1997, 2000, chmn. spl. exhbns. 1998), Q Artists (chmn. exhbns. 1995-99), Waterworks Artists, Internat. Soc. Exptl. Artists, Nat. Watercolor Soc., Pa. Watercolor Soc., Phila. Watercolor Soc. (signature mem.), La. Watercolor Soc. (assoc.), N.W. Watercolor Soc. (assoc.), San Diego Watercolor Soc. (assoc.), Taos Soc. Watercolorists (signature), Watercolor Art Soc. Houston, Watercolor West (assoc.), Western Colo. Watercolor Soc., Internat. Soc. Exptl. Artists (Merit award) and many others. Home: 3621 E Pasadena Ave Phoenix AZ 85018-1511

STONE, JANE BUFFINGTON, artist, writer; b. Madison, Wis., Dec. 1, 1942; adopted d. Marshall Buffington and Alvaretta (Smith) Atkinson; 1 child, Anthony Thomas. Student pub. schs., Eau Claire, Wis. Apprentice Karl Haagedorn, St. Paul, 1960-65; art instr. Head Start Program, St. Paul, 1965-67, Walker Art Inst., Mpls., 1967-69; founding mem., instr. Southside Free Sch., Mpls., 1968-69; free-lance artist Minn. and Oreg., 1965-73; art instr. Fairview Tng. Ctr., Salem, Oreg., 1974-77; founder, dir. 3 C's Sch. of Basic Carpentry, Salem, 1978-79; founder, pres. J. Stone Cards, Inc., Silverton, Oreg., 1980—. Author: Curriculum For Basic Carpentry Instruction, 1976. Newsletter editor NAACP, St. Paul, 1965-67, crisis counselor Mpls. Free Clinic, 1968-70, produce coord. Westbank Food Co-op, Mpls., 1968-70, counselor Womanspace, Salem, Oreg., 1978-80. Recipient Louie award Greeting Card Assn., N.Y.C., 1989. Mem. Am. Watercolor Assn., Oreg. Watercolor Assn. Unitarian Universalist. Avocation: foreign travel to remote tropical regions. Office: J Stone Cards Inc One J Stone Pla Silverton OR 97381

STONE, JUANITA JANE, telecommunications engineer; b. Wichita, Kans., June 8, 1955; d. Charles Junior and Helen Juanita (Coursey) S.; children: Amy Arminda Williams, Angela Kaye Williams; life partner: Ken Robinson. BSEET, DeVry Inst. of Tech., 1996. Temporary instr. Lewisville Ind. Sch. Dist., 1985-89; electron technician Kroger Food Stores, Keller, Tex., 1994; cons. engr. MCI Telecomms., Richardson, 1994-95; installation design engr. DSC Comms., Plano, Tex., 1995-98; owner, pres., design engr. JJS Services, Plano, Tex., 1997—; cons. engr. Citizens Comm., Dallas, Tex., 1998-99; proposal engr. Fujitsu Network Comms., Richardson, Tex., 1999—. Vol. Jr. Achievement, Richardson, 1996, 99; spkr. NMA Mini-CMC Conf., North Tex. Coun., 1997; co-dir. Praise Explosion, The Colony, Tex., 1983-94; dir. Children's Choir, The Colony, 1985-93, PTA, The Colony, 1985-94, Trinity River Mission, Dallas, 1994-95; troop leader Girl Scouts, The Colony, 1987-94, cross country track booster club, Plano, 1997—. Mem. Nat. Mgmt. Assn., Toastmasters Internat. (v.p. edn. 1996,98, pres. 1998, v.p. membership 1998-99, ATM Bronze 1997), Rich-Tones, Sweet Adelines. Avocations: computers, space program, gardening, music, competition shooting. Home: 1724 17th St Plano TX 75074-6415 Office: 1724 17th St Plano TX 75074-6415 E-mail: juanita@jjs-services.com.

STONE, JUDITH ELISE, artist, English educator; b. Boston, Sept. 15, 1940; d. Morris Joseph and Frances (Maletz) Tissenbaum; m. Donald Ivan Promish; m. Edward Johnson Stone, Aug. 24, 1964 (div. Mar. 1974); children: David Benjamin, Sylvia Beth. BA magna cum laude, Vassar Coll., 1962; MA in Tchg., Harvard U., 1965; MFA, U. Colo., Boulder, 1977. Adj. prof. Temple U., Phila., 1979-87, St. Joseph's U., Phila., 1983—, Coll. of Textiles, Phila., 1984—; tchr. Temple U., Japan, 1986-87; lectr. contemporary art history U. Vt., Burlington, 1999—. Lectr. various colls., univs. and confs. Contbr. articles to profl. jours.; one-person shows include Grimaldis Gallery, Balt., 1985, Hinoki Gallery, Tokyo, 1987, University City Sci. Ctr. Gallery, Phila., 1983, 89, Lancaster (Pa.) Mus. of Art, 1996, Caelum Gallery, N.Y.C., 2001, l'Espace 234, Montreal, 2002, Caelum Gallery, NYC, 2003, So. Vt. Art Ctr., Manchester, 2003; exhibited in group shows at Denver Mus. of Art, 1977, Boulder (Colo.) Fine Arts Ctr., 1978, Sebastian Moore Gallery, Denver, 1979, U. Colo. Art Galleries, Boulder, 1979, Allentown (Pa.) Mus., 1986, Pa. State Mus., Harrisburg, 1994, Stephen F. Austin U., Nacogdoches, 1995, Phila. Mus. Art, 1995, 100 Women/100 Works, Rochester, N.Y., 1996, San Diego Art Inst. (Grand prize), Gallery B.A.I., N.Y.C., 1997, Caelum Gallery, N.Y.C., 2000, So. Vt. Art Ctr., Manchester, 2002; represented in permanent collections at University City Sci. Ctr., Phila., St. Joseph's U., Phila., Balt. Gulf and Electric, Toyoda Internat. Sales, Inc., Tokyo, Design Studios, Tokyo, Idaho Nat. Bank, Boise. MacDowell colony resident fellow, 1992. Mem. AAUP, ACLU. Democrat. Jewish. Avocations: reading, travel, film watching, bicycle riding, photography. Home: 68 Richardson St Burlington VT 05401-5026 Office: Univ Vt Dept Art Williams Hall Burlington VT 05405 Office Phone: 802-656-2014. E-mail: DonaldPromish@cs.com.

STONE, KAREN, theater director; b. Horsforth, Yorkshire, England, 1952; Degree, Royal Academy of Music, 1970—73, Conservatorio di Musica "Santa Celilia", 1973—76. Asst. dir. Freiburg Opera, 1982—85; dir. English Nat. Opera, 1985—86; prod. and dir. various organizations including Maggio Musicale Fiorentino (Italy), Brighton Festival (Eng.), Royal Opera House (Covent Garden), Teatro Lirico di Parma (Italy), Glyndebourne Festival Opera (Eng.), et al, 1986—94; dep. dir. Cologne Opera, Germany, 1995; gen. mgr. Theaters of Graz, Austria, 2000—03; gen. dir. Dallas Opera, 2003—. Office: Dallas Opera 909 1st Ave Dallas TX 75210

STONE, LISA MURPHY, elementary school educator, music educator; b. Anderson, S.C., Mar. 22, 1959; d. William Ray and Frankie Watson Murphy; m. Fred G. Stone, May 27, 1978; children: David William, Michael Paul. BA in Music Edn., Erskine Coll., 1979; elem. edn. cert., Clemson U., 1990. Cert. tchr. S.C. Asst. buyer Pier I Imports Corp. Office, Ft. Worth, 1979—82; pvt. piano tchr. Lisa's Piano Studio, Seneca, SC, 1986—93; tchr. lang. arts 6th and 7th grade Seneca Mid. Sch., 1990—93; tchr. 1st grade Oconee Christian Acad., 1993—94; tchr. music preK-8th Thornwell Sch., Clinton, SC, 1994—96; tchr. 1st grade Liberty (S.C.) Elem. Sch., 1997—99; tchr. music grades K-5 McKissick Elem. Sch., Easley, SC, 1999—. Chair Pickens County Tchr. Forum Sch. Dist. Pickens County, Easley, 2002—03. Mem.: Music Educators Nat. Conf. Baptist. Avocations: gardening, cooking, piano. Home: 104 Harvest Dr Easley SC 29640 Office: McKissick Elem Sch 156 McKissick Rd Easley SC 29640

STONE, MARILYN, foreign language educator, consultant; b. N.Y.C., Jan. 14, 1935; d. Paul Ference Moskowitz and Anna Schwartz; m. Joseph Stone, Aug. 30, 1959; children: Sara Jean, Edward, Hillary, Daniel. BA in Spanish/French, Queens Coll.; MA in Spanish Lit., Columbia U.; PhD in Spanish Lit., NYU. Cert. Spanish/English translator, medieval/modern paleography profl. Spanish/English interpreter Nassau County Ct., 1985-86; Spanish lang. cons. Fine Arts Mus. of L.I., Hempstead, N.Y., 1986-87; Spanish instr. Dominican Coll., Blauvelt, N.Y., 1987, Nassau C.C., Blauvelt, N.Y., 1987, 92; instr. in translation methods NYU, N.Y.C., 1990—; ind. lang. cons. Chase Manhattan Bank, Bergen Lang. Inst., Teaneck, N.J., 1991—; asst. prof. transl. NYU. Presenter papers in field; adj. asst. prof. Spanish, Kingsborough C.C., CUNY, 1987-90; lectr. in field. Author: A Handbook of Courtroom Terms in Spanish and English, 1981, Marriage and Friendship in Medieval Spain, 1990, Women at Work in Spain From the Middle Ages to Early Modern Times, 1998; contbr. articles to profl. jours.

STONE, MARSHA L. music educator; b. Louisville, Ky. d. Robert Stone, Jr. and Delores Elliot Stone. B in Mus. Ed., Univ. of Louisville, Sch. of Music, Louisville, Ky., 1976; MEd elem., Univ. of Louisville, Sch. of Edn., Louisville, Ky., 1986. Music tchr., choral Jefferson County Pub. Sch., Lassiter Mid., Louisville, 1979—; singer, actress Music Theatre of Louisville, Louisville, 1993. Dir. Mag. St. S.D.A., Louisville, 1979—99. Ch. soloist St. Francis Episc. Ch., Louisville, 1980—81, 4th Ave. Meth. Ch., Louisville, 1981—2003. Recipient Music Scholarship, Jefferson Cmty. Coll. Music Program/Louisville, Ky., 1970—71, Outstanding Musical Talent, Ctrl. HS, 1970; grantee Academic Grant, Univ. of Louisville/Ky., 1971—75. Mem.: Jefferson County Tchr. Assn., Weightwatchers Internat. (leader 1980—), Weight Watchers NACO (leader 1979—), Louisville Bach Soc. (mem. 1979—80). Achievements include Nat. Assn. of Tchr. of Singing semi-finalist, 1971; soloist with the Louisville Orch., 1993. Avocations: singing, love to inspire individuals to better themselves by losing weight.. Home: 3612 Hurstbourne Ridge Louisville KY 40299 Office Phone: 502-485 8288.

STONE, NIKKI, motivational speaker, retired Olympic athlete; b. Princeton, N.J., Feb. 4, 1971; BS in Psychology magna cum laude, Union Coll., 1997. Motivational spkr. Podium Enterprises. Freestyle aerial skier. Winner Olympic Gold Medal in aerials, Nagano, 1998, World Championship Gold Medal, 1995, World Cup title, 1995, 1 World Cup events. Address: PO Box 680332 Park City UT 84068-0332 E-mail: nikkistone@compuserve.com.

STONE, SHARON, actress; b. Meadville, Pa., Mar. 10, 1958; d. Joe and Dorothy S; m. Michael Greenburg, 1984 (div. 1987); m. Phil Bronstein, 1998; 1 son. Student, Edinboro U. Model Eileen Ford Modeling Agy. Appeared in films Stardust Memories, 1980, Deadly Blessing, 1981, Irreconcilable Differences, 1984, King Solomon's Mines, 1985, Allan Quatermain and the Lost City of Gold, 1986, Cold Steel, 1987, Police Academy 4, 1987, Action Jackson, 1988, Above the Law, 1988, Beyond the Stars, 1989 (Personal Choice award), Total Recall, 1990, Year of the Gun, 1991, Diary of a Hitman, 1991, He Said/She Said, 1991, Scissors, 1991, Basic Instinct, 1991, Where Sleeping Dogs Lie, 1992, Last Action Hero, 1993, Sliver, 1993, Intersection, 1994, The Specialist, 1994, (also co-prodr.) The Quick and the Dead, 1995 (also co-prodr.), Casino, 1995 (Golden Globe award for best actress in film 1996, Acad. award nominee for best actress 1996), Diabolique, 1996, Last Dance, 1996, Sphere, 1998, The Mighty, 1998 (Golden Global nominee), Antz, 1998 (voice), Gloria, 1999, The Muse, 1999, Simpatico, 1999, Beautiful Joe, 2000, Picking Up the Pieces, 2000, Cold Creek Manor, 2003; TV appearances include Not Just Another Affair, 1982, Bay City Blues, 1983, Calendar Girl Murders, 1984, The Vegas Strip Wars, 1984, War and Remembrance, 1988, Tears in the Rain, 1988, (guest) The Larry Sanders Show, 1994, Big Guns Talk: The Story of the Western (tv spl.), 1997; narrator: Harlow: The Blond Bombshell, 1993, If These Walls Could Talk 2, 2000, Harold and the Purple Crayon, 2001. Office: Care Guy McElwaine PO Box 7304 North Hollywood CA 91603-7304

STONE, SUSAN A. lawyer; BA summa cum laude, Yale U., 1983; JD cum laude, Harvard U., 1987. Bar: Calif. 1987, U.S. Dist. Ct. (no. dist.) Calif. 1987, U.S. Ct. Appeals (9th cir.) 1987, U.S. Dist. Ct. (ctrl. dist.) Calif. 1988, Ill. 1990, U.S. Dist. Ct. (no. dist.) Ill. 1990, U.S. Ct. Appeals (7th cir.) 1990. Asst. U.S. atty. U.S. Dept. Justice, L.A.; law clk. to Judge William J. Orrick, U.S. Dist. Ct. for No. Dist. Calif.; ptnr. Sidley & Austin, Chgo. Former adj. prof. trial practice DePaul U. Coll. Law, Chgo. Named one of Top Young Litigators Under 40, Ill. Legal Times. Mem. Ill. Bar Assn., Calif. State Bar, Phi Beta Kappa. Office: Sidley & Austin 1 S First National Plz Chicago IL 60603-2000 Fax: 312-853-7036. E-mail: sstone@sidley.com.

STONE, SUSAN RIDGAWAY, marketing educator; b. Coronado, Calif., Oct. 30, 1950; d. Lester Jay and Marguerite Ridgaway (King) Stone; m. Martin Zachary Sipkoff, Oct. 27, 1984; 1 child, Benjamin. AB, Wilson Coll., 1977; MBA, Shippensburg U., 1980; DBA, George Washington U., 1992. Assoc. prof. mgmt. and mktg. Shippensburg (Pa.) U., 1983—; dir. mktg. VSP Wastewater Tech., Gettysburg, Pa., 1982; pres. Ridgaway Rose Internat., Inc., 1999—. Mktg. cons. Svcs. Unltd., Gettysburg, 1975—; lectr. in field. Author: (with Stephen J. Holoviak) Managing Human Productivity: People are Your Best Investment, 1987, 2nd printing 1991; contbr. articles to profl. jours. Recipient Excellence in Tchg. award, Corning Found., 1993, Outstanding Svc. award, 1994, 2002, Sprint Tchg. Excellence award, 1998, Orrston Bank Tchg. Excellence award, 2001, Panhellenic Coun. Tchg. award, 1999, Martin Babinee Outstanding Adv. award, 2003; fellow John L. Grove Rsch. fellow, 2002. Mem.: DAR, NOW, Southwest Acad. of Mgmt., S.E. Acad. Mgmt., Am. Mktg. Assn., Acad. Mktg. Sci., Survivors, Inc., Mensa, Adams County Literacy Coun., Nat. Hist. Trust, Kappa Kappa Gamma, Beta Gamma Sigma. Democrat. Episcopalian. Avocations: gardening, writing, sailing. Office: Shippensburg Univ 1871 Old Main Dr Shippensburg PA 17257-2299 E-mail: srston@ship.edu.

STONE, THERESA M. communications executive; b. Boston, 1944; Grad., Wellesley Coll.; grad. studies Cornell U.; MS, Sloan Sch. Mgmt., Mass. Inst. Tech., 1976. With Chubb Corp., 1990—97; pres., CEO Chubb Life Ins. Co. Am., 1994—97; with Morgan Stanley & Co., 1976—90; pres. Jefferson Pilot Comm., Greensboro, NC, 1997, exec. v.p., CFO, 1997—. Mem.: Burlington Industries Bd., Fed. Res. Bd., Richmond Br., MIT Corp., Greensboro United Way 1999 Campaign (pacesetters chair), Greensboro C. of C. Office: Jefferson Pilot Corp PO Box 21008 Greensboro NC 27420

STONER, CONNIE KAY, special education educator; b. Versailles, Mo., Apr. 18, 1949; d. Norman Francis and Helen Pauline (Kreissler) Schnirch; m. Gerald Alan Winter, Feb. 27, 1967 (div. 1971); children: Julie Marie Winter Stuart Brainard, Kimberly Lynn; m. Larry Dean Stoner, 1971; children: Grant, Colin. BS, Northeast Mo. State U., 1970, MA, 1971. Cert. speech pathology, audiology, Mo. Speech pathologist Cameron (Mo.) Pub. Schs., 1971-73, Independence (Mo.) Pub. Schs., 1973-78, self-contained lang. devel. tchr., 1978-96, speech pathologist, reading clinician, 1996—. Author: Language for Learners, 1981. Sec. Am. Field Svc.; v.p. Truman Music Boosters. Recipient Excellence in Teaching award, 1991; named Young Educator of Yr., Jaycees, 1986; HEW fellow, 1971. Mem. Mo. State Tchrs. Assn. (pres. 1997-99). Avocations: reading, aerobics, collecting music boxes. Office: Santa Fe Trail Elem 1301 Windsor St Independence MO 64055-1179 Home: 22608 NW Ashford Ct Blue Springs MO 64015-7330

STONER, OLIVIA HATCHETT, lawyer, financial planner; b. Phila., Oct. 2, 1947; d. Haywood and Vivian (Helton) Hatchett; m. Charles Timothy Stoner, Aug. 6, 1977; children: Tesha Nashan, Brenden Charles. BS, Wilberforce U., 1970; MA in Tchg., Antioch Putney Coll., 1971; JD, U. Pitts., 1978. Bar: Pa. 1983; CFP, 1992. Tchr. math. Sch. Dist. Phila., 1970-71; sales agt. Met. Life Ins. Co., Phila., 1971; juvenile probation officer Phila. Common Pleas Ct., Phila., 1972-75; trust and estate adminstr. investment mgmt. & trust dept. PNC Bank, Phila., 1980—99; CFO Synergy Devel. Group, Phila., 1990—; pvt. client advisor Wilmington Trust of Pa., 1999—2003; atty. Foley, Thompson and Dews, LLP, Phila. Contbg. editor: Paint Mag. Mem. bd. mggrs., chmn. nominating com. YMCA, Phila., 1991-93. Mem. Pa. Bar Assn., Philadelphia County Bar Assn., Urban Bankers Assn. (treas. 1995-96), Delaware Valley Soc. CFP's (bd. dirs. 1994-96), Phila. Astrological Soc. (treas. 1992-2003), Fin. Planning Assn. (bd. dirs. 1996-2003, editor newsletter). Democrat. Presbyterian. Avocations: drawing, painting, sculpting, astrology. Home: 3213 Wallace St Philadelphia PA 19104-2027

STONESIFER, PATRICIA Q. information systems executive; Degree, 1982. Editor-in-chief Que Corp., Indpls.; sr. mgr. Microsoft Press, 1988-89; gen. mgr. Microsoft Can., 1989-90; gen. mgr., then v.p. product support svcs. consumer divsn. Microsoft Corp., Redmond, Wash., 1990-93, sr. v.p. consumer divsn., 1993—. Office: Microsoft Corp 1 Microsoft Way Redmond WA 98052-8300

STONINGTON, EMILY S. state legislator; b. Oak Park, Ill., Jan. 12, 1947; m. Tim Swanson; 2 children. BA, Bennington Coll.; MA, U. Calif., Berkeley. Mem. Mont. Ho. of Reps., Mont. Senate, Dist. 15, Helena, 1996—. Home: 15042 Kelly Canyon Rd Bozeman MT 59715-9625 Office: Mont Ho of Reps State Capitol Helena MT 59620

STOPPEL, SHEREE' SUE, music educator; b. Colby, Kans., May 29, 1958; d. Donald Duane and Frances Mary Smith; m. Dwight Alan Stoppel, June 11, 1983; children: Kaleb Alan, Nickolas Lee, Blake Alexander. B in Music Edn., Kans. State U., 1980; M in Music Edn., Emporia (Kans.) State U., 1999. Cert. tchr. Kans. Music educator Unified Sch. Dist., Norton, Kans., 1980—82, Scott City, Kans., 1982—96; choir dir. Meth. Ch., Scott City, 1985—96, Osage City, Kans., 1996—; grad. asst. Emporia State U., 1997—99; music educator Unified Sch. Dist. 420, Osage City, 1999—. Named one of Outstanding Young Women of Am., 1982. Mem.: Kans. Music Educators Assn., Am. Choral Dirs. Assn., Music Educators Nat. Conf. Republican. Avocations: gospel singing, keyboard accompanist.

STORANDT, MARTHA, psychologist; b. Little Rock, June 2, 1938; d. Farris and Floy (Montgomery) Mobbs; m. Duane Storandt, Dec. 15, 1962; 1 child, Eric AB, Washington U., St. Louis, 1960, PhD, 1966. Lic. psychologist, Mo. Staff psychologist VA, Jefferson Barracks, Mo., 1967-68; asst. prof. to prof. Washington U., St. Louis, 1968—. Mem. nat. adv. council on aging Nat. Inst. on Aging, 1984-87; editor-in-chief Jour. Gerontology, 1981-86 Author: Counseling and Therapy with Older Adults, 1983; co-author: Memory, Related Functions and Age, 1974; co-editor: The Clinical Psychology of Aging, 1978, The Adult Years: Continuity and Change, 1989, Neuropsychological Assessment of Dementia and Depression in Older Adults: A Clinician's Guide, 1994. Recipient Disting. Service award Mo. Assn. Homes for the Aging, 1984. Fellow APA (pres. divsn. 20 1979-80, council rep. 1983-84, 86-88, Disting. Sci. Contbn. award divsn. adult devel. and aging 1988, Master Mentor award divsn. adult devel. and aging 2000, Disting. Contbns. to Clin. Geropsychology divsn. clin. psychology 2002), Gerontol. Soc. Am. Office: Washington U Dept Psychology Saint Louis MO 63130

STORCH, SUSAN BOROWSKI, lawyer; b. Jersey City, June 23, 1961; d. Raymond Edward and Clara Mary (Stryzek) Borowski; m. Michael John Storch, Feb. 9, 1985; children: Samantha Clare, Michael John Jr. BA, Rutgers U., 1983; JD, Seton Hall U., 1990. Bar: N.J. 1991. Corp. trust adminstr. Mfrs. Hanover Trust Co., N.Y.C., 1983-86; law clk. Congressman Dean Gallo, Washington, 1988, N.J. Supreme Ct. Com. on Complementary Dispute Resolution, Trenton, N.J., 1988; law clk. to asst. atty. gen. legis. affairs U.S. Dept. Justice, Washington, 1989; assoc. Rodino & Rodino, East Hanover, NJ, 1991—92; sr. assoc. Fragomen, Del Rey & Bernsen, Iselin, NJ, 1992—98, ptnr., 1998—2000; ptnr., chair corp. immigration practice group Sills Commis Radin Tischman Epstein & Gross, Newark, 2000—. Lectr. in field. Bd. dirs. Players Forum, N.Y.C., 1993-94; coord. Corp. Giving Coun., N.J. Women's Polit. Caucus, 1995; active various polit. fundraising campaigns. Recipient Commendation award Essex County Bd. Chosen Freeholders, N.J., 1990; Lyndon B. Johnson Congl. scholar, 1988. Mem.: ABA (labor and employment law sect. 1994—95), Exec. Women N.J. (nominations com.), Ctr. Study of Presidency, Psychology Assn. Am., Inst. Cont. Legal Edn. and Info. (N.J.), Coun. Internat. Personnel, Am. Immigration Lawyer Assn. (former press sec., former sec.), N.J. Bar Assn. (exec. bd. programs ctr. 1994—95). Democrat. Avocations: writing, sailing, golf. Office: Stills Cummis Radin Tischman Epstein & Gross PA One Riverfront Plaza Newark NJ 07102-5400

STORER, MARYRUTH, law librarian; b. Portland, Oreg., 1953; d. Joseph William and Carol Virginia Storer; m. David Bruce Bailey, 1981; children: Sarah, Allison. BA in History, Portland State U., 1974; JD, U. Oreg., 1977; M in Law Librarianship, U. Wash., 1978. Bar: Oreg. 1978. Assoc. law libr. U. Tenn., Knoxville, 1978-79; law libr. O'Melveny & Myers, L.A., 1979-88; dir. Orange County Pub. Law Libr., Santa Ana, Calif., 1988—. Mem. Am. Assn. Law Librs. (exec. bd. 1999-2002), So. Calif. Assn. Law Librs. (pres. 1986-87), Coun. Calif. County Law Librs. (sec./treas. 1990-94, pres. 1994-96), Arroyo Sero Libr. Network (chair 2000-03). Democrat. Episcopalian. Office: Orange County Public Law Library 515 N Flower St Santa Ana CA 92703-2304

STOREY, JOYCE R. writer, actress; arrived in US, 1993; d. Edison Bryar Storey and Emma Gertrude Tweedy; m. Thomas Alan Dowden, July 6, 1985 (div. 1996); m. Jeffrey Scott Wener, June 22, 1998; stepchildren: Allison Julie Wener, Erik Scott Wener. B in Music Edn., Acadia U., 1985; Prodrs. Diploma, Hollywood Film Inst., 2000; Filmmaker Diploma, Digital Film Acad., 2003. Cert. ind. filmmaker Hollywood Film Inst., 2000. Tchr. music Westwood Elem. Sch., Thompson, Canada, 1985—87; tchr. music, drama R.D. Parker Collegiate, Thompson, 1987—88; tchr. drama Glenlawn Collegiate Fine Arts Sch., Winnipeg, 1988—92; affiliate N.Y. Divsn. Westsun Internat. Inc., NYC, 1997—2000; prodn. mgr. Food for Thought, LLC, NYC, 2000; office mgr. High End Sys. Inc., NYC, 2001; gen. mgr. Stage Call Inc., NYC, 2002—. Mgr. Actor's Connection, NYC, 1993—; casting dir. Plato Films, Inc., Istanbul, 2003; sec. Bentley Prodns. Inc., NYC, 2003, Bink Inc., NYC, 2003. Columnist: Timeless Comm., 2000—, Front of House Mag., 2002—03; contbr. PLSN Mag., 2000—03; author: (poetry) Holding On To Forever, 2001 (Editor's Choice award, 2001), Pearls of the Past, 2002 (Editor's Choice award, 2002); actor: One Life to Live; (TV series) Guiding Light, As the World Turns, All My Children, The Sopranos, Sex and the City; (films) Amazing Grace, The Adulterer, Fire Storm Rising. Recipient Humanitarian award, Terry Fox Humanitarian Award program, 1984—85, Appreciation award, Allied Youth Internat., 1992. Avocations: ice skating, rollerblading, hiking, sewing, dance. Personal E-mail: joycestorey@aol.com.

STOREY, SUSAN LYNNE, investment banker; b. St. Louis, July 6, 1956; d. John George II and Rose Marie (Cahillane) S. BS, Boston Coll., 1984. Ptnr. Gray Shiftman & Storey, Boston, 1987—89, Recovery Mgmt., N.Y.C., 1989—93; pres. Capital Solutions Group, Inc., N.Y.C., 1992—; ptnr. Global Fin. Strategies/Corp. Recovery Svcs. Practice/KPMG; mng. dir. Nightingale Assocs., Getzler Henrich & Assocs. LLC, N.Y.C., 2003—. Chairwoman Modeta Sweater Club, Czech Republic, 1996—; dir. Dental a.s., Czech Republic, 1997-98. Charter mem. Internat. Women Insolvency Confedn., N.Y.V., 1994—; bd. dirs. Alliance Russian & Am. Women, N.Y.C., 1993—. Mem.: Turnaround Mgmt. Assn., Internat. Women in Insolvency and Restructuring Confederation, Am. Bankruptcy Inst., Phi Beta Kappa. Democrat. Roman Catholic. Office: Getzler Henrich & Assocs LLC 295 Madison Ave New York NY 10017

STORM, HANNAH, newscaster; b. Oak Pk., Ill., June 13, 1962; B in Polit. Sci. and Comm., U. of Notre Dame, 1983. Sports anchor, reporter KTXH-TV, Houston; Home Sports Entertainment; KNCN-FM Radio, Corpus Christi, Tex., WNDU-TV, South Bend, Ind., 1982—88; sports reporter, anchor WPQC-TV, Charlotte, NC, 1988—89; anchor CNN Sports Tonight, 1989—92; anchor, reporter NBC Sports, 1993—2002; anchor The Early Show, 2002—. Host NBC coverage of the NBA, 1997—2002, NBC coverage of Major League Baseball, 1995—2002, NBC coverage of Major League Baseball World Series, 1995, 97, 99. Author: (sports guide for parents) Go Girl!, 2002. Recipient Gracie Allen award, Am. Women in Radio and TV. Office: CBS News 524 W 57th St New York NY 10019

STORM, JACKIE, nutritionist, health education specialist; b. Halifax, N.S., Can., Sept. 20, 1943; d. Jack Charles Stone and Kathleen (Clow) Devisser. BA, NYU, 1979, MA, 1982, PhD, 1995. Cert. nutrition specialist. Nutrition educator N.Y. Health and Racquet Club, N.Y.C., 1973—; tchr. New Sch. Social Rsch., N.Y.C., 1980-87. Adj. prof. Kingsborough C.C., Bklyn., 1987-2001, St. Francis Coll., Bklyn., 1987; tchr. Acad. Med. Sys., 2001. Author: There's No Such Thing As A Fattening Food!, 1983. Mem. Am. Coll. Nutrition, Am. Nutraceutical Assn., Soc. nutrition Edn. Avocations: gardening, weight lifting. Office: 115 E 57th St New York NY 10022-2049 Office Phone: 212-220-0773. E-mail: jackiestorm@jackiestorm.com.

STORM, SUZANNE, state representative; b. Spokane, Wash., July 17, 1941; 1 child, Carmen. BA, William Jewell Coll., 1963; MS, U. Kans., 1984. Tchr. pub. schs., 1964—78; tchr., 1978—92; mem. Kans. Ho. of Reps., 1996—. Mem.: Shawnee Mission Edn. Found., Mainstream Coalition (bd. dirs. 1990—), Kans. Nat. Edn. Assn. (bd. dirs. 1990—96), NEA (pres. 1992—96). Democrat. Baptist. Office: 272-W State Capitol 300 SW 10th Ave Topeka KS 66612 Address: 8145 Mackey Overland Park KS 66204-3121

STORMER, NANCY ROSE, lawyer; b. Traverse City, Mich., Mar. 7, 1950; d. Benjamin Voice and Frances Rose (Gold) S.; m. Michael Charles Bagge, Aug. 1, 1985; children: Sean, Kiernan. AA, Harriman (N.Y.) Coll., 1973; BA magna cum laude, Marist Coll., 1977; JD, Antioch Sch. Law, 1981. Bar: N.Y. 1983, U.S. Dist. Ct. (no. dist.) N.Y. 1983, U.S. Supreme Ct. 1989. Staff atty. Legal Aid Soc. Mid N.Y., Utica, 1983-95, sr. atty., 1990-95; atty. in pvt. practice Utica, 1995—. Bd. dirs. Sister City Project, Utica, 1986-90, Salvation Army, Utica, 1988-89; mem. adv. coun. office for aging Oneida County Office for Aging, Utica, 1993-96; co-chairperson adv. coun. Hispanos Unidos, Utica, 1994. Named Profl. Woman of Yr. YWCA of Mohawk Valley, 1999. Mem. N.Y. State Bar Assn., Oneida County Bar Assn., Nat. Health Lawyers. Avocations: travel, reading, crafts. Home: 1314 Rutger St Utica NY 13501-2526 Office: 1325 Belle Ave Utica NY 13501-2615

STORRS, IMMI CASAGRANDE, sculptor; b. Aug. 2, 1945; d. Leo and Carla Maria Annie (Busch) Casagrande; m. Thomas Austin Storrs, Dec. 19, 1971 (div. 1983); 1 child, A. Maya. BA, U. Denver, 1968. Nessa Cohen grantee, 1981, 82, E.D. Found. grantee, 1989, 96; recipient Purchase award, Art Students League N.Y., Chaim Gross Found. award, 1989, Nat. Acad. Mus. Speyer prize, 1992. One-woman shows include Gallery 2, Woodstock, Vt., 1973, Fairwinds Gallery, Ferrisburg, Vt., 1974, Congress Hall, Timmendorferstrand, Germany, 1976, Amerika Haus, Hamburg, Germany, 1976, Cambridge Art Assn., Mass., 1978, Goethe Inst., Boston, 1980, 83, Sutton Gallery, N.Y.C., 1981, 82, 83, 86, Madison Gallery, 1987, Bologna-Landi Gallery, Easthampton, N.Y., 1987, 93, Vorpal Gallery, N.Y.C., 1989, 91, 92, La Posada, Santa Fe, 1989, Ruth Volid Gallery, Chgo., 1990, Bachelier-Cardonsky Gallery, Kent, Conn, 1996, Hurlbutt Gallery, Greenwich, Conn., 1997, Dillon Gallery, N.Y.C., 1997, 00; group shows include Fleming Mus., Burlington, Vt., 1973, ARtist Choice Mus., N.Y.C., 1983, Nat. Acad. Mus., N.Y.C., 1988, 92, 94, 95, 97, 99, 2001, 2003, Provincetown Art Assn. & Mus., Mass., 1988, Nat. Scultpure Soc., N.Y.C., 1989, 91, Elaine Benson Gallery, bridgehampton, N.Y., 1993, Sculptors Guild, Kyoto, Japan & Washington, 1993, N.Y.C., 1994, Cline Fine Art Gallery, Sante Fe, 1994, 95, Stamford Mus., Conn., 1996, Bachelier-Cardonsky Gallery, 1996, The White House, Washington, 1996, 97; represented in permanent collections at The Nat. Mus. Women in Arts, Washington, The Snite Mus., Nat. Acad. Mus., The Herbert Johnson Mus. at Cornell, numerous pvt. collections. Mem. Nat. Acad. Mus., Century Assn., Sculptors Guild. Avocations: skiing, tennis. Home: 169 E 78th St New York NY 10021-0485

STORY, AMY TAYLOR, music educator; b. Wilkes-Barre, Pa., Apr. 5, 1958; d. Robert Lee and Elen Jane Taylor; m. Brian Scott Story, June 16, 1979; children: Matthew Scott, Kathryn Jane. BS in Music Edn., Mansfield U., Pa., 1980; MS in Music Edn., Mansfield U., 1985. Cert. tchr. Pa, N.Y., 1980. Vocal music tchr. Arkport Ctrl. Sch., NY, 1980—89, Northside Blodgett Mid. Sch., Corning/Painted Post, NY, 1989—97, Canandaigua Acad., NY, 1997—. Cir. county, area all-state choruses various locations. Mem.: Steuben County Music Tchrs. Assn. (pres. 1994—95), Finger Lakes Music Educators Assn. (libr. 2002—), NY State Sch. Music Assn., Am. Choral Dirs. Assn., Delta Kappa Gamma. R-Conservative. Christian. Avocations: singing, travel, needlecrafts. Home: 3639 East Ridge Run Canandaigua NY 14424 Office: Canandaigua Academy 1 Academy Cir Canandaigua NY 14424 Office Phone: 595-396-3833. Personal E-mail: aschoirgirl@aol.com. E-mail: storya@canandaiguaschools.org.

STORY, ELLEN, state legislator; m. Ronald Story; 2 children. BA, U. Tex.; postgrad., U. Wis., SUNY, Stony Brook; MA, Cambridge Coll. County coord. Family Planning Coun. Western Mass., 1973, asst. exec. dir., 1981, assoc. exec. dir., 1984-92; mem. Mass. Ho. of Reps., Boston, 1992—. Founding mem. Hampshire County Human Svcs., Mass., 1974, past mem. prof. adv. com.; organizer Western Mass. Dems. and Independents for Frank Hatch for Gov., 1978; chmn. Barbara Griffith for Amherst Selectbd., 1982; coord. Evelyn Murphy for Lt. Gov., 1982; mem. Amherst Town Meeting, Mass.; pres., bd. dirs. Hampshire County Coun. Social Agencies, Mass.; bd. dirs. Hampshire Youth 2000 Coalition; charter mem. Friends of Amherst Recreation; co-founder, dir. Concerned Citizens for Quality Edn. Recipient Spl. Recognition award Hampshire County Coun. Social Agencies, 1991. Mem. Amherst Club, Rotary. Democrat. Office: Mass Ho of Reps State House Rm 167 Boston MA 02133

STORY, KENDRA, wholesale distribution executive; CFO Am. Bldrs. & Contrs. Supply Co., Inc., Beloit, Wis. Office: Am Bldrs & Contrs Supply One ABC Pkwy Beloit WI 53511 Office Fax: (608) 362-6215.

STORY, MARTHA VANBEUREN, retired librarian; b. Morristown, N.J., Mar. 6, 1940; d. John Mohlman and Jane de Peyster VanB.; m. William Ferguson Story, Oct. 19, 1963; children: Jessica, Alexandra. BA, Wellesley Coll., 1962; MLS, U. Md., 1975. Libr. Dewberry & Davis, Fairfax, Va., 1976-77, 80-84, Ashley Hall, Charleston, S.C., 1977-80, 85-86; cataloger Norfolk (Va.) Pub. Libr., 1987-90; dir. Mathews (Va.) Meml. Libr., 1990-99. Publicity chmn. Concerts By the Bay, 2001—; mem. lay visitors com. Kingston Parish, Mathews, Va., 1996—, scholarship com., 1996—, mem. 350th Anniversary com., 2001—02. Home: Holly Cove PO Box 117 Hudgins VA 23076-0117 E-mail: marthava88@yahoo.com.

STORY, SUSAN, merchant banker; b. Dublin; 1 child. Student, U. Coll., Dublin, Ireland, York U. From fgn. exchange trader to mng. dir. and head Global Trading Canadian Imperial Bank Commerce, Toronto, 1982—96, mng. dir. and head Global Trading, 1996—. Chmn. Canadian Com. Professionalism; pres. Forex Can. Chmn. Children's Miracle Found.; vice chmn. Children's Aid Found.; bd. dir. Ireland Fund. Office: BCE Place 161 Bay St PO Box 500 Toronto ON Canada M5J 2S8*

STOSKUS, JOANNA JORZYSTA, computer information systems educator; b. Newark, Feb. 10, 1947; d. Joseph B. and Anna Mary (Stopa) Jorzysta; m. Joseph Thomas Stoskus, Jr., Oct. 25, 1969; 1 child, Caryn Judith. BA in Math., Kean Coll. N.J., 1968; MA in Computer Sci., Montclair State U., 1985. Programmer, analyst Prudential Ins. Co., Newark, 1968-70, Bell Labs., Murray Hill, N.J., 1970-72; adj. instr. Middlesex County Coll., Edison, N.J., 1974-77; prof. engrng. tech. County Coll. of Morris, Randolph, NJ, 1977—. Avocation: golf. Office: County Coll Morris 214 Center Grove Rd Randolph NJ 07869-2007

STOTKA, JENNIFER LYNN, pharmaceutical executive, physician; b. El Paso, June 23, 1958; d. Victor Leonard and Theresa E. Stotka. BS in Chemistry and Biology, U. Hartford, 1980; MD, Wake Forest U., 1984. Diplomate Am. Bd. Internal Medicine, Am. Bd. Infectious Diseases. Assoc. clin. rsch. physician Eli Lilly & Co., Indpls., 1991-93, clin. rsch. physician, 1993-95, med. dir. infectious diseases, 1995-96, dir. U.S. regulatory affairs, 1996-97, dir. U.S. regulatory affairs & global ops., 1997-98, exec. dir. global clin. rsch., 1998—. Clin. instr. medicine U. Pitts., 1987-98; asst. prof. medicine Ind. U., Indpls., 1991-93; instr. Infectious Diseases/FDA, San Francisco, 1997. Contbr. articles to profl. jours. Vol. Damien Ctr. AIDS, Indpls., 1995, Freedom House, Richmond, Va., 1990, Rural Health Coalition, Winston-Salem, N.C., 1983. Recipient Lilly Pres.'s Recognition award; Postdoctoral fellow Nat. Found. Infectious Diseases, 1988. Fellow Infectious Diseases Soc. Am.; mem. Am. Acad. Pharm. Physicians, Am. Soc. Microbiology, Am. Coll. Physicians, Am. Women's Med. Assn., Drug Info. Assn. Avocations: canoeing, swimming, gardening, biking, reading. Office: Eli Lilly & Co Lilly Corp Ctr Indianapolis IN 46285-0001

STOTLER, ALICEMARIE HUBER, federal judge; b. Alhambra, Calif., May 29, 1942; d. James R. and Loretta M. Huber; m. James Allen Stotler, Sept. 11, 1971. BA, U. So. Calif., 1964, JD, 1967. Bar: Calif. 1967, U.S. Dist. Ct. (no. dist.) Calif. 1967, U.S. Dist. Ct. (ctrl. dist.) Calif. 1973, U.S. Supreme Ct. 1976; cert. criminal law specialist. Dep. Orange County Dist. Attys. Office, 1967-73; mem. Stotler & Stotler, Santa Ana, Calif., 1973-76, 83-84; judge Orange County Mcpl. Ct., 1976-78, Orange County Superior Ct., 1978-83, U.S. Dist. Ct. (ctrl. dist.) Calif., L.A., 1984—. Assoc. dean Calif. Trial Judges Coll., 1982; lectr., panelist, numerous orgns.; standing com. on rules of practice and procedure U.S. Jud. Conf., 1991-98, chair, 1993-98; chair 9th cir. Pub. Info. and Cmty. Outreach, 2000-; mem. exec. com. 9th Cir. Jud. Conf., 1989-93, Fed. State Jud. Coun., 1989-98, jury com., 1990-92, planning com. for Nat. Conf. on Fed.-State Jud. Relationships, Orlando, 1991-92, planning com. for We. Regional Conf. on State-Fed. Jud. Relationships, Stevens, Wash., 1992-93; chair dist. ct. symposium and jury utilization Ctrl. Dist. Calif., 1985, chair atty. liaison, 1989-90, chair U.S. Constn. Bicentennial com., 1986-91, chair magistrate judge com., 1992-93; mem. State Adv. Group on Juvenile Justice and Delinquency Prevention, 1983-84, Bd. Legal Specializations Criminal Law Adv. Commn., 1983-84, victim/witness adv. com. Office Criminal Justice Planning, 1980-83, U. So. Calif. Bd. Councilors, 1993-2001; active team in tng. Leukemia Soc. Am., 1993, 95, 97, 2000; legion lex bd. dirs. U. So. Calif. Sch. Law Support Group, 1981-83. Winner Hale Moot Ct. Competition, State of Calif., 1967; named Judge of Yr., Orange County Trial Lawyers Assn., 1978, Most Outstanding Judge Orange County Bus. Litig. Sect., 1990. Mem. ABA (jud. adminstrn. divsn. and litig. sect. 1984—, nat. conf. fed. trial judges com. on legis. affairs 1990-91), Am. Law Inst., Am. Judicature Soc., Fed. Judges Assn. (bd. dirs. 1989-92), Nat. Assn. Women Judges, U.S. Supreme Ct. Hist. Soc., Ninth Cir. Dist. Judges Assn., Calif. Supreme Ct. Hist. Soc., Orange County Bar Assn. (mem. numerous coms., Franklin G. West award 1984), Calif. Judges Assn. (mem. com. on jud. coll. 1978-80, com. on civil law and procedure 1980-82, Dean's coll. curriculum commn. 1981), Calif. Judges Found. Office: Ronald Reagan Fed Bldg & Courthouse 411 W 4th St Santa Ana CA 92701-4500

STOTLER, EDITH ANN, retired grain company executive, financial planner; b. Champaign, Ill., Oct. 11, 1946; d. Kenneth Wagner and Mary (Odebrecht) S. Student, Mary Baldwin Coll., 1964-66; BA, U. Ill., 1968. Asst. v.p. Harris Trust and Savs. Bank, Chgo., 1969-83; mgr. Can. Imperial Bank of Commerce, Chgo., 1983, sr. mgr., 1983-85, asst. gen. mgr. group head, 1985-88, v.p., dir. utilities, 1988-90; ptnr. Stotler Grain Co., Champaign, Ill., 1990—2002; pres. Homer Grain Co., Champaign, 1990-2000; pres., bd. dirs. S&I Grain Co., 1990-2000, SEMCO Energy Inc., 1987—2004. Bd. dirs., audit com., fin. com. SEMCO Energy Inc.; compensation com. Strategic Capital Bancorp, Inc., 2002—03. Past pres. liberal arts and scis. constituent bd., mem. pres.'s coun. U. Ill.; trustee, mem. fin. com. Countryside Sch., 1997—2000; dean's bus. coun. and exec. com. U. Ill. Bus. Coll., 1998—; bd. dirs. Champaign County YMCA, 2000—03; bd. dirs., treas. bd., chair investment and fin. coms. Champaign Pub. Libr. Found.; past mem. investment com., bd. trustees 4th Presbyn. Ch. Mem.: U. Ill. Found., Art Club (past pres., v.p.), Krannert Art Mus., Champaign Country Club (chair house com.), U. Ill. Found., Book Club. Avocations: needlepoint, reading, tennis, golf, cooking. Home: 900 N Lake Shore Dr Apt 2106 Chicago IL 60611-1522

STOTT, ANNETTE, art historian, educator; b. Madison, Wis., May 29, 1955; d. Peter and Huldah Pierce; m. Don W. Stott, Aug. 2, 1980. BA summa cum laude, Concordia Coll., Moorhead, Minn., 1977; MA, U. Wis., 1980; PhD, Boston U., 1986. Asst. prof. U. Maine, Orono, 1986-87, Winthrop Coll., Rock Hill, S.C., 1987-91, Denver U., 1991-94, assoc. prof., 1994—, dir. Sch. Art and Art History, 1999—. Author: Holland Mania: The Unknown Dutch Period in American Art and Culture, 1998; essayist: Gari Melchers: A Retrospective, 1990, Katwijk In De Schilderkunst, 1995; contbr. articles to profl. jours. Fulbright fellow, The Netherlands, 1983-84; Andrew Mellon Faculty fellow Harvard U., 1989-90; NEH fellow Winterthur, 1997-98; travel grantee Am. Coun. Learned Socs., Oxford, Eng., 1995. Mem. Am. Studies Assn., Assn. Historians Am. Art, Nineteenth Century Studies Assn., Coll. Art Assn. Office: Univ Denver Sch Art and Art History 2121 E Asbury Ave Denver CO 80208

STOTT, BARBARA PAXTON, volunteer; b. Greenville, Miss., July 30, 1925; d. Lawrence Lipscomb Paxton and Elizabeth Lloyd; widowed; children: Sheila Stott Gourlay, Pamela Stott Kendall, Barbara Stott McCoy. Student, Gulf Park Coll., 1943. Appeared in TV Spl. "A Day in the Life of America." Mem. Am. Women's Club, London, 1977-78, Am. Women's Assn., Singapore, 1983-85, Am. Women's Club Bermuda, 1982-83. Mem. DAR, Colonial Dames, Magna Charta Dames, Delta Debutante Club (bd. dirs.). Republican. Episcopalian. Home: Osceola Plantation RR 1 Box 351 Leland MS 38756-9801

STOUT, ELIZABETH WEST, foundation administrator; b. San Francisco, Mar. 4, 1917; d. Claudius Wilson and Sarah (Henderson) West; m. Bruce Churchill McDonald, Mar. 19 1944 (dec. 1952); children: Douglas, Anne; m. Charles Holt Stout, Oct. 27, 1958 (dec. 1992); stepchildren: Richard, George (dec.), Martha Stout Gilweit. Student, U. Nev., 1934-37; grad., Imperial Valley Coll., 1990. Cashier, acct. N.Y. Underwriters, San Francisco, 1937-42; sec. supply and accounts USN, San Francisco, 1942-44. Contbr. articles to profl. jours. Mem. adv. bd. Anza-Borrego Desert, Natural History Assn., 1974-84; founder Stout Paleontology Lab., Borrego Springs, Calif., 1982; found. trustee Desert Rsch. Inst., Reno, 1989—; active Black Rock Desert Project, 1989, Washoe Med. Ctr. League, 1953—, St. Mary's Hosp. Guild, 1953—. Named Disting. Nevadan U. Nev., 1993. Mem. Anza-Borrego Desert Natural History Assn. (dir. emeritus 1984), Soc. Vertebrate Paleontology, De Anza Desert Country Club, Kappa Alpha Theta. Republican. Episcopalian. Avocations: travel, writing, reading, golf.

STOUT, ELVA CAROLYN FRASER, elementary school educator; b. Independence, Mo., Oct. 20; d. Gertrude Alleen Warnke, Charles Allen Fraser; m. Forrest Eugene Stout; children: Sherri Jones, Karrie Henricks, F. Evan, Eric. BS, Appalachian State U., 1972; MEd, Augusta State U., 1978; postgrad., U. S.C., 1984—88. T-6 profl. tchg. cert. Tchr. T. A. Dugger Jr. High, Elizabethton, Tenn., 1972—74, A. C. Griggs, Augusta, Ga., 1974—75, Bel Air Elem., Evans, Ga., 1975—88, Lakeside Mid. Sch., Evans, 1988—92, Riverside Mid. Sch., Evans, 1992—. Field tester Am. Geol. Inst., 1999; evaluator Scope poster, 2000; reviewer, evaluator Astronomy Edn. Rev., 2002. Adult Sunday sch. tchr. First Bapt. Ch., Augusta, 1975—. Named Outstanding Sci. Tchr., Sigma Xi, 1994, AASTRA Tchr., Am. Astron. Soc., 1996, 1997, Rsch. Based Sci. Edn. Tchr., Nat. Optical Astronomy Observatories, 1999, Best Tchr. in Sci. and Math., 1991, Best Tchr. in Sci. and Tech., 1993—94. Mem.: Profl. Assn. Ga. Educators (membership coord. sch. 1980—91), Ga.'s Sci. Tchrs.' Assn., Nat. Earth Sci. Tchrs. Assn. (presenter), Nat. Assn. Geoscience Tchrs. (Ga.'s Outstanding Earth Sci. Tchr. 1996), Phi Delta Kappa (assoc.), Alpha Delta Kappa (assoc.; dist. chaplain 1980—82). Baptist. Avocations: fossil "hunter", amateur astronomer, painting, travel. Home: 4800 Woodbridge Pl Evans GA 30809 Office: Riverside Mid Sch 1095 Fury's Ferry Rd Evans GA 30809 Personal E-mail: TeacherES@aol.com. Business E-Mail: estout@ccboe.net.

STOUT, MARY WEBB, education program specialist; b. Richmond, Va., Dec. 24, 1947; d. Frank Edmond Webb and Edith Diuguid (Harris) Webb Steger; m. Teddy Alvin Stout, July 8, 1972. BA, Mary Washington Coll., 1970; MEd, U. Va., Charlottesville, 1972; Edn. Specialist, Coll. William and Mary, 1991, EdD, 1995; cert. in Multimedia Devel., George Mason U., 2003. Tchr. Harrisonburg City Sch., Va., 1970-71, Buckingham County Sch., Va., 1972-73; guidance counselor So. European Task Force US Army, Vicenza, Italy, 1973-78, edn. specialist Quartermaster Sch. Ft. Lee, Va., 1978-80, edn. specialist Tng. Support Ctr. Ft. Eustis, Va., 1980-82; edn. specialist Hdqs. Tng., Doctrine Command, Ft. Monroe, Va., 1982-83; edn. svc. specialist Combined Arms Ctr., Ft. Leavenworth, Kans., 1983-88; instrnl. systems specialist Hdqs. TRADOC, Ft. Monroe, 1988-98; supervisory edn. svc. specialist Hdqs. US Army Pers. Command, Alexandria, Va., 1998-2000; edn. program specialist OSD Office of Chancellor Edn. and Profl. Devel., Arlington, Va., 2000—; online faculty U. Phoenix, 2002—. Mem. devel. bd. Sch. Edn. Coll. William and Mary, 2002—. Legis. affairs rep. Running Man Homeowners Assn., Yorktown, Va., 1996—98; treas. Massanetta Springs Alumni Assn., Harrisonburg, Va., 1988—2002, membership chmn., 1998—2002, pres., 2002—. Recipient Alumni award Massanetta Springs Alumni Assn., 1996. Mem.: Am. Soc. for Tng. & Development, Am. Soc. for Tng. and Devel., Assn. for Instnl. Rsch., Am. Assn. for Adult and Continuing Edn., Mary Washington Coll. Alumni Assn., U. Va. Alumni Assn., Coll. William and Mary Alumni Assn., Assn. Advancement of Computing in Edn., Assn. Ednl. Comm. and Tech., Am. Assn. Higher Edn., Assn. Study Higher Edn., Kappa Delta Pi. Presbyterian. Avocations: running, red cross water safety instructor. Home: 6006 River Dr Mason Neck VA 22079-4127 Office: Dept Def Chancellor Edn and Profl Devel Civilian Pers Mgmt Svcs 1400 Key Blvd Ste B-200 Arlington VA 22209 Personal E-mail: MSTOUT8895@aol.com.

STOUT, PATRICIA A. communications educator; BA in Anthropology, U. Ariz., 1979; postgrad., U. Minn., 1979-81; PhD in Comm., U. Ill., 1985. Advt. mgr. alumni publ. U. Mont., Missoula, 1978-79; acct. mgmt. Judge Advt., Pub. Rels., Helena, Mont., 1979; tchg. asst., Sch. Journalism & Mass Comm. U. Minn., Mpls., 1979-80; project asst. Minn. Cmty. Prevention Program, 1980-81; vis. lectr. dept. advt. U. Ill., Urbana, 1981-84; asst. prof. dept. advt. U. Tex., Austin, 1984-90, assoc. prof. dept. advt., 1990—, assoc. dean acad. affairs Coll. Comm., 1996—. Vis. rsch. prof. Ctrs. for Disease Control and Prevention, Atlanta, 1993-94; vis. assoc. prof. dept. mktg. and internat. bus. U. Auckland, New Zealand, 1994; chmn. 5 doctoral coms., numerous masters theses, profl. reports U. Tex., Austin, mem., reader numerous others; dir. grad. studies dept. advt. U. Tex., Austin, Fall 1990, Summer 1993; ad hoc reviewer Jour. Advt., Jour. Consumer Rsch., Jour. Pub. Policy & Mktg., Journalism Quar., Critical Studies in Mass Comm., Jour. Bus. Rsch. Author: (with John D. Leckenby and Nugent Wedding) Advertising Management, (with Michael Solomon and Kim Rotzoll) The Advertising Around Us: A Consumer Perspective on Marketing Communications; editor procs. of 1990 Am. Acad. of Advt. Conf.; contbr. tech. papers, procs., articles to profl. jours.; presenter in field. Recipient cartoon caption contest first place award Olympia Beer Distbrs., Missoula, Mont., 1978-79, Jour. Advt. best article award Am. Acad. Advt., 1993, vis. rsch. prof. intergovernmental pers. act award Nat. AIDS Edn. and Info. Program, Ctrs. for Disease Control and Prevention, Atlanta, 1993-94; Pub. Health Svc. Tng. fellow Lab. Physiological Hygiene, U. Minn., 1980-81, Houston Harte Centennial Comm. fellow U. Tex., Austin, 1987-88, Am. Acad. Advt. Industry fellow Advt. Rsch. Found, N.Y., 1993-94; dissertation rsch. grantee U. Ill., 1984-85, summer rsch. grantee U. Tex., Austin, 1984-85, direct support grantee U. Tex., 1985-86, 86-87, rsch. grantee Am. Acad. Advt., 1985-86, rsch. grantee Teh Ogilvy Ctr. Rsch. and Devel., San Francisco, 1985-86, U. Rsch. Inst. spl. rsch. grantee U. Tex., 1988-89, 95-96, Columbia U. Tech. Studies Seminar grantee Freedom Forum Media Studies Ctr., 1992-93, immunization of Tex. children co-investigator grantee Tex. Dept. Health, 1995-96, an exploratory study on appropriate internet content and use standards for children co-investigator grantee Hogg Found. for Mental Health, 1996-97. Mem. Internat. Comm. Assn. (ad hoc reviewer), Am. Acad. Advt. (treas. 1989, v.p. 1990, pres. elect 1991, pres. 1992, past pres. 1993, publs. com. 1997—, ad hoc reviewer), Assn. Consumer Rsch. (ad hoc reviewer), Assn. Edn. in Journalism and Mass Comm., Soc. Consumer Psychology, Phi Kappa Phi, Kappa Tau Alpha, Alpha Delta Sigma. Home: 5508 Great Divide Dr Austin TX 78738-6123 Office: Univ Tex Dept Advt CMA 7142 Austin TX 78712

STOVAL, LINDA, political party official; b. Wyo. m. Tony Stoval. Ran 2 campaigns former Dem. Gov. Mike Sullivan; owner Solutions, Wyo.; chairperson Wyo. Dem. Party, 2001—. Office: 737 Kirk Ave Casper WY 82601-3324 Business E-Mail: stoval@trib.com.

STOVALL, CARLA JO, former state attorney general; b. Hardner, Kans., Mar. 18, 1957; d. Carl E. and Juanita Joe (Ford) Stovall. BA, Pittsburg (Kans.) State U., 1979; JD, U. Kans., 1982, MPA, 1993. Bar: Kans. 1982, U.S. Dist. Ct. Kans. 1982. Pvt. practice, Pitts., 1982—85; atty. Crawford County, Pitts., 1984—88; gov. Kans. Parole Bd., Topeka, 1988—94; atty. gen. State of Kans., Topeka, 1995—2002. Lectr. law Pittsburg State U., 1982—84. Mem. bd. govs. U. Kans. Sch. Law; Nat. Ctr. Missing and Exploited Children; Am. Legacy Found.; Nat. Crime Prevention Coun.; Coun. State Govts.; mem. bd. govs. Kans. Children's Cabinet; pres. NAAG, 2001—02, chmn. exec. com. midwest region, sexually violent predator com., 1995—96, bd. dirs., sec. Pittsburg Family YMCA, 1983—88. Named Outstanding Atty. Gen., Nat. Assn. Attys. Gen., 2001, Topeka Fraternal Order of Police's Amb. to Law Enforcement; recipient Champion award, Campaign Tobacco Free Kids, 2002, Adam Walsh Children's Fund Rainbow award, Nat. Ctr. Missing and Exploited Children, 2001, Kelley-Wyman award, Nat. Assn. Attys. Gen., 2001, Person of the Yr., Kans. Peace Officer Assn.'s Law Enforcement, Morton Baud Allied Profl. award, Nat. Orgn. Victim Assistance, Father Ken Czillinger award, Nat. Parents Murdered Children, Disting. Svc. to Kans. Children award, Kans. Children's Svc. League, Woman of Achievement award, Miss Kans. Pageant. Mem.: NAAG (pres. 2001—02), AAUW (bd. dirs. 1983—87), ABA, Bus. and Profl. Women Assn. (Young Careerist award 1984), Nat. Coll. Dist. Attys., Kans. County and Dist. Attys. Assn., Crawford County Bar Assn. (sec. 1984—85, v.p. 1985—86, pres. 1986—87), Kans. Bar Assn., Kans. Assn. Commerce and Industry (Leadership Kans. award 1983), Pittsburg Area C. of C. (bd. dirs. 1983—85, Leadership Pitts. award 1984), Pittsburg State U. Alumni Assn. (bd. dirs. 1983—88). Republican. Methodist. Avocations: travel, photography, tennis. Home: 138 S Blue Bells Ct Garden Plain KS 67050-9225*

STOVALL, FRANCES MIDDAGH, writer, preservationist; b. Lawrenceville, Ill., Dec. 7, 1921; d. John Judy and Rebecca (Fowler) Middagh; m. Jack N. Stovall, Aug. 16, 1941; children: Richard Middagh Stovall, Frances Judy S. Upchurch, John Fowler Stovall, Susan Calvert G. Carter. Student, McMurry Coll., 1938-41. Woman's Page editor Odessa (Tex.) News Times, 1937-40; reporter Abilene (Tex.) Reporter News, 1938-41. Author: Clear Springs and Limestone Ledges, A History of San Marcos and Hays County, 1986; editor: San Marcos Bicentennial Cookbook, 1976, Cottage Kitchen Cookbook, 1983, Cottage Kitchen, Second Helping, 1986, Twenty Years In Cottage Kitchen, 1996, Historical Markers in Hays County, 2003; columnist San Marcos Daily Record, 1988-2003. Founder Heritage Assn. San Marcos, 1975, bd. dirs., 1975-2003, hon. life mem., 1989—; chmn. City of San Marcos Bicentennial Commn., 1972-76, Hays County Hist. Commn., 1987-2003; initiator Main St. in San Marcos, 1988-89; founder Preservation Assocs., Inc., 1986, Friends of Hays County Hist. Commn., 1990-95. Named Woman of Yr. Beta Sigma Phi, San Marcos, 1976, 96, Vol. of Yr., Rotary Club San Marcos, 1995; recipient Tex. award for hist. preservation Tex. Hist. Commn., Austin, 1990, John Ben Shepperd Leadership award Tex. Hist. Commn., Austin, 1991, Lifetime Achievement award Tex. Hist. Commn., Austin, 1993; Preservation award named in her honor, 1999, The Frances Stovall Collection within the San Marcos City libr. dedicated in her honor, 2001. Mem. DAR, Nat. Trust for Hist. Preservation, Tex. Hist. Found., Tex. State Hist. Assn., Spring Lake Garden Club, Magna Charta Dames. Avocations: historic tours, historic research. Home: 20 Timbercrest St San Marcos TX 78666-3018

STOVALL, TERESA HILL, education educator, minister; b. Abilene, Tex., Jan. 17, 1964; d. Joe Mills Hill and Marilyn Barker MacDonald; m. Jay Marshall Stovall. BA, Tex. A&M U., 1986; MA, Southwestern Bapt. Theol. Sem., Ft. Worth, 1991, PhD, 2001. Min. edn. and adminstrn. Handley Bapt. Ch., Ft. Worth, 1988—95; min. to women Fielder Rd. Bapt. Ch., Arlington, Tex., 1995—2001; asst. prof. adult edn. and aging Southwestern Bapt. Theol. Sem., 2002—. Dir. women's program Southwestern Bapt. Theol. Sem., 2002—. Recipient Outstanding Rschr. award, So. Bapt. Conv., 2001. Mem.: Nat. Assn. Profs. Christian Edn., So. Bapt. Religious Educators Assn., Assn. Women's Ministry Profls., Nat. Assn. Ch. Bus. Adminstrn. (assoc.; cert.). Republican. Avocations: motorcycling, roller-coaster riding, travel. Office: Southwestern Bapt Theol Sem PO Box 22367 Fort Worth TX 76122 E-mail: tstovall@swbts.edu.

STOVER, CAROLYN NADINE, middle school educator; b. Martinsburg, W.Va., May 30, 1950; d. Norman Robert and Garnet Agnes (Zombro) Whetzel; m. James Stenner Stover Sr., Nov. 20, 1971; children: Heather N., James S. Jr. BA in Home Econs., Shepherd Coll., 1972; cert. in advanced studies, W.Va. U., 1978; cert. in tchg. methods, Marshall U., 1973; cert. in spl. edn., Shippensburg Coll., 1972. Cert. tchr., W.Va., N.Mex.; reg. EMT. Substitute tchr. Berkeley County Schs., Martinsburg, W.Va., 1972, adult edn. instr., 1972-77, home econs. instr., 1973-83; substitute tchr. Ruidoso (N.Mex.) Mcpl. Schs., 1984-90, child find coord. Region 9 edn. coop., 1990, life skills and at-risk educator, 1991—, coord. coun., 1991-93, mem. budget com., 1993. Elder First Presbyn. Ch., Ruidoso, 1984-90, 94-96, 2002--; sponsor Acad. Booster Club, Ruidoso, 1993—; instr. CPR, 1980. Named Outstanding Young Women of Am., 1981. Mem. NEA, Nat. Middle Sch. Assn., Ruidoso Edn. Assn. (reporter, membership chair), Ruidoso Bowling Assn. (sec. 1999-2001), Rotary (youth leadership councilor 1991—). Democrat. Avocations: cross-stitching, needlework, family, sports, youth. Home: Box 7837 PO Box 7837 Ruidoso NM 88355-7837 Office: Ruidoso Mid Sch 100 Reese Dr Ruidoso NM 88345-6016

STOVER, ELLEN L. health scientist, psychologist; b. Bklyn., Nov. 21, 1950; d. Ralph and Charlotte (Tulchin) Simon; m. Alan B. Stover, June 3, 1973; children: Elena Randall Simon, Randall Alan Simon, Samantha Anne Simon. BA with honors, U. Wis., 1972; PhD, Catholic U., 1978. Cons. NIMH, Rockville, Md., 1972-74, exec. sec. drug abuse rsch. review com., 1974-76, spl. asst. to assoc. dir. extramural programs, 1976-77, chief, small grants program, 1977-79, asst., acting & chief rsch. resources br., 1980-85, dep. dir., div. basic scis., 1985-88, dir. office AIDS, 1988-97, dir. divsn. mental disorders, behavioral rsch. and AIDS, 1997—; dir. Ctr. Mental Health Rsch. on AIDS. Co-chmn. AIDS rsch. behavioral coordinating com. NIH, 1993—. Recipient Superior Svc. award USPHS, 1987, 92, 93, Dir.'s award NIH, 1996, Presdl. Rank award, 2001. Mem. APA, Am. Psychol. Soc. Avocations: gardening, dance. Office: NIMH 6001 Executive Blvd Rm 6217 Bethesda MD 20892-0001

STOVER, LAURA ELKINS, artist; b. Exeter, N.H., Feb. 3, 1924; d. Ray Chase and Ina Laura (Nelson) Elkins; m. Alcot Haynes Stover, Nov. 23, 1944; children: Gregory Alcot Stover, Karyn Stover Lindsay, Andrew Nelson Stover. Grad. h.s., Hampton, N.H., 1942. Sec. War Prodn. Bd., Washington, 1942-43; asst. treas. Marjorie Webster Jr. Coll., Silver Springs, Md., 1943-44; sec. Dept. Agr., Washington, 1944-45; sec., asst. to curator Antique Sci. Instruments Harvard U., Cambridge, Mass., 1964-89. Founding mem. Saltbox Gallery, Topsfield, Mass., pres., 1998. Artist (books) Painting Flowers the Van Wyk Way, 2d edit., 1997, (Helen Van Wyk's) Successful Color Mixtures, rev. edit., Portraits in Oil, 1998. Mem. Topsfield Housing Authority, 1977-84. Mem. Newburyport Art Assn., Lynnfield Art Guild, Oil Painters of Am., Portrait Soc. Am., North Shore Arts Assn. (bd. dirs. 1979-87; Grumbacher Gold medal 1984, Marguerite S. Pearson Meml. award 1992, Emile A. Gruppe Meml. award 1996), Miniature Soc. Fla. (Third Place in oil Internat. Exhbn. 1996, First Place award Internat. Exhib., 2001). Avocations: braiding rugs, knitting, gardening, walking, hiking.

STOVICH, JOY, chemistry educator; b. Lubbock, Tex., July 25, 1963; d. A.L. and Doris Dean King; m. Laurence C. Stovich, Aug. 30, 1996; children: Jacob Morehead, Rebekah Morehead. BS in Chemistry, BS in Math. Edn., West Tex. State U., Canyon, 1985. Cert. environ. trainer, hazardous waste mgmt. Tchr. math. Canyon Jr. H.S., 1986-87; math./sci. tchr. San Jacinto Christian Acad., Amarillo, Tex., 1987-91; chemistry technician Mason & Hanger-Pantex, Amarillo, 1991-92, emergency response OSHA trainer, 1992-96, sect. mgr., 1996-97; instr. Traveling Chemistry Show West Tex. A&M U., Canyon, 1997—. Mem. Am. Chem. Soc., Nat. Sci. Tchrs. Assn., Sci. Tchrs. Assn. Tex. Avocations: scuba diving, reading, swimming. Home: 6403 Ridgewood Dr Amarillo TX 79109-6544 E-mail: chem4fun@cox-internet.com.

STOWE, MADELEINE, actress; b. L.A., Aug. 18, 1958; m. Brian Benben, 1982; 2 children. Films: Stakeout, 1987, Worth Winning, 1989, Tropical Snow, 1989, Revenge, 1990, The Two Jakes, 1990, Closetland, 1991, Unlawful Entry, 1992, The Last of the Mohicans, 1992, Another Stakeout, 1993, Short Cuts, 1993 (Best Supporting Actress award Nat. Soc. Film Critics), China Moon, 1993, Blink, 1994, Bad Girls, 1994, Twelve Monkeys, 1995, The Proposition, 1998, Playing By Heart, 1998, Dancing About Architecture, 1999, Impostor, 1999, The General's Daughter, 1999, We Were Soldiers, 2002, Avenging Angelo, 2002; TV movies: The Nativity, 1978, Beulah Land, 1980, The Gangster Chronicles: An American Story, 1981, Blood and Orchids, 1986, Magnificent Ambersons, 2002, Black Orchid (miniseries). Office: UTA care David Schiff 9560 Wilshire Blvd Ste 500 Beverly Hills CA 90212-2427

STOYAN, HORTENSIA RODRIGUEZ-SANCHEZ, library administrator; b. Yabucoa, P.R., June 9, 1917; d. Antonio and Juana (Sanchez) R.; m. Hector Aponte (dec.); children: Gloria, Jose. BA, U. P.R., Rio Piedras, 1943; MA, State Tchrs. Coll., 1946; MS, Columbia U., 1955. Cert. pub. librarian. Tchr. elem. and jr. H.S. Town of Juncos (P.R.) Dept. Edn., 1941-44; pub. libr. Bklyn. Pub. Library, Bklyn., 1954-58; head libr. John A. Howe Library, Albany, N.Y., 1958-65; asst. dir. Farmingdale (N.Y.) Pub. Library, 1967-77, ret., 1977. Author: History of Yabucoa, 1993; contbr. articles Cana Guarapo y Melao, 1995-98. Bd. dirs. Mentally Ill Assn., 1984-98. Mem. AAUW (bd. dirs. 1996, pres. Queens N.Y. br. 1999-2001). Avocation: writing poetry. Home: 43-01 208th St Bayside NY 11361

STRAAYER, CAROLE KATHLEEN, retired elementary education educator; b. Jackson, Mich., Jan. 4, 1934; d. Joseph and Maude Vivian (Whitney) Kerr; m. Richard Lee Straayer, Feb. 1, 1958; children: Steven Jay, Susan Kay Straayer Maxson. A, Jackson Community Coll., Mich., 1953; BS, Ea. Mich. u., 1957, MA, 1961. Cert. elem. tchr., Mich. Tchr. Napoleon (Mich.) Sch. Dist., 1954-56, Waterford (Mich.) Twp. Sch. Dist., 1957, Jackson (Mich.) Pub. Schs., 1957-98, ret., 1998—. Mem. choir 1st Presbyn. Ch., Jackson, 1983—; mem. Jackson Recycling Task Force, 2002-2003. Jackson Citizen Patriot scholar, 1971. Mem. NEA, AAUW (group leader 1989-92, chmn. edn. com. 1998-2000, program v.p. 1999-2001, pres. 2002-2004), Mich. ASCD (region 3 rep. 1989-90), Mich. Edn. Assn. (ret.), Jackson Edn. Assn. (bldg. rep., chmn. tenure com. 1974-00, mem. negotiating team 1995, bd. dirs. 1996), Jackson/Hillsdale Profl. Devel. (rep. 1988-90), Delta Kappa Gamma (pres. Beta Beta chpt. 1986-88, 98-2004, mem. state nominating com. 2001-03, state chmn. profl. affairs 2001-03, state chmn. personal growth and svcs. 2003-). Avocations: playing bridge, giving parties, tutoring at school and home. Home: 2220 Pioneer Dr Jackson MI 49201-8900

STRACK, ALISON MERWIN, neurobiologist; b. Midland, Mich., Apr. 19, 1963; d. William James and Alice (Armstrong) S. BS, U. Mich., 1985; PhD, Washington U., St. Louis, 1990. Asst. rsch. physiologist U. Calif. Sch. Medicine, San Francisco, 1990-97; rsch. fellow Merck Pharms., Rahway, NJ, 1997—. Contbr. articles to profl. jours. Grantee Am. Heart Assn., Calif. affiliate, 1993. Mem. Soc. Neurosci. Office: Merck Rsch Labs Dept Pharmacology R80Y-145 PO Box 2000 Rahway NJ 07065

STRADA, CHRISTINA BRYSON, retired humanities educator, librarian; b. Dunoon, Argyll, Scotland; d. Alexander Paul and Margaret (Spencer) Bryson; m. Joseph Anthony Strada (dec.); children: Michael, David, Elaine, Mary Margaret. AB, SUNY, Fredonia, 1968, MS, 1970; MLS, U. Buffalo, 1973. Library media specialist. Tchr. English Dunkirk (N.Y.) H.S., 1969-70, Cardinal Mindzenty H.S., Dunkirk, 1970-71, Lake Shore Cen. H.S., Angola, N.Y., 1971-72, libr., tchr., 1973-77; libr. dir. Darwin R. Barker Libr. and Mus., Fredonia, 1977-86; tchr., libr. Cassadaga (NY) Valley Sch. Dist., Fredonia, 1990—95; ret., 1995; instr. and librarian Fredonia (N.Y.) HS and BOCES Ednl. Ctr., Fredonia, 1995—2001. Instr. English composition, English lit., libr. rsch. Empire State Coll. N.Y., State Univ. Coll., Fredonia; cons. Friends of Barker Libr. and Mus., 1986—. Author short stories. Rschr. Fredonia Hist. Preservation Soc., 1986—; v.p. Friends of Barker Libr., 2001—; active Patterson Libr. Lit. Discussion Group; sec. NY State Victorian Soc., 2001—02; bd. dirs. Chautauqua County br. Lit. Vols. of Am., Dunkirk, NY, 1998—2001; bd. dirs., v.p. D.R. Barber Friends' Libr., 1997—2003. Mem. AAUW (chmn. telephone and reservations com. 1969—), NY State Libr. Assn., N.Y. State Tchr. Assn., LWV, Fredonia Shakespeare Club (v.p. 1988-89, pres. 1997-98, treas. 2002-03). Republican. Roman Catholic. Avocations: writing, reading, gardening, walking. Home: 15 Carol Ave Fredonia NY 14063-1207

STRADER, MARLENE KNOCKS, nursing educator; b. St. Louis; d. Charles Joseph and Julia (Motykaitys) Knocks; children: Ellen Marie Shocklee, Timothy James Shocklee Jr.; m. Richard P. Strader. ADN, St. Louis Comm. Coll., Meramec, Mo., 1972; BSN, St. Louis U., 1979, MSN, 1981, PhD, 1986. RN, Mo., Fla.; cert. health care risk mgr., Fla. Mem. nursing faculty So. U., Edwardsville, Ill., 1981-88, U. Mo., St. Louis, 1988-93; held rep., mem. faculty Joint Commn. on Accreditation of Health Care Orgns., Oakbrook Terrace, Ill., 1993-96. Mem. adv. bd. Compre-Health, St. Louis, 1985-96; nurse rschr. Midwest Nursing Rsch. Soc., St. Louis, 1988-91; cons. in field. Author: Role Transition to Patient Care Management, 1995. NIH grantee Nat. Ctr. for Nursing Rsch., Washington, 1990. Mem. ANA, Am. Nurses' Found. (grant 1988), Nursing Consortium St. Louis,Fla. Nurses' Assn., Sigma Theta Tau (grant 1988), Phi Kappa Phi. Avocation: gourmet cooking. Home and Office: 7226 Bryce Pt Pinellas Park FL 33782-4338

STRAHAN, JULIA CELESTINE, electronics company executive; b. Indpls., Feb. 10, 1938; d. Edgar Paul Pauley and Pauline Barbara (Myers) Shawver; m. Norman Strahan, Oct. 2, 1962 (div. 1982); children: Daniel Keven, Natalie Kay. Grad. high sch., Indpls. With Bechtel Nev./Lockheed Martin Nev. Techs., Las Vegas, 1967—; sect. head EG&G Co., 1979-83, mgr. electronics dept., 1984—. Recipient award Am. Legion, 1952, Excellence award, 1986. Mem. NAFE, Am. Nuclear Soc. (models and mentors), Internat. Platform Assn. Home: 5222 Stacey Ave Las Vegas NV 89108-3078 Office: EG&G PO Box 1912 Las Vegas NV 89125-1912 E-mail: jeweljcs@aol.com.

STRAIGHT, CATHY, editor; Dep. mng. editor Nashville Tennessean; with editor-development program Pioneer Press divsn. Knight Ridder; mng. editor features and sports St. Paul Pioneer Press, 2002—. Recipient Newsroom Supr. Recognition award, Gannett, 1999. Office: St Paul Pioneer Press 345 Cedar St Saint Paul MN 55101*

STRAIT, VIOLA EDWINA WASHINGTON, librarian; b. El Paso, Tex., Aug. 29, 1925; d. Leroy Wentworth and Viola Edwina (Wright) Washington; m. Freeman Adams, Mar. 6, 1943; 1 child, Norma Jean (Mrs. Louis Lee James); m. Clifford Moody, Jan. 8, 1950; 1 child, Viola Edwina III (Mrs. Paul M. Cunningham); m. Amos O. Strait, Dec. 9, 1972. Bus. cert., Tillotson Coll., 1946, BA, 1948; MS in Libr. Sci., U. So. Calif., 1954. Substitute tchr. El Paso Pub. Schs., 1948; sec., bookkeeper U.S.O.-YWCA, El Paso, 1948-50; libr. asst. Spl. Svcs. Libr., Ft. Bliss, Tex., 1950-53, libr., 1954-71; equal employment opportunity officer Ft. Bliss, 1971-72; dep. equal employment opportunity officer Long Beach (Calif.) Naval Shipyard, 1972-85; with Temp. Job Mart, Torrance, Calif., 1986-87; substitute tchr. Ysleta Ind. Sch. Dist., 1988-89; profl. libr. Eastwood Hts. Elem. Sch., 1989-90; sec. Shiloh Bapt. Ch., El Paso, 1991-92; br. mgr. El Paso Pub. Libr., 1992-96, retired, 1996. Host, prodr. (gospel music video with Viola Washington Strait), Time Warner TV, Cable Channel 15, 2003—04. Sec. Sunday sch. Bapt. Ch., 1956-66, 92-96, min. music, 1958-72, supr. young adult choir, 1966-72, pres. sr. choir, 1969-71; disc jockey Sta. KELP, El Paso, 1970-72; host radio show Sta. KTEP, U. Tex., El Paso, 1994-2004; hon. chmn. for ann. observance of Nat. Libr. Week, City of El Paso, 1970. Mem. ALA, Border Region Libr. Assn. (chmn. scholarship com. 1970), NAACP (sec. 1996), Alpha Kappa Alpha. Democrat. Baptist. Avocations: playing the piano and organ, public speaking, reading, ocean view dining. Home: 210 E Ocean Blvd Unit 1209 Long Beach CA 90802-4861

STRAND, JOAN H. law educator; b. 1950; BA, George Washington U., JD, 1975. Bar: D.C. 1976. Prof. law Nat. Law Ctr. George Washington U., Washington. Mem. ABA, D.C. Bar Assn. (pres.-elect, sec. 1993-94, bd. govs., family law sect., pub. svc. activities com.), D.C. Bar Found. (Jerrold Scoutt prize 1997). Office: George Washington U Nat Law Ctr Washington DC 20052-0001

STRAND, MARION DELORES, social service administrator; b. Kansas City, Mo., Dec. 19, 1927; d. Henry Franklin and Julia Twyman (Noland) Pugh; m. Robert Carmen Scipioni, Aug. 2, 1947 (dec. 1984); children: Mark, Brian, Roberta, Laura, Steven, Mary,Angela, Julie, Victor, Robert, Lawrence; m. Donald John Strand, Sept. 1, 1985. BA, U. Kans., 1948; MS, SUNY, Brockport, 1975; postgrad., Rochester Div. Sch., 1998—. Counselor N.Y. Dept. Labor, Rochester, 1971-75, 77-79; regulatory adminstr. N.Y. Dept. Social Svcs., Rochester, 1976-77, 79-81; pres. Greater Rochester Svcs., Inc. (doing bus. as Scribes & Scripts), 1982—. Founder Ctr. for Law Access and Document Preparation. Columnist, local newspaper. Active polit. campaigns for women candidates, 1981—; UN envoy Unitarian Ch., Rochester, 1988-92; fin. chair William Warfield Scholarship Com., Rochester, 1988-90; chair bd. govt. affairs Genesee Valley Arthritis Found., Rochester, 1988-90; mem. parade com. 95/75 Celebration of Monroe County, 1995; mem. Lyell Av. Revitalization Com.; Congl. candidate 28th Congl. Dist., N.Y., 1998; candidate 28th Congrl. Dist. N.Y., 1998; mem. Lead Free is Best for Me Coalition; sec., bd. dirs. Hidden Valley Homeowner's Assn.; active Choice and the Environment Task Force, First Unitarian Ch., Rochester; founding mem. Rochester Religious Coalition Equal Marriage. Mem. NOW (1st pres. Greater Rochester 1982-83, pres. child care com. Greater Rochester sect. 1987-88, current sec. and mem. local organizing com. 1998 Women's rights Conv. and Vision Summit, chair family issues task force), AAUW, Paralegals of Rochester, DAR, Greater Rochester C. of C. (legis. com., small bus. coun. 1987—, bd. dirs. women's coun. 1981-91, pres. 1989-90), Alliance Ind. Artists (treas.), Nat. Network Family Law Policy (organizing), Susan B. Anthony Rep. Women's Club (program com., 1st v.p. 1994, co-chair Greater Rochester Coalition for Choice 1994-95) Golden Girls Investment Club (founder), Phi Beta Kappa, Psi Chi. Avocations: tennis, golf, art, organ playing. Home and Office: Greater Rochester Svcs Inc 50 Hidden Valley Rd Rochester NY 14624-2301 E-mail: mstrand@rochester.rr.com.

STRANDJORD, M. JEANNINE, telecommunications industry executive; B in Acctg. and Bus. Adminstrn., U. Kans. CPA. V.p. fin. Macy's Midwest; with Kans. city Power & Light Co., Ernst and Whinney; v.p. fin. and distrbn. AmeriSource, Inc. (subs. Sprint), 1985—90, controller, 1986—90, sr. v.p., treas., 1990—98, sr. v.p. fin. global markets group, 1998—2003; sr. v.p. fin. svcs. Sprint Corp., 2003, sr. v.p., chief integration officer, 2003—. Bd. dirs. Am. Century Mutual Funds, DST Sys., Inc., Euronet Worldwide. Trustee Rockhurst U. Office: 6200 Spring Pkwy Overland Park KS 66251*

STRANG, HEIDI CORDOVA, art educator; b. Tacoma, Wash., Oct. 25, 1964; m. Michael Strang. BA, U. No. Colo., 1988; MA, U. Denver, 1996. Instr. Rocky Mountain Coll. Art & Design, Denver, 1997—; curatorial asst. Denver Art Mus., Denver, 1993—97; asst. curator Captiva Corp., Denver, 1993—95; instr. Aims C.C., Greeley, Colo., 1989—90, Met. State Coll., Denver, 2000; intern, Edn. Dept. Denver Art Mus., 1987. Group leader Artistic Italy, Independant, Denver, 2000—, Strang's City of Lights, Independant, Denver, 2001—; trainee EF Ednl. Tours, Paris, 2001; com. mem. Denver Art Mus., 1985—; mentor art students U. Denver, 2001; judge student exhbn. Mapleton Pub. Sch. Dist., Denver, 1999—2000, Weld County Sch. Dist., Greeley, 1999. Contbr. articles to profl. jours. Democrat. Avocations: dogs, travel, reading. Personal E-mail: Heidi_Strang@hotmail.com.

STRANG, RUTH HANCOCK, pediatric educator, pediatric cardiologist, priest; b. Bridgeport, Conn., Mar. 11, 1923; d. Robert Hallock Wright and Ruth (Hancock) S. BA, Wellesley Coll., 1944, postgrad., 1944-45; MD, N.Y. Med. Coll., 1949; MDiv, Seabury Western Theol. Sem., 1993. Diplomate Am. Bd. Pediat.; ordained deacon Episc. Ch., 1993, priest, 1994. Intern Flower and Fifth Ave. Hosp., N.Y.C., 1949-50, resident in pediat., 1950-52; mem. faculty N.Y. Med. Coll., 1952-57; fellow cardiology Babies Hosp., N.Y.C., 1956-57, Harriet Lane Cardiac Clinic, Johns Hopkins Hosp., Balt., 1957-59, Children's Hosp., Boston, 1959-62; mem. faculty U. Mich., Univ. Hosp., Ann Arbor, 1962-89, prof. pediatrics, 1970-89, prof. emeritus, 1989—; priest-in-charge St. Johns Episcopal Ch., Howell, Mich., 1994—. Dir. pediat. Wayne County Gen. Hosp., Westland, Mich, 1965-85; mem. staff U. Mich. Hosps., 1962-89; mem. med. adv. com. Wayne County chpt. Nat. Cystic Fibrosis Rsch. Found., 1966-80, chmn. med. adv. com. nat. found., Detroit, 1971-78; cons. cardiology Plymouth (Mich.) State Home and Tng. Sch., 1970-81. Author: Clinical Aspects of Operable Heart Disease, 1968; contbr. numerous articles to profl. jours. Mem. citizen's adv. coun. Juvenile Ct., Ann Arbor, 1968—76; mem. med. adv. bd. Ann Arbor Continuing Edn. Dept., 1968—77; v.p. Am. Heart Assn. Mich., 1989, pres., 1991; bd. dirs. Livingston Cmty. Hospice, 1995—99, Emrich Episcopal Conf. Ctr., 1998—; mem. Diocesan Com. for World Relief, Detroit, 1970—72; trustee Episcopal Med. Chaplaincy, Ann Arbor, 1971—96; mem. bishop's com. St. Aidan's Episc. Ch., 1966—69, sec., 1966—68, vestry, 1973—76, 1978—80, 1984—86, 1990—91, sr. warden, 1975—76, 1978, 1986, 1990; del. Episc. Diocesan Conv., 1980, 1991; mem. Congl. Life Circle Episcopal Diocese Mich., 1995—2001, mem. loans and grants com., 1995—99, mem. com. on reference ann. diocesan conv., 1995-98, chmn., 1996; mem. Diocese Mich. Clergy Family Project, 1996—98; co-dean Huron Valley area coun. Diocese Mich., 1998—2000; bd. trustees Ecumenical Theol. Sem., 1996—, chair acad. affairs com., 2000—; mem. Congl. Devel. Commn., 2001—03. Mem. AMA, Am. Acad. Pediat., Am. Coll. Cardiology, Mich. Med. Soc., Washtenaw County Med. Soc., N.Y. Acad. Medicine, Am. Heart Assn., Women's Rsch. Club (membership sec. 1966-67), Ambulatory Pediat. Assn., Am. Assn. Child Care in Hosps., Am. Assn. Med. Colls., Assn. Faculties of Pediat. Nurse Assn./Practitioners Programs (pres. 1978-81, exec. com. 1981-84), Episc. Clergy Assn. Mich., Northside Assn. Ministries (pres. 1975, 76, 79-80). Home: 4500 E Huron River Dr Ann Arbor MI 48105-9335 Office Phone: 517-546-3660. E-mail: sjec@cac.net.

STRANSKY, MARIA SOLEDAD, psychotherapist; d. Theodore Jere and Ana D. Stransky. BA, U. Notre Dame, 1996; MA, U. N.C., Charlotte, 1999. Cert. sex offender treatment provider Commonwealth of Va., 2002. Psychology intern Cleve. Ctr., Shelby, NC, 1997—98; grants devel. intern Mecklenburg County Health, Mental Health, and Cmty. Svcs., Charlotte, NC, 1998—99; psychologist Mental Health Unit, Brunswick Correctional Ctr., Lawrenceville, Va., 1999—2000; psychologist sr. Sex Offender Residential Treatment Program, Brunswick Correctional Ctr., Lawrenceville, Va., 2000—. Counselor Behavioral Awareness Ctr., Richmond, Va., 2002—. Mem.: APA (assoc.), Am. Correctional Assn., Assn. for the Treatment of Sexual Abusers. Office: Brunswick Correctional Ctr 1147 Planters Rd Lawrenceville VA 23868 Personal E-mail: msstrans@earthlink.net. E-mail: stranskyms@vadoc.state.va.us.

STRATA, JANE, music educator; b. Crestline, Ohio, Dec. 13, 1959; d. Arden Findlay and Janet Ellen High; m. Lewis Paul King, Apr. 21, 1985 (div. Aug. 1991); 1 child, John David King ; m. Jeffrey Lynn Strata, June 5, 1994; children: Melissa Strata Joseph, Michael, Alexandra, Nicholas. MusB, Heidelberg Coll. Substitute tchr. grades 5-6 Baumholder (Germany) Schs.; vocal music tchr. grades 4-12 Ayersville H.S., Defiance, Ohio. Home: 810 Washington Ave Defiance OH 43512-2851

STRATAS, TERESA (ANASTASIA STRATAKI), opera singer, soprano; b. Toronto, Ont., Can., May 26, 1938; Student of Irene Jessner, 1956-59; grad., Faculty Music, U. Toronto, 1959; LLD (hon.), McMaster U., 1986, U. Toronto, 1994; hon. degree, Juilliard Sch. Music, 1995, Eastman Sch. Music, 1998, U. Rochester, 1998. Winner Met. Opera auditions, 1959; major roles in opera houses throughout world include: Mimi in La Bohème; Tatiana in Eugene Onegin; Susanna in The Marriage of Figaro; Nedda in Pagliacci; Marenka in The Bartered Bride; Three Heroines in II Trittico; Violetta in La Traviata; title role in Rusalka; Jennie in Mahagonny; created title role in completed version of Lulu (Alban Berg), Paris Grand Opera, 1979; film appearances Kaiser von Atlantis, Seven Deadly Sins; Zefirelli's La Traviata, Salome, Lulu, Paganini, Zarewitsch, Eugene Oregin; Broadway debut in Rags, 1986; creator the role of Marie Antoinette Ghosts of Versailles world premiere Met. Opera, 1992; sang both female leading roles Il Tabarro, Pagliacci double bill opening Met. Opera, 1994, numerous recs. including Richard Strauss' Salomé, Songs of Kurt Weill. Decorated Order of Can.; recipient 3 Grammy awards, Emmy award, Drama Desk award, 1986, 3 Grammy nominations, Tony nomination, 1986, Tiffany award, 1994, Highest Paedeia award, 1996, Gemini award, 1997; named Performer of Yr., Can. Music Council, 1979. Address: The Ansonia 2109 Broadway New York NY 10023-2106

STRATE, JAN NICOLE (NIKI STRATE), contractor; b. Bassett, Nebr., Nov. 21, 1944; d. Howard Weir and Marian Evelyn (Wiese) Thompson; m. Paul Dean Peister, July 20, 1969 (div. Feb. 1984); children: Justin Paul, Jordan Nicole; m. James Richard Strate, Aug. 31, 1985. BA in Speech and Drama, Wayne State Coll., 1972, MS in Counseling magna cum laude, 1977. Clk. Meadowlark Gifts, Kearney, Nebr., 1965-66, Ransom House Gifts, Norfolk, Nebr., 1966-69; tchr. Norfolk Pub. Schs., 1970-84, Northeat C.C., Norfolk, 1970-84; supr. customer svc. Merchants Corp. Am., Buena Park, Calif., 1985-87; owner, v.p. Cal-Best Constrn. Co., Anaheim, Calif., 1987—. Republican. Episcopalian. Avocations: dance, acting, reading, cooking, entertaining, theatre, music. Home: 6519 E Joshua Tree Ave Orange CA 92867-2460

STRATING, SHARON L. elementary school educator, professional staff developer, educational consultant; b. Jamestown, ND, Jan. 20, 1949; d. Walter and Evelyn Darlene (Lang) Remmick; m. Rick Donald Strating, Dec. 24, 1978 (presently divorced); children: Heather Dawn, Amber Nicole, Ashley Renee. BS in Secondary Edn., S.W. Mo. State U., 1971; MEd in Sci. Edn., N.W. Mo. State U., 1992. Cert. elem. tchr., Mo. Tchr. Cassville R-III Sch., 1971-76, Savannah R-III Sch. Sys., Mo., 1976-91; instr. 4th grade Horace Mann Lab. Sch., Maryville, Mo., 1991—2003; profl. staff developer Regional Profl. Devel. Ctr., N.W. Mo. State U., Maryville, 2003—. Facilitator for Environ. Edn. Pilot Project Kans. U., Lawrence; co-chair EPA Pollution Prevention Adv. Task Force; mem. biol. sci. curriculum study Elem. Tchr. Module Project, 1993; instr. for coll. practicum students; Map 2000 Sr. Leader for performance-based assessment sys., Mo., 1994—. Author: Living the Constitution Through the Eyes of the Newspaper, 1987, Tabloid Teaching Tool, 6 edits., 1986-91; tchr. guides in lit. revised editions for Sadako and the Thousand Paper Cranes, The Kid in the Red Jacket, Missing Gator of Gumbo Limbo, Owls in the Family, Where the Waves Break: Life at the Edge of the Sea, 2000-2001; author: Open the Eyes of Children to the World of Literacy Through Comprehensive Literacy, Prof. Develop. Program, 2002. Chairperson March of Dimes, 1972-76, Cystic Fibrosis, 1972-78; scout leader Brownies, 1976-77; exec. bd. dirs. PTA, 1976-82, fund raising chairperson, 1976-83; program chairperson presch. PTA, 1976-80;chairperson community environ. activities, 1976—, Adopt a Hwy. Program, 1976-91; mem. Mo. Stream Team Effort, 1976—. Recipient Nat. Pres. Environ. Youth award, 1988, 89, Presdl. award State of Mo., 1992, 93, Nat. Presdl. award, 1992-93; named Mo. State Tchr. of Yr., 1990-91, Disney Salutes the Am. Tchr. award, 1995. Mem. Nat. Hist. Soc., Internat. Reading Assn., Nat. Bd. for Profl. Tching. Standards and Mid.-Age Child in Sci., Nat. Sci. Tchrs. Assn., Nat. Assn. Lab. Schs. (sec. 1994-95), Sci. Tchrs. Mo. Lutheran. Avocations: travel, ecology, creative writing, motivational speaking, arts and crafts. Office: Northwest Mo State U McKemy Ctr for Lifelong Learning Maryville MO 64468 Home: 3A Faustiana Pl Maryville MO 64468 Office Phone: 660-562-1515.

STRATMAN, DEBORAH, filmmaker, film and video educator; BFA, Sch. of the Art Inst. of Chgo., 1990; MFA, Calif. Inst. of the Arts, 1995. Adj. asst. prof. Film, Video and New Media, 1998; filmmaker and adj. asst., prof. film and video Sch. of Art Inst. of Chgo., 1998—. John Simon Guggenheim Meml. Found., 2003. Office: 37 South Wabash Chicago IL 60603-3103

STRATTON, EVELYN LUNDBERG, judge; b. Bangkok, Feb. 25, 1953; came to U.S., 1971 (parents Am. citizens); d. Elmer John and Corrine Sylvia (Henricksen) Sahlberg; children: Luke Andrew, Tyler John; m. Jack A. Lundberg. Student, LeTourneau Coll., Longview, Tex., 1971-74; AA, U. Fla., 1979, BA, U. Akron, 1976; JD, Ohio State U., 1978. Bar: Ohio 1979, U.S. Dist. Ct. (so. dist.) Ohio 1979, U.S. Ct. Appeals (6th cir.) 1983. Assoc. Hamilton, Kramer, Myers & Cheek, Columbus, 1979-85; ptnr. Wesp, Osterkamp & Stratton, 1985-88; judge Franklin County Ct. Common Pleas, 1989-96; justice Ohio State Supreme Ct., 1996—. Vis. prof. Nat. Jud. Coll., 1997—; spkr. legal seminars. Contbr. articles to profl. jours. Trustee Ohio affiliate Nat. Soc. to Prevent Blindness, 1989—, bd. dirs., trustee Columbus Coun. World Affairs, 1990-99, chmn. bd. dirs., 1999—; bd. dirs., trustee Dave Thomas Adoption Found., 1996—, ArChSafe Found., 1997—; mem. women's bd. Zephyrus League Cen. Ohio Lung Assn., 1989—; mem. Alliance Women Cmty. Corrections, 1993—. Recipient Gold Key award LeTourneau Coll., Gainesville, Fla., 1974, Svc. commendation Ohio Ho. of Reps., 1984, Scholar of Life award St. Joseph's Orphanage, 1998. Mem. ABA, ATLA, Columbus Bar Assn. (bd. govs. 1984-88, 90—, lectr.), Ohio Bar Assn. (jud. adminstrv. and legal reform com., coun. dels. 1992-96, Ohio Cmty. Corrections Orgn. (trustee 1995—), Columbus Bar Found. (trustee 1986-91, officer, sec. 1986-87, v.p. 1987-88), Am. Inns of Ct., Women Lawyers Franklin County, Phi Alpha Delta (pres. 1982-83). Office: Supreme Ct Ohio 30 E Broad St Fl 3 Columbus OH 43215*

STRATTON, JESSIE GRAY, state legislator; b. Swarthmore, Pa., Feb. 18, 1947; d. Caleb Allen and Jeannette (Poole) S.; m. Richard Arthur Stratton, 1970; children: Christopher Caleb, Susan Elise, David Pickett. BA, Earlham Coll., 1969. Tchr. social studies Olney Friends Sch., Barnesville, Ohio, 1970-76; mem. Canton Dem. Town Com., 1982—, vice chmn., 1987—; mem. Conn. Ho. of Reps., Hartford, 1989—. Del. Dem. Nat. Conv., 1984, 88. Del. Dem. Nat. Conv., 1984, 88; bd. dirs.,mem. exec. com. Sane/Freeze Campaign for Global Security, 1985-89. Home: 33 Bahre Corner Rd Canton CT 06019-2230 Office: Conn Ho of Reps State Capitol Hartford CT 06106

STRATTON, KATHLEEN R. medical association administrator; PhD. Dir. divsn. health promotion and disease prevention Inst. Medicine NAS, sr. program officer, 1999—2002; study dir. Immunization Safety Rev. Comm., Inst. of Medicine, 2002—. Office: Inst Medicine Foundry Bldg 1055 Thomas Jefferson St NW Washington DC 20007-5259 also: 2101 Constitution Ave NW Washington DC 20418-0007

STRATTON, MARGARET ADELE, psychologist; d. Maurice Gordon Smith and JoAnn Simpson; m. Steven L. Stratton, Aug. 10, 1973; children: Emily Diane, Brian Steven. D of psychology, Argosy U., ASPP, 1995—2002. Psychology extern Graydon Manor, Leesburg, Va., 1996—97, Balt. VA Hosp./ADTU, 1997—98; psychology intern CSPP/Quality Group Homes, Fresno, Calif., 1998—99; psychologist Westview Psychol. Services, Rockville, Md., 2000—. Mem.: APA. Immanuels Church. Avocations: running, travel, gardening, reading, writing. Office: Westview Psychological Services 932 Hungerford Dr Ste 27 Rockville MD 20850 Personal E-mail: maggielora@prodigy.net.

STRATTON, MARGARET ANNE, minister; b. Concordia, Kans., Oct. 10, 1940; d. Charles Edward and Marie Teresa Kier; m. Mick Stratton, June 9, 1973; children: James, Grace. BS in Home Econs., Kans. State U., 1973; M of Theology, Caribbean Comty. Ministerial Acad., Orlando, Fla., 1994; M of Divinity, So. Meth. U., 2000. Ordained elder United Meth. Ch., 2003. Pastor United Meth. Diamond Hill Parish and Mission, Ft. Worth, 2000—, also bd. dirs. Bd. dirs. Johnson Hill Children's Program, Eutaw, Ala., 1993—95. Recipient grants in field. Mem.: Nat. Assn. United Methodist Evangelists. Avocation: wood sculpting and carving. Office: Diamond Hill United Meth Ch and Mission 3005 Oscar Ave Fort Worth TX 76106 Office Phone: 817-626-0620. Office Fax: 817-626-0620.

STRATTON, MARIANN, retired naval nursing administrator; b. Houston, Apr. 6, 1945; d. Max Millard and Beatrice Agnes (Roemer) S.; m. Lawrence Mallory Stickney, nov. 15, 1977 (dec.). BSN, BA in English, Sacred Heart Dominican Coll., 1966; MA in Mgmt., Webster Coll., 1977; MSN, U. Va., 1981. Cert. adult nurse practitioner. Ensign USN, 1966, advanced through grades to rear adm., 1991; patient care coord. Naval Regional Med. Ctr., Charleston, S.C., 1981-83; nurse corps plans officer Naval Med. Command, Washington, 1983-86; dir. nursing svcs. U.S. Naval Hosp., Naples, Italy, 1986-89, Naval Hosp., San Diego, 1989-91; chief pers. mgmt. Bur. Medicine & Surgery, Washington, 1991-94; dir. USN Nurse Corps, Washington, 1991-94; ret. Oct. 1, 1994 USN, 1994. Decorated Disting. Svc. medal, Meritorious Svc. medal with two stars, Naval Achievement medal. Mem. Interagy. Inst. of Fed. Health Care Execs., Am. Volksporting Assn., Tex. Wanders, D'Vine Women, Garden Vols. of South Tex.

STRATTON, PAULINE A. former elementary education educator, alderman; b. Chgo., Feb. 18, 1946; d. Sam Costa and Helene (Lazaris) Stavrakas; m. George William Stratton, June 25, 1967; children: Gina Marie, Paul Kevin. B of Edn., Nat. Coll. Edn., 1967. Cert. tchr. grades K-9. Primary tchr. Worth (Ill.) Sch. Dist. # 127, 1967-70, substitute tchr., 1970-91, North Palos Sch. Dist. # 117, Palos Hills/Hickory Hills, Ill., 1976-87; alderman 2d ward City of Palos Hills, 1987—. Mem. lay adv. bd. S.W. Coop. Spl. Edn., Ill., South Met. Assn. Mem. sch. bd. North Palos Sch. Dist. # 117, Hickory Hills, 1983-91; vol., bd. dirs. Am. Cancer Soc.; vol. Diabetes Assn. Mem. Ill. Congress Parents and Tchrs. (cert. hon. life mem.), Maids of Athena (past grand pres.). Greek Orthodox. Avocations: walking, helping people. Home: 10315 S Alta Dr Palos Hills IL 60465-1705 Office: City of Palos Hills 10335 S Roberts Rd Palos Hills IL 60465-1929

STRAUB, SUSAN MONICA, special education educator; b. Tampa, Fla., Jan. 31, 1954; d. Paul Ferdinand and Betty Hew (Wellacott) S. AA, Hillsborough Community Coll., 1975; BA, U. S. Fla., 1978. Lifeguard, swimming instr. Tampa Recreation Dept., 1970-74 summers, pool mgr., 1975-76 summers, office asst. sec., 1977-78 summers; tchr. Hillsborough Assn. Retarded Citizens, Tampa, 1978-79, Hillsborough County Sch. Bd., Tampa, 1979—, Sch. of Hope, 1979-81, Mango Elem. Sch., 1981-85, Lopez Elem Sch., Seffner, Fla., 1985-93, Wilson Elem. Sch., Plant City, Fla., 1993-98, Mann Mid. Sch., Brandon, Fla., 1998-2000, Armwood H.S., Seffner, Fla., 2000—. Coach Spl. Olympics, Tampa, 1980, 2000—, games ofcl., 1982, steering com., Hillsborough County, 1984-92. Sec., treas. Superstar Bowling League for Handicapped, Tampa, 1988-89, 1st v.p., 1989-91. Recipient Spl. Olympics award Hillsborough County, State of Fla., 1980; named Vol. of Yr. Mass. Mutual, 1982, Coach of Yr. Hillsborough County Spl. Olympics, 1982, Tchr. of Yr. U. So. Fla. Alumni Assn., 1990. Mem. Coun. Exceptional Children (hospitality chair, Dept. Exceptional Student Edn. Person of Yr. 1987-88, Chpt. Tchr. of Yr. 1990), Soroptimist Internat. (1st v.p., 2d v.p. 1990-91, Team Leader 1985-91, 92-93). Democrat. Roman Catholic. Avocations: soccer, swimming. Home: 517 Somerstone Dr Valrico FL 33594- Office: Armwood H S 12000 Hwy 92 Seffner FL 33584-3418

STRAUMANIS, JOAN, academic administrator; b. N.Y.C., Feb. 10, 1937; d. Herbert S. and Mollie (Brandt) Cole; m. Irwin H. Pomerantz, June 25, 1956 (div. 1969); children: Rebecca, Joel; m. Eric R. Straumanis, June 7, 1969 (dec. 1996); 1 child, Andrei. BA Polit. Sci., Math., Antioch Coll., 1957; MS math., U. Colo.; PhD Philosophy, U. Md., 1974. Prof. Denison U., Granville, Ohio, 1971-82; acad. dean, prof. Kenyon Coll., Gambier, Ohio, 1982-86; dean faculty, prof. Rollins Coll., Winter Park, Fla., 1986-92; program officer Fund for Improvement of Postsecondary Edn. U.S. Dept. Edn., Washington, 1992—95; dean arts and scis. Lehigh U., Bethlehem, Pa., 1995—98; program officer Fund for Improvement of Postsecondary Edn. U.S. Dept. Edn., Washington, 1998—2002; pres. Antioch Coll., Yellow Springs, Ohio, 2002—. Office: Antioch Coll Pres Office 795 Livermore St Yellow Springs OH 45387*

STRAUS, A. SUSAN, volunteer; b. Chgo., Aug. 16, 1950; d. Herman and Ruth Krisky Straus. BA, Northeastern Ill. U., 1973; cert. paralegal, Roosevelt U., 1985. Cert. notary pub. Ill. Mail supr. Corboy and Demetrio, Chgo. Anti-war activist Peace Action, Chgo., 2000—. Mem.: NOW (pres. Chgo. chpt. 1997, 1998, v.p. Chgo. chpt. 1996, bd. dirs. 1997—, mem. edn. legal fund 2002—, sec. working women history project 2000—01, pres. working women history project 2002—).

STRAUS, KATHLEEN NAGLER, education administrator, consultant; b. N.Y.C., Dec. 3, 1923; d. Maurice and Mildred (Kohn) Nagler; m. Everet M. Straus, May 29, 1948 (dec. Nov. 1967); children: Peter R., Barbara L. BA in Econs., Hunter Coll., 1944; postgrad., Columbia U., 1944-45, Am. U., 1946-47, Wayne State U., 1976-78. Various positions, l944-50, 66; dep. dir. Model Neighborhood Agy., City of Detroit, l968-70; dir. social svcs. Southeastern Mich. Coun. Govts., Detroit, 1970-74; staff coord. Edn. Task Force, Detroit, 1974-75; exec. dir. People and Responsible Orgns. for Detroit, 1975-76; staff dir. edn. com. Mich. Senate, Lansing, 1976-79; assoc. exec. dir. Mich. Assn. Sch. Bds., Lansing, 1979-86; dir. community rels. and devel. Ctr. for Creative Studies, Detroit, 1986-87, pres., 1987-91; mem. Mich. Bd. Edn., 1992—, pres., 2003. Mem. Mich. Bd. for Pub. Jr. and C.C.s, Lansing, 1980-92, v.p., 1989, pres., 1991; cons. Met. Columbus (Ohio) Schs. Com., 1975-76; mem.. steering com. Mich. Edn. Seminars, 1979-86; mem. Adv. Com. on Higher Edn. Needs in S.W. Mich., 1971-72, Ad Hoc Com. on Equal Access to Higher Edn., 1970-71, Citizens Action Com. on Sch. Fin. Contbr. articles to profl. jours. Active numerous civic orgns.; vice chmn. downtown br. Met. Detroit YWCA, 1970-74; bd. dirs. Citizens for Better Care, Inc., 1973-78; mem. edn. com. New Detroit, Inc., 1972—; trustee Detroit Sci. Ctr., Inc., 1975—; founder, pres. Mich. Tax Info. Coun., 1982—; v.p. bd. dirs. Univ. Cultural Ctr. Assn., 1986-91; trustee Comprehensive Health Planning Coun. Southeastern Mich., 1977-78; mem. Wayne County Art and History Commn., 1988; co-chmn. Nat. Arts Program, 1987-88. Recipient Amity citation Congress, Detroit, 1966, Disting. Community Svc. award Am. Jewish Com., 1988, Disting. Community Svc. award Common Coun., Detroit, 1976, resolution Mich. Ho. of Reps., 1986, Mich. Senate, 1988, Educator of Yr. Wayne State U., 1999, Disting. Warrior award Detroit Urban League, 2000; named to Mich. Edn. Hall of Fame, 1997; inducted into Mich. Women's Hall of Fame, 2000. Mem. LWV (pres. Detroit 1961-63), Alpha Chi Alpha.. Democrat. Avocations: travel, theater, concerts. Home: 8801 Kingswood St Detroit MI 48221-1569 Office: State Bd Edn PO Box 30008 Lansing MI 48909-7508

STRAUS, LORNA PUTTKAMMER, biology educator; b. Chgo., Feb. 15, 1933; d. Ernst Wilfred and Helen Louise (Monroe) Puttkammer; m. Francis Howe Straus II, June 11, 1955; children: Francis, Helen, Christopher, Michael. BA magna cum laude, Radcliffe Coll., 1955; MS, U. Chgo., 1960, PhD, 1962. Rsch. assoc. dept. anatomy U. Chgo., 1962-64, instr., 1964-67, asst. prof., 1967-73, assoc. prof., 1973-87, prof., 1987—, asst. dean, then dean students Coll., 1967-82, dean admissions Coll., 1975-80, univ. marshal, 1999—. Trustee Radcliffe Coll., Cambridge, Mass., 1973-83; chmn. Cmty. Found., Mackinac Island Mich., 1994—. Recipient silver medal Coun. for Advancement and Support Edn., 1987. Mem.: North Ctrl. Assn. (commr. 1998—, pres.-elect 2001—02, pres. 2002—), Harvard U. Alumni Assn. (bd. dirs. 1980—83), Phi Beta Kappa. Avocations: travel, gardening. Home: 5642 S Kimbark Ave Chicago IL 60637-1606 Office: U Chgo 5845 S Ellis Ave Chicago IL 60637-1476 E-mail: l-straus@uchicago.edu.

STRAUSS, DOROTHY BRANDFON, marriage and family therapist; b. Bklyn. BA, Bklyn. Coll., 1932; MA, NYU, 1937, PhD, 1963. Diplomate Am. Bd. Sexology, Am. Psychotherapy Assn. Instr. Hunter Coll./CUNY, 1960-63; prof. Kean U., 1963-77; pvt. practice Bklyn. and, N.J., 1970—. Clin. prof. psychiatry Downstate Med. Ctr., SUNY, Bklyn., 1974-88; assoc. dir. Ctr. for Human Sexuality, 1974-82; mem. NIMH rsch. team U. Pa., 1973-82; guest lectr. Menninger Clinic, 1990. Contbr. chpts. to Understanding Human Behavior in Health and Illness; contbr. articles to profl. jours. and self help and psychol. web mags. Fellow Am. Assn. Clin. Sexologists (founding); mem. APA, Am. Assn. for Marital and Family Therapy (clin. mem. 1971—, supr. 1981—, presenter nat. confs., accreditation site vis.), Am. Assn. Sex Therapists, Counselors and Educators (chair task force on supervision 1984-86, chair supr. cert. com. 1986-93, chair cert. steering com. 1992-98, Disting. Svc. award 1998), Soc. for Clin. and Exptl. Hypnosis, Internat. Soc. Poets (Disting. Mem.), Kappa Delta Pi. Home and Office: 1414 Bay Shore Blvd Tampa FL 33611 E-mail: dbstrauss@aol.com.

STRAUSS, GWEN B. writer, editor; b. Deschapelles, Haiti, May 19, 1963; d. Julian Max Strauss and Katie Cowles Nichols; m. Jody Gerard Jenkins, June 22, 1996; children: Noah Jenkins, Sophie Jenkins, Eliza Jenkins. BA in Poetry, Hampshire Coll., 1986; MA in Edn., Wheelock Coll., 1987. Tchg. asst. Park Sch., Boston, 1986—87; freelance writer France, 1990—2003; editl. asst. Frank Books, Paris, 1992; editor Design Press, Savannah, Ga., 2002—. Editl. cons. So. Poetry Rev., Savannah, 2003. Author: (poetry book) Trail of Stones, 1989, (children's book) Night Shimmy, 1991; contbr. short stories and poetry to various lit. jours. Finalist Nat. Poetry Series, 1995, Allen Ginsburg Poetry prize, 2003; recipient hon. mention, Atlanta Rev., 2001. Mem.: Authors Guild, Amnesty Internat., Planned Parenthood. Democrat. Avocations: gardening, sailing. Office: Design Press SCAD Savannah GA 31404 E-mail: gbs0885@aol.com.

STRAUSS, HARLEE SUE, environmental consultant; b. New Brunswick, N.J., June 19, 1950; d. Robert Lemuel and Helene (Marcus) S. BA, Smith Coll., 1972; PhD, U. Wis., 1979. Postdoctoral fellow dept. biology MIT, Cambridge, 1979-81; congrl. sci. fellow U.S. House of Reps., Washington, 1981-83; spl. asst. Am. Chem. Soc., Washington, 1983-84; spl. cons. Environ. Corp., Washington, 1984-85; rsch. assoc. Ctr. for Tech., Policy and Indsl. Devel. MIT, Cambridge, 1985-86, rsch. affiliate, 1986-92; sr. assoc. Gradient Corp., Cambridge, 1986-88; pres. H. Strauss Assocs., Inc., Natick, Mass., 1988—. Exec. dir. Silent Spring Inst., Inc., 1994-95; adj. assoc. prof. Sch. Pub. Health, Boston U., 1990-94; lectr. Sch. Medicine, Tufts U., Boston, 1988-95; mem. steering com. Boston Risk Assessment Group, 1986-95. Co-editor, author: Risk Assessment in Genetic Engineering, 1991; author: Biotechnology Regulations, 1986; author book chpts. in field. Active Instl. Biosafety Com., Army Rsch. Lab., Natick, 1989—94, Army Sci. Bd., 1994—2001. Mem. AAAS, Am. Chem. Soc., Am. Soc. Microbiology, Assn. for Women in Sci. (chmn. com. New England chpt. 1986-88, co-chmn. legis. com. 1985-93), Biophys. Soc. (chmn. com. 1983-84, Congl. Sci. fellow 1981-83), Soc. for Risk Analysis (pres. New England chpt. 1991-92, pres.-elect 1995-2000). Jewish. Avocations: travel, hiking. Office: H Strauss Assocs Inc 21 Bay State Rd Natick MA 01760-2942 E-mail: hstrauss@aol.com.

STRAUSS, MARILYN SHEPERD, public relations executive; b. Cleve., Dec. 16, 1924; d. Reuben and Beatrice (Lichtenberg) Sheperd; m. Robert J. Kahn, Dec. 23, 1945 (div. Oct. 1990); children: Sheperd, Elizabeth; m. Robert W. Strauss, Nov. 15, 1991. Student, U. Ill., 1942-43. Pres. Guidance Sys., Cleve., 1985—. Democrat. Jewish. Home and Office: 3084 Richmond Rd Beachwood OH 44122-3247

STRAUSS, ROSEMARIE, medical/surgical nurse; m. Alfred John Strauss, Mar. 15, 1957; children: Kenneth John, Pamela Alice Gerth. BSN, Trenton State Coll., 1962. RN Germany, cert. sch. nurse, N.J.; tchr. N.J. RN USAF, Wiesbaden, 1955—56; RN, charge nurse St. Francis Hosp., Trenton, NJ, 1957—59; asst. nurse cons. Lovingston, Va., 1959—60. Scholar, U.S. Ballroom Championship, 1993. Republican. Avocations: poetry, singing, ballroom dancing, piano, guitar. Home: 10161 Regent Cir Naples FL 34109 Office: David Lawrence Ctr 6075 Golden Gate Pky Naples FL 34116 Personal E-mail: straussar@naples.net.

STRAVALLE-SCHMIDT, ANN ROBERTA, lawyer; b. NYC, Jan. 2, 1957; Grad. cum laude, Phillips Exeter Acad., 1975; student, Occidental Coll., 1975-78, Oxford Coll., Eng., 1976-77; BS cum laude, Boston Coll., 1980; JD, Boston U., 1987; MBA, Rensselaer Poly. Inst., 2002; grad., U. Phoenix Online. Bar: Conn. 1987, U.S. Dist. Ct. Conn. 1988, U.S. Supreme Ct. 1993. Consulting staff Arthur Andersen, Boston, 1980-82; supr. CID ops. Aetna Life & Casualty, Hartford, Conn., 1982-84; summer intern US Atty.'s Office, Boston, 1985; jud. clk. Hon. Judge Thayer III NH Supreme Ct., 1987-88; trial lawyer Day, Berry & Howard, Hartford, Conn., 1988-91; sr. lawyer comml. litig. and appellate practice Berman & Sable, Hartford, Conn., 1991-96; dir. maj. case unit Travelers Property and Casualty Corp., Hartford, Conn., 1996-98; sr. atty. Robinson & Cole, Hartford, Conn., 1998-2000; gen. counsel Conn. Resources Recovery Authority, Hartford, Conn., 2000—. Brief judge Nat. Appellate Advocacy Competition, 1996; online faculty U. Phoenix, 2002—, moot court judge, U. Conn., 1992, 2004. Mem. editl. bd. Conn. Bar Jour., 1990-99; contbr. articles to profl. jours. Mem. Hebron Dem. Town Com., Hebron Bd. Fin., 1995-99, Hebron Sch. Bldg. Com., 1997-99; justice of peace, 1997-99; apptd. mem. Hebron Bldg. Com., 1997-99; bd. dirs. Lawyers Without Borders, 2004 Hennessey scholar Boston U. Sch. Law, 1987. Mem. ABA, Conn. Bar Assn. (founder, chair appellate practice com. litigation sect. 1994-96, mem. exec. com. litigation sect., pro bono exec. com, 2004, chair pro bono initiative, corp. counsel sec., 2004), Am. Registry of Outstanding Professionals, 2003-. Home: 7 Don St Plainville CT 06062-1111 Office: Conn Resources Recovery Authority 100 Constitution Plz Ste 1700 Hartford CT 06103-1719 E-mail: astravalle@comcast.net.

STRAVINSKA, SARAH, dance educator; b. Pitts., Nov. 12, 1940; d. Robert Edwin Williams and Alice Elizabeth Markey Hildeboldt; m. George Lawrence Denton, May 10, 1959 (div. 1973); children: Kathryn, Michael, Laura, David. BFA in Dance, Fla. State U., 1977, MFA in Dance, 1979; Cert. in Ballet, Vaganova Inst., Leningrad, Russia, 1990; Cert., Raoul Gelabert Kinesiology Ins, N.Y.C., 1980. Dancer Ballet Russe, N.Y.C., 1957-58; dance choreographer Dutchess County Ballet, Beacon, N.Y., 1960-65; instr. Brevard C.C., Cocoa, Fla., 1969-73; chair dept. dance Randolph/Macon Woman's Coll., Lynchburg, Va., 1979-84; asst. prof. dance U. So. Miss., Hattiesburg, 1984-86; prof. and coord. dance U. La., Lafayette, 1986—. Dir. State of La. Danse Project, Lafayette, 1991-94. Choreographer original dance works: Mama! Stop the Bombs, 1989, The Yellow Wallpaper, 1990, Spring Night, 1998, Serrano!, 2002; reconstructor of classical ballets: Les Sylphides, 1991, Giselle, 1992, Swan Lake, 1993, Raymonda, Pas de Quatre, 1994. Dir. concerns for children La Danse with Acadiana Arts Coun., Lafayette, 1987-93; mem. Arts in Edn. Program, Lafayette, 1987—. Grantee Mellon Found., 1982. Mem. Am. Coll. Dance Festival Assn. (bd. dirs., festival coord. 1989-91), Dance History Scholars, CORPS de Ballet Internat. (founding mem.), Phi Kappa Phi. Episcopalian. Avocations: writing, music, reading, biking. Office: Univ of La PO Box 43690 Lafayette LA 70504-3690

STRAYHORN, CAROLE KEETON, comptroller; b. Sept. 13, 1939; d. Page Keeton; m. Barr McClellan (div. 1977); m. Hill Rylander (div. 1995); m. Ed Strayhorn, 2003; children from previous marriage: Mark, Scott, Brad, Dudley 1 stepchild. Govt. hons. grad., U. Tex., Austin. Pub. sch. tchr.; sch. bd. mem., pres., 1972—77; mayor, 1977—83; mem. Tex. R.R. Commn., 1994—98; state comptr. of rep. accounts Tex., 1998—. Recipient Friends of Tex. Taxpayers award, Citizens for a Sound Economy, 1999, Friend of Edn. award, Tex. Classroom Tchrs. Assn. Office: Tex Comptroller Capitol Station PO Box 13528 Austin TX 78711-3528*

STREEP, MERYL (MARY LOUISE STREEP), actress; b. Summit, N.J., June 22, 1949; d. Harry, Jr. and Mary W. Streep; m. Donald J. Grummer, 1978. BA, Vassar Coll., 1971; MFA, Yale U., 1975, DFA (hon.), 1983, Dartmouth Coll., 1981. Co-founder Mothers & Others for a Livable Planet. Appeared with : Green Mountain Guild; actress : (Broadway plays) Trelawny of the Wells, 1975; (plays) 27 Wagons Full of Cotton (Theatre World award); A Memory of Two Mondays; Henry V; Secret Service; The Taming of the Shrew; Measure for Measure; The Cherry Orchard; Happy End; Wonderland; Taken in Marriage; Alice in Concert (Obie award, 1981); (films) Julia, 1977; The Deer Hunter, 1978 (Best Supporting Actress award nat. Soc. film Critics, Acad. award nomination, 1978); Manhattan, 1979; The Seduction of Joe Tynan, 1979; Kramer vs. Kramer, 1979 (N.Y. Film Critics' award, Los Angeles Film Critics' award, both for best actress, Golden Globe award, Acad. award for best supporting actress); The French Lieutenant's Woman, 1981 (Los Angeles Film Critics award for best actress, Brit. Acad. award, Golden Globe award, Acad. award nomination, 1981); Sophie's Choice, 1982 (Acad. award for best actress, Los Angeles Film Critics award for best actress, Golden Globe award, 1982); Still of the Night, 1982; Silkwood, 1983 (Acad. award nomination); Falling in Love, 1984; Plenty, 1985; Out of Africa, 1985 (Los Angeles Film Critics award for best actress, Golden Globe award, 1985); Heartburn, 1986; Ironweed, 1987 (Acad. award nomination); A Cry in the Dark, 1988 (named Best Actress N.Y. Film Critics' Circle, 1988, Best Actress Cannes Film Festival, 1989, Acad. award nomination); She-Devil, 1989; Postcards From the Edge, 1990; Defending Your Life, 1991; Death Becomes Her, 1992; The House of Spirits, 1993; The River Wild, 1994; The Bridges of Madison County, 1995 (Acad. award nominee for best actress, 1996); Before and After, 1996; Marvin's Room, 1996; Dancing at Lugnasa, 1998; One True Thing, 1998; Music of the Heart, 1999 (Acad. award nominee for best actress); The Hours, 2002; Adaptation, 2002 (Southeastern Film Critics Assn. award for best supporting actress, 2002, Chgo. Film Critics Assn. award for best supporting actress, 2003, Golden Globe for best supporting actress, 2003); (TV films) The Deadliest Season, 1977; Alice at the Palace, 1982; (TV miniseries) Holocaust, 1978; Angels in America, 2003 (Golden Globe for best actress, 2004, Screen Actors Guild Award for best actress, 2004); (TV dramatic spls.) Uncommon Women and Others, 1979; First Do No Harm, 1997; Secret Service, 1977; voice : (films) Artificial Intelligence, 2001; narrator : (TV films) A Vanishing Wilderness, 1990; The Velveteen Rabbit, 1984 (Emmy award Best Children's Rec.). Recipient Mademoiselle award, 1976, Woman of Yr. award, B'nai Brith, 1979, Hasty Pudding Soc., Harvard U., 1980, Best Supporting Actress award, Nat. Bd. of Rev., 1979, Best Actress award, 1982, Star of Yr. award, Nat. Assn. Theater Owners, 1983, People's Choice award, 1983, 85, 86, 87, 1990, Women in Film Crystal award, 1998, Gotham award for Lifetime Achievement, 1999, Bette Davis Lifetime Achievement award, 1999. Office: Creative Artists Agy 9830 Wilshire Blvd Beverly Hills CA 90212-1825*

STREET, PATRICIA LYNN, retired secondary school educator; b. Lillington, N.C., May 3, 1940; d. William Banks and Vandalia (McLean) S.; m. Col. Robert Gest, June 2, 1962 (div. 1985); children: Robert, Roblyn Renee. BS, Livingstone Coll., 1962; MEd, Salisbury State U., 1974; postgrad., various, 1968—. Tchr. Govt. of Guam Marianas Island, Agana, Guam, 1962-64; sec., typist USAF, Glasgow AFB, Mont., 1964-65, Syracuse (N.Y.) U. AeroSpace Engring., 1966-67; tchr. Syracuse (N.Y.) City Sch. System, 1967-69; lectr. U. of Md., Eastern Shore, Princess Anne, Md., 1970-72; tchr. Prince George's County Pub. Schs., Upper Marlboro, Md., 1973—. Instr. U. Guam, Anderson AFB, 1963, U.S. Armed Forces Inst., Anderson AFB, 1963, Yorktowne Bus. Inst., Landover, Md., 1987-90, Cheseapeake Bus. Inst., Clinton, Md., 1983-89; asst. advisor student tchrs. U. Md. Ea. Shore, Princess Anne, 1972; adj. instr. Bowie State U., 1990—; conv. speaker. Mem. AAUW, NEA, ASCD, Am. Vocat. Assn., Md. Bus. Edn. Assn. (pres.-elect 1987-88, pres. 1988-89, Educator of Yr. 1989), Md. Vocat. Assn. (regional rep. 1986-89, audit chmn. 1987-89, Vocat.-Tech. Educator of Yr. 1989), Ea. Bus. Edn. Assn. (co-editor newsletter 1990-91, secondary exec. dir. 1991-94, pres.-elect 1997-98, pres. 1998-99), Md. State Tchrs. Assn., D.C. Bus. Edn. Assn., Nat. Bus. Edn. Assn., Nat. Bus. Edn. Assn. (exec. bd. dirs. 1998-99), Internat. Soc. for Bus. Edn., Md. Bus. Edn. Com., Prince George's County Edn. Assn., Delta Pi Epsilon. Democrat. Baptist. Avocations: sewing, singing, modern creative dancing. Home: 10107 Welshire Dr Upper Marlboro MD 20772-6204 Office: Prince George's Pub Sch Upper Marlboro MD 20772

STREET, PICABO, Olympic athlete; b. Triumph, Idaho, Apr. 3, 1971; Downhill skier U.S. Ski Team, 1994—. Biography Picabo: Nothing to Hide. Named World Cup Downhill Women's Champion, 1995, 1996; recipient Silver medal Women's Downhill Alpine Skiing, Plympic Games, Lillehammer, 1994, Bronze and Gold medals, World Championships, 1996, Gold medals (3) Woman's Super Giant Slalom Alpine Skiing, Nagano, Japan, 1998, Gold medal Super 6 Slalom, Winter Olympics, Nagano, Japan, 1998. Office: c/o US Ski and Snowboard Assn PO Box 100 Park City UT 84060-0100

STREET, TERRI EVANS, counselor, consultant; b. Marion, Va., Dec. 9, 1950; d. Edward Henry and Elizabeth (Burris) Evans; 1 child, Edward Brian Evans. BA in English and Edn., Emory and Henry Coll., 1972; MS in Edn. and Psychology, Radford Coll., 1977; MS in Counseling and Human Svcs., Radford U., 1992; cert. advanced grad. studies, Va. Poly. Inst. and State U., 1995, PhD in Counselor Edn., 1996. Nat. cert. counselor; cert. in secondary guidacce, speech, pub. speaking, English, grades 4-7, tchr. effectiveness and student achievement, Va. Tchr. social studies Austinville (Va.) Elem. Sch.cc, 1974-80; tchr. lang. arts Scott Meml. Elem. Sch., Wytheville, Va., 1980-85; tchr. English, speech and drama George Wythe H.S., Wytheville, 1985-91, counselor, 1991-94; grad. asst. Va. Poly. Inst. and State U. Coll. Edn., Blacksburg, 1995-96; counseling coord. Roanoke Valley Gov.'s Sch. for Sci. and Tech., Roanoke, Va., 1996—. Evening adminstr. Wytheville C.C., 1993; presenter in field, 1995—; mem. Wythe County Child Study Team, 1992-94; mem. steering com. Crossroads Tech. Prep. Consortium, 1991-94. Recipient presdl. citation U. Richmond Gov.'s Sch. for Visual and Performing Arts, 1990, 92. Mem. ACA, NEA, Nat. Assn. for Coll. Admission Counseling, Nat. Career Devel. Assn., Va. Edn. Assn. (resolutions com. 1983-85), Va. Career Devel. Assn., Va. Counselors Assn., Roanoke Edn. Assn., Roanoke Valley Counselors Assn., Wythe County Edn. Assn. (reporter 1976-77, 79-80, v.p. 1981-82, 92-93, treas. 1985-86), Chi Sigma Iota. Avocations: reading, spending time outdoors, theatre, dance. Home: 655 E Pine St Wytheville VA 24382-2019 Office: Roanoke Valley Gov's Sch for Sci and Tech 2104 Grandin Rd SW Roanoke VA 24015-3528

STREETEN, BARBARA WIARD, ophthalmologist, medical educator; b. Candia, N.H., Mar. 3, 1925; d. Robert Campbell Wiard and Gertrude Sarah Matheson; m. David Henry Palmer Streeten, Aug. 2, 1952; children: Robert Duncan, Elizabeth Anne, John Palmer. AB magna cum laude, Tufts U., 1945, MD cum laude, 1950. Diplomate Am. Bd. Ophthalmology. Jr.

resident in gen. pathology Mallory Inst., Boston City Hosp., 1951-52; fellow in ophthalmic pathology Mass. Eye and Ear Infirmary, Boston, 1952-53; resident in ophthalmology Wayne County Gen. Hosp., Eloise, Mich., 1953-56; from jr. to sr. clin. instr. ophthalmology U. Mich. Med. Sch., Ann Arbor, 1956-60; from asst. prof. to prof. ophthalmology SUNY Health Sci. Ctr. (now called SUNY Upstate Med. U.), Syracuse, 1964—, dir. eye pathology lab., 1966—; from asst. prof. to prof. pathology SUNY Health Sci. Ctr., Syracuse, 1968—. Contbr. more than 114 articles to profl. jours., chpts. to textbooks. Mem. vision study sect. Nat. Eye Inst., NIH, Bethesda, Md., 1977-80, mem. bd. sci. counselors, 1982-86; mem. editl. bd., mem. editl. adv. com. Ophthalmology jour., 1982-94; gen. editor Investigative Ophthalmology and Visual Sci., 1979-82, mem. editl. bd., 1987-92. Grantee Nat. Eye Inst., NIH, 1975—2002. Mem. Am. Assn. Ophthalmic Pathologists (charter, past pres., bd. dirs., Zimmerman medal 1997), Am. Acad. Ophthalmology (honor award 1990), Verhoeff Ophthalmic Pathology Soc. (past pres.), Assn. for Rsch. in Vision and Ophthalmology (past sect. chmn.), Internat. Soc. Ophthalmic Pathology (co-v.p. N.Am. 1990-92), Phi Beta Kappa, Alpha Omega Alpha. Episcopalian. Achievements include establishment of elastic system nature of the suspensory ligament of the ocular lens; ultrastructural and immunopathologic contributions to diseases of the ocular connective tissue matrix, particularly those related to cataract and glaucoma. Home: 334 Berkeley Dr Syracuse NY 13210-3000 Office: SUNY Upstate Med Univ WH Rm 2107 766 Irving Ave Syracuse NY 13210-1602 E-mail: streeteb@upstate.edu.

STREETER, CAROL, technology marketing executive; b. Radford, Va., Apr. 11, 1963; d. John Elliott Streeter and Nancy Mabry Christenson. Degree in elec. engring., Va. Poly. Inst., 1986; MBA in Fin., Loyola Coll., Balt., 1993. Electronics engr.-trainee U.S. Army, Aberdeen, Md., 1983-87; mem. tech. staff Command Ctr., Clarksburg, Md., 1987-88; svcs. mgr. Bell Atlantic, Harrisburg, Pa., 1988-93; dir. product mktg. Newbridge Networks, Herndon, Va., 1993-98, asst. v.p. product mktg., 1998—; dir. bus. devel. Interpath Comm., Raleigh, N.C., 1998; v.p. mktg. Newbridge Networks, Chantilly, Va., 1999-2000; v.p. solutions mktg. Alcatel USA, Chantilly, 2000—. Cons. mktg. devel., Gambrills, Md., 1998; presenter in field. Home: 2491 Wintergreen Way Gambrills MD 21054-1552 E-mail: carol.a.streeter@alcatel.com.

STREETER, LINDA V. music educator; b. Kingsport, Tenn., Mar. 3, 1959; d. Edith L. Vance; m. Jim M. Streeter, July 2, 1958; 1 child, J. Mark Jr. BS, U. Tenn., Knoxville, 1981. Cert. music tchr. K-12 Ga., 1987, Instrumental Music K-12 Tenn., 1982, gen. music Tenn., 1982, Instrumental Music K-12 Va., 1981. Elem. music tchr. Emmett Elem. Sch., Bristol, Tenn., 1984—87; gen. music exploratory mid. sch. tchr. E.T. Booth Mid. Sch., Woodstock, Ga., 1987—96; band dir. Lynchburg (Va.) City Schs., 1981—82; substitute tchr. Sullivan County and Kingsport City Schs., Blountville and Kingsport, Tenn., 1982—83; supply tchr./gen. music Holston Valley Mid. Sch., Briston, Tenn., 1983—84; band dir. Mountain Rd. Elem. Sch., Woodstock, Ga., 1996—. Asst. band dir./cons. Decatur (Ga.) City Schs., 1996—2002; cherub choir dir. Colonial Heights Presbyn. Ch., Kingsport, Tenn.; band dir. Kingsport (Tenn.) Cmty. Band, 1984—87; youth handbell dir. Covenant Presbyn. Ch., Marietta, Ga., 1990—93, cherub choir dir., 1988—90; handbell dir. Colonial Heights Presbyn. Ch., Kingsport, Tenn., 1984—87. Mem.: Gordon Inst. for Music Learning, Music Educators Nat. Conf., Presbyn. Assn. Musicians, Sigma Alpha Iota (treas. 1979—81, Sword of Honor 1981), Alpha Gamma Delta (social chmn. 1979—80). Presbyterian. Avocations: handbells, church choir, knitting, gardening, camping. Office: Mountain Road Elem Sch 615 Mountain Rd Woodstock GA 30188 E-mail: linda.streeter@cherokee.k12.ga.us.

STREETER, STEPHANIE ANNE, printing company executive; b. Boston, Sept. 19, 1957; d. Andrew Geoffrey Galef and Suzanne Jane (Cohen) Sidy; m. Edward Stanley Streeter, Feb. 22, 1980. BA in Polit. Sci., Stanford U., 1979. Mgr. market analysis Xerox Small Bus. System, Sunnyvale, Calif., 1980-81; regional sales mgr. Xerox Office Products Divsn., Sunnyvale, Calif., 1981-83; product mgr. Decision Data Computer Corp., Horsham, Pa., 1983-85; sr. product mgr. Avery Dennison Corp., Covina, Calif., 1985-88, bus. mgr. indexes, 1988-89, bus. mgr. computer supplies, 1989-90, dir. mktg., computer products, 1990-91, v.p. gen. mgr. label divsn. Diamond Bar, Calif., 1991-93, v.p., gen. mgr., Avery Dennison Brands, 1993—96, worldwide group v.p., 1996—2000; COO idealab!, Pasadena, Calif., 2000; pres., COO Banta Corp., Menasha, Wis., 2001—02, dir., 2001—, pres., CEO, 2002—. Bd. dirs. Wis. Mfrs. and Commerce. Fellow Internat. Women's Forum. Democrat. Avocations: bicycling, skiing. Office: Banta Corp 225 Main St Menasha WI 54952*

STREGE, KAREN, library director; State libr. Mont. State Libr., Helena, 1996—. Office: Mont State Library 1515 E 6th Ave PO Box 201800 Helena MT 59620

STREICH, CYNTHIA SUE, special education educator; b. South Bend, Ind., Sept. 4, 1952; d. Herbert Gustave and Marjory June (Scarfoss) Streich. B.Spl. Edn., Ind. U., South Bend, 1974; M.Spl. Edn., Ind. U., 1980, MS in Spl. Edn., 1997. Tchr. emotionally handicapped K-8th grade Madison Sch., South Bend, 1974—77; tchr. pre-vocat. edn. Jackson Sch., South Bend, 1977—92; tchr. categorial kindergarten Hamilton Sch., South Bend, 1992—93; tchr. cross categorial 7th-8th grades Navarre Sch., South Bend, 1993—96; tchr. cross categorial K-2d Studebaker Sch., South Bend, 1996—97; tchr. cross categorical 8th grade Navarre Sch., South Bend, 1997—2003; cross categorical 7th-8th grades Marshall Intermediate Ctr., South Bend, 2003—. Part-time retail clk. L.S. Ayres, South Bend, 1973—2000. Campaign/fund raising participant Dem. Party, South Bend, 1966—; bd. dirs. Firefighters Heritage Found., South Bend, 2002—, Somers Sq. Condo Assn., South Bend, 2003—. Named Labor Cmty. Hero, United Way AFL-CIO, South Bend, 2002, Advisor of the Yr., Jr. Achievement, 1986, Tchr. of the Yr., South Bend Tribune Newspaper, 2002, Hon. Group SBCSC, 1999; recipient Cmty. Svc. award for State of Ind., L.S. Ayres, 1992. Mem.: NEA (Cmty. Svc. award 2002), Ind. State Tchrs. Assn. (Cmty. Svc. award 2003). Democrat. Methodist. Home: 5808 Aberdeen Dr South Bend IN 46614-6360 Office: South Bend Cmty Sch Corp 635 S Main St South Bend IN 46601

STREIDL, ISABELLE ROBERTS SMILEY, economist; b. Glen Ridge, N.J., Nov. 7, 1913; d. Orton Ray and Louise Roberts (Speer) Smiley; m. Edward G. Streidl, Apr. 8, 1939 (dec. Sept. 1983); children: Nancy Louise, Linda Jeanne. BA cum laude, Mt. Holyoke Coll., 1935. Clk. VA, Washington, 1936; statis. clk. bur. of labor stats. U.S. Dept. Labor, Washington, 1936-39, sr. examining clk. children's bur., 1939-42, asst. child labor report analyst, 1942-45, child labor report analyst, 1945-46, labor economist women's bur., 1962-65, chief br. labor force rsch. women's bur., 1965-67, chief divsn. econ. status and opportunities, 1967-74. Mem. AAUW. Avocations: bridge, sewing, knitting. Home: 45 Strawberry Dr Carlisle PA 17013-4440

STREIFFER, JENNY, former soccer player; b. Metairie, La., May 25, 1978; Student, U. Notre Dame. Alt. U.S. Women's Olympic Soccer Team, 1996; mem. U-20 Nat. Team Nordic Cup championship, Denmark, 1997. Named Big East Rookie of Yr. and NSCAA 3d Team All-Am., freshman yr., U. Notre Dame. Achievements include scoring winning goal U-20 Nat. Team Nordic Cup championship, Denmark; midfield Notre Dame, NCAA championship freshman yr., undefeated regular season sophomore year. Office: US Soccer Fedn 1801-1811 S Prairie Ave Chicago IL 60616

STREISAND, BARBRA JOAN, singer, actress, director; b. Bklyn., Apr. 24, 1942; d. Emanuel and Diana (Rosen) S.; m. Elliott Gould, Mar. 1963 (div.); 1 son, Jason Emanuel; m. James Brolin, July 1, 1998. Grad. high sch., Bklyn.; student, Yeshiva of Bklyn. N.Y. theatre debut Another Evening with Harry Stoones, 1961; appeared in Broadway musicals I Can Get It for You Wholesale, 1962, Funny Girl, 1964-65; motion pictures include Funny Girl, 1968, Hello Dolly, 1969, On a Clear Day You Can See Forever, 1970, The Owl and the Pussy Cat, 1970, What's Up Doc?, 1972, Up the Sandbox, 1972, The Way We Were, 1973, For Pete's Sake, 1974, Funny Lady, 1975, The Main Event, 1979, All Night Long, 1981, Nuts, 1987; star, prodr. film A Star is Born, 1976; prodr., dir., star Yentl, 1983, The Prince of Tides, 1991, The Mirror Has Two Faces, 1996 (ASCAP Award for score, 1996) ; exec. prodr.: (TV movie) Serving in Silence: The Margarethe Cammermeyer Story, 1995; TV spls. include My Name is Barbra, 1965 (5 Emmy awards), Color Me Barbra, 1966; actress, prodr., dir. The Mirror Has Two Faces, 1996; rec. artist on Columbia Records; Gold record albums include People, 1965, My Name is Barbra, 1965, Color Me Barbra, 1966, Barbra Streisand: A Happening in Central Park, 1968, Barbra Streisand: One Voice, Stoney End, 1971, Barbra Joan Streisand, 1972, The Way We Were, 1974, A Star is Born, 1976, Superman, 1977, The Stars Salute Israel at 30, 1978, Wet, 1979, (with Barry Gibb) Guilty, 1980, Emotion, 1984, The Broadway Album, 1986, Til I Loved You, 1989; other albums include: A Collection: Greatest Hits, 1989, Just for the Record, 1991, Back to Broadway, 1993, Concert at the Forum, 1993, The Concert Recorded Live at Madison Square Garden, 1994, The Concert Highlights, 1995, Higher Ground, 1997, A Love Like Ours, 1999, Christmas Memories, 2001, The Essential Barbra Streisand, 2002. Recipient Emmy award, CBS-TV spl. (My Name Is Barbra), 1964, Acad. award as best actress (Funny Girl), 1968, Golden Globe award (Funny Girl), 1969, co-recipient Acad. award for best song (Evergreen), 1976, Georgie award AGVA 1977, Grammy awards for best female pop vocalist, 1963, 64, 65, 77, 86, for best song writer (with Paul Williams), 1977, 2 Grammy nominations for Back to Broadway, 1994; Nat. Acad. of Recording Arts & Sciences Lifetime Achievement Award, 1994, Cecil B. Demille Lifetime Achievement Award, 2000, Liberty & Justice Award, Rainbow/PUSH Coalition, 2001. Office: Barbra Streisand c/o Martin Erlichman Assoc Inc 5670 Wilshire Blvd Ste 2400 Los Angeles CA 90036

STREIT-WAITZ, KATHRYN THERESA, not-for-profit fundraiser; b. North Philadelphia, Pa., May 10, 1958; d. Charles William Streit, Jr. and Theresa Mary Fairchild; m. Robert John Waitz, May 3, 1985 (div. July 18, 1996); 1 child, Robert Charles Waitz. Postgrad. in MBA program, Phila. U., 2003—. Cert. Microsoft Office User Specialist-Technical ETI Internat., Pa., 2000. CEO, founder Esa Enterprise LLC, and Esa Way, Philadelphia, Pa., 1995—2003; tele/sales for Kimmel Cgtr. and Broadway at the Acad. Kimmel Ctr. Presents/Mktg Svcs., Inc., Phila. and El Segundo, Calif., 2003—. Dir. Gt. Arts and Comedy, Phila., 2002—; artist, web designer various not-for-profit orgns. Mem. On Cue Capital Group, Phila., 2003—. Recipient award, Inst. For Sci. and Bus. Edn., 1993—95. Mem.: Profl. Fin. Assocs. (assoc.; broker-id 1200693 b17 2000—03). Republican. Roman Catholic. Avocations: comedy critiques, painting, swimming, travel. Home: 3657 Frankford Ave Philadelphia PA 19134-2129 Office: Esa Enterprise llc/Esa Way Inc 3657 Frankford Ave Philadelphia PA 19134-2129 Personal E-mail: casicat76@aol.com. E-mail: esabiz@aol.com.

STRELAU, RENATE, historical researcher, artist; b. Berlin, Feb. 1, 1951; came to U.S., 1960; d. Werner Ernst and Gerda Gertrud (Bargel) S. BA, U. Calif., Berkeley, 1974; cert. Arabic lang. proficiency, Johns Hopkins U., 1976; MA, Am. U., 1985, MFA, 1991. Rsch. asst. Iranian Embassy, Washington, 1976-80. One-woman shows include Cafe Espresso, Berkeley, Calif., 1973, Riggs Bank, Arlington, Va., 1994-95; exhibited in group shows at Watkins Gallery, Washington, 1999, Khoja Gallery, Arlington, Va., 2002; represented in permanent collections C. Law Watkins Meml. Collection, Am. U. Mem. Am. Hist. Assn., Orgn. Am. Historians, Soc. for Historians Am. Fgn. Rels. (life). Office: PO Box 12655 Arlington VA 22219-2655 Office Phone: 703-862-9000. E-mail: strelau@renatestrelau.com.

STRICK, SADIE ELAINE, psychologist; b. Masontown, Pa, May 5, 1929; d. Michael and Mary (Oziemblowski) Wierzbicki; m. John Mackovjak, Dec. 31, 1947 (dec. Mar. 1972); children: Deborah, Susan; m. Ellis Strick, Aug. 11, 1974. BSW, U. Pitts., 1975, MEd, 1977, PhD, 1981. Lic. psychologist; fellow, diplomate Am. Bd. Med. Psychotherapists. Psychologist I Mayview State Hosp., Bridgeville, Pa., 1984-87; owner Counseling & Behavior Specialists, P.C., Pitts., 1981—. Mem. C.G. Jung Ednl. Ctr., Pitts., 1980-99; guest speaker Compassionate Friends, Pitts., 1986—. Womens Career Conv., Pitts., 1982. Bd. dirs. OAR/Allegheny, Pitts., 1981-82. Fellow Pa. Psychol. Assn.; mem. APA. Avocations: writing, walking, travel, gourmet cooking, reading, music. Home: 2160 Greentree Rd Apt 605W Pittsburgh PA 15220-1407 Office: Counseling and Behavior Specialists PC 429 Forbes Ave Ste 1614 Pittsburgh PA 15219-1604

STRICKER, MARY FRAN, music educator; d. Elmer George and Norma Jean Stricker; m. Robert J. Erny II. BA in Music Edn., McMurry U., 1979; degree in Med. Asst., Colo. Coll. Med. and Dental Assts., 1986. Cert. tchr. music Tex., 82, med. asst. Colo., 1986. Med. asst. Redwood Med. Lab., Rohnert Pk., Calif., 1990—95; music tchr. Stephenville (Tex.) Ind. Sch. Dist., 1996—. Bookkeeper Ross Stores, Rohnert Pk., 1993—95; sales Wal-mart, Granbury, Tex., 1994—96; substitute tchr. Granbury (Tex.) Ind. Sch. Dist., 1994—96; ind. vocalist, 1973—; pvt. voice and piano tchr., 1993—. Composer: (songs) Blue & Gold Song, 1999; performer (singer): (Operas) several companies, 1983—96. Mem. Cross Timbers Fine Arts Coun., 1999—; childrens choir dir. United Meth. Ch., Rohnert Pk., 1992—95; music dir. First Christian Disciples of Christ Ch., Stephenville, 2002—. Mem.: AAUW, Tex. Music Edn. Assn., Met. Opera Assn. (opera singer 1986—), Nat. Assn. Tchrs. Singing, Tex. Fedn. Tchrs. (campus rep. 2003—). Republican. Lutheran. Avocations: swimming, bowling, antiques. Home: 1361 N Garfield Ave Stephenville TX 76401 Office: Gilbert Intermediate School 950 N Dale Ave Stephenville TX 76401

STRICKLAND, BONNIE RUTH, psychologist, educator; b. Louisville, Nov. 24, 1936; d. Roy E. and Billie P. (Whitfield) S. BS, Ala. Coll., 1958; MS, Ohio State U., 1960, PhD (USPHS fellow), 1962. Diplomate: clin. psychology Am. Bd. Examiners in Profl. Psychology. From asst. to assoc. prof. psychology Emory U., Atlanta, 1962-73, dean of women, 1964-67; prof. emeritus psychology U. Mass., Amherst, 1973—, chmn. dept. psychology, 1976-77, 78-82, assoc. to chancellor, 1983-84. Mem. adv. coun. NIMH, 1984-87; Sigma Xi nat. lectr., 1991-93. Adv. editor numerous psychology jours., acad. pub. houses; contbg. author texts personality theory.; contbr. of numerous articles on social personality and clin. psychology to profl. jours.; contbg. author of two citation classics. Recipient Outstanding Faculty award Emory U., 1968-69; Chancellor's medal disting. service U. Mass., 1983. Fellow APA (pres. divsn. clin. psychology 1983, chmn. bd. profl. affairs 1980-83, chmn. policy and planning bd. 1983-85, pres. 1987, bd. dirs. 1986-87, Outstanding Leadership award 1992, Disting. Contbns. and Psychology in the Pub. Interest award 1999, Presdl. Citation 2001), Am. Psychol. Soc. (founder 1988, bd. dirs. 1989-93), New Eng. Psychol. Assn. (Disting. Contbns. award 2002), Am. Assn. Applied and Preventive Psychology (founder 1990, bd. dirs. 1990-94, pres. 1992-94), Acad. Clin. Psychology (chmn. 1982-83). Home: 558 Federal St Belchertown MA 01007-9754 Office: U Mass Dept Psychology Amherst MA 01003-7710

STRICKLAND, BRENDA B. music educator; b. Kansas City, Mo., Jan. 18, 1952; d. Dale Dillon and Martha Anne Bunch; m. John A.V. Strickland, Nov. 23, 1985. B Music Edn., U. Mo., Kansas City, 1974, M Music Edn., 1984. Music tchr. Shawnee Mission Schs., Overland Park, Kans., 1975-78, 79-85; sales rep. wordprocessing Xerox Corp., Overland Park, 1978-79; music tchr. Blue Valley Sch. Dist., Overland Park, 1985-92, Hanahau'oli Sch., Honolulu, 1992—2001, Arbor Montessori, Decatur, Ga., 2001—. Pres. Heart of Am. Orff Schulwerk Assn., Kansas City, 1990-91. Recipient Stanley Sch. Master Tchr. award, NEA, 1988, Dist. Master Tchr. award, 1991. Mem. Am. Orff Schulwerk Assn., Music Educators Nat. Conf. (named one of Top Ten Music Educators in Hawaii 1999), Greater Atlanta Orff Schulwerk Assn., Hawaii Orff Schulwerk Assn. (pres. 1994-96), Hawaii Music Educators Assn. (Outstanding Music Educator 2000). Mem. Unity Ch. Avocations: singing, piano, reading, church work. Home: 4469 Pineridge Cir Atlanta GA 30338-6538 Office: Arbor Montessori Sch 2998 LaVista Rd Decatur GA 30033

STRICKLAND, DOROTHY, education educator; BS, Newark State Coll.; MA, PhD, NYU. Elem. sch. tchr. N.J. pub. sch. sys., reading cons., learning disabilities specialist; prof. edn. Rutgers U., New Brunswick, NJ, 1985—, Samuel DeWitt Proctor Prof. Edn., 2002—. Active in numerous state and nat. adv. bds. Author: Language Literacy and the Child, Process Reading and Writing: A Literature Based Approach, The Administration and Supervision of Reading Programs, Educating Black Children: America's Challenge, Family Storybook Reading, Listen Children: An Anthology of Black Literature, Families: An Anthology of Poetry for Young Children, Teaching Phonics Today, 1998, Beginning Reading and Writing, 2000, Supporting Struggling Readers and Writers, 2002, Preparing Our Teachers, 2002, (Language Arts) Preparing Our Tchr., 2003, Learning & Tchg., 2004. Inducted into the Reading Hall of Fame, pres., 1997-98. Mem. Nat. Coun. Tchrs. English (Rewey Belle Inglis award for Outstanding Woman in English Education Annual Conv., rsch. award, Outstanding Educator in Lang. Arts award 1998), Internat. Reading Assn. (past pres., Outstanding Tchr. Educator of reading award). Home: 131 Coccio Dr West Orange NJ 07052-4121 Office: Rutgers U Dept Edn Grad Sch Edn New Brunswick NJ 08903

STRICKON, LINDA MELTZER, music educator; b. Bklyn., Dec. 8, 1946; d. Sidney and Helen Meltzer; m. Harvey Alan Strickon, July 2, 1972; children: Joshua Andrew, Meredith Cincy, Erica Stacey. BA, Syracuse (N.Y.) U., 1968; MusM in Edn., NYU, 1969. Cert. tchr. N.Y., 1969. Music tchr. N.Y.C. (N.Y.) Bd. of Edn., N.Y.C., 1969—; music coord. Cmty. Sch, Dist. 24, Queens, 1998—2004. Home: 11 West Brook Road Great Neck NY 11024-1219 Personal E-mail: lmstrick@optonline.net.

STRIDER, MARJORIE VIRGINIA, artist, educator; b. Guthrie, Okla. d. Clifford R. and Marjorie E. (Schley) S. BFA, Kansas City Art Inst., 1962. Faculty Sch. Visual Arts, N.Y.C., 1970-2001; artist-in-residence City U. Grad. Ctr. Mall, N.Y.C., 1976, Fabric Workshop, Phila., 1978, Grassi Palace, Venice, Italy, 1978. One-woman shows of sculpture, drawings and/or prints include Pace Gallery, N.Y.C., 1963-64, Nancy Hoffman Gallery, N.Y.C., 1973-74, Weather Spoon Mus., U.N.C., Chapel Hill, 1974, City U. Grad. Center Mall, 1976, Clocktower, N.Y.C., 1976, Sculpture Center, N.Y.C., 1983, Steinbaum Gallery, N.Y.C., 1983, 84, Andre Zarre Gallery, 1993, 95, Outdoor Installation, N.Y.C., 1997, Selby Gallery, Ringling Sch. of Art, Sarasota, Fla., 1998, Neuherzer Mus., Purchase, N.Y., 1999; exhibited in group shows at The Sculpture Center, N.Y.C., 1981, Drawing Biennale, Lisbon, Portugal, 1981, Newark Mus., 1984, William Rockhill Nelson Mus., Kansas City, 1985, Danforth Mus., Framingham, Mass., 1987, Delahoyd Gallery, N.Y.C., 1992; represented in permanent collections Guggenheim Mus., N.Y.C., U. Colo., Boulder, Albright-Knox Mus., Buffalo, Des Moines Art Center, Storm King (N.Y.) Art Center, Larry Aldrich Mus., Ridgefield, Conn., City U. Grad. Center, N.Y.C., Hirschhorn Mus. and Sculpture Garden, Washington, Santa Fe (N. Mex.) Mus. of Art, also pvt. collections. Nat. Endowment for Arts grantee, 1973, 80, Longview Found. grantee, 1974, Pollock-Krasner Found. grantee, 1990, Florsheim Art Fund grantee, 1998, 2000; Va. Ctr. for Creative Arts fellow, 1974, 92, Millay Colony for Arts fellow, 1992, Yaddo Colony, 1996, 97.

STRIEFSKY, LINDA A(NN), lawyer; b. Carbondale, Pa., Apr. 27, 1952; d. Leo James and Antoinette Marie (Carachilo) S.; m. James Richard Carlson, Nov. 3, 1984; children: David Carlson, Paul Carlson, Daniel Carlson. BA summa cum laude, Marywood Coll., 1974; JD, Georgetown U., 1977. Bar: Ohio 1977. Assoc. Thompson Hine LLP (formerly Thompson, Hine & Flory), Cleve., 1977-85, ptnr., 1985—. Loaned exec. United Way N.E. Ohio, Cleve., 1978; trustee ideastream, Mus. Theater Edn. Programming. Mem. ABA (real estate fin. com. 1980-87, vice chmn. leader liability com. 1993-97, mem. non-traditional real estate fin. com. 1987—), Am. Bar Found., Am. Coll. Real Estate Lawyers (bd. govs. 1994-98, treas. 1999), Internat. Coun. Shopping Ctrs., Nat. Assn. Office and Indsl. Parks, Urban Land Inst. (chmn. Cleve. dist. coun. 1996-2000), Cleve. Real Estate Women, Ohio Bar Assn. (bd. govs. real property sect. 1985-97), Greater Cleve. Bar Assn. (chmn. bar applicants com. 1983-84, exec. coun. young lawyers sect. 1982-85, chmn. 1984-85, mem. exec. coun. real property sect. 1980-84, Merit Svc. award 1983, 85), Pi Gamma Mu. Democrat. Roman Catholic. Home: 2222 Delamere Dr Cleveland OH 44106-3204 Office: Thompson Hine LLP 3900 Key Ctr 127 Public Square Cleveland OH 44114-1216 E-mail: linda.striefsky@thompsonhine.com.

STRIEGEL, NICOLE SUSETTE, director; d. Daniel Joseph and Maria Teresa Striegel. BS in Biology, U. New Orleans, 1997, MBA, 2000. Asst. dir. records and registration U. New Orleans, 1997—2000; dir. records and admissions Clovis C.C., N.Mex., 2000—01; v.p. mktg. Nexcor Techs., Atlanta, 2001—02; asst. dir. enrollment svcs. Pikes Peak C.C., Colorado Springs, Colo., 2002—.

STRIER, KAREN BARBARA, anthropologist, educator; b. Summit, N.J., May 22, 1959; d. Murray Paul and Arlene Strier. BA, Swarthmore Coll., 1980; MA, Harvard U., 1981, PhD, 1986. Lectr. anthropology Harvard U., Cambridge, Mass., 1986-87; asst. prof. Beloit (Wis.) Coll., 1987-89, U. Wis., Madison, 1989-92, assoc. prof., 1992-95, prof., 1995—, dept. chair, 1994-96. Panel mem. U.S. Dept. Edn., Washington, 1989—92. Author: (book) Faces in the Forest, 1999, Primate Behavioral Ecology, 2d edit., 2003; co-author: Planning, Purposing, and Presenting Science Effectively; mem. editl. bd.: Internat. Jour. Primatology, 1990—, Primates, 1991—, Yearbook of Phys. Anthropology. Recipient Presdl. Young Investigator award, NSF, 1989—94. Fellow: AAAS (coun. del. anthropology sect. 1998—2000), Am. Anthropol. Assn.; mem.: Animal Behavior Soc., Internat. Primatologcial Soc., Am. Assn. Phys. Anthropologists. Office: U Wis Dept Anthropology 5403 Social Sci Bldg 1180 Observatory Dr Madison WI 53706-1320 E-mail: kbstrier@facstaff.wisc.edu.

STRIKE, KIMBERLY THERESE, principal; d. Edward J. and Joan R. Kuper; m. Jeffery Brian Strike, Aug. 12, 1989; children: James, Jared, Elizabeth. BS in edn., Whitewater U., 1988; EdM, Nat. Louis, 1995; PhD, Marquette U., 2000. Tchr. Racine Unified, Racine, Wis., 1989—99; prin. Providence Cath., Union Grove, Wis., 1999—2002, Sacred Heart, Racine, Wis., 2002—. Vacation Bible Sch. Evang. United Meth., Racine, Wis., 1999—; chair mem., Eucharistic min. Sacred Heart Ch., Racine, Wis., 1983—; chair person Stuff the Bus Food Dr., Racine, Wis., 2000—. Recipient Marquette U. Scholarships, Milw., Wis., 1995—2000. Mem.: Nat. Cath. Educators Assn., Milw. Area Elem. Principal's Assn., Nat. Assn. Of Elem. Sch. Principals, Assn. of Supervision and Curriculum Devel., Phi Delta Kappa. Roman Catholic. Avocations: scrapbooks, reading, travel, photography, being mom.

STRINGER, C. VIVIAN, college basketball coach; b. Edenborn, Pa. m. William D. Stringer (dec.); children: David, Janine, Justin. Grad., Slippery Rock State Coll. Head coach Cheyney State Coll., 1971—83, U. Iowa, 1983—95, Rutgers U., 1995—. Head coach US Select Team tour China, 1980, World U. Games, Kobe, Japan, 1985, World Championship Zone Qualification Tournament, San Paulo, Brazil, 1989, US Pan-American Games, Havana, Cuba, 1991. Finalist Naismith Nat. Coach of Year award, 2000, 2001, 2003; named to Women's Basketball Hall of Fame, 2001;

recipient Phila. Sportswriters' Coach of Year, 1980, Phila. Sportswriters' Coach of Year, 1981, NCAA, Wade Trophy Women's Nat. Coach of Year, 1982, Converse Women's Nat. Coach of Year, 1988, Naismith award, Converse, Sports Illustrated, USA Today, Los Angeles Times and Black Coaches Assn. Women's Coach of the Year, 1993. Mem. Amateur Basketball Assn. U.S. (bd. dirs.). Achievements include 1st person (male or female) to lead 3 different schools to the NCAA final four.*

STRINGER, GRETCHEN ENGSTROM, consulting volunteer administrator; b. Pitts., Feb. 25, 1925; d. Birger and Gertrude Anne (Schuchman) Engstrom; m. Loren F. Stringer, Oct. 3, 1953 (dec. Sept. 1992); children: Lizbeth, Pamela, William E., Frederick E. BA, Oberlin Coll., 1946; Cert. in Teaching, U. Pitts., 1951, SUNY, Buffalo, 1964, M, 1996. Cert. vol. adminstr. Owner, founder, pres. Vol. Cons., Clarence, N.Y., 1979—; owner, founder, officer Non Profit Mgmt. Ctr., Buffalo, 1995-2000. Founding pres., bd. dirs. Ctrl. Referral Svc. Author: The Board Manual Workbook, 1980, rev., 1993, The Instructors Guide, 1982, A Magical Formula, 1980; co-author: Non Profit Management Education, 1998; contbr. articles to profl. jours. Exec. dir. Vol. Action Ctr., United Way Buffalo and Erie County, 1978-81; founding vice chair Erie County Commn. on Status of Women, 1989-2000; pres. Girl Scout Coun. of Buffalo and Erie County, chair, gen. mgr. cadette encampment; bd. dirs. Clarence Ctrl. Sch. Dist., 1976-86; chair, gen. mgr. Buffalo and Erie County Bicentennial Parade, 1976, Erie County Ski Swap; active Longview Protestant Home for Children Bd., Millard Fillmore Jr. Bd., Prevention is Primary, N.Y. Bd. State Foster Care Youth Ind. Project, others; Cmty. Hero Torch Bearer Summer Olympics, 1996; del. White House Conf. on Small Bus., 1995; vol. steering com. Martin House Restoration Corp., 1988—. Recipient Pinny Wilson Vol. award Buffalo and Erie County, 1981, Continuing Svc. award Mass. Mutual, 1987, Girl Scouts Thanks Badge, 1983, Susan Reid Greene Russell award Jr. League of Buffalo, 1994. Mem. Nat. Assn. Women Bus. Owners (bd. pres. Buffalo chpt. 1998-2000), N.Y. Assn. Vol. Ctrs. (founding exec. bd.), Vol. Admisntrs. Western N.Y. (founding pres. 1980), Buffalo Ambassadors of C. of C. (bd. dirs.), Women's Pavilion Pan Am. Centennial 2001 (founder, pres. bd. dirs. 1999-2001), Jr. League Buffalo, Inc. (sustainer v.p. 1998-2000), Assn. Vol. Adminstrn. (chair, gen. mgr. nat. conf. 1986, nat. trainer, re-cert. chair, subcom. vol. adminstrn. higher edn.). Office: Vol Cons 9015 Cliffside Dr Clarence NY 14031-1460 E-mail: gstringer@juno.com.

STRINGER, MARY EVELYN, art historian, educator; b. Huntsville, Mo., July 31, 1921; d. William Madison and Charity (Rogers) S. AB, U. Mo., 1942; AM, U. N.C., Chapel Hill, 1955; PhD (Danforth scholar), Harvard U., 1973. From asst. prof. art to prof. Miss. State Coll. for Women (now Miss. U. for Women), Columbus, 1947-91, prof. emeritus, 1991—. Regional dir. for Miss., Census of Stained Glass Windows in Am., 1840-1940. Bd. dirs. Mississippians for Ednl. Broadcasting; mem. Miss. com. Save Outdoor Sculpture, 1992-93. Recipient Medal of Excellence award Miss. U. Women, 2003; named Honored Artist Miss. Chpt. Nat. Mus. Women in Arts, 2003; scholar Fulbright Found., 1955-56; grantee Harvard U., 1966-67, NEH, 1980. Mem. AAUW (Medal of Excellence award Miss. chpt., 2003), Coll. Art Assn., Southeastern Coll. Art Conf. (dir. 1975-80, 83-89, Disting. Svc. award 1992, Miss. Hist. Soc. (Merit award 1995), Internat. Ctr. Medieval Art, Am. Birding Assn., Audubon Soc., The Nature Conservancy, Sierra Club, Phi Beta Kappa, Phi Kappa Phi. Democrat. Episcopalian.

STRINGFIELD, SHERRY, actress; b. Colorado Springs, Colo., June 24, 1967; m. Larry Joseph, 1998; 1 child. BFA, SUNY, Purchase, 1989. Theater appearances include Goose and Tom Tom, Hurly Burly, Devil's Disciple, A Dream Play, Hotel Baltimore, The Kitchen, Tom Jones; appeared in (TV series) Guiding Light, 1989-92, NYPD Blue, 1993, ER, 1994-96, 2001- (Emmy nominee Outstanding Lead Actress in a Drama Series, 1995), Going Home, 2000; (films) Burnzy's Last Call, 1995, 54, 1998, Borderline, 1998, Autumn in New York, 2000, Viva Las Nowhere, 2001; (TV movies) Border Line, 1999, Going Home, 2000; (TV appearances) Touched by an Angel, 1999, Third Watch, 2002.*

STRINGHAM, RENÉE, physician; b. Mpls., July 16, 1940; d. Clifford Leonard and Helen Pearl (Marcineak) Heinrich; children: Lars Eric, Leif Erik, Lance Devon. BS, St. Lawrence U., 1962; MD, U. Ky., 1972. Diplomate Am. Bd. Family Practice. Intern U. Fla., Gainesville, 1972-73; physician Lee County Coop. Clinic, Marianna, Ark., 1973-74; pvt. practice Coastal Health Practitioners, Lincoln City, Oreg., 1975-84; county med. officer Lincoln County Health Dept., Newport, Oreg., 1986-90; pvt. practice, 1984-90; student health Miami U., Oxford, Ohio, 1991-93; pvt. practice Macadam Clin., Portland, 1994; cons. student health Willamette U., 1994-95; contract physician West Salem Clinic, 1995-97; med. dir. Capital Manor, 1997-99; locum tenens, 1999—; physician Oreg. State Hosp., 2001—03. Trustee Coast Home Nursing, Lincoln County, 1984-86; expert witness EPA, 1980. Facilitator Exceptional Living, 1984-86. Fellow Am. Acad. Family Practice; mem. Lincoln County Med. Soc. (pres. 1984), Oreg. Med. Assn. Avocations: spontaneous music, folk dancing, sailing.

STRIPLING, BETTY KEITH, artist, medical/surgical nurse; b. Stephenville, Tex., Aug. 22, 1930; d. Fred Lancaster and Myrtle Ethel (Patton) Keith; m. Warren Lee Stripling, Mar. 22, 1952 (div. 1961); children: Keith, Kelley, David(dec.). Student, John Tarleton Agrl. Coll., 1948-50, Tarleton State U., 1980-85. LVN, Tex. Clk.-typist Kimbell-Food Products Co., Ft. Worth, 1950-52; LVN Stephenville Hosp. and Clinic, 1963, LVN floor duty, 1963-64, LVN surgery, 1964-66, Ft. Worth Osteo. Hosp., 1966-68; LVN, charge nurse Sunset Nursing Home, Stephenville, 1968-80, LVN, DON, 1973-78; LVN, charge nurse Cmty. Nursing Home, Stephenville, 1980-86, 89-94, pvt. duty nurse, 1986-89, cmty. nursing home LVN, 1998-99; freelance painter, 1999—2002. Democrat. Personal E-mail: bjstrip@ont.com.

STRIPLING, KAYE, school system administrator; BS in Health and Phys. Edn., Tex. Woman's U., 1962; EdM in Spl. Edn., U. Houston, 1967, ED in Curriculum and Instrn., 1985. Tchr. spl. edn. Houston Ind. Sch. Dist., 1964—75, prin. elem. and mid. schs., 1975—87, supt. Adminstrv. Dist. XIV, 1987—90, asst. supt. staff devel., 1990—94, supt. S.W. Adminstrv. Dist., 1995—2001, acting supt. schs., 2001, supt. schs., 2001—. Named Disting. Alumna, Tex. Woman's U., 2002. Office: Houston Ind Sch Dist 3830 Richmond Ave Houston TX 77027

STRIPLING BYER, KATHRYN, poet; Grad., Wesleyan Coll., Macon, Ga.; MFA, U. N.C., Greensboro. Poet-in-residence Western Carolina U., Cullowhee, NC. Author: The Girl in the Midst of the Harvest, 1986, Wildwood Flower, 1992 (Lamont Poetry Selection, 1992), Black Shawl, 1998; contbr. poems to jours., reviews and anthologies. Recipient Writing fellowship, Nat. Endowment for Arts, N.C. Arts Coun. Office: Western Carolina Univ Dept English Coulter Bldg Cullowhee NC 28723

STRISOWER, SUZANNE, clinical hypnotherapist, counselor; b. San Francisco, Oct. 27, 1956; d. Edward Herman and Beverly Gene (Boutell) S. BFA, JFK U., Orinda, Calif., 1988; MA, Pacifica Grad. Inst., 1994. Cert. clin. hypnotherapist; cert. counselor. Wallcovering installer, Orinda, Calif., 1974-82; interior designer Lyons, Hill & Ruga Inc., Pleasant Hill, Calif., 1983-85; project mgr. Wayne Ruga Inc., Martinez, Calif., 1985-88; exec. dir. Nat. Symposium for Healthcare Interior Design, Martinez, 1986-88; treatment counselor Youth Homes Inc., Walnut Creek, Calif., 1988-93; clin. hypnotherapist The Inner Journey, Walnut Creek, Calif., 1991—2000; aide and cmty. liaison to supr. Contra Costa County Dist. II, 1995—; social worker Youth for Change, Paradise, Calif., 2002—. Tchr. Acalanes Adult Edn. Ctr., Walnut Creek, 1992—; lectr. in field. Author: The Runes of the Four Realms, 2003. Child advisor, vice chairperson Contra Costa County Mental Health Commn., 1991-93; pres. Orgn. of Youth Svcs., 1991-94; mem. Juv. Justice Delinquency Prevention Commn. Contra Costa County, 1988-95, mem. family and children's trust com., mem. juv. sys. planning adv. com. Mem. Am. Coun. Hypnotist Examiners. Avocations: reading, hiking, travel, metaphysics. Home: 620 Mather Ln Oroville CA 95966

STROBEL, PAMELA B. energy executive; b. Chgo., Sept. 9, 1952; BS highest honors, U. Ill., 1974, JD cum laude, 1977. Bar: Ill. 1977, U.S. Dist. (ctrl. and no. dists.) Ill. 1977, U.S. Ct. Appeals (7th cir.) 1981, U.S. Claims Ct. 1983, U.S. Ct. Appeals (fed. cir.) 1985. Ptnr. Sidley & Austin, Chgo., 1988-93; exec. v.p., gen. counsel Commonwealth Edison Co., Chgo., 1993—2000; exec. v.p. Exelon Corp., Chgo., 2000—, exec. v.p., chief adminstrv. officer, 2003—; pres. Exelon Energy Delivery Co., Chgo., 2000—, vice-chair, 2000—01, CEO, vice-chair, 2001—02, chmn., CEO, 2002—03. Mem. Kappa Tau Alpha (staff 1975-77). Office: Exelon Corp PO Box 805398 Chicago IL 60680-5398

STROER, ROSEMARY ANN, real estate broker; b. N.Y.C., Oct. 1, 1934; d. Joseph and Rose Ann (Maguire) McBrien; m. Charles Stroer, Dec. 6, 1961 (dec. 1976). BA in English, CUNY, 1958, MA in English, 1973; MA, NYU, 1976. Dir. pub. relations PepsiCo, Purchase, N.Y., 1960-70; dir. student services and publs. N.Y.C. Bd. Edn., 1970-82; cons. pub. relations numerous orgns. including Ford Found., Architects for Social Responsibility, Cathedral St. John the Divine, Hampton Day Sch., Local TV, Inc., N.Y.C., 1975—; real estate broker, consultant Equity Analysis Internat. Inc., IT Properties, Inc., N.Y.C., 1986—. Author: Work as You Like It, 1979; editor: Holocaust: A Study in Genocide, 1977, Minimum Teaching Essentials, 1980. Spl. rep. Mayor's Task Force on Immunization, N.Y.C., 1982-83; spl. Dem. asst. campaign for Ho. of Reps., N.Y.C., 1972. Recipient Order of the Sun award govt. of Peru, 1964, numerous pub. service awards. Mem. Hunter Coll. Alumni Assn., Mus. Modern Art, UNICEF. Roman Catholic. Avocations: running, writing, landscaping. Home: 315 E 68th St New York NY 10021-5692

STROHMYER, DEB L. music educator, school librarian; d. Eugene Lee and Agnes Marie Fleming; m. Rick Allen Strohmyer, June 26, 1983 (div. May 9, 2003); children: Carl E., Heidi L. MusB in Edn., Mont. State U., 1976, MA, 1986; Libr. Sci. endorsement (summa cum laude), U. Mont., 1997. Adj. music educator Flathead Valley C. C., Libby, Mont., 1986—90; part-time substitute tchr. Libby Pub. Schs., K-12, Mont., 1986—90, Beaverhead Co. HS, Dillon, Mont., 1990—2000; adj. music educator U. Mont., Dillon, 1990—2000; choir dir., gen. music educator East Mid. Sch., Butte, Mont., 2000—01; K-8 music specialist Ramsay Elem. Sch., Mont., 2001—02; libr. K-8 Wisdom Elem. Sch., Mont., 2003; composer, choir dir, organist St. James Episcopal Ch., 1999—, St. Rose Cath. Ch., 1999—, First Luth., Dillon, Mont., 1990—. Performing arts task force bd. mem. U. Mont., 1994—98. Composer: (songs) Goin Home to Montana, 1989; singer (and poetry) Ignu Poetry Mag., 1992; poet, song writer: songs Rural Mont. Electric Co-opertive Mag., 1997; composer: 4 publ. works, 425 songs, 3 chamber works, 20 choral pieces, 30 instrumental pieces, 70 liturgical works. Campaign worker Mont. Dem. Party, Libby, 1986—90, Dillon, 1990—; lobbyist, activist parental rights Mont. Advocacy Program, Helena, 2000—03, Mont. Mental Health Ombudsman's Office, Helena, 2000—03. Mem.: Mont. Music Educator's Assn. Democrat. Lutheran. Avocations: radio announcer, accompanist, song writing. Home: 130 W Guadalupe Rd Apt 1078 Gilbert AZ 85233-3340

STROM, DORIS MARIE, music educator; b. Chgo., June 28, 1933; m. Edward R. McLaughlin. BA, U. Sioux Falls, 1953; MA, U. S.D., 1969. Tchr. music, English Sioux Falls, Philip Sch. Dist., Baltic Sch. Dist., Canton Sch. Dist., SD, 1955—73; ins. agt., exec. Prudential Ins. Co., Aberdeen, Rapid City, 1974—86; ednl. svcs. mgr., promotion mgr. Rapid City (S.D.) Jour., 1986—92. Adj. tchr. Nat. Am. U., Rapid City, 1980—89, 1999—, S.D. State U., Brookings, 1988—92; choir dir. 1st Congl. Ch., 1999—. Author: In the Village, 1996; co-author: Reflections, 1999. Avocations: gardening, cooking, reading.

STROMAN, SUSAN, choreographer, theater director; b. Wilmington, Del., Oct. 17, 1954; d. Charles and Frances Stroman; m. Mike Ockrent, 1996 (dec. Dec. 2, 1999); stepchildren: Ben, Natasha. Grad., U. Del. Choreographer Flora Roberts Inc. Dancer Chgo., 1977—78, Whoopee!, 1979, Richard III, 1980, Peter Pan, 1983, choreographer (off-Broadway) Broadway Babylon, 1984, Sayonara, 1987, Flora, the Red Menace, 1987, Shenandoah, 1988, Slasher, 1988, Rhythm Ranch, 1989, The Roar of the Greaspaint-The Smell of the Crowd, 1990, Gypsy, 1991, And the World Goes 'Round, 1991 (Outer Critics' Cir. award for choreography, 1991), A Christmas Carol, 1994, (Broadway plays) Crazy for You, 1992 (Tony award for best choreography, 1992, Drama Desk award for choreography, 1992, Outer Critics' Cir. award, 1992, Laurence Olivier award for choreography, 1993), Picnic, 1994, Show Boat, 1994 (Tony award for best choreography, 1995, Astaire award Theatre Devel. Fund, 1995), Big, 1996 (Tony nomination for best choreography, 1996), Oklahoma, 2002 (Laurence Olivier Award for choreography, 2002, Tony nomination for best choreography, 2002), (Operas) Don Giovanni, 1989, A Little Night Music, 1990, 100 in the Shade, 1992, (spl.) Liza Minnelli: Stepping Out at Radio City Music Hall, 1991 (Emmy nomination for choreography, 1993); choreographer, conceiver (Broadway plays) Steel Pier, 1997 (Tony nomination for best choreography, 1997), dir., choreographer The Music Man, 2000 (Tony nomination for best choreography, 2000, Tony nomination for best dir., 2000), The Producers, 2001 (Tony award for best choreography, 2001, Tony award for best dir., 2001, Drama Desk Award for best dir. musical, 2001), dir., choreographer, conceiver Contact, 2000 (Tony award for best choreography, 2000, Lucille Lortel Award for outstanding direction, 2000, Tony nomination for best dir., 2000), Thou Shalt Not, 2001; dir.: (Broadway plays) The Frogs, 2004; co-conceiver Trading Places, Equity Libr. Theatre Informals, 1983, dir., co-conceiver (off-Broadway) Living Color, 1986, co-conceiver, choreographer (TV spl.) Sondheim-A Celebration at Carnegie Hall, 1992, asst. dir., asst. choreographer (Broadway plays) Musical Chairs, 1980; dir.(TV spl.): An Evening With the Boston Pops-A Tribute to Leonard Bernstein, 1989. Recipient Disting. Achievement in Musical Theatre Award, Drama League, 2001. Address: Flora Roberts Agy Penhouse A 157 W 57th St New York NY 10019-2210

STROMBERG, JEAN WILBUR GLEASON, lawyer; b. St. Louis, Oct. 31, 1943; d. Ray Lyman and Martha (Bugbee) W.; m. Gerald Kermit Gleason, Aug. 28, 1966 (div. 1987); children: C. Blake, Peter Wilbur; m. Kurt Stromberg, Jan. 3, 1993; 1 child, Kristoffer Stromberg. BA, Wellesley Coll., 1965; LLB cum laude, Harvard U., 1968. Bar: Calif. 1969, D.C. 1978. Assoc. Brobeck, Phleger & Harrison, San Francisco, 1969-72; spl. counsel to dir. div. corp. fin. SEC, Washington, 1972-76, assoc. dir. div. investment mgmt., 1976-78; of counsel Fulbright & Jaworski, Washington, 1978-80, ptnr., 1980-96; dir. fin. instns. and market issues GAO, Washington, 1996-97; cons. Washington, 1997—. Mem. adv. panel on legal issues GAO, 1992—96; mem. NASD select com. on NASDAQ, 1994—96; trustee AARP Intestment Program and AARP Scudder Mut. Funds, 1997—2000; bd. dirs. Scudder Mut. Funds., Svc. Source, Inc., Mut. Fund Dirs. Forum. Dir. William and Flora Hewlett Found., 2000—; overseer Wellesley Ctrs. Women, 2003-. Mem. ABA (chmn. subcom. on securities and banks, corp. laws com., bus. sect. 1982-93), D.C. Bar Assn. (chmn. steering com. bus. sect. 1982-84), FBA (chair exec. coun., securities com. 1993-95), Am. Bar Retirement Assn. (bd. dirs. 1986-90, 94-96), Phi Beta Kappa. Home and Office: 3816 Military Rd NW Washington DC 20015-2704

STROMBOM, CATHY JEAN, transportation planner, consultant; b. Bremerton, Wash., Nov. 4, 1949; d. Paul D. and Carolyn (Snitman) Powers; m. David Glen Strombom, June 17, 1972; 1 child, Paul Davis. BA summa cum laude, Whitman Coll., 1972; M in City and Regional Planning, Harvard U., 1977; postgrad., U. Wash., 1982-84. Urban planner Harvard Inst. for Internat. Devel., Tehran, Iran, 1977; sr. transp. planner Puget Sound Coun. Govts., Seattle, 1978-84; asst. v.p., mgr. transp. planning/prin. profl. assoc. Parsons Brinckerhoff Quade and Douglas, Inc., Seattle, 1984—. V.p. Women's Transp. Seminar, Seattle, 1988-90 (Woman of Yr. 1989). Contbr. articles to profl. jours. Vol. U.S. Peace Corps, Marrakech, Morocco, 1973-75. Mem. Am. Inst. Cert. Planners (cert.), Am. Planning Assn., Inst. Transp. Engrs.,Leadership Tomorrow, Phi Beta Kappa. Home: 2580 W Viewmont Way W Seattle WA 98199-3660 Office: Parsons Brinckerhoff Quade and Douglas Inc 999 3rd Ave Ste 2200 Seattle WA 98104-4044

STROMMER, ANNE ELIZABETH RIVARD, retired librarian; b. Columbus, Ohio, Dec. 24, 1940; d. Edwin Kenneth Rivard and Alda Nathan (Olin) Rivard Willis; m. Mathias Adolf Strommer, Jan. 3, 1965; children: Elisabeth Anne, Mathias Edwin. BA, Kent (Ohio) State U., 1962; MA in Libr. Sci., U. Mich., 1964. Reference libr. Detroit Pub. Libr., 1962-65, Ft. Knox (Ky.) Mil. Libr., 1968-69, Houston Pub. Libr., 1978-80, branch mgr., 1980-81; tech. svcs. libr. North Harris County Coll., Houston, 1981-85, coord. tech. svcs., 1985-89, coord. tech. and automation svcs., 1990-93, coord. automated libr. svcs., 1993-96, dir. automated libr. svcs., 1996—2001. Mem. ALA, Tex. Libr. Assn., Freedom to Read Found. Home: 20718 Greymoss Ln Houston TX 77073-3108

STROMSWOLD, DOROTHY, retired secondary school educator; b. Mankato, Minn., Jan. 13, 1920; d. Andrew August and Mary Angela (Wachter) Farm; m. Stanley Andrew Stromswold, Oct. 30, 1942 (dec. Apr. 1998); 1 child, Carol. BS, Mankato State U., 1941; student, Mankato Comml. Coll., 1942. Cert. tchr., Minn. Tchr. high sch., Waldorf, Minn., 1942-43, 51-52, Worthington, Minn., 1945-46, Mankato Comml. Coll., 1942-45, 46-47; placement officer Sch. Journalism, U. Minn., Mpls., 1947-49; patent sec. Clark Equipment Co., Buchanan, Mich., 1952-59; book reviewer South Bend (Ind.) Tribune, 1978-93. Spkr. on travel and on the Supreme Ct. Elder, deacon Presbyn. Ch., Buchanan, 1974-81, 98—. Democrat. Avocations: supreme court, reading, giving informal talks. Home: PO Box 27 Buchanan MI 49107-0027

STRONACH, BELINDA, former retail executive; b. Newmarket, Ont., Can., May 2, 1966; d. Frank Stronach; m. Donald Walker, 1990 (div. 1995); children: Nikki 2 children ; m. Johann Olov Koss, 2000 (div. 2003). Student, York U., Toronto; JD (hon.), McMaster U. With Magna Internat. Inc., Aurora, Canada, 1985—2004, CEO, 2001—04, pres., 2002—04. Mem., bd. dirs. Magna Internat. Inc., 1988—2004, U.S. Chamber of Commerce; mem., Dean's Coun. J.F.K. Sch. Govt., Harvard U.; mem., Dean's Advisory Coun. Joseph L. Rotman Sch. Mgmt., U. Toronto; ran for leadership of Can. Conservative Party, 2004. Named Most Powerful Businesswoman in Can., Nat. Post, 2001.

STRONG, AUDREY FARONE, music educator; b. Syracuse, N.Y., Mar. 27, 1952; d. Salvatore Anthony and Agnes Josephine Farone; m. Roger William Strong, Oct. 5, 1974 (div. Jan. 3, 1997); children: Amanda M., Randal W. BA, SUNY, Brockport, 1974; Master of Arts and Humanities, SUNY, Buffalo, 1996. Cert. tchr. N.Y. Tchr. St. Paul's Sch., St. Paul's Roman Cath. Ch., Kenmore, NY, 1985—90; music educator Buffalo (N.Y.) Pub. Schs., 1990—94, North Tonawanda (N.Y.) City Schs., 1994—. Choral dir. Buffalo chpt. Soc. Preservation and Encouragement of Barbershop Quartet Singing Am., Inc., Buffalo, 2000—; cons. English Lang. Arts Tchrs. Edn., North Tonawanda, 2000—. Mem.: Friends of the Riviera Theatre Orgn., Eric-Niagara Sunrise Exch. Club, Alpha Delta Kappa (v.p. 2002—). Avocations: travel, quilting. Home: 35 Sutley Ct Tonawanda NY 14150 Office: North Tonawanda Schs-Ohio Elem 625 Ohio St North Tonawanda NY 14120 Office Phone: 716-807-3800 8112.

STRONG, CHRISTINA CORDAIRE, author, artist; b. Norfolk, Va., Aug. 21, 1932; d. Cordary Baker and Christina (Swann) Heiberger; m. Henry Hooker Strong, July 27, 1957 (dec. May 1972); children: Jonathan Hooker, Johanna Harrison. BA in French and Art, Woman's Coll./U. N.C., Greensboro, 1955; postgrad., Calif. State U., Fresno, 1976-79. Cert. tchr., Va. Designer custom kitchens Eastern Electric, Norfolk, 1950-51; tchr. Nofolk Pub. Schs., 1955-57; assoc. prof. Coll. William and Mary, Norfolk, 1956; v.p. Computron, Virginia Beach, Va., 1990; salesperson The Booke Shoppe, Elizabeth City, N.C., 1991-93; writer, 1991—. Author: (novels) Heart's Deception, 1992, Love's Triumph, 1993, Pride's Folly, 1993, Daring Illusion, 1994 (Holt medallion for Best Regency 1995). Mem. Romance Writers Am. (sec. Richmond chpt. 1990—), Chesapeake Romance Writers (treas. 1995), River City Romance Writers, Strawberry River Art Assn. (sec. 1997—), Tau Psi Omega, Theta Kappa Sigma (treas., pres. 1949-51), Nat. Soc. DAR, Daus. of the Confederacy (historian 1987, v.p. 1991—), Republican. Episcopalian. Avocations: dressage, trail riding, swimming, golf.

STRONG, MARCELLA LEE, music specialist, educator; b. East Liverpool, Ohio, Oct. 16, 1954; d. Carl and Ruth I. (White) Hinkle; m. David Lee Strong, Feb 19, 1977. BA magna cum laude, U. Toledo, 1976; MA in Early Childhood Edn., Kent State U., 1982. Cert. music, elem. tchr., Ohio. Music instr. Cardinal Local Schs., Parkman and Huntsburg, Ohio, 1977—. Choir dir. G.V. Nazarene Ch., Orwell, Ohio 1981-83; organist, mem. bd. deacons and stewardship com., sr. choir, jr. choir and ch. band dir. Huntsburg Congl. Ch., 1985—; mem., officer Orwell Farm Bur.; band dir. Kent State U. Coll. for Kids, 1995—. Mem. Cardinal Edn. Assn. (negotiator 1982, 84, 87, 90, 93, 96, 99, 2002, sec. 1983-84, treas. 1984-85, pres. 1985-86, 89-91, 1997-2002), Ohio Music Educators Assn., Kappa Delta Pi, Mu Phi Epsilon, Delta Kappa Gamma. Democrat. Avocations: spectator sports, traveling, reading, chess, member international trivia team. Home: 78 Chaffee Dr Orwell OH 44076-9526 E-mail: dlsmls@yahoo.com.

STRONG, SARA DOUGHERTY, psychologist, family therapist, custody mediator; b. Phila., May 30, 1927; d. Augustus Joseph and Orpha Elizabeth (Dock) Dougherty; m. David Mather Strong, Dec. 21, 1954. BA in Psychology, Pa. State U., 1949; MA in Clin. Psychology, Temple U., 1960, postgrad., 1968-72; cert. in family therapy, Family Inst. Phila., 1978. Lic. psychologist and family therapist, Pa. Med. br. psychologist Family Ct. Phila., 1960-85, asst. chief psychologist, 1985-88, chief psychologist, 1988-92; ret., 1992; pvt. practice, 1992—. Cons. St. Joseph's Home for Girls, Phila., 1963-84, Daughters of Charity of St. Vincent De Paul, Albany, N.Y., 1965-90, Pa. Counseling Svcs., Carlisle, 2001-. Mem. APA (assoc.), Am. Assn. Marriage and Family Therapists, Pa. Psychol. Assn., Nat. Register of Health Svc. Providers in Psychology, Family Inst. Phila. Democrat. Avocations: reading, dramatic productions, writing, yoga, dance. Office: 1 Greystone Rd Carlisle PA 17013-3743

STRONG, SUSAN CLANCEY, writer, communication consultant, editor; b. Cin., Nov. 10, 1939; d. William Power and Elizabeth (Browne) Clancey; m. Oliver Swigert, 1957 (div. 1972); children: Silvia, David Mack; m. Richard Devon Strong, 1977. BA, Northwestern U., 1965; MA, U. Calif., Berkeley, 1972, PhD, 1979. Tchr. Helen Bush Parkside Sch., Seattle, 1965-66, Taipei (Taiwan) Lang. Inst., 1967-68; acting instr. U. Calif., Berkeley, 1972-78, teaching fellow, 1979, lectr., 1979-84, St. Mary's Coll., Moraga, Calif., 1982-85; pvt. practice Orinda, Calif., 1985-90, 97—; sr. rsch. assoc. Ctr. for Econ. Conversion, 1990-96. Mem. Contra Costa County Conflict Resolution Panels, Calif., 1987-90; affiliate Support Ctr./CTD, San Francisco, 1987-90; del. UN Conf. on Econ. Conversion, Moscow, 1990; co-founder "The Who's Counting?" Project, 1996; founder The Metaphor Project, 1997. Author: The GDP Myth: How It Harms Our Quality of Life, and What Communities are Doing About It, 1995; editor Deficit Delirium, 1993, Shaping A New Conversion Agenda, 1995; author poetry; columnist, book reviewer, film reviewer. Mem. Bay Area Global Tomorrow Com., 1986; co-founder Peace Economy Working Group, 1988; co-founder Peace

Economy Campaign, 1988; mem. Peace Action Nat. Strategy Com., 1989-95, co-chair strategy com., 1992-93; conf. co-chmn. Nat. Sane/Freeze Congress, 1989-90, rep. nat. bd. advisors Nat. Peace Action, Washington, 1989-95; mem. bd. advisors Peace and Environ. Project, San Francisco, 1986-88; chmn. No. Calif. Sane Freeze, San Francisco, 1985-89; co-convenor The Natural Step Open Space Com. Conf., San Francisco, 1997. Mem. Phi Beta Kappa. Democrat. Episcopalian. Avocations: music, gardening. Mailing: PO Box 892 Orinda CA 94563-2124 Fax: 925-254-3304. E-mail: sstrong@metaphorproject.org.

STRONG, VIRGINIA WILKERSON, freelance writer, former educator; b. Vernal, Utah, Mar. 19, 1935; d. Arbun C. and Mildred (Wyman) Wilkerson; m. David Smith, Oct. 6, 1950 (div. Jan. 1960); children: Anna Smith Blyton, Dorothy Smith Wolf, Wendell Lee Smith, Ava Smith Eatman, Karen Smith Ritter; m. Lawrence D. Strong, June 1961 (div. May 1973); children: Lawrence D. Jr., Jeffrey A. BA, U. Miss., 1970, MEd, 1972; PhD, Ohio U., 1985. Cert. elem. edn. tchr., spl. edn. K-12 tchr., ednl. adminstrn. Rsch. asst. U. Miss., University, 1968-70, Utah State U., Logan, 1974-78; tchr. spl. edn. various schs., nr. Oxford, Miss., 1969-74; instr. spl. edn., project coord., rsch. asst. Ohio U., Athens, 1978-82; supr. spl. edn. Meigs County Bd. Edn., Pomeroy, Ohio, 1982-84; tchr. spl. edn., dept. chmn. L.A. Unified Sch. Dist., 1986-93, co-faciliator alcohol drug abuse, 1990-93; freelance writer, owner, mgr. Fenix Devel., Long Beach, Calif., 1990—. Early childhood adv. Utah Bd. Edn., Salt Lake City, 1976, evaluator edn. programs, Salt Lake City and Logan, 1976-77; acting dir. edn., cons. North Miss. Retardation Ctr., Oxford, 1993-94; curriclum developer Meigs County, 1982-84; dir. gifted edn. workshop Ohio U., 1980. Author: The Role of the Special Education Supervisor, 1985, (screenplays) To See the Elephant, Dark Encounters; contbr. articles to newspapers. Elector Dem. Party, Logan, 1976; religious instr. LDS Ch., various locations, 1953-97; docent Thoroughbred Hall of Fame, 2003—. U.S. Dept. Edn. grantee Utah State U., 1976. Mem. ASCD, Kappa Delta Pi, Phi Delta Kappa. Avocations: genealogy, gemology, photography, history buff, travel.

STRONGIN, BONNIE LYNN, English language educator; b. Chgo., Sept. 27, 1943; d. Arthur Caroll and Jennie Grace (Coffler) Bondy; m. Barry Michael Woldman, Jan. 27, 1965 (div. Aug. 1979); children: Scott, Erika, Jonathan; m. Stuart Jeffrey Strongin, Jan. 26, 1992. BA, Roosevelt U., 1964; MA, Concordia U., 1990. Cert. sec. English tchr., Ill. Core tchr. Dist. 15, Rolling Meadows, Ill., 1964—65, 1979—2004; English tchr., chair freshman level Leyden Twp. H.S., Franklin Park, Ill., 1965-69. Ednl. cons. French Internat. Sch. of Chgo., 1995; spkr. in field. Contbg. editor Collage Mag., 1980-82; contbr. articles to Collage Mag., Chgo. Tribune; guest Phil Donahue Show, 1984. Recipient Golden Apple State finalist award Golden Apple Found., Chgo., 1993, Excellence in English award English Speaking Union, Chgo., 1994, Tchrs. Who Care Enough to Challenge Award Ill. Math. and Sci. Acad., 2002. Fellow: Internat. Biographical Assn.; mem.: Ill. Assn. Tchrs. English, Ill. Edn. Assn., ASCD, NOW, NEA. Avocations: theater, opera, travel, film, art. Office: Plum Grove Jr HS 2600 Plum Grove Rd Rolling Meadows IL 60008-2042

STRONG-TIDMAN, VIRGINIA ADELE, marketing professional; b. July 26, 1947; d. Alan Ballentine and Virginia Leona (Harris) Strong; m. John Fletcher Tidman, Sept. 23, 1978. BS, Albright Coll., Reading, Pa., 1969; postgrad., U. Pitts., 1970-73, U. Louisville, 1975-76. Exec. trainee Pomeroy's divsn. Allied Stores, Reading, 1969-70; mktg. rsch. analyst Heinz U.S.A., Pitts., 1970-74; new products mktg. mgr. Ky. Fried Chicken, Louisville, 1974-76; dir. Pitts. office M/A/R/C, 1976-79; assoc. rsch. dir. Henderson Advt., Inc., Greenville, S.C., 1979-81; sr. v.p., dir. rsch. Bozell, Jacobs, Kenyon & Eckhardt, Inc., Dallas, 1981-86, 1981-86, sr. v.p., dir. rsch. and strategic planning Atlanta, 1986-88; sr. v.p., dir. mktg. svcs. Bozell, Inc., Atlanta, 1988-91; sr. v.p., mng. ptnr. Henderson Adv., Inc., 1991-95; prin. Ender-Ptnr., Inc., 1995-96; v.p. mktg. Booth Rsch. Svcs., Inc., 1996-98; COO Moore & Symons, Inc., 1998—. Cons. mktg. rsch. Greenville Zool. Soc., 1981; adj. prof. So. Meth. U., 1984-85. Mem. Am. Mktg. Assn. (Effie award N.Y. chpt. 1982). Republican. Episcopalian. Home: 140 River Ridge Ln Roswell GA 30075-4801

STROOPE, KAY, mathematician, educator; b. Odessa, Tex., Mar. 28, 1947; d. Cecil Clyde and Maurita Rosa Stroope. BS, Henderson U., 1970; MS in Edn., Delta State U., 1989; postgrad., U. Ark., 1987-88. Instr. math. Miller Jr. H.S., Helena-West Helena, Ark., 1970-79, Ctrl. H.S., Helena-West Helena, 1979-87, Benton (Ark.) Mid. Sch., 1987-89, Phillips C.C. U. Ark., Helena, 1989—. Basketball coach Miller Jr. H.S., 1977-81, Ctrl. H.S., 1981-86; math crusade trainer Dept. Higher Edn., Little Rock, 1993—, CMP trainer, 1995—. Co-author (handbook) Metrifacation for Teachers, 1975. Vol. Easter Seal, Helena, 1981-86, March of Dimes, 1987-95, Am. Cancer Soc., 1987—. Named Outstanding Young Educator Helena Jaycees, 1979. Mem. Nat. Coun. Tchrs. Ark., Ark. Coun. Tchrs. Math., Am. Assn. Two-Yr. Colls. Baptist. Home: 600 Galloway West Helena AR 72390-3223 Office: Phillips CC Univ Ark Campus Dr Helena AR 72342

STROSSEN, NADINE, legal association administrator, law educator; b. Jersey City, Aug. 18, 1950; d. Woodrow John and Sylvia (Simicich) S.; m. Eli Michael Noam, Apr. 25, 1980. AB, Harvard U., 1972, JD magna cum laude, 1975; LHD (hon.), U. Vt., 1992, U. R.I., 1992; JD (hon.), San Joaquin Coll. Law, 1996; LHD (hon.), Rpcky Mountain Coll., 1996, Mass. Sch. Law, 2000. Jud. clk. Minn. Supreme Ct., St. Paul, 1975-76; assoc. Lindquist & Vennum, Mpls., 1976-78, Sullivan & Cromwell, N.Y.C., 1978-83; prof. clin. law, supervising atty. Civil Rights Clinic, Sch. Law, NYU, 1984-88; prof. law N.Y. Law Sch., N.Y.C., 1988—; adj. prof. Columbia U., 1990—; pres. ACLU, N.Y.C., 1991—. Editor Harvard Law Rev., 1975; contbr. book chpts., articles to profl. jours.; author: In Defense of Pornography: Free Speech and the Fight for Women's Rights, 1995. Mem. Coun. Fgn. Rels., 1994—. Recipient Outstanding Young Person award Jaycees Internat., 1986; named one of Ten Outstanding Young Ams., U.S. Jaycees, 1986; adj. fellow Yale U. Calhoun Coll., 1997-. Mem. ACLU, Nat. Coalition Against Censorship (bd. dirs. 1988—), Human Rights Watch (exec. com. 1989-91), Harvard Club (N.Y.C.). Avocations: travel, skiing, singing. Office: NY Law Sch 57 Worth St New York NY 10013-2960 also: ACLU 125 Broad St 18th Fl New York NY 10004 E-mail: nstrossen@aclu.org.*

STROTHMAN, WENDY JO, book publisher; b. Pitts., July 29, 1950; d. Walter Richard and Mary Ann (Hodtum) S.; m. Mark Kavanaugh Metzger, Nov. 25, 1978; children: Andrew Richard, Margaret Ann. Student, U. Chgo., 1979-80; AB, Brown U., 1972. Copywriter, mktg. U. Chgo. Press, 1973-76, editor, 1977-80, gen. editor, 1980-83, asst. dir., 1983; dir. Beacon Press, Boston, 1983-95; v.p., pub. adult, trade and reference Houghton-Mifflin, Boston, 1995-96, exec. v.p. trade and reference divsn., 1996—. Trustee Brown U., 1990-96. Edtl. adv. bd. Scholarly Pub., 1993-94; bd. editors Brown Alumni Monthly, 1983-89; chmn., 1986-89. Bd. dirs. Editorial Project for Edn., trustee, 1987-91, treas., 1988-90. Fellow Brown U., 1997—. Mem. Renaissance Soc. (bd. dirs. 1980-83), Assn. Am. Pubs. (Freedom to Read com.), Pubs. Lunch Club (N.Y.C.), PEN New Eng. (adv. bd.), Examiner Club, NacRe Reins. Corp. (bd. dirs.). Office: Houghton Mifflin Co 222 Berkeley St Fl 7 Boston MA 02116-3764

STROUD, BETSY DILLARD, artist; b. Roanoke, Va., Aug. 12, 1940; d. Peter Hairston Dillard and Alice Elizabeth (Fitch) Madden; m. Ethan Beden Stroud, Dec. 29, 1979 (div. Mar. 1986); 1 child, John Hatcher Ferguson, III. BA, Radford Coll., 1968; MA, U. Va., 1970. Assoc. editor Internat. Artist mag., Scottsdale, Ariz., 1998-2001; profl. artist. Tchr. workshops through-out U.S.; judge art shows including those in Farmington, N.Mex., 1999, The Adirondacks Nat. Watermedia Exhbn., Old Forge, N.Y., 1996, Contemporary Watercolorists of Ariz., 1998, others. Contbr. articles to Am. Artist mag., 1987— and other profl. jours. Mem. S.W. Watercolor Soc. (pres. 1988-89, Edgar A. Whitney award 1989), Am. Watercolor Soc. (High Winds medal 1992, Artist Mag. award 1995), Nat. Watercolor Soc., Rocky Mountain Nat. Honor Soc. (Brass Cheque award 1992), Knickerbocker Artists, Ariz. Watercolor Soc. Avocations: piano, bridge, Scrabble, movies. E-mail: betsydillart@uswest.net.

STROUD, CARRIE HOGGARD, elementary school educator; b. Williamston, North Carolina, U.S.A., July 25, 1977; d. Michael Keith and Joanne Harden Hoggard; m. David Glenn Stroud, July 17, 1999; children: Christopher Damon Hoggard, Camden Michael. MUSB., East Carolina U., Greenville, NC., 1995—99. Tchr. Jacksonville Commons Mid. Sch., Jacksonville, NC, 1999—2000; pvt. music tchr. Crystal Coast Sch. of the Arts, Morehead, NC, 2000—01; tchr. Arthur W. Edwards Elem. Sch., Havelock, NC, 2001—. Safe and inviting goal team Arthur W. Edward Elem., Havelock, NC, 2002—03. Mem. Carteret County Sunshine Band, Morehead, NC, 2000—02; mem. Sigma Alpha Iota Music Frat. East Carolina U., NC, 1996—. Recipient North Carolina Tchr. Fellow, NC. Tchr. Fellow Comm., 1995—. Mem.: Music Educators N.C., N.C. Assn. Educators, Profl. Edn. N.C. Democrat. Baptist. Avocations: saxophone, piano, scrapbooks, reading. Home: 1908 Champion Dr Morehead City NC 28557 Office: Arthur W Edwards Elem 200 Education Ln Havelock NC 28532

STROUD, JACQUELINE LUCILLE, medical supply company executive; b. Carthage, Mo., Jan. 5, 1932; m. Herschel L. Stroud; children: Susan K. Stroud Milash, John L. Student, U. Mo., Kansas City, 1949-50, Sarachon Hooley Sec. Sch., 1950-51; BA in Spanish magna cum laude, Washburn U., Topeka, 1980. Pvt. sec. Recordak Corp., Chgo., 1951-54, Vance AFB, Okla., 1954-57, Hallmark Cards, Kansas City, Mo., 1957-61; adminstrv. asst., translator, export mgr. Munns Med. Supply (now MedVentures Internat. Inc.), Topeka, 1980—. Hist. lectr. Mid-19th Century Women, Civil War Medicine, U.S. San. Commn., recreation of Civil War era personages, 1995—; lectr. Associated Club Spkrs. Am., Knife and Fork Club, Inc. Officer, bd. mem. Internat. Ctr. Topeka, 1980's; bd. dirs. Girls' Club Topeka, 1980's; panelist Panel of Am. Women, 1967-75; Spanish translator Topeka Police Dept., 1981—; choir mem. St. David's Episcopal Ch., 1961—; participant, co-organizer Rejoice, Jubilee and Godspell folk masses, Blessing of the Animals at Topeka Zoo, 1968-96; columnist Westboro Neighborhood newsletter, 1975-98; mem. St. Francis Hosp. Aux. Recipient Outstanding Vol. award Jr. League Topeka, 1973, 1st pl. Mother-Dau. Nat. Equitable Ski Challenge, Keystone, Colo., 1972-73 Mem. ADA, Nat. Mus. Civil War Medicine, Am. Soc. Civil War Surgeons, Frontier Brigade of the 1st Western Divsn., Kans. Dental Auxs., Topeka Knife and Fork Club (pres. 1989-90), Minerva Lit. and Music Club (treas. 1999-2000), Kans. State Hist. Soc., Topeka Hist. Soc., Shawnee County Hist. Soc., N.E. Kans. Civil War Round Table, Kansas City Round Table (officer), Victorian Carthage. Avocations: hostess for kings of swing big band, snow skiing, spanish conversation classes, scuba diving, photography, civil war reenacments, church choir. Address: 3640 SW Drury Ln Topeka KS 66604-2550

STROUD, NANCY IREDELL, retired secondary school educator, freelance writer, editor; b. Raleigh, N.C., Apr. 10, 1943; d. John Johnson and Neffie (Mitchiner) Iredell. BA in English, Morgan State U., Balt., 1964; MEd in Adult and C.C. Edn., N.C. State U., 1976; postgrad., The Am. U., 1985. Tchr. history and English Pleasant grove Sch., Sampson County, N.C., 1964-65; social rsch. asst. N.C. State U., 1970; tchr. English Garner Consol. Sch., Wake County, N.C., 1965-67, Calumet H.S., Chgo., 1967-69, LeRoy Martin Jr. H.S., Raleigh, 1971-79, Needham B. Broughton H.S., Raleigh, 1979-84, The Chelsea Sch., Silver Spring, Md., 1984-85, Gaithersburg H.S., Montgomery County, Md., 1985-98; exec. editor Cypher mag., 1998-99. Former mem. adminstrv. bd. Trinity United Meth. Ch., mem. coun. on ministries, past chmn. ch. growth, former head liturgist worship com.; mem. United Meth. Women, Libr. Congress, Smithsonian Instn., Nat. Mus. women in the Arts, U.S. Holocaust Meml. Mus., Dem. Nat. Com., The Kennedy Ctr. Recognized as Outstanding Vol., Trinity United Meth. Ch., Germantown, Md., 1986-87. Mem. AAUW, ASCD, NEA, Md. Coun. of Tchrs. of English Lang. Arts, Md. State Tchrs. Assn., Montgomery County Debate League, Montgomery County Edn. Assn., Nat. Coun. Tchrs. English, Nat. Fedn. Interscholastic Speech and Debate Assn., Nat. Ret. Tchrs. Assn., Morgan State U. Alumni Assn., N.C. State U. Alumni Assn., Tchrs. of English in Montgomery County. Avocations: genealogy, classical and jazz music, reading, writing. Home: 349 Market St w Apt 117 Gaithersburg MD 20878-6447

STROUD, PEGGY ANN, secondary school educator; b. Batesville, Ark., Aug. 1, 1955; d. James Thomas and Marguerite E. Monk; m. M. Cole Elrod (div.). BS in Edn., U. Ctrl. Ark., Conway, 1977; MEd, Tex. Wesleyan U., Ft. Worth, 2002. Cert. tchr. Ark. Sub. tchr. Conway Pub. Schs., Ark., 1978—82; buyer Old Faculty House, Oklahoma City, 1982—85; buyer, R&D, TCBY, Little Rock, 1983—86; owner Hager's Jewelry Store, Conway, Ark., 1986—88; adminstrv. asst. to dir. Ark. Pks. and Tourism, Little Rock, 1988—91; tchr. Perry-Casa H.S., 1991—93, Heber Springs H.S., 1993—. Bd. dirs. Parents with Children with Disabilities, Conway, Ark. Bd. dirs., sec. Faulkner-Cleburne Regional Water Dist., Conway, Ark., 1985—91; mem. Faulkner County Reps., Conway, Ark., 1986—87; bd. dirs. First United Meth. Ch., Conway, Ark., 1988—90. Mem.: NEA, Ark. Ednl. Assn., Conway C. of C. Methodist. Avocations: arts and crafts, water sports. Office: Heber Springs HS 800 W Moore Heber Springs AR 72543

STROUD, RHODA M. elementary school educator; Tchr. Webster Magnet Elem. Sch., St. Paul. Apptd. mem. Minn. Bd. Edn. for State of Minn. Recipient State Tchr. of Yr. Elem. award Minn., 1992. Office: Webster Magnet Elem Sch 707 Holly Ave Saint Paul MN 55104-7126

STROUD, ELIZABETH FAYE, librarian; b. Tulsa, Mar. 25, 1939; d. Milton Earl and Lois (Buhl) S. BA in Philosophy, U. Wash., 1962, MLS, 1964. Intern Libr. of Congress, Washington, 1964-65; asst. dir. North Cen. Regional Libr., Wenatchee, Wash., 1966-69; reference specialist Congl. Reference div. Libr. of Congress, Washington, 1970-71, head nat. collections Div. for the Blind and Physically Handicapped, 1971-73, chief Congl. Reference div., 1973-78, dir. gen. reference, 1978-88; city libr., chief exec. officer Seattle Pub. Libr., 1988-96; exec. dir. Wash. Literacy, Seattle, 1996-99; reference coord. Timberland Regional Libr., Olympia, Wash., 1999—. Cons. U.S. Info. Svc., Indonesia, Feb. 1987. Mem. adv. bd. KCTS 9 Pub. TV, Seattle, 1988—; bd. visitors Sch. Librarianship, U. Wash., 1988—; bd. dirs. Wash. Literacy, 1988—. Mem. ALA (pres. reference and adult svcs. div. 1986-87, dir. bd. 1985-88), Wash. Libr. Assn., D.C. Libr. Assn. (bd. dirs. 1975-76), City Club, Ranier Club. Avocations: gardening, mountain climbing, reading. Office: Wash Literacy 220 Nickerson St Seattle WA 98109-1622

STROUP, KALA MAYS, educational alliance administrator, former state higher education commissioner; BA in Speech and Drama, U. Kans., 1959, MS in Psychology, 1964, PhD in Speech Comm. and Human Rels., 1974; EdD (hon.), Mo. Western State Coll., 1996; LHD (hon.), Harris-Stowe State Coll., 2000. V.p. acad. affairs Emporia (Kans.) State U., 1978-83; pres. Murray State U., Ky., 1983-90, S.E. Mo. State U., Cape Girardeau, 1990-95, Am. Humanics, Kansas City, Mo., 2002—; commr. higher edn., mem. gov.'s cabinet State of Mo., Jefferson City, 1995—2002. Pres. Mo. Coun. on Pub. Higher Edn.; mem. pres.'s commn. NCAA; cons. Edn. Commn. of States Task Force on State Policy and Ind. Higher Edn.; adv. bd. NSF Directorate for Sci. Edn. Evaluation; adv. com. Dept. Health, Edn. and Welfare, chair edn. com.; citizen's adv. coun. on state of Women U. S. Dept. Labor, 1974-76. Mem. nat. exec. bd. Boy Scouts Am., nat. exploring com., former chair profl. devel. com., mem. profl. devel. com., exploring com., Young Am. awards com., 1986-87, north ctrl. region strategic planning com., bd. trustees, nat. mus. chair; mem. Gov.'s Coun. on Workforce Quality, State of Mo.; bd. dirs. Midwestern Higher Edn. Commn.; chair ACE Leadership Commn.; mem. bd. visitors Air U.; v.p. Missourians for Higher Edn.; bd. dirs. St. Francis Med. Ctr. Found., 1990-95, Cape Girardeau C. of C., 1990-95, U. Kans. Alumni Assn.; pres. Forum on Excellence, Carnegie Found.; adv. bd. World Trade Ctr., St. Louis, Svc. Mems. Opty. Colls., 1997—; mem. Mo. Higher Edn. Loan Authority, 1995—, depts. econ. devel. & agrl. Mo. Global Partnership, 1995—, Mo. Tng. & Employment Coun., 1995-2002, Concordia U. Sys. Advancement Cabinet, State Higher Edn. Exec. Officers, 1995—, mem. com. workforce edn. and tng., 1996; bd. govs. Heartland's Alliance Minority Participation, 1995-2002; chair, mem. workforce devel. com. NPEC coun. U.S. Office of Edn., 1997—; bd. dirs. Midwestern Higher Edn. Com. Distributed Learning Workshop, 1998-2002, Dept. Natural Resources Minority Scholarship Adv. Bd.; chair Show Me Results sub-cabinet Educated Missourians; mem. Pub. Policy Initiative Stakeholder Com., 1999—; mem. Coun. Higher Edn. transfer and pub. interest com.; mem. access/diversity com. State Higher Edn. Exec. Officers; trustee, mem. adv. coun. Assn. Governing Bds. of Univs. and Colls. Ctr. for Pub. Edn., 2000—. ACE fellow; recipient Alumni Honor Citation award U. Kans., Award Distinction Profl. Black Men's Club, S.E. Mo., 1990, Dist. Svc. to Edn. award Harris-Stowe State Coll., 1996; named to U. Kans. Womans Hall of Fame, Ohio Valley Conf. Hall of Fame, 1997. Mem. Am. Assn. State Colls. and Univs. (past bd. dirs., mem. Pres.'s Commn. on Tchr. Edn., Task Force on Labor Force Issues and Implications for the Curriculum), Mortar Board, Phi Beta Kappa, Omicron Delta Kappa, Phi Kappa Phi, Rotary (found. Ednl. awards com.). Office: Am Humanics 4601 Madison Ave Kansas City MO 64112

STROUP, SALLY, federal agency administrator; b. Harrisburg, Pa. Grad., Ind. U. Pa., Loyola U. From staff atty. to sr. v.p. legal svcs. and chief counsel Pa. Higher Edn. Agy.; mem. profl. staff com. on edn. and the workforce U.S. Ho. of Reps., 1993—2001; dir. industry and govt. affairs Apollo Group Inc./U. Phoenix; asst. sec. postsecondary edn. Dept. Edn., Washington, 2001— Office: Dept Edn Office Postsecondary Edn 1990 K St NW Washington DC 20006

STROUSE, JEAN, writer; b. L.A., Sept. 10, 1945; d. Carl David and Louise (Friedberg) S. BA, Radcliffe Coll., 1967. Editl. asst. N.Y. Rev. of Books, 1967-69; freelance writer N.Y.C., 1969-72; editor Pantheon Books, N.Y.C., 1972-75; freelance writer N.Y.C., 1975-79, 1983—2003; book critic Newsweek Mag., N.Y.C., 1979-83, dir. Cullman Ctr. for Scholars and Writers N.Y. Pub. Libr., N.Y.C., 2003—. Selection com. J.S. Guggenheim Found., N.Y.C., 1995-97, trustee, 1987-94, 2001—, fellow, 1977, 86; exec. coun. Authors Guild; Ferris prof. journalism Princeton U., 1998; John J. Rhodes chair in Am. instns. and pub. policy Barrett Honors Coll., Ariz. State U., 2003. Author: Alice James, A Biography, 1980, Morgan American Financier, 1999; editor: Women & Analysis: Dialogues on Psychoanalytic Views of Femininity, 1974. Fellow NEH, 1976, 92, John D. and Catherine T. MacArthur Found., 2002—; recipient Bancroft prize Columbia U., 1981. Mem. Soc. Am. Historians (pres. 2001-02), Phi Beta Kappa (vis. scholar 1996 97).

STROUTH, LENORE EILEEN, music educator; b. Boise, Idaho, Oct. 25, 1970; d. Faith Ann and Bernard Francis Strouth. MusB, U. Iowa, 1994. Vocal music dir. United South Ctrl. Cmty. Schs., Wells, Minn., 1999—2002, Sibley East Cmty. Schs., Gaylord and Arlington, Minn., 2002—. Ch. musician St. Mary's Cath. Ch., Worthington, Minn., 1997—. Catechism tchr. Immaculate Conception Cath. Ch., Graettinger, Iowa, 1996—98. Mem.: Music Educators Nat. Conf., Am. Choral Dirs. Assn. Home: 10 8th St # 204 Gaylord MN 55334 Personal E-mail: lstrouth@mchsl.com. E-mail: lstrouth@sibley-east.k12.mn.us.

STRUBEL, ELLA DOYLE, advertising executive, public relations executive; b. Chgo., Mar. 14, 1940; d. George Floyd and Myrtle (McKnight) D.; m. Richard Craig G'sell, Apr. 26, 1969 (div. 1973); m. Richard Perry Strubel, Oct. 23, 1976; stepchildren: Douglas Arthur, Craig Tollerton. BA magna cum laude, U. Memphis, 1962; MA, U. Ill., 1963. Staff asst. Corinthian Broadcasting Co., N.Y.C., 1963-65; dir. advt. and pub. rels. WANE-TV, Ft. Wayne, Ind., 1965-66; asst. dir. advt. WBBM-TV, Chgo., 1966-67, mgr. sales promotion, 1967-69, dir. advt. sales promotion and info. svcs., 1969-70; dir. pub. rels. Waltham Watch Co., Chgo., 1973-74; mgr. advt. promotion and pub. rels. WMAQ-TV, Chgo., 1974-76; v.p. corp. rels. Kraft, Inc., Glenview, Ill., 1985-87; sr. v.p. corp. affairs Leo Burnett Co., Inc., Chgo., 1987-92, exec. v.p., 1992-98; mng. dir. EllaQuent Designs, 2002—. Mem. vis. com. U. Chgo. Harris Sch. Pub. Policy; pres. women's bd. Rehab. Inst. Chgo., 1982—84; chair Chgo. Network, 1994—95; trustee 4th Presbyn. Ch.; chair Rehab. Inst. Chgo., 1998—2001; bd. dirs. Chgo. Pub. Libr. Found., Rehab. Inst. Chgo. Named Outstanding Woman in Comms. in Chgo., YWCA, 1995, one of 100 Most Influential Women in Chgo., Crain's Chgo. Bus., 1996, Who's Who in Chgo. Bus., 2002. Mem. Casino Club, Econ. Club. Democrat. Presyterian. Home: 55 W Goethe St Chicago IL 60610-7406 Office: 737 N Michigan Ave Ste 1405 Chicago IL 60611-6654 Office Phone: 312-255-0235. E-mail: estrubel@aol.com.

STRUBLE, SUSAN C. artist, volunteer art therapist; b. N.Y.C., Jan. 4, 1939; d. Calvert Horton and Catherine (Snell) Crary; m. Robert Musser Struble, Mar. 30, 1985. BA, Carleton Coll., 1960. Art therapist Skills Inc., State College, Pa., 1995—, Adult Day Activities Ctr., State College, 1995—, adv. com., 2001—. Vol. art therapist Centre County Youth Ctr., Pa., 1990-93, Laurelton State Sch. and Hosp., 1973-74. Artist: works include Reclining Figure (1st prize Art Alliance Ctrl. Pa.), 1999. Asst. English tchr. Internat. Hospitality Coun., State Coll., 1995—; bd. dirs. friends Palmer Mus. of Art, Pa. State U., 1999—, sec., 2000—. Named Vol. of Yr. Ctrl. Counties Youth Ctr., 1993, Internat. Hospitality Coun., 1999, Adult Day Activities Ctr., 1999. Mem.: State Coll. Woman's Club (sec. art dept. 1998—99), Pa. Watercolor Soc. (sig. mem.), Am. Art Therapy Assn., Antique Automobile Club Am. Republican. Presbyterian. Avocations: art, music. E-mail: rmstruble@webtv.net.

STRUCK, NORMA JOHANSEN, artist; b. West Englewood, N.J., Feb. 17, 1929; d. Hans Christian and Amanda (Solberg) Johansen; m. H. Walter Struck, Aug. 21, 1955; children: Steven, Laurie. Student, N.Y. Phoenix Sch. Design, 1946-50, Art Students' League, N.Y.C., 1976-77. Staff artist Norcross, Inc., N.Y.C., 1950-60, free-lance artist, 1967-75; artist portraits, prints Scafa-Tornabene, Nyack, N.Y., 1976—; artist portraits, paintings U.S.N., U.S. Coast Guard, Washington, 1976—. Com. bd. mem. Navy Art Coop. Liaison, N.Y.C., 1976-80, Coast Guard Art Program, N.Y.C., 1980--. One-woman shows include Valley Cottage Gallery, N.Y., Bergen Co. Playhouse, Oradell, N.J., N.Y. Yacht Club, 2003, Nabisco Co., Fairlawn, N.J., 1987, Valley Cottage Gallery, N.Y., Bergen County Playhouse, Oradell, N.J.; exhibited in group shows Navy Hist. Mus., Washington, 1976, Navy Combat Art Gallery, Washington, World Trade Ctr., 1979, USCG, New Eng. Air Mus., Windsor Locks, Conn., 1984, Fed. Hall, N.Y.C., 1986, 93, 94, 95, 96, 97, Salmagundi Club, N.Y.C., Officers Club, Governor's Island, Hudson Valley Show, White Plains, N.Y., Intrepid Mus., N.Y.C., Alexander Hamilton U.S. Custom House, Newington-Cropsey Mus., N.Y., Bergen County Mus. Art & Sci., N.J.; represented in permanent collections U.S. Pentagon, Washington, Henie-Onstad Mus., Oslo, World Figure Skating Hall of Fame and Mus., Colorado Springs, Alexander Hamilton custom House, N.Y.C. Recipient Louis E. Seley award, Navy Art Program, 1979; Grumbacher award, Catherine Lorillard Wolfe, Nat. Arts Club, N.Y.C., 1978; George Gray award Coast Guard Art Program, Governors Island, N.Y., 1983, 89. Fellow Am. Artists Profl. League (pres.'s award 1979); mem. Portrait Soc. Am., Art Students League (life), Hudson Valley Assn. (bd. dirs. 1985-88, M. Dole award 1980), Soc. Illustrators, Salmagundi Club, Portrait Soc. Am., Inc. Avocations: antique collecting, gourmet cooking. Home: 910 Midland Rd Oradell NJ 07649-1904 E-mail: njstruck99@cs.com.

STRUHS, RHODA JEANETTE, civic and political worker; b. Fresno, Calif., Aug. 31, 1953; d. Edward Stanley and Mary Juanita (Pate) De Vere; m. Parry Leon Struhs, July 3, 1971; children: Jason, Lanisa. Grad. high sch., Fresno. Office mgr. Gunn McKay for U.S. Congress, Ogden, Utah, 1986; saleswoman Realty World-Simplified, Ogden, 1987-89; spl. edn. aide, substitute tchr. Weber Sch. Dist., Ogden, 1989-90; human svcs. aide Weber County Mental Health, Ogden, 1991; No. Utah field dir., office mgr. Pat Shea for Gov., Ogden, 1992; office adminstr. SHARE, INC., Ogden, 1993-97; mgr. cmty. resource-vol. ctr. Your Cmty. Connection, Ogden, 1997-99; Dem. adminstrv. asst. Utah Ho. of Reps., Salt Lake City, 1999—. Block leader Am. Heart Assn., March of Dimes, Easter Sales, 1979-93; troop leader, com. mem. Boy Scouts Am., Girl Scouts U.S.A., 1982-89; bd. dirs. Riverdale Elem. Sch. PTA, 1985-89, pres., 1987-88; bd. dirs. Women's Legis. Coun., 1989-91; conv. del. Weber County. Utah and Nat. Dem. Coms., 1981—; state sec. Utah Dem. Com., 1989-93; pres. Women's Legis. Coun. Weber County, 1993-95, parliamentarian, 1999-01; bd. dirs. Women's State Legis. Coun., 1993-97; vol. ctr. adv. com. Davis County United Way, 1989-99, Nat. Conf. State Legislatures, 1999—, Coun. State Govts., 1999—. Named Weber County Young Dem. of Yr., 1984, Dem. Vol. of Yr., 1986; recipient Extra Mile award Bonneville Coun. PTA, 1986, Disting. Svc. award Utah Dem. Com., 1993. Mem. Altrusa (pres. Ogden 1995-96, dist. membership chmn. 1997-99, dir. 1998-2002, Internat. Dist. Ten dir., 2001—). Avocations: handicrafts, camping, reading, travel. Home: 4312 S 700 W Ogden UT 84405-3404 Office: Utah Ho of Reps 318 State Capitol Salt Lake City UT 84114

STRUNA, NANCY L. social historian and American studies educator; b. Painesville, Ohio, May 24, 1950; d. Edward A. and Betty J. (Hoffacker) S. BS, U. Wis., 1972; PhD, U. Md., 1979. Social studies tchr. The Andrews Sch., Willoughby, Ohio, 1972-74; grad. asst. U. Md., College Park, 1974-76; tchr. 1-8 grades St. Mark's Elem., Adelphi, Md., 1976-78; instr. U. Md., College Park, 1978-80; asst. prof. U. Minn., Mpls., 1980-82; prof. dept. Am. Studies U. Md., College Park, 1982—, acting chair, 2001, exec. dir. univ. gen. edn., 2002—03. Spl. asst. to pres. women's issues, 1998-2000, fellow Acad. Affairs, 1998-99, campus legis. liaison, 1999. Author: People of Prowess, Sport, Leisure and Labor in Early America, 1996; contbr. articles to profl. jours., chpts. to books. Chair Pres. Commn. on Women's Issues U. Md., 1996—98; mem. Omohundro Inst. for Early Am. History, Culture and Soc. Named Disting. scholar Nat. Assn. Phys. Edn. in Higher Edn., 1993. Fellow Am. Acad. Kinesiology, N.Am. Soc. Sport History (pres. 1995-97), Orgn. Am. Historians, Am. Hist. Assn., Am. Studies Assn., U.S. Capitol Hist. Assn. Office: U Md 1102 Holzapfel Hall Coll College Park MD 20742-5620 Office Phone: 301-405-1357. Business E-Mail: nlstruna@umd.edu.

STRUTHERS, MARGO S. lawyer; BA, Carleton Coll., 1972; JD cum laude, U. Minn., 1976. Atty., shareholder Moss & Barnett, P.A. and predecessor firms, Mpls., 1976-93; ptnr. Oppenheimer Wolff & Donnelly, LLP, Mpls., 1993—. Mem. Am. Health Lawyers Assn., Minn. State Bar Assn (bus. law sect., former chair nonprofit com., former chair and former mem. governing coun. health law sect.). Office: Oppenheimer Wolff & Donnelly LLP Plaza VII 45 S 7th St Ste 3300 Minneapolis MN 55402-1614 E-mail: mstruthers@oppenheimer.com.

STUART, ALICE MELISSA, lawyer; b. N.Y.C., Apr. 7, 1957; d. John Marberger and Marjorie Louise (Browne) S. BA, Ohio State U., 1977; JD, U. Chgo., 1980; LLM, NYU, 1982. Bar: N.Y. 1981, Ohio 1982, N.Y. 1982, Fla. 1994, U.S. Dist. Ct. (so. dist.) Ohio, 1983, U.S. Dist. Ct. (so. and ea. dists.) N.Y. 1985. Assoc. Schwartz, Shapiro, Kelm & Warren, Columbus, Ohio, 1982-84, Paul, Weiss, Rifkind, Wharton & Garrison, N.Y.C., 1984-85, Kassel, Neuwirth & Geiger, N.Y.C., 1985-86, Phillips, Nizer, Benjamin, Krim & Ballon, N.Y.C., 1987—92; pvt. practice N.Y.C., 1992—98; atty. LeBoeuf, Lamb, Greene & MacRae, 1998—. Adj. prof. So. Coll., Orlando, Fla., 1997-98. Surrogate Speakers' Bur. Reagan-Bush Campaign, N.Y.C., 1984; mem. Lawyers for Bush-Quayle Campaign, N.Y.C., 1988; bd. dirs. Mayflower Soc. in State of NY, 1998-, counsellor, 2002-. Mem. ABA, N.Y. State Bar Assn., Winston Churchill Meml. Library Soc., Jr. League, Soc. Mayflower Descs. in State of N.Y. (bd. dirs. 1999-, counselor 2002--), Phi Beta Kappa, Phi Kappa Phi, Alpha Lambda Delta. Republican. Office: LeBoeuf Lamb Greene & MacRae 125 W 55th St New York NY 10019-5369

STUART, ANN, academic administrator, writer, educator; b. Madisonville, Ky., Dec. 22, 1935; d. Peter Frank and Laura (Hatchett) S.; m. Raymond R. Poliakoff, Aug. 22, 1980. BA in Edn., U. Fla., 1958; MA in English, U. Ky., 1962; PhD in English, So. Ill. U., 1976. Tchr. Maderia Beach Jr. High Sch., St. Petersburg, Fla., 1958-59, Bourbon County High Sch., Paris, Ky., 1959-60, Henry Clay High Sch., Lexington, Ky., 1960-62; prof. of English and tech. writing U. Evansville, Ind., 1962-89, asst. dean Coll. Arts and Scis., 1979-81, 86-87, adminstrv. coordinator writing programs, 1984-86; dean Sch. Arts and Scis. East Stroudsburg (Pa.) U., 1989-90; provost, v.p. acad. affairs Alma (Mich.) Coll., 1990-93; pres. Hartford (Conn.) Grad. Ctr., 1994—. Lectr. various regional and nat. profl. orgns.; dir. computer edn. Vanderburgh Sch. Corp., U. Evansville, Ball Communications, Inc., Evansville, 1985—; adminstrv. coordinator writing programs U. Evansville, 1985—; cons. various local, nat. bus., 1982—; vis. prof. computer tech. Purdue U., West Lafayette, Ind., 1987-88. Author: Writing and Analyzing Effective Computer System Documentation, 1984, Corresponding with Customers, 1985, The Technical Writer, 1987, Communication Guide For Corresponding with Students, Parents, Alumni and Donors, 1988. Bd. dirs. Evansville Arts and Edn. Council, 1972-75, Harlaxton Soc., Evansville, 1981-85. Mem. MLA, Ind. Corp. Sci. and Industry, Nat. Council Tchrs. English, Assn. Tchrs. Tech. Writing, Am. Coun. Edn., Am. Assn. Higher Edn., Am. Assn. Univ. Adminstrs., Rotary, Phi Kappa Phi, Delta Kappa Gamma. Clubs: Musicians of Evansville (pres. 1972-78). Avocations: art museums, performing arts, architecture. Office: Hartford Grad Ctr 275 Windsor St Hartford CT 06120-2910

STUART, CAROLE, publishing executive; b. N.Y.C., Feb. 22, 1941; d. Frank and Sally (Stern) Rose: m. Lyle Stuart, Feb. 4, 1982; 1 child, Jennifer Susan Livingston. Student, Bklyn. Coll. Pub. Lyle Stuart, Inc., Secaucus, N.J.; assoc. pub. Carol Pub. Group, N.Y.C.; pub. Barricade Books, Inc., N.Y.C. Author: Why Was I Adopted?, To Turn You On, 39 Sex Fantasies for Women, (with Claire Ciliotta), Why Am I Going to the Hospital?, I'll Never Be Fat Again, How To Lose 5 Pounds Fast, The Thank You Book. Mem. Authors Guild, Women's Media Group, Wine and Food Soc. N.Y.. Home: 1530 Palisade Ave Apt 6L Fort Lee NJ 07024-5402 Office: Barricade Books Ste 308A 185 Bridge Plz N Fort Lee NJ 02024

STUART, CYNTHIA MORGAN, university administrator; b. Harrisburg, Pa, June 29, 1949; d. Paul William and Bernice Leona (Boyer) M.; m. David Edward Stuart, June 14, 1971. Student, Elizabethtown (Pa.) Coll., 1967-69; BA, U. N.Mex., 1971, MPA, 1982, ABD in Ednl. Leadership, 2003. Admissions counselor U. N.Mex., Albuquerque, 1974-77, asst. dir. admissions, 1977-80, assoc. dir. admissions, 1980-83, dir. admissions, 1983—, Univ. articulation officer, 1989—, dir. student outreach svc. (secondary appointment), 1991-95, enrollment mgmt. team mem., 1998—. Mem. N.Mex. Coordinating Coun. Secondary Sch. and Coll., 1983-92; chair Coun. for Common Concerns, Albuquerque, 1987-95; mem. N.Mex. Articulation Com., Santa Fe, 1983-95; mem. adv. bd. Albuquerque Tech. Vocat. Inst., 1991—. Compiler, editor Statewide Statistical Profile Report, N.Mex. HS, 1983-90; cover photographer Prehistoric New Mexico, 2d edit., 1994, Glimpses of the Ancient Southwest, 1995. Coord. United Way, Albuquerque, 1980-81; elected del. N.Mex. Dem. Conv., 1982; mem. issues and advocacy com. Albuquerque Bus. Edn. Compact, 1991-93; mem. Am. Indian Edn. Initiative, Albuquerque, 1992—; Coll. Bd. del., 1991—. Recipient sys. devel. grant Commn. on Higher Edn., Santa Fe, 1995. Mem. Am. Assn. Collegiate Registrars and Admissions Officers (reporting officer of transfer credit N.Mex. 1979—), Rocky Mountain Assn. Collegiate Registrars and Admissions Officers (v.p. 1979-81, pres. 1983-84), N.Mex. Assn. Collegiate Registrars and Admissions Officers (sec.-treas. 1978-82, pres. 1991-92, Outstanding Svc. award 1990), N.Mex. Am. Coll. Testing Coun. (chair 1996-97, state rep. 1997—, trustee Am. Coll. Testing 1999-2002, del. to Coll. Bd. 1991—). Democrat. Avocations: photography, travel, drawing, music. Home: 423 Tulane Dr SE Albuquerque NM 87106-1417 Office: Univ New Mex Office of Admissions Student Svc Ctr Albuquerque NM 87131-0001 E-mail: cstuart@unm.edu.

STUART, DOROTHY MAE, artist; b. Fresno, Calif., Jan. 8, 1933; d. Robert Wesley Williams and Maria Theresa (Gad) Tressler; m. Reginald Ross Stuart, May 18, 1952; children: Doris Lynne Stuart Willis, Darlene Mae Stuart Cavalletto, Sue Anne Stuart Peters. Student, Calif. State U., Fresno, 1951-52, Fresno City Coll., 1962-64. Artist, art judge, presenter demonstrations at schs., fairs and art orgns., Calif., 1962—99; retired. Editor, art dir. Fresno High School Centennial 1889-1989, 1989; art advisor Portrait of Fresno, 1885-1985; contbg. artist Heritage Fresno, 1975; exhibited in group shows, including M.H. De Young Mus., San Francisco, 1971, Charles and Emma Frye Mus., Seattle, 1971, Calif. State U.-Fresno tour of China, 1974. Mem. adv. Ctrl. Calif. Women's Conf., 1989—, Patrons for Cultural Arts, Fresno, 1987-92, bd. dirs., 1991-92. Recipient 53 art awards, 1966-84; nominated Woman of the Yr., Bus./Profl. of Fresno, 1990. Mem. Soc. Western Artists (bd. dirs. 1968-74, v.p. 1968-70), Fresno Womens Trade Club (bd. dirs. 1986-93, pres. 1988-90), Fresno Art Mus., Fresno Met. Mus., Native Daus. Golden West Fresno. Republican. Avocations: world travel, photography, collecting art and dolls of different cultures. Home and Office: 326 S Linda Ln Fresno CA 93727-5737

STUART, GLORIA, actress; b. Santa Monica, Calif., July 14, 1910; m. Arthur Shekman, July 29, 1934 (dec. 1978); children: Blair Gordon Newell, Cylvia. Student, U. Calif., Berkeley. Film appearances include The Old Dark House, The Invisible Man, The Kiss Before the Mirror, My Favorite Year, 1982, Mass Appeal, 1984, Wildcats, 1986, Titanic, 1997 (Acad. award nomination for best supporting actress, Saturn award for best supporting actress, Golden Globe award for best performance by an actress in a supporting role, SAG award for outstanding performance by a female actor in a supporting role); appeared in numerous stage prodns.; one women shows (painting) in N.Y., Austria, Italy. Hollywood Walk of Fame-2000. Office: SAG 5757 Wilshire Blvd Los Angeles CA 90036-3635

STUART, JOAN MARTHA, fund raising executive; b. June 2, 1945; d. Ervin Wencil and Flora Janet (Applebaum) S. Student, Boston U., 1963-67. Cert. fund raising exec. Prodn. asst. Random House, N.Y.C., 1968-69; book designer Simon & Schuster, N.Y.C., 1969-71; feature writer Palm Beach (Fla.) Post, 1971-72; co-founder, comm. dir. Stuart, Gleimer & Assocs., West Palm Beach, 1973-84, pres., 1982—. Fin. devel. dir. YWCA Greater Atlanta, 1984-86, Ctr. for the Visually Impaired, Atlanta, 1986-90; ea. divsn. dir. City of Hope, 1990-94; devel. dir. Jewish Family Svcs., Atlanta, 1994-99, Ctr. for Visually Impaired, 1999-2002; dir. advancement The Epstein Sch., 2002—. Contbr. articles to profl. jours. Mem. crusade com. Am. Cancer Soc. Bd., 1981—; bd. dirs. Theatre Arts Co., 1980-81; cmty. svcs. chmn., bd. dirs. B'nai B'rith Women, 1980-82; chmn. publicity Leukemia Soc. Atlanta Polo Benefit, 1983; com. chmn. Atlanta Zool. Beastly Feast Benefit, 1984; mem. Atlanta Symphony Assocs.; chmn. Salute to Women of Achievement, 1987-90; founder, advisor Lauren's Run, 1992—; grad. Leadership Midtown, 2001. Recipient Nat. award B'nai B'rith Women, 1978, Regional award, 1979, Cert. of Merit, Big Bros./Big Sisters, 1976. Mem. Nat. Soc. Fund Raising Execs. (cert.), Diabetes Assn. (bd. dirs. 1990—), Jerusalem House (bd. dirs. 1991-94), Parent to Parent (bd. dirs. 1993-95). Democrat. Jewish. Office: 335 Colewood Way NW Atlanta GA 30328 Office Phone: 404-250-5636. E-mail: jstuart@epsteinatlanta.org.

STUART, LILLIAN MARY, writer; b. Chgo., Nov. 7, 1914; d. Ira and Katherine (Tries) Daugherty; m. Robert Graham Stuart, Aug. 7, 1936 (dec. Sept. 1969); 1 child, Mary Leone. Asst. to pres. Weisberger Bros., South Bend, 1933-42; head TWX distbn. Davis-Monthan AFB, Tucson, 1946-48; artist and music tchr., 1945-55; interviewer-counselor Ariz. State Employment Commn., Tucson, 1955-70; residence dir. YWCA, Tucson, 1970-71; tax preparer Tucson, 1971-72; U.S. census taker U.S. Govt., N.Mex., 1976, 80; mng. Luna County Rep. Party, Deming, 1976; tchr. YWCA, Tucson, 1969, El Paso Coll. Bus., 1972; tutor math, English, 1981. Travel lectr. various civic groups and clubs; radio reader Lighthouse for the Blind, El Paso, 1983—89; spkr. Internat. Women's Day Celebration, San Antonio, 1996, Lovington Rotary Internat., 1999, Kiwanis Internat., Lovington, 1999, Lovington Internat. Lions Club, 1999, Women's Club, Lovington, 2000, schs. in Lovington, 2002. Contbr. stories to The Quarterly; author: The Avestan, 1997; (series of biographies) Lighthouse for the Blind; actress Studebaker Players, South Bend, 1936-42, South Bend Theatre, 1936-42, (film) Extreme Prejudice, 1986; writer Centennial Mus. at U. Tex., El Paso, 1992-95; actress in commls., 1996-97. Counselor, vol. Crisis Ctr., Deming, 1975-77. Recipient plaques and prizes for various pieces of writing. Mem. Mensa, Rosicrucians. Avocations: travel, art. Address: 212 W Avenue A Lovington NM 88260-4120

STUART, LORI AMES, public relations executive; b. Hempstead, N.Y., Oct. 23, 1957; d. Henry Aschner and Janet (Hackel) Goldman; m. John Robert Ames, Jan. 30, 1982 (div. July 1990); 1 child, Robert Walter Ames; m. Robert John Stuart, July 27, 1991. BA, Hofstra U., 1979. Publicist Jane Wesman Pub. Rels., N.Y.C., 1980-84, v.p., 1991—; publicist, publicity mgr. William Morrow & Co., N.Y.C., 1984-89, publicity dir., 1989-90. Lectr., mentor NYU, 1994—. Jewish. Avocations: fishing, travel, reading, writing. Office: Jane Wesman Public Rels 322 8th Ave Ste 1702 New York NY 10001-6766

STUART, LYN (JACQUELYN L. STUART), judge; b. Sept. 23, 1955; m. George Stuart; children: Tucker, Shepard, Kelly. BA in Sociology and Edn., Auburn U., 1977; JD, U. Ala., 1980. Asst. atty. gen. State of Ala.; exec. asst. to commr. and spl. asst. atty. gen. Ala. Dept. Corrections; asst. dist. atty. Baldwin County; dist. judge, 1988—97; judge Ala. Cir. Ct., 1997—2001; justice Ala. Supreme Ct., 2001—. Republican. Office: 300 Dexter Ave Rm 3-215 Montgomery AL 36104-3741

STUART, MARIE JEAN, physician, hematologist, researcher; b. Bangalore, India, Sept. 11, 1943; came to U.S., 1967; d. Norman and Dorothy (Dias) S. BS, MB, Madras (India) U. Asst. prof. pediatrics SUNY Health Sci. Ctr., Syracuse, 1972-76, assoc. prof., 1976-81, prof. pediatrics, 1981-87; prof. chief hematology and oncology div. St. Christophers Hosp. for Children and Temple U., Phila., 1987-97; prof. thrombosis rsch. Temple U., 1987-97; dir. NIH Comprehensive Sickle Cell Ctr. Thomas Jefferson U., Phila., 1998—. Mem. nat. child health com. Nat. Inst. Child Health and Human Devel., Bethesda, Md., 1982-86; mem. nat. heart, lung and blood rsch. tng. com., NIH, Bethesda, 1993-2000; mem. NIH Sickle Cell Disease Adv. Coun., 2000—; mem. NIH Erythrocyte and Leucocyte Biology Study Sect., 2003—. Mem. editl. bd. Biology of the Neonate, 2000—; contbr. chpts. to books, articles to profl. jours. Docent in tng. Phila. Mus. Art. Recipient Rsch. award Temple U., 1997. Mem. Am. Fedn. Clin. Research. Am. Pediatric Soc., Soc. for Pediatric Research. Avocations: music, art. Home: 10B W Society Hill Towers Philadelphia PA 19106

STUART, NANCY RUBIN (NANCY ZIMMAN STETSON), journalist, author, writer, producer; b. Boston, Nov. 25, 1944; d. Stuart Wendell and Ethel (Rabinovitz) Zimman; m. William W. Stetson, Apr. 28, 2001; children: Elisabeth, Jessica. BA, Tufts U., 1966; MA in Teaching, Brown U., 1967; PhD (hon.), Mt. Vernon Coll., 1995. Playwright, dir. Equity Library Theatre, Roundabout, Joseph Jefferson and St. Clement's theaters, N.Y.C., 1971-74; freelance reporter Westchester-Gannett newspapers and mags., 1975-77, N.Y. Times, N.Y.C., 1977—. Faculty affiliate Bush Ctr. in Child Devel., Yale U., New Haven, 1981-86; mem. Westchester County Women's Adv. Bd., chair, 1988; bd. dirs. Women Writing Women's Lives Seminar; mem. faculty SUNY, Purchase, 1994-95, Fordham U., N.Y.C., 1996-99. Author: The New Suburban Women, Beyond Myth and Motherhood, 1982, The Mother Mirror: How a Generation of Women is Changing Motherhood in America, 1984, Isabella of Castile: The First Renaissance Queen, 1991, American Empress: The Life and Times of Marjorie Merriweather Post, 1995, Club Dance: The Show, The Steps, The Spirit of Country, 1998; writer, assoc. prodr: TV series America's Castles for A&E Network, 1996—99 (Telly award, 1999, Telly award (3), 2001, Writing Communicator award, 1999), The Gold Coast for The Grand Tour A & E TV, 1997, writer prodr., prodr.: TV series Restore America, 1999; writer prodr., prodr. (TV series) Restore America, 2001 (3 Telly awards); writer/assoc. prodr.: TV series Eccentrics, 1999 (Crystal award, Telly award), The N.Y. Times, 1977—2001, contbg. editor: Parents mag., 1987—91, : McCalls, Savvy, Travel & Leisure, Ladies Home Jour., 1980—92; theater critic : Stamford Advocate, 1994—96. Recipient Washington Irving award Westchester Libr. Assn., 1993, Telly award finalist, 2001; Time, Inc.-Bread Loaf Writers' Colony scholar, 1979. Fellow MacDowell Colony; mem. Author's Guild, Am. Soc. Journalists and Authors (Author of Yr. award 1992), PEN, Nat. Arts Club. Avocations: skiing, sailing, ballet and jazz dancing, classical music.

STUART, PAMELA BRUCE, lawyer; b. N.Y.C., Feb. 13, 1949; d. J. Raymond and Marion Grace (Cotins) S. AB with distinction, Mt. Holyoke Coll., 1970; JD cum laude, U. Mich., 1973. Bar: N.Y. 1974, D.C. 1975, U.S. Dist. Ct. D.C. 1979, U.S. Ct. Appeals (D.C. cir.) 1980, U.S. Supreme Ct. 1980, U.S. Dist. Ct. Md. 1989, Md. 1992, Va. 1993, U.S. Ct. Appeals (4th cir.) 1993, Fla. 1994, U.S. Dist. Ct. (ea. dist.) Va. 1994, U.S. Dist. Ct. (no. dist.) N.Y. 1996, U.S. Dist. Ct. (so. dist.) Fla. 1998, U.S. Dist. Ct. (so. dist.) N.Y. 1999, U.S. Dist. Ct. (ea. dist.) N.Y. 1999, U.S. Dist. Ct. (mid. dist.) Fla. 2001. Trial atty., deputy asst. dir. Bur. of Consumer Protection, FTC, Washington, 1973-79; asst. U.S. atty. U.S. Atty's Office, Washington, 1979-85; sr. trial atty. Office of Internat. Affairs, U.S. Dept. Justice, Washington, 1985-87; atty. Ross, Dixon & Masback, Washington, 1987-89; mem. Lobel, Novins, Lamont & Flug, Washington, 1989-92; pvt. practice, Washington, 1992—. Instr. Nat. Inst. for Trial Advocacy, Atty. Gen.'s Advocacy Inst., Legal Edn. Inst., Fed. Practice Inst.; mem. Jud. Conf. D.C., 1985-88, 1991-2004; mem. Jud. Conf., D.C. Cir., 1996, 98, 2000; assoc. mem. Consular Corps Washington; legal analyst CNN, MSNBC, Fox News, other TV networks. Author: The Federal Trade Commission, 1991; contbr. articles to profl. jours. Bd. dirs. Anacostia Econ. Devel. Corp., 1993—, Anacostia Holding Co., Inc., Anacostia Mgmt. Co., Inc., 1993—. Mem. ABA (internat. criminal law com., chmn., 1993-96, chmn. fed. crime rules subcom. white collar crime com. sect. criminal justice 1997-99), Bar Assn. D.C. (bd. dirs. 1995-2001, 2003-04), Asst. U.S. Attys. Assn. D.C. (exec. coun. 1993-99, pres. 1998-99), Assn. Trial Lawyers Am., Women's Bar Assn. D.C., Fla. Bar (exec. coun. real property probate and trust law sect. 1999—), Alumnae Assn. Mt. Holyoke Coll. (bd. dirs. 1986-89, 92-95, Alumnae medal of honor 1990), Edward Bennett Williams Inn of Ct. (master of bench), Fed. City Club (bd. govs. 1992—), Cosmos Club. Avocations: writing, interior design, investments, piano, art. Home: 5115 Yuma St NW Washington DC 20016-4336 Office: The J Raymond Stuart Bldg 1750 N Street NW Washington DC 20036 also: 111 Johns Island Dr Apt 7 Vero Beach FL 32963-3274 Office Phone: 202-835-2200. E-mail: pamstuart@aol.com.

STUART, SANDRA JOYCE, computer information scientist; b. Wheatland, Mo., Aug. 15, 1950; d. Asa Maxville and Inez Irene (Wilson) Friedley; m. John Kendall Stuart, Apr. 17, 1971; 1 child, Whitney Renee. Student, Cen. Mo. State U., 1968-69; AA (hon.), Johnson County C.C., 1980; BSBA cum laude, Avila Coll., 1992. Cert. Info. Sys. Security Profl. Statis. asst. Fed. Crop Ins. Corp., Kansas City, Mo., 1978-83; mgr. Fed. Women's Program, Kansas City, 1979-80; mgmt. asst. Marine Corps Fin. Ctr., Kansas City, 1983-85, analyst computer systems, 1985-88; computer programmer analyst Corps. of Engrs., Kansas City, 1988-91; regional program mgr. FAA, Kansas City, 1991—. Author: The Samuel Walker History, 1983. Asst. supt. Sunday sch. Overland Park (Kans.) Christian Ch., 1979-80, supt., 1980-82. Mem. Wheatland H.S. Alumni Assn. (pres. 1990-91), Mo-Kan High Tech. Crime Investigation Assn. (charter, 2d v.p. 1998-99, 1st v.p. 1999-2000, pres. 2000-2001), Kansas City Security Coalition. Avocations: needlework, genealogy, reading, travel.

STUART, TONI FREEMAN, priest; b. Bakerfield, Calif., Nov. 27, 1937; d. Jack Reginald Bice and Elinor Day Freeman; m. Arthur King Stuart, June 10, 1960 (div. 1974); children: Susan Reid Stuart-Shuman, Daniel King, Jane Elinor Edel. BA in English Lit., Stanford U., Calif., 1959; MA in Religion, Claremont Sch. Theology, Calif., 1989. Ordained priest Episcopal Ch. Advt. mgr. Vroman's Bookstore, Pasadena, 1959—69; field rep. City Dir. Robert White, Pasadena, 1971—74; exec. sec. Villa Park Neighborhood Improvement Assn., Pasadena, 1974—79; fund developer Pasadena Foothill Valley YWCA, Pasadena, 1979—84; sr. citizen coord. Jackie Robinson Ctr., City of Pasadena, 1984—86; neighborhood svcs. organizer Neighborhood Connections, Pasadena, 1986—89; assoc. priest All Saints Episc. Ch., Highland Park, L.A., Calif., 1989—91; asst. priest St. Paul's Episc. Ch., Pomona, Calif., 1991—92; interim priest St. Thomas Episc. Ch., Hacienda Hts., Calif., 1993; vicar Chapel of St. Francis, Atwater Village, L.A., Calif., 1993—2000; rector St. Matthews Episc. Ch., Sacramento, 2000—. Author: Adventures of the Soul, 2000. Mem. Sheriff Comdr.'s Cmty. Pride Com., Sacramento, 2001—, San Juan Unified Sch. Dist. Cmty. Commn., Sacramento, 2002—, Immaculate Heart Cmty., Dem. County Com., L.A.; dean Southeastern Deanery Episc. Diocese No. Calif., 2004—. Democrat. Episcopalian. Avocations: gardening, writing. Office: St Matthews Episcopal Ch 2300 Edison Ave Sacramento CA 95821

STUBBE, JOANNE, chemistry educator; Novartis prof. chemistry and biology MIT, Cambridge. Arthur C. Cope scholar award Am. Chemistry Soc., 1993. Mem. NAS. Office: MIT Dept Chemistry 77 Massachusetts Ave Dept Cambridge MA 02139-4307

STUBBS, KATRINA CHILDS, business consultant; b. Atlanta, Feb. 10, 1964; d. Theodore Roosevelt Childs and Jacqueline Louise (Clark) Childs-Taylor; children: Kayla Laranza, Kiara Danielle. BS in Chemistry, Dillard U., 1985; MBA, Albany State U., 1991. Med. specialist U.S. Army Res., Chamblee, Ga., 1981-87; technologist/chemist Miller Brewing Co., Albany, Ga., 1987-93; bus. cons. UGA Bus. Outreach Svc., Albany, 1993—; prin., owner Elite Profl. & Tutoring Svcs., Inc., 1999—. Minority student dir. UGA Bus. Outreach Svc., Albany, 1994-95. Named Vol. of Month, First Step Vol. Program, Albany, 1994. Mem. NAFE. Democrat. Baptist. Avocations: working with youths, aerobics, listening to gospel, reading. Office Phone: 229-446-8718. Personal E-mail: stubbs-kc@yahoo.com.

STUBBS, SUSAN CONKLIN, statistician; b. Washington, July 26, 1935; d. Maxwell Robertson and Marcia (Nye) Conklin; m. LeRoy Carter Hostetter, May 20, 1975 (div. 1988); m. Joel Richard Stubbs, Sept. 20, 1992. BA, Pa. State U., 1957. Economist Bur. of Census, Suitland, Md., 1973-74, Bur. of Labor Statistics, Washington, 1974-78, supervisory economist, 1978-84; statistician IRS, Washington, 1984-95, chief rschr. stats. of income divsn., 1989-92, coord. for indsl. classification, 1994-95; ret., 1995. Cons. joint com. on taxation U.S. Congress, 1992-94; OPM legis. fellow, 1988. Contbr. articles to profl. jours.; editor govtl. statis. publs. Leader, del., bd. dirs., v.p., chmn. nominating com. Nation's Capital coun. Girl Scouts U.S., 1968—; sec.-treas. Middlesex Beach Assn., Bethany, Del., 1991—94;

jobs. editor Caucus for Women in Stats., Washington, 1992—95; mentor Mentors Inc., Washington, 1992—94; treas. Smith Point Sea Rescue, 1997—2003; chmn., Christmas on Cockrell's Creek Reedville Fisherman's Mus., 2001—02, docent, 1997—, treas., 2003; active Boy Scouts Am. Campaign for Family Values; tutor and mentor People Helping People; fin. chmn., Christmas on Cockrell's Creek Reedville Fisherman's Mus., 2002; mem. Tax Economist Forum, 1990—97; treas. Rappahannock C.C. Found., 2003—; mentor Northumberland Middle Sch. in Tobacco grant program; treas. Region II, Episc. Diocese of Va., 1999—; bd. dirs. Rice's Hotel/Hughlett's Tavern Found., 1998—2000, Rappahannock C.C. Found., 2002—. Mem.: Am. Statis. Assn. (treas. 2003—), St. Stephen's Episcopal Ch. ECW (vice pres. 2002, treas. 2003—), Bus. and Profl. Women Essex County and No. Neck (sec. 1999—2001), Va. Federated Women's Clubs (pres. Northumberland County chpt. 1996—98, pres Ea. area Lee dist. 1998—2000), Rivers Bend Assn. (v.p., bd. dirs. 1996—98, chair bylaws com., chair long range planning com., chair fin. com. 1998—2001, v.p., bd. dirs., bd. mem. 2001—). Avocations: sailing, swimming, gardening, reading. Home: 776 Riverview Ln Heathsville VA 22473-4011

STUBER, IRENE ZELINSKY, writer, researcher; b. Cleve., Nov. 1, 1928; d. Joseph Frank and Marian (Kulchar) Zelinsky; m. Joseph Francis Stuber, Apr. 9, 1948 (div. Aug. 1954); children: Catherine, Geraldine, William. Student, Cleve. Coll., 1946-48. Editor Cleve. Kegler, 1954-60; publs. dir. Miami (Fla.)-Dade C. of C., 1963-65; staff writer Hollywood (Fla.) Sun-Tattler, 1966-67; urban affairs writer Ft. Lauderdale (Fla.) News, 1967-74; tech. editor Bell Aerospace, New Orleans, 1977-78; owner Kulchar's Jewelry, New Orleans, 1974-83, Hot Springs, Ark., 1983-90. Freelance writer. Rschr., writer (Internet newsletter) Women of Achievement and Herstory, 1994—, columnist; writer (Internet newsletter) Catt's Claws, 1995—. Mem. ctrl. com. Broward County (Fla.) Dem. Party, 1973-75, Garland County (Ark.) Dem. Party, 1996—; v.p. Va. Clinton Kelley Dem. Women's Club, Hot Springs, 1995-97. Recipient Pub. Svc. award City of Hollywood, 1967, Journalistic Excellence award AP, 1967, Recognition of Svcs. award Fla. Bar Assn., 1968. Mem. NOW (Ark. chpt. pres. 1993-94, Hot Springs chpt. pres. 1992-97), Harbor House (sec., bd. dirs. 1997-98), Women's Internet and Info. Network, Inc. (pres. 1997—). Avocation: "missionary" to introduce women to internet and women's history to internet. Home: PO Box 6185 Hot Springs National Park AR 71902-6185

STUCKEL, RUTH F. philosopher, educator, nun; b. St. Louis, Sept. 12, 1936; d. Oliver Conrad Stuckel and Helen Honora Mackin. BA, Fontbonne Coll., 1964; MA, Fordham U., 1966, Exeter (Eng.) U., 1971; postgrad. in PhD program, Kans. U., 1973. Asst. prof. philosophy Avila U., Kansas City, Mo., 1966—68, 1972—77, 1978—80, assoc. prof. philosophy, 1988—. Adj. prof. Harris Stowe State U., St. Louis, 1984—88; adj. vis. prof. Mt. St. Mary's Coll., Brentwood, Calif., 1977—78; bd. counselors, administrn. Sisters of St. Joseph of Carondelet, St. Louis, 1980—88; lectr. in field. Bd. dirs. Carondelet Health, Kansas City, 1989—2002, St. Teresa Acad., Kansas City, 2001—, St. Joseph Hosp., Kirkwood, Mo., 1980—88. Fellow Coolidge Rsch. Found. Colloquium, Episcopal Divinity Sch., Cambridge, Mass., 1992. Mem.: Midwest Bioethics Ctr., Kansas City Area Philos. Assn. (pres. 1993), Am. Cath. Philos. Assn. Democrat. Roman Catholic. Avocations: walking, films, travel, reading. Home: 11725 Wornall Rd Kansas City MO 64114 Office: Avila Univ 11901 Wornall Rd Kansas City MO 64145 E-mail: stuckelrf@mail.avila.edu.

STUCKER, ELEANOR MARIE, social worker, psychotherapist; b. Milledgeville, Ga., Oct. 4, 1951; d. Michael John Esposito and Leonora Marie Rossi-Esposito; m. Peter David Stucker, Dec. 16, 1990 (dec. Mar. 16, 1993). BA in Psychology, Rutgers U., 1974; MA in Rehab. Counseling, So. Ill. U., 1977; MSW, Columbia U., 1983. LCSW N.J., cert. social worker N.Y. Clin. social worker Jewish Bd. Children and Family Svcs., Linden Hill Sch., Hawthorne, NY, 1983—90; clin. social worker dept. psychiatry Hackensack (N.J.) Med. Ctr., 1990—99; clin. social worker Child Abuse Unit, Hackensack, 1999—; pvt. practice as psychotherapist Teaneck, NJ, 1996—. Fellow, So. Ill. U., 1974; scholar, State of N.J., Rutgers U., 1970. Mem.: NASW. Roman Catholic. Avocations: theater, travel. Home: 12D 2100 Linwood Ave Fort Lee NJ 07024 Office: Rm 8 362 Cedar Ln Teaneck NJ 07666

STUCKEY, DONNA SUE PINTAR, information services executive; b. Pittsburg, Kans., Oct. 20, 1960; d. Carl E. and Mary Ann (Bugni) Pintar; m. Donald Oris Stuckey, May 20, 1982 (div. Apr. 14, 1987); children: Banning W., Cassandra R., Heather D. BS in Math., BS in Computer Sci., Pittsburg State U., 1982, MS in Tech. Tchr. Edn., 2002. Asst. mgr. office info. svcs. Pittsburg State U., 1979-82, asst. office mgr. dept. computer sci., info. sci., 1979-82, coord. devel. info. svcs., 1988-92, dir. development info. svcs., 1992-98, bus. analyst/programmer Getty Oil Co., Tulsa, 1982-84; office mgr., sales asst. State Farm Ins. Co., Pittsburg, 1986-87; loan officer 1st Fed. Savs. & Loan, Pittsburg, 1987-88; programmer, applications analyst Office of Info. Svcs. Pitts. State U., 1998—. Asst. to grad. students, Pittsburg, 1988—; freelance installer PCs, Pittsburg, 1992-2004 Asst. troop leader Boy Scouts Am. Ozark Trails Coun., Pittsburg, 1989-2000, asst. troop leader Girl Scouts Am. Ozark Area Coun., 1990-2003; pres. home and sch. assn. St. Mary's Grade Sch., Pittsburg, 1995-97. Mem. Info. Tech. Adv. Coun., Pittsburg C. of C. (amb. com. 1995-98), Japan Karate-Do Genbu-Kai, Alpha Sigma Alpha, Omicron Delta Kappa, Kappa Mu Epsilon, Delta Mu Delta, Alpha Sigma Alpha Alumnae Assn. (pres., 1998-, Pittsburg chpt., treas., sec.), Phi Kappa Phi (pub. rels. chair), Pittsburg Kiwanis Club (editor, pub. rels. chair), Campus Girl Scouts of Pittsburg State U. (advisor). Roman Catholic. Avocations: Karate, walking, reading, gardening, pub. rels. event coordr.. Home: 707 N Highland St Pittsburg KS 66762-4521 Office: Pittsburg State U Office Info Svcs 1701 S Broadway St Pittsburg KS 66762-7500 E-mail: dstuckey@pittstate.edu.

STUCKEY, ELLEN MAE, music educator; d. Charles Franklin and Mary Dolores Hershberger; m. Joseph Bruce Stuckey, Jr., June 9, 1979; children: Laura L., Aaron N. BS in Music Edn., West Chester U., 1977; MEd in Music Edn., Pa. State U., 1981. Cert. music tchr. Pa. Dept. Edn. Music tchr. K-6 Everett (Pa.) Area Sch. Dist., 1977—82; pvt. music tchr. Martinsburg, 1982—; tchr. jr./sr. high vocal/gen. music Hollidaysburg (Pa.) Area Sch. Dist., 1988—89; music tchr. K-6 No. Bedford County Sch. Dist., Loysburg, Pa., 1990—. Dir. adult choir 1st Bapt. Ch. Altoona, Pa., 1977—87, Martinsburg Grace Brethren Ch., 1989—. Composer, lyricist: songs Hail to You, O Northern Bedford, 1995; contbr. to profl. mags.; composer 3 songs, co-author: mus. drama The Ark of Faith, 2003. Dir. luminary svc. Am. Cancer Soc., Martinsburg, 2002, 2003; mistress of ceremonies Little Miss pageant Roaring Spring (Pa.) Lions Club, 1996, 1997, 1998. Mem.: Nat. Guild Piano Tchrs., Am. Choral Dirs. Assn., Pa. Music Educators Assn. Republican. Grace Brethren. Avocations: spending time with family, gardening, photography, songwriting. Office: No Bedford County Sch Dist 217 NBC Dr Loysburg PA 16659 E-mail: estuckey@nbcsd.k12.pa.us.

STUCKY, JEAN SEIBERT, lawyer; b. Berkeley, Calif., Feb. 9, 1951; d. Edward Raymond and Frances Selma (Berg) S.; m. Scott Wallace Stucky, Aug. 18, 1973; children: Mary-Clare, Joseph. BA in Econs., Wellesley (Mass.) Coll., 1973; JD, Cornell U., 1978; MA in Econs., Trinity U., San Antonio, 1980; postgrad., George Washington U., 1991—95. Bar: DC 1978. Atty.-advisor Adminstrv. Conf. US, Washington, 1978-79, Divsn. Advice, NLRB, Washington, 1979-94; contractor labor counsel US Dept. Energy, Office Gen. Counsel, Washington, 1994—. Mem. Washington Cathedral Altar Guild, 1988—. Mem. DC Bar, Dames of Loyal Legion of US, Washington Wellesley Club (pres. 1992-94), Wellesley Coll. Alumnae Assn. (regional chmn. 1995-97). Republican. Episcopalian. Avocations: gardening, flower arranging. Home: 11004 Homeplace Ln Potomac MD 20854-1406 Office: US Dept Energy Office Gen Counsel 1000 Independence Ave SW Washington DC 20585-0001

STUCKY, NANCY L. special education educator; Tchr. spl. edn. Sandstone Elem., Billings, Mont. Recipient State Tchr. of Yr. Spl. Edn. award Mont., 1992.

STUDER, KATHY LYNN, music educator; b. Decatur, Ill., June 17, 1975; d. Stanley Lee and Renne Marie Walters; m. Daniel William Studer. BS Music Edn., U. Ill., Urbana-Champaign, 1997. Cert. IL Type 12 Tchg. Cert. 1997. Musician Busch Gardens Entertainment, Williamsburg, Va., 1993—94; band tchr. Kankakee Sch. Dist., Kankakee, Ill., 1997—98, Band for Today, Naperville, Ill., 1999—2000, Rondout Sch. Dist. 72, Lake Forest, Ill., 2000—03. Mem. cultural arts com. Rondout Sch., Lake Forest, Ill., 2001—02; coord. young authors Rondout Sch. Dist., Lake Forest, 2001—03. Musician Decatur (Ill.) Mcpl. Band, 1991—93; Vol. private instr. Univ. High Sch., Urbana, Ill., 1996—96. Mem.: NEA, Ill. Grade Sch. Music Assn., Music Educators Nat. Conf., Tech. Club (coord. 2002—03).

STUDEVANT, LAURA, medical association administrator; Pres. Nat. Environ. Health Assn., Denver; regional health mgr. Amtrak, Chgo. Address: Regional Pub Health Mgr Amtrak 210 S Canal Chicago IL 60606 Office: National Environ Health Assn 720 S colorado Blvd Ste 970S Denver CO 80246-1925

STUDIN, JAN, publishing executive; From acct. mgr. to v.p. Woman's Day, 1982—95, v.p., advt. dir., 1995—96; v.p., pub. Woman's Day Hachette Filipacchi Mags., Inc., N.Y.C., 1996—2002; v.p., pub. G+J USA's Parents Group, 2002—. Office: G+J USA Publishing 375 Lexington AVe New York NY 10017-5514

STUDLACK, CINDY JUNE, speech pathology/audiology services professional; b. Pottsville, Pa., Aug. 6, 1974; d. Howard L. and Diane E. Blankenhorn; m. John Paul Studlack, June 1, 2002. BS, Pa. State U., 1996; MS, Bloomsburg U., 1998. Cert. Clin. Competence Am. Speech & Hearing Assn., 1999, Pa. State Licensure in Speech and Language Pathology Dept. of State Bur. of Profl. & Occupl. Affairs, 1999, Profl. Tchg. Cert.: Level 2 Commonwealth of Pa, 2002. Camp counselor Easter Seals of Va., Falls Church, 1996; speech & lang. pathologist Schuylkill Intermediate Unit #29, Mar-Lin, Pa., 1998—. Contbr. case study Digital Laryngeal Massage. Mem.: Pa, State Edn. Assn., Am. Autism Soc., Pa. Speech and Hearing Assn., Am. Speech and Hearing Assn. (sch. based issues com.). Democrat. Lutheran. Home: 223 North 18th St Pottsville PA 17901 Office: Schuylkill Intermediate Unit #29 PO Box 130 17 Maple Ave Mar Lin PA 17951 Personal E-mail: jcstu@f-tech.net. E-mail: cstudlack@pgasd.com.

STUDLEY, JAMIENNE SHAYNE, lawyer, educator; b. N.Y.C., Apr. 30, 1951; d. Jack Hill and Joy (Cosor) Studley; m. Gary J. Smith, July 14, 1984. BA magna cum laude, Barnard Coll., 1972; JD, Harvard U., 1975. Bar: DC 1975, U.S. Dist. Ct. DC 1978. Assoc. Bergson, Borkland, Margolis & Adler, Washington, 1976—80; spl. asst., sec. U.S. HHS, 1980—81; assoc. Weil, Gotshal & Manges, Washington, 1981—83; assoc. dean law sch. Yale U., New Haven, 1983—87, lectr. law, 1984—87; syndicated columnist Am. Lawyer Media, 1990—91; exec. dir. Nat. Assn. for Law Placement, Washington, 1987—90, Calif. Abortion Rights Action League, 1992—93; dep. gen. counsel U.S. Dept. Edn., 1993—99, acting gen. counsel, 1997—99; pres. Skidmore Coll., Saratoga Springs, NY, 1999—2003; scholar-in-residence Carnegie Found. for the Advancement of Tchg., Palo Alto, Calif., 2003—04; pres. Pub. Advocates, Inc., 2004—. Vis. scholar adj. faculty U. Calif., Berkeley Law Sch., 1992; vis. com. Harvard Law Sch.; bd. dirs. Adirondack Trust Co., 1999—2003; vice chair for program, chair-elect The Annapolis Group, 2001—03; chair legis. com. Commn. on Ind. Colls. and Univs. N.Y. State, 2002—03. Pres. Conn. Women's Ednl. and Legal Fund, Hartford, 1986—87; co-founder Washington Area Women's Found., 1997; founding bd. dirs. Wood Art Collectors; mem. Jacob Javits fellowship bd. U.S. Dept. Edn., 2000—03; mem. policy com. Campus Compact, 2002—. Mem.: ABA (commn. on women in the profession 1991—94, chair editl. bd. Perspectives 1991—99, chair coord. coun. legal edn. 1996—97, com. on loan repayment and forgiveness 2001—03), Nat. Adv. Coun., First Book, Nat. Assn. for Ind. Colls. and Univs. (accountability com. 1999—2002), DC Bar Assn., Barnard in Washington (pres. 1977—78), Assn. Alumnae Barnard Coll. (bd. dirs. 1978—81), Phi Beta Kappa. Office: 131 Stewart St # 300 San Francisco CA 94105-1241

STUEWE, ISABEL, elementary school educator; BS in English, Concordia U. 5th grade tchr. St. John's Luth. Sch., Orange, Calif. Mem.: Luth. Edn. Assn. (past pres. Luth. elem. tchrs. dept.), Western Assn. Schs. and Colls. (commr.), Nat. Bd. for Profl. Tchg. Stds. (bd. mem. 1992—). Avocations: fishing, camping, reading. Office: St Johns Luth Sch 154 S Shaffer St Orange CA 92866

STUHR, ELAINE RUTH, state legislator; b. Polk County, Nebr., June 19, 1936; m. Boyd E. Stuhr, 1956; children: Cynthia (Stuhr) Zluticky, Teresa (Stuhr) Robbins, Boyd E., Jr. BS, U. Nebr. Tchr. jr. and sr. vocat. h.s. Nebr. schs.; senator Nebr. Unicameral, Lincoln, 1994—; chmn. Nebr. retirement sys. com.; vice chair natural resources com.; commr. edn. com. of states; farmer. Former asst. instr. U. Nebr., Lincoln; participant farmer to farmer assignment to Russia with Winrock, Internat., 1993, to Lithuania with Vol. Overseas Coop. Asistance, 1993; former pres. Agrl. Womens Leadership Network; former mem. bd. dirs. Feed Grains Coun., Nebr. Corn Bd.; agrl. adv. com. for Congressman Doug Bereuter. Past pres., bd. dirs. Found. for Agrl. Edn. and Devel.; former mem. exec. com. and bd. dirs. Agrl. Coun. Am.; nat. pres. Women Involved in Farm Econs., state pres.; mem. adv. com. Nebr. Extension Sv.; bd. dirs. Heartland Ctr. for Leadership Devel.; past chmn. Nebr. Agrl. Leadership Coun. Republican. Office: Nebr State Capitol Dist # 24 Lincoln NE 68509 E-mail: estuhr@unicam.state.ne.us.

STUKES, GERALDINE HARGRO, library and information scientist, educator; m. Marshall Willis Stukes, Jr., Dec. 24, 1964 (dec. May 2001); children: Marshall III, Stephen Edward. AAS, N.Y. Tech. Coll., 1968; BA, Bklyn. Coll., 1982; MLS, Pratt Inst., 1984; MA, Columbia U., 1994. Sch. sec. N.Y.C. Dept. Edn., Bklyn., 1974—86, sch. libr., 1986—2003; owner Egomi Info. Services Inc., 1989—. Adj. prof. libr. Medgar Evers Coll., CUNY, Bklyn., 1999—. Mem.: ALA, Am. Assn. of U. Women, NY Libr.Assn., Black Librs. Assn., African Am. Hist. and Geneaol. Assn. Home and Office: Egami Info Svcs Inc 69 Schenck Ave Brooklyn NY 11207

STUKES, REESIE, communications executive; b. Washington, D.C., Nov. 16, 1976; d. Alice Stukes. BS mktg., Hampton U., Hampton, Va., 1994—98. Comml. account exec. MCI, Raleigh, NC, 2000—, global svc. rep Cary, NC, 1999—2000. Mem.: Am. Mktg. Assn. Office: MCI 1000 St Albans Dr Ste 300 Raleigh NC 27609 Personal E-mail: rstukes@yahoo.com. E-mail: reesie.stukes@mci.com.

STULL, EVALYN MARIE, artist; b. Hays, Kans., June 7, 1949; d. Harold Kenneth Gossett and Helen Marie Loreg; m. Dennis Eugene Kincaid, Dec. 4, 1967 (div. 1968); children: Pamela Sue Kincaid, Mark Allen Kincaid; m. Kenneth Eugene Stull, Dec. 4, 1973 (div. 1983); children: Daniel Eugene, Carl Andrew. A in gen. studies, Morgan C.C., Fort Morgan, Colo. Owner Stull's Kinder Day Care, Fort Morgan, Colo., 1994, Paintings by Evalyn Stull, Chase, Kans., 2001—02. Home and Office: 201 Cedar/PO Box 134 Chase KS 67524

STUMBO, JANET LYNN, state supreme court justice; b. Prestonsburg, Ky. d. Charles and Doris Stanley Stumbo; m. Ned Pillersdorf; children: Sarah, Nancee, Samantha. BA, Morehead State U., 1976; JD, U. Ky., 1980. Bar: Ky. 1980, W.Va. 1982. Staff atty. to Judge Harris S. Howard Ky. Ct. Appeals, 1980—82; asst. county atty. Floyd County, 1982—85; ptnr. Turner, Hall & Stumbo, P.S.C., 1982—88; prosecutor Floyd Dist. Ct. and Juvenile Ct.; ptnr. Stumbo, DeRossett & Pillersdorf, 1989; judge Ct. Appeals, Ky., 1989—93, Supreme Ct. of Ky., 1993—. Named to Morehead State U. Alumni Assn. Hall of Fame, 1990, U. Ky. Coll. Law Alumni Hall of Fame, 1999; recipient Justice award, Ky. Women Advocates, 1991, Outstanding Just award, 1995, Bull's Eye award, Women in State Govt. Network, 1995. also: 311 N Arnold Ave Ste 502 Prestonsburg KY 41653-1279

STUMP, LISA DIAN, marketing professional, music educator; b. Columbia City, Ind., Aug. 11, 1958; d. Larry L. and Judith D. Thornburg; m. Claude D. Stump, June 21, 1980; children: Sarah D., Katlen M., Elizabeth A., Samantha J. BA in Music Edn., De Pauw U., 1980. Mktg. asst. Kathryn Beich Fundraising, Bloomington, Ill.; office mgr. Barry Skelton and Hoekstra, Bloomington; tchr. vocals dist. 87 Bloomington H.S.; tchr. Lavernia Sch. Dist., Tex.; edn. advisor USAF, Leipeim, Germany, Bent Waters, England. Home: PO Box 154 Arrowsmith IL 61722 Office: Kathryn Beich Fundraising # 2 Access Way Bloomington IL 61704

STUMP, M. PAMELA, sculptor; b. Detroit, July 8, 1928; d. Clarence Homer S. and Gladys Greening Bogue; m. David Everet Walsh, Aug. 1950 (div. 1975); children: Kimberly Klaerr, Sara Greening Walsh Munro, John Klaerr II; m. Richard Taylor White, March, 1989. B of Design, U. Mich., 1950, M of Design, 1951. Educator Ann Arbor (Mich.) Adult Edn., 1950-51, Saginaw (Mich.) Mus. Sch., 1963-68, Birmingham (Mich.) Bloomfield Art Assn., 1969, Washtenaw C.C., Ypsilanti, Mich., 1968-69, Cranbrook Ednl. Cmty., Bloomfield Hills, Mich., 1969-90. One-woman shows include Cranbrook Kingswood, Bloomfield Hills, 1969-90, Mich. Women's Hist. Ctr. & Hall of Fame, Lansing, 1994, Swann Gallery, Detroit, 1997; exhibited in group shows at Cranbrook Kingswood, 1950, 70, 87, City Art Mus., St. Louis, 1951, Terry Art Inst., Miami, Fla., 1951, Temple Israel, Detroit, 1951, 58, Ceceile Gallery, N.Y.C. (3rd prize), 1956, Pa. Acad. Fine Arts, Phila., 1958, Horace H. Rackham Sch. Grad. Studies, Detroit, 1960, Detroit Artists Market, 1961, R and R Robinson Gallery, Naples, Fla., 1962, Rubiner Gallery, West Bloomfield, Mich., 1963, Mich. Fine Arts Competition (Juror's award), 1983, 87, Slusser Gallery, U. Mich., 1989, Outdoor Sculpture II, III, Southfield, Mich., 1990, 91, N.Y. Acad. Scis., N.Y.C., 1991, Oakland U., 1991-92, Urban Park, Detroit, 1991, 92, Arc Gallery, Chgo., 1992, 1 Heritage Place, Southgate, Mich., 1993, Art Ctr., Sarasota, Fla.; prin. works include courtyard sculpture Kingswood Sch., steel sculpture Sister City, Tokushima, Japan, 10 bronze sculptures for Cranbrook Schs., Bloomfield Hills, Civic Ctr., Saginaw, bronze fountain at Presbyn. Ch., Grosse Ile, Mich, bronze sculpture of history of U. of Mich. Women, Ann Arbor, Mich. Bell Telephone Co., Saginaw, bronze sculpture at Providence Hosp., Southfield, meml. for poet T. Roethke Saginaw Valley State U., bronze sculpture at First Presbyn. Ch., Pompano Beach, Fla., Rochester Hills Libr., Saginaw Mus., Western Mich. U., Kalamazoo, numerous others. Mem. Emily's List, Planned Parenthood. Mem. ACLU, NOW, LWV, Nat. Assn. Women Artists, Nat. Mus. Women in Arts (charter), Detroit Artist Market, Detroit Inst. Arts Founders Soc., Internat. Sculptors. Avocations: reading, writing. Home: 19629 Parke Ln Grosse Ile MI 48138-1024 E-mail: mpamelastump@gatecom.com.

STUMP, PAMELA FERRIS, music educator; b. Roanoke, Va., May 1, 1955; d. Leo George and Virginia Belle (Garst) Ferris; m. John Gregg Stump, Sept. 20, 1975; children: John Jr., Matthew Todd, Carrie Michelle. BA in Music, Hollins Coll., 1991, MA, 1996. Cert. music tchr., Va. Pvt. piano tchr., Fincastle, Va., 1976. Organist Wheatland Luth. Ch., Buchanan, Va., 1981—, coun. mem., 1996-97, dir. children's choir, 1993—; pres., part-owner Tinkerview Swim Club Inc., Daleville, Va., 1992—; sec., part-owner Fincastle Motors Inc., 1996—, Fincastle Mulch and Stone, 1996—; instr. in music history Dabney Lancaster C.C., Clifton Forge, Va., 1997—; substitute music tchr. William Clark Middle Sch., Fincastle, 1996. Chmn. Va. Fedn. Music Clubs Festival, Roanoke, 1992-97; bd. dirs. Va. Luth. Homes Aux./Brandon Oaks, Roanoke, 1990-96; chapel and music vol. Brandon Oaks Health Ctr., Roanoke, 1990-96; chmn. ways and means Troutville (Va.) Elem. Sch. PTA, 1994-95. Anne Jett Rogers scholar Roanoke Symphony Assn., 1990, Dorminy Music scholar Hollins Coll., 1990. Mem. Roanoke Valley Music Tchrs. Assn. (pres. 1987-90), Va. Music Tchrs. Assn. (chmn. high sch. concerto 1990-92), Music Tchrs. Nat. Assn., Thursday Morning Music Club, Order Eastern Star. Avocations: swimming, computers, music. Home: 310 Blue Bird Ln Fincastle VA 24090-3201 Office: Dabney Lancaster CC Clifton Forge VA 24422

STUNJA, VALERIE ANN, aircraft dispatcher; b. Pitts., Aug. 3, 1956; d. Joseph Nicholas and Anna Jane (Mustatia) S. AAS, C.C. of Beaver County, Monaca, Pa., 1985, Aircraft Dispatcher, Kellmark Aeronautics, Miami, 1989. Comml. photographer, Pitts., 1978-80; ops. officer U.S. Air, Pitts., 1980-89, dispatcher, 1989—; flt. instr. Stensin Aviation, Monaca, Pa., 1984-85; real estate salesperson Northwood Realty, Pitts., 1993-94. Advanced ground instr. Beaver Aviation, Monaca, 1982, flt. instr., 1984, comml. pilot, 1984. Republican. Roman Catholic. Office: US Air Inc Ops Control Ctr 173 Industry Dr Pittsburgh PA 15275-1067

STURGES, SHERRY LYNN, recording industry executive; b. Long Beach, Calif., Dec. 11, 1946; d. Howard George and Alice Myrtle Fairbairn; m. Jeffery Alan Sturges, Dec. 30, 1969; children: Allisun Malinda, Jay. Grad. high sch., Las Vegas, Nev. V.p. Soultime, Inc., Las Vegas, 1968-69, Universe, Inc., Las Vegas, 1971-76; co-developer, owner Fun Trax Music Video and Audio Recording Studios, Westwood, Calif., 1986—. Creative cons. John Debella Show, 1990, M.T.V., L.A., 1990, KCET-TV, L.A., 1990,KTLA-TV, L.A., 1991. Co-writer song The Sharing of Love for TV series Murder, She Wrote, 1996, feature film The Ride, 1997; song writer (film) The Ride, 1997. Officer PTA, Woodland Hills, Calif., 1977-86, pres., 1984-86; vol. Connie Stevens Charity Orgn., Beverly Hills, Calif., 1980-84; vol. Crossroads Sch. for Arts and Sci., Westwood Meth. presch., West L.A. Bapt. Sch., Northridge United Meth. Ch., St. Vincent's Parents Coun., St. Joseph the Worker Sch., Chatsworth H.S., Sepulveda Nursery Sch., Nat. Neurofibromatosis Found., Life Steps Found., Westwood Village Assn., San Joaquin Valley Actors Repertory Co., 1997—. Recipient Outstanding Contribution award L.A. Unified Sch. Dist., Oxnard Unified Sch. Dist., 1998, 99. Mem. Am. Soc. Composers, Authors and Pubs. Republican. Avocations: collecting dolls, plates and figurines. Home: 29468Sequoia Rd Santa Clarita CA 91387-6246

STURGULEWSKI, ARLISS, state legislator, director; b. Blaine, Wash., Sept. 27, 1927; BA, U. Wash.; LLD (hon.), U. Alaska, Anchorage, 1993. Mem. Assembly Municipality of Anchorage; interim exec. dir. Alaska Sci. and Tech. Found., 1995. Vice chmn. New Capital Site Planning Commn., mem. Capital Site Selection Com.; chmn. Greater Anchorage Area Planning and Zoning Commn.; mem. Alaska State Senate, 1978-93; Rep. nominee Office Gov. Alaska, 1986, 90. Home: 2957 Sheldon Jackson St Anchorage AK 99508-4469 Office: 3201 C St Ste 405 Anchorage AK 99503-3967 E-mail: a.sturgulewski@swall.nacpas.com.

STURM, SHERRI CHARISSE, marketing and developmental researcher, actuary; b. Anoka, Minn., Dec. 27; d. George T. and Judith A. Tyler; m. Jeffrey M. Sturm, July 7, 1990. Student Russia, U. Minn., 1985, BS in Math., 1990. Various jobs in retai, hotel, food entertainment industry, Mpls., 1980-90; sr. actuary CNA Ins., Chgo., 1990-96; cons. Charisse Internat.,

Barrington, Ill., 1996—. Pvt. actuary practice, Barrington, 1991—. Avocations: skiing, ice skating, skateboarding, rollerblading. Home: 178 Bradwell Rd Barrington IL 60010-5831 E-mail: shersturm@msn.com.

STURMAN, GLORIDA J. lawyer; b. Cortez, Colo., June 26, 1957; BS cum laude, Ariz. State U., 1979, JD, 1982. Bar: Ariz. 1982, Nev. 1983. Atty. Edwards, Hale, Sturman, Atkin & Cushing, Ltd., Las Vegas. Mem.: ABA, So. Nev. Assn. Women Attys. (pres. 1988—89), Clark County Bar Assn. (pres. 1994), State Bar Nev. (pres. 2002—03, bd. govs.), State Bar Ariz. Office: Edwards Hale Sturman et al 415 S Sixth St Ste 300 Las Vegas NV 89101-6937

STURNS, DEBERA C. marketing professional; d. Riley L. and Ettie J. Sturns. BS in Home Econs., U. Tex., Austin, 1983. Sales / mktg. analyst Am. Airlines, Ft. Worth, 1985—2001; sales rep. Neiman Marcus, Dallas, 2002—. Mktg. cons. Advanced Design and Mktg., Oklahoma City, 2003—. Pub. rels. com. United Negro Coll. Fund, Ft. Worth, 2002—03; new members rels. team mem. The Potter's Ho., Dallas, 2002—03; fashion and cosmetic model CCASI Inc., Dallas, 2003. Avocations: travel, reading, spiritual enrichment.

STURTEVANT, BRERETON, retired lawyer, former government official; b. Washington, Nov. 24, 1921; d. Charles Lyon and Grace (Brereton) S. BA, Wellesley Coll., 1942; JD, Temple U., 1949; postgrad., U. Del., 1969-71. Bar: D.C. 1949, Del. 1950. Research chemist E.I. duPont DeNemours & Co., 1942-50; law clk. Del. Supreme Ct., 1950; gen. practice law Wilmington, Del., 1950-57; partner Connolly, Bove & Lodge, Wilmington, 1957-71; examiner-in-chief U.S. Patent and Trademark Office Bd. Appeals, Washington, 1971-88. Adj. prof. law Georgetown U., 1974-79 Trustee Holton-Arms Sch., Bethesda, Md., 1977-96, chmn. or mem. all coms., trustee emerita, 1997—. Mem. ABA, Exec. Women in Govt. (charter mem., chmn. 1978-79) Clubs: Wellesley College, Washington-Wellesley (pres. 1982-84). Episcopalian. Achievements include first woman law clerk, Delaware Supreme Court; first woman patent examiner-in-chief. Home: 1227 Morningside Ln Alexandria VA 22308-1042

STURZL, ALICE A. school library administrator; b. Marshfield, Wis., May 22, 1949; d. Aloysius F. and Lorraine R. (Wolk) Beyerl; m. Bruce R. Sturzl, Sr., June 9, 1973; stepchildren: Bruce R., Scott, Daniel, Ann, Todd, Timothy. BA, U. Wis., Oshkosh, 1971. Cert. tchr., Wis. Elem. libr. Sts. Peter and Paul Parish, Oshkosh, 1970-71; libr. Sch. Dist. of Laona, Wis., 1971-73; tchr. math. Our Lady of Perpetual Help, Glendale, Ariz., 1974-75, Most Holy Trinity Parish, Sunnyslope, Ariz., 1975-76; substitute tchr. Sch. Dists. of Laona and Wabeno, Wis., 1976-77; K-12 instructional media specialist Sch. Dist. of Laona, 1977—. Mem. Northeastern Wis. In-Sch. Telecomms. Adv. Bd., Green Bay, 1987-97, pres. 1989-97; trustee, v.p., pres. Wisconsin Valley Libr. Svc. Bd., Wausau, 1984-89, 2000—. Mem. Econ. Devel. Com., Town of Laona, 1987—; mem. parish coun. St. Leonard's Cath. Ch., Laona, intermittently 1983—; active Cmty. Soup and Homecoming/Laona Lions Club, 1983—. Mem. ALA, NEA, Wis. Libr. Assn. (sec. 1993-94, v.p. 1996, pres. 1997, past pres. 1998), Laona Edn. Assn. (sec.-treas.), Wis. Edn. Assn. (No. Tier UniServ), Wis. Ednl. Media Assn., Wis. Libr. Assn. Found. (v.p., sec.). Roman Catholic. Avocations: bowling, reading, travel, helping others, working with numbers. Home: 5170 E Silver Lake Rd Laona WI 54541-9255 Office: Sch Dist of Laona PO Box 100 5216 Forest Ave Laona WI 54541

STUTZMAN, DONNA J. minister; b. Lemoyne, Ohio, Apr. 29, 1936; d. David O. Kaser and Opal M. Stockwell; m. Darrell A. Stutzman, June 7, 1958 (dec. Sept. 1993); children: Denzel, Devon, Dawn, Dara, Desmond. BS in Child and Family Cmty. Svc., Bowling Green State U., Ohio, 1987; MA in Christian Psychology, Cornerstone U., Lake Charles, La., 1992. Ordained minister Nat. Conservative Christian Ch., 1999; lic. social worker Ohio. Pvt. piano tchr., Wauseon, Ohio, 1958—; case mgr. Fulton County Maumee Valley Guidance Ctr., Defiance, Ohio, 1987—89; assoc. pastor First Ch. of God, Wauseon, 1989—91; mental health profl. Fulton County Health Ctr., Wauseon, 1991—99; social worker, music coord. Fulton Manor Nursing Home, Wauseon, 1998—; hospice chaplain Cmty. Health Profls., Archbold, Ohio, 1999—; pastor Hope Christian Fellowship, Wauseon, 1991—. Vol. coord. Habitat for Humanity. Mem.: Am. Acad. Bereavement, Am. Assn. Christian Counselors, Nat. Christian Counselors Assn., Phi Upsilon Omicron. Avocations: reading, music. Home: 701 Burr Rd Unit 5 Wauseon OH 43567 E-mail: djstutzman@aol.com.

STUTZMAN, SANDRA LOUISE, advanced nurse practitioner; b. Ashland, Pa., Nov. 10, 1953; d. Mary (Tersavige) S. Diploma, Sacred Heart Hosp. Sch., Norristown, Pa., 1979; LPN, Pottstown Meml. Med. Ctr.; diploma, St. Joseph Sch. Nursing, Reading, Pa., 1983; BS, Pa. State U., Reading, 1991; MS, U. South Fla., 1994. Advanced RN practitioner. Staff nurse Pottstown Meml. Med. Ctr.; advanced RN practitioner Infectious Disease Ctr., Tampa (Fla.) Gen. Hosp.; advanced RN practitioner EverCare, Tampa, Fla., 1998-99, Sergio H. Vallejo, M.D., Lakeland, Fla., 1999—2002, Advent Christian Village, Dowling Park, Fla., 2002—. Mem. Am. Acad. Nurse Practitioners, Fla. Nurses Assn., Sigma Theta Tau.

STUTZMAN, SARAH E. music educator; b. Knoxville, July 11, 1980; d. Charles Joseph and Oleta Emery Stutzman. MusB in Music Edn., Maryville Coll., 2002. Cert. tchr. K-12 vocal/gen. Music theory/aural skills tutor Maryville (Tenn.) Conn., 1990—2002, music libr., 1999—2002, choir asst., 2000—02; youth choir/children's choir dir. Unity Bapt. Ch., Maryville, 2002—; music tchr/choir dir. Athens (Tenn.) City Schs. Substitute tchr. Sevier County Schs., Sevierville, Tenn., 1999—2003; substitute tchr. adventure club Ft. Craig SDL, Maryville, 2002—03; chorus mem. Knoxville Opera Co., 2001—. Recipient Concerto Contest winner, Maryville-Alcoa Coll./Cmty. Orch., 2001, 2002, Barraclough Choir award, Maryville Coll. Choir, 2002, Dorothy Barber Bushing award, Maryville Coll., 2001. Mem.: NEA, Tenn. Edn. Assn., Am. Choral Dir.'s Assn., Tenn. Music Educator's Assn., Music Educator's Nat. Conf., Delta Omicron. Southern Baptist. Avocations: singing, dance, acting, sewing, scrapbooks.

STYCOS, MARIA NOWAKOWSKA, adult education educator; b. Lwow, Poland, June 4, 1937; arrived in U.S., 1964; d. Marian Zygmunt Nowakowski and Julia Demska Nowakowska; m. Joseph Mayone Stycos; 1 child, Marek. BA, King's Coll. U. London, London, UK, 1958; MA, Cornell Univ., Ithaca, N.Y., 1967, PhD, 1977. Part time asst. prof. Ithaca Coll., NY, 1975—81; dir. Handwerker Art Gallery, Ithaca, NY, 1981—82; asst. prof. State U. of N.Y., Cortland, NY, 1982—86; sr. lectr. Cornell Univ., Ithaca, NY, 1986—. Cons. Cornell U., Costa Rica, 1987. Author: (contbg. articles in) Letras Project Femeninas, Revista / Rev., Interamericana P.R., Dictionary of the Lit. of the Iberian Peninsula, (book chap.) Transition to Democracy in Ea. Europe And Russia, 2002. Planning bd. mem. Village of Lansing, NY, 2002—. Mem.: faculty adv. com. Johnson Mus. of Art, Cornell U., MLA. Avocations: music, art, gardening, travel, reading. Office: Romance Studies Cornell Univ Ithaca NY 14853

STYER, SHARON LOUISE, music educator; b. Danville, Pa., July 6, 1958; d. Daniel Fredrick Breining, Jr. and Gertrude Josephine Breining; m. Kevin Brian Styer, Dec. 28, 2002. BS in Music, Messiah Coll., 1976—81. Music dir. Schuylkill Haven Sch. Dist., Schuylkill Haven, Pa., 1982—84; vocal music instr. Line Mountain Sch. Dist., Herndun, Pa., 1984—2003, Upper Dauphin Area Sch. Dist., 2003—. CD, Like Never Before, 1998, one-man shows include CD Christmas From The Heart, 2000. Dir., singer, dancer, actress Anthracite Citizen's Theater, Mt. Carmel, Pa., 1999—; prin. clarinet, asst. dir. Sunbury (Pa.) City Band, 1999—; mem. bd. Milton Area Cmty. Theatre, 2003—. Recipient nom. Disney Tchr. of Yr., Walt Disney World, 1999. Mem.: Order of Eastern Star. Republican. Protestant. Avocation: musical theatre. Home: RR 01 Box 505 Shamokin PA 17872 Office Phone: 717-362-6491.

STYLES, ANGELA B. federal agency administrator; BA with distinction, U. Va.; JD with honors, U. Tex. Legis. aide Congressman Joe Barton, Washington; counsel Miller & Chevalier, Washington; wigh gen. svcs. adminstrn. Office Govt.-Wide Policy and Pub. Bldgs. Svcs., 2001; counselor to the dir. Office Mgmt. and Budget; adminstr. for fed. procurement policy Exec. Office of the Pres., Washington, 2001—. Articles editor: Am. Jour. Criminal Law. Mem.: ABA (chair legis. coordinating com. sect. pub. contract law, vice chair acctg., cost and pricing com.), Order of the Coif. Republican. Office: Exec Office of the Pres Fed Procurement Policy EEOB 17th & Pennsylvania Ave NW Washington DC 20503

STYLES, BEVERLY (JUANITA ROBINS CARPENTER), entertainer, composer, musician; b. Richmond, Va., June 6, 1923; d. John Harry Kenealy and Juanita Russell (Robins) Carpenter; m. Wilbur Cox, Mar. 14, 1942 (div.); m. Robert Marascia, Oct. 5, 1951 (div. Apr. 1964). Studies with Ike Carpenter, Hollywood, Calif., 1965—98; student, Am. Nat. Theatre Acad., 1968—69; studies with Paula Raymond, Hollywood, 1969—70; diploma, Masterplan Inst., Anaheim, Calif., 1970. Freelance performer, musician, 1947-81; owner Beverly Styles Music, Yucca Valley, Calif., 1971—. V.p. spl. programs Lawrence Program of Calif., Yucca Valley, Calif.; talent coord., co-founder Quiet Place Studio, Yucca Valley, 1994; mem. exec. bd., awards dir. Am. chpt. Diogenes Process Group, 1996—. Composer, lyricist: (songs) Joshua Tree, 1975, Wow, Wow, Wow, 1986, World of Dreams, 1996, Thank You God, 1996, (music for songs) I'm Thankful, 1978, The Whispering, 1994; piano arrangements include Colour Chords and Moods, 1995, Desert Nocturne, 1996; records include The Perpetual Styles of Beverly, 1978; albums include The Primitive Styles of Beverly, 1977; tape cassettes include Gospel Diamonds, 1996; author: A Special Plan to Think Upon, The Truth as Seen by a Composer, 1978, A Special Prayer to Think Upon, 1983. Mem. ASCAP (Gold Pin award), Profl. Musicians Local 47 (life), Internat. Platform Assn. Republican. Avocation: creating abstract art. Home and Office: 7839 Aster Ave Yucca Valley CA 92284-4130

STYLES, MARGRETTA MADDEN, nursing educator; b. Mount Union, Pa., Mar. 19, 1930; d. Russell B. and Agnes (Wilson) Madden; m. Douglas F. Styles, Sept. 4, 1954; children: Patrick, Michael, Megan. BS, Juniata Coll., 1950; M. in Nursing, Yale U., 1954; Ed.D., U. Fla., 1968; hon. doctorate, Valparaiso U., 1986, U. Athens, Greece, 1991. Staff nurse VA Hosp., West Haven, Conn., 1954-55; instr. Bklyn. Hosp. Sch. Nursing, 1955-58; supr. North Dist. Hosp., Pompano Beach, Fla., 1961-63; dir. nursing edn. Broward Community Coll., Ft. Lauderdale, Fla., 1963-67; assoc. prof. Sch. Nursing Duke U., Durham, N.C., 1967-69, dir. undergrad. studies, 1967-69; prof., dean Sch. Nursing U. Tex., San Antonio, 1969-73; dean, prof. Coll. Nursing Wayne State U., Detroit; prof. nursing U. Calif., San Francisco, 1977—, dean Sch. Nursing, 1977-87; chairperson Com. for Study of Credentialization in Nursing, 1976-79; mem. adv. group div. nursing HEW, 1977. Asst. dir. nursing svcs. U. Calif. Hosps. and Clinics, 1978-87; mem. Nat. Commn. Nursing, 1980—; mem. Calif. Bd. Registered Nursing, 1985—; mem. Sec.'s Commn. on Nursing HHS, 1988—. Author: On Nursing: Toward a New Endowment (Am. Jour. Nursing Book of Yr. award 1982); co-author (with A. Affara) From Principle to Power: A Guidebook to Regulation in Nursing, 1992. Recipient Disting. Alumna award Yale U. Sch. Nursing, 1979; Am. Nurses' Found. 1st disting. scholar, 1983 Fellow Am. Acad. Nursing; mem. Nat. Acad. Scis., Am. Nurses Assn. (pres. 1986-88), Internat. Coun. Nurses (bd. dirs. 1989—), Sigma Theta Tau. Office: U Calif Sch Nursing PO Box N531C San Francisco CA 94143-0001

STYLES, TERESA JO, producer, educator; b. Atlanta, Oct. 19, 1950; d. Julian English and Jennie Marine (Sims) S. BA, Spelman Coll., 1972; MA, Northwestern U., 1973; PhD, U. N.C., Chapel Hill, 1998. Rschr. CBS News, N.Y.C., 1975-80, prodr., 1980-85; instr. mass comms. and English Savannah (Ga.) State Coll., 1985-89, asst. prof. English, 1990; asst. prof. mass comm. and women studies dir. Bennett Coll., Greensboro, NC, 1990-93; assoc. prof. mass comm., chmn. journalism and mass comm. N.C. A&T State U., Greensboro, 1993—. Researcher documentary CBS Reports: Teddy, 1979 (Emmy cert.); assoc. producer documentaries for CBS Reports: Blacks: America, 1979 (Columbia Dupont cert. 1979), What Shall We Do About Mother?, 1980 (Emmy cert.), The Defense of the U.S., 1980 (Columbia Dupont cert.). Adv. bd. Greensboro Hist. Mus., Eastern Music Festival, Women's Short Film Project. Mem. Writers Guild Am. (bd. dirs. east 1991-95), Dirs. Guild Am. (bd. dirs. east 1991-95), African Am. Atelier (Greensboro, N.C. bd. dirs.), Eastern Music Festival (bd. dirs.). Avocation: swimming. Home: 4400 Suffolk Trl Greensboro NC 27407-7842 Office Phone: 336-334-7900. E-mail: teresaj@ncat.edu.

STYNES, BARBARA BILELLO, integrative health professional, educator; b. N.Y.C., Apr. 24, 1951; d. Sylvester Francis and Jacqueline Marie (Giardelli) Bilello; m. Frank Joseph Stynes, Aug. 24, 1969; children: Christopher Francis, Jeremy Scott. BA, Rutgers U., 1976; MA in Health Studies, Antioch U., 1995. Cert. reiki practitioner. Mktg. rep. McNeil Consumer Products Co., Ft. Washington, Pa., 1979-82, Met Path Inc., Des Plaines, Ill., 1982-85; mktg. coord. Life program Meml. Hosp. and YMCA, Chattanooga, 1986-91; mem. Chattanooga Area Wellness Coun., 1986-91, Chattanooga Area Healthcare Coalition, 1986-91; dir. mktg. and comm., met. YMCA, Chattanooga, 1986-91, dir. internat. program, 1989-91, wellness cons., 1992-95; intern Mind/Body Inst., Affiliate Harvard Med. Sch., Deaconess Hosp, Columbus, Ohio, 1995—. Assoc. hospice residential care, 1995; therapeutic touch and presence facilitator, 1995—; lifestyle counselor, 1995—, Reiki practitioner, 1999—; program developer Set for Life, 1996; mindfulness based stress reduction facilitator, 1994—; fiber sculptor, 1975-77; weaver, 1976-79; wellness dir. Carolina Family Medicine & Wellness, Mooresville, N.C., 2000. Vol. comm. com. Am. Heart Assn., 1972-91, Spl. Olympics, Chgo., 1982-84; spkr. Tenn. Safety Belt coalition, 1986-91; clinic leader Am. Lung Assn., Chattanooga, 1986-88, YMCA cert. fitness specialist, 1986—, weight mgmt. specialist, 1987—; chairperson fundraising, trustee Pine Grove Coop. Sch., New Brunswick, N.J., 1977-78; sustaining bd. Choices, 1993-95; bd. dirs. Signal Mountain Newcomers Assn., Tenn., 1985-86; mem. sch. bd. Notre Dame H.S., 1989-91. Mem. NAFE, Omega: Inst. Holistic Studies, Inst. Noetic Scis., Am. Bus. Woman's Network Chattanooga (chair mem.), Fiber Arts Guild, Assn. Profl. Dirs., Kiwanis (chair internat. rels. com. Chattanooga chpt. 1990-91, publicity dir.), Gen. Bd. Newcomers, North Columbus, Sustaining Bd. Choices). Roman Catholic. Avocations: walking, yoga, gardening, travel, music. Home: 2706 Trent Pines Ct Sherrills Ford NC 28673-9132

SU, JUDY YA HWA LIN, pharmacologist; b. Hsinchu, Taiwan, Nov. 20, 1938; came to U.S., 1962; d. Ferng Nian and Chiu-Chin (Cheng) Lin; m. Michael W. Su; 1 child, Marvin. BS, Nat. Taiwan U., 1961; MS, U. Kans., 1964; PhD, U. Wash., 1968. Asst. prof. dept. biology U. Ala., Huntsville, 1972-73; rsch. assoc. dept. anesthesiology U. Wash., Seattle, 1976-77, acting asst. prof. dept. anesthesia, 1977-78, rsch. asst. prof., 1978-81, rsch. assoc. prof., 1981-89, rsch. prof., 1989—. Mem. surg. anesthesiology & trauma study sect. NIH, 1987-91; vis. scientist Max-Planck Inst. Med. Rsch., Heidelberg, West Germany, 1982-83; vis. prof. dept. anesthesiology Mayo Clinic, Rochester, Minn., Med. Coll. Wis., 1988; editorial bd. cons. Jour. Molecular & Cellular Cardiology, London, 1987—, European Jour. Physiology, Berlin, Germany, Muscle & Nerve, Kyoto, Japan, 1989—, Anesthesiology, Phila., 1987—, Molecular Pharmacology, 1988—, Jour. Biol. Chemistry, 1989—, Am. Jour. Physiology, 1990—; mem. rsch. study com. Am. Heart Assn., 1992-95. Contbr. articles to profl. jours. Grantee Wash. Heart Assn., 1976-77, 1985-87, Pharm. Mfrs. Assn. Found., Inc., 1977, Lilly Rsch. Labs, 1986-88, Anaquest, 1987—, NIH, 1978—; recipient Rsch. Career Devel. award NIH, 1982-87; rsch. fellowship San Diego Heart Assn., 1970-72, Max-Planck Inst., 1982-83. Mem. AAAS, Biophys. Soc., Am. Soc. for Pharmacology and Exptl. Therapeutics, Am. Physiol. Soc., Am. Soc. Anesthesiologists. Home: 13110 NE 33rd St Bellevue WA 98005-1318 Office: U Wash Dept Anesthesiology PO Box 356540 Seattle WA 98195-6540

SUAREZ-MURIAS, MARGUERITE C. retired language educator, retired literature educator; b. Havana, Cuba, Mar. 23, 1921; arrived in U.S., 1935, naturalized, 1959; d. Eduardo R. and Marguerite (Vendel) Suarez-Murias. AB, Bryn Mawr Coll., 1942; MA, Columbia U., 1953, PhD, 1957. Lectr. in Spanish Columbia U., 1954-56; pub. rels. officer med. divsn. Johns Hopkins U., 1957-58; asst. prof. Spanish and French Sweet Briar Coll., 1958-59; asst. prof. Hood Coll., 1960-61; lectr. Cath. U., 1960-63, asst. prof., summers 1960-62, assoc. prof., summers 1964-66; asst. prof. dept. langs. and linguistics Am. U., 1961-63, assoc. prof., 1963-66; prof. dept. classical and modern langs. Marquette U., Milw., 1966-68; prof. Spanish and Portuguese U. Wis., Milw., 1968—83, chmn., 1972-75; ret., 1983. Guest Milw. prof. U. South Africa, Pretoria, 1980. Author: (book) La Novela Romántica en Hispanoamérica, 1963, Antología Estilística de la Prosa Moderna Española, 1968, Essays on Hispanic Literature/Ensayos de Literatura Hispana, 1982; editor: Gironella's Los Cipreses Creen en Dios, 1969; contbr. articles to profl. jours.;. Mem.: Nat. Trust Historic Preservation. Roman Catholic. Achievements include designing, building and landscaping two homes. Home: 1315 Cold Bottom Rd Sparks MD 21152-9518

SUBER, DIANNE BOARDLEY, educational administrator; b. Tallahassee, May 22, 1949; d. John Wilkerson and Barbara Ann (Baker) Boardley; BS with honors, Hampton Inst., 1971; ME., U. Ill., 1973; postgrad. Hampton U.; MEd, Old Dominion U., doctoral studies Va. Poly. Insst. and State U.; children: Nichole Reshan, Raegan Latrese; m. Robert B. Suber. Elem. tchr. Greensboro (N.C.) Public Schs., 1971-72; tchr. Newport News (Va.) Public Schs., 1973-77, asst. prin., 1977-79, 80-82, acting prin., 1979-80; elem. prin. Williamsburg, Va., 1982-85; prin. Newport (Va.) News, 1986-89, 91—, program devel. specialist, 1989-91; owner/prin. DBS and Assocs.; adj. instr. Hampton U. grad. sch. edn., 1986—; owner Child Care Resources Inc.; guest lectr. Coll. William and Mary, Williamsburg; owner human resources devel. cons. DBS & Assoc.. Mem. Coalition for Good Govt. Mem. Nat. Assn. Elem. Sch. Prins., Nat. Assn. Edn. Young Children, Assn. Supervision and Curriculum Devel., Nat. Alliance Black Sch. Educators, Hampton Crusade for Votes League, Black Child Inst.; presenter nat. conf. Am. Assn. Sch. Adminstrs. State Dept. Edn., Va. and N.C. Mem. Am. Assn. Sch. Adminstrs. Democrat. Roman Catholic. Home: 12208 Penrose Trl Raleigh NC 27614-6804

SUBER, ROBIN HALL, former medical and surgical nurse; b. Bethlehem, Pa., Mar. 14, 1952; d. Arthur Albert and Sarah Virginia (Smith) Hall; m. David A. Suber, July 28, 1979; 1 child, Benjamin A. BSN, Ohio State U., 1974. RN, Ariz., Ohio. Formerly staff nurse Desert Samaritan Hosp., Mesa, Ariz. Lt. USN, 1974-80. Mem. ANA, Sigma Theta Tau.

SUBER, SHARON L. technology coordinator; BA, U. of Mass., Amherst, MA, 1982; Cert. in Computer Programming and Ops., Control Data Inst., New York, NY, 1982; Cert. in Videodisc Design and Prodn., U. of Nebr., Lincoln, NE, 1989. Cert. elem. edn. NJ, Massachusetts Elementary Education K-8 Mass. Tchr. St. Ann's Sch., Newark, 1976—81, Project Link Sch., Newark, 1979—81; adj. prof. Passaic County CC, Paterson, NJ, 1985—85; dir. of quality assurance Silver Burdett & Ginn, Morristown, NJ, 1983—89; mng. editor New Century Edn. Corp., Piscataway, NJ, 1989—91; computer cons. S3 Solutions, Maplewood, NJ, 1990—92; tchr. Newark Pub. Schools, Newark, 1992—2002, tech. coord., 2000—. Founder / dir. of after sch. program St. Ann's Sch., Newark, 1977—81; eighth grade class advisor Project Link Sch., Newark, 1979—81; faculty advisor and pub. of sch. newspaper Newark Pub. Schools, Newark, 1995—, asst. test coord. for schoolwide standardized testing program, 1996—98; sch. trainer, gender equality tng. program for students in grade 5 ASETS, Coll. of NJ, NJ, 1998—; facilitator of school-to-work program Newark Pub. Schools, Newark, 1997—99. Pub. of monthly cmty. mag., 1986—98; girl scout leader Essex County Coun., Essex, NJ, 1980—81. Mem.: AAUW, ASCD, NJ Assn. of Ednl. Tech., Nat. Coun. of Teachers of Math., Zeta Phi Beta. Home: 29 Galton Lane Willingboro NJ 08046

SUBKOWSKY, ELIZABETH, insurance company executive; b. New London, Conn., Feb. 17, 1949; d. Thomas and Matilda (Mastroianni) Logan; m. Robert A. Subkowsky, June 9, 1972. BA with honors and dist., U. Conn., 1971; MBA, DePaul U., Chgo., 1977. Cert. Project Mgmt. Profl. 2003, sr. advisor 2003. Asst. v.p. info. tech. CNA Ins., Chgo., 1973—2002; dir. The Tri Zetto Group, Albany, NY, 2003; v.p. info. tech. Bankers Life & Casualty, Chgo., 2003—. Mem. Highland Park (Ill.) Housing Commn., 1997-98; bd. dirs. Highland Park Hist. Soc., 1991-96, 1st v.p., 1993-96. Recipient De Paul U. Disting. Alumni award, 1999. Mem. Soc. for Info. Mgmt., Project Mgmt. Inst. Avocations: golf, bridge, reading. Office Phone: 312-396-6218. E-mail: esubkowsky@prodigy.net.

SUBSTAD LOKENSGARD, KATHRYN ANN, small business owner, career consultant; b. Mpls., Dec. 4, 1941; d. Arnold Torger and Ardis Louise (Klanderud) Substad; m. Arvid Luther Lokensgard, Nov. 23, 1963 (div. July 1982); children: Sara Kathryn Lokensgard Dickinson, Sigurd Arvid Lokensgard, Laura Ann Lokensgard. BA, St. Olaf Coll., 1963; postgrad., Pacific Luth. Theol. Sem., 1989. Tchr. Lookout Mountain (Tenn.) Elem. Sch., 1964-66; tchrs. aide Greenvale Elem. Sch., Northfield, Minn., 1974-76; substitute tchr. Incline Village (Nev.) K-12, 1978-80, asst. libr., 1980-82; fin. aid dir., fgn. student advisor Sierra Nevada Coll., Incline Village, 1982-85, asst. to pres., 1985-89; owner Tahoe Christian Bookstore, Tahoe Vista, Calif., 1993-2000; self-employed in home health svcs., 2000—. Substitute tchr., career cons., 1990-92; liaison to bd. Sierra Nevada Coll., 1985-88. Bd. dirs. ch. coun. Christ the King Luth. Ch., Tahoe City, 1986-89, local pub. TV sta., 1986-89; vol. tchr. ESL, 1991-98; active Nev. Literacy Coalition, 1991-98; bd. dirs. North Tahoe Reading Ctr.; deacon Incline Village Community Presbyn. Ch., 1992-95; trainer, leader Stephen Ministries, 1996-2000. Mem. PEO (social sec. 1988-89), AAUW, C. of C. (bd. dirs. 1988-89, Hospice 1991-98, Citizen of Month 1989). Avocations: tennis, hiking, skiing, sailing, swimming, knitting, porcelain doll-making.

SUCKIEL, ELLEN KAPPY, philosophy educator; b. June 15, 1943; d. Jack and Lilyan Kappy; m. Joseph Suckiel, June 22, 1973 AB, Douglass Coll., 1965; MA in Philosophy, U. Wis., 1969, PhD in Philosophy, 1972. Lectr. philosophy U. Wis., Madison, 1969-71; asst. prof. philosophy Fla. State U., Tallahassee, 1972-73, U. Calif., Santa Cruz, 1973-80, assoc. prof., 1980-95, prof., 1995—, provost Kresge Coll., 1983-89. Author: The Pragmatic Philosophy of William James, 1982, Heaven's Champion: William James's Philosophy of Religion, 1996, also articles, book introductions and chpts. Mem. Am. Philos. Assn., Soc. for Advancement Am. Philosophy Office: U Calif Stevenson Coll Santa Cruz CA 95064 E-mail: suckiel@ucsc.edu.

SUDANOWICZ, ELAINE MARIE, government executive; d. John Anthony and Helen Mary Sudanowicz. Student, Fontbonne Acad., Milton, Mass., 1974; BA, Boston State Coll., 1978; MPA, Suffolk U., Boston, 1986; grad. Exec. Leadership Devel. Program, Dept. of Def., 1993. Cert. level 2 contractor, level 3 in program mgmt., Mass. Pub. rels. office mgr. MacDonald & Evans Inc. Litho., Dorchester, 1974-78; rsch. asst. Nat. Commn. Neighborhoods, Washington, 1978; polit. cons. various nat., state and local polit. campaigns, 1974-86; telephonist supr., cons. ARC, Boston, 1980-81;

Chgo., 1972. Children's pub. libr., Mo., Md., Va., 1952-61; sch. libr. specialist Montgomery County (Md.) Pub. Schs., 1961-63; dir. Knapp Sch. Librs, Project, ALA, 1963-68, Jr. Coll. Libr. Info. Ctr., 1968-69; asst. prof. U. Pitts., 1971-73; dir. Office for Libr. Pers. Resources, ALA, Chgo., 1973-74; dean of students, assoc. prof. Grad. Libr. Sch., U. Chgo., 1974-77; asst. commr. for ext. svcs. Chgo. Pub. Libr., 1977-81; dean Coll. Profl. Studies, No. Ill. U., DeKalb, 1981-90; dir. univ. librs. No. Ill. U., 1990-92; exec. dir. ALA, 1992-94; assoc. Tuft & Assocs., 1995-98; dean Grad. Sch. Libr. and Info. Sci. Rosary Coll., 1995-97. Instr. grad. libr. edn. programs, 1958-73, UNESCO cons. on sch. librs., Australia, 1970; trustee Clarke Coll., 1969-72; sr. ptnr. Able Cons., 1987-92; cons. in field. Author: The O'Donnells, 1956, Many Names for Eileen, 1969, Problems in School Media Management, 1971, Carl H. Milam and the American Library Association, 1976, Opportunities in Library and Information Science, 1977, Realization: The Final Report of the Knapp School Libraries Project, 1968; co-author: Public Libraries: Smart Practices in Personnel, 1982. Mem.: ALA, Ill. Libr. Assn., Cath. Libr. Assn., Caxton Club, Chgo. Lit. Club. Roman Catholic. Home and Office: 2800 N Lake Shore Dr Apt 816 Chicago IL 60657-6202 E-mail: pslibcon@alumni.uchicago.edu.

SULLIVAN, PENELOPE DIETZ, computer software development company executive; b. Roanoke, Va., Dec. 29, 1939; d. Joseph Budding and Katherine Dietz; m. Thomas F. Sullivan, Sept. 7, 1963 (div. Mar. 1975); children: Courtney, Todd; m. Paul B. Hill, Mar. 31, 1990. BA, Colby Coll., 1961. Claims examiner Blue Cross/Blue Shield of D.C., Washington, 1961-66; self employed maker slipcovers and upholstery Springfield, Va., 1966-75; ins. sales Met. Life Ins. Co., Arlington, Va., 1975-76, Med. Pers. Pool Inc., Alexandria, Va., 1976-77; mktg. rep. IBM Corp., Washington, 1977-88, program mgr. Advanced Workstations Somers, N.Y., 1988-92; sales cons. IBM Open Sys., Washington, 1992-93; co-founder Open Sys. Assocs., Inc., Reston, Va., 1993—2001; v.p. bus. devel., co-founder Guru Networks Inc., 2001—. Avocations: golf, skiing, gardening, renovating houses. Office: 4100 Lafayette Ctr Chantilly VA 20151 E-mail: penny@gurunet.net.

SULLIVAN, RUTH ANNE, librarian; b. Portland, Maine, Jan. 15, 1955; d. Lawrence P. and Mary Louise (Gilman) S.; m. Charles H. Sullivan, May 1, 1982; children: Nora J., Ian J. BA, Wheaton Coll., 1979; MLS, U. Ariz., 1980. Serials ref. Mass. Bay Community Coll., Wellesley, 1980-81; asst. dir. Bristol Community Coll., Fall River, Mass., 1981-86, chief libr., 1986—. Office: Bristol Community Coll 777 Elsbree St Fall River MA 02720-7307

SULLIVAN, SANDRA LONG, retired human resources specialist; b. Cin., Ohio, Apr. 1, 1947; d. Thomas David and Alice Catherine Long; m. Daniel Joseph Sullivan, Jan. 17, 1944. AB, Thomas More Coll., Crestview Hills KY, 1969; MEd, Xavier U., Cin. OH, 1974. Case worker Hamilton Co. Dept. of Human Svcs., Cin., 1969—73; human svcs. coord. Xavier U., Cin., 1974—76; eap coord. Am. Airlines, Cin., 1988—2003; ret., 2003. Green Party. Avocations: travel, healing arts, recovery, animal rights, metaphysics. Home: 3636 Bellecrest Ave Cincinnati OH 45208 Personal E-mail: edanoul8@fuse.net.

SULLIVAN, SARAH LOUISE, management and technology consultant; b. Wilmington, Del., Sept. 24, 1954; d. Frederick William III and Ruth (Swavely) S. BS, Bowling Green U., 1975; MS, Ill. Inst. Tech., 1986, PhD, 1990. Programmer Computer Sci. Corp., Langley AFB, Va., 1975-77; sr. systems programmer JPLRCC, Perrysburg, Ohio, 1977-80; sr. systems engr. Kraft Inc., Glenview, Ill., 1980-83; project leader Siemens Gammasonics, Des Plaines, Ill., 1983-85; sect. mgr. Zenith Electronics, Glenview, Ill., 1985; mem. tech. staff AT&T Bell Labs., Naperville, Ill., 1986-87; cons., trainer Sarah L. Sullivan & Assocs., Morton Grove, Ill., 1987-90; instr. Ill. Inst. Tech., Chgo., 1988; asst. prof. dept. computer sci. North Cen. Coll., Naperville, 1988-89, Ind.-Purdue U., Ft. Wayne, 1990-94; prin. engr. Boeing Info. Svcs., Dayton, Ohio, 1995-96, Rockwell Collins, Cedar Rapids, Iowa, 1996-97; with Motorola, Schaumburg, Ill., 1997-98, Sys. Assessment Re-Engring. & Assurance Help, Columbus, Ohio, 1999—. Presenter in field. Mem. IEEE, Assn. for Computing Machinery, Oasis Ctr. for Human Potential.

SULLIVAN, SHIRLEY ROSS (SHIRLEY ROSS DAVIS), art collector; b. Berkeley, Calif. d. Edwin M. Ross; m. George Freeborn (dec.); children: George, Tita, Nelly, Mary; m. Thomas Davis (dec.); m. Charles Sullivan, Sept. 6, 1997. Interior designer, Woodside, Calif., 1963-90. Tchr., lectr., Woodside, 1965-70; art collector, Woodside and San Francisco, 1968—. Trustee San Francisco Mus. Modern Art, 1986—; pres. Collectors' Art Forum, San Francisco, 1983-85; mem. collectors' com. Nat. Gallery Art, 1998—. Office: ICMS 790 Laurel St San Carlos CA 94070-3164

SULLIVAN, TERESA ANN, law and sociology educator, academic administrator; b. Kewanee, Ill., July 9, 1949; d. Gordon Hager and Mary Elizabeth (Finnegan) S.; m. H. Douglas Laycock, June 14, 1971; children: Joseph Peter, John Patrick. BA, Mich. State U., 1970; MA, U. Chgo., 1972, PhD, 1975. Asst. prof. sociology U. Tex., Austin, 1975-76, assoc. prof. sociology, 1981-87, dir. women's studies, 1985-87, prof. sociology, 1987—, prof. law, 1988—, assoc. dean grad. sch., 1989-90, 1992-95, chair dept. sociology, 1990-92, vice provost, 1994-95, v.p., grad. dean, 1995—2002; asst. prof. sociology U. Chgo., 1977-81; exec. vice-chancellor for acad. affairs U. Tex. System, 2002—. Pres. Southwestern Sociol. Assn., 1988-89; mem. faculty adv. bd. Hogg Found. Mental Health, 1989-92; mem. sociology panel NSF, 1983-85. Author: Marginal Workers Marginal Jobs, 1978; co-author: As We Forgive Our Debtors, 1989 (Silver Gavel 1990), Social Organization of Work, 1990, 2d edit. 1995; co-author: The Fragile Middle Class, 2000; contbr. articles and chpts. to profl. jours. Bd. dirs. Calvert Found., Chgo., 1978, CARA, Inc., Washington, 1985; mem. U.S. Census Bur. Adv. Com., 1989-95, chmn., 1991-92; mem. sociology panel NSF, 1983-85; trustee St. Michael's Acad., 1996-2001. Leadership Tex. 1994. Fellow AAAS (liaison to Population Assn. Am. 1989-91, chair sect. K 1996), Sociol. Rsch. Assn., Am. Sociol. Assn. (sec. 1995—, editor Rose Monograph Series 1988-92), Philos. Soc. Tex., Soc. Study of Social Problems (chair fin. com. 1986-87), Population Assn. Am. (bd. dirs. 1989-91, chair fin. com. 1990-91), Assn. Grad. Schs. (pres. 2001-2002). Roman Catholic. Avocations: volkssporting, sci. fiction. Office: U Tex System 601 Colorado Ste 305 Austin TX 78701 E-mail: tsullivan@utsystem.edu.

SULLIVAN, VIRGINIA L. public affairs educator, consultant; b. Brookhaven, Miss., Oct. 12, 1950; d. Ernest and Loraine Headrick; children: Angelea, Sara. BS in Indsl. Tech., So. Ill. U., 1982; MA in Journalism, U. Colo., 1990. Enlisted USAF, 1975, advanced through grades to maj., 1995, pub. affairs officer, 1975-82, Colorado Springs, 1983-88, Montgomery, Ala., 1990-92, Ankara, Turkey, 1992-93, pub. affairs officer The Pentagon Washington, 1993-96, ret., 1996; pub. rels. instr. Ark. State U., Jonesboro, 1996—. Editor The Leader, 1991. Bd. dirs. Crowley Ridge Girls Scouts USA Coun., Jonesboro, 1997. Mem. Pub. Rels Coun. Ala. (student activities dir. 1991-92), Turkish Am. Assn. (ESL instr. 1993), Assn. Educators in Journalism and Mass. Comm., Pub. Rels. Soc. Am., Lions Club. Republican. Baptist. Avocations: tennis, writing poetry. Office: Ark State U Dept Journalism PO Box 1930 Jonesboro AR 72403-1930

SULLIVAN-SCHWEBKE, KAREN JANE, lawyer; b. Spokane, Wash., Feb. 25, 1955; d. John and Helen (Bartlett) Sullivan; m. Ethan K. Schwebke, Apr. 18, 1987; children: Noah, Eli. BA, U. Wash., 1978, MBA, JD, 1987. Exec. asst. to corp. controller Pay'n Save Corp., Seattle, 1980-83; tchg. asst. U. Wash. Coll. Bus., Seattle, 1984-85; law clk. Bogle & Gates Law Firm, Seattle, 1985, PACCAR, Inc., Bellevue, Wash., 1986, U. Wash. Law Sch., Seattle, 1987; dir. Boys and Girls Club Puget Sound, Everett, Wash., 1988-90; legal counsel Fla. State Human Rights Commn., 1995-97; exec. dir. Benton and Franklin Counties Wash. State Family Policy Coun., Kennewick, 1997-99; exec. dir., legal coun., CFO Mid-Columbia Regional Symphony and Ballet, Richland, Wash., 1999—2003; owner Art, History, Architure Tours of Centennial Kennewick, 2003—. Author: Guide to Centennial Kennewick, 2003. Chair Civil Svc. Commn., 1998-2003; mem. City Hist. Preservation Commn., 2003—; mem., chair City Centennial Commn., 2003—; mem. Leadership Tri-Cities Class 2001; bd. dirs. Women Helping Women Fund, 2001, Richland Opera Co., 2001—. Mem. NOW, Kappa Delta, U. Wash. Alumnae Assn. (dist. gov.), Rotary, DOVIA. Democrat. Avocations: reading, painting, interior decorating, gardening. Home: 2001 S Newport St Kennewick WA 99337-7811 E-mail: schweet4@msn.com.

SULZBACH, CHRISTI ROCOVICH, lawyer; b. L.A. BA, U. So. Calif., 1976; JD, Loyola U., 1979. Bar: Calif., 1980. Various to assoc. gen. counsel Tenet Healthcare Corp., Santa Barbara, Calif., 1983-99, exec. v.p., gen. counsel, 1999—2002, chief corp. officer, gen. counsel, 2002—. Mem. State Bar of Calif., ABA, FBA (bd. dirs. L.A. chpt.), Fedn. Am. Health Sys. (bd. dirs.), corp. adv. bd., U.S.C. Marshall Sch. Bus. Office: Tenet Healthcare Corp Corporate Office 3820 State St Santa Barbara CA 93105-3112 E-mail: christi.sulzbach@tenethealth.com.

SUMARYONO, KAREN L. secondary school educator, consultant; b. Framingham, Mass., Feb. 7, 1958; d. Chester C. and Joan M. Libucha; m. Widi Sumaryono, Dec. 31, 1989; 1 child, John W. BA in English and Journalism, U. Mass., 1980; MA in Linguistics, Ohio U., 1985. Cert. tchr. English lang. 5-12, tchr. English 9-12 Mass. H.s. english tchr. Peace Corps, Parakou, Benin, 1980—82; fgn. expert in linguistics Beijing Teachers Coll., 1985—86; tchr. trainer, supr. S.E. Asian Refugee Programs World Learning, Inc., 1988—91; tchr. ESL West Springfield (Mass.) H.S., 1992—. Tchr. cons., mem. exec. bd. Western Mass. Writing Project, Amherst, 1999—. Mem.: Mass. Assn. Tchrs. of Spkrs. of Others Langs. Home: 600 Federal St Belchertown MA 01007-9376 Office: West Springfield HS 425 Piper Rd West Springfield MA 01089

SUMMER, DONNA (LA DONNA ADRIAN GAINES), singer, songwriter, actress; b. Boston, Dec. 31, 1948; d. Andrew and Mary Gaines; m. Helmut Sommer (div.); 1 child, Mimi; m. Bruce Sudano; children: Brooklyn, Amanda. Has sold over 20 million records. Singer, 1967—; actress: (German stage prodn.) Hair, 1967-75, (Vienna Folk Opera prodns.) Porgy and Bess, (German prodns.) The Me Nobody Knows, (cable TV spl.) Donna Summer Special, 1980; recorded albums including The Wanderer, Star Collection, Love To Love You Baby, Love Trilogy, Four Seasons of Love, I Remember Yesterday, The Deep, Shut Out, Once Upon A Time, Bad Girls, On The Radio, Walk Away, She Works Hard For The Money, Cats Without Claws, All Systems Go, 1988, Another Place and Time, 1989, Mistaken Identity, 1991, Endless Summer, 1994, Christmas Spirit, 1994, I'm a Rainbow, 1996, Live & More Encore, 1999; subject My Life VH1 Concert, 1999; recorded theme song for Hunchback of Notre Dame, Disney; forerunner of disco style. Named Best Rhythm and Blues Female Vocalist, Nat. Acad. Rec. Arts and Scis., 1978, Best Female Rock Vocalist, 1979, Favorite Female Pop Vocalist, Am. Music Awards, 1979, Favorite Female Vocalist of Soul Music, 1979, Soul Artist of Yr., Rolling Stone mag., 1979; recipient Best Favorite Pop Single award, 1979, Best selling Black Music Album for Female Artist award Nat. Assn. Record Merchandizers, 1979, Ampex Golden Reel award for album On the Radio, 1979, Best-selling Album for Female Artist, 1980, Ampex Golden Reel award for single On the Radio, 1980, Ampex Golden Reel award for album Bad Girls, Best of Las Vegas Jimmy award for best rock performance, 1980, Grammy award for best inspirational performance, 1984. Office: 2401 Main St Santa Monica CA 90405-3515

SUMMER, JENA A. writer, artist, poet; 2 children. BA in Psychology, SUNY, Buffalo, 1981, BA in Theater, 1982; BA in Comm. cum laude, SUNY, Amherst, 1982. Car sales Kramer Motors Inc., Santa Monica, Calif., 1982—84; legal sec. Daniel Hartman Esq., Buffalo, 1986—88; v.p. asst. Orion Entertainment Co., Century City, Calif., 1992—94; tchr. lang. arts Page Pvt. Schs., Beverly Hills, Calif., 1996—97; tchr. English dept. Perutz Etz Jacob Hebrew Acad., L.A., 1997—2001; recreational asst. USAF, El Segundo, Calif., 2002—03. Intern AFTRA, Buffalo, 1991—2003; dist. intern edn. Hillcrest Elem. Sch. L.A. Unified Sch. Dist., 1994—95; mem., com. chair Infrastructure Pub. Regulated Resources, 2003—. Author: (novel) Publish America The Pact, 2002, poetry and short stories; exhbn., N.Y. Mus. Met., 1982. Com. leader Hollywood Heights West Neighborhood Coun., L.A., 2003; choir mem. St. Thomas the Apostle Episcopal, 1998—. Mem.: ACLU. Anglican. Home: 7367 Hollywood Blvd #213 Los Angeles CA 90046

SUMMERS, ANITA ARROW, public policy and management educator; b. N.Y.C., Sept. 9, 1925; d. Harry I. and Lillian (Greenberg) Arrow; m. Robert Summers, Mar. 29, 1953; children: Lawrence H., Richard F., John S. BA, Hunter Coll., 1945, DHL (hon.), 1995; MA, U. Chgo., 1947. Sr. econ. analyst Standard Oil Co. N.J., N.Y.C., 1947-54; asst. in econs. Yale U., New Haven, 1956-59; lectr. dept. econs. Swarthmore (Pa.) Coll., 1965-71; sr. economist Fed. Res. Bank Phila., 1971-75, research officer, 1975-79; adj. prof. pub. policy U. Pa., Phila., 1979-82, prof. pub. policy and mgmt., 1982—, dept. chair, 1983-88, univ. ombudsman, 2001—03, co-dir Wharton Urban Decentralization Project, 1987-97, dir. rsch. Wharton Real Estate Ctr., 2003—, sr. scholar Nat. Ctr. on the Edn. Quality of the Workforce, 1991—95. Expert witness schs. fin. Md., Mass., Va., 1980-85, Md., Va., 1996, Calif., 2003, bd. dirs. William Penn Found., Phila., 1993-98; chair bd. dirs. Mathematica Policy Rsch., Inc., Princeton, N.J., 1993—; mem. adv. com. Nat. Bd. Med. Examiners. Author: Economic Report on the Philadelphia Metropolitan Area, 1985, Economic Development within the Philadelphia Metropolitan Area, 1986, Local Fiscal Issues in the Philadelphia Metropolitan Area, 1987; editor: Urban Change in the United States and Western Europe, 1992, 99; contbr. articles to profl. jours. Chair econ. subcom. Pa. Three Mile Island Commn., Harrisburg, 1979; pres. Lower Merion (Pa.) LWV, 1963-65; mem. Mayor's Econ. Roundtable, Phila., 1984-88; mem. rsch. policy coun., 1992-94, Com. for Econ. Devel. Rockefeller Found. resident scholar, Bellagio, Italy, 1986. Mem. Am. Econ. Assn., Assn. for Pub. Policy and Mgmt. (policy coun. 1986), Phi Beta Kappa. Avocations: needlepoint, cooking. Home: 641 Revere Rd Merion Station PA 19066-1007 Office: U Pa Wharton Sch Dept Pub Policy and Mgmt Philadelphia PA 19104 E-mail: summers@wharton.upenn.edu.

SUMMERS, BARBARA JUNE, artist; b. Syracuse, N.Y., June 18, 1960; d. Judith Dawn (Yager) Austen-Myers. BFA, U. Tex., 1996. Served in USAF, Vandenburg AFB, Calif., 1981-82, Lakenheath AFB, U.K., 1982-84, Lackland AFB, Tex., 1984-85, Civil Svc., San Antonio, 1986-89; co-owner www.summerfineart.com. Freelance artist. Democrat. Home: 6811 Maple Lake St San Antonio TX 78244-1723 E-mail: BarbaraSummers@msn.com.

SUMMERS, CATHLEEN ANN, film producer; b. Chgo. d. Paul and Elizabeth Summers; m. Patrick Timothy Crowley. BA, U. So. Calif., 1973. Film editor, comml. producer, dir.'s asst. Roman Polanski, Rome, 1972; story editor Albert S. Ruddy Prodns. Paramount Pictures, L.A., 1973-74; exec. asst. Columbia Pictures, Burbank, Calif., 1974, story editor, 1974-76; devel. exec., v.p., producer Martin Ransohoff Prodns. Columbia Pictures, 1976; sr. v.p. Tri-Star Pictures, Century City, Calif., 1984-87; motion picture producer Cathleen Summers Prodns., L.A., 1989—; ptnr. ESN, Film Prodn. Resource Co. Motion picture producer, ptnr. Summers-Kouf Prodns., Burbank, 1986-87; motion picture producer Cathleen Summers Prodns., L.A., 1987, Summers-Quaid Prodns., Century City, Culver City, Calif., 1988—. Producer: (motion picture) Stakeout, 1987, DOA, 1991, Vital Signs, 1990, Mystery Date, 1991, Dogfight, 1991, The Sandlot, 1993, Stakeout II, 1993. Co-founder Diane Thomas Scholarship, UCLA, 1988—; bd. dirs. L.A. chpt. Nat. Parkinsons Found.; founding bd. dirs. U.S. Comedy Arts Festival, Aspen, Colo. Mem. Am. Film Inst. (pres. 3d Decade Coun. 1995, 96, 97).

SUMMERS, LORRAINE DEY SCHAEFFER, retired librarian; b. Phila., Dec. 14, 1946; d. Joseph William and Hilda Lorraine (Ritchey) Dey; m. F. William Summers, Jan. 28, 1984. BA, Fla. State U., 1968, MS, 1969. Ext. dir. Santa Fe Regional Libr., Gainesville, 1969-71; pub. libr. cons. State Libr. of Fla., Tallahassee, 1971-78, asst. state libr., 1978-84; dir. adminstrv. svcs. Nat. Assn. for Campus Activities, Columbia, S.C., 1984-85; asst. state libr. State Libr. of Fla., Tallahassee, 1985—2001, ret., 2001—. Bd. dirs., sec. Southeastern Libr. Network, Inc.; cons. in field. Contbr. articles to profl. jours. Del. Pres.'s Com. on Mental Retardation Regional Forum, Atlanta, 1975; del. Fla. Gov.'s Conf. on Libr. and Info. Svcs., 1978, 90. Mem. ALA (orgn. com. 1979-83, coun. 1982-84, 93-97, resolutions com. 1983-85, mem. legislation com. 1993-95, nominating com. 1996, awards com. 1998-99, Spectrum awards jury 1999-2000), Assn. Specialized and Coop. Libr. Agys. (dir. 1976-82, chmn. planning and orgn. com. 1976-80, chmn. nominating com. 1980-81, chmn. by laws com. 1985-86, exec. bd. state libr. agy. sect. 1983-86, pres. 1987-88, chmn. stds. rev. com. 1990-92), Southeastern Libr. Assn. (exec. bd. 1976-80, v.p., pres.-elect 1994-96, pres. 1996-98, past pres. 1998-2000, nominating com. 2000-02), Fla. Libr. Assn. (sec. 1978-79, dir. 1976-80, nominating com. 1995-96), Zonta (dir. 1992-95, sec. 1999-2001). Democrat. Methodist. Personal E-mail: lorsummers@worldnet.att.net.

SUMMERS, VANESSA, state legislator; m. Nicholas T. Barnes. Grad., Mid-Am. Coll. Funeral Svcs. State rep., mem. aged & aging, pub. policy, ethics, vet. affairs & urban affairs coms., chmn. interstate coop. com. Ind. Ho. of Reps., Indpls., 1991—; funeral dir. Summers Funeral Chapel. Named one of Top Ladies of Distinction. Mem. Alpha Kappa Alpha, Alpha Mu Omega. Democrat. Office: 1140 Brook Ln Indianapolis IN 46202-2255

SUMMERTREE, KATONAH See WINDSOR, PATRICIA

SUMMITT, APRIL, history educator; b. Knoxville, Tenn., Apr. 2, 1964; d. Ted E. and Connie L. (Westerberg) Summitt. BA in History and in English, Newbold Coll., 1987; MA in History, Andrews U., 1993; PhD, Western Mich. U., 2002. Adj. instr. Jordan Jr. Coll., Benton Harbor, Mich., 1988-93, Andrews U., 1990-92, asst. prof., 1996—. Doctoral assoc., lectr. Western Mich. U., 1993-96. Sec., bd. dirs. Berrien County Hist. Assn., 1997— . John F. Kennedy Libr. rsch. fellow, 1998. Mem. Am. Hist. Assn., Orgn. Am. Historians, Soc. for Historians of Am. Fgn. Rels., Phi Alpha Theta. Avocations: sailing, poetry, drama, cross-country skiing, piano. Office: Andrews U Dept History And Polit Sci Berrien Springs MI 49104-0001 Home: Apt 11 9766 Rosehill Rd Berrien Springs MI 49103-1287

SUMMITT, PATRICIA HEAD, basketball coach; b. Henrietta, Tenn., June 14, 1952; d. Richard and Hazel Head; m. R.B. Summitt; 1 child, Ross Tyler. BS in Phys. Edn., U. Tenn., Martin, 1974; MS in Phys. Edn., U. Tenn., Knoxville, 1975. Basketball player U. Tenn., Martin, 1970—74, head women's basketball coach Knoxville, 1974—. Head coach 1st U.S. Jr. Nat. team, 1977 (2 gold medals in internat. play), U.S. Nat. team William R. Jones Cup Games, 1979, World Championships, 1979, Pan Am. Games, 1979 (2 gold medals, 1 silver medal); asst. coach U.S. Women's Olympic Basketball team, 1980-84, head coach, 1984 (gold medal); assoc. athletics dir., U. Tenn.; past v.p. USA BASKETBALL; past Olympic rep. adv. com. to USA BASKETBALL; bd. trustees Basketball Hall of Fame; bd. dirs. Women's Basketball Hall of Fame. Active Big Bros./Big Sisters; Active spokesperson United Way, Race for the Cure, Juvenile Diabetes; hon. chair Tenn. Easter Seal Soc., 1985, 87, 88, 89; Tenn. chair Am. Heart Assn., 1994. Named Naismith Coach of Yr., 1987, 1989, 1994, 1997, Naismith Coach of Century, 2000, WBCA/Converse Coach of Yr., 1983—95; named one of Women of Yr., Women in Sports and Events, 1999; named to Women's Sports Foundation Hall of Fame, 1990, Nat. Assn. for Sport and Phys. Edn., 1996, Women's Basketball Hall of Fame, 1999, Basketball Hall of Fame, 2000; recipient silver medal, Olympic Games, 1976, gold medal, Pan Am. Games, 1975, silver medal, U.S. World Univ. Games, 1973, Wooden Award, 1997, ARETE Award for Courage in Sports, 1999. Mem. Chi Omega. Achievements include coach U. Tenn. women's basketball NCAA Championship teams, 1987, 89, 91, 96, 97, 98; coach U. Tenn. women's basketball SEC Championship teams, 1980, 85, 90, 93, 94, 95, 98, 99, 2000, 01, 02, 03.*

SUN, NORA CHI-JUN, pathologist; b. Shanghai, June 16, 1937; came to U.S., 1966; d. K.F. and S.W. Sun; m. David T. Sung; children: Thomas C.K. Lee, Anthony D. Sung. MD, Shanghai 2d Med. Coll., 1960; MS in Pathology, U. Minn., 1973. Demonstrator U. Hong Kong, 1964-66; rsch. biologist A.H. Robins Co., Richmond, Va., 1966-67; resident Med. Coll. Va., 1967—68; clin. teaching asst. Boston U. Sch. Medicine, 1968-70; resident Mallaory Inst. Pathology, 1968—70; fellow Mayo Clinic and Grad. Sch., 1970—73; asst. prof. pathology U. So. Calif., L.A., 1973-76; staff pathologist John Wesley Hosp., L.A., 1973-76; asst. prof. UCLA Sch. Medicine, L.A., 1976-82; staff pathologist, head hematopathology Harbor-UCLA Med. Ctr., Torrance, Calif., 1976—2002; assoc. prof. UCLA Sch. Medicine, L.A., 1982-88, prof. pathology, 1988—2002, prof. emeritus, 2002—. Recipient Women Achievement award Delta Kappa Gamma, Rochester, Minn., 1972, Disting. Svc. award Am. Soc. Clin. Pathologists, 1996. Mem. Internat. Assn. Chinese Pathologists (pres.-elect 1991-93, pres. 1993-95), Harbor-UCLA Med. Ctr. Faculty Soc. (pres.-elect 1990-91, pres. 1991-92). Office: Harbor UCLA Med Ctr 1000 W Carson St Torrance CA 90502-2004 E-mail: ncjsun@ucla.edu.

SUNDAY, MELVA DORA, elementary school educator; b. Balt., June 7, 1954; d. Henry Alfred Zeitschel Sr. and Emma Dora Wendesheim-Zeitschel; m. Steven Edward Sunday, Oct. 8, 1977; 1 child, Elizabeth Anne. BA, Bridgewater Coll., 1976; MEd, U. Md., 1981. Tchr. Crofton Woods Elem. Sch., Md., 1976—77, Belle Grove Elem. Sch., Brooklyn Park, Md., 1976—82, Overlook Elem. Sch., North Linthicum, Md., 1977—82, Hilltop Elem. Sch., Glen Burnie, Md., 1982—98, Rippling Woods Elem. Sch., Glen Burnie, 1998—2000, Folger McKinsey Elem. Sch., Glen Burnie, 2000—. Assoc. vocal/instrumental music Heritage Cmty. Ch., Severn, Md., 1988—2002. Mem.: Md. Music Educators, Music Educators Nat. Conf. Office: Folger McKinsey Elem Sch 175 Arundel Beach Rd Severna Park MD 21146 Office Phone: 410-222-6560.*

SUNDAYO, JUDY, psychologist, educator; b. Washington, Apr. 13, 1952; d. Granville N. and Thomasia (Smith) Moore; m. Guadalupe Gallegos, Mar. 25, 1978 (div. Nov. 1981); 1 child, Jaimah Aurora. BA in Psychology, Am. U., Washington, 1975; MA in Human Behavior, Internat. U., San Diego, 1983; MA in Counseling Psychology, Profl. Sch. Psychol. Studies, San Diego, 1982, PhD in Clin. Psychology, 1987. Lic. clin. psychologist, Calif. Adj. prof., group facilitator U. Ariz., 1985-88; adj. prof. U. La Verne, San Diego, 1987-89, San Diego State U., 1989-90; adminstrv. analyst June Burnett Inst., San Diego State U., 1988-89; evaluating clinician ERM Assocs. for NFL, San Diego, 1994—; pvt. practice psychology San Diego, 1992—; prof. San Diego Mesa Coll., 1989—. Contbr. poetry to anthologies, Words of Praise, 1984, Am. Poetry Anthology, 1982, Masterpieces of Modern Verse, 1985, Collectively Creatin', 1997. Mem. AAUW, APA, Assn. of Black Psychologists (life, historian 1998—, pres. 1996-98, chmn. membership com. 1990-96), Nat. Assn. of Colored Women. Avocations: writing, swimming, reading, crafts, hiking. Office: San Diego Family Inst 3235 4th Ave San Diego CA 92103-5701

SUNDEEN, SANDRA JOAN, mental health nurse; b. Jamestown, N.Y., Sept. 30, 1940; d. Harold E. and Helen (Carlson) S. BS, U. Rochester, 1966; MS in Psychiat. Nursing, U. Md., 1968. Asst. prof. U. Md. Sch. Nursing; chief psychiatric nursing Md. Dept. Health and Mental Hygiene, Balt. Rsch. in field. Author several books in field. Mem. ANA, Nat. League Nursing, Md. Nurses Assn., Md. League Nursing, Sigma Theta Tau, Phi Kappa Phi. Home: 790 Dividing Rd Severna Park MD 21146-4324

SUNDERLAND, HOLLY BROWN, church musician; b. KY; d. R. Kendall and Nancy B. Brown; m. Martin R. Sunderland. BMus, Westminster Choir Coll., NJ; MMus, U. Cinn. Choral music educator Va. Beach City Pub. Schs., Va.; music educator McAuley H.S., Cin., Summit Country Day Sch., Cin.; stock broker Charles Schwab, Cin. Mem.: NEA, Am. Choral Dirs. Assn., Music Educators Nat. Conf.

SUNDERLAND, JACKLYN GILES, former alumni affairs director; b. Corpus Christi, Tex., Oct. 21, 1937; d. Elbert Jackson and Mary Kathryn (Garrett) Giles; m. Joseph Alan MacInnis, Nov. 24, 1963 (div. Feb. 1982); children: Mary Kendall Brady, Joseph Alan MacInnis; m. Lane Von Sunderland, June 12, 1988. BA, U. Tex., Austin, 1960. Editor's asst. House & Garden mag., N.Y.C., 1962; reporter Corpus Christi Caller-Times, 1960, 69, Home Furnishings Daily, Fairchild Publs., N.Y.C., 1961, Houston Post, 1963; writer, rschr. Saudi Press Agy., Washington, 1980; writer/rschr. for V.P. U.S. White House, Washington, 1982-84; dir. pub. affairs President's Com. on Mental Retardation, Washington, 1984-85; dir. speakers bur. Commn. on Bicentennial U.S. Constn., Washington, 1985-87; speechwriter Sec. of HHS, Washington, 1987-88, U.S. Sec. of Labor, Washington, 1989; dir. alumni affairs Knox Coll., Galesburg, Ill., 1990-92. Campaign chmn. Am. Cancer Soc., Corpus Christi, 1961; liaison Am. Embassy, Copenhagen, 1965-68; docent, tchr. art Nat. Gallery and Smithsonian Mus., Washington, 1970-73; vestrywoman Grace Episcopal Ch., Galesburg, 1991; mem. Jr. League Washington, 1963-2003; vol. Hospice, 1996-97. Recipient Continental Marine citation for community svc., Camp Pendleton, Calif., 1977. Republican. Home: 185 Park Ln Galesburg IL 61401

SUNDHEIM, NANCY STRAUS, lawyer; B in History, U. Pa.; JD, Harvard U. With Arnold & Porter, Washington, Ropes & Gray, Boston, Dechert Price & Rhoads, Phila.; chief acquisitions counsel Unisys Corp., Blue Bell, Pa., 1987, dep. counsel, head corp. law group, 1990, corp. v.p., corp. sec., 1999, mem. exec. com., 1999—, sr. v., gen. counsel, 2001. Office: Unisys Corp Unisys Way Blue Bell PA 19424

SUNDICK, SHERRY SMALL, author, journalist, poet; b. Washington, July 17, 1946; d. Charles Haskell and Ruth (Behrend) Small; B.A., Am. U., 1970; m. Gary Norman Sundick, Aug. 3, 1969; children— Amy Beth, Suzanne Faye. Columnist, Today Newspapers, Rockville, Md., 1973-75; journalist The Jour. Newspapers, Chevy Chase, Md., 1975—, The Potomac Almanac, 1976-80. Recipient N.Am. Mentor Mag. Ann. Mentor Poetry award, 1973. Mem. Nat. League Am. Pen Women, Writers Center, World Poetry Soc. Jewish. Author: Celebration, 1977; (with Ruth Small) Potpourri, 1978; contbr. articles to various mags. and jours. including Md. Mag., No. Va. Mag. Design, Maine Life, Feelings, Smile, The Pen Women, Haiku Headlines, others. Address: 11809 Hunting Ridge Ct Potomac MD 20854-2152

SUNDQUIST, LEAH RENATA, physical education specialist; b. El Paso, Tex., July 22, 1963; d. Dominic Joseph and Patricia Ann (Manley) Bernardi; m. David Curtis Sundquist, June 23, 1990. AA, N.Mex. Mil. Inst., 1983; BS, U. Tex., El Paso, 1986; MEd in Curriculum and Instrn., City U., Bellevue, Wash., 1996. Field exec. Rio Grande Girl Scout Coun., El Paso, 1983-84; customer teller M-Bank, El Paso, 1984-85; soccer coach St. Clements Sch., El Paso, 1985; substitute tchr. El Paso Sch. Dist., 1986; commd. 2nd lt. U.S. Army, 1983, advanced through grades to maj., 1997, plans/exercise officer, 1990, ops. officer, 1990-1991; comdr. hdqs. Hdqs. Co. 141st Support Bn. U.S. Army N.G., 1996-97; dir. Childrens World Learning Ctr., Federal Way, Wash., 1992-94; phys. edn. specialist, tchr. K-6 Kent (Wash.) Elem. Sch., 1994-2001; health fitness tchr. Camas (Wash.) Mid. Sch., 2001—; ops. and tng. officer Bn S3, 1997-99; exec. officer, 1999—. Coord. NCCJ, El Paso, 1979-81; v.p. Jr. Achievement, El Paso, 1980-81; adult tng. vol. Girl Scout Coun., bd. dirs. Pacific Peaks coun., 1993-99, chair nominating com., 1996, jr. troop leater Totem coun. Girl Scouts U.S., 1996, chair program policies rev. com., 1997, trainer instrn. of adults, tng. coord. team mem., 1997—; bd. dirs. Jr. League Tacoma, 1993, 94, staff devel. coun. mem., 1997-2000, design com., 1998—. 3rd Res. Officer Tng. Corps scholar, 1981-83, H.P. Saunder scholar, 1982; recipient Humanitarian Svc. medal Great Fires of Yellowstone, U.S. Army, 1988, Gold award Girl Scouts U.S.A., 1981; decorated Nat. Def. Svc. medal Desert Storm; meritorius Svc. medal, 1991. Mem. NEA, Wash. Edn. Assn., Assn. U.S. Army, Oreg. Army Nat. Guard Assn., Assn. U.S. Army, Air Def. Artillery Assn., Zeta Tau Alpha (sec. 1983-85, house mgr. 1984-86). Republican. Roman Catholic. Avocations: soccer, fishing, hunting, skydiving, rafting. Home: 1315 SE 16th Ave Canby OR 97013

SUNDSTROM, BARBARA ANN, scriptwriter, film producer, educator; d. John and Norma Ballard; m. David Glenn Sundstrom; children: Erica Smith, Robert Kessler, Ann Kessler, Carly. BA, Baylor U., 1970; MA, U. of Houston, 1991. Cert. tchr. Tex., 1970. Tchr. Aldine Ind. Sch. Dist., Houston, 1971—72, Uvalde (Tex.) Consol. Ind. Sch. Dist., 1973—77, Cypress Fairbanks Ind. Sch. Dist., Houston, 1985—88; grad. tchg. asst. U. of Houston, Houston, 1989—91; dir. of promotion, playwright, actress A.D. Players Theatre Co., Houston, 1992—95; freelance writer Houston, 1995—2000; exec. dir. Cross Wind Productions, Houston, 2000—. Author: (plays) Doc in the Box, 1996 (Semi-Finalist Lamia Ink Internat. One Page Play Contest, 1996), The Hundred Penny Box, 1998, EST Marathon, 1998, (screenplays) Ky. Infidel, 1997, Sindone Treasure of Turin, 1999, Miss America in India, 2001 (Second Rounder Austin Film Festival, 2002); prodr.: (films) Holly's Story, 2003; singer: Houston (Tex.) Symphony Chorus, 1982—88. Spkr. evaluations United Way, Houston, 1990; coord. reading is fundamental program Jr. Svc. League, Uvalde, Tex., 1978—80; class missions coord. Second Bapt. Ch., Houston, 2001—04. Named Outstanding Grad. Student, Sch. of Comm. U. of Houston, 1991. Mem.: S.W. Alternative Media Project, The Dramatist Guild, Baylor U. Women, Pi Beta Phi. So. Baptist. Avocations: tap dancing, acting, swimming, skiing, camping.

SUNDVALL, SHEILA A. lawyer; b. Cleve., Jan. 21, 1963; BA, U. Mich., 1985, JD, 1988. Bar: Ill. 1988, U.S. Dist. Ct. (no. dist.) Ill. 1988, U.S. Ct. Appeals (7th cir.) 1989. Jud. clk. judge Richard D. Cudahy U.S. Ct. Appeals 7th Cir., Chgo., 1988-89; assoc. Sidley & Austin, Chgo., 1989-96, ptnr., 1996—. Lectr. in field. Mem. Legal Club Chgo., Phi Beta Kappa, Order of Coif. Office: Sidley & Austin 1 S First National Plz Chicago IL 60603-2000

SUPER, DEBORAH H. secondary school educator; d. Robin L. and Barbara J. Harvey; m. F. Joseph Super, Sept. 23, 1947; 1 child, Joseph F. BS, W.Va. U., 1974, MA, 1981, Marshall U., 1983. Tchr. Elkins Jr. High, Elkins, W.Va., 1974—84, 1987—93; adj. instr. Davis and Elkins Coll., Elkins, W.Va., 1982—85; tchr. Elkins H.S., Elkins, W.Va., 1984—85, 1993—2003, Clarke County H.S., Berryville, Va., 1985—86, Apple Pie Ridge Elem., Winchester, Va., 1986—87; adj. instr. Fairmont State Coll., Fairmont, W.Va., 1990—2003; work-based learning coord., vocat. integration specialist Randolph County Schs., 2003—. Supr. student tchrs. W.Va. U., Morgantown, W.Va., 1984, tchr. practicum supr., 1987—87; yearbook adviser Elkins H.S., W.Va., 1993—2003; accompanist Elkins High Madrigal Choir, W.Va., 1997—; gifted task force W.Va. State Dept. of Edn., Charleston, W.Va., 1997—2002; yearbook adv. bd. Walsworth Pub., Marceline, Kans., 1999—2001; yearbook judge Columbia Scholastic Press Assn., New York, NY, 1999—2001, Nat. Scholastic Press Assn., Kansas City, Mo., 2000—01; mentor tchr. Randolph County Schs., Elkins, W.Va., 2001—02; presenter at nat. yearbook conv. Columbia Scholastic Press Assn., New York, NY, 2001—02. Contbr. Idea mag. Adviser Teenage Republicans, Elkins, 1999—2003; music bd. First Bapt. Ch., Elkins, W.Va., 1987—2003, handbell dir., 1991—2003, pianist, organist, 1993—2003. Recipient Lang. Arts Tchr. of Yr., Randolph County Schs., 1987, 1992, 1994. Mem.: W.Va. Edn. Assn., Woman's Club (scholarship chmn. 2002—03), Delta Kappa Gamma (pres. 1990—92, chmn. state scholarship 1998—2000), Beta Sigma Phi (life; pres. 1990—94, Silver Cir. Award 2001). R-Conservative. Baptist. Avocations: piano, singing, reading. Home: 104 White Oak Ln Elkins WV 26241

SUPPA-FRIEDMAN, JANICE DESTEFANO, secondary school educator, consultant; b. Morristown, NJ, Apr. 27, 1943; d. Eugene Arthur and Isabella Vienna (Bottiglia) DeS.; m. Dennis Suppa, June 28, 1964 (div. May 1994); children: Julie Ann, Chad Dennis; m. Michael Jac Friedman, Oct. 7, 1995. BS in Edn., Bowling Green State U., 1964; MA in Edn., Va. Poly. Inst. & State U., 1977, cert. advanced grad. study, 1990. Cert. secondary tchr., Va. Tchr. English and reading Northwood (Ohio) Jr. High Sch., 1964—66; tchr. English and history Canaseraga (N.Y.) Ctrl. Schs., 1966—67; tchr. English and reading Marstellar Jr. High Sch., Manassas, Va., 1967—72; tchr. English Taylor Jr. High sch., Warrenton, Va., 1973—74; tchr. English and reading, lang. arts specialist, dept. head, lead tchr. Brentsville Dist. Mid.-Sr. High Sch., Nokesville, Va., 1975—99; reading specialist Graham Park Middle Sch., Dumfries, Va., 1999—2000; ednl. cons., 2000—. Ednl. cons. So. Region Coll. Bd., 2001—; reader for advanced placement literature and composition exam, 1996, 1998-2003; adj. prof. Old Dominion U., 1999, No. Va. C.C., 1992-94, George Mason U., 2004. Editor newsletter Spinning Wheel, 1991-94; contbr. articles to profl. jours. Va. English Bull. Tour guide George Washington Fredericksburg Found. at Kenmore Mansion and Plantation, Ferry Farms, Va., 2001—; officer of election Stafford County, 2001—03. Grantee Va. Comm. of the Arts, 1994-95, 2000, Prince William Edn. Found., 1996, 2000, Greater Washington Reading Coun., 1999, 2000, Va. Opera Assn., 2000, So. States Southland Corp., 2000. Mem. NATE (pres. 1992-1994), Nat. Coun. Tchrs. English (coord. Va. state Achievement in Writing awards 1995-2001, Va. state liaison 2001, judge Va. state forensics finals 2000-2003, judge Va. state excellence in lit. mags. 1998-2002), Va. Assn. Tchrs. English (exec. bd. 1992—, v.p. 2001-02, pres.-elect 2002-03, pres. 2004, Svc. award 1993), Phi Delta Kappa. Avocations: reading, music, hiking, swimming, biking.

SUPPES, CHRISTINE JOHNSON, publishing executive; b. LA, Mar. 3, 1953; d. Robert and Jane Johnson; m. Patrick Suppes; children: Alexandra Christine, Michael Patrick. Copygirl/editl. asst. San Francisco Examiner, 1972—73; pres. Gravure At Home, Stanford, Calif., 1997—2001; pub., editor-in-chief www.Fashionlines.com, Stanford, Calif., 1999—; chief designer Jewels by Christine, 2002—. Advt. cons. Clarum Corp., Palo Alto, Calif., 1997—, Gravure Corp., Dallas, 1997—2000; chief designer www.jewelsbyChristine.com, Stanford, Calif., 2003—. Author: Amanda Prescott, 1984, Clinic, 1985; contbr. revs. to San Francisco Chronicle, articles to SF Moda. Organizer, Teacher's Fund Bing School, Stanford, 1995—2001; mem. Peninsula Chpt. NARAL, Palo Alto, 1997—2000; supporter ARC, Palo Alto, 2001. Recipient Angel of Fashion com. award, N.Y.C., 1999—. Mem.: Fashion Group Internat., Camera Nazionale della Moda Italiana, Federation Francaise de la Couture. Office: Fashionlines 678 Mirada Ave Stanford CA 94305

SURECK, KAREN EILEEN, special education educator; b. Evansville, Ind., Dec. 8, 1949; d. Paul Edwin and Joyce Eileen (Marshall) Hachmeister; m. Gregory John Sureck, Apr. 18, 1981; children: John Gregory, Kate Elizabeth. BS, Murray State U., 1971; MA, U. Evansville, 1975. Lic. profl. educator. Tchr. spl. edn. Warrick County Sch. Corp., Boonville, Ind., 1971—. Dist. pres. United Meth. Women, Evansville, 1995—. Recipient Outstanding Young Educator award Jaycees, 1974, Outstanding Young Woman of Am. award, 1983. Mem. NEA, AAUW, Ind. State Tchrs. Assn., Warrick County Tchrs. Assn. Republican. Avocations: travel, reading, community involvement. Home: 766 S Rockport Rd Boonville IN 47601-9739 Office: Oakdale Elem Sch 802 S 8th St Boonville IN 47601-2000

SURINER, NOREEN P. rector, priest; d. Wayne A. and Priscilla P. Suriner; m. Robert Y. Phelan, Apr. 17, 2002. BA in Edn., Berkshire Christian Coll., Lenox, Mass., 1969; MEd, Am. Internat. Coll., Springfield, Mass., 1973; MDiv, Va. Theol. Sem., Alexandria, 1976. Ordination to Priesthood Episc. Ch., 1977, Ordination to Diaconate Episc. Ch., 1976; cert. tchr. Mass., 1969. Tchr. Berkshire Hills Regional Sch. Dist., Great Barrington, Mass., 1969—73; seminarian internship St. Columba's Episc. Ch., Washington, 1974—76, youth min. to priest in charge, 1976—80; assoc. The Ch. of the Redeemer, Balt., 1980—82; rector Christ the King Episc. Ch., Balt., 1982—95, Trinity Meml. Episc. Ch., Binghamton, NY, 1995—. Vice chair Ch. Pension Fund, N.Y.C., NY, 1991—; bd. mem. Consortium of Episc. Endowed Parishes, 2003—; nat. network of episc. clergy assns.; alternate dep. to gen. conv. Episc. Ch. of the USA. Contbr. chapters to books. Mem. Good Shepherd Found., Binghamton, NY, 2000—03, Binghamton Chpt. of Christmas In Apr., Binghamton, NY, 1998—99; chair of the bd. of directors Havan Afterschool Program, Binghamton, NY, 2003—. Mem.: Mayflower Soc. (life; mem.), Binghamton Club (corr.), Rotary (corr. Paul Harris Mem. 1999). Democrat. Episcopal. Achievements include first to First Woman ordained in Massachusetts; First ordained woman to serve on Pension Fund; First ordained woman to serve as Officer of the Fund; First woman to be called as Rector in Mid-Atlantic States; First Woman President of National Network of Clergy Association. Avocation: raising Scottish terriers. Office: Trinity Memorial Episcopal Church 44 Main St Binghamton NY 13905 E-mail: nsuriner@stny.rr.com.

SURLES, CAROL D. academic administrator; b. Pensacola, Fla., Oct. 7, 1946; d. Elza Allen and Versy Lee Smith; divorced; children: Lisa Surles, Philip Surles. BA, Fisk U., 1968; MA, Chapman Coll., 1971; PhD, U. Mich., 1978. Personnel rep. U. Mich., Ann Arbor, 1973-78, vice-chancellor-adminstrn. Flint, 1987-89; exec. asst. to pres., assoc. v.p. for human resources U. Ctrl. Fla., Orlando, 1978-87; v.p. acad. affairs Jackson State U., Miss., 1989-92; v.p. adminstrn. and bus. Calif. State U., Hayward, 1992-94; pres. Tex. Woman's U., Denton, 1994-99, Ea. Ill. U., Charleston, 1999—. Trustee Pub. Broadcasting Ch. 24, Orlando, 1985-87; bd. dirs. First State Bank, Denton, Tex., Tex.-N.Mex. Power Co., TNP-Enterprise. Recipient Outstanding Scholar's award Delta Tau Kappa, 1983. Mem. AAUW, Am. Assn. Colls. and Univs., Golden Key Honor Soc., Mortar Bd. Soc., Dallas Citizens' Coun., Dallas Women's Found., Coun. of Pres. (Austin, Tex.), Phi Kappa Phi, Alpha Kappa Alpha. Methodist. Avocation: playing piano and oboe. Office: Ea Ill U 600 Lincoln Ave Charleston IL 61920-3011

SURLEY, LESLIE K. marketing professional; d. O. C. and Virginia Louise Surley. BA, So. Meth. U., Dallas, Tex., 1990—94. Bus. devel. mgr. Intesol Internat. Corp., Long Beach, Calif., 2000—; vp/mgr. of ops., contbr. rels. Thomson Fin. (formerly I/B/E/S Internat., Inc.), New York, NY, 1996—2000. Project leader Coun. for Excellence in Govt., Washington, 1994—96. Prodr.: (political talkshow) Breakthrough. Mem.: Assn. for Women in Tech. (bd. mem. 2003—), CRM Assn. (co-founder of so. calif. 2003—). Methodist. Personal E-mail: lsurley@yahoo.com.

SURPRISE, JUANEE, chiropractor, nutrition consultant; b. Gary, Ind., Apr. 28, 1944; d. Glenn Mark and Willia Ross (Vasser) Surprise; m. Peter E. Coakley, Feb. 12, 1966 (div. Jan. 1976); children: Thaddeus, Mariah, Darius; m. Robert T.Howell, Feb. 24, 1984. RN, Phila. Gen. Hosp. Sch. Nursing, 1965; DrChiropractic summa cum laude, Life Chiropractic Coll, Marietta, Ga., 1981. Diplomate Nat. Bd. Chiropractic Examiners, Am. Chiropractic Bd. Nutrition, Am. Acad. Pain Mgmt.; bd. cert. naturopathic med. doctor; cert. clin. nutritionist, acupuncturist, Thompson technique, Nimmo receptor tonus technique. Staff nurse Children's Hosp., Balt., [illegible]; charge nurse Melrose (Mass.) Wakefield Hosp., 1967-80; hosp. adminstr. Animal Hosp. of Wakefield, Mass., 1967-79; chiropractor Chiropractic Clinic of Greenville, N.C., 1982-84, Family Med.-Chiropractic Clinic, Denton, Tex., 1984—; dean Sch. Nutrition Quantum-Veritis Interant. Univ. Sys.; dir. Ctr. Clin. Sci., Parker Coll. Chiropractic, Dallas, 1996-97, dir. diplomate and certification programs, 1997-2000. Mem. postgrad. faculty Tex. Chriopractic Coll., Northwestern U. Health Scis. Mem., chmn. Cmty. Planning Commn., North Reading, Mass., 1976-79; chmn. bldg. com. Immaculate Conception Ch., Denton, 1987-90, parish coun., 1990-92; v.p. Property Owners Assn., 2000-02. Fellow Am. Chiropractic Coll. Nutrition; mem. Am. Assn. Pain Mgmt., Am. Chiropractic Assn., Am. Coun. on Nutrition (pres.), Am. Chiropractic Bd. on Nutrition (past pres.), Tex. Chiropractic Assn. (chair nutrition coms.), Pi Tau Delta. Republican. Roman Catholic. Avocations: maine coon cat breeding, health education, camping. Office: Family Med and Chiropractic Rehab Clinic 1100 Dallas Dr Denton TX 76205-5121 E-mail: doctormunda@hotmail.com.

SUSKO, CAROL LYNNE, lawyer, accountant; b. Washington, Dec. 5, 1955; d. Frank and Helen Louise (Davis) S. BS in Econs. and Acctg., George Mason U., 1979; JD, Cath. U., 1982; LLM in Taxation, Georgetown U., 1992. Bar: Pa. 1989, D.C. 1990; CPA, Va., Md. Tax acct. Reznick Fedder & Silverman, P.C., Bethesda, Md., 1984-85; sr. tax acct. Pannell Kerr Forster, Alexandria, Va., 1985; tax specialist Coopers & Lybrand, Washington, 1985-87; supervisory tax sr. Frank & Co., McLean, Va., 1987-88; mem. editl. staff Tax Notes Mag., Arlington, Va., 1989-90; adj. faculty Am. U., Washington, 1989—; tax atty. Marriott Corp., Washington, 1993-94; sr. tax mgr. Host Marriott Inc., Washington, 1994-99, KPMG LLP, McLean, Va., 1999—. Mem. ABA, AICPAs, Va. Soc. CPAs, D.C. Soc. CPAs, D.C. Bar Assn. Office: KPMG LLP Ste 3064 1660 International Dr Mc Lean VA 22102-4832 E-mail: csusko@kpmg.com.

SUSMAN, SALLY, cosmetics executive; Student, London Sch. Econs.; BA, Conn. Coll. Legis. asst. U.S. Senate Com. Commerce, Sci. and Transp.; dep. asst. sec. legis. & intergovernmental affairs U.S. Dept. Commerce; pub. rels. Am. Express, 1995—97; sr. v.p. global comm. Estée Lauder Cos. Inc., N.Y.C., 2000—. Commr. N.Y.C. Commn. Women's Issues; bd. dirs. Nat. Partnership Women and Families, Parsons Sch. Design, Gina Gibney Dance; trustee Conn. Coll. Mem.: Arthur W. Page Soc. Office: Estée Lauder Co Inc 767 5th Ave New York NY 10153

SUSSE, SANDRA SLONE, lawyer; b. Medford, Ma., June 1, 1943; d. James Robert and Georgie Coffin (Bradshaw) Slone; m. Peter Susse, May 10, 1969 (div. May 1993); 1 child, Toby. BA, U. Mass., 1981; JD, Vt. Law Sch., 1986. Bar: Mass. 1986, U.S. Dist. Ct. Mass. 1988, U.S. Ct. Appeals (1st cir.) 1995. Staff atty. Western Mass. Legal Svcs., Springfield, 1986—. Mem. ABA, Women's Bar Assn. Mass. Avocations: hiking, german literature, films, skating. Address: Western Mass Legal Serv 127 State St Fl 4 Springfield MA 01103-1905 Office Phone: 413-781-7814. E-mail: ssusse@wmls.org.

SUSSKIND, EMILY H. broadcast executive; BA in Philosophy and Math., Wellesley Coll.; MBA in Fin., Wharton Sch., U. of Pa. With Salomon Brothers, Inc., 1985—96, dir.; sr. v.p., sys. devel. TELE-TV Systems, L.P., 1996—97; sr. v.p., tech. Dow Jones Markets, N.Y.C., 1997—98; sr. v.p., interactive services Sony Corp. of Am., N.Y.C., 1998—2000, pres., broadband services, 2000, exec. v.p., 2001—. Office: Sony Corp of Am 550 Madison Ave New York NY 10022

SUSSKIND, TERESA GABRIEL, publishing executive; b. Watford, Eng., Aug. 15, 1921; came to U.S., 1945; d. Aaron and Betty (Fox) Gabriel; m. Charles Susskind, May 1, 1945; children: Pamela Pettler, Peter Gabriel, Amanda. Ed., U. London, 1938-40. Profl. libr. Calif. Inst. Tech., Pasadena, 1946-48, Yale U., New Haven, 1948-51, Stanford (Calif.) U., 1951-52, SRI Internat., Menlo Park, Calif., 1953; founder, pres. San Francisco Press, Inc., 1959—. Active in cultural affairs; bd. govs. San Francisco Symphony, 1986-89. With Women's Royal Naval Svc., 1943-45. With Women's Royal Naval Svc., 1943-45. Mem. Town and Gown Club (Berkeley, Calif.; pres. 1984-85). Office: PO Box 426800 San Francisco CA 94142-6800

SUSSMAN, JANET I. social sciences educator; b. N.Y.C., Sept. 24, 1952; d. Joseph I. and Selma H. Sussman. BA, Douglas Coll., 1974. Pub. Harcourt Brace, N.Y.C., 1974—76, Van Nostrand Reinhold, 1975—77, Sky & Telescope Mag., Cambridge, Mass., 1977—80, Wholistic Edn. & Svcs., Inc., Charlotte, NC, 1984—90, No. Star Dimensions, 1986—; pub., cons. Time Portal Pubs., Fairfield, Iowa, 1993—. Author: Timeshift: The Experience of Dimensional Change, 1996; musician: (CD) Bridges, 2002. E-mail: timeport@kdsi.net.

SUSSMAN, LAUREEN GLICKLIN, junior high school educator; b. N.Y.C., Mar. 21, 1953; d. Harry and Ruth (Goldstein) G.; m. Alan Neil Sussman, May 30, 1977; children: David Efrem, Adam Jacob, Daniel Joshua. BA, Bklyn. Coll., 1974; MS, MSc, Hofstra U., 1998. Cert. tchr. nursery-6, spl. edn. tchr. all grades. Sec. McCann-Erickson, Inc., N.Y.C., 1974-75; adminstrv. asst., tour operator EasTours divsn. Fgn. Tours, N.Y.C., 1975-78; adminstrv. asst. Alan N. Sussman, CPA, Woodmere, N.Y., 1978-96; kindergarten tchr. Hebrew Acad. Long Beach (N.Y.), 1996-97; jr. high sch. tchr. Torah Acad. Girls, Far Rockaway, NY, 1997—. Participant Instrumental Enrichment/IRI Skylight, N.Y., 1995, 98, Dynamic Assessment project Touro Coll., N.Y.C., 1996; CSE parent rep., adv. Lawrence (N.Y.) Pub. Schs., 1992-97; trainer Life Tech., Cedarhurst, N.Y., 2004. Contbr. articles to profl. jours. Mem. Spl. Edn. PTA Lawrence Schs., 1986-2003, Sisterhood Congregation Bais Tefilah, 1990-2003; mem. Sisterhood East Meadow Jewish Ctr., chairperson social action, Israel affairs, 1979-81; mem. adv. bd. Kulanu of the South Shore of Nassau County, 2000—; mem. Sisterhood Kehillah Aish Kodesh, Emunah of Am. Mem.: AMIT Women (Masada chpt.), OTSAR (founder Nassau County chpt. 1987—, nat. bd. dirs., pres. Nassau chpt. 1987—2002). Democrat. Avocations: Israeli and simcha dancing, walking, reading, needlepoint. Office: Torah Acad Girls 444 Beach 6 St Far Rockaway NY 11691 E-mail: laughlick@aol.com.

SUSSMAN, MONICA HILTON, lawyer; b. N.Y.C., Apr. 2, 1952; BA cum laude, Syracuse U., 1973; JD, Hofstra U., 1977. Bar: Va. 1977, D.C. 1978. Legis. coun. N.Y. State Gov's. Office, Washington, 1977-79; spl. asst. to under sec. U.S. Dept. HUD, Washington, 1979-80, br. chief office State Agy. and Bond Fin. programs, 1980-82, office gen. counsel, 1982-83, also bd. dirs., 1988-95, v.p., 1989-93, treas. Nat. Housing Conf., 1990-93, also programs and regulations dep. gen. counsel; ptnr. McDermott, Will & Emery, Washington, Peabody & Brown, Washington, 1996-99, Nixon Peadoby LLP, Washington, 1999—. Pres. Nat. Housing Conf. Mem. D.C. Bar, Va. State Bar. Office: Nixon Peadbody LLP 401 9th St NW Ste 900 Washington DC 20004

SUSSMAN, WENDY RODRIGUEZ, artist, educator; b. N.Y.C., June 3, 1949; BA, Empire State Coll., 1978; MFA, Bklyn. Coll., 1980. Lectr. Touro Coll., N.Y.C., 1985-86, Pratt Inst., Bklyn., 1987-89; asst. prof. U. Calif., Berkeley, 1989-96, assoc. prof., 1996—. One-woman shows include Bowery Gallery, N.Y.C., 1982, 87, John Bergruen Gallery, San Francisco, 1992, D.P. Fong Gallery, San Jose, Calif., 1994, Platt Gallery U. Judaism, L.A., 1995, Jan Baum Gallery, L.A., 1996, The Jewish Mus., San Francisco, 1996; group shows include Bowery Gallery, 1980-88, Munson-Williams-Proctor Inst. Mus. Art, 1982, Reading (Pa.) Pub. Mus. and Art Gallery, 1983, Queens Mus., N.Y.C., 1983, Colby Coll. Mus. Art, Waterville, Maine, 1983, Butler Inst. Am. Art, Youngstown, Ohio, 1983, Bklyn. Coll., 1983,

Am. Acad. Inst. Arts and Letters, N.Y.C., 1984, Am. Acad. in Rome, 1987, John Berggruen Gallery, San Francisco, 1992, San Francisco Arts Commn. Gallery, 1992, 94, D.P. Fong Gallery, 1994, Boulder Mus. Art, 1995, Gallery Paule Anglin, San Francisco, 1996, 98, Jan Baum Gallery, L.A., 1996, U. Calif. San Diego Art Gallery, 1997. Rome Prize fellow in painting Am. Acad. in Rome, 1986-87, Visual Arts fellow NEA, 1989, Guggenheim fellow, 1998; Pollock-Krasner grantee Pollock-Krasner Found., 1988; recipient Max and Sophie Adler award Jewish Mus., Judah Magners Mus., 1996. Office: U Calif Berkeley Dept Art Berkeley CA 94720-0001

SUTCLIFFE, MARY OGDEN, clinical social worker; b. Chgo., June 9, 1928; d. Dana Presley and Vera Marie (Gassman) Ogden; m. Herbert Alfred Sutcliffe, Oct. 30, 1963; children: Stephen, Timothy, James, Penney Stahl. AA, Colby/Sawyer Coll., 1948; BS in Journalism, Syracuse U., 1950; MSW, Howard U., 1967. Cert. clin. social worker. Asst. editor House & Garden Mag., N.Y.C., 1949-51; reporter Bay News, East Meadow, N.Y., 1956-58; chief social worker Cmty. Mental Health Clinic, Manassus, Va., 1967-72, Children & Youth Health Ctr., Exeter, N.H., 1978-82, Rockingham Child and Family Svc., 1982-88; assoc. prof. psychology Garrett Coll., Oakland, Md., 1989-93; clin. social worker pvt. practice, Bethesda, Md., 1972-78, Durham, N.H., 1978-88, Oakland, Md., 1988-98; pvt. practice Durango, Colo., 1999—. Sec. Rep. Club, Port Washington, L.I., N.Y., 1972; v.p. Garrett County Alliance for Mentally Ill. Mem. AAUW (pres. 1961), Toastmasters (v.p. 1988), Pi Beta Phi. Avocations: triathlon, skiing, computers, rv travel, senior olympics.

SUTER, KAREN L. former state banking department administrator; b. July 4, 1956; Grad. with honors, Rutgers U., 1978, JD, 1981. Sr. dep. atty. gen., chief sect. for dept. banking and ins. Office of Atty. Gen.; with N.J. Banking & Instns. Dept., Trenton, 1988—2000, commr., 2000—01. Office: NJ Banking & Instns Dept PO Box 325 20 W State St Trenton NJ 08625-0040

SUTHERLAND, DAME JOAN, retired soprano; b. Sydney, Australia, Nov. 7, 1926; d. McDonald S.; m. Richard Bonynge, 1954; one son. Student, Royal Coll. Music, London, 1951. Appeared concert and oratorio performances, Australia; appeared in: opera Judith, Syndey Conservatory of Music; debut Covent Garden in Magic Flute, 1952; Italian debut in Handel's Alcina, Teatro la Fenice, Venice, 1960; Bellini's Puritani, Glyndebourne Festival, Sussex, Eng., 1960; Bellini's Beatrice di Tenda, La Scala, 1961, Rossini's Semiramide, La Scala, 1962; Meyerbeer's Les Huguenots, La Scala, 1962, N.Y. debut, Carnegie Hall, 1961; Opera debut Lucia, 1961; opened Sutherland-Williamson Opera Co. tour, Australia, 1965; appeared: Handel's Julius Caesar, Hamburg Opera, 1969; Bellini's Norma, Met. Opera, 1970; opened, Lyric Opera Chgo. with, Semiramide, 1971; San Francisco Opera with, Norma, 1972; San Francisco Opera with Trovatore, 1975; Met. Opera with I Puritani, 1976; Vancouver Opera with Le Roi de Lahore, 1977; premiered new prodn., Met. Opera in Tales of Hoffmann, 1973; first prodn. in Am. in eighty years Esclarmonde, Massenet, San Fancisco Opera, 1974; author: (with Richard Bonynge) The Joan Sutherland Album, 1986; A Prima Donna's Progress, 1997. Decorated Order of Merit, 1991; comdr. and dame comdr., Order Brit. Empire, 1979; Companion, Order Australia, 1975; recipient Grammy Award best classical vocal soloist, 1981. Fellow Royal Coll. Music. Office: Colbert Artist Mgmt. 111 W 57th St New York NY 10019-2211

SUTHERLAND, LISA JO, legislative staff member; b. Dayton, Ohio, Nov. 29, 1956; d. George H. and Gerene R. (Koepke) O.; m. Scott A. Sutherland, Aug. 29, 1987 BA, Drake U., Des Moines, 1979; JD, U. Wash., 1987. Legis. aide Alaska Rep. Steve Reiger, Juneau, 1986; assoc. Birch, Horton, Bittner and Perkins Coie, Anchorage, 1986; legis. aide, asst. majority leader U.S. Senate; legis. dir. U.S. Senator Ted Stevens, Washington, chief staff; dep. staff dir. com. appropriations U.S. Senate, 1997—. Cons. Bristol Bay Native Corp., Anchorage, 1984. Republican. Lutheran. Avocations: biking, gardening, politics. Office: US Senator Ted Stevens 522 Hart Senate Office Bldg Washington DC 20510-0001

SUTHERLAND, MARY (MARCUS), composer, musician, music company executive; d. T. Frederick Sholtis and Veronica Kuharik; m. Philip Selmar Marcus, Apr. 11, 1966 (div. 1979); children: Jennifer, Nancy; m. Howard Lawrence Sutherland, Apr. 6, 1997. MusB, DePaul U., 1967; MusM, U. Ky., 1978; postgrad., U. Memphis, 1978—80. Vocal coach, tchr., Memphis, 1978—94, St. Louis, 1994—; pianist Opera Memphis, Memphis Symphony Chorus, Regional Met. Opera, Memphis, 1980—94; composer, pianist, narrator The Sutherland Duo, 1992—; condr., art dir., mgr. devel. Midwest Chorale, 1994—2002; pianist Clayton H.S./MICDS, 1997—; music dir. Clayton (Mo.) Cmty. Theater, 2004—. Composer: (organ anthems) I Come with Joy, 1993, So Much to Sing About, 1993—94, (with cons. Dalton Baldwin) 21st Century Women Composers of Spiritual Music. Mentor Mentor St. Louis, 1996—2002; tutor Oasis, St. Louis, 2002—. Recipient Pres.'s doctoral fellowship, U. Memphis, 1978—80. Mem.: Internat. Alliance for Women in Music, Pi Kappa Lambda. Democrat. Avocations: reading, travel, theater. Home: 3104 Longfellow Blvd Saint Louis MO 63104 Office: The Sutherland Duo 3104 Longfellow Blvd Saint Louis MO 63104 Office Phone: 314-771-1054. E-mail: msongmaker@earthlink.net.

SUTHERLAND, SUSAN J. lawyer; b. Canton, Ohio, 1957; BA, Denison Coll., 1979; JD, NYU, 1982. Bar: N.Y. 1983. Ptnr. Skadden, Arps, Slate, Meagher & Flom, N.Y.C. Office: Skadden Arps Slate Meagher & Flom 4 Times Sq Fl 24 New York NY 10036-6595

SUTHERLAND-ABEL, ANNE ELIZABETH, pediatrician; b. Milwaukee, June 16, 1945; d. David Hollingsworth and Mildred June (Nees) Sutherland; m. Francis Lee Abel; one child, Jonathan Earl. BA, Pasadena Coll., 1967; MS, Ind. U., Indpls., 1969, MD, 1973. Diplomate Am. Bd. Pediat. Resident in pediat. Meth. Hosp., Indpls., 1973—75, Richland Meml. Hosp., Columbia, SC, 1975—76; pediatrician Moncrief Army Hosp., Ft. Jackson, SC, 1976—80; child and adolescent psychiatry fellow William S. Hall Psychiat. Inst., Columbia, SC, 1981—83, U. BC Vancouver Gen. Hosp., 1982; pvt. practice Columbia, SC, 1983—; pediatrician Children's Rehabilitative Svc., Orangeburg, SC, 1984—2000; chief med. sect. Columbia Area Mental Health Ctr., SC, 1987—92; assoc. prof. pediat., adj. assoc. prof. neuropsychiatry U. S.C., 1992—2000; mental health dir. Abuse Recovery Ctr., Columbia, SC, 1994—95; dir. Freddie Mac Child and Adolescent Protection Ctr., Children's Nat. Med. Ctr., Washington, 2001—. Cons. behavioral pediat. Epworth Children's Home, Columbia, S.C., 1983-86, 90-97; med. dir. Assessment and Resource Ctr., Columbia, 1996-2000; mem. med. adv. com., children's health rehabilitative svc. S.C. Dept. Health and Environ. Control, Columbia, 1986-92, mem. maternal and child health adv. com., 1989-91; behavioral devel. pediatrician Orangeburg Health Dept., 1994-96. Contbr. articles to profl. journals. Mem. S.C. Governor's Youth Unemployment Coun., Columbia, 1987. Recipient Alumni Award Pasadena Coll., 1977; Vol. of Yr. Award Mayor's Com. Employment Handicapped, 1988; grantee Ctr. Family Soc., U. S.C., 1993-95. Fellow Am. Acad. Pediat.; mem. AMA, Am. Profl. Soc. on Abuse of Children, Columbia Med. Soc. Avocations: music, boating, hiking, fishing, reading. Office: U S C Dept Pediat 4 Med Pk Ste 301 Columbia SC 29203 Personal E-mail: abela616@aol.com.

SUTLIN, VIVIAN, advertising executive; b. Chgo. d. Samuel E. and Doris (Weinberg) S. BA, Roosevelt U. V.p. creative group head Grey North Advt., Inc., Chgo.; v.p. creative dir., founder Pilot Products, Inc., Chgo.; TV writer, producer Grey Advt., Inc., NY; sr. writer Young and Rubicam, Inc., NY; v.p. creative dir. Dodge and Delano, NY; pres. Vivian Sutlin Advt., new products and consumer packaged goods specialist with full svc. TV and print, domestic and internat. ops.; creative supr. William Douglas McAdams, Inc., NY, Grey Med. Advt., Inc., NY; pres. Vivian Sutlin Comm. Cons. Consumer and Med./Pharm. Advt.; pres. Signature Products East, N.Y.C., Internat. Packaging, Printing and Promotional Products Co. Co-author: Industry Women Speak Out. Recipient Chgo. Fedn. Advt. Clubs award, Am. TV Commls. Festival award, TV award Art Dirs. Club Chgo., Triangle award Med. Advt. Print, Internat. Broadcasting award, Best of Decade award RX Club, Guacaipuro TV award. Avocations: jogging, aerobics, tennis, art.

SUTTER, ELEANOR BLY, retired diplomat; b. N.Y.C., Oct. 21, 1945; d. Samuel M. and Sylvia Gertrude Bly; children: Deborah Nelson, Willis. BA, Swarthmore Coll., 1966; MA, Am. U., 1978; diploma in strategic studies, U.S. Army War Coll., 1997. Instr. English Thammasat U., Bangkok and Udornthani Tchr. Tng. Coll., 1967-71, Lomonosov State U., Moscow, 1973-74; rschr. Kennan Inst. for Advanced Russian Studies, 1977-79; fgn. svc. officer Office Soviet Internal Affairs Dept. of State, 1979-80, fgn. svc. officer Office of Strategic Nuc. Policy, 1986-88, fgn. svc. officer Office of Soviet Union Affairs, 1988-90, office dir., 1997-99, sr. inspector Office Inspector Gen., 1999-2001, dir. Office of Proliferation Threat Reduction, 2001—02; fgn. svc. officer U.S. Embassy, Kinshasa, 1980-82, London, 1982-85, Moscow, 1990-92, charge d'affaires ad interim Bratislava, 1993, dep. prin. officer, 1993-95, dep. chief of mission, 1995-96. Exec. dir., exec. sec., advisor U.S. Del. to Nuclear and Space Talks, Geneva, 1987-91; teaching fellow Russian lit. The Am. U., 1976-77; escort interpreter and translator Dept. of State, 1976. Co-author: Final Report of the Kennan Institute's Soviet Research Institutes Project, 1981. Founder Camp Wocsom, Moscow, 1974. Mem. Am. Fgn. Svc. Assn. Avocations: music, folk dance. Office: care of Fgn Svc Lounge Dept State Washington DC 20520

SUTTER, JANE E. editor; b. Iowa; m. Gary Brandt. B Journalism, U. Mo., 1981. Reporter, then lifestyle editor Hawk Eye, Burlington, Iowa, 1981; lifestyle writer, editor Daily Courier-News, Elgin, Ill.; features editor, then dep. city editor Bradenton (Fla.) Herald, 1987—93; assigning editor The State, Columbia, SC, 1993—95; with corp. news divsn. Knight Ridder Inc., 1995—97; mng. editor Star-Gazette, Elmira, NY, 1997—98, exec. editor, 1998—2001; mng. editor Rochester (NY) Dem. and Chronicle, 2001—. Office: Rochester Dem and Chronicle 55 Exchange Blvd Rochester NY 14614-2001*

SUTTER, JANE ELIZABETH, science educator, writer, conservationist; b. St. Louis, Nov. 27, 1939; d. Richard A. and Elizabeth Henby Sutter. AB in Sociology and English, Vassar Coll., 1961; MA in Health Facilities Mgmt., Webster Coll., St. Louis, 1979. Healthcare analyst, Chgo. and St. Louis, 1966-83; asst. dir. radio, TV and motion picture dept. AMA, Chgo., 1966-67; staff coord., rsch. assoc. Chgo. water quality study and environ. health study Inst. of Medicine of Chgo., 1967-69; dir. environ. health planning Comprehensive Health Planning Inc., Chgo., 1969-73; planning assoc., spl. asst. to med. dir. Sutter Clinic, Inc., St. Louis, 1975-84; vol. activist, educator; founder, dir. for conservation and gardening for birds Wild Birds for the 21st Century Non-profit Ednl. Svcs., 1994—. Chmn. Opera Theatre of St. Louis Newsletter, Recitative, Vol. 1, No. 1, 1980, Vol. 1, No. 2, 1980; co-founder, com. mem. 1st Internat. Alewife Festival of Chgo., Chgo. Yacht Club, summer 1968; appointee Gov.'s Com. for Pure Air and Water, Chgo., 1968; spl. advocate N.Am. Migratory Birds particularly hummingbirds; mem. Ladue Chapel. Mem. Nat. Garden Clubs, Inc., Federated Garden Clubs of Mo., Inc., Clayton Garden Assn., Mo. Bot. Garden, St. Louis Artists' Guild (mem. artists' sect. 1992-95, portraitist), Inst. on Religion in an Age of Sci., Neotropical Bird Club (U.K.)., Univ. Club, Bradenton C. of C. Avocations: art, writing, gardening. Home: 7376 Pershing Blvd Saint Louis MO 63130-4206 E-mail: jesutteri@aol.com.

SUTTER, JEAN, sculptor; b. Chgo., Aug. 9, 1934; d. John H. and Lulu Kennedy Sutter; m. Paul W. Berg, Jan. 1, 1953 (dec. Mar. 1968); children: Mark, Julie, Karen;. B Visual Arts, Ga. State U., 1974, M Visual Arts, 1978. One-woman shows include: Lowe Gallery, Atlanta, 1989, U. Okla., Norman, 1984, Quinlan Art Ctr., Gainesville, Ga., 1981, Ga. State U., Atlanta, 1979, Auburn U., Ala., 1978; group shows include: Arts Connection, Atlanta, 1990, Jubilee-So. Festival of the Arts, Atlanta, 1987, Heath Gallery, Atlanta, 1985, Atlanta Arts Festival, 1980, 82, 84, Sculptural Arts Mus., 1982, Columbia Mus., S.C., 1982, Mus. of Touch, Atlanta, 1981, Am. Art Inc., Atlanta, 1981, Temple U., Phila., 1980, Cedar Crest Coll., Allentown, Pa., 1980-81, High Mus. Art, Atlanta, 1979, 78, others; collections include Ga. State U., New Life Covenant Ch., Atlanta, Macon (Ga.) State Coll., numerous pvt. parties. Home and Office: 18 Padsett Ct # 20334 Jasper GA 30143-7217

SUTTLE, DEBORAH S. state legislator; b. Charleston, W.Va., Dec. 28, 1945; m. James H. Suttle, June 4, 1966; children: Virginia Adele, Amber Karolyn. BS, W.Va. U., 1967; postgrad., U. Nebr., Omaha, 1989-91. Former RN; mem. Nebr. Legislature from 10th dist., Lincoln, 1997—. Vol. Douglas County election commr.; mem. United Meth. Ch., Omaha, League Women Voters, 1980—, Voices for Children; former mem. Omaha 2000 Task Force, Pulling Ams. Communities Together, Omaha Pub. Sch. Supt. Adv. Com., Nebr. Partnership Com., Douglas County Corrections Adv. Com.; mem. various PTA's, Omaha, 1976-93; former pres. LWV for Greater Omaha, 1991-93, Laura Dodge Elem. Parent-Tchr. Assn., 1978-79; vol. lobbyist Omaha PTA/PTSA Coun., 1980-91, Nebr. PTA, 1986-89; v.p. Optimist Internat., 1995-96; vol. lobbyist Nebr. LWV, 1994-96; vol. lobbyist, bd. dirs. PRIDE-Omaha, 1984-96. Mem. Nebr. Nurses' Assn. Home: 6054 Country Club Oaks Pl Omaha NE 68152-2009 Office: State Capitol Dist 10 PO Box 94604 Rm 1000 Lincoln NE 68509 Fax: 402-571-6901.

SUTTLE, HELEN JAYSON, retired education educator; b. Plattsburgh, N.Y., Dec. 13, 1925; d. Harold Lincoln Jayson and Blanche Rabideau Jayson Woods; widowed, 1993; 1 child, Adolphia Helen Suttle Blanton. BA in Edn., Limestone Coll., 1961; MA in Edn., Winthrop U., 1973. Cert. tchr., S.C. Tchr. Madden Elem. Sch., Spartanburg, S.C., 1961-71, West Jr. High Sch., Gaffney, S.C., 1971-81, L.L. Vaughn Elem. Sch., Gaffney, S.C., 1981-88; substitute tchr. Gaffney Dis. 1, 1988—. Vol. SC Budget Control Bd., Upstate Carolina Med. Ctr., Meals on Wheels, Literacy Assn., local soup kitchen; chmn. Cherokee County Rep. Com.; v.p. Ch. Women's Guild, pres., 1998—; dir. religious edn. Sacred Heart Ch., 2001—; pres. Sacred Heart Sr. Citizens Club; treas. ch. com. Greenville Deanery; pres.-elect Piedmont Deanery, 2002—; Eucharistic min., lector; mem. exec. bd. SC Coun. Cath. Ch. Women, 1998—, chair family commn., 1998—; pres. Piedmont Deanery, 2002—03; trustee Limestone Coll. Named woman of Yr., S.C. Coun. Cath. Women Greenville Deanery, 1996. Fellow Internat. Biog. Assn. (life, dep. gov. Am. chpt.), Limestone Coll. Alumni Assn. (pres., chpt. pres.), Fountain Club (charter mem.), Kalosophia Honor Soc. Roman Catholic. Avocations: writing, art, gardening, crafts. Home: 201 Trenton Rd Gaffney SC 29340-3626

SUTTON, BETTY, state legislator; married. BA, Kent State Univ., 1985; JD, Univ. Akron, 1990. Coun.-at-larte Barberton City Coun., 1990-91; v.p. Summit County Coun., 1991-92; state rep. Ohio Dist. 47, 1993—. Vice chmn. Judiciary & Criminal Justice Com., mem. Civil & Comml. Law, Ways & Means, Ins. Pub. Utilities & Elec. Twp. Com. Recipient Outstanding Performance in Const. Law Fed. Bar Assn., 1989, Am. Jurisprudence award, 1989. Mem. ABA, Akron Child Guidance Adv. Coun., Assn. Trial Lawyers Am., Ohio Acad. Trial Lawyers, Summit County Trial Lawyers, Fed. Dem. Women. Office: Ohio Ho of Reps State House Columbus OH 43215 Home: 13488 Walnut Trce Chardon OH 44024-9302

SUTTON, BETTY SHERIFF, elementary school educator; b. Orangeburg, S.C., Jan. 16, 1933; d. Luther Doyle and Mattie (White) Sheriff; m. William Bryan Nunn, June 19, 1954; 1 child, Lisbeth Sheriff Nunn (Mrs. William Reid Clark); m. James Carlton Sutton, Dec. 28, 1979 (dec., 1998). Student, Columbia Coll., 1949-52; BS, U. S.C., 1953. Tchr. grade 4 State of S.C. Pub. Sch., Blackville, 1953-54; tchr. grade 2 Dream Lake Elem. Sch., Apopka, Fla., 1954-64; tchr. spl. edn. Leon County Sch., Tallahassee, Fla., 1965-66; page mother Fla. Ho. Reps., Tallahassee, 1966-67; tchr. grade 3 Timberlane Elem. Sch./Leon County Schs., Tallahassee, 1967-71; tchr. grades 3 and 4 Golfview Elem. Sch./Brevard County Schs., Rockledge, Fla., 1972-86; tchr. grade 1 Cambridge Elem. Sch./Brevard County Schs., Cocoa, Fla., 1987-98; ret., 1998. Pres. Bits of Brevard, Inc., Rockledge. Chmn. Democrats for Conner, 1988, Keep Brevard Beautiful, 1990; active Brevard Symphony Orch. Guild, Brevard Mus. Guild, 1973—, Brevard Heritage Coun., Inc., Episcopal, St. Marks Guild. Recipient S.C. Forestry award State of S.C. Forestry Commn., 1977; ART grantee J. Paul Getty Ctr. for Edn. in the Arts, 1990. Mem. AAUW (pres. 1968-70), Apopka Woman's Club (pres. 1960-62), Apopka Garden Club, Brevard Reading Coun. (v.p. 1980-82), Am. Mothers, Inc., Columbia Coll. Column Club, Columbia Coll. Alumni Club. Ctrl. Fla., U. S.C. Alumni Club (life), Country Club of Rockledge, Delta Kappa Gamma (pres. 1992-94). Avocations: volunteering, reading, swimming, travel, farming. Home: 2201 Royal Oaks Dr Rockledge FL 32955-5440

SUTTON, BEVERLY JEWELL, psychiatrist; b. Rockford, Mich., May 27, 1932; d. Beryl Dewey and Cora Belle (Potes) Jewell; m. Harry Eldon Sutton, July 7, 1962; children: Susan, Caroline. MD, U. Mich., 1957. Diplomate Am. Bd. Pediat., Am. Bd. Psychiatry and Neurology. Rotating intern St. Joseph Mercy Hosp., Ann Arbor, Mich., 1958; resident in child psychiatry Hawthorne Ctr., Northville, Mich., 1958-62; resident in pediat. U. Hosp./U. Mich. Med. Ctr., Ann Arbor, 1959-61; resident in psychiatry Austin (Tex.) State Hosp., 1962-64, dir. children's svc., 1964-89, dir. psychiat. residency program, 1989—, dir. tng. and rsch., 1993-98. Cons. in field. Contbr. articles to profl. jours. Active numerous civic orgns. Recipient Outstanding Achievement award, YWCA, 1989, Jackson Day award, Tex. Soc. Child and Adolescent Psychiatry, 1989, Showcase award, Tex. Dept. Mental Health/Mental Retardation, 1990. Fellow Am. Acad. Child and Adolescent Psychiatry (life), Am. Psychiat. Soc., Am. Pediatric Assn.; mem. Tex. Soc. Child and Adolescent Psychiatry (pres. 1979-80), Tex. Soc. Psychiat. Physicians (Disting. Svc. award 1990), AMA, Tex. Med. Soc., Am. Genetics Soc. Office: Seton Shoal Creek Hosp 3501 Mills Ave Austin TX 78731 E-mail: bsutton@seton.org.

SUTTON, CECILIA (CECE SUTTON), bank executive; b. Charlotte, NC; B in Psychology, U. SC; MBA, Winthrop U. Branch manager First Union Corp., Raleigh and Cary, NC, consumer credit sales mgr. Charlotte, NC, 1984—86, consumer banking mgr. Greenville, SC, 1986—89, consumer bank training dir. Charlotte, NC, 1988—89, area exec. Rock Hill, SC, 1989—92, head SC Gen. Banking Group Greenville, SC, 1992—93, area exec. Rock Hill, SC, 1993—95, consumer banking exec., exec. v.p., 2001; exec. v.p., head retail Wachovia Corp. (merged with First Union Corp), Charlotte, 2001—. Office: Wachovia Corp 301 S Coll St Charlotte NC 28288-0018*

SUTTON, DOLORES, actress, writer; b. N.Y.C. BA in Philosophy, NYU. Appeared in broadway plays including Man With the Golden Arm, 1956, Career, 1958, Machinal, 1960, Rhinoceros, Liliom, She Stoops to Conquer, Hedda Gabler, Anna Karenina, Eccentricities of a Nightingale, Brecht on Brecht, Young Gifted and Black, Luv, The Friends, The Web and the Rock, The Seagull, Saturday, Sunday, Monday, The Little Foxes, What's Wrong With This Picture, The Cocktail Hour, My Fair Lady (Broadway revival), 1994, My Fair Lady (nat. tour), 1993-94; films include The Trouble With Angels, Where Angels Go, Trouble Follows, Crossing Delancey, Crimes and Misdeameanors, Tales of the Darkside; TV appearances include Studio One, Hallmark Hall of Fame Prodn. An Wilderness, Theatre Guild of the Air: Danger, Suspense, Gunsmoke, Valiant Lady, General Hospital, From These Roots, As the World Turns, Edge of Night, F. Scott Fitzgerald in Hollywood, Patty Hearst Story, All in the Family, Bob Newhart Show, All My Children, others, (TV writer) Lady Somebody, 1999, The Secret Storm, Loving; playwright: Down at the Old Bull and Bush, The Web and the Rock, Company Comin', Born Yesterday, 1995, A Perfect Ganesh, 1995, Detail of a Larger Work, 1995, The Front Page, 1996, The Exact Center of the Universe, 1997, A Drop in the Bucket, 1997, Spring Storm (newly discovered Tennessee Williams play), 1997, Signs and Wonders, 1998, It Gives Me Great Pleasure, 2001; prodns. Free Ascent, 2001, Burial Society, 2001, The Find, 2002. Mem. League of Profl. Theatre Women (bd. dirs.), Ensemble Studio Theatre (bd. dirs.).

SUTTON, G. KATHERINE HALLETT, nurse; b. Denver, Mar. 9, 1920; d. Lucius Felt Hallett and Genevieve Folsom (Pfeiffer) Taylor; m. John B. Sutton, Feb. 26, 1949 (dec. Mar. 1957); children: John, Lawrence, Stephen, Katherine Anne, Minou. BA, La. State U. Nurse ob-gyn. Glen Cove (N.Y.) Hosp.; head nurse N.Y. Neurol. Inst., N.Y.C.; floor nurse Jefferson-Hillman Hosp., Birmingham, Ala.; nurse ICU Highland Hosp., Shreveport, La.; supr. Schumpert Hosp., Shreveport, La. Mem. Order of Daus. of the King. Episcopalian. Avocation: church. Home: 600 E Flournoy Lucas Rd Apt J-6 Shreveport LA 71115-3839

SUTTON, JULIA, musicologist, dance historian; b. Toronto, July 20, 1928; d. Samuel L. and Anne R. (Rubin) Sumberg. AB summa cum laude, Cornell U., 1949; MA, Colo. Coll., 1952; PhD, U. Rochester, 1962. Instr. music history New Sch. for Social Rsch., 1962-63; instr. music Queens Coll., CUNY, 1963-66; instr. music history and musicology New Eng. Conservatory Music, 1967—90, instr. and prof. musicology, 1967—90, chmn. dept. music history and musicology, 1971-90, chmn. faculty senate, 1971-73, prof. emerita, 1992. Vis. asst. prof. George Peabody Coll. for Tchrs., 1966-67; instr. NYU, summers 1963, 64; pvt. tchr. piano, 1949-65; lectr., rsch. dir. in musicology, music as related to the dance; presenter numerous workshops and summer insts. on Renaissance dance. Dance dir. N.Y. Pro Musica prodn. An Entertainment for Elizabeth, Caramoor, N.Y., Saratoga, N.Y., U. Ariz., Stanford U., UCLA, 1969, ann. nationwide tours, 1970-1973; dance dir. Descent of Rhythm and Harmony, Colorado Springs, Colo., 1970, Renaissance Revisited, Phila., 1972, An Evening of Renaissance Music and Dance, York U., Toronto, 1974; author: Jean Baptiste Besard's Novus Partus 1617, 1962; editor: Thoinot Arbeau: Orchesography 1588, 1967; translator, editor: Fabritio Caroso: Nobiltà di dame 1600, 1986, reprinted 1995; producer, co-dir. (tng. video) Il Ballarino, 1991; contbr. numerous articles to profl. jours. and Internat. Ency. of Dance, The New Grove Dictionary of Music and Musicians 1st and 2d edit., Die Musik in Geschichte und Gegenwart, 1st edit. Mem. Am. Musicological Soc., Soc. of Dance History Scholars, Phi Beta Kappa.

SUTTON, JULIA ZEIGLER, retired special education educator; b. Greenville, Ala, July 24, 1935; d. Floyd Millard and Edith Nettles Zeigler; m. William G. Sutton, June 16, 1956; children: William F., Joseph S., Julia N., John M. BS in Edn., 1958. Cert. spl. edn./mental retardation tchr., Ala. Tchr., DIAL III vol. Huntsville City Sch., Ala., 1966, spl. edn. tchr., 1973—98; tchr. Christian Women's Job Corps, Huntsville, 1999—. Mem. adv. bd. Coll. Edn., U. Ala., Tuscaloosa, 2001—. Mem. Civic Club Coun., Huntsville, 1967—68, Huntsville Hosp. Aux., 1965—73, pres., 1967—68; mem./ choir and various positions First United Meth. Ch., Huntsville, 1975—; life mem. Huntsville Hosp. Angel; chmn. Spl. Ministries FUM Ch., 1982—85; vol. DIAL III readiness testing in city and county sch., 2000—. Named one of Outstanding Young Women of Am., 1968; recipient Listed in Who's Who of Am. Women, 2002—03. Mem.: DAR (Twickenham Town chpt. 1st vice regent 2002—), Organizing mem. of Hunts./Madison Co. Panhellenic, Huntsville Alpha Gamma Delta Alumnae Club (past pres.

1962), Coll. of Edn. Capstone Soc., Camellia Soc. (organizing pres. 2001—02), Huntsville Bot. Garden and Garden Guild, Early Works Soc. (chmn. mem. event 1998—), Twickenham Hist. Preservation (bd. dir. 1975—2000, dist. assn. sec. 1985—2000). Methodist. Avocations: cooking British tea foods, heraldry-painting coats of arms, aerobics, community volunteering, collecting teapots and tea china.

SUTTON, KAREN E. administrator; b. New Brunswick, N.J., Aug. 26, 1952; d. Alfred Michael and Carmen (Collado) Sutton; children: Sloane, Brooke, Devon, Megan, Christopher. BA, Hofstra U., 1974; postgrad., NYU, 1987—89. Asst. to dir. Mus. Am. Folk Art, N.Y.C., 1975-76, acting dir., 1976-77, bd. dirs., exec. com. officer, 1980-88, gallery dir., 1989-92, dir. ops., 1992-94, dep. dir. planning and adminstrn., 1994-95; v.p. Sotheby's, N.Y.C., 1995-96, sr. v.p. adminstrn., 1996-2001, sr. v.p. worldwide mktg., 2001—. Bd. dirs. Family Dynamics, N.Y.C., 1976-80. Mem. Cosmopolitan Club (younger members chmn). Democrat. Episcopalian. Home: 4 Sutton Pl New York NY 10022 Office: Sotheby's 1334 York Ave New York NY 10021-4806 Office Phone: 212-606-7410. E-mail: Karen.Sutton@sothebys.com.

SUTTON, LOUISE NIXON, retired mathematics educator; b. Hertford, N.C., Nov. 4, 1925; d. John Calhoun and Annie Mariah (McNair) Nixon. BS, N.C. A&T State U., 1946; MA, NYU, 1951, PhD, 1962. Cert. tchr. sci. and math., N.C. Tchr. math./sci. Willis Hare H.S., Pendleton, N.C., summer 1946; tchr. math. Dudley High Sch., Greensboro, N.C., 1946-47; instr. math. N.C. A&T State U., Greensboro, 1947-57; asst. prof. math. Del. State U., Dover, 1957-62; assoc. prof. to prof. and dept. head math. Elizabeth City (N.C.) State U., 1962-87, prof. emeritus, 1987—. Adv. com. math. cert. Del. State Bd. Edn., Dover, 1961-62, adv. com. cert. in math. and sci., 1959-61. NAACP rep. adv. com. N.C. Bd. Social Svcs., Raleigh, 1969—71; mem. fin. bd. Pearson St. YWCA, Greensboro, 1954—56; AME Zion rep. com. on Christian edn. of exceptional persons Nat. Coun. Chs., N.Y.C., 1963—65; rep. 150th Anniversary Advance, Am Bible Soc., 1964—66; trustee St. Paul AME Zion Ch., 1972—73, ch. treas., 1997—98; bd. dirs. Perquimans County Indsl. Devel. Corp., Hertford, 1967—72; bd. dirs. divsn. higher edn. N.C. Assn. Educators, 1969—72. Recipient Disting. Tchr. award Elizabeth City (N.C.) State U. Gen. Alumni Assn., 1974, Tchr. of Yr., 1980, Woman of Yr. award NAUW, 1976, Plaque St. Paul AME Zion Ch., 1999; honoree Daughter of Isis, Arabia Ct. # 23, 1998, Elizabeth City State U. Gen. Alumni Assn., 1997. Mem. NAUW (pres. 1974-80, regional dir. 1976-80), NAACP (life), Nat. Coun. Tchrs. Math. (life), N.C. Coun. Tchrs. Math. (v.p. colls. 1979-80), Order Ea. Star (grand assoc. dean 1993-95, worthy matron 1994-97), George Washington Carver Floral Club (pres. 1991-99), Daus. of Isis, Delta Sigma Theta (life, pres. Dover, Del. and Elizabeth City Alumnae chpts.). Republican. Avocations: mini-golf, bowling, quilting, crochet, fishing. Home: PO Box 364 Hertford NC 27944-0364

SUTTON, LYNN SORENSEN, librarian; b. Detroit, July 31, 1953; d. Leonard Arthur Edward and Dorothy Ann (Steele) Sorensen. AB, U. Mich., 1975, MLS, 1976. Dir. Med. Libr. South Chgo. Cmty. Hosp., 1976-77; corp. dirs. librs. Detroit-Macomb Hosp. Corp., Detroit, 1977-86; dir. librs. Harper Hosp., Detroit, 1987-88; dir. Sci. and Engring. Libr. Wayne State U., Detroit, 1989-95, dir. undergrad. libr., 1996—. Cons. Catherine McAuley Health Sys., Ann Arbor, Mich., 1993. Contbr. articles to profl. jours. Mem. ALA, Assn. Coll. and Rsch. Librs. (budget and fin. com. 1995—), Mich. Health Scis. Librs. Assn. (pres. 1987-88), Met. Detroit Med. Libr. Group (pres. 1983-84), Phi Beta Kappa, Beta Phi Mu. Office: Wayne State U Undergrad Libr Detroit MI 48202-3918

SUTTON, NANCY THURMOND, music educator; b. Fresno, Calif., Nov. 26, 1981; d. A. L. Thurmond and Rosetta Irene (Posey) Thurmond-Hale; m. Geoffrey Coe Sutton, June 25, 1977 (div. 1999); 1 child, Brittany Bradford. BMus, U. Memphis, 1969, MusM, 1979; cert., Royal Sch. Ch. Music, Croydon, Eng., 1994; D of Musical Arts, U. Calif., L.A., 2000. Organist, choirmaster St. Paul's Episcopal Ch., Memphis, 1965—68; organist, dir. music St. George's Episcopal Ch., Germantown, Tenn., 1968—97; dir. choral activities U. N.C., Charlotte, NC, 2000—. Dir. St. George's Festival of Music, Germantown, 1982—97; music instr. U. Memphis, 1975—76; faculty Sewanee Music Conf., 1995; tchr., mentor Memphis City Schs., 1969—73. Conductor Andrew Lloyd Webber's Requiem, 1986, Arvo Part's Miserere, 1990, Lalo Schifren's Cantos Aztecas, 1992, pub. Sun Splendor, 2000. Organist, choirmaster St.Christopher's Cath. Ch., Dickson, Tenn., 2003—; dir. choral workshops Roman Cath. Dioceses, Tenn. Grantee, Musician Artist Trust Fund, 1980—97. Mem.: Orch. League, Assn. Anglican Musicinas (conv. chair 1982), Am. Guild Organists (dean 1980—81). Episcopalian. Avocations: horseback riding, walking, reading, water skiing, snow skiing.

SUTTON, SHARON MARIE, emergency services nurse; b. Niskayuna, N.Y., Dec. 16, 1952; d. John Arthur Bond Sutton and Marie Regina Coyle; m. Jeffrey Glenn Schneider, Jan. 13, 1972 (div. Mar. 1975); 1 child, David Matthew. AAS in Nursing, Hudson Valley C.C., Troy, N.Y., 1973; BA in Polit. Sci./Econs., Union Coll., Schenectady, N.Y., 1988. RN, N.Y. Staff nurse/nursing supr. Hallmark Nursing Ctr., Schenectady, 1974-78; staff nurse St. Clares Hosp., Schenectady, 1977-84, Albany (N.Y.) Med. Ctr., 1985, Tri-Cities Nurses Registry, Latham, N.Y., 1985-87; gen. staff nurse Ellis Hosp., Schenectady, 1987—2000; pres. Internat. Commerce Group, 1989—; assoc. nurse mgr. Ellis Hosp., Schenectady, 1995-97; nurse emergency dept. Good Hope Hosp., Erwin, NC, 2001—. Mktg. cons., 1988—. Co-chair Schenectady County AIDS Task Force, 1994—99; vol. Talking with Kids about HIV/AIDS, Schenectady County/Cornell Coop., 1994—99, bd. dir., 1996—99, sec., 1997—99; adminstrv. bd. Meth. Ch. Am. Assn. Critical Care Nurses. Methodist. Avocations: gardening, reading, walking, swimming, bicycling.

SUVARI, MENA, actress; b. Newport, RI, Feb. 9, 1979; d. Ando and Candance Suvari; m. Robert Brinkmann, 2000. Actor: (TV films) Atomic Train, 1999; (TV series) Six Feet Under, 2004—; (films) Nowhere, 1997, Snide and Prejudice, 1997, Kiss the Girls, 1997, Slums of Beverly Hills, 1998, The Rage: Carrie 2, 1999, American Pie, 1999, American Beauty, 1999, American Virgin, 2000, Loser, 2000, Sugar & Spice, 2001, American Pie 2, 2001, The Musketeer, 2001, Sonny, 2002, Spun, 2002, Trauma, 2004. Office: c/o Gersh Agy 232 N Canon Dr Beverly Hills CA 90210*

SVADLENAK, JEAN HAYDEN, museum consultant; b. Wilmington, Del., Mar. 4, 1955; d. Marion M. and Ida Jean (Calcagni) Hayden; m. Steven R. Svadlenak, May 26, 1979. BS in Textiles and Clothing, U. Del., 1977; MA in History Mus. Studies, SUNY, Oneonta, 1982; postgrad., U. Calif., Berkeley, 1982. Curatorial asst. The Hagley Mus., Wilmington, 1976-77; curator of costumes and textiles The Kansas City (Mo.) Mus., 1978-82, chief curator, 1982-84, assoc. exec. dir. for collection and exhibits mgmt., 1984-86, interim pres., 1986-87, pres., 1987-89. Researcher, guest curator N.Y. State Hist. Assn., Cooperstown, 1980; grant reviewer Inst. for Mus. Svcs., 1985-89; ad hoc faculty U. Kans., 1991-2001, U. Mo., Kansas City, 1992-98. Mem. Am. Assn. Mus. (surveyor mus. assessment program 1985-89, accreditation vis. com. 1990—), Am. Assn. State and Local History, Heritage League Kansas City (bd. dirs. 1987-89), Midwest Mus. Conf. (coun. 1992-94), Mo. Mus. Assocs. (pres. 1992-94), Com. on Mus. Profl. Tng. (2d v.p. 1994-96, at-large rep. 1997-2000). Avocation: cooking. Home: 624 Romany Rd Kansas City MO 64113-2037

SVETLOVA, MARINA, ballerina, choreographer, educator; b. Paris, May 3, 1922; came to U.S. from Australia, 1940; d. Max and Tamara (Andreieff) Hartman. Studies with Vera Trefilova, Paris, 1930-36, studies with L. Egorova and M. Kschessinska, 1936-39; studies with A. Vilzak, N.Y.C., 1940-57; D honoris causa, Fedn. Francaise de Danse, 1988. Ballet dir. So. Vt. Art Ctr., 1959-64; dir. Svetlova Dance Ctr., Dorset, Vt., 1965-95; prof. ballet dept. Ind. U., Bloomington, 1969-92, prof. emeritus, 1992—, chmn. dept., 1969-78. Choreographer Dallas Civic Opera, 1964-67, Ft. Worth Opera, 1967-83, San Antonio Opera, 1983, Seattle Opera, Houston Opera, Kansas City Performing Arts Found. Ballerina original Ballet Russe de Monte Carlo, 1939-41; guest ballerina Ballet Theatre, 1942, London's Festival Ballet, Teatro dell Opera, Rome, Nat. Opera, Stockholm, Sweden, Suomi Opera, Helsinki, Finland, Het Nederland Ballet, Holland, Cork Irish Ballet, Paris Opera Comique, London Palladium, Teatro Colon, Buenos Aires, others; prima ballerina Met. Opera, 1943-50, N.Y.C. Opera, 1950-52; choreographer: (ballet sequences) The Fairy Queen, 1966, L'Histoire du Soldat, 1968; tours in Far East, Middle East, Europe, S.Am., U.S.; performer various classical ballets Graduation Ball; contbr. articles to Debut, Paris Opera. Mem. Am. Guild Mus. Artists (bd. dirs.), Conf. on Ballet in Higher Edn., Nat. Soc. Arts and Letters (nat. dance chmn.) Office: 2100 E Maxwell Ln Bloomington IN 47401-6119

SVOBODA, JOANNE DZITKO, artist, educator; b. Dec. 24, 1948; d. John Richard and Joanna Frances (Rygiel) Dzitko; m. Peter W. Svoboda, Sept. 3, 1972; children: Kimberly Anne, Lauren Anne. Student, Parsons Sch. Design, 1966, Kean Coll., 1970; BA, Jersey City State Coll., 1970, MA, 1975; postgrad., Tchrs. Coll., Columbia U., 1972, Chubb Inst., 1983-84. Art tchr., Jersey City, 1966-70, Henry Snyder H.S., Jersey City, 1970-80; tng. specialist Johnson & Johnson Baby Products, Skillman, N.J., 1984-89; cons., 1989—; pres. Mgmt. Strategies Internat., 1991—. Computer instr. Raritan Valley C.C., 1999—. Exhibited Courtney Gallery, Jersey City State Coll., 1970, 74, Long Valley, 1979-80; contbr. articles in field to various publs. Trustee Jersey City Mus. Assn., 1973-79, chmn. fine arts dept., 1972-79; mem. curriculum revision com. Jersey City Bd. Edn., 1976; mem. Washington Twp. Shade Tree Commn., 1979-81, chmn., 1981; mem. Washington Twp. Hist. Heritage Commn., 1981-85; active encouraging establishment of hist. zone Long Valley, landmarks, Jersey City and Washington Twp. Grantee N.J. State Dept. Edn., 1973; recipient awards N.J. Fedn. Jr. Woman's Clubs: black and white photography, 1979, crafts, 1979, 1st pl. color photography, 1980, free form, 1981. Mem. Am. H.S. Assn. (asst. exec. dir. 1997-99, 2000-), Inst. Raritan Valley CC. (2000-). Office: PO Box 336 Oldwick NJ 08858-0336 Office Phone: 908-823-0909.

SWABY, BARBARA EMILIE, music educator; b. Anchorage, Mar. 23, 1948; d. Elmer Frank and Emilie Barbara (Willie) Senkbeil; m. Gordon George Swaby, June 16, 1973; 1 child, Meredeth Andrea. BA in Music Edn., Concordia Coll., Moorehead, Minn., 1970. Cert. tchr. Mont., 1970. Mid. sch. music tchr. Sch. Dist. #1, Gt. Falls, Mont., 1970—75, elem. music tchr., 1975—76, voice tchr. pvt. voice studio, 1976—, HS choir tchr., 1979—84, 1993—. String bass player Gt. Falls Symphony, 1970—; soprano Gt. Falls Symphonic Choir, 1970—; soloist Gt. Falls Recital Series, 1985—. Organist various places, Gt. Falls, Mont., 1970—; choir dir. Peace Luth. Ch., Gt. Falls, Mont., 1973—85. Mem.: Am. Choral Dirs. Assn., Music Educators Nat. Conf., Nat. Assn. Tchrs. Singing. Lutheran. Avocations: sewing, knitting, crocheting, doll making. Home: 1808 15 Ave S Great Falls MT 59405 Office: CM Russell HS 228 17th Ave NW Great Falls MT 59404 E-mail: krikos2@yahoo.com.

SWAIN, JOYE RAECHEL, writer; b. Oklahoma City, Jan. 1, 1940; d. Enos Gerald and Opal Cowan (Boulton) Garland; m. Dwight Vreeland Swain, Feb. 12, 1969 (dec. Feb. 1992); children: Rocio, Antonia, Ronald (dec.), Gina, Jefferson, Diane, Michael, Enos, Gerald. BS in Math., Oklahoma City U., 1960; MA in Romance Langs., U. Okla., 1963. Freelance writer, lectr., Norman, Okla., 1965—. Instr. French U. Okla., Norman, 1962-65; assoc. prof. French U. Sci. and Arts of Okla., Chickasha, 1965-68; coord. Spanish lang. program Instituto Allende, San Miguel de Allende, Guanajuato, Mex., 1971-74; tchr. French George Lynn Cross Acad., Norman, 1982-83; tchr. CESL U. Okla., Norman, 1990-93; exec. dir. Okla. Profl. Writers Hall of Fame. Co-author: Scripting for Video and AV, 1981, Film Scriptwriting, 1988. Mem. Mystery Writers Am., World Sci. Fiction (Liaison with Latin Am.), Okla. Writers' Fedn., Inc. (pres. 1992-93), Okla. Pen Woman (pres. 1988-90), Norman Galaxy of Writers (pres. 1991-92). Avocations: swimming, travel, theatre. Home: 5008 N State St Warr Acres OK 73122-5213 E-mail: joyeraechel@hotmail.com.

SWAIN, JUDITH LEA, cardiovascular physician, educator; b. Long Beach, Calif., Sept. 24, 1948; m. Edward W. Holmes. BS in Chemistry with deptl. honors, UCLA, 1970; MD, U. Calif., San Diego, 1974. Diplomate Am. Bd. Internal Medicine, cardiovasc. disease; lic. physician Calif., Pa., N.C. Intern in medicine Duke U. Med. Ctr., 1974-75, resident in medicine, 1975-76, fellow in cardiology, 1976-80, assoc. in medicine, 1979-81, from asst. prof. medicine to assoc. prof. medicine, 1981-91, asst. prof. physiology, 1981-88, assoc. prof. microbiology & immunology, 1988-91, Herbert C. Rorer prof. med. scis., prof. genetics, 1991-92, mem. molecular biology grad. group, 1991-92, chief cardiovasc. divsn., 1991-92; chair dept. medicine Stanford (Calif.) U., 1996—. Vis. asst. prof. dept. genetics Harvard Med. Sch., Boston, 1985-86; mem. search com. for dir. Ctr. for Aging, Duke U. Med. Ctr., 1991—, mem. exec. com. deptl. awards selection, 1992—, chmn. combined degree dir. search com., 1993, mem. clin. rsch. ctr. adv. com., 1993-94, mem. grad. student admissions com., 1993, mem. search com. for chief cardiovasc. surgery, 1992, dept. medicine intern selection com., 1992—; mem. instnl. rev. com. Pa. Muscle Inst., 1993; cardiology adv. com. Nat. Heart, Lung, & Blood Inst., 1989-93; dir. USA-Russia Cardiovasc. Rsch. Program, 1992—; mem. NIH Task Force on Heart Failure, 1992-93, dirs. standing com. on clin. rsch. NIH, 1995—; cons. Netherlands Rsch. Initiative in Molecular Cardiology, 1993; external adv. com. Ctr. for Prevention of Cardiovasc. Disease, Harvard Sch. Pub. Health, 1993—; adv. coun. NHLBI, 1995—, Friends of NHLBI com., 1996—, lectr. in field. Exec. editor: Trends in Cardiovascular Medicine, 1990-93; mem. editl. bd. Circulation Rsch., 1991—, Circulation, 1991—, Jour. Clin. Investigation, 1992—; cons. editor: Circulation, 1993—; contbr. articles to med. jours. Mem. exec. com. Coun. on Basic Sci., Am. Heart Assn., 1986-93, chmn. Katz Prize Award Com., 1989-92, rsch. rev. com., 1990-93, fellowship rsch. com., 1992—, program com., 1992—, mem. Levine Young Investigator Awards Com., Coun. on Clin. Cardiology, 1994—, mem. Basic Sci. Coun.; bd. dirs. Southeastern Pa. Heart Assn., 1992—. Recipient Bristol-Myers Squibb Cardiovasc. Achievement award, 1992, also numerous rsch. grants. Fellow Am. Coll. Cardiology (internat. edn. com. 1994—, chair cardiovasc. rsch. com. 1996—), Coll. Physicians of Phila.; mem. Assn. Univ. Cardiologists, Assn. Am. Physicians, Assn. Prof. of Cardiology, Am. Soc. Cell Biology, Am. Fedn. Clin. Rsch., Am. Soc. Clin. Investigation (pres.-elect 1994—, councilor 1991—), Internat. Soc. Heart Rsch. (councilor 1988—), Interurban Clin. Club, Clin. and Climitol. Soc., John Morgan Soc. Office: Stanford U 300 Pasteur Dr Palo Alto CA 94304-2203

SWAIN, MARY ANN PRICE, university official; b. Chardon, Ohio, Apr. 20, 1941; d. A. David and Mary A. Price; m. Donald B. Swain, June 27, 1964; children: Judy, Brenda. BA in Psychology, DePauw U., 1963; MA in Psychology, U. Mich., 1964, PhD in Psychology, 1969. Dir. Sch. Nursing Doctoral Program U. Mich., Ann Arbor, 1975—76, chmn. dept. nursing rsch., 1977—82, assoc. v.p. acad. affairs, 1983—93, interim co-dir. pers., 1986—88, interim dir. affirmative action, 1988—89, interim v.p. student svcs., 1990—92; provost and v.p. acad. affairs SUNY, Binghamton, 1993—. Evaluation site visotor U. Balt. Sch. Law, 1996—97, Tes. Wesleyan U., 1998—99, U. Va. Sch. Nursing, Charlottesville, 1994—95; chmn. coun. acad. affairs Nat. Assn. State Univs. and Land Grant Colls., 1998—99. Co-author (with H. Erickson and E. Tomlim): Modeling and Role-modeling: A Theory and Paradigm for Nursing, 1983. Chmn. campaign United Way Broome COunty, Binghamton, 1998—99; pres. bd. dirs. Vis. Nurses Assn. Huron Valley, Ann Arbor, 1989—92. Fellow Woodrow Wilson fellow, 1963. Mem.: Am. Psychol. Soc., Am. Assn. Higher Edn., Am. Soc. Quality Control, Sigma Theta Tau, Phi Beta Kappa, Golden Key Hon. Soc. Office: Couper Administration Bldg PO Box 6000 Binghamton NY 13902-6000 E-mail: mswain@binghamton.edu.

SWAIN, SUSAN MARIE, communications executive; b. Phila., Dec. 23, 1954; d. Samuel B. Swain and Marie (Baeder) Paget. BA in Comms. magna cum laude, U. Scranton, Pa., 1976, Doctorate (hon.), 2000. Reporter Sta. WDAU-TV, Scranton, 1975-76; pub. rels. staff Up With People, Inc., Tucson, 1976—78; supr. Raytheon Service Co., Cambridge, Mass., 1978-80; research assoc. Nat. Counsel Assocs., Washington, 1980-82; producer C-SPAN Cable Network, Washington, 1982-83, dir. pub. relations, 1983-87, v.p. corp. communications, mem. exec. mgmt. com., 1987-89, sr. v.p., 1989—, exec. v.p., co-chief oper. officer; also creator & host "American Writers", C-SPAN. Officer The Nat. Cable Satellite Corp.; bd. mem. C-SPAN Ednl. Found., Talbot's Inc. Moderator (TV program) C-SPAN Viewer Call-In, 1982—; editl. mgr. Booknotes, 1997, Booknotes: Life Stories, 1999, Booknotes: Stories from History, 2001. Trustee U. Scranton, 1992—2000. Recipient Alumni award U. Scranton, 1976, Disting. Achievement award, 1991. Mem. Cable Telecom. Adminstrn. and Mktg., Mus. TV and Radio, Cable TV Pub. Affairs Assn. (bd. dirs. 1986-90, sec. 1988-89), Washington Cable Club, Alpha Sigma Nu. Roman Catholic. Avocations: sailing, biking. Office: C-SPAN 400 N Capitol St NW Ste 650 Washington DC 20001-1550

SWALLUM, MARYANN, musician, music educator; b. L.A., Sept. 6, 1944; d. Robert James and Alice Agasteen S. BM, Immaculate Heart Coll., L.A., 1966; MM, Northwestern U., 1972. Registered tchr., trainer Suzuki piano. Dir. piano program Our Lady of the Holy Rosary Sch., Sun City, Calif., 1964-66; music dir. N.W. Suburban Aide for Retarded Adults, Park Ridge, Ill., 1970-72; piano instr. Elmhurst (Ill.) Coll., 1972-79; founder, dir. Swallum Music Sch., Wilmette, Ill., 1974-79; music dir. Montessori sch., Park Ridge, Ill., 1975-79; music dir. Suzuki piano Dunbarton Sch., Hamilton, Bermuda, 1993-94; chair, instr. prep. dept. Coll. St. Scholastica, Duluth, Minn., 1994—. Piano instr., clinician Suzuki Inst. U. Wis., Stevens Point, 1978-82, U. We. Ont., London, 1980-82; dist. chair Am. Music Scholarship Competition, Cin., 1976-78; founder, dir. piano workshop for children; piano judge Ill. State Music Tchrs. Assn., Winnetka, 1977-78, Minn. State Music Tchrs., Duluth, 1980-92. Presdl. scholar The White House Commn., 1985; grantee to study with Daniel Pollack Steinway Recording Artist, 1989. Mem. Music Tchrs. Nat. Assn., Cecilian Soc. (sec. 1991-92, founder, dir. 1998), Suzuki Assn. Am. Avocations: hiking, snow skiing, snow shoeing.

SWAN, BETH ANN, nursing administrator; b. Phila., Nov. 11, 1958; d. John H. and Elizabeth A. Jenkins; m. Eric J. Swan, Apr. 11, 1987. BSN, Holy Family Coll., Phila., 1980; MSN, U. Pa., 1983, PhD in Nursing, 1996. RN, Pa.; cert. adult nurse practitioner ANCC. Nursing adminstr. spl. project s U. Pa., Phila., 1980—. Mem.: ANA, Am. Acad. Ambulatory Nursing Care, Pa. Nurses Assn., Assn. Health Svcs. Rsch., Sigma Theta Tau.

SWAN, SHANNA HELEN, epidemiologist, researcher; d. Rudolf Michael and Diana Ray Wittenberg; m. Steven Ravett Brown, Feb. 2, 1996; children: Deborah Ruth Lustig, Joshua Michael Freedman, Christopher Henry. BS in Math., CCNY, 1958; MS in Biostatistics, Columbia U., 1960; PhD in Stats., U. Calif., Berkeley, 1963. Chief reproductive epidemiology program Calif. Dept. Health Svcs., Berkeley, 1981—98; rsch. prof. family and cmty. medicine U. Mo., Columbia, 1998—, adj. prof. stats., 2002—. Recipient Ward Medal in Logic, CCNY, 1958; grantee, Nat. Inst. Environ. Health Scis., 1998—2002, U.S. EPA, 2001—. Mem.: NAS (com. on hormonally related toxicants 1995—99), Am. Statis. Assn., Soc. for Epidemiol. Rsch., Phi Beta Kappa. Democrat. Office: Univ Mo-Columbia Medical Sciences Building (MA306) Columbia MO 65212 E-mail: swans@health.missouri.edu.

SWANER-SMOOT, PAULA MARGETTS, clinical psychologist; b. Salt Lake City, Nov. 23, 1927; d. Sumner Gray and Pauline (Moyle) Margetts; m. Leland Scowcroft, May 22, 1951; children: Leland S., Jr., Sumner Margetts, Paula June Swaner-Sargetakis; m. Stephen P. Smoot, Sept. 25, 1997. BA in Eng. Lit., U. Utah, 1949, MA in Eng. Lit., 1972, MS in Ednl. Psychol., 1978, PhD in Clin. Psychology, 1986; postgrad., Washington Sch. Psychiatry, 1991, Mill Valley Calif. Acad., 1990; MA, in Mythological Studies, Pacifica Grad. Inst., 2003. Lic. clin. psychologist, Utah. Psychotherapist Granite Mental Health Ctr., Salt Lake City, 1978-80; intern Mental Health Unit, Juvenile Ct., Salt Lake City, 1984-87; pvt. practice Salt Lake City, 1986—. CEO Evergreen Coalition, 1993—2002; faculty Internat. Inst. Object Rels. Therapy, Chevy Chase, Md., 1996—, dir., Salt Lake City, 1996, founder, 2000; dir. Infant Observation Teleconferencing Satellite Program, 2000; established master tchrs. svcs. IIORT Videoconf. Supervision and Clin. Application Program, 2001. Chair Swaner Nature Preserve Found., 1993-2002; established Rock Mountain Psychol. Ctr. for Therapy and Tng., 2003. Mem.: APA, Utah Psychol. Assn. Democrat. Avocations: hiking, cross-country skiing, swimming.

SWANK, ANNETTE MARIE, software designer; b. Lynn, Mass., Nov. 9, 1953; d. Roland Paterson and Rita Mary (Edwards) S. BSEE and Computer Sci., Vanderbilt U., 1975; M of Engring. Sci., Pa. State U., 2003. Lead programmer GE, Phila., 1975-80; system analyst SEI Corp., Wayne, Pa., 1980-82; mgr., designer Premier Systems, Inc., Wayne, Pa., 1982-85, dir., 1985-88, tech. advisor, 1988-90, tech. architect, 1990-92, Funds Assocs. Ltd., Wayne, 1992-99; sr. bus. analyst First Data Investor Svcs. Group, Berwyn, Pa., 1999; prin. bus. analyst PFPC Inc., Berwyn, 1999-2000, v.p., mng. dir. SURPAS bus. unit, 2000—. Designer: (programming lang. and data dictionary) Vision, 1985. Treas. Master Singers, Plymouth Meeting, Pa., 1987-88. Mem. Assn. for Computing Machinery, Gamma Phi Beta (com. chmn. alumna Phila. 1986-87). Avocations: singing, dance, bowling, bridge, wine tasting. Home: 136 Pinecrest Ln King Of Prussia PA 19406-2368 Office: PFPC Inc 760 Moore Rd King Of Prussia PA 19406

SWANK, HILARY ANN, actress; b. Bellingham, WA, July 30, 1974; m. Chad Lowe, Sept. 28, 1997. Appeared in feature films: Buffy the Vampire Slayer, 1992, The Next Karate Kid, 1994, Sometimes They Come Back...Again, 1996, Kounterfeit, 1996, The Way We Are, 1997, Heartwood, 1998, Boys Don't Cry, 1999 (Golden Globe award for Best Actress, 2000, Oscar award for Best Actress, 2000), Affair of the Necklace, 2000, The Gift, 2000; (tv movies) Cries Unheard: The Donna Yaklich Story, 1994, Terror in the Family, 1996, Dying to Belong, 1997, The Sleepwalker Killing, 1997; (tv series) Camp Wilder, 1992, Beverly Hills, 90210, 1997-98, Leaving L.A., 1997; (tv appearances): Growing Pains, 1985, Evening Shade, Harry and the Hendersons, 1991. Avocations: sky diving, river rafting, skiing, swimming. Office: William Morris Agy 151 S El Camino Dr Beverly Hills CA 90212

SWANN, LOIS LORRAINE, writer, editor, educator; b. N.Y.C., Nov. 17, 1944; d. Peter J. and Edith M. (De Rose) Riso; m. Terrence Garth Swann, Aug. 15, 1964 (div. 1979); children: Peter Burgess, Polly Swann Coward; m. Kenneth E. Arndt, Sept. 3, 1988. BA, Marquette U., 1966. Editor Peat, Marwick, Mitchell & Co., N.Y.C., 1980-81; publs. cons. Mfrs. Hanover Trust, N.Y.C., 1981-88. Cons. bus. writing, 1988—; tchr. West H.E.L.P., Mt. Vernon, NY, 1991; tchr. nontraditional age students writing; founder, reader Calliope's Chamber, 1995—. Author: (novels) The Mists of Manittoo, 1976 (Ohioana Libr. award for 1st novel, 1976), Torn Covenants, 1981; contbr. articles to mags. Election insp. Dem. Party, Bronxville, NY, 1990—. Mem.: Poets and Writers, Authors Guild. Avocation: interior design. Home and Office: 270 Bronxville Rd Bronxville NY 10708

SWANN, MELISSA LYNNE, psychologist; b. Albuquerque, Aug. 25, 1962; d. Jimmie Gleen and Medgie (Nix) Swann. AA, Hinds C.C., Raymond, Miss., 1986; BA, Belhaven Coll., Jackson, Miss., 1989; MEd, Miss. Coll., Clinton, 1992; PhD, Southwest U., Kenner, La., 2000. Cert. emergency med. technician; lic. psychometrist. Youth counselor Cath. Charities, Jackson, 1991-92; psychologist Miss. State Hosp., Whitfield, 1992—. With Miss. Air N.G., 1985—. Named to Outstanding Young Women of Am., 1997. Mem. VFW, Am. Legion. Office: Miss State Hosp Psychology Dept Whitfield MS 39193

SWANSEN, DONNA MALONEY, landscape designer, consultant; b. Green Bay, Wis., July 8, 1931; d. Arthur Anthony and Ella Marie Rose (Warner) Maloney; m. Samuel Theodore Swansen, June 27, 1959; children: Jessica Swansen Bonelli, Theodor Arthur Swansen, Christopher Currie Swansen. AS in Integrated Liberal Studies, U. Wis., 1956; AS in Landscape Design, Temple U., 1982. Bridal cons. Richard W. Burnham's, Green Bay, 1951-54, 57-58; asst. buyer Shreve Crump & Low, Boston, 1958-59; buyer Harry S. Manchester, Madison, Wis., 1959-62; ptnr. Corson Borie & Swansen, Ambler, Pa., 1976, Swansen & Borie, Ambler, 1977-82; owner, operator Donna Swansen/Design, Ambler, 1983—. V.p. Energy Islands Internat. Inc., East Troy, Wis., 1963-94. Editor: Internat. Directory Landscape Designers, 1993. Co-founder Friends of Rising Sun, Ambler, Ambler Area Arts Alliance, 1975—76; founder, 1st pres. Plant Ambler, 1973—83, 1997—; chair Do It, Dig It exhibit Temple U., 1987; judge Temple U., 2002, Bucks County Beautiful Flowers Show, 2002, Assn. Profl. Landscape Designers, 2002; Dem. candidate for judge elections, 1988; active Gwynedd (Pa.) Monthly Meeting of Friends, 1974—; judge Del. Valley Coll., Doylestown, Pa., 2002; search com. for chair dept. landscape arch. and horticulture Temple U., 1987, curriculum rev. com., 1993; adv. com. Green Bay Bot. Garden, 1993—, Del. Valley Coll., Doylestown, Pa., 2000—, adv. bd., 2000—. Recipient Key to the Borough, Borough of Ambler, 1972; winner urban beautification project Roadside Coun. Am., Ambler, 1975, Athena award Wissahickon Valley C. of C., 1996. Mem. Assn. Profl. Landscape Designers (cert., co-founder, 1st pres. 1989-91, bd. dirs. 1989-95, 1st pres. Landscape Design Network Phila. 1978-85, Distinction award 1996, judge internat. design competition 2002, 03), Sigma Lambda Alpha (charter mem.). Democrat. Avocations: encouraging women, travel, gardening. Home and Office: 221 Morris Rd Ambler PA 19002-5202

SWANSON, CAROLYN RAE, news reporter, counselor; b. Riverton, Wyo., Nov. 10, 1937; d. Leonard Rae Swanson and Ruby Francis Mulholland Laliberte; m. William Glenn (dec. 1959); children: Donald, Rocky, Laurel; m. Larry T. Hess, Nov. 23, 1962; children: Lance Hess, Aaron Hess. AA, West Valley Coll., Saratoga, Calif., 1970; BA, San Jose State U., 1975. Cert. substance abuse counselor. Counselor, program dir. Carson Regional Coun., Carson City, Nev., 1977-82; Women's Internat. News Gathering Svc. news reporter Radio for Peace Internat., Costa Rica, 1988-89; reporter Nevada City, Calif., 1990-97; dir. Innovative Voices, Paradise, Calif., 1990—. Mem. adv. bd. UN U. of Peace, Costa Rica, 1988-89; bd. dirs. No. Nev. Lang. Bank, 1978-80; cons. Intertribal Coun., Nev.-No. Calif., 1977-80; mem. exec. bd. Grandparent State Coun., Calif., 1992-96. Coord. shelter for battered women, Carson City, 1979; U.S. del. Soviet-Am. dialog, Washington, 1988; N.Am. del. Peace Conf., Costa Rica, 1989; leader Fellowship of Reconciliation, Chico-Paradise area, 1991-92; Butte County contact Green Party, 1991—; Humboldt County coord. Postcorporate World, 1999—; adv. com. Children's Theater, Arcata, Calif., 2003—; Docent Arcata Museum, Yosemite, 2000. Recipient Promoting Arts award Villa Montalvo Theatre, Saratoga, Calif., 1975, award Nat. Inst. on Drug Abuse, Utah, 1978. Avocations: reading, travel, hiking, theatre, writing. Home: 2255 Alliance Rd Apt 2 Arcata CA 95521-5180

SWANSON, CELIA, retail executive; BA in Fashion Merchandising, U. Nebr., 1977. Sr. v.p. human resources and adminstrn. PACE Membership Warehouse, Inc., Denver; dr. dir. people group Sam's Club, 1994—95, v.p. people group, 1995—97, sr. v.p. membership, mktg. and adminstrn., 1997—2000, exec. v.p. membership, mktg. adminstrn., 2000—. Bd. govs. Children's Miracle Network, 2000—. Mem.: Nebr. Alumni Assn. (bd. dirs. 1999—). Office: Wal-Mart Stores Inc 702 SW Eighth St Bentonville AR 72716*

SWANSON, DIANE L. business management and economics educator, researcher; b. Manhattan, Kans., Oct. 6, 1950; d. Harold Albin Swanson and Betty Jo Lusby; m. Michael Dale Scott, Aug. 5, 1970 (dec. July 19, 1975); 1 child, Christopher William Scott. BS in Mgmt. and Fin., Avila, Kansas City, Mo., 1980; MA in Econs., U. Mo., Kansas City, 1982; PhD in Bus. Adminstrn., U. Pitts., 1996. Instr. econs., interim dir. Inst. Mgmt. Old Dominion U., Norfolk, Va., 1984—86; asst. prof. fin. Hampton (Va.) U., 1987—88; asst. prof. bus. econs. U. Pitts., 1988—89; assoc. prof. mgmt. Robert Morris Coll., Pitts., 1989—97, Kans. State U., Manhattan, 1997—, von Waaden prof. bus. adminstrn., founder and chair Bus. Ethics Edn. Initiative, 2002—. Mem. Pres.'s Commn. on Women Kans. State U., 2000—01, mentor Developing Scholars Program for Minority Students, 2000—01; presenter confs. and media broadcasts in field; Disting. Spkr. on bus. ethics edn. Book rev. editor, consulting editor: Internat. Jour. Orgnl. Analysis, 1994—; contbg. editor: Managing Ego Energy, 1994—; spl. issue editor: Jour. Individual Employment Rights, 2002—03; contbr. articles to profl. jours., chapters to books. Co-founder Nat. Campaign to Improve Bus. Ethics Edn., 2002—; bd. dirs. Women's Intercultural Network, San Francisco, 1994—2002, People's Coop., Manhattan, 1998—2000, All Acad. Task Force on Mentoring, 2002—. Recipient nat. award for tchg. excellence, Bell and Howell, 1982, award for entrepreneurial leadership, Advances in Mgmt. Conf., 1996, Best Article on Bus. and Soc. award, Internat. Assn. for Bus. and Soc. and Calif. Mgmt. Rev., 1999; fellow, David Berg Family Found. in Bus. Ethics, 1994; grantee, Beard Ctr. for Ethics, Duquesne U., 2000, Australian Grad. Sch. Mgmt., 2000—01; internat. grantee for exec. leadership. Mem.: Nat. Acad. Mgmt. (governing bd. Social Issues in Mgmt. 1998—), Beta Gamma Sigma. Democrat. Avocations: yoga, meditation, travel, gardening, cats. Office: Kans State U 101 Calvin Hall Manhattan KS 66506

SWANSON, DOLORES, special education educator, musician; b. Omaha, Sept. 5, 1931; d. Oswald Adelord Albert Hawkins and Mary Margaret Franckewicz; m. Emory Wilkins Bridgeford (div. July 1970), children: Emory Wilkins Jr., Lenora, Joseph, Mary, Irwin, Peter, Jeannette, Patrick, Mark, Gerard; m. Conrad John Swanson, Oct. 15, 1970 (div.). B Music Edn., U. Nev., Reno, 1985. Cert. spl. edn. tchr., generalist resource, Nev. Sec. Natelson's Women's Apparel, Omaha, 1949-50; sec.-stenographer U.S. Army Chem. Corps, Denver, 1952-54; singer, entertainer in midwest and western U.S., 1964-79; co-founder, instr. adult basic edn. Truckee Meadows C.C., Reno, 1989-91, 93-95; tchr. music Washoe County Sch. Dist., Reno, 1986-87, tchr. spl. edn., 1991—. Bd. dirs. No. Nev. Bus. Inst., Reno, 1971-72; choir dir. Our Lady of Wisdom Newman Ctr., Reno, 1996—. Recipient Fred and Anna Stadtmuller Meml. award U. Nev., 1987; Command scholar U. Nev., 1983-84. Mem. NEA, Coun. for Exceptional Children, Nev. Tchrs. Assn., Washoe County Tchrs. Assn. Democrat. Roman Catholic. Avocations: sewing, crafting, ceramics, crocheting, gardening. Office: Marvin Picollo Sch 900 Foothill Rd Reno NV 89511-9427

SWANSON, DONNA KAY, elementary school educator, writer; d. John Worley and Margaret Olive Ruth Elisabeth Carson-Worley; m. John McCord Swanson, June 10, 1956; children: Melynda Beth Leak, Melyssa Lynn Leak, Melanie Ann, John McCord Jr. Tchr., adminstrv. sec. Williamsport Day Sch., 1998—. Instr. writer workshops Learning Ctr., Williamsport, 2003. Author: (nonfiction) Mind Song, (poem and documentary film) Minnie Remembers (Golden Eagle Film award CINE, 1977), (novels) Rachel's Daughters, 2000, Angel World Trilogy, 2001. Tchr. Williamsport Christian Ch., 1970—2000. Republican. Avocations: wood sculpture, music, birdwatching, crafts, computer graphics. Home: 289W 300 N Williamsport IN 47993 Office: Williamsport Day Sch 448 E 4th St Williamsport IN 47993 E-mail: swanson@mindsongbooks.com.

SWANSON, ELIZABETH ANN, special education educator, researcher; d. Michael Jack McGuffin and Mary Ann Kraemer; m. Brett Alan Swanson. BS in Applied Learning and Devel., U. Tex., 1997, MEd in Spl. Edn., 2003. Cert. tchr. K-8 Tex., tchr. spl. edn. Tex. Tchr. Andrews Elem. Sch., Austin Ind. Sch. Dist., 1997—2002; grad. rsch. asst. U. Tex. Ctr. Reading and Lang. Arts, Austin, 2002—03, project coord., 2003—; instr. alternative cert. program Huston-Tillotson Coll., Austin, 2003. Contract writer Steck-Vaughn Pub., Austin, 2003—; adj. prof. Huston-Tillotson Coll., Austin, 2004. Mem.: Internat. Reading Assn., Coun. Exceptional Children, Kappa Delta Pi. Office: U Tex 1 University Station D4900 Austin TX 78712 Personal E-mail: eswan24@yahoo.com.

SWANSON, JEANNIE MARIE, special education educator; b. Bellevue, Wash., July 26, 1961; d. Mary Genieve O'Donnell and Delmar Theodore Swanson, Jr.; life ptnr. Barbara Lynn Silver. BS in Phys. Edn., Calif. Poly. U., Pomona, 1995; MS in Spl. Edn., Nat. U., Stockton, Calif., 1997. Profl. Clear Learning Handicap Credential Spl. Edn. Calif. Commn. on Tchr. Credentialing, 1999, Profl. Clear Multiple Subject Teaching Credential Calif. Commn. on Tchr. Credentialing, 1999, Clear Crosscultural Lang. and Acad. Devel.Certificate Calif. Commn. on Tchr. Credentialing, 1998. Tchr. 6th grade San Bernadino (Calif.) Unified Sch. Dist., 1991—92; tchr. 4th grade St. Anne's Cath. Sch., Lodi, Calif., 1992—97; spl. day class tchr. 4-6th grade Manteca (Calif.) Unified Sch. Dist., 1997—. Sci. instr. Orange County Dept. of Edn., Costa Mesa, Calif., 1988—95; daycare dir. k-4th YMCA, Long Beach, Calif., 1989—90; summer camp dir., Catalina Island Girl Scouts, L.A., Calif., 1986—88; homework assistance program tutor City of Lathrop, Calif.; girls' basketball coach Manteca (Calif.) Unified Sch. Dist., 1997—. Foster parent Human Svcs. Agy., Stockton, Calif.; vol. Spl. Olympics, Stockton, 1997. Mem.: NEA, Manteca Teachers Assn., Calif. Tchrs. Assn. Democrat. Avocations: sports, gardening, movies, bicycling. Office: Lathrop Elem Sch PO Box 32 Lathrop CA 95330-0032

SWANSON, KARIN, hospital administrator, consultant; b. New Britain, Conn., Dec. 8, 1942; d. Oake F. and Ingrid Lauren Swanson; m. B. William Dorsey, June 26, 1965 (div. 1974); children: Matthew W., Julie I., Alison K.; m. Sanford H. Low, Oct. 14, 1989. BA in Biology, Middlebury Coll., 1964; MPH, Yale U., 1981. Biology tchr. Kents Hill (Maine) Sch., 1964-66; laboratory instr. Bates Coll., Lewiston, Maine, 1974-78; asst. to gen. dir. Mass. Eye and Ear Infirmary, Boston, 1979-80; v.p. profl. services Portsmouth (N.H.) Hosp., 1981-83; v.p. Health Strategy Assn. Ltd., Chestnut Hill, Mass., 1983-85; v.p. med. affairs Cen. Maine Med. Ctr., Lewiston, 1986-89; health care mgmt. cons. Cambridge, Mass., 1989-91; CEO Hahnemann Hosp., Brighton, Mass., 1991-94; adminstr. Vencor Hosp., Boston, 1994-95; pres., CEO The Laser Inst. New Eng., Newton, Mass., 1996-97; health care mgmt./real estate devel. cons. Newcastle, Maine, 1997—. Mem. Phi Beta Kappa. Avocations: reading, gardening, walking. Home and Office: PO Box 1281 Damariscotta ME 04543-1281

SWANSON, MARY CATHERINE, educational reform program founder; b. Kingsburg, Calif., Sept. 3, 1944; d. Edwin Elmore and Corrine (Miller) Jacobs; m. Thomas Edward Swanson, Aug. 27, 1966; 1 child, Thomas Jacobs. BA in English and Journalism, Calif. State U., San Francisco, 1966; standard teaching credential in secondary edn., U. Calif., 1966; MA in Edn., U. Redlands, 1977; DHL (hon.), U. San Diego, 2002, U. LaVerne, 2003. Svc. adminstrv. credential, Calif.; specialist learning handicapped, Calif.; gifted cert., Calif. Tchr. English and journalism Woodland (Calif.) High Sch., 1966-67, Armijo High Sch., Fairfield, Calif., 1967-69, Moreno Valley High Sch., Sunnymead, Calif., 1969-70, Clairemont High Sch., San Diego, 1970-86; coord. San Diego County Office Edn., 1986-90, dir. AVID project, 1990-92; founder, exec. dir. AVID Ctr., 1992—. Newspaper and yearbook advisor Moreno Valley High Sch., Moreno Valley Sch. Dist., 1969-70; reading program coord. Clairemont High Sch., 1974-80, project English coord. and site plan coord., 1975-80, English dept. chairperson, 1978-86, coord. Advancement Via Individual Determination and WASC accreditation, 1980-86, in-sch. resource tchr., 1982-86; mem. numerous positions and coms. San Diego City Schs., 1974-91; mem. com. univ. and coll. opportunities commn. Calif. State Dept. Edn., 1981-82; mem. adv. com. tchr. edn. program Pt. Loma Coll., 1982-83, tchr. English methods course for tchrs. secondary edn., 1986-87; mem. accreditation vis. com. WASC, 1983, integration monitoring team Crawford High Sch., 1984, adv. com. San Diego Area Writing Project, 1987—; developer numerous curricular programs, 1967—. Community leader Olivenhain Valley 4-H Club, 1981-90; founder Olivenhain Valley Soccer Club, 1982; coord. Clairemont High Sch./Sea World Adopt-A-Sch., 1982-84. Named Headliner of Yr.-Edn./Creative Tchg., San Diego Press Club, 1991, Headline of Yr.-Cmty. Activist, 2002, Woman of Vision, LWV-San Diego, 1992, Nat. Educator of Yr., McGraw Hill, 2001, America's Best Tchr., Time Mag. and CNN, 2001; named to Pres.'s Forum on Tchg. as a Profession, Am. Assn. Higher Edn., 1991; recipient EXCEL award for excellence in tchg., 1985, Exemplary Program award, Nat. Coun. States on Insvc. Edn., 1990, Pioneering Achievement in Edn. award, Charles A. Dana Found., 1991; grantee, BankAmerica Found., 1980, UCSD Acad. Support Svcs., 1980, San Diego Gas and Elec. Found., 1984. Mem. Nat. Coun. Tchrs. English (Nat. Ctr. Excellence award 1985-87), Calif. Coun. Tchrs. English, Calif. Assn. Gifted Edn., Golden Key Nat. Honor Soc. (hon. mem.), Phi Kappa Phi. Office: San Diego County Office Edn 6401 Linda Vista Rd Rm 623 San Diego CA 92111-7319 also: AVID Ctr 5120 Shoreham Pl Ste 120 San Diego CA 92122 E-mail: mcswanson@avidcenter.org.

SWANSON, PATRICIA KLICK, foundation administrator; b. St. Louis, May 8, 1940; d. Emil Louis and Patricia (McNair) Klick; 1 child, Ivan Clatanoff. BS in Edn., U. Mo., 1962; postgrad., Cornell U., 1963; MLS, Simmons Coll., 1967. Reference librarian Simmons Coll., Boston, 1967-68, U. Chgo., 1970-79, sr. lectr. Grad. Library Sch., 1974-83, 86-88, head reference service, 1979-83, asst. dir. for sci. libraries, 1983-93, acting asst. dir. for tech. svcs., 1987-88, assoc. provost, 1993-98; program officer MacArthur Found., 1999—. Project dir. Office Mgmt. Svcs., Assn. Rsch. Librs., 1982-83; speaker in field; cons. on libr. mgmt., planning and space. Author: Great is the Gift that Bringeth Knowledge: Highlights from the History of the John Crerar Library, 1989; contbr. articles to profl. jours. Office: John D and Catherine T MacArthur Found 140 S Dearborn St Ste 1100 Chicago IL 60603-5202

SWANSON, PEGGY EUBANKS, finance educator; b. Ivanhoe, Tex., Dec. 29, 1936; d. Leslie Samuel and Mary Lee (Reid) Eubanks; m. B. Marc Sommers, Nov. 10, 1993. BBA, U. North Tex., 1957, M. Bus. Edn., 1965; MA in Econs., So. Meth. U., 1967, PhD in Econs., 1978. Instr. El Centro Coll., Dallas, 1967-69, 71-78, bus. div. chmn., 1969-71; asst. prof. econs. U. Tex., Arlington, 1978-79, asst. prof. fin., 1979-84, assoc. prof., 1984-86, chmn. dept. fin. and real estate, 1986-88, prof. fin., 1987—, interim dean Coll. Bus. Adminstrn., 1999—2000. Expert witness various law firms, primarily Tex. and Calif., 1978—; cons. Internat. Edn. Program, 1992-99; curriculum cons. U. Monterrey, Mexico, 1995, New Saudi Arabia U., 1999. Contbr. articles to acad. profl. jours. Vol. Am. Cancer Soc., Dallas, Arlington, 1981—, Meals on Wheels, Arlington, 1989—; mem. adv. bd. Ryan/Reilly Ctr. for Urban Land Utilization, Arlington, 1986-88. Mem. Fin. Exec. Inst. (chmn. acad. rels. 1987-88), Internat. Bus. Steering Com. (chmn. 1989-91), Am. Fin. Assn., Am. Econ. Assn., Fin. Mgmt. Assn. (hon. faculty mem. Nat. Honor Soc. 1985-86, program com. 1998-99), Southwestern Fin. Assn. (program com. 1987-88, 96), Midwest Fin. Assn. (program com. 1997-98, 98-99), Acad. of Internat. Bus. (program com. 1992-95), Acad. Disting. Tchrs., Phi Beta Delta (membership com. 1987-89). Republican. Episcopalian. Avocations: tennis, gardening. Home: 4921 Bridgewater Dr Arlington TX 76017-2729 Office: U Tex at Arlington PO Box 19449 Arlington TX 76019-0001 E-mail: swanson@uta.edu.

SWANSON, SHIRLEY JUNE, emergency room nurse, travel nurse, adult education educator; b. Dade City, Fla., Feb. 26, 1942; d. Alan John and Ollie Mae (Jackson) S.; m. James A. Whatley, 1960 (div. 1962); 1 child, Marsha L. Glunt; m. Jerald Ward Steen, Sr., June 7, 1963; children: Linda A. Stanley, Jerald Ward, Jr., Jerald Wagner. AA, Hillsborough C.C., 1974; BA, U. South Fla., 1975; AS, Gupton-Jones Coll., 1992, No. Maine Tech. Coll., 1996; postgrad., St. Joseph's Coll., Windham, Maine, 2001—. RN; cert. in elem. and adult edn. scis., Maine; mortician. Personal life underwriter Home Ins. Co., N.Y.C., 1979-82; with L.L. Bean, Freeport, Maine, 1988-90; tchr. biology Caribou (Maine) Adult Edn., 1994-96. Owner Alan's Dau.'s Place, 1988—, Angel Quilts, 1996—; spkr. in field. Author, editor Coffee Break, 1963-64. Ofcl. spinner Fla. State Fair, Tampa, 1984-85; spinner East Animal Farm/Westshore Mall, Tampa, 1984-85; guest spinner Town of Westfield (Maine) Jubilee Days, 1995; hospice vol. Vis. Nurses of Aroostook County, Caribou, 1995—. Billerica, Mass. O.E.S. scholar, 1975, Am. Bd. Funeral Svc. Edn. scholar, 1992, Caribou Adult Edn. Sys. scholar, 1995. Mem. Phi Theta Kappa, Pi Sigma Eta. Roman Catholic. Avocations: wool spinning, commision quilting, tutoring, weaving, amateur radio w4efm. Home: 1584 Woodland Ctr Rd Perham ME 04766-3314 Office: Caribou Adult Edn Ctr Sweden St Caribou ME 04736

SWANTON, SUSAN IRENE, retired library director; b. Rochester, N.Y., Nov. 29, 1941; d. Walter Frederick and Irene Wray S.; m. Wayne Holman, Apr. 12, 1969 (div. June 1973); 1 child, Michael; ptnr. James Donald Lathrop; children: Kathryn, Kristin. AB, Harvard U., 1963; MLS, Columbia U., 1965. Libr. dir. Warsaw (N.Y.) Pub. Libr., 1963-64, Gates Pub. Libr., Rochester, NY, 1965—2003; ret., 2003. Pres. Drug and Alcohol Coun., Rochester, 1985-91, mem. adv. coun., 1992-94; bd. dirs., co-chair info. svcs. Rochester Freenet, 1995—; sec. Gates Hist. Preservation Commn., 2000-03; chair Gates Dem. Com., 2004—. Mem. Gates Hist. Soc. (bd. dirs., pres. 1998—2002, v.p. 2002—03), Gates-Chili C. of C. (pres. 1982, sec. 1990-94, bd. dirs. 2003, Citizen of Yr. 1994), Harvard Club of Rochester (mem. adv. bd.). Home: 284 Gatewood Ave Rochester NY 14624-1622 E-mail: sswanton@ggw.org.

SWANTON, VIRGINIA LEE, writer, publishing executive; b. Oak Park, Ill., Feb. 6, 1933; d. Milton Wesley and Eleanor Louise (Linnell) Swanton. BA, Lake Forest (Ill.) Coll., 1954; MA in English Lit., Northwestern U., 1955; cert. in acctg., Coll. of Lake County, Ill., 1984. Editorial asst. Publs. Office, Northwestern U., Evanston, Ill., 1955-58; reporter Lake Forester, Lake Forest, 1959; editor Scott, Foresman & Co., Glenview, Ill., 1959-84; copy editor, travel coord. McDougal Littell/Houghton Mifflin, Evanston, 1985-94; sr. bookseller B. Dalton Bookseller, Lake Forest, Ill., 1985—2004; author, pub. Gold Star Publ. Svcs., Lake Forest, 1994—. Contbr. articles to profl. jours.; author: numerous poems. Former sec. bd. dirs., newsletter editor Career Resource Ctr., Inc., Lake Forest; current events discussion vol. Lake Forest/Lake Bluff Sr. Ctr.; mem. bd. deacons First Presbyn. Ch. Lake Forest. Mem.: Lake Forest/Lake Bluff Hist. Soc. (vol.), Chgo. Women Pub., Deerpath Art League. Presbyterian. Avocation: gardening. Office: Gold Star Publ Svcs PO Box 125 Lake Forest IL 60045-1333

SWARD, ANDREA JEANNE, musician, librarian; b. Hackensack, N.J., June 25, 1951; d. George Frederick and Carol Jeanne (Snoad) Lankow; m. Jeffrey Edwin Sward, June 7, 1975. Student, U. Minn., Duluth, 1969-72; BA in Psychology, Calif. State U., Fullerton, 1973, MLS, 1974, MS in Edn., 1976; cert. Bus. Intelligence and Data Ware, U. Calif. Irvine, 2003. Librarian, prof. Calif. State U., Fullerton, 1972—97; violist Anaheim (Calif.) Cultural Arts Ctr. Orch., 1978-80, Anaheim Civic Light Opera, 1978-80, Calif. European Tour Orch., Fullerton, 1978-79, Fullerton Cmty. Orch., 1978—86; computer programmer, analyst Hughes Aircraft, Fullerton, 1980-81, Smith-Kline/Beckman, Fullerton, 1981-83, ConAgra/Hunt-Wesson, Irvine, 1983—; librarian Downey (Calif.) City Library, 1985, Orange (Calif.) Pub. Library, 1985—90, Huntington Beach (Calif.) Library, 1985—. Editor Vis À Vis; An Interdisciplinary Journal, 1972-74. Contbr. articles profl. jours. and mags., 1977-79. Mem., contbr. Newport Harbor Art Mus., Newport Beach, Calif., 1975—, Los Angeles County Mus. of Art, 1975—, ACLU, 1976—, Cousteau Soc., 1978—, Audubon Soc., 1985—, Amigos de Bolsa Chica, 1985—, Spl. Olympics, 1987—; wildlife rehabilitator Wetlands and Wildlife Care Ctr., Orange County, 1999—. Fridley (Minn.) Edn. Assn. scholar, 1969, Spl. Edn. Assn. scholar, 1972; Edwin Carr fellow, 1976; Ptnrs. in Excellence grantee, 1979. Mem. ALA, Assn. for Computing Machinery, Calif. Library Assn., Calif. Reading Assn., Reading Educators Guild, Penguini Poets and Philosophers Guild of Placentia (co-founder). Democrat. Avocations: sports, reading, dance, theater, art. Home: PO Box 7019 Huntington Beach CA 92615-7019 E-mail: ajsward@yahoo.com.

SWARTHWORTH, SHARON T. military officer; b. Providence, Nov. 8, 1959; Enlisted U.S. Army, 1977; pers. adminstrn. specialist 50th Signal Bn., Ft. Bragg, NC, 304th Signal Bn., Republic of Korea; legal specialist 16th Signal Bn., Ft. Hood, Tex., 1981—82; legal specialist/ct. reporter 110th JAG Detachment, Ft. Carson, Colo., 1st Army, Ft. Meade, Md., sgt. 1st class; legal adminstr. Judge Advocate Gen.'s Corps, 1984; tng., advising and counseling officer Warrant Office Cand. Sch., Ft. McCoy, Wis.; IMA legal adminstr. Spl. Forces Command, Ft. Bragg, NC; legal adminstr. Legal Assistance Task Force/Desert Storm, Office of Judge Advocate Gen., Washington, Legal Svc. Study Group, Office of Gen. Counsel, Washington, Presidio of San Francisco, U.S. Army Litigation Ctr., Arlington, Va., U.S. Army Legal Svcs. Agy.; dir. ops. for legal tech. Office of Judge Advocate, Arlington, Va.; warrant officer Judge Advocate Gen.'s Corps, 1999—. Decorated Meritorious Svc. medal with 3 oak leaf clusters, Army Commendation medal with 6 oak leaf clusters, Army Achievement medal, numerous others. Office: Office of Judge Advocate General US Pentagon Washington DC 20310-1500

SWARTZ, LINDA Z. lawyer; b. Pitts., Mar. 22, 1962; d. William E. and Virgina N. Swartz. BA in Psychology, Bucknell U., 1984; JD, U. Pa., 1987. Bar: N.Y. 1988. Assoc. Milbank, Tweed, Hadley & McCloy, N.Y.C., 1987—95; sr. atty. Cravath, Swaine & Moore, N.Y.C., 1995—99; ptnr., co-chair tax dept. Cadwalader, Wickersham & Taft, N.Y.C., 1999—. Contbr. articles to profl. jours. Mem.: N.Y. State Bar Assn. (mem. exec. com. 1995—2001, 2003—). Office: Cadwalader Wickersham & Taft 100 Maiden Ln New York NY 10038 Office Phone: 212-504-6062. Business E-Mail: linda.swartz@cwt.com.

SWARTZ, ROSLYN HOLT, real estate executive; b. Los Angeles, Dec. 9, 1940; d. Abe Jack and Helen (Canter) Holt; m. Allan Joel Swartz, June 2, 1963. AA, Santa Monica (Calif.) Coll., 1970; BA summa cum laude, UCLA, 1975; MA, Pepperdine U., 1976. Cert. cmty. coll. instr., student-pers. worker, Calif. Mgr. pub. rels. Leader Holdings, Inc., L.A., 1968-75, pres., 1991—, sec., treas. North Hollywood, Calif., 1975-81, pres., 1981-91; CEO Beverly Stanley Investments, L.A., 1979—. Pres. Leader Properties, Inc., The Leader Fairfax, Inc., Leader 358, Inc., Leader 359, Inc., Leader Ventura, Inc., 1996—. Condr. An Oral History of the Elderly Jewish Community of Venice, Calif. at Los Angeles County Planning Dept. Library, 1974. Founder Pres.'s Cir. L.A. County Mus. Art; founder Gold Circle Music Ctr.; mem. The Blue Ribbon, Club 100; charter mem. Ctr. Dance Assn.; mem. Music Ctr. L.A. County; founder West Alumni Ctr.; chair UCLA Affiliates Sch. of Medicine Scholarship Com., 2004; capital patron Simon Wiesenthal Ctr.; past trustee Odyssey Theatre Ensemble; hon. chmn. bus. adv. coun. Nat. Rep. Congl. Com.; bd. dirs. House Ear Inst.; hon. bd. dirs. West L.A. Symphony. Mem.: NAFE, KCET Womens Coun.,

Comml. Real Estate Women, Am. Pharm. Assn., Nat. Mus. of Women in the Arts (So. Calif. coun.), UCLA Las Donas (exec. bd.), UCLA Chancellor's Assocs., Santa Monica Coll. Alumni Assn. (life), Town Hall (life), UCLA Alumni Assn. (life), Friends of Fox, Women's Guild Cedars-Sinai Med. Ctr., UCLA Prytanean Alumnae Assn., Friends of Robinson Gardens, Fashion Circle of Costume Coun., Order Eastern Star, Phrateres Internat., Phi Beta Kappa (Bicentennial fellow), Pi Lambda Theta, Pi Gamma Mu, Phi Delta Kappa, Alpha Kappa Delta, Alpha Gamma Sigma, Phi Alpha Theta. Avocation: horticulture. Office: PO Box 241866 Los Angeles CA 90024-9666

SWARTZ, SHARON MARIE, physician assistant; b. Lancaster, Ohio, June 4, 1964; d. Robert Lee and Nancy Louise Swartz. BA, Ohio State U., 1988; physician asst. cert., Wake Forest U., 1995. Cert. physician asst. Nat. Commn. Cert. Physician Assts. Physician asst. dermatology Nalle Clinic, Charlotte, NC, 1999—2000, Mecklenburg Dermatology Assocs., PA, Charlotte, 2000—. Fellow: Am. Acad. Physician Assts. Democrat. Jewish. Avocations: travel, swimming, music, movies. Home: 2832 Wimbledon Dr Gastonia NC 28056 Office: Mecklenburg Dermatology Assocs PA 1928 Randolph Rd Ste 316 Charlotte NC 28207 Business E-Mail: sswartz@meckderm.com.

SWARTZMILLER, MILDRED M. art gallery owner; b. Flint, Mich., June 23, 1924; d. John and Anna Eva (Hrabinec) Chludil; m. John M. Bila, June 25, 1945 (div. June 1970); children: David, Sharon, Marsha; m. Joseph F. Swartzmiller, Nov. 5, 1987 (dec. Mar. 1996). Grad. h.s., Muskegon Heights. Sec. Swartzmiller Lumber, Chesaning, Mich.; treas. Chesaning Area Arts; owner Artist's Alley, Chesaning, 1997—. Contbr. poetry to anthologies. Vol. Chesaning Garden Club, 1984-94. Recipient Best Writing award AAUW, 1942. Home: 319 S Wood St Chesaning MI 48616-1355

SWATZELL, MARILYN LOUISE, nurse; b. Johnson City, Tenn., July 31, 1942; d. Dallas Fred and Minnie Thelma (Clark) S. BS cum laude, East Tenn. State U., 1966, MS, 1967; BSN, U. Tenn., 1974. Chmn. pediatric nursing Meth. Hosp. Sch. Nursing, Memphis, 1978—80; head nurse Le Bonheur Children's Med. Ctr., Memphis, 1981—83; dir. maternal child nursing Jackson (Tenn.) Madison County Gen. Hosp., 1985—88; staff nurse Vanderbilt U. Hosp., Nashville, 1988—90; supr. Meth. Hosp. Lexington, Tenn., 1990—2003; dir. case mgmt. Henderson County Cmty. Hosp., Tenn., 2003—. Contbr. articles on care plans to profl. jours. Mem. ANA, Tenn. Nurses Assn., Tenn. Orgn. Nurse Execs., N.W. Assn. Case Mgrs. Home: 231 Law Ln Lexington TN 38351-6048

SWAYSLAND, JANET, advertising executive; BA in social sci., edn., Wake Forest U. Pres. Brodeur Worldwide, 2000—, gen. mgr. U.S. ops., 1999; co-dir. pub. rels. group Mullen Advt. & Pub. Rels.; v.p. U.S. divsn. The Body Shop, Inc. Chair U.S. exec. team Brodeur Worldwide. Office: Brodeur Worldwide 855 Boylston St Boston MA 02116

SWAZEY, JUDITH POUND, academic administrator, sociomedical science educator; b. Bronxville, N.Y., Apr. 21, 1939; d. Robert Earl and Louise Titus (Hanson) Pound; m. Peter Woodman Swazey, Nov. 28, 1964; children: Elizabeth, Peter. AB, Wellesley Coll., 1961; PhD, Harvard U., 1966. Rsch. assoc. Harvard U., 1966-71, lectr., 1969-71, rsch. fellow, 1971-72; cons. com. brain scis. NRC, 1971-73; staff scientist neuroscis. rsch. program MIT, Cambridge, 1973-74; assoc. prof. dept. socio-med. scis. and cmty. medicine Boston U., 1974-77, prof., 1977-80, adj. prof. Schs. Medicine and Pub. Health, 1980—; exec. dir. Medicine in the Pub. Interest, Inc., Boston and Washington, 1979-82, 89-93; pres. Coll. of the Atlantic, Bar Harbor, Maine, 1982-84, Acadia Inst., Bar Harbor, 1984-2001, founding pres., sr. scholar, 2001—. Mem. Army Sci. Bd., 1987-92. Author: Reflexes and Motor Integration, the Development of Sherrington's Integrative Action Concept, 1969, (with others) Human Aspects of Biomedical Innovation, 1971, (with R.C. Fox) The Courage to Fail, a Social View of Organ Transplants and Hemodialysis, 1975, rev. edit., 1978 (hon. mention Am. Med. Writers Assn., C. Wright Mills award Am. Sociol. Assn.), Chlorpromazine in Psychiatry, a Study of Therapeutic Innovation, 1974, (with K. Reeds) Today's Medicine, Tomorrow's Science, Essays on Paths of Discovery in the Biomedical Sciences, 1978; editor: (with C. Wong) Dilemmas of Dying, Policies and Procedures for Decisions Not to Treat, 1981, (with F. Worden and G. Adelman) The Neurosciences: Paths of Discovery, 1975, (with R.C. Fox) Spare Parts, Organ Replacement in American Society, 1992, (with C. Messikomer and A. Glicksman) Society and Medicine. Essays in Honor of Renée Fox, 2002; assoc. editor IRB: A Jour. of Human Subjects Rsch., 1979-2000; mem. editl. bd. Sci. and Engring. Ethics, 1994—; contbr. articles to profl. jours. Mem. Maine Dept. Human Svcs. Bioethics Adv. Com. (chair 1991-94); mem. Commn. on Rsch. Integrity, 1994-95; bd. dirs. Maine Bioethics Network, 1994-99. Wellesley Coll. scholar, 1961; Wellesley Coll. Alumnae fellow Harvard U., 1966, NIH predoctoral fellow, 1966, Radcliffe Coll. Coll. grad. fellow, 1966. Fellow AAAS (sci. freedom and responsibility com. 1986-89), Inst. Medicine of NAS (mem. health scis. policy bd. 1986-89, com. on nominations 2002—), Grad. Record Exam. (bd. dirs. 1987-91), Phi Beta Kappa, Sigma Xi. Office: PO Box 243 Bar Harbor ME 04609-0243 Office Phone: 207-288-3295.

SWEANEY, DONNA, state representative; b. Steubenville, Ohio, June 18, 1943; m. William James Ballantyne. BA, Youngstown State U., 1966; MEd, U. Hartford, 1974. Sch. counselor; rep. Vt. Ho. of Reps., 1996—. Chmn. Windsor Selectboard, 1986-87. Trustee Mt. Ascutney Hosp. Mem. NEA, Am. and Vt. Counseling Assns., Vt. Sch. Counselors. Office: 20 N Main St Windsor VT 05089-1307

SWEAT, LYNDA SUE, cooking instructor, catering company owner, deaconess; b. Phoenix, Apr. 5, 1949; d. Troy Eugene and Patricia June (Tignor) Lauchner; m. Doyle Dwayne Sweat, Feb. 7, 1976; children: Shannon Sue, Derek Dwayne. BA in Am. Studies, Ariz. State U., 2001, M in Religious Studies, Diploma Barrett Honors Coll., Ariz. State U, 2002. Leasing sec. Coldwell, Banker, Phoenix, 1968-74; exec. sec. Santa Anita Devel., Phoenix, 1974-78; prin., owner Tummy Yummy's, Phoenix, 1989—. Instr., Women's Seminars for Chs. on Christian Hospitality, 1984—; deaconess Palmcroft Bapt. Ch., Phoenix, 1989—, dir. fellowship com., editor and writer newsletter. Mem. Ariz. Bar Assn. Women's Aux., Maricopa County Bar Assn. Women's Aux., Southwestern Bible Coll. Women's Aux., Women in Food and Wine in Ariz. Club, Piecemakers (pres.). Republican. Avocations: crafting, quilting, porcelain doll making. Home: 19937 N Denaro Dr Glendale AZ 85308-5648

SWEED, PHYLLIS, publishing executive; b. N.Y.C., Dec. 6, 1931; d. Paul and Frances (Spitzer) S.; m. Leonard Bogdanoff (dec. Oct. 1975); children: Patricia Romano (dec. June 1994), James Alan. BA, NYU, 1950. Asst. buyer Nat. Bellas Hess, N.Y.C., 1950; assoc. editor Fox-Shulman Pub., N.Y.C., 1951-57; significant products and components editor Product Engring. mag. McGraw-Hill Pub., N.Y.C., 1957-61; mng. editor Haire Pub., N.Y.C., 1962-66; editor Gifts & Decorative Accessories Mag., 1966-78; sr. v.p. Geyer-McAllister Pub., N.Y.C., 1978-98, editor, co-pub., 1978-95, editor-in-chief, co-pub., 1995-98; dir. editl. devel. Gifts & Decorative Accessories, N.Y.C., 1998-99; prin. P.S. Comms. & Mktg., 1999—; editor-in-chief, pub. Gift Executive, 1999—. Bd. dirs. Frances Hook Scholarship Fund, 1989-96. Recipient Editl. Excellence award Indsl. Mktg., 1964, Nat. Assn. Ltd. Edit. Dealers award, 1993, 96, MagWeek Excellence award, 1992, Dallas Mktg. Ctr. award, 1969, 80, 82. Mem. Nat. Assn. Ltd. Edit. Dealers (assoc.), Internat. Furnishings and Design Assn. Avocations: gardening, collecting antique Belleek. Office: 505 LaGuardia Pl Ste 17D New York NY 10012-2004

SWEENEY, ANNE M. cable television company executive; b. Nov. 4, 1957; m. Philip Miller; 2 children. BA, Coll. of New Rochelle, N.Y., 1979; EdM, Harvard U., 1980. With Nickelodeon/Nick at Nite, 1981-93, sr. v.p. program enterprises; chmn., CEO Fx Networks, N.Y.C., 1993-96; exec. v.p. Disney/ABC Cable Networks, pres. Disney Channel Walt Disney Co., 1996—98, pres. Disney/ABC Cable Networks, Disney Channel, 1998—2000, pres. ABC Cable Networks Group, Disney Channel Worldwide, 2000—04, co-chair Media Networks divsn., pres. Disney/ ABC TV, 2004—. Bd. trustees Coll. of New Rochelle, Harvard U. Ptnrs. Coun.; hon. chair Cable Positive; bd. dirs. Walter Kaitz Found, Spl. Olympics Internat. Recipient Chair Award, Caucus for TV Prodrs., Writers, and Dirs., 2003. Mem. Nat. Acad. Cable Programming (bd. dirs.), Women in Cable (founding mem.) N.Y. Women in Cable (Exec. of Yr. 1994), Am. Women in Radio and TV (Star award 1995), Am. Advt. Fedn. (inducted in Hall of Achievement). Office: The Walt Disney Co 500 S Buena Vista St Burbank CA 91521

SWEENEY, EMILY MARGARET, prosecutor; b. Cleve., May 2, 1948; d. Mark Elliot and Neydra (Ginsburg) Mirsky; m. Patrick Anthony Sweeney, Dec. 30, 1983; 1 child, Margaret Anne. BA, Case Western Res. U., 1970; JD, Cleve. Marshall Coll. Law, 1981. Bar: Ohio 1981. Tchr. English Cleve. Pub. Schs., 1970; plant mgr. Union Gospel Press Pub. Co., Cleve., 1971-73; publ. specialist Cleve. State U., 1973-82; asst. U.S. atty. Dept. Justice, Cleve., 1982—93; U.S. atty. Cleve., 1993—2003. Precinct committeeman, Woodmere, Ohio, 1978; mem. Atty. Gen.'s Adv. Com. U.S. Attys., 1993—96, 1998—99, chmn. office mgmt. and budget subcom., 1993—2001, mem. asset forfeiture, civil issues, controlled substances and drug demand reduction, LECC/victim witness subcoms., 1993—2001; chmn. law enforcement coord. com. No. Dist. Ohio, 1993—2003. Recipient Eddy award for graphic design, 1977, Spl Achievement award U.S. Dept. Justice, 1985. Mem.: Fed. Bar Assn. Democrat. Office: US Atty's Office 1800 Bank One Ctr 600 Superior Ave E Ste 1800 Cleveland OH 44114-2600 also: US Attorneys Office 801 W Superior Ave Ste 400 Cleveland OH 44113

SWEENEY, JOYCE C. state representative; b. Colchester, Vt., July 23, 1928; 3 children. Grad., Edmunds H.S., Burlington, Vt. State rep. State of Vt., 2003—. Chairperson Bd. of Authority, 1999—; commr. Cemetery, Colchester; mem. Bd. of Auditors, Colchester, Bd. of Listers, Colchester; assessor Colchester; town clk.; treas.; past treas. United Ch. of Colchester, fin. sec. Mem.: Colchester Cemetery Assn. (clk., treas.). Republican. Protestant. Office: 1228 Main St Colchester VT 05446 E-mail: TheChoiceisJoyce@aol.com.

SWEENEY, LUCY GRAHAM, psychologist; b. Davenport, Iowa, Nov. 14, 1946; d. B. Graham and Dorothy (Lawson) S.; m. Richard N. Tiedemann, Dec. 2, 1978 (div. 1989); 1 child, Susan Lee; m. Rogers Stolen, June 28, 1997. AA, William Woods Coll., 1966; BA with honors, U. Denver, 1968; MA in Devel. Psychology, Columbia U., 1977; PsyD, Rutgers U., 1990. Cert. family therapist. Profl. actress, 1968-73; dir. therapeutic play and recreation program St. Luke's Med. Ctr., N.Y.C., 1973-78; child life coord. St. Francis Hosp., Hartford, Conn., 1978-80; clinician Resolve Community Counseling Ctr., Scotch Plains, N.J., 1981-84; staff psychologist women's inpatient unit Lyons (N.J.) VA Med. Ctr., 1990; psychologist women's treatment program Fair Oaks Hosp., Summit, N.J., 1990-92; cons. Kessler Inst. for Rehab., East Orange, N.J., 1992-94, Resolve Community Counseling Ctr., Scotch Plains, N.J., 1992—; pvt. practice Westfield, N.J., 1993-99, Blacksburg, Va., 1999—. Author: (plays) Hard Times Blues, 2003; contbr. articles to profl. jours. Recipient John Weyandt award for Outstanding Student in Theatre U. Denver, 1968. Mem.: APA. Home: 704 Cedarview Dr Blacksburg VA 24060-5906

SWEENEY, PATRICE ELLEN, health administration executive; b. Denver, Sept. 19, 1953; d. Floyd L. and Martha Lou (Ray) S.; m. Steven Michael Wilk, June 25, 1977; children: Adam, Kristen, Ryan. AB, Princeton U., 1975; MHA, Duke U., 1977. Adminstrn. resident U. Hosp. Jacksonville, Fla., 1977-78; fellow Am. Hosp. Assn., Blue Cross Blue Shield, Chgo., 1978-79; from dir. corp. svcs. to sr. corp. planner Md. Health Care System, Balt., 1979-82; spl. asst. to pres. Am. Hosp. Assn., Chgo., 1982-85; from dir. hosp. rels. to asst. v.p. hosp. rels. Premier Hosps. Alliance, Westchester, Ill., 1985-89, v.p. hosp. rels., 1989-95; v.p., owner, affiliate svcs. Premier, Inc., Westchester, 1996-99, sr. v.p. relationship mgmt., 1999—. Contbr. articles to profl. jours. NCAA wrestling announcer Princeton (N.J.) U., 1975, 81; nursing home visitor Manor Care, Balt., 1980-81; head room mother Lane Sch., Hinsdale, Ill., 1990-98; Sunday Sch. tchr. Union Ch., Hinsdale, 1992-96; bd. dirs. Rape Crisis Ctr., Balt., 1980-82. Population Inst. fellow, 1976-77; King Edward's Hosp. Fund fellow, 1977. Avocations: gardening, piano, cooking, needlework. Office: Premier Inc 700 Commerce Dr Oak Brook IL 60523

SWEENY, ANNE, broadcast executive; m. Philip Miller; 2 children. BA, Coll. New Rochelle; EdM, Harvard U. Sr. v.p. program enterprises Nickelodeon/Nick at Nite; chmn., CEO FX Networks, Inc., 1993; pres. Disney Channel, exec. v.p. Disney/ABC Cable Networks, 1996, pres., 1998—, Disney Channel, 1998—; pres. ABC Cable Networks Group, pres. Disney Channel Worldwide Walt Disney Co., Burbank, Calif., 2000—. Bd. dirs. Spl. Olympics, Walter Kaitz Found. Recipient Advocate Leader award, So. Calif. chpt. Women in Cable and Telecomms., 1998, STAR award, Am. Women in Radio and TV, 1995. Mem.: Women in Cable and Telecomms. (founder, Exec. of Yr. 1994, Woman of Yr. 1997). Office: 3800 W Alameda Ave Burbank CA 91505*

SWEET, LYNN D. journalist; b. Chgo., May 15, 1951; d. Jason and Ione Dover S. AB, U. Calif., Berkeley, 1973; MS in Journalism, Northwestern U., Evanston, Ill., 1975. Reporter Independent-Register, Libertyville, Ill., 1975-76, Chgo. Sun-Times, 1976-93, polit. writer, bur. chief Washington bur., 1993—; bur. chief Wash. bur. Chgo. Sun Times. Bd. dirs. Northwestern Univ.'s Medill Sch. of Journalism Alumni Bd., 1990-93. Office: Chgo Sun Times 1206 National Press Building Washington DC 20045-2200

SWEET, PORTIA ANN, retired human resources specialist; b. Charleston, W.Va., Jan. 14, 1939; BA, U. Houston, 1973. Sr. profl. in human resources. Adminstrv. mgr. Great Am. Ins. Co., Houston, Cin., Denver, 1973-81; cons., owner Sweet Encounters, Greeley, Colo., 1982-89; risk mgmt. splst. Hi/LO Auto Supply, Houston, 1991-94; human resources mgr. Chevron Products/MKTG, Houston, 1994-2000; ret., 2000. Vol. dir. Greeley Conv. Bur., 1986; bd. dirs. Women's Resource Ctr., Durango, Colo., 1988-89; vol. Houston Area Women's Ctr., 1990-91. Recipient Cert. Appreciation A Woman's Place, 1981. Mem. NAFE, NOW, Human Resources Mgmt. Assn. (bd. sec. 1995-96), Soc. Human Resources Mgmt., Houston Human Resources Mgmt. Assn., Risk and Ins. Mgmt. Soc., Ind. Ins. Agents (Big I). Episcopalian. Avocations: needlework, flower gardening, classical music. Home: 5800 Lumberdale Rd Apt 80 Houston TX 77092-1512 Office: Chevron Products Co 5959 Corporate Dr Houston TX 77036-2302

SWEETLAND, LORAINE FERN, librarian, educator; b. Morristown Corners, Vt., Aug. 13, 1933; d. William Eric and Sylbil Bedina (Bailey) Bloomfield; m. Ronald David Sweetland, July 1, 1950; children: Kathy L. (dec.), Dale J. Bettis. BS in Elem. Edn., Columbia Union Coll., 1968; MS in LS, Syracuse U., 1973. Tchr. 1st and 2d grade Beltsville (Md.) Seventh-day Adventist Sch., 1960-67; asst. libr., cataloger Vt. Tech. Coll., Randolph Ctr., 1968-69; middle sch. libr. Barre (Vt.) City Schs., 1970-74; tchg. prin. Cen. Vt. Seventh-day Adventist Sch., Barre, 1974-76, Brooklawn Seventh-day Adventist Sch., Bridgeport, Conn., 1976-81; med. libr. Washington Adventist Hosp., Takoma Park, Md., 1981-85; dir. libr. svcs. Seventh-day Adventists World Hdqs., Silver Spring, Md., 1985-95. Med. libr. cons., Balt., 1983-95; pres. Oasis, 1993-94; tchr. Home Study Internat., Silver Spring, Md., 1995-98, IPS-Info. Problem Solvers, Crossville, Tenn., 1998—. Book reviewer Libr. Jour., 1990-98. Trustee Randolph (Vt.) Pub. Library, 1970-71; sec. Nat. Area Hosp. Council, Washington, 1985; treas. Plateau Food Buying Club, 1999—. Mem. Laurel Rotary Club (bull. editor 1990-94). Republican. Avocations: gardening, computers, internet. E-mail: lauriefern@charter.net.

SWEETSER, SUSAN W. lawyer, advocate, former state legislator; b. Dec. 13, 1958; d. Robert Joseph and Lucretia Rose (Donnelly) Williams. BA in Polit. Sci./Environ. Adminstrn. with high honors, Johnson (Vt.) State Coll., 1982; JD magna cum laude, Vt. Law Sch., 1985; MBA, U. Pa., 2002. Bar: N.Y. 1986, Vt. 1986, U.S. Dist. Ct. Vt. 1989; CLU, ChFC, CFP. Confidential law clk. Appellate div. N.Y. Supreme Ct., Albany, 1985-86; assoc. Gravel & Shea, Burlington, Vt., 1986-90; atty. Nat. Life Ins. Co., Montpelier, Vt., 1990—2002; mem. Vt. State Senate, 1992-96; 2nd v.p. women's markets MassMutual Fin. Group. Victims rights adv. Essex Junction, Vt., 1980—; adj. prof. bus. law St. Michael's Coll., Winooski, Vt., 1991—, Johnson State Coll., 1995-97; justice of peace Town of Essex, 1991-95; chair judiciary com., 1994-96; mem. Health and Welfare Com.; former mem. Appropriations Com.; mem. Housing and Conservation Trust Fund Study Com., Civil Rights Study Com., Adoption Law Reform Study Com. Author articles on victims rights. Trustee Vt. State Colls., Waterbury, 1979-81, Univ. Health Ctr., 1992-94, bd. dirs.; mem. ethics com. Fanny Allen Hosp., Winooski, Vt., 1989-92; v.p. Lyric Theatre, Burlington, 1989-95; mem. Vt. Rep. State Com., Montpelier, chmn. Rep. State Conv., 1988, 92, 96; founder, pres. Survivors of Crime, Inc. Recipient Achievement award Vt. Law Enforcement Coordinating Com., 1990, Vt. Ctr. for Prevention and Treatment of Sexual Abuse and The Safer Soc. Program, 1991, Nat. recognition for victims rights work The Giraffe Project, 1991, award Nat. Found. for Improvement of Justice, 1993; named 754th Point of Light by former Pres. George Bush, 1992, Am. Heroine Ladies Home Jour., 1991, Legislator of Yr. Nat. Rep. Legislators Assn., 1995, Working Mother Mag. Working Mother of Yr., 1998. Fellow AAUW, Life Mgmt. Inst.; mem. Vt. Bar Assn., N.Y. State Bar Assn., Internat. Assn. Fin. Planners (chmn. legis. affairs Greater Vt. chpt. 1988-91). Roman Catholic. Avocations: skiing, flower gardening, running, camping, horseback riding. Office: 15 Cindy Ln Essex Junction VT 05452-3307

SWEIG, CHERRY ELIZABETH, artist, painter; BA in Art with honors and distinction, San Diego State U., 1978. Art dir. JT Racing, National City, Calif., 1980—82; computer graphics artist Copley Videotex/Time Inc., San Diego, 1982—83; video game designer Sega Electronics, San Diego, 1983; sr. art dir. Ashley Wayne Advt., San Diego, 1983—86; artist Gyotaku by Cherry Sweig, San Diego, 1986—, Artworks by Cherry Sweig, San Diego, 1986—. Curator art Chula Vista (Calif.) Nature Ctr., 1995—. Exhibitions include Chula Vista Nature Ctr. (Nat. Wildlife Refuge Sys. Award of Merit, 1997). Art cons. Chula Vista Nature Ctr., 2001—03. Mem.: Nature Printing Soc. (assoc.).

SWEIGART, ANNE B. communications company executive; With D&E Comms., Inc., Ephrata, Pa., 1936—, exec. v.p., 1981—85, CEO, 1985—2001, chmn. bd., pres., 1985—. Mem. bd. dirs. D&E Comms., Inc., 1952—. Office: D&E Communications Inc 124 E Main St Ephrata PA 17522

SWENSEN, MARY JEAN HAMILTON, graphic artist; b. Laurens, S.C., June 25, 1910; d. Elvin A. and Della (Brown) Hamilton; m. Oliver Severn Swensen, Mar. 3, 1943 (dec.). BS, Columbia U., 1956, MA, 1960; Cert. Notable, U. Madrid, Spain; postgrad., Ariz. State U., 1974-80. Mem. 1st USSA sr. internat. cross-country skiing team. One person shows at Colo. Fed. Savs. and Loan Assn., Denver, 1978, Panoras Gallery, N.Y.C., 1963; exhibited in group shows at Soc. Western Artist, M.H. de Young Mus., San Francisco, 1964, Nat. Art Roundup, Las Vegas, 1965, Fine Arts Bldg., Colo. State Fair, Pueblo, 1965, Duncan Gallery, Paris, 1974, Colo. Fed. Savs. & Loan Assn., Denver, 1978; graphics arts in pub. collections at Met. Mus. Art, N.Y.C., Nat. Graphic Arts Collection, Smithsonian Inst., Laurens (S.C.) Pub. Libr., N.Y.C. Pub. Libr. Assoc. Libr. of Congress, Archael. Inst. Am., Smithsonian Instn., Johns Hopkins. Recipient Duncan Gallery Prix de Paris, 1974, Notable award M.H. de Young Mus., 1964, YWCA of U.S.A. Gold Medal as most admired athlete of yr., 1977, USSA Nat. Vets. X-Country Racing Team Gold, Silver and Bronze medals for downhill, giant slalom, slalom, and cross-country sr. citizen and vet. races, 1963-79. Mem. Internat. Platform Assn., Am. Mensa, Columbia Club N.Y., Delta Phi Delta.

SWENSON, CONSTANCE N. artist; b. Mpls., Aug. 7, 1920; d. Marion Edward and Myrtle Evelyn Norman; widowed June, 1994; children: Norman, David Erik, Stephen Scott. Student, Mpls. Sch. Art, Gustavus Adolphus Coll. Home: 1722 Lakeview Dr SW Rochester MN 55902-4228

SWENSON, DIANE KAY, lawyer; b. Sioux Falls, S.D., June 16, 1952; d. Clarence Donald and Mildred Ann (Meyer) S. BA magna cum laude, Augustana Coll., 1974; JD, Hamline U., 1981. Bar: Minn. 1981. Tchr. Malvern (Iowa) Pub. Schs., 1974-76, Rosemount Pub. Schs., Apple Valley, Minn., 1976-78; legis. asst. to Senator Larry Pressler, U.S. Senate, Washington, 1981-86; exec. v.p. Am. Tort Reform Assn., Washington, 1986-99, Nat. Assn. Fed. Credit Unions, Washington, 1999—. V.p. Emmanual Luth. Ch., Bethesda, Md., 1997. Mem. ABA. Republican. Lutheran. Avocation: skiing. Home: 6140 Stonehenge Place Rockville MD 20852-5807 Office: Nat Assn Fed Credit Unions 3138 10th St N Arlington VA 22201-2149 Business E-Mail: dswenson@nafcunet.org.

SWENSON, SUE, foundation administrator, former health and education administrator; married; 3 children. BA, MA, U. Chgo.; MBA, U. Minn. Mktg. mgr. Barr Engring., Minn. Heart and Lund Inst., U. Minn.; commr. Adminstrn. on Developmental Disabilities, 1998—2001; exec. dir. Joseph P. Kennedy Jr. Foundation, Washington, 2001—. Cons. subcom. on disability policy U.S. Senate, Washington. Fellow Joseph P. Kennedy Jr. Found., 1996. Office: Joseph P Kennedy Jr Found 1325 G St NW Ste 500 Washington DC 20005

SWENSON, TREE (HOLLY), poet; Undergrad., U. Calif., 1969—72; MPA in Nonprofit Mgmt., Harvard U., 1996. Co-founder, exec. dir., pub. Copper Canyon Press, Port Townsend, Wash., 1972—93; dir. programs Mass. Cultural Coun., 1997—2002; exec. dir. Acad. Am. Poets, N.Y.C., 2002—. Art dir. Graywolf Press, 1984—93; lectr. Emerson Coll., 1993—97; coord. PEN New Eng., 1993—97; book designer W.W. Norton, 1993—97, Graywolf Press, 1993—97, Ecco Press, 1993—97, Sarabande Books, 1993—97, New Directions, 1993—97; cord. pub. module grad. writing seminars Bennington Coll., 1993—2002; grant fellowship panel Nat. Endowment for Arts, N.Y. State Coun. on Arts, Wash. State Arts Commn., Ill. Arts Coun.; mem. leadership devel. com. Nat. Assembly State Arts Agys., 1999—2002. Grantee grantee, Nat. Endowment for Arts, Lila Wallace-Reader's Digest Fund, Andrew W. Mellon Found. Office: Acad Am Poets 584 Broadway Ste 604 New York NY 10012-3210

SWENSSON, EVELYN DICKENSON, conductor, composer, librettist; b. Woodstock, Va., Sept. 18, 1928; d. Glenn Gilmer and Evelyn Christine (Ring) Dickenson; m. Sigurd Simcox Swensson, June 9, 1949; children: Lisë, Karen, Erik, Jon. Cert. in piano, Ward-Belmont Coll., 1946; BA in Piano and Voice, Hollins Coll., 1949; MusM, Westchester U., 1972. Condr. Aldersgate Meth. Ch., Wilmington, Del., 1969—2002, Brandywiners Ltd., Kennett Sq., Pa., 1973-86, Opera Del., Wilmington, 1974—, Bi-Centennial Chorus, Wilmington, 1976; guest condr. Del. Symphony Orch., Wilmington, 1977; condr. Ardensingers, Wilmington, 1978-80; condr. 200th Anniversary Meth. Ch. Am., Balt., 1984. V.p. Opera for Youth Inc.; dir. family opera theater Opera Del., Wilmington, 1974—. Condr.: inaugural concert for Gov. P.S. duPont IV, 1977, Sleeping Beauty (Respighi), 1977, The Zoo (Sullivan and Rowe), 1980, The Lion, the Witch and the Wardrobe (John McCabe), 1980, celebration of Swedes Landing, 1988, The Boy Who Grew Too Fast (Menotti), 1982, Charlotte's Web (Strouse), 1989, A Wrinkle in Time (Larsen), 1992, composer, condr.: The Enormous Egg, 1993, The Adventure of Beatrix Potter, 1994, The Jungle Book, 1995, Anne of Green Gables, 1996, The Homecoming, 1997, The Legend of Redwall Abbey, 1998, All Through the Night, 1999, The Trumpet of the Swan, 2000, The Mixed-Up Files of Mrs. Basil E. Frankweiler, 2002, "Billy Lee" Washington, 2003, The Secret of NIMH, 2004. Recipient W. W. Laird Music award, Opera Del., Wilmington, 1987, Internat. Reading Coun. Literacy award, 1989, Disting. Alumna award, West Chester U., 1989, 5 competition awards, Nat. League Am. Pen Women, 2000, Outstanding Svc. award, Nat. Opera ASsn., 2004. Mem.: Am. Guild Organists (choir master). Home: 166 Heyburn Rd Chadds Ford PA 19317

SWERDLOW, ROBERTA DYAS, educational consultant; d. Sandford Miller and Hyn Lee Dyas; m. Arthur Mayer Swerdlow, Jan. 20, 1979; 1 child, Jonathan Dyas Sysel. BSc, U. of Nebr., 1962—66; MA, Colo. State U., 1967—69. Chief, info. mgmt. br. U.S. Dept. of Agr., Washington, 1990—2001; pres. IPC Corp., Arlington, Va., 2001—. Dir. of english as a second lang. Armenian Agrl. Acad., Yerevan, Armenia, 1998—99. Recipient Secretary's Award of Excellence, U.S. Dept. of Agr., 1988. Avocation: travel. Office: IPC Corporation 6312 Seven Corners Ctr#115 Falls Church VA 22044 E-mail: raswerdlow@hotmail.com.

SWERGOLD, MARCELLE MIRIAM, sculptor; b. Antwerp, Belgium, Sept. 6, 1927; Student, NYU, Arts Students League, Sculptors Workshop. Sculptor, 1965—. One woman exbhns. include: Studio 12, N.Y.C., 1980, 82, 86, Nat. Fedn. Temple Sisterhoods, 1984; group exbhns. include Farleigh Dickinson U., Teaneck, N.J., 1972, Womanart Gallery, 1977, 78, Audubon Artist Ann., N.Y.C., 1978, 86, 88, 89, 90, 91, 92, 93, Am. Friends of Hebrew U., 1978, Internat. Treasury Fine Arts, Plainview, N.Y., 1979, Studio 12, 1980, 82, 86, New Britain (Conn.) Mus., 1980, also Cork Gallery, Lincoln Ctr., N.Y.C., Allied Artists Nat. Acad. Galleries, N.Y.C., U.S. Custom House, N.Y.C., others; represented in permanent collection New Britain Mus. Am. Art, in sculpture garden of Yad Vashem-Holocaust Mus., Jerusalem, Monument in the Park of the City of Ma'aleh Adumim, Israel, Sculpture in lobby at Fairlawn (N.J.) Jewish Ctr., Holocaust Meml. in lobby of Jewish Ctr., N.Y., Shaare Zedek Med. Ctr. in Jerusalem; represented in pvt. collection of Master Moshe Castel, Israel, Norman Levy, Harts Mountain Industries, Inc., Imri Rosenthal, Rosenthal and Rosenthal, N.Y., Itzrak Devier, Tel-Aviv, Mudge, Rose, Guthrie & Alexander, N.Y., Sylvian Sternberg, Jerusalem, others. Recipient Best in Show award for Tetons, Woman's Art Gallery, N.Y.C., 1977, 1st prize for sculpture Stanley Richter Assn. Arts, 1985, Vincent Glinski Meml. award Aububon Artists, 1986. Mem. N.Y. Soc. Women Artists (pres. 1979-81, exec. v.p. 1981—), Artists Equity, Contemporary Artists Guild. Home: 450 W End Ave New York NY 10024-5307 Studio: 246 W 80th St New York NY 10024-5705

SWETKIS, DOREEN L. advocate, educator, writer; b. Cleve., Oct. 13, 1969; d. Julius and Dolores Rita Swetkis; m. Marc R. Greenwald. B of Liberal studies, Bowling Green State U., Ohio, 1991; MEd, Cleve. (Ohio) State U., 1998. Rsch. asst. Met. Strategy Group, Cleve. Heights, Ohio, 1995—96; fair housing enforcement Cuyahoga Plan of Ohio, Inc., Cleve., 1996—98; grad. asst. Cleve. (Ohio) State U., 1997—2002, adj. prof., 2000—. Assoc. dir. Housing Advocates, Inc., Cleve., 2002—; cons. in field. Vol. Cuyahoga Plan of Ohio, Inc., Cleve., 1998—99. Mem.: Urban Affairs Assn., Pub. Adminstrn. Rsch. and Therapy, Am. Soc. Pub. Adminstrn. Office: Housing Advocates Inc 3655 Prospect Ave Cleveland OH 44115

SWETNAM, RUTH E. DANGLADE, curriculum director; b. Marion, Ind., Jan. 27, 1940; d. Harold Davis and Elizabeth (Lake) Neel; m. James K. Danglade, Sept. 2, 1961 (div. Nov. 1979); children: Annette, John, Douglas, Adam, Matthew; m. Gary L. Swetnam, June 19, 1993. BS, Ball State U., 1961, MA, 1964. Cert. elem., secondary bus., spl. edn. and speech pathology tchr., sch. adminstrn., Ind. Tchr. orthopedically handicapped Muncie (Ind.) Community Schs., 1961-67, tchr. of multiply handicapped, 1969-74, tchr. learning disabled, 1976-79; spl. edn. instr. Ball State U., Muncie, 1974-79; asst. dir. spl. edn. Delaware County Spl. Edn. Coop., Muncie, 1979-91; dir. curriculum Muncie Community Schs., 1991-98; dir. Inst. Cmty. Edn. Devel. and Sch. Improvement Ball State U., Muncie, 1998—2000; dir. Profl. Devel. Schs., Ball State U., 2000—; profl. devel. cons., 1998—. Sci. curriculum cons. NSF, Muncie, 1976-78; learning disabilities instr. Ball State U., 1974-80. Bd. dirs. Delaware County Easter Seal Soc., Minnetrista Cultural Found., Inc.; chairperson adv. coun. Ball State U. Coll. Bus., 1985-90; mem. adminstrv. bd. High St. United Meth. Ch., Muncie, 1984-88, youth coord., 1985-88; mem. adv. bd. Delaware County 4-H, 1991-98; chair allocations panel United Way of Delaware County, chmn. budget panel; mem. Muncie StarPress Ptnrs. for Literacy Adv. Bd. Mem. Coun. Exceptional Children (past pres. Delaware County chpt. 1977-78), Nat. Staff Devel. Coun., Ind. Staff Devel. Coun., Muncie-Delaware County C. of C. (bus. edn. partnership), Phi Delta Kappa, Pi Beta Phi. Methodist. Avocations: music, reading, traveling, walking, hiking. Office: Ball State U Teachers College 1003 Muncie IN 47306-0001 E-mail: rswetnam@bsu.edu.

SWIERBUT, WENDI MARIE, electrochemist; b. Youngstown, Ohio, Apr. 13, 1966; d. James Richard and Marie Elana (Evans) Price; m. Roger Allen Swierbut II, Sept. 25, 1993. BS cum laude, Youngstown State U., 1992; postgrad., U. Notre Dame. Product devel. engr. Energizer Battery Co., Westlake, Ohio, 1992-95; product mgr. Radiometer Am. Inc., Westlake, 1995-97; regional sales mgr. EG&G Instruments, Inc., Oak Ridge, Tenn., 1997—. Course dir. Exec. Women's Golf League, Cleve., 1994-96. Mem. Women in Sci., Electrochem. Soc., Nat. Assn. Corrosion Engrs. Republican. Roman Catholic. Achievements include 3 U.S. patents, 1 Taiwanese patent, numerous patents pending. Office: EG&G Instruments Inc 100 Midland Rd Oak Ridge TN 37830-9102 Home: 13058 Acacia Dr Grand Haven MI 49417-8888

SWIFT, JANE MARIA, former governor; b. North Adams, Mass., Feb. 24, 1965; d. John Maynard and Jean Mary (Kent) S.; m. Charles T. Hunt III, Feb. 19, 1994. BA in Am. Studies, Trinity Coll., Hartford, Conn., 1987. Exec. mgmt. trainee G. Fox. & Co., Hartford, 1987-88; adminstrv. aide Sen. Peter C. Webber, Boston, 1988-90; mem. Mass. State Senate, Boston, 1991-96, 3d asst. minority leader, 1993-96; coord. strategic devel. of regional airports Mass. Port Authority, Boston, 1997; dir. consumer affairs and bus. regulation Commonwealth of Mass., lt. gov., 1999-2001, gov., 2001—03. 3d asst. minority leader, 1993-96. Republican. Roman Catholic.*

SWIFT, KATHARINE I. cytotechnologist; b. Providence, Sept. 17, 1946; d. Oscar and Mary (Polly) Bergstrom; children: James P., Suzanne. BS, Empire State Coll., 1996. Cert. cytotechnologist. Cytology supr. St. James Hosp., Hornell, NY, 1986—93, Noyes Meml. Hosp., Dansville, NY, 1988—2000, Corning (N.Y.) Hosp., 1993—. Worked with Pan Am. Med. Mission setting up lab in San Cosme, Mex. Elder, United Presbyn. Ch., Hornell, 1993—; vol. case worker Tri County Housing, Steuben County, N.Y., 1994-99; case worker Interfaith Caregivers, Steuben County, 1996—; mem. Red Cross Disaster Team, Steuben County, 1999—, outreach caseworker, Red Cross, Ground Zero, N.Y.C., 2002; literacy vol., Steuben County, 1993-97; mem. peacemaking com. Geneva Presbytery, 2000—; mem. subcom. on mission to Mex., 1999—. Mem. Am. Soc. Cytology, Upper N.Y. State Soc. Cytology, Student Alumni Assn. Empire State Coll. (v.p. 1996-99, bd. govs. 1999—). Avocations: restoring homes, cross country skiing, travel. Address: Evening Tribune Maple City Dr Hornell NY 14843 Home: 5235 Nipher Rd Bath NY 14810

SWIFT, MARILYN K. artist, educator; b. Derby, Conn., Dec. 3, 1945; d. Andrew J. and Mary Jasinski Dudik; m. Lawrence A. Swift, July 19, 1969; children: David L., Kathryn A. BA, Coll. of New Rochelle, 1963—67. Art tchr. Norwood Pub. Schools, Norwood, Mass., 1967—70. Mem. of bd. of governors Rockport Art Assn., Mass., 1980—85; sec. New Eng. Watercolor Soc., Boston, 1993—96, Cape Ann Artisans, Gloucester, Mass., 2002—. Fellow: Hudson Valley Arts Assn.; mem.: Am. Artists Profl. League, Academic Artists of Springfield, North Shore Arts Assn., The Copley Soc. of Boston (life), Rockport Art Assn., New Eng. Watercolor Soc. Independent. Roman Catholic. Office: Swift Studio 20 rear Highland St Gloucester MA 01930 E-mail: mswiftstudio@adelphia.net.

SWIFT, MARY LOU, art dealer, financial consultant; b. Syracuse, N.Y., July 25, 1942; d. Andrew G. Swift and E.R. Ensle. BA, Sarah Lawrence Coll., Bronxville, N.Y., 1964; postgrad, U. Pa., 1964-66, NYU Bus. Sch., 1967-69, N.Y. Inst. Finance, 1967-69. Registered stockbroker N.Y. Stock Exch. and Nat. Assn. Securities Dealers. Adminstrv. head of syndicate dept. Drexel Harriman Ripley, N.Y.C., 1966-71; product mgr. Fieldcrest Mills, N.Y.C., 1971-74; acct. supr. advtg. Rosenfeld Sirowitz Lawson, N.Y.C., 1974-76, BBDO, N.Y.C., 1976-78, Cavalieri, Kleier, Pearlman, N.Y.C., 1978-79; bus., mktg. cons. Mary Lou Swift & Co., N.Y.C., 1979-81; instnl. stockbroker Mabon Securities, N.Y.C., 1981-91; Gerard Klauer Mattison, N.Y.C., 1992-93; pvt. art dealer internat. modern and contemporary art Mary Lou Swift Fine Arts, N.Y.C., 1994—. Cons. Miller Tabak & Co., Inc., 1994—. Recipient Undergraduate Fellowship (2) Am. Mus. Nat. History, 1962, 63. Avocations: golf, travel, languages. Office: Mary Lou Swift Fine Arts 148 W 23d St New York NY 10011

SWIFT-HOWARD, ALICE LORRAINE, school system administrator; b. Huntington Valley, Pa., Oct. 1, 1965; d. Robert Pink Swift Sr. and Beatrice Yvonne Swift; m. Lewis Dwayne Howard, Jan. 6, 2001; 1 child, Jordan Pink Lewis Howard. BA in Speech Curriculum, U. Md., 1990; M of Curriculum & Supv., Trinity Coll., 2003. From tchr., rschr., evaluator to asst. prin. Largo High Sch., Upper Marlboro, Md., asst. prin., 2004—. Mem.: Alpha Kappa Alpha. Avocations: reading, dollhouses, home decorating, travel, writing. Home: 331 Atwater Dr Annapolis MD 21401 Office: PGCPSS/Largo High Sch 505 Largo Rd Upper Marlboro MD 20772 Office Phone: 301-808-8880 x262. E-mail: alice.swift@pgcps.org.

SWIG, ROSELYNE CHROMAN, community consultant; b. Chgo., June 8, 1930; m. Richard Swig, Feb. 5, 1950 (dec.); children— Richard, Jr., Susan, Marjorie, Carol. Student, U. Calif.-Berkeley, UCLA; MFA (hon.), DHL (hon.), San Francisco Art Inst., 1988. Founder, pres. Roselyne C. Swig Artsource, San Francisco, 1977-94; apptd. by Pres. Clinton as dir. Art in Embassies Program U.S. Dept. of State, 1994-97; founder, pres. Comcon Internat., 1998—. Founder Ptnrs. Ending Domestic Abuse, San Francisco. Trustee San Francisco Mus. Modern Art, U. Art Mus., Berkeley, Calif.; ex officio bd. mem. Jewish Mus. San Francisco; bd. dirs., former treas. Am. Jewish Joint Distbn. Com.; vice chair fine art adv. panel Fed. Res., Washington; past trustee Mills Coll., Oakland, Calif.; past past pres., bd. dirs. Jewish Cmty. Fedn. San Francisco, the Peninsula, Marin and Sonoma Counties; past commr. San Francisco Pub. Libr.; past bd. dirs. San Francisco Opera, Am. Coun. for Arts, KQED Broadcasting Sys.; past. pres. Calif. State Summer Sch. Arts, past chair bd. trustees San Francisco Art Inst.; past pres. San Francisco Arts Commn.; past nat. v.p. Am./Israel Pub. Affairs Com.; past trustee United Jewish Appeal; past chair bd. trustees Univ. Art Mus. Mem. Women's Forum West (bd. dirs.), Internat. Women's Forum. Avocations: skiing, boating, tennis, fishing.

SWIGART, JOAN B. artist, art consultant; b. Peoria, Ill., Jan. 30, 1930; d. Claude S. and Elvera V. (Seeber) Bradley; m. Lynn S. Swigart, Mar. 30, 1952; children: Christopher, Paul Tag, Ann, Leigh. Student, Bradley U., 1948-50, 79-81, Ill. State U., Normal, 1981-84. Dir. multimedia arts inst. Bradley U., Peoria, 1973, 74, program dir. Econs. Fair, 1976, 77; artist-in-residence for several Ill. sch. dists. Ill. Arts Coun., Chgo., 1983, 84, 85. Vice pres. bd. dirs., chair cultural outreach Peoria Arts and Sci. Coun., 1986—88; chair pub. art com. Peoria City Beautiful Commn., 1986—88; bd. dirs. Peoria Art Guild, 1969—88; chair resident artist coun. Westport (Conn.) Art Ctr., 1990—92; bd. dirs. Gloucester (Mass.) Cultural Coun., chmn., 2002—. Exhibited in numerous solo, 2-person and group exhbns., 1980—. Dir. Sch. of Art, Peoria Art Guild, 1972-76; bd. dirs. Peoria Arts Festival, 1987-88, Urban League, Peoria, 1970-76, Planned Parenthood, Peoria, 1981-86; mem. edn. com. Lakeview Mus., 1985-88. Grantee Ill. Arts Coun., 1983, 84, 85. Democrat. Home: 13 Marble Rd Gloucester MA 01930-4324 Office: Swigart Studios 123 Main St Gloucester MA 01930-4324

SWIGER, ELINOR PORTER, lawyer; b. Cleve., Aug. 1, 1927; d. Louie Charles and Mary Isabelle (Shank) Porter; m. Quentin Gilbert Swiger, Feb. 5, 1955; children: Andrew Porter, Calvin Gilbert, Charles Robinson. BA, Ohio State U., 1949, JD, 1951. Bar: Ohio 1951, Ill. 1979. Sr. assoc., now of counsel Robbins, Schwartz, Nicholas, Lifton & Taylor, Ltd., Chgo., 1979—. Author: (book) Mexico for Kids, 1971, Europe for Young Travelers, 1972, The Law and You, 1973 (Literary Guild award), Law in Everyday Life, 1977, Careers in the Legal Professions, 1978, Women Lawyers at Work, 1978. Mem. Glenview (Ill.) Fire and Police Commn., 1976—86; chmn. Glenview Zoning Bd. Appeals, 1987—97. Mem.: Chgo. Bar Assn. (chmn. legis. exec. com. 1990—92), Women Bar Assn. Ill., Ill. Coun. Sch. Attys. (past chmn.), Ohio State U. Coll. Law Alumni Coun., Soc. Midland Authors. Republican. Home: 1933 Burr Oak Dr Glenview IL 60025 Office: Robbins Schwartz Nicholas Lifton & Taylor 20 N Clark St Ste 900 Chicago IL 60602-4115

SWIGER, ELIZABETH DAVIS, chemist, educator; b. Morgantown, W Va, June 27, 1926; d. Hannibal Albert and Tyreeca Elizabeth (Stemple) Davis; m. William Eugene Swiger, June 2, 1948 (dec.); children: Susan Elizabeth Swiger Knotts-Case, Wayne William. BS in Chemistry, W.Va. U., 1948, MS in Chemistry, 1952, PhD in Chemistry, 1964. Instr. math. Fairmont State Coll., 1948-49, instr. math. and phys. sci., 1956-57, instr. chemistry, 1957-60, from asst. prof. to assoc. prof., 1960—66, prof., 1966-92, chmn., divsn. sci., math, and health careers, 1991-92; NSF fellow rsch. W.Va. U., Morgantown, 1963-64, prof. emerita, 1992. Advisor Am. Chem. Soc. student affiliates, 1965-88. Author: Morton Family History, 1984-98, Davis-Winters Family History, 1994—, Civil War Letters and Diary of Joshua Winters, 1991, 2d edit., 1996; contbr. articles to profl. jour. Chmn. Blacks Chapel Meml. Found., 1993—; rep. adv. coun. to Bd. Regents Fairmont State Coll., Charleston, W.Va., 1977—78, rep. instl. bd. advisors, 1990—92. NSF grantee, 1963; named Outstanding Prof. W.Va. Legislature, Charleston, 1990. Mem.: Am. Chem. Soc. (advisor student affiliates 1965—88, sec. chmn. North W.Va. 1975—83), W.Va. Acad. Sci. (life; pres. 1978—79, exec. com. edn. chmn. 1990—93), Nature Conservancy (bd. dir. W.Va. chpt. 1970—86, chmn. 1980—82), Marion County Hist. Soc. (life), Prickett's Fort Meml. Found. (life; bd. dir. 1988—2000, chmn. elect 1990—92, chmn. 1992—96, bd. dir 2002—), Morning Gardeners Garden Club (pres. 1999—, 1999—2003). Republican. Methodist. Avocations: local history, local history, genealogy, gardening, computers, quilting. Home: 1599 Hillcrest Rd Fairmont WV 26554-4807 also: 242 Laird Dr Freeport FL 32439

SWILDENS, KARIN JOHANNA, sculptor; b. Amsterdam, The Netherlands, June 22, 1942; arrived in U.S., 1979; d. Petrus Bernardus Swildens and Ceclia Thecla Maria Vernimmen; m. Gilles Roger Basset, Mar. 25, 1963 (div. Jan. 1968); children: Eric Gilles Basset, Laurent Patrice Basset; m. Claude Maurice Gaignaire, June 28, 1972; 1 child, Gazelle Gaignaire. Diploma in art, L'Ecole des Arts Decoratifs, Paris, 1963. Exhibitions include Speak Easy Gallery, L.A., Waldo Collection, West Hollywood, Calif., Trios Gallery, Solana Beach, Calif., Tops, Malibu, Calif., Hamilton Gallery, Santa Monica, Calif., Glass Garage Gallery, West Hollywood, Calif., The Figurative Gallery, La Quinta, Calif. Vol. instr. Brentwood Unified Sci. Magnet Sch., 1979—82. Recipient Daumier Sculpture award, 1993. Home and Office: 1872 Midvale Ave Apt 303 Los Angeles CA 90025-6349 E-mail: karinswildens@earthlink.net.

SWING, MARCE, producer, publisher; b. Wichita, Kans., Dec. 3, 1943; d. Eldon Derry and Ruth (Biddle) S. Bus. mgr. Old Westport Med. Assn., Kansas City, Mo., 1972-73; dept. chmn., instr. Ft. Bragg (N.C.) Nursery and Kindergarten, 1965-66, Luth. Schs., Tex. Dist., Irving, 1966-68, Kansas City (Kans.) Sch. Dist. 500, 1973-78, Extension Dept. U. Calif., Northridge, 1979-82, Pima Coll., Tucson, 1983-84, Kinder Care, Lake Buena Vista, Fla., 1989-90; TV/motion picture exec. producer, dir., writer Swing Prodns., Orlando, Fla., 1989—; owner, pres. Swing Enterprises/Swing Prodns., Orlando, 1978—, Living for Edn., Inc., Orlando, 1994—; owner Edn. in the New Millennium, Inc., 2002; founder, pres. Digital Media Arts Incubator Lab, Inst. Ind. Filmmakers, Orlando, Fla.; projects prodr. read24-7.com. Exec. mgmt., acctg. andmktg. cons. to major internat. corps.; lectr., seminar instr., guest speaker, anchorperson, moderator, panelist. Exec. producer, dir., writer, featured talent on-air live and taped programming for networks, network affiliates and cable, feature motion pictures, on air internationally and web sites, interactive TV episodes, with mdse, 34 children's books and CD ROMS, puppets and collectables, V series, mini series, 30 celebrity profiles, 36 documentaries, 14 televents, 45 pub. svc. spots, 30 minute infomat, 12-hour entertinment Christmas Eve project; developer entertainment informational, ednl. and indsl. TV programs and videos; contbr. articles to profl. jours. Corp. adminstr., TV exec. producer, dir., fundraiser nat. hdqrs. March of Dimes, White Plains, N.Y., 1984-86, Arthritis Found., Atlanta, 1985; ofcl. hostess Seattle World's Fair; mem. Nat. Task Force for Child Care, Nat. Task Force for Youth Suicide, Nat. Task Force for Child Abuse; mem. Ariz. Commn. on Arts. Recipient local, regional and nat. art and craft awards. Mem. NEA, NAFE, AAUW, Am. Mgmt. Assn., Nat. Assn. Women Artists, Profl. Assn. Producers and Dirs., Nat. Printmaker's Assn., Nat. Thespian Soc., Thousand Oaks Art Assn., Internat. Digital Media Arts Alliance (founding mem.), Orange County, Fla. Govt. Arts and Cultural Affairs, Coun. Art Edn. and Resources, Show of Hands Gallery, Nat. Youth Camps. Lutheran. Avocations: reading, writing, photography, cooking, mural painting.

SWING, MARILYN S. metropolitan clerk; b. Nashville, Tenn., Aug. 21, 1949; BA, St. Mary of the Woods, Terre Haute, Ind., 1976. Adminstr. metro clerks office Govt. City of Nashville, Davidson County, Nashville, 1976—, metro clerk, 1984—. Bd. dirs. Municipal Clerks Edn. Found., 1992-99. Mem. Internat. Inst. Municipal Clerks. Office: Metropolitan Government of Nashville and Davidson County Metro Clerk 205 Metro Courthouse Nashville TN 37201-5026

SWINNEY, CAROL JOYCE, secondary school educator; Langs. tchr. Hugoton (Kans.) High Sch., 1972-98; dir. distance learning S.W. Plains Regional Svcs. Ctr., Kans., 1998—. Named Kans. Tchr. of Yr., Disney for Lang. Tchr. of Yr., 1993, Milken Nat. Educator, 1992. Office: PO Drawer 1010 Sublette KS 67877-1010

SWINNEY, JEANNE LYN, music educator; b. Maywood, Calif., July 30, 1964; d. Kenneth Earl and Sylvia Jeanne Nickels; m. Kirby Cleveland Swinney Jr., July 1, 1989; children: Adrian, Caitlyn. BA, Northeastern State U., Tahlequah, Okla., 1988. Cert. tchr. Okla. Vocal and instrumental music tchr. Barnsdall (Okla.) Pub. Schs., 1988—95; elem. music tchr. Shawnee (Okla.) Pub. Schs., 1995—. Mem. Jubilee Club, Barnsdall, 1988—92; 2d chair trombonist Bartlesville (Okla.) Symphony Orch., 1990—95. Named one of Outstanding Young Women of Am., 1997; grantee Music Tech., Shawnee Edn. Found., 1999, 2003. Mem.: Shawnee Assn. Classroom Tchrs. (pres. 2001—03), Okla. Edn. Assn., Okla. Music Educators Assn. Democrat. Methodist. Avocations: music, oil painting.

SWINTON, SONYA DEVONNE, government agency administrator; b. Muskogee, Okla., Dec. 3, 1957; d. Billy Clarence Swinton and Edna Lonetta Atkinson (Eggleston) Swinton. BS, U. Ark., 1980; MEd, Pa State U., 1982. Mgmt. divsn. Corp. For Cmty. and Nat. Svc., Washington, 1994—; cable tv coord. Cablevision, Inc.- Govt. Channel, New Carrollton, Md., 1987—94; edn. adminstr. USMC, Quanitico, Japan, 1982—86. Dir. Children's Cable TV Workshop-Entertainment Divsn., New Carrollton, 1987—90; exec. dir. Cmty. TV USA Network, Washington, DC, 1990—; v.p. advt. & mktg. Swinton Internat. Enterprises, Washington, 2000—. Author: (book) STAR POWER: Internet Celebrity, 2002, ROYAL DESTINY: USA, 2003. Chief executor Royal Swinton Soc., Washington, 2002. Sgt. USMC, 1982—86, Okinawa,Japan and Quanitco, VA. Named disting. alumna award, Nat. Assn. for Equal Opportunity in Higher Edn., 1998; recipient Cmty. Svc. Award, Taste of DC Festival Commn., 2001. Mem.: Soc. of Motion Picture & TV Engineers, Royal TV Soc. of N.Am., Nat. Acad. of TV Arts & Sciences (awards com. 1998), Am. Women In Radio TV (photographer 1998), Nat. Acad. of Rec. Arts & Sciences (assoc.; musicare bd. 1999), Royal Photographic Soc. of Gt. Britain. Baptist. Avocation: photography, sports and writing. Office: Community TV USA Network L'EnFant Plaza PO 23722 Suite 400 Washington DC 20026 Office Phone: 202-945-8716. Business E-Mail: SonyaS@ctvnusa.com.

SWIRE, EDITH WYPLER, music educator, musician, violist, violinist; b. Boston, Feb. 16, 1943; d. Alfred R. Wypler Jr. and Frances (Glenn) Emery Wypler; m. James Bennett Swire, June 11, 1965; 1 child, Elizabeth Swire Falker. BA, Wellesley (Mass.) Coll., 1965; MFA, Sarah Lawrence Coll., Bronxville, N.Y., 1983; postgrad., Coll. of New Rochelle, 1984-85; student prof. studies master prog. in health advocacy, Sarah Lawrence Coll., 2000—. Tchr. instrumental music, viola, violin The Windsor Sch., Boston, 1965-66; tchr., dir. The Lenox Sch., N.Y.C., 1967-76; music curriculum devel. The Nightingale-Bamford Sch., N.Y.C., 1968-69; head of fine arts dept. The Lenox Sch., N.Y.C., 1976-78, head of instrumental music, 1978-80; founder, dir., tchr. of string sch. Serpentine String Sch., Larchmont, 1981—96. Mem. founding com. Inter Sch. Orch., N.Y.C., 1972, trustee, 1976—; panelist Nat. Assn. Ind. Sch. Conf., N.Y.C., 1977. Mem. music and worship com., Larchmont Ave. Ch., 1978-82, 88. Mem. Westchester Musicians Guild, N.Y. State Music Tchrs. Assn., Music Tchrs. Nat. Assn., Music Tchrs. Coun. Westchester (program com.), Violin Soc. Am., Wellesley in Westchester, Am. String Tchrs. Assn., The Viola Soc. of N.Y. Avocations: chamber music, mind/body connections. Home and Office: 11 Serpentine Trail Larchmont NY 10538-2618

SWIT, LORETTA, actress; b. N.J., Nov. 4, 1939; Student, Am. Acad. Dramatic Arts, Gene Frankel Repertoire Theatre, N.Y.C. Broadway appearances include Same Time Next Year, Any Wednesday, Mame, The Mystery of Edwin Drood, Shirley Valentine, Chgo. (winner Sarah Siddons award 1990); films include Stand Up and Be Counted, 1972, Freebie and the Bean, 1974, Race with the Devil, 1975, S.O.B, 1980, Beer, 1985, Whoops Apocalypse (U.K.), 1987, Forest Warrior, 1996, Boardheads, 1999; star TV series M*A*S*H, 1972-83 (Emmy awards 1979, 81); TV movies include Shirts/Skins, 1973, The Last Day, 1975, Mirror, Mirror, 1979, Valentine, 1979, Friendships, Secrets and Lies, 1979, Cagney and Lacey, 1981, Games Mother Never Taught You, 1982, First Affair, 1983, The Execution, 1985, Dreams of Gold: The Mel Fisher Story, 1986, My Dad Can't Be Crazy, Can He?, Hell Hath No Fury, 1992, A Killer Among Friends, 1993, Forest Warrior, 1996; star on major dramatic shows and musical variety shows, including Bob Hope Christmas Special, Perry Como, The Muppets. Mem. AFTRA, Screen Actors Guild, Actors Equity. Address: Artists Group Ltd 10100 Santa Monica Blvd Los Angeles CA 90067-4003

SWITLO, JANICE GEORGINA ALICE E. barrister, solicitor, mediator, legal and business consultant, strategist; b. Vancouver, B.C., Can., Jan. 10, 1959; d. Alexander Donald and Mary (Shutka) Switlo; married; 1 child. LLB, Osgoode Hall, Toronto, 1986; B.Commerce, U. B.C., 1981. Mgmt. cons. Control Data Can. Ltd., Vancouver, 1981-83; articled student Ladner Downs, 1986—87; barrister, solicitor Aydin & Co., Vancouver, 1987-88; legal counsel Dept. Justice of Can., Vancouver, 1989-93; gen. counsel Westbank Indian Band, Westbank, B.C., 1993-94; barrister, solicitor, cons. Switlo & Co., Peachland, B.C., 1993-97; candidate fed. election Okanagan-Coquihaila, 1997; legal advisor Ministry Aboriginal Affairs, Govt. N.W.T., 1999-2000. Mem. adv. coun. on multiculturalism, adv. coun. to Minister of Multiculturalism, B.C., 1996-98; presenter in field. Author: (book/screenplay) Sookinchute, 2001, (treatise) Trick or Treaty?, 1995, Apple Cede: First Nations Land Management Regime, 1999, In a perfect world...Modern day colonialism in Canada, 2001, The River Forks Here: Canada's attempt to execute the 1969 White Paper and Indigenous Peoples, 2002, (book) Gustafsen Lake: Under Seige, 1997. Dir. B.C. Parents in Crisis Soc., Vancouver, 1991—93, Orpheum Kids Club Soc., Vancouver, 1991, Vancouver Youth Theatre, 2001. Named one of 2000 Outstanding Intellectuals of the 21st Century, Internat. Biog. Ctr., 500 Living Legends; recipient univ. scholarships. Mem. Internat. Bar Assn., Internat. Commn. Jurists (Can. sect.), Can. Counsel on Internat. Law, York U. Alumni Assn., U. B.C. Commerce Alumni Assn., Phi Delta Phi. Office: Switlo & Co 141-6200 McKay Ave Ste 955 Burnaby BC V5H 4M9 Canada E-mail: janice@switlo.com.

SWITZER, CAROLYN JOAN, artist, educator; b. Petoskey, Mich., Apr. 20, 1931; d. Eugene Constant and Burnis Hazel (Lower) S. Student, Wayne State U., 1954-55, St. John's Coll., Santa Fe, N.Mex., 1993; BA, Mich. State U., 1953, MA, 1964. Cert. tchr., Mich. Art tchr. Ferndale Bd. of Edn., 1953-56, Birmingham Bd. of Edn., Mich., 1956-96; pvt. tchr. drawing and painting. Exhbns. include state and local shows, galleries and pvt. collections. Cons. Girl Scouts U.S., Birmingham, Petoskey, Mich.; mem. Crooked Tree Arts Coun., Petoskey Recipient recognition award for svc. to community, Birmingham Edn. Assn. Coun., 1967, Outstanding Sr. Woman Lantern Night MSU, 1953. Mem. AAUW (scholar, Mich. State U., 1962), Nat. Art Edn. Assn., Mich. Art Edn. Assn., Mich. Edn. Assn., Detroit Inst. Art, Nat. Mus. for Women in Arts, Mich. Coun. for Arts, Art Study Club of Petoskey, Zonta Internat., Crooked Tree Arts Ctr. Petoskey. Avocations: music/singing, reading, exercise class, walking, photography. Home: 805 Lindell Ave Petoskey MI 49770-3159

SWITZER, KAREN BELLE RINGERS, music educator; d. Joseph Ringers Jr. and Ella (Kiss) Ringers; 1 child, Derek Joseph. Bachelor of Music Edn., Shenandoah Conservatory of Music, 1971; Master of Music Edn., Pa. State U., 1978. Cert. tchr. music. Tchr. gen. and vocal music Newport Sch. Dist., Pa., 1972—. Dir. show choir Innovation, Newport, 1975—; advisor chpt. 1434 Modern Music Masters, Newport, 1976—. Music coord. Inaugural Ceremony for Gov. Ed Rendell, Harrisburg, Pa., 2003. Mem.: NEA, Music Educators Nat. Conf., Pa. State Edn. Assn. (treas. 1990—94), Am. Choral Dirs. Assn. Avocations: sewing, crafts, reading, swimming. Office: Newport HS 300 N Sixth St Newport PA 17074

SWITZER, TOCCOA, artist; b. Clinton, S.C., Dec. 14, 1930; d. Hercules Milledge and Mercer Bailey (Vance) Wise; m. James Layton Switzer, Feb. 20, 1954 (dec.); children: James Layton Jr., Toccoa Bailey, Paul Kent III; m. Paul Kent Switzer, Jr., Oct. 12, 1990. AA, Stephens Coll., Columbia, Mo., 1951; BFA, Ohio State U., Columbus, 1953. Chmn. Switzer/Wise Investment LP, Union, S.C., 1989—. Bd. dirs. M.S. Bailey and Son, Bankers, Clinton, Clinton Investment Co.; mem. adv. bd. Anchor Fin. Corp., Myrtle Beach, S.C. Den mother Cub Scouts Am., Union, 1962-65; vol. ARC, Union, 1968—; Sunday Sch. tchr. Grace United Meth. Ch., Union, 1954-95, chmn. bldg. com., 1976-77, bd. trustees 1985—; bd. dirs. Great Town Program, Union, 1976-82; bd. dirs. Union Main St. Program, 1983-84; mem. bldg. com. Union Carnegie Libr., 1983-85; bd. mem. Union County Health Care Found., Union, 1993—; bd. trustees Wofford Coll., Spartanburg, S.C., 1990—; bd. dir. Bailey Found., Clinton, 1989—; bd. mem. U. S.C.-Union Partnership Bd., 1989—. Recipient Founder Day award U.S.C., Union, 1999. Mem. Friends of the Libr., Union Cotillion Club (pres.), Book and Garden Club (pres. 1989-90), Union County C. of C. (pres. 1981-82). Methodist. Avocations: painting, gardening, reading.

SWOBODA, MELANIE RUTH, elementary school educator, music educator; b. Ft. Knox, Ky., Jan. 19, 1974; d. James William and Violet Joyce Cowden; m. Joseph Wilford Swoboda, Jan. 13, 1996; children: Josie Nicole, Brendan Joseph. BS in Edn. summa cum laude, Western Ky. U., 1996. Tchr. 3d grade Sand Creek Elem. Sch., Colorado Springs, 1998—2000; tchr. music Waldo Pafford Elem. Sch., Hinesville, Ga., 2000—03. Recipient Ogden Trustees award, Western Ky. U., Bowling Green, 1996. Mem.: Profl. Assn. Ga. Educators, Ga. Music Educators Assn. Avocations: motorcycling, scrapbooks.

SWOOPE, JANICE ROBINS, music educator; b. Bayshore, NY, Oct. 13, 1953; d. Edwin Robins, Jr. and Blanche Louisa Robins; m. Eli Swoope, Jr., July 3, 1983. B in Music Edn., Keene State Coll., 1976; student, Meredith Coll., 1989. Tchr. Long Beach (NY) City Schs., 1972—83; coord. orch. Cumberland County Schs., Fayetteville, NC, 1990—94, dir. orch., 2003—; tchr. music Synder Bapt. Ch., Fayetteville, 2001—03. Guest clinician Harnett County Schs., Dunn, NC, 1996, Wake County Schs., Raleigh, NC, 1997, Roeboson County, Red Springs, 2003, Onslow County, Jacksonville, 2003; violinist Fayetteville Symphony, 1985—94, Raleigh Symphony, 1985—94, Wilson (NC) Symphony, 1985—94, Synder Bapt. Ch., Fayetteville, 1993—2003. Min. of music Abney Chapel SDA Ch., Fayetteville, 1996—2003. Mem.: NC Music Educators Assn. (audition chair 1992, all state chair 1996—2000). Avocations: walking, aerobics, reading, gardening. Home: 2913 Peacock St Hope Mills NC 28348 Office: Reid Ross Classical Sch 3200 Ramsey St Fayetteville NC 28301

SWOOPES, SHERYL DENISE, professional basketball player; b. Brownfield, Tex., Mar. 25, 1971; d. Louis Swoopes; m. Eric Jackson; 1 child, Jordan. Student, South Plains Jr. Coll., Tex.; BA, Tex. Tech. U., 1993. Basketball player USA Women's Nat. Team, 1995—96, Houston Comets, 1997—. Mem. Pan Am. Games Womens Basketball Team, 1995, WNBA Championship Team Houston Comets, 1997—99. Named S.W. Conf. Player of Yr., 1992, S.W. Conf. Newcomer of Yr., 1992, Nat. Player of Yr., 1993, Most Valuable Player, NCAA Final Four, 1993, 1997, WNBA, 2000, 2002, Defensive Player of Yr., 2000, 2002; named to All-WNBA First Team, 1998—2000, 2002; recipient Bronze medal, World Championship Team, 1994, Gold medal, Women's Goodwill Games Team, 1994, Women's Pro Basketball Player of Yr. award, ESPY, 2001. Achievements include having Nike basketball shoe named in her honor. Office: Houston Comets Two Greenway Plz Ste 400 Houston TX 77046 Address: 908 E Felt St Apt 111 Brownfield TX 79316-3703

SWOPE, FRANCES ALDERSON, retired librarian; b. Richmond, Va., Dec. 5, 1911; d. Joseph Newman and Frances (Richardson) Alderson; m. Kenneth Dabney Swope, Dec. 27, 1958; stepchildren: Jeanne Weikel, Lee Smith. BA, U. Ky., Lexington, 1933; BS in Libr. Sci., U. Ill., 1939; postgrad., U. Va., U. Mich., U. London. Tchr. Alderson (W.Va.) H.S., 1933-39; ext. libr. Circleville (Ohio) Pub. Libr., 1939-41, Kanawha County Pub. Libr., Charleston, W.Va., 1941-43; alt. custodian comdt.'s confidential and secret files 3rd Naval Dist. Hdqrs., N.Y.C., 1943-45; cataloguer Yale U. Libr., New Haven, 1946-47; chief ext. libr. Kanawha County Pub. Libr., 1947-67; archivist Greenbrier Hist. Soc., Lewisburg, W.Va., 1969-97. Named W.Va. History Hero, 1997. Mem. Nat. Trust Historic Preservation, Nat. Soc. Colonial Dames in Am., W.Va. Libr. Assn. Lt. USNR, 1943-45. Democrat. Presbyterian. Avocation: walking. Home: 1130 Highland Pl Apt 303 Harrisonburg VA 22801

SWORD, TERESA LE, music educator; b. Ontario, Oreg., July 8, 1965; d. Richard A. and Esther L. Long; m. Vern E. Sword, June 27, 1992. B in Edn., Evangel U., 1991; MS in Edn., Southwest Mission, 1999. Music tchr. Schell City (Mo.) Sch., 1991—92, Delta (Mo.) Sch., 1993—95, Koshkonong (Mo.) Sch., 1995—99, Gainesville (Mo.) Sch., 1999—2001; music tchr., libr. Hume (Mo.) Sch., 2001—. With Army Nat. Guard, 1998. Mem.: Music Educators of Mo., Mo. State Tchrs. Assn., Mo. Band Masters Assn., Orff Assn., The Nat. Assn. Music Edn., Assn. Supervision Curriculum Devel. Republican.

SWYSTUN-RIVES, BOHDANA ALEXANDRA, dentist; b. Kopychynci, Ukraine, Jan. 31, 1925; came to U.S., 1951; d. Peter and Maria (Ottawa) Swystun; m. John Rives, June 20, 1952 (div. 1960); 1 child, Peter A. DMD, Ludwig Maximillians Universitat, Munich, 1951; DDS, NYU, 1960. Dentist Dr. Joseph Matriss, East Rutherford, N.J., 1960-61; gen. practice dentistry Clifton, N.J., 1961-99. Vol. dentist Felician Sisters Orphanage, Lodi, N.J., 1982—; mem. Presdl. Task Force, Washington. Mem. ADA (award for commitment to professionalism and health), Ukrainian Med. Assn., Ukrainian Nat. Assn., Ukrainian Inst. Am., Clifton-Pasaic (N.J.) C. of C. Republican. Ukrainian Catholic. Avocations: reading, fgn. langs., walking, gold jewelry. Home: 149 Village Circle Glasgow KY 42141-7038

SYCKS, LINDA B. music educator; b. Ridgewood, NJ, Dec. 21, 1965; d. Robert John and Jean Delores (Hearn) Braden; m. David Brent Sycks, July 15, 1989; children: Jane Ellen, Emily Elizabeth, Megan Elaine. MusB, Capital U., 1988. Tchr. Eaton (Ohio) City Schs., 1988—91, Vandalia (Ohio) Butler Schs., 1991—94; instr. Ohio No. U., Ada, 1995—, Bluffton (Ohio) Coll., 1995—2003. Oboist Whitewater Opera Co., Richmond, Ind., 1989—91, Sinclair Wind ensemble, Dayton, Ohio, 1991—94, Miami Valley Symphony Orch., Dayton, 1992—94, Lima (Ohio) Symphony Orch., 1997—2003. Mem.: Ohio Music Adn. Assn., Internat. Double Reed soc., Kodaly Educators N.W. Ohio (pres. 1998—2002). Office: Ohio No Univ 525 S Main St Ada OH 45810

SYDNEY, DORIS S. sports touring company executive, interior designer; b. N.Y.C., Feb. 18, 1934; d. Morris and Frances (Terrace) Steinman; m. Herbert P. Sydney, Oct. 20, 1957; children: Madeleine Jane, Peter Samuel. Student, Vassar Coll., 1950-52; BS, Columbia U., 1952-55; postgrad., NYU, 1956-57, N.Y. Sch. Interior Design, 1974. Cert. documentor Equitable Life Ins. Co., N.Y.C., 1955-57; rschr. Fairchild Publs., N.Y.C., 1957-58; furniture sales Steinman's Inc., N.Y.C., 1958-60; interior designer, prin. Doris S. Sydney Interiors, Armonk, N.Y., 1975; exec. asst. Tennis Europe Inc., Conn., 1984—. Pres. Coman Hill Sch. PTA, 1971-72, Byram Hills H.S. PTA, 1977-79, also chair; pres. Byram Hills Scholarship Fund, 1980-82, Non-partisan Nominating Com., 1982-84; coun. del. Vassar Coll. Alumni Assn., Poughkeepsie, N.Y., 1973-77; chair Fred Caruolo Meml. Fund, 1979-81; pres. bd. trustees North Castle Pub. Libr., 1981-90; v.p. Friends North Castle Pub. Libr., 1993—; treas., pres. Armonk Hadassah, 1980—. Recipient Friend of Yr. award, N. Castle Libr., 2001, Pat Bresha award for cmty. svc., Lions Club, North Castle, 2003. Republican. Jewish. Home: 65 Windmill Rd Armonk NY 10504-2833 E-mail: dorissyd@aol.com.

SYER, FONTAINE, theater director; Degree, Mt. Holyoke Coll., 1969; MFA, U. Del., 2003. Co-founder, artistic dir. Theatre Project Co., 1975—89; various positions, 1989—92; assoc. dir. Oreg. Shakespeare Festival, 1992—96; artistic dir. Del. Theatre Co., Wilimington, Del., 1998—. Office: Delaware Theatre Co 200 Water St Wilmington DE 19801

SYGEEL, CRYSTAL RENEE, minister, consultant; d. David Richard and Joanne Williams Sygeel. BS, Old Dominion U., 1992; MDiv, Union Theol. Sem., 1996; MA in Christian Edn., Presbyn. Sch. Of Christian Edn., 1996. Ordained reverend The Va. Ann. Conf. of the United Meth. Ch., 1998. Youth counselor United Meth. Family Svcs, Richmond, Va., 1996—97, chaplain, 1997—2001; ministries coord. First United Meth. Ch. Bellevue, Seattle, 2001—. Artist Good Shepherd United Meth. Ch., Richmond, 1994—97; cons. in field. Author: The United Methodist Worship Planner, Fall Edition of Homeletics Magazine, 1997, Broken And Spilled Out, Curriculum for Sexual Misconduct Training for Planned Parenthood. Mem. task force Ch. Coun. Greater Seattle, 2002—03; active Reconciling Ministries Network, Seattle, 2001—03. Scholar, Union Theol. Sem., 1992—96. Mem.: Pacific N.W.Annnual Conf. United Meth. Ch., Va. Ann. Conf. United Meth. Ch. Methodist. Avocations: travel, dance, photography, creative writing, painting. Office: First United Methodist Church of Bellevue 1934 108th Ave NE Bellevue WA 98004 E-mail: csygeel@comcast.net.

SYGNECKI, CHRISTINA, sales executive; b. Forest Hills, N.Y., Aug. 30, 1954; d. Rene Julien and Marie Helene (Popovic) S.; m. Mark Spencer Conroy, May 22, 1977 (div. Dec. 1988). BA, U. Miami, 1974. Outside sales mgr. Cream of the Valley, Sacramento, 1983-84; dept. mgr. Oakville Grocery, San Francisco, 1984-85; store mgr. La Ferme Beaujolaise, San Francisco, 1985-86; chef, owner Nina Rent-A-Chef, San Francisco, 1986-88; mdse. coord. Carnival Cruise Lines, Miami, 1988-93; sales mgr. duty free Greyhound Leisure Svcs., Miami, 1993-95; sales mgr. cruise ships Weitnauer Am. Trading, Miami, 1995-96; mgr. Pertex Textile Products, Bloomfield Hills, Mich., 1996-97; metro mgr. Artisans and Estates of Kendall Jackson Winery, Santa Rosa, Calif., 1997—2002; territory mgr. Corterra Wines of Kendall Jackson Winery, 2002—. Mem. Seigneurs de Corbieres, France. Mem. Chaine des Rotisseurs (vice echanson, Merit award 1996), Sommelier Guild (v.p. 1993—), Ordre des Canardiers. Republican. Roman Catholic. Avocations: yoga, travel, wine collecting, literature, music. Home and Office: 6559 Harvey Ave Pennsauken NJ 08109-2459

SYKES, BARBARA, state legislator, state representative; b. Holly Grove, Ark., Apr. 12, 1955; married; 2 children. BA in Social Work, MPA, U. Akron. Rep. Ohio State Ho. Reps., Columbus, 2000—. Mem. econ. devel. and tech. com. Ohio State Ho. Reps., mem. pub. utilities com., mem. ways and means com. Mem.: NAACP, Friends of Maple Libr., PTA Firestone HS. Democrat. Office: Ohio State House Reps 77 South High Street 10th Floor Columbus OH 43215-6111

SYKES, DIANE S. state supreme court justice; b. Milw. children: Jay, Alexander. B, Northwestern U., 1980; JD, Marquette U., 1984. Reporter Milw. Jour.; law clk. to Hon. Terence T. Evans; assoc. Whyte & Hirschboeck S.C.; judge Milw. County Ct., 1992, Wis. Supreme Ct., Madison, 1999—. Office: Wis Supreme Ct PO Box 1688 Madison WI 53702

SYKES, JOLENE, former publishing executive; BS, East Carolina U. Mgr. corp. sales devel. Time Inc., 1990—91, S.E. regional mgr. corp. sales and mktg., 1991—93; S.E. dir. regional sales Sports Illus., 1993—96; pub. Fortune mag. Time, Inc., N.Y.C., 1996—99, pres. Fortune mag., 1999—2001; mem. bd. dirs. Resource Connection, Inc., 2002—. Office: Resources Connection Inc 695 Town Center Dr Ste 600 Costa Mesa CA 92626

SYKORA, BARBARA ZWACH, state legislator; b. Tracy, Minn., Mar. 5, 1941; d. John M. and Agnes (Schueller) Zwach; m. Robert G. Sykora, 1965; children: Mona, John, Kara, Mary. BA, St. Catherine Coll., 1963. Tchr. Springfield (Mass.) Sch., 1963-64, Roseville (Minn.) Sch., 1964-66; mem. Minn. Ho. of Reps., St. Paul, 1994—. Bd. dirs. Beacon Bank. Vice chmn. 2d Congl. Dist. Rep. Com., Minn., 1978-82; chmn. 6th Congl. Dist. Rep. Com., 1982-86; [illegible] Durenberger Campaign, 1980-82; Senator Pillsbury Campaign, Wayzata, Minn., 1980; chair Ind. Rep. State Com., Minn., 1987-93; dist. dir. Office Congressman Rod Grams, 1993-94; bd. dirs. Animal Humane Soc. Hennepin County, Minn. Acad. Excellence Found.; chair Family and Early Childhood Edn. Com., 1999-2002, Edn. Policy, 2003—; chair Legis. Commn. on IEcon. Status of Women, 2001—; asst. majority leader Rep. State Com., Minn. 2003—. Mem. Excelsior C. of C., Minnetonka Rotary. Republican. E-mail: bsykora@uswestmail.net.

SYLER, RENE, newscaster; b. Scott AFB, Belleville, Ill., Feb. 17, 1963; m. Buff Parham; 2 children. BA in Psychology, Calif. State U., Sacramento, 1987. Weekend reporter KTVN-TV, Reno, 1987—89; weekend anchor KOLO-TV, Reno, 1989—90, WVTM-TV, Birmingham, 1990—92; anchor WFAA-TV, Dallas, 1992—97, KTVT-TV, Dallas, 1997—2002; anchor, The Early Show CBS, 2002—. Recipient TV Personality of the Yr., Am. Women in Radio and TV, 1997. Mem.: Nat. Assn. of Black Journalists, Dallas-Ft. Worth Assn. of Black Communicators. Office: c/o CBS News The Early Show 524 W 57th St New York NY 10019

SYLVERS, ARLENE MARDER, clinical psychologist; b. Bklyn., June 2, 1938; d. Harry Isadore and Helen (Yurkowitz) Marder; m. Schuyler Sylvers, June 2, 1957 (div. 1970); children: Steven Eric, Lee Alan. BA in Psychology, Calif. State U., Northridge, 1972, MA in Psychology, 1974; PhD in Clin. Psychology, Internat. Coll., 1984. Lic. marriage, family and child counselor, Calif.; cert. adminstrv. svc. credential, std. designated svc. credential, pupil pers. svcs., sch. psychology, psych. ccmty. coll. tchg., Calif.; lic. psychologist, Calif. Tchr. spl. edn. Eleby Hall, 1972; dist. psychologist Newhall (Calif.) Sch. Dist., 1974-81, coord. spl. svcs., 1978-81, dir. spl. svcs. dept., 1981-98; pvt. practice marriage, family and child therapy, 1980—. Chmn. dirs. coun. Spl. Edn. Local Plan Area, Santa Clarita, Calif., 1976—; instr. dept. edn. Calif. Luth. Coll., part-time 1976-80; presenter in field to cmty. adv. couns. and univs. Pub. spkr. for various parent and cmty. groups. Mem. Am. Assn. Marriage and Family Therapists, Assn. Calif. Sch. Adminstrs., Calif. Assn. Marriage and Family Therapists, Alpha Gamma Sigma, Sigma Tau Sigma, Psi Chi, Phi Delta Kappa. Avocations: writing poetry, travel, yoga, theater, opera. Office: 23550 Lyons Ave Ste 207 Newhall CA 91321-5756

SYLVESTER, NANCY KATHERINE, management consultant; b. Evansville, Ind., July 17, 1947; d. Leonard Nicholas and Marjorie (Moore) Jochim; m. James Andrew Sylvester, Aug 21, 1971; children: Marcy Dee, Holly Nicole. BS, Ind. State U., 1969; MA, U. Mich., 1970. Registered profl. parliamentarian; cert. prof. parliamentarian; leadership/team/meeting mgmt. specialist; cert. tchr. of parliamentary procedure. Prof. speech Rock Valley Coll., Rockford, Ill., 1970-2001, prof. emeritus speech, 2001—. Chmn. bd. First Fed. Savs. Bank, Belvidere, Ill., 1996-98. Author: Handbook for Effective Meetings, 1993, Basics of Parliamentary Procedure, 1997, Complete Idiots Guide to Roberts Rules, 2004; contbr. articles to profl. jours. Bd. dirs. Jr. League Rockford, 1974-78, Rock River Homeowners Assn., 1990-91; pres. Children's Devel. Ctr. Aux. Bd., Rockford, 1984-85; parliamentarian Winnebago County Dem. Caucus, 1991; vice-chmn. Commn. on Am. Parliamentary Practice, 1989-90, chmn., 1990-91; nat. parliamentarian Girl Scouts U.S., 1996-97, bd. dirs. Rock River coun., 1979-81. Recipient Jardene medal Ind. State U., 1969, RVC Faculty of Yr. award, 1994, Athena award Rockford Area C. of C., 1999, Alta Hulett award for the professions YWCA, 2001; Rockham scholar U. Mich., 1969-70. Mem.: Royal Neighbors of Am. (parliamentarian 2001—), Am. Speech-Lang.-Hearing Assn. (parliamentarian 1994—), Info. Sys. Audit and Control Assn. (parliamentarian 1994—98), Ind. Accts. Assn. Ill. (parliamentarian 1990—2000), Am. Soc. Pain Mgmt. Nurses (nat. parliamentarian 1994—97), Phi Rho Pi (region 4 v.p. 1972—73, nat. v.p. 1973—74), Rockford C. of C. (ex-officer bd. dirs., Athena award 1999), Nat. League Nursing (parliamentarian 1995), Coun. Better Bus. Burs. (parliamentarian 1993), Speech Commn. Assn., Nat. Assn. Parliamentarians (chmn. nat. nominating com. 1997—99, bd. dirs. 1997—, chmn. bylaws com. 1999—2001, nat. parliamentarian 2001—03), Nat. Assn. Ins. Women (parliamentarian 1983—91), Am. Assn. Nurse Anesthetists (parliamentarian 2000—), Ill. Assn. Parliamentarians, Am. Vet. Med. Assn. (parliamentarian 1998—), Nat. Coun. State Bds. Nursing (parliamentarian 1992—99), Am. Women Soc. CPAs (parliamentarian 1991—96), Am. Soc. Women Accts. (parliamentarian 1980—), Am. Inst. Parliamentarians, Am. Bowling Congress (parliamentarian 2003—), Women's Internat. Bowling Congress (parliamentarian 2003—). Home and Office: 4826 River Bluff Ct Loves Park IL 61111-5836 Fax: 815-877-5290. E-mail: nancy@nancysylvester.com.

SYMENS, MAXINE BRINKERT TANNER, marketing professional; b. Primghar, Iowa, June 12, 1930; d. George Herman and Irene Marie (Dahnke) Brinkert; m. Jack Frederiksen Tanner, Dec. 28, 1950 (dec. Oct. 1976); m. Delbert Glenn Symens, Sept. 26, 1981. BS magna cum laude, Westmar Coll., 1970. Cert. tchr., Iowa. Elem. tchr. Rural Sch. O'Brien Co., Primghar, 1949-54, Gaza (Iowa) Com. Sch., 1954-60; secondary tchr. Primghar Com. Sch., 1960-81; fitness salon owner Slim 'N' Trim, George, Rock Rapids, Iowa, 1982-87; restaurant owner George Cafe, 1985-90, Pizza Ranch, 1988-96; with network mktg. divsn. Espial, 1997-99; dir. Coastal Vacations, 2000—03. Advt. sales cons. Internet advt., 1997-99, Antique & Gift Shop, 1998-2000. Pres. Primghar Edn. Assn., 1970-71. Mem. George C. of C., George Kiwanis Club (sec. 1991-95), Delta Kappa Gamma. Lutheran. Home: 307 Dell St NE George IA 51237-1030

SYMINGTON, GAYE R. state representative; b. Boston, Apr. 20, 1954; m. Charles M. Lacey; three children. BA, Williams Coll., 1977; MBA, Cornell U., 1983. V.p. Vt. Cmty. Loan Fund; rep. Vt. Ho. of Reps., 1996—. Treas. Vt. Cmty. Enterprise Fund; bd. dirs. Jericho Ctr. Preservation Assn. Chair Jericho Ctr. Preservation Assn. Mem. Vt. Health and Edn. Fin. Agy. Unitarian Universalist. Office: 324 Browns Trace Rd Jericho VT 05465-9780

SYMONDS, STACEY GABRIELLE, marketing professional; d. Richard Alan and Norma Rae Erth; m. Keith Andrew Symonds, May 27, 2001. BS in Textile/Apparel Mgmt., Cornell U., 1992; MA in Applied Social Rsch., U. Mich., 1996. Forecast analyst Gen. Motors Corp., Warren, Mich., 1996—97, market analyst Detroit, 1997—98, product devel. rsch. mgr. Warren, 1998—2000, mgr. strategic market analysis Detroit, 2000—02; mktg. rsch. mgr. Capital One Fin., McLean, Va., 2002—03, group mktg. rsch. mgr., 2003—. Mentor Pine Spring Elem. Sch., Annandale, Va., 2002—. Mem.: Am. Assn. for Pub. Opinion Rsch., Am. Mktg. Assn. (bd. mem., v.p. internal comm. 2003—, chair adminstrv. com. 2002—03), Cornell Club Mich. (chair book award 1999—2002). Avocations: hiking, reading, singing, volunteering. Office: Capital One Fin 1680 Capital One Dr Mc Lean VA 22102

SYMONETTE, LYS, foundation executive, musician, writer; b. Mainz, Germany, Dec. 21, 1920; came to U.S., 1936; d. Max Weinschenk and Gertrude (Metzger) Honheisser; m. Randolph Symonette, Sept. 1, 1949; 1 child, Victor. Student, Curtis Inst., Phila., 1937-39. Piano accompanist to internat. singers, 1940—. Musical asst. to Kurt Weill and L. Lenya, 1945-81; tchr. Curtis Inst., Phila., 1976—; musical exec., v.p. Kurt Weill Found., N.Y.C., 1981—. Translator operas from English to German and German to English, 1945—; co-editor Speak Low, Family Letters, 1996. Mem. Am. Fedn. Musicians, Alumni Assn. Curtis Inst. Music. Home: 160 W 73rd St New York NY 10023-3012 Office: Kurt Weill Found for Music 7 E 20th St New York NY 10003-1106

SYMS, HELEN MAKSYM, educational administrator; b. Wilkes Barre, Pa., Nov. 12, 1918; d. Walter and Anna (Kowalewski) Maksym; m. Louis Harold Syms, Aug. 16, 1947; children: Harold Edward, Robert Louis. BA, Hunter Coll., 1941; MS, Columbia U., 1947; teaching credentials, Calif. State U., Northridge, 1964. Statis. clk. McGraw Hill Pub. Co., N.Y.C., 1941-42; acct. Flexpansion Corp., N.Y.C., 1943-47, Oliver Wellington & Co., N.Y.C., 1947-48, Broadcast Measurement Bur., N.Y.C., 1948-51; tchr. Calif. State U., Northridge, 1964, Burbank (Calif.) Unified Sch. Dist., 1964-79; chmn. bus. edn. dept. Burbank H.S., 1974-79; docent, acct. arts coun. Calif. State U., Northridge, 1979—; tchr. MEND-Meet Each Need with Dignity Learning Ctr., Pacoima, Calif., 1987-89; assoc. dir. M.E.N.D. (Meet Each Need with Dignity) Learning Ctr., Pacoima, Calif., 1989-96. Mem. Phi Beta Kappa, Delta Kappa Gamma (pres. 1972-74, treas. Xi chpt. 1982-90, 92-2002, treas. area IX 1975-78). Home: 9219 Whitaker Ave Northridge CA 91343-3538

SYMS, MARCY, retail executive; MS in Pub. Rels., Boston U.; postgrad., Harvard U.; D (hon.), Bryant Coll. Pres. Syms Corp., Secaucus, N.J., 1983, chief operating officer, 1992-97, CEO, 1998—. Bd. dirs. Stanley Blacker, Inc., Am. Materials, Eau Claire, Wis. Author: Mind Your Own Business, Keep it in the Family; columnist Family Bus. Mag. Founding bd. dirs. Sy Syms Sch. Bus. Yeshiva U., 1985—. Recipient Disting. Bus. Leader of Yr. award Monmouth U., Marvin Feldman award Fashion Inst. Tech., Disting. Alumni award boston U., Good Citizen award Coun. Sr. Ctrs. & Svcs. of N.Y.C., Inc. Mem. Young Pres.' Orgn., Com. of 200, Intenrat. Women's Forum, Econ. Club N.Y. Office: Syms Corp One Syms Way Secaucus NJ 07094

SYNNESTVEDT, KIRSTIN, musician, educator; b. Bryn Athyn, Pa., Jan. 8, 1940; d. Raymond Harvey and Katherine Riefstahl Synnestvedt. Student, Tanglewood Berkshire Mus. Ctr., Lenox, Mass., 1956-59; BS, Juilliard Sch., 1963; MusM, Syracuse U., 1966; D of Musical Arts, U. Iowa, 1979. Coll. organist, instr. music Doane Coll., Crete, Nebr., 1966-69; ch. organist, choir dir., solo recitalist Chgo., 1973—. Organ concert broadcasts Sta. WNIB, Chgo., Sta. WDCB, Glen Ellyn, Ill., Sta. WMWA, Glenview, Ill.; adjudicator organ contests, Lincoln, Nebr., Des Moines, Iowa, Chgo. Creator, performer one-woman show of hats. Mem. Fire Buffs of Ill., Chgo., Ill. Fire Safety Alliance, Mt. Prospect, Ill.. Hon. scholar Juilliard Sch., 1961-63. Mem. Nat. Assn. Tchrs. Singing, Music Tchrs. Nat. Assn., Am. Guild Organists, Soc. for Preservation and Appreciation of Antique Motorized Fire Apparatus, 5-11 Club, Chgo. Club Women Organists (pres. 1980-82, 87-90), Pi Kappa Lambda (hon. mem.). Avocations: creative writing, cooking, gardening, modern dance, fast walking.

SYNNOTT, MARCIA GRAHAM, history educator; b. Camden, N.J., July 4, 1939; d. Thomas Whitney and Beatrice Adelaide (Colby) S.; m. William Edwin Sharp, June 16, 1979; children: Willard William Sharp, Laurel Beth Sharp. AB, Radcliffe Coll., 1961; MA, Brown U., 1964; PhD, U. Mass., 1974. History tchr. MacDuffie Sch., Springfield, Mass., 1963-68; instr. U. S.C., Columbia, 1972-74, asst. prof., 1974-79, assoc. prof. history, 1979-97, dir. grad. studies history dept., 1990-92, prof. history, 1997—. Author: The Half-Opened Door, 1979, contbr. essays to books. Active university-wide cmty. svc. projects. Fulbright scholar, 1988; Am. Coun. Learned Socs. grantee, 1981. Mem. Am. Hist. Assn., So. Hist. Assn., Orgn. Am. Historians (membership com. 1990-93), S.C. Hist. Assn. (pres. 1994-95), History of Edn. Soc. (mem. editl. bd. 1996, 97, 98, bd. dirs. 2000-02). Avocations: historic sites and museums, snow skiing, walking. Office: U SC Dept History Columbia SC 29208-0001

SYPHERS, MARY FRANCES, music educator; b. Floresville, Tex., Sept. 26, 1912; d. Little Fleming and Lillian Frances (Herrington) Spruce; m. Ansel James Syphers, July 23, 1959 (dec. 1972). BA in English, U. Tex., 1938; MEd, So. Meth. U., Dallas, 1950; studied voice with Dr. Wilcox, studied composition with Roy Harris,, 1947, studied Music Edn. with Augustus Zansig. Cert. high sch. music tchr., cert. elem. tchr., Tex. Tchr. music Ehlers Country Sch., Poth, Tex., 1931-35, Poth Ind. Sch. Dist., 1936-40, Sinton (Tex.) Ind. Sch. Dist., 1941, Stephen J. Hay Sch., Dallas, 1942-50, Alamo Sch., Dallas, 1951—, Edwin J. Kiest Sch., Dallas, 1955—, Lakewood Elem., Dallas, 1976-81. Voice, drama tchr. Poth Ind. Sch. dist., 1936-40. Contbg. author: New England To Texas, 1986. Choir dir. 1st Meth. Ch., Sinton, Tex., 1941-42; soloist, jr. choir dir. Oaklawn Meth. Ch., Dallas, 1942-43; soloist 1st Presbyn. Ch., Dallas, 1943-46, Highland Park Presbyn. Ch., Dallas, 1946-47; symphony chorus Dallas Music Staff, 1944-60; mem. choir St. Michael and All Angels Episocpal Ch., Dallas, 1949-91; organizer jr. female vols. USO, Dallas, 1960-70, coordinator jr. female vols. anniversary celebration, Dallas, 1966; mem. publicity com. So. Meml. Assn., Dallas, 1981; life mem. PTA; mem. Shakespeare Study Club. Recipient Citation as member of concert choir Am. Culture and Lang. Ctr., Salzburg, Austria, 1987. Mem. New Eng. Women (pres. Tex. chpt. 1985-87), Dallas Coun. World Affairs, Dallas Inst. Humanities (sponser), Buckland Hist. Soc. (life), Nat. Soc. Colonial Dames (chmn. 1981-90), DAR (Jane Douglas chpt.), Standard Club Dallas (recreation sec. 1981-91), Delta Kappa Gamma (pres. Epsilon chpt. 1960-62). Democrat. Episcopalian. Avocations: genealogy, book binding, picture taking, reading, family history. Home: 2729 Laurel Oaks Dr Garland TX 75044-6939

SYPOLT, DIANE GILBERT, federal judge; b. Rochester, N.Y., June 14, 1947; d. Myron Birne and Doris Isabell (Robie) Gilbert; m. Dwight Douglas Sypolt; children: Andrew, David Weinstein. BA, Smith Coll., Northampton, Mass., 1969; postgrad., Stanford U., 1977-78, Georgetown U., 1978; JD, Boston U., 1979. Bar: D.C. 1979, Mass. 1979. Law clk. to judge D.C. Ct. Appeals, Washington, 1979-80; assoc. Peabody, Lambert & Meyers, Washington, 1980-83; asst. gen. counsel Office of Mgmt. and Budget, Washington, 1983-86; dep. gen. counsel U.S. Dept. Edn., Washington, 1986-88, acting gen. counsel, 1988-89; legal counselor to V.P. of U.S., White House; counsel Pres.'s Competitiveness Coun., Washington, 1989-90; judge U.S. Ct. Fed. Claims, Washington, 1990—. Bd. dirs. Democracy Devel. Inst. Recipient Young Lawyer's award Boston U. Law Sch., 1989. Mem. Fed. Am. Inn of Ct. (Master), Federalist Soc. Office: US Ct Fed Claims 717 Madison Pl NW Washington DC 20439-0002 Office Phone: 202-219-9655. Business E-Mail: diane_sypolt@ad.uscourts.gov.

SYSYN, MARY A. alderman; b. Manchester, N.H., Mar. 8, 1930; d. James J. Bolos and Vasiliki Caragianis; children: Julia, William, Catherine, Susan. BA in Early Edn., U. N.H., 1973. Tchr. Manchester Sch. Dist., 1967—73; from mgr. to owner Mr. Steak Restaurant, 1970—93; rep. Avon Products Inc., 1993—. Alderman City of Manchester, 1993—; bd. dirs. Manchester Neighborhood Housing, 1996—. Democrat. Greek Orthodox. Home: 208 Lowell St Manchester NH 03104

SYTEK, DONNA P. former state legislator; b. Haverhill, Mass., Dec. 14, 1944; m. John Sytek; 1 child. AB, Regis Coll., 1966, MA. Chmn. rules com. N.H. Ho. of Reps., Concord; mem. N.H. Ho. of Reps. (dist. 26), Concord; chmn. Jud. Conduct Commn., Bow, NH, 2001—. Chmn. N.H. Rep. Com., 1982-84; pres. Nat. Rep. Legislators Assn., 1992-93; del. to Rep. Nat. Conv., 1980, 84, 88, 84 Const. Conv., Assembly on the Legislature, chmn., 1991-92; mem. exec. com. NCSL, 1990-94, 97-98, Coun. State Govt., 1989—. Mem. Dist. Nursing Assn. (bd. dirs. 1989—), Boys and Girls Club (bd. dirs. 1989-97). Republican. Roman Catholic. Avocation: travel. Office: Jud Conduct Commn 501 South St Bow NH 03304-3413

SZABLYA, HELEN MARY, writer, language professional, lecturer; b. Budapest, Hungary, Sept. 6, 1934; came to U.S., 1963; d. Louis and Helen (Bartha) Kovacs; m. John Francis Szablya, June 12, 1951; children: Helen, Janos, Louis, Stephen, Alexandra, Rita, Dominique-Mary. Diploma in Sales, Mktg., U.B.C., 1962; BA in Fgn. Lang., Lit., Wash. State U., 1976. Freelance writer, translator, 1967—; columnist Cath. News, Trinidad, West Indies, 1980-91; adult educator TELOS Bellevue (Wash.) C.C., 1987-89; adult educator Pullman-Spokane (Wash.) C.C., 1976-80; faculty Christian Writers' Conf., Seattle, 1983-88, Pacific N.W. Writers' Conf., Seattle and Tacoma, 1987—92; hon. consul for Wash., Oreg., Idaho Republic of Hungary, 1993—. Lectr. Washington Commn. for Humanities, 1987-89. Author: (with others) Hungary Remembered, 1986 (Guardian of Liberty award, 1986, George Washington Honor medal, Freedoms Found. award 1988), 56-os Cserkészcsapat, 1986, (with others) The Fall of the Red Star, 1996, Hungarian translation 1999, (1st prize Wash. Press Assn., 1st prize Nat. Fedn. Press Women); pub., editor Hungary Internat. newsletter, 1990-93; columnist Hungarian Bus. Weekly, 1994-95; translator: Emlékezünk, 1986, Mind Twisters, 1987. Recipient Nat. 1st place editl. Nat. Fedn. Press Women, 1987, Senator Tom Martin Meml. award Pacific N.W. Writers Conf., 1979; grantee Hungarian Am. Assn. Wash., 1986, Wash. Com. for Humanities, 1986; named Cmty. Woman of Yr. Am. Bus. Women Assn., 1990. Mem. AAUW, Wash. Press Assn. (pres. 1987-88, 1st and 2nd place awards, several editl. and profile awards 1983, 87, 89, 90, 91, 92, 96, Communicator of Achievement award 1987), Nat. Fedn. Press Women (Affiliate Pres.' award 1988, bd. dirs. edn. fund N.W. quadrant, mem. 21st century planning com.), Authors Guild, Am. Translators Assn., Arpad Acad. (Gold medal 1987), Nat. Writers Club, Internat. PEN Club, Sigma Delta Chi (editl. award 1989). Avocations: children, reading, dance, swimming, traveling. Home and Office: PO Box 578 Kirkland WA 98083-0578 Office Phone: 425-739-0631. E-mail: szablyahj@aol.com.

SZAKSZTYLO, KATHEE, design technologist; b. Chgo., Nov. 19, 1969; d. Casimir and Lillian Marie Szakszytlo. Film studies internship, Moscow U., 1992; BA in cinema, photography, So. Ill. Univ., 1993; MFA in tng., edn., Roosevelt U., Schaumburg, Ill., 1998. Program dir. Vill. of Hawthorn Woods (Ill.), 1988—94; sales support mgr. Corporate Computing, Bannockburn, Ill., 1994—96; tng. coord. W.W. Grainger, Inc., Lincolnshire, Ill., 1996—98, tng. specialist Lake Forest, Ill., 1998—2001, tech. tng. specialist, 2002, design technologist, 2003—. Mem. Chgo. Data Processing Edn. Coun. Roman Catholic. Avocations: painting, writing, environmental, landscaping. Home: 3451 N Carriage Way Dr Arlington Heights IL 60008 Office: WW Grainger Inc 100 Grainger Pkwy Lake Forest IL 60045-5201

SZALKOWSKI, DEBORAH, music educator; b. Ithaca, N.Y., Nov. 25, 1956; d. Leslie Rudy and Mary Jane Worden; m. Mark James Szalkowski, July 21, 1990. MusB, Ithaca Coll., 1977; MEd, SUNY, Albany, 1982. Profl. tchg. cert. Fla., N.Y. Tchr. vocal music Marathon (N.Y.) Ctrl. Schs., 1977—78; tchr. Voorheesville (N.Y.) Sr. H.S., 1978—80, Troy (N.Y.) City Schs., 1980—85; choir dir. Guilderland (N.Y.) Ctrl. Sch., 1985—95; tchr. Pinellas County Schs., Tarpon Spring, Fla., 1995—96, choir dir. Largo, Fla., 1996—. Choral arranger:. Mem.: Pinellas County Music Educators, Fla. Vocal Assn., Fla. Music Educators Assn. (25 Yr. Svc. award 2002), Music Educators Nat. Assn. Avocations: travel, boating. Home: 10111 Tarpon Dr Treasure Island FL 33706 Office: Pinellas Pk HS 6305 118th Ave N Largo FL 33773 Personal E-mail: debchoir1@cs.com.

SZE, SARAH, sculptor; b. Boston, Mass. BA, Yale U., 1991; MFA, Sch. of Visual Arts, N.Y., 1997. One-man shows include, Mus. of Contemporary Art, Chgo, Mus. of Fine Arts, Boston, Inst. of Contemporary Art, London, The Found. Cartier, Paris, exhibited in group shows, The Whitney Mus. of Am. Art, N.Y.C., The Carnegie Mus. of Art, Pitts., The Akademie deer Kunste, Berlin, 48th Venice Biennial. Fellow John D. and Catherine T. MacArthur Found, 2003.

SZEGO, CLARA MARIAN, cell biologist, educator; b. Budapest, Hungary, Mar. 23, 1916; arrived in U.S., 1921, naturalized, 1927; d. Paul S. and Helen (Elek) S.; m. Sidney Roberts, Sept. 14, 1943. AB, Hunter Coll., 1937; MS, U. Minn., 1939, PhD, 1942. Instr. physiology U. Minn., 1942-43; Minn. Cancer Rsch. found. fellow, 1943-44; rsch. assoc. OSRD, Nat. Bur. Stds., 1944-45, Worcester Found. Exptl. Biology, 1945-47; rsch. instr. physiol. chemistry Yale U. Sch. Medicine, 1947-48; mem. faculty UCLA, 1948—, prof. biology, 1960—. Author (pseudonym Marian Steele) poetry pub. in small lit. presses and anthologies; contbr. articles on steroid protein interactions, mechanisms of hormone action and lysosome participation in normal cell function. Garvan fellow U. Minn., 1939; Guggenheim fellow, 1956; named Woman of Year in Sci. Los Angeles Times, 1957-58; named to Hunter Coll. Hall of Fame, 1987. Fellow AAAS; mem. Am. Physiol. Soc., Am. Soc. Cell Biology, Endocrine Soc. (CIBA award 1953), Soc. for Endocrinology (Gt. Britain), Biochem. Soc. (Gt. Britain), Internat. Soc. Rsch. Reproduction, Phi Beta Kappa (pres. UCLA chpt. 1973-74), Sigma Xi (pres. UCLA chpt. 1976-77). Home: 1371 Marinette Rd Pacific Palisades CA 90272-2627 Office: U Calif Dept Molecular Cell & Devel Biology Los Angeles CA 90095-1606 E-mail: cmszego@ucla.edu.

SZEREMETA-BROWAR, TAISA LYDIA, endodontist; b. Geneva, N.Y., Mar. 21, 1957; d. Swiatoslaw Bohdan and Stefania (Melnyk) Szeremeta; m. Andrew Wolodymyr Browar, Sept. 19, 1981. BS in Dentistry, Case Western Res. U., 1978, DDS, 1980; cert. specialty endodontics magna cum laude, U. Ill., Chgo., 1982. Pvt. practice Hinsdale (Ill.) Periodontics and Endodontics, 1982—; asst. clin. prof. Northwestern U. Dental Sch., Chgo., 1986-97, clin. prof., 1997—. Counselor, mem. Plast-Ukrainian Scouting, 1963—; presenting team Worldwide Marriage Encounter, Chgo., 1985-94; mem. parish coun. Sts. Volodymyr and Olha, Chgo., 1985-94. E. Wach rsch. grantee U. Ill., Chgo., 1980. Mem. ADA, Am. Assn. Endodontists, Am. Coll. Stomatologic Surgeons, Ukrainian Med. Assn. (chair membership 1983-88), Ill. Assn. Endodontists (pres. 1990-91), Ill. State Dental Soc., Chgo. Dental Soc. (sec. table clinic 1990, vice chair 1991, chair 1992), Hinsdale C. of C. Ukrainian Catholic. Avocations: embroidery, marriage enrichment, marriage preparation, theology. Office: Hinsdale Periodontics & Endodontics 40 S Clay St Ste 111W Hinsdale IL 60521-3280

SZETO, YVONNE, architectural firm executive; b. Hong Kong, July 4, 1956;, naturalized; BArch, U. Minn., 1977; MArch, Harvard U., 1979. Registered N.Y., cert. Nat. Coun. Archtl. Registration Bds. With I.M. Pei & Ptnrs., 1977—89, Pei Cobb Freed & Ptnrs., 1989—99; ptnr. Pei Cob Freed & Ptnrs., N.Y.C., 1999—. Guest critic Yale U.; panel mem. Bilbao: The Transformation of the City Art Inst. Chgo.; jury Bus. Week/Archtl. Record Awards, 2000. Mem.: AIA (medal and Cert. of Merit 1977). Office: Pei Cobb Freed & Ptnrs LLP 88 Pine St New York NY 10005

SZILAGYI-HAWKINS, ELIZABETH MARIA, social services administrator; b. Chgo., Dec. 28, 1949; d. Bernard and Elizabeth (Szombathy) Szilagyi; m. Robert Lee Hawkins. BS in Social Welfare, Olivet Nazarene U., 1973. Lic. social worker, Ill. Social worker Proviso Council on Aging, Bellwood, Ill., 1980-84, dir. sr. citizen services, 1984—. Mem. Older Adults Job Fair com. Operation Able, Oak Park, Ill., 1983-86, Gottlieb Hosp. Home Health Adv. Bd., 1988—. Mem. Proviso Coord. Com. (sr. com., pres. 1986-87, 959-96), Family Care Sr. Companion Adv. Coun. (v.p. 1985-86, pres. 1986-87). Avocations: bicycling, swimming, sewing. Office: Proviso Coun on Aging 439 Bohland Ave Bellwood IL 60104-1833

SZKODY, PAULA, astronomy educator, researcher; b. Detroit, July 17, 1948; d. Julian and Pauline (Wolski) S.; m. Donald E. Brownlee, Mar. 19, 1976; children: Allison, Carson. BS in Astrophysics, Mich. State U., 1970; MS in Astronomy, U. Wash., 1972, PhD in Astronomy, 1975. Rsch. asst. Observatoire de Geneve, 1969, Kitt Peak Nat. Obs., 1970; rsch., teaching asst. U. Wash., Seattle, 1970-75, rsch. assoc., lectr., 1975-82, sr. rsch. assoc., 1982-83, rsch. assoc. prof., 1983-91, rsch. prof., 1991-93, prof., 1993—. Part-time mem. faculty Seattle U., 1974-75, 82, Bellevue Coll., 1975-77; vis. scientist Kitt Peak Nat. Obs., 1976; vis. instr. UCLA, 1977, adj. asst. prof., 1980, 81; vis. asst. prof. U. Hawaii, 1978; vis. asst. prof. Calif. Inst. Tech., 1978-79, 80, mem. XTE users com., 1996-99; mem. users com. Internat. Ultraviolet Explorer, 1983-85, 93-97; mem. A.J. Cannon adv. com. AAUW, 1986-91, chmn. 1988-90; mem. mgmt. ops. working group on Ultraviolet/Visual/Relativity, NASA, 1988-91. Contbr. numerous articles to profl. jours. Recipient Annie J. Cannon award, 1978. Fellow AAAS (mem. nominating com. 1990-93, chairperson 1993, mem.-at-large 1995-99); mem. Am. Assn. Variable Star Observers, Am. Astron. Soc. (councilor 1996-99), Internat. Astron. Union; mem. commn. 42 organizing com. 1991-97, v.p. 1997-00, pres. 2000—), Astron. Soc. Pacific (bd. dirs. 1988-92), Phi Beta Kappa. Office: U Wash Dept Astronomy PO Box 351580 Seattle WA 98195-1580 E-mail: szkody@astro.washington.edu.

SZOSTAK, M. ANNE, bank executive; b. London, 1950; BA in sociology, Colby Coll., Waterville, Maine, 1972; student, Husson Coll., 1992. Pres. Fleet Nat. Bank, Providence, 1980—82; sr. VP Fleet Nat. Bank, 1982—85, exec. VP, 1985—88, corp. VP, head human resources, 1988—91; pres., COO Fleet Bank Maine, 1991—94; sr. VP human resources FleetBoston Fin. Corp., 1994—98, exec. VP, dir. human resources and diversity, 1998—; chmn., CEO Fleet RI, RI, 2001—. Bd. dirs. Providence Energy Corp., New England Bus. Svcs. Chmn. Boys & Girls Clubs of Am., 2003—; bd. mem. United Way Women's Leadership Com. Named to Human Resources Honor Roll, Human Resources Exec. Mag., 2001; recipient Disting. Alumni Award, Colby Coll., Leadership Award, New England Coun., 1993, Athena Award, YWCA Outstanding Women's Gala, 2002. Office: Fleet Boston Fin 1 Federal St Boston MA 02110-2012

SZYMANSKI, EDNA MORA, dean; b. Caracas, Venezuela, Mar. 19, 1952; came to U.S., 1952; d. José Angel and Helen Adele (McHugh) Mora; m. Michael Bernard, Mar. 30, 1973. BS, Rensselaer Poly. Inst., 1972; MS, U. Scranton, 1974; PhD, U. Tex., 1988. Cert. rehab. counselor. Vocat. evaluator Mohawk Valley Workshop, Utica, N.Y., 1974-75; vocat. rehab. counselor N.Y. State Office Vocat. Rehab., Utica, 1975-80, sr. vocat. rehab. counselor, 1980-87; rsch. assoc. U. Tex., Austin, 1988-89; asst. prof. U. Wis., Madison, 1989-91, assoc. prof., 1991-93, assoc. dean sch. edn., 1993-97, dir. rehab. rsch. and tng. ctr., 1993-96, prof. rehab. psychology and spl. edn., 1997—99, chair dept. rehab. psychology and spl. edn., 1997-99, fellow tchg. acad., 1997; dean Coll. Edn. U. Md., College Park, 1999—. Cons. Rsch. Assocs. Syracuse, N.Y., 1988-90. Co-author various book chpts.; co-editor: Rehabilitation Counseling Basics and Beyond, 1992, 98; co-editor Work and Disability, 1996, 2003, Rehabilitation Counseling Bull., 1994-2000; contbr. articles to profl. jours. Mem. Pres.'s Com. on Employment of People with Disabilities, Washington, 1987-97. Recipient Rsch. award Am. Assn. Counselor Edn. and Supr., 1991. Mem. ACA (chair rsch. com. 1992-94, Rsch. awards 1990, 93, 95), Am. Rehab. Counseling Assn. (pres. 1985-86, rsch. award 1989, 94, Disting. Profl. award 1997, James F. Garrett award for disting. career in rehab. rsch. 1999), Coun. Rehab. Edn. (chair rsch. com. 1990-95, v.p. 1993-95, 97), Nat. Coun. Rehab. Edn. (chair rsch. com. 1992-99, Rehab. Edn. Rschr. of Yr. 1993, New Career in Rehab. Edn. award 1990). Office: U Md Coll Edn 3119 Benjamin Bldg College Park MD 20742-1100 Office Phone: 301-405-2336. E-mail: ednas@umd.edu.

SZYMANSKI, THERESE, marketing professional, writer; b. Southfield, Mich., Dec. 22, 1968; d. Alphonse and Virginia Szymanski. BA, Mich. State U., East Lansing, 1987—91. Copywriter, media buyer/planner, rschr. J.K. Kidd & Co., Bingham Farms, Mich., 1993—96; media buyer/planner, rsch. dir. Mars Advt., Southfield, 1996—98; mktg. cons. Media Power, Farmington Hills, 1998—99; mktg. comm. specialist Creative Solutions, Dexter, Mich., 1999—2000; found. gifts mgr. Nat. Gay and Lesbian Task Force (NGLTF), Washington, 2000—01; project mgr. Wendt Ctr. for Loss and Healing, Washington, 2002—03. Freelance designer, 1999—; freelance writer, 1987—; mktg. cons., 1998—. Author: (novel) When Evil Changes Face, 2000 (Finalist for a Lambda Lit. Award, 2002), When Good Girls Go Bad, 2003, When Some Body Disappears, When the Dead Speak, 1998, When the Dancing Stops, When the Corpse Lies, 2004; author and director: play Office Politics, 1998, And Divided We Fall, 1994 (Undergraduate Playwrighting Award-Winner, 1992); actor: (play) This Brooding Sky, 1996; contbr. novella in anthology Once Upon a Dyke; author (director): (play) Just a Phase: A Sapphic Tale, 1997 (Undergraduate Playwrighting Award-3rd Pl., 1992), Some Body's in the Closet; editor: (anthology) Back to Basics: A Butch/Femme Erotic Journey, 2004; contbr. short stories to jours. and collections. Bd. mem. South East Mich. Pride, Inc., Detroit, 1993—95; vol. Mautner Project, Washington, 2000—03; playwright in residence Pissed Off Wimmin Theatre Troupe, Detroit, 1994—98. Mem.: Sisters in Crime. Avocations: skiing, backpacking, weightlifting. Personal E-mail: tsszymanski@worldnet.att.net.

SZYMECZEK, PEGGY LEE, contract specialist; b. Piqua, Ohio, Jan. 31, 1953; d. Titus Taft and Veda Eura (Carpenter) Hooley; m. Fredrick Jones, Oct. 5, 1978 (div. Nov. 1985); 1 child, Fredrika; m. Larry D. Szymeczek, Jr., June 12, 1994. BA, Judson Coll., 1976; MPA, Golden Gate U., 1987. Telephone operator Dept. of the Army, Ft. Huachuca, Ariz., 1984-87; mgmt. asst., 1987-89; maint. svcs. asst., 1989-92; contract splst., 1992—. Adj. prof. German Cochise Coll., Sierra Vista, Ariz., 1983-84. Fin. chair Advance Planning Briefing for Industry, Ft. Huachuca, 1999. Splst. 4 U.S. Army, 1976-78. Recipient Army Achievement Medal; named Hon. mem. 54th Signa Bn., 1995. Mem. AAUW, Nat. Contract Mgmt. Assn. (sec. Coronado chpt. 1994-96, Robert Drew meml. award 1996, treas. 1998, officer S.W. region, functional dir. membership 1996-97). Avocations: reading, music. Office: USACECOM Acquisition Ctr AMSEL-AC-CC-S-RT-C Bldg 61801 Rm 3413 Fort Huachuca AZ 85613-5000 Home: 132 Kingsbridge Dr Goose Creek SC 29445-6645

SZYMKOWIAK, MARY L. non-profit organization administrator; b. Buffalo, Oct. 31, 1961; d. Edward and Patricia Marie (Kobielski) S.. BA, Cornell U., 1984. Asst. treas. Union Bank of Switzerland, N.Y.C., 1985—88; asst. v.p. 1st Am. Bank N.Y., N.Y.C., 1989—90; mgr. Union Sq. Cafe, N.Y.C., 1993—94; controller Gramercy Tavern, N.Y.C., 1994—96; mgr. Kaufman-Dahl, Inc., N.Y.C., 1996—98; nat. coord. The Human Adventure Corp., N.Y.C., 1998—, CFO, bd. dirs., 1998—. Bd. dirs. Resources, Inc., Bklyn., sec., 1998—. Roman Catholic. Office: The Human Adventure Corp 420 Lexington Ave # 2754-55 New York NY 10170

SZYMONIAK, ELAINE EISFELDER, retired state senator; b. Boscobel, Wis., May 24, 1920; d. Hugo Adolph and Pauline (Vig) Eisfelder; Casimir Donald Szymoniak, Dec. 7, 1943; children: Kathryn, Peter, John, Mary, Thomas. BS, U. Wis., 1941; MS, Iowa State U., 1977. Speech clinician Waukesha (Wis.) Pub. Sch., 1941-43, Rochester (N.Y.) Pub. Sch., 1943-44; rehab. aide U.S. Army, Chickasha, Okla., 1944-46; audiologist U. Wis., Madison, 1946-48; speech clinician Buffalo Pub. Sch., 1948-49, Sch. for Handicapped, Salina, Kans., 1951-52; speech pathologist, audiologist, counselor, resource mgr. Vocat. Rehab. State Iowa, Des Moines, 1956-85; mem. Iowa Senate, Des Moines, 1989—2000; ret., 2000. Bd. dir. On With Life, Terrace Hill Found. Adv. bd. Iowa State Inst. for Social and Behavioral Health; mem. Child Care Resource and Referral Cmty. Empowerment Bd., Greater Des Moines Coun. for Internat. Understanding, United Way, 1987—88, Urban Dreams, Iowa Maternal and Child Health com.; pres. Chrysalis Found., 1997; mem. City-County Study Commn.; Mem. Des Moines City coun., 1978—88; bd. dirs. Nat. League Cities, Washington, 1982—84, Civic Ctr., House of Mercy, Westminster House, Iowa Leadership Consortium, Iowa Comprehensive Health Assn. Named Woman of Achievement, YWCA, 1982, Visionary Woman, 1993, Young Women's Resource Ctr., 1989; named to Iowa Women's Hall of Fame, 1999; named Des Moines Woman of Influence, Bus. Record, 2000. Mem. Am. Speech Lang. and Hearing Assn.; Iowa Speech Lang. and Hearing Assn. (pres. 1977-78), Nat. Coun. State Legislators (fed. state com. on health, adv. com. on child protection), Women's Polit. Caucus, Nexus (pres. 1981-82, mem.

Supreme Ct. Select Com.), Wellmark Found. (adv. bd.), Des Moines (Iowa) Women's Club (bd. dir. 2003—). Avocations: reading, traveling, swimming, whitewater rafting. Home: 2116 44th St Des Moines IA 50310-3011 E-mail: ElaineSzy@aol.com.

SZYSZKA, ROSWITA EVELYN, artist; b. Chgo., Apr. 5, 1955; d. John and Regina (Rizinger) Schilli; m. Michael C. Szyszka, Jan. 29, 1977; children: David M., Eric S. AA, Am. Acad. Art, 1976. Illustrator The World Healing Book; artist: Looking Out, Looking In; featured Woodstock Colony of Arts Web Site (Top 100 artists of the 20th Century). Mem. Woodstock Artist Assn., The Woodstock Guild. E-mail: RoswitaSzyszka@hotmail.com.

TABAKA, SANDRA LEE, medical/surgical nurse; d. Elmer William and Elaine Verba Viehmann; m. John Lawrence Tabaka, Oct. 8, 1960 (div. Nov. 1985); children: James Lawrence, Anthony Michael, Theresa Lynn. ADN, St. Mary's Coll., O'Fallon, Mo., 1978; BSN, Webster U., 1993. RN Mo. Staff nurse St. Luke's Hosp., Chesterfield, Mo., 1978—82, assoc. head nurse, 1982—94, staff nurse, 1994—. Founding mem. St. Charles Countians Against Hazardous Waste, 1982—84; bd. mem. Cedar Groves Townhomes Assn., St. Charles, 1999—2002. Mem.: Oncology Nursing Soc. (oncology cert. nurse). Home: 244 Cedar Grove Dr Saint Charles MO 63304

TABER, MARGARET RUTH, retired electrical engineering technology educator, electrical engineer; b. St. Louis, Apr. 29, 1935; d. Wynn Orr and Margaret Ruth (Feldman) Gould Stevens; m. William James Taber, Sept. 6, 1958 B of Engring. Sci., BEE, Cleve. State U., 1958; MS in Engring., U. Akron, 1967; EdD, Nova Southeastern U., 1976; postgrad., Western Res. U., 1959-64. Registered profl. engr., Ohio; cert. engring. technologist. From engring. trainee to tng. dir. Ohio Crankshaft Co., Cleve., 1954-64; from instr. elec.-electronic engring. tech. to prof. Cuyahoga C.C., Cleve., 1964-79, chmn. engring. tech., 1977-79; assoc. prof. elec. engring. tech. Purdue U., West Lafayette, Ind., 1979-83, prof., 1983-2000, prof. emeritus, 2000—. Lectr. Cleve. State U., 1963-64; mem. acad. adv. bd. Cleve. Inst. Electronics, 1981—; cons. in field. Author: (with Frank P. Tedeschi) Solid State Electronics, 1976; (with Eugene M. Silgalis) Electric Circuit Analysis, 1980; (with Jerry L. Casebeer) Registers, 1980; (with Kenneth Rosenow) Arithmetic Logic Units, 1980, Timing and Control, 1980, Memory Units, 1980; 6809 Architecture and Operation, 1984, Programming I: Straight Line, 1984; contbr. articles to profl. jours. Bd. dirs. West Blvd. Christian Ch., deaconess, 1974-77, elder, 1977-79; deacon Federated Ch., 1981-84, 86-89, Stephen Leader, 1988—; mem. Cancer Support Group; vol. Lafayette Reading Acad., 1992—; ednl. resource vol., vol. tchr. Sunburst Farm Rainbow Acres, Inc., Ariz., 1988—. Recipient Helen B. Schleman Gold Medallion award Purdue U., 1991, The Greater Lafayette Cmty. Survivorship award, 1994, Outstanding Alumni award U. Akron Coll. Engring., 1994, Disting. Alumni award, Cleve. State U., 2002; Margaret R. Taber Microcomputer Lab. named in her honor Purdue U., 1991; NSF grant, 1970-73, 78; Rainbow Acres Computer Lab named The Marge Taber Computer Lab., 2002. Fellow Soc. Women Engrs. (counselor Purdue chpt. 1983-94, Disting. Engring. Educator award 1987); mem. IEEE (life sr.), Am. Cancer Soc. (co-chair svc. and rehab com. 1992-94, vol. coord. CanSurmount 1993-98, chair Cmty. Connections, mem. Resource, Info. and Guidance CoreTeam, 1994-98, v.p. Tippecanoe bd. dirs. 1996-98, relay for life hon. chair 1999), Am. Bus. Women's Assn. (ednl. chmn. 1964-66), Am. Soc. Engring. Edn., Am. Tech. Edn. Assn., Tau Beta Pi (hon.), Phi Kappa Phi. Avocations: robotics; camping; housekeeping. Home: 3036 State Rd 26 W West Lafayette IN 47906-4743 Office: Purdue U Elec Engring Tech Dept Knoy Hall Tech West Lafayette IN 47907

TABLEMAN, CLAUDETTE, principal; b. Flushing, N.Y., Nov. 22, 1949; d. Carmine Avena and Angela Ostuni; m. Kevin G. Tableman, July 30, 1972; children: Lauren Leigh, Carley Jeanne. BA, CUNY, 1971; MS, St. John's U., Jamaica, N.Y., 1975; EdD, Columbia U., N.Y.C., 2003. Tchr. Ind. Sch. Dist. 25, Flushing, NY, 1971—89; asst. prin. Parsons Jr. H.S. 168, Flushing, 1989—92, Ryan Jr. H.S. 216, Fresh Meadows, NY, 1992—95; prin. Bayside Sch., NY, 1995—96, Woodmere Mid. Sch., Hewlett, NY, 1996—. Bd. dirs. New Horizons Clinic, Ozone Park, NY, 1977—97. Scholar Danforth scholar, Harvard U., 1988, Chancellor's scholar, CUNY-Queens Coll., 1968. Mem.: AAUW, ASCD, Nat. Assn. Secondary Sch. Prins.

TABLER, SHIRLEY MAY, retired librarian, artist; b. Washington, Mar. 18, 1936; d. Howard Leon and Ella May (Miles) Bosley; m. Edward Charles Sepelak, July 30, 1954 (div. 1965); children: David Edward, Linda May, William Bryan; m. Carlton Byard Tabler, June 27, 1968 (dec. May 1993); stepchildren: Roger Byard, Charlotte Virginia. BS in Art Edn., U. Md., 1977, BA in Libr. Sci., 1978, MA in Art Edn., 1981, MLS, 1990. Sec. Nat. Capital Housing Authority, Washington, 1954-55; clk. Vitro Corp., Silver Spring, Md., 1956-57; hostess, cashier Hot Shoppes, Wheaton, Md., 1960-63; new accounts sec. State Nat. Bank, Bethesda, Md., 1966-68; media aide, art tchr. Montgomery County Pub. Schs., Rockville, Md., 1968-86, libr., cataloguer, computer tech., 1986-93. Exhibited in group shows at Arts Club, Washington, 1990, 91, 92, 93, 94, 95, 96, 97, Rockville Mcpl. Gallery, 1992, 93, 94, 95, 97, 98, 99, 2000, 02, Sugar & Fricht Gallery 1994, 95, Ten Oaks Gallery-Clarksville, 1994, 95, 97, 98, 99, 2000, Town Ctr. Gallery, 1994, Kensington Gallery, 1994, 95, 96, 97, 98, 99, 2000, 01, 02, Strathmore Hall, 1998, 99, 2000, 01, 02, 03, World-Wide Internat. Miniature Art Show, Eng., 1995, Hobart, Tasmania, 2000, Sandy Spring Mus. Art Gallery, 2000, Rockville Unitarian Gallery, 2001, Washington Area Printmakers Calendar, 1997, 98, 99, 2000, 01, 02, 03; one-person shows include Rockville Mcpl. Gallery 1989, Landon Gallery, Bethesda. Md., 1990, Washington Printmakers Gallery, 1994, 97, 2000, 02, Galleries at Savage Mill, 1996, 97, Cafe Monet Gallery, 1997, 98, 99, 2000, 02. Leader, advisor Girl Scouts U.S., Rockville, 1964-82. Mem. ALA, Soc. Librs. Internat., Am. Art League, Nat. League Am. Pen Women (past pres. Chevy Chase, pes. 2000-02), Md. Printmakers, Miniature Painters, Sculptors and Gravers Soc., D.C., Cider Painters Am., Art Gallery of Fells Point, Miniature Art Soc. Fla., Olney Art Assn. (newsletter editor 1984-91, show chmn. 1993, 98, libr. show chmn. 1992-94, program chmn. 1995, 96, 97, 98, joint show chair 1998), Rockville Art League, Phi Kappa Phi. Democrat. Methodist. Avocations: camping, leather tooling, painting, quilting, ceramics. Home: 123 Charles St Rockville MD 20850-1510 Office: Genevieve Roberts Studio 17521 Shenandoah Ct Ashton MD 20861-9774 E-mail: ladybugtab@juno.com.

TABLER, SUSAN BEIDLER, lawyer; b. Quakertown, Pa., Nov. 13, 1943; d. Henry Landis and Pauline Henrietta Beidler; m. Bryan Grant Tabler, Dec. 28, 1968 (div. July 1987); children: Justin Elizabeth, Gillian Gardner. BA, Wellesley Coll., 1965; JD summa cum laude, Ind. U., Indpls., 1975. Intern BBC, London, 1965-67; examiner Ednl. Testing Svc., Princeton, N.J., 1967-69; adminstrv. assoc. Long Wharf Theatre, New Haven, 1969-72; assoc. Ice Miller Donadio & Ryan, Indpls., 1975-81, ptnr., 1982—. Bd. dirs. Ind. Sports Corp., Indpls. Pres. bd. dirs. Julian Ctr., Indpls., 1975-80; bd. dirs. Cathedral Arts, Indpls., 1975-79. Fellow Ind. Bar Found.; mem. ABA (chmn. standing com. on Gavel awards 1985-88, labor law div. vice chair gen. practice sect. 1988-91), Ind. State Bar Assn., Indpls. Bar Assn., Ind. U. Alumni Assn. (bd. dirs. 1989—). Office: Ice Miller Donadio & Ryan 1 American Sq Indianapolis IN 46282-0020

TABOR, LINDA J. performing arts educator; b. Bridgeport, Conn., May 10, 1965; d. James Atwood Tabor and Ruth Paula Sykes. BFA magna cum laude, U. Bridgeport, 1999. Tchr. drama and dance Music and Arts Ctr. for the Handicapped, Bridgeport, 1987-2000, co-coord. new visions dance project, 1989-91; tchr. drama and dance Charles D. Smith Jr. Found., Bridgeport, 1993-94. Tutor Literacy Vols. of Am., Bridgeport, 1995-96. Mem. Phi Kappa Phi. Avocations: music, reading, t'ai chi, writing children's books.

TABRISKY, PHYLLIS PAGE, physiatrist, educator; b. Newton, Mass., Aug. 28, 1930; d. Joseph Westley and Alice Florence (Wainwright) Page; m. Joseph Tabrisky, Apr. 23, 1955; children: Joseph Page, Elizabeth Ann, William Page. BS, Douglass Coll., 1952; MD, Tufts U., 1956. Cert. phys. medicine and rehab. Intern U. Ill. Hosp., Chgo., 1956-57; phys. medicine and rehab. residency U. Colo. Sch. Medicine, Denver, 1958-60; gen. med. officer dept. pediatrics and medicine Coco Solo Hosp., Panama Canal Zone, 1961-62; staff physician dept. pediatrics Ft. Hood (Tex.) Army Hosp., 1963; instr. dept. rehab. medicine Boston (Mass.) U. Sch. Medicine, 1964-66; asst. prof. phys. medicine and rehab. U. Colo. Sch. Medicine, Denver, 1966-68; staff physician VA Med. Ctr., Long Beach, Calif., 1968-71, acting chief phys. medicine and rehab., 1971-73, asst. chief rehab. med. svcs., 1973-91, chief phys. medicine & rehab. svc., 1992—. Asst. clin. prof. phys. medicine and rehab. U. Calif. Coll. Medicine, Irvine, 1970-75, assoc. clin. prof., 1975-80, prof., 1980—, vice chair dept. phys. medicine and rehab., 1985—, dir. residency tng., 1982—. Fellow Am. Acad. Phys. Medicine and Rehab. (mem. accreditation coun. grad. med. com. 1993—); mem. Am. Congress Rehab. Medicine, Assn. Acad. Physiatrists (bd. trustees 1995-97), Alpha Omega Alpha. Republican. Episcopalian. Avocation: U.S. history. Office: VA Med Ctr 5901 E 7th St Long Beach CA 90822-5201

TACHA, ATHENA, sculptor, educator; b. Larissa, Greece, Apr. 23, 1936; came to U.S., 1963; MA, Nat. Acad. Fine Arts, Athens, Greece, 1959; MA in Art History, Oberlin Coll., 1961; PHD, U. Paris, 1963. Curator modern art Allen Art Mus., Oberlin, Ohio, 1963-73; prof. art Oberlin Coll., 1973-2000; adj. prof. art U. Md., College Park, 1999—. One-woman shows include Zabriskie Gallery, N.Y., 1979, 81, Max Hutchinson Gallery, N.Y., 1984, High Mus. Art, Atlanta, 1989, Franklin Furnace, N.Y., 1994, Beck Ctr., Cleve., 1998-99, Found. for Hellenic Culture, N.Y., 2001, also numerous other exhibits throughout the world, 1966—; prin. pub. commns. include sculptures at Am. Airlines Ctr., Dallas., City of Phila., Dept. Environ. Protection, Trenton, N.J., Case-Western Res. U., Cleve., Low Water Dam Riverfront Pk., Tulsa, Dept. of Transp., Hartford, Conn., City of Sarasota, Fla., Ecology Dept. U. Minn., St. Paul; collections include Hirshhorn Mus., Washington, Albright-Knox Art Gallery, Buffalo, Mus. Fine Arts, Houston, Nat. Coll. Fine Arts, Washington, Cleve. Mus. Art, Munson-Williams-Proctor Inst., Uttica, Nelson-Atkins Mus. Art, Kansas City, Allen Art Mus., Oberlin, Speed Art Mus., Louisville; author: (as A. T. Spear) Rodin Sculpture in the Cleveland Museum of Art, 1967, Brancusi's Birds, 1969; contbr. articles to profl. jours.; subject of book Cosmic Rhythms: Athena Tacha's Public Sculpture (E. McClelland), 1998, Dancing in the Landscape: The Sculpture of Athena Tacha, 2000. Recipient 1st prize May Show, Cleve. Mus. Art, 1968, 71, 79; NEA grantee, 1975; Bogliasco Found./Liguria Study Ctr. fellow, 2003. Home: 3721 Huntington St NW Washington DC 20015-1817 E-mail: atacha@umd.edu.

TACHA, DEANELL REECE, federal judge; b. Jan. 26, 1946; BA, U. Kans., 1968; JD, U. Mich., 1971. Spl. asst. to U.S. Sec. of Labor, Washington, 1971—72; assoc. Hogan & Hartson, Washington, 1973, Thomas J. Pitner, Concordia, Kans., 1973—74; dir. Douglas County Legal Aid Clinic, Lawrence, Kans., 1974—77; assoc. prof. law U. Kans., Lawrence, 1974—77, prof., 1977—85, assoc. dean, 1977—79, assoc. vice chancellor, 1979—81, vice chancellor, 1981—85; judge U.S. Ct. Appeals (10th cir.), Denver, 1985—; U.S. sentencing commr., 1994—98; chief judge U.S. Ct. Appeals (10th cir.), Denver, 2001—.

TACKE, ELEANOR, archivist; b. Highland Park, Mich., Feb. 13, 1939; d. Harold Starr and Margaret Eleanor (Gillett) Atherton; m. Carl Ewald Tacke, Nov. 24, 1961; children: Lisa Kathleen, Paul Christopher. B Gen. Studies, Wayne State U., 1991, M of Libr. Info. Sci., 1998. Sec. Gen. Motors Corp., Warren, Mich., 1961-65, exec. sec., 1979-95; tng. archivist Wayne State U., Detroit, 1996-97, grad. rsch. asst., 1997-98; photog. archivist Schroeder Info. Sys., Inc., Detroit, 1998—2000; archivist papers of James Beardsley Hendryx Leelanau Hist. Mus., Leland, Mich., 2003. Pres., Warren Coop. Nursery, 1971-72, Friends of Interlochen Pub. Libr.; trustee Interlochen Pub. Libr., 2002—; dir. Women's History Project N.W. Mich., Traverse City. Mem. AAUW, LWV of Grosse Pointe (v.p. 1995-2000), Mich. Archival Assn., Soc. Am. Archivists. Avocations: swimming, reading, travel, going to concerts and plays. Home: 5713 Bush Rd Interlochen MI 49643-9592

TACKETT, MARESA D. medical technician; b. Bogalusa, La., July 23, 1975; Cert. surgical technician Tenn. Tech. Ctr. of Memphis, 2000, laproscopic specialist. Surgical technologist Baptist Hosp., Collerville, Tenn., 2000—01; cert. surg. technologist O.R., Inc., Memphis, 2001—. Home: 180 Stonewall Rd Byhalia MS 38611

TACKWELL, ELIZABETH MILLER, social worker; b. Caney, Kans., Mar. 14, 1923; d. Jesse Winfield and Mattie (Shuler) Miller; m. Joseph J. Tackwell, Dec. 13, 1946 (dec. Mar. 1988); children: Steven, Tiana Tackwell David, Christy Tackwell. BA cum laude, U. Okla., 1953, MSW, 1962. Bd. cert. diplomate Am. Bd. Examiners in Clin. Social Work; lic. social worker, Okla. Social worker Dept. Pub. Welfare, Tulsa/Cleve./Okla. County, Okla., 1958-59, med. social analyst, 1960-61; assoc. John Massey M.D. Clinic, Oklahoma City, 1964-69; clin. asst. prof. Okla. U. Sch. Social Work, Oklahoma City, 1964—; asst. prof., clin. instr. dept. psychiatry/behavioral scis. Okla. U. Health Scis. Ctr., Oklahoma City, 1963—; psychiat. social worker VA Med. Ctr., Oklahoma City, 1961-97, chief mental health sect., 1976-97, adminstrv. dir. day treatment ctr., 1993-97; pvt. practice Oklahoma City, 1971—. Psychiat. surveyor Health Care Fin. Adminstrn., Dept. Human Svcs., Washington, 1985—. Recipient Svc. Commendation award DAV, 1980, Awards Am. Ex-Prisoners of War, 1994, 95, 96. Mem. NASW (diplomate in clin. social work, pres. Okla. chpt. 1971-73, Social Worker of the Yr. Western Okla. chpt. 1975, Lifetime Achievement award Okla. chpt. 1997), Am. Psychotherapy Assn. (cert. diplomate), Acad. Cert. Social Workers, Okla. Health and Welfare Assn. (conf. chmn. 1975—), Pi Gamma Mu. Home and Office: 1328 Tarman Cir Norman OK 73071-4846

TADEO, ELVIA, artist; b. Ensenada, B.C., Mex., Nov. 21, 1970; d. Austreberto and Consuelo (Tadeo) T. Student art, Rafael Contreras, Ensenada, 1986-89, Lorraine M. Rowley, San Diego, 1990-96, Silvia Moonier, 1997-98, Edward Mores, 1998-99. Represented by The Gallery on Broadway, San Diego. Juror La Jolla Art Assn., 1999-2001, Del Mar Fair, Calif., 2001—. Contbg. artist pastel painting: Baja 4 You, 1999; poetry pub. in Art Venues Mag., Newsletter of Pastel Soc. San Diego, Pastel Soc. West Coast; exhibited at LaJolla (Calif.) Art Assn. Gallery, 1997-2001, Galerias Internacionales of Hotel Hyatt Regency, Guadalajara, Mex., 1996-98, Gallery of Pastel Soc. of West Coast, Camino, Calif., 1997, Ceudonium de la Mujer, Ensenada, 1999-2001, Galeria de la Ciudad de Ensenada, B.C., Mex., 2000, Giorgio Santini's Gallery of Fine Arts, Rosarito, Mex., 2000-2001, El Centro Cultural San Angel, Mexico City, 2000, Centro Cultural Riviera, Ensenada, 2000, Centro Cultural Siglo 21, Mexico City, 2001, Hosp. Tembre, Mexico, 2001, Teatro la Cjuda-deia, Mexico, 2001, Hosp. of Pemex City, 2002, House of Reps., Mexico City, 2002, The Gallery on Broadway, San Diego; rep. Gallery on Broadway, San Diego, Gallery Giorgio Santini, Rosarito, San Diego Mus. of Art, Artist Guild, 2002-03. Art cons. Cultural Ctr. of Ensenada, 2000—; nat dir. Mexican Rep. in the Art Miles project, United Nations U.S.A. rep., 2002-03. Recipient 1st place Del Mar Fair, 1996, Spl. award, 1996. Mem. LaJolla Art Assn. (publicity chair 1999-2001), Pastel Soc. of West Coast, Degas Pastel Soc., Pastel Soc. San Diego, Carlsbad and Oceanside Art League, Internat. Assn. Pastels, Directorio Enciclopedico de las Artes Plasticas, Directorio of Artistas Plasticos de la Cordinacion Nacional de Artes Plasticas de Bellas Artes. Roman Catholic. Avocations: horseback riding, hiking. Office: PO Box 2229 Vista CA 92085 E-mail: elviatadeo@aol.com.

TADLOCK, ANITA CONNER, volunteer; b. New Orleans, Sept. 11, 1944; d. Marion and Lorena (Dobyns) Conner; m. Norman Edward Tadlock, June 25, 1966; children: Edward Scott, Stephanie Lee, Elizabeth Conner, Stephen Dobyns. BMusic, Queens Coll., Charlotte, N.C., 1966; student, U. Vienna, 1964, Colegio de Espana, Salamanca, Spain, 1993. Social worker Bur. Children's Svcs., Morristown, N.J., 1966-67, 69-70; pvt. piano tchr. N.J., 1966-82. Donations chair Am. Women's Assn. Singapore, 1992, chair cmty. svcs. com., 1993, 1st v.p., 1994, pres., 1994-95; bd. dirs. Am. Assn. of Singapore, 1994-95; chair in charge of food George Washington Ball com., 1996-97; bd. dirs. Am. Club of Singapore, 1994-96, membership chair, 1996-97; docent Singapore Nat. History Mus., 1995-97; mem. fin. com. Trinity United Meth. Ch., Hackettstown, N.J., 1998-2000; active Jr. League of London, 1984-91, non-resident sustainer, 1991—; active Boy Scouts Am., Girl Scouts U.S.; pres. PTA, 1982-84. Recipient Outstanding Vol. award Am. Assn., Singapore, 1996, Am. Women's Assn., Singapore, 1996. Mem. DAR, Jr. League of London, Delta Omicron, Kappa Delta. Methodist. Avocations: travel, reading, antiquing.

TAFOYA, MICHELE, sports reporter; Talk show host Minn. Vikings Talk Radio, KFAN, 1993—94; reporter CBS Sports, 1994—2000, ESPN, 2000—, NBA on ABC, 2003; sideline reporter Sunday Night NFL, ESPN, 2002—04, Monday Night Football, ABC, 2004—. Office: 77 W 66th St New York NY 10023*

TAFT, FRANCES PRINDLE, art history educator; b. New Haven, Dec. 12, 1921; d. William Edwin and Mildred (Bradley) Prindle; m. Seth Chase Taft, June 19, 1943; children: Frederick Irving, Thomas Prindle, Cynthia Bradley, Seth Tucker. BA with honors, Vassar Coll., 1942; MA, Yale U., 1948. Rsch. asst. Yale Med. Sch., New Haven, 1942; instr. comms. USN Officer Sch., Northampton, Mass., 1943-45; tchr. anatomy and art The Gateway Sch., New Haven, 1943-44; prof. art history Cleve. Inst. Art, 1950—. Bd. trustees Cleve. Mus. Art, mem. women's coun., lectr., 1950—; bd. trustees Karamu Art Ctr., Cleve., 1949-65; mem., bd. dirs. Vassar Art Gallery, Poughkeepsie, N.Y., 1972—. Chmn. bd. overseers Case Western Res. U., Cleve., 1984-86; trustee Michelson-Morley Ctr., Cleve., 1986-87; trustee Laurel Sch., 1950s— past pres.; mem. adv. com. Martha Holden Jennings Found., Cleve., 1973-91; pres. alumni/alumnae Assn. Vassar Coll., Poughkeepsie, 1966-72. Named Career Woman of Achievement, Cleve. YWCA, 1993; recipient Cleve. Arts prize, 1995, medal for excellence Cleve. Inst. Art, 1994, Spl. Citation award 1996; Frances Prindle Taft scholarship named in her honor Cleve. Inst. Art, 2003. Mem. Coll. Art Assn., Cleve. Soc. Archtl. Historians (past pres. local chpt.), Cleve. Archaeol. Soc. (past pres.), Print Club Cleve. Avocation: tennis player with national ranking since 1965. Home: 6 Pepper Ridge Rd Cleveland OH 44124-4904 Office Phone: 216-721-7301. E-mail: frannytaft@aol.com.

TAGGART, HELEN M. adult education educator, nurse; b. Savannah, Ga., Dec. 6, 1946; d. Thomas Anthony and Ruth Elizabeth (Sisson) McKenzie; m. Thomas Robert Taggart, Mar. 9, 1968; children: Kathleen Taggart Swanner, Thomas Robert Jr. BSN, Armstrong State Coll., 1978; MSN, Ga. So. U., 1992; postgrad., U. Ala., Birmingham, 1995—. Staff nurse St. Joseph's Hosp., Savannah, 1967-68, 77-89, head nurse, 1971-74, St. Mary's Hosp., Athens, Ga., 1968-71; instr. Armstrong State Coll., Savannah, 1989-92; asst. prof. Armstrong Atlantic State U., Savannah, 1992—. Profl. adv. com. Nat. Multiple Sclerosis Soc., Atlanta, 1992-96; bd. mem. Ga. Bd. Nursing, Atlanta, 1994—; mem. Clin. Simulation Task Force Nat. Coun. State Bds. Nursing, Chgo., 1996-99. Editor, contbr.: Adult Nursing in Acute Community, 1998; contbr. articles to profl. jours. and chpts. to books. Counselor Multiple Sclerosis Support Group, Savannah, 1989-97. Nat. Assn. Orthop. Nurses rsch. grantee, 1996, U. Ala. (Birmingham) traineeship grantee, 1997, Armstrong Atlantic State U. rsch. grantee, 1997-98. Mem. Nat. League Nurses (exec. bd. 1996-98), Assn. Bus. Women Am. (exec. bd. 1994-96), Nat. Assn. Orthop. Nurses (rsch. com. 1995-99), Ga. Nurses Assn. (exec. bd. 1992-96). Avocations: gardening, swimming, snow skiing. Home: 6 Mulberry Bluff Dr Savannah GA 31406-3226 Office: Armstrong Atlantic State Univ 11935 Abercorn St Savannah GA 31419-1989

TAGHIZADEH, GEORGEANNE MARIE, medical/surgical nurse, diagnostic cardiac sonographer; b. Cleve., July 14, 1969; d. George Dennis Hancsak, Ellyn Marie (Liedtke) Hancsak; m. Touraj Taghizadeh, Sept. 19, 2000; children: Alex children: Darius. AAS, Cuyahoga C.C., Cleve., 1993, AS, 1995; nursing diploma, Fairview Gen. Hosp. Sch. Nursing, 1995. RN Ohio, registered diagnostic cardiac sonographer. Cardiac sonographer U. Hosps. Cleve., 1993—96, staff nurse, clin. nurse sonographer, 1997—98, advanced practice nurse/cardiac sonographer, 1998—. Mem.: Soc. Diagnostic Med. Sonographers, Am. Coll. Cardiovasc. Nursing, Ohio Nurses Assn., Am. Soc. Echocardiography. Roman Catholic. Avocations: jogging, travel. Home: 22184 Horseshoe Ln Strongsville OH 44149 Personal E-mail: Georgetouraj@ameritech.net.

TAGIURI, CONSUELO KELLER, child psychiatrist, educator; b. San Francisco; d. Cornelius H. and Adela (Rios) Keller; m. Renato Tagiuri; children: Robert, Peter, John. BA, U. Calif.-Berkeley; MD, U. Calif.-San Francisco. Diplomate Am. Bd. Psychiatry and Neurology. Resident psychiatry Mass. Gen. Hosp., Boston; staff psychiatrist Children's Hosp., Boston, 1951-59; med. dir. Gifford Sch., Weston, Mass., 1965-85; chief psychiatrist Cambridge (Mass.) Guidance Ctr., 1961-84; mem. faculty dept. psychiatry Harvard Med. Sch., 1965—2002; cons. early childhood program Children's Hosp., 1985—. Contbr. articles in field to books. Fellow Am. Orth. Psychiat. Assn., Mass. Med. Soc., New Eng. Coun. Child Psychiatry.

TAGLE, HILDA GLORIA, former judge; b. Corpus Christi, Dec. 18, 1946; d. Manuel Cisneros and Dolores (Cipriano) T.; 1 child, Santiago. AA, Del Mar Coll., Corpus Christi, 1968; BA, East Tex. State U., 1969; MLS, North Tex. State U., 1971; JD, U. Tex., 1977. Bar: Tex. 1977, U.S. Dist. Ct. (so. dist.) Tex. 1989, U.S. Supreme Ct. 1985. Asst. city atty. City of Corpus Christi, 1977-78; asst. county atty. Nueces County, 1978-79; asst. dist. atty. Nueces County Dist. Atty., 1979-81; pvt. practice law Corpus Christi, 1981-85; judge Nueces County Ct. at Law No. 3, Corpus Christi, 1985—. Mem. State Commn. on Jud. Conduct, Austin, Tex., 1989—; mem. Gov's. Commn. for Women; mem. jud. edn. exec. com. Supreme Ct. Tex., Austin, 1987-89. Recipient Good Gals award Tex. Women's Polit. Caucus, 1990. Mem. Corpus Christi Bar Assn. (chmn. lawyers for literacy com. 1989-90, Women Lawyers of Coastal Bend, State Bar Tex. (co-chmn. ann. meeting planning com. 1991), Alpha Lambda Sigma. Mem. Christian Ch. (Disciples Of Christ). Office: Nueces County Ct at Law 3 901 Leopard Ste 703 Corpus Christi TX 78401

TAGLIENTE, JOSEPHINE MARLENE, artist; b. Chisholm, Minn., Nov. 23, 1939; d. Joseph and Carmela (DeLuca) T.; m. Wayne W. Brown, May 28, 1960 (div. 1972); children: Michael Anthony, Troy Tagliente, Roben Tagliente, Angela Monique, Ninon Terese, Anina Maria (dec.). Student, Mpls. Coll. Art and Design, 1957-59, Mankato State Coll., 1966, Kansas City Art Inst., 1972; MFA, U. Guanajuato, Mex., 1974. Artist-in-residence Jewish Cmty. Ctr., Wilmington, 1969; illustration chairperson, mem. faculty Ray Coll. of Design, Chgo., 1980-87; adj. faculty Paradise Valley C.C., Phoenix; spkr. in field. One-woman exhbn. Natalini Gallery, Chgo., 1986; group exhbns. include Windbell Gallery, Wilmington, Del., Newark (Del.) Gallery, Galeria San Miguel, Mex., Galeria Osman, Mex., Galeria Condor, Mex., Torres Gallery, Albuquerque, Dartmouth Gallery, Albuquerque, Edith Lampert Gallery, Santa Fe, La Luna Nueva, Santa Fe,

Herberger Theatre, Phoenix Little Theatre, Artesimo Gallery, Scottsdale, Ariz., Del. Art Mus., Wilmington, Sky Harbor Airport, 1994, Westaff, UK-Ariz., Canticles: Sight and Sound, 2002, others; represented in corp. collections Collins, Miller & Hutchins, Chgo., Mt. Sinai Hosp., N.Y.C.; also pvt. and pub. permanent collections; represented by Artisimo Gallery, Scottsdale; illustrations published in books; poetry published in anthologies; inventor garden products, office implements. Vol. art educator St. Anne's Intercity, Wilmington, 1967-68, Recreation Intercity, Chgo., 1978-79; cultural advocate for homeless Cultural Labor Party, Chgo., 1980-87, cultural advocate for minority concerns, 1985-88. Recipient Fine Art award Artist's Guild of Chgo., 1977, Print Drawing award, 1978, Educator/Svcs. award Sauk Area Career Ctr., 1984. Mem. Nat. Mus. Women in Arts, The Drawing Soc., Soc. Children's Book Writers and Illustrators, Statue of Liberty-Ellis Island Found. Social Democrat. Avocations: writing, digital painting, raising turtles and studying their habitat. E-mail: joyfulsunrise@qwest.net.

TAHIR, MARY ELIZABETH (LIZ TAHIR), marketing professional, consultant, speaker, writer; b. Greenwood, Miss., Dec. 14, 1933; d. Mahmoud Ibrahim and Mary Constance Tahir. Student, U. Miss., 1951-53. Cert. Profl. Cons., Acad, Profl. Cons. and Advisors. Mgmt. trainee Neiman-Marcus Co., Dallas, 1954-56; asst. buyer D.H. Holmes Co. Ltd., New Orleans, 1956-58, buyer, 1958-65, assoc. divisional mdse. mgr., 1965-67, divisional v.p., 1969-79, corp. v.p., gen. mdse. mgr., 1979-89; pres. Liz Tahir & Assocs., New Orleans, 1990—. Author: Mexico's Cosmetic and Fragrance Market: Past, Present and Future Opportunities, 1991, The Changing World of Mexican Retail Opportunities, 1991, Mexico: Window of Opportunity, 1991, Art of Negotiating, 1993, Negotiating More Profitable with Your Suppliers, Customers and Employees, 1994, Sizzling Customer Service, 1998. Bd. dirs. Vieux Carre Property Owners Assn., New Orleans, 1990, 2002, YWCA, 1996-2002. Recipient Role Model award YWCA, 1990, Woman Bus. Owner of the Yr. award, 1996. Mem. Women's Profl. Coun. (pres. 1998, chmn. New Choices 1989), Fashion Group Internat. (Alpha award 1987-88, Lifetime Achievement award 1993), Nat. Spkrs. Assn., Am. Mktg. Assn. (bd. dirs. 1996—, pres. 1997), Am. Assn. Profl. Cons., Am. Mgmt. Assn., Fgn. Rels. Assn. (bd. dirs. 1992—, pres. bd. dirs. 1994-96), Nat. Retail Fedn. Avocations: art collecting, textiles collecting. Home: 817 Esplanade Ave New Orleans LA 70116-1940 Office: Liz Tahir & Assocs 201 Saint Charles Ave Ste 2500 New Orleans LA 70170-2500 Office Phone: 504-569-1670. Personal E-mail: liz@liztahir.com.

TAI, ELIZABETH SHI-JUE LEE, library director; b. Si-Ann, China, Aug. 12, 1942; came to the U.S., 1965; d. Jun-Yee Lee and Fang-Yee Liu; m. Hsiang Tai, Dec. 29, 1969; children: Alan C., Victoria C., Brian C. BA in English Lang. and Lit., Nat. Cheng Kung U., Taiwan, 1965; M in Libr. and Info. Sci., Tex. Woman's U., 1967. Sr. libr. Queens (N.Y.) Borough Pub. Libr., 1967-73; asst. regional libr. Cin. Pub. Libr., Libr. for Blind and Physically Handicapped, 1973-75; libr. Ga. State Libr., Atlanta, 1975-78; dir. Poquoson (Va.) Pub. Libr., 1979—. Vol. Va. chpt. ARC-York County, 1980—; vice-chair Peninsula Ret. Sr. Vol. Program Coun., Newport News, Va., 1994—99, chair, 2000; mem. York County (Va.) Sch. Sys. Extend Program Coun., 1997; mem. Va. social svcs. bd. York County/City of Poquoson, 2002—; bd. dirs. Peninsula Ret. Sr. Vol. Program Coun., Newport News, Va., 2001—. Named City Employee of Yr., City of Poquoson, Va., 1989; recipient Letter of Commendation, Va. Gov. James Gilmore III, 2001, Unsung Hero/Heroine award Nat. Cheng Kung U. N.Am. Alumni and Found., 2003. Mem. ALA, Va. Libr. Assn., Va. Pub. Libr. Dirs. Assn. (region 3 rep. 2003—, Outstanding Pub. Rels. award 1998, Outstanding Facility award 1998, Outstanding Young Adult Program award 1999, Outstanding Children's Program award 1999, Outstanding Pub. Rels. Project award 2001, Outstanding Pub. Rels. Project award 2002, Outstanding Libr. Staff award 2003), Tidewater Area Libr. Dirs. Coun., Peninsula Chinese Am. Assn. (bd. mem., 2004—), Kiwanis Club of Tabb (charter mem.). Avocations: reading, gardening, swimming, tennis. Home: 129 Loblolly Dr Yorktown VA 23692-4254 Office: 500 City Hall Ave Poquoson VA 23662-1996 Office Phone: 757-868-3066. E-mail: etai@ci.poquoson.va.us.

TAINATONGA, ROSIE R. former director of education; b. Guam; BS in Bus. Adminstrn., U. Guam. Dir. of edn. Coun. of Chief State Sch. Officers, Washington, 1999—2003.

TAIT, HEATHER JEAN, artist; b. Silver Springs, Md., Apr. 17, 1975; BA, Gannon U., Erie, Pa. Profl. artist Silence Speaks, Atlanta, 1997—. E-mail: contact@silencespeaks.com.

TAKAMURA, JEANETTE CHIYOKO, dean; b. Honolulu, Aug. 1, 1947; d. Jiro and Jane Chiseko (Ishida) Chikamoto; m. Carl Takeshi Takamura, May 17, 1974; 1 child, Mari Leigh. BA, U. Hawaii, 1969, MSW, 1972; PhD, Brandeis U., 1985. Program dir. Moiliili Community Ctr., Honolulu, 1972-74; instr. sch. medicine and social work U. Hawaii, Honolulu, 1975-78, asst. prof., 1982-86; dir. exec. office on aging Office of Gov., Honolulu, 1987-94; dep. dir. State Dept. of Health, Honolulu, 1995-97; asst. sec. for aging U.S. Dept. HHS, Washington, 1997—2002; endowed chair in applied gerontology and pub. svc. Calif. State U., L.A., 2001—02; dean, Sch. Social Work Columbia U., N.Y.C., 2002—. Ptnr. Browne/Takamura, Honolulu, 1985-86. Contbr. articles to profl. jours. and chpts. to books; editorial bd.: Aging Today, 1991—. Adv. com. long term care Milbank Meml. Fund; adv. com. on aging issues World Econ. Forum. Grantee NIMH, 1982-84, U.S. Dept. HHS, 1985, 86, 89-90, 91. Mem. Nat. Assn. Statute Units on Aging (2d v.p. 1991-92), Am. Soc. on Aging (program planning com. 1992-93, exec. com. 1996—, nat. adv. bd. White House Conf. on Aging, 1995), Gerontology Soc. Am., Futurist Soc. Congregationalist. Avocations: travel, reading, walking. Office: Columbia U Sch Social Work McVickar Hall Rm 204 622 W 113th St New York NY 10025

TAKANISHI, RUBY N. foundation administrator, researcher; d. Kazuo and Misae Takanishi; m. Louis L. Knowles, Aug. 23, 1969; 1 child. AB in Psychology with honors, Stanford U., 1968; AM, U. Mich., 1969; postgrad., U. Chgo., 1969-70; PhD, Stanford U., 1973; postgrad., Harvard U., 1978-79. Teaching asst. Bing Nursery Sch. Stanford U., 1968, teaching asst. Sch. Edn., 1972, 73; asst. prof. dept. edn. Grad. Sch. Edn. UCLA, 1973-80, acting head early childhood devel. specialization, 1974, faculty Bush Tng. Program in Child Devel. and Social Policy, 1978-80, assoc. prof., 1980-86; exec. dir. Carnegie Coun on Adolescent Devel Carnegie Corp., N.Y., 1986—. Vis. asst. prof. dept. psychology Yale U., 1980; adj. assoc. prof. Tchrs. Coll., Columbia U., 1981-82; exec. dir. Fedn. Behavioral, Psychol. and Cognitive Scis., Washington, 1982; co-investigator Asian-Am. Edn. Project, 1973-76; bd. dirs. Grantmakers for Children, Coun. Founds.; rsch. assoc. Stanford Ctr. for Rsch. and Devel. in Teaching, Stanford U., 1973; adv. bd. Ms. Found. for Women, 1992, divsn. biobehavioral scis. and mental disorders Inst. Medicine, 1992; U.S. rep. UNESCO Mexico Conf., 1972; Harvard-Henry A Murray Ctr., Cambrige, Mass., 1997, Agy. Health Care Rsch. and Quality/U.S. Dept. Health and Human Svcs., Washington, 1997—; cons. to numerous insts. Assoc. editor: Am. Psychologist; consulting editor: Rehab. Psychology, Young Children; mem. editorial bd. Early Childhood Rsch. Quar.; mem. bd. reviewing editors: Ednl. Researcher; reviewer Am. Ednl. Rsch. Journ., Child Devel., Health Psychology, Psychology of Women Quar., Rev. Ednl. Rsch.; contbr. articles to profl. jours., chpts. to books; co-author: Preparing Adolescents for the 21st Century, 1997. Bd. trustees St. Augustine-by-the-Sea Sch., Santa Monica, Calif., 1976-77; mem. child care com. Calif. LWV, 1975-77; legis. asst. Office of Senator Daniel K. Inouye, Washington, 1980-81. Named one of Outstanding Young Women of Am., 1978. Mem. AAAS, APA (fellow, dir. office sci. affairs 1984-86, adminstrv. officer for children, youth and family policy office of nat. policy studies 1982-83, pub. interest, ethnic minority), APHA, Am. Ednl. Rsch. Assn. (program chair learning and devel. 1978, program chair spl. interest group in early edn. 1980), Nat. Assn. Edn. Young Children (chair com. orgnl. history and archives 1976-78), Soc. Rsch. in Child Devel. (program com. 1985-89, governing coun. 1989-95), Soc. Rsch. in Adolescence, Phi Beta Kappa. Avocation: volunteering for community service.

TAKIS, STEPHANIE, state senator; Ret.; Dem. rep. dist. 36 Colo. Ho. of Reps., 1996-2000; Dem. senator dist. 25 Colo. State Senate, 2000—; fin. specialist FEMA, Denver, 1992—94; rep. AtLarge City Coun., Aurora, Colo., 1989—93; mgmt. analyst U.S. Army, Aurora, Colo., 1983—92; congl. rels. Dept. Commerce, Washington, 1980—82; asst. to sen. Housing & Urban Devel. Com., Washington, 1979—80. Mem. bus. affairs and labor and fin. coms. Colo. Ho. of Reps.; mem. govt., vets. and mil. rels. and transp. and legis. audit coms. Colo. State Senate, bus., labor and fin. com. Office: Colo State Senate State Capitol 200 E Colfax Denver CO 80203

TALBERT, DOROTHY GEORGIE BURKETT, social worker; b. Rison, Ark.; d. Booker T. and Dorothy (Ragan) Burkett; m. Ernest Talbert, May 14, 1949; children— Ernest George, Dorothy Ernette. A.B., Ark. State A. M. and N. Coll., 1946; M.S.W., Atlanta U., 1948; postgrad. U. Pa., 1962, Tulane U., 1965. Caseworker child welfare services Miss. Dept. Pub. Welfare, 1948-49, Ill. Pub. Aid Commn., Chgo., 1951-53; probation counselor Family Ct. Del., 1956-58; with Del. State Dept. Pub. Welfare, Dover, 1958-71, unit supr., 1962-64, supr. licensing and day care services, 1964-67, chief program devel. Child Welfare Services, 1967-68, chief services to families and children, 1968-71; asst. dir. family services, div. social services Del. Dept. Health and Social Services, 1971-78, dep. dir. adult and spl. services, 1978-82, adult crisis intervention coordinator, Newark, 1982—, staff tng./resource developer, 1985— ; instr. continuing edn. program U. Del.; part time 1968—, ret. 1989—; mem. social services adv. com. Del. Adolescent Program, 1969-75, bd. dirs., 1969-75; mem. State Adv. Council on Alcoholism, 1972-76; mem. Del. Devel. Disabilities Planning Council, Del. Adv. Council for Coordination of Services to Handicapped; social work edn. adv. com. Del. State Coll., 1978— . Bd. dirs. United Way of Del., 1979. Mem. Nat. Assn. Social Workers, Am. Pub. Welfare Assn., Nat. Council Pub. Welfare Adminstrs., Black Profl. Forum (sec. 1979), Nat. Caucus Black Aged, NAACP, Delta Sigma Theta. Home: 3007 W 3rd St Wilmington DE 19805-1703 Office: Div State Service Ctrs 501 Ogletown Rd Newark DE 19711-5403

TALBOT, DEBORAH ANN, assistant principal; b. Nyack, Mar. 30, 1962; d. William Jospeh and Barbara Arline Johnstone; m. Joseph Patrick Talbot; children: Jessica Lauren, Joseph William. BA, SUNY, Binghamton, 1984; MS in Urban Edn., Iona Coll., 1990; MS in Sch. Adminstrn. and Supervision, Coll. New Rochelle, 1995. Cert. secondary Spanish tchr. N.Y., sch. adminstr. N.Y., supr. N.Y., sch. dist. adminstr. N.Y. Tchr. Sacred Heart HS, Yonkers, NY, 1988—90, Mahopac (N.Y.) HS, 1990—2001, asst. prin., 2001—. Mem.: ASCD. Office: Mahopac HS 421 Baldwin Place Rd Mahopac NY 10541 Business E-Mail: talbotd@mahopac.k12.ny.us.

TALBOT, MARTHA HAYNE, conservationist, biologist; b. San Francisco, Aug. 3, 1932; d. Francis Bourn and Anna (Walcott) Hayne; m. Lee Merriam Talbot, May 16, 1959; children: Lawrence Hayne, Russell Merriam. BA, Vassar Coll., 1954. Co-founder, asst. dir. student conservation program U.S. Nat. Parks, 1955-59; co-dir. East African Ecol. Rsch. Project, Kenya and Tanzania, 1959-63; asst. dir. S.E. Asia Project, Internat. Union for Conservation of Nature/Natural Resources, 1964-65; asst. coord. Internat. Biol. Programme, London, 1966; rsch. assoc. Smithsonian Instn., Washington, 1966-75; mem., treas. Fairfax County Park Authority, Fairfax, Va., 1973-77; sec.-treas. Talbot Racing Assocs., McLean, Va., 1983—; owner, dir. Talbot Hayne Vineyard, St. Helena, Calif., 1988—; sec.-treas. Lee Talbot Assocs. Internat., McLean, 1991—. Bd. dirs. Student Conservation Assn., 1966-78, 83-87, hon. dir., 1987— (Svc. Honor award), Defenders of Wildlife, 1974-77, Audubon Naturalist Soc., 1975-78, Rachel Carson Coun., 1975-94, treas., 1994-98, v.p., 1998—. Co-author: Introduction to the Landscape, East Africa, 1961, (monograph) The Wildebeest in Western Masailand East Africa, 1963, Renewable Natural Resources in the Philippines, 1964, Conservation of the Hong Kong Countryside, 1966; co-editor: Conservation in Tropical South East Asia, 1968; contbr. numerous articles to sci. jours. Cub Scout troop leader Boy Scouts Am., Geneva, 1978-83, transp. coord., McLean, 1989-95. Recipient Outstanding Pub. award The Wildlife Soc., 1963, Cinema Golden Eagle award Documentary Film, 1968, Disting. Alumna award Katharine Branson Sch., 1981, Conservation Svc. award U.S. Dept. Interior, 1986, Bd. Tribute to co-founder, Student Conservation Assn., 1984, Resolution of Honor, 1999; N.Y. Zool. Soc. grantee, 1961. Mem. Soc. Women Geographers (bd. dirs. 1972-75, treas. 1984-89, treas. Washington group 1990-96), Napa Valley Grape Growers Assn. Avocations: hiking, backpacking, bicycling, skiing, travel. Home: 6656 Chilton Ct Mc Lean VA 22101-4422

TALBOT, PAMELA, public relations executive; b. Chgo., Aug. 10, 1946; BA in English, Vassar Coll., 1968. Reporter Worcester, Mass. Telegram and Gazette, 1970—72; account exec. Daniel J. Edelman, Inc., Chgo., 1972—74, account supr., 1974—76, v.p., 1976—78, sr. v.p., 1978—84, exec. v.p., gen. mgr., 1984—90; pres. Edelman West, Chgo., 1990—95; pres., COO Edelman U.S., 1995—. Office: Edelman Pub Rels 200 E Randolph Dr Ste 6300 Chicago IL 60601-6436 E-mail: pam.talbot@edelman.com.

TALBOT, PHYLLIS MARY, reading educator; b. Chgo., Mar. 14, 1949; d. James Joseph Watson and Sylvia (Slyk) Parker; m. Laurel Curtis Talbot, Oct. 6, 1967; children: Bill, Dennis, Mary, Anna, Tim. BS, Northwest Mo. State U., 1991, MEd, 1993, EdS, 1994. Cert. early childhood, elem., reading K-12, elem. adminstrn., adult basic edn. Literacy coord. Northwest Mo. Literacy Coun., Maryville, 1994-95; Title I reading tchr. St. Clair Sch. Dist., Appleton City, Mo., 1995—99; prin. Montrose, Mo., 1999—2002; supt., Title I reading tchr., spl. edn. tchr. Ballard (Mo.) Sch. Dist., 2003—. Mem. AAUW, Mo. State Tchrs. Assn., Internat. Reading Assn. Roman Catholic. Home: 409 W Miller St Appleton City MO 64724-1523 Office: Ballard Sch Dist Ballard MO

TALBOT-ELLIOTT, SUSAN, artist; b. Budapest, Hungary, July 12, 1954; arrived in US, 1969; d. Louis and Victoria (Talbot) Kovacs; m. James W. Elliott, Dec. 22, 1979; children: Shawn, Christopher. BA magna cum laude, Marymount Manhattan Coll., N.Y.C., 1977; MSBA cum laude, Boston U. Italy ext., Vicenza, Italy, 1983. Represented by Cudahy's, Richmond, Va., 1994—, Studios on the Square Gallery, Roanoke, Va., 1996—2001, The Little Gallery, Moneta, Va., 2000—, Fisher Galleries, Washington, 1994—99. Solo exhibns. include Lynchburg (Va.) Fine Art Ctr., 1996, Studios on the Square Gallery, Roanoke, 1997, Nat. Arts Club, N.Y.C., 1995, Knickerbocker Artists Signature, Scottsdale, Ariz., 1997, Fraser Gallery, Washington, 1999, commd. portraits. Recipient Award of Excellence, Arts Coun. Blue Ridge, 1994. Mem.: Oil Painters of Am., Knickerbocker Artists USA, Portrait Soc. Am., Allied Artists Am. E-mail: talbotelliott@earthlink.net.

TALBOTT, JANET K. information technology executive; d. Ernest Leon and Juanita Sullivant Dunning; children: Frank Robert, Ernest Lee. MBA in Mgmt., Webster U., 1982, D in Mgmt. Work, 1990. Cert. enterprise integrator Soc. Mfg. Engrs., 1999. Adj. faculty Lindenwood U., St. Charles, Mo., 1983—84, So. Ill. U. at Carbondale, Ill., 1983—2000; staff mgr., acctg. and info. systems Southwestern Bell Tel. Co., St. Louis, 1979—80; engr. Combustion Engring., St. Louis, 1980—82, GM, Wentzville, Mo., 1982—85; mfg. systems engring. mgr. McDonnell Douglas (Boeing), Wentzville, Mo., 1985—91; advanced mgmt. cons. A. T. Kearney / Electronic Data Systems (EDS), Chgo., 1991—98; key oper. exec. info. tech. Woods Equipment Co., Oregon, Ill., 2000—00; CEO Janet K. Talbott, Bethalto, Ill., 2001—. Commr. Accreditation Bd. for Engring. and Tech., N.Y.C., NY, 1984—89; U.S. Congl. appointee NRC, Washington, 1999—2001; bd. of assessment - panel mem., NIST, Gaithersburg, Md.; industry bd. advisors, Coll. Engring. U. of Mo., Columbia, Mo., 1983—90, Rolla, Mo., 1982—89; chair, computer logistics edn. industry subcom. U.S. Dept. Def., 1989—90. Author: Managing Your Growth Oriented Development; editor: Automating Die Management Systems, Manufacturing Engineering Wheel (Soc. of Mfg. Engring. - Blue Book Award, 1998). Elder New Wine Ch.; active Jesus Food Pantry Ministries. Recipient Meet the Competition award, Instn. of Indsl. Engrs., 1989. Mem.: NAFE, ASME (hon.; subcom. chair, product data exch. std. 1987—89), Internat. Orgn. of Stds. (chair subcom. 1985—89), Assn. Integrated Mfg. Tech. (chair 1985—85, numerous), Inst. Indsl. Engineers (chair 1985—86, numerous), Soc. Mfg. Engrs. (chair, Computer and Automated Sys. Assn. 1997—98, Young Engr. of the Yr. Nominee 1984), Nat. Assn. Women Bus. Owners. Achievements include development of Product Data Exchange Specification (PDES) Commitee Chair; research in United States Air Force Letter of Achievement for work in Computer Aided Logistics Support. Office: Janet K Talbott 3 Cypress St Bethalto IL 62010-1020 E-mail: ceo@ijanet.com.

TALBOTT, NANCY COSTIGAN, science educator; b. Hutchinson, Kans., July 26, 1941; d. Loyd L. and Dorothy I. (Scheele) McQuilliam; m. James I. Costigan (dec. May 1991); children: James T. Costigan, Jayne Costigan Inlow, Jeanne Costigan, Jennifer Costigan Burr; m. William C. Talbott, Sept. 24, 1994. BS in Edn., Ft. Hays Kans. State U., 1963, MS in Comm., 1991. Tchr. Unified Sch. Dist. 489, Hays, Kans., 1963-64, 77—. Keynote spkr. Phi Delta Kappa, Kans., 1992-96; state leadership team Operation Phys. Sci., Kans., 1992—; nat. leadership team Operation Primary Phys. Sci., 1993—; assembly presenter Physics Is Fun, Kans., Okla. and Colo., 1990—. Bd. dirs., pres. Parish Coun., Immaculate Heart of Mary, 1991—; emcee Gov.'s Scholars Award Program, Topeka, 1994; state leadership team Kans. Excellence in Edn., Topeka, 1994—. Named Milken Nat. Educator, Milken Family Found., 1993, Kans. Tchr. of Yr., Kans. Bd. of Edn., 1994; recipient Ann. Award for Excellence in Tchg., Nancy Landon Kassebaum, 1993; Christa McAuliffe fellow, 1990-91; Eisenhower grantee, 1991, 92, 96. Mem. NEA, (nat. rep. local and state chpts. 1980—), Kans. Assn. Tchrs. of Sci. (bd. dirs., dist. rep. 1989-95), Univ. Alumni Assn. (bd. dirs. 1991—), Phi Kappa Phi. Roman Catholic. Avocations: golf, traveling, reading, bridge. Office: Kennedy Mid Sch 1309 Fort St Hays KS 67601-3742

TALESE, NAN AHEARN, publishing company executive; b. N.Y.C., Dec. 19, 1933; d. Thomas James and Suzanne Sherman (Russell) Ahearn; m. Gay Talese, June 10, 1959; children: Pamela Frances, Catherine Gay. BA, Manhattanville Coll. of Sacred Heart, 1955; LHD (hon.), Manhattanville, 2003. Fgn. exchange student 1st Nat. City Bank, London and Paris, 1956; editorial asst. Am. Eugenics Soc., N.Y.C., 1957-58, Vogue mag., N.Y.C., 1958-59; copy editor Random House Pub., N.Y.C., 1959-64, assoc. editor, 1964-67, sr. editor, 1967-73, Simon & Schuster Pubs., N.Y.C., 1974-81, v.p., 1979-81; exec. editor, v.p. Houghton Mifflin Co., N.Y.C., 1981-83, v.p., editor-in-chief, 1984-86, v.p., pub., editor-in-chief, 1986-88; sr. v.p. Doubleday & Co., N.Y.C., 1988-90; pres., pub., editorial dir. Nan A. Talese Books, 1990—. Home: 109 E 61st St New York NY 10021-8101

TALIAFERRO, ELLEN, medical educator; Grad., U. Okla. Sr. rsch. scientist dept. advanced biotech. and power McDonnel Douglas Astronautics Co.; staff emergency physician, dir. emergency svcs. Santa Monica Hosp. Med. Ctr.; dir. ambulatory care and emergency svcs. St. Joseph Hosp., Denver; assoc. clin. prof. medicine, chmn. dept. emergency medicine Kern Med. Ctr./UCLA, Bakersfield; faculty physician emergency medicine Parkland Meml. Hosp.; assoc. clin. prof. dept. surgery U. Calif., San Francisco; assoc. prof. surgery U. Tex. Southwestern Med. Sch.; faculty physician emergency svcs. San Francisco Gen. Hosp.; med. dir. Violence Intervention and Prevention Ctr. Co-founder Physicians for a Violence-free Soc. Recipient James D. Mills award for outstanding contbn. to emergency medicine. Office: Univ Tex Southwestern Med Sch # 106 5323 Harry Hines Blvd Dallas TX 75390

TALL, CAROL DAILEY, special education educator, speech pathology/audiology services professional; d. L. J. and Edith Mills Dailey; m. Mark Derek Tall, Aug. 27, 1994. BA in Speech, Lang. & Hearing, U. Southwestern La., 1993; MEd in Spl. Edn. Curriculum, Materials, McNeese State U., 2000. Lic. speech lang. pathologist La., 1983. Speech lang. pathologist asst. Acadia Parish Sch. Bd., Crowley, La., 1983—2000; tchr. tng. facilitator Acadia Parish Sch. Bd. Spl. Edn., Crowley, 2000—. Bd. dirs. Internat. Rice Festival Assn., Crowley, 1996—2003, children's activity chmn., 1996—2003. Mem.: Coun. of Exceptional Children. Baptist. Avocations: reading, continuous learning. Office: Acadia Parish School Board P O Drawer 309 Crowley LA 70527-0309 E-mail: ctall@acadia.k12.la.us.

TALL, CHERYL A. artist, art educator; b. Atlantic City, Mar. 21, 1946; d. William and Lorena Wilson; m. Ronald Brown, Sept. 20, 1964 (div. Dec. 1971); 1 child, Christopher Brown ; m. Bruce W. Tall, Dec. 25, 1977; children: Michael, Nicholas. BA, U. Ctrl. Fla., 1974; MFA, U. Miami, 1995. Artist, sculptor Sculpture Studio, Miami, Fla., 1985—95, Stuart, Fla., 1995—2000, Solana Beach, Calif., 2001—; adj. instr. Indian River C.C., Ft. Pierce, Fla., Palm Beach C.C., West Palm Beach, Fla., U. Fla., Gainesville, Vero Beach (Fla.) Ctr. for Arts. Dir. programs Crisis Intervention Ctr., Orlando, Fla., Jewish Home for Aged, Miami, Fla.; arts and crafts instr. Miami Mus. Sci.; arts and crafts instr. aftersch. programs Dade County, Miami, Alachua County, Fla.; leader workshops in field; resident artist Internat. Workshop for Ceramic Art, Tokohame, Japan, 1996; asst. Watershed Ctr. for Ceramic Arts, Newcastle, Maine, 1998; creative resident Art Sch. of Aegean, Samos, Greece, 1999; ceramic art resident Venasque, Provence, France; Levy/Polyocan Kilm God Award resident Watershed Ctr. for Ceramic Arts, Newcastle, Maine, 2001; creative arts resident Banff (Canada) Ctr. for Arts, 2003. One-woman shows include Duncan Gallery of Art, Stetson U., Deland, Fla., 1998, Douglas Gallery, New Smyrna Beach, Fla., 1999, Eissey Art Gallery, Palm Beach C.C., 1999, Schmidt Gallery, Boca Raton, Fla., 1999, Manatee Art League, Bradenton, Fla., 1999, Rotunda Gallery, City of Orlando, 2000, Ctr. for Arts, Vero Beach, 2000, Metro-Dade Cultural Resource Ctr., Miami, 2000, Gov.'s Club, West Palm Beach, 2001, 621 Gallery, Tallahassee, Fla., 2001, Orlando Mus. of Art Store, 2001, Wash. State U. Gallery, Pullman, 2002, Brevard Mus. Art, Melbourne, Fla., 2002, Sherwood Gallery, Laguna Beach, Calif., 2002, Bonita (Calif.) Hist. Mus., 2003, numerous others, exhibited in group shows at Deland Mus. Art, 1998, San Angelo (Tex.) Mus. Art, 1998, Arts on Douglas, New Smyrna Beach, Fla., 1998, Clay Arts Ctr., Port Chester, NY, 1998, Guilford (Conn.) Handcraft Ctr., 1999, Hyde Gallery, Grossmont Coll., El Cajon, Calif., 1999, Elements of Art Gallery, Columbus, Ohio, 1999, LeMoyne Art Found., Tallahassee, 1999, Boca Mus. Art, Boca Raton, 1999, Airport Gallery, Tallahassee, 1999, Ct. House Cultural Ctr., Stuart, Fla., 1999, New Art Space, Denver, 2000, A.I.R. Gallery, N.Y.C., 2000, Gallery on the Hudson, Irvington, NY, 2000, Denver Internat. Airport, 2000, First Union Bank, Charlotte, NC, 2001, Helen Day Art Ctr., Stowe, Vt., 2001, No. Trust Bank, Stuart, 2002, Jayne Gallery, Kansas City, Mo., 2002, Onda Gallery, Portland, Oreg., 2002, Ringling Sch. Art, Sarasota, Fla., 2002, Santa Fe (N.Mex.) Clay Gallery, 2002, Town and Country Hotel, San Diego, 2003, Mesa Coll. Art Gallery, 2003, Ramsden Morrison Gallery, 2003, Trios Gallery, Solana Beach, Calif., 2003, Arts Coll. Internat., 2003, Cannon Art Gallery, Love Libr., Carlsbad, Calif., 2003, Represented in permanent collections Brevard Art Mus., Burroughs-Chapin Art Mus., Myrtle Beach, SC, Bapt. Hosp. Miami Found., Bercu Ins. Agy., Ohio, Marx-Saunders Gallery, Chgo., Carol Korn Interiors, Boca Raton, Chapin Meml. Libr., Myrtle Beach, Coconut Grove Ctr., Clifford Tall Law Assoc., Myrtle Beach, Fla. Atlantic U., Boca Raton, Fisher Island Properties,

Miami, art published, reproduced in numerous publs., catalogues. Bd. dirs. Martin County Pub. Arts Bd., Stuart, 1999—2001; chmn. Ct. House Cultural Ctr. Exhibition Com., Stuart, 1996—99. Recipient Best of Show, Court House Cultural Ctr., 1998, 3d Place, 1998, award of merit, Wustum Mus. Art, 1998, Best of Show, LeMoyne Art Found., 1999, Mus. Art, Boca Raton, 1999, Court House Cultural Ctr., 1999, Juror's award, New Art Space, 2000, 2d place, Court House Cultural Ctr., 2000, 3d place sculpture award, Backus Gallery, 2001, 2d place, Court House Cultural Ctr., 2001, 1st place ceramics award, Del Mar Art Ctr., 2001, Best of Show 3D, 1st place ceramics, 2d place sculpture, Del Mar Fair, 2002, award of merit, San Diego County Fair, 2003, numerous other awards. Mem.: Nat. Conf. for Edn. of Ceramic Arts, San Diego Art Inst., Artists Guild. Democrat. Mem. Unity Ch. Avocations: travel, reading, medieval studies, dance, foreign films. Home: 4563 Chancery Ct Carlsbad CA 92008 Office: Sculpture Studio 217 N Acacia Ave Solana Beach CA 92075 E-mail: chryltal1829@yahoo.com.

TALLCHIEF, MARIA, ballerina; b. Fairfax, Okla., Jan. 24, 1925; d. Alexander Joseph and Ruth Mary (Porter) Tallchief; m. Henry Paschen, Jr., June 3, 1956; 1 child, Elise Paschen. DFA (hon.), Lake Forest (Ill.) Coll., Colby Coll., Waterville, Maine, 1968, Ripon Coll., 1973, Boston Coll., Smith Coll., 1981, Northwestern U., Evanston, Ill., 1982, Yale U., 1984, St. Mary-of-the-Woods (Ind.) Coll., 1984, Dartmouth Coll., 1985, St. Xavier Coll., 1989, U. Ill., 1997. Ballerina Ballet Russe de Monte Carlo, 1942-47; with N.Y.C. Ballet Co., 1947-65, prima ballerina, 1947-60; founder Chgo. City Ballet, 1979; now ballet dir. Lyric Opera Chgo., 1979—. Ballerina Ballet Russe de Monte Carlo, 1942—47, N.Y.C. Ballet Co., 1947—65, prima ballerina, 1947—60; founder Chgo. City Ballet, 1979; dir. ballet Lyric Opera Chgo., 1979—. Performer: (films) Presenting Lily Mais, 1943, Million Dollar Mermaid, 1953. Named Hon. Princess, Osage Indian Tribe, 1953; named to Nat. Women's Hall of Fame, 1996, Internat. Women's Forum Hall of Fame, 1997; recipient Disting. Svc. award, U. Okla., 1972, Dance Mag. award, 1960, Jane Addams Humanitarian award, Rockford Coll., 1973, Order of Lincoln award, 1974, Bravo award, Rosary Coll., 1983, award, Dance Educators Am., 1956, Achievement award, Women's Nat. Press Club, 1953, Capezio award, 1965, Nat. Medal of Arts, Pres. Clinton, 1999. Mem.: Nat. Soc. Arts and Letters. Office: Lyric Opera Ballet 20 N Wacker Dr Ste 860 Chicago IL 60606-2874

TALLENT, BRENDA COLENE, social worker, psychotherapist; b. Albany, Ky., Nov. 29, 1939; d. Hubert Lesco Denney and Roxie Mae Cowan-Denney; m. Norman Kenneth Tallent, Feb. 27, 1958 (dec. June 1975); children: Norma Houch, Delores, Sheila Weaver, Terry. BA Social Work, Ea. Ky. U., 1973; MPS, Western Ky. U., 1980; MSSW, U. Louisville, 1991. LCSW. Food stamp eligibility worker Cabinet for Human Resources, Frankfort, Ky., 1973—75, care home inspector, 1975—78, family svcs. clinician, 1978—88; mental health therapist Lake Cumberland Clinician Svcs., Somerset, 1988—90; county mgr. mental health svc. Adanta Clinical Svcs., 1990—94, site supr. mental health, 1994—96; CEO Expanding Horizons Counseling Ctr., 1996—. Cons. in field. Author poems. Mem.: NASW, Am. Fedn. Women, Nat. Acad. Social Workers, Albany Lions Club. Republican. Baptist. Avocations: writing, interior decorating, gardening, cooking, travel. Home: 1006 Ravenway PO Box 412 Albany KY 42602 Office: Expanding Horizons Counseling Ctr 1006 Allen St Albany KY 42602

TALLERICO, DELMA DOLORES, elementary school educator; b. Pricedale, Pa., May 2, 1952; d. Thomas Delmar Hepple and Elizabeth Theresa (Katchmark) Ambler; m. Samuel Joseph Tallerico, Aug. 9, 1975; children: Robert Peter, Michael James, Patrick Joseph. BA, Seton Hill Coll., 1974; MA in Tchg., U. Pitts., 1975; diploma, Inst. Children's Lit., 1994. Lic. real estate broker, Pa. Counselor Youth Corps, Greensburg, Pa., 1972-74; intern Greensburg (Pa.)-Salem, 1974-75; tchr. St. James Elem., Pitts., 1975-80; real estate agt. Metro Realty, Pitts., 1989-92; mus. tchr. Frick Art and Hist. Ctr., Pitts., 1993—99; computer tchr. St. Sebastian Sch., 2002—. Mem. St. Mary's Choir. Mem.: Cath. Bus. and Women's Profl. Assn. Republican. Roman Catholic. Avocation: piano.

TALLET, MARGARET ANNE, theatre executive; b. Binghamton, N.Y., Feb. 14, 1953; d. George Francis and Wilma Ann (Wagner) T.; m. Peter A., Myks, July 6, 1991. BA, St. Mary's Coll./U. Notre Dame, 1975; MBA, SUNY, 1979. Asst. dir. Parrish Art Mus., Southampton, N.Y., 1979-81; assoc. dir. devel. Detroit Inst. Arts Founders Soc., 1981-92; v.p. Franco Pub. Rels. Group, Detroit, 1992-96; pres. Music Hall Ctr. for the Performing Arts, 1996—. Bd. dirs. Aid for AIDS Rsch., 1987-92, Detroiters at Heart, 1992—; mktg. com. Mich. Cancer Found., Detroit, 1992—, Cultural adv. comm. city of Detroit, Adv. bd.:Arts Serve MI. Mem. Pub. Rels. Soc. Am. Roman Catholic. Office: Music Hall Ctr for Performing Arts 350 Madison St Detroit MI 48226-2290

TALLETT, ELIZABETH EDITH, biopharmaceutical company executive; b. London, Apr. 2, 1949; d. Edward and Edith May (Vickers) Symons; m. James Edward Wavle Jr.; children: James Edward Tallett, Alexander Martin Tallett, Christopher Andrew Wavle. BS with honors, U. Nottingham (Eng.), 1970. Ops. rsch. analyst So. Gas Bd., 1970-73; mgmt. svcs. mgr. Warner-Lamber (UK), Eastleigh, Eng., 1973-77, strategic planning mgr., 1977-81; internat. dir. strategic planning Warner-Lambert, Morris Plains, N.J., 1981-82, corp. dir. strategic planning, 1982-84; dir. mktg. ops. Parke-Davis, Morris Plains, 1984-87; exec. v.p. therapeutic products Centocor, Malvern, Pa., 1987-89, pres. pharms. div., 1989-92; pres., CEO Transcell Techs., Inc., Monmouth Junction, N.J., 1992-96, Dioscor, Inc., Stockton, 1996—2003; prin. Hunter Ptnrs. LLC, 2002—. Bd. dirs. Prin. Fin. Group, Inc., Varian, Inc., Coventry Health Care, Inc., IntegraMed Am. Inc., Immunicon Inc., Varian Semi Conductor Equipment Assoc. Inc.; dir. Biotech. Coun. N.J., NJ Ctr. Life Sci. Contbr. articles to profl. jours. Avocations: acting, badminton, travel, skiing.

TALLEY, CAROL LEE, newspaper editor; b. Bklyn., Sept. 10, 1937; d. George Joseph and Viola (Kovash) T.; children— Sherry, Jill, Scott. Student, U. Ky., 1955-57, Ohio U., 1957-58. Reporter Easton (Pa.) Daily Express, 1958-60; reporter N.J. Herald, 1962-64, edn. editor, 1964-66; reporter Daily Advance, Dover, N.J., 1966-68, polit. editor, investigative reporter, from 1969, mng. editor, 1974-81; editor Evening Sentinel, Carlisle, Pa., 1982—. Mem. A.P. Task Force N.J., 1970, Pa. Associated Press Mng. Editor's Bd. Dirs. Past bd. dirs. Helen Stevens Cmty. Mental Health Ctr. (chair), Carlisle; past pres. bd. dirs. Stevens Mental Health Ctr., Carlisle. Recipient pub. service awards Nat. Headliners, 1971, Sigma Delta Chi, 1971, George Polk Meml. award for local reporting, 1974, Dew Meml. award Pa. Newspaper Pub.'s Assn., 1985. Mem. Pa. Newspaper Editors Soc., Kiwanis Club. Office: 457 E North St Carlisle PA 17013-2655

TALLMER, MARGOT SALLOP, psychologist, psychoanalyst, gerontologist; b. NYC, Sept. 8, 1925; d. Harry and Mildred (Schifrin) Sallop; m. Jonathan Tallmer, Apr. 12, 1949 (dec.); children[00bf] Mary, Megan, Jill, Andrew. MS, NYU, 1948; MA, Yeshiva U., 1962, PhD, 1967; postgrad., NYU, 1976. Faculty dept. psychol. founds. Hunter Coll., NYC, 1969-76, assoc. prof., 1976-79, prof., 1979—94, prof. emeritus; staff psychologist Mt. Sinai Hosp., NY, 1967-68; post grad. Ctr. for Mental Health, 1968-69; pvt. practice NYC, 1967—2004; faculty, trustee, bd. dir. Nat. Psychol. Assn. for Psychoanalysis; faculty NY Ctr. for Psychoanalytic Tng., NY. Author: Sex in Later Life, 1996; editor: Sex and Life Threatening Illness, HIV Testing Positive, The Child and Death, Sexuality and the Older Adult; co-author: Suicide in the Elderly; mem. editl. bd. Current Issues in Psychoanalysis, Psychoanalytic Rev.; contbr. chpts. to textbooks, articles to profl jours. Mem. APA, Boston Soc. Gerontologic Psychiatry, N.Y. State Psychol. Assn. (past pres. divsn. adult devel. and aging). Address: 515 E 85th St New York NY 10028-0246 E-mail: mamadoc4@nyc.rr.com.

TALLY, LURA SELF, state legislator; b. Statesville, NC, Dec. 9, 1921; d. Robert Ottis and Sara (Cowles) Self; m. J.O. Tally Jr., Jan. 30, 1943 (div. 1970); children: Robert Taylor, John Cowles. AB, Duke U., 1942; MA, NC State U., 1970. Tchr., former guidance counselor Fayetteville (NC) city schs.; mem. NC Ho. of Reps. from 20th Dist., 1971—83, chmn. com. higher edn., 1975, 1980—83, vice-chmn. com. appropriations for edn., 1973—86; state senator from 12th Dist. NC, 1983—95; chmn. NC Senate Com. of Natural Resources, Cmty. Devel. and Wildlife, 1987, Environment and Natural Resources, 1989—94. Past pres. Cumberland County Mental Health Assn., NC Historic Preservation Soc.; trustee Fayetteville Tech. Inst., 1981—94; active Legis. Rsch. Com. Mem.: Am. Pers. and Guidance Assn., Fayetteville Woman's Club (past pres.), Fayetteville Bus. and Profl. Women's Club, Kappa Delta, Delta Kappa Gamma. Methodist. Office: W Jones St Raleigh NC 27601

TALUS, DONNA J. secondary school educator; b. Salem, Oreg., Sept. 13, 1931; d. Ralph V. and Estella R. (Barber) Sebern; m. Hank M. Talus, June 5, 1955 (dec.); children: Dottie Hofford, Steve, Stacy. BA in PE, Willamette U., 1953. Cert. ARC First Aid instr., travel agent. Secondary tchr. Langlois (Oreg.) H.S., Oreg., 1953-54, Heppner H.S., 1954-55; tchr. Stanfield (Oreg.) H.S., Oreg., 1955-57, Riverside (Oreg.) H.S., 1960; also bd. mem. Oreg.; secondary tchr. Myrtle Creek (Oreg.) H.S., 1960-67; caseworker Grant County Ctrl. Sch. Dist., John Day, Oreg., 1967-68; tchr. Prairie City (Oreg.) H.S., 1968-69; secondary tchr. Grant Union H.S., John Day, Oreg., 1969-75, Mt. Vernon (Oreg.) H.S., 1975-86, North Marion H.S., Aurora, Oreg., 1992-94; water fitness instr. Salem (Oreg.) Family YMCA, 1990—. Pres. PTA, Myrtle Creek, Oreg., 1966-67; Camp Fire guardian, Roseburg-John Day, Oreg., 1966-79; den mother Boy Scouts Am.; tchr. Meth. Ch. Sch. Camp, Oreg. Mem. NEA, AAUW (del. UN seminar 1982, pres. Oreg. State 1983-85). Republican. Methodist. Avocations: music, water fitness, bowling, line dancing. Home: 29650 SW Courtside Dr # 22 Wilsonville OR 97070-7482

TAMAREN, MICHELE CAROL, educational consultant, writer, retired special education educator; b. Hartford, Conn., Aug. 2, 1947; d. Herman Harold and Betty (Leavitt) Liss; m. David Stephen Tamaren, June 8, 1968; 1 child, Scott. BS in Elem. Edn., U. Conn., 1969; MA in Spl. Edn., St. Joseph Coll., West Hartford, Conn., 1976. Cert. elem. and spl. edn. tchr. Conn., Mass. Tchr. N.Y. Inst. Spl. Edn., Bronx, 1971-74; ednl. cons. Renbrook Sch., West Hartford, 1975-78; grad. instr. St. Joseph Coll., 1978; elem. tchr. Acton (Mass.) Pub. Schs., 1969-70, tchr. spl. edn., 1978-94, inclusion and behavioral specialist, 1996-2000; learning specialist and writer Educators Pub. Svc., Cambridge, Mass., 1994-96. Ednl. cons. to schs., parents, orgns., pubs., 1980—2000. Author: (book) I Make a Difference, 1992; contbr. articles to profl. jours. Bd. dirs. United Way, Acton-Boxborough, 1996—99. Grantee, Mass. Gov.'s Alliance Against Drugs, 1992; Horace Mann grantee, Mass. Dept. Edn., 1987, 1988. Mem.: Kappa Delta Pi, Phi Kappa Phi. Avocations: travel, writing, reading, distance walking. Home and Office: 34 Constitution Way Apt D Marblehead MA 01945-4652 E-mail: to_life@earthlink.net.

TAMARKIN, KATE, conductor; b. Newport Beach, Calif. Student, Academia Musicale Chigiana, Siena, Italy; MusB magna cum laude, Chapman U.; MusM, Northwestern U.; MusD, Peabody Conservatory. Conducting fellow Tanglewood Music Festival, 1987, L.A. Philharm. Inst., 1988-89; music dir. Fox Valley Symphony, Appleton, Wis., 1982-90, Vt. Symphony Orch. Assn., Inc., Burlington. Music dir. E. Tex. Symphony Orch.; guest condr. Okla. City Philharm., Riverside Symphony N.J., Okla. Sinfonia, Tulsa Philharm., Grant Pk. Festival Orch., Chgo., others; vis. assoc. prof. orchestral studies U. Minn.; assoc. condr. Dallas Symphony, 1989-94; vis. condr. U. Minn. Sch. Music, 1997-98. Appeared in numerous TV prodns. including Christmas concerts, 1993, 94, CNN-TV, (CBS-TV) Today Show. Recipient Alunni Merit award Northwestern U., Alumni of Yr. award Chapman U., 1997. Office: Vt Symphony Orch Assn Inc 2 Church St Burlington VT 05401-4445

TAMBARO, MARIE GRACE, health specialist, nursing educator; b. N.Y.C., June 28, 1946; d. Louis Vincent and Jeanette (Motto) Nunziato; m. Arthur Michael Tambaro, Sept. 20, 1964; children: Celeste, Joseph, Arthur Michael Jr., Louis Derek. BSN with honors, CUNY, 1981; postgrad., Seton Hall U., 1985. CCRN, ACLS. Critical care staff nurse Richmond Meml. Hosp., S.I., N.Y., 1980-83; nursing insgr. Brookdale C.C., Lincroft, N.J., 1983—; health specialist Holmdel (N.J.) Bd. Edn., 1990—. Apptd. to Holmdel Twp. Bd. of Health, 1989—, Holmdel Bd. of Edn. Dist. Instrnl. Coun., 1994; chair Holmdel Drug and Alcohol Commn., 1986-88; rep. to N.J. State Drug and Alcohol Commn., 1987. Mem. AAUW. Republican. Roman Catholic. Avocations: reading, gourmet cooking, fitness. Home: 15 Seven Oaks Dr Holmdel NJ 07733-1924 Office: Holmdel Twp Bd Edn 4 Crawfords Corner Rd Holmdel NJ 07733-1908

TAMBLYN, AMBER ROSE, actress; b. Santa Monica, Calif., May 14, 1983; d. Russ and Bonnie Tamblyn. Actor: (TV series) General Hospital, 1995—2001; (TV miniseries) Joan of Arcadia, 2003—; (films) Live Nude Girls, 1995, Rebellious, 1995, Johnny Mysto: Boy Wizard, 1996, The Ring, 2002, (guest appearances): Buffy the Vampire Slayer, 2001, Boston Public, 2002, Twilight Zone, 2002, CSI: Miami, 2002, Without a Trace, 2003, Punk'd, 2003, Late Show with David Letterman, 2004, Sharon Osbourne Show, 2004, Wayne Brady Show, 2004. Office: 8383 Wilshire Blvd Ste 530 Beverly Hills CA 90211*

TAMEN, HARRIET, lawyer; b. Yonkers, N.Y., May 17, 1947; d. Saul and Lily (Balglau) T. AB, Bryn Mawr Coll., 1969; JD, George Washington U., Washington, 1973. Bar: N.Y. 1974, U.S. Dist. Ct. (so. dist.) N.Y. 1975. Atty. W.T. Grant, N.Y.C., 1974-76, City of N.Y. Office Econ. Devel., divsn. Real Property, N.Y.C., 1977-81, Credit Lyonnais Bank, N.Y.C., 1981-86, Chase Manhattan Bank, 1986-89; v.p., counsel internat. corp. fin. Citibank, 1989-92; ptnr. Claugus Tamen & Orenstein, 1992-93; pvt. practice N.Y.C., 1994—. Bd. dirs. Dromenon Theatre, N.Y., 1980-86, Nat. Dance Inst., N.Y., 1982, chmn. bd. dirs., 1984-87; chmn. bd. dirs. Theatre & Dance Alliance, 1989-90; del. exch. program Women in Law, South Am., 1987—; mem. campaign staff Ed Koch for Mayor, N.Y.C., 1977; mem. steering com. Soviet Am. Banking Law Working Group, 1991—; guest lectr. Moscow Conf. on Banking, 1992, Ulaan Baatar, Mongolia, 1993-94, 96, Harriman Inst. of Columbia U., 1994; co-chair N.Y. Lawyers Com. for Clinton-Gore; mem. adv. coun. U.S. Export Import Bank, 2000. Mem. ABA, Assn. of Bar of City of N.Y.

TAMEZ, MYRIAM, poet; b. Pontiac, Mich., Sept. 25, 1969; d. Homero Tamez and Angelica Zambrano. Student, Ohio State U., 1989; BA in English and Music, Albion Coll., 1991; postgrad., U. Tex.-Pan-Am., Edinburg, 1991-93, Bennington Coll., 1993. English tchr. Donna (Tex.) Ind. Sch. Dist., 1991-92, Weslaco (Tex.) Ind. Sch. Dist., 1992-93; poet, 1991—. Contbr. poems to profl. publs. Mem. First Spanish-Am. Bapt. Ch., Pontiac, 1974-95. Avocations: singing, drawing. Home and Office: 274 W Columbia Ave Pontiac MI 48340-1710

TAMMINGA, CAROL ANN, neuroscientist; b. Grand Rapids, Mich., Jan. 26, 1946; d. Samuel William and Freda (Hekman) T.; children: Cristan Fredericka, Bonnie Michael. BS, Calvin Coll., 1966; student, U. Tubingen, Fed. Republic of Germany, 1966-67; MD, Vanderbilt U., 1971. Lic. physician, Ill., Md. Vivian Allen fellow Vanderbilt Med. Sch., 1968-71; intern in medicine Blodgett Meml. Hosp., Grand Rapids, Mich., 1971-72; resident in psychiatry U. Chgo., 1972-74, chief resident in psychiatry, 1974-75, instr. dept. psychiatry, 1975-77, asst. prof. psychiatry, 1978-79; assoc. prof. psychiatry U. Md., Balt., 1979-85, chief inpatient rsch. program, 1979—, prof. psychiatry, 1985—. Chief clin. investigator Manteno (Ill.) State Hosp., 1975-79; chief clin. biochemsitry unit Nat. Inst. Neurologic & Communicative Diseases & Stroke NIH, Bethesda, Md., 1979-85; mem. treatment devel. and assessment rsch. rev. com. NIMH, 1981-85, 90-94, 96-99; mem. FDA Psychopharm Adv. Com., 1990-92, 97—, chair, 1991-92, 98—; mem. Inst. Medicine, NAS, 1998—; cons. in field. Author: Schizophrenia: Scientific Progress, 1988, Schizophrenia Research, 1989; editorial bd. Am. Jour. Psychiatry, Biol. Psychiatry, Jour. Nervous and Mental Diseases, Schizophrenia Bull., Schizophrenia Rsch., Functional Neurology, Progress in Neuroendocrinimmunology, Progress in Neuro-Psychopharmacology and Biol. Psychiatry; contbr. articles to Archive Gen. Psychiatry Sci., Am. Jour. Psychiatry, Jour. Neural Transmission, Lancet, Physiol. Behavior, and other. Recipient McAlpin award Nat. Assn. Mental Health, 1979, Dean award, 1995; Beauchamp scholar, 1971; Found. for Rsch. in Psychiatry fellow, 1975-76, NIMH fellow, 1978-79. Mem. AAAS, Am. Psychiatric Assn., Am. Coll. Neuropharmacology, Internat. Psychoneuroendocrine Soc., Soc. Neurosci., Biol. Psychiatry. Achievements include research in schizophrenia. Office: U Md PO Box 21247 Baltimore MD 21228-0747 E-mail: ctamming@MPRC.umaryland.edu.

TAMONY, KATIE, editor-in-chief; m. Patrick Tamony; children: Sara, Caitlin. BA in History, U. Calif., Berkeley, 1989. Mng. editor No. Calif. Home and Garden mag.; copy editor Sunset mag., N.Y.C., 1994—97, editl. dir., 1997—98, dir. custom pub., 1998, v.p., 1998, editor in chief, 2001—. Author: Your Second Pregnancy: What to Expect This Time, 1995. Office: Sunset Time and Life Bldg 20th Fl 1271 Avenue of the Americas New York NY 10020

TAMOR-AMODO, FLORENCE MARIE, medical technologist; b. Honolulu, Hawaii, June 7, 1965; d. Gervacio Tenorio and Gertrudiz Cadiz Tamor; m. Steven Michael Acob Amodo, July 24, 1993; 1 child, Megan Puanani Amodo. BS, U. Manoa, Hawaii, 1988. Cert. med. technologist ASCP, 1989. Med. technologist Kaiser Permanente, Honolulu, 1989—. Pianist, Waipahu, Hawaii; children's choir dir. Avocation: piano.

TAMSETT, SUSAN O. architect, artist; b. Balt., Oct. 29, 1948; d. John Fredrick and Evelyn Imogene (White) Ott; m. Stephen James Tamsett, July 8, 1967 (div. Aug. 28, 1998); children: Anne Marie, Stephen James Jr., Alison Marie. Student, U. Ga., 1966—69; BFA in Architecture, R.I. Sch. Design, 1986, BArch, 1987. Asst. to prin. Architects Design Group II, Wellesley, Mass., 1988—89; assoc. Ann Beha Assocs., Boston, 1989—90; freelance design cons., freelance illustrator Ridgefield, Conn., 1990—95; sr. designer, project mgr. Shope Reno Wharton, Greenwich, Conn., 1995—96; prin. Studio 584, LLC, Ridgefield, 1996—. Exhibited in group shows at Art Students League, N.Y. (Best of contemporary Printmakers of N.Y.C., 02), Cork Gallery, Lincoln Ctr., N.Y., 2002—03, Silvermine Guild Arts Ctr. Nat. membership chair Interfaith Forum on Religious Art and Architecture, Washington, 1992—94; mem. Archtl. Adv. Com., Ridgefield, 1999—; founding mem. Sexual Assault Recovery and Healing, St. Barts of N.Y.C., 2000—; project coord. Documentation and Conservation Modern Movement Modern House Survey, New Canaan, Conn., 2001—. Mem.: AIA (assoc.; bd. dirs. profl. interest area on religious architecture 1994—98), Alpha Lambda Delta. Congregationalist. Avocations: rowing, kayaking, painting, 3-D construction pieces. Office: Studio 584, LLC PO Box 675 Ridgefield CT 06877

TAN, AMY RUTH, writer; b. Oakland, Calif., Feb. 19, 1952; d. John Yueh-han and Daisy Ching (Tu) T.; m. Louis M. DeMattei, Apr. 6, 1974. BA in Linguistics and English, San Jose (Calif.) State U., 1973, MA in Linguistics, 1974; LHD (hon.), Dominican Coll. San Rafael, 1991. Specialist lang. devel. Alameda County Assn. for Mentally Retarded, Oakland, 1976-80; project dir. M.O.R.E. Project, San Francisco, 1980-81; free-lance writer, 1981-88. Author: The Joy Luck Club, 1989 (Nat. Book Critics Circle award for best novel nomination 1989, L.A. Times Book award nomination 1989, Gold award for fiction Commonwealth Club 1990, Bay Area Book Reviewers award for best fiction 1990), The Kitchen God's Wife, 1991, The Moon Lady, 1992, The Chinese Siamese Cat, 1994, The Hundred Secret Senses, 1995, The Bonesetter's Daughter, 2001, The Opposite of Fate: A Book of Musing, 2003; also numerous short stories and essays; screenwriter, prodr.: (film) The Joy Luck Club, 1993. Recipient Best Am. Essays award, 1991. Office: care Ballantine Publ Publicity 201 E 50th St New York NY 10022-7703

TAN, LI-SU LIN, accountant, insurance executive, investment consultant; b. Keelung, Taiwan, Republic of China, Mar. 7, 1956; came to U.S. 1985; d. I-Chang and Sung-Mei (Chen) Lin; m. Bert T. Tan, Aug. 19, 1985; children: Patricia Tan, Peter Puwen Tan, Lotus Tan. BBA, Nat. Taiwan U., 1978; MBA, Ill. Inst. Tech., 1991. CPA, Ill., Taiwan; lic. ins. agt., Ill.; registered investment advisor. Asst. mgr. T.N. Soong & Co. (mem. firm of Arthur Anderson & Co., SC), Taipei, 1978-85; practitioner Li-Su Lin, CPA, Taipei, 1981-85, Li-Su Lin Tan, CPA, Naperville, Ill., 1988-90; pres. Lisu L. Tan & Co., Ltd., CPAs, Naperville, Ill., 1990—; agt. Mut. of Omaha Co., Lombard, Ill., 1991-94, Met. Life and Affiliated Cos., Bloomingdale, Ill., 1993-98, GE Fin. Assurance, Oak Brook, Ill., 1999—. Chair family Naperville Chinese Assn., 1990; bd. dirs. Amitabha Buddhist Libr. in Chgo., 2003—, pres., 2003—. Mem.: AICPA (tax divsn., quality control program), Ill. Soc. CPAs, Amitabha Buddhist Libr. in Chgo. (pres. 2003—, bd. dirs. 2003—), Buddha's Light Internat. Assn. (Chgo. chpt. pres. 2002—, bd. dirs. 2002—), Chinese Am. Culture Found. (bd. dirs. 2000—, pres. 2001—), Nat. Taiwan U. Alumni Assn. Greater Chgo. (bd. dirs. 1999—), World Taiwanese C. of C. (dep. treas. 1998—99), Taiwanese C. of C. N.Am. (treas. 1998—99, bd. dirs. 2002—), Greater Chgo. Area Taiwanese Am. C. of C. (bd. dirs. 1995—), Taipei First Girls High Alumni Assn. (treas. 1990—94). Buddhist. Avocations: travel, art collecting, photography. Office: Lisu L Tan & Co Ltd CPAs 6S235 Steeple Run Dr #200 Naperville IL 60540-3754 Office Phone: 630-416-9422. E-mail: lisu@lisutancpas.com.

TANAKA, KAY, genetics educator; b. Osaka, Japan, Mar. 2, 1929; came to U.S., 1969; d. Kumaji and Fusa (Nakamae) T.; m. Tomoko Hasegawa, Nov. 5, 1954; children: Atau, Elly Margaret. MD, U. Tokyo, 1956, Dr. Med. Sci., 1961; MA (hon.), Yale U., 1983. Asst. prof. medicine Harvard Med. Sch., Boston, 1969-73; sr. rsch. scientist Yale U., New Haven, Conn., 1973-82, prof. genetics, 1983-94, prof. emeritus, 1995—. Mem. biochemistry study sect. NIH, Bethesda, Md., 1983-84. Contbr. numerous articles to sci. jours., chpts. to books. Grantee NIH, 1971-95, March of Dimes, 1974-92. Mem. Am. Soc. Biol. Chemistry, Am. Soc. Human Genetics, Soc. Inborn Metabolic Disorders. Office: Yale U Dept Genetics 333 Cedar St New Haven CT 06510-3289

TANAKA, PATRICE AIKO, public relations executive; b. Hawaii; BA, U. Hawaii, 1974. Editor Hawaii Press Newspapers, 1974-77; dir. pub. rels. Hotel Inter-Continental Maui, 1977-79; from acct. exec. to sr. v.p. and creative dir. Jessica Dee Comm., N.Y.C., 1979-87, exec. v.p., gen. mgr., 1987-90; CEO, creative dir. PT&Co., N.Y.C., 1990—. Featured in books: American Dreamers, Visionaries and Entrepreneurs, 1995, The Art of Public Relations, 2002. Bd. dirs. Greater N.Y. coun. Girl Scouts U.S., U.S. Fund for UNICEF, Family Violence Prevention Fund. Named one of nation's 500 Most Influential Asian Ams., Avenue mag., 1996; recipient Mothering That Works award, Working Mother mag., 1994, Women Mean Bus. award, Bus. and Profl. Women USA, 1999, Paul M. Lund award for pub. svc., Pub. Rels. Soc. Am., 2002. Mem.: Asian Women in Bus. (bd. dirs.), Coun. Pub. Rels. Firms (founding bd. dirs.), Women Execs. in Pub. Rels., N.Y. Women in Comm. (pres. 2001—02, 2002—03, Matrix award for pub. rels. 1996), Asian Pacific Am. Women's Leadership Inst. (founding bd. dirs.), Women's Forum N.Y., U. Hawaii Alumni Assn. (bd. dirs. N.Y. chpt.). Home: One River Pl #2610 New York NY 10036 Office: Patrice Tanaka & Co Inc 320 W 13th St Fl 7 New York NY 10014-1200

TANDY, KAREN P. government agency administrator; b. Ft. Worth, Tex. married; 2 children. Grad., Tex. Tech. U., Tex. Tech. Law Sch., 1977. Asst. U.S. atty. ea. dist., Va., 1979—90; asst. U.S. atty. western dist., 1979—90; supr. dept. drug and forfeiture litig. Criminal Divsn. of Dept. Justice, 1990—99; assoc. dep. atty. gen., dir. Organized Crime Drug Enforcement Task Forces, 1999—2003, mgr., 2001—03; adminstr. Drug Enforcement Adminstrn., 2003—. Chief asset forfeiture unit U.S. Attys. Office Western Dist., Wash., 1988—90; clk. Chief Judge of No. Dist., Tex.; dep. chief Narcotics and Dangerous Drug Sect. Recipient Atty. Gens. award for disting. svc., Award for Extraordinary Achievement, Dept. Justice, Award for Superior Svc., U.S. Atty. Dir. Office: Drug Enforcement Adminstrn 2401 Jefferson Davis Hwy Alexandria VA 22301*

TANDY, KISHA RENEE, curator; b. Indpls., July 21, 1975; d. Floyd Allen Tandy, Shirley Ann Tandy. BA in Am. History, postgrad., Ind. Purdue U., 1997—. Summer asst. Ind. Hist. Soc., Indpls., 1997—97, 1998—98, 1999—99, exhbns. asst., 1998—98, edn. and pub. programming intern, 2000—01; collections intern Ruth Lilly Spl. Collections and Archives, Indpls., 1998—99, Morris-Butler House Mus., Indpls., 1999—2000; summer intern Riley Old Home Soc., Greencastle, Ind., 2000—00; asst. curator Ind. State Mus., Indpls., 2001—. Author: (essay) "W.E.B. DuBois, Feminism, and African American Women", 1997 (Preston Eagleson Award, second place, 1997); contbr. articles to profl. jours. Scholar, Indpls. Found., 1993—97, Minority Achievement scholar, Ind. U. Purdue U. Indpls., 1996—97, Zora Neale Hurstson-Mari Evans scholar, Ind. U. Purdue U. Sch. Liberal Arts, 1997—2000. Mem.: FIESTA Indianapolis, Inc., Ind. State Mus. Found., Ind. Hist. Soc., Ind. Freedom Trails, Ind. African Am. Genealogy Group, Hist. Landmarks Found. Ind., Am. Assn. for State and Local History. Avocation: reading. Office: Ind State Mus 650 W Washington St Indianapolis IN 46204 Business E-Mail: ktandy@dnr.state.in.us.

TANE, SUSAN JAFFE, retired manufacturing company executive; b. N.Y.C. d. Irving and Beatrice (Albert) J.; m. Irwin R. Tane; children by previous marriage: Robert Wayne, Stephen Mark. BS, Boston U., 1964; postgrad., Hofstra U., C.W. Post U. Elem. sch. tchr., Long Beach, N.Y., 1964-67; pres. Fashions by Appointment, Glen Cove, N.Y., 1967-71; adminstrv. asst. Peerless Sales Corp., Elmont, N.Y., 1967-71; from sales mgr. to mktg. dir. United Utensils Co., Inc., Port Washington, N.Y., 1973-78; v.p. ops. and control United Molded Products divsn. United Utensils Co., Inc., Port Washington, 1978-80; v.p. mktg. Utensco, Port Washington, 1980-88. Bd. dirs. Peerless Aerospace Corp. Co-inventor plastic container and handling assembly. Life mem. Ronald McDonald House; mem. Friends of the Arts-L.I. U., friend N.Y. Pub. Libr.; pres. Susan Jaffe Tane Found.; fellow Morgan Libr.; trustee, sr. v.p. Am. Jewish Congress; life mem. Hadassah; chair Commn. for Women's Equality/Am. Jewish Congress; bd. dirs. Poe Found. Mem. Boston U. Alumni Assn., Lotos Club (mem. libr. com.). Home: 12 Sands Light Rd Sands Point NY 11050-1228

TANENBAUM, LEORA, writer, editor; b. Bronx, N.Y., June 3, 1969; d. Saul Martin and Sheila (Siegel) T.; m. Jonathan Ari Lonner. BA in Modern Culture and Media, Brown U., 1991. Rsch./editl. asst. author Gail Sheehy, N.Y.C., 1991-94; assoc. editor Hadassah Women's Zionist Orgn. Am., N.Y.C., 1995—. Author: Slut! Growing Up Female With A Bad Reputation, 1999, Houper Perennial, 2000, Catfight: Women and Competition, 2002, Catfigh: Rivalries Among Women-From Diets To Dating, From the Boardroom To The Delivery Room, 2003; contbg. writer Boston Phoenix, 1994-96, contbr. numerous articles to profl. publs. Vol. Big Bros./Big Sisters N.Y.C., 1995—. Mem. Nat. Writers' Union, Phi Beta Kappa. Democrat.

TANG, ESTHER DON, development consultant, retired social worker; b. Tucson, Mar. 5, 1917; d. Don Wah and Yut (Gnan) Fok; m. David W. Tang, June 14, 1942; children: Patricia Karen Tang Crowley, Diana Cheryl Tang Simoes, David. Jr., Elizabeth Carol. Student, Draughn's Bus. Sch., San Antonio, 1936, U. Ariz., 1938-41, DHL (hon.), LHD (hon.), U. Ariz., 1992. Owner, operator supermarket, Tucson, 1940-66; exec. dir. Pio Decimo Ctr., Cath. Diocese, Tucson, 1966-85; cons., ptnr., vice chmn. bd. Netwest Devel. Corp., Tucson, 1985—. Mem. Tucson Airport Authority, 1975—, Pima County Crime and Pub. Safety Coun., 1999; chmn. Tucson-Taichung Sister Cities, 1979-91; chmn. Tucson Sister Cities Steering Com., 1984—, Sister Cities Assn. Tucson, 1990, Ariz. Pers. Bd.; chmn. bd. dirs. Pima Community Coll., 1975-85; pres. bd. dirs. Pima Coun. on Aging, 1986-90; coord. U.S. Bicentennial, Tucson; mem. adv. bd. Ariz. Dept. Econ. Security; master of ceremonies to welcome Pres. Clinton, City of Tucson, 1999. Named Woman of Yr., City of Tucson, 1955, Woman of Yr. in Adminstrn., 1968, Lady Comdr. the Holy Sepluchre Jerusalem; recipient Disting. Friend of the Humanities award Nat. Adv. Bd., 1989, Jefferson award Ariz. Daily Star, 1987, Svc. award Pima Coun. on Aging, 1987-89, Disting. Svc. award U. Pima C.C. Found., 1988, Roots and Wings Comty. award, 1988, Rosie award So. Ariz. Ctr. Against Sexual Assault, 1990, Lifetime Achievement award YWCA, 1992, 93, La Doña de los Descendientes del Precido de Tucson, 1997-98, centennial alumni award U. Ariz., 1998, Pan-Asian Cmty. Leadership award, 1999, Arthritis Humanitarian award, 1999, Altrusa Women in Svc. award, 2000, Asia Am. Times Devel. Mgmt. Excellence award, 2000, Voices into the Millennium award Ariz. Border Patrol, Dynamic Duo—Pointing Lives in New Directions award Compass Health Care, Congl. Recognition, 2002, Lulac Nat. Presdl. citation, 2002, award Agave Ariz. Hist. Tape TV, 2002, Lifetime award U. Ariz. Coll. Agr. and Life Sci., 2002; Learning Svc. Bldg. and Gallery named in her honor, U. Ariz., 2001; named Ariz. History Maker State of Ariz. Hist. League, 2003, 15th annual cath. Found. Honoring Ester Don Tang, 2004. Mem. Soroptimist (hon., Women Who Helped Build Tucson award), Rotary Club Tucson (4 way test award 1998) Cath. Found. Diocese of Tucson (honorale mention). Roman Catholic. Avocations: travel, cooking, golf. Home: 701 E Camino De Los Padres Tucson AZ 85718-1921 Office: Netwest Devel Corp 2221 E Broadway Blvd Ste 211 Tucson AZ 85719-6032

TANGMAN, RUTH S. educational administrator; b. Cin., Mar. 3, 1944; d. George Trowbridge and Georgiana (Hollingworth) Strong; m. Edward P. Tangman, Mar. 27, 1971 (div. June 1993); children: David James, Michael Dennis, Elena Pilar. BS in Social Welfare, George Mason U., 1973; MSEd, Va. Polytech. Inst., 1977; EdD, U. N.Mex., 1998. Program analyst Nat. Adv. Coun. on Vocat. Edn., Washington, 1974-77; assoc. dir. employment and tng. Nat. Gov.'s Assn., Washington, 1977-78; dir. vocat. rsch. Westinghouse Nat. Issues Ctr., Arlington, Va., 1978-79; dir., sole propr. Inst. for Program Assistance, Santa Fe, 1979-82; exec. dir. N.Mex. Vocat. Assn., Santa Fe, 1981-83; work program coord., adminstrv. asst. to cabinet sec. Human Svcs. Dept., Santa Fe, 1983-87; dir. occupl., adult, and continuing edn. U. N.Mex., Los Alamos, 1987-89; assoc. v.p. for instrn. Albuquerque Tech.-Vocat. Inst., 1989—98, Cornell U., Ithaca, NY, 1999—2001; sr. mgr. U. N. Mex., Albuquerque, 2001—. Instl. rep. Leadership Coun., Character Counts, Albuquerque, 1995-98, exec. bd. mem. Teach and Learn Ednl. TV Channel, Albuquerque, 1993-95; cons. Cornell Coop. Extension, L.I., 1995; founding mem. N.Mex. Lit. Coalition, 1990. Contbr. articles to profl. jours. Mgmt. com. Albuquerque Bus.-Edn. Compact, 1989-98; appointed commr. Albuquerque Goals Commn., 1990-93; co-chair Greater Albuquerque C. of C., bus. growth and devel. divsn., 1992; mem. Work-Force Devel. Task Force, Albuquerque, 1995-98 Recipient Leadership Recognition award, Tech.-Vocat. Inst. Dir. Outreach and Transition, 1994; named Master Tchr., Nat. Inst. for Staff and Orgn. Devel., Austin, Tex., 1993; recipient Achievement award Greater Albuquerque C. of C., 1992. Mem. Am. Assn. Cmty. Colls., Nat. Coun. of Instrnl. Adminstrs., Nat. Coun. on Cmty. Svcs. and Continuing Edn., Nat. Tech. Prep Network, Albuquerque Sch.-to-Work Steering Com. Democrat. Avocations: gardening, interior decorating, music and art appreciation. Office: Univ New Mex Albuquerque NM 87131

TANGUAY, JANET, expressive arts therapist, writer, filmmaker; b. Newport, Vt., Oct. 27, 1964; d. Marcel Maurice and Nancy Carol Tanguay. BA, u. Vt., 1986. Talk show prodr. WKXE-FM, White River Junction, Vt., 1986; asst. prodr. Northland Video Prodn., Lebanon, Vt., 1987-89, Mount View Prodns., Schenectady, N.Y., 1989-91; owner, pres. Studio J, Schenectady, 1991-94; mktg. rep. Adirondack Scenic, Glens Falls, N.Y., 1994; br. mgr. Manpower, Troy, N.Y., 1994—. Author: (children's book) Dustbunnies Don't Eat Carrots, 1998; screenwriter: Phoenix, 1999; prodr. promotional video. Mem., tutor Literacy Vols. Am., Schenectady, 1998—; mem. Sch.-to-Work Com., Troy, 1998—; mem. Voluntary Simplicity, Troy, 1998—. Mem. Rensselaer C. of C. (membership com. 1997-99), Upstate Inds. Avocations: tennis, film tai chi, yoga, weightlifting. Home: 17 State St Apt 4B Troy NY 12180-3829

TANIS, JANET ELEANOR, museum administrator, retired elementary school educator; b. Elizabeth, N.J., Oct. 24, 1921; d. Jacob Tanis and Hazel Cecilia Pellens; m. Layton Wolfram, Dec. 26, 1943 (dec.); m. Edwin Geckeler, Feb. 26, 1961 (dec.). BS, Douglass Coll., 1943; EdM, Rutgers U., 1957; postgrad., Drew U., 1963, Fairleigh Dickinson U., 1963—64, Rutgers U., 1963, U. Colo., 1968, postgrad., 1974, Kean Coll. of N.J., 1972—78, Chaminade U. of Honolulu, 1978. Cert. tchr. sci., phys. sci., secondary, home econs. 5-12, elem. K-8 N.J., supr. gen. and supr. sci. N.J., tchr., elem., 1-6, sci., 7-9, 9-12; home econs, 7-12 Fla. Tchr. home econs. 7-12 Roselle (N.J.) H.S., 1943—44; clk. Calco Chem. Corp., Bound Brook, NJ, 1944; substitute tchr. Hampton (N.J.) Pub. Sch., 1944—45; clk.-typist Somerville (N.J.) Quartermaster Depot, 1945; asst. hostess Woodlawn, Douglass Coll. Alumnae Ho., New Brunswick, NJ, 1945—48; home econs. advisor Pub. Svc. Electric and Gas Co., Plainfield and New Brunswick, NJ, 1948—53; asst. foods editor Woman's Home Companion mag., N.Y.C., 1953—54; tchr. Aldene Sch., Roselle Park, NJ, 1954—57, Washington Sch., Summit, NJ, 1957—58; elem. sch. sci. coord. Summit, 1958—62; sci. coord. K-9, 1962—75; tchr. grade 6 Lincoln Sch., Summit, 1975—76; tchr. earth sci. Summit Jr. H.S., 1976—79; tchr. sci. grades 8 and 9 Benjamin Sch., North Palm Beach, Fla., 1980—81; substitute tchr. Palm Beach County Pub. Schs., 1981—82; salesperson Harold Grant, North Palm Beach, 1984—89; asst., dir., dir. edn. Hibel Mus. Art, Palm Beach and Jupiter, Fla., 1987—. Tchr. Rutgers Grad. Sch. Edn., 1958, 59, 60, 1961—65, 1964; sci. writer, curriculum developer, substitute tchr. The Sch. Bd. of Palm Beach County, 1982—84; tchr. Fairleigh Dickinson U., Madison, NJ, 1972—73; instr. Nova U., Ft. Lauderdale, Fla., 1984; del. to U. Bristol (Eng.) Nat. Sci. Tchrs. Assn., 1968—69. Author: The Festival of Animals Coloring Book, 1991. Rep. for Hibel Mus. Art Palm Beach Cultural Coun., 1989—, Palm Beach County Attractions Assn., 1989—; vol. Am. Cancer Soc., West Palm Beach, 1985; sec., mem. Friends of the Lake Park (Fla.) Libr., 1986. Recipient Disting. Svcv. award, N.J. Sci. Suprs. Assn., 1982; grantee, IBM Corp., 1968—69. Fellow: N.J. Sci. Tchrs. Assn.; mem.: Mus. Educators of S.E. Fla., Nat. Sci. Tchrs. Assn. (life Fellowship award 1978), Rutgers Alumni Assn., Douglass Coll. Alumnae Assn., Kappa Delta Pi. Republican. Episcopalian. Avocations: reading, research, photography, painting, cooking. Home: 907 Lake Shore Dr # 310 Lake Park FL 33403 Office: Hibel Mus Art 5353 Parkside Dr Jupiter FL 33458

TANKOOS, SANDRA MAXINE, court reporting services executive; b. Bklyn., Nov. 12, 1936; d. Samuel J. and Ethel (Seltzer) Rich; m. Kenneth Robert Tankoos, Mar. 17, 1957; children: Robert Jon, Gary Russell, Jenine Sheryl. AA, Stenotype Inst., 1957; BA, Queens Coll., 1969; MA, C.W. Post Coll., 1973. Cert. stenotype reporter, 1959. Ct. reporter free lance, N.Y.C., 1957-70; tchr. Spanish various high schs., L.I., 1970-76; pres. Tankoos Reporting, N.Y.C., 1976—, Ar Ti Recording, Mineola, N.Y., 1977—, Sterling Reporting Svc., 2000—. Author: (children's book) Ettie and the Evil Eye; contbr. articles to profl. jours. Past pres., bd. dirs. Temple Sinai, Roslyn Hts., N.Y., 1989-91, Am. Jewish Acad., West Hempstead, 1984-94, LWV, Roslyn, 1969-75, NOW, Nassau County, 1975-77, bd. dirs. Religious Action Ctr., Washington, 1995—, ARZA, 1997—. Avocations: writing, piano. Home: 77 Shepherd Ln Roslyn Heights NY 11577-2508 Office: Ar-Ti Recording Inc 142 Willis Ave Mineola NY 11501-2613 also: Tankoos Reporting Co 305 Madison Ave New York NY 10165 E-mail: sandra@tankoos.com.

TANNEN, DEBORAH FRANCES, writer; b. Bklyn., June 7, 1945; d. Eli S. and Dorothy (Rosen) T. BA, SUNY, Binghamton, 1966; MA, Wayne State U., 1970, U. Calif., Berkeley, 1976; PhD, U. Calif., 1979. English instr. Mercer County C.C., Trenton, N.J., 1970-71; lectr. in acad. skills CUNY, Bronx, N.Y., 1971-74; asst. prof. Georgetown U., Washington, 1979-85, assoc. prof. linguistics, 1985-90, prof. linguistics, 1989-91, univ. prof., 1991—. McGraw disting. lectr. in writing Coun. for Humanities and dept. anthropology Princeton U., fall 1991; visitor Inst. for Advanced Study, Princeton, spring 1992; fellow Ctr. for Advanced Study in Behavioral Scis., Stanford, Calif., 1992-93. Author: Lilika Nakos, 1983, Conversational Style: Analyzing Talk Among Friends, 1984, That's Not What I Meant!: How Conversational Style Makes or Breaks Your Relations With Others, 1986, Talking Voices: Repetition, Dialogue and Imagery in Conversational Discourse, 1989, You Just Don't Understand: Women and Men in Conversation, 1990, Gender and Discourse, 1994, Talking From 9 to 5: Women and Men in the Workplace: Language, Sex and Power, 1994, The Argument Culture: Moving from Debate to Dialogue, 1998, The Argument Culture: Stopping America's War of Words, 1999; editor: Analyzing Discourse: Text and Talk, 1982, Spoken and Written Language: Exploring Orality and Literacy, 1982, Coherence in Spoken and Written Discourse, 1984, Perspectives on Silence, 1985, Linguistics in Context: Connecting Observation and Understanding, 1988, Gender and Conversational Interaction, 1993, Framing In Discourse, 1993, (play) An Act of Devotion, 1994. Rockefeller Humanities fellow, 1982-83; grantee NEH, 1980, 85, 86; recipient Elizabeth Mills Crothers prize U. Calif., 1976, Dorothy Rosenberg Meml. prize U. Calif., 1977, Joan Lee Yang Meml. Poetry prize U. Calif., 1977, Shrout Short Story prize, 1978, Emily Chamberlain Cook prize, 1978. Office: Georgetown U Lang & Linguistics ICC Bldg Rm 471 37th & O St NW Washington DC 20057-0001

TANNEN, RICKI LEWIS, lawyer, psychologist, educator; b. N.Y.C., Apr. 29, 1952; d. Paul and Lillian (Singer) Lewis; m. Marc Jay Tannen, Aug. 25, 1972; children: Laine Amy, Adam Jesse. BA in Social Scis., U. Fla., 1975, MEd in Psycholinguistics, JD with honors, U. Fla., 1981; LLM, Harvard U., 1991; PhD, Pacifica Grad. Inst., 2002. Bar: Fla. 1982. Tchr., guidance counselor Oak Hall Pvt. Sch., Gainesville, Fla., 1976-79; atty., jud. clk. U.S. Dist. Cts., Miami, Fla., 1981-82; rep. assoc. Ft. Lauderdale (Fla.) News, Sun-Sentinel newspaper, Ferrero, Middlebrooks, Strickland & Fischer, 1982-88; of counsel Klein & Tannen, Hollywood, Fla., 1990-91; mem., 1992—. Mem. gender bias study commn. Fla. Supreme Ct., 1986, apptd. commr., reporter, 1987—; adj. prof. women and the law, media law, rhetoric, comm. law Fla. Atlantic U., 1984-88, 1995—; mem. faculty Chautauqua Instn., 1995-98; co-chmn. Fla. Bar Media Law Conf., 1996; rsch. coord. Ctr. for Govtl. Responsibility, Gainesville, 1979-81. Editor: Elderly Law in Florida, 1982; author: Report of the Florida Supreme Court Gender Bias Commn.; contbr. articles to profl. jours. Pres. Ctr. for Jungian Studies, 2002—; dir. Inner Work Studies Program, 1995—; dir. Communitas. Mem. APA, ABA, AAUW, NOW, Nat. Coun. Jewish Women, Fla. Bar Assn. (com. on equal opportunity 1988—), Fla. Assn. women Lawyers, Assn. Psychol. Type, Assn. Transpersonal Psychology. Office: 1007 S North Lake Dr Hollywood FL 33019-1314 E-mail: rtannen@gate.net.

TANNENBAUM, BERNICE SALPETER, national religious organization executive; b. N.Y.C. d. Isidore and May Franklin; 1 child, Richard Salpeter. BA, Bklyn. coll. Chmn. Commn. on the Status of Women of the World Jewish Congress; mem. exec. bd. Am. sect. World Jewish Congress; chmn. internat. affairs com.; mem. Zionist Gen. Coun.; active Exec. World Zionist Orgn. Bd. dirs., mem. gen. assembly Jewish Agy.; bd. dirs., v.p. United Israel Appeal; mem. exec. com. Am. Zionist Movement; former chair Hadassah mag.; nat. pres. Hadassah, 1976-80; nat. chmn. Hadassah Internat., 1984-95; liaison Hadassah Found.; sec. Jewish Telegraphic Agy.; bd. govs. Hebrew U. Office: Hadassah 50 W 58th St New York NY 10019-2590

TANNENBAUM, JUDITH NETTIE, writer, educator; b. Chgo., Feb. 13, 1947; d. Robert and Edith (Lazaroff) Tannenbaum; 1 child, Sara Rachel Press. BA, U. Calif., Berkeley, 1968; MA, Sonoma State U., 1979. Cert. c.c. tchr. Calif. Artist-in-residence San Quentin State Prison, Tamal, Calif., 1986—89, Calif. Arts Coun., Albany, 1993—96, Albany Schs., 1996—2001; tng. coord. WritersCorps, San Francisco, 1993—. Author: Disguised as a Poem: My Years Teaching Poetry at San Quentin, 2000, Teeth Wiggly as Earthquakes: Writing Poetry in the Primary Grades, 2000. Mem.: PEN West, Calif. Poets in the Schs. Home: 3120 Yosemite El Cerrito CA 94530

TANNENBAUM, KAREN JEAN, library services supervisor; b. Evansville, Ind., Mar. 5, 1962; d. William J. and Mary Katherine Doom. MLS, Ind. U., 1995. Dir. youth svcs. Knox County Pub. Libr., Vincennes, Ind., 1996—98; supr. youth svcs. Evansville(Ind.) Vanderburgh Pub. Libr., Ind., 1998—. Reviewer: Sch. Libr. Jour., 2001. Mem. edn. com. Evansville Philharm. Guild; part-time cantorial soloist Temple Adath B'nai, Evansville, 2001—. Mem.: ALA-Young Adult Libr. Svcs. Assn. (mem. young adult outreach com.), ALA-Assn. Libr. Svcs. for Children (mem. presch. and parent edn. com. 2000—03, best books for young adults com. 2003—, mem. best books for young adults com.), AAUW (Evansville br., pres. 2000—02), Goodwill Ladies Aux., Hadassah (life; bd. dirs. 2001—, pres. 2002, Evansville chpt.). Jewish. Avocations: cantoring, travel, creative writing, reading. Office: 55 SE 5th St Evansville IN 47708-1603

TANNENWALD, LESLIE KEITER, rabbi, justice of peace, educational administrator, chaplain; b. Boston, May 5, 1949; d. Irving Jules and Barbara June (Caplan) Keiter; m. Robert Tannenwald. BA, Brandeis U., 1971, MA, 1976; MA in Edn. and Counseling, Simmons Coll., Boston, 1972. Cert. social worker, tchr., Mass.; justice of the peace. Sr. assoc. Combined Jewish Philanthropies of Greater Boston, 1977-84; ednl. cons. Bur. Jewish Edn., Boston, 1985-87; ednl. dir. Congregation Shalom Emeth, Burlington, Mass., 1987-92; religious sch. dir. Falmouth (Mass.) Jewish Congregation, 1993-99; pres. Jewish Life Svcs., Newton, Mass., 1993—; rabbi Temple Emmanuel, Chelsea, 2001—. Cons. Selected Ednl. Orgns., Boston, 1972; chaplain, rabbi to local nursing home facilities. Author: Curriculum, Male and Female, 1979 (Honors award 1971), Understanding the Holocaust, 1990, Awakening: Alternative Creative Learning Techniques, 1995. Officer, bd. dirs. Combined Jewish Philantropies of Greater Boston, 1972—; mem. Am. Jewish Congress, Boston, 1976—; rabbi, religious leader Sherborn Congregation, 1995—97, Congregation Agudath Achim (Medway), 1999—2001; title of damsel Imperial Order St. John Ecumenical Found. Recipient Leadership award Inst. Leadership Devel. and Fund Raising Mem. Nat. Alliance Profl. & Exec. Women, Alumni Assn. Benjamin S. Hornstein Program of Jewish Communal Svc., Assn. Jewish Community Personnel. Democrat. Avocations: swimming, watercolor painting, music. Home: 6 Clifton Rd Newton MA 02459-3147 Office Phone: 617-559-9746. E-mail: rabbiles18@aol.com.

TANNER, GLORIA TRAVIS, state legislator; b. Atlanta, Ga., July 16, 1935; d. Marcellus and Blanche Arnold Travis; m. Theodore Ralph Tanner, 1955 (dec.); children: Terrance Ralph, Tanvis Renee, Tracey Lynne. BA, Met. State Coll., 1974; MUA, U. Colo., 1976. Office mgr. Great Western Mfg. Co., Denver, 1965-67; writer Rage mag., 1969-70; reporter, feature writer Denver Weekly News, 1970-75; dir. East Denver Cmty. Office, 1974—; also real estate agt.; mem. Colo. Ho. of Reps., 1985-94; mem. from dist. 33 Colo. Senate, 1994—. Minority caucus chairwoman; mem. appropriations, bus. affairs, labor coms. Dist. capt. Denver Dem. Com., Colo., 1973-75; chairwoman Senatorial Dist. 3 Dem. Com., 1974-82; adminstrv. aide Colo. State Senator Regis Groff, Denver, 1974-82; alt. del. Dem. Nat. Conv., 1976, del., 1980; commr. Colo. Status of Women, 1977—; chairwoman Colo. Black Women for Polit. Action, 1977—; exec. asst. to Lt. Gov., 1978-79; mem. adv. bd. United Negro Coll. Fund, Colo. State Treas. Served USAF, 1952-55. Recipient Outstanding Cmty. Leadership award Scott's Meth. Ch., 1974, Tribute to Black Women award, 1980; named Woman of Yr., Colo. Black Women Caucus, 1974. Mem. Colo. Black Media Assn. (pub. dir. 1972—), Reginas' Civic Club (founder, first pres. 1959—, Outstanding Woman of Yr. 1975), Nat. Assn. Real Estate Brokers. Roman Catholic. Democrat. Home: 2841 Colorado Blvd Denver CO 80207-3015 Office: State Senate 200 E Colfax Ave Ste 274 Denver CO 80203-1716

TANNER, HELEN HORNBECK, historian, researcher; b. Northfield, Minn., July 5, 1916; d. John Wesley and Frances Cornelia (Wolfe) Hornbeck; m. Wilson P. Tanner, Jr., Nov. 22, 1940 (dec. 1977); children: Frances, Margaret Tanner Tewson, Wilson P., Robert (dec. 1983) AB with honors, Swarthmore Coll., 1937; MA, U. Fla., 1949; PhD, U. Mich., 1961. Asst. to dir. pub. rels. Kalamazoo Pub. Schs., 1937-39; with sales dept. Am. Airlines Inc., N.Y.C., 1940-43; tchg. fellow, then tchg. asst. U. Mich., Ann Arbor, 1949-53, 57-60, lectr. ext. svc., 1961-74, asst. dir. Ctr. Continuing Edn. for Women, 1964-68; project dir. Newberry Libr., Chgo., 1976-81, rsch. assoc., 1981-95, sr. rsch. fellow, 1995—. Expert witness in Indian treaty litig., 1963—; dir. D'Arcy McNickle Ctr. for Indian History, 1984-85; cons., expert witness mus. exhibits, documentary films; mem. Mich. Commn. Indian Affairs, 1966-70. Author: Zespedes in East Florida 1784-1790, 1963, 89, General Green Visits St. Augustine, 1964, The Greeneville Treaty, 1974, The Territory of the Caddo Tribe of Oklahoma, 1974, The Ojibwas, 1992; editor: Atlas of Great Lakes Indian History, 1987, The Settling of North America: An Atlas, 1995. NEH grantee, 1976, fellow, 1989; ACLS grantee, 1990. Mem. Am. Soc. Ethnohistory (pres. 1982-83), St. Augustine Hist. Soc., Conf. L.Am. History, Soc. History Discoveries, Chgo. Map Soc., Hist. Soc. Mich. Home: 5178 Crystal Dr Beulah MI 49617-9618 E-mail: hhtanner@charter.net.

TANNER, LAUREL NAN, education educator; b. Detroit, Feb. 16, 1929; d. Howard Nicholas and Celia (Solovich) Jacobson; m. Daniel Tanner, July 11, 1948; m. Kenneth J. Rehage, Nov. 25, 1989. BS in Social Sci, Mich. State U., 1949, MA in Edn., 1953; EdD, Columbia U., 1967. Pub. sch. tchr., 1950-64; instr. tchr. edn. Hunter Coll., 1964-66, asst. prof., 1967-69; supr. Milw. Pub. Schs., 1966-67; mem. faculty Temple U., Phila., 1969—, prof. edn., 1974-89, prof. emerita, 1993—; prof. edn. U. Houston, 1989-96. Vis. professorial scholar U. London Inst. Edn., 1974-75; vis. scholar Stanford U., 1984-85, U. Chgo., 1988-89; curriculum cons., 1969—; disting. vis. prof. San Francisco State U., 1987. Author: Classroom Discipline for Effective Teaching and Learning, 1978, La Disciplina en la enseñanza y el Aprendizaje, 1980, Dewey's Laboratory School: Lessons for Today, 1997 ; co-author: Classroom Teaching and Learning, 1971, Curriculum Development: Theory into Practice, 1975, 3d edit., 1995, Supervision in Education: Problems and Practices, 1987, (with Daniel Tanner) History of the School Curriculum, 1990; editor Nat. Soc. Study Edn. Critical Issues in Curriculum, 87th yearbook, part 1, 1988. Faculty rsch. fellow Temple U., 1970, 80, 81; recipient John Dewey Rsch. award, 1981-82, Rsch. Excellence award U. Houston, 1992, Outstanding Writing award Am. Assn. Colls. Tchr. Edn., 1998; Spencer Found. rsch. grantee, 1992. Mem. ASCD (dir. 1982-84), Soc. Study Curriculum History (founder, 1st pres. 1978-79), Am. Edn. Rsch. Assn. (com. on role and status of women in edl. R & D 1994-97), Profs. Curriculum Assn. (Factotum 1983-84, chair membership com. 1994-95), Am. Ednl. Studies Assn., John Dewey Soc. (bd. dirs. 1989-91, pres. 2000-01), Alumni Coun. Tchrs. Coll. Columbia U.

TANNER, LOIS, magazine editor; BA in English, Buffalo State U., 1977. Prodn. asstn. Harcourt Brace Jovanovich, N.Y.C., 1980-86; assoc. editor Rolling Stone Mag., N.Y.C., 1980-86; contract rsch. editor N.Y. Times, N.Y.C., 1986-92; assoc. editor, staff writer Working Woman Mag., N.Y.C., 1992-93; editor Her New York, N.Y.C., 1993-94, editor-in-chief Where Mag., N.Y.C., 1994—. Free-lance rschr., reporter Health, Self, Premiere, Entertainment Weekly, Seventeen mags., 1986-92. Mem. Am. Soc. Mag. Editors. Office: Where Mag 475 Park Ave S Ste 200 New York NY 10016-6901

TANNER, LYNN, actress; b. NYC, Mar. 22, 1953; d. Harry J. and Barbara Sylvia (Hirschman) Maurer; m. Allen Barry Witz, Aug. 31, 1975. BS, NYU, 1975; JD, DePaul U., 1980. Bar: Ill. 1980. Actress, various, 1980—. Actor: (films) Human Error, 1987, Another Time, Another Place, 1988, Twisted, 1995; (TV series, pilot) Hollywood Flat; (plays) Pack of Lies, Back at the Blue Dolphin Saloon, Toyer, Burying Rose, Dolores and Her Loved Ones, Final Placement, Facing the Dragon, The Workroom, Sign in Sidney Brusteins Window, Summer and Smoke, The Maids, Under Milkwood, Dark at the Top of the Stairs, Rosa; co-author: (screenplays) Wrong Turn, Tessa Deare, Reasons; co-prodr.: Hollywood Flat; dir.: (plays) Dickens, A Christmas Story, 2003. Mem. SAG, AFTRA, Actors Equity Assn., Women in Film, Women in Theatre, Ill. Bar Assn. E-mail: lynnjettstar@adelphia.net.

TANNER-OLIPHANT, KAREN M. family and consumer science educator; children: Christopher Oliphant, Michael Oliphant. BS mgana cum laude, Hampton U., 1977. Cert. home econ. edn. NJ. Tchr. family and consumer sci. Paterson (N.J.) Bd. Edn., 1977—82; mktg. specialist IBM Corp, Dallas, 1983—93; tchr. family and consumer sci. Roselle (N.J.) Bd. Edn., 1993—. Named Tchr. of Yr., NJ Assn. Family and Consumer Scis., 2000; recipient Role Model award, NAACP, 2004. Mem.: Family, Cmty. Career, Leaders of Am. (advisor), Am. Assn. Family and Consumer Scis. (bd. trustees 1995—), The Links, Inc. (past chpt. pres., past chmn. com.), Alpha Kappa Mu, Alpha Kappa Alpha (past officer, chmn. com.). Avocations: sewing, designing, cooking. Office: Roselle Bd Edn 710 Locust St Roselle NJ 07203

TANNERY, GINGER, art educator; b. Dallas, May 15, 1956; d. William Adam McCommas and Lenora (Bothwell) Vilbig; m. Myron Kent Tannery, Oct. 13, 1986 (div. May 1999); children: Heather Elizabeth, Kyle Adam, Clayton. BS in Horticulture, Stephen F. Austin State U., 1988, MEd, mid mgmt. cert., Stephen F. Austin State U., 2000. Cert. tchr. Stephen F. Austin State U. Art tchr. Diboll (Tex.) Ind. Sch. Dist., 1994—. Strategic planning bd. Diboll Ind. Sch. Dist., 1997-98, tech. com., 1997—, lead tchr., 1999-2000. Recipient scholarship Houston Livestock and Rodeo, Tex., 1987-88, scholarship Delta Tau Alpha Agr. Honor Soc., 1986-88. Mem. Tex. State Tchrs. Assn., Assn. for Supervision and Curriculum Devel., Tex. Computer Edn. Assn., Bus. and Profl. Women's Assn., Phi Delta Kappa. Roman Catholic. Avocations: watercoloring, jewelry, teaching sunday school, working out, extra-curricular school activities. Home: 3906 Maid Marion Ln Nacogdoches TX 75965-2324 Office: Diboll Jr HS 403 Dennis St Diboll TX 75941-2123 E-mail: gtannery@diboll.esc7.net.

TANOUE, DONNA A. bank executive, former federal agency administrator; BA, U. Hawaii, 1977; JD, Georgetown U., 1981. Spl. dep. atty. gen. Dept. Commerce and Consumer Affairs, Hawaii, 1981-83; commr. financial inst. State of Hawaii, 1983-87; ptnr. Goodsill Anderson Quinn & Stifel, Hawaii, 1987-98; chmn. FDIC, Washington, 1998—2002; vice chmn. Bank of Hawaii Investment Svcs. Group, 2002—. Office: PO Box 2900 Honolulu HI 96846-6000

TANUR, JUDITH MARK, sociologist, educator; b. Jersey City, Aug. 12, 1935; d. Edward Mark and Libbie (Berman) Mark; m. Michael Isaac Tanur, June 2, 1957; children: Rachel Dorothy, Marcia Valerie. BS, Columbia U., 1957, MA, 1963; PhD, SUNY, Stony Brook, 1972. Analyst Biometrics Rsch., N.Y.C., 1955-67; lectr. SUNY, Stony Brook, 1967-71, from asst. prof. to prof. sociology, 1971-94, disting. teaching prof., 1994—. Cons. NBC, N.Y.C., 1976—89, Lang. of Data Project, Los Altos, Calif., 1980—89, Inst. for Rsch. on Learning, 1994—95; mem. com. on nat. stats. NAS, 1980—87, com. on applied and theoretical stats., 1997—2000; trustee NORC, U. Chgo., 1987—; bd. dirs. Social Sci. Rsch. Coun., 2000—; mem. adv. com. SBE, NSF, 2000—. Author: The Subjectivity of Scientists and the Bayesian Approach, 2001; editor: Statistics: A Guide to the Unknown, 1972, Internat. Encyclopedia of Statistics, 1978, Cognitive Aspects of Survey Methodology, 1984, Questions About Questions, 1991, Cognition and Survey Research, 1999, Internat. Ency. of Social Scis., 1963—67; contbr. articles to sci., stats., and social sci. jours. Bd. dirs. Vis. Nurse Svc., Great Neck, N.Y., 1970-2000; bd. govs. Gen. Soc. Survey, Chgo., 1989-92. Sr. rsch. fellow, Am. Statis. Assn./NSF/Bur. Labor Statistics, 1988-89. Fellow AAAS, Am. Statis. Assn. (Founders award 1997); mem. Internat. Statis. Inst., Phi Beta Kappa. Home: PO Box 280 Montauk NY 11954 Office: SUNY Dept Sociology Stony Brook NY 11794-4356

TAN-WANG, GRACE, aeronautical engineer; married; children: Kelly, Marisa. Grad., MIT. Champollion mission engr. NASA; dep. system engrng. mgr. Mars Exploration, Jet Propulsion Laboratory, La Canada, Calif.; dep. mgr. spacecraft system engrng. Mars Exploration Rover Mission, 2003. Avocations: travel, bicycling, volleyball. Office: NASA Jet Propulsion Lab 4800 Oak Grove Dr M/S T1723 Pasadena CA 91109-8099*

TAPP, MAMIE PEARL, educational association administration; b. Aiken, S.C., July 20, 1955; d. Willie Lee and Nancy (Madison) Garrett; m. Anthony Karl Tapp, Aug. 13, 1983; children: Anthony K. II, Barry Garrett, Myles Jarvis. BA, CUNY, 1977; MA, New Sch. for Social Rsch., 1984; postgrad., Nova Southeastern U., 1994—. Flight attendant Capitol Airlines, Jamaica, N.Y., 1976-81; pers. assoc. Cmty. Svc. Soc., N.Y.C., 1982-83; pers. specialist Marriott Hotel, Tampa, Fla., 1983-84; dir. placement Tampa Coll., 1984-86, facility coord., 1986-87, compliance officer, 1987-88; career counselor Alpha House, Tampa, 1988-91; career specialist U. Tampa, 1991-96, adj. prof., 1992-93; career specialist Jr. Achievement Greater Tampa, Inc., Tampa, 1996—, tchr. asst. program adv. com. mem., 1996-98. Tchr. asst. program adv. com. Hillsborough H.S., 1996-97; sr. edn. svc. mgr. Jr. Achievement, 1997—. Author: (novels) Resumes, 1992, Cover Letters, 1991, Thank You Letters, 1992, (poetry) Inner Peace, 1999; co-editor: I Cried, 2001, Life, 2002. Bd. dirs. Children's Mus. Tampa, 1992-94; com. mem. United Way, Tampa, 1994-95; mem. bd. St. Peter Claver Cath. Sch., Tampa, 1995-99, exec. com. Glee Club, 1995; vol. Scout troop leader, 1997-98. Recipient Outstanding Bus. Woman award Am. Bus. Women's Assn., Tampa, 1987, Cmty. Svc. award Tampa Connections, 1993, Editor's Choice award Internat. Libr. of Poetry, 1999. Mem.: AAUW, Fla. Assn. Women in Edn., Am. Vocat. Assn. Roman Catholic. Avocations: reading, sewing. Office: Jr Achievement Central Maryland Inc 10711 Red Run Blvd Ste 110 Owings Mills MD 21117 E-mail: mtapp@earthlink.net.

TAPPER, JOAN JUDITH, magazine editor; b. Chgo., June 12, 1947; d. Samuel Jack and Anna (Swoiskin) T.; m. Steven Richard Siegel, Oct. 15, 1971. BA, U. Chgo., 1968; MA, Harvard U., 1969. Editor manuscripts Chelsea House, N.Y.C., 1969-71, Scribners, N.Y.C., 1971; editor books Nat. Acad. Scis., Washington, 1972-73; assoc. editor Praeger Pubs., Washington, 1973-74; editor New Rep. Books, Washington, 1974-79; mng. editor spl. pubs. Nat. Geog. Soc., Washington, 1979-83; editor Nat. Geog. Traveler, Washington, 1984-88; editor-in-chief Islands, internat. mag., Santa Barbara, Calif., 1989—; editl. dir. Islands Pub. Co., Santa Barbara, 1996—. Recipient Pacific Asia Travel Assn. Journalist of the Yr. award, 1995. Mem. Am. Soc. Mag. Editors, Soc. Am. Travel Writers (editors' coun.), Channel City Club. Democrat. Jewish. Avocations: travel, reading, tennis. Home: 603 Island View Dr Santa Barbara CA 93109-1508 Address: 6309 Carpinteria Ave Carpinteria CA 93013-2901

TAPPERT, TARA LEIGH, art historian, archivist, researcher; b. Detroit, Jan. 9, 1950; d. Herman Henry and Carol Louise (Zannoth) T.; m. Clarke Foster Dilks, Oct. 18, 1975 (div. Apr. 9, 1980). BA in History, Hope College, 1973; MSLS in Libr. and Archives Adminstrn., Wayne State U., 1976; PhD in Am. Civilization, George Washington U., 1990. Law libr. U.S. Dist. Ct. (ea. dist.), Detroit, 1973-77, Sullivan & Cromwell, Washington, 1977-83; editor Am. Studies Internat. George Washington U., Washington, 1983-85; curatorial asst., researcher Nat. Mus. Am. Art, Washington, 1987; curatorial asst. Nat. Portrait Gallery, Washington, 1988-90, guest curator, 1990-96; curator exhbns. and collections Roanoke (Va.) Mus. Fine Arts, 1990; guest curator Borghi & Co., N.Y.C., 1991-93; rsch. assoc. Am. Craft Mus., N.Y.C., 1992-98; pvt. practice Roanoke, Va., 1990-97, Washington, 1998—. Libr. cons. Nat. Press Club Libr., Washington, 1984-85; fine arts bibliographer Nat. Trust Brit. Libr., Cambridge, Mass., 1985-86; fine arts cons. Pa. Acad. Fine Arts, Phila., 1987; curatorial researcher, writer Detroit Inst. Arts, 1995; adj. faculty Parsons Sch. Design, Masters Program in the History of Dec. Arts at the Smithsonian Assocs., 1999—; arts cons. Scheurer Hosp.-Hueschen Arts Coll., Pigeon, Mich., 1999-2001, Glen Burnie Mus., Winchester, Va., 2002. Author: (exhbn. catalogue) The Emmets: A Generation of Gifted Women, 1993, (exhbn. catalogue) Craft in the Machine Age: 1920-45, 1995, (exhbn. catalogue) Cecilia Beaux and the Art of Portraiture, 1995, Aimee Ernesta and Eliza Cecilia - Two Sisters, Two Choices, 2000; guest co-editor spl. issue on Cecilia Beaux for Pa. Mag. of History and Biography, 2000; writer, rschr. Williams Coll. Mus.. Art, 2001, Biggs Mus. of Am. Art, 2002; author: William Sartain and Cecilia Beaux: The Influences of a Teacher, Pa. Cultural Landscape: The Sartain Family Legacy 1830-1930, 2000. Archivist, editor Roanoke Network for Profl. and Managerial Women, Roanoke, Va., 1992-93. Libr. Congress fellow George Washington U., 1985-86, Smithsonian pre-doctoral fellow, 1986-87, Beverly R. Robinson doctoral fellow Winterthur Mus., 1988. Mem. Am. Assn. Mus., Am. Studies Assn. (student 1985-87), Coll. Art Assn., Mid-Atlantic Archives Conf. (local arrangements 1991), Women's Caucus for Art (pres. 2002-03 Washington chpt., chapt. coun. 2003—), Art Librs. Soc. of N.Am. (John Benjamins award 1999), Nat. Coalition of Ind. Scholars. Democrat. Mem. Soc. Of Friends. Office: 3000 7th St NE Ste A Washington DC 20017-1401 Office Phone: 202-635-0869. E-mail: t_tappert@yahoo.com.

TARAKI, SHIRLEE, librarian; b. Chgo., Apr. 25, 1922; d. Frank and Leah (Simon) Heda; m. Mohamed Rasul Taraki, June 3, 1944 (dec. Aug. 1972); children: Lisa, Yosuf. BA in Psychology, U. Chgo., 1943, MA in Edn., 1947. Instr. English, Ministry of Edn., Kabul, Afghanistan, 1947-65, materials technician, 1965-72; libr. asst. Northwestern U., Evanston, Ill., 1973-90; libr. Ctr. for Women's Health St. Francis Hosp., Evanston, 1990-95. Mem. Evanston Com. on Aging, 1999—. Producer slide presentation An American Woman in Afghanistan, 1974—. Election judge Democrats of Evanston, 1991—, voting registrar, 1992—; vol. Wagner Health Ctr., Evanston, 1993—; mem. Evanston Comm. on Aging, 1999—. Mem. NOW (Evanston-North Shore chpt., founder), Circle Pines Ctr., Afghanistan Reconstrn. Support Com. (co-chair), Afghan Women's Task Force (founder, chair), Amnesty Internat., Phi Beta Kappa. Avocations: bicycling, travel, music, needlework. Home: 1864 Sherman Ave #7NW Evanston IL 60201-3738

TARAVELLA, ROSIE, actress; b. Mt. Morris, N.Y., July 8, 1962; d. Charles James and Carrie (Sardinia) T.; m. Michael Anthony Valerio, May 27, 1994. BA in Dramatic Arts, San Diego State U., 1985. Entertainment dir., staff trainer Johnny Rockets, Inc., L.A., 1986-98; staff writer, voice talent The Rick Dees Weekly Top 40, L.A., 1990-93; freelance writer, voice talent The Premiere Comedy Radio Network, L.A., 1992-98; actress L.A., 1992—; writer L.A. Times Calendar Live! Website, 1999—. Theatrical prodr., cons. The Tamarind Theater, L.A., 1993-94. Author (plays) Rose's Bowl-O-Rama, 1992, The Wives, 1994, Pa's Funeral, 1995; (with Diane Kelber) Blue Grass, 1999; screenwriter: Carlo's Wake, 1997; actress (commls.) AT&T, Dial, Radio Shack and others, 1992—, (TV) Who's the Boss, Ellen, Full House, Married with Children, The Client, Almost Perfect, Brooklyn South, Sinatra, Norma Jean and Marilyn, George and Leo, Roswell; actress, co-writer (film) Carlo's Wake, 1999. Pres. Boards and Boards Prodns., North Hollywood, Calif., 1994-98. Recipient Am.'s Best Sitcom Writing Competition award, 1999. Mem. Mus. TV and Radio, KCRW-Nat. Pub. Radio, Am. Soc. Prevention Cruelty Animals, Nat. Geog. Soc. Democrat. Roman Catholic. Avocations: cooking, genealogy, internet, film and tv history. Office: Broads and Boards 12828 Victory Blvd Ste 334 North Hollywood CA 91606-3013

TARAZON, MAUREEN REEVES, landscape artist, conservator; b. London, Eng., Feb. 20, 1934; arrived in U.S., 1955; d. Archibald Butterworth and Georgina Dorothy Reeves; m. Louis Cadena Tarazon, June 21, 1954; children: Glenda, Donella, Louis Jr. Student, London Polytechnic, London, Eng., 1949—51. Carpet designer Bontor and Wells, London, 1949—53; picture conservationist Sigoloff Gallery, San Antonio, 1975—91; landscape painter pvt. studio, San Antonio, 1970; artist picture restoration Tarazon Prodn., San Antonio, 1991—2004. Gallery artist Sigoloff Gallery, San Antonio, 1970—91, Salado Galleries, Tex., 1987—2003. Lmtd. edit. prints, Lullaby, Ondine, illustrator, Raucous Dorcus, 1998, one-woman shows include Sigoloff Galleries, San Antonio, Tex., 1973—91, Middleton Galleries, Annapolis, Md., 1988, exhibited in group shows at Green House Gallery, San Antonio, Tex., 1992, Represented in permanent collections oil paintings, watercolors and mural, over 1000 recorded works thoughout the world. 6 landscape paintings Benefit Juvenile Diabetes Found., 1990; artist in action demonstrations Zonta Club of San Antonio, Tex., 1986. Mem.: San Antonio Art League Mus. Meth. Avocations: art, history, gardening, plein-air paint outs. Home and Studio: 9517 Stillforest San Antonio TX 78250

TARBUCK, BARBARA JOAN, actor; b. Detroit, Jan. 15, 1942; d. George and Ruth Erma (Fillmore) T.; m. James Denis Connolly, May 17, 1980; 1 child, Jennifer Lane. B of Philosophy, Wayne State U., 1963; MA, U. Mich., 1965; postgrad., Ind. U., 1965-66. Author: (children's play) Who Am I?, 1972; Author/actor: They Call Me Dr. Greer, 1994; Actress:(TV movies) The Cracker Factory, 1979, Mrs. R's Daughter, 1979, A Christmas Without Snow, 1980, Between Two Loves, 1982, Victims for Victims: The Theresa Saldana Story, 1984, Out of Time, 1988, David, 1988, I Know My First Name is Steven, 1989, Death of the Incredible Hulk, 1990, A House of Secrets and Lies, 1992, A Child Lost Forever: The Jerry Sherwood Story, 1992, Jack Reed: Badge of Honor, 1993, Moment of Truth: Eye of the Stalker, 1995, Seduced by Madness: The Diane Borchardt Story, 1996, Before He Wakes, 1998, Mr. Murder, 1998, Just Ask My Children, 2001; (films) Short Circuit, 1986, Big Trouble, 1986, Curly Sue, 1991, Midnight Witness, 1993, Scanner Cop II, 1995, Tie That Binds, 1995, Legend of Razorback, 2002, Tulse Luper Suitcases: The Moab Story, 2003, Walking Tall, 2004; guest appearances: (TV shows) include M*A*S*H*, 1982, Cagney & Lacey, 1983-84, Falcon Crest, 1986-87, The Golden Girls, 1997, Knots Landing, 1979, Quantum Leap, 1992, Picket Fences, 1992, The Practice, 1997 ER, 1999, CSI, 2000, Judging Amy, 2001, Crossing Jordan, 2001, Six Feet Under, 2002, Without a Trace, 2003, Cold Case, 2003; Broadway shows include Brighton Beach Memoirs, Water Engine, Landscape and Silence; nat. tours: Broadway Bound, America Hurrah!. Fulbright grantee, 1966-67; recipient L.A. Drama Critics award, 1985. Mem. Zeta Phi Eta. Democrat.

TARDOS, ANNE, artist, writer, composer; b. Cannes, France, Dec. 1, 1943; d. Tibor and Berthe (Steinmetz) T.; m. Oded Halahmy, Nov. 6, 1976 (div. Dec. 1979); m. Jackson Mac Low, Jan. 20, 1990; step-children: Mordecai-Mark Mac Low, Clarinda Mac Low. Student, Acad. für Musik und Darstellende Kunst, Vienna, Austria, 1961—63, Art Students League NY, 1966—69. Guest tchr. Sch. Visual Arts, NYC, 1974-87, SUNY Albany, 1980, U. Calif., San Diego, 1990, Schule für Dichtung in Wien, Vienna, Austria, 1992-96. Author: Cat Licked the Garlic, 1992, Mayg-shem Fish, 1995, Uxudo, 1999, The Dik-dik's Solitude: New & Selected Works, 2002, A Noisy Nightingale Understands the Tiger's Camouflage Totally, 2003; composer: (CD) Museum Inside the Telephone Network, 1991, Chance Operation: Tribute to John Cage, 1993, Open Secrets, 1993, (cassette) Gatherings, 1980, Songs and Simultaneities, 1985; exhibitions include Jack Tilton Gallery, N.Y.C., 1989, Mus. Modern Art, Bolzano, Italy, 1989, Venice Biennale, 1990, Galerie 1900-2000, Paris, 1990, Mus. Modern Art, N.Y.C., 1993; author: (radio plays) Stimmen, 1986, Phoneme Dance for John Cage, 1986, Among Men, 1996. E-mail: annetardos@att.net.

TARGOVNIK, SELMA E. KAPLAN, physician; b. N.Y.C., Apr. 22, 1936; d. Harry A. and Helen (Goodstein) Kaplan; m. Jerome H. Targovnik, Dec. 2, 1961; children: Nina Rebecca, Labe Eric (dec.), Diane Michelle. BA, NYU, 1957; MD, Albert Einstein Col. Medicine, 1961. Diplomate Am. Bd. Dermatology. Intern Kaiser Found. Hosp., San Francisco, 1961-62; resident in internal medicine Bellevue Hosp., NYU Med. Ctr., 1962-63, U. Colo. Med. Ctr., Denver, 1963-64; rsch. fellow, resident in dermatology Boston U. Med. Ctr., 1964-66, mem. staff, 1968-69, NYU Med. Ctr., 1966-68; practice medicine specializing in dermatology Phoenix, 1969-98; ret. Part-time staff Carl Hayden VA Hosp., Phoenix, 1998—; mem. staff St. Joseph's Hosp., Phoenix, St. Luke's Hosp., Phoenix, Columbia Hosp., Phoenix; mem. staff Good Samaritan Hosp., Phoenix, chief divsn. dermatology, 1985-90; adj. assoc. prof. Midwestern U. Coll. Medicine, Glendale, Ariz., 1998—; clin. asst. prof. dermatology Kirksville Coll. Osteopathic Medicine, 2000--. Bd. dirs. ACLU, Ariz., 1973-78, 83-94, Congregation Beth El, Phoenix, 1971-75, Flagstaff Festival of the Arts, 1984-86; active Jewish Nat. Fund. Fellow Am. Acad. Dermatology, Assocs. for the Weizmann Inst. Sci., Assocs. for the Technion Inst.; mem. Am. Technion Soc. (bd. dirs. 1988-92, pres. Ariz. divsn. 1990-92), Dermatology Found., Sonoran Dermatologic Soc., Southwestern Dermatologic Soc., Pacific Dermatologic Soc., Noah Worcester Dermatologic Soc., Phi Beta Kappa, Mu Chi Sigma, Pi Delta Phi, Beta Lambda Sigma. Democrat. Jewish. Home: 3706 E Rancho Dr Paradise Valley AZ 85253 E-mail: selmaderm@cox.net.

TARITAS, KAREN JOYCE, customer service administrator; b. Ft. Wayne, Ind., June 5, 1957; d. George and Patricia Louise (Smith) T. BS, Purdue U., 1988; AAS, Ind. U., 1980. Cert. managed healthcare profl. Billing rep., experience analyst Lincoln Nat. Life Ins. Co., Ft. Wayne, 1974-82; customer svc. rep., underwriting asst. K&K Ins. Co., Ft. Wayne, 1984-86; telemarketing mgr. Stanley Steemer Carpet Cleaner, Ft. Wayne, 1990-98; svc. cons. AETNA U.S. Healthcare, Ft. Wayne, 1998—2002; with Ins. & Risk Mgmt., 2002, customer svc. rep., 2002—03. Mem. Nat. Geographic Soc., Am. Mus. Nat. History, Smithsonian Instn., Purdue U. Alumni Club, Ind. U. Alumni Club, Delta Sigma Pi. Avocations: collecting music boxes, cross stitch/needlepoint. Home: 4414 Hanna St Fort Wayne IN 46806-4744

TARNOFSKY-OSTROFF, DAWN, broadcast executive; V.p. dev. Kushner-Locke Co., 1984-89; pres. Michael Jacobs Prodns.; sr. v.p. creative affairs 20th Century Fox TV, 1989-96; sr. v.p. programming, prodn. Lifetime TV, N.Y.C., 1996-99, exec. v.p. entertainment, 1999—. Office: Lifetime TV 309 W 49th St Fl 16 New York NY 10019-7316

TARNOVE, LORRAINE, medical association executive; b. Atlantic City, July 26, 1947; d. Leonard Robert Tarnove and Jeanne Tarnove Yudkin; m. Steven B. Friedman, June 1, 1969; children: K. Brooke, Ari-Benjamin. BA, U. Md., 1969. Pres. Lorraine Tarnove Consulting, Columbia, Md., 1985-93; exec. dir. Am. Med. Dirs. Assn., Columbia. Contbr. chpt. to book. Office: AMDA 10840 Little Patuxent #760 Columbia MO 21044

TARRANT, SUSAN KATHRYN, art educator; b. Terre Haute, Ind., Apr. 7, 1951; d. Samuel Joseph and Mary Rose Tarrant. Student, Ind. State U., 1970; BA, St. Mary-of-the-Woods Coll., 1973; postgrad., Tex. Tech. U., 1983—89. Sec., bookkeeper trainee Tarrant Tile Inc., Terre Haute, Ind., 1968—72; math. tchr. Faulk Intermediate Sch., Brownsville, Tex., 1973—74; art tchr. Hanna H.S., Brownsville, 1974—80, fine arts dept. chair, 1980—93; fine arts dept. chair, fine arts magnet program dir. The Fine Arts Acad. at Lopez H.S., Brownsville, 1993—. Evaluator So. Assn. Colls. and Schs., McAllen, Tex., 1982; co-chair, advisor An Artistic Discovery 27th Congl. Dist. Tex., Corpus Christi, Brownsville, 1987—; judge Scholastic Art Awards, Lubbock, Tex., 1996. Active Clean Brownsville Com., 1978—82, St. Luke Parish Coun., Brownsville, 1977—84. Mem.: Tex. Art Edn. Assn. (parliamentarian 1981—90), Soc. N.Am. Goldsmiths, Nat. Art Edn. Assn. Roman Catholic. Avocations: cooking, reading, crafts. Home: PO Box 3721 Brownsville TX 78523-3721 Office: Lopez High Sch 3205 S Dakota Brownsville TX 78521

TARRODY, JANET FAULSTICH, retired congressional executive; BA in English, Coll. of William and Mary, 1964. Staff asst. Congressman James Roosevelt, Washington, 1965; office mgr. Congressman Thomas M.. Rees, Washington, 1966-76; chief of staff Congressman Anthony C. Beilenson, Washington, 1977-96.

TARR-WHELAN, LINDA, policy center executive; b. Springfield, Mass., May 24, 1940; d. Albert and Jane Zack; m. Keith Tarr-Whelan; children: Scott, Melinda. BSN, Johns Hopkins U., 1963; MS, U. Md., 1967. Program dir. AFSCME AFL-CIO, Washington, 1968-74, union area dir., 1974-76; adminstrn. dir. N.Y. State Labor Dept., Albany, N.Y., 1976-79; dep. asst. to pres. Carter White House, Washington, 1979-80; dir. govt. rels. NEA, Washington, 1980-86; CEO, pres. Ctr. for Policy Alternatives, Washington, 1986—, bd. dirs., 1985—. Apptd. U.S. rep. UN Commn. on Status of Women, 1996—. Bd. dirs. Benton Found., Adv. Inst., Ind. Sector; pres. State Issues Forum; mem. Freddie Mac Affordable Housing Adv. Bd. Recipient Disting. Grad. award Johns Hopkins U., 1981, Breaking the Glass Ceiling award, 1996; leadership fellow Japan Soc., 1987-88. Democrat. Avocations: walking, travel. Home: 3466 Roberts Ln Arlington VA 22207-5335

TARTAGLIONE, CHRISTINE M. state legislator; b. Phila., Sept. 21, 1960; Grad., Pierce Coll., 1980. Legal asst. to City Councilwoman Joan Krajewski, 1986—89; sr. exec. asst. to state treas., 1989—92; bus. rep. United Food and Comml. Workers Union, Phila., 1992—94; mem. from Dist. 2 Pa. Senate, Harrisburg, 1994—, Dem. chair labor and industry com. Democrat. Office: State Legislature Rm 458 Main Capitol Bldg Harrisburg PA 17120 also: 1061 Bridge St Philadelphia PA 19124-1824

TARVER, PAULA DIANN, marketing professional; b. Natchitoches, La., Nov. 3, 1945; d. Willie Marcus Smith and Annie Pearl Smith-Driever; m. Milton Lane Tarver, Jan. 27, 1967; children: Edwin Phillip, Mary Lane. BA, North Western State Coll., 1967; student, Oreg. State U., 1968. Sales and mktg. staff Rockwell Collins, Pamona, Calif., 1983—99, 2003—. Recipient Lifetime Achievement award, World Airline Entertainment Assn., 1995. Mem.: NARAS (Grammy award 1978). Democrat. Achievements include patents for first live TV on airplanes. Home: 201 E Chapman Ave 72N Placentia WA 98270 Office: Rockwell Collins 2001 W Mission Blvd Pomona CA 91766

TASKER, MOLLY JEAN, lawyer; b. Cumberland, Md., Feb. 13, 1945; d. Samuel Paul Tasker and Peggy Evelyn Purinton; m. Richard Mark Curtis, June 7, 1985. AA, Santa Fe Jr. Coll., 1968; BA, Fla. Atlantic U., 1970; JD,

Fla. State U., 1973. Bar: Fla. 1973, U.S. Supreme Ct. 1992, U.S. Dist. Ct. (mid. dist.) Fla. 1997. Atty., advisor CIA, Washington, 1974-82, asst. gen. counsel, 1983-95, chair publs. rev. bd., 1993-95; ptnr. Tasker & Stephens, PA, Indian Harbour Beach, Fla., 1996—. Bd. dirs. Brevard County Emergency Med. Svc. Found., Melbourne, Fla., Cmty. Housing Initiative, Melbourne; guest lectr. Fla. So. Coll., Lakeland, 1997-01. Exec. sec. Brevard County (Fla.) Juvenile Justice Coun., 1997—; vice-chair Brevard County Dem. Exec. Com., 1997-98; chair govtl. affairs com. C. of C., Melbourne, 1998-99. Recipient Spl. Recognition award Brevard County Legal Aid, Inc., Fla., 1997, 2000; Fulbright Travel grant Fla. State U. Ctr. for Slavic and East European Studies, 1972. Mem. AAUW, LWV, Phi Alpha Delta, Phi Gamma Nu. Lutheran. Avocations: photography, reading, tennis, boating. Home: 4050 Carolwood Dr Melbourne FL 32934-7179 Office: 244 E Eau Gallie Blvd Indian Harbor Beach FL 32937-4874

TASMAN, ALICE LEA MAST, not-for-profit fundraiser; d. Clarence Kurtz Mast and Florence Larue Barkley; m. William S. Tasman, Nov. 8, 1962; children: James B., W. Graham, Alice. BA, Barnard Coll., 1956; postgrad., U. Pa. Tchr. Am. Cathedral, Paris, 1953—54; asst. dir. pub. rels. Phila. Art Mus., 1956—61; pub. rels. exec. WUHY-FM, 1976—77; cons. Franklin Mint, 1991—94; fundraising, corp. devel. exec. Wills Eye Hosp., 1996—. Author: Wedding Album: Customs & Lore Through the Ages, 1981, Adam, A Three Island Cat, 1984. Women's bd. Thomas Jefferson U. Hosp., 1983—; chmn. Art in City Hall, 1995—2003; fundraising com., spl. events Recording for Blind, 1993—95; devel. com., trustee Woodmere Art Mus., 1994—2003; mem. Associated Svcs. for Blind; originator, chmn. annual exhibit Form in Art, 1987—; vol. Phila. Mus. Art, 1984—; annual concert and ball com. Phila. Orch., 1972—75; libr. Chestnut Hill Acad. and Springside Sch., 1977—78; antiques show com. U. Pa., 1972—75; coord. long-term patient care Chestnut Hill Hosp., 1981; fundraising and publicity chair Project Orbis, 1982; fundraiser Am. Diabetes Assn., 1982; vol. Chestnut Hill Hosp., 1978—87; hon. chair fundraising Overbrook Sch. for Blind, 1989; fundraiser Am. Indian Fund, 1989; hon. chair symposium, fundraiser 1st Nat. Inst. Blind Artists, 1990; internat. ambassador City of Phila., 1993; bd. dirs. Chestnut Hill Presbyn. Ch., 1989—93, Nat. Exhibits by Blind Artists, 1987—, Chestnut Hill Women's Com. Phila. Orch., 1965—, Chestnut Hill Cmty. Ctr. and Women's Exchange, 1978—; bd. dirs. coun. visual arts Chestnut Hill Acad., 1997—; bd. dirs. Art in City Hall, 1993—2003, Hitchcock Found., 1982—83. Recipient Cert. of Appreciation, Phila. Arts Fest., 1959, Wills Eye Hosp., 1994, Overbrook Sch. for Blind award, 1989, Louis Braille award, Associated Svcs. for Blind, 1993, Founder's award, Nat. Exhibits by Blind Artists, Disting. Daughters of Pa. award, Gov. and Mrs. Tom Ridge, 1997, Lady of Dumbarton award, Nat. Soc. Colonial Dames, 1999, Lifetime Achievement award, Little Rock Found., 2001. Mem.: Friends Vielles Maisons Francaises, Am. Ophthalmology Soc. (chair pres. dinner 1989—), Am. Bd. Ophthalmology (chair 75th anniversary dinner 1992), Am. Acad. Ophthalmology (chair Christian med. dental luncheon 1991—92), French Huguenot Soc., Chestnut Hill Hist. Soc. (pres. 1972—74, program chair 1974—75, fundraising and spl. events chair 1981—), Nat. Soc. Colonial Dames Commonwealth Pa. (house com. 1980—89, garden com. 1987, house com. 1993—94, chair program com. 1993—96, first v.p. 1998—2002, co-chair capital campaign fund 1999—2001, pres. 2002—), Rotary, Jr. League. Avocations: travel, skiing, painting, crafts, gardening.

TASSINARI, MELISSA SHERMAN, toxicologist; b. Lawrence, Mass., Sept. 26, 1953; m. R. Peter Tassinari; children: Michael, Emily, Sara. AB, Mt. Holyoke Coll., 1975; postgrad., U. St. Andrews, Scotland, 1973-74, PhD, Med. Coll. Wis., 1979. Diplomate Am. Bd. Toxicology. Rsch. asst. in orthopedic surgery., Lab. Human Biochemistry Children's Hosp. Med. Ctr., Boston, 1981-83; rsch. affiliate in toxicology Forsyth Dental Ctr., Boston, 1983-86, staff assoc. dept. toxicology, 1986-89; asst. prof. cell biology U. Mass. Med. Ctr., Worcester, 1989-91; head reproductive and developmental toxicology Pfizer Global R&D, Groton/New London, Conn., 1991—99, group dir. worldwide safety scis., 2001—02, group dir. sr. tech. advisors, 2002—04, sr. dir. regulatory panel and intelligence, 2004—. Rsch. fellow oral biology Harvard Sch. Dental Medicine, Boston, 1978-81, instr. oral biology and pathophysiology, 1981-83; asst. prof. biol. scis. Wellesley Coll., Mass., 1985-91, biology Simmons Coll., Boston, 1986-87. Contbr. abstracts, articles to profl. jours. Mem. Teratology Soc. (coun. 2000—, v.p. 2004), Neurobehavioral Teratology Soc., Mid. Atlantic Reprodn. and Teratology Assn. (steering com. 1994), Midwest Teratology Assn., Soc. Toxicology. Office: Pfizer Inc 50 Pequot Ave New London CT 06320

TASSONE, GELSOMINA (GESSIE TASSONE), metal processing executive; b. N.Y.C., July 8, 1944; d. Enrico and A. Cira (Petriccione) Gargiulo; children: Ann Marie, Margaret, Theresa, Christine; m. Armando Tassone, Mar. 20, 1978. Student, Orange County Community Coll., 1975-79, Iona Coll., 1980—. Head bookkeeper Gargiulo Bros. Builders, N.Y.C., 1968-72; pres., owner A&T Iron Works, Inc., New Rochelle, N.Y., 1973—. Recipient Profl. Image award Contractors Coun. Greater N.Y.C., 1986; named Businesswoman of Yr., Contractors Coun. Greater N.Y.C., 1985, N.Y. State Small Bus. Person of Yr., 1988, Entrepreneur of Yr. Inc. mag., 1990; company named a Successful Small Bus. Co. Westchester County C. of C./BSBA, 1986-88. Mem. Nat. Ornamental and Miscellaneous Metal Assn., Builders Inst. Westchester and Putnam County, Westchester Assn. Women Bus. Owners, Profl. Women in Constrn., Westchester C. of C. Office: A&T Iron Works Inc 25 Cliff St New Rochelle NY 10801-6803 Office Phone: 914-632-8992.

TASSOS, ALICE CROWLEY, writer; b. Dallas, June 19, 1925; d. Thomas Francis and Geneiva Edna (Lee) Crowley; m. John Tassos, Mar. 4, 1950 (div. June 1960); 1 child, Penelope Geneiva Tassos Grima. BA in English, French, BS in Journalism, So. Meth. U., 1945, BA in Psychology, 1960; MA in French, Columbia U., 1947. Solo pilot cert. Sec. to fashion editor Vogue Mag., N.Y.C., 1945-46; airline stewardess Trans-Caribbean Airline, N.Y.C., 1946; embassy libr. U.S. Info. Svc. Fgn. Svc. Dept. State, Athens, Greece, 1947-49; jr. exec. J. Walter Thompson Co., N.Y.C., 1950-51; city side reporter Miami Daily News, 1952; pub. rels. exec. Boca Raton (Fla.) Hotel & Club, 1953; pvt. practice writer, linguist Dallas, 1960—. Author poems. Canvasser Am. Heart Assn., New Canaan, Conn., 1959; office sec. Easter Seals, Dallas, 1960-61; vol. recreational therapy asst. Timberlawn Psychiat. Hosp., Dallas, 1961-64; vol. March of Dimes, Dallas, 1997. Sr. scholar So. Meth. U., Dallas Woman's Club, 1944-45; consumer price index pub. svc. commendation Dept. Commerce, Dallas, 1999. Mem. AAUW, NAFE, Cmty. of the Holy Spirit (assoc.), Daus. of the King, Alpha Theta Phi, Theta Sigma Phi, Psi Chi. Episcopalian. Avocations: skin diving, swimming, cycling, walking.

TATE, ALICIA SALEMME, special education educator; b. West Haven, Conn., Dec. 22, 1967; d. Robert Joseph and Mary Ann Furman Salemme; m. John David Tate, May 20, 1989; children: Mary Catherine, Daniel Joseph. BS, East Carolina U., 1989; postgrad., U. N.C., Greensboro. Cert. tchr. mentally retarded, learning disabled N.C. Spl. edn. tchr. Rockingham County Schs., Wentworth, NC, 1990—92; spl. edn. tchr., facilitator Scotland County Schs., Laurinburg, NC, 1992—; nat. bd. cert./needs specialist, 2000. Nat. bd. candidate support coord. Scotland County Schs., 2001—; participant, mem. Tchg. Am. About Accomplished Tchg. Coach Spl. Olympics, Laurinburg. Bright Ideas grant, 2002. Mem.: N.C. Assn. Educators, N.C. Coalition for Quality Tchg., Coun. for Exceptional Children (assoc.), Pi Lambda Theta. Avocations: swimming, reading, cooking. Home: 12961 Randomwoods Dr Laurinburg NC 28352 Office: Scotland County Schs 322 S Main St Laurinburg NC 28352 Personal E-mail: atate@scsnc.org.

TATE, DIANNE EVANS, program coordinator; b. Rockwood, Tenn., Apr. 1, 1947; d. Tom Harper and Myrle Lena (Marrs) Evans; m. J.B. Tate. BS in Edn., Kennesaw State Coll., 1988. Cert. tchr., Ga. Art tchr. Monroe County Schs., Madisonville, Tenn., 1968-69; dir. student ctr. Sanford U., Birmingham, Ala., 1969-73; sec. Cobb County Sch., Marietta, Ga., 1974-85; asst. state dir. vols. Ga. Dept. Corrections, Atlanta, 1988-92; adj. instr. North Metro Tech., Acworth, Ga., 1992—. Mem. Peach Bd., Cartersville, Ga., 1992—. Block capt. Neighborhood Watch, Catersville, 1995; bd. dirs. YWCA, Marietta, 1981-87; mayor pro tem Cartersville, 2003—. Mem. AAUW, Etowah Hist. Soc. (preservation chair 1992-95, chair tour of homes 1994). Avocations: hiking, reading, wheel thrown pottery. Home: 402 W Main St Cartersville GA 30120-3458 Office: North Metro Tech 5198 Ross Rd Acworth GA 30102-3132

TATE, HORENCENA, state legislator, software company executive; BS in Edn., U. Ga., 1977; M Ednl. Adminstrn., Atlanta U., 1988; PhD in Ednl. Adminstrn., Clark-Atlanta U., 1992. With Ga. Dept. Labor, Atlanta, from 1977, United Airlines, Atlanta, Apollo Travel Svcs., Atlanta; pres. Tate, Marsh and Assocs., Inc., software-mgmt. tng., Atlanta; mem. Ga. Senate, Atlanta, 1999—. Sec. state and local govtl. ops. com., mem. health and human svcs. com., retirement com., transp. com. Former del. Ga. Dem. Conf.; former computer literacy advisor Butler St. YMCA, Atlanta; vol. software instr. for local chs.; Clark-Atlanta U. del. to Internat. Cmty. Edn. Conf., Trinidad; spkr. to Atlanta pub. schs.; v.p. Rosalie Wright Cmty. Coun.; active Cascade United Meth. Ch., Atlanta. Mem. United Meth. Women. Office: Ga Senate Legislative Office Bldg 18 Capitol Sq SW Ste 320B Atlanta GA 30334-2000

TATE, SHEILA BURKE, public relations executive; b. Washington, Mar. 3, 1942; d. Eugene L. and Mary J. (Doherty) Burke; m. William J. Tate, May 2, 1981 (dec. Aug. 1998); children: Hager Burke Patton, Courtney Paige Patton Manzel. BA in Journalism, Duquesne U., 1964; postgrad. in mass comm., U. Denver, 1975—76. Rsch. asst. Westinghouse Air Brake Co.; asst. account exec. Falhgren and Assocs.; copywriter Ketchum, MacLeod and Grove, 1964—66; account exec. Burson-Marsteller Assocs., Pitts., 1967, sr. v.p. Washington, 1985—87; public rels. mgr. Colo. Nat. Bank, Denver, 1967—70; account exec. Hill and Knowlton, Inc., Houston, 1977—78, v.p. Washington, 1978—81; dep. to the chmn. Hill and Knowlton Inc., Washington, 1987—88; press sec. to First Lady White House, Washington, 1981—85; press sec. George Bush for Pres. Campaign, 1988; press sec. to Pres.-elect George Bush, 1988—89; vice chmn. Cassidy and Assocs. Pub. Affairs, Washington, 1989—91; pres. Powell Tate, Washington, 1991—99, vice-chmn., 1999—. Bd. dirs., former mem. Corp. for Pub. Broadcasting, vice chmn., 1990—92, chmn., 1992—94; bd. dirs. Ethics Resource Ctr., Washington, Guest Svcs. Corp., Fairfax, Va. Chmn. pub. affairs adv. bd. U.S. Mil. Acad.; mem. adv. bd. Ronald Reagan Inst. Emergency Med., George Washington Univ. Hosp., Washington; mem. nat. adv. bd. The Salvation Army; bd. dirs. First Tee of Greater Washington; adv. bd. Am. Acad. Family Physicians, Kansas City, Kans. Mem.: Nat. Press Club, Belfair Club, Farmington Country Club, Washington Golf and Country Club, Duquesne U. Century Club. Office: Powell Tate 700 13th St NW Ste 1000 Washington DC 20005-5926 E-mail: state@webershandwick.com.

TATE, SHEILA DIANE, music educator; d. Claude Tate, Sr. and Emily Tate. BA, Va. Union U., 1982—86; MusM, Westminster Choir Coll., 1989—91; student, Regent U., 2002—03. Teacher Certification Va., 1986. Instr. of music Va. Union U., Richmond, 1991—2000, asst. prof. of music, 2000—01; music tchr. Richmond Pub. Sch., Va., 2001—02; choir dir. Charles City H.S., Va., 2002—. Music dept. coord. Va. Union U., Richmond, 2000—01, freshman orientation coord., 1992—2001, u. choir dir., 1994—2001. Editor: (freshman orientation textbook) Virginia Union University: A Road to Success. Workshop presenter No. Neck Youth Conv., Montross, Va., 1999; singing historian African Am. Heritage Chorale, Richmond, Va., 1992—98; tchr. Richmond Christian Ctr., Richmond, Va., 2000—03; dir. Daughters of Grace Dance Ministry, Richmond, Va., 1997—2003; music coord. RCC Healing Ministry, Richmond, Va., 2000—03; workshop presenter St. Stephen's Episcopal Ch., Richmond, Va., 1999—99, Mt Nebo Bapt. Ch., West Point, Va., 1999—99.

TATLOCK, ANNE M. trust company executive; b. White Plains, NY, July 1, 1939; d. John and Kathleen (McGrath) McNiff; m. William Tatlock, Apr. 29, 1967; children: Julina, Kerry, Christopher. BA, Vassar Coll., 1961; MA in Econs., NYU, 1968. 1st v.p. Smith Barney Harris Upham, N.Y.C., 1962-84; exec. v.p. Fiduciary Trust Internat., N.Y.C., 1984-94, pres. NYC, 1994—99, pres., CEO, 1999—2000, chmn., CEO, 2000—. Bd. dirs. Fortune Brands, Lincolnshire, Ill., 1996—, Franklin Resources, San Mateo, Calif., 2001—, Merck, NJ, 2000—. Trustee Am. Ballet Theatre, NYC, 1994-, (pres., 1999-2001), Vassar Coll., 1994—, The Teagle Found., NYC, 1995—, Andrew W. Mellon Found., N.Y.C., 1995—, chmn., 2003—, Cultural Instns. Retirement Sys., NYC, 1989—, (chmn., 1995-99), Howard Hughes Med. Inst., Md., 2000—, The Conf. Bd., NYC, 2001—, Mayo Found., Minn., 2002—.

TATNALL, ANN WESLAGER, reading educator; b. Uniontown, Pa., June 1, 1935; d. Clinton Alfred and Ruth Georgia (Hurst) Weslager; m. George Gress Tatnall, Oct. 8, 1954; children: Peggy Ann, George Richardson. BS in Edn., U. Del., 1967; MA in Edn., Glassboro State Coll., 1978. Cert. reading specialist, cert. supr., cert. elem. tchr., N.J. Tchr. reading Oldmans Twp. Bd. of Edn., Pedricktown, N.J., 1972-78, reading specialist, 1978-95, reading supr., 1981-95. Mem. N.J. Dept. of Edn. Minimum Basic Skills Test Devel. Com., Trenton, N.J., 1981-82; mem. Quad-Dist. Reading Coordination Com., Salem County, N.J., 1987-95; chairperson Adminstrv. Com. of Oldmans Twp. Schs., Pedricktown, N.J., 1993-95. Chair Woodstown (NJ) Candlelight House Tour, 1983-99, homes chair, 2000—; pres. Pilesgrove-Woodstown Hist. Soc., 1994-99, v.p., 1999-2001, pres. 2002-03, trustee, 2003; v.p. Pilesgrove Libr. Assn., 1994-2002, pres., 2003; sec. Hist. Preservation Commn., Woodstown, 1989—; mem. jr. bd. Wilmington (Del.) Med. Ctr., 1969—, treas. Thrift Shop, 1970-75; trustee United Way of Salem County, 1997-99; mem. Salem County Cultural and Heritage Commn., 1997—. Recipient Gov.'s Tchr. Recognition Program award Gov. of N.J., 1988; selected Hands Across the Water, Russian/USA Tchr. Exchange, 1990-91; named Salem County Woman of Achievement, 1998. Mem. AAUW, Internat. Reading Assn., N.J. Reading Assn., Woman's Club of Woodstown. Avocations: travel, reading, Univ. of Del. football, restoration of historic houses, granddaughters. Home: 209 N Main St Woodstown NJ 08098-1227

TATOR, ADRIENNNE MARIA, director; b. Jersey City, Jan. 23, 1947; d. Vincent and Marie Del Colle; m. David Tator; children: Brennan, Andre, Kevin, Michaela. BA, Coll. St. Elizabeth, Morristown, N.J., 1968; MA, Kean U., Union, N.J., 1997; EdD, Seton Hall U., South Orange, N.J., 2002. Tchr., adminstr. St. Pius X H.S.; tchr., French and English Rahway H.S., NJ; adj. prof. Fairleigh Dickinson U., Coll. St. Elizabeth; pvt. ednl. cons.; supr. world langs. Millburn (NJ) Sch. Dist. Mem.: ASCD (program dir.), Kappa Delta Pi. Home: 1 Hillview Terr Summit NJ 07901 E-mail: tator@millburn.org.

TATROW, KRISTIN, research scientist; b. Perth Amboy, N.J., Aug. 22, 1973; BA, Lake Forest Coll., 1995; PhD, SUNY, Albany, 2002. Project coord./rsch. asst. Ctr. for Stress and Anxiety Disorders, Albany, 1997—2001; intern N.J. VA Hosp., East Orange, 2001—02; postdoctoral fellow Mt. Sinai Sch. Medicine, N.Y.C., 2002—. Contbr. articles to profl. jours. Scholar Rsch. Assistantship, U. Albany, 1997—2001; Travel scholar, Assn. Applied Psychophysiology and Biofeedback Travel, 2000, Grad. Student Orgn. Rsch. grantee, U. Albany, 2000, Grad. Student Orgn. Travel grantee, 2000, Psychology Dept. Grad. Student Rsch. grantee, 2000. Mem.: APA (assoc.), Assn. Applied Psychophysiology and Biofeedback, Assn. Advancement Behavioral Therapy (assoc.).

TATUM, BEVERLY DANIEL, psychology and education educator; b. Tallahaassee, Sept. 27, 1954; d. Robert Alphonse and Catherine Faith (Maxwell) Daniel; m. Travis James Tatum, July 28, 1979; children: Travis Jonathan Daniel, David Alexander Daniel. BA, Wesleyan U., Middletown, Conn., 1975; MA in Psychology, U. Mich., 1976, PhD, 1984. Lic. clin. psychologist. From asst. prof. to assoc. prof. dept. psychology Westfield (Mass.) State Coll., 1983-89; assoc. prof. dept. psychology and edn. Mt. Holyoke Coll., South Hadley, Mass., 1989—; pvt. practice Northampton, Mass., 1989—. Lectr. dept. black studies U. Calif., Santa Barbara, 1980-83, counseling psychologist, 1979-83; vis. scholar Stone Ctr., Wellesley (Mass.) Coll., 1991-92; chair, bd. dirs. Equity Inst., Emeryville, Calif., 1987-89. Author: Assimilation Blues, 1987. Predoctoral fellow APA Minority Program, 1976-79, dissertation fellow U. Calif., 1980-81, postdoctoral fellow Ford Found., 1991. Mem. APA, Am. Psychol. Soc., Ea. Psychol. Assn., Mass. Psychol. Assn., Assn. Women in Psychology, Assn. Black Psychologists. Office: Mount Holyoke College Dept Psychology And Ed South Hadley MA 01075

TATUM, CARLA MARIA, elementary school educator; b. Gainesville, Ga., Apr. 18, 1970; d. Charles Linton and Judy Ann Tatum. BS, North Ga. State U., 1992, EdM, 1993; EdS, Brenau U., 1996. Cert. tchr. support specialist Profl. Practices Commn., 2000. Tchr. Mashburn Elem., Cumming, Ga., 1993—2002, Settles Bridge Elem., Suwanee, Ga., 2002—. Dir. Settles Bridge After Sch. Program, Suwanee, 2002—. Facilitator Kids Voting USA, Suwanee, Ga., 2000—00. Outdoor Classroom grant, Environ. Edn. Alliance Ga., 2001. Mem.: Profl. Assn. Ga. Educators (assoc.), Assn. Supervision and Curriculum Devel. (assoc.). Avocations: gardening, researching, reading, real estate. Office: Settles Bridge Elem 600 James Burgess Rd Suwanee GA 30024 Personal E-mail: cmtatum@charter.net.

TATUM, JACKIE, former parks and recreation manager, municipal official; b. Kansas City, Mo., June 11, 1932; 2 children. BS in Phys. Edn., U. So. Calif. Tchr., Calif. With Ctrl. Recreation Ctr. Parks and Recreation Ctr. City of L.A., 1955; recreation dir. various recreation ctrs.; prin. recreation supr.; asst. gen. mgr. Valley Region, 1989-92; gen. mgr., 1992-98; cons. City of L.A., Dept. Recreation and Parks, 1998—. Chair nat. exec. com., creator, developer Wonderful Outdoor World (WOW); presenter in field. Contbr. articles to profl. jours.; appearances in tv, radio shows. Recipient Ticket to Life award Inner City Games; named Woman of the Yr. World Ops. Internat., 1976, City Employee of Yr. All City Employees Benefits Svc. Assn., 1992., One of Ten Most Powerful Black Women in L.A. Mem. Nat. Recreation and Parks Assn. (Disting. Svc. award 1997, tchr. Pacific Mktg. and Revenue Sources Mgmt. Sch.), Chi Kappa Rho (v.p., pres., past pres. Helen I. Pontius Nat. award of merit). Office: City of Los Angeles Recreation 200 N Main St Rm 1330 Los Angeles CA 90012-4110

TAUBIN, DAWN, film company executive; Staff prodr., cable television programming Warner Amex Cable Comms., Ohio; dir., publicity and promotion Nat. Amusements Inc., Boston, 1983—85; west coast regional publicity/promotion rep. to v.p., publicity MGM, 1985—89; v.p., publicity Warner Bros. Pictures, 1989—93, v.p., advt. and publicity, 1993—96, sr. v.p., advt. and publicity, 1996—99, exec. v.p., mktg., 1999—2001, pres., domestic mktg., 2001—. Office: Warner Bros Pictures 4000 Warner Blvd Burbank CA 91522-0001

TAUBMAN, JANE ANDELMAN, Russian literature educator; b. Boston, Oct. 23, 1942; d. Hyman M. and Esther (Rosenthal) Andelman; m. William Chase Taubman; children: Alexander, Phoebe. BA, Radcliffe Coll., 1964; MA, Yale U., 1968, PhD, 1972. Instr. Russian Smith Coll., Northampton, Mass., 1968-72; asst. prof. Russian Amherst (Mass.) Coll., 1973-83, assoc. prof. Russian, 1983-89, prof. Russian, 1989—. Author: A Life Through Poetry: Marina Tsvetaeva's Lyric Diary, 1989, (Russian transl. 2001), Cinetek: Asthenic Syndrome, 2000; co-author: Moscow Spring, 1989; co-editor: Marina Tsvetaeva: One Hundred Years, 1994; contbr. articles to profl. jours. Woodrow Wilson Found. fellow, 1964—, Am. Coun. Learned Socs.-SSRC, 1974, trustee-faculty fellow Amherst Coll., 1978, fellow Nat. Def. Title VI, 1965-68; grantee Am. Philos. Soc., 1975, Amherst Coll., 1991, 94, IREX grantee USSR, 1988. Mem. AAUP, Modern Langs. Assn., Am. Assn. Tchrs. Slavic and East European Langs., Am. Assn. Slavic Studies, Am. Coun. Tchrs. of Russian, Am. Assn. Tchrs. of Slavic and East European Langs. Office: Amherst Coll Dept Russian Amherst MA 01002 Office Phone: 413-542-2047.

TAUBMAN, JENNY, museum program director; b. Sofia, Bulgaria; m. Nicholas F. Taubman; children: Marc, Lara. Pres. Personal Image Consulting, 1981—97; chmn. capital campaign Art Mus. Western Va., Roanoke. Va. Israel adv. bd. Commonwealth of Va.; chmn. Brotherhood Week; coord. Bravo Arts, Inc.; bd. dirs. Temple Emmanuel; past pres. Hadassah and Temple Emanuel Sisterhood; bd. dirs. Va. Mus. Fine Arts, Richmond, Art Mus. Western Va., Western Va. Found. for Arts and Scis., Roanoke Symphony Aux., Roanoke City Arts Commn. Non-commd. officer Israeli Army. Avocations: art, tennis, design. Office: Art Mus Western Va Ctr in the Sq One Market Sq Roanoke VA 24011-1436

TAURASI, DIANA, college basketball player; Student, U. Conn., 2000—. Guard women's basketball U. Conn., 2000—. Named Big East Preseason Rookie of the Yr., 2000—01, Most Outstanding Player of the NCAA East Region, 2000—01, Big East Championship Most Outstanding Player, 2000—01, Kodak All-Am. and AP Second Team All Am., 2001—02, Naismith Player of the Yr., 2001—02, 2003, NCAA Final Four and East Regional Most Outstanding Player, 2003, USBWA Nat. Player of the Yr., 2003, Big East First Team Performer, 2002—03, Preseason All-Am., 2003; named to Big East All-Rookie Team, 2000—01, NCAA Mideast Region All-Tournament Team, 2001—02, All Big-East First Team, 2002, Big East All Tournament Team, 2002, Big East All-Tournament Team, 2003; recipient winner, Nat. Championship with U. Conn., 2002, 2003, 2004, Honda award for Women's Basketball Finalist, 2001—02, Honda Trophy Award, 2003, Wade Trophy, 2003. Office: Univ of Connecticut Harry A Gampel Pavilion Storrs CT 06269*

TAUSCHER, ELLEN O. congresswoman; b. Newark, N.J., 1951; m. William Y. Tauscher; 1 child, Katherine. BS in early Childhood Edn., Seton Hall U., 1974. With Bache Securities, N.Y.C., N.Y. Stock Exchange; dir. Tauscher Found.; mem. U.S. Congress from 10th Calif. dist., 1997—; mem. house armed svcs. com., house transp. com. U.S. Ho. Reps. Founder The ChildCare Registry; bd. regents Seton Hall U.; co-chair Delaine Eastin's State Supt. Pub. Instrn. Campaign, 1994; transp. and infrastructure com., surface transp. and water resources and environ. Author: The ChildCare Sourcebook, 1996. Active The Coalition, New Dem. Coalition, Bipartisan Freshman Campaign Fin. Reform Task Force, House Cancer Awareness Working Group, Congl. Caucus on the Arts; vice-chair Calif. Dem. Del. Democrat.*

TAUSSIG, MARGARET C. artist; b. Boston, Jan. 11, 1922; d. George Herbert Crocker, Jr. and Elsie Tyler Goodhue; m. William M. Taussig, Apr. 7, 1945 (dec. July 1980); children: Margo Pinkerton Zann, William Murray Taussig, Jr. Cert. secretarial course, Copley Secretarial Inst., Boston, 1941; cert. mech. drawing, Newton Trade Sch., 1943. Sec. rsch. Dr. Burton Hamilton, Boston, 1941; sec., lab. technician Dr. Irving and Dr. Winsor, Boston, 1942; draftsman ink lettering Reece Buttonhole Machine Co., Boston, 1942—45; painter Pigsty Studio, Canaan, NH, 1979—. Mem.: N.H. Art Assn., Ava Gallery, Chaffee Ctr. for the Arts, Sharon Art Ctr., N.H. Art Assn. (asst. to exec. dir. for office work 1997—2002, 1st prize watercolor

1988), So. Vt. Art Ctr., The Copley Soc. Boston. Episcopalian. Avocations: cross country skiing, hiking, sewing, interior decorating. Home and Office: Margaret Taussig Studio 543 Canaan St Canaan NH 03741

TAVARAS, TASHA NEANDA, writer; b. Atlanta, July 15, 1979; d. Debra Tavaras. Owner, CEO Poethnic Artistic Venue, Atlanta; asst. editor What's Within You Mag., Atlanta, 1998—. Home: 560 John Wesley Dobbs Ave NE #B Atlanta GA 30312-1638 E-mail: Poethnic@aol.com.

TAVARES, CHARLETA B. former state legislator; Student, Spelman Coll., Ohio State U. Mem. Ohio Ho. of Reps., Columbus, 1993-98; council mem. City of Columbus, OH. Mem. Met. Human Svc. Commn. Vol. Huckleberry House, Literacy Initiative. Recipient award Black Students in Comm. Ohio State U., 1992, Ctrl. Comty House award, 1992, Pub. Children's Svc. Assn. award, 1993; named Franklin County Dem. Women's Club Sweetheart, 1993. Mem. LWV, Far East Dem. Women's Club, Columbus Area Women's Polit. Caucus, Coalition of 100 Black Women.

TAYLER, IRENE, English literature educator; b. Abilene, Tex., July 13, 1934; d. B. Brown Smith and Madeline (Bowron); m. Edward W. Tayler, June 3, 1961 (div. 1971); children: Edward Jr., Jesse; m. Saul Touster, Jan. 14, 1978. BA in Philosophy, Stanford U., 1956, MA in Am. Lit., 1961, PhD in English Lit., 1968. Tchr. Breadloaf Sch. of Eng., Middlebury, Vt., 1970, 71, 75, 76; teaching asst. Stanford U., Calif., 1958-60; lectr. Columbia U., N.Y., 1961-71; asst. prof. CUNY, 1971-73, assoc. prof., 1973-76, MIT, Cambridge, 1976-82, prof., 1982-96, sec. of the faculty, 1993-95, retired, 1996. Chair gov. com. The English Inst., 1981. Author: Blake's Illustrations to the Poems of Gray, 1971, Holy Ghosts: The Male Muses of Emily and Charlotte Bronte, 1990; contbr. articles to profl. jours. Internat. Inst. Edn. fellow U. Munich, 1957-58; Wilson fellow Stanford U., 1961-62; ACLS study grantee, 1968-69; Faculty Rsch. Found. grantee CUNY, 1972-73; NEH sr. scholar fellow, 1980; Mac Vicar faculty fellow MIT, 1993-2003. Mem.: St. Botolph Club (Boston) (pres. 2000—03). E-mail: itayler@mit.edu.

TAYLOR, ANN, human resources specialist, educator; b. Gordonville, Pa., Feb. 28, 1940; d. Gideon S. and Elizabeth L. Stoltzfus; m. James R. Taylor III, Feb. 18, 1983 (dec. Sept. 1995). BA, Ea. Mennonite U., 1966; MEd, Millersville (Pa.) U., 1979; EdD, Temple U., 1995. Caseworker Lancaster (Pa.) Welfare Dept., 1969-72, Lancaster County Probation Parole Dept., 1967-69; parole agent Pa. Bd. Probation, Parole, Harrisburg, 1972-85; human resource cons., trainer Taylor Assocs., Lancaster, 1985—. Adj. prof. bus. mgmt. Pa. State U., Lancaster, 1979-2000; spkr. in field; free lance trainer Hamilton Bank, Lancaster, 1985-91, Armstrong World Industries, Lancaster, 1987, 91; adv. com. staff trainer Vantage Drug and Alcohol Facility, Lancaster, 1983-85. Co-author: Fire Up Your Brilliance; co-author articles to profl. jours. Vol. Lancaster County Mental Health Ctr., 1983-94; seminar leader Fulton County (Pa.) C. of C., 1985-86, York County (Pa.) C. of C., 1985-86, Lancaster County C. of C., 1985-88. Mem. Am. Counseling Assn. Democrat. Episcopalian. Avocations: travel, reading, gardening, hiking. Office: 214 E King St Lancaster PA 17602 Office Phone: 717-394-6859. E-mail: brilliance@comcast.net.

TAYLOR, ANNA DIGGS, federal judge; b. Washington, Dec. 9, 1932; d. Virginius Douglass and Hazel (Bramlette) Johnston; m. S. Martin Taylor, May 22, 1976; children: Douglass Johnston Diggs, Carla Cecile Diggs. BA, Barnard Coll., 1954; LLB, Yale U., 1957. Bar: D.C. 1957, Mich. 1961. Atty. Office Solicitor, Dept. Labor, W, 1957-60; asst. prosecutor Wayne County, Mich., 1961-62; asst. U.S. atty. Eastern Dist. of Mich., 1966; ptnr. Zwerdling, Maurer, Diggs & Papp, Detroit, 1970-75; asst. corp. counsel City of Detroit, 1975-79; U.S. dist. judge Eastern Dist. Mich. Detroit, 1979—. Hon. chair United Way, Cmty. Found., S.E. Mich.; trustee emeritus Detroit Inst. Arts; co-chair, vol. Leadership Coun.; vice-chair Henry Ford Health Sys. Mem. Fed. Bar Assn., State Bar Mich., Wolverine Bar Assn. (v.p.), Yale Law Assn. Episcopalian. Office: US Dist Ct 740 US Courthouse 231 W Lafayette Blvd Detroit MI 48226-2700

TAYLOR, BARBARA ALDEN, public relations executive; b. Dallas, Aug. 21, 1943; d. Harold Earl and Sally Alden (Howard) T. BA, Smith Coll., 1965; MA, Antioch Coll., 1971. Vol. Peace Corps., India, 1966-68; tchr. Upper Merion Sch. Dist., King of Prussia, Pa., 1969-70, Cheltenham Sch. Dist., Elkins Park, Pa., 1970-74; pub. rels. dir. Princess Hotels Internat., N.Y.C., 1974-75; chmn. Taylor & Hammond Ltd., N.Y.C., 1975-84; pres. Doremus/Marketshare, 1984-86; exec. v.p. Porter/Novelli, N.Y.C., 1986-90; sr. v.p. Hill and Knowlton, Inc., N.Y.C., 1990-93; sr. v.p. corp. comm. Lancaster Group Worldwide, 1993-95; sr. v.p. Coty Inc. and Benckiser Group, 1995-97; exec. v.p. Edelman Pub. Rels. Worldwide, N.Y.C., 1997—. Bd. dirs. Madison Square Boys' and Girls' Club N.Y., 1978—, also mem. women's bd. Boys' Club N.Y. Named to Acad. of Women Achievers YWCA, 1985; bd. dirs. Up With People, Tucson, 1990—; trustee Smith Coll., 1999—. Mem. Women in Comms., Pub. Rels. Soc. Am. (counselors acad.), Internat. Women's Forum, Advt. Women N.Y., Cosmetic Exec. Women, Fashio Group, Doubles Internat., Smith Coll. Alumnae Assn. (bd. dirs. 1993-96), Club N.Y., Lyford Cay Club, Jr. League City N.Y. Avocations: tennis, walking. Office: Edelman Pub Rels Worldwide 1500 Broadway Ste 504 New York NY 10036-4048

TAYLOR, BARBARA ANN OLIN, writer, educational consultant; b. St. Louis, Feb. 8, 1933; d. Spencer Truman and Ann Amelia (Whitney) Olin; m. F. Morgan Taylor Jr., Apr. 5, 1954; children: Frederick M. III, Spencer O., James W., John F. AB, Smith Coll., 1954; M in Mgmt., Northwestern U., 1978, PhD, 1984; LHD, U. New Haven, 1995. Mem. faculty Hamden (Conn.) Hall Country Day Sch., 1972-74; cons. Booz, Allen & Hamilton, Inc., Chgo., 1979; program assoc. Northwestern U., Evanston, Ill., 1982; co-founder, exec. dir. Nat. Ctr. Effective Schs. R&D, Okemos, Mich., 1986-89, rsch. assoc., 1987; chmn. Nat. Ctr. for Effective Schs. Resource and Devel. Found., 2002—03; cons. on effective schs. rsch. and reform Nat. Ctr. Effective Schs. R&D U. Wis., Madison, 1990-96; pres. Excelsior! Found., Chgo., 1994—. Mem. exec. com. Hudson Inst., New Am. Schs. Devel. Corp. Design Team, 1990-94; Danforth Disting. lectr. U. Nebr., Omaha, 1993. Co-author: Making School Reform Happen, 1993, Keepers of the Dream, 1994, The Revolution Revisited: Effective Schools and Systemic Reform, 1995; editor: Case Studies in Effective Schools Research, 1990; contbr. articles to profl. jours. Pres. Jr. League of New Haven, 1967-69; pres. NCCJ, New Haven, 1971-73; co-chair Coalition Housing and Human Resources, Hartford-New Haven, 1970-73; co-chair steering com. Day Care Conn., Hartford, 1971-73; trustee U. New Haven, 1961-71, Smith Coll., Northampton, Mass., 1984-90, Choate Rosemary Hall Sch., 1973-78, Lake Forest Coll., 1996—, Hudson Inst., 1989-97, Northwestern U., 1998-2002. Recipient Humanitarian award Mt. Calvary Bapt. Ch., 1988, Outstanding Alumna award John Burroughs Sch., 1994, Pres.'s award U. New Haven. Mem. ASCD, Nat. Commn. Citizens Edn. (bd. dirs. 1980-86), Nat. Staff Devel. Coun., Phi Delta Kappa (Internat. award for Outstanding Svc. 2000). Episcopalian. Office: Nat Ctr Effective Schs Rsch & Devel 1124 Lake Rd Lake Forest IL 60045-1723

TAYLOR, BETH L. counselor; b. Fort Hood, Tex., Oct. 8, 1951; d. Lytle Louis and Arthur Marie Taylor. BS, So. Conn. State U., 1973; MS in Edn., U. Dayton, 1975; JD, Tex. So. U., 1985. Tchr., Tex., 1974—89; counselor San Antonio ISD, 1989—, Pearland (Tex.) ISD, 1989—; adminstrv. aide Former State Rep. Frank Tejeda, San Antonio, 1990—92. Chair com. Martin Luther King Meml. City/County Commn., San Antonio, 1988—97. Mem.: Brazoria County Counselling Assn. Home: 1707 Starboard Shores Ct Missouri City TX 77459-1721

TAYLOR, BEVERLY LACY, musician, educator, stringed instrument restorer; b. Denver, Mar. 1, 1928; d. Frederick Thurlow and Ruth (Rogers) Lacy; m. Arthur D. Taylor, Mar. 18, 1967. BA, Wheaton Coll., Norton, Mass., 1949; postgrad., U. Denver, 1951-53, U. Colo., 1953. Scenic designer, tech. dir. Piper Players, Idaho Springs, Colo., 1949-51; art instr. Denver Art Mus., 1952; craft and speech instr. Wallace Sch., Denver, 1953; illustrator dept. native art Denver Art Mus., 1954-56; designer, owner The Art Studio, Santa Fe, 1956-58; instr., owner Classic Guitar Studio, Santa Fe, 1959—; instr. classical guitar Santa Fe Conservatory of Music, 1966-67, Coll. Sante Fe, 1971-72; stringed instrument restorer Lacy Taylor Studio, Santa Fe, 1967—. One-woman shows of mosaic panels include Mus. N.Mex., Santa Fe, 1959; exhibited in group shows at Mus. New Mex., 1962, 63; executed mosaic panels Denver Art Mus. Bd. mem. Renesan, Elderhostel Inst. Network. Recipient Miriam Carpenter Art prize Wheaton Coll., 1949, prize N.Mex. State Fair, 1959, 61. Mem. Guild Am. Luthiers, Assn. String Instrument Artisans. Avocations: drawing, gardening, dog training, horse therapy programs for handicapped adults and children. Home: 1210 Canyon Rd Santa Fe NM 87501-6128

TAYLOR, BRANDY MILLER, music educator; b. Decatur, Ala., Nov. 15, 1973; d. Patricia N. Miller; m. T. Brian Taylor, June 9, 2001. B in Music Edn., U. Montevallo, 1997, MusM, 1999. Orff-Schulwerk Nat. Orff-Schulwerk Assn. Tchr. music, dir. choir John E. Bryan Elem. Sch., Morris, Ala., 1997—. Mem.: Jefferson County Edn. Assn. (assoc. rep. 2002—), Ala. Edn. Assn., Ala. Orff-Schulwerk Assn., Ala. Music Educators' Assn. (publicity mgr. 2003—), Music Educators Nat. Conf. Office: John E Bryan Elementary School 600 Kimberly Cut-Off Road Morris AL 35116 Personal E-mail: muscmaker@yahoo.com.

TAYLOR, CAROLYN KAY, music educator; b. Protection, Kans., Mar. 30, 1938; d. Thomas George and Ruby D. Boone; m. Joseph Taylor; children: Corinne K. Maloch, Holly D. Peter, Daren K. Degree in Liberal Studies, Calif. State U., Chico, 1981. Life credential in music Calif. C.C., 1976, cert. multiple subject K-8 Calif., 1991. Instr. Butte C.C., Oroville, Calif., 1976—98; fine arts and music specialist Chico Unified Sch. Dist., Calif., 1985—. Handbell choir dir. First Christian Ch., Chico, 1976—94; choir and handbell choir dir. Bidwell Meml. Presbyn. Ch., Chico, 1979—81; choir dir. Aldersgate United Meth. Ch., 1998—. Musician: Touring Handbell Choir, 1980. Grantee, Kappa Delta Pi, Calif. State U., Chico, 1981. Mem.: Calif. Music Educators' Assn. (treas. exec. bd. 1994—98, sec. exec. bd. 1998—2001), Am. Orff-Schulwerk Assn. (pres. 1987—89, sec. 1999—2001), Mt. Lassen Chapter, American Orff-Schulwerk Association, California Music Educators' Association, Northern Section. Methodist. Avocation: music. Office: Chapman Sch 1071 E 16th St Chico CA 95928 Office Fax: 530-891-3294.

TAYLOR, CELIANNA ISLEY, information systems specialist; b. Youngstown, Ohio; d. Paul Thornton and Florence (Jacobs) Isley; divorced; children: Polly, Jerry, Jim. BA in Philosophy, Denison U., 1939; MLS, Western Res. U., 1942. Worked in several pub. librs. and univ. librs., 1939-50; head Libr. Cataloging Dept. Battelle Mem. Inst., Columbus, Ohio, 1951-53; head pers. office, assoc. prof. libr. adminstrn. Ohio State U. Librs., Columbus, 1954-65; coord. info. svcs., assoc. prof. libr. adminstrn. Nat. Ctr. for Rsch. in Vocat. Edn., Ohio State U., Columbus, 1966-70; sr. rsch. assoc., adminstrv. assoc., assoc. prof. libr. adminstrn. dept. computer and info. sci. Ohio State U., Columbus, 1970-86, assoc. prof. emeritus Univ. Librs., 1986—. Mem. Task Force on a Spl. Collections Database, Ohio State U. Librs., Columbus, 1988-89, comm. systems and recs. coord. Ohio State U. Retirees Assn., Columbus, 1992-93, info. specialist, MacForum, Ohio State U., Columbus, 2001—; cons. for several profl. orgns. including Ernst & Ernst CPA's and Oreg. State Sys. of Higher Edn., 1961-82. Author: (with J. Magisos) Guide for State Voc-Tech Edn. Dissemination Systems 1971, (with A.E. Petrarca, and R.S. Kohn) Info. Interaction 1982; editor Highlights-Coun. for Ethics in Econs., 1997—; contbr. several articles to profl. jours.; designer info. sys.: CALL Sys., 1977-82, Channel 2000 Proj. Home Info. Svc., 1980-81, Continuing Education Info. Ctr., 1989-90, Human Resources (HUR) Sys., 1976-77,1979-82, DECOS, 1975-86, Computer-asst. libr. Sys., Optical Scan Sys., 1972-73, ERIC Clearinghouse for vocat. edn., 1966-70. Bd. dirs. Columbus Reg. Info. Svc., 1974-78, Cmty. Info. Referral Svc., Inc. 1975-81; chmn. subcom. on design, info. and ref. com. Columbus United Cmty. Coun., 1972-73; dir. Computer Utility for Pub. Info. Columbus, 1975-81; acct. coord. Greater Columbus Free-net, 1994-98; info. specialist, coord. LWV Met. Columbus Website Com., 2001-02. Mem. ALA, Assn. Computing Machinery (Ctrl. Ohio chpt.), Am. Soc. Info. Sci. and Tech., Assn. Faculty and Profl. Women Ohio State U., Columbus Metro Club, Coun. for Ethics in Econs., World Future Soc., Olympic Indoor Tennis Club. Avocations: bicycling, bird watching, gourmet cooking, tennis, water aerobics. Home and Office: 3471 Greenbank Ct Columbus OH 43221-4724

TAYLOR, COLLETTE, public relations executive; Sr. v.p. human resources Golin/Harris Internat., Chgo., 1998, chief adminstrv. officer, 1998—. Office: Golin/Harris Internat 111 E Wacker Dr Chicago IL 60601-3713

TAYLOR, CONNIE, minister; b. Parma, Mo., Sept. 15, 1944; d. Louis Connie and Floy Ray (Lively) Edging; m. Richard H. Taylor, May 26, 1966; children: Jeffrey, Scott. BA, Evangel U., Springfield, Mo., 1966; postgraduate, St. Paul's Theol., Kansas City, Mo., 1999. Ordained elder United Meth. Ch., 2003. Tchr. Grand Blanc (Mich.) Pub. Schs., 1966—68; self-employed caterer Ft. Worth area, 1968—72; exec. asst. Evangelistic Temple, Tulsa, Okla., 1977—80; v.p. program svcs. David Livingston Found., Tulsa, 1980—91; pastor United Meth. Ch., Delaware, Okla., 1992—96, Waukomis, Okla., 1966—2002, Meml. United Meth. Ch., Chelsea, Okla., 2002—. Author: Quilt Block Bible Study, 2002. Office: Meml United Meth Ch 441 W 6th St Chelsea OK 74016 E-mail: revct@aol.com.

TAYLOR, CONNIE J. real estate company executive; b. Pilot Point, Tex., Oct. 24, 1938; d. William Samuel and Mattie Prentiss Williams; m. Brooks A. Taylor, Sept. 1, 1955; 1 child, Theresa Lynn Kellam. Grad., Pilot Point (Tex.) H.S., 1956. Gri, Crb, Abr Nat. Assn. of Realtors, Tex., 1974. Realtor Ebby Halliday, Arlington, Tex., 1977—82; dir. Century 21 Contemporary Living, Arlington, 1982—84; sales and mktg. dir. Arnold-Burkhardt, Arlington, 1984—86; broker, owner Connie Taylor Realtors, Arlington, 1985—89; v.p., gen. mgr Century 21-Herman Boswell Realtors, Arlington, 1989—95; pres., broker/owner The Win Team, Arlington, 1995—. Dir. Arlington Bd. Realtors, 1992—94. Elder Westminister Presbyn. Ch., Arlington, 1968—72. Mem.: Arlington Bd. Realtors (assoc. Safesperson of Yr. 1978), Tex. Assn. Realtors (assoc.), Nat. Bd. Realtors (assoc. cert. GRI, CRB, ABR 1974). D-Conservative. Protestant. Avocations: golf, travel, fishing, bridge.

TAYLOR, DONNA BUESCHER, marriage and family therapist; b. Andalusia, Ala., Sept. 16, 1953; d. Robert C. and Mary Kate (Vickers) Bush; m. Davis H. Buescher, Nov. 22, 1973 (div. Feb. 1992); children: Tracy Marie, Robert Davis, Kyle Moore; m. Thomas W. Taylor, Apr. 30, 1994. BA, Samford U., 1975; MA in Psychology, Austin Peay State U., 1989; postgrad., Tex. Woman's U., 1989-90. Tchr. Liberty Hall Acad., Williston, Fla., 1977, Bunnell Elem. Sch., Williston, Fla., 1978; tchr. geography Flagler-Palmcoast (Fla.) H.S., 1979; tchr. St. Joseph's Sch., Lakeland, 1980, St. Alban's Sch., Waco, Tex., 1981-83; sch. psychologist Dallas Ind. Sch. Dist., 1989-94, Plano (Tex.) Ind. Sch. Dist., 1994-96; marriage and family therapist Plano, 1994-98; pvr. practice Cleveland, Miss., 1998—. Parent educator Practical Parent Edn., Plano, 1996-98; adj. instr. Delta State U., Cleveland, 1999—; program dir. Early Learning Mentoring Program. Tchr. Sunday sch. So. Bapt. Orgn., 1973—; mem. nominating com. 1st Presbyn. Ch., Cleveland. Fellow Christian Athletes; mem. NASP, Tex. Assn. Sch. Psychologists, Collin County Psychol. Assn., Delta State Faculty Wives, Garden Club. Republican. Home: 1010 College St Cleveland MS 38732-3111

TAYLOR, DONNA BLOYD, vocational rehabilitation consultant; b. Louisville, Ky., July 15, 1958; d. Donald Ray Bloyd and Georgia Carmen (Bryant) Whitehead; 1 child, Stephanie Micah Taylor. BS, U. Louisville, 1981, MEd, 1982. Lic. profl. counselor, qualified rehab. provider, Ohio; lic. mental health counselor, Ind.; cert. rehab. counselor U.S. Dept. Labor; qualified rehab. coord., Ky.; cert. disability mgmt. specialist; cert. case mgr., vocat. evaluator, nat. counselor; diplomate Am. Bd. Vocat. Experts; qualified mental retardation profl., qualified rehab. provider, Fla; cert. vocat. evaluator, RAS. Program coord. Hazelwood ICF-MR, Louisville, 1981-83; lead vocat. therapist Rehab. Ctr. Southeastern Ind., Clarksville, 1983-85; regional supr., vocat. cons. Rehab. Coords., Inc., Louisville, 1985; asst. mgr., rehab. cons. Nat. Rehab. Cons., Cin., 1985-88; dist. mgr., vocat. cons. Recovery Unlimited, Inc., Cin., 1988-92; pvt. practice, Ft. Myers, Fla., 1992—. Vocat. expert Social Security Adminstrn.; officer Vets. County Svc., 2002—. Co-author: (with Timothy Field and others) Study Guide to the CIRS Exam, 1992, The St. Thomas Resource on Certification, Ethics and Training for Private Sector Rehabilitation, 1993, CCM Study Guide, 1994, Rehabilitation Consultants in the Courtroom, 1997, Study Guide for the Certified Disability Management Specialist Exam, 1998, (with Timothy Field and others) A Resource for the Rehabilitation Consultant on the Daubert and Kumho Rulings, 2000, Comprehensive Study Guide, 2001. Vol. Am. Cancer Soc., mem. Rape Crisis Intervention Team. Mem. ACA, Internat. Assn. Rehab. Providers (past pres. Ky. chpt., SCRB com., co-chair internat. affairs divsn.), Nat. Rehab. Assn., Nat. Forensic Ctr., Nat. Disting. Svc. Registry, Individual Case Mgmt. Assn., U. Louisville Alumni Assn., Disability Network Ohio-Solidarity, Rehab. Referral Network, Rehab. Internat., Phi Kappa Phi. Democrat. Meth. Home and Office: 11595 Kelly Rd Ste 211 Fort Myers FL 33908-2539 Office Phone: 239-482-0556.

TAYLOR, EDNA JANE, retired employment program counselor; b. Flint, Mich., May 16, 1934; d. Leonard Lee and Wynona Ruth (Davis) Harvey; children: Wynona Jane MacDonald, Cynthia Lee Zellmer. BS, No. Ariz. U., 1963; MEd, U. Ariz., 1967. Tchr. high sch. Sunnyside Sch. Dist., Tucson, 1963-68; employment program counselor employment devel. State of Calif., Canoga Park, 1968-98, ret., 1998. Mem. adv. coun. Van Nuys Cmty. Adult Sch., Calif., 1983-96, steering com., 1989-91, leadership coun., 1991-92; mem. adv. coun. Pierce C.C., Woodland Hills, Calif., 1979-81; first aid instr., recreational leader ARC. Mem. NAFE, Internat. Assn. of Pers. in Employment Security, Calif. Employment Counselors Assn. (state treas. 1978-79, state sec. 1980), Delta Psi Kappa (life). Avocations: writing, tennis, health and fitness, gardening. E-mail: tauchi2@mindspring.com.

TAYLOR, ELINOR ZIMMERMAN, state legislator; b. Norristown, Pa., Apr. 18, 1921; d. Harold I. and Ruth A. (Rahn) Zimmerman; m. William M. Taylor, 1947; 1 child, Barbara. BS, West Chester State Tchrs. Coll., 1943; student, Columbia U., 1944, U. Del., 1955; MEd, Temple U., 1958. Tchr. Ridley Park (Pa.) H.S., 1943-46, West Chester (Pa.) H.S., 1946-50; prof. West Chester State Coll., 1955-68, adminstr., 1968-76, now. prof. emeritus; mem. Pa. Ho. of Reps., 1977—. Chmn. subcom. on higher edn.; sec. Rep. Caucus; bd. dirs. Pa. Higher Edn. Assistance Agy.; active Gov. Commn. on Funding Higher Edn., Women; in Politics and Polit. Action Com.; Rep. chmn. Health and Welfare Com.; trustee Charles S. Swope Found.; founding trustee Bd. Chester County Edn. Found. Councilwoman Borough of West Chester, Pa., 1974-77, mem. recreation com., 1974-77. Named West Chester Citizen of Yr., 1985, Legislator of Yr. Pa. Assn. Home Health Agys., 1993; recipent Hon. award Pa. State Assn. for Health, Phys. Edn. and Recreation, 1962, Hon. Umpires award U.S. Field Hockey Assn., 1967, Disting. Alumni award West Chester State Coll., 1977, alumni award Temple U., 1982, Love of Children of Greater West Chester Golden Heart award, Achievement cert. Pa. Fedn. of Bus. and Profl. Women's Club, George Washington Honor award Valley Forge Freedom Found., Guardian of Small Bus. award, 1993-94, cert. of appreciation Am. Legion, 1995, Margaret Hoover Brigham award Chester County Emergency Med. Svc., 1995, Police Athletic League award, 1995; named to Henderson H.S. Hall of Fame, 1994. Mem. AAUW (former pres.), Nat. Assn. Women Legislators, Chester County Art Assn., Pa. Paramedice Assn. (hon.). Republican. Presbyterian. Office: Pa Ho of Reps 315-G Main Capitol Bldg House Box 20202 Harrisburg PA 17120-2020

TAYLOR, ELISABETH COLER, retired secondary school educator; b. N.Y.C., Jan. 24, 1942; d. Gerhard Helmut and Judith Coler; m. Billie Wesley Taylor II, Jan. 27, 1960; children: Letitia Rose, Billie Albert. Student, Wilmington Coll., 1959-60; BS, Wayne State U., Detroit, 1969; MS, The Ohio State U., 1980; postgrad., Wright State U., Dayton, Ohio, 1989—. Cert. home economist. H.s. tchr. home econs., computer sci., lang. arts Dayton (Ohio) City Schs., 1972-99. Bd. dirs. Camp Fire Girls, 1970-71, vol. Detroit Mus. of Art, 1970-71, group leader Camp Fire Girls, Boy Scouts, Dayton, 1968-74. Mem. AAUW (life), Am. Mensa Ltd. (life). Avocations: birding, travelling, needlework. Home: 131 Snow Hill Ave Dayton OH 45429-1705

TAYLOR, ELIZABETH ANN (BETH TAYLOR), advertising and marketing executive, video producer; b. New Orleans, Oct. 14, 1954; d. Rita Joy (Bova) T.; divorced. BS in Journalism, La. State U., 1977. Polit. cons. La. Rep. Party, New Orleans, 1972-75; gen. assignment reporter The Times-Picayune, New Orleans, 1975-76; asst. news dir. WRBT-TV, Baton Rouge, 1976-78; sports anchor/reporter WDAM-TV, Hattiesburg, Miss., 1978-85, bur. chief, 1985-86, assignments editor, 1986-89; dir. admissions/mktg. Pine Grove Psychiat. Hosp., Hattiesburg, 1989-91; owner, CEO Letter B Prodns., Hattiesburg, 1991—. Facility adv. coun. mem. Miss. Vocat.-Rehab. Dept., Laurel, Miss., 1988-89; mem. adv. com. Miss. Blood Svcs., Laurel, 1986-88; mem. women's adv. bd. Forrest Gen. Hosp., Hattiesburg, Miss., 1988-90; rsch. bd. adv. Am. Biog. Inst., 1991—. Author, creator video/mktg. promotions. Mem. comm. bd. United Way of Pine Belt Region, Laurel, 1985-88, United Way of S.E. Miss., Hattiesburg, 1988-90; mem. adv. bd. Hattiesburg Edn. Literacy Project, Hattiesburg, 1989-95; bd. dirs. Domestic Abuse Family Shelter, Laurel, 1988-95, Gulf Pines Girl Scout Coun., Hattiesburg, Miss., 1998—, DREAM, Hattiesburg, 1997—, South Ctrl. Miss. Red Cross, 1997-2000; grad. Leaders for a New Centry, 1999; appointed Mayor's Youth Coun., 2003, Hattiesburg. Mem.: La State U. Alumni Assn. (pres. Hattiesburg chpt.). Avocations: walking/hiking, whitewater rafting, camping, canoeing, golf. Office: Letter B Prodns 222 Sherwood Dr Hattiesburg MS 39401 E-mail: letterb@comcast.net.

TAYLOR, ELIZABETH ROSEMOND, actress; b. London, Feb. 27, 1932; d. Francis and Sara (Sothern) Taylor. Student, Byron House, Hawthorne Sch., Metro-Goldwyn-Mayer Sch. Actress : (films) There's One Born Every Minute, 1942; Lassie Come Home, 1943; The White Cliffs of Dover, 1944; Jane Eyre, 1944; National Velvet, 1944; Courage of Lassie, 1946; Cynthia, 1947; Life with Father, 1947; A Date with Judy, 1948; Julia Misbehaves, 1948; Little Women, 1950; Conspirator, 1950; The Big Hangover, 1950; Father of the Bride, 1950; Father's Little Dividend, 1951; A Place in the Sun, 1951; Callaway Went Thataway, 1951; Love is Better Than Ever, 1952; Ivanhoe, 1952; The Girl Who Had Everything, 1953; Elephant Walk, 1954; Rhapsody, 1954; Beau Brummel, 1954; The Last Time I Saw Paris, 1954; Giant, 1956; Raintree County, 1957; Cat on a Hot Tin Roof, 1958; Suddenly Last Summer, 1959; Scent of Mystery, 1960; Butterfield 8, 1960 (Acad. award Best Actress, 1960); Cleopatra, 1963; The V.I.P.'s, 1963; The Sandpiper, 1965; Who's Afraid of Virginia Woolf?, 1966 (Acad. award Best Actress, 1966); The Taming of the Shrew, 1967; The Comedians, 1967; Reflections in a Golden Eye, 1967; Dr. Faustus, 1967; Boom!, 1968; Secret Ceremony, 1968; The Only Game in Town, 1970;

Under Milkwood, 1971; X, Y and Zee, 1972; Hammersmith is Out, 1972; Night Watch, 1973; Ash Wednesday, 1973; That's Entertainment, 1974; The Driver's Seat, 1974; Blue Bird, 1975; Winter Kills, 1977; A Little Night Music, 1977; The Mirror Crack'd, 1980; Young Toscanini, 1988; The Flintstones, 1994; The Visit, 1999; appearances include : (TV films) Divorce His/Divorce Hers, 1973; Victory at Entebbe, 1977; Return Engagement, 1979; Between Friends, 1982; (TV series) Hotel (series), 1984; (TV films) Malice in Wonderland, 1986; (TV miniseries) North and South, 1986; (TV films) There Must Be a Pony, 1986; Poker Alice, 1987; Sweet Bird of Youth, 1989; theatre appearances include : (Broadway plays) The Little Foxes, 1981; Private Lives, 1983; narrator : (documentaries) Genocide, 1981; co-author (with Richard Burton): (novels) World Enough and Time, 1964; author Elizabeth Taylor, 1965, Elizabeth Taylor Takes Off: On Weight Gain, Weight Loss, Self Esteem and Self Image, 1988; lic. (fragrances) Elizabeth Taylor's Passion, Passion for Men, White Diamonds/Elizabeth Taylor, Elizabeth Taylor's Diamonds & Emeralds, Diamonds and Rubies, Diamonds & Sapphires, Elizabeth Taylor Black Pearls. Active philanthropic, relief, charitable causes internationally, including Israeli War Victums Fund for the Chaim Sheba Hosp., 1976, UNICEF, various children's hosps., med. clinics, Botswana; initiated Ben Gurion U. - Elizabeth Taylor Fund for Children of the Negev, 1982; supporter AIDS Project, L.A., 1985; founder, nat. chmn. Am. Found. for AIDS Rsch. (AmFAR), 1985—, internat. fund, 1985—; founder Elizabeth Taylor AIDS Found., 1991—. Named Comdr. Arts Letters, France, 1985, an honoree with dedication of Elizabeth Taylor Med. Ctr. Whitman - Walker Clinic, Washington, 1993; recipient Legion of Honor (for work with AmFAR), France, 1987, Aristotle S. Onassis Found., 1988, Jean Hersholt Humanitarian Acad. award (for work as AIDS advocate), 1993, Life Achievement award, Am. Film Inst., 1993.*

TAYLOR, ESTELLE WORMLEY, English educator, dean; b. Washington, Jan. 12, 1924; d. Luther Charles and Wilhelmina Wormley; m. Ivan Earle Taylor, Dec. 26, 1953. BS magna cum laude, Miner Tchrs. Coll., 1945; MA, Howard U., 1947; PhD, Cath. U. Am., 1969. Instr. English Howard U., 1947-52; tchr. Langley Jr. H.S., Washington, 1952-55, Eastern Sr. H.S., Washington, 1955-63; from instr. to prof. D.C. Tchrs. Coll., 1963-91, prof. English emerita, 1991—, acad. dean, 1975-76; assoc. provost Fed. City Coll., Washington, 1974-75; prof. Howard U., 1976-91, chmn. dept. English, 1976-85; assoc. dean Howard U. Coll. Liberal Arts, 1985-86; dir. expository writing program Grad. Sch. Arts and Scis., 1988-91. Mem., sec. Edn. Licensure Commn. of D.C., 1993—; mem. Commn. on Higher Edn., Mid. States Assn. Colls. and Schs., 1984-87, 88-90, co-chair steering com. to revise Characteristics of Excellence, 1992-93; mem. ctrl. exec. com. Folger Inst. Renaissance and 18th Century Studies, 1982-91; adv. bd. Humanities Inst. Montgomery Coll., 1997—. Contbg. editor A Howard Reader, 1997. 1st v.p. Order Daus. of King Episc. Ch. Diocese, Washington, 1994-98; commr. Edn. Licensure Com. of D.C., 1993—, also sec., vice chmn., 1995—; trustee U. D.C., 1979-83, vice chmn., 1983; mem. D.C. Cmty. Humanities Coun., 1990-91; co-chmn. planning com. Centennial Celebration of the Andrew Rankin Chapel Howard U., 1994, adv. bd. Coll. Arts and Scis., Howard U., 2002—; mem. selection bd. Fgn. Agrl. Svc., 2002. Named Disting. Alumni, Howard U., 1995, Alumni award for Disting. Postgrad. Achievement in Edn. and Lit., 1997, [illegible] fellow, 1980-83, [illegible] 1978-79. Mem. MLA (del. assembly 1994—), Nat. Assn. for Equal Opportunity in Higher Edn., Coll. Lang. Assn., Shakespeare Assn. Am., Pub. Mems. Assn. Fgn. Svc. Dept. of State, Links (v.p. Capital City chpt. 1979-81, corr. sec. 1989, rec. sec. 1991-93, 95—). Democrat. Home: 3221 20th St NE Washington DC 20018-2421

TAYLOR, FANNIE TURNBULL, social education and arts administration educator; b. Kansas City, Mo., Sept. 11, 1913; d. Henry King and Fannie Elizabeth (Sills) Turnbull; m. Robert Taylor, Dec. 2, 1938 (div. 1974); children: Kathleen Muir Taylor Isaacs, Anne Kingston Taylor Wadsack. BA, U. Wis., 1938; LHD (hon.), Buena Vista Coll., Storm Lake, Iowa, 1975. Mem. faculty U. Wis., Madison, 1941—, prof. social edn., 1949—, emerita, 1979—. Dir. Wis. Union Theater, 1946-66, coord. univ. systems arts coun., 1967-70, assoc. dir. Ctr. Arts Adminstrn., 1970-72, coord. Consortium for Arts, 1976-84; cons. in field. Author: The Arts at a New Frontier: The National Endowment for the Arts, Wisconsin Union Theater: Fifty Golden Years (Book award of Merit, State Hist. Soc. Wis. 1990); contbr. articles to profl. jours. Program dir. music Nat. Endowment Arts, 1966-67, program info. dir., 1972-76; bd. dirs. Wis. Arts Coun., 1964-72, Wis. Found. Arts, 1976-91, Madison Civic Music Assn., 1976-84, Madison Children's Mus., 1983-96, Elvehjem Mus. Art Coun., 1976—, chair 1983-86; Madison Civic Ctr. Found., 1981-94; hon. chair Wis. Union Theater Program Endowment Fund, 1985—; bd. dirs. Wis. chpt. Nature Conservancy, 1963-84, chmn. 1976-77; bd. dirs. Shorewood Hills Found., 1976—, pres., 1976-81. Recipient Oak Leaf award Nature Conservancy, 1981, Wis. Gov.'s award in Support of the Arts, 1992, Madison Cmty. Found. Asset Builders Leadership award, 2002; named Woman of Distinction, Madison YWCA, 1994. Fellow Wis. Acad. Scis., Arts and Letters; mem. Assn. Performing Arts Presenters (founder, exec. dir. 1957-72, 1st recipient Fannie Taylor award 1972), Am. Assn. Dance Cos. (bd. dirs. 1967-72), Nat. Assn. Regional Ballet (bd. dirs. 1975-77), Nat. Guild Cmty. Music Schs. Arts (bd. dirs. 1977-80), Women in Comm. (Writers' Cup 1980), U. Wis. Found., U. Wis. Alumni Assn. (Disting. Svc. award 1979), Madison Civics Club (pres. 1969-70), Univ. Club (pres. 1982-85), Blackhawk Club. Home: 8301 Old Sauk Rd Apt 303 Middleton WI 53562-4393 E-mail: ftaylor@facstaff.wisc.edu.

TAYLOR, FELICIA, newscaster; BS in Comm., Northwestern U. Prodr., field reporter WLS-TV, Chgo.; anchor, prodr., writer Fin. News Network; anchor bus. shows Fin. Times; London corr. CNBC, Ft. Lee, N.J., 1992-93, co-anchor Today's Bus., anchor This Morning's Bus., 1993—98, co-anchor MarketWatch; co-anchor Weekend Today in New York NewsChannel4, N.Y.C., NY, 1998—2003, co-anchor NewsChannel 4 at 6 and 11, 2003—. Office: NBC News 30 Rockefeller Plaza New York NY 10112*

TAYLOR, GRACE ELIZABETH WOODALL (BETTY TAYLOR), law educator, law library administrator; b. Butler, N.J., June 14, 1926; d. Frank E. and Grace (Carlyon) Woodall; m. Edwin S. Taylor, Feb. 4, 1951 (dec.); children: Carol Lynn Taylor Crespo, Nancy Ann Filer. AB, Fla. State U., 1949, MA, 1950; JD, U. Fla., 1962. Instr. asst. librarian U. Fla., 1950-56, asst. law libr. Coll. Law, 1956-62; dir. Legal Info. Ctr., 1962—2003, prof. law, 1976—2003; Clarence J. TeSelle prof. of law U. Fla., 1994—2003, historian, archivist Call-Law, 2003—. Trustee Nat. Ctr. for Automated Rsch., N.Y.C., 1978-96; past chmn. joint com. on LAWNET, Am. Assn. Law Librs., Am. Assn. Law Schs. and ABA, 1978—; cons. to law librs., 1975—; mem. adv. com. N.E. Regional Data Ctr., U. Fla., 1990—. Co-author: American Law Publications, 1986, 21st Century: Technology's Impact, 1988, Law in the Digital Age: The Challenge of Research in Legal Information Centers, 1996, also articles. Recipient 1st Disting. Alumni award Fla. State U. Libr. Sch., 1983, 2d Marya Lange/C.Q. award law and polit. sci. sect. ACRL and Congl. Quar., 1997; Lewis Scholar Fla. Legislature, 1947-50; grantee NEH, 1981-82, Coun. Libr. Resources, 1984-86; Dist. Svc. award, Florida Library Assn., 2000. Mem.: ABA (Law Libr. Congress facilities com. 1991—97), Am. Assn. Law Schs. (accreditation com. 1978—81), Am. Assn. Law Librs. (exec. bd. 1981—84, Marian Gould Gallagher Disting. Svc. award 1997, Aspen Law and Bus. Rsch. grant 1997), OCLC Users Coun. (pres. 1983—86), Beta Phi Mu, Phi Beta Kappa (v.p. U. Fla. chpt. 1994—95, pres. 1995—96). Democrat. Methodist. Avocations: computers, genealogy, crafts, gardening, grandchildren. Office: U Fla Legal Info Ctr Gainesville FL 32611 E-mail: Taylor@law.ufl.edu.

TAYLOR, GWENDOLYN BARNETT, school system administrator; b. Elizabeth City, N.C., Apr. 25, 1955; d. Willis and Mary Belle Barnett; m. Gordon Wayne Taylor, Feb. 7, 1976 (div. Sept. 1995); children: Kimberly, Tracey. BS in Music Edn., Norfolk (Va.) State U., 1977, MusM, 1986. Tchr. Portsmouth (Va.) Pub. Schs., 1978—81; contract specialist U.S. Govt., Richmond, Va., 1982—83; tchr. Portsmouth Pub. Schs., 1983—98, supr., 1998—. Bd. dir. Cmty. Conservatory of Arts, Portsmouth; instr. Angelos Bible Coll., Portsmouth, 2000—. Block chmn. Am. Heart Assn., 1998—, Am. Lung Assn., 1998—; min. music St. Mark Missionary Bapt. Ch., Portsmouth, 1995—. Recipient Black Outstanding Educator award, Delicados, Inc., 1998, VH1 Save the Music award, Cox Cable, 2001. Mem.: ASCD, AAUW, NEA, Va. State Reading Assn., Chorus Am., Am. Choral Dirs. Assn., Orgn. Am. Kodaly Educators, Music Educators Nat. Conf., English Handbell Choristers Guild, Alpha Kappa Alpha (Outstanding Female Arts Educator award 2000). Baptist. Avocations: gardening, reading. Home: 1217 Tazewell St Portsmouth VA 23701 Office: Portsmouth Pub Schs IRC 3651 Hartford St Portsmouth VA 23707

TAYLOR, GWENDOLYN NADINE, elementary school educator; d. Jessie and Mabel Oderis Taylor; m. Arthur Woods, June 8, 1968 (div. Sept. 1984); children: Twyla Renee Woods, Akil Omari Woods. BA, U. Md., Adelphi, 2003. Deli clk. Shoppers Food Warehouse, Lanham, Md., 1991—98; long term substitute tchr. Prince George County Schsch., Upper Marlboro, Md., 2000—; adminstrv. assistance Phoenix Group, Lanham, 2002—02. Vol. Prince George Cmty. Ctr., Capitol Heights, Md., 2002—03. Giant Foods Merit grantee. Democrat-Npl. Baptist. Avocations: travel, tennis, reading, cooking, writing.

TAYLOR, HEATHER MARIE, director; b. Park Ridge, Ill., May 21, 1974; d. Kent Emil and Rebecca Jo Buchholz; m. Christopher Lee Taylor, Jan. 13, 2001. BA in English and Secondary Edn., No. Ill. U., 1996; MS in Integrated Mktg. Comm. summa cum laude, Roosevelt U., 2000. Writer corp. comm. 360 Comm., Chgo., 1995—96; tchg. asst. No. Ill. U., DeKalb, 1995—96; tchr. Streamwood (Ill.) H.S., 1996—97; sr. mktg. mgr. Hanley-Wood, LLC, Addison, Ill., 1997—2002; owner, pres. Pro Writer Ltd., Portage, Ind., 2000—; dir. comms. for admissions, fin. aid and mktg. Valparaiso (Ind.) U., 2002—, adj. prof., 2003—. Adj. prof. Roosevelt U., Chgo., 2001—. Contbr. Of Diamonds and Rust, 1989, Great Poems of the Western World Vol. 2, 1990, articles to profl. jours. Mem.: NEA, Am. Mktg. Assn., Roosevelt Adj. Faculty Orgn., Sigma Tau Delta, Phi Kappa Phi, Golden Key. Lutheran. Avocations: photography, writing, travel. Home: 5683 Dovedale Ave Portage IN 46368 Office: Valparaiso U 1700 Chapel Dr Valparaiso IN 46383

TAYLOR, JACQUELINE ANN, systems administrator; b. Chgo., May 11, 1950; d. John R. and Edna Madigan; m. Richard LaVern Taylor, Aug. 19, 1972; children: Kristen Nicole, John William. BS in Math., No. Ill. U., 1972. Cert. Novell adminstr. Systems adminstr., acct. Am. Roofing Supply, Evansville, Ind., 1986-88; sr. acct. Challenge Dairy Products, Dublin, Calif., 1988-89; systems adminstr., asst. acctg. mgr. [illegible], Carlsbad, Calif., 1989-90; systems adminstr., acting mgr. La Jolla (Calif.) Surgi Ctr. Carson M. Lewis, M.D., 1990-92; systems adminstr., collections adminstr. Coleman Floor Co., Rolling Meadows, Ill., 1993-95; systems adminstr., info. sys. mgr. Village of Glen Ellyn, Ill., 1995—. Pres. Oblis Consultants, Barrington, Ill., 1994—. Mem. NAFE. Democrat. Roman Catholic. Avocations: skiing, knitting. Home: 205 Rue Touraine Barrington IL 60010-3721

TAYLOR, JANE ELLEN, elementary school educator; b. Port Clinton, Ohio, Feb. 2, 1955; d. Santo Thomas and Martha Zelma (Finefrock) Cipti; m. William Michael Taylor, Apr. 30, 1976; children: Aaron, Molly. BS in Edn., Ohio State U., 1979; MEd in Curriculum and Instrn., Ashland U., 1995. Paralegal cert. Am. Paralegal Assn. Mid. sch. team leader Discovery Sch., Mansfield, Ohio, 1979-82; tchr. 3rd/4th grade St. Edward's Sch., Ashland, Ohio, 1984-86; tchr. 4th grade St. Joseph's Sch., Libertyville, Ill., 1987-88; tchr. 2nd grade South Jordan (Utah) Elem. Sch., 1990-91; tchr. 1st grade Bataan Elem. Sch., Port Clinton, 1995-96, tchr. 2nd grade intervention class, 1996—, tchr. 3rd grade, 1997-98, tchr. 1st grade, 1998-99, tchr. 2nd grade, 1999—. Com. mem. Blue Ribon Com., Port Clinton, 1996—. Author: Mrs. T. and the Can-Do Kids, 1997. Active Bataan Parent/Tchr. Orgn., Bataan Sch., 1997—. Recipient Wal-Mart Tchr. of the Yr. award, 1997. Mem. Future Educators Am. (co-advisor 1996—), Port Clinton Athletic Boosters, Port Clinton Music Boosters, Port Clinton Acad. Boosters. Republican. Roman Catholic. Avocations: reading, swimming, computers, home decorating, family activities. Office: Bataan Elem W 6th St Port Clinton OH 43452

TAYLOR, JANET DROKE, legal secretary; b. Bristol, Tenn., Feb. 26, 1961; d. Jimmie D. and Nancy Bell (Sluder) Droke; m. Terry E. Taylor; children from previous marriage: Leslie Ann, Laurie Elizabeth. AA, East Tenn. State U., 1980; student, Milligan Coll., Johnson City, Tenn., 1988-89. With Sullivan County Election Commn., Blountville, Tenn., 1978; legal sec. Boarman & Vaughn, Johnson City, 1980-84; legal asst. Bob McD. Green and Assocs., Johnson City, 1985-89; fed. jud. sec. to U.S. cir. judge U.S. Ct. Appeals (4th cir.), Abingdon, Va., 1989—2003; jud. asst. to U.S. dist. judge U.S. Dist. Ct. (we. dist.) Va., Roanoke, 2003—. Adv. bd. legal asst. program Milligan Coll., Johnson City, 1988—89. Mem.: Fed. Jud. Secs. Assn. (4th cir. rep. 1998—2000), Appalachian Paralegal Assn., Tenn. Paralegal Assn. (treas. 1989, pub. rels. dir. 1990). Republican. Avocations: reading, piano, travel. Home: PO Box 727 Bluff City TN 37618-0727 Office: care Hon Glen E Conrad US Dist Judge PO Box 2822 Roanoke VA 24001

TAYLOR, JANET R. mayor; b. 1942; m. Duane Taylor; 5 children. Student, Chemeketa C.C. Lic. pvt. pilot. Co-founder, exec. Taylor Metal Products, Salem, Oreg. Mayor City of Salem, Oreg., 2003—; past chairwoman Salem Econ. Devel. Corp., S.E. Mill Creek Neighborhood Assn.; mem. Willamette River Bridge Task Force; sponsor A.C. Gilbert Discovery Village. Mem.: Salem Area C. of C. (v.p.), Salem Futures, Salem City Club, Salem Downtown Rotary. Office: Taylor Metal Products 3796 Turner Rd SE Salem OR 97302-2047

TAYLOR, JEAN ELLEN, mathematics researcher and educator; b. San Mateo, Calif., Sept. 17, 1944; d. Richard Lachlan and Donna Taylor; m. John Mark Guckenheimer, Apr. 18, 1969 (div.); m. Frederick J. Almgren, Oct. 6, 1973 (dec. 1997); 1 child, Karen Taylor Almgren stepchildren: Ann Almgren, Robert Almgren; m. William T. Golden, July 8, 2001. AB summa cum laude, Mt. Holyoke Coll., 1966, DSc (hon.), 2001; MS in Chemistry, U. Calif., Berkeley, 1968; MS in Math., U. Warwick, Coventry, Eng., 1971; PhD, Princeton U., 1973. Instr. MIT, Cambridge, Mass., 1972-73; asst. prof. Rutgers U., New Brunswick, N.J., 1973-77, assoc. prof., 1977-82, prof., 1982-87, prof. II, 1987—2002, prof. emeritus, 2002—; vis. scholar Courant Inst., NYU, 2002—. Mem. Inst. for Advanced Study, Princeton, N.J., 1974-75, 77-78, 85, 95-96; Miller vis. prof. U. Calif., Berkeley, 1999; vis. scholar Stanford (Calif.) U., 1989; visitor Princeton U., 1980-81; mem. Geometry Computing Group (permanent faculty of the Nat. Sci. and Tech. Ctr. for Computational and Visualization of Geometric Structures); cons. Nat. Bur. Standards, Gaithersburg, Md.; guest expert 3-2-1 Contact program Children's TV Workshop, 1978; mem. exec. com. Conf. Bd. of the Math. Scis., 2000-2002; lectr. in field. Contbr. articles in math., physics and materials sci. to profl. jours. Recipient Presdl. Pub. Svc. award Rutgers Coll. Class of 1962, 1999; Sloan Found. fellow, 1976-78; NSF grad. fellow, 1966-72, hon. fellow Woodrow Wilson Found.; rsch. grantee NSF, 1973—, Air Force Office Sci. Rsch., 1987-94. Fellow: AAAS (bd. dirs. 1995—99, chair sect. A 2003—), Assn. for Women in Sci., Am. Acad. Arts and Scis.; mem.: Soc. for Indsl. and Applied Math., Materials, Mining and Metall. Soc., Assn. for Women in Math. (pres. 1999—2001, nominating com. chair 2003—), Math Assn. Am., Materials Rsch. Soc., Am. Math. Soc. (nominating com. 1977—78, coun. 1984—89, exec. com. 1985—88, v.p. 1994—97, trustee 2003—), Assn. Princeton Grad. Alumni (governing bd. 1999—), Phi Beta Kappa. Democrat. Achievements include proof, in the context of Geometric Measure Theory, that the singular set in a mathematical model for soap bubble clusters and soap films on wire frames is what is physcally observed, thereby solving a 100 year old problem; development of mathematical models for treating shapes of surfaces and interfaces for crystalline materials and use of them to model crystal growth. Office: Courant Inst 251 Mercer St New York NY 10012 Business E-Mail: jtaylor@cims.nyu.edu.

TAYLOR, J(OCELYN) MARY, museum administrator, zoologist, educator; b. Portland, Oreg., May 30, 1931; d. Arnold Llewellyn and Kathleen Mary (Yorke) T.; m. Joseph William Kamp, Mar. 18, 1972 (dec.); m. Wesley Kingston Whitten, Mar. 20, 2001. BA, Smith Coll., 1952; MA, U. Calif., Berkeley, 1953, PhD, 1959. Instr. zoology Wellesley Coll., 1959-61, asst. prof. zoology, 1961-65; assoc. prof. zoology U. B.C., 1965-74; dir. Cowan Vertebrate Mus., 1965-82, prof. dept. zoology, 1974-82; collaborative scientist Oreg. Regional Primate Research Ctr., 1983-87; prof. (courtesy) dept. fisheries and wildlife Oreg. State U., 1984-95; dir. Cleve. Mus. Nat. History, 1987-96, dir. emerita, 1996—. Adj. prof. dept. biology Case Western Res. U., 1987-96. Assoc. editor Jour. Mammalogy, 1981-82. Contbr. numerous articles to sci. jours. Trustee Benjamin Rose Inst., 1988-93, Western Res. Acad., 1989-94, U. Circle, Inc., 1987-96, The Cleve. Aquarium, 1990-93, Cleve. Access to the Arts, 1992-96; corp. bd. Holden Arboretum, 1988-98, The Cleve. Mus. Natural History, 1996—, The Catlin Gabel Sch., 1998-2000, The Inst. for the Northwest, 1999—2001. Recipient Lake County Environ. award, Lake county metro parks.; Fulbright scholar, 1954-55; Lalor Found. grantee, 1962-63; NSF grantee, 1963-71; NRC Can. grantee, 1966-84; Killam Sr. Rsch. fellow, 1978-79 Mem. Soc. Women Geographers, Am. Soc. Mammalogists (1st v.p. 1978-82, pres. 1982-84, Hartley T. Jackson award 1993, hon. mem. 2001), Australian Mammal Soc., Cooper Ornithol., Assn. Sci. Mus. Dirs. (v.p. 1990-93), Rodent Specialist Group of Species Survival Commn. (chmn. 1989-93), Sigma Xi. Home: 2718 SW Old Orchard Rd Portland OR 97201-1637 E-mail: taylorjm@teleport.com.

TAYLOR, KAREN ANNETTE, mental health nurse; b. Kinston, N.C., Oct. 7, 1952; d. Emmett Green and Polly Ann (Taylor) Tyndall; m. Paul Othell Taylor Jr, June 24, 1979 (div. 1996); 1 child, Clarissa Anne. AA, Lenoir C.C., Kinston, 1972; Diploma, Lenoir Meml. Hosp. Sch. of, Nursing, 1984; student, St. Joseph's Coll., Windham, Maine, 1993-94. RN NC. Staff nurse Lenoir Meml. Hosp., 1984-86; staff nurse, relief patient care dir. Brynn Marr Hosp., Jacksonville, N.C., 1987-90; staff nurse, quality assurance Naval Hosp., Camp Lejeune, N.C., 1990-92. Recipient Meritorious Unit Commendation, Am Fedn Govt Employees, 1992. Baptist. Avocations: reading, crocheting. E-mail: karent@earthlink.net.

TAYLOR, KATHERINE, social service administrator; b. Milw., Feb. 26, 1958; d. James Albert Sr. and Cordelia Taylor; 1 child, Alyssa K. degree in correctional adminstrn., degree in sociology, U. Wis., [illegible]. Coord. summer youth program Milw. County Econ. Devel., Milw., 1981—82, sr. compliance monitor, 1982—83; asst. dir. planning Opportunities Industrialization Ctr. Greater Milw., 1983—84, dir. planning, 1985—88, asst. to sr. v.p., 1989—90, mgr. transp. programs, placement and employee svcs., 1991—93; asst. adminstr. Family House, Inc., Milw., 1994—. Bd. dirs., sec. African World Festivals, Milw., Family House, Inc., Family House Med. Assesment Referral Ctr., Milw. Recipient Love in Action award, Cmty. Youth Devel. Milw., 2001. Mem.: African Am. Coalition Empowerment. Avocations: reading, cooking. Office: Family House Inc 3269 N 11th St Milwaukee WI 53206 E-mail: familyhouseinc@cs.com.

TAYLOR, KATHLEEN (CHRISTINE TAYLOR), physical chemist, researcher; b. Cambridge, Mass., Mar. 16, 1942; d. John F. and Anna M. (Maloney) T. BA in Chemistry, Douglass Coll., New Brunswick, N.J., 1964; PhD in Phys. Chemistry, Northwestern U., 1968. Postdoctoral fellow U. Edinburgh, Scotland, 1968-70; assoc. sr. rsch. chemist Gen. Motors Rsch. Labs., Warren, Mich., 1970-74, sr. rsch. chemist, 1974-75, asst. phys. chemistry dept. head, 1975-83, environ. sci. dept. head, 1983-85, phys. chemistry dept. head, 1985-96; physics and phys. chemistry dept. head Gen. Motors Global Rsch. & Devel. Operations, Warren, Mich., 1995-98, materials and protesses dir., 1998—2002. Recipient Mich. Sci. Trailblazer award Detroit Sci. Ctr., 1986. Fellow AAAS, mem. NAE, Am. Chem. Soc. (Garvan medal 1989), Materials Rsch. Soc. (treas. 1984, 2d v.p. 1985, 1st v.p. 1986, pres. 1987), Soc. Automotive Engrs., The Catalysis Soc., Sigma Xi.

TAYLOR, KATHLEEN N. state legislator; b. Nyack, N.Y., May 28, 1942; 6 children. Student, U. N.H. Mem. N.H. Ho. of Reps. (dist. 11), Concord, 1996—; mem. mcpl. and county govt. com. N.H. Ho. of Reps., Concord, 1996—. Mem. Dover City Coun., 1996-98, mayor pro tem, 1997. Roman Catholic.

TAYLOR, KATHY DEANNE, marketing executive, consultant; b. Peoria, Ill., Sept. 20, 1951; d. Chas S. and Carol A. (McDonough) Guynn; m. Harold N. Taylor Jr. (dec. Nov. 1982); 1 child, Shawn. AA in Bus., Ill. Cen. Coll., Peoria; student in mktg. mgmt., Sangamon State, Springfield. Mgr. sales Credit Bur. Accounts, Inc., Peoria, 1986-87; sales exec. Rsch. Inst. Am., N.Y.C., 1987-93, mem. adv. coun., 1989, pres. bd., 1990-91; sales exec. Paramount Comm., Waterford, Conn., 1993-95; govt. sales cons. West Group Thompson Legal Pub., 1995—2001; pres. bd. Million Dollar Club, 1998, 2 Million Dollar Club, 2000; owner A Sweet Arrangement, 1999—; sales exec. Lexis-Nexis, 2001; propr. A Sweet Arrangement, 2000—. Dir. cardiac ctr. Proctor Community Hosp., 1972-81, risk mgmt. coord., 1981-83; pres. Cen. Ill. Risk Mgmt., Inc., 1983-86. Chmn. bd. Tri-County Heart Assn., Peoria, 1987-88, pres., 1986-87; div. and regional mgr. Am. Heart Assn., Ill. affiliate, Springfield, 1985-89, mem. speakers bur., risk factor com., 1972-81; bd. dirs. Dept. Rehab. Svcs., 1989-91; active ARC hospice tng. Meth. Med. Ctr. Vol. Svcs.; asst. CE dir. Springfield Rd. Bapt. Ch., 2001-02. Mem. NAFE, Am. Inst. Banking, Peoria Jaycee Women (v.p. 1984), Ill. Jaycee Women (state chaplain, mgr. family life program 1984-85), Morton Jaycettes (pres. 1980). Republican. Home and Office: 4709 N Prospect Rd Peoria Heights IL 61616-6439

TAYLOR, KOKO, singer; Albums include The Earthshaker, from the Heart of a Woman, I Got What It Takes, Queen of the Blues, 1985, Koko Taylor, 1987, Live From Chicago: An Audience with the Queen, 1987, Teaches Old Standard New Tricks, Jump for Joy, 1990, What It Takes: The Chess Years, 1991, Force of Nature, 1994. Office: Alligator Records care Nora Kinnally PO Box 60234 Chicago IL 60660-0234

TAYLOR, L. ANN, financial analyst; BS, Cornell U.; postgrad., Simmons Grad. Sch. Mgmt. Human resources mgr. Shearson Lehman, N.Y.C., 1986-87; database mgr. Thomson Fin./Securities Data, Newark, 1987-91; asst. treas. Bankers Trust, NYC, 1991—92; nat. adminstr. NAACP Econ. Devel., Balt., 1992-94; asst. v.p., sr. project mgr. US Trust, Boston, 1994—99; prin. cons., sr. project mgr. Razorfish, NYC, 1999—2001; sr. project mgr. Hollywood Entertainment, 2002—. V.p. Cornell Black Alumni Assn., NYC, 1992—93. Avocations: gardening, travel.

TAYLOR, LESLI ANN, pediatric surgery educator; b. N.Y.C., Mar. 2, 1953; d. Charles Vincent Taylor and Valene Patricia (Blake) Garfield. BFA, Boston U., 1975; MD, Johns Hopkins U., 1981. Diplomate Am. Bd. Surgery. Surg. resident Beth Israel Hosp., Boston, 1981-88; rsch. fellow Pediatric Rsch. Lab. Mass. Gen. Hosp., Boston, 1984-86; fellow pediatric surgery Children's Hosp. of Phila., Phila., 1988-90; asst. prof. pediatric surgery U. N.C., Chapel Hill, 1990-97, assoc. prof. pediat. surgery, 1997—.

Author: (booklet) Think Twice: The Medical Effects of Physical Punishment, 1985. Recipient Nat. Rsch. Svc. award NIH, 1984-86. Fellow Am. Coll. Surgeons; mem. AMA, Am. Acad. Pediatrics, Am. Pediat. Surg. Assn. Achievements include research on organ preservation for pediatric liver transplantation and short bowel syndrome. E-mail: lataylor@med.unc.edu.

TAYLOR, LESLIE CAROLE, minister; b. Augsburg, Germany, Mar. 29, 1959; d. William Wesley and Sue Ann Taylor. BA, Grinnell Coll., 1981; MDiv, Chgo. Theol. Sem., 1988. Cert. childcare adminstr. Ohio. Min. for constituency relationships Coordinating Ctr. for Women, United Ch. of Christ, N.Y.C., 1988—90, min. for planning and denom. relationships United Ch. Bd. for Homeland Ministries, Cleve., 1990—96; dir. Neighborhood Ho., Inc. Women's Resource Ctr., Columbus, Ohio, 1996—99; interim pastor Bethany Christian Ch., Columbus, 1999—2001; asst. dir. David's Extended Care, Canal Winchester, Ohio, 1999—2003; pastor Trinity United Ch. of Christ, Thornville, Ohio, 2001—. Moderator Ohio Conf., Columbus, 2000—01, chairperson racial ethnic empowerment com., 2002—; proxy United Ch. of Christ Pension Bds., N.Y.C., 2002—; spiritual dir. Epiphany Ministries of Ohio, Columbus, 2002—. Parlimentarian Nat. Coalition of 100 Black Women, Columbus, 1999—2002; cons., spkr. Ctr. for Prevention of Sexual and Domestic Violence, Seattle, 2002; mem., spkr. Ohio Religious Coalition for Reproductive Choice, Columbus, 2003. Democrat. Avocations: gardening, walking, reading, home remodeling. Office: Trinity United Ch of Christ 20 S West St Thornville OH 43076 Personal E-mail: leslietaylor@columbus.rr.com. E-mail: trinityuccthornville@columbus.rr.com.

TAYLOR, LINDA RATHBUN, investment manager; b. Rochester, N.Y., May 25, 1946; d. Lewis Standish and Elizabeth (Florence (Hunt) Rathbun; m. Donald Gordon Taylor, Mar. 1, 1975; children: Alexander Standish, Abigail Elizabeth, Elizabeth Downing. BA, Vassar Coll., 1968; MBA, Harvard U., 1973. Cert. CFA Assn. of Investment Mgmt. and Rsch., 1981. Assoc. corp. fin. Donaldson, Lufkin & Jenrette, N.Y.C., 1973-75; cons. IBRD, Washington, 1975; fin. analyst U.S. Treas. Dept., Washington, 1976-78; chief investment officer United Mine Workers Fund, 1978-85; investment mgr. Cen. Pension Fund Internat. Union Oper. Engrs., Washington, 1985-86; investment banker Saranow Co., 1986-89; pvt. investor, 1990—; mng. ptnr. Sakonnet Mgmt., LLC, 1998-2000. Pres. Boundary Farm Inc.; CEO CMAC, LLC, 2001—03; bd. dirs. J.P. Morgan Venture Capital Investors, J.P. Morgan Corp. Fin. Investors, 1998—; dir. Legg Mason Instnl. Funds, 1999—2002; bd. dirs. Fauquier Hosp. Found. Devel. Coun., 2002—. Contbr. articles to profl. jours. Trustee Montgomery County (Md.) Employees' Retirement Sys., 1987-93; bd. dirs. Washington Internat. Horse Show, 1995-2003; com. mem. Vassar Coll. Endowment Fund, 1992—; elder Bradley Hills Presbyn. Ch., 1992-95; dir. bd. pensions Presbyn. Ch. U.S.A., 1996-99; dir. Va. Horse Shows Assn. Found., 1998—. Recipient Disting. Alumni award Carolina Day Sch., 1996. Mem. Jr. League Washington, Washington Soc. Investment Analysts (bd. dirs. 1984-85), Assn. Investment Mgmt. and Rsch. Republican. E-mail: lrtaylorcfa@aol.com.

TAYLOR, LYDA REVOIRE WING, artist, gallery owner; b. Oakland, Calif., Jan. 25, 1952; d. Clinton Harold and Lettie Chaffey Wing; m. Kevin Bradford Taylor, June 22, 1985; children: Jeffrey, Heather, Jessica. BA, U. Calif., Davis, 1974. Founder, owner, artist Valley Arts Faire Gallery, Los Olivos, Calif., 1978-92; owner, artist The Taylor Collection, Angels Camp, Calif., 1999. Asst. dir. Peppertree Ranch Western Art Show, Santa Ynez, Calif., 1976-85. Represented in White House collection; exhbns. include Valley Arts Gallery, 1978-89, Bill Dodge Gallery, Carmel, 1985-90, Donlee/Lee Yougman Gallery, Calistoga and Los Olivos, 1985-99, Taylor Collection Gallery, Angels Camp, 1999—; official artist Easter at the White House, 1986. Set designer, painter Summer Funner Children's Theatre, San Diego, 1992-94, Michelson Drama Club-Childrens Theatre, Murphys, Calif., 1995-99; sec., treas., girls divsn. organizer Ebbetts Pass Youth Soccer, Murphys, 1995-2001. Mem. Calaveras County Arts Coun. (grantee 1998), Angels Camp Bus. Assn. Republican. Avocations: walking, gardening, children's sports. Office: 1234 S Main St Angels Camp CA 95222-1303

TAYLOR, MARETTA MITCHELL, state legislator; b. Columbus, Ga., Jan. 25, 1935; BS, Albany State, 1957; MS, Ind. U., 1966. Mem. Ga. Ho. of Reps., 1991-92, 93—; mem. edn., retirement, state planning and cmty. affairs coms.; co-owner, mgr. Designers Ltd., 1987—. Democrat. Baptist. Home: 1203 Bunker Hill Rd Columbus GA 31907-6718 Office: Ga House of Reps State Capitol Atlanta GA 30334

TAYLOR, MARGARET TURNER, clothing designer, architectural designer, economist, writer, planner; b. Wilmington, N.C., May 7, 1944. A.B. in Econs., Smith Coll., 1966; M.A. in Econ. History, U. Pa., 1970, now Ph.D. candidate in City and Regional Planning. Tchr. Jefferson Jr. High Sch., New Orleans, 1966-69; instr. econs. U. Tex.-El Paso, 1974-75; adj. prof. econs., Salisbury State U., Md., 1976-78; prin. mgr., designer Margaret Norriss, women's clothing, Salisbury, Md., 1980-95; owner Functional Design Ideas, Inc., 1995—; planner at Wharton Ctr. Applied Research, Phila., 1985-86; planning cons., writer.

TAYLOR, MARGARET WISCHMEYER, retired language educator; b. Terre Haute, Ind., Aug. 5, 1920; d. Carl and Grace (Riehle) Wischmeyer; m. John Edward Taylor, Sept. 5, 1942 (dec. 1988); children: Deborah Ann, Tobin Edward (dec. 2002), Mary Leesa. BA magna cum laude, Duke U., 1941; MA, John Carroll U., Cleve., 1973. Feature writer Dayton (Ohio) Daily News, 1945-53; freelance writer Cleve., 1953—; asst. to Dr. Joseph B. Rhine Duke U. Parapsychology Lab., Durham, NC, 1941; asst. prof. English and journalism Ea. Campus, Cuyahoga CC, Cleve., 1973-92, prof. emeritus, 1992—, advisor campus newspaper, 1973-84, dir. Writers Conf., 1975-90. Writing cons., editor various cos. and pubs., Cleve., 1973—; founder, operator Grammar Hot Line, 1987-92. Author: Crystal Lake Reflections, 1985, English 101 Can Be Fun, 1991, The Basic English Handbook, 1995. Recipient top state honors Ohio Newspaper Women's Assn., 1947, award for best ednl., best overall stories Am. Heart Assn., 1970, Besse award for tchg. excellence, 1980, Profl. Excellence award, 1985, Provost's Pride award, 1987, Nat. Tchg. Excellence award Coun. for Advancement and Support of Edn., 1989; named Ohio Outstanding Citizen, Ohio Ho. Reps., 1987, 89, Innovator of Yr., League for Innovations in C.C.s, 1988, Pres.'s award Cuyahoga C.C., 1992. Mem. Mensa, Phi Beta Kappa, Pi Beta Phi. Presbyterian. Avocations: grammar consulting, reading, writing. Home: 27900 Fairmount Blvd Cleveland OH 44124-4616 E-mail: taylorstock@ameritech.net.

TAYLOR, MARILYN JORDAN, architectural firm executive; m. Brainerd O. Taylor; children: Brainerd I., Alexis. Degree in govt. and urban affairs, Harvard Coll., 1969; MArch, U. Calif., Berkeley; postgrad., MIT. Joined Skidmore, Owings and Merrill LLP, Washington, 1971, urban designer, dir. design stations program of N.E. Corridor Improvement Project, 1978—85, chief urban design and planning practice N.Y.C., 1985—2001, chmn., 2001—. Past pres. N.Y.C. chpt. AIA; chmn. Nat. AIA Regional and Urban Design Com.; vis. prof. Harvard Grad. Sch. Design; David Rockefeller fellow N.Y.C. Partnership, fellows adv. com. Key projects include N.J. Performing Arts Ctr., Newark, Riverside South, Manhattan, NYNEX Hdqs., Battery Park City, Penn Sta. Redevelopment Project, various airports, many others. Bd. dirs. N.Y.C. Bldg. Congress (chmn. 2002-04), Comml. Real Estate Women N.Y., Inst. for Urban Design. Named Woman of Yr., Comml. Real Estate Women N.Y., 1998; named one of Most Influential Women in Am. Real Estate, GRID mag., 2001; named to List of Most Influential Women, Crain's N.Y., 1996, 2000; recipient Profl. Leadership award, Profl. Women in Constrn., 2001. Office: Skidmore Owings and Merrill LLP 14 Wall St New York NY 10005*

TAYLOR, MARILYN LEVERE, management consultant, educator; b. Hamilton, Ontario, Can., Apr. 27, 1942; arrived in U.S.A., 1956; d. Dwight S. and Reta (Finch) Levere; m. Robert E. Taylor, Apr. 1963; children: Theresa, Christopher. BA, U. So. Fla., 1967; MBA, Harvard U., 1971, DBA, 1979. Program dir. U. So. Fla., Tampa, Fla., 1967—72; from asst. prof. to prof. U. Kans., Lawrence, Kans., 1977—87, prof., 1987—94; Gottlieb/Mo. chair strategic mgmt. U. Mo., Kans. City, Mo., 1994—2000, dir. exec. MBA program, 1995—2000, faculty dir. Students in the City (svc. learning program), 2002—. Bd. dir. European Case Clearing House Babson Coll., Wellsley, Mass., The Workman Found., Leavenworth, Kans.; cons. in field, 1975—. Mem. editl. bd.: Case Rsch. Jour., 1988—; contbr. articles to profl. jours.; co-author (with Greg Dess & Thomas Lumpkin): Strategic Management: Text and Cases, 2003—. Adv. bd. Initiative for Competitive Inner City-Kans. City, Kans. City, 1995—; local adv. bd. Local Initiative Support Corp., Kans. City, 1999—. Recipient Faculty Pioneer award, Aspen Inst. & World Resources Inst., 2001; scholar, The Ewing Marion Kauffman Found., 2001—. Fellow: No. Am. Case Rsch. Assn. (v.p. membership 1986—88, v.p. programs 1989—90, pres. 1991—92); mem.: Mid West Acad. Mgmt. (founding track chmn. 1998—2000, case rsch. com. 1998—2000), Nat. Bus. Sch. Network (steering com. 1998—2001, C.R. Christensen award 2000, Nat. finalist field studies project 2001, Nat. winner field studies project 2000, Outstanding Leadership award 2001), Acad. Mgmt. Avocations: piano, walking, reading, swimming, travel. Office: Bloch School Bus & Pub Administration Univ Mo 5110 Cherry Kansas City MO 64110 Office Phone: 816-235-5774.

TAYLOR, MARTHA MCCLINTOCK, marriage and family therapist, researcher; b. Ruston, La., Sept. 2, 1944; d. Robert Stephen and Sallie Lou (Colvin) McClintock; m. Robert Adlis Taylor, Oct. 14, 1994. AA cum laude, Nat. U., 1990, BA in Behavioral Sci. magna cum laude, 1992; MA in Counseling, U. San Francisco, 1994. Lic. marriage and family therapist assoc., N.C. Med. asst. Kaiser Permanente, Sacramento, 1972-94; intern in marriage, family and child counseling San Juan Sch. Dist., Carmichael, Calif., 1993-95; pvt. practice, Benson, N.C., 1997—. Co-facilitator Bereavement Support Group, Sacramento, Calif., 1990-92, Depression Support Group, Benson, N.C., 1997—; intern, instr. parenting classes, Carmichael, Calif., 1994-95. Pres. Civitans, Benson, N.C., 1997-98; mem. ch. counsel Luth. Ch. Our Redeemer, Sacramento, 1992-95, pres., 1995; elder Benson Presbyn. Ch., 1998—, clk. of session, 1999—. Mem. DAR, Am. Assn. Marriage and Family Therapy (assoc.), Assn. Play Therapy, The Sandtray Network, N.C. Assn. Marriage and Family Therapy, Civitan. Avocations: gardening, genealogy. Office: Rose Cottage Counseling Ctr Inc 4691 NC 50 N Benson NC 27504

TAYLOR, MARY, state representative; M in Taxation, U. Akron. CPA. Sr. mgr. Bober, Markey, Fedorovich & Co.; state rep. dist. 43 Ohio Ho. of Reps., Columbus, 2002—, vice chair, homeland security, engring. and archtl. design com., mem. econ. devel. and tech., edn. and ways and means comms., fed. grant rev. and edn. oversight subcom. Councilwoman, fin. com. chair, mem. rules & pers. and intergovtl. and utilities coms. Green (Ohio) City Coun., 2001—. Republican. Office: 77 High St llth fl Columbus OH 43215-6111

TAYLOR, MARY LEE, retired college administrator; b. Amarillo, Tex., Nov. 13, 1931; d. David Kelly and Bessie F. (Peck) McGehee; m. Lindsey Taylor, Sept. 13, 1950 (dec. Aug. 1985); children: Gary, Kent, Ronald. BS, W. Tex. State U., 1959; MEd, Tex. Tech U., 1975. Tchr. Mesquite (Tex.) Pub. Schs., 1961-63; resource tchr. Amarillo Pub. Schs., 1971-79, supr., 1979-80; reading instr. Amarillo Coll., 1981-88, asst. prof. reading, 1988-93, assoc. prof., 1994-95. Project dir. Tex. Edn. Agy., Austin, 1984-85, 85-86, Amarillo Coll., 1988-89. Instr. GED Ctr. for Neighborhood Ministries, Phoenix, 2001—02. Mem. Tex. Assn. for Children with Learning Disabilities (meritorious svc. award 1985), Coll. Reading and Learning Assn. (spl. interest group leader 1987-89, cert. 1988, editor newsletter 1987-89), Am. Assn. Cmty. and Jr. Colls., North Plains Assn. for Learning Disabilities (pres. 1987-88, coord. accessibility svcs. 1993—), Tex. Assn. Developmental Educators (membership chmn. 1992-93), Assn. of Higher Edn. and Disabled Students. Avocations: camping, hiking. Home: 587 Greenfield Cir W Grand Junction CO 81504-4965 E-mail: mlltaylor@aol.com.

TAYLOR, MARY ROSS, art administrator; b. Pine Bluff, Ark., Jan. 26, 1945; d. Pinchback Taylor Jr. and Betty (Strickland) Abbott. BA, Vanderbilt U., 1967; MA, U. Tenn., 1969; postgrad., U. Tex., 1969-72; MA, John F. Kennedy U., Orinda, Calif., 1995. Propr., mgr. The Bookstore, Houston, 1973-83; exec. dir. Through the Flower Corp., Benicia, Calif., 1983-85, 1985-90, Lawndale Art and Performance Ctr., Houston, 1991—97; dir. www.artwomen.org, 2000—. Mem. adv. bd. Nat. Mus. Women in Arts, Washington, 1991—. Mem. Tex. Gov.'s Commn. on Women, 1991-93. Mem. Leadership Am. Assn. (pres. 1989). Home: PO Box 2765 Wimberley TX 78676 Office Phone: 512-924-2149.

TAYLOR, MICHELLE Y. human resources consultant; b. L.A., Aug. 23, 1965; d. Lucille S. Taylor, Rodney A. Taylor. B in Comm., U. San Diego, 1987; M in Orgnl. Mgmt., U. Phoenix, San Diego, 1994. Asst. program dir. Partnerships With Industry, San Diego, 1987—88; placement dir. Eldorado Coll., Escondido, Calif., 1988—89; supr. Kelly Staffing Svcs., San Diego, 1989—91; office mgr. Scripps Hosp., La Jolla, Calif., 1991—93; supr. Remedy Staffing Svcs., San Diego, 1993—94; corp. edn. mgr. U. Phoenix, San Jose, Calif., 1994—95; staffing mgr. Superior Design, San Jose, 1995—96; dir. human resources SV Probe, Inc., San Jose, 1996—98; v.p. human resources San Jose Nat. Bank, 1998—2000; cons. Michelle Y. Taylor Consulting, San Diego, 2000—01; sr. human resources cons. Paychex, Inc., San Diego, 2001—. Mem. Employment Advisory Coun., San Jose, 1998—2000. Scholar, U. San Diego, 1983. Mem.: Soc. for Human Resources Mgmt. Avocations: books on tape, fitness, collecting modern art, travel.

TAYLOR, MILDRED D. author; b. Jackson, Miss., Sept. 13, 1943; d. Wilbert Lee and Deletha Marie (Davis) Taylor. BA in Edn., U Toledo, 1965; MA, U Colo., 1969. Vol., tchr. English and history Peace Corps, Ethiopia, 1965-67, then recruiter, 1967-68; study skills coord. black edn. program U. Colo., 1969-71. Author: (children's fiction) Song of the Trees, 1975, Roll of Thunder, Hear My Cry, 1976, Let the Circle Be Unbroken, 1981, The Gold Cadillac, 1987, The Friendship and Other Stories, 1987, Mississippi Bridge, 1990, The Road to Memphis, 1990, The Well, 1995 (winner Jane Addams book award, 1996), The Land, 2001. Address: care Dial Books For Young Readers 375 Hudson St New York NY 10014-3658

TAYLOR, MILLICENT RUTH, elementary school educator; b. Kingston, Jamaica, Nov. 18, 1944; came to U.S., 1981; m. Henry Taylor; children: T'ousant, Howard, Annette, Kerry-Ann. BE, U. West Indies, 1981; MS, U. Miami, 1991. Cert. elem. edn. tchr., secondary social sci. tchr., Fla. Chairperson dept. history Mays Middle Sch., Miami, Fla., 1987—, peer tchr., 1987—; clin. tchr., 1990—; seminar presenter Mays Middle Sch., Miami, Fla., 1987-88, clin. tchr., 1990—. Leader, trainer Global Edn., Miami, Fla. 1989, sponsor History Bee, Miami, 1988-90, Geography Bee, 1988-90, 2003. Recipient State award for tchg. econs. Dade County Sch., 1992, Nat. award for tchg. econs. Joint Coun. Econ. Edn., 1991, State award for Gov. Awards for Excellence, 1995, Nat. award for tchg. econs. Nat. Coun. Econ. Edn., 1995. Mem. ASCD, Seventh Day Adventist. Avocations: reading, travel, sewing, photography. Home: 19834 SW 118th Ave Miami FL 33177-4435 Office: Mays Middle Sch Goulds FL 33170

TAYLOR, MINNA, lawyer; b. Washington, Jan. 25, 1947; d. Morris P. and Anne (Williams) Glushien; m. Charles Ellett Taylor, June 22, 1969; 1 child, Amy Caroline. BA, SUNY, Stony Brook, 1969; MA, SUNY, 1973; JD, U. So. Calif., 1977. Bar: Calif. 1977, U.S. Dist. Ct. (cen. dist.) Calif. 1978. Extern to presiding justice Calif. Supreme Ct., 1977; field atty. NLRB, L.A., 1977-82; dir. employee rels., legal svcs. Paramount Pictures Corp., L.A., 1982-85, v.p. employee rels. legal svcs., 1985-89; dir. bus. and legal affairs Wilshire Ct. Prodns., L.A., 1989-91; sr. counsel Fox Broadcasting Co., L.A., 1991-92, v.p. legal affairs, 1992-97, sr. v.p. legal affairs, 1997—. Webmaster www.ifcome.com, 2001—. Editor notes and articles: U. So. Calif. Law Rev., 1976-77. Mentor MOSTE, L.A., 1986-87, 88-89; pres. Beverly Hills chpt. ACLU, L.A., 1985. Fellow ABA, Calif. State Bar (mem. copyright subcom. 1994-95), L.A. County Bar Assn.; mem. Beverly Hills Bar Assn., L.A. Bead Soc. (membership sec. 1992-94, mem. bd. dirs. 1994-95), Order of Coif. Office: Fox Broadcasting Co 10201 W Pico Blvd Los Angeles CA 90064-2606

TAYLOR, NANCY ALICE, mechandiser, buyer; b. Sept. 25, 1956; AA, Santa Fe C.C., Gainesville, Fla., 1977; BS, Fla. State U., Tallahassee, 1979. Asst. to dir. of mdse. and design Nanlien Internat. Corp., L.A., 1980; fashion designer LV Industries, L.A., 1981-86; ptnr., mgr., designer Benz The Sun Society, Venice, Calif., 1982-85; fashion designer, mdse. mgr. Asics, Santa Ana, Calif., 1986-88, Ocean Pacific Lifestyles, Tustin, Calif., 1988-89; owner, mgr., buyer Century West Car Wash, Inc., L.A., 1989-99; owner, mgr. Nantex Recycling LLC, Cocoa Beach, Fla., 1999; merchandiser, clothing buyer Cocoa Beach Surf Co., 2000—. Mem. Solid Waste Assn. N.Am. Office: 2210 S Atlantic Ave Cocoa Beach FL 32931 E-mail: taylor.n.a@att.net.

TAYLOR, NATHALEE BRITTON, retired nutritionist; b. Lubbock, Tex., June 8, 1941; d. Nathaniel E. and Dessie Pauline (Moss) Britton; children by previous marriage: Clay H., Bret N. Courtney. BS in Home Econs., Tex. Tech U., 1963. Home economist Pioneer Gas, Lubbock, Tex., 1963-65; dietitian Tex. Tech U., Lubbock, 1966-71; home economist South Plains Electric Co-op., Lubbock, 1986; mgr. quality control Rip Griffins Enterprises, Lubbock, Tex., 1987; sales rep. Time Chem., Lubbock, 1987—2003; with Sentry, Lubbock; mktg. rep. Dodson Group Ins., Lubbock, Farmers Ins., Lubbock, Southwestern Bell Wireless; ret., 2003. Co-author: (cookbook) From Our House to Yours, 1975; columnist: Lubbock Lights mag.; presenter TV show Southwestern Cooking Sta. KTXT. Bd. dirs. Am. Heart Assn., Lubbock, 1985-87; mem. Home Economist in Bus. (pres. Lubbock chpt., 1985); culinary co-chmn. Lubbock C. of C. Arts Festival, 1982, 83, 84. Named Lincoln County Fair Queen. Mem. Tech. Home Econs. Alums (sec./treas.), Am. Home Econs. Assn. (v.p., sec./treas.), Bd.-Cove, Soroptomist (v.p. Lubbock club). Democrat. Avocations: gardening, writing, cooking, horseback riding.

TAYLOR, NICOLE RENÉE, model; b. Miami, Fla. d. Ken and Barbara T. With Irene Marie, Miami, 1989. Contracts with L'Oreal, 1990-92, Cover Girl Makeup; appeared in Seventeen (cover girl) 1989, Vogue, Elle, Mademoiselle, Harper's Bazaar; modeled for Yves Saint Laurent, Karl Lagerfeld; modeled swimsuit Sports Illus., 1997. Office: IMG Models 170 5th Ave Fl 10 New York NY 10010-5911

TAYLOR, RENEE, actress, writer; m. Joseph Bologna; 1 child, Gabriel. Grad., Acad. Dramatic Arts. Actress (films) The Errand Boy, Last of the Red Hot Lovers, A New Leaf, The Detective, Lovesick, White Palace, Delirious, End of Innocence, (stage) Three Sisters, Machinal, Annie Get Your Gun, Li'l Abner, Wish Your Were Here; writer (film) Lovers and Other Strangers (Academy award nomination), (TV) Paradise, (HBO spl.) Bedrooms (Writers Guild award); author: My Life On A Diet. Address: 16830 Ventura Blvd Ste 326 Encino CA 91436-1725

TAYLOR, ROSE PERRIN, social worker; b. Lander, Wyo., Feb. 11, 1916; d. Wilbur Rexford Perrin and Agatha Catherine (Hartman) Perrin DeMars; m. Louis Kempf Kugland, Sept. 1942 (div. 1951); children: Mary Louise, Carolyn Kugland McElhany; m. Wilfred Taylor, Oct. 13, 1962 (dec. 1991). AB, U. Mich., 1937; MSW, U. Denver, 1956; student, Columbia U., 1936, Santa Rosa Jr. Coll., 1974-93, Coll. of Marin, 1995-98. Group worker Dodge Cmty. House, Detroit, 1937-38; case worker Detroit Welfare Dept., Detroit, 1938-40; child welfare worker Fremont County Welfare Dept., Lander, Wyo., 1940-42; worker children's svcs. Laramie County Welfare Dept., Cheyenne, Wyo., 1951-57, dir., 1957-58; supr. San Mateo (Calif.) County Health & Welfare, 1958-74; dir. Fed. Day Care Project, San Mateo, 1964—. Tchr. Sch. Pub. Health Nursing, U. Wyo., 1951-55; tchr. Sch. Social Work, U. Calif., San Jose, 1962-63; workshop leader NIMH, Prescott, Ariz., 1961, Ariz. State U., Phoenix, 1962, Oreg. State Welfare Dept., Otter Crest, 1973; cons. day care workshops. Contbr. articles to profl. jours. Adminstrv. vol. Buck Ctr. for Rsch. in Aging, Marin County, 1994-95, vol. epidemiol. rschr. nutrition validation study for people in their 80's and 90's, 1995; bd. dirs. Friends of Redwoods, 2000-03; task force on programs and svcs. Redwood Bd., 2002-03; vol. aux. bd. Redwoods, 2003, 2004, leader low vision program, 2003; bd. dirs. United Ch. of Christ, 2002-03. Recipient Resolution of Commendation, Calif. State Senate, 1974; Annual Rose Taylor award San Mateo Child Care Coordinating Coun., 1982, Founder's Recognition award, 1997. Mem. NASW. Democrat. Mem. United Ch. of Christ. Avocations: artist, writer children's fiction, poetry. Home: The Redwoods # 10105 40 Camino Alto Mill Valley CA 94941-2943 E-mail: rosept@kugland.net.

TAYLOR, ROSEMARY, artist; b. Joseph, Oreg. d. Theodore and Sarah A. (Lambright) Resch; m. Robert Hull Taylor; children: Barbara Taylor Ryalls, Robert H. Student, Cleve. Inst. Art, 1937-40, NYU, 1947. Tchr. pottery Rahway (N.J.) Art Ctr., 1950-55. Pottery cons. McCalls Mag., 1962-72. One woman shows include Paterson (N.J.) Coll., 1964, Westchester (Pa.) Coll., 1970, Gallery 100, Princeton, N.J., 1967, George Jensen's, N.Y.C., 1972, Artisan Gallery, Princeton, 1974, Am. Crafts (Ohio), 1979-99, Guild Gallery, 1986-91, Little Art Gallery, N.C., 1985-99, Olde Queens Gallery (N.J.), 1987, N.J. Designer Craftsmen, 1990, 97, 98, 99 (bd. dirs. 1986-87, std. chmn. 1994), Creative Hands, 1995, 97, 98, 99, Princeton, 1994; group shows include Mus. Natural History, N.Y.C., Newark Mus., Trenton (N.J.) Mus., Montclair (N.J.) Mus., Phila. Art Alliance, Pa. Horticulture Soc., 1988, Nat. Design Center, N.Y.C., Michener Mus., Pa., 1996; represented in permanent collection Westchester Coll. Bd. dirs. Solebury Cmty. Sch.; mem. Fulbright award com., 1982, 83. Mem. LWV (pres. Plainfield, N.J. chpt.), Am. Craft Coun., N.J. Designer-Craftsmen, Phila. Craft Group, Bucks County (Pa.) C. of C., Visual Artists and Galleries Assn., Nat. Assn. Am. Penwoman, Michener Mus., Doylestown, Pa., Women in the Arts (charter). Democrat. Unitarian Universalist. Home: 10 Ingham Way New Hope PA 18938 Office: PO Box 282 Stockton NJ 08559-0282 E-mail: romy282@nni.com.

TAYLOR, RUTH ANNE, lawyer; b. Honolulu, Feb. 18, 1961; d. Gerald Lou and Charlotte Anne (Nelson) Allison; m. Thomas Scott Taylor, Dec. 28, 1985; children: Kyle Thomas, Kelly Gerald, Kory Scott. BA in Journalism, U. So. Calif., 1984; JD, N.Y. Law Sch., 1987. Bar: Calif. 1987, U.S. Dist. Ct. (so. dist.) Calif., U.S. Ct. Appeals (9th cir.). Assoc. Carlsmith, Wichman, Case Mukai & Ichiki, L.A., L.A., 1987-89, Christensen, White, Miller, Fink & Jacobs, L.A., 1989-93; assoc. gen. counsel Warner Bros. Records, Inc., 1993-98, v.p. legal and bus. affairs, 1998—. Mem. Los Angeles County Bar Assn., Beverly Hills Bar Assn. Republican. Avocations: scuba diving, skiing, photography, cooking.

TAYLOR, RUTH ARLEEN LESHER, marketing educator; b. Riverton, Iowa, Mar. 7, 1941; d. Clyde Almond and Bernice Emogene (Graves) Lesher; m. Leslie (Milburn) Taylor, Aug. 10, 1963; children: Treg Anthony,

John Leslie II. BS in Home Econs. Edn. magna cum laude, U. Houston, 1975; MEd, Tex. Christian U., 1977; PhD, U. N. Tex., 1981. Prof. mktg. Tarrant County C.C., Ft. Worth, 1977-78, North Tex. State U., Denton, 1978-81, Southwestern U., Georgetown, Tex., 1982-87, S.W. Tex. State U., San Marcos, 1981-82, 87—. Dir. travel to China, Japan, Hong Kong, Costa Rica, Morocco, Europe, Eng., Mex., Dominican Republic, Venezuela, Chile, Peru; faculty intern Tex. Dept. Econ. Devel. and Tex. Sec. of State Office; collaborator STAT-USA and Internat. Catalog Exhbn. U.S. Dept. Commerce. Author: Text Maps Study Guides, 1994—; contbg. author: The Psychology of Fashion, 1985, Ethics in Accounting, 1994; contbr. articles to profl. jours. Mem. Lost Creek Garden Club, Austin, Tex., 1985—, v.p.; vol. Bob Bullock State Hist. Mus. Grantee Merrick Found., 1991. Mem.: DAR, Am. Soc. for Competitiveness, Winthrop Soc., French Huguenot Soc., Colonial Dames, Internat. Hospitality Coun. (bd. dirs.), Mayflower Soc., Mktg. Mgmt. Assn., Western Mktg. Educators Assn., Am. Mktg. Assn., Alpha Mu Alpha, Alpha Kappa Psi, Phi Delta Kappa, Phi Epsilon Omicron, Beta Gamma Sigma. Avocations: travel, gardening, reading, entertaining. Office: Texas State University 601 University Dr San Marcos TX 78666-4685

TAYLOR, SANDRA E. public relations executive; BA in French, JD, Boston U.; grad., Colo. Women's Coll. Atty., Colo., 1975-77; internat. economist overseas and State Dept. U.S. Fgn. Svc., 1978; legis. asst. internat. trade and fin. staff Sen. John H. Chafee, 1984; v.p. pub. affairs govt. rels., media rels., crisis comms., comty. rels. Imperial Chem. Industries PLC Britain, 1988; v.p., dir. comms., pub. affairs fed., state, local, internat. govt. rels. Eastman Kodak Co., Washington, N.Y., 1996. Mem. Meridian Internat. Ctr. (bd, trustees, exec. com.), Martha's Table, Keystone Ctr., Atlantic Coun., Bus.-Govt. Rels. Coun., The Choral Arts Soc., Nat. Coun. UN Assn., U.S. South Africa Bus. Devel. Com.., Internat. Women's Forum. Office: Eastman Kodak Co 1250 H St NW Ste 800 Washington DC 20005-5936

TAYLOR, SHELLEY E. psychology researcher and educator; b. Mt. Kisco, N.Y., Sept. 10, 1946; d. Charles Fox and Pearl May (Harvey) T.; m. Mervyn Francis Fernandes, May 1, 1972; children: Sara F., Charles F. AB magna cum laude in Psychology, Conn. Coll., 1968; PhD in Social Psychology, Yale U., 1972. Asst. prof. psychology and social rels. Harvard U., Cambridge, Mass., 1972-77, assoc. prof., 1977-79; assoc. prof. psychology UCLA, 1979-81, prof., 1981—. Mem. vis. faculty dept. adminstrv. scis. Yale U., New Haven, 1971-72, vis. Sloane fellow, 1978; mem. basic sociocultural rsch. rev. com. NIH, 1979-83; Katz-Newcomb lectr. U. Mich., 1982; cons. to pub. houses and TV producers. Author: Social Cognition, 1986, 2d edit., 1991, Health Psychology, 1986, 3d edit., 1995, 5th edit., 2002. Positive Illusions: Creative Self-Deception and the Healthy Mind, 1989, The Tending Instinct: How Nurturing is Essential to Who We Are and How We Live, 2002; contbr. numerous articles to sci. publs. Active numerous charitable and fund-raising orgns. including Curtis Sch. PTA and U. So. Calif./Norris Cancer Ctr. Recipient Rsch. Scientist Devel. award NIMH, 1981-86, 86-91, MERIT award, 1987, Donald Campbell award for disting. sci. contbn. to sociology, 1995; numerous rsch. grants in field; Winthrop scholar, 1967; Woodrow Wilson fellow, 1968, NIMH fellow, 1969-72. Fellow APA (Sci. Weekend lectr. 1988, Disting. Sci. award 1980, Outstanding Sci.Contbn. award Divsn. 38, 1994), Brit. Psychol. Soc. (flying fellow), Acad. Behavioral Medicine Rsch., Soc. Psychol. Study Social Issues, Soc. Behavioral Medicine; mem. AAAS, Soc. Exptl. Social Psychology, Western Psychol. Assn. (pres. 1993-94). Office: UCLA Dept Psychology Franz 4611 Box 951563 Los Angeles CA 90095-1563*

TAYLOR, SHERRI KEARISE, obstetrician, gynecologist, writer; b. Balitmore, Maryland, July 11, 1975; d. Charles Avon and Shiela Vanessa (Caldwell) Taylor. BS, U. Md., Balt., 1992—98; MD, post baccalaureate, Mich. State Univ., 1998—99. Academic tutor UMBC athletics excel program, Balt., 1996—98; residential tutor UMBC classic upward bound, Balt., 1997—98; academic tutor Mich. State U., dept. of anatomy, East Lansing, Mich., 1999—2000; grad. asst. Mich. State U., office of state of affairs, East Lansing, Mich., 1999—2000; academic tutor Mich. State U., ABLE prog., East Lansing, Mich., 2000—01; resident Dr. Lehigh Valley Hosp., Allentown, Pa., 2003—. Author: (rsch.) NIH Sci. Reports, 1995, 1996, (anthology) Am. at the Millenium, 2000. Vol. Vol. of Am., Lansing, Mich., 1999—2000. Recipient Johnson Award for Excellence in Art of Med., Kalamazoo Ctr. for Med., 2003, Women in Med. Award, Mich. State U., Coll. of Human Med., 2000—01. Mem.: Student Nat. Med. Assn., Minority Med. Student Assn., Am. Coll. of ob-gyn. Avocations: crocheting, travel, hiking, piano, classical music. Office: Lehigh Valley Hosp Cedar Crest / 1-78 Allentown PA 18105

TAYLOR, SHERRY MICHELLE MILLS, elementary school educator; b. Atlanta, Nov. 15, 1932; d. Albert Fleming and Idolan Elizabeth (Clements) Mills; m. James Philip Taylor, May 18, 1974; children: David Lee, Laura Anne. Student, North Ga. Coll., 1973; BS in Edn., Mary-Hardin Baylor Coll., 1975; M in Early Childhood Edn., Francis Marion U., 1992. Cert. Nat. Bd. Profl. Tchg. Cert. Tchr. Florence Dist. 4 Timmonsville (S.C.) H.S., 1978—80; tchr. Florence (S.C.) Dist. 1 Schs., SC, 1987—. Mem.: NEA, S.C. Art Edn. Assn. (Outstanding Elem. Art Educator 2001). Roman Catholic. Avocations: reading, drawing, pottery making, horseback riding. Home: 962 Farm Quarter Rd Florence SC 29501 Office: Savannah Grove Elem Sch 2348 Savannah Grove Rd Effingham SC 29541 E-mail: staylor@fsd1.org.

TAYLOR, SUE ANN, film producer, television producer; b. Sanford, Maine, Sept. 29, 1954; d. Sidney M. Hall Jr.; m. Roy H. Taylor III, May 27, 1984; children: Michael, Katharine, Jessica. Student, U. Maine, 1972-74, Vt. Coll. Creative dir. Ad Lib Graphics, Mt. Laurel, N.J., 1976-80; pres. Hall-Yusem Advt., Phila., 1980-86, Hollyberry Post and Prodns., Allentown, Pa., 1986-93; ptnr. Finestkind Film & Video, Wells, Maine, 1993-94; pres. Natural Resources . . . A Wealth of Wellness, Canton, Ga., 1994—, Tapestry Prodn. Ga., Canton, 1996-2000; exec. dir. WILD Weekend, Canton, 1996—, Blue Heron Films, 2000. Mem. adv. bd. WILD Found., 1998—. Pub. Back to One Mag., 1999—. Founder Consumer Choice in Dental Care Project, Washington, 1996—. Recipient 7 Videographer awards, 2000, 9 Telly awards, 5 Communicators awards, 2000, 1 Emmy nomination, 2000. Mem. NATAS, Soc. Profl. Journalists (pres.). Avocations: biking, conservation activities, reading, travel. Home: 360 E Marietta St Canton GA 30114-3017 Office: 807 Ammons Dr Waleska GA 30183-3515

TAYLOR, SUSAN S. communications executive; b. Minneapolis, Oct. 17, 1945; d. Lucius O. and Mary Elizabeth (McNaughton) T. BS in Edn., U. Minn., 1967; MS in Ednl. Rsch. & Testing, Fla. State U., Tallahassee, 1971, PhD in Instl. Sys., 1974. Cert. tchr., Minn., Mo. Tchr. Minnetonka (Minn.) Pub. Schs., 1967—68; tchr./author CAI Lab.-Kansas City Pub. Schs., 1968-70; grad. asst. Fla. State U., Tallhassee, 1970-74; cons./mgr. Control Data Corp., 1974-88; tech. dir. WICAT Sys., Orem, Ut., 1989-90; owner/cons. SST Enterprises, Bloomington, Minn., 1990—. Presenter in field. Author: (book chpt.) CREATE: A Computer-Based Authorizing Curriculum, 1979. Sec. Minn. Episcopal Cursillo Coun., Minn., 1998—2001. Mem. Internat. Soc. Performance Improvement (co-chair independent cons., past pres., treas. Minn. chpt.), Am. Soc. Tng. & Devel. Avocations: gardening, genealogy, reading, walking, crafts. Office: SST Enterprises 7430 Autumn Chace Dr Ste 203 Bloomington MN 55438-1115 E-mail: sstenterprises@aol.com.

TAYLOR, SUSAN VOGEL, cultural organization administrator; d. Nathaniel David Vogel and Evelyn Paula Hoffman. BA, U. of S.C., 1963; postgrad., Montgomery St. Tech. Sch., Sydney, Australia, 1971—72, Holden Sch. of Art, Charlottesville, Va., 1972—73, Tex. Christian U., Ft. Worth, 1973—80. Founder, dir. Neighborhood Artist Network, Ft. Worth, 1980—83; founder, coord. Borders Poetry Group, Ft. Worth, 1996—; founder, prodr. SawGrass Poetry Performance Troupe, Ft. Worth, 1997—; founder, host Barnes and Noble Poetry Group, Ft. Worth, 1998—. Tchr. Centro Cultural de las Americas, Ft. Worth, 2002—; tchr. ESL for adults Fort Worth Ind. Sch. Dist., 2003—. Five day performance art piece at TCU, Rags to Riches and Faraway Dreams; contbr. poetry to lit. pubs. and anthologies. Participant Dialogue Among Civlizations through Poetry, Ft. Worth; coord. art and poetry Magnolia St. Arts Festival. Recipient award for contbn. to poetry cmty., Four Star Writing Workshop, 2002, Ft. Worth Slam Team, Inc., 2002. Mem.: Ft. Worth Haiku Soc., Poets of Tarrant County. Avocations: weight training, science fiction. Home: 2260 Ridgmar Plz No 63 Fort Worth TX 76116

TAYLOR, SUZONNE BERRY STEWART, real estate broker; b. Memphis, Sept. 27, 1926; d. Andrew Cleveland and Sue Hodge (Berry) Stewart; m. Robert Allen Taylor, Sr., June 15, 1946; children: Robert A. Jr., Suzonne Stewart Taylor Davids. Student, Rhodes Coll., 1948, U. S.C., 1969. Cert. residential specialist CRS Coun., 1996; grad. Realtors Inst.; cert. real estate broker; accredited buyer's rep. Am. Bd. Realtors. Sales agt. E. Roy Stone Realtors, Greenville, S.C., 1967-69; real estate broker Aven Assoc. Realtors, Dover, Del., 1970-80, Emerson & Co. Realtors, Dover, 1980—2000; realtor ERA Harrington Realty, 1998—. Active Cresent Music Club, Greenville, 1955, Wildwood Garden Club, Greenville, 1960; mem., costume chmn. Greenville Little Theater, Jr. League Greenville, 1956-66, sustaining mem., 1966—, Jr. League Wilmington, Del., 1999—, dir., 1999. Mem. Nat. Bd. Realtors, Del. Bd. Realtors, Kent County Bd. Realtors, Del. Hist. Soc., Biggs Mus., Alpha Omicron Pi. Republican. Episcopalian. Home: 517 Greenhill Rd Dover DE 19901-3766 Office: Emerson ERA Harrington 1404 Forest Ave Dover DE 19904 E-mail: suetaylor@doverhouses.com.

TAYLOR, TERESA, communications executive; BS, U. Wis., LaCrosse. Joined US West (now Qwest), 1988; exec. v.p. wholesale markets group Qwest Comm. Internat., Inc., 2003—, exec. v.p. products and pricing group, 2000—03. Bd. dirs. Colo. Inst. Tech., Colo. Children's Campaign. Office: Qwest Comm Internat Inc 1801 California St Denver CO 80202

TAYLOR, TERESA MARIE, realtor; b. San Antonio, Tex., Nov. 21, 1949; d. Willie G. and Theresa (Page) Murillo; m. Ralph W. Taylor, June 30, 1972 (div. 1979); children: Lisa, Phillip; m. Michael Brock Toon, Nov. 29, 1997. Grad., Exec. Sectl. Sch., 1969; student, Richland Coll., 1989, Brookhaven Coll., 1990. Lic. real estate agt., Tex. Sec. to controller Steak and Ale Restaurants, 1969-73; sec. Henry S. Miller Co., 1974-75; exec. sec. to sr. v.p. of fin. Jet Fleet Corp., 1976-78; exec. sec. to exec. v.p. and sr. v.p. J.L. Williams & Co., Inc., 1978-80; exec. sec. U.S. Lend Lease Inc., 1980-82; exec. sec. to gen. mgr. Melrose Hotel, 1982-83; exec. sec. to dir. North Tex. sales MCI Telecommunications, 1986-91; leasing agt. Lou Smith Realtors, Dallas, 1988; sales assoc. Christensen Realtors, Dallas, 1988-97; adminstrv. asst. to info. tech. group, pntr. Kenneth Leventhal & Co., Dallas, 1991-95; adminstrv. asst. to regional v.p. Bristol Hotel Co., 1995-98; sales assoc. Henry S. Miller Realtors, 1997—2001, Coldwell Banker, 2001—. Active Profl. Members League, Dallas Mus. Art, 1993-95; bd. dirs., v.p. fund raising Am. Kidney Fund, 1989-93, chmn. for ann. fund raiser; bd. dirs. Restart Orgn., 1990-93; fundraiser Nat. Marrow Donor Program, 1995-97; vol. KERP Channel 13, 1994—. Named Multi-Million Dollar Prodr. Mem.: Greater Dallas Assn. Realtors (Paint the Town participant 1989—92, Leadership alumni 2000—), Tex. Assn. Realtors, Nat. Assn. Realtors, Am. Bus. Women's Assn. (bull. editor 1987—88, publicity editor 1988—90, program chmn. 1989—90, hostess chmn. Dallas area coun. 1988—90, chn. pub. rels. com. 1990—92, Woman of the Yr. 1990). Republican. Roman Catholic. Avocations: tennis, snow skiing, cooking, needlepoint. Home: 4149 Republic Dr Frisco TX 75034-6327

TAYLOR, TERRY R. editor, educator; b. Valley Forge, Pa., Oct. 4, 1952; d. Thomas R. and Anna P. (Bystrek) T. BA in Journalism, Temple U., 1974. Reporter gen. assignments, sch. news Charlotte (N.C.) News, 1974-77; supr., writer AP, Phila., 1977-81, supr., writer sports desk N.Y.C., 1981-85, asst. editor sports, 1985-87, dep. editor sports, 1987-91, asst. chief bur., 1991-92, editor sports, 1992—; asst. editor sports N.Y. Times, 1991. Assoc. in journalism Columbia U., N.Y.C., 1991-95; adv. bd. Honda Awards, 1996—. Recipient John A. Domino Meml. award St. Bonaventure U., 1996, Founder's award Temple U., 1999; inductee Delaware County Sports Hall of Fame, 1998. Roman Catholic. Achievements include first woman sports editor at the AP. Office: AP Sports 50 Rockefeller Plz New York NY 10020-1605

TAYLOR, VESTA FISK, real estate broker, educator; b. Ottawa County, Okla., July 15, 1917; d. Ira Sylvester and Judie Maude (Garman) Fisk; m. George E. Taylor, Aug. 17, 1957 (dec. Oct. 1963); stepchildren: Joyce, Jean, Luther. AA, Northea. Okla. A&M, 1936; BA, N.E. State U., Tahlequah, Okla., 1937; MA, Okla. State U., 1942. Life cert. Spanish, English, history, elem. Tchr. rural sch. grades 1-4, Ottawa County, Okla., 1931-33; tchr. rural sch. grades 1-8, 1933-38; tchr. H.S. Spanish, English Wyandotte, Okla., 1938-42; tchr. H.S. Spanish, English, math. Miami, Okla., 1942-57; tchr. H.S. Spanish Jacksonville, Ill., 1960-65; tchr. H.S. Spanish, English Miami, 1965-79; owner, broker First Lady Realty, Miami, 1979—; tchr. real estate for licensing N.E. Okla. Vocat.-Tech., Afton, 1980-94. Radio spellmaster weekly-county groups Coleman Theater Stage, 1954-57; radio program weekly 4-H, Miami, 1953-57; weekly radio program telling story of Pilot Club Internat., Jacksonville, Ill., 1960-61. Author: (poem) The Country School, 1994. Vol. sec. Ottawa County Seniors' Ctr., 1993—; mem. restoration com. Friends of Theater, 1993—; mem. Friends of the Libr., 1994—. Named Outstanding Coach Ottawa County 4-H Clubs, Miami, 1955, 67, Outstanding Alumnus All Yrs. H.S. Reunion, Wyandotte, Okla., 1992, Champion Speller N.E. Okla. Retirees, Oklahoma City, 1991. Mem. AAUW (pres. 1978-80, treas. 1994-98), Ottawa Coutny Ret. Educators (treas. 1990-95, corr. sec. 1995—), Miami Classroom Tchr. (v.p. 1973-77), Tri-state Travel Club (purser 1989-95), Kappa Kappa Iota (pres. 1988-92, treas. 1986-88). Democrat. Baptist. Avocations: gardening, reading, travel, volunteering. Office: First Lady Realty 821 Jefferson St Miami OK 74354-4910 Home: 59501 E 100 Rd Miami OK 74354-4533

TAYLOR, VIRGINIA S. lawyer; b. Quitman, Ga. d. Allen Candler and Anne (Sanderson) Smith; divorced; children: Anne Taylor Hendry, Thomas Fielding. AB, Smith Coll., 1961; JD with distinction, Emory U., 1977. Bar: Ga. 1977, U.S. Dist. Ct. (no. dist.) Ga. 1977, U.S. Dist. Ct. (mid. dist.) Ga. 1979, U.S. Dist. Ct. (ea. dist.) Mich. 1988, U.S. Ct. Appeals (fed. cir.) 1982, U.S. Supreme Ct. 1981. Assoc. Kilpatrick & Cody, Atlanta, 1977-83, ptnr., 1983—, Kilpatrick & Stockton, L.L.P., Atlanta. V.p. Olmstead Parks Soc., Atlanta, 1985-93; bd. dirs. Piedmont Park Conservancy, Atlanta, 1991—, YWCA Metro. Atlanta, 1989-92, Leadership Atlanta, 1990. Mem. Ga. State Bar (chair patent, trademark and copyright sect. 1985-86), Order of Coif, Lawyer's Club Atlanta, Internat. Trademark Assn. (mem. publs. bd. 1995—, chair internat. forums subcom. 1992-95, bd. dirs. 1991-93, chair pub. com. 1988-90). Democrat. Methodist. Avocations: gardening, travel, reading, fly fishing. Office: Kilpatrick & Stockton LLP 1100 Peachtree St NE Ste 2800 Atlanta GA 30309-4530

TAYLOR-DUNN, CORLISS LESLIE, marriage and family therapist; d. Hilary Oliver and Sally Wilkins Taylor; m. David Charles Dunn, Aug. 2, 1975 (dec. Apr. 6, 2001). BA in Performing Arts, classically trained dramatic soprano, Ctrl. State U., 1971; MA in Marriage & Family Therapy, Azusa (Calif.) Pacific U., 1995; student in Counseling for the Ministry, Biola U., 1991—93. Lic. marriage & family therapist Bd. of Behavioral Scis., Calif., 2000. Psychotherapist Helicon Youth Ctr., Riverside, Calif., 1998—2001, Genesis Counseling Svcs., San Bernardino, Calif., 2002—02; pvt. practice Fort Garland, Colo., 2003—; pres., CEO, tchr. The Dunn Ctr. of Ft. Garland, Fort Garland, 2002—. Pres., ceo, nationwide safe ho. planter, tchr. The David Charles Dunn Found., Fort Garland, 2002—; tchr. music, drama and dance Cmty. Ctr. Author: (plays) (with Sandra Reaves-Phillips) Musical, Opening Night, 1981—82 (nominated for 3 off-Broadway Audelco awards, 1983); composer; dir.: Musical, Opening Night; author: (plays) Sojourner; The Story of an Ex-Slave (The Brody Art award Calif.Commn. Nat. Edn. Arts Assn., 1987); actor: (plays, Broadway) Ella, Bubbling Brown Sugar, 1977, Rockette Spectacular, Pin 'N Needles, Don't Bother Me I Can't Cope, (Broadway tour) Ruth in Raisin, 1976, 1988—89; prodr.: (TV films) Safehouse. Mem. Friends of the Fort support com. Fort Garland (Colo.) Mus.; founder Buffalo Soldiers Essay Contest Colorado Schs.; mem. steering com. Rural Philanthropy Days; bd. dirs. Cmty. Revitalization Com., Neighborhood Action Group, Marketing Com. Friends of the Fort. Mem.: Am. Assn. Marriage and Family Therapists (licentiate), Calif. Assn. Marriage and Family Therapists (licentiate), Costilla County C. of C. (mktg. com. 2003). Republican. Avocations: gardening, travel, acting, interior decorating, dance, ballet, jazz. Office: The David Charles Dunn Foundation 611 Macdonald Place Fort Garland CO 81133 Personal E-mail: ctaylordunn@aol.com.

TAYLOR-KIDDER, PAMELA SUE, special education educator; b. Conway, Ark., Jan. 9, 1969; d. Ben and Della Mae (Trammell) Taylor. AA Gen. Edn., N. Ark. C.C., 1989; BS in Edn., U. Ctrl. Ark., 1992. Cert. tchr. Ark. Spl. edn. tchr. Witts Spring (Ark.) Sch., 1993—99, St. Joe Pub. Sch., Ark., 1999—. Ednl. trainer Ark. Pediatric Facility, North Little Rock, 1993. Mem.: Coun. for Exceptional Children, Order of Eastern Star. Baptist. Avocations: sports, crafts.

TAYLOR-PICKELL, LAVONNE TROY, editor; b. Riverside, Calif., May 20, 1941; d. Troy Virgil Bradstreet and R. Victoria (Freeman) Chambers; m. Robert Martin Taylor, May 15, 1958 (div. 1975); children: Dana Freeman, Timothy Rene; m. Herman Pickell, Feb. 14, 1985; children: Marianne, Barry, David. Cert. personal trainer Am. Coun. on Exercise, 2003. Reporter Thousand Oaks (Calif.) Chronicle; with prodn. News Chronicle, Thousand Oaks, prodn. supr., 1979-81; with prodn. Ind. Jour., Thousand Oaks, Herald Examiner, L.A., L.A. Times; asst. mgr. Publ. Typography, Agoura, Calif., 1981-85; owner Excellence Enterprises, L.A., 1982—; sr. editor arts Glencoe/McGraw-Hill Sch. Pub., Mission Hills, Calif., 1987-96; actress, 1997—; copy chief Shape mag., 1997—. Spkr. various writers clubs. Editor, pub. L.A. My Way, 1991, On the Wings of Song, 1994; mng. editor The BookWoman, 1991-93. Mem. pub. rels. com. Conejo Players Theatre, Thousand Oaks, 1970-75, Betty Mann for 38th Assembly Dist., Agoura, 1975-76. Mem. NAFE, Am. Coll. Sports Medicine, Nat. Writers Club (pres. 1990-91, Merit Svc. award 1991), Women's Nat. Book Assn. (L.A. chpt. pres. 1992-93, newsletter editor, bd. dirs.). Avocations: reading, writing, gardening, music, art.

TAYLOR SONG, STEPHANIE INGRAM, nutritionist; b. Greenwich, Conn., Oct. 14, 1965; d. Edwin Douglas Taylor, Lois Johnstone Taylor. BA in French Lit., Dartmouth Coll., 1987; MS in Applied Physiology, Nutrition Edn., Tchrs. Coll. Columbia U., 1990, approved preprofl. practice program, 1991. Cert. Diabetes Educator 2001; registered dietitian 1991. Clin. dietitian Meadowlands Hosp. Med. Ctr., Secaucus, NJ, 1992—95, Hackensack U. Med. Ctr., Hackensack, NJ, 1995—2002; nutritionist Midtown Nutrition Care, N.Y.C., NY, 2001—03; owner, v.p., nutritionist Omni Health Profls., LLC, Saddle Brook, NJ, 2003—. Mem.: Am. Coll. Sports Medicine, No. Dist. N.J. Dietetic Assn. (pres. 2001—02, historian 1996—99, co-chair programming 1997—2000, mem. nominating com. 1998—99, chair pub. rels. 1999—2000), N.J. Dietetic Assn. (chair nominating com. 2000—01, Recognized Young Dietitian of Yr. 2001), Am. Dietetic Assn. (Recognized Young Dietitian of Yr. 2001). Episcopalian. Avocations: travel, skiing, tennis, scuba diving, swimming.

TAYMOR, JULIE, theater, film and opera director and designer; b. Newton, Mass., 1952; d. Melvin L. and Betty Taymor. BA in folklore and mythology, Oberlin Coll., 1974; attended, L'Ecole Mimet Theatre in Paris, France, Herbert Berghof Studio, N.Y.C. Founder Teatr Loh. Dir. Way of Snow, The Transposed Heads, 1984, The Tempest, 1986, Liberty's Taken, 1985, Juan Darién, 1988, Fool's Fire, 1992, Titus Andronicus, 1994, Oedipus Rex, 1992, The Magic Flute, Salomé, The Flying Dutchman, The Lion King, 1997, (Tony awards for best director and costume design 1998), operas, classical plays and exptl. theater projects; prodr. Shakespeare plays and operas; designer puppets, masks, imaginative costumes and other visual elements. MacArthur grantee, Watson fellow, 1974-79, Obie awards, 1988. Office: Internat Creative Mgmt 40 W 57th St New York NY 10019-4001*

TCHAIKOVSKY, LESLIE J. federal judge; b. 1943; BA, Calif. State Univ., Hayward, 1967; JD, Univ. of Calif., Berkeley, 1976. Law clk. to Hon. John Mowbray Nev. Supreme Ct., 1976-77; with Dinkelspiel, Steefel, Leavitt & Weiss, 1977-80, Gordon, Peitzman & Lopes, 1981, Dinkelspiel, Donovan & Reder, 1981-88; bankruptcy judge U.S. Bankruptcy Ct. (Calif. no. dist.), 9th circuit, Oakland, 1988—. Office: US Courthouse 1300 Clay St Oakland CA 94612-1425

TEAGUE, DEBORAH GANT, elementary school educator; b. Mankato, Minn., Jan. 23, 1952; d. Dorsett H. and Gwynlyn (Himmelman) Gant; m. William Lial Teague, June 7, 1991. AA, Meramec C.C., Kirkwood, Mo., 1972; BS, U. Mo., 1974, Edn. Specialist, 1989; MS, U. Minn., 1982. Tchr. Mexico (Mo.) Pub. Sch., 1977—. Recipient Presdl. Award in Excellence in Math. and Sci., NSF and Nat. Sci. Tchr. Assn., 1993; Fulbright Exch. fellow, 1985; Mo. State Incentive grantee Mo. State Dept. Edn., 1987, 88. Mem. Nat. Sci. Tchrs. Assn., Coun. of Elem. Sci. Teaching Internat., Assn. Presdl. Awardee Sci. Tchrs., Mo. Sci. Tchrs. Assn., N.E. Mo. State Tchrs. Assn. (exec. com. 1992-94), Phi Delta Kappa. Avocations: walking, swimming, travel. Home: 701 Ringo St Mexico MO 65265-1220 Office: Mexico Public Sch 1250 W Curtis St Mexico MO 65265-1855

TEAGUE, SHARON BEASLEY, state legislator; b. Feb. 15, 1952; married. AA, Ind. Coll. Bus. and Tech. Mem. Ga. Ho. of Reps., 1992—, mem. motor vehicles com., regulated beverages and state inst. and property com.; realtor. Cmty. activist. Baptist. Democrat. Home: PO Box 988 Red Oak GA 30272 Office: Ga House of Reps 504 Legis Office Bldg Atlanta GA 30334

TEAHAN, KATHLEEN M. state legislator, educator; b. Brockton, Mass., June 11, 1947; d. Joseph and Florence (Mahoney) Keras; m. Robert S. Teahan, 1971; children: Anne Teahan Berry, Jean, Robert J., John. BA, Bridgewater State Coll., 1969. Mem. Mass. Ho. of Reps., Boston, 1997—, mem. health care com., mem. state adminstrn. com.; tchr. Whitman Sch. Mem. Plymouth County Dem. League, Whitman Dem. Town Com., Whitman Sch. Com., Whitman-Hanson Regional H.S. Com.; mem. coun. Holy Ghost Parish Coun., 1993-97; pres. Whitman-Hanson Citizens Scholarship Found., 1979; mem. family selection com. Whitman Habitat for Humanity, 1994-95. Mem. Nat. Coun. Tchrs. English, Mass. Tchrs. Assn. Democrat. Office: Mass State Legis Rm 540 State House Boston MA 02133

TEAHON, JEAN ANN, county official; b. Dunning, Nebr., June 19, 1936; d. Norman Arthur and Margaret Elsa (Terwilliger) Linder; m. Charles Gerald Teahon, Aug. 31, 1958; children: Geri Ann, Peggy Lynn, Tedd Norman. AA, Kearney State Coll., 1958. Cert. assessor Nebr. Elementary tchr. Compton Sch., Valentine, Nebr., 1956, Calamus Valley Sch., Ainsworth, Nebr., 1956-57, Willow Lake Sch., Elsmere, Nebr., 1957-59, German Valley Sch., Brewster, Nebr., 1968-72; dep. county clk. Blaine County, Brewster, 1980-90, county clk./assessor, 1995—; office mgr. Ctrl. Sandhills Area Ext., Thedford, Nebr., 1992-94. Author: Blaine County

History, 1988. Active Dunning United Ch. of Christ, 1949—, memorial chair, 1992—. Mem. Nat. Assn. County Ofcls., Nebr. Assn. County Ofcls. Democrat. Office: Blaine County # 1 Lincoln Ave Brewster NE 68821 E-mail: jteahon@yahoo.com.

TEAL, ARABELLA W. lawyer, former state attorney general; b. N.Y.C., Jan. 1961; m. Gary Teal; 2 children. BA, Harvard Coll., 1984; JD, Georgetown U. Law Ctr., 1987. Law clerk for sr. judges D.C. Superior Court, 1987—88; section chief General Litigation Section I, 1996—99; acting prin. dep. corp. counsel D.C., 1999—2000, prin. dep. corp. counsel, 2000—02, interim corp. counsel, 2002—03; atty. McCabe & Mack LLP, Poughkeepsie, 2003—. Office: McCabe & Mack LLP 63 Washington St PO Box 509 Poughkeepsie NY 12602-0509*

TEATER, DOROTHY SEATH, retired county official; b. Manhattan, Kans., Feb. 11, 1931; d. Dwight Moody and Martha (Stahnke) Seath; m. Robert Woodson Teater, May 24, 1952; children: David Dwight, James Stanley, Donald Robert, Andrew Scott. BS, U. Ky., 1951; MS, Ohio State U., 1954. Home econs. tchr. Georgetown (Ky.) City Schs., 1951-53; extension specialist Ohio Coop. Extension, Columbus, 1967-73; consumer affairs adminstr. City of Columbus, 1974-79, Bank One Columbus NA, 1980-85; councilmember Columbus City Coun., 1980-85; commr. Franklin County, Columbus, Ohio, 1985-2000; ret. Mem. Columbus Met. Area Cmty. Action Orgn.; mem. adv. bd. Ohio Housing Trust; chairwoman Franklin County Children's Cabinet; pub. mem. Ohio Bd. Pharmacy, 2000—. Bd. dirs. BBB;, Silesian Boys and Girls Club, Rickenbacker-Woods Mus.; mem. hon. adv. bd. Girl Scouts. Recipient Outstanding Alumnus award U. Ky., 1989, Women of Achievement award YWCA, 1995, Disting. Svc. award Ohio State U., 1997; named Disting. Alumni, Ohio State U., 1977. Mem. County Commrs. Assn. Ohio (pres. 1994), Columbus Met. Club, Greater Columbus C. of C. (Columbus award 1997). Republican. Methodist. Avocations: gardening, sewing.

TEATER, TRICIA L. human resources specialist; b. Des Moines, Iowa, Dec. 3, 1956; d. Harold Lord and Patricia Mae Teater. BA in Journalism, Drake U., 1982; MPA, Roosevelt U., 1991. Legis. asst. Alderman David Orr, Chgo., 1984-85; exec. asst. to commr. City of Chgo., Dept. Human Svcs., 1985-89; dir. human resources Cook County Clk.'s Office, Chgo., 1990—. Vol. chaplain Ind. Dept. Corrections, Michigan City, Ill. Dept. Corrections; vol. ethics com. Horizon Hospice, Chgo.; bd. dirs. Prologue Alternative H.S., Chgo. Mem. ASPA, Soc. for Human Resources Mgmt. Democrat. Buddhist.

TEBBS, CAROL ANN, secondary school educator, academic administrator; b. Columbus, Ohio, Sept. 9, 1939; d. John Arthur and Ann Laurie (Wickham) Williams; m. Ronald Daniel Tebbs, Mar. 31, 1957; children: Kimberly Ann, Ronald Dan. BA in English, Whittier Coll., 1963, MA in English and Edn., 1972. Cert. tchr. K-adult Calif. Tchr. art and English Hacienda La Puente Unified Sch. Dist., Hacienda Heights, Calif., 1963-84; tchr. advanced placement English, acad. decathlon advisor, yearbook advisor Glen A. Wilson H.S., Hacienda Heights, 1984—2000. Mentor tchr. Hacienda La Puente Sch. Dist., Hacienda Heights, 1988—2000; reader, tchr. trainer advanced placement English Coll. Bd., 2000—; bd. dirs. Kepler Coll., Lynnwood, Wash., pres., 2003—; bd. dirs., tchr. Online Coll., 2000—. Author (e-books): Beyond Basics: Moving the Chart in Time, Beyond Basics: Tools for the Consulting Astrologer; writer (jour.) Kosmos, Mountain Astrologer, 1995—. Named Tchr. of the Yr., Nat. Walmart Stores Found., 1998; recipient D. Fedderson Cmty. Svc. award, PTA, 1970, Teacher of the Year, 1971, Glen A. Wilson Faculty Tchr. of Yr. award, 1999—2000. Mem.: United Astrology Congress (program chair 1986, 1989, 1992, coord. 1995, bd. chmn. 1995—99, co-founder), Internat. Soc. Astrol. Rsch. (pres. 1988—95, bd. dirs. 1995—2004), Delta Kappa Gamma. Methodist. Home and Office: 56870 Jack Nicklaus Blvd La Quinta CA 92253-5074 E-mail: Caroltebbs@aol.com.

TEBEDO, MARYANNE, state legislator; b. Denver, Oct. 30, 1936; m. Don Tebedo; children: Kevin, Ronald, Linda, Thomas, Christine. Mem. Colo. Ho. of Reps., Denver, 1982-88, Colo. Senate, Denver, 1988-. Profl. parliamentarian. Republican. Office: Colorado State Senate State Capitol Bldg 200 E Colfax Ave Ste 346 Denver CO 80203-1716

TEDD, MONIQUE MICHELINE, artist; b. Sotteville-les-Rouen, France, Jan. 25, 1943; came to U.S., 1968; d. Maurice Joseph and Dolly Jeanne (Carpentier) T.; m. Asiat A. Ali, Dec. 23, 1967; 1 child, Asiat Allum Ali. MFA in Painting, Beaux-Arts Sch. of Rouen, Seine Rouen Maritime, France, 1967. Art tchr. Vernon, France, 1967-68; advt. Hahn J. Shoes, Washington, 1968-69, Magrams, Burlington, Vt., 1974—. Set decorator Lyric Theater, Burlington, Vt., 1975. One-woman shows include St. Michael's Coll., Winooski, Vt., 1972, 91, Peel's Gallery, Danby, Vt., 1978-79, Gov.'s Corridor, State Capital, Montpelier, Vt., 1980, The Living and Learning Ctr., U. Vt., Burlington, 1982, Passepartout Gallery, Winooski, 1983, Gallery Two, Woodstock, 1984; exhibited in group shows at The Gallery, Washington, 1969, N.Y. First Internat. Art Show, 1970, Galerie des Trois Arts, Burlington, Vt., 1970-71, Fleming Mus., Burlington, 1972, Frog Hollow, Middlebury, 1973, The Four Winds Gallery, North Ferrisburg, Vt., 1975, Norwich U. Armory Show, Hanover, N.H., 1976, Old Bergen Art Guild Touring Exhibit, 1978-80, Stratton Art Festival, Stratton, Vt., 1979, Women's Ednl. Ctr., Essex Junction, Vt., 1981-82, Pocketbook Wood Gallery, Montpelier, 1981-82, Window, a Women's View, Burlington, 1981-82, Passepartout Gallery, 1985, Smith Coll., 1985, Wood Art Gallery, Montpelier, 1985, 86, 87, Helen Day Ctr., Stowe, Vt., 1986-87, Gallery Two, 1991, Shelburne Mus., 1996, Beaux Arts Studio, Essex Junction, Vt., 1998—; selected for exhibit and calendars Paysage de France, a 12-city exhibit, 1965. Recipient 1st prize Rouen C. of C., 1964, 3rd prize Grand Prix Internat. of Deauville, 1987, open studio 7th Vt. Craft Coun., 2000. Home: 9 Seneca Ave Essex Junction VT 05452-3521 E-mail: teddali@verizon.net.

TEDFORD, DEBORAH J. lawyer; b. Dec. 1950; Grad. cum laude, Yale U., 1972; grad., Boston U., 1976. Ptnr. Tedford, Gianni & Jensen, P.C., Mystic, Conn. Bd. dirs. Hospice Southeastern Conn. Fellow: Conn. Bar Found., Am. Coll. Trust and Estate Counsel; mem.: Southeastern Conn. Estate and Tax Planning Coun. (past pres.), Conn. Bar Assn. (chair legal problems of the elderly 1990—92, chair estates and probate sect. 1997—, sec. 1999—2000, pres. 2002—03, founding editor Estates and Probate Newsletter), Mystic Rotary Club (past pres.). Office: PO Box 350 30 Bank St New Britain CT 06050

TEDLOCK, BARBARA HELEN, anthropologist, educator, academic administrator; b. Battle Creek, Mich., Sept. 9, 1942; d. Byron Taylor and Mona Gerteresse (O'Connor) McGrath; m. Dennis E. Tedlock, July 19, 1968. BA in Rhetoric, U. Calif., Berkeley, 1967; MA in Anthropology, Wesleyan U., 1973; PhD in Anthropology, SUNY, Albany, 1978. Lectr. in music Tufts U., Medford, Mass., 1977-78, asst. prof. anthropology, 1978-82, assoc. prof., 1982-87; assoc. prof. anthropology SUNY, Buffalo, 1987-89, prof. anthropology, 1989—, disting. prof., 2003, chair dept. anthropology, 1998—2000, 2002—03, assoc. dean undergrad. edn., 2000—01. Vis. mem. Inst. for Advanced Study, Princeton, 1986. Author: Time and the Highland Maya, 1982, The Beautiful and the Dangerous Encounters with Zuni Indians, 1992, The Woman in the Shaman's Body: Reclaiming the Feminine in Religion and Medicine, 2003; editor: Dreaming: Anthropological and Psychological Interpretations, 1987; co-editor: Teaching From the American Earth, 1975; assoc. editor Jour. of Anthropol. Rsch., 1987-93; sr. editor Dreaming, 1990-95; assoc. editor Latin Am. Rsch. Rev., 1992—; mem. editl. adv. bd. Encyc. Cultural Anthropology, 1993-95, Handbook of Qualitative Research, 1998—. Adv. bd. Mus. of Indian Arts, Santa Fe, 1991-95; mem. Roycrofters-at-large East Aurura, N.Y., 1989—; mem. Cultural Survival, 1980—; mem. humanities panel WGBH, Boston, 1983-84; judge pottery Southwestern Assn. on Indian Affairs, Santa Fe, 1981-83. Fellowships NEH, 1986, 93, sr. fellowship Am. Coun. of Learned Socs., 1994, Weatherhead fellowship Sch. of Am. Rsch., 1980, sr. fellowship Ctr. for the Study of World Religions/Harvard U., 1998; Sabbatical fellow Am. Philos. Soc., 2002-03; recipient Charles Bordon, Geoffrey Bushnell Juan Cosmos prize in linguistics Internat. Congress of Americanists, 1979. Fellow Am. Anthropol. Assn. (bd. dirs. 1991-93, editor-in-chief Am. Anthropologist 1994-98, Pres.'s award for leadership 1997), Soc. for Cultural Anthropology, Am. Philosophical Soc.; mem. AAUW, PEN (elected), Soc. for Humanistic Anthropology (pres. 1991-93, Writing prize 1986), Soc. for Psychol. Anthropology (bd. dirs. 1993-96), Assn. for Study of Dreams (bd. dirs. 1990-95), Soc. for Ethnohistory (exec. bd. 1980-82), Am. Studies Assn. (exec. bd. 1983-85), Assn. on Am. Indian Affairs. Avocations: skiing, running, swimming, dancing, videoing. E-mial. Office: SUNY Buffalo Dept Anthropology Buffalo NY 14261-0001 E-mail: tedlockb@acsu.buffalo.edu.

TEE, VIRGINIA, lawyer; b. Damariscotta, Maine, Aug. 7, 1956; d. Lawrence Edward and Rosamond (Stetson) Tee; m. David A. Danaee, Oct. 29, 1982; children: Christina Nicole Danaee, Erica Michelle Danaee. BA in English, Fla. State U., 1978; JD, U. Puget Sound, 1992. Bar: Fla. 1992, Wash. 1994. Corp. counsel AT&T Wireless Svcs., Inc., Redmond, Wash., 1993-99; asst. gen. counsel drugstore.com,inc., Bellevue, Wash., 1999—. Mem. editl. adv. bd. Wash. State Bar News, 1996-98; mem. MCLE Bd., 1998—, chair, 2000-01. Mem. Wash. State Bar Assn., Fla. State Bar Assn. Office: drugstore dot com 13920 SE Eastgate Way Bellevue WA 98005-4440 Home: 5984 Senegal Dr Jupiter FL 33458-3473

TEEGARDEN, NICOLEE, art educator; d. Charles Whitney and Mary Lucille (Neiman) Webster; m. Ernest Allen Teegarden, Sept. 2, 1962 (div. May 1970); m. Joseph John Rozman, Jr., Dec. 26, 1973 (div. July 1986); m. Clark Love, Aug. 1986 (div. Dec. 1989). BFA in Art Edn., Drake U., 1967; MS in Painting, U. Wis., 1972, MFA in Painting, 1980. Relief house parent Evang. Children's Home, St. Louis, 1962; elem. art specialist Kenosha (Wis.) Unified Sch. Dist., 1969—71; tchr. Tremper H.S., 1971—2001, chair dept. art, 1978—79, 1984—99; instr. drawing Advanced Placement Studio Art, 1992—2000; instr. advanced drawing Kenosha Inst. Arts, 2002—03; pres. N.Am. Sintered Metal Corp., Kenosha, 2003—. Instr. Coll. Lake County, Grayslake, Ill., 1970. One-woman shows include Carthage Coll. Art Gallery, Kenosha, 1971, Daken Gallery, Waukegan, Ill., 1971, David Barnett Gallery, Milw., 1972, U. Wis. Fine Arts Gallery, 1972, Marine Bank Gallery, 1980, Upstairs/Downstairs Gallery, Kenosha, 1980, Ctr. City Espresso, Racine, Wis., 1991, Racine Visitors and Conv. Bur., Racine, 1996. Mem. adv. com. Milw. Art Mus., 1980—94, com. chair, 1990—94. Named Scholastic Art Awards Disting. Alumni, Milw. Art Mus., 1993; recipient Lakefront Festival Arts award, 1981, Regional Scholastic Art awards; Nat. Art Inst. scholar, Alliance Ind. Colls. Art and Design, 1988. Mem.: Nat. Art Edn. Assn. Home: 1701 Wisconsin Ave Racine WI 53403 Office: N Am Sintered Metal Corp 3301 63d St Kenosha WI 53142 Office Phone: 262-652-1600.

TEEL, JOYCE RALEY, retail executive; b. 1930; m. James Teel. Dir. Raley's, West Sacramento, 1950—; co-chmn. bd. dirs. Raley's, Bel Air Markets, Food Source, Nob Hill Foods, No. Calif., Nev., NMex., 1991—. Dir. non-profit Food for Families. Office: Raleys & Belaire 500 W Capitol Ave West Sacramento CA 95605-2696

TEELE, CYNTHIA LOMBARD, lawyer; b. Boston, Oct. 11, 1961; d. John Hughes and Patricia Jeanne (Linder) T. AB in Urban Studies magna cum laude, Brown U., 1983; JD, U. Va., 1986. Bar: Calif. 1986. Assoc. Lillick McHose & Charles, L.A., 1986-87, Wyman Bautzer Kuchel & Silbert, L.A., 1987-91; sr. atty. Paramount Pictures Corp.-TV Divsn., Hollywood, Calif., 1991-92, dir., legal, 1992-94, v.p., legal, 1994—. Home: 3644 Berryman Ave Los Angeles CA 90066-3306

TEEPLE, FIONA DIANE, librarian, lawyer; b. St. Thomas, Ont., Can., Jan. 9, 1943; d. William Lloyd and Grace (Hathaway) T. BA, U. Western Ont., London, 1964; BLS, U. B.C., Vancouver, 1965; MLS, U. Toronto, Ont., 1976; LLB, York U., Toronto, 1980. Bar: Ont., 1985. Asst. law librarian U. Western Ont., London, 1965-70; reference librarian York U. Law Library, Toronto, 1971-77; adminstrv. asst. Ont. Legis. Library, Toronto, 1980, exec. asst., 1981-83; chief librarian Supreme Ct. of Can., Ottawa, 1983-90, dir. libr., 1990—2003, spl. advisor libr. and info. svcs., 2004—. Editor: Practitioner's Desk Book, 1976-80; mng. editor CALL Newsletter, 1973-75; features editor Canadian Law Libraries, 2001—; chair Supreme Ct. of Can. 125th Ann. commemorative Book com., 1999-2000; contbr. articles, revs., book chpts. in field. Mem. Can. Assn. Law Librs., Law Soc. Upper Can., Assn. Can. Ct. Adminstrs. Mem. United Ch. Can. Mem. United Ch. Can.

TEETERS, NANCY HAYS, economist, director; b. Marion, Ind., July 29, 1930; d. S. Edgar and Mabel (Drake) Hays; m. Robert Duane Teeters, June 7, 1952; children: Ann, James, John. AB in Econs., Oberlin Coll., 1952, LLD, 1979; MA in Econs., U. Mich., 1954, postgrad., 1956-57, LLD, 1983, Bates Coll., 1981, Mt. Holyoke Coll., 1983. Tchg. fellow U. Mich., 1954-55, instr., 1956-57, U. Md. Overseas, Germany, 1955-56; staff economist govt. fin. sect. Bd. Govs. of FRS, Washington, 1957-66, mem. bd., 1978-84; economist (on loan) Coun. Econ. Advs., 1962-63; economist Bur. Budget, 1966-70; sr. fellow Brookings Instn., 1970-73; sr. specialist Congl. Rsch. Svc., Library of Congress, Washington, 1973-74; asst. dir., chief economist Ho. of Reps. Com. on the Budget, 1974-78; v.p., chief economist IBM, Armonk, N.Y., 1984-90. Bd. dirs., trustee Prudential Mut. Funds, 1985—2003. Author: (with others) Setting National Priorities: The 1972 Budget, 1971, Setting National Priorities: The 1973 Budget, 1972, Setting National Priorities: The 1974 Budget, 1973; contbr. articles to profl. publs. Recipient Comfort Starr award in econs. Oberlin Coll., 1952; Disting. Alumnus award U. Mich., 1980 Mem. Nat. Economists Club (v.p. 1973-74, pres. 1974-75, chmn. bd. 1975-76, gov. 1976-79), Am. Econ. Assn. (com. on status of women 1975-78), Am. Fin. Assn. (dir. 1969-71) Democrat. Home: 243 Willowbrook Ave Stamford CT 06902-7020

TEFLIAN, PAMELA JANE, lyricist, photographer; b. Salt Lake City, Apr. 23, 1955; d. Samual and Angeline Pallis Teflian. AS in Advanced Computer Graphic Design with highest honors(hon.), Platt Coll., Aurora, Colo., 1997; postgrad., U. Colo., Denver, 2002. Prodn. coord. The Bus. Word, Inc., Englewood, Colo., 1997—98; website content design and devel./webstie adminstr., circulation mgr. Pandata Corp., Englewood, 1998—2002; prodn. staff Telluride Internat. Film Festival, Englewood, 2003—; booking agt. for bands and performers Englewood, 2003—; performance coord. The Boulder New Renaissance Festival. Arts and entertainment reviewer Boulder Style Mag.; lyricist Am. Assn. Songwriters, Louie B. Pub. (BMI). Author: (book of poetry) The Violet Silence, 1987; contbr. poetry to profl. jours. Vol. Arapahoe County Sherif's Programs/Jehovah's Witnesses, Englewood, Colo., 1998—2002. Mem.: Audio Engring. Soc., Internat. Soc. Poetry (Award of Merit 2002, Editor's award). Avocations: playing drums and piano, weightlifting, swimming, audio engineering. Office: 4174 South Granby Cir Aurora CO 80014 Home: 7992 S Buchanan Way Aurora CO 80016-7104

TEGGE, PATRICIA ANN, administrative assistant; b. Milw., Oct. 25, 1922; d. Edmund Finegan and Norma Berthe (Kussel) Jones; m. Lloyd Frederick Tegge, Oct. 23, 1946 (dec. 1994); 1 child, Mark. B in Philosophy and Journalism, Marquette U., 1945. Adminstrv. sec. Family Svc. of Waukesha, Wis., 1966-91; ret., 1991. Mem. adv. bd. Salvation Army, past chmn. Recipient Outstanding Svcs. award Salvation Army 1983-85. Mem. DAR, Women in Communications (Southeastern Wis. chpt.), Nat. Assn. Parliamentarians (past pres. Wis. chpt.), Wis. Regional Writer's Assn. (chmn.), Wis. Soc. ([illegible] 1990—), [illegible] Club of Waukesha, Waukesha Women's Club (past pres.), Wis. Fedn. Women's Clubs (dist. pres. 1990—), Waukesha County Geneal. Soc. (newsletter editor 1997-2000). Republican. Lutheran. Home: 120 Corrina Blvd Apt 205 Waukesha WI 53186-3845

TEHRANI, FLEUR TAHER, electrical engineer, educator, researcher; b. Tehran, Iran, Feb. 16, 1956; came to U.S., 1984; d. Hassan and Pourandokht (Monfared) T.; m. Akbar E. Torbat, June 16, 1997. BS in Elec. Engring., Arya-Mehr U. of Tech., Tehran, 1975; DIC in Comm. Engring., Imperial Coll. Sci. and Tech., London, 1977; MSc in Comm. Engring., U. London, 1977, PhD in Elec. Engring., 1981. Registered profl. engr., Calif. Comm. engr. Planning Orgn. of Iran, Tehran, 1977-78; lectr. A elec. engring. Robert Gordon's Inst. Tech., Aberdeen, U.K., 1982-83; lectr. II elec. engring. South Bank U., London, England, 1983—84; asst. prof. elec. engring. Calif. State U., Fullerton, 1985-91, assoc. prof. elec. engring., 1991-94, prof. elec. engring., 1994—, dir. pharm. engring. program, 1999-2001. Vis. assoc. prof. elec. engring. Drexel U., Phila., 1987-88; sys. cons. Telebit Corp., Cupertino. Calif., 1985; engring. cons. PRD, Inc., Dresher, Pa., 1989-92; mem. NASA/Am. Soc. Engring. Edn. summer faculty Jet Propulsion Lab., Calif. Inst. Tech., Pasadena, 1995, 96. Contbr. articles to profl. jours.; patentee in field. Recipient Best Rsch. Manuscript award Assn. for the Advancement of Med. Instrumentation, 1993, NASA/Am. Soc. Engring. Edn. Recognition award for rsch. contbns., 1995, 96. Fellow Inst. for Advancement of Engring.; mem. IEEE, Women in Sci. and Engring. (chair Calif. State U. chpt. 1990-91), Assn. Profs. and Scholars of Iranian Heritage (pres. 1991-92), Sigma Delta Epsilon. Avocations: music, literature, poetry, stamp collecting. Office: Calif State U Coll Engring & Computer Sci 800 N State College Blvd Fullerton CA 92831-3547 E-mail: ftehrani@fullerton.edu.

TEICHER, STACY ELLEN, publishing executive; b. Bklyn., Feb. 16, 1196; d. Ernest and Lois T.. BA, Pa. State U., State College. Adminstrv. asst. Harcourt Brace Jovanovich, N.Y.C.; list rental sales Bill Comms., N.Y.C.; sales mgr. Raben Publ., N.Y.C.; advtsg. dir. Fancy Publs., N.Y.C.; publ. Lehigh Valley Mag., Bethlehem, Pa. Comms. mentor March of Dimes, Allentown, Pa., 2000, Habitat for Humanity, Allentown, 2002—. Mem.: Exec. Women Internat, Gtr. Lehigh valley Chamber. Avocations: reading, photography, travel, kayaking, walking. Office: Lehigh Valley Mag 910 13th Ave Bethlehem PA 18018

TEICHMAN, EVELYN, antiques appraiser, educator, estate liquidator; b. N.Y.C., Mar. 13, 1929; d. Bernard and Minnie (Goldenberg) Mensch; m. Milton Teichman, Jan. 16, 1949; children: David, Jeb, Sondra. Student, CUNY, 1946-49. Tchr. Bergen County Adult Schs., N.J., 1976—; freelance appraiser Paramus, N.J., 1978—; house contents and estate sale coord. Home: 56 Bush Pl Paramus NJ 07652-4004 Fax: 201-262-9552. E-mail: yonkiel@cs.com.

TEICHMAN, RUTH, state senator; m. Dennis Teichman; 4 children. Student, Kans. State U. Farmer; banker; mem. Kans. Senate, 2001—. Mem. Stafford Edn. Found.; founding mem. Sout Ctrl. Cmty. Found.; mem. Stafford Bd. Edn. Mem.: Stafford Drama Guild, Stafford Booster Club. Republican. Home: 402 N Union Stafford KS 67578

TEICHNER, MARTHA ALICE, network television news correspondent; b. Traverse City, Mich., Jan. 12, 1948; d. Hans H. and Miriam G. (Greene) Teichner. BA in Econs., Wellesley Coll., 1969; postgrad., U. Chgo., 1976-77. Gen. assignment reporter, newscaster WJEF radio, Grand Rapids, Mich., 1971-72; gen. assignment, city hall reporter WZZM TV, Grand Rapids, 1972-73; gen. assignment reporter WTVJ TV, Miami, Fla., 1973-75, WMAQ-TV, Chgo., 1975-77; news corr. CBS News, Atlanta, 1977-80, London, 1980-84, Dallas, 1984-87, Johannesburg, 1987-89, London, 1989-94; corr. CBS News "Sunday Morning", N.Y.C., 1994—. Atlanta assignments include El Salvador (first woman corr. sent by CBS), Panama: the Shah in Exile, United Mineworkers Strike, Cuban Boatlift, numerous disasters; London, Lebanon War (first woman corr. sent to Beirut by CBS), No. Ireland hunger strikes, Royal Wedding (Charles and Diana), Iran Hostage release; Dallas, Collapse oil industry, real estate, banks, Challenger crash, numerous disasters; Johannesburg, Mozambique civil war, significant racial, polit. issues; London, coverage former Yugoslavia (Slovenia, Croatia, Bosnia), Gulf War, Kuwait war aftermath, Romanian Revolution, Mandela release, polit. changes Ea. Europe, Mid. East, Royals, Clinton inauguration; N.Y.C., host series Conversations With..., Spoleto Festival, U.S.A., 1995, 97—; mem. coun. fgn. rels. Bd. mem., Simon Found., Chgo. Recipient Robert F. Kennedy Journalism award, Robert F. Kennedy Meml. Found., 1981, Breakthrough award Women, Men and Media, 1991, Emmy awards Am. Acad. TV Arts and Scis., 1996, (2), 1998, 2002, Excellence in Broadcasting award James Beard Found., 2002. Mem. DAR (Walter Hines Page Chpt.), Internat. Womens Media Found., Reform Club London. Avocations: food, wine, theater, music. Office: CBS News 524 W 57th St New York NY 10019-2924

TEITZ, BETTY BEATRICE GOLDSTEIN, retired interior designer; b. Mar. 10, 1914; d. Albert Stanley and Dora (Finestone) Gould; m. Milton A. Nusbaum, Apr. 10, 1943 (dec. Nov. 1956); 1 child, Alberta Joyce Nusbaum Duckman ; m. Harry Teitz, Dec. 28, 1959. Student, Rochester Bus. Inst., 1932—34, Rochester Inst. Tech., 1950—51, Columbia U., 1957—58. Owner design studio, Rochester, 1957; trainee WJ. Sloane, 1958; head design dept. Mason Furniture Co., Fall River, Mass., 1959; pvt. practice Providence, 1961—65; pres. Indesign Inc., Newport, RI, 1974—2003. Designer guest house The White House, Washington, U.S. War Coll., Newport, 1969—70; redesigned R.I. Corp. Rooney Plotkin & Willey, Newport, 1992, Providence, 92; designed the beginning restoration of Touro Synagogue, Newport, 94; interior designer Bryant Coll., Smithfield, RI, 2001—02; lectr. Navy Wives U.S.A. Staff asst. Motor Corps Grey Lady Rochester chpt. ARC Rochester, 1941—46, active Newport chpt.; Gray Lady vol. Genesee Hosp., Rochester, 1945—55; mem. Rochester Planned Parenthood, 1945—48; active Mental Health Clinic Citizens Adv. Com., Newport, 1967—78; yachting com. Am.'s Cup Race, 1950. Recipient Centennial Pageant Scenic award, Rochester, 1948, ARC awards, 1943—53, 10 yr. svc. pin, Genesee Hosp., 1955, Blue Ribbon award for flower show arrangements, 1950, 1952, 1955. Mem.: Preservation Soc. Newport R.I. (ednl. reproduction com. 1990—2000), Constrn. Specifications Inst. R.I. (sec.), Am. Inst. Interior Designers, Flower City Garden Club (past v.p. Rochester), Newport C. of C. (bldg. com.). Home: Apt 73 24 Tabor Xing Longmeadow MA 01106-1756

TEJEDA-BROWN, MARY LOUISE, artist; b. L.A., Jan. 11, 1921; d. Francisco Tejeda and Elizabeth (Kramis) Tejeda; m. William Reynold Brown, Oct. 26, 1946 (dec. 1991); children: Marie, Reynold, Franz, Elisa, Cristina, Regina, Marta, Mariane. Student, Frank Wiggens Trade Sch. Artist Raymond Advt. Co., L.A., 1938-40, No. Am. Aviation, Inglewood, Calif., 1941-46; freelance artist Whitney, Nebr., 1989—. Represented by Elaine's Art Gallery, Alliance, Nebr., Shamon Gallery, Hot Spring, S.D. One-woman shows include Mus. of Nebr. Arts, Kearney, 1998-99, Lee Dam Art Ctr., Kans., 1998, West Nebr. Arts Ctr., Scottsbluff, 1998, Chase County Art Ctr., Imperial, Nebr., 2000, U. Place Art Ctr., Lincoln, Nebr., 2001, Elaine's Fine Art Gallery, Aliance, Nebr., 2001; exhibited in shows at Gallery East, Loveland, Colo., 1991, Chadron (Nebr.) State Coll., 1989, 91, 93, 2003, West Nebr. Arts Ctr., 1992, 94, 95, Ft. Robinson Art Show, Nebr., 1991, 92, 93, Dakota Art Gallery, 1994, Agate Beds Nat. Monument, Nebr., 1994, Pastel Soc. Am., N.Y.C., 1994, Univ. Pl. Art Gallery, 1995, Gov.'s Mansion, Lincoln, Nebr., 1995, 2003, Mus. of Nebr., 1995, Colo. History Mus.,

Denver, 1998, Dakota Art Gallery, Rapid City, S.D., 2001, Mid-Am. Pastel Soc., 2002, Carnegie Arts Ctr., Alliance, Nebr., 2003 (Best of Show award); featured in Pastel Artist Internat. Mag., 2000; contbr. articles to profl. jours. Mem. Mid-Am. Pastel Soc., Pastel Soc. Am. (assoc.). Avocations: reading, travel. Home: 379 Bethel Loop Rd Whitney NE 69367-1730

TEJEDOR, MARCELA ALEJANDRA, sales executive, consultant; b. Buenos Aires, Dec. 23, 1964; arrived in U.S., 1994; d. Juan Tejedor and Carmen Ayala-Tejedor; 1 child from previous marriage, Kassandra Akouri-Tejedor. Student, MDCC Wolfson, Miami, 1999—. Creative svcs. dir. Elite Brands Internat. Exports, Miami, 1990—95, export dir. advisor, 1990—95; counter mgr. Burdines Cosmetics, Miami, 1995—98; territory sales mgr. Cameron Ashley Building Products, Pompano Beach, Fla., 1998—. Marketing cons. Verges Import & Export, Miami, 1994—98. Chairperson Annunciation Cath. Sch., Hollywood, Fla., 2001—. Mem.: FCA Coalition for Peace and Justice, 20-20 Vision Org., Internat. Hurrican Protection Assn., Aluminum Assn. Fla. SE chap. (sec.), Internat. Feng Shui Guild, Earth Save Org., Phi Theta Kappa. Roman Catholic. Avocations: preservation of environment, organic gardening, art festivals, art galleries, musical events.

TE KANAWA, KIRI, opera and concert singer; b. Gisborne, N.Z., Mar. 6, 1944; d. Thomas and Eleanor Te Kanawa; m. Desmond Park, Aug. 30, 1967 (div. 1997); children— Antonia Aroha, Thomas Desmond. Student, St. Mary's Coll., Auckland, N.Z., 1957-60, London Opera Centre, 1966-69; DMus (hon.), Oxford U., Dundee U., 1983, Warwick U., Auckland U., Waikato U., Nottingham U., Chgo. U., Durham U., Cambridge U. Joined Royal Opera House, London, 1971; appeared in role of Countess in Le Nozze di Figaro, 1971; U.S. debut in Santa Fe Festival, 1971; Met. Opera debut as Desdemona in Otello, 1974; appearances with all major European and Am. opera houses, including Australian opera cos., Royal Opera House, Covent Garden, London, Paris Opera, Munich Opera, La Scala, others; opera appeareances include Boris Gudonov, Carmen, Don Giovanni, the Magic Flute, Eugene Onegin, La Boheme, Manon Lescaut, many others; appeared in film Don Giovanni as Elvira, 1979; recs. include Blue Skies, 1986, Kiri Sings Gershwin, 1987, Kiri Te Kanawa: Italian Opera Arias, 1991, Kiri Her Greatest Hits, Ave Maria, Kiri on Broadway, The Kiri Selection, Kiri Side Tracks, My Fair Lady, Maori Songs; PBS appearance: Great Performances: West Side Story, 1985; author: Land of the Long White Cloud, 1989, Opera for Lovers, 1996. Decorated comdr. Order Brit. Empire, 1973, Dame Comdr. Brit. Empire, 1983, Order of Australia, 1990, Order of New Zealand, 1995. Mem.: Royal Acad. Music (hon.). Address: care Nick Grace Mgmt Ltd 69 Sheen Rd Richmond TW9 1YJ England

TELFER, MARGARET CLARE, internist, hematologist, oncologist; b. Manila, Apr. 9, 1939; came to U.S., 1941; d. James Gavin and Margaret Adele (Baldwin) T. BA, Stanford U., 1961; MD, Washington U., St. Louis, 1965. Diplomate Am. Bd. Internal Medicine, Am. Bd. Hematology, Am. Bd. Oncology; lic. Ill., Mo. Resident in medicine Michael Reese Hosp., Chgo., 1968, fellow in hematology and oncology, 1970, assoc. attending physician, 1970-72, dir. Hemophilia Ctr., 1971—, interim dir. div. hematology and oncology, 1971-74, 81-84, 89—, attending physician, 1972—, Rush-Presbyn. St. Luke's Hosp., 1999—, Olympia Fields (Ill.) Hosp., 1999—, Cook County Hosp., Chgo., 2000—, asst. prof. medicine U. Chgo., 1975-80, assoc. prof. medicine, 1980-85, assoc. prof. clin. medicine, 1985-89; assoc. prof. medicine U. Ill., Chgo., 1990-2001, Rush U., Chgo., 2001—. Mem. med. adv. bd. Hemophilia Found. Ill., 1971, chmn., 1972—83, lectr. annual symposium, 1978—84, mem. med. adv. bd. State of Ill. Hemophilia Program; dir. hematology-oncology fellowship program Michael Reese Hosp., 1971—75, 1981—84, 1989—2000, lectr. and mem. numerous coms.; lectr. Cook County Grad. Sch. Medicine, 1980—85, U. Chgo., ARC. Contbr. articles to profl. jours. Fellow ACP; mem. Am. Soc. Clin. Oncology, Am. Assn. Med. Colls., Am. Soc. Hematology, World Fedn. Hemophilia, Blood Club (Chgo.), Thrombosis Club (Chgo.). Office: Florsheim Bldg 29th & Ellis Chicago IL 60616

TELLEEN, JUDY, counselor; b. Chgo., Dec. 13, 1942; d. Kurt Theodore and Gertrude Lillian Lockwood Johnson; m. David Roger Telleen; June 15, 1964; children: Karin, Kirstin, Erik. BA, Lawrence U., 1964; MA, U. Mich., 1967, PhD, 1970. Program dir. counseling svcs. Asian Human Svcs., Chgo., 1994-95, coord. of counseling svcs., 1995-96, coord. of case mgmt., 1997-98; adj. prof. Governor's State Univ., University Park, Ill., 1995-99; counselor Arlington Heights, Ill., 1999—. Adv. com. mem. Bd. Suprs. and Sch. Bd., Va., 1993; mem. Pub. Policy and Legis. com. Ill. Counseling Assn., 1994, mem. governing coun., 2000—. Author: (book) A Predictive Model of the Cumulative Academic Achievement of Indian Students, 1970, (monograph) Gridance Factors Influencing Indian Students to Attend the University of Michigan, 1971; mem. editl. bd. (periodical) Ill. Counseling Assn. Quarterly, 1995—98. Youth advocate Bridge Youth & Family Svcs., Palatine, Ill., 1994—96; chairperson learning com. All Saints Lutheran Ch., Palatine, 1993—2001. Mem. Am. Counselor's Assn., Ill. Counselor's Assn., Ill. Assn. of Couples & Family Couns. (pres.), Ill. Assn. for Multicultural Counseling, Ill. Assn. of Mental Health Counselors, Assn. for Multicultural Counseling Develop., Internat. Assn. of Marriage & Family Counselors, Internat. Assn. of Addictions & Offender Counselors, Pi Lambda Theta, Phi Kappa Phi. Lutheran. Office: Ste 102 1040 S Arlington Heights Rd Arlington Heights IL 60005-3162

TELLEM, NANCY REISS, broadcast executive; b. Dec. 1952; m. Arn Tellem. Joined Warner Bros. TV, 1987, exec. v.p. bus. and fin. affairs; exec. v.p. bus. affairs CBS Entertainment, exec. v.p. CBS Prodns. CBS, 1997—98, pres. CBS Entertainment, 1998—; mem. bd. of dir. ThirdAge Media, 2000—. Office: CBS Entertainment 7800 Beverly Blvd Los Angeles CA 90036

TELLEM, SUSAN MARY, public relations executive; b. N.Y.C, May 23, 1945; d. John F. and Rita C. (Lietz) Cain; m. Marshall R.B.. Thompson; children: Tori, John, Daniel. BS, Mt. St. Mary's Coll., L.A., 1967. Cert. pub. health nurse; RN. Pres. Tellem Pub. Rels. Agy., Marina del Rey, Calif., 1977-80, Rowland Grody Tellem, L.A., 1980-90; chmn. The Rowland Co., L.A., 1990—; pres., CEO Tellem, Inc., L.A., 1992-93. Instr. UCLA Extension, 1983-97; adj. prof. Pepperdine U., 1999—; speaker numerous seminars and confs. on pub. rels. Editor: Sports Medicine for the '80's, Sports Medicine Digest, 1982-84. Bd. dirs. Marymount High Sch., 1984-87, pres., 1984-86; bd. dirs. L.A. Police Dept. Booster Assn., 1984-87; mem. Cath. Press Coun.; mem. pres.'s coun. Mus. Sci. and Industry. Mem. Am. Soc. Hosp. Mktg. and Pub. Rels., Healthcare Mktg. and Pub. Rels. Assn., Pub. Rels. Soc. Am. (bd. dirs. 1994—), L.A. Counselors, PETA, Am. Lung Assn. (chair comm. com. L.A. chpt.) Soc. for Prevention of Cruelty to Animals (chair PetSet), Sports Club (L.A.). Roman Catholic. Avocations: reading, tennis, aerobic dance. Office: 23852 Pacific Coast Hwy # 928 Malibu CA 90265-4879 Fax: 310-589-6101.

TELLER, SUSAN ELAINE, lawyer; b. San Diego, Calif., May 27, 1953; d. Jack and Joan (Mayer) T.; m. Donald F. Austin, July 6, 1980; children: Greg Austin, Cary Austin, Jack Austin. BA, Calif. State U., Sonoma, 1975; JD, Hastings Coll. of Law, 1979. Bar: Calif. 1980, Oreg. 1994, Wash. 1994. Assoc. Shapiro and Thorn, San Francisco, 1981-83; ptnr. Silverman and Teller, Alameda, Calif., 1983-93; assoc. Gevurtz, Menashe, et. al., Portland, Oreg., 1993-95; ptnr. Demary & Teller, Portland, 1995—; pvt. practice. Bd. dirs. Bus. and Profl. Women, Alameda; pres. PTA, Alameda. Named Woman of the Yr. Bus. Owner, Alameda Bus. and Profl. Women, 1988. Mem. Soroptimist Internat., AAUW, Oreg. Women's Lawyers, Queen's Bench, Soroptimist Internat. (bd. dirs. 1989). Office: 1123 SW Yamhill St Portland OR 97205-2106

TELLEZ, CORA, healthcare company executive; BA, Mills Coll.; MPA, Calif. State U. Various exec. positions to v.p., regional mgr. Hawaii Region Kaiser Found. Health Plan, 1978-94; sr. v.p., regional CEO Blue Shield, Calif., 1994-97; pres., chairwoman Prudential Health Care Plan of Calif., Inc., 1997-98; pres. CEO Health Net Foundation Health Systems, Inc., 1998—. Bd. mem. Golden State Bancorp Ince., Inst. Med. Quality, Calif. Assn. Health Plans, Holy Names Coll., Asian Cmty. Mental Health Svcs., Inst. for the Future. Mem. Phi Beta Kappa. Office: Health Net 21600 Oxnard St Ste 2000 Woodland Hills CA 91367-4969

TELLIER, JEN EMILY, psychologist, educator; b. Denver, Dec. 6, 1949; d. Stanley Edward and Patricia Susan Tellier; m. Paul Mark Sullivan, Jr., June 24, 1972 (div. 1986); m. George Michael Van Treeck, Dec. 24, 1992. BA, Colo. Women's Coll., 1972; EdM, Cambridge Coll., 1990; D in Psychology, Wright Inst., 1998. Cert. clin. psychologist Calif. Co-pres. ATA Assocs., Medway, Mass., 1988—90; rsch. coord. Taunton (Mass.) State Hosp., 1990—92; rsch. asst. U. Calif. San Francisco/San Francisco Gen. Hosp., 1993—95; neuropsychologist John Muir Med. Ctr., Walnut Creek, Calif., 1997—, Rehab. Without Walls, San Jose, Calif., 2000—. Adj. prof. Wright Inst., Berkeley, Calif., 2000—02, clin. supr., 2000—02; dir. clin. tng., prof. Argosy U., Point Richmond, Calif., 2002—; supr., cons. Family Mosaic, San Francisco, 2000—; cons. Probation Dept., San Francisco, 2001—; presenter Women's Health Ctr., Walnut Creek, Calif., 2001—, ARC, Alameda, Calif., 2003. Postdoctoral fellow, Wright Inst., 1998—2000, Kaiser Found. Rehab., 1999—2000. Mem.: APA (pres. 2001—02), Alameda County Psychol. Assn., Nat. Coun. for Schs. Profl. Psychology. Avocation: travel. Office: Argosy Univ 999-A Canal Blvd Point Richmond CA

TELNAES, ANN, cartoonist; b. Stockholm, 1960; m. David Lloyd. BFA, Calif. Inst. Arts. Animator and layout designer for various animation studios in London, L.A., Taiwan and N.Y.C., Warner Bros., Walt Disney Imagineering; editorial cartoonist. Bd. dirs. Cartoonists Rights Network. Named Best Cartoonist, Population Inst. XVIIth Global Media awards, 1996, Best Editl. Cartoonist, 6th Ann. Environ. Media Awards, 1996; recipient Nat. Headliner award for Editl. Cartoons, 1997, Pulitzer prize, 2001, Berryman award, Nat. Press. Found., 2003. Mem.: Assn. Am. Editl. Cartoonists (past v.p.).

TEMA-LYN, LAURIE, management consultant; b. Bklyn., Mar. 25, 1951; d. Morton and Jeanne (Lite) Carlin. BA, Bklyn. Coll., 1972. Mgmt. supr. Rapp & Collins, Inc., N.Y.C., 1972-78, v.p., 1978-80; assoc. Synectics, Cambridge, Mass., 1980-83; founder, gen. ptnr. IdeaScope Assocs., Cambridge, 1983-95; prin. Practical Imagination Enterprises, Carlisle, Mass., 1995—. Presenter European Conf. on Innovation and Creativity, 1987, 94. Performer: VOICES Chorale; contbr. articles to profl. jours. Bd. dirs. Arica Inst., N.Y.C., 1979-80; pres. bd. dirs. Savoyand Light Opera Co.; bd. mem., performer Voices Chorale. Mem. Creative Problem Solving Inst. (presenter, leader), Am. Mktg. Assn., Direct Mktg. Assn. (presenter), Product Devel. Mgmt. Assn., Creative Edn. Found., New Eng. Bus. Assn. for Social Responsibility, Qualitative Rsch. Cons. Assn., Boston Womens Network, Mgmt. Roundtable, Sharing a New Song. Office: Practical Imagination Enterprises 18 Losey Rd Ringoes NJ 08551-1206 E-mail: laurie@practical-imagination.com

TEMELKOFF, VONDA LEE, counselor, therapist; b. Sharon, Pa., July 12, 1937; d. Edward Hopkins and Alberta; m. Thomas B. Temelkoff, Nov. 10, 1956; children: Linda Temelkoff Schuller, Thomas C., Timothy B., Todd A. BS in Edn., Youngstown State U., 1970, MS in Edn., 1986; postgrad., Kent State U., 1981, 90, 92, Akron State U., 1981, Mt. St. Joseph, Cin., 1987, Bowling Green State U., 1989, Ashland Coll., 1990, Drake U., 1990. Cert. sch. counselor, Ohio tchr., Ohio; nat. bd. cert. counselor; nat. bd. cert. sch. counselor; lic. profl. counselor, Ohio; diplomate Am. Psychotherapy Assn. Tchr. elem. Woodside Elem. Sch., Austintown, Ohio, 1971-84; tchr. Am. history Austintown Middle Sch., 1984-85; tchr. math. and sci. Frank Ohl Middle Sch., Austintown, 1986-87; guidance counselor five elem. schs. Austintown, 1987-99; children's therapist Regional Assocs. in Counseling, Canfield, Ohio, 1987-91; child adolescent and family counselor Ctr. for Family Studies, 1999—. Presenter, parent workshop coord., cons. elem. counseling; intern NEOUCOM Cancer rsch. Ctr., Rootstown, summer 1986. Writer, prodr. (video) It's Your Choice, 1986. Youngstown State U. scholar, 1985-86, Jennings scholar, 1993-94; named Educator of Yr. Austintown, 1991. Mem. AAUW (bd. dirs. 1987, program v.p. 1988), ACA, Ohio Assn. for Counseling and Devel., Internat. Reading Assn. (bd. dirs. membership com. 1989), Friends of Am. Art, Chi Sigma Iota, Delta Kappa Gamma Soc., Phi Delta Kappa. Republican. Episcopalian. Avocations: swimming, golf, reading. E-mail: tomvon235@aol.com.

TEMIN, DAVIA B. marketing executive; b. Cleve., June 5, 1952; d. J.T. and Sylvia (Black) T.; m. Walter T. Kicinski, Aug. 10, 1991. BA, Swarthmore Pa./Coll., 1974; MA, Columbia U., 1976. Cmty. svcs. specialist Commonwealth Mass., Boston, 1975; editor-in-chief, founder Hermes mag. Columbia U. Bus. Sch., N.Y.C., 1976-79, dir. publ. affairs, 1979-83; v.p., dir. mktg. Citicorp Global Investment Bank, N.Y.C., 1983-86; v.p., dir. corp. mktg. Scudder, Stevens & Clark, N.Y.C., 1986-89; pres. The Temin Group, N.Y.C., 1989-90; v.p., dir. mktg. Schroder Wertheim & Co., Inc., N.Y.C., 1990-96; corp. v.p., head corp. mktg. GE Capital, N.Y.C., 1996-98; pres. Temin and Co., Inc., N.Y.C., 1998—. Exec. prodr. The Night & The Music Prodns., 1994—; bd. dirs. Soma Found.; chmn., bd. dirs. Mark Taylor Dance Co.; advisor to pres. Swarthmore Coll., 1994—, trustee, 1995—99, chair long range planning task force on ednl. leadership and visibility, devel. com., 1995—; bd. advisors Knight-Bagelot Fellowship Journalism Sch. Columbia U., 1995—; pres. bd. dirs., exec. com. Pub. Rels. Soc., N.Y.; bd. advisors Office.com, 2000—; trustee The Women's Leadership Fund; bd. dirs. The White House Project, Women's E-News; adv. bd. Goldman Sachs Investment Mgmt. Fin. Rsch. Initiative, Breakthrough TV. Chair Women's Counseling Project, 1978-81, Beth Cachet Dance Co., 1980-90; bd. trustees The Elaine Kaufman Cultural Ctr., 2000—. Recipient Meritorious Svc. award Commonwealth of Mass., 1976. Mem. Fgn. Policy Assn., Fin. Women's Assn., Women Pres.'s Orgn., Nat. Investor Rels. Inst., Women Inc., Nat. Arts Club, Strategic Adv. Bd., Devel. Com., Comm. Com., Columbia Bus. Sch. Club, Swarthmore Club, Princeton Club. Home: 530 E 90th St Apt 5K New York NY 10128-7860 Office: Temin and Co Inc Ste 1700 136 E 57th St New York NY 10022-2707

TEMME, MARCIA E. See HARDCASTLE, MARCIA E.

TEMPEL, JEAN CURTIN, venture capitalist; b. Hartford, Conn., Mar. 23, 1943; d. John J. and Sally (Miller) Curtin Jr.; m. Louis J. Tempel, Nov. 23, 1968 (div. 1978); m. Peter A. Wilson, May 10, 1980. BA in Math., Conn. Coll., 1965; MS in Computer Sci., Rensselaer Poly. Inst., 1972; advanced mgmt. program cert., Harvard U., 1979. Various sr. mgmt. positions Conn. Bank and Trust Co., 1965-80; mgr. strategic planning and mktg. Bank New Eng., 1980-82; sr. v.p., mgr. of custody The Boston Co., 1983, pres. Boston Safe Clearing Corp., 1984-90, exec. v.p., chief ops., info. officer, 1985, exec. v.p., COO, 1988-90; prin. Tempel Ptnrs. Inc., Boston, 1991; pres., COO Safeguard Scientifics Inc., Wayne, 1992-93, bd. dirs.; gen. ptnr. TL Ventures LP, Boston, 1994-96, spl. ltd. ptnr., 1997-99; founder, mng. ptnr. First Light Capital Inc., 2000—. Bd. dirs. Cambridge (Mass.) Tech. Ptnrs., Cambridge, Mass., 1991-98, Centocor, Malvern, Pa., Sonesta Internat. Hotels, Inc., Boston; trustee Scudder Funds, Boston, Northeastern U., Conn. Coll. Trustee Northeastern U., Conn. Coll. Mem. Internat. Women's Forum (dir.). Avocations: skiing, bicycling, sailing. Office: First Light Capital Inc 60 State St Fl 11 Boston MA 02109

TEMPERATO, SUSAN, mental health counselor, clinical supervisor; b. Buffalo, N.Y., Mar. 14, 1948; d. Anthony F. and Rose M. (Iraci) T. BA in Psychology, Daemen Coll. (Rosary Hill Coll.), Buffalo, N.Y., 1971; MS in Counselor Edn., Canisius Coll., Buffalo, 1985. Cert. clin. mental health counselor, nat. counselor, approved clin. supr., hypnotherapist. Tchr. Psychology, Sociology Mount St. Joseph Academy, Buffalo, 1970-71; mgmt. trainee Adam, Meldrum & Anderson, Buffalo, 1971-72; child care social worker Tiny Tot Child Devel. Ctr., Buffalo, 1972-83; supportive advocate for rape and sexual assault Suicide Prevention and Crisis Svcs., Buffalo, 1985-87, emergency admissions designee, 1985-87; program dir., clin. mental health counselor Horizon Health Svcs.-Hertel Elmwood Clinic, Buffalo, 1987—. Part time pvt. practice, 1989—; mental health del. to People's Rep. of China People to People Citizen Amb. Program, 1994. V.p. N.Y. State Mental Health Counselors Assn., 1987-89. Mem. Am. Counselor's Assn., Am. Mental Health Counselors Assn. (nat. membership chair 1991-92, Profl. Svc. award 1992), N.Y. State Assn. for Counseling and Devel., N.Y. State Mental Health Counselors Assn. Avocations: music, reading. Office: 699 Hertel Ave Ste 350 Buffalo NY 14207-2341

TEMPLETON, ANN, artist, educator; b. Houston, July 2, 1936; d. Lawrence L. and Marie L. (Bergeron) St. Pe'; m. James D. Templeton, Nov. 19, 1955; children: Pamela A., Donna M., James D. II, Donald L. Student, Massey Bus. Coll. Sec. A.M. Lockett Inc., Houston; owner Studio I and Gallery II, Houston; self-employed artist, instr. Ann Templeton Arts Inc., Houston, Ruidoso Downs, N.Mex. Instr. workshops and seminars, 1983—; juror at numerous art shows; instr. Okla. Christian Coll., Norman, 1997, Grayson County Coll., Tex., 1986, Jackson Jr. Coll., Tenn., 1983, 86, Lufkin Jr. Coll., Tex., 1986, San Juan Coll., Farmington, N.Mex., 1988, 90, 92, Ea. N.Mex. U., Ruidoso, 1994; artist-in-residence Fairmont (W.Va.) State Coll., 1998; represented by Brazier Fine Arts, Richmond, Va., Mahon Fine Arts, Ruidoso, Total Arts Gallery, Taos, N.Mex., Riverbend Gallery, Marble Falls, Tex., Rich Designs, Colorado Springs, Colo., Rice Gallery, Denver. Exhibited in group shows at Colony Show, Ruidoso, 1990-91, Tex. Arts Festival, Lubbock, 1990, 96, N.Mex. State Arts Fair, 1990-91, Knickerbocker N.Y., 1990, Mus. of the Horse, Ruidoso, 1992-95, 97, Shasta County Western Invitational, 1993, Tres Amigoes, Ruidoso, 1993-97, N.Mex. State Capitol, 1994, Roby Mills Exhbn., Colorado Springs, Colo., 1995, Permian Basin Art Inst., Odessa, Tex., 1995-96, Lafayette Art Assn., 1996, N.Mex. Pastel Soc., 1996, N.W. Pastel Soc., Washington, 1996, Pratt Gallery, San Diego, 1996, 98-99, Bardean Gallery, Albuquerque, 1997-98, Allied Artists Am., 1997, Brazier Fine Arts, Richmond, Va., 1998, Carlsbad (N.Mex.) Mus., 1998, Fairmont State Coll., W.Va., 1998, Heart Inst., Magnolia, Ark., 1998, Quinlan Art Ctr., Gainsville, Ga., 1999; represented in permanent collections at San Juan C.C., Farmington, N.Mex., Brownsville (Tex.) Art Mus., Hill Country Arts Found., Ingram, Tex., Coupeville (Wash.) Arts Ctr., Ellen Noe'l Art inst. of Permian Basin, Odessa, Carlsbad Art Mus., also corp. and pvt. collections. Recipient Best and Brightest award Scottsdale Artists Sch., 1989, awards N.Mex. Art League, 1993, Franklin Sq., N.C., Merit award J.R. Mooney Debut, 1994, Harbor County competition, 1995, Grumbacher Gold medal Lafayette Art Assn., 1996, 2d pl. award Mus. of the Horse, 1997, Slide Registry award Internat. Assn. Pastel Socs., 1998, 2d pl. award EuroFare Internat. Art Competition. others. Mem. N.Mex. Art Guild (life, hon.), Gulf Coast Art Guild (pres.), Pasadena Gulf Coast Art Soc. (hon., past pres.), Women in Arts, N.Mex. State Arts Assn., N.Mex. Art League (hon., award 1993), Oil Painters Am. (assoc.), Allied Artists Am. (assoc.), Pastel Soc. Am. (signature), Knickerbocker Artists USA (signature), Kans. Soc. Oil Painters (signature, award 1987). Roman Catholic. Avocations: music, books. Home: PO Box 651 Ruidoso Downs NM 88346-0651

TEMPLETON, FIONA, performance artist, writer, director; Performances include: L'Ile, 2003, Recognition, 1996, She Held Her Peace: 'Twas Strange!, 1994, Realities/Metamorphosis, 1992, Articulate Architecture, 1992, Be Our Guest, 1992, Where on Earth, 1990, Delirium of Interpretations, 1990, 91, You-The City, 1988—, Strange to Relate, 1989, Experiments in the Destruction of Time, 1983, Thought/Death, 1980, Defense, 1982, Cupid and Psyche, 1981, Out of My Way, 1988, A/Version, 1985, Against Agreement, 1981-82, Under Paper Spells, 1981-82, The Seven Deadly Jealousies, 1981-82, There Was Absent Achilles, 1981-82, The Hypothetical Third Person, 1987, Out of the Mouths, 1984, The New Three-Act Piece, 1983; co-founder, Theatre of Mistakes, London, 1975; author: Elements of Performance Art, 1976, London, 1984, You-The City, 1990, Cells of Release, 1997, Delirium of Interpretations, 2003; co-editor: Shattered Anatomies, 1995. Home: 100 Saint Marks Pl Apt 7 New York NY 10009-5822

TEMPLETON, HILDA B. psychiatrist, educator; BA in Biology, Rutgers U., Newark, 1962, MS in Biol. Scis., 1965; MD, U. Medicine and Dentistry N.J., 1978. Diplomate Am. Bd. Psychiatry and Neurology. Tchg. asst. in physiology Rutgers U., 1963-65; field dir. state of La. Med. Com. for Human Rights, 1965; dir. health and welfare The Urban League of Essex County, N.J., 1965-67; rsch. asst. dept. anatomy U. Medicine and Dentistry N.J., 1970-71; tchr. Ctrl. Mid. Sch., Orange, N.J., 1971-74; intern N.J. Med. Sch., 1978-79; resident Med. Sch. Rutgers U., 1978—81, chief resident Med. Sch., 1981; sr. resident Princeton (N.J.) Med. Ctr., 1982; pvt. practice Livingston, 1982—; clin. asst. prof. psychiatry and behavioral medicine N.Y. Coll. Osteo. Medicine, 1998—2001. Attending physician dept. psychiatry, dept. ob-gyn. St. Barnabas Med. Ctr., Livingston, 1982—, chair dept. psychiatry, 1997-2000, clin. chief dept. psychiatry, 1986-90, 91-93, 95-97, assoc. clin. chief dept. psychiatry, 1985-86, acting chair dept. psychiatry, 1986-87, mem. various hosp. coms.; clin. instr. dept. psychiatry U. Medicine and Dentistry of N.J., 1987-97; cons. Kessler Inst. for Rehab., 1982-91, Cmty. Psychiat. Inst., 1982-85, Jewish Vocat. Svcs., 1982-88; med. dir. interim out-patient program East Orange (N.J.) Gen. Hosp., 1982-83; mem. assoc. med. staff Fair Oaks Hosp., Summit, N.J., 1980-82; lectr. in field. Chair Newark Arts and Scis. Devel. Coun. Rutgers U. Found., 1995—98; mem. leadership com. Campaign for Cmty., Diversity and Ednl. Excellence, 1994—96; nat. bd. dirs. Down Syndrome Soc., 2001—; mem. med. adv. bd. No. N.J. chpt. Nat. Multiple Sclerosis Soc., 1982—86; mem. governing bd. The Cmty. Mental Health Ctr. of the Oranges, Maplewood and Millburn, 1983—84. Mem. AMA, Am. Soc. Psychosomatic Ob-Gyn., Am. Psychiat. Assn., Med. Women's Assn., Post Partum Internat., Depression After Delivery, N.J. Acad. Medicine, N.J. Psychiat. Assn., Tri-County Med. Soc., Essex County Med. Soc. (chmn. com. mental health 1998—). Office: 22 Old Short Hills Rd Ste 217 Livingston NJ 07039-5605 E-mail: hbtmdl@msn.com.

TEMPLETON, KAREN SCHROER, music educator; b. St. Paul, Oct. 18, 1954; d. James Richard and Nola Moring Schroer; m. Bradford Hopkins Templeton, July 30, 1988; 1 child, Douglas James. B in Music Edn., Wittenberg U., 1976; MusM, Ithaca (N.Y.) Coll., 1984. Permanent cert. music tchr. N.Y. Vocal music tchr. Pittsford (N.Y.) Ctrl. Schs., 1978—; dir. Eastman Children's Choir and Eastman Youth Chamber Chorale Eastman Sch. Music, U. Rochester, NY; music dept. leader Pittsford Mid. Sch. Dir. musical theater Pittsford Mid. Sch., Pittsford Summer Enrichment Inst., 1986—; site based instr. choral music methods Eastman Sch. Music, U. Rochester, dir. Music Horizons choir. Mem.: N.Y. State Sch. Music Assn. (past state mid. sch. chairperson, clinician music edn., guest condr. all-county music festival choruses), Music Educators' Nat. Conf., Am. Choral Dirs.' Assn., Parent Tchr. Student Assn. (life), Sigma Alpha Iota. Office: Pittsford Ctrl Schs Sutherland St Pittsford NY 14534 Personal E-mail: ktemplet@rochester.rr.com. E-mail: karen_templeton@pittsford.monroe.edu.

TENENBAUM, INEZ MOORE, superintendent of education; b. Hawkinsville, GA; m. Samuel J. Tenenbaum. Bsc, U. Ga., 1972, MEd, 1974; JD, U. S.C., 1986. Tchr. Elementary Sch.; dir. rsch. S.C. House Reps., 1977-83;

attorney Sinkler & Boye, P.A., 1986-92; supt. edn. S.C. Dept. Edn., Columbia, 1999—. Founder S.C. Ctr. Family Policy. Office: South Carolina Dept Edn Rutledge Bldg 1429 Senate St Columbia SC 29201-3730

TENER, CAROL JOAN, retired elementary school educator; b. Cleve., Feb. 10, 1935; d. Peter Paul and Mamie Christine (Dombrowski) Manusack; m. Dale Keith Tener, Feb. 13, 1958 (div. Aug. 1991); children: Dean Robert, Susan Dawn Tener Belair. Student, Cleve. Mus. Art, 1948-53, Cleve. Art Inst., 1953-54; BS in Edn. cum laude, Kent State U., 1957; MS in Supervision, Akron U., 1974; postgrad., Kent State U., 1964, 81, 88-90, Akron U., 1975, 79, John Carroll U., 1982, 83, 85-86, Ohio U., 1987, Baldwin Wallace Coll., 1989. Cert. permanent K-12 tchr., Ohio; cert. vol. counselor for Ohio sr. health ins. Ohio Dept. Ins. Stenographer Equitable Life Iowa, Cleve., 1953-54; tchr. elem. art Cuyahoga Falls (Ohio) Bd. Edn., 1957-58, 62-63, 65-68, tchr. jr. high sch., 1968-69; tchr. high sch. Brecksville (Ohio)-Broadview Heights Sch. Dist., 1969-94; chmn. dept. art Brecksville-Broadview Heights (Ohio) H.S., 1979-94, chmn. curriculum devel., 1982, 89; ret., 1994. Instr. for children Kent State U., 1956; advisor, prodr. cmty. svc. in art Brecksville Broadview Heights Bd. of Edn., 1969-94; former tchr. recreation and adult art edn. City of Cuyahoga Falls, 1967-68; com. mem. North Ctrl. evaluation com. Nordonia H.S., Nordonia City, Ohio, 1978, Solon H.S., Solon City, Ohio, 1989; chmn. north ctrl. evaluation com. Garfield Heights H.S., 1991; chair pilot program curriculum devel. com. in art/econs. Brecksville-Broadview Heights H.S., 1985-86, 86-87. Contbr. articles to newspapers, brochures, mags.; commd. artist for mural Brecksville City's Kids Quarters, 1994, Christopher Columbus/John Glen portraits in relief commemorating Columbus Day, 1961, Wooster (Ohio) Products Co.; editor Greater Cleve. chpt. Ohio Ret. Tchrs. Assn., 1998-2002; contbr. to Resources for You, 2003, Ohio Sr. Health Ins. Info. Program, Ohio Dept. Ins., 2001—. Chmn. Artmart Invitational Exhibit PTA, 1982-94; active Meals on Wheels program in Brecksville and Broadview Hts., 1995-98, Heart Disease collection, 1995, Stow-Glen Assisted Living Visitations, 1994-95, NCR Assisted Living transp. provision to hosps. and dr. in neighboring county; trustee, sec. Gettysburg Devel. Block Group Parma, 1995-96, Kids Quarters, 1994; Med Save fraud vol. Cuyahoga County Dept. Sr. and Adult Svcs., 2000-2002, spkrs. bur.; sr. health ins. info. program, cert. vol. counselor of OSHIIP under the Dept. of Insurance, Ohio Dept. Ins., 2001—. Recipient Ohio Coun. on Econ. Edn. award, 1985-86, award for significant svc. to cmty. Ret. and Sr. Vol. Program of USA, 1996, Svc. award Greater Cleve. Chpt./Ohio Ret. Tchrs. Assn., 1998, Outstanding Svc. award Sr. Medicare Patrol Projects, Cert. of Appreciation, U.S. Dept. Health and Human Svcs. Adminstrn. on Aging, 2002; Pres.'s scholar Kent State U., 1954-57; Resolution to thank a Med-Save Project Vol. signed by Cuyahoga County Commrs. Tim McCormack, pres., Jimmy Dimora, v.p., and Peter Lawson Jones, commr. Mem.: NAFE, ASCD, NEA (life), AAUW, S.W. Area Ret. Educators (co-chair 1996—98, program chair 1996—98, program coord. 1999—2000), Nat. Mus. Women in Arts, Cleve. Mus. Art, Acad. Econ. Edn., Brecksville Edn. Assn., Internat. Platform Assn., Nat. Art Edn. Assn., Ohio Ret. Tchrs. Assn. (life; registration chair 1997—98, pres.-elect Cleve. chpt. 1998, program chair 1998, interim editor 1998, circulation mgr. 1998—2002, chpt. pres. 1999, editor 1999—2002, trustee 2000, guest spkr. on newsletter writing and pub. 2000, nominating chair 2000—01, by-law chair 2000—01, Pub. Rels. awards 1999—2002), Phi Delta Kappa Pi. Roman Catholic. Avocations: photography, collecting books on architecture, painting. Home: 7301 Sagamore Rd Parma OH 44134-5732

TENER, LISA C. writer; b. N.Y.C., Apr. 2, 1963; d. Martin J. and Elizabeth C. (Berger) T. BS, Mass. Inst. Tech., 1984, MS, 1989. Fin. modeling analyst Pacific Gas & Electric, San Francisco, 1984-87; programming analyst Fidelity Investments, Boston, 1987-88; nat. acct. exec. AT&T, Boston, 1989-90; exec. dir. The Hospitality Program, Boston, 1990—2000; ednl. counselor MIT, Cambridge, 1991—; writer, creativity coach, 2003. Ednl. counselor Mass. Inst. Tech., Cambridge, 1991-96. Co-author: Good and Mad: Transform Anger Using Mid, Body, Soul and Humor, 2003. Mem. Women in Devel. (newsletter com. 1990-93, mentor 1994). Avocations: dance, writing, yoga. Home: 101 Waterway Rd Saunderstown RI 02874-3904

TEN EYCK, DOROTHEA FARISS, real estate agent; b. Pulaski County, Va., Dec. 2, 1923; d. Orel Cronk and Esther Mildred (Rexroad) Fariss; m. George Ten Eyck, Jan. 4, 1949 (dec.); m. John S. Kreeger, Aug. 27, 1965 (dec.); m. Robert L. Ten Eyck, Oct. 30, 1994. Student, Ind. U. Market rsch. Proctor & Gamble, Cin., 1944-47; sales real estate Lockwood Doeuch, Cin., 1963-65; sales Pines Door, Cin., 1991-93. Pres. women's com. Cin. Art Mus., mem. adv. com., docent emeritus; mem. Elder Indian Hill Ch. Independent. Presbyterian. Avocations: golf, skiing, gardening, travel, grandchildren. Home: 3032 Alpine Ter Cincinnati OH 45208-2925

TENHOUSE, GAYLE DENISE, secondary school educator; b. Oak Lawn, Illinois, Oct. 13, 1963; d. Henry Joesph and Janice Gaydos; m. Steven Loyd Tenhouse, June 25, 1988; children: Allison, Breanne. BS, Quincy U., Quincy, Ill., 1985; MS, Western Ill. U., Macomb, Ill., 1996. Band dir. Ctrl. Sch., Camp Point, Ill., 1985—94, Payson Sch., Ill., 1994—; supr. student teachers Western Ill. U., Macomb, Ill., 1998; adminstrv. asst. Payson Jr. and Sr. High Sch., Ill., 1998—; music tchr. Quincy Pk. Dist., Ill., 2003—. Treas. Miss. River Brass Band, Quincy, Ill., 1995—; trustee Am. Fedn. of Musicians, Local 265, Quincy, Ill., 2001—. Truancy com. Adams County Juvenile Justice Coun., Quincy, Ill., 2003—. Recipient Who's Who Among Am. Teachers, 2000, 2002, Tchr. of the Yr., CUSD Number Three, Camp Point, Ill., 1990, Recognition Award, Ill. Principals Assn., 1990—91. Mem.: Ill. Principals Assn., Assn. for Supervision Curriculum Devel., Music Educators Nat. Conf. Avocations: music, reading, family activities. Office: Payson Seymour High Sch 420 W Brainard Payson IL 62360 Personal E-mail: gtenhse@hotmail.com.

TENNANT, DIANE P. editor; m. Tom Tennant; 2 children. BA in English, Syracuse U.; MA in English Edn., SUNY, Binghamton. With Sarasota (Fla.) Herald-Tribune, 1982, part-time advt. clk., various positions features dept., asst. mng. editor, 1999—2002, interim mng. editor, 2002, mng. editor, 2003—. Office: Sarasota Herald-Tribune 801 S Tamiami Tr PO Box 1719 Sarasota FL 34230*

TENNEY, JANE MORRIS, real estate developer; d. Mendel Morris and Floreine Welch; m. Mark William Tenney, June 1, 1974; m. Daniel Marston Shepherd, Mar. 16, 1957 (div.); children: Daniel Vincent Shepherd, David Morris Shepherd. BS, U. Ky., 1962. Sales rep. IBM, South Bend, 1975—80; pres. Technivest, Inc., South Bend, Ind., 1980—88; mgr. bus. incubator Control Data, South Bend, 1984—89; owner, pres. Tenney Assocs., Inc, Niles, Mich., 1992—. Land developer Longmeadow Residential and Comml. Cmty., Niles, Mich., 1997—. Elected del. White Ho. Conf. of Small Bus., Washington, 1984—84. Recipient Demonstration Project on Watershed Devel. Design, Conservation Fund, 1997, Women of Yr., Four Flags C. of C., 2003. Mem.: Nat. Assn. of Realtor, Nat. Home Builders Assn. Office: Tenney Associates Inc 2110 Niles Buchanan Rd Niles MI 49120 E-mail: sales@longmeadow.info.

TENNEY, SARAH G. music educator; b. N.Y.C., Apr. 30, 1948; d. John Wool Griswold and Margaret Brett Tenney. BA, Bennington Coll., 1971; MusM, New Eng. Conservatory, 1976. Founder Spectrum Young Audiences Trio, Boston, 1976-80; marimba, percussion tchr. Rivers Music Sch., Weston, Mass., 1976-80, 85—, St. Ann's Sch., Bklyn., 1980-85; founder, dir. Marimba Magic, Weston, 1987—; tchr. improvisation Northeastern U., Boston, 1991-95. Percussionist on 6 Revel records; percussionist/timpanist in Christmas Revels, 1980—; presenter in field; concert performer Clarimba, 2002—. Composer: (composition/musical) Gamelon Dream, 1989, Mysterious Waltz, 1991, Whole Tone Dream, 1996, Adventures, 1999, Machines, 2000, Jaja Mani Dreams, 2001, Drum Circle, 2002, 3 Canons, 2003, Moving Music, 2004. Concert performer Concerts for Children, 1976-80, Cambridge World's Fair, 1997, 98, Clarimba Duo, 2002—. Recipient Am. Composers Forum grant. Mem. Music Tchrs. Nat. Assn. (conf. presenter 1991), Musicians Union, Music Educators Nat. Conf. (presenter ea. conf. 1992, 96), Percussive Arts Soc. (presenter internat. conv. 1989, 97), Orff Schulwerk Assn. (presenter nat. conf. 1996) presenter European Piano Tchrs. Assn., Internat. Conf., Budapest, 2000, Internat. Marimba Conf., Belgium, 1992. Office: The Rivers Music Sch 337 Winter St Weston MA 02493-1072 Office Phone: 781-235-6840.

TENNYSON, LOUISE H. artist; d. Floyd Tennyson and Maggie Marie Noell; m. B. G. Pierce (div. 1962); children: Eric, Gary; m. Floyd Q. Goble, Jr., Aug. 9, 1966. Student, El Camino Jr. Coll., Coll. of Dessert Harbor Jr. Coll. Bookkeeper various orgs., Calif., 1955—75; artist Richard Danskin Gallery, Palm Desert, Calif., 1983—. Avocations: dance, painting, photography, travel, animals. Home and Office: 6143 Mashie Rd Palm Springs CA 92264

TENOPIR, CAROL, information science educator; Grad. with highest honors, Whittier Coll., 1974; MS in Libr. Sci., Calif. State U., Fullerton, 1975; D in Libr. and Info. Scis., U. Ill., 1984. Supervisory libr. Cibbarelli and Assocs., Huntington Beach, Calif., 1976—77, v.p. ops., 1978—79; systems libr. U. Hawaii, Manoa, 1979—81; asst. prof. U. Hawaii Sch. Libr. and Info. Studies, Manoa, 1983—88, assoc. prof., 1988—93, prof., 1993—94; 1prof. U. Tenn. Sch. Info. Scis., Knoxville, 1994—. Grad. rsch. asst. Info. Retrieval Rsch. Lab. U. Ill., Urbana-Champaign, 1981—83; mem. grad. faculty U. Hawaii, Manoa, 1987—94, adj. prof. dept. comm., 1988—94, chair doctoral dissertation coms., mem. various coms.; adj. prof. coll. comm. U. Tenn., Knoxville, 1995—. Mem. editl. bd.: Online, 1986—; editor: Database Searching Series, Librs. Unltd., 1988—. Named one of Leaders of the Online Industry, Online Mag., 1987; recipient Doris Banks Publs. award, Calif. State U. Libr. Sci. Alumni Assn., 1983; fellow Univ. fellow, U. Ill., 1981—82, Josie B. Houchens fellow, 1982—83. Mem.: Assn. Records Mgrs. and Adminstrs., Spl. Librs. Assn., Hawaii Libr. Assn. (Disting. Libr. 1994), Am. Soc. Info. Scis. (Doctoral Dissertation Scholarship award 1983, Outstanding Info. Sci. Tchr. award 1993), Beta Phi Mu, Phi Kappa Phi. Office: U Tenn Sch Info Scis 804 Volunteer Blvd Knoxville TN 37996-0001

TENSER, BETH HILLARY, graphics designer, art director; b. Baltimore, Md., Nov. 11, 1968; d. David Elliott and Myrna Pruzon Tenser. BA, Adelphi U., 1991; MA, N.Y. Inst. Tech., 1993. Dir. art Island Art & Restoration, Elmont, NY, 1991—96, Bond Distbg. Co., Balt., 1997—. Pres. Adelphi's Resident Student Assn., Garden City, L.I., NY, 1989—91. Poster Competition, 1989 (Honorable Mention, 1989), Liver Let Die, 1991 (Honorable Mention, 1991). Recipient Academic Excellence in Leadership, Provosts, 1991. Mem.: The Babe Ruth Mus. Democrat. Avocations: singing, sports, travel, community advocate. Home: 2 High Stepper Ct #102 Baltimore MD 21208 Office Phone: 410-945-5600 139. Personal E-mail: btenser@bcpl.net.

TENUTA, LUIGIA, lawyer; b. Madison, Wis., June 4, 1954; d. Eugene P. and Nancy (Gardner) T. AB in Internat. Studies with honors, Miami U., Oxford, Ohio, 1976; JD, Capital U., 1981; postgrad., Pontifical Coll. Josephinum, 1987-88. Bar: Ohio 1981. With internat. mktg. dept. Dresser Industries, Columbus, Ohio, 1976-80, analyst strategic planning, 1980, mgr. internat bus. planning Stratford, Conn., 1981; pvt. practice law Columbus, 1981—. Former mem. devel. com. Miami U. Mem. Ohio Bar Assn., Columbus Bar Assn. Roman Catholic. Office: 6400 Riverside Dr Dublin OH 43017-5197

TEPERA, KAREN DENISE, real estate company executive; b. Cameron, Tex., Aug. 6, 1960; d. Raymond Tepera and Eileen Ann DiDominic; m. Tod Franklin; children: Kameron Frances Tepera Franklin, Logan Tod Tepera Franklin. Student, Tex. A&M U., 1978—82. Cert. property mgr. Inst. Real Estate Mgmt., 1994, apt. property supr. Nat. Apt. Assn., 1988. V.p. First Worthing, Dallas, 1985—94; exec. v.p. Westdale Asset Mgmt., Dallas, 1994—. Mem. bd. adjustments City of Dallas, 1995—97. Mem.: Apt. Assn. Greater Dallas (bd. dirs. 2001—03). Office: Westdale Asset Management 3300 Commerce Dallas TX 75226

TEPPER, ARIELLE, theater producer; d. Martin Tepper and Susan Levin. BFA, Syracuse U., 1996. Prodr.: (Broadway plays) Dance of the Vampires, Harlem Song, (off-Broadway plays) The Last Five Years (2 Drama Desk awards); (Broadway plays) A Class Act (5 Tony award nominations), James Joyce's The Dead (Tony award), Freak (2 Tony award nominations), Sandra Bernhard's I'm Still Here...Damn It, (off-Broadway plays) De La Guarda Villa Villa, Goodnight Children Everywhere (Olivier award for best play, 2000), Trainspotting; (films) 30 Days, 2000.

TEPPER, MARCY ELIZABETH, drug education director; b. Salt Lake City, Aug. 22, 1949; d. Warren Roswell and Rosemary Tepper. PhD, U. Ariz., Tucson, Ariz., 1983; MEd, U. Utah, Salt Lake City, Utah, 1972; Filosfia Y Letras, U. Valencia, Valencia, Spain, 1971; BA, San Francisco Coll. for Women, San Francisco, Calif., 1971. Cert. principal, mathematics, spanish tchr. 1990. Adjunct asst. prof. U. Arizona, Tucson, 1983—86; dir., owner 1.2.1 Tutoring, Tucson, 1984—90; counselor Teton County Sch. Dist., Jackson, Wyo., 1990—94; lectr. Ariz. State U., Tempe, Ariz., 1995—98; tchr. Santa Fe Public Schools, Santa Fe, 1998—99; coun. Safe Sch. Healthy Students Grant, Ethete, Wyo., 1999—2001; mid. sch. coord. Fremont County Schools #14, Ethete, Wyo., 2001—. Bd. mem. Ariz. Women Mathematics Sci., Tempe, 1997—98. Recipient Nat. Outdoor Leadership Sch. (NOLS) scholarship, 2003. Mem.: Interagy. Coord. Coalition (v.p. 2000—01, pres. 2001—03), Teton County Task Force (bd. 1992—94). Office: Wyoming Indian Sch 638 Blue Sky Highway Ethete WY 82520 Personal E-mail: marcyet@mail.trib.com. Business E-Mail: marcyt@fremont14.k12.wy.us.

TERADA, ALICE MASAE, retired elementary school educator; b. Hilo, Hawaii, Nov. 13, 1928; d. David Matsuo and Mitsuko (Sekido) Marutani; m. Harry T. Terada, Aug. 25, 1951; children: Suzanne T. Henderson, Keith Y., Lance S. Diploma, Queen's Hosp. Sch. Nursing, 1950; BS, We. Res. U., 1953; MEd, U. Hawaii, 1971. Cert. tchr., Hawaii. Registered nurse County Meml. Hosp., Hilo, Hawaii, 1950-51, U. Hosps., Cleve., 1952-53; lang. arts tchr. Dept. Edn., Honolulu, 1967-68; reading tchr. Reading Ctr., Honolulu, Hawaii, 1968-82; ret. Author: Under the Starfruit Tree, 1989, The Magic Crocodile, 1994. Mem. AAUW, Internat. Reading Assn., Zonta Club Internat., Zonta Club Honolulu (bd. dirs. 1996-97). Avocations: art, art history, porcelain antiques, yoga, swimming.

TERBORG-PENN, ROSALYN MARIAN, historian, educator; b. Bklyn., Oct. 22, 1941; d. Jacques Arnold Sr. and Jeanne (Van Horn) Terborg; 1 dau., Jeanna Carolyn Terborg Penn. BA in History, Queens Coll. CUNY, 1963; MA in History, George Washington U., 1967; PhD in Afro-Am. History, Howard U., 1978. Daycare tchr. Friendship House Assn., Washington, 1964-66; program dir. Southwest House Assn., Washington, 1966-69; adj. prof. U. Md.-Balt. County, Catonsville, 1977-78, Howard C.C., Columbia, Md., 1970-74; prof. history Morgan State U., Balt., 1969—, project dir. oral history project, 1978-79, coord. grad. programs in history, 1986—. Project dir. Assn. Black Women Hist. Rsch. Conf., Washington, 1982-83. Author: (with Thomas Holt and Cassandra Smith-Parker) A Special Mission: the Story of Freedman's Hospital, 1862-1962, 1975, African American Women in the Struggle for the Vote, 1850-1920, 1998; editor: (with Sharon Harley) The Afro-American Woman: Struggles and Images, 1978, 81, 97, (with Darlene Clark Hine and Elsa Barkley Brown) Black Women in America: An Historical Encyclopedia, 1993, 94, (with Sharon Harley and Andrea Benton Rushing) Women in Africa, 1987, (with Andrea Benton Rushing) Women in Africa and the African Diaspora: A Reader, 1996, (with Janice Sumler-Edmond) Black Women's History at the Intersection of Knowledge and Power, 2000; history editor Feminist Studies, 1984-89; mem. editl. bd. Md. Hist. Mag., 1988-94. Founding mem. Howard County Commn. for Women. Ford Found. fellow, 1980-81, Smithsonian Instn. fellow, 1982, 94-95; Howard U. grad. fellow in history, 1973-74, recipient Rayford W. Logan Grad. Essay award Howard U., 1973, Letitia Woods Brown Meml. prize for best article, 1988, Anna Julia Cooper award for disting. scholarship Sage Women's Ednl. Press, 1993, Letitia Woods Brown Meml. Book prize, 1998, Disting. Black Marylander in Edn. award, Towson Univ., 2003. Mem. Assn. Black Women Historians (co-founder, 1st nat. dir. 1980-82, nat. treas. 1982-84, cert. outstanding achievement 1981, Lorraine A. Williams Leadership award 1998), Am. Hist. Assn. (mem. com. on women historians 1978-81, Joan Kelly Prize com. 1984-86, chair com. on women historians 1991-94), Orgn. Am. Historians (mem. black women's history project adv. com. 1980-81), Alpha Kappa Alpha (mem. Internat. Archives and Heritage com. 1994-96). Office: Morgan State U 1700 E Cold Spring Ln Baltimore MD 21251-0002

TERESI, CINDY, music educator; d. Merton Keith and Jodie (Hale) Prior; m. J. Christopher Teresi, July 25, 1986; children: Michelle Susanne, Joseph Anthony Teresi, II, Rachel Christine. BA, Calif. State U., Sacramento, 1984. Cert. Single Subject Tchg. Calif., 1985, Multiple Subject Tchg. Calif., 1990, Orff-Schulwerk Am. Orff-Schulwerk Assn., 1992. HS band and choir tchr. San Juan Unified Sch. Dist., Carmichael, Calif., 1985—86, elem. music specialist; dir. Music & Movement for Young Children, Fair Oaks, Calif., 1992—2004; adj. prof. of music Am. River Coll., Sacramento; elem. music tchr. Loomis Union Sch. Dist., 2003—. Musician: (orchestra player) Local cmty. theatre orgn. Mem.: Am. River Orff-Schulwerk Assn., Am. Orff-Schulwerk Assn., Calif. Music Educators Assn., Nat. Assn. of Music Educators, Sierra Nev. Wind Orch., Rep. Women-Federated. R-Consevative. Catholic. Avocations: travel, baking, playing music.

TERHAAR, JOYCE, editor; b. Minn. m. Geoff Long; 2 children. Grad. magna cum laude, U. St. Thomas, 1981. Reporter Herald, Grand Forks, ND; reporter, bus. editor Santa Rosa (Calif.) Press Dem., 1984—88; bus. reporter Sacramento Bee, 1988—91, asst. met. editor, 1991—93, city editor, 1993—99, mng. editor, 1999—. Office: Sacramento Bee 2100 Q St PO Box 15779 Sacramento CA 95852*

TERNBERG, JESSIE LAMOIN, pediatric surgeon; b. Corning, Calif., May 28, 1924; d. Eric G. and Alta M. (Jones) T. AB, Grinnell Coll., 1946, Sc.D. (hon.), 1970; PhD, U. Tex., 1950; MD, Washington U., St. Louis, 1953; Sc.D. (hon.), U. Mo., St. Louis, 1981. Diplomate: Am. Bd. Surgery. Asst. resident in surgery Barnes Hosp., St. Louis, 1954-57, resident in surgery, 1958-59; rsch. fellow Washington U. Sch. Medicine, 1957-58; practice medicine specializing in pediatric surgery St. Louis, 1966—; intern Boston City Hosp., 1963—64; instr., trainee in surgery Washington U., 1959-62, asst. prof. surgery, 1962-65, assoc. prof. surgery, prof., 1965-71, prof. surgery, 1971-96, chief divsn. pediatric surgery, 1972-90, prof. emeritus, 1996—; mem. staff Barnes Hosp., 1959—90; gen. surgeon in chief Children's Hosp. of St. Louis, 1974-90. Mem. staff Children's Hosp., dir. pediatric surgery, 1972-90. Contbr. numerous articles on pediatric surgery to profl. jours. Trustee Grinnell Coll., 1984—. Recipient Alumni award Grinnell Coll., 1966, Faculty/Alumni award Washington U. Sch. Medicine, 1991, 1st Aphrodite Jannopaulo Hofsommer award, 1993. Fellow AAAS; mem. SIOP, Am. Pediatric Surg. Assn., We. Surg. Assn. (2d v.p. 1984-85), St. Louis Med. Soc., Soc. Surgery of the Alimentary Tract, Am. Acad. Pediatrics, Soc. Pelvic Surgeons (v.p. 1991-92), Brit. Assn. Paediatric Surgeons, Assn. Women Surgeons (disting. mem. 1995), Mo. State Surg. Soc., St. Louis Surg. Soc. (pres. 1980-81), St. Louis Pediatric Soc., Soc. Surg. Oncology, Pediatric Oncology Group (chmn. surg. discipline 1983-96), St. Louis Childrens Hosp. Soc. (pres. 1979-80), Acad. Sci. St. Louis (Trustees award 2002), St. Louis Met. Med. Soc. (hon., councilor, trustee), Barnes Hosp. Soc., Phi Beta Kappa, Sigma Xi, Iota Sigma Pi, Alpha Omega Alpha. Office: St Louis Childrens Hosp 1 Childrens Pl Saint Louis MO 63110-1002 E-mail: ternbergj@msnotes.wustl.edu.

TERNOVITZ, RUTH, mathematics and computer educator; b. Podmokly, Czechoslovakia, 1947; came to U.S., 1959; d. Moses and Nellie (Farkas) T. BA in Psychology, Bklyn. Coll., 1967, MA in Edn., 1970, MA in English Lit., 1978; postgrad., CUNY, 1978-83. Elem. sch. tchr. Pub. Sch. 115, Bklyn., 1968-85; computer documenter Malam Inc., Jerusalem, 1986-88; computer tchr. Pub. Sch. 219, Bklyn., 1989-96; math. tchr. Pub. Sch. 104, Bklyn., 1996—. Jewish. Avocations: oil and watercolor painting, drawing, travel, photography. E-mail: rternovitz@aol.com.

TERNUS, MARSHA K. state supreme court justice; b. Vinton, Iowa, May 30, 1951; BA, U. Iowa, 1972; JD, Drake U., 1977. Bar: Iowa 1977, Ariz. 1984. With Bradshaw, Fowler, Proctor & Fairgrave, Des Moines, 1977—93; justice Iowa Supreme Ct., Des Moines, 1993—. Editor-in-chief: Drake Law Rev., 1976—77. Mem.: Polk County Bar Assn. (pres. 1984—85), Order of Coif, Phi Beta Kappa. Office: Iowa Supreme Ct Jud Br Bldg 1111 E Court Ave Des Moines IA 50319-0001*

TERPENING, VIRGINIA ANN, artist; b. Lewistown, Mo., July 17, 1917; d. Floyd Raymond and Bertha Edda (Rodifer) Shoup; m. Charles W. Terpening, July 5, 1951; 1 child by previous marriage, V'Ann Baltzelle Deatrick. Student, William Woods Coll., Fulton, Mo., 1936-37, Washington U. Sch. Fine Arts, St. Louis, 1937-40. Lectr. on art; jurist for selection of art for exhibits Labelle (Mo.) Centennial, 1972; chmn. Centennial Art Show, Lewistown, 1971, Bicentennial, 1976; dir. exhibit high sch. student for N.E. Mo. State U., 1974; supt. ann. art show Lewis County (Mo.) Fair, 1975-90. One-woman shows include Culver-Stockton Coll., Canton, Mo., 1956, Creative Gallery, N.Y.C., 1968, The Breakers, Palm Beach, Fla., 1976, others; group shows include Mo. Ann. Show, City Art Mus., St. Louis, 1956, 65, Madison Gallery, N.Y.C., 1960, Ligoa Duncan Gallery, N.Y.C., 1964, 78, Two Flags Festival of Art, Douglas, Ariz., 1975, 78-79, Internat. Art Exhibit, El Centro, Calif., 1977, 78, Salon des Nations, Paris, 1985, UN World Conf. of Women, Narobi, Kenya, 1985, William Woods Coll., Fulton, Mo., 1992-95, La Junta Coll. Art League Internat., 1992, 94, Coffret Musée, Paris, 1995; represented in permanent collection Nat. Mus. of Women in Art, 1990; executed Mississippi RiverBoat oil painting presented to Pres. Carter by Lewis County Dem. Com., Canton, 1979. Mem. Lewistown Bicentennial Hist. Soc.; charter mem. Canton Area Arts Coun. of N.E. Mo. Recipient Cert. of Merit Latham Found., 1960-63, Mo. Women's Festival of Art, 1974, Bertrand Russell Peace Found., 1973, Gold Medallion award Two flags Festival of Art, 1975, Safeco purchase award El Centro (Calif.) Internat. Art Exhibit, 1977, 1st Pl. award LaJunta (Colo.) Fine Arts League, 1981, diploma Univ. Delle Arti, Parma, Italy, 1981, Purchase award Two Flags Art Festival, 1981, award Assn. Conservation and Mo. Dept. Conservation Art Exhibit, 1982, Purchase award Canton Area Arts Coun., 1988, Colorado Springs Art Festival, 1989; paintings selected for Competition '84 Guide by Nat. Art Appreciation Soc., 1984, 1st Pl. award New Orleans Internat. Art Exhibit, 1984, Two Flags Festival of Art, 1986, Sunflower Judges award Harlin Mus., West Plains, Mo., 1994, Key to City, Lifetime award, 1998; named artist laureate, Nepenthe Mondi Soc., 1984. Mem. Artist Equity Assn., Internat. Soc. Artists, Internat. Platform Assn., Nat. Mus. Women in Art (charter), Animal Protection Inst. Mem. Christian Ch. (Disciples Of Christ). Address: 105 S Vine St PO Box 117 Lewistown MO 63452-0117

TERR, LENORE CAGEN, psychiatrist, writer; b. N.Y.C., Mar. 27, 1936; d. Samuel Lawrence and Esther (Hirsch) Cagen; m. Abba I. Terr; children: David, Julia. AB magna cum laude, Case Western Res. U., 1957; MD with honors, U. Mich., 1961. Diplomate Am. Bd. Psychiatry and Neurology, Subspecialty Bd. Child and Adolescent Psychiatry. Intern U. Mich. Med. Ctr., Ann Arbor, 1961-62; resident Neuropsychiat. Inst. U. Mich., Ann Arbor, 1962-64, fellow Children's Psychiat. Hosp., 1964-66; from instr. to asst. prof. Case Western Res. U. Med. Sch., Cleve., 1966-71; pvt. practice Terr Med. Corp., San Francisco, 1971—; from asst. clin. prof. to clin. prof. psychiatry Sch. Medicine U. Calif., San Francisco, 1971—. Lectr. law, psychiatry U. Calif., Berkeley, 1971—90, Davis, 1974—88; dir. Am. Bd. Psychiatry and Neurology, 1988—96, chair psychiatry coun., 1996. Author: Too Scared to Cry, 1990, Unchained Memories, 1994, Beyond Love and Work, 1999; contbr. articles to profl. jours.; exhibited works in art show at Canessa Gallery, San Francisco, 2002. Named to Cleveland Heights H.S. Disting Alumni Hall of Fame, 2003; recipient Career Tchr. award, NIMH, 1967—69, Child Advocacy award, APA, 1994; grantee, William T. Grant Found., 1986—87, Leon Lowenstein Found., 2002; scholar-in-residence, Rockefeller Found., Italy, 1981, 1988, project grantee, Rosenberg Found., 1977. Fellow: Am. Acad. Child and Adolescent Psychiatry (coun. 1984—87), Am. Coll. Psychiatrists (program chair 1991—92, Bowis award 1993), Am. Psychiat. Assn. (Child Psychiatry Rsch. award 1984, Clin. Rsch. award 1987, Marmor Sci. award 2002); mem.: Phi Bet Kappa, Alpha Omega Alpha. Avocations: piano, walking, travel, gardening, needlepoint. Office: Terr Med Corp 450 Sutter St Rm 2534 San Francisco CA 94108-4204 Office Phone: 415-433-7800.

TERRANOVA, ELIZABETH (ELISA) JO, artist; b. Monrovia, Liberia, Jan. 15, 1954; (parents Am. citizens); d. Joseph and Joy Alice Terranova; life ptnr. Mark Gerard Domzalski, Oct. 19, 1996; life ptnr. Russell James Sether (div.); m. John Kenneth Mayes (div.). BFA in Art Edn., Ariz. State U., Tempe, 1987, MFA in Painting, 1993. Fine artist, 1980—; founder / pres. Sacred Heart Studios, Folsom, Calif., 1995—. Art film maker Twenty-three Degrees, Sacramento, 2001—; lectr. / guest spkr. colls., univs., fine art galleries. Short animated film, Trompe L'oeil, exhibitions include Orlando (Fla.) Mus. Art, Florence (Italy) Internat. Biennale, 2003, one-woman shows include U. Club Gallery, Winter Park, Fla., Women Image Now Gallery, Ariz. State U., Tempe, 1986, 1987, Harry Wood Gallery, Ariz. State U., Tempe, 1989, Student Union Art Gallery, San Francisco State U., 1993, James Kaneko Galler, Am. River Coll., Sacramento, 1994, Sheppard Fine Arts Gallery, U. Nev., Reno, Ridley Gallery, Sierra Coll., Rocklin, Calif., 2001; artist (invitational group shows) Ctr. Contemporary Art, Sacramento, (internat. juried group shows) Sacramento Fine Arts Ctr. (Excellence award, Merit award), (group shows) Crest Theater, Sacramento, 2002, (video group shows) Gallery Horse Cow, (group shows) Fortezza da Basso, Florence, 2003, Toyroom Gallery, Sacramento, 2004. Phelps Dodge scholar, 1990—91. Achievements include In collaberation with the United Nations and Italy, I have been nominated and accepted as one of the US representatives to display my artwork at the Florence International Biennale 2003, Italy; I was selected to participate in a juried exhibition at the Orlando Museum of art. The exhibit traveled to the Rotunda Building at the US capitol in Washington, D.C, development of my art serves as a visual diary that describes the human condition as told from the perspective of a quadriplegic. Like the works of Frida Kahlo and The Diary of Anne Frank; I hope to inspire this message that great things can be achieved against all odds. Avocations: art history, digital animation, computer animation, gardening. Office: Sacred Heart Studios Folsom CA [illegible]

TERRAS, AUDREY ANNE, mathematics educator; b. Washington, Sept. 10, 1942; d. Stephen Decatur and Maude Mae Bowdoin. BS with high honors in Math., U. Md., 1964; MA, Yale U., 1966, PhD, 1970. Instr. U. Ill., Urbana, 1968-70; asst. prof. U. P.R., Mayaguez, 1970-71, Bklyn. Coll., CUNY, 1971-72; asst. prof. math. U. Calif.-San Diego, La Jolla, 1972-76, assoc. prof., 1976-83, prof., 1983—. Prin. investigator NSF, 1974-88; vis. positions U. Aachen, Germany, 1998, Tsuda Coll., Tokyo, 1999, MIT, fall 1977, 83, U. Bonn (W.Ger.), spring 1977, Inst. Mittag-Leffler, Stockholm, winter, 1978, Inst. Advanced Study, spring 1984, Math. Scis. Rsch. Inst., Berkeley, Calif., winter 1992, spring 1995, CRM, U. Montreal, 1999, others; dir. West Coast Number Theory Conf., U. Calif.-San Diego, 1976, AMS joint summer rsch. conf., 1984; lectr. in field. Author: Harmonic Analysis on Symmetric Spaces and Applications, Vol. 1, 1985, Vol. II, 1988, Fourier Analysis on Finite Groups and Applications, 1999; editor: The Selberg Trace Formula and Related Topics, 1986; contbr. chapters to books, articles to profl. jours. Woodrow Wilson fellow, 1964, NSF fellow, 1964-68; NSF grantee Summer Inst. in Number Theory, Ann Arbor, Mich., 1973. Fellow: AAAS (nominating com. math. sect. project 2061); mem.: Assn. for Women in Sci., Assn. for Women in Math. (travel grants com. 1996), Soc. Indsl. and Applied Math., Math. Assn. Am. (program com. for nat. meeting 1988—90, chair joint program com. Am. Math. Soc. and Math. Assn. Am. 1991), Am. Math. Soc. (com. employment and ednl. policy com. on coms., coun., trans. editor, com. for the yr. 2000, western sect. program com., assoc. editor book revs. Bull., assoc. editor Notices). Achievements include research in harmonic analysis on symmetric spaces and number theory. Office: U Calif San Diego Dept Math La Jolla CA 92093 0112

TERRELL, ANN, artist, educator; b. Houston, June 9, 1942; d. Joseph Daniel Terrell and Albina Martha Kostohryz; m. Charles Gene Williams, Dec. 30, 1959 (div. Nov. 1965); 1 child, Lynn Ann Williams ; m. Arthur Louis Fernandez, Aug. 26, 1967 (div. Mar. 1975); 1 child, Jose Travis Fernandez. BA cum laude in Anthropology, Calif. State U. L.A., 2000. Copy editor Calif. State U., L.A., 1997—98; asst., guide L.A. County Mus. of Art, 1999—2001; substitute tchr. spl. edn. L.A. Unified Sch. Dist., 2001—; artist L.A., 1990—94. Recipient Calif. Goldmedal, Vocat. Indsl. Clubs Am. Skill Olympics, 1990. Mem.: Highland Park Heritage Trust, Friends of Arroyo Seco Libr., Golden Key Nat. Honor Soc., Phi Kappa Phi. Avocations: painting, genealogy. Home: 486 Museum Dr Los Angeles CA 90065 Office Phone: 323-223-3617.*

TERRELL, JANICE, language educator; b. Conway, Ark., Oct. 28, 1947; d. Cecil Ivan and Thelma Arlene Garrison; m. Frank Birdwell, Jr., Aug. 25, 1971 (div. Feb. 1981); m. Charles Henry Terrell, Apr. 1, 1983. BS in Edn., U. Ctrl. Ark., 1968; MA, U. Ark., 1970. Tchr. Arcadia Valley Pub. Sch., Ironton, Mo., 1970—71, Hampton (Va.) City Schs., 1971—81; bilingual tchr. Port Arthur (Tex.) Ind. Sch. Dist., 1981—2002; instr. Lamar State Coll., Port Arthur, 1992—. Sec. Port Arthur Tchrs. Assn., 1995, v.p., 96, v.p. membership, 1999—2002. Bd. dirs., sec. Port Arthur Little Theatre, 1996—2002, Tex. Artists Mus., Port Arthur, 2000—; organist First Ch. God. King Juan Carlos scholar, Madrid, 1992. Mem.: City Coun. PTA (2nd v.p. 2000—02), Soc. for Creative Anachronism (ct. baroness), Alpha Delta Kappa (chaplain 2001, historian 2001—02). Home: 4240 Dryden Rd Port Arthur TX 77642

TERRIS, LILLIAN DICK, psychologist, association executive; b. Blooomfield, N.J., May 5, 1914; d. Alexander Blaikie and Herminia (Doscher) Dick; m. Louis Long, Apr. 22, 1935 (dec. Sept. 1968); 1 son, Alexander Blaikie Long; m. Milton Terris, Feb. 6, 1971 (dec. Oct. 2002). BA, Barnard Coll., 1935; PhD, Columbia U., 1941. Diplomate Am. Bd. Examiners in Profl. Psychology. Instr. psychology Sarah Lawrence Coll., Bronxville, N.Y., 1937-40; jr. pers. tech. SSA, Washington, 1941; sr. pers. clk. OWI, N.Y.C., 1941-43; dir. profl. examination svc. Am. Pub. Health assn., N.Y.C., 1943-70; pres., 1970-79; pres. emeritus, 1979—. Assoc. editor: Jour. Pub. Health Policy, 1979—; contbr. articles to profl. jours. Recipient Nat. Environ. Health assn. award, 1976, Cert. Svc. award Bd. Preventive Medicine, 1979. Fellow Am. Psychol. Assn., Am. Coll. Hosp. Adminstrs. (hon.); mem. Am. Pub. Health Assn., N.Y. State Psychol. Assn., Phi Beta Kappa, Sigma Xi. Home: 1450 Post St 506 San Francisco CA 94109 Office: 475 Riverside Dr New York NY 10115-0122 E-mail: jphpterris@aol.com.

TERRIS, SUSAN, physician, cardiologist; b. Morristown, N.J., Sept. 5, 1944; d. Albert and Virginia Terris. BA in History, U. Chgo., 1967, PhD in Biochemistry, 1975, MD, 1976. Diplomate in internal medicine, endocrinology and metabolism, cardiovasc. disease Am. Bd. Internal Medicine. Resident in internal medicine Washington U., Barnes Hosp., St. Louis, 1976-78; fellow in endocrinology and metabolism U. Chgo., 1978-80, fellow cardiology, 1980-83, U. Mich., Ann Arbor, 1983-85, instr. cardiology, 1985-86; head cardiac catheterization lab., head cardiology Westland (Mich.) Med. Ctr., 1985. Contbr. articles to Jour. Biol. Chemistry, Am. Jour. Physiology, Am. Jour. Cardiology, Jour. Clin. Investigation, other profl. publs. Grantee Juvenile Diabetes Found., 1978-80, NIH, 1978-79. Mem. AAAS, Am. Heart Assn., N.Y. Acad. Sci. Achievements include rsch. demonstrating dependence of intracellular degradation of insulin upon its prior receptor-mediated uptake by liver; studies on the electrophysiologie effect of cathecholamimes on sheep Parkinje fibers and on the hemodynamic effects of various drugs on the human circulatory system.

TERRITO, MARY C. health facility administrator, oncologist, educator; BS in Biology, Wayne State U., 1965, MD, 1968. Intern/resident in internal medicine Parkland Hosp., Dallas, 1971-73; fellow in hematology/oncology Harbor-U. Calif., L.A., 1973-74, UCLA, 1974-75; rsch. assoc. Wadsworth VA Hosp., L.A., 1975-81; asst. prof. dept. medicine UCLA, 1975-81, assoc. prof., 1981-96, prof., 1996—, dir. bone marrow transplant program Ctr. Health Scis., 1981—. Contbr. articles to profl. jours. Office: UCLA Bone Marrow Transplantation Program Ctr 42-121 CHS 10833 Le Conte Ave Los Angeles CA 90095-3075

TERRY, BARBARA L. human services administrator; b. Cin., Mar. 17, 1955; d. Robert H. and Elizabeth (Addison) Akers; m. Dennis P. Terry. BA, Bowling Green State U., 1977; MS, Mich. State U., 1987. Registered social worker 1979, credentialed substance abuse counselor 1988. Program dir. Jackson-Hillsdale Mental Health, Jackson, Mich., 1977—84; program adminstr. Damar Homes, Indpls., 1984—85; exec. dir. Student Assistance Programs, Jackson, Mich., 1988—90; divsn. dir. Kent County Health Dept., Grand Rapids, Mich., 1990—97, dep. health dir., 1997—2001; v.p. Heart of West Mich. United Way, Grand Rapids, Mich., 2001—. Vol. mentor Grand Rapids Pub. Schs., 2001—. Recipient Profl. Svc. to Children award, Kent County Coun. for the Prevention of Child Abuse and Neglect, 1994, Outstanding Contbn. to Student Assistance award, South Ctrl. Mich. Substance Abuse Commn., 1990, Exceptional Svc. to Children award, Wood County Children's Services Assn., 1977. Mem.: Healthy Kent, Kent County Emergency Needs Task Force (Health Subcommittee Chair; Funding Chair 2000—01), Kent County Child & Family Coordinating Coun. (Executive Committee Member 1998—99). Avocations: travel, reading.

TERRY, DORIS D. music educator; b. Forrest City, Ark., Aug. 23, 1936; d. Samuel and Elizabeth Phillips; m. Ronald E. Terry; 5 children. BA, Adams State Coll., Alamosa, Colo., 1960, EdM, N. Tex. State U., Denton, 1970; postgrad. studies, Ga. Coll., Milledgeville, 1985; Honorary (hon.), Trinity Coll., Birmingham, Ala., 1985. Tchr. Mary Holmes Coll., West Point, Miss., Sims H.S., Holly Springs, Miss.; choral dir. LaVega H.S., Waco, Tex.; music tchr. Sheridan Middle Sch., Mpls.; choral dir. Southwest H.S., Macon, Ga.; dir. music Bibb County Schs, Macon, Ga. Mus. dir. Cherry Blossom Concert, Macon, Ga.; mem. Arts Alliance, Macon. Mem.: Ga. Music Educators (25 Yr. Svc. Plaque), Am. Choral Dirs. Assn., Music Educators Nat. Conf. Home: 1490 New Castle Dr Macon GA [illegible]

TERRY, ELIZABETH HAYS, needlepoint designer; b. Bryn Mawr, Pa., July 29, 1935; d. James Franklin and Mary Ellen (Carmichael) Hays; m. Charles L. Terry, III, Feb. 8, 1958; children: Elizabeth Harllee Carmichael Terry Moran, Charles L. IV. AB, Smith Coll., 1957. Asst. to profs. Harvard U., Cambridge, Mass., 1957-58; art tchr. Exeter (N.H.) Day Sch., 1968-72; asst. editor Phillips Exeter Acad. Alumni Quarterly, 1972-75, dir. alumni records, 1975-85; owner Elizabeth Terry, Needlepoint Design, Exeter, N.H., 1980—. Tchr. needlepoint Guild of Strawbery Banke, Portsmouth, N.H. Dir. for Town of Exeter-Save Our Shores, 1972. Mem. Smith Coll. Class of 1957 (class fund agt. 1972-77, alumnae fund com. 1977-80, class bequest chair 1982—, com. on deferred giving 1990—), N.H. Colonial Dames (pres. 1989-92, nat. historian 1992-94, nat. v.p. 1994-2000). Episcopalian. Avocations: tennis, needlepoint, historic preservation. Home and Office: 77 Brookside Dr Stratham NH 03885-2128 Office Phone: 603-772-8942. E-mail: ceterry@rcn.com.

TERRY, KAY ADELL, marketing executive; b. Portland, Oreg., July 11, 1939; d. Langdon Alcott and Emma Francis (Meyer) Howard; m. Frank F. Terry, Aug. 31, 1963 (div. Mar. 1988); 1 child, Kimberly Sue. CPC, CIPC. Office mgr. Merck Sharp & Dohme, Portland, 1959—63; asst. dir. admissions Seattle Pacific U., Seattle, 1963-66; owner United Personnel Svc., Seattle, 1966-86; pres., CEO Ram Force Cos., Seattle, 1986-91; pres. N.W. region Robert Half Internat., Seattle, 1991-93; pres., CEO Terry & Assocs., Seattle, 1993—; CEO Key Staff, LLC, 1996—2003. Bd. dirs. Ram Force Cos., Seattle Acctg. Force, Inc., Seattle, Office Force, Inc., Seattle, Data Force, Inc., Seattle. Contbr. articles to profl. jours. Vol. Spl. Olympics, Seattle. Named 16th Fastest Growing Co. in Wash. State, 1999, 2000; recipient Best Co. to Work for award, Wash. CEO mag., 1996—2000; fellow, Seattle Pacific U., 1989. Mem. Women Bus. Owners, Nat. Assn. Accts. (bd. dirs. 1985-87, Mem. Achievement award 1987, Disting. Svc. award 1987), Nat. Staffing Pers. Svcs. Assn. (vice-chmn. 1993), Wash. Athletic Club, Washington Software Assn., Nat. Tech. Svcs. Assn., Desert Falls Country Club, Columbia Tower Club. Republican. Avocations: travel, tennis, swimming, golf. E-mail: KTerry1010@aol.com., Kay@Keystaff.com.

TERRY, MELINDA LEE, elementary school educator; b. San Francisco, July 5, 1946; d. John Frederick Shaw and LeOta Louise Marpé; m. Ronald S. Terry, July 11, 1970 (div. 1983); children: Amber Melayne, Susannah Marpé. BA in Social Studies and Elem. Edn., San Jose State U., 1969; MA in Elem. Edn., U. Colo., 1986. Tchr. Montrose (Colo.) County Schs., 1969—70, Aurora (Colo.) Pub. Schs., 1983—97, Edmonds (Wash.) Sch. Dist., 1997—99, Everett (Wash.) Pub. Schs., 1999—. Home: 13504 48th Pl W Edmonds WA 98026-3415

TERRY, PAMELA MAYS, psychology educator; b. Macon, Ga., Oct. 20, 1949; d. Thomas Littleton and Nancy Valyne Smith M.; m. Stephen Wesley Terry, Feb. 4, 1984; 1 child, Valyne Kathryne. AB, U. Ga., 1971, MS, 1974, PhD, 1975. Rsch. psychologist U.S. Army Rsch. Inst., Fort Benning, Ga., 1976-92; asst. prof. psychology Gordon Coll., Barnesville, Ga., 1999—. Tech. cons. U.S. Army Infantry Sch., Ft. Benning, 1986-92, U.S. Army Basic Tng. Task Force, Ft. Benning, 1983-85; spl. equal employment opportunity officer Fort Benning, 1985. Mem. Forsyth Womens Club, 1996-98. Fellowship NSF, U. Ga., 1972-75. Mem. Am. Psychol. Soc., Ga. Sociol. Assn., Phi Beta Kappa, Sigma Xi, Phi Kappa Phi. Southern Baptist. Avocations: playing piano, genealogy. Home: 22 Brooklyn Ave Forsyth GA 31029 Office: Gordon Coll Divsn Bus and Social Sci 419 College Dr Barnesville GA 30204

TERRY, SANDRA ELEANOR, visual artist; b. Clifton Forge, Va., May 23, 1947; d. Robert B. and Grace J. (Amante) T. BA, Mary Baldwin Coll., 1990; MFA, Ind. State U., 1994; MA in Liberal Studies, New Sch. for Social Rsch., N.Y., 1998. Cert. tchr., Ind. Substitute tchr. Seymour (Ind.) Pub. Sch. Sys., 1990; tchg. asst., instr. Ind. State U., Terre Haute, 1991-94, tutor humanities Student Acad. Svcs., 1992-95. Baker, pastry chef, Different Drummer Restaurant, Staunton, Va., White Star Mills Restaurant, Staunton, McCormicks Restaurant, Staunton, Rising Sun Bakery, Charlottesville, Va., Claire's Restaurant, Charlottesville, South Street Restaurant, Charlottesville, Toast Restaurant, Broadway, N.Y., 2001-02; gallery docent Anderson Gallery, Seattle, 1967-70, Manolides Gallery, Seattle, 1967-70, Polly Friedlander, Seattle; lectr. in field. One-woman shows include Arts Illiana Exhbn. Space, Terre Haute, 1993, Turman Gallery, Ind. State U., 1994; exhibited in group shows at Turman Gallery, 1991-92, 94, Sheldon Swope Art Mus., Terre Haute, 1991, 92, 93, Bare-Montgomery Meml. Gallery, Ind. State U., 1992, Broad St. Gallery, New Castle, Ind., 1992, Coffee Grounds Gallery, Terre Haute, 1993, Saint Mary-of-the-Woods Coll., Ind., 1993, Shircliff Gallery of Art, Vincennes (Ind.) U., 1993, 69th Nat. Juried Print Exhbn. Soc. Am. Graphic Artists, 2002, Art Students League, N.Y., 2002, 03, 04, (honorable mention award); permanent collections include Bratislava Sch. Art, Slovakia, U. Manitoba, Winnipeg, Canada, Mary Baldwin Coll., Staunton, Va., Ind. State U., Terre Haute; prodr., host Bluegrass music WTJU-FM, Charlottesville, 1983-87, WMRA-FM, Harrisonburg, Va., 1983-87; bassist Ham & Eggs Bluegrass Band, 1978-88, Blue Horizon, 1978-88; graphic designer KRAB-FM program guide, 1968-70. Mem.: Soc. Am. Graphic Artists (newsletter graphic designer, newsletter mng. dir., exhbn. catalogue graphic designer).

TERRY-LEONARD, BRENDA L. psychologist, consultant; d. John and R. Ledora Terry; m. Gary Norman Leonard, July 11, 1998. BS, Howard U., 1988, MEd, 1990, PhD, 1999. Lic. psychologist Md., Washington. Psychology intern Wichita (Kans.) State U., Counseling & Testing Ctr., 1996—97; cons. Lorraine Brannon & Associates, Washington, 1997—2000; instr. Bowie (Md.) State U., 1999—2000; contract therapist Reginald S. Lourie Ctr., Rockville, Md., 1998—2001; therapist III City of Alexandria, Va., 1998—2001; lic. psychologist Kingsbury Ctr., Washington, 2001—, Bowie Counseling Svcs., Md., 2003—. Rueben tribe co-leader Prince George's Cmty. Ch., Springdale, Md., 2003. Mem.: APA (assoc.), Zeta Chi Omega (chair scholarship com. 2002—03). Avocations: literary book club participant, travel. Office: Kingsbury Ctr 5000 14th St NW Washington DC 20011-6926 Business E-Mail: bterryleonard@kingsbury.org. E-mail: terryleonardb@hotmail.com.

TERTELING-PAYNE, CAROLYN ANN, city official; b. Buhl, Idaho, Dec. 20, 1936; d. Carl Treva and Ann Christine (Witt) Edwards; m. Joseph Loyd Terteling, June 20, 1959 (div. Sept. 1991); children: Joseph Nixon, Steven Loyd, Thomas Edward, Andrew James; m. Frank Adrian Payne, May 13, 1995. BA with highest honors, U. Idaho, Moscow, 1959. Grad. tchg. asst. Ariz. State U., Phoenix, 1959-60; mem. Boise City Coun., 1993—, pres., 1996—2003; mayor City of Boise, Idaho, 2003—. Sustainer Boise Jr. League; mem. Collector's Forum, Boise Art Mus.; trustee, mem. exec. com., mem. bldg. and planning com. St. Lukes Regional Med. Ctr.; pres. Boise Pub. Libr. Found.; dir., past pres. U. Idaho Found.; dir. Fundsy Charitable Found., Boise River Festival; mem. adv. bd. Lit. Lab, Warm Springs Counseling Ctr.; hon. bd. Idaho Zool. Soc.; emeritus dir. Boise Philharmonic; past dir. Boise Mus. Art, Boise Bicentennial Commn., Boise Sch. Vols., Idaho Hist. Preservation Coun., Morriso Ctr. for Ars, Endowment Dr., Women's Life at St. Lukes, Idaho Law Found.; mem. adv. bd. Children at Risk Evaluative Svcs.; past dir. area coun. 11 Western states, Assn. Jr. Leagues Am.; past pres. St. Lukes Hosp. Aux., U. Idaho Found., Boise Jr. League; past chair symposium Albertson Coll. Idaho, Grand Opening of Morrison Ctr. for Arts, Sun valley, Arts and Humanities Benefit, Alternate Mobility Adventure Seekers, Boise State U. Named Idaho Statesman Disting. Citizen, 1979, Woman of Yr., C. of C., 1986; recipient Woman of Today and Tomorrow award Girl Scouts, 1992, Disting. Svc. award Idaho State Bar, 1992, Cultural Heritage award Coll. Letters and Sci. U. Idaho, 1994. Mem. U. Idaho Alumni Assn., Hillcrest Country Club (past dir.), PEO, Phi Beta Kappa, Gamma Phi Beta. Avocations: golf, tennis, gardening, reading. Home: 2050 Table Rock Rd Boise ID 83712-6663 Office: City Hall 150 N Capitol Blvd Boise ID 83702-5920 Mailing: PO Box 500 Boise ID 83701 0500

TERWILLEGAR, JANE CUSACK, librarian, educator; b. Warsaw, N.Y., Nov. 7, 1935; d. James Scott and Estella B. (Ackerman) Cusack; m. Gordon H. Terwillegar, July 26, 1958 (div. Mar. 1989); children: Sarah Ann Terwillegar Smedley, Arne Matthew. BA, Elmira (N.Y.) Coll., 1957; MLS, SUNY, Geneseo, 1960; EdS, U. Ga., 1977. Cert. tchr., Fla. Instr. U. Ga., Athens, 1975-81; libr. Palm beach County Libr., West Palm Beach, Fla., 1981-83, Palm Beach County Schs., Royal Palm Beach, Fla., 1983-94, dist. libr. media svcs. mgr. West Palm Beach, 1994—2000; dir. Lake Park Public Libr., 2000—. Lectr. Sch. Libr. and Info. Sci., U. South Fla., Tampa, 1987—, Nova U., Ft. Lauderdale, Fla., 1995—; task force mem. SUNLINK project Fla. Dept. Edn., 1995-2000; mem. adv. coun. Fla. Libr. Svcs. and Tech. Act., 1999—. Co-author: Commonsense Cataloging, 3d edit. 1983, 4th edit. 1990; reviewer Sch. Libr. Jour., 1986—; contbr. articles to profl. jours. Pres. Staff Assn. Palm Beach Sch. Dist., 1997-99. Mem. ALA, AAUW (pres. No. Palm Beach br. 2001-), Am. Assn. Sch. Librs. (exec. bd. 1990-94), Assn. for Libr. Svc. to Children (Newbery com. 1988-89), Fla. Assn. Media in Edn. (sec. 1988-89, bd. dirs. 1997—, pres. 1999-2001), Ednl. Media Assn. Fla. (pres. 1988), Kiwanis Club of Lake Park, Delta Kappa Gamma, Phi Beta Kappa, Delta Kappa Phi, Phi Delta Kappa. Avocations: scuba diving, sports cars. Home: 911 Oak Harbour Dr Juno Beach FL 33408-2173 Office: Lake Park Public Libr 529 Park Ave West Palm Beach FL 33403-

TERZIAN, GRACE PAINE, publisher; b. Boston, Oct. 19, 1952; d. Thomas Fite and Grace Hillman (Benedict) Paine; m. Philip Henry Terzian, Oct. 20, 1979; children: William Thomas Hillman, Grace Benedict Paine. BA in Art History, Williams Coll., 1974. Art dir. The New Republic, Washington, 1976-78; asst. editor The Chronicle of Higher Edn., Washington, 1978-79; rsch. editor Archtl. Digest, L.A., 1982-85; pub. The Women's Quar., Arlington, Va., 1994—. Editor Ex Femina, 1996—; sr. v.p. Ind. Women's Forum. Mem. Soc. Colonial Dames in Am., Phi Beta Kappa. Episcopalian. Home: 10505 Adel Rd Oakton VA 22124-1605 Personal E-mail: gterzian@radix.net., gterzian@cox.net.

TESAR, PATRICIA MARIE, academic coordinator; b. Cleve., Oct. 7, 1955; d. John Joseph and Florence Louise Tesar. BA in Interpersonal Com., Cleve. State U., 1982; MA in Rehab. Counseling, Gallaudet U., 1986; PhD in Spl. Edn. Adminstrn., Gallaudet U., 2002. Ind. living counselor ind. living program Health Hill Hosp., Cleve., 1982-83; practicum rehab. counselor for the deaf Va. Dept. Rehabilitative Svcs., Springfield, 1985; career counselor student spl. svcs./career ctr. Gallaudet U., Washington, 1984-90, coord. spl. svcs. Office for Students with Disabilities, 1990—. Co-chair subcom. adult employment Developmental Disabilities State Planning Coun. D.C., 1997—. Recipient Mima Bravo Counseling award, 1986, U.S. Congl. award of achievement, 1986, 92, Nat. Disting. Svc. Registry Counseling award, 1990; Quota Internat. fellow, 1986; Mary Pickford scholar, 1985; Gallaudet U. Pres.'s scholar, various yrs. Mem. ASCD, Am. Deafness and Rehab. Assn. (sec. met. Washington chpt. 1986-88, pres. 1988-90, 90-92), Am. Assn. Counseling and Devel., Nat. Rehab. Assn., Nat. Assn. for Deaf, Am. Assn. for Deaf-Blind, Md. Career Devel. Assn., Md. Rehab. Counseling Assn., Washington Consortium of Univs. Career Devel. Group, Washington Consortium of Univs. Student Support Svcs. Coalition (regional conf. coord.), Met. Washington Assn. Deaf-Blind, Coll. Placement Coun., Registry of Interpreters for the Deaf, Assn. Higher Edn., Coun. Exceptional Children, Kappa Delta Pi. Baptist. Avocations: reading, sign language interpreting. Home: 6500 Alexis Dr Bowie MD 20720-4755 E-mail: Patricia.Tesar@gallaudet.edu.

TESCH, MARIE LOUISE, music educator, artist; b. Watertown, SD, Apr. 8, 1952; d. Arthur Herman Tesch and Anna Mae Cook; m. Patrick Lee Dobbs, Aug. 25, 1990. BA, SD State U., 1970—74, MA, 1977—79. Language Arts Tchr. SD Dept. of Edn., 1974. Owner/operator Marie Louise Tesch Piano Studio, Rapid City, SD, 2000—. Fine artist Dakota Artists Guild, Rapid City, SD, 2002—. Exhibitions include Bayleaf Gallery, Spearfish, SD, Sturgis (SD) Area Arts Coun. Creator, dir. dramatic chorus

Rapid City Club for Boys, SD, 2002—03. Recipient Outstanding Young Woman in Am., 1981, First Pl. Newspaper Typography & Design, SD Press Assn., 1987, First Pl. in Newspaper Gen. Excellence, 1986; Grad. Tchg. Asst. in Speech scholar, SD State U., 1977—79. Office: Marie Louise Tesch Bingo Studio 3036 [illegible] Rapid City SD [illegible] E-mail: marietesch@rushmore.com.

TESORI, JEANINE, composer; b. 1961; m. Michael Rafter; 1 child. Composer: (Broadway plays) How to Succeed in Business Without Really Trying, 1995, Violet, 1997, Dream, 1997, Twelfth Night, 1998 (Tony nominee best original musical score, 1999), Swing!, 1999, Thoroughly Modern Millie, 2002 (Tony nominee best original musical score, 2002), Caroline, or Change, 2004 (Tony nominee best original musical score, 2004). Office: Eugene O'Neill Theatre 230 W 49th St New York NY 10019*

TESSENEER-STREET, SUSAN, photographer, artist, writer; b. Murray, Ky., Dec. 14, 1939; d. Ralph Athen and Susan Geneva (Kirkland) Tesseneer; m. Robert Beni Street Sr., Jan. 16, 1939 (div.); children: Robert Beni II, Ralph Calvin Sr. Student, Blue Mountain Coll. for Women, 1959—61, Memphis State U., 1963—66; BA, S.E. Mo. U., 1974; student, Harvard U., 2002. Tchr., 1974-79; bus. owner, 1977-85; writer, 1984-86; photographer, 1990—; artist, 1998—. Author: (book) Gift in Celebration of Women. Mem. Sikeston Art League, 1980—, pres., 1990-94; sec., treas., organizer Cmty. Concert, Sikeston, 1989. Mem. AAUW (charter), Profl. Photographers Am., Am. Soc. Portrait Artists, Hemingway Soc., Nat. Writers Club, Women in the Arts (charter), Am. Soc. Portrait Painters, Impressionist Soc., Nat. Writers Assn., Hemingway Soc., Nat. Assn. Women Writers, Nat. Women's History Mus. (charter). Office: Susan Tesseneer-Street Studio Gallery 1003 Allen Blvd Sikeston MO 63801-4711

TESSEREAU, LINDA ANN, music educator; b. Belleville, Ill., July 10, 1973; d. Elmer Richard and Sharon Sue Fehlhaber; m. Mark Alan Tessereau, June 26, 1998; children: Carleigh Nicole, Vanessa Skye. BME, Ill. U., 1997. Cert. music tchr. So. Ill. U., 1997. Asst. dir. bands Collinsville (Ill.) HS, 1996—97; dir. bands Harmony-Emge Dist. 175, Belleville, Ill., 1997—2003; dir. music Wolf Br. Mid. Sch., Belleville, 2003—. Instrumentalist USAF Nat. Guard, St. Louis, 1993—, tng. mgr., 1993—. Mem.: MENC, St. Clair County Music Assn., Ill. Grade Sch. Music Assn. (host band/chorus contest 1998—2002), Ill. Music Educators Assn., Am. Legion (mem. patriotic band 2003). Avocations: bowling, softball, jogging, travel. Home: 3206 Stonebridge Drive Belleville IL 62221 Office: Wolf Branch Middle School Huntwood Rd Swansea IL 62226

TESTA, DONNA MARIE, physician; b. Hershey, Pa., July 6, 1948; d. Emidiu Sebatino and Maria L. Josephine Testa; m. Joseph Laus, Apr. 25, 1970 (div. 1986). BS, Indiana U. of Pa., 1970; MD, Med. Coll. of Pa., 1975. Diplomate Am. Bd. Family Practice, Am. Bd. Geriatric Medicine, Nat. Bd. Med. Examiners, cert. ACLS. Tchr. biology and earth sci. Fox Chapel (Pa.) H.S., 1970—71; intern in psychiatry Albert Einstein Med. Ctr. North, Phila., 1975—76, resident in internal medicine, 1976—77; clinician Pontiac (Mich.) State Hosp., Pontiac, 1977—78; resident in family practice M.S. Hershey Med. Ctr., Pa. State U., 1978—80, instr. dept. family and cmty. medicine, 1980—81, asst. prof. family and cmty. medicine, 1981—85, 1990—2000, assoc. prof., 2000—; pvt. practice Office of Dr. Sandra Harmon-Weiss, Conshohocken, Pa., 1985—86, 1987; asst. dir. Kline Family Practice Ctr., Polyclinic Med. Ctr., Harrisburg, Pa., 1987—90. Lectr., presenter in field. Contbr. articles to profl. jours. Mem.: Physicians Com. for Responsible Medicine, Am. Acad. Family Physicians, Am. Geristric Soc., Alumnae Assn. Med. Coll. Pa. Office: MS Hershey Med Ctr 500 University Dr Hershey PA 17033

TESVICH, LISA KAY, industrial and organizational psychologist; b. New Orleans, July 21, 1965; d. Peter J. and Ann S. Tesvich; m. Rich Bonora. BA in Pers. Psychology, U. Calif., Santa Barbara, 1987; MS, Tulane U., 1992, PhD, 1994. Tchg. asst. Tulane U., New Orleans, 1989-94; assoc. Drake, Beam, Morin, New Orleans, 1992-94, Coopers & Lybrand, Chgo., 1994-95, cons., 1995-97; sr. cons. PricewaterhouseCoopers, Chgo., 1997—2002; assoc. prin. Buck Cons., 2002—. Mem. APA, Soc. for Human Resource Mgmt., Soc. Indsl./Orgnl. Psychology, Golden Key Honor Soc., Phi Beta Kappa. Avocations: travel, shopping, football, volleyball. Home: 4839 Almondwood Way San Diego CA 92130-2785 E-mail: ltesvich@san.rr.com.

TETELMAN, ALICE FRAN, small business owner; b. N.Y.C., Apr. 15, 1941; d. Harry and Leah (Markovitz) T.; m. Martin A. Wenick, Dec. 7, 1980. BA, Mt. Holyoke Coll., South Hadley, Mass., 1962. Rsch. and info. asst. Edn. and World Affairs, N.Y.C., 1963-67; legis. asst. U.S. Sen. Charles Goodell, Washington, 1968-70; land use and energy specialist Citizens Adv. Com. on Environ. Quality, Washington, 1973-74; sr. assoc. prog. mgr. Linton & Co., Washington, 1971-73, 75-76; pub policy cons. Washington, 1977-78; adminstrv. asst. U.S. Congressman Bill Green (N.Y.), Washington, 1978-81; cons. The Precious Legacy Project, Prague, Czechoslovakia, 1982-83; Rep. staff dir. Select Com. on Hunger, U.S. Ho. of Reps., Washington, 1984-85; dir. State of N.J. Washington Office, 1986-90; exec. dir. Coun. of Gov.'s Policy Advisors, Washington, 1991-94; dir. Washington Office, The City of N.Y., 1994-98. Pres. Italian Vacation Villas, Washington. Bd. dirs. Republican Women's Task Force, Nat. Women's Polit. Caucus, 1976-80, Women in Senate and House (WISH) List, 1998-2001. European Community grantee, 1975. Mem. Ripon Soc. (nat. exec. com. 1971-73). Office: Italian Vacation Villas PO Box 9586 Washington DC 20016-9586

TETEN, MELODY-LEIGH, library media specialist; b. Hazen, N.D., Nov. 3, 1954; d. Kenneth E. and Bertie-Leigh Compaan; m. Johann H. Teten, June 24, 1978; children: Theodore, Brian, Jennifer. BS in Elem. Edn., Kans. State U., 1976; MS in Spl. Edn., U. Ctrl. Okla., 1985. Title I tutor Unified Sch. Dist. #295, Jennings, Kans., 1976—77; title I tutor/elem. vocal and band Unified Sch. Dist. #352, Goodland, Kans., 1977—78; spl. edn. tchr. Sulphur Springs (Tex.) Ind. Sch. Dist., 1979—81; spl. edn. tchr. grade 6, 5th and 6th split tchr. Lawton (Okla.) Pub. Schs., 1983—88; 4th grade tchr. Chandler (Okla.) Pub. Schs., 1990—94; spl. edn. tchr. Newcastle (Okla.) Pub. Schs., 1995—97, libr. media specialist, 1997—. Mem.: NEA, Okla. Libr. Assn. Republican. Methodist. Avocations: reading, sewing, cross stitch, skiing.

TETRAULT, JEANNE L. building inspector; b. St. Petersburg, Fla., Dec. 10, 1944; d. Edgar N. and Irene C. Tetrault; life ptnr. Jan Zaitlin. Attended, Vassar Coll., 1963—65; student, Laney Coll., Oakland, Calif., 1999—2001. Cert. bldg. inspector, mech. inspector, combination residential inspector. Farmer, Albion, Calif., 1970—75; writer, 1975—82, 1970—75; carpenter, bldg. contractor 7 Sisters Constn., Berkeley, Calif., 1980—94; self-employed carpenter, designer Berkeley, 1994—96; carpenter, supr. U. Calif., Berkeley, 1996—97; bldg. inspector level 2 Contra Costa Bldg. Dept., Martinez, Calif., 2001—. Mem. adv. bd. Spinsters Inc.-Aunt Lute, San Francisco, 1984—85; workshop tchr. in field. Author: (books) Countrywomen: A Handbook for the New Farmer, 1976, A Woman's Carpentry Book, 1980; founding editor Countrywomen Mag., 1975—80, Tradeswomen Mag., 1980—81. Vol., designer accessible residential projects Rebuilding Together/Christmas in April. Mem.: Internat. Conf. Bldg. Officials. Green Party. Avocations: writing, horseback riding. Office: Contra Costa Bldg Dept 651 Pine St Martinez CA 94553 E-mail: savsarah@ix.netcom.com.

THACHER, BARBARA AUCHINCLOSS, history educator; b. Oyster Bay, N.Y., July 27, 1918; d. Hugh and Frances Coverdale (Newlands) Auchincloss; m. Thomas Thacher, Aug. 4, 1942; children: Barbara Burrall Thacher Plimpton, Elizabeth Coverdale Thacher Hawn, Thomas Day II, Hugh Auchincloss, Peter Anthony, Andrew. BA cum laude, Bryn Mawr Coll., 1940; MA in History, Columbia U., 1965. Editl. rschr. Newsweek, N.Y.C., 1940-41, 44; writer N.Y. Times Sunday Mag., News of Week Rev., N.Y.C., 1941-43; co-editor Christmas Booklist for Children Harper's Mag., [illegible]; asst. history dept. Barnard Coll., N.Y.C., 1964-65; rsch. asst. Ctr. Urban Edn., N.Y.C., 1966. Bd. dirs. Bryn Mawr Coll., 1966-88, chair bd. trustees, 1980-87, emeritus, 1988—, City Univ. of N.Y., trustee, 1970-73, WNET-TV-Channel 13, trustee, 1978-88; active Sheltering Arms Children's Svc., Istanbul Women's Coll., Leake & Watts Children's Home Svcs., Yonkers and N.Y.C., 1961-83, emeritus, 1983—, N.Y.C. Park Assn., Riverdale Girls Sch.; trustee Tchrs. Coll. Columbia U. Mem. Cosmopolitan Club (gov.), North Haven Casino. Democrat. Presbyterian. Home: Apt 311 88 Notch Hill Rd North Branford CT 06471-1852

THALER, LINDA KAPLAN, communications executive; m. Fred Thaler; children: Michael, Emily. BA magna cum laude, MA in music, CCNY. Former music instr. CCNY; with J. Walter Thompson, most recently as exec. v.p., exec. group creative dir.; exec. v.p., exec. creative dir. Wells Rich Greene BDDP, 1994—97; founder, CEO, chief creative officer Kaplan Thaler Group Ltd., N.Y.C., 1997—. Former mem. comedy improv troupe. Author: (jingle) I Don't Want to Grow Up, I'm a Toys 'R' Us Kid, Eastman Kodak-Because Time Goes By, (book) BANG! Getting Your Message Head in a Noisy World, 2003. Named Advertising Women of Yr., Advertising Women of N.Y., 2001; recipient 13 Clio awards. Office: Kaplan Thaler Group Ltd 58 W 40th St New York NY 10018*

THARNISH, ROSE MARIES LEHMAN, veterinarian; b. Greenville, Miss., Sept. 23, 1942; d. Isadore Hyman Lehman and Leatha Josephine Haynes; m. Robert Earley (div.); m. Larry Leslie Tharnish, Feb. 3, 1981. Student, N.W. Jr. Coll., Delta State U.; B, Memphis State U. N.Y.; JD, U. Tenn. Pres., owner Faith Ministry, Walls, Miss. Chmn. adv. bd. Rep. Nat. Com.; pres., bd. dirs. ACLU. Mem. Gardening Club, Audio Club, Book Club, Sierra Club, VFW, NAPCA. Avocation: scuba diving. Home: 5491 Adams Cir Walls MS 38680-8935

THARP, MARY THERESE, elementary school educator; b. Englewood, NJ, Sept. 11, 1970; d. John J. Campbell and Eileen A. Kelly; m. Jade Vincent Tharp, May 26, 1996; children: Bailey Douglas, Bradey Colleen. BA, Curry Coll., 1992; MEd, Brenau U., 2002; degree in ednl. specialist, Lincoln Meml. U., 2003. Tchr. St. John the Bapt. Sch., Hillsdale, NJ, 1992—93, East Hall Mid. Sch., Gainesville, Ga., 1999—. Mem.: Kappa Delta Pi. Avocations: dance, swimming, mothering. Office: East Hall Mid Sch 4120 E Hall Rd Flowery Branch GA 30542 E-mail: mttharp@lycos.com.

THARP, TWYLA, dancer; b. Portland, Ind., July 1, 1941; m. Peter Young (div.); m. Robert Huot (div.); 1 child, Jesse Huot. Student, Pomona Coll.; BA in Art History, Barnard Coll., 1963; D of Performing Arts (hon.), Calif. Inst. Arts, 1978, Brown U., 1981, Bard Coll., 1981; LHD, Ind. U., 1987; DFA, Pomona Coll., 1987; studied with Richard Thomas, Merce Cunningham, Igor Schwezoff, Louis Mattox, Paul Taylor, Margaet Craske, Erick Hawkins. Dancer Paul Taylor Dance Co., 1963-65; freelance choreographer with own modern dance troupe and various other cos. including Joffrey Ballet and Am. Ballet Theatre, 1965-87; founder, choreographer Twyla Tharp Dance Found., N.Y.C., 1965-87; artistic assoc., resident choreographer Am. Ballet Theatre, N.Y.C., 1987-91; teaching residencies various colls. and univs. including U. Mass., Oberlin Coll., Walker Art Ctr., Boston U. Choreographer White Oak Dance Project. Choreographer Tank Dive, 1965, Re-Moves, 1966, One Two Three, 1966, Forevermore, 1967, Generation, 1968, Medley, 1969, After Suite, 1969, Dancing in the Streets of London and Paris, 1969, The One Hundreds, 1970, The Fugue, 1970, The Bix Pieces, 1971, Eight Jelly Rolls, 1971, The Raggedy Dances, 1972, Deuce Coupe, 1973, As Time Goes By, 1974, Sue's Leg, 1975, Ocean's Motion, 1975, Push Comes to Shove, 1976, Once More Frank, 1976, Mud, 1977, Baker's Dozen, 1979, When We Were Very Young, 1980, Nine Sinatra Songs, 1982, The Catherine Wheel, 1982, Bach Partita, 1984, The Little Ballet, 1984, with Jerome Robbins Brahms Handel, 1984, At the Supermarket, 1984, In the Upper Room, 1987, Ballare, 1987, Stations of the Crossed, 1988, Everlast, 1989, Quartet, 1989, Bum's Rush, 1989, The Rules of the Game, 1990, Brief Fling, 1990, Grand Pas: Rhythm of the Saints, 1991, Deuce Coupe II, 1992, The Men's Piece, 1992, with Mikhail Baryshnikov Cutting Up, 1992—93, Demeter and Persephone, 1993, Waterbaby Bagatelles, 1994, Demeter and Persephone, 1994, Red, White & Blues, 1995, How Near Heaven, 1995, I Remember Clifford, 1995, Jump Start, 1995, Americans We, 1995, (films) Hair, 1979, Ragtime, 1981, Amadeus, 1984, White Nights, 1985, Valmont, 1989, I'll Do Anything, 1994, video spls. Making Television Dance, 1977, CBS Cable Confessions of a Corner Maker, 1980, (Broadway plays) Sorrow Floats, 1985, Singin' in the Rain, 1985, TV Baryshnikov by Tharp, 1985 (Emmy award for Outstanding Choreography, 1985, Emmy award for Outstanding Writing of Classical Music/Dance Programming, 1985), The Catherine Wheel, 1982 (Emmy award nomination for Outstanding Choreography, 1982); author (autobiography): When Push Comes to Shove, 1982. Recipient Creative Arts award, Brandeis U., 1972, Dance Mag. award, 1981, Univ. Excellence medal, Columbia U., 1987, Lions of the Performing Arts award, N.Y. Pub. Libr., 1989, Samuel M. Scripps award, Am. Dance Festival, 1990; MacArthur Found. fellow, 1992.

THAYER, EDNA LOUISE, medical facility and nursing administrator; b. Madelia, Minn., May 21, 1936; d. Walter William Arthur and Hilda Engel Emily Ann (Geistfeld) Wilke; m. David LeRoy Thayer, Aug. 30, 1958; children: Scott, Tamara, Brenda. Diploma in nursing, Bethesda Luth., 1956; BS in Nursing Edn., U. Minn., 1960; MSN, Washington U., St. Louis, 1966; MS in Counseling, Mankato (Minn.) State U., 1972. Cert. nursing adminstr. advanced ANA. Nurse Bethesda Luth. Hosp., St. Paul, 1956-58, U. Minn. Hosp., Mpls., 1958; from nurse to asst. head nurse supr., edn. dir. Fairmont (Minn.) Community Hosp., 1959-63; instr. Alton (Ill.) Meml. Hosp., 1963-66; from nursing instr. to assoc. prof. and dean Sch. Nursing Mankato State U., 1966-77; asst. adminstr. Rice County Dist. One Hosp., Faribault, Minn., 1977-89; RN, adminstrv. supr. St. Peter (Minn.) Regional Treatment Ctr., 1990-96; spkr., 1996—. Nurse surveyor Minn. Dept. Tech. Edn., St. Paul, 1980-93; mem. adv. co. LPN and MA programs Tech. Inst., Faribault, 1977-2001. Mem. Rice County Ext. Bd., Faribault, 1986-91, adult leader 4-H Club, Rice County and St. Paul, 1971-97; advisor Med. Explorers, Faribault, 1977-89; mem. Rep. Rodosovich Health Com., Faribault, 1984-94; coun. mem. Our Savior's Luth. Ch., Faribault, 1984-87; mem. Rep. Boudreau Health Care Adv. Com., 1996-2001. Recipient alumni award Nat. 4-H Club, 1983, Disting. Friend of Nursing award Mankato State U., 1995. Mem. Minn. Orgn. Nurse Execs. (bd. dirs. 1989-92), Dist. F Nursing Svc. Adminstrs. (pres. 1980-82), Minn. Nurses Assn. (bd. dirs. 1982-87, Pres.'s award 1983, pres. 5th dist. 1974, 75, pres. 13th dist. 1984-86), AAUW, Sigma Theta Tau, Delta Kappa Gamma (pres. Pi chptr. 1982-84, Woman of Achievement award 1985), Hosp. Aux. Republican. Avocations: crafts, volunteer work, theater, plays. Home: 7 Roots Beach Ln Elysian MN 56028-9731 Office Phone: 507-267-4588. Personal E-mail: dethayer@myclearwave.net.

THAYER, JANE See WOOLLEY, CATHERINE

THAYER, MARILYN, political organization executive, civic worker; married; 2 children. Fellow Inst. Politics, Loyola U., New Orleans. Former pres. women's aux. Vols. of Am.; past mem. bd. dirs. Sophie Gumble Guild; past v.p. and program chmn. Women for Better La.; pres. La. Fedn. Rep. Women, 1987-91; former nat. treas., mem.-at-large exec. com., and chmn. membership com. Nat. Fedn. Rep. Women, Alexandria, Va., pres., 1996-97, immediate past pres., 1997-98; immediate past nat. committeewoman for La., Rep. Nat. Com., also past mem. various coms.; co-chmn. vol. com., mem. host com. Rep. Nat. Com., 1988, mem. platform com., chmn. com. on human resources, 1984, 88; co-chmn. parish campaign, then co-chmn. state campaign Reagan-Bush Campaign. Office: Nat Fedn Rep Women 124 N Alfred St Alexandria VA 22314-3011 Fax: 703-548-[illegible]

THEE, CYNTHIA URBAN, psychotherapist; b. Phila., Feb. 12, 1960; d. Francis Joseph Jr. and Barbara (Fierro) Urban; m. Michael Gerard Thee, Oct. 26, 1991; children: Michael, Chelsea, Julia, Janelle, Eric. BA in Econs., Georgetown U., 1982; MSW, Syracuse U., 1985. Lic. social worker, Pa. Asst. coord. recreation/socialization pilot program Sussex County (N.J.) Welfare Bd., 1984; family-based social worker Youth Svcs., Inc., Phila., 1985-87; family therapist Family Preservation Svcs., Hudson and Camden County, N.J., 1987-89; individual and family therapist CORA Svcs., Inc., Phila., 1989-90; asst. mgr. for EAP ACORN Psychol. Mgmt. Corp., Phila., 1990-91; pvt. practice psychotherapist Feasterville, Pa., 1991—. Pvt. clin. cons. Penn Valley Cons. Assn., Lansdale, Pa., 1991-92, Main Line Health Psychiat. Group, Ardmore, Pa., 1991-92, Starting Point of N.J., Westmont, 1991-92, ACORN Psychol. Mgmt. Corp., 1989-92. Counselor Mother Teresa's Home for the Destitute and Dying, Calcutta, India, 1982-83, Damien Leprosy Social Welfare Ctr., Bihar, India, 1982-83. Named to Citizen Ambassador Program, 1994, 98; recipient Commendation for Leadership, ARC, 1982, Outstanding Citizen award Twp. of Ogdensburg, 1974. Mem. NASW, Acad. Cert. Social Workers. Democrat. Roman Catholic. Avocations: gardening, painting, photography, music, biking. Home and Office: 1841 Buck Rd Feasterville Trevose PA 19053

THEIS, KRISTINE LYNN, family practice nurse practitioner; b. Boise, Idaho, July 26, 1968; d. Robert Frederick and Beryl Annette Kring; m. Steven Robert Theis, Aug. 13, 1990; 1 child, Marina Janiece. BS in Biology, Oreg. State U., 1990; MSN, Vanderbilt U., 1992. RN Idaho, cert. family nurse practitioner, Am. Nurses Creditating Ctr. Nurse practitioner VA Med. Ctr., Boise, 1992—. Chmn. Idaho Nurse Practitioners Conf. Group, Boise, 1995—96; mem. VA Nurse Profl. Stds. Bd., Boise, 1995—2003; chmn. Idaho Commn. on Nursing and Nursing Edn., Boise, 2000—01; legis. chmn. new laws for nurse practitioners Nurse Practitioners Conf. Group, Boise, 1996—2001, 2003—04. Author, dir. mgr. (video) NPs in Idaho - 25 Year Celebration, 1996, pub. svc. announcements for state of Idaho, 2000. Recipient Nurse Excellence award, Boise, Idaho, 2004, VISN20, 2004. Mem.: ANA, Idaho Nurses Assn. (legis. chmn. 2000). Avocations: cooking, reading, singing, travel, shopping. Office: VA Med Ctr 500 W Fort St 116 Boise ID 83702 Office Phone: 208-422-1145. E-mail: theis.kristine@med.va.gov.

THEISS, GENA LEE, genealogist, researcher; b. Caneyville, Ky., May 16, 1925; d. Clarence Harbon Johnson and Gracie Higdon; m. Robert Maple Hunt, Nov. 9, 1946 (div. May 1948); 1 child, Nancy Jane; m. George William Theiss, July 15, 1949; children: Patricia Sue, Donna Lee, Martha Rhea. Grad. h.s., Caneyville, Ky., 1943. Bookkeeper Lincoln Bank & Trust Co., Louisville, 1944-47, Citizens Nat. Bank, Louisville, 1948-56, First Nat. Bank, Louisville, 1957-84. Author, editor: Christian Weedman and his Descendants 1735-1986, 1986, revised edit., 1989, Descendants of John Higdon and Millicent, 1998, Update on Christian Weedman and his Descendants, 2002, Possible Update on John Higdon and Millicent, 2002. Active Hillview Cumberland Presbyn. Ch. Mem. Ky. Hist. Soc., DAR, Ea. Star Chpt. 154. Republican. Avocations: genealogy, quilting, photography, stamp collecting, traveling. Home: 8417 Burlingame Rd Louisville KY 40219-5205

THEISS, PATRICIA KELLEY, public health researcher, educator; b. Atlanta, Dec. 12, 1934; d. Charles Henry and Susie Carlota (Tate) Kelley; m. Erich Albert Theiss (div. Aug. 1996). BA, Wellesley Coll., 1956; MS, Howard U., 1958, Cert. in Secondary Edn., 1959. Rsch. asst. Armed Forces Inst. Pathology, Washington, 1959-61; heath edn. phone coord. Howard U. Cancer Ctr., Washington, 1977-81; program assoc. D.C. Lung Assn., Washington, 1981-85; co-project dir. Know Your Body Evaluation Project Georgetown U. Sch. Medicine, Washington, 1985-87; coord. minority health grant for cancer cultivation Commn. Pub. Health, Washington, 1988-89, coord. data-based intervention rsch., 1989-93, protocol coord. immunization protocol NIH-DC initiative, 1994-97; pub. health advisor Dept. Health State Ctr. Health Stats. Inst. Minority Health Statistics Initiative, Washington, 1997—; coord. D.C. Healthy People 2010 Plan Initiative, 1998—; state contact U.S. Office Minority Health, Washington, 1999—. Mem. task force for substance abuse use Abuse Edn. for D.C. Pub. Schs., 1984-85; mem. Health Mothers/Health Babies Coalition, 1985-89. Contbr. articles to profl. jours. Chair health and welfare com. D.C. PTA, 1986-89; coord. AIDS awareness edn. State PTA, D.C., 1987-89. Recipient Cmty. Svc. award D.C. Assn. Health, Recreation and Dance, 1987. Mem. APHA, Met. Washington Pub. Health Assn. (pres. 1987-88). Democrat. Congregationalist. Avocations: oil painting, horseback riding. Home: 2501 Calvert St NW #902 Washington DC 20008 Office: DC Dept Health SCHS 825 N Capitol St NE Washington DC 20002-4210 E-mail: patricia.theiss@dc.gov.

THELANDER, BEVERLY, oil company executive; BS, MBA in Fin., UCLA. Variuos fin. positions ARCO, 1981-98, v.p. comm. pub. affairs & investor rels., 1998—. Office: ARCO 333 S Hope St Los Angeles CA 90071-1406

THEODOLI, KATRIN, manufacturing executive; m. Filippo Theodoli. Mng. dir. Magnum Marine Motor Yachts, Aventura, Fla., until 1990, CEO, pres., 1990—. Office: Magnum Marine 2900 NE 188th St Miami FL 33180-2998 Fax: 305-931-0088.

THEODORE, CRYSTAL, artist, retired educator; b. Greenville, S.C., July 27, 1917; d. James Voutsas and Florence Gertrude (Bell) T. AB magna cum laude, Winthrop Coll., 1938; MA, Columbia U., 1942, EdD, 1953; postgrad., U. Ga., 1947. Instr. art Winthrop Coll., 1938-43; prof. art, head dept. Huntingdon (Ala.) Coll., 1946-52, E. Tenn. State U., 1953-57, Madison Coll., 1957-68; vis. prof. art World Campus Afloat Chapman Coll., Calif., 1967; prof. art James Madison U., Harrisonburg, Va., 1968-83, prof. emeritus, 1983—. Contbr. articles to profl. jours.; paintings in regional and nat. art exhbns. Bd. dirs. Rockingham Fine Arts Assn., 1980—85, 1989, Citizens for the Downtown, 1989, Women's Coop. Coun. Harrisonburg and Rockingham County, 1976—79, Valley Coun. of the Arts, 1998—99, Shenandoah Coun. of the Arts, 1996—, pres., 1996—2002; founder OASIS Co-op Gallery, 2000. Served with USMC, 1944—46. Gen. Edn. Bd. of Rockefeller Found. fellow, 1952-53; recipient award Carnegie Found. Advancement of Tchg., 1947, 48, 49, 50; Ednl. Found. Program grantee AAUW, 1981-82; rsch. grantee Ednl. Radio and TV Ctr., 1956. Mem.: AAUW (cultural interests rep., nat. dir. 1980—82), Va. Mus., Va. Watercolor Soc., Mensa, Pi Lambda Theta, Eta Sigma Phi, Kappa Pi. Democrat. Lutheran. Home: 150 Bear Wallow Ln Harrisonburg VA 22802-0153

THERIOT, LISA MARIE, social worker; b. St. Martinville, La., Apr. 18, 1964; d. Harry Pierre Theriot, Sr. and Jeanette Marie Theriot. BA in Psychology, U. Southwestern La., 1988; MSW, La. State U., 1991. LCSW. Psychotherapist Philip Rowden, M.D., Baton Rouge, 1991—92; home health med. social worker Capital Home Health, Baton Rouge, 1992—96; psychotherapist Leinweber & Assoc., Baton Rouge, 1995—97; home health med. social worker Profl. Healthcare Svcs., Baton Rouge, 1997—99; social svcs. dir. and recreational dir. St. James Pl., Baton Rouge, 1999—2000; med. social worker Our Lady of the Lake, Baton Rouge, 2000—01; clin. mgr. Profl. Healthcare Svcs., Hammond, La., 2001—. Mem.: NASW. Avocations: writing songs, playing guitar, gospel singing, woodworking, home theater. Office: Profl Healthcare Svcs 1605 N Morrison Blvd Hammond LA 70401

THERN, PEGGY HUANG, literature educator, small business owner; d. Lin Yun and Wei Qing Huang; m. Kenneth Lawrence Thern, June 23, 1964; 1 child, Phillip Yung. BA, Kwong Hwa U., Shanghai, China, 1945—49. Cert. Real Estate Agent Hawaii, 1980. Clk. Civil Air Transport, Taipei, China, 1951—64; restaurateur, owner Paradise Garden, Honolulu, 1970—84; real estate agt. Honolulu, 1980—95; English tchr. McKinley Cmty. Sch., Honolulu, 1986—; sec. Chinese Luth. Ch., Honolulu, 1987—92. Mem. vol. tchr. First Chinese Ch. of Christ, Honolulu, 1994—. Author: (book) Sui Yue Liu Ying. Recipient Cert. of Svc., Civil Air Transport, 1957, Cert. of Appreciation, Chinese Luth. Ch., Honolulu, 1992.

THERON, CHARLIZE, actress; b. Benoni, South Africa, Aug. 7, 1975; d. Charles and Gerda Theron. Studied dance, Joffrey Ballet, N.Y.C. Actor: (films) Children of the Corn III, 1995, 2 Days in the Valley, 1996, That Thing You Do!, 1996, The Devil's Advocate, 1997, Trial and Error, 1997, Celebrity, 1998, Mighty Joe Young, 1998, The Astronaut's Wife, 1999, The Cider House Rules, 1999, Reindeer Games, 2000, The Yards, 2000, Men of Honor, 2000, The Legend of Bagger Vance, 2000, Sweet November, 2001, 15 Minutes, 2001, The Curse of the Jade Scorpion, 2001, Trapped, 2002, Waking Up in Reno, 2002, The Italian Job, 2003, Monster, 2003 (Golden Globe for best dramatic actress, 2004, Screen Actors Guild Award for best actress, 2004, Acad. Award for best actress, 2004); (TV films) Hollywood Confidential, 1997. Address: United Talent Agy Ste 500 9560 Wilshire Blvd Beverly Hills CA 90212*

THETFORD, FRANCES ALICIA, social services group administrator; b. Marlow, Okla., June 9, 1943; d. Lester Glenn and Cumi Frances (Shields) Jensen; m. Billy Eugene Thetford, June 23, 1964 (div. May 1989); children: Alicia, Bill. AB, Lewis & Clark Coll., 1974; BSBA, So. Ill. U., 1981. Acct. Nat. Marine & Rivertronics, Alton, Ill., 1967—84; CEO Gmeni, Inc., St. Louis, 1984—92; freelance constrn. & home sales St. Louis, 1992—2001; dir. bus. Salvation Army, St. Louis, 2001—02. Diabetes chair St. Louis Lions Club, 1995; pres. Hampton Lions Club, St. Louis, 2000; mem. social justice com. Archdiocese of St. Louis, 1998—; acolyte, tour guide Cath. Basilica, St. Louis, 2002—03. Nominee Poet of the Yr., Internat. Soc. Poets, 2002, 2003. Home: 12160 Plainsman St Saint Louis MO 63146

THEUT-TOPLYN, ELIZABETH ANN, psychologist; b. Ann Arbor, Mich., Apr. 30, 1963; d. C. Peter and Judith T. Theut; m. Glenn Allen Toplyn, Oct. 7, 2001. BA, U. Mich., 1985; MA, New Sch. Social Rsch., 1989, PhD, 1997. Lic. psychologist. Psychologist, N.Y.C., 1993—98, Lakeside Family Svcs., Bklyn., 1993—95; psychotherapist Met. Ctr. for Mental Health, N.Y.C., 1994—2000; psychologist Cath. Charities, Bklyn., 1998—99, N.Y. Foundling, Bronx, 1999—; pvt. practice psychologist N.Y.C., 2000. Pro bono psychologist Childrens Psychotherapy Project, 2001—. Mem.: APA, N.Y. State Psychol. Assn., Manhattan Psychol. Assn. (bd. mem. 2002—). Democrat. Avocations: pottery, reading, knitting, drawing. Office: 310 E 75th St #5K New York NY 10021

THEVENOT, MAUDE TRAVIS, retired home economist; b. Many, La., Dec. 31, 1914; d. Rennie L. and Fairy D. (Minter) Travis; m. Aubrey J. Thevenot, July 4, 1952 (dec. Sept. 1981); 1 stepchild, Peter A. BA, Northwestern State U., 1939; MS, La. State U., 1963. Tchr. home econs. Bienville Parish High Sch., Jamestown, La., 1940-41; parish home mgmt. supr. Farmers Home Adminstrn., USDA, Natchitoches, Oak Grove, Winnefield, La., 1942-47, state home mgmt. supr. Alexandria, La., 1948-52, social worker La. Dept. Pub. Welfare, New Roads, Alexandria, Marksville, La., 1952-56; home economist La. State U.-La. Coop. Extension Svc., Makrsville, Alexandria, 1957-74, specialist expanded food & nutrition edn. program Baton Rouge, 1975-79. Co-advisor in home econs. Ptnrs. of Am. La./El Savador and La. Home Econs., 1975. Author: Central District Louisiana Home Economics Association, 1984 Louisiana Federation of Chapters of the National Association of Retired Federal Workers, 1989; co-author: A Taste of Yesterday, 1988. Mem. Kent Plantation House, Inc., Alexandria, 1970—, com. mem. for orgn., 1970, exec. bd., 1985-88, cookbook chmn., 1985-90; mem. Friendship House-Adult Day Care Ctr., Alexandria, 1982-90, exec. bd., 1982-88, organizer, pres. vol. orgn., 1978-90; advisor Anchors as Pilot Club of Alexandria Outreach Com., Anchor Club of Pineville (La.) High Sch., 1978-90; mem. La. Avoyelles & Rapides Parish Farm Bur., Marksville, Alexandria, 1967-90, Avoyelles & Rapides Cowbelles, Alexandria, Marksville, 1967-70; mem. Calvary Bapt. Ch., leader Sunday Sch. class, mem. sr. group decoration com. for monthly luncheons, leader Dottie Hayes Bible Study Group. Recipient Plaque for Svc. Rapides Parish Coun. on Aging, Alexandria, 1971, Plaque for Outstanding Leadership & Svc., Rapides Parish Homemakers Coun., Alexandria, 1974, Plaque of Appreciation as Coord., Expanded Food and Nutrition Ednl. Program La. State U., Baton Rouge, 1978, 11 Certs. of Appreciation, Anchor Club of Pineville High Sch., 1980-90, Cert. of Recognition (3) Friendship House-Day Care for Adults, 1983, 84, 85, Plaque for Outstanding Svc., Rapides Coun. on Aging 20th Ann., 1967-87. Mem. Internat. Fedn. Home Econs., Am. Assn. Family and Consumer Sci., La. Home Econs. Assn. (v.p. 1972-73, Disting. Home Economist 1979-80), Am. Assn. Family and Consumer Svcs. (Wiley-Berger award 1995), Cen. Dist. Home Econs. (pres. 1972-73, Disting. Svc. award 1967, hon. mem. 1985), Nat. Assn. Extension Home Economist, La. Assn. Extension Home Economist, AAUW, La. Assn. Nat. Assn. Retired Fed. Employees (past pres., v.p. region VI, Meritorious Svc. plaque and cert. of citation 1988-89, Meritorious Svc. award 1992-93, life), CENLA (past pres.), Am. Assn. Retired Persons, La. State U. Alumni, La. State U. Home Econs. Retiree, Northwestern State U. Alumni, La. Retired Tchrs. Assn. (life), Pilot Club Internat., Epsilon Sigma Phi (life), Gamma Sigma Delta (Extension award of merit 1978). Democrat. Avocations: traveling, voluntary activities. Home: 507 Tanglewood Dr Alexandria LA 71303-3354

THEX, ALBERTA HUGHES, secondary education educator; b. Havre, Mont., Jan. 25, 1949; d. Albert Patrick and Florence Evangeline (Moe) Hughes; m. Tim Houston Thex, Nov. 25, 1972; children: David Scott, Kelly Marie. BA, Mont. State U., 1972; MS, Oreg. State U., 1995. Cert. tchr., Oreg. Tchr. Umpqua C.C., Roseburg, Oreg., 1975, Roseburg Sch. Dist., 1975-76, Salem (Oreg.)-Keizer Sch. Dist., 1980-87, Archdiocese of Portland, Stayton, Oreg., 1987-94; speech dir. St. Mary Sch., Stayton, Oreg., 1987-95; tchr. Salem-Keizer Sch. Dist., 1995-96; tchr., dir. lang. arts Falls City H.S., 1996—. Trainer Willamette Curriculum Coalition, 1997—; rep. Summer Design Inst.; site coun. Falls City Schs., 1997-2004, textbook com., 2000, yearbook adviser, 1996-2004. Author: Flood of '96, 1996; editor (poetry) Am. Anthology of Poetry, 1996, FCHS Writing Svc. Project, 2003-2004. Dir. talent show Schirle Elem. Sch., Salem, 1986; re-election com. Rep. Party, Salem, 1980-81; leader Girl Scouts Am., Salem, 1988-91; mem. com., band booster Sprague Band, Salem, 1991-2000. Recipient Pell grant Mont. State U., 1968-72, Eisenhower fellowship Oreg. State U., 1993-95, Speech Coach Recognition award Cathedral Sch., Portland, 1993. Mem. NEA, Nat. Coun. Math. Tchrs., Oreg. Edn. Assn., Oreg. Coun. Math. Tchrs., Oreg. Math. Edn. Coun., Oreg. Talented and Gifted Bd. (bd. dirs. 1989-92), Salem Edn. Assn., 21st Century Oreg. Assessment (coun. rep. 1995). Lutheran. Avocations: writing, traveling, creative crafts, fishing. Home: 595 Valleywood Dr SE Salem OR 97306-1691 Office: Falls City High Sch 111 N Main St Falls City OR 97344-9776

THIBAUDEAU, PATRICIA, state legislator; BA, Whitman Coll.; MSW, Smith Coll. Mem. Wash. Senate, Dist. 43, Olympia, 1995—; chair legis. and long term care com. Wash. Legislature, Olympia, 1999, Dem. caucus vice chair, 1997, Dem. asst. whip, 1994, mem. jud. com., mem. ways and means com. Mem. King's County Women's Polit. Caucus; mem. adv. com. Youth Care Bd.; mem. Wash. Ceasefire. Recipient award N.W. Women's Law Ctr., Bailey Boushay Citizen's award Youth Care Outstanding Cmty. Advocate, 1995, Cert. Recognition Wash. Alliance for Mentally Ill. Mem. AAUW. Democrat. Office: 414 John Cherberg Bldg Olympia WA 98504-0001

THIBIDEAU, CAROLYN C. musician, educator; d. Emery Spencer and Elizabeth Anne Cartwright; m. Robert James Thibideau, Dec. 28, 1958; children: Stephen Robert, Michael Charles, Richard Dayton, Peter John. BS, Oakland U., 1974; MusM, U. Mich., 1980. Cert. tchr. Mich., registered music educator Music Educators Nat. Conf. Music tchr. West Bloomfield (Mich.) Schs., 1975—2003. Organizing dir. Orchard Lake (Mich.) Music Series; composer, arranger, conductor, performer organ, piano, trumpet. Music dir., organist Orchard Lake (Mich.) Cmty. Ch., 1971—85, 1st Presbyn. Ch., Pontiac, Mich., 1994—. Finalist Tchr. of the Yr., Mich. Dept. of Edn., 1992. Mem.: Am. Guild English Handbell Ringers (past Mich. chairperson, clinician, conductor, past Mich. chair, clinician, conductor), Am. Guild Organists (assoc.; nat. conv. program com. 1980—86, bd. dirs. 1986—89, performer). Avocations: music, opera. Office: Antioch Pub Box 225 Oden MI 49764 Personal E-mail: carolynct1@aol.com.

THIBIDEAU, REGINA, retail executive, social worker; b. Quincy, Mass., Sept. 18, 1943; d. Roy John Joseph Robicheau and Cora Drew Cross; m. Bruce Edward Maranda, Aug. 27, 1966 (div. June 1980); children: Hathaway Jakobsen, Kenseth Thibideau; m. Ronald William Joseph Thibideau, Sept. 24, 1984. BA, U. Vt., 1965; MEd, No. Ariz. U., 1998. Sec. clin. psychology office U. Mass., Amherst, 1966-67; social worker Mass. Dept. of Welfare, Amherst, 1967-69, East Boston, 1969-70, Quincy, Mass., 1971-73; CPR coord. Am. Heart Assn., Hyannis, Mass., 1978-80; child advocate Office for Children, Hyannis, 1980; owner, retailer Maggie O'Shaughnessy's, Sun City West, Ariz., 1983—2002. Facilitator Mercy Otis Warren Women's Ctr., Hyannis, 1980-81. Contbg. writer T.J. Reid's Newsletter, Amite, La., 1999; writer Maggie's Newsletter, Sun City West, 1996—2002. Organizer Mother's Day Celebration, 1999, 2000; mem. Litchfield Park Libr. Assn., 1985-98; vol. French tutor, Barnstable Middle Sch.; vol. Save Our Sound in Hyannis; cmty. liaison vol. Elder Svcs. Cape Cod. Named Top 10 Boutiques in Ariz., Ariz. Woman mag., 1999, 2000, 2001, 02, One of Top Bus. in Ariz., 2000, 01, 02. Mem. AAUW, Sundome Merchants Assn. Avocations: travel, painting, computers, reading, walking. Home: PO BOX 191 Cotuit MA 02635 E-mail: reginathibideau@earthlink.net.

THIBODEAU, PATRICIA LEONA, medical librarian; b. Nashua, N.H., Jan. 6, 1952; d. Wilfred James and Leona Rosa (Buxton) Thibodeau; m. Steven Jay Melamut, Jan. 14, 1983. BA, U. N.H., 1974; MLS, U. R.I., 1976; MBA, Western Carolina U., 1991. Instr., cataloger R.I. Coll., Providence, 1976-77; dir. health scis. info. ctr., rsch. adminstrn. Women Infants Hosp. R.I., Providence, 1977-83; dir. info. media resources Mountain Area Health Edn. Ctr., Asheville, N.C., 1983-93; assoc. dir. Duke U. Med. Ctr. Libr., Durham, NC, 1993—2000; acting dir. Duke U. Med. Ctr., Durham, 2000—01, assoc. dean for libr. svcs. and archives, 2001— Instr. grad. libr. sch. U. R.I., Kingston, 1982; spkr. in field. Contbr. articles to profl. jours. Bd. dirs. Western N.C. Regional Child Abuse Ctr., Asheville, 1988-93; mem. allocations panel United Way, Asheville, 1988-93; chair Cancer Rsch. Com. Inst. Rev. Bd., Asheville, 1989-93. mem. Leadership Asheville X, 1991-92. Mem.: ALA, MLA (gov. task force 1996—97, bd. dirs. 1996—99, chmn. sect. coun. 1996—99, pres. 2003—04, disting. mem. acad. health info. profls.), Spl. Librs. Assn. Home: 202 Westbury Dr Chapel Hill NC 27516-9149 Office: Duke U Med Ctr Libr Box 3702 Seeley G Mudd Bldg 103 Durham NC 27710

THIBODEAU, VIRGINIA DURBIN, artist; b. Toledo, Ohio, Dec. 12, 1912; d. Charles Cleophas and May Gertrude (Stoeckle) Durbin; m. Robert E. Thibodeau, Aug. 10, 1935 (dec. Aug. 1983); children: Bernadette Judith, Joseph Henry. Student, Wayne State U., Coll. Creative Studies, Detroit, Cranbrook Acad. Arts, Bloomfield Hills, Mich., 1950. Comml. artist Toledo and Detroit Dept. Stores, 1930's and 40's; head art dept. Conventos Sacred Heart, Religious of Sacred Heart, Grosse Pointe, Mich., 1950-69; artist in residence Grosse Pointe Acad., 1979—. Exhibited in group show Toledo Mus. Art, 1945. Recipient art awards, Cannes, France, Nat. Miniature Show, Washington, Toledo Mus. Art, 1945-56, award Internat. Ecclesiastical Art Show, Detroit. Mem. Nat. Miniature Painters and Sculptors, Scarab Club, Women in the Arts, Grosse Pointe Artist Assn. (pres., awards 1949-92), Toledo Area Artists (juror 1936), Hilliard Soc. Roman Catholic. Home: 1729 Broadstone Rd Grosse Pointe Farms MI 48236-1948 Office: Grosse Pointe Acad 171 Lake Shore Rd Grosse Pointe Farms MI 48236-3760

THIELE, GLORIA DAY, retired librarian, small business owner; b. L.A., Sept. 4, 1931; d. Russell Day Plummer and Dorothy Ruby (Day) Plummer Thi; m. Donald Edward Cools, June 13, 1953 (div.); children: Michael, Ramona, Naomi, Lawrence, Nancy, Rebecca, Eugene, Maria, Charles. MusB, Mt. St. Mary's Coll., L.A., 1953. Libr. asst. Anaheim (Calif.) Pub. Libr., 1970-73, head Biblioteca de la Comunidad, 1973-74, children's libr. asst., 1974-76, childre's br. specialist, 1976-78, children's libr., 1978-81; head children's svcs. SantaM Maria (Calif.) Pub. Libr., 1981-85; cons. Organizationsl Ch.-Sch. Libr., L.A., 1980; owner, founder Discovery Garden, Grass Valley, Calif., 1989-93. Guest lectr. children's lit. Allan Hancock Coll., Santa Maria, 1981-85; cons. children's libr. programs, 1986 ; profl. storyteller, 1989— Contbr. poems to Amherst Soc.'s Am. Poetry Ann., 1988. Libr. liaison Casa Amistad Cmty. Svc. Group, Anaheim, 1973-74; mem. outreach com. Santiago Libr. System, Orange County, 1973-74, mem. children's svcs. com., 1971-81; mem. Cmty. Svcs. Coord. Coun., Santa Maria, 1982-85; chair children's svcs. com. Black Gold Libr. System, 1983-84; Allegro Alliance vol. for music in mountains, 1994-98; vol. Oasis Sr. Ctr., 1998-2002; mem. steering com. Cmty. Svcs. Dist. Status, Orcutt, 1999-2002; rep. 4th supervisorial dist. adv. com. Santa Barbara County Libr., 1999-2002. Mem. So. Calif. Coun. Lit. for Children and Young People, Kiwanis (sec., publicity chair, newsletter editor 1996-98, sec. Orcutt 1999-2000, Central Coast Winds & Waves, 2000—, bd. dirs. 2000-2001), Orcutt Friends of Libr. (v.p. 1999-2000, pres. 2000), P.E.O. Sisterhood (rec. sec. chpt. VZ 2002-03), Delta Epsilon Sigma. Republican. Roman Catholic.

THIELEN, CYNTHIA HENRY, lawyer, state legislator; Student, Stanford U., 1951-52, UCLA, 1952-53; BA with high honors, U. Hawaii, 1975, JD, 1978. Staff atty. Legal Aid Soc. Hawaii, 1979-84; staff atty. planning and zoning com. Honolulu City Coun., 1984-85; sr. litigation assoc. Brown, Johnston & Day, 1985-88; pvt. practice Honolulu, 1988—. Editor Windward Community Newspaper, 1969-71; mem. U. Hawaii Law Rev. Mem. State Ho. of Reps., 1990—, minority floor leader, 1992-97, co-chair women's caucus, 1997—; mem. State Hwy Safety Coun., 1977-81, State Environ. Coun., 1984-87, Nature Conservancy, Hist. Hawai'i; bd. dirs. Hanahauoli Sch., 1976-86, Hawaii Women's Polit. Action League, 1987—; candidate for lt. gov., Hawaii, 1986; v.p. State Helicopter and Tour Aircraft Adv. Bd., 1986-88, Kailua Neighborhood Bd., 1987-89; pres. Hawaii Children's Mus. Arts, Sci. and Tech., 1987-88, mem., 1987-90; chair Mayor's Adv. Task Force on the Environ., 1989-90. Sixth generation direct descendant of Patrick Henry. Mem. LWV, ABA, Hawaii Bar Assn., Hawaii Women Lawyers (chartered), Stanford Club. Office: State Capitol 415 S Beretania St Rm 443 Honolulu HI 96813-2407

THIEN-STASKO, VICKI LYNN, civil engineer technician; b. Scott Air Force Base, Ill., Apr. 22, 1953; d. Cordell Albert Knepper and Erna Rose (Studnicka) Knepper; m. Michael Lee Stasko, Nov. 19, 1988; stepchildren: Julie Stasko, Elliott Stasko ; m. William Frederick Thien, Mar. 12, 1971 (div.); 1 child, Kyle Thien. Associates of Arch., Belleville Area Coll., 1982, Associates of Applied Sci., 1988; BSC cum laude, Greenville Coll., 1998. Civil engr. tech. St. Clair County Hwy. Dept., Belleville, Ill., 1982—2002; part-time real estate agent Better Homes & Gardens /Strano, Belleville, Ill., 1993—94; part-time cosmetic cons. Christian Dior, Belleville, Ill., 1995—97; part-time census enumerator U.S. Dept. Commerce-Census Dept., Belleville, Ill., 2000—01. Co-chmn. "Operation Bag-It", Belleville, 1998—2002. Exhibitions include gingerbread creations/gingerbread scene Not a Creature was Stirring, 1996 (Best of Show, 1996), exhibitions include gingerbread creation/3'tall gingerbread Nutcracker Nuts Anyone?, 1997 (Merchant's award, 1997), exhibitions include gingerbread creation Frosty the Gingerbread Snowman, 1998 (Downtown Merchant's award, 1998), Mr. G. Shops Downtown Belleville, 2000 (Best of Show, 2000), exhibitions include gingerbread Crayola Factory, 2002 (first place profl. divsn.). Precinct committeewoman Dem. Party, Belleville, 1978—91; sec. Belleville Dem. Orgn., Belleville, 1979—91; mayoral appointment/mem. Belleville Re-develop. Com., Belleville, 1982—84; member St. Clair County Hist. Soc., Belleville, 2000—02; ch. sch. bd. mem., tchr. Christ United Ch. of Christ, Belleville, 1987—91. Recipient Ill. Gov.'s Hometown award, State of Ill., 1999. Protestant. Avocations: gardening, remodeling, travel. Office: St Clair County Hwy Dept 1415 N Belt W Belleville IL 62226

THIERRY, LAUREN, anchor; Grad. in English, Sarah Lawrence Coll.; MS in Journalism, Columbia U. Writer South China Morning Post, Hong Kong, 1984; writer, field prodr. Sta. WTNH-TV, New Haven, Conn., 1984-86; anchor, gen. assignment reporter Sta. WKRN-TV, Nashville, 1987-89, Sta. WBZ-TV, Boston, 1989-91, Sta. KCAL-TV, L.A., 1991-92; corr. King World T.V., N.Y.C., 1993-95, CNBC, Ft. Lee, N.J., 1995-96; anchor CNN Fin. News, N.Y.C., 1996—. Recipient H.W. Sackett award for Excellence in 1st Amendment Law. Office: CNN 5 Penn Plz Fl 20 New York NY 10001-1810

THIES, HEIDI MARIE, music educator; b. Denison, Iowa, July 12, 1975; d. Harvey Wayne and Lynette Marie Thies. BS, Wayne State Coll., 1997. Instr. vocal music 6-12 Sioux Ctrl. Cmty. Sch., Sioux Rapids, Iowa, 1998—. Lutheran. Avocations: travel, music, exercising. Office: Sioux Ctrl Cmty Sch 4440 US Hwy 71 Sioux Rapids IA 50585 Office Phone: 712-283-2571.*

THIESFELDT, SHEILA M. artist, educator, small business owner; b. San Juan, San Juan, Puerto Rico, Aug. 14, 1973; d. Edmund Thiesfeldt and Margarita Gonzalez. BFA, Jersey City State Coll., Jersey City, New Jersey, 1998. Art tchr. Art Ctr. No. Nj, New Milford, NJ, 1998—2001; camp art dir. Overpeck Riding Acad., Leonia, NJ, 1998—2001, camp dir., 2002—, bus. owner after sch. art sch., 2001—. Exhibited in group shows, N.J., P.R. Established Equine Art program, Leonia, NJ. Avocations: skiing, horseback riding. Office: Overpeck Fine Art 40 Fort Lee Road Leonia NJ 07605 E-mail: start125@aol.com.

THIMMIG, DIANA M. lawyer; b. Germany, May 5, 1959; BA cum laude, John Carroll U., 1980; JD, Cleve. State U., 1982. Bar: Ohio 1983, U.S. Dist. Ct. (no. dist.) Ohio 1983, U.S. Ct. Appeals (6th cir.) 1983, U.S. Supreme Ct. 1983, U.S. Ct. Appeals (3d cir. 1996); cert. Am. Bankruptcy Bd. for Consumer and Bus. Bankruptcy. Ptnr. Roetzel & Andress, Cleve. Contbr. articles to profl. jours. Hon. consul of Germany, 1988—; trustee Geauga United Way Svcs. Coun., 1992-96, Altenheim, 1992-97, Internat. Svcs. Ctr., 1998—2004; trustee Cuyahoga County Bar Assn., 1993—2004, pres.-elect, 2004—; trustee Legal Aid Soc., 1998—, pres., 2003—. Mem. Women's City Club Cleve. (pres. 1995-97). Office: Roetzel & Andress 1375 East Ninth St One Cleveland Ctr Ninth Floor Cleveland OH 44114

THOMA, COLLEEN ANN, educator; b. North Tonawanda, Ny, Dec. 29, 1939; d. Frank Victor and Helen Bursik; m. Michael Harry Thoma, Oct. 6, 1962; 1 child, Christopher Michael. BA, SUNY, Buffalo, 1986; PhD, Ind. U., 1997. Residential dir. Allegheny East MH/MR Ctr., Pitts., 1987—88; behavior cons. NISAR, Inc., Pitts., 1988—89; case mgr. No./SW MH/MR Ctr., Pitts., 1989—90, program supr. Pressley Ridge Schs., Pitts., 1990—93; grad. asst. U. Pitts., 1993—94, Ind. U., Bloomington, 1995—96, adj. asst. prof. Indpls., 1996—97; asst. prof. U. Nev., Las Vegas, 1997—2002, Va. Commonwealth U., Richmond, 2002—. Cons. in field; presenter in field. Co-author: (book) Transition Assessment: Wise Practices for Quality Lives; contbr. chapters to books, articles to profl. jours. Mem. bd. adv. U. Affiliated Program, U. Nev., Reno, 1997—2002, Opportunity Village, Las Vegas, 1998—2000, Transition Svcs., Las Vegas, 1999—2000. Grantee Initial Career award, U.S. Dept. Edn., Office Spl. Edn. Programs., 1999—2002, Va. Dept. Edn., 2003; U. fellow, Ind. U., 1995—97. Mem.: TASH (Alice H. Hayden award 1996, Positive Approaches award 1999), Am. Ednl. Rschrs. Assn., Coun. for Exceptional Children (sec. 2003—, divsn. on career devel. and transition, Disting. Mentor award Las Vegas chpt. 2001), Assn. for Persons in Supported Employment (pres. Nev. chpt., regional rep. 1997—2003), Am. Assn. on Mental Retardation. Democrat. Roman Catholic. Achievements include research in preparing special educators to facilitate self-determination in students with disabilities in transition; Key testimony to New Jersey Legislative Committee on Matthew's Law (positive behavior approaches/anti-aversive legislation); and to Nev. Legislature Com. on A.B. 280 (positive approaches/anti-aversive legislation). Avocations: travel, swimming, reading, computers, hockey. Office: Virginia Commonwealth Univ Box 842020 1015 W Main St Richmond VA 23284-2020 E-mail: cathoma@vcu.edu.

THOMAS, ANGELA M. marketing professional; b. Quincy, Mass., Oct. 19; d. Robert and Beverly Thomas. BS in Comm., Suffolk U., Boston, 1985. Music dir. WCOZ Radio, Boston, 1981, WILD Radio, Boston, 1982—86; N.E. regional promotion mgr. MCA Records, N.Y.C., 1986—89; assoc. dir. product mktg. Columbia Records, N.Y.C., 1989—90, dir. product mktg./Def Jam Venture, 1990—92, sr. dir. product mktg., 1992—93; v.p. artist devel. Columbia Records, Sony Music, 1993—95; v.p. urban music Capitol Records, EMI Music Group, N.Y.C., 1995—96; sr. v.p. mktg. and artist devel. Island Records, Polygram, N.Y.C., 1996—99; v.p. mktg., artist devel. RCA Records, BMG, N.Y.C., 2000—01; pres. Prana Mktg., Englewood, NJ, 2001—. Expert witness Universal Music, N.Y.C., 2003—, Proskauer Rose, N.Y.C., 2003—. Bd. dirs. Seeking Harmony in Neighborhoods Every Day (SHINE), N.Y.C.

THOMAS, ANN VAN WYNEN, law educator; b. The Netherlands, May 27, 1919; came to U.S., 1921, naturalized, 1926; d. Cornelius and Cora Jacoba (Daansen) Van Wynen; m. A.J. Thomas Jr., Sept. 10, 1948. AB with distinction, U. Rochester, 1940; JD, U. Tex., 1943; post doctoral degree, So. Meth. U., 1952. U.S. fgn. svc. officer, Johannesburg, South Africa, London, The Hague, The Netherlands, 1943-47; rsch. atty. Southwestern Legal Found., Sch. Law So. Meth. U., Dallas, 1952-67; asst. prof. polit. sci. So. Meth. U. Sch. Law, Dallas, 1968-73, assoc. prof., 1973-76, prof., 1976-85, prof. emeritus, 1985—. Author: Communism versus International Law, 1953, (with A.J. Thomas Jr.) International Treaties, 1950, Non-Intervention—The Law and its Import in the Americas, 1956, OAS: The Organization of American States, 1962, International Legal Aspects of Civil War in Spain, 1936-1939, 1967, Legal Limitations on Chemical and Biological Weapons, 1970, The Concept of Aggression, 1972, Presidential War Making Power: Constitutional and International Law Aspects, 1981, An International Rule of Law—Problems and Prospects, 1974. Chmn. time capsule com. Grayson County Commn. on Tex. Sesquicentennial, 1986-88; co-chmn. Grayson County Commn. on Bicentennial U.S. Constn., 1988-93; co-chmn. com. Grayson County Sesquicentennial, 1994-97; co-chmn. Grayson County Commn. on the Millenium, 1997—. Recipient Am. medal Nat. DAR Soc., 1992. Mem. Tex. Bar Assn., Am. Soc. Internat. Law, Grayson County Bar Assn. Home: Spaniel Hall 374 Coffee Cir Pottsboro TX 75076-3164

THOMAS, BETTY, director, actress; b. St. Louis, July 24, 1948; BFA, Ohio U. Former sch. tchr.; co-star Hill St. Blues, from 1981. Joined Second City Workshop, Chgo.; appeared on Second City TV, 1984; appeared in after sch. spl. The Gift of Love, 1985, Prison of Children, 1986. Appeared in The Fun Factory game show, 1976; (TV film) Outside Chance, 1978,

Nashville Grab, 1981, When Your Lover Leaves, 1983, The Late Shift, 1996 (Dirs. Guild Am. dramatic spl. award 1996); star TV series Hill Street Blues, 1981-87 (Emmy nominations 1981, 82, 83), (Emmy award, 1985); dir.: (TV) Dream On: "For Peter's Sake" (Emmy award, Outstanding Individual Achievement in Directing in a Comedy Series 1995), 1995, Male Pattern Baldness, 1998; (films) Troop Beverly Hills, 1989, The Brady Bunch Movie, 1995, Private Parts, 1997, Doctor Dolittle, 1998, 28 Days, 1999; prodr.: Can't Hardly Wait, 1998. Recipient Women in Film Crystal award, 2001.

THOMAS, BEVERLY IRENE, special education educator, educational diagnostician, substance abuse counselor; b. Del Rio, Tex., Nov. 12, 1939; d. Clyde and Eve Whistler; m. James Thomas, Jan. 28, 1972; children: Kenneth (dec.), Wade, Robert, Darcy, Betty Kay, James III, Debra, Brenda, Michael. BM summa cum laude, Sul Ross State U., 1972, MEd, 1976, MEd in Counseling, 1992, MEd in Mid. Mgmt., 1996. Cert. music, elem. edn., music edn., learning disabilities, spl. edn. generic, ednl. diagnosis, ednl. counseling, spl. edn. counseling and mid. mgmt. Tchr. Pecos-Barstow-Toyah Ind. Sch. Dist., 1974—92, 1999—2000; edn. diagnostician West Tex. State Sch., Tex. Youth Commn., ret., 1999; tchr. spl. edn. and enhanced 5th grade Pecos-Barstow-Toyah Ind. Sch. Dist., 1999-2000; youth counselor Tex. Workforce Ctr., Pecos, 2000; substance abuse counselor Reeves County Detention Ctr., 2001—. Gifted-talented coordinator 5th grade, Pecos-Barstow-Toyah Ind. Sch. Dist., 1999-2000. Mem. AAUW, ASCD, NEA, MENSA, Assn. for Children with Learning Disabilities (local sec. 1974), Tex. State Tchrs. Assn. (treas. 1991-94), Tex. Ednl. Diagnosticians Assn., Tex. Profl. Ednl. Diagnosticians, Reeves County Assn. of Children with Learning Disabilities, Nat. Coun. Tchrs. of Maths., Nat. Coun. Tchrs. English, Learning Disabilities Assn., Nat. Coun. for Geog. Edn., Learning Disabilities Assoc., Tex., Coun. for Exceptional Children, Tex. Counseling Assn., Am. Correctional Assn., Alpha Chi, Kappa Delta Pi, Chi Sigma Iota.

THOMAS, CAROL F. educational association administrator; MA in Ednl. Psychology, San Francisco State U.; PhD in Edn., U. Calif., Berkeley. Sr. program dir. S.W. Regional Lab., Los Alamitos, Calif., 1989—95; assoc. exec. dir. N.W. Regional Edn. Lab., Portland, Oreg., 1995—2001, CEO, 2001—. Office: NW Regional Ednl Lab Ste 500 101 SW Main St Portland OR 97204

THOMAS, CAROL LEE, massage therapist; b. Pawtucket, R.I., Dec. 4, 1954; d. Italo Adrian and Lenora Cecelia Costantino; m. David Michael Thomas, Nov. 13, 1982; children: Michelle, James. BA, R.I. Coll., 1978; cert., Massage Inst. of N.E., Boston, Mass., 1998. Lic. massage therapist R.I. Med. lab. technician R.I. Hosp., Providence, 1985—89, Drs. Sambandam & Colbert, Cranston, RI, 1990—92; pvt. practice RI, 1998—2000; loan officer Affordable Funding, Johnson, RI, 2003—. Scholar, R.I. State, 1973. Mem.: Am. Assn. Clin. Pathologists, Am. Massage Therapy Assn. Republican. Home: 14 Cedar St Johnston RI 02919

THOMAS, CAROL MARIE, business manager, lawyer; b. Milw., June 28, 1954; d. Howard John and Elfriede Marie (Wachcic) Schuh; m. Gerald Bernard Thomas, July 1, 1978; children: Gerald, James, Michael, Kathryn. BA, Ariz. State U., 1976; MA, Mich. State U., 1978; JD, Thomas M. Cooley Law Sch., 1997; postgrad., Wayne State U., 1997—. Bar: Mich. 1997. Head resident advisor Mich. State U., Lansing, 1977; counselor, instr. Mort. C.C., Flint, Mich., 1978; admissions coord. Delta Coll., Mich., 1978-80; bus. mgr. Dr. G. Thomas, Saginaw, Mich., 1980-97. Pres. Saginaw Newcomers Club, 1986; v.p. North Saginaw Twp. Little League, 1993-95, Saginaw County Med. Aux., 1987. Mem. State Bar Mich. Republican. Roman Catholic. Avocation: piano. Home: 4691 Hamlet Dr S Saginaw MI 48603-1988 Office: 6420 Normandy Dr Saginaw MI 48603-4354

THOMAS, CHERRYL T. former federal agency administrator; b. Oct. 31, 1946; BS Biology & Chem., Marquette U.; MS Physiology, U. Illinois, Chicago. Dir., mgmt. services Dept. Aviation, 1983—89; dir., personnel policy & utilization Dept. Water, 1989—92; deputy chief of staff Mayor Richard M. Daley City of Chgo., 1992—94, commr. Dept. Bldgs., 1994-98, chmn. U.S. Railroad Retirement Bd., 1998—2003. Mem., bd. trustees U. Chgo., 2000—. Home: 5020 S Lake Shore Dr Apt 2716N Chicago IL 60615-3220

THOMAS, CHRISTINE A. writer, editor, educator; b. Honolulu, 1974; BA, U. Calif., Berkeley, 1996; MA, U. East Anglia, Norwich, Eng., 2001. Freelance writer The Queen's Med. Ctr., Honolulu, 1996—97, Honolulu Weekly, 1996—97; staff writer Hawaii Hospitality Mag., Honolulu, 1998—98; contract feature writer Hawaii Food Industry Mag., Honolulu, 1998—98; freelance writer This Week Oahu Mag., Honolulu, 1998—98; book reviewer The Times Lit. Supplement, London, 2001—01; freelance editor The Life Transition Inst., Honolulu, 2001—01; writing workshop leader Thorpe Hamlet Mid. Sch., Norwich, England, 2001—01; book reviewer San Francisco Chronicle, 2001—; freelance editor Mich. State U. Press, East Lansing, 2002—02; book reviewer Phila. Inquirer, 2002—, Miami (Fla.) Herald, 2002—, The N.Y. Times, N.Y.C., 2002—03; freelance writer Environment News Svc. Online, 2002—03; guest lectr. journalism So. Conn. State U., New Haven, 2002—02; freelance reporter Bus. New Haven, 2002—02; book reviewer Women's Rev. Books, Wellesley, Mass., 2003—, Am. Book Rev., Normal, Ill., 2003—; adj. instr. Corinthian Colleges Inc., Santa Clara, Calif., 2003—; freelance editor PUKAR, Mumbai, India, 2003. Contbr. short fiction to mags.

THOMAS, CLARA MCCANDLESS, retired English language educator, biographer; b. Strathroy, Ont., Can., May 22, 1919; d. Basil and Mabel (Sullivan) McCandless; m. Morley Keith Thomas, May 23, 1942; children: Stephen, John. BA, U. Western Ont., London, 1941, MA, 1944; PhD, U. Toronto, 1962; DLitt (hon.), York U., 1986, Trent U., 1991; LLD (hon.), Brock U., 1992. Instr. English U. Western Ont., London, 1947-61, U. Toronto, 1958-61; asst. prof. English York U., Toronto, 1961-68, prof., 1969-84, prof. emeritus, Librs. Can. Studies Rsch. fellow, 1984—; acad. adv. panel Social Scis. and Humanities Research Council, 1981-84; mem. Killam Awards Selection Bd., 1978-81; rsch. fellow York U. Librs. Can. Studies, 1984—. Author biography of Anna Jameson, 1967, of Egerton Ryerson, 1969, of Margaret Laurence, 1969, 75, (with John Lennox) of William Arthur Deacon, 1982; Literary criticism (Can.), 1946, 72, 94, Memoir, 1999; mem. editl. bd. Literary History of Can., 1980—, Collected Works of Northrop Frye, 1993—. Recipient Internat. Coun. of Can. Studies prize No. Telecom, 1989; grantee Can. Coun., 1967, 73, Social Sci. and Humanities Rsch. Coun. Can., 1978-80 Fellow Royal Soc. Can.; mem. Assn. Can. Univs., Tchrs. English (pres. 1971-72), Assn. Can. and Que. Lit., Bus. and Profl. Women's Club, Assn. for Can. Studies. New Democratic. Office: York U 305 Scott Libr 4700 Keele St Downsview ON Canada M3J 1P3

THOMAS, CYNTHIA C. mortgage company executive; d. John H. and Barbara A. (Durtka) Thomas; m. Joseph F. Fessler, May 13, 1983 (div. Oct. 1989). BS, Ea. Mich. U., 1988; MPA, Wayne State U., 1995. Affordable housing project coord. Shorebank, Chgo., 1993—97; econ. devel. coord. Dept. Econ. Devel. City of Chgo., 1997—2001; cons. econ. devel. Chgo., 2002—; sr. loan officer Enterprise Mortgage Investments, Chgo., 2003—. Profl. cons. writer, Barcelona, 2000—02, Chgo., 2000—; prin. Thomas and Tabing, Inc.: Words that Work, Chgo., 2002—. Dep. registrar voter registration drive, Chgo., 1999—2000; tutor ESL Erie Neighborhood House, Chgo., 2002—; career coach welfare-to-work Bottomless Closet, Chgo., 2002—03. Avocations: yoga, languages. Office: Enterprise Mortgage Investments Inc 120 S Riverside Plz Fl 15 Chicago IL 60606

THOMAS, DARLENE JEAN, state employee; b. Latrobe, Pa., May 26, 1951; d. John George and Elizabeth C. (West) T.; children: Frank Joseph, Amy Marie Starry. AA, Westmoreland C.C., Youngwood, Pa., 1994. Residential svcs. aide Pa. Dept. Pub. Welfare, 1981-88; corrections officer I Pa. Dept. Corrections, Cresson, 1988-93, corrections officer II Somerset, 1993-94, corrections unit mgr., 1994—, adj. instr. Harrisburg, 1990—, mgmt. devel. com., 1996—, affirmative action com. Somerset, 1993—. Co-founder Women's Support Group, Somerset, 1993; co-facilitator Impact of Crime on Victims, Somerset, 1995. Mem. Phi Theta Kappa. Roman Catholic. Office: SCI Somerset 1590 Walters Mill Rd Somerset PA 15510-0004

THOMAS, DEBI (DEBRA J. THOMAS), ice skater; b. Poughkeepsie, N.Y., Mar. 25, 1967; d. McKinley and Janice Thomas; m. Christopher Bequette, Nov. 1996; children: Christopher Jules II, Luc. BS, Stanford U.; MD, Northwestern U., 1997. Competitive figure skater, 1976-88. Winner U.S. Figure Skating Championship, 1986, 88, World Figure Skating Championship, 1986, World Profl. Figure Skating Championship, 1988, 89, 91. Recipient Am. Black Achievement Award, Ebony mag., named Women Athlete of Yr., 1986; winner Bronze medal Olympic Games, 1988; named to U.S. Figure Skating Hall of Fame, San Jose Sports Hall of Fame. Address: Mentor Mgmt 5610 Town Center Dr # 5 Granger IN 46530-

THOMAS, DENE, academic administrator, educator; 3 children. B Lit., S.W. State U., cert. in secondary edn., 1978; PhD English, U. Minn., 1984; course, Bryn Mawr's Women in Higher Edn. Adminstrn. program, 1990. Vice provost acad. affairs to tchr., dept. chmn., dean U. Idaho; pres. Lewis-Clark State Coll., 2001—. Office: Lewis-Clark State Coll 500 8th Ave Lewiston ID 83501

THOMAS, DORIS AMELIA, family practice nurse practitioner; b. Somerville, N.J., Sept. 6, 1933; RN, Martland Med. Ctr., 1954; AA, Thomas Edison State Coll., 1992. Pub. health nurse Ocean Co. Health Dept., Toms River, 1976—94; RN staff nurse Camp Tapanemus, Freehold, 2001; RN supr. Kensington Manor, Toms River, 2002—03. Founder and pastor St. Thomas AME Ch., 1980—2001. Author: Points of Excellence, 2002. Home: 1724 Fairfield St Toms River NJ 08757 Office: St Thomas AME Ch 285 Whitesville Rd Jackson NJ 08527

THOMAS, ELAINE FREEMAN, artist, educator; b. Cleve., July 21, 1923; d. Daniel Edquard and Ellen Douglas (Wilson) Freeman; m. Frederick Lindel Thomas, June 28, 1943 (dec. May 1969); children: Janet Thomas Sullen, Frederick L. III. BS, Tuskegee (Ala.) U., 1945; MA, NYU, 1949; postgrad., U. Paris, 1966, U. Poona, India, 1973, Columbia U., 1970. Fellow Northwestern U., Evanston, Ill., 1944; Rosenwald fellow Black Mountain (N.C.) Coll., 1945; faculty, art dept. chair Tuskegee U., 1945-89. Fellow Berea (Ky.) Coll., 1956, U. of Ams., Mexico City, 1956; curator George Washington Carver Mus., Tuskegee Inst., 1962-77; mem. Fulbright-Hays Faculty Rsch., Senegal and LaGambia, Africa, 1989; panelist expansion arts Nat. Endowment of Arts, Washington, 1977-79; fgn. svc. officer evaluator U.S. Dept. State, Washington, 1979; mem. exec. com. Ala. Coun. Arts, Montgomery, 1986-91; numerous TV appearances. One-woman exhbn. Hallmark Greeting Cards, Crown Ctr., Kansas City, Mo.; participant TV documentary, 1974, 77, 82, 85, 87, 91, 94; set up George Washington Carver Exhbn., White House. Chmn. nat. screening com. Fulbright Grad. Fellows in Design, Inst. Internat. Edn., N.Y.C.. Named A Woman of Distinction, Auburn (Ala.) U., Ms. Sr. Am. of Ala., 1994, 1st runner up Ms. Sr. Am., 1994; recipient Disting. Svc. award U.S. Dept. Interior, Nat. Park Svc., Bicentennial award Pres. Gerald Ford, Resolution HR 274 award State of Ala. Ho. of Reps., Ms. Sr. Ala. award, 1994; named to 1995 Ala. Sr. Citizens Hall of Fame. Mem. Nat. Mus. of Women Artists, Optimists, Tau Beta Sigma, Delta Sigma Theta, Zeta Phi Beta (Woman of Yr. award 1978). Avocations: music, fashion, cross cultural consulting, retired senior volunteer. Home: 202 Rush Dr Tuskegee AL 36083-2707

THOMAS, ELEANOR SHEPHERD, health facility administrator; b. Brookfield, Mo., Sept. 18, 1925; d. John Davis Shepherd and Abbie Lou Gilman; m. Marvin E. Thomas, Mar. 27, 1971 (dec. Feb. 1987). Mem. staff AAB Rosecrans Field, St. Joseph, Mo., 1943—45; radio show host KUSN, St. Joseph, 1945—75; adminstrv. asst. Saxton Riverside Care Ctr., St. Joseph, 1987—. Arts educator Riverside & Woods Saxton Riverside Care Ctr., 1998—, Country Squire, 1998—, St. Francis Resdl., 1998—, Chilton Pl., 1998—. Adv. bd. Salvation Army, St. Joseph, 1990—. Named 20 Who Count, St. Joseph News Press, 2001; recipient Mayor's Arts award, City of St. Joseph, 2001, Golden Slipper award, Nat. Shoe Inst., N.Y., 1996, Silver Slipper awards, 1964, 1965, 1966. Mem.: PEO Sisterhood (pres. reciprocity). Avocations: puppet show performer/creator, ventriloquist, artist. Home: Ladybug Chalet 1701 Weisenborn Rd Saint Joseph MO 64507-2530 Office: Saxton Inc 1616 Weisenborn Rd Saint Joseph MO 64507 Office Phone: 816-232-9874.

THOMAS, ELIZABETH MARSHALL, writer; b. Boston, Sept. 13, 1931; d. Laurence K. and Lorna (McLean) Marshall; m. Stephen Thomas, 1956; children: Stephanie, Ramsay. Student, Smith Coll.; BA in English, Radliffe Coll., 1954. Writer, 1954—. Author: The Harmless People, 1959, Warrior Herdsmen, 1965, Reindeer Moon, 1987, The Animal Wife, 1990, The Hidden Life of Dogs, 1993, The Tribe of Tiger, 1994, Certain Poor Shepherds, 1998, The Social Lives of Dogs, 2000. Office: 80 E Mountain Rd Peterborough NH 03458-2318

THOMAS, ELLEN LOUISE, school system administrator; b. Doylestown, Pa., Nov. 30, 1940; d. Edward Martin and Evelyn Graham (Axenroth) Happ; m. Eugene Greene Leffever, June 30, 1963 (dec. Nov. 1978); children: Eugene Greene II, Jeanette Ellen Dellaripa; m. William Dewey Thomas, Sept. 15, 1981; 1 child, Jeremiah David. BA in Edn., Immaculata (Pa.) Coll., 1962; postgrad., Pa. State U., 1962-67. Pvt. practice tutor, Doylestown, 1958-65; tchr. Cen. Bucks Sch. System, Doylestown, 1962-65; adminstr. The Curiosity Shoppe, Doylestown, 1965—, The Toddler Ctr., Doylestown, 1979—; exec. dir. Camp Curiosity, Doylestown, 1984—, Thomas Lea Equestrian Ctr., Doylestown, 1988—. Tchr. trainer Confortunity of Christian Doctrine, Doylestown, 1965-78; cons. early childhood Am. Sch. in Hong Kong, 1981-84; lectr. in early childhood Bucks County Community Ctr., Newtown, Pa., 1978-90; workshop facilitator Head Start, Phila., 1990; cons. day care Cen. Bucks C. of C., Doylestown, 1989-90; ednl. coord. Forest Grove Presbyn. Ch., 1984-90. Mem. U.S. C. of C., Washington, Bucks County C. of C., Doylestown, Nat. Fedn. of Ind. Bus., Washington; children's ministry coord. Jesus Focus Ministry, 1995—; trainer Pa. Child Care, 1995—; pres. Pa. Day Camp Assn., 1998-2000; Sunday sch. tchr. Hilltown Bapt. Ch., 1995-2000; mem. Am. Camping Assn., 1994-, Plumstead Christian Sch. Bd., 1995-2001; varsity tennis coach, Plumstead Christian Sch.-boys, 1998-2003, girls, 2001-03; children's chmn. Central Bucks Village Fair, 2001-03. Mem. ASCD, Assn. for Childhood Edn. Internat., United Pvt. Acad. Schs. Assn., Bucks County Assn. Edn. Young Children (pres. 1974-78). Office: The Curiosity Shoppe 4425 Landisville Rd Doylestown PA 18901-1134 E-mail: FaxThomdew@aol.com.

THOMAS, ENOLIA, nutritionist, educator; b. Little Rock, Ark., June 1, 1938; d. Calvin - and Bernice Thomas. BS, Lincoln U., Jefferson City, Mo., 1960. Hosp. dietician Dept. Health, Christiansted, Saint Croix, Virgin Islands, 1969—72; chief nutritionist Dept. Social Welfare, St Croix. Virgin Islands, 1972—83; hosp. dietician Vets Administrn., Kerrville, Tex., 1984—85; rsch. dietician King Fasial Specialist Hosp. and Rsch. Ctr., Riyadh, Saudi Arabia, 1985—96; nutritionist Denver Dept. Human Svcs., 1996—. Contbr. articles to profl. jours. Vol. libr. docent Denver Pub. Libr., 1997—. Major USAF, 1960—69. Recipient Title 7 Older Americans Act/ Virgin Islands Elderly Nutrition Program, Commission On Aging, 1973 - 1983. Mem.: Nat. Assn. Commodity Supplemental Food Program (bd. dirs. 1999—2001), Am. Dietetic Assn., Stiles African Am. Heritage Ctr. (bd. dirs. 2001—04), Girl Scouts of Am. (life; troop leader 1962 - 83), Toastmasters Internat. (Toastmaster of the Yr. 1995), Alpha Kappa Alpha, Inc. (life; pres. 1978—82, Outstanding Woman in the Field of Nutrition). Home: 2298 S Kenton Way Aurora CO 80014 Office: Denver Food Assistance Program 80 South Santa Fe Dr Denver CO 80223 Office Fax: (720) 944-3418.

THOMAS, EVELYN B. agricultural products supplier; Sec., treas., bookkeeper Brandt Fertilizer, Pleasant Plains, Ill., 1953—; co-owner Har Brand, 1963-67, Brandt Chemical, 1967; sec./treas. Brandt Consolidated, Pleasant Plains, Ill. Office: Brandt Consolidated PO Box 277 Pleasant Plains IL 62677-0277 Fax: 217-626-1927. E-mail: bcadmin@brandtconsolidated.com.

THOMAS, FAYE EVELYN J. elementary and secondary school educator; b. Summerfield, La., Aug. 3, 1933; d. Reginald Felton and Atlee (Hunter) Johnson; m. Archie Taylor Thomas, Sept. 8, 1960; 1 child, Dwayne Andre. BA, So. U., 1954; student, Tuskegee Inst., 1958, student, 1969, U. Detroit, 1961, student, 1962, student, 1963, Ctrl. Mich. U., 1965; MS, U. Ctrl. Ark., 1971, Cleve. State U., 1979. Tchr. Cullen (La.) Elem. Sch., 1957; tchr. English and social studies Charles Brown H.S., Springhill, La., 1957—70; tchr. English, Upward Bound Program, Grambling State U., 1968; tchr. English, Springhill H.S., 1970; elem. intermediate tchr. Riveredge Elem. Sch., Berea, Ohio, 1971—93; tchr. 7th grade English, Ford Mid. Sch., 1993—94; program dir. Teen Pregnancy Prevention Program, 2003—04. Tchr. asst. elem. coun. curriculum and instrn. Berea Sch. Dist., 1984—85. Author: When the Time Is Right, Move On, A Journey to the Mountain Top, 2003. Grantee, EDPA, 1970—71, Internat. Paper Found., 1958, 1960, NDEA, 1965; scholar Martha Holden Jennings scholar, 1984—85. Mem.: NEA, Assn. Supervision and Curriculum Devel., N.E. Ohio Tchrs. Assn., Berea Edn. Assn., Ohio Edn. Assn., Ohio Motorists Assn., Charles Brown Soc. Orgn. (trustee 1984—), Black Caucus NEA, People United to Save Humanity, Toastmasters, Order Eastern Star. Democrat. Baptist. Office: 311 Henrietta White Blvd Springhill LA 71075-8407

THOMAS, GEORGIE A. state official; BA, Cornell U., 1965; MBA, Columbia U., 1973. Asst. portfolio mgr. Money Mgmt. dept. R.W. Pressprich & Co. Inc., N.Y.C., 1968-71; portfolio analyst Bache & Co., N.Y.C., 1971-72; with Exxon Corp., N.Y.C., 1973-76, consolidation analyst Treas. dept., 1975-76; treas. Penntech Papers Inc., N.Y.C., 1976-79; budget dir. Yankee Publishing Inc., Dublin, N.H., 1982-85; treas. State of N.H., Concord, 1985—. Mem. econ. growth and productivity and tech. coms. Bus. Research Adv. Council of Bur. Labor Statistics, 1978-79; mem. alumni counseling bd. Columbia U. Bus. Sch., 1973-79 Editor: Jour. World Bus., Columbia Bus. Sch. Mem. Fin. Women's Assn. N.Y. (mem. exec. bd. 1977-78), Womens Econ. Roundtable Clubs: Cornell of Fairfield County (Conn.). Home: PO Box 1317 Campton NH 03223-1317 Office: State NH State House Annex Rm 121 Concord NH 03301

THOMAS, HANNAH H. retired educator; b. Florence, Ala. d. Everett Napoleon and Evernee Hawkins; m. Monroe Thomas, June 11, 1945. BS, A&M U., Huntsville, Ala., 1951; MEd, U. Cin., 1964. Tchr. 4th, 5th and 6th grades Lauderdale Sch. Sys., Florence, 1948-55, tchr. sci. and biology, 1955-57, tchr. 4th and 5th grades, 1957-58; tchr. 4th, 5th and 6th grades Cin. Sch. Sys., 1958-74, remedial tchr. 4th, 5th and 6th grades, 1974-80. Organizer, dir. Sojourner Truth Theater, Cin., 1985—, African-Am. Heritage Day, Cin., 1988—. Named Woman of Yr., Cin. Enquirer, 1992, Tchr. of Yr. Lauderdale County Tchr., 1956, Woman of Yr., Zeta Phi Beta, 1998, one of 200 Great Cincinnatians, Cin. Bicentennial, 1988. Mem. Harriet Beecher Stowe Hist.-Cultural Assn. (pres. 1980—), NAACP, AARP, CH Forum. Baptist. Avocation: reading writing poetry and songs. Home: 1059 Loiska Ln Cincinnati OH 45224-2731

THOMAS, HAZEL BEATRICE, state official; b. Franklin, Tenn. d. William Henry Fuller and Mattie Betty (Covington) Fuller Young; m. Charles B. Thomas (dec. 1969); children: Charles Bradford Jr., Deborah Carlotta (dec.). BA, Fisk U., 1946; MA, Tenn. State U., 1972. Cert. elem. and secondary tchr., Tenn. Tchr. elem. Met.-Nashville Sch., 1954-87; rsch. assoc. Johns Hopkins U., Balt., 1978-79, Marquette U., Milw., 1979-86; exec. asst. to commr. edn. Tenn. Dept. Edn., Nashville, 1987—. Cons. Peer Mediated Learning System, Nashville, 1980-82; instr. Met. Sch. Tchr. Ctr., Nasvhville, 1985-87; mem. tech. assistance team for high sch. that work, So. Regional Edn. Bd., 1998-99; nat. disseminator student team learning rsch. project, Johns Hopkins U., 1978-1979. Author training modules Substitute Teaching, Tchr. Aides. Pres. Davidson County Dem. Women, Nashville, 1985-87; v.p. Tenn. Fedn. Dem. Women, 1989-91, pres., 2001—; pres. elect Nashville Women's Polit. Caucus, 1991—; pres. Tenn. Women's Polit. Caucus, 1994-95; mem. adminstrv. com. of bd. Nat. Women's Polit. Caucus, 1993-95, v.p., 1995—, v.p. edn. and tng., 2001—; mem. Tenn. Leadership, Inc., 1992—; spkr., polit. trainer US Info. Agy., Nairobi, Kenya, 1997; mem. exec. bd. Citizen's Com. for Ann. Gov.'s Prayer Breakfast, 1992—; mem. exec. com. Tenn. Dem. Party, 2001—; chmn. edn. com. Bellevue C. of C.; pres. Tenn. Fedn. Dem. Women, 2001-03; v.p. Nat. Fedn. Dem. Women, 2002—; mem. pub. edn. and govt. com. Metro. Govt. Nashville, Tenn., 2002-03. Recipient Svc. to Edn. and Teaching Profession award Nat. Coun. Negro Women, 1988; Nat. Def. Edn. Act scholar, 1965, 67. Mem. Am. Bus. Womens Assn. (charter), Tenn. Edn. Assn. (pres. dept. classroom tchr. 1974-75, state dept. affiliate, pres. 1988-Ed. c90), Bellevue C. of C. (bd. govs. 1990-91, edn. chair 2002-03), Assn. Classroom Tchr. (pres. S.E. region 1975-76), Met. Nashville Edn. Assn. (exec. bd. 1971-77), Bellevue Sertoma Club (life, pres. 1990-91), Nat. Women's Polit. Caucus (v.p. 1995—), Nat. Assn. Dem. Women (v.p., 2003-05, named Woman of Distinction for Tenn., 2002, 03), Nat. Fedn. Dem. Women (v.p. 2003). Democrat. Baptist. Avocations: reading, bridge. Office: Tenn Dept Edn Andrew Johnson Tower 710 James Robertson Pkwy Nashville TN 37243-1219 E-mail: hazel.thomas@state.tn.us.

THOMAS, HELEN A. (MRS. DOUGLAS B. CORNELL), newspaper bureau executive; b. Winchester, Ky., Aug. 4, 1920; d. George and Mary (Thomas) T.; m. Douglas B. Cornell. BA, Wayne U., 1942; LLD, Ea. Mich. State U., 1972; LHD, Wayne State U., 1974; LLD, Ferris State Coll., 1978; LHD, U. Detroit, 1979; LLD (hon.), Brown U., 1986, St. Bonaventure U., 1988, Franklin Marshall U., 1989, No. Mich. U., 1989, Skidmore Coll., 1992, Susquehanna U., 1993, Sage Coll., 1994, U. Mo., 1994, Northwestern U., 1995, Franklin Coll., 1995, Mich. State U., 1996, Potsdam U., 1998, A. Willenberg Univ., 1999; BA in Law, Mount Vernon Coll., 1999; LLD (hon.), Milliken U., 2002, Am. U. Beirut, 2003. With UPI, 1943-2000, wire svc. reporter, 1943-74, White House bur. chief, 1974-2000; columnist Hearst Newspapers, 2000—. Author: Dateline White House. Recipient Woman of Yr. in Comm. award, Ladies Home Jour., 1975, 4th Estate award, Nat. Press Club, 1984, Journalism award, U. Mo., Al Newharth award, 1990, Ralph McGill award, 1995, Lifetime award, Internat. Media Found., Internat. Women's Press Found., 1996, White House Corr. Assn., 1998, Lowell Thomas award, Marist Coll., 2001, Kahlil Gibran award, 2003, NOW award, 2003, Torch Bearer award, Planned Parenthood award, Physician Social Responsibility award. Mem. Women's Nat. Press Club (pres. 1959-60, William Allen White Journalism award), Am. Newspaper Women's Club (past v.p.), White House Corrs. Assn. (pres. 1976, Lifetime Achievement award 1998), Nat. Newspaper Assn. (Lifetime award 2002), Gridiron Club (pres. 1993), Sigma Delta Chi (fellow, Hall of Fame), Delta Sigma Phi (hon.). Home: 2501 Calvert St NW Washington DC 20008-2620 Office Phone: 202-263-6437. E-mail: helent@hearstdc.com.

THOMAS, HELEN HAZER, electrical engineer; b. Tehran, June 23, 1964; came to U.S., 1984; d. Abbas and Hajar (Youssefi) Hazer; m. Johnny

R. Thomas, Jan. 1, 1997. BSEE, U. Nev., 1988, MSEE, 1991. Tchr. asst. U. Nev., Las Vegas, 1988-89; sr. elec. engr. Fiber Chem. Inc., Las Vegas, 1989—. Recipient grant Army Rsch. Office, U. Nev., 1988-89. Mem. Phi Kappa Phi. Achievements include rsch. in high electron mobility transistors. Office: Fiber Chem Inc 1181 Grier Dr Ste B Las Vegas NV 89119-3746 Home: PO Box 530897 Henderson NV 89053-0897

THOMAS, JACQUELINE MARIE, journalist, editor; b. Nashville, Aug. 31, 1952; d. John James and Dorothy Jacqueline (Phillips) T. BA, Briarcliff Coll., 1972; M.Internat. Affairs, Columbia U., 1974. Reporter Chgo Sun-Times, 1974-85; assoc. editor Courier-Jour. and Louisville Times, 1985-86, Detroit Free Press, 1986-93; deputy bureau chief, news editor Detroit News, Washington Bureau, 1993-94, bur. chief, 1994-97; editl. page editor The Balt. Sun, 1997—. Instr. Roosevelt U., Chgo., 1983 Nieman fellow Harvard U., 1983 Mem. Chgo. Assn. Black Journalists (Print Journalist of Yr. 1982), Nat. Assn. Black Journalists, Nat. Press Found. (bd. mem., vice chair), Am. Soc. Newspaper Editors, Nat. Assn. Minority Media Execs., Nat. Conf. Editl. Writers. Office: Balt Sun 501 N Calvert PO Box 1377 Baltimore MD 21278-0001

THOMAS, JACQUELYN MAY, librarian; b. Mechanicsburg, Pa., Jan. 26, 1932; d. William John and Gladys Elizabeth (Warren) Harvey; m. David Edward Thomas, Aug. 28, 1954; children: Lesley J., Courtenay J., Hilary A. BA summa cum laude, Gettysburg Coll., 1954; student, U. N.C., 1969; MEd, U. N.H., 1971. Libr. Phillips Exeter Acad., Exeter, N.H., 1971-77, acad. libr., 1977—. Chair governing bd. Child Care Ctr., 1987-91; chair Com. to Enhance Status of Women, Exeter, 1981-84; chair Loewenstein Com., Exeter, 1982—; pres. Cum Laude Soc., Exeter, 1984-86; James H. Ottaway Jr. prof., 1990—; mem. bldg. com. Exeter Pub. Libr., 1986-88; chair No. New Eng., Coun. for Women in Ind. Schs., 1985-87; chmn. Lamont Poetry Program, Exeter, 1984-86. Editor: The Design of the Library: A Guide to Sources of Information, 1981, Rarities of Our Time: The Special Collections of the Phillips Exeter Academy Library; pub.: Memorial Minutes, Phillips Exeter Academy, 1936-2002. Libr. trustee, treas. Exeter Day Sch., 1965-69; bd. Exeter Hosp. Vols., 1954-59; mem. Exeter Hosp. Corp., 1978—; bd. dirs. Greater Portsmouth Cmty. Found., 1990—; active AAC&U, On Campus with Women, Wellesley Coll. Ctr. for Rsch. on Women; mem. People to People Amb. Program, sch. and youth svcs. libr. del. to People's Rep. China, 1998. Grantee N.H. Coun. for Humanties, 1981-82, NEH, 1982; recipient Lillian Radford trust award, 1989. Mem. ALA, Internat. Assn. Sch. Librs., New Eng. Libr. Assn., N.J., Ednl. Media Assn., New Eng. Assn. Ind. Sch. Librs., Am. Assn. Sch. Librs. (chmn. non-pub. sch. sect.), Phi Beta Kappa. Home: 17 Eagle Dr Newmarket NH 03857 Office: Class of 1945 Libr Phillips Exeter Acad 20 Main St Exeter NH 03833-2460 Fax: 603-777-4389. E-mail: jthomas@exeter.edu.

THOMAS, JANEY SUE, elementary school principal; b. Clarksville, Tenn., Feb. 10, 1949; d. James Ernest and Ethel Mae (Evans) Kirkland; m. Tony Lee Thomas, Oct. 9, 1965; children: Jeff, Kelli. BS in Elem. Edn., Austin Peay State U., 1979, MA in Elem. Edn. Adminstrn., 1982, postgrad., 1987-89. Tchr. Charlotte (Tenn.) Jr. High Sch., 1979-86; prin. Vanleer (Tenn.) Elem. Sch., 1986-91, Oakmont Elem. Sch., Dickson, Tenn., 1991—. Ednl. rep. Concerned Citizens for Edn., Dickson County, 1988; mem. com. United Way Med. Tenn., Dickson County, 1990-91, bd. dirs., 1992-93. Recipient Nat. Sch. of Recognition award U.S. Dept. Edn., 1990. Mem. NAESP (Excellence in Edn. award 1989-90), Tenn. Assn. Elem. Sch. Prins. (Nat. Exemplary Sch. award 1989-90), Dickson County Edn. Assn. (pres. 1989-90). Baptist. Avocations: reading, traveling, shopping. Home: 226 Druid Hills Dr Dickson TN 37055-3331 Office: Oakmont Elem Sch 630 Highway 46 S Dickson TN 37055-2552

THOMAS, JEANETTE MAE, public accountant; b. Minn., Dec. 19, 1946; d. Herbert and Arline Harmon; m. Gerald F. Thomas, Aug. 9, 1969; children: Bradley, Christopher. BS, Winona State U., 1968; postgrad., Colo. State U.; CFP, Coll. for Fin. Planning, Denver, 1985. Enrolled agt.; cert. fin. planner; registered rep. NASD; registered investment advisor; accredited tax advisor. Tchr. pub. schs. systems, Colo., N.Mex., Mich., 1968-72; adminstrv. asst. Bus. Men's Svcs., Ft. Collins, Colo., 1974-75; tax cons. Tax Corp. Am., Ft. Collins, Colo., 1972-80; chief acct. Jayland Enterprises, La Porte, Colo., 1981—; pres., CEO Thomas Fin. Svcs. Inc., Ft. Collins, 1980—. Contbr. articles to newspapers and profl. newsletters. Bd. dirs. local PTO, 1984-85; treas. Boy Scouts Am., 1985-88; master food safety advisor coop. ext. Colo. State U., 1988—; spkr., steering com. AARP Women's Fin. Info. Program, 1988-98; past chair adv. bd. Larimer County Coop. Ext., Colo. State U.; quality rev. com., sch. to career adv. bd. Poudre R-1 Schs.; judge county fairs. Mem. Internat. Assn. Fin. Planning (past officer), Am. Soc. Women Accts. (bd. dirs. 1984-86, 96-98), Workforce Investment Bd. (chair 1994-95), Nat. Soc. Accts., Colo. Soc. Pub. Accts., Inst. CFPs, Am. Notary Assn., Ft. Collins C. of C. (red carpet com. bus. assistance coun. 1989-96). Avocations: sewing, bread baking, food preservation, fly fishing, golf. Office: 400 S Howes St Ste 2 Fort Collins CO 80521-2802 Home: PO Box 559 Hale MI 48739-0559

THOMAS, JENNIFER BUTLER, special education educator, coach; b. Cleveland, Ohio, Apr. 2, 1975; d. Charlene E. and R. Richard Butler, Clayton G. (Stepfather) and Elaine Butler(Stepmother); m. Jamie W. Thomas, July 26, 2003. BS in Edn., Ashland U., Ashland, Ohio, 1993—97. Cert. tchr. of develpmentally handicapped Ohio, 1997, early edn. handicapped children Ohio, 1997, specific learning disablities Ohio, 1997. Varied exceptionalities tchr. Lee County Schools, Fort Myers, Fla., 1997—98; learning resource tchr. Gahanna Jefferson Schools, Gahanna, Ohio, 1999—2002; intervention specialist Wadsworth City Schools, Wadsworth, Ohio, 2002—. Gymnastics instr. YMCA, Fort Myers, Fla., 1997—98; academic tutor Gahanna Jefferson Schools, Gahanna, Ohio, 1998—2002; gymnastics instr. YMCA, Columbus, Ohio, 1998—99; h.s. cheerleading coach Gahanna Jefferson Schools, Gahanna, Ohio, 1999—2002; mid. sch. cheerleading coach Wadsworth (Ohio) City Schools, 2003—. Mem.: Assn. Supervision and Curriculum Devel., Coun. For Exceptional Children, Phi Mu Frat. Alumnae Chpt. Home: 600 Trease Rd Wadsworth OH 44281

THOMAS, JO, journalist; b. Long Beach, Calif., Dec. 7, 1943; d. Guy O'Neil DeYoung, Jr. and Josephine (Bradley) DeYoung; m. William L. Thomas III, June 12, 1965 (div. Sept. 1969); m. William F. Kelleher Jr., Dec. 19, 1985; children: Susan Elizabeth Kelleher, Kathleen DeYoung Kelleher. BA summa cum laude, Wake Forest U., 1965; MA, U. N.C., 1967. Reporter Cin. Post and Times-Star, 1966-70, Detroit Free Press, 1971-77; from Washington corr. to writer N.Y. Times, 1977—2001, writer, 2001—02; assoc. prof. U. Ill., Urbana, Ill., 1987—94, asst. chancellor, 2003—. Contbr. articles to newspapers and mags. Recipient Outstanding Reporting award Detroit Press Club, 1974-75, Robert F. Kennedy award, 1973; Nieman fellow Harvard U., 1970-71. Mem. Phi Beta Kappa, Kappa Tau Alpha. Office: U Ill Swanlund Adminstrn Bldg 601 E John St Champaign IL 61820 E-mail: jothomas@uiuc.edu.

THOMAS, KAREN P. composer, conductor; b. Seattle, Sept. 17, 1957; BA in Composition, Cornish Inst., 1979; MusM in Composition and Conducting, U. Wash., 1985. Condr. The Contemporary Group, 1981-85; condr., music dir. Wash. Composers Forum, 1984-86; artistic dir., condr. Seattle Pro Musica, 1987—. Conducting debut Seattle, 1987; composer: Four Delineations of Curtmantle for Trombone or Cello, 1982, Metamorphoses on a Machaut Kyrie for Strong Orch. or Quartet, 1983, Cowboy Songs for Voice and Piano, 1985, There Must Be a Lone Range for Soprano and Chamber Ensemble, 1987, Brass Quintet, 1987, Four Lewis Carroll Songs for Choir, 1989, (music/dance/theater) Boxiana, 1990, Elementi for Clarinet and Percussion, 1991, (one-act children's opera) Coyote's Tail, 1991, Clarion Dances for Brass Ensemble, 1993, Roundup for Sax Quartet, 1993, Three Medieval Lyrics for Choir, 1992, Sopravvento for Wind Quartet and Percussion, 1994, When Night Came for Clarinet and Chamber Orch. or Clarinet and Piano, 1994, Over the City for Choir, 1995, also numerous others. Recipient Composers Forum award N.W. Chamber Orch., 1984, King County Arts Commn., 1987, 90, Artist Trust, 1988, 93, 96, Seattle Arts Commn., 1988, 91, 93, New Langton Arts, 1988, Delius Festival, 1993, Melodious Accord award 1993; fellow Wash. State Arts Commn., 1991; Charles E. Ives scholar AAAI. Mem. Am. Choral Dirs. Assn., Broadcast Music, Am. Music Ctr., Internat. Alliance for Women in Music, Soc. Composers, Chorus Am., Conductors Guild. Office: 4426 1st Ave NW Seattle WA 98107-4306 E-mail: kpthomas1@aol.com.

THOMAS, KATHERINE CAROL, special education educator; b. Alice, Tex., June 15, 1943; d. Charles Anthony Sr. and elvira (Garcia) Rogers; m. Richard Harold Jr. Thomas, Aug. 9, 1980; 1 child, Rhonda Crystal. BS in Edn., Tex. A&I U., 1965; MS in Edn., Anticoch U., 1975. Tchr. Salazar Elem. Sch., Alice, Tex., 1965-73; supr. Alice Indetification and Referral System, 1975-78; supr. bilingual edn. Alice (Tex.) Sch. Dist., 1978-80, tchr., supr. migrant edn., 1980-83, tchr. spl. edn., 1983—. Sec.-treas. Slazar PTA, 1965-75; mem. com. Water Authority Commn., Alice, 1981. Mem. Tex. Tchrs. Assn., NEA, Am. Tchrs. Prins. Assn., Childhood Edn. Assn. (treas. 1968-74), AAUP, Spl. Edn. Assn. Democratic. Roman Catholic. Home: PO Box 3132 Alice TX 78333-3132

THOMAS, KATHERINE JANE, magazine and newspaper columnist; b. Bryan, Tex., Mar. 22, 1942; d. William Holt Jr. and Mary Anne (McCasland) Oliver; m. Robert Wayne Thomas, June 1, 1968; children: Jennifer Ann, Michael Frederick. BA, U. Tex., 1964. News reporter Abilene Reporter, Tex., 1964-67; with Ralston Purina Co., 1967-68; journalist The Eagle, Bryan, Tex., 1969-72, Wall St. Jour., Houston Bus. Jour., 1976-80; bus. columnist Houston Post, 1980-95. Sr. bus. columnist; features editor Hart's Energy Markets; electric power editor Oil & Gas Jour. Online. Judge Houston Area Inc. Mag. Entrepreneur of Yr., 1995; vol. judge out-of-state journalism competitions. Recipient Writing awards Tex. Press Assn., 1978-79, AP, 1966, 88, 91, Dallas Press Club Katie Finalist, 1990, 94, Matrix, 1989-90, Press Club of Houston, 1987, 89, 90, 91, 95, 96, Sierra Club of Houston, 1989, St. Louis United Fund, 1968, Abilene C. of C., 1965. Mem. Press Club of Houston (bd. dirs., sec. 1991), Press Club of Houston Ednl. Found. (treas. 1991, bd. dirs.). Episcopalian. Avocations: sailing, entertaining, walking, reading. Office: 1700 West Loop S Ste 1000 Houston TX 77027-3007 E-mail: katet@ogjonline.com.

THOMAS, LEONA MARLENE, health information educator; b. Rock Springs, Wyo., Jan. 15, 1933; d. Leonard H. and Opal (Wright) Francis; children: Peter, Paul, Patrick, Alexis. BA, Govs. State U., 1982, MHS, 1986; cert. med. records adminstrn., U. Colo., 1954. Staff assoc. Am. Med. Records Assn., Chgo., 1972-77, asst. editor, 1979-81; statistician Westlake Hosp., Melrose Park, Ill., 1982-84; asst. prof. Chgo. State U., 1984—, acting dir. health info. adminstrn. program, 1991-92; acting dir. health info. Internat. Coll., Naples, Fla., 1994; dir. health info. adminstrn. program Chgo. State U., 1994—. Mem. adv. com. Wellness Ctr., mem. adv. com. occupl. therapy program Chgo. State U. Mem. Assembly on Edn., Am. Health Info. Mgmt. Assn., APHA, Chgo. and Vicinity Med. Records Assn., Ill. Assn. Allied Health Profls., Gov.'s State Alumni Assn. Democrat. Methodist. Home: 6340 Americana Dr Apt 1101 Willowbrook IL 60527 Office: Chgo State U Coll Health Scis 95th at King Dr Chicago IL 60628

THOMAS, LISA, food service executive; Co-founder Kali's Sweets and Savories (now Clif Bar, Inc.), 1986—, CEO, 1996—. Office: Clif Bar Inc 1610 5th St Berkeley CA 94710-1715

THOMAS, LISE-MARIE, actress; b. Dallas, June 16, 1963; d. Robet Harold and Camilla Delores (Wicks) T.; m. Dietmar Rudolf Wertanzl, Aug. 1, 1992; 1 child, Sterling Alexa. BA in Liberal Studies, San Francisco State U., 1997. Actress/singer Beach Blanket Babylon, San Francisco, 1983-84, So. Az. Light Opera Co., Tucson, Az., 1991-95, Crystal Cruises, Inc., L.A., 1991-95; actress Soap Operas, L.A., 1988-99; asst. dir. Crystal Cruises, Inc., L.A., 1995-99; dir. various cabaret artists, L.A., 1999-2000. Principal Sterling Cons. Co., L.A., 1999; original cast mem. Tune the Grand Up (cabaret gold award), 1985. Mem. Phi Beta Kappa. Avocations: reading, skiing, travel, motherhood. Address: 3545 Park Ln Miami FL 33133-6824

THOMAS, LOIS C. organist, music educator; b. Ft. Worth, Oct. 15, 1932; d. Walter Scott and Margaret Alice Dawn Cook; m. Richard Wallace Thomas, Nov. 5, 1988. BA in Organ Performance, Tex. Christian U., 1986; postgrad., SWBT Sem. Organist Western Hills Bapt. Ch., Ft. Worth, 1959-69, 1st Ch. of Christ, Scientist, Ft. Worth, 1969-84, First Congl. Ch., Ft. Worth, 1985-87; organist, dir. St. Charles Martyr Anglican Ch., Grand Prairie, Tex., 1989—. Priest Communion of Evang. Episcopal Chs. Composer choral anthems. Fin. officer USCG Aux., Grapevine, Tex., 1989-95, sec., Grand Prairie, Tex., 1995. Mem. Am. Guild Organists (svc. playing cert., mem. phone com.), Arlington Music Tchr. Assn. (mem. phone com.). Home: 1501 Connally Ter Arlington TX 76010-4514

THOMAS, LYDIA WATERS, research and development executive; b. Norfolk, Va., Oct. 13, 1944; d. William Emerson and Lillie Ruth (Roberts) Waters; m. James Carter Thomas (div. 1970); 1 child, Denee Marrielle. BS in Zoology, Howard U., 1965, PhD in Cytology, 1973; MS in Microbiology, Am. U., 1971. Pres., CEO Mitretek Sys., McLean, Va., 1996—. Appointee Strategic Environ. R&D Sci. Adv. Bd., 1995-98; bd. dirs. Cabot Corp., George Washington U., U.S. Energy Assocs.; mem. Labs., Inc. Author: Automation Impacts on Industry, 1983; contbr. First World Energy Demand, 1996. Mem. Environ. Adv. Bd., U.S. C.E., 1980-82; expert witness, Senate. U.S. govt. pub. hearings, Washington, 1985; House of Reps., 1994; mem. adv. bd. George Wash. U. Va. campus; mem. Supt.'s Bus./Industry Adv. Coun. Fairfax County Pub. Schs.; mem. Va. Rsch. and Tech. Adv. Commn. Recipient Tribute to Women in Internat. Industry YMCA, 1986, EBONE Image award Coalition of 100 Black Women, 1990, Dean's award Black Engineer of Yr., 1991. Mem. AAAS, AIAA, Am. Soc. Toxicology, Nat. Def. Indsl. Assn., Teratology Soc., U.S. Energy Assn., Conf. Bd., Alpha Kappa Alpha. Office: Mitretek Systems 3150 Fairview Park Dr Falls Church VA 22042-4504

THOMAS, M. ANN, bank executive; m. Tony Singer, Aug. 31, 2001. JD, Ohio No. U., 1985. Atty. Bracewell & Patterson; exec. v.p. Woodforest Nat. Bank, Houston, 1995—99, COO, 1999—2001, pres., COO, 2001—. Named one of 25 Women to Watch, US Banker Mag., 2003. Office: Woodforest Nat Bank 13301 E Fwy Houston TX 77015*

THOMAS, MARCIA MARKOWITZ, library director, educator; b. Fort Worth, Dec. 2, 1944; d. Samuel and Davida Shosid Markowitz; m. Rickard James Thomas, Sept. 1, 1978 (div. July 1982); children: Aaron, James; m. John Katchmarik, Dec. 2, 1994. BA, U. Mo., 1968, MA, 1975. Libr. asst. Kansas City (Mo.) Pub. Libr., 1968—73; libr. dir. Ruth R. Cleveland Meml. Libr., Kansas City, 1976—. Prof. human biology Cleve. Chiropractic Coll., Kansas City, 1996—, faculty coun. pres., 1993—95, Kansas City, 1997—99, Kansas City, 2001—03, chair instl. rev. bd., 1979—. Co-author: Chiropractic: An Annotated Bibliography, 2000; contbr. articles to profl. jours. Rep. Southtown Neighborhood Coun., Kansas City; campus coord. Heart of Am. United Way, 1999—; bd. dirs. Astor Place Homes Assn., Kansas City; mem. task force sch. governance Kansas City Consensus. Mem.: ALA, MLA (chiropractic librs. sect., chair, program chair, bylaws com.), Chiropractic Libr. Consortium (pres., treas., sec.), Kansas City Libr. Network (treas., archivist), Midwest Bioethics Ctr., Med. Libr. Assn. (sect. coun. rep.). Liberal. Jewish. Avocations: bioethics, music, neighborhood advocacy. Office: Ruth R Cleveland Meml Libr 6401 Rockhill Rd Kansas City MO 64131 Business E-Mail: marcia@cleveland.edu.

THOMAS, MARGARET ANN, educational administrator, art educator; b. Waukesha, Wis., June 19, 1951; d. Melvin Michael and Elizabeth (Brewer) T.; m. Bruce Fiedler; 1 child, James. BA in Art Edn., Beloit Coll., 1974; MA in Art, U. Wis., Whitewater, 1981, MA in Ednl. Psychology, 1985; MS in Ednl. Adminstrn., U. Wis., 1995, PhD in Ednl. Adminstrn., Ednl. Psychology. Cert. K-12 art tchr., Wis., elem. and H.S. prin., curriculum dir. K-12, supt. Tchr. art Beloit (Wis.) Pub. Schs., 1974—; adj. prof. Beloit Coll., 1992—; prin. Mclenegan Elem. Sch., Beloit, 1999—2001, adminstr. grants, 2001—02, adminstr. acad. reporting sys., 2002—; adminstr. Synectics Mid. Charter Schs., 2003—. Muralist instr. Beloit Coll., summers, 1985-91, adj. prof., 1993—; adj. prof. Nat. Louis U., 1994—; adminstr. Charter Schs., 2003. Author: Effective Teachers; Effective Schools, 1989; contbr. articles to profl. jours. Bd. dirs. Wis.-Gate Found., 1985-87, Wis. Racquetball Assn., 1986-87, Wis. Future Problem Solving, 1986-87; pres. bd. dirs. YWCA, 1987-91; dir. Beloit and Vicinity Art Show, Beloit Coll., 1982-84, Rock Prairie Showcase Festival; founder Summer Explorers Beloit Coll. Mem. Wis. Coun. for Gifted and Talented (bd. dirs. 1984-87, v.p. 1985-86, pres. 1986-87). Home: 4421 Ruger Ave Janesville WI 53546-9780 E-mail: mathomas@sdb.k12.wi.us.

THOMAS, MARGARET ANN, not-for-profit developer; b. Milw., Sept. 12, 1946; m. John Thomas. Bachelor's Degree, U. Wis., 1973; Master's Degree, DePaul U., 1979. Pers. dir. Goodwill Rehab. Ctr., Milw., 1974—80; exec. dir. Hagerstown Goodwill Industries, 1980—84; pres. Goodwill Industries of Southeastern Pa., Inc., 1984—91, Goodwill Industries of the Gulf Coast, Inc., 1991—94, Goodwill Industries of the Chesapeake, Inc., 1994—. Chair leadership devel. task team Goodwill Industries INternat., mem. exec. coun., bd. mem.; mem. workforce investment bd. City of Balt.; mem. adv. bd. Schaefer Ctr., U. Balt. Trustee, chair planning com. Anne Arundel County Cultural Art Found.; co-chair Opera Gala Annapolis Opera Co.; bd. mem. Scholarships for Scholars. Recipient Mayor's Bus. Recognition award, 1998, Bus. 2000 award, Network 2000 and The Daily Record, 1999, Svc. Above Self award/Outstanding Non-Profit Agy., Rotary Club Woodlawn-Westview, 1999. Mem.: Md. Works (sec.), Md. Assn. Non-Profits (treas.). Office: Goodwill INdustries Chesapeake Inc 222 E Redwood St Baltimore MD 21202

THOMAS, MARIANNA, volunteer community activist, writer, speaker; b. Greenville, Ohio, Dec. 9, 1927; d. John Darl and Eva Jane (Hill) Munn; m. Harold D. Krickenbarger, Aug. 31, 1947 (div.); children: Harold Jr., Jane, Maryln, John; m. Lowell J. Thomas, Jan. 5, 1977 (dec.); 1 stepchild Lowell J. Student, Dayton (Ohio) Art Inst.; MA (hon.), Union (Ky.) Coll., 1978. Farmer Holstein Show Herd, Arcanum, Ohio, 1947-68; advt., broadcasting sta. work and writing positions Arcanum Times; sales and decorating positions Lowe Bros., Greenville, Ohio; exec. dir./fundraising Help for Children in the Holy Land/Spafford Children's Ctr., N.Y.C., 1969-76. Author: Catitudes, 1987, The Second Mrs. Lowell Thomas, 2002; mem. bd. contbrs. Dayton Daily News. Founder Citizens for Moral War peace orgn., 1967-70; mem. coun. Freedoms Found. at Valley Forge, 1982-84; nat. bd. dirs. Family Svc. Assocs. Am., N.Y.C., 1979-85, Am. Judicature Soc., 1978-80; founder, chmn. U.S. Civil Responsibilities, Dayton, 1988-93. Mem. Dayton Engrs. Club (hon.). Avocations: oil painting, poetry, swimming, cooking. Home: PO Box 626 Dayton OH 45405-0626 E-mail: MARIANNAMUNN@aol.com.

THOMAS, MARIANNE GREGORY, school psychologist; b. N.Y.C., Dec. 10, 1945; BS, U. Conn., 1985; MS, So. Conn. State U., 1987; cert. advanced studies, ednl. adminstrn., NYU, 1998. Cert. sch psychologist Conn, NY. Sch. psychology intern Greenwich (Conn.) Pub. Schs., 1986-87, sch. psychologist Hawthorne (N.Y.)-Cedar Knolls, U.F.S.D., 1987-88, Darien (Conn.) Pub. Schs., 1988—. Adj. instr. Coll. New Rochelle, 2002. Mem.: APA, NASP (cert), Conn Asn Sch Psychologists, Kappa Delta Pi, Phi Delta Kappa. Home: 154 Indian Rock Rd New Canaan CT 06840-3117

THOMAS, MARY AUGUSTA, library administrator; b. Washington, Mar. 15, 1951; d. Abram Henry and Mary Agnes Rosenfeld; m. George D. Thomas Jr., Nov. 9, 1991. AB cum laude, Mt. Holyoke Coll., 1973; MSLS, Cath. U., Washington, 1978. From rare book libr. to mgr. planning and adminstrn. Smithsonian Libr., Washington, 1976-91, asst. dir., 1991—2002, assoc. dir., 2002—. Author: An Odyssey in Print: Adventures in the Smithsonian Libraries/ Smithsonian Press, 2002; editor: Information Imagineering, 1998; contbr. mags. to librs. Recipient Smithsonian Inst. Sec.'s award for Excellence in Equal Employment Opportunity, 2000. Mem. ALA (chair editl. adv. bd. LA & M, 1998-2002, councilor 1999-2003, chair com. on resolutions), D.C. Libr. Assn. (pres. 1999, Disting. Svc. award 2001), Fed. Librs. and Info. Ctrs. (adv. bd. 1997-99), Libr. Adminstrn. and Mgmt. Assn. (chair bus. and fiscal officer discussion group 1998-2000, chair, editl. adv. bd. 1999-2002), Beta Phi Mu. Avocations: cooking, writing. Office: Smithsonian Librs Nhb 22 Washington DC 20560-0001

THOMAS, NADINE, state senator, nurse; b. Fort Myers, Fla., May 14, 1952; d. Marvin Lee and Carrie Lee (North) Dixon; m. Jolivet Aurelious Thomas, Jan. 15, 1977 (div. 1982); children: Nadia Joli, Doris Silas, Dorothy Silas. A, Edison Community Coll., 1974; student, Ga. State U., 1978-82. RN, Ga. Nursing unit coord. Crawford Long Hosp., Atlanta, 1977-90; nursing supr. S.W. Hosp. and Med. Ctr., Atlanta, 1990-92; mem. Ga. Senate from 10th dist., Atlanta, 1992—. Chmn. Changed Living Recovery, Decatur, Ga., 1991-92; bd. dirs. Ctr. for Drug Rehab. Mem. DeKalb Dem. Party Exec. Com., Decatur, 1988-90; pres. Brookwood and Knollwood Community Assn., Atlanta, 1988-92; state rep. Ga. Ho. Reps., Atlanta, 1990-92; co-pres. Sky Haven Pres. PTA, Atlanta, 1991-92. Mem. ANA, Ga. Nurses Assn. (Nurse Excellence award 1991). Avocations: golf, walking, music and dancing. Home: 3679 Talonega Trl Ellenwood GA 30294-1158 Office: Ga State Senate Rm 304 121H State Capitol Atlanta GA 30334

THOMAS, NANCY HINCKLEY, special education educator; b. Los Angeles, Calif., Mar. 7, 1939; d. Barton Armin and Helen (Ferguson) Hinckley; children: Gregory Dean, Garold Daniel, Deanna Nancy, Barton William, Deborah Hinckley, Bryan Joseph. AB, Stanford U., Calif., 1959. Resource Specialist Calif. Dept. head K-Mart Corp., Petaluma, Calif., 1982—89; spl. edn. tchr. R-House, Santa Rosa, Calif., 1994—2004, resource specialist, 1998—. Mem. Commonwealth Club, San Francisco, 1996—2004. Mem.: AAUW (treas. 1965—67), Smithsonian Instn. Avocations: reading, gardening. Home: 724 Bassett St Petaluma CA 94952

THOMAS, OUIDA POWER, music educator; b. Louisville, Miss., Nov. 25, 1939; d. Robert Alvin and Mavis (Simpson) Power; m. Charles Victor Thomas, Aug. 4, 1962; children: Karla Victoria, Sylvia Katharine Thomas White, Charles Gregory. BS in Bus. Edn. with highest honors, Miss. State U., Starkville, 1963; M Music Edn., Delta State U., 1993; postgrad., U. Memphis, 1996—. Nat. cert. tchr. of music. Ind. music tchr. piano and organ, Grenada, Miss., 1963—; classroom gen. music tchr. Kirk Acad., Grenada, 1977-87. Adjudicator auditions Federated Music Clubs, Oxford, Miss., 1990—. Accompanist musical prodns. Grenada Fine Arts Playhouse, 1979-81; organist, choirmaster All Saints' Episcopal Ch., Grenada, 1977—; mem. music and liturgy com. Episcopal Diocese of Miss., 1996-99. Mem. Am. Guild Organists, Nat. Guild Piano Tchrs. (chmn. local auditions 1977—, adjudicator auditions 1993—), Music Tchrs. Nat. Assn. (cert. in piano and organ), Miss. Music Tchrs. Assn. (cert. in piano and organ, exec. bd. 1993-94, state chair pre-coll. student activities 1995-96, chair state cert. 1999-2000, adjudicator auditions 1993—), Grenada Area Music Tchrs. Assn. (v.p. 1995—). Avocations: gardening, needlework. Home: 1985 Wooded Dr Grenada MS 38901-4073

THOMAS, PATRICIA ANNE, retired law librarian; b. Cleve., Aug. 21, 1927; d. Richard Joseph and Marietta Bernadette (Teevans) T. BA, Case Western Res. U., 1949, JD, 1951. Bar: Ohio, 1951, U.S. Supreme Ct., 1980. Libr. Arter & Hadden, Cleve., 1951-62; asst. libr., libr. IRS, Washington, 1962-78; libr. dir. Adminstrv. Office U.S. Cts., 1978-93, ret., 1993. Mem. Am. Assn. Law Librs., Soc. D.C. (pres. 1967-69), Soc. Benchers (Case Western Res. Law Sch.)

THOMAS, PATRICIA GOODNOW, journalist; b. Framingham, Mass., Dec. 28, 1924; d. Charles Frederick and Dorothy (Eaton) G.; m. Roy Condit Thomas, Oct. 7, 1961. BS, Simmons Coll., 1946; MAT, Rollins Coll., 1971. News reporter-writer Radio Station WCOP, Boston, 1946-52; editorial specialist Central Intelligence Agy., Washington, 1952-54; asst. editor Hood Milk Corp., Boston, 1954-55; sr. writer/editor Voice of America, Washington, 1955-61; writer Orlando Mag., Orlando, Fla., 1964-72; tchr. French, Eng. Oviedo (Fla.) H.S., 1965-66; prof. of journalism Seminole Cmty. Coll., Sanford, Fla., 1972-88; freelance writer Blairsville, Ga., 1988—. Editor: From Sky to Sea, 1993; contbr. articles to profl. jours. Mem. Fla. Freelance Writers Assn., Kappa Delta Pi.

THOMAS, PEGGY RUTH, public contract and procurement consultant; b. Granite, Okla., Dec. 19, 1933; d. Sidney Durrell and Ruth Mae (Tuley) Coffman; m. Charles Donald Gustafson, Nov. 28, 1953 (dec. Apr. 1959); children: Gene L., Richard L.; m. Donald Edward Thomas. Student, U. Okla., 1951-52, Okla. S.W. State U., 1952-53. Cert. purchasing mgr. Nat. Assn. Purchasing Mgmt. Contracting/procurement officer Fed. Govt., various locations, 1953-87, U. Alaska, Anchorage, 1988-93; CEO XPRT Cons., Anchorage, 1985—. Mem. Mensa. Avocation: travel. Home and Office: Xprt Cons 9701 Brien St Anchorage AK 99507-6670 E-mail: prthomas@gci.net.

THOMAS, RAMONIA, political organization executive, civic worker; Former mgr. customer svc. dept. Ariz. Pub. Svc. Co., Phoenix; now program adminstr. Ariz. Dept. Econ. Security, Phoenix. Ariz. del. Rep. Nat. Conv., 1992; past pres. Cactus Wren Rep. Women; past chmn. Ariz. African Am. Rep. Com.; precinct committeewoman dist. 25 Phoenix Rep. Com.; vol. numerous state and county level campaigns; pres. Ariz. Fedn. Rep. Women, 1996-97; mem.-at-large exec. com. Nat. Fedn. Rep. Women, Alexandria, Va., 1997—, also regent and dir. region 8; bd. dirs. Phoenix Parks and Recreation Dept.; mem. Ariz. State Arts Commn.; grad. Valley Leadership; former mem. Ariz. Gov.'s Coun. for Non-traditional Employment Women, Ariz. Women's Town Hall; past chmn. and mem. bd. dirs. Metro Youth Ctr.; past mem. bd. dirs. League United L.Am. Citizens, Ariz. NAACP. Mem. Maryvale C. of C. (past bd. dirs.), Soroptimists (past pres. Camelback chpt.). Office: Nat Fedn Exec Women 124 N Alfred St Alexandria VA 22314-3011 Fax: 703-548-9836.

THOMAS, REGENA L. secretary of state; BA in U. Studies, Morehead State U. Cons. Dem. Gov.'s Assn.; legislative analyst Legislative Research Commn., KY State Legislature, 1980—85; ptnr. IEM Mesage mgmt., Inc.; served Torricelli for Senate, 1996, McGreevey for Gov., 1997, Corzine for Senate, 2000; Sec. of State State of N.J., 2002—. Prin. liaison non-govtl. orgns., key Dem. constituencies; dep., dir. Constituent Svcs. Govt. Dist. Columbia; legis. analyst Legis. Rsch. Commn. Ky. State Legislature; with Nat. Rainbow Coalition and its founder, Rev. Jesse L. Jackson. Office: PO Box 300 Trenton NJ 08625-0300*

THOMAS, REGINA D. state legislator; m. Ervin J. Thomas Sr.; four children. Student, C.C. Balt. Mem. Ga. Ho. of Reps., 1995-98, asst. majority whip, 1997-98; mem. Ga. State Senate, Atlanta, 2000—, sec. def., sci. and tech. com., sec. vets. and consumer affairs com., mem. appropriations com., edn. com., reapportionment com.; tax assoc. H&R Block. Mem. com. for pathway to tchg. Savannah State U.; vol. Ralph Mark Gilbert Civil Rights Mus., Chatham-Savannah Citizen Adv.; active Liberty City Ch. of Christ, Savannah. Office: 1406 E 35th St Savannah GA 31404 also: 323-A Legislative Office Atlanta GA 30334 Office Fax: 404-463-7783. E-mail: rthomas@legis.state.ga.us.

THOMAS, RHONDA ROBBINS, marketing educator, consultant; b. Houston, Dec. 15, 1958; d. George B. and Barbara (Lillich) R.; m. Fred Holt Thomas, Aug. 22, 1981 (div. 1991); children: Brian P., Paige A.; m. Michael G. Florimbi, Oct. 18, 1997; 1 child, Allegra F. BA, U. Tex., 1980; MBA, So. Meth. U., 1989; PhD, U. Tex., Arlington, 1994. Profl. interior designer. Pres., CEO Design Austin, Tex., 1984-90; pres. Denova, Austin, 1988-93; prin. MarketShare Cons., 1993-95; asst. prof. mktg. Suffolk U., Boston, 1996-98; vis. prof. mktg. Sellinger Sch. Bus. Loyola Coll., Balt., 1998—; sr. mgr. e-bus. Deloitte Consulting, 2000—. Cons. SABRE Decision Techs., 1995-98; vis. asst. prof. mktg. U. Tex. Arlington, 1990-95, Loyola Coll., Balt., 1998-99; adj. mem. mktg. faculty Cox Sch. So. Meth. U., 1993-95. Bd. dirs. Children's Cancer Ctr., Austin, 1987-88, Dallas Mus. Art, 1990-94. Lester Johnson Grad. fellow Inst. Bus. Designers Found., 1990, Lakawanna Leather fellow, 1991. Mem. DAR, Am. Soc. Interior Designers (Design Excellence award 1985, 87, 88), Inst. Bus. Designers, Austin C. of C.

THOMAS, SARA R. state legislator; b. Indianola, Miss., Apr. 21, 1941; m. Arthur Lee Thomas. Student, Miss. Valley State U., Delta State U. State legislator Miss. Ho. of Reps., Jackson, 1996—. Mem. edn., municipalities, penitentiary, pub. bldgs., state libr. coms. Miss. Ho. of Reps. Mem. NEA, Miss. Assn. of Educators, Miss. Ret. Tchrs., Miss. Valley State U. Alumni Assn., Regulette Civic and Social, Crepe Myrtle Garden Club, Delta Uniserv Region, Phi Delta Kappa, Alpha Kappa Alpha. Democrat. Baptist. Home: 512 B King Rd Indianola MS 39367 Office: State Capitol Bldg PO Box 1018 Jackson MS 39215-1018 E-mail: sthomas@mail.house.state.ms.us.

THOMAS, SHARON M. city official; b. New Bedford, Mass., June 23, 1969; d. Tony C. and Rosemary F. (Couto) Teixeira; m. David Alan Thomas, July 25, 1992; 1 child, David A. Thomas II. Grad. h.s. Asst. coun. sec. New Bedford City Coun., 1987-89, city coun. sec., 1989-96, asst. coun. clk., office mgr., 1996—. Home: 64 Snow St New Bedford MA 02740-1431 Office: New Bedford City Coun 133 William St New Bedford MA 02740-6132

THOMAS, SHEILA FAYE, pediatric nurse practitioner; b. Lima, N.Y., Sept. 21, 1933; d. Vernon Arthur Wemett and Vivian Mary Louise Wright; m. Charles Edwin Thomas; children: Timothy, Gary, Trent, Karen. Diploma in Nursing, Highland Hosp. Sch. Nursing, 54; cert. in Pediat. Nursing, U. Rochester, 1972; student, Empire State Coll., 1972—86. With Highland Hosp., Rochester, NY, 1955—98; retired, 1998. Tchr. Am. Red Cross, Canandaigua, NY, 1955—58. Pres. Livingston County Cancer Soc., Geneseo, NY, 1973—74; mem. com. West Bloomfield (N.Y.) Rep. Party, 1994—2000; bd. dir. Ontario County Cancer Soc., Canandaigua, 1976—78, Hospice Serenity House, Victor, NY, 1994—2000. Mem.: ANA, Bloomfield Garden Club (vice chmn. 1980, pres. 1980, named in Book of Recognition 1989—). Avocation: quilting. Home: 8042 Wesley Rd Bloomfield NY 14469

THOMAS, SHIRLEY, author, educator, business executive; b. Glendale, Calif. d. Oscar Miller and Ruby (Thomas) Annis; m. W. White, Feb. 22, 1949 (div. June 1952); m. William C. Perkins, Oct. 24, 1969. BA in Modern Lit., U. Sussex, Eng., 1960, PhD in Comm., 1967; diploma, Russian Fedn. Cosmonautics, 1995. Actress, writer, producer, dir. numerous radio and TV stas., 1942-46; v.p. Commodore Prodns., Hollywood, Calif., 1946-52; pres. Annis & Thomas, Inc., Hollywood, 1952—; prof. technical writing U. So. Calif., L.A., 1975—. Hollywood corr. NBC, 1952-56; editor motion pictures CBS, Hollywood, 1956-58; corr. Voice of Am., 1958-59; now free lance writer; cons. biol. scis. communication project George Washington U., 1965-66; cons. Stanford Rsch. Inst., 1967-68, Jet Propulsion Lab., 1969-70. Author: Men of Space vols. 1-8, 1960-68, Spanish transl. 1961, Italian, 1962; Space Tracking Facilities, 1963, Computers: Their History, Present Applications and Future, 1965; The Book of Diets, 1974. Organizer, chmn. City of L.A. Space Adv. Com., 1964-73, Women's Space Symposia, 1962-73; founder, chmn. Aerospace Hist. Soc. Inc.; chmn. Theodore von Karman Postage Stamp Com., 1965—, stamp issued 1992; bd. dirs. World Children's Transplant Fund, 1993—, Achievement Rewards for Coll. Scients. Recipient Aerospace Excellence award Calif. Mus. Found. 1991, Nat. Medal Honor DAR, 1992, Yuri Gagarin Medal Honor, 1995. Fellow Brit. Interplanetary Soc.; mem. AIAA, AAAS, Internat. Acad. Astronautics, Internat. Soc. Aviation Writers, Air Force Assn. (Airpower Arts and Letters award 1961), Internat. Acad. Astronautics, Nat. Aero. Assn., Nat. Asn. Sci. Writers, Soc. for Tech. Communications, Am. Astronautical Soc., Nat. Geog. Soc., Am. Soc. Pub. Adminstrn. (sci. and tech. in govt. com. 1972—), Achievement Awards for Coll. Scientists, Theta Sigma Phi, Phi Beta. Home: 8027 Hollywood Blvd West Hollywood CA 90046 Office: U So Calif Profl Writing Program University Park Wale Phillips Hall 404 Los Angeles CA 90089-0001 E-mail: snowtech@pacbell.net.

THOMAS, SHIRLEY JEAN, assistant principal; b. Huntsville, Tex., July 9, 1955; d. George William and Norma Pauline Hunt; m. John Daniel Thomas; children: Monica Christine, Anna Danielle. BA, Sam Houston State U., 1977; MEd, Northwestern State U., Natchitoches, La., 1981; MS in Edn. Mgmt., U. of Houston Clear Lake, Houston, TX, 2003. Tchr. Conroe (Tex.) Ind. Sch. Dist., 1977—78, Natchitoches Parish (La.) Ind. Sch. Dist., 1979—83, La Porte (Tex.) Ind. Sch. Dist., 1983—2001; asst. prin. Young Learners Charter Sch., Houston, 2001—02; spl. edn. team leader Clear Creek Ind. Sch. Dist., League City, Tex., 2002—03, asst. prin., 2003—. Lead tchr. La Porte Ind. Sch. Dist., 1991—94. Com. mem. Rep. Party, Deer Park, Tex., 1988—92; tchr. Ch., Pasadena, Tex., 1995—97. Mem.: Assn. Supervision of Curriculum and Devel. (corr.). Republican. Avocations: travel, history. Home: 3413 Greenwood Place Deer Park TX 77536 Personal E-mail: sjthomas@sbcglobal.net.

THOMAS, SPRING URSULA, not-for-profit developer, educator, photographer; b. N.Y.C., Apr. 20, 1946; d. Everett John and Ursula (Reich) Voeglie; m. Raymond Tillman Gibson, July 4, 1972 (dec. Apr. 15, 1975); 1 child, Rick Tillman ; m. Michael Alan Thomas, June 15, 1991; stepchildren: Cheryl Ritzel, Jennifer Adams. Degree in tchg., Seattle U., 1976, BA Magna Cum Laude, 1977. Cert. ESL tchr. Cons. Seattle U., 1977—84, Kodiak (Alaska) Childcare Ctr., 1977; co-owner Convention Photographers N.W., Seattle, 1985—92; program dir. Earth Corps (formerly Cascadia Quest), Seattle, 1992—94; co-founder The IronStraw Group, Ellensburg, Wash., 1994—, also. pres. bd. dirs. Contbg. photographer (book) Seattle Tashkent Internat. Sister Cities, 1990. Citizen diplomat Seattle Tashkent Peace Park, 1988; developer Seattle Tashkent Children's Art Exch., 1989; com. mem. Ellensburg C. of C., 2003. Recipient Ptnrs. Participating Edn. award, 1987, World Citizen's Award, Physicians for Social Responsibility, 1988, Founders of a New Northwest, Pioneering Achievement award, Sustainable N.W., 2000. Avocations: philanthropy, the arts, nature. Office: IronStraw Group 607 E 5th Ave Ellensburg WA 98926 Home: 805 E 2nd Ave Ellensburg WA 98926 Business E-Mail: spring@ironstraw.org.

THOMAS, SUSAN WISKEMANN, music educator; b. Natrona Heights, Pa., Apr. 21, 1970; d. Harriette Marie and Ronald Glenn Wiskemann; m. Matthew Dale Thomas, Oct. 4, 1997; 1 child, Andrew Connor. MS in Music Edn. summa cum laude, Cert. of Dalcroze, Orff & Kodaly, Towson U., 2003; BS in Music Edn., Ind. U. Pa., 1994. Music educator Balt. County Pub. Schs., Towson, Md., 1995—. Mem.: Music Educators Nat. Conf., Md. Music Educators Assn. Office: Dogwood Elementary School 7215 Dogwood Road Baltimore MD 21244 E-mail: sthomas3@bcps.org.

THOMAS, SUZANNE WARD, public relations executive, communications educator, radio personality; b. Akron, Ohio, Sept. 21, 1954; d. Kendall Kramer and Margaret Ann (Owen) Ward; m. James Michael Thomas, Oct. 20, 1980; children: Seth Evin, James Kendall. BS in Edn., Miami U., Oxford, Ohio, 1977; MA in Comm., Regent U., Virginia Beach, Va., 1980. Writer, prodr. Sta. WVIZ, PBS, Cleve., 1980-82; dir. pub. rels. Sta. WOAC-TV, Canton, Ohio, 1982-83, hostess children's show, 1982-84; v.p. Thomas Video Prodns., Canal Fulton, Ohio, 1987-90; dir. pub. rels., instr. comm. Malone Coll., Canton, 1990—, editor The Malone Mag., 1990—; co-host morning radio show Sta. WNPQ-FM, 2001—. Co-hose morning radio program 95.9 FM-WNPQ, 2001—, host radio cmty. affairs program, 2001—. Author: (children's book) The Miracles of Jesus, 1991, also manuals. Hostess pub. affairs program Community TV Consortium, Canton, 1987; subcom. chmn. Govt. Day, Leadership Canton, 1987; v.p. Right to Life Ednl. Found., Canton, 1990; chmn. pub. rels. Jr. League Canton, 1986-87, rec. sec., 1987-88; bd. dirs. PTO, 1989-90; mgmt. assistance program United Way, 1998-99. Recipient Sparkler award Jr. League Canton, 1986, Pub. Rels. award, 1987, Addy awards Canton Advt. Club, 1992, 96. Mem. Sales and Mktg. Execs. (bd. dirs. Stark County chpt. 1989), Assn. Jr. Leagues Internat., Pub. Rels. Soc. Am. (accredited in pub. rels. 1995, bd. dirs.). Republican. Avocations: reading, tennis, aerobics, golf, writing. Office: Malone Coll 515 25th St NW Canton OH 44709-3823

THOMAS, SYLVIA ELIZABETH, artist; b. Amarillo, Tex., Apr. 18, 1931; d. Orville Alvie and Erah (Cearley) Blankenship; m. Allen Ralph Thomas, June 21, 1953 (dec. Nov. 1984); children: Michael Allen, Melanie Kay Thomas-Singleton, Terry Neal, Kelly Andrew. BA in Fine Art, West Tex. State Coll., 1953. Cert. life tchg. cert., Tex. Jr. H.S. art tchr. Dumas (Tex.) Pub. Schs., 1953; art tchr. Amarillo Pub. Sch. 5, 1973-76. Vol. art tchr. Sr. Citizen Assn., Amarillo, 1992-96. One-woman shows include Lost Circus Gallery, Amarillo, 1989, Carson County Square House Mus., Panhandle, Tex., 1991, 98, XIT Mus. Art Gallery, Dalhart, Tex., 1992, Junction City (Kans.) Arts Coun., 1993, Crabb Art Ctr., Dumas, Tex., 1993, 98, Kathleens Art Cafe, Dallas, 1994; exhibited in group shows at Carson County Sq. House Mus., 1995, Jamboree of Arts, Amarillo, 1995 (Best of Show), Colony Gallery, Amarillo, 1998, numerous others; permanent collections include Carson City Square House Mus., Crabb Art Ctr.; represented in numerous pvt. collections in Tex., Kans., Colo., N.Mex. Mem. Lone Star Pastel Soc. (pres., founder 1995-96), Pastel Soc. S.W. (show chmn. 1983-84, PSA plaque 1984, Gold Grumbacher medal 1989, 2d place award 1994), Artists and Craftsmen, Pastel Soc. Am.(signature mem., Sauter Margulies award 1992), Pastel Soc. N.Mex., Amarillo Fine Arts Assn. (Best of Show award 1986, 2d pl award 1988, 95, 1st place award 1991). Republican.

THOMAS, TAMMY LOUISE, medical/surgical nurse, writer; b. Chgo., May 7, 1960; d. Samuel Lewis and Flovesta Ellis; m. Gary L. Thomas, Apr. 7, 1979; children: Samuel Cedric, Brian Gary, Sarah Louise. AA, Kankakee (Ill.) CC, 1992. LPN, Ill. Patient instr. Gericare Providers, Englewood, Colo., 1999—2001; physician's asst. Midwest Eye Assocs., Kankakee, 1995—99; customer svc. assoc. Cigna Healthcare, Bourbonnais, Ill., 2001—. Mem.: Phi Theta Kappa. Home: 933 S 7th Ave Kankakee IL 60901 Personal E-mail: writinglife@hotmail.com.

THOMAS, TERESA ANN, microbiologist, educator; b. Wilkes-Barre, Pa., Oct. 17, 1939; d. Sam Charles and Edna Grace T. BS cum laude, Coll. Misericordia, 1961; MS in Biology, Am. U., Beirut, 1965; MS in Microbiology, U. So. Calif., 1973; cert. in ednl. tech., U. Calif., San Diego, 1998. Tchr., sci. supr., curriculum coord. Meyers HS, Wilkes-Barre, 1962-64, Wilkes-Barre Area Public Schs., 1961-66; rsch. assoc. Proctor Found. Rsch. in Ophthalmology U. Calif. Med. Ctr., San Francisco, 1966-68; instr. Robert Coll. of Istanbul, Turkey, 1968-71, Am. Edn. in Luxembourg, 1971-72, Bosco Tech. Inst., Rosemead, Calif., 1973-74, San Diego C.C. Dist., 1974-80; prof. microbiology and ecology Sch. Math Sci. and Engring. Southwestern Coll., Chula Vista, Calif., 1980—; mem. [illegible] Baja Studies EcoMundo team internat. program Southwestern Coll., mem. staff devel. com., 2001—. Pres. acad. senate, 1984-85, del., 1986-89; chmn., coord., steering com. project Cultural Rsch. Ednl. and Trade Exch., 1991-2000, Southwestern Coll.-Shanghai Inst. Fgn. Trade; coord. Southwestern Coll. Great Teaching Seminar, 1987, 88, 89, coord. scholars program, 1988-90; steering com. Southwestern Coll.; exec. com. Acad. Senate for Calif. C.C.s, 1985-86, Chancellor of Calif. C.C.s Adv. and Rev. Coun. Fund for Instrnl. Improvement, 1984-86; co-project dir. statewide, coord. So. Calif. Biotech. Edn. Consortium, 1993-95, steering com., 1993-98; adj. asst. prof. Chapman Coll., San Diego, 1974-83, San Diego State U., 1977-79; chmn. Am. Colls. Istanbul Sci. Week, 1969-71; adv. bd. Chapman Coll. Cmty. Ctr., 1979-80; cons. sci. curriculum Calif. Dept. Edn., 1986-89; pres. Internat. Rels. Club, 1959-61; mem. San Francisco World Affairs Coun., 1966-68, San Diego World Affairs Coun., 1992—; v.p. Palomar Palace Estates Home Owners Assn., 1983-85, pres., 1994-99, v.p., 1999-2003, pres., 2003—; mem. Rsch. Conf. on Undergrad. Microbiology Edn., Conn. Coll., 1999; bd. dir. US Orgn. Med. Ednl. Needs, US Internat. Boundary and Water Commn. Citizens Forum; presenter in field. NSTA Jour. of Coll. Sci. Tchg. Life mem. Chula Vista Nature Ctr.; mem. Internat. Friendship Commn., Chula Vista, 1985-95, vice chmn., 1989-90, chmn., 1990-92; mem. US-Mex. Sister Cities Assn., nat. bd. dir., 1992-94, gen. chair 30th nat. conv., 1993; active City of Chula Vista Resource Conservation Commn., 1996—, chmn. 2002—; active Chula Vista Bd. Ethics, 1999-2000; co-organizer Chula Vista People-to-People Sister City Dels. to Odawara City, Japan, 1991, 94, 99; cmty. adv. com. San Diego Mus. Man, 2000-2003; mem. County San Diego Solid Waste Hearing Panel, 2000—; citizens forum bd. US Internat. Boundary and Water Commn., 2002-; steering com. Chula Vista Gen. Plan Update, 2002—; hon. coach SWC Jaguars Basketball Team, 2003; com. mem. Chula Vista Environ., Open Space and Sustainable Devel., 2002—. Rsch. grant Pa. Heart Assn., 1962; NSF fellow, 1965, USPHS fellow, 1972-73; recipient Nat. Tchg. Excellence award Nat. Inst. Staff and Orgnl. Devel., 1989; named Southwestern Coll. Woman of Distinction, 1987; Hon. Coach Southwestern Coll. Ladies Basketball Apaches, 2001. Mem.: NEA, NIH (mentor Bridges to the Future program Southwestern Coll. and San Diego 1993—98, steering com.), Faculty Assn. Calif. C.C.s (state policy com. 2003—), Am. Assn. Cmty. and Jr. Colls., Calif. Tchrs. Assn., Nat. Sci. Tchrs. Assn. (coord. internat. honors exch. lectr. competition 1986, internat. com.), Am. Soc. Microbiology (So. Calif. Microbe Discovery Team 1995—99), Calif. Sci. Tchrs. Assn. (life), Nat. Assn. Biology Tchrs. (life), Chula Vista-Odawara (Japan) Sister Cities Assn. (founding pres. 1994—), Am. U. Beirut Alumni and Friends of San Diego (1st v.p. 1984—91), San Diego Zool. Soc., Japan Soc. San Diego and Tijuana (life), Japanese Hist. Soc. San Diego (life), Am.-Lebanese Assn. San Diego (1st v.p. 1984—91, pres. 1988—93, chmn. scholarship com.), Am. Lebanese Syrian Ladies Club (pres. 1982—83), Lions Internat. (bull. editor 1991—93, 2d v.p. 1992—93, 1st v.p. 1993—94, editor Roaring Times Newsletter 1993—94, chmn. dist. internat. rels. and cooperations com. 1993—95, pres. S.W. San Diego County chpt. 1994—95, Sweetwater Zone chmn. dist. 4-L6 1996—97, pub. rels. 1997—98, Best Bull. award 1992—93, named S.W. San Diego County Lion of Yr. 2000), Delta Kappa Gamma (Outstanding Pub. Svc. award Gamma Omicron chpt. 2003), Phi Theta Kappa, Sigma Phi Sigma, Kappa Gamma Pi (pres. Wilkes-Barre chpt. 1963—64, pres. San Francisco chpt. 1967—68), Alpha Pi Epsilon (life; advisor Southwestern Coll. chpt. 1989—90, founder).

THOMAS, VIOLETA DE LOS ANGELES, real estate broker; b. Buenos Aires, Dec. 21, 1949; came to U.S., 1967; d. Angel and Lola (Andino) de Rios; m. Jess Thomas, Dec. 23, 1974; 1 child, Victor Justin. Student, Harvard U. and U. Buenos Aires, 1967—73. Mgr. book div. Time-Life, N.Y.C., 1985-94; real estate broker First Marin Realty, Inc., Mill Valley, Calif., 1996-97; assoc. broker Trump Corp., N.Y.C., 1997—, Brown Harris Stevens, N.Y.C., 1997—. Rep. N.Y.C. Bd. dirs. Alliance Francaise, St. Louis, 1995-96, City of Tuburon, Calif., 1987-93, Art and Heritage Commn., Tiburon. Named Woman of Yr., City of Buenos Aires, 1977, Broker of Yr., Marin County and San Francisco, 1987-92. Mem. Principia Coll. Club (pres. 1997—). Office: Brown Harris Stevens 655 Madison Ave Fl 3 New York NY 10021-8056 E-mail: violetathomas@aol.com.

THOMAS, YVONNE SHIREY, family and consumer science educator; b. Jenner Cross Roads, Pa., Dec. 1, 1938; d. Edward Merle and Orphabel (Shaffer) Shirey; m. William Edward Thomas, Dec. 23, 1961; children: Scott Forrest, Matthew David. BS, Indiana U. of Pa., 1960; MS, Hood Coll., 1987. Home econs. educator Bristol (Pa.) Jr. Sr. High Sch., 1960-64; elem. educator Barbers Point Elem. Sch., Ewa Beach, Hawaii, 1964-65; guidance counselor Workman Jr. High Sch., Pensacola, Fla., 1966-68; mid. sch. educator Broadfording Christian Acad., Hagerstown, Md., 1973-76; home econs. educator Hancock (Md.) Jr. Sr. High Sch., 1986-88, Springfield Middle Sch., Williamsport, Md., 1988—; ret., 2001. Consumer affairs intern Citicorp Credit Svcs., Inc, Hagerstown, 1986; career day coord. Springfield Middle Sch., Williamsport, 1988-92. Bd. mem. Washington County Commn. for Women, Hagerstown, 1989-96, Cedar Ridge Ministries, Hagerstown, 1990-95, 96-2002. Recipient Judith Ruchkin Rsch. award Md. ASCD, Balt., 1987, award Md. Nutrition Adv. Coun., 1997-99; named Washington County Home Econs. Tchr. of Yr., Md. Home Econs. Assn., Hagerstown, 1989, Women-on-the-Move, The Herald Mail Co., Hagerstown, 1991; winner Md. Nutritional Adv. Coun. State, 1998-99, Mid Atlantic Nutrition Adv. Coun., 2000-01. Mem. AAUW (chair edn. fund 1989-90, v.p. membership 1990-92, grant 1992, pres.-elect 1992-93, pres. 1993-94, grantee 1994, chair Md. state edn. fund 1990-92, ednl. equity chair 1994-2000), NEA, Md. Tchrs. Assn. (Dorothy Lloyd Women's Rights award 1996), Am. Assn. Family and Consumer Scis. (cert. family life educator 1990-98), Soroptimist Internat. (Women of Distinction award 1996, Regional Woman of Distinction 1996), Delta Zeta (pres. 1959-60). Republican. Grace Brethren. Avocations: watercolor painting, quilting, hiking, traveling. Home: 19001 Rock Maple Dr Hagerstown MD 21742-2458

THOMAS-CAPPELLO, ELIZABETH, arts administrator; b. Bridgeport, Conn., Apr. 12, 1970; d. Leon Evan Thomas III and Mary Guccione Olson; 1 child, Chandler John Hunt; m. John Christopher Cappello, Jan. 2, 1999; 1 child, Camille Cappello. BS, So. Ill. U., Carbondale, 1993; MS, U. Ill., Springfield, 1996. Asst. to the dir. Univ. Mus., Carbondale, 1994; asst. dir. Peoria (Ill.) Art Guild, 1995; devel. Springfield Art Assn., 1995; exec. dir. Arts Coun. Orange County, Middletown, N.Y., 1996-97; cons. Dutchess County Arts Coun., Poughkeepsie, N.Y., 1997—; substiture art tchr. Valley Ctrl. Sch. Dist., Montgomery, N.Y., 1999—. Bd. dirs. Newburgh Ctr. for the Arts, chair, 1998—; bd. dirs. Museum Village, 1997-99; mem. Leadership Orange, 1998—. Home: 78 Ulster Ave Walden NY 12586-1442

THOMAS-GRAHAM, PAMELA, communications executive; m. Lawrence Otis Graham; 1 child. grad., JD, Harvard Coll. Ptnr. McKinsey & Co., 1989—99; pres., CEO CNBC.com, 1999—2001; pres., COO CNBC, Burbank, Calif., 2001, pres., CEO, 2001—. Author: Ivy League Mystery Series, (novels) A Darker Shade of Crimson, Blue Blood; editor: Harvard Law Rev. Bd. dirs. N.Y. Opera, Am. Red Cross, NY, Inner-City Scholarship Fund. Named Woman of Yr., Finl. Women's Assn.; named one of Forty Under Forty Rising Young Bus. Leaders, Crain's N.Y. Bus., Top 20 Women in Fin., Global Fin. Mag., Top 10 Cons. in Am., Cons. Mag.; recipient Matrix award, N.Y. Women Comm., 2001. Mem.: Phi Beta Kappa. Office: CNBC 3000 W Alameda Ave #C296 Burbank CA 91523*

THOMASHOW, LINDA SUZANNE, microbiologist; b. Norwood, Mass. d. John Michael and E. Jean (Cole) Ravinski. BS, U. Mass., 1968; PhD, UCLA, 1979. Asst. prof. Wash. State U., Pullman, 1983-84; rsch. geneticist

USDA Agrl. Rsch. Svc., Pullman, 1985—. Adj. prof. dept. plant pathology Wash. State U. Editorial bd. Applied & Environ. Microbiology, Washington, 1990—; contbr. articles to profl. jours. Mem. Am. Soc. Microbiology, Am. Phytopathol. Soc. (Ruth Allen award 1997), Internat. Soc. for Molecular Plant-Microbe Interactions. Achievements include research in production of antibiotics by beneficial bacteria that live in association with the roots of plants, structure, function and regulation of genes involved in antibiotic synthesis by bacteria, the ecological significance of antibiotic production in natural environments. Office: Wash State Univ PO Box 646430 Dept Plant Pathology Pullman WA 99164-6430

THOMAS-JOHN, YVONNE MAREE, artist, interior designer; b. Leeton, New South Wales, Australia, Sept. 8, 1944; came to U.S., 1966; d. Percy Edward and Gladys May (Markham) Thomas; m. Michael Peter John, Aug. 20, 1966; children: Michael Christian, Stephen Edwin Dennis. Student, Buenaventura Coll., 1969, U. Calif., Santa Barbara, 1975; cert., United Design Guild, 1975; AA, Interior Design Guild, 1976. Designer Percy Thomas Real Estate, Leeton, 1960-66; cosmetologist, artist Bernard's Hair Stylists, Ventura, Calif., 1966-67, 74-73; cosmetologist Banks Beauty Salon, Chgo., 1968-69; owner, mgr. Yvonne Maree Designs, Ventura and Olympia, Wash., 1978—. Owner, cosmetologist Mayfair Salon, Leeton, 1962-66; owner, mgr. Y.M. Boutique, Griffith, Australia, 1965-66. Contbr. numerous short stories and poems to newspapers; numerous pen and ink drawings, one-woman shows include Royal Mus. Sydney, Australia, 1954, exhibited in group shows at Ventura County Courthouse, 1970, Wash. Women in Art, Olympia, 1990, Timberland Libr., 1990, Maska Internat. Gallery, Seattle, 1991, Nat. Hdqrs. of Am. Soc. Interior Designers, Washington, 1992, Michael Stone Collection, 1992, Funding Ctr., Alexandria, Va., 1992, Mus. Modern Art, Bordeaux, France, 1993, Abbey Galleries, N.Y.C., 1993, Mus. Modern Art, Miami, 1993, Hargus Unique Gallery, Pomona, Calif., 1994, Gallery Brindabella, Oakville, Ont., Can., 1996, Art Comm. Internat., Phila., 1996, World Bank, Washington, 1996—97, UN Fourth World Conf. on Women, Beijing, China, 1995, others, 1st release of ltd. edit. prints, 1992, exhibitions include Hargus Unique Gallery, Pomona, Calif., 1994, Represented in permanent collections Royal Mus. Sydney, O'Toole Coll., Melbourne, Nat. Mus. Women in Arts, Washington, Patterson Collection, Mich., Witherow Collection, Washington, Samaniego Collection, Calif., Ronald Reagan Collection, Calif. Artist Ventura County Gen. HOsp. Artist Ventura County Gen. Hosp., 1970's. Recipient Cash and Cert. awards Sydney Newspapers, 1950's, Ribbon awards Sydney County Fairs, 1950's, 1st round winner painting Hathaway Competition, Ventura, Calif., 1970's. Mem. Am. Platform Assn. Avocations: swimming, tennis, walking, books, music. Office: Yvonne Maree Designs PO Box 2143 Olympia WA 98507-2143 E-mail: ymaree@ix.netcom.com.

THOMASON, LYNNE, councilwoman, medical laser technician; b. St. Paul, Aug. 2, 1953; d. Glenn O. and Helen M. Thomason. laser electro-optics diploma, laser marking cert., laser engraving cert., Hennepin Tech. Coll., 1996. Cert. direct endorsement underwriter U.S. Dept. HUD. Sr. closer Knutson Mortgage, Mpls., 1991-94; sr. med. laser technician Latis, Inc., Mpls., 1997—. Cons. Illumenex Corp., Mpls., 1998—; auditor, underwriter RMS, Mpls., 1998—. Vol. counselor North Heights Counseling Clinic, St. Paul, 1994-98; coun. mem. City of Mounds View, Minn., 1998—; commr. Mounds View Econ. Devel. Authority, 1999; coun. liaison Mounds View Econ. Devel. Commn., 1999; bd. dirs. N.W. Youth and Family Svcs. Mem. North Suburban C. of C. (assoc.). Lutheran. Avocations: reading, interior design, volunteer counseling. Office: City Mounds View 2041 Hwy 10 Mounds View MN 55112

THOMASON, NOLA FAYE, critical care-emergency supervisor; b. East St. Louis, Ill., May 23, 1957; d. Noel Noble and Dorothy Bernice (Burkett) Manring; m. Paul David Thomason, Mar. 23, 1979; children: Paula Faye, Rachel Elisabeth. ADN, Frontier C.C., Fairfield, Ill., 1986; Mobile Intensive Care Nurse/Emergency Care RN, Good Samaritan Hosp., Mt. Vernon, 1992; Trauma Nurse Specialist, Carbondale Meml. Hosp., 1996; EMT Basic, Frontier C.C., 1997. Cert. mobile intensive care nurse, mobile intensive care instr., emergency nursing care pediatric core curriculum, 1997. Charge nurse Rest Haven Manor, Albion, Ill., 1986—; staff nurse Kimberly Quality Care, Belleville, 1986—87; staff nurse emergency room Clay County Hosp., Flora, 1987—88; RN, supr. Good Samaritan Hosp., Mt. Vernon, 1990—92, Crossroads Cmty. Hosp., 1988—91; night supr. Fairfield (Ill.) Meml. Hosp., 1993—. Home: RR 3 Box 86 Fairfield IL 62837

THOMASON, NORMA JEAN, librarian; b. Roswell, N.Mex., Jan. 16, 1950; d. George Frederick and Frances Helen Lindaley; m. James Roy Thomason Jr., Oct. 29, 1983. BS, So. Colo. State Coll., 1972; MLS, La. State U., 1975. Eligibility worker La. Health & Human Resources, Baton Rouge, 1975-78, libr., 1979-82, rsch. statistician, 1984-86; libr. St. John's United Meth. Ch., Baton Rouge, 1998—. Treas. St. John's United Meth. Ch.-Ruth Cir. of United Meth. Women, 1994—. Mem. AAUW, La. Libr. Assn., Phi Kappa Phi. Home: 1222 Quail Hollow Dr Baton Rouge LA 70810-5186 Office: Saint Johns United Meth Ch 9375 Highland Rd Baton Rouge LA 70810-4024

THOMASON, SUZANNE IRENE, health services professional, researcher; b. Terry, Mont., May 3, 1953; d. Eldred Charles and Lillie Dolatta Thomason; m. Argan Neil Johnson Jr., Mar. 16, 1974 (div. Nov. 1986); children: Meris Elsie, Sam Argan Nels. BS, Mont. State U., 1975. Cert. Med. Technologist Am. Soc. Clin. Pathologists (ASCP), family support specialist. Family support specialist Develop. Ednl. Assistance Program, Mont., 1999—. Co-editor: The Wheels Keep Rolling Across Montana'a Prairie, 2001. Tour guide Prairie County Mus., Terry, 1995—; fundraiser Sr. Housing Bd., Terry, 1999—. Avocations: music, sign language. Address: 2200 Box Elder St Miles City MT 59301-2899

THOMASON-MUSSEN, JANIS FAYE, human services administrator; b. Rome, N.Y., Oct. 6, 1946; d. Howard Irving and Marjorie Ellen (Thomason) Mussen; children: John Kennedy Pratt, Wendy Jo Pratt Bowen, Amara Jo Pratt. BA in Journalism, Syracuse U., 1983. Reporter, columnist Oneida (N.Y.) Daily Dispatch, 1983-85; editor Coll. Graphic Arts and Photography Rochester (N.Y.) Inst. Tech., 1985-87; freelance writer, editor, photographer Rochester, 1987-88; exec. dir. Come-Unity Ctr., Inc. Wayne County Rural Ministry/Come-Unity Ctr., Inc., Williamson, N.Y., 1988—. Founder Wayne County (N.Y.) Coalition of Migrant Farmworker Svcs., 1991—; mem. Wayne County Task Force on In-Home Svcs. for Elderly, 1989—. Scholarship Gannett News Svc., 1982, 83; named Woman of Excellence Seven Lakes Girl Scout Coun., 1995. Mem. Sigma Delta Chi. Home: PO Box 698 Williamson NY 14589-0698 Office: Wayne County Rural Ministry PO Box 73 Williamson NY 14589-0073

THOMASOS, DENYSE, artist; b. Trinidad, 1964; BA in Painting and Art History, U. Toronto, 1987; student, Skowhegan Sch., 1988; MFA in Painting and Sculpture, Yale U., 1989. Asst. prof. painting Tyler Sch. Art Temple U., Phila., 1990—95; asst. prof. painting visual and performing arts Rutgers U., Newark, 1995—. One-woman shows include Fleisher Art Meml. Gallery, Phila., 1993, Olga Korper Gallery, Toronto, Ont., Can., 1994, 1998, Queens (N.Y.) Mus. Art, Bulova Corp. Ctr., 1997, Lennon, Weinberg Gallery, N.Y.C., 1997, 1999, exhibited in group shows at Alpha Gallery, Boston, 1989, A Space, Toronto, 1992, Vox Populi, Phila., 1993, Mercer Union, Toronto, 1994, Ottawa (Ont.) Art Gallery, 1994, Lennon, Weinberg Gallery, N.Y.C., 1996, 1998, Newhouse Ctr. Contemporary Art, Snug Harbor Cultural Ctr., S.I., 1997, Art Gallery North York, N.Y., 1997, Fine Arts Ctr. Galleries, U. R.I., Kingston, 1999, others; curator (exhibitions) Art in Gen., Gallery 6, N.Y., 1998. Recipient Joan Mitchell Found. award, 1998; grantee Exploration grantee, Can. Coun., 1990, "B" Nat. grantee, 1994, Visual Arts fellow in painting, Pa. Coun. on Arts, Phila., 1994, Mid-Atlantic Regional grantee, NEA, 1994; Pew fellow in Arts, Phila., 1995, Guggenheim Found. fellow, 1997. Office: care Lennon Weinberg Inc 560 Broadway Rm 308 New York NY 10012-3945 Fax: 212-941-0098.

THOMASSEN, PAULINE FRANCES, medical and surgical nurse; b. Cleve., Jan. 19, 1939; d. Henry Clifford and Mabel Pauline (Hill) Nichols; m. Ruben Thomassen, Nov. 10, 1979; children: Rhonda, Terry, Diana, Philipp, Jody, Barbara. AA in Nursing, So. Colo. State Coll., 1974, BA in Psychology with distinction, 1975; BSN magna cum laude, Seattle Pacific U., 1986. RN Wash. Staff nurse III orthopedic unit, clin. spine educator Swedish Hosp. Med. Ctr., Seattle, 1975—, preceptor orientation of RNs and student RNs, 1975—, clin. spine educator, 1998—2002; ret., 2002. Mem. planning task force and faculty Nat. Nurses Conf., The Nurse and Spinal Surgery, Cleve.; lectr. Coll. of Nursing, Raleigh Fitkin Meml. Hosp., Manzini, Swaziland, South Africa, 1999, St. Petersburg, Russia, 2003; mem. med. mission to assist in clinic for street children, Satipo, Peru, 00, Honolulu Police Dept., 2001; mem. med. mission, Philippines, 04; med. mission ofcl. Camp Nurse Camp Li-WA, Fairbanks, Alaska, 2002; guest spkr. degenerative lumbar spinal techniques, cadaver workshop U. Wash., Seattle, 2001; guest spkr. Am. Acad. Orthop. Surgeons, Dallas, 2002, Dallas, 02. Author: Spinal Disease and Surgical Interventions, 1995. Mem.: Nat. Assn. Orthop. Nurses. Office: Swedish Health Ctr 747 Broadway Seattle WA 98122-4379

THOMAS-WILLIAMS, PAMELA RAE, publishing executive, writer; b. La Crosse, Wis., July 30, 1955; d. Dale Richard and Betty Jean (Clark) Thomas; m. Richard G. Williams, Oct. 30, 1987. BA in Journalism, Marquette U., 1977. Pres. Visual Concepts, ltd., La Crosse, 1979-85, Books By Pamela, Ltd., La Crosse, 1985—. Dir. developmental resources Cath. Cmty. Svcs., Las Vegas, Nev., 1990-91; cons., fundraiser Cath. Charities, La Crosse, 1985-91, U.S. Dept. Commerce-Census Bur., 1999—; co-owner Williams Properties. Author: From My Pallet of Winter, Let Me Paint Your Spring, 1978, The Bride's Guide-A Complete Guide on How to Plan Your Wedding, 7th edit., 2000, (Spanish translation Bridal Guide) Guía Nupcial, 1994, Wedding Showers for Couples, 2nd edit., 2000, Elvis Lives--The Business of Being Elvis, 2003. Mem. area VFW aux., 1992—. Mem. Pub. Rels. Soc. Am., Sigma Delta Chi. Republican. Lutheran. Avocations: reading, collecting antiques and handguns. Office: Books By Pamela Ltd 2820 Leonard St La Crosse WI 54601-

THOMERSON, ANNE SPACH, counselor; b. Recife, Brazil, July 17, 1953; d. Jule Christian and Nancy (Clendinin) Spach; m. E. Harvey Thomerson, July 23, 1976; children: Alexander, Julia. MEd, Ga. State U., Atlanta, 1992. Author: In Defense of the Wolf, 1979. Mem. ACA, ASCA, Phi Beta Kappa. Democrat. Presbyterian. Avocations: writing, horseback riding, hiking, art, travel.

THOMPSON, ADRIENNE, secondary school educator; Tchr. advanced placement art history Sch. for Creative and Performing Arts, Cin. Mem. arts assessment steering com. Ohio Art Coun. Named Music Educator of the Yr., Ohio Art Edn. Assn. Mus. Divsn., 2000; recipient Ohio Govs. award for excellence in tchg., 1998, Outstanding Excellence award, Cin. Pub. Schs., 1999. Mem.: Nat. Bd. for Profl. Tchg. Stds. (bd. mem.). Office: Sch for Creative and Performing Arts 1310 Sycamore St Cincinnati OH 45202

THOMPSON, ANA CALZADA, secondary education educator, mathematician; b. Sanderson, Tex., Nov. 29, 1940; d. Leopoldo G. and Maria Deo Gracia (Sandoval) Calzada; m. Tommy Salinas Thompson, July 1, 1962; children: Tommy Michael, Anthony Jude, Ana Marie. BS, Sul Ross State U., Alpine, Tex., 1966; MEd, S.W. Tex. State U., 1980. Tchr. Poteet (Tex.) Ind. Sch. Dist., 1965-67, Northside Ind. Sch. Dist., San Antonio, 1967-68; tchr. math. N.E. Ind. Sch. Dist., San Antonio, 1968-97, chmn. dept., 1976-97. Prof. math. St. Philips Coll., San Antonio, 1986—; mem. Region 20 Tchr. Ctr., San Antonio, 1978-82; pres. S.W. Tchr. Ctr., San Marcos, Tex., 1970-82. Contbg. author: Graphing Power, 1995. Sec., La Vernia (Tex.) Ind. Sch. Dist., 1977-87, mem. bd., 1978-87; del. Tex. Dem. Conv., Houston, 1988, Ft. Worth, 1992, Dallas, 1996, El Paso, 2002; del. Guadalupe County Dem. Com., Seguin, Tex., 1988, 92, 96, 2002. Mem. NEA, Nat. Coun. Tchrs. Math., Tex. Tchrs. Assn., Alamo Dist. Coun. Tchrs. Math. Roman Catholic. Avocations: reading, knitting, travel, gardening.

THOMPSON, ANDREA, TV host former newscaster and actress; b. Dayton, Ohio, 1959; m. David Guc, 1987 (div. 1990); m. Jerry Doyle, 1995 (div. 1997); 1 child, Alec. Correspondent KRQE-TV, Albuquerque, 2000—01; news anchor, Headline News CNN, 2001—02. Films include Wall Street, 1987, Doin' Time on Planet Earth, 1988, Delirious, 1991, Lost Valley, 1998, A Gun, A Car, A Blonde, 1998, Rocket's Red Glare, 2000; TV series include Falcon Crest, 1989-90, Babylon 5, 1994-95, JAG, 1995-96, NYPD Blue, 1996-2000; host: Court TV, Saturday Night Line Up, 2002.

THOMPSON, ANNE ELISE, federal judge; b. Phila., July 8, 1934; d. Leroy Henry and Mary Elise (Jackson) Jenkins; m. William H. Thompson, June 19, 1965; children: William H., Sharon A. BA, Howard U., 1955, LLB, 1964; MA, Temple U., 1957. Bar: D.C. bar 1964, N.J. bar 1966. Staff atty. Office of Solicitor, Dept. Labor, Chgo., 1964-65; asst. dep. public defender Trenton, N.J., 1967-70; mcpl. prosecutor Lawrence Twp., Lawrenceville, N.J., 1970-72; mcpl. ct. judge Trenton, 1972-75; prosecutor Mercer County, Mercer County, Trenton, 1975-79; judge U.S. Dist. Ct. N.J., Trenton, 1979—. Vice chmn. Mercer County Criminal Justice Planning Com., 1972; mem. com. criminal practice N.J. Supreme Ct., 1975-79, mem. com. mcpl. cts., 1972-75; v.p. N.J. County Prosecutors Assn., 1978-79; chmn. juvenile justice com. Nat. Dist. Attys. Assn., 1978-79 Del. Democratic Nat. Conv., 1972. Recipient Assn. Black Women Lawyers award, 1976, Disting. Service award Nat. Dist. Attys. Assn., 1979, Gene Carte Meml. award Am. Criminal Justice Assn., 1980, Outstanding Leadership award N.J. County Prosecutors Assn., 1980, John Mercer Langston Outstanding Alumnus award Howard U. Law Sch., 1981; also various service awards; certs. of appreciation. Mem. Am. Bar Assn., Fed. Bar Assn., N.J. Bar Assn., Mercer County Bar Assn. Democrat. Office: US Dist Ct US Courthouse-4000 402 E State St Trenton NJ 08608-1507

THOMPSON, ANNE KATHLEEN, entertainment journalist; b. N.Y.C., Aug. 10, 1954; d. Charles Torrington Thompson and Eleanor Josephine (Callahan) Dekins; m. David Christopher Chute, Oct. 23, 1983; 1 child, Nora Thompson Chute. BA in Cinema Studies, NYU, 1976. Assoc. editor Film Comment, N.Y.C., 1981-82; West Coast editor Film Comment Mag., N.Y.C., 1982-96; publicity dir. Twentieth Century Fox Pictures, 1983-85; columnist Risky Bus., L.A. Weekly, L.A. Times Syndicate, 1985-93, Inside Film, 1988-90; U.S. editor Empire Mag., London, 1989-91; sr. writer Entertainment Weekly, 1993-96; west coast editor Premier Mag., 1996—. Account exec. P/M/K Pub. Rels., N.Y.C., 1979-81; publicist United Artists, N.Y.C., 1976-79; asst. mgr. Bleecker St. Cinema, N.Y.C., 1975-76. Unit publicist Terms of Endearment, The Adventures of Buckaroo Banzai, 1983; contbr. Entertainment Weekly, 1991—, (weekly variety) 7 Days mag., 1990, N.Y. Times, 1992—. Mem. Nat. Writer's Union, Women in Film. Office: Premiere 1990 S Bundy Dr Ste 250 Los Angeles CA 90025-5244

THOMPSON, ANNIE FIGUEROA, retired academic director, educator; b. Río Piedras, P.R., June 7, 1941; d. Antonio Figueroa-Colón and Ana Isabel Laugier; m. Donald P. Thompson, Jan. 23, 1972; 1 child, John Anthony. BA, Baylor U., 1962; MSLS, U. So. Calif., 1965; AMD, Fla. State U., 1978, PhD, 1980. Educator Mayan Sch., Guatemala City, Guatemala, 1962-63; cataloger libr. sys. U. P.R., Río Piedras, 1965-67, head music libr., 1967-81, assoc. prof. librarianship, 1981-85, dir. grad. sch. libr. info. sci. Rio Piedras, 1986-93, prof., 1986-96; ret., 1996. Author: An Annotated Bibliography About Music in Puerto Rico, 1975; co-author: Music and Dance in Puerto Rico from the Age of Columbus to Modern Times, An Annotated Bibliography, 1991; contbr. articles to profl. jours.; performed song recitals Inst. of P.R. Culture and U. P.R. Artist Series, 1974-78; soloist with P.R. Symphony Orch., San Juan, 1978; performed in opera, on radio and TV, San Juan, 1968-81. Sec. P.R. Symphony Orch League, San Juan, 1982-84; mem. pub. libr. adv. com. Adminstrn. for Devel. of Arts and Culture, P.R., 1982-84, Pub. Libr. Adv. Bd., 1989-94. Recipient Lauro a la Instrucción Bibliotecaria Sociedad de Bibliotecarios de P.R., 1985, Lauro a la Bibliografía Puertorriqueña, 1993. Mem. Sarasota Rotary (bd. dirs. 2000-02), Sociedad de Bibliotecarios de P.R. (pres. 1994-96), Music Libr. Assn. (bd. dirs. 1982-84, asst. conv. mgr. 2002-04, conv. mgr. 2004-), Sarasota Rotary Found. (bd. dirs.), Sigma Delta Kappa, Mu Phi Epsilon, Beta Phi Mu. Episcopalian. Home: 435 S Gulfstream Ave Sarasota FL 34236-6736 E-mail: annietmla@aol.com.

THOMPSON, BARBARA STORCK, state official; b. McFarland, Wis., Oct. 15, 1924; d. John Casper and Marie Ann (Kassabaum) Storck; m. Glenn T. Thompson, July 1, 1944; children— David C., James T. BS, Wis. State U., 1956; MS, U. Wis., 1959, PhD, 1969; L.H.D. (hon.), Carroll Coll., 1974. Tchr. pub. schs., West Dane County, Mt. Horeb, Wis., 1944-56; instr. Green County Tchrs. Coll., Monroe, Wis., 1956-57; coordinator curriculum Monroe Pub. Schs., 1957-60; instr. U. Wis., Platteville, 1960; supr. schs. Waukesha County Schs., Wis., 1960-63, supt. schs., 1963-65; prin. Fairview Elem. Schs., Brookfield, Wis., 1962-64; adminstrv. cons. Wis. Dept. Pub. Instrn., Madison, 1964-72, state coordinator, 1971-72; instr. U. Wis., Madison and Green Bay, 1972; supt. pub. instrn. Madison, Wis., 1973—81. Mem. Wis. State Bd. Vocat. Edn., 1973-81, Wis. Edn. Comm. Bd., 1973-81, Univ. Wis. Sys. Bd. Regents, 1973-1981. Author: A Candid Discussion of Critical Issues, 1975; Mem. editorial bd.: The Education Digest, 1975— ; Contbr. articles to profl. jours. Mem. White House Conf. Children, 1970, Gov.'s Com. State Conf. Children and Youth, 1969-70, Manpower Council, 1973-81; bd. dirs. Vocational, Tech. and Adult Edn., 1973-81, Ednl. Communications, 1973-81, Higher Edn. Aids, 1973-81, Agy. Instructional TV, 1975-81; mem. nat. panel on SAT score decline; bd. regents U. Wis., 1973-81, U.S. office f Edn. Visiting Sch. Team - England, GErmany, Sweden, Poland, Iran, Syria, India, and Japan. Recipient State Conservation award Madison Lions CLub, 1956; Waukesha Freeman award, 1961 Mem. Nat. Coun. Adminstrv. Women in Edn. (named Woman of Year 1974), Nat. Coun. State Cons. in Elem. Edn. (pres. 1974-75), Wis. Assn. Sch. Dist. Adminstrs., Assn. Supervision and Curriculum Devel., Wis. Assn. Supervision and Curriculum Devel., Southwestern Wis. Assn. Supervision and Curriculum Devel., Southeastern Wis. Assn. Supervision and Curriculum Devel. (mem. exec. council 1972-73), Dept. Elem. Sch. Prins., Wis. Elementary Sch. Prins. Assn., NEA, Wis. Edn. Assn. (pres. local chpt. 1970-71); life mem. So. Wis. Edn. Assn., Wis. Ednl. Rsch. Assn., Dept. Elem.-Kindergarten-Nursery Edn., Assn. Childhood Edn. Internat., Assn. Childhood Edn., Coun. Chief State Sch. Officers, Edn. Commn. of States, Nat. Coun. State Cons. in Elem. Edn. (pres. 1974-75), Am. Assn. Sch. Dist. Adminstrs. (chmn. policy com. 1963-81), Madison Ctrl. Internat. Lions Club, U. Wis. Alumni Orgn. (Sarasota, Fla. and Madison), U. Wis. League (Madison chpt.), Delta Kappa Gamma, Pi Lambda Theta. Office: Apt 123 325 S Yellowstone Dr Madison WI 53705-4301

THOMPSON, BERNIDA LAMERLE, principal, consultant, educator; b. Tuskegee, Ala., July 5, 1946; d. Barry James Sr. and Doris LaMerle (Askey) T.; m. Rolando Amerson, June 15, 1968 (div. Aug. 1988); children: Afriye Amerson, Mwando Amerson. BS in Elem. Edn., Cen. State U., 1968; MEd in Adminstrn. and Curriculum, Miami U., Oxford, Ohio, 1971; EdD in Early and Mid. Childhood Edn., Nova U., 1992. Classroom elem. sch. tchr. Dayton Pub. Schs.; asst. prin., intern St. James Cath. Sch., Dayton, Ohio; tchr. St. Augustine Cath. Sch., Washington; sci. resource tchr. D.C. Pub. Schs., Washington; founding tchr., prin. Roots Activity Learning Ctr., Washington, 1977—, Roots Pub. Charter Sch., 1999—. Multicultural advisor HBJ 1992 Reading Textbook. Author: Black Madonnas and Young Lions a Rite of Passage for African American Adolescents, 1992, rev. edit., 1998, Africentric Interdisciplinary Multi-Level Hands On Science, 1994, rev. edit., 2001; contbr. articles to profl. jours. Mem. Nat. Assn. Edn. Young Children, World Coun. Curriculum Instrn., Coun. Ind. Black Inst., Inst. Ind. Edn., Nat. Black Child Devel. Inst. Office: Roots Pub Charter Sch 15 Kennedy St NW Washington DC 20011-5201 Office Phone: 202-882-8073. Business E-Mail: bthompson@rootspcs.org.

THOMPSON, BERTHA BOYA, retired education educator, antique dealer and appraiser; b. New Castle, Pa., Jan. 31, 1917; d. Frank L. and Kathryn Belle (Park) Boya; m. John L. Thompson, Mar. 27, 1942; children: Kay Lynn Thompson Koolage, Scott McClain. BS in Elem. & Secondary Edn., Slippery Rock State Coll., 1940; MA in Geography and History, Miami U., 1954; EdD, Ind. U., 1961. Cert. elem. and secondary edn. tchr. Elem. tchr., reading specialist New Castle (Pa.) Sch. System, 1940-45; tchr., chmn. social studies Talawanda Sch. System, Oxford, Ohio, 1954-63; assoc. prof. psychology and geography, chair edn. dept. Western Coll. for Women, Oxford, 1963-74; assoc. prof. edn., reading clinic Miami U., Oxford, 1974-78, prof. emeritus, 1978—; pvt. antique dealer, appraiser Oxford, 1978—. Contbr. articles to profl. jours. Mem. folk art com. Miami U. Art Mus., Oxford, 1974-76; mem. adv. com. Smith libr., Oxford Pub. Libr., 1978-81. Mem. AAUP, Nat. Coun. Geographic Edn. (exec. bd. dirs. 1966-69), Nat. Soc. for Study Edn., Assn. Am. Geographers, Soc. Women Geographers, Nat. Coun. for the Social Studies, Pi Lambda Theta, Zeta Tau Alpha, Pi Gamma Mu, Gamma Theta Upsilon, Kappa Delta Pi. Avocations: antique collecting, reading, travel, tennis. Home: 6073 Contreras Rd Oxford OH 45056-9708

THOMPSON, BIRGIT DOLORES, civic worker, writer; b. Jamestown, N.Y., Apr. 7, 1930; d. Oscar Einar and Karin Johanna (Videll) Wolff; m. William Andrew Thompson, Jan. 26, 1952 (div. June 1978); children: William A., Christina A., Michael J., Timothy A., Kathleen S., Jeffrey B. AB summa cum laude, SUNY, Fredonia, 1974. Exec. dir. Fenton Hist. Ctr., Jamestown, 1975-82; fin. dir. Amicae, Inc., Fredonia, 1983-90; office mgr. JEM Counseling Ctr., Jamestown, 1990-93; resource/info. person Audubon Nature Ctr., Jamestown, 1993—. Author: Illustrated History of Jamestown and Chautauqua County, 1983; musician Jamestown String Quartet, violist local orchestras, 1970-2000; contbr. articles to newspapers. Historian City of Jamestown, 1978—; bd. dirs., chair scholarship com. Mozart Club, 2001—; play selection com. Lucille Ball Little Theatre of Jamestown, 1976—, pit orch.; mem. steering and fin. coms. Underground Railroad Tableau Project; bd. dirs. Jamestown YWCA, Chautauqua Regional Youth Symphony, pres., 1996—2001; com. mem. Jamestown Audubon Soc., newsletter editor, 1982—98. Mem. AAUW (chmn. What's New Fair Jamestown 1988-94, legislative breakfast 1995—, bd. dirs., pres. 1988-92, co-pres. 2000—, named gift award 1987), Interclub Coun. Jamestown (treas. 1998—, Woman of Yr. award 1992). Avocations: museums, concerts, reading, gardening. Home: 13 Lamont St Jamestown NY 14701-2021 E-mail: musicat@netsync.net.

THOMPSON, CAROLINE WARNER, film director, screenwriter; b. Washington, Apr. 23, 1956; d. Thomas Carlton Jr. and Bettie Marshall (Warner) T.; m. Alfred Henry Bromell, Aug. 28, 1982 (div. 1985). BA summa cum laude, Amherst Coll., 1978. Film dir., screenwriter William Morris Agy., Inc., Beverly Hills, Calif. Author: First Born, 1983; screenwriter: (films) Edward Scissorhands, 1990, The Addams Family, 1991, Homeward Bound: The Incredible Journey, 1993, The Secret Garden, 1993, Tim Burton's The Nightmare Before Christmas, 1993; screenwriter, dir.: Black Beauty, 1994, Buddy, 1997. Mem. Phi Beta Kappa. Avocation: horseback riding. Office: William Morris Agency Inc 151 S El Camino Dr Beverly Hills CA 90212-2775

THOMPSON, CARRIE LORRAINE, volunteer; b. Portsmouth, Va., Sept. 1, 1953; d. Gordon Howard and Marjorie Lorraine Hausenfluck; m. Rickie Lee Thompson, Oct. 13, 1972; children: Katynia Lorraine Speight, Vicktrie Leighanne Tucker, Brandon Lee, Mariah Lynnette. AA, Eastfield Jr. Coll., Mesquite, Tex., 1973. With Meals on Wheels, [illegible] Food Bank at Norwich Worship Ctr., Norwich, 1992—. Home: 21 Winchester St Norwich CT 06360 Office: Conn Food Bank Lawler Ln Norwich CT 06360

THOMPSON, CHARLOTTE ELLIS, pediatrician, educator, writer; d. Robert and Ann Ellis; divorced; children: Jennifer Ann, Geoffrey Graeme. BA, Stanford U., 1950, MD, 1954. Diplomate Am. Bd. Pediat. Intern Children's Hosp., San Francisco, 1953-54; resident UCLA, 1960-61, L.A. Children's Hosp., 1962-63; pvt. practice La Jolla, Calif., 1963-75; dir. Muscle Disease Clinic Univ. Hosp.-U. Calif. Sch. Medicine, San Diego, 1969-80, asst. clin. prof. pediat., 1969—; dir. Ctr. for Handicapped Children and Teenagers, San Francisco, 1981—2004. Cons. U.S. Naval Hosp., San Diego, 1970-91; dep. dir. Santa Clara County Child Health and Disability, Santa Clara, Calif., 1974-75; dir. Ctr. for Multiple Handicaps, Oakland, Calif., 1976-81; co-dir. Muscle Clinic Children's Hosp., San Diego, 1963-69; dir. muscle program U. Rochester, 1957-60. Author: Raising a Handicapped Child: A Helpful Guide for Parents of the Physically Disabled, 1986, 4th edit., 1991, rev., expanded edit., 2000, Allein leben: Ein umfassendes Handbuch für Frauen, 1993, Making Wise Choices: A Guide for Women, 1993, Raising a Child with a Neuromuscular Disorder, 1999, Raising A Handicapped Child, 1999; contbr. articles to med. jours., including Clin. Pediat., New Eng. Jour. Medicine, Neurology, Jour. Family Practice, Mothering, Jour. Pediatric Orthopedics, Pediatrician, Am. Baby, Pediatric News, also chpts. to books. Mem. Calif. Children's Svc. Com., 1977—. Fellow Am. Acad. Pediat. Avocations: tennis, ice skating, opera. Office: 8070 La Jolla Shores Dr # 514 La Jolla CA 92037 E-mail: cetmd@earthlink.net.

THOMPSON, CLAIRE LOUISA, nurse, educator; b. Columbus, Ohio, Sept. 29, 1938; d. Harry Edgar and Clara Etta (Brackenbusch) McKeever; m. Roger Lee Thompson, Dec. 20, 1958 (div. 1988); children: Jeffrey, Michael. Diploma, Bethesda Hosp. Sch. Nursing, Cin., 1959; student, Ball State, 1970, Ind. U., 1981, Purdue U., 1982-83. RN, Ohio, Ind., Calif.; cert. ins. rehab. specialist, case mgr.; cert. health occupl. level tchr., Ind. Oper. rm./emergency rm. nurse Greene Meml. Hosp., Xenia, Ohio, 1959-60; med.-surg. nurse, charge nurse Bethesda Hosp., 1960-64; med.-surg. nurse Porter Meml. Hosp., Valparaiso, Ind., 1965-66; staff and charge nurse Mercy Hosp., Elwood, Ind., 1968-74; gen. practice nurse W. A. Scea, MD, Elwood, 1970-74; exec. dir. Vis. Nurse Assn., Elwood, 1974-78; analyst Blue Cross/Blue Shield of Indpls., 1978; supr. Meth. Hosp. Clinic, Indpls., 1979-80; DON Upjohn Health Care, Indpls., 1980; staff nurse Americana Health Care Ctr., Indpls., 1981; instr. health occups. Washington Twp. Schs., Indpls., 1981-84; br. mgr. health & rehab. Crawford & Co., Indpls., 1984-88, regional med. svcs. advisor western region San Francisco, 1988-92; br. mgr. Crawford & Co., Health Care Mgmt., Modesto, Calif., 1992-94; ret., 1994. Developer in case mgmt. nursing svcs., 1974-94. Founder Meals on Wheels, Elwood, 1975, Vis. Nurses Assn., Elwood, 1976. Mem. NLN, Assn. Rehab. Nurses (pres. Ind. chpt. 1987-88), Nat. Ins. Womens Assn., Case Mgmt. Soc. Am., San Francisco Ins. Womens Assn., Rehab. Ins. Nurses Group. Episcopalian. Avocations: family, the arts, photography, cats.

THOMPSON, DAYLE ANN, small business owner, consultant; b. Grand Forks, N.D., Jan. 6, 1954; d. Duane Theodore and Anna Mae (Desautel) T.; m. Michael Gary Sciulla, Aug. 6, 1977 (div. Sept. 1980); m. Manfred Hans von Ehrenfried II, June 11, 1982. Secretarial degree, Aaker's Bus. Coll., Grand Forks, 1973; Masters Cert. in Project Mgmt., George Washington U., 1995. Receptionist U.S. Rep. Norman F. Lent U.S. Ho. of Reps., Washington, 1973-74; office mgr., personal sec. U.S. Rep. Les AuCoin, U.S. Ho. of Reps., Washington, 1975-78; bus. mgr., bookkeeper Virgin Islands POST, St.Thomas, USVI, 1978; office and pers. mgr. Internat. Energy Assocs. Ltd., Washington, 1978-82; program support mgr. MSI Svcs. Inc., Washington, 1982-84; pres., treas., chief exec. officer Tech. and Adminstrv. Svcs. Corp., Washington, 1984-2000; acctg. mgr. Carolyn Kinder, Inc., Clearwater, Fla., 1997—2002; pres. Get Taxes Back, Inc., St. Petersburg, Fla., 2000—. Hosp. vol. ARC, Arlington, Va., 1987. Recipient Group Achievement award NASA, 1984, 93, Commendation Letter, NASA, 1985, 87, 88, 91, 93, 94, Small Bus. Prime Contractor of Yr. award Small Bus. Adminstrn. Region 5, 1994, Adminstr. award for Excellence. Mem. Washington Space Bus. Roundtable (sponsor-benefactor 1990-92). Republican. Roman Catholic. Avocations: boating, fishing, reading. Home and Office: 4250 42d Ave S Saint Petersburg FL 33711-4231 Business E-Mail: dthompson@gettaxesback.com.

THOMPSON, DEBORAH CARPENTER, private school educator; b. Rutland, Vt., Feb. 22, 1943; d. Edwards Shinville and Frances (Howley) Carpenter; m. Hall Thompson, Sept. 4, 1965; children: Anne, Joel. BA, U. Vt., 1965; MEd, Boston U., 1968. Pres. Gtr. Portland (Maine) Childbirth Edn. Assn., 1973-78; assoc. in parish adminstrn. Congregational Ch. Cumberland (Maine), 1980-87; tutor English, history North Yarmouth Acad., Yarmouth, Maine, 1988—. Mem. Congregational Ch. Cumberland, 1976—. Mem. Maine Audubon Soc., Portland (Maine) Mus. Art, Portland Country Club, Val Halla Golf Course (chair bd. trustees 1987-93, greens com. 1997—). Avocations: golf, gardening, cross country skiing, politics, art. Home: 240 Greely Rd Cumberland Center ME 04021-9379

THOMPSON, DEBRA ANNE, speech pathology/audiology services professional, educator; b. Camden, N.J., June 21, 1958; d. Donald Charles and Barbara Anne Schuck; m. Matthew Joseph Thompson; children: Brian, Christopher. BA in Speech Pathology, Coll. of N.J., Trenton, 1979, MA in Speech Pathology, 1981. Cert. speech/lang. pathologist 1981; presch. handicapped tchr. 1992, tchg. hearing impaired 1994, nat. bd. cert. tchr. 2001, instrnl. tech. Speech pathologist East Greenwich Twp. Schools, Mickleton, NJ, 1980—82, Dillon (S.C.) Dist. 2 Schs., 1988—92, Pub. Schs. of Robeson County, Lumberton, NC, 1990—92, presch. handicapped tchr., 1992—94, tchr. of hearing impaired, 1994—2002; dir. instrnl. tech. U. N.C., Pembroke, 2002—. Tech. trainer Tanglewood Elem. Sch., Lumberton, NC, 1998—2002; sec., bd. mem. Acad. Booster Club Lumberton H.S., 1999—2002. Coach, scorekeeper Robeson Rockers Baseball Team, Lumberton, 2001. Mem.: Coun. for Exceptional Children (Spl. Educator award 2001), N.C. Assn. Ednl. Comm. and Tech., Amateur Athletic Union. Roman Catholic. Avocations: running, computers, golf. Office: UNCP Sch Education PO Box 1510 Pembroke NC 28372 Personal E-mail: dt0621@yahoo.com. Business E-Mail: debra.thompson@uncp.edu.

THOMPSON, DIANE E. lawyer; married; 2 children. Grad., Vassar Coll.; JD, George Washington U., 1976. Ptnr. Rogers, Joseph, O'Donnell and Quinn, 1981-83; counsel San Francisco Human Rights Commn., 1981-83; mem. Mondale for Pres. Compaign, 1984; gen. counsel NOW, 1985; adminstrv. asst., legis. dir. to Barbara Mikulski of Md., U.S. Ho. of Reps., Washington, 1986; chief to staff to Senator Mikulski of Md., U.S. Senate, Washington, 1987-89; ptnr. Foreman and Heidepriem, 1992-93; assoc. commr. for legis. affairs FDA, HHS, Rockville, Md., 1994—. Mem. adj. faculty Hastings Coll. Law, U. Calif. Office: US EPA 1200 Pennsylvania Ave NW Washington DC 20460-0001

THOMPSON, DOREEN, public relations executive; b. Somerville, Mass., Mar. 26, 1955; 2 children. BA in Mass. Comm., U. N.H., 1977; MA in Speech Comm., Emerson Coll., 1982. Account exec. Arnold Pub. Rels., Boston, 1984-85; account exec., account supr., v.p. Ingalls, Quinn & Johnson Pub. Rels., Boston, 1985-88; v.p., then sr. v.p. The Weber Group, Cambridge, Mass., 1988-98, exec. v.p., 1998—. Trustee Lasell Coll., Newton, Mass., 1990—; pro bono work Gang Peace, Boston, 1994. Recipient Regional award CIPPRA, 1993, Bellringer award Publicity Club, 1994. Office: The Weber Group 101 Main St Ste 3 Cambridge MA 02142-1527

THOMPSON, DOROTHEA KATHLEEN, microbiologist; b. Bellefonte, Pa., May 25, 1963; d. Charles Carr and Deborah Ann (Evenson) T. BA in English and Microbiology, U. Tenn., 1986; MS in Microbiology, Va. Polytechnic Inst./State U., 1989; MA in English, Pa. State U., 1992; PhD in Microbiology, Ohio State U., 1997. Grad. rsch. asst. dept. anaerobic microbiology Va. Tech., Blacksburg, 1986-89; grad. tchg. asst./lectr. dept. English Pa. State, University Park, Pa., 1990-92; grad. rsch. and tchg. assoc. dept. microbiology Ohio State, Columbus, 1992-97; ORISE postdoctoral fellow FDA/CBER divsn. bacterial products, Rockville, Md., 1998—99; rsch. assoc. environ. scis. divsn. Microbial Genomics Group, Oak Ridge Nat. Lab., Tenn., 1999—2002; rsch. staff scientist Oak Ridge Nat. Lab., 2002—. Tchg. asst. Howard Hughes Scholars Inst. in Genetics, University Park, 1992; vice-speaker Va. Tech. Grad. Student Assembly, Blacksburg, 1987-88; grad. student rep. Coun. on Rsch. and Grad. Studies, Columbus, 1993-94; departmental del. Ohio State Coun. Grad. Students, 1993-94. Contbr. articles to profl. jours. Mem. Am. Soc. Microbiology, Phi Beta Kappa, Phi Kappa Phi. Avocations: world travel, hiking, creative writing, tennis, guitar. Home: 5306 Amherst Woods Ln Knoxville TN 37921 Office: Oak Ridge Nat Lab Environ Sci Divsn PO Box 2008 Oak Ridge TN 37831-6038 Office Phone: 865-574-4815.

THOMPSON, DOROTHY BARNARD, elementary school educator; b. Flushing, NY, Aug. 14, 1933; d. Henry Clay and Cecelia Minnie Theresa (La Pardo) Barnard; m. Norman Earl Thompson, Aug. 12, 1956 (dec.); children: Greg, Scot, Henry, Marc (dec.), Matthew. BSEd, SUNY, New Paltz, 1953; MS, Hofstra U., 1984. Cert. elem. tchr. K-6th grades, reading specialist K-12th grades, NY. Adjunct prof. Suffolk Community Coll., Brentwood, NY, 1987—; adj. prof. Nassau Cmty. Coll., Uniondale, NY, 1986—; adj. prof., instr. Ctr. for Acad. Achievement Long Isl. U., Greenvale, NY, 1984-92; tchr. reading, 1st and 2nd grades Long Beach Pub. Sch., NY, 1988—. Mem. founding group Parent/Tchr., The Learning Tree, Garden City, NY, 1971; founder parent coop. Happy Day Nursery Sch., Bellmore, NY, 1975; parent-tchr. Commonwealth Sch., Bay Shore, Oakdale, 1976-82. Office: 456 Neptune Blvd Long Beach NY 11561-2400 E-mail: anetco01@aol.com.

THOMPSON, ELEANOR DUMONT, nurse; b. Derry, N.H., May 26, 1935; d. Louis Arthur and Florence Berthae (Gendreau) D.; m. Carl Hugh Thompson, Aug. 22, 1959; children: Justine, Julie. Student, Dartmouth Hitchcock Nur. Sch., 1956; BA, New Eng. Coll., 1977; MS, Drake U., 1984. Registered art therapist. Pediatric instr. Hanover (N.H.) Sch. Practical Nursing, 1958-61; pub. W.B. Sanders Co., Phila., 1962-95; pediatric instr. St. Joseph Hosp., Nashua, N.H., 1978-81; cert. clin. nurse specialist Mercy Hosp. Med. Ctr., Des Moines, 1987-90; clin. nurse specialist Portsmouth (N.H.) Regional Hosp., 1991-2000; pvt. practice Silverman & Assoc., Inc., 1991-93. Puppeteer St. Joseph's Hosp. Sch. Nursing, Nashua, 1981-82; created and conducted shows on hospitalization for children; nursing cons. Hospice Cen. Iowa, Des Moines, 1982-89; cons. art therapy N.H. Hosp., 2001—. Author: Pediatric Nursing An Introductory Text, 1965, 6th edit., 1992, (translations in Spanish, Italian and Portuguese), Introduction to Maternity and Pediatric Nursing, 1990, 2d edit., 1995. Vol. nurse Vietnam Vets. Ctr., Des Moines, 1985-87, Camp Apanda Childrens Cancer Camp Boone, Iowa, 1984-86; organist Holy Trinity Ch. Des Moines, 1982, St. Pius Ch., Des Moines, 1982. Mem. ANA, Am. Art Therpy Assn. (past pres.), N.H. Art Therapy Assn., N.H. Nurses Assn. Democrat. Roman Catholic. Avocations: horseback riding, playing piano and organ, travel. Home: 13 Sherman Ave Brentwood NH 03833-6225

THOMPSON, EVE KATHERINE, literature educator, department chairman; b. Woodland, Calif., Mar. 8, 1948; d. Lawrence Edward and Mariam Moore McArdell; m. Floyd Arthur Pratt, July 15, 1978 (div. July 1980); 1 child, Amber Louise Pratt ; m. Jay William Thompson, Aug. 4, 1984. BA in English, U. Calif., Berkeley, 1970; MA in Creative Writing, Calif. State U., Sacramento, 1981; PhD in Multicultural Edn., Union Inst. and U., 1998. Libr. asst. Calif. State U., Sacramento, 1975—77, English instr., 1984—85; substance abuse counselor The Aquarian Effort, Sacramento, 1977—84; English instr. Sacramento City Coll., 1980—84, Sierra Coll., Rocklin, Calif., 1984—85; lit. coord. Read Project, South Siskiyou County, Calif., 1985—89; English instr., dept. chair Coll. of the Siskiyous, Weed, Calif., 1985—. Curriculum developer Coll. of the Siskiyous, Weed, 1985—2003, faculty advisor for Phi Theta Kappa, 1988—92, chair profl. stds. com., 1994—98. Author: (plays) Read Radio Drama Series, 1989, Initiations, 1994, Faces of Siskiyous County, 2001, (poetry) Portfolio North, 2001, 2002. Troop leader Girl Scouts, Mt. Shasta, Calif., 1985—88; participant, spkr. Rotary Club, Weed, 1985—87; bd. mem. Sisson PTA, Mt. Shasta, 1987—92; active Coll. of the Siskiyous Found. Bd., 1992—94; profl. mentor, 1998—2003. Recipient Best Poetry award, Rouge River Writer's Conf., 1993, Cert. of Appreciation, AAUW, 1994. Mem.: Calif. Tchrs. Assn., Coll. Siskiyous Faculty Assn. Avocations: writing, painting, bicycling, kayaking, hiking.

THOMPSON, EWA M. foreign language educator; b. Kaunas, Lithuania; came to U.S., 1963; d. Jozef and Maria Majewski; m. James R. Thompson. BA in English and Russian, U. Warsaw, Poland, 1963; MFA in Piano, Sopot Conservatory Music, 1963; MA in English, Ohio U., 1964; PhD in Comparative Lit., Vanderbilt U., 1967. Instr. Vanderbilt U., Nashville, Tenn., 1964-67; asst. prof. Ind. State U., Terre Haute, 1967-68, Ind. U., 1968-70, Rice U., Houston, 1967-73, assoc. prof., 1974-79, prof., 1979—, chair, 1987-90; assoc. prof. U. Va., Charlottesville, 1973-74. Cons. NEH, 1973—, The John D. and Catherine T. MacArthur Found., The John Simon Guggenheim Found., U.S. Dept. Edn.; vis. cons. Tex. A&M U.; seminar dir. NEH Summer Inst., Southeastern La. U., 1990; chair Russian lit. conf. Rice U., 1989; lectr. various colls. and univs. Author: Russian Formalism and Anglo-American New Criticism: A Comparative Study, 1971, Witold Gombrowicz, 1979, Polish transl., 2002, Understanding Russia: The Holy Fool in Russian Culture, 1987 (Chinese transl. 1995, 2nd Chinese edit. 1998), The Search for Self-Definition in Russian Literature, 1991, Imperial Knowledge: Russian Literature and Colonialism, 2000, Polish transl., 2000; editor the Sarmatian Rev., (www.ruf.rice.edu/[]sarmatia) 1988—; contbr. articles to profl. jours., chpts. to books. Mellon grant, 1990, Rice U. grant 1990, Internat. Rsch. and Exchanges Sr. Scholar grant, 1991; Hoover Inst. fellow, 1988; scholar Vanderbilt U., 1964-67; recipient Silver Thistle award Houston's Scottish Heritage Found., 1988. Roman Catholic. Home: 142 Stoney Creek Houston TX 77024 Office: Rice Univ 6100 S Main St MS 32 Houston TX 77005-1892 E-mail: ethomp@rice.edu.

THOMPSON, G. NANETTE, state agency administrator; m. Bill Cooke; 5 children. BA in Internat. Rels., Stanford U., 1978; JD, U. Washington, 1982. Bar: Washington 1982, Alaska 1983. Pvt. practice, 1982—99; chmn. Regulatory Commn. Alaska, Anchorage, 1999—; asst. atty. gen. State of Alaska. Mem. fed.-state joint conf. on delivery advanced svc. FCC, 1999, state chmn. fed.-state joint conf. on delivery advanced svc., 1999—2001, mem. universal svc. joint bd., 2000—01, chmn. universal svc. joint bd., 2001—. Booth home adv. bd. Salvation Army, 1989—94, pres. booth home adv. bd., 1994; bd. dir. Campfire Boys & Girls, 1995—2000. Office: RCA 701 West 8th Ave Ste 300 Anchorage AK 99501

THOMPSON, GLORIA MATTHEWS, marketing and statistics educator; b. Havre De Grace, Md., Apr. 22, 1947; d. Henry and Elsie Matthews; children: Christina Laureen, Michael Gene. BA in music edn., Cath. U. Am., 1969; MBA, York Coll. Pa., 1999; D in bus. adminstrn., Nova S.E. U., 2004; MA in edn., U. Phoenix, 2003. Dept. chair, grad. bus. and mgmt. U. Phoenix, Phila. campus, Wayne, Pa., 2000—; owner/mgr. Country Fabrications, York, Pa., 1984—99; music tchr. Prince George's County Schools, Upper Marlboro, Md., 1969—78. Mktg. rsch. project dir. York Coll. Pa, 1999; academic program [illegible] U. Phoenix, 2001—02, curriculum devel., 2002, assessment devel., 02; adj. faculty Harrisburg Area CC, Pa., 1999—2000; adj. prof. Ctrl. Pa. Coll., Summerdale, 1999—2000. Mem.: SHRM (Soc. Human Resource Mgmt.), Mktg. Mgmt. Assn., Am. Mktg. Asociation. Office: U Phoenix Phil 170 S Warner Rd Ste 200 Wayne PA 19087 E-mail: gloria.thompson@phoenix.edu.

THOMPSON, HOLLEY MARKER, lawyer, marketing professional; b. Jamestown, NY, Jan. 30, 1947; d. Burdette James and Mary (Novitske) Marker; m. Lawrence D. Thompson; children: Jennifer Kristen Simos, Kendra Elise Blair, Jennifer Lynn, Stephanie Lynn. AAS, Jamestown C.C., 1966; BS, Ohio U., 1969; MA, W.Va. U., 1974, JD, 1980. Bar: W.Va. 1980, U.S. Dist. Ct. (so. dist.) W.Va. 1980, Pa. 1982, U.S. Dist. Ct. (we. dist.) Pa. 1982. Tchr. math. various pub. schs., Santa Ana (Calif.), Lakewood (N.Y.) and Morgantown (W.Va.), 1970-77; atty. for students W.Va. U., Morgantown, 1980; assoc. libr., lectr. W.Va. U. Coll. Law, Morgantown, 1980-83; assoc., libr. Jackson, Kelly, Holt & O'Farrell, Charleston, W.Va., 1983-86; cons. Hildebrandt, Inc., Somerville, NJ, 1986-94; sr. v.p. mktg. LexisNexis, Dayton, Ohio, 1994—. Spkr. in field. Contbr. articles to profl. jours. Mem.: ABA, Legal Mktg. Assn., N.J. Assn. Law Librs., Am. Assn. Law Librs., Spl. Libr. Assn., Phi Delta Phi. Office: LexisNexis 9443 Springboro Pike Miamisburg OH 45342 E-mail: holley.thompson@lexisnexis.com.

THOMPSON, JACQUELINE, air force officer, retired; b. Racine, Wis., Apr. 22, 1936; d. Edward Joseph and Gwenneth Ione (Wells) Sack; m. Claude Edward Osbourn, Dec. 17, 1955 (div. 1967); children: Jaime Edward, Rochelle Ione, Shannon Gaye, Desiree Patrice, Forest Kendall; m. George Wiley Glenn, Nov. 7, 1967; children: Brent Landry, Breanna Laura, Zane Aaron. AA, Gainesville Jr. Coll., Oakwood, Ga., 1982; DARB, USAF, Marietta, Ga., 1996. Joined USAF, 1972; supt. 94th Mobility Squadron, 1993-96; ret., 1996. Mem. NARFE (sec.-treas.), C. of C., Villa Rica Hist. and Mineral. Soc. (sec. 1997-99). Libertarian. Roman Catholic. Avocation: tracing ancestry. Home: 78 Southside Dr Villa Rica GA 30180-5109

THOMPSON, JANE ANN, elementary school educator, researcher; b. Dallas, Tex., Oct. 22, 1940; d. Mary Helen Hazelwood and Bert Cooper; m. Bob Joe Thompson, Oct. 16, 1959; children: Caryn Jones, Dana Finch, Perri Lawrence. EdB, U. North Tex., Denton, Tex., 1985, Med Reading Specialist, 1989. Cert. Elem. Self-Contained Tex., 1985, Learning Resource Endorsement Grades PK-12 Tex., 1998, Reading Specialist PK-12 Tex., 1989, Elem. English Grades 1-8 Tex., 1985, Elem. Reading Grades 1-8 Tex., 1986, Secondary English Grades 1-8 Tex., 1991. Tchr./curriculum developer Lewisville Ind. Sch. Dist., Lewisville, Tex., 1973—92; tchr. Carroll Ind. Sch. Dist., Southlake, Tex., 1992—94; instr. Dallas County C.C., Farmers Br., Tex., 1988—92, Tex. A&M at Commerce, Commerce, Tex., 2001—; cons. Region 10 Edn. Svc. Ctr., Richardson, Tex., 1994—2003; instr. Dallas County C.C. Sys., Dallas, 1989—92. Organizer and pres. Lewisville Area Reading Coun., Lewisville, Tex., 1989—90, founder and pres., 1988—92; chairperson of student media com. Tex. State Libr. Assn., Statewide, Tex., 1998—99; chairperson intellectual freedom com. Tex. State Reading Assn., Statewide, Tex., 1988—89; chmn. of intellectual freedom com. Tex. Reading Assn., Tex.; chairperson of student media com. Tex. State Libr. Assn., Tex.; trainer N.J. Writing Project of Tex. Mem.: ALA, Nat. Coun. of Teachers of English, Tex. Assn. for Gifted & Talented, Internat. Reading Assn., Tex. State Reading Assn., Tex. Computers Educators Assn., Tex. State Assn. of Sch. Librarians, Am. Assn. of Sch. Librarians, Tex. State Libr. Assn. (assoc.). R-Liberal. Bapt. Office: TAMU-Commerce Sowers Bldg Elementary Edu Commerce TX 75428 Office Phone: 903-886-5537.

THOMPSON, JAYNE CARR, public relations and communications executive, lawyer; b. Oak Park, Ill., Apr. 7, 1946; d. Robert Edward and Laurette (Rentner) Carr; m. James R. Thompson, June 19, 1976; 1 child, Samantha Jayne. BA, U. Ill., Chgo., 1967; JD, Northwestern U., 1970; degree (hon.), Lincoln (Ill.) Coll., 1990, St. Xavier U., Chgo., 1995, Ill. Coll., 1995. Assoc. in litigation McDermott, Will & Emery, Chgo., 1970; asst. atty. gen. State of Ill., Chgo., 1970-77, chief of criminal appeals divsn., 1972-77, dep. chief prosecution assistance bur., 1975-76, dep. chief criminal divsn., 1976-77, acting chief criminal divsn., 1977; of counsel Brown, Hay & Stephens, Springfield, Ill., 1977-78, Silets & Martin, Chgo., 1983-84; house counsel and v.p. devel. Nat. Coll. Edn., Evanston, Ill., 1984-85; atty. Lydon & Griffin, Chgo., 1989-91; prin. Dilenschneider Group Inc., Chgo., 1999-2000, mng. prin., 2000—02; CEO, pres. Jayne Thompson and Assocs. Ltd., 2002—. Contbr. chpt. to book, articles to profl. jours. First Lady of Ill., Springfield, 1977-91; mem. Ill. Commn. on Status of Women, 1997-2001; pres. bd. dirs. Chgo. Pub. Libr., 1998—; mem. women's bd. Northwestern U., 1978—; bd. dirs. Chgo. Pub. Libr. Found., 1998—; mem. adv. bd. for Ill. Treas. for Women's Issues, 2002—; mem. chmn.'s adv. coun. Lincoln Pk. Zoo, 2002—; mem. Met. Planning Coun., 2002--. Mem. Ill. State Bar Assn., Execs. Club (Chgo.), Coun. on Fgn. Rels. (Chgo. com.), Econ. Club (Chgo.). Avocations: reading, cooking, tennis. Office: Jayne Thompson & Assocs Ltd 33 N Dearborn St Ste 2200 Chicago IL 60602 E-mail: jthompson@jaynethompson.com.

THOMPSON, JEAN TANNER, retired librarian; b. San Luis Obispo, Calif., June 15, 1929; d. Chester Corey and Mildred (Orr) T.; 1 child, Anne Marie Miller Student, Whitworth Coll., Spokane, Wash., 1946-49; AB, Boston U., 1951; postgrad., U. Wis., Eau Claire, 1964-67; MSL.S., Columbia U., 1973; Ed.M., U. Va., Charlottesville, 1978. Asst. social sci. librarian Univ. Libraries Va. Polytechnic Inst. and State U., Blacksburg, 1973-77, head social sci. dept. Univ. Libraries, 1977-83; head reference dept. Meml. Library U. Wis., Madison, 1983-86, asst. dir. reference and info. svcs., 1986-91, ret. Contbg. editor: ALA Guide to Information Access, 1994; mem. editorial bd. RQ, 1984-89. Mem. ALA, Assn. Coll. and Research Libraries (edn. and behavioral sci. sect. vice chmn. 1985-86, chmn. 1986-87), Wis. Library Assn., Wis. Assn. of Acad. Librarians. Presbyterian. Home: 4929 High Grove Rd Tallahassee FL 32309-2957

THOMPSON, JENNIFER B. Olympic swimmer; b. Dover, N.H., Feb. 26, 1973; Student in Med. Sch., Columbia U. 5th place 50 m. freestyle Olympic Games, 1992, Silver medallist 100 m. freestyle, 1992, Gold medallist 4 x 100 m. freestyle relay, 1992, 1996, 2000, Gold medallist 4 x 100 m. medley relay, 1992, 1996, 2000, Gold medallist 4 x 200 m. freestyle relay, 1996, 2000, Bronze medallist 100 m. freestyle, 2000, fifth place 100 m. butterfly, 2000, set 4 world records; winner numerous U.S. Nat. Titles and Short Course World Championships, 1997—2000; medallist Goodwill Games, 1998, Pan Am. Games, 1987, Pan Pacific Championships, 1989—99, World Championships, 1991—98. Active Swim Across Am. Named Sportswoman of Yr., Women's Sports Found., 2000, Swimmer of Yr., USA Swimming, 1993, 1998; recipient Spring Nationals Kiphuth award, 1993, Performance of Yr. award, USA Swimming, 1999. Achievements include being the most decorated olympic female athlete in U.S. history.

THOMPSON, JILL LYNETTE LONG, federal agency administrator, former congresswoman; b. Warsaw, Ind., July 15, 1952; BS, Valparaiso U., 1974; MBA, Ind. U., 1978, PhD, 1984. Mgmt. cons. Campbell and Pryor, 1985-86; mem. 101st-103rd Congresses from 4th Ind. dist., 1989-95; mem. agrl. com.; mem. vets. affairs com.; under sec. for rural development USDA, 1995—. Asst. instr., lectr. Indiana U., Bloomington; adj. prof. Indiana U.-Purdue U. Ft. Wayne,; asst. prof. Valparaiso U. Councilwoman City of Valparaiso, Ind., 1984; chair Congrl. Rural Congress. Democrat. Methodist. Office: FSA State Office 101 SW Main St Stee 1300 Portland OR 97204-3221

THOMPSON, JOSIE, nurse; b. Ark., Apr. 16, 1949; d. James Andrew and Oneda Fay (Watson) Rhoads; m. Mark O. Thompson, Feb. 14, 1980. Diploma, Lake View Sch. Nursing, 1970; student, Danville C.C., 1974-75, St. Petersburg Jr. Coll., 1979. RN Ill., Wyo., cert. Devel. Disabilities Divsn., N.Y. Staff nurse St. Elizabeth Hosp., Danville, Ill., 1970-78, Osteopathetic Hosp., St. Petersburg, Fla., 1980-81, Wyo. State Hosp., Evanston, 1981-83, Wyo. Home Health Care, Rock Springs, 1984—, adminstr., 1986-95; pres. Home Health Care Alliance Wyo., 1991-92; staff nurse home health Interim Health Care, Cheyenne, Wyo., 1996-97; staff nurse Rocky Mountain Home Health Care, Green River, Wyo., 1997—, dir. nursing, 2000-01; staff nurse Sageview Care Ctr., 2001, S.W. Wyo. Rehab. Ctr. for Mentally and Physically Handicapped Persons, Rock Springs, Wyo., 2001—03; pvt. practice nursing, case mgmt., rehab., respite care Respito, ISC, 2004—. Mem. nursing program adv. bd. Western Wyo. C.C.; mem. Coalition for the Elderly, Spl. Needs Com. Sweetwater County, 1992-93. Home: PO Box 1154 Rock Springs WY 82902-1154 Office Phone: 307-362-3144.

THOMPSON, JOYCE LURINE, retired information systems specialist; b. White Oak Twp., Mich., Mar. 5, 1931; d. Orla Jacob and Ethel Inita (Thayer) Sheathelm; m. Robert E. Thompson, Dec. 10, 1949 (div. 1972); children: Wendy, Robin, Kristen (dec.). Student, Mich. State U., 1972-78, Lansing (Mich.) Community Coll, 1976-77. Programmer, analyst Mich. State U., East Lansing, 1966-73; tech. programmer Mich. State Police, East Lansing, 1973-77; database coord. Mich. Dept. Treasury, Lansing, 1977-79; systems engr. 4-Phase Systems, Grand Rapids, Mich., 1979-81; mktg. rep. Motorola, Grand Rapids, 1981-84; data analyst Whirlpool Corp., Benton Harbor, Mich., 1984-88, data adminstr., 1988—; owner, propr. Thompson House, South Haven, Mich., 1994—. Activity chmn. Girl Scouts U.S.A., East Lansing; leader 4-H Clubs, East Lansing; vol. Stepping Stones South Haven, ADA Com., Lake Mich. Maritime Mus., Scott Club South Haven, 2000—, treas., 2001-2004. Mildred Erickson fellow Mich. State U., EAst Lansing, 1974-78. Mem. Assn. Systems Mgmt. (sec. 1984), Data Adminstrn. Mgmt. Assn. Avocations: photography, music, beach combing, antiques.

THOMPSON, JUDITH KASTRUP, nursing researcher; b. Marstal, Denmark, Oct. 1, 1933; came to the U.S., 1951; d. Edward Kastrup and Anna Hansa (Knudsen) Pedersen; m. Richard Frederick Thompson, May 22, 1960; children: Kathryn Marr, Elizabeth Kastrup, Virginia St. Claire. BS, RN, U. Oreg., 1958, MSN, 1963. RN, Calif., Oreg. Staff nurse U. Oreg. Med. Sch., Eugene, 1957-58, Portland, 1958-61, head staff nurse, 1960-61; instr. psychiat. nursing U. Oreg. Sch. Nursing, Portland, 1963-64; rsch. asst. U. Oreg. Med. Sch., Portland, 1964-65, U. Calif., Irvine, 1971-72; rsch. assoc. Stanford (Calif.) U., 1982-87; rsch. asst. Harvard U., Cambridge, Mass., 1973-74; rsch. assoc. U. So. Calif., L.A., 1987—. Contbg. author: Behavioral Control and Role of Sensory Biofeedback, 1976; contbr. articles to profl. jours. Treas. LWV, Newport Beach, Calif., 1970-74; scout leader Girl Scouts Am., Newport Beach, 1970-78. Named Citizen of Yr. State of Oreg., 1966. Mem. Soc. for Neurosci., Am. Psychol. Soc. (charter), ANA, Oreg. Nurses Assn. Republican. Lutheran. Avocations: art collecting, travel, tennis. Home: 28 Sky Sail Dr Corona Del Mar CA 92625 1436 Office: U So Calif University Park Los Angeles CA 90089-0001 Office Phone: 213-740-7350. E-mail: judith@neuro.usc.edu.

THOMPSON, JULIA ANN, physicist, educator; b. Little Rock, Mar. 13, 1943; d. Erwin Arthur and Ruth Evelyn (Johnston) T.; m. Patrick A. Thompson, Mar. 22, 1964 (div. 1974); 1 child, Diane E.; m. David E. Kraus, Jr., June 22, 1976; children: Vincent Szewczyk, Larry Lynch. BA, Cornell Coll., Mt. Vernon, Iowa, 1964; MA, Yale U., 1966, PhD, 1969. Research assoc. Brookhaven Lab., Upton, N.Y., 1969-71; research assoc./assoc. instr. U. Utah, Salt Lake City, 1971-72; asst. prof. physics U. Pitts., 1972-78, assoc. prof., 1978-85, prof., 1986—, dir. undergrad. rsch. program, 1992—. Mem. users coms. Brookhaven Nat. Lab., 1983-86; condr. expts. Inst. Nuclear Physics, Novosibirsk, USSR, Ctr. Europeene Recherche Nucleaire, Switzerland, Brookhaven Natl. Lab., L.I.; spokesperson hyperon decay expt BNL, 1972-80; leader PhysMcVan, Cape Town, South Africa, 2001-03; adj. prof. physics U. Mo., St. Louis, Mo., 2002—; dir. Pitt/U. Mo. St. Louis Quarknet site, 2002—. Contbr. articles to profl. jours. Bd. dirs. 1st Unitarian Ch., Pitts., 1980-83; zone councillor Soc. Physics Students, 1986-88; with Nat. Acad. Sci. Exch. to USSR, 1989-90. Fellow Am. Phys. Soc. (com. on status of women in physics 1983-86, exec. com. forum on physics and soc. 1990-93, com. on minorities 1995-98). Democrat. Unitarian Universalist. Avocations: promoting effective science education, hiking, reading, music. Achievements include research with W.E. Cleland and D.E. Kraus in optical triggering; with the collaboration with AFS and HELIOS expt. in direct photon and lepton production, leading to modified understanding of the gluon function, and limits on anomalous electron production; with collaborators at Brookhaven National Laboratory in New York and Budker Institute of Nuclear Physics in Novosibirsk, Russia, studies of rare and semi-rare kaon decays.

THOMPSON, KAREN MARIE, art educator; d. Carl Henry and Bernice Pearson Pohle; m. Stanley Wendell Thompson, May 1, 1957 (dec. Nov. 11, 2001); children: Jay Scott, Karilyn Lee Thompson-Starks. MA in Art History, U. Hawaii, 1984. Assoc. dir. U. Hawaii Art Gallery, Honolulu, 1984—91; curator of edn. Honolulu Acad. Arts, 1991—. Bd. dirs., adv. com. Applied History of Art and Architecture Ednl. Found., Honolulu, 2001—; advisor U. of Hawaii Coll. of Edn., Tchr. Edn. Com. for Art, Honolulu, 1995—2000. Author: (exhbn. booklet for children) First Emperor of China: A Search for Immortality, 1995, Art All Around, 1998, Discovering the Art of Ancient Egypt, 2000, A Visit to Grandfather's House, 2003; co-author: (exhbn. catalogue) Jean Charlot: Artist and Scholar, 1991; contbr. exhbn. catalogue: A Hawaii Treasury: Masterpieces from the Honolulu Academy of Arts, exhbn. catalogue: The Art of Asian Costume, exhbn. catalogue: Greek and Russian Icons; curator (art exhibition) Tales from The Tomb, 2000, Dream Worlds/Real Worlds of William Joyce, 2002, (art exhbn.) Russia Through the Eyes of Children, 2003. Mem.: Hawaii Mus. Assn., Hawaii Alliance for Arts Edn., Nat. Art Edn. Assn. (Hawaii Art Educator of Yr. 2003). Office: Honolulu Acad Arts 900 South Beretania St Honolulu HI 96814 Business E-Mail: kthompson@honoluluacademy.org.

THOMPSON, KATHLEEN SHAMBAUGH, marriage and family counselor; b. Bakersfield, Calif., Oct. 22, 1945; d. Stephen W. and Marilyn L. Shambaugh; m. John W. Thompson, June 10, 1967 (dec. Mar. 1971); children: Stephen, Charles. Student, Colo. Women's Coll., 1964; BA in English, U. Colo., 1968; MA in Counseling, U. Denver, 1976. Tchg. credential U. Colo., 1971, lic. marriage and family counselor. Tchr., Denver, 1971—76; marriage, family and child counselor, 1982—. Editor, proofreader, 1977—80. Author: Going Through Life-A Collection of Poems, 2000, Coping with Grief and the Death of Loved Ones, 2002, An American Girl in Canada, 2002, A Life Filled With Poetry, 2003, Counseling Helps, 2004, Professional Guides: The Case Study, Human Sexuality in Marriage, Crime and Rehabilitation, Introducing the Gap Theory, 2003, A Car Accident, Different Kinds of Pain, and Surgery 5 Years Later, 2003, A Journey Through the Triangle of Canada, Britian, and America, 2004, Writers and Writing, 2004, Brown Flowers, 2004, Landscaping a Small Lot, 2004. Named one of Best Poets of 2000, Internat. Libr. Poetry, 2001. Mem.: Internat. Soc. Poets (Internat. Poet Merit 2000), Delta Delta Delta. Presbyterian. Avocations: stamp collecting, doll collecting, art, collectibles, gardening. Home and Office: 1655 W Ajo Way # 170 Tucson AZ 85713

THOMPSON, KATHY C. bank executive; From. sr. v.p. to exec. v.p. Stock Yards Bancorp Inc, Louisville, 1992—96, exec. v.p., 1996—. Named No. 3 Fast Tracker in the Industry, U.S. Bankers Mag., 2003. Office: Stock Yards Bancorp Inc 1040 East Main St Louisville KY 40206*

THOMPSON, LAURA JILL, curator, educator; b. Queens, N.Y., Sept. 24, 1967; d. George and Alice Rachel Dickstein; m. Thompson Roger Marvin, Sept. 3, 2000. BS in Art Edn., SUNY, New Paltz, 1989; MA in Liberal Studies, NYU, 1992; EdD in Art Edn., Columbia U., 2001. Mgr. student and tchr. svcs. Mus. of the City of N.Y., 1991—98; faculty creative arts lab. Columbia U. Tchrs. Coll., N.Y.C., 1998—2000; dir. edn. and pub. programs Schenectady (N.Y.) Mus., 2000—02; assoc. curator exhibits and edn. Kidspace at Mass. MoCA, North Adams, Mass., 2002—. Com. mem. N.Y.C. Mus. Edn. Roundtable, 1994—; v.p. for mus. edn. N.Y.C. Art Tchrs. Assn., 1998—2000; arts and mus. edn. cons., NY, 1998—; com. mem. Clifton Park (N.Y.) Art Adv. Coun., 2002—. Mem.: N.Y.C. Mus. Educators Roundtable, Nat. Art Edn. Assn., Coll. Art Assn., Internat. Soc. for Edn. Through the Arts, Am. Assn. Mus. (edn. com.). Avocations: gardening, painting, travel.

THOMPSON, LAVERNE ELIZABETH THOMAS, college official; b. Bklyn., July 17, 1945; d. Roscoe Lee and Mary Elizabeth (Blackwell) Thomas (dec.). BA in English, Bluffton Coll., 1967; MS in Edn. Adminstrn./Supervision, U. Dayton, 1977; PhD in Higher Edn., U. Toledo, 1991. Cert. sch. prin., secondary sch. supr., realtor, Ohio. Tchr. English and speech Piqua (Ohio) Ctrl. H.S., 1967—68; instr. Lima (Ohio) Sr. H.S., 1968—77, Shawnee H.S., Lima, 1977—86; grad. asst. U. Toledo, 1986—91, interim counselor, adminstr. student support svcs., 1989, interim adminstrv. asst. multicultural student devel., 1990; dir. pre-svc. edn./urban tchr. program Wayne County C.C., Detroit, 1996—2002; chief acad. officer N.W. campus Wayne County C.C. Dist., Detroit, 2002—. Real estate agt. Alberta Lee Realty, Lima, Ohio, 1978-82, Slonaker Realty, Lima, 1982-84, Gooding Co., Lima, 1985-90; substitute English tchr., Maumee (Ohio) City Schs., 1996; adj. prof., acad. coord. alternative edn. Spring Arbor Coll., Lambertville, Mich., 1995-96; reviewer Eisenhower Grants for Higher Edn., Mich. Dept. Edn., 1997, 98, 99, 2000, 01; stakeholder Skillman Found. project Child Care Coord. Coun. Greater Detroit, Wayne County, 1998-2001; mem. exec. bd. Young Educators Soc. Mich., 1999—. Editor Higher Edn. newsletter, 1987. Participant 17th ann. Nat. Conf. on Citizenship, Washington, 1962; co-chair Brotherhood Dinner Sr. H.S., Lima, 1976; bd. dirs. Lima YWCA, 1971. Mem. Va. Assn. New Homemakers Am. (state pres. 1962, nat. pres. 1963), All God's Children Collectors' Club, Belleek Collectors' Internat. Soc., Harmony Kingdom Collectors Club, Boyd's Bears Friends Collectors Club. Avocations: periodical reading, writing, walking. Home: 13851 Sibley Rd Riverview MI 48192-7759

THOMPSON, LEA, actress; b. Rochester, Minn., May 31, 1961; m. Howard Deutch. Actress: (films) Jaws 3-D, 1983, All the Right Moves, 1983, The Wild Life, 1984, Red Dawn, 1984, Back to the Future, 1985, Howard the Duck, 1986, Space Camp, 1986, Some Kind of Wonderful, 1987, Casual Sex, 1988, The Wizard of Loneliness, 1988, Going Undercover, 1988, Back to the Future II, 1989, Back to the Future III, 1990, Article 99, 1991, Dennis the Menace, 1993, The Beverly Hillbillies, 1993, The Little Rascals, 1994, The Right to Remain Silent, 1996 (TV movies) Nightbreaker, 1989, Montana, 1990, Stolen Babies, 1993, The Substitute Wife, 1994, The Unspoken Truth, 1995, The Unknown Ciclist, 1997, (TV series) Tales from the Crypt, 1989, Robert Wuhl's World Tour, 1990, Caroline in the City, 1995—, (TV miniseries) A Will of Their Own, 1998. Pa. Ballet Co. scholar, Am. Ballet Theatre scholar, San Francisco Ballet scholar. Office: care NBC PO Box 5617 Burbank CA 91523-0001

THOMPSON, LOIS JEAN HEIDKE ORE, psychologist; b. Chgo., Feb. 22, 1933; d. Harold William and Ethel Rose (Neumann) Heidke; m. Henry Thomas Ore, Aug. 28, 1954 (div. May 1972); children: Christopher, Douglas; m. Joseph Lippard Thompson, Aug. 3, 1972; children: Scott, Les, Melanie. BA, Cornell Coll., Mt. Vernon, Iowa, 1955; MA, Idaho State U., 1964, EdD, 1981. Lic. psychologist, N.Mex. Tchr. pub. schs. various locations, 1956-67; tchr., instr. Idaho State U., Pocatello, 1967-72; employee/orgn. devel. specialist Los Alamos (N.Mex.) Nat. Lab., 1981-84, tng. specialist, 1984-89, sect. leader, 1989-93; pvt. practice indsl. psychology and healthcare, Los Alamos, 1988—. Sec. Cornell Coll. Alumni Office, 1954-55, also other orgns.; bd. dirs. Parent Edn. Ctr., Idaho State U., 1980; counselor, Los Alamos, 1981-88. Editor newsletter LWV, Laramie, Wyo., 1957; contbr. articles to profl. jours. Pres. Newcomers Club, Pocatello, 1967, Faculty Womens Club, Pocatello, 1968; chmn. edn. com. AAUW, Pocatello, 1969. Mem.: APA, N.Mex. Soc. Adlerian Psychology (pres. 1990, treas. 1991—97, bd. dirs. 1996—), N.Mex. Psychol. Assn. (bd. dirs. divsn. II 1990, 1999, sec. 1988—90, chmn. 1990, 1999—2000). Mem. Lds Ch. Avocations: racewalking, backpacking, skiing, tennis, biking. Home and Office: 340 Aragon Ave Los Alamos NM 87544-3505

THOMPSON, LORI RAQUEL, marriage and family therapist, consultant; b. Branson, Mo., July 23, 1970; d. Dennis Gene and Claudette Elaine Reagan; m. Matthew Alan Thompson, Jan. 9, 1999. BA, U. Mo., Columbia, 1993; MS, Okla. State U., Stillwater, 1997. Lic. marriage and family therapist Okla., 1999. Sr. counselor Stillwater Domestic Violence Svcs., 1997—99; home based counselor Family & Children's Svcs., Tulsa, 1999—2000; trainer and cons. Nat. Resource Ctr. Youth Svcs., Tulsa, 2000—03; family counselor Youth Svcs. Tulsa, 2003—. Bd. mem. Okla. Assn. Marriage and Family Therapists, 2001—03, pres.-elect, 2003—. Mem.: ASTD. Democrat. Methodist. Avocations: bicycling, skiing, reading, gardening. Home: 913 S Winston Tulsa OK 74112 Office: Nat Resource Ctr Youth Svcs Bldg 4W 4503 E 41st St Tulsa OK 74135 Office Phone: 918-272-4969. E-mail: lthompson@yst.org.

THOMPSON, LULA AVERHART, retired educator; b. Farmersville, Ala. d. Frank and Octavia (Reese) Averhart; m. Oscar Lee Thompson. AB cum laude, Paine Coll., 1939; postgrad., U. Ala., 1942, Western Res. U., 1950; MEd, Ala. State Coll., 1959; tchr. trainer cert., Fla. State U., 1966; EdS, Auburn U., 1972, double AA prof. tchg. cert., 1973. Tchr. home econs. Fairfield Bd. Edn., 1939-49, tchr. math., 1950-63, tchr. social studies, 1963-73. Life mem., Sunday sch. tchr., former sec. Sunday sch., former dir. youth programs Mars Hill Bapt. Ch., Democrat. Avocations: ceramics, designing and making personal clothing and hats, reading, traveling. Home: 4500 Mcclain St Bessemer AL 35020-1848

THOMPSON, MARGARET M. physical education educator; b. Merrifield, Va., Aug. 1, 1921; d. Lesley L. and Madeline (Shawen) T. BS, Mary Washington Coll., 1941; MA, George Washington U., 1947; PhD, U. Iowa, 1961. Tchr., supr. phys. edn. Staunton (Va.) City Schs., 1941-44; tchr. jr. high sch. phys. edn. Arlington County, Va., 1944-47; instr. women's phys. edn. Fla. State U., Tallahassee, 1947-51; instr., asst. prof., assoc. prof. phys. edn. Purdue U., Lafayette, Ind., 1951-65, dir. gross motor therapy lab., 1963-65; assoc. prof. phys. edn. U. Mo., Columbia, 1965-68, prof., 1968-71, dir. Cinematography and Motor Learning Lab. Dept. Health and Phys. Edn., 1965-71; prof. phys. edn. U. Ill., Champaign-Urbana, 1971-87, prof. emeritus, 1987—. Vis. prof. Escola de Educacão Fisica, U. de São Paulo, Brazil, 1985; vis. prof. phy. edn. Inst. Bioscis. de Rio Claro, U. Estadual Paulista, Brazil, 1991. Author: (with Barbara B. Godfrey) Movement Pattern Checklists, 1966, (with Chappelle Arnett) Perceptual Motor and Motor Test Battery for Children, 1968, (with Barbara Mann) An Holistic Approach to Physical Education Curriculum: Objectives Classification System for Elementary Schools, 1977, Gross Motor Inventory, 1976, revised edit., 1980, Developing the Curriculum, 1980, Setting the Learning Environment, 1980, Sex Stereotyping and Human Development, 1980; also film strips, articles. Mem.: AAHPER. Home and Office: 1311 Wildwood Ln Mahomet IL 61853-9770 E-mail: mmthomps@uiuc.edu.

THOMPSON, MARGIE ANN, artist; b. LA, Nov. 5, 1934; d. John William Jr. and Odessa Addie Meek; m. Donald Leroy Thompson, June 29, 1956; children: Mark(dec.), Laurie, Donna, Lee. Grad. high. sch., LA. Various office positions, Calif., 1952—80; freelance graphic designer, 1980—88; advt. designer The Signal, Saugus, 1988—89; watercolor artist Quartz Hill, Calif., 1990—. Mem.: Antelope Valley Allied Arts Assn. (various positions 1990—97). Republican.

THOMPSON, MARGUERITE MYRTLE GRAMING (MRS. RALPH B. THOMPSON), librarian; b. Orangeburg, S.C., Apr. 23, 1912; d. Thomas Laurie and Rosa Lee (Stroman) Graming; m. Ralph B. Thompson, Sept. 17, 1949 (dec. Oct. 1960). BA in English cum laude, U. S.C., 1932, postgrad., 1937; BLS, Emory U., 1943. Tchr. English pub. high schs., S.C., 1932-43; libr. Rockingham (N.C.) High Sch., 1943-45, Randolph County (N.C.) Libr., Asheboro, 1945-48, Colleton County (S.C.) Libr., Walterboro, 1948-61; dir. Florence (S.C.) County Libr., 1961-78. Sec. com. community facilities, svcs. and instns. Florence County Resources Devel. Com., 1964-67; vice chmn. Florence County Coun. on Aging, 1968-70, exec. bd. 1968-82, bd. treas., 1973-75, bd. sec., 1976-77, bd. v.p., 1979; mem. Florence County Bicentennial Planning Com., 1975-76; mem. rels. and allocations com. United Way, 1979-80. Named Boss of Yr. Nat. Secs. Assn., 1971. Mem. ALA (coun. 1964-72), Southeastern Libr. Assn., S.C. Libr. Assn. (pres. 1960, chmn. assn. handbook revision com. 1967-69, 80, sect. co-chmn. com. standards for S.C. pub. librs. 1966-75, fed. rels. coord. 1972-73, planning com. 1976-78), Greater Florence C. of C. (women's div. chmn. 1969-70, bd. dirs. 1975-77), S.E. Regional Conf. Women in C. of C. (bd. dir. 1970-71), Florence Bus. and Profl. Women's Club (2d v.p. 1975-76, Career Woman of Yr. 1974, parliamentarian 1980-81, chmn. scholarship com. 1981-82), Delta Kappa Gamma (county chpt. charter pres. 1963-65, treas. 1966-70, chmn. com. on expansion 1977-80, 82-84, state chpt. chmn. state scholarship com. 1967-73, state 2d v.p. 1971-73, state 1st v.p. 1973-75, state pres. 1975-77, chmn. policy manual 1977-81, chmn. adv. coun. 1978-85, chmn. fin. com. 1981-83, parliamentarian 1987-91, adminstrv. bd. 1987—, chmn. nominations com. 1989-91, dir. S.E. Region 1978-80, coord. S.E. Regional Golden Anniversary Conf. 1979, internat. scholarship com. 1970-74, internat. exec. bd. 1975-77, 78-80, internat. adminstrv. bd. 1978-80, internat. constn. com. 1980-82, internat. achievement award com., 1986-88), Florence Literary Club (sec. 1964-66, 79-82, pres. 1970-72). Methodist (chmn. ch. libr. com. 1965-71, chmn. com. ch. history, 1968-69, sec. adminstrv. bd. 1979-82). Home: 1000 Live Oaks Dr SW # 8B Orangeburg SC 29115-9600

THOMPSON, MARI HILDENBRAND, medico-legal and administrative consultant; b. Washington, Apr. 26, 1951; d. Emil John Christopher Hildenbrand and Ada Lythe (Conklin) Hildenbrand-Kammer; m. R. Marshall Thompson, Sept. 27, 1970 (div. June 1981); 1 child, Jeremy Marshall. BA in Secondary Edn., BA in Performing Arts, Am. U., 1976. Cert. med. staff coord.; cert. profl. credentialing specialist. Employment interviewer Scripps Meml. Hosp., La Jolla, Calif., 1977-81; office mgr. Jacksina & Freedman Press Office, N.Y.C., 1982-83; staffing coord., med. staff asst. Am. Med. Internat. Clairemont Hosp., San Diego, 1983-85; adminstrv. asst. Am. Med. Internat. Valley Med. Ctr., El Cajon, Calif., 1985-88; med. staff coord. Sharp Meml. Hosp., San Diego, 1988-92; adminstrv. asst. Grossmont Hosp., La Mesa, Calif., 1992-93, coord. Sharp family practice residency program, 1993-94; mgr. Sharp Meml. Hosp. med. staff svcs., San Diego, 1994-96; cons. med. staff svcs. San Diego Rehab. Inst., 1997. Cons. and adminstrv. support for Legal Support, Inc., 1989—, St. Charles Med. Ctr., 1998—, cons. Legal Support N.W., LLC, 1999—; coord. Deschutes Ct Defenders, 1999—; wardrobe mistress various cmty. theatres, San Diego, 1978-79, actress, San Diego, 1979-81. Co-founder N.Y.C. Playreaders Group, 1981-83, N.J. Shakespeare Theatre, Madison, 1982, Good Humor Improv Co., N.Y.C., 1982-83; contbg. writer to Poetry Revival: An Anthology, 1994. Active Dem. Nat. Com., 1996—; vol. Cascades Theatre Co., 1997—. Named one of Outstanding Young Women of Am., 1986. Mem. AFTRA. Democrat. Buddhist. Avocations: writing poetry, horseback riding, swimming, gardening, fishing. Home: 22925 Superior Ct Bend OR 97702-9271 E-mail: marutz@buddhist.com.

THOMPSON, MARIE ANGELA, computer engineer, consultant; b. Sheffield, Yorkshire, Eng., Aug. 8, 1951; came to U.S., 1979. d. Leslie Arthur and Gloria Mabel (Sheldon) Findley; m. Stephen J. Thompson, Feb. 10, 1990. BS with honors, U. Leeds, 1973; MS, U. Reading, 1975. Software engr. ITT, London, 1975-79, GTE, Northlake, Ill., 1979-80, St. Petersberg, Fla., 1980-82, Reston, Va., 1982-83; dir. rsch. Northcor, Hamden, Conn., 1985-90; mgr. spl. projects SAC of Am., Ridgefield, Conn., 1990-98; cons. Universal Solutions 2000, Ridgefield, Conn., 1998, Thompson, Findley & Co., Hampton Bays, N.Y., 1998—. Cons. Ivy League Corp., Ridgefield, Conn., 1995-98, Digital Network 1, Ridgefield, 1995-98, First Frontier Capital Corp., Great Neck, 1999—, East End Trading Co., Hampton Bays, N.Y., 1999—. Dir. concessions Pop Warner Football, Ridgefield, 1993, 94, dir. registration, 1994, 95, 96, 97, dir. fundraising, 1996-98. Recipient Bob Scalzo Meml. award Ridgefield Pop Warner Football, 1997. Mem. AAUW, AAAS, Am. Inst. Chem. Engrs., Conn. Assn. for the Gifted, N.Y. Acad. Scis., Conn. Business and Industry Assn., Ridgefield C. of C., Mensa. Avocations: tennis, Go, computing, skiing, reading. Office: Thompson Findley & Co 14 Rutland Plz #301 Rutland VT 05701

THOMPSON, MARSHA, newscaster; married; 4 children. News dir. WLBT, Jackson, Miss., health reporter. Bd. dirs. Miss. Leukemia Soc., Madison County Cultural Ctr. Named Investigative Reporter of Yr., Miss. AP, 1998; recipient Fannie Lou Hamer award, NAACP, Sple. Svc. award, Miss. Commn. for Prevention of Child Abuse. Mem.: Miss. AP Broadcasters Assn., Ctrl. Miss. Med. Alliance Aux., Miss. Women's Club (past pres.). Avocation: sailing. Office: WLBT 715 S Jefferson St Jackson MS 39201

THOMPSON, MARY KOLETA, sculptor, non-profit organization management consultant; b. Portsmouth, Va., Dec. 27, 1938; m. James Burton Thompson, May 5, 1957; children: Burt, Suzan, Kate, Jon. BFA, U. Tex., 1982; postgrad., Boston U.; MA in Philanthropy and Devel., St. Mary's U. Minn., 1999. Cert. non-profit mgmt. Pres., CEO The Planning Resource People, Lampasas, Tex., 1990—; Tex. fin. devel. specialist ARC Tex., 1994-98; devel. dir. Very Spl. Arts Tex., 1991-92; dir. devel. ARC, Austin, 1992-94; pub. affairs adminstr. Pink Palace Mus. and Memphis Mus. Inc., Memphis, 1998; CEO Lamapasas C. of C., Lampasas, TX, 1998-99; pres., CEO Assn. Non-Profit Orgns., 1998—, Tex. Assn. Bed and Breakfast Innkeepers, 1998; pres. A Little Cottage B&B, 1999—2004; owner Heritage Sta. Antiques, 1999—. Dir. Tex. Children's Mus., Fredericksburg, 1987-88, Internat. Hdqrs. SHAPE Command Arts and Crafts Ctr., 1985-86; com. chmn. Symposium for Encouragement Women in Math. and Natural Sci., U. Tex., Austin, 1990; instr. nonprofit mgmt., fin. devel., bd. leadership, grant proposal writing Ctrl. Tex. Coll., 2002—. Sculptor portrait busts. Bd. dirs. Teenage Parent Coun., Austin, 1990-92, ARC. Named U.S. Vol. of Yr., Belgium, 1986; grantee NEA, 1988. Mem.: AAUW (life; pres. 1990—92), Women in Comm. (co-chmn. SW regional conf.), Lometa Lions Club (pub. rels. com. 1999—), Heritage Station Antique Vehicle Show (founder), Heritage Station Antiques Show and Sale (founder), Leadership Tex. (life), U. Tex. Ex-Student Assn. (life), Heritage Station Antiques Forum (founder), Raleigh Tavern Soc. (founder), Leadership Tex. Alumnae Assn. (bd. dir.), Tex. Hist. Found (life). Avocations: writing, lecturing, meeting and strategic planning. Office: 100 W 190 PO Box 10 Lometa TX 76853-0010

THOMPSON, MARY B. writer, illustrator; b. Corpus Christi, Tex., Dec. 11, 1929; d. Henry Charles and Marjorie Murray Keller. BA in Psychology, So. Meth. U., 1957; MA in Secondary Edn., MA in Creative Writing, NYU, 1961, ABD in Higher Edn. Adminstrn., 1969. Cert. secondary edn. English N.Y. Rschr. Ruder & Finn Inc., N.Y.C., 1958—60; TV script writer Philco Corp., N.Y.C., 1961, Phila., 1961; faculty The New Lincoln Sch., N.Y.C., 1961—64, So. Meth. U., Dallas, 1964—68; freelance writer, 1968—81; freelance writer pub. rels., 1981—85; real estate developer, 1985—90; author, pub. Melior Press, Leesburg, Fla., 1997—2000; author, illustrator

The Lighthouse Press, Deerfield Beach, Fla., 2000—. Mem. curriculum com. So. Meth. U., Dallas, 1966; vol. tchr. advanced English classes Leesburg H.S. Author: (novella) Closed Circuit, 1961, (book) B.S. Detecting, 1999, illustrator: B.S. Detecting: Success Possible Communicating, 2000-2004. Mem.: LWV, Nat. Writers Union, Defenders of Wildlife, South Lake Animal League, Sierra Club, Kappa Delta Pi. Avocations: gardening, recreational vehicle travel. Home: 6623 Hopi Trail Leesburg FL 34748

THOMPSON, MARY EILEEN, chemistry educator; b. Mpls., Dec. 21, 1928; d. Albert C. and Blanche (McAvoy) T. BA, Coll. St. Catherine, 1953; MS, U. Minn., 1958; PhD, U. Calif., Berkeley, 1964. Tchr. math. and sci. Derham Hall H.S., St. Paul, 1953-58; mem. faculty Coll. of St. Catherine, St. Paul, 1964-69, prof. chemistry, 1969-2000, chmn. dept., 1969-90, prof. emeritus, 2000—. Project dir. Women in Chemistry, 1984-98. Contbr. articles to profl. jours. Mem. AAAS, Am. Chem. Soc. (chmn. women chemists com. 1992-94, award for encouraging women into chem. scis. careers 1997), Coun. Undergrad. Rsch. (councillor 1991-96), N.Y. Acad. Scis., Chem. Soc. London, Sigma Xi, Phi Beta Kappa (senator 1997-2003). Democrat. Roman Catholic. Achievements include research interests in Cr(III) hydrolytic polymers, kinetics of inorganic complexes, Co(III) peroxo/superoxo complexes. E-mail: methompson@stkate.edu., MTHOM17349@aol.com.

THOMPSON, MARY LOU, elementary school educator; b. Cambridge, Mass., Dec. 29, 1933; BS in edn., Framingham (Mass.) State Tchrs. Coll., 1956; MEd, Boston U., 1962; postgrad., Simmons Coll., Boston, Lesley Coll., Cambridge, Mass., Fitchburg (Mass.) State Coll. Elem. tchr. Burlington (Mass.) Pub. Sch., 1956—61, Sudbury (Mass.) Pub. Sch., 1961—2001; substitute tchr. Maynard Pub. Schs. Tutor learning disabled adults, 1997—99. Author curr. materials. Edn. liaison state senate campaign, Sudbury, Mass., 2002. Recipient sculpture placed in Sudbury Libr. in honor, by staff and parents of Israel Loring Sch., 2001. Mem.: NEA, Mass. Tchr. Assn. Avocations: art hist., reading, gardening, home maintenance, photography. Home: 4 DeMarco Rd Sudbury MA 01776-2036

THOMPSON, NANCY, art director; b. Mobile, Ala., Apr. 19, 1953; d. leon and Roas C Wiggins; m. John Michael Thompson, Mar. 14, 1956; 1 child, Laine Michael. BS in music edn., U. Ala., 1975; MEd, U. S. Ala., 1985. Cert. admin. U. S. Ala., 1998. Band dir. Mobile County Sch. Sys., Ala., 1976—2001, asst. prin., 2001, fine arts supr., 2002—. Presenter, cons. Mobile County Sch. Sys., 2001—03. Contbr. articles various profl. jours. Pres. Mobile County Pub. Sch. Bands, 2001. Named Worthy Maton, Order of Easton Star. Mem.: Music Edn. Nat. Conf., US Sports Acad., Vol. of Am., Order of LaShe's (pres. 1998), Kappa Kappa Iota (pres. 1985). Meth. Avocations: music, fishing, painting. Home: 2681 D'Iberville Dr Mobile AL 36695 Office: Mobile County Pub Sch Sys 504 Gov St Mobile AL 36602 E-mail: nthompson@mcpss.org.

THOMPSON, NANCY P. state legislator; b. Sioux Falls, S.D., Oct. 26, 1947; m. James Thompson, July 4, 1970; children: Kevin, Matthew, Cynthia, Joseph. BA, Creighton U., 1969, MA, 1982. Dist. staff mem. U.S. Rep. John Cavanaugh; dep. chief of staff Gov. Ben Nelson; former tchr.; mem. Nebr. Legislature from 14th dist., Lincoln, 1997—. Former exec. dir. Omaha Cmty. Partnership; mem. Sarpy County Bd. Commrs. Home: 1302 Western Hills Dr Papillion NE 68046-7036 Office: State Capitol Dist 14 PO Box 94604 Rm 1117 Lincoln NE 68509-4604 E-mail: nthompson@unicam.state.ne.us.

THOMPSON, PAMELA A. nurse administrator; b. Silsbee, Tex., Apr. 7, 1949; d. John David and Peggy Gean (Gholson) Austin; m. Robert Laurence Thompson, May 26, 1979; children: Garrett Austin, Durete Abdella. BSN, U. Conn., 1971; MSN, U. Rochester, 1979. RN. Dir. maternal and child health Copley Meml. Hosp., Aurora, Ill., 1980-82; dir. emergency svcs. and pediatrics LaGrange (Ill.) Cmty. Hosp., 1982-86; v.p. Dartmouth Hitchcock Med. Ctr., Lebanon, N.H., 1986—. Pres. bd. Behavioral Health Network, Concord, N.H., 1997-99; chair Ctrl. and Eastern Europe Nursing Task Force, Washington, 1994-98. Sec., Andover (N.H.) After Sch. Program, 1994-96. Mem. ANA, Am. Coll. Healthcare Execs., Am. Orgn. Nurse Execs. (bd. dirs. 1997-98), N.H. Orgn. Nurse Execs. (pres. 1992-96), N.H. Hosp. Assn. (pres. bd. 1997-98), Ctr. for Nursing Leadership (mem. coun. 1998—). Democrat. Roman Catholic. Avocations: cooking, horseback riding, reading, sewing. Office: Dartmouth Hitchcock Med Ctr One Medical Center Dr Lebanon NH 03756 Home: 10524 Knollwood Dr Manassas VA 20111-2834

THOMPSON, PAMELA J. nurse; b. Hutchinson, Minn., Feb. 5, 1959; d. James Sidney and Frances Helen (Boller) Orloff; m. Philip Ernest Thompson, July 5, 1979 (div. Apr. 1993); 1 child, Amber, Renee. Student, Kans. State U., 1991-94; BSN magna cum laude, Washburn U., 1996. RN Kans. Mech. welding inspector Daniel Internat. Corp., Burlington, Kans., 1981-84, Braidwood, Ill., 1984-85; quality specialist Eval. Rsch. Corp., Glen Rose, Tex., 1985-87; multi disciplinary quality inspector Fluor Daniel, Mineral, Va., 1988-89, Surry, Va., 1989-90, quality engr. Boss, Mo., 1990-91; nurse asst. Manor Care Health Svc., Topeka, 1995-96, charge nurse, 1997-98, asst. dir. nurses, 1998—. Vol. Sr. Ctr., Topeka, 1996, Rescue Mission, Topeka, 1995, ARC, 1989—. Mem. ANA, Phi Kappa Phi, Sigma Theta Tau. Republican. Avocations: crochet, history, reading, embroidery, cooking. Office: Manor Care Health Svcs 2515 SW Wanamaker Rd Topeka KS 66614-5269 Home: 600 N Kansas Ave Topeka KS 66608-1240

THOMPSON, PAMELA PADWICK, public relations executive; b. Columbus, Ohio, June 13, 1943; d. Frank John and Tiami Judith (Padwick) T.; stepfather, James William Bampton; m. Fairman Rogers Thompson, Jan. 10, 1942; children: Ryder McNeal, Darby McNeal. BA, U. Louisville, 1994; MA, U. Dayton, 1998. Ptnr. Crutcher, Kelly and Assocs., Louisville, 1979-83; owner Transl. Co., Louisville, 1981-83, Technigraphics, Louisville, 1984-87; v.p. dir. individual support Grtr. Louisville Fund for the Arts, Louisville, 1989-92; v.p. comms. John Templeton Found., Radnor, Pa., 1997—. Adj. prof. U. Louisville, 1997. Contbr. articles to profl. jours. including Small Group Behavior. Chair pub. rels. com. Keene Valley Libr., 2000-01; bd. dirs. Louisville Nature Ctr., 1996-97; mem. ad hoc com. State Ky. Biodiversity Coun., Louisville, 1996-97; city commr. City of Rolling Fields, Louisville, 1991-94; alliance bd. dirs. J.B. Speed Art Mus., Louisville, 1986-92. Mem. APA, Soc. for Consumer Psychology, Pub. Rels. Soc. Am., Jr. League Phila., Cosmo. Club Phila., Ausable Club. Episcopalian. Avocations: hiking, gardening, tennis, travel. Home: 4 Porter Ln Rose Valley PA 19086 Office: John Templeton Found Five Radnor Corp Ctr Ste 100 Radnor PA 19087 Fax: (610) 687-8961. E-mail: pthompson@templeton.org.

THOMPSON, PATRICIA A. lawyer; b. Waco, Tex., Apr. 28, 1952; d. George R. and Thelma M. (Franco) T.; m. Neil H. Korbas, Apr. 23, 1993. BA, Wash. State U., 1974; JD, St. Mary's U., 1977. Bar: Wash. 1978. From juvenile dep. to dep. prosecuting atty. Spokane County, Wash., 1978-97; asst. atty. gen. State of Wash., Spokane, 1997—. Bd. dirs. Northeast Wash. Treatment Alternatives, Spokane, 1985—, Spokane County Domestic Violence Consortium, 1994-96. Mem. Am. Bus. Women's Assn. (pres., sec. 1982—, woman of yr. 1986), Catholic Bus. & Profl. Women (sec. 1988—), Action Women's Exch. (treas. 1994—), Sacred Heart Parish Coun. Roman Catholic. Avocations: needlework, travel, reading. Home: 4111 S Perry St Spokane WA 99203-4239 Office: Asst Atty Gen 1116 W Riverside Ave Spokane WA 99201-1106

THOMPSON, PATRICIA RATHER, literature educator, department chairman; b. Houston, Nov. 27, 1939; d. Daniel Irvin and Veda Byrl (Page) R.; m. Bobby Dean Thompson, Sept. 3, 1960; children: Troy, Byron, Mark. BA, Sam Houston State U., 1962, MA, 1980. Tchr. Houston Ind. Sch. Dist., 1962-65; tchr., dept. chair Klein (Tex.) Ind. Sch. Dist., 1980—. Tchr. North Harris Montgomery County C.C., Conroe, Tex., 1993-96, 2001--; writing cons., Spring, Tex., 1990—; online communication cons., 1997—. Contbr. poetry and articles to profl. jours. Mem. ASCD, Tex. Gifted and Talented, Tex. State Tchrs. English. Home: 210 Shannondale Ln Spring TX 77388-5965 Office: Klein High Sch 16715 Stuebner Airline Rd Klein TX 77379-7394

THOMPSON, PHYLLIS DARLENE, retired elementary school educator; b. West Milton, Ohio, May 21, 1934; d. Howard Luther and Dorothy Mae (Heisey) Yount; m. Joel Kent Thompson, Aug. 22, 1954 (div. Feb. 1981); children: George Kevin, Jolanna Renee, Howard Kraig. BS in Edn., Manchester Coll., 1956; MEd, LaVerne U., 1977. Cert. tchr., Ill. Tchr. Dist. 83, North Lake, Ill., 1956-59; missionary, tchr. Ambon (Indonesia) U., 1961-62; tchr. Dist. Unit 46, Elgin, Ill., 1969—2000. Organizer Mother Goose Day Care Ctr., Elgin, 1970s. Choir mem. Highland Ave Ch. of the Brethren, Elgin, 1964—, bd. chair, 1980-83, ch. bd., 1997-98. Recipient Ednl. Excellence award State of Ill., 1978, Disting. Educator award Kane County, 1978. Mem. NEA, Ill. Edn. Assn., Elgin Tchrs. Assn. (bldg. rep. 1994-96), Alpha Delta Kappa (pres., v.p., sec. 1972—). Democrat. Avocations: letter writing, reading, cross stitching, walking. Home: 11 Kensington Loop Elgin IL 60123-2720

THOMPSON, RONELLE KAY HILDEBRANDT, library director; b. Brookings, S.D., Apr. 21, 1954; d. Earl E. and Maxine R. (Taplin) Hildebrandt; m. Harry Floyd Thompson II, Dec. 24, 1976; children: Clarissa, Harry III. BA in Humanities magna cum laude, Houghton Coll., 1976; MLS, Syracuse U., 1976; postgrad., U. Rochester, 1980, 81; cert., Miami U., 1990. Libr. asst. Norwalk (Conn.) Pub. Libr., 1977; elem. libr. Moriah Ctrl. Schs., Port Henry, NY, 1977—78; divsn. coord. pediat. gastroenterology and nutrition U. Rochester (N.Y.) Med. Ctr., 1978—81, cons., pediat. housestaff libr. com., 1980—81; dir. Medford Libr. U. S.C., Lancaster, 1981—83; dir. Mikkelsen Libr., Libr. Assocs., Ctr. for Western Studies, mem. libr. com. Augustana Coll., Sioux Falls, SD, 1983—, adminstrv. pers. coun., 1989—94, 1997—. Presenter in field. Contbr. articles to profl. jours. Mem. S.D. Symphony; advisor pers. dept. City of Sioux Falls. Recipient leader award YWCA, 1991; Gaylord Co. scholar Syracuse U., 1976; named S.D. Libr. of Yr., 1998. Mem. ALA, AAUW, Assn. Coll. and Rsch. Librs. (nat. adv. coun. coll. librs. sect. 1987—), Mountain Plains Libr. Assn. (chair acad. sect., nominating com. 1988, pres. 1993-94), S.D. Libr. Assn. (chair interlibr. coop. task force 1986-87, pres. 1987-88, chair recommended minimum salary task force 1988, chair local arrangements com. 1989-90, 2002—), S.D. Libr. Network (adv. coun. 1986—, exec. com. 1992-96, 1998-2000, chair adv. coun. 1994-96, 98-2000). Office: Augustana Coll Mikkelsen Libr 29th & Smt Sioux Falls SD 57197-0001 Office Phone: 605-274-4921. E-mail: ronelle_thompson@augie.edu.

THOMPSON, SADA CAROLYN, actress; b. Des Moines, Sept. 27, 1927; d. Hugh Woodruff and Corlyss Elizabeth (Gibson) T.; m. Donald E. Stewart, 1949; 1 dau., Liza. BFA, Carnegie Inst. Tech., 1949; DFA, Carnegie Mellon, late 1970's. Speech tchr. 92d St YMHA, N.Y.C. Stage debut in The Time of Your Life at Carnegie Inst. Tech. Drama Sch., 1945; co-founder Univ. Playhouse, Mashpee, Mass., 1947, appeared at Pitts. Playhouse, The Playhouse, Erie, Pa., summer stock prodns. at Henrietta Hayloft Theatre, Rochester, N.Y., Cambridge, Mass.; New York debut in Under Milk Wood, at YMHA, 1953; appeared in Off-Broadway revival at Circle in the Sq. Theatre, 1961, and Nat. Edn. Television presentation, 1966; appeared in plays The Clandestine Marriage, Provincetown Playhouse, N.Y.C., 1954, The White Devil and, The Carefree Tree at, Phoenix Theatre, N.Y.C., 1955, The Misanthrope, Off Broadways Theatre East, 1956, The River Line, Carnegie Hall Playhouse, 1957; joined Am. Shakespeare Festival, Stratford, Conn., 1957 appearing in Othello, Much Ado About Nothing, 1957-58, The Merry Wives of Windsor, Alls Well That Ends Well, 1959, Twelfth Night, The Tempest and, Antony and Cleopatra, 1960; appeared in Off Broadway prodn. of Chekhov's Ivanov, 1958, Broadway prodn. of Juno and the Paycock, 1959, Tartuffe at Lincoln Center Repertory Theatre, 1965, Johnny No-Trump, 1967, The American Dream, 1968, The Effect of Gamma Rays on Man-in-the-Moon Marigolds, 1970, Twigs, 1971, Mourning Becomes Electra, 1971, Sat.Sun.Mon early 1980's, Any Given Day 1995; motion pictures include You Are Not Alone, 1961, Desperate Characters, 1971, The Pursuit of Happiness, 1971; starred in TV series: Sandburg's Lincoln, 1974-76, Family, 1976-79 (Emmy award for outstanding actress in a dramatic series); TV spl. The Entertainer, 1976; appeared in TV mini-series Marco Polo, 1982, Princess Daisy, 1983, Queen, 1993, (TV movies) Adventures of Huckleberry Finn, 1985, My Love, 1986, Fatal Confession: A Father Dowling Mystery, 1987, Home Fires Burning, 1987, Fear Stalk, 1989, The Skin of Our Teeth, 1980's, Painting Churches, 1980's, Andre's Mother, 1990, Indictment: The McMartin Trial, 1995. Recipient Tony award 1972, New York Drama Critics award for best actress of year Variety 1971-72, 2 Obie awards, Atlanta Drama Critics Mask award as best actress for performance in The Vinegar Tree 1978; Any Mother's Son, 1997; The Patron Saint of Liars, 1998, tv.; Pollock, 1999, film. Office: Richard Bauman & Assocs 5757 Wilshire Blvd Ste 473 Los Angeles CA 90036-3635 Address: PO Box 490 Southbury CT 06488-0490

THOMPSON, SALLY ENGSTROM, state official; b. Spokane, Wash., Feb. 17, 1940; d. Logan C. and Ava Leigh (Phillips) Engstrom; m. Donald Edward Colcun, 1981; children: Lauri Thompson, Tom Thompson, Tami Thompson, Sheri Colcun Trumpfheller. BS magna cum laude, U. Colo., 1975. CPA, Colo. 1976, Kans. 1986. Audit mgr. and mgmt. cons. Touche Ross & Co., Denver, 1975-82; v.p., mgr. planning and fin. analysis United Bank, Denver, 1982-85; pres., chief oper. officer Shawnee Fed. Svgs., Topeka, 1985-90; treas. State of Kans., 1991-98; CFO, acting asst. sec. for adminstrn. USDA, Washington, 1998—. Past editorial advisor New Accountant mag. Bd. dirs. Everywoman's Resource Ctr., Topeka, 1988-92, Community Svc. Found. Kans., Kids Voting Kans. (hon.); v.p., bd. dirs. Downtown Topeka Inc., YWCA, Topeka, 1986-93, Woman of Achievement award, 1984; mem. fin. com. Girl Scouts U.S., Kaw Valley, various coms., United Way of Greater Topeka; chmn. art auction com. KTWU-TV, summer concert, Topeka Civic Theatre. Recipient Disting. Community Leadership award Topeka Pub. Schs., 1989, Disting. Leadership award Nat. Assn. Community Leadership, 1991, 1991 Class Leadership Kans. Mem. AICPAs, Am. Soc. Women Accts., Kans. Soc. CPAs, Kansas C. of C. and Industry, Greater Topeka C. of C. (bd. dirs. 1989-92), Emporia State U. Bus. Sch. Adv. Bd., Nat. Assn. State Auditors, Controllers and Treas., Nat. Assn. State Treas. (v.p., Midwest regional chair), Women Execs. in Govt., Beta Alpha Psi. Democrat. Office: USDA 1400 Independence Ave SW Washington DC 20250-0002

THOMPSON, SANDRA LEE, library administrator; b. Dover, Ohio, Jan. 23, 1968; d. Robert Leonard and Gwendolyn Ruth Stewart; m. Alan McKinney Thompson, Sept. 9, 1990; children: LeeAnna, Alisha, James. BS in Edn., Ohio U., 1989; M of Libr. Info. Sci., U. S.C., 2001. Tchr. Harrison Hills City Sch. Dist., Hopedale, Ohio, 1989-90; asst. dir. Puskarich Pub. Libr., Cadiz, Ohio, 1990-97, dir., 1998—. Mem. Ohio Libr. Coun., Columbus, 1994—; bd. dirs. Southeastern Ohio Libr. Orgn., Caldwell, 1997—, Ohio Pub. Libr. Info. Network. Mem.: Cadiz Rotary Assocs. (trustee), Am. Libr. Assn. Office: Puskarich Pub Libr 200 E Market St Cadiz OH 43907-1200 E-mail: sthompson@oplin.org.

THOMPSON, STEPHANIE DENISE, newspaper columnist, radio host; b. Tulsa, Sept. 19, 1961; d. Richard Harvey and Judith Carol (Holtzinger) Welcher; m. Jeffery Lee Taylor, June 16, 1990 (div. July 1992); m. Dennis Ray Buckley, Oct. 30, 1995 (div. Feb. 1997); m. Michael Floyd Thompson, Feb. 14, 2002; 1 child, Micah Faith. BS, Okla. State U., 1983; MA, U. Okla., 1994. News anchor Sta. KOSU-FM, Stillwater, 1981, Sta. KRXO-FM, Stillwater, 1982; asst. producer Sta. KTVY-TV, Oklahoma City, 1983-84; anchor/reporter Sta. KTEN, Ada, Okla., 1985-86; producer Am.'s Shopping Channel, Oklahoma City, 1987; pub. rels. coordinator S.W. Med. Ctr. Okla., Oklahoma City, 1988-89, pub. rels. assoc., 1990-91, mgr. pub. rels. and devel., 1991-93; exec. dir., CEO Neighborhood Alliance, Oklahoma City, 1994-95; cmty. devel. assoc. Integris Health, Oklahoma City, 1995-99; host State of Change radio talk show, 2000—. Cons. on brochure, Woman to Woman, 1990; radio talk show and syndicated columnist, 2000—. Contbr. Chicken Soup for the Gardener's Soul, 2001, God Allows U-Turns, 2001. Mem. comms. com. United Way, Oklahoma City, 1989-90; bd. dirs. Nat. Clown and Laughter Hall of Fame, 1989-97; bd. dirs. HUGS, 1992-94, Firesafe Found., 1994-96, Internat. Ctr. for Humor and Health, 1995-97, Contact, 1996-97; bd. dirs. Youth Build Oklahoma City, 1996; mem. jr. hospitality Xanadu, 1996-2002, auction chmn., 1998, acquisitions chmn., 1999, bd. dirs., 1999—. Recipient Good Guy award, KTVY-TV, 1988, 89. Mem. Women in Comms. (v.p. 1981-82), Am. Hosp. Assn., Okla. Hosp. Assn., Am. Soc. Health Care Mktg. and Pub. Rels., Pub. Rels Soc. Am., Oklahoma City C. of C., South Oklahoma City C. of C., Lions Internat., Am. Bus. Clubs (bd. dirs.), Rotary Internat. (group study exch. to Queensland, Australia 1995), West Oklahoma City Rotary Club (bd. dirs. 1999-2000), Oklahoma City Carefree Rose Garden Club, Toastmasters. Methodist. Avocations: writing, photography, modeling. Office: PO Box 1502 Edmond OK 73083-1502

THOMPSON, TARA D. writer, career advisor, educator, illustrator; b. Borger, Tex., June 7, 1962; d. Sammy Jo and Jeannean (Johansen) T. AA, Tex. State Tech. Inst., 1982; AAS, Richland Coll., 1991; BA, U. Tex., Dallas, 1993; MA in Counseling, Amber U., 1995. Art dir. Dalco Athletic Lettering, Garland, Tex., 1983-85; office mgr. Jean West Enterprises, Dallas, 1985-86; dept. adminstr. Dean Witter Reynolds, Inc., Dallas, 1986-87; info. specialist, pub. relations asst. Anderson Fischel Thompson Advt., Dallas, 1986-87, office mgr., 1987-89, traffic mgr., 1989-90; writer, illustrator Garland, Tex., 1990—; intern Richland Coll., Dallas, 1994-95; career cons. Career Dimensions, Dallas, 1995—97. Adj. faculty mem. Richland Coll., Dallas, 1995—2003; facilitator Career Fitness Workout, 1996-97; acad. career advisor Richland Coll., 1997-. Vol. listener Dallas Ind. Sch. Dist., 1991-92. Mem. NACADA, Nat. Employment Counseling Assn., Nat. Career Devel. Assn., Undergrad. Psychology Assn. U. Tex. (treas. 1992), Toastmasters (pres. 1992-93, v.p. pub. rels. and membership Speaking Scholars, CTM 1993, Thunderducks,2003-04), People for the Ethical Treatment of Animals. Avocations: roller skating, motorcycling, bicycling, hiking, motocross. Office: 12800 Abrams Rd Dallas TX 75243-2199 E-mail: TDT8401@DCCCD.EDU.

THOMPSON, TERESA ACKERMAN, special education educator; b. Elkhart, Ind., June 11, 1971; d. Robert Lee and Mary Marie Ackerman; m. Tedd Bennett Thompson, Sept. 20, 1996. BA in Social Scis., Mich. State U., 1995; tchg. cert., Olivet Coll., 1996; M in Edn., Grand Valley State U., 2001. Tchr. Mich. State U., E. Lansing, 1994-96, Okemos H.S., Mich., 1996-97, Holt H.S., Mich., 1997—. Presenter in field. Vol. Mich. Rschrs. Assn., Spl. Olympics, Holt, Mich., 1999—. Democrat. Roman Catholic. Avocations: reading, hiking, travel, boating, walking. Office: Holt HS 1784 Aurelius Rd Holt MI 48842-1920 E-mail: ttbytwo@aol.com.

THOMPSON, TERRIE LEE, graphic designer; b. Myrtle Creek, Oreg., Apr. 22, 1960; d. Claud Willie and Blanche Bernice Thompson. Student, Umpqua C.C., 1983-84; BFA, Pacific N.W. Coll. Art, 1988. Freelance graphic designer Terrie Thompson Design, Portland, 1987-90; graphic designer Promotion Products Inc., Portland, 1989-90, L. Grafix Inc., Portland, 1990-91, Warn Industries, Milwaukie, Oreg., 1991-92; pres. Thompson Typographics Inc., Portland, 1990—; typography contractor Nike Inc., Beaverton, Oreg., 1992—. Typography trainer for various design firms and agys., Portland, 1992-98, pres. Seeing Spots, Inc., 1998—. Work published in various design publs., including The Best in Catalogue Design, Comm. Arts Design Ann., How Mag. Computer Art and Design Ann.; creator cartoon character "Spot", 1989. Vol. graphic designer Washington Park Zoo, Portland, 1990; vol. art dir. Portland Mac Users Group, Portland, 1995; vol. beach clean-up crew Stop Oreg. Litter and Vandalism, 1990—. Recipient Bronze award Optima Design Awards, 1995, Digital Art and Design Ann. award Print Mag., 1997, Regional Design Ann. award Print Mag., 1997, Applied Arts Annual, 1997, 98, Good Neighbor award Forest Park Neighborhood Assn., 1999. Avocations: hiking, travel, camping, photography, music. Home and Office: Thompson Typographics Inc PO Box 83327 Portland OR 97283-0327

THOMPSON, THELMA BARNABY, English educator, university dean; b. Jamaica, West Indies, July 22, 1940; d. Claude Noel and Elaine Jordan (Robertson) Barnaby; m. Winston Lloyd Thompson, June 15, 1976; 1 child, Lisa Valdeen. BA, Howard U., Washington, D.C., 1970; MA, Howard U., 1972, PhD, 1978; diploma, Bethlehem Tchrs. Coll., Malvern, Jamaica, West Indies, 1960. Lectr. CUNY, 1972-74; asst. prof. Bowie (Md.) State Coll., 1974-76; assoc. prof., asst. chmn. English dept. U. D.C., Washington, 1976-88, dean Sch. Arts and Letters, 1988-90, Norfolk State U., 1990—. Asst. dean U. D.C., Washington. Author: The Seventeenth Century English Hymn; also articles. Recipient Bethlehem Coll. Medal of Distinction, scholarship and grad. fellowship. Mem. MLA, Coll. Lang. Assn. (pres., chmn. com. high sch./coll. rels.), South Atlantic MLA, Middle Atlantic Writers, Phi Beta Kappa, Phi Delta Kappa (award for disting. svc. and commitment to excellence in edn. 1991). Home: 1708 Handcross Way Virginia Beach VA 23456-5445 Office: Norfolk State U Sch Arts and Letters Bos 4600 2401 Corprew Ave Norfolk VA 23504

THOMPSON, TINA, professional basketball player; b. Feb. 10, 1975; B of Sociology, U. S.C., 1997. Forward WNBA - Houston Comets, 1997—. Played in WNBA All-Star Games (1999,2000,2001). Named Pac-10 Freshman of Yr., 1994, AP All Am. 2d Team, Kodak Dist. All-Am. Team, All-Pac-10 First Team, 1996-97; named to All-WNBA 1st Team, 1997, 98, All-WNBA 2nd Team, 1999-2002; named to WNBA All Star Team, 1999-2002; named MVP, WNBA All-Star game, 2000; won 1997, 98, 99 WNBA championship with Houston. Office: Houston Comets 2 E Greenway Plz Ste 400 Houston TX 77046-0202

THOMPSON, TRACY LEE, bank executive, voice educator; d. Tanya Lee Woodward and Carl Lance Lee; m. Mark Peter Thompson, Nov. 28, 1998. BBA Internat. Econs., Sam Houston State U., Huntsville, Tex., 1993. Br. mgr. Wells Fargo Bank, San Ramon, Calif., 2002—03, premier banker Concord, Calif., 2003—. Singer (vocal instructor): (bel canto training) Vocal Instructions. Mem.: NAFE (assoc.), Am. Bus. Women's Assn. (assoc.; sec. 2000—01, v.p. 2001—02). R-Consevative. Achievements include Member of SHSU Opera Troupe. Avocations: singing, reading, politics. Home: 1820 Harvest Road Pleasanton CA 94566 Office: Wells Fargo Bank 2190 Willow Pass Road Concord CA 94520 Personal E-mail: tleethomp@earthlink.net.

THOMPSON, VETTA LYNN SANDERS, psychologist, educator; b. Birmingham, Ala., Sept. 7, 1959; d. Grover and Vera Lee (King) S.; m. Cavelli Andre Thompson, May 27, 1990; children: Olajuwon, Malik Rashad, Kimberlyn, Assata Iyana. BA, Harvard U., 1981; MA, Duke U., 1984, PhD, 1988. Cert. psychologist and health svc. provider, State of Mo. Com. Psychologists. Psychology intern Malcolm Bliss Mental Health Ctr., St. Louis, 1985-86; psychotherapist, testing coord. Washington U. Child Guidance Clinic, St. Louis, 1986-87; psychologist, treatment team coord. Hawthorn Children's Psychiatric Hosp., St. Louis, 1987-89; asst. prof. U. Mo., St. Louis, 1989-95, assoc. prof., coord. black studies, 1995—. Tchg. asst. Duke U., Durham, N.C., 1982-84, rsch. asst., 1984-85; chair monitoring com. crisis access sys. Ea. Regional Adv. Coun. Dept. Mental Health,

St. Louis, 1995-97; chair African Am. Task Force on Mental Health, Jefferson City, Mo., 1995-97; chair budget and planning com. Ea. Regional Adv. Coun., Dept. Mental Health, St. Louis, 1996-97, pres. Ea. Regional Adv. Coun., 1997-99; mem. children's mental health planning group St. Louis Mental Health Bd., 1996-97. Mem. editl. adv. bd. A Turbulent Voyage: Readings in African American Studies, 1995-96; mem. bd. editl. advisors Gt. Plains Rsch.; contbr. articles to profl. jours. Mem. adv. com. on violence prevention and investment in youth Mo. House, Jefferson City, 1995; mem. managed care steering com. Dept. Mental Health, Jefferson City, 1995—96, mem. strategic planning adv. coun., 1997; mem. Mo. Bd. for Respiratory Care, 1997; mem. state com. for psychologists Mo., 1997—; chair, 2000—02; sec., chair discipline com., 1999—2000; bd. dirs. St. Louis Mental Health Assn., sec., 2000—02, chair planning com., 2002, 2d v.p., 2002, pres., 2003. Kellogg Found.-Mo. Youth Initiative fellow, 1991-93; Ctr. for Great Plains Studies fellow U. Nebr., 1995—; recipient Disting. Svc. award Mental Health Assn. St. Louis, 1998, 99. Mem. APA (divsns. 1, 45), Assn. Black Psychologists, Am. Orthopsychiat. Assn. Methodist. Avocations: aerobics, walking, jazz. Office: U Mo 8001 Natural Bridge Rd Saint Louis MO 63121-4401

THOMPSON, WANDA DAWSON, music educator; b. Lakeland, Fla., Apr. 13, 1948; d. Fuller Leon and Nell Davis Dawson; m. Richard Louis Jackson, June 5, 1970 (div. 1980); 1 child, Lea Jackson Poole ; m. Glenn Edward Thompson, Sept. 1, 1984; children: Ashley Carol, Cline Davis. BS in Music Edn., U. Ala., 1970; MA in Music Edn., U. N.Ala., 1977. Musical dir. Morgan County High, Hartselle, Ala., 1970—80; choral dir. Hartselle High, 1980—95, choral dir. and tchr. gen. music, 1999—; tchr. gen. music grades K-5 Barkley Bridge Elem., Hartselle, 1995—99. Choral dir. Hartselle Jr. High, 1970—74; tchr. gen. music grades K-5 Burleson Elem., Hartselle, 1979—81; choral dir. Calhoan C.C., Decatur, Ala., 1994—2001. Named Ala. Outstanding Young Educator, Ala. Jaycees, 1981. Mem.: Music Educators Nat. Conf., Ala. Edn. Assn., Am. Choral Dirs. Assn. Democrat. Avocation: sewing. Home: 709 Celia Dr SE Hartselle AL 35640 Office Phone: 256-773-5427.

THOMPSON-DRAPER, CHERYL L. electronics executive, real estate executive; b. Houston, Dec. 11, 1950; d. J. R. and Mary Claude Thompson; m. John T. Draper, Aug. 17, 1991; children: Mary-Catherine, John M., Tom. Student, Houston C.C., Massey Bus. Coll. Various positions Warren Electric Group hdqrs., 1970-85; mgr. Warren Electric Co., 1985-89, v.p., bd. dirs., sec., 1990-92; chmn. bd., CEO, owner Warner Electric Co., 1992—, Warren Electric Del Caribe, 1992—, Warren Electric of La., 1992—, Warren-Dominican Republic, 1992—, Warren Electric of Tex., 1992—; mgr., CEO, owner Warren Electric Telecomms.-Utility Co., 1995—; chmn., pres., CEO, owner Warren Electric Group Ltd.; chmn. bd., CEO, pres., owner Thompson Real Estate Ltd., 1995—. Cons. in field. Contbr. articles to profl. jours. Bd. dirs., v.p. San Jacinto coun. Girl Scouts U.S., chmn. fundraiser Urban Campout 1995-96, Houston Sports Found.; vice chmn. Theatre Under the Stars, 1997-2001, chmn. bd., 2001—; bd. dirs. Houston Livestock Show and Rodeo, 1994—; mem. spkrs. and internat. com. All Those Texans, pres., 1997; bd. dirs., mem. exec. com. Greater Houston Partnership, 1996—; mem. Tex Fedn. of Rep., Montgomery County Fair Adv. Bd., 1996—; bd. dirs. Nat. Edn. Found., mem. med. adv. coun. and vet. med. adv. coun. Tex. A&M U., mem. tech. adv. coun. Coll. Engring.; chmn. indsl. distbn. adv. coun. U. Houston Coll. Engring.; mem. Am. Leadership Forum-Houston, 2000. Recipient Texan of Yr. award All Those Texans, 1994, Mktg. Excellence award-Indsl. Sales, Affiliated Distbrs., 1994, Woman on the Move award City of Houston, 1995, Outstanding Family Owned Bus. award State of Tex., 1995, 1st Largest Woman-Owned Bus. award Houston Bus. Jour., 1998, 99, 2000, 01, Warner Cable's Hometown Hero award, 1996, 3rd Largest Woman-Owned Bus. award State of Tex, Woman Enterprise Mag., 1996, 1997, Disting. Svc. award Houson Elec. League, 1996, Leadership Tex 1997 Class, Cora Bacon Foster award, 1997, 1998, Cmty. Svc. award Houston Bus. Jour., 1997, Indsl. Distbn. award of Distinction, Texas A&M U., 1997, Honeywell's Supplier of Yr. award, 1998. Fellow Paul Harris Rotary Club of Houston (bd. dirs.); mem. Nat. Assn. Elec. Distbrs. (bd. dirs., v.p. 1999-00); mem. NAFE, U.S. C. of C. (internat. com.), Am. Alliance of Family Bus., Nat. Assn. Corp. Dirs., Tex. Exec. Women, Exec. Women Internat., DAR, Petroleum Club of Houston, Pasadena C. of C., Women's C. of C. of Tex., Women's Contractor Assn. Republican. Methodist. Office: Warren Electric Group PO Box 67 Houston TX 77001-0067 Fax: 713-236-2188. E-mail: cheryltd@warrenelectric.com.

THOMPSON-LORENZO, ANGELA CHRISTINE, music educator; b. Pitts., Oct. 6, 1956; d. Dante Lorenzo and Mary Louise DeMarco; m. Gilbert Ross Thompson, Oct. 18, 1986; 2 children. MusB in Edn., Seton Hill Coll., 1978. Masters equivalency Md., advanced profl. tchg. cert. Tchr. Holy Family Sch., Latrobe, Pa., 1978—80; music tchr. Montgomery County (Md.) Pub. Schs., 1982—. Pvt. voice tchr. and vocal cons., 1978—. Exec. bd. mem. Rockville (Md.) Musical Theatre, 1990. Avocations: reading, cooking, walking, theater.

THOMS, JEANNINE AUMOND, lawyer; b. Chgo. d. Emmett Patrick and Margaret (Gallet) Aumond; m. Richard W. Thoms; children: Catherine Thoms, Alison Thoms. AA, McHenry County Coll., 1979; BA, No. Ill. U., 1981; JD, Ill. Inst. Tech., 1984. Bar: Ill. 1984, U.S. Dist. Ct. (no. dist.) Ill. 1984, U.S. Ct. Appeals (7th cir.) 1985; cert. mediator 19th Jud. Cir. Ill. Assoc. Foss Schuman Drake & Barnard, Chgo., 1984-86, Zukowski Rogers Flood & McArdle, Crystal Lake and Chgo., 1986-92, ptnr., 1992—. Arbitrator 19th Jud. Ct. Ill., 1991—. Mem. women's adv. coun. to Gov. State of Ill.; mem. McHenry County Mental Health Bd., 1991—98, v.p., 1993—94, pres., 1995—98; mem. governing coun. Good Shepherd Hosp., Barrington, Ill., 2001—; mem. adv. com. McHenry County Found., 2004—. Mem.: LWV, ABA, Acad. Family Mediators (cert.), Am. Trial Lawyers Assn., McHenry County Bar Assn., Chgo. Bar Assn., Ill. State Bar Assn. (coun. trust and estates sect. 2000—01, Ill. legis. dist. scholarship com. 2001, 2002—03), Phi Alpha Delta. Office: Zukowski Rogers Flood & McArdle 50 N Virginia St Crystal Lake IL 60014-4126 also: 100 S Wacker Dr Chicago IL 60606-4006

THOMS, JOSEPHINE BOWERS, artist; b. Lansing, Mich., Sept. 14, 1922; d. Raymon Lyon and Adele (Hammond) Bowers; m. Bert Thoms, June 4, 1945 (dec.); 1 child, Adele Lucile Thoms; m. Peter Blackford Lauck, May 10, 1983. BA, Hillsdale Coll., 1944; MA, Md. Inst. Coll. Art, 1977. Instr. modern dance Hillsdale (Mich.) Coll., 1943-44; artist-in-residence St. John's Coll., Annapolis, Md., 1953-55, 68-70; instr. art Washington and Jefferson Coll., Washington, Pa., 1956, Bethany (W.Va.) Coll., 1963-65; illustrator Md. Dept. Natural Resources, Annapolis, 1977-95. Joint owner Onset Bay Gallery and Studio, Onset, Mass., portrait artist, colorist; instr. Washington Art Assn., 1958-69; art dir. Md. Fedn. Art, Annapolis, 1970-72, pres., 1972-74. Illustrator: Federal Prose, 1947; executed murals: History of Electricity, Hillsdale, 1942, The Harbor at Annapolis, Crownsville, Md., 1989. Mem. Caritas Soc. at St. John's Coll., 1969—, Md. Peace Action, Annapolis, 1983—. Recipient 1st prize for Exhbn. of Nature-Related Art, Adkins Arboretum, Tuckahoe State Pk., Denton, Md., 1995. Mem. Md. Soc. Portrait Painters (cert., exhibits chairperson 1995—), Annapolis Watercolor Club (1st prize 1993). Democrat. Episcopalian. Avocations: swimming, aerobics, piano, needlepoint design. Home: 61 Southgate Ave Annapolis MD 21401-2829

THOMSEN, PEGGY JEAN, mayor, educator, councilman; b. St. Louis, Feb. 28, 1940; d. Harold Herman and Crystal Mary (Margolf) Levora; m. John Henry Thomsen, Dec. 1, 1961; children: Dianna, James, Robert. BA, Calif. State U., Fresno, 1961, MA with honors, 1968; PhD, U. Calif., Berkeley, 1997. Gen. secondary credential, Calif. Instr. Ctrl. Tex. Coll., 1980-83, City Colls. Chgo., 1983-86, Heald Colls., San Francisco, 1987; mayor, coun. mem. City of Albany, 1997—. Mem. East Bay Econ. Alliance, 1997—, Nat. Mayors Conf., 1998-99, Alameda County Mayor's Conf., 1998-99; bd. alt. Waste Mgmt. Authority, 1999—; bd. dirs. Alameda County Congestion Mgmt. Agy., 1997—. Editor City of Albany (Calif.) Newsletter, 1987. Mem. sch. bd. Albany Unified Sch. Dist., 1978-97, pres. sch. bd., 1980-81, 85-86; pres. PTA, Albany, 1976-78, 69-71; leader Girl Scouts U.S.A., Albany, 1970-82; mem. fund-raising team YMCA, Albany, 1981-88; bd. dirs., sec. Bay Area chpt. March of Dimes, San Francisco, 1979-88, chmn., 1985-86, chmn. Alameda County chpt., 1985-88; mem. adminstrv. code Rev. com. Calif. Dept. Edn., 1981-83, chmn. sch. improvement program selection panel, 1981, mem. fin. com., 1982, state budget com., 1982; Acorn Br. Assoc. Children's Hosp., Oakland. Recipient Svc. award Jaycees, Albany, 1970, Svc. awards Calif. PTA, 1971, 78, Vol. of Yr. award March of Dimes, Alameda County, 1984; named Sta. KABL Citizen of Day, 1984. Mem. NEA, LWV, Nat. Sch. Bds. Assn., Calif. Sch. Bds. Assn., Calif. Elected Women's Edn. Asn., League Calif. Cities (pres.-bd. mem. East Bay divsn. 1997—), Calif. Elected Women's Assn. for Edn. and Rsch., Congestion Mgmt. Agy. (bd. mem. 1997—), Pi Gamma Mu. Democrat. Avocations: needlework, editing, reading. Home: 757 Pierce St Albany CA 94706-1033 Office: City of Albany 1000 San Pablo Ave Albany CA 94706-2226

THOMSON, AUDREY SHIRE, volunteer; b. Paterson, NJ, Nov. 21, 1929; d. Gerald John Shire, Maybelle Conover; m. Norman B. Thomson, Oct. 17, 1954 (div. May 1985); children: Norman B., Christine de Armas, Scott B. BA, Coll. of St. Elizabeth, Morristown, N.J., 1950; MPA, NYU, 1990. Jr. pharmacologist Hoffman LaRoche, Nutley, NJ, 1950—55; exec. asst. Am. Cancer Soc. Nat. Office, N.Y.C., 1983—86; exec. asst. to pres. United Fedn. Tchrs., N.Y.C., 1986—89; asst. to pres. Grand Ctrl. Partnership, N.Y.C., 1990—93, 34th St. Bus. Improvement Dist., N.Y.C., 1990—93, Bryant Park Restoration Corp., N.Y.C., 1990—93; asst. to founding ptnr. Edison Project, N.Y.C., 1992—93. Mgr. "first night" events Pierpont Morgan Libr., N.Y.C., 1992—93. Editor: (newsletter) Mus. Pieces, 1978—81; contbr. articles to profl. jours. Fundraiser Coll. of St. Elizabeth, 1995—2000, capital campaign com., 2003—, mem. steering com., 2003—, class chmn., 2003—; active various polit. campaigns Miami, Fla. Mem.: AAUW (program organizer 1994—2004, bd. dirs., ednl. equity chmn., fundraising chmn. 1994—2004, fundraiser task force 2002—04, Eleanor Roosevelt Ednl. Found. award 1999, Platinum award 1997—2001, Rosborough Meml. award, Silver award 2002). Roman Catholic. Avocations: reading, sewing, walking Civil War battlefields. Home: 7600 Central Ave Savannah GA 31406

THOMSON, HELEN LOUISE, artist; b. Lewiston, Ill., Nov. 28, 1928; d. Clyde Arthur Pomeroy and Myrtle Lynch Cluney; m. William Edward Thomson, 1950; children: Persephone Ann, Lucinda Renee, Cynthia Louise. Student, Western Ill. U., 1972, 78, 85, U. Ill., 1972; diploma, North Light Art Sch. Artist, Table Grove, Ill., 1970—. Adj. prof. Western Ill. U., Macomb, 1985-94; mem. spkrs. roster Spoon River Coll., Canton, Ill., 1986-94; exec. dir. Two Rivers Arts Coun., Macomb, 1985-94. Exhibited in numerous one woman and group exhbns.; contbr. art to calendars United Fed. Savs. & Loan, 1980, 86. Pres. Spoon River Coll. Found., Canton, Ill., 1979-85, Fulton County Arts Coun., Canton, 1973-83; bd. dirs. Regional Arts Adv. Coun., Western Ill. U., 1978-83; mem. adv. panel Ill. Arts Coun., Chgo., 1980-83; officer PTA, Table Grove, 1957-85. Recipient Ruth Watts Svc. award Performing Arts Soc., Western Ill. U., 1994, award Two Rivers Arts Coun., 1994; selected for feature stories on pub. TV sta. WMEC, 1997, Canton Daily Ledger, Macomb Jour., Peoria (Ill.) Jour. Mem. PEO Sisterhood (pres., sec., chpalain, v.p.), Ill. Art League (exhbn. awards), Ill. Watercolor Soc., Galesburg Civic Art Ctr. (exhbn. awards), Chgo. Art inst. Avocations: antiques, antique dolls, family history, travel. Home: 404 S Broadway St Table Grove IL 61482-0163

THOMSON, KATHLEEN KEPNER, state agency administrator, researcher; b. Raton, N.Mex., Mar. 30, 1929; d. John C. Kepner and Ruth Edna Whitford; m. George William Thomson, June 23, 1979 (dec. Nov. 17, 1996). BA in Social Studies, U. N.Mex., 1951; MS in Polit. Sci., U. Wis., 1955. Cert. tchr. N.Mex. Rschr. budget Office of Gov., Madison, Wis., 1954; rsch. assoc. Wis. Legis. Reference Bur., Madison, 1954—64, Wis. Taxpayers Alliance, Madison, 1964—66; sr. rsch. assoc. Citizens Rsch. Coun. Mich., Detroit, 1966—86; ret. Chair Mich. Natural Resources Coun., 1990—94. Recipient Disting. Svc. award, Mich. Botanical Club, 1999. Mem.: Govt. Rsch. Assn. (hon.), Mich. Bot. Club (pres. S.E. chpt. 1995—2001), Mich. Cactus and Succulent Soc., Archaeology Conservancy. Unitarian Universalist. Avocations: music, conservation, reading. Home: 5066 Elmhurst Ave Royal Oak MI 48073-1102

THOMSON, SONDRA K. secondary school educator; b. Audubon, Iowa, Aug. 24, 1940; d. Merlyn Franklyn and Leona Marie Peterson; m. Alan Richard Thomson, Sept. 3, 1989; children from previous marriage: Paul Spiegel, Joni Spiegel, Steve Spiegel. BA magna cum laude, Calif. State U., Hayward, 1988; MA in Spl. Edn., Chapman U., 2000. Cert. resource specialist, learning handicapped credential, social sci. credential. Co founder, assoc. editor Am. Remnant Mission, Pleasant Hill, Calif., 1977—84; substitute tchr. Mt. Diablo Sch. Dist., Concord, Calif., 1985—90; spl. day class tchr. Antioch Sch. Dist., Antioch, Calif., 1997—99; resource specialist Deer Valley HS, Antioch, Calif., 1999—, mem. adv. coun., 2002—03. Adv. coun. Deer Valley HS, 2002, 2003—04. Contbr. articles to mags. Office: Deer Valley HS 4700 Lone Tree Way Antioch CA 94509

THOMSON, THYRA GODFREY, former state official; b. Florence, Colo., July 30, 1916; d. John and Rosalie (Altman) Godfrey; m. Keith Thomson, Aug. 6, 1939 (dec. Dec. 1960); children— William John, Bruce Godfrey, Keith Coffey. BA cum laude, U. Wyo., 1939. With dept. agronomy and agrl. econs. U. Wyo., 1938-39; writer weekly column Watching Washington pub. in 14 papers, Wyo., 1955-60; planning chmn. Nat. Fedn. Republican Women, Washington, 1961; sec. state Wyo. Cheyenne, 1962-86. Mem. Marshall Scholarships Com. for Pacific region, 1964-68; del. 72d Wilton Park Conf., Eng., 1965; mem. youth commn. UNESCO, 1970-71, Allied Health Professions Council HEW, 1971-72; del. U.S.-Republic of China Trade Conf., Taipei, Taiwan, 1983; mem. lt. gov.'s trade and fact-finding mission to Saudi Arabia, Jordan, and Egypt, 1985 Bd. dirs. Buffalo Bill Mus., Cody, Wyo., 1987—; adv. bd. Coll. Arts and Scis., U. Wyo., 1989, Cheyenne Symphony Orch. Found., 1990—. Recipient Disting. Alumni award U. Wyo., 1969, Disting. U. Wyo. Arts and Scis. Alumna award, 1987, citation Omicron Delta Epsilon, 1965, citation Beta Gamma Sigma, 1968, citation Delta Kappa Gamma, 1973, citation Wyo. Commn. Women, 1986; named Internat. Woman of Distinction, Alpha Delta Kappa, Keith and Thyra Honors Convocation in her honor Coll. of Arts and Scis. U. Wyo., 1997. Mem. N.Am. Securities Adminstrs. (pres. 1973-74), Nat. Assn. Secs. of State, Council State Govts. (chmn. natural resources com. Western states 1966-68), Nat. Conf. Lt. Govs. (exec. com. 1976-79) Republican. Home: 3102 Sunrise Rd Cheyenne WY 82001-6136

THOMSON, VALERIE ANNE, artist, art gallery owner; b. Mason, Mich., May 4, 1959; d. Duanne Carlton and Margaret Mary Thomson; children: Kasey, Emily. AA, Kendall Sch. of Design, Grand Rapids, Mich., 1980. Graphic designer Mitchell St. Graphics, Petoskey, Mich., 1980—81, Wainright and Raber, Mishawaka, Ind., 1981—82, Malec & Assocs., Arlington, Tex., 1982—83, Point Comm., Dallas, 1983—99, Unigraphics, Dallas, 1983—99; impressionist painter Petoskey; owner Valerie Studio & Fine Art Gallery, Petoskey, 1999—. Aerobic instr. Exhibitions include Art Expo, N.Y., 2001. Recipient Fine Arts award, Crooked Tree Arts Ctr., Dallas Tops Award, 1983. Mem.: Aerobic Fitness Assn. of Am., Oil Painters of Am. Avocations: reading, bicycling. Office: Valerie Studio & Fine Art Gallery 219 E Lake St Petoskey MI 49770

THON, MELANIE RAE, writer; b. Kalispell, Mont., Aug. 23, 1957; d. Raymond Albert and Lois Ann (Lockwood) T. BA, U. Mich.; MA, Boston U., 1982. Instr. U. Mass., Boston, 1988-91, Emerson Coll., Boston, 1988-93, Harvard U., Cambridge, Mass., 1989-93; prof. Syracuse (N.Y.) U., 1993-96, Ohio State U., 1996—2000, U. Utah, 2000—. Author: Meteors in August, 1990, Girls in the Grass, 1991, Iona Moon, 1993, First, Body, 1997, Sweet Hearts, 2000. Avocations: hiking, swimming, snow shoeing, skiing.

THORBURN, LISA A. acoustical consulting company executive; BS in Scientific & Tech. Comm., Mich. Tech. U. With Sisters of St. Dominic, Anshen & Allen, IWERKS Entertainment, Don Dommer Assocs., STUDIOS Architecture, Harveys Resort Hotel/Casino, South Lake Tahoe, Helsing Group, Brava, Inc.; prin. designer Thorburn Assocs., Castro Valley, Calif. Contbr. tech. articles to profl. jours. Mem. AIA, NAFE, Soc. Tech. Comm., Soc. Mktg. Profl. Svcs., Constrn. Specifications Inst. Office: 2867 Grove Way Castro Valley CA 94546-6709

THORN, SUSAN HOWE, interior designer; b. Washington, Apr. 22, 1941; d. James Bennett Cowdin and Lois (Fiesinger) Howe; m. William D. Thorn, June 22, 1963; children: Melissa Ann, William David. Lighting design, Parsons Sch. Design, 1975-77; BA, Syracuse U., 1962; AB, N.Y. Sch. Interior Design, 1995. Owner, designer Susan Thorn Interiors, Inc., Cross River, N.Y., 1965—. Designer total bldg. Cooper Labs, Bedford Hills, N.Y., 1973, total redesign Nycrest Corp., Cold Spring, N.Y., 1973-75, showrooms, model rooms stylist and coordinator France Voiles Co. Inc., N.Y.C., 1976, total design new corp. hdqrs. in Gen. Dynamics Bldg. (with Marjorie Borradaile Helsel), Robert E. Eastman Co., N.Y.C., 1967, Cummin & Friedland Capital Corp., 1982; designer offices, stores, employee areas comml., public, residential clients, including Waccabuc (N.Y.) Country Club, 1969, S. Salem (N.Y.) Library, St. Vincent's Hosp., N.Y.C., 1996; instr. adult edn. dept. John Jay High Sch.; spkr. civic orgns. Mem. Am. Soc. Interior Designers (profl.), Internat. Assn. Lighting Designers (assoc.), Decorators Club, Club of N.Y., Waccabuc Country Club. Episcopalian. Home: 88 N Salem Rd Cross River NY 10518 E-mail: thorninteriors@earthlink.net.

THORNBURG, LINDA A. writer; b. Denver, Aug. 8, 1949; d. William J.R. Thornburg and Marjory Smith. BA, U. Colo., 1973. Pres., prin. Word Wizards, Woodbridge, Va., 1990—. Author: (book series) Cool Careers for Girls, 1999—2004; editor: iLinx Society for Human Resource Management, 2000—03. Mem.: AAUW (br. sec. 2000—02, br. program chair 2004), Washington Ind. Writers. E-mail: wordwzrds@aol.com.

THORNE, KRISTAN, newscaster; BJ, La. Tech. Broadcaster, La.; talk-radio show host; reporter ABC Affiliate, Alexandria, La., show anchor; DJ, news anchor KZMS; news dir. KXKZ-Radio, Ruston, La.; reporter WSAV-TV3, Savannah, Ga. Mem. state Bd. AP. Recipient 15 awards, AP. Avocations: scuba diving, skydiving, working out, pet Border Collie. Office: WSAV-TV3 1430 E Victory Dr Savannah GA 31404

THORNTON, FELICIA, food service executive, corporate financial executive; BSc Econs., Santa Clara U.; MBA Corp. Fin., Mktg., U. So. Calif. V.p., corp. planning and acctg. Ralphs Grocery Co., v.p., admin., 1998, group v.p., fin. and adminstrn., 1999—2001; group v.p. retail ops. Kroger Co., 2000—01; exec. v.p., CFO Albertson's, Inc., 2001—. Various mgmt. positions in fin. and adminstrn., retail ops. and corp. planning. Office: Albertson's Inc 250 Park Ctr Blvd Boise ID 83726*

THORNTON, GLENDA ANN, librarian; b. Chickasha, Okla., Aug. 11, 1949; d. G. Van and Clara Maude (Lister) Long; m. Phillip Wynn Thornton, Sept. 18, 1970; children: Edward D., Jonathan C. BA, U. Okla., 1971, MLS, 1973; PhD, U. North Tex., 1993. Reference libr. Aurora (Colo.) Pub. Libr., 1974-75; tech. svcs. libr. Adams State Coll., Alamosa, Colo., 1975-80; collection devel. libr. Henderson State U., Arkadelphia, Ark., 1980-85, acting dir. libr., 1984; head material acquisitions libr. U. North Tex., Denton, 1985-91; assoc. dir. libr. svc. Auraria Libr. U. Colo., Denver, 1991—98; dir. Cleve. State U. Libr., 1998—. Co-author: AHE Vendor Directory, 1988; editor: Collection Management, vols. 26-27, 2000-03; revs. editor Tech. Svcs. Quar., 1997—; contbr. articles to profl. jours. Mem. Ohio LINK Libr. Adv. Coun., 1998—. Mem. ALA, Libr. Adminstrn. and Mgmt. Assn., Assn. Coll. and Rsch. Librs., Acad. Libr. Assn. Ohio, Cleve. Area Met. Libr. Assn. (bd. dirs. 2002—), Beta Phi Mu. Avocation: gardening. Office: 2121 Euclid Ave RT 501 Cleveland OH 44115-2214

THORNTON, JERRY SUE, community college president; BA, MA, Murray (Ky.) State U.; PhD, U. Tex.; DHL, Coll. St. Catherine, St. Paul. Tchr. jr. high sch., Earlington, Ky., Murray H.S., Triton Coll., RiverGrove, Ill., dean arts ans scis.; pres. Lakewood C.C., White Bear Lake, Minn., 1985-92, Cuyahoga C.C., Cleve., 1992—. Bd. dirs. Nat. City Bank, Applied Indsl. Techs. Author books, book chpts. and articles. Bd. dirs. Greater Cleve. Growth Assn., Greater Cleve. Roundtable, Urban League of Greater Cleve., United Way Svcs., Rock and Roll Hall of Fame and Mus., Cleve. Found. Mem. Alpha Kappa Alpha. Office: Cuyahoga CC Office of Pres 700 Carnegie Ave Cleveland OH 44115-2833

THORNTON, KATHRYN C. physicist, astronaut; b. Montgomery, Ala., Aug. 17, 1952; d. William C. and Elsie Cordell; m. Stephen T. Thornton; children: Carol Elizabeth, Laura Lee, Susan Annette; stepchildren: Kenneth, Michael. BS in Physics, Auburn U., 1974; MS in Physics, U. Va., 1977, PhD, 1979. Physicist U.S. Army Fgn. Sci. & Tech. Ctr., Charlottesville, Va., 1980-84; with NASA, 1984—, astronaut Lyndon B. Johnson Space Ctr., 1985—, mission specialist Space Shuttle Discovery flight STS-33, 1989-96; prof. University of Virginia Sch of Engineering, VA, 1996—. Aboard maiden flight Space Shuttle Endeavor, 1992. Nato post-doctoral fellow Max Planck Inst. Nuclear Physics, 1979-80. Mem. AAAS, Am. Phys. Soc., Sigma Xi, Phi Kappa Phi. Office: U Va Charlottesville VA 22903

THORNTON, NANCY FREEBAIRN, psychotherapist, consultant, military officer; b. Mexico, Mo., Feb. 9, 1949; d. John Arthur Black Sr. and Pauline Cearley Black; children: Marinda Jane, William Thomas IV, Ann Elizabeth. BS, Ariz. State U., 1971; MA, U. Okla., 1978; PhD in Clin. Psychology, Forest Inst., 1990. Lic. Psychotherapist Ala., 1988. Commd. U.S. Army, 1971—85, advanced through grades to major, 1983, company cmdr. engr. basic tng., 1976—77; tactical officer U.S. Mil. Acad., West Point, NY, 1978—81; ret. U.S. Army, 1983; pvt. practice Cullman, 1988—. Cons. in field. Vol. Girl Scouts Am., 1957—. Named Subject of Paul Harvey Rest of Story radio show, 1983; named one of Top 35 Adults Under 35, U.S. Mag., 1980; named to featured story in, Esquire Mag., 1983; recipient Unsung Hero award, Cullman Times, 1998. Mem.: Cullman Women's League (officer). Achievements include first female engineer officer in the U.S. Army. Home: 1809 Loch Ave Cullman AL 35055

THORNTON, PAULINE CECILIA EVE MARIE SUZANNE, special education educator; b. L.A., July 1, 1951; d. John Woodrow Thornton and Pauline Lucia DeWolfe; children: Patrick Ellis Hooker-Wafford, Damien Charles Wafford. Student, L.A. City Coll., 1969—71; BA in English, UCLA, 1975; MA in Spl. Edn., Calif. State U., Bakersfield, 2003. Profl. clear multiple-subjects credential/profl. clear learning Calif. State Dept. Edn., 1999. Reading tutor L.A. Unified Sch. Dist., 1970—71, instrnl. asst., 1975, tchrs. asst., 1975—78; childcare worker Children's Home Soc. Bakersfield, 1981—84; instrnl. technician Nat. Assn. for People with Disabilities, 1981—85; instrnl. aide I Bakersfield City Sch. Dist., 1981—85, substitute tchr., 1985—94, cert. spl. edn. tchr., 1994—. Author: (poetry) Internat. Soc. Poetry Anthologies, 2000—03, (anthology) Theatre of the Mind, 2003. Mem.: CTA, NEA, AARP, So. Poetry Law Ctr., Folgers Shakespeare Libr., Am. Acad. Poets, Internat. Soc. Poets, Nat. Writers'

Union, others, ACLU Alumni, Amnesty Internat., Peace and Freedom Party, Internat. Soc. for Krishna Consciousness, Muslim Peace Fellowship, Nuc. Peace Orgn., The Wisdom Fund, United Lodge Theosophists, Sigma Tau Delta. Roman Catholic. Avocations: science fiction, jazz, philosophy, movies. Home: 5805 Hartman [illegible]

THORNTON, YVONNE SHIRLEY, physician, author, musician; b. N.Y.C., Nov. 21, 1947; d. Donald E. and Itasker F. (Edmonds) T.; m. Shearwood McClelland, June 8, 1974; children: Shearwood III, Kimberly Itaska. BS in Biology, Monmouth Coll., 1969; MD, Columbia U., 1973, MPH, 1996; DSc (hon.), Tuskegee U., 2003. Diplomate Am. Bd. Ob-gyn. Resident in ob-gyn Roosevelt Hosp., N.Y.C., 1973-77; fellow maternal-fetal medicine Columbia-Presbyn. Med. Center, N.Y.C., 1977-79; commd. lt. comdr. M.C. USN, 1979; asst. prof. ob-gyn Uniformed Svcs. U. Health Scis., 1979-82; assoc. prof. Cornell U. Med. Coll., N.Y.C., 1989-92; dir. clin. svcs. dept. ob-gyn N.Y. Hosp.-Cornell Med. Center, 1982-88; asst. attending N.Y. Lying-In Hosp., 1982-89; assoc. clin. prof. ob-gyn. Columbia P&S, 1995-98, assoc. clin. prof., 2001—02; clin. prof. ob-gyn. U. Medicine and Dentistry N.J., 1998-2000; prof. clin. ob-gyn. Med. Coll. Cornell U., 2003—. Dir. Chorionic Villus Sampling Program, 1984-92; dir. perinatal diagnostic testing ctr. Morristown Meml. Hosp., 1992-2000, divsn. maternal-fetal medicine St. Luke's Roosevelt Hosp. Ctr., 2000-02; vice chair ob-gyn, dir. maternal-fetal medicine, Jamaica Hosp. Med. Ctr., 2002—; staff Nat. Naval Med. Ctr., Bethesda, Md.; saxophonist Thornton Sisters ensemble, 1955-76; vis. assoc. physician The Rockefeller U. Hosp., 1986-96; prof. clinical OB/GYN Cornell U. Med. Coll., 2003—; examiner Am. Bd. Ob-Gyn, 1997—; vice chmn. Dept. Ob-Gyn. Jamaica Hosp. Med. Ctr. Author: The Ditchdigger's Daughters, 1995, (named best books for young adults ALA, Excellence in Lit. award, N.J. Edn. Assn., nominated for Pulitzer Prize 1995) Primary Care for the Obstetrician and Gynecologist, 1997, Woman to Woman, 1997. Recipient Excellence in Literature award, N.J. Edn. Assn., 1996, winner Daniel Webster Oratorical Competition, Internat. Platform Assn., 1996; nominated Pulitzer Prize, 1995. Fellow: ACOG, ACS; mem.: AMA, Am. Fedn. Musicians, Soc. Maternal-Fetal Medicine, Assn. Women Surgeons, N.Y. Acad. Medicine. Democrat. Baptist. Office: 8900 Van Wyck Expressway New York NY 11418

THORNTON-ARTSON, LINDA ELIZABETH, psychiatric nurse; b. Balt., Dec. 27, 1956; d. Herbert and Helen (Thornton) Powell; m. Michael C. Artson, Oct. 28, 1983; children: Michelle Cherise, Mia Charmain. AA in Psychology, Community Coll. of Balt.; BSN, Coppin State Coll. Cert. gerontol. nurse; cert. psychiat. nurse; cert. nurse cons. in case mgmt.; cert. med.-legal cons. Charge nurse Melchor Nursing Home, 1973-83; med./surg. nurse North Charles Gen. Hosp., Balt., 1975-80; psychiat. nurse Wyman Park Psychiat. Hosp., Balt., 1980-84; dir. nurses Lebran Nursing Home, Cin., 1984-85, George A. Martin Gerontology Ctr., Cin., 1983-84; staff nurse Walter P. Carter Psychiat. Hosp., Balt., 1986-90; pvt. cons. Woodbridge, Va., 1999. Expert witness in elderly abuse, head injury, and myofacial pain syndrome; instr. for med. tech. nursing assistance counrse in cert. nursing assts. for Va.; med.-legal cons. for Suder & Suder Lar Firm; lectr. in field psychiat. nursing and gerontology nursing; cons. long-term care; cons. for law firms, nursing students, case mgmt. for ins. cos.; mem., supporter AIDS Fuond., Whitman-Walker Clinic Inc., Washington; v.p. Artson Ent., 1985—. Co-author: Warehouse of the Living Dead, 1989; appeared on nat. TV as expert on elderly abuse; contbr. articles to profl. jours. Mem. NAFE, ANA, ABA, Nat. League for Nursing, Am. Heart Assn., Md. Nurses Assn., WHO, Nat. Found. for Depressive Illness Inc., Nat. Headache Found., Nat. Cleft Palate Soc., Psychiat. Nurse Soc., Back Pain Assn. Am., Am. Pain Soc., Am. Acad. Pain Mgmt., Am. Chronic Pain Assn., Pain Found., Arthritis Found., Head Injury Found., Va. Nursing Assn., Head Injury Svc. Partnership, Fibromyalgia Assn. Washington, Coppin State Coll. Alumni Assn., Brain Injury Assn. of Va., Am. Chronic Pain Assn. (leader Woodbridge Va. chpt.), Head Injury Partnership Va., Am. Bd. Forensic Nursing (diplomate), Am. Coll. of Forensic Examiners, Am. Assn. Legal Nurse Consultants, Nat. Assn. Legal Assistants, Am. Assn. Nurse Attys., Internat. Assn. Forensic Nurses, Va. Inst. Forensic Sci. Med. Avocations: reading, cooking, art, travel, head injury advocacy. Address: PO Box 194 Woodbridge VA 22194

THORP, CAROL LYN, elementary school music educator; b. Cumberland, Md., May 11, 1950; d. Phares Lynn and Dorothy Jane Hostettler; m. Albert Lindsay Thorp; children: Amy, Allison. B of Music Edn., W.Va. Wesleyan Coll., 1972; M in Edn., W.Va. U., 1982. Cert. permanent music and elem. edn. Tchr. Wood County Bd. of Edn., Parkersburg, W.Va., 1993—. Pres. Madison Elem. Faculty Senate, Parkersburg, 2001—03, Parkersburg High A Cappella Choir Boosters, 2000—01; facilitator Weigh Down Workshop, Parkersburg, 1997—2002; dir. Puppet Ministry Stout Meml. United Meth. Ch., Parkersburg, 1993—2002; mem. Chancel Choir Stout Meml. United Meth. Ch., Parkersburg, 1993—2002. Grantee Tech. grantee, Bell Atlantic, 1997. Mem.: Music Educators. Office: Wood County Board of Edn 13th St Parkersburg WV 26101

THORPE, JANET CLAIRE, judge; b. Bklyn., Dec. 8, 1953; d. Burton Walter and Phyllis Claire (Read) T.; m. David Frank Palmer, Aug. 26, 1978 (div. Aug. 1988); children: Katherine Elaine, Jennifer Claire; m. James Francis Box, June 29, 1991; children; Melissa Richelle, Maergrethe Cashel. Student, Boston U., 1972-74; BA in Polit. Sci. & History with honors, Union Coll., 1975; postgrad., Western New Eng. Sch. Law, 1975-76; JD, Emory U., 1978. Bar: Ga. 1978, U.S. Ct. Appeals (5th and 11th cirs.) 1978, 80, Fla. 1987, U.S. Dist. Ct. (mid. dist.) Fla. 1987. Law clk. to judge U.S. Dist. Ct., Atlanta, 1978; regional atty. Comptroller of Curency, Atlanta, 1978-80; assoc. corp. counsel Trust Co. Ga., Atlanta, 1980-86; dir. Trusco Properties, Inc., Atlanta, 1981-86; gen. counsel, corp. sec. SunTrust Banks Fla., Inc., Orlando, 1986-2000; gen. counsel SunTrust Bank N.A., Orlando, 1986-2000; group v.p. SunTrust Banks, Inc., 1995-2000; cir. ct. judge State of Fla. (9th cir.), Orlando, Fla., 2000—. Mem. Coun. Battered Women, Atlanta, 1983-86, bd. dirs., 1986; bd. visitors Cornell Mus. Fine Art, Rollins Coll., 1990-96; mem. bd. zoning variances City of Orlando, 1996-99; bd. dirs. Orange County Cmty. Alliance, 2000-03. Mem. Ga. Bar Assn., Fla. Bar Assn., Assn. Bank Holding Cos (lawyers com. 1983-90), Am. Corp. Counsel Assn. (bd. dirs. ctrl. Fla. chpt. 1991-99), Am. Diabetes Assn. (bd. dirs. Fla. chpt. 1989-97), Leadership Orlando. Episcopalian. Avocations: gardening, child rearing, house renovation, photography. Office: Orange County Courthouse 425 N Orange Ave Orlando FL 32801

THORSEN, CHRISTINE MAE, music educator; b. Mendota, Ill., Feb. 13, 1972; d. Harold Erwin and Sally LaDonne Thorsen. BS cum laude, North Ctrl. U., 1995. Cert. elem. classroom grades K-9 Ill., music classroom K-12 Ill., elem. classroom grades K-6 Minn. Kindergarten tchr. Ottawa (Ill.) Christian Acad., 1995—97; reading aide Sheridan (Ill.) Grade Sch., 1997—98; music tchr. Earlville (Ill.) Grade Sch./H.S., 1998—2000, Cmty. Unit Dist. #2, Serena, Ill., 2000—. Pvt. piano instr., Ottawa, Ill., 1995—; Suzuki piano tchr. Suzuki Music Schs., Ottawa, Peru and Princeton, Ill., 1999; ch. musician Praise Ctr. Assembly of God, Ottawa, 1995—98, Freedom Luth. Ch., Ottawa, 1998—2003. Vocalist: albums Whispering Hope, 2001, vocalist, pianist: albums Voice in the Wilderness, 2001. Accompanist Cmty. Choir, Sheridan, 2000—02. Mem.: Cmty. Unit #2 Tchrs. Assn. (treas. 2003—), Ill. Grade Sch. Music Assn., Music Educators Nat. Conf. Avocations: sewing, folk music, world music, world drumming. Office: Cmty Unit Dist #2 Serena HS Quincy St Serena IL 60549

THORSEN, MARIE KRISTIN, radiologist, educator; b. Milw., Aug. 1, 1947; d. Charles Christian and Margaret Josephine (Little) T.; m. James Lawrence Troy, Jan. 7, 1978; children: Katherine Marie, Megan Elizabeth. BA, U. Wis., 1969; MBA, George Washington U., 1971; MD, Columbia Coll. Physicians and Surgeons, 1977. Diplomate Am. Bd. Radiology. Intern. Columbia-Presbyn. med. Ctr., N.Y.C., 1977-78, resident dept. radiology, 1978-81; asst. prof. radiology Med. Coll. Wis., 1982-84, assoc. prof., 1984-89, prof., 1989-94; dir. computed tomography Waukesha Meml. Hosp., 1994—. Contbr. articles to profl. jours. Fellow computed body tomography Med. Coll. Wisc., Milw., 1981-82; Am. Coll. Radiology, Radiol. Soc. N. Am., Wis. Radiologic Assn. (sec., treas. 2001—). E-mail: mkthoren@aol.com.

THORSEN, NANCY DAIN, real estate broker; b. Edwardsville, Ill., 1944; d. Clifford Earl and Suzanne Eleanor (Kribs) Dain; m. David Massie, 1968 (div. 1975); 1 child, Suzanne Dain Massie; m. James Hugh Thorsen, May 30, 1980. BSc in Mktg., So. Ill. U., 1968, MSc in Bus. Edn., 1975; grad., Realtor Inst., Idaho, 1983. Cert. residential and investment specialist, fin. instr., luxury home mktg. specialist, 2004; designated real estate instr. State of Idaho; accredited buyer rep. Personnel officer J.H. Little & Co. Ltd., London, 1969-72; instr. in bus. edn. Spl. Sch. Dist. St. Louis, 1974-77; mgr. mktg./ops. Isis Foods, Inc., St. Louis, 1978-80; asst. mgr. store Stix, Baer & Fuller, St. Louis, 1980; assoc. broker Century 21 Sayer Realty, Inc., Idaho Falls, Idaho, 1981-88, RE/MAX Homestead Realty, 1989—. Spkr. in field; real estate fin. instr. State of Idaho Real Estate Commn., 1994; founder Nancy Thorsen Seminars, 1995. Bd. dirs. Idaho Vol., Boise, 1981-84, Idaho Falls Symphony, 1982; pres. Friends of Idaho Falls Libr., 1981-83; chmn. Idaho Falls Mayor's Com. for Vol. Coordination, 1981-84; power leader Power Program, 1995; mem. Mtn. River Valley Red Cross, chair capital campaign, cmty. gifts chair ARC. Recipient Idaho Gov.'s award, 1982, cert. appreciation City of Idaho Falls/Mayor Campbell, 1982, 87, Civilian Disting. Pres. award, 1990, Bus. Women of the Yr. award C. of C., 1998; named to Two Million Dollar Club, 1987, 88, Four Million Dollar Club, 1989, 90, Top Investment Sales Person for Eastern Idaho, 1985, Realtor of Yr. Idaho Falls Bd. Realtors, 1990, Outstanding Realtors Active in Politics, Mem. of Yr. Idaho Assn. Realtors, 1991, Women of Yr. Am. Biog. Inst., 1991, Profiles of Top Prodrs. award Real Estate Edn. Assn., Above the Crowd award 1997; named Western Region Power Leader, Darryl Davis Seminars. Mem. Nat. Spkrs. Assn., Idaho Falls Bd. Realtors (chmn. Orientation 1982-83, chmn. edn. 1983, chmn. legis. com. 1989, 95—, chmn. program com. 1990, 91), Idaho Assn. Realtors (pres. Million Dollar Club 1988-2001, edn. com. 1990-93), Women's Coun. Realtors, Am. Bus. Women's Assn., So. Ill. U. Alumni Assn., Idaho Falls C. of C. (Bus. Woman of the Yr.-Professions, 1997), newcomers Club, Civitan (pres. Idaho Falls chpt. 1988-89, Civitan of Yr. 1986, 97, Outstanding Pres. award 1990, Hall of Fame 1998), Real Estate Educators Assn. Office: RE/MAX Homestead Inc 1301 E 17th St Ste 1 Idaho Falls ID 83404-6273 E-mail: thorsen@srv.net.

THORTON, ANGELICA, newscaster; b. Mass. BA in Broadcast Journalism, Emerson Coll. Anchor, reporter KECI-TV, Missoula, Mont.; gen. assignment reporter NBC 17, Raleigh, NC, 1999—. Recipient award, Soc. Profl. Journalists, 1999. Avocations: skiing, hiking, soccer. Office: NBC 17 Studios 1205 Front St Raleigh NC 27609

THOYER, JUDITH REINHARDT, lawyer; b. Mt. Vernon, N.Y., July 29, 1940; d. Edgar Allen and Florence (Mayer) Reinhardt; m. Michael E. Thoyer, June 30, 1963; children: Erinn Thoyer Rhodes, Michael John. AB with honors, U. Mich., 1961; LLB summa cum laude, Columbia U., 1965. Bar: N.Y. 1966, D.C. 1984. Law libr. U. Ghana, Accra, Africa, 1963-64; assoc. Paul, Weiss, Rifkind, Wharton & Garrison, N.Y.C., 1966-75, ptnr., 1975—. Mem. TriBar Opinion Com., 1995—. Bd. visitors Law Sch. Columbia U., N.Y.C., 1991—; bd. dirs. Women's Action Alliance, N.Y.C., 1975-89, pro bono counsel, 1975-97; mem. Women's Coun. Dem. Senatorial, campaign com., 1993-97; organizing com. Alumnae Columbia Law Sch., 1996—. Recipient medal for excellence, Columbia Law Sch., 2003. Mem. N.Y. County Lawyers Assn. (mem. securities and exchs. com. 1976-79), Assn. of Bar of City of N.Y. (mem. securities regulation com. 1976-79, mem. recruitment of lawyers com. 1980-82, mem. com. on mergers, acquisitions and corp. control contests 1996—). Home: 1115 5th Ave Apt 3B New York NY 10128-0100 Office: Paul Weiss Rifkind Et Al 1285 Ave of Americas New York NY 10019-6028

THRALL, EILEEN FOWLER, real estate broker, government staff official; b. Washington, July 20, 1943; d. Edward Earl and Violet Wells (Ashford) Fowler; m. William Anthony Thrall, Feb. 2, 1963; children: James Edward, Jennifer Dianne, John Joseph. AS in Bus. Adminstrn., Am. U., 1964; BSBA, George Mason U., 1985. Cert. real estate broker. Girl Friday property mgmt. rental cashier The Carey Winston, Co., Washington, 1964-65; adminstrv. asst., asst. rental mgr. Reston, Va., Inc., 1965-67; cmty. columnist Potomac News, Woodbridge, Va., 1981-85; realtor, salesperson Old Mill Properties ERA Tatum, Inc., Prince William, Va., 1985-92; realtor, assoc. broker ERA Tatum, Inc., Better Homes Realty, Prince William, 1992—; asst. to chmn. bd., county supr. Prince William County Govt., Prince William, 1992-99. Bd. dirs. Prince William County Pub. Schs., 1991-92; mem. magisterial dist. chair Prince William County Dem. Com., 1975-2001; mem. steering com. No. Va. C.C. Tech. Consortium, Woodbridge, Va., 1991-98; mem. various offices Dumfries Meth. Ch., 1977—; mem. Bd. Zoning Appeals, 2002-, Prince William. Mem. Nat. Assn. Realtors, Va. Assn. Realtors, Prince William Assn. Realtors. Democrat. Methodist. Avocations: reading, bicycling, boating, camping, cooking. Home: 18312 Possum Point Rd Dumfries VA 22026-2817 Office: Better Homes Realty Inc 16150 Country Club Dr Dumfries VA 22026-1633

THRASH, PATRICIA ANN, educational association administrator; b. Grenada, Miss., May 4, 1929; d. Lewis Edgar and Weaver (Betts) T. BS, Delta State Coll., 1950; MA, Northwestern U., 1953, PhD, 1959; cert. Inst. Edn. Mgmt., Harvard U., 1983; EdD (hon.), Vincennes U., 1997; DHL, Drake U., 1997, Adrian Coll., 1998. Tchr. high sch. English, Clarksdale, Miss., 1950-52; head resident Northwestern U., 1953-55, asst. to dean women, 1955-58, asst. dean women, 1958-60, lectr. edn., 1959-65, dean women, 1960-69, assoc. prof. edn., 1965-72, assoc. dean students, 1969-71; asst. exec. sec. Commn. on Instns. Higher Edn., North Central Assn. Colls. and Schs., 1972-73, assoc. exec. dir., 1973-76, assoc. dir., 1976-87, exec. dir., 1988-96; exec. dir. emeritus, 1997—. Mem. adv. panel Am. Coun. on Edn., MIVER program evaluation mil. base program, 1991-94; mem. nat. adv. panel Nat. Ctr. Postsecondary Tchg., Learning & Assessment, 1991-95. Author (with others): Handbook of College and University Administration, 1970; editor Jour. Northwestern U. Inst. for Learning in Retirement, 2000-02; contbr. articles to ednl. jours. Bd. dirs. Delta State U. Found., 2000-2002. Mem. Nat. Assn. Women Deans and Counselors (v.p. 1967-69, pres. 1972-73), Ill. Assn. Women Deans and Counselors (sec. 1961-63, pres. 1964-66), Am. Coll. Pers. Assn. (editl. bd. jour. 1971-74), Coun. Student Pers. Assns. in Higher Edn. (program nominations com. 1974-75, adv. panel Am. Coll. Testing Coll. Outcome Measures project 1977-78, staff Coun. on Postsecondary Accreditation project for evaluation nontraditional edn. 1977-78, mem. editl. bd. Jour. Higher Edn. 1975-80, guest editor Mar.-Apr. 1979, co-editor NCA Quar. 1988-96, vice-chair regional accrediting dirs. group 1993, exec. com. Nat. Policy Bd. for Higher Edn. Inst. 1993-95), Mortar Bd. (hon.), Phi Delta Theta, Pi Lambda Theta, Alpha Psi Omega, Alpha Lambda Delta. Methodist. Home: 2337 Hartrey Ave Evanston IL 60201-2552

THRASHER, DIANNE ELIZABETH, mathematics educator, computer consultant; b. Brockton, Mass., July 11, 1945; m. George Thomas Thrasher, Jan. 28, 1967; children: Kimberly Elizabeth, Noelle Elizabeth. BA in Math., Bridgewater State Coll., 1967, diploma in computer sci., 1987. Cert. secondary math., history tchr. Tchr. math. Plymouth/Carver Regional Schs., Plymouth, Mass., 1976-78, Alden Sch., Duxbury, Mass., 1980-82, Marshfield (Mass.) H.S., 1982-84; computer cons. TC2I-Thrasher Computer Cons. and Instrn., Duxbury, Mass., 1988—; dir., owner Internat. Ednl. Franchise, 1991-95; owner Duxbury Math. Ctr. K-Adult, 1995—. Owner New Eng. Regional Kumon Ednl. Franchise, 1991-95, 2000—; Mass. State approved profl. point devel. provider for tchr. cert., 1996. Active U.S. Figure Skating Assn., Colorado Springs, 1978-85; 2d reader First Ch. Christ Scientist, Plymouth, 1971-73; bd. govs. Skating Club of Hingham, Mass., 1978-86, [illegible], dir. Learn to Skate program, 1983-85, mem. First Ch. Christ Scientist, Boston, 1964—; with New Eng. Regional Kumon Franchise Owners, 1991-95; charter mem. Nat. Adv. Coun. of the U.S. Navy Meml. Found., 1992, Mary Baker Eddy Libr. for the Betterment of Humanity, Boston, 2002. Recipient Presdl. Nomination for Excellence in Tng. Math., NSF, 1992, Ed Taylor Meml. Vol. Svc. award Skating Club Hingham, 1995, Amateur Photo award Internat. Libr. Photography, 1999. Mem. NAFE, AAUW, Math. Assn. Am., Am. Math. Soc., Am. Nat. Coun. Tchrs. Math, Duxbury Bus. Assn., Bostonian Soc., Nat. Hist. Trust and Preservation Soc., Smithsonian, Internat. Soc. Photographers (Amateur Photo award 1999). Avocations: antiques, bicycling, skating, sailing. Home: 140 Toby Garden St Duxbury MA 02332-4945 E-mail: sumizumi@aol.com.

THRASHER, FAY C. clinical psychologist; b. Wynne, Ark., Dec. 17, 1935; d. Andrew J. and Joy M. (Charles) Thrasher; children: Jeffrey K. Mitchell, Sidney J. Guidroz Jr. MEd, McNeese State U., 1963; MA, La. State U., 1967, PhD, 1970. Lic. psychologist. Chief psychologist Cmty. Mental Health, Lake Charles, La., 1970-73; clin. psychologist VA Hosp., Salisbury, N.C., 1973-76; chief psychologist VA Opt Clinic, San Antonio, 1976-77, Alvin C. York VA Med. Ctr., Murfreesboro, Tenn., 1977-87; clin. psychologist VA Med. Ctr., Alexandria, Va., 1990-95, chief psychologist, 1995—. Bd. dirs. Oasis Ministry, Pineville, La.; cons. to freedom cons., 1996—; bd. dirs. New Beginning Acad., Alexandria, treas., 1997—; cons. Bunkie Adolexcent Ctr., Bunkie Gen. Hosp., 1993—97. Chmn. Combined Fed. Campaign, Murfreesboro, 1985—86. Mem.: APA, Am. Coll. Forensic Examiners, Nat. Register. Avocations: duplicate bridge, antique collector, renovation of old homes, art, music. Home: 303 Rain Tree Pl Pineville LA 71360-5472 Office: Freedom Counseling Ctr 2809 Donahue Ferry Rd Pineville LA 71360-4513 Office Phone: 318-473-0010 x 2626.

THRASHER, JENNIFER NICHOLS, music educator; b. Greenville, S.C., Apr. 14, 1976; d. T. Farrell and Alice Williamson Nichols; m. Daniel Gregory Thrasher, Dec. 7, 1996; children: Taylor Elizabeth, Hunter Gregory. B in Music Edn., Ga. Coll. and State U., 1999. Primary music educator Worth County Primary Sch., Sylvester, Ga., 1999—2000; sch. sec. Baldwin H.S., Milledgeville, Ga., 2000—01; elem. music educator Midway Elem. Sch., Milledgeville, 2001—; ch. music min. Manley Meml. Bapt. Ch., Eatonton, Ga., 2000—. Mem.: Profl. Assn. Ga. Educators, Ga. Music Educators Assn. Republican. Avocations: singing, reading, water sports, religious Bible study. Home: 105 S Oak St Haddock GA 31033 Office: Midway Elem Sch 101 Carl Vinson Rd SE Milledgeville GA 31061 Business E-Mail: jthrasher@baldwin.k12.ga.us.

THRASHER, ROSE MARIE, critical care nurse, community health nurse; b. Urbana, Ohio, Jan. 19, 1948; d. Jesse and Anna Frances (Clark) T. Student, Mercy Med. Ctr. Sch. Med. Tech., Springfield, Ohio, 1966—67, Wittenberg U., 1969—70; BSN, Ohio State U., 1974, BA in Anthropology, 1994, BA in Art History, 1997, BA in Geography, 2002. RN, Ohio; bd. cert. cmty. health nurse ANA; cert. provider BCLS and ACLS, Am. Heart Assn., CCRN, AACN; cert. asthma mgmt. edn. Am. Lung Assn. Ohio. Pub. health nurse Columbus (Ohio) Health Dept., 1977-78; critical care nurse VA Med. Ctr., San Francisco, 1981, Staff Builders Health Care Svc., Oakland, Calif., 1975-76, 81-85; supr., case mgr., home health nurse, passport program and intermittent care program Interim Health Care (formerly Med. Pers. Pool), Columbus, 1976-77, 85—, chart reviewer, 1996-98; IRP nurse Ohio State U. Hosps. East, Columbus, 1999—2003; ind. home health nurse, provider med. svcs. State of Ohio Dept. Human Svcs., 1999—. Chart reviewer Interim Health Care Support Svcs., Columbus, 1997. Acad. scholar Wittenberg U., Ohio State U. Mem. AACN, ANA (coun. cmty. health nursing), AAUW, AAAS, Internat. Union Anthrop. and Ethnol. Scis., N.Y. Acad. Scis., Ohio Nurses Assn., Intravenous Nurses Soc., Ohio State U. Alumni Assn., Am. Anthrop. Assn., Midwest Art History Soc., Coll. Art Assn., Nat. Mus. Women in Arts, Nat. Women's Hall of Fame, Ohio Acad. Sci., Ohio State U. Coll. of Nursing Alumni Soc. Business E-Mail: thrasher.2@osu.edu.

THREADCRAFT, KELLI KING, speech pathology/audiology services professional; b. Huntsville, Ala., Jan. 25, 1976; d. Marion Bierne and Carol Freeman King; m. Joshua Howard Threadcraft, May 20, 2000. B in Comm. Disorders, Auburn (Ala.) U., 1998; M, U. Montevallo, 2000. Cert. clin. competence in speech-lang. pathology. Speech-lang. therapist Montevallo (Ala.) Elem. Sch., 2000—01; spl. edn. tchr. Tarrant (Ala.) Elem. Sch., 2001—; pvt. practice speech-lang. therapy Birmingham, Ala., 2003. Mem.: Speech and Hearing Assn. Ala., Am. Sppech and Hearing Assn., Jr. League. Avocations: walking, smocking.

THRIFT, JULIANNE STILL, academic administrator; b. Barnwell, S.C. m. Ashley Ormand Thrift; children: Lindsay, Laura. BA, MEd, U. S.C.; PhD in Pub. Policy, George Washington U. Formerly asst. exec. dir. Nat. Assn. Coll. and Univ. Attys.; ombudsman U. S.C.; exec. dir. Nat. Inst. Ind. Colls. and Univs., 1982-88; exec. v.p. Nat. Assn. Ind. Colls. and Univs., Washington, 1988-91; pres. Salem Acad. and Coll., Winston-Salem, N.C., 1991—. Office: Salem Coll Office of the President Winston Salem NC 27108-0548

THURMAN, KAREN L. former congresswoman, lobbyist; b. Rapid City, S.D., Jan. 12, 1951; d. Lee Searle and Donna (Altfillisch) Loveland; m. John Patrick Thurman, 1973; children: McLin Searl and Liberty Lee. BA, U. Fla., 1973. Mem. Dunnellon City Coun. (Fla.), 1975—83; mayor of Dunnellon Dunnellon, 1979-81; mem. Monroe Regional Med. Ctr. Governancy Com., Comprehensive Plan Tech. Adv. Com., Fla. State Senate, 1983—93, U.S. Congress from 5th Fla. dist., 1993—2002, ways and means com ., 1996—2002, House agrl. comm., comm. on gov. reform and oversight; lobbyist eAppeals, Miami, 2004—, Freedom Healthcare, Hollywood, 2004—. Del. Fla. Dem. Conv., Dem. Nat. Conv., 1980; mem. Regional Energy Action com. Recipient Svc. Above Self award Dunnellon C. of C., 1980, Regional Coun. Appreciation for Svc. award. Mem. Dunnellon C. of C. (dir.), Fla. Horseman's Children's Soc. (charter). Democrat. Episcopalian.

THURMAN, MARY ANNE, foundation administrator; b. Dallas, Dec. 17, 1937; d. Lon B. and Lottie Belle Evans; m. Billy R. Thurman, June 21, 1956; children: Steven M., Todd E. Grad., Honey Grove (Tex.) High Sch. Regional supr. Capital Healthcare, Dallas, 1973—83; exec. v.p. Hall-Voyer Found., Honey Grove, Tex., 1985—. Mem. Texoma Coun. Govt. Econ. Devel. Coun., Sherman, Tex., 2000—; dir. Friends of Libr., Honey Grove, 1986—2000. Mem.: Honey Grove C. of C. (pres., sec. 1988—2002), Oakwood Cemetery Assn. (pres. 1996—2000, sec. 2001), Red River Valley Tourism Assn. (bd. dirs. 1989—92), Kiwanis (dir. 1998—2000). Avocations: reading, piano. Office: Hall Voyer Found PO Box 47 Honey Grove TX 75446 E-mail: thruman@honeygrove.org.

THURMAN, UMA KARUNA, actress; b. Boston, Apr. 29, 1970; d. Robert and Nena (von Schlebrugge) T.; m. Gary Oldman, 1990 (div. 1992); m. Ethan Hawke, 1998; 2 children. Appeared in films Kaze no tani no Naushika, 1984, Kiss Daddy Good Night, 1987, Johnny Be Good, 1988, Dangerous Liaisons, 1988, The Adventures of Baron Munchausen, 1989, Where the Heart Is, 1990, Henry and June, 1990, Cheerleader Camp II, 1990, Final Analysis, 1992, Jennifer Eight, 1992, Mad Dog and Glory, 1993, Even Cowgirls Get the Blues, 1993, Pulp Fiction, 1994 (Acad. award nom. Best Supporting Actress), A Month By the Lake, 1995, The Truth About Cats and Dogs, 1996, Beautiful Girls, 1996, Les Miserables, 1997,

The Avengers, 1997, Batman & Robin, 1997, Gattaca, 1997, Vatel, 1999, Sweet and Lowdown, 1999, Tape, 2001, Chelsea Walls, 2001, Kill Bill: Volume 1, 2003, Paycheck, 2003, Kill Bill: Volume 2, 2004; TV movies include Robin Hood, 1991, Duke of Groove, 1996, The Golden Bowl, 2000, Hysterical Blindness, 2002 (also exec. prodr.). Office: Creative Artists Agy care Brian Lourd 9830 Wilshire Blvd Beverly Hills CA 90212-1804*

THURNER, AGNES H. retired administrative secretary; b. Manistique, Mich., July 21, 1934; d. Joseph and Elise Kaulfuerst; m. James C. Wegner, June 5, 1954 (div. 1969); children: Robin, Leonard; m. Maximilian Franz Joseph Thurner, May 29, 1993. Dir. Statesman's Club of First Federal Savings, 1969—79; pres. Sq. Dance Assn., Milw., 1987-2000; ret., 2000. Author: Square Dancing in Wisconsin, 1998. Pollworker Ozaukee County, Mequon, Wis., 1995—. Mem. Wis. Regional Writers Assn. Lutheran. Avocations: reading, music, crafts, dance, composer/lyricist.

THURSTON, BONNIE BOWMAN, religious educator, minister, poet; b. Bluefield, W.Va., Oct. 5, 1952; d. Ernest Venoy and Eleanor Sabina (King) Bowman; m. Burton Bradford Thurston, May 29, 1980 (dec. Nov. 1990). BA summa cum laude, Bethany Coll., 1974; MA, U. Va., 1975, PhD, 1979; postgrad. Harvard Div. Sch., 1983, Eberhard Karls U., Fed. Republic Germany, 1983-84, Ecole Biblique, Jerusalem, 1993. Ordained to ministry Disciples of Christ Ch., 1984. Instr., asst. dean U. Va., Charlottesville, 1979-80; adj. prof. Wheeling Coll. (name now Wheeling Jesuit U.), W.Va. 1980-81, asoc. prof., chair dept. theology, 1985—95, assoc. prof. N.T. Pitts. Theol. Sem., 1995-99, William F. Orr prof., 1999—2002, Orr chair, 2002—; asst. prof. Bethany Coll., W.Va., 1981-83; vis. scholar Harvard U. Div. Sch., Cambridge, 1983; tutor Inst. Study of Christian Origins, Tübingen, Fed. Republic Germany, 1983-85; co-pastor Knoxville Ch., Pitts., 1982-83, Taylorstown Christian Ch., 1985-88, Chapel Hill Christian Ch., 1994-97, First Christian Wheeling, 2003; lectr. Sch. Religion, Council of Chs., Wheeling, 1980-81, 85-90. Author: The Widows, 1989, Wait Here and Watch., 1989, Spiritual Life in the Early Church, 1993, Women in the NT, 1998, To Everything a Season, 1999, Preaching Mark, 2002, (vols. of poetry) The Heart's Land, 2001, Hints and Glimpses, 2004; assoc. editor: Catholic Biblical Quarterly; contbr. articles to profl. jours., poetry to jours. Dupont fellow U. Va., 1975-76. Mem. Cath. Bibl. Assn., Soc. Bibl. Lit., Internat. Thomas Merton Soc. (bd. dirs.), Soc. for Buddhist-Christian Studies, Disciples Hist. Soc. Avocations: gardening, music, cooking. Office: PO Box 2258 Wheeling WV 26003

THURSTON, KATHLEEN, academic administrator; Project mgr. Ideal Constrn., Inc., Honolulu, v.p. ops., pres., Thurston Pacific, Inc., Honolulu, 1997—; commr. Dept. Hawaiian Home Lands; mem. bd. regents U. Hawaii, Honolulu, 2001—. Bd. dirs. Bishop Mus., Office of Hawaiian Affairs Native Hawaiian Revolving Loan Fund. Mem.: Gen. Contrs. Assn. of Hawaii (past pres.). Office: University of Hawaii 2444 Dole St Honolulu HI 96822

THURSTON, SALLY A. lawyer; b. Glens Falls, N.Y., 1961; BS, Cornell U., 1983; JD, Harvard U., 1986. Bar: N.Y. 1987. Ptnr. Skadden, Arps, Slate, Meagher & Flom, N.Y.C.; v.p., tax counsel NDC, Inc., N.Y.C., 1997. Office: Skadden Arps Slate Meagher & Flom 4 Times Sq Fl 24 New York NY 10036-6595

THURSTON, TINA L. archaeologist, educator; b. N.Y.C., Sept. 11, 1958; d. Ted Thurston and Danya Krupska; m. Nestor Enrique Zarragoitía. BA, MA in Anthropology, Hunter Coll., CUNY, 1990; PhD in Anthropology, U. Wis.-Madison, 1996. Archaeologist Wis. State Hist. Soc., Madison, 1994—96; asst. prof. Millsaps Coll., Jackson, Miss., 1997—99; dir. Thy Archaeol. Project, Thisted, Denmark, 1998—; asst. prof. Baylor U., Waco, Tex., 1999—2002, dir. Inst. of Archaeology, 2000—02; asst. prof. SUNY, Buffalo, 2002—. Author: Landscapes of Power, Landscapes of Conflict, 2001. Fellow, NSF, 1990—92; grantee, 1992—93, 1998, 2000—02, 2003—. Mem.: North Atlantic Biocultural Orgn., Am. Anthrop. Assn., Soc. Am. Archaeology.

TIBBS, MARTHA JANE PULLEN, civic worker; b. Memphis, Feb. 12, 1932; d. John Thomas Jr. and Martha Frances (Gragg) Pullen; m. Eugene Edward Tibbs; children: Martha Katherine, Eugene Edward Jr. BSBA, U. Tenn., 1953; MA Edn., U. Memphis, 1958. Cert. tchr., social worker, Tenn. Tchr. Lausanne Sch., Memphis, 1954-55, Millington H.S., Memphis, 1955-56, Presbyn. Day Sch., Memphis, 1956-57, St. Mary's Episcopal Sch., Memphis, 1958-60; social worker Tenn. Dept. Pub. Welfare, Memphis, 1962-63. Author geneal. works. Mem. Memphis Vol. Svc. Bd., 1963-64; mem. Shelby County Hist. Comm., 1983-97, commr., 1983—; block worker Cancer, Kidney and Heart Fund, Memphis, 1984—; sec., treas. Eastland Presbyterian Ch. Mem.: DAR (past chpt. regent, sec.-treas. regents coun.), AAUW, NEA, Tenn. Geneal. Soc., Tenn. Tchrs. Assn., Tenn. Soc. Pres. Founders and Patriots of Am., Soc. Descendants of Knights Most Noble Order of Garter, Colonial Order of Crown, Tenn. State DAR (transp. chmn. 2001—), Cleve. Jr. Aux., Cleve. Med. Aux. (sec./treas.), West Tenn. Hist. Soc., Chicasaw Dist. DAR Sch. (Tenn. state vice chmn. DAR schs., parliamentarian Zachariah Davies chpt., chmn. Zachariah Davies chpt.), Nat. Registrar Daus. of Founders and Patriots Am. (v.p. Tenn. chpt., past Tenn. state registrar), Tenn. State Registrar Founders and Patriots (pres. 2003—), Nat. Soc. Colonial Dames XVII Century (1st v.p., pres. 2003—, 2d v.p. past treas. Chucaqua chpt.), Nat. Soc. So. Dames Am. (historian 2001—02, sec. 2002—, past pres. Memphis chpt., past state pres.), Colonial Dames Am., Tenn. State Dames of Ct. of Honor (pres. 2003—, historian, 1st v.p., nat. def. chmn.), Sovereign Colonial Soc. Ams. Royal Descent, Memphis Scottish Soc., Am. Clan Donald Soc., Am. Clan Gregor Soc., Family of Bruce Soc., Planetgenet Soc., Nat. Soc. Magna Charta Dames and Barons (past state sec. 2000—02, past Magna Carta sec. West Tenn. chpt. 2001—02, treas. West Tenn. chpt. 2002—), Cleve. Garden Club (past pres.), U. Club Memphis, Early Settlers Shelby County (registrar 1988, bd. dirs. 1992—, sec. 1998—, pres. 2002—), Nineteenth Century Club (newsletter editor 1985—88, sec. 1993—95, corr. sec. 1999—), Racquet Club, Cleve. Women's Club, Alpha Omega Pi. Republican. Presbyterian. Avocations: art, genealogy, computers, dance, tennis. Home: 2008 Massey Rd Memphis TN 38119-6404

TIBBS, SUE, state representative; b. Tulsa, Okla., Oct. 6, 1934; d. Clyde and Frances (VanSlyke) Sloan; m. Milton Homer Tibbs; children: Debra West, Kelli Dodd. Student, Tulsa Jr. Coll. Mem. Okla. Ho. of Reps., 2001—. Named Woman of Yr. Republican. Office: State Capitol 2300 N Lincoln Blvd Rm 323 Oklahoma City OK 73105

TICE, PAMELA PARADIS, scientific editor, writer; b. Hutchinson, Minn., Sept. 1, 1955; d. Paul Edward, Sr. and Mary LaVerne (Hebert) Paradis; m. Jeffrey Johns Powell, June 17, 1977 (div. July 1982); m. Christopher Allen Tice, Aug. 25, 1997. BA, Coll. of St. Scholastica, 1977. Statis./sec. U. Tex. M.D. Anderson Cancer Ctr., Houston, 1978-87; data coord. Baylor Coll. Medicine, Houston, 1987-88, editl. asst., 1988-90, sr. editor, 1992-2000, rsch. assoc., 2000—; dept. editor U. Tex. Med. Sch., Houston, 1990-91; editor, Houston medicine HCA Ctr. for Health Excell., Houston, 1991-92; exec. asst. U. Tex. Sch. Nursing, Houston, 1991-92. Mem. scope and mandate task force, Coun. of Sci. Editors, Chgo., 1996. Editor-in-chief: Am. Med. Writers Assn. Jour., 1992-95 (Apex awards 1995, 96, 97, Matrix award 1996, 2000, 2001, others). Recipient Presdl. Alumni award, Coll. of St. Scholastica, 2003. Mem. AAAS, Am. Med. Writers Assn. (chpt. sec. 1989-90, chpt. treas. 1990-92, chpt. pres.-elect 1992-93, chpt. pres. 1993-94, chpt. past pres. 1994-95, chpt. dir.-at-large 2001-2003, chair McGovern Award com. 2003-04, Chpt. Svc. award 1994, Assn. Pres. award 1993, Assn. Leadership award 1995), Coun. of Sci. Editors, Bd. of Editors in the Life Scis. (diplomate 2002), Assn. for Women in Comm. Office: Baylor Coll Medicine Dept Family & Cmty Medicine 3701 Kirby Dr Ste 600 Houston TX 77098-3926 E-mail: ptice@bcm.tmc.edu.

TICER, PATRICIA, state senator; m. Jack Ticer; 4 children. Grad., Sweet Briar Coll. Councilwoman City of Alexandria, Va., 1982-84, vice mayor, 1984-90, appointed mayor, 1991-92, mayor, 1992-95; state senator Commonwealth of Va., 1995—. Mem. Agrl., Conservation and Natural Resources Com., Rehab. and Social Svcs. Com., Local Govt. Com., 1995—; vice chair, Joint Com. on Tech. and Sci., former chair Metro Washington Coun. of Govts.; former mem., bd. dirs. No. Va. Transp. Commn., chmn., 1994; bd. trustees Land Conservation Found. commn. on Early Childhood and Child Day Care Programs. Office: City Hall 301 King St Alexandria VA 22314-3211 Also: Va Senate 429 Gen Assembly Bldg Richmond VA 23219 E-mail: patsy@tidalwave.net.

TICER, TERRI JEAN, sales executive; b. Childress, Tex., Apr. 15, 1955; d. Jerry H. and J. Colene (Eudey) T. AA, Clarendon Jr. Coll., 1977; BS, W. Tex. State U., 1979. Human svcs. dir. S. Plains Coll., Plainview, Tex., 1979-81; sales rep. Avon Products, N.Y.C., 1981-2001. Contbr. articles to profl. jours. Vol. Hospice of Plains, Plainview, 1985—2002, Meals on Wheels, 1997—98, 2003—, Hale County Crisis Ctr., 2002; mem. Faith in Sharing House, 1985—89, 1995, Friends of Libr., Plainview, 1986—91, Humane Soc., Plainview, 1987—92; chmn. Youth Group Reunion, 1990—91; mem. disaster team ARC, 1997—2000; vol. Muscular Dystrophy Jailathon, 1997—2002; mem. W. Tex. State U. Alumni Assn., 2002—; bd. dirs. Big Bros./Big Sisters, 1986—88, City of Plainview Blue Eyes, 2002—. Mem.: AAUW (membership v.p. 1987—89, chmn. edn. found. 1989—92, hosp. aux. 1992—98), Plainview Writers Guild (treas. 1993—96), Austin Writers League (mem. 1993—96), Toastmasters (v.p. 2002—03, sergeant-at-arms 2004—), Plainview Lions Breakfast Club (treas. 1995—97, newsletter ed. 1995—98, bd. dirs. 1998—), Plainview/Hale County Insate Hands Program (co-dir. 2002—), Plainview C. of C. (mem. 2002—). Avocations: reading, writing short stories, photography, weights. Home: 2503 W 13th St Apt 5 Plainview TX 79072-4869

TICHY, SUSAN HASTINGS, music educator; d. John and Jean Hastings; m. Rudolph S. Tichy, July 27, 1985; children: Mary Sue, Matthew. MusB, SUNY, Fredonia, 1981; MusM, MFA, SUNY, Buffalo, 1985. Cert. tchr. N.Y., 1985. Music tchr. Batavia (N.Y.) City Schs., 1981—83; grad. tchg. asst. SUNY, Buffalo, 1983—85, lectr. music edn., 1985—99; music tchr. Iroquois Ctrl. Schs., Elma, NY, 1999—. Editor: (music contest manual) New York State School Music Association Manual. Bd. dirs. Lancaster (N.Y.) Town Band, 1991, Amherst Symphony. Mem.: Erie County Music Educators' Assn., N.Y. State Sch. Music Assn. (adjudicator 1985—). Avocations: musical performance, church volunteer work. Office: Iroquois Central Schools Box 32 Elma NY 14059 E-mail: sue_tichy@iroquois.wnyric.org.

TICKNOR, CAROLYN M. computer company executive; BA in Psychology, U. Redlands, Calif.; MA in Indsl. Psychology, San Francisco State U.; MBA, Stanford U. From programming ops. mgr. to pres., CEO Hewlett-Packard Co., Palo Alto, Calif., 1977-94, pres., CEO laser jet imaging sys., 1994—. Office: Hewlett Packard Co 300 Hanover St Palo Alto CA 94304

TIDBALL, M. ELIZABETH PETERS, physiologist, educator, science administrator, researcher; b. Anderson, Ind., Oct. 15, 1929; d. John Winton and Beatrice (Ryan) Peters; m. Charles S. Tidball, Oct. 25, 1952. BA, Mt. Holyoke Coll., 1951, LHD, 1976; MS, U. Wis., 1955, PhD, 1959; MTS summa cum laude, Wesley Theol. Sem., 1990; DSc (hon.), Wilson Coll., 1973, Trinity Coll., 1974, Cedar Crest Coll., 1977, U. of South, 1978, Goucher Coll., 1979, St. Mary-of-The-Woods Coll., 1986; LittD (hon.), Regis Coll., 1980, Coll. St. Catherine, 1980, Alverno Coll., 1989; HHD (hon.), St. Mary's Coll., 1977, Hood Coll., 1982; LLD (hon.), St. Joseph Coll., 1983; LHD (hon.), Skidmore Coll., 1984, Marymount Coll., 1985, Converse Coll., 1985, Mt. Vernon Coll., 1986. Tchg. asst. physiology dept. U. Wis., 1952-55, 58-59; rsch. asst. anatomy dept. U. Chgo., 1955-56, rsch. asst. physiology dept., 1956-58; USPHS postdoctoral fellow NIH, Bethesda, Md., 1959-61; staff pharmacologist Hazleton Labs., Falls Church, Va., 1961, cons., 1962; assoc. in physiology George Washington U. Med. Ctr., 1960-62, asst. rsch. prof. dept. pharmacology, 1962-64, assoc. rsch. prof. dept. physiology, 1964-70, rsch. prof., 1970-71, prof., 1971-94, prof. emeritus, 1994—; asst. dir. M of Theol. Studies program Wesley Theol Sem., 1993-94; disting. rsch. scholar Hood Coll., Frederick, Md., 1994—, co-dir. Tidball Ctr. for Study of Ednl. Environments, 1994—. Lucie Stern Disting. vis. prof. natural scis. Mills Coll., 1980; scholar in residence Coll. Preachers, 1984, Salem Coll., 1985, Wesley Theol. Sem., 1992; Disting. scholar in residence So. Meth. U., 1985; vis. trustee prof. Skidmore Coll., 1995; cons. FDA, 1966-67, assoc. sci. coord. sci. assocs. tng. programs, 1966-67; com. on NIH tng. programs and fellowships NAS, 1972-75; faculty summer confs. Am. Youth Found., 1967-78; founder, dir. Summer Seminars for Women Am. Youth Found., 1987-95; cons. for instl. rsch. Wellesley Coll., 1974-75; exec. sec. com. on edn. and employment women in sci. and engrng. Commn. on Human Resources, NRC/NAS, 1974-75, vice-chmn., 1977-82; cons., staff officer NRC/NAS, 1974-75; cons. Woodrow Wilson Nat. Fellowship Found., 1975-99, NSF, 1974-91; bd. mentor Assn. Governing Bds. of Univs. and Colls., 1991—, Gale Fund for the Study of Trusteeship Adv. Comm., 1992-98; cons. Women's Coll. Coalition Rsch. Adv. Com., 1992—; Single Gender Schooling Working Group, U.S. Dept. Edn., 1992-94, women's colls. roundtable, 1998; rep. to D.C. Commn. on Status of Women, 1972-75; nat. panelist Am. Coun. on Edn., 1983-90; panel mem. Congl. Office of Tech. Assessment, 1986-87; fellows selection com., fellows mentor Coll. Preachers, 1992—. Lead author: Taking Women Seriously, 1999; columnist Trusteeship, 1993-95; mem. editl. bd. Jour. Higher Edn., 1979-84, cons. editor, 1984—; mem. editl. bd. Religion and Intellectual Life, 1983—; contbr. articles to profl. jours. Trustee Mt. Holyoke Coll., 1968-73, vice chmn., 1972-73, trustee fellow, 1988—; trustee Hood Coll., 1972-84, 86-92, exec. com., 1974-84, 89-92, trustee emerita, 1997—; overseer Sweet Briar Coll., 1978-85, dir. emerita, 2003—; trustee Cathedral Choral Soc., 1976-90, pres. bd. trustees, 1982-84, hon. trustee, 1991—; trustee Skidmore Coll., 1988—, mem. exec. com., 1993—, trustee Bishop Claggett Ctr., 2003—; mem. governing bd. Coll. of Preachers, 1979-85, chmn., 1983-85; mem. governing bd. Protestant Episcopal Cathedral Found., 1983-85, mem. exec. com., 1983-85; bd. vis. Salem Coll., 1986-93; ctr. assoc. Nat. Resource Ctr., Girls Club Am., 1983-90; mem. governing bd. Buckinham's Choice Residents' Assn., 1999-2002. Named Outstanding Grad., The Penn Hall Sch., 1988; recipient Alumnae medal Honor, Mt. Holyoke Coll., 1971, Outstanding Svc. award, Am. Youth Found., 1975, Valuable Contbns. Gen. Alumni Assn. award, George Washington U., 1982, 1987, Pres.'s medal, 1999, Chestnut Hill medal Outstanding Achievement, Chestnut Hill Coll., Phila., 1987, Lifetime Svc. and Schoalrship award, Bd. Women's Coll. Coalition and Nation's Women's Coll. Presidents, 1998, Order of Merit, Cathedral Choral Soc., 2000, Shattuk fellowship, 1955—56, Mary E. Woolley fellowship, Mt. Holyoke Coll., 1958—59, postdoctoral fellowship, USPHS, 1959—61. Mem. AAAS, Am. Physiol. Soc. (chmn. task force on women in physiology 1973-80, com. on coms. 1977-80, mem. emeritus 1994—), Am. Assn. Higher Edn., Mt. Holyoke Alumnae Assn. (dir. 1966-70, 76-77), Histamine Club, Sigma Delta Epsilon, Sigma Xi. Episcopalian. Home: 4100 Cathedral Ave NW Washington DC 20016-3584 also: 3200 Baker Cir # I-235 Adamstown MD 21710

TIDD, JOYCE CARTER, etiquette educator; b. Chipley, FL, May 29, 1932; d. Brown Carter and Gussie Gurtrude Tiller; m. Matthew Heywood Tidd, Jan. 27, 1951; 1 child, Michael Heywood. Diploma, U. Ext. Conservatory, Chgo., 1971. Ch. choir dir. Hamp Stevens Meth. Ch., Columbus, Ga., 1949—50; co-chmn. of music Morningside Presbyn., Columbus, Ga., 1965—72; founder, owner Joyce Tidd Music Studio, Columbus, Ga., 1956—2001; founder, tchr. Sherwood Etiquette Sch., Columbus, Ga., 1996—2001. Home: 5846 Eula Ave Columbus GA 31909

TIEDGE-LAFRANIER, JEANNE MARIE, editor; b. N.Y.C., July 24, 1960; d. Richard Frederick and Joan Jean (Gerardo) Tiedge; m. John Daniel Lewis Lafranier, Oct. 8, 1989; children: Katelyn Ellen, John Richard. BA, Drew U., 1982. Asst. Denise Marcil Lit. Agy., N.Y.C., 1982-84; sr. editor New Am. Libr., N.Y.C., 1984-87, Warner Books, N.Y.C., 1987-95; editor corp. comm. Disticor, Ajax, Ont., Can., 1995—. Avocations: marathoner, equestrian.

TIEFEL, VIRGINIA MAY, librarian; b. Detroit, May 20, 1926; d. Karl and June Garland (Young) Brenkert; m. Paul Martin Tiefel, Jan. 25, 1947; children: Paul Martin Jr., Mark Gregory. BA in Elem. Edn., Wayne State U., 1962; MA in Library Sci., U. Mich., 1968. Librarian Birmingham Schs., Mich., 1967-68; librarian S. Euclid-Lyndhurst Schs., Cleve., 1968-69; acquisitions-reference librarian Hiram Coll., Ohio, 1969-77; head undergrad. libraries Ohio State U., Columbus, 1977-84, dir. library user edn., 1978-95, faculty outreach coord., 1995-98. Contbr. articles to profl. jours. Recipient Disting. Alumnus award U. Mich. Sch. Info. and Libr. Studies, 1993. Mem. ALA (v.p. Ohio sect. 1973-74, pres. 1974-75, Miriam Dudley Bibliographic Instrn. Librarian of Yr. 1986), Acad. Library Assn. Ohio (Outstanding Ohio Acad. Librarian 1984), Assn. Coll. and Research Libraries (chmn. bibliographic instrn. sect. com. on research 1983-84, chmn. com. on performance measures 1984-90). Lutheran. Home: 4711 Oak Bluff Ct Eau Claire WI 54701 E-mail: vtiefel@aol.com.

TIEFENTHAL, MARGUERITE AURAND, school social worker; b. Battle Creek, Mich., July 23, 1919; d. Charles Henry and Elisabeth Dirk (Hoekstra) Aurand; m. Harlan E. Tiefenthal, Nov. 26, 1942; children: Susan Ann, Daniel E., Elisabeth Amber, Carol Aurand. BS, Western Mich. U., 1941; MSW, U. Mich., 1950; postgrad., Coll. of DuPage, Ill., 1988-90. Tchr. No. High Sch., Flint, Mich., 1941-44, Cen. High Sch., Kalamazoo, 1944-45; acct. Upjohn Co., Kalamazoo, 1945-48; social worker Family Svc. Agy., Lansing, Mich., 1948-50, Pitts., 1950-55; sch. social worker Gower Sch. Dist., Hinsdale, Ill., 1962-70, Hinsdale (Ill.) Dist. 181, 1970-89, cons., 1989—; sch. social worker Villa Park (Ill.) Sch. Dist. 45, 1989; addictions counselor Mercy Hosp., 1990-92; asst. prof. sch. social work, liaison to pub. schs. Loyola U., Chgo., 1990-98, ret., 1998. Field instr. social work interns U. Ill., 1979-88; impartial due process hearing officer; mem. adv. com. sch. social work Ill. State Bd. Edn. approved programs U. Ill. and George Williams Coll.; speaker Nat. Conf. Sch. Social Work, Denver, U. Tex. Joint Conf. Sch. Social Work in Ill.; founder Marguerite Tiefenthal Symposium for Ill. Sch. Social Work Interns. Co-editor The School Social Worker and the Handicapped Child: Making P.L. 94-142 Work; sect. editor: Sch. Social Work Quarterly, 1979. Sec. All Village Caucus Village of Western Springs, Ill., mem. village disaster com.; deacon Presbyn. Ch. Western Springs, Sunday sch. tchr., mem. choir; instr. Parent Effectiveness, Teacher Effectiveness, STEP; trainer Widowed Persons Service Tng. Program for Vol. Aides AARP. Recipient Ill. Sch. Social Worker of Yr., 1982. Mem. Nat. Assn. Social Workers (chmn. exec. council on social work in schs.), Ill. Assn. Sch. Social Workers (past pres., past conf. chmn., conf. program chmn.), Ladies Libr. Assn., Sch. Social Workers Supervisors Group (del. to Ill. Commn. on Children), Programs. for Licensure of Social Work Practice in Ill., Ladies Libr. Assn. (Kalamazoo), LWV, DKG, PEO. Avocation: sewing. Home: 4544 Grand Ave Western Springs IL 60558-1545 also: 3151 West B Ave Plainwell MI 49080

TIEMANN, BARBARA JEAN, special education educator; b. Gothenberg, Nebr., Jan. 22, 1955; d. Thurl L. Rogge and Betty R. (Kent) Van Eperen; m. Robert L. Tiemann, June 3, 1977; children: Erich, Hans, Robin (dec.) BS in Elem. Edn., U. Nebr., 1987, MEd, 2000, MEd with severe/profound endorsement. Cert. tchr. Nebr., Fla. Kindergarten tchr. Ft. Pierce (Fla.) Elem. Sch., 1988-89, devel. kindergarten tchr., 1989; psychol. svcs. asst. Beatrice State Devel. Ctr., 1993—2000; resource tchr. Lincoln (Nebr.) Schs., 2000—. Mem. Creighton Parents Assn., Humanities Coun. Mem. NEA, Eastern Star, Lincoln Edn. Assn., Nebraska Edn. Assn., After 5, U. Nebraska Alumni, Compassionate Friends.

TIEMANN, JEANNINE E. music educator; b. Florissant, Mo., Nov. 24, 1970; d. Lambert Owen and Janet Evelyn T. BA in Music Edn., So. Ill. U. Edwardsville, 1994, MA in Music Edn., 1996. Cert. special tchr. K-12. Pvt. piano/voice instr. So. Ill. U., Edwardsville, 1991-99; choral dir. Edward A. Fulton Jr. High, O'Fallon, Ill., 1996—. Mem. Am. Choral Dirs. Assn., Music Educators Nat. Conf., Ill. State Music Tchrs. Assn., Ill. Music Educators Assn. (chmn. dist. 6 1999—), Sigma Alpha Iota (mem. award 1994, sword of honor 1994, sec. 1992-93, treas. 1993-94, v.p. mem. 1998-2000, sec. 2000-). Republican. Luth. Avocations: bowling, counted cross stitch. Office: Edward A Fulton Jr High 307 Kyle Rd O Fallon IL 62269-6611 E-mail: jtiemann@ofallon90.net.

TIENDA, MARTA, demographer, educator; b. Tex. PhD in Sociology, U. Tex., 1977. From asst. prof. to prof. rural sociology U. Wis., Madison, 1976—87; vis. prof. Stanford U., 1987; Ralph Lewis prof. sociology U. Chgo., 1994—97, chmn. dept. sociology, 1994—96; prof. sociology and pub. affairs Princeton U., NJ, 1997—, dir. office population rsch., 1998—2002, Maruice P. During '22 prof. demographic studies, 1999—. Rsch. assoc. office population rsch. Princeton U., 1997—; bd. dirs. Fed. Res. Bank N.Y. Co-author: Hispanics in the U.S. Economy, 1985, Hispanic Population of the United States, 1987, Divided Opportunities, 1988, The Color of Opportunity, 2001, Youth in Cities, 2002; contbr. articles to profl. jours. Trustee Jacobs Found. of Switzerland; bd. dirs. Princeton Med. Ctr. Guggenheim fellow. Fellow: AAAS, Am. Acad. Political Social Sci., Ctr. Advanced Study Behavioral Scis.; mem.: Internat. Union for Sci. Study of Population, Population Assn. Am. (past pres.), Am. Econ. Assn., Am. Sociol. Assn. Office: Office Population Rsch Princeton U 247 Wallace Hall Princeton NJ 08544-2091

TIERNEY, MAURA, actress; b. Boston, Feb. 3, 1965; m. Billy Morrissette, 1994. Student, NYU, Cir. in the Sq. Theatre Sch. Actor: (TV series) 704 Hauser St., —, News Radio, 1995—2000, ER, 2000—; (TV films) Flying Blind, 1990—, Out of Darkness, —, Student Exchange, —, Crossing the Mob, —, (guest appearance): (TV series) Growing Pains; (TV films) Family Ties; (TV series) Law & Order, The Van Dyke Show, : (films) Dead Women in Lingerie, 1991, The Linguini Incident, 1991, White Sands, 1992, Fly By Night, 1993, The Temp, 1993, Primal Fear, 1996, Primary Colors, 1997, Liar, Liar, 1997, Primary Colors, 1998, Forces of Nature, 1999, Instinct, 1999, Welcome to Mooseport, 2004. Office: c/o CAA 9830 Wilshire Blvd Beverly Hills CA 90212*

TIETJEN, MILDRED CAMPBELL, librarian, college official; b. Rome, Ga., May 26, 1940; d. William Franklin and Willie (Bohannon) Campbell; m. William Leighton Tietjen, Dec. 15, 1968; 1 child, William Campbell. AB, Berry Coll., Mt. Berry, Ga., 1961; M.A in L.S., Peabody Coll., Nashville, 1962. Librarian Gordon Lee High Sch., Chickamauga, Ga., 1962-64; dir. library Ga. Southwestern Coll., Americus, 1964-83, assoc. dean for acad. affairs, 1984—. Contbr. articles to profl. publs. Mem. Sumter Hist. Preservation Soc., Americus, 1985 Council on Library Resources fellow, 1975 Mem. ALA, Southeastern Library Assn., Ga. Library Assn. (scholarship chmn. 1982—), Bus. and Profl. Women (sec. Americus and Sumter County 1984, parliamentarian 1985, Woman of Achievement award 1982), DAR (historian Council of Safety chpt. 1984-85), Beta Phi Mu, Kappa Delta Pi, Alpha Epsilon, Delta Kappa Gamma (pres. 1976), Alpha

Chi Clubs: Ga. Southwestern Coll. Faculty Women (pres. 1982-83). Presbyterian. Home: Rte 2 RR 2 Box 192 Plains GA 31780-9802 Office: Georgia Southwestern College Wheatley St Americus GA 31709-3700

TIFFANY, SANDRA L., state legislator; b. Spokane, Wash., June 30, 1949, m. Ross M. Tonkens; 1 child, Courtney. Student, U. Calif. Mem. Nev. Assembly, 1993—. Mem. Nev. Rep. State Ctrl. com., Clark County Rep. Ctrl. com.; mem. adv. bd. Boys and Girls Club of Henderson; bd. dirs. Desert Rsch. Inst. Mem. Nat. Assn. Women Bus. Owners, Nat. Conf. State Legislatures, Nat. Orgn. Women Legislators, Am. Legis. Exchange coun., Nat. Rep. Leadership Assn., Exec. Devel. Assn., Henderson C. of C. (mktg. and tourism com., issues com.), Nev. Rep. Women's Club, Green Valley Cmty. Assn., Variety Club. Home: 2156 Sun Swept Way Henderson NV 89074-4273

TIFT, MARY LOUISE, artist; b. Seattle, Jan. 2, 1913; d. John Howard and Wilhelmina (Pressler) Dreher; m. William Raymond Tift, Dec. 4, 1948. BFA cum laude, U. Wash., 1933; postgrad., Art Ctr. Coll., L.A., 1945-48, U. Calif., San Francisco, 1962-63. Art dir. Vaughn Shedd Advt., L.A., 1948; asst. prof. design Calif. Coll. Arts & Crafts, Oakland, Calif., 1949-59; coord. design dept. San Francisco Art Inst., 1959-62. Subject of cover story, Am. Artist mag., 1980, studio article, 1987; one-woman shows, Gumps Gallery, San Francisco, 1977, 1986, 90, Diane Gilson Gallery, Seattle, 1978, Oreg. State U., 1981, Univ. House, Seattle, Frye Art Mus., Seattle, 2000; exhibited in group shows including Brit. Biennale, Yorkshire, Eng., 1970, Grenchen Triennale, Switzerland, 1970, Polish Biennale, Crakow, 1972, Nat. Gallery, Washington, 1973, Madrid Biennale, 1980, U.S.-U.K. Impressions, Eng., 1988; represented in permanent collections, Phila. Mus. Art, Bklyn. Mus., Seattle Art Mus., Library Congress, Achenbach Print Collection, San Francisco Palace Legion of Honor, San Diego Mus. Art, U.S. Art in Embassies. Served to lt. USNR, 1943-45. Mem. Print Club Phila., World Print Council, Calif. Soc. Printmakers, Phi Beta Kappa, Lambda Rho. Christian Scientist. Studio: 4400 Stone Way N Apt 521 Seattle WA 98103-7487

TIGELEIRO, SUSANA, corporate financial executive; b. Newark, Mar. 2, 1967; d. Armando and Helena (Ferreira) T. BS, Seton Hall U., 1989, MBA, 2000. CPA, cert. mgmt. acct., N.J. Sr. acct. Arthur Andersen, Roseland, N.J., 1989-91; sr. auditor Johnson & Johnson, New Brunswick, N.J., 1991-94; sr. analyst Ethicon, Inc., Somerville, N.J., 1994-95, Ortho-McNeil Pharm., Raritan, N.J., 1995-97; sr. analyst internat. strategic planning Johnson & Johnson, New Brunswick, 1997—2001, dir. bus. devel. mergers and acquisition, 2001—. Telethon vol. Children's Miracle Network, Somerville, N.J., 1992-94. Mem. AICPA, Inst. Mgmt. Accts. Roman Catholic. Avocations: travel, cooking, reading. Office: Johnson & Johnson Johnson & Johnson Plaza New Brunswick NJ 08901-2021

TIGETT-PARKS, ELIZABETH, arts administrator; b. Houston, Apr. 29, 1971; d. Joel Ray and Zane Ann Tigett; m. Christopher Dylan Parks, July 10, 1999. BA in Art History magna cum laude, Rollins Coll., 1993; MA in Visual Arts Admin. summa cum laude, NYU, 1999. Property contr. Christie's East, N.Y.C., 1993-95; adminstr. contemporary art Christie's Inc., N.Y.C., 1995-97; asst. to the dir. Diane Upright Fine Arts, N.Y.C., 1997-99; dir. Bronwyn Keenan Gallery, N.Y.C., 1998-99; contemporary art specialist eArtGroup.com, N.Y.C., 1999-2000; sr. account exec. artnet.com, 2000—. Contbr. articles to profl. jours. Mem. MOMA (jr. assoc.). Democrat. Christian. Avocations: painting, in-line skating, hiking, scuba diving, writing. Home: 276 Otter Rock Dr #rear Greenwich CT 06830-7045 E-mail: LParss@artnet.com.

TIGHE, MARY ANN, real estate company executive; m. David Hidalgo; 1 child from previous marriage, Aaron. BA in art history, Cath. U.; MA in art history, U. Md. Staff mem. Smithsonian Instn.; arts adv. to v.p. Walter Mondale; dep. chmn. Nat. Endowment Arts; v.p. Am. Broadcasting Co.; sales assoc. Edward S. Gordon Inc. (name changed to Insignia/ESG Inc. 1997), 1984; exec. mng. dir. Insignia/ESG Inc., NYC, 1993—99, vice chmn., 1999—2002; pres., CEO NY Tri-State Region CB Richard Ellis, NYC, 2002—. Dir. Imperial Parking Corp. Bd. dirs. NYC Ballet, Parrish Art Mus., The New 42nd St., Joan's Legacy: The Joan Scarangello Found. to Conquer Lung Cancer. Recipient Woman Yr., Comml. Real Estate Women NY, 2001. Mem.: Real Estate Bd. NY (exec. com. bd. govs. 2001—, Henry Hart Rice award 1997, 2002, Robert T. Lawrence award 1992, 1998). Office: CB Richard Ellis Group Inc 200 Park Ave New York NY 10166*

TIGHE-MOORE, BARBARA JEANNE, electronics executive; b. Wadsworth, Ohio, Jan. 12, 1961; d. Norton Raymond and Laura Alida (Frank) Tighe; m. Derek William Moore, June 26, 1982. Student, Hocking Tech. Coll., 1981, Sinclair Coll., 1986; BBA Honors Coll. magna cum laude, Kent State U., 1988. Lic. amateur radio operator. Tech. writer computer dept. Sinclair Coll., Dayton, Ohio, 1983; project mgr. O'Neil & Assocs., Dayton, 1983-84; biomed., bio-acoustic real-time flight simulation tempest developer Systems Rsch. Labs., Dayton, 1984-86; computer specialist Kent State U. Press, 1987-88; mgmt. analyst Electronic Warfare Frontier Engring. Inc., 1988-89; supr. small computer tech. svcs. Frontier Engring., Inc., 1989-90, project engr., 1990-92; ptnr., bd. dirs. MKCC, Dayton, 1990—, SDCC, Dayton, 1992—; regional mgr. User Tech. Assocs., Dayton, 1993-96; pres., owner Lida Ray Techs., Dayton, 1978—. Mem. graphics steering com., mem. sanctioned UNIX software adv. team Aero. Sys. Divsn.; program chair IEEE Internat. Wireless LAN Conf.; mem. Engring. Application Support Environ. Security Working Group, pres., 2000; proceedings chmn. Nat. Aerospace & Electronics Conf., 1995, 96, 97, bd. dirs., pres., 2000; bd. dirs. MKCC, Dayton, 1993—, Cin. Digital Women, SDCC; pres, bd. dirs. NAECON, 2000; spkr. Govt. Land Mobile Commn. Conf., 1993, Internat. Engring. Mgmt. Cons., 1994, Wireless '93, Calgary, Alta., Nat. Aerospace & Electronics Conf., 1995, 96, 97. Author: Job Search Strategies for the 90's, 1993, Through the Glass Ceiling, 1997, Riding the 5:15, 2000, Convergence of Socio-Economic and Technology Factors, 2001; co-author: Women on a Wire, 1996, Women on a Wire, vol. 2, 2001; editor: Graphics Directions, 1990—91; pub.: Team Advisor, SDCC Cleaning Times, IEEE Update; contbr. poetry to mags. and anthologies, papers, articles to profl. jours. Counselor Kwam's Kinder Kamp; tchr. Bible Sch.; cook Meals on Wheels; organizer/cook funeral Svcs. Dinners. Recipient Vol. Citizen award Wadsworth C. of C, 1979, Ohio Essayist award, 1979, Virginia Perryman award, 1979, Disting. Leadership award, 1990, 91. Mem.: IEEE (former treas., sec. Dayton sect., bd. dirs. 1995—97, chmn. bd. dirs. Dayton sect. 1999, region 2 chpt. coord. 2000—), Equestrian Team (point rider 1977—87), Armed Forces Comms. and Electronics Assn. (judge sci. fair western dist. 1992—), Internat. Film Soc. (pres. 1986—88), Assn. Internat. Students Econs. & Commerce (pres. 1986—87), Def. Planning Analysis Soc. (exec. bd.), Assn. Computer Machinery, Data Processing Mgmt. Assn., Tech. and Soc. of IEEE, Engring. Mgmt. Soc. of IEEE, Computer Soc. of IEEE (sec. 1991—92, vice chmn. 1992—93, chmn. 1994—95), Mortar Bd., Fencing Club, Beta Gamma Sigma, Omicron Delta Kappa, Phi Theta Kappa. Avocations: travel, investing, equestrian show jumping, soccer. Home: 729 Kyle Dr Tipp City OH 45371-1435 Office Phone: 937-667-4972. Business E-Mail: bjmoore@lidaray.com. E-mail: lidaray@siscom.net.

TIGUE, VIRGINIA BETH (GINNY TIGUE), volunteer; b. Owosso, Mich., Sept. 10, 1945; d. Joseph Frederick and Florence Marion Sahlmark; m. Joseph James Tigue Jr., Aug. 12, 1967; children: James Christopher, Molly Elizabeth. BS, cert. in phys. therapy, U. Mich., 1967. Registered phys. therapist, Mich., Calif. Phys. therapist at hosps., rehab. ctrs. and pvt. practice. Co-owner Tigue Property Co.; former co-owner Tex. Toyota of Grapevine. Councilman Pl. 5 City of Colleyville, 1998—2004, mayor pro tem, 2000—04, bond steering com., 1991, master plan revision com., 1997-98, chmn. cmty. ctr. adv. com. 1998; mem. Art Coun. Ft. Worth and Tarrant County Bd., Ft. Worth, 1997—, Tarrant County College Found. Bd., 2001-; founding bd. dirs. Grapevine-Colleyville Ind. Sch. Dist. Edn. Found., 1998—; bd. dirs. Colleyville C. of C., 1991—, chmn., 1994; founding chmn. Harris Hosp., 1992, 93, mem. women's adv. bd., 1992—, bd., HEB Hosp. trustees, 1999—, bd. Meth. Health Harris Found. 2001-; bd. dirs. Arts Coun. N.E. Tarrant, 1991-98, chmn., 1995-96; bd. dirs. Origins Mus., 1998—, v.p. 2000-2001; bd. dirs. Vol. Ctr. of Tarrant County, 1998-2002, chmn. 2000; bd. dirs. Dallas Mus. Art League, 1999-2000, United Way of Met. Tarrant County, 2000—, bd. dirs., 2002—; bd. dirs. N.E Leadership Forum, 1999—04, chmn., 2004; sustaining mem. Dallas Jr. League, 1991—; founding bd. dirs. Tarrant County Coll. Found., 2001—; sr. advisor Nat. Charity League, 1994,; bd. dirs. N.E. Tarrant County divsn. Am. Heart Assn., 1993-94, co-chmn. gala 1997; fund raising chmn. Friends of Colleyville Libr., 1992—; home tour com. Colleyville Women's Club, 1990, 93, 96, fashion show chmn., 1996; mem. adv. bd. Women's Shelter, 1996-98; mem. Women Leader's Summit, Washington, 1995, 96, 98, 99; mem. Women's Policy Forum, 1999—, Women's Found. of Tarrant County, 2000—. Named Most Influential Bus. Woman, The Bus. Press, 1997, Vol. of Yr., City of Colleyville, 1997, Colleyville Citien of Yr., 2001; recipient Legacy of Women award The Women's Shelter, 1995, Herman J. Smith Leadership award Colleyville C. of C., 1994, Proclamation as Outstanding Citizen of Colleyville, 1995. Mem. Colleyville Area C. of C. (bd. dirs. 1990-98, pres.-elect 1993, pres. 1994, vice-chmn. membership devel. 1997, vice-chmn. cmty. devel. 1998, 2003, vice chmn. bus. devel. 2004, Citizen of Yr. 2001, exec. bd. 2003-), Tex. Congress Parents and Tchrs. (hon. life mem.). Republican. Methodist. Avocations: golf, traveling, reading, the arts. Home: 4415 Meandering Way Colleyville TX 76034-4513

TILGHMAN, SHIRLEY MARIE, academic administrator, biology educator; b. Toronto, Can. 2 children. PhD in Biochemistry, Temple U., 1975. Prof. molecular biology Princeton U., 1986—, Howard A. Prior prof. in life scis., 1986—2001, pres., 2001—. Investigator Howard Hughes Med. Inst., 1988-2001; bd. dirs., Brookhaven Sci. Lab., 2001-; trustee The Jackson Lab., 1994-2003, mem. of corp., 2003-. Mem.: NAS, Am. Acad. Arts and Scis., Royal Soc. London, Inst. of Medicine, Am. Philos. Soc. Office: Princeton U Office of Pres One Nassau Hall Princeton NJ 08544-0001

TILL, BEATRIZ MARIA, international business consultant, translator; b. Havana, Cuba, Sept. 27, 1952; came to U.S., 1961; d. Thomas Emanuel and Gladys Manuela (Loret de Mola) Alexander; m. John Edwin Till, Oct. 30, 1976. Student, U. Fla., 1970-71, 72-74, U. Ariz., 1988. Translating sales sec. Rozier Machinery, Tampa, Fla., 1976-78; paralegal, interpreter-translator, 1979-83; pres. Beatriz M. Till Translations, 1983—. Interpreter-translator Office of Worker's Compensation, State of Fla., Tampa, pvt. attys., 1979—; spl. advisor to Sec. of Commerce, State of Fla.; surveillance audio/video transcription specialist Fed. Ct. State of Fla. (middle dist.); interpreter for Pres. Ronald Reagan, 1983; also, expert witness on tape recording transcriptions and translations. Active World Trade Ctr.; adv. bd. mem. Neighborhood Justice Ctr. Mem. Internat. Platform Assn., Nat. Assn. Judiciary Interpreters and Translators, Fla. C. of C., Riverview C. of C., Tampa Bay Internat. Trade Coun.,Fla. Coun. Internat. Devel. Republican. Avocations: reading, photography, cooking, gardening. Home: 12301 Pathway Ct Riverview FL 33569-4122 Office: Beatriz M Till Translations 12301 Pathway Ct Riverview FL 33569-4122 E-mail: bmtilltran@aol.com.

TILLERY-KRISKE, CHARLENE, art educator; d. Richard W. Tillery. BFA cum laude, Kent State U., 1975. Cert. tchr. Kans., 1991. Art educator Kansas City (Kans.) Schs., 1978—79, Ft. Scott (Kans.) Schs., 1991—. Art therapist pub. schs., Fort Scott, Kans., 1991—2002. Exhibitions include Bourbon County Arts Coun., 1998 (best of show, 1998), Albrecht Kemper Mus. Art, 2002, Grand Nude Exhbn., 2002, Verdigris Valley Juried Exhbn., 2002. Art educator, art advisor, therapy Pub. and Pvt. Schools, Many, 1975—2002. Various art grants, 1976, 1998. Mem.: Kans. City Artist Coalition (assoc.). Achievements include first to Art for Exceptional Children. Avocations: travel, horseback riding, ranching, birdwatching. Home and Studio: Charlene Maker of Marks 23916 Valley Rd LaCygne KS 66040

TILLEY, TANA MARIE, pharmaceutical executive; b. Athens, Ga., Dec. 28, 1955; d. Harry Sanford Pierce and Shirley Joanne Webster; m. Scott David Tilley, Aug. 28, 1977; children: Christopher Scott, Lauren Brooke. AD in Nursing, U. S.C., 1980, BS in Nursing cum laude, 1990. Asst. mgr. Brook's Fashions, 1975-78; staff nurse labor and delivery Spartanburg Regional Hosp., 1980-84, head nurse labor and delivery, 1984-89, staff nurse emergency rm., 1989-90; profl. sales rep. L'Nard & Assocs., 1989-90, TAP Pharm., 1990-92, regional hosp. liaison, 1992-95, dist. mgr., hosp. acct. execs., 1995-96, dist. mgr., 1996, 1997-2000, regional sales mgr., 2000—. Methodist. Home: 605 Shade Lake Ct Alpharetta GA 30004 Office: TAP Pharmaceuticals 1050 Crown Point Ste 1445 Atlanta GA 30338 E-mail: tanatilley@tap.com.

TILLMAN, BARBARA ANN, education educator, consultant; b. Waterbury, Conn., Oct. 20, 1945; d. Jehue and Carrie Lee Tillman. BSBA, Loyola, Paris, 1978; MA in Behavior Sci., Calif. State U., Dominguez Hills, 1994. Program mgr. Barclay Career Schs., New Port Beach, Calif., 1984-90, dir. edn. L.A., Cypress, Calif., 1984-90; vocat. rehab. counselor Am. Interant. Health and Rehab., L.A., 1990-92, Cascade Rehab. Co., Inc., L.A., 1992-94, Career Transition Ctr., Long Beach, Calif., 1994-96; instr. Nat. U., Costa Mesa, Calif., 1996—; ednl. cons. Fred Jefferson Foster Agy., Compton, Calif., 1996—. Cons. County L.A. Mem. Nat. Rehab. Assn., Internat. Assn. Personnel Employment Security, So. Calif. Mediation Soc. Democrat. Roman Catholic. Avocations: story telling, cooking. Office: Nat U 3390 Harbor Blvd Costa Mesa CA 92626-1502 Fax: 714-773-4644.

TILLMAN, MARY NORMAN, urban affairs consultant; b. Atlanta, Jan. 31, 1926; d. Mary Nellie Shehee; m. James A. Tillman Jr., Apr. 11, 1952; children: James A., Gina G. BA, Morris Brown Coll., 1947; postgrad., U. Minn., 1964, Old Dominion U., 1975—. Asst. bus. mgr. Morris Brown Coll., Atlanta, 1947-53; race rels. and urban affairs cons. Tillman Assocs. Cons. Social Engrs., Atlanta and Syracuse, N.Y., 1963—, sr. ptnr., treas., from 1965, now pres. Bd. dirs. The Tillman Inst. of Human Rels., Inc.; clin. prof. United Theol. Sem., New Brighton, Minn.; adj. prof. Gordon-Conwell Theol. Sem., South Hamilton, Mass. Author: What is Your Racism Quotient?, 1964, A Common Sense Approach to Racism and Other Exclusivities, 1998, (with James A. Tillman, Jr.) Why America Needs Racism and Poverty, 1972, Black Intellectuals, White Liberals and Race Relations: An Analytic Overview, 1973; What is your Exclusivity Quotient, 1978, A Common Sense Approach to Racism and Other Exclusivities, 2001; also articles. Mem. adv. coun. to urban ministries dept. So. Bapt. Conv., Cmty. Rels. Commn., Atlanta; bd. dirs. Christian Coun. Met. Atlanta, Tillman Inst. Human Rels. Mem. Tidewater Assn. Pub. Adminstrs. (dir.), Am. Acad. Cons., Nat. Black Writers Consortium (v.p.), Joint Ctr. for Polit. Studies. Office: 1765 Glenview Dr SW Atlanta GA 30331-2307

TILLMAN, MERCIA V. musician; b. Chatham, England; Singer Sid Mills band, London, 1932—39; club hostess/catering mgr. US Military Officer Clubs, 1955—69; owner Mercia Tillman Wedding Cons. & Catering, Manassas, Va., 1972—73; dir. svcs. Innisbrook Resort, Tarpon Springs, Fla., 1975—76; columnist West Coast Publs., Largo, Fla., 1977—78; owner Mercia Tillman Prodns., 1996—. Author: (songs) Florida, My State of Dreams, 1996, Walk Around the Mall, 1996, Goodbye Little Princess, 1998, Hello, My Love, Hello, 2000; author and pub.: Little Gems, 2004. Named Ms. Fla. Sr. Am., 1996; recipient Vol. Woman of Yr., Soroptimist Internat., Fla., 1997, Blue Cross/Blue Shield Ageless Hero award, State of Fla., 1999, 2000, Inductee Sr. Hall of Fame, City of St. Petersburg, Fla., 2000, KFC Col.'s Way award, State of Fla., 2000. Mem.: WWII Meml. Soc. (charter), Ms. Sr. Am. Fla. Queen Club.

TILLMAN, SHIRLEY, retired military officer; b. Poplarville, Miss., Mar. 23, 1950; d. L. S. Collins and Pairlee (Goines) Flowers. AB, Jones County Jr. Coll., 1970; BSc in Mgmt., Park Coll., 1990. Desert 300 Runner cert. U.S. Army, 1991. Enlisted US Army, 1972, advanced through grades to sgt. major, 1993; personnel records specialist Fitzsimmons Gen. Hosp., Denver, 1972—73; unit clk. Fitzsimmons Army Med. Ctr., Denver, 1973—79, 10th Co., Ft. Benning, Ga., 1979—80; various personnel positions US Army, various, 1980—94; divsn. sgt. major FORSCOM, Ft. McPherson, Ga., 1995—97; pers. sgt. major Ft. Rucker, Ala., 1997—2000; ret. US Army, 2000. Youth vol. various, 1972—. Avocations: painting, ceramics, fishing, hunting, sewing.

TILLMAN, TAMRA (TAMMY) K. secondary school educator; b. Scottsbluff, Nebr., June 19, 1953; d. Alvin and Mabel Hagen; m. Terry L. Tillman, June 5, 1971; children: Chad Michael, Andy Jay. BS, Bemidji State U., 1975; MS, Chadron State Coll., 1986. Adminstrv./tchr. cert. Nebr. Dept. Edn., 1975. Educator/coach Dist. #73, Bayard, Nebr., 1975—77, McGrew (Nebr.) Pub. Schs., 1977—86; educator (secondary math.)/ coach Bayard Pub. Schs., 1986—. Curriculum specialist Bayard Pub. Schs., 1994—, north ctrl. accrediation internal chairperson, 1997—. Moderator Nebr. Dept. Edn. Policy Forums, Lincoln, 2003. Named Outstanding Young Educator, Nebr. Jaycees, 1991; recipient Christa McAullffe prize, Lincoln Star Jour., 1991, Wall of Tolerance award, Nat. Campaign of Tolerance, 2001. Mem.: NEA, Nat. Coun. Math. Tchrs., Bayard Edn. Assn. (pres. 1999—2001), Nebr. State Edn. Assn. (Scotts Bluff County Tchr. of Yr. 1981). Republican. Presbyterian. Avocations: motorcycling, sewing, reading, gardening. Home: 340638 County Road N Minatare NE 69356 Office: Bayard Public Schools East 8th PO Box 607 Bayard NE 69356 Office Phone: 308-586-1700.

TILLMAN, VICKIE A. diversified financial services company executive; BA in comm., MPA in fin., U. Pitts. With Standard & Poor's, 1977—, exec. mng. dir. pub. fin. ratings dept., exec. v.p. structured fin. ratings, 1994—99, exec. v.p., 1999—, mem. exec. com. Office: Standard & Poor's 55 Water St New York NY 10041*

TILLOTSON, MARY, cable television host; BA in Journalism, U. Ala. Anchor WSB-Radio, Atlanta; news anchor WMAL-Radio, Washington; reporter, anchor WTTG-TV, Washington; congl. reporter Ind. TV News Assn., Washington; news anchor Mutual Radio Network, Washington; reporter CNN, 1981-85, White House corr., 1985-88, Capitol Hill corr., 1988-91; TV talk show host CNN & Co. Atlanta, 1991—. Nominee CableACE award for best talk show interviewer, 1996. Office: Cable News Network One CNN Ctr 1 Cnn Ctr NW Atlanta GA 30303-2762

TILNEY, ELIZABETH A. marketing executive; B, U. Va; MBA, Dartmouth U. With media planning Benton & Bowles Advt., N.Y.C., 1979-81; with acct. mgmt. Ogilvy & Mather Advt., N.Y.C. and Houston, 1983-87; formerly with Russell Reynolds Assocs.; sr. v.p. mktg. comm. and adminstrn. Enron, Houston, 1996-99; sr. v.p. mktg. comm. and human resources Energy Svcs. subsidiary Enron, Houston, 1999—. Office: Enron Corp 1400 Smith St Houston TX 77002-7327

TIMCENKO, LYDIA TEODORA, biochemist, chemist; b. Beograd, Yugoslavia, July 4, 1951; arrived in U.S., 1975; d. Teodor Pavle and Branislava (Spasojevic) Timcenko; m. Ghazi Youssef, June 16, 1980 (div. Oct. 1989); children: Ali Alexander Youssef, Kareem Misha Youssef; m. Peter Porzio, Mar. 11, 1996. BS in Chemistry, U. Belgrade, Yugoslavia, 1975; MS, Wayne State U., 1977, PhD, 1984. Grad. asst. Wayne State U., Detroit, 1976-78, 81-84, rsch. assoc., 1986—88, lectr. in chemistry, 1989; postdoctoral fellow Mich. Cancer Found., Detroit, 1985; postdoctoral fellow Sch. Medicine Wayne State U., 1986—88; lectr. in chemistry Lawrence Tech. U., Southfield, Mich., 1989, 90-91; biochemist Strohtech, Inc., Detroit, 1990—91; prof. chemistry Sussex County Coll., Newton, NJ, 1997—99; asst. prof. chemistry N.Y. Techol. Coll., City U. Bklyn., 1999—; sci. tchr. New Milford (NJ) H.S., 2002, Newton (N.J.) H.S., 2002—; adj. prof. Pace Univ., N.Y.C., 2004—. Prin. investigator, rsch. scientist ICN Galenika Inst., Clin. Ctr. Serbia, Belgrade, 1991—96; rsch. scientist, mktg. cons. Huet Biol., Birmingham, Mich., 1987—91; adj. prof. chemistry Kean Coll.; adj. prof. dept. chemistry and chem. biology Stevens Inst. Tech., Castle Point on Hudson, Hoboken, NJ; adj. assoc. prof. organic chemistry Pace U., N.Y.C., 2002—. Contbr. articles to profl. jours. Mem.: Am. Chem. Soc., Am. Soc. Microbiology, Phi Lambda Upsilon. Achievements include research in in shigella toxin in shigella and E. coli; mitoch GPO in advenal cortex; liberation of labile sufur from ferredoxins; adhesion shigella to HCTH and HELA; localization of GST and GP in adrenal. Home: 306 State Route 94 Columbia NJ 07832-2771

TIMLIN-SCALERA, REBECCA MARY, neuropsychologist; b. Hartford, Conn., Aug. 20, 1972; d. Thomas Francis and Rosalie Marie Timlin; m. Thomas Michael Scalera, June 11, 1999. BA in Psychology, Fairfield U., 1994; MS in Edn., Fordham U., 1997, profl. diploma in sch. psychology, PhD in Counseling Psychology, Fordham U., 2001. Lic. psychologist Conn., NY, cert. neurofeedback provider. Bilingual vocat. counselor Easter Seals Rehab. Ctr., Hartford, Conn., 1994—95; extern psychologist Bellevue Hosp. Ctr., N.Y.C., 1998—99; intern psychologist NYU Med. Ctr.-Risk Inst., N.Y.C., 2000—01, fellow psychologist, 2001—02; neuropsychologist Neuropsychology Cons., LLC, Norwalk, Conn., 2002—. Cons. neuropsychologist Norwalk (Conn.) Hosp., 2002—, St. Joseph's Manor, Trumbull, Conn., 2002—; adj. prof. U. Conn., Stamford, 1999—2002, Fairfield (Conn.) U., Fairfield, 2000. Author: articles in field; contbr. articles to numerous mags., including Cosmopolitan. Vol. vocat. counselor Pacific House Men's Shelter, Stamford, 1999—2001. Mem.: APA, Conn. Psychol. Assn., Psi Chi (Regional Rsch. award 1997). Avocations: tennis, acting, travel, yoga, piano. Office: Neuropsychology Cons LLC 111 East Ave Ste 313 Norwalk CT 06851

TIMM-BROCK, BARBARA, chief product officer; b. St. Paul, Minn., Oct. 18, 1960; married; two children. BS in Chem. Engring., MS in Mgmt. of Tech., U. Minn. Sr. dir. Grand Metropolitan PLC/Pillsbury Co., 1982-92, Pizza Hut Inc., 1992-96; v.p. The Olive Garden, 1996-98; chief product officer Bakery Cafe Group, AFC Enterprises, 1998—. Avocation: golf. Office: Bakery Cafe Group 5555 Glnrdg Ctr N Atlanta GA 30342

TIMMER, BARBARA, state agency administrator; b. Holland, Mich., Dec. 13, 1946; d. John Norman and Barbara Dee (Folensbee) T. BA, Hope Coll., Holland, Mich., 1969; JD, U. Mich., 1975. Bar: Mich. 1975, U.S. Supreme Ct. 1995. Assoc. McCrosky, Libner, VanLeuven, Muskegon, Mich., 1975-78; apptd. to Mich. Women Commn. by Gov., 1976-79; staff counsel subcom. commerce, consumer & monetary affairs Ho. Govt. Ops. Com., U.S. Ho. of Reps., 1979-82, 85-86; exec. v.p. NOW, 1982-84; legis. asst. to Rep. Geraldine Ferraro, 1984; atty. Office Gen. Counsel Fed. Home Loan Bank Bd., 1986-89; gen. counsel Com. on Banking, Fin. and Urban affairs U.S. Ho. of Reps., Washington, 1989-92; asst. gen. counsel, dir. govt. affairs ITT Corp., Washington, 1992-96; sr. v.p., dir. govt. rels. Home Savs. of Am., Irwindale, Calif., 1996-99; ptnr. Manatt, Phelps & Phillips, Washington, 1999—; gen. counsel MyPrimeTime, Inc., San Francisco, 2000-01; asst. sec. U.S. Senate, 2001—02, asst. sgt. at arms, 2003; chief info. officer Calif. Dept. Transp., Sacramento, 2003—. Mem. info. tech. coun. Women's Transp. Seminar, Calif., 2004—. Editor: Compliance With Lobbying Laws and Gift Rule Guide, 1996. Bd. dirs. Women's HIgh Tech Coalition. Named to Acad. of Women Achievers, YWCA, 1993; recipient

Affordable Housing award, Nat. Assn. Real Estate Brokers, 1990, Disting. Alumni award, Hope Coll., 2003. Mem. ABA (bus. law sect., electronic fin. svcs. subcom.), FBA (chair exec. coun. banking law com.), Exchequer Club, Women in Housing and Fin. (bd. dirs. 1992-94, gen. counsel 1994-98, Calif. state CIO coun. 2004—), Supreme Ct. Bar Assn., Supreme Ct. Hist. Soc., Mich. Bar Assn., Bar of D.C. Episcopalian. Office: 2629 Main St PMB 115 Santa Monica CA 90405 E-mail: btimmerdc@earthlink.net.

TIMMINS, MARYANNE, real estate accountant, educator; b. Hackensack, N.J., Feb. 15, 1975; d. Paul Langerfeld and Loretta Timmins. BS, Rutgers U., 1997. CPA Am. Inst. CPA's. Personal banking rep. PNC Bank, Hackensack, 1996-97, personal banking rep. supr. Lyndhurst, N.J., 1997-98; auditor Valley Nat. Bank, Wayne, N.J., 1998-99, Summit Bancorp, Ridgefield Park, N.J., 1999-2000; fin. instr. Ctr. Fin. Tng., Clifton, N.J., 1999—; sr. acctg. assoc. Prudential Real Estate Investors, Parsippanny, NJ, 2000—. Religious instr. Queen of Peace Ch., North Arlington, N.J., 1997—. Samuel and Marcella S. Geltman scholar Rutgers U., 1997. Mem. AICPA, N.J. Soc. CPAs. Avocations: computers, step aerobics, reading, gardening. Home: 74 Birchwood Dr North Arlington NJ 07031-5130 Office: Prudential Investment Mgmt 8 Campus Dr 4th Fl Parsippany NJ 07054-4409 E-mail: maryanne.timmins@prudential.com.

TIMMINS, REBECCA JOANNA, educational association administrator; b. Metairie, La., Nov. 23, 1974; d. Amy Elizabeth Wolfe and William Michael Fraught(Stepfather). BS in bus. adminstrn., U. of So. Miss., 1998; Med in Coll. Student Pers. Services, U. of SC., 2000. Tips Aramark/Ga., 2003. Photographer FLASH/Magnolia Composites, Hattiesburg, Miss., 1997—98; sr. photographer Alan Anderson Photography, Columbia, SC, 1998—2000; grad. asst. U. of SC., Columbia, 1998—99; mktg./spl. projects grad. asst. U. of SC. Housing, Columbia, SC, 1999—2000; u. 101 co-instructor U. of SC., 1999; so. regional dir. Golden Key Internat. Honour Soc., Atlanta, 2000—03, cmty. svc. coord., 2001—02; assoc .dir. U.S. Ops., 2003—. Regional tng. conf. Golden Key, Atlanta, 2000—. Metro area regional adminstr. Ga. Dist. Bd. of Cir. K Internat., Atlanta, 2003; divsn. rally planning com. mem. Ga. Dist. of Kiwanis - Divsn. 16, Atlanta, 2002—03; sec. Metro Dekalb Kiwanis Club, Decatur, Ga., 2000—. Recipient J.B. Guillory Most Outstanding Chpt. Pres. award, LAMISSTENN Cir. K Dist. Bd., 1994, Soc. of Disting. Collegians, Cir. K Internat., 1995, Carolinas Dist. Most Outstanding Chpt. Pres., 2000; LAMISSTENN Cir. K Dist. scholarship, 1995, Bob and Sandy Boothe Mgmt. scholarship, USM Coll. of Bus., 1996, Leslie Van Iten Grad. scholarship, Alpha Delta Pi Found., 1999, Carolinas Cir. K Dist. scholarship, Cir. K Internat., 1999. Mem.: Am. Coll. Pers. Assn. (program reviewer 2002—03), Cir. K Internat. (chartering pres., dist. chair 1993—96, Weatersby Soc. (Hall of Fame) 2003), U. of So. Miss. Alumni Assn. (life), U. of SC. Alumni Assn. (life), Golden Key Internat. Honour Soc. (life; chpt. pres. 1995—97, So. Regional Leadership Award 1997 (first annual)), Gamma Sigma Alpha (life; chartering pres. 1997—98), Order of Omega (life), Omicron Delta Kappa (life; pub. rels. 1997—98), Beta Gamma Sigma Alumni Assn. (life), Alpha Delta Pi (life; alumnae comm. dir. and internat. officer 1999—2002, Shining Diamond Leadership award 1994, 1998). Catholic. Achievements include first female member of the Mandeville High School Key Club in Mandeville, LA. Avocations: photography, travel, web design, community service. Office: Golden Key Internat Honour Soc 621 North Ave NE Bldg C Ste 100 Atlanta GA 30308 Personal E-mail: rebeccatimmins@hotmail.com.

TIMMONS, DEBRA, surgical technologist; b. Toledo, Ohio, Aug. 13, 1954; d. Kenneth and Christene Moulton; m. Wilmer Timmons; children: Marikate, Matthew, Meaghan. BS in Speech Pathology/Audiology, Bowling Green State U., 1978. Cert. surg. technologist. New accts. rep. Nat. City Bank, Norwalk, Ohio, 1981—2000; cert. surg. technologist Fisher Titus Med. Ctr., Norwalk, Ohio, 2001—. Mem.: Assn. Cert. Surg. Technologists, Nat. Vocat.-Technol. Honor Soc. Personal E-mail: dtimmortek@msn.com.

TIMMONS, EVELYN DEERING, pharmacist; b. Durango, Colo., Sept. 29, 1926; d. Claude Elliot and Evelyn Allen (Gooch) Deering; m. Richard Palmer Timmons, Oct. 4, 1952 (div. 1968); children: Roderick Deering, Steven Palmer. BS in Chemistry and Pharmacy cum laude, U. Colo., 1948. Chief pharmacist Meml. Hosp., Phoenix, 1950-54; med. lit. rsch. librarian Hoffman-LaRoche, Inc., Nutley, N.J., 1956-57; staff pharmacist St. Joseph's Hosp., Phoenix, 1958-60; relief mgr. various ind. apothecaries, Phoenix, 1960-68; asst. then mgr., dir. compounding Profl. Pharmacies, Inc., Phoenix, 1968-72; mgr. Mt. View Pharmacy, 1972-76, owner/mgr., 1976—; pres. Ariz. Apothecaries, Ltd., 1976—. Mem. profl. adv. bd., bereavement counselor Hospice of Valley, 1983-96; mem. profl. adv. bd. Upjohn Health Care and Svcs., Phoenix, 1984-86; bd. dirs. Am. coun. on Pharm. Edn., Chgo., 1986-92, v.p., 1988, 89, treas., 1990-91; mem. expert adv. bd. compounding pharms. U.S. Pharmacoepial Conv., 1992—; preceptor U. Ariz., 1965—, Midwestern Coll. Pharmacy, Ariz. Campus, 1998—; chief cons. bioidentical hormone replacement therapy and safety; disease mgmt. specialist; lectr. on NHRT and BHRT. Mem. editl. adv. bd. Internat. Jour. Pharm. Compounding, 1997-2000; author poetry; contbr. articles to profl. jours. Mem. Scottsdale (Ariz.) Fedn. Rep. Women, 1963-68; various other offices Rep. Fedn.; mem. platform com. State of Ariz., Nat. Rep. Conv., 1964; asst. sec. Young Rep. Nat. Fedn., 1963-65; active county and state Rep. coms.; adv. bd. Internat. Jour. of Pharm. Compounding, 1996-2001; fin. chmn. Internat. Leadership Symposium: Women in Pharmacy, London, 1987; treas. Leadership Internat. Women Pharmacy, 1991-2001; mem. founders circle Gladys Taylor McGarey Med. Found., 1996—. Named Outstanding Young Rep. of Yr., Nat. Fedn. Young Reps., 1965, Preceptor of Yr., U. Ariz./Syntex, 1984; recipient Disting. Pub. Svc. award Maricopa County Med. Soc., 1962, Disting. Alumni award Wasatch Acad., 1982, Career Achievement award Kappa Epsilon, 1983, Leadership and Achievement award Upjohn Labs., 1985-86, Outstanding Achievement in Profession award Merck, Sharp & Dohme, 1986, award of Merit Kappa Epsilon, 1988, Disting. Coloradoan award U. Colo., 1989, Vanguard award Kappa Epsilon, 1991, Unicorn award Kappa Epsilon, 1993, Compounding Pharmacist of the Yr. award Profl. Compounding Corp. of Am., 1994, 96, Healing Heart award Gladys Taylor McGarey Found., 1998, 50 Yr. Certificate U. Colo., 2000. Fellow Am. Coll. of Apothecaries (v.p. 1982-83, pres. elect 1983-84, pres. 1984-85, chmn. bd. dirs. 1985-86, adv. coun. 1986-92, Chmn. of Yr. 1980-81, Victor H. Morganroth award 1985, J. Leon Lascoff award 1990), Internat. Acad. of Compounding Pharmacists (bd. dirs. 1993-2000); mem. Ariz. Soc. of Hosp. Pharmacists, Am. Pharm. Assn. (Daniel B. Smith award 1990), Ariz. Pharmacy Assn. (Svc. to Pharmacy award 1976, Pharmacist of Yr. 1981, Bowl of Hygeia 1989, 1st Innovative Pharmacy award 1994, 50 Yr. Practice and Membership award 2001), Maricopa County Pharmacy Assn. (pres. 1977, Svc. to Pharmacy award 1977), Am. Soc. of Hosp. Pharmacists, Am. Aircraft Owners and Pilots Assn., Air Safety Found., Nat. Assn. of Registered Parliamentarians, Civinettes (pres. Scottsdale chpt. 1960-61), Kappa Epsilon (recipient Career Achievement award 1986, Vanguard award 1991, Unicorn award 1993). Avocations: flying, skiing, swimming, hiking, writing. Office: Mt View Pharmacy 10565 N Tatum Blvd Ste B-118 Scottsdale AZ 85253-1095 Office Phone: 480-948-7065. E-mail: evelyn@mountainviewpharmacy.com.

TIMPANO, ANNE, museum director, art historian; b. Osaka, Japan, June 17, 1950; d. A.J. and Margaret (Smith) T. BA, Coll. William and Mary, 1972; MA, George Washington U., 1983. Program mgmt. asst. Nat. Mus. Am. Art, Washington, 1977-86; dir. The Columbus (Ga.) Mus., 1986-93, DAAP Galleries, U. Cin., 1993—. Grant reviewer Inst. Mus. Svcs., Washington, 1988—, Ga. Coun. for Arts, Atlanta, 1988-91. Mem. 1992 Quincentenary Commn., Columbus, 1987-92. Recipient David Lloyd Kreeger award George Washington U., 1980. Mem. Am. Assn. Mus. (surveyor mus. assessment program), Assn. of Coll. and Univ. Mus. and Galleries, Coll. Art Assn., Midwest Mus. Conf. Roman Catholic. Home: 85 Pleasant Ridge Ave Fort Mitchell KY 41017-2861 Office: U Cin PO Box 210016 Cincinnati OH 45221-0016 E-mail: anne.timpano@uc.edu.

TINCHER-THRELKELD, MARSHA LEA, music educator; b. Cin., Aug. 29, 1964; d. Leo and Joyce Ann Tincher; m. David Milton Threlkeld, July 5, 1998; 1 child, Jazzlyn Lachelle Threlkeld. B in Music Edn., Cumberland Coll., 1987; M in Music Edn., Ea. Ky. U., 1992; cert. rank I supr., Union Coll., Barbourville, Ky., 1997. Music tchr. Jackson County HS, McKee, Ky., 1987—; chorus dir. Sue Bennet Coll., London, Ky., 1991—92; flute instr. Cumberland Coll., Williamsburg, Ky., 1996—99. Flute player London Cmty. Orch., 1998—. Music min. 1st United Meth. Ch., London, 1992—. Mem.: Nat. Flute Soc., Ky. Music Educators Assn., Music Educators Nat. Conf. Home: 265 Park Estate Ln London KY 40744 Office: Jackson County HS US Hwy 421 Mc Kee KY 40447

TINDALL, JANICE CLOUGH, family physician; b. Glens Falls, N.Y., Feb. 7, 1945; d. Harold Arthur Clough and Carol Irene (McKernon) Smith; m. Robert Cook Tindall, June 18, 1966; children: Leslie Carol, Ami Catherine, Kelley Rae. BA in Biology, U. Rochester, 1966; BS in Edn., Pa. State U., 1968; MD, Hahnemann U., 1980. Lic. physician, Pa. Lab. rsch. asst. Pa. State U., State College, 1966-69; salesperson, mgr. Tupperware, Laramie, Wyo., 1971-75, mgr. Gap, Pa., 1975-76; resident family medicine Lancaster (Pa.) Gen. Hosp., 1980-83; family physician County Line Med. Ctr., Gap, 1983—; emergency "fast care" physician Lancaster Gen. Hosp., 1994—. Mem. vestry St. Johns Episcopal Ch., Gap. Mem. AMA, Am. Acad. Family Practice, Pa. Acad. Family Practice, Pa. Med. Soc., Lancaster City and County Med. Soc. Avocations: reading, gardening, bird watching, travel, skiing. Office: County Line Med Ctr 5275 Lincoln Hwy Gap PA 17527-9427

TINNER, FRANZISKA PAULA, social worker, artist, apparel designer, educator, entrepreneur; b. Zurich, Switzerland, Sept. 18, 1944; arrived in U.S., 1968; d. Siegfried Albin and Gertrude Emilie (Sigg) Maier; m. Rolf Christian Tinner, Dec. 19, 1976; 1 child, Eric Francis. Student, U. Del., 1973-74, Va. Commonwealth U., 1974; BFA, U. Tenn., 1984; BA of Arts, U. Ark., Little Rock, 1991, postgrad. Lic. real estate broker. Dominican nun, Ilanz, Switzerland, 1961-67; waitress London, 1967-68; governess Bryn Mawr, Pa., 1969; saleswoman, 1970-90; model, 1983; artist, designer Made For You, Kerrville, Tex. and Milw., 1984-90; realtor Century 21, Milw., 1987-91; owner, entrepreneur Exquisite Treasures by Swiss Miss, 1998—. Intern Birch Community Ctr., 1992-93. Designer softsculptor doll Texas Cactus Blossom, 1984; author: (poems) The Gang (recorded by Nat. Libr. of Poetry), 1996, Cry Out for Help, 1998 (pres. choice award 1999), Springtime, 2000 (contest finalist). Ombudsman Action 10 Consumerline, Knoxville, Tenn., 1983—84; foster mother Powhatan, Va., 1976—81; vol. ARC, Knoxville, 1979; Va. Home for Permanently Disabled, 1975; vol., counselor Youth ofr Understanding-Fgn. Exch., Powhatan, 1975—77; tchr. pager/archiving host, mentor, area expert on Am. On Line, 1992—98; vol. Interactive Ednl. Svc., Ark., 1999—; vol. infant intensive care Ark. Children's Hosp., 1999—; vol. Online Internet Emotional/Psych Support BB (WWW), 1999—. Recipient Art Display award U. Knoxville, 1983, Prof. Choice of Yr. award, 1983, Outstanding Achievemnt award TV Channel 10, Knoxville, 1984, 1st place award for paintings and crafts State Fair Milw. [illegible] 1st place award Nat. Dollmakers, 1985, finalist Best of Coll. Photography, 1991, Achievement award Coll. Scholar in Am., 1991, Achievement cert. in technique of anger therapy, 1993, Achievement cert. in crisis response team tng., 1994, Achievement cert. vol. work tchg. AOL. Mem. NASW, NAFE, Milw. Bd. Realtors, Homemakers Club (pres. 1979-80), Newcomers Club, Bowlers Club (v.p.), Internat. Platform Assn. Avocations: art, cooking, teaching, writing, helping disabled and mentally ill. E-mail: elfqueenz@aol.com.

TINNEY, HARLE HOPE HANSON, museum administrator, owner; b. Providence, Apr. 15, 1941; d. Frederick Charles and Grace Alma (Williamson) Hanson; m. Donald Harold Tinney, Dec. 2, 1960. Student, Albion Coll., 1959—60, Brown U., 1960. Tour guide Belcourt Castle, Newport, RI, 1959-60, mus. ptnr., owner, 1972—; stained glass crafter St. Luke Studio, Providence, 1961-89. Sec. founder Royal Arts Found., Newport, 1969—, events planner, 1984—, treas., 1996—; donor svcs. Mosaic Club, Newport, 1984-2000, Shake-A-Leg, Newport, 1980-1989, Newport Music Festival, 1964—; ch. organist St. Declan Chapel, 1998-2001. Mem. Sovereign Order Knights Hospitaller St. John Jerusalem (asst. editor newsletter 1998—), Royal Arts Found. (exec. dir. 2002-). Avocations: music, cello, church organ, antique restoration. Home: Belcourt Castle 657 Bellevue Ave Newport RI 02840-4280

TINSLEY, ADRIAN, college president; b. N.Y.C., July 6, 1937; d. Theodore A. and Mary Ethel (White) Tinsley. AB, Bryn Mawr Coll., 1958; MA, U. Wash., 1962; PhD, Cornell U., 1969. Asst. prof. English U. Md., College Park, 1968-72; dean William James Coll., Grand Valley State, Allendale, Mich., 1972-80; assoc. vice chancellor acad. affairs Minn. State U., St. Paul, 1982-85; exec. v.p., provost Glassboro (N.J.) State Coll., 1985-89; pres. Bridgewater (Mass.) State Coll., 1989—2002, pres. emerita, 2002—. Coord. women higher edn. adminstrn. Bryn Mawr & Hers Summer Inst., Bryn Mawr, Pa., 1977—. Editor: Women in Higher Education Administration, 1984. Office: Boyden Hall Bridgewater State Coll Bridgewater MA 02325-0001

TINSLEY, NIKKI LEE, federal agency administrator; b. Apr. 23, 1948; BS in Bus. Admistrn., Ohio State U./Va. Commonwealth U., 1970; MS in Bus. Admistrn., U. Colo./U. No. Colo., 1981. Ednl. program asst. Office of Edn., Wash., 1971; bookstore mgr. U.S. Govt. Printing Office, Denver, 1971-76; auditor U.S. GAO, Denver, 1976-82; supervisory auditor Dept. of Interior, Minerals Mgmt. Svc., Lakewood, Colo., 1982-90; divsnl. insp. gen. EPA, Kansas City, Kans., 1990—95, dep. insp. gen. Washington, 1995-96, acting insp. gen., 1997-98, insp. gen., 1998—. Chair human resources com. Pres.'s Coun. on Integrity and Efficiency, 2002—04; mem. Adv. Coun. on Gobt. Auditing Stds., Comptroller Gen.'s Domestic Working Group. Recipient Bronze medal for commendable svc. EPA, 1995. Mem.: Colo. Soc. CPAs, Inst. Internal Auditors, Assn. Govt. Accts. (Disting. Fed. Leadership award 2004). Office: EPA MC 2410 1200 Pennsylvania Ave NW Washington DC 20460-0001

TINSMAN, MARGARET NEIR, state legislator; b. Moline, Ill., July 14, 1936; d. Francis Earl and Elizabeth (Lourie) Neir; m. Robert Hovey Tinsman Jr., Feb. 21, 1959; children: Robert Hovey III, Heidi Elizabeth, Bruce MacAlister. BA in Sociology, U. Colo., 1958; MSW, U. Iowa, 1974. Health care coord. Community Health Care, Inc., Davenport, Iowa, 1975-77; assoc. dir. Scott County Info., Referal, and Assistance Svc., Davenport, Iowa, 1977-79; county supr. Scott County Bd. Suprs., Davenport, Iowa, 1978-89; mem. Iowa Senate from 21st dist., Des Moines, 1989—, asst. minority leader, 1992—96. Chair Iowa Adv. Commn. on Inter-govt. Rels., 1982—84; U.S. country rep. to the German-Am. Symposium German Marshall Plan, 1983; commr. Iowa Dept. Elder Affairs, Des Moines, 1983—89. Chair planning com. Quad City United Way, Davenport; bd. dirs. Bi-State Met. Planning Commn., Davenport, 1981-89, Quad City Devel. Group, Davenport, 1988-90; mem. structure commn. Nat. Episcopal Ch. Named Iowa Social Worker of Yr., NASW, 1978. Mem. Am. Lung Assn. of Ill.-Iowa (bd. dirs. 1989—), Davenport C. of C. (local/state govt. com. 1989—), Nat. Assn. Legislators, Nat. Assn. of Counties (bd. dirs. 1984-89, pres. Women Ofcl. 1984-89), Iowa State Assn. of Counties (bd. dirs. 1983-89, chair), Jr. League (sustaining mem. 1989), Vol. Action Ctr. (pres. 1989), Phi Beta Kappa. Republican. Avocations: tennis, golf, sailing, water and snow skiing. Home: 2865 Hickory Hill Ln Bettendorf IA 52722 Office: 3541 E Kimberly Rd Davenport IA 52807-2552

TIPTON, MELANIE CAROL, music educator; b. Jacksonville, Ark., May 13, 1972; d. John David and M. Carol Odell; m. Adam Robert Tipton, June 11, 1994. B of Vocal Music, Ouachita Bapt. U., 1996; postgrad., So. Bapt. Theol. Sem., 1996, postgrad., 2000—01. Piano/vocal coach Bader Music Village, Louisville, 1996—2000; music min. Midlane Park Bapt. Ch., Louisville, 1999—2001; music tchr. Graceland Bapt. Sch., New Albany, Ind., 2000—01, Christian Acad. Louisville, 2002—. Owner Melanie's Melodies, Louisville, 2001—03. Composer: (songs) David's Song, 2002. Recipient Tchr. award, Star Sys., 2002. Mem.: Ky. Music Educators Assn. (superior/excellent ratings 2003), Music Educators Nat. Corp. Southern Baptist. Avocations: scrapbooks, walking, gardening.

TIRELLI, MARIA DEL CARMEN S. retired realtor; b. Rio Grande, PR, Apr. 8, 1919; d. Carmelo Siaca Pacheco and Luisa Guzman Berrios; m. Francesco Tirelli, Dec. 20, 1947 (dec. Oct. 2002); children: Rose, Frank, Marie, Angelo. BS, U. P.R., 1941; MS, U. Chgo., 1944; JD, InterAm. U., 1978. Cert. home econs. tchr., N.Y., Spanish tchr., N.Y.C.; registered dietitian/nutritionist; cert. realtor, counselor. Home econs. tchr. Dept. Edn., San Juan, P.R., 1941-43; nutritionist USDA, San Juan, 1944-45, Dept. Health, San Juan, 1946-47; sch. lunch supr. III & IV Dept. Edn., San Juan, 1948-55; dietitian Good Samaritan Hosp., West Islip, N.Y., 1961-62; food svc. dir. N.Y. Dept. Mental Hygiene, Islip, N.Y., 1964-74; sch. lunch dir. North Babylon (N.Y.) Schs., 1964-74; realtor C-21, Watson, Coldwell Banker, Brandon, Fla., 1982-00; realtor, assoc. Coldwell Banker, Brandon, 1985—95; ret., 2000. Pres. P.R. Dietetic Assn., San Juan, 1951-52, L.I. (N.Y.) Dietetic Assn., 1973; cons. dietitian various nursing homes, L.I., 1973-75; ad honorem lectr. U. P.R., Rio Piedras, 1955. Contbr. articles to profl. jours. Mem. Nativity Ch. Chorale, 1982-00. Recipient scholarship U. P.R., San Juan, 1943, grant U. Chgo., 1943. Mem. Nat. Assn. Realtors, Fla. Assn. Realtors., Tampa Board of Realtors (realtor assoc., mem. legis. title com. 1983), Legion of Mary (Brandon, sec. 1983-91). Republican. Roman Catholic. Avocations: music, piano, chorale. Home: PO Box 667 Valrico FL 33595-0667

TIRELLO, MARIA EUGENIA DUKE, artist; b. San Salvador, El Salvador, Sept. 27, 1947; arrived in U.S., 1980, permanent resident, 1993, naturalized, U.S., 2000; d. Carlos Alberto Duke Tomasino and Ana Maria (Ruiz-Flores) Duke; m. Mario Ernesto Tirello Hill, Nov. 7, 1970; 1 child, Juan Antonio Tirello Duke. Diploma in computer programming, Charron Williams Coll., 1983; diploma exec. sec., Elinor Smith, 1986; studied art with Victor Manuel Rodriguez Preza, El Salvador; studied with some of the finest nat. and internat. artists, U.S. Lic. real estate 1992. Lectr. in field. Artist (one-woman shows) Common Market, Miami, 1990, Sky Gallery, 1996, Nicaragua C. of C. Gala, Miami, 2002; Exhibited in group shows at Met. Mus., Coral Gables, 1989, Wirtz Gallery, South Miami, 1989, 1993, 1996, 2001, One Brickell Sq. Lobby Gallery, Miami, 1989, 1992, 1993, 1994, 1996, 1997, 1998, 2000, 2001, 2003, Pioneer Mus. Depot, Fla. City, 1990, 1991, 1992, Coral Gables Fed., 1993, Am. Assn. Salvadorenos Profls., Miami, 1994, 1996, 1997, Am. Arts Profl. League, Miami, 1994, 1996, 1999, Heim Am. Gallery, Fisher Island, 1995, Galeria 1-2-3, El Salvador, 1995, Coconut Grove Conv. Ctr., 1995, Mus. Sci. and Space Transit Planetarium, Miami, 1995—2001, Fla. Mus. Hispanics and Latin Am. Art, Miami, 1995 (Honorable Mention, 1997), 1997, SunTrust Bank Lobby Gallery, Miami, 1996, 1997, 1999, 2000, Art Expo N.Y., 1996, Historia Fine Art Gallery, Coral Gables, Fla., 1996, One Datra Ctr. Lobby Gallery, Miami, 1996, Royal Poncian Fiesta, Miami, 1996 (Honorable Mention, 1996), Union Planters Bank Lobb Gallery, Miami, 1996, Ctr. Art Gallery Alvaro Gomez Hurtado, Miami, 1997, IV Congreso Continental de la Mujer Americana, Miami, 1997, Salon de Pintoras Latinoamericanas, Miami, 1997, Europe Gallery, Miami, 1998—99, South Dade Regional Libr., Miami, 1998, Brickell Key Day, Miami, 2000 (3d pl., 2000), Lift Ctr. Gallery, Miami, 2000 (Honorable Mention, 2000), Bet Breira Gallery, Miami, 2000 (Honorable Mention, 2000, 2002), 2001, 2002, Ann Kolb Nature Ctr., Hollywood, Fla., Represented in permanent collections SunTrust Bank, Miami, Merrill Lynch, Miami, Arimar Corp., Fla., BANCORP, El Salvador, BanCo, El Salvador, Industrias Cristal, El Salvador, M.A. Lima Assoc. S.A. de C.V., El Salvador. Mem.: Waterworks, Gold Coast Watercolor Soc., Fla. Profl. Artists Guild (Merit award 2000, SunTrust Bank Purchase award 2001, hon. mention Amerkan award 2003, Honorable Mention 2003), Fla. Watercolor Soc., Miami Watercolor Soc. (3d place 1995, Merrill Lynch Purchase award 1995, Salis Internat. award 1998, Color Q, Inc. award 1999, Best in Show 2001, Outstanding award 2001, Merit award 2002). Roman Catholic. Avocations: art, music, movies. E-mail: MTirello@aol.com.

TIRONE, BARBARA JEAN, health insurance administrator; b. Celina, Ohio, Nov. 19, 1943; d. Vincent James and Theresa Barbara (Goettermoeller) G. BA, Miami U., 1965; MBA, U. Chgo., 1977. Asst. dir. for internat. trade State of Ill., Chgo., Brussels, Hongkong and Sao Paulo, Brazil, 1973-76; dir. office of mgmt. and planning Office Human Devel. Svcs., Chgo., 1976-79; dep. regional adminstr. Health Care Financing Adminstrn., Chgo., 1979-82, regional adminstr., 1982-87, dir. bur. of prog. ops. Balt., 1987-92; dir. health stds. and quality bur. Health Care Fin. Adminstrn., Balt., 1992-96; pres., CEO AdminaStar, Inc., Indpls., 1996-2001. Recipient Presdl. Disting. Rank award 1988, 94, Presdl. Meritorious Rank award 1987, 92; named Fed. Exec. of Yr., 1987. Home: 11212 Appaloosa Dr Reisterstown MD 21136 E-mail: bgagel@comcast.net.

TIRSCHWELL-NEWBY, KATHY ANN, events production company executive; b. Hudson, Wis., Jan. 8, 1961; d. Walter Haskell and Doris Hilda (Dornfeld) T. DDS (hon.), Roth/Williams Ctr., 1993. Traffic dir. Sta. KRKC, King City, Calif., 1978-79; office mgr. Cable TV of King City/Greenfield, 1979-82; lead cashier Del Webb's High Sierra Hotel & Casino, Lake Tahoe, Nev., 1982-84; acctg. analyst Hyatt Hotels, Burlinghame, Calif., 1984-87; v.p., owner Computer Diagnostic Info Inc., Burlingame, 1987-93; exec. dir. Roth/Williams Ctr., Burlingame, 1990-93; event support mgr. Stuart Rental Co., Sunnyvale, Calif., 1994-96, Cheskin & Masten/ImageNet, Redwood Shores, Calif., 1996; adminstr. Bayshore Animal Hosp., San Mateo, Calif., 1996-97; event sales mgr. Stuart Rental Co., Sunnyvale, 1997-2000; prodr. sports and corp. events E2k/Olmstead Prodns., Palo Alto, Calif., 2000—. Pres. Jr. Fairboard, Salinas Valley Fair, King City, Calif., 1979-80. Mem.: Internat. Spl. Events Soc. (1st v.p. No. Calif. chpt. 2003, pres.). Office: e2k/Olmstead Prodns 801 High St Palo Alto CA 94301 Office Phone: 650-838-0800. Personal E-mail: katjtn@aol.com.

TISCHHAUSER, KATHERINE JETTER, music educator, cellist; b. Raleigh, N.C., May 25, 1968; d. Frederick Robert and Glenda Bagwell Jetter; m. Andreas P. Tischhauser, Oct. 13, 1996. BM in Cello Performance, BA in Applied Math., E. Carolina U., 1991; M in Cello Performance, Fla. State U., 1993, D in Cello Performance, 2002. Tchg. asst. Fla. State U., Tallahassee, 1991—96; assoc. prof. cello & music theory Ft. Lewis Coll., Durango, Colo., 1996—. Dir. student honors orch. Ft. Lewis Coll., 2002. Performer: (prin. cellist) Showcase Chamber Orch., 1996—, San Juan Symphony, 1996—, (recital soloist) Ft. Lewis Coll., 1996—2003, (ensemble) Shelly/Tischhauser, 2001—. Mem.: ISB, ASTA (state sec. 1999—2003), Phi Kappa Phi (life). Avocations: gardening, sewing, cooking, bicycling. Office: Ft Lewis Coll Music Dept 1000 Rim Dr Durango CO 81301 E-mail: cellokate@music.org.

TISCHLER, JUDITH BLANCHE, retired music publishing executive, educator; b. N.Y.C., May 14, 1933; d. Max and Anna (Drescher) Zucker; m. Alfred Tischler, Dec. 14, 1958; children: Marva, Mira, Gary. MA, CCNY, 1975; PhD, Jewish Theol. Sem., 1989. Editor, dir. Transcontinental Music Publs., N.Y.C., 1981—2000. Prof. music Jewish Theol. Sem., H.L. Miller

Cantorial Sch. French hornist various concerts worldwide, 1952-71. Office: HL Miller Cantonal Sch Jewish Theol Sem of Am 3080 Broadway New York NY 10027 E-mail: tisch33@netvision.net.il., judithtischler@hotmail.com.

TISHNER, KERI LYNN, visual art education consultant; b. Santa Ana, Calif., June 1, 1964; d. Albert John, Jr. and Barbara Ann (Milner) Geverink; m. David Jackson Tishner, Apr. 27, 1985. BA in Art with distinction, Calif. State U., Long Beach, 1988, tchg. credentials, 1991; postgrad., Calif. State U., San Bernardino, 1994—99. State D coaching license Calif. Youth Soccer Assn. Art tchr. Apple Valley (Calif.) H.S., 1991—99, Granite Hills H.S., Apple Valley, 1999—2002, dept. chair visual and performing arts, 1999—2002; visual art edn. cons. DrawPaintCreate.com, 2002—. Mentor tchr., 1998—2000. Presenter in field of art. Participant Calif. Arts Project, San Bernardino, 1995. Mem. NEA, Nat. Art Edn. Assn., Calif. Tchrs. Assn., Calif. Art Edn. Assn., Los Angeles County Mus. Art, Norton Simon Mus. Art. Avocations: inline skating, ski boarding, art, computers, skiing. E-mail: keri@drawpaintcreate.com.

TISINGER, CATHERINE ANNE, history and economics educator; b. Winchester, Va., Apr. 6, 1936; d. Richard Martin and Irma Regina (Ohl) T. BA, Coll. Wooster, 1958; MA, U. Pa., 1962, PhD, 1970; LLD (hon.), Coll. of Elms, 1985. Provost Callison Coll., U. of Pacific, Stockton, Calif., 1971-72; v.p. Met. State U., St. Paul, 1972-75, interim pres., 1976-77; dir. Ctr. for Econ. Edn., R.I. Coll., Providence, 1979-80; v.p. acad. affairs Ctrl. Mo. State U., Warrensburg, 1980-84; pres. North Adams State Coll., Mass., 1984-91; dean arts and scis.. Shenandoah U., Winchester, Va., 1999—2001, prof. history and econs., 2001—, Disting. prof., 2001—. Cons. North Cen. Assn. Colls. and Schs., 1980-84, New Eng. Assn. Schs. and Colls., 1978-79, 85—, Minn. Acad. Family Physicians, 1973-77; mem. adv. bd. First Agrl. Bank, North Adams, 1985-91; pres. No. Berkshire Cooperating Colls., 1986-91; v.p. Coll. Consortium for Internat. Studies, 1989-90; cons. Inst. for Experiential Learning, 2002—. V.p. Med. Simulation Found., 1986-88; bd. dirs. Williamstown Concerts, 1988-91, Shawnee coun. Girl Scouts U.S.A., 1992-93, Parents' Choice, 1997-98, Parents Guide to Children's Media, Inc., 1998-2004. Mem. No. Berkshire C. of C. (bd. dirs. 1984-89, v.p. 1986-89). Avocations: fiber and textile arts, photography. Office: Shenandoah U 1460 University Dr Winchester VA 22601-5195 E-mail: ctisinge@su.edu.

TITLE, GAIL MIGDAL, lawyer; b. Waldenberg, Germany, May 31, 1946; AB, Wellesley Coll., 1967; JD, U. Calif., Berkeley, 1970. Bar: Calif. 1971. Mng. ptnr. Katten Muchin Zavis (formerly Katten Muchin & Zavis), Beverly Hills. Adj. prof. law Loyola U., 1976-96; trustee Ctr. for Law in the Pub. Interest. Mem. ABA (litigation sect., forum com. entertainment), Assn. Bus. Trial Lawyers, State Bar Calif. (standing com. pub. interest law 1976—), L.A. County Bar Assn. (del. conf. dels. 1974-76, 88-89), Beverly Hills Bar Assn., L.A. Copyright Soc. (trustee), Office: Katten Muchin Zavis 1999 Ave Of Stars Ste 1400 Los Angeles CA 90067-6115

TITO, MAUREEN LOUISE, educational administrator; b. Long Beach, Calif., Mar. 14, 1946; d. Francis Bowen and Marie Louise (Hogan) Barrett; m. Jose D. Tito, July 4, 1971; children: Yvonne, Russell, Daryl, Nathan. AB in Polit. Sci., Holy Name Coll., Oakland, Calif., 1969; MA in Linguistics, Ateneo de Manila, Philippines, 1985; PhD in Edn., U. Philippines, 1987. English lang. cons. Lang. Internat., Manila, 1979-85; English dept. coord. Maryknoll Coll. High Sch., Manila, 1981-85; edn. specialist Farrington Community Sch., Honolulu, 1985-91; English lang. cons. Job Preparation Program, Honolulu, 1990-91; project trainer U. Hawaii, Honolulu, 1989-90; edn. dir. Dept. of Pub. Safety, Honolulu, 1990-91, state dir. correctional edn., 1991—. Cons. in field. Contbr. articles to profl. jours. Trainer AIDS for ARC, 1991-93. Mem. AAUW, Nat. Assn. Adult Learners with Spl. Needs, Am. Assn. Adult and Continuing Edn., Hawaii Assn. Counseling and Devel., Correctional Edn. Assn., Nat. Assn. State Correctional Edn. Dirs. Office: Dept Pub Safety 919 Ala Moana Blvd Honolulu HI 96814-4920 E-mail: res1ipflb@verizon.net.

TITTLE, VICKI MARKS, healthcare business manager; b. Johnson City, Tenn., Apr. 23, 1959; d. James and Nancy Lee (Swartz) Marks; m. Terry L. Johnson, Dec. 20, 1976 (div. Jan. 1984); 1 child, E. Reneé Johnson; m. Troy Lee Tittle, Jan. 12, 1993. BS in Comms., East Tenn. State U., 1989. Admissions rep., cashier Woodridge Psychiat. Hosp., Johnson City, 1985-89; patient accounts rep. Johnson City Med. Ctr., 1989-90; ops. mgr. Uniform Temp. Svc., Johnson City, 1990-91; ctr. mgr. Family Medicine Assocs. & Quillen Coll. of Medicine, Johnson City, 1991-92; patient accounts mgr. Cardiology Assn. of East Tenn., Knoxville, 1992-93; mgr. Zemp Health Svcs., Louisville, Tenn., 1993; bus. mgr. Ambulatory Care of Tenn., Knoxville, 1993-95; fin. dir. Assoc. Therapeutics, Inc., Knoxville, 1995-97; corp. bus. mgr. Wake Emergency Physicians Priority Care, Cary, N.C., 1997; office mgr. Cary Dermatology Ctr., 1997—. Mem. pers. and budgeting com. dept. family practice Quillen Coll. of Medicine, Johnson City, 1991-92. Del., grad. Leadership Cary, 1997; vol., campaigner Young Reps., Johnson City, 1980-85. Mem. Cary C. of C. (amb. 1997—). Democrat. Baptist. Avocations: studying forensic pathology and psychology, writing fiction, english history. Office: Cary Dermatology Ctr 101 SW Cary Pkwy Ste 210 Cary NC 27511-5588

TITUS, ALICE CESTANDINA (DINA TITUS), state legislator; b. Thomasville, Ga., May 23, 1950; m. Thomas Clayton Wright. AB, Coll. William and Mary, 1970; MA, U. Ga., 1973; PhD, Fla. State U., 1976. Prof. polit. sci. U. Nev., Las Vegas, 1977—; mem. from dist. 7 Nev. Senate, 1989—, minority fl. leader, 1993—, mem. Legislative commn., 1991—. Chmn. Nev. Humanities Com., 1984-86; mem. Eldorado Basin adv. group to Colo. River Commn.; active Gov. Commn. Bicentennial of U.S. Constn.; former mem. Gov. Commn. on Aging. Author: Bombs in the Backyard: Atomic Testing and American Politics, 1986, Battle Born: Federal-State Relations in Nevada during the 20th Century, 1989. Mem. Western Polit. Sci. Assn., Clark County Women's Dem. Club, Amer. Pen Women, Aquavision, PEO. Greek Orthodox. Home: 1637 Travois Cir Las Vegas NV 89119-6283 Office: Nev Senate 401 S Carson St Rm 114F Carson City NV 89701-4747

TITUS, MICHELE R. state legislator; m. Eric DeBarry; 2 children. Grad., Albany Law Sch., 1998. Edn. lawyer, Brklyn.-Queens, NY, 1998—; state rep. State of N.Y., 2002—. Former exec. dir. N.Y. State Black and Puerto Rican Legis. Caucus. Democrat. Office: 19-31 Mott Ave Rm 301 Far Rockaway NY 11691

TITUS, SUSAN ANNE, association executive; b. L.A., Mar. 2, 1944; d. Clifford E. and Thelma A. (Chambers) T. BA in English, U. N.C., 1965; MSW, Wayne State U., 1968. Asst. dir. Edgemont Cmty. Ctr., Durham, N.C., 1965-66; group activities specialist City of Detroit Dept Parks and Recreation, 1968-70; program dir. Operation Friendship, Detroit, 1970-72; camping svcs. adminstr. Girl Scout Met. Detroit, 1972-74; adminstrv. asst. to coun. mem. Maryann Mahaffey Detroit City Coun., 1974-77; exec. dir. Citizens for Better Care, Detroit, 1977—98, Mich. Parkinson Found., 1998—2002, Transp. Riders United, 2002—. Mem. Mich. Dept. Social Svcs., 1973-80, adult cmty. placement adv. com., 1973-78, chairperson, 1976-78, chairperson, 1976-79, adult svcs. adv. com., 1976-80; mem. Comprehensive Health Planning Coun. of S.E. Mich., 1976-87, bd. dirs., 1977-87, plan implementation com., 1977-87, commn. to reduce excess hosp. capacity, 1978-87, vice chairperson, 1979-80; mem. Dept. Mental Health Adv. Com. on the Office of Recipient Rights, 1976-82, vice chairperson, 1977-80; part-time faculty dept. sociology and social work U. Detroit, 1978-79; part-time faculty Wayne State U. Sch. Social Work, Detroit, 1979-80, 2003—; mem. New Detroit Health Com., 1979-93; mem. Fed. Emergency Mgmt. Adminstrn., U.S. Fire Adminstrn. Task Force on Fires in Boarding Homes, 1981-82; mem. adv. com. to med. dist. region 14 VA, 1983-86; apptd. mem. Mental Health and Aging Adv. Coun., 1990-96; presenter in field. Mem. editl. bd. Bd. and [illegible] Quality Forum, [illegible]-99. Mem., chairperson Mich. State Health Corod. Coun., 1978-87; mem. spkrs. bur. United Found. Met. Detroit, 1980-98; mem., treas. Voight Park Neighborhood Security Com., 1988-90; mem. fin. com. Chateaufort Place Cooperative, 1990-97, sec. 2002-03, treas., 2003—; apptd. mem. Detroit Sr. Citizens Commn., 1994, 96; pub. mem., corp. mem., bd. dirs. Greater Detroit Area Health Coun., 1994—. Recipient Demmy award United Found. Met. Detroit Spkrs. Bur., 1982, Disting. Recognition award Detroit City Coun., 1989, Spl. Tribute, Mich. State Ho. of Reps., 1989, Sidney Rosen Life Long Achievement award for cmty. svc. Detroit Area Agy. on Aging, 1995. Mem. ACLU (Mich. state bd. dirs. 1988—, Met. Detroit br. bd. 1989—, treas. 1990-92, NASW (cert., Detroit Met. chpt. bd. mem. at large 1967-70, v.p. 1971-73, pres. 1973-77, Mich. chpt. v.p. 1977-81, Met. Detroit area chpt. Social Worker of Yr. 1989), Nat. Citizens Coalition for Nursing Home Reform (nominating com. chairperson 1979-82, treas. 1984-86, v.p. 1986-88, pres. 1988-94, Advocacy Meml. award 1994), Coun. Exec. Officers (treas. 1990-96), Women Execs. (founder), Consumer Health Coalition (founder). Home: 1528 Chateaufort Pl Detroit MI 48207-2717 Office: WSU SSW 400 Thompson Hall Cass Ave Detroit MI 48207

TITUS-DILLON, PAULINE YVONNE, associate dean academic affairs, medical educator; b. Petersfield, Jamaica, Jan. 1, 1938; came to U.S., 1954; d. Ernest H. Titus and Vera I. (Tate) Harvey; m. Owen C. Dillon, Nov. 29, 1963. Student, Pratt Inst., 1954-57; BS in Chemistry summa cum laude, Howard U., 1960, MD, 1964. Diplomate Nat. Bd. Med. Examiners, Am. Bd. Internal Medicine. Intern Freedmen's Hosp. (name now Howard U. Hosp.), Washington, 1964-65, asst. resident, 1965-67, resident, chief resident, 1967-68, family practice physician, 1971, attending, 1971—; fellow in endocrinology and metabolism Georgetown U. Hosp., Washington, 1968-69; postdoctoral fellow NIH, Bethesda, Md., 1975-77; outpatient clinic physician Vets.' Adminstrn. Hosp., Columbia, S.C., 1969-71; from asst. prof. to assoc. prof. dept. medicine Howard U. Coll. Medicine, Washington, 1971-81, prof. internal medicine, 1981—, assoc. dean acad. affairs, 1980—2000; chief med. officer, residency prog. dir. Howard U. Med. Svc. D.C. Gen. Hosp., Washington, 1977-80, attending, 1977-80; sr. assoc. dean Howard U. Coll. Medicine, Washington, 2000—. Cons. Malawi, Africa project of Dept. Cmty. Health and Family Practice, 1989, Nat. Bd. Med. Examiners, 1995, Ednl. Commn. for Fgn. Med. Grads., 1997; Howard U. Coll. Medicine rep. Am. Assn. Med. Colls., 1980—, coord. activities, presenter, 1982-83, exec. devel. seminar for women, 1983, mem. Nat. Identification Prog. for Advancement of Women in Higher Edn., 1985, others; exec. chief proctor Nat. Bd. Med. Examiners, 1983—, liaison rep. for Howard U. Coll. Medicine, 1987—, mem. steering com. for liaison rep., 1989—, prin. investigator for Computer Based Exams. project, 1989—, mem. bd., 1997—; mem. numerous hosp., coll. coms., subcoms., reviews; lectr., presenter confs., workshops, symposiums. Contbr. articles to profl. jours. Recipient Joseph L. Johnson physiology award, 1961-62, Jacobi Soc. cert. of merit for proficiency in pediatrics, 1964, James E. Simpson Meml. prize Howard U., 1964, psychiatry prize, 1964, dept. surgery prize, 1964, Matilda Davis-Cunningham award, 1964, Am. Acad. Dental Medicine award, 1964, Daniel Hale Williams internship award, 1966, Daniel Hale Williams residency award, 1968, Nat. Rsch. Svc. award, 1975-77, inspirational leadership award Student Coun. Coll. of Medicine, 1979, superior performance as Chief Med. Officer award Howard U. Med. Svc., D.C. Gen. Hosp., 1980, student coun. award Howard U. Coll. Medicine, 1995, Pearl A. Watson award for excellence in delivery of health care Caribbean Am. Intercultural Orgn., 1996; ; named Doctor of Year, D.C. Gen. Hosp., 1980; Alma Wells Givens scholar, 1962-63. Fellow ACP; mem. AMA, Nat. Med. Assn., Am. Med. Women's Assn. (liaison officer Howard U. Coll. Medicine, v.p. br. 1 Washington chpt. 1991-92, pres. 1992-93, Janet M. Glasgow Meml. award 1964), Nat. Bd. Med. Examiners, N.Y. Acad. Scis., D.C. Med. Soc., Phi Beta Kappa, Sigma Xi, Beta Kappa Chi, Alpha Omega Alpha (sec., treas. 1977-98, Gamma chpt. of Washington, councillor 1998—). Avocations: sewing, crochet, aerobics. Office: Howard Univ Coll Medicine 520 W St NW Washington DC 20059-0001 Fax: 202-806-7934.

TITZMAN, DONNA M. energy executive; BBA in Acctg., U. Tex. CPA. Acct. natural gas liquids Valero Energy Corp., San Antonio, 1986—89, various positions with fin. dept., 1989, v.p., treas., 1999—. Office: Valero Corp Hdqs 1 Valero Pl San Antonio TX 78212-3186*

TLOUGAN, JESSICA ELISE, music educator; b. Waseca, Minn., May 19, 1977; d. Leslie Benjamin and Karen Louise (Hauschildt) Tlougan. Degree in Instrumental Music, Gustavus Adolphus Coll., 1999. Band dir. Stewartville (Minn.) HS, 1999—2002, South St. Paul (Minn.) Pub. Schs., 2002—03, Stewartville (Minn.) HS, 2003—. Democrat. Luth. Office: Stewartville HS 500 4th St SW Stewartville MN 55976 Home: 925 41st St NW Apt 221 Rochester MN 55901-4267

TOAL, JEAN HOEFER, state supreme court chief justice; b. Columbia, S.C., Aug. 11, 1943; d. Herbert W. and Lilla (Farrell) Hoefer; m. William Thomas Toal; children: Jean Hoefer Eisen, Lilla Patrick. BA in Philosophy, Agnes Scott Coll., 1965; JD, U. S.C., 1968; LHD (hon.), Coll. Charleston, 1990; LLD (hon.), Columbia Coll., 1992, The Citadel, 1999, Francis Marion U., 1999, U. S.C., 2000. Bar: S.C. Assoc. Haynsworth, Perry, Bryant, Marion & Johnstone, 1968-70; ptnr. Belser, Baker, Barwick, Ravenel, Toal & Bender, Columbia, 1970-88; assoc. justice S.C. Supreme Ct., Columbia, 1988-00, chief justice, 2000—. Mem. S.C. Human Affairs Commn., 1972-74; mem. S.C. Ho. of Reps., 1975-88, chmn. house rules com., constitutional laws subcom. house judiciary com.; mem. parish coun. and lector St. Joseph's Cath. Ch.; chair S.C. Juvenile Justice Task Force, 1992-94; chair S.C. Rhodes Scholar Selection Com., 1994. Mng. editor S.C. Law Rev., 1967-68. Bd. visitors Clemson U., 1978; trustee Columbia Mus. Art; bd. trustees Agnes Scott Coll., 1996—. Named Legislator of Yr. Greenville News, Woman of Yr., U. S.C. Mortar Bd.,1989; recipient Disting. Svc. award S.C. Mcpl. Assn., Univ. Notre Dame award, 1991, Algernon Sydney Sullivan award U. S.C., 1991, John W. Williams award, Richland County Bar Assn., 1994, Jean Galloway Bissell award, S.C. Women Lawyers Assn., 1995, Agnes Scott Coll. Outstanding Alumna award, 1991. Mem. ABA, S.C. Women Lawyers Assn., John Belton O'Neill Inn of Ct., Phi Beta Kappa, Mortar Bd., Order of the Coif. Office: Supreme Ct SC PO Box 11330 Columbia SC 29211-2456 E-mail: jtoal@sccourts.org.

TOAY, THELMA M. columnist, poet; b. Anamosa, Iowa, Feb. 22, 1915; d. Frank Leroy and Edna May Stoughton; m. John S. Toay; 3 children. Student, St. Lukes Sch. Nursing, Davenport, IA, 1933, Highland Coll., 1966—67, Famous Writer's Course, Westport, CT; AA in Journalism, N.E. Iowa CC, Peosta, 1995—97. Contbr. various newspapers, Freeport, Ill., 1962—; contbr. Julien's Jour., Dubuque, Iowa, 1995—2003. Author: Bittersweet, 1979, Places for the Heart - Profiles of Life, 2001. Avocations: theater, music, reading, flower gardening.

TOBACH, ETHEL, retired curator; b. Miaskovka, USSR, Nov. 7, 1921; came to U.S., 1923; d. Ralph Wiener and Fanny (Schechterman) Wiener Idels; m. Charles Tobach, 1947 (dec. 1969). BA, Hunter Coll., 1949; MA, NYU, 1952, PhD, 1957; DSc (hon.), L.I. Univ., 1975. Lic. psychologist, N.Y. Rsch. fellow Am. Mus. Natural History, N.Y.C., 1958-61, assoc. curator, 1964-69, curator, 1969-90, emerita curator; rsch. fellow NYU, N.Y.C., 1961-64. Adj. prof. psychology and biology CUNY, N.Y.C., 1964—; disting. cons. faculty Saybrook Inst., San Francisco, 1998—. Co-editor: (series) T.C. Schneirla Conference Series, 1981, Genes & Gender Series, 1975; editor: International Jour. Comparative Psychology, 1987-93; assoc. editor: Peace and Conflict: Jour. of Peace Psychology, 1994—. Recipient Disting. Sci. Career, Assn. Women in Sci., 1974, NIHH Career Devel. award, 1964-74, Disting. Sci. Publ., Assn. for Women in Psychology, 1982, Kurt Lewin award Soc. for Psychol. Study of [illegible], [illegible]; Gustavus Myers award for outstanding pub. on human rights in N.Am., 1996, Lifetime Peace Activity award Soc. for Study Peace, Conflict and Violence, 1999, Lifetime Achievement Psychology in Pub. Interest Gold Medal award Am. Psychol. Found., 2003. Fellow APA (pres. comparative psychology divsn.. 1985, peace psycology divsn., 2003); mem. Internat. Soc. Comparative Psychology (sec. 1988-92, pres. (hon.)), Ea. Psychol. Assn. (pres. 1987, bd. dirs. 2001—, mem. exec. com. 2002—), N.Y. Acad. Scis. (v.p. behavioral scis. 1973-76), Psychologists for Social Responsibility, Soc. for Study of Peace, Conflict and Violence. Office: Am Mus Natural History Central Pkwy 79th St New York NY 10024-5192

TOBEN, DOREEN A. corporate financial executive; b. Curacao; m. Ed Toben; 2 children. AB Polit. Sci., MBA Fin. and Mktg. . Dir. corp. planning AT&T, 1972; exec. dir. mktg. Bell Atlantic Enterprises Internat., Inc., 1989; various positions equipment engring., ops., and small bus. and consumer market mgmt. Bell Atlantic, Pa.; dir. fin. Bell Atlantic, 1983; divsn. mgr. strat. planning Bell Atlantic, 1984; asst. v.p.-comptroller Bell Atlantic, N.J., 1992; CFO Bell Atlantic, 1993; v.p. corp. fin. Bell Atlantic, vice pres., controller, 1995; mem. com. Bell Atlantic, v.p., CFO telecomm. network; sr. v.p., CFO telecomm. group Verizon, exec. v.p., CFO, 2002—. Office: Verizon 1095 Avenue of Americas New York NY 10036

TOBER, BARBARA D. (MRS. DONALD GIBBS TOBER), editor; b. Summit, N.J., Aug. 19, 1934; d. Rodney Fielding and Maude Starkey; m. Donald Gibbs Tober, Apr. 5, 1973. Student, Traphagen Sch. Fashion, 1954-56, Fashion Inst. Tech., 1956-58, N.Y. Sch. Interior Design, 1964. Copy editor Vogue Pattern Book, 1958-60; beauty editor Vogue mag., 1961; dir. women's services Bartell Media Corp., 1961-66; editor-in-chief Bride's mag., N.Y.C., 1966-94; chmn. Mus. Art and Design; pres. Acronym, Inc., N.Y.C., 1995—, The Barbara Tober Found., 1995—. Sec.-treas., dir. Sugar Foods Corp.; adv. bd. Traphagen Sch.; coord. SBA awards; Am. Craft Coun., 1983—, benefit food com. chmn., 1984-87. Author: The ABC's of Beauty, 1963, China: A Cognizant Guide, 1980, The Wedding . . . The Marriage . . . And the Role of the Retailer, 1980, The Bride: A Celebration, 1984 Mem. Nat. Council on Family Relations, 1966; nat. council Lincoln Center Performing Arts, Met. Opera Guild; mem. NYU adv. bd. Women in Food Service, 1983; NYU Women's Health Symposium: Steering Com., 1983—. Recipient Alma award, 1968, Penney-Mo. award, 1972, Traphagen Alumni award, 1975, Diamond Jubilee award, 1983, Disting. Women award Northwood U., 1997. Mem. Fashion Group, Internat. Furnishings and Design Assn. (v.p., program chmn.), Am. Soc. Mag. Editors, Am. Soc. Interior Designers (press mem.), Intercorporate Group, Women in Communications (60 yrs. of success award N.Y. chpt. 1984), Nat. Assn. Underwater Instrs., Pan Pacific and S.E. Asia Women's Assn., Asia Soc., Japan Soc., China Inst., Internat. Side Saddle Orgn., Millbrook Hounds, Golden's Bridge Hounds, Wine and Food Soc., Chaines des Rotisseurs (chargée de press) (bd. dirs.), Dames d'Escoffier, Culinary Inst. Am. Home and Office: 620 Park Ave New York NY 10021-6591

TOBIAS, ANITA, publishing executive; V.p. U.S. syndication L.A. Times Syndicate, 1998—. Office: Los Angeles Times Syndicate Times Mirror Sq 145 S Spring St Fl 10 Los Angeles CA 90012-3601

TOBIAS, DOROTHY BURTON, retired elementary school music educator, consultant; b. Columbia, S.C., Jan. 6, 1936; d. Joseph Nathaniel Burton and Dorothy Simons Bryan; m. William Raymond Tobias, Aug. 16, 1957 (dec. Nov. 25, 1994); children: William Raymond Jr., Dorothy Burton Tobias Yeley, Lawerence Hodge. BS Vocal performance and Music Edn., Winthrop Univ., Rock Hill, S.C., 1957; MHDL, Univ. N.C., Charlotte, 1981. Music specialist Orff Schulwerk master classes levels I, II and II Charlotte City Sch., 1957—58; elem. music specialist Charlotte-Mecklenburg Sch., 1975—80; devel. dir. WFAE Pub. Radio, Univ. N.C., Charlotte, 1980—81; elem. gen. music specialist Charlotte-Mecklenburg Sch., 1981—2001. Ch. choirs, childrens choir various orgn.; conf. presenter various workshops. Contbr. chapters to books. Precinct chair Dem. Party, Charlotte, 1970; mem., arts chair Jr. Women's league, Charlotte, 1965—72; bd. mem. Friends of the Arts Davidson Coll. Found., Davidson, NC, 1989—91, Friends of Music Queens Univ., Charlotte, 1994—, Golden Cir. Theatre, Charlotte, 1978—82; pres. of aux. Theatre Charlotte, 1974—75. Recipient Tchr. of the Yr., Charlotte-Meck Sch. Spl. Area, 1989; grantee N.C. Music Edn. Grant Winner, 1994, Charlotte-Mecklenburg Arts & Sci. Grant Winner, 1993, 1994, 1995; fellowship to study with Royal Shakespeare Co., Stratford, London, Eng., 1984. Mem.: Am. Orff Schulwerk Assn. (Piedmont chpt. sec., v.p. 1982, 1983, 2001, pres. 1984, nat. adv. bd. 1984), Music Educators Nat. Conf., N.C. Music Edn. Assn. (bd. chair elem. sect. 1994). Democrat. Meth. Avocations: antiques, cooking, travel, reading. Home: 2248 Colony Rd Charlotte NC 28209-1712

TOBIAS, JUDY, university development executive; b. Pitts. d. Saul Albert Landau and Bess (Previn) Kurzman; m. Seth Tobias (dec. May 1983); children: Stephen Frederic, Andrew Previn; m. Lewis F. Davis, 1990. Student, Silvermine Artists Guild, 1951-55; BA (hon.) (hon.), New Coll. of Calif., 1989. Art cons. Westchester Mental Health Asn., White Plains, N.Y., 1968-69; cons. sch. social work NYU, 1973-74, devel. exec., 1976—. Conf. coord. Today's Family: Implications for the Future, N.Y.C., 1974-75; cons. Playschools, Inc., N.Y.C., 1975; majority counsel mem. Emily's List, 1991—. Mem. Gov.'s Commn. on Continuing Edn., Albany, N.Y., 1968-70, Nat. Coun. on Children and Youth, Washington, 1974-75, Manhattan Inter-Hosp. Group on Child Abuse, 1975-76; chmn. N.Y. met. com. for UNICEF, 1976-77; mem. exec. com. Town Hall Found., N.Y.C., 1979—, vice chmn., 1986-90; founder, bd. dirs. N.Y. chpt. WAIF, Inc., 1961-99, nat. pres., 1978-82, nat. bd. dirs., 1978-2000; pres. emeritus, 1993-99; bd. dirs. Citizen's Com. for Children, City of N.Y., 1975—, v.p., 1983-90, 97-99; bd. dirs. Am. br. Internat. Social Svc., 1965-80; bd. dirs. Andrew Glover Youth Program, 1986-89, mem. adv. coun., 1989—; bd. dirs. Goddard Riverside Cmty. Ctr., 1985—, Dance Mag. Found., 1986-92, St. John's Place Family Ctr., 1987-93, Capitol Hall Preservation Corp., 1989-93, Inst. for Cultural Diversity; steering com. The Leadership Connection, 1992—. Recipient Nat. Humanitarian award, WAIF, 1990, Millennium Honoree award, NYU Sch. Social Work, 2000. Mem. Child Study Assn. Am. (bd. dirs. 1963-71, pres. 1969-71, bd. dirs. Wel-Met Inc. 1972-85), Brookings Instn. (coun. mem. 1998—), Emily's List (majority coun. 1990—), Women Matter (bd. chmn. 2003—). E-mail: ajtdavis@aol.com.

TOBIAS, SHEILA, writer, educator; d. Paul Jay and Rose (Steinberger) Tobias; m. Carlos Stern, Oct. 11, 1970 (div. 1982); m. Carl T. Tomizuka, Dec. 16, 1987. BA, Harvard Radcliffe U., 1957; MA, Columbia U., 1961, MPhil, 1974; PhD (hon.), Drury Coll., 1994, Wheelock Coll., 1995; PhD (hon.), SUNY, Potsdam, 1996, Mich. State U., 2000, Worcester Polytech, 2002. Journalist, W. Germany, U.S. and Fed. Republic Germany, 1957-65; lect. in history C.C.N.Y., N.Y.C., 1965-67; univ. adminstr. Cornell U., Wesleyan U., 1967-78; lect. in women's studies U. Calif., San Diego, 1985-92; lect. in war, peace studies U. So. Calif., 1985-88. Cons. sci. and bus. U. Amsterdam, Leiden, Netherlands, 1995—98; pres. Outreach Coord. Sci. Master's Initiative, 1997—; vis. prof. U. Amsterdam, U. Leiden, 1994—97. Author: Overcoming Math Anxiety, 1978, rev. edit., 1994, Succeed with Math, 1987, Revitalizing Undergraduate Science: Why Some Things Work and Most Don't, 1992, Science as a Career: Perceptions and Realities, 1995; co-author: The People's Guide to National Defense, 1982, Women, Militarism and War, 1987, They're Not Dumb, They're Different, 1990, (with Carl T. Tomizuka) Breaking the Science Barrier, 1992, Rethinking Science as a Career, 1995, (with Jacqueline Raphael) The

Hidden Curriculum, 1997, Faces of Feminism, 1997. Exec. v.p. Vet. Feminists of Am., 2002—. Fellow AAAS; mem. Am. Assn. Higher Edn. (bd. dirs. 1993-97). Avocations: outdoor hiking, skiing. E-mail: Sheila@SheilaTobias.com.

TOBIASSEN, VIRGINIA HEGE, editor, author; b. Winston-Salem, N.C., Apr. 18, 1959; d. Fredrick Pfohl and Dorothy Alice (Baker) Hege; m. William Edward Tobiassen, June 11, 1988; 1 child, Thor Hege Tobiassen. BA in English, U. N.C., 1981. Editor John F. Blair, Publisher, Winston-Salem, N.C., 1983-85, McFarland & Co., Inc. Publishers, Jefferson, N.C., 1985-89; asst. dir. for press activities Appalachian Consortium, Boone, N.C., 1989; freelance editor, author Boone, 1990-96; editor McFarland & Co., 1996—2002, editl. devel. chief, 2002—. Author: (book) Am I Glowing Yet?, 1995, The Gift of the Magi Retold in Rhyme, 2002. Democrat. Moravian.

TOBIN, AILEEN WEBB, educational administrator; b. Milford, Del., July 9, 1949; d. Wilson Webster Webb and Dorothy Marie (Benson) Rust; m. Thomas Joseph Tobin, Jr., July 31, 1971. BA cum laude, U. Del., 1971, MEd, 1975, PhD, 1981. Cert. tchr. secondary edn., cert. reading specialist, cert. reading cons., Del. Dir. Del. Tutoring Ctr., Wilmington, 1971-74; grad. teaching asst. U. Del., Newark, 1974-81, instr. Coll. Edn., 1978-82; ednl. specialist U.S. Army Ordnance Ctr. & Sch., Aberdeen Proving Ground, Md., 1982-85, chief internal eval. br., 1985-88, chief evaluation divsn., 1988, chief standardization and analysis div., 1988-90, dir. quality assurance, 1990-94, dir. tactical support equipment dept., 1994-98, dir. command planning office, 1998—. Cons. Dorchester County Sch. Dist., Dorchester County, Md., 1977-80; rsch. assoc., Ctr. for Ednl. Leadership, Newark, 1981-82; staff assoc., Rsch. for Better Schs., Inc., Phila., 1981-84. Author: (book chpt.) Approaches Informal Eval. of Reading, 1982, Dialogues in Literary Research, 1988, Cognitive & Social Perspectives for Literary Research & Instruction, 1989; contbr. articles to profl. jours. Recipient Silver award Fed. Exec. Bd., 1992, Comdr.'s award for Civil Svc. Dept. Army, 1994, 96, Order of Samuel Sharpe award Ordnance Corps Assn., 1994, Superior Civil Svc. award Dept. Army, 1995, 98. Mem. Internat. Reading Assn., Nat. Reading Conf., Am. Ednl. Rsch. Assn., Am. Evaluation Assn., Ordnance Corps Assn., Kappa Delta Pi. Methodist. Avocations: travel, reading, tennis, sailing. Home: 2515 Boston St # 205 Baltimore MD 21224 Office: US Army Ordnance Ctr & Sch ATSL CP Aberdeen Proving Ground MD 21005

TOBIN, BARBARA KAY, minister; b. Davenport, Iowa, Oct. 9, 1943; d. Robert Thomas Myers and Frances Louella Davis; m. Richard James Tobin, Feb. 12, 1966; 1 child, Mary Beth Tobin Peter. B.Humanities, Social Sci. and Edn., Purdue U., 1966; BEd, Ball State U., 1968; MDiv, Colgate Rochester Div. Sch., 1994. Cert. tchr. N.Y., ordained to ministry Presbyn. Ch., 1994. Fgn. lang. tchr. West Irondequoit Schs., Rochester, NY, 1968—93; chaplain Strong Meml. Hosp., Rochester, 1993—94; pastor of visitation First Presbyn. Ch., Pittsford, NY, 1994—96; assoc. pastor Perinton Presbyn. Ch., Fairport, NY, 1995—2000; pastor Irondequoit Presbyn. Ch., Rochester, 2000—. Sec., bd. dirs. Irondequoit Sr. Transp. Ministry, Rochester, 2002—; mem. com. on ministry Genesee Valley Presbytery, 2001—. Mem.: N.Y. State Ret. Tchrs. Assn., Purdue U. Alumni Assn. (life; pres.'s coun. 1993—). Presbyterian. Avocations: reading, travel, sailing. Office: Irondequoit Presbyn Ch 2881 Culver Rd Rochester NY 14622 Office Phone: 585-266-3370. Personal E-mail: bottei66A@aol.com.

TOBIN, LOIS MOORE, home economist, educator, retired; b. Johnstown, Pa., Oct. 8, 1928; d. William B and Ida L. (Diehl) Moore; m. Warner E. Tobin, June 7, 1953 (dec.); children: Brian W., Robert E. BS, Indiana State Tchrs. Coll., Pa., 1951; postgrad., U. Pitts., 1952, U. Colo., 1953; MEd, Pa. State U., 1967; postgrad., Indiana U. of Pa., 1977-85. Tchr. Allegheny Valley Joint Sch. Dist., Springdale, Pa., 1951-53, Kittanning (Pa.) Sch. Dist., 1953-55, Carlisle (Pa.) Joint Sch. Dist., 1964-66, State Coll. (Pa.) Sch. Dist., 1967-73; mem. faculty dept. food and nutrition Indiana U. of Pa., 1974, 76-77, mem. faculty home econs. edn., 1979-82, coord. Single Parent-Homemaker Svc. Ctr. Vocat. Pers. Prep., 1984-91. Mem. adv. com. Indiana Area Vocat.-Tech. Sch., 1981-94; presenter in field. Author: (booklet) Home Economics Education Bibliography on Special Needs, 1982, Teaching Special Needs Individuals in Home Economics, 1982; contbr. articles to profl. newsletters. Sec. Indiana County Human Svcs. Coun., 1990—91; vol. Bloodmobile, 1986—; tour guide Breezedale Restoration, 1986—; pres. Calvary Ch. Women's Club, 1975—76, Indiana County Newcomers Club, 1974, 1975; elder, session mem. Calvary Presbyn. Ch., 1996—2002. Grantee Dept. Edn. Bur. Vocat. Edn., 1980-82, 86-91, Human Svcs. Devel. Fund, 1989-91. Mem. Am. Vocat. Assn., Pa. Vocat. Assn., Nat. Trust for Hist. Preservation, Indiana County Hist. and Geneal. Soc., Indiana U. of Pa. Ret. Faculty Assn. (treas. 1998-2002), Indiana County Alumni Assn. (bd. dirs.), Pa. Home Econs. Assn. (treas. 1975-77), Pa. Vocat. Home Econs. Educators (sec. 1990-91). Avocations: swimming, travel, church choir. Home: 896 White Farm Rd Indiana PA 15701-1254

TOCHTROP, LOIS, state legislator, nurse consultant; b. St. Louis, Jan. 31, 1942; d. Walter Louis Werner and Elizabeth Louise Brante; m. Paul Frederick Tochtrop, Oct. 14, 1961; children: Tony, Scott, Timothy. BSN and Health Care Adminstrn., Metro State Coll., 1988. RN; lic. nursing home adminstr. Staff nurse City Hosp., St. Louis, 1963-67; head nurse St. Louis U. Hosp., 1967-70; staff nurse Meml. Hosp., Jefferson City, Mo., 1970-75, nurse supr., 1975-79; office nurse, asst. DON Craig (Colo.) Med. Clinic, 1979-83; staff nurse Willowbrook Care, Denver, 1984-88, DON, 1988-90, Park Forest Care Ctr., Denver, 1990-98, nursing cons., 1998—. Pres. Colo. Nurses Assn. Dist. 23, 1992-96; legis. affairs specialist Abate of Co., 1993-96. Named Legislator of Yr., AARP, Denver, 1999, Colo. Sr. Lobby, Denver, 1999, Colo. Cancer Soc., Denver, 1999. Democrat. Roman Catholic. Avocations: reading, walking, word games, motorcycling. Home: 10452 Dale Cir Denver CO 80234-3533

TOCIO, MARY ANN, association executive; MS, Simmons Coll. Sch. Mgmt. Sr. v.p. ops. Health Stop Med. Mgmt., Inc., Boston; CEO Bright Horizons Family Solutions Family Ctrs., Cambridge, Mass. Office: Bright Horizons Family Solutions One Kendall Sw Bldg 200 Cambridge MA 02139

TODD, CHERYL, art educator; b. Winston-Salem, N.C., Nov. 9, 1947; d. Dwight Lionel and Betsy Ann Gordon; m. David Gary Todd, June 27, 1970; children: Kevin, Tate. BS, East Carolina U., 1970; MEd, U. S.C., 1989. Chairperson fine arts dept., art and English tchr. Myrtle Beach (S.C.) H.S., 1972-99. Sponsor Interact, sr. class sponsor, cheerleeding Myrtle Beach H.S.; shag dance instr. Myrtle Beach Recreation Dept. Avocations: watercolor painting, snorkeling, biking. Home: 3900 Oak Cir Myrtle Beach SC 29577-0870 E-mail: ctodd@mbh.sccoast.net.

TODD, J. C. See COOPER, JANE

TODD, JUDITH F. lawyer; b. Chgo., Jan. 25, 1946; Student, Vassar Coll.; AB, U. Mich., 1968; JD cum laude, U. Miami, 1972. Bar: Fla. 1972, Ill. 1977, Ala. 1981. With Sirote & Permutt PC, Birmingham, Ala., now ptnr. Assoc. editor U. Miami Law Review, 1971-72. Fellow Am. Coll. Trust and Estate Counsel; mem. ABA, Fla. Bar, Ill. State Bar Assn. Office: Sirote & Permutt PC 2311 Highland Ave S Birmingham AL 35205-2972

TODD, KATHLEEN GAIL, physician; b. Portland, Oreg., Aug. 31, 1951; d. Horace Edward and Lois Marie (Messing) T.; m. Andrew Richard Embick, March 31, 1980; children: Elizabeth Todd Embick, Margaret Todd Embick. BA, Pomona Coll., 1972; MD, Washington U., St. Louis, 1976. Diplomate Am. Bd. Family Practice. Resident U. Wash. Affiliated Hosps., Seattle, 1976-79; pvt. practice Valdez (Alaska) Med. Clinic, 1980—; chief of staff Valdez Community Hosp., 1986—. Mem. AMA, AAFP, Am. Acad. Family Practice, Alaska State Med. Assn. (counselor-at-large 1986-87). Democrat. Episcopalian. Avocations: skiing, kayaking, camping, music. Office: Valdez Med Clinic PO Box 1829 Valdez AK 99686-1829

TODD, KIM A. actress; d. Edward W. and Mary F. Nissen. BFA, U. Iowa. Co-owner Video Assocs.; owner Player's Studios Ltd., N.Y.C. Mem., performer Potter's Field, Mo Ming Mime Troupe, Player's OE of Second City, Chgo. Mem.: NAFE, AFTRA, SAG, Actors Equity Assn. Home: 65 Nassau #4A New York NY 10028

TODD, LINDA MARIE, nutrition researcher, circulation manager, financial consultant, pilot; b. LA, Mar. 30, 1948; d. Ithel Everette and Janet Marie Fredricks; m. William MacKenzie Cook, Jan. 11, 1982 (div. Oct. 1989); m. Robert Oswald Todd, Apr. 8, 1990; 1 child, Jesse MacKenzie Todd. BA in Psychology and Sociology, U. Colo., 1969; student in Psychology, U. No. Colo., 1970. Pilot lic., weather cert., FCC lic., Calif. life ins. lic., coll. teaching credential; registered with Nat. Assn. Securities Dealers. Counselor Jeffco Juvenile Detention Ctr., Golden, Colo., 1969-71; communications Elan Vital, Denver, 1971-81; legal sec. Fredman, Silverberg & Lewis, San Diego, 1980-82; escrow supr. Performance Mktg. Concepts, Olympic Valley, Calif., 1982-85; mgmt. commn. instr. Sierra Coll., Truckee, Calif., 1986-87; regional mgr. Primerica Fin. Svcs., Reno, 1987-91; air traffic, weather advisor Truckee Tahoe Airport Dist., Calif., 1986-96; circulation mgr. Tahoe World Newspaper, 2001—03, Sierra Sun, 2001—. Student tour leader, air show organizer Truckee (Calif.) Tahoe Airport, 1986-96; fin. cons. Primerica Fin. Svcs., Truckee, 1987-91; gen. agt. TTS Fin., 1992—; co-founder Todd Nutrition, 1995—; co-owner Todd Aero, 1990—; bd. dirs. Pacific Crest Fin. Corp., 1996—. Editor: (newsletter) Communications, 1975. Chorus mem. operas and musicals, 1960s-70s; prodn. crew mem. Lake Tahoe Summer Music Festivals, 2000—; sec. gen. Arapahoe H.S. Model UN, Littleton, Colo., 1965; del. State Model UN, Colo., 1966; conv. del. Elan Vital, The Ninety-Nines, Inc.; pub. affairs officer CAP. Recipient Univ. scholarship Littleton (Colo.) Edn. Assn., 1966, flight scholarship The Ninety-Nines Inc., Reno, 1990; named Recruiter of Month, Al Williams Primerica, Reno, 1987. Mem. CAP, Elan Vital, Plane Talkers, The Ninety Nines, Planetary Soc. Avocations: hiking, skiing, swimming, flying, soaring. Home and Office: PO Box 1303 Truckee CA 96160-1303

TODD, MARY BETH, medical oncologist, researcher; b. Tulsa, Okla., June 10, 1951; d. Earl K. and Edith (Beaty) T. BA, Okla. City U., 1972; postgrad., U. Tulsa, 1973-74; DO, Okla. State U., 1978. Assoc. rsch. scientist Yale Sch. Medicine, New Haven, 1984-86; dir. outpatient svc. Yale Medical Sch., New Haven, 1986-93; asst. prof. Sch. Medicine Yale U., New Haven, 1986-91, assoc. prof., 1991-93; assoc. prof. medicine UMDNJ-RWJMS, New Brunswick, 1993—2002, prof. medicine, 2002—, deputy dir. The Cancer Inst. N.J., New Brunswick, NJ, 1993—. Scientific adv. panel for immunology svcs. Food & Drug Adminstrn., Washington, 1991-95; scientific adv. bd. HEM Pharmeceuticals Corp., 1991-93; external medical adv. bd. Conn. Hospice, 1990-92; co-chair N.J. Working Group to Improve Outcomes in Cancer Patients. Recipient grants Nat. Inst. Health, 1989-98. Mem. Am. Coll. Physicians, Am. Fedn. Clinical Rsch., Am. Soc. Clinical Oncology, Am. Assn. Cancer Rsch., Am. Soc. Hemetology, Internat. Soc. Interferon and Cytokine Rsch. Office: The Cancer Inst NJ 195 Little Albany St New Brunswick NJ 08901-1914

TODD, NORMA ROSS, retired government official; b. Butler, Pa., Oct. 3, 1920; d. William Bryson and Doris Mae (Ferguson) Ross; m. Alden Frank Miller, Jr., Apr. 16, 1940 (dec. Feb. 1975); 1 child, Alden Frank III; m. Jack R. Todd, Dec. 23, 1977 (dec. Sept. 1990). Student, Pa. State U., 1944-46, Yale U., 1954-57. Exec. mgr. Donora (Pa.) C. of C., 1950-57, pres., 1972; exec. mgr. Donora Cmty. Chest, 1950-57; office mgr. Donora Golden Jubilee, 1951; staff writer Donora Herald-American, 1957, city editor, 1957-70; assoc. editor Daily Herald, Donora, 1970-73; svc. rep. Pitts. Telesvc. Ctr., Social Security Adminstrn., HHS, 1977-83. Mem. Mayor's Adv. Coun., Donora, 1965-69, Citizens' Adv. Coun., Donora, 1965-69; mem. Donora Bd. Edn., 1954-60, pres., 1960; mem. Donora Borough Coun., 1970-72; bd. dirs. Mon Valley chpt. ARC, 1964-99, sec. bd., 1964-97, chmn. bd. dirs., 1997-99, mem. lifetime adv. bd., 2000; bd. dirs. Washington County Tourism Agy., 1970-90, sec., 1972-90; bd. dirs. Washington County History and Landmarks Found., 1971-80, 91-92, sec., 1975-80, 91-93, hon. life mem., 1996; bd. dirs. Mon Valley YMCA, 1960-66, Mon Valley coun. Camp Fire Girls, 1965-79, Mon Valley Drug and Alcoholism Coun., 1971-78; hon. life mem. Pa. Congress PTAs; bd. dirs. United Way Mon Valley, 1973-82, chmn. pub. rels., 1973-74. Recipient Fine Arts Festival of Pa. Poetry first prize award Fedn. Women's Clubs, 1987, 1st and 2d pl. awards for photography Washington County Fine Arts Festival, County Fedn. Women's Clubs, 1990, Disting. Svc. award Donora Rotary Club, 1997, Millenium Peace award, India, 2001, Two World Poets awards J. Mark Press, 2002, U.S. Rep. Senatorial Medal of Freedom, 2003, Congl. Order Merit, 2003; pub. in Best Poems of 1995 Nat. Libr. of Poetry, Best Poems of 1996, Best Poems of 1997, Outstanding Poets of 1998, Am. at the Millennium The Best Poets of the 20th Century, The Best Poems and Poets of 2001, The Best Poems and Poets of 2002, and numerous anthologies in U.S., Italy, Great Britain and India. Mem. AAUW, Svc. Corps Retired Execs. (sec. 1998—), Pa. Soc. Newspaper Editors, Pitts. Press Club, Donora C. of C. (pres. 1971-72), DAR (regent Monongahela Valley chpt. 1974-77, treas. 1992-2001), Internat. Platform Assn. (finalist Acad. of Poets Competition, 2001), World Poetry Soc. Internat., Internat. Poets Acad., Famous Poet Soc., U.S. Poets, Metverse Muse, Washington County Poetry Soc. (pres. 1967-69), Donora Hist. Soc. (curator 1990—), Family of Bruce Soc. (descendants of King Robert the Bruce of Scotland 1987—), Washington County Fedn. Women's Clubs (rec. sec. 1964-66, pub. rels chmn. 1990-92), Order Ea. Star (worthy matron 1966-67, treas. 1986-94, 98—2003, bd. dirs. Western Pa. Eastern Star Home 1997-98, adv. bd. Masonic Eastern Star Home-West 1998-2000), White Shrine of Jerusalem (high priestess 1973-74, treas. 1995-2001), Order of Amaranth (royal matron 1966, dist. dep. 3 times, grand rep. W.Va. 1979-80), Donora Forecast (pres. 1957-59), Donora Unidon (pres. 1965-66, 56-57), Clan Ross Assn. U.S. Avocation: genealogy. Home: Overlook Ter Donora PA 15033 also: 1310 Mckean Ave Donora PA 15033-2200

TODD, PAMELA SUE, music educator; b. Easton, Pa., Dec. 11, 1956; d. Harry William Campbell, Jr. and Dorothy Wagner Campbell; m. Kenneth Wayne Todd, Aug. 29, 1980; 1 child, Jonathan Robert. MusB in Edn., Houghton Coll., 1978. Tchr. jr. high music Bethlehem Area Sch. Dist., Pa., 1978—80; sec. to music dir. Tremont Temple Bapt. Ch., Boston, 1981—83; profl. accompanist 22d St. Bapt. Ch., Tucson, 1992—98, Palo Verde Christian Sch., Tucson, 1992—98, tchr. instrumental, vocal music, 1994—2000; tchr. instrumental music grades 7-12 Pusch Ridge Christian Acad., Tucson, 2000—01; profl. accompanist St. Gregory Coll. Prep. Sch., Tucson, 2001—. Pvt. music tchr., Tucson, 1974—; vocal dir. Oswego Choral Soc., NY, 1987—92; music tchr. Zion Luth. Sch., Oswego, 1990—92; prin. horn Catalina Foothills Philharm., Tucson, 1996—; asst. prin. horn Ariz. Symphonic Winds, Tucson, 2000—02, French horn player, 2000—. Coord. worship for children's ch. El Camino Bapt. Ch., Tucson, 2003. Conservative-R. Baptist. Achievements include Nominated to Disney Outstanding Teachers 2001. Avocations: sewing, travel, gardening, painting. Home: 145 NE Slope Loop Tucson AZ 85748 Personal E-mail: ziggyboo@cox.net.

TODD, RUTH, artist; b. Sanford, N.C., Nov. 10, 1909; m. Judson Cornelius and Flora Thomas; m. Littleton Todd, May 19, 1934. Student, Anderson Coll., 1927-28, U. Miami, 1930-31, Colorado Springs Coll., 1954. One-woman shows Morris Gallery, N.Y.C., 1958, Bodley Gallery, N.Y.C., 1962, Internat. House, Denver, 1964, U. Colo., Boulder, 1968, Joseph Magnin Gallery, Denver, 1975, Merrill-Chase Galleries, Chgo., 1977, West End Gallery, Winston-Salem, N.C., 1979, also others; exhibited in numerous group shows, including Santa Fe Mus., Sweat Meml. Art Mus., Portland, Maine, Creative Galleries, N.Y.C., N.Y.C. Ctr. Gallery, N.C. State Mus. Art, Raleigh, Mulvane Art Ctr., Topeka, Denver Art Mus., U. N.Mex., Albuquerque, Colorado Springs (Colo.) Fine Arts Ctr., La Galléria Escondido, Taos, N.Mex.; represented in permanent collections Princeton U., NYU, also corp. and pvt. collections. Recipient awards for art including Soc. Four Arts Mus., Palm Beach, Fla., Nelson Adkins Gallery, Kansas City (Mo.) Mus., George Walter Vincent Smith Art Mus., Springfield, Mass., Joslyn Art Mus., Omaha, Okla. Fine Arts Ctr., Oklahoma City; 1st award Nat. Space Art Exhibit, 1969, 3d award, 1975. Episcopalian.

TODD, SHIRLEY ANN, school system administrator; b. May 23, 1935; d. William Leonard and Margaret Judy (Simmons) Brown; m. Thomas Byron Todd, July 7, 1962 (dec. July 1977). BS in Edn., Madison Coll., 1956; MEd, U. Va., 1971. Cert. tchr. Va. Elem. sch. tchr. Fairfax County Sch. Bd., Fairfax, Va., 1956—66, mid. sch. tchr., 1966—71; guidance counselor James F. Cooper Mid. Sch., McLean, Va., 1971—88, dir. guidance, 1988—96; chmn. mktg. Lake Anne Joint Venture, Falls Church, Va., 1979—81, mng. ptnr., 1980—82. Del. Fairfax County Rep. Conv., 1985. Fellow: Fairfax Edn. Assn. (bd. dirs. 1968—70, profl. rights and responsibilities commn. 1970—72); mem.: ASCD, NEA, Va. Sch. Counselors Assn., Va. Counselors Assn., Va. Counselors Assn. (exec. com. 1987), No. Va. Counselors Assn. (exec. bd. 1982—83, hospitality and social chmn.), Va. Edn. Assn. (state com. on local assns. and urban affairs 1969—70), Vintage Ladies of No. Va. (newsletter editor 2002—03), Women's Golf Assn. (pres. 1997—98), Welcome Club of No. Va. (pres. 2003—04), Chantilly Nat. Golf and Country Club (v.p. social 1981—82). Baptist. Avocations: golf, tennis. Home: 6543 Bay Tree Ct Falls Church VA 22041-1001

TODD COPLEY, JUDITH A. materials and metallurgical engineering educator; b. Wakefield, West Yorkshire, Eng., Dec. 13, 1950; came to U.S., 1978; d. Marley and Joan Mary (Birkinshaw) Booth; m. David Michael Todd, June 17, 1972 (div. June 1981); m. Stephen Michael Copley, Aug. 3, 1984; 1 child, Amy Elizabeth. BA in Materials Sci., Cambridge (Eng.) U., 1972, MA, PhD in Metall./Materials Sci., 1977. Rsch. asst. Imperial Coll. Sci. and Tech., London, 1976-78; rsch. assoc. SUNY, Stonybrook, 1978; rsch. engr. U. Calif., Berkeley, 1979-81; asst. prof. materials sci. and mech. engring. U. So. Calif., L.A., 1982—90; assoc. prof. metall. and materials engring. Ill. Inst. Tech., Chgo., 1990-97, assoc. chair mech. materials and aerospace engring., 1995—2001, prof. materials and mech. engring., 1997—2002, assoc. dean rsch. Armour Coll. Engring. and Sci., 2001—02; P.B. Breneman dept. head chair chair dept. engring. sci. and mechanics Pa. State U., University Park, 2002—. Mem. task force Materials Property Coun., N.Y.C., 1979—89; prof. Iron and Steel Soc., 1996—2002; mem. editl. bds. Contbr. articles to profl. jours.; patentee in field. Recipient Brit. Univs. Student Travel award, 1972, Brit. Fedn. Univ. Women award, 1979, Faculty Rsch. award Oak Ridge (Tenn.) Nat. Lab., 1986, Vanadium award British Inst. Materials, 1990; Kathryn Kingswell Meml. scholar, 1972, Julia Beveridge Award, IIT, 1998, Cert. Appreciation Am. Soc. Mech. Engrs., 1995, 97, Forging Industry Ednl. Rsch. Found., 1993, Booz-Allen and Hamilton Award for Tchg. and Svc., Ill. Inst. Tech., 1996, Mary Ewart Traveling Scholarship, Cambridge Univ., 1972, Sci. Rsch. Coun. Fellowship and Overseas Travel Award, 1972. Fellow ASME Internat. (chmn. materials and fabrication com. 1993-97, pressure vessel and piping divsn. membership chair PVP divsn., 1997-2001, assoc. editor Jour. Pressure Vessel and Piping Tech., 1994-2001, mem. exec. com. PVP divsn. 2001—, v.p. mfg. group 2002—, bd. on women and miniorites award 1997), Fellow Assn. Women in Sci., Fellow ASM Internat. (chmn. L.A. chpt. 1986-87, coun. mem. materials sci. divsn. 1984-89); mem. AIME (Rsch. award 1983), ASTM, Soc. Women Engrs. (sr.), Electron Microscopy Soc., Hist. Metallurgy Soc., Nat. Soc. Corrosion Engrs. (Seed grant award 1983), Microbeam Analysis Soc., Soc. Mfg. Engrs., Am. Assn. Univ. Women, Instn. Metall., Chartered Engr. Status, Minerals, Metals, Materials Soc. of the Am. Inst. Mining, Metall. Petroleum Engrs., Am. Ceramics Soc., Ill. Microscopical Soc. Avocation: archaeometry. Office: Pennsylvania State Univ Dept Engring Sci and Mechanics 212 Earth-Engring Sci Bldg University Park PA 16802-6812 E-mail: jtodd@psu.edu.

TODORO, MARY ELIZABETH, process engineer; b. Buffalo, N.Y., Apr. 21, 1980; d. Carl Arthur and Peggy Ann Todoro. BSChemE, U. S.C., 2002. EIT S.C. Bd. Registration for Profl. Engrs. and Land Surveyors, 2003. Process engr. asst. Alcoa, Inc., Goose Creek, SC, 2000—01, process engr., 2002—. Orgn. pres. U. S.C. Newman Club, Columbia, 2000—02. Mem.: Am. Chem. Soc. Office: Alcoa - Mt Holly PO Box 1000 Goose Creek SC 29445

TODOROVA-MORENO, ILINA, psychologist, educator; arrived in U.S., 1996; children: Barbara Cvejik, Simonida Cvejic. PhD, U. Belgrade, 1987. Lic. psychologist Mo. Prof. U. Chyril and Methodius, Skopje, 1975—96, St. Louis U., 2000—. Exec. dir., psychotherapist, founder CARE MHS, St. Louis, 2002—; pres., founder Harmony in Life, St. Louis, 2002—. Author: (book) My Drawings-My Truth: Psychology of Children's drawings, 1997, Wake Up Your Creative Mind: Psychology of Creative Thinking, 1994, Psychology, 1996. Mem.: APA. Office: Care MHS 5629 Gravois Ave Saint Louis MO 63116 Personal E-mail: ilinam@aol.com.

TOELKES, DIXIE E. state legislator; m. Roger Toelkes. Educator; mem. from dist. 53 Kans. State Ho. of Reps., Topeka. Address: 3811 SE 33rd Ter Topeka KS 66605-3077 Office: Kans House of Reps State House Topeka KS 66612

TOENSING, VICTORIA, lawyer; b. Colon, Panama, Oct. 16, 1941; d. Philip William and Victoria (Brady) Long; m. Trent David Toensing, Oct. 29, 1962 (div. 1976); children: Todd Robert, Brady Cronon, Amy Victoriana; m. Joseph E. diGenova, June 27, 1981. BS in Edn., Ind. U., 1962; JD cum laude, U. Detroit, 1975. Bar: Mich. 1976, D.C. 1978. Tchr. English, Milw., 1965-66; law clk. to presiding justice U.S. Ct. Appeals, Detroit, 1975-76; asst. U.S. atty. U.S. Atty.'s Office, Detroit, 1976-81; chief counsel U.S. Senate Intelligence Com., Washington, 1981-84; dep. asst. atty. gen. criminal div. Dept. Justice, Washington, 1984-88; spl. counsel Hughes Hubbard & Reed, Washington, 1988-90; ptnr. Cooter and Gell, Washington, 1990-91; ptnr., co-chmn. nat. white collar group Manatt, Phelps and Phillips, Washington, 1991-95; founding ptnr. diGenova & Toensing, Wasington, 1996—. Mem. working group on corp. sanctions U.S. Sentencing Commn., 1988-89; co-chairperson Coalition for Women's Appts. Justice Judiciary Task Force, 1988-92; spl. counsel for Teamsters investigation, U.S. Ho. of Reps., Subcom. on Oversight and Investigations of com. on Edn. and the Workforce, 1997-98. Author: Bringing Sanity to the Insanity Defense, 1983, Mens Rea: Insanity by Another Name, 1984; contbg. author: Fighting Back: Winning The War Against Terrorism, Desk Book on White Collar Crime, 1991; contbr. articles to profl. jours. Founder, chmn. Women's Orgn. To Meet Existing Needs, Mich., 1975-79; chmn. Republican Women's Task Force, 1979-81; bd. dirs. Project on Equal Edn. Rights, Mich., 1980-81, Nat. Hist. Intelligence Mus., 1987-95, America's Talking Legal Analyst, 1995; MSNBC legal analyst, 1998-99. Recipient spl. commendation Office U.S. Atty. Gen., 1980, agy. seal medallion CIA, 1986, award of achievement Alpha Chi Omega, 1992; featured on cover N.Y. Time Mag. for anti-terrorism work, April 1991. Mem. ABA (mem. standing com. on law and nat. security, mem. coun. criminal justice sect., mem. adv. com. complex crimes and litigation, vice chmn. white collar crime com., chmn. subcom. on corp. criminal liability). E-mail: dt@digenovatoensing.com.

TOEPFER, SUSAN JILL, editor; b. Rochester, Minn., Mar. 9, 1948; d. John Bernard and Helen Esther (Chapple) T.; m. Lorenzo Gabriel Carcaterra, May 16, 1981; children: Katherine Marie, Nicholas Gabriel. BA, Bennington Coll., 1970. Mng. editor Photoplay Mag., N.Y.C., 1971-72; freelance writer N.Y.C., 1972-78; TV week editor N.Y. Daily News, N.Y.C., 1978-79, leisure editor, 1979-82, features editor, 1982-84, arts and entertainment editor, 1984-86, exec. mag. editor, 1986-87; sr. writer People Mag., N.Y.C., 1987-89, sr. editor, 1989-91, asst. mng. editor, 1991-94, exec. editor, 1994-00, dep. mng. editor, 2000—02; editor-in-chief Rosie Mag., 2002; editor-at-large G+J USA, N.Y.C., 2003—. Office: G+J USA 375 Lexington Ave New York NY 10017-5514

TOFF, NANCY ELLEN, book editor; b. Greenburgh, N.Y., Aug. 29, 1955; d. Ira N. and Ruth (Bluthenthal) T. AB, Harvard U., 1976. Editor, prodr. Music Minus One, N.Y.C., 1973-75; rschr. Time-Life Books, Alexandria, Va., 1976-80; editor, asst. prodr. Time-Life Music, Alexandria, Va., 1980-84; prodn. mgr. Vanguard Recording Soc., N.Y.C., 1984-86; editor Grove's Dictionaries of Music, N.Y.C., 1984-85; v.p., editor-in-chief Chelsea House Pubs., N.Y.C., 1986-89, v.p., dir. book devel., 1990; editl. dir. Julian Messner/Silver Burdett Press, Englewood Cliffs, N.J., 1990-91; editl. dir. children's and young adult books Oxford U. Press, N.Y.C., 1991-98, editl. dir. young adult reference, 1998—, v.p., 1999—. Editorial cons., Music Div. Lib. of Congress, 1983; hist. cons., Dept. of Musical Instruments, Met. Mus. of Art, N.Y.C., 1986. Author: The Development of the Modern Flute, 1979, The Flute Book, 1985, 2d edit., 1996, Georges Barrère and the Flute in America, 1994; cons. editor Flutist Quar., 1990-99; contbr. articles to profl. jours.; curator Georges Barrère and the Flute in America, N.Y. Pub. Libr., 1994. Bd. dirs., Radcliffe Coll. Alumnae Assn. 1979-80. Recipient Dena Epstein award Music Libr. Assn., 1997; Sinfonia Found. rsch. grantee, 1999. Mem. Nat. Flute Assn. (asst. sec. 1988-89, sec. 1989-90, bd. dirs. 1990-92), N.Y. Flute Club (bd. dirs. 1986—, sec. 1991-92, 98-2000, pres. 1992-95, 1st v.p. 1995-98). Home: 425 E 79th St Apt 6F New York NY 10021-1011 Office: Oxford U Press 198 Madison Ave New York NY 10016-4341 E-mail: toffn@oup-usa.org.

TÖGEL, CORNELIA (CONNI) D. artist; b. Winfield, Ill., July 24, 1965; d. Heinrich and Lisa Scherz; m. Peter Horst Tögel, Apr. 1, 1989; children: Jamie-Lee, Holly, Annie-Mae. Grad. Kolping Coll. Applied Graphics, Stuttgart, Germany, 1993. With Charisma Art, Colorado Springs, Colo. Author: Briefe die das Leben schrieb; exhibitions include Magnum Opus XIV, Sacramento Fine Arts Ctr., Pandora's Box, Manitou Springs Bus. Art Ctr., Represented in permanent collections George W. Bush, prin. works include various mags. Mem.: Am. Watercolor Soc., Nat. Watercolor Soc., Watercolor West, Pikes Peak Watercolor Soc. (assoc.), AskART.com. Office: Charisma Art 3165 Windjammer Dr Colorado Springs CO 80920 Personal E-mail: conni@charisma-art.com. Business E-Mail: conni@charisma-art.com.

TOKER, KAREN HARKAVY, physician; b. New Haven, Oct. 23, 1942; d. Victor M. and Nedra (Israel) Harkavy; m. Cyril Toker, Sept. 1, 1968; children: David Edward, Rachel Lee. BS in Chemistry, Coll. William and Mary, 1963; MD, Yale U., 1967. Diplomate Am. Bd. Pediat., 1974. Intern dept. pediat. Bronx Mcpl. Hosp. Ctr., Albert Einstein Coll. Medicine, N.Y., 1967-68, asst. resident dept. pediat., 1968-69, sr. resident dept. pediat., 1969, 70-71, attending pediatrician, 1971-72, 73-76; pediatrician Montgomery Health Dept., Silver Springs, Md., 1976-83; pediatric cons. Head Start Program Montgomery County Pub. Schs., Rockville, Md., 1976-83; pvt. practice gen. pediat. Rockville, 1983-89; pediatrician Nemours Children's Clinic, Jacksonville, Fla., 1991-95; med. dir. Pearl Plaza Pediatrics, Duval County Pub. Health Unit, 1995-97; instr. pediat. Albert Einstein Coll. Medicine, N.Y., 1971-74, asst. prof. pediat., 1974-76; clin. asst. prof. U. Fla., 1995—2003; med. dir. Ctr. for Women and Children, Duval County Health Dept., 1997—2003; pediatric cons. Urban Child Health, 2003—. Exec. bd. sec. Congregation Har Shalom, Potomac, 1989-91. Fellow Am. Acad. Pediat.; mem. Fla. Med. Assn., Duval County Med. Soc., Ambulatory Pediatric Assn. Democrat. Jewish. Avocations: piano, opera, ballet, swimming. Home and Office: 6030 Oakbrook Ct Ponte Vedra Beach FL 32082 Office Phone: 904-285-6851.

TOKHEIM, SARA ANN, writer, information technology professional; b. Cedar Rapids, Iowa, Dec. 15, 1941; d. George Elmer and Helen Clay (Blessing) Tokheim. Programmer Westinghouse Learning Corp., Iowa City, Iowa, 1969-75; cons. U. Iowa, 1976-81, Davis Thomas & Assocs., Mpls., 1982-86, IBM, Mpls., 1986-92. Ind. cons., 1992-96, State of N.Mex., 1996—. Author: (play) The Hand, 1998. Pres., SCORE, Santa Fe, 1997-98. Mem City Different Bus. and Profl. Orgn. (treas.). Avocations: softball, writing screenplays and poetry. Office: 4491 Cerrillos Rd Santa Fe NM 87507-9721

TOLBERT, MARGARET A. geochemistry educator; Prof. dept. chemistry U. Colo., Boulder. Recipient James B. Macelwane Young Investigator medal Am. Geophys. Union, 1993. Office: U Colo Dept Chemistry PO Box 215 Boulder CO 80309-0215

TOLCHIN, JOAN GUBIN, psychiatrist, educator; b. N.Y.C., Mar. 10, 1944; d. Harold and Bella (Newman) Gubin; m. Matthew Armin Tolchin, Sept. 1, 1966; 1 child, Benjamin. AB, Vassar Coll., 1964; MD, NYU, 1972. Diplomate Am. Bd. Gen. Psychiatry, Am. Bd. Child Psychiatry. Rsch. asst. Albert Einstein Coll. Medicine, N.Y.C., 1964-68; instr. psychiatry med. coll. Cornell U., N.Y.C., 1977-78, clin. instr., 1978-86, clin. asst. prof., 1986—. Contbr. articles to profl. jours., chapters to books. Fellow: Am. Acad. Child and Adolescent Psychiatry; mem.: N.Y. Coun. Child and Adolescent Psychiatry (bd. dirs. 1992—96, pres. 1994—95, bd. advisors 2001—), Am. Acad. Psychoanalysis and Dynamic Psychiatry (sec. 1998—2001), Alpha Omega Alpha (mem. disaster psychiatry outreach). Office: 35 E 84th St New York NY 10028-0871

TOLCHIN, SUSAN JANE, public administration educator, writer; b. N.Y.C., Jan. 14, 1941; d. Jacob Nathan and Dorothy Ann (Markowitz) Goldsmith; m. Martin Tolchin, Dec. 23, 1965; children: Charles Peter, Karen Rebecca. BA, Bryn Mawr Coll., 1961; MA, U. Chgo., 1962; PhD, NYU, 1968. Lectr. in polit. sci. CCNY, N.Y.C., 1963-65, Bklyn. Coll., 1965-71; adj. asst. prof. polit. sci. Seton Hall U., South Orange, N.J., 1971-73; assoc. prof. polit. sci., dir. Inst. for Women and Politics, Mt. Vernon Coll., Washington, 1975-78; prof. pub. adminstrn. George Washington U., Washington, 1978-98; prof. pub. policy Sch. Pub. Policy George Mason U., Fairfax, Va., 1998—. Disting. lectr. Indsl. Coll. Armed Forces, 1994. Author: The Angry American: How Voter Rage is Changing the Nation, 1996, 2d edit., 1998; author: (with Martin Tolchin) To the Victor: Political Patronage from the Clubhouse to the White House, 1971, Clout--Womanpower and Politics, 1974, Dismantling America--The Rush to Deregulate, 1983, Buying Into America--How Foreign Money Is Changing the Face of Our Nation, 1988, Selling Our Securit--The Erosion of America's Assets, 1992, Glass Houses--Congressional Ethics and the Politics of Venom, 2001. Bd. dirs. Cystic Fibrosis Found., 1982—; county committeewoman Dem. Party, Montclair, N.J., 1969-73. Recipient Founder's Day award NYU, 1968, Trachtenberg award for rsch. George Washington U., 1998; named Tchr. of Yr., Mt. Vernon Coll., 1978; Dilthey fellow George Washington U., 1983, Aspen Inst. fellow, 1979. Fellow Nat. Acad. Pub. Adminstrn.; mem. Am. Polit. Sci. Assn. (pres. Women's Caucus for Polit. Sci. 1977-78), Am. Soc. Pub. Adminstrn. (chair sect. natural resources and environ. adminstrn. 1982-83, Marshall Dimock award 1997). Democrat. Office: Inst Pub Policy George Mason U Fairfax VA 22030 E-mail: tolchin@gmu.edu.

TOLDALAGI, MARIANNE, foundation administrator; Bd. dirs. Am. Womans Econ. Devel. Corp., N.Y.C. Sr. v.p./gen. mgr. Leisure Travel, Am. Express. Office: Am Womans Econ Devel Corp 71 Vanderbilt Ave Ste 320 New York NY 10169-0005

TOLER, PENNY, former professional basketball player, sports team executive; b. Mar. 24, 1966; B of Psychology, Long Beach State U., 1989. Guard, Montecchio, Italy, 1989—91, Pescara, Italy, 1991—94, Sporting Flash, Greece, 1994—96, Ramat HaSharon, Israel, 1996—97, Los Angeles Sparks, (WNBA), 1997—99; gen. mgr. L.A. Sparks, 1999—. Mem. U.S. Basketball Olympic Com., 1999—. Founder Points from Penny Program, 1998. Named All-Am. & Co-Player of Yr./Big West, 1988, 1989. Achievements include scored first ever basket in WNBA history. Avocations: table tennis, tennis, craps. Office: LA Sparks Great Western Forum 555 N Nash St El Segundo CA 90245-2818

TOLF, GALE MAUREEN, artist, educator; b. Joliet, Ill., Dec. 2, 1953; d. Arthur C. Tolf and Helen C. Kelly Tolf. AA, Joliet (Ill.) Jr. Coll., 1973; BA in Art, So. Ill. U., 1976; student in Art Therapy, U. Ill., 1976; MA in Gifted Edn., N.E. Ill. U., 1982; student, Govs. State U., 1984—87; cert. in Elem. Edn., U. St. Francis, 1984; student, C.G. Jung Inst., 1996—. Cert. tchr. Ill., 1983. Art therapist Pacific Grove/Monterey (Calif.) Adult Schs., 1978—83; tchr. St. Mary Magdelene Sch., Joliet, Ill., 1985—86; tchr. reading Joliet (Ill.) Job Corps., 1986—89; art therapist South Ctrl. Cmty. Svcs., Chgo., 1989—94; part time art tchr., 1994—. Exhibitions include over 35; author: 38 poems, 12 plays; 170 published illustrations, one-woman shows include Allyn Gallery So. Ill. U., Carbondale, Ill., 1975, Clay People Gallery, 1976, Tillie Gorts Cafe, Pacific Grove, Calif., 1980, Mandala Gallery, 1981, Carmel Valley (Calif.) Cafe, Carmel Valley, Calif., 1982, Carl Cherry Found., Carmel, Calif., 1982, Lewis U., Romeoville, Ill., 1990, Bicentennial Theater, Joliet, Ill., 1990, Marquette Pk., Chgo., Ill., 1999, Bean Counter Cafe, Evanston, Ill., 2000, N.E. Ill. U., Chgo., Ill., 2001, Cafe Express, Evanston, Ill., 2001, Kent (Conn.) Cmty. Playhouse, Kent, Conn., 2002, Koki, Evanston, Ill., 2002; editor: Joliet Job Corps Poetry and Art Rev., 1986—88. Recipient Best of Show award Ceramics, Monterey Art Fair, 1980, Best of Show award Photography, 1982; scholar, Ill. State U., 1971—73, Joliet (Ill.) Kiwanis, 1973—76, Joliet (Ill.) Bus. and Women's Club, 1973—76. Mem.: Chgo. (Ill.) Artist Coalition, Phi Beta Kappa, Mensa. Home: 1406 Chicago Ave Evanston IL 60201

TOLIA, VASUNDHARA K. pediatric gastroenterologist, educator; b. Calcutta, India; came to U.S., 1975; d. Rasiklal and Saroj (Kothari) Doshi; m. Kirit Tolia, May 30, 1975; children: Vinay, Sanjay. MBBS, Calcutta U., 1968-75. Intern, resident Children's Hosp. Mich., Detroit, 1976-79, fellow, 1979-81, dir. pediat. endoscopy unit, 1984-90, dir. pediat. gastroenterology and nutrition, 1990—; instr. Wayne State U., Detroit, 1981-83, asst. prof., 1983-91, assoc. prof., 1991-97, prof., 1997—. Mem. editl. bd. Inflammatory Bowel Diseases, 1999— Am. Jour. Gastroenterology, 1999, Rev. of World Lit. in Pediatrics, 1999—; contbr. articles to profl. jours. Named Woman of Distinction, Mich. chpt. Crohn's and Colitis Found. Am., 1991. Fellow Am. Coll. Gastroenterology (chair ad-hoc com. pediat. gastroenterology 1998-2000), Am. Acad. Pediats.; mem. Am. Gastroenterology Assn., N.Am. Soc. Pediat. Gastroenterology and Nutrition, Soc. Pediat. Rsch. Office: Childrens Hosp Mich 3901 Beaubien St Detroit MI 48201-2119

TOLIAS, LINDA PUROFF, music educator; b. Dearborn, Mich., Nov. 26, 1954; d. Nick Puroff and Milka Stoycheff; m. Peter Elias Tolias, June 26, 1988. MusB in Music Edn. with honors, U. Mich., 1976; MusM in Music Performance, Wayne State U., 1992. Tchr. music El Dorado (Ark.) Pub. Schs., 1976-77, Ferndale (Mich.) Pub. Schs., 1979-83; tchr. bands and orch. Dearborn Pub. Schs., 1983—. Founder, condr. El Dorado Youth Symphony, 1976-77; instr. Oakland U. Summer Music Camp, Rochester, Mich., 1982-84; condr., string clinician Oakland U. Youth Orch., Rochester, 1982-84; string clinician Dearborn Pub. Schs., 1983-96, Farmington Pub. Schs., 1994-96; music performer Detroit Symphony Orch., 1978-83, Mich. Opera Theatre, 1977-90; prin. violinist U. Mich. Philharm. Orch., 1975-77, South Ark. Symphony, 1976-77, Detroit Symphony Civic Orch., 1977-79; mem. Las Palmas Internat. Opera Orch. '76 Tour; mem. Internat. Musicians Local 5, 1978. Sponsor City Beautiful Commn., Dearborn, 1983—. Fellowship U. Mich., 1975-76; recipient Roberta Siegel award for Opera, 1975-76, Music Educator of Yr. award 1998. Mem. NOW, Mich. Educator's Nat. Conf., U. Mich. Alumni Assn., Am. String Tchrs. of Am. Democrat. Greek Orthodox. Avocations: music, reading, dance, cooking. Home: 32267 Auburn Dr Beverly Hills MI 48025-4234 Office Phone: 313-730-3998.

TOLKOFF, ESTHER PHYLLIS, writer, magazine editor; b. Bronx, N.Y., Nov. 13, 1947; d. Isadore and Muriel (Zimmerman) Tolkoff. BA, CCNY, 1968; MA in L.Am. Lit., U. Wis., 1969. Writer, editor, 1969—; writer, TV and radio pub. affairs N.Y.C. Bd. Edn., 1970-73; adjunct instr. Spanish Lehman Coll., Bronx, 1971-73; writer Telegeneral Studios, N.Y.C., 1973-74, CUNY Courier, N.Y.C., 1974-76, Yeshiva U., N.Y.C., 1977-79; assoc. editor The N.Y. Tchr., N.Y. State United Tchrs., N.Y.C., 1979—93; editor The Alumnus Mag. CCNY Alumni Assn., 1995—99, editor The Communicator, 1994—; regular contbr., feature writer, theatre critic Back Stage Mag., 1994—. Contbr. articles to periodicals, chpts. to book. Recipient recognition Best Feature Article, Internat. Labor Comm., Washington, 1989, Best Single Article, Met. Labor Press Coun., N.Y.C., 1990, Best Writing, 1981, 89, Award for Excellence Feature Article, APEX, 2000. Mem. AFTRA (editl. bd. N.Y. local 1994-2000), Nat. Writers Union, Internat. Mus. Theatre Alliance, N.Y. Women in Comm., N.Y. Coalition of Profl. Women in Arts and Media, Editl. Freelancers Assn., CCNY Alumni Assn. (bd. dirs. 2000-), Comm. Alumni Group CCNY (first v.p., 2000-, bd. dirs. 1993—). Democrat. Avocation: acting. Home: 315 E 21st St New York NY 10010-6512 Office Phone: 212-254-3723. E-mail: ETolkoff@avantguild.com.

TOLL, BARBARA ELIZABETH, art gallery director; b. Phila., June 8, 1945; d. Joseph M. and Evelyn Toll BA, Goucher Coll., 1967; MFA, Pratt Inst., 1969. Asst. dir. jr. coun. Mus. Modern Art, N.Y.C., 1969-70; dir. Hundred Acres Gallery, N.Y.C., 1971-76; curator David Rockefeller Collection, N.Y.C., 1975-81; pres., dir. Barbara Toll Fine Arts, N.Y.C., 1981-94, dir., 1994—. Mem. Corp. Yaddo; curator Focus: Donald Judd Furniture, Parrish Art Mus., Southampton, NY, 1996, Friendships in Arcadia: Writers and Artists at Yaddo in the 90s, 2000, Follies: Fantasy in the Landscape, Parrish Art Mus., 2001, Reconfiguring Space: Blueprints for Art in Gen., 2003. Trustee Ind. Curators Internat.; nat. bd. dirs. ArtTable, 2001—04. Avocation: gardening. Office: 138 Prince St New York NY 10012-3135

TOLLE, MELINDA EDITH, engineer, scientist; b. N.Y., Aug. 8, 1964; d. Robert Dale and Mildred Elva Tolle. BS in Physics, BS in Geophysics, U. Utah, 1986, MS in Mech. Engring., 1988. Cert. quality engr. Am. Soc. for Quality; cert. quality mgr. Am. Soc. for Quality. Engr. assoc. Thiokol, Brigham City, Utah, 1987-88, sr. engr. assoc., 1988-90, engr., 1990-92, sr. scientist, sr. engr., 1992-98, prin. scientist, prin. engr., 1998-2000; sr. prin. scientist, sr. prin. engr. Alcoa, Brigham City, Utah, 2000—. Adj. instr. Weber State U., Ogden, Utah, 1996—. Mem. AIAA (regional dep. dir. Meb 2000—, Utah sect. chair-elect 1998-99, chair 1999—), Am. Soc. for Quality (sect. chair 1997-98, mem. chair 1995-96, vice chair 1996-97, strategic mgmt. plan chair 2000—), Am. Nuc. Soc., Utah Engring. Coun. (bd. dirs. 1998—), Alpha Nu Sigma (pres. 1988). Office: Thiokol PO Box 707 Brigham City UT 84302-0707

TOLLIVER, DOROTHY, librarian; b. N.Y.C., Apr. 10, 1937; d. Morris and Rose (Poliner) Lamm; m. Robert F. Tolliver, Sept. 3, 1956; children: Craig Lee, Marc Alan. BA, Ind. U., 1958; MSLS, U. Ill., Champaign-Urbana, 1973. Inter-libr., reference libr. L.A. County Libr., 1958-59; dir. libr. Temple City (Calif.) Pub. Libr., 1959-60; reference, young adult libr. Burbank (Calif.) Pub. Libr., 1960-62; PTA libr. Roselawn Elem. Sch., Danville, Ill., 1970-72; reference libr. Danville Area C.C., 1970—72, head libr. 1973—88; libr. dir. Kahului Pub. Libr., 1988—89, head libr. UH Maui C.C., Kahului, 1989—. Cons. Ill. Office Edn., 1980-88, Hawaii Dept. Edn., 1992—. Mem. Commn. Status of Women, 1992—98; sec. Maui County Com. Status of Women, 1991—96; dir. Jewish Arts and Edn. Coun. Maui, 1996—99; mem. Hawaii Book Acad., judge Ka Pala Pala Po'okela awards, 2002—; chair Maui County Women's Conf., 1993; vice chair Maui County Commn. Persons with Disabilities, 1996—2001; pres. S&M Katz Jewish Libr. of Maui, 1996—, Hawaii Ctr. for the Book, 2002—; bd. dirs. Congregation Gan Eden, 1990—, pres., 1991—95; bd. dirs. Congregation Israel, pres., 1983—87; bd. dirs. Maui Cmty. Theater, 1997—; actor, dir. Voices on the Wind Readers' Theater, 1992—. Recipient Little Red Schoolhouse award Danville Schs. Citizens Com., 1972, Hawaii State award for leadership in promoting postive soc. change, edu. and womens equity, 1997. Mem.: AAUW (pres. Maui chpt. 1993—97, state bd. dirs. 1993, Hawaii State award), ALA, Am. Coll. and Rsch. Librs., Maui County Libr. Assn. (pres. 1990—96), Hawaii Libr. Assn. (bd. dirs.), Phi Beta Mu (alpha chpt.). Jewish. Avocations: reading, theatre, travel. Office: Maui Community Coll 310 W Kaahumanu Ave Kahului HI 96732-1617 Office Phone: 808-984-3583. E-mail: tolliver@hawaii.edu.

TOLLIVER, LORRAINE, language educator, writer; d. Elbert and Maggie Tolliver; m. Gerald Levin, 1974 (div. 1986); 1 child from previous marriage, Roger Anthony Regensburg (dec.). BA, Calif. State U., Northridge, 1963; MA, U. Calif. L.A., 1966. Radio and TV writer WHIO, Dayton, Ohio, 1954—57, WCPO, Cin., 1953—54; reporter and editl. writer Advertiser - Press Newspapers, Hawthorne, Calif., 1971; instr. English upper divsn. Chapman Coll. Residence Ctr., Riverside, Calif., 1968—69; instr. English Long. Beach (Calif.) City Coll., 1969—89; prof. English Compton Coll., Calif., 1971—2000; instr. English West L.A. Coll., Culver City, Calif., 1974—. Instr. and coord. Compton Coll. Work Experience Program, 1974—75; pub. reader, presenter. Author: (books) Sibelius, 2002 (Dance of the Sun Pubs. award); poet: poem Feelings of the Heart, 2001 (2d pl., 2001), front cover poem Scroll Original Artist mag., 2002, Freshwater Poetry mag., 2003 (Spl. Recognition award, 2003). Mem.: AFT. Achievements include over two hundred poems published in literary jours. in approximately thirty states, mostly on the east and west coasts. A few have been published in Can. Avocations: hiking, travel, hosting cultural groups, theater, creative writing workshops. Home: 3873 Woodside Dr Richmond IN 47374

TOLMACH, JANE LOUISE, community activist, municipal official; b. Havre, Mont., Nov. 12, 1921; d. Robert Francis and Veronica (Tracy) McCormick; m. Daniel Michael Tolmach (Dec.), Sept. 9, 1946; children: James, Richard, Eve Alice, Adam, Jonathan. AB, UCLA, 1943; M in Social Scis., Smith Coll., 1945; JD, S. We. U., L.A., 1981. Social worker ARC Field Svcs. Corona Naval Hosp., Norco, Calif., 1945-46; chmn. bd. dirs. Camarillo (Calif.) State Hosp., 1959-68; mem. bd. trustees Oxnard (Calif.) Union High Sch. Dist., 1965-72; mem. state reclamation bd. Calif., 1981-82; mem. bd. govs. Calif. C.C., 1982-87; mem. bd. St. John's Regional Hosp., Oxnard, 1986-89; mem. bd. of assessment appeals County of Ventura, Ventura, Calif., 1992—2002, transp. commr., 2002—. Chmn. fin. com. Ventura County Grand Jury, 1958; mem. Oxnard (Calif.) Planning Commn., 1957-62; exec. mem. So. Calif. Assn. Govts., L.A., 1975-76. Author: Smith Studies, 1945. Chmn. Ventura County Dem. Com., 1959-62; alternate or del. Dem. Nat. Convs., 1960, 68, 76, 88, 92, alt. 1956, 64; Women'schm. S. Calif. Dem. Com., 1966-70; nominee state assembly, 36th dist., Ventura, Calif., 1976; elected Oxnard City Coun. 1970-78, mayor, 1973-74. Home: 656 Douglas Ave Oxnard CA 93030-4614 E-mail: jane.tolmach@oxn.net.

TOLMACHOFF, WILLADENE, accountant, auditor; b. Mt. Vernon, Ky., July 13, 1945; d. Willie and Wanda Thacker; m. Innokenty Tolmachoff, July 27, 1968. MS, George Washington U., 1978; M. in Gen. Adminstrn., U. Md., 1994. Cert. fin. mgr. Audit mgr. USDA, Washington, 1987-97; dir. performance audits Office of Inspector Gen., Washington, 1998-2000; cash mgmt. dep. project mgr. Office of Fin. and Sys., Washington, 2000—01, internal audit/internal security audit mgr., 2001—. Adj. prof. Strayer U., 1997—. Mem.: Assn. Govt. Accts. Avocations: walking, bicycling, reading. Home: 1010 Rhode Island Ave NE Washington DC 20018 Office: Rm 367 810 1st St NE Washington DC 20002 E-mail: tolmachev@aol.com.

TOLSTEDT, BUFFY D. music educator, musician; b. Las Cruces, N.Mex., Feb. 23, 1975; d. Richard Dean and Sharon Ann T.. B in Music Edn., Ea. N.Mex. U., Portales, 1998; M in Music Edn., U. Miss., Oxford, 2000. Lic. tchr. N.M. Tchr. Farmington (N.Mex.) Mcpl. Schs., 2000—. Flutist San Juan Coll. Orch., Farmington, 2001—; saxophonist San Juan Coll. Jazz Band, Farmington, 2002—. Musician: performed with Ernie Watts. Named concerto competition winner, San Juan Coll., 2001; recipient Red Apple award for tchg. excellence, Found. Edn. Excellence, 2001. Mem.: N.W. N.Mex. Music Educators Assn., Music Educators Nat. Conf. Avocations: cycling, racquetball.

TOLSTEDT, CARRIE L. bank executive; BS in Bus. Adminstrn., U. Nebr.; degree in Banking, U. Wash. From credit tng. program to corp. banking officer United Bank Denver, corp. banking officer; from v.p. corp. banking to sr. v.p. downtown Omaha (Nebr.) retail banking Norwest Bank Nebr., Omaha, 1986—95; sr. v.p. corp. retail FirstMerit Corp., Akron, Ohio, 1995—96, pres., CEO Citizens Nat. Bank and Peoples Nat. Bank, 1996—98, exec. v.p., 1996—98; with Norwest Corp., 1998; regional pres. Ctrl. Calif. Wells Fargo & Co., San Francisco, 1998—2001, exec. v.p. regional banking, 2001—. Bd. dirs. The Cmty. Coll. Found. Mem.: Consumer Bankers Assn. (bd. dirs.), U. Nebr. Alumni Assn. (bd. dirs.), Calif. C. of C. (bd. dirs.). Office: Wells Fargo & Co 420 Montgomery St San Francisco CA 94163*

TOM, GAIL, business educator; b. Rock Springs, Wyo., July 18, 1952; d. Edward Young and Ruby (Wong) T.; m. Calvin Tong, July 24, 1977; children: Ryan Tom Tong, Stephanie Tom Tong. BA, U. Calif., Davis, 1972, MS, 1974, PhD, 1978; MA, Calif. State U., Sacramento, 1973, U. Calif., Riverside, 1977. Grad. teaching asst. Calif. State U., Sacramento, 1973, prof., 1978—; rsch. asst. U. Calif., Davis, 1974-77, adj. prof., 1985—. S. U.S. Bankruptcy Ct., Sacramento, 1994-95, Calif. State Employment Devel. Dept., Sacramento, 1992-94, Silverado Broadcasting, Sacramento, Stockton, Calif., 1995—; reviewer Coll. Textbook Pubs., 1985—. Author: Applications of Consumer Behavior, 1982, Understanding Consumer Behavior, 2001; contbr. articles to profl. jours. JC Penney Retail grantee Brigham Young U., 1994; Dir. Mktg. Assn. fellow, 1986, 96. Mem. Am. Mktg. Assn., Assn. Consumer Rsch., Western Mktg. Educators Assn. (bd. dirs. 1995—). Avocations: classical music, mystery books, movies, cycling, walking. Office: Calif State U Sch Bus 6000 J St Sacramento CA 95819-2605

TOM, LAUREN, actress, singer; b. Chgo., Aug. 4, 1959; d. Chan and Nancy (Dare) T.; m. Glenn Lau-Kee, Oct. 23, 1982. Student, Northwestern U., 1977; BA, NYU. Plays include A Chorus Line, 1978-79, The Music Lessons, 1980, Family Devotions, 1981, Doonesbury, 1983-84, Hurlyburly, 1985, (film) Nothing Lasts Forever, 1982, (TV shows) The Facts of Life, 1982, ABC Afterschool Special, 1984, CBS Afterschool Break, 1984. Supporter Asia Inst., Washington. Mem. Actors' Equity Assn., Screen Actors Guild, AFTRA.

TOMAINO, LEAH KARRATOGLOU, artist; b. Denville, N.J., May 24, 1965; d. Peter Karratoglou and Edith (Dardick) Cefaloni; m. Francis Joseph Tomaino, Mar. 23, 1989; children: Francesca, Marcus. BFA, The Cooper Union, 1987; postgrad., Studio Art Sch. of the Aegean, Samos, Greece, 1987; MA, The William Paterson U., 2002. One-person shows include The Atlantic Gallery, N.Y.C., 1994, 95, 96, 97, 2000, The Randolph (N.J.) Twp. Free Pub. Libr., 1995, Children's Mus. of Arts, N.Y., N.Y., 1999, The Clifton (N.J.) Arts Ctr., 2003, Morris County Libr., N.J., 2003; two-person shows include The West Wing Gallery, Ringwood, N.J., 1989, The Atlantic Gallery, N.Y.; exhibited in group shows at Ringwood State Park, 1987, The Barn Gallery, Ringwood State Park, 1987, 88, Arts Coun. Gallery, Cobleskill, N.Y., 1993, The Atlantic Gallery, N.Y.C., 1993—, City Without Walls, Newark, 1994-95, New Work Corner, City Without Walls, Newark, 1995, William Paterson U., Wayne, N.J.; represented in permanent collections Dover (N.J.) Mcpl. Bldg., Polizzotto & Polizzotto, Bklyn., various pvt. collections. Mem. The Atlantic Gallery (v.p. 1993—, exhbn. coord. 1994-95), N.Y. Artist's Equity (grantee 1996—). Home: 12 Charles St Randolph NJ 07869-1408

TOMAN, MARY ANN, federal official; b. Pasadena, Calif., Mar. 31, 1954; d. John James and Mary Ann Zajec T.; m. Milton Allen Miller, Sept. 10, 1988; 1 child, Mary Ann III. BA with honors, Stanford U., 1976; MBA, Harvard U., 1981. Mgmt. cons. Bain and Co., Boston, 1976-77; brand mgr. Procter & Gamble Co., Cin., 1977-79; summer assoc. E.F. Hutton, N.Y.C., 1980; head corp. planning The Burton Group, PLC, London, 1981-84; pres., founder Glenclair Ltd., London, 1984-86; pres. London Cons. Group, London, Beverly Hills, Calif., 1987-88; mem. U.S. Presdl. Transition Team, Bus. and Fin., 1988-89; dep. asst. sec. commerce, automotive affairs, consumer goods U.S. Dept. Commerce, Washington, 1989-93; commr., chmn. L.A. Indsl. Devel. Authority, 1993-95; dep. treas. State of Calif., Sacramento, 1995-99. Bd. dirs. U.S. Coun. of Devel. Fin. Agencies, 1994-97. Founder, chair Stanford U. Fundraising, London, 1983-88; chair Reps. Abroad Absentee Voter Registration, London, 1983-88; bd. dirs. Harvard Bus. Sch. Assn., London, 1984-87; vol. Bush-Quayle Campaign, 1988; trustee Bath Coll., Eng., 1988—; apptd. by Gov. Wilson to State of Calif. Econ. Devel. Adv. Coun., 1994-97, Jobs Tng. Coordinating Coun., 1998-2000; first vice chmn. Rep. Party L.A. County, 1996-99; chmn. Republican Party Los Angeles County, 1999—; mem. exec. bd. Coun. Calif. County Chairmen, 1999—; mem. U.S. Presdl. Transition Team, 2000-2001; Rep. candidate for Calif. State Treas., 2002. Named Calif. Mother of Yr., 1997. Mem. Stanford Club U.K. (pres. 1983-88), Harvard Club N.Y., Harvard Club Washington, Nat. Assn. of Urban Rep. County Chmn. Roman Catholic. Home: 604 N Elm Dr Beverly Hills CA 90210-3421 Office: PO Box 71483 Los Angeles CA 90071-0483 Office Phone: 310-274-4822.

TOMASKY, SUSAN, corporate officer; b. Morgantown, W.Va., Mar. 29, 1953; m. Ron Ungvarsky; 1 child, Victoria. BA cum laude, Univ. Ky., 1974; JD (hons.), George Washington Univ., 1979. Staff mem. House Com. Interstate and Fgn. Commerce, Washington, 1974—76; with FERC's Office of Gen. Counsel., Washington, 1979—81; assoc. Van Ness, Feldman & Curtin, Washington, 1981—86; ptnr. Van Ness, Feldman & Curtis, Washington, 1986—93; gen. coun. Federal Energy Regulatory Commn., Washington, 1993—97; 1997ptnr. 1998Hogan & Harts, Washington, 1997-98; senior v.p., gen. coun. & Sec. Am. Electric Power Svc. Corp., Columbus, Ohio, 1998—2000, exec. v.p., gen. counsel, sec., 2000—01, exec. v.p., CFO, 2001—. Staff mem. George Washington U. Law Rev., 1979. Trustee Columbus Symphony Orch., Columbus Sch. for Girls; co-chair Keystone Energy Bd. Mem. Greater Columbus C. of C., Phi Beta Kappa.

TOMASULO, VIRGINIA MERRILLS, retired lawyer; b. Belleville, Ill., Feb. 10, 1919; d. Frederick Emerson and Mary Eckert (Turner) Merrills; m. Nicholas Angelo Tomasulo, Sept. 30, 1952 (dec. May 3, 1986); m. Harrison I. Anthes, Mar. 5, 1988. BA, Wellesley Coll., 1940; LLB (now JD), Washington U., St. Louis, 1943. Bar: Mo. 1942, U.S. Ct. Appeals (D.C. cir.) 1958, Mich. 1974, U.S. Dist. Ct. (ea. dist) Mo. 1943, U.S. Supreme Ct. 1954, U.S. Tax Ct. 1974, U.S. Ct. Appeals (6th cir.) 1976. Atty. Dept. of Agr., St. Louis and Washington, 1943-48; Office of Solicitor, Chief Counsel's Office IRS, Washington and Detroit, 1949-75; assoc. Baker & Hostetler, Washington, 1977-82, ptnr., 1982-89, of counsel, 1989, ret., 1989. Sec. S.W. Day Care Assn., Washington, 1971—73; state bd. mem., dir. region IV Fla. Life Care Residents Assn., 2002—04; mem. adv. bd. Brede-Wilkins Scholarship Found., 2002—. Mem.: FBA, ABA, Mo. Bar, Village on the Green Residents Assn. (mem. coun. 1998—2000, chair health care com. 1999—2001, mem. fin. com., chair fin. com. 2004—), Wellesley Club (Ctrl. Fla.). Episcopalian. Home: 570 Village Pl Apt 300 Longwood FL 32779-6037

TOMASZESKI, JOSEPHINE GALLAS, retired nursing educator; b. Manchouli, Manchuria, China, Jan. 18, 1919; d. Paul Fedorovich Kislitzin and Barbara Matveevna (Borodeev) Kislitzin-Meisel; m. John Joseph Gallas, Jan. 22, 1953 (dec. Feb. 1966); m. Julian Stephen Tomaszeski, June 10, 1972; stepchildren: Julie Ann, Mary Jane, Wayne Michael (dec.), John William. Have 16 step-grandchildren (July, 2002). Student, Mary Washington Coll., 1937; diploma, St. Mary's Coll. Nursing, 1941; BS in Pub. Health Nursing, Cath. U. Am., 1943; MSN, U. Calif., Berkeley and San Francisco, 1960. RN, Calif.; cert. pub. health nurse, tchr., Calif. Nurse, charge nurse Children's Hosp., Washington, 1941-43; pub. health nurse Dept. Pub. Health, Washington, 1943-45; dir. outpatient clinic, nurse instr. Mary's Help Hosp., San Francisco, 1946-49; nurse, pub. health nurse, nurse instr. VA Med. Ctr. and Gen. Clinics, San Francisco, 1949-54; nurse instr. St. Mary's Hosp., San Francisco, 1954-55; asst. prof. nursing U. San Francisco, 1954-72; medicine and treatment nurse Schutz Am. Sch., Alexandria, Egypt, 1972-73; newspaper corr. Representative, Calmar, Alta., Can., 1975-81; medicine and treatment nurse Hillhaven Convalescent Hosp., San Rafael, Calif., 1982. Vol. nurse County Health Dept., Sausalito, Calif., 1956-63; vol. pollworker City of Sausalito, 1962-65; vol. city coun. campaigns, Sausalito, 1962-65; vol. Santa Venitia Cmty. Orgn., San Rafael, Calif.; vol. Ladies Aux. Can. Legion; substitute tchr. religious classes. Fed. Nursing grant Cath. U. Am., 1942-43; Fed. scholar U. Calif., Berkeley, 1959-60. Mem. ANA, AAUP, Nursing Alumni Bd. U. San Francisco (voting vol. 1982-94), NLN (sec. 1956-60), Ch. Womens Club, Calmar Royal Can. Legion Women's Aux. (exec. com. 1999--), Sigma Theta Tau, Alpha Phi Sigma. Republican. Roman Catholic. Continue to pay for licensure as (inactive) nurse, @ Bd. of Nurse examiners in Calif. Home: 5114 49 Ave PO Box 444 Calmar AB Alberta Canada TOC 0V0

TOMB, CAROL E. retail executive; b. Balt., Nov. 3, 1952; d. Richard John and Doris Elaine Tomb; children: Kurt M., Kristen E., Kevin R. AS, Harcum Coll., 1973; cert., Inst. Cert. Fin. Planners, 1988; BA, Simpson Coll., 2001. Various retail mgmt. positions, N.Y. and Iowa, 1973-78; pres. Nouveau Riche, Ltd., Des Moines, 1986-95; mgr. bookstore ops. Knowledge Knook Bookstore Des Moines Area C.C., Ankeny, Iowa, 1998—. Mem. Des Moines Civic Ctr., People to People Internat. Avocation: international travel. Office: Knowledge Knook Bookstore Des Moines Area CC 2006 S Ankeny Blvd Ankeny IA 50021-8995 E-mail: cetomb@dmacc.edu.

TOMB, DIANE LENEGAN, federal agency administrator; Grad., Mt. St. Mary's, Md. Assoc. dir. Office Bus. Liaison U.S. Dept. Commerce, 1991—93, dir. pub. affairs for Internat. Trade Adminstrn.; dir. pub. affairs practice, mktg. dir. Washington regional office Burson-Marsteller, 1994—97; sr. v.p. for comm. Fannie Mae Found.; asst. sec. for pub. affairs Dept. HUD, Washington, 2002—. Office: Dept HUD Pub Affairs 451 7th St SW Washington DC 20410-9000

TOMBE, SHEILA JOAN, language educator, editor; b. Belfast, Northern Ireland, Mar. 6, 1959; d. J. Gordon Tombe. BA English and Spanish, U. Strathclyde, Glasgow, Scotland, 1983; MA Comparative Lit., U. S.C., Columbia, S.C., 1987; PhD Comparative Lit., U.S.C., Columbia, S.C., 1992. Esl asst. Instituto Nacional Mixto Numero Dos, Madrid, 1981—82; esl and spanish instr. Four Seasons Lang. Sch. and Cultural Ctr., Hamamatsu, Japan, 1987—89; vis. asst. prof. English U. S.C., Columbia, SC, 1992—93, assoc. prof. English Beaufort, SC, 1993—. Editor Apostrophe: USCB Jour. of the Arts, Beaufort, SC, 1996—. Author: (plays) Lost in the Moonlight (New Voices Drama Award, 1991), (poem) Rosebud, Velazquez pinta en color por primera vez (Gival Press TriLanguage Award in Spanish, 2000); actor: (plays) Macbeth, Shirley Valentine. Actor, dir. LowCountry Shakespeare, Beaufort, SC, 1996—2003; actor, organizer SC Playwrights Conf., Beaufort, SC, 1996—2000. Grantee Regrant, Arts Coun. of Beaufort County, 1997; scholar Stevenson Scholarship, U. Edinburgh, 1981, Internat. Student Exch. Bursary, CIES, 1981; Rsch. Found. Fellowship, U. S.C., 1992. Mem.: AAUP (assoc.), Acad. of Am. Poets (assoc.). Office: Univ S C Beaufort 801 Carteret St Beaufort SC 29902 Office Phone: 843-521-4158. E-mail: sjtombe@gwm.sc.edu.

TOMBERS, EVELYN CHARLOTTE, lawyer, law educator; b. Phila., Nov. 7, 1956; d. Gerold G. and Margot (Ort) Knauerhase; m. Peter C. Tombers. AS, Temple U., 1976, BA, 1977; JD, Thomas M. Cooley Law Sch., 1991. Bar: Mich. 1991. Dist. intake counselor Fla. Dept. Health Rehab. Svc., Naples, 1985-87; satellite dir. Youth Shelter S.W. Fla., Naples, 1987-88; adj. prof. Thomas M. Cooley Law Sch., Lansing, Mich., 1991-92; jud. law clk. to Justice Patricia J. Boyle Mich. Supreme Ct., Detroit, 1992-94; assoc. Harvey, Kruse, Westen and Milan, Troy, Mich., 1994-95, Bowen, Radabaugh, Milton & Brown, Troy, Mich., 1995-99, Morrison Mahoney & Miller LLP, Southfield, Mich., 1999—2000. Chmn. State Bar Mich. Appellate Practice Sect., 2001-2002. Named one of Outstanding Women Grads., Women Lawyers Am., 1991. Avocation: golf. Home: 1289 Tracilee Dr Howell MI 48843 Office: Thomas M Cooley Law Sch 300 S Capitol Ave Lansing MI 48901

TOME, CAROL, corporate financial executive; V.p., treas. Riverwood Internat. Corp.; sr. v.p. fin. Home Depot, CFO, 2001—. Office: Home Depot 2455 Paces Ferry Rd Atlanta GA 30339-4029

TOMEI, CAROLYN, state representative; m. Gary Michael. BS in Psychology, MSW, Portland State U. State rep., dist. 41 Oreg. House Rep., Salem, 2001—; mayor City of Milwaukie, Oreg.; child devel. specialist Portland Pub. Schs. Vice-chair Health and Human Svcs. Com.; mem. Water Com.; instr. Portland C.C. Democrat. Office: 900 Court St NE H-388 Salem OR 97301 Office Phone: 503-986-1441.

TOMICH-BOLOGNESI, VERA, engineering executive; b. L.A. d. Peter S. and Yovanka (Ivanovich) T.; m. Gino Bolognesi, July 12, 1969. AA, John Muir Jr. Coll., Pasadena, Calif., 1951; BA in Polit. Sci., UCLA, 1953, MEd, 1955, EdD, 1960. Cert. secondary tchr., Calif.; cert. secondary sch. adminstrn., Calif.; cert. jr. coll. tchr., Calif. Tchg. asst. dept. edn. UCLA, 1956; tchr., dept. chmn. Culver City (Calif.) Unified Sch. Dist., 1956-91; rschr., writer U.S. Dept. Edn., Washington, 1961, del. to Yugoslavia, 1965; co-owner, exec. Metrocolor Engring., San Gabriel, Calif., 1973—. Cons., Continental Culture Specialists, Inc., Glendale, Calif., 1985-92; rsch. asst. Law Firm of Driscoll & Tomich, San Marino, Calif., 1989—. Author: Education in Yugoslavia and the New Reform, 1963, Higher Education and Teacher Training in Yugoslavia, 1967; screenplay editor 1990—. Bd. trustees St. Sava Serbian Orthodox Ch., San Gabriel, 1975—, mem., 1960—. Named an Outstanding Young Women of Am., 1966; recipient Episcopal Gramata, Serbian Orthodox Ch. of Western Am., 1996, 2002. Mem. NEA (life), Calif. Tchrs. Assn., UCLA Alumni Assn., Alpha Gamma Sigma, Pi Lambda Theta. Home: 100 E Roses Rd San Gabriel CA 91775-2343 Office: Metrocolor Engring 5110 Walnut Grove Ave San Gabriel CA 91776-2026

TOMKOW, GWEN ADELLE, artist; b. Detroit, May 16, 1932; d. Galen A. and Edythe Christine (Barr) Roberts; m. Michael Tomkow, Nov. 14, 1953; children: Eric Michael, Thomas Edward, Nikola Christine, Kit Adair. A of Bus., Detroit Bus. Inst., 1952; student, Birmingham Bloomfield Art Assn., Assn., Mich., 1985-87, Visual Art Assn., Livonia, Mich., 1984-89. Tchr. watercolor Visual Art Assn., Livonia, 1989—; tchr. watercolor workshop Village Fine Art Assn., Milford, Mich., 1996; tchr. workshop Ella Sharp Mus. Jackson Civic Art, Mich., 1996—2003; slide lectr. Livonia Artist Club, 1995, Palette and Brush Club, Southfield, Mich., 1995, Pontiac (Mich.) Oakland Artists, 1995, Ea. Mich. U. Watercolor Soc., 1994; tchr. watercolor workshop Ann Arbor Women Painters U. Mich. Art Sch., 1997; slide lectr. Western Ohio Water Color Soc., 1999; tchr. watercolor workshop Awakening Artist Inside Art Imporium, 2004. Artist-in-residence Farmington Art Commn., Farmington Hills, 1988; slide lectr. Springfield (Ohio) Art Mus; mem. Framington Hills Art Commn., 2002 . Artist (exhibitions) Joppich's Bay St. of Northport, 1988—98; exhibitions include Joppich's Bay St. of Northport, 2000—03, Cary Gallery, 1995, 1997, Art Corridor, 1998, Cary Gallery, 2003, Represented in permanent collections E. Carothers Dunnegan Gallery of Art Mus., Bolivar, Mo., Atrium Gallery, Northville, MI. Recipient Purchase awards U.S.A. Springfield (Mo.) Art Mus., 1990, 93, 94, Watercolor U.S.A., 1999, 1st prize Helen de Roy Competition, Oakland C.C., Farmington, Mich., 1988, 92, Grumbacher Gold medal Farmington Artists Club, 1992, 2001, Farmington Hills, Mich., 1995, 98. Mem. Nat. Watercolor Soc. (signature, Alex Nepote Meml. award 1998), Mich. Watercolor Soc. (Meml. award 1992), Farmington Art Assn. (pres. 1987-89), Detroit Soc. Women Painters Sculptors (sec. 1994-95, award 1999), Palette and Brush (v.p. 1982-83), Founders Soc. Detroit Inst. Arts, Nat. Mus. Women in the Arts. Presbyterian. Avocations: tennis, golf, choir singer, theater.

TOMKO-WOODDELL, THERESA MARIE, music educator; b. Warren, Ohio, May 24, 1966; d. William Thomas and Linda Joyce Totten; m. Christopher John Tomko, July 5, 1990 (div. Apr. 24, 1997); m. Thomas G. Wooddell, Nov. 16, 2003; 1 child, Zachary Thomas Wooddell. MusB in Edn., Youngstown State U., Ohio, 1989. Cert. tchr. Va. Band dir. Fairfax County Pub. Schs., Herndon, Va., 1990—. Band dir. Herndon Area Honors Band, Va., 1995—. Mem.: Am. Recorder Soc., Va. Music Educators Assn., Va. Band and Orch. Dirs. Assn., Women's Band Dirs. Internat., Am. Fedn. Tchrs., Music Educators Nat. Conf. Avocations: early music (recorders), reading, nature walks. Home: 202 Winter Frost Ct Sterling VA 20165 Office: Dranesville Elem Sch 1515 Powells Tavern Pl Herndon VA 20170

TOMLIN, JEANNE BRANNON, real estate broker, small business owner; b. Carroll, Iowa; d. James Leonard and Mary Agnes (Cavenaugh) Brannon; widowed; children: David, Elizabeth; m. James W. Tomlin; stepchildren: Angela, Julie, Lori, Fran. A in Archtl. Tech., Ind. U. Purdue U., Indpls., 1970, student. Lic. real estate broker. Salesperson F.C. Tucker, Indpls.; mgr. Dan Nichols Builder, Greenwood, Ind.; asst. mgr. Carpenter Better Homes and Gardens, Carmel, Ind., sales broker, 1989-92, Tomlin Realtors, Greenwood, 1992-97, pres., CEO, 1997—. Mem. com. Nat. Handicapped Sports, Indpls., 1986-88; mem tech. task force Met. Indpls. Bd. Realtors, 1993-94, mem. comm. com., 1998—. Mem. Indpls. C. of C., Greenwood C. of C., Golden Key Nat. Honor Soc., Alpha Sigma Lambda. Avocations: scuba diving, skiing. Office: Tomlin Realtors 243 S Madison Ave Greenwood IN 46142-3123

TOMLIN, LILY, actress; b. Detroit, Sept. 1, 1939; Student, Wayne State U.; studied mime with Paul Curtis, studied acting with Peggy Feury. Appearances in concerts and colls. throughout U.S.; TV appearances include The Music Scene, 1969-70, Laugh In, 1970-73, Lily Tomlin, CBS Spls., 1973, 81, 82; 2 ABC Spls., 1974, 75, Edith Ann Animated Specials, ABC, 1994, The Magic School Bus, 1994 (voice), Murphy Brown, 1996-98, The West Wing, 2002-; motion picture debut in Nashville, 1975 (N.Y. Film Critics award); also appeared in The Late Show, 1977, Moment by Moment, 1978, The Incredible Shrinking Woman, 1981, Nine to Five, 1980, All of Me, 1984, Big Business, 1987, Shadows and Fog, 1992, The Player, 1992, Short Cuts, 1993, The Beverly Hillbillies, 1993, And the Band Played On, HBO, 1993 (Best Supporting Actress Emmy nominee - Special, 1994, Emmy nominations guest appearance Homicide, 1996), Getting Away with Murder, 1995, The Celluloid Closet, 1995, Blue in the Face, 1995, Flirting With Disaster, 1996, Reno Finds Her Mom, 1997, Get Bruce, 1999, Krippendorf's Tribe, 1998, Tea with Mussolini, 1999, Picking Up the Pieces, 2000, The Kid, 2000, Orange County, 2002; exec. prodr. TV Series Citizen Reno, 2001; one-woman Broadway show Appearing Nitely, 1977 (Spl. Tony award), The Search for Signs of Intelligent Life in the Universe, 1985 (Drama Desk award, Outer Critics Circle award, Tony award 1986); recs. include This is a Recording, And That's The Truth, Modern Scream, On Stage. Recipient Grammy award 1971, 5 Emmy awards for CBS Spl. 1973, 81, Emmy award for ABC Spl. 1975, Emmy award Magic Sch. Bus, 1995, Peabody award Celluloid Closet, 1997, Peabody Edith Ann's Christmas, 1997, Cable Ace award The Search for Signs of Intelligent Life in the Universe, 1992.*

TOMLINSON, FEROL MARTIN, reading and learning center media specialist; b. Woodstock, Ill., Sept. 21, 1931; d. Clinton E. and Minnie Ada (Tremere) Martin; m. Henry Sawyer Tomlinson, June 27, 1953; children: Lynn Tomlinson Lenker, Lee Eleanor Baseley. BS, U. Ill., 1953; cert. reading specialist, Nat. Coll. Edn., 1966. Cert. learning ctr. media specialist, 1977. Tchr. McHenry (Ill.) Sch. Dist., 1953-55, Johnsburg Sch. Dist. 12, 1958-91, tchr. remedial reading, 1965-67, dir. learning ctr., 1970-83; head tchr. Ringwood (Ill.) Sch., 1977-91; dir. Dist. 12 Summer Sch., 1965-68. Active McHenry Choral Club, 1953-72, 4-H; sec.-treas.; assoc. Milk Producers Ill., 1967-75; sec.-treas. McHenry County Lamb and Wool Prodrs., 1978-81; trustee Ringwood Meth. Ch., 1990-98, Ringwood Cmty. Cemetary, 1990-97. Named Outstanding Delta Zeta Alumnae U. Ill. 1968; recipient Svc. award Assoc. Milk Prodrs. Ill., 1974; named Dist. 12 Tchr. of Yr., 1978, Disting. grad. McHenry Cmty. H.S., 1989, Ringwood Sch. Libr. dedicated as Ferol M. Tomlinson Learning Ctr., 1991. Mem. U. Ill. Alumnae Assn., NEA, Ill. Edn. Assn., Johnsburg Tchr. Assn. (past officer), DAR (Becky Thatcher award Ill. DAR), Order Eastern Star, Delta Kappa Gamma (sec. 1972-76, v.p. 1980-82, pres. 1986-88, Ill. Achievement award 1988), Delta Zeta (past chpt. pres. 1951-53). Republican. Methodist. Office: 4700 School Rd Ringwood IL 60072-9606 Home: 2501 N Martin Rd Mchenry IL 60050-9001

TOMLINSON-KEASEY, CAROL ANN, university administrator; b. Washington, Oct. 15, 1942; d. Robert Bruce and Geraldine (Howe) Tomlinson; m. Charles Blake Keasey, June 13, 1964; children: Kai Linson, Amber Lynn. BS, Pa. State U., 1964; MS, Iowa State U., 1966; PhD, U. Calif., Berkeley, 1970. Lic. psychologist, Calif. Asst. prof. psychology Trenton (N.J.) State Coll., 1969-70, Rutgers U., New Brunswick, N.J., 1970-72; prof. U. Nebr., Lincoln, 1972-77, U. Calif., Riverside, 1977-92, acting dean Coll. Humanities and Social Scis., 1986-88, chmn. dept. psychology, 1989-92, vice provost for academic planning and pers. Davis, 1992-97, vice provost for academic initiatives, 1997-99, chancellor, 1999—. Author: Child's Eye View, 1980, Child Development, 1985; also numerous chpts. to books; articles to profl. jours. Recipient Disting. Tchr. award U. Calif., 1986. Mem. APA, Soc. Rsch. in Child Devel., Riverside Aquatics Assn. (pres.). Office: PO Box 2039 Merced CA 95344

TOMLJANOVICH, ESTHER M. retired judge; b. Galt, Iowa, Nov. 1, 1931; d. Chester William and Thelma L. (Brooks) Moellering; m. William S. Tomljanovich, Dec. 26, 1957; 1 child, William Brooks Tomljanovich. AA, Itasca C.C., 1951; BSL, St. Paul Coll. Law, 1953, LLB, 1955. Bar: Minn. 1955, U.S. Dist. Ct. Minn. 1958. Asst. revisor of statutes State of Minn., St. Paul, 1957-66, revisor of statutes, 1974-77, dist. ct. judge Stillwater, 1977-90; assoc. justice Minn. Supreme Ct., St. Paul, 1990—98, ret., 1998. Adv. bd. women offenders Minn. Dept. Corrections, 1999—; leadership com. So. Minn. Legal Svcs. Corp., 1999—. Former mem. North St. Paul Bd. Edn., Maplewood Bd. Edn., Lake Elmo Planning Commn.; trustee William Mitchell Coll. Law, 1995—2004, Legal Rights Ctr., 1995—2004, pres., 1999; bd. dirs. Itasca C.C. Found., 1996—2004, Medica Health Ins. Co., 2001—, vice chair, 2003—. Recipient Centennial 2000 award William Mitchell Coll., Disting. Alumna award; named one of One Hundred Who Made a Difference William Mitchell Coll. Law Mem. Minn. State Bar Assn., Bus. and Profl. Women's Assn. St. Paul (former pres.), Minn. Women Laywers (founding mem.). Office: 8533 Hidden Bay Trail Lake Elmo MN 55042

TOMMELEIN, IRIS DENISE, construction engineering and management educator, consultant; b. Brussels, Mar. 16, 1962; m. James Warren Lovekin, July 22, 1995. Grad. in Civil Engring., Free U. Brussels, 1984; MSCE, Stanford U., 1985, MS in Computer Sci., PhD in Civil Engring., 1989. Registered profl. engr., Belgium. Asst. prof. U. Mich., Ann Arbor, 1989-95, assoc. prof., 1995-96, U. Calif., Berkeley, 1996—2001, prof., 2001—; rsch. assoc. Lean Constrn. Inst., 1997—. Fellow Belgian Am. Ednl. Found.; mem. ASCE (assoc.), Internat. Group for Lean Constrn. Office: Univ Calif Berkeley 215 McLaughlin Hall Spc 1712 Berkeley CA 94720-1712 Office Phone: 510-643-8678.

TOMPKINS, JULIE LYNBERG, market research consultant; b. Monterey Park, Calif., Mar. 14, 1953; d. Leland Dwayne and Vivian Joanne (Share) Lynberg; m. Terry Cady Tompkins, Mar. 11, 1978; children: Jeffrey, Devon, Christopher. BA in Human Biology, Stanford U., 1974; MBA in Mktg., U. Santa Clara, 1979. Chemist Syntex Corp., Palo Alto, Calif., 1974-78; market rsch. analyst Syntex Labs., Palo Alto, 1978-80, mgr. new product planning, 1980-85, mgr. market analysis, 1985-86; pres., founder Medsearch Inc., Cupertino, Calif., 1986—. Mem. Med. Mktg. Assn., Pharm. Market Rsch. Group. Avocations: stained glass, needlework.

TOMPKINS, SUSIE, apparel company executive, creative director; children: Quincey, Summer. Design cons. Esprit de Corp, San Francisco. Office: Esprit de Corps Internat 3 Embarcadero Ctr Ste 2290 San Francisco CA 94111-4045 also: 1370 Broadway Fl 16 New York NY 10018-7302

TOMPSON, MARIAN LEONARD, professional society administrator; b. Chgo., Dec. 5, 1929; d. Charles Clark and Marie Christine (Bernardini) Leonard; m. Clement R. Tompson, May 7, 1949 (dec. 1981); children: Melanie Tompson Kandler, Deborah Tompson Frueh, Allison Tompson Fagerholm, Laurel Tompson Davies, Sheila Tompson Doucet, Brian, Philip. Student public and parochial schs., Chgo. and Franklin Park, Ill. Co-founder La Leche League (Internat.), Franklin Park, 1956, pres., 1956-80, dir., 1956—, pres. emeritus, 1990—; exec. dir. Alternative Birth Crisis Coalition, 1981-85; founder, exec. dir. AnotherLook, Inc., 2000—. Cons. WHO; bd. dirs. N.Am. Soc. Psychosomatic Ob-Gyn, Natural Birth and Natural Parenting, 1981-83; mem. adv. bd. Nat. Assn. Parents and Profls. for Safe Alternatives in Childbirth, Am. Acad. Husband-Coached Childbirth; mem. adv. bd. Fellowship of Christian Midwives; mem. profl. adv. bd. Home Oriented Maternity Experience; guest lectr. Harvard U. Med. Sch., UCLA Sch. Pub. Health, U. Antioquia Med. Sch., Medellín, Columbia, U. Ill. Sch. Medicine, Chgo., U. W.I., Jamaica, U. N.C., Nat. Coll. of Chiropractic, Am. Coll. Nurse Midwives, U. Parma, Italy, Inst. Psychology, Rome, Rockford (Ill.) Sch. Medicine, Northwestern U. Sch. Medicine, NGO Forum/4th World Conf. on Women, Beijing; mem. family com. Ill. Commn. on Status of Women, 1976-85; mem. perinatal adv. com. Ill. Dept. Pub. Health, 1980-83; mem. adv. bd. Internat. Nutrition Comm. Svc., 1980—; bd. cons. We Can, 1984—; exec. adv. bd. United Resources for Family Health and Support, 1985-86; mem. internat. adv. coun. World Alliance of Breast Feeding Action, 1996. Author: (with others) Safe Alternatives in Childbirth,

1976, 21st Century Obstetrics Now!, 1977, The Womanly Art of Breastfeeding, 6th edit., 1997, Five Standards for Safe Childbearing, 1981, But Doctor, About That Shot..., 1988, The Childbirth Activists Handbook, 1983; author prefaces and forwards in 11 books; columnist La Leche League News, 1958-80; columnist People's Doctor Newsletter, 1977-80, mem. adv. bd., cons., 1988-92; assoc. editor Child and Family Quar., 1967—; mem. med. adv. bd. East West Jour., 1980—; also articles. Mem. adv. bd. Shelters for Healthy Environments, 1998—2002, The Beginning Project, 2000. Recipient Gold medal of honor Centro de Rehabilitacao Nossa Senhora da Gloria, 1975, Night of 100 Stars III Achiever award Actors Fund Am., 1990, N.Y. Soc. Ethical Culture Ethical Humanist award, 1999, 100 Women Making a Difference Today's Chgo. Woman. Mem. Nat. Assn. Postpartum Care Svcs. (adv. bd.), Chgo. Cmty. Midwives (adv. bd.), World Alliance for Breast Feeding Action (mem. internat. adv. coun. 1997). Office: 1400 N Meacham Rd Schaumburg IL 60173-4808 Office Phone: 847-869-1278. E-mail: m.tompson@comcast.net.

TOMS, JUSTINE WILLIS, educational organization executive; b. Evanston, Ill., Oct. 16, 1942; d. Robert Jacques and Ruth (Herzfeld) W.; m. Donald Carroll Welch, Nov. 1962 (div. 1969); 1 child, Robert Gregory Welch; m. Michael Anthony Toms, Dec. 16, 1972. BS, Auburn U., 1967. Elem. sch. tchr. Sylacauga (Ala.) Sch. System, 1966-69; exec. dir. New Dimensions Radio, Ukiah, Calif., 1973—. Seminar leader in field. Co-author: True Work: Doing What You Love and Loving What You Do, 1998; editor (quar. jour.) New Dimensions Jour., 1987—. Democrat. Buddhist. Avocations: horseback riding, drumming.

TONACK, DELORIS, elementary school educator; Elem. tchr. math. and sci. Goodrich Jr. High Sch., 1996—. Recipient Nebr. State Tchr. of Yr. award math./sci., 1992. Office: Sci Focus Program 1222 S 27th St Lincoln NE 68502-1832

TONAK, LORETTA JEAN, music educator, librarian; b. Sioux Falls, S.D., July 11, 1951; d. Harven and Irene Caroline Brass; children from previous marriage: Benjamin, Rebecca, Timothy. BS, Dakota State U., Madison, S.D., 1973; post grad., 1973—. Cert. tchr. Wyo., S.D. Tchr. elem. music Clark (S.D.) Schs., 1973—86, tchr. 7-12 art, 1973—86; tchr. elem. music Washakie County Schs., Worland, Wyo., 1986—87, Crook County Dist. 1 Schs., Sundance, Wyo., 1987—96; tchr. mid. sch. band Sheridan (Wyo.) Dist. 2 Schs., 1996—. Smart Classroom grant, 2000. Mem.: Assn. of Am. Educators, Wyo. Music Educators Assn. (v.p. elem. music 1995—97, 25 Yr. award 1998), Delta Kappa Gamma. Baptist. Avocations: children's librarian, pianist. Home: 731 Dunnuck St Sheridan WY 82801 Office: Central Mid Sch 25 S Custer Sheridan WY 82801 Office Phone: 307-674-6545.

TONEY, ANGELA M. medical administrator and educator; b. Southbridge, Mass., June 1, 1970; d. Alvin Darryl Toney; 1 child, Meghan. BS i Biology, BA in English, Harvard U., 1993, MPH, 1996. Med. asst., Boston, 1989-96; emergency med. technician EMT-I Boston EMS, 1991-95; rschr. Premier Rsch. Worldwide, Phila., 1997-98; med. instr. Star Tech. Inst., Upper Darby, Pa., 1997—, asst. dir., 1997-98, med. dir., 1998—, U. Pa., 1998—. Advisor Delaware County Intermediate Unit, 1997—; Disaster Health Svcs. vol. ARC, Phila., 1998—, vol. trainer, 1997—; med. exam. proctor NCCT, Overland Park, Kans., 1997—. Mem. Am. Assn. Med. Assts., Internat. Congress Med. Profls., Am. Soc. Clin. Lab. Sci., Tri-County Chpt. Med. Assts., Delaware County Computer Assn. (dir. pub. rels. 1998—), Delaware County C. of C., Alpha Beta Kappa Delta Pa. Democrat. Ropman Catholic. Avocations: black and white photography, travel, classical literature, foreign films. Office: Star Tech Inst 1570 Garrett Rd Upper Darby PA 19082-4500 also: U Pa 3400 Spruce St Philadelphia PA 19104-4206 E-mail: Angeland45@yahoo.com.

TONEY, AVIA VERNET, medical products manufacturer; b. New Smyrna Beach, Fla., Jan. 23, 1947; d. Albert Lewis and Willie Mae (Williams) Thompson; m. Livingston Toney (div. Sept. 1985); 1 child, Carla. BS, Fla. A&M U., 1971. Pharmacist Medics Drug Mart, Atlanta, 1971-72; asst. dir. pharmacy Fla. A&M U., Tallahassee, 1972-75; asst. research scientist Am. McGaw, Irvine, Calif., 1975-76; dept. head CD Med., Miami Lakes, Fla., 1976-82; supr. process control Coulter Electronics, Hialeah, Fla., 1982-83; mgr. regulatory affairs Ross Labs., Columbus, Ohio, 1983-94; dir. quality assurance and regulatory affairs Command Med. Products, Ormond Beach, Fla.; mgr. regulatory affairs Bausch & Lomb Pharm. Divsn., Tampa, Fla.; with SIMS Protex, Ft. Myers, Fla., 1994—. Bd. dirs. Open Door Clinic, Columbus, 1983-86; active mem. Urban League, Columbus, 1985—088. Mem. Am. Soc. Quality Control, NAACP, Nat. Assn. Female Execs. (network dir. 1987—), Regulatory Affairs Profl. Soc. Roman Catholic. Home: PO Box 592104 Orlando FL 32859-2104 Office: SIMS Portex 5100 Tice St Fort Myers FL 33905-5208

TONEY, CREOLA SARAH, minister; b. Darlington, S.C., Mar. 29, 1920; d. Lonnie John and Mary Rosella (Marsh) Staton; m. Calvin William Toney, Jr., May 16, 1937 (dec. 1985); children: Calvis Loretta, Donald Wallace, Johnnie, Joyce, Paula, Anthony, Creola, Mildred, Luwanna, Philip. AA, Wayne Community Coll., Detroit, 1986; BSW, Wayne State U., Detroit, 1992. Lic. social worker, Mich. With Chartered Greyhound Bus Svcs., 1964-80, 84-85; pastor Faith Temple Ch. of God in Christ, Detroit, 1984—; tchr. Sleepy Hollow Schs., Detroit, 1986-87. Local, dist. and state pres., nat. rep., prayer and Bible band aux. Ch. of God in Christ Inc., S.W. Mich., 1960-83. Vol. Wayne County Dept. Social Svcs., Detroit; founder, organizer Vols. for Christ Visitation Group; state sec. women's sect. Examining Bd., 1974-86; active Met. jail ministry, hosp. ministry; notary pub. Wayne County State of Mich., 1972-92. Recipient cert. of recognition and letter Wayne County Sheriff's Dept., 1988, 89, cert. of recognition Wayne County Execs., 1990, Mich. William Milliken, 1977, 78, 82, Spirit of Detroit award City Coun., 1991. Avocations: sewing, interior decorating, baseball, bicycling, horse shoes. Home: PO Box 4310 Detroit MI 48204-0310

TONG, KAITY, anchor; BA, Bryn Mawr Coll.; MA, Stanford U. Street reporter various West Coast radio/tv networks; anchor WABC Eyewitness News, WB-11 News at 10/WPIX-TV, N.Y.C. Recipient Exceptional Achievement award, Disting. Woman award, Star award, Edward R. Murrow award. Acitve United Cerebral Palsy, Children's Mus. of Manhattan, Juvenile Diabetes Found., Friends for Life, League for the Hard of Hearing. Office: WPIX-TV/Tribune Co 220 E 42d St New York NY 10017

TONG, ROSEMARIE, medical humanities and philosophy educator, consultant and researcher; b. Chgo., July 19, 1947; d. Joseph John and Lillian (Nedued) Behensky; m. Paul Ki-King Tong, Aug. 15, 1971 (dec. Apr. 1988); children: Paul Shih-Mien Tong, John Joseph Tong; m. Jeremiah Putnam, Aug. 1, 1992. BA, Marygrove Coll., 1970; MA, Cath. U., 1971; PhD, Temple U., 1978; LLD (hon.), Marygrove Coll., 1987; LHD (hon.), SUNY, Oneonta, 1993. Asst. and assoc. prof. philosophy Williams Coll., Williamstown, Mass., 1978-88; vis. disting. prof. humanities Davidson (N.C.) Coll., 1988-89, Thatcher Prof. in med. humanities and philosophy, 1989-99; prof. humanities and philosophy U. N.C., Charlotte, 1999—; dir. Ctr. for Profl. and Applied Ethics, Charlotte, 2002—. L. Stacy Davidson vis. chair in liberal arts U. Miss., Oxford, 1998; Louise M. Olmstead vis. prof. philosophy and women's studies, Lafayette Coll., Easton, Pa., 1993; disting. prof. health care ethics U. N.C., Charlotte, 1999—; manuscript reviewer Wadsworth Pub. Co., 1985-92; curriculum reviewer philosophy dept. Carlton and Bowdoin Colls., 1986; honors examiner Hobart and William Smith Colls., 1990; dissertation dir., adj. faculty The Union Inst., 1992-93; cons., judge, panelist, organizer and speaker in field; mem. numerous U. coms. Author: Women, Sex and the Law, 1984, Ethics in Policy Analysis, 1985, Feminist Thought: A Comprehensive Introduction, 1989, Feminist Philosophies: Problems, Theories, and Applications, 1991, Feminine and Feminist Ethics, 1993, Feminist Thought: A More Comprehensive Introduction, 1998, (with Larry Kaplan) Controlling Our Reproductive Destiny, 1994, Feminist Philosophy: Essential Readings in Theory, Reinterpretation and Application, 1994, Feminist Bioethics, 1997, Feminist Thought: A More Comprehensive Ethics, 1998, Globalizing Feminist Bioethics: Crosscultural Perspectives, 2000; contbr. numerous articles to profl. jours.; mem. various editl. bds. Project reviewer Annenberg/CPB Project, Washington, 1986; policy writer dvsn. health svcs. rsch. and policy U. Minn., 1988, Frank Graham Porter Early Childhood Ctr., U. N.C. Chapel Hill, 1988; mem. Charlotte task force Congl. Task Force Health Care, Congressman Alex McMillan, 1991, standards and ethics com. Hospice N.C., 1991, resource and ethics coms. McMillan-Spratt Task Force Health Care Policy, 1992, pastoral care com. Carolinas Med. Ctr., 1990—, ethics com. Presbyn. Hosp., 1990—, N.E. Regional Hosp., 1991, Nat. Adv. Bd. Ethics in Reproduction, Washington, 1993; active Hastings Ctr. Project Undergrad. Values Edn., Briarcliff Manor, N.Y., 1993, N.C. Found. Humanities and Pub. Policy; mem. bioethics Resource Group, 1992—; mem. feminist approaches to bioethics network, 1996—; dir. med. humanities program Davidson Coll., 1988-98. Named Prof. of Yr., Carnegie Found. and Coun. Advancement and Support of Edn., 1986. Mem. Internat. Assn. for Feminist Approaches to Bioethics Network (coord. 1999—), Internat. Assn. Bioethics (chair 2003—), Am. Assn. for Bioethics and Humanities, Am. Cath. Philos. Assn., Am. Philos. Assn. (ad hoc com. computers, pub. and role of Am. Philos. Assn. 1984, adv. com. to program com. 1986-88, nomination com. 1989-91, nat. com. on status of women 1989-93, 2003—), Am. Legal Studies and Assn., Am. Soc. Pol. and Legal Philosophy, Am. Soc. Law and Medicine, Nat. Coun. Rsch. on Women, Nat. Women Studies Assn., Internat. Assn. Philosophy Law and Social Philosophy, Assn. Practical and Profl. Ethics, Society Christian Ethics, Soc. Women in Philosophy, Soc. Philosophy and Tech., Soc. Philosophy and Pub. Affairs, Soc. Study of Women Philosophers, Network Feminist Approaches to Bioethics, The Hastings Ctr., Triangle Bioethics Group, So. Soc. Philosophy and Psychology. Avocations: aerobics, boating, hiking. Office Phone: 704-687-2850.

TONKENS, REBECCA ANNETTE, maternal/women's health nurse, rehabilitation nurse; b. Searcy, Ark., Dec. 17, 1943; d. William T. and Velda M. (Goodloe) McAfee; m. Richard E. Morris, June 24, 1960 (div. Nov. 1980); children: Terri L. Morris Bomar, Toni L. Morris Carroll; m. Solvin W. Tonkens, Dec. 22, 1986. LPN, Area Vocat. Tech. Sch., Kansas City, Kans., 1973; ADN, Kansas City C.C., 1980; BSN, Webster U., 1992. RN, Kans., Mo. Area Vocat. Tech. Sch.; staff nurse Providence-St. Margaret Hosp., Kansas City, 1973-80; indsl. nurse, office mgr. Kansas City Indsl. Clinic, 1980-81; staff nurse Bethany Med. Ctr., Kansas City, 1981-1999; retired, 1999; outreach nurse specialist Quintiles Phase I Svcs., 2000—. Active community rels. diabetes unit Bethany Med. Ctr., 1983-86. Officer, v.p., bd. dirs. Cambridge Townhouse Assn., Leawood, Kans., 1989-92; chaperone Rose Bud (Ark.) Band at Presdl. Inauguration, Washington, 1992; mem. adv. bd. Kansas City Kans. C.C. Day Care Ctr.; vol. Habitat for Humanity, Salvation Army, others. Recipient Cert. of Appreciation, Salvation Army, 1994, Korean Am. Sr. Citizen Soc. Kans. City, 2001, Ctrs. for Medicare and Medicaid Svc., 2002, U.S. Dept. Health and Human Svcs., 2002. Mem. ANA, Am. Coll. Occupational and Environ. Medicine (aux.), Mo.-Kans. Assn. Medicine Shoppes, Inc. (flu prevention coord.), Assn. Osteo. Physicians and Surgeons (aux.), Optimist Club. Episcopalian. Home and Office: 314 Westhills Way Hamilton MT 59840-9365 E-mail: flunurse@aol.com.

TOOLE, JOAN TRIMBLE, financial consultant; b. Ipswich, Mass., Apr. 3, 1923; d. Dana Newcomb and Barbara (Campbell) T.; m. John R. Marchi, Dec. 28, 1943 (div. Aug. 1959); children: Jon, Jael, Charis, Peter; m. Kenneth Ross Toole, Apr. 22, 1960 (dec. Aug. 1981); children: Dana O'Keefe, David Campbell. BA, Antioch Coll., Yellow Springs, Ohio, 1946; MS in Fin., U. Mont., 1976; MPA, Harvard U., 1985. Rancher J/J and KJ Ranches, 1955-82; Mont. legis. asst., researcher, 1981-83; cons. Mont. Dept. Revenue, 1985-87, U. Mont. Biol. Sta., 1987-89; pvt. practice, 1987—. State coord. Cranston for Pres., 1983-84; lobbyist Office Pub. Instrn., 1989-90; mem. tax appeals bd. Ravalli County, 1981-84; mem. Mont. Bd. Natural Resources and Conservation, 1986-90; bd. dirs. Forever Wild Endowment; active LWV, Mont. Environ. Info. Ctr., No. Plains Resource Coun.; bd. dirs., treas. Mont. Conservation Voters, 1992—; mem. Lewis & Clark City/County Health Bd., 1994-98, treas. Montanans for Coal Trust, 1999—. Mem. AARP (vol. income tax preparer 1993—), Harvard Club (bd. dirs. ch. schs. and scholarships). Democrat. Episcopalian. Home: Apt 1 1205 E Broadway St Helena MT 59601-5152 Office: Apt 1 1205 E Broadway St Helena MT 59601-5152

TOOMAN, STEPHANIE, performing arts educator; BFS, Julliard Sch.; MFA, Purchase Coll. Rehearsal dir. Neta Pulvermacher, Errol Grimes, The Purchase Dance Corps; dancer, rehearsal dir. Kazuko Hirabayashi, Tokyo; tchr. dance Alvin Ailey Am. Dance Ctr., the Netherlands Dance Theatre, 1st and 2d Cos., the Hague, Netherlands, The Rotterdam Dance Acad., The Inst. del Theatre, Barcelona; with Merian Soto/Pepatian, EarlMosley Diversity of Dance, Nathan Trice, Errol Grimes Dance Group; collaborator, dancer Reggie Wilson, 1989—.

TOOMEY, JEANNE ELIZABETH, animal activist; b. NYC, Aug. 22, 1921; d. Edward Aloysius and Anna Margaret (O'Grady) Toomey; m. Peter Terranova, Sept. 28, 1951 (dec. 1968); children: Peter Terranova (dec.), Sheila Terranova Beasley. Student, Hofstra U., 1938-40; student law sch., Fordham U., 1940-41; BA, Southampton Coll., 1976; postgrad., Monmouth Coll., 1978-79. Reporter, columnist Bklyn. Daily Eagle, 1943-52; with The Fitzgeralds, NBC Radio, N.Y.C., 1952-53; reporter, writer King Features Syndicate, N.Y.C., 1953-55; reporter, columnist N.Y. Jour.-Am., N.Y.C., 1955-61; newsman AP, N.Y.C., 1963-64; stringer; columnist News Tribune, Woodbridge, N.J., 1976-86; editor Calexico (Calif.) Chronicle, 1987-88; editor community sect. Asbury Park (N.J.) Press, 1988; pres., dir. Last Post Animal Sanctuary, Falls Village, Conn., 1989—. Author: Murder in the Hamptons, 1994, Assignment Homicide, 1998. Named Woman of the Yr. N.Y. Women's Press Club, 1960. Mem. Newswomen's Club of N.Y., Overseas Press Club, N.Y. Press Club, Silurians. Roman Catholic. Address: PO Box 259 Falls Village CT 06031-0259 Office: 95 Belden St Falls Village CT 06031 Office Phone: 860-824-0831. Office Fax: 860-824-5460.

TOOMEY, KATHLEEN ELIZABETH, state agency administrator; b. Aspinwall, Pa., Nov. 21, 1951; AB in biology cum laude, Smith Coll., 1973; MPH, MD, Harvard U., 1979. Diplomate Am. Bd. of Family Practice, Nat. Bd. of Med. Examiners. Resident dept. family medicine U. Wash., Seattle, 1979-82; clin. dir. Alaska Native Hosp., Kotzebue, 1982-85; Pew Health Policy fellow Inst. for Health Policy Studies, U. Calif. Sch. Medicine, San Francisco, 1985-87; Epidemic Intelligence Svc. officer Nat. Ctr. for Prevention Svcs., Ctrs. for Disease Control, Atlanta, 1987-89; legis. asst. on health issues to Senator John Chafee, U.S. Senate, Washington, 1991; asst. to dir. for external rels., 1989-90; state epidemiologist, dir. epidemiology and prevention br. Divsn. of Pub. Health, Ga. Dept. of Human Resources, 1993-97, dir., 1997—. Adj. assoc. prof. in epidemiology Rollins Sch. of Pub. Health, Emory U.; clin. assoc. prof. Morehouse U. Sch. Medicine, Emory U.; mem. Statewide Child Fatality Rev. Panel, 1998; mem. Bd. Health Promotion and Disease Prevention, Inst. of Medicine, 1998—; mem. Tech. Adv. Group on Devolution and Federalism, Nat. Health Policy Forum, George Washington U., 1998—. Mem. task force The Nat. Campaign to Prevent Teen Pregnancy, 1996-99. Fulbright scholar, 1973-74. Mem. Am. Acad. Family Physicians, Am. Pub. Health Assn. (governing coun. Ga. state chpt. rep. 1997-99), Am. Sexually Transmitted Diseases Assn., Assn. State and Territorial Health Ofcls. (exec. com. 1998—), Ga. Acad. Family Physicians, Ga. Pub. Health Assn., Med. Assn. Atlanta, Med. Assn. Ga. (pub. health and preventative health care com. 1997—). Office: Divsn of Pub Health 2 Peachtree St NW Ste 15-470 Atlanta GA 30303-3142 E-mail: [illegible]

TOOTE, GLORIA E. A. real estate developer, lawyer, columnist; b. N.Y.C. d. Frederick A. and Lillie M. (Tooks) Toote Student, Howard U., 1949-51; JD, NYU, 1954; LLM, Columbia U., 1956. Bar: N.Y. 1955, U.S. Dist. Ct. (so. and ea. dists.) N.Y. 1956, U.S. Supreme Ct. 1956. With firm Greenbaum, Wolff & Ernst, 1957; mem. editorial staff Time mag., 1957-58; asst. gen. counsel N.Y. State Workmen's Compensation Bd., 1958-64; pres. Toote Town Pub. Co. and Town Sound Studios, Inc., 1966-70; asst. dir. Action Agy., 1971-73; asst. sec. Dept. HUD, 1973-75; vice chmn. Pres.'s Adv. Council on Pvt. Sector Initiatives, 1983-85; housing developer, 1976—; pres. Trea Estates and Enterprises, Inc.; newspaper columnist. Chairperson The Policy Coun. Former bd. dirs. Citizens for the Republic, Nat. Black United Fund, Fed. Exec. Women in Govt., Am. Arbitration Assn., Consumer Alert; bd. overseers Hoover Inst., 1985-95; vice chair Nat. Polit. Congress of Black Women, 1984-92; former mem. Coun. Econ. Affairs, Rep. Nat. Com.; pres. N.Y.C. Black Rep. Coun.; exec. trustee Polit. Action Com. for Equality; mem. NYNEX Consumer Adv. Coun., 1995-98. Recipient citations Nat. Bus. League, Alpha Kappa Alpha, U.S. C. of C., Nat. Assn. Black Women Attys. Mem. N.Y. Fedn. Civil Svc. Orgns., Nat. Assn. Real Estate Brokers, Fed. Nat. Mortgage Assn. (bd. dirs. 1992-94), Nat. Citizens Participation Coun., Nat. Bar Assn., Delta Sigma Theta, others. Address: 282 W 137th St New York NY 10030-2407

TOOTHE, KAREN LEE, elementary and secondary school educator; b. Seattle, Dec. 13, 1957; d. Russell Minor and Donna Jean (Drolet) McGraw; m. Edward Frank Toothe, Aug. 6, 1983; 1 child, Kendall Erin. BA in Psychology with high honors, U. Fla., 1977, MEd in Emotional Handicaps and Learning Disabilities, 1979. Cert. behavior analysis Fla. Dept. Profl. Regulation, behavior analyst Nat. Behavior Analyst Bd. Alternative edn. self-contained tchr. grades 2 and 3 Gainesville Acad., Micanopy, Fla., 1979; emotional handicaps self-contained tchr. Ctr. Sch. Alternative Sch., Gainesville, Fla., 1979-80; learning disabilities resource tchr. grades 2 and 3 Galaxy Elem. Sch., Boynton Beach, Fla., 1980-81, learning disabilities self-contained tchr. grades 1-3, 1981, varying exceptionalities self-contained tchr. grades 3-5, 1981-83, chpt. one remedial reading tchr. grades 3 and 4, 1982-83; sec. and visual display unit operator Manpower, London, 1983-84; dir. sci./geography/social studies program Fairley House Sch., London, 1984-86, specific learning difficulties self-contained tchr. ages 8-12, dir. computing program, 1984-89; specific learning difficulties resource tchr. ages 8-16 Dyslexia Inst., Sutton Coldfield, Eng., 1990; behavior specialist, head Exceptional Student Edn. dept. Gateway High Sch., Kissimmee, Fla., 1990, behavior specialist, head ESE dept., 1991, resource compliance specialist, head ESE dept., 1991-93, tchr. summer youth tng. and enrichment program, 1993, Osceola High Sch., Kissimmee, 1992; resource compliance specialist, program specialist for mentally handicapped, physically impaired, occupational and phys. therapy programs St. Cloud (Fla.) Mid. Sch., 1993-96, local augmentative/assistive tech. specialist, 1995—; resource compliance specialist, program specialist physically impaired occupl./phys. therapy programs, local augmentative/assistive tech. specialist Hickory Tree Elem. Sch., 1996-97, program specialist assistive tech., occpl., and phys. therapy, physically impaired programs, 1997-99, program specialist assistive tech., 1999—. Sch. rep. CREATE, Alachua County, Fla., 1979-80, Palm Beach County South Area Tchr. Edn. Ctr. Coun., 1980-83, chmn., 1982-83; mem. writing team Title IV-C Ednl. Improvement Grant, Palm Beach County, Fla., 1981; mem. math. curriculum writing team Palm Beach County (Fla.) Schs., 1983; mem., co-dir. Fairley House Rsch. Com., 1984-90; co-founder, dir. Rsch. Database, London, 1984-89; co-chmn. computer and behavior/social aspects writing teams Dyslexia Inst. Math., Staines, Eng., 1990; lectr., course tutor Brit. Dyslexia Assn., Crewe, Eng., 1990; mem. Vocat.-Exceptional Com., 1991-93; mem. Osceola Reading Coun., 1991-98; mem. sch. adv. com. Gateway High Sch., 1991-93, St. Cloud Mid. Sch., 1993-96; mem. sch. adv. com. Hickory Tree Elem. Sch., 1999-2000, Ctr. for Ind. Living Assitance for Tech. Divsn.; presenter in field. Mem. bd. assistive tech. divsn. Ctr. for Ind. Living. Named Mid. Sch. Profl. of Yr. Osceola chpt. Coun. Exceptional Children, 1995, 96, Profl. Recognized Spl. Educator, 1997; winner Disney's Teacherific Spl. Judges award, 1997; recipient Outstanding Svcs. to Coun. for Exceptional Children award, 2002, 2003, Outstanding Related Svcs. Tchr. of Yr., 2003, Outstanding Support Svcs. award, 2003. Mem. CEC (named local chpt. Mid. Sch. Profl. of Yr. 1995, 96, exec. com. 1997—, C.A.N. rep. 1997-99, pres.-elect 1999-2000, pres. 2000-01, Outstanding Svcs. to CEC award 2002, 03, Outstanding Related Svcs. Tchr. of Yr. 2003, Outstanding Support Svcs. award 2003), Fla. Soc. for Augmentative and Alt. Comm., Phi Beta Kappa. Avocations: traveling, reading, physical fitness, scuba diving, arts and crafts. Home: 2175 James Dr Saint Cloud FL 34771-8830 Office: Osceola Dist Schs ESE Adminstrv Annex 805 Bill Beck Blvd Kissimmee FL 34744-4492 Office Phone: 407-348-2984. Business E-Mail: toothek@osceola.k12.fl.us.

TOPALIAN, NAOMI GETSOYAN, writer; b. Beirut, Jan. 26, 1928; came to the U.S., 1953; d. Avedis S. and Zarouhi T. (Yezegelian) G.; m. Paul G. Topalian, Sept. 18, 1954; children: Andrew P., Janet Z. Topalian Moffatt. Diploma, Am. U. Hosp. Sch. Nursing, Beirut, 1952; BS, Boston U., 1967. RN, Mass. Pediat. nurse Children Med. Ctr., Boston, 1954-55; inservice edn. supr. Winchester (Mass.) Hosp., 1967-70; tchr. nursing Northeastern Vocat. H.S., Wakefield, Mass., 1970-72; med. and surg. nurse various tchg. hosps., Boston, 1973-87. Author: Dust to Destiny, 1986, People, Places and Moultonborough, 1989, Legacy of Honor, 1995; contbr. Personality and Presidency: A Scientific Inquirey, 1998, Breaking the Rock of Tradition, 2000; contbr. articles to profl. jours. Supt. primary divsn., Sunday sch. tchr., mem. pulpit com., co-pres. couples club Armenian Meml. Ch., Watertown, Mass.; Armenian lang. tchr. First Armenian Ch. of Belmont; active Belmont Coun. Chs., chair religious edn. com.; pres. Armenian Women's Edn. Club. Mem. Armenian Internat. Womens Assn. Avocations: needle work, knitting, counseling the bereaved. Home: 46 Circle Rd Lexington MA 02420-2926

TOPELIUS, KATHLEEN ELLIS, lawyer; b. July 15, 1948; BA, U. Conn., 1970; postgrad., U. Md., 1971-74; JD, Cath. U. Am., 1978. Bar: D.C. 1978, U.S. Supreme Ct. 1988. Atty. office of gen. counsel Fed. Home Loan Bank Bd., 1978-80; ptnr. Morgan, Lewis & Bockius, Washington, 1985-93, Bryan Cave, Washington, 1993—. Recipient Alpha award Fed. Home Loan Bank Bds., 1979. Office: Bryan Cave 700 13th St NW Fl 7 Washington DC 20005-5921 Business E-Mail: ktopelius@bryancave.com.

TOPHAM, SALLY JANE, ballet educator; b. N.Y.C., June 2, 1933; d. William Holroyd Topham and Marian Phyllis (Thomas) Topham Halligan; m. Joseph Vincent Ferrara, Dec. 27, 1958 (div. 1977); children: Gregory Paul, Mark Edward. Student Ballet Theatre Sch., Royal Acad. Dance, London; trained in Europe. Freelance profl. dancer ballet, opera ballet, summer stock, 1956-59; founder, dir. Monmouth Sch. Ballet, N.J., 1963-83; dir. Shore Ballet Theatre Sch., 1986-95; freelance tchr., choreographer, 1996—. Tchr., dir. Mount Allison U. Summer Sch., New Brunswick, Canada, 1973—77; dir. Westfield Sch. Ballet, NJ, 1976—77; artistic dir. Shore Ballet Co., 1977—; prof. ballet Monmouth Coll., West Long Branch, NJ, 1981—83; founder Ctrl. Jersey Acad. Ballet, Red Bank, NJ, 1983—85; dir. Acad. of Shore Ballet, 1995—2000; cons. formulation dance curriculum for N.J. pub. schs. State Bd. Edn., 1997; tchr. Colts Neck Dance Acad., 2000—03, Middletown Dance Acad., 2003, Spring Lake Sch. Dance, 2003—. Choreographer (ballet) Coppelia, 1981, 90, 96, Shubert Songs, 1980, Homage to Bournonville, 1977, Nutcracker, 1985, Cinderella, 1988; staged many ballets and opera ballets. Bd. dirs. Monmouth Arts Found., Red Bank, 1972—, Shore Ballet Co., Red Bank, 1976—; founder, bd. dirs. Monmouth Civic Ballet, Red Bank, 1972-75. Mem.: English Speaking

Union (bd. dirs., treas. 2004), Am. Acad. Ballet (assoc.), Royal Acad. Dance (assoc.; reg. tchr., advanced tchg. diploma 1979). Avocations: theater, music, books, travel. Office: Shore Ballet Co 8 Hunt St Rumson NJ 07760-1428

TOPINKA, JUDY BAAR, state official, political organization worker; b. Riverside, Ill., Jan. 16, 1944; d. William Daniel and Lillian Mary (Shuss) Baar; 1 child, Joseph Baar. BS, Northwestern U., 1966. Features editor, reporter, columnist Life Newspapers, Berwyn and LaGrange, Ill., 1966-77; with Forest Park (Ill.) Rev. and Westchester News, 1976-77; coord. spl. events dept. fedn. comm. AMA, 1978-80; rsch. analyst Senator Leonard Becker, 1978-79; mem. Ill. Ho. of Reps., 1981-84, Ill. Senate, 1985-94; treas. State of Ill., Springfield, 1995—; chmn. State Rep. Party, 2002—. Former mem. judiciary com., former chmn. senate health and welfare com.; former mem. fin. instn. com.; former co-chmn. Citizens Coun. on Econ. Devel.; former co-chmn. U.S. Commn. for Preservation of Am.'s Heritage Abroad, serves on legis. ref. bur.; former mem. minority bus. resource ctr. adv. com. U.S. Dept. Transp.; former mem. adv. bd. Nat. Inst. Justice. Founder, pres., bd. dirs. West Suburban Exec. Breakfast Club, from 1976; chmn. Ill. Ethnics for Reagan-Bush, 1984, Bush-Quayle 1988; spokesman Nat. Coun. State Legislatures Health Com.; former mem. nat. adv. coun. health professions edn. HHS; mem., GOP chairwoman Legis. Audit Commn. of Cook County; chmn. Riverside Twp. Regular Republican Orgn., 1994—. Recipient Outstanding Civilian Svc. medal, Molly Pitcher award, Abraham Lincoln award, Silver Eagle award U.S. Army and N.G. Office: Office of Ill State Treasurer 100 W Randolph St Ste 15-600 Chicago IL 60601-3232*

TOPLITT, GLORIA H. voice educator, singer, actress; b. St. Louis, May 22, 1925; d. Wade Fitzgerald Hamilton and Neyneen Farrell Pires; m. James Parnell, 1942 (div. July 1949); 1 child, Dennis James Parnell; m. Abraham Toplitt, Aug. 19, 1968. Student, Guy Bates Post Acad. Dramatic Arts, L.A., 1941-43. Stage performer, N.Y.C., 1944-59; dir. entertainment Holland Am. Lines, 1959-61; tchr. voice North Hollywood (Calif.) Conservatory, 1965-67; pvt. voice tchr. North Hollywood, 1968-95; music specialist outreach program NASA Space Sci. and Tech., Inc., Springfield, Va., 1997—. Dir. Workshop Theatre Program, North Hollywood, 1968-78; coach for impaired voices, North Hollywood, 1968—. Author, composer: Parade of Planets, 1998, Space Challenge, 1999 actor: (plays, N.Y. stage prodns.) appeared as leading lady Oklahoma, Chocolate Soldier, Lend an Ear, Courtin' Time, Showboat, Take Me Along, Auld Lang Syne, Three Musketeers, Carousel, Oh! Captain, Brigadoon, Guys and Dolls, Hit the Deck, Finian's Rainbow, others. Mem. election bd. Office of Voter Registrar, North Hollywood, 1996-98. Avocations: poetry, travel, theatre, elderhostel classes, reading. Home: 4405 Carpenter Ave North Hollywood CA 91607-4110

TOPOLEWSKI-GREEN, MARY JO THERESE, small business owner; b. Toledo, Ohio, June 29, 1969; d. Leonard Martin and Carol Ann Topolewski; m. Robert Wendell, Jr. Green, Oct. 12, 2000. Student, Davenport U., 2002, Bowling Green State U., Ohio, 1987—90. Office adminstr. Mich. Dept. Transp., 1993—95; adminstrv. asst. Schrader Ent., Fairview, Mich., 1997—2001, Reliance Heating and Cooling, Mio, Mich., 1998—99; co-owner Sunfish Studios, Fairview, 1999—; adminstrv. asst. Otsego Meml. Hosp., Gaylord, Mich., 2002—. Freelance profl. dance instr.; web site designer and cons.; audio/video prodn. and sound recording cons. Mem.: Internat. Thespian Soc. (life; chpt. pres. 1986—87). Avocations: dance, singing, computers.

TOPOLSKI, CATHERINE, science educator; b. Bridgeport, Conn., Feb. 23, 1948; d. Edward Joseph and Jean (Skierski) Topolski; m. Richard A. Hoffman, Feb. 1970 (div. June 1981); children: Alan Hoffman, Alexandria Hoffman, Aaron Hoffman. BS, Sacred Heart U., Fairfield, Conn., 1984; MS, So. Conn. State U., 1993. Sci. tchr. Emmett O'Brien Vocat. Tech. H.S., Ansonia, Conn., 1985—2002, Bullard Havens Vocat. Tech. H.S., Bridgeport, Conn., 2002—. Class advisor, ski club advisor, student assistance team peer mediator Emmett O'Brien Vocat. Tech. H.S., 1987—. Organizer Emmett O'Brien River Cleanup Naugatuck River Watershed Assn., Conn., 1994—. Mem.: Conn. Sci. Tchrs. Assn., New Eng. Sci. Tchrs. Assn., Sacred Heart Alumni Assn. Roman Catholic. Avocations: reading, exploring nature, volleyball.

TOPPING, AUDREY RONNING, photojournalist; b. Camrose, Alta., Can., May 21, 1928; arrived in U.S., 1967; d. Chester Alvin and Inga Marie (Horte) Ronning; m. Seymour Topping, Nov. 10, 1949; children: Susan, Karen, Lesley, Robin, Joanna. Student, Augustana Univ., Camrose, 1943-46, Nanking (China) U., 1947-48, Berlin Art Sch., 1956-58, U. B.C., 1949-50; D of Arts (hon.), Rider Coll., N.J., 1983. Freelance journalist N.Y. Times Mag., N.Y.C., 1966—2001; writer, photographer Nat. Geographic, Washington, 1971-79; columnist Earth Times, N.Y.C., 1996—; spl. corr. Houston Chronicle, 1997—2001; photjournalist-at-large Earthuman Mag., 2002—. Advisor U.S.-China Arts Exch., 1997—; commentator, writer Great Wall Across The Yangtze (PBS), Homecoming (Chinese TV), 2002; TV scriptwriter China Mission, 1975. Author: Dawn Wakes In the East, 1972, The Splendors of Tibet, 1981, Charlie's World, 2000; A Day in the Life of Can., 1986, two children's books, photo essays, N.Y. Times, Nat. Geographic, Readers Digest, Time, Life, Geo, Sci. Digest, Earth Times, others, exhibitions include Royal Ont. Mus., Toronto, 1980, Hallmark Gallery, N.Y.C., 1973, Overseas Press Cub, 1975, Westchester C.C., 1989, 2004, Libby Gallery, Purchase, N.Y., 2004. Recipient Alumni award Augustana Univ. Coll., 1989, Medallion award Westchester C.C., 1989, Greenway Winship award Internat. Ctr. Journalists, 2000. Mem.: Coun. of Fgn. Relations, Soc. Woman Geographers, Asia Soc., Fgn. Policy Assn., Fox Meadow Tennis Club, Jr. Fortnightly. Avocations: sculpture, painting, tennis, skiing, exploring. Home and Office: 5 Heathcote Rd Scarsdale NY 10583-4413 E-mail: topaud@aol.com.

TORCHIN, MIMI, periodical editor; Founder, editor-in-chief Soap Opera Weekly, N.Y.C, 1989—. Office: Soap Opera Weekly 261 Madison Ave Fl 9 New York NY 10016-2303

TORDIFF, HAZEL MIDGLEY, education director; b. Columbia Station, Ohio, Sept. 24, 1920; d. Joseph and Mary Ceclia (Vitovec) Midgley; m. Joseph F. Tordiff, Nov. 13, 1946; children: Cathy, Joseph F. Tordiff Jr., John C. BS, Kent State U., 1942; student, U. Va., 1968, Catholic U., 1975. Instr. Warren (Ohio) Bus. Coll., 1942-44; exec. sec. to plant mgr. GE, Warren, 1943-44; adminstrv. asst. Fgn. Svc., Dept. State, and Am. Embassy, Stockholm and Lisbon, Portugal, 1947-52; dir. tng. Washington Bus. Sch., Vienna, Va., 1969—2000; ret., 2000. Leader Girls Scouts U.S., Bonn, Germany, 1960—64; den mother Cub Scouts Am., Bonn, 1962—66; scorekeeper Little League Baseball, Bonn, Vienna, 1960—70. Sgt. WAC U.S. Army, 1944—47. Named Outstanding Bus. Tchr. in U.S., Assn. Ind. Schs. and Colls., 1984. Mem.: Profl. Secs. Internat. (faculty sponsor 1981—84). Avocations: bowling, gardening, sports spectator. Home: 1302 Ross Dr SW Vienna VA 22180-6724

TORGERSON, KATHERINE P. diversified business media company executive; Now v.p. human resources and exec. adminstrn. Penton Media, Inc., Cleve., with. Office: Penton Media Inc Ste 316 1300 E 9th St Cleveland OH 44114-1503

TORIBARA, MASAKO ONO, voice educator; b. Fresno, Calif., Sept. 8, 1925; d. Mataichi Harry and Sawo Ono; m. Taft Y. Toribara, Aug. 28, 1948; children: Lynne Suzanne, Neil Willard. B Music Edn. magna cum laude, U. Mich., 1946, MusM in Voice, 1949. Instr Bowling Green (Ohio) State U., 1946-48, Hochstein Music Sch., Rochester, N.Y., 1965-66; instr. to lectr. Eastman Sch. Music, Rochester, 1965—, prof. emerita, 1999—. Mem. Opera Under the Star, Rochester, 1954-56; judging panel Rochester Philharmonic Young Artist Audition, 1986, 98, 99; adjudicators various competitions. Soprano soloist Dewey Ave. Presbyn. Ch., Rochester, 1953-59, 1st Bapt. Ch. Rochester, 1961-77, Ars Antigua, Rochester, 1961-65. Den mother Brownie Scouts, Rochester, 1959; co-pres. Jr. High Family Faculty Forum in Mid. Sch. in Gates Sch., Rochester, 1964-66. Mem. Music Tchrs. Nat. Assn. (state and nat. cert.), Nat. Assn. Tchrs. Singing, Pi Kappa Lambda, Phi Beta Kappa, Phi Kappa Phi, Mu Phi Epsilon. Avocations: reading, travel, attending musical events, cooking. Home: 54 Timpat Dr Rochester NY 14624-2928 Office: Eastman Sch Music 26 Gibbs St Rochester NY 14604-2599

TORKELSON, JODIE RAE, charitable organization executive; b. Cudahy, Wis., May 13, 1958; d. Wallace Keith and Delores Helen (Hagen) T. BA in Polit. Sci., Moorhead State U., 1980. Staff asst. Congressman Richard Nolan, Washington, 1980-81; office mgr. Congressman Leon E. Panetta, Washington, 1981-86, adminstrv. asst., 1988-89; acting exec. dir. Life Underwriters for Lutheran Charities, Mpls., 1986-88; dir. adminstrn. com. on budget U.S. Ho. of Reps., Washington, 1989-93, assoc. dir. for adminstrn. Office of Mgmt. and Budget, 1993-94; asst. to pres. for mgmt. and adminstrn. The White House, Washington, 1994-97; chief of staff, sr. advisor to dir. Voice of Am., Washington, 1997-99; v.p. ops. Children's Def. Fund, Washington, 2000. Lutheran. Office: Children's Def Fund 25 E St NW Washington DC 20001-1591

TORME, MARGARET ANNE, public relations executive, communications consultant; b. Indpls., Apr. 5, 1943; d. Ira G. and Margaret Joy (Wright) Barker; children: Karen Anne, Leah Vanessa. Student, Coll. San Mateo, 1961-65. Pub. rels. mgr. Hoefer, Dieterich & Brown (now Chiat-Day), San Francisco, 1964-73; v.p., co-founder, creative dir. Lowry & Ptnrs., San Francisco, 1975-83; pres., founder Torme and Lauricella Comms., San Francisco, 1983—. Cons. in communications. Mem. Coun. Pub. Rels. Firms, San Francisco C. of C. (Outstanding Achievement award for Women Entrepreneurs 1987), Jr. League (adv. bd.), Pub. Rels. Orgn. Internat. (v.p., dir.). Office: 847 Sansome St San Francisco CA 94111-2908 E-mail: margaret@torme.com.

TORNBLOM, CLAUDIA L. civilian military employee; BSc, Iowa State U.; MPA, U. Minn.; graduate, Nat. Defense U., 1992. From fiscal programs mgmt. officer to dep. asst. sec. U.S. Army Civil Works Program, Washington, dep. asst. sec. mgmt. & budget. Office: Office of Secretary of Army for Civil Works Army Pentagon Washington DC 20310-1500

TORNEDEN, CONNIE JEAN, bank officer; b. Tonganoxie, Kans., Sept. 14, 1955; d. Byron Calvin and Edna Jeannette (Keck) Swain; m. Lawrence Dale Torneden, Sept. 18, 1976; 1 child, James Milton. Bus. cert., Kansas City (Kans.) C.C., Kans., 1974, student, Nat. Compliance Sch., Norman, Okla., 1984; Mortgage Lending Diploma, ABA Am. Inst. Banking, 1997. Adminstrv. sec. to chmn. of bd., pres. First State Bank and Trust, Tonganoxie, 1974-80, asst. cashier, 1981-83, asst. v.p. and compliance officer, 1984-97, bank security officer, 1989-95, loan ops. officer, 1998, loan prodn. specialist, 1999—2002, loan asst., 2002—. Lobbyist, treas. 24 40 Hwy. Task Force, Leavenworth, Kans., 1989-91; bd. dirs. sec. Reno Cemetery Assn., Tonganoxie, 1986—; co-founder Tonganoxie Days, chmn., 1986, 88-93, 95-2004; grad. 30. Leavenworth County Leadership [illegible], 1991; sec.-treas. Maple Grove Cemetery Assn., 1995—, Reno Twp. Fire Dept., 1996—. Mem. Am. Bus. Women's Assn. (treas. 1986-87, sec. 1997-98, 2001-03, Woman of Yr. award Twilight chpt. 1994), Mid-Am. Dairymen Assn. (sec. 1978-80), Nat. Assn. Old West Gunfighter Teams (nat. champions 1989, 90), Linwood Grange (5th and 6th degrees 1978), Tonganoxie C. of C. (sec. 1983-86, 92-94, pres. 1986, 88, 89, 96, v.p. 1995, treas. 1997, Mem. of Yr. award 1990, 92, Citizen of Yr. award 2001), Tonganoxie Jaycees (sec. 1991). Democrat. Mem. Soc. Of Friends. Avocations: music, fossil collecting, stamp collecting, coin collecting, writing poetry and short stories. Office: First State Bank and Trust PO Box 219 Tonganoxie KS 66086-0219

TORNESE, JUDITH M. financial institution executive; b. Pitts., Aug. 26, 1942; d. Ilario and Rose Mary Tornese; m. Jerry E. Winters. Student, U. Pitts., Golden Gate U. CPCU. Various positions Transam Corp., San Francisco, 1971-81; dir. risk mgmt. TransAm. Corp., San Francisco, 1981-87; dir. X.L. Ins. Co., 1987-92; v.p. risk mgmt. TransAm. Corp., San Francisco, 1987—; dir., chair devel. com. St. Vincent de Paul Soc., 1994—. Dir. San Francisco Suicide Prevention, 1984-90; mem. Earthquake Ins. and Recovery Fin. Com. of Seismic Safety Commn., 1988-91. Named Risk Mgr. of Yr. Bus. Ins. Mag., 1992. Mem. Risk and Ins. Mgmt. Soc. (soc. dir. 1981—, chair nominating com. 1987-92, strategic planning com., 1996—), Mfr.'s Alliance Productivity and Innovation (risk mgmt. coun. 1981-85). Office: Transam Corp 600 Montgomery St San Francisco CA 94111-2702

TORNEY, ANNE, architectural firm executive; MA arch., Univ. of Calif., Berkeley, Calif.; BA arch., Princeton Univ. Lic. David Baker & Assoc., San Francisco, Calif. Ptnr. Solomon ETC, San Francisco, 1994—99, prin., 2000—02, project arch./mgr., 2002—. Achievements include design of projects included: Vermont Village Plaza, the mixed-use complex in So. Ctrl. LA, the 50-unit Alcantara Court in San Francisco, 101 San Fernando and 324 apt. currently under construction in San Jose. Office: Solomon ETC 1328 Mission St 4th Fl San Francisco CA 94103

TORNOW, BARBARA, academic administrator; b. Buffalo, Feb. 17, 1943; d. Elmer Henry and Elizabeth Jane S. Tornow; m. Charles Jack Sheehan, Sept. 1987 (dec. 1992); stepchildren: Charles, Jacquelyn. BA summa cum laude, William Smith Coll., 1965; MA in Polit. Sci., U. Pa., 1966, postgrad., 1966-70. Residence dir. Phila. Coll. Art, 1969-72, asst. dir. fin. aid./housing, 1972-77; dir. fin. aid Clark U., Worcester, Mass., 1977-79, Brandeis U., Waltham, Mass., 1979-86; dir. fin. assistance Boston U., 1986-96, exec. dir. fin. assistance, 1996—2002, sr. advisor, v.p. enrollment, 2002—. Trustee, admissions com. chair Hobart and William Smith Colls., Geneva, 1994—; mem., bd. dirs. TERI, Boston, 1985—, chmn., 1985—88. Chair Action Ctr. Ednl. Svcs. & Scholarships, Boston, 1998-99, mem., 1986-99; participant U.S. Dept. Edn. Negotiated Rulemaking, Washington, 1999, Project EASI, 1996-98. Mem.: Student Loan Mktg. Assn. (adv. com. 1995—), Mass. Assn. Student Fin. Aid Adminstrs. (pres. 1982—83, chair 1994—96, Svc. to Profession 1991), Nat. Assn. Student Fin. Aid Adminstrs. (bd. dirs. 1994—97), Phi Beta Kappa. Democrat. Avocations: horseback riding, travel. Office: Boston U 881 Commonwealth Ave Boston MA 02215-1300 Office Phone: 617-353-9258. E-mail: btornow@bu.edu.

TOROK, MARGARET LOUISE, insurance company executive; b. Detroit, June 22, 1922; d. Perl Edward Ensor and Mary (Seggie) Armstrong; m. Leslie A. Torok, Aug. 14, 1952; 1 child, Margaret Mary Ryan. Lic. Ins. Agy. From ins. agt. to corp. officer Grendel-Wittbold Ins., Southgate, Mich., 1961-72, pres. of corp., 1972—2001. Bd. dirs. Ind. Ins. Agts. of Mich., Lansing, 1984-92, Ind. Ins. Agts. of Wayne County, Dearborn, 1967—, pres. 1978. Bd. dirs. So. Wayne County C. of C., Taylor, 1975—, CEO, chmn. bd. dirs., 1997-98; bd. dirs. City of Southgate Tax. Increment Fin. Authority Dist. and Econ. Devel. Commn., 1987—, YMCA, mem. endowment coun., Wyandotte, 1978—, chmn. Leadership, 1980-88; bd. dirs. Downriver Cmty. Alliance, 1990-94; lay chmn. Cath. Svc. Appeal for Archdiocese of Detroit, 1989; co-chair fundraiser Sacred Heart Ch.; mem. bd. MESC Employers Com., 1991-95; com. mem., bd. dirs. New Workforce Devel. Com., gov. appt., charter mem.; hon. chmn. Art Ambience, 2002; chmn. bd. MESC com., 1991-95. Recipient Capital award Ind. Ins. Agts. of Mich., 1988, Lifetime Achievement award, Amb. award, 1994, Woman of Yr. AAUW, 1994, Salute to Excellence award Downriver Coun. of Arts, 1993-94, Chmn. of Yr. award MESC Job. Svc. Employers Com., 1991, Robert Stewart award Wyandotte Svc. Club Coun., 1994, Partnership award The Info. Ctr., 1996, 2001, W.O. Hildebrand award Mich. Assn. Ins. Agts., 1997; named to Ins. Hall of Fame, Olivet Coll., 1998. Mem.: Mich. Assn. Ins. Agts., Soroptimist Club of Wyandotte Southgate Taylor (pres. 1984—86, Advancing Status Women award 1988, Soroptimist of Yr. award 1993—94), Wyandotte Yacht Club. Roman Catholic. Office: Grendel Wittbold Agy Inc 12850 Eureka Rd Southgate MI 48195-1344 Office Phone: 734-284-4740.

TORONTO, ELLEN LESLIE KAYLOR, psychologist; b. Kenton, Ohio, Nov. 6, 1944; d. Harry Irvin and Gladys Lucille (Smith) Kaylor; m. Robert Sharp Toronto, Dec. 29, 1969; children: Aaron, Matthew, Daniel, David. BA summa cum laude, Miami U., Oxford, Ohio, 1967; PhD, U. Mich., 1973. Lic. psychologist. Tchr. Head Start, Kenton, 1965-67; rsch. asst. V.A. Hosp., Ann Arbor, Mich., 1968-73; clin. psychology intern Lafayette Clin., Detroit, 1973-74; chief psychologist/outpatient unit Ypsilanti (Mich.) Regional Psychiat. Hosp., 1974-80; clin. psychologist Adrian (Mich.) Psychotherapy Assocs., 1985-90; pvt. practice Ann Arbor, 1980—. Chmn. affirmative action Mich. Psychoanalytic Coun., East Lansing, 1990—, co-founder women's study group, Ann Arbor, 1982—. Contbr. articles to profl. jours. Den leader Cub Scouts/Boy Scouts Am., Ann Arbor, 1981, 83, 85, 89—; tchr. women's orgn. LDS Ch., Ann Arbor, 1969-80; mem. Ann Arbor Civic Theatre, 1988—. Recipient fellowship NSF, 1967-70. Mem. Am. Psychol. Assn., Mich. Psychol. Assn., Mich. Soc. for Psychoanalytic Psychology (chmn. affirmative action 1985-90), Phi Beta Kappa. Democrat. Avocations: dance, acting, doll collecting. Office: 2360 E Stadium Blvd Ann Arbor MI 48104-4887

TORPEY, TARA JANE, sales executive; d. William Thomas and Wendy Susan Torpey. BS, Towson U., 1995. Sales staff Am. Online, San Francisco, 1998—2001; nat. accounts mgr. Lawyers Weekly Publs., Boston, 2001—. Vol. Boston Cares, 2003. Office: Lawyers Weekly Publs 41 West St Boston MA 02111

TORRENCE, GWEN, Olympic athlete; b. Atlanta, June 12, 1965; m. Manley Waller Jr.; 1 child, Manley Waller III. BA, U. Ga., 1987. Runner Olympic Games, Atlanta, 1996. Named 2d pl., NCAA 100, 1985, 7th pl., USA/Mobil 100, 1985, 5th pl., USA/Mobil 200, 1985, champion, NCAA 100, 1987, NCAA 200, 1987, winner, Pan Am. Games 200, 1987, USA/Mobil 200, 1991, winner 100 meters, 200 meters, USA/Mobil Track & Field Championships, 1995, 5th pl., U.S. World Championships 200, winner, Sprints WOrld Univ. Games; recipient 3d pl. in both 100 and 200 trials, Olympic Games, 1988, 2d pl. USA/Mobil 100, 1991, Gold medal 200 Meter, Barcelona Spain, 1992, Gold medal 100 Meters, World Track & Field Championships, Gutenborg, Sweden, 1995, winner 100 Meters, World Athletic Championships, 1995, Gold medal 100 meters, 200 meters, Goodwill Games, 1995, Gold medal 4 X 400 meter relay, Atlanta Olympic Games, 1996, Bronze medal 100 meters, 1996. Achievements include ranked 5th in the world at 200 meters Track & Field News, 1987; ranked number 3 sprinter in the world, 1991; ranked 3d place in the workd in the 100, 1993; ranked 2d place in the work in the 200, 1993; ranked 4th place in the work in the 400, 1993. Address: US Track & Field 1 RCA Dome Ste 140 Indianapolis IN 46225-1023

TORRENCE, MARGARET ANN JOHNSON, company executive, consulting paralegal, therapist, human resources manager, training instructor; b. Memphis, Apr. 25, 1946; d. Simon Robert and Earline Juanita (Parker) Johnson; m. Tony Horace Robinson, Oct. 16, 1965 (div. 1968); 1 child, Veronica Antoinette; m. David Torrence, Feb. 16, 1968 (div. Jan. 1997); 1 child, Erika Joyce. BSBA, Pacific Western U., L.A., 1989; MS in Counseling and Human Svcs., Pacific Western U., 1991; PhD, Kensington U., Glendale, CA, 1993. Paralegal Torrence Lawn Care, Rialto, 1985—91, contract adminstr., 1985—91; pres. Torrence Scholarship Svc., 1986—89; CEO Torrence Group Home, Inc., San Bernardino, Calif., 1990—95; tng. specialist, data conversion operator, group leader U.S. Postal Svc., 1995—. Author: Abuses in Am. Soc., 1991, Children of Abuse-A Continuing Cycle-Past, Present, Future, 1993. With USAF, 1964-65. Mem. NAFE (Natl. Assn. of Female Execs.), Am. Acad. Profl. Coders, Women in Mil. Svc. Am. Meml. Found., Inc., Nat. Mgmt. Assn. Avocations: reading, tennis, swimming, travel.

TORRENCE-THOMPSON, JUANITA LEE, public relations executive; b. Brockton, Mass., Nov. 08; d. James Lee Torrence and Zylpha Odyselle Mapp-Robinson; m. Hugh Warren Thompson, Dec. 19, 1965; 1 child, Derek Rush. BS in Bus. & Comm., Empire State Coll., Old Westbury, N.Y., 1983; MA in Comm., Fordham U., 1989. Newsletter editor UN Internat. Sch., 1976-77; pub. rels., editl. asst. Nat. Assn. Theatre Owners, 1979-80; asst. acct. exec. Richard Weiner, Inc., 1984; newsletter editor SUNY Empire State Coll., 1985-87; editor Dorf & Stanton Comm., Inc., 1987-88; pub. rels. exec. pvt. practice, 1988—. Adj. prof. pub. rels. Coll. New Rochelle, N.Y., 1997. Author: Spanning The Years, Wings Span to Eternity, Celebrating a Tapestry of Life, Spanning the Years Wing Span to Eternity; contbr. articles, poems, short stories, essays to mags., newspapers and newsletters. Bd. dirs. So. Queens Park Assn., Jamaica, N.Y., 1988-91; mem. parent faculty soc. UN Internat. Sch., N.Y.C., 1976-80; pub. rels. cons. UN Coll. Fund, N.Y.C., 1994. Recipient Feature Article award Writers Digest, 1985, Meritorious Svc. award United Negro Coll. Fund, 1994, Editors Choice award Nashville Newsletter, 1994, Robins Nest Mag., 1996, First prize N.Y. Pub. Libr. Contest, 1996, Outstanding Achievement award SUNY, Empire State Coll., Old Westbury, honoree SUNY, Margaret A. Walker Short Story Competition award 1999, 2000. Mem. AAUW, Nat. Assn. Black Journalists, Poetry Soc. Am., Acad. Am. Poets, Native Am. Journalists Assn., Black Ams. in Pub., Poets and Writers, Fresh Meadows Poets. Avocations: travel, theatre, films, opera, concerts. Office: PO Box 751205 Forest Hills NY 11375-8805 E-mail: poetrytown@earthlink.net.

TORRES, BARBARA WOOD, technical services professional; b. Coudersport, Pa., Sept. 18, 1945; d. Ken and Myrna Wood; m. James Torres, July 3, 1965; children: James C, William D. BS in Physics, U. N.Mex., 1969, MS in Physics, 1972. Mem. staff Quantum Systems, Inc., Albuquerque, 1967-72, EG&G, Albuquerque, 1972-76, Mission Rsch. Corp., Albuquerque, 1977-78; from staff mem. to v.p. test engrng. BDM, Albuquerque, 1978-97; dir. test engrng. Northrop Grumman Mission Sys. (formerly TRW), Albuquerque, 1998—2000, divsn. dir. ethics and bus. conduct, 2001—. Mem. N.Mex. State Sci. and Tech. Commn., 1983—86; mem. com. NEWTEC Joint Venture, N.Mex., 1998—2004. Mem. adv. bd. N.Mex. Comprehensive Regional Ctr. Minorities, 1993—96; judge N.Mex. Regional and State Sci. Fair, 1986—; bd. dirs. N.Mex. Network for Women in Sci., 1988—92, 2003—. Named Outstanding Grad., Rio Grande H.S., 1995; recipient Gov. Award for Outstanding N.Mex. Women, 1988. Mem.: IEEE, Soc. for Internat. Affairs, Ethics Officers Assn., Inst. Test and Evaluation Assn., Am. Bus. Women's Assn. (dist vpres 1995—96, nat secy 1996—97, One of Top 10 Bus Women 1982), Am. Phys. Soc. Avocations: travel, mystery and spy novels, walking. Home: PO Box 478 Tijeras NM 87059-0478 Office: Northrop Grumman Mission Sys 100 Sun Pl NE Ste 300 Albuquerque NM 87109

TORRES, CYNTHIA ANN, banker; b. Glendale, Calif., Sept. 24, 1958; d. Adolph and Ruth Ann (Smith) T.; m. Michael Victor Gisser, Mar. 11, 1989; children: Spencer Williams Gisser, David Westfall Torres Gisser. AB, Harvard U., 1980, MBA, 1984. Research assoc. Bain & Co., Boston, 1980-82; assoc. Goldman, Sachs & Co., N.Y.C., 1984-88, v.p., 1988, First Interstate Bancorp, L.A., 1989-92; dir. Fidelity Investments Mgmt. (H.K.) Ltd., Hong Kong, 1993-96; pres. Integrity Investments Consultants, Ltd., 1996—99; dir. mktg. Diamond Portfolio Advisors LLC, Santa Monica, Calif., 1999—. Mem. judiciary rev. bd. Bus. Sch. Harvard U., Boston,

1983-84. Rockefeller Found. scholar, 1976; Harvard U. Ctr. for Internat. Affairs fellow, 1979-80; recipient Leadership award Johnson and Johnson, 1980; by Council for Opportunity in Grad. Mgmt. Edn. fellow, 1982-84. Mem.: Fin. Women's Assn. Hong Kong (past pres.), Asia Soc., Acad. Polit. Sci., Harvard-Radcliffe Club So. Calif. (exec. v.p.). Office: Diamond Portfolio Advisors LLC 10940 Wilshire Blvd Ste 600 Los Angeles CA 90024 Personal E-mail: cynthiatorres@earthlink.net.

TORRES, DARA, Olympic athlete; b. Beverly Hills, Calif., Apr. 15, 1967; Degree in broadcasting, U. Fla. Intern CNN and NBC Sports; commentator TV sports NBC, ESPN, TNT, Fox News, Fox Sports; ret. swimmer TV reporter: Good Morning America, Inside Edition; host Oxygen Sports. Spokesperson Tae Bo workout tapes. Host sci. and tech. show Discovery Channel. Recipient Gold medal (2) 4 x 100-meter freestyle, 4 x 100-meter medley (team), Bronze medal (3) 50 and 100-meter freestyle, 100-meter fly Sydney Olympics, 2000, Gold medal 100-meter freestyle, 4 x 100-meter freestyle, 4 x 100-meter relay (team) Pan Pacific Championships, 1987, Gold medal 4 x 100-meter freestyle relay (team) L.A. Games, 1984, Bronze medal 4 x 100-meter freestyle relay (team), Silver medal 4 x 100-meter medley (team), 1988, Gold medal 4 x 100-meter free relay (team) Barcelona Olympics, 1992; 12-time nat. champion; former world-record holder 50-meter freestyle, Am.-record holder 50-meter freestyle and 100-meter fly, 1991 Summer Nationals Kiphuth award, 1991, Summer Nationals Comeback award Achievements include first american to swim in four Olympics, five time US Open champion, seven time National A team member, two time All Star team. Office: USA Swimming 1 Olympic Plz Colorado Springs CO 80909-5746

TORRES-MABASA, VIRGINIA MARIA, physician assistant; b. Red Bluff, Calif., Sept. 16, 1969; d. Ben Alvarado Torres, Maria Beatriz Velez-Topete; m. Rodrigo Icawalo Mabasa, July 29, 1991; 1 child, Kiara Marie Mabasa. AA in Biology cum laude, Miracosta Coll., 1998; BS in Physician Asst. Practice with honors, U. So. Calif., L.A., 2001. Cert. surg. technologist Liaison Coun. for Certification for Surg. Tech., 1994, physician asst. Med. Bd. Calif., 2002, Nat. Commn. Certification for Physician Assts., 2002. Surg. technologist Scripps Meml. Hosp. Surgery Ctr., La Jolla, Calif., 1995—98, Virginia Beach (Va.) Ambulatory Surgery Ctr., Va., 1998—99; physician asst. primary care program Keck Sch. Medicine U. So. Calif., 1999—2001; physician asst. Pasadena Rehab. Inst., Pasadena, Calif., 2002—. Asst. instr. Spanish Primary Care Physician Asst. Program U. So. Calif. Keck Sch. Medicine, L.A., 2000—00. V.p. Future Physician Assts. Am., Miracosta Coll., Oceanside, 1997—98. E-4 USN, 1989—94. Decorated Navy Achievement medal USN. Mem.: Assn. Surg. Technologists, Calif. Acad. Physician Assts., Am. Acad. Physician Assts., Phi Theta Kappa (life), Gamma Beta Phi (life; sec. 2000—01). Avocations: travel, reading, skating.

TORRESYAP, PEARL MARIE, surgical nurse; b. Cleve., Oct. 1, 1930; d. Clyde E. and Pearl C. (Flanagan) Callender; m. Fortunato Torresyap, Oct. 30, 1953; children: Joy, Gay, Fay. Diploma, Luth. Hosp. Sch. Nursing, 1951. Cert. nurse in oper. rm. Staff nurse Lakewood (Ohio) Hosp., 1951-54, Choate Hosp., Woburn, Mass., 1976-78; thoracic charge nurse Boston VA Med. Ctr., 1979-94, orthopedic charge nurse in oper. rm., 1994-96, ret., 1996. Contbr. articles to jours. in field. Vol. Mus. Sci. Human Body Connection, 1996—; bd. dirs. Vol. Svc. League, 2002--, Mus. of Sci., 2002—. Mem. ANA, Assn. Oper. Rm. Nurses (pres. Mass. chpt. I 1988-89, book reviewer for jour.), Mass. Coun. Nursing Orgns. (rep. 1989-93), Mass. Nurses Assn., Internat. Toastmasters (treas. 1989-90). E-mail: beanblossom@aol.com.

TORREY, BARBARA BOYLE, research council administrator; b. Pensacola, Fla., Nov. 27, 1941; d. Peter F. and Elsie (Hansen) Boyle; m. E. Fuller Torrey, Mar. 23, 1968; children: Michael, Martha. BA, Stanford U., 1963, MS, 1970. Vol. Peace Corps, Tanzania, 1963-65; fiscal economist Office Mgmt. and Budget, Washington, 1970-80; dept. asst. sec. HHS, Washington, 1980-81; dir. Ctr. for Internat. Rsch. Census Bur., Washington, 1984-92; pres. Population Reference Bur., Washington, 1992-93; exec. dir. Commn. on Behavioral and Social Scis. and Edn. NRC, NAS, Washington, 1993—. Bd. dirs. Luxembourg Income Study. Co-editor: The Vulnerable, 1987, Population and Land Use, 1992; contbr. articles to profl. jours. Fellow AAAS; mem. Population Assn. Am. (bd. dirs. 1993—). Office: Population Ref Bur 1875 Connecticut Ave NW Ste 520 Washington DC 20009-5728

TORREY, CLAUDIA OLIVIA, lawyer; b. Nashville, June 10, 1958; d. Claude Adolphus and Rubye Mayette (Prigmore) T. BA in Econ., Syracuse U., 1980; JD, N.Y. Law Sch., 1985. Bar: NY 1988. Legal intern Costello, Cooney & Fearon, Syracuse, NY, 1979; legal clk. First Am. Corp., Nashville, 1981; legal asst. James I. Meyerson, N.Y.C., 1982-85; jud. law clk. N.Y. State Supreme Ct., N.Y.C., 1985; interim project supr., legal asst. CUNY Ctrl. Office, 1985-86; legal analyst Rosenman & Colin Law Firm, N.Y.C., 1986-87; asst. counsel N.Y. State Legis., Albany, 1988-90; atty., cons. pvt. practice, Nashville, Cookeville, Tenn., 1991—. Bd. dirs. Children's Corner Day Care Ctr., Albany, 1989-90. Author column Health Law Jour. of N.Y. State Bar Assn., 1996—; co-author Legal Manual for New York Physicians, 2003. Ch. rep. FOCUS exec. coun. Westminster Presbyn. Ch., Albany, 1990; mem. PDS/USN Alumni Bd., Nashville, 2001—; interim chair Synod of Living Waters COR Com., Presbyn. Ch. (U.S.A.), 2002. Mem. ABA (young lawyers divsn. liaison to ABA forum on health law 1994-96), Internat. Platform Assn., N.Y. State Bar Assn. (chmn., mem. sub-com. on non-resident mems. 2004-, chmn. health law sect. study group on health info., privacy and confidentiality 1998-99), Alpha Kappa Alpha (treas., pres., corr. sec. Iota Upsilon Chpt. Syracuse U.) Avocations: singing, reading, harp, travel, art. Home and Office: PO Box 150234 Nashville TN 37215-0234 Office Phone: 931-528-4280. E-mail: jewel3@prodigy.net.

TORREZ, CAROLINE HERMINIA, recreation director; d. Philip Hernandez and Lucy Mercedes Rivera; m. Robert Pierre Torrez, June 10, 1995. BA, Calif. State U., Fullerton, 1975. Export parts specialist C.B.S. Musical Inst., Fullerton, 1976—77; bilingual interviewer Orange County Housing Authority, Santa Ana, Calif., 1977—79, field rep., 1979—83, mktg. rep., 1983—87; recreation dir. City of Anaheim (Calif.) Parks and Recreation, 1985—87; Home Investment Partnership Act coord./county rep. Housing and Cmty. Devel. Orange County, Santa Ana, 1987—99; v.p. internal ops. CHAMP, Inc., Santa Ana, 2000—. Charter mem. Brea (Calif.) Jaycee Women, 1980; dist. dir. Region 8 Orange County Jaycees, 1987; pres. Fountain Valley (Calif.) Jaycees, 1989; with Men-On-Missions-Eastside Christ Ch.; bd. dirs. Alliance/Mentally Ill. Orange County, Tustin, Calif., 1988—89; coord. Hands Across Am., 1986. Mem.: SAG, Nat. Assn. Exec. Women. Avocations: acting, viola, dance, singing, opera. Office: CHAMP Inc 633 Young St Santa Ana CA 92706

TORRIANI-GORINI, ANNAMARIA, microbiologist, educator; b. Milan, Dec. 19, 1918; came to U.S., 1955, naturalized, 1962; d. Carlo and Ada (Forti) Torriani; m. Luigi Gorini (dec. Aug. 1976); 1 child, Daniel. PhD, U. Milan, Italy, 1942. Research assoc. Istituto Ronzoni Chimica-Biochimica, Milan, 1942-48; charge de recherche Institut Pasteur, Paris, 1948-56; research assoc. NYU, 1956-58, Harvard U., Cambridge, Mass., 1958-60, MIT, Cambridge, 1960-71, assoc. prof. microbiology, 1971-76, prof., 1976—; prof. emerita, 1989. Recipient NIH Career award, 1962-72; Fulbright fellow, 1956-58. Mem. Am. Soc. Microbiology, Soc. Française de Microbiologie (hon.). Home: 115 Longwood Ave Brookline MA 02446-6625 Office: MIT Dept of Biology 68-371 Cambridge MA 02139 E-mail: Pho@mit.edu.

TORSON, DIANNA MAY, small business owner; b. San Diego, Dec. 29, 1940; d. Eugene Henry Torson and Dolores Elaine Seaton; life ptnr. John Alexander Barney; children: Patricia Ann, Kim Elaine Zilverberg, Scott Ruel Randall. BA, S.D. State U., 1988, MA, 1990. Instr. Sinte Gleska U., Mission, SD, 1990—99, chair arts and scis., 1992—94, dean arts and scis., 1994—96; dir. student devel., Native Am. advisor Dakota State U., Madison, SD, 1996—2000; co-owner, v.p. LeadingEducation.com, Brookings, SD, 2000—. With Humanities Spkrs. Bur., S.D. Humanities Coun., Brookings, 1990—96; coord., instr. summer teacher's inst. Sinte Gleska U. and S.D. State U., Brookings and Mission, 1992—95; advisor Sinte Gleska Lit. Coun., Mission; coord. Sinte Gleska U. Bush Faculty Devel. Com., Mission, 1993—94. Recorder and transcriber (narrative non-fiction) Salt Camp: HerStory Lakota Living Treasure Ollie Napesni, 2003; contbr. poetry to Leaning Into the Wind, Woven on the Wind, poetry and photography to mags. Mem.: Phi Kappa Phi (life). Democrat. Avocations: horseback riding, walking, bicycling, reading, environmental affairs. Office: LeadingEducation.com 46850 221st St Brookings SD 57006 E-mail: torsond@itctel.com.

TORSTRICK, REBECCA LEE, anthropologist, educator; b. Louisville, Ky., Dec. 17, 1954; d. Donald Lee Torstrick and Dolores King; m. Jeffrey David Sutter; 1 child, Maia Sutter. AB, U. Ill., 1972—76; MEd, Wash. U., 1979—81, PhD, 1984—93. From asst. prof. to assoc. prof. Ind. U., South Bend, Ind., 1996—2002, assoc. prof. anthropology, 2002—. Vis. asst. prof. Wash. U., St. Louis, 1994—96. Author: (book) The Limits of Coexistence: Identity Politics in Israel, 2000. Mem.: Assn. Rsch. Motherhood, Am. Ethnol. Soc., Assn. Polit. and Legal Anthropology, Am. Anthrop. Assn., Mid. E. Sec.- AAA. Office: Ind U South Bend 1700 Mishawaka Ave South Bend IN 46634-7111

TORTORA, LESLIE C. finance company executive; With Goldman Sachs & Co., N.Y.C., 1984—, ptnr., 1992—, mng. dir., 1996—, mem. mgmt. com., 1999—. Office: Goldman Sachs & Co 85 Broad St New York NY 10004-2456

TORUÑO, RHINA M. Literature educator, researcher, writer; b. San Salvador, El Salvador; came to U.S., 1981; d. Juan Felipe and Juana (Contreras) Toruño; m. Henriquez Trujillo, Nov. 4, 1967 (div.); children: Mario Felipe, José Rodrigo; m. Hector-Neri Castañeda (dec.). Grad., Santa Ines Coll., Nueva San Salvador, El Salvador, 1961; BA in Philosophy, Nat. U .El Salvador, 1971; MA in Philosophy, Cath. U. Louvain, Belgium, 1973, PhD in French Contemporary Philosophy, 1978; MA in Hispanic and Latin Am. Lit., Nat. U. Paris/Sorbonne, 1976; PhD in Latin Am. Lit., Ind. U., Bloomington, 1994. Tchr. asst. Nat. U. El Salvador, San Salvador, 1968-71, prof. philosophy, 1976-81; vis. scholar Sch. Edn. Stanford U., Palo Alto, Calif., 1981-82; vis. asst. prof. Fla. State U., 94-95; asst. prof. U. Tex. of the Permian Basin, Odessa, 1995-97, assoc. prof., 1997-00, prof., 01—, Kathlyn Cosper Dunagan prof. humanities, Spanish area coord., 1997—. Cons. for edn. com. Mexican-Am. Network of Odessa, 1997—. Author: Time, Destiny and Oppression on the Work of Elena Garro, 1996, 2d edit., 1998; assoc. editor Chiricu, Ind. U., Bloomington, 1985-90, Third Woman, Berkeley U., 1986-87; author more than 50 articles on literary criticism in English, French, Spanish. Recipient Ednl. Rshc. award, Pan Am. Round Table, Odessa, Tex., 1996, Internat. Prize Emmanuel Mounier, French Assn. of Friends of Emmanuel Mounier, Paris, 1974, Damas de Oro, Odessa, Tex., 2000; grantee U Tex., Odessa, 2000, 02, 03; fellow Internat. Fedn. Univ. Women, Geneva, 1981-82. Mem. Soc. des Amis d'Emmanuel Mounier, Fedn. Internat. des Femmes Deplomees de Univs. Internat., Salvadoran Acad. Scis. (1st female mem.), Salvadoran Acad. Lang. (Royal Acad. of Spain br.), Pan Am. Round Table, Spanish Book Club (pres. 1996—), Hispanic C. of C. Democrat. Roman Catholic. Avocations: reading short stories for children, aerobics, gardening, travel. Home: 4305 Buck Pl Odessa TX 79762-4650 Office: U Tex Permian Basin 4901 E University Blvd Odessa TX 79762-0001 E-mail: toruno_r@utpb.ed.

TOSHACH, CLARICE OVERSBY, real estate developer, former computer executive; b. Firbank, Westmoreland, Eng., Nov. 21, 1928; came to U.S., 1955; d. Oliver and Nora (Brown) Oversby; m. Daniel Wilkie Toshach, July 30, 1965 (dec. Aug. 1992); 1 child, Duncan Oversby Toshach; 1 child from previous marriage, Paul Anthony Beard. Textile designer Storeys of Lancaster, Eng., 1949-55; owner, operator Broadway Lane, Saginaw, Mich., 1956-70; pres., owner Clarissa Jane Inc., Saginaw, 1962-70, Over-Tosh Computers, Inc. dba Computerland, Saginaw and Flint, Mich., 1983-95; mgr., ptnr. Mich. Comml. Devel. L.L.C., Saginaw, 1995—. Trustee Saginaw Gen. Hosp., 1977-83, Home for the Aged, 1978-80; bd. dirs. Vis. Nurse Assn., pres., 1981-83; bd. dirs. Hospice of Saginaw, Inc., v.p., 1981-83; mem. long range planning com. United Way of Saginaw, 1982-83; cmty. advisor Jr. League of Saginaw, 1982-83; pres. Saginaw Gen. Hosp. Aux., 1972-82, pres., 1976-77.

TOSI, LAURA LOWE, orthopaedic surgeon; b. N.Y.C., Mar. 25, 1949; d. Jerome Richard T. and Deborah Thornton (Prouty) Rogers; m. David S.C. Chu, Apr. 1, 1978. BA, Boston U., 1971; MD, Harvard U., 1977. Orthop. surgeon Children's Nat. Med. Ctr., Washington, 1984—, chief pediat. orthop. surgery, 2000—03; assoc. prof. orthop. surgery George Washington U., Washington, 1984—. Trustee Orthopaedic Rsch. and Edn. Found., 1995-2002, sec. bd. trustees, 2000-2002. Fellow: Am. Acad. Orthop. Surgeons (bd. dirs. 1994—95, 2003—), Am. Acad. Cerebral Palsy and Devel. Medicine; mem.: Ruth Jackson Orthop. Soc. (treas. 1987—90, v.p. 1990—91, pres. 1991—92), Pediat. Orthop. Soc. N.Am. (bd. dirs. 1990—91, sec. elect 2000, sec. 2001—), Acad. Orthop. Soc. (bd. dirs. 1998—2002), Am. Orthop. Assn. Office: Children's Nat Med Ctr 111 Michigan Ave NW Washington DC 20010-2916

TOSSI, ALICE LOUISE, special education educator; b. St. Augustine, Fla., Feb. 25, 1941; d. Hubert Parker and Marie Francis (Mecca) Hahn; m. Donald Joseph Tossi, Feb. 19, 1966; children: Kevin, Craig, Raymond. BA, Rollins Coll., 1978. Cert. elem. tchr., Fla. Sec. Diocese of St. Augustine, Fla., 1958-59, Fla. East Coast Ry., St. Augustine, 1959-60; legal sec. Mahon & Stratford, Jacksonville, Fla., 1960-61; sec. comptroller's dept. Esso Standard Oil S. A., Ltd., Coral Gables, Fla., 1962-63; sec. Kelly Temporary, Maitland, Fla., 1976-78; tchr. All Souls Elem., Sanford, Fla., 1979-81, Harbor Elem., Maitland, 1981-82; sec., tech. asst. physically impaired Seminole County Sch. Bd., Sanford, 1983—; chorus pars profl. Sweet Adelines show Lakeview Mid. Sch., 1957—2003; asst. Highlands Elem. Sch., Winter Springs, Fla. Bd. dirs. Seminole County Dem. Assn., 1983. Mem. Coun. of Exceptional Edn. (sec. 1986-90, Placque 1987), Seminole County Sch. Bd. Assn. (sec. polit. action com.). Roman Catholic. Home: 114 W Woodland Dr Sanford FL 32773-5706

TOTENBERG, NINA, journalist; b. N.Y.C., Jan. 14, 1944; d. Roman and Melanie (Shroder) T.; m. Floyd Haskell, Feb. 3, 1979 (dec.); m. H. David Reines, 2000. Student, Boston U.; LLD (hon.), Haverford Coll., Chatham Coll., Gonzaga U., Northeastern U., St. Mary's, SUNY; LHD, Lebanon Valley Coll., Westfield State Coll., Pa. State U., Pine Manor Coll., De Paul U., Simmons Coll. Reporter Boston Record Am., 1965, Peabody Times, 1967, Nat. Observer, 1968-71, Newtimes, 1973, Nat. Pub. Radio, Washington, 1974—, Inside Washington, 1992—; reporter Nightline ABC, 1993-98. Contbr. articles to N.Y. Times Mag., Harvard Law Rev., Christian Sci. Monitor, N.Y. Mag., Parade. Recipient Sidney Hillman award, 1983, Alfred I. Dupont award Columbia U., 1988, 91, George Foster Peabody award, 1991, George Polk award, 1991, Joan Barone award, 1991, Silver Gavel award ABA, 1968-98, Woman of Courage award Women in Film, 1991, Athena award, 1994, Presdl. Commendation, Radcliffe Coll., 1998; named outstanding broadcast journalist of yr. Nat. Press Found., 1999. Mem. Sigma Delta Chi (award 1991). Office: NPR 635 Massachusetts Ave NW Washington DC 20001-3740

TOTER, KIMBERLY MROWIEC, nurse; b. Chgo., Apr. 22, 1956; d. A. Kenneth and Megan Dawson (Schiefer) Mrowiec; m. William Frank Toter, Dec. 16, 1978; children: William Kenneth, Kimberly Helen, Tod Frank, Matthew Jonathan, Haley Victoria, Tonia Megan. BS in Biology, Millikin U., 1978; cert. sch. nursing, Decatur (Ill.) Meml. Hosp., 1978. RN operating room nurse., Ill. Oper. room nurse Riddle Meml. Hosp., Media, Pa., 1979-89; pres., chief exec. officer Towic Med., Inc., Park Ridge, Ill., 1986—; staff nurse oper. room Luth. Gen. Hosp., Park Ridge, 1991; perioperative nurse, 1991—. Instr. Delaware Community Coll., Media, 1986; reviewer, cons. Perioperative Nursing Care Planning; speaker laparoscopy seminar Luth. Gen. Hosp., 1992, 93; cheerleading coach St. Paul of the Cross, 1993-96, volleyball coach, 1997—. Contbg. author: Decision Making in Perioperative Nursing, 1987; also articles; patentee gastric drainage system. Cheerleading coach St. Paul of the Cross, 1993-96, volleyball coach, 2000—. Recipient Young Alumnus of Yr. award Millikin U., 1991. Mem. Assn. Operat. Rm. Nurses (v.p. Southeast Pa. chpt. 1983-85, pres.-elect 1985-86, pres. 1986-87, ednl. chmn. 1983-85, chmn. bylaw and policy com. 1987—89, bd. dirs. 1983-89, chmn. 1987-88, bd. dirs. NW suburban chpt. 1995—), Pa. Coun. Oper. Rm. Nurses, Am. Tech Mgmt. (bd. dirs. 1989), Pi Beta Phi. Roman Catholic. Avocations: jogging, swimming, aerobic dance, photography, volleyball.

TOTH, SUSAN IRENE, surgeon, educator; b. Rome, N.Y., May 27, 1963; d. John Edward and Patricia Ann Toth; life ptnr. Nancy Jane Peirce. BA, Rollins Coll., 1985; MD, U. Miami Sch. Medicine, 1989. Resident in surgery U. Wis., 1989—94; surgeon Physicians Plus Med. Group, 1994—98; clin. asst. prof. U. Wis. Med. Sch., Madison, 1998—, gen./laparoscopic surgeon, 1994—. Mem. Physicians Plus Med. Group, Madison, 1994—98. Fellow: ACS; mem.: Wis. Surg. Soc., Soc. Laparoendoscopic Surgeons, Assn. Women Surgeons, Soc. Am. Gastrointestinal Endoscopic Surgeons. D-Liberal. Avocations: motorcycling, bass guitar. Office: U Wis Health 1 S Park St Madison WI 53715 Personal E-mail: sitoth@wisc.edu. E-mail: sitoth@wisc.edu.

TOTTEN, MARY ANNE, internist; b. Topeka, May 22, 1946; d. Frederick Eugene Totten and Mildred Roberta (Johnson) Black. BA in Microbiology, U. Kans., 1968, MD, 1972; MPH, Boston U., 1984. Diplomate Am. Bd. Internal Medicine with added qualifications in geriatrics, Nat. Bd. Med. Examiners, cert. med. dir. in long term care. Intern in internal medicine Hosp. of St. Raphael, New Haven, 1972-73; resident New Eng. Deaconess Hosp., Boston, 1973-75; fellow in endocrinology and metabolism Lahey Clinic Found., Burlington, Mass., 1975-76; fellow in diabetes Joslin Clinic, Boston, 1976-77; instr. medicine Boston U. Med. Ctr., 1977-83, asst. clin. prof., 1983-84; staff physician in gen. internal medicine Boston City Hosp., 1977-80; staff physician endocrinology Boston Hosp., 1977-84; dir. diabetes treatment and rehab. unit Mattapan (Mass.) Hosp., 1982-84; staff physician St. Joseph's Hosp., Parkersburg, W.Va., 1984—2002, chmn. dept. internal medicine, 1989-91, med. dir. skilled nursing unit, 1992—97, 2000—02, advisor to diabetes care task force, 1994-97, pres. med. staff, 1995-97; fellow in geriatrics UMPC Shadyside Hosp., Pitts., 1998-2000; specialist in geriatrics rehabilitation Health South Rehab Hosp., Parkersburg, W.Va., 2000—02. Med. dir., Elliot Hosp. Sr. Health Ctr, Manchester, NH, 2002—; mem. del. diabetes educators People to People Tour, USSR and China, 1987. Author, editor: Case Studies for Nurses and Nurse Practitioners, 1990; contbr. articles to med. jours. Recipient Physician Recognition award, AMA, 1987, 1990, 1997, 2001, Trailblazing Women of the Yr. award, YWCA and Altrusa, 1988, Leadership Devel. award, Parkersburg C. of C., 1990. Fellow ACP (mem. Gov.'s Coun. W.Va. 1990-91); mem. Am. Med. Dirs. Assn. Methodist. Avocations: swimming, bicycling, photography, music. Office: Senior Health Primary Care 138 Webster St Manchester NH 03104-4027 E-mail: mtotten@elliot-hs.org.

TOTTON, GAYLE, professional sports team executive; CEO Sacramento (Calif.) Sirens. Office: Sacramento Sirens PO Box 15920 Sacramento CA 95813-9998*

TOUBY, KATHLEEN ANITA, lawyer; b. Miami Beach, Feb. 20, 1943; d. Harry and Kathleen Rebecca (Hamper) T.; m. Joseph Thomas Woodward; children: Mark Andrew, Judson David Touby. BS in Nursing, U. Fla., 1965, MRC in Rehab. Counseling, 1967; JD with honors, Nova U., 1977. Bar: Fla. 1978, D.C. 1978. Counselor Jewish Vocat. Svc., Chgo., 1967-68; rehab. counselor Fla. Dept. Vocat. Rehab., Miami, 1968-70; spl. asst., asst. U.S. atty. U.S. Dept. Justice, Miami, 1978-80; assoc. Pyszka & Kessler, P.A., Miami, 1980-83; ptnr. Touby & Smith, P.A., Miami, 1983-89, Touby, Smith, DeMahy & Drake, P.A., Miami, 1989-94, Touby & Woodward, P.A., Miami, 1994—. Chmn. adv. exec. bd. Paralegal Edn. program Barry U., 1986-87; lectr. Food and Drug Law Inst., 1987-89, 91; lectr. environ. law Exec. Enterprises, 1987-88; lectr. trial techniques, Hispanic Nat. Bar Assn., St. Thomas Law Sch.; adj. prof. product liability Can. Govt., U.S. Trade and Mktg. Dept., 1989-95. Co-author: The Environmental Litigation Deskbook, 1989; contbr. chpts. to books, articles to profl. jours. Mem. ABA, Am. Inns of Ct. (pres. 1998-99, pres.-elect St. Thomas Law Sch. chpt. 1997-98, pres. 1998-99), Dade County Bar Assn. (legal aid, pub. svcs. com. 1988), Fed. Bar Assn. (bd. dirs. 1989—, v.p. 1991-92, pres.-elect So. Fla. chpt. 1992-93, pres. 1993-94), Cuban-Am. Bar Assn., Phi Delta Phi (province pres. 1982-85, bd. dirs. 1985-87). Roman Catholic. Home: 4150 Bay Point Rd Miami FL 33137-3352 Office: Touby & Woodward PA 250 Bird Rd Ste 308 Miami FL 33146-1424

TOUBY, LINDA, artist; b. Bklyn. d. Nat and Cele Touby; m. Barry Michael Schwartz, Dec. 24, 1964 (div. 1981); 1 child, Jaqueline. BFA, Pratt Inst., 1964; postgrad., Nat. Acad., N.Y.C., 1976, Art Students League, 1990. Pvt. tchr. Art, N.Y.C., 1990—. Author, illustrator (children's books): Sasaphras, 1974, Up, Up and Away, 1980; illustrator: Glimmerings (Zack Ragow), 1978; one-woman shows: Tribeca Gallery, N.Y.C., 1992, 93, La Mama La Galleria, N.Y.C., 1993, 95, Novart Gallery, Madrid, 1996; exhibited in numerous group shows, including Mus. Realism and Atheism, Lvov, Ukraine, 1990, La Mama Gallery, N.Y.C., 1991, Alex Gallery, 1991-2003, Provincetown (Mass.) Art Assn. and Mus., 1992-2004, Albert-Knox Art Gallery, Buffalo, 1995, Tribeca Gallery, 1992, 93, Rice/Polak Gallery, Provincetown, 1992-2004, Gallerie Roseg, St. Moritz, Switzerland, 1993, Eva Cohon Gallery LTD., Chgo., 1993, 94, Mus. Gallery, Boca Raton, Fla., 1993, Madelyn Jordon Gallery, Scarsdale, N.Y.C., 2003, 2004, Artspace/Virginia Miller Galleries, Coral Gables, Fla., 2000, 2002, 2004, Goya Art Gallery, N.Y.C., 1995, Kouros Gallery, N.Y.C., 1995, 98, Bill Hodges Gallery, N.Y.C., 1998, 99, 2000, 2004, Gallery de Arte Novart, Madrid, 1996, Blanvar Gallery de Arte, Majorca, Spain, 1996, Casa de Agua, Polencia, Spain, 1997, Timothy Yarger Fine Art, Bangkok, Thailand, 2003, 2004, Timothy Yarger Fine Art, Beverly Hills, Calif., 2004, Iandor Fine Art, Newark, 2002, 2003, 2004, Gallerie Rieder, Munich, Germany, 2000, 2001, Gen. Motors Corp., Phillips, Corp., Profl. Indemnity Agy., Inc., Bertholon-Rowland Corp., U.S. State Dept.; permanent collections: Antonio Morales, Correo del Arte Publisher, Spain, Danforth Mus. Fine Arts, Framingham, Mass., Richard Erdman, ALgiers, John Danlovich, San Jose, Calif., Rust Deming, Tunis, Tunisia, William Melam, Islamabad, Pakistan. Grantee Change, Inc., 1995. Avocations: photography, writing. Studio: 500 W 52nd St New York NY 10019-5060 Office Phone: 212-245-6521.

TOUHILL, BLANCHE MARIE, retired university chancellor, history-education educator; b. St. Louis, Mo., July 1, 1931; d. Robert and Margaret (Walsh) Van Dillen; m. Joseph M. Touhill, Aug. 29, 1959. BA in History, St. Louis U., 1953, MA in Geography, 1954, PhD in History, 1962. Prof. history and edn. U. Mo., St. Louis, 1965-73, assoc. dean faculties, 1974-76, assoc. vice chancellor for acad. affairs, 1976-87, vice chancellor, 1987-90, chancellor, 1991—2002, chancellor emeritus, 2002—. Bd. dirs. Peabody Energy, Inc. Author: William Smith O'Brien and His Irish Revolutionary Companions in Penal Exile, 1981, The Emerging University UM-St. Louis,

1963-83, 1985; editor: Readings in American History, 1970, Varieties of Ireland, 1976. Named Outstanding Educator St. Louis chpt. Urban League, 1976; recipient Leadership award St. Louis YWCA, 1986. Mem. Nat. Assn. State Univs. and Land Grant Colls. (exec. com. 1988—), Am. Com. on Irish Studies (pres. 1991—), Phi Kappa Phi, Alpha Sigma Lambda. E-mail: j_touhill@hotmail.com.

TOULANTIS, MARIE, retail executive; V.p. The Chase Manhattan Bank, New York, NY, 1987-96, sr. v.p., 1996-97; exec. v.p. fin. Barnes & Noble Inc., N.Y.C., 1997-99, CFO barnesandnoble.com Inc., 1999—. Office: Barnesandnoble dot com Inc 76 9th Ave Fl 11 New York NY 10011-5201

TOURTET, CHRISTIANE ANDRÉE, writer, human rights activist, photojournalist, reporter; b. Grenoble, France, June 18, 1945; came to U.S., 1965; d. André and Maria Tourtet. Cert. completion humanistic psychology, Fla. Jr. Coll., Jacksonville, 1969, AS with high honors, 1973, AA with high honors, 1974; BA with honors, Jacksonville U., 1975. Hostess interpreter-translator Credit Lyonnais, Grenoble, 1963-65; instr. French Albany (N.Y.) Acad. for Girls, 1965-66; instr. French, asst. lang. lab. Coll. of St. Rose, Albany, 1966-67; instr. French Bartram Sch., Jacksonville, 1970; instr. French and modeling Fla. Jr. Coll., Jacksonville, 1971-74; producer-dir., radio personality edn1. French program Sta. WFAM FM radio, Jacksonville, 1977-79; interpreter, translator French Lang. Bank, Jacksonville, 1980-83. Tutor pvt. and small group classes in French; model for publicity ads, brochures in major mags., newspapers; lectr. in field. Author: Fruits of Life (Silver medal Arts Scis. Letter, Paris, 1977); editor, contbr. New Leaf News, Fla. Flambeau, Back to School Mag.; editor, pub., contbr. Environ. Med. and Disability Corner, Tallahassee Area Ch. News, FSView, AARP Newsletter, Tallahassee Alliance with Disabilities Newsletter; recs. Flamingo Studios, Tallahassee, Fla., 1986-87 (Internat. Woman of Yr., 1991-29, 1996-97, Internat. Woman of Millenium 2000, International Personality of the Year, 2001; exhibited in group shows at North Fla. Fair, Tallahassee, 2002 (1st, 2d, and 3d pl. in photography, 2d pl. 2003); paintings exhibited in France, Monte Carlo and U.S.; photography exhibited in galleries, pub. in mags. including Today's Photographer; guest appearance Phyllis Fauricker Show, Jacksonville, Fla.; actrees in over 28 TV commls. Pres. Le Cercle Francais, Albany, 1965. Named Woman of Yr., Romanian Prince Paltin Sturdza, Princess Cornelia Sturdza and Prince Michael Sturdza, 1995; named to Millenium Hall of Fame; recipient 1st prize Solfège Artistic Competition, 1957, 1st prize, Accordion Acad. Grenoble, 1958, Bronze medal accordion solo, Cup of France, City of Lyon, 1958, Gold medal Cup of France, 1959, Cup of Europe, 1959, 2d prize in singing, City of Grenoble, 1961, medal of City of Grenoble, 1977, medal of Dauphine County, 1977, medal of Chevalier of Order of Merit, Paris, 1976, medal of Chevalier of French Courtesy, 1977, medal of Nat. Merit, 1976, Silver medal honor, Twentieth Century Achievement award, 1993, U.S. flag flown over Capitol in her honor, Washington, 1999—2001, Internat. Woman of Yr., Romanian Prince Paltin Sturdza, Princess Cornelia Sturdza and Prince Michael Sturdza, 1996—97, Lifetime Distinction of Honor for Photographic Achievement, Am. Image Press, Meritorious Achievement award. Mem. NAFE, APHA, Am. Acad. Environ. Medicine (assoc.), Environ. Illness Assn. Tallahassee (founder, pres. 1989—), Chem. Injury Info. Network (judge arts and talent contest 1999), Nat. Ctr. Environ. Strategies, Share, Care, Prayers, H.E.A.L., Am. Med. Writers Assn., Internat. Platform Assn., Nat. Assn. Sci. Writers, Freelance Media Svcs., India Assn. Tallahassee (publicity officer, fashion show judge), Internat. Freelance Photographers Orgn., World Nat. Congress (senator 2003—), Am. Image Press, Phi Theta Kappa. Address: PO Box 20517 Tallahassee FL 32316-0517 E-mail: tourtet@yahoo.com.

TOUSSAINT, T. NICOLETTE, writer, nonprofit organization official; b. Chgo., Nov. 11, 1951; d. Richard A. Slusser and Myra J. Toussaint-Devine; m. Mason A. Ingram. BA in English, BS in Journalism, U. Colo., 1974; MS in Publ. Design, Ill. Inst. Tech., 1979. Copywriter Spiegel Catalog, Chgo., 1974-75, Doug Gotthoffer Advt., Palo Alto, Calif., 1983; pub. rels. specialist NOW, 1975; mgr. advt. and creative svcs. GE/Calma, Calif., 1980-82; sr. copywriter Lowe Marschalk, San Francisco, 1983-85; creative supr. NW Ayer, L.A., 1986; creative dir. Sound Ideas Prodns., San Francisco, 1987-90; mgr. creative svcs. Rides for Bay Area Commuters, San Francisco, 1989-93; sr. comm. cons. Comm. Techs., San Francisco, 1993; pres. Pub. Rels. for Social Change, San Francisco, 1994-96; media dir. The Utility Reform Network (TURN), San Francisco, 1996-98; comm. dir. Hewlet-Annenberg Challenge for Pub. Sch. Reform, 1998—. Author: (ednl. video series) Broken Wings: Women and Domestic Violence, 1996; one-woman shows in graphics Chgo. Pub. Libr., 1978. Regional coord. Clothesline Project, San Francisco, 1993-95; mem. nat. program bd. Unitarian Univesalists Acting To Stop Violence Against Women, 1995-96; publicist Women and Cancer Walk, San Francisco, 1995, 96, Dangerous Promises, anti-violence campaign, L.A. and San Francisco, 1995, 96; mem. adv. com. Vanguard Pub. Found., San Francisco, 1996-97. Recipient 1st place award for graphics Ravinia Festival, Ill., typography award N.Y. Art Dirs. Club, 1978, award San Francisco Advt. Club, 1984, 85, Am. Advt. Fedn., 1985, One of 10 Best Nat. Bus.-to-Bus. Campaigns award Bus. and Profl. Advt. Assn., 1985, One of Top 10 Nat. Nonprofit Ann. Reports award Bus. Pub. mag., 1992, Cindy award for Apple Computer interactive disk ednl. program, 1988; award for coordinating Bay Area Clothesline Project, San Francisco Bd. Suprs., 1994, Woman Who Makes a Difference award San Francisco Commn. on Status of Women, 1995. Mem. NOW (chmn. task force on violence against women San Francisco chpt. 1994, v.p. pub. rels. 1995-96, pres. 1996-97, immediate past pres. 1997—), Sierra Club. Avocations: watercolor painting, sweater design, growing roses. Office: Bay Area Sch Reform Collaborative 730 Harrison St San Francisco CA 94107-1271

TOUSSIENG, YOLANDA, make-up artist; Television work includes: (movies) Fallen Angel, 1981, 1981, Blue de Ville, 1986, (series) Pee-wee's Playhouse, 1986, (mini-series) North and South, Book II, 1986, films include Blue City, 1986, No Man's Land, 1987, Beetlejuice, 1988, Gross Anatomy, 1989, Three Fugitives, 1989, Farewell to the King, 1989, Edward Scissorhands, 1990, Flatliners, 1990, Everybody Wins, 1990, Hoffa, 1992, Batman Returns, 1992, Mrs. Doubtfire, 1993, Ed Wood, 1994 (Acad. award for Best Make-up, 1994), Being Human, 1994, Junior, 1994. Office: IATSE Local 706 11519 Chandler Blvd North Hollywood CA 91601-2618

TOWE, A. RUTH, retired museum director; b. Circle, Mont., Mar. 4, 1938; d. David and Anna Marie (Pedersen) James; m. Thomas E. Towe, Aug. 21, 1960; children: James Thomas, Kristofer Edward. BA, U. Mont., 1960, MA, 1970; postgrad., Am. U., 1964. Bookkeeper, copywriter Sta. KGVO, Missoula, Mont., 1960-61; grad. asst. Sch. of Journalism U. Mont., Missoula, 1961-62; editorial asst. Phi Gamma Delta mag., Washington, 1964; reporter The Chelsea (Mich.) Standard, 1965-66; dir. Mont. Nat. Bank, Plentywood, 1966-73; bookkeeper, legal sec. Thomas E. Towe, Atty. of Law, Billings, Mont., 1967-68; dir. Mont. Nat. Bank, Browning, 1972-73; mus. exec. dir. The Moss Mansion Mus., Billings, 1988—2003; ret., 2003. Bd. dirs. Billings Depot, Inc., sec., 1999—. Mem. Mont. Coun. of Family Rels. & Devel., 1970; pres. Mont. Assn. of Symphony Orchs., 1987-88; sheriff Yellowstone Corral of Westerners, Billings, 1993; pres. Yellowstone Hist. Soc., 1998-2000; vice-chmn. Yellowstone Dem. Ctrl. Com., Billings, 1983-84; mem. Billings Friends Mtg., 1986—. Mem. AAUW, PEO, Mont. Assn. Female Execs., Mus. Assn. Mont. (pres. 1990-92, bd. dirs. 1989-96), Jr. League, Theta Sigma Phi (hon.). Avocation: gardening. E-mail: r.towe@bresnan.net.

TOWE, LINDA MILLER, music educator; b. Madison, Tenn., Nov. 18, 1940; d. David Rhea Miller and Reu Elma Parrish Miller-Pate; m. Allen Mason Henson (div. Apr. 1973); children: Chris Henson, Angela Henson; m. William Harding Towe. BA, Belmont U., 1962; MusM, Murray State U., 1967. Music tchr. Orange County, Orlando, 1962—63, Craken County, Paducah, Ky., 1964—71, Lakeside Elem., Hendersonville, Tenn., 1971—84, Hawkins Mid. Sch., Hendersonville, 1985—89; choral dir. Hendersonville (Tenn.) HS, 1989—. Freshmen chorus chmn. Mid. Nashville, 1996—98, all state chorus chmn., 1998—2000. Mem.: Tenn. Music Edn. Assn., Am. Choral Dirs. Assn., Music Edn. Nat. Conv., Concert Chorale of Nashville, First Bapt. Ch., Hendersonville, Alpha Delta Kappa Tchr's. Sorority. Home: 136A Hatcher Ln Hendersonville TN 37075 Office: Hendersonville HS 123 Cherokee Rd Hendersonville TN 37075

TOWNE, KRISTINE MARIE, title company executive; b. Fond du Lac, Apr. 1, 1969; d. Thomas John and Dianne Jeanne Towne; 1 child, Michael Christopher. Attending, Lakeshore Tech. Coll. Lic. Title Ins. Agent State Wis., 1993; Real Estate Agent Moraine Pk. Tech. Coll., 2001. Teller Green Lake (Wis.) State Bank., 1989—91; collections teller Nat. Exch. Bank. and Trust, Fond du Lac, 1991—92; examiner Guaranty Title Inc., Fond du Lac, 1992—96, Green Lake, 1992—96, First Title Fond du Lac, Inc., 1996—98; mgr. Wis. Title Inc., Fond du Lac, 1998—. Mem. bd. Home Builders Assoc., Fond du Lac, 2001—02. Hon. chmn. Bus. Adv. Coun., Washington, 2003—. Nominee Fond du Lac Leadership Program, COC, 2003. Mem.: NFIB (Nat. Fedn. Independent Bus.), Wis. Land Title Assoc., COC, Home Bldrs. Assoc., Bd. Realtors. Roman Catholic. Avocations: golf, swimming, painting, volleyball, snowboarding. Office: Wis Title Inc 21 E 2nd St Fond Du Lac WI 54935 E-mail: krist@wititleinc.com.

TOWNE, RUTH H. state legislator; b. Manchester, Conn., June 17, 1928; m. Roderick E. Towne (dec.); 2 children. BS, U. Conn., 1949. Dairy farmer, Berlin, Vt.; rep. Dist. 5 State of Vt., 1977—. Breeder Morgan horses; mem. U-32 H.S. Bd. Dirs., chairwoman; treas. Washington Ctrl. Supervisory Union; consumer mem. Bd. Vet. Registration and Exam.; mem. Vt. Ext. Svc., 1949-52; rep. dist. 4-2 Barre City Berlin. Named Woman of Yr. Vt. Farm. Bur., 1989. Mem. DAR Marquis de Lafayette chpt., Vt. Farm Bur., Washington County 4-H Club (agt.), Berlin Hist. Soc. (v.p. 1985-2000). Home: Box 4285 523 Three Mile Bridge Rd Berlin VT 05602-9288 Office: Vt House of Reps Office Of House Mems Montpelier VT 05602

TOWNER, MARGARET ELLEN, retired minister; b. Columbia, Mo., Mar. 19, 1925; d. Milton Carsley and Dorothy Marie (Schloeman) Towner. BA, Carleton Coll., 1948; MDiv, Union/Auburn Theol. Sem., 1954; MA in Guidance and Counseling, Western Mich. U., 1967; DDiv (hon.)., Carroll Coll., 1989. Ordained to ministry Presbyn. Ch., 1956. Dir. Christian edn. Takoma Park (Md.) Presbyn. Ch., 1954-55; min. of edn. 1st Presbyn. Ch., Allentown, Pa., 1955-58, assoc. pastor Kalamazoo, Mich., 1958-69, Northminster Presbyn. Ch., Indpls., 1970-72; exec. dir. Kalamazoo YWCA, 1969-70; co-pastor Kettle Moraine Parish, Waukesha County, Wis., 1973-90; ret., 1990. Mem. Christian edn. and youth coms. Western Mich. Presbytery, So. Mich. Presbytery; chair synod sch. com. Synod of Mich.; mem. nominating com. Whitewater Presbytery, Ind.; mem. adv. com. discipleship and worship Gen. Assembly Mission Coun., commr., 1965—81; vice moderator, mem. spl. com. to study nature ch. and practice governance; chair Synod of Lakes and Prairies Comprehensive Rev. Com., mem. coun. advisors Dubuque Theol. Sem.; vice moderator gen. assembly Presbyn. Ch., 1982; records and overtures Peace River Presbyn. Ch.; parish assoc. Siesta Key Chapel, Sarasota, Fla. Contbr. articles, photographs to profl. publs. Pres. Timberlake Homeowners Assn., Sarasota, 1992—95, Lakes Maintenance Bd., Sarasota, 1994—96; chair bd. trustees Camp Brainerd, Pa., 1955—56; mem. Sch. Faith Com., Faculty Greater Washington Coun. Chs., radio-TV, C.E. and youth coms., pub sch. com.; mem. cmty. com. UNICEF; bd. dirs. Planned Parenthood; mem. inter-agy. exec. com. HEW, Kalamazoo; vol. chaplain emergency rm. Waukesha Meml. Hosp., Meml. Hosp. Oconomowoc, Wis.; dean, dir. Coun. Chs. Leadership Schs., Kalamazoo; mem. Japan Internat. Christian U. Indpls. Com. Recipient Disting. Alumnus award, Carleton Coll., 1983. Mem.: PEO (guard, historian 1972—), Nat. Assn. Presbyn. Clergywomen. Avocations: golf, photography, travel, environmental studies. Home and Office: 7333 Scotland Way # 2120 Sarasota FL 34238-9852

TOWNS, DEBI, state legislator; b. Feb. 12, 1956; MSE, U. Wis., Whitewater, 1999. Dairy farm owner; former fin. cons. and sch. adminstr.; mem. Wis. State Assembly, Madison, 2002—, vice chair com. on edn., mem. agr. com., mem. coll. and univ. com., mem. edn. reform com., mem. fin. instns. com. Republican. Office: State Capitol Bldg Rm 302 N PO Box 8953 Madison WI 53708 Address: 7930 N Eagle Rd Janesville WI 53545

TOWNSEND, ALAIR ANE, publisher, municipal official; b. Rochester, N.Y., Feb. 15, 1942, d. Harold Eugene and Dorothy (Sharpe) T.; m. Robert Harris, Dec. 31, 1970 (div. 1994). BS, Elmira Coll., 1962; MS, U. Wis., 1964; postgrad., Columbia U., 1970-71. Assoc. dir. budget priorities Com. on Budget, U.S. Ho. of Reps., Washington, 1975-79, dep. asst. sec. for budget HEW, 1979-80, asst. sec. for mgmt. and budget, 1980-81; dir. N.Y.C. Office Mgmt. and Budget, 1981-85; dep. mayor for fin. and econ. devel. City of N.Y., 1985-89; pub. Crain's N.Y. Bus., N.Y.C., 1989—. Bd. dirs. Armor Holdings, Inc.; bd. overseers Tchrs. Ins. and Annuity Assn.-Coll. Retirement Equities Fund; former mem. adv. bd. Ford Motor Credit Corp. Former vice-chmn., trustee Elmira Coll.; former mem. Coun. Fgn. Rels.; former bd. govs. Am. Stock Exch.; chmn. Am. Woman's Econ. Devel. Corp.; former chmn. N.Y.C. Sports Commn.; former chmn. Consol. Corp. Fund of Lincoln Ctr.; bd. dirs. Lincoln Ctr.; vice-chmn. Buffalo Fiscal Stability Auth. Mem. Women's Forum, Partnership for NYC (bd. dirs.), N.Y. State Bus. Coun. (past vice chmn.), Econ. Club N.Y. (bd. dirs.). Office: Crain's NY Bus 711 3d Ave New York NY 10017

TOWNSEND, ANN VAN DEVANTER, foundation administrator, art historian; b. Washington, June 20, 1936; d. John Ward and Ellen Keys (Ramsey) Cutler; m. Willis Van Devanter, Dec. 27, 1958 (div. May 1974); 1 child, Susan Earling Van Devanter (Mrs. John Philip Newell); m. Lewis Raynham Townsend, Dec. 10, 1983. BA, Brown U., 1958; MA, George Washington U., 1975. Grantsmanship ctr. cert. Guest curator Balt. Mus. Art, 1971-77; dir. cultural affairs Chevy Chase (Md.) Savs. & Loan, Inc., 1978-81; dir. spl. partnership projects NEA, Washington, 1982-83; founding pres. The Trust for Mus. Exhbns., Washington, 1984—. Organizer over 60 nat. and internat. mus. exhbns. for more than 240 mus. Co-author: Self-Portraits of American Artists, 1670-1973, 1974; author: Anywhere So Long As There Be Freedom, 1975, Two Hundred Years of American Painting, 1976; contbr. articles to mags. U.S. commr. Cagnes-Sur-Mer Internat. Afts Festival, France, 1977, 78; mem. women's com. Washington Opera, 1993—; bd. dirs. Friends of Corcoran Gallery of Art, Washington, 1975-76, Strathmore Hall Arts Ctr., Rockville, Md., 1978-80, Am. Swedish Hist. Mus., Phila., 1987-89, U.S. World Fedn. Friends of Mus., 1995—. Acad. grad. fellow Johns Hopkins Sch. Advanced Internat. Studies, 1958. Mem. Nat. Soc. Arts and Letters, Soc. Women Goegraphers, Am. Assn. Mus., Internat. Coun. Mus., Am. Friends of the Hermitage Mus., Am. Friends of French Heritage, Cir. of the Nat. Gallery of Art, Sulgrave Club, Cosmos Club. Episcopalian. Avocations: backgammon, gourmet cooking, ballroom dancing, bridge. Office: The Trust for Mus Exhbns 1424 16th St NW Ste 600 Washington DC 20036-2239 E-mail: atownsend@tme.org.

TOWNSEND, BRENDA S. educational association administrator; Dir. profl. devel. Internat. Reading Assn., Newark, Del., 1992—, dir. con. and affiliate svcs. Mem. adv. bd. The Gooding Inst. Rsch. in Family Literacy. Office: Internat Reading Assn 800 Barksdale Rd PO Box 8139 Newark DE 19714-8139

TOWNSEND, ELIZABETH, state legislator; Mem. from dist. 31 Maine State Ho. of Reps., 1993-95, mem. from dist. 36, 1995—. Address: 44 Country Ln Portland ME 04103-6206 Office: Maine Ho of Reps State Capitol Augusta ME 04333-0001

TOWNSEND, FRANCES FRAGOS, federal agency administrator; m. John Townsend; 2 children. BA, BS, Am. U., 1982; JD, San Diego U., 1984. Asst. dist. atty., Bklyn., 1985—88; chief to staff to asst. atty. gen. criminal divsn. Dept. Justice, 1993—95, acting dep. asst. atty. gen., 1997—98, counsel Office of Intelligence Policy and Re., 1998—2001; asst. commandant for intelligence U.S.C.G., Dept. Homeland Security, 2001—03; dep. asst. to Pres. Bush, dep. nat. security advisor for combating terrorism Nat. Security Coun., 2003—. Office: Eisenhower Exec Office Bldg Rm 313 17th St & Pennsylvania Ave NW Washington DC 20504

TOWNSEND, IRENE FOGLEMAN, accountant, tax specialist; b. Birmingham, Ala., May 29, 1932; d. James Woods and Virginia (Martin) Fogleman; m. Kenneth Ross Townsend, Mar. 18, 1951; children: Marietta Irene, Martha Shapard, Kenneth Ross Jr., Elizabeth Buchanan. BSBA, East Carolina U., 1980. CPA, N.C., Va. Acct. Norwood P. Whitehurst & Assocs., Greenville, N.C., 1981-86; asst. v.p. Tenet Healthcare Corp., Vienna, Va., 1995—; v.p. NME Psychiatric Hosps., Inc., Vienna, Va., 2001—. Fellow AICPA, N.C. Assn. CPAs, D.C. Inst. CPAs, Va. Soc. CPAs; mem. DAR, N.C. Soc. Daus. of Colonial Wars, Colonial Dames 17th Century. Democrat. Episcopalian (lay reader, chalice bearer). Avocations: bicycling, genealogy. Home: 2521 Paxton St Woodbridge VA 22192-3414 Office: Tenet Healthcare Corp 501 Church St NE Ste 301 Vienna VA 22180-4734 E-mail: irene_townsend@hotmail.com.

TOWNSEND, JANE KALTENBACH, biologist, educator; b. Chgo., Dec. 21, 1922; BS, Beloit Coll., 1944; MA, U. Wis., 1946; PhD, U. Iowa, 1950. Asst. in zoology U. Wis., 1944-47, asst., project assoc. in pathology, 1950—53; asst., instr. U. Iowa, 1948-50; rsch. fellow Wenner-Grens Inst. Am. Cancer Soc., Stockholm, 1953—56; asst. prof. zoology Northwestern U., 1956-58; asst. prof. to assoc. prof. zoology Mt. Holyoke Coll., South Hadley, Mass., 1958-70, prof., 1970-93, chmn. biol. scis., 1980-86, prof. emeritus, 1993—. Fellow AAAS (sec. sect. biol. sci. 1974-78); mem. Am. Assn. Anatomists, Am. Inst. Biol. Scis., Soc. Integrated Comparative Biology, Soc. Exptl. Biology and Medicine, Soc. Devel. Biology, Corp. of Marine Biol. Lab., Sigma Xi, Phi Beta Kappa. Office: Mount Holyoke Coll Dept Bio Scis South Hadley MA 01075 Business E-Mail: jtownsen@mtholyoke.edu.

TOWNSEND, JULIE RAE, artist, educator; b. Davenport, Iowa, Oct. 26, 1964; d. Richard Earl and Gladys Imogene Crow; m. Kelvin Leroy Townsend, Sept. 26, 1989; children: Stephanie Allisson, Elliott Russell. BFA, St. Ambrose U., Davenport, Iowa, 1983—87, BA in Art Edn. K-12, 2001—02. Cert. tchr. Iowa, 2003. Tchr. Davenport Mus. Art, 2002, Lincoln Fundamental Elem., Davenport, Iowa, 2003; tchr. Kaleidoscope program Augustana Coll., Rock Island, Ill. Presenter Ea. Iowa Writing Project workshop. Commissions, exhibitions include 700 sq. ft. mural 1st Presbyn. Ch., Davenport, exhibitions include Dubusque Mus. Art, Tri-Ann. Tri-City Exhbn., Moline's Reher Gallery, Ill., prin. works include charcoal Rapunzel's Bad Hair Day (Hon. Mention, 1995), prin. works include drawing Still Life (Scholastic Achievement Award, 1982); contbr. articles to profl. jours. Vol. Midcoast Fine Arts, Rock I., Ill., 1995—2003; vol. Friends of Catich St. Ambrose U., Davenport, Iowa, 2003—; leader Girl Scouts (Miss. Valley coun.), Davenport, Iowa, 1997—2003; vol. First Presbyn. Ch., Davenport, Iowa. Named 1st Best 2D Artist Quad Cities, River Cities Reader, 2003; recipient 3d Best 2D Artist Quad Cities, 2001, 2d Best 2D Artist Quad Cities, 2002. Mem.: Ea. Iowa Writing Project Adv. Com., Iowa Talented and Gifted Assn. (co-pres. Davenport chpt.), Nat. Art Edn. Assn. (assoc.), Davenort Mus. of Art (assoc.), Nat. Oil Painter's Soc. (assoc.), Midcoast Fine Arts (life; vol. various jobs 1996—2003). Home: 1131 E Columbia Ave Davenport IA 52803 Office Phone: 563-323-6838. Personal E-mail: julesart@netexpress.net.

TOWNSEND, KATHLEEN KENNEDY, former lieutenant governor; b. Greenwich, Connecticut, July 4, 1951; d. Robert F. and Ethel S. Kennedy; m. David Townsend; children: Meaghan, Maeve, Kate, and Kerry. BA cum laude, Harvard Univ., 1974; JD, U. N.Mex., 1978. Instr. Dundalk Cmty. Coll., 1985-86, Essex Cmty. Coll., 1986-87, U. Pa., 1987-88; exec. dir. Md. Student Svc. Alliance, State dept. of Edn., 1987—93; dep. asst. atty. gen. U.S. Dept. Justice, Washington, 1993-94; lt. gov. State of Md., 1995—2003; pres. Operation Respect, 2003; adj. prof. Georgetown's Sch. of Pub. Policy, 2003. Chair so. region Nat. Conf. Lt. Gov., chair oversight com. Johns Hopkins U., Peabody Inst., 1995-96; nat. adv. bd. Export-Import Bank U.S.; bd. adv. Johns Hopkins U. Sch. Advanced Internat. Studies, Inst. Human Virology U. Md; chair, State House Trust, 1995-2003, Adv. Bd., After-School Opportunity Programs, 1999-, co-chair, Safe Schools Interagency Steering Com., 1999-2003; Delegate, Dem. Party Nat. Conv., 1988, 1996, 2000; chair, Dem. Caucus of Lt. Gov. Editor U. N.Mex. Law Rev.; contbg. articles to profl. jour. and newspapers. Founder Robert F. Kennedy Human Rights Award; chair Cabinet Coun. Criminal and Juvenile Justice, 1995-2003; chair Cabinet Coun. for Bus. and Econ. Devel.; chair Md. del. Pres. Summit Am. Future, 1997; chair State Sys. Reform Task Force for Children and Youth Reform, 1996, Task Force to study increasing availability of substance abuse programs, 1998-2001, Gov.of the Yr. 2000 Pub. Info.; chair adv. bd. after sch. opportunity programs; co-chair Md. Family Violence Coun.; bd. dir. John F. Kennedy Libr. Found., Nat. Inst. Women's Policy Rsch.; chair external adv. bd. Kennedy Krieger Inst. Early Infant Transition Ctr.; sr. advisor, Appropriations Com., House of Delegates, 1984-85; asst. Atty. Gen., Md., 1985-86; bd. ptnr. Radcliffe Coll. Recipient 4 hon. degrees; Visionary Leadership Award, Healthy Families Am., 2000, Clinton Ctr. Award for Leadership, Dem. Leadership Coun., 2002. Mem., Econ. Devel. Commn., Baltimore County, 1987, Gov. Exec. Coun., Gov. Commn. on Svc. and Volunteerism, 1998-. Democrat. Office: Operation Respect 5th Fl 2 Penn Plaza New York NY 10121*

TOWNSEND, LINDA LADD, mental health nurse; b. Louisville, Apr. 26, 1948; d. Samuel Clyde and Mary Elizabeth Ladd; m. Stanley Allen Oliver, June 7, 1970 (div. 1978); 1 child, Aaron; m. Warren Terry Townsend Jr., Jan. 1, 1979; children: Mark, Amy, Sarah. Student, Catherine Spalding Coll., 1966-67; BSN, Murray State U., 1970; MS in Psychiat./Mental Health Nursing, Tex. Woman's U., 1976. RN, Tex., Ky.; lic. advanced practice RN, profl. counselor, marriage and family therapist, Tex.; cert. group psychotherapist. Charge nurse med. and pediatric units Murray (Ky.)-Calloway County Hosp., 1970-71; team leader surg./renal transplant unit VA Hosp., Nashville, 1971-73; team leader, charge nurse gen. med.-surg. unit Providence Hosp., Waco, Tex., 1973-74; outpatient therapist Mental Hygiene Clinic, Ft. Hood, Tex., 1975-76; outpatient nurse therapist Ctrl. Counties Ctr. for Mental Health/Mental Retardation, Copperas Cove & Lampasas, Tex., 1977-80; psychiat. nurse clin. specialist, marriage/family therapist Profl. Counseling Svc., Copperas Cove, 1979—. Cons. Metroplex Hosp. and Pavilion, Killeen, Tex., 1980—. Founding mem. Family Outreach of Coryell County, 1986—, past pres. and past sec.; founding memd. Partnership for a Drug and Violence-Free Copperas Cove; advocate Tex. Peer Assistance Program for Nurses, Walk to Emmaus, 1993; disaster mental health svc. counselor ARC, 1998. Recipient Mary M. Roberts Writing award Am. Jour. of Nursing, 1970; named Mem. of Yr.-Vol., Family Outreach of Coryell County. Mem. ANA (cert. clin. specialist in adult psychiat. and mental health nursing, cert. clin. specialist in child and adolescent psychiat. and mental health nursing), Tex. Nurses Assn., Am. Group Psychotherapy Assn. (cert.), Inst. for Humanities at Salado, Sigma Theta Tau. Democrat. Methodist. Avocations: genealogy, camping, nature activities, music, sports. Office: Profl Counseling Svc 806 E Avenue D Ste F Copperas Cove TX 76522-2231

TOWNSEND, MARJORIE RHODES, aerospace engineer, business executive; b. Washington, Mar. 12, 1930; d. Lewis Boling and Marjorie Olive (Trees) Rhodes; m. Charles Eby Townsend, June 7, 1948; children: Charles Eby Jr., Lewis Rhodes, John Cunningham, Richard Leo. BEE, George Washington U., 1951. Electronic scientist Naval Rsch. Lab., Washington, 1951-59; rsch. engr. to sect. head Goddard Space Flight Ctr.-NASA, Greenbelt, Md., 1959-65, tech. asst. to chief systems divsn., 1965-66, project mgr. small astronomy satellites, 1966-75, project mgr. applications explorer missions, 1975-76, mgr. preliminary systems design group, 1976-80; aerospace and electronics cons. Washington, 1980-83; v.p. systems devel. Space Am., 1983-84; aerospace cons. Washington, 1984-90; dir. space systems engring. BDM Internat., Inc., Washington, 1990-91; dir. space applications BDM ESC, Washington, 1991-92; sr. prin. staff mem. BDM Fed., Inc., Washington, 1992-93. Aerospace cons., Washington, 1993—. Patentee digital telemetry system. Decorated Knight Italian Republic Order, 1972; recipient Fed. Women's award, 1973, EUR award for Culture, 1974, Engr. Alumni Achievement award George Washington U., 1975, Gen. Alumni Achievement award George Washington U., 1976, Exceptional Svc. medal NASA, 1971, Outstanding Leadership medal NASA, 1980, Eye-of-the-Needle award NASA, 1991. Fellow IEEE (chmn. Washington sect. 1974-75), AIAA (chmn. nat. capitol sect. 1985), AAAS (coun. del. 1985-88), Washington Acad. Sci. (pres. 1980-81); mem. Internat. Acad. Astronautics, Am. Geophys. Union, Soc. Women Engrs., Wing of Aerospace Med. Assn., Inc. (hon.), DAR, Daus. Colonial Wars, Mensa, Sigma Kappa, Sigma Delta Epsilon (hon.). Republican. Episcopalian. Home and Office: 3529 Tilden St NW Washington DC 20008-3122 E-mail: mrtownsend@aol.com.

TOWNSEND, SANDRA L. state representative; b. Buffalo, Okla., Dec. 25, 1936; 3 children. County clk., chief dep. San Juan County, Aztec, N.Mex., 1967—91; ret., 1991; state rep. dist. 3 N.Mex. State Legis., Santa Fe, 1995—. Mem. Agr. and Water Resources com. N.Mex. State Legis., Santa Fe, mem. Appropriations and Fin. com. Republican. Methodist. Home: PO Box 1292 Aztec NM 87410 Office: New Mexico State Capitol Rm 201B Santa Fe NM 87504

TOWNSEND, SUE JOYCE, retired air traffic controller; b. Delhi, N.Y., June 1, 1941; d. John and Ida Frances (Turner) Mostert; m. Burdette David Townsend, June 28, 1986 (dec. Nov. 1997). BGS, George Washington U., 1977. Cert. paralegal; lic. real estate salesperson, N.Y., Fla.; lic. real estate broker, Fla. Air traffic controller, instrument instr. Ross Aviation Inc., Ft. Rucker, Ala., 1966-68; air traffic controller Eastern region FAA, 1968-91. Flow controller N.Y. TRACON, Westbury, 1982-83, tng. instr., 1983-84; FAA supr. Binghamton (N.Y.) Tower, 1984-88. Chair Town of Delhi Zoning Bd., 1991-93; mem. Delaware County Planning Bd., Delhi, 1992—; pres. Delhi Beautification Com., 1999—. Served with U.S. Army, 1959-66. Recipient Legis. Resolution, N.Y. state Senate, 1999. Mem. Am. Legion (post 190 Delhi), Profl. Women Controllers (co-founder, 1st pres.), Kiwanis (pres. Delhi). Avocations: golf, bicycling, swimming, travel, camping. Office: Harry W Hawley Realty 4 Court St Delhi NY 13753-1082 also: ERA Mt Vernon Sarasota FL 34234 Home: 4997 Stonecastle Dr Venice FL 34293-8203 E-mail: susiet@Catskill.net.

TOWNSEND, SUSAN STOCKSTILL, elementary school educator, music educator; b. Washington, June 24, 1955; d. Frank Irwin Stockstill and Sue Carol Carr; m. William Frank Townsend, Nov. 23, 1997; children: Claire Emerson Stevens, Anna Catherine Stevens. B of Music Edn., East Carolina U., 1977. Chorus and gen. music tchr. Hope Mills (N.C.) Jr. H.S., 1977—84, Stedman (N.C.) Mid. Sch., 1995—96; chorus and drama tchr. Max Abbott Mid. Sch., Fayetteville, NC, 1996—. Quiz bowl competition team coach Max Abbott Mid. Sch., Fayetteville, 1997—, music dept. chairperson. Asst. music dir. Village Bapt. Ch., Fayetteville, 1986—2002. Grantee, Jr. League Fayetteville, 1996, 1997. Mem.: N.C. Music Educators Assn. (assoc.; site chairperson East #3 choral festival mid. sch. choral sect. 1999—, tchr. of the yr. coord. mid. sch. choral sect. 2000—, exec. bd. mid. sch. choral sect.), Sigma Alpha Iota (life), Delta Zeta (life; rec. sec. 1975—76). Conservative. Baptist. Avocations: travel, skiing, reading, singing, golf. Home: 4236 Huntsfield Rd Fayetteville NC 28314 Office: Max Abbott Middle School 590 Winding Creek Rd Fayetteville NC 28305 Personal E-mail: sjst624@aol.com. E-mail: susantownsend@ccs.k12.nc.us.

TOWNSEND, TERRY, publishing executive; b. Camden, N.J., Dec. 14, 1920; d. Anthony and Rose DeMarco; m. Paul Brorstrom Townsend, Dec. 8, 1961; 1 child, Kim. BA, Duke U., 1942; LHD (hon.), Dowling Coll., 1991. Pub. rels. dir. North Shore U. Hosp., Manhasset, N.Y., 1956-68; pres. Theatre Soc., L.I., 1967-70, Townsend Comm. Bur., L.I., 1970-98; ptnr. L.I. Communicating Svc., Bellport, 1977—; sales rep. Zere Comml. Real Estate Svcs., 2003—. Pub. L.I. Bus. News, 1979-98, pub. emeritus, 1998—; v.p. ParrMeadows Racetrack, Yaphank, N.Y., 1977; mem. Bellport Archtl. Rev. Bd., 1997—. Columnist, writer L.I./Bus., Ronkonkoma, 1970-75. Assoc. trustee North Shore U. Hosp., 1968—; bd. govs. Adelphi U. Friends Fin. Edn., 1978-85; chmn. ann. archtl. awards competition N.Y. Inst. Tech., 1970-83; trustee Dowling Coll., 1984-2000; trustee L.I. Fine Arts Mus., 1984-85; pub. broadcasting PBS Sta. WLIW TV, Garden City, L.I., N.Y., 1990-93; bd. dirs. Family Svc. Assn. Nassau County, 1982-92; dinner chmn. L.I. 400 Ball, 1987; trustee L.I. Mus. Art, 1994-2003; pres. Bellport Women's Golf Club, 2004. Recipient Media award 110 Ctr. Bus. and Profl. Women, 1977, Enterprise award Friends of Fin. Edn., 1981, L.I. Loves Bus. Showcase Salute, 1982, Cmty. Svc. award N.Y. Diabetes Assn., 1983, Disting. Long Islander in Comm. award L.I. United Epilepsy Assn., 1984, Spl. award Dowling Coll. Spring Tribute, 1989, Disting. Svc. award Episcopal Health Svcs., 1989, Disting. Citizen award Dowling Coll., 1991, Gilbert Tilles award Nat. Assn. Fundraising Execs., 1994, Hadassah Cmty. Svc. award, 1996, Golden rule award Little Village Sch., 1997, Lifetime Achievement award L.I. Assn., 1998, Promote L.I. Achievement award, 1998, Lifetime Achievement award Advancement for Commerce & Industry, 1999; named 1st Lady of L.I., L.I. Pub. Rels. Assn., 1973, L.I. Woman of Yr. L.I. Assn. Action Com., 1989; honoree Suffolk County Girl Scouts, 2004; Paul and Terry Townsend Sch. of Bus., Dowling Coll., designated in her honor, 2004. Mem.: Bellport Women's Golf Club (pres. 2003—04). Office: LI Communicating Svcs PO Box 915 Bellport NY 11713-0915 E-mail: terytowns@aol.com.

TOWNSEND, WENDY, marketing executive; b. N.Y.C., Nov. 28, 1942; d. Paul Brorstrom Townsend and Ruth Grace (Moerchen) Burgess; m. Robert Joe Baker, Aug. 2, 1970; children: Lynn Baker, Robert Baker, Michelle Townsend. BS, Boston U., 1965; MA, Antioch U., Seattle, 1993. Comm. specialist GE Co., Lynn, Mass., 1964-67; pub. rels. dir. Unitarian-Universalist Svc. Com., Boston, 1967-70; comm. specialist Gen. Foods Co., Sydney, Australia, 1974-75; pub. rels. devel. dir. Seattle-King County Coun. of Camp Fire, 1976-83; east reg. pub. rels. mgr. Group Health Coop., Seattle, 1983-85; v.p. mktg. Wash. Credit Union, Lynnwood, 1986-96; prin. Townsend Assocs. West, Seattle, 1996—2000; v.p. mktg. Washington's Credit Union, Mountlake Terrace, Wash., 2000—. Nat. tng. staff Camp Fire, 1979-80; bd. dirs. Victory Hts. Cmty. Coun., Seattle, 1992-94; cons. strategic planning EarthSave, Seattle, 1994-97; mem. mktg. com. Youth Care, Seattle, 1997. Mem. AAUW (pres. 1971), Pub. Rels. Soc. Am. (accredited, chpt. pres. and bd. dirs. 1996, assembly del. 2000—, Totem award 1980), Mktg. Comm. Execs. Internat. (bd. dirs. 1992-96), Women in Comm. (chpt. pres. 1981-82, bd. dirs. 1980-86). Episcopalian. Avocations: hiking, yoga, creative writing. Home: 10312 17th Ave NE Seattle WA 98125-7661 Office: Washingtons Credit Union 6920 220th St SW Ste 202 Mountlake Terrace WA 98043 E-mail: wendyt@washingtonscredit.union.org.

TOWNSEND-BUTTERWORTH, DIANA BARNARD, educational consultant, author; b. Albany, N.Y., Dec. 12; d. Barnard and Marjorie (Bradley) Townsend; m. J. Warner Butterworth, Jan. 23, 1969; children: James, Diana. AB, Harvard-Radcliffe Coll., 1960; MA, Tchrs. Coll., Columbia U., 1971. Tchr. St. Bernard's Sch., N.Y.C., 1963-78, head of lower sch. English, 1965-71, head of jr. sch., 1971-78; assoc. dir. Early Care Ctr., N.Y.C., 1984-87; acad. advisor Columbia Coll., N.Y.C., 1987-88; ednl. cons., lectr. N.Y.C., 1988—. Dir. parent involvement initiative Ctr. Ednl. Outreach & Innovation, Tchrs. Coll., Columbia U., 1996, chmn. devel. com. alumni coun. Tchrs. Coll., 1994-98; chmn. sub-com. Harvard schs. com. Harvard Coll., Cambridge, Mass., 1975—. Author: Preschool and Your Child: What You Should Know, 1995, Your Child's First School, 1992 (Parent's Choice award 1992), (book chpt.) Handbook of Clinical Assessment of Children and Adolescents; contbr. articles to ednl. publs. and jours. Mem. women's health symposium steering com. N.Y. Hosp., N.Y.C., 1988—. Mem. Assn. Lower Sch. Heads (co-founder 1975), Alumni Coun. Tchrs. Coll. (com. chair 1993-98), Harvard Faculty Club. Avocations: skiing, hiking, swimming, theatre, reading. Home: 1170 5th Ave New York NY 10029-6527

TOWSLEE, JANET L. special education educator; b. Louisville, Apr. 4, 1942; d. James and Juanita (Flowers) T.; m. Donald Collier, Aug. 28, 1964; children: Richard Louis, Rebecca Elizabeth. BS in Russian Studies, Fla. State U., 1963; MA in Spl. Edn., U. Louisville, 1967; EdD in Spl. Edn., Ind. U., 1974. Cert. tchr. spl. edn. Tchr. Jefferson County Schs., Louisville, 1963-69; teaching asst. Ind. U., Bloomington, 1969-72; with dept. spl. edn. Ga. State U., Atlanta, 1972—, assoc. dean, dir. ednl. field svcs. dean's office, 1978-91; faculty dept. spl. edn. Clayton State Coll., 1992—. Instr. edn. U. Louisville, 1966-67, 69; tchr. basic adult edn. Jefferson County Bd. Edn., 1963-69. Author: Future Educator of America Handbook, 1989, 91, 93; editorial cons. Profl. Educator, 1986—; contbr. articles, book revs. to profl. jours. Bd. dirs. Tommy Nobis Ctr., 1987—, also twice pres. Recipient Outstanding Svc. award Tommy Nobis Ctr., 1987; named Disting. Adminstr. of Yr. Mortar Bd. Ga. State U., 1983. Mem. Assn. Tchr. Educators (one of 70 Leaders Tchr. Edn. 1990, pres. 1987-88, Pres. award for Svc. 1983, 86, Honor Roll 1984), Comparative and Internat. Edn. Soc., Nat. Coun. States Insvc. Edn., U.S.-China Tchr. Edn. Consortium, Assn. Spl. Edn. Tech., Coun. Exceptional Children Internat. (divs. mental retardation, tchr. edn., career devel. internat. edn. and svcs.), Am. Assn. Colls. Tchr. Edn. (NCATE exec. bd.), S.E. Regional Assn. Tchr. Educators, Ga. Assn. Tchr. Educators, Ga. Staff Devel. Coun., Ga. Coun. Exceptional Children, Met. Atlanta Tchr. Edn. Group. Home: 1194 W Nancy Creek Dr NE Atlanta GA 30319-1644

TOWSNER, CYNTHIA MERLE, vocational school educator; b. Washington, Apr. 23, 1939; d. Philip and Edith Towsner; married, 1963; children: Scott David Garrison, Katrina L. Goldband. BS, U. Md., 1961, postgrad., 1964-65, Am. U., 1987. Adv. cert. contracting officer's tech. rep. U.S. Dept. Edn. Tchr. Montgomery County Pub. Schs., Rockville, Md., 1961-66, 72-80; spl. asst. to commr. rehab. svcs. adminstrn. U.S. Dept. Edn., Washington, 1981-85, spl. asst. to the dir. Office Intergovtl. & Interagy. Affairs, 1985-87, acting dir. intergovtl. affairs office, 1987, ednl. program specialist Office Bilingual Edn. & Minority Languages Affairs, 1987-93, edn. program specialist Bilingual Vocat. Tng., 1993-96, nat. coord. family literacy and literacy vols. for adults, 1996—. Pres. Office Vocat. Adult Edn., U.S. Dept. Edn., Educare Programs, Inc., Chevy Chase, Md., 1988—; cons. R.J. Comer Comm., Inc., Jacksonville, Fla., 1995-97; v.p. Dalmahoy Group Internat., Chevy Chase, 1997-99. Photographer Project Education Reform: Time for Results, vol. 1, 1987. Vol. Holy Cross Hosp., Silver Spring, Md., 1969-74; asst. to pres. for edn. issues, chair nominating com., chair cmty. directory Rock Creek Hills Civic Assn., Kensington, 1968-85; v.p. D.C., Md. and Va. region, chair youth rally, chair radiothon publicity St. Jude's Children's Rsch. Hosp., Aiding Leukemia Stricken Am. Children, Memphis, 1969-81; chair internat. festival Larchmont Elem. Sch. PTA, Montgomery County, MD, 1976-78; bd. dirs., mem., chair Citizens for Edn., Montgomery County, Md., 1977-82; active Renaissance Women, Washington, 1983-87; chair corp. and bus. contbns. Hosp. Relief Fund for the Caribbean, Chevy Chase, 1989-91, annual ball com., 1989-94; vol. tutor Laubach Literacy Action and Literacy Vols. Am., Chevy Chase, 1989-93. Recipient Meritorious Svc. medal Am. Automobile Assn., Washington, Honors award Rock Creek Hills Civic Assn., Kensington, Md., 1979, Pres.'s award Combined Fed. Campaign, Washington, 1987, Hammer award V.P. of the U.S., Washington, 1996, 1st place ribbon in photography Montgomery County Agrl. Fair, Gaithersburg, Md., 1998, 1st, 2nd and 3rd place ribbons in photography Montgomery County Agrl. Fair, Gaithersburg, 1999, 1st and 2nd place ribbons in photography Md. State Fair, Timonium, 1999, 1st pl. award Md. State Fair, 2000. Mem. AAUW, Internat. Freelance Photographers Orgn. (named Master Photographer 2002, life), Assn. for Career and Tech. Edn., Soc. Govt. Meeting Profls., Nat. Trust for Scotland, Nat. Mus. Women in the Arts (founding mem.). Avocations: photography, reading, traveling. Home: 4620 N Park Ave Apt 1404E Chevy Chase MD 20815-4563 E-mail: cindymt@comcast.net.

TOZER, ELIZABETH FARRAN, interior and floral designer; b. Cleve., Jan. 25, 1942; d. Charles and Irma (Gaensslen) Farran; m. W. James Tozer Jr., July 30, 1965; children: Farran Tozer Brown and Katherine Tozer Roddy. BFA, Ohio Wesleyan U., 1964. Residential and comml. interior and floral designer Elizabeth Farran Tozer Design, N.Y.C., 1982—. Interior design cons. N.Y. Found. for Sr. Citizens, N.Y.C., 1982—; pres. The Flower Svc. Store, N.Y.C., 1972-92; spokesperson Am. Florists Mktg. Coun., 1987; appeared in numerous radio, TV, and newspaper interviews in eleven maj. U.S. cities. Author: The Art of Flower Arranging, 1981; contbr. articles to profl. publs. Chmn. N.Y. Flower Show, 1996; mem. exec. com., mem. nominating com. Mus. of the City of N.Y., 1994—; vice chmn., chmn. nominating com., bd. dirs. N.Y. Found. for Sr. Citizens, 1980-; mem. nominating com. Sch. Am. Ballet, Lincoln Ctr., 1977—; chmn. more than 30 maj. fundraising events in N.Y.C. and Dutchess County, N.Y., 1977—; mem. adv. bd. Nat. Acad. Design, 1999-; chmn. Inst. Ecosys. AldoLeopold Soc., 2001-. Recipient award Mcpl. Arts Soc., 1997, award YWCA Acad. Women Achievers, 1995, Pillars of Industry award, Best Srs. Mid-Rise Bldg. award Nat. Assn. Home Builders, 1995, Spl. Merit award Associated Builders and Owners of Greater N.Y., 1993. Mem. N.Y. Hort. Soc. (nominating com.). Avocation: raising miniature horses. Office: EFT Design Ltd 1112 Park Ave # 6A New York NY 10128-1235

TRABULSI, JUDY, advertising and marketing executive; b. Houston; d. Richard Joseph and Genevieve (Jamail) T. BS in Comm., U. Tex., 1971. Exec. v.p., exec. media dir. Gurasich, Spence, Darilek & McClure, Austin, Tex., 1971—. Mem. nat. adv. coun. SBA, Washington, 1994-96; adv. coun. U. Tex. Comm. Sch., Austin, 1996—; adv. mem. 21st Century Dems., 1996. Office: Gurasich Spence Darilek & McClure 828 W 6th St Austin TX 78703-5420

TRACEY, PATRICIA A. career officer; b. Bronx, N.Y. m. Richard Metzer. Grad., Women Officers Sch., 1970; BA in Math., Coll. New Rochelle; MS in Ops. Rsch., Naval Postgrad. Sch. Ensign USN, 1970; advanced through grades vice admiral; cmd. ctr. officer naval space surveillance sys.; staff tour of comdr. in chief Pacific fleet; bur. naval personnel placement officer; extended planning analyst sys. analysis divsn. chief naval ops. staff, 1980-82, exec. officer recruiting dist., 1982-84, manpower and personnel analyst program appraisal divsn., 1984-86; comdr. Naval Tech. Tng. Ctr. Treasure Is., 1986-88; head enlisted plans, cmty. mgmt. br. Chief Naval Personnel, 1988-90; comdr. Naval Sta. Long Beach (Calif.), 1990; fellow chief naval ops.'s strategic studies group Naval War Coll.; dir. manpower and personnel J-1 joint staff, 1993-95; comdr. Naval Tng. Ctr., 1995-96; chief naval edn. and tng., dir. naval tng. chief naval ops. Pensacola, Fla., 1996-98; dep. asst. sec. of def., 1998—. Decorated 3 Legions of Merit, Def. Disting. Svc. medal, Navy Disting. Svc. medal, 3 Meritorious Svc. medals. Office: Dep Asst Sec of Def Mil Personnel Policy 4000 Defense Pentagon 3E767 Washington DC 20301-4000

TRACHUK, LILLIAN ELIZABETH, music educator; b. Monroe, Wis., July 28, 1921; d. William John Blair and Stella Mae Harness-Blair; m. Max A. Trachuk, Dec. 21, 1949 (dec. Sept. 1983); children: Thomas Max, William Anton. Piano tchr., Newport News, Va., 1964—. Home: 101 Burnham Pl Newport News VA 23606

TRACY, JANET RUTH, legal educator, librarian; b. Denison, Iowa, July 16, 1941; d. L. M. and Grace (Harvey) T.; m. Rodd Mc Cormick Reynolds, Feb. 15, 1975 (dec. June 1993); children: Alexander, Lee. BA, U. Oreg., 1963; ML, U. Wash., 1964; JD, Harvard U., 1969. Bar: NY 1970. Reference libr. Harvard Coll. Librs., Cambridge, Mass., 1964-66; assoc. Kelley Drye & Warren, N.Y.C., 1969-71; dir. data base design Mead Data Ctrl., Inc., N.Y.C., 1971-75; dir. rsch. Mvpl. Employees Legal Svc. Fund, N.Y.C., 1975-76; from asst. to assoc. prof. N.Y. Law Sch., N.Y.C., 1976-82; asst. libr. dir. Law Libr. Columbia U., N.Y.C., 1982-86; prof., law libr. dir. Fordham U., N.Y.C., 1986—. Chmn. Conf. Law Librs. Jesuit Univs., 1988-89. Co-author: Professional Staffing and Job Security in Academic Law Libraries, 1989. Recipient Catalog Automation award Winston Found., 1990, 91, 92. Home: 285 Riverside Dr New York NY 10025-5276 Office: Fordham U Sch of Law 140 W 62nd St New York NY 10023-7407 E-mail: jtracy@law.fordham.edu.

TRACY, JOHN PATRICK, state legislator; b. Springfield, Vt., Apr. 12, 1952; m. Lynn Richardson Pitcher; five children. BA, U. Vt., 1984. Rep. State Vt., 1995—. Restaurant mgr. Vice chair Burlington & Chittenden County Dem. Coms.; mem. Ward 5 Dem. Com.; active Burlington Waterfront Bd. Mem. VFW. Address: 92 Park St Burlington VT 05401-4327

TRACY, SAUNDRA J. academic administrator; m. Doug Tracy; children: Steve, Elaine. BA in Spanish, Carroll Coll., Waukesha, Wis., 1968; M Ed in Fgn. Lang. Instrn., U. Pitts., 1971; PhD in Edn. Adminstrn., Purdue U., West Lafayette, Ind., 1981. Dir. Greater Cleve. Adminstr. Assessment Ctr., 1968—88; asst. to assoc. prof. edn. Cleve. State U., 1981—88; exec. dir. sch. study coun. Lehigh U., 1989—91, dir. ednl. programs Lee Iacocca Inst., 1990—92, assoc. prof. to prof. edn., 1988—94; dean of coll. of edn. Butler U., 1994—98; v.p. acad. affairs Mt. Union Coll., 1998—2001; pres. Alma Coll., 2001—. Fellow, Am. Coun. of Edn., 1992—93. Office: Alma Coll 614 West Superior St Alma MI 48801-1599 Office Phone: 989-463-7146.

TRAFFORD, ABIGAIL, columnist, editor, writer; b. N.Y.C., July 14, 1940; d. William Bradford and Abigail (Sard) T.; children: Abigail Brett Miller, Victoria Brett. BA cum laude, Bryn Mawr Coll., 1962. Researcher Nat. Geog. Soc., Washington, 1964-67; tchr. Hermansberg Mission, Northern Ter., Australia, 1967-68; spl. corr. Time mag., The Washington Post, Houston, 1969-74; writer, asst. mng. editor U.S. News & World Report, Washington, 1975-86; health editor The Washington Post, 1986-00, columnist Second Opinion, 2000—. Author: Crazy Time: Surviving Divorce and Building a New Life, 1982, revised edit., 1992, My Time: Making the Most of the Rest of Your Life, 2004. Journalism fellow Harvard Sch. Pub. Health, 1980. Mem. Washington Press Club Found. (bd. mem. 1989—, pres. 1993-95). Home: 2600 Upton St NW Washington DC 20008-3826 Office: The Washington Post 1150 15th St NW Washington DC 20071-0002

TRAGESER, THERESA HELEN, project manager; b. Kettering, Ohio, Sept. 5, 1963; d. James Henry and Judith Theresa (Schrein) T. Word processor Mooney-Lettieri, San Diego, 1983-85; adminstrv. asst. Jerde Partnership, San Diego, 1985-87; asst. project mgr. Del Mar Partnership, Del Mar, Calif., 1987-89; project coord. Collins Gen. Contractors, San Diego, 1989-90; dir. of ops. JK Palmer Cons., San Marcos, Calif., 1990-92; project mgr. Coded Communications, Carlsbad, Calif., 1992-95; sr. project mgr. U.S. Pub. Technologies, San Diego, 1995-97, Coded Communications, Carlsbad, Calif., 1997—. Adminstrv. subcom. Orchids and Onions Design Awards, San Diego, 1985-89. Mem. Sports Car Club Am. (sec. San Diego region 1995-96). Democrat. Roman Catholic. Avocations: skiing, auto racing, fitness, fine wines, art and literature. Office: Coded Communications Corp 884 N Market St # 904 Wilmington DE 19801-3011

TRAINES, ROSE WUNDERBAUM, sculptor, educator; b. Monroeville, Ind., Sept. 13, 1928; d. Louis and Leah (Fogel) Wunderbaum; m. Robert Jacob Traines, June 25, 1949; children: Claudia Denise Traines Lang, Monica Rae Traines Martin. Student, Ind. State Tchr.'s Coll., 1946—48, Mich. State U., 1948—49; BS, Ctrl. Mich. U., 1951. Lectr. in field. One person shows include Ctrl. Mich. U., Mt. Pleasant, 1964, Alma Artmobile, Mich., 1972, Ctrl. Mich. Homecoming, Mount Pleasant, Mich., 1982, Internat. Inst. Scrap Iron and Steel, Inc., Washington, 1983, Fontainebleau Hotel, Miami Beach, Fla., 1983, Elliott Mus. Art Gallery, Stuart, Fla., 1988, 98, Walt Kuhn Gallery, Cape Neddick, Maine, 1988, Coll. Club of Boston, 1990, Brass Latch Gallery, Montpelier, Ind., 1991, 96, 98, Vero Beach Ctr. for the Arts, Fla., 1992, Maritime and Yachting Mus., Stuart, Fla., 1997, Mid-Mich. Regional Med. Ctr., Healing Arts Gallery, Midland, 1997, Northwood Gallery, Midland, Mich., Commerca Bank Art Series, Palm Beach Gardens, 2002, Gallery Five, Tequesta, Fla., 2002, Michigan U. Park Libr. Gallery, 2002, Art Reach of Mid. Mich., Mt. Pleasant, 2002, Arthur Glick Jewish Cmty. Ctr., Indpls., Ind., 2004; two-person shows include Gallery One, North Palm Beach, 1973, Midland Ctr. for the Arts, Mich., 1976, Springfield Art Mart, Ohio, 1977, Hillel Student Ctr. Gallery-U. Cin., 1993, others; exhibited in group shows including Saginaw Mus. Art, Mich., 1965, Grand Rapids Mus., Mich., 1966, Kalamazoo Mus., Mich., 1967, Kellogg/Kresge Art Ctr., Mich. State U., East Lansing, 1967, Art Reach Mid-Mich., Mount Pleasant Mich., 1987, Salmagundi Club, N.Y.C., 1988, 91-92, 96, Copley Soc., Boston, 1990, 95, Allied Artists of Am., Inc., N.Y.C., 1995-96, Self Family Arts Ctr., Hilton Head Island, S.C., 1996-97, Palm Beach Gardens Fla. City Hall, 2003, Plam Beach Gardens Cmty. Ctr., 2003, others; represented in permanent collections at Dow-Corning Corp. Collection, Midland Ctr. for the Arts, Elliott Mus., Stuart, Fla., Walt Kuhn Gallery, Maine, Norman Cousins, Tom Keating, Donny Mersee, Alden Dows, Carl Gerstackers, Coll. Club Boston, Pullen Elem. Sch., Isabella Bank and Trust Co., Ctrl. Mich. U., Blake Libr, Stuart, Fla., La Belle Mgmt. Corp., Morey Bandit Industries, Mich., Ctrl. Mich. Cmty. Hosp., Northwood U., The Vets. Meml. Libr., Brass Latch Gallery, Northville (Mich.) Pub. Libr, others, also pvt. collections. Tchr. Jewish Sunday Sch., Mt. Pleasant, 1955-70; officer Child and Youth Study Clubs, Mt. Pleasant, 1963-73; mem. City Recreation Commn., Mt. Pleasant, 1963-73, Area Health Planning Coun., Mt. Pleasant, 1974-80; pres., vol. Hosp. Aux. Med. Care, Red Cross Blood Bank, United Fund Cancer Dr., Mt. Pleasant, 1960-80; storyteller pub. libr., Mt. Pleasant, 1957-79. Recipient Northwood U. Artist award, Midland Ctr. for Arts, Mich., 2002. Mem.: Brass Latch Gallery, Art Reach of Mid-Mich., Hilton Head Art League S.C. (Lifetime of Creative Excellence award 1998), Copley Soc. Boston (signature mem.), Allied Artists of Am. (Mems. award of merit 1996, Raymond H. Brumer Meml. award 1999), Nat. Mus. of Women in Arts (charter), Salmagundi Club (Philip Isenberg award 1993, Pamela Singleton award 1997, Elliot Liskin Meml. award 1998, Anonymous award 1998, Peters Sculpture Materials award 2001, Alphaeus P. Cole Meml. award 2001, Mems. Meml. award 2003). Jewish. Avocations: lecturing, community work, tennis, presenting humorous programs, drums. Home: 1217 North Dr Mount Pleasant MI 48858-3226

TRAMMELL, JEAN EHRHART, real estate agent, secondary school educator; b. Newark, N.J., July 21, 1952; d. Dale K. and Jean R. (Carter) Erhart; m. Thomas B. Trammell; children: Thomas, Thor, Arthur, Tristan. Assoc. in Theatre Arts, Manatee C.C., 1973; BA in Theatre and Comm. Arts, U. West. Fla., 1975. Cert. tchr. K-14 Fla., lic. real estate agt. Fla. Pres. The Venice Company/Comml. Properties Downtown Venice. Pres. Erhart Family Found., Venice, 1997—; bd. dirs., chmn. mktg. com., mem. fundraising and steering coms., v.p. bd. dirs. Venice Area Beatification, Inc., 2001—03; past mem. Econ. Devel. Adv. Bd., Airport Master Plan Rev. Com. City of Venice; mem. Venice Comty. Ctr. Rev. Com., 2000—01, City Tax Oversight Com., Venice, 2000—. Mem., past pres. Friends of Venice Libr.; sec., 2d v.p. of arts and edn., dir. Stage II and Theatre Camp, guest artistic dir. Venice Little Theatre, pres. bd. dirs., 2000—; numerous offices including past pres., bd. drs. Venice MainStreet, Inc., chmn. mktg. com., 2002—03; v.p., guest instr. and dir. P.J. Prodns. Children's Theatre, Venice, 1992—, founding dir., guest artistic dir., 1987—2001; mem. jury Arts in Pub. Places, Venice, 2000—02; chmn. strengthening parenting com. The Substance Abuse Prevention Coalition of Sarasota County, Inc., 2001—03; past. bd. dirs. 20/20 Steering and Visioning Bd., Venice; Arts and Culture Alliance, 1998—. Named Woman of Impact, Sarasota County Commn. on Status of Women, 1997; named to Venice Little Theatre Vol. Hall of Fame; recipient Pres. award, Venice (Fla.) Little Theatre, 1985—86, Pillar of Our Comty. award, City of Venice, Nat. Leadership award, Nat. Rep. Congl. Com., 2001, Bus. Person of Yr., 2003, and many other awards. Mem.: Quota Internat. of Venice Area (charter pres. 1995—97, treas. and publicist 1997—99, dist.(27) sec.-treas. 1999, v.p. (27) 2001, lt. gov. (27) 2000—02, gov. (27) 2002—04), Venice Area C. of C. (bd. dirs. 1995—2001, past chmn. several coms., past task force project dir. Interlocal Peforming Arts Ctr. Study, Marie Kaufman Pres. award 1998), Venice Area Historic Soc. (pres. 1999—2001, past pres. 2001—02, chmn. hist. plaque com. 2000—03), Fla. Theatre Conf. (life), Venice Rotary Club (Doc Matson award 2003). Office: The Venice Co 101 W Venice Ave Venice FL 34285

TRAMPUSCH, CHRISTINE ANN, music educator; b. Menomonee Falls, Wis., Apr. 4, 1977; d. Joseph and Susan Gertrude Trampusch. MusB, Carroll Coll., Waukesha, Wis., 1996—2000. Cert. Music Educator Wis., 2000. Diet clk. Cmty. Meml. Hosp., Menomonee Falls, Wis., 1993; instrumental music tchr. Hartford Jt.#1 Sch. Dist., Hartford, Wis., 2000—. Mem.: MENC (Music Educators Nat. Conf.). Personal E-mail: ct2456@aol.com.

TRAN, NGUYET T. accountant; b. Hanoi, Vietnam, Sept. 23, 1930; came to U.S., 1964; d. Huong Van and Chin Thi Tran; divorced; 1 child, Minh C. Nguyen. BSBA, San Francisco State U., 1980; MBA, U. Phoenix, 1987. Lang. tchr. U.S. Dept. Def., Presidio of Monterey, Calif., 1966-71; bookkeeper Nathan B. Siegel, CPA, San Francisco, 1971-76; sr. acct. Nat. Med. Enterprises, San Francisco/San Rafael, Calif., 1976-80; staff acct. Hillhaven Inc., Tacoma, 1980-93; acct., bus. mgr. Guardian Med. Hill Rehab. Ctr., Oakland, Calif., 1993—, dir. adminstrv. svcs., acct., 1998—. Sec. to ambassador Vietnam Mission to UN, N.Y.C., 1964-66; press and info. sec. govt. Ministry of Fgn. Affairs, Saigon, Vietnam, 1956-64. Mem. NAFE, AARP, Nat. Notary Assn., Smithsonian Inst. (assoc.), Am. Cancer Soc. Republican. Buddhist. Avocations: reading, gardening, knitting. Home: 2 Davenport Hercules CA 94547-3626 Office: Amer Baptist Homes of the West Piedmont Gardens 110 41st St Oakland CA 94611-5250

TRANSOU, LYNDA LOU, advertising art administrator; b. Atlanta, Dec. 11, 1949; d. Lewis Cole Transou and Ann Lynette (Taylor) Putnam; m. Lue Gregg Loso, Oct. 25, 1991. BFA cum laude, U. Tex., 1971. Art dir. The Pitluk Group, San Antonio, 1971, Campbell, McQuien & Lawson, Dallas, 1973-74, Bozell & Jacobs, Dallas, 1974-75; art dir., ptnr. The Assocs., Dallas, 1975-77; art dir. Belo Broadcasting, Dallas, 1977-80; creative dir., v.p. Allday & Assocs., Dallas, 1980-85; owner Lynda Transou Advt. & Design, 1986—. Recipient Merit award, N.Y. Art Dirs. Show, 1980, Gold award, Dallas Ad League, 1980, Silver award, 1980, 1981, 1982, 2 Merit awards, Houston Art Dirs. Club, 1978, Dallas Ad League, 1986, Merit award, Broadcast Designers Assn., 1980, Merit awards, Dallas Ad League, 1978, 1987, Silver award, Houston Art Dirs. Show, 1982, Gold award, Tex. Pub. Rels. Assn., 1985, N.Y. One Show, 1982, Creativity awrd, Art Direction mag., 1986, Print award, Regional Design Annual, 1988, 2 Gold Adrian awards, 1997, Katy award, Dallas Press Club, 2001. Mem. Am. Inst. Graphic Arts, Dallas Soc. Visual Comm. (Bronze award 1980, Merit award 1978-86), Delta Gamma (historian 1969-70).

TRAPP, MARY JANE, lawyer; b. Columbus, Ohio, July 6, 1956; AB cum laude, Mount Holyoke Coll., 1978; JD, Case Western Reserve U., 1981. Bar: Ohio 1981, U.S. Supreme Ct. 1987. Ptnr. Apicella and Trapp, Cleve. Commr. Supreme Ct. Ohio Bd. Commrs. on Unauthorized Practice of Law, 1986—89; mem. Supreme Ct. Rules adv. com., 1997—2002. Fellow: Ohio State Bar Found., Am. Bar Found.; mem.: Cleve. Bar Assn. (trustee 1995—98), Cuyahoga County Bar Assn. (trustee 1986—93, 1999—), Ohio Acad. Trial Lawyers, Ohio State Bar Assn. (pres. 2001—02), ABA. Office: Apicella and Trapp 1200 Penton Media Bldg 1300 E 9th St Cleveland OH 44114-1503

TRAUDT, MARY B. elementary school educator; b. Chgo., Jan. 1, 1930; d. Lloyd Andrews Haldeman and Adele Eleanor (MacKinnon) Haldeman-Oliver; m. Eugene Peter Traudt, Dec. 6, 1952 (dec.); 1 child, Victoria Jean. BS, Cen. Mich. U., 1951; MA, Roosevelt U., 1978; postgrad., U. Ill., 1982. Asst. editor Commerce Clearing House, Chgo., 1951-53; tchr. Cleve. Elem. Sch., 1954-56, Chgo. Sch. System, 1956-57, Community Consolidated # 54, Hoffman Estates, Ill., 1957-64, Avoca Elem. Sch., Wilmette, Ill., 1964—; ret., 1995. Recipient Computer award Apple Computer Co. Mem. NEA (life), Ill. Assn. of Ret. Tchrs. (life), North Shore Assn. of Ret. Tchrs. (life), Avoca Edn. Assn. (v.p. 1986-91), Alpha Psi Omega. Presbyterian. Avocations: reading, sewing, music, travel, gardening. Home: 512 N McClurg Ct #2201 Chicago IL 60611-5357

TRAUGER, ALETA ARTHUR, judge; BA in English magna cum laude, Cornell Coll., Iowa, 1968; MAT, Vanderbilt U., 1972, JD, 1976. Tchr., Tenn., Eng., 1970-73; assoc., law clk. Barrett, Brandt & Barrett, P.C., Nashville, 1974-77; asst. U.S. atty., first asst., chief of criminal divsn. Mid. Dist. Tenn., 1977-82, No. Dist. Ill., 1979-80; assoc. Hollins, Wagster & Yarbrough, P.C., Nashville, 1983-84; legal counsel Coll. of Charleston, S.C., 1984-85; counsel, ptnr. Wyatt, Tarrant, Combs, Gilbert & Milom, Nashville, 1985-91; judge Tenn. Ct. of the Judiciary, 1987-93; chief of staff Mayor's Office, Nashville, 1991-92; bankruptcy judge U.S. Bankruptcy Ct. (mid. dist.) Tenn., Nashville, 1993-98; dist. judge U.S. Dist. Ct. (mid. dist.) Tenn., Nashville, 1998—. Mem. hearing panel bd. profl. responsibility Tenn. Supreme Ct., 1983-84, mem. adv. com. on rules of civil and appellate procedure, 1989-96; lectr. Vanderbilt U. Sch. Law, 1986-88, mem. Law Sch. alumni bd., 1989-92; master of bench Harry Phillips Am. Inn of Ct., 1990-94; mem. Internat. Women's Forum, 1993—, v.p. Tenn. chpt., 1996-97; mem. Nat. Conf. Bankruptcy Judges, 1994-98, chmn. ethics com., 1994-98; trustee Cornell Coll., 1998—. Bd. dirs. Nashville Inst. for Arts, 1992-99, Miriam's Promise (adoption agy.), 1995-98, Renewal House, 1996-98. Fellow: Nashville Bar Found., Tenn. Bar Found. (life), Am. Bar Found. (life); mem.: FBA (v.p. 1983—84, 1985—86), ABA, Fed. Judges Assn., Nat. Assn. Women Judges (liaison to ABA commn. on the status of women in the profession 2000—01), Tenn. Lawyers Assn. for Women (v.p. 1988—89, pres. 1989—90, bd. dirs. 1990—91), Lawyers Assn. for Women (pres. 1982—83, bd. dirs. 1983—84, 1986—88), Nashville Bar Assn. (bd. dirs. 1984, 1989—91). Office: 825 US Courthouse 801 Broadway Nashville TN 37203-3816 Office Phone: 615-736-7143.

TRAUGOTT, ELIZABETH CLOSS, linguist, educator, researcher; b. Bristol, Eng., Apr. 9, 1939; d. August and Hannah M. M. (Priebsch) Closs; m. John L. Traugott, Sept. 26, 1967; 1 child, Isabel. BA in English, Oxford U., Eng., 1960; PhD in English lang., U. Calif., Berkeley, 1964. Asst. prof. English U. Calif., Berkeley, 1964-70; lectr. U. East Africa, Tanzania, 1965-66, U. York, Eng., 1966-67; lectr., then assoc. prof. linguistics and English Stanford (Calif.) U., 1970-77, prof., 1977—2003, chmn. linguistics dept., 1980-85, vice provost, dean grad. studies, 1985-91, mem. grad. record examinations bd., 1989-93, mem. test of English as a fgn. lang. bd., 1990—92, chmn. test of English as a fgn. lang. bd., 1991—92. Mem. higher edn. funding coun. Eng. Assessment Panel, 1996, 2001. Author: (book) A History of English Syntax, 1972; author: (with Mary Pratt) Linguistics for Students of Literature, 1980; author: (with Paul Hopper) Grammaticalization, 1993, rev. edit., 2003; author: (with Richard Dasher) Regularity in Semantic Change, 2002; editor (with ter Meulen, Rielly, Ferguson): On Conditionals, 1986; editor: (with Heine) Approaches to Grammaticalization, 2 vols., 1991; series co-editor: Topics in English Linguistics; contbr. articles to profl. jours. Am. Coun. Learned Socs. fellow, 1975—76, Guggenheim fellow, 1983—84, Ctr. Advanced Study Behavioral Scis. fellow, 1983—84. Fellow: AAAS; mem.: AAUW, AAUP, MLA, Internat. Pragmatics Assn. (bd. dirs. 2000—), Internat. Soc. Hist. Linguistic (pres. 1979—81), Linguistic Soc. Am. (pres. 1987, sec.-treas. 1994—98). Office: Stanford Univ Dept Linguistics Bldg 460 Stanford CA 94305-2150 Business E-Mail: traugott@stanford.edu.

TRAUTHWEIN, CHRISTINA, editor-in-chief; Asst. editor Archtl. Lighting Mag., 1989, editor-in-chief. Mem.: IESNA (mem. N.Y. Designer's Lighting Forum), IALD (mem. press affiliate, co-chair awards com.). Office: 770 Broadway New York NY 10003

TRAUTMAN, ALTA LOUISE, nurse, funeral director, writer; b. McKeesport, Pa., Oct. 30, 1954; d. Ernest Bernhardt and Eleanor Jeannette (Runge) Trautman. AAS in Nursing, Cmty. Coll. Allegheny County, West Mifflin, Pa., 1974; Diploma Grad. Funeral Dir., Pitts. Inst. Mortuary Sci., 1989. RN Pa.; lic. funeral dir. Pa. Staff nurse U. Pitts. Med. Ctr., McKeesport, 1974-80, emergency room nurse, 1981-2001; flight nurse Allegheny Gen. Hosp., Pitts., 1980-81; arranger, embalmer D.J. Heatherington Funeral Home, 1990-91; funeral dir. Teichart-Gracan Funeral Home, 1999; quality assurance and process improvement coord. Three Rivers Family Hospice, White Oak, Pa., 2000—01; staff nurse, emergency dept. and indsl. nursing Nurse Finders, 2001—03; asst. recovery of flight 93 Shanksville, Pa., 2001; infusion specialist Integrated Health Care Advantage, North Huntington, Pa., 2002—; emergency dept. nurse Jefferson Regional Med. Ctr., 2003. Cons. in emergency and forensic nursing. Mem.: Am. Assn. of Legal Nurse Consultants. Lutheran. Avocations: cooking, needlecrafts, altar designs. E-mail: rnfd@libcom.com.

TRAVER, JANICE WEYGANDT, horse breeder; b. Lakewood, Ohio, Oct. 3, 1926; d. Ross Shannon and May Eloise (Fritz) Weygandt; m. Dolph Rodgers Traver II, Nov. 27, 1956; 1 child, Patrice Grandy; stepchildren: Dolph III (dec.), Pamela Robbins, Ninon Ruscher, Francine Johnson, Melinda Leaver, Celeste Correia. Student, Miami U., Oxford, Ohio, 1945-46, Coll. of Wooster, 1945-47, I.A.S., 1951-52. Accts. payable/advt. U.S. Fabricators, Wooster, Ohio, 1948-49, clk. Sel. Svc. System, Wooster, Ohio, 1950-52; asst. bookkeeper John B. Kelly, Inc., N.Y.C., 1952-54; acct. Meyers Label Co., Inc., N.Y.C., 1954-55; chief acct. Taylor Furniture Co., New Orleans, 1956-58; planning [illegible] Warrenton, Va., 1977-87; horse breeder Bealeton, Va., 1966—. Author, editor (mag.) The Spanish Bit, 1974-79. Bd. dirs. Fauquier Hosp. Aux., co-chair vols., 1967—; mem. Concerned Citizens Fauquier County, Warrenton, 1969—, bd. dirs., v.p.; pres. So. Fauquier Assn., Bealeton, 1985-95; vice chmn., chmn. Fauquier County Planning Commn., 1978-82. Mem. NOW, Am. Andalusian Horse Assn. (pres. 1973-83), Am. Cancer Soc. (pres. 1973-75), Am. Heart Assn. (bd. dirs. 1984-90), Sierra Club, Common Cause, Habitat Humanity, World Wildlife Fund, Amnesty Internat. Democrat. Presbyterian. Avocations: gardening, painting, zoology, politics, needlework. Home: PO Box 1511 Belton TX 76513-5511

TRAVERIA, BETH M. mental health counselor; b. Canton, Ohio, Sept. 21, 1954; d. Carl Halter and Theresa (Manning) Anderson; m. Kenneth V. Draime, Dec. 7, 1974; children: Rory, Aaron, Andrew; m. Roy J. Traveria, May 7, 1992. BS in Med. Tech., Akron U., 1975; MS in Mental Health Counseling, St. Thomas U., Miami, Fla., 1995; postgrad., Walsh U., North Canton, Ohio, 1997. Med. technologist Aultman & Timken Mercy & Massillon Hosps., Massillon and Canton, Ohio, 1974-92; mental health counselor Cath. Cmty. Svcs. of Stark County, Canton, 1995—. Mem. ACA, Am. Soc. Clin. Pathologists. Office: Catholic Community Svcs Stark County 625 Cleveland Ave NW Canton OH 44702-1805

TRAVIS, TRACY LEIGH, emergency physician; b. Lynchburg, Va., Aug. 27, 1957; d. Charles C. Jr. and Mildred (Lindsay) T.; m. David Stephens; children: Jennifer Koecke, Travis Stephens. BS in Biology, Lynchburg Coll., 1979; MD, Eastern Va. Med. Sch., 1982. Diplomat Am. Bd. Emergency Medicine. Resident Butterworth Hosp., Grand Rapids, Mich., 1987; emergency physician Mary Washington Hosp., Fredericksburg, Va., 1988-93, ExpressCare, Stafford, Va., 1992-96, Inova Emergency Care, Fairfax, Va., 1996—, Inova Fairfax Hosp., 1998—. Fellow Am. Coll. Emergency Physicians; mem. Phi Kappa Phi. Home: 10856 Meadow Pond Ln Oakton VA 22124-1446 Office: Emergency Physicians No Va Ltd 3300 Gallows Rd Falls Church VA 22042-3307

TRAXLER, EVA MARIA, marketing professional; b. Phorzheim, Germany, June 1, 1955; d. Wayne Delmar and Ruth Lydia (Mischak) Frasure; m. Richard John Traxler, Mar. 25, 1986. BS, U. Minn., 1980; MBA, U. St. Thomas, 1987. Ops. control planner Gen. Mills, Mpls., 1981; asst. prodn. planner Pillsbury, Mpls., 1982-87, planning specialist, 1987-88; new products planner Land O'Lakes, Mpls., 1988-89, mktg. asst., 1989-90; sr. product mgr., mgr. mdse. svcs. Newell/Rubbermaid, St. Paul, 1990-94; mktg. mgr. Jostens, Mpls., 1995-96; brand mgr. Metacom, 1996-98; mgr. sml. bus. mktg. Am. Express, 1998—, advice mgr., 2001—. Big sister Big Bros./Big Sisters, St. Paul, 1982-89, bd. mem., 1986-92, Courage Ctr., 1998—. Avocations: fitness, travel, old house renovation. E-mail: evatraxler@hotmail.com.

TRAYLOR, ANGELIKA, stained glass artist; b. Munich, Bavaria, Germany, Aug. 24, 1942; Came to U.S., 1959; d. Walther Artur Ferdinand and Berta Kreszentia (Boeck) Klau; m. Lindsay Montgomery Donaldson, June 10, 1959 (div. 1970); 1 child, Cameron Maria Greta; m. Samuel William Traylor III, June 12, 1970. Student, Pvt. Handelsschule Morawetz Jr. Coll., Munich, 1958. Freelance artist, 1980—. Works featured in profl. jours. including the Daylily Jour., 1987, Design Jour., South Korea, 1989, The Traveler's Guide to American Crafts, 1990, Florida Mag., 1991, Florida Today, 1993, Adventures in Art, vol. 3, 1993, Melbourne Times, 1994, The Orbiter, 1996, The Glass Collector's Digest, 1996, (TV appearances) Focus on History, 1993, Focus, 1998, Space Coast Press, 1999, Weekend Decorating Projects - Women's Day, 1999, Pen Women, 1999, Stained Glass for the First Time, 2000, Creative Stained Glass; represented in permanent collections White House Christmas Ornament Collection, 1993, 97, Holmes Regional Med. Ctr., Melbourne, Fla., other pvt. and corp. collections. Recipient Fragile Art award Glass Art mag., 1982, 1st Yr. Exhibitor award Stained Glass Assn. Am., 1984, 2d pl. Non-figurative Composition award Vitraux des USA, 1985, Best of Show Stained Glass Assn. Am., 1989, 3d pl., 1989, Merit award George Plimpton All-Star Space Coast Art Open, 1994; named Hist. Woman of Brevard, Brevard Cultural Alliance, 1991, one of 200 Best Am. Craftsmen Early Am. Life mag., 1994, 95, 97, 98, 2000. Home and Office: 100 Poinciana Dr Indian Harbor Beach FL 32937-4437

TRAYLOR, GAYLA S. music educator, composer; d. Ronald and Ann Howland; m. David Traylor, June 26, 1982; children: Andrew Ryan, Daniel Mckenna. B in elem. music edn., Whitworth Coll., 1981; MA in Tchg. and Learning, Nova Southeastern U., 2002. Cert. profl. acad. Wash., 1981, Hawaii, 1990. Pvt. piano instr., Hawaii, 1975—; music educator Kamehameha Elem. Sch., Honolulu, 1983—. Clinician Hawaii Chpt. of Suzuki Violin Instrn., 1987—88. Music arranger, composer:. Mem.: Nat. Piano Tchrs. Guild, Hawaii Piano Tchrs. Assn., Hawaii Music Tchrs. Assn. (state chmn.), Hawaii Music Educators Assn. (rec. sec., clinician 2003), Hawaii Orff-Schulwerk Assn. (members-at-large 2003). Conservative-R. Protestant. Avocations: reading, tennis, cooking.

TREACY, SANDRA JOANNE PRATT, artist, educator; b. New Haven, Aug. 5, 1934; d. Willis Hadley Jr. and Gladys May (Gell) P.; m. Gillette van Nuyse, Aug. 27, 1955; 1 child, Jonathan Todd. BFA, R.I. Sch. Design, 1956; student, William Paterson Coll., 1973-74. Cert. elem. and secondary tchr., N.J. Tchr. art and music Pkwy. Christian Ch., Ft. Lauderdale, Fla., 1964-66; developer Pequannock Twp. Bd. of Edn., Pompton Plains, N.J., 1970-72, tchr. art, 1972-76; vol. art tchr. Person County Bd. of Edn., Roxboro, N.C., 1978-80, tchr. art, 1980-91, So. Jr. High Sch., Roxboro, 1989-91, Woodland Elem. Sch., Roxboro, 1989-93; tchr. Helena Elem. Sch., Timberlake, N.C., 1991-93. Tchr. elem. art Bethel Hill Sch., Roxboro, 1974-79, vol. art tchr., 1979-80; tchr. basic art, vol. all elem. schs. Person County, Roxboro, 1977-80; tchr. arts and crafts, summers 1981-882; tchr. art home sch. So. Mid. Sch., 1993—, Person H.S., 1993-94. Artist, illustrator. Mem. Roxboro EMTs, 1979-81; bd. dirs. Person County Arts Coun., 1980--81, 93-95, pres., 1981-82; piano and organ choir accompanist Concord United Meth. Ch., 1981—; leader Morgan Trotters, 1992-94, asst. dir., 1993-96, bd. dirs.; coach, horseback riding for handicapped. Mem. NEA, Nat. Mus. of Women in the Arts (continuing charter), Smithsonian Assocs., N.C. Assn. Arts Edn., N.C. Assn. Educators, N.C. Art Soc. Mus. of Art, Internat. Platform Assn., Womans Club (tchr. Pompton Plains chpt. 1974-79), Person County Saddle Club (rec. sec. 1981-84), Puddingston Pony Club (dist. sec. 1974-75 Montville Twp. chpt.), Roxboro Garden Club (continuing, commr. 1980-82, pres. 1982-84, 87—, sec. 1993-94, 97-98, v.p. 1993-95, pres. 1995—), Roxboro Woman's Club (arts dept.). Republican. Avocations: horseback riding, swimming, sailing, reading, playing piano and organ. Home: 1345 Kelly Brewer Rd Leasburg NC 27291-9622 Office Phone: 336-599-6995 ext. 404.

TREADWAY, JESSICA, writer, educator; b. Albany, N.Y., Mar. 21, 1961; d. Ralph Stephen and Ann Olivia (Olson) T. BA, SUNY, Albany, 1982; MA, Boston U., 1985. Lectr. Ext. Sch. Harvard U., Cambridge, Mass., 1994-98; lectr. Tufts U., Medford, Mass., 1994-98; dir. MFA program, asst. prof. Emerson Coll., Boston, 1998—. Author: Absent Without Leave, 1993 (John C. Zacharias award 1993). Fellow Radcliffe Coll., 1993, Mass. Cultural Coun., 1996, NEA, 1998. Mem. AAUW, PEN/New Eng. (coun. 1998—). Office: Emerson Coll 120 Boylston St Boston MA 02116-4624 Home: 16 Jersey Ln Manchester MA 01944-1429

TREADWAY, SANDRA GIOIA, library director; b. Jersey City, N.J., Jan. 15, 1950; d. Robert Peter and Essey Grace (Graham) Gioia; m. John David Treadway, Sept. 4, 1976 (div. 2003); 1 child, Robyn Grace. BA in History, Manhattanville Coll., 1971; MA in History, U. Va., 1972, PhD in History, 1978. Instr. history Va. Polytech Inst. & State U., Blacksburg, 1976-78; editor Va. State Libr., Richmond, 1978-91, dir. pubs., 1991-96; deputy dir. [illegible], 1996—. Author: Women of Mark, 1995; co-author: The Common Wealth: Treasures from the Collections of the Library of Virginia, 1997; co-editor: Dictionary of Virginia Biography, vol. 1, 1999, vol. 2, 2001. Mdm. bd. St. Mary Sch., Richmond, 1988-96. Mem. Am. Hist. Assn., Orgn. Am. historians, So. Historical Assn., So. Assn. Women Historians (pres. 2002), Va. Hist. Soc., Va. Libr. Assn., Serra Internat. (bd. dirs. 1985—). Roman Catholic. Avocations: reading, travel. Home: 8201 Gaylord Rd Richmond VA 23229-4121 Office: Libr LVa 800 E Broad St Richmond VA 23219-1905

TREADWELL-RUBIN, PAMELA A. lawyer; b. Arlington, Tex., Dec. 15, 1960; BA in Polit. Sci., U. Ariz., 1982, JD, 1985. Bar: Ariz. 1985. Prosecutor, Tucson City, 1985—87; dep. atty. Pima County, 1987—93; atty. Moeller, Gage & Treadwell-Rubin, PC, Tucson. Mem. Ariz. Juvenile Justice Adv. Coun., 1993—96. Fellow: Ariz. Bar Found. (bd. dirs. 1991—94, chair victims' rights pro bono panel 1992—93); mem.: Pima County Bar Assn. (bd. dirs. 1989—90, pres. Young Lawyers divsn. 1989—90, bd. dirs. 1996—), Ariz. Women Lawyers Assn., State Bar Ariz. (bd. govs. 1994—95, pres. Young Lawyers divns. 1994—95, cert. specialist worker's compensation 1995—, bd. govs. 1996—, pres. 2003—, Outstanding Young Lawyer 1997). Office: Moeller Gage and Treadwell-Rubin 2606 E 10th St Tucson AZ 85716

TREANOR, BETTY MCKEE, interior design educator; b. Tooele, Utah, Oct. 2, 1938; d. Oscar Hart and Mable Genevieve (Smith) McK.; m. James Treanor, Dec. 27, 1978. BA, Brigham Young U., 1966; MA, Iowa State U., 1970. Instr. Brigham Young U., Provo, Utah, 1966-68; grad. teaching asst. Iowa State U., Ames, 1968-70, instr. Ariz. State U., Tempe, 1972-74; asst. prof. U. Tex., Austin, 1974-80; assoc. prof. S.W. Tex. State U., San Marcos, 1980—, coord. interior design program, 1999—2002. Freelance designer, artist craftsman, 1972—; comml. interior designer, Phoenix, 1970-72; interior design program coord., S.W. Tex. State U., 1999-2002. Editor: Comprehensive Bibliography for Interior Design, 1984, 87. Fellow Interior Design Educators Coun. (southwest regional chair 1977-88), Internat. Interior Design Assn., Am. Soc. Interior Designers, Found. for Interior Design Edn. Rsch. (chmn. bd. 1990, 92, trustee 1986-94, accreditation com. 1979-86), Irish Georgian Soc., Tex. Assn. for Interior Design (edn. rep. 1985-90). Home: 10806B Pinehurst Dr Austin TX 78747-1621 Office: SW Tex State U FCS 601 University Dr San Marcos TX 78666-4685

TREASURE-TERRELL, SUZANNE MARIE, marketing and sales professional, writer, poet, lyricist; b. Chgo., Aug. 18, 1963; d. James Allen Olejarz and Christeen Joy Lindblom; adopted by James DuWayne and Mary Frances (Urban) T.; m. Kenneth Dwayne Terrell, Apr. 1, 2000. Student part time, Dallas Bapt. U., 1988-99. Toll assistance operator Southwestern Bell Tel./AT&T, Dallas, 1982-88; bus. office clk. Southwestern Bell Tel., Dallas, 1988-93, drafting clk., 1993-94, svc. rep., 1994-2000; ret., 2000; customer svc. rep. Blockbuster Video, Dallas, 1994-95; sales rep. Up in Smoke Tobacco Shop, Dallas, 1995-96; sec. bd. Irving Writers Connection, 1994. Telefundraiser Stephen Dunn & Assoc., Myerson Symphony Ctr., Dallas, 1992-93; mem. V.I.P. security staff Tex. Rangers Ballpk., Arlington, 1993-94; job steward Comm. Workers of Am., Dallas, 1982-2000, ret. mem., 2000—; cons., advisor participative mgmt. and employee interactive com., Dallas, 1991-93; owner Treasured Thoughts; co-owner The Revolving Door Inn. Contbr. poetry to Amherst Soc., Am. Poetry Ann. (Poetic Achievement award 1994); contbr. articles to newsletters, Alzheimer's Assn., Tex. Scottish Rite Hosp. for Children, Irving Writers Connection, SBC PM/EI Com.; lyricist for Fatal Fate. Fundraiser United Way, Dallas, 1992-93; cert. ct. appointed advocate Dallas CASA, 1992—; cert. tel. counselor Contact 214, Dallas, 1995-97; press ops. rep. World Cup USA 94, Dallas. Recipient award of merit World of Poetry, Sacramento, 1987, 91, Editor's Choice award The Nat. Libr. of Poetry, Owings Mills, Md., 1998, Commendation Letter Pres. Bill Clinton for positive contbn. and dedication to volunteerism in local cmty., Dallas, 1993; named Famous Poet for 1998, 99, 2003, Famous Poets Soc., Hollywood, Calif., Talent, OR, 1998, 99, 2003; nominee Golden Rule award JC Penney, Dallas, 1993. Mem. Comm. Workers of Am. (job steward 1982-2000, CWA-COPE Platinum Quorum 1993-96, Outstanding Contbn. award 1994, CWA-COPE Triple Quorum 1996-97, Outstanding Contbn. award 1996, 99), Tel. Pioneers of Am. (life mem.), Irving Writers Connection (sec. bd. 1994), Allen Area Rep. Women's Club. Methodist. Avocations: writing poetry and short stories, arts and crafts, volunteering for children-oriented organizations, illness-related orgns. and nat. events. Home: 514 Bending Bough Dr Spring TX 77388-6102 also: PO Box 1171 Ozark MO 65721-1171

TREAT, SHARON ANGLIN, state legislator; b. Brattleboro, Vt., Jan. 30, 1956; d. Robert Sherman and Mary Lou (Strassburger) T. AB, Princeton U., 1978; JD cum laude, Georgetown U., 1982. Bar: Maine, N.J. Asst. dep. pub. adv. N.J. Dept. of the Pub. Adv., Trenton, 1982-85; assoc. atty. Ball, Livingston & Tykulsker, Newark, 1985-86; staff atty. Natural Resources Coun. Maine, Augusta, 1986-90; state rep. Maine State Legis., Augusta, 1991-96; mem. dist. 18 Maine Senate, Augusta, 1997—; pvt. practice Gardiner, Maine, 1991—. Leader Ctr. for Policy Alternatives, Washington, 1992—; house chair Human Resources Com., 1993-94, Judiciary Com., 1995-96; senate chair natural resources com., 1997—; mem. labor com. 1997—, mem. Adv. Commn. on radioactive Waste, 1997—. Bd. dirs. N.J. Environ. Lobby, Trenton, 1984-86, Maine People's Resource Ctr., Augusta, 1991—, N.E. Citizen Action Resource Ctr., Hartford, Conn., 1992—, Maine Assn. Conservation Commns., 1994—; co-founder, dir. Alliance, Portland, Maine, 1987; trustee Class of 1978 Found., White Plains, N.Y., 1988—; mem. adv. bd. Augusta Area Rape Crisis Ctr., 1992—; mem. adv. coun. Divsn. of Deafness, 1994—; mem. Natural Resources Coun. Maine, Maine Women's Lobby. Mem. Gardiner Libr. Assn., Rotary. Democrat. Office: PO Box 12 Gardiner ME 04345-0012 also: Maine State Senate 3 State House Sta Augusta ME 04333-0003

TREFTS, JOAN LANDENBERGER, retired educator, administrator; b. Pitts., Jan. 31, 1930; d. William Henry III and Eleanore (Campbell) Landenberger;m. Albert Sharpe Trefts Sr., June 20, 1952 (dec.); children: Dorothy, Albert Jr., William, Deborah, Elizabeth. AB, Western Coll. for Women, 1952; M, John Carroll U., 1982, M, 1984. Lic. and cert. home economist, cert. prin., N.Y., Ohio, supr., biol. sci., econs., voact. edn., pre-kindergarten edn. Summer sch. prin. John Adams H.S., Collinwood and South High, Cleve., 1972-95. Cons. Cleve. Partnership Program. Trustee Chautauqua Literacy and Sci. Cir., Presbyn. Assn. Chautauqua, NY. Named Tchr. of Yr., Cleve., 1994. Mem.: DAR (state officer 2000—), Ohio Vocat. Assn. (bd. dirs.), Am. Vocat. Assn. (nat. com.), Am. Home Econs. Assn., Presbyn. Assn. (trustee), Dames of Ct. of Honor (pres. gen. 2001—), Colonial Daus. of 17th Century (nat. officer), Daus. Am. Colonists (state officer), Nat. Officers Colonial Clergy (nat. officer, chancellor), Colonial Dames Am. (pres. chpt. 18, nat. officer ct. honor), U.S. Daus. of 1912, Colonial Dames of XVII Century, New Eng. Soc. of Western Res. (pres.), Clearwater Country Club, Cleve. Skating Club, Union Clubs. Republican. Presbyterian. Avocations: curling, rug hooking, needlepoint. Home: 20101 Malvern Rd Shaker Heights OH 44122-2825

TREGO, NANCY REMINE, not-for-profit fundraiser; b. Richmond, Va., Feb. 18, 1948; d. James Andrew and Miriam Franklin (Bruce) ReM.; m. Geoffrey Garrett Trego, Sept. 26, 1982 (div. 1995); children: James Neal, Garrett Douglas. BA in Govt., William and Mary, 1970. With U.S. Dept. Labor, Washington, 1970-73, Nat. Assn. Counties, Washington, 1973-82, dep. assoc. dir., 1978-82; policy analyst Nat. Commn. Employment Policy, Washington, 1983—87; grants mgr., dir. fund devel. & fin. Bon Secours-St. Mary's Health Care Found., Richmond, 1994—2000; devel. dir. Richmond (Va.) SPCA, 2000—01; prin., owner Trego and Assocs., LLC, Richmond, 2002—. Mem. Capital Area Pvt. Industry Coun., Richmond, 1994-2000; past pres. Children's Health Involving Parents, Richmond, Va.; presenter U. Richmond Inst. on Philanthropy, 2003-04. Mem. Healthy Families Task Force, Henrico County, 1995-98; vestry, jr. warden St. Matthew's Episcopal Ch. Mem. Richmond (Va.) Assn. Fundraising Profls. (bd. dir.), Va. PTA (life).

TREICHEL, DIXIE ANN, composer, sound designer, consultant; b. Oshkosh, Wis., Apr. 30, 1956; d. Leona and Carl Treichel. Student, U. Wis., Oshkosh, 1974—76, Vienna Internat. Music Centre, Austria, 1976—77; BMus in Composition, U. Ill., 1980; postgrad., U. Chgo., 1987—88. Ind. artistic cons., composer, sound designer, theater technician, tchr. Creative Collaborations, 1980—; founder, dir., composer Unique Sounds Ensemble, Mpls., 2000—. Producing cons., technician, condr. Phoenix Spring Ensemble, San Francisco, 1990—97; pres., festival dir. New Music Chgo., Chgo., 1986—87; co-founder, artistic dir. Diverse Arts Ensemble, Urbana, Milw., Chgo., 1979—86. Composer (musician): (interdisciplinary performance) Morphos, Internat. Exptl. Intermedia Festival, (exploratory music) Portal, Internat. Exptl. Intermedia Festival; composer: (string quartet) Pointed Quarks (Onyx String Quartet Competition Award, 1997); sound designer (theatrical sound design) Street Car Named Desire (Drama-Logue Award, 1996); prodr.: (interdisciplinary performance) Seeds (Producing Grant, 1980). Radio host KFAI, Fresh Fruit, Mpls., 1998—. Fellow Edn. Fellowship, U. of Chgo., 1987-1988. Mem.: New Music Chgo., Am. Composers Forum, Internat. Assn. Women in Music. Achievements include invention of experimental musical instruments. Avocations: swimming, bicycling, reading, writing poetry, philosophy.

TREJO, JOANN, medical researcher; b. Stockton, Calif., Jan. 23, 1964; BS, U. Calif., Davis, 1986; PhD, U. Calif., San Diego, 1992. Postdoctoral fellow Cardiovasc. Rsch. Inst., U. Calif., San Francisco, 1992—2000; asst. prof. pharmacology U. N.C., 2000—. Undergrad. rsch. asst. Lawrence Berkeley Lab. Divsn. Biology and Medicine, 1983—86; tchg. asst. dept. environ. toxicology U. Calif., Davis, 1986, dept. pharmacology, San Diego, 1988—91, dept. biology, 1989. Contbr. articles to profl. jours. Recipient Nat. Hispanic Scholarship Fund award, 1990—91, Minority Scientist Career Devel. award, Am. Heart Assn., 1995; fellow San Diego and Grad. Opportunity, 1986—88, Dissertation, Nat. Rsch. Coun. Ford Found., 1991—92, Pres.'s Postdoctoral, U. Calif., 1993—95; grantee Tng., NIH/NHLBI Cardiovasc. Rsch. Inst., 1992—93; scholar Katherine Larcara, 1982, Jack O'Keefe, 1982, Kiwanis Club Undergrad., 1982. Mem.: LWV, AAAS, Am. Soc. Cell Biology, Soc. Advancement of Chicanos and Native Americans in Sci. Home: 303 Lorraine St Carrboro NC 27510-1121 Office: UNC-Sch Medicine Dept Pharmacology 1106 Mary Ellen Jones Bldg Chapel Hill NC 27514

TREMAGLIO, MICHELLE T. merchant banker; b. Berea, Ohio, Sept. 10, 1973; BA, Baldwin Wallace, 1995, MBA, 2000. Br. mgr. Nat. City Bank, Cleveland, 1997—2003. Com. chair Twinsburg C. of C., 2003. Mem.: Nat. Assn. Female Execs., Alpha Phi.

TREMBLAY, GAIL ELIZABETH, art educator; b. Buffalo, N.Y., Dec. 15, 1945; d. Roland Gilbert and Leela Mae Tremblay. BA in Drama, U. N.H., 1967; MFA in English, U. Oreg., 1969. Lectr. Nathaniel Hawthorne Coll., Antrim, NH, 1969—70, U. N.H., Durham, NH, 1971, Keene State Coll., Keene, NH, 1971—77; asst. prof. U. Nebr., Omaha, 1977—80; mem. faculty The Evergreen State Coll., Olympia, Wash., 1981—. Author: Annex 21 #3 Talking to the Grandfathers, 1979, Indian Singing in 20th Century America, 1991, Indian Singing, 2000. Bd. dir. Women's Caucas for Art, N.Y.C., 1988—2000, pres. bd., 1999—2000; pres. bd. dir. Indian Youth Am., Sioux City, Iowa, 1980—; bd. dir. Wash. Commn. for Humanities, Seattle, 1998—2003. Recipient Alfred E. Richards Poetry prize, U. N.H., 1966, Kathe Kollowitz award, Seattle Women's Caucus for Art, 2000, Gov.'s Art award, Wash. State, 2001, Pres. award of achievement in the Arts, Nat. WCA, 1993. Mem.: Coll. Art Assn. Avocations: gardening, Scrabble, flower arranging. Office: The Evergreen State College SEM 3127 Olympia WA 98505

TREMBLAY, JOAN LOUISE, district manager; b. Peabody, Mass., Dec. 4, 1953; d. Robert A. and Elizabeth L. (Lyons) T.; m. Peter R. Linskey, Nov. 27, 1976 (div. 1985); 1 child, Kristin L. AS, North Shore C.C., 1973, AS, 1980. Cert. dangerous goods tng. Inventory control rep. Stop & Shop, Salem, Mass., 1969-79; customs inspector U.S. Customs, Boston, 1979-87; ops. mgr. Randy Internat., Boston, 1987-92; perishable sales Boston Bay Brokers, 1992-95; perishable mgr. Thyssen Haniel Logistics, Boston, 1995-99, dist. mgr., 1999—. Orientation leader North Shore C.C., Beverly, Mass., 1971-73, ad hoc screening com., 1971-73, program coun., 1971-73, v.p. student senate 1972-73, chmn. budget com. 1972-73, sec. bus. club, 1972-73; mem. Immaculate Conception Rockettes Drum & Bugle Corps, 1961-73; basketball coach Salem Youth, 1989; drill instr. Salem H.S. band, 1975-79; cheerleading coach Salem Pop Warner football, 1988-91. With USN, 1975-77. Recipient Gregory Venturo award NSCC, 1973. Mem. Air Cargo Club. Roman Catholic. Avocations: horseback riding, dance, bowling, gardening, golfing. Home: 132 Essex St Saugus MA 01906-4370 Office: Thyssen Haniel Logistics 135 Bremen St Boston MA 02128-1737

TRENHAILE, JENNIFER ANN, music educator; b. Albion, Nebr., Aug. 11, 1968; d. Paul Joseph and Marilyn Jo (Hellbusch) Schuele; m. William Dale Trenhaile, Aug. 12, 1989; children: Heather, Eathan, Emily, Sidney, Noah. BFA in Edn., Wayne State Coll., 1990. Tchr. Neligh (Nebr.)-Oakdale Sch., 1990—93, Pope John XXIII HS, Elgin, Nebr., 1996—98, St. John Bapt. Sch., Petersburg, Nebr., 1998—99, Emerson (Nebr.)-Hubbard Cmty. Sch., 2000—. Mem.: Nebr. Bandmasters Assn., Music Educators Nat. Conf., Emerson (Nebr.)-Hubbard Edn. Assn. (pub. rels. 2003). Avocations: piano, walking.

TRENKLER, TINA LOUISE, nuclear engineer; b. Poughkeepsie, N.Y., Nov. 11, 1964; d. Irene Elfrede Rockelmann Donahue. BS in Nuclear Engring., U. Cin., 1987; postgrad., U. Ariz., 1987-88, Ga. Inst. Tech., 1994-96; MBA, U. Wash., 2001. Engring. aide U.S. NRC, Washington, 1984-86; mgr. environ. health physics Foster Wheeler Environ., Bellevue, Wash., 1988-96; v.p. trading card games Wizards of the Coast, Renton, Wash., 1996—2003; founder, CEO, Verveline LLC, Seattle, 2003—; v.p. Kirner Cons., Olympia, Wash., 1996—. Spkr. in field. Vol. Chicken Soup Brigade, Seattle, 1990-97, Master Home Environmentalist Program, Seattle, 1996-2000; pres. Pike Lofts Condominium Assn., 2002—. Scholar Inst. Nuclear Power Ops., 1984. Mem. Health Physics Soc., Am. Nuclear Soc., Soc. for Risk Analysis, NOW. Office: Verveline LLC 1122 E Pike St # 840 Seattle WA 98122-3934

TRENSE, SHARON, state legislator; b. Nov. 23, 1939; m. Charles Trense; 2 children. Student, Northwestern U. Owner Sharons of Dunwoody; mem. Ga. Ho. of Reps., 1992—. Mem. edn., human rels. and aging coms., mem. state inst. and property coms. Republican. Methodist. Office: Ga Ho of Reps State Capitol Atlanta GA 30334 Home: 2296 Littlebrooke Dr Atlanta GA 30338-3154

TRENT, TIFFANY LEONE, English educator, writer, editor; b. Roanoke, Va., Aug. 9, 1973; d. Dennis Alvin and Maxine Vandervort Musselman; m. Jewel Andrew Trent, July 3, 1995. MA, Va. Tech, 1997; MFA, MS, U. Mont., 2002. Tech. writer/editor Energy Savers Unltd., Inc., Blacksburg, Va., 2000; editor-in-chief/sr. pubs. officer Kadoorie Farm and Botanic Garden, Hong Kong, 2000—01; tech. comm. editor Va. Bioinformatics Inst., Blacksburg, 2001—03; instr. English Va. Tech, Blacksburg, 2003—. Freelance editor/writer, Blacksburg, Va., 2000—03. Author: (literary nonfiction) Smashing the Tiger: Wildlife in Hong Kong (Goldfarb fellow, 2002), The House that Jack Built (AWP intro to jours. award, 1997). Facilitator Blacksburg Writer's Workshop, 2003. Mem.: Coun. Sci. Editors, Assn. Studies Lit. and Environ., Associated Writing Programs, Sigma Tau Delta. Avocations: writing, reading, learning about chinese culture. Office: English Dept Va Tech Shanks Hall 0112 Blacksburg VA 24061 E-mail: ttrent@vt.edu.

TREPPLER, IRENE ESTHER, retired state senator; b. St. Louis County, Mo., Oct. 13, 1926; d. Martin H. and Julia C. (Bender) Hagemann; student Meramec Community Coll., 1972; m. Walter J. Treppler, Aug. 18, 1950; children: John M., Steven A., Diane V. Anderson, Walter W. Payroll chief USAF Aero. Chart Plant, 1943-51; enumerator U.S. Census Bur., St. Louis, 1960, crew leader, 1970; mem. Mo. Ho. of Reps., Jefferson City, 1972-84; mem. Mo. Senate, Jefferson City, 1985-96; chmn. minority caucus, 1991-92. Active Gravois Twp. Rep. Club, Concord Twp. Rep. Club; alt. del. Rep. Nat. Conv., 1976, 84; mem. Mo. Adv. Coun. on Hist. Preservation, 1998—; gov. apptd. Mo. Adv. Coun. on Hist. Preservation, 1998—. Recipient Spirit of Enterprise award Mo. C. of C., 1992, appreciation award Mo. Med. Assn., Nat. Otto Nuttli Earthquake Hazard Mitigation award, 1993, Disting. Legislator award Cmty. Colls. Mo., 1995; named Concord Twp. Rep. of Yr., 1992. Mem. Nat. Order Women Legislators (rec. sec. 1981-82, pres. 1985), Nat. Fedn. Rep. Women. Mem. Evangelical Ch.

TRESCOTT, SARA LOU, water resources engineer; b. Frederick, Md., Nov. 17, 1954; d. Norton James and Mabel Elizabeth (Hall) T.; m. R. Jeffrey Franklin, Oct. 8, 1983. AA, Catonsville C.C., Balt., 1974; BA in Biol. Sci., U. Md., Balt., 1980. Sanitarian Md. Dept. Health & Mental Hygiene, Greenbelt, 1982; indsl. hygienist Md. Dept. Licensing & Regualtion, Balt., 1982-85; from water resources engr. to chief dredging div. Md. Dept. Natural Resources, Annapolis, 1985-92, chief navigation div. Stevensville, 1992-96, chief ops. & maintenance, 1996, dir. maintenance engring. ops., 1996—. Chair adv. bd. EEO, Annapolis, 1990-92; tech. com. Nat. Mgmt. Info. Systems, Balt., 1983. Contbr. articles to profl. jours. Mem. ASCE, County Engrs. Assn. Md. Democrat. Achievements include research in beneficial uses of dredged material; development of technology for hydrographic surveying, providing Md. with an improved waterway transportation network. Home: PO Box 22 Woodbine MD 21797-0022 Office: DNR 580 Taylor Ave Annapolis MD 21401 Office Phone: 410-260-8904.

TRESTON, SHERRY S. lawyer; BA, Dominican U., 1972; MS, Purdue U., 1973; MBA, U. Chgo., 1979; JD with honors, DePaul U., 1983. Bar: Ill. 1983. With trust dept. 1st Nat. Bank Chgo.; with sys. dept. Sears Bank & Trust Co., Chgo.; with planning dept. Fed. Res. Bank, Chgo.; assoc. Sidley Austin Brown & Wood, Chgo., 1983—91, ptnr., 1991—. Trustee Dominican U. Office: Sidley Austin Brown & Wood 1 S Bank 1 Plz Chicago IL 60603-2000 Fax: 312-853-7036.

TRETHEWEY, NATASHA, poet, literature educator; b. Gulfport, Miss., 1966; BA in English, U. Ga.; MA in English and Creative Writing, Hollins U.; MFA in Poetry, U. Mass. Instr. Auburn U.; poet, assoc. prof. English Emory U., Atlanta, 2001—. Author: Domestic Work, 2000 (Cave Canem Poetry prize, 1999, Miss. Inst. of Arts and Letters Book prize, 2001, Lillian Smith award for peotry, 2001), Bellocq's Ophelia; contbr. poetry to publs. Recipient Disting. Young Alumna award, U. Mass., Julia Peterkin award, Converse Coll., Grolier Poetry prize, Grolier Bookstore, Cambridge, Mass., Margaret Walker award for poetry, Poets and Writers mag. and QBR: The Black Book Rev., Jessica Nobel-Maxwell Meml. award for poetry, Am. Poetry Rev.; fellow, John Simon Guggenheim Meml. Found., 2003, Nat. Endowment for the Arts, Ala. State Coun. on the Arts, Money for Women/Barbara Deming Meml. Fund; Bunting fellow, Radcliffe Inst. for Advanced Study, Radcliffe U., 2000—01. Office: Emory Univ Creative Writing Program 537 Kilgo Cir Atlanta GA 30322

TRETTIN, ROSEMARY ELIZABETH, fraternal organization administrator; b. Appleton, Wis. d. August W. and Elizabeth C. (Etten) T. BA, Mt. Mary Coll., Milw., 1945. Tchr., forensic coach Pulaski (Wis.) High Sch., 1947-51, Freedom (Wis.) High Sch., 1951-60, St. Mary Cen. High Sch., Menasha, Wis., 1960-79; forensic coach Xavier High Sch., Appleton, 1979-86; pres. St. Mary Ct. Nat. Catholic Soc. Foresters, Appleton, 1953-86, 91—, nat. dir., 1974-78, nat. v.p., 1978-86, pres., 1986-90; sec. Green Bay (Wis.) Diocesan Assn., 1974-78, pres., 1978-86. Mem. Nat. Cath. Comms. Found., N.Y.C., nat. dir., 1986-89, exec. v.p., 1989-90; dir. Wis. Fraternal Congress, 1982-83, Ill. Fraternal Congress, 1989-90; co-leader Fish Cmty. Svc., Civic Leaders Am., Nat. Cath. Soc. Foresters (Fraternalist of Yr. 2002). Eucharistic min. St. Mary Ch., coord. leisure club, 1993—. Named to Hall of Fame, Wis. Forensic Coaches Assn., 1994. Mem. Nat. Cath. Forensic League (sec., pres.), Nat. Forensic League (Double Diamond Key award 1983), Cath. Daus. Am., Outagamie County Hist. Soc., Monté Alverno Retreat Guild (treas. and pres.), Optimist (Neenah-Menasha Breakfast Club), St. Joseph Fraternity of Secular Franciscans (sec.), Christ Child Soc., Monte Alverno Retreat Guild (v.p., 2003). Roman Catholic. Avocations: gardening, travel.

TREUTING, EDNA GANNON, retired nursing administrator, retired nursing educator; b. New Orleans, Dec. 16, 1925; d. Alphonse Joseph and Clara Josephine (David) Gannon; m. August Raymond Treuting, Sept. 4, 1948 (dec.); children: Keith, Karen Treuting Stein, Madeline Treuting LeBlanc, Jaime Treuting Gonzales, Jay (dec.). Diploma, Charity Hosp. Sch. Nursing, New Orleans, 1946; BS in Nursing Edn., La. State U., 1953; MPH, Tulane U., 1972, DPH, 1978. RN, La.; cert. family nurse practitioner Tulane U. Head nurse premature nursery Charity Hosp., New Orleans, 1946-47, head nurse pediatrics, 1947-49; instr. pediatrics Charity Hosp. Sch. Nursing, New Orleans, 1949-52, 54, instr., LPN, 1953; pvt. duty Touro, Hotel Dieu, New Orleans, 1957-59; instr. maternal and child health La. State U. Sch. Nursing, New Orleans, 1960, 65, 69-71; from instr. to prof., sect. head Tulane Sch. Pub. Health and Tropical Medicine, New Orleans, 1972-83; dean, prof. Our Lady Holy Cross Coll. Nursing Div., New Orleans, 1983-84; chief nurse Dept. Health and Hosp., New Orleans, 1987-94. Region IV nurse practitioner Baylor U., Health Edn. and Welfare, 1974-76; citizen amb. to South Am. People to People, 1979; presentor U. Hawaii Pub. Health and Nursing, 1977; planner, advisor, reviewer continuing edn. U. Tenn., Memphis, 1990-95. Author, editor: Occupation Health Nursing, 1979; sect. head, prin. investigator Practitioner Programs Family and Pediatric, 1973-83; item writer Nurse Practitioners, Community Health and Occupational Nursing, 1974-80; mem. editl. bd. to sci. jours. and Nurse Practitioner Jour. Pres. Oti-Mrs. Internat., New Orleans, 1955-68; sponsor bd. dirs. Holy Cross H.S. Treuting Scholarship, New Orleans, 1966—; hurricane and disaster nurse ARC, New Orleans, 1966-77; v.p. Pandora Carnival Club, New Orleans, 1968-78; alternate state health dept. Commn. Nursing Supply and Demand by Legislation, 1991-94; planner, presentor La. State Rsch. Day, 1990-92. Named outstanding woman in the mainstream world's fair women of achievement, 1984. Mem. AARP (pres. 2001—), New Orleans Dist. Nurses Assn. (First J.B. Hickey Meml. Cmty. award 1985, Great 100 Nurse-First Yr. 1987), La. Pub. Health Assn. (Dr. C.B. White Merritorious Diligent Svc. 1990), La. Nurse Practitioners Assn.(Edna Treuting scholarship named in her honor), AARP (sr. mem., chpt. pres. 2001—), Tulane U. Alumni Assn. (past pres.), Tulane Med. Alumni Assn. (past pres.), New Image Club of Mandeville (chmn. 1986-2003), Mandeville Rep. Women, Young at Heart, Delta Omega (nat. and chpt. past pres.), Sigma Theta Tau. Republican. Roman Catholic. Avocations: traveling, dance, swimming, photography, reading. Home: 1914 Marlin Dr Mandeville LA 70448-1069

TREVENS, FRANCINE LINDA, writer, publishing executive; b. Bklyn., Aug. 2, 1932; d. Philip and Celia (Cohen) Freedman; m. Bruce Trevens, June 4, 1955 (div. 1978); children: Janine Robin, Melissa Thea DiGenova. Writer dinner theater segment Best Plays Ann., N.Y.C.; advtsg. copywriter Allied Advt., Boston, 1955—59; theater critic Springfield (Mass.) Daily News, 1968—77; press agent ATPAM-Off Broadway, N.Y.C., 1980—2000; producing dir. Hasselfree Mysteries, N.Y.C., 1990—2001; pub. TnT Classic Books, N.Y.C., 1994—. Freelance writer. Dir.(freelance): various plays, 1952—; author: Fairies, Elves and Little People, 1978; contbr. Giant Story Book, 1978, Big Story Book, 1978, McGraw-Hill World Ency. of Drama, 1981; dir.: N.Y.C. premier William Gibson's Butterfingers Angel, 1982. Recipient Best Poem award, Boston Globe, 1950. Mem.: Dramatists Guild, Greater N.Y. Ind. Pubs. Assn. (sec. 2001—02, pres. 2002—), Assn. Theater Press Agts. and Mgrs. Avocations: gardening, antique doll collecting, reading. Office: TnT Classics 360 W 36 St # 2 NW New York NY 10018-6412 E-mail: tntclassics@aol.com.

TREVOR, LESLIE JEAN, special education educator; b. Texas City, Tex., Mar. 22, 1957; d. William Giles and Betty Jo (Langhammer) Hill; m. Stephen Lynn Trevor, June 11, 1988. BS in Elem. Edn., U. Tex., 1979. Tchr. reading Wiederstein Elem. Sch., Cibolo, Tex., 1979-82; tchr. compensatory Olympia Elem. Sch., Universal City, Tex., 1992—, lead tchr., dept. head spl. educators, 1996-97. Decision making team Olympia Elem., 1994-97. Chmn. Jr. League San Antonio, 1994—; vol. Botanical Gardens Childrens Saturday Classes, 1996-97. Mem. Assn. Tex. Profl. Educators, U. Tex. Austin Alumni Assn. (life), No. Hills Country Club, Gamma Phi Beta (pres. 1979-80), Gamma Phi. Republican. Lutheran. Home: 8646 Park Olympia Universal City TX 78148-3262 Office: Olympia Elem Sch 8439 Athenian Dr Universal City TX 78148-2601

TREYBIG, EDWINA HALL, sales executive; b. Ft. Worth, Dec. 12, 1949; d. George Edward and Lillian Wanita (Herring) Hall; m. Jerry Kenneth Treybig, Sept. 20, 1980; children: Allison Lindsey, Gifford Carl, Brick Edward. BS in Home Econs., Tex. Tech U., 1972. Office mgr. Am. Internat. Rent-A-Car, Dallas, 1973, gen. mgr., 1973-74; sales rep. Martinez Mud Co., Denver, 1977-80, Am. Mud Co., Denver, 1980-83, Robinson Construction Co., Denver, 1983-87, Dig-It, Inc., N.Y.C., 1987-88; sales rep., corp. sec. Treybig Enterprises, Littleton, Colo., 1984—. Organizer Mile High Golf Tournament, Denver, 1980-84; mem. subcom. Colo. Devel. Disabilities Planning coun., Denver, 1989-90; mem. Coalition to Insure the Uninsurable, Denver, 1989-90; founder Littleton Acad., 1996-97; founder, pres. governing bd. Littleton Prep. Charter Sch., 1998-2001. Mem. Soc. Petroleum Engrs. (organizer golf tournament), Internat. Assn. Drilling Contractors, Ind. Producers Assn. Mountain States, Assn. Retarded Citizens, Denver Petroleum Club (organizer golf tournament), Alpha Chi Omega (social chmn. 1970-72). Republican. Mem. Ch. of Christ. Avocations: doll and bear collecting, down-hill skiing. Home and Office: 7397 S Fillmore Cir Littleton CO 80122-1942

TRIANA, GLADYS, artist; b. Camaguey, Cuba, Nov. 17, 1937; came to U.S., 1974; d. Jose Daniel Triana and Francisca Maria Perez; m. Manuel Angel Malleiro, Apr. 11, 1974. Student, Oriente U., Santiago de Cuba, 1957; B in Art summa cum laude, Mercy Coll., 1976; MEd, L.I. U., 1977. Art educator N.Y.C. Bd. Edn., 1978—. Exhbn. cons. Salute to Bklyn.'s Creative Youth Exhbn., The Bklyn. Art Coun., Children's Gallery at Bklyn. Mus., 1986—; created and implemented Children Expressions Mural Program at Cmty. Sch. Bd. Dist. #2, N.Y.C., 1987—. One women shows include Lyceum Gallery, Havana, Cuba, 1962, 63, Tramontana Gallery, 1971, Intar Gallery, 1975, Cuban Mus. Art and Culture, Miami, Fla., 1988, Mus. Contemporary Hispanic Art, N.Y., 1990, Mus. Modern Art, Santo Domingo, 1991, Nader Gallery Fine Arts, Santo Domingo, Bronx Mus. Arts, 1995, Jeux De Memoire, Espace Nesle, Paris, Trapecio Gallery, Lima, Peru, 1997; exhibited in group shows at Palacio de Bellas Artes Mus., 1962, 91, Sala de Arte Gallery, Madrid, 1971, Mus. Sci., Chgo., 1975, Inst. de Cultura Puertoriquena, Museo de Ponce, P.R., 1976, 92, Queens Coll., 1979, Meeting Point Gallery, Miami, 1982, Todd Capp Gallery, N.Y., 1986, Mus. Contemporary Hispanic Art, N.Y., 1988, Warehouse Gallery, N.Y.C., 1989, Stratus Gallery, N.Y.C., 1989, L.I. U., 1989, Mus. Contemporary Art, Caracas, Venezuela, 1990, Discovery Mus., Bridgeport, Conn., 1990, Modern Art Latin Am., Washington, 1990, Humphrey Gallery, N.Y.C., 1992, Paine Weber Art Gallery, N.Y.C., 1992, Artspace, New Haven, Conn., 1992, Adriana Landon Gallery, N.Y.C., 1993, Sotavento Gallery, Caracas, 1995, Nat. Libr. Can., Ottawa, Ont., 1996, Mexic-Art Mus., Austin, Tex., 1997, Espace Nesle, Paris, Trapeio Gallery, Lima, 1998, Tampa Mus. Art; contbr. articles to profl. publs.; illustrator in field. Mem. Mus. of Women, Washington, 1990—, Women of Caucus, N.Y.C., 1992—, Ctr. for Books of

Art, N.Y.C., 1993—. Recipient Art Competition 3rd prize Ateneo de Marianao Gallery, Havana, Cuba, 1964, Ednl. scholarship Nat. Clairol Loving Care Art Program, 1974, Hon. mention Mus. of Sci., Chgo., 1975, Spl. mention The N.Y.C. Bd. Edn. Masters and Apprentices Exhibit, 1990, Outstanding Achievement in Visual Arts award The Queens Borough Pres. of City of N.Y., 1990, Cintas fellowship, 1993. Mem. NOW, Mus. Modern Art, Met. Mus. Avocations: music, ballet, opera, tennis, bicycling.

TRIANTAPHYLLOU, H. H. plant pathologist; b. Fuerth, Bavaria, Germany, Jan. 16, 1927; came to U.S., 1954; d. Friedrich and Ferdinandine (Schonleben) Hirschmann; m. Anastasios Christos Triantaphyllou, July 9, 1960; 1 child, Christos F. PhD, U. Erlangen, Erlangen, Germany, 1951. From tech. asst. to prof. N.C. State Univ., Raleigh, N.C., 1954-92; ret. Contbr. articles to profl. jours., chpts. to books in field. Recipient rsch. award Soc. Sigma Xi, 1962, Ruth Allen award Am. Phytopathol. Soc., 1993, Soc. Nematologists fellowship, 1981. Mem. Helminthological Soc. Wash., Soc. European Nematologists, Soc. of Nematologists, Soc. Sigma Xi. Avocations: sailing, music, piano. Office: N C State U Dept Plant Pathology PO Box 7616 Raleigh NC 27695-0001

TRIBBLE, PAMELA GAIL, special education educator; b. Richmond, Ky., Aug. 2, 1953; d. Emmett Darwin Stone and Jewell Dean Saylor; m. Donald Joseph Tribble, Jan. 11, 1973; children: Kimberly Jo, Donald Jacob. AS in Nutrition Mgmt., Ea. Ky. U., 1994, BS in Dietetics, 1997. Teaching Certification and Rank II Ky. Dept. of Edn., 2003, cert. tchr. and rank II Ky. Nutrition mgr. Fayette County Schs., Lexington, Ky., 1994—2000; spl. edn. tchr. Franklin County H.S., Frankfort, Ky., 2000—. Clin. dietary technician Lexington Country Pl., 1997—2000. Coach and fundraiser Spl. Olympics, Richmond, 1986—96. Roberta Hill Scholarship award, Ea. Ky. U., 1996—97. Mem.: NEA (assoc.), Phi Upsilon Omicron (assoc.; v.p. and pres. 1995—97). Liberal. Baptist. Avocations: bluegrass music, camping, violin, drawing, archaeology. Home: 295 Harris Rd Richmond KY 40475 Office: Franklin County High School 1100 East Main St Frankfort KY 40601 Office Phone: 502-875-8400. Personal E-mail: cusa349ab@aol.com. Business E-Mail: ptribble@franklin.k12.ky.us.

TRICASE, ELIZABETH, gymnast; b. Elmhurst, Ill., July 26, 1986; d. Pino and Sheila. Gymnast Ill. Gymnastics Inst./U.S. Natl. Team, 2001—; competed in U.S. Gymnastics Championships, Cleve., 2001, 2002, 2003, Spring Cup, Burlington, Canada, 2002, Pacific Alliance Championships, Vancouver, Canada, 2002, U.S. Classic, Pomona, Calif., 2001, Virginia Beach, Va., 2002, San Antonio, 2003, FL Gym Open, Luxembourg City, Luxembourg, 2004, Am. Classic, Ontario, Calif., 2004, Nat. Elite Podium Meet, NYC, 2004. Named U.S. Nat. Vault Champion, 2002; recipient 1st place vault, U.S. Gymnastics Championships, 2002, FL Gym Open, 2004. Avocations: soccer, basketball, running track. Office: 145 Plaza Dr Westmont IL 60559*

TRIECE, ANNE GALLAGHER, magazine publisher; b. Bklyn., July 1, 1955; d. Anthony J. and Mary Ann (Clines) Gallagher; m. David Mark Triece, Nov. 3, 1990; 1 child, Elizabeth Renee. BBA cum laude, CUNY, 1978. Media planner Isidore Lefkowitz Elgort, N.Y.C., 1978-80; sr. media supr. Ted Bates Advt., N.Y.C., 1980-83; account mgr. Prevention mag., N.Y.C., 1983-85; N.Y. mgr. Home mag., N.Y.C., 1985-92; assoc. pub. Met. Home mag., N.Y.C., 1992—. Coord. Arts Program for Homeless, N.Y.C., 1994. Recipient advt. excellence award Knapp Comm., 1985. Mem. Advt. Women N.Y. (commendation 1985). Roman Catholic. Avocations: scuba diving, tennis, skiing.

TRIEDMAN, KAREN, design educator, consultant; b. N.Y.C., Dec. 15, 1957; AB in Am. Civilization, Brown U., 1975; MA in Arts, SUNY, Albany, 1982; MFA in Painting, U. Chgo., 1984. Tchg. asst., instr. drawing SUNY, 1980-82; instr. visual merchandising C.C. of R.I., Warwick, 1990-91; instr. visual merchandising, design, color theory RISD, Providence, 1988—. Cons. on exhibit design, visual merchandising, store design and color. Co-author: Colorgraph8cs The Power of Color in Graphic Design, 2002; contbr. articles to profl. jours. Treas. Miriam Hosp. Women's Assn., Providence, 1986-89; chmn. design com. The Tomorrow Fund at Hashbro Children's Hosp., Providence, 1996; mem. edn. com. Gordon Sch., East Providence, R.I., 1995-97. Grantee U. Chgo., 1982-84. Mem. Coll. Art Assn., Color Mktg. Group. Office: Visimark 12 Sheldon St Providence RI 02906-1016

TRIFOLI-CUNNIFF, LAURA CATHERINE, psychologist, consultant; b. L.I., N.Y., June 8, 1958; d. Peter Nicholas and Susan Maria (Graziano) T.; m. John Kevin Cunniff, June 6, 1992; children: James Peter, Capri Susan. BA, Hofstra U., Uniondale, N.Y., 1980, MA, 1982, PhD, 1986. Founder, prin. Quality Cons., West Islip, N.Y., 1980-87; sr. tng. officer Norstar Bank, Garden City, N.Y., 1985-87; asst. v.p. mgmt. devel. First Boston Corp., N.Y.C., 1986-90; mgr. exec. devel. Merrill Lynch, N.Y.C., 1990-91; pres. The Exec. Process, 1991—. Cons. Am. Mgmt. Assn., N.Y.C., 1981 83, AT&T, Basking Ridge, N.H., 1982-83, The First Boston Corp., 1991—, Goldman Sachs, 1991—, Merrill Lynch & Co., 1991—, Union Bank of Switzerland, 1991—, Sanford C. Bernstein & Co., 1992—, Alexander & Alexander, 1993—, S.G. Warburg, 1994; instr. dept. psychology Hofstra U., 1983-85. Author: Vietnam Veterans: Post Traumatic Stress and its Effects, 1986; contbr. articles to profl. publs. Shift coord. Islip Hotline, 1976-78; eucharistic min. Hofstra U. Cath. Soc., 1980-85, Good Samaritan Hosp., West Islip, N.Y., 1988—. Scholar, Hofstra U., 1978-81, fellow, 1980, 81. Mem. Am. Psychol. Assn., Am. Soc. Tng. and Devel., Nat. Psychol. Honor Soc., Internat. Platform Soc. Roman Catholic. Avocations: equestrian sports, art, music. Office: 2906 Bree Hill Rd Oakton VA 22124-1212

TRIGOBOFF, SYBELLE, artist, art educator, lecturer; b. Brooklyn, NY, Feb. 20, 1932; d. Sol and Esther Devorah (Novack) Rosenberg; m. Harold Trigoboff, 1950; children: Norman Jed, Sharon Malva, Hinda Leah. Curator, artist Amontrigallery, N. Bellmore, NY, 1964-66; lectr., critique Greenbriar Art Workshops, N. Bellmore, NY, 1970—, Drawing From Life Model Workshops, N. Bellmore, NY, 1975—. Vis. lectr. art assn., pub. libr., coll., LI, NY, 1970—, B.O.C.E.S. Cultural Arts Ctr., Syosset, NY, 1990-91; mem. art adv. com. N Bellmore Pub. Libr., 1972-77; owner, cons. Atrigart, LI, NY, 1980—; curator Nat. Com. Furtherance of Jewish Edn., 1997. Designer artist 18 ft. menorah commd. by Nat. Com. for Furtherance of Jewish Edn., Nassau County, 1984; contbg. artist (on-line video, internet gallery installation) World's Women, 1995-96; contbg. author: Total Immersion, 1995; curated and exhibited: "Images & Words--Women's Voices" at SUNY - Stoney Brook, NY, 1999; exhibited: Women's Caucus for Art at Phoenix Gallery - NYC, 2000, "Artists Invite Artists" at Graphic Eye Gallery" Port Washington, NY, 2003. Pres. LWV, Town of Hempstead, NY, 1965-67; adv., LI rep., Bais Chana Women Internat., 1994—. Recipient Spl. Opportunity stipend grant, NY Found. Arts and East End Arts Coun., 1997; Sarah Domb Jewish Ed. Award at 59th Nat. Awards Dinner of NCFJE - NYC, 1999. Avocations: gardening, grand-parenting. Home: 1272 Greenbriar Ln North Bellmore NY 11710-2306

TRIIPAN, MAIVE, library director; b. Virumaa County, Estonia, Jan. 4, 1942; d. Osvald and Minna (Olesk) Triipan; m. Kalle Dobkevich, Mar. 6, 1971 (div. June 4, 1974); 1 child, Raul. B. of Libr., Tartu U., Tartu, Estonia, 1967. Rsch. mgmt. asst. Libr. of Estonian Acad. Sci., Tallinn, Estonia, 1967-74, asst. dir. rsch. work, 1974-84, dir., 1984—. Mem. State Libr. Coun., Tallinn, 1974-87, State Libr. Coun. at Dept. of Culture and Edn., Tallinn, 1989—, Tech. U. Coun., Tallinn, 1993—, Estonian Nat. Libr. Coun., Tallinn, 1994—; fin. mgr. Merelaug, 1998-99; project mgmt. Scis. Dept. Estonian Inst. Pub. Adminstrn.; project mgmr. Style Wear, Tallinn, 2000-01; specialist further edn. Astangu Vocat. Rehab. Ctr., Tallinn, 2000, head dept. IT and staff tng., 2002-. Editl. bd. Estonian Retrospective, 1975; mng. pub. National Bibliography 1525-1940, 1993. Mem. Estonian Librs. Assn. Avocations: literature, music, art. Business E-Mail: maive@astrangu.ee.

TRINCHERO, AGNES THERESA, social services consultant, administrator, educator; b. Niles, Calif. d. Louis Jacob and Theresa Marie (DeMattei) T. BA, San Jose State U.; MSW, U. Calif., Berkeley; DSW, U. So. Calif., L.A. Lic. clin. social worker Calif. Fulbright lectr. U.S. Dept. of State, Italy; pvt. practice Laguna Beach, Calif., 1993—. Bd. dirs. Calif. Social Welfare Archives, LA. Recipient Silver medallion, YWCA of North Orange County, Child Advocacy award, Child Welfare League Am. Mem. NASW (Daniel Koshland Leadership award Calif. chpt.), Laguna Art Mus., L.A. County Mus. Art, Nat. Cathedral Assn. Democrat. Roman Catholic. Avocations: travel, theater, dance, writing, gardening.

TRIPLETT, ARLENE ANN, management consultant; b. Portland, Oreg., Jan. 21, 1942; d. Vincent Michael and Lorraine Catherine (Starr) Jakovich; m. William Karrol Triplett, Jan. 27, 1962; children: Stephen Michael, Patricia Ann. BA, U. Calif., Berkeley, 1963. Budgets and reports analyst Cutter Labs., Berkeley, 1963-66; controller Citizens for Reagan, 1975-76; dir. adminstrn. Republican. Nat. Com., 1977-80; asst. sec. Dept. Commerce, Washington, 1981-83; assoc. dir. mgmt. Office Mgmt. and Budget, Exec. Office of Pres., Washington, 1983-85; prin. assoc. McManis Assocs., Inc., 1985-87, v.p., 1987-89, sr. v.p., 1989-93; from v.p. to exec. v.p. Am. Tours Internat., Inc., L.A., 1993-97; prin. McManis Assoc., Manhattan Beach, Calif., 1997-98, IBM, Manhattan Beach, Calif., 1999—2002; mgmt. cons. to govt. orgns., 2002—. Roman Catholic.

TRIPLETTE, LAURANCE DALTROFF, art advisor and appraiser; b. Memphis, Mar. 22, 1951; d. Louis S, and Mary Elizabeth (Thurmond) Daltroff; m. C. Jeffery Triplette, June 2, 1973; children: Gabrielle, Joshua. BA, Salem Coll., 1973; MA, Vermont Coll. Norwich Univ., 1985. Intern reporter Winston-Salem Journal, Winston-Salem, N.C., 1973; editorial asst. R.J. Reynolds Tobacco, 1973-75; asst. PR rep. RJR Industries, Inc., 1975-77, art program coord., curator, 1977-83; intern curator Sawtooth Ctr. for Visual Art, 1983; pres. Laurance Triplette, Inc., Winston-Salem, 1983—. Adj. instr. art dept. Appalachian State Univ., 1986, 87; lectr. N.C. A&T Univ., 1988, River City Festival of Arts, 1986, Nat. Glass Collector's Conf., 1985, Internat. Spring Furniture Market/Design Ctr., 1984, Am. Crafts Coun., 1983, Mint Mus. Art Southeastern Art Conf., 1980; curator N.C. Gov.'s Bus. Awards in the Arts & Humanities, 1981-98; appraiser, cons. to various arts couns. Group shows include Zone One Contemporary Art Gallery, 1995, Urban Arts of Winston-Salem, 1985, Sawtooth Ctr. for Visual Arts, 1983, Tobacco Festival, 1982-83, Spoleto Festival, 1978-83, Carolina Street Scene, 1978-83, Delta Fine Arts, N.C. Arts Coun., City of Winston-Salem, Raleigh Arts Commn.; contbr. articles to profl. jours. Precinct voting asst. Mecklenburg County, Charlotte, N.C., 1996, precinct voting Dem. judge, 1997 99. Recipient Feature and News Writing awards Internat. Assn. Bus. Communications, 1975, 76, 77, Cert. of Award Printing Industry of Am., 1979, Creativity Cert Art Direction Mag., 1979. Mem.: Am. Soc. Appraisers (dep. state dir. 1998—99, bd. examiners 1999—, dep. dist. dir. 2000—02, dep. state dir. 2001—, sr. accreditation mem., former chpt. officer). Methodist. Avocation: vocalist. Office: PO Box 472232 Charlotte NC 28247-2232 Fax: (704) 541-6003. E-mail: ldtriplett@aol.com.

TRIPP, AILI MARI, political science educator; b. Middlesbrough UK, May 24, 1958; came to US, 1974; d. Lloyd William Frederick and Marja-Liisa (Aro) Swantz; m. Warren Earl Tripp, Aug. 28, 1976; children: Lloyd Max, Leila Mari. BA, U. Chgo., 1983, MA, 1985; PhD, Northwestern U., Evanston, Ill., 1990. Assoc. prof. dept. polit. sci. and womens studies program U. Wis., Madison, 1992—2002; dir. Women's Studies Rsch. Ctr., 2000; assoc. dean Internat. studies Northwestern U, Evanston, Ill., 2003—. Author: Changing the Rules: The Politics of Liberalization and the Urban Informal Economy in Tanzania, 2001, Women and Politics in Uganda, 2001. Am. Coun. of Learned Soc. fellow, 1991; grantee Inst. for the Study of World Politics, 1988, John D. and Catherine T. MacArthur Found., 1993, AAUW, 1993, Social Sci. Rsch. Coun., 1995, UN World Inst. for the Study of Devel. Econ. Rsch., 1987, Am. Scandinavian Found., 1999. Mem. Am. Polit. Sci. Assn. (Victoria Schuck award 2001), African Studies Assn.

TRIPP, APRIL, special education services professional; BS, Calif. State U., Fullerton, Calif., 1981; MA with hons., Calif. State U., Long Beach, Calif., 1985; MS, Johns Hopkins U., 1994; PhD with hons., Tex. Woman's U., 1989. 1st coord. adapted physical edn. Balt. County Pub. Schs.; assoc. prof. U. Ill., Urbana-Champaign, Ill. Chmn. adapted physical edn. section Md. AHPERD; mem. Nat. Cert. for Adapted Physical Edn. Standards Com., Spl. Olympics. Recipient Excellence in Edn. award-Spl. Tchr. of Yr. Balt. County, Mabel Lee award Am. Alliance Health, Phys. Edn., Recreation and Dance, 1994; grantee Nat. Handicapped Sports. Mem. Nat. PTA (hon. life award 1993), ARAPCS (mem. adapted physical activity coun. exec. com.) Office: Dept Kinesiology Univ Ill Louise Freer Hall 906 S Goodwin Ave Urbana IL 61801 E-mail: atripp3@uiuc.edu.

TRIPP, KAREN BRYANT, lawyer; b. Rocky Mount, NC, Sept. 2, 1955; d. Bryant and Katherine Rebecca (Watkins) Tripp; m. Robert Mark Burleson, June 25, 1977 (div. 1997); 1 child, Hamilton Chase Tripp Barnett. BA, U. NC, 1976; JD, U. Ala., 1981. Bar: Tex. 1981, US Dist. Ct. (so. dist.) Tex. 1982, US, Ct. Appeals (fed. cir.) 1983, US Dist. Ct. (ea. dist.) Tex. 1991, US Supreme Ct. 1994, US Dist. Ct. (no. dist.) Tex. 1998, US Ct. Appeals (5th and 9th cirs.) 2000, US Ct. Appeals (3d cir.) 2001. Law clk. Tucker, Gray & Espy, Tuscaloosa, Ala., 1978-81; law clk. to presiding justice Ala. Supreme Ct., Montgomery, Ala., summer 1980; atty. Exxon Prodn. Rsch. Co., Houston, 1981-86, coord. tech. transfer, 1986-87; assoc. Arnold, White and Durkee, Houston, 1988-93, shareholder, 1994-98; shareholder, head intellectual property sect. for Houston office Winstead, Sechrest & Minick, Attys. at Law, Houston, 1998; pres. Blake Barnett & Co., 1996—; pvt. practice, 1999—. Creator, program planner, master of ceremonies 1st and 2d intellectual property law confs. for women corp. counsels. Editor: Intellectual Property Law Rev., 1995—2003; contbr. articles to profl. jour. Chair U. Houston and Houston intellectual Property Law Assoc. Fall CLE Inst. on Intellectual Property, 2000. Mem. ABA (intellectual property law sect., ethics com. 1992-96), Houston Bar Assn. (interprofl. rels. com. 1988-90), Houston Intellectual Property Law Assn. (outstanding inventor com. 1982-84, chmn. 1994-95, sec. 1987-88, treas. 1991-92, bd. dir. 1992-94, 98-2000, nominations com. 1993, 96, chmn. fall CLE Inst. 2000), Tex. Bar Assn. (antitrust law com. 1984-85, chmn. internat. law com. intellectual property law sect. 1987-88, internat. transfer tech. com. 1983-84, planning com. continuing legal edn. conf. on intellectual property 2003), planning comm. for 2003 CLE Inst. on Intellectual property Law, Tex. Exec. Women, Women's Fin. Exch., Am. Intellectual Property Lawyers Assn. (patent law com. 1995), Intellectual Property Owners Assn. (copyright com.), Women in Tech. (founder), Lil Eli's Club (founder), Phi Alpha Delta. Republican. Episcopalian. Office: PO Box 1301 Houston TX 77251-1301 E-mail: ktripp@tripplaw.com.

TRIPP, LINDA A. LYNN, court reporter; b. Patterson, Ga., Nov. 11, 1946; d. Bert L. and Jelain (Crews) Lynn; m. J. Randolph Tripp, Sept. 25, 1977. Student, South Ga. Coll., 1964-67, Pitt Community Coll., Greenville, N.C., 1977-78; cert. real estate broker, East Carolina U., 1979, BS, 1980, MA, 1981. Adminstr. State of N.C., Greenville, 1968-79; pres. Tripp Diet Ctrs., Inc., Greenville, 1979-92; co-owner, dir. AmeriCom Prodn. Group, Inc., 1989—; CEO Carolina Ct. Reporters, Inc., 1999—. Charter mem. Greenville Aquatics and Fitness Ctr.; chmn. bd. Am. Prodn. Group, Inc., Carolina Ct. Reporters. Contbr. articles to profl. jours. Vol., adv. bd. Pitt C.C., Greenville, 1984; vol. Greenville Parks and Recreation, 1987; active St. Timothy's Episc. Ch., Greenville, Greenville Mus. Art; v.p. Performing Arts and Friends of the Theater, 2002-; dirs. cir. summer theater, art enthusiast East Carolina U.; co-chair Pitt County Heart Gala, 2002; chair Performing Arts Valentines Gala, 2002; mem. Art Enthusiasts of ECU, Dir.'s Circle ECU Summer Theater; mem. Chancellor's Soc., E. Carolina U. Mem. Nat. Steno Verbatin Reporters Assn., N.C. Verbatim Reporters Assn., Am. Pers. and Guidance Assn., N.C. Real Estate Commn., Ayden (N.C.) Country Club, Pirate Club of East Carolina U. (dir.), Ironwood Golf and Country Club, The Jockey Club (mem. adv. bd.), Pi Omega Pi. Republican. Avocations: golf, tennis, swimming. Office: Carolina Ct Reporters Inc 105 Oakmont Profl Plz Greenville NC 27858

TRIPP, MARIAN BARLOW LOOFE, retired public relations executive; b. Lodgepole, Nebr., July 26; d. Lewis Rockwell and Cora Dee (Davis) Barlow; m. James Edward Tripp, Feb. 9, 1957; children: Brendan Michael, Kevin Mark. BS, Iowa State U., 1944. Writer Dairy Record, St. Paul, 1944-45; head product promotion divsn., pub. rels. dept. Swift & Co., Chgo., 1945-55; mgmt. supr. pub. rels. J. Walter Thompson Co., N.Y.C. and Chgo., 1956-76, v.p. consumer affairs Chgo., 1974-76; pres. Marian Tripp Communications Inc., Chgo., 1976-94. Mem. Am. Inst. Wine and Food, Confriere de la Chaine des Rotisseriers (officer Chgo. chpt.), Mayflower Soc., Daughters of the Am. Revolution, Les Dames D'Escoffier. Episcopalian. Office: 100 E Bellevue Pl Chicago IL 60611-1157 E-mail: mbtripp.@aol.com.

TRIPP, SUSAN GERWE, museum director; b. Balt., Dec. 28, 1945; d. Earl Joseph and Maria Elizabeth (Wise) Gerwe; m. David Enders Tripp, June 9, 1977. BS, U. Md., 1967. Home econs. tchr. Balt. County Pub. Sch. Sys., 1967-74; curator of art Johns Hopkins U., Balt., 1974-76, curator of art, archivist, 1976-78, instr. evening coll., 1978-84, dir. univ. collections, 1979-91; supr., instr. art history Goucher Coll., Notre Dame U., Balt., 1977-86; dir. docent tng. Homewood Mus., Balt., 1987-89; exec. dir. Old Westbury (N.Y.) Gardens, 1992-96; writer Stuyvesant, N.Y., 1996—. Dir. Homewood Restoration Adv. Com., 1983-92, Evergreen Restoration Adv. Com., 1988-92, Advancement Basilica Hist. Trust, Inc., 2000-2001; lectr. in field. Co-author: The Garrett Collection of Japanese Art, 1993 (NEA Grant 1980), Contbr. articles to profl. jours. Bd. dirs. Columbia County Hist. Soc., 1996-2002, 2003—, pres. bd. dirs., 1997-2002, sec., 2003—; trustee Regional and Cmty. Hist. Preservation Benefit Plan, 2002—; chmn. Vanderpoel house restoration Columbia County Hist. Soc., 2002-03; judge Hist. Hudson Preservation Awards, 2000—; bd. trustees Am. Numismatic Soc., 2003—. Recipient Hist. Preservation award Balt. Heritage, Inc., 1988, 91, Rsch. award Am. Soc. Interior Designers, 1991. Fellow Am. Numismatic Soc. (standing com., libr., trustee 2003—); mem. Brit. Mus. Soc., Oriental Ceramic Soc., Balt. Mus. Art, Furniture History Soc., Hist. Hudson, Am. Assn. Mus. Columbia County Hist. Soc. (bd. dirs. 2003—, sec. bd. dirs. 2003—), Omicron Nu. Avocations: architecture, archaeology, chinese ceramics, historical restoration. Office: PO Box G Stuyvesant NY 12173-0009

TRIVETTE, SUSAN BROWN, music educator; b. Salisbury, N.C., Apr. 24, 1953; d. Howard Wesley and Anne Thomas Brown; m. Bobby Ray Trivette, June 29, 1975; children: Kathryn Ann, Daniel Charles. B in Music Edn., U. N.C., Greensboro, 1975. Tchr. Rowan-Salisbury (N.C.) Schs., 1978—2003. Piano instr.n, Granite Quarry, NC, 1975—84; freelance musician, NC, 1975—2003; flute instr., Salisbury, 1990—95; vis. instr. Catawba Coll., Salisbury, 1995—96. Musician Salisbury Symphony Orch., 1975—2003. Organist First United Ch. of Christ, Salisbury, 1990—2003. Mem.: Profl. Educators N.C., N.C. Music Educators Assn. (dist. pres. 1991—93, 2001—03), Alpha Delta Kappa (state music chair 1992—96, 1998—2000, v.p.). Republican. Methodist. Home: 1620 Shive Rd Salisbury NC 28146 Office: Rowan-Salisbury Schs 118 Walnut St Granite Quarry NC 28072 E-mail: SusanTSbt@aol.com.

TROESTER, WALTRAUD, artist, graphic designer, consultant; b. Wilhelmshaven, Germany, June 26, 1942; came to U.S., 1987; d. Johannes and Gertrud (Mueller) T. Diploma, Higher Comml. Sch., Opladen, Germany, 1961; student, U. Tex.-Pan Am., Edinburg, 1988-90; student of reflexology, 1997. Exec sec. Dresdner Bank AG, Lueckenhaus Co., Hermanns Co., others, Germany, 1961-86; multi-media artist including fine art, graphic design, lettering, McAllen, Tex., 1990—. Reflexologist, McAllen and Wimberley, Tex., 1997—. Exhibited in solo exhbns. at McAllen Internat. Mus., 1995, South Tex. Symphony Assn., McAllen, 1996, U. Tex.-PanAm, 1998; exhibited in numerous nat. and internat. juried exhbns.; works include X-ray series, hand-lettered portraits. Recipient Best of Show and Purchase awards. Mem. Internat. Inst. Reflexology, Phi Kappa Phi. Home: 304 Eagles Nest Dr Wimberley TX 78676 E-mail: langes@io.com.

TROGE, DARLENE I. director; d. Peter A. Silva and Loretta A. Hunter; m. Martin David Troge, Sept. 0, 1987; children: Tela L., Alexander D. Congl. intern U.S. Congress, Washington, 1978—78; dir. native am. history programs Shinnecock Speakers Bur., Riverhead, 1982—99; dir. ops. Riverhead Charter Sch., Calverton, NY, 2000—03, chief compliance officer, 2003—. Trustee Hassanamisco Found., Worcestor, Mass., 1979—; pres. bd. trustees Riverhead Charter Sch., Calverton, 1999—2000. Achievements include first to leader in school reform through charter school legislation with a return to traditonal education with a hands on project based approach and high expectaitons for students of all backrounds. Office: Riverhead Charter School 3685 Middle Country Rd Calverton NY 11933 E-mail: dtroge@edisonschools.com.

TROHKIMOINEN, JUDITH LORRAINE, elementary school educator; b. Sheridan, Wyo., Oct. 16, 1964; d. John Raymond and Jeanette Elaine Trohkimoinen; m. Vernon Thomas Trowbridge, Mar. 26, 1994. AA, Casper Coll., 1985; MusB, U. No. Colo., 1988; MS in Tchg., Portland State U., 1998. Cert. tchr. Oreg., Wyo. Elem. music specialist Baker Sch. Dist. 5J, Baker City, Oreg., 1989—. Choir dir. 1st Presbyn. Ch., Baker City, 1994—, Sing-it-Yourself Messiah, 1996—; music dir. Baker's Dozen, 1991—99. Arranger: songs The Vacant Chair, 1995, The Water is Wide, 1995; composer (performer): Judy Laurie, 1992. Clk. session 1st Presbyn. Ch., 1994—99; bd. dirs. People for Improvement Edn., 2001—. Named state winner, Oscar Mayer Schoolhouse Jam Talent Search, 2002; recipient Pres.'s citation Leadership, Oreg. Edn. Assn., 2003. Mem.: Crossroads Assn. Arts, Music Educators Nat. Conf., Baker Edn. Assn. (pres. 1999—2003). Democrat. Avocations: singing, reading, baking, bicycling. Home: 1620 Plum St Baker City OR 97814-4042

TROJAHN, LYNN, academic administrator; b. Ft. Smith, Mar. 30, 1962; m. Craig William Trojahn, May 25, 1989; 1 child, Rachel. B of Internat. Rels. & Spanish, Colgate U.; MBA, Am. Grad. Sch. Internat. Mgmt., 1986. Devel. Breakthrough Found., San Francisco, 1984-91, Emergency Housing, San Jose, Calif., 1991-92, U. N.Mex. Gen. Libr., Albuquerque, 1993—. Author Libr. Devel. mag., 1997. Mem. Nat. Soc. Fundraising Execs. (v.p. 1993—), Acad. Libr. Advancement & Devel. Network (founder), Kiwanis, Phi Eta Sigma. Avocations: reading, golf, volunteering, public speaking, horseback riding. Office: U N Mex Zimmerman Libr Tale At Roma Albuquerque NM 87131-0001

TROLL, KITTY, actress, writer; b. N.Y.C., Dec. 18, 1950; d. Hans and Lillian Holland (Ellman) T.; m. Douglas Getchell (div.); 1 child, Wyatt Theodore. Student, Cambridge Sch. of Weston; studied with Lee Strasberg, Michael Howard, N.Y.C. Instr. drama Pacific (Calif.) High Sch.; founder Mixed-Media Theatre, Dallas. Appeared in (stage prodns.) A Grape for Seeing, The Night of the Iguana, Blues for Mr. Charlie, A Midsummer Night's Dream, Spoon River Anthology, The Moon is Blue, Day of the Races, Old Wives Tale, Bandits, Survivors, Beggar's Choice, Much Ado

About Nothing, (films) Stardust Memories, 1980, The Last to Know, 1981, Sun and Moon, Permanent Wave, 1986, (TV) As the World Turns, All My Children, For Richer, for Poorer, Texas; author (screenplay) Holding the Bag, (teleplay) Malpractice, (book) The Party Book. Mem. Actors' Equity Assn., Screen Actors Guild, AFTRA.

TROMBETTA, ANNAMARIE, artist; b. Bklyn., Aug. 5, 1963; d. Philip and Maryann (Lepere) T. Student, Bklyn. Mus. Sch. Fine Arts, 1980-83, Parsons Sch. Design, N.Y.C., 1983-86, Nat. Acad. Sch. Fine Arts, 1989-93; cert., N.Y. Acad. Art, N.Y.C., 1986-89. One-woman show Liederkrantz Club, N.Y.C., 1993, Hist. Richmondtown Mus., 2001, Garibaldi-Meucci Mus., 2002, Wagner Coll., 2003, The Dana Discovery Ctr., 2003, Staten Island Inst. Arts & Sciences, 2004; exhibited in group shows Bklyn. Mus., 1983, Parsons Sch. Design Art Gallery, 1985, Salamagundi Club, N.Y.C., 1988, 92, 93, 94, 95, 96, NAD, 1990, 93, Columbia U., 1990, Lincoln Ctr., 1991, 92, Union League Club, N.Y.C., 1991, Atlantic Gallery, N.Y.C., 1993, 95, 97, First Street Gallery, N.Y.C., 1994, Nat. Arts Club, N.Y.C., 1994, Pakistan Mission, N.Y.C., 1997, 98, Nat. Arts Club Grand Gallery, Godwin-Ternbach Mus., 2001, also others; group exhbns. include Arnot Art Mus.; art provided for Prasad Art Auction,Manhattan Studios, 1998; represented in pvt. collections, mural executed S.I. Ctr., 1981. Recipient Philip Isenberg Meml. award, 1991, Frank Dumond Meml. award, 1991, John and Anna Lee Stacey award, 1992, Valerie Delacorte Scholarship award, 1992, Philip Isenberg award, 1992, Arthur and Melville Philips award, 1993, Frank Duveneck Meml. award, 1994, Julius Allen award, 1996, Jacqueline Fowler award, 1996, Inga Denton award, 1997, Award-winning photo-feature Manhattand Arts Internat. mag., 1997; scholar 1983-93; Premier Grant, Coun. Arts & Humanities Staten Island, 2001, Encore Grant, 2004; Edwin Austin Abbey Mural Workshop Scholarship, 2002. Mem. William Butler Yeats Soc. N.Y. (bd. dirs. 1991—, scholarship to W.B. Yeats Summer Sch., Sligo, Ireland 1990), Salmagundi Art Club N.Y. (com. 1996), Theosophical Soc., Painting Group in Soho, Pastel Soc. of Am. Avocations: writing poetry, running, cooking, biking. Home and Office: 175 E 96th St Apt 14P New York NY 10128-6207 Office Phone: 212-427-5990. E-mail: trombettaart@yahoo.com.

TROMBLEY, DEBORAH PELKEY, crossword puzzle constructor; b. Plattsburgh, N.Y., June 12, 1950; d. Euclid Francis and Mary Dorothy (Rondeau) Pelkey; m. Edward John Trombley; 1 child, Jay Jessica. BA in English, SUNY, Plattsburgh, 1973, postgrad., 1985-87. Tchr. Adirondack Correctional, Treatment and Evaluation Ctr., Dannemora, N.Y., 1973-75; crossword puzzle constructor N.Y. Times, Simon & Schuster, Dell Champion, Penny Press, Games Mag., 1986—. Pres.-elect bd. dirs. Planned Parenthood, Plattsburgh, 1979; mem. exec. com. Rape Resources, Plattsburgh, 1977-79, Women, Inc., Plattsburgh, 1977-79; vol. United Way, Plattsburgh, 1978-79. Mem. Coll. Found./SUNY Plattsburgh, Kappa Delta Pi. Democrat. Avocations: boating, skiing, gardening, computers, chess.

TRONTELL, MARIE CELESTINE, dean; Diploma, Rutgers State U., 1969, MD, 1976. Diplomate Am. Bd. Internal Medicine (chief proctor exam 1988, 89, 90, 91), Am. Bd. Pulmonary Diseases. Intern in internal medicine, resident in internal medicine Coll. Medicine and Dentistry of N.J.-Rutgers Med. Sch. Hosp., 1976-79, med. chief resident, 1978-79, fellow in pulmonary disease, 1979-81; asst. chief medicine for tng. Robert Wood Johnson Univ. Hosp., New Brunswick, 1980-96, dir. resident tng., 1982-96, chief inpatient svcs., 1987-96; asst. prof. medicine UMDNJ-Robert Wood Johnson Med. Sch., New Brunswick, 1981-87, program dir. internal medicine residency, 1983-96, acting chief divsn. gen. internal medicine, 1986-87, assoc. prof. medicine, 1987-96, assoc. chmn. dept. medicine, 1991—, prof. clin. medicine, 1996—, assoc. dean acad. affairs Piscataway, 1996—. Mem. editl. adv. bd. Info Trends: Medicine, Law, and Ethics; contbr. articles to profl. jours.; spkr. in field. Fellow ACP (mem. grad. med. edn. com. N.J., mem. career change task force 1994), Am. Coll. Chest Physicians; mem. Am. Thoracic Soc., Assn. Behavioral Scis. and Med. Edn., Assn. Program Dirs. in Internal Medicine (nat. coun. mem., mem. membership svcs. com., mem. program planning com.), N.J. Thoracic Soc., Soc. Gen. Internal Medicine., Phi Beta Kappa, Alpha Omega Alpha. Home: 1111 S Branch Dr Whitehouse Station NJ 08889-3234 Office: 675 Hoes Ln # R-102 Piscataway NJ 08854-5627 also: UMDNJ Robert Wood Johnson Med Sch Dept Acad Affairs 675 Hoes Ln Piscataway NJ 08854-5627

TROP, SANDRA, museum administrator; b. Bklyn. BS, NYU, 1955; cert. in arts adminstrn., Harvard U., 1978. From assoc. dir. to dir. Everson Mus. Art, Syracuse, NY, 1974—95, dir., 1995—. Adminstr. edn. dept. Everson Mus. Art, 1972, adminstr. docent program, 1968-72, advt. copy writer, 1965-68; adj. prof. Syracuse U., 1973-75. Mem. founding bd. dirs. Lowe Art Ctr., Syracuse U., Salt City Playhouse, Folk Art Gallery, Syracuse Landmark Theatre; mem. Internat. Com. for Museums and Collections of Modern Art; mem. Literacy Vols. Am.; appointed to Mayor's Commn. on Fin. Planning for City of Syracuse. Mem. Am. Arts Alliance, Am. Assn. Museums, N.E. Regional Mus. Conf., Internat., Syracuse Fedn. Women's Clubs, Corinthian Found. Office: Everson Museum Art 401 Harrison St Syracuse NY 13202-3091

TROPIANO, JOANN ALMA, librarian, library director; b. Bridgeton, N.J., Mar. 7, 1947; d. Herbert Robert and Estenna Dolores (Bell) Gould; m. Robert Lee Carney, June 24, 1970 (div. 1981); children: Robert Christian, Jacqueline Estenna; m. Anthony Tropiano, Jr., May 28, 1990 (dec. Jan. 1995). BA, Glassboro State Coll., 1970; MLS, Rutgers U., 1981. Cert. profl. libr., permanent tchr., ednl. media specialist, N.J. Elem. sch. libr. Nutley (N.J.) Pub. Schs., 1970-77, high sch. libr., 1977—2001; dir. Nutley Free Pub. Libr., 1996—, trustee, 1987-96. Mem. Nutley Mcpl. Alliance, 1997—, Nutley Hall of Fame Com. Recipient Outstanding Educator award Nutley Jaycees, 1995. Mem. ALA, Rutgers-Sch. Comm. Info. and Libr. Svcs. Alumni Assn., N.J. Libr. Assn., Essex County Libr. Dirs. Assn., Nutley Rotary Club, LWV. Democrat. Episcopalian. Avocations: travel, reading. Office: Nutley Free Pub Libr 93 Booth Dr Nutley NJ 07110-2706

TROSS-TANNER, MARSHA LYNN, elementary school educator; b. New Orleans, May 29, 1962; d. Ernest Tross, Sr. and Edna Selena (Johnson) Bush; m. Charles Wallace Tanner Sr., Apr. 4, 1998. BA Vocal Music Edn., Dillard U., 1985; postgrad., So. U. New Orleans, 2000—. Tchr., substitute McDonogh #32 Sch., New Orleans, 1987—90; tchr. math., sci., reading Immaculate Heart of Mary Sch., 1990—2002; choir dir. St. Stephen Bapt. Ch., 1995—, Beautiful Zion Bapt. Ch., 1983—; tchr. St. Cletus Cath. Sch., Gretna, La., 2002—. Assoc. dir. min. music Westside Bapt. Assn., New Orleans, 2001—. Democrat. Baptist. Avocations: piano, computers, singing. Home: 1539 Kabel Dr New Orleans LA 70131 Office: St Cletus Cath Sch 3610 Claire Ave Gretna LA 70053

TROST, EILEEN BANNON, lawyer; b. Teaneck, N.J., Jan. 9, 1951; d. William Eugene and Marie Thelma (Finlayson) Bannon; m. Lawrence Peter Trost Jr., Aug. 27, 1977; children: Lawrence Peter III, William Patrick, Timothy Alexander. BA with great distinction, Shimer Coll., 1972; JD cum laude, U. Minn., 1976. Bar: Ill. 1976, U.S. Dist. Ct. (no. dist.) Ill. 1976, Minn. 1978, U.S. Tax Ct. 1978, U.S. Supreme Ct. 1981. Assoc. McDermott, Will & Emery, Chgo., 1976-82, ptnr., 1982-93; v.p. No. Trust Bank Ariz. N.A., Phoenix, 1993-95; ptnr. Sonnenschein Nath & Rosenthal, Chgo., 1995—. Mem. Am. Coll. Trust and Estate Coun., Minn. Bar Assn., Internat. Acad. Estate and Trust Law, Chgo. Estate Planning Coun. Roman Catholic. Office: Sonnenschein Nath & Rosenthal 8000 Sears Tower Chicago IL 60606 Office Phone: 312-876-8149. E-mail: etrost@sonnenschein.com.

TROTT-BACKUS, ELAINE ERIKA ALDRICH, gerontologist, educator; d. Carl Emil and Helen Eugenia (Johnson) Bender; m. Stephen Wiley Aldrich, Sept. 17, 1961 (div. 1969); children: Rebecca Aldrich, Rachel Aldrich, Sarah Aldrich, Hannah Aldrich; m. Philip Anson Trott, Dec. 17, 1980 (dec. Nov. 26, 2000); 1 child, Rose Trott ; m. Raymond Clark Backus, Mar. 17, 2002. Cert. in interior design, R.I. Sch. Design, 1959; BS, MS, U. R.I., 1973; cert. in bus. adminstrn., Trinity U., San Antonio, 1975; postgrad., Nat. Grad. U., Washington, 1976—77; [illegible] foods from U.S. FDA, N.C. State U., 1989. Owner Aldrich & Aldrich Interior Design, Providence, 1959—69; exec. dir. Ctrl. Geriat. Ctr., Warwick, RI, 1973—85; co-owner, now owner Victorian Emporium, Westerly, R.I. and Stonington, Conn., 1989—. Adj. prof. gerontology U. R.I., Providence Coll., R.I. Coll., R.I. Jr. Coll., 1973—85, Simmons Coll., Tufts U., Northeastern U., Mary Immaculate, Boston, 1978—80; guest lectr. Harvard U., Boston, 1979; cons. U.S. Senate Subcom. on Aging, Washington; incorporator Nat. Inst. Adult Day Care-Nat. Coun. on Aging, Washington, 1979; mem. Gov.'s Long Term Care Planning Com., State of R.I., Providence. Author: The Herb Vinegar Cookbook, 1990. Mem. Sr. Transp. Com. of Groton (Conn.) Social Svcs., 1999—2000; mem. scholarship com. Groton Sr. Ctr., 1998—. Mem.: Internat. Order Rebekahs (vice grand mem.), Phi Kappa Phi (elected 1973), Omicron Nu (elected 1972). Unitarian-Universalist. Avocations: creating art in paper, pressed flowers and collage, gardening, travel, birding. Address: PO Box 777 Stonington CT 06378

TROUT, GWENN LOUISE, minister; b. Gettysburg, Pa., July 5, 1958; d. Thomas Arthur and Nancy Ruth (Shanebrook) Trout. BA in Speech Comms., Theatre, U. Pa., Mansfield, Pa., 1980; MDiv Luth. Theol. Sem. at Gettysburg, 1997. Ordained to min. of Word and Sacrament Evangel. Luth. Ch. in Am., 1997. Mng. dir. Profl. Summer Theatre, Harrisburg Area C.C., Harrisburg, Pa., 1980; asst. to the dir. and coun. PA Coun. on the Arts, Harrisburg, Pa., 1980—86; publs. design cons. Pa. Dept. of Gen. Svcs., Harrisburg, 1986—93; student helper, pub. rels. and devel. Gettysburg Luth. Sem., Gettysburg, 1993—97; vicar Trinity Luth. Ch., Taneytown, Md., 1996—97; pastor St. James Luth. Ch., Columbia, Pa., 1997—. Mem. synod coun. Lower Susquehanna Synod, 2001—. Mem.: Greater Harrisburg Sweet Adelines Internat. Lutheran. Avocation: singing, photography, travel, theatre. Home: 138 Colonial Crest Dr Lancaster PA 17601 Office: St James Luth Church 655 S 10th St Columbia PA 17512

TROUT, LINDA COPPLE, state supreme court chief justice; b. Tokyo, Sept. 1, 1951; BA, U. Idaho, 1973, JD, 1977; LLD (hon.), Albertson Coll. Idaho, 1999. Bar: Idaho 1977. Judge magistrate divsn. Idaho Dist. Ct. (2d jud. divsn.), 1983-90, dist. judge, 1991-92, acting trial ct. adminstr., 1987-91; justice Idaho Supreme Ct., 1992—, chief justice, 1997—. Instr. coll. law U. Idaho, 1983, 88. Mem. Idaho State Bar Assn., Clearwater Bar Assn. (pres. 1980-81).*

TROUT, MARGIE MARIE MUELLER, civic worker; b. Apr. 27, 1923; d. Albert Sylvester and Pearl Elizabeth (Jose) Mueller; m. Maurice Elmore Trout, Aug. 24, 1943; children: Richard Willis, Babette Yvonne. Student, Webster Coll., 1944-45. Cert. genealogist Bd. Cert. Genealogy. Sec. offices Robertson Aircraft Corp., St. Louis, 1942; speed lathe and drill press operator Busch-Selzer Diesel Engine Co., St. Louis, 1942-43; Cub Scout den mother Vienna, Austria, 1953-55, Mt. Pleasant, Mich., 1955, London, 1956-57; leader Nat. Capitol coun. Girl Scouts U.S.A., Bethesda, Md., 1963-65; co-chmn. Am. Booth YWCA and Red Cross Ann. Bazaars, Bangkok, 1970-72; worker ARC, Vientiane, Laos, 1959-60, Bangkok, 1970-72; activities co-chmn., exec. bd. mem. Women's Club Armed Forces Staff Coll., Norfolk, Va., 1975-77. Mem. Am. Women's Clubs, Embassy Clubs, Internat. Women's Clubs Vienna, 1952-55, London, 1956-59, Vientiane, 1959-61, Munich, Germany, 1965-69, Bangkok, 1969-72, Norfolk, 1975-77. Crochet articles exhibited Exhbn. of Works of Art by the Corps Diplomatique, London, 1958. Home: 6203 Hardy Dr Mc Lean VA 22101-3114

TROUTMAN, VICTORIA EVANS, elementary school educator, artist; b. Shreveport, La., Dec. 15, 1944; d. Charles Morris and Dorothy Marie (Dunn) Evans; m. Donald Leroy Troutman, Apr. 26, 1969. BS in Elem. Edn., Elizabethtown Coll., 1966; MS in Edn., Pa. State U., 1981. Cert. tchr. Pa., 1969. 2d grade tchr. Wilson Sch. Dist., West Lawn, Pa., 1966—69, Reading (Pa.) Sch. Dist., 1970—76, 1st grade tchr., 1976—99; assoc. artist Art Plus Gallery-Publicity Ch., West Reading, Pa., 2000—. One-woman shows include L. J. Fitness, Womelsdorf, exhibitions include Hard Bean Cafe, West Reading, Fire & Ice, Jewish Cmty. Ctr., Reading, Berks Art Alliance Show, Reading Area C.C., Wyomissing Art Inst., Reading Mus., Berks Art Alliance Show, 2001—03, Lebanon Valley Coll., Annville, 2002, others. Mem.: AAUW (pres. Reading br. 2003—04), Wyomissing Inst. Arts, Berks Art Alliance, Ret. Pennsylvanians, Ret. Reading Area Tchrs., Order Ea. Star. Republican. Lutheran. Avocations: painting, photography, travel, reading, hiking.

TROUTT POWELL, EVE, historian, educator; m. Timothy Powell; children: Jibreel, Gideon. BA in history and lit., Harvard U., 1983, MS in middle ea. studies, 1988, PhD. in middle ea. studies, 1995. Reporter trainee The N.Y. Times; assoc. prof. of history U. of Ga., Athens, Ga., 1995—. Author: (book) A Different Shade of Colonialism: Egypt, Great Britian and the Mastery of the Sudan, 2003; co-editor: The African Diaspora in the Mediterranean Lands of Islam, 2001. Fellow, Inst. for advanced Study, Princeton U., 1999, Lilly Tchg. Fellow, U. of Ga., John D. and Catherine T. MacArthur Found., 2003. Office: Univ of Georgia dept of History LeConte Hall Rm 220 Athens GA 30602

TROXELL, LUCY DAVIS, management consultant; b. Cambridge, Mass., Apr. 25, 1932; d. Ellsworth and Mildred (Enneking) Davis; m. Charles DeGroat Bader, June 13, 1952 (div. Aug. 1974); children: Christie P. Walker, Mary Bader Montgomery, Charles D. Bader Jr., David Bradford Bader; m. Victor Daniel Shirer Troxell, Aug. 1974. BA, Smith Coll., Northampton, Mass., 1952; grad., Inst. Paralegal Training, Phila. Cert. employee benefit specialist, assoc. in risk mgmt. Paralegal O'Melveny & Myers, L.A., 1976-77; acct. exec. Olanie Hurst & Hemrich, L.A., 1977-78; asst. to trustee Oxford Ins. Mgmt., L.A., 1978-80; dir. corp. svcs., asst. corp. sec. Consolidated Elec. Distbrs., Inc., Westlake Village, Calif., 1980-93; pres. MONMAK LDT, Westlake Village, 1993—. Vol. Friends of the Westlake Village Libr., 2000—, ARC; clk. St. Mathew's Parish Vestry, Pacific Palisades, Calif., 1988, sr. warden, 1989—90; lic. lay eucharistic min. Episcopal Ch.; sustaining bd. dirs. Jr. League, Hartford, Conn., 1952—58, L.A., 1952—60; bd. dirs. Smith Coll. Club, Hartford, 1952—58, Nat. Charity League, L.A., 1964—68, Theatre Palisades, 1960—74; bd. dirs., treas. HOA Lakeshore Cmty. Assn., 1999—2002. Sophia Smith scholar. Fellow: Risk and Ins. Mgmt. Soc. (program chmn. L.A. chpt. 1985—86), Internat. Soc. Cert. Employee Benefit Specialists (bd. dirs., sec., treas. 1988—89, pres. 1989—90, edn. chmn. L.A. chpt. 1986—88). Republican. Avocations: finance, acting, music, art. Home: 450 Puerto Del Mar Pacific Palisades CA 90272-4233 Office: MONMAK LDT 32001 Viewlake Ln Westlake Village CA 91361

TROXLER, WILLIE THOMASENE, retired elementary school educator; b. Raleigh, N.C., Sept. 3, 1925; d. Charles Gilmer Cates and Addie Gaye Long; m. Roger Vernon Troxler, Mar. 18, 1950; children: Bonnie Lynn, Teri. BA, St. Mary's Jr. Coll., Raleigh, 1945; BA in Journalism, U. N.C., 1947; MA in Lang. Arts, U. Charlotte, 1976. Reporter State Advt. Divsn., NC, 1947—48; assoc. editor Carolina Road Builders Trade Mag., NC, 1948—50; elem. sch. tchr. Salisbury (N.C.) City Schs., 1961—78. Exhibited in group shows at Page Walker Arts and History Ctr., Cary, NC, 1999, Rowan Regional Hosp., Salisbury, NC, 1999, Davidson County Mus. Art, Lexington, NC, 1999, others, one-woman shows include Depot Visual Arts Ctr., Mooresville, NC, 1997, Rowan Pub. Libr., Salisbury, NC, 1982, Chatham County Hosp., Asheboro, NC, 1982, Salisbury Pub. Sch. Supplementary Ctr. Art Gallery, 1982. Active Salisbury Symphony Guild; 2nd v.p. Rep. Women, Salisbury. Mem.: Stanley County Art Guild, Davidson County Art Guild (judges commendation 1986, Pres. Choice Stuffer Myer's Meml. award 1995, Third pl. 1998, First pl. 2002), Mooresville Art Guild, Waterworks Visual Art Works, Watercolor Soc. N.C. (Fifth pl. Fall Show 1997, Merit award Spring Show 1999), Carolina Artist (past pres.). Home: 131 Richmond Rd Salisbury NC 28144-2847

TROY, NANCY J. art history educator; BA magna cum laude with honors in art, Wesleyan U., 1974; MA, Yale U., 1976, PhD, 1979. Gallery asst. Waddington Galleries, London, 1973; rsch. asst. Soc. Anonyme Collection, Yale U., New Haven, 1975, tchg. asst. history of art dept., 1975-76; asst. prof. dept. history of art Johns Hopkins U., Balt., 1979-83; asst. prof. dept. art history Northwestern U., Evanston, Ill., 1983-85, assoc. prof., 1985-92, prof., 1992-93, chmn. dept., 1990-92; vis. prof. UCLA, 1994; vis. prof. art history U. So. Calif., L.A., 1994-95, prof., 1995—, chmn. dept., 1997—. Scholar-in-residence Getty Rsch. Inst. for History Art and Humanities, L.A., 1993-96, organizer Work in Progress lecture series, 1993-98; series co-editor Histories, Culturs, Contexts, Reaktion Book, London; curatorial coord., spl. cons. to Ilya Bolotowsky Retrospective, Solomon R. Guggenheim Mus., N.Y.C., summers 1972-74; asst. to curator French paintings Nat. Gallery Art, Washington, summer 1975, bd. advisors Ctr. for Advanced Study in VisualArts, 1999-2002; guest curator Yale U. Art Gallery, 1979; mem. fine arts accessions com. and com. on collections Balt. Mus. Art, 1979-82; cons. De Stijl: 1917-1931, Visions of Utopia exhbn. Walker Art Ctr., Mpls., Washington, The Netherlands, 1982; cons. amplifying art program Art Inst. Chgo., 1984-85; mem. vis. com. Harvard U. Art Mus., Cambridge, Mass., 1992-98; lectr., chmn., moderator numerous symposia, 1980—; numerous invited lectures, 1975—, including U. Brighton, Eng., U. London, Middlesex U., London, Royal Coll. Art, London, U. Toronto, Mt. Holyoke Coll., Barnard Coll., Columbia U., Newcomb Coll., Tulane U., Los Angeles County Mus. Art, Art Inst. Chgo., Terra Mus. Am. Art, Chgo., N.C. Mus. Art, Raleigh, McGill U., Montreal, Vassar Coll; mus. projects peer rev. panelist NEH, 1991; peer reviewer Woodrow Wilson Ctr., Washington, 1994, 96; external reviewer dept. art history U. Mich., 1987; bd. dirs. Nat. Com. for History Art, 1998—; peer reviewer for promotion and tenure Boston U., Lake Forest Coll., Middlesex U., Occidental Coll., U. Mo., Columbia, U. Va., 1996-98. Author: The De Stijl Environment, 1983, Modernism and the Decorative Arts in France: Art Nouveau to Le Corbusier, 1991, (exhbn. catalog) Mondrian and Neo-Plasticism in America, 1979; editor: (with Eve Blau) Architecture and Cubism, 1997; mem. editl. bd. Art Bull., 1993—; contbr. articles and book revs. to profl. jours., including Decorative Arts Soc. Jour., Design Issues, Art Bull., October, Archithese, Arts mag., Portfolio, Design Book Rev., chpts. to books. Mem. Md. Coun. on Arts, 1981-82; trustee Wesleyan U., 1994-97. Recipient Disting. Alumna award Wesleyan U., 1991, postdoctoral tchg. award Lilly Endowment, 1985; Fulbright-Hays grantee, The Netherlands, 1977-78, travel grantee Kress Found., summer 1976, spring 1977, grantee Am. Coun. Learned Soc., summers 1981, 91, 98-99; grantee Graham Found. for Advanced Studies in Fine Arts, 1982, publ. grantee, 1989; grantee NEH, 1982-83, Am. Philos. Soc., 1986, Inst. for Advanced Study Sch. Hist. Studies, 1987, Getty Rsch. Inst. for History Art and Humanities, 1989-90, Zumberge Faculty Rsch. and Innovation Fund, U. So. Calif., 1998-99, Guggenheim Found., 1998-99; AT&T rsch. fellow Northwestern U., 1992-93. Mem. Coll. Art Assn. Am. (nominating com. 1990, bd. dirs. 1992-97, ann. meeting local host com. L.A. 1998-99), Soc. Archtl. Historian (sec. Chgo. chpt. 1984-85, peer reviewer Jour. 1996). Office: U So Calif Dept Art History University Park 104 Watt MC 0293 Los Angeles CA 90089-0001

TRUCKENBRODT, YOLANDA BERNABE, retired air force officer, consultant; b. Manila, June 17, 1952; d. Nestor Leynes and Zenaida Bernabe Javier; m. Edmund Phillip Truckenbrodt, July 27, 1972. BA, Far Ea. U., Manila, 1971; AAS, C.C. of the Air Force, 1979; MBA, Angelo State U., 1980; MPA, U. West Fla., 1987; D of Pub. Adminstrn., Nova Southeastern U., 2000; diploma, Air Command and Staff Coll., 1995. Cert. Dept. of Def.'s Acquisition Profl. in Program Mgmt., USAF Software Quality Assurance. Enlisted USAF, 1974, advanced through grades to maj., ret., 1998; program mgr. KC-135 Reengine Dep. for Airlift and Trainer Sys., Wright-Patterson AFB, Ohio, 1980-84; electronic warfare program mgr. Tactical Sys. Divsn., Eglin AFB, Fla., 1985—89; program mgr. Airborne Warning and Control Sys. Elec. Sys. Ctr., Hanscom AFB, Mass., 1989—92; program analyst ballistic missile def. hdqs. Air Force Materiel Command, Wright-Patterson AFB, 1992-94; congl. liaison staff officer Plans and Programs Divsn., Wright-Patterson AFB, 1995-98. Flight comdr. detachment 847 Res. Officers Tng. Corps, San Angelo, Tex., 1978—80; chairperson Asian-Am. Pacific Islander Heritage Com., Eglin AFB, 1986—87; officer-in-charge Air Force Assn. Nat. Acquisiton Symposium, Wright-Patterson AFB, 1993—94; student-in-residence Def. Sys. Mgmt. Coll., Ft. Belvoir, Va., 1994; staff officer Directorate of Plans and Programs, Wright-Patterson AFB, 1995—98; guest spkr. Nat. Bus. and Profl. Assn., San Angelo, 1993. Contbr. articles to profl. jours. Pres. Filipino-Am. Assn., Fort Walton Beach, Fla., 1987; vol. Air Force Mus., Dayton, Ohio, 1995—96; vol. reading tutor Ohio Reads Program, 2002—; vol. Nightingale Ho., Wright-Patterson AFB, 1996—98; vol. income tax preparer Ret. Officers Assn., Wright-Patterson AFB, 1999—; vol. social worker United Way, Dayton, 1982—84; bd. dirs. Filipino-Am. Assn., Ft. Walton Beach, Fla., 1987, Filipino-Am. Coun. N.W. Fla. Nominee Lt. Robert Sullivan Meml. award, Eglin AFB, 1985; named Airman of the Quarter, Air Weather Svc. Comm. Squadron, 1975, Career Woman of Yr., Gayfers Career Club of Okaloosa County, Fla., 1987, Jr. Officer of the Quarter, Airlift and Trainer Sys., Wright-Patterson AFB, 1983, Airborne Warning and Control Systems, Hanscom AFB, 1991, winner State of Ohio Summer Biathlon Series Championship Cup, 2002, 2d Pl. Overall winner for half-marathon, 4th Internat. Marathon on Great Wall, China, 1999, winner numerous race awards in track and field and Summer Biathlons; named one of Outstanding Young Women of Am., 1983; recipient Appreciation and Recognition award, Dyess AFB Human Rels. Coun., 1976, 1977, Air Force Res. Tng. Corps (ROTC) Leadership award, 1979, Arnold Air Soc. Outstanding Pledge award, 1979, Drill Commandant of Yr. award, 1978; Robert G. Carr scholar, Detachment 847 ROTC, Angelo State U., 1978, 1980. Mem. Women in Mil. Svc. for Am. Meml. (charter), Air Force Women Officers Assoc., Angelo State U. Alumni Assn. (Disting. ROTC Alumnae of Yr. 2002), Ohio River Rd. Runners Club, Sigma Beta Delta (life). Avocations: travel, arts and music, summer biathlons, marathons, photography.

TRUCKSIS, THERESA A. retired library director; b. Hubbard, Ohio, Sept. 1, 1924; d. Peter and Carmella (DiSilverio) Pagliasotti; m. Robert C. Trucksis, May 29, 1948 (dec. May 1980); children: M. Laura, Anne, Michele, Patricia, David, Robert, Claire, Peter; m. Philip P. Hickey, Oct. 19, 1985 (dec. May 1993). BS in Edn., Youngstown Coll., 1945; postgrad., Youngstown State U., 1968-71; MLS, Kent State U., 1972. Psychometrist Youngstown (Ohio) Coll., 1946-49; instr. ltd. svc. Youngstown State U., 1968-71; libr. Pub. Libr. Youngstown & Mahoning County, Youngstown, 1972-73, asst. dept. head, 1973-74, asst. dir., 1985-89, dir., 1989-97, NOLA Regional Libr. System, Youngstown, 1974-85. Contbr. articles to profl. jours. Mem. bd. Hubbard Sch. Dist., 1980-85. Mem. ALA, Ohio Libr. Assn. (bd. dirs. 1979-81), Pub. Libr. Assn. Address: 133 Viola Ave Hubbard OH 44425-2062

TRUDEAU, SUSAN (SMOKY TRUDEAU), writer; b. Aurora, Ill., Nov. 28, 1956; d. James Lee and Mary Ziegler Houff; m. Phillip Landon, Aug. 5, 1975 (div. Dec. 1986); 1 child, Steven Landon ; m. Robert W. Trudeau, Aug. 27, 1988; 1 child, Robin. AA, Kendall Coll., 1975; BA cum laude, N. Ctrl. Coll., 1988. Freelance feature writer The Sun, Naperville, Ill., 1992—97, The Beacon-News, Aurora, Ill., 1993—96; instr. cmty. edn. Parkland C.C., Champaign, Ill., 1998—, Heartland C.C., Normal, Ill., 2003—, Ill. Valley C.C., Oglesby, 2003—; freelance feature writer The News-Gazette, Champaign, 2003—. Writer and cons. Forest Preserve Dist. DuPage County,

Wheaton, Ill., 1996—97; writing coach pvt. clients, Champaign, 2000—; writer in residence Mary Anderson Ctr., Mt. St. Francis, Ind., 2001—03. Author: (novels) Redeeming Grace, 2003, short stories; contbr. articles to mags. and newspapers. Troop leader Girl Scouts Am., Champaign, 1997—2002. Nominee Pushcart prize, 2003; recipient Commendation for comprehensive reporting of med. issues in DuPage County, DuPage County Med. Soc., 1994. Avocations: camping, piano, sculpting. E-mail: smoky@smokytrudeau.com.

TRUDELL, CYNTHIA, automotive executive; b. St. John, Can., 1953; married; 2 children. Degree in chemistry, U. Wolfville, Can.; D of Phys. Chemistry, U. Windsor, Ont., Can., 1978. Chem. process engr. Ford Motor Corp., Windsor, Can., 1979-81; sr. engring. supr., supt. mfg. GM, Windsor, Can., 1981-87, engring. mgr. Willow Run transmission complex Ypsilanti, Mich., 1987-89, ops. mgr., 1989-90; chief engr. process techs. Powertrain Advanced Mfg. Systems, St. Catherines, Ont., Can., 1990-92, mgr. engine & foundry ops., 1992-95; plant mgr. Wilmington (Del.) Assembly Ctr., 1995; pres. Saturn, Spring Hill, Tenn., 1995—, chmn., 1997—. Office: Saturn Corp 100 Saturn Pkwy Spring Hill TN 37174-2493

TRUE, JEAN DURLAND, entrepreneur, oil industry executive, gas industry executive; b. Nov. 27, 1915; d. Clyde Earl and Harriet Louise (Brayton) Durland; m. Henry Alfonso True Jr., Mar. 20, 1938; children: Tamma Jean (Mrs. Donald G. Hatten), Henry Alfonso III, Diemer Durland, David Lanmon. Student, Mont. State U., 1935-36. Ptnr. True Drilling Co., Casper, Wyo., 1951—94, True Oil Co., Casper, 1951-94, Eighty-Eight Oil LLC, 1955-94, True Geothermal Energy Co., 1980—, True Ranches, 1981-94. Officer, dir. White Stallion Ranch, Inc., Tucson, Smokey Oil Co., Casper. Mem. steering com. YMCA, Casper, 1954-55, bd. dirs., 1956-68; mem. bd. dirs. Gottsche Rehab. Ctr., Thermopolis, Wyo., 1966-93, mem. exec. bd., 1966-93, v.p., 1983-90; mem. adv. bd. for adult edn. U. Wyo., 1966-68; mem. Ft. Casper Commn., Casper, 1973-79; bd. dirs. Mus. of Rockies, Bozeman, Mont., 1983-87, mem. Nat. Adv. Bd., 1997-2000; bd. dirs. Nicolaysen Art Mus., 1988-93, Nat. Cowboy and We. Heritage Mus., 1997-2002, dir. emeritus, 2002--; mem. Nat. Fedn. Rep. Women's Clubs; dep. Rep. Nat. Conv., 1972; trustee Trooper Found., 1995—. Mem. Casper Area C. of C., Alpha Gamma Delta, Casper Country Club, Petroleum Club. Episcopalian. Office: PO Box 2360 Casper WY 82602-2360

TRUE, KATIE, state legislator; Pa. state rep. Dist. 37, 1993—. Republican. Office: 143 East Wing PO Box 202020 Harrisburg PA 17120-2020

TRUESDALE, CAROL A. music educator; b. Rochester, N.Y., June 24, 1949; d. Ralph Edward and Bernice Elizabeth Truesdale. BA in English/Edn., SUNY, Geneseo, 1972, MA in English, 1977. Cert. tchr., N.Y. Tchr. Churchville-Chili Ctrl. Schs., North Chili, N.Y. Author: The Ancient Ones, 1998; lyricist Maybe We Can, 1988, Ted E. Bear, 1981, New Shoes Blues, 1989. Mem. Rep. Com., City of Rochester; mem. edn. com. Martin L. King Found., Rochester, 1995—. Fellow Robert W. MacVittie Soc.; mem. ASCAP. Avocations: travel, history, reading, volunteering. Home: 2470 East Ave Rochester NY 14610-2509

TRUEX, DOROTHY ADINE, retired university administrator; b. Sedalia, Mo., Oct. 6, 1915; d. Chester Morrison and Madge (Nicholson) T. AB, [illegible] 1937; EdD, Columbia U., 1956. Asst. dean women N.W. Mo. State U., Maryville, 1939-43, dean women, 1943-45, Mercer U., Macon, Ga., 1945-47, U. Okla., Norman, 1947-69, assoc. prof., 1969-72, dir. rsch. and program devel., 1969-74, prof. edn., 1972-74, dir. grad. program in student pers. svcs., 1969-74; vice chancellor for student affairs U. Ark., Little Rock, 1974-83, alumni specialist, 1983-84, acad. adviser, 1984-87. Exec. bd. N. Cen. Assn. Schs. and Colls., 1977-83. Author 7 novels. Mem. Nat. Assn. Women Deans, Adminstrs. and Counselors (pres. 1973-74), So. Coll. Pers. Assn. (pres. 1970), Okla. Coll. Pers. Assn. (pres. 1972-73), William Jewell Coll. Alumni Assn. (pres. 1970-73), WOman's City Club (pres. 2000-2001), Pi Beta Phi, Alpha Lambda Delta, Mortar Bd., Sigma Tau Delta, Cardinal Key, Gamma Alpha Chi, Kappa Delta Pi, Pi Lambda Theta, Alpha Psi Omega, Pi Gamma Mu, Delta Kappa Gamma, Phi Delta Kappa, Phi Kappa Phi. (nat. v.p. 1986-89) Avocation: writing. Home: 14300 Chenal Pkwy Apt 7422 Little Rock AR 72211-5819

TRUGLIA, CHRISTEL, state legislator; b. Germany; m. Anthony D. Truglia (dec.); 3 children. Student, Darien (Conn.) H.S. Mem. Conn. Ho. of Reps., Hartford, 1973-84, 88—, Conn. Senate, Hartford, 1984-87. Mem. appropriations, human svcs., substance abuse prevention coms, L.I. task force, children at risk task force and gray haired caucus; mem. Dem. Leadership Coun., 1991—, Nat. Order of Women Legislators, 1991—, Lower Fairfield County Conf./Exhbn. Authority, 1992—, Com. on Edn. Excellence, 1992—. Vice chmn. Stamford (Conn.) Dem. City Com., 1976-78; bd. dirs. Com. on Tng. and Employment, 1990—; mem. exec. com. Lower Fairfield County Action Against Chem. Dependency, 1991—; active Coun. on Probate Jud. Conduct, 1976-88, Stamford Com. on Aging, 1978-88, Child Care Ctr. of Stamford, Family Re-entry, Inc., 1990—, Aide for Retarded Inc. Aux. Recipient Hannah G. Solomon Cmty. Svc. award Nat. Coun. Jewish Women, 1987, Spl. award Family Re-entry, 1990, Friend of Edn. award Conn. Coun. for Am. Pvt. Edn., 1991, Adv. Leadership award, 1991, Appreciation cert. Conn. Acad. Physicians Assts., 1991, Cmty. Svc. award Coun. Chs. and Synagogues, 1991, Law Day Liberty Bell award Stamford-Norwalk Regional Bar Assn., 1992, United Srs. in Action award Conn. Gen. Assembly, 1992, Child Adv. Legis. Leadership award Conn. Coalition for Children, 1992, Spl. Recognition award Coalition of 100 Black Women of Lower Fairfield County, 1992, Bd. dirs. Jewish Home for Elderly, 1992; named Child Adv. Legislator, State Coalition for Children and State Commn. on Children, 1990, Legis. Advisor of Yr., Conn. Youth Svcs. Assn., 1990. Mem. Rippowan Bus. and Profl. Women's Club (Woman of Yr. 1991). Democrat. Home: 7 Gypsy Moth Landing Stamford CT 06902-7725 Office: Conn Ho of Reps State Capitol Hartford CT 06106-1591

TRUITT, ANNE DEAN, artist; b. Balt., Mar. 16, 1921; d. Duncan Witt and Louisa Folsom (Williams) Dean; m. James McConnell Truitt, Sept. 19, 1947 (div.); children— Alexandra, Mary McConnell, Samuel Rogers. BA, Bryn Mawr Coll., 1943; postgrad., Inst. Contemporary Art, Washington, 1948-50. Exhibited in one woman shows at Andre Emmerich Gallery, N.Y.C., 1963, 65, 69, 75, 80, 86, 91, Danese Gallery, N.Y.C., 1998, 2001, Minami Gallery, Tokyo, 1964, 67, Balt. Mus. Art, 1969, 75, 92, Pyramid Galleries, Washington, 1971, 73, 75, 77, Whitney Mus. Am. Art, N.Y.C., 1973-74, Corcoran Gallery, Washington, 1974, Osuna Gallery, Washington, 1979, 81, 86, 89, 91-92, Neuberger Mus., Purchase N.Y., 1986, Georgia O'Keefe Mus., Santa Fe, 2000; exhibited in group shows at Balt. Mus. Art, 1970, 72-73, 82, Whitney Mus. Am. Art, 1970-71, 72, 77, Phillips Collection, Washington, 1971-72, Pyramid Galleries, 1972, 73, Mus. Contemporary Art, Chgo., 1974, 77, Indpls. Mus. Art, 1974, Nat. Gallery Art, Washington, 1974, Corcoran Gallery Art, Washington, 1975, numerous others; translator: (with C.J. Hill) Marcel Proust and Deliverance from Time (Germaine Brée), 1955; author: Daybook: The Journal of an Artist, 1982, Turn: The Journal of an Artist, 1986, Prospect: The Journal of an Artist, 1996. Guggenheim fellow, 1970; Nat. Endowment for Arts fellow, 1971, 77; Australia Council for Arts fellow, 1981 Home: 3506 35th St NW Washington DC 20016-3114

TRUITT, KAREN RENEÉ, special education educator; b. Wausau, Wis., Mar. 29, 1963; d. Harold Ray and Wilma Jean Driskell; m. John B. Truitt, Aug. 10, 1991; 1 child, Kendra Pearl. AA, Ill. Ctrl. Coll., 1990; EdB, Kans. State U., 1993, EdM, 2000. Cert. elem. tchr., lic. spl. edn. tchr. Adminstrv. specialist U.S. Army, Ft. Stewart, Ga., 1984—87; substitute tchr. Unified Sch. Dist. 475, Junction City, Kans., 1993—94; tchr. emotionally disturbed Ft. Riley (Kans.) Mid. Sch., 1994—99, spl. edn. coord., 1999—; continuous improvement monitor Unified Sch. Dist. 475, 2001—03, spl. edn. task force, 2001—03. With U.S. Army, 1984—87. Mem.: Kans. Edn. Assn., Golden Key. Democrat. Office: USD 475 Ft Riley Middle Sch 4020 1st Divsn Rd Fort Riley KS 66442

TRUITT, SUZANNE, real estate broker; b. Lewes, Del., Aug. 20, 1943; d. James Shockley and Dorothy Virginia (Shockley) T. Student, U. Del., 1961-62; AA, Goldey Beacom Coll., 1964; grad., Realtors Inst., 1988. Cert. in real estate brokerage mgmt., real estate appraiser, residential specialist; accredited buyers rep. Notary public State of Del., Dover, 1976—; property and casualty ins. agt. J. A. Montgomery Inc., Wilmington, 1984—; real estate broker C-21/Mann Moore Assocs., Inc., Rehoboth Beach, Del., 1988—; mktg. mgr. Long Neck Village, Millsboro, Del., 1991; broker of record, mgr. Gull Point, Patterson Schwartz Real Estate, Millsboro, 1991-93; with C-21/Mann Moore Assocs., Inc., Rehoboth Beach, Del., 1993—, Atlantic Appraisal, Rehoboth Beach, 1993—. Mem. NAFE (life), Am. Soc. Notaries, Ins. Women Sussex County, Women's Coun. Realtors. Republican. Methodist. Avocations: boating, fishing, walking, reading, golf. Home: 8 Sheffield Rd Rehoboth Bch DE 19971-1400 Office: C21 Mann & Sons Inc 4343 Coastal Plz Rehoboth Beach DE 19971-1147 Office Phone: 410-430-5748. E-mail: suetruitt@dmv.com.

TRUJILLO, ANGELINA, endocrinologist; b. Long Beach, Calif. BA in Psychology, Chapman Coll., 1974; postgrad., U. Colo., 1974-75, MD, 1979. Resident in internal medicine Kern Med. Ctr., Bakersfield, Calif., 1979-82; fellow in endocrinology UCLA, Sepulveda, Calif., 1982-84, chief resident dept. internal medicine, 1985-86; chief diabetes clinic Sepulveda (Calif.) VA Med. Ctr., 1986-89; physician specialist Olive View Med. Ctr., Sylmar, Calif., 1989; chief divsn. endocrinology U.S.D. Sch. Medicine, Sioux Falls, 1990—2001; ACOS R&D Royal C. Johnson VA Med. Ctr., Sioux Falls, 1998—2001. Adj. instr. UCLA, 1982-84, adj. asst. prof. medicine, 1985-89, clin. asst. prof. family medicine, 1994-2001; asst. prof. U. S.D. Sch. Medicine, 1990-94, assoc. prof., 1994—, assoc. dir. internal medicine residency program, 1992-95; spkr. in field. Pub. spkr. in diabetes, women and heart disease. Grantee NIH, 1986-89, Am. Diabetes Assn., 1985-87, Pfizer, Inc., 1990-91, Nat. Heart, Lung, and Blood Inst., 1994—, Bristol-Myers Squibb, 1994-2001 Mem. ACP, Am. Fedn. Clin. Rsch. (med. sch. rep., endo/metabolism subspecialty coun.), Am. Soc. Hypertension, Am. Diabetes Assn., Assn. Program Dirs. in Internal Medicine, Assn. Clerkship Dirs. in Internal Medicine, S.D. State Med. Assn., Seventh Dist. Med. Soc., Wilderness Med. Soc. (mem. environ. coun.). Office: U SD Sch Med 1400 W 22nd St Sioux Falls SD 57105-1505

TRUJILLO, ANNA, food company administrator, city official; b. Brownsville, Tex., Mar. 5, 1945; d. Santos S. and Minerva C. Saldivar; m. Jose Antonio Trujillo, June 5, 1964 (div. 1971); children: Michael A., Joeanna K., David A., Sandra A. AA in Sociology, N.Mex. Jr. Coll. Notary pub., State of N.Mex., 1990-94. Office mgr., osner La Poblanita Foods, Lovington, N.Mex., 1964-96; officer mgr. N.Mex. Trujillo Foods, Lovington, 1995—; city commr. City of Lovington, 1988—. Bd. dirs. Lea County Extraterritorial, Lovington, 1992—, Lea County Registration, Lovington, 1985-87. Vice chair Lovington Dem. Party, Hobbs, N.Mex., 1983; mem. com. N.Mex. State Ctrl. Com., 1984. Named Outstanding Lea County Woman, 1991, Lea County Pioneer, 1994; recipient Leadership award Dem. [illegible] 1996. Mem. Lovington Women's Club (sec. 1981-82), Altar Soc., Rebecca Lodge. Democrat. Roman Catholic. Avocations: reading, [illegible] painting, bike riding, gardening. Home: 400 N East St Lovington NM 88260-3628 Office: Trujillo Foods 721 N Main Ave Lovington NM 88260-3417

TRULOVE, SARAH CHAPPELL, humanities educator; b. LA, Feb. 10, 1936; d. J. Edgar Chappell and Dorothy Kober; m. Donald Trulove (div.); children: Ann Marie, Paul Chappell; m. James W. Woelfel, Nov. 24, 1982; stepchildren: Skye Hamilton, Allegra Joerke, Sarah Gowen. EdB, Washburn U., 1971; MA in Religious Studies, U. Kans., 1982. State coord. Religious Coalition for Abortion Rights, Lawrence, Kans., 1979—83; asst. dir. Hall Ctr. for the Humanities U. Kans., Lawrence, 1983—87; instr. in charge Ind. Study Western Civilization, Lawrence, 1993—; lectr. humanities and western civilization U. Kans., Lawrence, 1997—. Co-dir. humanities and western civilization semester abroad in Florence or Paris U. Kans., 2001; founding mem. Highlands Inst. for Am. Religious Thought, 1988. Contbr. Patterns in Western Civilization, 1991; co-editor: Patterns in Western Civilization, 1991, 3rd edit., 2003; assoc. editor: Am. Jour. Theology & Philosophy, 1988—95; contbr. articles to profl. jours. Democrat. Home: 808 Alabama St Lawrence KS 66044 Office: Humanities & Western Civilization Program U Kans Lawrence KS 66045

TRUMAN, MARGARET, author; b. Independence, Mo., Feb. 17, 1924; d. Harry S (32nd Pres. U.S.) and Bess (Wallace) T.; m. E. Clifton Daniel Jr., Apr. 21, 1956; children: Clifton T., William, Harrison, Thomas. LHD, Wake Forest U., 1972; HHD, Rockhurst Coll., 1976. Concert singer, 1947-54, actess, broadcaster, author, 1954—; author: Souvenir, 1956, White House Pets, 1969, Harry S. Truman, 1973, Women of Courage, 1976, Murder in the White House, 1980, Murder on Capitol Hill, 1981, Letters from Father, 1981, Murder in the Supreme Ct., 1982, Murder in the Smithsonian, 1983, Murder on Embassy Row, 1985, Murder at the FBI, 1985, Murder in Georgetown, 1986, Bess W. Truman, 1986, Murder in the CIA, 1987, Murder at the Kennedy Center, 1989, Murder in the National Cathedral, 1990, Murder at the Pentagon, 1992, Murder on the Potomac, 1994, First Ladies, 1995, Murder in the National Gallery, 1996, Murder in the House, 1997, Murder at the Watergate, 1998, Murder in the Library of Congress, 1999, Murder at Foggy Bottom, 2000, Murder in Havana, 2001, Murder at Ford's Theatre, 2002, The President's House, 2003; editor: Where the Buck Stops: The Personal and Private Writings of Harry S. Truman, 1989. Trustee and v.p. Harry S. Truman Inst.; sec. bd. trustees Harry S. Truman Found.

TRUMBLEY, BETTY JO WILSON, retired purchasing executive; b. Haleyville, Ala., Mar. 15, 1933; d. William Emmett and Mona Pauline (Wilson) Brown; Harvey Earl Trumbley, Sept. 28, 1957 (div. 1976); 1 child, Hellen Lucia. Grad. H.S., West Haven, Conn. Prodn. mgr. methods engr. Vanguard Systems, Stamford, Conn., 1975-78; printed cir. design mgr. Data Svc. Co., Stamford, 1978-79; acctg. technician Mil. Dept., Hartford, 1979-82; prodn. and purchasing mgr. Digital Diagnostic Corp., Hamden, Conn., 1982—97, ret., 1997. With WAC U.S. Army, 1952-54, USAR, 1954-58, Conn. Army N.G., 1975-93. Mem. NRA, NAFE, AMVETS, Am. Legion, Non-Commissioned Officers Club. Mem. Ch. of Christ. Avocations: coins, stamps, home and family video tapes, repair electronic toys. Home: 48 Wade St West Haven CT 06516-1931

TRUMBO, CYNTHIA L. counselor educator; b. Dallas, Aug. 9, 1955; d. John Reinhardt and Carolyn Harvey (Herbert) Taylor; m. Dana Andrew Bulter, June, 4, 1977 (div. June 1979); m. Floyd Michael Trumbo, Feb. 13, 1988; 1 daughter, Jennifer Lynn. BS, Kans. State U., 1977; MS, Iowa State U., 1982, PhD, 1987. NCC Nat. Cert. Counselor, lic. profl. clin. counselor Ky. Asst. program coord. Lubbock (Tex.) Regional Mental Health/Retardation Ctr., 1979, program coord., 1979-81; counseling grad. asst. Iowa State U., 1982-83, adminstrv. grad. asst., 1983-87; asst. prof. Western Ky. U., Bowling Green, 1987-89, adj. prof., 1989-91, 1997—. Pvt. cons., 1990. Mem. Ky. Assn. Counselors. Republican. Baptist.

TRUMBULL, VIRGINIA HARDESTY, retired special education educator; b. Watertown, N.Y., Sept. 16, 1936; d. Paul Walter and Alice Virginia (Cole) Hardesty; m. David Trumbull, June 21, 1958 (dec. Apr. 20, 1972); children: Rebecca, Jonathan, Gwendolyn. BA, Antioch Coll., 1959; MEd, Keene State Coll., 1969; EdD, U. Va., 1975. Sci. tchr. Stockbridge (Mass.) Sch., 1959; biology tchr. Stockbridge Pub. Sch., 1960—62; co-dir. Spl. Edn. Program, Brattleboro, Vt., 1968—72; spl. edn. prof. Keene (N.H.) State Coll., 1974—99; ret. Cons. State of N.H. Edn., NH, 1974—99. Co-author: Making the Grade, 0197. Dir. Tchr. Corps. project, NH. Mem.: SAVVY Investment Club (pres. 1990—92). Democrat. Unitarian/Universalist. Avocations: hiking, gardening, reading, cooking. Home: 57 Wildwood Rd Spofford NH 03462

TRUMP, MARTHA LINDLEY BLAINE BEARD, philanthropist; m. Robert Trump, 1984; 1 child, Christopher. Student, U. Tokyo. Clothing line creator Am. Classics by Blaine Trump, QVC, 1999. Fundraiser Am. Ballet Theatre, Meml. Sloan-Kettering Cancer Ctr.; vice-chair God's Love We Deliver. Named one of 50 Most Beautiful People World, People mag., 1998; recipient Marietta Tree award for pub. svc., Citizen's Com. for NYC, 1998. Achievements include all proceeds from clothing line Am. Classics by Blaine Trump go to God's Love We Deliver. Office: God's Love We Deliver 166 Ave of the Americas New York NY 10013*

TRUMPENER, KATIE, literature educator; Student, U. Freiburgh, West Germany; BA with honors, U. Alberta, Can.; MA in Eng. and Am. Lit., Harvard U.; PhD in Comparative Lit., Stanford U., 1990. Assoc. prof. germanic studies U. Chgo., 1990—. Author: Bardic Nationalism: The Romantic Novel and the British Empire, 1997 (MLZ prize for a First Book, 1998, British Acad. Rose Mary Crawshay prize, 1998); co-editor: Modern Philology. Office: Univ Chgo Eng Dept Gates-Blake 324 1050 E 59th St Chicago IL 60637 E-mail: ktrumpen@midway.uchicago.edu.

TRUPE, MARY-ANN, secondary school educator; b. Trenton, NJ, Jan. 6, 1939; d. Norman Louis Green and Jean Hortense Lurvey; m. Robert Arthur Barclay, Nov. 28, 1955 (dec. July 2, 1965); children: Mary Ann, Alison Jean; m. Titus Weidman Trupe, Dec. 30, 1966; children: Amy Suzanne, Sara Diana. BA, Houghton Coll., 1960; French cert., Millersville U., 1981, Spanish cert., 1985; Sign lang. cert., Deaf & Hearing Sch., Lancaster, Pa., 2001. Pvt. elem. reading tchr., 1955—59; tchr. Erlton Elem. Sch., NJ, 1955—59; tchr. French and Spanish lang. St. Joseph Acad., Columbia, Pa., 1981—91; tchr. English Lancaster Cath. H.S., Lancaster, 1991—, chair English dept., 1993—2003. Troop leader Girl Scouts Am., Horseheads, NY, 1967—73; Sunday Sch. tchr. Horseheads Presby. Ch., 1974—77, youth leader, 1975—77. Recipient Nat. Gold Apple Tchr. award, Scholastic, 2001. Mem.: AAUW (pres. 1973—75), Lancaster Lit. Guild. Republican. Presbyterian. Avocations: gardening, painting, reading, travel, piano. Home: 1038 Hearthstone Rd Lancaster PA 17603

TRUSDELL, MARY LOUISE CANTRELL, retired state educational administrator; b. Chandler, Okla., Oct. 24, 1921; d. George Herbert and Lois Elizabeth (Bruce) Cantrell; m. Robert William Trusdell, Jan. 7, 1943, children— Timothy Lee, Laurence Michael. BA, Ga. So. Coll., 1965; MEd, U. Va., 1974. Dir. specific learning disabilities program Savannah Country Day Sch., Ga., 1960-65; learning disabilities tchr. Richmond pub. schs., Va., 1966-73; dir. New Community Sch., Richmond, 1974-75; dir. Fed. Learning Disabilities Project, Dept HEW, Mid. Peninsula, Va., 1975-76; supr. programs for learning disabled Va. Dept. Edn., Richmond, 1976-86; bd. dirs. Learning Disabilities Council, Richmond, Very Spl. Arts- Va., 1986-91; mem. adv. com. Learning Disabilities Research and Devel. Project, Woodrow Wilson Rehab. Ctr., Fisherville, Va., 1983. Co-editor: Understanding Learning Disabilities: A Parent Guide and Workbook, 1989, 3d [illegible] Retarded Children, 1957-60, Meml. Guidance Clinic, Richmond, 1966-69. Named Tchr. of Yr., Learning Disabilities Ctr., Richmond, 1972. Mem. Orton Dyslexia Soc. (pres. capital area br. 1968-70, nat. bd. dirs. 1970-72, Va. br. 1986-91), Alliance for the Mentally Ill. Cen. Va. (pres. 1991-93). Presbyterian. Avocations: travel, theater, reading.

TRUSTY, SHARON, state legislator; b. Oregonia, Ohio, Aug. 27, 1945; children: Katherine Doberstein, Jonna Patterson, Jessica Zachary. Mem. Ark. State Senate, 2001—. Bd. dirs. Simmons First Bank. Co-chair Ark. Rep. Party, 1984-86; bd. mem. Ark. Dept. Workforce Edn., 1997-98; staff mem., legis. liason Gov. Mike Huckabel, 1999; commr. Ark. Dept. Econ. Devel.; chair bd. dirs. St. Mary's Regional Med. Ctr. Republican. Baptist. Office: 8 Pine Forest Russellville AR 72801 also: State Capitol Rm 320 Little Rock AR 72201 E-mail: trustys@arkleg.state.ar.us.

TSAI, RUTH MAN-KAM, nurse; b. China, Aug. 9, 1942; came to U.S., 1963; d. William Y.S. and Dorris (Young) T.; m. James Migaki, Aug. 19, 1967 (div. Aug. 1975); children: Grace, Paul; m. Patrick Joseph McFaden, July 24, 1982 (div. June 1997). BSN, Biola U., 1979. RN Calif. Vis. nurse Vis. Nurses Assn., Long Beach, Calif., 1987-88; mental health nurse VA Med. Ctr., Loma Linda, Calif., 1988-89, 92-93, W. Los Angeles, 92-93; home health care nurse Interhealth, Inc., Whittier, Calif., 1990-91; vocat. nurse instr. Pacific Coast Coll., Santa Ana, Calif., 1991-92; nurse evaluator II Dept. Health Svcs., L.A., 1994-95; home health nurse Procel Internat. Corp., Hermosa, Calif., 1995-96; mental health nurse Premiere Nursing Svcs., Long Beach, 1995—; vocat. nurse instr. Concorde Career Inst., Garden Grove, 1999—2001; charge nurse Harbor View Adolescent Ctr., Long Beach, Calif., 2001—. Quality rev. coord. Calif. Med. Audit, Arcadia, 1997; disability analyst, mem. Am. Bd. Disability Analysts, 1998. Lions & Kiwanis Clubs scholar, 1964, Blue Cross scholar, L.A., 1975. Republican. Evangelical. Avocations: crafts, movies, ping-pong, walking, reading.

TSALIKIAN, EVA, physician, educator; b. Piraeus, Greece, June 22, 1949; came to U.S., 1974; d. Vartan and Arousiak (Kasparian) T.; m. Arthur Bonfield, Apr. 8, 2000. MD, U. Athens, 1973. Rsch. fellow U. Calif., San Francisco, 1974-76; resident in pediats. Children's Hosp., Pitts., 1976-78, fellow in endocrinology, 1978-80; rsch. fellow Mayo Clinic, Rochester, Minn., 1980-83; asst. prof. pediats. U. Iowa, 1983-87, assoc. prof. pediats., 1987—, dir. pediat. endocrinology, 1988—. Fellow Juvenile Diabetes Found., 1978-80, Heinz Nutrition Found., 1980-81; recipient Young Physician award AMA, 1977. Mem. Am. Diabetes Assn. (mem. bd. mid Am. sect.), Endocrine Soc., Soc. Pediat. Rsch., Lawson Wilkins Soc. for Pediat. Endocrinology, Internat. Soc. Pediat. and Adolescent Diabetes. Home: 206 Mahaska Dr Iowa City IA 52246-1606 Office: U Iowa Dept Pediatrics 2856 JPP Iowa City IA 52242

TSCHETTER, KRIS, professional golfer; b. Detroit, Dec. 30, 1964; m. Kirk Lucas. BA in Radio, T.V., Film, Tex. Christian U., 1987. Mem. Ladies Pro Golf Assn., 1987—. Tour victories include 1991 J.C. Penney Classic, 1992 Northgate Computer Classic. Office: c/o Ladies Pro Golf Assn 100 International Golf Dr Daytona Beach FL 32124-1082

TSE, MAN-CHUN MARINA, educational association administrator; b. Kai-Ping, China, Dec. 14, 1948; came to U.S., 1972; d. Sun-Poo and Su-ling Cheung. BA in English, U. Chinese Culture, Taipei, Taiwan, 1970; MS in Spl. Edn., U. So. Calif., 1974; leadership program diploma, Harvard U., 2003. Cert. tchr., spl. edn. tchr., Calif. Rsch. asst. lit. U. Chinese Culture, 1970-72; English tchr. Tang-Suede Mid. Sch., Taiwan, 1970-72; instr. Willing Workers, Adult Handicapped Program L.A. Sch. Dist., 1976-77; instr. ESL Evans Adult Sch., L.A., 1977—82; instr. ESL and polit. sci. Lincoln Adult Sch., L.A., 1986—94; spl. edn. tchr. Duarte (Calif.) Unified Sch. Dist., 1977—2000; prin. assoc. under sec. Office of English Lang. Acquisition, Lang. Enhancement and Acad. Achievement for Limited English Proficient Students U.S. Dept. Edn., 2000—. Commr., program co-chair Calif. Spl. Edn. Adv. Commn., Sacramento, 1994-96; mem. Calif. State Bd. Edn., 1996-99; mem. Calif. State Summer Sch. for the Arts, 1998-99; coun. mem. L.A. County Children Planning Coun., 1995—; com. mem. L.A. County Sci. & Engring. Fair Com., 1993—; hon. adv. bd. Asian Youth Ctr., San Gabriel City, Calif., 1992—; exec. bd. Pres. Com. on

Employment of People with Disabilities (U.S.), 1997—; com. mem. tchr. devel. project Nat. Assn. State Bd. Edn., 1977—; mem. Calif. State Supts. Art Task Force, 1997-98; advisor Calif. Coun. Tech., 1996-99; mem. Calif. Rehab. Coun. Appeared on numerous TV and radio programs. Bd. trustee Bruggemeyer Libr., Monterey Park, Calif., 1993-99; pres. L.A. County Coun. Rep., 1994—, mem. Calif. Statewide Focus Group Diversity, Sacramento, 1995-97; chair Chinese Am. Edn. Assn., 1993—; co-chair, co-founder Multi-Cultural Cmty. Assn., 1992—; bd. dirs. Rosemead-Taipei Sister City, 1993—, San Gabriel Valley Charity Night Com., 1992—; chmn. Los Angeles County-Taipei County Friendship Com., 1996—. Recipient Recognition cert. Duarte Edn. Found., 1990, Calif. Legis. Assembly, 1993, cert. Valley View Sch., 1991, award State Calif., 1991, Appreciation award City Rosemead, 1992, Commendation cert. Alhambra Sch. Dist., 1992-93, Edn. award Asian Youth Ctr., 1992, 1992, Commendation cert. City L.A., 1992, commendation County L.A., 1992, award U.S. Congress, 1993, Proclamation City Alhambra, 1993, Chinese Am. PTA award, 1993, John Anson Ford award L.A. County Human Rels. Com., 1993, Appreciation cert. Chinese Consolidated Benevolent Assn., 1994, City Monterey Park, 1995, Recognition cert. Calif. State Senate, 1994, Spl. Achievement award Calif. Spl. Edn. Adv. Commn., 1997, Duarte United Edn. Ctr., 1997, Outstanding Comm. Svc. award City of Duarte, Calif., 1997, Disting. Woman of Yr. award Calif. 24th Dist. Sen.'s Office, 1997, Svc. award Calif. Fedn. Exceptional Children Coun., 1998, Calif. Sanitorial award, 1999, L.A. County Bd. Suprs. Outstanding Svc. award, 1999, Monterey Park City award, 1999. Mem. Calif. Tchr. Assn., Chinese Edn. Assn., Internat. Platform Assn., Nat. Assn. State Bds. Edn. Office: US Dept Edn Mary Switzer Bldg 330 C St SW Rm 5082 Washington DC 20202-6510

TSENG, ROSE, academic administrator; BS, Kansas State U.; MS, PhD Nutrition, U. Calif., Berkeley. Registered dietician. Prof., chair, dir., assoc. dean San Jose State U., 1970—86, dean Coll. Applied Scis. and Arts, 1986—93; chancellor, CEO West Valley-Mission C.C., Calif., 1993—98; chancellor U. Hawaii-Hilo, 1998—. Office: U Hawaii-Hilo 200 W Kawili Hilo HI 96720-4091

TSOH, JANICE YUSZE, clinical psychologist, researcher; b. Hong Kong, May 26, 1968; d. Ka Kuk Tsoh and Chung Mei Lee; m. Dave Lee, July 26, 1997. BA, SUNY, Binghamton, 1990; MA, U. R.I., 1993, PhD, 1995. Rsch. asst. Cancer Prevention Rsch. Consortium, U. R.I., Kingston, 1990-94; psychology resident U. Miss., VA Med. Ctrs., Jackson, 1994-95; postdoctoral fellow U. Tex, MD Anderson Cancer Ctr., Houston, 1995-97, U. Calif., San Francisco, 1997-99, asst. rsch. psychologist, 1999-2000, asst. adj. prof., 2000—; attending med. staff Langley Porter Psyc. Inst., 2001—. Cons. Lifescan Inc., Militas, Calif., 1999-2001, Am. Cancer Soc., 2001, nat. Asian Women's Health Orgn., 2000—. Mem. rev. bd. Am. Jour. Health Behaviors, 1996—99, reviewer Addiction Jour. Drug and Alcohol Dependence, Jour. Consulting and Clin. Psychology, Health Psychology, CNS Drugs, Jour. Abnormal Psychology, Jour. Substance Abuse Treatment; contbr. articles. Recipient Travel award Nat. Inst. on Drug Abuse, 1998, New Investigator award Tobacco-Related Rsch. Program, 1999—2003, Pilot Study Fund U. Calif. Treatment Rsch. Ctr., San Francisco, 1999, Career Devel. award Nat. Inst. Drug Abuse, 2000—; fellow Univ. Found. U. Tex. MD Anderson Cancer Ctr., Houston, 1996-97. Mem. APA, Soc. Behavioral Medicine, Soc. for Rsch. on Nicotine and Tobacco, Nat. Asian Women's Health Orgn., Phi Beta Kappa, Psi Chi. Office: U Calif Dept Psychiatry LPP I 401 Parnassus Ave 0984-TRC San Francisco CA 94143-0984

TSOODLE-MARCUS, CHARLENE, education educator, school system administrator; b. May 8, 1947; d. Charles and Patrita (Lujan) Tsoodle; m. Joe David Marcus, July 29, 1976; 1 child, Keith Eagle Marcus. AA in Police Sci., Monterey Peninsula Coll., 1968; BA in Criminal Justice, N. Mex. State Univ., 1971. Indian justice specialist planner Gov. Coun. on Criminal Justice, Santa Fe, 1972-80; records adminstr. N. Mex. Corrections Dept., Santa Fe, 1980-93; govs. asst. Taos Pueblo Govs. Office, N.Mex., 1993-94; coord. Taos County Gov. Planning Dept., 1994-95, Northern Pueblos Inst., Northern N. Mex. C. C., Esponola, N.Mex., 1995—2001; jail adminstrn. Taos County Detention Ctr., 2001—. Chmn., housing commr. No. Pueblos Housing Authority, Santa Fe, 1993—; bd. mem. Rocky Mountain Youth, Taos, 1998—; steering com. mem. Rio Arriba Environ. Health, Espanola, 1999—. Photo feature Nat. Geog., 1994. Vice chair, com. mem. Taos County Tax Adv., 1993—95; vol. Indian Culture Clubs, Santa Fe, 1980—93, Taos Indian Bapt. Ch., Taos, 1980—93. Mem.: Am. Indian Sci. & Engring. Soc. (adv. 1999—), Nat. Congress Am. Indians (life), Phi Theta Kappa, Alpha Iota Sigma. Avocations: jewelry making, Indian pottery, arts and crafts. Office: Taos County Adult Detention Ctr Jail Adminstr 105 Albright St Ste J El Prado NM 87529

TSUI, SOO HING, educational research consultant; b. Hong Kong, Aug. 2, 1959; came to U.S., 1985; d. Sik Tin and Yuk Kam (Cheung) T. BSW cum laude, Nat. Taiwan U., 1983; MSW cum laude, Columbua U., 1987, postgrad., 1992—. Cert. social worker, N.Y. Dir. cmty. handicapped ctr., Taipei, Taiwan, 1983-85; dir. youth recreational program, 1986; social work dept. supr. St. Margaret's House, N.Y.C., 1987-89; chief bilingual sch. social work N.Y.C. Bd. Edn., 1990—, rsch. cons., 1993—; rschr. Columbia U., N.Y.C., 1991-95; chief rsch. cons. N.Y.C. Dept. Transp., 1993-96; cheif rschr. immigrant social svcs. N.Y.C. Bd. Edn., 1996—. Bilingual social worker Nat. Assn. Asian/Am. Edn., 1989—; union social work regional rep. N.Y.C. Bd. Edn., 1990-93, citywide bilingual social work rep., 1991-93, citywide social work budget allocation comms. rep., 1992-93; mem. conf. planning com. bd. Amb. For Christ, Boston, 1991-93; coord. doctoral colloquial com. bd., 1991-93, Scholarships Coun. Social Work Edn., Columbia U., N.Y.C., 1992-94; mem. planning com. social work bd. Asian Am. Comms., N.Y.C., 1991-95; exec. dir. alumni bd. Columbia U. Sch. Social Work, 1995—, exec. dir. bd. Columbia newsletters Columbia U. Sch. Social Work, 1996—; exec. bd. dirs. Chinese for Christ, 1993-95. Recipient Nat. Acad. award, 1979-83; Nat. Acad. scholar, 1987-88; Nat. Rsch. fellow Sch. Coun. on Social Work Edn., 1992-94. Home: 65-38 Booth St Apt 2B Rego Park NY 11374

TUAN, DEBBIE FU-TAI, chemist, educator; b. Kiangsu, China, Feb. 2, 1930; came to U.S., 1958; d. Shiau-gien and Chen (Lee) T.; m. John W. Reed, Aug. 15, 1987. BS in Chemistry, Nat. Taiwan U., Taipei, 1954, MS in Chemistry, 1958, Yale U., 1960, PhD in Chemistry, 1961. Rsch. fellow Yale U., New Haven, 1961-64; rsch. assoc. U. Wis., Madison, 1964-65; asst. prof. Kent (Ohio) State U., 1965-70, assoc. prof., 1970-73, prof., 1973—; vis. scientist Yeshiva U., N.Y.C., summer 1966; rsch. fellow Harvard U., Cambridge, 1969-70; vis. scientist SRI Internat., Menlo Park, Calif., 1981; rsch. assoc. Cornell U., Ithica, N.Y., 1983. Vis. prof. Acad. Sinica of China, Nat. Taiwan U. and Nat. Tsing-Hwa U., summer 1967, Ohio State U., 1993, 95. Contbr. articles to profl. jours. Recipient NSF Career Advanced award, 1994—; U. Grad. fellow Nat. Taiwan U., 1955-58, F.W. Heyl-Anon F fellow Yale U., 1960-61, U. Faculty Rsch. fellow Kent State U., 1966, 68, 71, 85; Pres. Chiang's scholar Chinese Women Assn., 1954, 58, Grad. scholar in humanity and scis. China Found., 1955. Mem. Am. Chem. Soc., Am. Phys. Soc., Sigma Xi. Office: Kent State U Chemistry Dept Williams Hl Kent OH 44242-0001

TUBB, BETTY LOU, music educator; b. Oklahoma City, Oct. 6, 1932; d. Eugene Woodrow Freeze and Otha Merle Perkins; m. Boyd Junior Bryce, Aug. 6, 1948 (dec. June 1965); children: Donna Bryce Lacquement, DiAnn Bryce Neff; m. Curtis O'Connor Tubb, Dec. 30, 1969; 1 child, Tara Elizabeth. BMus in Piano, Oklahoma City U., 1966. Pvt. music tchr., Oklahoma City, 1960—69; with Tonsmeire Sch. Music, Mobile, Ala., 1969—71; music tchr. Mobile Christian Sch., 1971—80; pvt. music tchr. Cross City, Fla., 1980—85; music tchr. Wrights Girls Sch., Mobile, 1985—2001. Mem.: Music Tchrs. Nat. Assn., Ala. Music Tchrs. Assn., Nat. Guild Piano Tchrs. (adjudicator 1965—99, treas., chair scholarship com.), Mobile Music Tchr. Assn. (pres. 1972—74, treas. 2001—02, scholarship chmn.), Sigma Alpha Iota. Republican. Mem. Church Of Christ. Avocation: heritage.

TUBBS, VIRGINIA CAROL, music director; b. Butte, Mont., Mar. 28, 1944; d. Lester Edmond and Irma Louise Braun; m. James Walter Tubbs, July 16, 1972. BA, Andrews U., Berrien Springs, Michigan, 1966, MA, 1967. Music tchr. Bakersfield Acad., Bakersfield, Calif., 1967—68; piano tchr. Pvt. Studio, Bloomington, Ind., 1968—75, Walla Walla, Wash., 1976—78; piano and organ tchr. Garden State Acad., Hackettstown, NJ, 1978—80, Pvt. Studio, Christiansburg, Va., 1987—91; piano tchr. Vt. Coll. Sch. of Music and Dance, Vt., 1994—98, Pvt. Studio, Eau Claire, Wis., 1998—; organist First Ch. of Christ Scientist, Walla Walla, Wash., 1976—78; music dir. First United Presbyn. Ch., Succasunna, NJ, 1978—80; asst. organist / dir. St. Anthony Cath. Ch., Baltimore, Md., 1982—86; organist / dir. St. Michael Luth. Ch., Perry Hall, Md., 1982—86; organist First Congl. Ch., Burlington, Vt., 1992—93; organist / dir. First Bapt. Ch., Barre, Vt., 1994—98; music dir. First Presbyn. Ch., Eau Claire, Wis., 1999—. Pianist / asst. dir. The Johns Hopkins U. Choral Soc., 1983—86; pianist / organist Choraleers, Barre, Vt., 1995—98; recital organist Mable Tainter Theater, Menomonie, Wis., 2000—02; music dir. Barre Opera Ho., Barre, Vt., 1995. Recipient Nat. Honor Roll, Nat. Guild of Piano Teachers, 1990, 1991. Mem.: Chippewa Valley Rag Soc. (frequent performer 2000—03), Music Teachers Assn. (treas., recital chariman, sec., state theory chair 1976—2003), Am. Guild of Organists (sub-dean, profl. concerns chmn., newsletter, performer 1978—2002, dean 2000—03, colleague). Avocations: antiques, cats, bicycling. Home: 1719 Laurel Avenue Eau Claire WI 54701 Office: FIrst Presbyterian Church 1221 Rudolph Road Eau Claire WI 54701 Personal E-mail: tubbsvc@hotmail.com.

TUCCERI, CLIVE KNOWLES, science writer and educator, consultant; b. Bryn Mawr, Pa., Apr. 20, 1953; d. William Henry and Clive Ellis (Knowles) Hulick; m. Eugene Angelo Tucceri, Sept. 1, 1984 (div. Nov. 1991); 1 child, Clive Edna. BA in Geology, Williams Coll., 1975; MS in Coastal Geology, Boston Coll., 1982. Head sci. dept. Stuart Hall Sch., Staunton, Va., 1975-77; mem. sci. faculty William Penn Charter Sch., Phila., 1977-79, Tower Sch., Marblehead, Mass., 1982-86, Bentley Coll., Waltham, Mass., 1986-88; adminstrv. dir., co-founder Stout Aquatic Libr. Nat. Marine and Aquatic Edn. Resource Ctr., Wakefield, R.I., 1982-89; mem. sci. faculty Mabelle B. Avery Sch., Somers, Conn., 1989-90; mem. faculty, head sci. dept. MacDuffie Sch., Springfield, Mass., 1992-93; mem. sci. faculty East Hampton (Conn.) Middle Sch., 1993—, sci. team leader, 1994-95, sci. chairperson grades K-12, 1995—, 8th grade advisor, 2000—01. Cons. Longmeadow (Mass.) Pub. Schs., 1989-94, Addison-Wesley Pub. Co., Menlo Prk, Calif., 1986-94; cons., freelance writer Prentice-Hall Inc., Needham, Mass., 1991. Co-head class agt. Williams Coll. Alumni Fund, 2000—, vice chair, 2003—; admissions rep. Williams Coll., 2001—; vol. The Bushnell Ctr. for Performing Arts, 2001—; mem. search com. Christ Ch., Middle Haddam, Conn., 2000—01, mem. vestry, 2002—; bd. dirs. People Against Rape, Staunton, 1976—77. Mem.: AAUW (bd. dirs., br. pres.-elect 1975—77, v.p. 1985—86, sec. 1986—87), NEA, NSTA, Cousteau Soc., Conn. Edn. Assn., Conn. Sci Tchrs. Assn., Conn. Sci. Suprs. Assn., Mass. Environ. Edn. Soc. (bd. dirs. 1985—88), Mass. Marine Educators (pres. 1987—89, bd. dirs. 1983—91, editor Flotsam and Jetsam MA Marine Educators newsletter 1991—97), Southeastern New Eng. Marine Educators (publs. chair Nat. Conf. com.), Nat. Mid. Level Sci. Tchrs. Assn., Nat. Marine Edn. Assn. (sec. 1986—87, chpt. rep. 1987 1989), Sigma Xi. Episcopalian. Avocations: renovating old homes, sailing, gardening, reading. Home: 12 Birchwood Dr East Hampton CT 06424-1312

TUCHOLKE, CHRISTEL-ANTHONY, artist, educator; b. Leczyca, Poland, Mar. 2, 1941; arrived in U.S., 1952; d. Alfred and Eleonore Marie (Mundt) T.; m. Anthony C. Stoeveken, June 9, 1967; children: Jennifer, Joshua. BS in Art Edn., U. Wis., Milw., 1964, MS in Fine Arts Drawing and Painting, 1965. Grad. tchg. asst. U. Wis., Milw., 1964-65; art instr. Milw. Pub. Schs., 1965-66; univ. instr. Western Carolina U., Cullowhee, N.C., 1966-67; print curator Tamarind Lithography WK, L.A., 1968; artist, 1970—. Vis. artist, designer Artists Ltd. Edits., Kohler (Wis.) Co., 1989. Exhibited in over 91 shows; commns. include Wis. Arts Bd., Miller Brewing Co., Northwestern Mut. Life. Mem. Profl. Dimensions (hon. mem.). Home: 8535 W Mequon Rd Mequon WI 53097-3101

TUCK, AMY, lieutenant governor; b. Starkville, Miss., July 8, 1963; d. Grady William and Mary (Boykin) Tuck. BA in Polit. Sci., Miss. State U., Starkville, 1985; postgrad., Miss. State U., Miss. State U., Starkville, 1992—; JD, Miss. Coll., 1989. Legal asst. Ben. F. Hilburn Jr., Atty. at Law, Starkville, Miss., 1984-85; grad. asst. dept. polit. sci. Miss. State U., Starkville, 1986-87; law clk. Minor Buchanan, Jackson, Miss., 1987-88, Deposit Guaranty Nat. Bank, Jackson, 1988-89; state senator dist. 15 State of Miss., Jackson, 1990-99, lt. gov., 2000—. Adj. prof. Wood Jr. Coll., Mathiston, Miss., 1990-95. Mem. Oktibbeha County Voter Re-Registration Com., Oktibbeha County Fedn. Dem. Women; bd. dirs. Oktibbeha County Am. Cancer Soc., 1991-92; mem. local rels. com. Children and Family Svcs.; assoc. mem. Nat. Mus. Women in the Arts, 1992-93. Mem. NAFE, Am. Legis. Exch. Com., Am. Soc. Pub. Adminstrs., Nat. Conf. State Legislature, Nat. Order Women Legislators, Miss. State U. Alumni Assn., Starkville Area Bus. and Profl. Women's Club, Oktibbeha County C. of C., Gamma Beta Phi, Pi Sigma Alpha, Omicron Delta Kappa, Phi Delta Phi (vice-magister 1988, historian 1988-89). Democrat. Methodist. Office: Office of the Lt Gov PO Box 1018 Jackson MS 39215-1018

TUCK, CAROLYN WEAVER, middle school educator; b. Petersburg, Va., Nov. 18, 1947; d. Fred William Weaver and Virginia Evelyn (Fick) Lang; m. Michael Lewis Jones, Dec. 27, 1969 (div. 1991); children: Kristen Michelle Jones, Kara Denise Jones; m. Richard Harper Tuck, July 30, 1994. BS, Radford U., 1970, MS, 1971; adminstrv. cert., William and Mary Coll., 1991, George Washington U., 1991. Cert. secondary sch. prin., English and history tchr., Va. English tchr. Galax (Va.) City Schs., 1971-72, Waynesville (N.C.) Schs., 1973-75; circulation libr. Western Carolina U., Cullowhee, N.C., 1972-73; English and history tchr. Poquoson (Va.) City Schs., 1975—81, 1985—2002; acting asst. prin. Poquoson (Va.) Mid. Schs., 1989; libr. media specialist Poquoson (Va.) Mid. Sch., 2002—. Rep. to state MS conf. Va. Bd. Edn., Poquoson, 1991. Writer advanced social studies/English curriculum; contbr. articles to profl. jours. Solicitor Am. Cancer Soc., Poquoson, 1992-98, Mother's March of Dimes, 1996-2000; bible sch. tchr. Tabernacle Meth. Ch., Poquoson, 1994. Mem. NEA, Va. Edn. Assn., Poquoson Edn. Assn. (v.p. 2000—), Nat. Mid. Sch. Assn., Pi Gamma Mu, Sigma Tau Delta. Avocations: bridge, travel, doll collecting, genealogy. Home: 105 Shallow Lagoon Yorktown VA 23693-4111 Office: Poquoson Mid Sch 985 Poquoson Ave Poquoson VA 23662-1799

TUCKER, ANNE WILKES, curator, photography historian and critic, lecturer; b. Baton Rouge, Oct. 18, 1945; AAS in Photographic Illustration, Rochester Inst. Tech., 1968; BA in Art History, Randolph-Macon Women's Coll.; MFA in Photographic History, SUNY-Buffalo, 1972. Rsch. asst. Internat. Mus. Photography at the George Eastman House, Rochester, NY, 1968—70; rsch. assoc. Gernsheim Collection U. Tex., Austin, 1969, 1979; curatorial intern dept. photography Mus. Modern Art, N.Y.C., 1970—71; photography cons. Creative Artists Pub. Svc. Program, N.Y.C., 1971—72; vis. lectr. New Sch. for Social Rsch., 1973; dir. photography lecture series Cooper Unionn Forum, N.Y.C., 1972—75; lectr. Cooper Union for Advancement of Arts and Sci., 1972—75; vis. lectr. Phila. Coll. Art, 1973—75; affiliate artist U. Houston, 1976—80; curator photography Mus. Fine Arts, Houston, 1976—; Gus and Lyndall Wortham cur., photographic historian and critic, lectr. Trustee Visual Studies Workshop, 1980—2000, Houston Ctr. Photography, 1991—96, Houston Foto Fest, 1988—; visual arts panel The Houston Festival, 1981—83; adv. bd. Randolph-Macon Woman's Coll. Art Gallery, 1982—84; dir. numerous exhbns. and workshops; lectr. in field; mem. numerous juries and panels. Author: (books and catalogues) The Woman's Eye, 1973; author: (with William [illegible]) The Target Collection of American Photography, 1977; author: Target II: 5 American Photographers, 1981, Target III: In Sequence, 1982; author: (with Philip Brookman) Robert Frank: New York to Nova Scotia, 1986; author: (with Maggie Olvey) The Sonia and Kaye Marvins Portrait Collection, 1986, 1995; author: Photo Notes and Filmfront, 1977; author: (with other curators) The Museum of Fine Arts, Houston: A Guide to the Collection, 1981; author: Unknown Territory: Photography by Ray K. Metzker, 1957-83, 1984, Fifth Annual International Fine Art Photography Exposition, 1984; author: (with Andy Grundberg) American Prospects: The Photographs of Joel Slernfeld, 1987, 1994; author: (with Willie Morris) American Classroom: The Photographs of Catherine Wagner, 1988; author: (with Pamela Allara) Crosscurrents/Crosscountry, 1988; author: (with other authors) Money Matters: A Critical Look at Bank Architecture, 1990; author: The Blue Moon: Photographs by Keith Carter, 1990; author: (with Pete Daniel) Carry Me Home: Photographs by Debbie Fleming Caffery, 1990; author: George Krauze, 1991, Tradition and the Unpredictable: The Allan Chasanoff Photographic Collection, 1994, Quest for the Moon, 1995, (exhbns. and catalogues) Brassai: Eye of Paris, 1999, Louis Faurer, 2002, History of Japanese Photography, 2003; co-prodr. (video) Fire in the East: The Portrait of Robert Frank, 1986; editor: (books and catalogues) The Anthony G. Cronin Memorial Collection, 1979, (manual) Susanne Bloom and Ed Hill, 1980, The Photo League, 1987, Czech Modernism 1900-1945, 1990, Paul Strand: Essays on His Life and Work, 1991, George Krause, 1992; contbr. articles to profl. jours. and mags. Recipient Third Ann. Publ. award, Internat. Ctr. Photography, 1987, John Simon Guggenheim Meml. Alumna Achievement award, Randolph-Macon Woman's Coll., 1993; fellow Found. fellow, 1983—84; grantee Nat. Endowment Arts grantee, 1976, 1986, 1989. Mem.: Houston Ctr. for Photography, Art Table, Inc., Coll. Art Assn., Soc. Photographic Edn. (nat. bd. dirs. 1976—80, sec. 1977—79). Office: Mus Fine Arts PO Box 6826 Houston TX 77265

TUCKER, BERNADINE, patient registrar; b. Feb. 27, 1945; d. Erie Wendell and Ethel M. Tucker; children: Andrew Edwards II, Alicia Edwards. Student, U. Md., Madrid, 1970—71, U. Mass., 1976—77; Cert. in Mgmt., Hampshire Coll. Med. transcriptionist Glens Falls (N.Y.) Hosp., 1965—66, Physicians Hosp., Plattsburgh, NY, 1966—67; outreach worker Ednl. Opportunity Ctr., Chicapee, Mass., 1975; asst. dir. fin. aid U. Mass., Amherst, 1975—79; patient registrar Glens Falls Hosp., 2001—. Outreach YWCA, Springfield, Mass., 1975; facilitator Coll. Fair, Springfield, Mass., 1975. Recipient award, Internat. Yr. of Women, 1975. Democrat. Avocations: poetry, needlework, sketching, painting, journals. Home: 196 Ridge St Glens Falls NY 12801

TUCKER, BEVERLY SOWERS, information specialist; b. Trenton, N.J., Dec. 1, 1936; d. Eldon Jones and Verbeda Eleanor (Roberts) Sowers; m. Harvey Richard Tucker, Dec. 27, 1958 (div. Nov. 1983); children: Randall Richard, Brian Alan. BS in Chemistry with distinction, Purdue U., 1958; MS in Geology, No. Ill. U., 1985; MA in Library and Info. Sci., Rosary Coll., 1989. Asst. rsch. librarian CPC Internat., Argo, Ill., 1958-62; chem. patent searcher Chgo., 1962-66; info. specialist C. Berger & Co., Wheaton, Ill., 1986, Amoco Corp., Naperville, Ill., 1987-99, Baxter Healthcare, Round Lake, Ill., 1999—; faculty Coll. Du Page, Glen Ellyn, Ill., 1989—; with Baxter Healthcare, Round Lake, Ill., 1999—. Mem. Spl. Libraries Assn., Ill. Fedn. Women's Club (treas. 5th dist. 1979-81, Outstanding Jr. Clubwoman award 1979-80), Garden Club Council Wheaton (pres. 1981-82), Wheaton Jr. Woman's Club (pres. 1977-78, Single Parent scholar 1984), Gardens Etc. Club (pres. 1978-79), Alpha Lambda Delta, Delta Rho Kappa, Theta Sigma Phi, Alpha Chi Omega (grantee 1985). Republican. Presbyterian. Avocations: bridge, needlework, gourmet cooking. Home: 1507 Paula Ave Wheaton IL 60187-6135

TUCKER, CALANTHIA RALLINGS, school administrator; b. Chgo., Oct. 22, 1946; d. Donnell and Exie Bernettia (Williams) Rallings; m. Joseph Tuckerm June 25, 1967; children: La Canas Yvette, Tahirah Michelle Tucker Elliott. BS, Tenn. State U., 1968; MS, Va. Poly. and State U., 1978; EdD, Vanderbilt U., 1992. Tchr. Fairfax County Pub. Sch., Alexandria, Va., 1969-72, 1976-82, human rels. specialist, 1982-85; asst. prin. Robert E. Lee H.S., Springfield, Va., 1985-90; prin. Mt. Vernon H.S., Alexandria, 1990—; adminstrv. officer Fairfax County Pub. Schs. Supts. Office, 1999—. Cons. U. Va., 1984, Red Clay Sch. Dist., Wilmington, Del., 1997; guest lectr. George Washington U., Washington, 1996-98; mem. nat. safety focus group on sch. violence U.S. Dept. Edn., Calif., 1993. Exec. bd. mem. Gum Spring Cmty. Corp, Alexandria, 1994; mem. Mt. Vernon Cmty. Coalition, Alexandria, 1993—. Recipient Disting. Edn. Leadership award Washington Post, 1996-97, E.L. Patterson Cmty. Svc. award Urban League, Inc., 1997, Edn. award NAACP, Va., 1997; named Prin. of the Yr. Fairfax County Pub. Schs., 1996-97, Minority Achievement Prin. of the Yr., 1996. Mem. ASCD, Am. Assn. Sch. Adminstrs., Fairfax County H.S. Prins. Assn., Black Women United Action (Among Most Admired Women 1996), Phi Delta Kappa (historian), Delta Kappa Gamma. Democrat. Church of Christ. Avocations: art, reading, jogging. Home: 11106 Lakenheath Way Oakton VA 22124-1912 Office: Burkholder Adminstrv Ctr 10700 Page Ave Fairfax VA 22030-4006 E-mail: ctucker@burkholder.fcps.K12.va.us.

TUCKER, CATHERINE L. financial advisor; b. Rochester, N.Y., Feb. 20, 1955; d. Arthur R. and Teresa M. (Mazza) LaPietra; m. Robert P. Smithson, Jan. 1, 1982 (div. May 1996); m. Curtis C. Tucker, Sept. 9, 2000. AAS in Dental Hygiene, Erie C.C., Buffalo, 1975; BS in Health Edn., SUNY, Brockport, 1978; MS in Tchr. Prep., Allied Health, SUNY, Buffalo, 1980. CFP, 2001. Dental hygienist various dentists, Rochester, 1975—80; educator Owens Tech. Coll., Dayton, Ohio, 1980—82; travel agt. Triangle Travel, Middletown, Ohio, 1991—92; owner New Directions Travel, Middletown, Ohio, 1992—96; fin. advisor Am. Express Fin. Advisors, Middletown, 1996—. With USAR, 1977—79. Mem.: Mid Miami Valley C. of C. (bd. dirs. 1999—, exec. com. 1999—2002), Am. Bus. Women's Assn., Soroptimist Internat. Avocation: racquetball. Home and Office: 4509 Rosewood Ct Middletown OH 45042 Office Phone: 513-727-9990. E-mail: catherine.l.tucker@aexp.com.

TUCKER, CYNTHIA ANNE, journalist; b. Monroeville, Ala., Mar. 13, 1955; d. John Abney and Mary Louise (Marshall) Tucker; m. Michael Pierce, Dec. 26, 1987 (div. 1989). BA, Auburn U., 1976. Reporter The Atlanta Jour., 1976-80, editorial writer, columnist, 1983-86; reporter The Phila. Inquirer, 1980-82; assoc. editorial page editor The Atlanta Constitution, 1986-91, editorial page editor, 1992—. Bd. dirs. ARC, 1989-93, Families First, 1988—, Internat. Women's Media Found., 1994—. Nieman fellow Harvard U., 1988-89; Pullitzer Prize finalist for commentary, 2004. Mem.: Coun. Fgn. Rels., Nat. Assn. Minority Media Execs., Nat. Assn. Black Journalists, Am. Soc. Newspaper Editors (Disting. Writing award 2000). Mem. United Ch. Christ. Office: Atlanta Constitution 72 Marietta St NW Atlanta GA 30303-2804*

TUCKER, CYNTHIA DELORES NOTTAGE (MRS. WILLIAM M. TUCKER), political party official, former state official; b. Phila., Oct. 4, 1927; d. Whitfield and Captilda (Gardiner) Nottage; m. William M. Tucker, July 21, 1951. Student, Temple U., Pa. State U., U. Pa.; student hon. degrees, Villa Maria Coll., Erie, Pa., 1972, Morris Coll., Sumter, S.C., 1976; DHL (hon.), U. D.C. Sec. of state Commonwealth of Pa., Harrisburg, 1971-77; nat. pres. Fedn. Democratic Women, 1979-81; v.p. Pa. chpt. NAACP, nat. v.p. bd. trustees; mem. nat. adv. bd. Nat. Women's Polit. Caucus; now chair Black Caucus Nat. Dem. Com. Mem., vice chair Pa. Black Dem. Com., 1966—; chair Women for Dem. Action, 1967—; nat. chair Nat. Polit. Congress of Black Women, Inc., 1992—; sec., mem. Phila.

Zoning Bd. Adjustment, 1968-70; vice chair Pa. Dem. State Com., 1970-76; mem. exec. com. Dem. Nat. Com., 1972-76; Dem. candidate lt. gov., Pa., 1978; v.p. Phila. Tribune Newspaper; del. Dem. Nat. Conv., Pa., 2000. Del. to White Ho. Conf. on Civil Rights; bd. dirs. Phila. YWCA, New Sch. Music, Martin Luther King Ctr. for Social Change; pres., founder Phila. Martin Luther King Assn.; mem. Commonwealth bd. Med. Coll. Pa.; bd. assocs. Messiah Coll.; founder, pres. Bethune-DuBois Fund; bd. mem. Del. Valley Coll.; mem. adv. bd. Parents TV Coun.; spl. contbn. fund trustee NAACP. Recipient Freedom Fund award NAACP, 1961, Svc. and Achievement award NAACP, 1964, Phila. Tribune Charities Ann. award, Cmty. Svc. award Opportunities Industrialization Ctr., Emma V. Kelley Achievement award Nat. Elks, 1971, Thurgood Marshall award, 1982, Lincoln U. Nat. Leadership award, 1993, Cmty. Svc. award Quaker City chpt. B'nai B'rith; named Best Dressed Woman of Yr., Ebony mag., One of 100 Most Influential Black Ams., 1973-77; included in 1996 People mag.'s list of Twenty-Five Most Intriguing People; George Gallup Inst. fellow. Mem. Nat. Assn. Secs. State (v.p.), Pa. Bd. Property, Commn. Interest Coop., Gov. Affirmation Act Coun., Nat. Assn. Real Estate Brokers, Bus. and Profl. Women's Club, Links (dir.), Alpha Kappa Alpha (hon.). Achievements include first to to be an African-American president of the National Federation for Democratic Women. Home: 6700 Lincoln Dr Philadelphia PA 19119-3155

TUCKER, EUNICE JONES, secondary school educator, educator; b. Abbeville, Ala., Jan. 17, 1930; d. Drew and Emma Lee Jones; m. Percy Lee Ashford, Dec. 24, 1954 (div. Aug. 1976); 1 child, Randall Alonzo; m. Willie Zdvie Tucker, Nov. 18, 1985. BS, Ala. A&M U., 1954, MS, 1969. Tchr. biology Dixon Mills (Ala.) H.S., 1954-57; clk. Ala. A&M U., Normal, 1958-66; adminstr. Drake Tech. Coll., Normal, 1966-67; tchr. reading Moulton (Ala.) H.S., 1967-70; tchr. English Edd White Mid. Sch., Huntsville, Ala., 1970-71; tchr. sci. Whitesburg Mid. Sch., Huntsville, 1971-79, Stone Mid. Sch., Huntsville, 1979-92. Mem. Ala. Dem. Conf., Huntsville, 1993-96; mem. women's coalition Equality for Women, Huntsville, 1991—. Named to Nat. Women's Hall of Fame, 1994. Mem. AAUW (bd. dirs. 1994—), Nat. Libr. of Congress Assocs. (charter). Apostolic Holiness. Avocations: reading, decorating, basketball, walking, church work. Home: 2126 Pisgah Dr Huntsville AL 35810

TUCKER, JULIE ROBYN, illustrator, art educator; b. Nashville, Apr. 23, 1977; d. Walter Franklin and Jennifer Lynn (Thomas) Houdeshell; m. Kenneth Wayne Tucker, Nov. 2, 2002. BFA in Illustration with Art History minor, Savannah Coll. Art and Design, 1999. Freelance illustrator, Nashville, 1999—; art tchr. DeLand Mus. Art, Fla., 1999; art tchr. Harris House Atlantic Ctr. for the Arts, New Symrna, Fla., 2000; art tchr. Frist Ctr. for the Visual Arts, Nashville, 2001; art instr. Sarratt Ctr. Vanderbilt U., Nashville, 2001; art tchr. and visual arts studio mgr. Renaissance Ctr., Dickson, Tenn., 2001—. Artist in residence Williamson County Pks. and Recreation, various schs. in Williamson County. 14 illustrations, Florida Quest Educational Reading Guide, 2000; designer (cover art) Renaissance Ctr. Program Guide, lead artist and instr. (mural beautification project) Renaissance Ctr. Art tchr. at children's tent Tenn. Arts and Crafts Assn., Nashville, 2001—03; art tchr. for celebration of cultures Scarrit Bennett Ctr., Nashville, 2002. Mem.: Bd. Mus. Advs. (art tchr. African Am. St. Festival 2003). Conservative. Methodist. Avocations: singing, dance, acting. Office: The Renaissance Center 855 Highway 46 South Dickson TN 37055 E-mail: julie.tucker@rcenter.org., tuckerillustrations@earthlink.net.

TUCKER, MAUREEN ANN, musician; b. Jackson Heights, N.Y., Aug. 26, 1944; d. James Thomas and Margaret Mary (Daly) T.; divorced; children: Kerry, Keith, Austen, Kate, Richard. Grad., Levittown (N.Y.) Meml. H.S., 1962. Drummer Velvet Underground, 1965-71; guitarist, songwriter, singer Moe Tucker Band, 1989—. Recordings include (singer, guitarist, songwriter) Playin Possum, 1981, Life in Exile After Abdication, 1986, (prodr., arranger) I Spent a Week There The Other Night, 1990, Dogs Under Stress, 1993; drummer Lou Reed Band, Japan, 1990, European tours with Velvet Underground, 1993, Moe Tucker Band, 1989—. Tchr. English St. Pauls Hispanic Ministry, Douglas, Ga., 1990—. Inducted into Rock & Roll Hall of Fame, 1996. Roman Catholic. Office: Maureen Tucker Music PO Box 2357 Douglas GA 31534-2357

TUCKER, NINA ANGELLA, hospital administrator; b. Miami, Fla., June 6, 1965; d. Joseph John and Diane (Accolla) A.; 1 child, Ryan. BA, Emory U., Atlanta, Ga., 1987; MA in Health Adminstrn., MBA, U. Fla., Gainesville, 1990. Asst. adminstr. Med. City Dallas, 1990-92, Meml. Hosp. West, Pembroke Pines, Fla., 1992-95; adminstr. Joe DiMaggio Children's Hosp. Women's Svcs. at Meml. Regional Hosp., Hollywood, Fla., 1995—. Pres. Meml. Employees Fedl. Credit Union, 1993—. Recipient Regents award Am. Coll. Healthcare Execs., 1996. Roman Catholic. Avocations: walking, water skiing. Office: Meml Regional Hosp 3501 Johnson St Hollywood FL 33021-5487

TUCKER, RHONDA RENEÉ, music educator; b. Gallapolis, Ohio, Apr. 11, 1959; d. Jimmy Gene and Margaret June Tucker. BME, Birmingham-So. Coll., 1981; MusM in Edn., Samford U., 1990. Cert. tchr. Ala., nat. bd. cert. tchr. Music tchr. Southside Baptist Ch. Early Childhood Ctr., Birmingham, Ala., 1981—82, Shades Cahaba Elem. Sch., Homewood, Ala., 1982—. Author: Words to Play By, 2001. Nominee Disting. Tchr., Birmingham Post Herald, 1998—99. Mem.: NEA, Ala. Music Educator's Assn. (pres. elect 2001—03, pres. 2003—), Am. Orff-Schulwerk Assn. (pres. 1993—95). Republican. Methodist. Avocations: musical theatre, singing, playing piano, playing flute, tap dancing. Office: Shades Cahaba Elementary School 3001 Montgomery Hwy Homewood AL 35209

TUCKER, SHIRLEY LOIS COTTER, botany educator, researcher; b. St. Paul, Apr. 4, 1927; d. Ralph U. and Myra C. (Knutson) Cotter; m. Kenneth W. Tucker, Aug. 22, 1953. BA, U. Minn., 1949, MS, 1951; PhD, U. Calif., Davis, 1956. Asst. prof. botany La. State U., Baton Rouge, 1967-71, assoc. prof., 1971-76, prof., 1976-82, Boyd prof., 1982-95, prof. emerita, 1995—. Adj. prof. dept. biology U. Calif., Santa Barbara, 1995—. Co-editor: Aspects of Floral Development, 1988, Advances in Legume Systematics, Vol. 6, 1994; contbr. numerous articles on plant devel. to profl. jours. Recipient, Outstanding Alumni Achievement award U. Minn., 1999; fellow Linnean Soc., London, 1975—, Fulbright fellow Eng., 1952-53. Mem. Bot. Soc. Am. (v.p. 1979, program chmn. 1975-78, pres.-elect 1986-87, pres. 1987-88, Merit award 1989), Am. Bryological and Lichenological Soc., Brit. Lichenological Soc., Am. Inst. Biol. Scis., Am. Soc. Plant Taxonomists (pres.-elect 1994-95, pres. 1995-96), Phi Beta Kappa, Sigma Xi. Home: 3987 Primavera Rd Santa Barbara CA 93110-1467 Office: U Calif Dept Biology EEMB Santa Barbara CA 93106 Business E-Mail: tucker@lifesci.ucsb.edu.

TUCKER, SUSAN CAROL, state legislator; b. Winfield, Kans., Nov. 7, 1944; d. Allen and Jeanne (Lawrence) Shaffer; m. Mike A. Tucker, Dec. 2, 1967; children: Mark, David. Student, U. Nigeria, 1965; BA magna cum laude, Mich. State U., 1966. English tchr. Lexington (Mass.) High Sch., 1966-69; legis. aide Mass. Legislature, Boston, 1980-82; mem. Ho. of Reps. Mass. Great and Gen. Ct., Boston, 1983-92, vice chair edn. com., chair spl. commn. on child abuse, mem enery com., ethics com.; mem. Mass. Senate, Boston, 1998-. Chair Mass. Caucus Women Legislators. V.p. Mass. LWV, Boston, 1977-80. Recipient Environ. Achievement award Environ. Lobby Mass., 1984, Legislator of Yr. for Victim's Rights award, 1990. Mem. Nat. Women's Polit. Caucus. Democrat. Office: Mass Senate R 416-A State House Boston MA 02133

TUCKER, TANYA DENISE, singer; b. Seminole, Tex., Oct. 10, 1958; d. Beau and Juanita Tucker; children: Presley, Beau Grayson. Singer Tanya Tucker Inc., 1959—. Regular on Lew King Show; rec. artist formerly with Columbia Records, MCA Records, Capital Records; albums include Tear Me Apart, Chagnes, Delta Dawn, Dreamlovers, Here's Some Love, TNT, Girls Like Me, Greatest Hits, 1989, Greatest Hits (1972-75), Greatest Hits Encore, 1990, Greatest Country Hits, 1991, Greatest Hits 1990-92, 1993, Love Me Like You Use To, 1987, Strong Enough to Bend, 1988, Tanya Tucker Live, Tennesee Woman, 1990, What Do I Do With Me, 1991, (with Delbert McClinton) Can't Run From Youself, 1992, Soon, 1993, Fire to Fire, 1994, (with T. Graham Brown, Delbert McClinton) Tanya, 1995, Christmas with Tanya Tucker and Suzy Bogguss, 1995, The Best of My Love, 1995, Love Songs, 1996, Complicated, 1997, Little Things, 1997, Super Hits, 1998; TV appearances include A Country Christmas, 1979, The Georgia Peaches, 1980; actress: (mini-series) The Rebels, 1979, (film) Jeremiah Johnson, 1968. Recipient: Country Music Assn. award, 1991, female vocalist of the year; 2 Grammy nominations, 1994. Office: Tanya Tucker Inc 109 Westpark Dr Ste 400 Brentwood TN 37027-5032

TUCKNER, MICHELLE, newscaster; b. Hudson, Wis. BS in Journalism/Broadcast News, U. Kans. Weekend news reporter KTKA, Topeka; anchor/reporter WEAU-TV Channel 13, 2000—. Recipient award, Kans. Assn. Broadcasters, William Randolph Hearst Journalism awards; scholar, Assn. for Women in Sports Media, 1999. Office: WEAU PO Box 47 Eau Claire WI 54702

TUDOR, BRENDA S. retail company executive; CPA. Acct. Strand, Skees, Jones & Co., Asheville, N.C.; gen. acctg. mgr. Ingles Markets, Inc., Black Mountain, N.C., 1984-88; controller, sec., 1988-98; v.p., CFO, 1998—; also bd. dirs. Office: Ingles Markets Inc 1560 Hwy 70 E Black Mountain NC 28711

TUDRYN, JOYCE MARIE, professional society administrator; b. Holyoke, Mass., July 27, 1959; d. Edward William and Frances Katherine (Bajor) T.; m. William Wallace Friberger III, Sept. 18, 1982; 1 child, Kristen. BS in Comm., Syracuse U., 1981. Asst. editor Nat. Assn. Broadcasters, Washington, 1981-83; dir. programs Internat. Radio and TV Soc. Found., N.Y.C., 1983-87, assoc. exec. dir., 1988-94; exec. dir. Internat. Radio and TV Soc., N.Y.C., 1994-97, pres., 1997—. Spkr. in field; nat. adv. bd. Alpha Epsilon Rho Broadcasting Soc., 1988-91, 93-94, hon. trustee, 1994-98, officer, 1999-2001; v.p. Corp. for Ednl. Radio and TV, 1988-94; adv. bd. Marist Coll. Sch. Comm., 1999—, Syracuse U. Newhouse Sch. Pub. Comm., 1999—; vice chmn. edn. iEmmy Festival, 1999; guest prof. U. Scranton, 2000. Columnist TV Facts, Figures and Film mag., 1983-88; one-woman photography exhbn. Synchronicity Space, N.Y.C., 1998. Recipient Disting. Edn. Svc. award Broadcast Edn. Assn., 2003; named one of Most Influential Women in Radio, Radio INK Mag., 2003; inducted into Syracuse U. Newhouse Sch. Profl. Wall of Fame Gallery, 2000. Mem. N.Y. Media Roundtable, Gamma Phi Beta. Avocation: photography. Office: Internat Radio and TV Soc Found 420 Lexington Ave Ste 1601 New York NY 10170-1799

TUETING, SARAH, professional hockey player; b. Winnetka, Ill., Apr. 26, 1976; Degree in neurobiology, Dartmouth Coll. Goal keeper U.S. Nat. Women's Hockey Team, 1996—. Recipient Ice hockey Gold medal Olympic Games, Nagano, Japan, 1998. Avocations: soccer, tennis, playing piano and cello. Office: c/o USA Hockey 1775 Bob Johnson Dr Colorado Springs CO 80906

TUFT, MARY ANN, executive search firm executive; b. Easton, Pa., Oct. 11, 1934; d. Ben and Elizabeth (Reibman) T. BS, West Chester (Pa.) State Coll., 1956; MA, Lehigh U., 1960. Cert. assn. exec. Nat. trainer Girl Scouts U.S.A., N.Y.C., 1965-68; cons. Nat. League for Nursing, N.Y.C., 1968-69; exec. dir. Nat. Student Nurses Assn., N.Y.C., 1970-85; mem. Commn. on Dietetic Registration, Am. Dietetic Assn., 1981-85; pres. Specialized Cons. Ltd., 1983-85; exec. dir. Radiol. Soc. N.Am., Oak Brook, Ill., 1985-88; pres. Tuft & Assocs., Inc., 1989—. Trustee, Found. of the Nat. Student Nurses Assn., 2001—; adv. bd. Cognitive Neurology and Alzheimer's Disease Ctr. of Northwestern Univ./Feinberg Sch. of Medicine. Bd. dirs. Nurses House, Inc., 1981-85, Am. Friends of Hebrew U., Midwest Region, 2000—; bd. dirs. Chgo. Sinai Cong., 1987-91, v.p., 1988. Recipient Disting. Alumnus award West Chester State Coll., 1979; Mary Ann Tuft Scholarship Fund named in her honor Found. Nat. Student Nurses Assn.; Kepner-Tregoe scholar, 1966. Mem. ALA (pub. mem. com. on accreditation 1993-95), Am. Soc. AAssn. Execs. (bd. dirs. 1980-83, trustee for cert. 1980-83, vice chmn. 1983-84), N.Y. Soc. Assn. Execs. (pres. 1978-79, bd. dirs. 1975-78, 1st Outstanding Exec. award 1982), Continuing Care Accreditation Assn. (bd. dirs. 1983-85), Specialized Cons. in Nursing (faculty). Office Phone: 312-642-8889. E-mail: matuft@tuftassoc.com.

TUFTE, VIRGINIA JAMES, humanities educator, writer; b. Meadow Grove, Nebr. d. Micah Dickerson and Sarah Elizabeth (Bartee) James; m. Edward E. Tufte; 1 child, Edward Rolf. BA, U. Nebr., 1944; PhD, UCLA, 1964. Prof. English Renaissance lit. U. So. Calif., L.A., 1964-89, disting. prof. of English emerita, 1993—. Cons. Milton Studies and other jours., MLA, Ednl. Testing Svc., NEH. Co-author: Remembered Lives, 1992; co-editor: Changing Images of the Family, 1979; contbr. articles to profl. jours.; author: The Poetry of Marriage, 1970, Grammar as Style, 1971; co-author: Exercises in Creativity, 1971; author, prodr. (video) Reaching for Paradise: The Life and Art of Carlotta Petrina, 1994; editor: High Wedlock Then Be Honoured, 1970. Fellow William Andrews Clark Libr., L.A., 1963-64. Mem. MLA, AAUP, Renaissance Soc. Am., Renaissance Conf. So. Calif., Nat. Mus. Women in Arts, Phi Beta Kappa. Avocations: visual arts, illustrated books, life histories.

TUFTON, JANIE LEE (JANE TUFTON), dental hygienist, animal rights lobbyist, activist; b. Allentown, Pa., Jan. 6, 1949; d. Robert Harry and Jean Lorraine (Seng) T. BS in Edn., Indiana U. Pa., 1979; postgrad. in English, 1979-82. Registered dental hygienist, Pa., N.J., Calif.; cert. tchr., Pa. Dental hygienist pvt. dental practices, Pa., N.J., Calif., 1976-90. Author bd. game for dental health edn., 1974. Lobbyist, activist for animal rights; bd. dirs. and pub. rels. Lehigh Valley Animal Rights Coalition, 1984-93; active civil rights movement, cultural events, literacy programs, detoxification units for drug and alcohol abuse, venereal disease clinics, practical-life workshops for the cognitively impaired, suicide hotlines, YWCA, Girl Scouts U.S. Recipient recognition Pa. Dental Hygienists Assn., 1974 Mem. Am. Anti-Vivisect. Soc., Nat. Humane Edn. Soc., The Fund for Animals, The Humane Soc. of the U.S., Nat. Alliance for Animals, Internat. Soc. for Animal Rights, Physicians Com. for Responsible Medicine, Culture and Animals Found., Animal Legal Def. Fund, People for the Ethical Treatment of Animals, Farm Animal Reform Movement, Farm Sanctuary, Com. to Abolish Sport Hunting, Animal Rights Mobilization, In Def. of Animals, United Animal Nations, Internat. Platform Assn., Internat. Network for Religion and Animals, Humane Religion, Performing Animal Welfare Socs., Disabled and Incurably Ill for Alternatives to Animal Rsch., United Poultry Concerns, Am. Soc. for Prevention of Cruelty to Animals. Avocations: photography, tennis, reading, environmental issues, women's studies. Home: 2102 S Lehigh Ave Whitehall PA 18052-5532

TUGEND, ALINA NURIT, journalist; b. L.A., Sept. 23, 1959; d. Thomas and Rachel Tugend; m. Mark Andrew Stein; children: Benjamin Tugendstein, Gabriel Tugendstein. BA, U. Calif., Berkeley, 1981; MS in Law, Yale U., 1987. Staff writer UPI, Providence, 1982—83, Education Week, Washington, 1985—86, L.A. Herald Examiner, 1987—89; environ. writer Orange County Register, Santa Ana, Calif., 1989—94; London corrs. Chronicle Higher Edn., London, 1994—2000; freelance writer NY, 2000—. Jewish.

TUGEND, JENNIE LEW, film producer; b. L.A., Dec. 13, 1948; d. Jack W.F. and Angela (Huang) Lew; m. James Tugend, Dec. 31, 1987. Film prodr. JLT Prodns., L.A. Mentor Peter Stark Producing Program, U. So. Calif. Prodr. Lethal Weapon, 1987, Scrooged, 1988, (with Steve Perry) Lethal Weapon 2, 1989, Lethal Weapon 3, 1992; (with Dale R. de la Torre, Jim Van Wyck) Radio Flyer, 1992, (with Lauren Shuler-Donner) Free Willy, 1993, Free Willy 2, 1995, Free Willy 3, 1997, Star Kid, 1998, Return to Me, 2000. Mem. SAG, Prodrs. Guild Am., Acad. Motion Picture Arts and Scis.

TUISKU, MARY JOAN, volunteer, advocate; b. Laurium, Mich., May 30, 1946; d. Allwin Eugene Dina Joseph and Gladys Muriel Prideaux; m. Richard H. Tuisku, June 24, 1967; children: Tammy Ann Bricker, Jason Christian, Jodi Marie. Assoc. Degree, No. Mich. U., 1966. Customer svc. Sears, Houghton, Mich., 1966—68, D&N Bank, Hancock, Mich., 1982—91. Cons. TU-Mar Broadcasting, Houghton, 1993—. Active Hancock Recreation Commn., 1980—94, Sister Cities Com., 1988—2003, Hancock Finnish Theme Com., 1990—2003, Hancock Planning Commn., 1990—95, Hancock Hist. Preservation Commn., 1992—95, Quincy Area Adv. Coun., Hancock, 1992—95, Mich. Tech. U. Multi-cultural Com., Houghton, Hancock Pub. Schools Libr. Adv. Com.; chairperson Hancock Ordinance Revision Com., 1990—93; commr. Western Upper Peninsula Planning & Devel. Region, Houghton, 1990—95, Keweenaw Nat. Hist. Pk. Adv. Commn., Calumet, Mich., 1993—97; city councilor City of Hancock, 1982—2003, mayor, 1990—95; chairperson new ch. bldg. com. Glad Tidings, Hancock; chairperson Mich. Technol. U. Cmty. Adv. Coun., Houghton, 1992—95; panelist Mich. Coun. for the Arts and Cultural Affairs, Lansing. Named Civic Leader of the Yr., Keweenaw Peninsula C. of C., 1994, Citizen of the Yr., Salvation Army. Mem.: Omicron Delta Kappa. Independent. Avocations: reading, travel, music, sports, art. Home: 939 Lynn St Hancock MI 49930 Office: MJET Consulting 939 Lynn St Hancock MI 49930 Office Phone: 906-482-7368. E-mail: mtuisku@up.net.

TULIN, MARNA, psychotherapist; b. N.Y.C., Feb. 23, 1930; d. Irving Bernsohn and Gloria Bernsohn Turner; m. Harold Klingbeil, Feb. 14, 1948 (dec. May 1952); 1 child, Deborah Klingbeil Tulin-Donnell; m. Stephen Wise Tulin, Jan. 31, 1959; children: Douglas Wise, Andrea Wise, Houlihan. BA, NYU, 1960; MSW, Columbia U., 1962; PhD in Psychology, Tulane-Pacific Western U., 1988. LCSW N.Y., Vt., diplomate social work. Caseworker Cmty. Svc. Soc., N.Y.C., 1962-63, Jewish Child Care Assn., N.Y.C., 1964-67; psychotherapist Jewish Child Care Psychiat. Clinic, N.Y.C., 1967-70; cons. pre-K, spl. needs program, home learning Mamaroneck (N.Y.) Sch. Sys., 1976-80; pvt. practice psychotherapist N.Y.C., Westchester, 1980-92, North Ferrisburg, Vt., 1993—; cons. parents place Mamaroneck (N.Y.) Sch. Sys., 1980-81; cons. Stamford (Conn.) Sch. Sys., 1981, Bank St. Coll. Edn., N.Y.C., 1987; pvt. practice North Ferrisburg, 1993—. Chmn. bd. Louise Wise Svc., N.Y.C., 1991—93, dir. emeritus; trustee Howard Ctr. for Human Svcs., Burlington, Vt., 1997—; mem. profl. adv. com. Mental Health Assn. N.Y., 1993—2000. Mem. AAUW, Internat. Conf. for Advancement Pvt. Practice Social Workers, Pi Sigma Alpha. Democrat. Jewish. Avocation: antique dealing. Home and Office: 100 Champlin Hill Rd North Ferrisburg VT 05473-4076 Fax: 802-425-3384.

TULL, THERESA ANNE, retired diplomat; b. Runnemede, N.J., Oct. 2, 1936; d. John James and Anna Cecelia (Paull) T. BA, U. Md., 1972; MA, U. Mich., 1973; postgrad., Nat. War Coll., Washington, 1980. Fgn. svc. officer Dept. State, Washington, 1963, Brussels, 1965-67, Saigon, 1968-70; dep. prin. officer Am. Consulate General, Danang, Vietnam, 1973-75; prin. officer Cebu, Philippines, 1977-79; dir. office human rights, 1980-83; charge d'affaires Am. Embassy, Vientiane, Laos, 1983-86; Dept. State Senior Seminar, 1986-87; ambassador to Guyana, 1987-90; diplomat-in-residence Lincoln U., Pa., 1990-91; dir. office regional affairs, bur. East Asian & Pacific affairs Dept. State, Washington, 1991-93; amb. to Brunei Bandar Seri Begawan, 1993-96. Recipient Civilian Service award Dept. of State, 1970, Superior Honor award, 1977 Mem. Am. Fgn. Svc. Assn., Women's Civic Club. Address: 3500 Boardwalk Apt 726N Sea Isle City NJ 08243

TULLIS, TRICIA M. marketing professional; b. Green Bay, Wis., Dec. 20, 1965; d. Lee Peter and Mary Lou Roffers. BS in mktg., Edgewood Coll., Wis. Assoc. mktg. mgr. Rayovac Corp., Madison, Wis., 1996—98, channel mktg. mgr., 1998—2001, nat. account mgr., 2001—. Vol. Habitat for Humanity, Madison, Wis. Mem.: Women's Insight Network. Office: Rayovac Corp 601 Rayovac Dr Madison WI 53711 E-mail: tullis@rayovac.com.

TULLOS, BARBARA WADDELL, art educator; b. Nassawadox, Va., July 31, 1947; d. Henry Marsden and Geraldine Payne Waddell; m. Charles Gilbert Tullos, Mar. 10, 1973; children: Sara Ansley, Anna Whitney, Elizabeth Brownrigg. BA, Fla. State U., 1969; MEd, Troy State U., 1989. Graphic designer Baton Bursten and Osborne, Atlanta, 1969—71, Ga. State U., Atlanta, 1972—76; art educator Carver Creative and Performing Arts Ctr., Montgomery, Ala., 1989—92, Montgomery Acad., 1992—. Contbr. chapters to books Imaginative Learning, The Arts: Design for Understanding, Weaving Arts into the Curriculum. Task force children's mus. Jr. League, Montgomery, 1985—88; treas. Ala. Alliance Art Edn., 1998—2000, mem. exec. bd., 2000—. Recipient Ala. Elem. Divsn. Art Educator of the Yr., Ala. Art Edn. Assn., 1997; Fulbright-Hays fellow, U.S. Ednl. Commn., 1998, Fulbright fellow, Japan-U.S. Ednl. Commn., 1999. Mem.: Ala. Art Edn. Assn. (elem. divsn. chmn. 2001—03, bd. dir. 1994—, J. Eugene Grigsby Jr. award 1998). Episcopalian. Avocations: travel, pastel drawing. Home: 741 Thorn Pl Montgomery AL 36106 Office: Montgomery Acad 1550 Perry Hill Rd Montgomery AL 36106 E-mail: tullos.b@montgomeryacademy.org.

TULLY, SUSAN BALSLEY, pediatrician, medical educator; b. San Francisco, July 12, 1941; d. Gerard E. Balsley Sr. and Norma Lilla (Hand) Carey; m. William P. Tully, June 19, 1965; children: Michael William, Stephen Gerard. BA in Premed. Studies, UCLA, 1963, MD, 1966. Diplomate Am. Bd. Pediat. with subsplty. in pediatric emergency medicine. Intern L.A. County-U. So. Calif. Med. Ctr., 1966-67, jr. resident pediat., 1967-68; staff pediatrician, part-time Permanente Med. Group, Oakland, Calif., 1968; sr. resident pediat. Kaiser Found. Hosp., Oakland, 1968-69, Bernalillo County Med. Ctr., Albuquerque, 1969-70, chief resident pediatric outpatient dept., 1970; instr. pediat., asst. dir. outpatient dept. U. N.Mex. Sch. Medicine, Albuquerque, 1971-72; asst. prof. pediat., dir. ambulatory pediat. U. Calif., Irvine, 1972-76, asst. prof. clin. pediat., vice chair med. edn., 1977-79; staff pediatrician Ross-Loos Med. Group, Buena Park, Calif., 1976-77; assoc. prof. clin. pediat. and emergency medicine U. So. Calif. Sch. Medicine, 1979-86; dir. pediatric emergency dept. L.A. County/U. So. Calif. Med. Ctr., 1979-87; prof. clin. pediat. and emergency medicine U. So. Calif. Sch. Medicine, 1986-89; dir. ambulatory pediat. L.A. County/U. So. Calif. Med. Ctr., 1987-89; clin. prof. pediat. UCLA, 1989-93, vice chair pediat., 1996-97, prof. clin. pediat., 1993-97, prof. emeritus, 1997—; dir. ambulatory pediat. Olive View-UCLA Med. Ctr., 1989-96, chief pediat., 1996-97, cons. pediatrician, 1997—. Mem. survey team pediatric emergency svcs. L.A. Pediatric Soc., 1984—86; mem. adv. bd. preventive health project univ. affiliated program Children's Hosp. L.A., 1981—83; lectr. nursing pediat. nurse practitioner program Calif. State U., L.A., 1997—; pediat. toxicology cons. L.A. County Regional Poison Control Ctr. Med. Adv. Bd., 1981—97; clin. faculty rep. pediatric advancement and promotion com. UCLA Sch. Medicine, 1992—93; pediatric liaison dept. emergency medicine Olive View/UCLA Med. Ctr., 1989—96, dir. lead poisoning clinic, 1993—99; mem. quality assurance com. Los Angeles County Cmty.

Health Plan, 1986—89. Author: (with K.E. Zenk) Pediatric Nurse Practitioner Formulary, 1979; (book chpt. with W.A. Wingert) Pediatric Emergency Medicine: Concepts and Clinical Practice, 1992, 2d edit., 1997; (with others) Educational Guidelines for Ambulatory/General Pediatrics Fellowship Training, 1992, Physician's Resource Guide for Water Safety Education, 1994, reviewer Pediatrics, 1985-89; editl. cons. Advanced Pediatric Life Support Course and Manual, 1988-89, Archives of Pediatrics and Adolescent Medicine, 1996—; dept. editor Pediatric Pearls Jour. Am. Acad. Physician Assts., 1989-94; tech. cons., reviewer Healthlink TV Am. Acad. Pediatrics, 1991; reviewer Pediatric Emergency Care, 1992—; question writer sub-bd. pediatric emergency medicine Am. Bd. Pediatrics, 1993-98; assoc. editor: Curriculum for the Training of General Pediatricians, 1996; cons. to lay media NBC Nightly News, Woman's Day, Sesame Street Parents, Parenting, Los Angeles Times; author numerous abstracts; contbr. articles to profl. jours. Cons. spl. edn. programs Orange County Bd. Edn., 1972-79; mem. Orange County Child Health Planning Coun., 1973-79; co-chairperson Orange County Child Health and Disability Prevention Program Bd., 1975-76; mem. Orange County Child Abuse Consultation Team, 1977-79; mem. project adv. bd. Family Focussed "Buckle Up" Project, Safety Belt Safe, U.S.A., 1989-96. Fellow Am. Acad. Pediat. (life, active numerous sects. and coms., active Calif. chpt.); mem. APHA, Ambulatory Pediatric Assn., L.A. Pediatric Soc. (life). Democrat. Avocations: art needlework, reading. Office: Olive View UCLA Med Ctr Pediatrics 3A108 14445 Olive View Dr Sylmar CA 91342-1495

TUMPSON, JOAN BERNA, artist; BA with highest distinction, Northwestern U., 1969; JD, Yale U., 1973. Bar: N.Y. 1974, U.S. Dist. Ct. (so. and ea. dists.) N.Y. 1974, U.S. Ct. Appeals (2d cir.) 1975, U.S. Dist. Ct. (no. dist.) Ohio 1977,. U.S. Supreme Ct., 1977, Ohio 1980, Fla. 1980, U.S. Dist. Ct. (so. dist.) Fla. 1981. Gen. assignment reporter, rewriteman AP, N.Y. Bur., A.P. Stringer, Yale U., 1970-72; assoc. Debevoise Plimpton Lyons & Gates (now Debevoise & Plimpton), N.Y.C., 1973-77; staff atty., lectr. law Cleve. Marshall Law Sch., Cleve. State U., 1977-78; vis. asst. prof. law Case Western Res. U., Cleve., 1978-79; assoc. Sage Gray Todd & Sims, Miami, Fla., 1980-82; ptnr. Tumpson & Astbury, Miami, 1982-92, Tumpson & Charchat, Miami, 1993-98; artist, 1998—. Class of 73 sec. Yale Law Sch.; bd. dirs. Greater Miami Jewish Fedn. Cable TV, Inc., 1988-92, long term planning com.; trustee Dade County Art in Pub. Places Trust, 1989-93; host south Fla. talk show One to One Sta. WAXY-AM, 1994-98; active Dem. Bus. Coun., 1996-97. Mem. Fla. Bar, Yale Club Miami Studio: 535 SW 12th Ave Miami FL 33135 E-mail: Tumpson@aol.com.

TUNHEIM, KATHRYN H. public relations executive; b. Sacred Heart, Minn., 1956; BA in Polit. Sci., U. Minn., 1979. Staff asst. U.S. Senator Wendell Anderson, 1977-79; mgr., bus. planning NCR Comten, 1979-81; corp. pub. rels. mgr. Honeywell, 1981-84, dir. corp. pub. rels., 1985-86; v.p. pub. rels. and internal comm. Honeywell Inc., 1987-90; pres., CEO Tunheim Santrizos, Mpls., 1990—. Office: Tunheim Santrizos 1100 Riverview Tower 8009 34th Ave S Minneapolis MN 55425-1608

TUNNELL, CLIDA DIANE, air transportation specialist; b. Durham, N.C., Nov. 20, 1946; d. Kermit Wilbur and Roberta (Brantley) T.; m. Michael A. Murphy, May 24, 1997. BS cum laude, Atlantic Christian Coll., 1968; pvt. pilot rating, instr. rating, Air Care, Inc., 1971, 83. Cert. tchr. Tchr. Colegio Karl C. Parrish, Barranquilla, Colombia, 1968-69, Nash County Schs., Nashville, N.C., 1969-86; ground sch. instr. Nash. Tech. Coll., Nashville, 1984-85; specialist Am. Airlines, Dallas-Ft. Worth Airport, Tex., 1987—, A300 lead developer in flight tng. program devel., 1988-89, with flight ops. procedures flight ops. tech., 1990—, F100-fleet splst. flight ops. tech., 1990—98, 737 fleet splst., 1998—2002, mgr. flight ops. procedures, 2003—. Ednl. cons., Euless, Tex., 1989—; profl. artist. State Tchrs. Scholar N.C., 1964-68, Bus. and Profl. Women Scholar, 1980-81. Mem. 99, Internat. Orgn. Women Pilots (various offices), AMR Mgmt. Club. Avocations: flying, painting, writing, traveling. Home: PO Box 234 Euless TX 76039-0234

TUNSTALL, DOROTHY FIEBRICH, early childhood educator; b. Elizabeth City, Va., Sept. 18, 1939; d. Louie Ludwig and Nancy Julia (Drafts) Fiebrich; m. Frank S. Clark Jr., June 11, 1961 (div. 1970); children: Sherri Ann D'Alessio, Debra Sue Pate, Frank S. Clark III; m. Jim Tunstall, June 1987 (div. 1995). BA in Elem. Edn., Stetson U., 1961, MA in Edn., 1963; Ed. Spec. in Edn. Adminstrn., U. S.C., 1991, PhD in Early Childhood, 1993. Cert. tchr. Fla., S.C. Substitute tchr. Broward County Schs., Ft. Lauderdale, Fla., 1963-70, EABE tchr., 1972-80; title I, tchr. for fed. govt. South Fla. State Hosp., Pembroke Pines, Fla., 1970-72; tchr. spl. edn. Richland Sch. Dist. #2, Columbia, S.C., 1980-81; COBOL programmer Comptr. Gen.'s Office, Columbia, 1982-85; tchr. spl. edn. Calhoun County Schs., St. Matthews, S.C., 1985-88; tchr. kindergarten Fairfield County Schs., Winnsboro, S.C., 1989-92; dir. St. Paul's Child Care Ministry, Columbia, SC, 1997—2000, Good Shepherd Day Sch., Columbia, 2001—. Adj. prof. U. S.C., Columbia, 1994—. Active Lexington County Adolescent Pregnancy Prevention Bd., 1999—, Lexington County First Steps Bd., 2001—03; v.p. unit 7 Am. Legion Aux., 2000—02, pres. unit 7, 2002—. Mem.: AAUW (pres. 1998—2002), Mental Health Assn. in Mid-Carolina (v.p. 1992—93, bd. dirs., Pres. award 1993), Lexington County Arts Assn. (pres. 1992—93, Newcomer's award 1981), Wildlife Action Inc. (pres. 1991—93), Beta Sigma Phi (Girl of Yr. 1967). Avocations: reading, gardening. Home: 159 Corley Mill Rd Lexington SC 29072-7600 Office: Good Shepherd Day Sch 3909 Forest Dr Columbia SC 29204 E-mail: directorgsds@aol.com.

TURCOT, MARGUERITE HOGAN, medical researcher; b. White Plains, N.Y., May 19, 1934; d. Joseph William (dec.) and Marguerite Alice (dec.) Barrett) Hogan; children: Michael J., Susan A. Turcot, William R. Student, Syracuse U., 1951-54; BSN, U. Bridgeport, 1968. RN, Conn., N.C. Nurse Park City Hosp., Bridgeport, Conn., 1968-69, Meml. Mission Hosp., Asheville, N.C., 1969-70; instr. St. Joseph's Hosp., Asheville, 1970-71, oper. rm. nurse, 1973-77, charge nurse urology-cystoscopy, 1977-85; tchr. Asheville-Buncombe Tech. Coll., Asheville, 1971-72, Buncombe County Child Devel., Asheville, 1972-73; rschr. VA Med. Ctr., Asheville, 1988—; owner Reed House Bed & Breakfast, Asheville, 1985—2001. Bd. dirs. RiverLink, Quality Foreward. Charter mem. French Broad River Planning Com., Asheville, 1987—, Biltmore Village Hist. Mus.; mem. Asheville Bicentennial Commn., 1990-93. Recipient Griffin award, 1994, Friend of the River award, Land of Sky Regional Coun., 1995, Sondley award, Hist. Resources Commn. Asheville and Buncombe County, 1996, Vol. of Yr. award, RiverLink, 2001, Critical Link award, 2003; grantee U. Bridgeport, 1967—68; scholar Syracuse U. Faculty, 1951—54. Mem. Am. Urology Assn. (presenter VA urology workshop Asheville chpt. 1981, nat. meeting allied), Am. Bd. Urologic Allied Health Profls., Nat. Trust for Hist. Preservation, Preservation Found. N.C., Blue Ridge Pkwy. Assn., Preservation Soc. Asheville and Buncombe County (bd. dirs., past pres.), Asheville Newcomers Club (founder, 1st pres.), Earthwatch, Friends of Blue Ridge Pkwy. Inc. Republican. Roman Catholic. Avocations: preservation, history, architecture, sewing, hiking. Home: 130 School Rd Asheville NC 28806-1532 Office: VA Med Ctr Tunnel Rd Asheville NC 28805-1233

TURCZYN-TOLES, DOREEN MARIE, pharmaceutical consultant; b. Chelsea, Mass., Aug. 5, 1958; d. Francis Henry and Rosalie (Lomba) Turczyn. BA cum laude, Boston U., 1981; MA, U. Chgo., 1984. Programming subcontr. Abbott Labs., Abbott Park, Ill., 1983-84; programmer, analyst Nat. Opinion Rsch. Ctr., Chgo., 1984-88; statis. computing analyst G.D. Searle & Co., Skokie, Ill., 1988-90; supr. Parke-Davis Pharms., Ann Arbor, Mich., 1990-92; mgr. applications programming Univax Biologics, Inc., Rockville, Md., 1993-95; asst. project dir. Apache Med. Sys., Inc., McLean, Va., 1995-96; group mgr. Westat, Inc., Rockville, Md., 1996—2002. Mem. NAFE, NOW. Democrat. Presbyterian.

TUREK, SONIA FAY, journalist; b. N.Y.C., Aug. 2, 1949; d. Louis and Julia (Liebson) T.; m. Gilbert Curtis, June 18, 1995. BA in English, CCNY, 1970; MSLS, Drexel U., 1972; MS in Journalism, Boston U., 1979. Children's libr. Wissahickon Valley Pub. Libr., Ambler, Pa., 1973; supr. children's svcs. Somerville Pub. Libr., Somerville, Mass., [illegible] The Watertown (Mass.) Sun, 1979, The Bedford (Mass.) Minuteman, 1979; reporter The Middlesex News, Framingham, Mass., 1979-83, The Boston Herald, 1983, asst. city editor, city editor, 1983-86, asst. mng. editor features, 1986-89, asst. mng. editor Sunday, 1989-93, dep. mng. editor, arts and features, 1993-99, wine columnist, 1984—. Tchr. Cambridge (Mass.) Ctr. for Adult Edn., 1982, 83; adj. prof. Boston U., 1986; travel writer The Boston Herald, 1984—. Avocations: wine and food, travel, sailing. E-mail: sfturek@aol.com.

TURETSKY, JUDITH, librarian, researcher; b. Bklyn., Jan. 19, 1944; d. Samuel and Ruth (Moskowitz) Turetsky. BS, Boston U., 1965; MS, Long Island U., 1969. Tchr. Trumbull (Conn.) Bd. Edn., 1965-66; libr. Darien (Conn.) Bd. Edn., 1968-69, Albert Einstein Coll., Bronx, 1969-74; researcher Koskoff, Koskoff & Bieder, Bridgeport, Conn., 1977-86. Author: (book and micro film), The History and Development of the D. Samuel Gottesman Library of Albert Einstein College of Medicine. Mem.: AMIT (life), Med. Libr. Assn., Yeshiva U. Women's Orgn. (life), Hadassah U. Women's Orgn. (life). Democrat. Avocations: reading, classical music, crocheting, doll collecting. Home and Office: 62 Gate Ridge Rd Fairfield CT 06825-

TURK, ELIZABETH ANN, music educator; b. N.Y.C., July 10, 1957; d. William Robert Turk, Elizabeth Ann Brittingham. BA in Music and History, Dowling Coll.; MA in German Lang. and Lit., Hofstra U.; MA in European History, SUNY Stony Brook; MA in Music Libr. Sci., Columbia U. Tchg. asst SUNY, Stony Brook, 1986—88; lectr. music Dowling Coll., Oakdale, NY, 1988—91; tchr. music Amityville Pub. Schs., Amityville, NY, 1991—; dir. theater arts and music dir. Miller Pl. H.S.; music dir. Amityville H.S., Commack H.S. South, Carriage House Players, Kids for Kids Theater, Inc. Tchr. vocal music Miller Place Pub. Sch., Miller Place, NY, Hewlett Woodmere Pub. Sch., Hewlett, NY; pvt. tchr. and vocal coach, Massapequa, NY. Singer (soloist): Rome Opera Festival, 1989, 1990; performer: Tchaikovsky Competition, 1978, 1982, 1986, Minn. Opera, 1979, 1980, 1981, L.I. Youth Orch. Summer Tours; dir.: Sleeping Beauty, Sound of Music, Fiddler on the Roof, Little Shop of Horrors, Cinderella, Oliver, numerous others; choreographer Fiddler on the Roof, Sound of Music, Little Shop of Horrors, Oliver, Grease. Recipient award for further study, Met. Opera, 1981—90, Herald award for choreography and music dir. Mem.: Suffolk County Music Educator's Assn., Music Educators Nat. Conf., Suffolk County Wrestling Assn. (tournament dir. league V 1974—, numerous awards), White Star Triangle (Beloved Queen 1973—74), Order Ea. Star (various offices, assoc. condr.). Home: 90 Clock Blvd Massapequa NY 11758

TURKOVA, HELGA, library director; b. Prague, Czech, Apr. 20, 1942; d. Johann Turek and Anna (Kusbachová) Turková. Grad., Charles U., Prague, Czech, 1964, PhD, 1969. Diploma in librarianship. Libr. Czechoslovak Acad. of Scis., Prague, Czech, 1964-65, Prague Info. Svc., Prague, Czech, 1965-67; ind. spez. libr. Dept. of Hist. Castles Libr. Nat. Mus. Libr., Prague, Czech, 1967-90, dir., 1990—. Co-author: (book) Rilke and Kraus and Vrchotovy J., 1985, (catalogue) Catalog incunabula in Castle Libraries, 1992, 2001; editor: Sborník Národního muzea-rada C-literární historie, 1990—. Mem coun Friends Old Prague, 1963—, Soc R M Rilke, 1992—. Mem.: Literary Sci Soc Sci Acad Czech Republic, Spolecnost Národního muzea, Asn Librarians. Roman Catholic. Avocations: history of Prague, history, art. Office: Knihovna Národni muzeum Václavské náměsti 68 115 79 Prague 1 Czech Republic E-mail: helga.turkova@nm.cz.

TURLINGTON, CHRISTY, model; b. Walnut Creek, Calif., Jan. 2, 1969; d. Dwain and Elizabeth T. With Ford Models, Inc., 1985; model Calvin Klein, 1986, Calvin Klein's Eternity Fragrance, 1988; with Maybelline Cosmetics, 1992; co-creator, skin care line Sundari, 2000—. Beauty spread with Vogue, 1987; has worked with Herb Ritts, Patrick Demarchelier, Steven Meisel; has worked for Anne Klein, Michael Kors, Chanel, Perry Ellis; appeared in George Michael's "Freedom" video. Author: Living Yoga. Spokesperson for anti-smoking CDC. Office: United Talent Agy 9560 Wilshire Blvd Ste 500 Beverly Hills CA 90212-2427 also: 344 E 59th St New York NY 10022-1513

TURLINGTON, PATRICIA RENFREW, artist, educator; b. Washington, Sept. 14, 1939; d. Henry Wilson and Anne Ruth (Bright) Renfrew; m. William Troy Turlington III, June 3, 1963 (div. Oct. 1971); children: William Troy IV, David Yelverton; m. William Archie Dees, Jr., June 4, 1994. Student, Meredith Coll., 1957, Washburn U., 1965-66, N.C. State UY., 1969-72. Comml. artist Adlers Inc. & McJoseph's, Raleigh, N.C., 1959-62; exec. dir. Goldsboro (N.C.) Art Ctr., 1973-78; elem. art tchr. Wayne Country Day Sch., Goldsboro, 1979-86; art prof. Wayne C.C., Goldsboro, 1986—. Artist-in-residence Edward Laredo Inst. of the Humanities, Cochabamba, Bolivia, summer 1988; vis. artist Va. Western C.C., Roanoke, Va., 1986, Wake Forest U., Winston Salem, 1987, Catawba Valley C.C., Hickory, N.C., 1989, Salem Coll., Winston Salem, N.C., 1992. Works represented in permanent colections Blue Cross-Blue Shield, Durham, N.C., Duke Med. Ctr., Mint Mus., Charlotte, U. N.C., Chapel Hill, Wachovia Bank and Trust Co., Winston-Salem; corp. and pub. brick sculpture commissions Brick Assn. N.C., Greensboro, Cohn Enterprises, Lenoir, N.C., Cordova Elem. Sch., Rockingham, N.C., Wilkes C.C., Wilkesboro, N.C., Hocker Bros. Brick and Tile Co., Inc., Green Bay, Wis., Kincaid Brick Co., Tampa, Fla., Koontz Masonry, Lexington, N.C., McDonald's Restaurants, Knoxville, Tenn., Jonesville, N.C., Cary, N.C., Gastonia, N.C., Knightdale, N.C., Fayetteville, N.C, N.Y.C. Transit Authority, N.Y.C., North Dr. Elem. Sch., Goldsboro, N.C., Rowan Meml. Hosp., Salisbury, N.C. Atlantic Ctr. for the Arts fellow, New Smyrna Beach, Fla., 1986; Pntrs. of the Ams. grantee, U.S. Info. Agy., Washington, 1988. Home: 709 Park Ave Goldsboro NC 27530-3834 Office: Turlington Brickworks PO Box 8 Goldsboro NC 27533-0008 Office Phone: 919-731-7273. E-mail: turlingtondees@nc.rr.com.

TURNAGE, KAREN L. medical technologist; b. Bethel, N.C., Oct. 19, 1957; d. Lionel Anderson and Lula Jane Turnage; m. Frederick Zeno Mills, Dec. 24, 1982 (div. 1992); 1 child, Travis Colby Mills. BS, Fairleigh Dickinson U., 1980. Med. technologist Duke U. Med. Ctr., Durham, N.C., 1980-81; sr. med. technologist Univ. Health Sys. Eastern N.C., Greenville, 1981-87; displayer/decorator Home Interiors, Dallas, 1987-89; med. technologist supervisor Univ. Health Sys. Eastern N.C., 1987—. Pres. PTA E.B. Aycock Sch., 1998-99; women's day pres. Mt. Calvary Bapt. Ch., Greenville, 1994-95. Mem. Am. Soc. Clin. Pathologists. Democrat. Avocations: acting, gardening, weightlifting, snow skiing, decorating. Home: 107 Fox Run Cir Greenville NC 27858-9730

TURNBULL, ANN PATTERSON, special educator, consultant, research director; b. Tuscaloosa, Ala., Oct. 19, 1947; d. H. F. and Mary (Boone) Patterson; m. H. Rutherford Turnbull III, Mar. 23, 1974; children: Jay, Amy, Kate. BS in Edn., U. Ga., 1968; MEd, Auburn U., 1971; EdD, U. Ala., 1972. Asst. prof. U. N.C., Chapel Hill, 1972-80; prof., co-dir. Beach Ctr. U. Kans., Lawrence, 1980—. Cons. Dept. Edn., Washington, 1987—, Australian Soc. for Study of Intellectual Disability, Adelaide and Washington, 1990. Author: Free Appropriate Public Education, 2000, Exceptional Lives: Special Education in Today's Schools, 2001, Families, Professionals and Exceptionality, 2001. Recipient Rose Kennedy Internat. Leadership award, Kennedy Found., 1990, 20th Century award in Mental Retardation, 1999; Joseph P. Kennedy Jr. Found. fellow, 1987-88. Mem.: Internat. League Socs. for Persons with Mental Handicaps (com. chair 1986—90), The Arc-U.S. (named Educator of Yr. 1982), Am. Assn. on Mental Retardation (bd. dirs. 1986—88, v.p. 2001, pres.-elect 2002, pres. 2003—04). Democrat. Avocations: travel, exercise. Home: 1636 Alvamar Dr Lawrence KS 66047-1714 Office: Univ Kans Beach Ctr 3136 1200 Sunnyside Dr Lawrence KS 66045-7534 E-mail: turnbull@ku.edu.

TURNBULL, DANA, psychologist; d. Bonnie and Royce Turnbull; m. Robert Franklin, Apr. 25, 1999; children: Hey Dude, Persephone, Kierra. BA, East Tex. State U., Commerce; MA, McNeese State U., Lake Charles, La.; MS, PhD, Pacific Grad. Sch. of Psychology, Palo Alto, Calif. Lic. clin. psychologist Tex., 2000. Correctional psychologist Montford Unit, Lubbock, Tex., 1998—2000; clin. psychologist Vericare, San Diego, 2000—; pvt. practice Bedford, Tex., 2002—. Author: (manual) Reducing Relocation Stress. Mem.: APA, Dallas Psychol. Assn., Ft. Worth Area Psychol. Assn., Metroport Rotary Club (dir. vocat. svcs. 2003—). Independent. Avocations: travel, Renaissance jewelry, Muay Thai, gardening, animal rights. Office: Dana Turnbull PhD Clinical Psycholog 2600 Tibbets Dr Suite B Bedford TX 76022 E-mail: dana@drdanaturnbull.com.

TURNBULL, MARJORIE REITZ, foundation executive, former state legislator; b. Madison, Wis., July 4, 1940; d. J. Wayne anf Frances H. (Millikan) R.; m. Augustus Bacon Turnbull, Nov. 26, 1965 (dec. Nov. 1991). Student, Agnes Scott Coll., 1958-60; BA, U. Fla., 1962; MA, U. Ga., 1968. Legis. analyst Fla. Ho. of Reps., Tallahassee, 1973-85, staff dir. com. on health and rehab. svcs., 1975-78, exec. asst. to speaker, 1978-80; asst. dir. Devel. Svc. Program Office, Tallahassee, 1980-82; dep. asst. sec. Health Planning State Fla., 1982-84; ind. cons. legis. mgmt. and planning, Tallahassee, 1984-95, state rep., 1994-2000; exec. dir. Tallahassee C.C. Found., 1995—. County commr. Leon County, Tallahassee, 1988-94; bd. dirs. Fla. Assn. Counties, Tallahassee, 1993-94, Tallahassee Symphony Orch., 1992—, Apalachee coun. Girl Scouts U.S., Tallahassee, 1988—. Recipient Outstanding Svc. in Govt. award Delta Kappa Omega, Tallahassee, 1996; named Woman of Yr., AAUW, Tallahassee, 1991, County Champion in the Legislature, Fla. Assn. Counties, 1995, Legislator of Yr., Fla. Assn. Sch. Supts., 1999; recipient Girl Scout Woman of Distinction award, 1999, Disting. Svc. award Fla. Student Assn., 2000, Disting. Citizens award Boy Scout Coun., 2000, Meritorious Achievement award Fla. A&M U., 2000, Legis. Advocacy award Fla. Coalition Against Domestic Violence, 2000, Freedom from Violence Leadership awrd, 2000, Model of Achievement award Tallahassee C.C., 2001. Mem. Rotary (program com. 1992—), Zonta Internat., Fla. Blue Key. Democrat. Presbyterian. Avocations: scuba diving, travel, cultural activities. Home: 3221 E Lakeshore Dr Tallahassee FL 32312-2062 Office: Tallahassee C C 444 Appleyard Dr Tallahassee FL 32304 E-mail: turnbulm@tcc.fl.edu.

TURNBULL, MARY REGINA, secondary school educator; b. Phila., Aug. 27, 1935; d. Thomas Lawrence and Mary Catherine (Shaughnessy) T. BA in Humanities, Villanova U., 1965; MA in Theology/Adolescent Psychology, LaSalle U., Phila., 1969. Cert. tchr., Pa. Tchr. elem. sch., suburban Phila., 1953-64, secondary sch., Warminster, Pa., 1964-69; supr. State Farm Ins., Springfield, Pa., 1969-73; optometric asst. Dr. Ellis S. Edelman, Newtowne Square, Pa., 1973-76; tchr. vocat. h.s., Phila., 1976-80, secondary sch., Drexel Hill, Pa., 1980—2003. Roman Catholic. Office: Msgr Bonner HS 263 Lansdowne Ave Drexel Hill PA 19026

TURNBULL, VERNONA HARMSEN, retired residence counselor, education consultant; b. Teeds Grove, Iowa, Dec. 6, 1916; d. Henry Ferdinand and Ida Amelia (Dohrmann) Harmsen; m. Alexander Turnbull, Oct. 12, 1961. BA, Cornell Coll., Mt. Vernon, Iowa, 1939; MEd, U. Colo., Boulder, 1947, profl. cert. edn., 1955. Cert. secondary and h.s. tchr. Tchr. English, Latin and phys. edn. Winslow (Ill.) H.S., 1939-45; dir. women's activities, instr. Trinidad (Colo.) State Jr. Coll., 1947-53; counselor women, assoc. prof. edn. Western State Coll., Gunnison, Colo., 1953-54; instr., residence counselor Stephens Coll., Columbia, Mo., 1955-61; ret., 1961. Active Salvation Army Aux. Mem. AAUW, Am. Assn. Ret. Persons (corr. sec. 1986-87), Kena Kampers Camping Club. Avocations: photography, camping, art, dance, baking.

TURNER, AILEEN ARCHUNDE, artist; b. Seboyeta, N.Mex., Dec. 9, 1941; d. Valentin Archunde and Euphemia Jaramillo; m. Robert Leroy Turner, Dec. 1, 1962; 1 child, Eric Ian Darrow. BA in Spanish Lit., U. Colo., Denver, 1987. Spanish tchr. Notre Dame Cath. Sch., Denver, 1985—88; ESL instr. Front Range C.C., Denver, 1985—86; ESL tutor St. Thomas Sem., Denver, 1986—87; ESL instr. C.C. Denver, 1988—88, Truckee Meadows C.C., Reno, 1989—92, N.Mex State U., Alamogordo, 1992—93, U. N.Mex, Valencia Campus, Tome, 1997—2001. Exhibitions include Rocky Mountain Nat. Watermedia Exhbn. (Century Award of Merit, 1976), Am. Watercolor Soc. (Helen Gapen award, 1980), N.Mex. State Fair (First Pl. in Oils, 1998). Mem.: Rocky Mountain Nat. Watermedia Soc. (life). Republican. Roman Catholic. Avocations: reading, children's literature, genealogy, cooking, movies. Home: 309 Star Dr Belen NM 87001 Office: 309 Star Dr Belen NM 87002 Personal E-mail: turnerbelen@juno.com.

TURNER, ALICE KENNEDY, editor; b. Mukden, Manchuria; d. William Taylor and Florence Bell (Green) T. BA, Bryn Mawr Coll., 1962. Sr. editor Holiday mag., N.Y.C., 1969-70; assoc. editor Publishers Weekly, N.Y.C., 1972-74; sr. editor Ballantine Books, N.Y.C., 1974-76, New York mag., N.Y.C., 1976-80; fiction editor Playboy mag., Chgo., N.Y.C., 1980—2001. Author: Yoga for Beginners, 1973, The History of Hell, 1993; co-author: The New York Woman's guide, 1975; editor: Playboy Stories, 1993, The Playboy Book of Science Fiction, 1996; co-editor: Snake's Hands: The Fiction of John Crowley, 2002. Home: 2 Charlton St New York NY 10014-4909

TURNER, BARBARA A. former dance company executive; b. Louisville; BA, U. Ky.; MA, U. Louisville. Dir. devel. Ballet Internat., Indpls., now mng. dir. Office: Ballet Internat 502 N Capitol Ave Ste B Indianapolis IN 46204-1204

TURNER, BERNICE HILBURN, recording industry executive; b. Black Rock, Ark., Jan. 13, 1937; d. Floyd W. and Clementime (Higgins) Hilburn; m. Doyle Turner, Feb. 28, 1957 (div. Jan. 1980); children: Johnny, P.J., Danny, Jill, Robby. PhD in Applied Psychology, 1974. Musician Hank Williams Sr., Nashville and Montgomery, Ala., 1950-52, 1952-76; owner Onyx Recording Studio, Memphis, 1985—, Turner Limousine Svc., Memphis, 1988—. Named Pioneer in Country Music, United Music Heritage of Tenn., 1989. Mem. Unity Ch. Home: 1646 Bonnie Dr Memphis TN 38116-5732

TURNER, BONESE COLLINS, artist, educator; b. Abilene, Kans. d. Paul Edwin and Ruby (Seybold) Collins; m. Glenn E. Turner; 1 child, Craig Collins. BS in Edn., MEd, U. Idaho; MA, Calif. State U., Northridge, 1974. Instr. art L.A. Pierce Coll., Woodland Hills, Calif., 1964—. Prof. art Calif. State U., Northridge, 1986-89; art instr. L.A. Valley Coll., Van Nuys, 1987-89, Moorpark (Calif.) Coll., 1988-98, Arrowmont Coll. Arts & Crafts, Gatlinburg, Tenn., 1995-96; advisor Coll. Art and Arch. U. Idaho, 1988—; juror for art exhbns. including Nat. Watercolor Soc., 1980, 91, San Diego Art Inst., Brand Nat. Watermedia Exhbn., 1980, 96-97, prin. gallery Orlando Gallery, Tarzana, Calif. Represented in permanent collections Smithsonian Inst., Olympic Arts Festival, L.A.; one-woman shows include Angel's Gate Gallery, San Pedro, Calif., 1989, Art Store Gallery, Studio City, Calif., 1988, L.A. Pierce Coll. Gallery, 1988, Brand Art Gallery, Glendale, Calif., 1988, 93, 2000, Coos (Oreg.) Art Mus., 1988, U. Nev., 1987, Orlando Gallery, Sherman Oaks, Calif., 1993, 98, 2002, Burbank (Calif.) Creative Arts Ctr., 2000, Village Sq. Gallery, Montrose, Calif., 2002; prin. works in pub. collections The Smithsonian Inst., Hartung Performing Arts Ctr., Moscow, Idaho, Robert V. Fulton Mus. Art, Calif.

State U., San Bernardino, Calif., Home Savs. and Loan, San Bernardino Sun Telegram Newspapers, Oreg. Coun. for the Arts, Newport, Oreg. Pub. Librs., Brand Libr., Glendale, Calif., Lincoln (Nebr.) Pub. Lib., Indsl. Tile Corp., Lincoln, Nebr. Recipient Springfield (Mo.) Art Mus. award, 1989, 2002, 1st prize Brand XXVIII, 1998, Glendale, Calif., Butler Art Inst. award, 1989, 1st award in graphics Diamond Jubilee Exhibit/Pasadena Soc. Artists, 2002, Nat. award Acrylic Painters Assn. Eng. and U.S.A., 1996. Mem. Nat. Acrylic Painters Assn. of Eng. (award 1996), Nat. Mortar Bd. Soc., Nat. Watercolor Soc. (life, past pres., Purchase prize 1979), Watercolor U.S.A. Honor Soc. (award), Watercolor West. Avocations: bicycling, music, singing.

TURNER, BRACHA, Naive Landscape painter; b. Jerusalem; Exhbns. include 55 solo exhbns. and numerous juried exhbns.: J.F. Kennedy Art Gallery, Montreal, New Eng. Fine Arts Inst., Boston, Internat. Women in the Arts Conf., Beijing; permanent display of paintings include Hadassah Hdqtrs., N.Y., ZOA House, Tel-Aviv, Nat. Coun. of Jewish Women, N.Y., Ichilov Hosp., Tel-Aviv, Office of the Mayor of Jerusalem, Israel, The Bible Mus. Tel Aviv, Office of the Mayor N.Y.C., Rambam Hosp., Haifa, Israel, others; painting reproduced on cards by Hadassah; contbr. drawings to Sara's Daughters Sing, 1989.

TURNER, BRENDA KAYE, state legislator; b. Oak Ridge, Mar. 14, 1948; d. James Bookie and Virginia (Sivley) T. BA, U. Tenn., Chattanooga, 1974; MA, U. Ala., Tuscaloosa, 1977. Asst. to clk. Ala. Ho. of Reps., Montgomery; pub. info. specialist Tuscaloosa Park and Recreation Authority; resource tchr. spl. edn. Catoosa County, Ga.; mem. Tenn. Ho. of Reps., Nashville. Mem. AAUW, Epilepsy Found., Chattanooga C. of C. Address: 3425 Audubon Dr Chattanooga TN 37411-4402

TURNER, ELAINE S. allergist, immunologist; b. Glen Cove, N.Y., 1947; MD, Med. Coll. Pa., 1974. Diplomate Am. Bd. Allergy & Immunology, Am. Bd. Internal Medicine. Intern Michael Reese Hosp., Chgo., 1974-75; resident in internal medicine Cleve. Clinic, 1976-78; fellow in allergy & immunology Northwestern U., Chgo., 1978-80; with St. Mary's Hosp., Va., Henrico Drs. Hosp., Va. Mem. ACP, Am. Acad. Allergy, Asthma and Immunology, Va. Allergy Soc., Richmond Acad. Medicine. Office: Va Adult & Pediat Allergy & Allergy Ste 103 7605 Forest Ave Richmond VA 23229-4936

TURNER, ELIZABETH ADAMS NOBLE (BETTY TURNER), real estate company executive; b. Yonkers, N.Y., May 18, 1931; d. James Kendrick and Orrel (Baldwin) Noble; m. Jack Rice Turner, July 11, 1953; children: Jay Kendrick, Randall Ray. BA, Vassar Coll., 1953; MA, Tex. A&I U., 1964. Ednl. cons., Tex. sales mgr. Noble & Noble Pub. Co., N.Y.C., 1956-67; psychometrist Corpus Christi Guidance Ctr., 1967-70; psychologist Corpus Christi State Sch., 1970-72, dir. programs, asst. supt., 1972, dir. devel. and vol. svcs., 1972-76, dir. rsch. and tng., 1977-79; psychologist Tex. Mental Health and Mental Retardation, 1970-79, program cons., 1979-85; pres. Turner Co., 1975-82; mayor pro tem Corpus Christi, 1981-85; mayor, 1987-91; CEO, pres. Corpus Christi C. of C., 1991-94; pres. Betty Turner Real Estate, 1999—. V.p. bus. and govt. rels. ctrl. and south Tex. divsns. Columbia Healthcare Corp., 1994-99. Dir. alumni Corpus Christi State U., 1976-77; coord. vols. Summer Head Start Program, Corpus Christi, 1967; chmn. spl. gifts com. United Way, Corpus Christi, 1970; mem. Corpus Christi City Coun., [illegible] and Noble, N.Y.C.; founder Com. of 100 and Goals for Corpus Christi; pres. USO; bd. dirs. Coastal Bend Coun. Govts., Corpus Christi Mus., Harbor Playhouse, Cmtys. in Schs., YWCA, Y-Teen Sponsor, Del Mar Coll. Found., Tex. A&M at Corpus Christi Pres.' Coun., Food Bank, Hispanic C. of C., TAMACC Corp. Ptnrs., Salvation Army, Jr. League, Coun. Deaf Silent Found.; bd. Southside Cmty. Hosp., 1987-93, Gulfway Nat. Bank, 1985-92; strategic planning com. Meml. Hosp., 1992, Tex. Capital Network Bd., 1992-95, Humana Hosp., Physician Relocation and Condo Sales, Rehab. Hosp., dir. of vols., South Tex., Admiral Tex. Navy; bd. dirs. Pacific Southwest Bank, 1997-2000, St. David's/Austin and Medth. Healthcare Sys., San Antonio, 1997-99; apptd. Gov.'s Commn. for Women, 1984-85, Leadership Tex. Class I, Corpus Christi, Class II; founder Goals for Corpus Christi, Bay Area Sports Assn., Assn. Coastal Bend Mayor's Alliance; founder Mayor's Commn. on the Disabled, Mayor's Task Force on the Homeless; active Port Aransas Cmty. Ch., U. Tex. Sch. Nursing Adv. Coun., 1998-99; bd. dirs. Del Mar Coll. Found., 1998—, Am. Heart Assn., 1999-2000, Bethune Day Care Nursery, 1999—, Jr. League Cmty. Adv. Coun., 1999-2000, Strategic Planning Com., 2000—, Silent Found., 2001—, 21st Century Charter Sch., 2001-2002, Boys and Girls Club of Corpus Christi, 2002—, Nat. AARP, 2002-04; pres.-elect Food Bank, 2002—; elder Cmty. Presbyn. Ch. Named Corpus Christi Newsmaker of Yr., 1987; recipient Love award, YWCA, 1970, Y's Women and Men in Careers award, 1988, Recognition award, Rotary, 1991, Comdr.'s award for pub. svc., U.S. Army, Scroll of Honor award, Navy League, award, Tex. Hwy Dept., Road Hand award, Tex. Hwy. Commn., Women of Distinction award, Girl Scouts Tex. Mem. NAACP (life), Tex. Psychol. Assn. (pres., mem. exec. bd.), Psychol. Assn. (pres., founder), Tex. Mcpl. League (bd. dirs.), Jr. League Corpus Christi, Tex. Bookman's Assn., Tex. Assn. Realtors, Corpus Christi Town Club, Corpus Christi Yacht Club, Jr. Cotillion Club, Kappa Kappa Gamma. Home: 403 Blue Heron Dr Port Aransas TX 78373 Office Phone: 361-877-1111. E-mail: bettytyrner@centurytel.net.

TURNER, ELNORA CRANKFIELD, special education educator and administrator; b. Anniston, Ala., June 16, 1953; d. Willie B. Watts and Elmira (Turnre) Crankfield Watts; m. Edward Ell Turner; children: Joseph Hawkins Jr., Nicholas (dec.), Quincy, Demetrius. BS, Jacksonville (Ala.) State U., 1975, MS, 1983, EdS, 1994, adminstrv. cert., 1995. Tchr.'s aide Anniston City Schs., 1978-83, tchr., 1983-95, supr. spl. edn., 1995—, dir. parent support group, 1996—. Pub. spkr. Bapt. Ch. Avocations: working with children, sewing, speaking, church. Home: PO Box 1082 Anniston AL 36202-1082

TURNER, FLORENCE FRANCES, ceramist; b. Detroit, Mar. 9, 1926; d. Paul Pokrywka and Catherine Gagal; m. Dwight Robert Turner, Oct. 23, 1948; children: Thomas Michael, Nancy Louise, Richard Scott, Garry Robert. Student, Oakland C.C., Royal Oak, Mich., 1975-85, U. Ariz., Yuma, 1985, U. Las Vegas, 1989—. Pres., founder Nev. Clay Guild, Henderson, 1990-94, mem. adv. bd., 1994-2000, v.p., 2000—02. Workshop leader Greenfield Village, Dearborn, Mich., 1977-78, Plymouth (Mich.) Hist. Soc., 1979, Las Vegas Sch. System, 1989-90, Detroit Met. area, 1977-85. Bd. dirs. Las Vegas Art Mus., 1987-91; corr. sec. So. Nev. Creative Art Ctr., Las Vegas, 1990-94. Mem.: Nev. Camera Club, Las Vegas Gem Club, So. Nev. Rock Art Enthusiasts, Phi Kappa Phi. Avocations: photography, collecting gems, travel.

TURNER, GWENDOLYN MARIE, band director, musician; b. Dillon, S.C., Mar. 25, 1957; d. G. Maurice and Marguerite Phillips Turner. Student, Winthrop Coll., 1977; BS in Music cum laude, U. N.C., Pembroke, 1980. Cert. tchr. N.C. Band dir. Lewis Chapel Mid. Sch., Fayetteville, NC, 1980—2003, Pine Forest Mid. Sch., Fayetteville, 2003—. Chair N.C. All-State Mid. Sch. Band, Greensboro, 1993—94; condr., clinician Cumberland (N.C.) All-County Band, 1984, S.E.D.B.A. All-Dist. Band, NC, 1993, U. N.C.-Pembroke Invitational Band, 1995; clarinetist Snyder Meml. Bapt. Ch. Orch., Fayetteville, 1982—, Cumberland Oratorio Singers Orch., Fayetteville, 1991—, Cape Fear Regional Theatre Orch., Fayetteville, 1998—2002. Named one of Outstanding Young Women of Am., 1987. Mem.: So. Dist. Bandmasters Assn. (v.p., recording sec. 1995—97, pres. 1997—99), Profl. Educators of N.C., N.C. Bandmasters Assn. (Award of Excellence 1998), Music Educators Nat. Conf. Avocations: gardening, reading, needlecrafts, collecting. Office: Pine Forest Mid Sch 6901 Ramsey St Fayetteville NC 28311 Office Phone: 910-488-2711.

TURNER, JANET SULLIVAN, painter, sculptor; b. Gardiner, Maine, Nov. 15, 1935; d. Clayton Jefferson and Frances (Leighton) Sullivan; m. Terry Turner, Oct. 6, 1956; children: Lisa Turner Reid, Michael Ross, Jonathan Brett. BA cum laude, Mich. State U., 1956. Rep. Am. Women in Art, UN World Conf. on Women, Nairobi, Kenya, 1985. One-woman shows include San Diego Art Inst., 1971, St. Joseph U., Phila., 1981, Villanova (Pa.) U. Gallery, 1982, Pa. State U., Middletown (Pa.), 1985, Temple U. (Pa.), 1986, Widener U. Art Mus., Chester, Pa., 1987, 94, Rosemont Coll., Pa., 1995, Sande Webster Gallery, Phila., 1998, 2000; exhibited in group shows at Del. Art Mus., Wilmington, 1978, Woodmere Art Mus., Phila., 1980, 2000, Port of History Mus., Phila., 1984, Allentown Art Mus., 1984, Trenton (NJ) City Mus. Ellarslie Open VIII, 1989, Ammo Gallery, Bklyn., 1989, Pa. State Mus., Harrisburg, 1990-94, Galeria Mesa, Ariz., 1991, Del. Ctr. for Contemporary Arts, Wilmington, 1992, Holter Mus., Helena, Mont., 1992, S.W. Tex. State U., San Marcos, 1993, Fla. State U. Mus., Tallahassee, 1993, Newark Mus., 1993, U. Del., 1994, 1st St. Gallery, NYC, 1994, Noyes Mus., NJ, 1995, Sande Webster Gallery, Phila. 1995-2003, Phila. Art Mus., 1997, Krasdale Gallery, White Plains, NY, 2001, Moore Coll. of Art, Phila. Sculptors, Phila. Pa., 2002; represented in permanent collections Nat. Mus. Women in Arts, "American Album", Wash. D.C., Kresge Art Mus., East Lansing, Mich, ARA Svc. Inc., Phila., Blue Cross/Blue Shield, Phila., Am. Nat. Bank and Trust co., Rockford, Ill., Burroughs Corp., Lisle, Ill., State Mus. Pa., Harrisburg, Bryn Mawr (Pa.) Coll., Rosemont Coll., Villanova (Pa.) Coll., LaSalle U. Art Mus., Phila., Noyes Mus., NJ, Nat. Liberty Mus., Phila., Kimmel Ctr., Phila. Bd. dirs. Rittenhouse Sq. Fine Arts Ann., Phila., 1984—86. Recipient 2d pl. award San Diego Art Inst. 19th Ann. Exhbn., 1971, award of merit Pavilion Gallery, Mt. Holly, N.J., 1991, 3d pl. Katonah Mus. of Art, N.Y., 1992, purchase award State Mus. of Pa., Harrisburg, 1992. Mem. Artists Equity (pres. 1987-88), Nat. League of Am. Pen Woman, Phila. Watercolor Club, Delta Phi Delta. Republican. Roman Catholic. Home: 88 Cambridge Dr Glen Mills PA 19342-1545

TURNER, JEAN-LOUISE, public relations executive; b. Washington, Sept. 29, 1942; d. Fletcher Wood and Mary Louise (Gant) T.; student Howard U., 1959-62; B.A., Fed. City Coll., 1970, M.A., 1972; children—Nathaniel Anthony Landry, Mark Andrew Landry. Coordinator public relations Sta. WRC-TV, Washington, 1969, Howard Univ., 1997-; adminstr. prodn., 1970-72; mgmt. trainee NBC, Washington, 1972; producer spls. Sta. WRC-TV, 1972-76, asso. producer documentaries, 1972-76; mgr. community affairs and public affairs, host Sta. WRC/WKYS, Washington, 1976-78, producer WRC 1978-79; media rep. PEPCO, Washington, 1979-81; press aide D.C. City Council, 1981-82; dir. pub. relations LaMancha, Inc., 1983-84; v.p. Talisman Assocs., 1984—; prin., owner Millennium Tours; mgr. Jafra Skin Care, 1994; judge Gabriel awards; mem. media panel D.C. Arts and Humanities Commn.; bd. dirs. Epilepsy Found. Am.; pres. parish coun. St. Francis de Sales Roman Cath. Ch., 1993, 94—; career role model St. Anthony's High Sch. Recipient Hallmark award Jr. Achievement, 1976, Public Service award Washington Area Council Alcoholism and Drug Abuse, 1977; Public Interest award Council Better Bus. Burs. Inc., 1977. Mem. Capital Press Club, Washington Assn. Black Journalists, Nat. Acad. TV Arts and Scis., Nat. Assn. Public Continuing Adult Edn., Anchor Mental Health Assn. (bd. dirs., chmn. 1992-94, Award of Appreciation 1994), Washington Women's Forum (charter), Nat. Assn. Program Dirs., Citizens Bd. Providence Hosp. (1998-), Alpha Kappa Alpha. Roman Catholic. [illegible] 1979-81. Home: 4314 12th Pl NE Washington DC 20017-3823 Office: 4314 12th Place NE Washington DC 20017

TURNER, KAREN, psychotherapist, educator; b. Compton, Calif., Feb. 11, 1945; d. Charles Wilson and Luciel Spratt. Bachelor's, Calif. State U., L.A., 1970, Master's, 1972. Lic. Marriage and Family Therapist. Pvt. practice, Denver, 1970—; prof. JFK U., Orinda, Calif., 1980—87. Group/staff facilitator Ctr. Attitudinal Healing, Sausalito, Calif., 1991—93, Spirit Rock Meditation Ctr.; lectr. in field. Contbr. articles to profl. jours. Mem.: Assn. Transpersonal Psychology, Am. Assn. Psychotherapists (diplomate), Am. Assn. Marriage and Family Therapists. Office: 1776 S Jackson St Ste 616 Denver CO 80210 Office Phone: 303-300-4502. E-mail: silverstreak55@earthlink.net.

TURNER, KATHLEEN, actress; b. Springfield, Mo., June 19, 1954; m. Jay Weiss, 1984; 1 child, Rachel Ann. Student, Cen. Sch. of Speech and Drama, London, Southwest Mo. State U.; BFA, U. Md. Various theater roles, Broadway debut: Gemini, 1978, Cat on a Hot Tin Roof, 1990, Indiscretions, 1995; appeared in TV series The Doctors, 1977, Style and Substance, 1996; TV movies inlcude Friends At Last, 1995, Moonlight and Valentino, 1995; films include Body Heat, 1981, A Breed Apart, 1982, The Man With Two Brains, 1983, Crimes of Passion, 1984, Romancing the Stone, 1984, Prizzi's Honor (Golden Globe award for best actress), 1985, The Jewel of the Nile, 1985, Peggy Sue Got Married, (D.W. Griffith award for best actress, Oscar nomination for best actress) 1986, Julia and Julia, 1988, Switching Channels, 1988, Who Framed Roger Rabbit, 1988, Accidental Tourist, 1988, The War of the Roses, 1989. V.I. Warshawski, 1991, Undercover Blues, 1993, House of Cards, 1993, Serial Mom, 1994, Naked in New York, 1994, A Simple Wish, 1997, (TV movie) Love in the Ancient World, 1997, (TV movie) Legalese, 1998, The Real Blonde, 1998, The Virgin Suicides, 1999, Prince of Central Park, 1999, Love and Action in Chicago, 1999, Baby Geniuses, 1999; dir. (Showtime Cable movie) Leslie's Folly, 1994; also performed in radio shows with the BBC, 1992, 93; voice: Bad Baby, 1997, Beautiful, 2000. Office: ICM care Chris Andrews 8942 Wilshire Blvd Beverly Hills CA 90211-1934

TURNER, KATHY ANN, mental health services professional; b. Cinn., May 16, 1962; d. James Robert and Alice Louise Taylor; m. Michael Arcia Turenr, Jr., June 1, 1985; children: Joseph Paul, Christopher James, Sarah Alyse. AA, Riverside C.C., 1998; BS in Edn., Lewis Clark State Coll., 2002. Spl. edn. asst. Corona-Norco Unified Sch. Dist., Norco, Calif., 1996—98; direct care provider devel. disabilities Inclusion North, Inc., Grangeville, Idaho, 1998—2000; tech. for tchrs. asst. Lewis Clark State Coll., Lewiston, Idaho, 2000—01; sub. tchr. Prairie Sch., Idaho, 2001—03; psychol. social rehab. provider Frontier Journeys, Grangeville, Idaho, 2002—; specialist devel. disabilities Opportunities Unltd., Inc., 2004—. Counselor Hope Pregnancy Ctr., Grangeville, 2003—. Portrait, Liz (2nd pl. award Idaho County Art Competition, 1998). Daffodil days chmn. Am. Cancer Soc., Corona, Calif., 1995—98. Named Woman of the Yr., Norco C. of C., 1995. Mem.: Coun. for Exceptional Children, Kappa Delta Pi (pres. 2001—03). R-Consevative. Avocations: baking, canning, fishing, card playing, calligraphy. Home: 408 E North St Grangeville ID 83530 Office: Frontier Journeys Counseling 304 State St Grangeville ID 83530 Office Phone: 208-983-0309.

TURNER, LETITIA RHODES, artist; b. Media, Pa., Aug. 17, 1923; d. Samuel Noblit and Letitia (Eves) Rhodes; m. Ellwood Jackson Turner Jr., Aug. 1, 1942; children: Rue Baronsky, Letitia Mayo, Elizabeth Rorke. Diploma, Cowanova Sch. Dancing, 1941. Dance instr. Cowanova Sch. Dancing, 1939—41; sec., treas. Rose Tree Realty Inc., Media, Pa., 1961-81. Dance tchr., 1939, 40, 41. Portrait painter (Portrait of Mary 3d pl. 1990, Portrait of Brett 2d pl. 1987) Pres. Am. Legion Aux., Media, 1991-2002, photographer, 1992, sec., 1993—; sec. Del. County Am. Legion Aux., 1994, historian, 1995; 1st v.p. Woman's Aux. Media Presbyn. Ch., Media, 1963; mem. D.A.R.E., Media, 1983-91, 92, 93—. Mem. Artist Guild Delaware County, Art League Delaware County, Artist Guild of Riddle Village, Am. Legion Aux. (sec. Del. County 1993, historian 1994). Republican. Avocations: needlepoint, holiday spa, art design for ch. bulletin covers. Home and Office: Riddle Village L-302 Media PA 19063

TURNER, LISA PHILLIPS, human resources executive; b. Waltham, Mass., Apr. 10, 1951; d. James Sinclair and Virginia Turner. BA in Edn. and Philosophy magna cum laude, Washington Coll., Chestertown, Md., 1974; AS in Electronics Tech., AA in Engring., Palm Beach Jr. Coll., 1982; MBA, Nova U., 1986, DSc, 1989; PhD, Kennedy Western U., 1990. Cert. Sr. Profl. in Human Resources, quality engr.; lic. USCG capt.; lic. pvt. pilot FAA. Founder, pres. Turner's Bicycle Svc., Inc., Delray Beach, Fla., 1975-80; electronics engr., quality engr. Audio Engring. and Video Arts, Boca Raton, 1980-81; tech. writing instr. Palm Beach Jr. Coll., Lake Worth, Fla., 1981-82; adminstr. tng. and devel. Mitel Inc., Boca Raton, 1982-88; mgr. communications and employee rels. Modular Computer Systems, Inc., Ft. Lauderdale, Fla., 1988-89; U.S. mktg. project mgr. Mitel, Inc., Boca Raton, Fla., 1990-91; v.p. human resources Connectronics, Inc., Ft. Lauderdale, Fla., 1991-93; sr. mgr. human resources Sensormatic Electronics Corp., Boca Raton, Fla., 1993-98, dir. human resources, 1998—2001; chief tng. officer, dir. human resources Tyco Fire and Security Svcs., Inc., Boca Raton, Fla., 2001—. Contbg. author Kitplanes Mag. With USCG Aux. Recipient Human Resources Profl. Excellence award, Soc. Human Resource Mgmt., 1999. Mem. Soc. for Human Resource Mgmt., Internat. Assn. Quality Cirs., Am. Soc. Quality Control, Fla. Employment Mgmt. Assn., Am. Acad. Mgmt., Employment Assn. Fla., Am. Capts. Assn., Citizens Police Acad., Aircraft Owners and Pilot's Assn., Exptl. Aircraft Assn., Fla. Aero. Club. Achievements include being the first female to construct, complete and fly a pulsar XP aircraft. Home: 1358 Fairfax Cir E Boynton Beach FL 33436-8612 Office: Tyco 1 Town Center Rd Boca Raton FL 33436-1010 Office Phone: 561-989-7979. E-mail: llsaturner@prodigy.net., lisaturner@tycoint.com.

TURNER, LYNDA L. secondary educator, English; b. Corbin, Ky., Apr. 29, 1949; d. W. A. and Frances B. (Marshall) Turner. BA, Berea Coll., 1971; MA, U. Ky., 1973, MSLS, 1990; postgrad., Western Ky. U., 1993. Cert. tchr., Ky. Instr. German U. Ky., Lexington, 1971-73; actress, singer Wilderness Road, Berea, Ky., 1973-78; instr. German, English, theatre, libr. Frederick Fraize H.S., Cloverport, Ky., 1975—. Author: (poetry) Persona, 1990. Mem. ACLU, Louisville, 1990—. Grantee NEA, 1983, 90. Mem. ALA, NEA, AAUW, Am. Assn. Tchrs. German, Ky. Edn. Assn. Office Phone: 270-788-3388. E-mail: lturner@cport.k12.ky.us.

TURNER, MABEL CROUGHAN, retired microbiologist; b. Macomb, Ill., Jan. 13, 1920; d. Walter Wilson and Mary Frances (Miner) Wilson Johnson; m. Claire Malloy Croughan, July 18, 1940 (dec.); children: Jack, Caitlin, Shelley Booth, Timothy, Mary Minihane-Croughan, Matthew; m. Hubert Edwards Turner, Jan. 16, 1996. AA, UCLA, 1939; B Arts and Sci., U. Calif., Berkeley, 1940. Cert. pub. health lab. technician, pub. health bacteriologist, clin. lab. technician, clin. lab. technologist, Dept. Health, State Calif.; cert. approval dairy bacteriology Dept. Agr., State Calif. Lab. dir. Santa Cruz (Calif.) County Hosp., 1945-46, Campbells Clin. Lab., Santa Cruz, 1946-50; clin. technologist Marin Med. Lab., San Rafael, Calif., 1954-55, 1961-66; lab. dir. Ross Gen. Hosp. Lab., Kentfield, Calif., 1955-56, Ross Valley Doctors Lab., Kentfield, 1956-57, Doctors Clin. Lab., El Dorado, Kans., 1958-61, Pub. Health Lab. Marin County, San Rafael, 1966-88; ret. Trustee Novato Unified Sch. Dist., 1973-90; cook, hostess, supr. Homeless Shelter, Presbyn. Ch., Novato, 1980; state com. on tchr. credentials State of Calif., Sacramento, 1987-89; elder, mem. nominating com. for pastor Novato Presbyn. Ch., 1992-95; liason com. Cmty. Buck Ctr. on Aging, Novato, 1994—; active Commn. on Aging, County of Marin, San Rafael, 1995-96. Named Life Member PTA and Outstanding Parent, 1954, 65, Woman of the Yr. and Woman of [illegible] Club, 1983-95, Sr. Citizen of Yr., Calif. State Senate and Assembly, 1993. Achievements include co-discovery of new virus "Marin Agent" which causes diarrhea and vomiting in patients. Home: 8 Haverhill Ct Novato CA 94947-2037

TURNER, MARTA JONES, public affairs professional; V.p. pub. affairs Flowers Industries, Inc., Thomasville, Ga., 1998—. Office: Flowers Industries Inc 1919 Flowers Cir Thomasville GA 31757-1137

TURNER, MYRTLE INEZ, training facility director, research scientist; b. Munich, Oct. 2, 1962; d. James Edward and Evelyn Virginia Turner; 1 child, Jennifer Brandice Jones. BS in Biology, Ga. State U., 1984; MPH in Cmty. Health, Emory U., 1986; PhD in Higher Edn.-Occupl. Studies, Ga. State U., 2000. Cert. environ. trainer Nat. Environ. Tng. Assn. Virology lab. student aide Ga. Dept. Human Resources, Atlanta, 1983; lab. scientist newborn screening and virology Ga. Dept. Human Resourses, 1984—85; poison info. specialist Ga. Poison Control Ctr., Atlanta, 1985—89; indsl. hygienist Haztech, Inc., Decatur, Ga., 1987; environ. health scientist Williams-Russell and Johnson, Inc., Atlanta, 1987—89; indsl. hygienist U.S. Dept. Labor, OSHA, Methuen, Mass., 1989—90, Atlanta, 1990—91; Region IV indsl. hygienist U.S. Gen. Svcs. Admin., Atlanta, 1991—93; rsch. scientist II, indsl. hygienist Ga. Inst. Tech., Atlanta, 1993—2001, assoc. dir. OSHA Tng. Inst. Edn. Ctr., 2001—. Mem. Emory U. Rollins Sch. Pub. Health, Atlanta, 1998—2002. Mem. Nat. Adv. Com. on Occupl. Safety and Health, Washington, 2000—02. Mem.: Sigma Gamma Rho (pres. Zeta Alpha Sigma chpt. 2000—03). Home: PO Box 491212 College Park GA 30349 Office: Ga Inst Tech O'Keefe Bldg 151-6th St Rm 022C Atlanta GA 30332-0837 Personal E-mail: miturnerphd@netscape.net. E-mail: myrtle.turner@gtri.gatech.edu.

TURNER, NATALIE A. retired small business owner, consultant; b. Vancouver, B.C., Can. d. Walter P. and Jenny (Ferley) Koohtow; m. George M. Turner, Jr. BS, McGill U., 1949. Internat. clearance officer Gillette Co., Boston; mgr. internat. ops., chemist program mgr. Chemist-Blood Bank, Can. Red Cross Blood Transfusion Svc.; rsch. asst. in neurophysiology Allen Meml. Inst., Montreal; owner, sole propr. SUMIDAR, North Easton, Mass. Cons. Damon Biotech, 1988-89. Co-author rsch. publs. in field. Bd. dirs. Children's Mus. in Easton, 1989—. Mem. NAFE, Internat. Congress Physiology, Am. Chem. Soc., Soc. Cosmetic Chemists (cert., nat. bd. dirs., U.S. rep. to exec. bd. Internat. Fedn.), New Eng. Women Bus. Owners, Kappa Alpha Theta (life). Avocations: sewing, golf, portraits in fabric.

TURNER, PATRICIA BUTLER, mental health nurse, educator, consultant; b. Galesburg, Ill., Aug. 31, 1943; d. Allen Dale and Mary Lacky; m. Glen William Butler, Mar. 14, 1964 (div. Apr. 1974); children: Scott Lewis, Andrew William, Suzanne Elizabeth; m. Keith Warren Turner, Oct. 13, 1992. AA in Nursing/Journalism, Sacramento City Coll., 1965; BS in Sociology/Psychology, SUNY, Albany, 1992. Clin. nurse Mercy Gen. Hosp., Sacramento, Sacramento Med. Ctr.; Davis (Calif.) Cmty. Hosp.; clin. nurse Woodland (Calif.) Meml. Hosp., 1965-74; dir. nurses Woodland Skilled Nursing, 1978-79; head nurse/psychiatry St. Croix Mental Health, Christiansted, U.S. V.I., 1974-79; clin. program coord. Yolo County Mental Health, Woodland, 1980—. Instr. Yuba C.C., Marysville, Calif., 1988—. Author curriculum; mem. editl. adv. bd. Daily Democrat. Bd. dirs. Concilio of Yolo County, Woodland, 1984-87; mem. Red Cross Nat. Disaster Mental Health, 1996—. Recipient Bell award Mental Health Assn. Yolo County, 1993; NIMH grantee, 1989-90. Mem. LWV (recording sec. 1997, 98, co-pres. 1999—), Calif. Elected Women's Assn. Edn. & Rsch., Virgin Islands Nurses Assn., Forensic Mental Health Assn. Calif. (sec. 1991-93, conf. planning 1990-91, dir. edn. and tng. 1996-98, West award 1999), Rotary Internat. Democrat. Roman Catholic. Avocations: diving, boating, travel, golf. Home: McKinney-Rubicon Rd Homewood CA 96141 Office: Yolo County Mental Health 213 W Beamer St Woodland CA 95695-2510

TURNER, PEGGY ANN, graphics designer, artist, educator; b. Memphis, Jan. 17, 1951; d. James Patrick and Margaret Helen (Brastock) Turner. BFA, U. Tenn., 1974, MFA summa cum laude, 1992. Art dir. Turner Design, Knoxville, 1972-84; designer, illustrator Creative Displays, Knoxville, 1974-75; designer alumni affairs U. Tenn., Knoxville, 1975-81, grad. tchg.

asst. dept. art, 1989-91; sr. art dir. Whittle Comm., Knoxville, 1982-85; creative dir. Sullivan-St. Clair Advt., Mobile, Ala., 1985-89; prof. graphic design Savannah (Ga.) Coll. Art and Design, 1991-92; asst. prof. graphic design Va. Poly. Inst. and State U., 1992-96; owner True G.R.I.T. Graphics Inc., Paper Whites Custom Invitations, 1996-99; assoc. prof. Tusculum Coll., Greeneville, Tenn., 1999-2000, adj. prof. Pellissippi State Tech. CC, Knoxville, 1999-2000. Assoc. faculty Tasculum Coll., Knoxville, Greenville; adj. faculty Pellissippi St. Tech. CC; sr. lectr. Wanganui (New Zealand) Sch. Design, 2000—. One-woman shows include S. Morris Gallery, Savannah, 1992, Ewing Gallery, Knoxville, 1992, Armory Art Gallery, Va. Poly. Inst. and State U., 1993, Gallery 303, Ga. So. U., 1994, Littman-White Gallery, Portland (Oreg.) State U., 1996, Allison Gallery, Tusculum Coll., Greeneville, 1999, exhibited in group shows at Women's Art Works III, Rochester, N.Y., Nat. Expos II, Chgo., 1993, Current Works, Kansas City, Mo., 1993, U. W. Fla., 1994, Paper Stars, San Francisco, 1994, Nat. Exposures, Winston-Salem, N.C. Recipient nat. citation, Coun. Advancement Edn., 1981, award, Warren Paper Co., 1984; grantee, Va. Poly. Inst. and State U., 1992, 1993, Women's Rsch. Inst., 1993, 1995; Fred M. Roddy scholar, 1970, Blinn scholar, 1991. Mem.: Alpha Lambda Delta. Democrat. Episcopalian. Avocations: world hunger, women's rights, art censorship.

TURNER, SANDRA CHUCALO, music educator; b. Scranton, Pa., Nov. 1, 1948; d. Marcus and Frances Biesecker Chucalo; m. Ronald A. Turner, Aug. 9, 1968; 1 child, Alison Rebecca. BA summa cum laude, Charleston So. U., 1970; MMus, Converse Coll., 1973; M in Ch. Music, So. Bapt. Theol. Sem., Louisville, 1976, DMA, 1987. Instr. So. Bapt. Theol. Sem., 1974—87, adj. prof., 1987—93, prof., 1994—. Organist Deer Park Bapt. Ch., Louisville, 1974—97, Louisville, 2002—, Broadway Bapt. Ch., Louisville, 1997—2002. Grantee, Musicians' Union, 1982, 1984. Mem.: So. Bapt. Conf. Ch. Musicians, Am. Guild of Organists, Music Tchrs. Nat. Assn., Royal Coll. Music (assoc.). Southern Baptist. Avocations: bicycling, hiking. Home: 2313 Carolina Ave Louisville KY 40205 Office: So Bapt Theol Seminary 2825 Lexington Rd Louisville KY 40280

TURNER, SHIRLEY KERSEY, state legislator; BS, Trenton State Coll.; MA, Rider U.; postgrad., Rutgers State U., 1976-80. Health & phys. edn. tchr. Bd. Edn., Trenton, 1966-70; asst. dir., coun. equal opportunity program Rider U., Lawrenceville, N.J., 1970-73, assoc. dir. office career devel. & placement, 1973—; assemblywoman N.J. Gen. Assembly, 1994-97; mem. N.J. Senate, Dist. 15, Trenton, 1997—. Founding mem. mentoring program Rider U., 1990, Mercer County Sch.-Age Child Care; mem. senate edn. com., state bd. canvassers, NJ Black and Latino caucus, commn. bus. efficiency pub. schs., NJ task force child abuse and neglect; bd. mem. Troy Vincent Found., Kid's Bridge, Inc. Elected Mercer County Freeholder, 1983, Freeholder v.p., 1986; chairwoman Mercer County Dem. Party. Mem. NAACP Metro. Trenton, N.J. Placement Group, Mid. Atlantic Placement Assn., Nat. Assn. Higher Edn., Am. Assn. Counseling & Devel. Office: NJ State Senate 1440 Pennington Rd Ewing NJ 08618-2662

TURNER, TINA (ANNA MAE BULLOCK), singer; b. Brownsville, Tenn., Nov. 26, 1939; m. Ike Turner, 1956; children: Craig, Ike Jr., Michael, Ronald. Singer (with): Ike Turner Kings of Rhythm, and Ike and Tina Turner Revue; appeared in (films) Gimme Shelter, 1970, Soul to Soul, 1971, Tommy, 1975, Sgt. Pepper's Lonely Hearts Club Band, 1978, Mad Max Beyond Thunderdome, 1985, Break Every Rule, 1986, Last Action Hero, 1993, concert tours of Europe, 1966, Japan and Africa, 1971, Showtime TV concert Wildest Dreams, albums with Ike Turner Hunter, 1970, Ike and Tina Show II, Ike and Tina Show, 1966, Ike and Tina Turner, Bad Dreams, 1973, Ike and Tina Turner Greatest Hits, vol. 1,2 and 3, 1989, Greatest Hits, 1990, Proud Mary, 1991, The Ike and Tina Turner Collection, 1993, solo albums Let Me Touch Your Mind, 1972, Tina Turns the Country On, 1974, Acid Queen, 1975, Love Explosion, 1977, Rough, 1978, Airwaves, 1979, Private Dancer, 1984, Break Every Rule, 1986, Tina Live In Europe, 1988, Foreign Affair, 1989, Simply the Best, 1991, What's Love Got to Do With It? (soundtrack), 1993, recordings Sixties to Nineties, with others, 1994, Wildest Dreams, 1996, Twenty Four Seven, 2000; performer (with USA): for Africa on song We are The World, 1985; author: (autobiography) I, Tina, 1985. Nominee Grammy (Best Pop Female Vocal) for "I Don't Wanna Fight", 1994; named to Rock and Roll Hall of Fame, 1991; recipient Grammy award, 1972, 1985, 1986.

TURNER-WARWICK, MARGARET, physician, educator; b. Nov. 19, 1924; d. William Harvey and Maud Kirkdale (Baden-Powell) Moore; m. Richard Trevor Turner-Warwick, Jan. 21, 1950; children: Gillian, Lynne. MA, BM, BCh, Oxford (Eng.) U., 1950, DM, 1956; PhD, London U., 1961; DSc (hon.), NYU, 1985, Exeter U., 1990, U. London, 1990, Hull U., 1991, U. Sussex, 1992, U. Oxford, 1992, U. Cambridge, 1993, U. Leicester, 1997. Clin. tng. U. Coll. Hosp., Brompton Hosp., 1950-61; cons. physician Elizabeth Garrett Anderson Hosp., 1961-67, Brompton and London Chest Hosps., 1967-72; prof. medicine Brompton and Cardio Thoracic Inst., London, 1972-87; dean Cardiothoracic Inst., London, 1984-87; pres. Royal Coll. Physicians, London, 1989-92. Chmn. UKCCCR, London. Author: (book) Immunology of Lung, 1979. Non-exec. mem. Royal Brompton Governing Body, London; chmn. Royal Devon Exeter Healthcare Trust, 1992-95. Decorated dame comdr. Brit. Empire; recipient Osler medal Oxford, 1996, Pres. award European Respiratory Soc., 1997. Fellow: ACP (hon.), Royal Coll. Radiology, Acad. Med. Sci. (founder 1998), Royal Coll. Physicians Ireland, Royal Coll. Physicians and Surgeons Glasgow, U. Coll. London, Faculty Pub. Health Medicine, Faculty Occupl. Medicine, Royal Australian Coll. Physicians, Bencher Mid. Temple (hon.), Royal Coll. Physicians and Surgeons Can. (hon.), Royal Coll. Anaesthetists (hon.), Coll. Medicine South Africa (hon.), Royal Coll. Pathologists (hon.), Imperial Coll. London (hon.), Royal Coll. Gen. Practitioners (ad enundum), Royal Coll. Physicians Edinburgh, Royal Coll. Gen. Practitioners, Green Coll. Oxford (hon.), Lady Margaret Hall Oxford (hon.), Girton Coll. Cambridge (hon.); mem.: Brit. Thoracic Soc. (pres. 1982, President's medal 1999), Acad. Malaysia, South German and Australasian Thoracic Socs. (hon.), Assn. Physicians Gt. Britain and Ireland (hon.), Alpha Omega Alpha. Avocations: gardening, violin, country life, watercolor painting. Home: Pynes House Thorverton Nr Exeter Devon EX5 5LT England

TURNEY, SHARON JESTER, retail executive; b. 1958; BA in Bus. Edn., U. Okla. With Foley's, 1979—88, Neiman Marcus, 1989—2000, sr. v.p. gen., mgr. gen. merchandise, 1997—98, exec. v.p. merchandising, creative prodn., advt. and pub. rels., 1998; pres., CEO Neiman Marcus Direct, 1999—2000; CEO, pres. Victoria's Secret Catalogue, 2000—. Office: Victorias Secret Direct LLC 3425 Morse Crossing Columbus OH 43219*

TURNEY, VIRGINIA, writer; b. Raton, N.Mex., Oct. 14, 1929; d. Otto and Lillian G. Olson; m. Eugene T. Turney Jr., July 17, 1962 (dec. Oct. 1979); children: Dianne Bohannan, Djinee Turney Jeffrey, Tore Nils and Nils Tore (twins); m. William M. Adams. BA, UCLA, 1950; DPsy, U. Miami, Fla., 1966. V.p. Anodyne, Inc., 1967-78; founder, pres., chmn. Ginni Lee All Sports, 1973—; chmn., pres. E.T. Turney, Inc., 1978—; pres. ToysCraftsGames, Islamorada, Fla., 1985—. Psychologist People's Ct. for Handicapped Teens. Author: Cuban Spy for Freedom, 1981, Operation Truth, 1988. Mem. Save-A-Turtle Found., Whale Protection Assn., Gorilla Found. Mem. Miami Jockey Club, Palm Bay Rolls Royce Owners Club, Rolls Royce Enthusiasts, Key West Garden Club, Island Fishing, Club, Internat. Women's Fishing Club, Catskill Fly Fishing Club, West Palm Beach Fishing Club. Home: PO Box 14266 108 S 29th St Mexico Beach FL 32456

TURNLUND, JUDITH RAE, nutritionist; b. St. Paul, Sept. 28, 1936; d. Victor Emanuel and Vida Mae (Priddy) Hanson; m. Richard Wayne Turnlund, Nov. 9, 1957; children: Michael Wayne, Mark Richard, Todd Hanson. BS in Chemistry and Psychology, Gustavus Adolphus Coll., 1958; PhD in Nutrition, U. Calif., Berkeley, 1978. Registered dietitian. Postdoctoral fellow U. Calif., Berkeley, 1978-80, lectr., 1984-92, adj. assoc. prof., 1989-97; rsch. nutrition scientist Western Regional Rsch. Ctr./Western Human Nutrition Ctr., USDA, San Francisco, Albany, and Davis, Calif., 1980—; rsch. leader Western Human Nutrition Ctr. USDA, San Francisco, 1993-96; adj. prof. nutrition U. Calif., Davis, 2000—. Vis. asst. prof. Am. U. Beirut, Lebanon, 1979, 80. Editor: Stable Isotopes in Nutrition, 1984; contbr. articles to profl. jours. Recipient Cert. of Merit, USDA/ARS, 1984, 93, 98, Disting. Alumni citation Gustavus Adolphus Coll., 1988, Am. Inst. Nutrition's Lederle award in Human Nutrition, 1996; USDA grantee, Nat. Dairy Coun. grantee. Fellow Am. Soc. Nutritional Scis.; mem. Am. Soc. Clin. Nutrition, Am. Dietetic Assn. Home: 2276 Great Hwy San Francisco CA 94116-1555 Office: U Calif USDA/ARS Western Human Nutrition Rsch One Shields Ave Davis CA 95616 E-mail: jturnlun@whnrc.usda.gov.

TURO, JOANN K. psychoanalyst, psychotherapist, consultant; b. Westerly, R.I., Feb. 13, 1938; d. Angelo and Anna Josephine (Drew) T. BS in Biology and Chemistry, U. R.I., 1959; MA in Human Rels. and Psychology, Ohio U., 1964; postgrad., NYU, 1966-71, N.Y. Freudian Inst., N.Y.C., 1977-85, Mental Health Inst., 1977-80. Rsch. asst. biochemistry studies on schizophrenia Harvard U. Med. Sch., Boston, 1959-60; indsl. psychology asst. studies on managerial success N.Y. Telephone Co., N.Y.C., 1964-66; staff psychologist Testing and Advisement Ctr. NYU, 1966-70; psychology intern Kings County Hosp., Bklyn., 1970-71; staff psychologist M.D.C. Psychol. Svcs., N.Y.C., 1971-72; clin. dir. Greenwich House Substance Abuse Clinic, N.Y.C., 1973-76; cons. psychotherapist Mental Health Consultation Ctr., N.Y.C., 1977-82; pvt. practice N.Y.C., 1981—. Mental health cons. Bklyn. Ctr. for Psychotherapy, 1976-78; with Psychoanalytic Consultation Svcs., 1994—; presenter in field. Mem. Internat. Psychoanalytic Assn. (cert.), Soc. for Personality Assessment (cert.), N.Y. Freudian Soc. (cert., co-chmn. grad. com. 1985-86, mem. continuing edn. com. 1986—, pub. rels. com. 1992-93, psychoanalytic consult svc. 1994—, tng. and supr. psychoanalyst 1995—, ethics com. 1999—, tng. analyst panel 2000—, chair 2002-2003, presenter 2002, bd. dirs. 2003-06), N.Y. Coun. Psychoanalytic Psychotherapists (cert.), Met. Assn. for Coll. Mental Health Practitoners (cert.). Office: 175 W 12th St Apt 15A New York NY 10011-8211

TUROCK, BETTY JANE, library and information science educator; b. Scranton, Pa., June 12; d. David and Ruth Carolyn (Sweetser) Argust; m. Frank M. Turock, June 16, 1956; children: David L., B. Drew. BA magna cum laude (Charles Weston scholar), Syracuse U., 1955; postgrad. (scholar), U. Pa., 1956; MLS, Rutgers U., 1970, PhD, 1981. Library and materials coordinator Holmdel (N.J.) Public Schs., 1963-65; story-teller Wheaton (Ill.) Public Library, 1965-67; ednl. media specialist Alhambra Public Sch., Phoenix, 1967-70; br. librarian, area librarian, head extension service Forsyth County Public Library System, Winston-Salem, NC, 1970—73; asst. dir., dir. Montclair (N.J.) Public Library, 1973—76; asst. dir. Monroe County Library System, Rochester, N.Y., 1978-81; asst. prof. Rutgers U. Sch. Comms., Info. and Libr. Studies, 1981-87; assoc. prof. Rutgers U. Sch. Comm. Info and Libr. Studies, 1987-93, prof., 1994—, dept. chair, 1989-95, dir. MLS program, 1990-95, assoc. dean, 2002—. Vis. prof. Rutgers U. Grad. Sch. Library and Info. Studies, 1980-81; adviser U.S. Dept. Edn. Office of Libr. Programs, 1988-89. Author: Serving Older Adults, 1983, Creating a Financial Plan, 1992; editor: The Bottom Line, 1984-90; contbr. articles to profl. jours. Trustee Raritan Twp. (N.J.) Pub. Libr., 1961—62, Keystone Coll., 1991—, Freedom to Read Found., 1994—97, Librs. for the Future, 1994—97, Fund for Am.'s Librs., 1995, Trejo Found., 1995—; trustee Bd. Am. Libr., Paris, 1999—; mem. Bd. Edn. Raritan Twp., 1962—66; ALA coord. Task Force on Women, 1978—80; mem. action coun.; treas. Social Responsibilities Round Table, 1978—82. Charles Weston scholar Syracuse U., 1955; recipient N.J. Libr. Leadership award, 1994; named Woman of Yr. Raritan-Holmdel Woman's Club, 1975. Mem. AAUP, Am. Soc. Info. Sci., Assn. Libr. and Info. Sci Edn., Am. Libr. Assn. (pres. 1995-96, pres.-elect 1994-95, exec. bd. 1991-97, coun. 1988-97, equality award 1998), Rutgers U. Grad. Sch. Library and Info. Studies Alumni Assn. (pres. 1977-78, Disting. Alumni award 1994, Extraordinary Libr. Advocate of 20th Century award 2000), Phi Theta Kappa, Psi Chi, Beta Phi Mu, Pi Beta Phi. Unitarian Universalist. Home: 39 Highwood Rd Somerset NJ 08873-1834 Office: Rutgers U 4 Huntington St New Brunswick NJ 08901-1071 E-mail: bturock@scils.rutgers.edu.

TUROCK, JANE PARSICK, nutritionist; b. Peckville, Pa., Apr. 15, 1947; d. Paul Charles and Elizabeth Dorothy (Mistysyn) Parsick; m. Michael John, July 12, 1968; children: Eric Matthew, Nathan Andrew, J. Seth, Melanie Kay. BS, Marywood Coll., Scranton, 1969; MS, Marywood Coll., 1982. Registered dietitian; cert. nutrition specialist. Registered dietitian Jane P. Turock, Scranton, Pa., 1985—; founder and chief dietitian Gastric Bubble, Scranton, Pa., 1986—; prof. Penn State Coll., Scranton, Pa., 1987—; dietitian & presenter WNEP TV Healthwatch, Avoca, Pa., 1988—; dir. & chief dietitian Vascular Inst. of Northeast Pa., Pa., 1989—; owner, mgr. Nutrition...Plus/Fitness Unlimited, Scranton, Pa., 1991—. Cons. Home Health Care Assn., Clarks Summit, 1985—; dietitian Clarks Summit, 1985—; founder Nat. Nutrition Month Bakeoff; dir. Camp Jane. Treas. Lackawanna County Med. Soc. Aux., 1974-76, pres., 1979-80, bd. dirs., 1980-81; allocations com. United Way Lackawanna County, 1990—; mem. bd. dirs. Lupus Found., 1995, St. Francis of Assissi Kitchen, 1995. Mem. Am. Dietic Assn., Northeast Dist. Pa. Dietic Diet Therapy, Consulting Nutritionists in Pvt. Practice, Am. Diabetic Assn., Northeast Womens Network, Allied Wedding Firm. Republican. Roman Catholic. Avocations: skiing, tennis, gourmet cooking, jogging, swimming. Office: Nutrition Plus/Lady Jane Fitness 375 N 9th Ave Scranton PA 18504-2005 also: Abington Family Svcs 211 N State St Clarks Summit PA 18411-1087 also: Lady Jane Inc dba The Ski Habit Union Dale PA 18470 also: Nate's Outdoor Sports Ctr 611 State St Clarks Summit PA 18411 also: Jane P Turock MSRD 397 N 9th Ave Scranton PA 18504-2005 Office Phone: 570-357-0104. E-mail: janeturock@excite.com.

TUROCY, CATHERINE, performing company executive; BFA magna cum laude, Ohio State U., 1974. Tchr. Baroque dance STEPS Dance Studio, N.Y.C., 1991—95; tchr. The Baroque Ballet Workshop, Calif., 1995—, Baroque Dance Workshops, 1996—; dancer Cleve. Ballet Co., 1967—70, Modern Dance Troupe, Ohio State U., 1971—74, The Baroque Dance Ensemble, 1972—80, The Auk Mime and Dance Troupe, 1974—75, The Max Co., 1976—77, The Mitchell Rose Dance Co., 1977—78, Court Dance Co. N.Y., 1977—79; dancer, artistic dir. The N.Y. Baroque Dance Co., 1976—. Guest choreographer; vis. lectr.; vis. artist. Creator (video) The Art of Dancing: An Introduction to Baroque Dance, 1979 (Dance Film award, 1979); author: Moving History/Dancing Cultures: A Dance History Reader, 2001, Dance Masters: Roseman, Janet Lynn, 2001; dancer numerous videos, TV, plays, stage, choreographer numerous musicals, modern dance, stage. Named Chevalier in Order of Arts and Letters, French Govt., 1995; recipient N.Y. Dance and Performance award, 2001, Jerome Found. award for choreographic creation, 1985; fellow, Nat. Endowment for Arts, 1980—81, 1987, N.Y. Found. for Arts, 1990, Nat. Endowment for Arts Choreography, 1980, 83, 84, 86-88, 90, 94-96, 96-97; grantee, Nat. Endowment for Arts Heritage and Preservation, 1997—98; scholar, Getty, 1997. Mem.: Alpha Lambda Delta. Home: 6901 Gaston Ave Dallas TX 75214

TURQUETTE, FRANCES BOND, editor; b. Atlanta, Sept. 25, 1931; d. Sewell Hinton and Lavonia DeLay Dixon; m. Charles Eugene Bond, Sept. 12, 1952 (div. Jan. 1969); children: Turner D., Laura S., L. Irene, Cynthia D., Nelson K.; m. Atwell Rufus Turquette, Dec. 27, 1998. Student, Wesleyan Coll., 1948—50; BA in Journalism, U. Ga., 1952; MA in Art History, U. Ill., 1971. Editl. asst. Meth. Pub. Ho., Nashville, 1952-53, Rsch. Press, Champaign, Ill., 1972-73; editing supr. McGraw-Hill Book Co., N.Y.C., 1974-80; publs. editor pub. affairs U. Ill., Urbana, 1974, 80-88; editor Nat. Ctr. for Supercomputing Applications, Champaign, 1988-96. Vis. faculty, editor Coll. of Commerce, U. Ill., Urbana, 1970-71, [illegible] com., Editorial and Composition Standards McGraw Hill Book Co., N.Y.C., 1975-77; editor, writer access, 1988-96. Mem. program chair, liaison, bd. govs. Channing Murray Found., Urbana, 1982-92; mem. adv. bd. to freeze nuclear weapons 15th Congrl. Dist., 1982-87; co-pres. SANE/Freeze, Champaign County, 1992-94. Mem. Nat. Assn. Sci. Writers, Art Inst. Chgo. (nat. assoc.), Lyric Opera Chgo., Theta Sigma Phi. Unitarian Universalist. Avocations: travel, writing, gardening, photography. Home: 914 W Clark St Champaign IL 61821-3328 E-mail: aturquette1@iopener.net.

TURTURRO, AIDA, actress; b. NYC, Sept. 25, 1962; Grad., State U. NY, New Paltz, 1984. Actor: (films) Life with Mikey, 1993, Money Train, 1995, Sleepers, 1996, Fallen, 1998, Celebrity, 1998, Deep Blue Sea, 1999, Mickey Blue Eyes, 1999, Bringing Out the Dead, 1999, Play It to the Bone, 1999, Crocodile Dundee in Los Angeles, 2001; (TV series) As the World Turns, 1998, The Soprano's, 2000—; (Broadway plays) A Streetcar Named Desire, 1992, (guest appearance): (TV series) Law and Order, 1990. Office: 1100 Ave of the Americas New York NY 10036*

TURYN, NOREEN AUDREY, television news anchor, reporter; b. St. Louis, July 19, 1962; d. Victor and Eileen Dorothy (Simpson) T. BS in Broadcast Journalism, U. Md., 1984. Rschr./investigator WJLA-TV, Washington, 1984-85; news stringer WAMT/WAJX Radio, Titusville, Fla., 1985-86; prodr./technician Balt. Radio Reading Svc., 1986-88; assignment editor WMAR-TV, Balt., 1988-90; reporter/anchor WSET-TV, Lynchburg, Va., 1990—. Mem. com. Woman's Resource Ctr., Lynchburg, 1994-95; bd. dirs. Big Bros./Big Sisters, Lynchburg, 1996; mem. pub. rels. com. ARC, Lynchburg, 1995; bd. dirs. Ellington Fellowship Playhouse, 2002—. Recipient Nat. Scripps Howard award for Excellence in Journalism, Regional Edward R. Murrow award, Meritorius award, Va. Assn. of Broadcasters. Mem. Delta Delta Delta. Office: WSET-TV 2320 Langhorne Rd Lynchburg VA 24501-1547 Office Phone: 434-528-1313.

TUSHMAN, J. LAWRENCE, wholesale distribution executive; Ptnr., mgr. Sherwood Food Distbrs., Detroit. Office: Sherwood Food Distributors 18615 Sherwood St Detroit MI 48234-2813

TUSKEY, LAURA JEANNE, music educator, pharmacologist; b. Virginia Beach, Va., May 7, 1966; d. Cromer Lee Ishmael and Annabell E. Eschbach; m. John Phillip Tuskey, June 26, 1998. Student, Old Dominion U., Norfolk, Va., 1984—86. Cert. pharmacy technician Pharmacy Technician Certification Bd., 2003. Pianist Cath. Ch. of St. Mark, Virginia Beach, Va., 1991—; office mgr. CompuGeek, L.L.C., Chesapeake, Va., 2002—03; pharmacy technician Farm Fresh, Inc., Virginia Beach, Va., 2002—, Phar Mor, Inc., Norfolk and Virginia Beach, Va., 1991—98; music therapist Our Lady of Perpetual Health, Virginia Beach, Va., 1999—2000. Aromatherapy educator, Hampton Roads, Va., 2000—. Contbr. articles to profl. jours. Mem.: Alzheimer's Assn. (chmn. memory walk com. 2001), Nat. Pastoral Musicians Assn. R-Liberal. Roman Catholic. Avocations: aromatherapy, musical events, reading, travel. Office: Catholic Church of St Mark 1505 Kempsville Rd Virginia Beach VA 23464

TUTTLE, ASHLEY, dancer; b. Columbia, SC; Student, Sch. Am. Ballet. Mem. Am. Ballet Theatre, N.Y.C., 1987—, soloist, 1992—, prin. ballerina, 1997—. Roles include Mathilda Kchessinska in Anastasia, Callipe and Polyhymnia in Apollo, Nikiya in La Bayadere, mother/sweathear in Billy the Kid, Cinderella and the Spring Fairy in Cinderella, Prayer in Copellia, Gulnare and the pas de deux in Le Cosaire, the Queen of the Driads, Amour and flower girl in Don Quixote, others, featured roles in Ballet Imperial, Cruel World, Drink to Me Only With Thine Eyes, The Leaves are Falling, leading roles in Brahms-Haydn Variations, The Elements, Jump Start, Piece D'Occasion. Office: Am Ballet Theatre 890 Broadway New York NY 10003

TUTTLE, MARCIA, retired elementary school educator, music educator; b. Spirit Lake, Iowa, Dec. 30, 1945; d. Frank Ewing and Ann Parsons Tuttle; 1 child, Amy Beth Gould. BA in English, Elem. Edn., U. Iowa, 1969, MA in Reading Disabilities, 1975; BA in Piano Pedagogy summa cum laude, Mt. Mercy Coll., 1985. Cert. tchr. Iowa. Elem. tchr. Cedar Rapids (Iowa) Cmty. Schs., 1969—2001; piano tchr. Cedar Rapids, 1981—2001, Salmon Creek Piano Studio, Vancouver, Wash., 2002—. Composer, performer Iowa Composers Concerts, Cedar Rapids, 1983—85; adjudicator Pvt. Music Teachers Assn. Competition, Cedar Rapids, 1994—95, Kalina Piano Studio Competition, Cedar Rapids, 1996—2000. Composer: Tempus Suite, Sibelius Publication. Coord. Cedar Rapids Cmty. Sch. Dist. Music Contest, 1987—92; big sister Big Bros./Big Sisters Assn., Cedar Rapids, 1986—; vol. HOSTS Reading Readiness, Vancouver, Wash., 2002—; music dir., pianist Living Branch Luth. Ch., Woodland, Wash., 2002—. Named honoree, Belin-Blank Ctr. for Gifted Edn., U. Iowa, 1996, 1998; recipient Outstanding Music Grad. award, Mt. Mercy Coll., 1985, Hero award, Big Bros./Big Sisters, Cedar Rapids, 2000. Mem.: Music Tchrs. Nat. Assn., Wash. Music Tchrs. Assn., Clark County Music Tchrs. Assn. (2d v.p. 2003—), S.W. Wash. Watercolor Soc., Beethoven Club. Avocations: watercolor painting, music, travel. Home: 2115 NW 143d Cir Vancouver WA 98685

TUTTLE, MARTHA BENEDICT, artist; b. Cin., Feb. 4, 1916; d. Harris Miller and Florence Stevens (McCrea) Benedict; m. Richard Salway Tuttle, June 3, 1939; children: Richard, Jr., McCrea Benedict (dec.), Martha (dec.), Elisabeth Hall. Grad. high sch., Cin.; student, Art Acad. Cin., 1934-38. V.p. Barq Bottling Co., Inc., Cin., 1948-80. One-woman shows include KKAE Gallery, 1963, Univ. Club, 1967, Miller Gallery, 1971, St. Clements, N.Y., 1973, Livingston Lodge, 1974, Holly Hill Antiques, 1979, Peterson Gallery, 1983, Art Acad. Cin., 1984, Closson Gallery, 1986, Camargo Gallery, 1992; represented in permanent collection Cin. Art Mus. Tchr. Sunday sch. Grace Episcopal Ch. and Indian Hill Ch., Cin., 1953-75; shareholder Cin. Art Mus.; founder partnership to save the William and Phebe Betts House; donor with partnership to The Nat. Soc. Colonial Dames of Am. the William and Phebe Betts House for establishing a Rsch. Ctr. Mem. Soc. Colonial Dames Am. (bd. dirs. 1976-89), Camargo Club, Univ. Club. Republican. Home: # 3C 2401 Ingleside Ave Cincinnati OH 45206-2118

TUTWILER, MARGARET DEBARDELEBEN, federal agency administrator; b. Birmingham, Ala., Dec. 28, 1950; d. Temple Wilson and Margaret (DeBardeleben) Tutwiler, II. Student, Finch Coll., 1969-71; BA, U. Ala., 1973. Sec. Ala. Rep. Party, Birmingham, 1974; scheduler Pres. Ford Com., Birmingham, 1975-78; exec. dir. Pres. Ford Com. Ala., Birmingham, 1976; pub. rels. rep. Nat. Assn. Mfrs. for Ala. and Miss., Birmingham and Washington, 1977-78; dir. scheduling George Bush for Pres. Com., Houston and Washington, 1978-80; spl. asst. to Pres. Reagan and exec. to Chief of Staff The White House, Washington, 1981-85; asst. sec., pub. affairs & public liaison U.S. Dept. Treasury, 1985-88; sr. advisor transition team U.S. Dept. State, Washington, 1988-89, asst. sec. pub. affairs, spokesman, 1989-92, U.S. amb. to Morocco Rabat, 2001—03, under sec., pub. diplomacy & pub. affairs Washington, 2003—; ptnr. Fitzwater & Tutwiler, Inc., Washington, 1993—2001. Dep. chmn. Bush-Quayle '88, Washington, 1988. Recipient Woman of Yr. award Wake Forest U., 1986, Alexander Hamilton award, 1988, Am. Ctr. for Internat. Leadership's Marshall award for outstanding leadership Birmingham Sothern's GALA 10, 1991. Republican. Episcopalian. Office: US Dept State Harry S Truman Bldg 2201 C St NW Rm 7261 Washington DC 20520*

TUZEE, MICHELLE, newscaster; m. Craig Tuzee; 2 children. BA in journalism, U. So. Calif. Prodr., anchor, reporter KJCT-TV, Grand Junction, Colo.; reporter WBAY-TV, Wis.; anchor, reporter WFTX-TV, Fort Myers, Fla.; co-anchor, Today in Florida, 7 News at Noon WSVN, Miami; co-anchor, Eyewitness News at 4, 6 and 11pm KABC 7, Los Angeles, 1997—. Office: ABC7 Broadcast Ctr 500 Circle Seven Dr Glendale CA 91201*

TUZEL, TULIN, food service executive; b. Istanbul, Turkey, Jan. 26, 1950; came to the U.S., 1967; m. Turhan Tuzel; children: Erin, Sasha, Armand. BSChemE, CCNY; MSChemE, N.Y. Poly. Inst.; MBA, U. Conn. Rsch. engr. Olin Corp., La.; rschr. Nestle, N.J.; v.p. R&D Sara Lee Corp., Chgo.; sr. v.p. R&D, chief tech. officer Burger King Corp., Miami, Fla. Avocation: tennis. Office: Burger King Corp PO Box 020783 17777 Old Cutler Rd Miami FL 33157-6347

TWAIN, SHANIA (EILLEEN REGINA EDWARDS), country musician; b. Windsor, Ontario, Can., Aug. 28, 1965; d. Sharon and Jerry Twain(Step-father), Clarence Edwards; m. Robert John Lange, Dec. 28, 1993; 1 child, Eja. Recs. Beginnings, 1989—90, 1999, Shania Twain, 1993, The Woman in Me, 1995 (Acad. Country Music Assn. Award for Album of Yr., 1995, ABC Radio Networks Country Music Award for Female Video Artist of Yr., 1995, Billboard Music Award for Country Album of Yr., 1996, Grammy award for Best Country Album, 1996), These Blues are Mine, 1996, Come on Over, 1997, Star Profile, 1999, Maximum Shania, 2000, Complete Limelight Sessions, 2001, Up!, 2002 (Can. Country Music Assn. Award for Album of Yr., 2003, Billboard Music Award for Country Album of Yr., 2003). Recipient Country Music TV (Europe) Rising Star award, 1993, Am. Music Award for Favorite New Country Artist, 1995, Can. Country Music Assn. Award for female vocalist of yr., 1995, Acad. of Country Music Award for Top New Female Vocalist, 1995, Best Country Album Grammy award, 1995, Blockbuster Entertainment Award for Favorite New Country Artist, 1996, Country Music TV (Europe) award for Female Artist of Yr., 1996, Juno Award for Country Female Vocalist of Yr., 1996, Juno Award for Entertainer of Yr., 1996, World Music Award for World's Best Selling Country Artist, 1996, Favorite New Artist award, Am. Music Awards, 1996, Am. Music Award for Best Female Country Artist, 1997, Juno Award for Country Female Vocalist of Yr., 1997, Juno Award for Internat. Achievement, 1997, Am. Music Award for Favorite Female Country Artist, 1998, Billboard Music Award for Female Artist of Yr., 1998, Country Music Assn. Award for Entertainer of Yr., 1999, Acad. Country Music Award for Entertainer of Yr., 1999, Am. Music Award for Favorite Female Country Artist, 1999, Am. Music Award for Favorite Female Pop/Rock Artist, 1999, Blockbuster Entertainment Award for Favorite Overall Single, 1999, Juno Award for Country Female Vocalist of Yr., 1999, Grammy Award for Best Female Country Vocal Performance (You're Still The One), 1999, Grammy Award for Best Country Song (You're Still The One), 1999, Juno Award for Best Songwriter, 2000, Juno Award for Best Country Female Artist, 2000, Grammy Award for Best Female Vocal Country Performance (Man!I Feel Like A Woman), 2000, Grammy Award for Best Country Song (Come On Over), 2000, Acad. Country Music Award for Entertainer of Yr., 2000, Billboard Music Award for Top County Artist of Yr., 2003, Billboard Music Award for Country Album Artist of Yr., 2003, Juno Fan Choice Award, 2003, Juno Award for Artist of Yr., 2003, Juno Award for Country Rec. Yr. (I'm Gonna Getcha Good), 2003, Can. Country Music Assn. Award for Video of Yr. (I'm Gonna Getcha Good), 2003, Can. Country Music Assn. Award for Female Artist of Yr., 2003. Office: Mercury Records 66 Music Sq W Nashville TN 37203-4315 Address: Shore Fire Media c/o Georgette Pascale 32 Court St Fl 16 Brooklyn NY 11201-4404*

TWARJAN, COLLEEN ANN, dental hygienist; b. Manchester, N.H., Jan. 1, 1956; d. Robert Francis and Josephine Margaret (O'Brien) H.; m. John Paul Twarjan Jr., Oct. 9, 1982; children; Jesse, Max, Sam. AA, N.H. Tech. Inst., Concord, 1977. Dental hygienst Dr. Steven Christenson, Concord, N.H., 1977-78, Dr. Joseph Maroun, Salem, N.H., 1978-83, Dr. Christos Giotopoulos, Manchester, 1978-84, Lindner Dental Assocs., Bedford, 1997—. Mem. Smyth Rd. PTO, Manchester, N.H., 1988—, treas. 1989-96, v.p., 1996, pres., 1997-99; v.p. Hillside PTO, 1999-2000, pres. 1997-98. Roman Catholic. Avocation: gardening. Office: Lindner Dental Assocs Bedford NH 03110

TWIGG, NANCY L. nursing association administrator; Exec. dir. State of N.Mex. Bd. Nursing, Albuquerque. Office: State NMex Bd Nursing 4206 Louisiana Blvd NE Ste A Albuquerque NM 87109-1841

TWISS, WANDA MAY, interior designer; b. Marengo, Ind., Oct. 28, 1934; d. Gamford Ingle and Anjie Pearl (Beld) Tate; m. Eugene Clyo Twiss, Nov. 27, 1952; children: Sheryll Lynn, Carol Ann. Student pub. schs., Newcastle, Ind. Decorator, Interiors by Decorating Den, Leesburg, Fla., 1970-85, franchise owner, 1983—, regional coordinator, instr., 1984—, designer, 1985—. Mem. Am. Soc. Interior Designers (allied mem.). Mem. Ch. of Nazarene. Home: 38840 Ella Dr Lady Lake FL 32159 Office: Interiors by Decorating Den 1031 W Main St Leesburg FL 34748-4965

TWOMEY, ELIZABETH ANN MOLLOY, education educator; b. Lynn, Mass. d. Hugh E. and Theresa A. (Callahan) Molloy; children: Ann, Paula, Charles. AB, Emmanuel Coll., 1959; MEd, Mass. State Coll., 1964; EdD, Boston Coll., 1982; LLB (hon.), Notre Dame, Manchester, N.H., 1984; LHL (hon.), Emmanuel Coll., 1998. Elem. sch. tchr. Lynn (Mass.) Pub. Schs., 1959-63; English tchr. Reading (Mass.) Pub. Schs., 1973-75, prin., 1975-81, vice prin., 1981-82; supt. Lincoln (Mass.) Pub. Schs., 1982-88; assoc. commr. Dept. Edn., Quincy, Mass., 1988-92, dep. commr. Concord, N.H., 1992-94, commr., 1994—2000. Adj. prof. Lynch Sch. Edn. Boston Coll., 2000—. Trustee Emmanuel Coll., Boston, 1975-85, U. N.H., Durham, 1994—. Recipient Disting. Alumni award Emmanuel Coll., 1984. Avocations: walking, reading, gardening. Office: Lynch Sch Education Boston Coll Concord NH 02467

TWYMAN, NITA (VENITA TWYMAN), music educator; b. Beloit, Wis., July 14, 1948; d. W.R. and Geneva L. (Goodman) Corvin; m. Dennis D. Twyman, Aug. 16, 1969; children: Christopher Grant, Kevin Scott. AA with honors, Southwestern Coll., Oklahoma City, 1968; B Music Edn. cum laude, So. Nazarene U., 1971; postgrad., U. Okla., 1970-71, 91-94; MMus, Oklahoma City U., 1975. Piano instr. Oklahoma City Southwestern Coll., 1968-70; pvt. music instr. Twyman Piano Studio, Oklahoma City, 1968—. Adj. faculty mem. Redlands C.C., El Reno, Okla., 1995—, Rose State Coll., Oklahoma City, 2003—; creative cons. Great Start in Music ednl. music video; choir dir. Ctrl. Ch., Oklahoma City, 1989; staff accompanist Oklahoma City First Pentecostal Holiness Ch., 1966-68. Solo performances at local churches. Mem. Nat. Guild Piano Tchrs. (nat. tchr. cert., nat. adjudicator), Music Tchrs. Nat. Assn. (nat. cert. in piano and music theory, Piano Technicians Guild grantee 1991), Okla. Music Tchrs. Assn. (adjudicator), Ctrl. Okla. Music Tchrs. Assn. (sec., parliamentarian, treas., mem. various coms.), Okla. Fedn. Music Clubs (adjudicator), Oklahoma City Pianists Club (performer), Phi Kappa Lambda. Avocations: scuba diving, bicycling, water skiing, snow skiing. Office: Nita Twyman Piano Studio 5915 NW 23rd St Ste 107 Oklahoma City OK 73127-1254

TYDINGCO-GATEWOOD, FRANCES MARIE, judge; b. Oahu, Hawaii, Jan. 21, 1958; d. Daniel J. and Francesca S. Tydingco; m. Robert Gatewood; children: Daniel Gatewood, Michael Gatewood, Stephen Gatewood. BA in Polit. Sci., Marquette U., 1980; JD, U. Mo., Kansas City, 1983. Law clk. to Hon. Forest W. Hanna Jackson County Cir. Ct., Kansas City, 1983—84; asst. atty. gen. Govt. of Guam, 1984—88, chief prosecutor, 1990—94; asst. prosecutor Jackson County Prosecutor's Office, Mo., 1988—90; trial judge Superior Ct. Guam, 1994—2002; assoc. judge Supreme Ct. Guam, 2002—. Profl. Tech. scholar, Govt. of Guam. Office: Supreme Ct Guam Guam Jud Ctr Ste 300 120 W O'Brien Dr Hagatna GU 96910 Home: 222 Chalan Santo Papa Ste 222 Hagatna GU 96910 Business E-Mail: ftgate@guamsupremecourt.com.

TYLER, ANNE (MRS. TAGHI M. MODARRESSI), writer; b. Mpls., Oct. 25, 1941; d. Lloyd Parry and Phyllis (Mahon) T.; m. Taghi M. Modarressi, May 3, 1963 (dec. Apr. 1997); children: Tezh, Mitra. BA, Duke U., 1961; postgrad., Columbia U., 1962. Author: If Morning Ever Comes, 1964, The Tin Can Tree, 1965, A Slipping-Down Life, 1970, The Clock Winder, 1972, Celestial Navigation, 1974, Searching for Caleb, 1976, Earthly Possessions, 1977, Morgan's Passing, 1980, Dinner at the Homesick Restaurant, 1982, The Accidental Tourist, 1985, Breathing Lessons, 1988 (Pulitzer Prize for fiction 1989), Saint Maybe, 1991, (juvenile) Tumble Tower, 1993, Ladder of Years, 1995, A Patchwork Planet, 1998, Back When We Were Grownups, 2001, The Amateur Marriage, 2004; contbr. short stories to nat. mags. Home: 222 Tunbridge Rd Baltimore MD 21212-3422*

TYLER, CECILIA KAY, career officer US Army; b. McCall, Idaho, May 18, 1956; d. Cecil Edward and Ruby Ilene (Wine) Oatney; m. Nelvin Eugene (Gene) Tyler Jr., Dec. 24, 1991. BBA in Acctg., Idaho State U., 1978; MS in Econs. and Ops. Research, Colo. Sch. Mines, 1987; MS in Nat. Resourcing Strategy, Nat. Def. U., 2000; student, Command and Gen. Staff Coll., Leavenworth, Kans., 1989—90, Indsl. Coll. Armed Forces Nat. Def. U., Ft. McNair, Washington, 1999—2000. Commd. 2d lt. U.S. Army, 1978, advanced through grades to col., 2000, platoon leader A, B and C Cos. 8th Signal Battalion, 1978-81, logistics officer, 1981; promoted to capt., 1982; divsn. radio officer 2AD U.S. Army, Ft. Hood, Tex., 1982—83, comdr. C co. 142d Signal Battalion, 1983—85, chief market analysis 6th Recruiting Brigade Ft. Baker, Calif., 1987-89; promoted to maj., 1990; chief strategic systems plans br. 5th Signal Command U.S. Army, Fed. Republc of Germany, 1990-91, chief plans & programs div., 1991, exec. officer 509th Signal Battalion Camp Darby Italy, 1991-92, exec. officer office dep. chief staff, info. mgmt. Heidelberg, Germany, 1992-94, promoted to lt. col., 1994; dep. brigade comdr. 2d Sig BDE, Mannheim, Germany, 1994—96; comdr. 504th Signal Battalion, Fort Huachuca, Ariz., 1996-98; chief current ops. divsn. Army Signal Command, Fort Huachua, Ariz., 1998-99; dep. dir. Coalition Warfare, Internat. Cooper. Office of Under Sec. of Def. Acquisition, Tech. & Logistics, Pentagon/Washington, Va., 2000—; promoted to col., 2000. Pres. 4-H Club, Valley County, Idaho, 1973-74. Mem. Armed Forces Communication-Electronics Assn., Assn. U.S. Army. Avocations: skiing, sewing, reading, fishing. Home: 8661 Pohick Forest Ct Springfield VA 22153 Office: OUSD (AT&L)/IC 3070 Defense Pentagon Rm 2E173A Washington DC 20301 E-mail: tylercg@cox.net., cecilia.tyler@osd.mil.

TYLER, DANA, anchor; b. Columbus, Ohio; BA in Mktg. and Broadcast Journalism, Boston U. Intern WBNS-TV, Columbus, gen. assignment reporter, 1981—83, co-anchor weekday newscasts, 1983—90; weekend co-anchor/corr. WCBS-TV, N.Y.C., 1990—. Lectr. in field. Vol. N.Y.C. Sch. Vol. Programs. Honored by Harlem YMCA, Y of Greater N.Y.; recipient Emmy award for outstanding anchor, 1987, Emmy award for outstanding newscast, 1996, Emmy award for coverage of NYC Blackout, 2004. Office: WCBS-TV/CBS Corp 524 W 57th St New York NY 10019-2924*

TYLER, GAIL MADELEINE, nurse; b. Dhahran, Saudi Arabia, Nov. 21, 1953; (parents Am. citizens); d. Louis Rogers and Nona Jean (Henderson) T.; m. Alan J. Moore, Sept. 29, 1990; 1 child, Sean James. AS, Front Range C.C., Westminster, Colo., 1979, BSN, U. Wyo., 1989. RN, Colo. Ward sec. Valley View Hosp., Thornton, Colo., 1975-79; nurse Scott and White Hosp., Temple, Tex., 1979-83, Meml. Hosp. Laramie County, Cheyenne, Who., 1983-89; dir. DePaul Home Health, 1989-91; field staff nurse Poudre Valley Hosp. Home Care/Poudre Care Connection, 1991-98, Rehab. and Vis. Nurses Assn., Fort Collins, Colo., 1999—2003; resource pool nurse Poudre Valley Hosp., Fort Collins, Colo., 2003—. Mem., parish nurse Rocky Mountain Health Ministry. Avocations: doll collecting, sewing, reading, travel. Office: Poudre Valley Hosp 1024 S Lemay Ave Fort Collins CO 80524

TYLER, JANET IRENE, music educator; b. Topeka, June 30, 1965; d. John Thomas and Norma Jean Robinson; m. Michael Ray Tyler, Oct. 3, 1997. MusB, MusM, U. Kans., 1992. Grad. tchg. asst. U. Kans., Lawrence, 1990—92; dir. choir Garside Mid. Sch., Las Vegas, Nev., 1993—95, Eldorado H.S., Las Vegas, 1995—. Composer (vocal composition): Just Look at Us Now, 2002. Mem.: Music Educators Nat. Conf., Am. Choral Dirs. Assn. (chair vocal jazz 1993—), Internat. Assn. Jazz Edn. (pres. 2002—). Democrat. Avocations: dog breeding, organist, interior design. Office: Eldorado H S Choral Music Dept 1139 N Linn Ln Las Vegas NV 89110 Office Phone: 702-799-7200 4050.*

TYLER, LIV, actress; b. Portland, Maine, Jan. 7, 1977; d. Steven Tyler (lead singer: Aerosmith) and Bebe Buell. Motion picture actress and print model. Actress (films): Silent Fall, 1994, Empire Records, 1995, Stealing Beauty, 1996, Inventing the Abbotts, 1997, Armageddon, 1998, Onegin, 1999, The Little Black Book, 1999, Cookie's Fortune, 1999, Plunkett & MaCleane, 1999, One Night at McCool's, 2001, Lord of the Rings: The Fellowship of the Ring, 2001, The Lord of the Rings: The Two Towers, 2002, The Lord of the Rings: The Return of the King, 2003, Jersey Girl, 2004.; appeared in Aerosmith's music video, Crazy, 1994. Office: c/o CAA 9830 Wilshire Blvd Beverly Hills CA 90212-1804

TYLER, PAYNE BOUKNIGHT, museum executive; b. Johnston, S.C., Mar. 11, 1933; d. William Miller and Frances Payne (Turner) B.; m. Harrison Ruffin Tyler, July 19, 1958; children, Harrison Ruffin Jr., Julia Gardiner Tyler Samaniego, William Bouknight. BA, U. S.C., 1955; postgrad., N.Y. Sch. Interior Design, 1956. Pres. Historic Sherwood Forest Corp., Charles City, Va., 1975—. Author: James River Plantations Cookbook, 1983, Virginia Presidents Cookbook, 1989. Jr. bd. mem., pres. Jr. Bd. of Hist. Richmond Found., 1960-61; mem. Planning Commn., Charles City, 1988-97; coun. Va. Mus. Fine Arts; others. Mem. U.S. Polo Assn., Nat. Soc. Colonial Dames of Am., Jamestowne Soc., Jr. League Richmond, Deep Run Hunt Club (Richmond), Princess Anne Hunt Club (Charles City), Santa Fe Hunt Club (Rancho Santa Fe, Calif.), Rancho Santa Fe Polo Club, Country Club Va. (Richmond), Richmond Cotillion and Va. Creepers (Richmond), Soixant Plus, Rancho Santa Fe Country Club, Two Rivers Country Club, Garden Club of Va. Episcopalian. Avocations: fox hunting, polo, painting, writing, historical bldg. restoration. Home: 5416 Tuckahoe Ave Richmond VA 23226-2336 also: Sherwood Forest Plantation Charles City VA 23226

TYLER, PEGGY LYNNE BAILEY, lawyer; b. Seattle, Oct. 15, 1948; d. John Thomas and Doris Mae (Lindgren) Bailey; m. Tom Kenneth Newton, May 25, 1975 (div. 1980); m. Allan Gregory Lambert, Aug. 3, 1980 (div. May 1996); m. Charles Kevin Tyler, Sept. 12, 1997; children: Eli Raven, Joshua Alec. BA in Psychology, Beloit Coll., 1970; MS in Counseling Psychology, Ill. Inst. Tech., 1973; JD, Syracuse (N.Y.) U., 1978. Bar: D.C. 1983. Mental health specialist Ill. Dept. Mental Health, Chgo., 1971-72; mem. rsch. faculty Cornell U., Ithaca, N.Y., 1973-75; assoc. O'Connor, Sovocool, Pfann and Greenburg, Ithaca, 1978, Dacy, Richin & Meyers, Silver Springs, Md., 1979-81; ins. adminstr. Nat. Assn. Broadcasters, Washington, 1981-86, dir. ins. programs, 1986-90; assoc. Architect of the Capitol, Washington, 1990—. Co-author, editor: Broadcaster's Property and Liability Insurance Buying Guide, 1989. Bd. dirs. Hartford-Thayer Condominium Assn., 1994—, pres., 1995-96, sec., 1996-2000, treas., 2000—. Mem. D.C. Bar Assn. (mem. steering com. of arts entertainment, sports law sect. 1989-90, sect. editor newsletter 1989-90). Independent. Jewish. Avocations: antiques, gourmet cooking, ballet. Office: Architect of the Capitol Office of Employment Counsel Rm H2-202 Ford House Office Bldg Washington DC 20515-0001 Office Phone: 202-226-0680. E-mail: ptyler@aoc.gov.

TYLER, RACHEL, finance specialist; BA in Comm., Legal Instns., Econs., and Govt., BS in Math., Am. U., 1998, MSc in Fin., 2002. Fin. sys. analyst Bur. Pub. Debt, Washington, 1998—2002, fixed income mkt. specialist, 2002—03.

TYMESON, JODI, state official; b. Boone, Iowa, June 27, 1955; BA, U. No. Iowa; MPA, Drake U. Tchr.; state rep., 2001—. Mem. edn. com.; mem. human resources com.; mem. oversight and comms. com.; vice chair appropriations com.; mem. ways and means com. Inspector gen. Iowa N.G. Republican. Office: State Capital E 12th and Grand Des Moines IA 50319

TYNDALL, GAYE LYNN, secondary school educator; b. Reno, Apr. 21, 1953; d. Chris H. and Ellen (Hutchinson) Gansberg; m. Dave Tyndall, Mar. 17, 1973; children: Jody, Dave. BS, U. Nev., Reno, 1987, postgrad. Cert. secondary tchr. Tchr. math, sci. Douglas High Sch., Minden, Nev., 1987—. Treas. Nev. Sci. Project, Reno, 1990—; presenter Reading and Writing in the Math Classroom Internat. Reading Assn., Nat. Sci. Tchrs., Assn., 1990-92. Recipient Nev. State Tchr. of Yr. award Nev. Bd. Edn., 1993. Mem. Nat. Coun. Tchrs. Math., Calif. Math Coun. Avocations: momming, rodeo, family activities. Office: Douglas High Sch PO Box 1888 Minden NV 89423-1888

TYNER, BESSIE HUBBARD, mechanical engineer, mathematician; b. Fayetteville, N.C., Sept. 23, 1961; d. Kenneth Brigman and Ellen Merle H.; m. Kenneth Blake Tyner. BSME, N.C. State U., 1983, MME, 1985, BS in Applied Math., 1989, M in Pub. Admin., 1993. Registered profl. engr., N.C. Mech. engr. N.C. State U., 1985-98, asst. phys. plant dir. for design svcs., 1994-95, supr. capital improvement svcs., 1995-98; dir. design and constrn. U. N.C., Pembroke, 1998—. Mem. faculty Indsl. Ventilation Conf., N.C. State U. Author: Marriage and Death Notices, 1991, vol. II, 1997; (with others) NCSU Guidelines for Construction, 1988, 91, 97. Editor Cumberland County Geneal. Soc., Fayetteville, 1991-93. With Coast Guard Aux. Recipient Disting. Svc. award N.C. State U., 1994. Mem. DAR (sec. 1991-93), ASHRAE, NSPE, ASME (chpt. historian 1987-88), N.C. Soc. Engrs. (Order of Engr. 1987), Order of Crown of Charlemagne, Jamestowne Soc. (N.C. Co. treas. 1994—), Nat. Soc. Daus. Colonial Wars, Nat. Soc. Daus. Founders and Patriots Am. (N.C. v.p. 1997—), Nat. Soc. Descs. Colonial Clergy, Nat. Soc. Dames Ct. of Honor, U.S. Daus. of 1812 (v.p. 1997—), USCG Pipes and Drums, Colonial Dames XVII Century (recording sec. 1999—), Women Descs. Ancient Honorable Artillery Co. Mass. (organizing pres., N.C. ct.), FSA Scot, Tau Beta Pi, Pi Alpha Alpha. Republican. Avocations: history, genealogy, calligraphy, electronics, marquetry. Home: PO Box 3636 Pembroke NC 28372-3636 Office: U NC Pembroke Phys Plant PO Box 1510 Pembroke NC 28372-1510

TYNER, LEE REICHELDERFER, lawyer; b. Annapolis, Md., Mar. 12, 1946; d. Thomas Elmer and Eleanor Frances (Leland) Reichelderfer; m. Carl Frederick Tyner, Aug. 31, 1968; children: Michael Frederick, Rachel Christine, Elizabeth Frances. BA, St. John's Coll., 1968; MS, U. Wash., 1970; JD, George Washington U., 1975. Bar: Wash., D.C., U.S. Dist. Ct. (D.C.), U.S. Ct. Appeals (4th cir., 1st cir., 9th cir., D.C. cir., 5th cir., 8th cir., 11th cir., 10th cir.), U.S. Ct. Claims, U.S. Supreme Ct. Profl. staff U.S. Senate Commerce Com., Washington, 1970-72; trial atty. Land and Natural Resources div. U.S. Dept. Justice, Washington, 1975-85; atty. Office of Gen. Counsel U.S. EPA, Washington, 1985—. Bd. dirs. Grace Episcopal Day Sch., Silver Spring, Md., 1987-89, vestry Grace Episcopal Ch., 1997—2003; den leader, cubmaster Boy Scouts Am., Silver Spring, 1987-91. Recipient Bronze medals, U.S. EPA, 1988, 92, 2002, 2003. Mem. Order of the Coif. Episcopalian. Home: 1416 Geranium St NW Washington DC 20012-1518 Office: US EPA 2366A 1200 Pennsylvania Ave NW Washington DC 20460 E-mail: skildpadde@aol.com., tyner.lee@epa.gov.

TYNG, ANNE GRISWOLD, architect; b. Kuling, Kiangsi, China, July 14, 1920; d. Walworth and Ethel Atkinson (Arens) T.; 1 child, Alexandra Stevens. AB, Radcliffe Coll., 1942; M of Architecture, Harvard U., 1944; PhD, U. Pa., 1975. Assoc. Stonorov & Kahn, Architects, 1945-47; assoc. Louis I. Kahn Architect, 1947-73; pvt. practice architecture Phila., 1973—; adj. assoc. prof. architecture U. Pa. Grad. Sch. Fine Arts, 1968-96. Assoc. cons. architect Phila. Planning Commn. and Phila. Redevel. Plan, 1954; vis. disting. prof. Pratt Inst., 1979-81, vis. critic architecture, 1969; vis. critic architecture Rensselaer Poly. Inst., 1969, 78, Carnegie Mellon U., 1970, Drexel U., 1972-73, Cooper Union, 1974-75, U. Tex., Austin, 1976; lectr. Archtl. Assn., London, Xian U., China, Bath U., Eng., Mexico City, Hong Kong U., 1989, Baltic Summer Sch., Architecture and Planning, Tallinn, Estonia, Parnu, Estonia, 1993, Alicante U., Spain, 1997, Barcelona U., Spain, 1997; panel spkr. Nat. Conv. Am. Inst. Architects, N.Y.C., 1988, also numerous univs., throughout U.S. and Can.; asst. leader People to People Archtl. del. to China, 1983; vis. artist Am. Acad., Rome, 1995. Subject of films Anne G. Tyng at Parsons Sch. of Design, 1972, Anne G. Tyng at U. of Minn., 1974, Connecting, 1976, Forming the Future, 1977; work included in Smithsonian Travelling Exhbn., 1979-81, 82, Louis I. Kahn: In the Realm of Architecture, 1990-94, Mus. Contemporary Art Travelling Exhbn., L.A., 1998—; author, editor: Louis Kahn to Anne Tyng, The Rome Letters 1953-1954, 1997; contbr. articles to profl. publs.; prin. works include Walworth Tyng Farmhouse (Hon. mention award Phila. chpt. AIA 1953); builder (with G. Yanchenko) Probability Pyramid, 1984. Fellow Graham Found. for Advanced Study in Fine Arts, 1965, 79-81. Fellow AIA (Brunner grantee N.Y. chpt. 1964, 83, dir., mem. exec. bd. dirs. Phila. chpt. 1976-78, John Harbeson Disting. Svc. award Phila. chpt. 1991); mem. Nat. Acad. Design (nat. academician), C.G. Jung Ctr. Phila. (planning com. 1979-97), Form Forum (co-founder, planning com. 1978-85). Democrat. Episcopalian. Home and Office: 2511 Waverly St Philadelphia PA 19146-1049 E-mail: agtyng@aol.com.

TYRER-FERRARO, POLLY ANN, music instructor, software developer; b. St. Louis, Mo., Aug. 25, 1964; d. Jack Harold and Elizabeth (Neff) Tyrer; m. Joseph Scott Ferraro, Aug. 12, 1994; 1 child, Maria Ann Ferraro. BM, Cen. Meth. Coll., 1986; MM, Southern Meth. Univ., 1988. Ind. piano tchr., Dallas, 1988—; ptnr., owner Concert Master, Dallas, 1993—; owner Keynote Studio. Adv. bd. Dallas Southwest MTA, De Soto, Tex., 1990-97, Jr. Pianist Guild, Dallas, 1996-97, Dallas Music Tchr., 1990-92; mem. tchr.'s evaluation panel Hal Leonard, Milw., 1996; presenter Tex. Music Tchr. Conv., 1994. Author: Technique TIme, 1997; composer (music): Various Ensembles, 1995-97; arranger various Technique Disks, 1994-97; contbr. articles to profl. jours. Active Downwinders, Dallas, 1996—, Planned Parenthood, Dallas, 1992—. Recipient Nat. Honor Roll award Nat. Guild Music Tchrs., 1994. Mem. Dallas Southwest Music Tchrs. (pres. 1991-92, treas. 1997-98), Jr. Pianist Guild (v.p. 1996-98), World of Music Com. Avocations: cats, music, doll houses. Home: 1308 Carriage Creek Desoto TX 75115-3637 Office: The Keynote Studio 1308 Carriage Creek Dr Desoto TX 75115-3637

TYRIE, TINA NAPIER, music educator; b. Newport News, Va., Jan. 27, 1957; d. John Gilbert and Juanita Spears Napier; m. Robert Stanley Tyrie, June 14, 1980. MusB, Western Ky. U., 1979, MA in Edn., 1981. Exec. dir. March of Dimes, Bowling Green, Ky., 1981—82; band dir. Warren East High Sch., 1982—87, Broadway Meth. Ch., 1983—88, Bowling Green High Sch., 1987—. Tchr. clarinet pvt. practice, Bowling Green, 1975—2000. Performer (clarinetist): So. Ky. Concert Band, 1993—2003; performer: cmty. musicals, 1983—2003. Mem. choir Broadway Meth. Ch., Bowling Green, 1982—2003. Mem.: Ky. Band Assn., Nat. Band Assn.,

Music Educators Nat. Conf., Ky. Music Educators Assn. (solo and emsemble adjudicator 1982—2003, Outstanding Mid. Sch. Tchr. 1991—92), Delta Omicron (pres., advisor 1979—83), Phi Beta Mu. Avocations: horseback riding, reading. Home: 417 Shaker Mill Rd Bowling Green KY 42103 Office: Bowling Green Ind Sch Dist 1211 Center St Bowling Green KY 42101

TYRRELL, LILIAN, craftsperson, artist; b. London, 1944; One-woman shows include Akron (Ohio) Art Mus., 1984, 1991, Coll. Wooster (Ohio) Art Mus., 1986, Massillion (Ohio) Mus., 1989, Ctr. for Tapestry Arts, N.Y.C., 1990, U. Mo., St. Louis, 1991, St. Mary's Coll., Notre Dame, Ind., 1992, Mus. for Textile, Toronto, 1992, Richmond (Ind.) Art Mus., 1993, Va. Ctr. Craft Arts, Richmond, 1993, Cleve. Mus. Art, 1994, Ins. Devel. Co., Columbus, Ohio, Pepper Pike Place Assocs., Cleve., Jacob, Visconsi and Jacob. Named 1st visual artist of yr., Cleve. Arts, 1993; individual artists fellow, Ohio Arts Coun., 1982—83, 1985—86, 1988—89, 1990—91, 1992—93, regional visual arts fellow, Arts Midwest/NEA, 1989—90, visual arts fellow, NEA, 1994—95.

TYRRELL, MARY MARGARET, community health educator; b. Superior, Wis., Apr. 1, 1943; d. Frank J. and Elsie Mary (Erbeck) O'Brien; m. Joseph Mark Tyrrell, Aug. 16, 1969 (div. Jan. 1975); children: Corey, Megan. BSN, Coll. of St. Scholastica, 1965; M of Pub. Health, U. Minn., 1979. RN, Minn. Patient edn. coord. Internat. Diabetes Ctr., Mpls., 1969; edn. intern Minn. Comprehensive Epilepsy Program, Mpls., 1978-79; dir. aging edn. A.H. Wilder Found., St. Paul, 1979-81; supr. St. John's Hosp. Home Care, St. Paul, 1981; cmty. health nurse coord. VA Med. Ctr., St. Cloud, Minn., 1982-88; asst. dir. Minn. Bd. of Nursing, St. Paul, 1988-92; study coord. Mpls. Med. Rsch. Fedn., Mpls., 1992-95; pres. Memoirs Inc., St. Paul, 1994—. Contbr. articles to profl. publs. Mem. Stearns County Health Adv. Bd., St. Cloud, 1983-89, chair, 1984-87; mem. Minn. West Ctrl. Adv. Bd., St. Cloud, 1983-86, chair 1984-87; mem. Eartwatch-Indonesian Health Care, Jakarta, Indonesia, 1992. Lt. USN, 1963-68. Named Outstanding Alumna award Coll. of St. Scholastica, 1990. Mem. Minn. Gerontol. Soc. (treas. 1991-93), Minn. Elders Coalition (exec. com. 1992-96), Am. Pub. Health Assn., Am. Gerontol. Soc., Sigma Theta Tau (com. chair 1991). Home and Office: 1669 Ford Pkwy Saint Paul MN 55116-2138 Office Phone: 612-698-1158. E-mail: maryobtyrr@aol.com.

TYRRELL, ROSEMARY, performing company executive, educator; d. Rosemary Tyrrell; m. Mark Alan Robertson, Oct. 6, 1957. BA, Youngstown State U.; MA, U. Kans. Exec. dir. Icarus Puppet Co., San Diego, 1990—. Instr., faculty mentor Fashion Inst. of Design and Merchandising, San Diego, 1998—. Dir.(actor): (original play) The Crane Daughter; author (director, actor): (original play) Many Voices (grant Nat. Endowment for the Arts), The Adventures of Masha, Thief of Dreams/La dron de Suenos. Recipient Charles I. Jenney award, Kelsey-Jenney Bus. Coll., 1991, Living Legacy award, Women's Internat. Ctr., 1999. Mem.: Union Internationale de la Marionnette, Puppeteers Am., San Diego Performing Arts League.

TYRRELL-MEIER, CASSANDRA B. banker; b. Compton, Calif., May 15, 1942; d. Edwin Rudolph and Katherine Jahn; m. Harlan Meier, May 27, 2000; children: Dennis, Debra, Cassandra, Daniel, Michael; stepchildren: Jeffrey L. Meier, Chris H. Meier, Julie F. Moser, Vickie K. Hess. Degree in banking, Am. Inst. Banking, Denver, 1958; certificate, Dale Carnegie, 1979. Proof operator Internat. Bank & Trust, Denver, 1958-89, First Nat. Bank, Denver, 1959-61; motor bank supr. Jefferson Bank & Trust, Lakewood, Colo., 1972-76; head teller United Bank of Broomfield, Colo., 1976-79; auditor Western Nat. Bank, Denver, 1980-82; sr. v.p., cashier North Valley Bank, Thornton, Colo., 1982—. Asset/liability mgmt. North Valley Bank, 1988—, 401(K) trustee, 1988—, also mem. investment com. Mem. North Metro C. of C., Fin. Mgmt. Soc., Fin. Women Internat., Western Ind. Bankers and CFOs, Colo. Disaster Back-up Assn., Am. Mgmt. Assn., Ind. Banker Network. Roman Catholic. Home: 14850 E 120th Ave Brighton CO 80603-6905 E-mail: ctyrrell@nvbank.com.

TYSON, CHARLOTTE ROSE, software development manager; b. San Mateo, Calif., Aug. 14, 1954; d. Herbert Parry and Rose (Goldner) T.; m. Edward Phillip Sejud, Aug. 11, 1979; children: Laura Rose, Elizabeth Ann. AA in Physics, DeAnza Coll., 1974; BS in Elec. Engring., U. Calif.-Berkeley, 1976; MS in Computer Info. Systems, U. Denver, 1992. From engr. to engr. to mgr. software mfg. ops. IBM, Boulder, Colo., 1976—93; systems devel. and program mgr. Storage Tek, Louisville, Colo., 1993—, mgr. software solutions integrated svcs., 1996-97, mgr. multiplatform solns devel., 1997-98, mgr. client server tape software, 1999-2000, dir. storage solutions integration ctr., 2000—02, dir. storage solutions ops., 2002—. V.p. corp. adv. bd. women in engring. program U. Colo., 2000—; women in tech. com. 2001 Women's Summit, 2001—; corp. rep. to bd. dirs. Colo. Software and Internet Assocs., 2002—. Leader Mountain Prairie Coun. Girl Scouts U.S., 1992-94; fund raiser Longmont Symphony Guild, 1994; team mgr., treas. girls competitive soccer St. Vrain Express, 1995-96; dir. Longmont Lightning Girls Competitive Basketball League, 1997-99; host gardener Longmont Garden Tour, 1999; gen. mgr. girls basketball Longmont H.S., 2000— Mem.: IEEE (chmn. Denver sect. 1982—83, Debt of Gratitude award 1981, 1982, 1983), AAUW, Electromagnetic Compatability Soc. (chmn. Boulder chpt. 1979—91, registration chmn. EMC internat. symposium 1981, bd. dirs. 1985—90, awards and membership chmn. 1986—90, treas. 1998, EMC symposium 1996—99), Soc. Women Engrs. (sr.; life), St. Vrain Hist. Soc. Office: Storage Tek One StorageTek Dr Louisville CO 80028-0001 E-mail: charlotte_tyson@storagetek.com.

TYSON, CICELY, actress; b. N.Y.C., Dec. 19, 1933; d. William and Theodosia Tyson; m. Miles Davis, 1981 (div.). Student, N.Y. U., Actors Studio; hon. doctorates, Atlanta U., Loyola U., Lincoln U. Former sec., model. Co-founder Dance Theatre of Harlem; bd. dirs. Urban Gateways Tage appearances include: The Blacks, 1961-63, off-Broadway, Moon on a Rainbow Shawl, 1962-63, Tiger, Tiger, Burning Bright, Broadway; films include: Twelve Angry Men, 1957, Odds Against Tomorrow, 1959, The Last Angry Man, 1959, A Man Called Adam, 1966, The Comedians, 1967, The Heart is a Lonely Hunter, 1968, Sounder, 1972 (Best Actress, Atlanta Film Festival, Nat. Soc. Film Critics, Acad. award nominee, Best Actress, Emmy award, Best Actress in a spl., 1973), The Blue Bird, 1976, The River Niger, 1976, A Hero Ain't Nothin' but a Sandwich, 1978, The Concorde-Airport 79, 1979, Bustin' Loose, 1981, Fried Green Tomatoes, 1991, Jefferson in Paris, 1995, The Grass Harp, 1996, Aftershock, 1999; TV appearances include: (series) East Side, West Side, 1963, Sweet Justice, 1994-95, Road to Galveston, 1996; (films) Marriage: Year One, 1971, The Autobiography of Miss Jane Pittman, 1974, Just an Old Sweet Song, 1976, Wilma, 1977, Roots, 1977, A Woman Called Moses, 1978, King, 1978, The Marva Collins Story, 1981, Benny's Place, 1982, Playing With Fire, 1985, Samaritan: The Mitch Snyder Story, 1986, Acceptable Risks, 1986, Intimate Encounters, 1986, The Women of Brewster Place, 1989, Heat Wave, 1990 (Cable Ace award 1991), Winner Takes All, 1990, The Kid Who Loved Christmas, 1990, When No One Would Listen, 1992, Duplicates, 1993, House of Secrets, 1993, Oldest Living Confederate Widow Tells All, 1994 (Emmy Awd., Best Supporting Actress - Miniseries), Mama's Flora Family, 1998 (Image award 1999), Always Outnumbered, 1998, Ms. Scrooge, 1997, The Price of Heaven, 1997, Riot, 1997, Bridge of Time, 1997, A Century of Women, 1994, ; other appearances include: Wednesday Night Out, 1972, Marlo Thomas and Friends in Free to Be...You and Me, 1974, CBS: On the Air, 1978, Liberty Weekend, 1986, The Blessings of Liberty, 1987, Without Borders, 1989, Visions of Freedom: A Time Television Special, 1990, Clippers, 1991, A Century of Women, 1994 Trustee Human Family Inst.; trustee Am. Film Inst. Recipient Vernon Price award, 1962; also awards NAACP Nat. Council Negro Women; Capitol Press award. Office: More/Medavoy Mgmt Dirs Guild of Am Bldg 7920 W Sunset Blvd Ste 401 Los Angeles CA 90046-3300

TYSON, CYNTHIA HALDENBY, academic administrator; b. Scunthorpe, Lincolnshire, Eng., July 2, 1937; came to U.S., 1959; d. Frederick and Florence Edna (Stacey) Haldenby; children: Marcus James, Alexandra Elizabeth. BA, U. Leeds, Eng., 1958, MA, 1959, PhD, 1971; DHL (hon.), Mary Baldwin Coll., 2003. Lectr. Brit. Council, Leeds, 1959; faculty U. Tenn., Knoxville, 1959-60, Seton Hall U., South Orange, N.J., 1963-69; faculty, v.p. Queens Coll., Charlotte, N.C., 1969-85; pres. Mary Baldwin Coll., Staunton, Va., 1985—2003, pres. emerita, 2003—; pres. Robert Haywood Morrison Found., 2002—. Contbr. articles to profl. jours. Mem. Va. Internat. Trade Commn., Richmond, 1987; trustee Am. Frontier Culture Mus., Va.; mem. Va. Lottery Bd., 1987-94; chair selection com. State of Va. Rhodes Scholarship Competition, 1993-97; bd. dirs. Cmty. Found. Staunton, Augusta County and Waynesboro, 1993-98. Fulbright scholar, 1959; Ford Found. grantee Harvard U., 1981; Shell Oil scholar Harvard U., 1982. Mem.: Assn. Presbyn. Colls. and Univs. (bd. dirs. 1998), So. Assn. Colls. and Schs. (vice chair 1998, pres.-elect 2001, pres. 2002), Assn. Va. Colls. and Univs. (pres. 1997—98), So. Assn. Colls. for Women (pres. 1980—81), Mary Baldwin Coll. (hon.), Phi Beta Kappa. Republican. Office: Robert Haywood Morrison Found 1373 East Morehead St Ste 2 Charlotte NC 28204-2979

TYSON, EDITH SLOSSON, retired librarian, writer; b. Richmond, Va., Apr. 11, 1935; d. Preston William Slosson and Lucy Chase (Denny) Wright; m. Ivan Maurice Aron, Mar. 24, 1967 (dec. May 1968); m. Dean Eyster Tyson, July 23, 1976 (dec. Dec. 1995); stepchildren: David Dean, Mary Jane Tyson Strickler. BA with distinction, U. Mich., 1966, MA in Comparative Lit., 1967; MLS, Clarion U. of Pa., 1984. Tchr. asst. in English U. N.Mex., Albuquerque, 1966-67; post-H.S. tchr. Milan (Mich.) Fed. Prison, 1967-68; tchr. program in religious studies U. Mich., Ann Arbor, 1972-79; cmty. resource tchr. Cmty. H.S., Ann Arbor, 1976-79; religious edn. dir. Knox (Pa.) Parish, 1979-84; librarian ref. and young adult svcs. Warren (Ohio)/Trumbull County Pub. Libr., 1985-99; ret., 1999. Author: Books for Teens: Stressing the Higher Values, 1993, Orson Scott Card: Writer of the Terrible Choice, 2003; contbr. articles to to profl. jours. Mem.: Ch. and Synagogue Libr. Assn (Lectr. workshop leader 1987). Democrat. Presbyterian. Avocation: family. Home: Apt 430 1216 Fifth Ave Youngstown OH 44504 E-mail: edithtyson@yahoo.com.

TYSON, GAIL L. health federation administrator; b. Havre de Grace, Md, Dec. 28, 1954; d. William Alva Way and Virginia Lorena Tyson; m. Joseph Matthew Pease, May 17, 1986; 1 child, Loren Juliette Tyson Pease. BA, Dickinson Coll., 1976. Dir. edn. Harrisburg Area Rape Crisis Ctr., Pa., 1976-77; cmty. info. specialist CONTACT Harrisburg, 1978-81, asst. dir., 1981-85; pub. info. coord. Dauphin County Human Svcs., Harrisburg, 1985-87; unit exec. dir. Am. Cancer Soc., Harrisburg, 1988-92; exec. dir. Nat. Voluntary Health Agys. Pa. Com., Harrisburg, 1992-99; pres., CEO Cmty. Health Charities of Pa., Harrisburg, 2000—. V.p. Human Svc. Program, 1987; chmn. Nat. Voluntary Health Agy. Coun. State Affiliates, 1997, 98. Mem. adv. com. Harrisburg Area C.C., 1985-87; mem. adv. bd. Ret. Sr. Vol. Program, Harrisburg, 1986-88, sec., 1987; lifetime mem. Girl Scouts US, bd. dir. Hemlock coun., 1977-91, v.p., 1982-88, pres., 1988-91, chmn. diversity task force, 1992. Recipient Thanks badge Hemlock coun. Girl Scouts US, 1991. Mem. Wheel and Chain Hon. Soc. Methodist. Office: Community Health Charites of Pa 2213 Forest Hills Dr Ste 3 Harrisburg PA 17112-1090

TYSON, LAURA D'ANDREA, dean, economist, educator; b. Bayonne, N.J., June 28, 1947; BA, Smith Coll., 1969; PhD, MIT, 1974. Prof. econ. and bus. adminstrn. U. Calif., Berkeley, 1978-98, BankAmerica dean Haas Sch. Bus., 1998—; chmn. Pres.'s Coun. Econ. Advisors, Washington, 1993-95; nat. econ. advisor to Pres. U.S. Nat. Econ. Coun., Washington, 1995-96. Prin. Law and Econs. Consulting Group; bd. trustees Asia Found.; mem. adv. bd. Barter Trust, Epiphany, Shorenstein Co. LP, G7 Group, Inc. Editor: (with John Zysman) American Industry in International Competition, 1983, (with Ellen Comisso) Power, Purpose and Collective Choice: Economic Strategy in Socialist States, 1986, (with William Dickens and John Zysman) The Dynamics of Trade and Employment, 1988, (with Chalmers Johnson and John Zysman) Politics and Productivity: The Real Story of How Japan Works, 1989, Who's Bashing Whom? Trade Conflict in High Technology Industries, 1992; mem. adv. bd.: Jour. Econ. Perspectives; mem. bd. editors: Am. Prospect and Calif. Mgmt. Rev.; econ. viewpoint columnist: Bus. Week mag.; commentator: Nightly Bus. Report; author domestic and internat. econ. policy matters in Washington Post, N.Y. Times, and other nat. and internat. syndicated newspapers and mags. Mem. Nat. Bipartisan Commn. Future Medicare, 1997—99. Mem.: Trilateral Commn., New Am. Found., Morgan Stanley, Dean Witter, Discover & Co., Inst. Internat. Econs., Human Genome Scis., Inc., Healtheon Corp., Fox Entertainment Group, Inc., Eastman Kodak Co., Coun. Fgn. Rels., Ameritech Corp. Office: Haas Sch Bus 545 Student Srvs # 1900 Berkeley CA 94720-0001

TYSON, LISA N. food products executive; Assoc. atty. corp. securities group Winstead, Sechrest & Minick, 1991—98; v.p., asst. gen. counsel Suiza Foods, 1998—2002; sr. v.p., dep. gen. counsel, asst. sec. Dean Foods, 2002—. Office: Dean Foods 2515 McKinney Ave Ste 1200 Dallas TX 75201-1945*

TYSON, LUCILLE R. health facility administrator, geriatrics nurse; b. North Wales, Pa., Feb. 14, 1939; d. Edwin Shelly and Marion (Wenhold) Rosenberger; m. Ronald Saylor Tyson, June 29, 1963; children: Bryan, Bruce. AS, Middlesex County Coll.; BA, Wheaton Coll.; MSW, Rutgers U. Cert. gerontol. nurse; lic. social worker; RN. Dir. N.J. Parkinson Info. & Referral Ctr. Robert Wood Johnson U. Hosp., New Brunswick, N.J.; human svcs. planner Middlesex County Dept. Human Svcs., New Brunswick; dir., right to know regulations Roosevelt Hosp., Edison, N.J.; dir., quality assurance Cen. N.J. Jewish Home for Aged, Somerset, N.J. Mem. Piscataway (N.J.) Twp. Coun., 1990—; mem. rev./appeals com. Middlesex County Dept. Human Svcs., 1992—; bd. dirs. Metlar Ho. Found.; mcpl. dir. Piscataway Rep. Orgn., 1995—; county committeewoman Middlesex County Rep. Orgn., 1995—2001; rep. exec. committeewoman Greenville County, SC, 2001-. Mem. ANA, NASW, Nat. Soc. DAR, N.J. Nurses Assn., Assn. Quality Assurance Profls. N.J., Geriatric Inst. N.J., Rep. Exec. Comm.

TYTLER, LINDA JEAN, communications and public affairs executive, retired state legislator; b. Rochester, N.Y., Aug. 31, 1947; d. Frederick Easton and Marian Elizabeth (Allen) T.; m. George Stephen Dragnich, May 2, 1970 (div. July 1976); m. James Douglas Fisher, Oct. 7, 1994. AS, So. Va. Coll., Buena Vista, Va., 1967. Spl. asst. to Congressman John Buchanan, Washington, 1971-75; legis. analyst U.S. Senator Robert Griffin, Washington, 1975-77; ops. supr. Pres. Ford Com., Washington, 1976; office mgr. U.S. Senator Pete Domenici Re-election, Albuquerque, 1977; pub. info. officer S.W. Cmty. Health Svc., Albuquerque, 1978-83; cons. pub. rels. and mktg. Albuquerque, 1983-84; account exec. Rick Johnson & Co., Inc., Albuquerque, 1983-84; dir. mktg. and comm. St. Joseph Healthcare Corp., 1984-88; mktg. and bus. devel. cons., 1987-90; dir. comm. and pub. affairs Def. Avionics Systems, Honeywell Inc., 1990-2000, dir. comms., 2000—02; dep. dir. pub. affairs Los Alamos Nat. Lab., 2002—. Capt. N.Mex. Mounted Patrol, 1998-2002; bd. dirs. Jobs for N.Mex.; mem. N.Mex. Ho. of Reps., Santa Fe, 1983-95, ret. 1995, vice chmn. appropriations and fin. com., 1985-86, chmn. Rep. Caucus, 1985-88; chmn. legis. campaign com. Rep. Com.; co-chair del. to Republic of China, Am. Coun. Young Polit. Leaders, 1988. Bd. dirs. N.Mex. chpt. ARC, Albuquerque, 1984. Recipient award N.Mex. Advt. Fedn., Albuquerque, 1981, 82, 85, 86, 87, Honeywell Cmty. Svc. award, 1997. Mem. Am. Soc. Hosp. Pub. Rels. (cert.), Nat. Advt. Fedn., Soc. Hosp. Planning and Mktg., Am. Mktg. Assn., N.Mex. Assn. Commerce and Industry (bd. dirs., exec. com. 1996-2002). Republican.

TYUS-SHAW, TINA, newscaster; Grad., Tenn. State U. Reporter, Macon, Ga.; anchor WSAV-TV, Savannah, Ga., 1992—, field anchor, 1995, co-anchor, lead Healthwatch corr. Recipient torchbearer, Olympic Torch Run (Ga.), 1996, Office: WSAV-TV3 1430 E Victory Dr Savannah GA 31404

UBEL, OLIVE JANE, retired secondary school educator; b. Newton, Kans., June 20, 1932; d. Arnold Jantz and Emma Decker; m. Jake Ralph Ubel, Dec. 20, 1953 (dec. Dec. 1995); children: Mary Colleen, Douglas Ralph. BS, Kans. State U., 1953, MS, 1975. Tchr. home econs. and sci. Westmoreland (Kans.) H.S., 1954—56; tchr. art Highland Park Jr. High, Topeka, 1956—58; sec. U.S. Borax and Chem. Corp., Topeka, 1958—70; tchr. art and home econs. Shawnee Heights Unified Sch. Dist. 450, Tecumseh, Kans., 1970—93; cons./ret. Kans. Assn. Family and Consumer Scis. Trustee Human Ecology Found. Bd. Kans. State U., Manhattan, 1995—2003; trustee Kans. State U. Found. Bd., Manhattan, 2002—. Mem. woman's bd. Mulvane Art Mus., Washburn U., Topeka, 1993—; elder Trinity Presbyn. Ch., Topeka, 1967—69, 1980—82, 1994—96; bd. dirs. Presbyn. Manor, Topeka, 1996—2002, Aux. League Topeka Symphony, 1998—. Mem.: PEO Internat. (chaplain, v.p. 2002—03, pres. 2003—), AAUW, Topeka Assn. Family and Consumer Sci., Kans. Assn. Family and Consumer Sci., Am. Assn. Family and Consumer Sci. (cert. family and consumer scis., programs chair), Am. Legion Aux. (Topeka chpt.), Women of the Moose, Phi Kappa Phi, Phi Delta Kappa, Kappa Omicron Nu, Delta Delta Delta, Alpha Delta Kappa. Avocations: sewing, dance, gardening, drawing and painting, design.

UCCELLO, VINCENZA AGATHA, artist, director, educator emerita; b. Hartford, Conn., May 11, 1921; d. Salvatore and Josephine (Bordonaro) U. BS, St. Joseph Coll., West Hartford, Conn., 1956; DHL, St. Joseph Coll., 2000; MA in Liberal Studies, Wesleyan U., 1961; MFA, Villa Schifanoia, Florence, Italy, 1963. Tchr. art Glastonbury High Sch., Conn., 1957-61, East Hartford Pub. Schs., Conn., 1963-64; prof. fine arts St. Joseph Coll., 1964—, chmn. dept. fine arts, 1967-85, acting curator, dir. coll. art collections, 1978—, dir. Art Gallery, 2000—02. One-woman shows Villa Schifanoia, Florence, 1963, St. Joseph Coll., 1965, 81, Pump House Gallery, Hartford, Conn., 1986; group shows Am. Painters in Paris Exhbn., Nat. Print and Drawing Exhbn., Ohio U., Athens, Ball State U., Muncie, Ind., Austin Art Ctr., Trinity Coll., Hartford, Munson Gallery, New Haven; represented in permanent collections St. Joseph Coll., N.Y. Pub. Libr., Ctr. for Book Arts, Conn. Nat. Bank, Hartford; pvt. collections. Trustee West Hartford Art League. Recipient Harper Meml. award in painting, 1969, 2d prize Atria Gallery Blues Show, Disting. Alumnae award St. Joseph Coll., Dist. Adv. award Conn. Art Educators Assn.; fellow Venice Artists Workshop, 1965; Yale U. fellow Andrew U. Mellon Found., 1980. Mem. Coll. Art Assn. Am. Conn. Women Artists (pres. 1974-76), Am. Assn. Mus., Assn. Colls. and Univ. Mus. and Galleries. Home: 51 Hilltop Dr West Hartford CT 06107-1434

UCHIDA, JANICE YUKIKO, plant pathologist/mycologist, researcher; b. Kealakekua, Hawaii, Jan. 17, 1949; d. Tamotsu Tom and Misao (Oshima) Kadooka; m. Raymond Sueyoshi Uchida; children: Duane, Janelle. BA in Botany, U. Hawaii, 1970, MS in Bot. Sci., 1972, D in Bot. Sci. in Plant Pathology, 1984. Instr. dept. gen. sci. U. Hawaii, Honolulu, 1972-76, rsch. assoc. dept. plant pathology, 1976-87, asst. plant pathologist dept. plant pathology, 1987-94, assoc. plant pathologist dept. plant and environmental protection scis., 1994—. Contbr. rsch. articles and papers to sci. jours. Coord. Urata Music, Honolulu, 1995—. Ednl. Challenge grantee USDA, 1997-99; grantee State of Hawaii, 1980-, USDA, 1999—; Mentor NSF scholar, 1995-96. Mem. Am. Phytopathol. Soc., Mycol. Soc. Am., Phi Kappa Phi, Gamma Sigma Delta (sr. editor: Plant Disease, 2004-, Excellence in Rsch. award 2000). Office: U Hawaii Dept Plant and Eviron Protection Scis 3190 Maile Way Honolulu HI 96822-2232 Fax: 808-956-2832. E-mail: juchida@hawaii.edu.

UCHIDA, MITSUKO, pianist; b. Dec. 20, 1948; d. Fujio and Yasuko Uchida. Student, Hochschule für Musik, Vienna, Austria. Artist-in-residence Cleve. Orch., 2001—. Performer: performs regularly with Berlin Philharm., Vienna Philharm., Cleve. Orch., others, recs. include complete piano sonatas and concertos of Mozart, Beethoven's piano concertos, Debussy's Etudes, Schubert Sonatas and Impromptus, Schoenberg Piano Concerto, Carnegie Hall recital series Mitsuko Uchida: Vienna Revisited, 2002—. Recipient Gramophone award, 2001. Avocation: music. Address: Van Walsum Mgmt Ltd 4 Addison Bridge Pl London W14 8XP England E-mail: inro@vanwalsum.com.

UCKO, BARBARA CLARK, writer; b. Cambridge, Mass., Mar. 27, 1945; d. Hugh Kidder and Marie (Folsom) Clark; m. David Alan Ucko, Aug. 13, 1972; 1 child, Aaron Mark. BA in Art History, Oberlin Coll., 1967; MA in English, U. Mo., Kansas City, 1992. Copywriter Bantam Books, N.Y.C., 1974—76; promotion dir. Pocket Books, N.Y.C., 1976—77, Antioch Bookplate, Yellow Springs, Ohio, 1977; instr. composition Sch. of Chgo. Art Inst., Chgo., 1986; mgr. corp. comm. Sprint, Westwood, Kans., 1992—98; pvt. piano tchr. Kansas City, Mo., 1998—2001. Author: (novels) Family Trappings, 1985, Scarlett Greene, 1987, (short stories) Laurel Review, Nit and Wit, Open, Artful Dodge and Chatelaine. Various libr. bds., sch. vol. and hosp. bds. Calif., Mo., Washington D.C. Recipient 1st pl. award, Barbara Storck Short Fiction Competion, U. Mo., 1991, 2d pl., 1992. Mem.: Soc. Midland Authors. Democrat. Avocations: crafts, crossword puzzles, piano, walking, reading.

UEBELHOR, TARA LEIGH, financial analyst; b. Huntingburg, Ind., May 19, 1974; d. Ronald Roman and JoAnn Uebelhor. BA, Ind. U., 1997. Law Enforcement Certification Ind., 1995. Client/fertility helper case coord. Internat. Fertility Ctr., Indpls., 1999—2000; sec. Am. United Life Ins. Co., Indpls., 2000—01, mortgage loan adminstr., 2001—02, mortgage prodn. analyst, 2002—. Curator Am. United Life Ins. Co., Indpls., 2000—. Office: American United Life Insurance Company One American Sq Indianapolis IN 46206

UEHLING, BARBARA STANER, educational administrator; b. Wichita, Kans., June 12, 1932; d. Roy W. and Mary Elizabeth (Hilt) Staner; children: Jeffrey Steven, David Edward. BA, U. Wichita, 1954; MA, Northwestern U., 1956, PhD, 1958; hon. degree, Drury Coll., 1978; LLD (hon.), Ohio State U., 1980. Mem. psychology faculty Oglethorpe U., Atlanta, 1959-64, Emory U., Atlanta, 1966-69; adj. prof. U. R.I., Kingston, 1970-72; dean Roger Williams Coll., Bristol, R.I., 1972-74; dean arts scis. Ill. State U., Normal, 1974-76; provost U. Okla., Norman, 1976-78; chancellor U. Mo.-Columbia, 1978-86, U. Calif., Santa Barbara, 1987-94; sr. vis. fellow Am. Council Edn., 1987; mem. Pacific Rim Pub. U. Pres. Conf., 1990-92; exec. dir. Bus. and Higher Edn. Forum, Washington, 1995-97. Cons. North Ctr. Accreditation Assn., 1974-86; mem. nat. educator adv. com. to Compt. Gen. of U.S., 1978-79; mem. Commn. on Mil.-Higher Edn. Rels., 1978-79, Am.Coun. on Edn., bd. dirs. 1979-83, treas., 1982-83, mem. Bus.-Higher Edn. Forum, 1980-94, exec. com. 1991-94; Commn. on Internat. Edn., 1992-94, vice chair 1993; bd. dirs. Coun. of Postsecondary Edn., 1986-87, 90-93, Meredith Corp., 1980-99; mem. Transatlantic Dialogue, PEW Found., 1991-93. Author: Women in Academe: Steps to Greater Equality, 1979; editorial bd. Jour. Higher Edn. Mgmt., 1986-95; contbr. articles to profl. jours. Bd. dirs., chmn. Nat. Ctr. Higher Edn. Mgmt. Sys., 1977-80; trustee Carnegie Found. for Advancement of Teaching, 1980-86, Santa Barbara Med. Found. Clinic, 1989-94; bd. dirs. Resources for the Future, 1985-94; mem. select com. on athletics NCAA, 1983-84, also mem. presdl. commn.; mem. Nat. Coun. on Edn. Rsch., 1980-82. Social Sci. Research Council fellow, 1954-55; NSF fellow, 1956-57; NIMH postdoctoral research fellow, 1964-67; named one of 100 Young Leaders of Acad. Change Mag. and ACE, 1978; recipient Alumni Achievement award Wichita State U., 1978, Alumnae award Northwestern U., 1985, Excellence in Edn. award

Pi Lambda Theta, 1989. Mem. Am. Assn. Higher Edn. (bd. dirs. 1974-77, pres. 1977-78), Western Coll. Assn. (pres.-elect 1988-89,k pres. 1990-92), Golden Key, Sigma Xi. E-mail: bcharlton3@hotmail.com.

UEHLING, JUDITH OLSON, artist, painter, printmaker, sculptor; b. Chgo., Apr. 3, 1935; d. Raymond and Virginia (Ericsson) Olson; m. David Theodore Uehling, June 19, 1959 (div. Nov. 1983); children: Mark David, Greta Lynn, Mary Birgit. BA, Smith Coll., 1957; postgrad., Sch. Art Inst., Chgo., 1957—58. Vis. artist Peacock Printmakers, Aberdeen, Scotland, 1982; hon. sec. Printmakers Coun., London, 1985—91; exhbn. commr. Valetta, Malta, 1991; tchr. painting Sommerakademie, Marburg, Germany, 2001—03; lectr. in field. One-woman shows include Fanny Garver Gallery, 1976, 1979, 1981, Ripon (Wis.) Coll., 1978, Novi Sad Art Gallery, Yugoslavia, 1983—84, Am. Ctr. U.S. Internat. Comm. Agency, Belgrade, 1983—84, Meml. Union U. Wis., Madison, 1984, Peacock Printmakers, Aberdeen, 1984, Galerie Bremer, Berlin, 1988, A.I.R. Gallery, N.Y.C., 1999, Galerie in der Tu, Marburg, Germany, 2002, 2002, exhibited in group shows at Lemon Geranium Gallery, N.Y.C., 1973, Hansen Galleries, 1975, Internat. Exhbn. Graphic Art, Frechen, Germany, 1976, Internat. Biella (Italy) Prize for Prints, 1976, Invitational Bicentennial Art Competition, Milw., 1976, Grafik aus Amerika, Leverkusen, Germany, 1976, 1977, 3d Norwegian Internat. Print Biennial, Fredrikstad, Norway, 1976, 4th, 1978, Gallery Marronier, Kyoto, Japan, 1979, Utubo Gallery, Osaka, Japan, 1979, State Capitol Bldg., Madison, Wis., 1982, Royal Scottish Acad., Edinburgh, 1983, 11th, 12th, 14th, and 15th Internat. Biennial of Graphic Art, Ljubljana, Yugoslavia, Parrish Art Mus., Southampton, N.Y, 1999, Just Art Galerie, Berlin, Germany, 2000, Ben Shahn Ctr., William Patterson U., N.J, 2000, Brownson Coll., Manhattanville Coll., N.Y., Bolton Mus. & Art Gallery, Eng., Represented in permanent collections Mus. of City of N.Y., Gallery of Yugoslav Portrait, Tuzla, Bosnia, Graves Art Gallery, Sheffield, Eng., Lovell, White, Durrant, Eng., Victoria and Albert Mus., Whitworth Art Gallery, Manchester, Eng., Wiltshire County Museums, Eng., Bank of Am., U. Wis., Madison, Columbus (Ga.) Mus., Washington County Mus. of Fine Arts, Md., Continental Bank, Chgo., commissions, Wis. Telephone Co., 1977, Affiliated Bank Madison, 1978, Lovell, White Durrant, London, 1990, Allied Dunbar, 1991, Eagle Ins., London, 1993; contbr. articles to profl. jours. Vol. Artists Talk on Art, N.Y.C., 1995-98. Recipient Fellowship award Hereward Lester Cooke Found., 1976, Chmn. Action grant Wis. Arts Bd., 1982, Acquisition prize 10th Internat. Exhbn. of Original Drawings, Rijeka, Yugoslavia, 1986, Artist by Appt. grant Frans Masereel Centrum, Belgium, 1987-89, Best of Show award 18th Ann. Metro Show, City Without Walls, Newark, N.J., 1999, Best Abstract Painting Guild Hall Mems. Exhbn., East Hampton, N.Y., 2003. Mem. Chelsea Arts Club (London), Print Europe Orgn., Coll. Art Assn. (internat. com.). Avocations: studying German language, walking. Home and Office: Deep View Studio PO Box 143 Wainscott NY 11975-0143 Office Phone: 631-329-6661. E-mail: juehling@earthlink.net.

UFFEN, ELLEN SERLEN, editor, writer; b. N.Y., N.Y. d. Jack and Anne Calbor Serlen; m. Robert J. Uffen, Feb. 21, 1977; children: Jordan Serlen, Elizabeth Serlen. BA, CCNY, 1966; MA, SUNY, 1969, PhD, 1975. Assoc. prof. Mich. State U., East Lansing, Mich., 1975—92; mng. editor The ASHA Leader Am. Speech-Lang.-Hearing Assn., Rockville, Md., 1993—. Author: Strands of the Cable, 1990. Office: American Speech Lang Hearing Assn 10801 Rockville Pike Rockville MD 20852

UGGAMS, LESLIE, entertainer; b. N.Y.C., May 25, 1943; d. Harold Coyden and Juanita Ernestine (Smith) Uggams; m. Grahame John Kelvin-Pratt, Oct. 16, 1965; children: Danielle Nicole Pratt, Justice Harolde John Kelvin-Pratt. Student, Juillard Sch. Music, 1961-63; degree (hon.), Jarvis Coll., Tyler, Tex., Wilberforce (Ohio) U. Appeared on (TV series) Beulah, 1949, featured on Sing Along with Mitch, 1961—64, starred in (Broadway plays) Hallelujah Baby, 1967 (Tony award, 1968), Her First Roman Broadway Musical, 1968, star of (weekly TV variety show) The Leslie Uggams Show, 1969, appearances in nightclubs top TV mus. variety shows, appeared in films Two Weeks in Another Town, Black Girl, 1962, Skyjacked, 1972, Poor Pretty Eddie, 1973, appeared in (TV miniseries) Roots, ABC-TV, 1977 (Critics Choice award as best supporting actress, 1977), (TV films) Sizzle, 1981, Harlem, 1993, Star (Broadway musicals) Blues in the Night, 1982, (Broadway musical) Jerry's Girls, 1985, Anything Goes, 1987, star (off-Broadway) The Old Settler, 1999 (Audelco award as best actress), (dramatic play), 1999, (musical play) King Hedley II, 2001 (nominated Tony award best actress, 2001), Thunder Knocking on the Door, 2002 (Audelco award best actress, 2002), (TV miniseries) Backstairs at the White House, 1979, co-host (TV series) Fantasy TV, 1982—83 (Emmy award 1983, 1983); author: The Leslie Uggams Beauty Book, 1966. Founding mem. BRAVO chpt. City of Hope, Los Angeles, 1969, treas., 1969—79. Named best singer on TV, 1962—63; recipient Drama Critics award, Newspaper and TV critics, 1968, Tony award, 1968, Emmy award, 1993. Mem.: SAG, NARAS, AFTRA, Actors' Equity Assn. Democrat. Presbyterian. Avocations: needlepoint, knitting, tennis, squash, exercising. Office: The Gage Group Inc care Phillip Adelman 315 W 57th St Frnt 4H New York NY 10019-3158 E-mail: leslie@leslieuggams.com.

UHLENBECK, KAREN KESKULLA, mathematician, educator; b. Cleve., Aug. 24, 1942; d. Arnold Edward and Carolyn Elizabeth (Windeler) Keskulla; m. Olke Cornelis, June 12, 1965 (div.) BS in Math., U. Mich., 1964; PhD in Math., Brandeis U., 1968. Instr. math. MIT, Cambridge, 1968-69; lectr. U. Calif., Berkeley, 1969-71; asst. prof., then assoc. prof. U. Ill., Urbana, 1971-76, assoc. prof., then prof. Chgo., 1977-83; prof. U. Chgo., 1983-88; Sid W. Richardson Found. Regents' Chair in Math. U. Tex., 1988—. Spkr. plenary address Internat. Conress Maths., 1990; mem. com. women on sci. and engring. NRC, 1992-94; mem. steering com., dir. mentoring program for women Inst. for Advanced Study/Park City Math. Inst. Author: Instantons and Four Manifolds, 1984. Contbr. articles to profl. jours. Recipient Common Wealth award for Sci. and Invention, PNC Bank, 1995; NSF grad. fellow, 1964-68, Sloan Found. fellow, 1974-76, Mac-Arthur Found. fellow, 1983-88. Mem. AAAS, NAS, Alumni Assn. U. Mich. (Alumnae of Yr. 1984), Am. Math. Soc., Assn. Women in Math., Phi Beta Kappa. Avocations: gardening, canoeing, hiking. Office: U Tex Dept Math Austin TX 78712

UKEN, MARCILE RENA, music educator; b. Avon, S.D., Sept. 16, 1931; d. Martin Andrew and Helen (Janssen) Bertus; m. Emil Jaden Uken, Dec. 8, 1953 (dec. 1990). BS, Southern State Coll., 1952. Cert. secondary sch. tchr., Nebr. Tchr. pub. sch., Delmont, S.D., 1952-53, Carroll (Nebr.) Pub. Sch., 1954-56; spl. edn. tchr. State of Nebr., Wayne, 1953-60; piano tchr. pvt. studio, Wayne, 1955. Co-chairperson Am. Cancer Soc., Wayne, 1964-76; mem. Federated Women's Club, Wayne. Fellow Nat. Fedn. Music Clubs, Music Tchrs. Nat. Assn., Nebr. Music Tchrs., Siouxland Music Tchrs.; mem. Bus. and Profl. Women. Avocations: exercise group, bible studies, music concerts, Nebr. Huskers football, working with youth groups.

UKPONMWAN, LUCY, elementary school educator; BA, U. Ife, Nigeria, 1981; MPA, Suffolk U., 1985. Tchr. EDO Coll., Benin, Nigeria, 1981-82; substitute tchr. Yonkers (NY) Bd. Edn., 1985-89, tchr. sixth grade, 1997—, N.Y.C. Bd. Edn., 1990—97. Vol. Bronx Mcpl. Hosp., 1989. Mem. ASCD. Office: CES 64X 1425 Walton Ave Bronx NY 10452-6901

ULEN, GENE ELDRIDGE, elementary school educator; b. Detroit, June 13, 1939; d. James Swan and Dorothy Benson Eldridge; m. Ian Paul Ulen, Aug. 10, 1933; children: Heather Jean, Lori Dorothy. BA in Edn., Mich. State U., 1960, MA in Edn., 1961; adminstrv. credential, Point Loma U., 1987. 2nd grade tchr. San Diego Unified Schs., San Diego, 1962—70; 6th grade tchr. Crown Pointe Elem. Sch., San Diego, 1971—86; 4th-5th gifted class tchr. Cadman Elem. Sch., San Diego, 1987—2000; substitute tchr. All Saints Sch., San Diego, 2000—. Active San Diego Nat. Women Polit. Group, 1995—2000; sec. LaJolla (Calif.) Dem. Club, 2000—02. Mem.: LWV, LaJolla Book Club, Phi Delta Kappa (bd. mem. 1986—2000). Episcopalian. Avocations: roses, sailing, bridge, tennis. Home: 5840 Cozzens St San Diego CA 92122

ULLAS, YVONNE LEE, primary school educator; AA, Yakima Valley C.C., 1979; BA in Edn., Ctrl. Wash. U., 1981, postgrad., 1991, Antioch U., 1992; MEd, Heritage Coll., 1995. Parent educator Yakima Sch. Dist., 1975-79; camp dir. Yakima Parks and Recreation, 1979-86; tchr. St. Joseph's Grade Sch., Yakima, 1981-86, Naches Primary Sch., 1988—. Commr. Gov.'s commn. on Early Learning, 1998-2000; bd. dirs. Gov.'s Profl. Educator Standards bd. Named Tchr. of Month, KAPP TV, 1993, US West Washington State Outstanding Tchr., 1994, Wash. State Tchr. of Yr., 1998; recipient Christa McAuliffe Excellence in Edn. award, 2000; grantee Share 105 Tech., 1997. Mem. NEA, Wash. Edn. Assn., Naches Edn. Assn. (dist. del.), Naches Edn. Assn. (bldg. rep.), Yakima Valley C.C. Alumni Assn., Ctrl. Washington U. Alumni Assn., Heritage Coll. Alumni Assn., Retired Tchrs. Assn., N.W. Regional Ednl. Lab., Nat. State Tchr. of Yr. Assn., Parent, Tchr., Student Assn. Office: Naches Valley Primary Sch 2700 Old Naches Hwy Yakima WA 98908-8900 Home: 1615 S 13th Ave Yakima WA 98902

ULLIAN, ELAINE S. health facility administrator; b. Jan. 3, 1948; MPH, U. Mich., 1973; BA, Tufts U., 1969. Pres., CEO Faulkner Corp./Faulkner Hosp., 1987-94; v.p. clinical ops New England Med Ctr, 1984-86; dir. strategic planning consult. FinReport Systems/Amherst Assoc., 1982-84; dir of planning assist. admin. Boston U. Med Ctr Hosp, Boston, 1976-82; dir. Hill Burton Prog. Mass. Dept of Health, Boston, 1974-76; advocate planner, comm. organizer Eastern Middlesex Opportunities Council, 1969-72; assoc. prof. Boston U. Sch of Public Health, Boston, 1994—; lecturer Harvard Sch of Public Health, 1987—; vice chair Conference of Boston Tching Hosp., 1993—; pres. ceo Boston Med Ctr, Boston, 1996—. Recipient: Maimonides award for Outstanding Leadership in Health Care of the Anti-Defamation League, 1989; Abigail Adams award for Political Leadership of the Mass. Women's Political Caucus, 1992; Mass. Health Council award for Outstanding Leadership in Public Health, 1994; The Boston Club Achievement award, 1995; Fifth Anniversary Community Service award, Bostonian Club, 1995. Bd of dirs.: Greater Boston Chamber of Commerce, Corp. Advisory Bd Pine Manor Junior Coll.; mem., Governor's Council on Economic Growth and Tech., Mayor's Special Advisory Comm. on Health Care, 1994-95, chair, Health, Family, Youth servs comm., Menino Transition Team, 1993-94, Health and Human Servs comm., Weld Transition Team, 1990, chair, Metropolitan Boston Hosp. Council, 1988-90, bd mem. Mass. Hosp. Assoc., 1988-90, mem., Regional Policy Board, Amer. Hosp Assoc., 1990-93, Tufts Associated Health Plan, 1987-94, Celebrate Discovery Inc., Mass. Taxpayers Found., 1992-, Mass. Health Research Inst., 1987-94. Office: Boston Med Ctr Exec Ofc Talbot 1 1 Boston Medical Ctr Pl Boston MA 02118-2908

ULLMAN, NELLY SZABO, statistician, educator; b. Vienna, Aug. 11, 1925; came to U.S., 1939; d. Viktor and Elizabeth (Rosenberg) Szabo; m. Robert Ullman, Mar. 20, 1947 (dec.); children: Buddy, Wiliiam John, Martha Ann, Daniel Howard. BA, Hunter Coll., 1945; MA, Columbia U., 1948; PhD, U. Mich., 1969. Rsch. assoc. MIT Radiation Lab, Cambridge, Mass., 1945; instr. Polytechnic Inst. of Bklyn., 1945-63; from asst. prof. to prof. Ea. Mich. U., Ypsilanti, 1963—2002, prof., 2002; ret., 2002. Author: Study Guide To Actuarial Exam, 1978; contbr. articles to profl. jours. Mem. Am. Math. Assn., Am. Assn. Univ. Profs. E-mail: nullman@emich.edu.

ULLMAN, TRACEY, actress, singer; b. Slough, Eng., Dec. 30, 1959; m. Allan McKeown, 1984; children: Mabel Ellen, John Albert Victor. Student, Itaia Conti Stage Sch., London. Appeared in plays Gigi, Elvis, Grease, The Rocky Horror Show, Four in a Million, 1981 (London Theatre Critics award), The Taming of the Shrew, 1990, The Big Love, (one-woman stage show) 1991; films include The Young Visitors, 1984, Give My Regards to Broad Street, 1984, Plenty, 1985, Jumpin' Jack Flash, 1986, I Love You To Death, 1990, Household Saints, 1993, I'll Do Anything, 1994, Bullets over Broadway, 1994, Ready to Wear (Prêt-à-Porter), 1994, Everybody Says I Love You, 1996; Brit. TV shows include Three of a Kind, A Kick Up the Eighties, Girls on Top; actress TV series: The Tracey Ullman Show, from 1987-90 (Emmy award Best Performance, Outstanding Writing, 1990, Golden Globe award Best Actress, 1987), Tracey Takes On, 1996— (four Emmys including Outstanding Music, Comedy and Variety Show 1997, Cable Ace award for best comedy variety series 1996); album You Broke My Heart in Seventeen Places (Gold album). Recipient Brit. Acad. award, 1983, Am. Comedy award, 1988, 90, 91, Emmy award for Best Performance in a Variety/Music Series for "Tracey Ullman Takes on New York", 1994. Office: IFA Talent Agy 8730 W Sunset Blvd Ste 490 Los Angeles CA 90069-2248

ULLRICH, LINDA J. medical technologist; b. Rockford, Ill., May 10, 1944; d. Glenn H. and R. Catherine (Mathews) Person; m. John R. Brody, June 11, 1966 (div. July 1978); children: Kevin R. Brody, Keith A. Brody; m. Sterling O. Ullrich Sr., Mar. 10, 1979 (dec. Oct. 1999); stepchildren: Sterling O. Jr., Eugene, Lee Anna, Michelle. BA, Thiel Coll., 1966; MPA, Kent State U., 1993, postgrad., 1996—. Cert. med. tech. Am. Soc. Clin. Pathologists, specialist in hematology. Staff med. tech. Sharon Gen. Hosp., Pa., 1966—76; supr. hematology, coagulation, urinalysis sects. Sharon Regional Health Sys. (formerly Sharon Gen. Hosp.), 1976—96, lab. mgr., 1996—2003; lab cons. Condell Med. Ctr., Chgo., 2003—. Edn. coord. Beaver County C.C., Pa., 1976-80; tech. supr. lab. Cancer Care Ctr., Hermitage, Pa., 1993-2003; adj. prof. Thiel Coll., Greenville, Pa., 1994-95, 97-99, Youngstown State U., 2003—; com. mem. Sharon Regional Health Sys., 1990-2003. Merit badge counselor, com. mem. Troop 67 Boy Scouts Am., Newton Falls, Ohio, 1982-95; hospice vol., 2002-03. Lutheran. Avocations: bicycling, hiking, knitting, reading. Office: Condell Acute Care 3440 Grand Ave Gurnee IL 60031

ULLRICH, ROXIE ANN, special education educator; b. Ft. Dodge, Iowa, Nov. 10, 1951; d. Rocco William and Mary Veronica (Casady) Jackowell; m. Thomas Earl Ullrich, Aug. 10, 1974; children: Holly Ann, Anthony Joseph. BA, Creighton U., 1973; MA in Teaching, Morningside Coll., 1991. Cert. tchr. Iowa, cons. in spl. edn. Iowa. Tchr. Corpus Christi Sch., Ft. Dodge, Iowa, 1973-74, Westwood Community Schs., Sloan, Iowa, 1974-80, Sioux City Community Schs., 1987—. Cert. judge Iowa High Sch. Speech Assn., Des Moines, 1975—; supt. Woodbury County Fair; leader 4H Club; mem. Westwood Cmty. Sch. Bd., Sloan, Iowa. Mem. Am. Paint Horse Assn., Am. Quarter Horse Assn., Sioux City Hist. Assn., Sioux City Art Ctr., M.I. Hummel Club, Red Hat Soc., Phi Delta Kappa. Avocations: doll collector, plate collector, horse-back riding. Home: PO Box W 819 Brown St Sloan IA 51055

ULMEN, KATHRYN T. neuroscience clinical nurse specialist; b. Green Bay, Wis., Dec. 23, 1952; d. Joseph H. and Dorothy M. (Gavronski) Ulmen. RN, Holy Family Hosp. Sch. Nursing, Manitowoc, Wis., 1976; BSN, U. Wis., 1980; MS, Tex. Woman's U., Dallas, 1981. CNRN. Staff nurse U. Wis. Hosp., Madison; neurosci. clin. nurse specialist St. Vincent Hosp., Green Bay. Mem.: ANA, Am. Heart/Stroke Assn., Nat. Stroke Assn., Am. Assn. Neurosci. Nurses, Am. Brain Tumor Assn., Am. Assn. Neurol. Surgeons, Sigma Theta Tau.

ULMER, EVONNE GAIL, health science facility executive; b. Bagley, Minn., Sept. 12, 1947; d. John Ferdinand and Elsie Mabel (McCollum) Lundmark; m. G. Bryan Ulmer, Jan. 11, 1969; 1 child, G. Bryan. Diploma, St. Luke's Hosp., Duluth, Minn., 1968; BS, St. Joseph's Coll., N. Windam, Maine, 1981; MHA, U. Minn., 1984; JD, T.M. Cooley Law Sch., Lansing, Mich., 1997. Bar: Mich. 1997. Staff nurse Baton Rouge Gen., 196970, St. Luke's Hosp., Duluth, Minn., 1968-69, 71-72; asst. adminstr. Hickory Heights Care Ctr., Metarie, La., 1972-73; asst. head nurse Eisenhower Hosp., Colorado Springs, Colo., 1973-74; dir. pt. care svcs. St. Vincent's Gen. Hosp., Leadville, Colo., 1974-78; insvc., quality assurance dir. Watsatch Hosp., Heber City, Utah, 1979; adminstr. Prospect Park Living Ctr., Estes Park, Colo., 1982-84; asst. adminstr. Estes Park Med. Ctr., Colo., 1979-84; CEO Weston Co. Hosp. and Manor, Newcastle, Wyo., 1984-92, Ionia (Mich.) County Meml. Hosp., 1992—; pres. Ionia County Health Sys., 1995—. Mem. Am. Hosp. Assn. Chgo. (trustee 1998-01, past tech. small and rural governing coun., past del. region and policy bd., past chair small and rural governing com., mem. leadership com.), Medicare Geog. Reclassification Rev. Bd., Mich. Health and Hosp. Assn. (bd. dirs.). Republican. Lutheran. Home: 536 Skyview Dr Ionia MI 48846-9776 Office: Ionia County Meml Hosp Ionia MI 48846 E-mail: evonneulmer@hotmail.com.

ULMER, FRANCES ANN, former lieutenant governor; b. Madison, Wis., Feb. 1, 1947; m. Bill Council; children: Amy, Louis. BA in Econs. and Polit. Sci., U. Wis.; JD with honors, Wis. Sch. Law. Polit. advisor Gov. Jay Hammond, Alaska, 1975-81; former mayor City of Juneau, Alaska; mem. Alaska Ho. of Reps., 1986-94, minority leader, 1992-94; lt. gov. State of Alaska, 1995—2002; U.S. rep. to North Pacific Anadramous Fish Commn., 1994—; disting. prof. U. Alaska, Anchorage, 2003—. Democrat. E-mail: affau@uaa.alaska.ed.*

ULRICH, JODY L. accountant; b. Marshfield, Wis., Mar. 18, 1969; d. Robert Harold and Donetta Marie (Oertel) U.; m. Harley Hastings Thomas IV, July 23, 1994 (div. Aug. 1998). BS, Marquette U., 1991. Cost acct. Schwarz Pharm., Mequon, Wis., 1992-93, Wis. Dairies Coop., Baraboo, 1993-94, Acme Die Casting, Inc., Racine, Wis., 1994-97; sr. cost acct. Bosch Automation Tech., Racine, Wis., 1997-2001; gen. acctg. supr. Bosch Rexroth Corp., Sturtevant, Wis., 2001; budget analysis mgr. Unifund, Cin., 2001—02, mgr. budgets and fin. analysis, 2002—03. Mem. Inst. Mgmt. Accts., Kiwanis (bd. dirs. 1999, nominating com. 1999). Republican. Avocations: volleyball, golf, skiing, piano/music, gardening. Home: 4869 Rialto Ridge West Chester OH 45069

ULRICH, LAUREL THATCHER, historian, educator; b. Sugar City, Idaho, July 11, 1938; d. John Kenneth and Alice (Siddoway) Thatcher; m. Gael Dennis Ulrich, Sept. 22, 1958; children: Karl, Melinda, Nathan, Thatcher, Amy. BA in English, U. Utah, 1960; MA in English, Simmons Coll., 1971; PhD in History, U. N.H., 1980. Asst. prof. humanities U. N.H., Durham, 1980-84, asst. prof. history, 1985-88, assoc. prof., 1988-91, prof., 1991-95; prof. history and women's studies Harvard U., Cambridge, Mass., 1995—, James Duncan Phillips prof. early Am. history, 1997—, dir. Charles Warren Ctr., 1997—. Audiocourse cons. Annenberg Found.; cons., participating humanist numerous exhibits, pub. programs, other projects; project humanist Warner (N.H.) Women's Oral History Project; bd. editors William & Mary Quar., 1989-91, Winterthur Portfolio, 1991—. Author: Good Wives: Image and Reality in the Lives of Women in Northern New England, 1650-1750, 1982, A Midwife's Tale: The Life of Martha Ballard Based on Her Diary, 1785-1812, 1990 (Pulitzer Prize for history 1991), The Age of Homespun: Objects and Stories in the creation of an American Myth, 2001; contbr. articles, abstracts, essays and revs. to profl. publs. Coun. mem. Inst. Early Am. History and Culture, 1989-91, trustee Strawbery Banke Mus., 1987-93. NEH fellow, 1982, 84-85, MacArthur Fellowship award, 1992-97, John Simon Guggenheim fellow, 1991-92; women's studies rsch. grantee Woodrow Wilson Fellowship Found., 1979; co-recipient Best Book award Berkshire Conf. Women's Historians, 1990; recipient Best Book award Soc. for History of Early Republic, 1990, John S. Dunning prize and Joan Kelly Meml. prize Am. Hist. Assn., 1990, Bancroft Prize for Am. History, 1991. Mem. Orgn. Am. Historians (nominating com. 1992—, ABC-Clio award com. 1989), Am. Hist. Assn. (rsch. coun. 1993-96). Office: Harvard U Charles Warren Ctr Emerson Hall 4th Fl Cambridge MA 02138*

ULRICH, LORI LORRAINE, primary school educator; b. St. Louis, Mo., Mar. 9, 1976; d. Ronald George and Patricia Ann Brune; m. Kevin James Ulrich, July 24, 1999. AA, East Ctl. C.C., 1994—96; BS in edn., Ctrl. Mo. State U., 1996—99; MS in edn., SW Bapt. U., 2000—02. Kindergarten tchr. Sullivan Primary Sch., Sullivan, Mo., 1999—. Mem.: Mo. State Teachers Assn. Avocations: reading, sport activities, outdoor activities, swimming, travel.

ULSHAFER, SHARON A. accountant, educator; b. Greensburg, Pa., Nov. 3, 1975; d. Stephen Eugene and Connie Louise Billey; 1 child, Victoria. BS summa cum laude, West Chester U. of Pa., 1998; MBA, Alvernia Coll., 2003. Restaurang mgr. Your Place Restaurant, Shillington, Pa., 1998; bookkeeper Easter Seal Soc., Reading, Pa., 1998—99; acctg./bus. instr. PACE Inst. Bus. Coll., Reading, 1998—2001, 2003—; sr. acct. Parsons Energy & Chems. Group, Inc., Reading, 2001—. Vol. Easter Seal Soc., Reading, 1999, mem. health/safety com., 1998—99, vol. Gov. Mifflin Pre-Sch. PTA, treas., 2000—03; coach Gov. Mifflin Broncos Cheerleading, 2003—04; mem. com. Parsons United Way, 2002—. Mem.: Inst. Mgmt. Accts. Democrat. Roman Catholic. Avocation: travel. Home: 417 Grove Ave Mohnton PA 19540 Office: 2675 Morgantown Rd Reading PA 19607

UMAN, SARAH DUNGEY, editor; b. Dayton, Ohio, July 22, 1942; d. Arthur Bertram and Lucretia M. (Nash) Dungey; children: Michael Uman, Sebastian Rosset. Student, New Sch. for Social Rsch., 1962-64. Editl. assoc., publicity dir. Grove Press, Inc., N.Y.C., 1970-79; sr. editor Playboy Paperbacks, N.Y.C., 1979-81, Berkley Pub., N.Y.C., 1982-85; exec. editor Consumer Reports Books, Yonkers, N.Y., 1985-94; dir. Red Bear Editl. Svcs., N.Y.C., 1996—.

UMANSKY, DIANE, publishing executive; B in journalism, U. RI. Corr. Bergen Record; writer various teen publs. including Scholastic; mng. editor Nickelodeon; sr. editor First for Women; editor-in-chief MediZine Guidebook, 1995—. Freelance writer First for Women, SELF, Family Circle, American, Harper's Bazaar, Working Mother, Good Housekeeping, Weight Watchers. Office: MediZine 298 Fifth Ave 2nd Fl New York NY 10001

UMEH, MARIE ARLENE, English language educator; b. Bklyn., Aug. 29, 1947; d. Rudolph Vasper and Erma Eunice (Hinds) Linton; m. Davidson C. Umeh, Jan. 7, 1976; children: Ikechukwu, Uchenna, Chizoba, Ugochukwu. BA, St. John's U., Jamaica, N.Y., 1970; MS, Syracuse U., 1972; MPS, Cornell U., 1977; MA, U. Wis., 1980, PhD, 1981. Instr. SUNY, Brockport, 1972-74, Oneonta, 1974-75; asst. instr. Cornell U., Ithaca, N.Y., 1976-77; prin. lectr. Anambra State Coll., Awka, Nigeria, 1982-89; substitute assoc. prof. Medgar Evers Coll., CUNY, Bklyn., 1989; adj. prof. Hostos C.C., CUNY, Bronx, 1990—2003, Queens Coll., CUNY, Flushing, N.Y., 1990; assoc. prof. English John Jay Coll., CUNY, 1990—, faculty advisor, 1989—. Adj. prof. SUNY, Stony Brook, 2000—. Editor: Flora Nwapa, 1998, Buchi Emecheta, 1996; editor Rsch. in African Lit., 1995, Who's Who Among American Teachers, 1998; contbg. editor: Who's Who in Contemporary Women's Writing, 2001. Recipient Africademic award, John Jay Coll. African Students Assn., 1996, Dominican Students award, 1993, PSC-CUNY award, 1998, 1999, Gender Studies award, John Jay Coll-,CUNY, 2001; fellow, NEH, 1991, Summer Tchrs. Workshop, 2003. Mem.: AAUW, MLA (African Lit. Divsn. exec. 1999—2001), Virginia Woolf Soc., N.Y. African Studies Assn., African Lit. Assn. Avocations: reading, writing, aerobics, jazz. Office: CUNY John Jay CollCriminal Justice Dept English 445 W 59th St New York NY 10019-1104 Office Phone: 212-237-8726. E-mail: msumeh@aol.com.

UMHOEFER, AURAL M. retired dean, educational consultant; b. Wausau, Wis., May 11, 1942; d. Mark John Vladick, Alice Marion Vladick; m. Paul Anthony Umhoefer. MS, U. Wis., 1965; BA in French, Rosary Coll., 1964—64. Head libr. Green Bay ctr. U. Wis., 1965—68, dir. learning resource ctr., 1968—80, dean, campus exec. officer Baraboo/Sauk county campus, 1980—2002, ret. 2002, Cons. U. Wis. Sys., 2003—. Bd. dirs. Wells Fargo, Baraboo; bd. dirs. Hist. Sites Found. Circus World Mus., Baraboo, 1984—90; bd. dirs. Wis. Correctional Ednl. Assn., 1990—98. Bd. dirs. Al Ringling Theatre, Friends of Campus, Inc., Boy Scouts Am., Madison, 1985—97; mem. devel. coun. St. Clare Hosp., Baraboo, 1993—97. Named Outstanding Young Women of Am., 1975, Aural M. Umhoefer bldg. in her honor, U. Wis., Baraboo, 2002; recipient Outstanding Alumni award, Newman H.S. - Wausau, Wis., 1992, Citation from Senate, State of Wis., 1991, 2002, Pub. Svc. award, Fed. Bur. Prisons, 1991, 2002, Appreciation award, Circus World Mus., 1986, Citation from Govt., State of Wis., 2002. Mem.: AAUW (corp. rep. 1985—97, Wis. Women Leaders in Edn. award 1986, 1989), Wis. Correctional Edn. Assn. (v.p., pres. 1994—98), U. Wis. Alumni Assn. (pres. 1984—86, Spark Plug award 1992), Rotary Internat. (vocat. chair, bd.dirs.). Avocations: cooking, reading, travel, gardening. Home: 700 Effinger Rd Baraboo WI 53913 Office: University of Wisconsin 1006 Connie Rd Baraboo WI 53913 Office Phone: 608-263-1953. Personal E-mail: pauralum@julmet.com. Business E-Mail: aumhoefe@uwsa.edu.

UNDERWOOD, BRENDA S. information specialist, microbiologist, grants administrator; b. Oak Ridge, Tenn., Mar. 19, 1948; d. William Henry Hensley and Maudell Townsend; m. Thomas L. Janiszewski, Feb. 14, 1984; 1 child, Thomas Zachary Janiszewski. BS, U. Tenn., 1970; MS, Hood Coll., 1980; MBA, Mt. St. Mary's Coll., 1993. Scientist I chem. carcinogenesis Frederick (Md.) Cancer Rsch. Ctr., 1977-84; microbiologist NCI/NIH, Bethesda, Md., 1984-86; sci. tech. writer Engring. and Econs. Rsch., Germantown, Md., 1987-88; spl. asst. to dir., program dir. grants div. Cancer Biology Diagnosis Ctrs., NCI/NIH, Bethesda, 1988-91; indexer, divsn. extramural activities Rsch. Analysis and Evaluation br. NCI/NIH, Bethesda, 1991—, sect. chief for rsch. documentation sect., supr. tech. info. specialist, 1991—2002; br. chief, referral and program analysis br. NICHD/NIH, 2002—. Vol. Riding for the Handicapped, Frederick, 1990-96; mem., recreational sec. Capitol Hill Equestrian Soc., Washington, 1988. Mem. AAAS, Am. Soc. for Microbiology, Am. Assn. for Cancer Rsch., Women in Cancer Rsch., Federally Employed Women. Avocations: english riding, hiking, swimming, biking, gardening. Office: NCI-NIH RAEB Divsn Extramural Activ Bethesda MD 20892-0001

UNDERWOOD, CAROLE ANN, English and Spanish language educator; b. Toledo, Ohio, May 9, 1943; d. Alton Ellsworth and Ruth Lillian (Hoefflin) Bahnsen; m. Winston Dale Underwood, Sept. 7, 1963; children: David, Shawna. BA in edn., Heidelberg Coll., 1966. Tchr. Lakota Local Schs., Sandusky County, Ohio, 1965-68, Bettsville (Ohio) Local Schs., 1970—98; ret., 1998. Author: Walden North, 1980. Mem. The Hemingway Soc., The Mich. Hemingway Soc.(bd. dirs. 1995—). Republican. Lutheran. Avocations: reading, writing, embroidery, quilting. Home: 820 Central Ave Fostoria OH 44830-4704

UNDERWOOD, JANE HAINLINE HAMMONS, anthropologist, educator; b. Ft. Bliss, Tex., Oct. 30, 1931; d. Frank and Lydia (Williams) Hammons; m. Van K. Hainline, Oct. 20, 1947 (div. 1966); children: Michael K., Susan J.; m. John W. Underwood, July 4, 1968; 1 dau., Anne K. AA, Imperial Valley Coll., 1957; BA, U. Calif., Riverside, 1960; MA, UCLA, 1962, PhD, 1964. Asst. prof. U. Calif., Riverside, 1963-68; research anthropology Yap Islands, 1964, 65-66; prof. anthropology U. Ariz., Tucson, 1968-99, prof. emeritus, 1999—, assoc. dean Grad. Coll., 1979-80, asst. provost for grad. studies, 1980-82, acting dir. Sch. Health Related Professions, 1980-82, asst. v.p. research, assoc. dean Grad. Coll., 1982-87; assoc. Micronesian Area Rsch. Ctr., 1987—. Contbr. articles to profl. jours. Woodrow Wilson fellow, 1960-61; UCR Jr. Faculty fellow, 1968 Fellow AAAS; mem. Am. Assn. Phys. Anthropologists (v.p. 1980-82), Assn. Study Human Biology, Pacific Sci. Assn. (life), Assn. for Study Social Biology (bd. dirs. 1996-99), Sigma Xi (pres. U. Ariz. chpt. 1991-92). Home: 2228 E 4th St Tucson AZ 85719-5118 E-mail: kammagar@prodigy.net.

UNDERWOOD, LUCINDA JEAN, poet, playwright, small business owner, researcher; b. Troy, Mich., Aug. 1, 1964; d. Harold L. and Betty Jo (Arms) U. Grad. high sch., Livingston, Tenn., 1982. With Dawn Wells, Nashville, 1976-80; owner, mgr. Cindy's Critter Care, Cookeville, Tenn., 1986—. Author: (poetry) The Mystic, 1996; songwriter. Mem. Nat. Pony Express Assn. Office: Cindy's Critter Care 836 Bray St Apt B Cookeville TN 38501-3733

UNGAR, ROSELVA MAY, primary and secondary school educator; b. Detroit, Oct. 31, 1926; d. John and Elva Rushton; m. Kenneth Sawyer Goodman, Dec. 26, 1946 (div. 1950); m. Fred Ungar, June 22, 1952 (div. 1977); children: Daniel Brian, Carol Leslie, Lisa Maya. Student, U. Mich., 1946-48; BA, UCLA; MA, Pacific Oaks Coll. Cert. elem. tchr.; cert. early childhood; bilingual cert. of competency in Spanish. Recreation dir. Detroit City Parks and Recreation, 1946-50, L.A. Unified Sch. Dist., 1950-52, tchr., 1984—2001, mentor tchr. elem. edn., 1988-94, ret., 2001; tchr. head start Found. Early Childhood Edn., L.A., 1965-73; staff organizer Early Childhood Fedn. Local 1475 AFT, L.A., 1973-79; staff rep. Calif. Fedn. Tchrs., L.A., 1979-83. Contbr. articles to profl. jours. Mem. Gov.'s Adv. Com. Child Care, L.A., 1980-83; mem. Sierra Club, 1978—; mem. So. Calif. Libr. Social Studies, L.A., 1989—; charter mem. Mus. Am. Indian Smithsonian Inst., Womens Internat. League for Peace and Freedom, ACLU, So. Poverty Law Ctr., Food First, Meiklejohn Civil Liberties Inst.; bd. dirs., pres. Found. for Early Childhood Edn., 1997—, Coalition Progressive L.A. Mem. Nat. Assn. Multicultural Edn., Calif. Assn. Bilingual Edn., So. Calif. Assn., Edn. Young Children, Early Childhood Fedn. (pres. emeritus 1979—), United Tchrs. L.A. (chpt. chair 1984-96, east area dir. and UTLA bd. dirs. 1996-99), L.A. Coalition Labor Union Women (charter; bd. dirs. 1980-86). Avocations: guitar, folk songs, hiking. E-mail: roselvau@yahoo.com.

UNGARO, SUSAN KELLIHER, magazine editor; BA, MA, William Patterson Coll. From mem. staff to editor-in-chief Family Circle mag., N.Y.C., 1976—94, editor-in-chief, 1994—. Mem.: Am. Soc. Mag. Editors (bd. dir. 1998—, pres. 2003—). Office: Gruner & Jahr 375 Lexington Ave New York NY 10017-5514

UNGARO-BENAGES, URSULA MANCUSI, federal judge; b. Miami Beach, Fla., Jan. 29, 1951; d. Ludivico Mancusi-Ungaro and Ursula Berliner; m. Michael A. Benages, Mar., 1988. Student, Smith Coll., 1968-70; BA in English Lit., U. Miami, 1973; JD, U. Fla., 1975. Bar: Fla. 1975. Assoc. Frates, Floyd, Pearson et al, Miami, 1976-78, Blackwell, Walker, Gray et al, Miami, 1978-80, Finley, Kumble, Heine et al, Miami, 1980-85, Sparber, Shevin, Shapo et al, Miami, 1985-87; cir. judge State of Fla., Miami, 1987-92; U.S. dist. judge U.S. Dist. Ct., Miami, 1992—. Mem. Fla. Supreme Ct. Race & Ethnic & Racial Bias Study Commn., Fla., 1989-92, St. Thomas U. Inns of Ct., Miami, 1991-92; mem. Jud. Resources Com. Jud. Coun. U.S.; chmn. Ct. Svcs. Com. So. Dist. Fla., chmn. Magistrate Judge Com. Bd. dirs. United Family & Children's Svcs., Miami, 1981-82; mem. City of Miami Task Force, 1991-92. Mem. ABA, Fed. Judges Assn., Fla. Assn. Women Lawyers, Dade County Bar Assn., Eugene Spellman Inns of Ct. U. Miami. Office: US Dist Ct 301 N Miami Ave Fl 11 Miami FL 33128-7702

UNGER, BARBARA, poet, retired educator; b. N.Y.C., Oct. 2, 1932; d. David and Florence (Schuchalter) Frankel; m. Bernard Unger, 1954 (div. 1976); m. Theodore Sakano, 1987; children: Deborah, Suzanne. BA, CCNY, 1955, MA, 1957; advanced cert., NYU, 1970. Grad. asst. Yeshiva U., 1962-63; edn. editor County Citizen, Rockland County, NY, 1960-63; tchr. English N.Y.C. Pub. Schs., 1955-58, Nyack (N.Y.) H.S., 1963-67; guidance counselor Ardsley (N.Y.) H.S., 1967-69; prof. English Rockland C.C., Suffern, NY, 1969—95, ret., 1995, Poetry fellow Squaw Valley Cmty. of Writers, 1980; Writer-in-residence Rockland Ctr. for Arts, 1986. Author: (poetry) Basement, 1975, Learning to Fox Trot, 1989, The Man Who Burned Money, 1980, Inside the Wind, 1986, Blue Depression Glass in Troika One, 1991, (fiction) Dying for Uncle Ray, 1990; co-author (with Lloyd Ultan): (non-fiction) Bronx Accent: A Literary and Pictorial History of the Borough, 2001 (N.Y. Soc. Libr. Book award for borough history, 2001, J.M. Kaplan Furthermore grant); contbr. Anthology Mag. Verse, Yearbook Am. Poetry, 1984, Anthology Mag. Verse, Yearbook Am. Poetry, 1989, poetry and fiction to more than 75 lit. mags. Ragdale Found. fellow, 1985, 86, 89, SUNY Creative Writing fellow, 1981-82, Edna St. Vincent Millay Colony fellow, 1984, Djerassi Found. fellow, 1991, Hambidge Ctr. for Creative Arts and Scis. fellow, 1988; NEH grantee, 1975; recipient Goodman Poetry award, 1989, Anna Davidson Rosenberg award Judah Magnes Mus., 1989, Roberts Writing award, 1990, New Letters Lit. awards, 1990; finalist Am. Fiction Competition, 1982, John Williams Narrative Poetry Competition, 1992; honorable mention Chester Jones Nat. Poetry Contest. Mem.: PEN, Authors' Guild, Acad. Am. Poets, Poets and Writers. Office Phone: 845-357-1683.

UNGER, LAURA SIMONE, lawyer, commissioner; b. N.Y.C., Jan. 8, 1961; d. Raymond and Susan Marie (Vopata) Simone; m. Peter Van Buren Unger, June 29, 1991. BA in Rhetoric, U. Calif., Berkeley, 1983; JD, N.Y. Law Sch., 1987. Bar: Conn. 1987, N.Y. 1988. Mem., bd. dirs. MBNA Corp., 2004- Recipient Performance award SEC, N.Y., 1988, D.C., 1989. Mem. ABA (subcom. on civil litigation and SEC enforcement matters and subcom. on SEC adminstrn., budget and legislation of the ABA bus. law sect. com. on federal regulation of securities), Fed. Bar Assn., Jr. League Washington, Decade Soc., Women in Housing and Fin. Roman Catholic. Avocations: tennis, jogging, movies, concerts, music. Office: US SEC 450 5th St NW Ms 6/8 Washington DC 20549-0001

UNGER, ROBERTA, architect; BArch, Kent State U. Registered Ga. Prin. Arch. Group, Atlanta, 1991—. Adv. bd. So. Poly. Inst., 1999—2000; commr. Dekalb County Historic Preservation Commn.; bd. dirs. North Ga. Arch. Found. Fellow: AIA (dir. 1987—89, sec. 1990, v.p. 1991, pres. 1993, bd. dirs. 1994, Ivan Allen award 1995, Bronze medal 1995, Svc. to Profession award 1994); mem.: Dekalb C. of C. Office: 381 Venable St Atlanta GA 30313

UNGER, SUZANNE EVERETT, music educator, musician; b. Valdosta, Ga., Oct. 19, 1959; d. Robert Wayne and Susan Pendleton Everett; m. Gary Phillip Unger; children: Andrew, Sara. BA in Music Edn., Tift Coll., 1981; postgrad., Valdosta State U. Cert. Orff Schulwerk level 1, Performance Based Tchg.-4 level tchr. Music educator Dougherty County Schs., Albany, Ga., 1981—84, Lee County Elem. Sch., Leesburg, Ga., 1984—89, 1994—99, Lee County Primary Sch., Leesburg, 1986—; Pianist/Organist 1st United Meth. Ch., Albany, Ga., 1991—; accompanist Albany (Ga.) Chorale, 1999—. Accompanist All State Choir, 1997. Grantee for Creation Station, LeeFocus, 2001. Mem.: Music Educators Nat. Conf. (gen. music chair dist. 2 1996—98). Methodist. Avocations: cross stitch, computer use, collecting Precious Moments figurines. Home: 309 Northampton Rd Leesburg GA 31763 Office: Lee County Primary Sch 282 Magnolia St Leesburg GA 31763 Personal E-mail: gsunger@earthlink.net. Business E-Mail: ungersu@lee.k12.ga.us.

UNGERLEIDER, DOROTHY FINK, educational therapist; b. Chgo., Apr. 22, 1934; d. Theodore I. and Florence R. (Jacobson) Fink; m. J. Thomas Ungerleider, Dec. 19, 1954; children: John, Margot Ellen. BSEd in Spl. Edn. with honors, U. Mich., 1955; MA in Spl. Edn. with honors, Calif. State U., Northridge, 1975. Cert. ednl. therapist; cert. elem. and spl. edn. tchr., Calif. Edn. therapist in pvt. practice, Encino, Calif., 1968—. Lectr. in field; mentor schs. attuned program L.A. Unified Schs., 1999—. Author: Reading, Writing and Rage, 1985, 2d edit., 1996; contbr. articles to profl. jours. Pro bono cons., ednl. therapist Juvenile Justice Connection Project, New Directions for Youth, Van Nuys H.S. Tech. Program. Fellow Assn. Ednl. Therapists (founding pres. 1979-82, chair adv. bd. 1983—, honoree Ann. Conf. 1994). Avocations: hiking, speed walking, adventure travel, skiing. Office: Assn Ednl Therapists 1804 W Burbank Blvd Burbank CA 91506-1315 E-mail: dotrwr@earthlink.net.

UNGERLEIDER, LESLIE G. neuroscientist; b. N.Y.C., Apr. 17, 1946; d. Albert and Frieda (Mandel) Cohen; m. Robert Desimone, Sept. 6, 1982; 1 child, Matthew David. BA magna cum laude, SUNY, Binghamton, 1966; PhD, NYU, 1970. Asst. prof. psychology Okla. State U., Oklahoma City, 1970-72; postdoctoral fellow Dept. Psychology Stanford (Calif.) U., 1972-75, Neuropsychology Lab. NIMH, Bethesda, Md., 1975-78, staff fellow, 1978-80, sr. staff fellow, 1980-85, rsch. psychologist, 1985-91, chief sect. neurocircuitry, 1992—95, chief lab brain and congnition, 1995—. Mem. editorial bd. Neuropsychologia, 1990—, J. Neurosci, 1996—, Cerebrol Cortex, 1998—, Human Brain Mapping, 1993—; contbr. articles to profl. jours. Fellow AAAS, APA, Am. Psychol. Soc.; mem. Soc. Neurosci., NAS Inst. Medicine. Achievements include basic research on nonhuman primates revealing neural mechanisms and cortical circuitry underlying visual perception and memory. Office: NIH Bldg 10 / Rm 4C104 10 Center Dr Bethesda MD 20892-0001

UNGRICHT, YVETTE SCHARFFS, musician, music educator; b. Salt Lake City, Dec. 30, 1960; d. Gilbert Woodrow Scharffs and Laura Virginia Smith; m. Albert Lon Ungricht, Mar. 6, 1984; children: Andrew Lon, Mary Katherine, Emilie Laura, Amy Elizabeth. BMus in Piano, U. Utah, 1981, MMus in Theory and Composition, 1983; postgrad., Boston U., 1983—86. Grad. tchg. asst. U. Utah, Salt Lake City, 1981—83, Boston U., 1983—84; asst. mgr. Nashville Symphony, 1984—86; pvt. piano tchr. Salt Lake City, Boston, Nashville, 1978—; ch. organist LDS Ch., various locations, 1974—; theory and composition instr. Salt Lake C.C., Salt Lake City, 1998—. Adv. bd. Joy Rubin Piano Competition, Salt Lake City, 1998—2000; choir dir. LDS Ch., Salt Lake City, 1982—84, Salt Lake City, 1988—91; instr. Governors Sch. for the Arts, Nashville, 1985—86; mem. music cir. adv. bd. Sch. Music U. Utah, 2001—, chmn. take a seat capital campaign, 2001—. Composer: various choral, vocal, piano and organ compositions, 1978—; designer needlework, 2000—. Del. Rep. Conv., Salt Lake City, 1988—91; Primary and Relief Soc. tchr. LDS, Salt Lake City, 1974—; bd. dirs. PTA, Salt Lake City, 1999—2001. Mem.: Utah Music Tchrs. Assn., Am. Musicol. Soc., Bonsai Club of Utah (publicity chmn. 1991—), Owl and Key, Phi Kappa Phi. Mem. Lds Ch. Avocations: bonsai, needlework, painting, hiking, gardening. Home: 2725 Moraine Cir Salt Lake City UT 84109

UNITHAN, DOLLY, visual artist; b. Kelantan, Malaysia; arrived in US, 1976; Postgrad., Brit. Coun. Fine Arts Exch., 1974, Ecole Nationale des Beaux Arts de Nancy, France, 1974; BFA, Hornsey Coll. Art, 1975; MFA, Pratt Inst., 1978. Summer intern Guggenheim Mus, NYC, 1976; panelist, artist in residence Asian Am. Arts Ctr., 1993; lectr. in field. One-person shows include Internat. Art Ctr., London, 1975, Am. Assn. State Colls. and Univs., Orlando, Fla., 1977, Sloan Gallery, Lock Haven State Coll., Pa., 1978, Permanent Mission of Malaysia to UN, NYC, 1987, Kerr Gallery, NYC, 1987, Lyman Allyn Art Mus., New London, Conn., 1990, UN Secretariat, NYC, 1991, Gracie Mansion, NYC, 1994, Angel Orensanz Found., NYC, 1995, Cathedral of St. John the Divine, NYC St. Boniface Chapel Gallery, 1996; exhibited in group shows including Palace of Westminster, Hos. of Parliament, London, 1978, City Mus. and Art Gallery, Gloucester, Eng., 1978, Mus. Art, Hove, Eng., 1978, Contemporary Gallery, Warsaw, Poland, 1978, BWA Gallery, Wroclaw and Szczecin, Poland, 1978, Arts Coun. Gallery, Belfast, No. Ireland, 1978, Parrish Art Mus., Southampton, NY, 1979, Modern Art Ctr., Guadalajara, Mex., 1979, Alternative Mus., NYC, 1981, Nat. Mus. Fine Arts, Havana, Cuba, 1986, Hillwood Art Mus., Brooklyn, NY, 1988, P S 1 Mus., NYC, 1990, Nat. Art Gallery, Kuala Lumpur, 1991-92, League of Nations Archives, Palais des Nations, Geneva, 1993, Jewish Mus., Vienna, Austria, 1993, Peace Mus., Remagen, Germany, Westbeth Galleries, NYC, Tweed Courthouse Gallery, NYC, 1994, China Art Mus., Beijing, 1995, Raiffeisenkasse, Ulrich bei Steyr, Peace parish, Austria, 1996, Ctrl. Children's and Youth Arts Palace, Samarkand, Uzbekistan, 1997; Palais des Nations, United Nations Office, Geneva, 1998, Firehouse, NYC, 1999, Cathedral of St. John the Divine Synod Hall, NYC, 2002, Asian Am. Arts Ctr., NYC, 2002; represented in permanent collections including Lock Haven State Coll., Pa., Alternative Mus., NYC, Am. Assn. State Colls. and Univs., Washington, Permanent Mission of Malaysia to UN, Wilfredo Lam Ctr., Havana, Malaysian Embassy, Washington, Spirit Found., NYC, Asian Am. Arts Ctr., NYC, World Bank, Washington; artwork included in (jours.) Multicultural Edn., 1994, Artspiral, 1994, (book) Sculpture, Technique, Form, Content, Imagine Strawberry Fields. Named grad. scholar, Mara, Malaysia, 1976—78, Archives of Contemporary Arts, Venice Biennale, 1990; recipient Artist award, Rainbow Art Found., NYC, 1985, Art award ArtQuest '88, Internat. Art Competition, Calif., 1988; grantee, Lee Found., Singapore, 1972, 1976, Pollock-Krasner Found., 1991—92. Avocation: collecting antiques. Personal E-mail: dollyunithan@yahoo.com.

UNSAL-TUNAY, NURAN, geological engineer, researcher; b. Igdir, Turkey, Dec. 26, 1956; came to U.S., 1995; d. Kamil and Feride (Gunay) Tunay; m. Ilhan Unsal, Oct. 28, 1979; 1 child, Volkan. Diploma in Geol. Engring., Earth Sci. Geol. Engring., Turkey, 1982; cert. in Civil Engring., Min. of Pub. Works, Ankara, Turkey, 1985. Geol. engr. Gen. Directorate of Bank of Provinces, Konya-Ankara, Turkey, 1982-84, Gen. Directorate of Hwy., Kayseri-Ankara, Turkey, 1984-89, Adminstrn. Pub. Works, Manisa, Turkey, 1989-95. Cons. Pub. Works, Manisa, Turkey, 1989-95; adv. bds. Pub. Works, Municipality, Civil Cts., Manisa, Turkey, 1992-94. Inventor: Adaptation of Stabilized Hydrated Lime, Publication of the Chamber of Geol. Engring. of Turkey, 1993. Recipient of presentations 46th Congress of Geology of Turkey, Ankara, 1993. Fellow Geol. Assn. Can.; mem. Geol. Soc. Am., Chamber of Geol. Engrs. of Turkey. Achievements include the soil improvement with hydrated lime stabilization; applied in the area of Manisa Teachers House Buildings, was one of the first applications in Turkey. Home: 30-69 Hobart St Apt 1N Flushing NY 11377

UNTERBERGER, BETTY MILLER, history educator, writer; b. Glasgow, Scotland, Dec. 27, 1923; d. Joseph C. and Leah Miller; m. Robert Ruppe, July 29, 1944; children: Glen, Gail, Gregg. BA, Syracuse U., N.Y., 1943; MA, Harvard U., 1946; PhD, Duke U., 1950. Asst. prof. E. Carolina U., Greenville, 1948-50; assoc. prof., dir. liberal arts ctr. Whittier Coll., Calif., 1954-61; assoc. prof. Calif. State U.-Fullerton, 1961-65, prof., chmn. grad. studies, 1965-68; prof. history Tex. A&M U., College Station, 1968—. Vis. prof. U. Hawaii, Honolulu, summer 1967, Peking U., Beijing, 1988; vis. disting. prof. U. Calif., Irvine, 1987—, Patricia and Bookman Peters prof. history, 1991—; vis. prof. Charles U., Prague, Czechoslovakia, summer 1992, Regents prof., 2000—; mem. adv. com. fgn. rels. U.S. Dept. State, 1977-81, chair, 1981; mem. hist. adv. com. U.S. Dept. Army, 1980-82, USN, 1991—; mem. Nat. Hist. Publs. and Records Commn., 1980-84; mem. history rev. panel to Dir. of CIA, 1999—. Author: America's Siberian Expedition 1918-1920: A Study of National Policy, 1956, 69 (Pacific Coast award Am. Hist. Assn. 1956); editor: American Intervention in the Russian Civil War, 1969, Intervention Against Communism: Did the U.S. Try to Overthrow the Soviet Government, 1918-20, 1986, The United States, Revolutionary Russia and the Rise of Czechoslovakia, 1989, paperback edit. with a 2000 yr. perspective, 2000; contbr.: Woodrow Wilson and Revolutionary World, 1982, The Liberal Persuasion, 1997, The United States and the Russian Civil War, microfilm edit., 25 reels, 2001; mem. editl. adv. bd. The Papers of Woodrow Wilson, Princeton U., 1982-92, Internt. History, 1999—; bd. editors: Diplomatic History, 1981-84, Red River Valley Hist. Rev., 1975-84. Trustee Am. Inst. Pakistan Studies, Villanova U., Pa., 1981—, sec., 1989-92; mem. League of Women Voters. Woodrow Wilson Found. fellow, 1979; recipient Disting. Univ. Tchr. award State of Calif. Legislature, 1966. Mem. LWV, NOW, AAUW, Am. Hist. Assn. (chair 1982-83, nominating com. 1980-83), Orgn. Am. Historians (govt. relations com.), Soc. Historians of Am. Fgn. Relations (exec. council 1978-81, 86-89, govt. relations com. 1982-84, v.p. 1985, pres. 1986, co-winner Myrna F. Bernath prize 1991), Am. Soc. for Advancement Slavic Studies, Coordinating Com. on Women in Hist. Profession, Rocky Mountain Assn. Slavic Studies (program chair 1973, v.p. 1973-74), So. Hist. Assn., Asian Studies Assn., Assn. Third World Studies, Czechoslovak Soc. Arts and Scis., Czechoslovak History Conf., Women in Nat. Security, Women's Fgn. Policy Coun., Beyond War, Peace History Soc., Sierra Club, Phi Beta Kappa, Phi Beta Delta. Office: Tex A&M U Dept History College Station TX 77843-0001 E-mail: bettymu@tamu.edu.

UNTERBURGER, AMY L. editor; b. Detroit, 1957; d. George W. and Mary L. (Wilkerson) U.; m. David E. Salamie, Oct. 14, 1989; 1 child, Claire. BA in Polit. Sci., Olivet (Mich.) Coll., 1979. Editl. asst. Gale Rsch., Detroit, 1983-84, asst. editor, 1984-86, sr. asst. editor, 1986-87, assoc. editor, 1987-88, editor, 1988-94; ptnr. InfoWorks Devel. Group, 1995—. Editor: Who's Who in Technology, 6th edit., 1989, Who's Who among Hispanic Americans, 1st edit., 1991, 2nd edit., 1992, 3rd edit., 1994, Who's Who among Asian Americans, 1994, Actors and Actresses vol. International Dictionary of Films and Filmmakers, 3rd edit., 1996, Women Filmmakers and Their Films, 1998. Avocation: gardening. Office: InfoWorks Devel Group 2801 Cook Creek Dr Ann Arbor MI 48103-8962

UNVERFERTH, BARBARA PATTEN, small business owner; b. Hartford, Conn., Sept. 27, 1945; d. Leslie A. and Mildred B. (Owen) Patten; m. Robert L. Gerbig, June 1968 (div. 1977); children: Patricia G. Toohey, R. Braden Gerbig, Jo Ann Gerbig; m. Donald Unverferth, Dec. 29, 1978 (deceased); children: Katherine J. Unverferth, Megan M. Unverferth. BA cum laude, Ohio Wesleyan U., 1967; MS in Zoology, Ohio U., 1969; MS in Pathology, Ohio State U., 1980. Rsch. asst. Scripts Inst., LaJolla, Calif., 1969-70; tchr. biology Mariemont H.S., Cin., 1970-71; rschr. dept. cardiology Ohio State U., Columbus, 1980-84; gen. ptnr. Art Access, Columbus, 1993—. Founder, pres. Unverferth House Inc., Columbus, 1988—; mem. dirs. cir. Wexner Ctr., Columbus, 1995—. Author (book chpt.) Dilated Cardiomyopathy, 1985. Corr. sec. Jr. League, Columbus, 1974; corr. sec., mem. exec. bd. Childhood League, Columbus, 1980-85; sec. womens bd. Mus. of Art, Columbus, 1992-93; mem. Columbus AIDS Task Force, 1998. NSF grantee, 1966, NSF fellow, 1968; named Woman of Yr. Rotary Club Upper Arlington, Ohio, 1993. Mem. Kappa Alpha Theta (pres. alumni club 1976). Avocations: tennis, skiing. Office: Art Access 540 S Drexel Ave Bexley OH 43209 E-mail: unvi@aol.com.

UPADHYAY, WENDY SCHUTT, psychotherapist; b. San Antonio, Oct. 9, 1967; d. Norman Leslie and Patricia Toman Schutt; m. Christopher Leroy Johnson, Sept. 28, 1991 (div. Apr. 2001); m. Nishant Rasesh Upadhyay, Feb. 16, 2002. BA in Psychology, Miami U., 1989; MA in Profl. Counseling, Ill. Sch. Prof. Psychology, 1996; PsyD in Clin. Psychology, Ill. Sch. Profl. Psychology, 2002. Human resources generalist Arthur Andersen & Co., Chgo., 1990—96; doctoral intern counseling and consultation svcs. U. Wis., Madison, 1999—2000, after-hours crisis counselor counseling and consultation svcs., 2000—03; psychotherapist St. Agnes Hosp., Fond du Lac, Wis., 2003—. United Way campaign peer rep. coord. and mem. steering com. Arthur Andersen, Chgo., 1991—96. Contbg. author: Visible and Invisible Disabilities, 2003; creator and editor (cookbook) Taste of Andersen: Simply the Best, 1995. Vol. Planned Parenthood, Madison,

2001—03. Mem.: APA, Wis. Psychol. Assn. Democrat. Unitarian Universalist. Avocations: photography, reading, pottery, skiing, travel. Office: St Agnes Hosp 430 E Division St PO Box 385 Fond Du Lac WI 54936 E-mail: wendyay@charter.net.

UPBIN, SHARI, theatrical producer, director, agent, educator; b. N.Y.C. children: Edward, Elyse, Danielle. Master tap instr. Talent mgr. Goldstar Talent Mgmt., Inc., N.Y.C., 1989-91. Faculty Nat. Shakespeare Conservatory, N.Y. Asst. dir. : (plays, 1st Black-Hispanic Shakespeare prodn.) Julius Ceasar, 1979; dir.(choreographer): (plays) Matter of Opinion, 1980, Side by Side, 1981; prodr.(dir.): Vincent, The Passions of Can Gogh, 1981, : (Broadway plays) Bojangles, TheLife of Bill Robinson, 1984; dir.: Captain America, 1996; (plays) Fiddler of the Roof, Cabaret, Life with Father, Roar of the Grease Paint, 1979—82, Feminist Movements, 1997; co-prodr.: One Mo' Time; prodr.(dir): Flypaper, 1991—92, Women on Their Own, Things My Mother Never Told Me, How Could Cupid Be So Stupid!, 1999, (dir.) Timeless Divas, 2003, 20th Ann. One Mo' Time, 2000, Vintage 2001, Timeless Divas! Salute to Women in Cabaret, Broadway Over 40. Founder Queens Playhouse, N.Y., Children's Theatre, Flushing, N.Y.; mem. Willy Mays' Found. Drug Abused Children. Recipient Jaycees Svc. award Jr. Miss Pageants Franklin Twp., N.J., 1976. Mem. League Profl. Theatre Women (past pres.), Soc. Stage Dirs. and Choreographers, Coalition of Women in Arts & Media (bd. dirs.), Actors Equity Assn., Villagers Barn Theatre (1st woman pres.), N.Y. Womens Agenda (bd. dirs.). E-mail: shariupbin@earthlink.net.

UPCHURCH, ELOUISE K. vocational counselor; b. Tulsa, Okla., Dec. 22, 1937; d. Clarence Harvey and Oneta Pearl Kinion; m. James Oliver Upchurch, Aug. 6, 1960; children: Kevin James, Karana Upchurch Carroll. BS, Anderson Coll. (now Anderson U.), 1960; M Health, Phys. Edn. & Recreation, Portland State U., 1969; D, Miss. State U., 1990. Tchr. phys. edn., English Crown Point Ind. Schs., Ind., 1960—61; tchr. phys. edn. Yazoo City Pub. Schs., Miss., 1969—78, vocat. counselor, 1981—; ret., 2003. Counselor Manchester Acad., Yazoo City, Miss., 2003—04. Mem. lic. bd. Lic. Profl. Counselors, Jackson, Miss., 1994—97. Mem.: Miss. Counseling Assn. (treas., Sch. Counselor of Yr. 1989), Am. Sch. Counselors Assn. (pres.).

UPDIKE, HELEN HILL, investment manager, financial advisor; b. N.Y.C., Mar. 27, 1941; d. Benjamin Harvey and Helen (Gray) Hill; m. Charles Bruce Updike, Sept. 7, 1963 (div. 1989); m. Asa Rountree, Oct. 10, 1998. BA, Hood Coll., 1962; PhD, SUNY, Stony Brook, 1978; postgrad., Harvard U., 1986. Lectr. SUNY, Stony Brook, 1969-75; asst. prof. U. Mass., Boston, 1975-77, Hofstra U., Hempstead, NY, 1978-85, assoc. prof., 1985-90, chmn. dept. econs. and geography, 1981-84, assoc. dean Hofstra Coll., 1984-87; pres. Interfid Capital Corp., 1987—2001; prin. Bridgewater Advisors, N.Y.C., 2001—. Cons. econ. policy, 1973—; vis. asst. prof. SUNY, Stony Brook, 1977—78; commentator WNYC Radio, 1997—; bd. dirs. Faberge, McCrory Corp. Author: (book) The National Banks and American Economic Development, 1870-1900, 1985. Trustee Madeira Sch., Greenway, Va., 1984—88, Literacy, Inc., 1997—2002; mem. nat. adv. bd. Outward Bound, 1986—92; trustee, v.p. L.I. Forum Tech., 1979—85; trustee Outward Bound, 1988—97. Mem.: AAAS. Office: Bridgewater Advisors 452 Fifth Ave New York NY 10018

UPDIKE, LINDA S. personnel placement firm executive; b. Detroit, May 22, 1956; d. Arthur E. Nowak and Loraine J. (Zalewski) Jacks; m. Keith N. Updike, June 19, 1981; children: Elizabeth A., Jason J. AS in Bus. Mgmt., Macomb Cmty. coll., 1983. Adminstrn. clk. Graham Mortgage, Southfield, Mich., 1974-78; sec. Conveyor Engring., Detroit, 1978; sec. product sales dept.l Haden Uniking, Troy, Mich., 1978-83; mem. sales dept. Rapid Installations, Louisville, 1983, Harcon Engring., Madison Heights, Mich., 1984-86; adminstrv. asst. Design Systems Inc., Farmington Hills, Mich., 1987-94; gen. mgr. Staff Resources Inc., Farmington Hills, 1994; pres. GBL Resources Inc., Troy, 1994—. Mem. NAFE. Avocations: golf, travel. Office: GBL Resources Inc 6966 Crooks Rd Ste 20 Troy MI 48098-1798

UPHAM, ESTHER J. music educator; b. Chgo., July 17, 1973; d. Thomas Carlton and Diantha June Upham. MusB, U. Tenn., 1995, MusM, 1997. Cert. tchr. music. Piano tchr. pvt. practice, North Judson, Ind., 1987—91; tchr. Camp Danbee, Pittsfield, Mass., 1994; tchr. piano pvt. practice, Knoxville, 1991—97; tchr. English YMCA, Taichung, Taiwan, 1997—98; assoc. lectr. Ind. U., South Bend, 1999; tchr. piano Shirk's Piano, 1999. Tchr., accompanist U. Notre Dame, South Bend, Ind., 2000—02. Accompanist Starke County Choir, Knox, 1987. Mem.: South Bend Music Tchrs. Assn. (v.p. 2000—02), Music Tchrs. Nat. Assn., Phi Kappa Phi. Avocations: travel, studying languages, reading.

UPMEYER, LINDA, state official; b. July 1952; married. Bachelor's degree, U. Iowa, 1997; M in Nursing, Drake U., 1999. Family nurse practitioner; state rep., 2003—. Mem., vice-chair edn. appropriation subcom.; mem. human resources standing com., mem. environ. protection standing com.; mem. appropriations standing com. Mem.: Iowa Nursing Assn. (chair polit. action com.), Sigma Theta Tau (mem. Gamma chpt.). Office: State Capitol E 12th and Grand Des Moines IA 50319

UPRIGHT, DIANE WARNER, art dealer; b. Cleve. d. Rodney Upright and Shirley (Warner) Lavine. Student, Wellesley Coll., 1965-67; BA, U. Pitts., 1969; MA, U. Mich., 1973, PhD, 1976. Asst. prof. U. Va., Charlottesville, 1976-78; assoc. prof. Harvard U., Cambridge, Mass., 1978-83; sr. curator Ft. Worth Art Mus., 1984-86; dir. Jan Krugier Gallery, N.Y.C., 1986-90; sr. v.p., head contemporary art dept. Christie's, N.Y.C., 1990-95; pres. Diane Upright Fine Arts, N.Y.C., 1995—. Author: Morris Louis: The Complete Paintings, 1979, Ellsworth Kelly: Works on Paper, 1987, various exhbn. catalogues; contbr. articles to art jours. Mem. Art Table, Inc. Office: Diane Upright Fine Arts 188 E 76th St New York NY 10021-2826

UPSHUR, CAROLE CHRISTOFK, psychologist, educator; b. Des Moines, Oct. 18, 1948; d. Robert Richard and Margaret (Davis) Chistofk; 1 child, Emily. AB, U. So. Calif., 1969; EdM, Harvard U., 1970, EdD, 1975. Lic. psychologist, Mass. Planner Mass. Com. on Criminal Justice, Boston, 1970-73; licensing specialist, planner, policy specialist Mass. Office for Children, Boston, 1973-76; asst. prof. Coll. Pub. and Cmty. Svc. U. Mass., Boston, 1976-81, assoc. prof., 1982-93, prof., 1993-2001, chmn. Ctr. for Cmty. Planning, 1979—81, 1984—86, 1995—96; prof., interim assoc. dean family medicine and cmty. health Grad. Sch. Biomed. Scis. U. Mass. Med. Sch., Boston, 2004—. Sr. rsch. fellow Maurice Gaston Inst. Latino Pub. Policy, 1993—, Ctr. Social Devel. & Edn., 1991-2001, Gerontology Inst., 1996-2001, McCormack Inst. for Pub. Affairs, dir. PhD in Pub. Policy program, 1995-2001; cons. to govt. and cmty. agys.; assoc. in pediat., sr. rsch. assoc. U. Mass. Med. Sch., 1983-94; adj. prof. Heller Sch. Social Welfare, Brandeis U., 1985-98; prof. family medicine and cmty. health U. Mass. Med. Sch. and Meml. Health Care, 2004-; interim assoc. dean, Clin. and Population Health Rsch. Grad. Sch., U. Mass. Med. Sch., 2004—. Contbr. articles to profl. jours. Mem. Brookline Human Rels.-Youth Resources Commn., 1988-91, Gov.'s Commn. on Facility Consolidation, 1991-92, Mass. Healthcare Adv. Com., 1993—. Fellow Mass. Psychol. Assn.; mem. APA, APHA, Soc. Tchrs. of Family Medicine. Office: U Mass Med Sch Dept Family Med 55 Lake Ave N Worcester MA 01655

UPSON, HELEN RENA, retired history educator; b. Southington, Conn., Aug. 18, 1912; BA, Grinnell (Iowa) Coll., 1958; MA, U. Iowa, 1960, PhD, 1969. Commd. USN, 1943, advanced through grades to lt. comdr., ret., 1958; adminstrv. officer math., scis. divsn. Office of Naval Rsch., Washington, 1949-50; instr. Armed Forces Info. Sch., Carlysle, Pa., Ft. Slocum, N.Y., 1950-53; tng. officer Naval Air Sta., Hutchinson, Kans., 1953-55; pub. info. officer 17th Naval Dist., Kodiak, Alaska, 1955-57, Office of Chief of Info., Office of Sec. Navy, Washington, 1957-58; grad. asst. instr. U. Iowa, 1958-65; assoc. prof. Am. and European history Calif. Western U./U.S. Internat. U., San Diego, 1965-76, adj. prof. Am. econ. history and internat. European problems, 1976-81. Author: Order and System: Charles Frances Adams Jr. and the Railroad Problem, 1970, The western Odyssey of Nin Connecticut Brothers: An Intimate History of American Enterprise, 1989. Mem. Tierrasanta Cmty. Coun., San Diego and chmn. lit. com., 1982-83. Mem. AAUW, Nat. Ind. Scholars, Am. Hist. Soc. Unitarian Universalist. Avocations: swimming, hiking, skiing, photography, travel. Home: 183 3rd Ave Apt 310 Chula Vista CA 91910-1822

UPTON, BARBARA, hypnotherapist, small business owner; b. Utica, N.Y., Sept. 10, 1948; d. Nelson Crandle Upton and Mary Catherine Jones; m. John Horvath, Apr. 8, 1972 (div. 1982); children: Bryce Horvath, Ian Horvath. BA cum laude, SUNY, Albany, 1970. Devel. officer Rehab. Programs, Poughkeepsie, NY, 1981—88; v.p. United Way of Dutchess County, Poughkeepsie, 1988—97; hypnotherapist Poughkeepsie, 1997—2003; founder Waking Planet, New Paltz, NY, 2001—03. Organizer, workshop leader Truessence Creations, 1995—2003. Columnist Freetime Newspaper, 1999, curator The Magical Feminine, 2001, 2003; editor: Waking Planet Chronicles, 2002—03. Mem. Women in Black, New Paltz, 2001—03. Mem.: Internat. Assn. Counselors and Therapists, Tivoli Artists Group. Home: PO Box 955 New Paltz NY 12561 E-mail: barbara@wakingplanet.com.

UR, ROSE-MARIE, member of parliament; b. Ekfrid Twp., Canada; m. Louis Ur; children: Terry, Michelle. RN asst. Strathroy-Middlesex Gen. Hosp.; mktg. mgrt., pub. rels. mgr. mktg. firm produce; farmer, owner, operator of family farm; constituency asst. for provincial M.P.P. Douglas Reycraft Toronto (Provincial), Ottawa, 1986-88; sr. constituency asst. for fed. M.P. Hon. Ralph Ferguson House of Commons, Ottawa, 1988-93, M.P. for Lambton-Middlesex, 1993—2002, M.P. for Lambton-Kent-Middlesex, 1997—. Bd. dirs. Strathroy Area Assn. Cmty. Living; tax preparation cmty. vol. Dept. Nat. Revenue; mem. fundraising com. Caradoc Cmty. Centre, Mount Brydges, Ont. Mem. Ont. Fedn. Agr., Ont. Vegetagle Growers, Strathroy Lioness Club (charter), Ind. Order Oddfellows and Rebekahs. Office: House of Commons 449 Confederation Bldg Ottawa ON Canada K1A 0A6

URAHN, SUSAN K. foundation administrator; BA in Sociology, D of Policy & Adminstrn., U. Minn. With rsch. dept. Minn. Ho. Reps.; dir. planning & evaluation Pew Charitable Trusts, Phila., 1994—. Rschr. in field. Contbr. tech. reports to profl. pubs. Office: Pew Charitable Trusts 2005 Market St Ste 1700 Philadelphia PA 19103-7017

URANGA, JEAN R. lawyer; b. West Point, N.Y., Sept. 30, 1949; BA, Western Wash. U., 1971; JD, Willamette U., 1975. Bar: Idaho 1975, U.S. Dist. Ct. Idaho 1975, U.S. Ct. Appeals (9th cir.) 1980. Atty. Uranga & Uranga, Boise, Idaho. Mem.: Idaho State Bar (continuing legal edn. com. 1987—90, discipline hearing com. 1983—86, Supreme Ct. com. on child custody mediation 1989—, bankruptcy and family law sects., bar commr. 1990—93, pres. 1992). Office: Uranga and Uranga PO Box 1678 714 N Fifth St Boise ID 83701-1678

URATO, BARBRA CASALE, [illegible] 10, 1941; d. Dominick Anthony and Concetta (Castrichini) Casale; m. John Joseph Urato, June 20, 1965; children: Concetta U. Graves, Gina E., Joseph D. Student, Seton Hall U., 1961-63. File clk. Martin Gelber Esquire, Newark, 1956-58; policy typist Aetna Casualty Ins., Newark, 1959-61; sec. to dean Seton Hall U., South Orange, N.J., 1961-63; paralegal sec. Judge Robert A. McKinley, Newark, 1963-65, Joseph Garrubbo, Esquire, Newark, 1965-66; office mgr. Valiant I.M.C., Hackensack, N.J., 1971-73; asst. pers. mgr. Degussa Inc., Teterboro, N.J., 1975-78; night mgr. The Ferryboat Restaurant, River Edge, N.J., 1976-78; mgr. Fratello's and Ventilini's, Hilton Head, S.C., 1978-80; day mgr. Ramada Inn Restaurant, Paramus, N.J., 1980-81; mgr. Gottlieb's Bakery, Hilton Head, 1982-83; asst. mgr. closing dept. Hilton Head Mortgage Co., 1983-84; owner, mgr. All Cleaning Svc., Hilton Head, 1984—; owner Hilton Head Investigations, 1990-93, 1990-92, Aaction Investigators, 1992-94. Mem. NAFE, Profl. Women of Hilton Head, Assn. for Rsch. and Enlightenment, Rosicrucian Order. Roman Catholic. Avocations: metaphysics, music, gardening, learning.

URBAN, A. GREG M. health facility administrator; b. Richmond, Va., May 23, 1943; d. A. E. Maroney and Martha J. Talbott; children: Steven T., Jeffrey B., Elizabeth U. Hirsh. Grad. h.s., Colonial Heights, Va. Teletype oper. Sears Roebuck, Petersburg, Va., 1959—61; with CIT Credit Corp., Petersburg, 1961—63; med. staff sec. Petersburg Gen. Hosp., 1963—64; asst. dir. Comfort Keppers, Jacksonville Beach, Fla., 2002—03, coord., 2003—. Pres. C.H. Jaycettes, Colonial Heights, 1967—68; mem. Women of the Symphony, Washington, 1979; assoc. mem. Wolf Trap, Vienna, Va., 1980. Mem.: Rep. Club, Info. Club of Washington, Coun. of Garden Clubs, Fed. Woman's Club. Republican. Episcopalian. Avocations: golf, tennis, gardening. Home: 43 Ramona St Ponte Vedra Beach FL 32082 Office: Comfort Keepers 233 N 3d St Jacksonville Beach FL 32250

URBAN, AMANDA (BINKY URBAN), literary agent; m. Ken Auletta, 1977; 1 child. BA in English, Wheaton Coll., Mass. Gen. mgr. N.Y. mag.; editl. mgr. Esquire mag.; literary agent Internat. Creative Mgmt., N.Y.C., v.p., co-dir. lit. dept., 1988—98, co-head, 1999—. Office: Internat Creative Mgmt 40 W 57th St New York NY 10019*

URBAN, CARRIE, computer specialist; b. Summit, N.J., Nov. 30, 1969; BS in Fin., U. Colo., Colorado Springs, 1994, MBA in Info. Systems, 1996; grad. child psychology, Stratford Career Inst., Washington, 1999, grad. sewing and dressmaking, 2000. Sys. operator Celestial Light BBS, Colorado Springs, 1984-98, Country Estate BBS, Casa Grande, Ariz., 1999; freelance computer cons. Casa Grande, 1998—. Intern Interactive Mgmt. Systems, Colorado Springs, 1997; tech. support profl. Gateway Computers, Colorado Springs, 1998; computer tutor Judith Crawford, Colorado Springs, 1998-99; computer troubleshooter Summit Home Health Care, Colorado Springs, 1999, Millie Forbush, Casa Grande, 2000. Writer newsletter column Transgender Connection, 1996-97, Transgender Jour., 1998-99; writer Ground Zero, Colorado Springs, 1996-97. Mem. adv. coun. Equality Colo., Colorado Springs, 1998-99. Mem. Nat. Rifle Assn. (cert. personal protection course), Christian Broadcasting Network, Concerned Women of Am., Humane Soc. U.S. Republican. Baptist. Avocations: reading, bowling, singing, writing. Home: 1728 E Catalina Ave Casa Grande AZ 85222-5716 E-mail: carrieu@cybertrails.com.

URBAN, CATHLEEN ANDREA, graphic designer; b. Elizabeth, N.J., June 7, 1947; d. Emil Martin and Susan (Rahoche) Cupec; m. Walter Robert Urban, Nov. 5, 1966; children: Karen Louise, Kimberly Ann. Student, Rutgers U., 1965-66, 91-94; AS in Bus. Adminstrn., AAS in Computer Programming, Raritan Valley C.C., North Branch, N.J., 1990. Office mgr. K-Mart Corp., Somerville, N.J., 1987-90; software developer Bellcore, Piscataway, N.J., 1990-93, sys. tech. support cons., 1993-94, software developer, 1994-96, software quality assurance tester, 1996-97, project mgr., 1997—; graphic designer, owner CathiCards, Inc., Neshanic Station, N.J., 1995—. Leader Somerset County 4-H Program, Bridgewater, 1978-87. Mem. NAFE, AAUW, Nat. Space Soc., Internat. Platform Assn., Project Mgmt. Inst., Internat. Guild Candle Artisans, Golden Key Honor Soc., Mensa, Phi Theta Kappa. Roman Catholic. Avocations: science fiction, reading, dog shows, candle making. Office: Bell Comm Rsch 444 Hoes Ln Piscataway NJ 08854-4104 Home: 570 Amwell Rd Hillsborough NJ 08844-3404

URBINA, FEBE GLORIA, elementary school principal; b. Nuevo Laredo, Tamaulipas, Mexico, Aug. 25, 1942; came to U.S., 1947; d. Manuel Urbina and Irene Salce de Urbina. BA, Howard Payne Coll., 1965; MEd, U. Houston, 1975. Cert. tchr., adminstr., biling. educator, spcl. edn., mid mgmt., ednl. diagnostician, Tex. Cashier Weingarten Grocery, Houston, 1960-64; social worker Neighborhood Ctrs. Assn., Houston, 1965-68; elem. sch. tchr. Houston Ind. Sch. Dist., 1968-70, curriculum coord., 1970-2000, prin., 1973—. Adj. instr. Adult Edn. Houston C.C., 1965-71; mem. Legal United L.Am. Citizens Ednl. Adv. Bd., Houston, 1975-76; adj. English tchr. Harris County C.C., Pasadena, Tex., 1986-88; mem. supt.'s adv. bd. Houston Ind. Sch. Dist., 1990-97; presenter Conv. of Excellence, 1988, 90, 95, 98, Conv. Sch. External Funds, 1998, Lightspan Conv., 1998. Co-author: (book) Strategies for Bilingual/ESL Teachers, 1968. Sunday Sch. Tchr. Southmain Bapt. Ch., Houston, 1970-76; ch. pianist Heights Bapt. Temple, Houston, 1976-86; mem. Meadowbrook Civic Club, Houston, 1987-98. Recipient Mary Hill Davis award Home Mission Bd., Atlanta, 1961; named Hispanic Principal of Yr., Houston Ind. Sch. Dist. 1975, Principal of Yr. 1994. Mem. ASCD, Houston Assn. for Sch. Adminstrs. Avocations: travel, music, mission trips, translating, reading. Home: 899 Old Genoa Red Bluff Rd Houston TX 77034-4010 Office: Bonner Elem Sch 8100 Elrod St Houston TX 77017-5216

URDANG, ALEXANDRA, book publishing executive; b. N.Y.C., June 29, 1956; d. Laurence Urdang and Irena (Ehrlich) Urdang de Tour. BA in English Lit., U. Conn., 1977. Customer svc. and fulfillment mgr. Universe Books, N.Y.C., 1978-79, sales mgr., assoc. mktg. mgr., 1980-82; asst. v.p., dir. spl. sales Macmillan Pub. Co., N.Y.C., 1982-88; v.p. new markets Warner Books, Inc., N.Y.C., 1988-97. Avocations: architecture, art, antiques. Office: Apt 2A 201 E 69th St New York NY 10021-5472

URIBE, CLAUDIA PATRICIA, psychologist, educator; b. L.I., N.Y., May 5, 1968; d. Jorge and Rocio Uribe. AA in Journalism, Miami-Dade C.C., 1990; BS in Criminal Justice, Fla. Internat. U., 1992, BA in Sociology/Anthropology, MS in Criminal Justice, Fla. Internat. U., 1995; MS in Clin. Psychology, Miami Inst. Psychology, 1999; PhD of Clin. Psychology, Carlos Albizu U., 2001; postgrad., Nova Southeastern U. Cert. tchr. Fla. Case mgr. Child Support Divsn. State Atty.'s Office, Miami, Fla., 1992—96; dir. social svcs. Centro Mater Child Care Ctr. Cath. Cmty. Svcs., Inc., Miami, 1996—97; exec. dir. One Nation, Miami, 1997—99; ednl. specialist Miami Dade County Pub. Schs., Miami, 1999—. Med. disability specialist U.S. Dept. Labor, Miami, 1993—96; adj. prof. Miami Dade C.C., Miami, 2002—. Mem.: ACE (Fla. chpt.), LWV, APA, Rep. Nat. Hispanic Assembly, Miami-Dade C. of C. (Immigration com. 1997), Coconut Grove Women Rep., Brest Cancer Found., Hist. Found. Republican. Roman Catholic. Avocations: scuba diving, yoga, spinning, pilates. Office: Miami Dade County Pub Schs 1450 NE 2d St Rm 843 Miami FL 33132*

URIBE, JENNIE ANN, elementary school educator; b. National City, Calif., Apr. 17, 1958; d. Robert and Alice (Packard) U. BA, San Diego State U., 1981, cert. teacher, 1982; MB, Nat. Univ., 2000. Tchr. Langdon Ave. Sch., L.A. Unified Sch. Dist., Sepulveda, Calif., 1984-94, tchr. potentally gifted students class, 1987-94; tchr. Spreckels Elem. Sch., San Diego City Schs., 1994—97, Rosa Elem., 1997—. Tchr./advisor for student govt., 1987-93; guide tchr., 1997—; prof. deve. advisor, 1997—. Mem. adv. coun. Sch. Site, 1992-1997. Avocations: tennis, music, movies, reading. Home: 2259 Peach Tree Ln Spring Valley CA 91977-7046 Office: Rosa Parks Elem Sch 4510 Landis St San Diego CA 92103

URIS, PATRICIA FIRME, health science association administrator; b. Muskegon, Mich. BSN, U. Colo., 1974, MS in Psychiatric/Mental Health Nursing, 1978, PhD in Nursing, 1993. Staff nurse Colo. Mental Health Inst., Denver, 1984-76; on-call staff Bethesda PsycHealth Sys., Denver, 1977; clin. specialist Pk. E. Comprehensive Cmty. Mental Health Ctr., Denver, 1978; asst. exec. dir. Colo. Nurses Assn., Denver, 1979-80; project co-dir. Western Interstate Commn. Higher Edn., Boulder, Colo., 1980-85; project dir. Western Inst. Nursing/Western Soc. Rsch. Nursing, Boulder, 1987-90, assoc. dir., 1987-90, spl. cons., 1990-94; program devel., mgmt. cons. Arvada, Colo., 1994-95; asst. prof. U. Colo. Health Scis. Ctr., Denver, 1995-99; program adminstr. Bd. Nursing Colo. Dept. Regulatory Agys., Denver, 1999—. Guest lectr. U. Colo. Health Scis. Ctr., 1979-82, 80-83, 94-97, Metro. State Coll., 1979-82; cons. U. Alaska, 1982, Wyo. Dept. Health and Social Svcs., 1982, Utah Dept. Health, 1982; reviewer Appleton-Century-Crofts Pub. Co., 1985, Colo. Dept. Health and Environment, 1996, 97, Nat. Assn. Sch. Nurses, Inc., 1997, HHS, 1997, 98, 99. Cons. Rocky Mountain Ctr. Healthcare Ethics; mem. clin. adv. bd. ONEDAY/The Family AIDS Project, Denver; mem. stds. based edn. com. Arvada W. Sch. Improvement Leadership Team, Jefferson County, Colo. Recipient NIH stipend, 1976-78; Calloway scholar U. Colo. Health Scis. Ctr. Mem. ANA, Am. Psychiatric Nurses Assn., Assn. Child and Adolescent Psychiatric Nurses, Soc. Edn. and Rsch. Psychiatric-Mental Health Nursing, Nat. Assn. Sch. Nurses, Colo. Nurses Assn. (ANA del. 1982, 84, mem. commn. social and legis. concerns 1981-85, chair 1981-83, Virginia S. Paulson award 1981), Colo. Mental Health Assn. (pro bono vol.), Sigma Theta Tau (chpt. bd. dirs. 1993-96, mem. rsch. com. 1995-99, chmn. 1995-96, Henrietta Loughran scholar 1993).

URISTA, DIANE JEAN, music educator, researcher; b. Mpls., Mar. 28, 1957; d. Joseph and Jean Helen (Sanzenbach) U.; m. Peter John Quehl, June 1, 1985 (div. Sept. 1994); m. Jonathan Jaye Niefeld, July 6, 1996. MusB, Concordia Coll., Moorhead, Minn., 1979; MusM, Northwestern U., 1990; MPhil, Columbia U., 1996. Coord. Children's Music Program Am. Conservatory Music, Chgo., 1986-90; instr. music humanities Columbia U., N.Y.C., 1993—; instr. music theory NYU, N.Y.C., 1997—. Foster parent, Plan Internat., Honduras, 1985— Mellon fellow Columbia U., 1993-97. Mem. AAUW (Am. Dissertation fellow 1997), Coll. Music Soc., Soc. Music Theory, Mu Phi Epsilon. Avocations: reading, poetry, ice skating, movies.

URQUHART, SALLY ANN, environmental scientist, chemist, educator; b. Omaha, June 8, 1946; d. Howard E. and Mary Josephine (Johnson) Lee; m. Henry O. Urquhart, July 31, 1968; children: Mary L. Urquhart Kelly, Andrew L. BS in Chemistry, U. Tex., Arlington, 1968; MS in Environ. Scis., U. Tex., Dallas, 1986. Cert. chemistry and composite H.S. sci., Tex.; lic. asbestos mgmt. planner, Tex. Rsch. asst. U. Tex. Dallas, Richardson, 1980-82; H.S. sci. tchr. Allen (Tex.) Ind. Sch. Dist., 1983-87; hazardous materials specialist Dallas Area Rapid Transit, 1987-90, environ. compliance officer, 1990-94, environmental compliance coordination officer, 1994-95; pres. Comprehensive Environ. Svcs. Inc., Dallas, 1995—2000; tchr. chemistry Richardson Tex. Ind. Sch. Dist., 1998—, tchr. advanced placement chemistry, 2000—. Contbr. articles to Tech. Tchr. Pres. Beacon Sunday Sch. Spring Valley United Meth. Ch., Dallas, 1987, adminstrv. bd. dirs., 1989, com. status and role of women, 1992; mem. conservation commn. EnviroMentor Program, 1997-2000. Scholar Richardson (Tex.) Br. AAUW, 1980; recipient dir.'s award Soc. Tex. Environ. Profls., 1997. Mem. Assn. Chemistry Tchrs. Tex., Sci. Tchrs. Assn. Tex., Assn. Tex. Profl. Educators., U. Tex.-Dallas Alumnae Assn. (com. 1992-94). Avocations: jewelry design, counted cross stitching. Home: PO Box 833597 Richardson TX 75083

USHENKO, AUDREY ANDREYEVNA, painter, art historian, educator; b. Princeton, July 28, 1945; d. Andrew Pavlevitch and Fay (Hampton) U.; m. S.M. Harcaj; 1 child, Emily. Student, Sch. of Art Inst., 1963-64; BA, Ind. U., 1965; MA, Northwestern U., Evanston, Ill., 1967, PhD, 1979. Instr. Valparaiso (Ind.) U., 1968-73, asst. prof., 1978-79; instr. Alan R. Hite Inst. U. Louisville, 1973-74; asst. prof. Northwestern U., Evanston, Ill., 1974-75; vis. faculty Columbia Coll., 1980-88; assoc. prof. Ind.-Purdue U., Ft. Wayne, Ind., 1988—. Gallery artist Gruen Gallery, Chgo., 1983—, Denise

Bibro Gallery, N.Y.C., 1993—, Yvonne Rapp Gallery, Louisville, 1989—; artist oil paintings Bacchus & Ariadne III, 1987 (NAD Clark prize), Social Security, 1987 (Purchase prize 1989), Chgo. Art Expo, 1996, Marriage Project-Travelling Exhbn., 1996, Conviviality, 1997 (NAD Isidor Medal 1997), Fort Wayne Mus. of Art, 1998; curator exhbn. N.Y.C., 1998-99. Mem. AAUP (sec. local chpt. 1990—), NAD. Democrat. Orthodox. Avocations: reading, music. Home: 2519 East Dr Fort Wayne IN 46805-3612

USHER, ANN L. music educator; d. Richard D. and Margaret L. Miller; m. Thomas E. Usher, Aug. 12, 1989; children: Kelsey M., Adam T., Logan R. MusM, Kent (Ohio) State U., 1993. Permanent tchg. cert. Ohio. Music educator Parma (Ohio) City Schs., 1990—92, Solon (Ohio) City Schs., 1992—2000; asst. prof. music U. Akron, Ohio, 2000—. Dir. Cleve. Orch. Children's Chorus. Office: U Akron Guzzetta Hall 366 Akron OH 44325-1002 Office Phone: 330-972-6923. Business E-Mail: ausher@uakron.edu.

USHER, BETHANY MCKAY, biological anthropology educator; b. Richmond, Va., July 11, 1970; d. Cecil H. and Elizabeth M. Usher; m. Jaimin David Weets. PhD, Pa.State U., 2000. Archaeologist, graphics mgr. R. Christopher Goodwin & Assoc., Inc., Frederick, Md., 1991—93; tchg. and rsch. asst. Ariz. State U., Tempe, 1993—95, Penn State U., 1995—2000; asst. prof. anthropology Shippensburg (Pa.) U., 1999—2000; asst. prof. biol. anthropology SUNY, Potsdam, NY, 2000—. Scholar Fulbright Fgn. scholar, Fulbright Assn., 1997—98. Mem.: Am. Assn. Phys. Anthropologists. Office: SUNY Coll at Potsdam 118A MacVicar Hall Potsdam NY 13676 Office Phone: 315-267-2051. Business E-Mail: usherbm@potsdam.edu.

USHER, CHARLENE LYNETTE, lawyer; d. Connie Usher and Barbara A. Montgomery. BS, Calif. Poly. U., Pomona, 1991; JD, U. Calif., San Francisco, 1996. Bar: Calif. 1997. Staff counsel Liberty Mut. Ins. Co., San Francisco, 1998—99; assoc. Seyforth, Shaw et al, L.A., 2000, Waters & Robinson, Diamond Bar, Calif., 2001; founder, mng. atty. Usher Law Group, Diamond Bar, 2001—. Mem.: ABA, John M. Longton Bar Assn., Calif. Assn. Black Lawyers, Black Women Lawyers of L.A., Nat. Bar Assn., City Club on Bunker Hill. Avocations: skiing, tennis, golf, travel, reading. Office: Usher Law Group # 375 1142 S Diamond Bar Blvd Diamond Bar CA 91765 E-mail: clusher@usherlawgroup.com.

USHER, NANCY SPEAR, retired language arts educator; b. Malden, Mass., Mar. 13, 1938; d. George Alonzo and Mary Elizabeth (York) Spear; m. Walter Lansley Whitlock, June 13, 1959 (div. Oct. 1961); m. Frederic Laurence Usher, Apr. 19, 1970 (dec. April 1998). BS in Edn., U. So. Maine, 1960; postgrad., Boston U., Salem State Coll., 1964-68. 5th grade tchr. Melrose (Mass.) Sch. Dept., 1961-63, 7th grade English tchr., 1963-65, 71-97, 7th grade spl. needs tchr., 1965-70; ret., 1997. Freshman girls' basketball coach Melrose High Athletic Dept., 1973-77. Mem. U. So. Maine Alumni Assn. Avocations: golf, boating, reading. E-mail: nusher38@aol.com.

USHER, PHYLLIS LAND, state official; b. Winona, Miss., Aug. 29, 1944; d. Sandy Kenneth and Ruth (Cottingham) Land; m. William A. Usher (dec. Dec. 1993). BS, U. So. Miss., 1967; MS, U. Tenn., 1969; postgrad., Purdue U., Ind. U., Utah State U. Libr. Natchez (Miss.) - Adams County Schs., 1967-68; materials specialist Fulton County Bd. Edn., Atlanta, 1969-71; cons. divsn. instructional media Ind. Dept. Pub. Instrn., Indpls., 1971-74, dir. divsn., 1974-82, dir. fed. resources and sch. improvement, 1982-85; acting assoc. supt. Ind. Dept. Edn., 1985, sr. officer Ctr. Sch. Improvement, 1985-96, asst. supt., 1996—. Pres. bd. dirs. INCOLSA, mcpl. corp., 1980-82; pres., owner Usher Funeral Home, Inc.; pres. NU Realty Corp.; mem. task force sch. Libraries Nat. Commn. Libraries and Info. Sci.; cons. in field. Bd. dirs. Hawthorne Cmty. Ctr.; mem. Gov. Inst. Conf. Children and Youth Task Force. Recipient citation Internat. Reading Assn., 1975; Title II-B fellow, U. Tenn., 1968-69. Mem. ALA, Nat. Assn. State Ednl. Media Profls., West Deanery Bd. Edn., Indpls. Archdiocese, Delta Kappa Gamma. Office: State House Rm 229 Indianapolis IN 46204-2728

USHIJIMA, JEAN M. retired city official; b. San Francisco, Feb. 14, 1933; d. Toyoharu George and Frances Fujiko (Misumi) Miwa; m. Tad E. Ushijima; 1 child, Carol M. BS, U. San Francisco, 1981. City clk. City of Beverly Hills, Calif., 1973—94; ret., 1994. Bd. dirs. West L.A. Japanese Am. Citizens League, 1979—, pres., 1988—91, also chmn. bd.; bd. dirs. Leadership Edn. for Asian Pacifics, 1985—90. Mem.: Internat. Inst. Mcpl. Clks. (bd. dirs. 1988—91), League Calif. Cities (adminstrv. svcs. com. 1982—86, 1993—), Calif. Women in Govt. (program chmn. 1978—79), City Clks. Assn. Calif. (pres. 1986, City Clk. of Yr. award 1989), Acad. Advanced Edn., Beverly Hills C. of C. (Employee of Yr. award 1990). Avocations: reading, Japanese dancing.

USHRY, ROSELYN, minister; b. Balt., Dec. 23, 1943; d. Lawrence and Dorothy Louise (White) Blake; m. Wyman Ushry, Jr., Dec. 23, 1970; m. Charles C. Jones (div. Sept. 1970). AA, Balt. C.C., 1977; BS, Morgan State U., 1980; postgrad. in M Theology program, St. Mary's Sem. U., Balt. Ordained evangelist United Coun. Christian Cmty. Chs. of Md., 1977. Caseworker assoc. I-II Dept. Social Svcs., Balt., 1972—80; adminstrv. asst. Dept. Child Support Enforcement, Balt., 1980—83; asst. dir. Child Support Adminstrn., Balt., 1983—89, dir., 1989—97, Customer Svc. Child Support, Balt., 1997—99; pastor Wilson Park Christian Cmty. Ch., Balt., 1989—. Exec. sec. Christian Cmty. Coun., Balt., 2000—. Featured Lift Every Voice and Sing, WMAR TV, 2000—01. Dir. summer camp, Balt., 1999—2001; instr. GED classes, Balt., 1999—; mem. bd. neighborhood assn., Balt., 1989—; ordained elder United Coun. Christian Cmty. Chs. of Md. and Vicinity, 1985—. Recipient Outstanding Pastor award, WWIN Spirit 1400, 2001—02, Most Inspirational Person award, Balt. City Pub. Schs., 2001. Avocation: missionary work in foreign countries. Home: 1515 Winston Ave Baltimore MD 21212

USINGER, MARTHA PUTNAM, counselor, educator, dean; b. Pitts., Dec. 10, 1912; d. Milo Boone and Christiana (Haberstroh) Putnam; m. Robert Leslie Usinger, June 24, 1938 (dec Oct. 1968); children: Roberta Christine (dec.), Richard Putnam. AB cum laude, U. Calif., Berkeley, 1934, postgrad., 1935—36, Oreg. State U., 1935—37, U. Ghana, 1970, Coll. Nairobi, 1970. Tchr. Oakland (Calif.) Pub. Schs., 1936-38, Berkeley (Calif.) Pub. Schs., 1954-57, dean West Campus, counselor, 1957-78. Lectr., photographer in field. Author: Ration Books and Christmas Crackers, 1989, Threading My Way, 3 vols., 2003; contbg. author: Robert Leslie Usinger, Autobiography of an Entomologist, 1972. Mem. DAR, Berkeley Ret. Tchrs., U. Calif. Emeriti Assn., U. Calif. Alumnae Assn., Prytanean Alumnae Assn. (alumnae pres. 1952-54), Berkeley Camera Club, Mortar Bd., Am. Friends of Puttenham, P.E.O., Delta Kappa Gamma. Avocations: photography, slide shows and lectures, ethnic textiles, travel, geneology.

USSERY, REBECCA ALICE, secondary school educator; b. Lubbock, Tex., Sept. 4, 1969; d. Bennie D. Ussery and Joyce Ann Rowe; 1 child, Stephen Neil. AS, South Plains Coll., 1990; BA in History, Tex. Tech U., 1995, postgrad., 2003. Tex. educator's cert. - secondary social studies composite Tex. State Bd. Tchr. Certification, 1999. Tchr. Wedgwood Sixth Grade Sch., Ft. Worth, 1999—2000, Lubbock H.S., 2000—03. Faculty advisor Key Club Lubbock H.S., 2000—03. Mem.: Texas-Oklahoma Dist. Key Club (region 1 advisor 2003), Kiwanis Club Lubbock. Avocations: camping, hockey, travel, music.

UTLEY, JANE BESON, poet; b. Houston, Dec. 14, 1954; d. John Mark and Frances Ester (Rupert) Beson; m. Ronald Gene Utley, June 29, 1985. Asst. mgr. McCoy Devel. Corp., Houston, 1978-81; with accounts receivable dept. Arpco Office Supply, Houston, 1981; payroll analyst Toshiba Internat., Houston, 1981-86. Songwriter Jeff Roberts Pub., 1996-97. Contbr. poems to Best Poems of the 90's, 1996, American Poetry Annual, 1997, Word Weaver, 1997, Treasure the Moment, vol. X, 1997, A Celebration of Poets 1997, (audio tape) Internat. Libr.'s The Sound of Poetry, anthologies; pub. comml. song Majestic Records and Countrywine Pubs. Mem. Top RecordsSongwriters Assn. Avocations: writing, fishing, gardening, reading. Office: Flooring Cons PO Box 1610 Brookshire TX 77423-1610 E-mail: jutley3169@aol.com.

UTTERBACK, BETTY HARRIS, writer; b. Coalmont, Ind., July 30; d. Earl Daniel and Esther Jane (Bosley) Harris; student in journalism Ind. U., 1945-47; BA in Cultural Studies, Empire State Coll., 1988; m. Max Gene Utterback, Aug. 10, 1947; children: Pamela Kim Utterback Tyminski, Max Andrew. Pub. relations ofcl. Purdue U., 1947-50; free lance writer, 1950-69, 84—; with Gannett Rochester (N.Y.) Newspapers, 1969-84, TV editor, 1973-80, feature writer, 1980-84, columnist Gannett News Service, 1973-80. Co-author: (with John Robertson) Suddenly Single, 1986. Bd. dirs. Literacy Vols. Am., Rochester, 1984-87. Recipient 1st prize for feature N.Y. State AP, 1977. Republican. Presbyterian. Home: 80 E Jefferson Rd Pittsford NY 14534-2320

UTZ, HEIDI M. writer; b. Pompton Lakes, N.J., Oct. 26, 1962; d. Lois Cook and Donald Lowrey Utz. BA, Drew U., 1983. Account exec., media mgr. Gilbert, Whitney & Johns, Inc., Whippany, NJ, 1983—84; pub. rels. dir. Utz Engring., Inc., Clifton, NJ, 1985—88; owner Abiquiu East Pub. Rels., Morristown, NJ, 1989—91; acquisitions, periodicals libr. Coll. of Santa Fe, 1991—92; arts writer Albuquerque Tribune, 1994—96; writer, reviewer, columnist Crosswinds, Santa Fe, 1994—2000; book editor self employed, Santa Fe, 1994—; assoc. editor Mothering Mag., Santa Fe, 1996—98, Outside Mag., Santa Fe, 1998—2000; arts editor, writer Pasatiempo, Santa Fe New Mexican, 2000—01; film critic, columnist Santa Fe Reporter, 2001—02; writer, editor Bechtel Nev. Corp., Los Alamos, 2001—; owner Heidi Utz Media, Santa Fe, 2001—. Submissions juror Santa Fe Film Festival, 2001—02. Co-author: (book) Montezuma: The Castle in the West, 2002. Bd. dirs., constrn. vol. Morris County Habitat for Humanity, NJ, 1990—91; ESL instr. Literacy Volunteers of Am., Santa Fe, 1992—93; mentor Bechtel Nev., 2001—. Avocations: hiking, films, writing children's books, music. Personal E-mail: utzutzutz@aol.com.

UTZ, SARAH WINIFRED, nursing educator; b. San Diego; d. Frederick R. and Margaret M. (Gibbons) U.; BS, U. Portland, 1943, EdM, 1958; MS, UCLA, 1970; PhD, U. So. Calif., 1979. Clin. instr. Providence Sch. Nursing, Portland, Oreg., 1946-50, edn. dir., 1950-62; edn. dir. Sacred Heart Sch. Nursing, Eugene, Oreg., 1963-67; asst. prof. nursing Calif. State U., L.A., 1969-74, assoc. prof., 1974-81, prof., 1981—, assoc. chmn. dept. nursing, 1982—; cons. in nursing curriculum, 1978—; healthcare cons., 1991—; past chmn. ednl. adminstrs., cons., tchrs. sect. Oreg. Nurses Assn., past pres. Oreg. State Bd. Nursing; mem. rsch. program Western Interstate Commn. on Higher Edn. in Nursing; chmn. liaison com. nursing edn. Articulation Coun. Calif. Author articles and lab manuals. Served with Nurse Corps, USN, 1944-46. HEW grantee, 1970-74, Kellogg Found. grantee, 1974-76, USDHHS grantee, 1987—; R.N., Calif., Oreg. Mem. Am. Nurses Assn., Calif. Nurses Assn. (edn. commr. region 6 1987—, chair edn. interest group region 6, 1987—), Am. Ednl. Rsch. Assn., AAUP, Phi Delta Kappa, Sigma Theta Tau. Formerly editor Oreg. Nurse; reviewer Western Jour. Nursing Rsch. Home: 1409 Midvale Ave Los Angeles CA 90024-5454 Office: 5151 State University Dr Los Angeles CA 90032-4226

UVA, SHELLEY ANNE, not-for-profit fundraiser, writer; b. Bklyn., July 7, 1950; d. Jack and Isabel Abramowitz; m. Kenneth Joseph Uva, May 4, 1975; children: Diana Vincenza, Katharine Elizabeth. BA, Boston U., 1972; MA, NYU, 1974. Editl. asst. The New Yorker, N.Y.C., 1972—73; writer, editor East Side Courier, N.Y.C., 1975—77, Am. Jour. of Nursing, N.Y.C., 1978—79; grantwriter NYU, N.Y.C., 1979—82, dir. prospect rsch., 1982—83; fundraising cons. N.Y.C., 1984—2001; dir. of devel. FIND Aid for the Aged (Project FIND), N.Y.C., 2001—. Author: (history textbook) The United States in the Making, 1979, rev., 1986, (short stories) Lost and Found, 1997. Democrat. Jewish. Avocations: reading, movies, theater. Personal E-mail: shelu@aol.com. E-mail: suva@projectfind.org.

UZDILLA, LAURA ANGELINE, radiation oncology technician, researcher; b. Wilkes-Barre, Pa., Nov. 29, 1977; d. Benjamin Charles Uzdilla and Angela Marie Thompson. BS Genetic Engring. magna cum laude, Cedar Crest Coll., Allentown, Pa., 2000. Rsch. technician radiation oncology dept. U. of Md., Balt., 2000—03. Named Best Jr. Handler, English Setter Nat. Soc., 1994. Mem.: English Setter Assn. Am., Northestern Md. Kennel Club, Alpha Mu Gamma, Tri Beta (sec. 1999—2000). Democrat. Roman Catholic. Avocations: dog handler/trainer, dog breeder of English setters, swimming. Home: Apt 4 501 Eastview Ter Abingdon MD 21009

UZMAN, BETTY BEN GEREN, pathologist, retired educator; b. Fort Smith, Ark., Nov. 17, 1922; d. Benton Asbury and Myra Estelle (Petty) Geren; m. L. Lahut Uzman, Dec. 17, 1955 (dec.); 1 dau., Betty Tuba. Student, Fort Smith Jr. Coll., 1939-40; BS, U. Ark., 1942; MD, Washington U., 1945; postgrad., M.I.T., 1948-50; MA (hon.), Harvard U., 1967. Intern Childrens Hosp., Boston, 1945-46; resident in pathology Barnes Hosp., St. Louis, 1946-48; Am. Cancer Soc. research fellow MIT, Cambridge, Mass., 1948-50; chief biol. ultrastructure and exptl. pathology Children's Cancer Research Found., Boston, 1950-71; instr. Harvard Med. Sch., Boston, 1949-53, assoc., 1953-56, research assoc., 1956-67, assoc. prof., 1967-71, prof., 1971-72; head research dept. Sparks Regional Med. Center, Fort Smith, 1972-74; prof. pathology La. State U., Shreveport, 1974-77, U. Tenn., Memphis, 1978-89. Assoc. chief staff rsch. VA, Shreveport, 1974-77; staff pathologist VA, Memphis, 1978-89, chief lab. svc., 1986-87; chief field ops., spl. asst. to dir. VA Central Office, Washington, 1978-79, dir. med. rsch. svcs., 1979-80; chmn. pathology A Study sect. NIH, 1973-76; cons. to sci. dir. Children's Cancer Rsch. Found., Boston, 1971-73; mem. adv. com. on prevention, diagnosis and treatment Am. Cancer Soc., 1970-73, 77-80; mem. adv. bd. Office Regeneration Rsch., VA, 1985-89; disting. vis. investigator Inst. Venezolano Investigation Cientificas, Caracas, 1972-74 Decorated Order of Andres Bello 1st class Venezuela; recipient Weinstein award United Cerebral Palsy, 1964; Am. Cancer Soc. research fellow, 1948-50 Mem. AAAS (emerita), Am. Soc. Cell Biology, Soc. Devel. Biology, Am. Acad. Neurology (assoc.), Am. Soc. Neurochemistry, Microscopy Soc. Am. (Diatome poster award 1985), Internat. Acad. Pathology, Am. Assn. Neuropathology (assoc.), Soc. Neurosci., Am. Assn. Cancer Rsch. Home and Office: Geren Farm 16048 E State Highway 197 Scranton AR 72863-0048 E-mail: bguzman@aol.com.

UZZELL-BAGGETT, KARON LYNETTE, career officer; b. Goldsboro, N.C., Apr. 28, 1964; d. Jesse Lee and Ernestine Smith Uzzell; m. Ronald Walter Baggett, July 26, 1990; 1 child, Kathleen; stepchildren: Christina, Brian, Adam. BS, U. N.C., 1986; postgrad., U. Md., 1993-96. Commd. 2nd lt. USAF, 1986, advanced through grades to lt. col., 1990, exec. officer 6ACCS, 1986-88, ops. tng. officer 7393MUNSS Murted AFD, Turkey, 1988-89, command and control officer 52FW Spangdahlem AB, Germany, 1989-92, SENEX mission dir. 89AW Andrews AFB, Md., 1992-95, dep. chief classified control Office Sec. Def., 1995-97, chief classified control Office Sec. Def., 1998-99, flight comdr., dir. ops. 82TRSS Sheppard AFB, Tex., 1999-2001; detachment comdr. USAFE MSS, Vicenza, Italy, 2001—02; comdr. 78MSS, Robins AFB, Ga., 2002—04, 416EMSS, Karshi-Khanabad, Uzbekistan, 2003—04. Emergency med. technician Orange County Rescue Squad, Hillsborough, N.C., 1985-86; treas. Melwood PTA, Upper Marlboro, Md., 1994-97; meml. vol. Women in Mil. Svc., Washington, 1993—; entitlements vol. Whitman Walker Clinic, Washington, 1993-98. Mem. Women in Mil. Svc. for Am., So. Poverty Law Ctr. Democrat. Baptist. Avocations: running, weightlifting, sewing, cross stitching, gardening. Home: 121 Spring Chase Cir Kathleen GA 31047

VACCARIELLO, CAROL POLIZZI, b. Cleveland, Ohio, Nov. 02; d. Raymond Joseph Polizzi and Frances Mary Samartano; m. Frank Joseph Vaccariello, Dec. 31, 1985. D of ministry, Ecumenical Theol. Sem., 1989—92. Lic. Profl. Counselor State of Mich., 1992. Sr. min. and bridge builder First Christian Ch., El Paso, Tex., 1999—2001; cert. programs, co-dir. U. of Creation Spirituality, Oakland, Calif., 2001—. Sr. min. and spiritual companion North Oakland Christian Ch., Orion, Mich., 1991—99. Internat. gen. bd. Christian Ch., Disciples of Christ, Indpls., 1988—92. Mem.: ACA (assoc.). Office: University of Creation Spirituality 2141 Broadway Oakland CA 94612 E-mail: carol.vacc@csnet.org.

VACCARO, ANNETTE ANDRÉA, music educator; b. Port Chester, N.Y., June 12, 1957; BS in Music Edn., Mercy Coll., 1980; cert. in Tchg., Manhattanville Coll., 1980; MS in Music Edn., We. Conn. State U., 1984; PhD in Adminstrn. and Supervision, Fordham U., 1990. Music tchr. Lakeland Ctrl. Schs., Shrub Oak, NY, 1980—, theatre dir., 1980—. Adj. prof. Mercy Coll., Yorktown Heights, NY, 1993—95; advisor Wig 'n' Whiskers Drama Club Lakeland HS, Shrub Oak, 1986—, mem. AIDS Awareness Com., 1990—93; guest condr. Dutchess County (N.Y.) Music Festival, 1991; adminstrn. mentoring com. Lakeland Sch. Dist., Shrub Oak, 2002—. Named Alumni of Yr., Lakeland (N.Y.) Edn. Found., 1999, Tchr. of Yr., Walmart Corp., 2001; recipient Nat. Theatre award, BRAVO Channel, 1999, Am. Tchr. award, The Walt Disney Corp., 2001; grantee, Lakeland (N.Y.) Edn. Found., 1999. Home: 129 Fields Lane Peekskill NY 10566 Office: Lakeland High School 1349E Main St Shrub Oak NY 10588

VACCARO, BRENDA, actress; b. Bklyn., Nov. 18, 1939; d. Mario and Christine (Pavia) V. Student, Neighborhood Playhouse, 1958-60. Appeared in Broadway plays: Everybody Loves Opal, 1961, The Affair, 1962, Tunnel of Love, 1962, Children from Their Games, 1963, Cactus Flower, 1965 (Tony award best supporting actress), The Natural Look, 1967, How Now Dow Jones, 1968 (Tony nomination best actress in mus. comedy), The Goodbye People, 1968 (Tony nomination for best actress in drama), Father's Day, 1971, California Suite with Neil Simon, The Odd Couple, 1985 with Sally Struthers, Jake's Women, 1992 with Alan Alda-A Neil Simon Play, Full Gallop (one woman show), 1998; motion pictures include: House by the Lake, 1977, Midnite Cowboy, 1969, Where It's At, 1969, I Love My Wife, 1970, Summer Tree, 1971, Going Home, 1971, Once Is Not Enough, 1975, Airport '77, 1977, Fast Charlie, 1977, Capricorn One, 1978, First Deadly Sin, 1980, Zorro, The Gay Blade, Supergirl, 1984, Water, 1986, Heart of Midnight, 1988, Cookie, 1988, Ten Little Indians, 1988, Masque of the Red Death, 1989, Love Affair, 1994, The Mirror Has Two Faces, 1996; TV appearances in The Greatest Show on Earth, 1963, Fugitive, 1963, Defenders, 1965, Doctors and Nurses, 1965, Coronet Blue, 1967, Naked City, The FBI, 1969, The Psychiatrist, 1971, Name of the Game, 1971, Marcus Welby, M.D, 1972, Banacek, 1972, McCloud, 1972, McCoy, Streets of San Francisco, Sara, 1976 (Emmy nomination for best dramatic actress), Paper Dolls, Dear Detective, 1979, The Pride of Jesse Hallam, 1980, A Long Way Home, 1981, Star Maker, 1981, Deceptions, 1985, St. Elsewhere, Murder She Wrote, 1990, Trials of Rosie O'Neil, 1991, Civil Wars, 1991, Flesh and Blood, 1991, The King of Queens, 1998, Ally McBeal, 1998, Friends, 1996; TV movie appearances in Travis Logan, D.A, 1971, What's A Nice Girl Like You, 1971, Honor Thy Father, 1973, Sunshine, 1973, The Big Ripoff, 1975, Julius and Ethel Rosenberg, 1978, Guyana Tragedy: The Story of Jim Jones, 1980, Paper Dolls, Dear Detective, 1989, Stolen: One Husband, Columbo, 1990, Once Is Not Enough (Academy award, Golden Globe award, People's Choice award), The Shape of Things (Emmy award for supporting actress), Golden Girls Ebbs Tide Revenge (Emmy award 1991), Red Shoe Diaries, 1991, Following Her Heart, 1994, Sing Me the Blues Lena, 1995, Touched by an Angel, 1996, Stolen One Husband, 1997, Johnny Bravo Show (voice over series animation), 1993-2000, When Husbands Cheat, 1998, Fat Girl (voice over series animation), 2001. Recipient Theatre World award, 1961-62, 3 Tony nominations, 2 Hollywood Fgn. Press Assn. nominations.

VACCARO, JOANN, psychologist; b. Queens, Aug. 17, 1973; d. Gaspare and Stella Ricovero; m. Emanuele Vaccaro, Sept. 16, 2000; 1 child, Gino Antonio. BA in Psychology, NYU, 1994; MA in Clin. Psychology, Hofstra U., N.Y., 1996, PhD in Clin. Psychology, 2000. Behavioral cons. The Working Orgn. for Retarded Children, Inc., Lake Success, NY, 1996—; sch. psychologist Oceanside (N.Y.) Pub. Schs., 1999—. Behavioral cons. Applied Behavior Analysis After Sch. Program, Lake Success, NY, 2001—. Mem.: Assn. for Advancement of Behavior Therapy, Am. Psychol. Assn. Avocations: teaching dance, bicycling. Office: Oceanside Pub Schs Sch #3 2852 Fortesque Ave Oceanside NY E-mail: JoannVaccaro@aol.com.

VACHHER, SHEILA ANN, information systems consultant; b. Trenton, N.J., May 27, 1966; d. Prehlad Singh and Margaret Mary Vachher. BA magna cum laude, U. Mich., 1988; MBA, Tex. A&M U., 1993. Retirement accounts rep. Gt. Lakes Bancorp., Ann Arbor, Mich., 1988-89, 91; strategic planning and fin. analyst Ricoh Corp., West Caldwell, N.J., 1993-95, sys. analyst, 1995-96, sr. tech. planning and control analyst, 1996-97, sr. systems analyst, 1997; sr. cons. Ernst & Young, Vienna, Va., 1997-98; prin. computer programmer Litton PRC, McLean, Va., 1998; cons. RCM Techs., Bethesda, Md., 1998-99; sr. database engr. Acuent Inc. (formerly Kinetic Techs., Inc.), Vienna, Va., 1999—. Career ctr. adv. coun. Tex. A&M U., College Station, 1993. Mem. Young Adult Cmty., Washington, 1998—, comms. officer, 2000—01; mem. Young Adult Ministry Coun., Washington, 1999—2000; bd. dirs. Tiburon Homeowners Assn., 1998—2000, dir., 1999—2000. Recipient Regents Alumni scholarship, 1984, Women's Club of Plymouth scholarship, 1984, James B. Angell scholar U. Mich., 1986-87, Otto Graf scholarship U. Mich., 1987-88, Lechner fellowship Tex. A&M U., 1991-92, scholarship Tex. A&M U. Coll. Bus. Adminstrn., 1992, Washington Campus scholarship Tex. A&M U., 1992. Mem. NAFE, Tex. A&M Club of N.Y.C. (v.p. 1994-97), Nat. Capital Tex. A&M Club. Avocations: photography, travel, arts, computers, bicycling. Home: 20601 Twelve Oaks Way Ashburn VA 20147 Office: Acuent Inc 1964 Gallows Rd Ste 210 Vienna VA 22182-3814 Business E-Mail: svachher@acuent.com.

VADER-MCCORMICK, NANCY JANE, humanities educator; b. Bay City, Mich., Feb. 2, 1955; d. Donald Neil and Jennie Lou Vader; m. John William McCormick, June 21, 1986; 1 child, Megan Rose. BS, We. Mich. U., 1976; MA, Ctrl. Mich. U., 1980; PhD, U. Fla., 1985. Asst. dean Delta Coll., Univ. Ctr., Mich., 1976—89, instr., 1989—90; adj. prof. Saginaw (Mich.) Valley State U., 1990—96; assoc. prof. Delta Coll., 1996—. Trainer Mich. Judicial Inst., 1990—2003; cons. Consumers Energy, Mich., 1989—, MV & Macnlow Assocs., Mich., 1989—2000. Author: Baby Doll and Friends, 1990, Creativity: From the Inside Out, 2002, Academic Service-Learning Handbook, 2003. Vol. Bay City (Mich.) Pub. Schs., 1993—, Am. Cancer Soc., Bay City, 1993—. Mem.: C.C. Humanities Assn., Nat. Comm. Assn., Phi Delta Kappa (pres. 1986—87). Avocations: running, writing, poetry, photography, travel. Home: 4718 Maplewood Drive Bay City MI 48706 Office Phone: 989-686-9458.

VADUS, GLORIA A. scientific document examiner; b. Forrestville, Pa. Diploma, Cole Sch. Graphology, Calif., 1978; BA in Psychology Counseling, Columbia Pacific U., 1981, MA in Psychology, 1982; diploma handwriting expert, Edith Eisenberg, Bethesda, Md., 1991. Diplomate Am. Bd. Forensic Examiners; cert. Am. Acad. Graphology, Washington, 1978, ct. qualified document examiner, registered graphologist 1978, cert. behavioral profiling and cert. questioned documents Am. Bd. Forensic Examiners. Pres., owner Graphinc, Inc., 1985—. Accredited instr. graphology Montgomery County Schs., Md., 1978—79; instr. Psychogram Centre, 1978—85, Coun. Graphol. Socs., 1980; testifier superior and probate cts.;

pub. forum panelist, lectr., rschr., script therapist pers. selection specialist; writer in field; cons. graphologist; developed Trilogy base for rsch. Am. Handwriting Analysis Found. Author: numerous studies and papers in field, also environ. papers. Chmn. Letter of Hope for POWs; vol. Montgomery County, 1987—88; bd. dirs., cmty. affairs chair East Gate I Civic Assn., Potomac, Md., 1985—87. Named one of 500 Leaders World Influence; recipient Spl. award, US/Japan Marine Facilities Panel Valuable Contbr. Japanese Panel UJNR/MFP, 1978—94, Gold Nib Analyst of Yr. award, Am. Handwriting Analysis Fedn., 1982, Dancing Fan award, Marine Tech. Soc., Tokyo chpt., 1991, Profound Contbr. to Soc. to the Yr., 2000, Internat. Peace prize, United Cultural Conv. of USA, 2003, Am. Bronze medal of Honor, 2001. Fellow: Am. Bd. Forensic Examiners (life; awards chair 1993—94, Meritorious award 1994, Outstanding Contbn. cert.); mem.: Coun. Graphical Socs. (bd. dirs. 1982—84), Soc. Francaise de Graphologie for Am. Handwriting Analysis Found., Nat. Assn Document Examiners (bd. dirs. 1985—92, ethics hearing bd. 1986, chmn. nominations com. 1987—88, elections chmn. 1988, parliamentarian 1988—92), Nat. Forensic Ctr., Am. Handwriting Analysis Found. (life; chmn. rsch. com., chmn. adv. bd. 1981—87, bd. dirs. 1981—91, pres. 1982—84, chmn. nominations com. 1985—86, officiator 1986, policy planning and ethics com. 1986—91, ethics chmn. 1989—91, chmn., past pres. adv. bd. 1989—91, hon. profl. women's adv. bd. 1999, cert.), Nature Conservancy, Charles F. Menninger Soc., IEEE-Distaff (internat. chmn. bd. dirs. 1969—72, fashion show chair 1969—72), Internat. Platform Assn., Nat. Wildlife Fedn., Nat. Capitol Jaguar Owners Club (judge 1975—78), Sierra Club, Henry Hicks Garden Club of the Westburys, N.Y. (v.p., pres. elect, judge, chair flower shows, bd. dirs. 1967—71), Soroptimist Internat. (internat. chair, v.p., Bethesda chpt. Montgomery County, bd. dirs. 1987—92), Nat. Writers Club. Home: 8500 Timber Hill Ln Potomac MD 20854-4237

VAHLE, LAURA MILES, marriage and family therapist, educator; b. NYC, June 10, 1953; d. William Herbert Miles and Carmen Helena Dell'Orefice; m. Robert Thomas Vahle, Aug. 1988 (div. Sept. 1998). BA in Sociology, U. Calif., LA, 1983; MS in Counseling, Calif. State U., Northridge, 1991. Lic. marriage & family therapist Bd. Behaviorial Sci., Calif., 1998, cert. rape crisis counselor. Consumer svc. coord. Regional Ctr. for Developmentally Disabled, Lancaster, Calif., 1995—98; lic. assessor San Fernando Valley Cmty. Mental Health Ctr., Palmdale, Calif., 2001—. Instr. Antelope Valley Coll., Lancaster, Calif., 2002—03. Contbr. articles to profl. jours.; author: (poem) Stars Twinkle. Mem.: Allied Arts (mentor 2003). Democrat. Episcopalian. Avocations: drawing, sculpting, quilting. Home: 44550 15th St E Unit 1 Lancaster CA 93535 Office: Cmty Svc Assessment Ctr San Fernando Vally Cmty Mental Health 2151 E Palmdale Blvd Ste B Palmdale CA 93550 also: Allied Arts Cedar Ctr 11857 Cedar St Ste 5 Lancaster CA 93534 Office Phone: 661-940-1289.

VAHRADIAN, MELINDA, fine artist; b. Ridgecrest, Calif., Nov. 20, 1956; d. Judson Calkins and Susan Frances (Huffaker) Smith; m. Scott Kendall Vahradian, July 11, 1987; children: Daniel Judson, Michael Joseph, Dylan Robert. BS in Social Ecology, U. Calif., Irvine, 1978. Cert. tchr. multiple subjects, cert. learning handicapped specialist, Calif. Learning handicapped specialist San Lorenzo Valley Unified Sch. Dist., Felton, Calif., 1984-91; artist, owner Not So Still Lifes, Santa Cruz, Calif., 1996—. Bd. dirs., leader Nursing Mothers Coun., Santa Cruz, 1990-99; leader Diabetes Support Group, Santa Cruz, 1999, participant [illegible] Cultural Coun., 1999-2003. Democrat.

VAIL, ELIZABETH FORBUS, volunteer; b. July 25, 1918; d. Sample Bouvard and Elizabeth J. (Buchtenkirk) Forbus; children: Judith Ashforth, Suzanne E. Vail Lander. Student, jr. coll., Washington, 1937—39. Copywriter, asst. to Pres. Kastor Chesley, Clifford & Atherton, Inc., N.Y.C.; 1st female airport mgr. Lebanon (N.H.) Airport, 1972. Mem. tourism and devel. com. Marathon (Fla.) City Coun., apptd. to City Code Enforcement Bd., apptd. to Marathon Aviation com.; vol. Monroe County Hurricane Ctr.; former mem. Monroe County Tourist Devel. Coun.; vol. Literacy Vols. of Am. Mem.: LWV, Am. Assn. Airport Execs., Internat. Platform Assn., Friends of Marathon Libr., Marathon Yacht Club. Avocation: reading. Home: 61 Sombrero Beach Rd Marathon FL 33050

VAIL, IRIS JENNINGS, civic worker; b. N.Y.C., July 2, 1928; d. Lawrence K. and Beatrice (Black) Jennings; grad. Miss Porters Sch., Farmington, Conn.; m. Thomas V.H. Vail, Sept. 15, 1951; children: Siri J., Thomas V.H. Jr., Lawrence J.W. Mem. exec. com. Garden Club Cleve., 1962—83; mem. women's coun. Western Res. Hist. Soc., 1960—, Cleve. Mus. Art, 1953—. Chmn. Childrens Garden Fair, 1966-75, Public Square Dinner, 1975; bd. dirs. Garden Center Greater Cleve., 1963-77; trustee Cleve. Zool. Soc., 1971-98, life trustee 1998—; mem. Ohio Arts Coun., 1974-76, pub. sq. com. Greater Cleve. Growth Assn., 1976-93, pub. sq. preservation and maintenance com. Cleve. Found., 1989-93, chmn. pub. sq. planting com., 1993. Hon. trustee Cleve. Bot. Garden, 2001. Recipient Amy Angell Collier Montague medal Garden Club Am., 1976, Ohio Gov.'s award, 1977. Mem. Chagrin Valley Hunt Club, Cypress Point Club, Kirtland Country Club, Colony Club, Women's City of Cleve. Club (Margaret A. Ireland award). Home: 14950 County Line Rd Chagrin Falls OH 44022-6800

VAINSCHTEIN, ARKADY, physics educator; b. Novokuznetsk, Russia, Feb. 24, 1942; MS in Physics, Novosibrisk U., 1964; Budker U., 1968. Prof. physics Novosibirsk, 1983-89; dir. theoretical physics inst. U. Minn., 1993-96, mem. theoretical physics inst., 1990—, Gloria Lubkin prof. physics, 1990—. Vis. prof. U. Minn., 1989-90. Mem. Am. Phys. Soc. Office: U Minn Sch Physics & Astronomy 116 Church St SE Minneapolis MN 55455-0149

VAITUKAITIS, JUDITH LOUISE, medical research administrator; b. Hartford, Conn., Aug. 29, 1940; d. Albert George and Julia Joan (Vaznikaitis) V. BS, Tufts U., 1962; MD, Boston U., 1966. Investigator, med. officer reproductive rsch. Nat. Inst. Child Health and Human Devel., NIH, Bethesda, Md., 1971-74; assoc. dir. clin. rsch. Nat. Ctr. Rsch. Resources NIH, Bethesda, Md., 1986-91, dir. gen. clin. rsch. ctr., 1986-91, dep. dir. extramural rsch., 1991, acting dir., 1991-92, dir., 1993—; from assoc. prof. to prof. medicine Sch. Medicine Boston U., 1974-86, assoc. prof. physiology, 1975-80, assoc. prof. ob-gyn., 1977-80, program. dir. gen. clin. rsch. ctr., 1977-86, prof. physiology, 1980-86; head sect. endocrinology and metabolism Boston City Hosp., 1974-86. Mem. internat. sci. adv. bd. Wellcome Trust-UIC. Author: Clinical Reproductive Neuroendocrinology, 1982; mem. edtl. bd. Jour. Clin. Endocrin. and Metabolism, 1973-80, Proc. Soc. Exptl. Biol. and Medicine, 1978-87, Endocrine Rsch., 1984-88; contbr. articles to profl. jours. Chair rev. com. Nat. Space Biomedical Rsch. Inst. Strategic Rsch. Plan Office of Biol. and Phys. Rsch., NASA, Washington, 2002; mem. NIH Stem Cell Task Force, 2002. Recipient Disting. Alumna award Sch. Medicine, Boston U., 1983, Mallincrodt award for Inv. Rsch. Clin. Radiossay Soc., 1980, Alumni award Boston U., 2003; named to Nat. Inst. for Child Health and Human Devel. Hall of Honor, 2003. Mem. Am. Fedn. Clin. Rsch., Endocrine Soc., Am. Soc. Clin. Rsch., Inst. Medicine-NAS. Office: Nat Ctr Rsch Resources NIH 31 B Center Dr MSc 2128 Bldg 31 Rm 3B11 Bethesda MD 20892-0001 E-mail: vaitukai@mail.nih.gov.

VALAKIS, M. LOIS, retired elementary school educator; b. Phila., Jan. 25, 1939; d. John Demosthenes and Blanche Antoinette Marquis Valakis. BS in Edn., Framingham (Mass.) State Tchrs. Coll., 1959. Elem. edn. tchr. Town of Framingham, 1959—98. Mem. ESEA Title III project, Framingham, 1969—70. Avocations: reading, music, photography. Home: 2 Concord Ter Framingham MA 01702

VALDÉS, KAREN W. art gallery director, educator; b. L.A., May 25, 1945; d. Richard Victor and Eleanor M. (Tomte) V.; m. Thomas E. Schwarz, Oct. 14, 1989. BFA, U. Calif., Irvine, 1968; MFA, Fla. State U., 1974. Dir. cultural events Fla. State U., Tallahassee, 1973-75; curator exhbn. Art Mus. So. Tex., Corpus Christi, 1975-76; assoc. prof., dir. gallery Miami (Fla.)-Dade Community Coll., 1976-84; dir. Gloria Luria Gallery, Miami, 1985; curator exhbn. Mus. Art, Ft. Lauderdale, Fla., 1985-89; assoc. prof., dir. univ. galleries U. Fla., Gainesville, 1989-95; gallery curator Arts Ctr. Galleries, Okaloosa-Walton C.C., Niceville, Fla., 1995—. Panelist NEA, Ft. Lauderdale, 1978-80, Dade County Art in Pub. Places, Miami, 1980-83, GSA Commn., 1982, Arts in State Bldgs., Gainesville, 1989—. Mem. Am. Assn. Mus., Coll. Art Assn., U. Fla. Hispanic Faculty Assn. Democrat. Avocation: sailing. Office: Arts Ctr Galleries Okaloosa-Walton CC 100 College Blvd E Niceville FL 32578-1347

VALDEZ, DENISE, newscaster; BA in TV broadcasting, Pepperdine U. Reporter KMIR-TV, Palm Springs, 1992; weekend anchor, reporter KCCN-TV, Monterey, Calif., 1992—93; co-anchor, reporter KSAT-TV, San Antonio, 1994—2001; weekend anchor, reporter KXAS-TV (NBC), Dallas/Ft. Worth, 2001—02; co-anchor, Channel 4 News with Furnell Chatman NBC4, Los Angeles, 2002—, interim co-anchor, Today in LA. Mem.: Nat. Assn. of Hispanic Journalists. Office: NBC 4 3000 W Alameda Ave Burbank CA 91523*

VALDEZ, DIANNA MARIE, language educator, consultant; b. Santa Fe, N.Mex., July 13, 1949; d. Delfino Julian and Margaret Erlinda Valdez. BSc, U. N.Mex., 1971, MA, 1981. Cert. Reading Tchr. N.Mex., 76, English as Second Lang. & Bilingual Tchr. N.Mex., 96. From classroom tchr. to instl. coach Albuquerque Pub. Sch., Albuquerque, 1971—2002, instl. coach, 2002—. Adj. instr. Lesley Coll., Cambridge, Mass., 1986—90; writing cons. San Felipe Elem. Sch., San Felipe Pueblo, N.Mex., 1998. Author, editor: Curriculum Integration Guide, 1984. Mem. ctrl. coord. coun. Title I Homeless Project, Albuquerque, 1998—2001; active supporter All Faith's Receiving Home, Albuquerque, 1995—2001. Recipient Achievement award, Theta State, 2001. Fellow: Nat. Writing Project-Rio Grande; mem.: Internat. Reading Assn. (pres. Camino Real coun. 1999—2000, Mem. of Yr. award 2001), Delta Kappa Gamma (state 1st v.p. 1982—2002, State Achievement award 2001). Republican. Roman Catholic. Avocations: needlecrafts, reading, writing, multimedia technology, trout fishing. Home: PO Box 1071 Corrales NM 87048 Office: Albuquerque Pub Schs Griegos Elem 4040 San Isidro NW Albuquerque NM 87107

VALDEZ, WANDA DANIEL, county official; b. Yuma, Ariz., May 11, 1950; d. Jose Pedro and Gloria Diaz (Otero) D.; m. Joe R. Valdez, June 26, 1976 (div. Nov. 1999); children: Kevin Lance, Kimberly Jo. Student, Pima Coll., 1978-96, Pepperdine U., Irvine, Calif, 1976-78. Office mgr. James K. Wilson Produce Co., Nogales, Ariz., 1977-96; chief dep. treas. Santa Cruz County, Nogales, 1997—. Alderwoman City of Nogales, 1996—, city councilwoman, 1997-2000, sec.-treas. Dem. Party, Nogales, 1990-96, vice chair 1999; PTC pres. A.J. Mitchell Sch., 1986-90, Little Red Sch., 1991-96, Lourdes H.S., 1993-94. Mem. Am. Bus. Women's Assn. (sec. 1992-95). Roman Catholic. Home: 668 W Noon St Nogales AZ 85621-2550 Office: Santa Cruz County Treasurers 2150 N Congress Dr Nogales AZ 85621

[illegible], DEBORAH, communications executive; m. Scott Snelgrove; 1 child, Helen Snelgrove. BA Journalism, The George Wash. U. Exec. dir. SASS Comm., GWU, Washington, 1989—. Mktg. chair Am. Assn. of U. Administrators, Washington. Office: SASS Communications - GWU 2121 I Street NW Suite 102/3 Washington DC 20052

VALE, MARGO ROSE, physician; b. Balt., June 16, 1950; d. Henry and Pauline Esther (Koplow) Hausdorff; m. Michael Allen Vale, Aug. 22, 1971; children: Edward, Judith. BA magna cum laude, Brandeis U., 1971; MD, Albert Einstein Coll. Medicine, 1975. Diplomate Am. Bd. Dermatology. Resident in internal medicine and dermatology NYU, N.Y.C., 1975-79, Bellevue Hosp., N.Y.C., 1975-79, VA Hosp., N.Y.C., 1975-79; staff physician HIP Greater N.Y., Bay Shore, 1979-81; pvt. practice medicine Huntington, N.Y., 1981—. Cons. in dermatology Huntington Hosp., 1981—, Gurwin Jewish Geriatric Ctr., Commack, N.Y., 1990—. Contbr. articles to profl. jours. Mem. Am. Acad. Dermatology, Med. Soc. State N.Y., Long Island Dermatology Soc., Suffolk County Med. Soc., Suffolk Dermatology Soc. (pres. 1990-92), Phi Beta Kappa. Avocations: cooking, photography, sketching, music. Office: 205 E Main St Huntington NY 11743-2923

VALEN, NANINE ELISABETH, psychotherapist, poet; b. N.Y.C., Nov. 7, 1950; d. Herbert and Felice Holman Valen; m. Gerald Charles Levinson, Nov. 17, 1971; children: Aaron Valen Levinson, Adam Valen Levinson. BA magna cum laude, Bryn Mawr Coll., 1971, MS, 1973, MSS, 1985. LCSW. Writer, producer Children's Television Workshop, N.Y.C., 1974—76; writer, prodr. KQED-TV, San Francisco, 1977; writer, producer WITF-TV, Harrisburg, Pa., 1981—82; child therapist Irving Schwartz Inst. Children and Youth, Phila., 1983—84; psychotherapist Pa. Friends Behavioral Health, 1996—, pvt. practice, Swarthmore, 1989—. Author: The Devil's Tail, 1978; co-author: The Drac: French Tales of Dragons and Demons, 1995, author of poems. Fellow, Va. Ctr. Creative Arts, 1978. Mem.: NASW, Greater Phila. Soc. Clin. Therapists. Avocations: singing, travel, hiking. Home and Office: 307 Maple Ave Swarthmore PA 19081

VALENCIA, MARGARITA, Spanish language educator; b. Bogotá, Colombia, Nov. 28, 1952; arrived in U.S., 1973; BA, MA in Polit. Sci., U. Calif., Santa Barbara. Profl. clear single subject tchg. credential in Spanish; cert. eligibility for Calif. prelim. adminstrv. svcs. credential. Tchr. Spanish Manual Arts H.S. L.A. Unified Sch. Dist., 1994—. Mem.: Acad. Polit. Sci. N.Y., L.A. World Affairs Coun., Sierra Club.

VALENCIA, MELANIE LAINE, music educator, performer; b. Oneonta, NY, Dec. 5, 1962; d. Jose Lardizabal and Marcell Jewell (Wiseman) V.; m. Frederick John Kelly, Mar. 18, 1990; children: Laine Valencia, Kelly, Frederick Alexander. Student, Ithaca Coll., 1981-85; BS in Music, Wells Coll., 1985; MFA, Carnegie Mellon U., 1988. Tchr. flute, staff mem. various music stores, Johnson City & N.Y.C., 1981—2002; conc. bookings and adminstrv. various non-profit agys., N.Y.C., 1988-94; flutist, founder Keeping Co. Ensemble, N.Y.C., 1989—2002; flutist, dir. Valencia Duo, N.Y.C. & Binghamton, 1993—; flutist, founder, dir. Contemporary Collaborative Ensemble, N.Y.C., 1993—; instr. toddler music class Vestal (N.Y.) Recreation Dept., 1995—2000; flutist Quintessence Woodwind Quintet, Binghamton, 1995—2000; piccoloist So. Tier Concert Band, Binghamton, 1995—2001; dir. elem. band Windsor (N.Y.) Sch. Dist., 1996—98; dir. small ensembles Binghamton H.S., 1998—2002; dir. West Mid. Sch. Bands and Ensembles Binghamton City Sch. Dist., 1998—. Mem. NEA, Nat. Flute Assn., N.Y. State United Tchrs., Broome County Music Educators Assn., N.Y. State Sch. Music Assn., N.Y. State Sch. Band Dirs. Assn., Internat. Assn. Jazz Educators, Am. Fedn. Tchrs., Music Educators Nat. Conf., Phi Beta Kappa. Avocations: cooking, travel, music collaborations, cross-country skiing, gardening. Home: 45 Lincoln Ave Binghamton NY 13905-4242 Office: West Mid Sch West Middle Ave Binghamton NY 13905-4242

VALENSTEIN, SUZANNE GEBHART, art historian; b. Balt., July 17, 1928; d. Jerome J. and Lonnie Cooper Gebhart; m. Murray A. Valenstein, Mar. 31, 1951. With dept. Asian Art Met. Mus. Art, N.Y.C., 1965—. Rsch. curator Asian Art. Author: Ming Porcelains: A Retrospective, 1970, A Handbook of Chinese Ceramics, 1975, rev. and enlarged, 1989, Highlights of Chinese Ceramics, 1975, (with others) Oriental Ceramics: The World's Great Collections: The Metropolitan Museum, 1977, rev., 1983, The Herzman Collection of Chinese Ceramics, 1992. Mem. Oriental Ceramic Soc. (London), Oriental Ceramic Soc. (Hong Kong). Office: Met Mus Art Dept Asian Art Fifth Ave at 82nd St New York NY 10028

VALENTI, BETTY JANET, resource specialist, educator; b. Detroit, Apr. 12, 1956; d. Beverly Rex and Mary Gracia (Nelson) McMinn; m. Nick Jonathon Valenti, Dec. 29, 1990; 1 child, Lindsay Elizabeth. Student, U. Calif., Irvine, 1985, credential resource specialist, 1991; BS in Spl. Edn., Ea. Mich. U., 1979. Specialisty physically handicapped Capistrano (Calif.) Unified Sch. Dist., 1980-90; spl. day tchr. Pasadena (Calif.) Unified Sch. Dist., 1990-91; resource specialist Kepple Union Sch. Dist., Pearblossom, Calif., 1991-92; early interventionist Palmdale (Calif.) Sch. Dist., 1996-97, resource specialist, 1994—. Parent cons. Nat. Parent to Parent Support and Info. Sys., Inc., Blue Ridge, Ga., Hemihypertrophy, Blue Ridge, 1996-97; spl. edn. rep. Sch. Site Coun.-Rep. Tumbleweed Sch., Palmdale, 1995-97; coord. Coordinated Compliance Rev., 1991-97. Educator specialist Coun. Adv. Com. for Spl. Edn. Antelope Valley Local Plan, Palmdale, 1996; Spl. Olympics coach Richard Henry Dana Sch., Dana Point, Calif., 1984, 85. Mem. AAUW, Calif. Assn. Resource Specialists, Nat. Parent to Parent Support and Info. Sys. Republican. Presbyterian. Avocations: drawing, reading, computer software research, swimming, traveling. Home: 5340 Allen Ct Palmdale CA 93551-1950

VALENTINE, CHERYL ANN WHITNEY, music educator; b. Newllton, La., June 25, 1956; d. Samuel Leon and Hazel Octavia (LeBlanc) Whitney; 1 child, Andante Latrese Valentine-Burton. BA, Va. Union U., 1981. Cert. tchr. Mich. Vocal music tchr. Detroit (Mich.) Pub. Schs., 1981—. Dir. music Sanctuary Fellowship Ch., Detroit, 1996—; validator Nat. Bd. Profl. Tchg. Stds., San Antonio, 2000—. Mem.: Detroit (Mich.) Assn. Negro Musicians, Am. Choral Dirs. Assn., Music Educators Nat. Conf., Mich. Vocal Music Assn. (dist. mgr. 2002—), Zeta Phi Beta. Democrat. Baptist. Home: 19453 Whitcomb Ave Detroit MI 48235 Office: Detroit High Sch Performing Arts 4333 Rosa Parks Blvd Detroit MI 48208 Office Phone: 313-494-2357 ext 251. Office Fax: 313-494-1506.

VALENTINE, DEBRA A. lawyer; b. Cleve., Apr. 16, 1953; AB magna cum laude in History, Princeton U., 1976; JD, Yale U. Law School, 1980. Bar: D.C., U.S. Dist. Ct. D.C., U.S. Ct. Appeals (D.C. Cir., 3d Cir., 11th Cir.), U.S. Supreme Ct. Law clk. Judge Arlin M. Adams, U.S. Ct. Appeals, 3d Cir., Phila., 1980-81; atty./advisor Office of Legal Counsel, Dept. of Justice, Washington, 1981-85; assoc. O'Melveny & Myers, Washington, 1985-91, ptnr., 1991-95; dep. dir. policy planning FTC, Washington, 1995-96, asst. dir. for internat. antitrust, 1996-97, gen. counsel, 1997-2001; ptnr., co-chair antitrust practice group O'Melveny & Myers, Washington, 2001—. Cons. Sec. of State's Adv. Com. South Africa. Bd. editors BNA Antitrust & Trade Regulation Reporter; contbr. articles to profl. jours. Adv. mem. bd. dirs. The Washington Ballet. Fulbright scholar, 1976-77. Mem. ABA, Internat. Bar Assn., Am. Law Inst., D.C. Bar, Coun. on Fgn. Rels., Phi Beta Kappa. Home: 2853 Ontario Rd NW Apt 605 Washington DC 20009-2246 Office: O'Melveny & Myers 1625 I St NW Washington DC 20006-4001 E-mail: dvalentine@omm.com.

VALENTINE, PHYLLIS LOUISE, counseling administrator; d. Harold Gray and Velma Eura Long; m. Samuel L. Valentine, Dec. 30, 1995. BA, St. Augustine's Coll., 1970; MEd, Bowie State U., 1992; student, Trinity Coll., 1974—77, Georgetown U., 1989, U. D.C., 1974—88. Cert. sch. counselor K-12, [illegible] Laton Reformatory Youth Ctr. II PSI Assocs., Washington, 1984—86; chpt. 1 reading/math. lab tchr. D.C. Pub. Schs., 1986—92, chpt. 1 resource asst., 1992—93; chpt. 1 CAI lab tchr./team coord. C.W. Harris Elem. Sch., Washington, 1992—95; sch. counselor J.C. Nalle Elem. Sch., Washington, 1995—. Mem. tchr. adv. bd. Ctr. for Artistry in Tchg., Washington, 1999—; dir., presenter J.C. Nalle Sch. Extended Day, 1998. V.p. Brandywine Sta. Townhouse Assn., Upper Marlboro, Md., 1990—97. Recipient Letter of Commendation, Exec. Dir. Chpt. 1 program, 1987, AIMs Pilot, Bryan Elem. Sch., 1984, HOST Corp., 1994, DCPS Parent Ctr. Incentive, 1997. Mem.: D.C. Sch. Counseling Assn., Am. Sch. Counseling Assn., Am. Counseling Assn., Tots & Teens Inc. (pres. 1985—93, corr. sec. 1985—93, youth leader 1987—91, D.C. chpt., award 1990—91), D.C. Counseling Assn. (pres.-elect 2001—02, pres. 2002, dedicated svc. plaque 1993), Phi Delta Kappa (mem. Beta chpt.), Nat. Sorority Phi Delta Kappa (Beta chpt.), Sigma Gamma Rho (recording sec., anti-basilus 1971—78). Avocations: gardening, listening to jazz music, dance. Business E-Mail: phyllis.valentine@k12.us.

VALERIO BARRAD, CATHERINE M. lawyer; BA, U. Calif., San Diego, 1982; MBA, UCLA, 1984; JD magna cum laude, Northwestern U., 1993. Ba: Calif. 1993, U.S. Ct. Appeals (9th cir.) 1994. Law clk. to Hon. Douglas H. Ginsburg, U.S. Dt. Appeals for D.C. Circuit, Washington, 1993-94; assoc. Sidley & Austin, L.A., 1994—. Contbg. author: Federal Appellate Practice Guide, Ninth Circuit, 1994; articles editor Northwestern U. Law Rev., 1992-93; contbr. articles to legal publs. Mem. Order of Coif. Office: Sidley & Austin 555 W 5th St Los Angeles CA 90013-1010 Fax: 213-896-6688. E-mail: cbarrad@sidley.com.

VALETTE, REBECCA MARIANNE, Romance languages educator; b. N.Y.C., Dec. 21, 1938; d. Gerhard and Ruth Adelgunde (Bischoff) Loose; m. Jean-Paul Valette, Aug. 6, 1959; children: Jean-Michel, Nathalie, Pierre. BA, Mt. Holyoke Coll., 1959, LHD (hon.), 1974; PhD, U. Colo., 1963. Instr., examiner in French and German U. So. Fla., 1961-63; instr. NATO Def. Coll., Paris, 1963-64, Wellesley Coll., 1964-65; asst. prof. Romance Langs. Boston Coll., 1965-68, assoc., 1968-73, prof., 1973—2003, prof. emeritus, 2003—. Lectr., cons. fgn. lang. pedagogy; Fulbright sr. lectr., Germany, 1974; Am. Coun. on Edn. fellow in acad. adminstrn., 1976-77. Author: Modern Language Testing, 1967, rev. edit., 1977, French for Mastery, 1975, rev. edit., 1988, Contacts, 1976, rev. edit., 1993, 97, 2001, C'est Comme Ça, 1978, rev. edit., 1986, Spanish for Mastery, 1980, rev. edit., 1989, 94, Album: Cuentos del Mundo Hispanico, 1984, rev. edit., 1992, French for Fluency, 1985, Situaciones, 1988, rev. edit., 1994, Discovering French, 1994, 97, 2001, A votre tour, 1995, Ventanas Uno, 1998, Images 1, 2, 3, 1999, Reflections on the Connolly Book of Hours, 1999, Weaving the Dance, 2000, Discovering French Nouveau, 2004; contbr. articles to fgn. lang. pedagogy and Native Am. art publs. Decorated officer Palmes Académiques, chevalier Ordre Nat. du Mérite (France). Mem. MLA (chmn. divsn. on tchg. of lang. 1980-81), Am. Coun. on Tchg. Fgn. Langs., Am. Assn. Tchrs. French (v.p. 1980-86, pres. 1992-94), Alliance Francaise of Boston and Cambridge (pres. 2002—), Phi Beta Kappa, Alpha Sigma Nu, Pi Delta Phi. Home: 16 Mount Alvernia Rd Chestnut Hill MA 02467-1019 Office: Boston Coll Lyons 304 Chestnut Hill MA 02467-3804 E-mail: valette@bc.edu.

VALETTI, LEOTA MAY, artist; b. St. Clair Shores, Mich., Oct. 14, 1926; d. Leo Clyde Williams and Jane Domenica Deldin; m. John Valetti (dec.); m. Earl Laws (div.); children: Eileen Joanne Cromer, Nancy Jane Laws. Grad. H.S., St. Clair Shores; grad., Famous Artists Schs., 1965. Avocations: art, piano, stamp collecting, writing, reading. Home: 21440 Lakebreeze Saint Clair Shores MI 48082

VALFRE, MICHELLE WILLIAMS, nursing educator, administrator, writer; b. Reno, Feb. 12, 1947; d. Robert James and Dolores Jane (Barnard) Williams; m. Adolph A. Valfre, Nov. 7, 1998. BSN, U. Nev., Reno, 1973; M Health Svc., U. Calif., Davis, 1977. RN, Oreg., Ariz. Staff nurse VA Hosp., Reno, 1973-77; family nurse practitioner Tri-County Indian Health Svc., Bishop, Calif., 1977-81; instr. nursing Rogue C.C., Grants Pass, Oreg., 1981-82; psychiat. nurse VA Hosp., Roseburg, Oreg., 1982; dir. edn. Josephine Meml. Hosp., Grants Pass, 1983-84; geriat. nurse practitioner Hearthstone Manor, Medford, Oreg., 1984-86; chmn. nursing dept. Roque

C.C., Grants Pass, Oreg., 1986-89, instr. social scis., 1997-98; prin. Health and Ednl. Cons. Inc., Dallas, Oreg., 1989—; DON Highland House Nursing Ctr., Grants Pass, 1990. Bd. dirs. Tri-County Indian Health Svc.; cons. for nursing svcs. in long-term care facilities. Author: Professional Skills for Leadership, Foundations of Mental Health Care, 2000, 3d edit., 2004; contbr. Fundamental Health Care Concepts and Skills. Mem. Josephine County Coalition for AIDS, Grants Pass, 1990. With USN, 1965-69. Mem. NAFE, Nat. League Nursing, Oreg. Ednl. Assn., Oreg. State Bd. Nursing (mem. re-entry nursing com. 1992-93). Office Phone: 503-831-2252. Personal E-mail: avalfre@mindspring.com.

VALLA, TERESSA MARIE, artist, textile designer; b. Lynchburg, Va., Nov. 23, 1957; d. James J. and Mary Theresa (Hopkins) V. BS, U. Vt., 1979; student, Studio Art Sch. Aegean, Samos, Greece, 1987, Art Students League, 1986-89, Vt. Studio Ctr., 1991. Vis. artist Carnegie Hall, N.Y.C., 1994; stage & prop designer Video-Pollack Meets Picasso, N.Y.C., 1993; artist in residence Prague (Czeck Republic) Painters Workshop, 1994, Graffiti Alternative-N.Y.C. Housing Authority 2000 Mural Project, Mural Painting Workshop, N.Y.C., 1997. Exhibitions include 80 Washington Square East Galleries, N.Y.C., 1990, Lincoln Ctr., N.Y.C., 1990, Glass Art Gallery, N.Y.C., 1991, Clocktower Gallery, N.Y.C., 1991, Home Contemporary Theater & Art, N.Y.C., 1991, Kampo Cultural Ctr., N.Y.C., 1991, Ape Gallery, N.Y.C., 1992, La Mama La Galleria, N.Y.C., 1992, Alleycat Gallery, N.Y.C., 1993, CBGB's 313 Gallery, N.Y.C., 1993, Tweed Gallery, 1993, Art Dirs. Club, N.Y.C., 1993, Gallery One Twenty Eight, N.Y.C., 1993, 99, Westbeth Gallery, N.Y.C., 1993-94, Artist Space, N.Y.C., 1993, Tompkins Sq. Pk., N.Y.C., 1994-95, World Fin. Ctr., N.Y.C., 1994, Palacio Pombal, Lisbon, Portugal, 1994, 450 B'way Gallery, N.Y.C., 1995, Tweed Gallery, N.Y.C., 1997, Soka gakkai Internat., N.Y.C., 1997, Traveling Exhbn., Germany, 1998, Dearte Magik, Pa., 1998, Provincetown (R.I.) Mus. and Art Assn., 1999, Atelier Colletivo in Olinda, Pernambuco, Brazil, 1999, Contemporary Mus., Balt., 2000, Mus. Modern Art, N.Y.C., 2002, Joy X-2 Gallery, Parallels, Pa., 2002, Gallery X, N.Y., 2002, Gallery K & S, Berlin, 2003, Sato Mus., Tokyo, 2003; permanent collections include Paterson (N.J.) Mus., Mid Hudson Arts & Sci. Ctr., Libr. of Congress, N.Y. Pub. Libr., New England Ctr. Contemporary Art, Brooklyn, Conn.; also pvt. collections. Vol. Earth Day, N.Y.C., 1994-95. Recipient Ezra Jack Keats Meml. award, 1988-89; grantee Art Students League, 1987-88, E.D. Found., 1994, 98, Mellon Found., 2001-02, N.Y. Found. for Arts/N.Y. Recovery Fund, 2002, Gottlieb Found Recovery Grant; Annenberg Challenge grantee, 2001-02. Mem. Women's Caucus Art, Orgn. Ind. Artists, Art Initiative. Home: 170 W 78th St Apt 2B New York NY 10024-6774

VALLBONA, RIMA-GRETEL ROTHE, foreign language educator, writer; b. San Jose, Costa Rica, Mar. 15, 1931; d. Ferdinand Hermann and Emilia (Strassburger) Rothe; m. Carlos Vallbona, Dec. 26, 1956; children: Rima-Nuri, Carlos-Fernando, Maria-Teresa, Maria-Luisa. BA/BS, Colegio Superior de Senoritas, San Jose, Costa Rica, 1948; diploma, U. Paris, 1953; diploma in Spanish Philology, U. Salamanca, Spain, 1954; MA, U. Costa Rica, 1962; D in Modern Langs., Middlebury Coll., 1981. Tchr. Liceo J.J. Vargas Calvo, Costa Rica, 1955-56; faculty U. St. Thomas, Houston, 1964-95, prof. Spanish, 1978-95, Cullen Found. prof. Spanish, 1989, head Spanish dept., 1966-71, chmn. dept. modern fgn. lang. 5, 1978-80, prof. emeritus, 1995—. Vis. prof. U. Houston, 1975-76, Rice U., 1974, 80-83, 95, U. St. Thomas, Argentina, 1972; vis. prof. U. St. Thomas, Merida program, 1987-95. Author: Noche en Vela, 1968, Yolanda Oreamuno, 1972, La Obra en Prosa de Eunice Odio, 1981, Baraja de Soledades, Las Sombras que Perseguimos, 1983, Polvo del Camino, 1972, La Salamandra Rosada, 1979, Mujeres y Agonias, 1982, Cosecha de Pecadores, 1988, El arcangel del perdon, 1990, Mundo, demonio y mujer, 1991, Los infiernos de la mujer y algo mas, 1992, (crit. edit.) Vida i sucesos de la Monja Alferez, 1992, Flowering Inferno-Tales of Sinking Hearts, 1994, La narrativa de Yolanda Oreamuno, 1996, Tormy, la Prodigiosa Gata de Donaldito, 1997, Tejedoras de sueños versus realidad, 2003; mem. (editl. bd.) Letras Femeninas, 1984—98, Alba de America, U.S., sec. (culture) Inst. Literario y Cultural Hispanico; co-dir.: Foro Literario, 1987—89; contbg. editor: The Americas Rev., 1989—95; contbr. numerous articles and short stories to lit. mags. Mem. scholarship com. Inst. Hispanic Culture, 1978, 79, 88, 91, chmn., 1979, bd. dirs., 1974-76, 88-89, 91-92, chmn. cultural activities, 1979, 80, 85, 88-89; bd. dirs. Houstoh Pub. Libr., 1984-86; bd. dirs. Cultural Arts Coun. Houston, 1991-92. Recipient Aquileo J. Echeverria Novel prize, 1968, Jorge Luis Borges Short Story prize, Argentina, 1977, Agripina Montes del Valle Novel prize, 1978, Constantin Found. grant for rsch., U. St. Thomas, 1981, Lit. award, S.W. Conf. Latin Am. Studies, 1982, Ancora Lit. award, Costa Rica, 1984, Civil Merit award, King Juan Carlos I of Spain, 1989, Children's Book award, Bay Area Writers League, 2003. Mem.: Nat. Writers Assn., Inst. Lit. y Cultural Hispanico, Casa Argentina de Houston, Inst. Hispanic Culture Houston, Latin Am. Writers Assn. Costa Rica, Inst. Internat. de Lit. Iberoam., Latin Am. Studies Assn., Academia Norteamericana de la Lengua Espanola (elected), S.W. Conf. Orgn. Latin Am Studies, South Ctrl. MLA, Houston Area Tchrs. Fgn. Lang., Houston Area Tchrs. Spanish and Portuguese, Am. Assn. Tchrs. Spanish and Portuguese, Sigma Delta Pi, Phi Sigma Iota. Roman Catholic. Home: 3706 Lake St Houston TX 77098-5522 E-mail: rvallbona@aol.com.

VALLEE, CATHERINE E. music educator; b. Troy, NY, Mar. 5, 1965; d. Robert Joseph and C. Earla Bills; m. David N. Vallee, May 14, 1988; children: Jennifer Margaret, Sean Robert, Samuel David, Jessica Lynn. MusB music edn., Coll. St. Rose, Albany, NY, 1983—87; MusM instrnl. tech., SUNY, Albany, NY, 1988—92. Cert. Music Tchr. NY, 1992. Mutuel clk. NY State Racing Assn., Saratoga Springs, NY, 1999—; music tchr. Cohoes City Sch. Dist., Cohoes, NY, 1987—. Band dir. marching, concert, jazz Cohoes City Sch. Dist., Cohoes, NY, 1987—; cheerleading coach Cohoes HS, Cohoes, NY, 1987—; music dept. coord. Cohoes City Sch. Dist., Cohoes, NY, 2002—; cub scout camp area dir. Boy Scouts of Am., Wakpominee, NY, 2003—. Mem.: Music Educator Nat. Conf. Roman Catholic. Home: 500 7th Avenue Watervliet NY 12189 Office: Cohoes City School District 7 Bevan Street Cohoes NY 12047

VALLEE, JUDITH DELANEY, environmentalist, writer, fundraiser; b. N.Y.C., Mar. 14, 1948; d. Victor and Sally Hammer; m. John Delaney, Apr. 9, 1974 (div. 1978); m. Henry Richard Vallee, May 15, 1987. BA, CUNY, 1976. Exec. dir. Save the Manatee Club, Maitland, Fla., 1985—. Apptd. U.S. Manatee Recovery Plan Team, Jacksonville, Fla., 1988-97, Fla. Manatee Tech. Adv. Coun., Tallahassee, 1989-2002, Save the Manatee Com., Orlando, Fla., 1985-92, World Conservation Union/Sirenia Specialist Group, Switzerland, 1996; advisor Save the Wildlife Inc., Chuluota, Fla., 1992-93; bd. dirs. Environ. Fund for Fla. Lobbyist Save the Manatee Club, 1989; vol. Broward County Audubon Soc., Ft. Lauderdale, 1983-84, Wild Bird Care Ctr., Ft. Lauderdale, 1984. Recipient Refuge Support award Chassahowitzka Nat. Wildlife Refuge, 1989. Democrat. Avocations: creative writing, antiques, wildlife observation, canoeing. Office: Save the Manatee Club Inc 500 N Maitland Ave Ste 210 Maitland FL 32751-4458 E-mail: jvallee@savethemanatee.org.

VALLES, JUDITH, mayor, former academic administrator; b. San Bernardino, Calif., Dec. 14, 1933; d. Gonzalo and Jovita (Lopez-Torices) V.; m. Chad Bradbury, Sept. 30, 1956 (dec. Sept. 1969); children: Edith Renella, Nohemi Renella, Chad; m. Harry Carl Smith, Oct. 13, 1985. BA in English, Redlands (Calif.) U., 1956; MA in Spanish Lit., U. Calif., Riverside, 1966; doctorate (hon.), U. Redlands, 2000. Instr. Spanish San Bernardino (Calif.) Valley Coll., 1963-84, head dept. fgn. lang., 1971-76, chair div. humanities, 1976-81, dean extended day, 1981-83, adminstrv. dean acad. affairs, 1983-87, exec. v.p. acad. and student affairs, 1987-88; pres. Golden West Coll., Huntington Beach, Calif., 1988—; mayor San Bernardino, 1998—. Mem. adv. com. Police Officers Standards and Tng. Commn., Sacramento, 1991—. Author fgn. lang. annals and sociol. abstracts. Speaker statewide edn. and community orgns., 1988—; bd. dirs. exec. coun. and chief exec. officers Calif. Community Colls., 1990—. Recipient Bishops award for diocese, Outstanding Pub. Svc. award NALEO, 2001; named One of Outstanding Women Orange County YWCA, 1990, Citizen of Achievement LWV, 1989, Woman of Distinction Bus. Press, 1998, Influential Latina of the Yr. Hispanic Lifestyle, 1998, State of Calif. Woman of the Yr., 1999, Humanitarian Yr. Cath. charities, 1999, Citizen Yr. Boy Scouts Am., 1999, Empire Woman Yr. State Assembly, 1999, Outstanding Cmty. Leader, Cmty. Found., 2002, Woman of Yr., State Senate, 2003; inducted into Hall of Fame, San Bernardino Valley Coll. Mem. Women's Roundtable Orange County, Conf. and Visitors Bur., C. of C. (Vanguard), Kiwanis, Charter 100. Avocations: opera, theater, reading, running. Office: Conf Mayors 300 N D St San Bernardino CA 92418-0001

VALLETTA, AMBER, model; b. Tulsa, Feb. 9, 1973; m. Hervé Le Bihan. With Boss Models, N.Y.C.; Elite Models, N.Y.C., 1996—. Office: Fl 2 300 Park Ave S New York NY 10010-5313

VALLIANOS, CAROLE WAGNER, lawyer; b. Phila., Aug. 19, 1946; d. F. Leonard Wagner and Helen Rose Pikunas; m. Peter Denis Vallianos, June 22, 1963; children: Kelly, Denis, Jamie Vallianos-Healy. BA, Calif. State U., Fullerton, 1981; JD, Southwestern U., 1995. Bar: Calif. 1997. Nonprofit cons., Manhattan Beach, Calif., 1982—; atty. in pvt. practice, 1997—. Non-profit cons. USIA, Turkey, 1997, Cyprus, 1997, Bosnia, 1998, India, 1999. Pres. LWV Calif., 1989—91; mem. com. on pvt. judging Calif. Jud. Coun., 1989—91, mem. com. on race and ethic bias in the cts., 1991—96, mem. com. on access and fairness in the cts., 1994—97, 2002—, mem. task force on jury sys. improvements, 1998—2003; mem. Women Lawyers L.A. Jail Project; mem. adv. bd. U. Fla. Marion Brechner Citizen Access Project, 2000—02; bd. dirs. LWV U.S., 1992—98, LWV Edn. Fund U.S., 1992—98, Harbor-UCLA Rsch. and Edn. Inst., 2002—, treas., 2003—. Mem. LWV Beach Cities (former pres.), Am. Judicature Soc. (bd. dirs. 1996—, exec. com. 2001—, sec. 2003), First Amendment Coalition Calif. (bd. dirs. 1995—), Coalition for Justice (v.p. 1993—), Pacific Coun. Internat. Policy, Benjamin Aranda Inn of Ct. (exec. com. 2002—). Avocations: travel, political memorabilia, literature.

VALVO, BARBARA-ANN, lawyer, surgeon; b. Elizabeth, N.J., June 7, 1949; d. Robert Richad and Vera (Kovach) V. BA in Biology, Hofsta U., 1971; MD, Pa. State U., 1975; JD, Loyola Sch. Law, 1993. Bar: La. 1993; diplomate Am. Bd. Surgery. Surg. intern Nassau County Med. Ctr., East Meadow, NY, 1975-76; resident gen. surgery Allentown (Pa.)-Sacred Heart Med. Ctr., 1976-80; asst. chief surgery USPHS, New Orleans, 1980-81; pvt. practice gen. surgery New Orleans, 1981-89; pvt. practice med. malpractice law, 1995—. Upjohn scholar, 1975. Fellow ACS; mem. ABA, Fed. Bar Assn., La. Bar Assn., La. Trial Lawyers Assn. Republican. Avocations: computers, raising animals. Office: 4130 Loire Dr Ste A Kenner LA 70065 Office Phone: 504-467-8762. E-mail: bavalvo@att.net.

VAN ALLEN, BARBARA MARTZ, marketing professional; d. Walter Atlee and Barbara Jean (Winebrenner) Martz; m. Peter Cushing Van Allen, Sept. 3, 1983; children: Caroline Kent, Peter Cushing Jr. BA with honors, U. N.C., 1976; MA, George Washington U., 1983; MBA, NYU, 1993. Legis. asst. U.S. Ho. of Reps., Washington, 1976-81, legis. dir., 1981-83; dir. ITT Corp., N.Y.C., 1984-90; pres. Van Allen Assocs., N.Y.C., 1990-93, 2000—; mng. dir. Cushman & Wakefield, Inc., N.Y.C., 1994-2000. Bd. dirs. Washington Nat. Cathedral Coll. Preachers, 2000—. Mem. N.Y.C. Jr. League, 1986—; mem. econ. devel. task force N.Y.C. Mayoral Campaign and Transition Team, 1994—95; bd. dirs. 801 West End Avenue Corp., N.Y.C., 1995—99. Recipient Star awards for print campaign and internal comm. Bus. Mktg. Assn., 1996, nat. pro-comm. profl. excellence award for radio, 1996, Pro Com. award, 1997, Impact award, 1998. Mem. NAFE, Internat. Assn. Bus. Communicators (Iris Merit award 1996, Ace Merit award 1996, Ace award of excellence for pub. 1997, Ace award of merit for Reporter's Handguide 1997, N.Y. Fest. award, BMA Pro Comm. award for Direct Mail: Soup to Nuts, 1998, APEX award for Real Estatements publ., 1998), Bus. and Profl. Women's Club, YWCA Acad. Women Achievers. Home: 4407 Hadfield Ln NW Washington DC 20007-2034

VAN ALLEN, VERONICA ELAINE, marketing and public relations professional; b. Jamaica, N.Y., May 6, 1936; d. William James and Florence Veronica (Lester) Van Allen; children: Veronica E. Davis, Valerie E. Boyd; m. Ian Helsby, July 4, 1998. BEd, U. Miami, 1963; cert., U.S. Chamber Inst. Orgn. Mgmt., Boulder, Colo., 1984-88. Cert. tchr., Fla. English, phys. edn. tchr. Dade County Sch. Sys., Miami, Fla., 1963-67; founder, coach girls' track team Acad. of the Holy Names, Tampa, Fla., 1972—74; exec. dir. Royal Palm Festival Inc., West Palm Beach, Fla., 1978-82; exec. v.p. No. Palm Beaches C. of C., Palm Beach Gardens, Fla., 1982-88; dir. mktg., pub. rels. Operation Explore, Palm Beach Gardens, Fla., 1993—. Exec. dir. World Trade Coun., 1983-86. Editor (newspaper supplement) Royal Palm Festival, 1978-82 (Advt. Club aw ard 1980), video pub., 1981 (Internat. Festival Assn. award 1981); editor (ann. chamber mag.) Guide to No. Palm Beaches, 1984-88, Air Show mag., 1987. Vice chmn. Tourist Devel. Coun. Palm Beach County, 1987, mem., 1983—88; vice chmn. Leadership Palm Beach County, 1985—86, bd. dirs., 1984—89; mem. mil. acad. screening com. Congressman Tom Lewis, Palm Beach Gardens, 1986—94; bd. dirs. Sun Fest, 1982—84; mem. Internat. Coun. Air Shows, 1981—86, Alumni Assn.LPBC, 1987—; coord. religious instrn. St. Paul of the Cross, North Palm Beach, Fla., 1977—80. Mem. U. Miami Alumni Assn., Internat. Festival Assn., Am. C. of C. Execs. Republican. Roman Catholic. Avocations: reading, snow skiing, theater, tennis, aerobics. Home: 170 Esperanza Way Palm Beach Gardens FL 33418

VAN ALSTYNE, JUDITH STURGES, retired language educator; b. Columbus, Ohio, June 9, 1934; d. Rexford Leland and Wilma Irene (Styan) Van Alstyne; m. Dan C. Duckham (div. 1964); children: Kenton Leland, Jeffrey Clarke. BA, Miami U., Oxford, Ohio, 1956; MEd, Fla. Atlantic U., 1967. Sr. prof. Broward CC, Ft. Lauderdale, Fla., 1967-88, spl. asst. women's affairs, 1972—88, dir. cmty. svcs., 1973—74, dir. cultural affairs, 1974—75; ret., 1988. Spkr., cons. Malaysian Coll., 1984; ednl. travel group tour guide, 1984—88; v.p., ptnr. Downtown Travel Ctr., Ft. Lauderdale, 1993—. Author: (book) Write It Right, 1980, Professional and Technical Writing Strategies, 6th edit., 2004; freelance writer travel articles: ; contbr. articles and poetry to profl. jours. Bd. dirs. Broward CC Found., Inc., Fla., 1973—2003, Broward Friends of Libr., Fla., 1994—98, Broward Friends Miami (Fla.) City Ballet, 1994—98, 2001—03; active Sister cities/People to People, Ft. Lauderdale, 1988—99; docent Ft. Lauderdale Mus. Art, 1988—, docent coun., 1999—2002, docent pres., 2001—03; officer, mem. Friends Mus., Ft. Lauderdale, 1992—, Broward Pub. Libr. Found., Fla., 1998; bd. govs. Mus. of Art, 2003—. Recipient award of achievement, Soc. Tech. Comm., 1986, award of distinction, Fla. Soc. Tech. Comm. Mem.: English-Speaking Union (bd. dirs. 1984—89), Travelers Century Club. Democrat. Episcopalian. Home and Office: # 265 1688 S Ocean Ln Fort Lauderdale FL 33316-3346 E-mail: ladyvanj@aol.com, judithvanalstyne@aol.com.

VAN ALTENA, ALICIA MORA, language educator; b. San Juan, Argentina, May 31, 1945; came to U.S., 1986; d. Francisco and Pilar (Garcia) Mora; m. William Foster van Altena, June 2, 1986. MA in Edn., Nat. U., San Juan, 1978. Prof. 2d lang. state colls. and high schs., San Juan, 1971-80; asst. prof. State U., San Juan, 1981-86; teaching asst. So. Conn. State U., New Haven, 1987-88; lectr. Yale U., New Haven, 1987-91, dir .beginners, 1992-94, lang. coord., 1993-94, sr. lectr., 1993—. Bd. dirs. Fedn. of Tchrs. of English, Argentina, 1983-86. Roman Catholic. Avocations: travel, photography, gardening. Home: 105 Swarthmore St Hamden CT 06517-1916 Office: Yale U Yale Spanish Dept 82 Wall St # 90 New Haven CT 06511-6605

VANALTENBURG, BETTY MARIE, lumber company executive; b. Tulsa, Dec. 27, 1963; d. Floyd Albert and Charolette Virginia (Quinton) V. BA in Comm., U. Tulsa, 1986. Adminstrv. supr. All Wood Products Co., Tulsa, 1986—. Bd. dirs. Tulsa Oklahomans for Human Rights, 1987-89, [illegible], mem. host com. Names Project, 1990, 93, 95, 97, 2000, regional rep., 1999—; co-dir. mdse. exec. bd. dirs. Names Project, Tulsa, 1998-99, co-chair ctrl. region logistics, Washington, 1996, quilt display coord., 1997—; bd. dirs. Follies Revue, Inc., Tulsa, 1993-97, v.p., 1994-97; vol. acctg. Children's Med. Ctr.-Children's Miracle Network Telethon, 1994, 95, 96, 97, 98, 99, 2000, 01, 02. Mem. Order of Eastern Star (worthy matron Tulsa chpt. # 133 1995-96, 98-99), Daus. of The Nile Zibiah Temple #102 (Princess Tirzah 1995-96, Princess Royal 1996-97, 2004—, Queen 1997-98, Supreme Appt. 2002-03), Honorable Order of Ken. Cols. Republican. Presbyterian. Avocations: model trains, reading, travel, fundraising, native american beadwork. Office Phone: 918-585-9739. E-mail: vancan@worldnet.att.net.

VAN APPLEDORN, MARY JEANNE, composer, music educator, pianist; b. Holland, Mich., Oct. 2, 1927; d. John and Elizabeth (Rinck) van A. MusB with distinction, Eastman Sch. Music, 1948, MusM, 1950, PhD in Music, 1966; postgrad., MIT, 1982. Chmn. music theory and music composition Tex. Tech. Univ., Lubbock, 1950—, chmn., founder symposium of contemporary music, 1951-82, chmn. grad. studies in music, 1970-81, Paul Whitfield Horn prof., 1989—. Mem. Ann. ASCAP Std. Panel AWards, 1980—2003. Author: Keyboard Singing and Dictation Manual, 1968; composer: Suite for Carillon (1st prize World Carillon Fedn. 1980), 1980, Cacophony for Band (Va. Coll. Band Dirs. Nat. Assn. award 1981), Lux: Legend of Sankta Lucia for Band, 1982, Liquid Gold for Saxophone and Tape (Premio Ancona award 1986), 1986, Four Duos for Viola and Cello (1st prize Tex. Composers Guild), 1987, Set of Seven (N.Y.C. Ballet), 1988, Sonatine for Clarinet and Piano, Weill Recital Hall, N.Y.C., 1988, 7th World Congress Women in Music, 1991, Concerto for Trumpet and Band, 1990, Festival a Kerkrade, Cantata: Rising Night After Night, 1990; music recorded by Vienna Modern Masters, Slovak Radio Orch. and Chorus, Bratislava, Czechoslovakia; composer: Terrestrial Music, a double concerto for violin and piano with string orch., 1997, Cycles of Moons and Tides for concert band, 1995, Rhapsody for Violin and Orch. recorded by Polish Radio Orch., 1997, Les hommes vides (T.S. Eliot's "The Hollow Men" in French translation by Pierre Leyris) for unaccompanied SATB choir, 1996, Symphony for Percussion Orchestra, 2000, Opus One CD177: Cycles of Moons and Tides for Symphonic Band, 1995, Passages (Brit. Trombone Assn. award 1996), Music of Enchantment for Native Am. flute, strings and percussion, 1997, Gestures for clarinet quartet, 1999, Miniatures for Trombone Quartet, 2000, Songs without Words for 2 coloratura sopranos and piano, 2000, Meliora, fanfare for orchestra, 2000, Soundscapes for bassoon and strings, 2002, Passages III for clarinet, violoncello and piano, 2003, A Symphony of Celebration for Orchestra, 2003, Musique for Trombone and Piano, 2003, Sonata for Solo Guitar, 2003. Commd. for carillon work Skybells Crystal Cath. Carillon, 1991. Recipient Internat. Trumpet Guild Brass Trio Competition award for Trio Italiano, 1996, Rhapsody for Violin and Orch., 1996, Incantations for Oboe and Piano, 1998, Five Psalms for Trumpet, Tenor Voice and Piano, 1998, Galilean Galaxies for Flute, Bassoon and Piano, 1998, Symphony for Percussion Orch., 2000, Festive Fanfare and Postlude for Trumpets, Snare Drums and Cymbals, 2000, A Symphony of Celebration, 2002, Meliora Symphony for Winds and Percussion, 2003; faculty rsch. grantee Tex. Tech. U ., 1982, MIT, 1982. Mem. ASCAP (mem. ann. std. panel awards 1980-2003), Soc. Composers Inc., Internat. League Women Composers, Delta Kappa Gamma (internat. scholar 1959-60), Mu Phi Epsilon, Alpha Chi Omega, Kappa Kappa Psi, Tau Beta Sigma. Home: 1629 16th St Apt 216 Lubbock TX 79401-4703 Office: Tex Tech U PO Box 42033 Lubbock TX 79409-2033 E-mail: mvanappl@ttacs.ttu.edu.

VAN ARENDONK, SUSAN CAROLE, elementary school educator; b. Marshalltown, Iowa, Feb. 16, 1954; d. Ernest Jerome and Alice Marjorie (Harmon) Groff; m. Wayne Alan Van Arendonk, Aug. 14, 1994. BS, Iowa State U., 1976; MS in Edn., U. Kans., 1981; EdS, U. Iowa, 2001. Professionally recognized spl. educator Coun. for Exception Children, 1999; nat. bd. cert. tchr. exceptional needs. Resource rm. aide Pinckney Elem., Lawrence, Kans., 1976-77; tchr. spl. edn. Booth Elem. Sch., Wichita, Kans., 1977-78; tchr. resource rm. Clinton (Iowa) Cmty. Schs., 1978-80; tchr. spl. edn. Henry Sabin Elem. Sch., Clinton, 1980-83; edn. specialist U. Iowa, 1984; cons. No. Trails Area Edn. Agy., Clear Lake, Iowa, 1984-86; tchr. resource rm. Tomiyasu Elem. Sch., Las Vegas, 1986-88, 90-92, tchr. 3d grade, 1988-90, 92-94; tchr. lang. arts, spl. edn. Haysville (Kans.) Mid. Sch., 1996-97; tchr. behavior disorders Heartspring, Wichita, Kans., 1997-98; tchr. spl. edn. Gammon Elem., Wichita, 1998-2000, Curtis Mid. Sch., Wichita, 2000—. Edn. specialist, student tchr. supr. U. Iowa, 1983, grad. asst. 1984; cons. Heartland Area Edn. Agy., Johnston, Iowa, 1994-96. Treas. State Rep. Campaign, Iowa, 1974, publicity chmn., 1974. Mem. Coun. Exceptional Children, Iowa State Alumni Assn. (life), U. Iowa Alumni Assn. (life), Humane Soc. Am., U. Kans. Alumni Assn., Phi Lambda Theta. Democrat. Jewish. Home: 2359 N Parkridge Ct Wichita KS 67205-2002 Office: Curtis Mid Sch 1031 S Edgemoor Wichita KS 67218 Office Phone: 316-973-7350. E-mail: wvanarendonk@cox.net.

VAN ARK, JOAN, actress; d. Carroll and Dorothy Jean (Hemenway) Van A.; m. John Marshall, Feb. 1, 1966; 1 child, Vanessa Jeanne. Student, Yale Sch. Drama. Appeared at Tyrone Guthrie Theatre, Washington Arena Stage, in London, on Broadway; performances include: (stage) Barefoot in the Park, 1965, School for Wives, 1971, Rules of the Game, 1974, Cyrano de Bergerac, Ring Round the Moon, A Little Night Music, 1994, Three Tall Women, 1995, Vagina Monologues, L.A., Denver, Colo., San Diego, Calif. 2001-2002, The Exonerated, N.Y.C. 2002, (TV series) Temperatures Rising, 1972-73, We've Got Each Other, 1977-78, Dallas, 1978-81, Knots Landing, 1979-92 (also dir. episodes Letting Go, Hints and Evasions), (voice) Santa Bogito, 1995; (TV movies) The Judge and Jake Wyler, 1972, Big Rose, 1974, Shell Game, 1975, The Last Dinosaur, 1977, Red Flag, 1981, Shakedown on the Sunset Strip, 1988, My First Love, 1989, Murder at the PTA, 1990, To Cast a Shadow, 1990, Always Remember I Love You, 1990, Grand Central Murders, 1992, Tainted Blood, 1992, Someone's Watching, 1993, When the Darkman Calls, 1994, Loyal Opposition: Terror in the White House, 1998, Intimate Portrait: Michele Lee, 1999, Intimate Portrait, Joan Van Ark, 2002. Tornado Warning, 2002; (TV miniseries) Testimony of Two Men, 1978, Knots Landing: Back to the Cul-de-Sac, 1997; dir., star ABC-TV Afterschool Spl. Boys Will Be Boys, 1993; films, Frogs, 1970 Held for Ransom, 2000, UP Michigan,2001, The Icemakers, 2002. Recipient Theatre World award, 1970-71, L.A. Drama Critics Cir. award, 1973, Outstanding Actress award Soap Opera Digest, 1986, 89. Mem. AFTRA, SAG, Actors Equity Assn., Dir. Guild of Am. Address: care William Morris Agy Inc c/o Sam Haskell 151 S El Camino Dr Beverly Hills CA 90212-2704

VANARSDALE, DIANA CORT, social worker; b. N.Y.C., Oct. 27, 1934; d. Arthur and Augusta Deutsch; m. Leonard VanArsdale, Sept. 17, 1978; children by previous marriage: Hayley, Daniel. BS, NYU, 1955; MSW, Colmbia U., 1957. Clinician Payne Whitney Clinic, N.Y. Hosp., N.Y.C., 1957-59; clinician psychiat. clinic Jewish Bd. Guardians, N.Y.C., 1959-61; founder, pres. Bix Six Towers Nursery Sch., N.Y.C., 1962-67; dir. intake and social svc. L.I. Consultation Ctr., Forest Hills, N.Y., 1966-84, clin. dir., coord. clin. svcs., 1984-86; supr. faculty mem. L.I. Inst. Mental Health, 1981-87; dir. Srs. Option Svc., Allendale, NJ, 1980—90. Author: Transitions: A Woman's Guide To successful Retirement, 1991. Mem. NASW, N.Y. Soc. Clin. Social Workers. Home: 47-30 61st St 18C Woodside NY 11377-5763

VAN ARSDEL, MARY MARGARET, actress, voice educator; b. Seattle, Sept. 5, 1953; d. Paul Parr and Rosemary (Thorstenson) Van A. BA magna cum laude, Bowdoin Coll., Brunswick, Maine, 1975; AA, Am. Acad. Dramatic Arts, N.Y.C., 1977. Asst. mng. dir. Theatre West, Inc., L.A., 1988-94, mng. dir., 1994-96; pvt. voice and speech tchr., L.A., 1996—. Former head coach, asst. head coach BC Cons., L.A., 1995-98; mng. dir. emeritus Theatre West, 1993—. Actress: (play) Survival of the Heart, 1990, (film) In the Line of Fire, 1994, (TV) L.A. Law, 1994, (TV pilot) Heart Attack and Vine, 1996, others. Recipient Outstanding Performance award Dramalogue, L.A., 1990, 92, 93, L.A. Drama Critics Circle award, 2000. Mem. AFTRA, SAG, Actors Equity Assn., The Musical Theatre Guild, Pacific Resident Theatre Ensemble. Avocations: hiking, travel, bicycling, singing, golden retrievers. Office: 514 N Catalina St Burbank CA 91505-3243 E-mail: MVsings@aol.com.

VANASDALAN, JOAN LOUISE, music educator, musician; b. Carlisle, Pa., Aug. 18, 1953; d. Charles William and Ruth Margaret (Koontz) Vanasdalan. BS in Music Edn., Gettysburg Coll., Pa., 1975; MA in Piano Performance, The Am. U., Washington, 1983. Music tchr. K-6 Long Branch Pub. Schs., NJ, 1975—77; music tchr. pre-K-6 Wash. Pub. Schs., 1981—93; tchr. Head Start-6 Gaithersburg Elem. Sch., Gaithersburg, Md., 1993—. Profl. piano accompanist, vocal coach, Wash., 1983—. Grantee Cafritz grantee, Cafritz Found. Mem.: Am. Orff-Schulwerk Assn., Music Educators Nat. Conf. Avocations: genealogy, reading, cross stitch. Home: 11112 Black Forest Way Gaithersburg MD 20879 Office: Gaithersburg Elem Sch 35 N Summit Ave Gaithersburg MD 20877

VAN AUKEN, SUE S. property manager, real estate broker; d. Harold Thomas and Edith Bernice Van Auken; 1 child, Thomas Earl. AA, Long Beach (Calif.) City Coll., 1985. Lic. Broker, Real Estate and Mortgages Dept. of Real Estate, State of Calif., 1985, cert. Notary Pub. State of Calif., 1998. Mgr., container yard Eagle Marine Services, Ltd., San Pedro, Calif., 1968—84; residential and investment real estate specialist Pridemark Realtors/Century 21 Pk., Huntington Beach/Long Beach, Calif., 1985—91; broker/owner RS Properties, RS Fin. Services and RS Property Mgmt., Anaheim, Calif., 1986—; sr. loan cons. Titan Fin./Stone Am. Fin., Fountain Valley/Irvine, Calif., 1991—93; dir. of mktg. Advanced Health Mgmt. Group, Inc., Los Alamitos, Calif., 1992—96; residential, investment, comml. real estate specialist Century 21 Dream Team, Tustin, Calif., 1996—98; sr. loan cons. Allstate Fin., Tustin, Calif., 1996—98; project mgr. Hunt Enterprises, Anaheim, Calif., 1997—98; CEO/pres. RS Companies, Inc., Anaheim, Calif., 1998—. V.p. Summerwind Homeowners Assn., Anaheim, Calif., 2002—, pres., 1995—2001. Mem.: Nat. Assn. Mortgage Brokers (assoc.), Calif. Assn. Realtors (assoc.), Nat. Assn. Realtors (assoc.), Nat. Notary Assn. (assoc.), Calif. Assn. Mortgage Brokers (assoc.), Pacific West Assn. Realtors (assoc.). Avocations: spending time with grandchildren, movies, reading. Office: RS Companies Inc 630 S Euclid St Anaheim CA 92802 Personal E-mail: suejan@pacbell.net.

VANAUKER, LANA, recreational therapist, educator; b. Youngstown, Ohio, Sept. 19, 1949; d. William Marshall and Joanne Norma (Kimmel) Speece; m. Dwight Edward VanAuker, Mar. 16, 1969 (div. 1976); 1 child, Heidi. BS in Edn. cum laude, Kent (Ohio) State U., 1974; MS in Edn., Youngstown (Ohio) U., 1989. Cert. tchr., Ohio; nat. cert. activity cons. Phys. edn. instr. St. Joseph Sch., Campbell, Ohio, 1973-75; program dir. [illegible] 1975-85; exercise technician Youngstown State U., 1985—86; health educator Park Vista Retirement Ctr., Youngstown, 1986-87; sch. tchr. Salem (Ohio) City Sch., 1987-88; recreational therapist Trumbull Meml. Hosp., Warren, Ohio, 1988—. Activity cons. Mahoning/Trumbull Nursing Homes, Warren, 1990-92; adv. bd. rep. Ohio State Bur. Health Promotion Phys. Fitness, 1996—; mem. adv. bd. Ohio State Executive Physical Fitness Dept. Health, 1996; tchr. Mohican Youth Ctr., Loudonville, Ohio, 1998-99. Producer chair exercise sr. video Excercise is the Fountain of Youth, 1993; photographer, choreographer; cover photography feature Mahoning County Med. Soc. Bull., 2000; exhibited in group show Forum Health, 1999. Vol. Am. Cancer Soc., 1980—, Am. Heart Assn., 1986—, Dance for Heart, 1980-86; mem. State of Ohio Phys. Fitness Adv. Bd., 1996-97. Youngstown State U. scholar, 1986-89; recipient 1st pl. Kodak Internat. Newspaper Snapshot award, 1998-99, 1st Place Internat. Libr. Photography, 2000. Mem.: AAHPERD, U.S. Amateur Ballroom Dance Assn. (v.p. 2002—03), Pa. Activity Profl. Assn. (pres., spkr. 2001), Resident Activity Profl. Assn. (pres. 1994—96, 2001—03), Youngstown Camera Club (social chair 1989—90, pres. 1993—95), Kappa Delta Pi. Democrat. Presbyterian. Avocations: photography, international dance, volleyball, aerobics, travel. Home: 4133 S Turner Rd Canfield OH 44406-8737 Office: 4N Unit Forum Health 1350 E Market St Warren OH 44483-6608 Office Phone: 330-841-9942.

VAN BARON, JUDITH E. college administrator; b. Mankato, Minn., Dec. 2, 1942; d. William Henry and Grace Eloise (Gerth) Appel; m. Clayton Junior Gorder, Dec. 22, 1962 (div. 1973); 1 child, Erika Gorder; m. Thomas William McCabe, Nov. 10, 1978. AA, Waldorf Coll., 1962; BA, Luther Coll., 1963; MA, U. Iowa, 1969, PhD, 1973. Tchr San Jose (Calif.) State U., 1976-77; exec. dir. Monmouth Mus., Lincroft, N.J., 1977-79; tchr. U.S. Mil. Acad. Prep. Sch., Ft. Monmouth, N.J., 1983-90; dir. Stefanotti Gallery, N.Y.C., 1979-82; v.p. acad. affairs Savannah (Ga.) Coll. Art and Design, 1992-96, v.p. external affairs, 1996—. Pres. N.Y. Art Critics Circle, N.Y.C., 1979-83; vis. com. Met. Mus. Art, N.Y.C., 1974-76; bicentennial adv. com. to Borough Pres. Robert Abrams, 1975-76. Exec. dir., curator Bronx (N.Y.) Mus. Arts, 1974-76; pres. Middletown (N.J.) Preservation Adv. Commn., 1982-83. Kress Found. fellow, 1971. Mem. AAUW, Nat. Coun. Art Adminstrs., Assn. Collegiate Schs. Arch., Coll. Art Assn., Nat. Assn. Women in Edn.

VAN BOCKSTAELE, ELISABETH JEANNE, neuroscientist, researcher; b. Paris, Jan. 4, 1965; d. Pierre Georges and Kathleen Mary (Garrish) Van B.; m. Erol Veznedaroglu, June 27, 1993; children: Lauren Kincal, Alec Tristan. BA, Sarah Lawrence Coll., Bronxville, N.Y., 1985; MS, N.Y.U., 1989; PhD, 1991. Grad. student N.Y.U., 1986-91; postdoctoral fellow Cornell U. Med. Coll., N.Y.C., 1991-93, instr. in Neuroscience, 1993-94, asst. prof. Neuroscience, 1994-96; asst. prof. Thomas Jefferson U., Phila., 1996-98, assoc. prof., 1998—. Author: Central Neural Mechanisms in Cardiovascular Regulation, 1991; contbr. articles to profl. jours. Named NARSAD Young Investigator Nat. Alliance for Rsch. on Schizophrenia and Depression, 1994-96; recipient NIDA First award Nat. Inst. on Drug Abuse, 1994-99, Established Investigatorship award Am. Heart Assn., 1996, a.e. Bennett award Soc. Biol. Psychiatry, 1999. Mem. Soc. for Neuroscience. Office: Thomas Jefferson Univ Dept Pathology & Cell Biol 1020 Locust St Rm 520 Philadelphia PA 19107-6731

VAN BOER, HELEN SHIRLEY, counselor, educator; d. Calvin Dudley Bush and Francesca Keen; m. Bertil Herman Van Boer, June 12, 1949; children: Bertil Jr., Eric, Kenton. BA, Vanderbilt U., 1947, MA, 1950; PhD, Fla. State U., 1960, Union U., 1983. Tchr. Nashville City Schs., 1947—51; prof. Pacific Union Coll., Angwin, Calif., 1960—65; tchr. Napa Coll., 1965—82; v.p. sch. bd. Tahoe-Truckee Sch. Dist., Truckee, Calif., 1982—85; counselor, instr. Sierra Nev. Coll., Incline Village, 1985—93; instr. Blue Ridge C.C., Hendersonville, NC, 1994—2003. Cons. Napa Valley Unified Sch. Dist.; family counselor pvt. practice, Hendersonville, 1994—2004; invited presenter Native Coast Poets, Crustal River, Fla., 2002, Sun Coast Poets, Soroptomists, Hendersonville, 2002; judge artist's awards Hendersonville City Arts Assn., 2001—02. Author of poems, editor. Program chair Friends Hendersonville County Libr. Mem.: Seasoned Poets Blue Ridge (founder), Western N.C. Genealogical Soc. (v.p. 2000—03, program chair), Western N.C. Pen Women (v.p. 2000—01, pres. 2002—). Republican. Avocations: music, art, gardening, travel. Home: 22 Horse Pasture Dr Hendersonville NC 28739 Office Phone: 828-697-6046.

VAN BOGAERT, CYNTHIA A. lawyer; BS in Math., U. Wis., 1980, JD, 1982; postgrad., U. Chgo., 1990-93. Bar: Wis. 1983, Ill. 1985. Atty. U.S. Steel Corp., Pitts. and Dallas, Peoples Gas, Chgo., Inland Steel Industries, Inc., Chgo., Adminstrv. Mgmt. Group, Arlington Heights, Ill., 1994-96, Boardman, Suhr, Curry & Field LLP, Madison, Wis., 1996—. Mem. WEB (pres. Madison, Wis. chpt. 1998-99, nat. dir.-at-large 1998-2000, nat. pres. 2000-02, past pres. 2002—), ABA, Wis. Bar Assn., Dane County Bar Assn., Chgo. Bar Assn., Legal Assn. Women.

VAN BORTEL, MARY CATHERINE, sales executive; d. Howard Van B. Sales mgr. John Holtz Mercedes Banz-BMW, until 1985; used car sales, 1985-91; owner Van Bortel Subaru, 1991—. Office: Van Bortel Motorcar Inc 6327 Rte 96 Victor NY 14564

VANBRUNT-KRAMER, KAREN, business administration educator; b. Milw., May 1, 1934; D. Roy Charles and Viola Marguerita (Yerges) VanBrunt; m. Allen Lloyd Weitermann (div. 1963); 1 child, Tera Lee Johnson; m. Keith Kramer (div. 1979); children: Holden Jon, Stafford James. BS, U. Wis., 1956; MA, NYU, 1976; PhD, Ohio State U., 1992. Owner Design By Karen Lee, Larchmont, N.Y., 1975-82; interior designer Maurice Vallency Design, N.Y.C., 1976-79; grad. rsch. assoc. Ctr. on Edn. and Tng. for Employment, Columbus, Ohio, 1987-92; assoc. prof. bus. adminstrn. St. Joseph Coll., West Hartford, Conn., 1992-99. Lectr. and curriculum developer entrepreneurship state vocat. schs., high schs., colls., and univs. throughout U.S. and Ea. Europe, 1987-92; instr. Berkeley Sch., White Plains, N.Y., 1968-82; adj. prof. N.Y.C. C.C., 1979-83, Milw. Area Tech. Coll., 1983-85, Columbus (Ohio) State C.C., 1986-90, Capital U., Columbus, 1998, U. Wis. Milw., Mt. Mary Coll., Milw.; participant Women in Soc. Citizen Amb. Program to China, 1997, leader Women in Exec. Mgmt. Bus., 1998; mem. Inst. World Affairs, U. Wis., Milw., 1999—. Mem. Wadsworth Atheneum, Hartford, 1992—99, West Hartford Art League, 1993—99; vol. U. Conn. Health Ctr., Farmington, Little Sisters of the Poor, St. Joseph Residence, Enfield, Conn., 1989—92, Milw. Art Mus.; docent Columbus Symphony Orch., 1986—92; mem. women's guild First Cmty. Ch., Columbus, 1985—92. Mem. AAUP (membership chair 1993-97), AAUW (past social chair Wis. br.), NAFE, World Affairs Coun., Am. Vocat. Assn., Ohio Vocat. Assn., Coalition for Effective Orgns., Am. Mktg. Assn., Am. Mgmt. Assn., Nat. Edn. Ctr. for Women in Bus., World Federalist Assn. (Milw. sec./treas. 2001—), Phi Beta Kappa, Phi Kappa Phi, Phi Lambda Theta, Phi Delta Kappa, Delta Pi Epsilon, Omicron Tau Theta. Avocations: theatre, art, music, photography, ice dancing. Home: 125 N University Dr Unit 322S West Bend WI 53095-2954

VAN BULCK, MARGARET WEST, accountant, financial planner, educator; b. Chgo., Nov. 25, 1955; d. Lee Allen and Margaret Ellen (Sauls) West; m. Hendrikus E.J.M.L. van Bulck, Aug. 7, 1976; children: Marcel Allen, Sydney Josette. BS in Mktg., U. S.C., 1978; MA in Econs., Clemson U., 1981. CPA, S.C. Econs. instr. St. Andrews Presbyn. Coll., Laurinburg, N.C., 1980-82; staff acct. L. Allen West, CPA, Sumter, S.C., 1982-84; ptnr. West & Van Bulck, CPAs, Sumter, 1984-88, Van Bulck & Co., CPA's, Sumter, 1989—. Part time instr. U. S.C., Sumter, 1985-87, mem. full time faculty, 1989-92. Contbr. articles to profl. jours. Treas. Make-A-Wish Found., Sumter, 1985-87, wish granting chmn. 1987-88; edn. found. chmn. Laurinburg/Scotland County chpt. AAUW, 1981-83; treas. Friends Sumter County Library, 1986-88, Sumter Gallery of Art, 1989-91; mem. Jr. Welfare League, Sumter, Circle Bible [illegible] tchr. beginning vol. 1990-92; deacon First Presbyn. Ch., 1994-97; den leader pack 86 Boy Scouts of Am., 1992-95, troop com. mem., advancement chair, 1998-2001, troop com. treas., 2000-. Recipient Sirrine Found. award, Clemson U., 1978, '79; grantee U.S. Dept. Labor, 1979-80. Mem. AICPA, S.C. Assn. CPAs, Internat. Assn. Fin. Planning, Sumter Estate Planning Coun. (past treas.), Trian Club (treas. 1998—), Carolinian Club, Omicron Delta Epsilon. Presbyterian. Home: 234 Haynsworth St PO Box 1327 Sumter SC 29151-1327 Office: Van Bulck & Co CPAs PO Box 1327 Sumter SC 29151-1327 Office Phone: 803-775-3000. E-mail: margaretvb@sc.rr.com., margaret@vanbulckCPAs.com.

VAN BUREN, ABIGAIL (JEANNE PHILLIPS), columnist, lecturer; b. Mpls., Apr. 10, 1942; d. Morton and Pauline (Friedman) Phillips, (the founder of the Dear Abby advice column in 1956). Student, U. Colo., 1960—62. Writer Dear Abby Radio Show, CBS, 1965—71; columnist Dear Abby, 1987—. Bd. mem. Planned Parenthood of Los Angeles, 1989—90; life-time cons. Group for Advancement of Psychiatry, 1995—; bd. adv. Alzheimers Assn. of Los Angeles, 1996—; bd. mem. Rose and Jay Phillips Found., 1991—, ACLU of So. Calif. Found., 1998—; adv. bd. L.A. Internat. Women's Media Found. Courage in Journalism, 2000—; bd. adv. UCLA Med. Ctr., Ctr. for Rsch. and Training in Humane and Ethical Med. Care (CHEC), 2000—. Lifetime cons. Group for Advancement of Psychiatry, 1995—; bd. advisors Alzheimer's Assn. of L.A., 1996—; adv. bd. L.A. Internat. Women's Media Found. Courage in Journalism, 2000—; bd. advisors UCLA Med. Ctr., Ctr. for Rsch. and Tng. in Humane and Ethical Care (CHEC), 2000—; bd. dirs. Planned Parenthood of L.A., 1989—90, Rose and Jay Phillips Found., 1991—, ACLU of So. Calif. Found., 1998—, MADD, 2003—, Children's Rights Coun., 2003—. Recipient Generations of Choice award, Planned Parenthood of L.A., 1999, Minority Organ/Tissue Transplant Edn. Program (MOTTEP) Key of Life award, Howard U., Wash. D.C., 2000, Award of Appreciation, U.S. Gen. Svcs. Adminstrn. Fed. Consumer Info. Ctr., 2000, Star on Hollywood Walk of Fame for Dear Abby Radio Show, 2001, Recognition by the Office of Nat. Drug Control Policy (ONDCP), award from the White House and Substance Abuse and Mental Health Svcs. Adminstrn. for help in launching Nat. Inhalants and Poisons Awareness Week, 2001, Erasing the Stigma Leadership award, Didi Hirsch Mental Health Ctr., 2001, MOTTEP Award of Excellence, 2001, Commendation for Operation Dear Abby and OperationDearAbby.net, Dept. Navy and USMC, 2002, Appreciation for support of the military svc. mems. of the U.S. for Operation Dear Abby and OperationDearAbby.net, Space and Naval Warfare Sys. Ctr. (SPAWAR), 2002, Alzheimer's Assn. Maureen Reagan Advocacy Award, 2003, Appreciation award, Overeaters Anonymous, 2003, Advocacy award, Alzheimer's Assn. L.A., 2003, award of Appreciation, U.S. GSA Fed. Citizen Info. Ctr., 2004. Syndicated in the U.S., Brazil, Mex., Japan, Philippines, Fed. Republic Germany, India, Holland, Denmark, Can., Korea, Thailand, Italy, Hong Kong, Taiwan, Ireland, Saudi Arabia, Greece, France, Dominican Republic, P.R., Costa Rica, U.S. Virgin Islands, Bermuda, and Guam; published on the Internet at DearAbby.com and OperationDearAbby.net for messages to the military. Office: Philips-Van Buren Inc Ste 2710 1900 Ave of the Stars Los Angeles CA 90067

VANBUREN, DENISE DORING, corporate communications executive; b. Troy, N.Y., May 15, 1961; d. James L. and Eunice A. (Myers) Doring; m. Steven Paul VanBuren, Apr. 1, 1989; children: Schuyler Paul, Troy James Doring, Brett Steven VanBuren. BA in Mass Comm. magna cum laude, St. Bonaventure U., 1983; MBA, Mount St. Mary Coll., 1997. Reporter, news anchor Sta. WGNY-AM-FM, Newburgh, NY, 1984; news dir., anchor NewsCtr. 6, Dutchess County, NY, 1985-90; dir. media rels. Ctrl. Hudson Gas & Electric, Poughkeepsie, NY, 1993—, mgr. corp. comms., 1998-99, asst. v.p. corp. comm., 1999-2000, v.p. corp. comm. and cmty. rels., 2000—. Adj. prof. Marist Coll., Poughkeepsie, NY. Co-author: Historic Beacon, 1998, Beacon Revisited, 2003. Councilwoman City of Beacon, 1992-93, chmn. 85th anniversary celebration; pres. Beacon Hist. Soc., 1989-94; bd. dirs. Locust Grove Hist. Site, Stony Kill Found., Inc. Recipient Salute to Women in Bus. & Industry award D.C. YWCA, 1990, 97, Outstanding Chpt. Regent award N.Y. State orgn. DAR, 1999; named Vol. of Yr. award, City of Beacon, 1999. Mem.: DAR (vice regent Melzingah chpt. 1990—98, regent 1998—2001, nat. chmn. PR 1999—, chmn. pub. rels. com. NY state), Greater So. Dutchess C. of C. (bd. dirs.), Nat. Soc. Daus. of Union Vets. of the Civil War, Exch. Club of So. Dutchess (bd. dirs.). Republican. Roman Catholic. Avocations: genealogy, needlework. Office: CH Energy Group Inc 284 South Ave Poughkeepsie NY 12601-4838

VAN BUREN, MARY LOU, retired religious organization administrator; b. Toledo, Feb. 1, 1929; d. Martin Clyde and Norma Adella (Speers) Van B. BA, DePauw U., 1951; MA in Religious Edn., Union Theol. Sem., Tchrs. Coll. Columbia U., 1952. Dir. Christian edn. Met. Meml. Meth. Ch., Washington, 1952-54, Bexley United Meth. Ch., Columbus, Ohio, 1954-68; exec. sec. women's divsn. Bd. Global Ministries United Meth. Ch., N.Y.C., 1968-89; program devel. Bd. Global Ministries, United Meth. Ch., N.Y.C., 1968-76; spiritual and theol. concerns, 1976-89. Nat. chairperson Meth. Dirs. Christian Edn., 1963-65; mem. alumni coun. Union Theol. Sem., N.Y.C., 1969-72. Author: (booklet) Retreats, An Introductory Manual, 1976, (with others) Spirituality in Ecumenical Perspective, 1993; contbr. articles to Response Mag. Recipient Alumna tribute Union Theol. Sem., 1992, Centennial Laity award in spiritual formation Scarritt-Bennett Ctr., 1992. Mem. Christian Educators Fellowship, Ecumenical Inst. Spirituality. Democrat. Home: 4831 Buck Hill Rd N Trumansburg NY 14886-9648

VAN CAMP, DIANA J. music educator; b. Washington, Oct. 24, 1946; d. Gordon Ashley and Gabrielle Marie-Anne Van Camp. B in Music Edn., Ind. U., 1969; MusM, Fla. State U., 1976; PhD in Music Edn., Ohio State U., 1989. Cert. tchr. music K-12 Ohio. Orch. tchr. Gainesville (Fla.) City Schs., 1969—72; orch. tchr., profl. violinist Memphis Symphony and Schs., 1975—79; music edn. and orch. tchr. Otterbein Coll., Westerville, Ohio, 1979—82; tchg. assoc. music edn. Ohio State U., Columbus, 1982—85; orch. dir. Bexley (Ohio) City Schs., 1985—86, Newark (Ohio) City Schs., 1987—. Pvt. violin studio, Newark, 1990—. Violinist: Southea. Ohio Symphony, 1992—, Welsh Hills Symphony, 1990—, Land of Legend Philharmonic, 1995—, Ctrl. Ohio Symphony, 2000—. Grantee, Nat. Endowment for the Arts, 1975—79. Mem.: Ohio Music Educators Assn., Music Educators Nat. Conf., Sigma Alpha Iota. Avocations: walking, hiking, swimming, church work. Home: 125 Beechtree Rd Whitehall OH 43213

VANCE, HELEN T. secondary school counselor; b. Fresno, Calif., Nov. 4, 1928; d. Edward Charles and Virginia Rohrbough Trainer; widowed; 1 child, Robert Keith. BA in Eng., Fresno State Coll., 1950; MEd, Cal Poly U., 1969. Tchr., counselor Coalinga (Calif.) Jr. H.S., 1951—76, counselor Coalinga H.S., 1977—92. Editor: Man From Devil's Den, 1994. Mem.: AAUW, Cal Poly Alumni, Fresno State Alumni, Coalinga Woman's Club. Lutheran. Avocations: reading, travel, gardening, organ, piano.

VANCE, MARY, academic administrator; b. Seoul, Korea, Nov. 16, 1957; d. Irwin F. and Mae Hoeft; m. Eric J. Vance. BA, U. Wis., 1979, MA, 1983; PhD, Mich. State U., 1993. From advisor to coord, Mich. State U., East Lansing, 1984-93; coord. Holmes Scholars Holmes Group, East Lansing, 1993-94; dir. edn. student svcs. Iowa State U., Ames, 1994-97; dir. acad. support and advising svcs. George Mason U., Fairfax, Va., 1997—. Adj asst. prof. Iowa State U., 1994-97; cons. Southeastern Assn. Edn. Opportunity Program Personnel, Memphis, 1993-94. Contbr. articles to jours. Mem. strategic planning steering com. Ames Cmty. Sch. Dist., 1995-96; mem. Leadership Ames, 1995; bd. dirs. YWCA, Ames, 1996; mem. Make A Wish, 1998—. Recipient Outstanding Asian Pacific Am. Faculty/Staff awards, 1985-93, All U. Diversity Photo award, 1992, Outstanding Grad. Woman Spl. Merit award, 1992, Appreciation, Southeastern Assn. Ednl. Opportunity Program Pers., 1992, [illegible] 1993, Holmes Scholars, 1994, Holmes Group, 1994, Cert. of Achievement, Leadership Ames, 1995, Cert. Recognition, Univ. Disability Group, 2000, Cert. Appreciation, Korean Quar., 2003, Woman of Color, UW Superior, 2003. Mem. Nat. Orgn. Acad. Advising Assn., Assn. Higher Edn. and Disability, Nat. Orientation Dirs. Assn., Asian Pacific Am. Women's Leadership Inst., Acad, Affairs Adminstrs., Nat. Assn. Colls. and Employers (chair acad. staff senate). Bapt. Avocations: reading, gourmet cooking, eating, movies, writing book reviews. Office: Wis Pub Liberal Arts Coll Univ Wisconsin 134 Old Main,Belknap&Catlin,PO Box2000 Superior WI 54880-4500 E-mail: mvance@uwsuper.edu.

VANCE, PATRICIA H. state legislator; b. Williamsport, Pa., Mar. 19, 1936; m. Charles D. Vance. RN, Harrisburg Hosp. Sch. Nursing, 1957. Mem. Pa. Ho. of Reps., Harrisburg. Home: 3806 Market St Camp Hill PA 17011-4327 Office: Pa Ho of Reps B-16 Main Capitol PO Box 202020 Harrisburg PA 17120-2020

VANCE SIEBRASSE, KATHY ANN, legislative staff member; b. Kansas City, Kans., Oct. 28, 1954; d. Donald Herbert Vance and Barbara June (Boris) Vance-Young; m. Charles Richard Siebrasse, Mar. 8, 1980; 1 stepson, Michael (dec.); 1 son, Bradley. BS in Journalism, No. Ill. U., 1976. Reporter Des Plaines (Ill.) Suburban Times and Park Ridge Herald, 1974-75, DeKalb (Ill.) Daily Chronicle, 1976-78; stringer Rockford (Ill.) Register Star, 1978; editor The MidWeek Newspaper, DeKalb, 1978-81, owner and pub., 1982—2001; legis. aide Ill. State Senator J. Bradley Burzynski, Sycamore, 2001—. Part-time journalist The Midweek, DeKalb, 2004—. Active No. Ill. U. Found., 1992-99, mem. exec. bd., 1994-99, chair bus. and industry for No. Ill. U. campaign, 1993-94; pres. DeKalb Athletic Barb Boosters, 1995-97; chair Kishwaukee Hosp. Health Coun., Comm. Com., 1984-92, DeKalb County Partnership for a Substance Abuse Free Environment, 1990-2001; bd. dirs. DeKalb Edn. Found., sec., 1987-89, pres., 1989-93, active, 1987-94; sponsor Big Bros./Big Sisters Bowl-a-Thon, food drive Salvation Army, 1990-2002; bd. mem. Am. Heart Assn., 2000—; active Relay for Life, Am. Cancer Soc., 1999-2001, Heart Walk, Am. Heart Assn., 2000—; chair capital campaign Tails Humane Soc., 2002; pres.-elect, publicity chair Joseph F. Glidden Homestead Found.; bd. dirs., chair fundraising campaign Suicide Prevention Svcs., Batavia, 2002—. Recipient Comty. Svc. award Nat. Assn. of Advt. Pubs., 1980, Athena award Oldsmobile, DeKalb C. of C., 1990, Bus. of Yr., 1994, Heritage award Kishwaukee Cmty. Hosp., 2003. Mem. Soc. Profl. Journalists, Ill. Press Assn., No. Ill. Newspaper Assn., Ind. Free Papers Am. (Cmty. Svc. award 1992-93, 2nd pl. nat. gen. excellence award 1996), DeKalb County Farm Bur., DeKalb and Sycamore C. of C. (editor Sycamore newsletter 1994-96, mem. DeKalb Athena award com., bd. dirs., v.p. DeKalb 1996, chair 1997, Sam Walton Bus. Leader of Yr. De Kalb chamber 1999). Avocations: photography, reading, swimming, skiing, sailing. Office: State Sen J Bradley Burzynski 505 DeKalb Ave Sycamore IL 60178

VAN CLEAVE, VICKI L. psychologist, educator; b. Lexington, Ky., July 4, 1964; d. Ruth Kilby and George William Van Cleave. BA, U. Colo., 1986; D of Clin. Psychology, Ill. Sch. Profl. Psychology, 1999. Mental health worker Boulder (Colo.) Psychiat. Inst., 1985—87, Longmont (Colo.) United Hosp., 1987—89; child protection caseworker III Denver Dept. Social Svcs., 1989—90, intensive services child protection worker III, 1990—91; placement alternative caseworker IV Adams County Dept. Social Svcs., Commerce City, Colo., 1991—93; extern Child and Family Counseling Ctr., Chgo., 1994—95; mental health counselor Univ. Hosp., Chgo., 1994—95; psychodiagnostician Iyamah Behavioral Health Care, Chgo., 1995—96; extern Creative Growth Psychotherapy, Chgo., 1995—96; intern Colo. State U., Ft. Collins, 1996—97; therapist, psychologist Mental Health Coun. Denver, 1997—99, program mgr., 1999—2000; pvt. practice therapist Denver, 1997—2000; clin. psychologist Golden Triangle Cmty. Mental Health Ctr., Havre, Mont., 2000—. Mem. child protection team Dept. Pub. Health and Human Svcs., Havre, 2000—; mem. adj. faculty Met. State Coll., Denver, 1999—2000, Mont. State U., Havre, 2000—02. Actor: (plays) Arsenic and Old Lace, No Sex Please We're British, God's Country; stage mgr. (plays) Rosencrantz and Gildenstern, tech. operator lighting London Suites, tech. operator sound Art. Mem. foster care rev. team Denver Dept. Social Svcs., 1990—91, mem. ct. liaison com., foster care issues com., 1991; bd. dirs. Ct. Appointed Spl. Advocates (CASA), Havre, 2002—03; foster parent Boulder County Dept. Social Svcs., 1989—90, Denver Alternative for Youth Svcs., 1990—93. Mem.: APA, Nat. Play Therapy Assn., Mont. Psychol. Assn. (sec. 2003—). Democrat. Avocations: swimming, walking, travel, reading, movies. Office: Golden Triangle Cmty Mental Health Ctr PO Box 1038 Havre MT 59501 E-mail: vickiv@gtc-mhc.org.

VAN CLEVE, RUTH GILL, retired lawyer, government official; b. Mpls., July 28, 1925; d. Raymond S. and Ruth (Sevon) Gill; m. Harry R. Van Cleve, Jr., May 16, 1952 (dec. Oct. 2001); children: John Gill, Elizabeth Webster, David Hamilton Livingston. Student, U. Minn., 1943; AB magna cum laude, Mt. Holyoke Coll., 1946, LLD, 1976; LLB, Yale U., 1950. Bar: D.C. 1950, Minn. 1950. Intern Nat. Inst. Pub. Affairs, 1946-47; atty. Dept. Interior, 1950-54, asst. solicitor, 1954-64; dir. Office Territorial Affairs, 1964-69, 1977-80, dep. asst. sec., 1980-81, acting asst. sec., 1993; atty. Solicitor's Office, 1981-93, FPC, 1969-75, asst. gen. counsel, 1975-77. Author: The Office of Territorial Affairs, 1974, The Application of Federal Laws to the Territories, 1993. Mem. Guam War Claims Rev. Commn., 2003—04. Recipient Fed. Woman's award, 1966, Disting. Svc. award Dept. Interior, 1968, Presdl. Rank award, Pres. U.S., 1989. Mem. Phi Beta Kappa. Unitarian. Home: 4400 Emory St Alexandria VA 22312-1321

VAN CURA, JOYCE BENNETT, librarian; b. Madison, Wis., Mar. 25, 1944; d. Ralph Eugene and Florence Marie (Cramer) Bennett; m. E. Jay Van Cura, July 5, 1986. BA in Liberal Arts (scholar), Bradley U., 1966; MLS, U. Ill., 1971. Libr. asst. Rsch. Libr. Caterpillar Tractor Co., Peoria, Ill., 1966-67; ref. libr., instr. libr. tech. Ill. Ctrl. Coll., East Peoria, Ill., 1967-73; asst. prof. Sangamon State U. (U. Ill.-Springfield), Springfield, Ill., 1973-80, assoc. prof., 1980-86; head libr. ref. and info. svcs. dept. Ill. Inst. Tech., 1987-90; dir. Learning Resources Ctr. Morton Coll., 1990—2003. Reviewer Libr. Jour., Am. Ref. Books Ann.; convenor Coun. II, Ill. Clearinghouse for Acad. Libr. Instrn., 1978; presentor 7th Ann. Conf. Acad. Libr. Instrn., 1977, Nat. Women's Studies Assn., 1983, others; participant Gt. Lakes Women's Studies Summer Inst., 1981, Nat. Inst. Leadership Devel. seminar, 1995. Contbr. articles to profl. jours. Pres. Springfield chpt. NOW, 1978—79; invited Susan B. Anthony luncheon, 1978, 1979; mem. adv. bd. Suburban Libr. Sys., 1992—94, Nat. Commn. Learning Resources; v.p. membership Riverside chpt. Lyric Opera Chgo., 1994—96, 1999—; active Riverside Arts Ctr.; Dem. precinct Committeewoman, 1982—85; vice-moderator Fourth Presbyn. Women, 1989—90; elder Riverside (Ill.) Presbyn. Ch., 1992—, mem. session, 1993—96, 2000—01, mem. adminstrn. com., 1993—2003, chmn. adminstrn. com., 1993—96, 1999, 2000—01, mem. endowment com., 1996—98; bd. dirs. Berwyn-Cicero Coun. on Aging. Ill. state scholar, 1962-66; recipient Citizenship award Am. Legion, 1962, Cert. of Recognition Ill. Bicentennial Commn., 1974. Mem.: AAUW (bd. dirs. Riverside br. 1992—94, 1997—99, chmn. standing com. on women Springfield br., com. on women Ill. state divsn.), ALA, Lyric Opera Chgo. Riverside Chpt. (v.p. 1995—), Ill. Libr. Assn. (presenter 1984), Nat. Assn. Women in C.C., Springfield Art Assn., No. Ill. Learning Resources Coop. (del. 1990—2003, steering com. West Suburban postsecondary consortium 1996—2000), Nat. Women's Studies Assn. (presenter 1983, 1984, 1995), Women in Mgmt., Am. Mgmt. Assn., No. Ill. Learning Resources Consortium Bd., Spl. Librs. Assn., Ill. Assn. Coll. and Rsch. Librs. (bibliog. instrn. com.), Libr. Info. and Tech. Assn., Libr. Adminstr. and Mgmt. Assn. (ref. and adult svcs. divsn.), Assn. Coll. and Rsch. Librs., Am. Opera Soc. of Chgo., Nat. Trust Hist. Preservation, Musicians Club of Women Chgo., Beta Phi Mu. Home: 181 Scottswood Rd Riverside IL 60546-2221

VAN DE BOVENKAMP, SUE ERPF, charitable organization executive; b. N.Y.C.; d. George Norton and Bettina Lions (Hearst) Mortimore; student Gardner Sch., Art Students League, Cooper Union; m. Armand Grover Erpf, 1965 (dec.); children: Cornelia Aurelia, Armand Bartholomew; m. Gerrit Pieter Van de Bovenkamp, Aug. 11, 1973 (div.). Pres. Armand G. Erpf Fund, N.Y.C., 1971—; founder, hon. chmn. Erpf Catskill Cultural Ctr., 1972—. Bd. advisors, founder N.Y. Zool. Soc., 1971—, 1001 Nature Trust, 1973, William Beebe fellow, 1983—; fellow in perpetuity Met. Mus. Art, 1977; life fellow Pierpont Morgan Libr., 1974—; mem. coun.of friends Whitney Mus. Am. Art, 1971-77; mem. Whitney Circle, 1978-93; bd. dirs. Catskill Ctr. for Conservation and Devel., 1983-86; mem. adv. coun., dept. art history and archaeology Columbia U., 1972—, established univ. seminar on uses of oceans, 1977, mem. adv. coun. Translation Ctr., 1986; life conservator N.Y. Pub. Libr., 1980; fellow Frick Collection; 1971—, Whitney fellow, 2994—; mem. coun. Agribus. Coun., Inc., 1979-87; founder, life mem. World Wildlife Fund, 1973—, bd. dirs., 1984-89; mem. pres.'s coun. Columbia U., 1973-78; life mem. Mus. City N.Y., 1972—, mem. pres.'s coun., 1971—. Mem. N.Y. Acad. Scis., The Planetary Soc., Mus. Natural History (life), Asia Soc. (pres.'s coun.), Wildlife Fedn. (adv.), African Wildlife Found. (pres.'s cir.). mem. Mus. of Natural Hist. pres., coun. of the Asia Soc. Office: The Armand G Erpf Fund 640 Park Ave New York NY 10021-6126

VANDEBUNTE, EILEEN J. health facility administrator; b. Sioux Falls, S.D., July 8, 1945; BA, Central Coll., 1967; MPA, Fairleigh Dickinson, 1998. Office: Monmouth Med Ctr 300 Second Ave Long Branch NJ 07740

VANDEL, DIANA GEIS, management consultant; b. San Antonio, Apr. 2, 1947; d. John George and Elma Ruth (Triplett) Geis; m. Jerry Dean Vandel, Apr. 17, 1976; 1 child, Jeremy Kyle. MusB, U. Tex., 1969. Cert. tchr., Tex. Tchr. music Zilker Elem. Pub. Sch., Austin, Tex., 1969-70, Isely Sch., Austin, 1986; asst. adminstr. Hillside Manor Nursing Home, Inc., San Antonio, 1970-76, 78-79, mgmt. cons., 1979-89, adminstr., 1988; mgmt. cons. Promoting Excellence Consultation, Austin, 1991-95, Winning Solutions, Austin, 1995—; owner Your Biggest Fan, 1999—. Owner, facilitator creative music and relaxation in motion classes, San Antonio, 1982-84; fine arts facilitator Cedar Creek Elem. Sch., Austin, 1988-91; seminar leader Movement Spiritual Inner Awareness, Austin, 1986—2003, min., 1989-2003. Austin rep. Peace Theol. Sem., L.A., 1988-93; exec. bd. Cedar Creek Booster Club, 1989-91. Avocations: photography, yoga, meditation, gardening, reading. Home: 916 Terrace Mountain Dr Austin TX 78746-2732 Office: Winning Solutions and Your Biggest Fan 916 Calithea Rd Austin TX 78746-2716 Office Phone: 512-328-3734. E-mail: dvandel@earthlink.net.

VANDEMARK, MICHELLE VOLIN, critical care, neuroscience nurse; b. Sioux Falls, S.D., Feb. 14, 1962; d. Verlynne V. and Suzanne (Cronin) Volin; m. Richard E. VanDemark, June 5, 1982; children: Andrew Porter, Hannah Elizabeth. BA in Biology, Lake Forest (Ill.) Coll., 1984; BSN, Northwestern U., Chgo., 1986; MS in Nursing, Loyola U., Chgo., 1990. RN, Ill., S.D.; cert. neurosci. nursing, CNRN, ACLS. Staff nurse neurosci. unit Evanston Hosp., Ill., 1986-90, staff nurse intensive care unit, 1990-93; neurosci. clin. nurse specialist Sioux Valley Hosp., Sioux Falls, S.D., 1995—. Mem. Am. Assn. Neurosci. Nurses (pres. Gt. Plains chpt. 1995-96, bd. dirs. 2000-03), Sigma Theta Tau, Alpha Sigma Nu. Home: 321 E 27th St Sioux Falls SD 57105-3032

VAN DEMARK, RUTH ELAINE, lawyer; b. Santa Fe, May 16, 1944; d. Robert Eugene and Bertha Marie (Thompson) Van D.; m. Leland Wilkinson, June 23, 1967; children: Anne Marie, Caroline Cook. AB, Vassar Coll., 1966; MTS, Harvard U., 1969; JD with honors, U. Conn., 1976; MDiv, Luth. Sch. Theology, Chgo., 1999. Bar: Conn. 1976, Ill. 1977, U.S. Dist. Ct. Conn. 1976, U.S. Dist. Ct. (no. dist.) Ill., U.S. Ct. Appeals (7th cir.) 1984, U.S. Supreme Ct. 1983; ordained to ministry, Luth Ch., 1999. Instr. legal rsch. and writing Loyola U. Sch. Law, Chgo., 1976-79; assoc. Wildman, Harrold, Allen & Dixon, Chgo., 1977-84, ptnr., 1985-94; prin. Law Offices of Ruth E. Van Demark, Chgo., 1995—2003; pastor Wicker Park Luth. Ch., Chgo., 1999—. Mem. rules com. Ill. Supreme Ct., 1999-2002, chair appellate rules subcom., 1996-2002; mem. dist. ct. fund adv. com. U.S. Dist. Ct. (no. dist.) Ill., 1997—. Assoc. editor Conn. Law Rev., 1975-76. Bd. dirs. Lutheran Soc. Svcs. Ill., 1998—, sec., 2000—02, chmn., 2002-; mem. adv. bd. Horizon Hospice, Chgo., 1978—, YWCA Battered Women's Shelter, Evanston, Ill., 1982-86; del.-at-large White House Conf. on Families, L.A., 1980; mem. alumni coun. Harvard Divinity Sch., 1988-91; vol. atty. Pro Bono Advs. Chgo., 1982-92, bd. dirs., 1993-99, chair devel. com., 1993; bd. dirs. Friends of Pro Bono Advs. Orgn., 1987-89, New Voice Prodns., 1984-86, Byrne Piven Theater Workshop, 1987-90, Luth. Social Svcs. Ill. (sec., 2000—), 1998—; founder, bd. dirs. Friends of Battered Women and Their Children, 1986-87; chair 175th Reunion Fund Harvard U. Div. Sch., 1992; dean Ctrl. Conf. Met. Chgo. Synod ELCA. Mem. ABA, Ill. Bar Assn., Conn. Bar Assn., Chgo. Bar Assn., Appellate Lawyers Assn. Ill. (bd. dirs. 1985-87, treas. 1989-90, sec. 1990-91, v.p. 1991-92, pres. 1992-93), Women's Bar Assn. Ill., Jr. League Evanston (chair State Pub. Affairs Com. 1987-88, Vol. of Yr. 1983-84), Chgo. Vassar Club (pres. 1979-81), Cosmopolitan Club (N.Y.C.). Home: 2046 W Pierce Ave Chicago IL 60622-1946 E-mail: revwplc@earthlink.net.

VANDENBERG, JOKA MARIA, physicist, researcher; b. Heemstede, The Netherlands, Jan. 24, 1938; came to the U.S., 1968; d. Antonius Vandenberg and Maria Elisabeth Van Amerongen; m. Rudolf Johannes Voorhoeve, May 11, 1968 (div. Aug. 1975); children: Lucy, Niels; m. James Charles Phillips, Mar. 1, 1996. B in Physics, State U., Leiden, The Netherlands, 1959, M in Phys. Chemistry, 1962, PhD in Solid State Physics, 1964. Tchg. asst. Lab. Inorganic Chemistry, Leiden, 1959-60; rsch. asst. Lab. Crystallography, Amsterdam, 1962-64; rschr. Royal Dutch Shell Lab., Amsterdam, The Netherlands, 1964-68; postdoctoral staff Bell Labs., Murray Hill, N.J., 1968-69, cons., 1972; mem. tech. staff Lucent Techs., Murray Hill, 1973-2001. Mem. affirmative action com. Bell Labs., Murray Hill, 1990-91. Mem. IEEE, Am. Phys. Soc., Royal Dutch Acad. Scis. (corr.). Achievements include patent for super conducting films. Home: 204 Springfield Ave Summit NJ 07901 E-mail: joka_berg@comcast.net.

VAN DEN BLINK, NELSON MOOERS, light industrial manufacturing executive; Chmn., CEO Hiliard Corp., Elmira, N.Y., 1982—. Chair Southern Tier Econ. Growth, Inc. Office: Hilliard Corp 100 W 4th St Elmira NY 14901-2190

VANDENBURG, KATHY HELEN, small business owner, career coach, resume writer; b. Clifton, N.J., Feb. 6, 1969; d. Milan and Helen (Derco) Suchanek; m. James Joseph Vandenburg III, Aug. 31, 1996. BA in Psychology, Montclair State U., 1991; MA in Edn., Seton Hall U., 1995; postgrad., Rider U., 1997-98. Cert. job and career transition coach Career Planning and Adult Devel. Network. Admissions counselor William Paterson U., Wayne, N.J., 1995-96; career counselor New Brunswick (N.J.) Pub. Schs., 1996-2000, Cornerstone Relocation Group, Warren, NJ, 2000-01; career tng. advisor Transitions Ctr. for Women, Warren County C.C., Washington, NJ, 2001—02, Transitions Ctr. for Women, NORWESCAP, Washington, NJ, 2002—. Mem.: Profl. Assn. Resume Writers and Career Coaches, Career Masters Inst., Nat. Resume Writers Assn., Hunterdon County C. of C. Avocations: swimming, travel, classical music, theatre, cooking.

VANDEN HEUVEL, KATRINA, magazine editor; b. N.Y.C., Oct. 7, 1959; d. William Jacobus and Jean Babette (Stein) Vanden H.; m. Stephen F. Cohen, Dec. 4, 1988; 1 child, Nicola Anna. BA summa cum laude in Politics, Princeton U., 1982. Prodn. assoc. ABC Closeup Documentaries, 1982-83; asst. editor The Nation, N.Y.C., 1984-89, editor-at-large, 1989-93, acting editor-in-chief, 1994-95, editor-in-chief, 1995—. Vis. journalist Moscow News, 1989; Moscow coord. Conf. Investigative Journalism After the Cold War, 1992; co-founder, co-editor Vyi i Myi, 1990—. Editor: The Nation, 1865-1990; The Best of the Nation, 1990-2000: Selections from the Independent Magazine of Politics and Culture, 2001, A Just Response: The Nation on Terrorism, Democracy and September 11, 2001, 2002; co-editor: Voices of Glasnost: Interviews with Gorbachev's Reformers, 1989, Taking Back America, 2004; contbr. articles to newspapers. Recipient Maggie award Planned Parenthood Fedn. Am., 1994. Mem. Correctional Assn. N.Y. (dir.), Inst. for Women's Policy Rsch. (bd. dirs.), Coun. Fgn. Rels., Inst. Policy Studies (trustee), Network of East-West Women (bd. advisors), Franklin and Eleanor Roosevelt Inst. (trustee), Moscow Ctr. for Gender Studies (mem. adv. com.), Century Assn., Avca Found. (bd. mem.). Office: The Nation 33 Irving Pl Fl 8 New York NY 10003-2332

VAN DE PUTTE, LETICIA, pharmacist, state legislator; b. Tacoma, Dec. 6, 1954; d. Daniel and Isabel (Aguilar) San Miguel; m. Henry P. Van de Putte, Jr., Oct. 223, 1977; children: Nichole, Vanessa, Henry, Gregory, Isabella, Paul. Student, St. Mary's U., San Antonio, 1973-74, U. Houston, 1975, 76-77, U. Tex., 1979; cert. JFK sch. exec. program, Harvard U., 1993. Registered pharmacist, Tex. Supr. MHMR T. L. Vordenbaument and Assocs., San Antonio, 1971-82; pharmacist in charge Botica Guadalupana, San Antonio, 1982-85; owner Loma Park Pharmacy, San Antonio, 1985-95. Panelist Eil Lilly & Co. Pham. Adv. Panel, 1989—. Mem. St. Joseph's Cath. Ch., 1977—; mem. YWCA, 1983—, bd. dirs., 1983-86; appointee City Coun. Commn. on Status of Women, San Antonio, 1985; sec. Mex.-Am. Legis. Caucus; mem. Tex. Ho. of Reps. Labor and Employment Commn., 1991-92, Human Svcs. Commn., 1991-94, Internat. Cultural Rels., 1993-94, Econ. Devel. Commn., 1995—, Juvenile Justice and Family Issues Commn., 1995-97, vice chmn. ins. commn., 1997—; mem. Alamo Area Coun. Govts., 1992—; chair Interagy. Child Abuse Network Com. Recipient Mother and Leader award LULAC, 1992, Mujeres Project award Mex.-Am. Unity Coun., 1992, Hermine Tobolowsky award for outstanding contributions to women's issues Bus. and Profl. Women, 1997, Lifetime Achievement award U. Tex., 1997, Ofcl. Advocate of Yr., 1997, Patient Advocacy award Tex. Acad. Family Physicians, 1997; Kellogg fellow Harvard/JFK Exec. Elected Ofcls. program, 1993; named Young Career Woman of Yr., Mex.-Am. Profl. Women's Club, 1983, Outstanding Women in Politics, San Antonio Express News, 1992, Tex. Assn. Regional Coun. award, 1995, Tex. Med. Assn. Medicine Best award, 1995, 97, Legislator of Yr., Tex. Assn. for Edn. of Young Children, 1999, one of 50 Most Influential Pharmacists, Am. Druggist Mag., 1999. Mem. Market Sq. Assn. (sec. 1985-86), Tex. Pharm. Assn. (coun. mem. 1987-90, Pharmacist of Yr. 1996), Bexar County Pharm. Assn., Nat. Assn. Retail Druggists, Women of the Moose. Democrat. Office: 3718 Blanco Rd Ste 2 San Antonio TX 78212-1330

VANDERBEKE, PATRICIA K. architect; b. Detroit, Apr. 3, 1963; d. B. H. and Dolores I. VanderBeke. BS in Architecture, U. Mich., 1985, MArch, 1987. Registered arch., Ill. Archtl. intern Hobbs & Black, Assocs., Ann Arbor, Mich., 1984-86, Fry Assocs., Ann Arbor, 1988; arch. Decker & Kemp Architecture/Urban Design, Chgo., 1989-92; prin., founder P. K. VanderBeke, Arch., Chgo., 1992—. Mem. adv. com. dept. arch., Triton Coll. Contbr. photographs and articles to Inland Arch. mag.; contbr. photographs to AIA calendar. Chair recycling com. Lake Point Tower Condo. Assn., Chgo., 1990—, chair. ops. com., 1993; mem. benefit com. The Renaissance Soc., U. Chgo., Redmoon Theater, Chgo. George S. Booth travelling fellow, 1992. Mem. AIA (participant 1st ann. leadership inst. 1997, 1st place nat. photog. contest award 1992, hon. mention 1994, membership com. Chgo. chpt.), Chgo. Archl. Club, hon. mention 2000 Burnham Prize Competition, The Cliff Dwellers (mem. arts com.). Office: 155 W Burton Pl Apt 16 Chicago IL 60610-1326

VANDERBILT, GLORIA MORGAN, artist, actress, fashion designer; b. N.Y.C., Feb. 20, 1924; d. Reginald Claypoole and Gloria (Morgan) V.; m. Pasquale di Cicco (div.); m. Leopold Stokowski, 1945 (div. 1955); children— Stanislaus, Christopher; m. Sidney Lumet, 1956 (div.); m. Wyatt Emory Cooper, 1963; children— Carter V. (dec.), Anderson H. Attended, Mary C. Wheeler, Miss Porter's schs.; studied acting with, dir. Sanford Meisner, beginning 1955. Exhibited in one-man shows at Rabun Studio, N.Y.C., 1948, Bertha Shaeffer Gallery, N.Y.C., 1954, Juster Gallery, N.Y.C., 1956, Hammer Gallery, N.Y.C., 1966, 68, Cord Gallery, N.Y.C., 1966, Washington Gallery Art, 1968, Neiman-Marcus, Dallas, 1968, Vestart Gallery, N.Y.C., 1969, Parish Museum, Southampton, N.Y., also in Nantucket, Mass., Houston, Reading, Pa., Monterey, Calif., Nashville; exhibited in group shows, Washington Gallery Art, 1967, Hoover Gallery, San Francisco, 1971, stage career; acted in summer stock prodn. The Swan; made Broadway debut in The Time of Your Life, 1955; other stage appearances include Picnic, 1955, The Spa, 1956, Peter Pan, 1958, The Green Hat; made TV debut in Tonight At 8:30; other TV appearances include Colgate Comedy Hour, 1955, Flint and Fire on U.S. Steel Hour, 1958, Family Happiness on U.S. Steel Hour, 1959, Very Important People; appeared in film Johnny Concho, 1955; dir. design film, Riegel Textile Corp., N.Y.C., from 1970; designer stationary and greeting cards, Hallmark Co., fabrics, Bloomcraft Co., bed linens, Martex Co., table linens, Peacock Co., Gloria Vanderbilt jeans; also china, glassware, scarves. Recipient Sylvania award 1959, Fashion award Neiman-Marcus 1969. Author: Love Poems, 1955, (with Alfred Allen Lewis) Gloria Vanderbilt Book of Collage, 1970, Woman to Woman, 1979, Once Upon a Time: A True Story, 1985, novel Never Say Good-Bye, 1989, The Memory Book of Starr Faithfull, 1994; author: (with Alfred Allen Lewis) play Three by Two, early 1960's, Black White, White Knight, 1987; poems and short stories. Mem. Actors Equity, Screen Actors Guild, AFTRA, Authors League Am., Am. Fedn. Arts.

VANDERBURG, KATHLEEN, surgical nurse; b. Milw., Feb. 2, 1951; d. Raymond Lawrence and Louise Mary (Jelich) Ksobiech; m. Richard John, July 27, 1975. Diploma, Mt. Sinai Hosp. Sch. Nursing, 1972; BS, Chapman Coll., 1979; BS in Nursing, McKendree Coll., 1988; MS, Health Sci. Chapman Coll., 1981. RN Fla. Supr. oper. room svcs. USAF, Langley AFB, Va., 1991—93, commd., 1974, advanced through grades to col., 1994, dir. oper. rm. and c.s.s. svcs., 1994—96; cmdr. 375th Aeromed. Evacuation Squadron, Scott AFB, Ill., 1996—97; chair dept. aerospace edn. and tng., assoc. dean Aerospace Nursing, Brooks AFB, Tex., 1998—2001; ret., 2001. Decorated Meritorious Svc. medal (6), Commendation medal (3), Legion of Merit. Mem. Air Force Assn., Assn. Operating Rm. Nurses. Home: 308 Miracle Strip Pky 12A Fort Walton Beach FL 32548

VANDERHEYDEN, CAROL, retired elementary school educator; b. Delhi, N.Y., Feb. 13, 1946; d. Harlan R. and Wilda D. Claypool; m. Larry J. VanderHeyden, Dec. 21, 1968; children: Robert, Amy. BS in Edn., Bethel Coll., 1968; student, St. Francis. Cert. tchr. Ind., 1968, Mich., 1968. Elem. tchr. Pean Harris Madison Corp., Mishawaka, Ind., Edwardsburg (Mich.) Pub. Sch. Author: A Touch of Class, 2003. Recipient Conservation Educator of Yr. award, Cass County Soil and Water Conservation Dist., 1996. Mem.: Ret. Tchrs. Assn., Green Thumbs Garden Club, Solivita Travel Club (treas. 2003—). Republican. Avocations: boating, painting, flower arranging, reading, photography. Home: 399 Lake Butler Drive Poinciana FL 34759

VANDER HEYDEN, MARSHA ANN, business owner; b. Milw., Sept. 15, 1942; d. Bernard Aloysius and Leona Adeline (Zimpel) Vander H. BA, Alverno Coll., 1964; postgrad., Layton Sch. Art, 1966; MFA, Cornell U., 1969; diploma in carpentry and cabinetmaking, Manhattan Trade Sch., 1975. Rschr. The Nigerian Mus., Lagos, 1970; tchr. The Cloisters/The Met. Mus. Art, N.Y.C., 1973-74; woodshop instr. The New Lincoln Sch., N.Y.C., 1973-75; tchr. Grand Street Settlement, N.Y.C., 1974-76; mgr., head tchr. The Woodsmith's Studio, N.Y.C., 1976-77; founder, pres. Trade Links, Inc. (runs Me Too Kids program), N.Y.C.; owner, operator Vander Heyden Woodworking, Inc., N.Y.C., 1977—, Tapestries etc. dba Vander Heyden Woordworking Inc., N.Y.C. Designer pet products under name Doggone Purrrty; patentee frame assembly. Mem. Urban-rural Coalition. Recipient award of excellence The Archtl. Woodwork Inst., Washington, 1989. Mem. Miniatures Industry Assn. Am. Avocations: gardening, her dog and cats, hiking, animal and human rights issues, reading. Home and Office: 151 W 25th St 8th Fl New York NY 10001-7204 E-mail: mymarsha@earthlink.net.

VAN DER HOEK, SHERRY A. counselor; b. Chgo., July 20, 1956; d. John Albert and Stella Rose (dec.) Troike; m. Herman Vanderhoek (dec.); stepchildren: Michiel, Martin. AAS, Prairie State Coll., 1992; BA, Govs. State U., 1994, MA, 1997. Lic. profl. counselor, Ill.; cert. counselor Nat. Bd. Cert. Counselors. Counselor South Suburban Coun. on Alcoholism, East Hazel Crest, Ill., 1990-93, South Suburban Family Shelter, Hazel Crest, Ill., 1996-97; facilitator Aunt Martha's Youth Svcs. Ctr., Inc., Park Forest, Ill., 1991-92; grad. asst. Govs. State U., University Park, Ill., 1995-97; pvt. practice counselor Matteson, Ill., 1998—. Mem.: ACA, Ill. Alcoholism and Drug Dependence Assn., Assn. Counselor Edn. and Supervision (Outstanding Grad. Student Scholarship award 1997), Internat. Assn. Addiction and Offender Counselors, Ill. Counselor Educators and Suprs. (Outstanding Grad. Student award 1996), Ill. Alcohol and Other Drug Profl. Cert. Assn., Ill. Counseling Assn. (founder Govs. State Chpt., pres. 1996, regional gov. 1997—2000), Chi Sigma Iota (chpt. sec. 1995), Psi Chi (chpt. founder, pres. 1997). Avocations: stained glass, cross-stitch, cooking. Home and Office: 3761 W 216th Pl Matteson IL 60443

VANDER HORST, KATHLEEN PURCELL, nonprofit association administrator; b. Glen Rock, NJ, Jan. 15, 1945; d. Thomas Ralph and Elizabeth Jeanne (Burnett) Purcell; m. John Vander Horst Jr., Feb. 12, 1972 (div. Oct. 1993). Dir. devel. svcs. Johns Hopkins U., Balt., 1968-71; dir. devel. Union of Colls. of Art, Kansas City, Mo., 1971-72; dir. pub. rels. Md. Ballet and Ctr. Stage, Balt., 1973-76; dir. program devel. Joint Ctr. for Polit. and Econ. Studies, Washington, 1976-90, v.p. program devel., 1990—2000, cons., 2001—. Dir., Roland Park Cmty. Found., Balt., 1990-2000, vice-chmn., 1998-99, chmn., 2000-02; dir., chair program com. Centro de la Comunidad, Balt., 1997-2001.

VANDERLINDEN, CAMILLA DENICE DUNN, telecommunications industry executive; b. Dayton, July 21, 1950; d. Joseph Stanley and Virginia Danley (Martin) Dunn; m. David Henry VanderLinden; Oct. 10, 1980; 1 child, Michael Christopher. Student, U. de Valencia, Spain, 1969; BA in Spanish and Secondary Edn. cum laude, U. Utah, 1972, MS in Human Resource Econs., 1985. Asst. dir. Davis County Community Action Program, Farmington, Utah, 1973-76; dir. South County Community Action, Midvale, Utah, 1976-79; supr. customer service Ideal Nat. Life Ins. Co., Salt Lake City, 1979-80; mgr. customer service Utah Farm Bur. Mutual Ins., Salt Lake City, 1980-82; quality assurance analyst Am. Express Co., Salt Lake City, 1983-86, quality assurance and human resource specialist, 1986-88, mgr. quality assurance and engring. Denver, 1988-91; mgr. customer svc. Tel. Express Co., Colorado Springs, Colo., 1991-97; dir. Call Ctr. United Membership Mktg. Group, Lakewood, Colo., 1997-98; telesvcs. industry mgr. Piton Found., Denver, 1998—; customer care and tng. dir. SafeRent, 2000—; pvt. call ctr. cons., 2000—; dir. quality assurance Tele-Servicing Innovations, 2000—02; ops. mgr. Bayaud Industries, 2002—. Mem. adj. faculty Westminster Coll., Salt Lake City, 1987-88. mem. adj. faculty, mem. quality adv. bd. Red Rocks C.C., 1990-91. Vol. translator Latin Am. community; vol. naturalist Roxborough State Park; internat. exch. coord. EF Fgn. Exch. Program. Mem. Internat. Customer Svc. Orgn. (officer call ctr. chpt.), Colo. Springs Customer Svc. Assn. (officer). Christian. Avocations: swimming, hosting foreign exchange students. Home: 10857 Snow Cloud Trail Littleton CO 80125-9211 Office Phone: 303-946-1235. E-mail: camillavan@usa.net.

VANDERLIP, ELIN BREKKE, philanthropic executive; b. Oslo, June 7, 1919; came to the U.S., 1934; m. Kelvin Cox, Nov., 1946 (dec. 1956); children: Kelvin Jr., Narcissa, Henrik and Katrina (twins). With Norwegian Embassy, Washington, Norwegian Fgn. Ministry, London, 1941-44, Red

Cross, Calcutta, India; pres. Friends of French Art, Portuguese Bend, Calif. Sponsor of charity art conservation fundraising events Friends of French Art; tour leader Ile de France, Anjou, Bordelais, Provence-Cote d'Azur, Alsace, Dordogne, Lyonnais-Isere, Brittany, Burgundy, Normandy, Languedoc, Loire, Gascony, Le Nord, Charente, Champagne, Eure et Loir, 1978-96, Route de Berry, Auvergne and Toulouse. Decorated Comdr. Order of Arts and Letters (France) Chevalier of the Legion of Honor. Home and Office: Villa Narcissa 100 Vanderlip Dr Palos Verdes Peninsula CA 90275-5920 Fax: (310) 377-4584. E-mail: VillaCissa@aol.com.

VANDER NAALD EGENES, JOAN ELIZABETH, small business owner, educator; b. Des Moines, Feb. 13, 1936; d. Bert and Cathryn Alice (Bunger) Vander Naald; m. David Iddings Grant, July 25, 1959 (div. Oct. 1984); children: Jeffrey, Pamela, Elizabeth, Jennifer. BA, U. Iowa, 1958. Cert. profl. in edn., Iowa, Colo.; cert. travel agt., Iowa. Instr. St. Katherine's Sch., Davenport, Iowa, 1958-59, Iowa Ctrl. C.C., Fort Dodge, 1959-61; city councilwoman Boone, 1980-86; instr. Des Moines Area C.C., Boone Campus, 1983; founder, owner, importer Global Ednl. Svcs., Des Moines, 1992-97; receptionist, sec. Automobile Club of So. Calif., West Los Angeles, 1997-2001. Bd. mem. Iowa Psychology Bd. Examiners, Des Moines, 1984-93; rsch. interviewer Iowa State U., Ames, 1984; resource tchr., workshop presenter about Russia, 1988-94; freelance photographer, 1988—. Lifetime mem. Rep. Senatorial Inner Circle, Washington, 1987—; pres. Iowa 4th Dist. Rep. Women, 1990-91, Polk County (Iowa) Rep. Women, 1994; precinct chair 12, ward 01, Des Moines, 1995-97; pres. Des Moines Metro Opera Guild, 1996-97, coun. sec., 1995-97; extensive vol. activities, including various fundraising chairs. Recipient 1st prize Youth Projects, Iowa Devel. Commn., 1983, Women Helping Women award for volunteerism, Boone, 1983; named Entrepreneur of Yr. in Iowa award GE, 1995. Republican. Avocation: swimming. Home: 36047 Palomino Way Palm Desert CA 92211

VANDERSLICE, ELLEN, architect; b. Ann Arbor, Mich., Oct. 8, 1953; d. Ralph L. Vanderslice, Carolyn G. Vanderslice; married. MArch Coll. Architecture and Urban Planning, U. Mich., 1983, BS, 1981. Lic. Architect, Oreg., 1996. Pres. America Walks, Portland, Oreg., 1996—2003; project mgr. Office of Transp., City of Portland, 1994—99, 2003—; project designer David Giulietti and Assocs., Portland, 1990—94. Pres. Willamette Pedestrian Coalition, Portland, 2001—03; mem. com. on pedestrians Transp. Rsch. Bd., Washington, 2001—04; mem. adv. com. Pub. Rights-of-Way Access, Washington, 1999—; co-treas. Portland chpt. Women's Transp. Seminar, 1997—97; prin. Ellen Vanderslice AIA, Portland, 1999—2003. Composer (CD): Once in a Blue Moon, 2000, The Standard Vanderslice, 2001, Don't Look Before You Sing, 2003. Sec. Northwest Dist. Assn., Portland, 1986—88. Recipient Pl. Planning award for Portland Pedestrian Master Plan and Pedestrian Design Guide, Environ. Design and Rsch. Assn., 2000, Exemplary Svc. to Pedestrian Transp. Program and Unwavering Commitment to Advocacy of Walking award, Portland Office of Transp. Engring. and Devel., 1999, Outstanding Project award for Portland Pedestrian Design Guide, Inst. Transp. Engrs. Oreg. Sect., 1999, Reclaiming Our Streets All-Star award, City Commr. Earl Blumenauer, 1991, Northwest Traffic Circulation Project Leadership award, Neighbor Newspaper, 1987, 1st prize jazz, USA Songwriting Competition, 2002. Mem.: AIA (sec. Portland chpt. 1998—99, Nehemiah Housing Project award of excellence Portland chpt. 1993), Assn. Pedestrian and Bicycle Profls., Women's Transp. Seminar (co-treas. Portland chpt. 1997, Woman of Yr. Portland chpt. 2000), Nat. Assn. Watch and Clock [illegible], Oreg., Portland Songwriters Assn. (1st pl. Blues/Jazz/R&B Category 1999, 2000, 2001, 2003). Avocations: restoring eight-day clocks, canoeing, hiking. Office: 1120 SW 5th Ave Rm 800 Portland OR 97204 Business E-Mail: ellen.vanderslice@pdxtrans.org.

VANDERSLICE, STEPHANIE M. humanities educator; b. Queens, N.Y., Feb. 4, 1967; d. William Muller and Maureen Pettei; m. John Vanderslice, July 2, 1993; children: Jackson H., Wilson A. MFA, George Mason U., 1992; PhD, U. La., 1997. Asst. prof. writing U. Ctrl. Ark., Conway, 1997—. Dir. Nat. Writing Project of Ctrl. Ark., Conway, 1999—; grantee vis. writers program Ark. Arts Coun., 1999; grantee, Nat. Writing Project, 1999—. Contbr. articles to profl. jours.; editor: profl. vols. Grantee Deep South Writing Conf. Program grantee, La. Arts Coun., 1995,1996. Mem.: MLA, Conf. on Coll. Composition and Comm., Nat. Coun. Tchrs. of English. Avocations: travel, walking, collecting children's books. Office: Univ Ctrl Arkansas 201 Donaghey Ave, Thompson 336 Conway AR 72035 Business E-Mail: stephv@uca.edu.

VANDERSYPEN, RITA DEBONA, guidance counselor, academic administrator; d. Sam S. and Myrtle (Genova) DeBona; m. Robert Louis Vandersypen, Aug. 17, 1974; children: Regina Marie, Ryan Matthew. BA summa cum laude, La. Coll., 1975; MEd, La. State U., 1980, postgrad., 1982; EdS, Northwestern State U., Natchitoches, La., 1993. Eligibility worker Rapides Parish Office Family Svcs., Alexandria, 1975-78; welfare social worker Rapides Parish Foster Care Svcs., Alexandria, 1978-79; tchr. A. Wettermark High Sch., Boyce, La., 1979-84; tchr. English English Alexandria Sr. High Sch., 1984-92, guidance counselor, 1992-2000; asst. prin., curriculum coord. Brame Jr. H.S., Alexandria, La., 2000—. Pres. Andersen Fire Protection Inc. Contbr. to handbook and curriculum guide. Sponsor Future Voters Am. Club, 1984-89, 4-H Club, 1988-97. Mem. Rapides Assn. Principals, Rapides Fedn. Tchrs., La. Assn. Principals, La. Vocat. Assn., La. Mid. Sch. Assn., Rapides Livestock Club, Belgian-Am. Club, Am. Quarter Horse Assn., Phi Kappa Phi, Kappa Delta Pi. Roman Catholic. Office: Brame Jr HS 4800 Dawn St Alexandria LA 71301-3301

VANDERTIE, SUZAN MARY, music educator; d. Jule Joseph and Lucille Young Vandertie. MusB, Seton Hill Coll., Greensburg, Pa., 1967; MusM edn., Duquesne U., Pitts., Pa., 1968—71, Multimedia Tech. Cert. Program, 1996—97. Cert. Multimedia Tech. Duquesne U., 1997; K-12 Profl. Music Tchr. Dept. of Edn./Pa., 1967. Elem. band dir. Moon Area Sch. Dist., Moon Twp., Pa., 1967—75, HS orch. dir., 1967—75, elem./mid. sch. orch. dir., 1975—2003; unified arts dept. chair Moon Area Mid. Sch., Moon Twp., Pa., 1990—95; k-12 music coord. Moon Area Sch. Dist., Moon Twp., Pa., 1995—2003; adj. prof. Point Park U., Pittsburgh, 2004—. Substitute bell choir dir. Coraopolis United Meth. Ch., Coraopolis, Pa., 1989; comm. com. mem. Moon Edn. Assn., Moon Twp., Pa., 1998—2000; advocacy and awareness task force mem. Arts Edn. Collaborative, Pitts., 2001—; comm. com. chairperson Moon Edn. Assn., Moon Twp., Pa., 2001—03; new tchr. mentor Moon Area Sch. dist., Moon Township, Pa., 2002—03; mentor, gov. inst. for arts educators Dept. of Edn., Harrisburgh, Pa., 2003—. Editor: (newsletter) PAPERMOON (Pa, State Edn. Assn. Internal Communication Award, 2002), Moon Middle School MUSIC NEWS (Pa, Sch. Pub. Rels. Assn. Hon. Mention newsletter category, 1995); photographer (professional education magazine) Mid. Sch. Jour. - photographic submission (second Pl. award for student photography, 1990). Recipient Hon. Mention - cmty. rels./publicity, Pa, Sch. Pub. Rels. Assn., 1995; grantee Emerging Tech. Award For Educators, AT&T Broadband, 2002, 20,000 Funding grant, Digital Assessment Group, 2003. Mem.: Tech. Inst. for Music Educators, Pa., State Edn. Assn., Pa., Music Edn. Assn. Avocations: digital graphic design, digital videography, photography, folk fiddling, arts education research. Home and Office: 719 Seventh Avenue Coraopolis PA 15108 Personal E-mail: svandertie@comcast.net.

VANDERTUUK-PERKINS, JENNIFER ELIZABETH, counselor, psychologist; d. Rodney Roy Perkins and Jill Ellen VanDerTuuk-Perkins; m. Joe Allen Behun II, Aug. 22, 1997; children: Lucile Elizabeth Perkins-Wagel, Gabriel Theodore Perkins-Behun, Madeline Emilie Joy Perkins-Behun; m. Ashley Allen Wagel, Dec. 26, 1993 (div. Aug. 20, 1997). MA in Ednl. and Devel. Psychology, Andrews U., Berrien Springs, MI, 1996, MA in Cmty. Counseling, 1999; PhD in Counseling Psychology, Cambridge State U., Honolulu, Hawaii, 2000; Grad. Cert. in Forensic Clin. Psychology, Capella U., Mpls., Minn., 2003. Lic. Limited Lic. Psychologist Mich., 2002; registered Social Worker Mich., 2003; Diplomate of the Bd.- Clinical Forensic Counseling Am. Coll. of Forensic Counselors, 2003, cert. counselor Nat. Bd. for Cert. Counselors, 1999, lic. profl. counselor Mich., 2001. Counselor/legal adv. Safe Shelter, Inc., Benton Harbor, Mich., 1996—97; teen pregnancy dir. Women In Renewal, Niles, Mich., 1997—2000; dir.,cons. Theragogy.com, Grand Rapids, Mich., 1997—; clin. program supr., early impact Bethany Christian Svcs., Grand Rapids, Mich., 2001—; prof. Spring Arbor U., Grand Rapids, Mich., 2002—. Autism cons. Bethany Christian Svcs., Grand Rapids, Mich., 2001—; joint planning com. mem. Family Independence Agy., Grand Rapids, Mich., 2001—. Author: (book) The Religious Experience of Asperger's Syndrome, (children's book) Life With Gabriel (A Sibling's Perspective of Autism), (volume of poetry) When You Were Young; contbr. scientific papers. Mem. P21! Family Independence Agy. - Kent County, Grand Rapids, Mich., 2001—03. Mem.: ACA (licentiate), APA (assoc.). D-Liberal. Non-Denominational. Achievements include research in Choroid Plexus Cysts and Autism; development of Online Counseling resource library for therapists. Avocations: painting, writing, photography. Office: Bethany Christian Svcs 901 Eastern NE Grand Rapids MI 49503

VANDERVALK, CHARLOTTE, state legislator; b. Allentown, Pa., July 31, 1937; Mem. coun., Montvale, N.J., 1980-85; freeholder, Bergen County, N.J., 1986-91; mem. N.J. Gen. Assembly, Trenton, 1991—, asst. majority leader, 1992-95. Asst. majority leader N.J. State Assembly, 1992—. Bd. dirs. United Way of Bergen County, 1989—; vol. Bergen County Juvenile Fire Prevention Bd. Recipient disting. cmty. svc. award Bergen County Med. Soc., 1988, untiring support award Bergen County Juvenile Fire Prevention, 1989. Home: 220 Kinderkamack Rd Ste E Westwood NJ 07675-3601 Office: NJ Gen Assembly State House Trenton NJ 08608

VANDER VEER, SUZANNE, aupair business executive; b. Phila., Sept. 21, 1936; d. Joseph Bedford Vander Veer and Ethel K. Short; m. James Robb Ledwith, Nov. 29, 1958 (div. Sept. 1978); children: Cheryl Day, James Robb Jr., Scott Wiley; m. Herbert Keyser Zearfoss, Nov. 14, 1992. AA, Colby Sawyer Coll., 1957; postgrad., State U. Iowa, 1957-58. Tchr. Booth Sch., Bryn Mawr, Pa., 1958; profl. tour guide Cities of Phila., N.Y.C. and Washington, D.C., 1976-89; regional dir. Transdesigns, Woodstock, Ga., 1979-87; area rep. Welcome Wagon Internat., Tenn., 1987-93, mem. local bd., 1987-93; condo. complex mgr. St. Davids, Pa., 1990-93; area dir. E.F. Aupair, Cambridge, Mass., 1993—. Art cons., 1979—. Chair host family program Internat. House of Phila., 1966-74; mem. women's com. Pa. Hosp., 1966-71; mem. com. Phila. Antique Show, 1995—; docent Phila. Mus. of Art, 1974-80; bd. dirs. Plays for Living, Phila., 1966-84, Kynett Found., 2002—; chair congl. care coun. Office of Deacon Bryn Mawr Presbyn. Ch., 1997-2002. Mem. PEO (past pres.), Jr. League of Phila. (bd. dirs., sustainer chair 1993-95, Pres.' Cup 1995, sustainer bd. 1985—, Sustainer of the Yr. award 2001), Kynett Found., Merion Cricket Club, Cosmopolitan Club of Phila. Home: 532 Candace Ln Villanova PA 19085-1702

VAN DERVEER, TARA, university athletic coach; b. Niagara Falls, N.Y., June 26, 1953; Grad., Indiana U., 1975. Coach women's basketball Stanford U. Cardinals, 1985—, U.S. Nat. Women's Team, 1995-96. Coach gold medalist Women's Olympic Team, 1996. Achievements include champions NCAA Divsn. 1 A, 1990, 92. Office: Stanford U Women's [illegible] Athletics Stanford CA 94305

VANDERWALKER, DIANE MARY, materials scientist; b. Springfield, Mass., Nov. 1, 1955; BS, Boston Coll., 1977; PhD, MIT, 1981. NATO fellow U. Oxford, Eng., 1981-82; asst. prof. SUNY, Stony Brook, 1983-85; materials rsch. engr. Army Rsch. Lab. (formerly U.S. Army Materials Tech. Lab.), Watertown, Mass., 1986-94. Cons. IBM, Yorktown Heights, N.Y. Contbr. articles to profl. publs. Mem. N.Y. Acad. Scis. Roman Catholic.

VANDER WEIDE, CHERI DEVOS, sports team executive, marketing professional; b. Grand Rapids, Mich., Feb. 3, 1961; m. Robert A. Vander Weide. BA in Bus. Adminstrn., Hope Coll. Dir. health and beauty mktg. Amway Corp., Ada, Mich., v.p. corp. affairs, mem. policy bd.; exec. vice-chmn. gov. bd. Orlando Magic Basketball. Trustee United Arts of Ctrl. Fla.; chmn. children's hosp. com. Butterworth Hosp. Office: Orlando Magic 2 Magic Place 8701 Maitland Summit Blvd Orlando FL 32810-5915

VAN DEUSEN, CHERYL A. business educator, consultant; b. Sarasota, Fla. BS, Va. Tech. U., 1979; MBA, Appalachian State U., 1989; PhD, U. S.C., 1997. Cert. hotel adminstr., hotel educator. Vis. asst. prof. Hawaii Pacific U., Honolulu, 1997—98; assoc. prof. U. North Fla., Jacksonville, 1998—. Internat. cons. Cultural Assets Mgmt., 1992—. Contbr. articles to refereed jours. Cmty. svc. coord. Jr. Achievement, Jacksonville, 1998—2003; vol. leader Coronado of Silver Sands 4-H, Daytona and New Smyrna Beach, 1996—2003; faculty advisor Soc. for Human Resource Mgmt., Jacksonville, 1999—2003. Grantee Rsch. and Tchg. grantee, U.S. Dept. of Edn., 2000—02. Fellow: UNF Ctr. for Internat. Bus. Studies (rsch. assoc. 1999—2003); mem.: Acad. of Mgmt., Internat. Assn. for Bus. and Soc., Acad. of Internat. Business-S.E. USA (vice-chair 1999—2002, chair 2003—). Office: U North Fla Coggin Coll of Business 4567 St Johns Bluff Rd Jacksonville FL 32224

VANDEVER, JUDITH ANN, county official; b. Hemstead, N.Y., Aug. 6, 1941; d. John Anthony Klym and Kathryn M. (Lane) Trexler; children: Garret, Kimberlee Vandever Johnson. Dep. recorder Clark County Recorder, Las Vegas, Nev., 1979-91, chief dep. recorder, 1991-93, asst. recorder, 1993-94, county recorder, 1995—. State chair Nev. Young Woman of the Yr., 1991; mem. S.M.A.R.T. Team Clark County Sch. Dist., 1994—95; mem. ctrl. com. State/County Dem. Ctrl. Com., 1988—; state dir. Women Ofcls. Nat. Assn. Counties, 1997—. Recipient Leadership Dedication award Amigos De HIP, 1996, Women Elected Ofcls. Spotlight award Women's Dem. Club, 1996. Mem. ASPA, Nat. Assn. County Recorders and Clks. (bd. dirs. 1999—), Nat. Assn. County Recorders, Election Ofcls. and Clks. (bd. dirs. 1999-02), Assn. of Profl. Mortage Women,Assn. of Recorders Mgrs. and Adminstrs., U. Nev.-Las Vegas Jean Nidetch Women's Ctr. (original founder), Leadership Las Vegas Alumni Assoc., Las Vegas C. of C. (bd. of trustees, cmty. coun. 1995-98). Office: Clark County Recorder 500 S Grand Central Pkwy Las Vegas NV 89106-4506

VAN DE VYVER, SISTER MARY FRANCILENE, academic administrator; b. Detroit, Sept. 6, 1941; d. Hector Joseph and Irene Cecilia (Zygaildo) V. BA, Madonna Coll., 1965; MEd, Wayne State U., 1970, PhD, 1977. Joined Sisters of St. Felix of Cantalice, Roman Cath. Ch., 1959. Tchr. Ladywood High Sch., 1967-71, Gabriel Richard H.S., 1971-74; adminstrv. asst. to pres. Madonna Coll., Livonia, Mich., 1974-75, acad. dean, 1975-76; now pres. Madonna U., Livonia, Mich. Office: Madonna U Office of President 36600 Schoolcraft Rd Livonia MI 48150-1176

VAN DE WATER, READ, former federal agency administrator; b. Charlotte, NC; m. Mark Van de Water; 3 children. Degree, U. South, 1986; M, George Washington U.; JD, Georgetown U. Appropriations assoc., legis. asst. Congressman Tom DeLay, Tex., 1987—91; legis. coun., dir. govt. affairs Northwest Airlines, 1991—97; legis. coun. internat. trade and investment Bus. Roundtable, 1997—99; founder Carson King Cons., 2000; asst. sec. aviation & internat. affairs U.S. Dept. Transp., Washington, 2001—03. Mem. Nat. Mediation Bd., Washington, 2003—. Republican. Office: Nat Mediation Bd 1301 K St NW Ste 250 E Washington DC 20005-7011*

VAN DE WATER, SUSAN D. physiatrist; BA in Biology, Oberlin Coll., 1974; PhD, U. Rochester, 1979; MD, U. Tex., San Antonio, 1986. Diplomate Am. Bd. Physical Medicine and Rehabilitation. Postdoctoral fellow U. Tex. Med. Br., Galveston, 1979-81; resident Rehab. Inst. Chgo., 1986-90; med. dir. Meml. Rehab. Hosp., Midland, Tex., 1990-94; physiatrist, assoc. med. dir. Health South Rehab. Hosp., Midland, 1994—. Chmn. phys. medicine and rehab. com. Meml. Hosp. and Med. Ctr., Midland, 1991-92, 93-94, Med. Ctr. Hosp., Odessa, Tex., 1990-92; mem. med. adv. bd. Tex. Rehab. Commn., 1994—. Contbr. articles to profl. jours. Louise Barekman Meml. scholar Tex. Med. Assn., 1985, Bowen-Vogt Med. scholar, 1984, J. Belcher Trust scholar, 1983, So. Med. Assn. scholar 1982; Grad. fellow NSF, 1974-77, Rush Rhees Grad. fellow U. Rochester, 1974-77. Fellow Am. Acad. Phys. Medicine and Rehab.; mem. AMA, Assn. Acad. Physiatrists, Tex. Soc. Phys. Medicine and Rehab., Tex. Med. Assn., Midland County Med. Assn., U. Tex. San Antonio Alumni Assn., Alpha Omega Alpha, Phi Beta Kappa. Office: PO Box 4766 Midland TX 79704-4766

VANDIVER, BETTY JEAN, protective services professional; b. Harrodsburg, Ky., Sept. 27, 1950; d. Cecil Raymond and Ruby Marie (Hawkins) VanD. AA, Ea. Ky. U., 1971, BS, 1993—. Juvenile counselor, juvenile correctional officer Cabinet for Human Resources, Waddy, Ky., 1981—91; dir. admissions, adminstrv. asst. dept. mental health Ky. Correctional Psychiat. Ctr., LaGrange, Ky., 1991—94; ct. designated worker Cabinet of Justice-53rd Jud. Dist., various cities, Ky., 1994—2003; living instr. Best House Group; telecom. officer Unit 194 Harrodsburg Police Dept., Harrodsburg, Ky., 2003—. Bd. mem. Local Interagy. Coun., Shelbyville, Ky., Youth Adv. Coun., Shelbyville, Taylorsville, Drug and Alcohol Adv. Coun., Shelbyville.Private Childcare, Christian Children's Homes of Kentucky; supr. Christian Children's Homes Ky., Danville, Ky. Mem. NAFE, NRA, Ea. Star (Hamilton chpt. 293). Avocations: sky diving, horseback riding, fishing, rifle/handgun competition. Address: PO Box 79 Burgin KY 40310-0079 Home: 102 W Court St Burgin KY 40310 Office: Harrodsburg Police Dept 411 N Greenville St Harrodsburg KY 40330

VANDIVER, DONNA, public relations executive; BJ, MBA in Mgmt. Pres. Vandiver Group, St. Louis, 1993—. Bd. dirs. Am. Heart Assn.; mem. adv. bd. Pky. Edn. Found. Named Small Bus. Person of the Yr. SBA, 1998; recipient Quest award Nat. Fedn. Press Women, 1999. Mem. Nat. Assn. Women Bus. Owners (Bd. dirs. St. Louis chpt., Disting Women Bus. Owner of the Yr. award 1999), Assn. Corp. Growth, St. Louis Press Club, Downtown St. Louis Partnership, St. Louis Regional Commerce and Growth Assn., Media Club. Office: Vandiver Group 10411 Clayton Rd Saint Louis MO 63131-2928

VANDIVER, PAMELA BOWREN, science educator; b. Santa Monica, Calif., Jan. 12, 1946; d. Roy King and Patricia (Woolard) Evans; m. J. Kim Vandiver, Aug., 1968 (div. 1984); 1 child, Amy. BA in Humanities and Asian Studies, Scripps Coll., 1967; postgrad., U. Calif., Berkeley, 1968; MA in Art, Pacific Luth. U., 1971; MS in Ceramic Sci., MIT, 1983, PhD in Materials Sci. and Near Eastern Archeology, 1985. Instr. in glass and ceramics Mass. Coll. of Art, Boston, 1972; lectr. MIT, Cambridge, 1973-78, rsch. assoc., 1978-85; rsch. phys. scientist Conservation Analytical Lab., Smithsonian Instn., Washington, 1985-89; sr. scientist in ceramics and glass Smithsonian Ctr. for Materials Rsch. and Edn., Washington, 1989—2002, dir., 2003; prof. materials sci. and engring. U. Ariz., Tucson, 2004—. Instr. semester-at-sea U. Pitts., spring 1995; vis. prof. Northwest U. of Sci. & Tech., Xianyang, China, 1996; bd. dirs. [illegible], guest rschr. Nat. Inst. Stds. and Tech., Gaithersburg, Md., 1989-91. Co-author: Ceramic Masterpieces, 1986; co-editor: Materials Issues in Art and Archaeology, vol. 1 1988, vol. 5, 1997, vol. 6, 2002; bd. editors Archeomaterials, 1986-93; contbr. over 100 numerous articles to profl. jours. Sponsor mentorship program Thomas Jefferson H.S. of Sci. and Tech., Alexandria, 1992. Recipient Disting. Alumna Achievement award Scripps Coll., 1993. Fellow Am. Anthrop. Assn.; mem. AAAS, Am. Inst. Archeology, Soc. Am. Archeology, Internat. Inst. of Conservation, Soc. for History of Tech., Am. Ceramics Soc. (ancient ceramics com. 1978—), Materials Rsch. Soc. (guest editor bull. 1992, 2001), Am. Chem. Soc., Annapolis Yacht Club, Cosmos Club, Sigma Xi. Avocations: sailing, diving, photography. Office: Smithsonian Inst Ctr Materials Rsch and Edn 4210 Silver Hill Rd Suitland MD 20746 Office Phone: 520-400-2077. E-mail: vandiver@mse.arizona.edu.

VANDIVER, RENEE LILLIAN AUBRY, interior designer, architectural preservator; b. New Iberia, La., Nov. 7, 1929; d. Harold George and Josephine Fortier (Brown) Aubry; m. Arthur Roderick Carmody, Jr., Jan. 1952 (div. 1979); children: Helen Bragg Carmody Stroud, Renee Josephine Carmody Mathews, Arthur Roderick III, Patrick Gerard, Timothy H.A., Mary Joellyn, Virginia Caroline, Joseph Barry; m. Frank Everson Vandiver, Mar. 21, 1980. BFA, Sophie Newcomb Coll. Tulane U., 1951; postgrad., U. Paris, 1951-52, Centinary Coll., 1966-68, La. State U., Shreveport, 1978. Designer, supt. art New Iberia Parish Elementary Schs., 1951; archtl. drafter and designer Perry L. Brown, Inc., Baton Rouge, 1950-52; tchr. art St. Joseph's Elem. Sch., Shreveport, 1960-69; designer, illustrator, saleswoman Stierwalt Interiors, Shreveport, 1974-78; design cons. for president's homes and gardens North Tex. State U., Tex. A&M U., Denton, College Station, 1980-88; design cons., planner, saleswoman, pres. Renee Aubry Vandiver Interiors, College Station, Tex., 1980—; design cons. Am. U. in Cairo, 1997—; proofreader, editor, rschr., asst. Office of Frank E. Vandiver, College Station, 1998—. Interior design and house constrn. cons. Heritage Antiques and Interiors, New Iberia, 1972—; interior design cons., Tenn., La., S.C., 1980—; invited student Middle Eastern master painter Sabri Raghab; involved with consultations and contruction large new campus, pres.'s home grounds Am. U., Cairo. Editl. and illustrations collaborator works on gen. mil. history with Frank E. Vandiver, 1990—; works include design constrn. of new Pres.'s Home on campus of Am. U. of Cairo, 2004. Mem. NAFE, DAR, Constrn. Specifications Inst., Dallas Market Ctr., Houston Market Ctcr., Jr. League, Textile Mus., Mus. Women in Arts, Tex. A&M U. Women's Club (hon. pres. 1981—), Fedn. Tex. A&M U. Mother's Club. Avocations: painting, playing piano, gardening, travel, reading. Home: PO Box 10600 College Station TX 77842-0600

VAN DOREN, HENRIETTA LAMBERT, nurse, anesthetist; b. Birmingham, Ala., Sept. 21, 1946; d. Martin Lee and Maude Elizabeth (Land) Lambert; m. Terry Lee Van Doren, Oct. 14, 1969; children: Terry Lee Jr., Timothy Wayne. AA in Nursing, Meridian (Miss.) Jr. Coll., 1968; cert., Charity Hosp. Sch. Anesthesia, New Orleans, 1971; PhD in Health Svcs./Nursing Adminstrn., Columbia Pacific U., 1982. RN, cert. registered nurse anesthetist; hypnotherapist Am. Bd. Hypnotherapy. Registered hypnotherapist, chief nurse anesthetist Riley Meml. Hosp. HMA, Meridian, Miss., 1972—2000; self-employed, 2000—. Mem.: Am. Assn. Hypnotherapy, Am. Assn. Nurse Anesthetists. Republican. Baptist. Home: 2551 Campground Rd Lauderdale MS 39335-9621

VAN DOVER, KAREN, middle and elementary school educator, curriculum consultant, language arts specialist, lecturer; b. Astoria, N.Y. d. Frederick A. and Frances L. (Thomas) Van D. BA, CUNY; MALS, SUNY, Stony Brook; postgrad., St. John's U., Jamaica, N.Y. Cert. permanent N-6 tchr., art tchr. K-12, sch. adminstr., supr., N.Y. Tchr., sch. dist. adminstr. St. James (N.Y.) Elem. Sch.; tchr. Nesaquake Intermediate Sch., St. James, lead tchr. English, 1984-92, Smithtown Mid Sch., St. James, 1992-93, curriculum specialist, 1993—. Leader staff devel. and curriculum devel. workshops Smithtown Sch. Dist., 1984—, mem. supt.'s adv. com. for gifted and talented, mem. supt. adv. com. for lang. arts assessment, mem. textbook selection coms. site-based mgmt. team, 1994—, chair 1996-99, master tchr. bd. Prentice Hall, Englewood Cliffs, N.J., 1990—, chair ELA com. for curriculum and the stds., 2000. Contbg. author: Prentice Hall Literature

Copper, 1991, 94. Corr. sec. Yaphank Taxpayers and Civic Assn., 1984-86, Nesaquake Sch. PTA, 1990-91, mem., 1977-92; mem. Smithtown Mid. Sch. PTA, 1992—. Mem. ASCD, Am. Ednl. Rsch. Assn., Nat. Assn. Secondary Sch. Prins., Nat. Assn. Elem. Sch. Prins., L.I. Lang. Arts Coun., Nat. Coun. Tchrs. English, Internat. Reading Assn., Nat. Middle Schs. Assn., N.Y. State English Coun., Internat. Platform Assn., Phi Delta Kappa. Home: 8 Penn Commons Yaphank NY 11980-2025 Office: Smithtown Middle Sch 10 School St Saint James NY 11780-1800 E-mail: kvandover@smithtown.k12.ny.us.

VAN DUSEN, DONNA BAYNE, communications consultant, educator, researcher; b. Phila., Apr. 21, 1949; d. John Culbertson and Evelyn Gertrude (Godfrey) Bayne; m. David William Van Dusen, Nov. 30, 1968 (div. Dec. 1989); children: Heather, James. BA, Temple U., 1984, MA, 1986, PhD, 1993. Instr. Kutztown (Pa.) U., 1986—87, Ursinus Coll., Collegeville, Pa., 1987—96; cons., rschr. Comm. Rsch. Assoc., Valley Forge, Pa., 1993—96; assoc. prof. MS in Mgmt. program Regis U., Denver, 1998—. Rschr. Fox Chase Cancer Ctr., Phila., 1985-86; adj. faculty Temple U. Law Sch., 1994-97, LaSalle U., 1994-96, Wharton Sch., U. Pa., 1994-95; asst. prof. Beaver Coll., Glenside, Pa., 1995-96; faculty Jones Internat. U., 1996-99, Metro State U., Denver, 1997-99; cons. Human Comm. Resources and Solutions, 1997—, acad. coun. chair, 2002-. Writer Mountain Connection, 1998—. Vol. Friends in Transition; vol. mediator Victim Offender Reconciliation Program. Recipient Excellence in Tchg. award, 2003. Mem.: Nat. Comm. Assn. Avocations: oil painting, creative writing, sailing, gardening, reading. Home: 2589 Alkire St Golden CO 80401 E-mail: dvanduse@regis.edu.

VAN DUSEN, LANI MARIE, psychologist; b. Alexandria, Va., July 23, 1960; d. Arthur Ellsworth and Ann Marie (Brennan) Van D. BS magna cum laude, U. Ga., 1982, MS, 1985, PhD, 1988. Cert. secondary tchr., Ga. Tchr. Henry County Sch. Sys., McDonough, Ga., 1982-83; rsch. psychologist Metrica Inc., Bryan, Tex., 1988; asst. prof. psychology U. Ga., Athens, 1988-89, chmn. Conf. for Behavioral Scis., 1987; assoc. prof. psychology Utah State U., Logan, 1989—. Cons. Western Inst. for rsch. and Evaluation, Logan, 1990—; bd. dirs. Human Learrning Clinic, Logan, 1990—, Ctr. for Sch. of Future; reviewer William C. Brown Pubs., 1990, Dushkin Pub. Group Inc., 1990-91. Contbr. articles to profl. jours. Fellow Menninger Found.; mem. APA, Psychonomic Soc., Am. Ednl. Rsch. Assn., AAUP, ASCD. Republican. Avocations: hiking, tennis, skiing, knitting, swimming. Home: 1633 N 1200 E North Logan UT 84341-2102 Office: Vandusen Consulting Ste 210 550 North Main Logan UT 84321

VAN DUYN, MONA JANE, poet, educator; b. Waterloo, Iowa, May 9, 1921; d. Earl George and Lora G. (Kramer) Van D.; m. Jarvis A. Thurston, Aug. 31, 1943. BA, U. No. Iowa, 1942; MA, U. Iowa, 1943; D.Litt. (hon.), Washington U., St. Louis, 1971, Cornell Coll., Iowa, 1972, U. No. Iowa, 1991, U. of the South, Sewanee, Tenn., 1993, George Wash. U., 1993; LHD, Georgetown U., 1993. Instr. in English U. Iowa, Iowa City, 1943-46; instr. in English U. Louisville, 1946-50; lectr. English Univ. Coll., Washington U., 1950-67; poetry editor, co-pub. Perspective, A Quar. of Lit., 1947-67. Lectr. Salzburg (Austria) Seminar Am. Studies, 1973; adj. prof. poetry workshop Washington U., Spring 1983; vis. Hurst prof., 1987; poet-in-residence Sewanee Writers Conf., 1990, Breadloaf Writing Conf., Mass., 1974. Author: Valentines to the Wide World, 1959, A Time of Bees, 1964, To See, To Take, 1970, Bedtime Stories, 1972, Merciful Disguises, 1973, Letters from a Father and Other Poems, 1983, Near Changes, 1990 (Pulitzer Prize for poetry 1991), Firefall, 1993, If It Be Not I, 1993, Selected Poems, 2002. Recipient Eunice Tietjens award, 1956, Helen Bullis prize, 1964, 76, Harriet Monroe award, 1968, Hart Crane Meml. award, 1968, Borestone Mountains 1st prize, 1968, Bollingen prize, 1970, Nat. Book award, 1971, Sandburg prize Cornell Coll., 1982, Shelley Meml. prize Poetry Soc. Am., 1987, Lilly prize for poetry, 1989, Mo. Arts award, 1990, Golden Plate award Am. Acad. Achievement, 1992, Arts and Edn. Coun. St. Louis award, 1994; grantee Nat. Coun. Arts, 1967, NEA, 1985; Guggenheim fellow, 1972. Fellow Acad. Am. Poets (chancellor 1985-99); mem. NAAS, Nat. Acad. Arts and Letters (Loines prize 1976), Acad. Arts Scis. Achievements include first woman to be named United States poet laureate, 1992.*

VAN DYCK, WENDY, dancer; b. Tokyo; Student, San Francisco Ballet Sch.; BA in Performing Arts, St. Mary's Coll., 2003. With San Francisco Ballet, 1979—96, prin. dancer, 1987—96, instr., tchr., 1996; co-dir. Lawrence Pech Dance, San Francisco, 1996—. Performances include Forgotten Land, The Sons of Horus, The Wanderer Fantasy, Romeo and Juliet, The Sleeping Beauty, Swan Lake, Concerto in d: Poulenc, Handel-a Celebration, Menuetto, Intimate Voices, Hamlet and Ophelia pas de deux, Connotations, Sunset, Rodin, In the Night, The Dream: pas de deux, La Sylphide, Beauty and the Beast, Variations de Ballet, Nutcracker, The Comfort Zone, Dreams of Harmony, Rodeo, Duo Concertant, Who Cares; performed at Reykjavik Arts Festival, Iceland, 1990, The 88th Conf. of the Internat. Olympic Com., L.A., 1984, with Kozlov and Co. Concord Pavilion; guest artist performing role Swan Lake (Act II), San Antonio Ballet, 1985, Giselle, Shreveport Met. Ballet, 1994; featured in the TV broadcast of Suite by Smuin. Mailing: PO Box 1 Littleriver CA 95456

VAN DYKE, WENDY JOHANNA, artist; b. Moline, Ill., July 22, 1955; d. Kreger D. and Sara K. (Weeks) Emry; m. Mikel P. Van Dyke, Feb. 11, 1978; children: Benjamin, Jonathan. BS in Bus. Adminstrn with highest honors, U. Ill., 1977. Mgr. Stringer Art Factory and Gallery, Davenport, IA, 1977-78, Warren L. Langwith, Inc., Davenport, IA, 1977-78. V. chmn. visual arts com. Quad Cities Arts Coun., Rock Island, Ill., 1979-80. Exhibited in group shows at Davenport Mus. of Art, 1977, 84, 88, 95, Muscatine (Iowa) Art Ctr., 1980, 83, 88, 90, Blanden Mem. Art Gallery, Ft. Dodge, Iowa, 1980, Graceland Coll., Lamoni, Iowa, 1980, Waterloo (Iowa) Mcpl. Art Galleries, 1980, Carrol (Iowa) Arts Coun., 1981, Clinton (Iowa) C.C., 1981, Algona (Iowa) H.S., 1981, Art Guild of Burlington, Iowa, 1981, 96, 2003, Woodbine Comm. Schs., Iowa, 1981, Cen. Coll., Pella, Iowa, 1981, Augustana Coll. Art Gallery, Rock Island, Ill., 1996, 98, 2001, Quad City Arts, Rock Island, Ill., 2003, 04. Mem. fine arts com. Buchanan Sch. PTA, Davenport, 1983-92; mem. arts adv. com. Davenport Cmty. Schs., 1986-89; active Devel. of State of Iowa Art Curriculum, Des Moines, 1991-92; bd. dirs. Quad Cities Arts Coun., Rock Island, Ill., 1979-80; mem. artist adv. coun., exhbns. and acquisitions com Davenport Mus. Art, Figge Art Ctr., 2003-. Mem. Quad City Arts, Bi-State Literacy Coun., Friends of Davenport Pub. Libr., Art Inst. Chgo. (nat. assoc.), U. Ill. Alumni Assn. (life), Phi Kappa Phi, Beta Gamma Sigma, Alpha Lambda Delta, Phi Gamma Nu. Avocations: reading, writing, biking, yoga. Home: 2517 W 43rd St Davenport IA 52806-4913

VAN DYKEN, AMY, Olympic athlete; b. Engelwood, Colo., Feb. 15, 1973; d. Don and Becky Van Dyken; m. Alan McDaniel, Oct. 1995. Student, Colo. State U. Swimmer U.S. Nat. Resident Team, Colorado Springs, Colo., 1994, U.S. Olympic Team, Atlanta, 1996, Sydney, 2000; ret. Named Female NCAA Swimmer of Yr., 1994, Assoc. Press Female Athlete of the Yr., 1996, USOC Sports Woman of the Yr., 1996, Woman's Sports Found. Woman of the Yr., 1996, USA Swimming Swimmer of the Yr., 1996, Phillips Performance of the Yr. award, 1996; named one of Glamour's Top Ten Women of the Yr., 1996; recipient Bronze medal, World Championships, 1994, Triple Gold medals, Pan Am. Games, 1995, Silver medal, 1995, Gold medal 50 meter freestyle, Atlanta Olympic Games, 1996, Gold medal 100 meter butterfly, 1996, Gold medal 4x400 meter freestyle relay, 1996, Gold medal 4x100 meter medley relay, 1996, Gold medal 4x400 freestyle, Sydney Olympic Games, 2000, ESPY award, best female athlete, 1997. Achievements include 1st American women to win 4 gold medals in any event during a single Olympic game.

VAN DYNE, MICHELE MILEY, information engineer; b. Harrisburg, Pa., Sept. 8, 1959; d. Joseph Lawrence Miley and Tina Theresa (Dudash) Smollack; m. David Franklin Buck, Aug. 8, 1981 (div. July 1984); m. David George Van Dyne, Sept. 9, 1989. BA in Psychology, U. Mont., 1981, MS in Computer Sci., 1995; PhD in elec. engring., U. Kans., 2003. Div. sr. tech. programmer, analyst Allied-Signal Aerospace, Kansas City, Mo., 1985-89; knowledge engr. United Data Svcs., Inc., United Telecom, Overland Park, Kans., 1989-90; pres. IntelliDyne, Inc., Kansas City, Mo., 1990—. Cons. Comprehensive Devel. Ctr., Missoula, Mont., 1984; speaker Sigart, Kansas City, 1988; chmn. Expert-Systems-Kans. and Mo. (ESKaMo), 1990-92. Vol. Planned Parenthood Greater Kansas City, 1986. United Bldg. Ctrs. scholar, 1976. Mem. IEEE Computer Soc., Am. Assn. for Artificial Intelligence, Internat. Neural Network Soc., Instrnl. Tech. Network (steering com. 1990-92), Women in Tech. Network (steering com. 1990-91, chmn. pub. rels. com. 1991-92), Alpha Lambda Delta. Democrat. Episcopalian. Avocations: reading, decorating, kayaking, sewing, home remodeling. Home and Office: 6040 Wornall Rd Kansas City MO 64113-1418 E-mail: mvandyne@worldnet.att.net.

VANE, DENA, magazine editor-in-chief; Editor-in-chief First for Women, Englewood Cliffs, NJ. Office: First for Women Bauer Pub Co 270 Sylvan Ave Englewood Cliffs NJ 07632-2521

VANE, SYLVIA BRAKKE, anthropologist, writer, publishing executive, researcher; b. Fillmore County, Minn., Feb. 28, 1918; d. John T. and Hulda Christina Brakke.; m. Arthur Bayard Vane, May 17, 1942; children: Ronald Arthur, Linda, Laura Vane Ames. AA, Rochester Jr. Coll., 1937; BS with distinction, U. Minn., 1939; postgrad, Radcliffe Coll., 1944; MA, Calif. State U., Hayward, 1975. Med. technologist Dr. Frost and Hodapp, Willmar, Minn., 1939-41; head labs. Corvallis (Oreg.) Gen. Hosp., 1941-42; dir. lab. Cambridge (Mass.) Gen. Hosp., 1942-43; staff Peninsula Clinic, Redwood City, Calif., 1947-49; vice pres. Cultural Systems Rsch. Inc., Menlo Park, Calif., 1978—; pres. Ballena Press, 1981—. Cons. cultural resource mgmt. So. Calif. Edison Co., Rosemead, 1978-81, San Diego Gas and Elec. Co., 1980-83, Pacific Gas and Elec. Co., San Francisco, 1982-83, Wender, Murase & White, Washington, 1983-87, Yosemite Indians, Mariposa, Calif., 1982-91, San Luis Rey Band of Mission Indians, Escondido, Calif., 1986-89, U.S. Ecology, Newport Beach, Calif., 1986-89, Riverside County Flood Control and Water Conservation Dist., 1985-95, Infotec, Inc., 1989-91, Alexander & Karshmer, Berkeley, Calif., 1989-92, Desert Water Agy., Palm Springs, Calif., 1989-90, Met. Water Dist., 1992-2001, Nat. Park Svc., 1992-2001, Applied Earthworks, Inc., 1997-2001, N.W Econ. Assocs., 2002—, County of Riverside, 2002-03. Author: (with L.J. Bean), California Indians, Primary Resources, 1977, rev. edit., 1990, The Cahuilla and the Santa Rosa Mountains, 1981, The Cahuilla Landscape, 1991, Ethnology of the Alta California Indians, vol. I Pre Contact, vol. II POst Contact, 1992, Spanish Borderlands Sourcebooks, vols. 3, 4; contbr. chpts. to several books. Bd. dirs. Sequoia Area coun. Girl Scouts U.S., 1954-61; bd. dirs., v.p., pres. LWV, South San Mateo County, Calif., 1960-65. Fellow Soc. Applied Anthropology, Am. Anthropology Assn.; mem. Southwestern Anthropology Assn. (prog. chmn. 1976-78, newsletter editor 1976-79), Soc. for Am. Archaeology, Soc. Calif. Archaeology (Martin A. Baumhoff Spl. Achievement award 1998). Mem. United Ch. of Christ. Office: Ballena Press 823 Valparaiso Ave Menlo Park CA 94025-4206

VAN EKEREN, YBI, artist; b. Zwolle, Overysel, The Netherlands, Aug. 2, 1927; arrived in Can., 1951; came to U.S., 1960; AA, Riverside City Coll., 1968; BA, Fullerton State U., 1977. Exhibited in group shows at Riverside (Calif.) Art Mus., 1969 (1st award for graphics, 3rd award for sculpture), Arlington (Calif.) Art Guild, 1970 (2nd Place award for graphics), Nat. Orange Show, San Bernardino, 1994 (2nd Place award), Calif. Mid-State Fair, Paso Robles, 1996 (2nd Place award), Printmaker Show, San Luis Obispo, 1996 (Merchant's award), Fine Arts Inst., San Bern, Calif., 1999, 34st Internat. Exhibit (hon. mention), Fine Arts Inst. San Bern, 2001 (2d award). Mem. Cayucos Art Assn., San Luis Obispo Art Assn., San Luis Obispo Printmakers, Nat. Mus. of Women in the Arts (Washington). Office: Studio Art Gallery 731 Santa Ysabel Ave Los Osos CA 93402-1137

VAN ELLA, KATHLEEN E. fine art consultant; b. Flint, Mich., Apr. 16, 1943; d. Wallace Joseph Werich and Helen Catherine Gutenkanf; m. James Eugene Van Ella, Aug. 8, 1964 (div. Apr. 1975); children: Aleen Janette Malloy, Erica Kathleen Krzyszkowski. BS in History and English Lit., Loyola U., Chgo., 1967; postgrad., Ray-Vogue Sch. Design, 1977—80. Founder, pres., dir. Portraits/Chgo. Inc.-Fine Portrait Painting and Sculpture, Lake Forest, Ill., 1980—. First program coord. Common Ground, Deerfield, Ill., 1975—77; dir. sales, mktg., pub. rels. for Chinese artists East-West Contemporary Art Gallery, Chgo., 1986—92. Recipient award of spl. merit for pub. art, Young Lawyers Group of Chgo. Bar Assn., 1995. Mem.: Wedgwood Soc., Lake Forest C. of C. Roman Catholic. Avocations: writing, travel, nature walking, swimming, reflecting. Home: 780 Greenview Pl Lake Forest IL 60045 Office: Portraits/Chgo Inc 780 Greenview Pl Lake Forest IL 60045

VAN EMBURGH, JOANNE, lawyer; b. Palmyra, N.J., Nov. 18, 1953; d. Earl Henry and Clare (Kemmerle) Van E.; m. Samuel Michael Surloff, July 6, 1993. BA summa cum laude, Catholic U., 1975; JD cum laude, Harvard Law Sch., 1978. Bar: Calif. 1978. Assoc. atty. Agnew Miller & Carlson, L.A., 1978-82; ptnr. Sachs & Phelps, L.A., 1982-91, Heller, Ehrman, White & McAuliffe, L.A., 1991-93; mng. council Toyota Motor Sales, USA, Inc., Torrance, 1993—, asst. gen. coun., 2000—. Mem. ABA. Avocations: reading, cooking, sports. Office: Toyota Motor Sales USA Inc 19001 S Western Ave Torrance CA 90501-1106

VAN ERT, HEIDI, gifted education educator, artist, art therapist; b. Honolulu, Jan. 4, 1955; d. Willard Lee and Gretchen (Schubert) Van E.; m. Thomas Patrick Casey, July 29, 1978 (div.); 1 child, Christopher Michael. BA in Humanities for Elem. Tchrs., Colo. Coll., 1976; MS in Spl. Edn., U. Utah, 1987, PhD in Gifted Edn., 1993, MA in Art Therapy, 1994. Cert. tchr. with gifted endorsement, Utah. Instr. and coach skiing Snowbird Learn-To-Race Program, Salt Lake City, 1971-73; assoc. jr. high sch. ministries 1st Presbyn. Ch., Colorado Springs, Colo., 1977-78; elem. tchr. Lincoln Consol. Schs., Ypsilanti, Mich., 1979-81, Willow Canyon Elem. Sch., Sandy, Utah, 1981-83, Rowland Hall-St. Mark's Sch., Salt Lake City, 1983-88; clin. instr. spl. edn. U. Utah, Salt Lake City, 1987-94; tchr. gifted and talented Peruvian Park Elem. Sch., Sandy, 1994-97; 6th grade tchr. Uintah Elem. Sch., Salt Lake City, 1997-98; 4th and 5th grade tchr. Bonneville Elem. Sch., Salt Lake City, 1998—99; asst. prof. sch. edn. Westminster Coll., Salt Lake City, 1999—. Art therapist, Salt Lake City, 1994—; counselor Essex Sch. for Gifted, Columbus, Ohio, 1985; team mem. rural staff devel.Ea. Utah region Utah Office Edn., 1989-91; edn., devel. and creativity cons. Black Bottoms, Salt Lake City, 1994; coord. Youth Acad. Excellence, U. Utah, 1995-97; presenter in field; mem. planning com. Regional Art Therapy Conf., Salt Lake City, 1991-92. Contbr. articles to profl. publs.; one-woman show Petersen Art Ctr., 1995, Oasis Cafe, 1997, 99, Salt Lake Libr., 2001, Wasatch Frame Shop and Gallery, 2003. Vol. with Navajo and Winnebago tribes 1st Presbyn. Ch., 1974, 76; trustee Realms of Inquiry Sch., Salt Lake City, 1991-92; hospice vol. Salt Lake Cmty. Nursing Svcs., 1993-96. Named Tchr. of Month, Sandy C. of C., 1996; Steffensen-Cannon scholar U. Utah, 1990-92, leadership tng. grantee, 1992-93, rsch. fellow, 1992-93. Mem. Nat. Assn. Gifted Children, Am. Art Therapy Assn. (profl. art therapist), Mensa. Avocations: painting, reading, cross-country skiing, writing, camping. Home: 3842 Salt River Way Unit 3 Salt Lake City UT 84119-7483 Office: Westminster Coll Sch of Edn 219 Carleson Hall 1850 S 1300 E Salt Lake City UT 84105 Office Phone: 801-832-2483. E-mail: hvanert@westminstercollege.edu.

VANGELLOW, DEBORAH SOPHIA, sports educator, administrator; b. Rochester, N.Y., Dec. 20, 1962; d. George and Catherine Sophia (Sarantis) V. BA, U. No. Iowa, 1986; MS, Miami (Ohio) U., 1988. Spl. events asst. U. No. Iowa, Cedar Falls, 1981-86, asst. track/field coach, 1985-86, advisor student athletic bd., 1989-92, mem. core com student athlete assistance program, 1989-92, head coach women's golf, 1991-92; grad. intern Office Recreational Sports, Miami U., Oxford, Ohio, 1986-88; program coord. Japanese "Superlady" Project Kathy Whitworth Golf Acad., West Columbia, Tex., 1992-94; teaching asst. Columbia Lakes Sch. of Golf, West Columbia, 1992-94; golf projects coord. Heritage of Golf Corp., Houston, 1994-96; golf sch. coord., instr. Heritage Sch. of Golf, Houston, 1994-96; LPGA teaching profl. Cullen & Co. Golf Instrn., 1996—. Instr. wellness program U. No. Iowa, 1983-86, coord. residence hall, 1989-92, instr. health and phys. edn., 1990-92; instr. health and phys. edn. K-12, No. U. H.S., Cedar Falls, 1986, asst. softball coach, 1987; adj. instr. dept. ednl. leadership Miami U., 1986-89, coord. summer conf. halls, 1988, freshman acad. advisor, residence hall dir., 1988-89; asst. dir. Golf Digest Jr. Instrnl. Schs., Hueston Woods, Ohio, summers 1988-92; activity dir. Columbia Lakes Jr. Sch. of Golf, West Columbia, summers 1991-92; faculty Rice U., 1997—. Active Annunciation Greek Orthodox Cathedral, 1993—, Big Brothers/Big Sisters Northeast Iowa, 1990-92; vol. Spl. Olympics, 1982-86; instr. first aid and CPR, ARC, 1989-92, mem., 1989—; instr. cancer prevention program Am. Cancer Soc., 1990-92, bd. dirs., 1991-92. Recipient Mabel M. Wright Meml. Scholarship award, 1985-86; named one of Outstanding Young Women of Am., 1988, Top Flite Golfwoman of Yr., 1995; named coach golf team traveling to Holland, Internat. Sport for Understanding Program, 1996, Favorite Golf Instr., Golf for Women Mag., 1996. Mem. AAUW, LPGA, NAFE, Womensport Internat., Am. Coll. Pers. Assn., U.S. Golf Assn., Nat. Assn. Profl. Organizers, Nat. Assn. Golf Educators, Nat. Strength and Conditioning Assn., Women's Sports Found., No. Iowa Alumni Assn., U. No. Iowa Athletic Club, Omicron Delta Kappa, Alpha Chi Omega. Avocations: mountain biking, racquetball, music, movies, books. Home and Office: 4144 Greystone Way Apt 707 Sugar Land TX 77479-3014

VAN GINKEL, BLANCHE LEMCO, architect, educator; b. London, 1923; d. Myer and Claire Lemco; m. H. P. Daniel van Ginkel, 1956; children: Brenda Renee, Marc Ian. B.Arch., McGill U., 1945; M.C.P., Harvard U., 1950. Tech. asst. Nat. Film Bd. Can., 1943-44; mgr. City Planning Office, Regina, Sask., Can., 1946; architect Atelier Le Corbusier, Paris, 1948; asst. prof. architecture U. Pa., 1951-57; ptnr. van Ginkel Assocs., Montreal, Que., Can., also Toronto, Ont., Can., 1957[00bf]; prof. architecture U. Toronto, 1977—92, dir. Sch. Architecture, 1977-80, dean faculty architecture and landscape architecture, 1980-82. Vis. critic Harvard U., 1958, 70; adj. prof. U. Montreal, McGill U., others; curator exhbns. RCA, U. Toronto, others. Contbr. articles to profl. jours. Mem. Nat. Capital Planning Com., Ottawa, Art Adv. Com., Ottawa; mem. adv. com. Nat. Mus.'s Corp.; mem. Que. Provincial Planning Commn.; founder, v.p. Corp. of Urbanists of Que., 1963-65; bd. dirs. Montreal Internat. Film Festival, 1961-66. Decorated Order of Can.; recipient Internat. Fedn. Housing and Planning Grand Prix award, 1956, Massey medal for arch., 1962, Mademoiselle Mag. award, 1957, Queen's Silver Jubilee medal, 1977, Citizenship citation Can. Govt., 1991, Queen's Golden Jubilee medal, 2002, award of Order of Urbanists of Que., 2003. Fellow AIA (hon.), Royal Archtl. Inst. Can. (exec. com. 1971-74), Toronto Soc. Arch.; mem. Can. Inst. Planners (bd. dirs. 1961-64), Assn. Collegiate Schs. Architecture (bd. dirs. 1981-84, v.p. 1985-86, pres. 1986-87, Disting. Prof. award 1989), Royal Can. Acad. Art (bd. dirs. 1992—2000), Internat. Archive of Women Architects (bd. dirs. 1985-2001), Ont. Assn. Arch. (life), Order of Can. Office: 38 Summerhill Gardens Toronto ON Canada M4T 1B4

VAN GOETHEM, NANCY ANN, painter, educator; b. Detroit, June 27, 1950; d. Walter and Margaret E. (Cook) Van G.; m. Lawrence M. Joseph, Apr. 10, 1976. BFA, Pratt Inst., Bklyn., 1983. Artist Detroit Free Press, Detroit, 1972-81; ind. artist, 1983-92; instr. Parsons Sch. of Design, N.Y.C., 1992—. Artist in various jours. including Ontario Review, fall 1995, 2003, The Male Body U. Mich., 1994, Poetry East, fall 1993; exhbn.: History of Women in Am. Schlesinger Libr., 1994-95, Marygrove Coll., 2001. Grantee, Santa Fe Art Inst., 2002. Mem. Women's Caucus for Art, Coll. Art Assn. Home: Apt 33N 355 S End Ave New York NY 10280-1005

VAN HOESEN, BETH MARIE, artist, printmaker; b. Boise, Idaho, June 27, 1926; d. Enderse G. and Freda Marie (Soulen) Van H.; m. Mark Adams, Sept. 12, 1953. Student, Escuela Esmaralda, Mexico City, 1945, San Francisco Art Inst., 1946, 47, 51, 52, Fontainbleau (France) Ecole des Arts, Acad. Julian and Acad., 5Grande Chaumier, Paris, 1948-51; BA, Stanford U., 1948; postgrad., San Francisco State U., 1957-58. One-Woman shows include, De Young Mus., San Francisco, 1959, Achenbach Found., Calif. Palace Legion of Honor, San Francisco, 1961, 74, Santa Barbara (Calif.) Mus., 1963, 74, 76, Oakland (Calif.) Mus., 1980, John Berggruen Gallery, San Francisco, 1981, 83, 85, 88, 91; traveling exhibit Am. Mus. Assn., 1983-85; group shows include, Calif. State Fair, Sacramento, 1951 (award), Library of Congress, Washington, 1956, 57, San Francisco Mus. Modern Art, 70 (award), Boston Mus. Fine Arts, 1959, 60, 62, Pa. Acad. Fine Arts, Phila., 1959, 61, 63, 65, Achenbach Found., 1961 (award), Bklyn. Mus., 1962, 66, 68, 77, Continuing Am. Graphics, Osaka, Japan, 1970, Hawaii Nat. Print. Exhbn., Honolulu, 1980 (award), Oakland Mus., 1975 (award); represented in permanent collections, including, Achenbach Found., San Francisco, Fine Arts Mus., Bklyn. Mus., Mus. Modern Art, N.Y.C., Oakland Mus., San Francisco Mus. Modern Art, Victoria and Albert Mus., (London), Chgo. Art Inst., Cin. Mus., Portland (Oreg.) Art Mus. (Recipient award of Honor, San Francisco Art Commn. 1981); author: Collection of Wonderful Things, 1972, Beth Van Hoesen Creatures, 1987, Beth Van Hoesen: Works on Paper, 1995, Beth Van Hoesen Teddy Bears, 2000. Mem. Calif. Soc. Printmakers (award 1993), San Francisco Women Artists. Office: c/o John Berggruen 228 Grant Ave Fl 3D San Francisco CA 94108-4612

VAN HOOSER, PATRICIA LOU SCOTT, art educator; b. Springfield, Mo., Oct. 4, 1934; d. Arthur Irving and Isoline Elizabeth (Jones) Scott; m. Buckley Blaine Van Hooser, Mar. 28, 1956 (div.); children: Buckley Blaine II, Craig Alan. BA, Drury U., 1956; MS in Art, Pittsburg (Kans.) State U., 1968. Society writer Springfield News & Leader & Press, 1955—56; hostess radio program Sta. KSEK, Pittsburg, Kans., 1962—63; tchr. art and home econs. Hurley (Mo.) HS, 1956—57; art supr. elem. sch. Mountain Grove, Mo., 1960; tchr. art Hickory Hills Sch., Springfield, 1960—61; tchr art and English jr. and sr. schs., Baxter Springs, Kans., 1965—75; art coord. Joplin (Mo.) Elem. Sch. Dist., 1975—. Lectr. in field; chmn. for S.W. Mo., Nat. Youth Art Month. Bd. dirs. Spiva Art Ctr.; sec. Parents without Ptnrs., CV & FE Credit Union; bd. recorder S.W. Mo. Credit Unions. Mem.: ASCD, NEA, AAUW (2d v.p. Joplin br.), Epsilon Sigma Alpha, Pittsburg State U. Alumni Assn. (sec., pres. Joplin br.), Joplin Cmty. Concert Assn., S.W. Mo. Mus. Assn., Mo. Edn. Assn., S.W. Mo. Dist. Art Tchrs., Mo. Art Edn. Assn., Nat. Art Edn. Assn., Assn. Childhood Edn. Internat. (pres. Joplin br., pres. Mo. state), Writers of Six Bulls, Joplin Writer's Guild, Cafe au Lait Club. Methodist. E-mail: Pvanhooser6@cs.com.

VAN HOUTEN, ELIZABETH ANN, corporate communications executive, painter; b. Washington, Feb. 22, 1945; d. Raymond R. and Marian Edna (Hovemann) Van H. BA, Mary Washington Coll., 1966. Analyst U.S. Gov., Washington, 1966-68; dep. chief of publs. Found. for Coop. Housing, Washington, 1968-72; editor Nat. League of Savs. Inst., Washington, 1972-76; dir. pub. relations Fed. Nat. Mortgage Assn., Washington, 1976-83; v.p. communications & investor relations Sallie Mae (Student Loan Mktg. Assn.), Washington, 1983-93; v.p. corp. and investor rels. Sallie Mae, Washington, 1993-95; ret., 1995; curator Monhegan (Maine) Hist. and Cultural Mus., 1995-98; painter. Apptd. by city coun. to Master Plan Task Force, Alexandria, Va., 1987—92; sec. Monhegan Assocs., 1995—97, trustee, 1998—2001, mem. nominating com., 1999—2002; mem. campaing com. for Del Pepper, Alexandria, 1987; bd. dirs. Washington Studio Sch., 1995—99; mem. bd. dirs. Watergate of Alexandria, 1985—93, pres., 1988—89, chmn., 1991—93; chmn. emeritus Liz Lerman Dance Exch. Mem.: Women Artists of Monhegan Island, Monhegan Artists Open Studio List. Avocations: walking, music, visual arts, reading. Home: PO Box 61 Monhegan ME 04852-0061

VANI, ANITA H. music educator, voice educator; b. Lapua, Finland, Sept. 6, 1963; arrived in U.S., 1965; d. Aimo K. and Mirja M. Riihiaho; m. Michael T. Vani, July 16, 1988; children: Eric M., Alissa H. BA Music Edn., Palm Beach Atlantic Univ., W. Palm Beach, Fla., 1988. Nat. Bd. Cert. EMC/Music 2002. Music specialist Haverhill Elem., W. Palm Beach, Fla., 1988—89; pvt. voice instr. Jimmy Ferraro's Performing Arts Sch., New Port Richey, Fla., 1989—92; elem. music specialist Lee Elem./Carrollwood Elem. and Mitchell Elem., Tampa, Fla., 1989—92; owner pvt. voice studio New Port Richey, Ill., 1992—; elem. music specialist Citrus Pk. Elem., Tampa, Fla., 1992—. Composer (CD recordings) Songs of Immigrant Finns, 2001, singer, 2001; composer, singer: Säteet Auringon, 1989 (top 10 listing in Finland). Founding bd. mem. Juanita Haines Charitable Found., New Port Richey, Fla. Mem.: Nat. Educators Assn., Fla. Educators Assn., Fla. Elem. Music Educators Conf., Hillsborough Elem. Music Coun., Music Educators Nat. Conf.

VANIER, JERRE LYNN, art director; b. Phoenix, June 11, 1957; i. Jerry Dale Barber and Betty Jane (Brady) Barber Hughes; m. Kent Douglas Wick, May 4, 1979 (div. June 1994); 1 child, Jared Kent Wick; m. Jay David Vanier, June 6, 1994; 1 child, Jolie Jacqueline. BA in Art History magna cum laude, Ariz. State U., 1978, MA in Humanities. Chmn., vice chmn. Internat. Friends of Art, Scottsdale, Ariz., 1990-96; dir. 19th and 20th century art Joy Tash Gallery, Scottsdale, 1996-97; dir. estate art Vanier Fine Art, Ltd., Scottsdale, 1997-98, dir., 1998—, Vanier Galleries on Marshall, Scottsdale, 1999—. Mem. pub. art collection adv. bd. Scottsdale Cultural Coun., 1990—, Phoenix Jr. League, Art Renaissance Initiative Faces of Ariz. Mem. DAR (Ariz. page continental congress 1993, Ariz. vice chmn. Jr. Am. Citizen com. 1998, 3d vice regent Camelback chpt. 1993), Colonial Dames Am., Daus. Republic of Tex. (non-resident), Nat. Soc. Arts and Letters (Valley of Sun chpt. bd. dirs. 1988-92, art chmn. 1988-90, membership chmn. 1990-92), Jr. League Phoenix, Alpha Delta Pi, Phi Kappa Phi. Republican. Avocations: genealogy, collecting contemporary art. Office: 7106 E Main St Scottsdale AZ 85251-4316

VAN MARTER, LINDA JOANNE, pediatrician, educator, neonatologist, researcher; d. Neal Dahl and Martha Erickson Van Marter. BS, U. Pitts., 1976, MD, 1980; MPH, Harvard U., 1985. Resident in pediatrics Children's Hosp. Med. Ctr., Boston, 1980—83; fellow in neonatal perinatal medicine Joint Program in Neonatology, 1983—86; from instr. pediat. to asst. prof. pediat. Harvard Med. Sch., Boston, 1986—2002, assoc. prof. pediatrics, 2002—. Reviewer Pediat., Jour. of Pediat., Am. Jour. Pub. Health, New Eng. Jour. Medicine. Recipient Richard L. Day award in pediat. U. Pitts. Sch. Medicine, 1980. Fellow Am. Acad. Pediats. (perinatal sect. exec. com. 1999—, neoprep working group 1996—, chair 2001-03); mem. Am. Pediat. Soc., Perinatal Rsch. Soc., Ea. Soc. for Pediat. Rsch. (coun. 1998-2003), Soc. for Pediat. Epidemiol. Rsch. (sec., treas. 1987-91, pres. 1992-93), Soc. for Pediat. Rsch., Alpha Omega Alpha. [illegible] Medicine 300 Longwood Ave Boston MA 02115-5737

VANMETER, VANDELIA L. retired director; b. Seibert, Colo., July 17, 1934; d. G.W. and A. Pearl Klockenteger; m. Victor M. VanMeter, Jan. 21, 1954; children: Allison C., Kristopher C. BA, Kansas Wesleyan U., 1957; MLS, Emporia State U., 1970; PhD, Tex. Woman's U., 1986. Cert. libr. media specialist. Tchr. Ottawa County Rural Sch., Kans., 1954-55; social scis. tchr. McClave (Colo.) High Sch., 1957-58, Ellsworth (Kans.) Jr. High Sch., 1959-68; libr., media specialist Ellsworth (Kans.) High Sch., 1968-84; asst. prof. libr. sci. U. So. Miss., Hattiesburg, 1986-90; chair dept. libr./info. sci. Spalding U., Louisville, 1990-96, libr. dir., 1991-99. Cons. to sch., pub. and spl. librs., Kans., Miss., Ky., 1970-99; mem. Ky. NCATE Bd. Examiners. Author: American History for Children and Young Adults, 1990, World History for Children and Young Adults, 1992, America in Historical Fiction, 1997; editor: Mississippi Library Media Specialist Staff Development Modules, 1988, Library Lane Newsletter, 1991-99; contbr. chpts. to books; contbr. articles to profl. jours. Active City Coun., Ellsworth, Kans., 1975-79, Park Bd., Ellsworth, 1975-79; bd. dirs. Robbins Meml. Libr., 1977-79. Grantee Kans. Demonstration Sch. Libr., 1970-72, Miss. Power Found., 1989, Project Technology Enhances Curriculur Instrn., 1996-97; named Women of Yr. Bus. and Profl. Women of Ellsworth, Kans., 1976. Mem. ALA, Assn. Coll. and Rsch. Librs., Ky. Libr. Assn., Assn. for Libr. and Info. Sci. Educators.

VAN METRE, LAUREN, foundation administrator; M of Russian Studies, Georgetown U.; postgrad., Johns Hopkins U. Mem. policy planning staff Office Internat. Security Affairs, Pentagon, Washington; program officer rsch. & studies U.S. Inst. Peace, Washington. Contbr. articles to profl. jours. Office: US Inst Peace 1200 17th St NW Ste 200 Washington DC 20036-3011

VAN METRE, MARGARET CHERYL, artistic director, dance educator; b. Maryville, Tenn., Nov. 24, 1938; d. Robert Fillers and Margaret Elizabeth (Goddard) Raulston; m. Mitchell Robert Van Metre II, Aug. 25, 1956; 1 child, Mitchell Robert. Elem., intermediate and advanced tchg. certs. Dir. Van Metre Sch. of Dance, Maryville, 1958-96; artistic dir. Appalachian Ballet Co., Maryville Coll., 1972-96; founding dir. Appalachian Ballet Co., 1972; dir. Van Metre Arts Mgmt., S.C., 1996—. Chmn. dance panel Tenn. Arts Commn., 1973-74; chmn. Bicentennial Ballet Project, Tenn., 1975-76; mem. Nat. Bd. Regional Dance Am., 1997-2003; owner Van Metre Arts Mgmt., Edisto Island, S.C., 1996—. Choreographer ballets: Delusion, 1965, Hill Heritage Suite, 1972, Dancing Princesses, 1983. Mem. Tenn. Assn. of Dance (pres. 1972), Southeast Regional Ballet Assn. (pres. 1996, 97, 98, 99, 2003-04). Democrat. Episcopalian. Home: 2103 Myrtle St Edisto Island SC 29438-3437

VANN, LORA JANE, reading educator, retired; b. Chgo. d. Amos Alva and Mary Prudie (Ellery) V. BA, Marian Coll., Indpls., l958; MA, Ball State U., l963, EdD, l985. Cert. life tchr., reading specialist, supr., Ind. Elem. tchr., asst. prin. Indpls. Pub. Schs., l959-7l; instr. dept. edn. William Woods Coll., Fulton, Mo., 1972-73; tchr. reading, supr. Washington Twp. Schs., Indpls., 1973—2002; ret., 2002. Teaching fellow Ball State U., Muncie, Ind., l980-8l; cons. Advanced Tech., Inc., Indpls., 1987; vis. cons. North Cen. Assn., Bloomington, Ind., 1988, Peace Pole Project Ideas, 2001. Author: Self-Concept and Parochial School Children, 1985, Sigma's Outstanding Women of the 20th Century, 3 vols., l986, 88, 25th Anniversary (1965-90) History of the Life Membership (NAACP) Committee, 1990; co-author: Multi-Cultural Global Awareness African-American Resources, 1992; editor newsletters Reading Timely Topics, l974-80, AS News, l985-2002. Pres. St. Rita Bd. Edn., Indpls., 1987-89; founder Afro-Am. Children's Theatre, 1987. Cath. Interracial Coun. scholar, 1954; NDEA grantee, 1964, 65, Fulbright grantee, Birmingham, Eng., 1967-68, Ball State U. grantee, l980-8l. Mem Internat. Reading Assn., Nat. Coun. Negro Women (charter, sec. Cen. Ind. sect. l98l-84), Washington Twp. Edn. Assn. (chmn. polit. action com. 1987-88, co-chmn. 1988-89), AAUW, Fulbright Assn., Kappa Delta Pi, Phi Delta Kappa, Sigma Gamma Rho (treas. cen. region 1981-86, chpt. pres. 1986-90, 96-2000, trustee nat. edn. found.). Roman Catholic. Avocations: reading, walking, playing piano. Home: 2801 Hillside Ave Indianapolis IN 46218

VAN NESS, PATRICIA WOOD, religious studies educator, consultant, author; b. Peterborough, NH, Sept. 12, 1925; d. Leslie Townsend and Bernice E. (Coburn) Wood; m. John Hasbrouck Van Ness, June 13, 1953; children: Peter Wood, Stephen Hasbrouck, Timothy Coburn. BA, U. Wash., 1947; MA, Inst. Transpersonal Psychology, Palo Alto, Calif., 1993. Leader various workshops and retreats, 1979—; records mgr. dept. pub. rels. Std. Oil Co., NJ, (now Exxon Corp., NYC), 1948-50, sec. pub. rels. dept., 1951—53; sec. law dept. Johnson & Johnson, New Brunswick, NJ, 1953-54; reporter Hudson Valley Newspapers, Highland, NY, 1972-74; acting assoc. dir. office of pub. rels. SUNY, New Paltz, 1974; ednl. cons. Ulster County Assn. for Mental Health, Kingston, NY, 1973-76; Christian educator Meth. Ch., New Paltz, NY, 1976—78, White Plains Presbyn. Ch., NY, 1978—81; adminstrv. asst. Ctr. for Cont. Edn. Calif. Econ., Palo Alto, Calif., 1983-84; profl. rep. pvt. practice Palo Alto, 1984; adminstrv. asst. Inventory Transfer Systems Inc., Palo Alto, 1984-85; Christian Educator Bedford Presbyn. Ch., NH, 1986—88; coord. pub. rels., adminstrv. asst. Inst. Transpersonal Psychology, Menlo Pk., NJ, 1981-83. Workshop leader and cons. Author: Transforming Bible Study with Children, 1991; assoc. editor and writer Bible Workbench, 1993—; contbr. numerous articles to profl. jours. Trustee Peterborough (NH) Players, 1998—2001. Mem. Assn. Presbyn. Ch. Educators. Avocations: swimming, reading, contra dancing, theater. Home: 11 Jaquith Rd Jaffrey NH 03452-6406 E-mail: pwvn@monad.net.

VANNI, DEBORAH ANN, marriage and family therapist, educator; b. Redwood City, Calif., Sept. 22, 1960; d. Neil Anthony and Jeanette Jacqueline Vanni; life ptnr. Ralph Kent Turner, July 24, 1991. MA in marriage and family therapy/art therapy, Notre Dame de Namur U., 1999—2003; BA in English (minor in philosophy), Chico State U., 1982—84. Cert. secondary tchr. Calif., primary tchr. Calif. English tchr. Oroville H.S., Calif., 1986—87; health tchr. Pacific Grove H.S., Calif., 1987—88; fifth grade tchr. St. Emydius Sch., San Francisco, 1988—89; english tchr. SAEF Sch., Kurosio City, Japan, 1989—90, Monta Vista H.S., Cupertino, Calif., 1991—; counselor Support Network For Battered Women, Mountain View, Calif., 2001—. Field hockey coach Monta Vista H.S., Cupertino, Calif., 1991—2000; on-site interviewer Digital Clubhouse Network, Sunnyvale, Calif., 2000—. Prodr.: (video production) Student Videos (WAVE: Western Access Video Excellence, 1999, 2001, 2002); editor: (book of poetry) Reflections on a Polka-Dotted Sheep. Recipient Excellence in Rsch., Notre Dame de Namur U., 2003. Mem.: Calif. Teacher's Assn., No. Calif. Art Therapy Assn., Calif. Assn. of Marriage and Family Therapy, Fremont Edn. Assn., Delta Epsilon Sigma. Office: The Support Network for Battered Women 1975 West El Camino Real Suite 205 Mountain View CA 94040 Personal E-mail: vanturner2@att.net.

VAN NOORD, DIANE C. artist, educator; b. Muskegon, Mich., Dec. 12, 1950; d. Ernest Raymond and Judith Ann Olsen; m. Calvin G. Van Noord, Sept. 26, 1981; children: Tawn Star, Brian Calvin, Timothy John. BA, Hope Coll., 1991; MA, Western Mich. U., 1994. Artist, Holland, Mich., 1996—99; pvt. art tchr., 2000—. Guest lectr. Counterpart Assn., Grand Haven, Mich., 1997, Lakeland Painters, Grand Haven, 1997, Traverse City (Mich.) Art Assn., 1997, Holland Christian Schs., 1998, 99, 2000. Exhbns. include Neville Pub. Mus., Green Bay, Wis., 1994, Carillon Gallery, Ft. Worth, 1995, 97, Sedona (Ariz.) Arts Ctr., 1995, 96, 99, Holland Area Arts Coun., 1995, Pitts. Ctr. for the Arts, 1995, Miss. Mus. Art, Jackson, 1995, Unitarian Universalist Ch., Phoenix, 1996, Lakeland Painters, Grand Haven, Mich., 1996, Sun Cities Mus. Art, Sun City, Ariz., 1997, Art Inst. Phoenix, 1998, Hill Country Arts Found., Ingram, Tex., 1998, Mus. Tex. Tech. U., Lubbock, 1998, Dunton Gallery, Arlington Heights, Ill., 2000, Internat. Mus. Art, El Paso, 2000, among others; one-woman shows include Gallery Upstairs, Grand Haven, 1996, Moynihan Gallery, Holland, 1997, Trinity Presbyn. Ch., Denton, 1997, Show Sabbatical, 1998, 99, Freedom Village, Holland, 2000, Acad. Artists Assn., Springfield, Mass., 2001, Hilton Head Art League, 2001, Oil Painters Am., Chgo., 2002, Audubon Artists N.Y., 2002, Magnum Opus XIV, Sacramento, 2002, Am. Artists Profl. League, N.Y.C., 2002, Celebration of Western Art, San Francisco, 2002, Hilton Head Art League, 2003, 2004, Oil Painters Am., Taos, N.Mex., 2003, Scottsdale Artists Sch, 2004, Nat. Watercolor Soc., 2004, others; permanent collections in Fla., Ariz., Mich., Nebr., Ind.; contbr. articles to profl. jours. Recipient Merchant's award Lakeland Painters, 1996, No. Ariz. Watercolor Soc., Sedona Arts Ctr., 1999, Diane Parssinen Meml. award No. Ariz. Watercolor Soc., 2001, 2d prize Internat. Artist Mag., 2002, Honorable Mention, Artists Mag., 2002. Mem. Ariz. Watercolor Assn., No. Ariz. Watercolor Assn., Oil Painters Am. (assoc.), Nat. Watercolor Soc. (assoc.), Allied Artists (assoc.), Am. Women Artists (assoc.). Republican. Home: 6418 Oakridge Dr Holland MI 49423-8999 E-mail: dvn@dianevannoord.com.

VAN NORTWICK, BARBARA LOUISE, library director; b. Johnson City, N.Y., Jan. 3, 1940; d. Joseph John and Mary Louise (Hamzik) Goodwin; m. David Harry Van Nortwick, Nov. 17, 1962; children: Kimberly Lynn, Craig Michael. BA, Harpur Coll., 1961; MLS, SUNY, Albany, 1976; DA in Info. and Libr. Adminstrn., Simmons Coll., 1986. Coord. ednl. facilities Maine-Endwell (N.Y.) H.S., 1961-64; tchr. English, Guilderland (N.Y.) H.S., 1965-66; audiovisual libr. South Colonie (N.Y.) H.S., 1974-76; head libr. Westfield (Mass.) H.S., 1976-78, Columbia H.S., East Greenbush, N.Y., 1978-79; libr. dir. N.Y. State Nurses Assn., 1979-84; dir. com. on aging N.Y. State Senate, Albany, 1983-84, dir. select com. interstate coop., 1985-89; assoc. prof. govt. document and social scis. Skidmore Coll., Saratoga Springs, N.Y., 1989-94; libr. dir. New Lebanon (N.Y.) Jr.-Sr. H.S., 1994-98; dir. N.Y. State Legis. Libr. Albany, 1998—. Del. Mass. Gov.'s Conf. Librs. and Info. Svcs., 1978-79; trustee Capital Dist. Libr. Coun., 1990-95; cons. HEW grant on self-directed continuing edn. for nurses; adj. prof. Sch. Libr. and Info. Sci., SUNY, Albany, 1983-84; libr. adj. faculty Coll. of St. Rose, Albany, 1995-98. Mem. editl. bd. Coll. and Undergrad. Librs. Jour., 1992-94. U.S. Govt. Title II B fellow Simmons Coll. Mem. ALA, N.Y. Libr. Assn., Spl. Libr. Assn., Am. Assn. Law Librs. Methodist. Office: NY State Legis Libr Rm 337 The Capitol Albany NY 12224 Home: 14 Elizabeth Rd Harwich MA 02645-1007

VAN NOY, CHRISTINE ANN, restaurateur; b. Oakland, CA, Mar. 25, 1948; d. Julio Ceaser and Bernice Thelma (Rose) Lucchesi; m. David Craik Van Noy, July 10, 1971; children: James Allan, Joseph Julio. Student, U. Calif., Berkeley, 1971-73, U. Phoenix, 1994—. Exec. sec. Kaiser Permanente Med. Care Program, Oakland, 1966-76; owner Secret Closet Boutique, Moraga, Calif., 1972-82; owner, operator The Wordshop, Moraga, 1976-86; owner, cons. Van Noy & Assocs., Moraga, 1979—; exec. sec. to sr. v.p., regional mgr. Kaiser Permanente Med. Care Program, 1986-88, chmn., CEO, 1988-92, dir. adminstrv. svcs., 1992-98, v.p. adminstrv. svcs., 1999-2000; owner Giulio's Catering, 1999-2000; pres. Kaiser Permanente Internat.; owner Cafe Dolce, 2000—02; prin. Guillio's Catering, 2002—. Instr. U. Calif., Santa Cruz, 1983-84, Diablo Valley Coll., Concord, Calif., 1984; cons. Nat. Alliance Homebased Businesswomen, San Francisco, 1981-84. Author: Homebased Business Guide, 1982, (with others) Women Working Home, 1982. Mem. bd. Joaquis Moraga Sch. Dist., 1983-84, Calif. Federated Jr. Women's Clubs, 1972-77; bd. dirs. Orinda/Moraga Recreational Swimming Assn., 1984-85, St. Mark's United Methodist Ch., Moraga, 1983-84; pres. bd. Protect Our Nation's Youth Baseball Assn., 1987-90; dir. Ctr. for Living Skills, 1990—. Mem. Women Health Care Execs. Democrat. Roman Catholic. Avocations: graphic design, painting, writing. Home: 181 Paseo Del Rio Moraga CA 94556-1641 Office: Cafe Dolce 100 Pringle Ave #120 Walnut Creek CA 94596 E-mail: cafedolce@hotmail.com.

VAN ORDEN, PHYLLIS JEANNE, librarian, educator; b. Adrian, Mich., July 7, 1932; d. Warren Philip and Mabel A. Nancy (Russell) Van O. BS, Ea. Mich. U., 1954; AMLS, U. Mich., 1958; EdD, Wayne State U., 1970. Sch. librarian East Detroit (Mich.) Pub. Schs., 1954-57; librarian San Diego Pub. Library, 1958-60; media specialist Royal Oak (Mich.) Pub. Schs., 1960-64; librarian Oakland U., Rochester, Mich., 1964-66; instr. Wayne State U., Detroit, 1966-70; asst. prof. Rutgers U., New Brunswick, N.J., 1970-76; prof. library science Fla. State U., Tallahassee, 1977-91, assoc. dean for instrn., 1988-91; prof. libr. sci. program Wayne State U., Detroit, 1991-93; dir. Grad. Sch. of Libr. and Info. Sci. U. Wash., Seattle, 1993-96; cons. in field, 1996—. Editor: Elementary School Library Collection, 1974-77; author: Collection Program in Schools, 2001, Library Service to Children, 1992, Selecting Books for the Elementary School Library Media Center, 2000. Fla. State Libr. grantee, 1984, 86, 88; Lillian Bradshaw scholar Tex. Woman's U., 1993. Mem.: ALA (libr. resources and tech. svcs. divsn., Blackwell/N.Am. scholarship award 1983), Assn. for Libr. and Info. Sci. Edn. (pres. 1990, Svc. award 1997), Assn. Libr. Svc. to Children (past pres., Dist. Svc. award 2002), Pi Lambda Theta. Avocations: music, knitting, physical fitness, cooking, travel. E-mail: vanordp@u.washington.edu.

VAN OST, LYNN, physical therapist, Olympic team official; b. Englewood, N.J., Sept. 7, 1960; d. William Carlisle and Marijane Dorward Van Ost. BSN, West Chester State Coll., Pa., 1982; MEd, Temple U., Phila., 1987, BS in Phys. Therapy, 1986—88. RN Pa, 1982; cert. athletic trainer Nat. Athletic Trainer's Assn., 1984. Staff nurse Abington (Pa.) Meml. Hosp., 1982—84; nurse/ athletic trainer US Sports Acad., Mobile, Ala., 1984—85; sports medicine coord. Providence Hosp., Mobile, Ala., 1985—86; coord. of sports medicine Del. County Meml. Hosp., Drexel Hill, Pa., 1988—90; staff phys. therapist Hunterdon Phys. and Sports Therapy, Flemington, NJ, 1990—91, Sports Phys. Therapy, Somerset, NJ, 1991—92; clin. specialist, sports medicine Thomas Jefferson U. Hosp., Phila., 1992—98; asst. dir. Sports Phys. Therapy Inst., Princeton, NJ, 1998—90, dir. Flemington, 2000—02; clin. specialist, sports phys. therapy Hunterdon Med. Ctr., Flemington, 2002—. Vol. athletic trainer US Olympic Com., Colo. Springs, Colo., 1989—96, US Field Hockey, Colo. Springs, 1993—96, US Short Track Speed Skating, Lake Placid, NY, 1994—99. Author: (study guide) Athletic Training Student Guide to Success, 2003, (cd rom) Goniometry, 1999. Scholar Athletic Tng., Temple U., 1982-1984. Mem.: Nat. Athletic Trainer's Assn., Abbes' Soc., Panhellenic (pres. 1981—82), Alpha Phi (panhellenic rep. 1980—81). Achievements include patents for Athletic Tng. Jacket. Avocations: golf, travel. Home: 2 Riverview Drive West Trenton NJ 08628 Office: Hunterdon Med Ctr 2100 Wescott Drive Flemington NJ 08822-4604 Office Phone: 908 782-1095.

VAN OUWERKERK, ANITA HARRISON, reading educator; b. Oakdale, La., Feb. 16, 1942; d. Otto Joseph and Nora Land Harrison; m. Clyde Carter, Dec. 31, 1962; m. William Van Ouwerkerk, June 28, 1969 (dec.); children: Kathryn, Jeffrey, Joseph. BA, Northwestern State U., Natchitoches, La., 1963; student McNeese State U., 1965; MEd, U. New Orleans, 1968; student, Lamar State U., Beaumont, Tex., 1978—83. Cert. tchr. K-8 and mentally retarded La., 1963, Tex., 1979. Various tchg. and cons. positions, La., 1963—70; edn. cons. Allen Paris, Elizabeth, La., 1974—75; tchr. spl. edn. West Orange Cove Inst. Sch. Dist., Orange, Tex., 1978—95; instr. Lamar State Coll., Orange, Tex., 1988—2001; instr. reading Blinn Coll., Bryan, Tex., 2001—. Dir. Greater Orange Area Lit. Svc., Orange, 1999—2001, bd. dirs., 1998—2001. Fellow spl. edn., U. New Orleans, 1967—68. Mem.: Nat. Assn. Devel. Educators, Tex. Coll. Reading and Learning Assn. (pres. elect 2001), League of Women Voters, Toastmasters, Delta Kappa Gamma (pres., sec. 1996—2000). Unitarian Universalist. Avocations: writing, singing, sewing. Home: 1506 Bennett St Bryan [illegible] Office: Blinn Coll PO Box 6030 Bryan TX 77802 Business E-Mail: avanouwerkerk@acmail.blinncol.edu.

VAN PELT, JANET RUTH, retired insurance company executive; b. Baltimore, Md., Jan. 28, 1948; d. John Francis and Helen Janet V. BA, Fla. State U., 1969, MA, 1972. Instr. Wayne State U., Detroit, Mich., 1971-72; promotion asst. Actors Theatre of Louisville, Ky., 1972-73; lecturer Towson State U., Towson, Md., 1973-75; workers' compensation Harry T. Campbell Sons' Co., Towson, 1973-74; claims representative Atlantic Mutual Companies, Hunt Vly., Md., 1974-78; claims supr. Atlantic Mut. Cos., N.Y., 1978-79; home office claims examiner Atlantic Mutual Co., N.Y., 1979-88; supr. home office excess claims Am. Home Assurance Co., East Orange, N.J., 1988, sr. supr. home office excess claims, 1989-90; claims mgr. GRE Ins. Group, Princeton, N.J., 1990-92, Elliston, Inc., New Hope, Pa., 1992—. Mem. Assn. of Research and Enlightment, Windsor Haven Condominium Assn. (pres.). Democratic. Episcopalian. Avocations: reading, swimming, flower arranging, travel. Office: Elliston Inc Buckingham House 9 Reeder Rd New Hope PA 18938-1015 Office Phone: 215-862-2010.

VANPOOL, CYNTHIA PAULA, special education educator, special services consultant; b. San Antonio, Dec. 8, 1946; d. Walter Foye and Pauline (Karger) Phillips; m. Darrell William Vanpool, Feb. 3, 1968; children: George Karger, William Davies. AB in English, Drury Coll., 1968; MS in Spl. Edn. Tchg., Pittsburg (Kans.) State U., 1987. Cert. tchr., Kans., Mo., Okla.; cert. instr. in Quest Skills for Adolescents. Tchr. lang. arts and journalism Miami (Okla.) Pub. Schs., 1968-69; dir. Christian edn./outreach ministries First Assembly of God, Miami, 1981-83; substitute tchr. Miami Pub. Sch. Dist., 1983-85, learning disabilities specialist, journalism sponsor/advisor, 1985-93, spl. svcs. cons., 1993—. Chair spl. edn. dept. Will Rogers Jr. H.S./Mid. Sch., Miami, 1988-94, nat. jr. honor soc. advisor, 1993-94; homebound instr.; cooperating educator for student tchr. practicum student supervision, supr. resident tchr.; cons., tutor, presenter in field; pvt. practice ednl. cons.; chairperson adv. bd. Joyful Learning Ctr. Child Care Sch. Recipient Cert. of Appreciation, Miami Evening Lions Club, 1987, Disting. Svc. award Okla. Lions Clubs, 1988, Internat. Presdl. Cert. of Appreciation for Humanitarian Svc., Lions Internat., 1988; Miami Pub. Sch. Enrichment Found. grantee, 1995, 97. Mem. Coun. for Exceptional Children, Divsn. for Learning Disabilities, Coun. for Children with Behavior Disorders, Phi Kappa Phi. Mem. Assembly of God. Ch. Avocations: reading, writing, entertaining, movies, music. Home: 6996 S 590 Rd Miami OK 74354-4500 Office: Miami Pub Schs 1930 B St NE Miami OK 74354-2117

VAN RAALTE, BARBARA G. retired realtor; b. Rochester, N.Y., Apr. 11, 1932; d. Maurice Harry and Estelle Belle (Breman) Goldman; m. John Alan Van Raalte, Sept. 5, 1954 (div. July 1974); children: John Alan Jr., Peter Baird, Thomas Douglas, Skye Van Raalte Herzog. BA in Econs. and Polit. Sci., Wellesley Coll., 1954; postgrad., Harvard Grad. Sch. Design, 1993, 95. Cert. buyer rep., N.C. Dir. devel. Stowe (Vt.) Sch., 1975-77; assoc. dir. devel. NYU Med. Ctr., The Rusk Inst. Rehab. Medicine, N.Y.C., 1977-80; dir. devel. Planned Parenthood of Vt., Burlington, 1980-83; realtor, sr. assoc. Foulsham Farms Real Estate, South Burlington, 1983-95, Trombley Real Estate, Burlington, 1995-97; sr. assoc. CBR Re/Max Preferred Real Estate, South Burlington, 1997-99; sr. assoc. Pall Spera Co. Real Estate, Stowe, Vt., 1999—2002, ret., 2002. Bd. dirs., treas. Hist. Soc., Stowe, 1974-75; bd. dirs. emeritus Katonah (N.Y.) Mus. Art, 1980—; mem. Nat. Spkrs. Bur., United Jewish Appeal, 1982-84; guide Shelburne (Vt.) Farms, 1994-, vol. Lake Champlain Maritime Mus. Mem. Hadassah (bd. dirs. Mid. East affairs 1996-98). Jewish. Avocations: architecture and city planning, landscape design, photography, travel, cross country skiing, bicycling. Home: 5 Southwind Dr Burlington VT 05401-5463

VAN RAALTE, POLLY ANN, reading and writing specialist, photojournalist; b. N.Y.C., Sept. 22, 1951; d. Byron Emmanuel and Enid (Godnick) Van R. Student, U. London, 1972; BA, Beaver Coll., 1973; MS in Edn., U. Pa., 1974, EdD, 1994, West Chester State Coll., 1977. Title I reading tchr. Oakview Sch., West Deptford Twp. Sch. Dist., Woodbury, N.J., 1974-75, title I reading supr., 1975 summer; lang. arts coord. Main Line Day Sch., Mitchell Sch., Haverford, Pa., 1975-76; reading supr. Salvation Army, Phila., summer 1976; reading Huntingdon Jr. H.S., Abington (Pa.) Sch.

Dist., 1976-78; reading specialist No. 2 Sch., Lawrence Pub. Sch., Inwood, N.Y., 1978-87; high sch. reading specialist Cedarhurst, N.Y., 1988-93, Lawrence (N.Y.) H.S., 1988-93; elem. reading specialist No. 5 Sch., 1992—; reading specialist Hewlett (N.Y.) Elem. Sch., Hewlett-Woodmere Pub. Sch., 1987-88, Lawrence Mid. Sch., 1993-95; instr. reading and spl. edn. dept. Adelphi U., 1973—. Columnist South Shore Record, featured columnist, 1992—; columnist Boulevard Mag., 1995-97; photojournalist Manhattan Reports, 1997-2002; feature columnist www.15minutesmagazine.com. Bd. dirs., mem. exec. bd. Five Towns Cmty. Ctr., 1991-93, co-chmn. ednl. youth svcs. edn. com., 1991-93; cons. to sch. dists.; advisor Am. Biog. Inst., Inc.; coord. Five Towns Young Voter Registration, Hewlett, N.Y., summer 1971; chmn. class fund Beaver Coll., also mem. internat. rels. com. U. Pa. scholar, 1977-78; mem. assoc. divsn. Jewish Guild for Blind; mem. N.Y. City Sports Commn.; co-chair youth svcs. com. Mem. Internat. Reading Assn., Wis. Reading Assn., Nat. Coun. Tchrs. English, Nassau Reading Coun., N.Y. Reading Assn., Coun. Exceptional Children, Coun. for a Beautiful Israel, Nat. Assn. Gifted Children, Am. Assn. of the Gifted, Nat./State Leadership Tng. Inst. on the Gifted and Talented, Children's Lit. Assembly, N.Y. State English Coun., Assn. Curriculum Devel., Am. Israel Pub. Affairs Com., New Leadership Com. of Jewish Nat. Fund, State of Israel Bonds New Leadership, Simon Wiesenthal New Leadership Soc., Nat. Polit. Action Com., Am. Friends of Hebrew U. (torch com.), Technion Soc., Am. Friends David Yellin Tchr.'s Coll., Am. Friends Israel Philharm., Am. Friends of Tel Aviv U., Am. Israel Cultural Found., Hadassah, Film Soc. Lincoln Ctr., U.S. Olympic Soc., Friends of N.Y.C. Sports Commn., Cooper-Hewitt Mus., Mus. Modern Art, Met. Mus. Art, Whitney Mus., Phila. Mus. Art, Smithsonian Inst., Friends of Carnegie-Hall, Friends of Am. Ballet Theatre, Friends of Am. Theatre Wing, Women's Am. Orgn. for Rehab. Through Tng. (citi women divsn. N.Y.C.), U. Pa. Alumni Assn. N.Y.C., Dorot Soc., Human Rels. Club (sec.), Actors' Fund, Pi Lambda Theta, Kappa Delta Pi (sec., Internat. Tennis Hall of Fame). Home: 26 Meadow Ln Lawrence NY 11559-1828 Office: #5 Sch Cedarhurst Ave Cedarhurst NY 11516

VAN REGENMORTER, WILLIAM, state legislator; m. Cheryl; four children. Mich. jud. com., econ. devel. com., energy com.; chmn. House Rep. Caucus, 84-90. Commr. Ottawa County Bd. Commrs., 1980-82; mem. Mich. Ho. of Reps., 1982-90, Mich. Senate from 22nd dist., Lansing, 1990—. Named legis. of yr. 1985 Mich. Sheriff's Assn., Mich. Assn. Police, 1988, Police Officer's Assn. Mich., 1989; recipient Santarelli award Nat. Orgn. for Victim Assistance, 1985, justice award Found. for Improvement of Justice, 1986, leadership award Nat. Sheriff's Assn., 1987. Office: Mich Senate State Capitol PO Box 30036 Lansing MI 48909-7536 Home: 5965 16th Avenue Hudsonville MI 49426

VAN RY, GINGER LEE, school psychologist; b. Alexandria, Va., June 26, 1953; d. Ray Ellsworth Hensley and Bernice Anne (Weidel) Wolter; m. Willem Hendrik Van Ry, Aug 23, 1986; 1 child, Anika Claire. AA, U. Nev., Las Vegas, 1973; BA, U. Wash., 1983, MEd, 1985. Cert. sch. psychologist (nationally). Psychometrist The Mason Clinic, Seattle, 1980-84, supr., psychology lab., 1984-86; sch. psychologist Everett (Wash.) Sch. Dist., 1986—. Mem. profl. ednl. adv. bd. U. Wash. Sch. Psychology, Seattle, 1995—; mem. early childhood devel. del. to China, 2000. Author: (with others) Wash. State Assn. of Sch. Psychologists Best Practice Handbook, 1993. Co-pres. Lake Cavanaugh Hghts. Assn., Seattle, 1994-95, chmn. long-range planning com., 1995—. Mem. AAUW, NEA, NASP (nationally cert. sch. psychologist), Wash. State Assn. Sch. Psychologists (chair profl. devel. com. 1995-2001), Wash. State Edn. Assn., U. Wash. Alumni Assn. Democrat. Avocations: reading, travel, fgn. cultures, woodworking, horticulture. Office: The Everett Sch Dist PO Box 2098 Everett WA 98203-0098

VAN SANT, JOANNE FRANCES, academic administrator; b. Morehead, Ky., Dec. 29, 1924; d. Lewis L. and Dorothy (Green) Van S. BA, Denison U., Granville, Ohio; MA, The Ohio State U.; postgrad., U. Colo. and The Ohio State U.; LLD (hon.), Albright Coll., 1975. Tchr., health and phys. edn. Mayfield (Ky.) H.S., 1946—47; instr. Denison U., Granville, Ohio, 1948; instr. women's phys. edn. Otterbein Coll., Westerville, Ohio, 1948-52, assoc. prof., 1955-62, dept. chmn., 1950-62, chmn. div. profl. studies, 1961-65, dean of women, 1952-60, 62-64, dean of students, 1964-93, v.p. student affairs, 1968-93; v.p., dean student affairs emeritus, 1993—; cons. Instnl. Advancement, 1993—. Co-pres. Directions for Youth, 1983-84, pres., 1984-85; bd. dirs. North Area Mental Health; trustee Friendship Village of Columbus, 1996—, pres. bd., 1998—; trustee Westerville Civic Symphony at Otterbein Coll., 1983-88; active numerous other community orgns.; ordained elder Presbyn. Ch., 1967. Named to hon. Order of Ky. Cols., 1957; recipient Focus on Youth award Columbus Dispatch, 1983, Vol. of the Yr. award North Area Mental Health Svcs., 1982, citation Denison U., 1996. Mem. Am. Assn. Counseling and Devel., Ohio Personnel and Guidance Assn., Ohio Assn. Women Deans, Adminstrs., Counselors (treas., exec. bd. 1972-73), Nat. Assn. Student Personnel Adminstrs., Ohio Coll. Personnel Assn., Mortar Bd. (hon.), Zonta Internat. (pres. Columbus, Ohio club 1978-80, dist. gov. 1988-90, internat. svc. chmn. 1996-98, internat. found. bd. 1997-2001), Vocal Arts Resource Network (chair bd. dirs. 1994-96), Cap and Dagger Club, Torch and Key Hon., Order Omega, Alpha Lambda Delta, Theta Alpha Phi, others. Avocations: musical and children's theater production, choreography. Home: 9100 Oakwood Pt Westerville OH 43082-9643 Office: Otterbein Coll Instnl Advancement Westerville OH 43081 E-mail: deanvan@aol.com., jvansant@otterbein.edu.

VAN SCHENKHOF, CAROL DOUGHERTY (CAROL DOVAN), soprano, music educator; b. Reading, Pa., Apr. 20, 1942; d. Harry Hammond Dougherty and Magdalen Mary Doviak; m. Mark Anton van Schenkhof, Feb. 18, 1995; m. John William Heierman, Sept. 4, 1965 (div. July 6, 1986). BA, Chatham Coll., Pitts., Pa., 1964; grad. studies, Julliard Sch., N.Y., 1964—65; MA Ethnomusicology, Hunter Coll., N.Y., 1970; grad. studies, Julliard Sch., N.Y., 1970; adv. studies in opera performance, Hunter Coll. Opera Theater, 1971; adv. studies, Mannes Coll., 1980; vocal pedagogy, Westminster Choir Coll., Princeton, N.J., 1992, vocal pedagogy, 1996, Oberlin Conservatory, Ohio, 2000, vocal pedagogy, 2002. Voice tchr. Chatham Coll. Lab. Sch. of Music, Pitts., 1964; resource profl. Lincoln Ctr., N.Y.C., 1972; vis. artist, lectr. Ewha Univ., Seoul, Republic of Korea, 1975, Emissora Nacional de Radioifusao, Lisbon, Portugal, 1976, Conservatorio Nacional, Lisbon, 1976; lectr. opera C.W. Post Coll., L.I. Univ., Greenvale, NY, 1982—83; profl. coord. Port Wash. Libr.-Music Adv. Coun., Port Wash., NY, 1985—87; voice tchr. Stony Brook Univ., NY, 1998—99, Carol Dovan-van Schenkhof Studios, Port Wash., NY, 1980—. Adjudicator Nat. Assn. Tchrs. of Singing Columbia Univ., N.Y., 1994, Westminster Choir Coll., Princeton, NJ, 1995, N. Y. Music Tchrs., 1997—98, Queens Coll., Flushing, NY, 2001; adjudicator N.Y. State Sch. Music Assn., L.I., NY, 1991—, Assoc. Music Tchrs. League, N.Y., 1993—. Singer: Rhodesia T.V. Ltd., 1974; performer: Rhodesia Organizations, 1974; singer: (recording artist) South African Broadcasting, 1974, Emissora Nacional de Radiodifušao, 1976, (soloist) Met. Opera Studio, 1971—72, Alice Tully Hall, 1983, recitals with composer Jeanne Singer, 1983—87, Nat. Grand Opera, 1983, (Operas) Best of Opera, Carnegie Hall (Placido Domingo-hon. dir.), 1982, La Boheme (Placido Domingo-hon. dir.), 1981, Ninth Symphony of Beethoven- Reading Sympony Orch., 1983, numerous others. Recipient 1st Pl. award, Competition Pitts. Musicians Club, 1962, Pitts. Concert Soc. Youth Auditions, 1962, Pitts. Concert Soc. Major Auditions, 1963; scholar, Chautauqua (NY) Inst. Music, 1962—63, Aspen (Colo.) Music Festival, 1964. Mem.: NY Singing Tchrs., Am. Guild Musical Artists, Nat. Assn. for Music Edn., Nat. Assn. of Tchrs. Singing, Associated Music Tchrs. League (exec. bd. 1994—). Epsic. Avocations: gardening, sailing. Home and Studio: 6 Hillview Ave Port Washington NY 11050

VAN SCHOIACK EDSTROM, LEIHUA CATHLEEN, psychologist, researcher; b. Portland, Oreg., Dec. 12, 1966; d. Larry Cecil and Joan Anna Van Schoiack; m. David Joseph Sylvester, Aug. 13, 1988 (div. Nov. 1, 1995); m. Christopher Emanuel Edstrom, Aug. 19, 2000; 1 child, Christian Emanuel Edstrom. BS in Psychology, U. Wash., 1988, MEd in Ednl. Psychology, 1994, PhD in Ednl. Psychology, 2000. Cert. sch. psychologist Wash. Rsch. scientist Com. for Children, Seattle, 1993—; resident in psychology Morrison Ctr., Portland, 1998—99; intern Seattle Mental Health, 2001—02. Sch. psychologist Sunset Elem., Shoreline, Wash., 1996—97. Recipient All-Am. Scholar Collegiate award, U.S. Achievement Acad., 1994; fellow, U. Wash., 1991—92; scholar, 1995. Mem.: NASP, APA. Pentecostal. Avocations: piano, singing, hiking, reading, sewing. Office: Com for Children 568 1st Ave Ste 600 Seattle WA 98104

VANSICKLE, SHARON DEE, public relations executive; b. Portland, Oreg., Nov. 10, 1955; BA in Mktg. and Journalism, U. Portland, 1976, postgrad., 1977-79. Reporter Willamette Week, Portland, 1976-77; dir. pub. rels. Tektronix, Portland, 1977-83; prin. pub. rels. KVD Pub. Rels., Portland, 1983-98; CEO KVO Pub. Rslc., Portland, 1999—. Chmn. Pinnacle Worldwide, bd. dirs. pub. rels. coun. Vice chair Portland Met. Area Reg. Arts and Culture Coun.; bd. dirs. CPRF, The Oreg. Entrepreneur's Forum, Pres.'s Coun. on Arts & Sci., U. Portland. Mem. Pub. Rels. Soc. Am. (pres. Portland chpt. 1994-95, chair-elect N. Pac. dist., mem. counsilor's acad., bd mem. and chair tech. com. 1999 Spring conf.). Office: KVO Pub Rels 200 SW Market St Ste 1400 Portland OR 97201-5741

VAN SITTERT, BARBARA C. retired classics educator, writer; b. Panora, Iowa, Dec. 14, 1935; d. Dean Leonard Culver and Lola Mae Rich; m. Logan Earl Van Sittert, June 9, 1957; 1 child, Todd. PhD, Ariz. State U., 1975, MA, 1962; BS, Iowa State U., 1958. Tchr., adminstr. Phoenix Coll., 1962—98. Dir. honors program Phoenix Coll., 1982—98, dir. founder classics program, 1990—98. Contbr. articles to profl. jours., 2000. Exec. com. Ariz. Commn. of Arts, Phoenix, 1976—82; chmn. Charter Govt. Commn., Phoenix, 1980—81; pres. Maricopa Coll. Faculty Assn., Phoenix, 1980—82. Mem.: Nat. Soc. Arts & Letters. Home and Office: 7007 N Wilder Rd Phoenix AZ 85021

VANSTONE, AMANDA, Australian government official; married. Cert. in mktg. studies, South Australian Inst. Tech., 1972, grad. diploma in legal practice, 1983; BA, U. Adelaide, Australia, 1981, LLB, 1983. Retailer, wholesaler; pvt. practice barrister and solicitor; mem. for South Australia Australian Senate, 1984—, shadow spl. min. of state, spokesperson on status of women; parliamentary sec. to dep. leader of the opposition; min. for employment, edn., tng. and youth affairs Australia, 1996-97; min. for justice, 1997-98; min. for justice and customs, 1998-2001; min. for family and cmty. svcs., 2001—03; min. assisting Prime Min. for the Status of Women, 2001—03; min. for immigration, multicultural and indigenous affairs, 2003—; min. assisting the Prime Min. for reconciliation, 2003—. Mem. Liberal-Nat. Party Coalition. Office: Ste MF 40 Parliament House Canberra ACT 2600 Australia

VANSTROM, MARILYN JUNE CHRISTENSEN, retired elementary school educator; b. Mpls., June 10, 1924; d. Harry Clifford and Myrtle Agnes (Hagland) Christensen; m. Reginald Earl Vanstrom, Mar. 20, 1948; children: Gary Alan, Kathryn June Vanstrom Marinello. AA, U. Minn., 1943, BS, 1946. Cert. elem. tchr NY, Ill. Tchr. Pub. Sch., St. Louis Park, Minn., 1946-47, Deephaven, Minn., 1947-50, Chicago Heights, Ill., 1950-52, Steger, Ill., 1964, substitute tchr. Dobbs Ferry, N.Y., 1965-72, Yonkers, N.Y., 1965-92. Mem. Ch. Women, Christ Meml. Luth. Ch. Mem. AAUW (life, pres. So. Westchester br. 1988-90, Ednl. Found. award 1990), Morning Book Club, Evening Book Club (Met. West br. Minn., So. Westchester br. N.Y.), Yonkers Fedn. Tchrs., U. Minn. Alumni Assn. Democrat. Avocations: painting, sketching, choir, piano, travel. Home: 12300 Marion Ln W Apt 2105 Minnetonka MN 55305-1317

VAN SUSTEREN, GRETA CONWAY, news anchor, lawyer; b. Appleton, Wis., June 11, 1954; d. Urban Peter and Margery (Conway) Van Susteren; m. John Purcell Coale, Oct. 12, 1987. BA in Econs, U. Wis., 1976; JD, Georgetown U., 1979, LLM, 1982. Bar: D.C. 1979, U.S. Supreme Ct. 1982, Md. 1985, Wis. 1987, U.S. Ct. Appeals (D.C., 2d and 4th cirs.). Ptnr. Milliken, VanSusteren & Canan, Washington, 1982—; with CNN, 1991—2002, co-host Burden of Proof, legal cons. The World Today; host On the Record With Greta Van Susteren Fox News, 2002—. Adj. prof. Georgetown Law Ctr., Washington, 1985—; lectr., panelist Jud. Conf., Washington, 1986. Bd. dirs. Stuart Stiller Found., Washington, 1982—. Stiller fellow, Georgetown Law Ctr., 1980. Mem.: ATLA (lectr. conf. 1986—), ABA, D.C. Bar Assn.

VAN TASSEL-BASKA, JOYCE LENORE, education educator; b. Toledo, July 28, 1944; d. Robert Rae and Eleanor Jane (Kenyon) Sloan; m. Thomas Harold Van Tassel, May 21, 1964 (div. 1975); m. Leland Karl Baska, July 25, 1980; 1 child, Ariel Sloan. BEd cum laude, U. Toledo, 1966, MA, MEd, 1969, EdD, 1981. Tchr. Toledo Pub. Schs., 1965-72, coord. gifted programs, 1973-76; dir. Ill. gifted program Ill. State Bd. Edn., Springfield, 1976-79; dir., area svc. ctr. Matteson (Ill.) Sch. Dist., 1979-82; dir. Ctr. for Talent Devel. Northwestern U., Evanston, Ill., 1982-87; Smith prof. edn. Coll. William and Mary, Williamsburg, Va., 1987—, dir. Ctr. for Gifted Edn., 1988—2002, exec. dir. Ctr. for Gifted Edn., 2002—. Mem. Va. Adv. Bd. on Gifted and Talented, 1988-2000; mem. State Ohio Adv. Bd. Gifted and Talented, 1975-76; mem. edn. coun. Nat. Bus. Consortium, 1981-84. Mem. editorial bd. Roeper Rev., 1980-82; pub. Talent Devel. Quar., 1983-87; manuscript rev. editor Jour. Edn. of Gifted, 1981—; mem. editorial adv. bd. Critical Issues in Gifted Edn. series; mem. editorial bd. Gifted Child Quar., 1984-97, Jour. Advanced Devel.; column editor Understanding the Gifted Newsletter, 1984-90: editor Gifted and Talented Internat., 1997—; book review ed., Gifted Child Quarterly, author 12 books; contbr. chpts. and over 260 articles to profl. jours. Bd. trustees Lourdes High Sch., Chgo., 1985-86. Recipient Outstanding Faculty award State Coun. Higher Edn. Va., 1993, 97; grantee U.S. Office Edn., 1977-78, 78-79, Ill. State Bd. Edn., 1979-82, 84-91, Richardson Found., 1986, 89, Fry Found., 1987-90, Va. State Coun. Higher Edn., 1987-89, 90-91, 93-95, Bur. Indian Affairs, 1989, Hughes Found., 1989-94, Va. State Libr., 1989-90, Va. State Dept. Edn., 1990-93, 93-95, Funding Agy. U.S. Dept. Edn., 1989, 90-93, 93-95, 96-99, 2000-02, 02—; eminent scholar Coll. William and Mary, 1987—, Nat. Ednl. policy fellow U.S. Office Edn., 1979-80, Paul Witty fellow in gifted edn., 1979, Outstanding Rsch. Paper award Mensa, 1995, Phi Beta Kappa Fac. Awd., 1995, Dist. Scholar, Nat. Assoc. Gifted Children, 1997. Mem. ASCD, Nat. Assn. Gifted Children (bd. dirs. 1984-90, Disting. Scholar award 1997), Coun. Exceptional Children, Assn. for Gifted (pres. 1980-81), World Coun. on Gifted, Am. Ednl. Rsch. Assn., Phi Beta Kappa, Phi Delta Kappa (pres. Northwestern chpt. 1986-87). Avocations: photography, tennis, writing. Home: 128 Harriet Cir Williamsburg VA 23185-5115 Office: Coll William and Mary Jones Hall Williamsburg VA 23185

VANTERPOOL, YVONNE ADELYN, elementary school educator; b. St. Kitts, St. Christopher and Nevis, Aug. 14, 1942; d. Robert and Mary (Delany) Shelford; m. William Gainesville Vanterpool, June 23, 1966; children: Carol, Ricky, Joy, Myron, Michael. BA, U. V.I., 1976; MS, Nova U., Ft. Lauderdale, Fla., 1986. Cert. elem. tchr., V.I. Elem. tchr. V.I. Dept. Edn., St. Thomas, 1977—; tchr. Houston Ind. Sch. Dist., 1987-88. Mem. ASCD, Am. Fedn. Tchrs., Internat. Reading Assn., St. Thomas/St. John Reading Coun.

VAN TILBURG, JOANNE, archaeologist, educator, foundation administrator; b. Mpls., Apr. 20, 1942; d. Everton George and Ruth (Butler) Becker; m. Johannes Franciscus Pieter Van Tilburg, Aug. 10, 1968; 1 child, Marieka Joanna. BS, U. Minn., 1965; MEd, UCLA, 1976, PhD, 1986. Rsch. assoc. Inst. Archaeology UCLA, 1980—, dir. Rock Art Archive, Cotsen Inst. Archaeology, 1996—; assoc. rschr. Inst. de Estudios U. de Chile, Isla de Pascua, 1986—. Lectr. Archaeol. Inst. Am., 1995—, Brit. Mus., 1990—; instr. UCLA Extension, 1990—. Author: Easter Island Archaeology, Ecology and Culture, 1994, H.M.S. Topaze on Easter Island, 1992; editor: Ancient Images on Stone, 1983; contbr. articles to profl. jours. Pres. Mana Found. Grantee Nat. Geog. Soc., 1989, Calif. Coun. for the Humanities, 1980, 95. Fellow Royal Geog. Soc.; mem. Archaeol. Inst. Am. (Golden Trowel campaign medallion 1999), Soc. for Am. Archaeology, Pacific Arts Assn. Office: UCLA Inst Archaeology Fowler Mus Cultural History 405 Hilgard Ave Los Angeles CA 90095-9000

VAN TUYL, LORAINE YVETTE, psychologist; arrived in U.S., 1983; d. Jules Tjien-Gie and Josta Lucretia Tjenalooi; m. Robert Johan Van Tuyl, Dec. 27, 1992; children: Terrance, Jade. BA in Spanish highest honors, U. Calif.; MS in Psychology, Pacific U., 1997, PhD, 1999. Lic. psychologist Calif. Family support specialist, mgmt. trainee Travis AFB Family Support Ctr., Fairfield, Calif., 1992—94; practicum counselor Gronowski Clinic, Palo Alto, Calif., 1995—95; bilingual English/Spanish counselor Alum Rock Counseling Ctr., San Jose, Calif., 1996—97; practicum counselor U. Calif. Davis Counseling Ctr., 1997—98, predoctoral intern, 1998—99, psychology fellow, victim counselor, 1999—2002; clin. psychologist Inner Balance Counseling, Albany, Calif., 2002—. Cons., facilitator multicultural immersion program U. Calif., Davis, 1999—2002, lectr. dept. sociology, 2002. Contbr. chapters to books. Sr. editor Students for Ethnic and Cultural Awareness, Palo Alto, Calif., 1996—97; v.p. Student Coun. Exec. Bd., Palo Alto, 1996—97; bd. mem. Bay Area Surinamese Assn., 1997—. Recipient Found. award, Calif. Psychol. Assn., 1995; Leroy Lucas Entering Minority Student scholar, Pacific Grad. Sch. Psychology, 1994. Mem.: APA, Asian Am. Psychol. Assn. Office: Inner Balance Counseling 902 Curtis St Albany CA 94507 Office Phone: 925-642-1716.

VAN UMMERSEN, CLAIRE A(NN), academic administrator, biologist, educator; b. Chelsea, Mass., July 28, 1935; d. George and Catherine (Courtovich); m. Frank Van Ummersen, June 7, 1958; children: Lynn, Scott. BS, Tufts U., 1957, MS, 1960, PhD, 1963; DSc (hon.), U. Mass., 1988, U. Maine, 1991. Rsch. asst. Tufts U., 1957-60, 60-67, grad. asst. in embryology, 1962, postdoctoral tchg. asst., 1963-66, lectr. in biology, 1967-68; asst. prof. biology U. Mass., Boston, 1968-74, assoc. prof., 1974—86, assoc. dean acad. affairs, 1975-76, assoc. vice chancellor acad. affairs, 1976-78, chancellor, 1978-79, dir. Environ. Sci. Ctr., 1980-82; assoc. vice chancellor acad. affairs Mass. Bd. Regents for Higher Edn., 1982-85, vice chancellor for mgmt. systems and telecom., 1985-86; chancellor Univ. System N.H., Durham, 1986-92; sr. fellow New Eng. Bd. Higher Edn., 1992-93; sr. fellow New Eng. Resource Ctr. Higher Edn. U. Mass., 1992-93; pres. Cleve. State U., 1993—2001; v.p., dir. Office of Women Am. Coun. Edn., 2001—. Cons. Mass. Bd. Regents, 1981-82, AGB, 1992—, Kuwait U., 1992-93; asst. Lancaster Course in Ophthalmology, Mass. Eye. and Ear Infirmary, 1962-69, lectr., 1970-93, also coord.; reviewer HEW; mem. rsch. team which established safety stds. for exposure to microwave radiation, 1958-65; participant Leadership Am. program, 1992-93; bd. dirs. Nat. Coun. Sci. Environment, 1998—, mem. subcom. for future and fin. Active N.H. Ct. Systems Rev. Task Force, 1989-90, Leadership Cleve. Class '95, Gov.'s Coun. on Sci. and Tech., 1996-98, Strategy Coun. Cleve. Pub. Schs., 1996-98, Cleve. Sports Commn., 1999-2001, Cleve. Mcpl. Sch. Dist. Bd., 1999-2001; New Eng. Bd. Higher Edn., 1986-92, exec. com., 1989-92, N.H. adv. coun., 1990-92; chair Rhodes Scholarship Selection Com., 1986-91; bd. dirs. N.H. Bus. and Industry Assn., 1987-93; governing bd. N.H. Math. Coalition, 1991-92; exec. com. 21st Century Learning Cmty., 1992-93; state panelist N.H. Women in Higher Edn., 1986-93; bd. dirs. Urban League Greater Cleve., 1993-2001, strategic planning com., chair edn. com., 1996-99, sec., exec. com., 1997-99; bd. dirs. Great Lakes Sci. and Tech. Ctr., 1993-2001, edn. com., 1995-2001; bd. dirs. Greater Cleve. Growth Assn., 1994-2001, Civic Vision 2000 and Beyond, Cleve., 1997-98; bd. dirs., exec. com. Sci. and Tech. Coun. Cleve. Tomorrow, 1998-99; rep. N.E. Ohio Tech. Coalition, 1999-2001; trustee Ohio Aerospace Inst., 1993-2001, exec. com., 1996-2001; strategic planning com. United Way, 1996-2000, chair environ. scan subcom. 1996-2001; leadership devel. com. ACE, 1995-98, women's commn., 1999-2001; bd. dirs. United Way, 1995-2001; co-chair Pub. Sector Campaign, 1997-98; bd. dirs. NCAA, divsn. 1, exec. com., 1999-2001; mem. AGB Ctr. for Pub. Higher Edn. Trusteeship and Goverance, 2001-03, Assn. Liaison Officers Adv. Com., 1998-2001. Recipient Disting. Svc. medal U. Mass., 1979, Woman of the Yr. Achievement award YWCA, 1998; Am. Cancer Soc. grantee Tufts U., 1960. Mem. Am. Coun. on Edn (com. on self-regulation 1987-91), Nat. Conf. Cmty. and Justice (program com. 1996-2001), Nat. Coun. for Sci. and the Environment (bd. dirs. 1999-, fin. and futures coms.), State Higher Exec. Officers (fed. rels. com., 1986-92, cost accountability task force, exec. com. 1990-92), ACE (com. leadership devel.), Nat. Assn. Sys. Heads (exec. com. 1990-92), Nat. Ctr. for Edn. Stats. (network adv. com. 1989-92), New Eng. Assn. Schs. and Colls. (commn. on higher edn. 1990-93), North Ctrl. Assn. Schs. and Colls. (evaluator 1993-2001, chair accreditation teams 1986-90), Greater Cleve. Round Table (bd. dirs. 1993-2001, exec. com. 1995-2001), Cleve. Playhouse (trustee 1994-2001), Nat. Assn. State Univs. and Land Grant Colls. (exec. com. on urban agenda, mem. commn. tech. transfer, state rep.), Am. Assn. State Colls. and Univs. (commn. on urban agenda 1996-2001, bd. dirs. 1996-99, mem. emerging issues task force 1996-98), Phi Beta Kappa, Sigma Xi. Office: American Coun on Edn One DuPont Cir NW Washington DC 20036-1193 Office Phone: 202-939-9390. E-mail: claire_van_ummersen@ace.nche.edu.

VAN VLECK, PAMELA KAY, real estate company officer; b. St. Cloud, Minn., Aug. 26, 1951; d. Kipp James Gillespie and Lorraine Marie (Johnson) Storck; m. Clinton Eugene Van Vleck, Jan. 29, 1985. Student, St. Cloud State U., 1969-70, Washburn U., 1971-72. Lic. pilot; lic. cmty. assn. mgr. Mgr., broker Coldwell Banker-Pioneer Realty, Jackson, Wyo., 1980-85; owner, broker Tri-Corp Realty, Ltd., Scottsdale, Ariz., 1985-87, Affiliated Properties Group, Inc., Phoenix, Las Vegas, Nev., 1987-91; mgr., broker Machan Hampshire Properties, Las Vegas, Nev., 1990-91; v.p. Affiliated Property Mgmt. Corp., 1990-92; retail properties specialist Grubb & Ellis, Tucson, 1991-92; dir., comml. broker Cameron Real Estate Svcs., Naples, Fla., 1992-98; dir. Lee County Cameron Real Estate Svcs., Inc., Ft. Myers, Fla., 1994-98, v.p., 1997-98; ptnr., dir. property mgmt. Grubb & Ellis, Ft. Myers, 1998—. Bd. dirs., owner Affiliated Properties Group Inc./Affiliated Property Mgmt. Corp., Phoenix, 1985-92; bd. dirs., cons. Realty Software Svcs. Ariz., Inc., Phoenix, 1986-91, MHP Realty & Mgmt., Inc., Las Vegas, 1989-91. Developer, copywriter computer software program REMMI (Real Estate Matching, Mktg. and Inventory). Grad. Leadership Lee County, 1996, chair steering com., 1997-98. Mem. NAFE, Women in Comml. Real Estate, Nev. Devel. Authority, Women's Comml. Sales Assn., Internat. Coun. Shopping Ctrs., Resl Estate Investment Soc., Exec. Womens Golf League. Republican. Avocations: reading, skiing, biking, golf, hiking. Office: 13131 University Dr Fort Myers FL 33907-5716 E-mail: pvanvleck@viprealty.com.

VAN VLIET, CAROLYNE MARINA, physicist, researcher; b. Dordrecht, Netherlands, Dec. 27, 1929; arrived in U.S., 1960, naturalized, 1967; d. Marinus and Jacoba (de Lange) Van V. BS, Free U. Amsterdam, Netherlands, 1949, MA, 1953, PhD in Physics, 1956. Rsch. fellow Free U. Amsterdam, 1950-54, rsch. assoc., 1954-56, asst. dir., 1958-60; postdoctoral fellow U. Minn., Mpls., 1956-57, faculty, 1957-58, 60-70, prof. elec. engring. and physics, 1965-70; prof. theoretical physics U. Montreal, Que., Can., 1969-95, sr. rschr. math. rsch. ctr., 1969-2000, prof. emerita, 1998—.

Vis. prof. U. Fla., 1974, 78-88; prof. elec. and computer engring. Fla. Internat. U., 1992-2000; adj. prof. physics U. Miami, 2001—. Contbg. author: Fluctuation Phenomena in Solids, 1965; contbr. articles to profl. jours. Rsch. grantee NSF, Air Force OSR, Nat. Sci. and Engring. Rsch. Coun., Ottawa. Fellow IEEE (life); mem. Am. Phys. Soc., N.Y. Acad. Scis., Associated Artists, Mid. Ea. Dance. Office: U Miami James L Knight Physics Bldg 1320 Campo Sano Dr Coral Gables FL 33146 E-mail: vanvliet@physics.miami.edu.

VAN VLIET, CLAIRE, artist; b. Ottawa, Ont., Can., Aug. 9, 1933; d. Wilbur Dennison and Audrey Ilene (Wallace) Van V. AB, San Diego State Coll., 1952; MFA, Claremont Grad. Sch., 1954; DFA (hon.), U. of the Arts, Phila., 1993, San Diego State U., 2002. Instr. printmaking Phila. Coll. Art, 1959-65; owner The Janus Press, 1954—; vis. lectr. printmaking U. Wis.-Madison, 1965-66. Mem. bd. advisors Hand Papermaking. One-man exhbns. include Print Club Phila., 1963, 66, 73, 77, Wiggin Gallery, Boston Pub. Libr., 1977, Rutgers U. Art Gallery, 1978, AAA Gallery, Phila., 1980, Dolan/Maxwell Gallery, Phila., 1984, 91, Mary Ryan Gallery, N.Y.C., 1986, Mills Coll., 1986, U. of the Arts, Phila., 1989, Victoria and Albert Mus., London, 1994, Ottawa Sch. of Art Gallery, Can., 1994, Bates Coll. Mus. of Art, Lewiston, Maine, 1994, 99, N.D. Mus. Art, 1999, Rosenwald Wolf Gallery Univ. Arts.Phila, 2001; group exhbns. include Bklyn. Nat., Phila. Arts Festival, Kunst zu Kafka, Germany, Paper as Medium, Smithsonian Instn., Washington, Paper Now, Cleve. Mus. Art, 1986, Boyle Arts Festival, Ireland, 1993, Libr. Congress, 1997—, N.D. Mus. Art, 1999; represented in permanent collections Nat. Gallery Art, Phila. Mus. Art, Boston Pub. Libr., Libr. of Congress, Cleve. Mus. Art, Montreal Mus. Fine Arts, Victoria and Albert Mus. London, Tate Gallery, London. NEA grantee, 1976-80, Ingram-Merrill Found. grantee, 1989; MacArthur fellow, 1989-94. Mem. NAD, Soc. Printers Boston, Vt. Arts and Scis. Address: 101 Schoolhouse Rd Newark VT 05871-9773

VANZANT, IYANLA, writer; b. Bklyn., 1953; married; 3 children. BS summa cum laude, Medgar Evers Coll., 1983; JD, Queens Coll. Law Sch., 1988. Host Iyanla (TV talk show), 2001; founder, exec. dir. Inner Visions Worldwide Network, Inc., Silver Spring, Md.; lawyer; ordained minister; inspirational spkr. Author: Tapping the Power Within: A Path to Self-Empowerment for Black Women, 1992, Acts of Faith: Daily Meditations for People of Color, 1993 (BlackBoard Book Yr., 1994), The Value in the Valley: A Black Woman's Guide Through Life's Dilemmas, 1995 (Black-Board Book Yr., 1995), Interiors: A Black Woman's Healing in Progress, 1995, Faith in the Valley: Lessons for Women on the Journey to Peace, 1996 (BlackBoard Book Yr., 1996), The Spirit of a Man: A Vision of Transformation of Black Men and the Women Who Love Them, 1997, The Big Book of Faith, 1997, Success Gems: Your Personal Motivation Success guide, 1997, In the Meantime: Finding Yourself and the Love You Want, 1998, One Day My Soul Just Opened Up: Forty Days and Forty Nights Toward Spiritual Strength and Personal Growth, 1998, Yesterday I Cried: Celebrating the Lessons of Living and Loving, 1999, Don't Give It Away: A Work Book of Self Awareness and Self Affirmation, 1999, The Good Company: A Woman's Journal for Spiritual Reflection, 1999, Daily Ghetto Mediations: Affirmations for the Ghetto in You, 1999, Until Today!: Daily Devotions for Spiritual Balance and Peace of Mind, 2001, Up from Here: Reclaiming the Male Spirit, 2002, Every Day I Pray, 2001, Living Through the Meantime, 2001. Nat. spokesperson Literacy Vol. Am. Recipient Alumni Yr., Nat. Assn. Equal Opportunity Edn., 1994, Oni award, Internat. Congress Black Women. Mailing: Inner Visions Worldwide Network Inc 926 Phila Ave Silver Spring MD 20910 Office Phone: 301-608-8750. Office Fax: 301-608-3813.*

VAN ZANT, SUSAN LUCILLE, principal; b. Torrance, Calif., Apr. 29, 1942; d. Paul McHenry and Lucille Eileen (McQuarrie) Mansfield; m. Jerry Brian Van Zant, Oct. 27, 1960; children: Steven Brian, Karen Daphne Van Zant Hosaka. BA in History and Social Sci., Calif. State U., Long Beach, 1966; MA in Curriculum, No. Ariz. U., 1974; EdD in Adminstrn., U.S. Internat. U., 1982. Cert. elem. tchr., kindergarten and secondary sch. adminstr., Calif. Tchr. Borrego Springs (Calif.) Unified Sch., 1967-69, Poway (Calif.) Unified Sch. Dist., 1969-76, prin., 1976—. Instr. community rels., law and fin. Nat. U., San Diego, 1987-92. Author: (with others) The Principal as Chief Executive, 1991; contbr. articles to profl. jours. Named Calif. Educator of Yr. Calif. State Dept. of Edn./Milken Found., 1989, Blue Ribbon Sch., U.S. Dept. of Edn., 1994; recipient Educator's award Freedom's Found., 1990. Mem. Nat. Assn. Elem. Sch. Prins. (bd. dirs., state leader, Disting. Prin. award 1988), Calif. Alliance for Edn. (coord.), Assn. Calif. Sch. Adminstrs. (chair elem. adminstrn.), Poway Assn. Sch. Mgrs. (pres. 1982), San Diego/Imperial County Adminstrs. (pres. 1993-94), Delta Kappa Gamma (pres. 1990-92). Baptist. Home: 16204 Quail Rock Rd Ramona CA 92065-7214 E-mail: suvanzant@aol.com.

VAN ZANTE, SHIRLEY M(AE), magazine editor; b. Elma, Iowa; d. Vernon E. and Georgene (Woodmansee) Borland; m. Dirk C. Van Zante. AA, Grandview Coll., 1950; BA, Drake U., 1952. Assoc. editor Mchts. Trade Jour., Des Moines, 1952-55; copywriter Meredith Pub. Co., Des Moines, 1955-60, book editor, 1960-67; home furnishings editor Better Homes and Gardens Spl. Interest Publs., Meredith Corp., 1967-74; home furnishing and design editor Better Homes and Gardens mag., 1974-89; writer, editl. cons., 1989-98. Named Advt. Woman of Yr. in Des Moines, 1961; recipient Dorothy Dawe award, 1971, 73, 75, 76, 77, Dallas Market Ctr. award, 1983, So. Furniture Market Writer's award, 1984. Mem. Alpha Xi Delta. Address: 1905 74th St Des Moines IA 50322-5701

VARA, KATHY, newscaster; d. George and Mary; m. Rene Vara. BA in radio/TV/film, North Tex. State U. Anchor, reporter KVII-TV, Amarillo, Tex., 1987—88; reporter KSAT-TV, San Antonio, 1988—91; morning anchor KARE-TV, Minneapolis, 1991—92; anchor WRC-TV, Washington, 1991—94, Today in LA, KNBC-TV, Los Angeles, 1994—2001, Eyewitness News 5 to 7am and 11am, KABC, Los Angeles, 2001—. Contbr. Arthritis Found. of Am., Lupus Found. Recipient Hispanic Heritage Award, President Clinton, 1997. Office: ABC7 Broadcast Ctr 500 Circle Seven Dr Glendale CA 91201*

VARDALOS, NIA, actress, screenwriter; b. Winnipeg, Can., Sept. 24, 1962; d. Constantine and Doreen Vardalos; m. Ian Gomez, 1993. Attended, Ryerson U. Actor: (films) No Experience Necessary, 1996, Men Seeking Women, 1997, Short Cinema, 1998, Meet Prince Charming, 1999, (also writer) My Big Fat Greek Wedding, 2002, (also writer, exec. prodr.) Connie and Carla, 2004, (voice): (TV series) Team Knight Rider, 1997, (guest appearance): High Incident, 1996, Common Law, 1996, The Drew Carey Show, 1997, Boy Meets World, 1998, It's Like, You Know, 1999, Two Guys, a Girl, and a Pizza Place, 1999, Curb Your Enthusiasm, 2000. Office: c/o Brillstein Grey Mgmt 9150 Wilshire Blvd Ste 350 Beverly Hills CA 90212*

VARE, ETHLIE ANN, journalist; b. Montreal, Que., Can., Mar. 8, 1953; d. Ben Herman and Shirley (Marder) Riley; 1 child, Russell. BA in World Lit., U. Calif., Santa Barbara, 1972. Columnist United Media, N.Y.C., 1979-91; chief West Coast bur. Syndicated Internat. Network, London, 1993—. Pres. L.A. Women in Music, 1987-89. Author: Adventurous Spirit, 1992 (Pub. Libr. award 1992); co-author: Mothers of Invention, 1988 (Am. Libr. award 1988), Patently Female, 1998; editor: (book) Legend: Frank Sinatra and the American Dream, 1995, Diva: Barbara Streisand and the Making of a Superstar, 1996, Rainbow: A Tribute to Judy Garland, 1997; exec. editor: Rock Mag., 1984-87. Recipient Maggie award for best editl. content Western Mag. Pubs. Assn., 1986. Mem. ACLU, AAUW, Women in Film, Amnesty Internat. Democrat. Jewish. Avocation: rock and roll.

VARELA, VICKI, state official; b. Aurora, Colo. m. Brett J. DelPorto: 2 children. Student, U. Colo., 1976; BA in English, Brigham Young U., 1978. Reporter Associated Press, Denver, Cheyenne, N.Y.C., 1978-79, Deseret News, Salt Lake City, 1979-83, edn. editor, 1983-86; asst. commr. higher edn. for pub. affairs Utah Higher Education Commn., Salt Lake City, 1986-92; dep. chief of staff to gov. State of Utah, Salt Lake City, 1992—. Exec. dir. Olympics Referendum Campaign, Salt Lake City, 1989. Vol. worker with Republican Inst. to train political candidates and campaign mgrs. in developing democracies (helped conduct seminar in Veronezh, Russia, 1995); mem. comty adv. com. First Presbyn. Ch. Restoration/Preservation Project; active in European Comty. Visitors' Program, 1996; studied in Germany, Spain, Brussels and Great Britain. Office: Office Gov 210 State Capitol Salt Lake City UT 84114

VARELLAS, SANDRA MOTTE, judge; b. Anderson, S.C., Oct. 17, 1946; d. James E. and Helen Lucille (Gilliam) Motte; m. James John Varellas, July 3, 1971; children: James John III, David Todd. BA, Winthrop U., 1968; MA, U. Ky., 1970, JD, 1975. Bar: Ky. 1975, Fla. 1976, U.S. Dist. Ct. (ea. dist.) Ky. 1975, U.S. Ct. Appeals (6th cir.) 1976, U.S. Supreme Ct. 1978. Instr. Midway Coll., Ky., 1970-72; adj. prof. U. Ky. Coll. Law, Lexington, 1976-78; instr. dept. bus. adminstrn. U. Ky., Lexington, 1976-78; ptnr. Varellas, Pratt & Cooley, Lexington, 1975-93, Varellas & Pratt, Lexington, 1993-97, Varellas & Varellas, Lexington, 1998—. Fayette County judge exec., Ky., 1980—; hearing officer Ky. Natural Resources and Environ. Protection Cabinet, Frankfort, 1984-88; bd. trustees Lexington Network 1994-98, 2002—, sec., 1994-98. Committeewoman Ky. Young Dems., Frankfort, 1977-80; pres. Fayette County Young Dems., Lexington, 1977; bd. dirs. Ky. Dem. Women's Club, Frankfort, 1980-84, bd. dirs., Bluegrass Estate Planning Coun., 1995-98; grad. Leadership Lexington, 1981; chairwoman Profl. Women's Forum, Lexington, Ky., 1985-86, bd. dirs., 1984-87, Aequum award com., 1989-92; mem. devel. coun. Midway Coll., 1990-92; co-chair Gift Club Com., 1992. Named Outstanding Young Dem. Woman, Ky. Young Dems., Frankfort, 1977, Outstanding Former Young Dem., Ky. Young Dems., 1983. Mem. Ky. Bar Assn. (treas. young lawyers divsn. 1978-79, long range planning com. 1988-89), Fla. Bar, Fayette County Bar Assn. (treas. 1977-78, bd. govs. 1978-80), LWV (nominating com. 1984-85), Greater Lexington C. of C. (legis. affairs com. 1994-95, bd.d irs. coun. smaller enterprises 1992-95), The Lexington Forum (bd. dirs. 1996-99), Lexington Philharm. Guild (bd. dirs. 1979-81, 86—), Nat. Assn. Women Bus. Owners (chmn. cmty. liaison/govtl. affairs com. 1992-93). Office: Varellas & Varellas 167 W Main St Ste 1310 Lexington KY 40507-1398

VARGA, DEBORAH TRIGG, music educator, entertainment company owner; b. Dayton, Ohio, Dec. 15, 1955; d. Ernest Cushman and Phyllis Ann (Martz) Trigg; m. Ali M. Abadi, Dec. 30, 1980 (div. July 1987); 1 child, Darren Vincent; m. Richard Charles Varga, June 25, 1994; 1 child, Kathryn Lenore. B of Music Edn. in Violin Performance, Converse Coll., Spartanburg, S.C., 1977. Music educator Seminole County Sch. Bd., Sanford, Fla., 1978-92, Howard County Pub. Schs., Ellicott City, Md., 1993—. Co-founder, co-owner Gold Star Entertainment, Inc., Orlando, Fla., 1984-86, Ctr. Stage Entertainment, Inc., Maitland, Fla., 1986-92; owner Varga Music Entertainement, Highland, Md., 1993—, Composer children's songs, 1990—, Martin Luther King Tribute, Human Rights Commn., Howard County, 1997-00. Mem. Am. Fedn. Musicians, Music Educators Nat. Conf., Am. String. Tchrs. Assn., Nat. Orch. Assn. Avocations: waterskiing, whitewater rafting, tennis, golf, reading. Home: 13464 Allnutt Ln Highland MD 20777-9743

VARGA, JEANNE-MARIE, women's healthcare company executive; BS in Med. Tech., Towson State U.; MA in Mgmt. and Supervision, Ctrl. Mich. U. Sr. sci. reviewer Ctr. for Devices and Radiol. Health, FDA, 1980-83; mgr. U.S. regulatory affairs Sorin Biomedica S.P.A., 1983-87; dir. quality assurance and regulatory affairs Baxter Diagnostics, Inc., 1987-92; v.p. worldwide regulatory and quality Sanofi Diagnostics Pasteur, Inc., 1992-98; v.p. regulatory affairs and quality sys. Women First HealthCare, Inc., San Diego, 1998—. Office: Women First HealthCare Inc 12220 El Camino Real Ste 400 San Diego CA 92130-2091 Fax: 619-509-1353.

VARGAS, DIANA LISA, television station executive; BA in Mass Media, Hunter Coll., 1983. Acct. exec. Sta. KTTV, L.A., 1988-90, sales, 1990-91, local sales mgr., 1991-94, v.p. gen. sales mgr., 1994-97, v.p. gen. mgr., 1997—. Office: Sta KTTV 1999 S Bundy Dr Los Angeles CA 90025-5203

VARGAS, MARTHA, government liaison; b. Bogota, Columbia; arrived in U.S. 1981. AA in bus. adminstrn., Miami-Dade Cmty. Coll. Asst. to pres. Cafecol Trading Corp., 1985; mktg. asst. Capitol/EMI Records, Miami, 1989; U.N. liasion Together Found., N.Y.C., 1991—. Mem. exec. com. UN DPI/NGO; bd. dirs. Soc. Internat. Devel., N.Y. chap. Office: Together Found 55 E 75th St New York NY 10021-2736 Fax: 212-628-4265.

VARGO, BETH COPELAND, writer; b. Fukuoka, Japan, Jan. 14, 1951; d. Edwin Luther and Louise Tadlock Copeland; m. Charles Joseph Vargo, Jan. 14, 1978; children: Sarah, Joseph. BA in English, St. Andrews Presbyn Coll., 1973; MFA in Creative Writing, Bowling Green State U., 1975. Author: (poetry) Traveling Through Glass, 2000 (Bright Hill Press Nat. Poetry Book award, 1999), Obi, 2001 (First Pl. in Poetry - Sixth Ann. Peregrine prize, 2001), (short stories) Painted Angels, 2000 (Sheila K. Smith Short Story award The Nat. League of Am. Pen Women, 2000), poetry. Mem.: Acad. of Am. Poets.

VARIS, JINA ALEKSANDRA, voice educator; b. Lithuania; came to U.S., 1948; d. Paulius and Kunigunda (Stanaitis) V.; 1 child, Vytas V. Vergeer. Student, Curtis Inst. Music, Juilliard Sch. Music; BA, Northeastern U., 1988; MM, Northwestern U., 1990, postgrad., 1997—. Instr. voice pvt. practice, Glenview, Ill., 1980—; instr. voice, music instr. Lake Forest (Ill.) Coll., 1990-93; instr. voice Highland Park (Ill.) High Sch., 1993-95, DePaul U., Chgo., 1994-95, Lake Forest High Sch., 1995—; asst. prof. music Goshen Coll., Ind., 1995; opera dir., concert and opera performer. Mem. Nat. Assn. Tchrs. Singing, Music Tchrs. Nat. Assn.

VARNELL, MAXINE ANN, minister; b. Knowles, Okla., May 4, 1916; d. Richard Newton and Ida Mae (Ferris) Rhoads; m. Carl Edwin Varnell, July 17, 1938. 9th gr., Timberview Sch., Helena, Okla., 1930. Ordained to ministry Living Way Ministerial Assn., 1954. Evangelist Living Way Ministerial Assn., Tulsa, Okla., 1954—70; pastor Living Way Pentacostal Ch., Chanute, Kans., 1954; chmn. True Gospel Temple, Inc., Tulsa, Okla., 1970—. Author (songs): Forever I'm Yours Dear, 1969, Give Me One Mora Chance Before We Part, 1969; author: (book) Bread for the Hungry by Hearing His Voice, 1976. Republican. Home: 2501 N Quincy St Enid OK 73701

VARNER, CHARLEEN LAVERNE MCCLANAHAN (MRS. ROBERT B. VARNER), nutritionist, educator, administrator, dietitian; b. Alba, Mo., Aug. 28, 1931; d. Roy Calvin and Lela Ruhama (Smith) McClanahan; student Joplin (Mo.) Jr. Coll., 1949-51; BS in Edn., Kans. State Coll. Pittsburg, 1953; MS, U. Ark., 1958; PhD, Tex. Woman's U. 1966; postgrad. Mich. State U., summer, 1955, U. Mo., summer 1962; m. Robert Bernard Varner, July 4, 1953. Apprentice county home agt. U. Mo., summer 1952; tchr. Ferry Pass Sch., Escambia County, Fla., 1953-54; tchr. biology, home econs. Joplin Sr. H.S., 1954-59; instr. home econs. Kans. State Coll., Pittsburg, 1959-63; lectr. foods, nutrition Coll. Household Arts and Scis., Tex. Woman's U., 1963-64, rsch. asst. NASA grant, 1964-66; assoc. prof. home econs. Central Mo. State U., Warrensburg, 1966-70, adviser to Colhecon, 1966-70, adviser to Alpha Sigma Alpha, 1967-70, 72, mem. bd. advisers Honors Group, 1967-70; prof., head dept. home econs. Kans. State Tchrs. Coll., Emporia, 1970-73; prof., chmn. dept. home econs. Benedictine Coll., Atchison, Kans., 1973-74; prof., chmn. dept. home econs. Baker U., Baldwin City, Kans., 1974-75; owner, operator Diet-Con Dietary Cons. Enterprises, cons. dietitian, 1973—, Home-Con Cons. Enterprises. Mem. Joplin Little Theater, 1956-60. Mem. NEA, Mo., Kans. state tchrs. assns., AAUW, Am., Mo., Kans. dietetics assns., Am., Mo., Kans. home econs. assns., Mo. Acad. Scis., AAUP, U. Ark. Alumni Assn., Alumni Assn. Kans. State Coll. of Pittsburg, Am. Vocat. Assn., Assn. Edn. Young Children, Sigma Xi, Beta Sigma Phi, Beta Beta Beta, Alpha Sigma Alpha, Delta Kappa Gamma, Kappa Kappa Iota, Phi Upsilon Omicron, Theta Alpha Pi, Kappa Phi. Methodist (organist). Home: PO Box 1009 Topeka KS 66601-1009

VARNER, CHILTON DAVIS, lawyer; b. Opelika, Ala., Mar. 12, 1943; d. William Cole and Frances (Thornton) Davis; m. K. Morgan Varner III, June 19, 1965; 1 child, Ashley Elizabeth. AB with distinction, Smith Coll., 1965; JD with distinction, Emory U., 1976. Assoc. King & Spalding, Atlanta, 1976-83, ptnr., 1983—. Trustee Emory U., Atlanta, 1995—; bd. dirs. Wesley Woods Healthcare, 11th Cir. Ct. Appeals Hist. Soc.; bd. trustees Product Liability Adv. Coun. Found., 1996—. Author: Appellate Handbook for Georgia Lawyers, 1995. Mem. Leadership Atlanta, 1984-85; asst. clk., elder, bd. elders Trinity Presbyn. Ch., Atlanta, 1985-88; exec. com. Ate Arts Alliance, Atlanta, 1981-85; mem. Atlanta Symphony Chorus, 1970-74. Recipient Disting. Alumna award Emory U. Law Sch., 1998. Fellow Am. Coll. Trial Lawyers; mem. ABA, Ga. Bar Assn., Atlanta Bar Assn., Order of Coif, Phi Beta Kappa. Office: King & Spalding 191 Peachtree St NE Ste 4900 Atlanta GA 30303-1740

VARNER, HELEN, communications educator; b. Biddeford, Maine, Jan. 21, 1946; d. E. Harold Kemper and Darlene Ruth (Marcus) Meeks; m. Foy E. Varner, Jr., May 26, 1977; children: Dawn Hedgpeth, Jennifer Thompson, Foy E. III. B in Applied Arts and Scis., Stephen F. Austin State U., 1981, MA, 1983; EdD, Tex. A&M U., 1990. Reporter Galveston (Tex.) Daily News, 1964-65; acct. exec. John Gilbert Advt. Agy., Miami, Fla., 1965-67; chief Correspondence Sch., U.S. Army Edn. Ctr., Mannhiem, Germany, 1967-70; coord. pub. info. Galveston Coll., 1970-74; pub. rels., advt. dir. Sea-Arama Marineworld, Inc., Galveston, 1974-77; owner, chief exec. officer The Varner Pub. Rels. & Advt. Agy., Galveston, 1977-81; instr. Stephen F. Austin State U., Nacogdoches, Tex., 1981-88; assoc. prof. journalism N.E. La. U., Monroe, La., 1988-90, Chaminade U. of Honolulu, 1990-91; assoc. prof. comm. Hawaii Pacific U., Honolulu, 1991—, v.p. univ. rels. and dean of comm., 1998. Pres. Galveston Conv. & Vis. Bur., Galveston, 1978-79. Pres. Galveston Press Club, 1977, ARC, Galveston Chpt., 1976, Nacogdoches Chpt., 1980; dir. Girl Scouts Am., Gulf Coast, Galveston, 1976. Named Outstanding Adviser Pub. Rels. Student Soc. Am., 1989, Outstanding Prof. Omicron Delta Kappa, 1989, Favorite Prof. Alpha Lambda Delta, 1988; recipient Mentor award Mortarboard Sr. Leadership Soc., 1990, Outstanding Adviser award Women In Communication, Inc., 1986-87, 85-86. Mem. Assn. for Edn. in Journalism and Mass Communication, Tex. Pub. Rels. Assn. (pres. 1987-88), Pub. Rels. Soc. Am., Pub. Rels. Assn. La. (sec. 1989), So. Pub. Rels. Fedn., Women In Communications (pres. Honolulu Profl. chpt. 1995-96), Orgn. of Women Leaders (Woman Leader of Yr. 1995-96), Pub. Rels. Found. Tex. Avocation: miniatures collection. Home: 46-082 Puulena St Apt 1224 Kaneohe HI 96744-3754 Office: Hawaii Pacific U 1132 Bishop St Ste 504 Honolulu HI 96813-2820 Office Phone: 808-544-0825. E-mail: hvarner@hpu.edu., communication@hpu.edu.

VARNER, JOYCE EHRHARDT, retired librarian; b. Quincy, Ill., Sept. 13, 1938; d. Wilbur John and Florence Elizabeth (Mast) Ehrhardt; m. Donald Giles Varner, Sept. 12, 1959; children: Amy, Janice, Christian, Matthew, Nadine. BA, Northeastern Okla. State U., 1980; MLS, U. Okla., 1984. Lab. analyst Gardner Denver Co., Quincy, 1956-60; sales rep. Morrisonville, Ill., 1963-69; libr. clk. U. Ill., Urbana, 1973-75; libr. tech. asst. Northeastern Okla. State U., Tahlequah, 1976-86; asst. reference libr. Muskogee (Okla.) Pub. Libr., 1986-90; libr. Jess Dunn Correctional Ctr., Taft, Okla., 1990-98; ret., 1998; field office supr. Census 2000 Dept. of Commerce, Welling, Okla., 1998. Editor Indian Nations Audubon Nature Notes, 1977-81, 96—; contbr. articles to newspaper. Vol. Lake-Wood coun. Girl Scouts U.S.A., 1975-98, bd. dirs. 1992-98, pres., 1995-96; sec.-treas. Cherokee County Rural Water Dist. 7, 1987—; edn. chmn. Indian Nations chpt. Nat. Audubon Soc., 1989-2000, pres., 2000—; project dir. Tahlequah Friends of the Libr., 2002—. Recipient Thanks Badge, Lake-Wood coun. Girl Scouts U.S.A., 1990. Mem. AAUW (chair diversity com. 2000), Okla. Libr. Assn. (nominating com. 1989), Okla. Acad. Sci., Okla. Ornithol. Soc. (chmn. libr. com. 1978-88, Award of Merit 1990, pres.-elect 1994, pres. 1995-96), Alpha Chi, Beta Beta Beta, Phi Delta Kappa (Found. rep. 1984-86, historian 1992—). Avocations: nature study, needlework, square dancing, genealogy. Home: 20582 S Welling Rd Welling OK 74471-2001

VARONA-LACEY, GLADYS MARIA, language educator; b. Cuba; arrived in USA, 1959; BA, Wells Coll., 1971; MA, U. Pitts., 1973, Cert. in Latin Am. Studies, 1976, PhD, 1983. Instr. MIT, Cambridge, Mass., 1978—81, Tufts U., Medford, Mass., 1978—83, asst. prof., 1983—86; vis. asst. prof. Boston U., 1986—87; preceptor in Romance langs. Harvard U., Cambridge, 1987—88; asst. prof. Ithaca (N.Y.) Coll., 1988—96, assoc. prof., chair to prof., 1996—2003, chair, 1998, prof., 2003—. Author: José María Arguedas: Más allá del indigenismo, 2000; editor: Introducción a al literatura hispanoamericana, 1997, Latin America: An Interdisciplinary Approach, 1999, Contemporary Latin American Literature, 2001. Councilwoman town bd., Danby, NY, 2000—. Office: Ithaca Coll 953 Danby Rd Ithaca NY 14850-7000

VARRO, BARBARA JOAN, retired editor; b. East Chicago, Ind., Jan. 25, 1938; d. Alexander R. and Lottie R. (Bess) V. BA, Duquesne U., 1959. Feature reporter, asst. fashion editor Chgo. Sun-Times, 1959-64, fashion editor, 1964-76, feature writer, 1976-84; v.p. pub. rels. Daniel J. Edelman Inc., Chgo., 1984-85; v.p. PRB/Needham Porter Novelli, Chgo., 1985-86; editor Am. Hosp. Assn. News, Chgo., 1987-94; editor spl. sects. Chgo. Tribune, 1995-2000; ret. Recipient awards for feature writing Ill. AP, 1978, 79, 80 Mem.: PEO.

VARTANIAN, ISABEL SYLVIA, retired dietitian; b. Duquesne, Pa. d. Apel and Mary (Kasparian) V. BS, U. Ala., 1957; MS, Columbia U., 1962. Registered dietitian. Dietetic intern N.Y. Hosp./Cornell Med. Ctr., N.Y.C., 1957-58; therapeutic dietitian Vets. Affairs Med. Ctr., Bronx, N.Y., 1958-60, adminstrv. dietitian, 1960-62, nutrition clinic dietitian, 1962-63, rsch. and nutrition clinic dietitian Coral Gables, Fla., 1963, nutrition clinic dietitian Richmond, Va., 1963-66, chief nutritional therapy edn. and rsch. sect., 1966-83, nutrition support dietitian, 1983-2000; ret. Bd. dirs. Richmond Cmty. Action Program, 1978—83, Hopewell Preservation, Inc.; mem. adv. com. Social Svcs., Hopewell, Va., 1991—2001; mem. Sr. Citizens Adv. Commn., 2000—; bd. trustee Appomattox Regional Libr. Sys., 2000—. Recipient Outstanding awards Vets. Affairs Med. Ctr., Superior Performance awards, Outstanding award. Mem. Richmond Dietetic Assn. (chair diet therapy sect. 1966-67, pres.-elect 1967-68, pres. 1968-70, chair Dial-A-Dietitian 1972-74, chair pub. rels. 1973-74, 78-81, chair Divsn. Cmty. Dietetics 1983-85, chair program planning com. 1985), Va. Dietetic Assn. (chair career guidance com. 1963-65, ednl. exhibits 1967, Dial-A-Dietitian 1972-74, pub. rels. 1982-84, visibility campaign 1984, exhibit com. 1984, program planning com. 1988, divsn. cmty. dietetic 1989-91), Va. Soc. Parenteral and Enteral Nutrition (chair program planning com. 1988-89, membership com. 1990), Am. Dietetic Assn. (life), Profl. Va. Dietetic Assn., Greater Richmond Assn. for Continuity of Care, Woodman World Lodge, Rotary, Am. Legion Aux., Ft. Lee Officers and Civilian Club (mem. adv. coun. 2000-03), Fort Lee Cmty. Action Coun. Home: 2005 Jackson St Hopewell VA 23860-3633

VARY, EVA MAROS, retired chemicals executive; b. Kecskemet, Hungary, Apr. 13, 1933; came to U.S., 1958; d. Anthony and Kathleen (Czencz) Maros; m. Eugen Szent-Vary, June 13, 1956 (div. 1958); 1 child, Susan Marie. Chem. engring. diploma, Tech. U. Budapest (Hungary), 1956; PhD in Phys. Chemistry, UCLA, 1966. Chem. engring. area supr. Ujpesti Textile Plant, Budapest, 1956-57; chemist geology dept. UCLA, 1958-65; rsch. chemist, staff chemist Fabrics and Finishes Dept. Dupont, Phila., 1966-71, rsch. supr., 1971-79, tech. area supt. Parlin, N.J., 1979-80, asst. plant mgr. Parlin, Toledo, 1980-85; product supt. mng. Tedlar plant Dupont Fabricated Products, Buffalo, 1985-87, environ. cons. Wilmington, Del., 1987-90; dir. product safety, regulatory affairs pigments div. Ciba-Geigy Corp., Newport, Del., 1990-98; ret., 1998. Inventor, patentee release coatings. Com. chair Zonta Internat., Toledo, 1984, Buffalo, 1987. Mem. Am. Chem. Soc. Roman Catholic. Avocations: tennis, skiing, travel, photography. Home: 1100 Lovering Ave Apt 1508 Wilmington DE 19806-3288 E-mail: varyeva@aol.com.

VARY, PATRICIA SUSAN, biologist, educator, retired geneticist; b. Wewoka, Okla, Nov. 20, 1941; d. Clayton Loring and Margaret Elizabeth Potter; m. James C. Vary Sr., Jan. 20, 1967 (div. Dec. 20, 1987); children: Catherine A. Vary, James C. Vary Jr. BS in Microbiology, Tex. Christian U., 1963, MS in Microbiology, 1965; MS in Biochemistry, U. Wis., 1967; PhD, Stanford U., 1969. Asst. prof. No. Ill. U., DeKalb, 1977—83, assoc. prof., 1983—90, full prof. biology, 1990—, chair dept. biol. sci., 1995—99. Cons. Abbott Labs., Chgo., 1988—95. Bd. mem. LWV, Wheaton, Ill., 1969—85, pres., 1976—77; adv. com. Wheaton Sch. Bd., 1980; violinist Cmty. Symphony; mem. Women's Chorus; mem. cunty Bd. dir. Dem. Precinct Com., DeKalb, 2000—. Fellow Fogarty internat. fellow, NIH, 1989—90; grantee, NSF, 1979—92, NIH, 1989—. Mem.: AAAS, J. Indus. Microbiotech (mem. editl. bd.), Soc. Indsl. Microbiology, Genetic Soc. Am., Am. Soc. Microbiology, Sigma Xi (local pres. 1992—93). Unitarian Universalist. Achievements include patents for plasmidless B.megaterium, lac-B.megaterium. Avocations: travel, bicycling. Office: No Ill Univ Dept Biol Sci Dekalb IL 60115

VASATURO, MARY ANN, school psychologist; b. Glendale, N.Y., Dec. 8, 1962; d. Anthony and Diane Vasaturo. BS in Fin., St. John's U., Queens, N.Y., 1984, MBA in Mktg., 1987; MA in Clin. Psychology, Biola U., 1997. Cert. sch. psychologist N.Y. Promotion planner Colgate-Palmolive, N.Y.C., 1989—92; mktg. cons. N.Y.C., 1992—95; counselor N.Y.C. Bd. Edn., 1998—2000; sch. psychologist United Cerebral Palsy, Bklyn., 2000—01, Dept. Edn., Honolulu, 2001—. Mem.: MIl. Child Edn. Coalition, Hawaii Assn. Sch. Psychologists (pres.-elect), Nat. Assn. Sch. Psychologists.

VASILEFF, LILI ALEXANDRA, financial planner; b. Flushing, NY, Feb. 26, 1955; d. Henry David and Martha Schober Vasileff; m. Stephen Penfield Kressen, Aug. 23, 1980 (div. Jan. 1, 1991); children: Nathaniel David Penfield Kressen, Alexandra Marta Kressen. BA cum laude, Mt. Holyoke Coll., 1977; M Internat. and Pub. Affairs, Columbia U., 1979; cert. in European rels., Inst. d'Etudes Politiques, Paris, 1976; cert. fin. planner, Coll. Fin. Planning, 1995. CFP, cert. divorce specialist. Internat. officer Am. Express Internat. Bank, N.Y.C., 1979—80; assoc. Arthur Andersen, Denver, 1980—81; officer Bank of Denver, 1981—84; v.p., internat. treas. Security Pacific Corp., L.A., 1984—89; owner Money Matters!, Woodbridge/Greenwich, Conn., 1991—. Adj. prof. Quinnipiac U., Hamden, Conn., 1993—96. Mem. adv. com. Children With Spl. Health Care Needs., New Haven, 1995—; mem. Conn. Coun. Divorce Mediation, 1997—; bd. dirs. Friends of Yale-New Haven Children's Hosp., New Haven, 1991—. Recipient Dr. Barbar award, Yale-New Haven Children's Hosp., 1996. Mem.: Sarah (ARC), Conn. Coalition for Inclusive Edn., Fin. Planning Assn. (co-pres.), Assn. Divorce Fin. Planners (bd. dirs. New Haven chpt.). Avocations: ballet, theater, travel, advocate for children with special health care needs.. Office: Money Matters! 26 Maple Vale Dr Woodbridge CT 06525 E-mail: lvasileff@aol.com.

VASILESCU, VASILICA, psychologist, consultant; b. Buzau, Romania, Nov. 18, 1947; arrived in U.S.A., 1988; d. Dumitru and Alexandrina Fratila; children: Mike, Gabriel. PhD in Psychology, U. Bucharest, 1993; PhD in Clin. Psychology, Alliant U., 2000. CPA Calif.; lic. psychologist Calif. Clin. psychologist Porterville (Calif.) Devel. Ctr., 2000—. Mem.: Calif. Psychol. Assn., Am. Psychol. Assn. Democrat. Orthodox. Home: 620 Village Green Porterville CA 93257 Office: Porterville Development Ctr PO Box 2000 Porterville CA 93257

VASILJEVIC, ELIZABETH AGNES, music educator, secondary school educator; b. Dover, Del., Jan. 11, 1973; d. Frank Phillip and Elizabeth Ellen Jelich; m. Vladan Vasiljevic, Nov. 11, 2000. BSc in Music Edn., West Chester U., 1994; MusM in Choral Condr., U. Ill., 1995. Cert. tchr. Del., 1994, Ill., 1996. Choral tchr. Normal (Ill.) Cmty. West HS, 1996—2000, Bremen HS, Midlothian, Ill., 2002—03. Choral dir. Women's Choir Westchester (Pa.) U., 1991—94. Recipient Distinction award, Fiest-Val Music Festival, Pidgeon Forge, Tenn., 1998. Mem.: Am. Choral Dirs. Assn., Music Educators Nat. Conf. Roman Cath. Avocations: gardening, reading. Home: 1422 Hemlock Knoll Terrace Northbrook IL 60062

VASLEF, IRENE, historian, librarian; b. Budapest, Hungary, Mar. 23, 1934; came to U.S., 1956, naturalized, 1960; d. Imre and Ilona (Selyebi-Kovats) Szabo; m. Nicholas P. Vaslef, Sept. 22, 1956; children— Suzanne, Steven. BA, San Jose (Calif.) State U., 1960; MS, Simmons Grad. Sch. Library Sci., Boston, 1963; postgrad., Columbia U., 1968, U. Colo., 1961-62, U. Munich, 1967-68; PhD, Catholic U. Am., 1984. Librarian, Cambridge, Mass., 1962-64; librarian Colorado Springs (Colo.) Sch. System, 1964-67; head catalog librarian Colo. Coll., Colorado Springs, 1968-72; librarian Dumbarton Oaks Rsch. Libr., Trustees for Harvard U., 1972—. Editor/compiler Am. Byzantine Bibliography in Byzantine studies/Etudes Byzantines, 1979—, Classica et Mediaevalia, 1986, Leyden: Brill, 1986; contbr. articles to profl. jours. Mem. Spl. Libraries Assn., Art Libraries Assn. N.Am., Phi Gamma Mu. Home: 4131 N River St Mc Lean VA 22101-5819 Office: Harvard U Dumbarton Oaks Rsch Libr 1703 32nd St NW Washington DC 20007-2934

VASQUES, VICTORIA L. federal agency administrator; m. Fabrice Vasques; 1 child, Alex. BS, Calif. State U., Fullerton; tchg. credentials, U. Calif., Irvine. Dir., Indian Edn. US Dept. Edn., Wash., 2002—; dir., Indian affairs US Dept. Energy, Wash.; edn. program spec. Off Indian Edn., Indian Reservation Econ., Wash., Pres. Commn. HIV Epidemic, Wash.; tech. asst. spec. Nat. Congress of Am. Indians; tribal liaison Com. for 50th Pres. Inaugural. Named Am. Indian Woman of Yr., 1986. Mem.: Decade Soc. Office: US Dept Edn Indian Edn 400 Maryland Ave SW FOB-6 Rm 3W205 Washington DC 20202 E-mail: victoria.vasques@ed.gov.

VASS, JOAN, apparel designer; b. N.Y.C., May 19, 1925; d. Max S. and Rose L.; children: Richard, Sara, Jason. Student, Vassar Coll., 1941; BA, U. Wis., 1946. Pres. Joan Vass, Inc., N.Y.C., 1977—, Vass-Ludacer, N.Y.C., 1993—. Recipient Prize de Cashet, Prince Machiabelli, 1980, Coty award, 1979, Disting. Woman in Fashion award Smithsonian Instn., 1980. Office: Joan Vass Inc 36 E 31st St New York NY 10016-6821 also: 214 W 39th St New York NY 10018-6850 E-mail: joanvass@worldnet.att.net.

VASSILOPOULOU-SELLIN, RENA, clinician investigator; b. Dec. 29, 1949; MD, Albert Einstein Coll. Medicine, 1974. Resident Montefiore Hosp., Bronx, 1974-77; fellow Northwestern U., Chgo., 1977-80; prof. Univ. Tex., Houston, 1980—. Fellow ACP, Am. Assn. Clin. Endocrinol.; mem. AAAS, AMA, Am. Soc. Bone and Mineral Rsch., Am. Diabetes Assn., Am. Soc. Clin. Oncology, Endo Soc. Office: Anderson Cancer Ctr 1515 Holcombe Blvd # 15 Houston TX 77030-4009

VASYLYEVA, ANNA, artist, writer; b. Kiev, Ukraine, Nov. 24, 1977; d. Tamara Balenko and Vladimir Vasylyev. Fine Art Degree, T.G. Shevchenko State Art Sch., 1993—97. Tchr. asst. KidsArt, Tarzana, Calif., 1999; designer, illustrator Pub. Ho. KM Academia, Kiev, Ukraine, 1996, All Electronics Corp., Van Nuys, Calif., 2002—; art tchr. Marina's Sch. of Music and Art, Northridge, Calif., 2001; lab asst. Calif. State U., Northridge, 2004—. Exhibitions include State Fall Exhbn. of Art, Los Angeles Mission Coll., Limner Gallery, Pacific Design Ctr., L.A., Art Assn. Harrisburg's 76th Ann. Juried Exhbn., Svitozor Gallery, Los Angeles Valley Coll., Art Acad. of Los Angeles, Art Gallery of the U. Kiev-Mogila Acad., First Internat. Exhbn. -Presentation of Periodical Publications about Pets; contbr. articles to mags. Recipient Biography Pub., The Nat. Dean's List, 2002—03; State U. Fee grant, Calif. State U., Northridge, 2003—, Campus Fee grant, 2003—. Christian. Avocations: reading, travel, horseback riding. Office: All Electronics Corporation 14928 Oxnard St Van Nuys CA 91411 Office Phone: 818-997-1806. Personal E-mail: anyav77@yahoo.com.

VAUCLAIR, MARGUERITE RENÉE, communications and sales promotion executive; b. Englewood, N.J., Jan. 26, 1945; d. Maurice Joseph and Yvonne Jeanne (Reynaud) V.; m. William Augustus Peeples II, (div. 1986). BS in Journalism, Bowling Green State U., 1967. Asst. promotion mgr. Internat. Herald Tribune, Paris, 1967-70; Europe promotion mgr. Vision-The European Bus. Mag., London, 1971; dir. programs and promotion Am. C. of C. in France, Paris, 1973-76; promotion and rsch. mgr. Johnston Internat. Pubs., N.Y.C., 1977-80; prin. Marguerite Vauclair Promotion-Pub. Rels.-Advt., 1981—; promotion mgr. L.A. Times Syndicate, 1985-88; advt. promotions and spl. sects. mgr. Soundings Publs. Inc., Essex, Conn., 1990. Collaborator on books, author: (guide) Guest Houses, Bed-and-Breakfasts, Inns and Hotels in Newport, R.I., 1982; contbr. travel articles and photographs to mags. and newspapers. Mem. Pub. Rels. Soc. Am. (Prisms awards com. L.A. 1988), Women in Comm. (bd. dirs. L.A. 1987-89), French-Am. C. of C. in U.S., Inc. (publs. com. 1993-98), Alliance Francaise de Westchester (bd. dirs. 2002—), Advt. Club of Westchester (bd. dirs. 1994-97), Fairfield County Pub. Rels. Assn., Conn. Press Club (bd. dirs. 2000—), Kappa Delta (bd. dirs. UCLA chpt. 1986-88, U. Conn. 1990-91). Office: 131 Purchase St Rye NY 10580-2139

VAUGHAN, BERNIECE MILLER, retired school system administrator, writer; b. Parkville, Mo., Jan. 24, 1913; d. Clarence Absalom and Elsa Alba (Duley) M.; m. George Lowell Vaughan, Aug. 12, 1935 (dec. 1980); children: Elsa Rae Pearce, Rosemary Anderson. BA with honors, Park Coll., Parkville, Mo., 1934; MA, U. of the Pacific, 1960. Tchr. various elem. schs., Platte County, Mo., 1935-39, Lodi (Calif.) elem. schs., 1948-60; tchr., adminstr. Lodi Elem. Sch. Dist., 1960—78; ret. Contbr. articles to various mags. Recipient Citations of Excellence Lodi Schs., San Joaquin County, State of Calif. Mem. DAR, Calif. Ret. Tchrs., San Joaquin Geneology Club, Tokay Antique Club (pres. 1982-83, sec. 1983-84). Democrat. Methodist. Avocations: autobiographical writing, geneological research. Home: 2044 Kenway Ct Lodi CA 95242-3218

VAUGHAN, LINDA, publishing executive; Pub. Soap Opera Digest, N.Y.C., 1993—, Soap Opera Weekly, N.Y.C., 1993—. Office: 110 Fifth Ave 4th Fl New York NY 10011

VAUGHAN, MARTHA, biochemist, educator; b. Dodgeville, Wis., Aug. 4, 1926; d. John Anthony and Luciel (Ellingen) V.; m. Jack Orloff, Aug. 4, 1951 (dec. Dec. 1988); children: Jonathan Michael, David Geoffrey, Gregory Joshua. Ph.B., U. Chgo., 1944; MD, Yale U., 1949. Intern New Haven Hosp., Conn., 1950-51; research fellow U. Pa., Phila., 1951-52, Nat. Heart Inst., Bethesda, Md., 1952-54, mem. research staff, 1954-68; head metabolism sect. Nat. Heart and Lung Inst., Bethesda, 1968-74; acting chief molecular disease br. Nat. Heart, Lung and Blood Inst., Bethesda, 1974-76, chief cell metabolism lab., 1974-94; dep. chief pulmonary and critical care medicine br. Nat. Heart, Lung, and Blood Inst., Bethesda, 1994—. Mem. metabolism study sect. NIH, 1965-68; mem. bd. sci. counselors Nat. Inst. Alcohol Abuse and Alcoholism, 1988-91. Mem. editl. bd. Jour. Biol. Chemistry, 1971-76, 80-83, 88-90, assoc. editor, 1992—; editl. adv. bd. Molecular Pharmacology, 1972-80, Biochemistry, 1989-94; editor: Biochemistry and Biophysics Rsch. Comms., 1990-91; contbr. articles to profl. jours., chpts. to books. Bd. dirs. Found. Advanced Edn. in Scis., Inc., Bethesda, 1979-92, exec. com., 1980-92, treas., 1984-86, v.p., 1986-88, pres., 1988-90; mem. Yale U. Coun. com. med. affairs, New Haven, 1974-80. Recipient Meritorious Svc. medal HEW, 1974, Disting. Svc. medal HEW, 1979, Commd. Officer award USPHS, 1982, Superior Svc. award USPHS, 1993. Mem. NAS, Am. Acad. Arts and Scis., Am. Soc. Biol. Chemists (chmn. pub. com. 1984-86), Assn. Am. Physicians, Am. Soc. Clin. Investigation. Home: 11608 W Hill Dr Rockville MD 20852-3751 Office: Nat Heart Lung & Blood Inst Nih Bldg 10 Rm 5N 307 Bethesda MD 20892-0001 E-mail: vaughanm@nih.gov.

VAUGHAN, NADINE, psychologist; b. Tampa, Fla., Aug. 30, 1947; d. Joseph Marcus and Velna Pearl (Jones) Williams; m. E.L. Vaughan III, 1966 (div. Aug. 1976); children: Edward L. Vaughan, Heather Vaughan Oyarzun, Melanie Sage; m. Richard S. Traum, Sept. 2002. BA in Criminal Justice, U. South Fla., 1974, MA with honors in Rehab. Counseling, 1975; PhD in Psychology, Saybrook Inst., 1990. Lic. clin. psychologist, Calif., Wash., Fla. Co-founder Women's Resource Ctr., Tampa and Nevada City, Calif., 1973—; cmty. and organizational devel. specialist State of Calif., Berkeley, Sacramento, 1978-82; cons., trainer N. Vaughan, PhD, 1982—; regional trainer APA Hope Program, 1994—; clin. dir. dist. 13, Fla. Camelot Cmty. Care divsn. Providence, 2002—03. Owner Living Theatre Co.; adj. prof. Rollins Coll., Valencia Coll. Mem. APA, Am. Coll. Forensic Examiners (diplomate psychol. spltys., med. psychology). Democrat. Avocations: theatrical directing and performance, scriptwriting. E-mail: psychespace@earthlink.net.

VAUGHAN, NANCY KING, educational consultant; b. Pampa, Tex., Feb. 23, 1957; d. Betty Morman and Ellis Leon King; m. Dennis Bruce Vaughan, Mar. 31, 1988; children: Gretchen, Jason, Jeffery. BS, U. Tex., 1979; MEd, Tex. A&M U., 1991, MS, 1993, EdD, 2002. Cert. spl. edn. tchr. Tex., elem. math. tchr. Tex., elem. reading tchr. Tex., mid. mgmt. adminstr. Tex., supt. Tex. Prin. Lancaster (Tex.) Ind. Sch. Dist., 1993—96; ednl. cons. Edn. Svc. Ctr. Region XI, Ft. Worth, 1996—. V.p. Pink Pink Rose, 2002—. Bd. advs. Tarrant County Courage to Teach, Ft. Worth, 1999—2003; mem. dist. ednl. improvement com. Keller (Tex.) Ind. Sch. Dist., 2000—03. Mem.: Tex. Coun. Women Sch. Execs. (v.p. 2003—), Assn. Compensatory Educators Tex. (pres. 2003—). Home: 5884 Echo Bluff Fort Worth TX 76137 Office: Edn Svc Ctr Region XI 3001 N Freeway Fort Worth TX 76106 Personal E-mail: nkvaughan@aol.com. Business E-Mail: nvaughan@esc11.net.

VAUGHN, CONNIE MARIE, marketing professional, writer; b. Cin., Mar. 10, 1965; d. Richard and Susan Harless Halley, William Edward and Carol Welling Vaughn. BA in Math. & Stats., Miami U., Oxford, Ohio, 1987; MA in Devel. Psychology, Loyola U., Chgo., 1993; MBA in Mktg. & Orgnl. Behavior, U. Chgo., 2001. Account dir. Epsilon Data Mgmt., Burlington, Mass., 1995—2000; brand planner Rapp Collins, Chgo., 2000—01; dir. strategic/database mktg. GSP Mktg., Chgo., 2001—02; modeling & database mktg. mgr. JC Whitney, Chgo., 2002—03; sr. mgr., mkt. devel. Quill Corp., Lincolnshire, Ill., 2004—. Contbr. articles and poems to jours. Scholar, Nat. Merit Scholarship Corp., 1983—84; Alumni scholar, Miami U. Ohio, 1983—87, Regents scholar, Ohio Bd. Regents, 1983—87, Dean's fellow, Loyola U. Chgo., 1989—92. Mem.: Guild Complex, Chgo. Songwriters Collective, Poetry Ctr. Chgo., Psi Chi, Pi Mu Epsilon. Home: 148 W Huron St Chicago IL 60610 Personal E-mail: cmvaughn1@aol.com.

VAUGHN, EULALIA COBB, retired science educator, mathematician; b. Smithville, Tenn., Aug. 1, 1926; d. Luther Leonidas Fuson and Allie Pearl Redmon; m. Lewis Latane Cobb, Aug. 14, 1944 (dec. 1980); children: Carl Cobb, Luther Fuson Cobb, Lewis Cobb Jr., James Cobb, David R. Cobb, John Winston Cobb; m. Floyce Vaughn, 1983. BS, Mid. Tenn. State U., 1946, MEd, 1980. Tchr. Secondary Sch., Tulahoma, Tenn., 1946, sci. and math. tchr., 1947, 1948, Pine Bluff, Ark., 1959, Birmingham, Ala., 1965, Nashville, 1965—91; ret. Chair dept. various schs., Tenn., 1967—91; pres. Dekalb County Ret. Tchrs. Assn., 1992—98; tchr. mission sch., 1996—; sponsor Sci. Olympiad Glencliff H.S., Nashville (state winner). Author: Poetry Book, 2001; contbr. articles to Nashville Tennesean. Voter registration Dem. Party, Smithville, 1995—2001, mem. steering com.; women's leader United Meth. Women, Cookeville, Tenn., 1991—2001, sec. comm., dist. pres., 1992—. Mem.: Family Cmty. Edn. (pres.). Democrat. Methodist. Avocation: family. Home: PO Box 132 1161 S Mountain St Smithville TN 37166

VAUGHN, GLORIA C. state representative; b. Corpus Christi, Tex., June 25, 1936; m. James M. Vaughn; children: James, Melodie. Student, Del Mar Jr. Coll., Salvation Army Coll., N.Mex. State U. State rep. dist. 51 N.Mex. State Legis., Santa Fe, 1996—. Mem. Bus. and Industry com. N.Mex. State Legis., Santa Fe, mem. Energy and Natural Resources com. Mem.: FEMA (bd. dirs.), LVA (bd. dirs.), ARC (sec.), Salvation Army, Salvation Army (pres.), Am. Cancer Bd., Boy Scouts Am., Habitat for Humanity (bd. dirs.), Alamogordo Women's Club. Republican. Home: 503 E 16th St Alamogordo NM 88310 Office: New Mexico State Capitol Rm 203 ICN Santa Fe NM 87503

VAUGHN, KATHY, municipal official; Pres. bd. commrs. Pub. Utility Dist., Everett, Wash. Home: PO Box 1107 Everett WA 98206-1107 Office: Office Bd Commrs Pub Utility Dist 2320 California St Everett WA 98201-3750

VAUGHN, LINDA M. municipal official; b. Moline, Ill., Aug. 6, 1947; d. Merwin Perry and Margaret Anne (Larson) Baker; m. Jeffery M. Vaughn, Aug. 16, 1969; children: Jason P., Eric M. Student, Moline Inst. Commerce, 1965. Data entry clk. Farmall (Internat. Harvester), Rock Island, Ill., 1973-75, Ingersoll, Rockford, Ill., 1975-87; trustee Village of Machesney Park (Ill.), 1987-89, clk., 1989—. Guest columnist Post Jour., 1997—. Charter mem. Chamber Women's Network, Loves Park, Ill., 1995; sec. GPAC Sr. Ctr., Loves Park, 1997—; sec., treas. NIMCA, Regional Clk. Assn., Ill., 1995—. Mem. Northwestern Ill. Mcpl. Clks. Assn. (sec. 1990-92, treas. 1997-99), C. of C. (ambassador 1987—). Democrat. Roman Catholic. Avocations: writing, fishing, reading, walking, grandchildren. Home: 9519 Shore Dr Machesney Park IL 61115-2058 Office: Village Machesney Park 300 Machesney Rd Machesney Park IL 61115-2495

VAUGHN, LISA DAWN, physician, educator; b. Ashland, Ky., May 10, 1961; d. Charles Clinton and Mildred Darlene (Cantrell) V. AS in Biology, U. Ky., 1981, BS in Zoology, 1983; DO, W.Va. Sch. Osteo. Medicine, 1988. Diplomate Nat. Osteo. Med. Bd.; cert. Am. Assn. Med. Rev. officer, 1996. Gen. intern Doctors Hosp. Inc., Massillon, Ohio, 1988-89, family practice resident, 1989-91; emergency room physician Coastal Emergency Svcs., Snowpark, Ohio, 1989-90; urgent care physician Acute Care Specialists, Akron, Ohio, 1991; physician Portage Family Practice Clinic, North Canton, Ohio, 1991-95, First Care Family Health & Immediate Care Ctr., Canton, Ohio, 1995-95; dir. occupl. medicine First Care, Canton, 1996, med. dir. urgent care sys., 1996-97; physician Mercy Health Ctr. Jackson, Ohio, 1997—. Clin. asst. faculty Ohio U. Coll. Medicine, Athens, 1990-91, adj. clin. faculty, 1992—; asst. dir. family practice residency Ohio U. Coll. Medicine-Doctors Hosp. Inc., Massillon, 1992-95; urgent CARE physician First Care, Canton, Ohio, 1995—; med. dir. family home health svc. Doctors Hosp., 1992-94, chmn. dept. family medicine, 1994-95; med. dir. Riczo and Co. Managed Care Orgn., 1997—;med. adv. to Canton City Schools, Med. Assisting Program; med. advisor Boy Scouts Med. Explorers, Massillon, 1989-90; med. career advisor Girl Scouts Career Day, Canton, 1990; affiliate physician Cleve. Clinic, 1991—; med. advisor Canton City Sch. Med. Assisting Program, 2002—. Contbr. poems. Col. Ky. Cols. Assn., Ashland, 1989—; vol. United Way of Stark County, 1990-91. Mem. Cleve. Clinic Found. (affiliate physician), AMA, Am. Coll. Osteo. Family Physicians, Am. Osteo. Assn. (cert.), Ohio State Med. Assn., W.Va. Soc. Osteo. Medicine, Stark County Med. Soc., Sigma Sigma Phi (sec. 1985-86). Democrat. Avocations: writing, horseback riding, poetry. Office: Statcare Jackson 7452 Fulton Dr NW Massillon OH 44646-9393

VAUGHN, SUSAN MARIE, journalist, educator; b. Hastings, Nebr., Apr. 22, 1945; d. Philip S. and Berta I. Abrahamson; m. Thomas P. Vaughn, May 1, 1966 (div. 1982); children: Jeanne, Matthew. BA, Coe Coll., Cedar Rapids, Iowa, 1967; MS in Journalism, Columbia U., 1992. Tchr. social studies, Columbia, Conn., 1967—68; reporter Hartford Courant, Manchester, Conn., 1968—69, 1971—75, Manchester (Conn.) Herald, 1976—79; mng. editor, reporter The Jours., Windsor, Conn., 1980—81; reporter, feature writer, copy editor Manchester Herald, 1984—87; news editor, reporter The Chronicle, Willimantic, Conn., 1987—91; reporter Jour. Inquirer, Manchester, Conn., 1992—97; news editor Bristol (Conn.) Press, 1997—98; copy editor The Advocate, Stamford, Conn., 1998—99; asst. prof. journalism Lynchburg (Va.) Coll., 2001—03. Mem. media careers adv. bd. Manchester C.C., 1989—94, mem. comm. program evaluation team, 1998; vis. asst. prof. journalism Iona Coll., New Rochelle, NY, 1999—2001; freelance writer New York Times, Newsday, Hartford Monthly, Living in Stanford mag., Blue Ridge Bus. Jour. Contbr. newspaper articles The Chronicle, 1987 (UP Internat. Bus. award, 1989, UP Internat. Cmty Svc. award, 1988). Vol. Hartford Stage, 1984—89, Christmas in Apr., 1995—2003, Habitat for Humanity, 2002; Vol. Bushnell Auditorium, Hartford, 1995—99; pres., mem. Manchester Arts Coun., 1986—90, Acad. Music Vol., Lynchburg, Va., 2002; tchr. English as a Second Lang. Literacy Vols. Am., Stamford, 1999—2001. Fellow journalism, Finland Ministry of Fgn. Affairs, 1992. Mem.: Assn. Educators Journalism and Mass Comm., Soc. for Profl. Journalists, Coll. Media Advisers, Scrivener's Writers Group. Avocations: hiking, dance, photography, travel, art. Office: Lynchburg Coll 1501 Lakeside Dr Lynchburg VA 24501 Home: 2811 Rivermont Ave Apt 4 Lynchburg VA 24503-1413 Business E-Mail: vaughn@lynchburg.edu.

VAUGHT, WILMA L. foundation executive, retired air force officer; b. Pontiac, Mich., Mar. 15, 1930; d. Willard L. and Margaret J. (Pierce) V. BS, U. Ill., 1952; MBA, U. Ala., 1968; postgrad., Indsl. Coll. Armed Forces, 1972-73; D Pub. Affairs (hon.), Columbia Coll., 1992. Cert. cost acct. Commd. 2d lt. USAF, 1957, advanced through grades to brig. gen., 1980, chief data services div. 306th Combat Support Group, 1963-67, mgmt. analyst Office Dep. Chief of Staff, comptroller Mil. Assistance Command Saigon, Vietnam, 1968-69, chief advanced logistics systems plans and mgmt. group Air Force Logistics Command Wright-Patterson AFB, Ohio, 1969-72, chief cost factors br., chief security assistance br. Washington, 1973-75, Directorate Mgmt. Analysis, Office of Comptroller, 1973-75, dir. program and budget Office Dep. Chief of Staff, comptroller Hdqrs. Air Force Systems Command Andrews AFB, Md., 1980-82, comdr. U.S. Mil. Entrance Processing Command North Chicago, Ill., 1982-85, ret., 1985; pres. Women in Mil. Svc. Meml. Found., Arlington, Va., 1987—. Pres. bd. dirs. Pentagon Fed. Credit Union, 1975-82; bd. regents Inst. Cost Analysis, 1979-83; Air Force sr. mil. rep. Def. Adv. Com. on Women in Services, 1982-85; chmn. Com. on Women in Armed Forces, NATO, Brussels, 1984-85. Bd. dirs. Air Force Retired Officer Community, 1986-90; mem. adv. bd. Jane Addams Conf.; mem. bd. trustees The Teller Found. Decorated Bronze Star medal, Def. Disting. Service medal, U.S. Air Force Disting. Service medal; recipient Ill. Achievement award U. Ill., 1983 Mem.

Internat. Women's Forum. Methodist. Home: 6658 Van Winkle Dr Falls Church VA 22044-1010 Office: Women in Mil Svc Meml Found 5510 Columbia Pike Ste 302 Arlington VA 22204-3123

VAYANIAN, SOLARA ZAKELI, artist, educator; b. Chgo., June 14, 1947; d. Ralph William Forst, Marion Elizabeth Engel; children: Michael Paul Catlett, Noel Thomas Catlett. BA in Phys. Edn. and Dance, San Diego State U., 1975. Founder, dir. Winged Fire Prodns., Sedona, Ariz., 1978—; founder, facilitator Kinesio-Emotional Release System, Sedona, 1978—; founder, dir. Compassionate Care Internat., Sedona, 2001—. Author: (novels) Time Dancer, 1972, The Stars Gave Passion, 1977, Octangle Blue, 1989, Time Out of Mind, 2000; author: (or co-author) (stage prodn.) Journey thru the Mask, The Doorway of the Heart. Founder, dir. care teams Emergency Relief Care Teams for victims, caregivers and rescuers followed by cmty. and/or personal rebuilding; founder, dir. care teams pilot program Kachina Point Rehab. and Healthcare Ctr., Sedona. Recipient Barbara Marx Hubbard Women of Vision award for innovative social action, 1996. Achievements include development of workable systems for healing, wholeness and human potential development through the arts, education, interactive community programs, performances and events. Avocations: reading, running, designing and sewing clothes, costumes. Office: Compassionate Care Internat PO Box 622 Sedona AZ 86339

VAZ, KATHERINE ANNE, language educator; b. Castro Valley, Calif., Aug. 26, 1955; d. August Mark and Elizabeth (Sullivan) Vaz; m. Michael Trudeau, May 1, 1994. BA, U. Calif., Santa Barbara, 1977; MFA, U. Calif., Irvine, 1991. Assoc. prof. English U. Calif., Davis, 1995-99; lectr. Harvard U. Briggs-Copeland, 2003—. Keynote spkr. Libr. of Congress, 1997; keynote spkr. lit. confs. U. Ariz., Ariz., U. Calif., Berkeley, U. Mass., Dartmouth U., Rutgers U.; mem. U.S. Presdl. del. to Expo 98/World's Fair, Lisbon, Portugal; Briggs-Copeland lectr. Harvard U., Cambridge, Mass., 2003. Author: (novels) Saudade, 1994, Mariana, 1997, (short stories) Fado & Other Stories, 1997 (Drue Heinz Lit. prize, 1997). Grantee, Nat. Endowment Arts, 1993, Davis Humanities Inst., U. Calif., Davis, 1998—99. Mem.: PEN, Portuguese-Am. Leadership Coun. U.S., Authors Guild. Democrat. Roman Catholic.

VAZIRANI-FALES, HEEA, legislative staff member, lawyer; b. Calcutta, India, Apr. 1, 1938; d. Sunder J. Vazirani; m. John Fales Jr., 1978; children: Deepika, Reetika, Ashish, Monika, Jyotika, Denise. AB, Guilford Coll., 1959; JD, Howard U., 1979. Staff/legis. dir. Montgomery County Del, Gen. Assembly of Md., 1981-87; legis. counsel to Congresswoman Constance A. Morella, US Ho. of Reps., Washington, 1987-94, counsel subcom. on postal svc. com. govt. reform, 1995—2000, dep. staff dir. and counsel subcom. on DC govt. reform, 2000—02, counsel subcom. on civil svc., 2003—. Mem. staff Vols. for Visually Handicapped, 1973-79, bd. dirs., 1979-81; bd. dirs. Manipal Edn. and Med. Found., 1970-92. Mem. Phi Delta Phi. Office: Subcom on Civil Svc B-373A Rayburn Bldg Washington DC 20515

VAZQUEZ, MARTHA ALICIA, judge; b. Santa Barbara, Calif., Feb. 21, 1953; d. Remigio and Consuelo (Mendez) V. BA in Govt., U. Notre Dame, 1975, JD, 1978. Bar: N.Mex. 1979, U.S. Dist. Ct. (we. dist.) N.Mex. 1979. Atty. Pub. Defender's Office, Santa Fe, 1979-81; ptnr. Jones, Snead, Wertheim, Rodriguez & Wentworth, Santa Fe, 1981-93; judge U.S. District Ct. N.Mex., Santa Fe, 1993—. Democrat. Roman Catholic. Office: US Courthouse PO Box 2710 Santa Fe NM 87504-2710

VEACO, KRISTINA, lawyer; b. Sacramento, Mar. 4, 1948; d. Robert Glenn and Lelia (McCain) V.; 1 child, Nina Katherine. BA, U. Calif., Davis, 1970, JD, Hastings Coll. Law, 1981. Legal adv. to commr. William T. Bagley Calif. Pub. Utilities Commn., San Francisco, 1981-86; sr. counsel Pacific Telesis Group, San Francisco, 1986-94; sr. counsel corp. and securities and pol. law AirTouch Comms., San Francisco, 1994-98; asst. gen. counsel, asst. sec. McKesson Corp., San Francisco, 1999—. Mem.: ABA, Am. Soc. Corp. Secs. (pres. San Francisco chpt. 2001—02, mem. adv. com. San Francisco chpt., nat. bd. dirs.), San Francisco Bar Assn., Phi Beta Kappa. Democrat. Episcopalian. Avocations: cooking, reading. Office: McKesson Corp 1 Post St Fl 33 San Francisco CA 94104-5233 E-mail: Kristina.veaco@mckesson.com.

VEDDER, NENA HELENE, music educator; b. Hamilton, N.Y., Nov. 2, 1977; MusB, SUNY, Potsdam, 1999; MMusEd, CUNY, Queens, 2001. K-8 music tchr. Berne-Knox-Westerlo Ctrl. Sch. Dist., Berne, NY, 1999—2000; music tchr. 3-5; grade 4 chorus Commack (N.Y.) Union Free Sch. Dist., 2000—. Musician: (vocal soloist) L.I. Masterworks and Philharmonic Choirs. Mem.: Suffolk County Music Educators Assn., Music Educators Nat. Conv., NY State Sch. Music Assn., Stony Brook Camerata, Sigma Alpha Iota (life; v.p. membership, corr. sec. 1997—98, Ruby Sword of Honor; Sword of Honor 1999).

VEECH, LYNDA ANNE, musician, educator; b. Montclair, N.J., July 19, 1969; d. Robert Gerald, Sr. and Josephine Veech. B in Music Edn., Rutgers U., New Brunswick, 1991, MA in Music History, 1995, MusM in Piano Performance and Pedagogy, Westminster Choir Coll., Princeton, N.J., 1998. Cert. tchr. N.J. Faculty mem. Westminster Conservatory, Princeton, 1995—2000; pvt. studio dir. Studio of Lynda A. Veech, Verona, NJ, 1995—; faculty mem. Essex County Coll., Woodbridge, NJ, 1996—98, Caldwell (N.J.) Coll., 2000—01; choral dir. Caldwell and West Caldwell Pub. Schs., 2000—02; music tchr. Bartle Elem. Sch., Highland Park, NJ, 2002—03, Morris Cath. HS, Denville, NJ, 2003—. Cons. freelance work, Verona, NJ, 1995—2002; participant Hands Across the Water Internat. Tchr. Exch. Program, Australia, 2002. Performer Ameropa Internat. Music Festival, Prague, Czech Republic, 2001. Bd. dirs. Music and More Booster Club, Caldwell, NJ, 2001—02; ch. musician 1st Bapt. Ch., Montclair, 2000—01; organist, choir dir. Calvary Luth. Ch., 2003—; vocalist Canticle AIDS Benefit Ensemble, NJ, 1999—2000. Grantee, Rutgers U., 1991—95, Westminster Choir Coll., 1995—97. Mem.: Music Edn. Assn. (co-founder 2000—), Nat. Conf. Piano Pedagogy, Piano Tchrs. Guild, N.J. Edn. Assn., Am. Choral Dir.'s Assn., Music Educator's Nat. Conf. (treas. 1987, v.p. 1991). Roman Catholic. Avocations: reading, swimming, ballet, writing poetry, playing music in sacred and secular settings. Home: 124 Sunset Ave Verona NJ 07044 Office: Morris Cath High Sch 200 Morris Ave Denville NJ 07834-1360 Personal E-mail: notenut@aol.com.

VEEDER, NANCY WALKER, social work educator; b. Albany, N.Y., Mar. 17, 1937; d. Harold Gerit and Alice (Walker) V. AB, Smith Coll., Northampton, Mass., 1959; MS, Simmons Sch. Social Work, Boston, 1963; PhD, Brandeis U., 1974; MBA, Boston Coll., 1990. Prof., grad. sch. social work Boston Coll., Chestnut Hill, 1968—. Home: 53 Lake Ave Newton Center MA 02459-2110 E-mail: veeder@bc.edu.

VEGA, MARYLOIS PURDY, journalist; b. Chgo., Nov. 4, 1914; d. William Thomas and Mary Helene (Buggy) Purdy; m. Carlos Juan Vega, Sept. 4, 1965. BA, U. Wis., Madison, 1935. With Time mag., N.Y.C., 1942-84; chief Letters to the Editor, 1951-67, chief editl. rsch., 1967-76, assoc. editor, 1976-84. Mem.: Overseas Press. Roman Catholic. Home: 303 Birchwood Southbury CT 06488-1378

VEGA, RAYNETTE NORMA, hotel official; b. Kohala, Hawaii, Feb. 26, 1962; d. Antone Tony and Ramona Mona Vega. Student, Fayetteville (N.C.) Tech. Sch., 1980-81, Youth with a Mission, Sunland, Calif., 1982-83. Christian counselor Centrum of Hollywood, Calif., 1983-84; security officer Hawaii Protective Assn., Kamuela, 1984-87, Puakea Bay Ranch, Kapaau, Hawaii, 1987-93; concierge Hyatt Regency Waikoloa, Hawaii, 1988-89. Youth Christian counselor New Covenant Ch., Waimea, Hawaii, 1985-86. Author: (poetry) Rainbows of Poems from Heaven Above, 1987, Heart Beat in Love, 1993. Recipient Golden Poet award World of Poetry, 1987-91, award Poetry Acad., 1993, Poet of Merit award Internat. Soc. Poets, 1993, Internat. Hall of Fame, 1996. Avocations: jogging, tennis, reading, writing poetry.

VEHRS, NANCY JOYCE, county official; b. Warrenton, Va., Mar. 19, 1958; d. Karl Heinz and Ellen Elizabeth Vehrs. BA in Econs., Coll. William and Mary, 1980. Cert. mcpl. clk. Clerical specialist Fairfax (Va.) County Dept. Pub. Works, 1980—81; office mgr., various adminstrv. positions Woodburn Ctr. for Cmty. Mental Health, Annandale, Va., 1981—86; budget analyst Fairfax County Police Dept., 1986—90; clk. to the bd. suprs. Fairfax County Govt., 1990—. Sec. Lake Jackson Garden Club, Manassas, Va., 1998—2000. Mem.: Va. Mcpl. Clks. Assn. (regional dir. 2001—03, 2d v.p. 2003—), Internat. Assn. Mpcl. Clks., Va. Native Plant Soc., Prince William Wildflower Soc. (pres. 1992—94, newsletter editor 1998—, pres. 2000—02). Avocations: gardening, hiking, bicycling, nature, travel. Home: 8318 Highland St Manassas VA 20110-3671 Office: Fairfax County Office of the Clk to the Bd Suprs Ste 533 12000 Govt Ctr Pkwy Fairfax VA 22035

VEIGA, JENNIFER, state representative; b. Long Beach, Calif., Oct. 10, 1962; BS, U. Colo., Boulder, 1987; JD with honors, George Washington U., 1987. Assoc. Hall & Evans, LLC, Denver; state rep. dist. 3 Colo. Ho. of Reps., Denver, 1996—, mem. joint com. on legis. con. Nat. del. Am. Coun. Young Polit. Leaders; student coord. Hart campaign U. Colo., 1984. Mem.: AB A, Colo. Women's Bar Assn. (co-chair task force on gender bias, chair pub. policy com.), Colo. Bar Assn., Denver Bar Assn. Democrat. Roman Catholic. Avocations: reading, golf, travel, basketball. Office: Hall & Evans LLC Ste 1700 1200 17th St Denver CO 80202 also: State Capitol # 222 200 E Colfax Ave Denver CO 80203

VEIT, CLAIRICE GENE TIPTON, measurement psychologist; b. Monterey Park, Calif., Feb. 20, 1939; d. Albert Vern and Gene (Bunning) Tipton; children: Steven, Barbara, Laurette, Catherine. BA, UCLA, 1969, MA, 1970, PhD, 1974. Asst. prof. psychology Calif. State U., L.A., 1975-77, assoc. prof. psychology, 1977-80; rsch. psychologist The Rand Corp., Santa Monica, Calif., 1977—. Rsch. cons. NATO Tech. Ctr., The Hague, The Netherlands, 1980-81; faculty Rand Grad Sch., Santa Monica, 1993—99. Developer subjective transfer function (STF) method to complex sys. analysis and the mental health inventory. Mem. NOW, Soc. Med. Decision-Making, L.A. Opera League. Avocations: mountain climbing, playing piano, travel, music, theatre. Office: The Rand Corp 1700 Main St Santa Monica CA 90401-3297 E-mail: veit@rand.org.

VEIT, GAE, construction executive; CEO, owner Shingobee Builders, Loretto, Minn., 1980—. Recipient Contractor Yr., Am. Public Works Assn., 1994, Supplier Yr., Alliant Techsystems, 1993, Nat. Female Entrepreneur Yr., Dept. Commerce, 1991. Office: Shingobee Builders PO Box 8 Loretto MN 55357-0008 Fax: 612-479-3267.

VELA, LAURIE STORY, illustrator, writer, publisher, producer; b. Sacramento, Calif., Nov. 17, 1962; d. Harry and Hazel May (Triglia) Vela; m. Daniel Murphy; 1 child, Jeremiah Vela-Murphy. AA in Comms., San Joaquin Delta Coll., Stockton, Calif., 1983; BA in Comms., U. Calif., Davis, 1990, MA in Edn., 1991. Tchg. asst. U. Calif., Davis, 1990—91; childcare specialist YMCA of the Redwoods, Boulder Creek, Calif., 1991—95; prin., performer, prodr. Laurie's Stories, Newtown Sq., Pa., 1992—, nat. performance tours, 1992—2000. Cons., educator Loma Prieta (Calif.) Ind. Home Study, 1995—98, Green Valley Parent Co-Op Preschool, Palo Alto, Calif., 1996—98; presenter in field; e-book pub. www-lauriestories.com, 2000—. Author, illustrator, prodr.: Leaping Literacy: Fun Phonics from A2Z, 1997, Laurie Story Audio Tapes, 1993—96, Environmental Musical Trilogy, 1992, author, illustrator, performer, prodr.Leaping: Literacy Video Series, 12 shows, 2001—, author, illustrator, performer, prodr.: Leaping Literacy Audio Series, 12 shows, 2002—03; author (illustrator, pub.): of more than 150 books (120 in the Leaping Literacy series). Recipient award for drama, Bank of Am., 1980. Mem.: Soc. Children's Book Authors and Illustrators, Children's Music Network, San Francisco Folk Music Club (children's activities coord. Camp Harmony 1994—). Avocations: nature, hiking, music, singing. Home and Office: Laurie's Stories 3514 Caley Rd Newtown Square PA 19073 E-mail: laurie@lauriestories.com.

VELARDE, HEIDE MARIE, publisher, writer, lyricist; b. Oahu Honolulu, May 16, 1953; d. Margaret Curette, Nicholas Curette; m. Arthur Charles Velarde; children: Ryan, Aaron, Devin, Tori. Sr. clk. typist Kelly Svcs., Kelly Girl Divsn., San Francisco, 1978—79; acctg. technician Health and Human Svcs., Divsn. of Acctg., Fiscal, and Budget Svcs., San Francisco, 1980—85; dataentry, clk., accts. payable Kelly Svcs., Kelly Girl Divsn., Hayward, Calif., 1989—92; publ., propr. Crookbook Press, Union City, Calif., 1999—; writer Amerecord, Hollywood, Calif., 2002—, Hilltop Records, Hollywood, Calif., 2002—. Author: A Fadeaway Dream of Justice to Redeem, 1999 (Certificate of Merit, 2000). Mem.: BMI. Avocation: reading, gardening, swimming. Home: 33244 Fourth Street Union City CA 94587-2104 Office: Crookbook Press 33244 Fourth Street Union City CA 94587-2104

VELASCO, ESDA NURY, speech and language professional; b. Cali, Colombia, Oct. 1, 1953; d. Florentino and Dominga (Castro) Rivera; m. William Lubin Velasco, July 29, 1972; children: Martin Hernando, Monica Marie, Jaime Mauricio, Christopher Michael. BA in Psychology and Spanish cum laude, Cleve. State U., 1989, MEd. Spanish tchr. Berlitz Sch. of Langs., Cleve., 1979-85; interpreter Fed. Ct., Cleve., 1980-87; founder, pres. ENV Global Comm. Inc., Cleve., 1987—, Spanish instr., interpreter, translator, 1987—. Interpreter various orgns., 1980-87. Mem. MLA, N.E. Ohio Translators Assn., Am. Translators Assn. (cert.). Roman Catholic. Avocations: music, reading, dance, horseback riding, camping. Office: ENV Global Comm 5005 Rockside Rd Ste 600 Cleveland OH 44131-6827

VELASCO, JODI MARIE, military lawyer; b. Elk Grove Village, Ill., July 19, 1969; d. John Edward and Margaret Ann Velasco; m. Anthony Michael Elavsky, Mar. 2, 1993. AA, U. Md., 1993; BA in Women's Studies, BA in Polit. Sci., U. Okla., 1997, JD, 2001. Enlisted U.S. Air Force, 1989, advanced through grades to sr. airman, 1993; asst. judge advocate, capt. USAF Res. 507th Air Refueling Wing, Tinker AFB, Okla., 2003—. Mem. NOW (state treas. 1996-98), ACLU (chpt. v.p. 1999-2000), Res. Officer Assn., Phi Alpha Delta (chpt. clk. 1999-2000, chpt. justice 2000-01), Pi Sigma Alpha. Democrat. Roman Catholic. Avocations: triathlon, feminism, vegetarianism, animal rights. Home: 2309 Carolyn Ct Norman OK 73071-2111 Office: 507 ARW/JA 7435 Reserve Rd Tinker Afb OK 73145 E-mail: jodi.velasco@tinker.af.mil.

VELASQUEZ, ROSE, realtor; b. N.Y.C., Feb. 27, 1947; d. Pascual Negrón and Maria Luisa Vazquez; (div. 1985); 1 child, Lisa Marie Velasquez. Student, Bronx C.C., 1994. Lic. notary N.Y.; lic. in real estate sales. Sec. Commonwealth P.R., N.Y.C., 1966-72; exec. sec. Combustion Equipment Assn., N.Y.C., 1972-81; group adminstr. for internat. Ruder Finn & Rotman, N.Y.C., 1981-86; v.p. adminstrn. GCI Group Internat., N.Y.C., 1986-91; sales agt./broker assoc., sales mgr. Metro-Star, Bronx, N.Y., 1992-97; broker, owner Rose Velasquez, Inc., Realtor, Bronx, 1998—. Sales assoc. rep. Century 21 Met. N.Y./L.I. Brokers Coun., 1993-95, team leader sales assocs. round table discussions, 1994. Fellow Nat. Notary Assn., N.Y. State Assn. Realtors, Bronx-Manhattan Assn. Realtors (grievance com. 1996—, MLS subcom. 1999). Democrat. Avocations: reading, gardening, family activities, theater. Office: Rose Velasquez Inc Realtor 1301 Allerton Ave Bronx NY 10469-5610

VELAZQUEZ, NYDIA M. congresswoman; b. Yabucoa, P.R., Mar. 28, 1953; Grad., U. P.R.; MA, NYU, 1976. Mem. 103rd-108th Congress from 12th N.Y. dist., Washington, 1992—; mem. banking and fin. svcs. com. 105th-108th Congress from 12th N.Y. dist., dem. mem. small bus. com. Ranking Dem. mem. of the Com. on Sml. Bus., 106th Congress. Democrat. Office: US Ho of Reps 2241 Rayburn HOB Washington DC 20515-0001*

VELDEY, BONNIE, special education educator; b. Mpls., Jan. 24, 1960; d. George Joseph III and Ethel Annette Acko;m. Steve Douglas Veldey, June 13, 1991; 1 child, Tyler George. AA, Inver Grove C.C., Inver Grove Heights, Minn., 1989; BA, Coll. St. Catherine, 1991; MA in Spl. Edn., U. St. Thomas, 1998. Sci. tchr. Roma (Tex.) Ind. Sch. Dist., 1991-92; spl. edn. tchr. Clark County Sch. Dist., Las Vegas, Nev., 1996-99; pvt. practice spl. edn. tchr. Mpls., 1999—2001; tchr. spl. edn. Mpls. (Minn.) Pub. Schs., 2001—. Democrat. Roman Catholic. Home: 4331 Minnehaha Ave Minneapolis MN 55406-3908

VELEZ-MITCHELL, ANITA, entertainer, writer; b. Vieques, P.R., Feb. 2, 1922; d. Francisco and Lucille Rieckehoff Velez; m. Pearse Mitchell (dec. July 1983); children: Gloria Vando, Jane; m. Erasmo Vaudo. Studied with, José Ferrer, Lajos Egri, Gene Frankel, Luigi, Katherine Dunham, Carlo Mazzone, Lydia Chaliapin, Peter Johl. Tchr. poetry for tchrs. & writers Pub. Schs.; instr. Am. Mus. Natural History, N.Y.C., 1975—80; tchr. jazz workshop Marina Svetlova Dance Ctr., Vt.; pvt. acting, pub. presentation, diction coach. Dir.: (plays) Salsa of Hispanic Women, The Sharks in West Side Story, The Perils of Chencha, U Are Who You Eat, Our Wonderful World, Butterflies Are Free (Dir.'s award), The Monkey's Paw (Dir.'s award); (films) Kids Want In; contbr. literary mags.; subject of documentary : Dancing Through Life (Gracie Allen award); performer: (poetry recitals) Columbia U., Bklyn. Coll., The Ctr. for Iberoamerican Writers, The Puerto Rican Heritage House, Writer's Place in Kans. City, The Vieques Mus., (TV series) Plain Clothes Man, (TV films) Lamp Unto My Feet, (TV series) Muscling In; performer: (with Anita Vélez Dancers) The Ed Sullivan Show, the Palace Theatre, Hilton Hotels; performer: (commercials) Dole Pineapple Girl, mambo for Coca Cola, Charmin; performer: (with Cantinflas-Mex.) Hilton Hotels; performer: Ringling Brothers Circus; composer: (films) If at First; dir.: various; author: The Cave Named EGO, 2003, Perils of Chencha, Ripples of the Mind, The Stoop; co-author: The Voice of an Angel, 2002 (Best Film Short award LA Film Fair, 2002); performer: (plays) Anita in West Side Story, (TV Comml.) Hilton Hotels. Spkr. for USMC in Vieques U.N., 2001—03. Named Mother of the Yr., Inst. Puerto Rican Culture, Poet of the Yr., Disting. Woman of Yr., Temas Mag.; recipient Director's award, Latin Am. Theatre Ensemble, Julia de Burgos award, INKY award, La MaMa, 3 Ibero-Am. awards, Tribute, Pan Am. Symphony, 2000; grantee, Thanks Be to Grandmother Winifred Found. Mem.: PEN, SAG, AFA, AGMA, AFTRA, Louis Logan Pleiade, Yale Poets, PEN Poets, The Heritage House P.R., 100 Hispanic Women, Nat. Assn. Puerto Rican Writers, 12th Night Club. Avocations: dance, acting, singing, writing, poet. Home and Office: Primavida Theatre Arts 171 West 57th St New York NY 10019

VELEZ SILVA, XENIA, Puerto Rican government official; Sec. of treasury Puerto Rico, 1999—. Office: Dept of Treasury PO Box 9024140 San Juan PR 00902-4140

VELICER, [illegible] [illegible] Cedar Rapids, Iowa, Aug. 27, 1941; d. Allan J. and Geraldine Frances (Stuart) Schafbuch; m. Leland Frank Velicer, Aug. 17, 1963 (dec. Dec. 2000); children: Mark Allan, Gregory Jon, Daniel James. BS, Iowa State U., 1963, MS, 1966; cert. Elem. Edn., Mich. State U., 1976. Tchr. chemistry Prendergast High Sch., Upper Darby, Pa., 1964-65; tchr. home econs. Cardinal O'Hara High Sch., Springfield, Pa., 1965-66; substitute tchr. Pa., Mich., 1967-76; elem. tchr. Winans Elem. Sch., Waverly, Mich., 1976-78, Wardcliff Elem. Sch., Okemos, Mich., 1978-94; tchr. gifted and talented alternative program grades 4 and 5 Hiawatha Elem. Sch., Okemos, 1994-95; tchr. grade 4 Wardcliff Elem. Sch., 1995-2001; ret., 2001. Computer coord., Great Books coord.; dist. com. mem. math, computer, substance abuse, cable TV, evaluation revision Okemos Pub. Schs., Instrnl. Coun.; del. Mich. Edn. Exch. Opportunity Program, Germany, 1999. Author: (video) Wardcliff School Documentary, 1982, The Integrated Arts Program of the Okemos Elementary Schools, 1983. Citizens adv. com. to develop a five-yr. plan, 1982-83, bldg. utilization adv. com., 1983-84, cmty. use of schs. adv. com., 1984-85, strategic planning steering com., 1989-90, taking our schs. into tomorrow com., 1990-91, bonding election steering com., 1991; chmn. wellness com. Okemos Pub. Schs., 1993-95; bd. dirs. Okemos Music Patrons, 1981-86, pres., 1984-86; faculty rep. PTO; leadership coun. Nat. Inst. Clin. Application Behavioral Medicine, 1998—; chaperone Okemos HS German Club Exch., 1987, Benton Cmty. HS Spanish Club Exch., Mex., 1995, Costa Rica, 1999, Spain, 2001, 03. Recipient Classrooms of Tomorrow Tchr. award Mich. Dept. Edn., 1990. Mem. NEA, NAFE, AARP, Nat. Ret. Tchrs. Assn., Mich. Edn. Assn., Okemos Edn. Assn. (exec. coun.), Mich. Coun. Tchrs. Math., Lansing Woman's Club, Phi Kappa Phi, Omicron Nu, Iota Sigma Pi. Democrat. Avocations: swimming, reading, hiking, travel, cultural events. Home: 2678 Blue Haven Ct East Lansing MI 48823-3804 E-mail: jvelicer@msu.edu.

VELLENGA, KATHLEEN OSBORNE, retired state legislator; b. Alliance, Nebr., Aug. 5, 1938; d. Howard Benson and Marjorie (Menke) Osborne; m. James Alan Vellenga, Aug. 9, 1959; children: Thomas, Charlotte Vellenga Landreau, Carolyn Vellenga Berman. BA, Macalester Coll., 1959. Tchr. St. Paul Pub. Schs., 1959-60, Children's Ctr. Montessori, St. Paul, 1973-74, Children's Ho. Montessori, St. Paul, 1974-79; mem. Minn. Ho. of Reps., St. Paul, 1980-94, mem. tax. com. and rules com., 1991—94, chmn. St. Paul del., 1987—90, chmn. criminal justice div., 1987—90, mem. Dem. steering com., 1981—94, chmn. judiciary, 1991, 92, chmn. edn. fin., 1993—94. Mem. St. Paul Family Svcs. Bd., 1994-95; exec. dir. St. Paul/Ramsey County Children's Initiative, 1994-2000. Chmn. Healthstart, St. Paul, 1987-91; mem. Children, Youth and Families Consortium, 1995-99, Macalester Coll. Bd. Alumni, 1995-2001; chair Minn. Higher Edn. Svcs. Coun., 2000—; mem. Citizens League Bd., Minn., 1999-2002, State Commn. Cmty. Svc., 2000—04; bd. dirs. Sexual Violence Ctr., 2004—. Mem. LWV (v.p. St. Paul chpt. 1979), Minn. Women Elected Ofcls. (vice chair 1994). Democrat. Presbyterian.

VELLUCCI, SHERRY LYNN, library and information science educator; b. Paterson, N.J., Nov. 14, 1948; d. Peter and Eleanor M. Vellucci; m. Robin A. Leaver, June 10, 1988. AB, Rutgers U., 1972; MS in Libr. Sci., Drexel U., 1983; D in Libr. Sci., Columbia U., 1995. Catalog libr. Princeton (N.J.) U., 1977-78; choral libr. Westminster Choir Coll., Princeton, 1978-83, libr. dir., 1983-92; asst. prof. St. John's U., Jamaica, N.Y., 1992-98, assoc. prof., 1998—, dir. divsn. of libr. info. sci.; dir., divsn. libr./info. sci. St. John's Univ. Author: Bibliographic Relationships in Music Catalogs, 1997; co-author: Notes in the Catalog Record, 1989; mem. editl. bd. Cataloging and Classification Quar., 1998—; contbr. chpts. to books and articles to profl. jours. Mem. Internat. Assn. Music Librs. (bd. dirs. 1996-98, pres. 1999—), Music Libr. Assn. (treas. 1986-90, bd. dirs. 1991-93, Spl. Achievement award 1998), Music Libr. Assn., Am. Libr. Assn. (Best of Libr. Resources and Tech. Svcs. award 2001), Spl. Libr. Assn., Beta Phi Mu. Office: St Johns Univ DLIS 8000 Utopia Pkwy Jamaica NY 11439-0001 E-mail: velluccs@stjohns.edu.

VENABLE, LISA ANITA, computer programmer; b. Durham, N.C., Jan. 21, 1963; d. Robert Nathaniel and Florence Rebecca (Daniel) V. BS, U. Ga., Athens, 1985, Fla. A&M U., 1988; MS, Fla. State U., 1999. Computer programmer, analyst I State of Fla. Dept. Edn., Tallahassee, 1990-93, computer programer, analyst II, 1993-99. Reading tutor Lit. Vols., Leon County, Fla., 1993-2001, vol. Leon County Pub. Libr., 2001. Avocations: sewing, reading, music. Home: 403 W 15th Ave Cordele GA 31015-2432

VENDELA, model; b. Sweden; With Ford Models, Inc., N.Y., 1986, Elizabeth Arden, [illegible]. Appeared on cover of Sports Illustrated Swimsuit Edition, 1993. Office: Ford Models Inc 344 E 59th St New York NY 10022-1513

VENDITTI, CLELIA ROSE See PALMER, CHRISTINE

VENDLER, HELEN HENNESSY, literature educator, poetry critic; b. Boston, Mass., Apr. 30, 1933; d. George and Helen (Conway) Hennessy; 1 son, David. AB, Emmanuel Coll., 1954; PhD, Harvard U., 1960, U. Oslo, 1981; DLitt (hon.), Smith Coll., 1980, Kenyon Coll., 1982, U. Hartford, 1985, Union Coll., 1986, Columbia U., 1987, Washington U., 1991, Marlboro Coll., 1989, Yale U., 2000; DHL (hon.), Fitchburg State U., 1990, Dartmouth Coll., 1992, U. Mass., 1992, Bates Coll., 1992, U. Toronto, Ont., Can., 1992, Trinity Coll., Dublin, Ireland, 1993, U. Cambridge, 1997, Nat. U., Ireland, 1998, Wabash Coll., 1998, U. Mass, Dartmouth, 2000, Yale U., 2000, U. Aberdeen, 2000, Tufts U., 2001, Amherst Coll., 2002, Colby Coll., 2003. Instr. Cornell U., Ithaca, NY, 1960-63; lectr. Swarthmore (Pa.) Coll. and Haverford (Pa.) Coll., 1963-64; asst. prof. Smith Coll., Northampton, Mass., 1964-66; assoc. prof. Boston U., 1966-68, prof., 1968-85. Fulbright lectr. U. Bordeaux, France, 1968-69; vis. prof. Harvard U., 1981-85, Kenan prof., 1985—, Porter U. prof., 1990—, assoc. acad. dean, 1987-92, sr. fellow Harvard Soc. Fellows, 1981-93; poetry critic New Yorker, 1978-99; mem. ednl. adv. bd. Guggenheim Found., 1991-2001, Pulitzer Prize Bd., 1991-99. Author: Yeats's Vision and the Later Plays, 1963, On Extended Wings: Wallace Stevens' Longer Poems, 1969, The Poetry of George Herbert, 1975, Part of Nature, Part of Us, 1980, The Odes of John Keats, 1983, Wallace Stevens: Words Chosen Out of Desire, 1984; editor: Harvard Book of Contemporary American Poetry, 1985, Voices and Visions: The Poet in America, 1987, The Music of What Happens, 1988, Soul Says, 1995, The Given and the Made, 1995, The Breaking of Style, 1995, Poems, Poets, Poetry, 1995, The Art of Shakespeare's Sonnets, 1997, Seamus Heaney, 1998; Coming of Age as a Poet, 2003. Bd. dirs. Nat. Humanities Ctr., 1989—93. Recipient Lowell prize, 1969, Explicator prize, 1969, award Nat. Inst. Arts and Letters, 1975, Radcliffe Grad. Soc. medal, 1978, Nat. Book Critics award, 1980, Keats-Shelley Assn. award, 1994, Truman Capote award, 1996; Fulbright fellow, 1954, AAUW fellow, 1959, Guggenheim fellow, 1971-72, Am. Coun. Learned Socs. fellow, 1971-72, NEH fellow, 1980, 85, 94, Overseas fellow Churchill Coll., Cambridge, 1980, Charles Stewart Parnell fellow Magdalene Coll., Cambridge, 1996, hon. fellow, 1996—. Mem. MLA (exec. coun. 1972-75, pres. 1980), AAAL, English Inst. (trustee 1977-85), Am. Acad. Arts and Scis. (v.p. 1992-95), Norwegian Acad. Letters and Sci., Am. Philos. Soc. (Jefferson medal 2000), Phi Beta Kappa. Home: 54 Trowbridge St # 2 Cambridge MA 02138-4113 Office: Harvard U Dept English Barker Center Cambridge MA 02138-3929 Office Phone: 617-496-6028.

VENEMAN, ANN M. secretary of agriculture; b. Modesto, Calif., June 29, 1949; d. John G. and Nita D. (Bomberger) V. BA in polit. sci., U. Calif., Davis, 1970; M in pub. policy, U. Calif., Berkeley, 1971; JD, U. Calif., 1976. Bar: Calif. 1976, U.S. Supreme Ct. 1981. Atty. San Francisco Bay Area Rapid Transit Dist., 1976-78; dep. pub. defender City of Modesto, 1978-80; ptnr. Damrell, Damrell & Nelson, Modesto, 1980-86; asst. to adminstr. Fgn. Agrl. Svc., 1986-87, assoc. adminstr., 1987-89; dep. undersec. Internat. Affairs and Commodity Programs, 1989-91; dep. sec. U.S. Dept. Agriculture, Washington, 1991-93; sec. Calif. Dept. Food and Agr., 1995—99, U.S. Dept. Agriculture, Washington, 2001—. Office: USDA Office Sec 14th & Independence Ave SW Washington DC 20250-0001*

VENERABLE, SHIRLEY MARIE, gifted education educator; b. Washington, Nov. 12, 1931; d. John Henry and Jessie Josephine (Young) Washington; m. Wendell Grant Venerable, Feb. 15, 1959; children: Angela Elizabeth Maria Venerable-Joyner, Wendell Mark. PhB, Northwestern U., 1963; MA, Roosevelt U., 1976, postgrad., 1985. Cert. in diagnostic and prescriptive reading, gifted edn., finger math., fine arts, Ill. Tchr. Lewis Champlin Sch., 1963-74, John Hay Acad., Chgo., 1975-87, Leslie Lewis Elem. Sch., Chgo., 1988-99, Robert Emmet Sch., Chgo., 1999—; self employed tutorial programs, 1999—. Sponsor Reading Marathon Club, Chgo., 1991—; co-creator Project SMART-Stimulating Math. and Reading Techniques John Hay Acad., Chgo., 1987-90, curriculum coord., 1985-87; creative dance student, tchr. Kathryn Duham Sch., N.Y.C., 1955-56; creative dance tchr. Doris Patterson Dance Sch., Washington, 1953-55; recorder evening divsn. Northwestern U., Chgo., 1956-62; exch. student tchr. Conservatory Dance Movements, Chgo., 1958-59; art cons. Chgo. Pub. Sch., 1967. Author primary activities Let's Act and Chat, 1991-94, Teaching Black History Through Classroom Tours, 1989-90. Solicitor, vol. United Negro Coll. Fund, Chgo., 1994; sponsor Ward Reading Assn. Marathon, Chgo., 1991-94, 99; active St. Giles Coun. Cath. Women, 1985-96; vol. REAC Ctr. Programs Books, Info., Literacy and Learning, 1997-98. Recipient Meritorious award United Negro Coll. Fund, 1990, 94, Recognition award Alderman Percy Giles, Chgo., 1993. Mem.: ASCD (assoc. Recognition of Svcs. award 1989), Internat. Reading Assn., Nat. Women of Achievement Assn. (Chgo. chpt.), Phi Delta Kappa, Sigma Gamma Rho (Delta Sigma grad. chpt. 1963—93, Sigma chpt. 1992, Eta Xi Sigma chpt.), Eta Xi Sigma (Pearl award for excellence in edn. 1997). Roman Catholic. Home: 1108 N Euclid Ave Oak Park IL 60302-1219

VENNUM, JOAN FAY, artist; b. Long Branch, NJ, July 12, 1929; d. John Bourke and Edna Frances (Fay) V.; m. Ted Naomi Kurahara, 1954; children: Mie, Thomas, Leon. BFA, Washington U., 1951; MFA, U. Ill., 1953. Represented by Sundaram Tagore Gallery, NYC. One-woman shows include Galleri Heland, Stockholm, Sweden, 1982, Columbia Univ., N.Y.C., 1984, Konstmuseet Galleri Astley, Uttersberg, Sweden, 1991, Gallieret, Eskilstuna, Sweden, 1992, Lilla Galleriet, Umeå, Sweden, Galleri Astley, Seattle, Wash., 1992, Konstmuseet Galleri, Astley, Uttersberg, Sweden, 1998, Cewe Konstforening, Nykoping, Sweden, 1998, Lilla Galleriet, Umea, Sweden, 1999, Galleri Sjohasten, Nykoping, Sweden, 2000, Sundarm Tagore Gallery, N.Y.C., 2001, 03; exhibited in group shows at Westbeth, N.Y.C., 1980, Fairleigh Dickenson U., 1981, Oil and Steel Gallery, N.Y.C., 1983, City Gallery, N.Y.C., 1984, Galleri Astley, Uttersberg, Sweden, 1985, 87, Grafiska Sallskapet, Stockholm, Selected Graphics, 1988, Maryland Inst., Balt., 1992, Anita Shopolsky Gallery, N.Y.C., Galleri Astley, Seattle, 1993, Printmaking Workshop Gallery, N.Y.C., 1994, Stockholm Art Fair, 1997, Gallery Astley, Uttersberg, Sweden, 1998, Sundaram Tagore Gallery, 2002, others; represented in public collections including Museo Civico Taverna, Italy, N.Y. Public Libr., City of Falun, Sweden, Bklyn. Mus., N.Y.C., Printmaking Workshop, N.Y.C., The Power Collection, Sydney, Australia, Lincoln Ctr. Libr., N.Y.C., Konstmuseet, Uttersberg, Skandia Forsakringsbolag, Stockholm; co-producer: (with Susan Brockman and Sally Gross) (film) Lee's Ferry, 1982. Studio: 78 Greene St New York NY 10012-5100 Office Phone: 212-966-2336.

VENRICK, KRISTIE LUND, mathematics educator; b. Longmont, Colo., Oct. 7, 1955; d. Myron Joseph and Christine Lorraine Thompson; m. James Thomas Venrick, Feb. 14, 1986; 1 child, Emily Lund. BS, Bethany Coll., 1977; MA, U. No. Colo., 2002. Tchr. St. Vrain Valley Schs., Longmont, Colo., 1978—2000, math. coord., 2000—. Named Educator of Yr., Longmont C. of C., 1996; recipient Presdl. award for Excellence in Math. and Sci. Tchg., White House and NSF, 2000. Mem.: AAUW, Nat. Coun. Suprs. Math., Nat. Coun. Tchrs. Math., Phi Delta Kappa. Republican. Lutheran. Home: 3567 Columbia Dr Longmont CO 80503 Office: St Vrain Valley Sch Dist 395 S Pratt Pky Longmont CO 80501

VENTO, M. THÉRÈSE, lawyer; b. N.Y.C., June 30, 1951; d. Anthony Joseph and Margaret (Stechert) V.; m. Peter Michael MacNamara, Dec. 23, 1977; children: David Miles, Elyse Anne. BS, U. Fla., 1974, JD, 1976. Bar: Fla. 1977, U.S. Dist. Ct. (so. and mid. dists.) Fla. 1982, U.S. Ct. Appeals (5th and 11th cirs.) 1981, U.S. Supreme Ct. 1985. Clk. to presiding justice U.S. Dist. Ct. (so. dist.) Fla., Miami, 1976-78; assoc. Mahoney, Hadlow & Adams, Miami, 1978-79, Shutts & Bowen, Miami, 1979-84, ptnr., 1985-95; founding ptnr. Gallwey Gillman Curtis & Vento, P.A., Miami, 1995—. Trustee Miami Art Mus., 1988—, v.p., 1999—; trustee The Beacon Coun., 1995-97, Law Sch. Alumni Coun., U. Fla., 1994—. Fellow Am. Bar Found.; mem. Dade County Bar Assn. (dir. young lawyers sect. 1978-83, editor newsletter 1981-83), Fla. Assn. for Women Lawyers, Fla. Bar Assn. (bd. govs., young lawyers div. 1983-85, civil procedure rules com. 1983-90, exec. coun. trial lawyers sect. 1996—), The Miami Forum (v.p. 1987-88, bd. dirs. 1989-91, co-pres. 2001-2002). Home: 3908 Main Hwy Miami FL 33133-6513 Office: Gallwey Gillman Curtis & Vento PA 200 SE 1st St Ste 1100 Miami FL 33131-1912 E-mail: TVento@GGCVH.com.

VENTRESS, MARY ELLEN, school system administrator; b. Lafayette, La., Feb. 8, 1943; d. James Andrew and Mary Eloise (Pace) Banfield; m. Vernon Mark Ventress Jr., Nov. 20, 1965; children: Mark Andrew, Jennifer Lyle. BA, La. State U., 1965; MEd, U. So. La., 1981. Tchr. East Baton Rouge Parish, 1965-67, Lafayette Parish, 1972-76; asst. prin. Lafayette Parish-Edgar Martin Sch., Lafayette, 1976-86; prin. Lafayette Parish-Broadmoor Elem. Sch., 1986-91, Lafayette Parish-Edgar Martin Mid. Sch., 1991—. Mem. Lafayette Parish Prin.'s Assn. (sec. 1986-87, v.p. 1987-88, pres. 1988-89), La. Assn. Computer Using Educators (Outstanding Computer Educator 1987, Nat. Excellence award 1989-90). Home: 103 Berwick Cir Lafayette LA 70508-6439 Office: Edgar Martin Mid Sch 401 Broadmoor Blvd Lafayette LA 70503-5201

VENTURA, JACQUELINE N. retired nurse, researcher; b. Chgo., Sept. 17, 1942; d. Frank Joseph and Ellen Sarah (Healey) Ventura. Diploma, St. Francis Sch. Nursing, Evanston, Ill., 1963; BS, DePaul U., Chgo., 1967; MS, U. Wis., 1972, PhD, 1975-80. RN, Ill. Staff nurse Hines VA Hosp., Maywood, Ill., 1963-67; team leader US AID, Vinh Long, Vietnam, 1967-69; staff nurse Childrens Meml. Hosp., Chgo., 1969-70; clin. nurse specialist U. Wis. Hosps. and Clinics, Madison, 1972-75; nurse cons., instr. U. Wis. Sch. Nursing, Madison, 1975-78; asst. prof. nursing U. Calif., San Francisco, 1981-89, nurse rschr. dept. radiology, 1989-95; clin. rsch. assoc. Dendreon Corp., Seattle and Mountain View, Calif., 1996—2002, ret., 2003. Recipient Civilian Svc. award Govt. of South Vietnam, 1969. Mem.: AAUW, Drug Info Assn., Women's Overseas League, Sigma Theta Tau. Home: 1530 5th Ave San Francisco CA 94122-3835

VENTURACCI, TONI MARIE, artist, substitute educator; b. Battle Mountain, N.V., Nov. 19, 1958; d. Tony Simone Ancho and Deanna Paul; m. Steven Louie Venturacci, July 28, 1979; children: Daniel Steven, Kassi Marie. A in Bus., W.N.C.C., Fallon, N.V., 1999. Substitute educator Churchill County Sch. Dist., Fallon, Nev., 1998—2001; pvt. art tchr. Nev., 2000—01. Organizer fundraisers Nev. State H.S. Rodeo, 1998—2001. Mem.: Am. Paint Horse Assn. (accomplished painter), Am. Qtr. Horse Assn. (accomplished breeder). Republican. Roman Catholic. Avocations: horses, art work, sewing, cooking, rodeoing. Home: 445 Venturacci Ln Fallon NV 89406

VENTURINI, TISHA LEA, professional soccer player; b. Modesto, Calif., Mar. 3, 1973; Degree in phys. edn., U. N.C. Mem. U.S. Women's Nat. Soccer Team. Mem. championship team CONCACAF, Montreal, 1994. Recipient Gold medal Centennial Olympic Games, 1996, Silver medal world Univ. Games, 1993, Hermann trophy, 1994; mem. championship team CONCACAF, Montreal, 1994; named Player of Yr. Mo. Athletic Club, 1994. Office: c/o US Soccer Fedn 1801 S Prairie Ave # 1811 Chicago IL 60616-1319

VENZER, DOLORES, artist; b. Atlanta, Ga., May 21, 1933; d. Simon Seymour I and Pearl Levy Moltack; m. Stanley Jerry Sater, June 1955; children: Robyn Degnan, Simon Sater, Denise Landwerlen; m. Alan Marvin Venzer, June 29, 1974; children: Sherrie Nowacki, Diane Ransen, Ellen Venzer. BFA, U. Ga., 1954. Artist 21st Century Gallery, Denver, Philinda Gallery, Edwards, Colo., Forms Gallery, Del Ray, Fla., Naked Horse Gallery, Scottsdale, Az., Artists Atelier of Atlanta, S.W. Accents Gallery, Woodstock, Vt., Hansen Gallery, Knoxville, Tenn. Co-owner past pres. Artist's Atelier of Atlanta, 1992-99; judge Callaway Garden's Art Exhibit, 1998. Recipient Merit award, Seasoned Eye 3, Modern Maturity Mag., 1990, Honorable Mention award, Grumbacher Hall of Fame, 1995, Artist's Choice award, Callaway Garden's, 1999, Grumbacher Choice Creative Artists Guild, Dalton, Ga., 1994. Mem. Ga. Coun. Arts, Artists Atelier Atlanta, Atlanta Arts Ctr., A.R.T. Station, S. Cobb Arts Alliance, Dekalb Coun. Arts. Republican. Jewish. Office: Artists Atelier Atlanta 800 Miami Cir NE Ste 200 Atlanta GA 30324-3048

VERANI, PATRICIA LEWIS, sculptor; b. L.I., N.Y., Jan. 2, 1927; d. Tracy Hammond Lewis and Esther Tufts Latting; m. Osvaldo Verani, Apr. 24, 1950; children: Michela E., Margherita, Daniela E., Giovanni M. Diploma with honors, Boston Mus. Sch. Fine Arts, 1948. Co-owner Verani's Restaurant, Manchester, N.H., 1955-65; sec. Verani Real Estate Londonderry, N.H., 1965-77; technician H&O Dental, Manchester, 1977-78; freelance sculptor Londonderry, 1978—. Commd. U.S. Capitol Hist. Soc. for Bill of Rights, 1991. Sculptor (8 ft. bronze statue) Fighting Black Bear of U. Maine, 1979; sculptor, designer U.S. Commemmorative Silver Dollar, 1987, Olympic U.S. Commemmorative Silver Dollar, 1988, Commemmorative Half Dollar for Congress, 1989, ; designer The Flagbearer Olympic Coin, 1996. Treas. Londonderry PTA, 1961-65; vol. artist Londonderry Hist. Soc., 1979, 94-97, 2003-04; vol. Save Outdoor Sculpture, N.H., 1994; advisor Londonderry Commons Com., 1995—. Mrs. David Hunt Traveling scholar Boston Mus. Sch., 1948, Mrs. Louis Bennet Bas Relief prize nat. Sculpture Soc., 1989. Fellow, New Eng. Sculptors Assn. (charter); Master, Copley Soc. Boston; Mem. Am. Numismatic Assn. (Gold medal for medallic excellence 1995), Nat. Sculpure Soc., N.H. Art Assn., Pen and Brush, Am. Medallic Sculpture Assn. Avocations: gardening, swimming, coin and stamp collecting. Home and Office: 77 Page Rd Londonderry NH 03053-2114

VERBESSELT, MARTINE CAROLE, primary school educator; b. Brussels, Oct. 20, 1955; arrived in U.S., 1977; d. Joseph Herkelboek and Jaenine Van den Branden; m. Yvan Verbesselt, July 20, 1977; 1 child, Virginie. Degree in tchg., Ecole Pedagogique Berkendael, Brussels, 1977; cert. 2d lang. specialist, U. Mons, Belgium, 1984; degree in elem. tchg., Xavier U., 1993. Cert. tchg. K-8. French tchr. CODOFIL, Lake Charles, La., 1977—80, 1982—87; immersion tchr. of French Kansas City (Mo.) Sch. Dist., 1987—88; partial and full immersion French tchr. Cin. Pub. Schs., 1989—. Mem. adv. bd. PTO/PTA Cin. Pub. Schs., 1989—2003. Recipient Active Mem. award, LSDMC, Cin., 2001—02. Mem.: Immersion Can. Avocations: technology, photography, snorkeling. Home: 6591 Pullman Ct West Chester OH 45069

VERDEHR, ELSA LUDEWIG (ELSA LUDEWIG VERDERBER), music educator; d. Stephan H. J. and Josephine Marie (Tetz) Ludewig; m. Walter Verdehr (Verderber), Sept. 11, 1971. MusB, MusB in Edn., Oberlin (Ohio) Conservatory, 1957; MusM, Eastman Sch. of Music, 1962; MusD, Eastman Sch. Music, 1962. Disting. prof. of music Mich. State U., East Lansing, 1962—. Clarinetist Verdehr Trio, East Lansing, Mich., 1972—; clarinetist Richards Wind Quintet Mich. State U., 1972—92; prin. clarinetist Grand Teton Music Festival Orch., 1974—. Musician: (CD's) 20 recordings of The Making of a Medium Series, (TV series) Verdehr Trio on major composers of today: Alan Hovhanness; Ned Rorem; Thea Musgrave, Joan Tower, Libby Larsen, Gian Carlo Menotti, Karel Husa, Leslie Bassett, Gunther Schulle, 50 nat. and internat. clarinet festivals; commd. over 160 new works for violin-clarinet-piano with husband Walter. Mem.: Internat. Clarinet Assn., [illegible] (hon.). Office: Mich State Univ Sch of Music West Circle Dr East Lansing MI 48824

VERDILL, ELAINE DENISE, artisan; b. Bellefontaine, Ohio, Nov. 5, 1955; d. Margaret (Miller) V. BS, Bowling Green State U., 1978. Coord. info. svcs. JILA, U. Colo., Boulder, 1990-96, budget analyst, 1996—. Mem. Hand-Weavers' Guild of Boulder. Avocation: photography. Office: JILA U Colo Cb 440 Boulder CO 80309-0001

VERDUIN, BERT M. real estate executive; b. Benton, Ark., Feb. 9, 1947; d. Elvis Lee and Helen Lee (McBride) Moses; m. Michael Hankins Verduin, May 23, 1970; children— Valerie Ann, Clinton Logan. AAS, Brookhaven Coll., 1982; BBA, U. North Tex., 1996; grad. real estate designation George Leonard Sch. Real Estate. Lic. real estate broker; CPA; housing credit cert. profl. Acct., Realty Devel. Corp., Dallas, 1970-77; owner, mgr. Tax Service, Dallas, 1977-83; sr. v.p., contr. Realty Devel. Corp., Dallas, 1983-87; pres. Strobe Mgmt. Svcs., Inc., Dallas, Tyler, 1987-94, controller Focus Asset Mgmt. Group, 1994-2002, sr. v.p., contr. Accolade Property Mgmt., 2002—. Mem. Apt. Assn. Greater Dallas. Republican. Mem. Ch. of Christ. Avocations: reading; crafts. Office: 621 Cowboys Pkwy 200 Irving TX 75063

VERED, RUTH, art gallery director, owner; b. Tel Aviv, Sept. 26, 1940; d. Abraham and Helen Rosenblum; children: Sharon, Oren. BA in Art History with honors, Bezalel U., Jerusalem, 1964. Freelance art cons., Israel and N.Y.C., 1965-75; dir. Vered Gallery, East Hampton, N.Y., 1977—. Exhibited at Vered Gallery. Sgt. paratroops Israeli Army, 1958-60. Home: 891 Park Ave New York NY 10021-0326 Office: Vered Gallery 68 Park Pl East Hampton NY 11937-2407 E-mail: vered@mindspring.com.

VERGANO, LYNN (MARILYNN BETTE VERGANO), artist; b. NYC, Nov. 14; d. George and Sis Anagnostis (Helaine Haas); children: Scott, Stephen, Sandy, Sefton. Student, Pratt Inst., 1959-60; BA, NYU, Heights, 1963; MA, NYU, 1964. Lectr. art Morris County Coll., 1982. Lectr. UN Pan Pacific and S.E. Asia Women's Assn., N.Y. chpt., 1996, 2001, AAUW, Caldwell, N.J. chpt. 1998, Nat. Soc. of Arts and Letters N.J. chpt. 1998, 2001, AAUW, Somerset Hills, N.J. chpt., 2001, Fortnightly Club, Summit, N.J., 2001, Somerset Art Assn., 2002, Summit Coll. Club, 2003; art judge, juror Sussex County Arts and Heritage Coun. Skylands, Sussex County C.C., N.J., 2003. Author, illustrator: Paintings by Lynn Vergano, 1980, Paintings by Lynn Vergano, 1998; one-woman shows include Paper Mill Playhouse, N.J., 1976, 79, 83, Fairleigh Dickinson U., N.J., 1977, Drew U., N.J., 1977, Rutgers U., N.J., 1978-79, Hong Kong Arts Ctr., 1980, Am. Univ. Alumni, Bangkok, Thailand, 1980, Caldwell Coll., N.J., 1980, União Cultural Brasil-Estados Unidos, São Paulo, Brazil, 1982, Galleria Fenice, Venice, Italy, 1985, St. Sophia Mus., Istanbul, Turkey, 1988, Nat. Arts Club, N.Y.C., 1989, Centreplace, Hamilton, New Zealand, 1990, Women's Nat. Rep. Club, N.Y.C., 1997, UN Pan Pacific and S.E. Women's Assn., 2001, Chang Gung Meml. Hosp., Kaohsiung, Taiwan, 2002, Internat. PUbl. Mofa News & Report, Ministry Fgn. Affairs, Taiwan, 2002; exhibited in group shows at Monmouth Mus., Lincroft, N.J., 1976, 77, 82, Morris Mus., Morristown, N.J., 1977, 78, 2003, N.J. State Capital Mus., Trenton, 1979, Nat. Audubon Artists, N.Y.C., 1981, Salmagundi Club, N.Y.C., 1981, World Trade Ctr., N.Y., 1981, Nat. Arts Club, N.Y.C., 1981—, Bergen Mus., Paramus, N.J., 1983, Macculloch Hall Hist. Mus., N.J., Morristown, 1984, 87, 89, 92, 96, Lincoln Ctr., N.Y.C., 1987, 2002, Bklyn. Botanic Gardens, N.Y., 1987, Seton Hall U., South Orange, N.J., 1998, Johnson & Johnson, New Brunswick, N.J., 2000, others; exhbn. UN Pan Pacific and S.E. Asia Women's Assn.-N.Y. chpt. N.Y. Acad. Sci., 1998, 2001, Nabisco World Hdqrs., Hanover, N.J., 1999, Reeves Reed Arboretum, Summit Coll. Club, 1999. Pres., chpt. charter mem., 1969-70, hon. mem. Welcome Wagon Club, Randolph, N.J., 1969—. Recipient UN 25th Anniversary Creative Writing award, 1970, John H. Miller award Morris County Coll., 1979, Grumbacher gold medallion, 1984, Torch award NYU, 1993. Mem. AAUW (hon.), Nat. Arts Club (exhibiting), Nat. Soc. Arts and Letters (exec. bd. N.J. chpt. 1979—), Federated Art Assns. N.J. (trustee 1982—, pres., chmn. bd. dirs. 1982-88, Heritage plaque 1989), N.Y. Acad. Scis., Kenilworth Art Assn. (hon.), Millburn-Short Hills Arts Ctr., Am. Soc. of Geolinguistics (bd. dirs. 2003-), Shanghai-Tiffin Club (hon., Disting. Svc. award 1998), Delta Kappa Gamma (N.Y.C. chpt., hon.).

VERGER, JOANNE, state representative; Attended, Northwestern State U., La. State U. Cert. speech therapist. State rep., dist. 9 Oreg. House Rep., Salem, 2001—; former mayor City of Coos Bay; co-owner Verger Chrysler. Mem. com. Rules, Restricting, and Pub. Affairs, Transportation. Mem. state bd. Oreg. Easter Seal Soc.; chair campaign United Way; mem. bd. Southwest Oreg. C.C. Found. Named One of Oreg.'s 6 Outstanding Women, 1993. Office: 900 Court St NE H-372 Salem OR 97301

VERGUN, OLGA VICTOROVNA, physiologist, researcher; b. Isilkul, Russia, Jan. 28, 1968; d. Victor V. and Alexandra I. Vergun. PhD, Ulyanovsk Pedagogical U., Russia, 1994. Sr. scientist Inst. of Gen. Pathology and Pathophysiology Russian Acad. of Med. Sci., Moscow, 1994—97; rsch. fellow Dept. Physiology, U. Coll. London, 1997—2000; rsch. assoc. Dept. Pharmacology, U. Pitts., 2000—. Fellow, Royal Soc./NATO, 1997—98, Wellcome Trust Internat., 1998—99. Mem.: Am. Soc. for Neuroscience, Am. Biophysical Soc., The Physiol. Soc. Achievements include research in the role of Mitochondria in Neurotoxicity. Office: Univ Pitts W1304 BST 200 Lothrop Str Pittsburgh PA PA152

VERHESEN, ANNA MARIA HUBERTINA, social worker; b. Heerenveen, Friesland, Netherland, Dec. 6, 1932; came to U.S., 1968; d. Hendrikus H. and Henrika C. (Kluessjen) V. BS, Mercy Coll. of Detroit, 1981; MA, Sienna Height, Adrian, Mich., 1992. Childcare worker Schiedam, Netherland, 1952-54; social worker Rotterdam Halfweg, Netherland, 1954-59; childcare worker Mt. St. Ann's Home, Worcester and Lawrence, Mass., 1968-70; chem. dependency social worker St. Vincent Med. Ctr., Toledo, Ohio, 1970-75; social worker St. Joseph Hosp., Nashua, N.H., 1975-78; vocation dir. Grey Nuns, Lexington, Mass., 1978-79; coord. community svcs. St. Vincents Med. Ctr., Toledo, 1981-91; pvt. practice clin. therapist Sylvania, Ohio, 1992—. Alcohol/drug addiction/mental health counselor for ex-prisoners; founder St. Vincent Med. Ctr. Alcoholism Detox and Rehab. Unit, Toledo, 1970-75. Co-founder Transitional Residences for the Homeless, Toledo, 1981-90, Ohio Coalition for the Homeless, Columbus, 1982-89; co-founder of a home for persons with AIDS; co-chair City of Toledo Housing Policy, 1985-90; coord. Housing Now, Toledo, 1988-90. Recipient Woman of Achievement award Women in Communication, Toledo, 1986, Spirit of '87 award N.W. Ordinance and U.S. Constn. Bicentennial Commn., Toledo, 1987, Gov.'s Spl. Recognition award, 1988, Man for Others award St. John's High Sch., 1991; named Woman of Toledo, St. Vincent Med. Ctr. Aux., 1988, Ohio Ho. of Reps., 1987; featured in various mags. Roman Catholic. Home: 2015 N Mccord Rd Apt 127 Toledo OH 43615-3071 Office: Elliott and Assocs Inc 5600 Monroe St Sylvania OH 43560-2731 E-mail: hubertina@buckeye-express.com.

VERHOEK, SUSAN ELIZABETH, botany educator; b. Columbus, Ohio, 1942; m. S.E. Williams; 1 child. Student, Carleton Coll., 1960-62; BA, Ohio Wesleyan U., 1964; MA, Ind. U., 1966; PhD, Cornell U., 1975. Herbarium supr. Mo. Bot. Garden, St. Louis, 1966-70; asst. prof. Lebanon Valley Coll., Annville, Pa., 1974-82, assoc. prof., 1982-85, prof., 1985—. Vis. researcher Cornell U., Ithaca, N.Y., 1982-83; content cons. Merrill Pub. Co., 1987-89; vis. profl. Chgo. Bot. Garden, 1991. Author: How to Know the Spring

Flowers, 1982; contbr. articles to profl. jours., newspapers, and bulls. Trustee Lebanon Valley Coll., Annville, 1979-82, 84-90, 92-98; dir. Lebanon Valley Coll. Arboretum, 1996—. Mem. Soc. for Econ. Botany (pres. 1985-86), Bot. Soc. Am., Am. Assn. Bot. Gardens and Arboreta. Office: Lebanon Valley Coll Dept Biology Annville PA 17003-0501 Office Phone: 717-867-6178. Business E-Mail: verhoek@lvc.edu.

VERI, FRANCES GAIL, musician, educator; b. Lancaster, Pa., Dec. 6, 1942; d. Frank Americus Veri and Ada Margaret Kirk; m. Michael George Jamanis, Aug. 29, 1964; 1 child, Michael Thomas Jamanis. BS, Juilliard Sch., 1964, MS, 1965. Faculty Hartt Coll. Music, Hartford, Conn., 1964—66, Lebanon Valley Coll., Annville, Pa., 1966—71; artist-in -residence Franklin Marshall Coll., Lancaster, 1971—74; duo-pianist Veri & Jamanis, Columbia Artists, NYC, 1974—88; co-founder Pa. Acad. Music, Lancaster, 1989, dean, 1991—; pres. Prince Prodns., Inc., Lancaster, 1999—. Advisor Nat. Fedn. Music Clubs, 1991—96. Walter Damrosch scholar, Fontainebleau Sch. Fine Arts, 1969. Mem.: ASCAP. Episcopalian. Avocations: poetry, writing. Home: 1109 Marietta Ave Lancaster PA 17603 Office: Pa Acad Music 42 N Prince St Lancaster PA 17603 E-mail: verijamanis@aol.com.

VERLEY, BARBARA ANN, music educator; b. Nashville, Tenn., Aug. 4, 1953; d. James Edward and Mary Leila Goodwin; m. Robert Alan Verley, Dec. 21, 1990. Elem./Jr. High Adminstrv. Lic., Ind. State U., 1994—96; BA, U. of Evansville, MS in sch. guidance and counseling, 1992—94, MA, 1976—79. Music tchr. Castle Jr. H.S., Newburgh, Ind., 1976—, Wash. Elem. Sch., Evansville, Ind., 1975—76. Choral condr. Castle Jr. H.S., Newburgh, Ind., 1976—92, teacher's credit union faculty rep., 1979—; castle h.s. summer band camp coach Castle H.S., 1984—86; academic bowl coach for dramatic interpretation, prose, and poetry Castle Jr. H.S., 1985—2001, talent show coord., 1987—; ind. state sch. music assn. judge ISSMA, Ind., 1988; student/tchr. sponsorship program leader for at-risk students Castle Jr. H.S., 1988—90, performance-based accreditation corre-late chair, 1988—90; orchestral musician Bethel Temple Cmty. Ch., Evansville, 1989—2002; faculty adv. chair Castle Jr. H.S., 1992—93, adminstrv. intern, 1993—94, reality store project co-chair, 1993—94; north ctrl. assn. team mem. Ind. State U., Terre Haute, 1993—94; profl. devel. com. mem. Castle Jr. H.S., Newburgh, Ind., 1999—2002, student discipline-free com. chair, 1999—2002; orchestral musician First Christian Ch., Newburgh, 2001—; student facilitator for strengthening families program Castle Jr. H.S., 2002—03, sect. 504 com. mem., departmental lead tchr., sch. improvement com. team mem., 2001. Musician Bethel Temple Cmty. Ch., Evansville, Ind., 1989—2002, First Christian Ch., Newburgh, Ind., 2001—02. Nominee Disney's Outstanding Tchr. of the Yr. award, Disney, 1998, 2001; recipient musician, All-American Youth Honor Band in Europe, 1971. Mem.: Ind. State Teacher's Assn. (assoc.; faculty rep. 1983—85), NEA (assoc.), Music Educators Nat. Conf. (assoc.), Phi Kappa Phi (assoc.), Chi Sigma Iota (assoc.), Sigma Alpha Iota (assoc.), Christian. Achievements include initiating student self-esteem programs. Avocations: computer, cars, flute, keyboards, bass. Home: 7377 Bosma DR Newburgh IN 47630-9625 Office: Castle Junior HS 2800 HWY 261 PO Box 677 Newburgh IN 47629-0677 Personal E-mail: bvgtp@msn.com.

VERLICH, JEAN ELAINE, writer, public relations consultant; b. McKeesport, Pa., July 5, 1950; d. Matthew Louis and Irene (Tomko) V.; m. S(tanley) Wayne Wright, Sept. 29, 1979 (div. June 1988). Student, Bucknell U., 1968-69; BA, U. Pitts., 1971. Pres. sec. Com. to Re-elect Pres., S.W. Pa., 1972; adminstrv. asst. Pa. Rep. James B. Kelly III, 1972-73; reporter Beaver (Pa.) County Times, 1973-74; proofreader Ketchum, MacLeod & Grove, Pitts., 1975-76; cmty. rels. specialist PPG Industries, Pitts., 1976-77; editor PPG News, 1977-79, sr. staff writer, 1979-84, comm. coord., 1984-85; pub. rels. assoc. Glass Group, 1986-87; mgr. pub. rels. Glass Group PPG Industries, 1987-92; account mgr. Maddigan Comm., Pitts., 1992-93; owner JV Comm., Pitts., 1993—. Mem. Internat. Assn. Bus. Communicators (bd. dirs. Pitts. chpt. 1981, v.p. pub. rels. Pitts. chpt. 1982, v.p. programs Pitts. chpt. 1985, pres. Pitts. chpt. 1986), Travelers Aid Soc. Pitts. (bd. dirs. 1992-95, v.p. 1994-95), Phi Beta Kappa, Delta Zeta, Automotive Pub. Rels. Coun. Office: JV Comm PO Box 11114 Pittsburgh PA 15237-0414 E-mail: jverlich@jvcommunications.com.

VERMEER, MAUREEN DOROTHY, sales executive; b. Bronxville, N.Y., Mar. 21, 1945; d. Albert Casey and Helen (Valentine Casey) Vermeer; m. John R. Fassnacht, Feb. 11, 1966 (div. 1975); m. George M. Dallas Peltz IV, Oct. 26, 1985. Grad., NYU Real Estate Inst., 1976. Lic. real estate broker, notary pub., N.Y. With Douglas Elliman, N.Y.C., 1965-74, mgmt. supr., 1974-78, v.p., 1978-83; real estate broker Rachmani Corp., N.Y.C., 1983-84; v.p. sales and mktg. Carol Mgmt. Corp., N.Y.C., 1984-90; v.p. mktg. The Sunshine Group, N.Y.C., 1990; v.p., sec., bd. dirs. H.J. Kalikow & Co., N.Y.C., 1991—. Mem. Real Estate Bd. N.Y. (bd. dirs., residential mgmt. com.), Assn. Real Estate Women (bd. dirs. charitable fund). Republican. Presbyterian. Avocations: skiing, scuba diving. Home: 111 Broadway Norwood NJ 07648-1412 Office: H J Kalikow & Co 101 Park Ave Fl 25 New York NY 10178-0002

VERMILLION, JULIA KATHLEEN, music educator; b. Beardstown, Ill., June 28, 1958; d. Beulah Mahalah and Charles Francis Warden; m. Danny Lee Vermillion, July 15, 1978; 1 child, Erica. BA, We. Ill. U., 1980. Tchr. Beardstown (Ill.) Cmty. Sch. Dist., 1993—; choir dir. Beardstown United Meth. Ch., 1992—. Cmty. choir dir. Beardstown Cmty. Choir, 1991—. Recipient Tchr. of Yr. award, Wal Mart, 1998, Tchr. of Month award, Beardstown Rotary Club, 1995. Mem.: Ill. Music Educators Assn. (dist. IV jr. high choral chair 1997—). United Meth. Avocation: travel. Home: 6256 Crooked Ln Beardstown IL 62618 Office: Beardstown Community Unit Sch Dist 200 East 15th St Beardstown IL 62618

VERNAZZA, TRISH BROWN (TRISH EILEEN BROWN), visual artist, art therapist, sculptor; b. Tampa, Fla., Mar. 22, 1958; d. Burrell Joseph and Katharine Stowell (Weekly) B. BFA in Art History, U. South Fla., 1993; MA in Clin. Feminist Psychology, New Coll. Calif., 1997; postgrad., U. Calif., Berkeley, 1997. Lic. marriage and family therapist, art therapist; older adult tchr. Flight attendant Pan Am. World Airways, N.Y.C., 1989-91; art therapist jail psychiat. svcs. Haight Ashbury Free Clinics, Tampa, 1997-99; art instr. to older and disabled adults, 1999—; program mgr. Mental Health Sys., 2002—; pvt. practice psychotherapy Oceanside, 2003—. Judge John's Seafood Festival, Madeira Beach, Fla., program mgr., Mental Health Sys., 2002—. Artist: worked with HIV Women/AIDS Artreach phase 3, sculpture, 1994; group shows include Centre Gallery, U. So. Fla., 1994, U. Mobile Ala., 1994, Ctr. for Contemporary Art, Tampa, 1994, Fla. State U. Gallery and Mus., Tallahassee, 1994, Valencia C.C., Orlando, Fla., 1993, Tandemn Art Ctr., Venice, Fla., 1993, 4th Ann. Fla. Biennal, Richmond Art Ctr., Calif., 1996, calendar Richmond Art Ctr., 1997, Sonoma Art Festival, 1997, Napa Valley Mustard Festival, 1998, Sebastopol Art Ctr., 1999; author: Women Art & Mental Illness; works included in pvt. collections; contbr. articles to profl. jours.; presenter festivals, confs. and workshops. Vol. art/crafts instr. Substance Abused Mothers Against Drugs, Tampa, 1993; vol. docent Salvador Dali Mus., St. Petersburg, Fla., 1986-88; mem. Women's Caucus for Art; active multicultural workshops arts & crafts for children, Clearwater, Fla., 1995; intersession instrs. arts & crafts for children, Alameda, Calif., 1995-98; vol. art therapist chronic mentally ill adults Berkeley Creative Living Ctr., 1996-97. Recipient Hillsborough County Emerging Artist award; named to Wall of Tolerance So. Poverty Law, Ala.; grantee Serpent Source Found. women, San Francisco. Mem. Women in Psychologyk, Calif. Assn. Marriage and Family Therapists, San Diego North County Assn. Marriage Family Therapists, North County African-Am. Women's Assn., Oceanside Mus. Art. Democrat. Avocations: art therapist and visual artist with a feminist, female and feminine voice addressing social, political and gender issues. E-mail: info@TrishV.com.

VERNERDER, GLORIA JEAN, retired librarian; b. Ft. Wayne, Ind., June 2, 1930; d. John Otto and Vergie W. (Geiger) Krieg; m. Carl Penrod Vernerder, Dec. 25, 1952 (dec. Sept. 1984); children: Carla Jeanne Vernerder Kelly, Nina Marie Vernerder Anderson. Grad., Midway (Ky.) Coll.; student, Ind. U., Ft. Wayne, U. Ky. Br. libr. Pub. Libr. of Ft. Wayne and Allen County, 1950-52; children's libr. La Grange (Ill.) Pub. Libr., 1952-59, Hinsdale (Ill.) Pub. Libr., 1961-68, head of youth svcs., 1969-95. Editor: Sunlight and Shadows, 1983, 87, 90, 92; contbr. articles to profl. jours. Mem. adminstrv. bd. First United Meth. Ch., La Grange, 1986-88, Stephen Ministry, 1986—, v.p. United Meth. Women, 1995-98, pres., 1998-2000, mem. adminstrv. coun., 1996-2000. Mem. ALA, Ill. Libr. Assn., Libr. Adminstrs. Conf. of No. Ill. (treas. 1969), La Grange Woman's Club (v.p. 1998-99, pres. 2000-01), Gen. Fedn. of Women's Clubs, Ill. Fedn. of Women's Clubs (6th dist. pres. 2002-04). Republican. Methodist. Avocations: storytelling, theater, reading. Home: 732 7th Ave La Grange IL 60525-6706

VERNON, ALISON F. nursing administrator, artist; b. Cortland, N.Y., June 6, 1957; d. Frank and Deborah Elizabeth Fogg Lambert; m. Mark Thomas Vernon; children: Jeremiah, Deborah, Arrolyn. BA in Sociology, U. Del., 1980; BSN summa cum laude, Colby-Sawyer Coll., 1990. RN; able bodied seaman. Staff RN New London (N.H.) Hosp., 1990—91; staff RN, charge RN Dartmouth-Hitchcock Med. Ctr., Lebanon, NH, 1991—94, cardiology rsch. coord., 1994—97; staff RN Lake Sunapee Region Vis. Nurse Assn., New London, 1997—98, cardiac resource specialist, 1997—, patient care coord., case mgr., 1998—. Exhibitions include New London Hist. Soc. Artshow, 1999—2002, New London Hosp. Day Art Show, 1999—2002, Sulloway and Hollis Gallery, 2000, Dartmouth Hitchock Med. Ctr., 2000—02. Chmn. bd. dirs. Kearsarge Youth Hockey, 1998—2000, bd. dirs., 1994—2000. Democrat. Baptist. Avocations: hiking, running, cooking. Office: Lake Sunapee Regional VNA 65 Pingree Rd New London NH 03257

VERNON, DORIS SCHALLER, retired writer; b. Petoskey, Mich., Mar. 7, 1915; d. Harve and Edna (Covey) Frederickson; m. William Albert Schaller, Oct. 18, 1938; children: Kirk, Karen, Brent. Student, Cleary Coll., 1936-37, North Cen. Mich. Coll., 1960-61, 66-69. Sec. Mr. Beebe, Dean Freshman Coll., Petoskey, Mich., 1934-35, Dr. Dean C. Burns, Burns Clinic, Petoskey, 1937-38; with Probate and Juvenile Ct. Register, Petoskey, 1956-60; sec. bd. No. Mich. Rev., Inc., Mich., 1960-93; ret., 1996. Bd. dirs., Petoskey Friendship Ctr., gardening com., 2001—. Contbr. travel stories to profl. publs. Cub scout leader, Petoskey; treas. Camp Daggett Bd.; pres. Bus. and Profl. Women's Club, Petoskey, 1974-75; state bd. Don't Waste Mich., Riga and Lansing, 1989—, bd. dirs. No. bd., 1988—; civic gardening chair Petoskey Area Garden Club, sec., 1986; program chair Keenagers, First Christian Ch.; choir mem. First Christian Ch.; dir. Friendship Chorus for Care Ctrs. Singing Monthly Programs, Emmet County; bd. dirs. Friendship Ctr. Petosky, Mich., 1997-2001. Recipient cert. of commendation Guardian of the Earth, No. Mich., 1997. Avocations: square dancing, quilting. Home: Apt 413 Independent Village 965 Hager Dr Petoskey MI 49770-3213

VERNON, LILLIAN, mail order company executive; b. 1927; d. Herman and Erna Menasche; m. Paolo Martino; children: Fred, David. DCS(hon.), Mercy Coll., Dobbs Ferry, N.Y., 1984, Coll. New Rochelle; DSc in Bus. Adminstrn. (hon.), Bryant Coll.; LLD (hon.), Baruch Coll., LHD (hon.), Old Dominion U.; DCS (hon.), Mercy Coll.; DCS Coll. New Rochelle (hon.); D. in Bus. Adminstrn. (hon.), Bryant Coll.; LLD (hon.), Baruch Coll. CEO Lillian Vernon, New Rochelle, NY, 1951—. Lectr. in field. Contbr. articles to profl. jours. Trustee Coll. Human Svcs., Bryant Coll.; mem. adv. bd. Giraffe Project Girl Scout Coun. Tidewater; mem. adv. bd. Women's News; mem. bd. overseers Columbia U. Bus. Sch., NYU; mem. adv. com. Citizens Amb. Program; mem. bus. com. Met. Mus. Art; bd. govs. The Forum; mem. nat. com. The Kennedy Ctr. for Performing Arts, Washington; active The Ellis Island Reopening Com.; Bd. dirs. Westchester County, Ctr. Preventive Psychiatry, Va. Opera, Children's Mus. Arts, Retinitis Pigmentosa Found. Named Va. Press Women Newsmaker of Yr., woman of Yr., Women's Direct Response Group and Westchester County Fedn. Women's Clubs, Hampton Rds. Woman of Yr., So. New Eng. Entrepreneur of Yr.; named to Acad. Women Achievers, YWCA, Direct Mktg. Assn. Hall of Fame, Conn. Women's Hall of Fame; recipient Disting. Achievement award, Lab. Inst. Merchandising, Entrepreneurial award, Women's Bus. Owners of N.Y., 1983, Bravo award, YWCA, Woman of Achievement award, Woman's NEws, Nat. Hero award, Big. Bros./Big Sisters, Legend in Leadership award, Emory U., A Woman Who Has Made a Differene award, Inter. Womens Forum, medal of honor, Ellis Island, Bus. Leadership award, Gannett Newspapers, Outstanding Bus. Leader award, Northwood Inst., Congl. Record Commendation award, Crystal award, Coll. Human Svcs., City of Peace award, Bonds of Israel, Svc. award, Sr. Placement Bur., Excellence award, Westchester Assn. Women Bus. Owners, Commendation in Cong. Record, Magnificent Seven award, Bus. and Profl. Women, Woman of Distinction award, Birmingham So. Coll. Mem.: Nat. Retail Fedn. (bd. dirs.), Women's Forum, Com. of 200, Am. Stock Exch. (listed co. adv. com.), Am. Bus. Conf. (dir.), Lotos Club. Office: Lillian Vernon Corp 1 Theall Rd Rye NY 10580-1450

VERNON, LISA JO, reading and special education educator; b. Alliance, Ohio, Feb. 26, 1968; d. Donna Rae and George Kenneth Vernon. BS in Edn., U. Akron, 1990; MA in Edn., Hampton U., 2000; PhD in Edn., Coll. of William and Mary, 2003. Educator Barberton (Ohio) City Schs., Barberton, Ohio, 1990—95, Norfolk (Va.) City Pub. Schs., Norfolk, Va., 1995—2000; grant coord. Coll. William and Mary, Williamsburg, Va., 2000—03; prof. edn. Hampton (Va.) U., 2002—. Ind. ednl. cons., Hampton, Va., 2000—. Mem.: Coun. for Learning Disabilities, Coun. for Children with Behavior Disorders, Tchr. Edn. Divsn. (CEC), Coun. for Exceptional Children. Office: Hampton U Phoenix Hall 111-B Hampton VA 23668 Home: 318 Washington St Hampton VA 23669 Office Phone: 757-727-5537. Office Fax: 757-727-5434. Personal E-mail: jovern@cox.net. E-mail: lisa.vernon@hamptonu.edu.

VERRETT, SHIRLEY, soprano; b. New Orleans, May 31, 1931; d. Leon Solomon and Elvira Augustine (Harris) V.; m. Louis Frank LoMonaco, Dec. 10, 1963; 1 dau., Francesca. AA, Ventura (Calif.) Coll., 1951; diploma in voice (scholarship 1956-61), Juilliard Sch. Music, 1961; MusD (hon.), Coll. Holy Cross, Mass., 1978. CPA, Cert. real estate broker. Faculty U. Mich. Sch. Music, 1996—, James Earl Jones disting. univ. prof. voice, 1999—. Mem. adv. bd. Opera Ebony. Recital debut Town Hall, N.Y.C., 1958; appeared as Irina in Lost in the Stars, 1958; orchestral debut Phila. Orch., 1960; operatic debut in Carmen, Festival of Two Worlds, Spoleto, Italy, 1962; debuts with Bolshoi Opera, Moscow, 1963, N.Y.C. Opera, 1964, Royal Opera, Covent Garden, 1966, Maggio Fiorentino, Florence, 1967, Met. Opera, 1968, Teatro San Carlos, Naples, 1968, Dallas Civic Opera, 1969, La Scala, 1970, Vienna State Opera, 1970, San Francisco Opera, 1972, Paris Opera, 1973, Opera Co. Boston, 1976, Opera Bastille, Paris, 1990; guest appearances with all major U.S. symphony orchs.; toured Eastern Europe and Greece with La Scala chorus and orch., 1981; TV debut on Ed Sullivan Show, 1963; TV performances include: Great Performances series, live performance of Macbeth at La Scala, Santuzza in Cavalleria Rusticana; film debut Maggio Musicale, 1989, Macbeth, 1986; rec. artist, RCA, Columbia, ABC (Westminster), Angel Everest, Kapp, Philips Records and Deutsche Grammophon. Recipient Marian Anderson award, 1955, Nat. Fedn. Music Clubs award, 1961, Walter Naumberg award, 1958, Blanche Thebom award, 1960; named Chevalier Arts and Letters (France), 1970, Commandeur, 1984; John Hay Whitney fellow, 1959; Ford Found. fellow, 1962-63; Martha Baird Rockefeller Aid to Music Fund fellow, 1959-61; grantee William Matteus Sullivan Fund, 1959; grantee Berkshire Music Opera, 1956; recipient Achievement award Ventura Coll., 1963, Achievement award N.Y. chpt. Albert Einstein Coll. Medicine, 1975; 2 plaques Los Angeles Sentinel Newspaper, 1960; plaque Peninsula Music Festival, 1963; Los Angeles Times Woman of Yr. award, 1969 Mem. Mu Phi Epsilon. Office: U Mich Sch Music 1100 Baits Dr Ann Arbor MI 48109-2085 E-mail: verrett@umich.edu.

VERSCH, ESTHER MARIE, artist; b. Santa Monica, Calif., May 27, 1927; d. Claro Contreras Santellanes and Juana Hernandez; m. Chester Ray Fraelich, Nov. 14, 1943 (div. Nov. 1964); children: Joe Fraelich, Diane Fraelich Foster Preston; m. Terry Lee Versch, June 21, 1969; stepchildren: Fred, Roman, Joseph, Terry Jr., Michael. Student, East L.A. Coll., Pasadena City Coll. Lic. vocat. nurse. Nurse pvt. dr.'s office, L.A., 1968-69, U. So. Calif. Med. Ctr., L.A., 1963-68; artist Altadena, Calif., 1972—. Artist: (front cover) Library Services L.A., 1983, Christmas card for Western Greeting Inc., (back cover) Moccasin Tracks, 1984-85; one woman shows include Republic Fed. Savings, Altadena, Calif., Pasadena Pub. Libr., Whites Art Store and Gallery, La Canada, Calif., 1979, Windmill Gallery, 1985; group exhibitions: Women Artists of the West Internat. Exhibition and Sale, Cody Western and Wildlife Classyc, 1979, Nat. Cowgirl Hall of Fame, Hereford, Tex., 1978, Beauty for the Beast Benefit, 1980, Ducks Unltd. Invitational Art Show, Taylor, Mich., 1986-87, Lawrence (Kans.) Indian Art Show, Mus. Anthropology, 1989-90, Snake River Showcase, Lewiston, Idaho, 1992, Women Artists of the West, 1992, 98, 99, Death Valley 49's Invitational Art Show, 1994-2000, 2001, George Ohr Cultural Arts and Cultural Ctr., Biloxi, Miss., 1998, Western and Wildlife Invitational Art Show, Estes Park, Colo., 2000, WAOW Art Show Pinedale, Wyo, 2002, Art and Music Festival, Dublin, Ohio, 2002; collections: Johnson Humrick House Mus., Coshocton, Ohio, and other private collections; illustrator back cover Moccasin Tracks, 1984-85. Vol. nurses aide City View Hosp., L.A., 1960-63; vol. Arroyo Rep., Pasadena, Calif., St. Luke Hosp., Pasadena, 1990-94, flu immunization ARC, 1977-78. Recipient Gold medal for watercolor San Gabriel Fine Arts, 1979, Best of Show award for watercolor Am. Indian and Western, 1990, Hon. mention San Gabriel Fine Arts, 1990, 3rd Place Watercolor Women Artists of the West Saddle Back Art Gallery, 1982. Mem. Women Artists of the West (emeritus mem., treas., asst. sec., editor West Wind, membership chmn.), Ohio Art League, Coshocton Art Guild. Republican. Roman Catholic. Avocations: walking, gardening, sewing. E-mail: everschart@newsguy.com.

VERSIC, LINDA JOAN, nurse educator, research company executive; b. Aug. 27, 1944; d. Robert and Kathryn I. (Fagird) Davies; m. Ronald James Versic, June 11, 1966; children: Kathryn Clara, Paul Joseph. RN, Johns Hopkins Sch. of Nursing, 1965; BS in Health Edn., Ctrl. State U., 1980; MS in Edn., Nova Southeastern U., 2000. Asst. head nurse Johns Hopkins Hosp., Balt., 1965—67, staff Nurse Registry Miami Valley Hosp., Dayton, Ohio, 1973—90; instr. Miami Jacobs Jr. Coll. Bus., Dayton, 1977—79; pres. Ronald T. Dodge Co., Dayton, 1979—86, chmn. bd., 1987—; chmn. bd. dirs. A-1 Travel, Inc. Instr. Warren County Career Ctr., Ohio, 1980—84, coord. diversified health occupations, 1984—2003, career pathways coord., 2003—. Coord. youth activities, mem. steering com. Queen of Apostles Cmty.; active Miami Valley Mil. Affairs Assn., Glen Helen, Friends of Dayton Ballet, Dayton Art Inst., Cin. Art Mus. Recipient Excellence in Tchg. award, 1992, award for Project Excellence, 1992. Mem.: Am. Vocat. Assn., Ohio Vocat. Assn., Welsh Soc. Cin., South Slavic Club of Greater Dayton, Johns Hopkins Club, Vocat. Indsl. Clubs Am. (chpt. advisor 1982—). Roman Catholic. Home: 1601 Shafor Blvd Dayton OH 45419-3103 Office: Ronald T Dodge Co PO Box 41630 Dayton OH 45441-0630

VERSTANDIG, TONI GRANT, federal agency administrator; b. Pitts., Jan. 15, 1953; d. Louis A. and Ruth M. (O'Block) Grant; m. Lee L. Verstandig, Feb. 20, 1982; 1 stepchild, Scott B.; 1 child, Grant L. BA, Boston U., 1974; AD, Stephens Coll., 1972. Legis. asst. subcom. on agrl. labor House Com. on Edn. and Labor, 1976-77; staff dir. subcom. on accts. House Adminstrn. Com., 1977-78; mem. profl. staff subcom. on internat. security/sci. affairs House Com. on Fgn. Affairs, 1978-86; mem. profl. staff Com. on Fgn. Affairs, 1986-93; dep. asst. sec. of state Near Ea. affairs U.S. Dept. of State, Washington, 1993—. Cons. to com. on fgn. affairs U.S. Ho. of Reps., 1978-93, staff dir. subcom. accts., com. on house adminstrn., prin. legis. asst. to Congressman John N. Dent. Vol. cons. on fgn. policy and nat. security Clinton-Gore Presdl. Campaign, 1992. Recipient Spl. Merit of Honor commendation Mayor Kevin White. Office: Dept of State Near Eastern Affairs 2201 C St NW Rm 6244 Washington DC 20520-0001

VER STEEG, DONNA LORRAINE FRANK, nurse, sociologist, educator; b. Minot, N.D., Sept. 23, 1929; d. John Jonas and Pearl H. (Denlinger) Frank; m. Richard W. Ver Steeg, Nov. 22, 1950; children: Juliana, Anne, Richard B. BSN, Stanford, 1951; MSN, U. Calif., San Francisco, 1967; MA in Sociology, UCLA, 1969, PhD in Sociology, 1973. Clin. instr. U. ND Sch. Nursing, 1962-63; USPHS nurse rsch. fellow UCLA, 1969-72; spl. cons., mem. adv. com. on physicians' assts. and nurse practitioner progs. Calif. State Bd. Med. Examiners, 1972-73; asst. prof. UCLA Sch. Nursing, 1973-79, assoc. prof., 1979-94, asst. dean, 1979-81, chmn. primary ambulatory care, 1976-87, assoc. dean, 1983-86, prof. emeritus, chair primary care, 1994-96, prof. emeritus, 1996—. Co-prin. investigator PRIMEX Project Family Nurse Practitioners, UCLA Ext., 1974—76; assoc. cons. Calif. Postsecondary Edn. Commn., 1975—76; spl. cons. Calif. Dept. Consumer Affairs, 1978; accredited visitor Western Assn. Sch. and Coll., 1985; mem. Calif. State Legis. Health Policy Forum, 1980—81; mem. nurse practitioner adv. com. Calif. Bd. RN, 1995—97; mem. Edn. Industry Interface, Info. Devel. Mktg. Sub Com., 1995—99, recruitment, 1999—2001; archivist Calif. Strategic Planning Com. Nursing/Colleagues in Caring Project, 1995—. Contbr. chpts. to profl. books, articles to profl. jours. Recipient Leadership award Calif. Area Health Edn. Ctr. Sys., 1989, Commendation award Calif. State Assembly, 1994; named Outstanding Faculty Mem., UCLA Sch. Nursing, 1982. Fellow Am. Acad. Nursing; mem. AAAS, AAUW, ANA (pres. elect Calif. chpt. 1977-79, pres. 1979-81, interim chair Calif. 1995-96), Nat. League Nursing, Calif. League Nursing, N.Am. Nursing Diagnosis Assn., Am. Assn. History Nursing, Stanford Nurses Club, Sigma Theta Tau (Alpha Eta chpt. Leadership award Gamma Tau chpt. 1994), Sigma Xi. Home: 708 Swarthmore Ave Pacific Palisades CA 90272-4353 Office: UCLA Sch Nursing Box 956917 Los Angeles CA 90095-6917

VERSTEGEN, DEBORAH A. finance educator; b. Neenah, Wis., Oct. 27, 1946; d. Gerald C. and Margaret A. (Lamers) V. BA, Loretto Heights Coll., 1969; EdM, U. Rochester, 1972; MS, U. Wis., 1981, PhD, 1983. Adminstr. Iditarod Area Sch. Dist., McGrath, Alaska, 1976-79; rsch. asst. Wis. Ctr. for Edn. Rsch., 1981-84; dir. asst. prof. mid-mgmt. program U. Tex., Austin, 1984-86; asst. prof. edn. fin. and policy U. Va., Charlottesville, 1986-91, assoc. prof. edn. in fin. and policy, 1992-99, prof., 2000—. Assoc. rsch. fellow Oxford U., Eng., 1991; adv. bd. U.S. Dept. Edn., 1989-92. Author over 250 books, reports, chpts., articles and revs., latest being The Impacts of Litigation and Legislation on Public School Finance, 1990, Spheres of Justice in Education, 1991; editor Jour. Edn. Fin., 1990-93, editor edn. policy, 1993—. Treas. LVW, 1986, mem. Va. state bd., 1995—97, Va. edn. chair, 1993—2001. Recipient Alumni Achievement award, U. Wis., Madison, 1997. Mem.: AAUP (exec. bd. Va. 1999—, pres.-elect 2003, pres. 2003—04), U. Coun. on Ednl. Adminstrn. (adv. bd. fin. ctr. 1991—, disting. svc. award 1991), Women Edn. Leaders Va. (chair 1998, pres. 1999—2000, founder), Am. Ednl. Rsch. Assn. (SIG chair fiscal issues and policy 2002—04), Am. Ednl. Fin. Assn. (bd. dirs. 1986—89,, disting. svc. award

1989), Phi Kappa Phi, Phi Delta Kappa. Home: 2156 Timber Mdws Charlottesville VA 22911-7231 Office: U Va Curry Sch Edn Ruffner Hall 405 Emmet St S Charlottesville VA 22903-2424 E-mail: dav3e@virginia.edu.

VERTEFEUILLE, CHRISTINE SIEGRIST, judge; b. New Britain, Conn., Dec. 10, 1950; BA in Polit. Sci., Trinity Coll., 1972; JD, U. Conn., 1975. Pvt. practice, 1975-89; judge Conn. Superior Ct., 1989—99; adminstrv. judge Waterbury Jud. Dist., 1994-99, complex litig. judge, 1999; judge Appellate Ct., 1999-2000; assoc. justice Conn. Supreme Ct., 2000—. Alternate mem. Waterbury and New Haven (Conn.) Grievance Panels, 1985-89; faculty Conn. Judges Inst., 1989-94. Recipient Jud. award Conn. Trial Lawyers Assn., 1995. Mem. Conn. Bar Assn. (mem. exec. com. real property 1988-89). Office: Supreme Ct Bldg 231 Capitol Ave Hartford CT 06106

VERTS, LITA JEANNE, university administrator; b. Jonesboro, Ark., Apr. 13, 1935; d. William Gus and Lolita Josephine (Peeler) Nash; m. B. J. Verts, Aug. 29, 1954 (div. 1975); 1 child, William Trigg. BA, Oreg. State U., 1973; MA in Lingustics, U. Oreg., 1974; postgrad., U. Hawaii, 1977. Librarian Forest Research Lab., Corvallis, Oreg., 1966-69; instr. English Lang. Inst., Corvallis, 1974-80; dir. spl. svcs. Oreg. State U., Corvallis, 1980-96, faculty senator, 1988-96; ret., 1996. Editor ann. book: Trio Achievers, 1986, 87, 88; contbr. articles to profl. jours. Precinct com. Rep. Party, Corvallis, 1977-80; adminstrv. bd. 1st United Meth. Ch., Corvallis, 1987-89, mem. fin. com., 1987-93, tchr. Bible, 1978—; bd. dirs. Westminster Ho., United Campus Ministries, 1994-95; adv. coun. Disabilities Svc., Linn, Benton, Lincoln Counties, 1990-99, vice-chmn., 1992-93, chmn. 1993-94; citizen adv. bd. on Transit, 1998—, intercity steering com., 1999—, Corvallis Downtown Parking Commn., 1999—; Oreg. Longterm Care Ombudsman, 1999—. Mem. N.W. Assn. Spl. Programs (pres. 1985-86), Nat. Coun. Ednl. Opportunities Assn. (bd. dirs. 1984-87), Nat. Gardening Assn., Alpha Phi (mem. corp. bd. Beta Upsilon chpt. 1990-96). Republican. Methodist. Avocations: gardening, photography, golf. Home: 530 SE Mayberry Ave Corvallis OR 97333-1866 E-mail: l.verts@comcast.net.

VERVILLE, ELIZABETH GIAVANI, federal official; b. N.Y.C., July 13, 1940; d. Joseph and Gertrude (Levy) Giavani. BA, Duke U., 1961; LLB, Columbia U., 1964. Bar: Mass. 1965, U.S. Supreme Ct. 1970, D.C. 1980. Assoc. Snow Motley & Holt, successor Gaston Snow & Ely Bartlett, Boston, 1965-67; asst. atty. gen. Commonwealth of Mass., Boston, 1967-69; atty. advisor for African affairs U.S. Dept. State, Washington, 1979-72, asst. legal adviser for East Asian and Pacific affairs, 1972-80, dep. legal adviser, 1980-89; dep. asst. sec. state Bur. Politico-Mil. Affairs Bur. Politico-Mil. Affairs, Washington, 1989-92, sr. coord., 1992-95; dir. for global and multilateral affairs Nat. Security Coun., Washington, 1995-98; dep. dir. Critical Infrastructure Assurance Office, Washington, 1998-2000; spl. rep. Bur. Narcotics and Law Enforcement, Washington, 2000-01; acting dep. asst. sec. Bur. Internat. Narcotics and Law Enforcement, Dept. State, Washington, 2001—02, sr. advisor, 2002—. Recipient presdl. rank of meritorious exec., 1985, 90, presdl. rank disting. exec., 1988. Mem. Am. Soc. Internat. Law, Coun. on Fgn. Rels. Home: 3012 Dumbarton Ave NW Washington DC 20007-3305 Office: Bur Internat Narcotics & Law Enforcement State Dept Washington DC 20520-0001 E-mail: vervilleeg@state.gov.

VESCOVO, DIANE KIRKLAND, federal judge; b. 1955; BA in History, U. Va., 1976; JD, Memphis State U., 1980. Bar: Tenn. 1980. Atty. Lloyd C. Kirkland, Jr., Memphis, 1981-87, Internat. Paper Co., Memphis, 1987-92, Wolff, Ardis, P.C., Memphis, 1992-95; magistrate judge U.S. Dist. Ct. (we. dist.), Memphis, 1995—. Mem. Phi Beta Kappa. Office: US Dist Ct 341 Federal Bldg 167 N Main St Memphis TN 38103-1816 Fax: 901-495-1387.

VESEY, MARY FRANCES, writer, educator; b. Providence, July 11, 1965; d. Joseph Rosario and Mary Alice Perroni. BA, W.Va. U., 1988; MA, R.I. Coll., 1997. Cert. tchr. secondary English R.I., Mass. Tchr. Bristol (R.I.) County Pub. Schs., 1989—94; English tchr. St. Mary Sch., Providence, 1994—96; tchr. Blessed Sacrament Sch., Providence, 1996—98. Facilitator ednl. studies Diocese Providence Cath. Schs., 1994—95, spelling bee judge, 1996—98; STAR team dirs., program dir. Greater Providence YMCA, 1995—96. Author: (book) The Confessions of citizen g, 2002, At the Corner of Central and Canal, 2002, Beyond the Corner of Central and Canal, 2003; contbr. poetry to publs. Fundraiser Greater Providence YMCA, 1994—98, United Way, Providence, 1995—96. Mem.: New Eng. Masters Swim Club (All-Am. swimmer 1996, World Ranked Masters swimmer 1996), Golden Key, Phi Beta Kappa.

VESPER, ETHEL ROSE, language educator, consultant; d. Eugene and Celia Blum; m. Donald Robert Vesper, Apr. 10, 1960 (div. 1980); children: Tina, Patrick. BS in Edn., U. Kans., 1960; MA in Linguistics, U. Calif., Davis, 1969; PhD in Anthropology, U. Mo., 1976; MA in Ministry, Seattle U., 1985. CEO, primary cons. NorWeskan Assocs., Seattle, 1978—; asst. prof. anthropology dept Phillips U., Enid, Okla., 1980—84, dir. ESL program, 1980—84; lead & trainer, panel maintenance Boeing Co., Seattle, 1986—96, edn., tng. DCAC/MRM, 1996—99, orgnl. devel. advisor, 1996—2000, coord., employee devel. Maintenance Engring. & Publs., 1999—2002; mem. faculty U. Phoenix, 2000—. Instr. Skagit Valley C.C., Langley, Wash., 1984—90, U. Phoenix, 1999—. Author: (book) Intro Linguistics: A Text for High School Students, 1965; author: (with Don R. Vesper) Change in language situation and attitudes in a multilingual society, 1975. Vol. chaplain Wash. State Reformatory, Monroe, 1984—; min. St. James Cath., Seattle, 2000—, mem. operation nightwatch, 1995—; coord., Eucharistic min. Cabrini Pastoral Care Swedish Hosp./St. James Cath., Seattle, 2001—; vol. chaplain Monroe Correctional Complex, Twin Rivers Unit. Named Vol. of the Yr., Wash. State, Dept. Corrections, 1999-2000; fellow Nat. Fgn. Lang., NSF, 1971-71; 1972-73, Grad. Traineeship, 1973-1974; grantee, 1974-76. Fellow: Am. Anthropology Assn. Roman Catholic. Personal E-mail: e.vesper@worldnet.att.net.

VESPER, ROSE, state legislator; m. Lee Vesper; children: Stephanie, Jennifer, Jessica. BA, Xavier U., 1960; MA, Midwestern U., 1967. Past mem. Ohio Valley Regional Devel. Commn., Ohio Water and Sewer Rotary Commn.; pres. Ohio Clermont County Farm Bur.; rep. Ohio State Ho. Reps. Dist. 72. Mem. Nat. Fedn. Rep. Women; chmn. Clermont County Rep. Party, 1990—, Southwestern Ohio Rep. Leadership; owner, operator beef cattle/crop farm. Named Clermont County Farm Woman of Yr., 1988; recipient Disting. Svc. award Ohio Med. Polit. Action Com., 1988, Coop. Ext. Agts. Assn. award, 1990, Frances Boltom award Ohio League Young Reps., 1990. Mem. Richmond Hist. Soc., Clermont, Brown and Clinton County C. of C., State Med. Assn., Farm Bur., Farmers Union. Home: 1174 Watkins Hill Rd New Richmond OH 45157-9504 Office: Ohio Ho of Reps State House Columbus OH 43215

VESPOLI, LEILA L. lawyer, energy executive; b. 1959; d. Zouhair Yassine and Carol Vespoli. BS, Miami (Ohio) U.; JD, Case Western Reserve U. Bar: Ohio 1984. From atty. to sr. atty. Ohio Edison, Akron, Ohio, 1985—97; assoc. gen. counsel First Energy Corp., Akron, Ohio, 1997—2000, gen. counsel, 2000—, v.p, 2000—01, sr. v.p., 2001—. Office: First Energy Corp 76 S Main St Akron OH 44308

VEST, GAYLE SOUTHWORTH, obstetrician, gynecologist; b. Duluth, Minn., Apr. 7, 1948; d. Russell Eugene and Brandon (Young) Southworth; m. Steven Lee Vest, Nov. 27, 1971; 1 child, Matthew Steven. BS, U. Mich., 1970. Diplomate Am. Bd. Ob-Gyn. Intern in ob-gyn. Milw. County Gen. Hosp., 1974-75, So. Ill. U. Sch. Medicine, 1975-78; pvt. practice Chapel Hill (N.C.) Ob-Gyn., 1978-80; asst. attending physician dept. ob-gyn. U. N.C. Sch. Medicine, Chapel Hill, 1978-80; clin. assoc. dept. ob-gyn. Duke U. Med. Ctr., Durham, N.C., 1978-80; pvt. practice Big Stone Gap (Va.) Clinic, 1980-88, Norwise Ob-Gyn. Assocs., Norton, Va., 1988—. Fellow: ACOG; mem.: Wise County Med. Soc., Med. Soc. Va., Va. Ob-Gyn. Soc., Christian Med. and Dental Assn., Am. Soc. Reproductive Medicine. Avocations: skiing, kayaking, travel. Office: Norwise Ob Gyn Assocs 102 15th St NW Ste 301 Norton VA 24273-1616

VESTAL, JOSEPHINE BURNET, lawyer; b. Iowa City, June 13, 1949; d. Allen Delker and Dorothy (Walker) V. Student, Williams Coll., 1970; BA, Mt. Holyoke Coll., 1971; JD, U. Wash., 1974. Bar: Wash. 1974, U.S. Dist. Ct. (we. dist.) Wash. 1974, U.S. Ct. Appeals (9th cir.) 1984, U.S. Ct. Appeals (D.C. cir.) 1984, U.S. Dist. Ct. (ea. dist.) Wash. 1993. Ptnr. Selinker, Vestal, Klockars & Andersen, Seattle, 1974-80; assoc. Williams, Kastner & Gibbs, Seattle, 1981-87; mem. Williams, Kastner & Gibbs, PLLC, Seattle, 1988—. Mem. ABA (labor and employment sect.), Def. Rsch. Inst. (labor and employment sect.), Wash. State Bar Assn., King County Bar Assn. Office: Williams Kastner & Gibbs PO Box 21926 Seattle WA 98111-3926 E-mail: jvestal@wkg.com.

VESTAL, MARILYN ANITA, writer, researcher, educator; b. Pitts., May 28, 1950; d. Elmo Foucheaux and Mary Alice (Hayes) Vestal; 1 child, Daven Remley. BS in Child and Family Devel., Va. Tech., 1974; MBA in Mgmt., Tex. Tech. U., 1980; PhD in Conflict Mgmt., Nova Southeastern U., 2001. Vol. Peace Corps, Dominican Republic, 1974-76; child devel. tng. specialist Tex. Tech. U., Lubbock, 1977-80; methods analyst supr. Cmty. Progress Coun., York, PA., 1980-81; program adminstr. East Coast Migrant Head Start Project, 1982-84; mgmt./fiscal specialist, data mgmt. project coord. Head Start Resource and Tng. Ctr., U. Md., 1984-87; exec. dir. Child Care Cons., Inc., Pa., 1987-90; mgmt. cons., mediator, 1990—. Assoc. prof. human resources mgmt. Webber Coll., 1993-97; assoc. prof. mgmt. orgn. devel. Ea. Mennonite U., 2000-; adj. prof. conflict resolution Nova Southeastern U., 2001-; cons. S.C. Ednl. TV, 1992-96, U. Md., Head Start Resource and Tng. Ctr., 1988-92, South Fla. C,C., 1995, Region IV Mgmt. Inst., Tuskeegee U., 1995, DHHS/Adminstrn. on Children and Families, Washington, 1991—, Wheelock Coll., 1997-98, Aspen Sys.; presenter numerous papers at confs., workshops. Mem. editl. bd.: 4th R, Assn .for Conflict Resolution, 2003—. Facilitator Wellspring Retreat, Family Enrichment Ctr., Archdiocese of Miami, 1998-2000; arbitrator Nat. Assn. Securities Dealers, 1998-; mem. Nat. Peace Corps Assn., Soc. for Human Resources Mgmt., 2001—, Consortium on Peace Rsch., Ed., Devel., 2000-02, Assn. for Conflict Resolutions, 1999-; mem., bd. dirs. Child Care Cons., Inc., York, 1990-91, bd. pres. Mediation Svcs. Conflict Resolution, 2000-02; bd. dirs. Atkins House, York, 1989-90. Recipient Margaret Sangar award Planned Parenthood, 1975, Beyond War award, 1987, Cert. Recognition Dept. Interior, 1976; Head Start Rsch. scholar, 1999-2000. Mem. Broward County Mediators Assn. Roman Catholic. Avocations: tennis, travel, culture. E-mail: vestala@suscom.net.

VETTER, ALLISON LEE, sociologist, educator; b. Dayton, Ohio, Jan. 29, 1971; d. David Joe and Rogean T. Vetter. BA in Sociology and Psychology, Doane Coll., 1994; MA in Sociology, U. Nebr., 1996, PhD in Sociology, 2001. Grad. asst. U. Nebr., Lincoln, 1994—99, 2000—01; vis. prof. Doane Coll., Crete, Nebr., 1999—2000; asst. prof. U. Ctrl. Ark., Conway, 2001—. Mem.: Ark. Sociol. and Anthrop. Assn. (v.p. 2003—04), Nat. Coun. Family Rels., Am. Sociol. Assn. Office: U Ctrl Ark 201 Donaghey Ave Irby 306 Conway AR 72035 Office Phone: 501-450-5587.

VETTER, NOELLE I. information technology manager; b. Poughkeepsie, N.Y., Jan. 10, 1968; d. Donald Anthony Panessa and Hollis Carol Robison-Krug. AS cum laude, Cazenovia (N.Y.) Coll.; BSBM, U. Phoenix. Project leader News Corp., Wilton, Conn., 2000—01; mgr. info. sys. MDF Sys., Inc., Bristol, Conn., 2001—. Freelance tech. cons., Bristol, 1991—2000. Mem.: NAFE (assoc.), Am. Soc. Quality (assoc.), Project Mgmt. Inst. (assoc.), Golden Key Internat. Honor Soc. (life), Phi Theta Kappa (life). Liberal. Roman Catholic. Avocations: classic cars, reading, travel. Home: 78 Dorset Way Bristol CT 06010 Personal E-mail: noelle_vetter@hotmail.com.

VEVERKA, RUTH TONRY, retired secondary school educator; b. Martinsburg, W.Va., June 24, 1918; d. James Charles and May Elizabeth (Matthews) Tonry; m. Rudolph Edward Veverka, Sept. 18, 1948; 1 child, Karen Elizabeth. BS in Home Econs., W.Va. U., 1940; MA, U. Nebr., 1950; postgrad., U. Nebr., Omaha, 1970. Cert. tchr., W.Va., Nebr. Tchr. Ft. Ashby (W.Va.) High Sch., 1940-41, Bunker Hill (W.Va.) High Sch., 1941-42; cryptanalyst USN, Washington, 1946-48; libr. sci. worker Westside Community Schs., Omaha, 1970-88. Mem. ARC, Arlington, Va., 1953-56, Navy Relief Soc., San Diego, 1959-61. Lt. USN, 1942-46. Mem. AAUW, Home Economists in Homemaking, Women Accepted for Vol. Emegency Svc., Feminine Vets. World War II, Order Ea. Star, 1918 Club, Phi Upsilon Omicron, Kappa Delta Pi, Pi Lambda Theta, Pi Mu Epsilon, Alpha Xi Delta. Republican. Lutheran. Avocations: reading, swimming, needlepoint.

VIAL, ALTA EULICE, retired music educator; b. Conroe, Tex., Jan. 20, 1930; d. Samuel Thomas and Alta Darl (Madeley) Hoke; 1 child, Laurie Vial Amsler. BS, Tex. Women's U., Denton, 1950; MEd, SHSTC, Huntsville, Tex., 1956. Cert. tchr. Tex. Tchr. health and phys. edn. Perryton H.S., Tex., 1950, Aldine Ind. Sch. Dist., Tex., 1952—56; tchr. music Conroe Ind. Sch. Dist., Tex., 1957—77, Willis Ind. Sch. Dist., Tex., 1978; pvt. classical guitar tchr. Conroe, 1980—90; pvt. voice tchr., 1955—80. Lectr. in field; performer harp, lute Tex. Renaissance Festival, 1976—2000; costume designer/maker 1450-1650 periods, 1979—2000. Mem.: Conroe Art League (charter), Montgomery County Choral Soc., Tex. State Tchrs. Assn., Tex. Music Educators Assn. (elem. music chmn. 1968—69), Delta Kappa Gamma (music chmn. 1970—80, chpt. achievement award 1979). Methodist. Avocations: oil painting, watercolors, reflexology, bridge. Home: 311 Lilly Conroe TX 77301-1365

VICK, FRANCES BRANNEN, publishing executive; b. Trinity, Tex., Aug. 14, 1935; d. Carl Andrew and Bess (courtney) B.; m. Ross William Vick Jr., June 23, 1956; children: Karen Lynn, Ross William III, Patrick Brannen. BA, U. Tex., 1958; MA, Stephen F. Austin State U., 1968; DHL, U. North Tex., 2000. Teaching fellow Stephen F. Austin State U., Nacogdoches, Tex., 1966-68, lectr., 1968-69, Angelina Coll., Lufkin, Tex., 1969-71, Baylor U., Waco, Tex., 1974-75, 77-78; vice prin. Vanguard Sch., Waco, 1975-77; pres. E-Heart Press, Inc., Dallas, 1979—; co-dir. UNT Press U. North Tex., Denton, 1987-89, dir., 1989—. Publisher 170 books; editor 50 books. Leadership coun. Ann Richards Com., Austin, 1990-94; amb. Inst. Texan Cultures; mem. Tex. Commn. on Arts, Lit., 1991. Named to Tex. Inst. of Letters. Mem.: AAUW, Rocky Mountain Book Pubs. Assn., Women in Scholarly Pub., Soc. Scholarly Pub., Pen Ctr. USA West, Tex. Inst. Letters (councilor 2002—), Philos. Soc. Tex., Western Lit. Assn., Tex. Humanities Resource Ctr. (bd. dirs. 1990—91, 2002—), Tex. Folklore Soc. (councillor 1991—93), Book Pubs. Tex. (v.p. 1990—96, pres. 1996), UNT League Profl. Women, Tex. Humanities Alliance, Leadership Am., Leadership Tex., East Tex. Hist. Assn. (life), Tex. State Hist. Assn. (life). Democrat. Episcopalian. Home: 3700 Mockingbird Ln Dallas TX 75205-2125

VICK, SUSAN, playwright, educator, director, actress; b. Raleigh, NC, Nov. 4, 1945; d. Thomas B. Jr. and Merle (Hayes) V. MFA, So. Meth. U., 1969; PhD, U. Ill., 1979. Prof. drama/theatre and dir. theatre WPI, 1981—; playwright Excuse Me For Living Prodns., Cambridge, Mass., 1989—, Festival Fringe, Edinburgh, 1989—. Playwright Ensemble Studio Theatre, N.Y.C., 1981-83; founder WPI Ann. New Voices Festival of Original Plays, 1982. Editor: (2 vols.) Playwrights Press, Amherst, 1988—; playwright: When I Was Your Age, 1982, Ord-Way Ames-Gay, 1982, Investments, 1985, Half Naked, 1989, Quandary, 1983, Meat Selection, 1984, Give My Love to Everyone But, 1989; appeared in plays including Rip Van Winkle, 1979, Why I Live at The P.O., 1982, The Play Group, 1984-85, Present Stage, 1985, Sister Mary Ignatius Explain It All, 19[illegible], [illegible], 1988, Bogus Joan, 1992-93; dir. play Give My Love to Everyone But, 1990 (Edinburgh Festival); theatre editor: Sojourner The Women's Forum, 1995-98; dramatist, script cons. Clyde Unity Theatre, Glasgow, Scotland, 1992-93, 1999-2000. Dir., Women's Community Theatre, Amherst, 1981-84, Upstart, Wis., 1994; head Kew Montessori Ctr. Faculty fellow U. Ill., 1976-77, Bd. of Trustees Award for Outstanding Tchg., WPI, 1997. Mem. U.S. Inst. for Theatre Tech., Nat. Assn. Schs. of Theatre, New Eng. Theatre Conf., Inc., Drama League, Dramatists Guild (assoc.), Soc. Stage Dirs. and Choreographers (assoc.), U.S. Inst. Theatre Tech., New England Theatre Conf., Nat. Assn. Schs. Theatre, Alpha Phi Omega (Svc. to Students award 1996). Avocations: puppets, frogs, travel. Office: WPI 100 Instit Rd Worcester MA 01609-2280 E-mail: svick@wpi.edu.

VICKERS, MARCIA, journalist; BA, Meredith Coll., 1983; MA, Columbia U. Grad. Sch. Journalism. Editor-in-chief On Wall St., Securites Data Pub./Thomson; contbr. NY Times Sunday Bus. Section, 1996—98; dept. editor markets and investments Bus. Week, 1999—2000, assoc. editor, prin. markets reporter, 2000—. Adj. prof.; appeared on Moneyline, CNNfn, ABC News' World News Tonight with Peter Jennings, Nat. Pub. Radio, Money Talks, WABC-TV, NY. Recipient Medill/Strong Fin. Writing award, 1999, 2000. Office: Bus Week 1221 Ave of the Americas 43rd Fl New York NY 10020 Office Phone: 212-512-2511.*

VICKERS, NANCY J. academic administrator; BA, Mt. Holyoke Coll., 1967, LHD (hon.), 1999; MA, Yale U., 1971, PhD, 1976. Prof. French and Italian Dartmouth Coll., 1973—87; prof. French, Italian, and comparative literature U. Southern Calif., 1987—97, dean curriculum and instrn. Coll. Letters, Arts and Scis., 1994—97; pres. Bryn Mawr Coll., 1997—. Vis. prof. Harvard U., U. Pa., UCLA; bd. dirs. Bryn Mawr Bank Corp.; bd. govs. U. Calif. Humanities Rsch. Inst., Coun. Dante Soc. Am. Recipient Presdl. medal Outstanding Leadership and Achievement, Dartmouth Coll., 1991; fellow vis. fellow, Princeton U. Office: Bryn Mawr Coll 101 N Merion Ave Bryn Mawr PA 19010-2899

VICKERY, ANN MORGAN, lawyer; b. Anderson, S.C., June 25, 1944; d. Joseph Harold and Doris (Rogers) Morgan; m. Raymond Ezekiel Vickery, Jr., June 23, 1979; children: Raymond Morgan, Philip Dickens. AB History, Mary Baldwin Coll., 1965; JD, Georgetown U., 1978. Bar: D.C. 1978. Elem. sch. tchr., Chesterfield County, Va., 1965-66; legal publs. specialist Nat. Archives and Record Svc., Washington, 1966-69; speech writing staff to Pres., rsch. asst., chief rschr., staff asst. The White House, Washington, 1969-74; summer clerk Graham & James, Washington, 1975; various positions Dept. Treasury, Washington, 1975-78; atty. Hogan & Hartson, LLP, Washington, 1978—. Health group dir. Hogan and Hartson, LLP, Washington, 1991—, exec. com., 1992-95, 96-99, Washington office mng. ptnr., 1999—; outside legal counsel Nat. Hospice and Palliative Care Orgn., 1982— (named Woman of the Yr. 1986); spkr. in field. Contbr. articles to profl. jours. Dir. Hospice No. Va., Arlington, 1987-93; trustee Nat. Hospice Found., 1996—. Mem. ABA, Am. Health Lawyers Assn., D.C. Bar, Health on Wednesday, Phi Alpha Theta. Office: Hogan & Hartson LLP Columbia Square 555 13th St NW Ste 12E-300 Washington DC 20004-1161

VICKREY, HERTA M. microbiologist; b. San Gregorio, Calif. m. William David Vickrey; children: Ellean H., Carlene L. Smith, Corrine A. Pochop, Arlene A.; m. Robert James Fitzgibbon, Dec. 28, 1979. BA, San Jose State U., 1957; MA, U. Calif., Berkeley, 1963, PhD in Bacteriology and Immunology, 1970. Cert. immunologist, pub. health microbiologist, clin. lab. scientist. Pub. health microbiologist Viral & Rickettsial Diseases Lab., Calif. State Dept. Pub. Health, Berkeley, 1958-60, 61-62, 1964; postgrad. rsch. bacteriologist dept. bacteriology U. Calif., Berkeley, 1963-64; bacteriologist Children's Hosp. Med. Ctr. No. Calif., Oakland, 1958-70; asst. prof. U. Victoria, B.C., Can., 1970-72; rsch. assoc. rsch. dept. Wayne County Gen. Hosp., Wayne, Mich., 1972-83; lab. supr. med. rsch. and edn. U. Mich., Ann Arbor, 1977-83; pub. health lab. dir. Shasta County Pub. Health Svcs., Redding, Calif., 1983-84; sr. pub. health microbiologist Tulare County Pub. Health Lab., Tulare, Calif., 1984—, rsch. supr. Visalia, Calif., 1992-93; med. technologist Hillman Health Clin. Lab., Tulare, Calif., 1994-96, clin. lab. scientist, 1996—. Vis. scientist MIT, Cambridge, 1982; organizer, lectr. mycology workshop Tulare County Health Dept. Lab., Visalia, 1988; USPHS trainee U. Calif., Berkeley, 1965, 66. Author: Isolation and Identification of Mycotic Agents, 1987-88; contbr. articles to profl. jours. Fundraiser Battered Women's Shelter, Redding, 1983, Real Opportunities for Youth, Visalia, 1985, 86, Open Gate Ministries, Dinuba, Visalia, 1987-94, 97-99, 2003. Fellow NIH, 1966-69, Dr. E.E. Dowdle rsch. fellow, U. Calif., 1969-70; grantee U. Victoria, 1970-72, Med. Rsch. and Edn. and Med. Adminstrn., U. Mich., 1973-83. Mem. No. Calif. Assn. Pub. Health Microbiologists, Calif. Scholarship Soc., Am. Soc. Clin. Pathologists (assoc.), Phi Beta Kappa, Delta Omega, Phi Kappa Phi, Beta Beta Beta. Avocations: biking, hiking, swimming. Home: 3505 W Campus Dr Apt 5 Visalia CA 93277-1869 Office: Tulare County Pub Health Lab 1062 S K St Tulare CA 93274-6421

VICTOR, LORRAINE CAROL, critical care nurse; b. Duluth, Minn., June 14, 1953; d. George E. and Phyllis M. (Pierce) Drimel; m. Robert G. Victor BA in Nursing, Coll. St. Scholastica, 1975; MS in Nursing, U. Minn., 1984; postgrad., Coll. St. Catherine. Cert. regional trainer for neonatal resuscitation program; cert. critical care clin. nurse specialist; cert. neonatal nurse practitioner. Staff nurse St. Mary's Hosp., Rochester, Minn., 1975-79, 81-00, U. Wis. Hosp., Madison, 1979-80, U. Minn. Hosps., Mpls., 1981-84, 85-86; clin. instr. neonatal ICU, Children's Hosp., St. Paul, 1984-86; clin. nurse specialist neonatal ICU, Orlando (Fla.) Regional Med. Ctr., 1986-88, Children's Hosp., St. Paul, 1988—2001; neonatal nurse practitioner Children's Hosp., St. Paul, 2001—. Mem. AACN (Critical Care Nurse of Yr.award Greater Twin Cities chpt. 1992), Nat. Assn. Neonatal Nurses, Acad. Neonatal Nursing, Sigma Theta Tau. Office: Children's Hosps & Clinics St Paul Birth Ctr 345 Smith Ave N Saint Paul MN 55102-2369

VICTORY, NANCY, federal agency administrator; BA, Princeton U.; JD, Georgetown U. Ptnr. Wiley, Rein & Fielding, Washington; asst. sec. for comm. and info. Dept. Commerce, Washington, 2001—, adminstr. Nat. Telecom. and Info. Adminstrn., 2001—. Office: Dept Commerce Nat Telecom and Info Adminstrn 14th & Constitution Ave NW Washington DC 20230

VIDAL, MAUREEN ERIS, theater educator, actress; b. Bklyn., Mar. 18, 1956; d. Louis and Lillian (Kaplan) Hendelman; m. Juan Vidal, June 25, 1974 (div. Sept. 1981); m. Guillermo Eduardo Uriarte, Dec. 22, 1986. BA, Bklyn. Coll., 1976, MS, 1981. From english tchr. to drama tchr. N.Y.C. Bd. Edn., 1976—2002, chair women's history dept., 1984—, dean, 1997—, drama tchr., 2002—. Mem PETA Humane Soc. Mem.: AFTRA, Gorilla Soc., Nat. Anti-Vivisection Soc. (mem. physicians' com. responsible medicine), Heights Players Theater Co. (arranger theatrical performance for residents of homeless shelters 1986—2003, exec. bd., sec. 1993—, actress), Doris Day Animal League, Delta Psi Omega. Avocations: travel, whitewater rafting, scuba diving, skydiving, theater. Home: 3380 Nostrand Ave Brooklyn NY 11229-4056 Office: I S 318 101 Walton St Brooklyn NY 11206-4311 also: Heights Players 26 Willow Pl Brooklyn NY 11201-4513 E-mail: MVidal4942@aol.com.

VIDAL-BROWN, SHERRY, psychologist; m. Roger Brown. BA, Baylor U., 1990; MBA, U. Houston, 2000; PhD in Psychology, Tex. A&M, 2000. Cons., Dallas, 2000—01; dir. orgnl. devel. Am. Airlines, Dallas, 2001—. Bd. dirs. Girls Inc., Dallas, 2002. Bank Am. scholar, U. Houston. Mem.: APA, Soc. Indsl. Psychologists. Office: Am Airlines PO Box 619616 Dallas TX 75261-9616

VIDAVER, ANNE MARIE, plant pathology educator; b. Vienna, Mar. 29, 1938; came to U.S., 1941; d. Franz and Klara (Winter) Kopecky; children: Gordon W.F., Regina M. BA, Russell Sage Coll., 1960; MA, Ind. U., 1962, PhD, 1965. Lectr. U. Nebr., Lincoln, 1965-66, rsch. assoc., 1966-72, asst. prof., 1972-74, assoc. prof., 1974-79, prof. plant pathology, 1979—, interim dir. Ctr. Biotech., 1988-89, 97-00, head dept. plant pathology, 1984-2000, 2003—; chief scientist USDA's NRICGP, 2000—02. Contbr. articles to profl. jours. and books; patentee in field. Recipient Pub. Svc. award Nebr. Agri-Bus., 1977, Sci. award for excellence NAMA, New Orleans, 1991. Fellow AAAS, Am. Phytopath. Soc., Am. Soc. Microbiology; mem. Intersoc. Consortium for Plant Protection, Internat. Soc. Plant Pathology, Alliance for Prudent Use of Antibiotics. Avocations: indoor gardening, reading. Office: U Nebr Dept Plant Pathology Lincoln NE 68583-0722 E-mail: avidaver1@unl.edu.

VIDERGAR, TERESA, music educator, musician; b. San Barnardino, Calif., Oct. 9, 1963; d. John August and Frances Vidergar. MusB in Piano Performance, Calif. State U., Fullerton, 1986; MusM in Piano Performance, Eastman Sch. Music, 1990. Cert. multiple subject tchr. 2003. Piano instr. Teresa Vidergar Piano Studio, Fontana, Calif., 1981—; staff accompanist Temple Beth Israel Synagogue, Pomona, Calif., 1984—87, St. Anne Cath. Ch., San Bernardino, 1986—87, accompanist San Barnardino, Calif., 1991—96; accompanist for diocese Holy Rosary Cathedral, San Bernardino, 1986—87; piano accompanist CCD Congress, Cath. Convention, Anaheim, Calif., 1987; piano soloist, recitalist city colls. and recital series, Calif. and NY, 1986—94; piano instr. Music Maker Music Sch., Anaheim, 1996—. Piano adjudicator South Western Youth Music Festival, Southern Calif., 2000—. Bd. dirs., chmn. regional festival So. Calif. Jr. Bach Festival, 2001—. Recipient 3d prize, Joanna Hodges Internat. Piano Competition, 1985, Cert. of Merit, So. Calif. Jr. Bach Festival. Mem.: Music Tchrs. Assn. Calif. (state adjudicator chmn. for Composers Today program 2001—, 2d v.p. San Bernardino br. 1997—, award for Young Artist Debut Concert 1985, award for performance at state conv. 1985, Cert. of Merit Piano Exams), Music Tchrs. Nat. Assn. Office: Music Maker Music Sch 5701 E Santa Ana Canyon Rd Anaheim CA 92807

VIDERMAN, LINDA JEAN, paralegal, corporate executive; b. Follansbee, W.Va., Dec. 4, 1957; d. Charles Richard and Louise Edith (LeBoeuf) Roberts; m. David Gerald Viderman Jr., Mar. 15, 1974; children: Jessica Renae, April Mae, Melinda Dawn. AS, W.Va. No. C.C., 1983; cert. income tax prep., H&R Block, Steubenville, Ohio, 1986. Cert. surg. tech., fin. counselor; lic. ins. agt. Food prep. pers. Bonanza Steak House, Weirton, W.Va., 1981—83; ward clk., food svcs. Weirton Med. Ctr., 1982—84; sec., treas. Mountaineer Security Systems, Inc., Wheeling, W.Va., 1983—86; owner, operator The Button Booth, Colliers, W.Va., 1985—; paralegal, adminstr. Atty. Dominic J. Potts, Steubenville, Ohio, 1987—92; gen. ptnr., executrix Panhandle Homes, Wellsburg, W.Va., 1988—96; sec.-treas., executrix Panhandle Homes, Inc., 1996—; ins. agt. Milico, Mass. Indemnity, 1991—92, L&L Ins. Svcs., 1992—94; paralegal Atty. Fred Risovich II, Weirton, 1991—93, [illegible] paralegal Cipriani & Paull, L.C., Wellsburg, W.Va., 1993—2004; owner Wellsburg Office Supply, 1993—94; owner, operator Viderman Child Care Svcs. Co., Wellsburg, 1997—; owner, dir. Viderman & Assocs., Wellsburg, 1997—; legal asst. Cassidy, Myers, Cogan, Voegelin, & Tennant, L.C., 2004—. Notary pub., 1991—. Contbr. articles to profl. jours.; author numerous poems. Chmn. safety com. Colliers (W.Va.) Primary PTA, 1985-87; founding mem. Brooke County Homeschoolers/Panhandle Homeschoolers Assn., 1999; editor Panhandle Homeschoolers Newsletter, 2000; mem., sec. LaLeche League, Steubenville, Ohio, 1978-80; vol. counselor W.Va. U. Fin. Counseling Svc., 1990—; IRS vol. Vol. Income Tax Assistance Program, 1991—. Mem. W.Va. Manufactured Housing Assn. (bd. dirs. 2001-), W.Va. Writers Assn., Legal Assts. of W.Va., Inc., Am. Affiliate of Nat. Assn. Legal Assts., W.Va. Trial Lawyers Assn., Wellsburg Art Assn., Brooke County Genealogical Soc., Phi Theta Kappa. Jehovah'S Witness. Avocations: christian ministry, home computing, camping, genealogy, home schooling. Home: RR2 Box 28 Wellsburg WV 26070-9500 Office: Panhandle Homes Inc RR 2 Box 27A Wellsburg WV 26070-9500 E-mail: lviderman@aol.com.

VIEIRA, MEREDITH, television personality; b. Providence, Dec. 30, 1951; m. Richard Cohen June 14, 1986; children: Benjamin, Gabriel, Lily Max. BA in English (magna cum laude), Tufts U., 1975. News announcer WORC-Radio, Worcester, Mass., 1975; reporter, anchor WJAR-TV, Providence, R.I.; reporter WCBS-TV, N.Y.C., 1979-82; from reporter to news correspondent CBS News, N.Y.C., 1982-93; chief correspondent ABC News, N.Y.C., 1993—; co-host The View, N.Y.C., 1997—; host Lifetime TV's Intimate Portrait, 1999—. Host The Miss America Pageant, 1998; narrator ABC TV special Open Sesame: The Making of Arabian Nights, 2000; host ABC special The Beatles Revelation, 2000, ABC TV Network's Countdown to Oscar, 2000, Who Wants to Be a Millionaire, 2002. Recipient Front Page award Newswoman's Club of N.Y., 1991, Robert F. Kennedy journalism award, 1995, Woman of Yr. award, City of Hope, 2001, six Emmy awards for reporting; honored by Anti-Defamation League; Found. Am. Women Radio and T.V., 1997. Office: ABC 320 W 66th St New York NY 10023-6304*

VIERRA, AMANDA ROSE, counselor; b. San Jose, Calif., Nov. 29, 1978; d. Elaine Margaret and Harold Joseph Vierra. BA in psychology, York U., 1998—2000. Teacher's aide Dom Dinis Preschool & Daycare, San Jose, Calif., 1993—96; devel. asst. Notre Dame H.S., San Jose, Calif., 2000—02; domestic violence group counselor Gardner Health Care - Proyecto Primavera Batterers Intervention Program, San Jose, Calif., 2001—02; after care specialist Family Supportive Housing San Jose (Calif.) Family Shelter, 2002—. Phys. therapy asst. Precision Biomechanics, Santa Barbara, Calif., 1998. Web designer (scholastic webpage) Adolescent Psychology. Avocations: hockey, web design, photography. Office: San Jose Family Shelter 1590 Las Plumas Ave San Jose CA 95133 Office Phone: 408-926-8885 111. Personal E-mail: madhadder45@yahoo.com.

VIGEN, KATHRYN L. VOSS, nursing administrator, educator; b. Lakefield, Minn., Sept. 24, 1934; d. Edward Stanley and Bertha C. (Richter) Voss; m. David C. Vigen, June 23, 1956 (div. 1977); children: Eric. E., Amy Vigen Hemstad, Aana Marie. BS in Nursing magna cum laude, St. Olaf Coll., 1956; MEd, S.D. State U., 1975; MS, Rush U., 1980; PhD, U. Minn., 1987. RN. Staff nurse various hosps., Mpls, Boston, Chgo., 1956-68; nursing instr. S.E.A. Sch. Practical Nursing, Sioux Falls, S.D., 1969-74; statewide coord. upward mobility in nursing Augustana Coll., Sioux Falls, S.D., 1974-78; cons./researcher S.D. Commn. Higher Edn., 1974-79; gov. appointed bd. mem. S.D. Bd. Nursing, 1975-79; RN upward mobility project dir., chair/dir. div. of nursing Huron Coll. S.D. State U., 1978-79, mobility project dir., 1980-84; head dept. nursing, assoc. prof. Luther Coll., Decorah, Iowa, 1984-94; prof. nursing Graceland Coll., Independence, Mo., 1994-2001; dir., dean Sch. Nursing, North Park U., Chgo., 2001—. Cons. in field; developer outreach MSN programs Graceland Coll.; governing bd. mem. Midwest Alliance in Nursing, S.D. and Iowa, 1984-92, Mo., 1998—; founder Soc. for Advancement of Nursing, Malta, 1992; developer Health Care in the Mediterranean Study Abroad Program, Greece and Malta, 1994, 96, 98; developer summer internship for Maltese nursing students Mayo Med. Ctr. and Luther Coll.; presenter on internat. collaboration with Malta for nursing leadership 2d Internat. Acad. Congress on Nursing, Kansas City, 1996; presenter in field. Author: Role of a Dean in a Private Liberal Arts College, 1992; devel. and initiated 3 nursing programs in S.D., 1974-84 (named Women of Yr., 1982). Lobbyist Nursing Schs. in S.D., 1974-79; task force mem. Sen. Tom Harkin's Nurse's Adv. Com., 1986-94. Fellow to rep. U.S.A. ANA cand. in internat. coun. nursing 3M, St. Paul, 1978; recipient Leadership award Bush Found., St. Paul, 1979; Faculty fellow Minn. Area Geriatric Edn. Ctr. U. Minn., 1990-91; Fulbright scholar to Malta, 1992; recipient Fulbright award Malta Coun. Internat. Exch. of Scholars, Washington, 1992—; named Disting. Alumna, St. Olaf Coll., 2003. Mem. AAUW, ANA, AACN (hon. mem.), Am. Assn. Colls. Nursing (hon., exec. devel. subcom. 1990—, Hon. Mem. award), Internat. Assn. Human Caring, Iowa Nurse's Assn. (bd. dirs. 1989-92, mem. nursing edn. com. 1989—, co-pres. 1989—), Midwest Alliance in Nursing (gov. bd. rep. Iowa 1989-92, chair membership com. 1989-92, Mo., 1998—, S.D. gov. bd. rep. 1984-86, Rozella Schlotfeldt Leadership award 1993), Iowa Acad. Sci., Iowa Assn. Colls. Nursing Soc., Gerontol. Soc. Am., Am. Assn. Colls. Mich., Rotary, Sigma Theta Tau. Democrat. Lutheran. Avocations: singing, travel and other cultures, meeting people, sailing, reading. Home: 5360 N Lowell Ave # 412 Chicago IL 60630 Office: North Park U 3225 W Foster Ave Chicago IL 60625 Office Phone: 773-244-5235.

VIGIL, DEBBIE SAXON, surgical technician; b. Lake Charles, La., Oct. 29, 1959; d. Odis McNeil and Mary Lou (Collins) Saxon; m. Johnny S. Vigil, May 17, 1980 (div. Aug. 1995); children: Johnny, Shawn. Home health aide Superior Home Health, Murry, Utah, 1996—98; surg. technologist U. Utah Hosp., Salt Lake City, 2000—. Home: 21 W Wasatch St Midvale UT 84047

VIGIL-GIRON, REBECCA, state official; b. Taos, N.Mex., Sept. 4, 1954; d. Felix W. and Cecilia (Santistevan) Vigil; 1 child, Andrew R. AA in Elem. Edn., N.Mex. Highlands U., 1978, BA in French, 1991. Sec., project monitor, customer svc. rep. Pub. Svc. Co. N.Mex., 1978-86; sec. of state N.Mex., 1987-90, 98—; exec. dir. N.Mex. Commn. Status of Women, 1991; electoral observer UN, Angola, Africa, 1992, Internat. Found. Electoral Sys., Dominican Republic, 1994, 1996, Washington, 1996. Participant AMPART, Mex., 1991. Dem. nominee U.S. Ho. Reps., 1990. Named among 100 Most Influential Hispanics in Nation, Hispanic Bus. Mag., 1990; recipient Trio Achievers award S.W. Assn. Student Assistance Programs, 1993, Gov.'s award Outstanding N.Mex. Women, 1994. Mem. Albuquerque Hispano C. of C. (membership rep., sr. sales mktg. rep., corp. rels. coord.) Democrat. Office: Office of the New Mexico Secretary of State State Capitol North Annex, Suite 300 Santa Fe NM 87503

VIGLIOTTI, PATRICIA NOREEN, welder, sculptor; b. Poughkeepsie, N.Y., May 13, 1955; d. James George and Florence Violet (Terwilligar) Dingee; Grad. h.s., Stratsbough. Welder Argos Inc., Brester, N.Y., 1989—; owner Vigliotti Sculpture Gallery & Studio, Balwinville, N.Y. One woman shows include Ward Lawrence, N.Y.C., Gallery 84; exhibited in group shows at Tannery Brook Collections Gallery, Woodstock, N.Y., Samagundi Club Galleries, New Rochell Art Assn. (hon. mention), Gregg Chlm Gallery, 1992, Comm. Acad. of Fine Arts, 1992, Orgn. of Ind. Artists, N.Y.C., represented in Providence Town of Mass. by Ester Lastique; featured as a sculptor in New Art International, 1997-98. Avocation: raising cockatiels and iguanas. Home: 8 Parker Dr E Mahopac NY 10541-2059

VIGORITO, ROSARIA SUSANNA, law librarian, adult education edu- [illegible] b. Long Branch, New Jersey, Apr. 28, 1959; d. [illegible] Armando and Aida Vigorito. BA cum laude(hon.), N.Y. Univ.; grad sch. of Arts and Sci., and Internat. Politics and Bus.1981, N.Y. Univ.1982; JD (hon.), Bkyln. Law Sch., 1985; LLM in Trade regulation (hon.), N.Y. Univ., 1987; MLS (hon.), Rutgers State Univ., 1995; MFA, N.Y. Acad. Art, Grad Sch. of Figurative Art, 2003. Bar: N.Y. 1986, N.Y. (So. and Ea. Dist) 1989, U.S. Supreme Court: 1997. Pub. policy assoc. Fed. of Protestant Welfare Agencies, N.Y., 1985—86; assoc. Duetsch, Klagsbrun, and Blasband, N.Y., 1987—91; evening ref. and ILL Libr. N.Y., 1992—95; assoc. prof., gov. docs., spl. collections Libr. Peter W. Rodino Law Libr. Seton Hall Univ. Sch. of Law, Newark, 1996—97; assoc. prof., internat. law,gov. docs., ref. libr., 1997—99; assoc. prof. internat. law and ref. libr. City Univ. of N.Y., N.Y., 1999—. Co-editor: Directory of Gov. Docs. Collections and Librarians, 1997; author: Computer Assisted Legal Rsch. for N.Y. Paralegals; Inst. for Paralegals Edn., 2002, (article) The Evolution and Establishment of the ICC, 2002. Bd mem. Actors Alliance, NY, 1988—91, Am. Cancer Soc. Lesbian, Bisexual and Transgender project, NY, 2002; exhibiting artist Am. Cancer Soc. Lesbian, Bisexual and Transgender project launch party, NY, 2002; breast walk NY, 1998—99; participating artist N.Y. Acad. of Art Grad. Exhbn., 2003. Mem.: N.J. Law Libr. Assn. (sec. 1996—97, v.p. and pres. elect 1997—99, pres. 1998—99, exec. bd. mem. 1999—2000), Law Libr. Assn. of Greater N.Y., Am. Soc. of Internat. Law, Am. Assn. of Law Libr., Am. Bar Assn. Achievements include fluent speaking and bacic reading Italian. Avocations: painting, art, sculpture, yoga, baseball, opera, literature, fgn. / ind. films, travel. Office: City Univ of NY Sch of Law 65-21 Main St Flushing NY 11228 E-mail: vigorito@mail.law.cuny.edu.

VIGUS, REBECKA ANN, education educator; b. Flint, Mich., Feb. 28, 1954; d. William and Donavee Vigus; 1 child, Jamie Renee Kline. BS, Ea. Mich. U., Ypsilanti, Mich., 1976; MA, Oakland U., Rochester, Mich., 1999. Cert. 30 hour Continuing Mich., 1990. Adj. faculty Kirtland C.C., Roscommon, Mich., 1992—2000; tchr. West Branch-Rose City Sch., West Branch, Mich., 1989—. Bldg. rep. WBRCEA, West Br., Mich., 2001—03; curriculum coun. rep West Br.- Rose City Schools, West Br., Mich., 2002—; 21st century cmty. learning ctr. grant team MSU Ext., West Br., Mich., 2001—; sch. improvement team Rose City Elem.-Mid. Sch., Rose City, Mich., 2002—; disney tchr. award nominee Disney Learning Partership, Burbank, Calif., 2001. Author poetry to profl. jour.; poet (poetry) Pals; editor: (newsletter for women) Lady Rebecka's Tea Room Tribune; poet (poetry) Reawakened. Vol. tutor Mich. Dyslexia Inst., West Br., Mich., 1994—97; booster WB-RC Athletic Boosters, West Br., Mich., 1989—94; music booster WBRC Music Boosters, West Br., Mich., 1989—94. Mem.: WBRCEA (region coun. del. 2003—), MEA-R (life), Am. Grant Writers Assn. (assoc.), Internat. Soc. of Poets (life). Personal E-mail: rebeckavigus@sbcglobal.net.

VILA, ADIS MARIA, lawyer, academic administrator, educator; b. Cuba, Aug. 1, 1953; d. Calixto Vila and Adis C. Fernandez. BA with distinction, Rollins Coll., 1974; JD with honors, U. Fla., 1978; LLM with high honors, Institut Universitaire de Hautes Estudes Internationales, Geneva, 1981; MBA, U Chgo., 1997. Bar: Fla. 1979, DC 1984. Assoc. Paul & Thomson, 1979-82; White House fellow Office Pub. Liaison, Washington, 1982-83; spl. asst. to sec. state for inter-Am. affairs Dept. State, Washington, 1983-86; dir. Office of Mex. and Caribbean Basin, Dept. Commerce, Washington, 1986-87; sec. Dept. Adminstrn., State of Fla., 1987-89; asst. sec. for adminstrn. USDA, Washington, 1989-91; vis. fellow Nat. Def. U., Washington, 1992-93; v.p. internat. devel. Vigoro Corp., Chgo., 1994-95; v.p. govt. affairs regulatory policy, Carribean & Latin Am. Nortel Networks, 1997-2000; pres., CEO Vila & Assocs., 2001—; prof. Huizenga Grad. Sch. Bus. Nova Southeastern U. Vis. asst. prof. Fla. Internat. U., 1993—94; mem. adv. bd. Ams. Global Asset Mgmt. Fund, 1999—; v.p. external affairs Miami Dade C.C., 2002—03; adj. prof. internat. bus. strategy and internat. law Nova Southeastern U., 2002—. Trustee So. Ctr. Internat. Studies, 1987—. Named one of 100 Most Influential Hispanics, 1988; Paul Harris fellow, Rotary Internat., 1983, U.S.-Japan Leadership fellow, 1991—92, Eisenhower Exch. fellow, Beca Fiore, Argentina, 1992. Mem.: Women Execs. in State Govt. (bd. dirs. 1987—89), Am. Coun. Young Polit. Leaders (bd. dirs. 1984—), Internat. Women's Forum, Coun. Fgn. Rels. (term mem. 1987—92), Dade County Bar Assn. (bd. dirs. young and lawyers sect. 1979—87). Republican. Roman Catholic. Avocations: tennis, skiing, golf, theater, art.

VILARDO, CAROLE, research association administrator; b. Bronx, N.Y., Mar. 11, 1941; d. Thomas and Victoria Vilardo. Cert., Tobe-Coburn Sch., 1960. Group mgr. Gimbel Bros., N.Y.C., 1960-63; gen. mgr. Showcase Shops, N.Y.C., 1963-71; owner Fashion Gallery, Las Vegas, Nev., 1971-79, Whatever, Ltd., Las Vegas, 1979-85; pres. Nev. Taxpayers Assn., Las Vegas and Carson City, 1986—. Pub. mem. Legis. Interim Tax Commn., Nev., 1979-81, 93-95; adv. mem. Gov.'s Health Care Study, Nev., 1996-98, Water Infrastructure Funding, Clark County,Nev., 1996-97. Contbr. articles to profl. publs.; editor rsch. papers in field. Bd. dirs. Winchester Town Bd., 1989-92; founding mem. Secret Witness, Clark County, 1979-92; bd. dirs. Nat. Kidney Found. of Nev., 1996—, v.p., 1992-93; bd. dirs. YMCA of So. Nev., 1992—. Recipient Free Enterprise award Las Vegas C. of C., 1981, Women of Achievement award Las Vegas C. of C., 1991, Homer Rodriquez award Nev. Assessors' Assn., 1997. Mem. Nat. Taxpayers Conf. (bd. dirs. 1995—). Avocations: gardening, cooking, reading. Office: Nev Taxpayers Assn 2303 E Sahara Ave Ste 203 Las Vegas NV 89104-4138

VILAS, FAITH, aerospace scientist; b. Evanston, Ill., Apr. 14, 1952; d. Jack Jr. and Faith McCrea (Lehman) V.; m. Larry Wayne Smith, July 5, 1986. BA, Wellesley (Mass.) Coll., 1973; MS, MIT, 1975; PhD, U. Ariz., 1984. Sr. rsch. asst. Cerro Tololo Inter-Am. Obs., La Serena, Chile, 1975-77; sr. assoc. scientist Lockheed Electronics Co., Houston, 1977-78; vis. rsch. scientist NRC, Johnson Space Ctr., Houston, 1984-85; space scientist NASA, Johnson Space Ctr., Houston, 1985—, chief planetary astronomy group, 2002—; discovery program scientist NASA Hdqs., Washington, 2001—02; chief planetary astronomy group Johnson Space Ctr., 2002—. Editor: (with C.R. Chapman and M.S. Matthews) Mercury, 1988; mem. editl. bd. Icarus, 2001—03. Bd. dirs. Vatican Observatory Found., 1996—. Mem. Am. Astron. Soc. (div. planetary scis. nominating com. 1988-91, sec. 1992-95, vice chmn. 1995-96, chmn. 1996-97, prize com. chmn. 1997-98), Johnson Space Ctr. Nat. Mgmt. Assn. (chair Am. enterprise com. 1987-88, Shield Excellence award 1988). Episcopalian. Avocations: traveling, flying, emergency medicine. Office: NASA Johnson Space Ctr Code SR Houston TX 77058 E-mail: Faith.Vilas-1@nasa.gov.

VILE, SANDRA JANE, leadership training educator; b. Oceanside, N.Y., Oct. 4, 1939; d. John Oliver and Roberta May (Wood) Ryan; m. Joseph Charles Vile, June 27, 1964; children: Jonathan Charles, Susan Jane. BS in Christian Edn. cum laude, Nyack Coll., 1961; MS in Edn., SUNY, Oneonta, 1963; diploma, Childrens Ministries Inst., Warrenton, Mo., 1974; Cert. in Visual Comm., Faith Venture Visuals, Inc., Lititz, Pa., 1979. Cert. elem. tchr., N.Y. Tchr. Hudson (N.Y.) City Sch. Dist., 1961-64, South Orangetown Ctrl. Sch. Dist., Orangeburg, N.Y., 1964-67; local dir. Child Evangelism Fellowship of Empire State, Afton, N.Y., 1972-88, state tng. instr., 1988-92; leadership tng. instr. Child Evangelism Fellowship, Inc., Warrenton, 1992—2002, vol. leadership tng. instr., 2002—. Vis. lectr. Nyack (N.Y.) Coll., 1967; tng. cons. Faith Venture Visuals, Inc., 1980-96. Contbr.: Children's Ministry Resource Bible, 1993. Lay leader Teen Missions, Inc., Merritt Island, Fla., 1982. Recipient Alumna of Yr. award Faith Venture Visuals, Inc., 1993. Mem. Pro Merito Soc., Logicians Soc. Avocations: computers, travel, counted cross-stitch. Home and Office: 270 Route 27B Hudson NY 12534-3919

VILIM, NANCY CATHERINE, advertising agency executive; b. Quincy, Mass., Jan. 15, 1952; d. John Robert and Rosemary (Malpede) V.; m. Geoffrey S. Horner, Feb. 16, 1992; children: Matthew Edward Cajda, Megan Catherine Cajda, Margaret Horner. Student, Miami U., Oxford, [illegible] Daniels Inc., Chgo., 1973-74; asst. buyer Campbell Mithun, Chgo., 1974-75; buyer Tatham, Laird & Kudner, Chgo., 1975-77; media buyer Adcom, Inc. div. Quaker Oats Corp., Chgo., 1977-79; media supr. G.M. Feldman, Chgo., 1979-81; v.p. media dir. Media Mgmt., 1981-83; v.p. broadcast dir. Bozell, Jacobs, Kenyon & Eckhardt, Chgo., 1983-88; v.p., media mgr. McCann-Erickson, Inc., 1989—2002; broadcast supr. OMD USA, Chgo., 2002—04; sr. media buyer GSD&M, Chgo., 2004—. Judge 27th Internat. Broadcast Awards, Chgo., 1987. Co-pres. Immaculate Conception Religious Edn. Parents Club, 1995-96. Recipient Media All Star awards Sound Mgmt. Mag., N.Y.C., 1987. Mem. Broadcast Advt. Club Chgo., Mus. Broadcast Communications, NAFE. Office: GSD&M 625 N Michigan Ave Chicago IL 60601

VILLACHICA, ANDREA LUISA, art educator; d. Carlos Alberto Villachica and Gloria Jean Taylor; m. Andrew Maxwell Taylor, July 17, 1997. BA, BFA, U. Colo., 1991, MA, 2001; educator license, Regis U., 1997. Box office mgr. Artist Series, Boulder, Colo., 1986—92; asst. dir. Macky Auditorium, Boulder, 1992—93; English tchr. Centro Mexicano Internacional, Morelia, Mexico, 1993—94; tchr. Commonwealth No. Marianas Pub. Schs., 1997—99; art educator Boulder Valley Pub. Schs., 1999—. Mem.: Nat. Assn. for Bilingual Edn., Nat. Art Edn. Assn. Avocations: ceramics, bicycling, languages.

VILLAGOMEZ, DEBORAH LYNN, medical/surgical nurse, horse breeder; b. Calumet, Mich., Sept. 29, 1962; d. Rudolph J. Kela and Lyla Lillian Seppala. Grad. in nursing, Coll. of Lake County, Grayslake, Ill., 1991. RN Wis., N.Mex. Arabian and Quarter Horse rancher, Edgewood, N.Mex. Home: 1138 Mountain Valley Rd Edgewood NM 87015

VILLA-KOMAROFF, LYDIA, molecular biologist, educator, university official; b. Las Vegas, N.Mex., Aug. 7, 1947; d. John Dias and Drucilla (Jaramillo) V.; m. Anthony Leader Komaroff, June 18, 1970. BA, Goucher Coll., 1970; PhD, MIT, 1975; DSc (hon.), St. Thomas U., 1996, Pine Manor Coll., 1997; PhD (hon.), Goucher Coll., 1997. Rsch. fellow Harvard U., Cambridge, 1975-78; asst. prof. dept. microbiology U. Mass. Med. Ctr., Worcester, 1978-81, assoc. prof. dept. molecular genetics micro, 1982-85; assoc. prof. dept. neurology Harvard Med. Sch., Boston, 1986-95; sr. rsch. assoc. neurology Children's Hosp., Boston, 1985-95, assoc. dir. mental retardation rsch. ctr., 1987-94; prof. dept. neurology Northwestern U., Evanston, Ill., 1995—2002, assoc. v.p. rsch., 1995-97, v.p. rsch., 1998—2002; v.p. for rsch., COO, Whitehead Inst. for Biomed. Rsch., Cambridge, Mass., 2003—; sr. lectr. Sloan Sch. Mgmt., MIT, 2003—. Mem. mammalian genetics study sect. NIH, 1982-84, mem. reviewers rsch., 1989, mem. neurol. disorders program project rev. com., 1989-94; mem. adv. bd. Biol. Sci. Directorate, NSF, 1994-99; bd. dirs. Nat. Ctr. Genome Rsch., 1995-2000, TransKaryotic Therapies, 2003—; mem. adv. coun. Nat. Inst. Neurol. Disorders and Stroke, NIH, 2000-04. Contbr. articles and abstracts to profl. jour.; patentee in field. Recipient Hispanic Engr. Nat. Achievement award, 1992, Nat. Achievement award Hispanic Mag., 1996; inducted Hispanic Engr. Nat. Achievement Hall of Fame, 1999;selected 50 most important Hispanics by "business & Tech., Hispanic Engr. & Info. Tech." mag. 2003; Helen Hay Whitney Found. fellow, 1975-78; NIH grantee, 1978-85, 89-96. Mem. AAAS (bd. dirs. 2000—), Am. Soc. Microbiology, Assn. for Women in Sci., Soc. for Neurosci., Am. Soc. Cell Biology, Soc. for Advancement Chicanos and Native Ams. in Sci. (founding, bd. dir. 1987-93, v.p. 1990-93). Office: Whitehead Inst Biomed Rsch 9 Cambridge Ctr Cambridge MA 02142 E-mail: luk@wi.mit.edu.*

VILLALON, DALISAY MANUEL, nurse, real estate broker; b. Angat, Bulacan, Philippines, Apr. 27, 1941; came to U.S., 1967; d. Federico Manuel and Librada (Garcia) Manuel; divorced; children: Ricky, May, Liberty, Derrick, Dolly Rose. BS in Nursing, Manila Cen. U., 1961; postgrad. in nursing, U. Ill., Chgo., 1972-74. RN, Ill. Instr. nursing Cen. Luzon Sch. Nursing, Philippines, 1966-67; staff nurse St. Alexis Hosp., Cleve., 1968-70, Augustana Hosp., Chgo., 1972-74; nurse mgr. Holy Child Med. Clinic, Chgo., 1976-80; nurse auditor 1st Health Care, Rosemont, Ill., 1982-83; dir. nurses North Shore Terr., Waukegan, Ill., 1983-90, Carlton House, 1991-94. Columnist Philippine News. Bd. dirs. Filipino Am. Coun., Chgo., 1978-80, v.p., 1980-82; bd. dirs. Asian Human Svcs., Chgo.; pres. Am.-Filipino Profl. Civic Alliance, Chgo., 1984-90, Philipino-Am. United for Svc.-Oriental Objective, 1991—; chmn. Philippine Week Com., 1979; past v.p. Filipino Ams. Concerned for Elderly; trustee Rizal-MacArthur Found.; past v.p. Filipino Svc. League, 1989-91; past exec. v.p. Asian Festival, Inc.; past chmn. various civic coms.; mem. Asian-Am. Adv. Coun. Mayor Daley, 1989-97. Recipient Cert. Appreciation Rizal-MacArthur Found., 1977, Most Outstanding Filipino in Midwest award Cavite Assn. Am., 1980, Outstanding Community Svc. Appreciation award Filipino Am. Coun., 1981, 89, NGHIA Sinh Internat., Inc., 1989, Outstanding Svc. award Asian-Am. Coaliton, 1989, Outstanding Contrn. award Dirs. Nursing and Adminstrs. Conf., 1988, Nat. Prism award 2003; named to Filipino Hall of Fame for comty. svc., 1996 Phil Reports TV. Mem. Ill. Nurses Assn. (bd. dirs., dist. senator 1989-91, human rights and ethics commn. 1990-91), Philippine Med. Assn. Aux. (pres. 1980, Outstanding Leadership award 1989), Chgo. Med. Soc. Aus. (v.p. 1980), Chgo. Philippine Lioness Club (pres. 1983-84, Outstanding Svc. award 1985), Filipino Woman's Club Chgo. (Outstanding Woman in Leadership 1992, Chgo. Filipino Hall of Fame award 1998), Filipino Am. Polit. Assn. Democrat. Roman Catholic. Home: 1070 Sanders Rd Northbrook IL 60062-2904 Office: Vitas Health Care Corp Vitas Innovative Care 700 N Sacramento Chicago IL 60612 Personal E-mail: delyvillalon@netzero.net.

VILLANI, LUISA, writer, educator; m. Michael Ray Yeager, Mar. 27, 1983 (dec. Jan. 1994); 1 child, David. MFA, MA, U. Pitt., 2000. Instr. Edinboro U. Pa., 2000—01, Indiana U. Pa., 2001—03. Coord., founder Project Chiapas, Northridge, Calif., 1994—97. Author: (book) On the Eve of Everything, 1998, Running Away From Russia, 2000. Pres. Amnesty Internat. CSUN, 1996—97. Grantee Bucknell Fellowship, Bucknell U., 1996, PCA Fellowship, Pa. Coun. Arts., 2002. Home: 10043 Wooaley Ave North Hills CA 91343

VILLARREAL, JUNE PATRICIA, sales consultant; b. Atlantic City, Sept. 26, 1929; d. Edmund N. and Dorothy R. (McDowell) Ricchezza; m. Ottavio Gelmi, Dec. 16, 1954 (div. 1964); 1 child, Alessandra; m. Robert Joseph McElroy, Oct. 16, 1970 (dec. May 1974); m. Carlos Castañeda Villarreal, Oct. 3, 2002. Student, Temple U., 1947-48, Georgetown U., 1951-53. Staff mem. Am. Consulate Gen., Milan, 1954; legis. asst. U.S. Senate, Washington, 1956; social sec. Amb. of Finland, Washington, 1958; adminstrv. asst., translator Roosevelt and Clark Lobbyists, 1958—59; legis. asst. to congressman Washington, 1960-65; sr. assoc. Gillmore M. Perry Co., Washington, 1965-76; sales exec., cons., 1980-87; ptnr. Mfrs. Representatives Internat., Washington, 1987-97; ret. Pres. Spanish-Portugese Study Group, 1994—95. Mem.: AAUW, Pan Am. Round Table, Equestrian Order Holy Sepulchre of Jerusalem (Lady Comdr. 2003—), Georgetown U. Alumni Assn., John Carroll Soc., Army Navy Club (Washington). Republican. Roman Catholic. Home: 4000 Cathedral Ave NW Apt 208B Washington DC 20016-5254

VILLASENOR, BARBARA, book publisher; b. L.A., Sept. 17, 1946; d. Charles Belmont and Zita (Lewis) Bloch; m. Victor Edmundo Villasenor, Dec. 29, 1974 (div. Dec. 1999); children: David Cuauhtemoc, Joseph Edmundo. BA in Sociology, U. Calif., Berkeley, 1967; postgrad., Radcliffe coll., 1967. Media buyer Diener Hauser Greenthal, L.A., 1971-76; editor Charles Pub., Oceanside, Calif., 1976-87, pub., 1987—. Ptnr. Strategies, San Diego, 1998—99; breath worker Heart to Heart, San Diego, 1988—94; event coord. Snow Goose Global Thanksgiving, Oceanside, 1992—; mem. Interfaith Alliance, San Diego, 1996—. Recipient award, Small Press Mag., 1996. Mem.: San Diego Publishers and Writers. Democrat. Avocations: creative expression, peace in the Mid. East. Office: Charles Publishing 1308 Stewart St Oceanside CA 92054-5448

VILLAVERDE, LEILA E. education educator; d. Jose Luis and Elba Villaverde; m. Roymeico A. Carter, Aug. 12, 2000. BS, Fla. Internat. U., 1994; MS, Ea. Va. Med. Sch., 1996; PhD, Pa. State U., 1999. Asst. prof. DePaul U., Chgo., 1999—2002, U. N.C., Greensboro, 2002—. Author: Secondary Education; co-editor: Rethinking Intelligence, 1999, Dismantling White Privilege, 2000; mem. editl. bd.: Taboo, 2001—, Greenwood Press, 2002—03. Mem.: Coll. Art Assn., Am. Ednl. Studies Assn., Am. Ednl. Rsch. Assn. Avocations: photography, art, writing. Office: UNCG Sch Edn 236 Curry Bldg Greensboro NC 27402

VILLEGAS, ALMA, theater director, actor, writer; d. Moisés Villegas and Antonia Fernández; m. Juan Sánchez, Mar. 13, 1987; 1 child, Liora Sánchez. BS in Home Econs., U. of PR, 1969; MS in Secondary Edn. & Biology, U. of Bridgeport, 1979; PhD in Ednl. Theater, NYU, 1995. Cert. prodr. Bklyn (N.Y.) Cmty. Access TV, 1999. Tchr. HS theater and sci. Dept. of Edn., Bayamón, PR, 1970—80; adj. prof. N.Y.C. (N.Y.) Tech. Coll., 1989; adj. asst. prof. CUNY, 1990; exec. and artistic dir. Música Against Drugs, Inc. The Art Ctr. for Cmty. Healing, Bklyn., 1995—. Artistic dir. Café Teatro Julia de Burgos, N.Y.C., 1992—94. Author: Intimate Voices; actor: Intimate Voices; dir.: (plays) Don Pedro Vive; author: (plays) Don Pedro Vive; dir., actor: (plays) Madre Selva: From Life to Spirit, Borinquén Mall: La Vitrina de las Américas; actor, prodr.: (plays) Julia de Burgos: Un Canto a la verdad sencilla. Mem. Christian Cultural Ctr., Bklyn., 1986—2003. Recipient Outstanding Work in Edn. & Theater award, Jardines de Caparra H.S., 1975, 1977, 1978, 1979, Best Direction and Performance award, Festival de la Lengua, Colegio Regional, de Bayamón, UPR, 1980; scholar, Instituto de Cultura Puertorriqueña, 1980—81. Mem.: NAFE, Soc. Stage Dirs. and Choreographers (assoc.). Home: 346 South Third Street Apt 1 Brooklyn NY 11211 Office: The Art Center for Community Healing 622 Broadway Brooklyn NY 11206 Office Phone: 718-218-7640. Personal E-mail: guariken@aol.com.

VILLEMAIRE, DIANE DAVIS, adult education educator; b. Burlington, Vt., Nov. 21, 1946; d. Ellsworth Quinlan and Elizabeth Charlotte (Galvin) Davis; m. Bernard Philip Villemaire, Aug. 16, 1969; 1 child, Emily Jane. BS, U. Vt., 1968, MA, 1994; PhD, McGill U., Montreal, Que., Can., 1999. Cert. secondary sch. tchr., Vt., nat. bd. profl. tchr. aya sci. Rsch. asst. U. Vt., Burlington, 1965-68; tchr. biology Burlington H.S., 1968-71, Harwood Union H.S., Moretown, Vt., 1971—. Adj. faculty U. Vt., 1998—; equity specialist Harwood Union HS, Duxbury, Vt., 2002—. Author: E.A. Burtt, Historian and Philosopher, A Biography of the author of the Metaphysical Foundations of Modern Physical Science, 2002. Mem. NEA, AAUW (discussion leader), Am. Assn. Biology Tchrs. (Outstanding Biology Tchr. award 1978), Soc. for Advancement of Am. Philosophy, Phi Alpha Theta. Democrat. Avocations: antique flowers, art, travel, science and scientific advancements. Office: Harwood Union HS Vt Rt 100 South Duxbury VT 05660-9404 Office Phone: 802-882-1174. E-mail: vilmaire@madriver.com.

VILLOCH, KELLY CARNEY, art director; b. Kyoto, July 22, 1950; d. William Riley and stepdaughter Hazel Fowler Carney; m. Joe D. Villoch, Aug. 9, 1969; children: Jonathan, Christopher, Jennifer. A in Fine Arts, Dade C.C., Miami, Fla., 1971; student, Metro Fine Arts, 1973-74, Fla. Internat. U., 1985-88. Design asst. Lanvin, Miami, 1971—74, Fieldcrest, Miami, 1974-77; art dir. Advercolor, Miami, 1977-78; art dir. copywriter ABC, Miami, 1978-89; writer Armed Forces Radio & TV Network; multimedia dir. ADVITEC, 1989-91; art dir. writer Miami Write, 1979—89; owner Beach Point Prodns., 1992—; editor-in-chief L'Avenue Mag., 1998—. Lectr. Miami Dade C.C., cons. Studio Masters, North Miami, 1979-89; writer Lucent Techs., Telephonetics, Algorhythm, Inter-tel, 1997—; creative mktg. dir. Raintree Media, 2000. Prin. works include mixed media, 1974 (Best of Show 1974), pen and ink drawing, 1988 (Best Poster 1988); writer, dir., editor, prodr. (video film) Bif, 1988, Drink + Drive = Die, 1994; scriptwriter (film) The Raft, 1994, (charity video) Rosie O'Donnell, 2002; writer, dir., prodr. (pub. svc. announcement) Reading is the Real Adventure, 1990; film editor Talent Times Mag.; author: Winds of Freedom, 1994; art dir., exec. com. Miami Hispanic Media Conf., 1992, 93, 94; editor-in-chief, film editor: In Grove Miami Mag., 1994-96; webmaster, web content provider, website design cons., writer, graphic artist Guru Comms., 1996; editor-in-chief L'Avenue Mag., Miami Mag., Fla. Journey and Miami Guide, 1998-99, Paladar mag., 2002, Decasa mag., 2002, Flash Animation: Passionate Nomad-A Journey Through Cairo, 2002; web content provider WEBCOM; webmaster Miami Metro Mag., 2000; sr. editor Channels Intl. Mag., 2001; web site designer, multimedia dir. State of Fla. grantee LimeLite Studios, Inc., 1990, William Douglas Pawley Found. grantee, Frances Wolfson scholar, Cultural Consortium grantee, 1993. Mem. Am. Film Inst., Phi Beta Kappa. Avocations: animation, printmaking, skin diving, boating, painting. E-mail: beachn@worldnet.att.net.

VINCENSI, AVIS A. sales executive, medical educator; b. Hazardville, Conn., July 10, 1949; d. George P. Vincensi and Hilda G. (Boucher) Vincensi(dec.). AS in Bus., Holyoke (Mass.) CC, 1987. Registered diagnostic med. sonographer, radiologic tech., radiography, mammography. X-ray technologist Baystate Med. Ctr., Springfield, Mass., 1969—73, Cooley Dickinson Hosp., Northampton, Mass., 1971—73, Holyoke Hosp., 1974—87, sonographer, 1973—82; sonographer, supr. Providence Hosp., Holyoke, 1982—87; sonographer Diagnostic Imaging, Springfield, Mass., 1987—90; product specialist/product mktg. sales Corometrics Med. Sys., Wallingford, Conn., 1991—96; diagnostic reagent rep. Sigma Diagnostics, St. Louis, 1996—2002; clin. adj. prof. Springfield Tech. CC, 1999—2002, assoc. prof., 2002—, bd. dirs., 1999—, assoc. prof., dept. chair diagnostic med. sonography, 2002—. Recipient 2 Gold medals and 1 Silver medal Tai Chi competition, 2002. Mem.: Am. Inst. Ultrasonic Medicine, Am. Registry Diagnostic Med. Sonographers. Home: 101 Acushnet Ave Springfield MA 01105-2218 E-mail: avincensi@stcc.edu.

VINCENT, VAL D. state legislator; b. Middlebury, Vt., June 15, 1948; m. John W. Vincent; 4 children. BA, Castleton State Coll., 1975. Tchr.; bus. owner; rep. State of Vt., 1991—. Bd. dirs. Small Bus. Devel. Ctr., Human Resources Investment Bd. Mem. Lund Family Ctr. Bd., Gov.'s Inst. Home: PO Box 131 Waterbury VT 05676-0131

VINE, NAOMI, museum administrator; b. Seattle; MA and PhD, U. Chgo., 1976; postgrad., Emory U., 1991—. Dir. of edn. Mus. of Contemporary Art, Chgo., 1980-86; chief curator Dayton (Ohio) Art Inst., 1986-88; assoc. dir. High Mus. of Art, Atlanta, 1988; chief exec. ofr., pres. Orange County Mus. of Art, Newport Beach, Calif. Address: Orange Cty Museum of Art 850 San Clemente Dr Newport Beach CA 92660

VINECOUR, ONEIDA AGNES, nurse; b. Port Arthur, Tex., Oct. 15, 1917; d. Ernest Eugene and Gertrude Mary (Wooldridge) Thorn; m. Seymour Vinecour, Jan. 14, 1943 (dec. 1976); children: Seymour Jacob, Rebecca Leah. Diploma, St. Mary's Hosp. Sch. Nursing, Port Arthur, 1939; postgrad., cert. Surg. Tech., Anesthesia, Cook County Hosp., 1939-40; postgrad. U. Chgo., 1939-40, Tex. Coll. Mines, 1943, U. Tex. Health Ctr. R.N., cert. occupational audiometric technician, occupl. spirometric technician. Operating room supr., instr. Schumpert Meml. Hosp., Shreveport, La., 1940-41; anesthetist St. Joseph Hosp., Albuquerque, 1941-42; operating room supr., instr. Lynn City Hosp. (Mass.), 1946-48; staff anesthetist St. Mary's Hosp., Port Arthur, Tex., 1951-53, in service dir., 1971-73; staff nurse Tyler County Hosp., Woodville, Tex., 1964-65; dept. head, supr. Park Pl. Hosp., Port Arthur, 1965-71; operating room supr. Mid-County Hosp., Nederland, Tex., 1973-81; staff nurse Baptist Meml. Hosp., Beaumont, Tex., 1973-81; part time staff Health Care Svcs., Port Arthur, 1983—; indsl. nurse Synpol Inc., 1984-86; staff nurse Texaco Chem. Plant, Port Arthur, 1986-92, Olsten Health Care Svcs., 1992—, staff nurse Huntsman Petro-Chem. Corp., 1996—. Served as officer U.S. Army Nurse Corps, 1942-46. Mem. Am. Nurses Assn., Mass. Nurses Assn., Tex. State Nurses Assn., Assn. Occupational Health Nurses. Republican. Methodist. Home: 2502 Glenwood Dr Port Arthur TX 77642-2639

VINITSKAYA, MARINA, language educator, education educator; b. Moscow, Sept. 27, 1956; d. Svetlana Maksimova and Mikhail Freinkel, Igor Maksimov (Stepfather); m. Gregory Vinitskiy, June 24, 1977; children: Mikhail Vinitskiy, Yelena, Mikhail Vinitskiy, Helen. MA in TESOL(hon.), Moscow City U., Russia, 1972—78; MSED, Baruch Coll., CUNY, 2000—03; student, Union Inst. and U. SAS NY State, 2003, cert. SDA NY State, 2003. Dir. of fgn. lang. dept. Canadian-Russian Joint Venture, Moscow, 1989—92; prof. Yeshiva U., NYC, 1994—96, Baruch Coll., CUNY, NYC, 1994—98, Fordham U., NYC, 1997—99; ell-iss NYC Dept. of Edn., 1997—. Course developer New Age Corp., Inc, NYC, 1999—; prof. Hunter Coll., NYC, LIU, Bklyn. Scholar New Visions Scholarship, 1998. Mem.: NY TESOL. Achievements include development of ESL programs for Adults. Home: 24 Blythe Place Staten Island NY 10306 Personal E-mail: vinitskaya@aol.com. E-mail: vinitskaya@aol.com.

VINSON, LEILA TERRY WALKER, retired gerontological social worker; b. Lynchburg, Va., July 28, 1928; d. William Terry and Ada Allen (Moore) Walker; m. Hughes Nelson Vinson, Aug. 11, 1951; children: Hughes Nelson, William Terry. Student, Agnes Scott Coll., 1946-48; BA, U. Ala., Tuscaloosa, 1950; postgrad., U. Ala., Birmingham, 1980-81, U. Va., 1950-51. Cert. gerontol. social worker, Ala. Tchr. English and Latin Marion County Bd. Edn., Hamilton, Ala., 1952-59; social worker I Marion County Dept. Pensions and Security, 1963-72, gerontol. social worker II, 1972-85; ret., 1985. Bd. dirs. Marion County Dept. Human Resources, 1985—; bd. mem. Clye Nix Libr., Bevill Coll. Cmty. Theatre, 1992—; spkr. gen. subjects. Recipient Ala. Woman Committed to Excellence award Tuscaloosa coun. Girl Scouts U.S., 1987; named Mrs. Marion County, PTA, Gwin, Ala., 1969, Woman of Yr. Town of Hamilton, 1980, New Retiree of Yr. Ala. Ret. State Employees Assn., 1988, Woman of Yr. BPW, 1985; Gessener Harrison fellow U. Va., 1950-51. Mem. AAUW, DAR (flag chmn. Bedford chpt. 1988-90), UDC, Bus. and Profl. Women's Club (dist. dir. 1984-86, Outstanding Dir. award 1986), Ala. Fedn. Women's Club. Home: PO Box 1112 Hamilton AL 35570-1112 also: Military Rd Hamilton AL 35570

VINSON, LYNETTE D. speech pathology/audiology services professional; b. St. Louis, May 24, 1958; d. Alfred Joseph Hanke and Mary Berliner; m. Mark T. Vinson, Dec. 18, 1983; children: Timothy Ross, Aaron Joseph, Hannah Lynne, Cassia Rose. BSE in Speech Pathology, Ctrl. Mo. State U., 1980, MS in Speech Pathology, 1983. Cert. speech pathologist Am. Speech-Lang. Hearing Assn., 1984, lic. Bd. Healing Arts, Mo., 1984. Speech pathologist Sedalia (Mo.) Sch. Dist., 1980—82, Francis Howell Sch. Dist., St. Charles, 1983—84, Rainbow Ctr. for Communication Disorders, Blue Springs, Mo., 1984—91; speech pathologist, rehab. mgr. Cheyenne Mountain Therapies, Oak Grove, Mo., 1996—98; speech pathologist Odessa (Mo.) R-7 Sch. Dist., 1991—95, Rehab. Choice, Inc., St. Charles, Mo., 1995—; rehab. mgr. Sundance Rehab., St. Louis, 1998—2000; speech-language pathologist Lexington (Mo.) R-V Sch. Dist., 2000—. Mem.: Mo. Speech-Lang. Hearing Assn., Am. Speech Lang. Hearing Assn. (Continuing Edn. award 2003). Home: 14004 Hwy U Odessa MO 64076 Office: LexingtonR-V School District S13 Hwy Lexington MO 64067 Personal E-mail: lvinson@accessmo.us. E-mail: lvinson@mail.lexington.k12.mo.us.

VINSONHALER, CHRIS, storyteller, musician, consultant; b. Ocala, Fla., Nov. 30, 1956; d. Henry and Dorothy (Hambrick) Martin; m. John S. Weldon, June 14, 1980 (div. 1989); children: Anna Margaret Vinsonhaler Weldon, Morgan Elaine Vinsonhaler Weldon. BS in English, U. Ga., Athens, 1978; MA in English, U. N.C., Chapel Hill, 1983; MLS, U. So. Miss., Hattiesburg, 1990. Cert. tchr. Miss. Reporter The Miss. Press, Pascagoula, 1987-88, The Sun Herald, Ocean Springs, Miss., 1988-90, bur. chief Jackson County, 1989-90; columnist The Clarion Ledger, Jackson, Miss., 1991-94; librarian Westminster Acad., Gulfport, Miss., 1991-93; assoc. Marian Wingo & Assocs., Ocean Springs, 1991—. Organizer, dir. Great Oaks Storytelling Festival, Ocean Springs, Friends of Folk, Camp Inspire. Performer (cassette tape) Wild & Crazy, 1993, Drench MY Soul, 1993, How To Survive School, 1996, Rain!, 1996; editor Pearls, Myths and Memories of Hancock County, The Renaissance Project. Mem. AAUW, Nat. Storytelling Assn. Democrat. Avocations: singing, writing, dance, poetry, sailing. Home: 1017 La Fontaine St Ocean Springs MS 39564-4933 E-mail: oakshade@cableone.net.

VIOLA, MARY JO, art history educator; b. Yonkers, N.Y., July 25, 1941; d. William F. and May (Cleary) O'Connor; m. Jerome Joseph Viola, June 21, 1967 (dec. Feb. 1990). BA in Fine Arts, Coll. of Mt. St. Vincent, 1963; MA in Art History, NYU, 1966; MPhil in Art History, CUNY, 1983, PhD in Art History, 1992. Art history tchr. Georgian Ct. Coll., N.J., 1965-66, Hollins Coll., Roanoke, Va., 1966-67, Marymount Coll., Tarrytown, N.Y., 1967-71, Baruch Coll., CUNY, N.Y.C., 1974-97, Bklyn. Coll., 1990-97, Parsons Sch. of Design, N.Y.C., 1991-93, Rutgers U., 1993-95, Bronx C.C. CUNY, 1997—. Curator exhbns. Baruch Coll. Gallery, N.Y.C., 1987-88. Editor: A World View of Art History, 1985; art exhibited at Tribes Gallery, N.Y.C., 1996; creater ednl. videos. Rschr. for ethnic festivals, N.Y.C., 1993—. Fellow Nat. Trust for Hist. Preservation, 1964, Marymount Coll., 1970, Boston Mus. Fine Arts/CUNY, 1978, Luce Found., 1988. Mem. Coll. Art Assn., Historians of Am. Art, City Lore. Avocations: tai chi, argentine tango, ballroom dance. Home and Office: 37 Roosevelt St Yonkers NY 10701-5823

VIOLANTE, PATRICIA, consultant, language expert, writer, translator/interpreter; b. Pescara, Italy, Dec. 13, 1950; came to U.S., 1956; d. Renato Osvaldo and Agata (Vento) V.; m. Guido Marco Cassetta, May 22, 1986. BA, U. Md., 1972; MS, Georgetown U., 1976. Lectr. in translation Georgetown U., Washington, 1976—2001; dir. grad. admissions Southeastern U., Washington, 1980-82; translator, interpreter Embassy of Italy, Washington, 1991—. CEO, Comalux, Inc., doing bus. as Trappings, Washington, 1981-86; voice talent; scriptwriter, cons. Cassetta/Hunt & Co., Washington, 1980—. Translator: The Goddess of Kisses, 2001, Women's Law Project, 2000, Italy in the Balkans, 1998, Happy Birthday, 1989, Dolce Susanna, 1992, Attidunal Survey: Sacred Heart of Jesus, 1977. Mem. Leadership Greater Washington. Mem. Nat. Assn. Jud. Interpreters and Translators, European Soc. for Translation Studies. Avocations: poetry, gardening, pasta cookery and menu planning. Home: 1409 Foxhall Rd NW Washington DC 20007-2006 Office: Embassy of Italy 3000 Whitehaven St NW Washington DC 20008-3612

VIOLENUS, AGNES A. retired school system administrator; b. N.Y.C., May 17, 1931; d. Antonio and Constance Violenus. BA, Hunter Coll., 1952; MA, Columbia U., 1958; EdD, Nova U., 1990. Tchr. N.Y. State Day Care, N.Y.C., 1952-53, N.Y.C. Bd. Edn., 1953-66; asst. prin. N.Y.C. Elem. and Jr. H.S., 1966-91; student tchr. supr. dept. edn., adj. lectr. CCNY, 1997—. Adj. instr. computer dept. continuing edn. divsn. York Coll., N.Y.C., 1985-88, Hunter Coll., N.Y.C., 1998—; adj. instr. tchr. mentor program grad. edn. divsn. CCNY, 1990-91; reviewer ednl. and instrnl. films; judge news and documentary Emmy awards NATAS, 1995, 97, 2000, 2002. Co-author: LOGO: K-12, 1980; contbr. articles to profl. jours. Mem. mid-Manhattan br. NAACP, mem. com. on Afro-Am. acad., cultural, and tech. olympics; life mem. Girl Scouts U.S., N.Y.C.; bd. visitors Manhattan Psychiat. Ctr., 1995, pres., 2000, chair 1999—; vol. advisor math., sci., computers Workshop Ctr., CCNY, 1995-97; bd. dirs. Hunter Coll. Scholarship and Welfare Fund. Recipient Dedicated Svc. award Coun. Suprs. and Adminstrs., Appreciation award Aerospace Edn. Assn., 1985, Significant Contbn. award Am. Soc. for Aerospace Edn., 1985, Leaders' Day Cert. of Appreciation, Girl Scouts U.S., 1997. Mem. ASCE, AAUW, Am. Ednl. Rsch. Assn., Assn. Advancement of Computing in Edn., Assn. Computers in Math. and Sci. Tchg., Soc. for Info. Tech. and Tchr. Edn., Assn. for Women in Sci., Nat. Tech. Assn., N.Y. Acad. Scis. (scientists in schs. program 1995), Nat. Assn. Negro Bus. and Profl. Women's Clubs (scholarship com. 1989—, family math. com. 1995, rec. sec. 1994-95, profl. award 1997), Nat. Black Child Devel. Inst. (bd. dirs. 1991—, sci. exhibit com. 1995, v.p. 1999, co-chair entering coll. zone program 1999, 2000, pub. policy com. 1991—, Bridge Bldr.'s award 1995), Schomburg Ctr. Rsch. in Black Culture Schomburg Corp. (vols. adv. com. 1992—, bd. trustee, co-chair corp. task force on African-Am. in math., sci. and tech. 1992—, pres. 1995-98, treas. 1999-2000), Doctorate Assn. N.Y. Educators, N.Y. Alliance Black Sch. Educators, Hunter Coll. Alumni Assn. (bd. dirs. 1993—, rec. sec. 1996-99, treas. 1999—2002, named to Hall of Fame 1998), Bank St. Alumni Coun. Greater N.Y. (asst. sect. 1991-93), Wistarians Alumni Hunter Coll. (exec. com. 1990—, pres. 1990-94). Democrat. Roman Catholic. Avocations: music, genealogy.

VIORST, JUDITH STAHL, writer; b. Newark, Feb. 2, 1931; d. Martin Leonard and Ruth June (Ehrenkranz) Stahl; m. Milton Viorst, Jan. 30, 1960; children: Anthony Jacob, Nicholas Nathan, Alexander Noah. BA, Rutgers U., 1952; grad., Washington Psychoanalytic Inst., 1981. Author: (children's books) Sunday Morning, 1968, I'll Fix Anthony, 1969, Try It Again Sam, 1970, The Tenth Good Thing About Barney, 1971 (Silver Pencil award 1973), Alexander and the Terrible Horrible No Good Very Bad Day, 1972, My Mama Says There Aren't Any Zombies, Ghosts, Vampires, Creatures, Demons, Monsters, Fiends, Goblins or Things, 1973, Rosie and Michael, 1974, Alexander, Who Used to Be Rich Last Sunday, 1978, The Good-Bye Book, 1988, Earrings!, 1990, The Alphabet from Z to A (with Much Confusion on the Way), 1994, Alexander, Who's Not (Do You Hear Me? I Mean It!) Going to Move, 1995, Super-Completely and Totally the Messiest, 2001; (poetry) The Village Square, 1965-66, It's Hard to Be Hip Over Thirty and Other Tragedies of Married Life, 1968, People and Other Aggravations, 1971, How Did I Get to Be Forty and Other Atrocities, 1976, If I Were in Charge of the World and Other Worries, 1981, When Did I Stop Being Twenty and Other Injustices, 1987, Forever Fifty and Other Negotiations, 1989, Sad Underwear and Other Complications, 1995, Suddenly Sixty and Other Shocks of Later Life, 2000; (with Milton Viorst) The Washington Underground Gourmet, 1970, Yes Married, 1972, A Visit From St. Nicholas (To a Liberated Household), 1977, Love and Guilt and the Meaning of Life, Etc., 1979, Necessary Losses, 1986, Murdering Mr. Monti, 1994, Imperfect Control, 1998, You're Officially a Grown-Up, 1999, Grown-up Marriage, 2003; (musical) Love and Shrimp (book and lyrics), 1990; (HBO children's movie) Alexander and the Terrible, Horrible, No Good, Very Bad Day (book and lyrics), 1990, children's stage musical, 1998, (musical) Alexander, Who's Not Not Not Not Not Gong to Move (book and lyrics), 2003. Recipient Emmy award for poems used in Anne Bancroft Spl., 1970. Jewish.

VIRES, JUDY DOAN, early childhood educator; b. London, Mar. 3, 1954; d. Chester Lee and Shirley Mae (Smith) Doan; m. Charles Edward Vires, June 2, 1973; children: Jordan Ross, Dylan Case. BS, West Ga. Coll., 1996; MEd in Reading, State U. West Ga., 2003. Dir. Great Atlanta Christian Sch., Peachtree City, Ga., 1987-92; tchr. 1st gr. Arlington (Ga.) Christian Sch., 1996—. Test adminstr. Arlington Christian Sch., Fairburn, Ga., 1992-96; reading endorsement, 2003, ESOL endorsement, 2003. Vol. vision screener Prevent Blindness Ga., Atlanta, 1994-96. Mem. Student Profl. Assn. Ga. Educators, Delta Gamma. Home: 748 Bridlepath Ln Peachtree City GA 30269-1808

VIROSTKO, JOAN, elementry school educator; b. Jackson Heights, N.Y., Feb. 6; d. John and Dorothy Veronica (Eckert) Virostko. Cert. of Studies, Oxford U., 1972, 73; B.S., St. John's U., 1968, M.S., 1970, P.D., 1972, 85, M.B.A., 1980, Ph.D., 1983, SAS, SDA, 1985. Cert. elem. tchr., N.Y.; cert. sch. bldg. adminstr., sch. dist. adminstr., N.Y. Educator Half Hollow Hills Paumanok Sch., Dix Hills, N.Y.; instr. Oxford U., England, summer 1985, 86; instr., 1987—. Contbr. Ellis Island Found, 1984-86; lector Sacred Heart Cath. Ch., Glendale, N.Y., 1986-87; sustaining mem. Rep. Nat. Com.,

1980—, sponsor 1980— . Recipient Disting. Dissertation award, 1983; named Educator of Yr., N.Y. State Assn. Tchrs., 1985, 92, 95, 99, 2001. Mem. N.Y. State United Tchrs. Assn., Kappa Delta Pi, Phi Delta Kappa, Alpha Sigma Alpha, Delta Sigma Chi. Republican. Avocations: traveling, music, water and snow skiing, water sports. Office: Half Hollow Hills Paumanok Sch 1 Seamans Neck Rd Dix Hills NY 11746-7114 Address: 5731 69th Ln Maspeth NY 11378-1918

VISOCKI, NANCY GAYLE, information services consultant; b. Dumont, N.J., May 13, 1952; d. Thomas and Gloria Visocki. BA in Math., Manhattanville Coll., 1974; MS in Ops. Rsch. and Stats., Rensselaer Poly. Inst., 1977. Rsch. asst. Coll. Physicians and Surgeons Columbia U., N.Y.C., 1974-75; programmer analyst R. Shriver Assocs., Parsippany, N.J., 1977-79; sr. tech. rep. GE Info. Svcs. Co., East Orange, N.J., 1979-81, mgr. project office Morristown, N.J., 1981-83, tech. dir., 1983-87, tech. mgr., 1988-89, area mgr. sys. devel. and consulting Parsippany, 1989-92, area tech. mgr. sys. devel. and cons., Fin. Info. Sys., 1992-93, sr. cons. info. svcs., 1993-98, project mgr. e-commerce sys. integration, 1998-2000; mgr. Major e-commerce Applications Practice, 2000—03. Active Western Hills Christian Ch., Tranquility, N.J., 1986—; vol. Women's Ctr., Hackettstown, N.J., 1989-93; class fundraising and gift chmn. Rensselaer Poly. Inst., Troy, N.Y., 1991-95; vol. Elfun Soc., 1981—. Manhattanville Coll. grantee, Purchase, N.Y., 1970-71; tuition fellow Rensselaer Poly. Inst., 1975-77. Mem. NAFE, Elfun, Women of Accomplishment. Avocations: tai chi, hiking, bicycling, reading, yoga.

VISSER, VALYA ELIZABETH, physician; b. Chgo., Oct. 2, 1947; d. Roy Warren and Tania Eugenia (Morozoff) Nelson; children: Kira Elizabeth Visser, Michael Philip Visser. BS, Iowa State U., 1968; MD, U. Iowa, 1973. Diplomate Am. Bd. Pediatrics, Sub-Bd. Neonatal-Perinatal Medicine. Resident pediatrics U. Iowa Hosps. and Clinics, Iowa City, 1976; fellow neonatology Children's Mercy Hosp., Kansas City, 1978; asst. prof. pediatrics U. Kans. Sch. Medicine, Kansas City, 1978-81; staff pediatrician U.S. Army Med. Corps., Ft. Bragg, N.C., 1981-83; attending neonatologist Carolinas Med. Ctr., Charlotte, 1983—. Chair dept. pediatrics Carolinas Med. Ctr., Charlotte, 1999—; conf. chair Extracorporeal Life Support Orgn., Ann Arbor, Mich., 1993-95. Major Med. Corps., 1981-83. Fellow Am. Acad. Pediatrics. Mem. Unitarian-Universalist Ch. Avocation: music. Office: Carolinas Med Ctr Dept Pediatrics PO Box 32861 Charlotte NC 28232-2861

VITAL, PATRICIA BEST, lawyer; b. Pitts., Mar. 26; d. Clarence D. and Billie Lorraine (Wilson) B.; m. Leo Vital, Mar. 30. BA magna cum laude, U. Tenn., Chattanooga, 1989; JD with honors, U. Tenn., 1992. Bar: Ga. 1994, Tenn. 1993, U.S. Dist. Ct. (ea. dist.) Tenn. 1993, U.S. Dist. Ct. (no. dist.) Ga. 1995, U.S. Ct. Appeals (6th cir.) 1993, U.S. Ct. Appeals (11th cir.) 1995, U.S. Supreme Ct. 1996. Legal asst. Gleason & Assoc. Law Firm, Rossville, Ga., 1981-82; med. staff coord. Hutcheson Med. Ctr., Ft. Oglethorpe, Ga., 1982-86; rsch. asst. U. Tenn. Law Coll., Knoxville, 1991-92; from law clk. to assoc. atty. Lusk, Carter & McGhehey, Chattanooga, 1990-93; pvt. practice Chattanooga, 1993—; mediator, arbitrator Vital Dispute Resolution Svcs., Chattanooga, 1996—. Law clk. Hamilton County Attys. Office, Chattanooga, summer 1990; devel. coun. co-chair class 1992 U. Tenn. Coll. Law, alumni network mentoring program, 1993—, deans cir., 1990—; pres. adult scholars program U. Tenn., Chattanooga, 1988-89, adult scholars program adv. coun., scholarship com., 1994—; presenter in field; adj. prof. pre-trial litigation, legal asst. studies program U. Tenn., fall, 1997; instr. Law Sch. Admission Test preparation course KAPLAN, Inc., 1999-2000; commn. continuing legal edn. and specialization Tenn. Supreme Ct., 1996-2001; panel mediator, arbitrator (Ea. and Mid. dists.) Tenn. Fed. Mediation Programs, Tenn. Supreme Ct. Rule 31 civil/family domestic violence mediator, U.S. Dept. Justice, Key Bridge Found., Am. with Disabilities, Chattanooga Better Bus. Bur., Coun. Better Bus. Burs. AutoLine Arbitration, Hamilton County Tenn. Divorce Mediation, Am. Health Lawyers ADR Svc.; mem. panel, chair arbitration panel NASD, U.S. Dept. Labor/AEIDR; mem. adv. bd. ProLex, LLC, 2003—. Co-author: Tennessee Alternative Dispute Resolution Handbook, 1997; contbr. articles to profl. jours. Mentor Hamilton County Bd. Edn., 1995-96; cmty. resource person Ooltewah Middle and Chattanooga Phoenix Middle Schs., 1994-96; capt. attys. team presch. phon-a-thon Siskin Found., 1994-95; mem. Chattanooga Chamber Found. Leadership Chattanooga Class, 1997-98; nat. adv. bd. Ctr. for Enterprise Edn., Peabody Coll. Edn., Vanderbilt U., 1998-2000. Mem. ABA (ethics 2000 adv. coun. 1998, dispute resolution sect. Boston Conf. Planning Com. 1998-2000, co-chair dispute resolution sect. State and Local Bar Com. 1998-2000), AAUW, Fed. Bar Assn., Nat. Inst. Dispute Resolution, Nat. Assn. Mediators in Edn., Am. Health Lawyers Assn., Nat. Assn. Women Bus. Owners (local chpt. bd. dirs. 1994), Am. Soc. Law, Medicine and Ethics, Tenn. Bar Assn. (com. chair, sec. and spkr. ho. of dels. 1995—, com. chair law related edn. 1996-97, bd. dirs. law office tech. and mgmt. 1994-96, sec-treas., chair-elect, chair dispute resolution sect. 1995-98, Merit award 1995, mem. editl. bd. TBALink), Mediation Assn. Tenn. (chair continuing mediation edn., curriculum com. 1996-98), Tenn. Trial Lawyers Assn., Tenn. Assn. Med. Staff Svcs., Nat. and Tenn. Assn. Ptnrs. in Edn., Ga. State Bar Assn., Chattanooga Bar Assn. (bd. govs. 1996-97, chair bd. govs. task force on the future Tenn. judicial sys. 1995-96, centennial planning com. 1996-97, chair continuing legal edn. com. 1994-95, chair ethics rules rev. com. 1998-99, chair dispute resolution com. 1998—, First Beyond the Call of Duty award 1995), Chattanooga Trial Lawyers Assn. (dir., gov. bd. 1995-2000), Southeast Tenn. Lawyers Assn. Women (dir. at-large 1996-97), Better Bus. Bur., S.E. Tenn. Coun. on Children & Youth, Chattanooga Area C. of C., Phi Delta Phi. Avocations: whitewater rafting, mountain hiking, aerobics, reading. Office: Vital Law Offc & Dispute Resolution Svcs James Bldg Ste 801 735 Broad St Chattanooga TN 37402-1804 Fax: (423) 267-2376. Office Phone: 423-267-2378. E-mail: best-law@mindspring.com.

VITETTA, ELLEN SHAPIRO, microbiologist educator, immunologist; BA, Conn. Coll.; MS, NYU, 1966, PhD, MD, 1968. Prof. microbiology Southwestern Med. Sch., U. Tex., Dallas, 1976—; dir. Cancer Immunobiology Ctr., U. Tex., Dallas, 1988—; Sheryle Simmons Patigian Disting. chair in cancer immunobiology Southwestern Med. Sch., U. Tex., Dallas, 1989—. Bd. sci. coun. NCI Cancer Treatment Bd., 1993; sci. adv. bd. Howard Hughes Med. Inst., 1992—; Kettering selection com. GM Cancer Rsch. Foun., 1987-88; task force NIAID in Immunology, 1989-90; mem. sci. bd. Ludwig Inst., 1983—. Mem. editl. bd.: Advances in Host Defense Mechanisms, 1983—, Annual Review of Immunology, 1991—, Bioconjugate Chemistry, 1989-93, Cellular Immunology, 1984-93, Current Opinions in Immunology, 1992—, FASEB Journal, 1987—, Internat. Jour. of Oncology, 1992—, Internat. Soc. Immunopharmacology, 1989—, Jour. of Immunology, 1975-78, Molecular Immunology, 1978-93; assoc. editor Cancer Research, 1986—; Immunochemistry sect. editor: Jour. of Immunology, 1978-82; co-editor in chief: Therapeutic Immunology, 1992—. Recipient Women's Excellence in Sci. award Fedn. Am. Soc. Exptl. Biology, 1991, Taittinger Breast Cancer Rsch. award Komen Found., 1983, Pierce Immunotoxin award, 1988, NIH Merit award, 1987—, U. Tex. Southwestern Med. Sch. Faculty Teaching awards 1989, 91, 92, 93, 94, FASED Excellence in Sci. award, 1991, Abbot Clinical Immunology award Am. Soc. Microbiologists, 1992, Past State Pres. award Tex. Fed. Bus. Profl. Women's Club, 1993, Richard and Hinda Rosenthal Found. award Am. Assn. Cancer Rsch 1995, Charlotte Friend award Am. Assn. Cancer Rsch., 1995. Mem. Am. Assn. Immunologists (pres. 1994), Nat. Acad. Scis., Am. Acad. Microbiology (hon.). Achievements include co-discovery of IL-4, development of immunotoxins and identification of IgD on murine B cells. Office: Univ Texas Cancer Immunobiol Ctr 6000 Harry Hines Blvd Dallas TX 75235-5303 Address: Scottdale Conference 6914 Pemberton Dr Dallas TX 75230-4260 E-mail: ellen.vitetta@utsoutheastern.edu.

VITO, MARILYN ELAINE, business educator; b. Louisville, Oct. 24, 1947; d. Gerald E. and Eleanor M. (Spencer) Bowles; m. Louis J. Vito, May 22, 1971; children: Louis Vito Jr., Linda, Sandra, Steven. BS in Bus., Stockton State Coll., 1980; MBA, Monmouth Coll., 1985; postgrad., Stonier Grad. Sch. Banking, 1989. CPA N.J., Pa., cert. mgmt. acct. Supr. Golden Nugget Casino/Hotel, Atlantic City, N.J., 1980-81; v.p., contr. Security Savs. & Loan, Vineland, N.J., 1981-85; sr. v.p., CFO Horizon/Marine Nat. Bank, Pleasantville, N.J., 1985-89; exec. v.p., CFO Meridian Mortgage Corp., Wayne, Pa., 1989-93; assoc. prof. bus. studies Richard Stockton Coll., Pomona, N.J., 1993—. Delegation leader Citizen Amb. Program Women Accts. to Ea. Europe, 1998. Mem. host com. Hillary Clinton/Tipper Gore reception Dem. Nat. Com.Women's Coalition, Phila., 1996. Grantee Disting. Faculty grant, Richard Stockton coll., 1996, NSF, 1999. Mem.: AICPA (campus liaison 1997—), N.J. Soc. CPA (bd. dirs. 1987—89), Am. Soc. Women Accts (Phila. chpt. pres. 1987—89, nat. pres. 1992—93, bd. dirs. South Jersey chpt. 1996—97, nat. nominating com. 1999). Home: 29 Clover Hill Cir Egg Harbor Township NJ 08234-7558 Office: Richard Stockton Coll PO Box 195 Pomona NJ 08240-0195 E-mail: mev@stockton.edu.

VITTETOE, MARIE CLARE, retired clinical laboratory science educator; b. Keota, Iowa, May 19, 1927; d. Edward Daniel and Marcella Matilda Vittetoe. BS, Marycrest Coll., 1950; MS, W.Va. U., 1971, EdD, 1973. Staff technologist St. Joseph Hosp., Ottumwa, Iowa, 1950-70; instr. Ottumwa Hosp. Sch. Med. Tech., 1957-70, St. Joseph Hosp. Sch. Nursing, Ottumwa, 1950-70; asst. prof. U. Ill., Champaign-Urbana, 1973-78; prof. clin. lab. scis. U. Ky., Lexington, 1978-94. Mem. Sisters of Humility of Mary, 1946—; chair Congregation of Humility of Mary. Author: Vittetoe Family Tree and Scrapbook, 2000, Peiffer-Berg Family Tree and Scrapbook, 2000, Lutz/Peiffer Family Tree Update, 2002, Vittetoe Family Tree Update, 2002; contbr. articles to profl. jours. Vol. hosp. labs., Haiti, 1999—. Recipient Kingston award for Creative Teaching; Recognition award for svc. to edn. Commonwealth of Ky. Coun. on Higher Edn., disting. grad. award Nat. Cath. Ednl. Assn., 1995, devel. of youth award Iowa 4-H Found., 1996; named Ky. Col.; Marie Vittetoe award for excellence in svc. named for her U. Ky., 1999. Mem. Am. Soc. for Med. Tech. (chmn. 1986-89, Profl. Achievement award 1991, Ky. Mem. of Yr. award 1994), Am. Soc. Clin. Lab. Scis., Am. Soc. Clin. Pathologists (assoc.), Alpha Mu Tau, Phi Delta Kappa, Alpha Eta. Avocations: walking, genealogy.

VIVELO, JACQUELINE JEAN, author, English language educator; b. Lumberton, Miss., Jan. 23, 1943; d. Jack and Virginia Olivia (Bond) Jones; m. Frank Robert Vivelo, June 19, 1965; 1 child, Alexandra J. BA, U. Tenn., Knoxville, 1965, MA, 1970. Caseworker N.Y.C. Dept. Welfare, 1965-66; instr. reading Knoxville Coll., 1968-70; instr. English Middlesex County Coll., Edison, N.J., 1970-72, U. Mo., Rolla, 1975-77, Middlesex County Coll., Edison, 1978-80, Lebanon Valley Coll., Annville, Pa., 1981-87, asst. prof. English, 1987-91. Author: Super Sleuth, 1985 (Best Book award), Beagle in Trouble, 1986, A Trick of the Light, 1987, Super Sleuth and the Bare Bones, 1988, Writing Fiction: A Handbook for Creative Writing, 1993, Reading to Matthew, 1993 (Best Book award), Mr. Scutter's Magic Spell, 1993, Chills Run Down My Spine, 1994, Have You Lost Your Kangaroo?, 1995, Chills in the Night, 1997, Miss Topple Walks on Air, 1998; editor: College Education Achievement Project's Handbook for College Reading Teachers, 1969; co-editor: American Indian Prose and Poetry, 1974: contbr. articles/short stories to various publs. Recipient Best Book award Am. Child Study Assn., 1985, Young Book Trust, U.K., 1994, Pa. Coun. of the Arts Fellowship award for Lit., 1992; NIMH grantee, 1969-70. Mem. Children's Lit. Coun. Pa. (v.p. 1991), Soc. Children's Book Writers, Mystery Writers Am., Sigma Tau Delta (sponsor Omicron Omicron chpt. 1988-90), Pi Lambda Theta. Home: 5117 Brittany Dr Old Hickory TN 37138-1262

VIVEROS, MARY L. principal; d. James Carroll and Anastasia O'Connell Swift; m. Carlos Viveros, Dec. 29, 1976; children: Anastasia, Sarah Maria, Carlos. MS, U. Kans., 1993, EdD, 2002. Cert. edn. adminstr. Kans. Tchr. J.C. Harmon H.S., Kansas City, Kans., 1990—97; asst. prin. Wash. H.S., Kansas City, 1997—2001; prin. Sumner Acad. Arts and Sci., Kansas City, 2001—. Mem.: ASCD, Phi Delta Kappa. Home: 5013 Howe Dr Roeland Park KS 66205

VIZZINI, CAROL REDFIELD, symphony musician, music educator; b. San Diego, Jan. 3, 1946; d. Ernest Sylvester and Eleanor Diana (Soneson) Redfield; m. Edward Tracy Browning (div. 1981); children: Victor, Charlotte; m. Joseph Russell Vizzini, Apr. 12, 1997. MusB, Phila. Musical Acad., 1968. Prin. cellist Somerset Hills Symphony, Basking Ridge, N.J., 1971-81, New Philharm. of N.W. N.J., Morristown, 1978-87; asst. prin. cellist Princeton (N.J.) Chamber Symphony, 1985-95; prin. cellist Orch. St. Peter-by-the-Sea, Point Pleasant, N.J., 1987-92; instr. in cello Westminster Conservatory, Rider U., Princeton, 1987—, head string dept., 1992—. Chamber music coach Vt. Music and Arts Ctr., Lyndonville, 1980-81; coach Greater Princeton Youth Orch., 1989-92; chamber music coach N.J. Youth Symphonies, Summit, 1989—; chamber music coord. Westminster Conservatory, 1991-98. Author: Cello Scales, Volume One (One and Two Octave Scales), 1997, Cello Scales, Volume Two (Three and Four Octave Scales), 2000. Mem. Am. String Tchrs. Assn., Am. Fedn. Musicians, Music Tchrs. Nat. Assn. (string coord. 1989-93). Avocations: gardening, fly fishing, travel. Office: Westminster Conservatory of Music Rider Univ 101 Walnut Ln Princeton NJ 08540-3819 E-mail: cjvizzini@earthlink.net.

VLADECK, JUDITH POMARLEN, lawyer; b. Norfolk, Va., Aug. 1, 1923; BA, Hunter Coll., 1945; JD, Columbia U., 1947. Bar: NY 1947, US Supreme Ct. 1962. Assoc. Conrad & Smith, N.Y.C., 1947-51; sole practice N.Y.C., 1951-57; mem. Vladeck, Elias, Vladeck & Engelhard P.C., N.Y.C., 1957—; sr. ptnr. Vladeck, Waldman, Elias & Englehard, P.C., N.Y.C. Adj. prof. Fordham Law Sch. Mem. adv. bd. Inst. for Edn. and Rsch. on Women and Work, Cornell U.; bd. dirs. NY Civil Liberties Union, 1963-68; bd. dir., counsel Tamiment Inst., Inc.; bd. dirs. lawyers' coordinating com. AFL-CIO; bd. mem. Non-Traditional Employment for Women. Recipient Hunter Coll. Profl. Achievement award, 1992, Edith Spivack award, 1998, Women of Power and Influence award NY NOW, 1998, ORT Jurisprudence award, 1996; elected to Hunter Coll. Hall of Fame, 1988; Non-Taditional Employment for Women named building Judith P. Vladeck Ctr. for Women, 1989; Margaret Brent Award, ABA 2002; Columbia Law Sch. Assoc. Medal for Excellence, 2003; NEW 25th Anniv. Equity Leadership Award, 2003. Fellow Am. Bar Found., Coll. of Labor and Employment Lawyers; mem. ABA (co-chmn. labor law and equal employment coms., NY State Bar Assn. (labor law com.), Assn. of Bar of City of NY, NY County Lawyers Assn., Fed. Bar Assn., Women's Bar Assn., Am. Arbitration Assn. (panel of arbitrators), Columbia Law Sch. Alumni Assn. (bd. dir.), Harlem Inst. Fashion (counsel, bd. dir.). Home: 115 Central Park W New York NY 10023-4153 Office: Vladeck Waldman Elias & Engelhard 1501 Broadway Ste 800 New York NY 10036-5560 E-mail: jvladeck@vladeck.com.

VOCE, JOAN A. CIFONELLI, retired elementary school educator; b. Utica, N.Y., Mar. 22, 1936; d. Albert and Theresa (Buono) Cifonelli; m. Eugene R. Voce Sr., Aug. 16, 1958; children: Eugene R. Jr., Lisa V. Stewart, Mark L., Daniel A. BS in Elem. Edn., Coll. St. Rose, Albany, N.Y., 1958; MS in Elem. Edn., SUNY, Cortland, 1981. Elem. tchr. Utica (N.Y.) Pub. Schs., 1958-59, 61-62, 64-67; tchr. Deerfield Elem. Sch., Whitesboro (N.Y.) Ctrl. Sch. Dist., 1968-91. Vol. Presbyn. Home for Ctrl. N.Y.; mem. St. Anne's Ch., Whitesboro, NY, Our Lady of Hope Ch., Port Orange, Fla. Mem. AAUW (Mohawk Valley br.), N.Y. State United Tchrs., Whitesboro Ret. Tchrs. Assn., Am. Assn. Ret. Persons, Oneida County Ret. Tchrs. Assn. (sec.), N.Y. State Ret. Tchrs. Assn., Coll. of St. Rose Alumni Assn., Utica Symphony League, Mohawk Valley Performing Arts, Pelican Bay Country Club (Daytona Beach, Fla.), Skenandoa Golf and Country Club (Clinton, NY), Alpha Delta Kappa (v.p. 1974-76, pres. 1976-78, corr. sec. 1972-74, rec. sec. 1986-88, 90-91). Avocations: reading, travel, golf, gourmet cooking, theatre. Home: 109 Birchwood Ln Whitesboro NY 13492-2517 Address: 201 Surf Scooter Dr Daytona Beach FL 32119 E-mail: jcvoce@webtv.net.

VOCE, PATRICIA MARIA, medical/surgical nurse; b. N.Y.C., May 20, 1965; d. James Joseph Massi and Patricia Elvira Bozza; m. Frank William Voce, Jr., Sept. 17, 1988; children: Frank IV, Christopher. BSN, Dominican Coll., 1987. RN N.Y. Staff nurse White Plains (N.Y.) Hosp., 1987—89; RN Nyack Hosp. Cmty. Health, Orangeberg, NY, 1989—; per-diem skills lab. instr. Rockland Boces and LPN Program, 2001—. Rec. sec. Rockland Rep. Women, New City, NY, 1999—. Home: 4 Foltim Way Congers NY 10920

VOEGELE, KAREN E. social worker; b. Summit, NJ, Dec. 30, 1973; d. James Paul Adorna and Shirley Ann (Schmidt) Ruppert; m. John Richard Voegele, Oct. 13, 2001. BA, U. Mass., 1996; MSW, U. Pa., 2000. Social worker Big Brothers Big Sisters, Eatontown, NJ, 1996—98; counselor Thomas Jefferson U., Phila., 2000—01; therapist Life Counseling Svcs., Paoli, Pa., 2001—02, Northwestern Human Svcs., 2000—. Home: 3799 Cresson St Philadelphia PA 19127 Office Phone: 215-836-3124. Personal E-mail: karenvoegele@hotmail.com.

VOEGTLIN-ANDERSON, MARY MARGARET, secondary school educator, music educator; b. Seattle, Wash. d. Joseph Walter and Veronica Margaret (Conroy) Voegtlin; m. Terry Lee Anderson, Mar. 19, 1977 (div. July 20, 1982). BA cum laude, Marylhurst U., 1963; postgrad., U. Wash., 1963—65, Oakland U., 1968, Seattle Pacific U., 1982—84. Cert. std. tchg. grades K-12 Wash. Profl. cellist Oreg. Symphony, Portland, 1962—63; tchr. music and humanities Chinook Middle Sch., Seattle, 1963—89, gifted edn. specialist, 1983—89; tchr. music, music dept. chair Highline H.S., Seattle, 1989—, tchr. honors English, 1989—. Contralto soloist Mt. Baker Pk. Presbyn. Ch., 1966—68, U. Congl. Ch., Seattle, 1968—73; profl. singer Seattle Opera Co., 1968—70; vocal coach, advisor Highline Jazz Ensemble, Seattle, 1990—2004; pvt. music and voice tchr., Seattle, 1991—; astronomy club advisor Highline H.S., Seattle, 1998—2004; dir. Highline Dist. Youth Orch., 2003—04, Burien Sr. Choir, 2003; trustee Sunlight Waters Corp., 2002—. Contbr. articles to profl. jours. Officer, sec. 46th Legis. Dist. Dem. Party, Seattle, 1974—78, chairperson Initiative 314 Campaign, 1975; Wash. state conv. del. Dem. Party, Olympia, 1976, Dem. precinct chairperson Seattle, 1976—77. Grantee Fulbright Scholarship grant, Nat. Tchrs. Performance Inst., Oberlin Coll., Ohio, 1970. Mem.: NEA, Nat. Coun. Tchrs. English, Seattle Astron. Soc., Music Educators' Nat. Conf. Roman Catholic. Avocations: astronomy, reading, bicycling, writing, hiking. Office: Highline HS 225 S 152nd St Seattle WA 98148

VOGEL, H. VICTORIA, psychotherapist, trauma, post-traumatic stress disorder and addiction recovery counselor and educator, author; BA, U. Md., 1968; MA, NYU, 1970, 75, MEd, Columbia U., 1982, postgrad., 1982, cert., Am. Projective Drawing Inst., 1983; CASAC, New Sch. U. for Social Rsch., 2000. Diplomate Am. Acad. Experts in Traumatic Stress; cert. addiction recovery counselor, expert in traumatic stress, alcohol and substance abuse counselor, addictions treatment, addiction counseling alcohol and substance abuse. Art therapist Childville, Bklyn., 1962-64; tchr. Montgomery County (Md.) Jr. H.S., 1968-69; with H.S. divsn. N.Y.C. Bd. Edn., 1970—; guidance counselor, instr., psychotherapist in pvt. practice. Guidance counselor, instr., psychotherapist in pvt. practice; clin. counseling cons. psychodiagnosis and devel. studies, art/play therapy The Modern Sch., 1984—; art/play therapist Hosp. Ctr. for Neuromuscular Disease and Devel. Disorders, 1986—; employment counselor-adminstr. N.Y. State Dept. Labor Concentrated Employment Program, 1971-72; intern psychotherapy and psychoanalysis psychiat. divsn. Ctrl. Islip Hosp., 1973-75, Calif. Grad. Inst., L.A.; intern psychol. counseling and rehab. N.J. Coll. Medicine, Newark, 1979. Author: The Never Ending Story of Alcohol, Drugs and Other Substance Abuse, 1992, Variant Sexual Behavior and the Aesthetic Modern Nudes, 1992, Psychological Science of School Behavior Intervention, 1993, Joycean Conceptual Modernism: Relationships and Deviant Sexuality, 1995, Electronic Evil Eyes, 1995 (U.S. Cert. of Recognition, 1996), Psychological Paradigms of Alcohol Violence Suicide Trauma Addiction Variant Pathologies PTSD and Schizophrenia, 1999. Mem. com. for spl. events NYU, 1989; participant clin. and artistic perspectives Am. Acad. Psychoanalysis Conf., 1990, participant clin. postmodernism and psychoanalysis, 1996; aux. police officer N.Y. Police Dept., 1994—; chair bylaws com. Columbia U., 1995—. Mem.: ACA, AAAS, APA, Tchrs. Coll. Adminstrv. Women in Edn., Assn. Humanistic Psychology (exec. sec. 1981), Art/Play Therapy, N.Y. Art Tchrs. Assn., Am. Acad. Experts Traumatic Stress (diplomate in expert traumatic stress), Am. Soc. Group Psychotherapy and Psychodrama (pubs. com. 1984—), Am. Orthopsychiat. Assn., Am. Psychol. Soc., Phi Delta Kappa (editor chpt. newsletter 1981—84, exec. sec. Columbia U. chpt. 1984—, chmn. nominating com. for chpt. officers 1986—, rsch. rep. 1986—, pub. rels. exec. bd. dirs. 1991, NYU chpt. v.p. programs 1994—).

VOGEL, LAURA C. M. psychologist; b. Dallas, Tex., Aug. 15, 1968; d. Esta B. and Charles L.L. Vogel; m. Jeffrey A. Zimerman, Jan. 7, 2000; children: Samuel A. Zimmerman, Morgan A. Zimmerman. BA, Austin Coll., Sherman, Tex., 1986—90; PhD, U. of No. Tex., Denton, Tex., 1992—98. Lic. Psychologist Tex. State Bd. of Examiners of Psychologist, 1999; registered Health Svc. Provider Nat. Register of Health Svc. Providers in Psychology, 2002. Pre-doctoral intern Ctrl. Tex. Veterans Health Care Sys., Temple, Tex., 1997—98; post doctoral fellow / staff psychologist Tex. Scottish Rite Hosp. for Children, Dallas, 1998—2001; staff psychologist Our Children's Ho. at Baylor, Dallas, 2001—. Sr. rsch. asst. U. of No. Tex. / Project HOW (Health Outcomes of Women) - Project Funded by the Centers for Disease Control, Denton, Tex., 1993—97; adj. prof. U. of No. Tex., Denton, Tex., 2001. Author: (jour. article) Jour. of Traumatic Stress, (poster presentation) Effects of Psychol. Abuse and Communal Orientation on Women;s Psychopathology, (dissertation) Predictors of posttraumatic stress disorder in a cmty. sample of women: Exam. of the role of violence and ethnicity, (poster presentation) Ethnicity and Predictors of Posttraumatic Stress Disorder Symptoms in Battered Women, (jour. article) Violence and Victims. Recipient Professing Women Award, U. of No. Tex. Women's Studies Roundtable, 1995—96. Mem.: APA. Avocation: gardening. Personal E-mail: drvogel@juno.com.

VOGEL, MALVINA GRAFF, video and infosystems specialist; b. N.Y.C., May 5, 1932; d. Daniel Louis and Rose Miriam (Kanarick) Graff; m. Seymour Vogel, Jan. 27, 1952 (div.); children: Howard Ferris, Hal Steven, Scott Leslie, David Michael, Lisa Gayle. AB, Hunter Coll., 1952, postgrad., 1953. Cert. tchr., N.Y., N.J. Tchr. Norwood (N.J.) Pub. Schs., 1952-53, Farmingdale (N.Y.) Pub. Schs., 1953-55; researcher, writer Sy Vogel Realty, Commack, N.Y., 1965-67; writer-editor E.D.L.-McGraw Hill, N.Y.C., 1967-73; writer ednl. programs Ednl. Concepts, Inc., Babylon, N.Y., 1973-75, Instructional Concepts, Inc., New Hyde Park, N.Y., 1973-75; editor-in-chief Waldman-Playmore Pub. Co., N.Y.C., 1976-83; v.p. creative services Kid Stuff/GameTek, Inc., North Miami Beach, Fla., 1983-90; owner, pres. MVP Writing/Editing Prodns., Sunrise, Fla., 1990-94; v.p. creative svcs. Herbko Internat., Hallandale, Fla., 1995—2001; owner, pres. MVP Writing/Editing Prodns., Aventura, Fla., 2001—. Author short stories, reading and social studies programs; adaptor lit. classics for children; editor over 200 books for children and adults, over 50 computer software and video cartridge programs for preschoolers, children, teens and adults, over 600 crossword puzzles. Pres. Old Bethpage Elem. Sch. PTA, 1967-71; founder, pres. women's aux. Plainview, N.Y. Little League, 1968; scholarship chair Plainview-Old Bethpage Scholarship Fund, 1972-73. Scholarship for children's writing, Hofstra U., 1975. Mem. Nat. Assn. Female Execs.,

Soc. Children's Book Writers, Women in Communications, Soc. Preservation of English Lang. and Lit. Avocations: stamp collecting/philately, reading, antiques, swimming. Home and Office: Apt 2614 3370 NE 190th St Miami FL 33180-2463

VOGEL, PAULA ANNE, playwright; b. Washington, Nov. 16, 1951; d. Donald Stephen and Phyllis (Bremerman) Vogel. BA, Cath. U., 1974; doctoral studies, Cornell U., 1974-77. Instr. theatre and women's studies Cornell U., Ithaca, N.Y., 1978-81; prodn. supr. Theatre on Film & Tape, N.Y.C., 1983-85; prof. Creative Writing Program, Brown U., Providence, 1985—. Author: (plays) Meg, 1977 (Nat. Playwright award Am. Coll. Theatre Festival), And Baby Makes Seven, 1984, Desdemona, 1985, The Oldest Profession, 1988, The Baltimore Waltz, 1992 (Obie award for best play, 1992), Hot 'N' Throbbing, 1994, The Mineola Twins, 1996, How I Learned to Drive, 1996 (Pulitzer prize, 1998, Obie award, 1997, N.Y. Drama Critics Drama Desk award for best play, 1997, Lucille Lortel award, 1997, Outer Critics' Circle award, 1997). Recipient Bunting award, Radcliffe-Harvard Colls., 1990, Pew Charitable Trust Sr. Residency award, 1995, Laura Pels award, 1999; grantee Fund for New Am. Plays, 1994; playwright fellow NEA, 1981, 1990, Guggenheim fellow, 1995. Fellow: McDowell Colony; mem.: New Dramatists. Office: Brown U PO Box 1852 Providence RI 02912-1852*

VOGEL, SALLY THOMAS, psychologist, social worker, educator; b. Joplin, Mo., July 3, 1925; d. Clyde Albert Thomas and Kathryn (Waite) Thompson; m. F. Lincoln Vogel, Sept. 4, 1946; children: Kathryn Duchin, Linda, Robert L. BA, Beaver Coll., 1947; MEd, North Adams State Coll., 1969; EdS, Seton Hall U., 1995. Case worker Pa. Dept. Welfare, Phila., 1947-48; high sch. tchr. Downington High Sch., Coatesville, Pa., 1969-71; sch. social worker Delaware Valley High Sch., Frenchtown, N.J., 1970-84; study team coord. Holland Twp. Sch., Milford, N.J., 1975-85, sch. social worker, 1975-90, guidance counselor, 1990-94; sch. psychologist Lake Shore Sch. Dist., St. Clair Shores, Mich., 1998—2002. Instr. in Parent Effectiveness and Tchr. Effectiveness, Hunt County Adult Edn., N.J., 1975-84; advanced trainee Edn. Tng. Inst., Calif., 1984-89; presenter in field. Acting exec. dir. Big Bros./Big Sisters (founder), Hunterdon County, N.J., 1976. Recipient Ed Kiley Svc. award Big Bros./Big Sisters, 1978. Mem.: AAUW, NASP, MASP. Office: Lake Shore Sch Dist Violet Sch 22020 Violet Saint Clair Shores MI 48081

VOGEL, SUSAN CAROL, nursing administrator; b. Hartford, Conn., Oct. 9, 1948; d. Morton B. and Esther (Riback) Worshoufsky. Diploma in nursing, Grace Hosp., New Haven, 1969; B in Healthcare Mgmt., U. La Verne, 1991, M in Health Adminstrn., 1994. RN, Calif.; cert. nephrology nurse, Nephrology Nurse Cert. Bd. Oper. rm. nurse New Britain (Conn.) Gen. Hosp., 1970-72; staff nurse oper. rm. Parkview Cmty. Hosp., Riverside, Calif., 1972-74; staff nurse dialysis, IV team Cedars-Sinai Med. Ctr., L.A., 1974-82; clin. nurse III dialysis UCLA, 1982-88; nurse mgr. inpatient dialysis UCLA Med. Ctr., 1988-93; adminstr. South Valley Regional Dialysis Ctr., Encino, Calif., 1993—; pres. Renal Replacement Therapies, Inc. Bd. dirs. End Stage Renal Disease Network 18, med. rev. bd., 1996—2000, treas. Author: (with others) Review of Hemodialysis for Nurses and Dialysis Personnel, 7th edit., 2002, Vascular Access, Principles & Practices, 4th edit., 2002; editor Nephrology Nursing Jour., 2000-02. Mem. med. rev. bd. End Stage Renal Disease Network 18, 1996-2000; pres. Calif. Dialysis Coun., 2002—. Mem. NAFE, Am. Nephrology Nurses Assn. (pres. L.A. chpt. 1990-92, 96-98, nat. chairperson hemodialysis spl. interest group 1993-95), Nat. Kidney Found. Avocations: traveling, skiing. Office: South Valley Regional Dialysis Ctr 17815 Ventura Blvd Ste 100 Encino CA 91316-3600

VOGELGESANG, SANDRA LOUISE, business executive, writer, consultant; b. Canton, Ohio, July 27, 1942; d. Glenn Wesley and Louise (Forry) Vogelgesang; m. Geoffrey Ernest Wolfe, July 4, 1982. BA, Cornell U., 1964; MA, Tufts U., 1965, MA in Law and Diplomacy, 1966, PhD, 1971. With Dept. State, Washington, 1975-97, policy planner for sec. state and European Bur., 1975-80, dir. Econ Policy Office, Orgn. Econ. Coop. and Devel., 1981-82, econ. minister U.S. Embassy, Ottawa, Can., 1982-86, dep. asst. sec. Internat. Orgn. Affairs Bur., 1986-89; dep. asst. adminstr. Office Internat. Activities Environ. Protection Agy., Washington, 1989-92; with Dept. State, Washington, 1992; sr. policy advisor Agy. for Internat. Devel., 1993; U.S. amb. to Nepal Dept. State, Washington, 1994-97; pres. Everest Assocs. and Himalaya, 1997—. Bd. dirs. Ctr. for Econ. Devel. and Population Activities; mem. women and conservation com. World Wildlife Fund, 1997—, mem. Nat. Coun., 1999—; bd. advisors Am.'s Soc., N.Y.C., 1986—89; mem. Pres.'s Coun. of Cornell Women Cornell U., 1998—; adv. com. Dept. of Treasury com. on Internat. Child Labor Enforcement, 1999—; writer, cons. internat. devel. issues. Author: Long Dark Night of the Soul, The American Intellectual Left and the Vietnam War, 1974, American Dream-Global Nightmare: The Dilemma of U.S. Human Rights Policy, 1980. Bd. dirs. Crafts Ctr., 1999-2000. Recipient Meritorious Service awards, 1973, 74, 82, 83, 86, Disting. Honor award, 1976 Dept. State, Pres.' Disting. Service award, 1985. Mem. Council on Fgn. Relations. Office: 9009 Charred Oak Dr West Bethesda MD 20817-1923 E-mail: everest.associates@erols.com.

VOGELZANG, JEANNE MARIE, professional society administrator, lawyer; b. Hammond, Ind., Apr. 15, 1950; d. Richard and Laura Ann (Vanderaa) Jabaay; m. Nicholas John Vogelzang, May 17, 1971; children: Nick, Adam, Tim. BA, Trinity Christian Coll., Palos Heights, Ill., 1972; MBA, U. Minn., 1981; JD, U. Chgo., 1987. Bar: Ill. 1987; CPA, Ill.; CAE. Tchr. Timothy Christian H.S., Elmhurst, Ill., 1972-74; tchg. assoc. in fin. U. Minn., Mpls., 1980-81; fin. analyst Quaker Oats Co., Chgo., 1982-84; assoc. Baker & McKenzie, Chgo., 1987-89, Jenner & Block, Chgo., 1989-91; pres., owner J.M. Vogelzang & Assocs., Western Springs, Ill., 1991-99; exec. dir. Structural Engrs. Assn. Ill., Chgo., 1992—, Nat. Coun. Structural Engrs. Assn., Chgo., 1996—; pub., editor Structure mag., 1996—. Com. mem. Western Springs Planning Commn., 1991—95; village trustee Village of Western Springs, 1995—99, chmn. fin., chmn. gen. govt. com.; adv. bd. Coll. DuPage Internat. Trade Ctr., Glen Ellyn, Ill., 1992—94; bd. dirs., acad. affairs com., planning com., exec. com. sec. Trinity Christian Coll., 1992—98; trustees' evaluation com. Christian Ref. Ch. N.Am., 1998—; treas. The Tower Party of Western Springs, 1999—2001; jud. code com. Christian Reformed Ch. N.Am., Grand Rapids, Mich., 1991—97; bd. dirs. Austin Christian Law Ctr., Chgo., 1989—92, Barnabas Found., Palos Heights, Ill., 1989—95, Ctrl. Park Chapel, Holland, Mich., 2002—. Fellow Ill. Lincoln Excellence in Pub. Svc., 1999. Mem. ABA, Am. Soc. Assn. Execs., Ill. Bar Assn., Chgo. Bar Assn., Elim Work Svcs. Bus. Roundtable. Mem. Christian Reformed Ch. Office: 203 N Wabash Ave Ste 2010 Chicago IL 60601-2418 Office Phone: 312-372-5708.

VOGT, KATHLEEN CUNNINGHAM, musician, music educator; b. Ellwood City, Pa., July 3, 1951; d. Joseph Edward and Dorothea Cunningham Vogt. BS summa cum laude in Music Edn., Duquesne U., 1973, M in Music edn., 1975. Cert. Tchr Nat. Bd., 2003. Tchr., band and choral dir. Diocese of Pitts. Schs., 1973—79; tchr., band dir. Carrick H.S., 1980—84; band dir., drama tchr. Hanahan (S.C.) H.S., 1984—. Instr. percussion Duquesne U., Pitts., 1975—79; adj. prof. Charleston So. U., SC, 2001—; guest clinician and conductor, 1975—. Musician: Pitts. Symphony Orch., Charleston Symphony Orch., Lowcountry Winds, Charleston (S.C.) Cmty. Band. Mem. Hanahan Area Arts Coun. Mem.: All Berkeley County Music Educators, Nat. Band Assoc., Nat. Baton Twirling Assn., Nat. Twirling Judges Bur. (Inducted into Baton Twirling Hall of Fame 2002), Am. Sch. Band Dirs. Assn., SC. Band Dirs. Assn. (S.C. State Marching Band Champions 1986, 1987, 1988, 1991, Outstanding Performance award 1985—2003), SC. Music Educators Assn., Music Educators Nat. Conf., Phi Beta Mu. Home: 504 Greenmeadow Rd Goose Creek SC 29445 Office Phone: 843-820-3710.

VOGT, MARTHA DIANE, lawyer; b. Albertville, Ala., Sept. 22, 1952; m. Robert A. Vogt, May 26, 1973. BA, Oakland U., 1974; JD, Wayne Law Sch., 1980. Bar: Mich. 1980, U.S. Ct. Appeals (4th cir.) 1985, Fla. 1988, U.S. Ct. Appeals (6th cir.) 1990, U.S. Ct. Appeals (11th cir.) 1996. Ptnr. Clark, Klein & Beaumont, Detroit, 1980-92, Bavol & Vogt, Tampa, Fla., 1992-95; pvt. practice Law Office of M. Diane Vogt, Tampa, Fla., 1995—. Adj. prof. Wayne Law Sch., Detroit, 1987-92; instr. U. South Fla., 1995. Author: The Silicone Solution, 1999; co-author: Lawyer Retention: Improving Job Satisfaction for Lawyers. Mem. ABA, DRI, State Bar of Mich. Assn., The Fla. Bar Assn. Office: 100 N Tampa St Ste 2100 Tampa FL 33602-5809

VOGT-DOWNEY, MARILYN JUNE, secondary education educator, Sovietologist; b. Fairbury, Ill., June 29, 1943; d. Horace William and Viola Gertrude (Munz) Goembel; m. William Paul Vogt, Dec. 1963 (div. 1972); 1 child, Erika Lynn; m. John Nicholas Downey, Mar. 11, 1983. BA in Russian Lang., Ill. State Normal U., 1966; MA in L.Am. Studies, Ind. U., 1971. Translator of Russian, Pathfinder Press, N.Y.C., 1972-74; adminstrv. sec. Robin A. Wilson, N.Y.C., 1975-80; pipefitter 2d class Coastal Drydock & Repair Corp., Bklyn., 1980-81; mem. tech. staff Internat. Viewpoint, Paris, 1982; sec. Merrill Lynch Capital Markets, N.Y.C., 1982-85, Olympia & York Battery Park Co., N.Y.C., 1985-86; tchr. social studies City-As-Sch. H.S., N.Y.C., 1986—. Author, editor: The USSR 1987-1991: Marxist Perspectives, 1993; translator: Notebooks for the Grandchildren, 1995; contbr. translator: Leon Trotsky Writings, 1929-40, 1972-80; editl. com., journalist Bull. in Def. of Marxism, 1986-96. Coord. Moscow Trials Campaign Com., N.Y.C., 1988-90, U.S.-Soviet Workers Info. Com., N.Y.C., 1990-93; mem. coordinating com. U.S. Com. for Dem. Human Rights in Russia, N.Y.C., 1991-93; mem. Internat. Coord. Com. for Study of Leon Trotsky's Legacy, Russia and N.Y., 1994—. Mem. United Fedn. Tchrs. (chpt. del. 2003—).

VOIGHT, ELIZABETH ANNE, lawyer; b. Sapulpa, Okla., Aug. 6, 1944; d. Robert Guy and Garnetta Ruth (Bell) Voight; m. Bodo Barske, Feb. 22, 1985; children: Anne Katharine, Ruth Caroline. BA, U. Ark.-Fayetteville, 1967, MA, 1969; postgrad., U. Hamburg (W.Ger.), 1966-67; JD, Georgetown U., 1978. Bar: N.Y. 1979, Munich 1997. Lectr. German Oral Roberts U., Tulsa, 1968-69; tchr. German D.C. pub. schs., 1971-73; instr. German Georgetown U., Washington, 1973-74, adminstrv. asst. to dean Sch. Fgn. Svc., 1974-77; law clk. Cole Corette & Abrutyn (now Alston & Bird LLP), Washington, 1977-78; atty. Alston & Bird LLP (formerly Walter, Conston, Alexander & Green, P.C.), N.Y.C., 1978-88, Alston & Bird, LLP, Munich, 1990—, CMS Hasche Sigle, Munich, 1990—. Author (with Dr. Martin Peltzer): German Law Pertaining to Limited Liability Companies, German-English Text, 4th edit., 2000, German Securities Acquisition and Takover Act, 2002, German Commercial Code, German-English Text, 5th edit., 2002; trans. (articles for profl. jours.). Chmn. regional screening Am. Field Svc., N.Y.C., 1981-86; founding mem. Am. Berlin Opera Found. German Acad. Exchange Program fellow, 1966-67; adv. coun. Georgetown U. BMW Ctr. German and European Studies. Mem. Assn. Bar City N.Y., Munich Bar Assn., Internat. Fiscal Assn., Internat. Bar Assn., Am. C. of C. in Germany (Munich hospitality com.), Phi Beta Kappa, Kappa Kappa Gamma. E-mail: elizabeth.voight@cmslegal.de., voight@camelot.de.

VOIGT, CYNTHIA, writer; b. Boston, Feb. 25, 1942; d. Frederick C. and Elise (Keeney) Irving; married, 1964 (div. 1972); m. Walter Voigt, Aug. 30, 1974; children: Jessica, Peter. BA, Smith Coll., 1963. High sch. tchr. English, Glen Burnie, Md., 1965-67; tchr. English Key Sch., Annapolis, Md., 1968-69, dept. chmn., 1971-79, tchr., dept. chmn., 1981-88. Author: Homecoming, 1981, Tell Me If the Lovers Are Losers, 1982, Dicey's Song, 1982 (John Newbery medal 1983), The Callender Papers, 1983 (Edgar award 1984), A Solitary Blue, 1983, Building Blocks, 1984, Jackeroo, 1985, The Runner, 1985 (Silver Pencil award 1988, Deutscher Jugend Literator Preis 1989, ALAN award 1989), Come a Stranger, 1986, Izzy, Willy Nilly, 1986 (Calif. Young Reader's award 1990), Stories About Rosie, 1986, Sons From Afar, 1987, Tree by Leaf, 1988, Seventeen Against the Dealer, 1989, On Fortune's Wheel, 1990, The Vandemark Mummy, 1991, Orfe, 1992, Glass Mountain, 1991, David and Jonathan, 1992, The Wings of a Falcon, 1993, When She Hollers, 1994, Bad Girls, 1996, Bad, Badder, Baddest, 1997, Elske, 1999, It's Not Easy Being Bad, 2000, Bad Girls in Love, 2002.*

VOIGT, ELLEN, literature educator; BA, Converse Coll.; MFA, U. Iowa. Prof. poetry MIT; prof. Goddard Coll., Warren Wilson Coll., Asheville, NC, 1981—. Tchr. Bread Loaf Writers' Conf., Aspen Writer's Conf., Ind. Writers' Conf., Napa Writer's Conf., Catskills Writers' Conf., RopeWalk Writers' Conf. Author: (poems) Claiming Kin, 1976, The Forces of Plenty, 1983, The Lotus Flowers., 1987, Two Trees, 1992, Shadows of Heaven, 2002, (sonnet) Kyrie, 1995 (Nat. Book Critics' Circle award finalist, Teasdale Poetry prize); co-editor (with Gregory Orr): Poets Teaching Poets: Self and the World; author: The Flexible Lyric, 2001. Fellow, Acad. Am. Poets, 2002; grantee, Vt. Coun. Arts, NEA, Guggenheim Found. Office: Warren Wilson Coll PO Box 9000 Asheville NC 28815

VOLANSKY, MICHELE, dramaturg, educator; b. Camden, N.J., Apr. 6, 1968; d. Robert George and Helena Suzanne Volansky. BA, Wash. Coll., Chestertown, Md., 1990; MA, Villanova, Phila., 1992. Asst. lit. mgr. Actors Theatre of Louisville, Louisville, 1993—95; dramaturg/ lit. mgr. Steppenwolf Theatre Co., Chgo., 1995—2000; dramaturg Phila. Theatre Co., 2000—. Artistic adv. bd. Theatre Forum Mag., San Diego, 1999—, Chgo. Dramatists, Chgo., 2001—. Author: (play) Whispering City, 1999; dramaturg (play) SPACE (Elliott Hayes award for Dramaturgy, 1999). Mem.: Lit. Mgrs. and Dramaturgs of the Ams. (pres. 2002—). Roman Catholic. Home: 2210 Myrtle Street Philadelphia PA 19130 Personal E-mail: volansky@yahoo.com.

VOLGMAN, ANNABELLE SANTOS, cardiologist, educator; b. Quezon City, The Philippines, Oct. 30, 1957; arrived in U.S., 1970; d. Raymundo Jocson and Purificacion Villatuya Santos; m. Keith Allen Volgman, Apr. 23, 1988; children: Robert Keith, Caroline Annabelle. BA, Barnard Coll., 1980; MD, Columbia U., 1984. Internal medicine resident U. Chgo. Hosps. and Clinics, 1984—87; cardiology fellow Northwestern Meml. Hosp., Chgo., 1987—90; asst. prof. Rush U., Chgo., 1990—2000, assoc. prof., 2001—. Cons. and spkr. in field. Contbr. articles to profl. jours. Fellow: Am. Coll. Cardiology; mem.: Am. Heart Assn. (bd. dirs. 2002—, med. chair Women's Legacy Luncheon 2000—02, Spl. Merit award 2001, 2002), Menomonee Club (bd. dirs. 2002—). Avocations: running, bicycling, triathlons, reading, swimming. Office: Rush Heart Inst Ste 1159 1725 W Harrison St Chicago IL 60612

VOLIN, SUZANNE, former laboratory administrator; b. Detroit, Sept. 27, 1921; d. Kean Leo and Mignonne Bader Cronin; m. Verlynne Vincent Volin, Sept. 8, 1945; children: Suzanna, James, Virginia, Mignonne, André, Richard, Michelle, John. BA, U. Western Ont., London, Can. With Providence Hosp., Detroit, Childrens Hosp., Detroit, Evanston (Ill.) Clin. Lab., Detroit. Fellowship grantee Sioux Falls Branch STate. Mem. AAWU (ednl. rsch. and project grantee), Am. Soc. Clin. Pathologists (cert. med. technologist). Republican. Roman Catholic. Avocations: bridge, traveling, golf, tennis. Home: 1325 S 2nd Ave Sioux Falls SD 57105-1907

VOLK, KRISTIN, advertising agency executive; b. Phila., Feb. 26, 1953; d. Richard H. and Doris (Colasanti) V. BS in Biology, Tufts U., 1976; MPH, Boston U. Sch. Med., 1981. Rsch. technician Beth Israel Hosp., Boston, 1976; rsch. asst. Dana-Farber Cancer Inst., Boston, 1976-78; sr. rsch. asst. Beth Israel Hosp., Boston, 1978-81, tech. supr. Schneider Parker Jakuc Advt., Boston, 1981-86; v.p., assoc. rsch. dir. HBM/Creamer, Boston, 1986-88, Della Femina McNamee, Boston, 1988-90; v.p., dir. rsch. Lawner Reingold Britton & Ptnrs., Boston, 1990-93; sr. v.p., dir. consumer insight group Arnold Fortuna Lawner & Cabot, Boston, 1993-95; exec. v.p., dir. consumer insight group Arnold Comm., Inc., Boston, 1995-99; exec. v.p., dir. strategic planning Deutsch Boston, 1999—2001; exec. v.p., chief mktg. officer Arnold Worldwide, N.Y.C., 2001—. Guest lectr. colls. and univs., Boston. Contbr. articles to profl. jours. Mem. Am. Assn. Advt. Agencies (account planning group com., chmn. conf. 1998), Ad Club N.Y. Home: 180 W 20th St Apt 10F New York NY 10011

VOLK, PATRICIA GAY, fiction writer, essayist; b. N.Y.C., July 16, 1943; d. Cecil Sussman and Audrey Elaine (Morgen) Volk; m. Andrew Blitzer, Dec. 21, 1969; children— Peter Morgen, Polly Volk BFA cum laude, Syracuse U., 1964; student, Sch. Visual Arts, N.Y.C., 1968, New Sch., 1975, Columbia U., 1977-88. Art dir. Appelbaum & Curtis, N.Y.C., 1964-65, Seventeen Mag., Triangle Publs., N.Y.C., 1966-68; copywriter Doyle, Dane, Bernbach, Inc., N.Y.C., 1969-88, also sr. v.p., creative mgr., 1969-87, sr. v.p.- assoc. creative dir., 1987-88; columnist N.Y. Newsday, 1995-96; fiction instr. Yeshiva Coll. Fiction instr. Playwrights Horizon Theater Sch., Marymount Coll. Author: The Yellow Banana, 1985 (Word Beat Press Fiction Book award 1984), White Light, 1987, All it Takes, 1990, Stuffed: Adventures of a Restaurant Family, 2001; contbr. articles to N.Y. Times mag., Redbook, Allure, Mirabella, Family Circle, The New Yorker, The Atlantic, Playboy, others; contbr. short stories to popular and small press publs. and anthologies. Recipient Stephen E. Kelly award, 1983, Various Andy, Clio, Effie and One Show awards, 1970—88, Yaddo fellow, 1983, 1999, 2001, MacDowell fellow, 1984, 2000. Mem.: PEN, Author's Guild, Juliana Berner's Anglers.

VOLKMANN, FRANCES COOPER, psychologist, educator; b. Harlingen, Tex., May 4, 1935; d. Edward O. and Elizabeth (Bass) C.; m. John Volkmann, Nov. 1, 1958 (dec.); children: Stephen Edward, Thomas Frederick. AB magna cum laude, Mt. Holyoke Coll., 1957; MA, Brown U., 1959, PhD, 1961; DSc, Mt. Holyoke Coll., 1987. Rsch. assoc. Mt. Holyoke Coll., South Hadley, Mass., 1964-65; lectr. U. Mass., Amherst, 1964-65, Smith Coll., Northampton, Mass., 1966-67, asst. prof., 1967-72, assoc. prof., 1972-78, prof. psychology, 1978—, dean faculty, 1983-88, Harold E. Israel and Elsa M. Siipola prof. psychology, 1988—, acting pres., 1991. Vis. assoc. prof. Brown U., Providence, 1974, vis. prof., 1978-82; vis. scholar U. Wash., Seattle, summer 1977. Contbr. articles to profl. jours. Trustee Chatham Coll., 1987-95; mem. City Coun., Northampton, 1998—. USPHS fellow, 1961-62; NSF grantee, 1974-78; Nat. Eye Inst. grantee, 1978-82 Fellow APA, AAAS, Optical Soc. Am.; mem. Ea. Psychol. Assn., Soc. Neurosci. Psychonomic Soc., Assn. Rsch. in Vision and Ophthalmology, New Eng. Assn. Schs. and Colls. (vice chair commn. instns. higher edn. 1991-93, chair 1993-95).

VOLKOW, NORA DOLORES, medical research center director; b. Mexico City, Mar. 27, 1956; m. Steven Adler. BA, Modern Am. Sch., Mexico City, 1974; MD, Nat. U. Mex., 1980; postgrad. in Psychiatry, NYU, 1980-84. Diplomate Am. Bd. Psychiatry and Neurology. Rsch. asst. Registro Nacional de Anat. Path., Mexico City, 1975-76, Miles Lab. Exp. Therap., Mexico City, 1977-78; intern St. Anne Psychiat. Hosp., Paris, 1979-80; residency NYU Dept. Psychiatry, 1981—84; asst. prof. U. Tex. Med. Sch., Houston, 1984-87; attending physician psychiat. unit Herman Hosp., Houston, 1985-87; assoc. scientist dept. medicine Brookhaven Nat. Lab., Upton, NY, 1987-89, assoc. chief of staff, Clinical Rsch. Ctr., 1990, dir. Nuclear Medicine, 1994—2003, dir, NIDA/DOE Imaging Ctr., 1997—2003, assoc. dir. life sciences, 1999—2003; assoc. prof. dept. psychiatry SUNY, Stony Brook, 1991—2003, assoc. dean, Sch. Med., 1997—2003; lecturer, Psychiatry Dept. Columbia Univ.; dir. Nat. Inst. on Drug Abuse (NIDA), Washington, 2003—. Mem. Adv. Com. for Minority Tng. in Psychiatry, Washington, 1991—; mem. study sect. in clin. neuroscis. NIH, Washington, 1992—; elected mem., Inst. Medicine, 2000. Co-editor: Positron Emission Tomography in Schizophrenia Research, 1991. Named Innovator of the Yr., U.S. News and World Report, 2000; recipient Premio Robins award, U. Mex., 1978, Premio Gabino Barrera award, 1981, Laughlin fellowship, Am. Coll. Psychiatry, 1984, Scanditronix scholarship, 1985, Paul C. Aebersold award, Soc. of Nuclear Medicine, 2003. Office: Nat Inst on Drug Abuse NIH 6001 Executive Blvd, Rm 5213 Bethesda MD 20892*

VOLLMER, HELEN, public relations executive; B Journalism, M Radio/TV/Film, U. Tex. Copywriter for maj. retail outlet; acct. exec. Ruder & Finn; v.p., mgr. client rels. Bozell & Jacobs Pub. Rels.; CEO Vollmer Pub. Rels. Office: Vollmer Pub Rels 800 Travis, Ste 501 Houston TX 77002-5706

VOLZ, ANNABELLE WEKAR, learning disabilities educator, consultant; b. Niagara Falls, N.Y., May 24, 1926; d. Fred Wekar and Margaret Eleanor (McGillivray) Wekar Treadwell; m. William Mount Volz, May 9, 1958; children: Amy D., William M. Jr. BA, Seton Hill Coll., 1948; MS in Elem. Edn., N.Y. State Univ. Coll., 1956. Cert. learning disabilities cons. N.J. Georgian Ct. Coll., 1981. Lab. technician Moore Bus. Forms Inc., Niagara Falls, 1948-50, Niagara Falls Health Dept., 1950-53; tchr. Niagara Falls Bd. Edn., 1953-56, Am. Dependent Sch., Ashiya, Japan, 1956-58, Mehlville Bd. Edn., St. Louis County, Mo., 1968-70, U.S. Dependent Schs. European Theatre, Weisbaden, Fed. Republic of Germany, 1970-74; paraprofl. Medford (N.J.) Bd. Edn., 1978-81; learning disabilities tchr., cons. Southampton Bd. Edn., Vincentown, N.J., 1981-91. Mem. Womens Fin. Info. Program, Burlington County, 1990-91. Mem. LWV (N.C. chpt., Winston-Salem chpt. 1993-99, sec. 1994-96, mem. chair 199 6-99, voter's guide chair 1996, 98, LWV Piedmont chpt.), AAUW (N.J. chpt. Medford chpt. 1982-91, N.C. Winston Salem chpt. 1992—, treas. 1993-2000), Nat. Retired Edn. Assn., N.J. Retired Edn. Assn., Assn. Learning Cons., Seton Hill Alumnae Assn., Kappa Delta Pi. Home: 5080 Mountain View Rd Winston Salem NC 27104-5110

VON BAILLOU, ASTRID, executive search consultant; b. Neutitschein, Czech Republic, Mar. 2, 1944; d. Karl von Baillou and Angela Stillfried; m. Dennis Hallam Bigelow, Oct. 21, 1967 (div. Oct. 1994). BA in English, Sweet Briar Coll., 1965. Creative dir. Freeman Advt., Washington, 1969-72; on-air reporter, prodr. PBS, BBC, London Weekend TV, N.Y.C., 1972-80; v.p. Sci. Program Group TV, Washington, 1980-82; pres. Cullen & Casey, N.Y.C., 1982-86; sr. v.p. Ruder Finn, N.Y.C., 1986-87; pres. Baillou Internat., N.Y.C., 1988-94; prin., mgmt. dir. Kinser & Assocs., N.Y.C., 1994-2000; ptnr. Kinser & Baillou, N.Y.C., 2000—. Home: 1245 Park Ave Apt 19F New York NY 10128-1740 Office Phone: 212-534-2161. E-mail: search@kinserbaillou.com.

VON BARGEN, SALLY, stock image photography company executive; BA in Psychology, U. Calif., Santa Cruz; MEd, Seattle U. Circulation dir. CommTek Comm.; founding v.p. sales and mktg. Netlink; cons. Gen. Instruments, Citicorp, Fingerhut and Viacom; advisor and orgnl. cons. to CEO and pres. Photo Disc, founding mem. mgmt. team, co-pres.; pres. Getty One, Seattle. Mem. Satellite Broadcasting Assn. (nat. bd. dirs.). Office: Getty Images Inc 701 N 34th St Ste 400 Seattle WA 98103-3415

VON BRANDENSTEIN, PATRIZIA, production designer; Prodn. designer The Mirisch Agy., L.A., 1978—. Prodn. designer films including Heartland, 1979, Breaking Away, 1979, Ragtime, 1981 (Academy award nomination best art direction 1981), Silkwood, 1983, Amadeus, 1984 (Academy award best art direction 1984), A Chorus Line, 1985, The Money Pit, 1986, No Mercy, 1987, The Untouchables, 1987 (Academy award nomination best art direction 1987), Working Girl, 1988, The Lemon Sisters, 1990, Postcards From the Edge, 1990, Billy Bathgate, 1992, Sneakers, 1992, Leap of Faith, 1993, Six Degrees of Separation, 1993, The Quick and the Dead, 1995, Just Cause, 1995, The People vs. Larry Flynt, 1996, A Simple Plan, 1998, Man on the Moon, 1999, Shaft, 2000, It Runs in the Family, 2002, The Emperor's Club, 2002; costume designer films including Between the Lines, 1977, Saturday Night Fever, 1977, A Little Sex, 1982.

VON BRAUNSBERG, MARY JANE, clinical psychologist; b. N.Y.C. d. Thomas Charles and Margaret Mildred (Bradley) V.; m. Charles A. Gealish; children: Justin, Jeffrey, Luke, Sheridan, Jenny, Joshua, Maria, Amy, Bryon, Jordan. BS, Syracuse U., 1985, MS, 1990, PhD, 1993. Licensed Clin. Psychologist, N.Y. State. Clin. psychologist Hutchings Psychiatric Ctr., Syracuse, N.Y., 1991—; clin. dir. Dissociative Disorders Diagnostic & Treatment Ctr., Syracuse, 1998—. Chairperson Ctr. Human Policy, Syracuse, 1978-80. Co-Author: Amy Maura, 1979, Hackett McGee, 1980, The Sneely Mouthed Snerds, 1980. Mem. Am. Psychological Assn., Internat. Soc. Study of Dissociative Disorders. Office: Dissociative Disorder Diagnos & Treatment Ctr 315 S Crouse Ave Syracuse NY 13210-1870

VONDRUSKA, ELOISE MARIE, librarian; b. Chgo., Sept. 13, 1950; d. George A. and Irene L. Klebba; m. Richard J. Vondruska, Aug. 11, 1972. BA, Loyola U., Chgo., 1972; MS, U. Ill., 1973. Acquisitions librarian Parkland Coll., Champaign, Ill., 1973-79, tech. svcs. librarian, 1979-83; serials cataloger Arlington Heights (Ill.) Meml. Library, 1983-85; authorities librarian Northwestern U., Evanston, Ill., 1985-87; rsch. adminstr. Dastrup/Vondruska Assocs., Chgo., 1987-91. Head catalog dept. Northwestern U. Sch. Law Libr., 1989-97, assoc. dir. for bibliog. svcs., 1997—. Ill. State scholar, 1968-72, DePaul U. scholar, 1968; Katharine L. Sharp fellow, 1972. Mem. ALA, Am. Assn. Law Librs., Chgo. Assn. Law Librs., Ill. Libr. Assn. (bd. dirs. 1983, 85-86), Beta Phi Mu. Avocations: travel, golf, films. Office: 357 E Chicago Ave Chicago IL 60611-3059

VON ESCHEN, LISA A. lawyer; BA, Coll. of William and Mary, 1986; JD, NYU, 1991. Bar: Calif. 1991. Mem. bd. dirs. Western Law Ctr. for Disability Rights. Mem.: Women Lawyers Assn. L.A., Assn. Bus. Trial Lawyers, L.A. County Bar Assn. (vol. Pro Bono Domestic Violence Project, mem. labor and employment sect.). Office: Latham and Watkins LLP 633 W Fifth St Ste 4000 Los Angeles CA 90071*

VON FETTWEIS, YVONNE CACHÉ, archivist, historian; b. L.A., Nov. 28, 1935; d. Boyd Eugene and Georgette Louisa (Tilmann) Adams; m. Maurice Lee Caché, Jan. 8, 1955 (div. 1962); children: Maurice C.B. II, Michele-Yvonne (Mrs. Vernon Young Sr.); m. Rolland Phillip von Fettweis, July 22, 1967. BA, Wagner Coll., 1954; postgrad, Am. U., 1973, Bentley Coll., 1981. Legal sec., asst. Judge, Davis, Stern, Orfinger & Tindall, Daytona Beach, Fla., 1961-66, head rec. sect., bd. dirs. 1st Ch. Christ Scientist, Boston, 1969-71, rsch. assoc., 1971-72, adminstrv. archivist, 1972-78, sr. assoc. archivist, 1979-84, records adminstr., 1984-91, div. mgr. records mgmt./orgnl. archives, 1991-92, divsn. mgr. ch. history, 1992-, divsn. mgr. ch. history and healing ministry, 1995; divsn. mgr. ch. history, 1995-96; ch. historian 1st Ch. Christ Scientist, Boston, 1996—. Cons. Christian Sci. Bd. Dirs., 1999—, pres. of Mother Ch., 2002-; mem. Religious Pub. Rels. Coun. Co-author: Mary Baker Eddy: A Lifetime of Healing, 1996, Mary Baker Eddy: Christian Healer, 1997, The New Woman and the New Church: The Lincoln Women, 2001. Trustee Ch. Hist. Trust, 1995—; exec. sec. Volusia County Goldwater campaign, Daytona Beach, 1964; mem. Christian Sci. Bd. Lectureship, 1998. Mem. Soc. Am. Archivists (editor The Archival Spirit), Automated Records and Techniques Task Force, Am. Mgmt. Assn., Orgn. Am. Historians, Ctr. for Study Presidency, Religious Pub. Rels. Coun., New Eng. Archivists, Assn. Records Mgrs. and Adminstrs. (bd. dirs. 1983—), Assn. Coll. and Rsch. Librs., Bay State Hist. League, Order Ea. Star, Order Rainbow (bd. dirs. 1972-77). Republican. Christian Scientist. Home: 147 Bosarvey Dr Ormond Beach FL 32176-6662 Office: 1st Ch Christ Sci 175 Huntington Ave # A240 Boston MA 02115-3117

VON FRAUNHOFER-KOSINSKI, KATHERINA, bank executive; b. N.Y.C. m. Jerzy Kosinski, Feb. 15, 1987 (dec. May 3, 1991). Student, St. Joseph's Convent, London, Clark's Coll. Various positions Robert W. Orr & Assocs., N.Y.C.; with traffic dept. Compton Advt., Inc., N.Y.C., 1956-63; acct. exec. J. Walter Thompson Co., N.Y.C., 1963-69; product mgr. Natural Wonder line Revlon Co., N.Y., 1969-71; pres. Scientia Factum, Inc., N.Y.C., 1971—, Polish Am. Resources Corp., N.Y.C., 1992—, pres., CEO, 1992—2002. Bd. dirs. DZ Bank Polska, Warsaw, 1997—2001, Warsaw, 2002—. Co-founder Westchester Sports Club. Assoc. fellow Timothy Dwight Coll./Yale U., 1997—. Avocations: skiing, horse/polo, swimming, photography. Home: 60 W 57th St New York NY 10019-3909

VON FRIEDERICHS-FITZWATER, MARLENE MARIE, health communication scholar and researcher; b. Beatrice, Nebr., July 14, 1939; d. Paul M. and Velma B. (von Friederichs) Fitzwater; children: Richard Nielson, Kevin T. Young, James L. Nielson, Paul M. Nielson. BS, Westminster Coll., 1981; MA, U. Nebr., Omaha, 1981; PhD, U. Utah, 1987; cert. in death edn., Temple U., 1982. Various pub. rels., writing and editing positions, 1957-78; teaching fellow in comm. U. Nebr., Omaha, 1978-83, U. Utah, Salt Lake City, 1978-83; asst. prof. mass comm. U. So. Colo., Pueblo, 1983-85; prof. comm. studies Calif. State U., Sacramento, 1985—, chair comm. studies, 1996-2000; assoc. clin. prof. family practice Sch. Medicine U. Calif., Davis, 1987—; adj. asst. prof. hematology and oncology UCD Sch. Med. Condr. workshops on communication skills for health care profls. Bergan Mercy Hosp., Omaha, 1980-81, Mercy Care Ctr., Omaha, 1980-81, Am. Cancer Soc., 1981-82, Hospice of Salt Lake, Utah, 1981-82; condr. seminars, workshops and courses on health communication, death and dying, patient edn. and compliance, other related topics, 1983—; presenter in health communication various profl. orgn. meetings and confs., 1981—; dir., co-founder The Health Communication Rsch. Inst., Sacramento, 1988—. Contbr. articles to profl. jours. Trainer United Way, Sacramento, project mgr., 1986—; pres. bd. dirs. Hospice Care Sacramento, Inc., 1986-87; instr. vol. tng. program Hospice Consortium Sacramento; hospice vol. 1980—. Recipient Lifetime Achievement award Sacramento Pub. Rels. Assn., also numerous state, regional and nat. awards for writing, editing, publ. design and photography. Fellow Am. Acad. on Physician & Patient; mem. Internat. Communication Assn. (health communication div., newsletter editor 1987-89, sec. 1989-91), AAUP, Assn. Behavioral Scis. and Med. Edn., Assn. Women in Sci., Pub. Rels. Soc. Am. (bd. dirs. Calif. Capital chpt. 1987-91), Soc. Tchrs. Family Medicine, Soc. Health Care Pub. Rels. and Mktg. No. Calif. Home: 5020 Hackberry Ln Sacramento CA 95841-4765 Office: Calif State U Communication Studies Dept 6000 J St Sacramento CA 95819-2605 E-mail: fitzwaterm@csus.edu., fitzm@heri.com.

VON FURSTENBERG, BETSY, actress, writer; b. Neiheim Heusen, Germany, Aug. 16, 1931; d. Count Franz-Egon and Elizabeth (Johnson) von F.; m. Guy Vincent de la Maisoneuve (div.); 2 children.; m. John J. Reynolds, Mar. 26, 1984. Attended Miss Hewitt's Classes, N.Y. Tutoring Sch.; prepared for stage with Sanford Meisner at Neighborhood Playhouse. Made Broadway stage debut in Second Threshold, N.Y., 1951; appeared in Dear Barbarians, 1952, Oh Men Oh Women, 1954, The Chalk Garden, 1955, Child of Fortune, 1956, Nature's Way, 1957, Much Ado About Nothing, 1959, Mary Mary, 1965, Paisley Convertible, 1967, Avanti, 1968, The Gingerbread Lady, 1970 (toured 1971), Absurd Person Singular, 1976; off Broadway appearances include For Love or Money, 1951; toured in Petrified Forest, Jason and Second Man, 1952; appeared in Josephine, 1953; subsequently toured, 1955; What Every Woman Knows, 1955, The Making of Moo, 1958 (toured 1958), Say Darling, 1959, Wonderful Town, 1959, Season of Choice, 1959, Beyond Desire, 1967, Private Lives, 1968, Does Anyone Here Do the Peabody, 1976; appeared in Along Came a Spider, Theatre in the Park, N.Y.C., 1985; appeared in film Women Without Names, 1950; TV appearances include Robert Montgomery Show, Ed Sullivan Show, Alfred Hitchcock Presents, One Step Beyond, The Mike Wallace Show, Johnny Carson Show, Omnibus, Theatre of the Week, The Secret Storm, As the World Turns, Movie of the Week, Your Money or Your Wife, Another World; writer syndicated column More Than Beauty; contbr. articles to newspapers and mags. including N.Y. Times Sunday Arts and Leisure, Saturday Rev. of Literature, People, Good Housekeeping, Art News, Pan Am Travel; co-author: (novel) Mirror, Mirror, 1988. Avocations: tennis, painting, photography.

VON FURSTENBERG, DIANE SIMONE MICHELLE, fashion designer, writer, entrepreneur; b. Brussels, Dec. 31, 1946; came to U.S., 1969; d. Leon L. and Liliane L. (Nahmias) Halfin; m. Eduard Egon von Furstenberg, July 16, 1969 (div.); children: Alexandre, Tatiana. Student, U. Madrid, 1965-66, U. Geneva, 1966-68. Founder, pres. Diane von Furstenberg Studio, L.P., N.Y.C., 1970—; pres. Diane Von Furstenberg Ltd., N.Y.C.; founder Salvy, Paris, 1985. Pioneer TV shopping with creative and live on-air selling Silk Assets collection, 1992; returns to retail as designer DIANE line of signature dresses, including the wrap, 1997. Author: Diane Von Furstenberg's Book of Beauty; Beds, 1991, The Bath, 1993, The Table, 1996, DIANE: A Signature Life, 1998; contbg. editor Vanity Fair mag., 1993. Recipient Ellis Island Medal of Honor, 1986.*

VON GENCSY, EVA, dancer, choreographer, educator; b. Csongrad, Hungary, Mar. 11, 1924; arrived in Can., 1948; d. Joseph and Valery Von G.; m. John S. Murray, May 13, 1957 (div. 1967). Student V.G. Troyanoff, Russian Ballet Acad., Budapest, Hungary, 1934-41, Szineszegyesuleti Iskola Theatre Sch., 1941-44; diploma, Royal Acad. Dance, London, 1953. Solo debut Salzburg (Austria) Landes Theatre, 1945-47; soloist Royal Winnipeg (Can.) Ballet, 1948-53; with Ballets Chiriaeff TV Co. (now Les Grands Ballet Canadiens), 1953-57, TV performer, 1957-70. Jazz instr. Banff Sch. Fine Arts, 1962-75; founder, dir. jazz workshop Saidye Bronfman Ctr., Montreal, Que., Can., 1965-72; with Les Grands Ballets Canadiens, 1962-72; co-founder, artistic dir., resident choreographer Les Ballets Jazz de Montreal Sch. and Co., 1972-79; guest tchr. Can., U.S.A., Europe, Malta, Marrocco, 1979-97; choreographer; adjudicator dance festivals. Past bd. dirs. Dance in Can. Recipient Best Dancer award French TV, 1967, Queen's medal, 1977, Lifetime Achievement award U. Que., Montreal, 1997, Rossetti Lifetime Achievement award, 1997. Mem.: Equity (hon.). Home: Apt 508 3650 Rue de la Montagne Montreal QC Canada H3G 2A8

VON GIZYCKI, ALKISTIS ROMANOFF, research scientist, educator, scholar, writer; b. Famagusta, Cyprus; arrived in U.S., 1967; d. Costas and Evangelia Lillian Victoria Kyprianou; m. Nicholas Romanoff, 1977 (dec.); m. Walter Von Gizycki, Sept. 19, 1981 (div. Dec. 1992); children: Bernard, Elsa. BA with honors, RMWC, Lynchburg, Va., 1967-71; MA in Psychology, New Sch. U., 1976-78. Educator, counselor Bilingual Bd. Edn., Nicosia, Cyprus, 1971-86, bus. devel. Bucci Trading Co., Nicosia, Cyprus, 1981-86; rschr., writer freelance, 1986—. Officer ch. bd. Fifth Ave. Presbyn. Ch. 1979—; vol. ch. and civic leader. Fulbright grantee; recipient Gen. Excellence award, valedictorian Am. Acad., Nicosia, Cyprus, 1967, Vol. award J.P. Morgan Chase Found., 1995, Outstanding Performance award J.P. Morgan Chase, 1997. Mem. NOW, AAUW, NY Acad. Sci. (assoc.), Am. Psychol. Assn. Avocations: theater, films, reading, music, ballet. E-mail: alk12345@aol.com.

VON HAKE, MARGARET JOAN, librarian; b. Santa Monica, Calif., Oct. 27, 1933; d. Carl August and Inez Garnet (Johnson) von Hake. BA, La Sierra U., 1955; MS in Library Sci., U. So. Calif., 1963. Tchr. Newbury Park (Calif.) Acad., 1955-60, librarian, 1957-60; circulation librarian Columbia Union Coll., Takoma Park, Md., 1962-67, library dir., 1967—, assoc. prof., 1990—. Mem. ALA, Md. Libr. Assn., Congress of Acad. Libr. Dirs. of Md. (exec. dir. 1999-00), Md. Ind. Coll.and Univ. Assn. Libr. Dirs. Round Table (chair 1996-98), Assn. Seventh Day Adventist Librs. (newsletter editor 1981-83, pres. 1989-90), Sligo Federated Music Club (pres. 1988-89, yearbook co-editor 2000—). Republican. Office: Columbia Union Coll 7600 Flower Ave Takoma Park MD 20912-7796

VONHERRLICH, PHYLLIS HERRICK, academic administrator; d. Phillip Carl and Elisabeth Lingberg Herrick; children: Charles Phillip children: Kaarin Elien. Cert. in Maine Studies, U. Maine, Orono, 2001, B in Univ. Studies, 2002. Adminstrv. staff Am. Heart Assn., Greater Boston Divsn., Brookline, Mass., 1972—77, Mass. Med. Soc., Waltham, 1983—88, Brookline (Mass.) Sch. Com., 1983—88, U. Maine Sys., Bangor, 1988—. Author: (monograph, web site) Augusta (Maine) Women's History Trail. Mem. Augusta (Maine) Hist. Preservation Commn. Mem.: Norlands Living History Mus., Friends of the Maine State Mus., Old Ft. Western, Kennebec Hist. Soc. (mem. hist. preservation com. 2002—03), Alpha Sigma Lambda. Democrat. Avocations: historical research on 19th century Maine women, writing, reading, walking, needlecrafts. Office: Univ So Maine Muskie Sch 295 Water St Augusta ME 04330 E-mail: phyllis.vonherrlich@maine.gov.

VON KAPPELHOFF, DORIS See DAY, DORIS

VON KELLENBACH, KATHARINA, religious studies and women's studies educator; b. Stuttgart, Germany, May 18, 1960; d. Karl and Brigitte Von Kellenbach; m. Björn Krondorfer, May 18, 1991; children: Zadekia S., Tabitha I. Student, Kirchliche Hochschule Berlin, 1979-83, Georg August U., Göttingen, Germany, 1983; MA, Temple U., 1984, PhD, 1990. Asst. prof. St. Mary's Coll. of Md., 1991—2000, assoc. prof., 2000—, chair dept. philos. and religious studies, 2002—. Vis. lectr. Lehigh U., Bethlehem, Pa., 1989, 90-91. Author: (book) Anti-Judaism in Feminist Religous Writings, 1994; author articles on the life and work of 1st ordained female rabbi, Regina Jonas, 1902-44, articles to profl. jours., chapters to books; co-editor (with Susanne Scholz) Zwischen-Räume: Deutsche Feministische Theologinnen im Ausland, 2000,(with Björn Krondorfer and Norbert Reck) Von Gott Reden im Land der Täter: Theologische Stimmen der dritten Generation nach der Shoah, 2001. Charlotte Newcombe fellow, Woodrow Wilson Found., Princeton, 1989-90, ACLS fellow, 2000; grantee Alexander von Humboldt Found., 2000. Mem. Am. Acad. Religion, Soc. for Values in Higher Edn., European Soc. for Women in Theol. Rsch. Home: PO Box 302 Saint Marys City MD 20686-0302 Office: St Marys Coll of Md Saint Marys City MD 20686

VON KEUDELL, RENATE, language educator; b. Lübeck, Germany; arrived in U.S., 1962; AA, William Rainey Harper Coll., 1974; BA, Elmhurst Coll., 1976; MA, Northwestern U., 1977. Instr. German, French, ESL William Rainey Harper Coll., Palatine, Ill., 1978—92, assoc. prof., chair German dept., 1993—, chair world lang. dept., 2002—. Author: (textbook) Exercies in German Grammar, 1995, A Journey in German, 1999. Mem. Bd. Higher Edn. State of Ill. Mem.: MLA, Chgo. Coun. Fgn. Rels., Goethe Inst. Chgo., Am. Assn. Tchrs. German. Avocations: reading, writing, travel, walking, opera. Office: William Rainey Harper Coll 1200 W Algonquin Rd Palatine IL 60067

VON MOSCH, WANDA GAIL, middle school educator; b. Richmond, Va., Jan. 21, 1952; d. Jesse James, Sr. and Thelma Arleen (Bruce) Perdue; m. Carl Allan Von Mosch, June 24, 1978; children: Carl Allan Jr., Sarah Ashley, Katie Danielle. BS, Longwood Coll., 1974; postgrad., Old Dominion U., 1991—. Tchr. pub. schs. City of Hampton, Va., 1974-77, City of Virginia Beach, Va., 1977—. Mem., planning coun., mem. faculty coun. Gt. Neck Mid. Sch., coord. ptnrs. edn., comm. liaison; coord., coach Odyssey of Mind, Gt. Neck, 1997—98. Sunday sch. tchr. Va. Marine Sci. Mus., Virginia Beach, 1983—, Bethel Bible grad., tchr., 1990—; participant Malcolm Baldridge TQM procedure U.S. Congress for Ind. Learning; mem. PTA; mem. adminstrv. bd. Francis Asbury United Meth. Ch., Virginia Beach, 1986—, supt., 1991. Named Tchr. of the Yr., Walmart, 2002, Gt. Neck, 2002; recipient PTA award for Disting. Svc., 1990. Mem.: NEA, Virginia Beach Tchr. Forum, Virginia Beach Reading Coun., Va. Math. League, Va. Reading Coun., Virginia Beach Edn. Assn., Va. Edn. Assn. Republican. Avocations: reading, cooking, music, board games, golf. Office: Great Neck Middle Sch North Great Neck Rd Virginia Beach VA 23454-1112

VON RAFFLER-ENGEL, WALBURGA (WALBURGA ENGEL), linguist, cross-cultural communications specialist, lecturer, writer; b. Munich, Sept. 25, 1920; came to U.S., 1949, naturalized, 1955; d. Friedrich J. and Gertrud E. (Kiefer) von R.; m. A. Ferdinand Engel, June 2, 1957; children: Lea Maxine, Eric Robert von Raffler. DLitt, U. Turin, Italy, 1947; MS, Columbia U., 1951; PhD, Ind. U., 1953. Free-lance journalist, 1949-58; mem. faculty Bennett Coll., Greensboro, NC, 1953-55, U. Charleston (formerly Morris Harvey Coll.), W.Va., 1955-57, Adelphi U., CUNY, 1957-58, NYU, 1958-59, U. Florence, Italy, 1959-60, Istituto Postuniversitario Orgn. Aziendale, Turin, Italy, 1960-61, Bologna Center of Johns Hopkins U., 1964; assoc. prof. linguistics Vanderbilt U., Nashville, 1965-77, prof. linguistics, 1977-85, prof. emerita, sr. rsch. assoc. Inst. Pub. Policy Studies, 1985—2002, dir. linguistics program, 1978—85; chmn. com. on linguistics Nashville U. Ctr., 1978—85; Italian NSF prof. Psychol. Inst. U. Florence, Italy, 1986-87; prof. NATO Advanced Study Inst., Cortona, Italy, 1988; pres. Kinesics Internat., 1988—. Vis. prof. linguistics Shanxi U., Peoples Republic China, 1988-2002; vis. prof. U. Ottawa, Ont., Can., 1971-72, Lang. Scis. Inst., Internat. Christian U., Tokyo, 1976, U. Paris, Sorbonne, 1965-67, 1978-79; grant evaluator NEH, NSF, Can. Coun.; manuscript reader Ind. U. Press, U. Ill. Press, Prentice-Hall; advisor Trinity U., Simon Frazer U.; dir. internat. seminar Cross-Cultural Comm., 1986-87; mem. Ctr. for Global Media Studies, 1999; State Dept. Italy del. to Congress of the Hague; lectr. in field; specialist in non-verbal comm.. Author: Il prelinguaggio infantile, 1964, The Perception of Nonverbal Behavior in the Career Interview, 1983, The Perception of the Unborn Across the Cultures of the World, Japanese edit., 1993, English edit., 1994 (transl. into Chinese), A Traveler's Guide to Cross-Cultural Business Communications, 2000; co-author: Language Intervention Programs, 1960-75; editor, co-editor 12 books; author films and videotape; contbr. of 500 articles to profl. jours. in Engish, Itialian, French, German, Chinese, Japanese. Grantee Am. Coun. Learned Socs., NSF, Can. Coun., Ford Found., Kenan Venture Fund, Japanese Ministry Edn., NATO, UNESCO, Finnish Acad., Meharry Med. Coll., Internat. Sociol. Assn., Internat. Coun. Linguists, Tex. A&M U., Vanderbilt U., others. Mem. AAUP, Internat. Linguistic Assn., Linguistic Soc. Am. (chmn. Golden Anniversary film com. 1974, emerita 1985—), Linguistic Assn. Can. and the U.S., Internat. Assn. for Applied Linguistics (com. on discourse analyses, sessions chmn. 1978), Lang. Origins Soc. (exec. com. 1985-97, chmn. internat. congress, 1987), Internat. Sociol. Assn. (rsch. com. for sociolinguistics, session co-chmn. internat. conf. 1983, session chmn. profl. conf. 1983), Internat. Coun. Psychologists, Internat. Assn. for Intercultural Comms. Studies, Internat. Assn. for Study of Child Lang. (v.p. 1975-78, chmn. internat. conf. Tuscan Acad. Scis., Florence, Italy 1972), Inst. for Nonverbal Comm. Rsch. (workshop leader 1981), Southeastern Conf. on Linguistics, 1980— (hon. mem. 1985—), Semiotic Soc. Am. (organizing com. Internat. Semiotics Inst. 1981), Nat. Assn. Scholars, Tenn. Assn. Scholars (bd. dirs. 1998-99), Internat. Assn. for Intercultural Comms. Studies (panel organizer 1999), United Europe Movement (sect. chmn. 1944-45), Internat. Comm. Assn., Internat. Pragmatics Assn. Achievements include being instrumental in forcing Vanderbilt U. to enroll women on an equal basis with men. Home and Office: 2455 Brighton Oaks San Antonio TX 78231

VON REDLICH, EMILY PAULETTE, music educator; b. Columbia, S.C., Nov. 23, 1951; d. Larry Sutton Shannon, Sr. and Sarah Alice Thaggard; m. Charles Edward Ambrose, Jr., July 14, 1973 (div. Mar. 1984); children: Jennifer A. Taylor, Dana C. Ambrose; m. Matthew Hamilton von Redlich, May 13, 1989. MusB in Edn., Miss. U. for Women, 1973; student, U. So. Miss., 1975, U. Miss., 1978—80; MusM, U. Ala., 1989. Cert. music tchr. Miss., 1973, Ala., 2001. Tchr. music St. Martin Elem. and Jr. H.S., Biloxi, Miss., 1974—75, Ocean Springs Jr. and Sr. H.S., Miss., 1975—76, Brookwood Elem. Sch., Tuscaloosa, Ala., 1988—90; instr. music and drama Tuscaloosa Acad., 1995—. Accompanist Theatre Dept. U. Ala., Tuscaloosa, 1988—96; dir. music ministries St. Mark United Meth. Ch., Northport, Ala., 1985—95; piano tchr., vocal coach, Tuscaloosa, 1969—97. Charter mem. Wall of Tolerance So. Poverty Law Assn., Montgomery, Ala., 1997—. Mem.: Am. Orff-Schulwerk Assn. (cert., Ala. chpt.), Nat. Assn. Tchrs. Singing, Nat. Assn. Music Educators, Fellowship United Meth. Music and Worship Arts. Republican. Methodist. Office: Tuscaloosa Academy 420 Rice Valley Rd N Tuscaloosa AL 35406*

VON RYDINGSVARD, URSULA KAROLISZYN, sculptor; b. Deensen, Germany, July 26, 1942; came to U.S., 1950; d. Ignacy and Konegunda (Sternal) Karoliszyn; m. Paul Greengard. BA, MA, U. Miami, Coral Gables, Fla., 1965; postgrad., U. Calif., Berkeley, 1969-70; MFA, Columbia U., 1975; PhD (hon.), Md. Inst. Art, 1991. Instr. Sch. Visual Arts, N.Y.C., 1981-82; asst. prof. Pratt Inst., Bklyn., 1978-82, Fordham U., Bronx, N.Y., 1980-82; assoc. prof. Yale U., New Haven, 1982-86; prof. grad. divsn. Sch. Visual Arts, N.Y.C., 1986—. One-woman shows include Laumeier Sculpture Gallery, St. Louis, 1988, Capp St. Project San Francisco, 1990, Lorence-Monk Gallery, N.Y.C., 1990-91, Zamek Ujazdowski Contemporary Art Ctr., Warsaw, Poland, 1992, Storm King Art Ctr., Mountainville, N.Y., 1992-94, Galerie Lelong, N.Y.C., 1994, Weatherspoon Art Gallery, Grensboro, N.C., 1994, Univ. Gallery, Amherst, 1995, Mus. Art, Providence, 1996, Mus. Art R.I. Sch. Design, Providence, 1996, Yorkshire Sculpture Pk., Wakefield, England, 1997, Nelson-Atkins Mus., Kansas City, Mo., 1998, Madison (Wis.) Art Ctr., 1998, Chgo. Cultural Ctr., 1998, Indpls. Mus. Art, 1999, The Contemporaty Mus., Honolulu, 1999, Barbara Krakow Gallery, Boston, 1999, Galerie Lelong, Zurich, 2000, N.Y.C., 2000, Doris C. Freedman Plz., Ctrl. Pk., N.Y.C., 2000, Neuberger Mus. Art, SUNY, Purchase, 2002; exhibited in group shows at Contemporary Arts Ctr., Cin., 1987, Damon Brandt Gallery, N.Y.C., 1989, Met. Mus. Art, N.Y.C., 1989-93, Whitney Mus. Contemporary Art, 1990, Cultural Ctr., Chgo., 1991, Ctrl. Bur. Art Exhbns., Warsaw and Krakow, Poland, 1991, The Cultural Space/Exit Art, N.Y.C., 1992, Galerie Lelong, N.Y.C., 1993, Denver Art Mus. and Columbus Art Mus., 1994—, others; outdoor exhbns include Pelham Bay Park, Bronx, N.Y., 1978, Neuberger Mus., Purchase, N.Y., 1979, Artpark, Lewiston, N.Y., 1979, Laumeier Sculpture Park, St. Louis, 1989-94, Walker Art Ctr., Mpls., 1990-93, Oliver Ranch, Geyserville, Calif., Storm King Art Ctr., Mountainville, N.Y., 1992-93; contbr. articles to profl. jours. Fulbright Hays travel grantee, 1975; grantee N.Y. State Coun. Arts, Am. the Beautiful Fund, Nat. Endowment for Arts, Creative Artists Program Svc.; Griswald traveling grantee Yale U., 1985; Guggenheim fellow, 1983-84; Nat. Endowment for Arts individual artists grantee, 1986-87; recipient Acad. award in Art, Am. Acad. Arts and Letters, 1994, Alfred Jurzykowski Found. Fine Arts award, 1996, Joan Mitchell award, N.Y., 1997. Studio: 429 S 5th St Brooklyn NY 11211-7425 E-mail: art@galerielong.com.

VONSCHLEGEL, PATRICIA, artist; b. Fayetteville, N.C., Aug. 3, 1941; d. Robert Blackburn and Margaret (Scull) Slagle; m. John Lee Jordan, July 16, 1960 (div. Feb. 1975); children: John Christopher Jordan, Lisa Nicole Jordan. B of Creative Arts, U. N.C., Charlotte, 1978. Tchr. aide Children's Adventure, Nederland, Colo., 1978; kindergarten tchr. Charlotte Acad., 1980-81; tchr., supr. San Francisco Head Start, 1981-82; art tchr. Our Lady of Consolation, Charlotte, 1982-83. Exhbns. include McKnight Gallery/U. N.C., 1978, Charlotte Printmakers, 1978, Princeton U., 1979, Davis (Calif.) Art Fair, 1982, Queens Gallery Group Show, Charlotte, 1983, Springs Mills Show, Lancaster, S.C., 1987, Art on the River, Savannah, Ga., 1989, Ann Gleason Interiors, Savannah, 1989, Spotlight on So. Artists, Atlanta, 1991, 92, 93, 94, 95, Coastal Nat., St. Simon Island, Ga., 1992, The Checkered Moon Gallery, 1993, Evening of the Arts/Hilton Head Island, S.C., 1992, 93, 94, 95, 96, Tin Can Alley Exhibit/Self Ctr.,Hilton Head, 1996; solo show at Patton and Howell, Savannah, 1990; contbr. to publd. Sanskrit, So. Accent. Roman Catholic. Avocations: theater, symphony, reading. Home: 322 E Taylor St Apt 1207 Savannah GA 31401-5059

VONSCHULZE-DELITZSCH, MARILYN WANDLING (LADY VONSCHULZE-DELITZSCH), artist, writer; b. Alton, Ill., May 16, 1932; d. Ralph Marion and Mary Mildred (Branson) W.; m. Sir Georg W.W. Herzog VonSchulze-Delitzsch; children: Jeffrey, Douglas, Pamela. Student, Monticello Coll., Godfrey, Ill, 1950-51, U. Ill., 1951-53; BA in Art, Webster U., St. Louis, 1968; MA Edn. in Art Edn., Washington U., St. Louis, 1975. Cert. tchr. art Kindergarten-Grade 12, Mo. 4th grade tchr. Alton (Ill.) Pub. Schs., 1961-62; art. buying dept. Gardner Advt. Co. Inc., St. Louis, 1962-63; art tchr. mid. sch. Lindbergh Sch. Dist., St. Louis, 1968-75; cons., designer V.P. Fair, Inc., St. Louis, 1982; adminstrv. asst. to headmaster, coll. counseling dept. John Burroughs Sch., St. Louis, 1979-82; dir. pub. rels. and advt. Dance St. Louis, 1983-85; freelance art and design St. Louis, 1970—; tchr. art mid. sch. St. Louis Pub. Schs., 1987-90, tchr. art Elem. Magnet Sch. for Visual and Performing Arts, 1990-98. Tchr. drawing and painting Summer Arts Inst., St. Louis Pub. Schs., 1992, graphic arts designer, cons. comty. affairs divsn., 1985-96, sch. vol. divsn., 1990-92, Webster Groves (Mo.) Sch. Dist., 1989-90, Pub. Sch. Retirement Sys., St. Louis, 1991; implementer classroom multi-cultural art edn. projects, 1987-98; summer participant Improving Visual Arts Edn., Getty Ctr. for Edn. in Arts, 1990; book illustrator-McGraw Hill Inter-Americana de Mexico, Mexico City, 1994-95, Simon & Schuster, Mexico City. Designer (cover and icons) English Language Teaching Text, 1996; designer Centennial Logo for St. Louis Pub. Schs. Sesquicentennial, 1988; painter, designer murals for Ctrl. Presbyn. Ch. Nursery, 1978-79, St. Nicholas Greek Orthodox Ch., 1980; designer two outdoor villages VP Fair, Arch Grounds, St. Louis, 1982; published writer. Patron St. Louis Symphony Orch. Recipient merit and honor awards Nat. Sch. Pub. Rels. Assn., 1990, 91, 92, 93, 95, Mo. Sch. Pub. Rels. Assn., 1989-90, 91, 92, 93. Mem. St. Louis Art Mus., PEO Sisterhood, Nat. Soc. DAR, Colonial Dames of 17th Cent., United Daus. of Confederacy, Chi Omega Alumnae. Avocations: Native American arts and culture, paintings, drawings, portraits. E-mail: tulipsaintlouis@earthlink.net.

VON STADE, FREDERICA, mezzo-soprano; b. Somerville, N.J., June 1, 1945; m. Peter Elkus, 1973 (div.); children: Jennie, Lisa; m. Michael G. Gorman, Jan. 1991. Student, Mannes Coll. Music, N.Y.C., Ecole Mozart, Paris; DMus (hon.), Yale U., 1985. Former nanny, salesgirl; sec. Am. Shakespeare Festival. Debut in Le nozec di Figaro with Met. Opera, 1970, later resident mem., Covent Garden debut, 1975; appeared with opera cos. including Paris Opera, San Francisco Opera, Salzburg Festival, London Royal Opera, Spoleto Festival, Boston Opera Co., Santa Fe Opera, Houston Grand Opera, La Scala; recital artist, soloist with symphony orchs.; appeared in operas The Marriage of Figaro, Faust, The Magic Flute, Don Giovanni, Tales of Hoffman, Rigoletto, Der Rosenkavalier, The Seagull, Werther, The Barber of Seville, The Dangerous Liasons, Le Nozze di Figaro; albums Frederica Von Stade Sings Mozart-Rossini Opera Arias, French Opera Arias, Pelleas and Melisande, Idomeneo, La Sonnambula, Simple Gifts with Mormon Tabernacle Choir, Songs of the Cat with Garrison Keillor; created roles of Nina in the Seagull (Pastieri), 1974, Tina in the Aspern Papers (Arganto), 1988; starred in Dominick Argento's Casa Guidi, 1985, Carnegie Hall, N.Y.C.; rec. artist EMI. Mem. Am. Guild Mus. Artists Roman Catholic. Avocations: tennis, skiing, dance. Office: Columbia Artists Mgt Inc Arbib/Treuhaft Div 165 W 57th St New York NY 10019-2201

VON THURN, JELENA, health science specialist; b. Skopje, Macedonia, Yugoslavia, Jan. 1, 1939; came to U.S., 1972; d. Miladin and Hedy (Hem) M.; m. Ernst Anzbock, Dec. 14, 1959 (div. 1971); children: Harald, Evelyn; m. Ranko Caric, Nov. 3, 1973 (div. 1980); 1 child, Peter. Student, Molloy Coll., 1979-81, L.I. U., 1981-82, Rockland C.C., 1985, Vt. Coll., 1985-86, Orange County C.C., 1988, Empire State Coll., 1990—. Ordained to ministry Universal Spiritualist Assn. U.S.A., 1985; lic., real estate agt., N.Y.; registered and cert. reflexologist, N.Y. Owner Walter's Bake Shop, 1973-79; nurse's aide Hillside Manor, 1980; clerical worker Molloy Coll., 1980-81, L.I. U., 1981-82; chiropractor asst. Steven R. Siegel D.C., 1982; owner Linden Motel, 1983; lectr. on Shiatsu and reflexology New Age Ctr., 1985-86; v.p., min. Universal Ctr. New Age Consciousness, Inc., Milford, Pa., 1985—; with Abatelli Realty, 1988; owner Athena Spa, 1993-94, Jelena's Skin Care and Anti-Aging Clinic, Carmel, Calif., 1998—; esthetician The Spa, Pebble Beach, Calif., 1999. Gen. agt. Intern Cons. Exchange, San Diego, Calif., 1986; spa and skincare therapist, Pebble Beach, Calif., 1995, Carmel Valley Ranch, 1995, Hyatt Regency, 1996. Mem. Alliance of Massage Therapists, Inc., Universal Spiritualist Assn., Assoc. Bodywork and Massage Profls., Carmel Art Assn. Avocations: oil painting, piano, guitar, dance, estate auctions.

VOORHESS, MARY LOUISE, pediatric endocrinologist; b. Livingston Manor, N.Y., June 2, 1926; d. Harry William and Helen Grace (Schwartz) V. RN, City Hosp. Sch. Nursing, Binghamton, N.Y., 1946; BA in Zoology, U. Tex., 1952; MD, Baylor Coll., Houston, 1956. Diplomate Am. Bd. Pediatrics and Pediatric Endocrinology. Rotating intern Albany (N.Y.) Med. Ctr., 1956-57, asst. resident pediatrics, 1957-58, chief resident pediatrics, 1958-59; rsch. fellow pediatric endocrinology and genetics SUNY Health Sci. Ctr., Syracuse, 1959-61, asst. prof. pediatrics, 1961-65, assoc. prof. pediatrics, 1965-70, prof. pediatrics, 1970-76, SUNY Sch. Medicine and Biomed. Scis., Buffalo, 1976-91, prof. pediatrics emeritus, 1991—; co-chief div. endocrinology Children's Hosp. Buffalo, 1976-91; retired, 1997. Ad hoc reviewer Jour. Pediatrics, Pediatrics, Am. Jour. Diseases Children, other. Contbr. sci. articles to profl. jours., chpts. to books. Mem. adv. bd. Interim Healthcare inc., 1991-97; mem. devel. coun. Children's Hosp. Buffalo Found., 1991-97; med. dir. Children's Growth Found., Buffalo, 1976-97; cmty. advisor Assn. for Rsch. Childhood Cancer, Buffalo, 1990-97. Recipient rsch. career devel. award Nat. Cancer Inst., 1961-71, Dean's award SUNY Sch. Medicine and Biomed. Scis., 1991. Fellow Am. Acad. Pediatrics, AAAS; mem. Soc. Pediatric Rsch. (emeritus), Am. Pediatric Soc. (emeritus), Endocrine Soc. (emeritus), Lawson Wilkins Pediatric Endocrine Soc. (emeritus), Phi Beta Kappa, Alpha Omega Alpha. Presbyterian. Home: 6311 Chiswick Park Williamsburg VA 23188-6369 E-mail: mlv6311@widomaker.com.

VOORHIS, LORI BETH, respiratory therapist; b. Lebanon, Ind., Sept. 7, 1959; d. Scott Hanen Hosier III and Sandra Kay Pock; m. Lester Alan Voorhis, Aug. 25, 1979 (div. Nov. 23, 2000); children: Emily Suzanne Burke, Jill Kathleen, Galan Jacob, Hannah Grace, Micah Jean. Cert. respiratory therapy, Meth. Hosp. Sch. Respiratory Therapy, Indpls., 1978; student, Marian Coll., 1998—. Cert. respiratory therapy Nat. Bd. Respiratory Therapy, 1987. Staff therapist, clin. instr., emergency rm. and ICU specialist; staff therapist, team leader, clin. instr., cardiac specialist St. Vincent Hosp., Indpls., 1989—2002; staff therapist Midtown Nursing and Rehab., Indpls., 2002—. Co-leader Girl Scouts Am., Zionsville, Ind., 1990—93; vol. Humane Soc., Indpls., 1995—96; mem. Ind. Ext. Homemakers, Lebanon, 1995—98. Career Advancement scholar, Ind. Ext. Homemakers, 2001, Adult Student scholar, Boone County Chpt. Zonta Internat., 2001. Mem.: Sigma Tau Delta (chpt. pres. 2001). Avocations: gardening, rock collecting, trivia, baking. Home: 109 N Adams St Brownsburg IN 46112-1232 Personal E-mail: lghvoorhis@netzero.net.

VOORLAS, STEPHANIE KATHERINE, freelance/self-employed writer, photographer; b. Racine, Wis., Apr. 1, 1951; d. Peter Harry Voorlas and Athena Callas. BA equivalent in Social Anthropology, U. Beirut, Lebanon, 1974; BA in Arabic Studies, U. Utah, 1993. Freelance writer, photographer. Contbr. articles to profl. publs. Tibetan Buddhist. Avocations: skiing, mountaineering. Home: PO Box 527 Silverton CO 81433

VOREACOS, SALLY A. social worker; b. Cleveland, Ohio, Feb. 16, 1929; d. William Ambrose Cahill and Laura Rebecca Bell; m. Paul Howard Voreacos, Dec. 15, 1951; children: Susan Ellicott, David Paul. BA cum laude, Radcliffe Coll., 1950; MSW, U. Md., 1968. LCSW Md., ACSW, NASW. Social worker VA Hosp., Balt., 1969—71; sr. social worker Johns Hopkins Hosp., Balt., 1975—90.

VOSE, KATHRYN KAHLER, marketing and communication executive; b. Denton, Tex., Aug. 18, 1953; d. James and Martha Kahler; m. William O. Vose, June 1, 1996. BA in Sociology, Sophie Newcomb Coll. Tulane U., 1975; MA in Mass Communications, U. Minn., 1977. Corr. newspapers, N.Y.C., Mpls.; nat. corr. Newhouse Newspapers, Washington; comm. dir. U.S. Dept. Edn.; v.p. comm. & mktg. Campaign for Tobacco-Free Kids, Washington. Panelist Washington Week In Review; vis. fellow Woodrow Wilson Nat. Fellowship Found; adviser World Health Orgn.; contbr. Nat. Acad. Scis. Recipient Crystal Medallion award AMA, Clarion award Assn. Women Comm., Silver Inkwell award Internat. Assn. Bus. Communicators, Mercury Grand award MerComm Internat., Thoth (2) awards Pub. Rels. Soc. Am., Assoc. Press Mng. Editors Pub. Svc. award. Mem. Nat. Press Club (pres. 1991, bd. govs.). Home: 3351 Tennyson St NW Washington DC 20015-2442 Office: Nat Ctr Tobacco Free Kids 1707 L St NW Ste 800 Washington DC 20036-4209

VOSEVICH, KATHI ANN, writer, editor, scholar; b. St. Louis, Oct. 12, 1957; d. William and Catherine Mildred (Kalinowski) V.; m. James Hughes Meredith, Sept. 6, 1986. AB with honors, St. Louis U., 1980, MA, 1983; PhD, U. Denver, 1988. Tchg. fellow St. Louis U., 1980-83, acad. advising fellow, 1983-84; tchg. fellow U. Denver, 1985-87; prof. ESL, BNM Talensch., Uden, The Netherlands, 1988-91; instr. English, mentor U. Ga., Athens, 1992-94; vis. asst. prof. Colo. Coll., Colorado Springs, 1994; sr. tech. writer and editor Titan Client/Server Techs., Colorado Springs, 1994-96, head documentation, libr., 1996-97; documentation mgr. Beechwood, Colorado Springs, 1997-98, tech. mgr., 1998-99; tech. writer Microsoft, Redmond, Wash., 1999-2000; documentation and process mgr. Sprint, Denver, 2000; practice and group mgr. e-bus. Sprint Corp., Denver, 2000—02, svc. launch mgr. Mobile Computing Svcs., 2002—03, strategic market mgr., 2003—. Forensic judge USAF Acad., Colo., 1987-88; edn. officer Volkel (The Netherlands) Air Base, 1988-91; instr. English European divsn. U. Md., The Netherlands and Belgium, 1989-91. Author: Customer Care User's Guide, 1996, Interview with Joseph Heller, 1999, Conversations with Joseph Heller in Understanding the Literature of World War II, 1999, Office Update, 1999-2000, Tutoring the Tudors, 2000, Sprint Takes Messaging into the Future, 2003; editor: Subscription Services System Documentation, 1996, Titan Process Documentation, 1994-96; copy editor: Language, Ideas, and American Culture; War, Literature and the Arts; contbr. over 100 electronic texts and articles to profl. jours. Colo. scholar U. Denver, 1985-86, grad. dean scholar, 1988; NEH fellow U. Md., 1994 Mem. MLA, Phi Beta Kappa, Alpha Sigma Nu. Roman Catholic. Avocations: writing, drawing, raising Bernese mountain dogs. Office: Sprint Ste 1400 1099 18th St Denver CO 80202

VOSKA, KATHRYN CAPLES, consultant, facilitator; b. Berkeley, Calif., Dec. 26, 1942; d. Donald Buxton and Ellen Marion (Smith) Caples; m. David Karl Nehrling, Aug. 15, 1964 (div. Nov. 1980); children: Sandra E. Nehrling, Barbara M. Nehrling, Melissa A. Nehrling-Holmgren; m. James Edward Voska, Aug. 31, 1985. BS, Northwestern U., 1964; MS, Nat.-Louis U., 1989. Cert. teacher, Ill.; cert. career mgmt. fellow practitioner Inst. Career Cert. Internat. Tchr. pub. schs., Northbrook and Evanston, Ill., 1964-65; acting phys. dir. YWCA, Evanston, Ill., 1975; quality control technician Baxter Travenol, Morton Grove, Ill., 1978-80; sr. quality assurance analyst Hollister Inc., Libertyville, Ill., 1980-85; info. ctr. trainer, tech. training mgr. Rand McNally, Skokie, Ill., 1985-92; cons., facilitator Capka & Assocs., Skokie and Kansas City, 1992—; dir. edn. Nat. Office Machine Dealers, 1992-94; career and mgmt. cons. Right Mgmt. Cons., Overland Park, Kans., 1994—. Pvt. practice estate conservator. Telephone worker Contact Chgo. Crisis Hotline, 1989-90; CPR instr. trainer Amer. Heart Assn., Chgo., 1977-89; aquatic dir. YMCA, Evanston, Ill., 1969-80; rep. Alumnae Panhellenic Coun., Evanston, 1969-75; grad. Leadership Overland Park, 1996, mem. 15th anniv. special task force. Mem. ASTD (bd. dirs. Kansas City chpt. 1997-99), ASCD, Soc. Human Resource Mgmt., Midwest Soc. Profl. Cons., Assn. for Mgmt. Orgn. Design, Chgo. Orgn. Data Processing Educators, Chgo. Computer Soc., Info. Ctr. Exch. of Chgo., Assn. Quality and Participation, Am. Soc. for Quality (teller N.E. Ill. sect. 1982-84), Internat. Soc. for Performance Improvement, Assn. Career Profls. Internat. founding pres. Kansas City chpt. 2002-04, nat. bd. dirs. 2000—, nat. bd. v.p., pres. elect 2002-04, pres. 2004—, nat. bd. pres. 2004—, chmn. internat. membership drive 2004), Learning Resource Network. Presbyterian. Avocations: scuba diving, swimming, hiking, camping, travel. Home: 1001 E 118th Ter Kansas City MO 64131-3828 Office: Right Mgmt Cons 7300 W 110th St Ste 800 Overland Park KS 66210-2387 Office Phone: 913-323-2309. Personal E-mail: kvoska@kc.rr.com. Business E-Mail: kathy.voska@right.com.

VOSS, JANICE E. astronaut; b. South Bend, Ind., Oct. 8, 1956; d. James R. and Voss. Student, U. Okla., 1973—75; BSc in Engring Sci., Purdue U., 1975; MSc in Elec. Engring., MIT, 1977; student, Rice U., 1977—78; PhD in Aero. & Astronautics, MIT, 1987. Co-op NASA, Houston, 1973—75, crew tnr., 1977—87; with Orbiatl Sci. Corp., 1987—90; astronaut NASA, 1991—. Astronaut space mission on STS-57, 1993, space mission on STS-63, 1995; payload comdr. space mission on STS-83, 1997; astronaut space mission on STS-94, 1997, space mission on STS-99, 2000. Fellow, NSF, 1976, Howard Hughes fellow, 1981, Zonta Amelia Earhart fellow, 1982. Mem.: AIAA. Avocations: reading, dance, volleyball, flying. Office: Astronaut Office CB NASA Johnson Space Center Houston TX 77058

VOZHEIKO WHEATON, LENA, music educator, pianist; b. Alma-Ata, Kazakhstan, Dec. 30, 1951; d. Vladimir Isidorovich and Enessa Vasilyevna Vozheiko; m. Charles S. Wheaton, Dec. 20, 1995; 1 child, Anton A. MS, Conservatory of Music, Frunze Kyrgyzstan, 1975; PhD in Piano Performance, Tchaikovsky Music Conservatory, Moscow, 1989. Instr. Conservatory of Music, Frunze, 1975-93. Accompanist at various nat. and internat. competitins; pianist for Carmina Burana, Vancouver Symphony, Washington, 1997. Author: Principles of Duo Piano Playing, 1992. Mem. Music Tchrs. Nat. Assn. Avocation: painting rock animal figures.

VRANCIK, BARBARA A. lawyer; BBA, U. Miami, 1976; JD, DePaul U., 1979. Bar: Ill. 1979, N.Y. 1985. Law clk. to Hon. Robert Eisen, Bankruptcy Ct. for No. Dist. Ill., Chgo., 1979-80; ptnr. Sidley & Austin, N.Y.C. Editor DePaul Law Rev., 1978-79. Office: Sidley & Austin 875 3d Ave New York NY 10022 Fax: 212-906.2021. E-mail: burancik@sidley.com.

VRATIL, KATHRYN HOEFER, federal judge; b. Manhattan, Kans., 1949; BA, U. Kans., 1971, JD, 1975; postgrad., Exeter U., 1971-72. Bar: Kans. 1975, Mo. 1978, U.S. Dist. Ct. Kans. 1975, U.S. Dist. Ct. (we. dist.) Mo. 1978, U.S. Dist. Ct. (ea. dist.) Mo. 1985, U.S. Ct. Appeals (8th cir.) 1978, U.S. Ct. Appeals (10th cir.) 1980, U.S. Ct. Appeals (11th dist.) 1982, U.S. Supreme Ct., 1995. Law clk. U.S. Dist. Ct., Kansas City, Kans., 1975-78; assoc. Lathrop Koontz & Norquist, Kansas City, Mo., 1978-83; ptnr. Lathrop & Norquist, Kansas City, 1984-92; judge City of Prairie Village, Kans., 1990-92. Bd. dirs. Kans. Legal Bd. Svcs., 1991-92; mem. adminstrv. com. Jud. Conf. of the U.S., 2000—. Bd. editors Kans. Law Rev., 1974-75, Jour. Kans. Bar Assn., 1992—. Mem. Kansas City Tomorrow (XIV); bd. trustees, shepherd-deacon Village Presbyn. Ch.; nat. adv. bd. U. Kans. Ctr. for Environ. Edn. and Tng., 1993-95; bd. dirs. Kans. Legal Svcs., 1991-92. Fellow Kans. Bar Found., Am. Bar Found.; mem. ABA (editl. bd. Judges Jour. 1996—), Am. Judicature Soc., Nat. Assn. Judges, Fed. Judges Assn., Kans. Bar Assn. (mem. bench bar com., 2000—), Mo. Bar Assn., Kansas City Met. Area Bar Assn., Johnson County Bar Assn., Assn. Women Judges, Lawyers Assn. Kansas City, Supreme Ct. Hist. Soc., Kans. State Hist. Soc., U. Kans. Law Soc. (bd. govs. 1978-81), Kans. U. Alumni Assn. (mem. Kansas City chpt. alumni bd. 1990-92, nat. bd. dirs. 1991-96, bd. govs. Adams Alumni Ctr. 1992-95), Chancellor's Club, Williams Ednl. Fund, Jayhawks for Higher Edn., Homestead Country Club Prairie Village (pres. 1985-86), Native Sons and Daus of Kans. (life), Jr. League Wyandotte and Johnson Counties, Order of Coif, Kans. Inn of Ct. (master 1993—, pres. 1999-2000), Phi Kappa Phi. Republican. Presbyterian. Office: 511 US Courthouse 500 State Ave Kansas City KS 66101-2403

VRBKA, JUDITH MARY, music educator; b. Osceola, Nebr., May 14, 1961; d. Charles Gregory and Wilomine Angela Kucera; m. Lynn James Vrbka, Aug. 13, 1988; 1 child, Michael Thomas. BFAE, Wayne State Coll., 1983; MusM in Elem. Edn., U. Nebr., 1991. Vocal and instrumental music tchr. Dix (Nebr.) Pub. Schs., 1984—85; vocal music tchr. Shelby (Nebr.) Pub. Schs., 1985—97, vocal and instrumental music tchr., 1997—98, Rising City Pub. Schs., 1997—98, Shelby (Nebr.) Pub. Schs., 1998—99; vocal music tchr. Wilber (Nebr.)-Clatonia Pub. Sch., 1999—. Home: PO Box 284 801 S Shimerda Wilber NE 68465

VREDENBURGH, JUDY, youth organization executive; m. Donald Vredenburgh; 1 child. BA, U. Pa., 1970; MBA, U. Buffalo, 1975. Various positions in retail; exec. v.p., gen. mdse. mgr. Sizes Unlimited/Lerner Women; CEO Chess King; sr. v.p. March of Dimes, 1993—99; CEO and pres. Big Brothers Big Sisters of Am., 1999—. Bd. dirs. Generations United. Big Sister; bd. overseers Sch. Arts and Sciences. U. Penn. Office: Big Brothers Big Sisters of Am Nat Office 230 N 13th St Philadelphia PA 19107*

VREDEVOE, DONNA LOU, research immunologist, microbiologist, educator; b. Ann Arbor, Mich., 1938; BA in Bacteriology, UCLA, 1959, PhD in Microbiology, 1963. USPHS postdoctoral fellow Stanford U., 1963-64; instr. bacteriology UCLA, 1963, postgrad. rsch. immunologist dept. surgery Ctr. Health Scis., 1964-65, asst. rsch. immunologist dept. surgery Ctr. Health Scis., 1964-67; asst. prof. Sch. Nursing, Ctr. Health Scis., 1967-70, assoc. prof., 1970-76, prof., 1976—, assoc. dean Sch. Nursing, 1976-78, acting assoc. dean Sch. Nursing., 1985-86, asst. dir. space planning Cancer Ctr., 1976-78, dir. space planning, 1978-90, cons. to lab. nuc. medicine and radiation biology, 1967-80, acting dean Sch. Nursing, 1995-96. Chair acad. senate UCLA, 1999—2000, vice chancellor acad. pers., 2001—. Contbr. articles to profl. publs. Postdoctoral fellow USPHS, 1963-64; Mabel Wilson Richards scholar UCLA, 1960-61; rsch. grantee Am. Cancer Soc., Calif. Inst. Cancer Rsch., Calif. divsn. Am. Cancer Soc., USPHS, Am. Nurses Found., Cancer Rsch. Coordinating Com. U. Calif., Dept. Energy, UCLA. Mem Am. Soc. Microbiology, Am. Assn. Immunologists, Am. Assn. Cancer Rsch., Nat. League Nursing (2d v.p. 1979-81), Sigma Xi, Alpha Gamma Sigma, Sigma Theta Tau (nat. hon. mem.) Office: UCLA Chancellor's Office 2147 Murphy Hall PO Box 951405 Los Angeles CA 90095-1405

VROMAN, BARBARA FITZ, writer, educator; b. Chgo., Mar. 31, 1933; d. William Edwin and Pearl Asenith (Coombs) Fitz; m. Dale Duane Vroman, June 30, 1951; children: Guy, Kim, Marc, Ryan. Grad. high sch., Plainfield, Wis. News editor Waushara Argus Newspaper, Wautoma, Wis., 1966-72; pub. Pearl-Win Pub. Co., Hancock, Wis., 1981-91; tchr. summer sessions The Clearing, Ellison Bay, Wis., 1989—; presenter pvt. seminars Rhinelander Sch. of Arts, U. Wis., 1975—. Novelist: Sons of Thunder, 1981, Linger Not at Chebar, 1992; co-author: Tomorrow is a River, 1977, (non-fiction) Samll Celebration Summer, 2003. Home: N4721 9th Dr Hancock WI 54943-7617 Office Phone: 715-249-5407.

VRUWINK, AMY SUE, state legislator; b. May 22, 1975; BS, Marion Coll., Fond du Lac, Wis., 1997. Former congl. aide; mem. Wis. State Assembly, Madison, 2002—, sec. Minority Caucus, 2003—. Democrat. Office: State Capitol Rm 412N PO Box 8953 Madison WI 53708 Address: 9425 Flower Ln Milladore WI 54454

VUCANOVICH, BARBARA FARRELL, retired congressman; b. Fort Dix, N.J., June 22, 1921; d. Thomas F. and Ynez (White) Farrell; m. Ken Dillon, Mar. 8, 1950 (dec. 1964); children: Patty Dillon Cafferata, Mike, Ken, Tom, Susan Dillon Anderson; m. George Vucanovich, June 19, 1965 (dec. Dec. 1998). Student, Manhattanville Coll. of Sacred Heart, 1938-39. Owner, operator Welcome Aboard Travel, Reno, 1968-74; Nev. rep. for Senator Paul Laxalt, 1974-82; mem. 98th-104th Congresses from 2d Nev. dist., 1983-96; chmn. appropriations subcom. on military construction; Rep. natl. committeewoman Nev. Rep. Party, 1996-2000. Pres. Nev. Fedn. Republican Women, Reno, 1955-56; former pres. St. Mary's Hosp. Guild, Lawyer's Wives. Mem.: Hidden Valley Country (Reno). Roman Catholic.

VUKMIR, LEAH, state legislator; b. Apr. 26, 1958; m. George Vukmir; children: Elena, Nicholas. BSN, Marquette U., Milw., 1980; MSN, U. Wis., 1983. Cert. pediat. nurse practitioner, RN Wis. Faculty nursing St. Mary's Med. Ctr., Children's Hosp. of Wis.; mem. Wis. State Assembly, Madison, 2002—, vice chair edn. reform com., mem. children and families com., mem. econ. devel. com., mem. criminal justice com., mem. health com. Lectr. in field; guest panelist Sunday Insight TV show; rsch. fellow Wis. Policy Rsch. Inst.; past pres. Parents Raising Ednl. Stds. in Schs. Contbr. articles to profl. jours. Vol. speedskating referee ASU; mem. stds. and assessment subcom. Gov. Tommy Thompson's Task Force on Edn. and Learning, Wis.; mem. English/lang. arts task force Coun. on Model Acad. Stds.; mem. choir Annunciation Greek Orthodox Ch. Recipient Alumni Achievement award, Brookfield East H.S., 2002, Unsung Hero award, Ctr. for Edn. Reform, Washington, 1998. Mem.: West Allis Speedskating Club. Republican. Greek Orthodox. Office: State Capitol Bldg Rm 307 N PO Box 8953 Madison WI 53708 Address: 2544 N 93d St Wauwatosa WI 53226

VULGAMORE, ALLISON, performing arts administrator; BMus, Oberlin Coll. Former gen. mgr., artistic adminstr., mgr. ops. Nat. Symphony Orch., Washington; former gen. mgr. N.Y. Philharm. Orch., N.Y.C.; pres. Atlanta Symphony Orch., 1993—. Bd. dirs. Oberlin Coll.; mem. arts challenge panel in music NEH. Bd. dirs. Midtown Alliance; mem. Vision 2000 Econ. Devel. Collaborative; Cultural Olympiad and opening ceremonies coord. Centennial Olympic Games, Atlanta, 1996. Am. Symphony Orch. League fellow, 1980. Mem. Atlanta Rotary. Office: Atlanta Symphony Orchestra Robert W Woodruff Arts Ctr 1293 Peachtree St NE Ste 300 Atlanta GA 30309-3552

VYDARENY, KAY HERZOG, radiologist, medical educator; b. Chgo., Nov. 26, 1942; MD, U. Mich., 1968. Diplomate Am. Bd. Radiology. Intern Blodgett Meml. Med. Ctr., Grand Rapids, Mich., 1968—69; resident in diagnostic radiology Mich. State U., Grand Rapids, 1975—80; prof. radiology Emory U., Atlanta; radiologist Emory U. Hosp., Atlanta. Mem.: Am. Roentgen Ray Soc., Am. Assn. Women in Radiology, Assn. Univ. Radiologists, Am. Coll. Radiology (pres. 2001—02), Radiol. Soc. N.Am.

WACHSTEIN, JOAN MARTHA, dental hygienist; b. Phila., Nov. 12, 1941; d. Milton and Mabel Louise (Friedman) Hertzfeld; m. Mortimer Berwyn Wachstein, July 14, 1962 (dec. 1989); 1 child, Esther Lynn. RDH, Temple U., Phila., 1961. Registered dental hygienist; cert. gerontology referral Union Am. Hebrew Congregations and Hebrew Union Coll. Jewish Inst. Religion. Dental hygienist Dr. M.B. Wachstein, Newark, Del., 1970-89; pres. Jewish Family Svc. of Del., 1992—94, Aux. of Miltion & Hattie Kutz Home, 1985—97; campaign mgr. Milton and Hattie Kutz Home for Capital Campaign, 1995; pres. Milton and Hattie Kutz Home, Inc., 1997—99. Bd. dirs. Jewish Fedn. Del., 1994—97, 1999, mem. exec. com., 1992—93, mem. Jewish Cmty. endowment com., 1993—99; mem. Mid-Atlantic coun. Union Am. Hebrew Congregations, 1981—, vice chair biennial program com., 1990—92, chair, 1992—94, bd. dirs., 1994—, v.p., 1992—98, pres., 1998—2002; trustee Union of Am. Hebrew Congregations, 1994—, mem. com. on Jewish family concerns, 1997—, mem. commn. on religious living, 1998, mem. outreach commn. exec. com., chair com. on older adults, 1996—2000, com. on small congregations, 2000—, biennial program com., 2000—, budget com., 2000—, chair task force adult care facilities, 2001; mem. Women of Reform Judaism, Fedn. Temple Sisterhoods, 1975—97, v.p., 1987—89, 1989—91, 1991—93, mem.-at-large bd. dirs., 1993—97; pres. Beth Emeth Sisterhood, 1968—70; mem. jr. bd. Christiana Care Del., Inc.; apptd. commn. adult entertainment establishments State of Del., 1993—2001; mem. N.Am. bd. World Union Progressive Judaism; mem. exec. com. Assn. Reform Zionists Am./World Union N Am., 1999—; v.p. Assn. Reform Zionists Am./World Union N.Am., 2004—; chair Women for Carper com. for Gov. State of Del., 1993—96; co-chmn. Women for Minner for Gov., State of Del., 2001—02; vol. ombudsman State of Del. Divsn. Svcs. for Aging Adults and Adults with Phys. Disabilities, 2000—03; bd. dirs. Assn. Jewish Families and Children, 1995—99. Recipient Community Builder award NCCJ, 1985, Keva cert. Ctrl. Conf. Am. Rabbis and Nat. Assn. Temple Educators. Mem.: AAUW, Orgn. for Ednl. Resources and Tech. Tng., Nat. Coun. Jewish Women, Jewish Women Internat., Hadassah, Temple U. Dental Hygiene Alumni Assn. Jewish. Home: 3331 Silverside Rd Wilmington DE 19810-4804 Fax: 302-478-5157. E-mail: JWachs3331@aol.com.

WACHT, LENY NOWAG, art educator; b. Mannheim, Germany, Sept. 14, 1912; arrived in U.S., 1930; d. Joseph and Katherine (Kramer) Nowag; m. Peter Wacht, Jan. 29, 1932 (dec. Nov. 1981); 1 child, Anita Batman. Tchrs. Degree, Froebel Sem., Germany, 1929. Tchr. art, Greenwood, Miss., 1950—95. Mem. Cotton Landia Mus., Greenwood. Mem.: Delta Art Assn (founder), Greenwood Women's Club (chmn.). Roman Catholic. Home: 216 W Adams Ave Greenwood MS 38930-3017

WACHTELL, WENDY, foundation administrator; b. White Plains, N.Y., May 5, 1961; d. Thomas and Esther Carole (Pickard) Wachtell; children: Jameson Myer Schine, Bradley Thomas Schine, Davis Berndt Schine. BA, Wellesley Coll., 1983; MA in Journalism, U. So. Calif., L.A., 1987. Legis. asst. U.S. House Reps., Washington, 1983-85, various positions KCBS TV, L.A., 1986-88; v.p. Joseph Drown Found., L.A., 1988—. Bd. dirs., co-chair L.A. Urban Funders, The Accelerated Sch., So. Calif. Assn. Philanthropy, U. So. Calif., Ctr. for Philanthropy and Pub. Policy, The John Thomas Dye Sch., Joseph Drown Found.; advisor Psychol. Trauma Ctr., L.A., 1988—90, Ctr. for Talented Youth, Glendale, Calif., 1989—98. Office: Joseph Drown Found Ste 2330 1999 Avenue Of The Stars Los Angeles CA 90067-6033

WACKER, SUSAN REGINA, creative design director; b. Red Bank, NJ, Apr. 29, 1954; d. Durward Richard and Margaret Rose (Williams) W. BFA, Pratt Inst., 1978, cert. computer graphics/electronic pub., 2001. Asst. art dir. Lesley-Hille Inc., NYC, 1975-79; art dir. Kasica, Lefton, Brown, Inc., NYC, 1979-80, Marinelli & Hnath Assoc., Inc., NYC, 1980-82; sr. design dir. Elizabeth Arden Co., NYC, 1982-99; art dir. L'Oreal Retail Divsn., NYC, 2000—02; design cons. SRW Design, Pittsfield, Vt., 2002—. Exhibited at The Nature of Diamonds, Mus. Natural History, NYC, 1997-98; patentee in field. Recipient (4) DESI awards, 1980, ANDY award, 1980, Fragrance Found. award, 1988, 91, 92, Silver award NJ Packaging Execs. Club, 1990, ADDY Excellence citation, 1991, Edison Best New Products Gold Medal award, 1991, (2) Gold awards Nat. Paperbox & Packaging Assn., 1992, (2) Gold awards, 1994, Silver award Paperboard Packaging Coun., 1993, Excellence award, 1993, Silver Excellence award Nat. Paperbox & Packaging Assn., 1993, (10) Silver Excellence awards, 1994, Mobius 1st Place Statuette award, 1995, Gold award Nat. Paperboard Coun., 1995, Prix Francois 1st de L'Emballage de Luxe, 1995, OMA Gold award, 1995, Oscar de L'Emballage Prestige à Lyon, 1995, Mobius award First Place Statuette for Elizabeth Taylor's Black Pearls perfume product line/package design, 1996, OMA Gold award for Elizabeth Arden's 5th Avenue tester display, 1996, OMA Bronze award for Elizabeth Taylor's Black Pearls tester display, 1996, Lagerfeld, Jako Mdsg., 1998, CPC "Package of the Month" (October), Elizabeth Arden's 5th Avenue fragrance line, 1996, Natl. Paperboard Packaging Conc. award, 1996, OMA Bronze award Lagerfeld JAKO Mdsg. Program, 1998. Mem. Internat. Perfume Bottle Assn., Cosmetic Exec. Women Found., Fashion Group Internat.(publ. com.), Annette Green Mus. at Fragrance Found. Avocations: skiing, tennis, horseback riding, photography. Office: SRW Design 19 Schoolhouse Dr PO Box 567 Pittsfield VT 05762 E-mail: srwacker@aol.com., srwdesign@comcast.net.

WADDING, TONIA J. multi-media specialist; b. Albert Lea, Minn., May 1, 1959; d. Elford Neil and Shirley Ann Magner; 1 child, Elizabeth Ann. MS, Abilene Christian U., Tex., 1982. Tchr. Dimmitt Mid. Sch., Tex., 1982—86; title I tchr. River Ridge Sch. Dist., Patch Grove, Wis., 1987—99, libr. media specialist, 1999—. Pres. GREAT, Patch Grove, 2001—03. Home: 123 Hwy 61 N Apt 1 Potosi WI 53820 Office: River Ridge Sch Dist 11165 Co P Patch Grove WI 53817 E-mail: wadding@rrsd.k12.wi.us.

WADDINGTON, BETTE HOPE (ELIZABETH CROWDER), violinist, educator; b. San Francisco; d. John and Marguerite (Crowder) Waddington. BA in Music, U. Calif., Berkeley, 1945, postgrad., Julliard Sch. Music, 1950, San Jose State Coll., 1955; MA in Music and Art, San Francisco U., 1953; studied with, Joseph Fuchs, Melvin Ritter, Frank Gittelson, Felix Khuner, Daniel Bonsack, D.C. Dounis, Naoum Blinder, Eddy Brown. Cert. gen. elem. and secondary tchr., Calif.; life cert. music and art for jr. coll.; cert. in librarianship for elem. sch. to jr. coll., Calif. Violinist Erie (Pa.) Symphony, 1950-51, Dallas Symphony, 1957-58, St. Louis Symphony, 1958-95. Toured alone and with St. Louis Symphony U.S., Can., Middle East, Japan, China, England, Korea, Europe, Africa; concert master Peninsula Symphony, Redwood City and San Mateo, Calif., Grove Music Soc., N.Y.C.; violinist St. Louis Symphony, 1958-95, violinist emeritus; numerous recs. St. Louis Symphony, 1958—. Julliard Sch. Music scholar 1950, San Jose State Coll. scholar 1955. Mem. Am. String Tchrs. Assn., Am. Musicians Union (life, St. Louis and San Francisco chpts.), U. Calif. Alumnae Assn. (life, Berkeley), San Francisco State U. Alumni Assn. (life), San Jose State U. Alumni Assn. (life), Sierra Club (life), Alpha Beta Alpha. Avocations: travel, art, archeology, history, drawing, painting. Office: St Louis Symphony Orch care Powell Symphony Hall 718 N Grand Blvd Saint Louis MO 63103-1011

WADDINGTON, IRMA JOANN, music educator; b. Nokomis, Ill., June 7, 1929; d. Albert William and Rose Minnie (Hueschen) Miller; m. Ralph Roger Waddington, Nov. 3, 1946; children: Joann, Janet, Jennifer. Cert. piano, organ Ill. State Music Tchrs. Assn. Music tchr. pvt. studio, Pana, Ill., 1957—2003; ch. organist, choir dir. St. Paul Luth. Ch., Pana, 1957—; keyboard player Waddington Trio, Pana, 1987—98, 2000—02. Composer: Memories of Kerri, 1983, Rejoice! Rejoice!, 1993, Praise! Praise!, 1993. Organist Rotary Club, Pana, 1985—, sr. citizens, Pana, 1970—, local nursing homes, Pana, 1974—. Named Best Piano Teacher, Decatur (Ill.) Herald & Review, 1987, Member of Yr. Decatur Area Music Tchrs. Assn., 1997. Mem. Am. Fedn. Musicians (pres., 1965-68), Music Tchrs. Nat. Assn., Decatur Area Music Tchrs. Assn. (pres. 1983, 84, 90, 94, 95, clinician, 1979—), Ill. Music Tchrs. Assn. (clinician 1991 conv.). Republican. Lutheran. Avocations: travel, golf. Home: 709A Kitchell Ave Pana IL 62557-1875

WADDY, PATRICIA A. architectural history educator; b. Cannelton, Ind., July 29, 1941; d. Luther and Gertrude Viola (Brandyberry) W. BA, Rice U., 1963; MA, Tulane U., 1965; PhD, NYU, 1973. Vis. lectr. Carnegie-Mellon U., Pitts., 1970-71, asst. prof., 1971-77; assoc. prof. archtl. history Syracuse U., NY, 1977-91, prof., 1991—2002, Disting. prof. architecture, 2002—. Vis. lectr. Cornell U., Ithaca, N.Y., 1977, vis. assoc. prof., 1980. Author: Seventeenth-Century Roman Palaces: Use and The Art of the Plan, 1990 (Alice Davis Hitchcock award 1992); co-author: (with D. DiCastro and A.M. Pedrocchi) Il Palazzo Pallavicini Rospigliosi e la Galleria Pallavicini, 2000; editor Nicodemus Tessin the Younger, Traicté dela decoration interieure (1717), 2002. Fulbright grantee, Rome, 1968-69; fellow Am. Acad. in Rome, 1970, Nat. Humanities Ctr., 1984-85, Samuel H. Kress sr. fellow Nat. Gallery Art, 1994-95, NEH fellow, 1998-99, Guggenheim fellow, 1999-00, Am. Coun. Learned Soc. fellow, 1978. Mem. Soc. Archtl. Historians (book rev. editor Jour. 1985-88, editor 1990-93, 2d v.p. 1993-94, 1st v.p. 1994-96, pres. 1996-98), Coll. Art Assn., Renaissance Soc. Am. Office: Syracuse U Sch Architecture Syracuse NY 13244-1250 E-mail: pwaddy@syr.edu.

WADE, BRENDA LYNN, chef; b. Shelby, Mich., Oct. 19, 1962; d. John and Marcella Wade. Student, Grand Rapid Jr. Coll. Chef Big Bear Brewing Co., Coral Springs, Fla., 1996—2003, West Boca Med. Ctr., Boca Raton, Fla., 2003—. C.A. Muer Corp. scholar, James Beard Found. scholar. Mem. Roundtable For Women in Food Svc. Home: 1332 SE 5th Ct Deerfield Beach FL 33441-4934

WADE, ERNESTINE, public health nurse; b. Franklin, La., Aug. 18, 1941; d. Phillip and Emma (Bettis) Miller; m. James Wade Jr., Dec. 25, 1965; 1 child, Kevin Troy. ASN, Lamar U., 1980. Nurse asst. U. Tex., Galveston, 1961, pharmacy technician St. Mary Hosp., Port Arthur, Tex., 1963-64, lic. vocat. nurse, 1967-80, RN, 1980-81, Bapt. Hosp., Beaumont, Tex., 1981-82, UpJohn Home Health Agy., Port Arthur, 1982-83, Pub. Health Dept., Port Arthur, 1983-96; dir. health Port Arthur City Health Dept., 1996—. Mem. Star Enterprise Corp., Port Arthur, 1996—, UpJohn Healthcare, 1981-83, Port Arthur Ind. Sch. Dist. Head-Start, 1994-96. Mem. Southeast Tex. Nursing Assn. Avocations: reading, walking. Home: 4918 Austin Ave Port Arthur TX 77640-2505 Office: Port Arthur City Health Dept 603 5th St Port Arthur TX 77640-6540

WADE, KAREN, federal agency administrator; b. Cortez, Colo. m. John W. Wade (div.). Student, U. Colo., 1960-62; B.Bus., Ft. Lewis Coll., 1962-64; postgrad., U. No. Ariz., 1973, U. Tenn., Knoxville, 1977. So. region trail coord. Appalachian Trail Project Nat. Park Svc., 1978-83; mgmt. asst. Shenandoah Nat. Park, Va., 1983-85; supt. Ft. McHenry Nat. Monument and Historic Shrine Hampton Nat. Hist. Park, Balt., 1985-87, supt. Guadalupe Mountains Nat. Park, Tex., 1987-90, Wrangell-St. Elias Nat. Park and Preserve, Alaska, 1990-94, Great Smoky Mountains Nat. Park, Gatlinburg, Tenn., 1994—, dir., 1999—. Office: Dir Intermountain Reg Nat Park Svc PO Box 25287 Denver CO 80225-0287 also: 12795 Alameda Pky Denver CO 80228 E-mail: karen_wade@nps.gov.

WADE, MAGGIE, newscaster; b. Crystal Springs, Miss. married; 2 children. Student, Jackson State U., Miss. Coll. Reporter WHJT-FM; radio announcer, mktg. rschr., weekend news anchor WJDX-MISS 103; anchor WLBT, Jackson, Miss.; adj. prof. Belhaven Coll., Jackson, Miss. Miss. rep. Presdl. Summit, 1997; mem. adv. bd. So. Christian Svcs. for Children and Youth; bd. dirs. Friends of Children's Hosp., U. Med. Ctr., Miss. Pub. Edn. Forum, Coun. on Reform and Excellence, Jackson Pub. Schs., United Way Ctrl. Miss.; Olympic Torchbearer; spkr. in field. Actor: (films) A Time to Kill, Ghosts of Mississippi. Active United Negro Coll. Fund, Easter Seals, Santa's Toy Chest; mem. Word of Faith Christian Ctr.; bd. dirs. Salvation Army, River Oaks Hosp., Diabetes Found. Miss. Named Outstanding Young Mississippian, Miss. Jr. C. of C., Woman of Yr., Alcorn State U., Outstanding Career Woman, Jackso9n Sales and Mktg. Execs., Woman of Yr., State Martin Luther King, Jr. Com.; named one of Outstanding Young Women in Am.; named to Hall of Fame, Miss. Families for Kids; recipient over 150 awards, Angel in Adoption award, Congl. Coalition on Adoption, Top 40 under 40 Bus. award, Miss. Bus. Journ., Svc. to Mankind award, Miss., Meritorious Leadership award, Tougaloo Coll., Vernon Dahmer award for svc. to children, State NAACP, Svc. to Edn. award, Jackson State U. Office: WLBT 715 S Jefferson St Jackson MS 39201

WADE, REBA, music teacher, pianist; b. Dresden, Tenn., Apr. 30, 1938; d. John Buford and Willie Ruth (Todd) Tilley; m. Ronald Lee Wade, July 22, 1956; children: Tony Lee, Randy Neal. Student, U. Tenn., Martin, 1976-80. Tchr. pvt. studio, Martin, 1962-70, 76—, Sharon (Tenn.) Sch., 1968, Westview H.S., Martin, 1976--79, Greenfield (Tenn.) Sch., 1984-86; mgr., dir. Wade Bros., Martin, 1965-71, High Variety Show Mems., Martin, 1994—. Tchr., accompanist for students, shows, groups, auditions and on radio and TV; profl. pianist; vice consul Internat. Biog. Ctr., 2002, 03, 04, advisor to dir.-gen., 2002. Prodr. Wade Bros. Rec., 1969, student recs., 1988-90, 97-2003; author lyrics, music original compositions including Little Cowboy, 1963, I Love My Jesus, 1963, Christmas Time, 1964, Happy Happy Day, 1964, Love, 1964, Oh How I Love You, 1965, Dear Mis-Fortune, 1965, Red Lace, 1965, Crazy Little Feeling, 1967, All Because of Christmas Day, 1968, Mean Mean Mama, 1968, God is Like This, 1979, Little Dreams, 1992, also tnr., prodr., 1988-90, 97-2001; performer Christmas music The White House, 1997-98, Pentagon Party, 1998; performer World Wide Air Show RAF, Fairford, Eng., London, 1999; recorded 3CDs (total 32 songs and pieces on piano), Nasville, Tenn., 2000, 2001, Christmas CD (9 songs), 2003; recorded 18 songs and pieces on piano, Hilltop Recording Studio, Nashville, Tenn., 2000, 12 others, 2001, 10 more songs, 2003; prodr. five reco. sessions Hilltop Recording Studio, Nashville, tenn., 2000; tnr. students Cerebral Palsy Telethon WBBJ TV, Jackson, Tenn., 1995-2002. Active in civic affairs, 1947-; judge music festival U. Tenn., Martin, 2000-01, 2002, fall performance, 2000-01, 2002-03, Kiwanis Club Talent Show, 2000-01; active Martin Elem. Chorus, 2001; fundraiser Big Cypress Tree State Park, 2000-01, Dickson (Tenn.) Police Dept., 2000, Relay for Life, 1992-; planner, tnr. fund raiser program local fire dept. to buy new fire truck, 2000, entertainment fund raiser local town to install new lights in town, 2000; vice consul Internat. Biog. Ctr., 2002-, advisor to dir. gen., 2002-. Recipient Vol. Svc. award State of Tenn. Recreation and Parks Assn., 2001; selected for the crowning of ABI World Laureate; nominated for Am. medal of Honor, 2002; recipient Companion of Honor award, 2002, Universal Award of Accomplishment, ABI, 2002; named Internat. Woman of the Yr., 2001 Fellow Internat. Biog. Assn. (life); mem. SAI (life, social chmn. 1979), Songwriters Guild Am., Music Tchrs. Nat. Assn., Philharm. Music Club (v.p. 1983-84, pres. 1985), Am. Coll. Musicians, Dem. Women. Baptist. Avocations: music writing, interior decorating and designing, travel, church and charity work, political and military entertaining. Home: 208 Melody Dr Martin TN 38237-5535

WADE, TYRA V. manufacturing executive; b. Cheyenne, Wyo., Jan. 8, 1957; d. Larry Emil Schieck and Wanda Frances Reimer. Student, South Mountain Coll., 1991-97. Cert. trainer/instr. Mgr. Holiday Inn, Homestead, Fla., 1977-80, Legion Club, Alliance, Nebr., 1980-87; supr. Motorola, Phoenix, 1987-2000; mgr. S.W. Traffic Systems, 2001—. Baptist. Avocations: art, computers, cooking. Home: 6833 S 18th St Phoenix AZ 85042-5706

WADLEY, FREDIA STOVALL, state commissioner; b. Winchester, Tenn. BS, Tenn Tech U., 1967; MD, U. Tenn., 1969; MSHPA, U. Cin., 1978. Diplomate Am. Bd. Pediats. Pediat. intern City of Memphis Hosp., 1970, pediat. resident, 1971-72; clin. instr. pediats. dept. pediats. U. Tenn. Ctr. for Health Scis., Memphis, 1973-74; pvt. practice Winchester, Tenn., 1974-75; instr. phys. assessment course dept. nursing U. Tenn., Chattanooga, 1975-76; dir. med. svcs. Dept. Health and Environ. Southeast Region, Chattanooga, 1975-80, regional dir., 1981-83; chief med. officer Dept. Health and Environ. Commr.'s Office, Nashville, 1984-87; dir. Met. Health Dept., Nashville, 1987-95; commr. Dept. Health, Nashville, 1995-97; state med. dir. Tenn. Health Srvcs. Bureau, 1997—; clin. asst. prof. dept. pediats. Meharry Med. Coll., 1985—; mem. faculty staff preventive medicine divsn. Quillen Dischner Med. Coll., 1985-87; now commr. Dept. Health, Nashville. Vol. faculty mem. dept. nursing U. Tenn. Ctr. for Health Scis., Memphis, 1977-83, U. Tenn., Knoxville, 1977-83; mem. preventive medicine resident adv. com. Meharry Family Medicine Dept., 1988—; adj. assoc. prof. nursing dept. family and cmty. health Vanderbilt U., 1988—; presenter in field. Contbr. articles to profl. jours. Mem. HSA III Task Force on Ambulatory Health Care Problems, 1977, HSA III Bd., 1981-82; mem. southeast Tenn. regional placement com. Tenn. Med. Loan Scholarship Program, 1978-79; bd. dirs. Southeast Tenn. Chpt. Kidney Found., 1981, Vol. Healthcare Sys., Inc., 1988-90, Vanderbilt AIDS Project, 1990, United Way Mid. Tenn., 1992-95, ARC, 1992; mem. Tenn. Sch. health Coalition, 1985—, Cmty. Coalition for Minority Health, 1988, Mayor's Substance Abuse Action Team, 1990; active Brentwood United Meth., Sunday Sch. tchr. 6th grade, 1984-87; chmn. Tenn. AIDS Adv. Com., 1987-88, Davidson County Child Fatality Rev. Team, 1994-95, others. Mem. AMA, APHA (Charles G. Jordan award for outstanding accomplishments in field of pub. health so. br. 1981), Southern Health Assn. (chmn. awards com. and governing coun. 1981-83, pres. 1989-90, spl. meritorious award for outstanding contbns. to orgn. and pub. health 1992), Tenn. Pub. Health Assn. (pres. 1990-91, spl. meritorious award 1993), Tenn. Health Officers, Tenn. Pediat. Soc., Tenn. Med. Assn., Nashville/Davidson County Acad. Medicine, Davidson County Pediat. Soc. Office: Health Svcs Bureau 425 5th Ave N Fl 3D Nashville TN 37247-0001

WADLEY, SUSAN SNOW, anthropologist; b. Balt., Nov. 18, 1943; d. Chester Page and Ellen Snow (Foster) W.; m. Bruce Woods Derr, Dec. 28, 1971 (div. July 1989); children: Shona Snow, Laura Woods; m. Richard Olanoff, July 4, 1992. BA, Carleton Coll., Northfield, 1965; MA, U. Chgo., 1967, PhD, 1973. Instr. Syracuse U., 1970-73, asst. prof., 1973-76, dir. fgn. and comparative studies program, 1978-83, prof., 1982, dir. So. Asia Ctr., 1985—, Ford-Maxwell prof. South Asian Studies, 1990—, chair anthropology dept., 1990-95, assoc. dean Coll. of Arts and Scis., 2003—. Trustee Am. Inst. Indian Studies, Chgo., 1984-93, exec. com., 1991-94; mem. joint com. South Asia Social Sci. Rsch. Coun., 1982-89. Author: Shakti: Power in the Conceptual Struture of Krimpur Women, 1975, Women in India: Two Perspectives, 1978, revised, 1989, 95, Struggling with Destiny in Karimpur, 1976-84, 1994; editor: Power of Tamil Women, 1980, Oral Epics in India, 1989, Media and the Transformation of Religion in South Asia, 1995. Pres. Edward Smith Parent Tchr. Orgn., Syracuse, 1988-89; pres. bd. dirs. Open Hand Internat. Mask and Puppet Mus., 2000-2003. Grantee NSF, 1967-69, U.S. Dept. Edn., 1983-84, Smithsonian Instn., 1983-84, Am. Inst. Indian Studies, 1989, Social Scis. Rsch. Coun., 1989, NEH, 1995, 98. Mem. Am. Anthropological Soc., Am. Folklore Soc., Assn. for Asian Studies. Home: 302 Carlton Dr Syracuse NY 13214-1906 Office: Syracuse U Maxwell Sch Syracuse NY 13244-0001 Business E-Mail: sswadley@maxwell.syr.edu.

WADLOW, JOAN KRUEGER, retired academic administrator, construction executive; b. LeMars, Iowa, Aug. 21, 1932; d. R. John and Norma I. (IhLe) Krueger; m. Richard R. Wadlow, July 27, 1958; children: Dawn, Kit. BA, U. Nebr., 1953, PhD, 1963; MA, Fletcher Sch. Law and Diplomacy, 1956; cert., Grad. Inst. Internat. Studies, Geneva, 1957. Mem. faculty U. Nebr., Lincoln, 1966-79, prof. polit. scis., 1964-79, assoc. dean Coll. Arts and Scis., 1972-79; prof. polit. scis., dean Coll. Arts and Scis., U. Wyo., Laramie, 1979-84, v.p. acad. affairs, 1984-86; prof. polit. sci., provost U. Okla., Norman, 1986-91; chancellor U. Alaska, Fairbanks, 1991-99. Cons. on fed. grants; bd. dirs. Alaska Sea Life Ctr., Key Bank Alaska; mem. Commn. Colls. N.W. Assn.; pres. Lan Constrn., Inc., 1999—. Author articles in field. Bd. dirs. Nat. Merit Scholarship Corp., 1988-97, Lincoln United Way, 1976-77, Bryan Hosp., Lincoln, 1978-79, Washington Ctr., 1986-99, Key Bank of Alaska, Alaska SeaLife Ctr.; v.p., exec. commr. North Ctrl. Assn., pres., 1991; pres. adv. bd. Lincoln YWCA, 1970-71; mem. def. adv. com. Women in the Svcs., 1987-89; mem. cmty. adv. bd. Alaska Airlines; mem. Univ. Pres.'s Mission to Israel, 1998; mem. bd. dirs. Netarts Occanside Sanitary Dist., 2002 . Recipient Mortar Board Tchg. award, 1976, Alumni Scholar Achievement award Rotary Internat., 1998, Alumni Achievement award U. Nebr., 2003; Seacrest Journalism fellow 1953-54, Rotary fellow, 1956-57, fellow Conf. Coop. Man, Lund, Sweden, 1956. Mem. NCAA (divsn. II pres. coun. 1997-99), Internat. Studies Assn. (co-editor Internat. Studies Notes 1978-91), Nat. Assn. State Univs. and Land-Grant Colls. (exec. com. coun. acad. affairs 1989-91, chair internat. affairs counsel 1996-97), Western Assn. Africanists (pres. 1980-82), Assn. Western Univs. (pres. 1993), Coun. Colls. Arts and Scis. (pres. 1983-84), Greater Fairbanks C. of C., Gamma Phi Beta. Republican. Congregationalist. Address: Chancellor Emerita PO Box 246 Oceanside OR 97134-0246 E-mail: wadlow@oregonvos.net.

WADSWORTH, JACQUELINE DORÈT, private investor; b. San Diego, June 15, 1928; d. Benjamin H. Dilley and Georgia E. (Elliott) Dilley Waters; m. Charles Desmond Wadsworth Jr., June 16, 1954 (dec. 1963); 1 child, Georgia Duncan Wadsworth Barber. BS, U. Oreg., 1950; MA, San Diego State U., 1952. Cert. tchr. Calif., Oreg. Dir. Jr. Red Cross, San Diego County chpt. ARC, 1952-59, asst. dir. leadership ctrs. for 8 western states, 1954-59; pvt. investor, comml. real estate and property devel., 1974—. Interior designer J. Wadsworth Interiors, La Jolla, Calif., 1990—2002. Vol. chair nat. conv. ARC, San Diego, 1966; vol., fundraiser San Diego Symphony Orch. Orgn., 1974-83; mem. Gold Ribbon Patron com. San Diego Symphony, 1995-99; friends mem., vol. San Diego Mus. Art, 1958—, Asian Arts Coun., 1996—; mem. Scripps Found. for Medicine and Sci., 1990—; life mem., fund raiser, bd. dirs., chmn. Scripps, Mercy Hosp. Aux., 1965—; life mem., chair, bd. dirs. Social Svc. Aux., 1968—. Recipient Svc. award Mercy Hosp. Aux., 1967-70. Mem. Japanese Garden Soc. of San Diego, Globe Gilders Theatre Aux. (activity chairperson 1966-85), San Diego Zool. Soc. (curator 1976—), Mingei Internat., Palladian Soc. (San Diego County chpt.), Mus. Contemporary Art San Diego, San Diego Natural History Mus. Republican.

WAELSCH, SALOME GLUECKSOHN, geneticist, educator; b. Danzig, Germany, Oct. 6, 1907; arrived in U.S., 1933, naturalized, 1938; d. Ilya and Nadia Gluecksohn; m. Heinrich B. Gluecksohn, Jan. 8, 1943; children: Naomi Barbara, Peter Benedict. Student, U. Konigsberg, Germany, U. Berlin, 1927—28; PhD, U. Freiburg, Germany, 1932; DSc (hon.), Columbia U., 1995. Rsch. assoc. in genetics Columbia U., 1936—55; assoc. prof. anatomy Albert Einstein Coll. Medicine, 1955—58, prof., 1958—63, prof. molecular genetics, 1963—, chmn. dept. genetics, 1963—76. Mem. study sects. NIH. Author: contbr. numerous articles on devel. genetics. Recipient Nat Medal of Sci., Pres. Clinton, 1993, Thomas Hunt Morgan medal, Genetics Society of America, 1999. Fellow: Am. Acad. Arts & Scis., AAAS;

mem.: The Royal Soc., Am. Soc. Human Genetics, Am. Soc. Naturalists, Soc. Devel. Biology, N.Y. Acad. Scis. (hon.), Genetics Soc., Am. Assn. Anatomists, Am. Soc. Zoologists, NAS, Sigma Xi. Office: Albert Einstein Coll Med 1300 Morris Park Ave Bronx NY 10461-1926 E-mail: gradus@aecom.yu.edu.

WAGEMAN, VIRGINIA FARLEY, editor, writer; b. Jersey City, N.J., Feb. 18, 1941; d. James Christopher and Charlotte Carter (Stebbins) Farley; m. Steven Lipson, Dec. 26, 1962 (div. 1964); 1 child, Melissa; m. James Carter Wageman, Apr. 22, 1968; children: Robinson Michael, Sarah Carter. BA, Bard Coll., 1964. Book editor, prodn. asst. AICPA, N.Y.C., 1964-67; prodn. mgr. U. Hawaii Press, 1967-68; asst. dir. office univ. rels. U. Md., Balt., 1968-70; dir. publs. art mus. Princeton U., 1971-81; writer, editor Hirshhorn Mus. and Sculpture Garden, Washington, 1982-86; freelance editor, from 1986; sr. editor Hudson Hills (N.Y.) Press, 1988—2002; mgr. publs. Coll. Art Assn., N.Y.C., 1989-96; editor, writer various publications, from 1996. Art critic Honolulu Advertiser, 1999-2002. Author: Essential Guide to Maui (Island Heritage), 2001, Essential Guide to Oahu, Waikiki and Honolulu (Island Heritage), 2002. Recipient Smithsonian Commendation for Exceptional Svc. Mem. Art Table, Assn. Freelance Art Editors (pres. 1984-86), Princeton Rsch. Forum, Coll. Art Assn. Died July 3, 2003.

WAGER, DEBORAH MILLER, researcher, consultant; b. Phila., Sept. 5, 1938; d. Albert S. and Pauline (Goldberg) Miller; m. Robert J. Wager, July 3, 1966; 1 child, James M. BA, Skidmore Coll., 1960; MAT, Columbia U., 1963. Editor Toy Quality and Safety Report, Washington, 1972-88; cons. Wager Rsch., Washington, 1989—. Devel. rschr. Sidwell Friends Sch., Washington, 1988-89, 92-98, 2003—, Georgetown Day Sch., 1995—; trustee Sheridan Sch., Washington, 1978-84. Author: Good Toys, 1986. Mem. Assn. Profl. Rschrs. Advancement. Office: Wager Rsch Consulting 4545 29th St NW Washington DC 20008-2144

WAGER, PAULA JEAN, artist; b. Lansing, Mich., Dec. 19, 1929; d. Mervin Elihu and Cora Della (Raymer) Fowler; m. William Douglas Wager, May 4, 1952; children: Pamela Ann, Scott Alan. Student, Mich. State U., 1949-52. Music tchr., Toledo, Ohio, 1968-72, Union Lake, Mich., 1972-76; tchr. art, artist Paula Wager's Art Studio, Commerce Twp., Mich., 1984—. Hostess Artistic Touch with Paula, Media Network of Waterford, 1999—, (Cable Comcast channel 44), Waterford, Mich., 1991-94, 96—, AT&T (formerly called TCI West Oakland), Walled Lake, Mich., Channel 10, 1991-94, Channel 14, 1996—. Exhibited in group shows including Village Art Supplies, 1982-88, Pontiac Oakland Soc. Artists, 1983—, Pontiac Galleria, 1983, 99, Oakland C.C., Commerce Twp., 1985, Red Piano Gallery, Hilton Head, S.C., 1985-89, Mich. State U., East Lansing, 1986, Silver Pencil Gallery, Pontiac, 1987-89, Wooden Sleight, Vestaburg, Mich., 1988-93, Art Pad, Keego Harbor, Mich., 1990-93, Local Color Gallery, Union Pier, Mich., 1992-94, Mich. Assn. Artists, Southfield Civ. Ctr. Mich. 1995, 97, 98, Swann Gallery, Detroit, 1995—, Kiva Gallery, Waterford, 1999, Southfield Ctr. arts, 1999; solo exhbns. include Waterford Pub. Lib., 1996, Waterland Pub. Libr., 1996—. Millers Artist Supplies, Ferndale, Mich., 1996, Waterford Twp. Hall, 1996, 99, Masonic Lodge, Milford, 1997, 98, 99, Livonia Libr., 1999; represented in pvt. collections; juror Village of Fine Arts Assn., 1996. Recipient Outstanding Achievement award in instructional programming Comcast Cable TV, Waterford, 1992, 1st place, Waterford Friends of the Arts Art Show, 1988, Pontiac Oakland Soc. Artists Cmty. Rm., 1990, Am. Biog. Inst. Woman of Yr. Commemorative medal, 1995; Waterford Cable Commn. grantee, 1991, 93, Charter Twp. of Waterford grantee, 1991-94, 98. Mem. Nat. Assn. Female Exec. Pontiac Oakland Soc. Artists, Waterford Friends of the Arts, Mich. Watercolor Soc., Birmingham Bloomfield Art Assn., Colored Pencil Soc. Am., Colored Pencil Soc. Detroit, Village Fine Arts Assn., Paint Creek Ctr. for the Arts. Avocations: music, art. Home: 1426 Birchwood Dr Okemos MI 48864-3033

WAGLE, SUSAN, state legislator, small business owner; b. Allentown, Pa., Sept. 27, 1953; m. John Thomas Wagle, Apr. 3, 1980; children: Julia Marie, Andrea Elizabeth, John Timothy, Paul Thomas. BA in Elem. Edn. cum laude, Wichita State U., 1979, post grad., 1979-82. Tchr. Chisholm Trail Elem., Kans., 1979-80; tchr. emotionally disturbed, special edn. Price Elem., Kans., 1980-82; real estate investor Kans., 1980—; prin. Wichita Bus. Inc., Kans., 1983—; mem. Kans. Ho. Reps. from 99th dist., Topeka, 1990, 92, 94-2000; speaker pro tem Kans. Ho. Reps., Topeka, 1994-2000; mem. Kans. Senate from 30th dist., Topeka, 2001—. Mem. Am. Legis. Exchange Coun. (state chmn., nat. bd. dirs., Outstanding Legis. of Yr. award 1994), Farm Bur., Nat. Fedn. Ind. Bus., Nat. Restaurant Assn., Wichita Ind. Bus. Assn. Home: 14 N Sandalwood St Wichita KS 67230-6612

WAGNER, ALYSON KAY (ALY WAGNER), professional soccer player; b. San Jose, Calif., Aug. 10, 1980; Majored in combined scis., Santa Clara U., Calif., 1999—2002. Soccer player, midfielder U.S. Women's Nat. Team, 1998—; team mem. San Diego Spirit, 2003—. No. 1 draft pick San Diego Spirit, WUSA, 2003. Finalist Hermann trophy, 2001, Mo. Athletic Club award, 2001; named second team All-Am, NSCAA, 2000, first team All-Am, 2001, first team All-Am., 2002, Offensive MVP, NCAA Final Four, 2001, Female Player of Yr., Soccer Am., 2001; recipient Top VII award, NCAA, 2002, Mo. Athletic Club Hermann trophy, 2002. Office: US Soccer Fedn 1801 S Prairie Ave Chicago IL 60616*

WAGNER, ANN, political organization executive; m. Ray Wagner; children: Raymond III, Stephen, Mary Ruth. BSBA, U. Mo., 1984. Mem. com. Lafayette Twp.; chmn. com. St. Louis County Republican Ctrl. Com.; mem. Mo. Fedn. Republican Women; dir. ho. and senate redistricting commn. Mo. Republican Party, 1991, chmn., 1999—; Mo. state exec. dir. Bush/Quayle Campaign, 1992; advisor Ashcroft for Senate Campaign, 1994; 2nd congl. dist. chair Dole for Pres. Campaign, 1996; co-chmn. Republican Nat. Com., Wash., 2001—. Chair Mo. Rep. Party. Mem.: Republican Nat. Conv. Midwestern State Chmn.'s Assn. (com. on arrangements 2000, del. 2000, del. chmn. 2000). Office: Mo Rep Party 204 East Dunklin Jefferson City MO 65101

WAGNER, ANNICE MCBRYDE, judge; BA, law degree, Wayne State U. With Houston and Gardner; gen. counsel Nat. Capital Housing Authority; people's counsel D.C.; assoc. judge Superior Court D.C., 1977-90, D.C. Ct. Appeals, 1990—, now chief judge. Mem. teaching team, trial advocacy workshop Harvard U. Office: Dist of Columbia Court of Appeals 500 Indiana Ave NW Ste 6000 Washington DC 20001-2131*

WAGNER, BARBARA ANN, accountant, writer; b. Atlantic City, N.J., Oct. 11, 1945; d. Francis Leon Wagner and Ethel Mae Thompson; m. Francis Xavier Geary, Sept. 7, 1969 (div. Sept. 1984); children: William Robert Geary, Andrea Dawn Geary, Cynthia Christine Geary. Student, L.A. City Coll., 1967—68, Ursinus Coll., 1985—94. Acct. Bank of Am., Hollywood, Calif., 1965—67; prodn. acct. Selmur Pictures, Hollywood, 1967—69; constrn. acct. Scott Paper Co., Phila., 1970—73; internal auditor Westover Cos., King of Prussia, Pa., 1984—86; mgr. Time and Billing Miller, Mason and Dickenson, Conshohocken, Pa., 1986—92; property acct. R Reef Funds, King of Prussia, 1992—96; acct. Camera Shop, Bryn Mawr, Pa., 1998—. Author (poems): Mad Poets Rev., 2000, 2001, 2002, Phila. Fringe Festival, 2002. Recipient Hon. Mention for Poetry, Phila. Writers Conf., 2002. Mem.: Pa. Poetry Soc., Mad Poets Soc.*

WAGNER, BARBARA LEE, musician; b. Lockport, N.Y., Feb. 5, 1937; d. Richard Lee and Flora May McCarthy; m. William George Wagner, June 15, 1957 (dec. Apr. 17, 2003); children: Molly Heller-Wagner, Carrie Martin. BFA, SUNY, Buffalo, 1958; studied with Raymond Harvey, Buffalo, 1988—95. Condr. Orchard Park (N.Y.) Chorale, 1975—79; dir. vocal activities Nichols Mid. Sch., Buffalo, 1977—97, Nichols Upper Sch., Buffalo, 1997—2001, Buffalo Sem., 2001—03; music. dir. Buffalo Gay Men's Chorus, 2001—. Music dir. Peace Odyssey Concert Choir, 1989; guest condr. City of Good Neighbors Chorale, 1992; condr. Freudig Singers, 1998. Condr.: premier of Requiem by Kurt Vonnegut and Edgar Grana, 1988; co-author: Singing the Living Tradition, 1993. Min. music Unitarian Universalist Ch., Buffalo, 1963—; music dir. Temple Beth Am. Choir, Williamsville, NY, 1964—78, Unitarian Universalist Gen. Assembly Choir, 1986, 1992. Recipient award for Choral Excellence, Buffalo Philharm. Orch., 2002, Erie County Music Educators, 2002. Mem.: Erie County Music Educators Assn., N.Y. State Sch. Music Assn., Music Educators Nat. Assn., Am. Choral Dirs. Assn., Am. Guild Organists (exec. bd.), Unitarian Universalist Musicians Network (former v.p., former exec. bd., chair new hymns supplement task force 2003), Chromatic Club (bd. dirs.). Democrat. Avocations: reading, gardening. Home: 9 John Brian Ln Buffalo NY 14227 Office: Unitarian Universalist Ch 695 Elmwood Ave Buffalo NY 14222 Personal E-mail: wagschoir@aol.com.

WAGNER, BRENDA MARCYEA, music educator, musician; b. McPherson, Kans., Nov. 3, 1961; d. Irvin Leroy and JoAnn Bielefeldt Wagner. MusB in Edn., U. Okla., 1984; MusM in Edn., U. Ctrl. Okla., 1997. Cert. instrumental music K-12 Okla. State Dept. Edn., 1985. Orch. dir. George Lynn Cross Acad., Norman, Okla., 1984—85; orch. dir./string specialist Oklahoma City (Okla.) Pub. Schs., 1985—90, Norman Pub. Schs., 1990—. Sect. violinist Lawton (Okla.) Philharm. Orch., 1983—91, Okla. Symphony Orch., Oklahoma City, 1984—89, Okla. Philharm. Soc., Oklahoma City, 1989—. Named one of 50 Directors Who Make a Difference (State of Okla.), Sch. Band and Orch. Mag., 2002. Mem.: NEA, Am. Fedn. Musicians, Okla. Edn. Assn., Am. String Tchrs. Assn., Okla. Music Educators Assn. (all-omea orch. chair 1997), Music Educators Nat. Conf., Pi Kappa Lambda, Mu Phi Epsilon (sec. 1983). Achievements include Conductor of High School Orchestra selected to perform at The Midwest Clinic in December 2002; Co-Conductor of High School Orchestra selected to perform at the National Music Educators Conference in April 1994. Avocations: travel, reading. Office: Norman North High School 1809 Stubbeman Norman OK 73069 Personal E-mail: bwagnerorch@earthlink.net.

WAGNER, CHARLENE BROOK, publishing consultant, elementary school educator; b. L.A. d. Edward J. and Eva (Anderson) Brook; children: Gordon, Brook, John. BS, Tex. Christian U., 1952; MEd, Sam Houston U., 1973; postgrad., U. Tex., Austin, 1975, Tex. A&M U., 1977. Sci. educator Spring Branch Ind. Sch. Dist., Houston, 1970-98; ret., 2000; dir. CompuKidZ, Houston, 1998—2000; cons. Scott Foresman, Addison Wesley, Ginn, Houston. Cons. Scott Foresman Pub. Co., Houston, 2000-01; owner Sci. Instrnl. Sys. Co., 1988—; dir. Compukidz. Mem. Houston Symphony League, 1992, Mus. Fine Arts, Mus. of Art of Am. West, Houston, 1989, Mus. Natural Scis., Women's Christian Home, Houston, 1991; mem. Houston Grand Opera Guild, mem. exec. bd. 1999-2000, rec./corr. sec.; social chmn. Encore, 1988; mem. Magic Circle Rep. Women's Club. Mem.: AAUW, NAFE, NEA, Internat. Platform Assn., Spring Branch Edn. Assn., Tex. State Tchrs. Assn., Heather and Thistle Soc., Wellington Soc. for Arts (Houston chpt.), Clan Anderson Soc., Art League Houston, Shepherd Soc., Watercolor Arts Soc. (Houston), Houston Highland Games Assn., Space City Ski Club. Episcopalian. Avocations: painting, watercolor media. Home: 2670 Marilee Ln Apt B54 Houston TX 77057-4264 E-mail: wagner2670@aol.com.

WAGNER, CHERI J. business owner; b. Mar. 9, 1963; Owner, mgr. Wagner Constrn., Lake Arrowhead, Calif., 1980-94, Blind Ambitions, Skyforest, Calif., 1994—. Mem. C. of C., Soroptimists, Nat. Fedn. Ind. Bus., Humane Soc., Arrowhead Bldg. Contractors Assn., Mountain Women's Assn. Office: PO Box 885 Skyforest CA 92385-0885 E-mail: poker4me247@msn.com.

WAGNER, CYNTHIA GAIL, editor, writer; b. Bethesda, Md., Oct. 3, 1956; d. Robert Cheney and Marjory Jane (Kletzing) W. BA in English, Grinnell Coll., 1978; MA in Comms., Syracuse U., 1981. Editl. asst. The Futurist/World Future Soc., Bethesda, Md., 1981—82, staff editor, 1982-85, asst. editor, 1985-91, sr. editor, 1991-92, mng. editor, 1992—. Editor: (newsletter) Futurist Update, 2000—; columnist: 3-2-1 Contact, 1994; contbr. Encyclopedia of the Future, 1995, The 21st Century, 1999. Mem. Theatre Comm. Group, Washington Shakespeare Reading Group. Avocation: theater. Office: The Futurist World Future Soc 7910 Woodmont Ave Ste 450 Bethesda MD 20814-3066 E-mail: cwagner@wfs.org.

WAGNER, DORIS WALKLING, volunteer, director; b. near Gamber, Md., Feb. 16, 1926; d. John Earl and Pearl Elizabeth (Flora) Walkling; m. William Edward McGrath, Jan. 22, 1947 (div. 1974); children: Ellen, Jane, Ann, Kevin, Mary, Timothy, Thomas, Brigid; m. George Everett Wagner, Oct. 20, 1979. Diploma, St. Agnes Hosp. Sch. Nursing, Balt., 1946. Lic. underwriter life and health ins. Md.; RN Md., 1947. Nurse, Westminster, Md., 1946—96; nurse case mgr. Home Call, Inc., Westminster, Md., 1979—89; asst. adminstr., nurse S. Carroll Adult Day Care, Eldersburg, Md., 1989—94, Eldersburg Adult Day Care, 1994—96; field ops. asst. Experience Works Inc. (formerly Green Thumb, Inc.), Westminster, Md., 2001—. Show sec. Columbia (Md.) Horse Show, 1968. Author: (Poetry) Lyrical Heritage, 1996 (Editor's Choice, 1996), The Best Poems of 1997, 1997 (Editor's Choice, 1997), (Anthology) Along the Way, 1999 (Best Poem of 1999). Pres., bd. dirs. Humane Soc. of Carroll County, Md., 1987—; mem. Sr. Provider Info. Network, Westminster, Md., 2001—. Recipient Stephen J. Cesare Pub. Svc. award, Experience Works, Inc., 2003. Fellow: Westminster Sr. Ctr. Republican. Roman Catholic. Avocations: bridge, gardening, painting, reading, writing. Home: 2360 Braddock Rd Mount Airy MD 21771

WAGNER, DOROTHY MARIE, retired senior creative designer, artist; b. Chgo., Jan. 12, 1926; d. William Christopher and Margaret Frances (Rowell) W. Student, Kalamazoo Coll., 1943-45; BS, Western Mich. U., 1947; BFA, Art Ctr. Coll. Design, L.A., 1962. Dir. electroencephalography lab. Bronson Hosp., Kalamazoo, 1945-51; dir. EEG lab. Terr. Hosp., Kaneohe, Hawaii, 1951-55, UCLA Med. Ctr., 1955-60; sr. creative designer GM Tech. Ctr. Styling, Warren, Mich., 1962-82. Cons. in EEG, Army Hosp., Honolulu, 1950-55; dir. sales and rental gallery Pt. Huron (Mich.) Mus., 1989-93, art and painting instr., 1992-96. Recipient Best of Show award Ea. Mich. Internat. Art Show, 1992, 1st pl. award, 1988, 89, 94. Mem. Blue Water Art Assn. (pres. 1990-96), Orion Art Ctr. Episcopalian. Avocations: horseback riding, showing in dressage, breeding and raising racing greyhounds, water color and acrylic painting, stained glass design and fabrication. Home: 14841 Pine Knoll Rd Capac MI 48014-1913 E-mail: dot@glis.net.

WAGNER, FRANCES RITA, secondary school educator; b. Pasadena, Calif., Feb. 8, 1947; d. Joseph Francis and Reta Clarice (Bell) Inco; m. Danny Eugene Wagner, Aug. 6, 1969; 1 child, Christine Marie Wagner Barth. BA, Calif. State Coll., 1969; Cert. Paralegal Studies, U. La Verne (Calif.), 1991; MA in Tchg., Grand Canyon U., 2001. Cert. instrumental music tchr., English lit. tchr., social scis. tchr. Calif. Tchr. La Canada (Calif.) Unified Sch. Dist., 1984-90, Covina Valley Unified Sch. Dist., Covina, Calif., 1991—, cons., 1996—, splst. at-risk students, 1997. Cons. Pasadena (Calif.) C.C., 1987. Author: poems. Mem. PTA South Hills H.S., Covina, Calif., 1991—. Grantee L.A. Opera Assn., 1997; recipient mini-grant Rotary Club Internat., 1996; named Hon. Life Mem. PTA South Hills H.S., 1996; Winner 1st Place Art PACE Art Found., 1995. Mem. Sigma Alpha Iota, Phi Delta Kappa. Avocations: writing, gardening, embroidery, art, baking. Office: South Hills HS 645 S Barranca St West Covina CA 91791-2943

WAGNER, GERALDINE MARIE, nursing educator, consultant; b. Renton, Wash., Apr. 12, 1948; d. Ernest F. and Vera P. (Temiraeff) W. AA, Pasadena City Coll., 1970; BA cum laude, Calif. State U., Northridge, 1977; BSN, Calif. State U., L.A., 1982; MEd summa cum laude, Azusa Pacific U., 1990; Cert. pub. health nurse, Calif. Dept. Health Svcs. In utilization mgmt. Blue Cross, Woodland Hills, Calif., 1987-88, Healthmarc, Pasadena, Calif., 1988-90; nursing educator, asst. dir. vocat. nursing program Casa Loma Coll., L.A., 1991-92, dir. program planning and devel., and coord. continuing edn. Lake View Terrace, 1992-93; dir. vocal. nursing program Glendale (Calif.) Career Coll., 1994-95; with patient care rev. svcs. U. So. Calif. U. Hosp., L.A., 1996—; med.-legal nurse cons., 2000—. Capt. Nurse Corp, U.S. Army, 1979-84. Mem.: VFW, Fellowship of Cath. Scholars, Nat. Assn. Cath. Nurses, Computer Using Educators, Nat. Coun. Tchrs. of Math., Am. Math. Soc., Soc. Cath. Social Scientists, Inst. of Religious Life, Assn. U.S. Army, Res. Officers Assn. of U.S., Army Nurse Corps. Assn., AMVETS, Cath. War Vets, U.S. Naval Inst., Mil. Officer Assn. Am., Order of Preachers, Assn. of Hebrew Catholics, Am. Legion, Sigma Theta Tau, Pi Lambda Theta. Roman Catholic. Home: 924 Rock Rose Ln Lompoc CA 93436 Office Phone: 805-735-3575. E-mail: srgmwagnerop@earthlink.net.

WAGNER, JODY M. treasurer; b. Canton, Ohio; m. Alan L. Wagner; children: Rachel, Jason, Elizabeth, Maxwell. Undergrad. degree in Econs., Northwestern U., Evanston, Ill., 1977; grad. degree in law, Vanderbilt U., Nashville, 1980. Bar: Tenn. 1980, Va. 1984. With Fautman and Canoles PC, Norfolk, Va., 1981—2002; state treas. Va., 2002—. Office: Commonwealth of Va Dept of Treasury 101 N 14th St Richmond VA 23218*

WAGNER, JUDITH BUCK, investment firm executive; b. Altoona, Pa., Sept. 25, 1943; d. Harry Bud and Mary Elizabeth (Rhodes) B.; m. Joseph E. Wagner, Mar. 15, 1980; 1 child, Elizabeth. BA in History, U. Wash., 1965; grad., N.Y. Inst. Fin., 1968. Registered Am. Stock Exch., N.Y. Stock Exch., investment advisor. Security analyst Morgan, olmstead, Kennedy & Gardner, L.A., 1968-71, Boettcher & Co., Denver, 1972-75; pres. Wagner Investment Mgmt., Denver, 1975—. Chmn. The Women's Bank, N.A., Denver, 1977-94, organizational group pres., 1975-77; chmn. Equitable Bankshares Colo., Inc., Denver, 1980-94; pres. Equitable Bank of Littleton, Colo., 1985; lectr. Denver U., Metro State, 1975-80. Author: Woman and Money series Colo. Woman Mag., 1976, moderator "Catch 2' Sta. KWGN-TV, 1978-79. Pres. Bit Sisters Colo., Denver, 1977-82, bd. dirs., 1972-83; bd. fellows U. Denver, 1985-90; bd. dirs. Red Cross, 1980, Assn. Children's Hosp., 1985, Colo. Health Facilities Authority, 1978-84, Jr. League Cmty. ADv. Com., 1979-82, Bros. Redevel., Inc., 1979-80; mem. agy. rels. com. Mile High United Way, 1978-81, chmn. United Way Venture Way, 1978-81, chmn. United Way Venture Grant com., 1980-81; bd. dirs. Downtown Dener, Inc., 1988-95; bd. dirs., v.p., treas. The Women's Found. Colo., 1987-91; treas., trustee, v.p., Graland Country Day Sch., 1990-97, pres., 1994-97; trustee Denver Rotary Found., 1990-95, Hunt Alternatives Fund, 1992-97; trustee The Colo. Trust, 1998—, chmn., 2003—. Recipient Making It award Cosmopolitan Mag., 1977, Women on the Go award, Savvy Mag., 1983, Minouri Yasoui award, 1986, Salute Spl. Honoree award, Big Sisters, 1987; named one of the Outstanding Young Women Am., 1979; recipient Woman Who Makes A Difference award Internat. Women's Forum, 1987,, Maverick Thinker award Urban Park, 2003. Fellow Assn. Investment Mgmt. & Rsch.; mem. Women's Forum Colo. (pres. 1979), Women's Found. Colo., Inc. (bd. dirs. 1986-91), Denver Soc. Security Analysts (bd. dirs. 1976-83, v.p. 1980-81, pres. 1981-82), Colo. Investment Advisors assn., Rotary (treas. Denver chpt. found., pres. 1993-94), Leadership Denver (Outstanding Alumna award 1987), Pi Beta Phi (pres. U. Wash. chpt. 1964-65). Office: Wagner Investment Mgmt Inc Ste 240 3200 Cherry Creek South Dr Denver CO 80209-3245

WAGNER, JULIA A(NNE), retired editor; b. Alexandria, Va., Feb. 15, 1924; d. Luigi and Domenica (Di Giammarino) Coppa; widowed. BA, George Washington U., 1948, MA, 1950. With U.S. Govt., Washington, 1941-55, publs. editor, 1951-55; editl. asst. Dell Pub. Co., N.Y.C., 1956-59, mng. editor, 1959-72, editor-in-chief, 1973-87; ret., 1987.

WAGNER, LEANA MOREE, computer executive, graphic designer, fine artist; b. San Diego, Nov. 19, 1957; d. Alan Daniel and Shirley Moree (Wright) W. Lab. asst. Kearney Field Sta., Parlier, Calif., 1975-76; forms processing equipment operator IRS, Fresno, Calif., 1983-87, data comms. technician, 1994, major sys. operator, 1987—. Portrait artist, Fresno, 1979—. Featured artist in article Artist's Mag., 2002. Recipient 2d pl. ribbon Fresno Fair Fine Art's Exhibit, 1989, People's Choice award, 1994. Avocations: ceramics, horticulture.

WAGNER, MARILYN SCHOEFER, writer; b. Glendale, Calif., Sept. 9, 1937; d. Ernest and Miriam Schoefer; m. Larry Richard Wagner, June 20, 1959; 1 child, Brock. BA, Stanford U., 1959, MA, 1960. Various sales and mgmt. positions Burbank Horticultural Svc., Calif., 1950—59; tchr. spl. program Burbank Pub. Schs., 1958; tchr. Greenhills Exempted Sch. Dist., Ohio, 1960—61, Green Bay Pub. Schs., Wis., 1961—64. Cons. on SAT and sch. placements Cin. Area Schs., 1980—87; family crisis counselor, 1963—2002. Author short stories, Pole Cats, 1997, Cat and Other Tales, 1999. Sec. Ft. Bragg Area Rep. Women Federated, 1993—2003; chmn. Expatriate Ball, Cin., 1980—82; pres. Internat. Study Group, Brussels, 1976—77, founder, pres., and lectr. Cin., 1978—88; bd. dirs. Mendocino Theatre Co., Calif., 1994; mem. steering com. Leadership Mendocino, 2000—02; docent and daughter of founders Mendocino Coast Botanical Gardens. Avocation: golf.

WAGNER, MARY KATHRYN, sociology educator, former state legislator; b. Madison, S.D., June 19, 1932; d. Irving Macaulay and Mary Browning (Wines) Mumford; m. Robert Todd Wagner, June 23, 1954; children: Christopher John, Andrea Browning. BA, U. S.D., 1954; MEd, S.D. State U., 1974, PhD, 1978. Sec. R.A. Burleigh & Assocs., Evanston, Ill., 1954-57; dir. resource ctr. Watertown (S.D.) Sr. High Sch., 1969-71, Brookings (S.D.) High Sch., 1971-74; asst. dir. S.D. Com. on the Humanities, Brookings, 1976-90; asst. prof. rural sociology S.D. State U., 1990-96; mem. S.D. Ho. of Reps., 1981-88, S.D. Senate, 1988—92. Mem., pres. Brookings Sch. Bd., 1975-81; chair fund dr. Brookings United Way, 1985; bd. dirs. Brookings Chamber music Soc., 1981-98, Advance and Career Learning Ctr. Named Woman of Yr., Bus. and Profl. Women, 1981, Legislator Conservationist of Yr., Nat. and S.D. Wildlife Fedn., 1988. Mem. Population Assn. Am., Midwest Sociol. Soc., Rural Sociol. Soc., Brookings C. of C. (mem. indsl. devel. com. 1988-98), PEO, Rotary. Republican. Episcopalian. Avocations: reading, gardening, music, golf, bridge. Home: 24497 N Playhouse Rd Keystone SD 57751-6653 E-mail: drswagnerrtmk@aol.com.

WAGNER, MARY MARGARET, library and information science educator; b. Mpls., Feb. 4, 1946; d. Harvey F.J. and Yvonne M. (Brettner) W.; m. William Moore, June 16, 1978; children: Lebohang Y.C., Nora M. BA, Coll. St. Catherine, St. Paul, 1969; MLS, U. Wash., 1973; PhD, U. Minn., 2003. Asst. libr. St. Margarets Acad., Mpls., 1969-70; libr. Derham Hall High Sch., St. Paul, 1970-71; youth worker The Bridge for Runaways, Mpls., 1971-72; libr. Guthrie Theater Reference and Rsch. Libr., Mpls., 1973-75; asst. br. libr. St. Paul Pub. Libr., 1975; assoc. prof. dept. info. mgmt. Coll. St. Catherine, St. Paul, 1975—. Del. Minn. Gov.'s Pre-White House Conf. on Librs. and Info. Svcs., 1990; mem. Minn. Pre-White House Program Com., 1989-90, Continuing Libr. Info. and Media Edn. Com. Minn. Dept. Edn., Libr. Devel. and Svcs., 1980-83, 87-2002; mem. cmty. faculty Met. State U., St. Paul, 1980—; mem. core revision com. Coll. St. Catherine, 1992-93, faculty budget adv. com., 1992-95, faculty pers. com., 1989-92, 2001—, acad. computing com. 1991-96, ednl. policies com., 1998-01; chair curriculum subcom. Minn. Vol. Cert. Com., 1993—. Contbr. articles to profl. jours. Bd. dirs. Christian Sharing Fund, 1976-80, chair, 1977-78.

Grantee U.S. Embassy, Maseru, Lesotho, Africa, Brit. Consulate, Maseru, Fed. Inst. for Mus. and Libr. Scis., various founds.; Upper Midwest Assn. for Intercultural Edn. travel grantee Assoc. Colls. Twin Cities. Fellow: Higher Edn Consortia for Urban Affairs (bd. dirs. 1998—); mem.: ALISE (chair internat. rels. com. 2001—03), ALA (libr. book fellows program 1990—91), Minn. Ednl. Media Orgn., Minn. Libr. Assn. (pres. 1981—82, chair continuing edn. com. 1987—90, steering com. Readers Adv. Roundtable 1989—91), Spl. Libr. Assn., Am. Soc. Indexers, Am. Soc. Info. Sci. Office: Coll St Catherine Dept Info Mgmt 2004 Randolph Ave Saint Paul MN 55105-1750 E-mail: mmwagner@stkate.edu.

WAGNER, MARY SUSAN, academic administrator; b. Troy, N.Y., Oct. 28, 1952; BS in Music Edn., Coll. St. Rose, 1974; MS, SUNY, 1977. Music educator South Colonie Sch. Dist., Albany, NY, 1974—95; elem. sch. prin. E. Greenbush CSDD, NY, 1995—. Mem.: NAFE, Nat. Assn. Elem. Sch. Prins., Assn. for Curr. Devel., N.Y.State Assn. Women Adminstrs. Office: Green Meadow Sch 234 Schuurman Rd Castleton On Hudson NY 12033 Office Phone: 518-477-6422. Business E-Mail: wagnerma@egesd.org.

WAGNER, MELINDA, musician, composer; b. Phila., 1957; m. James Saporito; children: Benjamin, Olivia. Grad., U. Chgo., U. Pa. Studied with Richard Wernick, George Crumb, Shulamit Ran, Jay Reise. Instr. U. Pa., Swarthmore Coll., Syracuse U., Hunter Coll. Works performed by: Chgo. Symphony, Am. Composers Orchestra, Chamber Music Soc. of Lincoln Ctr., Ill. Chamber Orchestra, Oakland East Bay Symphony; commissioned works: Barlow Found., Fromm Found. Harvard U., Mary Flagler Carey Charitable Trust, Chgo. Symphony Orchestra, N.Y. New Music Ensemble, Am. Brass Quintet; composer Falling Angels, commissioned by Chgo. Symphony Orchestra, premiered in 1993, performed by Am. Composers Orchestra, 1995, Chgo. Symphony, 1996, Concerto for Flute, Strings, and Percussion (Pulitzer prize in Music 1999), commissioned and premiered by Paul Lustig Dunkel and Westchester Philharmonic, 1998, Extremity of Sky, premiered by Emanuel Ax, Chicago Symphony Orch., 2003. Fellow Guggenheim Meml. Found., Howard Found., 1996; resident fellow MacDowell Colony, Yaddo; grantee Ill. Arts Coun., N.Y. State Coun. on Arts; recipient three ASCAP Found. Young Composer awards. Mem. ASCAP (panelist ASCAP Deems Taylor Competition, ASCAP Found. Morton Gould Grants to Young Composers Program; recipient numerous ASCAP Standard Special awards).*

WAGNER, MURIEL GINSBERG, nutrition therapist; d. Irving A. and Anna Ginsberg; 1 child, Emily Lucinda Faith. BA, MS, Wayne State U.; PhD, U. Mich., 1982. Registered dietitian. Nutritionist Merrill-Palmer Inst., Detroit; pvt. practice, nutritional therapist Southfield, Mich., 1976—. Cons. select com. on nutrition U.S. Senate, 1973-74, Ford Motor Co., Dearborn, Mich., 1975-78, Detroit Dept. Consumer Affairs, 1979—, adj. faculty mem. Wayne State U., Detroit, 1970-80, U. Mich., Dearborn, 1974-79. Author: (cookbook) Tun...ahhh, 1993; contbr. articles to profl. publs.; writer, publisher (newsletter) Eating Younger. Vol. Am. Heart Assn. of Mich.; also various local and nat. govtl. groups Recipient Outstanding Cmty. Svc. award Am. Heart Assn., 1990, named Outstanding Profl., Mich. Dietetic Assn., 1974. Fellow Am. Dietetic Assn. (organizer Dial-A-Dietitian); mem. Am. Diabetes Assn. Avocations: cooking, recipe development, gardening. Office: 4000 Town Ctr Ste 8 Southfield MI 48075-1401 Office Phone: 248-350-1190. E-mail: eatingyounger@ameritech.net.

WAGNER, NANCY HUGHES, secondary school educator, state legislator; b. Raleigh, N.C., Sept. 27, 1943; d. Eugene Anderson and Miriam St. Clair (Morgan) Hughes; m. Clarence Cobaugh Wagner II, Sept. 12, 1970; children: Morgan Anderson, Cobaugh Wagner III. BA, Salem Coll., Winston-Salem, N.C., 1965; MS, Wilmington (Del.) Coll., 1989. Tchr. Milford (Del.) Sch. Dist., 1965-66, Capital Sch. Dist., Dover, Del., 1966-70, 89—; job specialist Jobs for Del. Grads., Dover, 1987-89; rep. Del. Ho. of Reps., Dover, 1992—, former chair small bus., chair judiciary com., sch. to work coord., 1998—. Mem. parents bd. U. Del., Newark, 1991-93; bd. visitors Del. State U., Dover, 1995—; bd. dirs. Modern Maturity Ctr., Dover, 1995—, 801 House Aid in Dover, 1995—, Because We Care, Dover, 1995—; mem. Kent County Parks and Recreation Commn., Dover, 1990-92; pres. South Run Crossing Civic Assn., Springfield, Va., 1982-85, PTA Dover H.S., 1987-89; mem. Rep. State Com., Kent County Rep. Women's Club; bd. dirs. Murphy Sch., 1991—. Mem. AAUW, C. of C., Nat. Coun. State Legislators, Coun. of State Govts., Capital Edn. Assn., Del. Edn. Assn., Capital City Rotary Club, Delta Kappa Gamma Soc. Internat. Republican. Presbyterian. Avocations: reading, politics, travel. Home: 283 Troon Rd Dover DE 19904-2370 Office: House of Reps Legis Hall Rm 117 PO Box 1401 Dover DE 19903-1401

WAGNER, PATRICIA HAMM, lawyer; b. Gastonia, N.C., Feb. 1, 1936; d. Luther Boyd and Mildred Ruth (Wheeler) Hamm; married; children: David Marion, Michael Marion, Laura Marion. AB summa cum laude, Wittenberg U., 1958; JD with distinction, Duke U., 1974. Bar: N.C. 1974, Wash. 1984. Asst. univ. counsel Duke U., Durham, N.C., 1974-75, assoc. univ. counsel health affairs, 1977-80; atty. N.C. Meml. Hosp., 1975-77; assoc. N.C. Atty. Gen. Office, 1975-77, Powe, Porter & Alphin, Durham, 1980-81, prin., 1981-83; assoc. Williams, Kastner & Gibbs, 1984-86, Wickwire, Goldmark & Schorr, 1986-88; spl. counsel Heller, Ehrman, White & McAuliffe, 1988-90, ptnr., 1990—. Arbitrator Am. Arbitration Assn., 1978—; arbitrator, pro tem judge King County Superior Ct., 1986—; tchr. in field. Mem. bd. vis. Law Sch. Duke U., 1992-98; bd. dirs. Seattle Edn. Ctr., 1990-91, Metroctr. YMCA, 1991-94, Cmty. Psychiat. Clinic, Seattle, 1984-86; bd. dirs., sec.-treas. N.C. Found. Alternative Health Programs, Inc., 1982-84; bd. dirs., sec.-treas. N.C. Ctr. Pub. Policy Rsch., 1976-83, vice-chmn., 1977-80; mem. task force on commitment law N.C. Dept. Human Resources, 1978; active Def. Rsch. Inst. 1982-84; bd. dirs. Law Fund, 1992—, v.p., 1993-97, pres., 2000-01; mem. ADR Roundtable, 1996-2001. Fellow Am. Bar Found.; mem. ABA (mem. ho. dels. Seattle-King County Bar Assn. 1991-94, mem. litigation sect.), Am. Soc. Hosp. Attys., Am. Law Inst., Wash. State Bar Assn. (mem. domestic rels. task force 1991-93), Seattle-King Bar Assn. (mem. bd. trustees 1990-93, sec. bd. 1989-90, chair judiciary and cts. com. 1987-89, mem. King County Superior Ct. delay reduction task force 1987-89, mem. gender bias com. 1990-94, chair 1990-91), Wash. Def. Trial Lawyers (chmn. ct. rules and procedures com. 1987, co-editor newsletter 1985-86), Wash. State Soc. Hosp. Attys., Wash. Women Lawyers (treas. 1986, 87). Office: Heller Ehrman White & McAuliffe Ste 6100 701 5th Ave Seattle WA 98104-7098 E-mail: pwagner@hewm.com.

WAGNER, SALLY STERRETT, music educator; b. Pitts., Sept. 24, 1951; d. Walter Renwick and Dorothy Grimpe Sterrett; m. Michael David Wagner, June 15, 1991; children: Caroline Elaine, Michael David Wagner Jr. MusB, U. Del., 1973; M Music Edn., Mich. State U., 1980. Cert. tchr. Md. Tchr. gen. music Dover Air Force Base Schs., Del., 1973—74; dir. bands Smyrna High Sch., 1974—77; choir dir. Portland Mid. & High Schs., Mich., 1979—80; dir. bands Beltsville Jr. High Sch., Md., 1980—81, Eleanor Roosevelt High Sch., Greenbelt, 1981—. Adjudicator Heritage Festivals, Salt Lake City, 1987—. Contbr. articles to profl. jours. Dir. youth choir Laurel Presbyn. Ch., 1995—2002. Recipient Outstanding Educator award, Prince Georges County C. of C., 1985, Outstanding Music Educator award, Md. Music Educators Assn., 2001. Mem.: Music Educators Nat. Conf., Md. Band Dirs. Assn., Women Band Dirs. Internat. Avocations: reading, counted cross stitch, travel. Office: Eleanor Roosevelt High Sch 7601 Hanover Pky Greenbelt MD 20770 E-mail: sally_wagner@comcast.net.

WAGNER, SUSAN JANE, sales and marketing consulting company executive; b. Englewood, N.J., Aug. 11; d. Jules A. and Florence I. (Froeba) W.; m. Mark E. McKenna, May 4, 1984. MusB with honors, Syracuse U., 1974; MPA with honors, Fairleigh Dickinson U., 1983. Dir. music, theater dependant sch. U.S. Dept. Def., Fed. Republic Germany, 1976-82; grad. asst. Fairleigh Dickinson U., Rutherford, N.J., 1982-83; account exec. Katz Radio/Katz Communications, Inc., N.Y.C., 1983-85; account mgr. network Katz Radio Group, N.Y.C., 1985-87, v.p., dir. mktg., 1987-90, sr. v.p. dir.mktg., 1990-91; v.p. corp. mktg. Katz Comm., Inc., N.Y.C., 1992-93; owner Exec. Dynamics Inc., Mahwah, N.J., 1993—. Mem. Am. Women in Radio and TV, Electronic Media Mktg. Assn., Am. Mktg. Assn., Promotion Mktg. Assn. Am., Broadcast Promotion Mktg. Execs., Sigma Alpha Iota, Gamma Phi Beta. Avocations: sailing, skiing, singing. Office: Exec Dynamics 2 James Brite Cir Mahwah NJ 07430-2527 Office Phone: 201-327-9070 E-mail: edi1@iglide.net.

WAGNER, VIVIAN AUDREY, communications educator, writer; b. Woodland, Calif., July 12, 1967; BA in English, U. Calif., Irvine, 1989; MA in English, Ohio State U., 1991; PhD in English, U. Ill., 1996. Tchg. asst. Ohio State U., Columbus, Ohio, 1989—92, U. Ill., Urbana-Champaign, Ill., 1992—96; freelance writer New Concord, Ohio, 1997—. Vis. asst. prof. English Muskingum Coll., New Concord, Ohio, 2003—. Author: Aging and Elder Care, 2000, The One Hour Wiz Guide to Stock Option, 2001; contbr. articles to profl. jours. Mem.: Soc. Profl. Journalists, Assn. Writers and Writing Programs, Modern Lang. Assn. Home and Office: PO Box 265 New Concord OH 43762

WAGNER-WESTBROOK, BONNIE JOAN, management professional; b. Watertown, N.Y., July 18, 1953; d. Elmer Ethan and Joan Eleanor (Niedermeier) Wagner; m. John Drewry Westbrook Jr., Aug. 21, 1982. BS, SUNY, Geneseo, 1975, MS, 1981; EdD, Rutgers U., 1989. Tchr. elem. Rochester (N.Y.) Sch. for the Deaf, 1975-80; instr. adult basic edn. Rochester City Sch. Dist., 1981-82; profl. interpreter Nat. Tech. Inst. for the Deaf, Rochester, 1981-83; instr., interpreter Henrietta (N.Y.) Ctrl. Sch. Dist., 1983-84; intern Middlesex County Vocat. Tech. Schs., New Brunswick, N.J., 1985; adminstr. Pub. Svc. Electric and Gas Co., Newark, 1990-91; cons. on urban initiative for N.J. Dept. Edn. Rutgers U., New Brunswick, 1985-86, program specialist, 1987-88, rsch. assoc. for N.J. Commn. on Employment and Tng., 1988-89, also senator Grad. Sch. Edn., 1985-87, program dir. New Brunswick, 1991—, dir. leadership devel. and fin. programs. Cons. Blueprint Project, Hudson County C.C., 1992-93, Pub. Svc. Electric and Gas Co., Newark, 1986-89. Vol. Rochester Sch. for the Deaf, 1977; mem. Rochester Oratorio Soc., 1978-81, SUNY Geneseo Chamber Singers, 1971-75. Rutgers U. scholar, 1986; Rutgers U. fellow, 1987. Mem. Am. Coun. on Edn. of Deaf, Nat. Registry Interpreters for Deaf, Rochester Amateur Radio Assn., Rutgers U. Alumni Assn., Omicron Tau Theta. Republican. Avocations: photography, gardening, computers, music, hiking. Home: 327 Becker St Highland Park NJ 08904-2522 Office: Rutgers U Sch Mgmt & Labor Rels Ctr Mgmt Devel 94 Rockafeller Rd Ste 215 Piscataway NJ 08854-8054 Office Phone: 732-445-5448. E-mail: westbroo@cmd.rutgers.edu.

WAGNON, JOAN, banker, former mayor; b. Texarkana, Ark., Oct. 17, 1940; d. Jack and Louise (lucas) D.; m. William O. Wagnon Jr., June 4, 1964; children: Jack, William O. III. BA in Biology, Hendrix Coll., Conway, Ark., 1962; MEd in Guidance and Counseling, U. Mo., 1968. Sr. rsch. technician U. Ark. Med. Sch., Little Rock, 1962-64, sr. rsch. asst. Columbia, Mo., 1964-68; tchr. No. Hills Jr. H.S., Topeka, 1968-69, J.S. Kendall Sch., Boston, 1970-71; counselor Neighborhood Youth Corps, Topeka, 1973-74; exec. dir. Topeka YWCA, 1977-93; mem. Kans. Legislature, 1983-94; exec. dir. Kans. Families for Kids, 1994-97; mayor City of Topeka, 1997-2001; pres. Ctrl. Nat. Bank, Topeka, 2001—. Mem. Health Planning Rev. Commn., Topeka, 1984-85. Recipient Service to Edn. award Topeka NEA, 1979, Outstanding Achievement award, Kans. Home Econs. Assn., 1985, Equity in Action award Kans. B & PW Clubs, 1991, Disting. Svc. award Kans. Ct. Svcs. Officers, 1992, Womens Rights Star award NOW, 1994; named Woman of Yr. Mayors Council Status of Women, 1983, named one of Top Ten Legislators Kans. Mag., Wichita, 1986, Legislator of Yr., Kans. NASW, 1989. Mem. Topeka Assn. Human Svc. Execs. (pres. 1981-83), Topekans for Ednl. Involvement (pres. 1979-82), Women's Polit. Caucus (state chair). Lodges: Rotary. Democrat. Methodist. Avocations: music, swimming, boating. Office: City Hall 215 SW 7th St Topeka KS 66603-3732 Home: 4036 NE Kimball Road Topeka KS 66617

WAGONER, ANNA MILLS, prosecutor; BA, Agnes Scott Coll.; JD, Wake Forest U. Assoc. Woddson, Linn, Sayers, Lawther, Short and Wagoner, 1985—87, ptnr., 1987—90; judge Rowan County Dist. Ct., 1990—2001; U.S. atty. mid. dist. U.S. Dept. Justice, NC, 2001—. Office: PO Box 1858 Greensboro NC 27402

WAHBA, MARCELLE M. ambassador; b. Calif., Dec. 1948; m. Derek M. Farwagi; 1 child, Morwenna O. Farwagi. BA in Polit. Sci., Western Coll. for Women. Dep. policy officer Near East Office U.S. Info. Agy., 1987—88; press attaché, embassy spokesperson Dept. State, Cairo, 1988—91, pub. affairs officer Am. Embassy Cyprus Nicosia, 1991—95, counselor for press and cultural affairs Amman, Jordan, 1995—99, Cairo, 1999—2001, U.S. amb. to United Arab Emirates Washington, 2001—. Office: DOS Amb 6010 Abu Dhabi Pl Washington DC 20521

WAHLBERG, GRETCHEN MARIE, music educator; b. Milw., May 16, 1953; d. Arnold Oscar and Ruth Marie Wahlberg. M in Music Edn., Fla. State U., 1976. Music tchr. Sch. Bd. of Lee County, Ft. Myers, Fla., 1976—. Adj. prof. Fla. Gulf Coast U., Ft. Myers, 2000—, Barry U., Ft. Myers, 2003—. Composer: tchr. tng. level 1 children's songs (Golden Apple Tchr., 1996). Mem.: AOSA, Fla. Elem. Music Tchrs. Assn., Fla. Music Educators Assn., Phi Kappa Pi (life). Avocations: horseback riding, gardening. Home: 1528 Poinsettia Ave Ft. Myers FL 33901 Office: Mirror Lakes Elem Sch 525 Charwood Av S Lehigh Acres FL 33936

WAHLERS, LINDA ANN FORD, writer; b. Great Barrington, Mass., June 20, 1948; d. George Edward and Eugenie Evelyn (Peck) Ford; m. Herman Frederick Wahlers; 1 child, Heather. AA, Bay Path Coll., 1968. Co-founder, cons., mgr. Original Poetry Cir., NY and Kans., 1997—99; co-founder, web prodr. Poets Internat., U.S. and U.K., 1999—. Named one of Phenomenal Women of the Net, 1998—. Mem.: Rossendale Writers U.K., Lancashire Authors' Assn. U.K. (hon.). Avocation: genealogy, music. Home: 3132 County Rte 7 Copake NY 12516

WAHRMUND, PEGGY STIELER, artist, rancher; b. Kerry County, Tex., Sept. 22, 1927; d. Edgar and Anna W. Stieler; m. Emil T. Wahrmund, Oct. 14, 1950 (dec. Aug. 1998); 1 child, Warren. BS, Tex. Women's U., 1949; MA, N.Mex. Highlands U., 1960. One-woman shows include Southwest Tex. State U., Sam Marcos, 1961, Tex. Women's U., Denton, 1963, Springfield City Libr., Mass., 1964, Kernville Art Club, Tex., 1965, Hill County Arts Found., Ingram, Tex., 1968, Am. Embassy, San Salvador, El Salvador, 1978, Am. Internat. Quilt Assn., Frankfort, Germany, 1996, exhibited in group shows at Am. Crafts Coun., San Antonio, 1957, Austin, 1965, Lubbock, 1968, M.Mex. Highlands U., Las Vegas, 1960, Southwest Crafts Ctr., San Antonio, 1978, Hill Country Arts Found., Ingram, Tex., 1978, 1986, Kaffe Gallery, Corpus Christi, Tex., 1979, Bright Shawl Gallery, San Antonio, 1985, Am. Internat. Quilt Assn., 1986, Houston, 1995, 1995, Quilter's Guild East Tex., Tyler, 1987, Am. Quilt Assn., Houston, 1990, West Coast Quilters' Conf., Sacramento, 1991, City Mus., Marshall, Tex., 1993, Southwest Parks and Monuments Assn., Stonewall, Tex., 1994, Am. Internat. Quilt Invitational, Portland, 1995, Represented in permanent collections Jeep Collins Jewelry, San Antonio, Bank One, Fredericksburg, Tex., Security State Bank, Bass Anglers Sportsman Ssoc., Montgomery, Ala., James Avary Craftsman, San Antonio, Austin, Houston, Kernville, Tulsa, Southwest Tex. U. Art Dept., San Marcos, Am. Embassy, San Salvador. Mem.: Am. Quilters Soc., Internat. Quilt Assn. (award 1996). Home: 474 Cir Ranch Rd Fredericksburg TX 78624-6462

WAIDLER, BEVERLY MAE, music teacher; b. Eau Claire, Wis., Jan. 14, 1941; d. George Hiram and Myrtle Julianna (Gunderson) Gilbertson; m. Brian Edmund Waidler Sr., Aug. 12, 1961; children: Brian Edmund jr., Sonvy Kristina, Heidi Julianna. BS in Elem. Edn., U. Md., 1962, MEd in Music and Piano/Voice, 1976. Cert. elem. and music tchr. Tchr. 5th grade Pub. Schs. Prince George's County, Bladensburg, Md., 1962; GS 5 mortgage notes accts. clk. Fed. Housing Authority, Washington, 1963-64; 4th grade substitute tchr. Amidon Sch., Washington, 1966; music tchr. vocal and gen. Parkland Jr. H.S. Montgomery County Pub. Schs., Rockville, Md., 1966-67; pvt. piano tchr. Rockville, 1966-80; salesperson, then office worker Sears Montomery Mall, Bethesda, 1989-91; substitute tchr. Pub. Schs. D.C. and Montgomery County, Rockville, Gaithersburg, Washington, 1991-95; pvt. piano and voice instr. Rockville, 1995—. Singing recitals include Weisbaden, Germany, 1982, Kaiserslautern, Germany, 1982, Pirmasens, Germany, 1983. Election office worker Dem. gubinatorial race, Wheaton, 1992; unit pres. Ch. Women United, 1976-78, mem. 1997—; lobby participant Internat. Women's Year, 1975. Mem. AAUW, Phi Theta Delta, Friday Morning Music Club. Democrat. Baptist. Avocations: art appreciation, reading biographies, walking, yoga. Home: 7036 Wick Ln Rockville MD 20855-1963

WAINIO, MELODY F. dean; b. Coshocton, Ohio, Feb. 25, 1948; d. Francis W. and Dorothy M. Burkhart; m. Edwin A. Wainio, July 20, 1985; m. Robert H. Vaughn, Sept. 7, 1968 (div. 1983); children: Eric R. Vaughn, Bryan S. Vaughn. AA, Lakeland C.C., Mentor, OH, 1982; BS in Tech. Edn., U. Akron, 1987; MSEd, Capella U., 2003. Adj. instr. Bryant and Stratton Coll., Richmond Heights, Ohio, 1990—90, full-time instr., 1990—91, faculty advisor, 1991—98, assoc. dean instrn. Willoughby Hills, Ohio, 1998—2003, dean student svcs., 2003—. Mem.: ASCD, Nat. Acad. Advising Assn. Home: 181 Meriden Rd Painesville OH 44077 Office: Bryant and Stratton Coll 27557 Chardon Rd Wickliffe OH 44092 Personal E-mail: mwainio@ameritech.net. E-mail: mfwainio@bryantstratton.edu.

WAINTROOB, ANDREA RUTH, lawyer; b. Chgo., Dec. 23, 1952; d. David Samuel and Lees (Carson) W. AB, Brown U., 1975; JD, U. Chgo., 1978. Bar: Ill. 1978, U.S. Dist. Ct. (no. dist.) Ill. 1978, U.S. Dist. Ct. (cen. dist.) Ill. 1996, U.S. Ct. Appeals (7th cir.) 1982, U.S. Supreme Ct. 1989. Assoc. Vedder, Price, Kaufman and Kammholz, Chgo., 1978-84; ptnr. Vedder, Price, Kaufman, Chgo., 1984-94, Franczek Sullivan, P.C., Chgo., 1994—. Mem. Chgo. Bar Assn., Nat. Coun. Sch. Attys. Home: 5428 S Harper Ave Chicago IL 60615-5506 Office: Franczek Sullivan 300 S Wacker Dr Ste 3400 Chicago IL 60606-6708

WAINWRIGHT, CYNTHIA CRAWFORD, banker; b. N.Y.C., July 5, 1945; d. Townsend Wainwright and Rosalie deForest (Crosby) Gevers; m. Stephen Berger, Sept. 24, 1977; children: Robin Wainwright Berger, Diana Wainwright Berger. MBA, Columbia Bus. Sch., 1984. Sec., adminstrv. asst. Time-Life Broadcast, N.Y.C., 1965-68; adminstrv. asst. Downe Comms., N.Y.C., 1968-69, Office of the Mayor, N.Y.C., 1969-71; program mgr. Dept. of Correction, N.Y.C., 1972-73, dir. adminstrn., 1973-75, dep. commr., 1978-79; dir. of spl. projects N.Y. State Dept. Correctional Svcs., Albany, 1975-76; asst. dir. Offender-Based Transaction Svcs./Divsn. Criminal Justice, Albany, 1976-77; various positions Chem. Bank, N.Y.C., 1979-96, dir. corp. soc. resp. Chase Bank, N.Y.C., 1996—. Mem. adv. coms. N.Y. State Office of Parks, N.Y.C., 1986-95; bd. dirs., chmn. Hist. House Trust of N.Y.C., 1989—; bd. dirs., past pres. The Bridge, Inc., N.Y.C., 1984—; trustee, past pres. Preservation League of N.Y. State, Albany, 1984—; trustee The Chapin Sch., Ltd., N.Y.C., 1989—. Named Woman of the Yr. East Manhattan C. of C., 1984; recipient Mental Health award The Bridge, Inc., N.Y.C., 1992, award for acad. excellence Columbia Bus. Sch., N.Y.C., 1983. Avocations: horseback riding, tennis, cooking. Office: Chase Bank 600 5th Ave Fl 3 New York NY 10020-2302

WAINWRIGHT HENBEST, MARGARET A. state representative; b. L.A., Aug. 13, 1953; m. Michael Henbest; children: Ryan, Daniel, Kevin. BS in Health Scis., Oreg. U., 1976; MS, Calif. State U., Long Beach, 1984. Pediatric nurse practitioner, pvt. practice, 1984—86; pediatric nurse practitioner, Child Abuse Clinic St. Luke's Regional Med. Ctr., 1991—; asst. prof. nursing Boise State U., 1988—91; state rep. dist. 16A Idaho Ho. of Reps., Boise, 1996—, mem. revenue and taxation com.; mem. CHIPS task force, 1998; chmn. joint legis. oversight com., 2000—; mem. mental health interim com., 1996. Small benefit plan com. Idaho Dept. Commerce, 1994—95. Mem.: ASPAC, ANA, St. Joseph's Home & Sch. Assn. (pres.), Nat. Assn. Pediatric Nurse Practitioners and Assocs., Idaho Nurses Assn. (legis. com. chair nurse practitioner group 1990—), Child Abuse Law Mentors, Mountain States Group (bd. dirs., pres.), Kids Count (bd. dirs.), Discovery Ctr. Idaho (past bd.), Rotary. Democrat. Office: State Capitol PO Box 83720 Boise ID 83720-0038

WAITE, FRANCES W. librarian, professional genealogist; b. Newberrytown, Pa., Jan. 7, 1944; d. Jacob Kister and Mary Fisher (Conley) Wise; m. Arthur Owen Waite, May 22, 1937; children: Catherine Ann, Douglas Arthur, Mary Virginia. BS in Edn., Shippensburg U., 1964; MS, Kutztown U. Elem. sch. tchr. Cen. Bucks Sch. Dist., Doylestown, Pa., 1964-65, 67-68; receptionist Bucks County Hist. Soc., Doylestown, 1981-86, libr., 1987—. Lectr., tchr. family history rsch.; verifying genealogist for Nat. Soc. Colonial Dames of Am. Com. of Pa., 1998-2002. Co-author: (books) Bucks County Tax Records 1693-1778, 1982, Bucks County Declarations and Naturalizations 1802-1906, 1985; author: (books) Descendants of Thomas Connelly, 1980, Descendants of Hans Detweiler, 1976, expanded and updated edit., 1995, Desendants of Johannes Weiss of Dover, Pa., 1997, White Families of Lower Bucks, 1999, Anderson Families of Upper York County, Pa., 1999, Connelly-Conley Descendants of Thomas Connelly of Rapho Township Lancaster County PA, 2002, 2d edit., 2003; editor numerous geneal. reference books, 1980-99. Charter mem. Bucks County Choral Soc., Doylestown, 1972-99. Mem. Nat. Geneal Soc. (award of merit 1997), Geneal. Soc. of Pa. (past co-chair program com. 1991-97, publs. com. 1990-99), Bucks County Geneal. Soc. (founder, v.p., pres., newsletter editor 1981-90). Avocations: choral singing, travel, crocheting, gardening. Home: 649 S Chubb Dr Doylestown PA 18901-4547

WAITE, HELEN ELEANOR, funeral director; b. Richmond, Va., Aug. 7, 1947; d. Julia F. (Braxton) Candia; m. Malcolm L. Waite, July 24, 1982. AB, Va. State U., 1968, MA, 1977; degree in funeral svc., Northampton C.C., Bethlehem, Pa., 1994. Cert. tchr., Pa., N.J. Tchr. Westmoreland County Schs., Montross, Va.; tchr. English Rittenhouse Acad., Phila.; owner Helen E. Waite Funeral Service, Phila. Mem. Nat. Coun. Tchrs. English, Pa. Coun. Tchrs. English, Nat. Funeral Dirrs. Assn., Pa. Funeral Dirs. Assn. Home: 820 N 65th St Philadelphia PA 19151-3303 E-mail: waitefuneralsvc.@msn.com.

WAITE-FRANZEN, ELLEN JANE, academic administrator; b. Oshkosh, Wis., Feb. 17, 1951; d. Earl Vincent and Margaret (Luft) W.; m. Thomas H. Dollar, Aug. 19, 1977 (div. July 1984); m. Kent Hendrickson, Mar. 26, 1994 (div. Dec. 1995); m. Scott Franzen, Apr. 4, 1998. BA, U. Wis., Oshkosh, 1973; MLS, U. Wis., Milw., 1977. Head of cataloging Marquette U., Milw., 1977-82; head catalog libr. U. Ariz., Tucson, 1983-85; assoc. dir. libr. Loyola U., Chgo., 1985-86, acting dir. libr., 1986-87, dir. libr., 1987-94, v.p. acad. svcs., 1994-97; assoc. provost for info. svcs. U. Richmond, 1997-99, v.p. for info. svcs., 1999—2002; v.p. for computing and info. svcs. Brown U., Providence, 2002—. Cons. Loyola U., Chgo., 1984, Boston Coll., 1986, U. San Francisco, 1989; bd. trustees Online Computer Lib. Ctr., Dublin,

Ohio, 1994-2000. Contbg. author: Research Libraries and Their Implementation of AACR2, 1985; author: (with others) Women in LC's Terms: A Thesaurus of Subject Headings Related to Women, 1988. Mem. ALA. Avocation: photography. Office: Brown U Computing and Info Svcs Box 1885 Providence RI 02912-1885 E-mail: ewaite@brown.edu.

WAITES, CANDY YAGHJIAN, former state official; b. N.Y.C., Feb. 21, 1943; d. Edmund Kirken and Dorothy Joanne (Candy) Yaghjian; children: Jennider Lisa, Robin Shelley. BA, Wheaton Coll., Mass., 1965; MPA, U. S.C., 1997. County councilwoman, Richland County, SC, 1976—88; mem. S.C. Ho. of Reps., 1988—94; lectr. polit. sci., assoc. dean Leadership Inst. Columbia Coll., 1993—99; dir. divsn. children's svcs. Gov.'s Office, 1999—2003. Vice chmn. Adv. Commn. on Intergovtl. Rels., S.C., 1977-87; bd. dirs. Interagy. Council on Pub. Transp., S.C., 1977-85, Central Midlands Regional Planning Council, Columbia, S.C., 1977-84; dir. Wachovia Bank. V.p. bd. dirs. United Way of Midlands, 1977-89; trustee Columbia Mus. Art, 1982-88; bd. dirs. Rape Crisis Network, 1984-87, Nat. ATHENA Found., 1999-2001; chmn. County Coun. Coalition; mem. C. of C. Leadership Forum, S.C. Fedn. of Blind; mem. adv. bd. U. S.C. Humanities and Social Scis. Coll., Family Shelter, Nuturing Ctr.; pres. Trinity Housing Corp.; found. bd. palmetto Richland Meml. Hosp., 1995-2000; mem. Columbia Housing Authority Bd., 1997-2000. Named Outstanding Young Career Woman, Columbia YWCA, 1980, YWCA Hall of Fame, 1993, Columbia Housing Authority Bd., Outstanding Young Woman of Yr., Columbia Jaycees, 1975, Pub. Citizen of Yr. NASW; recipient Ann. Legis. award Common Cause S.C., 1990, 91. Mem. S.C. Women in Govt. (vice chmn. 1984-86), S.C. Assn. Counties (bd. dirs. 1982-88, Pres.'s award 1983, Legislator of Yr. award 1992), Columbia C. of C. (Athena award 1998), Network Female Execs., LWV (pres. 1973-76), Unic. Assocs. Club, Mortar Bd. (hon.), Omicron Delta Kappa. Democrat. Episcopalian. Avocations: exercising, drawing, gardening, walking. Home: 3419 Duncan St Columbia SC 29205-2705

WAIXEL, VIVIAN, journalist; b. Norfolk, Va., July 22, 1946; d. Julius and Julia (Heimann) W.; m. Steven E. Scharbach, Aug. 24, 1969. BS in Communication, Simmons Coll., 1967; MA in Communication, U. Wis., 1971; PhD in Journalism (hon.), Simmons U., 2002. Teaching asst. U. Wis., Madison, 1967-69; reporter Wis. State Jour., Madison, 1969-72, The Record, Hackensack, N.J., 1972-74, bus. editor, 1974-76, assignment editor, 1976-86, sports editor, 1986-88, chief news editor, 1988-92, mng. editor, 1992-97, editor, 1997-2000, v.p., exec. editor, 2000—, Herald News, West Paterson, N.J., 2000—. Recipient Tribute to Women and Industry award, YWCA, 1976. Avocations: snorkeling, fitness walking, music, reading. Office: The Record 150 River St Hackensack NJ 07601-7155*

WAJDA, SHIRLEY TERESA, historian; b. Warren, Ohio, May 28, 1958; d. Henry Walter Wajda and Erna Emilie Boenning. BA, Boston U., 1982; AM, U. Pa., 1989, PhD, 1992, cert. in mus. curatorship, 1984. Mng. editor Am. Quar., 1985—87; asst. prof. history and Am. studies (tenured) Boston U., 1991—94; vis. asst. prof. Am. studies U. Iowa, 1995; asst. prof. history and Am. studies (tenured) Kent (Ohio) State U., 1996—. Mem. coll.-level exam. program test devel. com. Am. History (I and II) Ednl. Testing Svc., Princeton, NJ, 1998—2001. Mem. editl. bd.: American Studies, 1997—; Mem. editl. bd. Kent State U. Press, 2002—; exhibitions include Designing Domesticity: Decorating the American Home Since 1876, 2001; contbr. articles to profl. jours., . Recipient Disting. Achievement award, Ednl. Press Am., 1990; fellow, NEH, 1994; Baird Soc. fellow, Smithsonian Instn., 2004—. Mem.: Berkshire Conf. Women Historians, Orgn. Am. Historians, Am. Studies Assn., Soc. for Historians of Early Am. Republic. Office: Kent State U Dept History 305 Bowman Hall 44242-0001

WAJSFELD, ANNIE R. volunteer; b. Antwerp, Belgium, Jan. 19, 1936; arrived in U.S., 1949; d. Szloma Chaskel and Hinda (Labin) Wajsfeld. BA, Bklyn. Coll., 1972. Cert.: Bklyn. Coll. (paralegal). With CUNY Grad. Ctr., N.Y.C., 1965—70, Kingsborough C.C., Bklyn., 1970—90, Bklyn. Coll., 1991—96. Del. Dem. Party, Bklyn., 1990, Nat. Coun. Young Israel, Manhattan, 1975—99; office mgr., treas. Young Israel Van-derveer Park Synogogue, Bklyn., maintained meml. book. Named Woman of the Yr., Young Israel Synagogue, 1988, 1996. Mem.: Dem. Club (inspector 41 assembly dist. 2000—). Jewish. Avocations: reading, outdoor activities, attending cultural events. Office: AMIT HQ 7th Ave New York NY

WAKATSUKI, LYNN Y. commissioner; Commr. fin. instns. divsn. fin. instns. Dept. Commerce and Consumer Affairs, Honolulu, 1995—. Office: Dept Commerce Consumer Affairs Divsn Fin Instns PO Box 2054 Honolulu HI 96805

WAKE, MADELINE MUSANTE, academic administrator, nursing educator; Diploma, St. Francis Hosp. Sch. Nursing, 1963; BS in Nursing, Marquette U., 1968, MS in Nursing, 1971; PhD, U. Wis., Milw., 1986. Clin. nurse specialist St. Mary's Hosp., Milw., 1971-74, asst. dir. nursing, 1974-77; from dir. continuing nursing edn. to provost Marquette U., Milw., 1977—2002, provost, 2002—. Mem. devel. team Internat. Classification for Nursing Practice, Geneva, 1991-99. Chmn. bd. dirs. Trinity Meml. Hosp., Cudahy, Wis., 1991-96. Recipient Profl. Svc. award Am. Diabetes Assn.-Wis. affiliate, 1978, Excellence in Nursing Edn. award Wis. Nurses Assn., 1989; named Disting. Lectr. Sigma Theta Tau Internat., 1991. Fellow: Am. Acad. Nursing; mem.: AAHE, Vis. Nurs Assn. wis. (bd. dirs.), Am. Assn. Coll. Nursing (bd. dirs. 1999—2002), ANA. Office: Marquette Univ O'Hara Hall Milwaukee WI 53201-1881

WAKE, MARVALEE HENDRICKS, biology educator; b. Orange, Calif., July 31, 1939; d. Marvin Carlton and Velvalee (Borter) H.; m. David B. Wake, June 23, 1962; 1 child, Thomas A. BA, U. So. Calif., 1961, MS, 1964, PhD, 1968. 1968Teaching asst./instr. U. Ill., Chgo., 1964, asst. prof., 1968—69; lectr. U. Calif., Berkeley, 1969—73, asst. prof., 1973—76, assoc. prof., 1976—80, prof. zoology, 1980—89, chmn. dept. zoology, 1985—89, chmn. dept. integrative biology, 1989—91, 1999—2002, assoc. dean Coll. Letters and Sci., 1975—78, prof. integrative biology, 1989—, Chancellor's prof., 1997—2000. Mem. NAS/NRC Bd. on Sustainable Devel., 1995-99, NSF Bio Adv. Commn., 1997—2002; Smithsonian Sci. Commn., 2001-2002. Editor, co-editor: Hyman's Comparative Vertebrate Anatomy, 1979, The Origin and Evolution of Larval Forms, 1999; co-author: Biology, 1978; contbr. articles to profl. jours. NSF grantee, 1978—; Guggenheim fellow, 1988-89. Fellow: AAAS (chair Biology Sect. G 1998), Calif. Acad. Sci. (trustee 1992—98, hon. trustee 1998—), Am. Acad. Arts and Scis.; mem.: Am. Inst. Biol. Sci. (pres.-elect 2004), World Congress of Herpetology (sec. gen. 1994—97), Internat. Union Biol. Scis. (U.S. nat. com. 1986—, chair 1992—95, sec. gen. 1994—2000, pres. 2000—04), Soc. Integrative Comparative Biol. (pres. 2001—03), Am. Soc. Ichthyologists and Herpetologists (bd. govs. 1978—, pres. 1984). Office: U Calif Dept Integrative Biology 3060 VLSB Berkeley CA 94720-3140

WAKEFIELD, MARIE CYNTHIA, performing arts educator, playwright, poet; b. Chgo., Feb. 11, 1945; d. Daniel Jesse Armstrong and Margaret M. Jenkins; m. Donald Wakefield; children: Adolphus Beal III, Donald Wakefield II, Walter McIntyre Jr., Michele McIntyre, Reyna, Candace. Student, Cortez W. Peters Bus. Coll., Chgo., 1962—63. Founder Creative Works, Etc., Inc., Inglewood, Calif. Poet/playwright: Quiet Storm, 1994. Named Poet of Yr., Famous Poets Soc., 1995, 1998, 2000. Avocations: writing, singing, producing plays. Office: Creative Works Etc 9717 S 8th Ave Inglewood CA 90305 Personal E-mail: mwake9717@aol.com.

WAKEMAN, MARTHA JANE, artist, educator; b. Bridgeport, Conn., Jan. 8, 1948; d. Norman Burr and Muriel (Evitts) Wakeman; m. Robert E. Proctor, Mar. 15, 1980; children: Rebecca Anne Proctor, Andrew Wakeman Proctor. BS, Skidmore Coll., 1970; MA, Villa Schifaroia-Rosary Coll., Florence, Italy, 1972, MFA, 1978. Cert. art tchr. K-12, Conn. Instr. art Gonzaga U. Jr. Yr. Abroad Program, Florence, 1974-79, Conn. Coll., 1980-81, instr. art Return to Coll. program, 1984—; instr. painting Umbra Inst., Pengra, Italy, 2002. Exhibited in one-woman shows in Milan, Florence, N.Y.C. and Conn., 1972-96; group shows include Alan Stone Gallery, N.Y.C., Skidmore Coll., Vangarde Gallery, New London, Conn., MS Gallery, Hartford, Conn., No-Ho Gallery, N.Y.C., Conn. Women Artists, New Haven; paintings included in more than 100 pvt. collections in Europe, U.S. and Can.; subject of articles. Class coord. St. Joseph Sch., New London, 1998-99, Pine Point Sch., Stonington, Conn., 1995-97; mem. parish coun. St. Joseph Ch., New London, 1993-96, lector, 1995—/ Democrat. Roman Catholic. Avocations: swimming, travel, studying foreign languages, reading. Home: 105 Oneco Ave New London CT 06320-4120 Office: Conn Coll Box 5573 New London CT 06320

WAKEMAN, OLIVIA VAN HORN, marketing professional; b. Starkville, Miss. d. Thomas Oliver and Mary Jeanne Wakeman. BA in Mgmt., Eckerd Coll., St. Petersburg, Fla., 1980; MIM in Mktg./Advt., Am. Grad. Sch. Internat. Mgmt., 1982. Bus. analyst Dun & Bradstreet, Tampa, Fla., 1980; mgmt. cons. Cardinal Mgmt. Assocs., L.A., 1982-83; asst. account exec. McCann-Erickson, N.Y.C., 1984-86; account exec. Hearst Mag., N.Y.C., 1986-87, Ribaudo & Schaefer, N.Y.C., 1987-88; dir. pub. affairs/bus. soc. and ethics program Carnegie Coun. on Ethics and Internat. Affairs, N.Y.C., 1989-93; mgr. client svcs. Burson-Marsteller, Inc., N.Y.C., 1994-97, Young & Rubicam, Inc., N.Y.C., 1994-99, Cohn & Wolfe, N.Y.C., 1997-99; sr. writer TManage, Inc., 2000—. Adult edn. mktg. prof. Touro Coll., N.Y.C., 1989; mktg. comm. cons. Hoffmann-La Roche, Inc., McGraw-Hill Inc., Daniel J. Edelman, Inc., Dilenschneider Group, Stingray Ptnrs., N.Y.C., 1993-94; sr. writer T Manage, Inc., 2000—. Reading vol. Vol. Svcs. for Children, N.Y.C., 1991-93. Episcopalian. Avocation: scuba diving. Home: c/o Tmanage Inc 7000 N Mopac #350 Austin TX 78731 Address: 2301 S Mo Pac Expy Apt 208 Austin TX 78746-7955

WAKOSKI, DIANE, poet, educator; b. Whittier, Calif., Aug. 3, 1937; d. John Joseph and Marie Elvira (Mengel) W. BA in English, U. Calif., Berkeley, 1960. Writer-in-residence Mich. State U., East Lansing, 1976—, Univ. disting. prof., 1990—. Vis. writer Calif. Inst. Tech., 1972, U. Va., 1972-73, Wilamette U., 1973, Lake Forest Coll., 1974, Colo. Coll., 1974, U. Calif., Irvine, 1974, Macalester Coll., 1975, U. Wis., 1975, Hollins Coll., 1974, U. Wash., 1977, Whitman Coll., 1976, Emory U., 1980-81, U. Hawaii, 1978. Author: books Coins and Coffins, 1962, Discrepancies and Apparitions, 1966, Inside The Blood Factory, 1968, The George Washington Poems, 1967, The Magellanic Clouds, 1969, The Motorcycle Betrayal Poems, 1971, Smudging, 1972, Dancing On The Grave of A Son Of A Bitch, 1973, Trilogy, 1974, Virtuoso Literature For Two and Four Hands, 1976, Waiting For the King of Spain, 1977, The Man Who Shook Hands, 1978, Cap of Darkness, 1980, The Magician's Feastletters, 1982, The Collected Greed: Parts I-XIII, 1984, The Rings of Saturn, 1986, Emerald Ice: Selected Poems 1962-87, 1988 (William Carlos Williams prize 1989), Medea The Sorceress, 1991, Jason the Sailor, 1993, The Emerald City of Las Vegas, 1995, Argonaut Rose, 1998, The Butcher's Apron: New & Selected Poems, 2000. Named Univ. Disting. Prof., Mich. State U., 1990, Author of Yr., Mich. Libr. Assn., 2003; recipient award, Mich. Arts Found., 1989, Disting. Faculty award, Mich. State U., 1989; grantee Cassandra Found., 1970, N.Y. State Cultural Coun., 1971—72, Guggenheim Found., 1972—73, Fullbright, 1984, Mich. Arts Coun., 1988. Office: Mich State U 207 Morrill Hall East Lansing MI 48824-1036 E-mail: dwakoski@aol.com., wakoski@pilot.msu.edu.

WALCHER, JENNIFER LYNNE, city official; b. Denver, Feb. 8, 1956; d. Donald Robert and Winifred Edmunde (O'Dell) W. AS in Adminstrn. of Justice, Arapahoe C.C., Littleton, Colo., 1984; BS in Criminal Justice, Columbia Coll., Aurora, Colo. and Columbia, Mo., 1986; AS in Occupl. Safety, Trinidad State Jr. Coll., 1994. Cert. water distbn. sys. technician, Colo. Security patrolman Mission Viejo, Highlands Ranch, Colo., 1983-84; security officer Denver Water Dept., 1985-87, water serviceman I, 1987-88, safety and loss control specialist, 1988—. Contbr. articles to profl. publs. Instr. CPR and first aid Colo. Safety Assn., Denver, 1988—; instr. defensive driving Nat. Safety Coun., 1988—. With USN, 1974-81. Mem. Am. Soc. Safety Engrs., Phi Theta Kappa. Lutheran. Avocations: golf, camping, fishing, ceramics, writing poetry. Home: 2720 S Newland St Denver CO 80227-3519 Office: Denver Water Dept 1600 W 12th Ave Denver CO 80204-3412

WALCHER, KATHLEEN, state official; b. Sept. 20, 1948; Clk. of ct. of Common Pleas, Huron County; civil sheriff deputy; deputy clk.; state rep. State of Ohio, 58th Dist., 2002—. Mem.: Juvenile and Family Law (vice-chair), Econ. Devel. and Tech., County and Twp. Govt., Agr. and Natural Resources. Republican. Office: 77 South High St 12th Fl Columbus OH 43215-6111

WALCZYK, EUGENIA C. music educator; b. Syracuse, N.Y., June 6, 1932; d. Francis E. and Henrietta M. Bulawa; m. Robert S. Walczyk (dec. July 1994); children: Robert Jr., Claire, Donald, Jeffrey, Karen, Daniel. BA, Syracuse Univ., 1953; MS, SUNY, Oswego, N.Y., 1983. Music tchr. Ctrl. Sq. (N.Y.) Schs., 1981—2003. Author: (book) Intro. to Keyboard, 1988; contbr. articles to profl. jours. Recipient Fulbright Mem. Fund Scholarship, Fulbright Mem. Found., 2002; grantee Grant, Life Touch Pictures, 1994—95. Mem.: Music Educators Nat. Conference, Sigma Alpha Iota. Avocation: gardening. Home: 5796 Albert Rd Brewerton NY 13029

WALD, FLORENCE, dean, nurse; b. 1916; Grad., Mt. Holyoke Coll.; degree, Yale U., 1941. Established first Hospice unit in U.S., 1971.

WALD, FRANCINE JOY WEINTRAUB (MRS. BERNARD J. WALD), physicist, academic administrator; b. Bklyn., Jan. 13, 1938; d. Irving and Minnie (Reisig) Weintraub; m. Bernard J. Wald, FEb. 2, 1964; children: David Evan, Kevin Mitchell. Student, Bklyn. Coll., 1955-57; BEE, CCNY, 1960; MS, Poly. Inst. Bklyn., 1962, PhD, 1969. Engr. Remington Rand Univac divsn. Sperry Rand Corp., Phila., 1960; instr. Poly. Inst. Bklyn., 1962-64, adj. rsch. assoc., 1969-70; lectr. N.Y. C.C., Bklyn., 1969, 70; instr. sci. Friends Sem., N.Y.C., 1975-76, chmn. dept. sci., 1976-94; instr. sci., chmn. dept. sci. Nightingale-Bamford Sch., N.Y.C., 1994-99. Adj. asst. prof. NYU. NDEA fellow, 1962-64. Mem. AAAS, Am. Phys. Soc., Am. Assn. Physics Tchrs., Assn. Tchrs. in Ind. Schs., N.Y. Acad. Scis., Nat. Sci. Tchrs. Assn., Sigma Xi, Tau Beta Pi, Eta Kappa Nu.

WALD, PATRICIA MCGOWAN, retired federal judge; b. Torrington, Conn., Sept. 16, 1928; d. Joseph F. and Margaret (O'Keefe) McGowan; m. Robert L. Wald, June 22, 1952; children: Sarah, Douglas, Johanna, Frederica, Thomas. BA, Conn. Coll., 1948; LLB, Yale U., 1951; HHD (hon.), Mt. Vernon Jr. Coll., 1980; LLD, LLD, Hofstra U., 1991, New Eng. Coll., 1991, Vermont Law Sch., 1995, Yale U., 2001. Bar: D.C. 1952. Clk. to Hon. Jerome Frank U.S. Ct. Appeals, 1951—52; assoc. Arnold, Fortas & Porter, Washington, 1952—53; mem. D.C. Crime Commn., 1964—65; atty. Office of Criminal Justice, 1967—68, Neighborhood Legal Svc., Washington, 1968—70; co-dir. Ford Found. Project on Drug Abuse, 1970, Ctr. for Law and Social Policy, 1971—72, Mental Health Law Project, 1972—77; asst. atty. gen. for legis. affairs U.S. Dept. Justice, Washington, 1977—79; judge U.S. Ct. Appeals (D.C. cir.), 1979—99, chief judge, 1986—91; judge Internat. Criminal Tribunal for Former Yugoslavia, The Hague, Netherlands, 1999—2001. Author: Law and Poverty, 1965; co-author: Bail in the United States, 1964, Dealing with Drug Abuse, 1973; bd. editors: ABA Jour., 1978—86; contbr. articles to profl. jours. Trustee Ford Found., 1972—77, Phillips Exeter Acad., 1975—77, Agnes Meyer Found., 1976—77, Conn. Coll., 1976—77; active Carnegie Coun. on Children, 1972—77. Mem.: ABA-Ctrl. and Ea. European Law Inst. (exec. bd. 1994—99), Inst. Justice Initiative, Am. Acad. Arts and Scis., Am. Law Inst. (coun. mem. 1979—, exec. com. 1985—99, 2d v.p. 1988—93, 1st v.p. 1993—98), Open Soc. Inst. (chair justice initiative 2002— chair), Phi Beta Kappa. Office: 2101 Connecticut Ave NW Washington DC 20008

WALD, SUSAN LORI, counseling administrator; b. Bklyn., Mar. 28, 1958; d. Sidney Bernard and Harriet Oppenheimer Weinberger; m. Jody Todd Wald, Oct. 26, 1985; children: Nathan, Jessica, Corey. BA, SUNY, Stony Brook, 1980; EdM, Boston U., 1981; PD, St. John's U., 1989. Cert. sch. counselor N.Y. Caseworker Angel Guardian Home, Bklyn., 1981—84; sch. counselor The Shield Inst., Queens, NY, 1984—88; guidance counselor N.Y. Bd. Edn., Queens, 1988—89; svc. coord. Cooper Kids Therapy Assocs., Syosset, NY, 1998—2001; guidance counselor N.Y.C. Bd. Edn., 2001—. Mem.: Am. Counselor Assn., Am. Sch. Counselor Assn.

WALD, SYLVIA, artist; b. Phila., Oct. 30, 1915; Ed., Moore Inst. Art, Sci. and Industry. One-woman shows include U. Louisville, 1945, 49, Kent State Coll., 1945, Nat. Serigraph Soc., 1946, Grand Central Moderns, N.Y.C., 1957, Devorah Sherman Gallery, Chgo., 1960, New Sch., 1967, Book Gallery, White Plains, N.Y., 1968, Benson Gallery, Bridgehampton, L.I., 1977, Knoll Internat., Munich, 1979, Amerika Havs, Munich, 1979, Aaron Berman Gallery, N.Y.C., 1981, Hirschltadler Gallery, 1994, New Britain (Conn.) Mus., 1994, Dongah Art Gallery, Seoul, Korea, 1995, Hanlim Art Gallery, Daejun, 1995-96, Kwanju City Art Mus, Pusanm Korea, Dong Shin U., Kwangju, 1996, Chosun U. Mus., Kwanju City, 2001, Chosun Univ. Mus. Art, Kwangsu, Korea, 2002, Tenri Gallery, N.Y.C., 2004; exhibited in group shows at Nat. Sculpture Soc., 1940, Sculpture Internat., Phila., 1940, Chgo. Art Inst., 1941, Bklyn. Mus., 1975, Library of Congress, 1943, 52, 58, Smithsonian Instn., 1954, Internat. Print Exhbn., Salzburg and Vienna, 1952, 2d Sao Paulo Biennial, 1953, N.Y. Cultural Center, 1973, Mus. Modern Art, N.Y.C., 1975, Benson Gallery, Bridgehampton, L.I., 1982, Dumon-Landis Gallery, New Brunswick, N.J., 1982-83, Suzuki Gallery, N.Y.C., 1982, Sid Deutch Gallery, N.Y.C., 1983, Aaron Berman Gallery, N.Y.C., 1983, Full House Gallery, Kingston, N.J., 1984, Nabi Gallery, Sag Harbor, N.Y., 1989, Worcester Mus., 1991, Boston Mus. Fine Arts, 1991, Hirschl & Adler Gallery, N.Y.C., 1993, Parrish Mus., Southampton, 2002, others; represented in permanent collections Aetna Oil Co., AAUW, Ball State Tchrs. Coll., Bibliotheque Nat., Paris, Bklyn. Mus., Howard U., State U. Iowa, Library of Congress, U. Louisville, Nat. Gallery, Mus. Modern Art, Phila. Mus., N.C. Mus., Rose Mus. Art at Brandeis U., Whitney Mus., N.Y.C., Finch Coll. Mus., N.Y.C., U. Nebr., Ohio U., U. Okla., Princeton, Victoria and Albert Mus., Walker Gallery, Worcester (Mass.) Art Mus., Guggenheim Mus., N.Y.C., Grunewald Mus., UCLA, Rutgers Mus., N.J., Aschenbach Collection Mus., San Francisco, Grunewald Coll. Mus. UCLA, Wellesley Coll.; acquisitions Yale U. Art Gallery, 1998, Cleve. Mus., 1998; Contbr. articles to profl. jours. Address: 417 Lafayette St New York NY 10003-7005

WALDBAUM, JANE COHN, art history educator; b. Jan. 28, 1940; d. Max Arthur and Sarah (Waldstein) Cohn. BA, Brandeis U., 1962; MA, Harvard U., 1964, PhD, 1968. Rsch. fellow in classical archaeology Harvard U., Cambridge, Mass., 1968-70, 72-73; from asst. prof. to assoc. prof. U. Wis., Milw., 1973-84, prof. art history, 1984—2002, chmn. dept., 1982-85, 86-89, 91-92, adj. prof. anthropology, 2002—. Dorot rsch. prof. W.F. Albright Inst. Archaeol. Rsch., Jerusalem, 1990-91; vis. scholar Hebrew U. Jerusalem, 1989-91. Author: From Bronze to Iron, 1978, Metalwork from Sardis, 1983; author (with others), co-editor: Sardis Report I, 1975; mem. editl. bd. Bull. Am. Schs. Oriental Rsch., 1994-98, Near Eastern Archaeology, 2000-2002; contbr. numerous articles to profl. jours. Woodrow Wilson Found. fellow, dissertation fellow, 1962-63, 65-66, NEH postdoctoral rsch., Jerusalem, 1989-90; grantee Am. Philos. Soc., 1972, NEH, summer 1975, U. Wis.-Milw. Found., 1983. Mem. Am. Schs. Oriental Rsch. (bd. trustees 2003—), Soc. for Archaeol. Sci., Israel Exploration Soc., Archaeol. Inst. Am. (exec. com. 1975-77, chmn. com. on membership programs 1977-81, nominating com. 1984, chmn. com. on lecture program 1985-87, acad. trustee 1993-98, 1st v.p. 1999—2002, pres. 2003-, com. profl. responsibilities 1993—, fellowships com. 1993-99, gold medal com. 1993-99, chair 1996-97, Near East Archaeology interest group 1993—, chair ann. meeting com. 1999—2002, chair regional meetings com. 1999—2002, pers. com., governance com., devel. com., fin. com.), W.F. Albright Inst. Archaeol. Rsch. (trustee 1996—, mem. governance com. 1996—), Wis. Soc. Jewish Learning (trustee 1993-99), Milw. Soc. Archaeol. Inst. (bd. dirs., pres. 1983-85, 91-95, 97-99), Phi Beta Kappa. Office: U Wis Dept Anthropology PO Box 413 Milwaukee WI 53201-0413 E-mail: JCW@uwm.edu.

WALDEN, ALICE, artist, educator; b. Billings, Mont., June 14, 1943; d. George John and Lilly (Sevick) Martin; m. Dee Edward Walden, June 23, 1962; children: San Dee Walden Russell, Kevin. BA, Mont. State U., 1980. Cert. art tchr., Mont. Bookkeeper 1st State Bank, Livingston, Mont., 1961-62, Gallatin Farmers Co., Bozeman, Mont., 1966-71; acctg. asst. Rowland Thomas & Co., Miles City, Mont., 1972-78, Don Winslow & Assocs., Miles City, 1979-80; home bound tchr. Sch. Dist. # 1, Miles City, 1980-81, gifted edn. tchr., 1981-86, art tchr., 1986—; profl. artist Miles City, 1991—; owner, mgr. Wool House Gallery, Miles City, 1994—. Executed various steel sculptures in pvt. collections, N.D., Wyo., Mont., Wash., Calif. Home: 419 N 7th St Miles City MT 59301-3117

WALDEN, CATHERINE JANE, not-for profit director, social worker, consultant; b. Fayetteville, Ark., Mar. 9, 1955; d. Betty Louise and Richard Marshall Walden. B in Social Work, U. Ark., Little Rock, 2000, MPA, 2002; cert. in life care planning, U. Fla./Intelicus, 2002. Mdse. buyer Campbell-Bell Dept. Stores, Fayetteville, Ark., 1979—81; asst. store mgr. M.M. Cohn's Dept. Store, Memphis, 1981—85; inventory shortage control mgr. Goldsmith's Dept. Stores, Memphis, 1985—90; assoc. dir. Am. Amputee Found., Inc., Little Rock, 1991—2001, exec. dir., 2001—, life care planner, 2002. Treas. Rape Crisis, Inc., Little Rock, 2001—02, adv., 1997—2002; project bus. leader Jr. Acheivement/Memphis City Sch. Sys., 1987—89; oncology ward vol. Meth. Hosp., Memphis, 1985—86. Mem.: NASW, Internat. Acad. Life Care Planners, Nat. Rehab. Assn., Phi Kappa Phi, Pi Alpha Alpha. Office: Am Amputee Found Inc PO Box 250218 Little Rock AR 72225

WALDEN, DANA, broadcast executive; BA in Comm., U. So. Calif. Formerly with Bender, Goldman & Helper; former v.p. mktg. Arsenio Hall Comm., Paramount; former sr. v.p. media and corp. rels. 20th Century Fox TV, v.p. current programming, 1994—96, former v.p. drama, former sr. v.p. drama, former exec. v.p. drama devel., co-pres., 1999—. Named to Women in Entertainment Power List, Hollywood Reporter, 1999—2003. Mem.: Hollywood Radio and TV Soc. (v.p. 2003—). Office: 20th Century Fox TV 10201 W Pico Blvd Bldg 88 Rm 29 Los Angeles CA 90035*

WALDEN, JANET C. lawyer; AB, Brown U., 1976; JD, NYU, 1979. Bar: N.Y. 1979. Assoc. Rubin Baum Levin Constant & Friedman, N.Y.C., 1979-86, Schulte, Roth & Zabel LLP, N.Y.C., from 1986, ptnr. Mem. ABA, Assn. Bar City N.Y. Office: Schulte Roth & Zabel LLP 900 #d Ave New York NY 10022 E-mail: janet.walden@srz.com.

WALDMAN, ANNE LESLEY, poet, performer, editor, publisher, educational administrator; b. Millville, N.J., Apr. 2, 1945; d. John Marvin and Frances (Le Fevre) W.; m. Reed Eyre Bye; 1 son, Ambrose. BA, Bennington Coll., 1966. Dir. The Poetry Project, St. Marks Ch. In-the-Bowery, N.Y.C., 1968-78; dir. Jack Kerouac Sch. of Disembodied Poetics at Naropa Inst., Boulder, Colo., 1974—. Adj. faculty Inst. Am. Indian Arts,

Santa Fe; bd. dirs. Com. for Internat. Poetry, Eye and Ear Theatre, N.Y.C.; poet-in-residence with Bob Dylan's Rolling Thunder Rev.; dir. Naropa Study Abroad in Bali, Indonesia, 1998; guest dir. Schule fur Dichtung, Vienna, 1999. Author: (poetry) On the Wing, 1968, O My Life, 1969, Baby Breakdown, 1970, Giant Night, 1970, No Hassles, 1971, Life Notes, 1973, Fast Speaking Woman, 1975, Journals and Dreams, 1976, Shaman, 1977, Countries, 1980, Cabin, 1981, First Baby Poems, 1982, Makeup on Empty Space, 1983, Invention, 1986, Skin Meat Bones, 1986, The Romance Thing, 1987, Blue Mosque, 1988, Helping the Dreamer: New and Selected Poems, 1989, Not a Male Pseudonym, 1990, Lokapala, 1991, Troubairitz, 1993, Iovis: All is Full of Jove, 1993, Kill or Cure, 1994, Iovis II, 1997; editor: Nice To See You: Homage to Ted Berrigan, 1991, The Beat Book, 1996, (anthologies) The World Anthology, 1969, Another World, 1972, Talking Poetics From Naropa Institute vol. 1, 1978, vol. 2, 1979, Out of This World, 1991, (with Andrew Schelling) Disembodied Poetics: Annals of the Jack Kerovac School, 1994, (with Anselm Hollo and Jack Collom) Polemics; translator (with Andrew Schelling) Sons & Daughters of the Buddha, 1996; publisher: anthologies Angel Hair Books, N.Y.C., Full Ct. Press, N.Y.C.; recordings: The Dial-a-Poem Poets Disconnected, Anne Waldman/John Giorno, Fast Speaking Woman, The Nova Convention, Big Ego, Uh-oh Plutonium!, 1982, Crack in My World, 1986, Assorted Singles, 1990; performance videos include Eyes in All Heads, 1990, Live at Naropa, 1991, Battle of the Bards, 1991; featured on nat. pub. radio show All Things Considered, also featured in the poetry documentary Poetry In Motion. Dir. summer writing program Naropa; organizer Surrealist, Objectivist, Feminist, Pan Am. Ecology, Performance Confs., and The Robert Creeley Symposium. Recipient Dylan Thomas Meml. award New Sch., N.Y.C., 1967, Blue Ribbon Am. Film Festival, Nat. Literary Anthology award, 1970; named Heavyweight Champion Poet, 1989, 90; Cultural Artists Program grantee, 1976-77; NEA grantee, 1979-80; recipient Shelley Meml. award, 1996. Mem. PEN Club, Amnesty Internat. Office: c/o Naropa Inst 2130 Arapahoe Ave Boulder CO 80302-6602

WALDO, ANNA LEE, retired science educator, writer; b. Great Falls, Mont., Feb. 16, 1925; d. Lee William Van Artsdale and Cecelia Anna Prayzek; m. Willis Henry Waldo; children: Judith Ann, Sara Kendall, Dale Frederick, Patricia Gwyn, Richard Kirk. BS in Chemistry, Mont. State Coll., 1946; MS in Organic Chemistry, U. Md., 1949. Biochemistry instr. U. Dayton, Ohio, 1950—55, Mercy Coll., Frontenac, Mo., 1964—73; sci. instr. St. Louis C.C.-Meramec, Kirkwood, Mo., 1975—85, Calif. Poly. Tech. U., San Luis Obispo, 1995—97. Author: Sacajawea, 1979, rev. edit., 1984, Prairie, 1986, Circle of Stones, 1999, Circle of Stars, 2001; contbr. articles to profl. jours. Recipient L. White Quest award for writing, Women of the Globe Dem. newspaper, 1980, Woman of Distinction award, AAUW, 2001. Mem.: Authors Guild, Alpha Chi Sigma. Republican. Home: 49 Los Palos Dr San Luis Obispo CA 93401 7725

WALDO, SUSAN LAUDERDALE, psychologist; b. Ft. Leonard Wood, Mo., Jan. 30, 1960; d. William Roy and Alvey Patricia Lauderdale; m. James P. Waldo, Dec. 18, 1982; children: Adrienne, Jay, Bethany, Claire, Brandan. BS in Psychology, Tex. A&M U., 1982, MEd in Elem. Edn., U. Houston, 1986; PhD in Edn. and Counseling Psychology, U. Mo., 1995. Lic. psychologist Mo. Pscyhol. resident Dr. Gary C. Kitto & Assocs., Sedalia, Mo., 1995—96, Psychol. Cons. Sedalia, 1996—97, psychologist, 1997—2000, Sedalia Psychol. Svcs., 2000—. Bd. dirs. Child Safe, Sedalia, 1998—, Salvation Army, Sedalia, 2000—, Pettis County Cmty. Partnership, Sedalia, 2000—; mem. Sedalia Critical Incident Stress Debriefing Team, 1998—; founding mem. Teen Pregnancy Prevention Coalition, Sedalia, 2001—03. Mem.: APA, Mo. Assn. Play Therapists. Republican. Avocation: theater. Home: 524 S Grand Ave Sedalia MO 65301 Office: Sedalia Psychol Svcs 103 E 4th Ste 201 Sedalia MO 65301

WALDRON, ALLENE, insurance group executive; b. Jamestown, N.Y., Apr. 27, 1944; d. Sheridan Travers and Frances Marian Buck; m. Alton Guy Waldron, Sept. 8, 1962; children: Kimberly A. Kinnear, Tammy M., Robert A., Dan A. Grad., Edinboro (Pa.) U. Cert. in gen. ins. Assembler Elgin Electronics, Waterford, Pa., 1969-70, insp., 1972-75, Cherry Hill Ethan Allen, Union City, Pa., 1976-81; demonstrator Stanley HomePro, Waterford, 1981-82; mail clk. Erie (Pa.) Ins. Group, 1982-83, customer svc. rep., 1983-90, endorsement specialist, 1990—. Chair parish Asbury United Meth. Ch., 1991-93, chair adminstrv. coun., 1993-95. Mem. Nat. Assn. Ins. Women (CPIW), Order Eastern Star (worthy matron), Order of Amaranth (royal matron, royal patron, dist. dep.). Democrat. Avocations: piano, crocheting, knitting, reading, clown. Home: 136 E 1st St Waterford PA 16441-9711 Office: Erie Ins Group 100 Erie Insurance Pl Erie PA 16530-0001

WALDRON, ANN W. writer; b. Birmingham, Dec. 14, 1924; d. Earl Watson and Elizabeth (Roberts) Wood; m. Martin Waldron (dec.); children: Peter, Thomas William, Martin III, Laura O'Brien. AB, U. Ala., 1945. Reporter Atlanta Constitution, 1945-47; reporter, columnist Tampa Tribune, Fla., 1957-60, St. Petersburg Times, Fla., 1960-65; book editor Houston Chronicle, 1970-75; editor Princeton (N.J.) U., 1978-89. Author: (books) The House on Pendleton Block, 1975, The Integration of Mary Larkin Thornhill, 1975 (Notable Book of the ALA, Best Book of the Child Study Assn.), The Luckie Star, 1977, Scaredy Cat, 1978, The French Detection, 1979 (Notable Book for Social Studies, Children's Book Coun.), The Blueberry Collection, 1981, True or False? The Detection of Art Forgeries, 1983, Close Connections: Caroline Gordon and the Southern Renaissance, 1987 (Nonfiction award Ala. Libr. Assn.), Claude Monet, 1991, Francisco Goya, 1992, Hodding Carter: The Reconstruction of a Racist, 1993, Eudora: A Writer's Life, 1998, The Princeton Murders, 2003, Death of a Princeton President, 2004.

WALDRON, KAREN, company executive; m. Shawn Ricci. Chairperson/sr. v.p. F&W Mgmt.; pres. Bent Tree Farm Ltd., The Ctr. at Walnut Grove; chairperson, CEO Fralin and Waldron, Inc., Roanoke, Va. Mem. bd. visitors Radford U.; mem. exec. bd. Roanoke Valley Horse Show; pub. bd. dirs., chair Va. Horse Ctr. Avocations: horse industry, Pilates instruction, yoga, dance. Office: Fralin and Waldron Inc Ste 200 PO Box 24018 3130 Chaparral Dr Roanoke VA 24018

WALDROP, ROSMARIE, writer; b. Kitzingen, Germany, Aug. 24, 1935; arrived in U.S., 1958; d. Josef and Friederike Sebald; m. Keith Waldrop, Jan. 20, 1959. Student, U. Wurzburg, 1954—56, U. Freiburg, 1957—58; MA, U. Mich., 1960, PhD, 1966. Asst. prof. Wesleyan U., 1964—70. Vis. writer Southeastern Mass. U., 1977; vis. lectr. Tufts U., 1979—81; vis. assoc. prof. Brown U., 1977—78, 1983, 97. Author: The Hanky of Pippin's Daughter, 1987, Reluctant Gravities, 1999, A Form of Taking It All, 2001, Blindsight, 2003, translator books and poems. Recipient Writer's award, Lila Wallace Readers Digest, N.Y.C., 1999—2002; fellow, NEA, 1994; grantee, Found. for Contemporary Performance Arts, 2003; scholar, Brown U. Mem.: PEN. Home: 71 Elmgrove Ave Providence RI 02906

WALDSTEIN, GAIL P. pediatric pathologist, writer; b. Bklyn., Apr. 9, 1942; d. Milton Herman Waldstein and Dorothea Schlegel; m. Mark Levine, June 1965 (div. Jan. 1976); children: Sarah Levine, Samantha Levine, Saul Levine; m. Bruce Hansen, Apr. 1990 (div. Sept. 1992). BA, Douglass Coll., 1964; MD, Temple U., 1968. Pediatric intern Univ. Colo. Hlth. Sci. Ctr., 1968—69, residency in path., 1971—72; residency in pediatric path. The Children's Hosp., Denver, 1969—72, assoc. pediat. pathologist, 1973—92; pediat. pathologist Toledo Hosp., 1993—95, Childrens Hosp. Mich., Detroit, 1995—97; part-time pediat. pathologist Presbyn. Med. Ctr., Denver, 1997—2001. Asst./assoc. prof. U. Colo. Sch. Medicine, Denver, 1973—92; assoc. pathologist Wayne State Med. Sch., Detroit, 1995—97; chair credentials com. Children's Hosp., Denver, 1982—90. Author poems, essays, short stories, novels. Fellow, Rocky Mountain Women's Inst., 1997—98, Colo. Coun. Arts, 2001, Helene Wurlitzer Found., 2002. Mem.: Colo. Author's League. Home: 180 Cook St #308 Denver CO 80206

WALDT, RISA, therapist, artist, educator; b. Tucson, Dec. 29, 1951; d. Carl J. W. and Jane D. S.. BA in Fine Arts, U. Ariz., 1973. Cert. Am. Soc. Experiential Therapists. Art therapist Miraflores ADL Facility, Tucson, 1993-94, Sierra Tucson Art Therapist, 1993-94; cons. and presenter in field. Author, artist: A Story of Being, Grand Canyon, A River Trip, others; featured in Artists of Arizona, Vol. I and II; one-woman shows include Rancho Linda Vista Gallery, others, 1973-; group shows include Tucson Mus. of Art, Rosequist Gallery, Tucson's Mountain Oyster Club. Facilitator Cir. of Friends--Job Corps, Tucson Mem.: Santa Cruz Valley Art Assn., So. Ariz. Watercolor Guild (pres. 2003—04), Ariz. Watercolor Soc., Nat. League Am. Pen Women, Nat. Watercolor Soc., Nat. Mus. Women in Arts, Am. Watercolor Soc., Sweat Lodge. Episcopalian. Home: PO Box 41625 Tucson AZ 85717-1625

WALENSKY, DOROTHY CHARLOTTE, language educator; b. N.Y.C., Mar. 23, 1941; d. Oliver L. and Henny T. (Schlesinger) Marton; m. Ernest Leonard Walensky, Aug. 17, 1968; 1 child. BA, Adelphi U., 1962; MA in Spanish, Middlebury Coll. and U. Madrid, 1963; MA in Teaching, Fairleigh Dickinson U., 1966. Bilingual sec. internat. div. Turner Jones Co., Inc., N.Y.C., 1963-64; prof. Spanish and German, Fairleigh Dickinson U., Teaneck, N.J., 1965—. Mem.: MLA, AAUP, Am. Assn. Tchrs. German, Am. Assn. Tchrs. Spanish and Portuguese, Delta Phi Alpha, Sigma Delta Pi. Avocations: travel, photography, stamp collector, tennis, ice skating. Office: Fairleigh Dickinson U 1000 River Rd Teaneck NJ 07666-1996

WALENTIK, CORINNE ANNE, pediatrician; b. Rockville Centre, N.Y., Nov. 24, 1949; d. Edward Robert and Evelyn Mary (Brinskele) Finno; m. David Stephen Walentik, June 24, 1972; children: Anne, Stephen, Kristine. AB with honors, St. Louis U., 1970, MD, 1974, MPH, 1992. Diplomate Am. Bd. Pediat., Am. Bd. Neonatal and Perinatal Medicine, cert. physician exec. Certifying Commn. on Med. Mgmt., Am. Coll. Physician Execs. Resident in pediat. St. Louis U. Group Hosps., 1974-76, fellow in neonatalogy, 1976-78; neonatalogist St. Mary's Health Ctr., St. Louis, 1978-79; from co-dir. to dir. neonatal unit St. Louis City Hosps., 1979-85; dir. neonatalogy St. Louis Regional Med. Ctr., 1985-96; asst. prof. pediat. St. Louis U., 1980-94, assoc. clin. prof., 1994-98, assoc. prof. pediat., 1998—2001, prof. pediat., 2001—. Supr. nursery follow-up program Cardinal Glennon Children's Hosp., St. Louis, 1979—, neonatologist, physician exec. for managed care and pub. policy, 1997—; chair provider svcs. adv. bd. St. Louis Regional Health Commn. Contbr. articles to profl. jours. Mem. adv. com. Mo. Perinatal Program., 1983-86; vice chair cmty. adv. bd. Mo. Found. for Health. Fellow: Am. Acad. Pediat. (pres.-elect Mo. chpt.), mem.: APHA, St. Louis Met. Med. Soc., Mo. State Med. Assn., Nat. Perinatal Assn. (coun. 1984—87), Mo. Perinatal Assn. (pres. 1983), Mo. Pub. Health Assn. (pres. St. Louis chpt. 1995—96). Roman Catholic. Avocations: bridge, baseball, sports. Home: 7234 Princeton Ave Saint Louis MO 63130-3027 Office: Cardinal Glennon Children's Hosp 1465 S Grand Blvd Saint Louis MO 63104-1003 Office Phone: 314-577-5612. E-mail: walentca@slu.edu.

WALHOUT, JUSTINE SIMON, chemistry educator; b. Aberdeen, S.D., Dec. 11, 1930; d. Otto August and Mabel Ida (Tews) S.; m. Donald Walhout, Feb. 1, 1958; children: Mark, Timothy, Lynne, Peter. BS, Wheaton Coll., 1952; PhD, Northwestern U., 1956. Instr. Wright City Community Coll., Chgo., 1955-56, asst. prof. Rockford (Ill.) Coll., 1956-59, assoc. prof., 1959-66, 81-89, prof., 1989-96, prof. emeritus, 1996—, dept. chmn., 1987-95; cons. Pierce Chem. Co., Rockford, 1968-69; trustee Rockford (Ill.) Coll., 1987-91. Contbr. articles to profl. jours. Mem. Ill. Bd. Edn., 1974-81. Mem. AAUW (Ill. bd. dirs. 1985-87), Am. Chem. Soc. (councilor 1993-99), Rockford LWV (bd. dirs. 1983-85, 2002-04), Sigma Xi. Presbyterian. Home: 320 N Rockford Ave Rockford IL 61107-4547 Office: Rockford Coll 5050 E State St Rockford IL 61108-2311

WALKER, ALICE, writer; b. Eatonton, Ga., Feb. 9, 1944; d. Willie Lee and Minnie (Grant) W.; m. Melvyn R. Leventhal, Mar. 17, 1967 (div. 1976); 1 dau., Rebecca Walker Leventhal. BA, Sarah Lawrence Coll., 1966; PhD (hon.), Russell Sage U., 1972; DHL (hon.), U. Mass., 1983. Co-founder, pub. Wild Trees Pr., Navarro, Calif., 1984-88. Writer in residence, tchr. black studies Jackson State Coll., 1968-69, Tougaloo Coll., 1970-71; lectr. literature Wellesley Coll., 1972-73, U. Mass., Boston, 1972-73; disting. writer Afro-American studies dept. U. Calif., Berkeley, 1982; Fannie Hurst Prof. of Literature Brandeis U., Waltham, Mass., 1982; cons. Friends of the Children of Miss., 1967. Author: Once, 1968, The Third Life of Grange Copeland, 1970, Five Poems, 1972, Revolutionary Petunias and Other Poems, 1973 (Nat. Book award nomination 1973, Lillian Smith award So. Regional Coun. 1973), In Love and Trouble, 1973 (Richard and Hinda Rosenthal Found. award Am. Acad. and Inst. of Arts and Letters 1974) Langston Hughes: American Poet, 1973, Meridian, 1976, Goodnight, Willie Lee, I'll See You in the Morning, 1979, You Can't Keep a Good Woman Down, 1981, The Color Purple, 1982 (Nat. Book Critics Circle award nomination 1982, Pulitzer Prize for fiction 1983, Am. Book award 1983), In Search of Our Mothers' Gardens, 1983, Horses Make a Landscape Look More Beautiful, 1984, To Hell With Dying, 1988, Living By the Word: Selected Writings, 1973-1987, 1988, The Temple of My Familiar, 1989, Her Blue Body Everything We Know: Earthling Poems, 1965-1990, 1991, Finding the Green Stone, 1991, Possessing the Secret of Joy, 1992, (with Pratibha Parmar) Warrior Marks, 1993, (with others) Double Stitch: Black Women Write About Mothers & Daughters, 1993, Everyday Use, 1994, Alice Walker Banned: The Banned Works, 1996, Everything We Love Can Be Saved: A Writer's Activism: Essays, Speeches, Statements and Letters, 1997, The Same River Twice, 1997; editor: I Love Myself When I'm Laughing... And Then Again When I'm Looking Mean and Impressive, 1979, By The Light of My Father's Smile, 1998, The Way Forward is With a Broken Heart, 2000, Absolute Trust in the Goddess of the Earth: New Poems, 2003. Recipient first prize Am. Scholar essay contest, 1967, O. Henry award for Kindred Spirits, 1986, Nora Astorga Leadership award, 1989, Fred Cody award for lifetime achievement Bay Area Book Reviewers Assn., 1990, Freedom to Write award PEN Ctr. USA West, 1990; Bread Loaf Writer's Conf. scholar, 1966; Merrill writing fellowship, 1967; McDowell Colony fellowship, 1967, 77-78; National Endowment for the Arts grantee, 1969, 77; Radcliffe Inst. fellowship, 1971-73; Guggenheim fellow, 1977-78. Address: Random House Inc 1745 Broadway #B1 New York NY 10019-4305

WALKER, ALICE R. mechanical engineer; b. Jackson, Wyo., May 19, 1965; d. Robert and Rosemary McIntosh; m. Kyle Walker; 2 children. BSME, U. Nev., 1991. Mech. engr. REECo., Las Vegas, 1991-92; sr. prodn. engr. Tyler Refrigeration MSD, Waxahachie, Tex., 1993-97; mech. engr. Sys. Engrng. & Labs., Tyler, Tex., 1997-2000; product engr. Carrier Corp., Tyler, Tex., 2000—. Registered engr. in tng. Mem. ASME (student v.p. 1990-91, 1st pl. speaking award 1991), Nat. Soc. Profl. Engrs. (assoc., pres.), Tex. Soc. Profl. Engrs. Avocations: horseback riding, camping, snow skiing, restoring classic pick-up, softball. Office: Carrier Corp 1700 E Duncan St Tyler TX 75702-2430

WALKER, AMY MELISSA, English as second language educator; b. Oct. 17, 1965; Student, U. Madrid, 1985-86; BA in Spanish, Elmira Coll., 1987; MS in Fgn. Lang. Edn., Syracuse U., 1989, MA in Linguistics, 1995. Tchr. Syracuse (N.Y.) City Sch. Dist., 1989-90; instr. English Lang. Inst., Syracuse U., 1990—. Sales assoc. Kaufmann's; beauty cons. Mary Kay Cosmetics. Photography exhibits at The Cmty. Folk Art Gallery, Syracuse, N.Y., 1998, Syracuse U. Cmty. Darkrooms Mems. Show, 1999. Mem. adult edn. com. May Meml. Unitarian Universalist Soc., Syracuse, 1993-99, mem. min.'s adv. com., 1995-96, mem. denominational affairs com., 1997-98. Mem. TESOL. Avocations: photography, writing, asian indian, middle eastern and african cooking, reading. Office: Syracuse U English Lang Inst 700 University Ave Syracuse NY 13210-1719

WALKER, ANNETTE, retired counseling administrator; b. Birmingham, Ala., Sept. 20, 1953; d. Jesse and Luegene (Wright) W. BS in Edn., Huntingdon Coll., 1974; MS in Adminstrn. and Supervision, Troy State U., 1977, 78, MS in Sch. Counseling, 1990, AA in Sch. Adminstrn., 1992; diploma, World Travel Sch., 1990; diploma in Cosmetology, John Patterson Coll., 1992; MEd in higher Edn. Adminstrn., Auburn (Ala.) U., 1995. Cert. tchr., adminstr., Ala.; lic. cosmetologist, Ala.; lic. funeral dir., Ala. Tchr. Montgomery (Ala.) Pub. Sch. System, 1976-89, sch. counselor, 1989—2000; lit. tchr. Fed. Bur. of Justice, 1997—2000; ret., 2000; acad. advisor Cmty. Coll. of Air Force; acad. counselor Maxwell Air Force Base, Ala. Tchr. Fed. Govt., 1997—, U.S. Bur. Justice, 1997—; gymnastics tchr. Cleveland Ave. YMCA, 1971-76; girls coach Montgomery Parks and Recreation, 1973-76; summer sch. sci. tchr. grades 7-9, 1977-88; chmn. dept. sci. Bellingrath Sch., 1987-90, courtesy com., 1987-88, sch. discipline com., 1977-84; recreation asst. Gunter AFB, Ala., 1981-83; calligraphy tchr. Gunter Youth Ctr., 1982; program dir. Maxwell AFB, Ala., 1983-89, vol. tchr. Internat. Officer Sch., 1985—, Adult Laubach Reading Prog., Ala. Goodwill Amb., 1985—, day camp dir., 1987, calligraphy tchr., 1988; trainer internat. law for sec. students, Ala., 1995—; leader of workshops in field; sales rep. Ala. World Travel, 1990—; behavior aid Brantwood Children's Home, 1996—; computer tchr. hs diploma program Montgomery County Sch., 1995—; behavior aide Brantwood Children's Home, 1995—; hotel auditor, 1995—; Am. del. to China, People to People Internat., 1998; acad. advisor C.C. of Air Force, Maxwell AFB, Ala., 2002—. Mem. CAP; tchr. Sunday sch. Beulah Bapt. Ch., Montgomery; vol. zoo activities Tech. Scholarship Program for Ala. Tchrs. Computer Courses, Montgomery, Ala.; bd. dirs. Cleveland Ave. YMCA, 1976-80; sponsor Bell-Howe chpt. Young Astronauts, 1986-90, Pate Howe chpt. Young Astronauts, 1991-92; judge Montgomery County Children Festival Elem. Sci. Fair, 1988-90; bd. dirs. Troy State U. Drug Free Schs., 1992—; chmn. Maxwell AFB Red Cross-Youth, 1986-88; goodwill amb. sponsor to various families (award 1989, 95); State of Ala. rep. P.A.T.C.H.-Internat. Law Inst., 1995; bd. dirs. People to People Internat., 2000. Named Tchr. of the Week, WCOV-TV, 1992, Ala. Tchr. in Space Program, summer, 1989, Local Coord. Young Astronaut Program, 1988, Citizen Amb. to China, People to People Internat., 1999; recipient Outstanding High Sch. Sci./Math. Tchr. award, Sigma Xi, 1989, Most Outstanding Youth Coun. Leader award, Maxwell AFB Youth Ctr., 1987, Outstanding Ala. Goodwill Amb. award, 1989, 1995, Tchr. of Yr. award, Paterson Sch., 1990, Career Infusion award (Most Appreciated Tchr. award), 1987, Montgomery Pub. Sch., 1982, 1984, Earthwatch Ednl. award, Israel, 1997, 20 Class award, Maxwell AFB Internat. Fgn. Officer Program, 25 Class award, 2003; Fulbright scholar, Japan, 1999. Mem. NEA, Internat. Platform Assn., People to People Internat. (founder, bd. trustees, organizer, pres. Ala. chpt. 1998), Nat. Sci. Tchrs. Assn., Ala. Sch. Counselors, Montgomery Sch. Counselors Assn., Montgomery County Ednl. Assn., Space Camp Amb., Huntingdon Alumni Assn. (sec.-treas.), Ala. Goodwill Amb., Montgomery Capital City Club, Young Astronauts, Ea. Star, Japan Friends of Fulbright Meml. Fund Tchr. Prog., Water Watch, Montgomery, AL, Zeta Phi Beta, Chi Delta Phi, Kappa Pi. Avocations: international travel, calligraphy, international food, cruising. Home: 2301 Westwood Dr Montgomery AL 36108 E-mail: awalker2001@yahoo.com.

WALKER, BERNICE BAKER, artist; b. Carbondale, Pa., Dec. 23, 1928; d. William Robert and Bernice Mary (Parry) Baker; m. Joseph Henry Walker, Sept. 13, 1952. Student, Richmond Profl. Inst., 1946-47; BFA, R.I. Sch. Design, 1952. Artist Highlights for Children, 1952-55, Studio K, Lancaster, Pa., 1959-64; tchr. Heintzelman Art Assn., Manheim, Pa., 1975-86; owner The Design Corner, Lancaster, 1989—2003. Tchr. Lancaster County Art Assn. Mem. Pa. Watercolor Soc., Lancaster Spinners & Weavers, Lancaster County Art Assn., Mid Atlantic Weavers, Village Art Assn., Lancaster Camera Club. Avocations: spinning, natural dyeing, reading, photography, bridge.

WALKER, BETSY ELLEN, consulting and systems integration company executive; b. Atlanta, Sept. 14, 1953; d. John Franklin and Betty Louise (Brown) W.; children: William Franklin, Samuel Elliott. BA summa cum laude, Duke U., 1974; MBA, Harvard U., 1978. Mgmt. trainee First Atlanta, 1974, officer, 1975-76; analyst Coca Cola, Atlanta, 1977; bus. analyst Am. Mgmt. Systems Inc., N.Y.C., 1978-80, prin., 1981, v.p., 1982-99, dir. fin. svcs. group, 1982-90, IBM Svcs. sector group, 1990-92, fin. strategic initiatives group, 1993; dir. fin. industry Strategic Alliance Group, 1994-96, area dep. dir. fin. industry groups, 1996-97; COO, bd. dirs. Security First Network Bank, Atlanta, 1999. Mem. mgmt. policy com. Am. Mgmt. Systems, 1988-99, mem. corp. operating group; pres. B.E. Walker Assoc., Inc., 1999-2003. J. Spencer Love fellow Harvard U., 1976-78. Mem. Alexandria North Ridge Citizens Assn. (exec. bd. 1994-96), Harvard Bus. Sch. Club (bd. mgrs. Madison Green 1990-91, treas.), Phi Beta Kappa, Pi Mu Epsilon. E-mail: bewalker@mindspring.com.

WALKER, BETTE, automotive executive; BS in Bus. Mgmt., U. NH; student, Bosotn U. Tech. dir. Latin Am. Digital Equip. Corp.; IT exec. auto. sector safety restraint sys. AlliedSignal, Inc.; v.p., CIO Delphi Corp., Troy, Mich., 1997—. Office: World Hdqrs 5725 Delphi Dr Troy MI 48098-2815*

WALKER, BRIGITTE MARIA, translator, linguistic consultant; b. Stolp, Germany, Sept. 20, 1934; came to U.S., 1957; d. Joseph Karl and Ursula Maria Margot Ehrler; m. John V. Kelley (div.); 1 child, John V. Jr.; m. Edward D. Walker, July 3, 1977. Grad., Erlangen Translator's Sch., Germany, 1956; grad. fgn. corres., Berlitz Sch., Germany, 1956. Bilingual sec., translator Spencer Patent Law Office, Washington, 1959-62; office mgr., translator I. William Millen, Millen and White, Patent Law, Washington, 1962-67; prin. Tech. Translating Bur., Washington, 1967-68, St. Petersburg Beach, Fla., 1968—. Cons. for patent law offices, Washington, 1962—; ofcl. expert for ct. Paul M. Craig, Patent Atty., Rockford, Ill., 1981; cons. to sci. editor Merriam-Webster, Inc., Springfield, Mass., 1987—. Author: German-English/English-German Last-Resort Dictionary for Technical Translators, 1991, (poetry) The Other Side of the Mirror, 1992 (Poetry award Nat. League Am. Pen Women 1994); co-translator: The Many Faces of Research, 1980; holder of trademark in field. Evaluator fgn. textbooks Pinellas County Sch. Bd., St. Petersburg, 1987, German judge, 1988. Recipient Recogninition award Pinellas County Sch. Bd., 1988, Meritorious Pub. Svc. award City of St. Petersburg Beach, 1987, poetry award Nat. League Am. Pen Women, 1994, 99, 2000, essay award, 1996, short story award, 1997, Grand prize for poem DDDD Publs., 1998. Mem. Mensa (Winner Nat. award Best Fiction 1996). Democrat. Lutheran. Avocations: swimming, aerobics, piano, painting. Home: Pasadena Apts #428 1885 Shore Dr S Saint Petersburg FL 33707-4746

WALKER, CARLENE MARTIN, state senator; BS, Brigham Young U., 1969. Supr. coding & data entry the Wirthlin Group, 1982-86; cons. D.K. Shifflet & Assocs., 1987-88; ptnr., mgr. Covecrest Properties, 1978-99; dir. adminstrn. Energy Lock, Inc., 1992-99; tech. recruiter Manpower Tech., 1999-2000; mem. Utah State Senate, Salt Lake City, 2001—. Cons. Wash. Times Newspaper, 1987-88. Bd., chair fundraising com. Granite Edn. Found., 1989-90; chmn., founder of the bd. Repub. Womens Political Action Com. Office: 4085 E Prospector Dr Salt Lake City UT 84121

WALKER, CAROLYN MAE, secondary school educator; b. Neptune, N.J., Apr. 29, 1941; d. Frank and Estella (Matutis) W. BA in Sci., Montclair State Coll., 1963; MA in Edn., Newark State Coll., 1970. Cert. tchr., N.J. Elem. tchr. Howell (N.J.) Twp. Bd. Edn., 1963-65, Englishtown (N.J.)-Manalapan Regional Schs., 1965-67, Freehold (N.J.) Borough Schs.,

1967-70, Freehold Regional H.S., 1970-73, North Brunswick (N.J.) Twp. Bd. Edn., 1975—. Mem. NSTA, N.J. Sci. Tchrs. Assn., N.J. Schoolwomen's Club, Alpha Delta Kappa (chair pres. 1972-74, state sec. 1974-76, state v.p. 1976-78). Roman Catholic. Avocations: cruising, dressmaking, needlework, gardening, classical/popular music. Office: North Brunswick Twp HS Raider Rd North Brunswick NJ 08902 E-mail: caramwalker@juno.com.

WALKER, CAROLYN PEYTON, English language educator; b. Charlottesville, Va., Sept. 15, 1942; d. Clay M. and Ruth Peyton. BA with distinction in Am. History/Lit., Sweet Briar Coll., 1965; cert. in French, Alliance Francaise, Paris, 1966; EdM, Tufts U., 1970; MA in Englisn and Am. Lit, Stanford U., 1974, PhD in English Edn., 1977. Tchr. elem. and jr. h.s., Switzerland, 1967-69; tchr. elem. grades Boston Sch. System, 1966-67, 69-70, Newark (Calif) Unified Sch. System, 1970-72; instr. divsn. Humanities Canada Coll., Redwood City, Calif., 1973, 76-78; instr. Sch. Bus. U. San Francisco, 1973-74; evaluation cons. Inst. Profl. Devel., San Jose, Calif., 1975-76; asst. dir. Stanford U. Learning Assistance Ctr., Calif., 1972—77, dir., 1977—84, supr. counselors, tutors and tchrs., 1972-84; lectr., dept. English Stanford U., 1977-84; lectr. Stanford U. Sch. Edn., 1975-84; pvt. practice corp. tng., 1983—; mem. faculty U. Calif., Santa Cruz, Berkeley, 1995—; prof. dept. English San Jose State U., 1984-93, dir. The Writing Ctr. dept. English, 1986—93, dir. Steinbeck Rsch. Ctr., 1986—87; cons. Advanced Micro Devices, Calif., 1996, CellNet Data Sys., 1996—98, Fujitsu, 1997, Proxim, 1997—98, AMP, 1997—98, Tech. Comm. Internat., 1997—2002, Inovant, Inc., 1999, VISA Internat., 1999—, Sun Microsystems, 2002. Condr. reading and writing workshops, 1972-1994; reviewer Random House Books, 1978-95, Rsch. in the Teaching of English, 1983-95, Course Tech., Inc., 1990; cons. Basic Skills Task Force, U.S. Office Edn., 1977-79, Right to Read, Calif. State Dept. Edn., 1977-85, Program for Gifted and Talented, Fremont (Calif). Unified Sch. Dist., 1981-82; bd. dirs. The Tech Mus. of Innovation, San Jose, 1983-84; head cons. to pres. to evaluate college's writing program, San Jose City Coll., 1985-87, cons. U. Texas, Dallas, 1984; cons. DeAnza Coll., 2000-01; cons. Stanford U., 1977-78, 84; cons., CCNY, 1979, U. Wis., 1980; numerous testing programs; cons. to pres. San Diego State U., 1982; Ednl. Testing Svc., 1985-88; English dept. Writing Ctr., 1986-93; spkr. numerous profl. confs.; cons. in field. Author: Handbook for Teaching Assistants at Stanford University, 1977, Learning Center Courses for Faculty and Staff: Reading, Writing, and Time Management, 1981, How to Succeed as a New Teacher: A Handbook for Teaching Assistants, 1978, ESL Courses for Faculty & Staff: An Additional Opportunity to Serve the Campus Community, 1983, (with Karen Wilson) Tutor Handbook for the Writing Center at San Jose State University, 1989, (with others) Academic Tutoring at the Learning Assistance Center, 1980, Writing Conference Talk: Factors Associated with HIgh and Low Rated Writing Conferences, 1987, Lifeline Mac: A Handbook for Instructors in the Macintosh Computer Classrooms, 1989, Communications with the Faculty: Vital Links for the Success of Writing Centers, 1991, Coming to America, 1993, Teacher Dominance in the Writing Conference, 1992, Instant Curriculum: Just Add Tutors and Students, 1993; editor newsletter Environ. Vols. Inc., Palo Alto, Calif., 1999-2003; contbr. chpts. to Black American Literature Forum, 1991; contbr. articles to profl. jours. Founding mem. Tech. Mus. of Innovation, San Jose, Calif., 1995; vol. fundraiser Peninsula Ctr. for the Blind, Palo Alto, Calif., 1982—2001, The Resource Ctr. for Women, Palo Alto, 1975—76, Pathways Hospice, 2002—; vol. Gamble Garden Ctr., 1989—. Recipient Award for Outstanding Contbns., U.S. HEW, 1979, award ASPPIRE (federally funded program), 1985, two awards Student Affirmative Action, 1986, award Western Coll. Reading & Leanring Assn., 1984, founding mem. Tech Museum of Innovation, 1995; numerous other awards and grants. Home: 2350 Waverley St Palo Alto CA 94301-4143

WALKER, DEBORAH SUE, nurse midwife, educator; b. Chillicothe, Ohio, Apr. 15, 1955; d. Wilbur Lee and Mary Anna W. ADN, San Joaquin Delta Coll., 1978; BSN, Sonoma State U., 1981; MS, U. Minn., 1989; DNSc, UCLA, 1994. RN, Calif., Hawaii, Mich; cert. nurse-midwife, ACNM, ob.-gyn. nurse practitioner NCC, FNP, ANSC. Nurse Scripps Meml. Hosp., LaJolla, Calif., 1978-79, Sonoma County Community Hosp., Santa Rosa, Calif., 1979-81; FNP Sonoma County Indian Health Project, Santa Rosa, Calif., 1981-83; ob.-gyn. nurse practitioner Kaiser Permanente, Honolulu, 1983-88, nurse mid-wife Bellflower, Calif., 1989-91; asst. clin. prof. Coll. of Medicine dept. ob-gyn U. Calif., Irvine, 1991—94; asst. prof. U. Missouri, 1994—96, U. Mich., 1996—2003; assoc. prof. Wayne State U. Coll. Nursing & OB/GYN, 2003—. Mem. ANA (cert.), AMA, ACOG, Am. Coll. Nurse Midwives (cert.), Calif. Coalition Nurse Practitioners, Sigma Theta Tau. Avocations: skiing, community theatre, golf. Office: Wayne State Univ Coll Nursing 5557 Cass Ave Detroit MI 48202 E-mail: dswalker@wayne.edu.

WALKER, HELEN SMITH, retired real estate broker; b. Grovania, Ga., Jan. 29, 1917; d. George Washington and Mattie (Ellis) Smith; m. James Lee Walker, Apr. 21, 1946; 1 child, James Kenneth. Student, Ga. Wesleyan Coll., 1934-35, U. Ga., 1935-36, Wesleyan Conservatory, 1936-37. Sales rep. Thornton Realty Co., Macon, Ga., 1959-68; owner, operator Klondike Farms, Houston County, Ga., 1960—; co-owner, v.p. Warno Corp., Macon, 1964-69; v.p. O'Neal-Willingham Realty, Macon, 1968-71; assoc. broker Fickling & Walker Realty, Macon, 1971-77; pres., co-owner Hibble, Walker & Douglas, Macon, 1977-82; assoc. broker Fickling & Walker, Macon, 1982-91; ret. Tchr. primary tng. Union Bapt. Ch., 1950-65; mem. Make Am. Better Commn., 1971; group capt. Am. Cancer Crusale, 1978; active Ga. Trust for Hist. Preservation, Macon Hist. Soc., Macon Symphony. Mem. Am. Forestry Assn., Wesleyan Alumnae Club (awards com. 1988-89, 91—), Civic Woman's Club Macon. Democrat. Avocations: reading, writing poetry, gardening, music.

WALKER, JOAN H. marketing and communications executive; m. George Walker. BA, Rutgers U., New Brunswick, 1968, MA in Sociology, 1973. Sr. exec. mktg. and govt. N.J. State Govt., 1973-83; pres. Richmann & Ptnrs., 1983-88; exec. v.p. Saatchi & Saatchi, 1988-90; mng. dir. mktg. comm. NYNEX Corp., 1990-93; pres., CEO Bozell Pub. Rels., N.Y.C., 1993-96; ptnr. Bozell Sawyer Miller Group, 1996; sr. v.p. corp. comm. Ameritech, Chgo., 1996-99; sr. v.p. global pub. affairs Monsanto (merged with Pharmacia & UpJohn, now Pharmacia), Skolie, Ill., 1999—2002; exec. v.p. corp. mktg. and comm. Qwest Comm. Internat., 2002—. Dir. Qwest Found.; mem. bd. trustees Colo. Symphony Orch. Office: Qwest Comm Internat 1801 California St Denver CO 80202 E-mail: Joan.H.Walker@am.pnu.com.

WALKER, JUANITA MOFFETT, retired elementary school educator; b. Edwards, Miss., Jan. 31, 1939; d. Fred Douglas and Matlean Allen Moffett; m. Tommy Lewis, June 11, 1962; children: Tommy Jr., Edward, Roland. AA, Utica (Miss.) Jr. Coll., 1959; BA, Jackson State U., 1961; MA, Purdue U., 1995; postgrad., Black Hills State U., Spearfish, S.D., Ind. U. Cert. tchr. Miss., S.D., counselor Ind. Tchr. Burgland H.S., McComb, Miss., 1961, Oglala Cmty. H.S., Pine Ridge, SD, 1962—69, Wirt H.S., Gary, Ind., 1969—71, West Side H.S., Gary, Ind., 1971—78; counselor Pulaski Mid. Sch., Gary, Ind., 1978—82, Bailly Mid. Sch., Gary, Ind., 1982—91, Edison Mid. Sch., Gary, Ind., 1991—2001. Testing coord. Bailly and Edison Mid. Schs., 1982—95; dept. chmn. Edison Mid. Sch., 1991—2001; chmn. guidance career day Bailly Mid. Sch., 1982—90. Author: Church Folk, 2001; co-host cable TV show. Historian Gary Civic Chorale, 1980—; founder, pres. Gary Writers Workshop, 2001—; mem. Friends of Libr., Gary, 2000—. Mem.: Lake County Ret. Tchrs. Assn., Alpha Kappa Alpha. Avocations: singing, playing keyboards, travel, public speaking, reading. Home: PO Box 4286 Gary IN 46404

WALKER, JULIET, alcohol/drug abuse services professional, educator; d. Harold Green and Elaine Walker. Student, Kennedy King Coll., 1968—70, Ill. Coll. Optometry, 1970—71; BS, Bradley U., 1974; postgrad., Chgo. State U., 1975—78, Olivet Nazarene Coll., 1979—80, Roosevelt U., 1980—81. Cert. alcohol and drug abuse counselor. Substitute tchr. Chgo. Pub. Sch. Sys., 1990—93, Rock Island (Ill.) Sch. Dist., 1994—97; alcohol and drug abuse counselor Brass Found., Chgo., 2000—02, Cornell/Interventions, Chgo., 2002, Dimensions of Recovery, Chgo., 2002—03, Family Guidance Ctr., Chgo., 2003—, Specialized Assistance Svcs., Chgo., 2002—. Avocations: drawing, reading, table tennis, hiking, birdwatching. Office: Specialized Assistance Svcs 2101 S Indiana Ave Chicago IL 60616

WALKER, KARA, artist; b. Stockton, Calif., Nov. 26, 1969; BA in Painting/Printmaking, Atlanta Coll. Art, 1991; MFA in Painting/Printmaking, R.I. Sch. Design, 1994. One-woman shows include Ctr. Curaltorial Studies, Bard Coll., Annandale-on-Hudson, N.Y., 1995, Nexus Contemporary Arts Ctr., Atlanta, 1995, Wooster Gardens/Brent Sikkema, N.Y.C., 1995, 1998, Bernard Toale Gallery, Boston, 1996, Huntington Beach (Calif.) Arts Ctr., 1997, U. Chgo., 1997, Contemporary Arts Ctr., Cin., 1997, Henry Art Gallery, U. Wash., Seattle, 1997, The Carpenter Ctr., Harvard U., Cambridge, Mass., 1997, San Francisco Mus. Modern Art, 1997, The Forum, St. Louis, 1998, Vienna State Opera House, Austria, 1998, The Print Ctr., Phila., 1998, Galleri Index, Stockholm, 1998, Contemporary Arts Mus., Houston, 1999, Calif. Coll. Arts and Crafts, Oliver Art Ctr., Oakland, 1998, Brent Sikkema, N.Y., 1998, Gallery 100, Atlanta, 1991, McKinney Ave. Contemporary, Dallas, 1999, exhibited in group shows at New Visions Gallery, Atlanta, 1991, exhibited in group shows, Atlanta, 1991, exhibited in group shows, MU Gallery, Boston, 1993, exhibited in group shows, Providence, 1994, exhibited in group shows, Paul Morris Gallery, N.Y.C., 1995, Mills Gallery, Boston, Inst. Contemporary Art, 1996, Greg Kucera Gallery, Seattle, 1997, Stephen Friedman Gallery, London, 1998, Elaine L. Jacob Gallery, Wayne State U., Detroit, 1999, numerous others; author: Freedom, A Fable, A Curious Interpretation of the Wit of a Negress in Troubled Times; contbr. articles to profl. jours. Recipient John D. and Catherine T. MacArthur Found.; fellow Individual Artist's fellow, Art Matters, Inc.; scholar Presdl. scholar, Atlanta Coll. Art, Ida Blank Ocko scholar. Office: care Brent Sikkema 530 West 22d St New York NY 10011

WALKER, KATHRYN A. telecommunications industry executive; B in Civil Engring., SD State U.; MS, degree in Engring., U. Mo. Asst. v.p. human resources Sprint Tech. Svcs., 1995—97; v.p. product mgmt. Sprint Bus., 1997—2002; sr. v.p. network svcs. global Markets group Sprint Corp., 2002—03, exec. v.p. network svcs., 2003—. Office: 6200 Sprint Pkwy Overland Park KS 66251*

WALKER, LINDA LEE, lawyer; b. Phila., Jan. 24, 1954; d. M. Lorenzo and Romaine Yvonne (Smith) W.; children: Jessica Marie McIntyre, Nicole Yvonne McIntyre. BA, U. Penn., 1975; JD, Yale U., 1978. Bar: N.Y. 1979, U.S. Dist. Ct. (so. and ea. dists.) N.Y. 1982, U.S. Ct. Appeals (1st cir.) 1982; NASD. Asst. regional atty. HHS, N.Y.C., 1978-82; assoc. Shea and Gould, N.Y.C., 1982-85; v.p., sr. assoc. counsel Chase Manhattan Bank, N.A., N.Y.C., 1985-89; v.p., assoc. gen. counsel Citicorp Credit Svc., N.Y.C., 1989-97; asst. gen. counsel Prudential Ins. Co. Am., Newark, 1997-2000, v.p., chief compliance officer for Prudential Retirement, 2000—. Mem., Phi Beta Kappa. Office: Prudential Ins Co Am 200 Wood Ave S Iselin NJ 08830 E-mail: linda.walker@prudential.com.

WALKER, LORENE, retired elementary school educator; b. Clovis, N.Mex., July 27, 1911; d. Jessie H. and Tille Eula (Harlan) Black; m. Carl Westley Walker, June 9, 1934; children: Wesley, Charles. BS, N.Mex. State U., 1933; M Family Life, Cen. Wash. U., 1959, postgrad., 1956-74. Tchr. home econs. Floyd Sch., near Portales, N.Mex., 1933-34, Navajo Meth. Mission, Farmington, N.Mex., 1947-48; home agt. extension svc. Wash. State Coop. Extension Svc., Yakima, 1948-56; family life, counseling tchr. West Valley Sch., Yakima, 1956-71, spl. elem. reading tchr., 1971-75; tour organizer, leader Mission Tour, Yakima, 1966-98; trainer missioners United Meth. Ch., Yakima, Wash., 1998—. Coord. 4-H camps, fairs and programs Wash. Coop. Extension Svc., Yakima, 1950-56. Chairperson Experiment for Internat. Living, Yakima Valley Rep. Women's Club, 1960-67; docent, tour leader Yakima Valley Mus., 1976—; trustee Found. Pacific Northwest United Meth. Ch., 1984—; pres. Columbia River dist. United Meth. Ch., 1987-88, chairperson global missions, 1993-94; chair Tour With a Mission, 1966-2003. Mem. AAUW (treas. 1962-66, bd. dirs., chair internat. rels. 1962-89; spl. honor award 1989), United Meth. Women (pres. 1987-89; spl. recognition 1989), Wesleyan Svc. Guild Meth. Women. (officer 1964-68), Alpha Delta Kappa (pres. 1967-69). Avocations: gardening, travel, needlework, international political and cultural news. Home: 101 N 48th Ave Apt 25A Yakima WA 98908-3179

WALKER, LUCY DORIS, secondary school educator, writer; b. Ridgeway, NC, May 6, 1951; d. Edgerton Verl and Mary Ellen (Williams) Plummer; m. William A. Walker Jr., June 21, 1969 (div. Aug. 1974); 1 child, Lucretia Marie. BA in English Edn., Fairleigh Dickinson U., 1975; MA in Theater Arts, Montclair State U., 1977. Cert. English and theater arts tchr., N.J. Tchr., dir., actor, writer Ctr. Modern Dance Edn., Hackensack, NJ, 1978; writer, dir. Am. Theater Actors, NYC, 1978-79; tchr. multicultural hub Ctr. Internat. Studies, Cultural Events, Teaneck HS, Teaneck, NJ, 1979—; coord. Teaneck Arts Acad. at Teaneck HS, Teaneck, NJ, 2002—. Artistic dir. Teaneck H.S. dance ensemble, 1989—; program coord. African and African-Am. Studies Resource Ctr., 1990—; instructional leader for fine and performing arts, coord. Teaneck Arts Acad.. Writer and choreographer various plays, 1979-95. Recipient Acad. Achievement award Fairleigh Dickinson U. Opportunities Program, 1974, Black Heritage award Nat. Assn. Negro Bus. & Profl. Women's Clubs, 1991. Mem. NEA, NJ Edn. Assn. Democrat. Baptist. Avocations: sewing, gardening, hiking, painting, music. Home: 363 Washington Pl Englewood NJ 07631-3232 Office: Teaneck HS 100 Elizabeth Ave Teaneck NJ 07666-4713 E-mail: walkplum@aol.com.

WALKER, MARGARET SMITH, real estate company executive; b. Lancashire, Eng., Oct. 14, 1943; came to U.S., 1964; d. Arthur Edward and Doris Audrey (Dawson) Smith; m. James E. Walker, Feb. 6, 1992. Lic. real estate agt., Hawaii. Broker Lawson-Worrall Inc. (now Mary Worrall/Sotheby), Honolulu, 1974-81; pres. Maggie Parkes & Assocs., Inc., Honolulu, 1981—. Bd. dirs. Aloha State Dressage Soc., Honolulu, 2001, Hawaii Opera Theatre, 2002—, com. chmn., chmn. Opera Ball, 1997. Mem. Am. Horse Shows Assn., Hawaii Horse Shows Assn., Outrigger Canoe Club. Episcopalian. Avocations: dressage riding, horse show management. Office: PO Box 25083 Honolulu HI 96825-0083

WALKER, MARTHA YEAGER, state senator, businesswoman; b. May 15, 1940; m. H. Jarrett Walker; children: Meredyth, Brent, Melissa. BS, W.Va. U. Mem. W.Va. Ho. of Reps., Charleston, 1990-92, W.Va. Senate, Charleston, 1993—. Mem. fin. com., govt. orgn. com., health and human resources com., pensions com., rules com., enrolled bills com.; with Byrd Inst. Studies, U. Charleston. Mem. W.Va. Dem. Exec. Com., Charleston Zoning Appeals Bd., Ctr. for Econ. Options, Byrd Inst. Govt. Studies, U. Charleston; former mem. Cabin Creek Health Ctr.; former treas. Kanawha County Pvt. Industry Coun.; active Literacy Vols. W.Va.; bd. dirs. Poison Control Ctr., Cabin Creek Health Ctr., Multiple Sclerosis Soc. W.Va., W.Va. Children's Health Policy Bd., Gov.'s Cabinet on Children and Families, Regional Contracting Assistance Ctr., Charleston Capitol Market, Literacy Vols. of Am.; sustaining mem. Jr. League Charleston; treas. PIC Kanawha County. Mem. Charleston C. of C., W.Va. U. Alumni Assn., Rotary. Democrat. Presbyterian. Office: WVa Senate 1900 Kanawha Blvd E Rm 439M Charleston WV 25305-0009 also: 11 Quail Cove Rd Charleston WV 25314-1634

WALKER, MARY L. federal agency administrator, lawyer; b. Dayton, Ohio, Dec. 1, 1948; d. William Willard and Lady D. Walker; 1 child, Winston Samuel. Student, U. Calif., Irvine, 1966-68; BA in Biology/Ecology, U. Calif., Berkeley, 1970; postgrad., UCLA, 1972-73; JD, Boston U., 1973. Bar: Calif. 1973, U.S. Supreme Ct. 1979. Atty. So. Pacific Co., San Francisco, 1973-76; assoc. Richards, Watson & Gershon, L.A., 1976-78, ptnr., 1979-82; dep. asst. atty. gen. lands div. U.S. Dept. Justice, Washington, 1982-84; dep. solicitor U.S. Dept. Interior, Washington, 1984-85; asst. sec. for environment, safety and health U.S. Dept. Energy, Washington, 1985-88; spl. cons. to chmn. bd. Law Engring., Atlanta, 1988-89; v.p., West Coast and the Pacific Law Environ., Inc., San Francisco, 1989; ptnr., head environ. law dept. Richards, Watson & Gershon, San Francisco, 1989-91; ptnr. Luce, Forward, Hamilton & Scripps, San Diego, 1991-94; ptnr. and head San Diego Environ. Practice Group Brobeck, Phleger & Harrison, LLP, San Diego, 1994—2001; gen. counsel air force U.S. Dept. Defense, Washington, 2001—. U.S. commr. InterAm. Tropical Tuna Commn., 1989—95; mem. adv. bd. Floresta, Inc. Bd. dirs. Endowment for Cmty. Leadership, 1987—2000, Global Involvement Through Edn., 1998—2001. Mem. Calif. Bar Assn., San Diego Bar Assn., BIOCOM (bd. dirs. 1991-2001, pres. 1994), Profl. Women's Fellowship-San Diego (co-founder, bd. dirs. 1996-2001, pres. 1996-97), World Affairs Coun., Renaissance Women. Republican. Office: US Dept Defense Gen Counsel 1740 Air Force Pentagon Washington DC 20330-1740

WALKER, MELISSA A. historian, educator; b. Maryville, Tenn., Sept. 13, 1962; d. Guy E. and Rachel E. (Lewellyn) W. BA in History, Maryville Coll., 1985; MA in History, Providence Coll., 1993; PhD in History, Clark U., 1996. Office mgr. Maryville Coll., 1985-86, dir. alumni rels., 1986-87; assoc. dir. alumni rels. Bryant Coll., Smithfield, R.I., 1987-92, asst. dir. devel. rsch., 1992-96; asst. prof. history Converse Coll., Spartanburg, SC, 1996—2002, assoc. prof., 2002—. Adj. prof. C.C. of R.I., Providence, 1995, Bryant Coll., 1996; cons. Alumni Job Fair Consortium, Boston, 1992-94. Author: All We Know Was to Farm, 2000, Southern Women at the Millenium, 2003, Country Women Cope With Herd Times, 2003; contbr. articles to profl. jours. Vol. United Way, Providence, 1988, 90, Maryville, 1986; mem. fundraising com. R.I. Women's Health Collective, Pawtucket, R.I., 1995-96. Recipient Outstanding Advisor award Bryant Coll., 1991, Don Sahli award Tenn. Edn. Assn., 1984; grantee Rockefeller Archives Ctr., 1994, Franklin Rsch. grant Am. Philos. Assn., 2003, So. Studies Rsch. grant U. N.C., 2003. Mem. Orgn. Am. Historians, So. Assn. Women Hisorians (exec. sec. 2000-, Willie Lee Rose Pub. prize 2001), So. Hist. Assn., Agrl. History Soc. Office: Converse College 580 E Main St Spartanburg SC 29302-0006 Office Phone: 864-596-9104.

WALKER, MINERVA E. GILARA, retail executive, poet; b. Dauphin County, Pa., June 23, 1924; d. Daniel Snavely Ensminger and Nora Alice Hostetter; m. Stanley Michael Gilara, July 11, 1942 (div. Aug. 1972); children: Jerry, Stanley, Paul, Connie; m. John Henry Walker, Nov. 25, 1976 (dec. June 1993); 1 child, Tina. Student, Harrisburg Area C.C. Freelance writer, reporter Lebanon (Pa.) Daily News, 1954—60; hostess, retail advt. Welcome Wagon Internat., Hummelstown, Pa., 1958—60; tour guide, pub. rels. Indian Echo Caverns, Hummelstown, 1967—72; staff writer Middletown (Pa.) Press and Jour., 1960—66; retail rep. Svc. Advantage, Indpls., 1994—2000, Office Max, Shaker Heights, Ohio, 2000—. Lutheran. Avocations: poetry, writing, art, travel, needlecrafts. Home: 28905 229th Pl SE Black Diamond WA 98010

WALKER, NANCY ANNE, small business owner, history educator, art educator; b. Palo Alto, Calif., May 27, 1942; d. John Clarence and Dorothy May (Mole) Cheney; 1 child, Shelley Marie. BS, U. Oreg., 1964; MA, San Fernando State U., 1968; PhD, U. Colo., 1975. Lic. real estate broker, Calif. Instr. U. Md., Fed. Republic Germany, 1970-74; instr. history Modesto Jr. Coll., Calif., 1977-80, 88-93; owner, pres. Lockeford Clock Co., Inc., Stockton, Calif., 1978—; lectr. Calif. State U., Stanislaus, 1992; art and history docent Haggin Mus., 2002—. Owner Lockeford Angiques, 1974—, Nancy Walker Rentals. Contbr. articles to jours. including The Pioneer, Lockeford-Clements News, East European Quar., among others. Mem. Mayor's Task Force on Affirmative Action, Stockton, 1984—; pres. San Joaquin chpt. Nat. Orgn. for Women, 1988; mem. Del Tor Excavation, Israel, summer 1985; area rep. Youth for Understanding, 1987, 88; activities chmn. 6th Ward Ch. of Jesus Christ of Latter-day Saints, 1984; mem. Stockton Opera Guild; bd. dirs. Stockton Beautiful, 2002. Austrian Govt. grantee, 1970. Mem. DAR, Daus. Am. Colonists, Soc. Mayflower Descendants, Am. Hist. Assn., Clements-Lockeford C. of C. (dir. 1977-79), Kappa Alpha Theta, Kiwanis. Avocations: writing local history, travel. Office: 18880 N Highway 88 Lockeford CA 95237-9519

WALKER, OLENE S. governor; b. Ogden, Utah, Nov. 15, 1930; d. Thomas Ole and Nina Hadley (Smith) W.; m. J. Myron Walker, 1957; children: Stephen Brett, David Walden, Bryan Jesse, Lori, Mylene, Nina, Thomas Myron. BA, Brigham Young U., 1954; MA, Stanford U., 1954; PhD, U. Utah, 1986; HHD (hon.), Weber State U., 1997. V.p. Country Crisp Foods, 1969-92; mem. Utah Ho. of Reps. Dist. 24; lt. gov. State of Utah, 1993—2003, gov., 2003—. Mem. Salt Lake Edn. Found. bd. dirs. 1983-90; dir. community econ. devel.; mem. Ballet West, Sch. Vol., United Way, Commn. on Youth, Girls Village, Salt Lake Conv. and Tourism Bd.; mem. adv. coun. Weber State U. Mem. Nat. Assn. Secs. of State (Western chmn., nat. lt. gov.'s conf., pres. 1997-98). Mem. Lds Ch. Office: Gov 210 State Capitol Building Salt Lake City UT 84114-1202*

WALKER, PATRICIA ANN DIXON, retired elementary school educator, real estate rehabilitator; b. Somerset, Pa., Nov. 26, 1937; d. Telford Miles and Bernice Irene Dixon; m. Paul J. Kuty, Nov. 2, 1957 (div. Nov. 1974); 1 child, Paul Dixon Kuty ; m. James William Walker, Mar. 23, 1991. BS in Elem. Edn., Ind. State Coll., 1960; MA in Elem. Edn., Trenton State Coll., 1966. Tchr. grade 1 Neshaminy Sch. Dist., Langhorne, Pa., 1960—93; real estate investor Phila., 1985—2003. Vol. tutor NAACP, Bucks County, Pa., 1967—68; mem. Levittown Hist. Preservation Com., 2002—04; committeewoman Dem. Party, Bucks County, 1974—78; chair Dem. Assn. Middletown Twp., Bucks County, 1974—75. Recipient Gift of Time tribute, Am. Family Inst. Valley Forge, 1992. Mem.: Homeowners Assn. Phila., Neshaminy Fedn. Ret. Tchrs., Pa. Assn. Sch. Retirees (mem. Bucks County chpt.). Avocation: travel. Home: 24 June Rd Levittown PA 19056

WALKER, ROSLYN ADELE, museum director; b. Memphis, Tenn., July 26, 1944; Student Gen. Studies, U. Poitiers, France, 1965; BS in Art Edn. with high honors, Hampton U., 1966; MA in History of Art, Indiana U., 1969, PhD in History of Art, 1991. Registrar Mus. African Art, Washington, 1968-69; coord. Univ. Art Gallery U. Mass., Amherst, 1969-70; temporary registrar Fed. Dept Antiquities Nat. Mus., Lagos, Nigeria, 1970; curator of collections Inst. African Studies U. Idaban, Nigeria, 1973-75; curator ethnographic art collection Univ. Mus. Ill. State U., Normal, 1975-81, interim adminstr., 1975, adminstr., 1975-77, dir., 1977-81; curator Nat. Mus. African Art Smithsonian Instn., Washington, 1981-93, sr. curator, 1993-97, dir., 1997—2002. Rsch. asst. Mus. Modern Art, N.Y.C., 1971-72, guest curator African Women/African Art, The African-Am. Inst., N.Y.C., 1976, Lakeview Mus. Arts and Scis., Peoria, Ill., 1981; instr. in primitive art U. Mass., Amherst, 1969-70, in African decorative art USDA Grad. Sch., Washington, 1984. in Art in Africa, Dept. Art History, U. Md., College Park, 1990; vis. lectr. Afro-Am. Art, Ind. U., Bloomington, 1970-71, lectr. 1971-72, summer program, U. Idaban, Nigeria, 1974; asst. prof. Art Dept., Ill. State U., Normal, 1975-81. Author: (with Roy Sieber) African Art in the

Cycle of Life, 1987, Olowe of Ise: A Yoruba Sculptor to Kings, 1998; contbr. catalogs for exhibitions of African Art to Royal Acad. of Arts, London, 1995, Guggenheim Mus. N.Y. and Afro-Am. Hist. and Cultural Mus., Phila., 1996; contbr., reviews, essays and articles to profl. jours. and mags. Mem. visual arts and crafts adv. panel Washington Commn. on the Arts. Recipient Ford Found. Fgn. Study grant, 1965, Faculty Rsch. grant, U. Mass., 1970, Fgn. Lang. fellowship Ind. U., Bloomington, 1971, Grant in Aid, Ind. U., 1972, Rsch. Fund grant (collections-based), Smithsonian Instn., Washington, 1994; named Twenty Yr. Student, Hampton U., 1986. Mem. Arts Coun. African Studies Assn. (past bd. dirs.), ArTable, Assn. Art Mus. Dirs.

WALKER, SALLY BARBARA, retired glass company executive; b. Bellerose, N.Y., Nov. 21, 1921; d. Lambert Roger and Edith Demerest (Parkhouse) W. Diploma, Cathedral Sch. St. Mary, 1939; AA, Finch Jr. Coll., 1941. Tchr. interior design Finch Coll., 1941-42; draftsman AT&T, 1942-43; with Steuben Glass Co., N.Y.C., 1943—, exec. v.p., 1959-62, exec. v.p. ops., 1962-78, exec. v.p. ops. and sales, 1978-83, exec. v.p., 1983-88, ret., 1988. Pres. 116 E. 66th St. Corp. Mem. Fifth Ave. Assn., Rockaway Hunting Club, Lawrence Beach Club, Colony Club, English-Speaking Union, Garden Club of Lawrence, City Garden Club of N.Y.C. Republican. Episcopalian. Home: 116 E 66th St New York NY 10021-6547

WALKER, SAVANNAH T. retired executive assistant, legislative assistant; b. Lubbock, Tex., Nov. 23, 1930; d. John Hansford and Lenore Belle (Muecke) Tunnell; m. Julius Waring Walker, Jr., July 29, 1956; children: Savannah Waring, Lucile Lenore, George Julius Stewart. BA, Tex. Tech. U., 1951; student, Radcliffe Coll., 1951. Cert. secondary sch. tchr., Tex. Tchr., English and journalism Phillips (Tex.) Ind. Sch. Dist., 1951-52; asst. to congressman Mahon U.S. Congress, Washington, 1952-54, adminstrv., exec. asst., 1954-58, 63-66; legis. asst. to chmn. House Appropriations U.S. Ho. of Reps., Washington, 1973-78; exec. asst. to v.p. Nat. Assn. Mfrs., Washington, 1985-89; exec. asst. to pres. Ogilvy Pub. Rels. Worldwide, Washington, 1990-99; sr. mgr. Pres. of the Americas, Ogilvy Pub. Rels. Worldwide, 2000—01. Vol., fundraiser for charitable orgns., Chad and Eng., 1966-73; pres. Am. Women in London, 1971-72, Am. Women in Liberia, Monrovia, 1979-80. Mem. AAUW, PEO, Am. Women in the Arts Mus., DAR, Internat. Women's Club (founder pres.) (Ouagadougou, Burkina Faso), Delta Delta Delta. Avocations: church work, bridge, reading, needlework, writing. Home: 3801 Jenifer St NW Washington DC 20015-1917 E-mail: julwalk@aol.com.

WALKER, SUZANNAH WOLF, language educator; b. Akron, Ohio, May 3, 1954; d. Robert Patton and Katherine Jane (Guglielmi) Wolf Jr.; m. Timothy Gordon Walker, Dec. 23, 1980 (div. Dec. 21, 1992). BA in Secondary Edn., U. Akron, 1976; MA in Pub. Rels., Kent State U., 1987. Tchr. English, Spanish Cuyahoga Falls (Ohio) City Sch., 1977—96; tchr. English DOD Dependents Sch., Wurzburg, Germany, 1981—82; tchr. English, Spanish Canton (Ohio) City Schs., 1999—. Mem. supt. adv. com. Cuyahoga Falls City Sch., 1995, bldg. rep., 1992—95, Canton City Schs., 2000—03. Pub. rels. intern Ronald McDonald House, Cleve., 1985. Mem.: NEA, Canton Profl. Educators Assn. (mem. exec. com. 2003—), N.E. Ohio Fgn. Lang. Assn., Ohio Fgn. Lang. Assn., Cuyahoga Falls Edn. Assn., Ohio Edn. Assn. Home: 3430 E Prescott Cir Cuyahoga Falls OH 44223 Office Phone: 330-454-7717.

WALKER, VICKI L. state senator; m. Steven Walker; children: Adam, Sara. Ct. reporting program, Lane C.C., 1980—83; BS in Polit. Sci., U. Oreg., 1978. State sen. Oreg. State Senate, Salem, 1999—; ct. reporter Salem, 1983—. Mem.: Oreg. Ct. Reporters Assn., Am. Found. for Suicide Prevention-NW. Democrat. Office: 900 Court St NE S-210 Salem OR 97301

WALKER, WANDA MEDORA, retired elementary school educator, consultant; b. San Diego, Aug. 28, 1923; d. Bryant Hereford and Anna Genevieve (Barnes) Howard; m. Elmer Manfred Walker, Nov. 23, 1949 (dec. Aug. 1978); children: Kathleen May Stewart (dec.), Mary Ellen Quessenberry, Sydney Edward, Jessie Ann Meacham. BA, San Diego State U., 1947; MA, U. Wash., 1948; PhD, Calif. Western U., 1967. Cert. (life) spl. secondary music tchr., elem. tchr., sch. adminstr. Elem. tchr. Lakeside (Calif.) Elem. Dist., 1948-50, La Mesa (Calif.) Sch. Dist., 1951-53, San Diego City Schs. Dist., 1953-57, cons. gifted, 1957-59, vice prin., 1959-62; prin. San Diego Schs. Dist., 1962-88. Rep. San Diego City Schs. War Against Litter, 1971—76; pres. Assn. Calif. Sch. Adminstrs. Ret., 1992—94. Recipient Am. Educators medal Freedoms Found. Valley Forge, 1973, Woman of Yr. award Pres. Coun. Women's Svc., Bus. & Profl. Clubs San Diego, 1980, Woman of Action award Soroptomists Internat. El Cajon, 1992. Mem.: AAUW (parliamentarian 1989—98, Appreciation award 1992), Sr. Resource Ctr. (adv. bd., vol. 1989—), Assn. Calif. Sch. Adminstrs. (pres.), San Diego City Sch. Adminstrn. Assn. (pres. 1976—77), Calif. Retired Tchrs., Singing Hills Women's Golf Club. Avocations: photography, painting, gardening, golf, music. Home: 13208 Julian Ave Lakeside CA 92040-4312

WALKER, YVONNE DENISE, research analyst; b. Warren, Ohio, Oct. 11, 1967; BA, Hiram (Ohio) Coll., 1990; MBA, SUNY, Albany. Budget analyst N.Y. State Divsn. of Budget, 1990-96; criminal justice and corrections rsch. analyst Ho. of Reps., Olympia, Wash., 1996—. Bd. dirs. Camp Thatcher Opportunities, Albany, 1994-96, Albany County Youth Burs., 1995-96; chair N.Y. State Divsn. of Budget Affirmative Action Com., 1991-96, Big Bros./Big Sisters, Thurston County, 1997—. Mem.: Nat. Assn. Blacks in Criminal Justice, Jr. League (v.p. fin. 1997—). Home: 11308 107th St SW Tacoma WA 98498-1412 Office: Criminal Justice & Corrections House Of Representatives Olympia WA 98504-0001

WALKER-GRIFFIN, DONNA FAY, information technology manager; b. Barbouville, Ky., Feb. 2, 1957; d. Theodore Reed; m. Mel Leon Griffin; children: Antuan Renard Walker, Andre Lamont Walker. BA, Ohio State U., 1981. Cert. help desk profl. STI Knowledge, Chgo., 2001. Clk. typist Office Comptr. Dept. Def., Columbus, Ohio, 1986—86, mgmt. asst. Office Comptr., 1987—88, program budget analyst Office Installation Svcs., 1988—97, program mgmt. analyst Office Corp. Performance, 1997—2000, computer specialist, info. technologist Def. Supply Ctr., 2000—. Ch. fin. adminstr. New Calvary Ministries Ch., Reynoldsburg, Ohio, 1999—. Min. New Calvary Ministries Ch., Reynoldsburg, 2002—03. Recipient Cert. of Appreciation for Mentorship, Broadleigh Elem. Sch., 8 Years. Mem.: Fed. Exec. Assn. (assoc.), Fed. Employed Women (assoc.), Blacks In Govt. (assoc.; treas.). Avocations: volleyball, ping pong/table tennis, singing, tennis, bowling. Home: 7391 Woodlow Drive Reynoldsburg OH 43068 Office: Dept Def (DSCC) 3990 E Broad St Columbus OH 43216-5000 Personal E-mail: newcalvary@itilink.com. E-mail: donnaf.walker@dscc.dla.mil.

WALKER-TAYLOR, YVONNE, retired academic administrator; b. New Bedford, Mass., Apr. 17, 1916; d. Dougal Ormonde and Eva Emma (Revallion) Walker; m. Robert Harvey Taylor (dec.) BS, Wilberforce U., 1936; MA, Boston U., 1938; Edn. Specialist, U. Kans., 1964; L.H.D. (hon.), Morris Brown Coll., 1985; Dr. Pedagogy (hon.), Medaille Coll., 1985, Northeastern Coll., 1985. Asst. acad. dean Wilberforce U., Ohio, 1967-68, v.p., acad. dean, 1973-83, provost, 1983-84, pres., 1984-88; Disting. Presdl. prof. Edn. Ctrl. State U., 1990-96. Bd. dirs. Nat. Commn. on Coop. Edn., 1977-82, 83-88, United Way, Xenia, Ohio, 1985-88; chmn. culture planning council Nat. Mus. Afro-Am. History; sec. Greene Oaks Health Ctr., 1983-87; bd. trustees, Dayton Art Inst; v.p. jud. coun. AME Ch.; mem. Ohio Humanities Coun., 1994—, Greene City Violence Bd. Named Woman of Yr., Met. Civic Women's Assn., Dayton, 1984, one of Top Ten Women, Dayton Newspapers-Women's Coalition, Dayton, 1984, Outstanding Woman of Yr., Iota Phi Lambda, Dayton, 1985; recipient Drum Major for Justice award So. Christian Leadership Conf., 1986; named to Greene County Hall of Fame, 1990. Mem. Com. on Ednl. Credit and Credentials of the Am. Council on Edn., Alpha Kappa Alpha, Phi Delta Kappa. African Methodist Episcopalian. Club: Links (past pres.) Avocations: reading, swimming, horseshoes, tennis, bicycling. Home: 1279 Wilberforce-Clifton Rd Wilberforce OH 45384-9999 Office: Wilberforce U Brush Row Rd PO Box 336 Wilberforce OH 45384-0336 E-mail: deonwt@aol.com.

WALKLEY, MARY L, voice educator, music educator; b. Storm Lake, Iowa, Oct. 17, 1947; d. Leonard Leroy Gustafson and Betty Angelyne Barnes; m. Robert Wayne Gustafson, Feb. 10, 1965 (div. Feb. 11, 1983); children: Robert Scot, Andrea Lynn Jenkins. MusB in performance, U. of Tampa, Fla., 1983. Cert. level V speech level singing Instr. Seth Riggs Speech Level Singing Internat., 2000. Founder and dir., pre-coll. music program U. of Tampa, Fla., 1983—93; founder and program dir. Pre-Coll. Music Program, 1983—93; fine arts dir. Tampa Prep. Sch., 1983—96, 1983—97; founder and music dir. The Broadway Theatre Project, 1990—; founder and program dir. The Speech Level Singing Inst., L.A., 1998—2002; guest artist and workshop presenter Internat. Thespian Assn., Tampa, 1998—. Vocal cons. Busch Gardens Entertainment, Tampa, Fla., 1998—. Musician (arranger): (vocal arrangements, orchestrations) Broadway Theatre Project. Grantee study with Seth Riggs, Benedict Found., 1997. Mem.: NARAS, Nat. Assn. of Teachers of Singing, Inc. Avocations: travel, reading, singing, piano. Home: 775 NE 76th Street Miami FL 33138 Office: FloridaSings 775 NE 76th Street Miami FL 33138 E-mail: mary@floridasings.com.

WALKUP, MARY ROE, state legislator; b. Kennedyville, Md., May 4, 1924; d. William Benjamin and Catharine Cooper (Roe) Groves; m. Harry Ernst Walkup, 1945; children: Mary Anne, Harry Ernst Jr., Margaret Louise, Robert Douglas. BSN, U. Md., 1945. RN, Md. Nurse U. Md. Hosp., Balt., 1945-46; mem. Md. Ho. of Dels., Annapolis, 1995—. Editor Kent Conservation News, 1972-78. Women's vice chmn. Md. 1st Congl. Dist. Rep. Com., 1970-74; legis. chmn. Md. Fedn. Rep. Women, 1970-72; spl. asst. to census chmn. Kent County, Md., 1970, census chmn., 1970, commr., 1978-86; pres. Rep. Women's Club Kent and Queen Anne's County, Md., 1973-77; sec. Md. Rep. Ctrl. Com., 1974-78; mem. citizens adv. com. Chesapeake Bay Program, 1988—, chmn., 1989-91; mem. Md. Water Quality Adv. Com., 1988—; charter mem., bd. dirs. Kent Conservation Inc., 1989—, sec., 1969-72, pres., 1972-74, 91-93; v.p. Nat. Wildlife Fedn., 1972-78, alt. del., 1977. Named Conservationist of Yr., Md. Wildlife Fedn., 1977, Outstanding Md. Rep. Woman of Yr. and Thomas Sone award Md. Rep. Ctrl. Com., 1977.

WALL, AUDREY G. secondary school educator; b. Concord, N.C., June 6, 1920; d. William Henry and Barbara (Golns) Gillis; m. Melvin Lloyd Wall, Sr., Nov. 7, 1973 (dec. Sept. 24, 1983); 1 child, Melvin Lloyd, Jr. BA, Barber-Scotia Coll., 1951; MS, A&T State U., 1958. Educator Stanly County Bd. Edn., Albemarle, N.C., 1962-65, Mecklenburg County Bd. Edn., Charlotte, N.C., 1965—. Reporter Stanly News & Press, 1951-53; feature writer Charlotte Post, 1982-85. Reader Am. Assn. for Blind, Charlotte, 1977-79; vol. Mercy Hosp., Charlotte, 1983-94; pres. Charlotte chpt. World Fedn. Meth. Women, 1986-88; vol. Carolinas Med. Ctr., 1994-97; planning com. Charlotte Women's Commn., 1995—; pres.-elect local chpt. Ch. Women United, Charlotte, 1994-96, pres., 1996-98, statewide comms. dir., 1998-99, state v.p., 1999—; moderator Presbyn. Women, 2000—. Mem. NEA (life), Order Eastern Star, Delta Sigma Theta. Home: 3115 Clearview Dr Charlotte NC 28216-3624

WALL, BARBARA WARTELLE, lawyer; b. New Orleans, Sept. 30, 1954; d. Richard Cole and Ruth Druhan (Power) Wartelle; m. Christopher Read Wall, June 21, 1980; 2 children. BA, U. Va., 1976, JD, 1979. Bar: N.Y. 1980, U.S. Dist. Ct. (so. and ea. dists.) N.Y. 1980. Assoc. Satterlee & Stephens, N.Y.C., 1979-85; asst. gen. counsel Gannett Co., Inc., Arlington, Va., 1985-90, sr. legal counsel, 1990-93, v.p., sr. legal counsel, 1993—. Mem. ABA (past chair forum on comm. law), N.Y. State Bar Assn., Assn. of Bar of City of N.Y. Republican. Episcopalian. Home: 5026 Tilden St NW Washington DC 20016-2334 Office: Gannett Co Inc 7950 Jones Branch Dr Mc Lean VA 22102-0320

WALL, BETTY JANE, real estate consultant; b. Wichita Falls, Tex., Mar. 23, 1936; d. Albert Willis and Winnie Belle (Goodloe) Beard; m. Richard Lee Wall, Feb. 21, 1959; 1 child, Cynthia Lynn. BS, Vocat.Home Econs. Edn, U. Okla., 1958; MEd, Midwestern U., 1959. Lic. real estate salesperson, Tex. Tchr. San Diego County Schs., 1959-60, Long Beach (Calif.) City Schs., 1960-61, Norman (Okla.) Kindergarten Assn., 1961-65; real estate salesperson WestMark Realtors, Lubbock, Tex., 1983-85; now ind. real estate salesperson Lubbock, 1985—. Coll. adviser Nat. Panhellenic Conf., Tex., 1979-91; judge talent and beauty pageants, Tex. N.Mex., Okla., 1984—. Treas. Lubbock Symphony Guild, 1985-87, v.p. ways and means com., 1987-88, chmn. ball, 1990, pres. elect, 1993-94, pres., 1994-95; bd. dirs. Tex. Assn. of Symphony Orchs., 1994-95, Ballet Lubbock, 1996-98, 2000—; bd. dirs. Miss Lubbock Pageant, 1992—; co-chmn. Performance Lubbock' 96, 1996; mem. Lubbock Arts Festival Com., 1997-98. Recipient Tex. Tech. U. Outstanding Greek Alumni award, 1994, Tex. Tech. Chancellor's Coun. Mem. Tex. Real Estate Assn., Jr. League Lubbock (treas. 1976-78, sustaining advisor fin. com. 1979-83, hdqrs. commn. advisor 1989-94), Mus. Tex. Tech. Univ. (chmn. planetarium com. 1996, trustee 1997—, bd. dirs., mus. league 1992-2002, pres. 2002, v.p. 2002-2003), Lubbock C. of C., Lubbock Women's Club (bd. dirs. 1996-2000, pres. 1999-2000, pres. hist. found. 1999-2000), Tex. Tech. U. Faculty Women's Club (v.p. and pres. 1967-69, Lubbock chpt. Achievement Rewards for Coll. Sci. bd. 1995-96), Alpha Chi Omega (nat. coun., nat. panhellenic del. 1978-83, 88-90, nat. v.p. membership 1985-88, nat. v.p. collegians 1990-92), Mus. Tex. Tech U. Assn. (v.p. mus. league 2002-2003), Lubbock Alumnae Panhellenic (pres. 2003-04). Avocations: needlepoint, travel, music. Home and Office: 3610 63rd Dr Lubbock TX 79413-5308

WALL, CAROLYN RAIMONDI, communications executive; b. Springfield, Mass., July 2, 1942; d. Amedio G. and Celestina F. (Penna) Raimondi; m. Peter M. Wall, Oct. 24, 1964 (div. 1972); children: Christina, Suzanne; m. Warren J. Keegan, June 17, 1984 (div. 1989). AB, Trinity Coll., Washington. Advt dir. Beldoch Industries, N.Y.C., 1972-74; promotion dir. Fairchild Pubs., N.Y.C., 1974-76; v.p., pub. Adweek, N.Y.C., 1976-83; assoc. pub. N.Y. Mag., N.Y.C., 1983-84, pub., 1984-85; exec. v.p. consumer div. Murdoch Mags., 1985-87; v.p., gen. mgr. Sta. WNYW, N.Y.C., 1987—92; dir. News America Holdings; exec. v.p. corp. devel. and sales News America, 1992—95; pres. Cowles Bus. Media, 1995-96, WBIS-TV, 1996-98; pub. Newsweek, 1998—2001, dir. mktg. and comms., 2001; ptnr. Quintacom, 2002—. Mem. bus. adv. bd. Lubin Schs. Bus., Pace U., 1982-88; bd. dirs. N.Y. Urban League, Found. for Minority Interests in Media, MacDuffie Sch., Internat. Radio and TV Found. Mem. Internat. Radio and TV Soc., N.Y. TV Acad. Arts and Scis., Advt. Women N.Y. (bd. dirs., pres. 1981-83). Mem. Advt. Women of N.Y. (bd. dirs., pres. 1981-83) Democrat. Roman Catholic.

WALL, DIANE EVE, political science educator; b. Detroit, Nov. 17, 1944; d. Albert George and Jean Carol Bradley. BA in History and Edn., Mich. State U., 1966, MA in History, 1969, MA in Polit. Sci., 1979, PhD in Polit. Sci., 1983. Cert. permanent secondary tchr., Mich. Secondary tchr. Corunna (Mich.) Pub. Schs., 1966-67, N.W. Pub. Schs., Rives Junction, Mich., 1967-73; lectr. Tidewater C.C., Chesapeake, Va., 1974-77; instr. Wayne State U., Detroit, fall 1980, Lansing (Mich.) C.C., 1981-83, Ctrl. Mich. U., Mt. Pleasant, 1982; prof. dept. polit. sci. Miss. State U., 1983—, undergrad. coord., 1993—. Pre-law advisor Miss. State U., 1990—93, chair, 1993—. Co-editor spl. issue Southea. Polit. Rev.; contbr. articles, revs. to profl. jours., chpt. to book, entry to ency. Evaluator Citizen's Task Force, Chesapeake, Va., 1977; panelist flag burning program Ednl. TV, Mississippi State, 1990, prayer in pub. sch., Starkville Cmty. TV, 1995; gubernatorial appointee Miss. Task Force on Local Govt. Info. Systems, 2003. Recipient Paideia award Miss. State U. Coll. Arts and Scis., 1988, Miss. State U. Outstanding Woman Tchg. Faculty award Pres.'s Commn. on Status of Women, 1994, Acad. Advising award Miss. State U., 1994, Outstanding Advisor award Nat. Acad. Advising Assn. and ACT, 1995, Miss. State U. Upper Level Undergrad. Tchg. award Miss. State U. Alumni Assn., 2000; Grad. Office fellow Mich. State U., 1980; Miss. State U. rsch. grantee, 1984. Mem. ASPA (exec. bd. Sect. for Women 1987-90, Miss. chpt. pres. 1992-93), LWV (Chesapeake charter pres. 1976-77), Miss. Polit. Sci. Assn. (exec. dir. 1991-93), Miss. State U. Soc. Scholars (pres. 1992-93), Miss. State U. Faculty Women's Assn. (v.p. 1985-86, pres. 1986-88, scholar 1987-89), Phi Kappa Phi (v.p. 1985-86, pres. 1986-88), Pi Sigma Alpha (Ann. Chpt. Activities award 1991). Democrat. Methodist. Avocations: dog obedience training, corvette activities, gardening. Office: Miss State U PO Drawer PC Mississippi State MS 39762 E-mail: dew1@ps.msstate.edu .

WALL, JANET G. state legislator; b. Portsmouth, N.H., Nov. 21, 1949; two children. BS, U. N.H., 1971. Rep. dist. 9 N.H. Ho. Reps. Water commr. Madbury, N.H., chmn. bd. dirs.; commr. Straf County exec. commn., 1989—, Straf County Coop. Extension Svc., 1992—; jud. com. N.H. Ho. Reps. Chmn. Heritage Collections Com., 1990—; govt. adv. commn. Peace Redevel.; dir. Madbury Hist. Preservation Project; project coord. Madbury Forum. Mem. Durham Hist.Soc. (past pres., bd. dirs., com. chair), Durham-Green Bay Rotary (dir. RADAR), Lee Hist. Soc., Durham Hist. Assn. Home: 4 Pudding Hill Rd Madbury NH 03820-7001 Office: NH State Senate State Capital Concord NH 03301

WALL, KATHY ELLIOTT, secondary school educator; b. Kershaw, S.C., Nov. 13, 1955; d. Alton Leonard and Myrtle Mildred Elliott; m. Ronald Lee Wall, June 19, 1976; children: Noel E., Elliott Lee, Oliver Lawrence. BMus, Furman U., Greenville, S.C., 1978; MEd, U. S.C., 1983. Cert. tchr. S.C. Tchr. Heath Springs (S.C.) Elem. Sch., 1978—85, Andrew Jackson Mid. Sch., Kershaw, SC, 1985—99, Andrew Jackson H.S., Kershaw, SC, 1992—. Keyboard accompanist Covenant Bapt. Ch., Lancaster, SC, 2001—; children and youth music dir. First Bapt. Sch., Kershaw, 1990 2001; interim music dir. Heath Springs Bapt. Sch., 1980—84. Vol. Meals on Wheels, Kershaw, 1999—. Mem.: Palmetto State Tchrs. Assn., Music Educators Nat. Conf. Home: PO Box 91 Kershaw SC 29067

WALL, SHERRY HODGES, elementary school educator; b. Meriwether County, Ga., Nov. 21, 1951; d. William Henry and Leta (Reeves) Hodges; m. Charles R. Wall, Feb. 15, 1970; children: Christiane, Kera Leigh. BA in Mid. Grades Edn. cum laude, LaGrange (Ga.) Coll., 1986; student, Upson County Vocat.-Tech. Sch., Thomaston, Ga., 1971; MEd in Mid. Grade Edn., Columbus (Ga.) Coll. Cert. mid. grades Math and English tchr., Ga. Tchr.'s aide, tchr. Flint River Acad., Woodbury, Ga.; tchr. 5th grade math. and English, Pike County Bd. Edn., Zebulon, Ga. 4th grade inclusion tchr. Nat. Coun. Tchrs. Math., Ga. Tchrs. Math., Nat. Coun. Tchrs. Sci. Mem. NEA, Ga. Assn. Educators.

WALL, SONJA ELOISE, nursing administrator; b. Santa Cruz, Calif., Mar. 28, 1938; d. Ray Theothornton and Reva Mattie (Wingo) W.; m. [illegible] 1960 (div. [illegible] 1968); children: [illegible] Lynn, Lance Edward; m. John Aspesi, Sept. 1969 (div. 1977); children: Sabrina Jean, Daniel John; m. Kenneth Talbot LaBoube, Nov. 1, 1978 (div. 1989); 1 child, Tiffany Amber; m. Charles Borsic, July 2002. BA, San Jose Jr. Coll., 1959; BS, Madonna Coll., 1967; student, U. Mich., 1968 70; postgrad., Wayne State U., 1967-68. RN, Calif., Mich., Colo. Staff nurse Santa Clara Valley Med. Ctr., San Jose, Calif., 1959-67, U. Mich. Hosp., Ann Arbor, 1967-73, Porter and Swedish Med. Hosp., Denver, 1973-77, Laurel Grove Hosp., Castro Valley, Calif., 1977-79, Advent Hosp., Ukiah, Calif., 1984-86; motel owner LaBoube Enterprises, Fairfield, Point Arena, Willits, Calif., 1979—; staff nurse Northridge Hosp., L.A., 1986-87, Folsom State Prison, Calif., 1987; co-owner, mgr. nursing registry Around the Clock Nursing Svc., Ukiah, 1985—; critical care staff nurse Kaiser Permanente Hosp., Sacramento, 1986-89; nurse Snowline Hospice, Sacramento, 1989-92; carepoint home care and travel nurse Hosp. Staffing Svcs. Inc., Placerville, Calif., 1992-94, interim home health nurse, 1994-95; nurse Finders Home Health Care, 1996; owner Sunshine Manor Resdl. Care Home, Placerville, Calif., 1995—, Rainbow Manor Residential Care Home, 2000; psychol. trauma RN Folsom State Prison, 2002—. Owner Royal Plantation Petites Miniature Horse Farm. Contbr. articles to profl. jours. Leader Coloma 4-H, 1987-91; mem. mounted divsn. El Dorado County Search and Rescue, 1991-93; docent Calif. Marshall Gold Discovery State Hist. Park, Coloma, Calif. Mem. AACN, NAFE, Oncology Nurses Assn., Soc. Critical Care Medicine, Am. Heart Assn. (CPR trainer, recipient awards), Calif. Bd. RNs, Calif. Nursing Rev., Calif. Critical Care Nurses, Soc. Critical Care Nurses, Alzheimers Aid Soc. No. Calif., Am. Motel Assn. (beautification and remodeling award 1985), Nat. Hospice Nurses Assn., Cmty. Residential Care Assn. Calif., Soroptimist Internat. Calif., Am. Miniature Horse Assn. (winner nat. grand championship 1981-83, 85, 89), DAR (Jobs Daus. hon. mem.), C. of C. of El Dorado County, Kiwanis, Cameron Park Country Club. Republican. Episcopalian. Avocations: pinto, paint and miniature horses, real estate development, swimming. Home and Office: Sunshine Manor Residental Care Home Care and Around Clock Nursing Svc 3112 Washington St Placerville CA 95667-5825 Fax: (530) 6222233. E-mail: sunshinemanor@directcon.net.

WALLACE, BARBARA BROOKS, writer; b. Soochow, China, Dec. 3, 1922; came to U.S., 1938; d. Otis Frank and Nicia Brooks; m. James Wallace Jr., Feb. 27, 1954; 1 child, James V. BA, UCLA, 1945. Script sec. Foote, Cone & Belding, Hollywood, Calif., 1946-49; tchr. Wright MacMahon Secretarial Sch., Beverly Hills, Calif., 1949-50; head fund drive Commerce and Industry Divsn. ARC, San Francisco, 1950-52. Author: Claudia, 1969 (Nat. League of Am. Pen Women Juvenile Book award 1970), Andrew the Big Deal, 1970, The Trouble with Miss Switch, 1971, Victoria, 1973, Can Do, Missy Charlie, 1974, The Secret Summer of L.E.B. (Nat. League of Am. Pen Women Juvenile Book award 1974), Julia and the Third Bad Thing, 1975, Palmer Patch, 1976, Hawkins, 1977, Peppermints in the Parlor, 1980 (William Allen White award 1983), The Contest Kid Strikes Again, 1980, Hawkins and the Soccer Solution, 1981, Miss Switch to the Rescue, 1981, Hello, Claudia, 1982, Claudia and Duffy, 1982, The Barrel in the Basement, 1985, Argyle, 1987, 92, Perfect Acres, Inc., 1988, The Twin in the Tavern, 1993 (Edgar award Mystery Writers Am. 1994), Cousins in the Castle, 1996, Sparrows in the Scullery, 1997 (Edgar award 1998), Ghosts in the Gallery, 2000, Secret in St. Something, 2001, Miss Switch Online, 2002, The Perils of Peppermints, 2003. Mem. Children's Book Guild of Washington, Alpha Phi. Episcopalian. Home and Office: 5100 Fillmore Ave 106 Alexandria VA 22311-5038 E-mail: jimbob4@comcast.net.

WALLACE, BARBARA FAITH, linguistics educator; b. NYC, Dec. 15, 1952; Diploma, U. London, 1977; MA, M Philosophy, CUNY, 1981. Tchr. descriptive linguistics Queens Coll., N.Y.C., 1979-80; tchr. African history John Jay Coll., N.Y.C., 1981-82; tchr. anthropol. linguistics CCNY, 1981-84; tchr. linguistics, math. coord., classroom and sci. Smart Process N.Y.C. Bd. Edn., 1986—; chief officer Barbara Co., 2001—. Artist's asst. Faith Ringgold, 1991—; co-chair Art with Kids grant selection com., Anyone Can Fly Found., Inc., 2003—. Editor: Faith Ringgold Story Quilts and Other Narratives, 2004; exhibitor; contbr. articles to profl. jours. Named Coun. Internat. Edn. Exchange grantee, 1974, Brit. Fedn. U. Women scholar, 1976, fellow CUNY, 1977-81, grant Fund for N.Y.C. Pub. Edn., 1992, grant Women Sports Found., 1993. Mem.: Barbara Faith Co. (chief officer and founder), Greenpeace. Avocations: computer, travel, photography. Home: 10 W 135th St Apt 11S New York NY 10037-2623 Office: John B Russwurm Sch 2230 5th Ave New York NY 10037-2196 also: Barbara Faith Co PO Box 246 New York NY 10037-0246

WALLACE, BECKY WHITLEY, protective services official; BA in Criminal Justice, Montgomery C.C. Police officer City of Troy (N.C.), 1974-75; deputy sheriff Montgomery County (N.C,), 1975-78, 82-94; alcohol law enforcement agt. N.C. Dept. Crime Control & Pub. Safety, Greensboro, 1978-82; U.S. marshal N.C., 1994—. Recipeint Leadership N.C. Stanley Frank award, Breaking the Glass Ceiling award Nat. Ctr. Women in Policing; named Disting. Woman of N.c., Coun. Women. Mem. Fed. Law Enforcement Officers' Assn., N.C. Women's Law Enforcement Assn., Nat. Sheriffs Assn., N.C. Sheriff's Assn., Montgomery County Law Enforcement Assn., Profl. Women's Assn. Office: US Post Office 324 W Market St Greensboro NC 27401-2544

WALLACE, BETTY JEAN, elementary school educator, lay minister; b. Denison, Tex., Dec. 5, 1927; d. Claude Herman and Pearl Victoria (Freels) Moore; m. Billy Dean McKneely, Sept. 2, 1950 (div. Nov. 1964); children: Rebecca Lynn, Paul King, David Freels, John Walker, Philip Andrew McKneely. Student, Tulane U., 1947; BA, Baylor U., 1949; postgrad., U. Houston, 1949-50, 74, 81, Rocky Mountain Bible Inst., 1959, U. Colo., 1969-70, U. No. Colo., 1965, 68, 72, U. St. Thomas, 1992, Autonomous U. Guadalajara, summer 1993; MEd, Houston Bapt. U., 1985. Cert. life profl. elem., high sch., life profl. reading specialist, secondary field ESL tchr., Tex. Tchr. Galena Park (Tex.) Ind. Sch. Dist., 1949-50, 52-53, 72-98, Corpus Christi (Tex.) Independent Sch. Dist., 1950-51, Denver Pub. Schs., 1953-54, 63-72, Wackenhut Cleveland (Tex.) Correctional Ctr., 1999—2003. Author: The Holy Spirit Today, 1989, Our God of Infinite Variety, 1991, God Speaks in a Variety of Ways, 1991. Sunday sch. tchr. So. Bapt. Conv. chs., Tex., 1946-50, Denver, 1952-56; tchr. kindergarten Emmanuel Bapt. Ch., Denver, 1956-59, 60-63; missionary, Queretaro, Mex., 1977, 78; mem. Rep. Senatorial Inner Circle, Washington, 1989-91, 2002, Round Table for Ronald Reagan, Washington, 1989-90; mem. Pres.' Club, 2002-03, founding mem. RNC Presdl. Trust; helper Feed the Poor, Houston, 1983-85; active Suicide Prevention, Houston, 1973-76, Literacy, Houston, 1978-81; rep. NEA, Denver, 1966-72; mem. Retirement Com., Denver, 1970-72; bd. advisors Oliver North, 1994. Recipient Rep. Senatorial medal of freedom, 1994, Rep. Senatorial medal of Victory, Justice, Freedom and Liberty, 2002, Congl. Order of Merit, 2003; grantee, NSF, 1969—70. Mem. Tex. Classroom Tchrs. Assn. (officer rep., pres. Galena Park chpt. 1988-91), Pres.'s Club, Delta Alpha Pi (pres. Waco chpt. 1948-49), Alpha Epsilon Delta. Republican. Avocations: writing, archeology, gardening, reading, gem/jewelry collecting and designing. Home: 14831 Anoka Dr Channelview TX 77530-3201

WALLACE, BONNIE ANN, biochemistry and biophysics researcher, educator; b. Greenwich, Conn., Aug. 10, 1951; d. Arthur Victor and Maryjane Wallace. BS in Chemistry, Rensselaer Poly. Inst., 1973; PhD in Molecular Biophysics and Biochemistry, Yale U., 1977; DSc (hon.), U. London, 1995. Postdoctoral rsch. fellow Harvard U., Boston, 1977-78; asst. prof. dept. biochemistry and molecular biophysics Columbia U., N.Y.C., 1979-86, assoc. prof., 1986; prof. dept. chemistry, dir. Ctr. for Biophysics Rensselaer Poly. Inst., 1987-92; reader in crystallography U. London, 1991—2001, prof. molecular biophysics, 2001—; dir. Ctr. for Protein and Membrane Structure and Dynamics, Daersbury Lab., 1999—. Vis. scientist MRC Lab. Molecular Biology, Cambridge, Eng., 1978; Fogarly sr. fellow Birkbeck Coll., U. London, 1990. Assoc. editor Peptide and Protein Letters; mem. editl. adv. bd. Biochemistry; contbr. numerous articles to profl. jours. and books. Jane Coffin Childs fellow, 1977-79; recipient Irma T. Hirschl award, 1980-84, Sci Web award, 1998; Camille and Henry Dreyfus tchr.-scholar, 1986; named Hot Young Scientist Fortune Mag., 1990; Subject of Documentary Film: Hypertension Research for the Future, 1995. Fellow: AAAS, Inst. Biology, Royal Soc. Chemistry; mem.: Biochem. Soc. Britain, Brit. Crystallographic Assn. (BSG award 1994), Biophysics Soc. (nat. coun., mem. internat. rels. com., Dayhoff award 1985), Phi Lambda Upsilon, Sigma Xi. Office: U London Birkbeck Coll Dept Crystallography London WC1E 7HX England

WALLACE, C. ELIZABETH MCFARLAND, retired association director; b. Cumberland, Md., Apr. 2, 1914; d. Frank Russel and Maude Sabine (McFarland) McFarland; m. David Henry Wallace, Aug. 17, 1938; children: David Henry Jr., Stephen McFarland, Douglas Cecil; m. Charles F. Pratt, Oct. 12, 1991 (dec. Dec. 1996). BS summa cum laude, U. Md., 1936, MA, 1937. Cert. tchr., Md. Tchr. math. and sci. Annapolis (Md.) Jr. and Sr. H.S., 1952-59; exec. dir. Shellfish Inst. N.Am., Annapolis and Sayville, N.Y., 1960-72; account exec. Manna Fin. Assn., Fairfax, Va., 1972-74; exec. dir. Marine Tech. Soc., Washington, 1974-75; sr. program analyst NSF, Washington, 1975-85. Rschr. Chesapeake Biol. Lab., Solomons Island, Md., 1931-41. Editor: (biweekly newspaper) Shellfish Soundings, 1959-71. Co-founder LWV, Annapolis, 1940—, recorder Leisure World, Silver Spring, Md., 1995—; dir. Mut. 16, Leisure World, 1986-88, treas.; rep. Mut. 16 to Leisure World Comty. Coun.; life mem. Md. PTA; active Meals on Wheels; lobbyist LWV, Anne Arundel County Tchrs. Assn., shellfish industry. Fellow U. Md., 1936. Mem. Am. Fisheries Soc. Democrat. Methodist. Avocations: reading, dance, traveling. Home: Leisure World 15501 Prince Frederick Way Silver Spring MD 20906-1318

WALLACE, CAROL, editor at large; b. Chgo. BS in Comm., U. Ill., 1971. With Phila. Daily News, Rochester Times-Union, Tribune Pub. Co., N.Y. Daily News, N.Y.C., 1979—82; sr. writer People Mag., N.Y.C., 1982—85, sr. editor, 1985—88, 1990—92, asst. mng. editor, 1991—94, dep. mng. editor, 1994—97, mng. editor, 1997—2002; editor at large Time Inc., N.Y.C., 2003—. Writer, host The Wallace Report for Daytime, Heart/ABC Women's Network, 1982—84; editor Us Mag., 1988—90. Co-author: The Portable Best Friend, 1996. Recipient Front Page award, Newswomen's Club N.Y., 1982. Office: Time Inc Rockefeller Ctr New York NY 10020-1393

WALLACE, EDNA MARIE, paralegal; b. Indpls., July 22, 1945; d. William T. and Agnes L. (Pierce) Branson; m. James Michael Wallace; children: Penny Sue Wallace-Steele, Brandi Michael Wallace-Coffin. Paralegal Cert., Am. Inst. Paralegal Studies, Oak Brook Terrace, Ill., 1988. Paralegal, office adminstr. Baldwin & Baldwin, Danville, Ind., 1985—90; paralegal Tucker, Surface, Fehribach, Indpls., 1990—92; paralegal, office adminstr. Hebenstreit & Moberly, 1992—96; paralegal Kroger, Gardis & Regas, 1996—2002, Whitham, Hebenstreit & Zubek, LLP, 2002—. Presenter in field. Paralegal adv. bd. St. Mary of the Woods Coll., 1999—. Mem. ABA (assoc.), Nat. Fedn. Paralegal Assns. (registered paralegal), Indpls. Bar Assn. (chair paralegal exec. com. 1998-2000, 2002-03, Legal Awareness com., Placement com., CLE comm., Paralegal of Yr. 1999), Ind. State Bar Assn. (paralegal com.), Ind. Paralegal Assn. (bd. dirs. legis. sect. chair 1999-2003, chair ethics sect. 2000-03, Lifetime Achievement award 2002), Bus./Profl. Women, Order Eastern Star, Job's Daus. (adult leader 1986-2000, bd. dirs. ednl. found. 1997-2000), Epsilon Sigma Alpha (pres. chpt. 1988-90). Republican. Baptist. Office: Whitham Hebenstreit & Zubek LLP 151 N Delaware St # 2000 Indianapolis IN 46204 E-mail: emw@whzlaw.com.

WALLACE, EVELINA VELVIA JOETHA, elementary school educator; arrived in U.S., 1979; d. Milton Rodon Cox Sr. and Leanna Sara Cox; m. Sydney Alexis Wallace IV, Dec. 9, 1989; children: Alexia Justina, Sydney Alexis V. AA, Miami Dade C.C., 1983; BS, Miami Fla. Meml. Coll., 1984. Tchr. S.C. Pherson High Sch., Nassau, The Bahamas, 1984—91, Bayharbor Elem. Sch., Miami, 1991—92, Oak Grove Elem. Sch., 1992—93, North Miami Mid. Sch., 1993—94, Lake Steven Elem. Sch., 1994—97, Meml. Mid. Sch., Orlando, 1997—98, Ctrl. Ave. Elem. Sch., Kissimmee, 1998—99, Kissimmee Elem. Sch, 1999—. Dir. women of region Caribbean Internat. Mins., Kissimmee, 1997, v.p., 1994, marriage counselor, 1994. Mem.: Arts Complete Edn., Fla. Music Educators Assn. Avocations: cooking, travel, singing. Home: 2080 Pine Needle Trail Kissimmee FL 34746 E-mail: evelinawallace@cim.com.

WALLACE, FANNIE MARGARET, minister, religious organization administrator; b. Corpus Christi, Tex., Apr. 20, 1942; d. Isaac Herron and Etha Lena Madison; m. William Taft Wallace, Nov. 1, 1973; children: Robert Terrance Hill, Prinston Damone Hill, Kevin Claudell Hill, Charisma Pitre. BTh, Cornerstone U. & Sem. of Jerusalem, Israel, 1994. Pastor, founder pvt. sch., adminstr., bus. developer Praise Assembly Ministries/Harbor Christian Acad., Del City, Okla., 1993—; CEO Praise Assembly Full Gospel Ministries, Del City, 1993—. Author: Prosperity Belongs to You, 1999, How To Go From Victory to Victory, 1999, Called to Separate, 2000, No More Issues, 2001, Next Level, 2002. Office: Praise Assembly Full Gospel Ministries 3540 SE 15th St Del City OK 73115 Office Phone: 405-677-3553. Business E-Mail: praiseassembly@sbcglobal.net.

WALLACE, GLADYS BALDWIN, librarian; b. Macon, Ga., June 5, 1923; d. Carter Shepherd and Dorothy (Richard) Baldwin; m. Hugh Loring Wallace Jr., Oct. 14, 1941 (div. Sept. 1968); children: Dorothy, Hugh Loring III. BS in Edn., Oglethorpe U., 1961; MLS, Emory U., 1966; EdS, Ga. State U., 1980. Libr. pub. elem. schs., Atlanta, 1956-66; libr. Northside HS, 1966-87, Episc. Cathedral St. Philip. Author: The Time of My Life, 1994, Glorious Grass, 2003. Mem. High Mus. Art, Madison-Morgan Cultural Ctr. Recipient Poet of Merit award, 1999; Ga. Dept. Edn. grantee, 1950, NDEA grantee, 1963, 65. Mem.: Am. Assn. Univ. Women, Atlanta Hist. Soc., Am. Assn. Ret. Persons, Atlanta Bot. Garden, Ga. Women of Achievement. Home: NC 6 136 Peachtree Memorial Dr NW Atlanta GA 30309-1096

WALLACE, HELEN MARGARET, pediatrician, preventive medicine physician, educator; b. Hoosick Falls, NY, Feb. 18, 1913; d. Jonas and Ray (Schweizer) W. AB, Wellesley Coll., 1933; MD, Columbia U., 1937; MPH cum laude, Harvard U., 1943. Diplomate Am. Bd. Pediat., Am. Bd. Preventive Medicine. Intern Bellevue Hosp., NYC, 1938-40; child hygiene physician Conn. Health Dept., 1941-42; successively jr. health officer, health officer, chief maternity and newborn div., dir. bur. for handicapped children NYC Health Dept., 1943-55; prof., dir. dept. pub. health NY Med. Coll., 1955-56; prof. maternal and child health U. Minn. Sch. Pub. Health, 1956-59; chief profl. tng. US Children's Bur., 1959-60, chief child health studies, 1961-62; prof. maternal and child health U. Calif. Sch. Pub. Health, Berkeley, Calif., 1962-80, 99; prof., head divsn. maternal and child health Sch. Pub. Health San Diego State U., Calif., 1980—; Univ. Rsch. lectr. San Diego State U., Calif., 1985—. Cons. WHO numerous locations, including Uganda, The Philippines, Turkey, India, Geneva, Iran, Burma, Sri Lanka, East Africa, Australia, Indonesia, China, Taiwan, 1961—, traveling fellow, 1989—; cons. Hahnemann U., Phila., 1993, Ford Found., Colombia, 1971; UN cons. to Health Bur., Beijing, China, 1987; fellow Aiiku Inst. on Maternal and Child Health, Tokyo, and NIH Inst. Child Health and Human Devel., 1994; dir. Family Planning Project, Zimbabwe, 1984-87; vis. prof. U. Calif., Berkeley, 1999, 00, prof. emeritus, 2000—; mem. adv. com., faculty APHA Com. on Continuing Edn. Author, editor: 20 textbooks; editor (sr.): Health and Social Reform for Families for the 21st Century, 2d edit., 2003, Health and Welfare for Families in the 21st Century, 2003 (award Am. Coll. Nursing, Am. Jour. Nursing); contbr. 335 articles to profl. jours. Mem. coun. on Disabled Children to Media, 1991; dir. San Diego County Infant Mortality Study, 1989—, San Diego Study of Prenatal Care, 1991. Recipient Alumnae Achievement award Wellesley Coll., 1982, U. Minn. award, 1985; Ford Found. study grantee, 1986, 87, 88; fellow World Rehab. Fund, India, 1991-92, Fulbright Found., 1992—, NIH Inst. Child Health and Human Devel., 1994, Aiiku Inst. of Maternal-Child Health, Tokyo, 1994. Fellow: APHA (officer sect., chmn. com. on internat. maternal and child health, mem. faculty and adv. com. maternal and child health program 2000, Martha May Eliot award 1978, award in Internat. Maternal and Child Health 2001), Am. Acad. Pediatrics (Job Smith award 1980); mem.: AMA, Am. Sch. Preventive Medicine, Ambulatory Pediatric Assn., Am. Acad. Cerebral Palsy, Assn. Tchrs. Maternal and Child Health. Home: 850 State St San Diego CA 92101-6046

WALLACE, JANE HOUSE, retired geologist; b. Ft. Worth, Aug. 12, 1926; d. Fred Leroy and Helen Gould (Kixmiller) Wallace. AB, Smith Coll., 1947, MA, 1949; postgrad., Bryn Mawr Coll., 1949-52. Geologist U.S. Geol. Survey, 1952-97; chief Pub. Inquiries Offices, Washington, 1964-72, spl. asst. to dir., 1974-97, dep. bur. ethics counselor, 1975-97, Washington liaison Office of Dir., 1978-97; ret., 1997. Recipient Meritorious Service award Dept. Interior, 1971, Disting. Svc. award, 1976, Sec.'s Commendation, 1988, Smith Coll. medal, 1992. Fellow Geol. Socs. Am., Washington (treas. 1963-67); mem. Sigma Xi (assoc.)

WALLACE, JEANNETTE OWENS, state legislator; b. Scottsdale, Ariz., Jan. 16, 1934; d. Albert and Velma (Whinery) Owens; m. Terry Charles Wallace Sr., May 21, 1955; children: Terry C. Jr., Randall J., Timothy A., Sheryl L., Janice M. BS, Ariz. State U., 1955. Mem. Los Alamos (N.Mex.) County Coun., 1981-82; cons. County of Los Alamos, 1983-84; chmn., vice chmn. Los Alamos County Coun., 1985-88; cons. County of Los Alamos, Los Alamos Schs., 1989-90; rep. N.Mex. State Legislature, 1991—. Mem. appropriations and fin. govt. and urban affairs, N.Mex., 1991—, legis. fin. com., Indian affairs, radioactive and hazardous materials, co-chmn. Los Alamos County's dept. energy negotiating com., 1987-88; mem. legis. policy com. Mcpl. League, N.Mex., 1986-88; mem. legis. fin. com. Info. Tech. and Energy Coun., radioactive & hazardous materials com., medicaid oversight com., legis. coun., info. tech., LANL oversight com., energy coun. Bd. dirs. Tri-Area Econ. Devel., 1988-94, 96—, Crime Stoppers, Los Alamos, 1988-92, Los Alamos Citizens Against Substance Abuse, 1989-94; mem. N.Mex. First, Albuquerque, 1989-2003; legis. chmn. LWV, 1990; mem. Los Alamos Rep. Women, pres., 1989-90; bd. dirs. Los Alamos Commerce and Devel., 1990—. Mem. Los Alamos Bus. & Profl. Women (legis. chmn. 1990), Los Alamos C. of C., Mana del Norte, Kiwamis. Methodist. Avocations: tennis, needlework, reading. Home: 1913 Spruce Los Alamos NM 87544-3041 E-mail: wallace@losalamos.com.

WALLACE, JOYCE IRENE MALAKOFF, internist; b. Phila., Nov. 25, 1940; d. Samuel Leonard and Henrietta (Hameroff) Malakoff; m. Lance Arthur Wallace, Aug. 30, 1964 (div. 1974); 1 dau. Julia Ruth; m. Arthur H. Kahn, Oct. 7, 1979 (div. 1986); 1 son, Aryeh N. Kahn. AB, Queens Coll., CUNY, 1961; postgrad., Columbia U., 1962-64; MD, SUNY, 1968. Diplomate Am. Bd. Internal Medicine. Intern St. Vincent's Hosp. Med. Ctr., N.Y.C., 1968-70; practice medicine N.Y.C., 1970-71; resident Manhattan VA Hosp., N.Y.C., 1972, Nassau County Med. Ctr., East Meadow, N.Y., 1972-73; practice medicine North Conway, NH, 1973—74; practice medicine specializing in internal medicine N.Y.C., 1976—; med. dir. FROST'D Primary Care, 1999—2003. Mem. attending staff Nassau County Med. Ctr., 1974, St. Vincent's Hosp. and Med. Ctr., N.Y.C., 1977— ; asst. prof. medicine Mt. Sinai Med. Sch., N.Y.C.; pres. Found. for Rsch. on Sexually Transmitted Diseases, Inc., 1986-89, exec. and med. dir., 1989-2003. Fellow ACP, N.Y. Acad. Medicine; mem. Am. Med. Women's Assn., N.Y. County, N.Y. State Med. Socs. Office: 32 W 18th St New York NY 10011

WALLACE, JULIA DIANE, newspaper editor; b. Davenport, Iowa, Dec. 3, 1956; d. Franklin Sherwood and Eleanor Ruth (Pope) W.; m. Doniver Dean Campbell, Aug. 23, 1986; children: Emmaline Livingston Campbell, Eden Jennifer Campbell. BS in Journalism, Northwestern U., 1978. Reporter Norfolk (Va.) Ledger-Star, 1978-80, Dallas Times Herald, 1980-82; reporter, editor News sect. USA Today, Arlington, Va., 1982-89, mng. editor spl. projects, 1989-92; mng. editor Chgo. Sun-Times, 1992-1996; exec. editor Statesman Jour., 1996—98; mng. editor Arizona Republic, Phoenix, 1998—2000, Atlanta Journal and Constitution, Atlanta, 2001—02, editor, 2002—. Mem. Am. Soc. Newspaper Editors. Mailing: The Atlanta Journal Constitution P O Box 4689 Atlanta GA 30302 Office: Atlanta Journal Constitution 72 Marietta St NW Atlanta GA 30303*

WALLACE, MARCIA GAYLE, art educator, theater educator, photographer; b. Cleve., Jan. 3, 1951; d. William Charles Wallace and Ruth Charlotte Andersen; life ptnr. Tom Carraway. BA in Art, Conn. Coll., 1973; MFA in Mixed Media Art, Ariz. State U., 1976; MA in Speech and Theater, Ark. State U., 1997. Vis. lectr. in art Phoenix Coll., 1977—78; exhibits designer coord. Omaha Children's Mus., 1978—79; project coord. photo preservation We. Heritage Mus., Omaha, 1980—81; artist-in-edn. Ark. Arts Coun., 1984—95; instr. art, speech, and theater Ozarka Tech. Coll., Melbourne, Ark., 1993—98, U. Ark. C.C., Batesville, 1998—. Presenter in field. Author: Theater as Nexus in Small Communities, 1997;, exhibitions include Ark. Arts Ctr., 1987, Lyon Coll., 1995, Hendricks Coll., 1996, corp. collections. Mem. Batesville Area Arts Coun., 1998—; bd. dirs. Batesville Cmty. Theater, 1999—. Artist Photography fellow, Ark. Arts Coun., 1986. Mem.: S.W. Theatre Assn. Avocations: home designing and building, gardening, scuba diving, travel, hiking. Home: 865 Brown Camp Rd Mountain View AR 72560 Office: U Ark CC at Batesville POB 3350 Batesville AR 72503 E-mail: mwallace@uaccb.edu.

WALLACE, MARY ELAINE, opera director, author; m. Robert House. BFA cum laude, U. Nebr., Kearney, 1940; MusM, U. Ill., 1954; postgrad., Music Acad. West, Santa Barbara, Calif., 1955, Eastman Sch. Music, 1960, Fla. State U., 1962. Prof. voice, dir. opera La. Tech. U., Ruston, 1954-62, SUNY-Fredonia, 1962-69, So. Ill. U.-Carbondale, 1969-79; dir. Marjorie Lawrence Opera Theatre, Opera on Wheels; adminstrv. adviser Summer Playhouse, Carbondale; stage mgr. Chautauqua Opera Co., N.Y., 1963; asst. mus. dir., condr. Asolo Festival, Sarasota, Fla., 1961; music editor, critic The Chautauquan Daily; adjudicator Met. Opera auditions; exec. sec. Nat. Opera Assn., 1981-91. Co-author: Opera Scenes for Class and Stage, 1979, (with Robert Wallace) More Operas Scenes for Class and Stage, 1990, Upstage Downstage, 1992. Founding mem. bd. dirs. Rockwall Alliance for the Arts, 2001; founding bd. dirs. Rockwall Musicfest, Rockwall, 2002. Recipient Lifetime Achievement award Nat. Opera Assn., 1998, disting. alumni award U. Nebr., 1998. Mem. Nat. Opera Assn. (pres. 1974, 75), Music Tchrs. Nat. Assn., Nat. Assn. Tchrs. Singing, AAUP, AAUW, Met. Opera Guild, Mortar Bd., Sigma Tau Delta, Pi Kappa Lambda, Phi Beta, Alpha Psi Omega, Delta Kappa Gamma Address: 3106 Lakeside Dr Rockwall TX 75087-5319 E-mail: mehouse@flash.net.

WALLACE, MARY COLETTE, architectural researcher, designer; m. Clay Wallace. BArch, BA in Philosophy, U. Okla., 1989. Design rschr. various architecture and design firms, 1989—97; pres. Wallace Rsch. Group, Bellevue, Wash., 1998—. Task force mem. NW Regional Sustainable Bldg. Action Plan, Seattle, 1998—99. Contbr. articles to profl. jours.; editor (author): The WRG Newsletter. Cons. Overlake Pk. Presbyn. Ch. /Habitat for Humanity Townhome Project, Bellevue, Wash., 1991—94. Mem.: MENSA, AIA (assoc.), Assn. of Ind. Info. Profls. (electronic comm. com. chair list coord. 2003—). Democrat. Presbyterian. Avocations: swimming, drawing. Office: Wallace Research Group POB 50128 Bellevue WA 98015 Office Phone: 425-637-9049. E-mail: info@wallaceresearch.net.

WALLACE, MICHELE, writer, educator; b. N.Y.C., Jan. 4, 1952; d. Robert Earl Wallace and Faith Ringgold; m. Eugene Nesmith, Dec. 22, 1989 (div. Nov. 2002). BA, CCNY, 1974, MA in English, 1990; PhD in Cinema Studies, NYU, 1998. Asst. prof. English CUNY, 1989—91; assoc. prof. English, women's studies and film CUNY and CUNY Grad. Ctr., 1991—97, prof., 1998. Pres. Art Without Walls, 1974. Author: Black Macho and the Myth of the Superwoman, 1979, Invisibility Blues: Pop to Theory, 1990, Black Popular Culture, 1992, Dark Designs and Visual Culture, 2004, Invisibility Blues: From Pop to Theory and Back Again, 2004; columnist: The Village Voice, 1996; contbr. to newspapers and popular mags. including Ms., The Village Voice, The Nation, The N.Y. Times, Art Forum, Art In America; editor: Women in Art, 1971; mem. editl. bd.: Social Identities, Women and Therapy. Founding mem. Nat. Black Feminist Orgn., 1974; pres. Women Students and Artists for Black Art Liberation, 1970—76. Mem.: PEN, MLA, Oscar Micheaux Soc., Soc. Cinema Studies, Am. Studies Assn., Phi Beta Kappa.

WALLACE, MICHELE, media company executive; Assignment editor Sta. WVUE-TV, ABC, New Orleans, News 12, all-news cable channel, L.I., N.Y.; with Medialink Inc., N.Y.C., 1989—; now v.p. global ops. Office: Medialink Inc 708 3rd Ave Fl Dave9 New York NY 10017-4201 E-mail: mwallace@medialink.com.

WALLACE, NORA ANN, lawyer; b. Phila., May 24, 1951; AB, Vassar Coll., 1973; JD cum laude, Harvard U., 1976. Bar: N.Y. 1977. Mem. Willkie Farr & Gallagher, N.Y.C. Trustee Vassar Coll., Bklyn. Acad. Music, Bklyn. Acad. Music Endowment Trust; pres. Harvard Law Sch. Assn. of N.Y.C.; bd. dirs. Joseph Collins Found. Office: Willkie Farr & Gallagher 787 7th Ave New York NY 10019-6099

WALLACE, PATRICIA ELLEN, minister; b. Rockville Centre, NY, July 29, 1950; d. Bertram Earl Wallace, Jr. and Lorraine Marie File; children: Russell, Ryan, Alicia, Richard, Peter, Jonathan. A in Theology and Missions, Cathedral Bible Coll., 1999. Lic. minister, pastor Pentecostal Holiness, ordained pastor Ch. of God. Evangelist, recording artist Patricia Wallace Ministries, NY, 1975—; pastor Burlington, Vt., 1981—84; pastor, counselor Pentecostal Holiness Ch., Lake City, SC, 1995—99; pastor, chaplain Ch. of God, Cleve., Tenn., 2000—. Performer: (albums) Hope in My Darkest Hours, 1992; author: Nine Steps to Being Whole, 2000, When the One You Love Hurts: A Guide to Aid in the Recovery of Domestic Abuse, 2003. Founder, chmn. bd. dirs. Six-Mile Crisis Intervention, Mt. Pleasant, SC, 1995—97; victims advocate, crisis counselor United Way-Turning Point Battered Woman's Shelter, Monroe, NC, 1999—; counselor West Main Crisis Counseling Ctr., Rock Hill, SC, 2000—. Recipient Cert. of Recognition, Calvary Protestant Ch., 1964, Baldwin Sr. H.S., 1968, United Way, 2002. Avocations: art, singing, guitar. Home: PO Box 754 Fort Mill SC 29716 Office: PO Box 952 Monroe NC 28111

WALLACE, PAULA S. academic administrator; 3 children. BA, Furman U.; MEd, EdS, Ga. State U. Co-founder Savannah Coll. Art and Design, 1979, pres., 2000—. Author of children's books. Mem. Skidaway Island United Meth. Ch., Savannah, Ga. Film and Videotape Commn., Ga. C. of C.; bd. dirs. B. B. & T. Bank, Nat. Mus. Women in the Arts. Recipient Oglethorpe Bus. and Profl. Women award, James T. Deason Human Rels. award; named Outstanding Young Woman of Am., Ky. Col.; named to Savannah Bus. Hall of Fame. Office: Savannah Coll Art and Design PO Box 3146 622 Drayton St Savannah GA 31402-3146

WALLACE, ROANNE, hosiery company executive; b. Greenwood, Miss., Dec. 18, 1949; d. Robert Carter and Lois Anne (Vick) Wallace. BM, U. Tenn., 1971; MA, U. NC, 1976; MBA, Wake Forest U., 1982. Exec. dir. Am. Bd. Clin. Chemistry, Winston, Salem, NC, 1977-78; adminstrv. officer Forsyth County Office Emergency Mgmt., 1978-79, sr. asst. dir., 1979-82; with Sara Lee, 1982—; mktg. dir. Hanes Her Way Intimates, Sara Lee Hosiery, Just My Size, 1988—; product mgr. L'eggs Products, Inc., 1986-88. Mem. adv. coun. Forsyth County Office Piedmont Emergency Mgmt., Winston-Salem, NC; bd. dirs. Piedmont Opera Theatre, Inc.

Recipient Miss University of Tenn., Tenn., 1970. Home: 803 Devon Ct Winston Salem NC 27104-1263 Office: Sara Lee Intimates 5650 University Pkwy Winston Salem NC 27105-1312

WALLACE, SARAH FITZGERALD, music educator; d. Roger Eugene Fitzgerald and Patricia Gail Finnell; m. Matthew Spaulding Wallace, July 25, 2000. MusB, Meredith Coll., 1997. Lic. tchr. K-12 music edn. N.C. Elem. gen. music educator Green Yr.-Round Elem., Raleigh, NC, 1997—99; choral dir. North Johnston H.S., Kenly, NC, 1999—2001; project assoc. The Copernicus Group Ind. Rev. Bd., Cary, NC, 2001—02; elem. gen. music tchr. Lead Mine Elem., Raleigh, 2002—03. Mem.: Music Educators Nat. Conf.

WALLACE, SARAH REESE, banker; b. Newark, Ohio, Apr. 30, 1954; m. John H. Wallace; children: Sarah Hollman, John Gilbert, John Gerald. MBA, Ind. U., 1979; BA, DePauw U., 1976. Mgmt. trainee City Nat. Bank, Columbus, Ohio, 1976-78; with First Fed. Savs. and Loan Assn., Newark, 1980—, pres., 1982-99, chmn., 1999—, also bd. dirs. Trustee Ohio Savs. and Loan League, 1987—94, Thomas J. Evans Found., Newark Campus Devel. Fund, 1999—, DePauw U., 2000—; pres., sec. Thomas J. Evans Found., 1980—; trustee, treas. exec. com. Licking County Found., 1993—95; trustee A Call to Coll., Ctrl. Ohio Tech. Coll., Newark. Recipient Woman of Achievement award, 1993, Oustanding Young Alumni award DePauw U., 1990. Office: PO Box 4460 Newark OH 43058-4460

WALLACE, SCYATTA A, public health researcher, program consultant; d. Alexander and Miama Wallace. BA, Yale U., New Haven, 1996; PhD Fordham U., Bronx, NY, 2002. Asst. rsch. scientist NYU Sch. Medicine, N.Y.C., 2000—02; postdoctoral fellow CDC, Atlanta, 2002—04; asst. prof. SUNY, 2004—. Evaluation cons. Evaluation Tech. Assistance Ctr. Columbia U., N.Y.C., 1998—2000; P.T.O. instr. Fordham U., Bronx, NY, 1999—2000; evaluation cons. Social Sci. Rsch. Coun., N.Y.C., 1998—; diversity cons. Allyn and Bacon Pub. Co., Boston, 2002—04. Mem. alumni schools com. Yale U., New Haven, 1997—. Fellow Ethics Edn., NSF, 1998-2001; grantee, Ctr. for Ethics Edn., 2000—02. Mem.: NIH (health dispatchers scholor 2003—), APHA, APA (Policy Fellow 2000), Soc. Rsch. in Child Devel., Assn. of Practical and Profl. Ethics, Sigma Xi, Delta Sigma Theta (v.p. then pres. 1994—96). Avocations: photography, painting, travel. Office Phone: 404-639-6158. Personal E-mail: scyatta@earthlink.net.

WALLACE, STEPHANIE ANN, music educator, conductor; b. Denver, Mar. 28, 1956; d. Carmen Reilly Sutley and Gladys Jane Stults; m. Brett Lee Wallace, July 28, 1979; children: Lindsey Annette, Robin Christine. Bachelor of Music Edn., Colo. U., Boulder, 1979. Cert. music tchr. grades K-12 Colo. Tchr. orch. Dist. 12 Five Star Schs., Northglenn, Colo., 1979—82; tchr. cello Broomfield, Colo., 1982—90, Boulder, 1982—90; tchr. orch. Boulder Valley Sch. Dist., 1990—. Condr. and music dir.: Front Range Youth Symphony Orchestras, 1991—, Auspices of the Arvada Ctr. for Arts and Humanities, —, cellist: Cameo String Quartet, 1980—, music arranger: string quartets and orchs., guest conductor:. Mem.: Music Educators Nat. Assn., Am. String Tchrs. Assn. (condr. all-state string orch. 2003), Pi Kappa Lambda (mem. Alpha Tau chpt.). Avocations: scuba diving, snorkeling, bicycling, hiking, fishing. Home: 4343 Eldorado Springs Dr Boulder CO 80303 Office: Boulder Valley Schs Fairview HS, Casey [illegible]

WALLACE-BRODEUR, RUTH MYRNA, writer; b. Springfield, Mass., Aug. 25, 1941; d. Emery Lincoln and Dorothy Helen (Blume) Wallace; m. Paul Henri Brodeur, Sept. 1, 1962; children: Jennifer Beth, Jeremy Ethan, Rachel Ruth, Sarah Blythe. Student, Andover Newton (Mass.) Theol.; BS in Psychology, U. Mass., Amherst, 1962. Psychologist Pineland Hosp.-Tng. Ctr., Maine, 1962—63; freelance writer various newspapers and mags., 1974—82. Spkr. in field. Author: The Kenton Year, 1980, One April Vacation, 1981, Callie's Way, 1984, Steps in Time, 1986, Stories from the Big Chair, 1989, Home by Five, 1992, The Godmother Tree, 1992, Goodbye Mitch, 1995, Blue Eyes Better, 2003 (End of Year Best Books List Publisher's Weekly Booklist, 2003). Hospice vol. Ctrl. Vt. Home Health Hospice; reading mentor Everybody Wins Montelier (Vt.) Elem. Sch.; tutor reading, ESL Adult Basic Edn., Montpelier. Mem.: Authors Guild, Inc., Soc. Children's Book Writers and Illustrators, Green Mountain Club. Democrat. Unitarian Universalist. Avocations: painting, gardening, sewing, kayaking, skiing.

WALLACE DOUGLAS, JEAN, conservationist; b. Des Moines, Iowa, June 30, 1920; d. Henry A. and Ilo Wallace; m. Wallace Leslie Douglas, Oct. 12, 1946; children: David, Joan, Ann. BA, Connecticut Coll., 1943. Pres. Wallace Genetic Found., Washington, D.C., 1965—. Past bd. dirs. America The Beautiful, Am. Bird Conservancy, Cornell Lab. of Ornithology, The Land Inst., Wallace House Birthplace, The Accokeek Found., Am. Farmland Trust, Concern, Henry A. Wallace Inst. for Alternative Agr. Office: Wallace Genetic Found Ste 220 4900 Massachusetts Ave NW Washington DC 20016-4358

WALLACE MCRAE, SHIRLEY ANN, retired secondary school educator; b. Jasper, Ala., Sept. 24, 1946; d. J.D. and Verna Mae Wallace; m. Don McRae (div.); 1 child, Barry Lynn McRae. AS, Judson Coll. for Women, 1965, Walker Coll., 1966; BS, Livingston U., 1968; MA, U. Ala., Birmingham, 1976, postgrad., 1977. Sci. tchr. Cordova (Ala.) H.S., 1968—99, head sci. dept., 1968—98; sci. tchr. Wallace State C.C., Hanceville, Ala., 1991—99; ret. Hanceville, Ala., 1999. Developer: ednl. and examination materials in field. Mem.: AAUW. Democrat. Baptist. Avocations: reading, collecting. Home: 89 Site B Rd Parrish AL 35580

WALLACH, ANNE JACKSON See JACKSON, ANNE

WALLACH, BARBARA PRICE, classicist, educator; b. Roanoke, Va., Aug. 31, 1946; d. Benjamin Thomas and Geneva Mae (Bittinger) Price; m. Luitpold Wallach, Aug. 22, 1970 (dec. Nov. 1986). BA in Latin, Mary Washington Coll., 1968; MA in Classics, U. Ill., 1970, PhD in Classical Philology, 1974. Summer vis. lectr. U. Ill., Urbana, 1977; vis. asst. prof. U. Pitts., 1979-80; asst. prof. U. Mo., Columbia, 1980-85, assoc. prof., 1985—. Author: Lucretius and the Diatribe, 1976; contbr. articles to profl. jours. Mem. Am. Philol. Assn., Classical Assn. Middle West and South, Internat. Soc. for the History of Rhetoric, Vergilian Soc., Phi Beta Kappa. Democrat. Avocations: music, flute, reading, sports. Office: U Mo Dept Classical Studies Columbia MO 65211-0001

WALLACH, MAGDALENA FALKENBERG (CARLA WALLACH), writer; b. Brussels; d. Carl Albert and Renee Antoinette (Meunier) Falkenberg; m. Philip Charles Wallach, Mar. 5, 1950. Student, Columbia U., Hunter Coll., New Sch. for Social Rsch. Ptnr. Williams-Falkenberg Advt. Assocs., Inc., N.Y.C., 1951-55. Author: Reluctant Weekend Gardener, 1971, Interior Decorating with Plants, 1976, Gardening in the City, 1976, Garden in a Teacup, 1978; contbr. articles to N.Y. Times, Glamour, Working Woman, Greenwich Time, Stamford Adv, others. Former bd. dirs. ARC, N.Y.C.; active Bruce Mus., 1987-2001, chmn. spl. events 75th anniversary gala, chmn. Renaissance Ball, bd. dirs., also other fundraising activities; former bd. dirs., v.p. Greenwich Adult Day Ctr. Mem. Nat. League Am. PEN Women (pres. Greenwich br. 1987-92, Owl award 1996), Authors Guild, Garden Writers Assn., English-Speaking Union (past bd. dirs. Greenwich br.), Alliance Francaise, Nat. Inst. Social Scis. Roman Catholic. Avocations: gardening, reading, travel, music, theater. Home: 126 W Lyon Farm Dr Greenwich CT 06831-4352

WALLACH, PATRICIA, councilwoman, retired mayor; b. Chgo. m. Ed Wallach; 3 children. Grad., Pasadena City Coll. Mem. city coun. City of El Monte, Calif., 1990-92, mayor, 1992-99, elected mem. of city coun., 2003—. Ret. tchr.'s aide Mountain View Sch. Dist. Past trustee El Monte Union High Sch. Dist., L.A. County High Sch. for the Arts; amb. of goodwill Zamora, Michoacan, Mex., Marcq-en-Baroeul, France, Yung Kang, Hsiang, Republic of China, Minhang, Peoples Republic of China; bd. dirs. Cmty. Redevel. Agy., El Monte Cmty. Access TV Corp.; mem. PTA, Little League Assns.; v.p. exec. bd., treas. Foothill Transit. Mem. League of Calif. Cities, San Gabriel Valley Coun. of Govts., Independent Cities Assn., U.S./Mex. Sister Cities Assn., Sister Cities Internat., Women of the Moose, El Monte Women's Club. Office Phone: 626-580-2001.

WALLACH-LEVY, WENDEE ESTHER, astrophotographer; b. N.Y.C., Dec. 29, 1948; d. Leonard Morris and Annette (Cohen) Wallach; m. David H. Levy, Mar. 23, 1997; 1 child, Nanette R. Vigil. BS in Edn., SUNY, Cortland, 1970; MA in Teaching, N.Mex. State U., 1975. Cert. tchr. N.Mex. Tchr. phys. edn. Las Cruces (N.Mex) Pub. Schs., 1970—96; mem. Shoemaker-Levy Observing Team, 1996—; dir. Jarnac Obs., Vail, Ariz., 1997—; mem. Jarnac Sky Survey Team, Vail, 2001—. Intramural and athletic coord. White Sands Sch., 1970—93; instr. swimming N.Mex. State U. Weekend Coll., Las Cruces, N.Mex., 1986—96; dir., coord. learn to swim program ARC, Las Cruces, N.Mex., 1970—96; instr. phys. edn., coach volleyball and track, athletic coord. Sierra Mid. Sch., 1993—96. Co-author: Making Friends with the Stars, Cosmic Discoveries, 2001; co-host (internet radio show) LetsTalkStars.com. Instr., trainer water safety ARC, 1973—98, instr., trainer CPR, 1974—98; instr., trainer life guard, health and safety specialist Doña Ana County, N.Mex., 1988—96, instr. trainer std. first aid, 1991—98; chair com. health and safety svcs. Doña Ana County Red Cross, N.Mex.; vol. MDA chairperson Telescopes for Telethon Fundraising Com., 1998—. Named Water Safety Instr. of the Yr., ARC, 1986, 1989, Asteroid 6485 in her honor, 1997; recipient 25 yr. Svc. award, ARC, 1992, 30 Yr. Svc. award, 1997. Mem.: AAHPERD, Nat. Intramural-Recreational Sports Assn., N.Mex. Alliance Health, Phys. Edn. Recreation and Dance (spkr., aquatic chmn. 1990—92), Internat. Dark Sky Assn. (life). Democrat. Jewish. Avocations: skywatching, swimming, needlework, astro photography.

WALLACK, RINA EVELYN, lawyer; b. Pitts.; d. Erwin Norman and Gloria A. (Schacher). AD in Nursing, Delta Coll., 1973; BS cum laude in Psychology, Eastern Mich. U., 1980; JD cum laude, Wayne State U., 1983. Registered nurse Mich.; bar: Calif. 1983. Psychiat. head nurse Ypsilanti (Mich.) State Hosp., 1973-77, instr., nursing educator, 1977-80; teaching asst. contracts Wayne State U., Detroit, 1981-83; legal asst. Wayne County Prosecutor's Office, 1982-83; atty. NLRB, L.A., 1983-86, dir. employee rels. legal svcs. Paramount Pictures Corp., L.A., 1986-89, v.p., 1989-98, v.p., sr. counsel, 1998-2002, sr. v.p., 2002-; Contbr. articles to profl. jours. Instr. ARC, Mich., 1978-80. Recipient Am. Jurisprudence Book award, 1983. Mem. ABA, L.A. County Bar Assn., Am. Trial Lawyers Assn., Mich. Bar Assn., Calif. Bar Assn., Order of Coif. Avocations: shooting, movies, dancing, reading, photography.

WALLEN, LINA HAMBALI, economics educator, consultant; b. Garut, West Java, Indonesia, Mar. 24, 1952; came to U.S., 1986; d. Mulyadi and Indra (Hudiyana) Hambali; m. Norman E. Wallen, Apr. 16, 1986. BA, IKIP, Bandung, Indonesia, 1975, DRA, 1984; PhD in Psychology, Columbia [illegible] U., 1993. Cert. tchr. Clk. PT Radio Frequency Communication, Bandung, 1972-74; adminstrv. mgr. CV Electronics Engring., Jakarta, Indonesia, 1974-76; exec. sec. PT Tanabe Abadi, Bandung, 1977-81; br. mgr. PT Ama Porta, Bandung, 1982-84; tchr. SMA Pembangunan, Bandung, 1976-83, Patuha Coll., Bandung, 1980-84. Faculty econ. dept. No. Ariz. U. Coll. Bus. Adminstrn., 2000—.

WALLER, PATRICIA FOSSUM, transportation executive, researcher, psychologist; b. Winnipeg, Man., Can., Oct. 12, 1932; d. Magnus Samuel and Diana Isabel (Briggs) Fossum; m. Marcus Bishop Waller, Dec. 27, 1957; children: Anna Estelle, Justin Magnus, Martha Wilkinson, Benjamin Earl. AB in Psychology cum laude, U. Miami, Coral Gables, 1953, MS in Psychology, 1955; PhD in Psychology, U. N.C., 1959. Psychology intern VA Hosp., Salem, Va., 1956; psychology instr. Med. Sch. U. N.C., Chapel Hill, 1957; USPHS postdoctoral fellow R.B. Jackson Lab., Bar Harbor, Maine, 1958-60; psychologist VA Hosp., Brockton, Mass., 1961-62; psychology lectr. U. N.C., Chapel Hill, Greensboro, 1962-67, assoc. dir. driver studies Hwy. Safety Rsch. Ctr. Chapel Hill, 1967-89, founding dir. Injury Prevention Rsch. Ctr., 1987-89; dir. Transp. Rsch. Inst. U. Mich., Ann Arbor, 1989-99, sr. rsch. scientist emerita, prof. emerita, 1999—; sr. rsch. scientist Ctr. for Transp. Safety, Tex. Transp. Inst. Tex. A&M U., 2002—. Bd. dirs. Intelligent Transp. Soc. Am., Washington, 1991—99, Traffic Safety Assn. Mich., Lansing, 1991—99; bd. advisors Eno Transp. Found., Inc., Lndnsdowne, Va., 1994—97; chair group 5 coun. Transp. Rsch. Bd. of NRC, Washington, 1992—95; chmn. Task Force Operation Regulations, 1974—76, mem. study com. devel. ranking rail safety R&D projects, 1980—82, chmn. group 3 coun. operation, safety and maintenance transp. facilities, 1980—83, mem. IVHS-IDEA tech. rev. panel, 1993—2000, chair workshop human factors rsch. in hwy. safety, 1992, chair ad hoc com. environ. activies, 92, mem. task force on elderly drivers, 1990—93, mem. com. vehicle user characteristics, 1983—86, mem. com. planning and adminstrn. of transp. safety, 1986—92, mem. com. alcohol, other drugs and transp., 1986—98, numerous other coms., mem. spl. coms. including Inst. Medicine Dana Award com., 1986—90, com. of 55MPH nat. maximum speed limit, 1983—84; mem. motor vehicle safety rsch. adv. com. Dept. Transp., Washington, 1991—94; reviewer JAMA, Jour. Studies on Alcohol, Jour. of Gerontology, Am. Jour. Pub. Health; apptd. Pres. Coun. Spinal Cord Injury, 1981; apptd. advisor Nat. Hwy. Safety Adv. Com. to Sec. U.S. Dept. Transp., 1979—80, 1980—83, chair nat. motor carrier adv. com., 1997—98; author numerous reports on transp. to govtl. coms. and univs. Author: (with Paul G. Shinkman) Instructor's Manual for Mogan and King: Introduction to Psychology, 1971; author: (with others) Psychological Concepts in the Classroom, 1974, Drinking: Alcohol in American Society—Issues and Current Research, 1978, The American Handbook of Alcoholism, 1982, The Role of the Civil Engineer in Highway Safety, 1983, Aging and Public Health, 1985, Young Driver Accidents: In Search of Solutions, 1985, Alcohol, Accidents and Injuries, 1986, Transportation in an Aging Society: Improving the Mobility and Safety for Older Persons, 1988, Young Drivers Impaired by Alcohol and Drugs, 1988; mem. editorial bd. Jour. Safety Rsch., 1979—; assoc. guest editor Health Edn. Quar., 1989; assoc. editor Accident, Analysis, and Prevention, 1978-84, mem. editorial bd., 1976-87; contbr. articles to profl. jours. Grantee HHS, 1982, 92-97, NIH; named Widmark laureate Internat. Coun. Alcohol, Drugs and Traffic Safety, 1995; Dist. Alumnus Awd., Dept. Psych., UNC Chapel Hill, 1997; recipient James J. Howard Trailblazer award Nat. Assn. of Govs. Hwy. Safety Reps., 1998, Svc. Awd., Intelligent Transportation Soc. of Amer., 1999; World Traffic Soc. Awd., 1999, World Safety Symposium, 1999; Lifetime Acheivement Awd., Mich. Traffic Safety Summit, 1999. Mem. AAAS, APA (Harold M. Hildreth award 1993), APHA (injury control and emergency health svcs. sect., Disting. Career award 1994, transp. rsch. bd., Roy W. Crum award for rsch. contbns. 1995), Assn. for the Advancement of Automotive Medicine (chmn. human factors sect. 1978-80, bd. dirs. 1979-82, pres. 1981-82), Coun. Univ. Transp. Ctrs. (exec. com. 1991-93), Transp. Rsch. Bd., Ea. Psychol. Assn., Sigma Xi. Democrat. Avocations: gardening, reading. Office: 1779 Crawford Dairy Rd Chapel Hill NC 27516 E-mail: pwaller@umich.edu.

WALLER, WILHELMINE KIRBY (MRS. THOMAS MERCER WALLER), civic worker, organization official; b. N.Y.C., Jan. 19, 1914; d. Gustavus Town and Wilhelmine (Claflin) Kirby; m. Thomas Mercer Waller, Apr. 7, 1942. Ed., Chapin Sch., N.Y.C. Conservation chmn. Garden Club Am., 1959-61, pres., 1965-68, chmn. nat. affairs, 1968-74, dir., 1969-71; mem. adv. com. N.Y. State Conservation Commn., 1959-70; mem. Nat. Adv. Com. Hwy. Beautification, 1965-68; trustee Mianus River Gorge Conservation Com. of Nature Conservancy, 1955—, Arthur W. Butler Meml. Sanctuary, 1955-79; dir. Westchester County Soil and Water Conservation Dist., 1967-74; adviser N.Y. Gov.'s Study Commn. Future of Adirondacks, 1968-70; adv. com. N.Y. State Parks and Recreation Commn., 1971-72; adv. com. to sec. state UN Conf. Human Environment, 1971-72; mem. Pres.'s Citizens Adv. Com. on Environ. Quality, 1974-78. Mem. planning bd., Bedford, 1953-57; mem. Conservation adv. coun., Bedford, N.Y., 1968-70, Westchester County Planning Bd., 1970-88; bd. govs. Nature Conservancy, 1970-78; Mem. Lyndhurst council Nat. Trust for Historic Preservation, 1965-74; bd. dirs. Scenic Hudson, Inc., 1985-88. Recipient Frances K. Hutchinson medal Garden Club Am., 1971, Holiday mag. award for beautiful Am., 1971, Conservation award Am. Motors Corp., 1975, Oak Leaf award Nature Conservancy, 1988. Mem. Nat. Soc. Colonial Dames, Huguenot Soc. Am., Daus. of Cincinnati Address: Tanrackin Farm Bedford Hills NY 10507

WALLER, WILMA RUTH, retired secondary school educator and librarian; b. Jacksonville, Tex., Nov. 15, 1921; d. William Wesley and Myrtle (Nesbitt) W. BA with honors, Tex. Woman's U., 1954, MA with honors, 1963, MLS with honors, 1976. Tchr. English Dell (Ark.) High Sch., 1953-54, Jefferson (Tex.) Ind. Schs., 1954-56, Tyler (Tex.) Ind. Schs., 1956-68; librarian Wise County Schs., Decatur, Tex., 1969-71, Thomas K. Gorman High Sch., Tyler, 1971-74, Sweetwater (Tex.) Ind. Sch. Dist., 1974-86; ret. Lectr., book reviewer for various clubs. Active in past as vol. for ARC, U. Tex. Health Ctr. Ford Found. fellow, 1959; recipient Delta Kappa Gamma Achievement award, 1992. Mem. UDC, Smith County Ret. Sch. Pers., Bible Study Group, Delta Kappa Gamma. Republican. Baptist. Avocations: reading, gourmet cooking, piano, writing letters. Home: 1117 N Azalea Dr Tyler TX 75701-5206

WALLEY, PAMELA KAYE, elementary school educator; b. Auburn, Ind., Aug. 1, 1969; d. Joseph S. and Margaret M. Witmer; m. Stephen Richard Walley. BS in Music Edn., Taylor U., 1992; MEd, Ind. Wesleyan U., 2000. Lic. tchr. in gen., choral and instrumental music grades K-12 Ind., 1992. Music educator Fairfield Elem. Sch., Fort Wayne, Ind., 1992—96, Croninger Elem. Sch., Fort Wayne, Ind., 1997—2001, Weisser Park Arts Magnet Sch., Fort Wayne, Ind., 2001—. Choral dir. Fort Wayne (Ind.) Children's Choir, 2000—; soprano Heartland Chamber Chorale, Fort Wayne, 2000—; choral dir. First Missionary Ch. Youth Chorale, Fort Wayne, 2001—; assoc. faculty Taylor U., Fort Wayne, 2001. Mem.: Ind. Music Educators Assn. (Circle the State coord. area 2 1997—99, elected rep. to IMEA bd. 1995—97), Am. Orff-Schulwerk Assn. Avocations: reading, gardening, cooking. Office: Weisser Park Arts Magnet Sch 902 Colerick St Fort Wayne IN 46806 Business E-Mail: Pamela.Walley@fwcs.k12.in.us

WALLHAUSEN, MILDRED CAROLYN, publisher; b. N.Y.C., Apr. 3, 1914; d. James Meroe and Frances (Bronson) Savell; m. Arthur Louis Wallhausen Sr., Sept. 25, 1936 (dec. Nov. 1969); children: Art L. Jr., Elizabeth Gail. Grad., Brown Bus. Coll., 1932. Proofreader Daily Am. Rep., Poplar Bluff, 1933-36; co-owner Enterprise-Courier, Charleston, 1936-69, pub., 1969—, East Prairie (Mo.) Eagle, 1969—. Illustrator: (children's book) Bobby Butterfly, 1986; watercolor artist. Mem. Mo. Gov.'s Adv. Coun., Comprehensive Health Planning Coun., 1969-73; mem. Bootheel CHP Coun., 1971-72, Charleston Park and Recreation Bd., 1972-77, Sr. Citizens Housing Project, 1973, Miss. County TB Assn., 1945-53, S.E. Mo. Regional Coun. Alcoholism and Drug Abuse, 1976-78, Miss. County Child Welfare Coun., 1974-77; bd. dirs. Miss. County Child Devel. Ctr., 1974-77; pres. Eugene Field Elem. Sch. PTA, 1948, Charleston H.S. PTA, 1935; chpt. mother FHA, 1955, 62; mem. Miss. County Cmty. Chs.; commr. East Prairie Housing Authority, 1992—; SEMO State U. Copper Dome Soc.(pres. coun.), mem. citizens adv. bd. S.E. U., Cape Girardeau KRCU-Public Radio, 1996-1999. Inducted Mo. Press Assn. Hall of Fame, 2000. Mem. NAACP, S.E. Mo. Press Assn (pres. 1981, historian 1982-), Miss. County Sheltered Workshops (bd. mem. 1985-), Am. Legion Aux, Citzens' Adv. Bd. 1997-99. Republican. Episcopalian. Office: Enterprise-Courier 206 S Main Charleston MO 63834

WALLIN, JEAN R. state legislator; b. Hibbing, Minn., Jan. 13, 1934; Student, U. Minn. Mem. N.H. Ho. of Reps., Concord, 1967-69, 75, N.H. Ho. of Reps. (dist. 15), Concord, 77-79, 96—; mem. local and regulated revenues com. N.H. Ho. of Reps., Concord, 1996—. Mediator. Chmn. N.H. Liquor Commn.; mem. Dem. Nat. Com.; pres. Nashua Bd. Edn., 1974-75. Mem. N.H. Mediators Assn. Unitarian Universalist. Office: NH Legis State House Concord NH 03301

WALLIN, MADGE MARIE, retired librarian, musician; b. Algona, Wash., Aug. 28, 1917; d. Samuel Gordon Felt and Lola Dorothy Woodruff; m. Charles Edward Wallin, Apr. 5, 1942 (dec. Mar. 6, 1991). Student in English lit., Seattle C.C., Seattle, 1948—49; student, U. Wash., Olympia (Wash.) Peninsula Coll., 1973—75. Lead clk. tool engring., libr. Boeing Hdqs., Seattle, 1950—64; libr. City of Port Townsend, Wash., 1943—45, 1948—62. Singer: Seattle Madrigal Soc., radio, TV, Seattle Opera Ho., others. Recipient internat. awards for flower arranging, 1986, 1988, 1989, Mary Johnson award. Fellow: DAR, Nat. Trust Historic Preservation (historic preservation award 1994), Port Townsend Garden Club (pres., bd. dirs., life judge, Gardener of Yr.); mem.: His. Soc. Jefferson County (arts and crafts bd. dirs.). Avocations: walking, sightseeing, birdwatching, gardening, writing. Home: 535 Fillmore St Port Townsend WA 98368

WALLING, DEBRA ANN, recreational therapist, director; b. Red Bank, N.J., Jan. 22, 1965; d. Charles James and Patricia Ann (Keane) W. BA, Slippery Rock U., 1988; postgrad., Georgian Ct. Coll. Recreational therapist Bayshore Health Care Ctr., Holmdel, N.J., 1988, 89-90, 1994-99, dir. recreation therapy, 1999—2001; pharmacy/I.V. tech. Bayshore Cmty. Hosp., Holmdel, 1988-89; co-mgr. Lane Bryant, Limited Inc., Ocean, N.J., 1990-92, store sales mgr., 1992-94; dir. recreation Meridian Nursing and Rehab., Red Bank, NJ, 2001—. Avocations: arts and crafts, travel, whitewater rafting, pet care, theater. Home: 120 Wilson Ave Apt 3 Port Monmouth NJ 07758-1553

WALLING, MARY JO ANNE, women's health nurse; b. L.A., Nov. 15, 1959; d. Armand Leo and Wilma Ceceila (Mathers) W.; m. Kevin M. McConnell, Dec. 26, 1981 (div. Dec. 1985); 1 child, Chelsey Christine Walling. BSN, Mount St. Mary's Coll., 1981; MICN, San Joaquin Delta, 1983; cert. early childhood edn., Strattford Career Inst., Wash. DC., 2001, cert. tchrs. aide, cert. child psychology, Strattford Career Inst., Wash. DC., 2002; cert. childcare mgmt., Edn. Direct, 2002; student, Strattford Career Inst., 2003—. RN Calif., Oreg.; cert. pub. health nurse, 1982, emergency nurse, Nat. Bd. Emergency Nursing, 1983. Nurse med. sur. St. Jo Sister of Providence, Burbank, Calif., 1981; nurse ICU, telemetry, emergency rm. St. Jo Med. Ctr., Stockton, Calif., 1982-85; nurse short-stay surg. Santa Marta Hosp., East L.A., 1987; nurse poison control U. Calif. Irvine Med. Ctr., Orange, 1987; nurse utilization review Provident Life and Accident, Chatanooga, Tenn., 1988; nurse labor, delivery Kaiser Permanente, L.A., 1990, Hollywood Presbyn./Queen of Angels Hosp., L.A., 1992; nurse labor, delivery and postpartum precel, Hermosa Beach, Calif., 1994—; nurse Fetal Testing Ctr. Glendale (Calif.) Meml. Hosp. and Health Ctr., 1996—. Mem. Nurses for World Peace Health Harmony, 1989—. Vol. L.A. Pediatric AIDS Network; leadership tng. Brownie Girl Scouts Am. Coun., 2000, leadership tng. jr. level, 2002; vol. L.A. Free Clinic, 2000, AIDS Walk, 1992, 1999,

2000, 2003; security vol. Nat. Dem. Conv., 2000; vol. Dem. State Conv., 2002; supporter Opn. USA. Mem. Emergency Nurses Assn., Am. Assn. Critical Care Nurses. Republican. Roman Catholic. Avocations: skiing, volleyball, basketball, music, golf.

WALLINGTON, PATRICIA MCDEVITT, computer company executive; b. Phila., July 29, 1940; d. James J. and Mary (Eschbach) McDevitt; m. William R. Wallington; 1 child, Colleen Xydis. BBA, U. Pa., 1975; MBA, Drexel U., 1978; postgrad. mgmt. devel., Harvard U., 1981. Project mgr. Fidelity Mut., Phila., 1965-72, Penn Mut. Ins. Co., Phila., 1972-77; mgr. info. systems Sun Info. Svcs., Phila., 1977-81; dir. info. systems Sun Exploration & Prodn. Co., Dallas, 1981-87; sr. v.p., chief info. officer Mass. Mut. Life Ins. Co., Springfield, 1987-89; corp. v.p., chief info. officer Xerox Corp., Rochester, NY, 1989—99; pres. CIO Assocs., Sarasota, Fla., 2000—. Mem. MBA adv. bd. Baylor U., Waco, Tex., 1986-88; bd. dirs. FINA, Inc., Middlesex Mut. P&C Co. Mem. adv. bd. Handicap Ctr.-HUP, Phila., 1978-80; v.p. fin. Girls Club Dallas, 1986-87. Named one of Top 100 Women in Tech., 1994, Hall of Fame, 1997, CIO mag., 1997. Mem. Soc. for Info. Mgmt.*

WALLIS, DEBORAH, curator; b. Salina, Kans., Mar. 17, 1971; BS, Kans. State U., Manhattan, 1993; MA in Mus. Studies, U. Nebr., Lincoln, 1994. Registrar Richrd Nixon Libr. and Birthplace, Yorba Linda, Calif., 1995—98; dir., curator Nat. Mus. of Roller Skating, Lincoln, Nebr., 2000—. Mem.: Nebr. Mus. Assn. (bd. mem. 2002—). Office: Nat Mus Roller Skating 4730 South St Ste 2 Lincoln NE 68506

WALLIS, DIANA LYNN, artistic director; b. Windsor, Eng., Dec. 11, 1946; d. Dennis Blackwell and Joan Williamson (Gatcombe) W. Grad., Royal Ballet Sch., Eng., 1962-65. Dancer Royal Ballet Touring Co., London, 1965-68; ballet mistress Royal Ballet Sch., London, 1969-81, dep. ballet prin., 1981-84; artistic coord. Nat. Ballet of Can., Toronto, 1984-86, assoc. artistic dir., 1986-87, co-artistic dir., 1987-89; free-lance prod., tchr. London; dep. artistic dir. English Nat. Ballet, London, 1990-94; artistic dir. Royal Acad. Dance, 1994—. Fellow Imperial Soc. Tchrs. Dancing. E-mail: lwallis@rad.org.uk.

WALLISCH, CAROLYN E. principal; b. Denver, Aug. 23, 1939; d. Morgan Franklin and Margaret C. (Kopf) White; m. Darrell Dean Wallisch, June 9, 1963; children: Michael Dean, Kerri Elise. BA in Elem. Edn., U. No. Colo., 1961, MA in Elem. Edn., 1965; postgrad., Denver U., 1989. Cert. tchr. grades K-8, adminstrn. grades K-12. Tchr. grade 1 San Jose Unified Sch. Dist., 1961-62, Greeley (Colo.) Pub. Schs., 1962-69; tchr. grades 2-8, dean of students Jefferson County Schs., Lakewood, Colo., 1984-94; prin. grades K-5 Littleton (Colo.) Pub. Schs., 1994—2001; ret., 2001. Adj. prof. dept. edn. Colo. Christian U., Lakewood, Colo. Contbr. articles to profl. jours. Leader 4-H Clubs of Am., Littleton, 1982-84, Girl Scouts U.S.A., Littleton, 1979-82; den leader Boy Scouts Am., Littleton, 1976-78; precinct committeewoman Littleton, 1984-90. Named one of Outstanding Young Women of Am., 1965, Model Tchr., ABC News Peter Jennings Who's Happening in Edn., 1993, Instr. Mag., 1993. Mem. ASCD, Internat. Reading Assn. (Colo. coun. 1989—), Colo. Coun. Tchrs. Math. (conf. presenter), Colo. Assn. Sch. Execs. (conf. presenter), PTO (v.p. 1994—), Kiwanis, Kappa Delta Pi (bd. dirs.), Sigma Sigma Sigma (bd. dirs.), Alpha Delta Kappa (bd. dirs.), Phi Delta Kappa (bd. dirs., rsch. chmn. 1987—). Republican. Avocations: tennis, golf. Home: 5549 W Hinsdale Ave Littleton CO 80128-7021 Office: Colo Christian U Sch Edn 180 South Garrison St Lakewood CO 80226

WALL-LIEVSAY, BONNIE LEE, human resources specialist, educator; b. Chicago, Ill., Feb. 13, 1949; d. Harry Joseph Burgess, Lois Elizabeth Burgess; m. David Ray Lievsay; 1 child, Diana Lievsay. BA, Antioch Coll., 1970; MPA, San Jose State U., 1979; MA, Fielding Inst., 1995, PhD, 1998. Internal orgnl. develop. cons. Portland Gen. Electric, Portland, Oreg., 1985—91; prin. cons. West Slope Cons., Portland, 1991—99; tng. coord. R.R. Donnelley & Sons Co., Salem, Va., 2000—01; sr. instrnl. designer The Performance Edge Inc., Hardy, Va., 2001—02; faculty Am. InterContinental U., 2003—, DeVry U., 2003—. Recipient The Golden Penguin for Orgnl. Innovation award, Am. Soc. Tng. and Develop., Portland chpt., 1987; fellow Donna Bushnell Meml. fellow, Fielding Inst., 1997. Mem.: Soc. Human Resources Mgmt., Orgnl. Develop. Network, Acad. Mgmt. Home: 5586 Highfields Rd Roanoke VA 24018 Personal E-mail: westslope@att.net.

WALLNER, AMANDA OBER, retired music educator; b. Corning, N.Y., Nov. 16, 1942; d. William Bertrand Ober and Louise Ober Jughulian; m. William Edward Wallner, June 27, 1964; children: Abbie, Christine. BS, Ithaca Coll., 1964; postgrad., Conn. Coll., 1988-89, U. Freiburg, Germany, 1972. Cert. tchr. Music educator Guilford (Conn.) Pub. Schs., 1978—. Founder, dir. Checkerberry Theater Prodns., Guilford, Conn., 1981-82. Performer Conn. Artist Prodns., 1977-82, Young Audiences Inc., 1974-75; recitalist, Mich. State U. Lansing C.C. Prodn., 1975-76. Founder, pres. E. Lansing (Mich.) Com. for Children's TV, 1973-76, founder Citizen's United for Better Broadcasting, E. Lansing, 1973; mem. adv. com. WGRS, WMNR Fine Arts Radio, 1996—. Recipient Resolution of Tribute, citation LVW, 1996, Diana award Senate Concurrent Resolution, East Lansing, 1975, Gen. Assembly Official Citation, the Conn. House, 1995, Celebration of Excellence, Conn. State Bd. of Edn., Hartford, 1995, Katherine Dunham award, Conn. Edn. Assn., Human and Civil Rights Com., Hartford, 1995, selected Internat. Festival Arts & Ideas Youth Summit, New Haven, 1996, Internat. Voice Contest, Vienna, 1972, Susan B. Anthony award Conn. Edn. Assn., 1997; Hilda Maehling grant Nat. Found. Improvement of Edn., 1995. Mem. AAUW, Guilford Edn. Assn. (rep. 1992). Democrat. Avocations: art, literature, opera, jazz.

WALLNER, MARY JANE, state legislator, director child care organization; b. St. Louis, Oct. 25, 1946; d. Arthur M. and Frances (Fulkerson) Bills; m. Nicholas Anthony Wallner, Mar. 10, 1967; children: Jenny, Jessy. BS in Child and Family, U. N.H., 1971; postgrad, Wheelock Coll., 1974-76. Child care worker Newmarket (N.H.) Day Care, 1967-69, dir., 1971-72; tchr. Exeter (N.J.) Head Start, 1969-70; dir. Merrimack Valley Day Care, Concord, N.H., 1973—; mem. N.H. Ho. of Reps. (dist. 24), Concord, 1980—. VISTA vol. Jane Adams Hull House, Chgo., 1966; bd. dirs. N.H. Womens Lobby, Concord, 1991—, Meritorious Svc. award, 1988; bd. dirs. N.H. Task Force for the Prevention Child Abuse, Concord, 1985-91; trustee Trust Fund for the Prevention Child Abuse, Concord, 1987-91. Recipient Friend of Children award N.H. Group Home Assn., 1988, Commitment to Young Children award N.H. Assn. for the Edn. Young Children, 1989, Voice for Children award Child and Family Svcs., 1990. Mem. Zonta (sec. 1980—). Democrat. Office: Merrimack Valley Day Care Svcs 19 N Fruit St Concord NH 03301-2989

WALLS, MARTHA ANN WILLIAMS (MRS. B. CARMAGE WALLS), publishing executive; b. Gadsden, Ala., Apr. 21, 1927; d. Aubrey Joseph and Inez (Cooper) Williams; m. B. Carmage Walls, Jan. 2, 1954; children: Byrd Cooper, Lissa Walls Vahldiek. Student pub. schs., Gadsden. Pres., dir. Walls Newspapers, Inc., 1969-70; sec., treas., dir. Summer Camps, Inc., Guntersville, Ala., 1954-69; CEO, pres., dir. So. Newspapers, Inc., Houston, 1970—; pres., dir. So. Newspapers of Ala., Inc., Scottsboro. V.p., dir. Ft. Payne (Ala.) Newspapers, Inc. Bay City (Tex.) Newspapers, Inc., Galveston Newspapers, Inc.; dir. Monroe (Ga.) Newspapers, Inc.; bd. dirs. Jefferson Pilot Corp., Greensboro, N.C., 1990-98, Jefferson-Pilot Life Ins. Co., 1990-98, Jefferson Pilot Comm., 1990-98. Bd. dirs. Montgomery Acad., 1970-74. Mem.: Soc. Profl. Journalists. Episcopalian. Office: So Newspapers Inc 1050 Wilcrest Dr Houston TX 77042-1608

WALRATH, PATRICIA A. state legislator; b. Brainerd, Minn., Aug. 11, 1941; d. Joseph James and Pansy Patricia (Drake) McCarvill; m. Robert Eugene Walrath, Sept. 1, 1961; children: Karen, Susan, David, Julie. BS, Bemidji State U., 1962; MS, SUNY, Oswego, 1975. Cert. secondary math. tchr., N.Y., Mass. Programmer analyst Control Data Corp., Mpls., 1962-65; crewleader dept. commerce U.S. Census, Middlesex County, Mass., 1979-80; selectman Town of Stow, Mass., 1980-85; tchr. math. Hale Jr. High Sch., Stow, 1981-82; instr. math. Johnson & Wale Coll. Hanscom AFB, Bedford, Mass., 1983-84, test examiner, 1983-84; state rep. 3d Middlesex dist. State of Mass., Boston, 1985—. Mem. ways and means com. Mass. Ho. of Reps., 1987—92, 1996, mem. joint coms. on local affairs, 1993—95, mem. pub. svc. com., 1993—96, mem. election law com., 1985—86, 1995—96, mem. sci. and tech. com., 1995—96, mem. commerce and labor com., 1996, mem. govt. regulations com., 96, chmn. com. long term debt and capital expenditures, 1997—2001, asst. whip, floor chair, 2001—. Chmn. Mass. Indoor Air Pollution Commn., Boston, 1987-88; mem. Stow Dem. Com., 1988—; merit badge counselor Boy Scouts Am., Stow and Hudson, Mass., 1990—. Recipient Disting. Svc. award Auburn N.Y. Jaycees, 1976. Mem. LWV (pres. 1973-76, dir. fin. 1977-78), Mass. Legislators' Assn., Mass. Dem. Leadership Coun. (v.p. 1991-92, co-chmn. 1993-94, treas. 1995-99), Mass. Women's Legis. Caucus (chair 1986). Roman Catholic. Avocations: gardening, stamp collecting, travel. Home: 20 Middlemost Way Stow MA 01775-1363 Office: State Capital RM481 Boston MA 02133 E-mail: Rep.PatriciaWalrath@hou.state.ma.us.

WALSH, BARBARA JEAN, music educator; b. Brookings, S.D., Sept. 19, 1959; d. Richard Carl and Jean Ann Graff; m. David Thorne Walsh, June 18, 1983. B in Music Edn., Colo. State U., 1981; MusM, U. Nev., 1989. Cert. tchr. Colo., Nev. Music tchr. Washoe County Sch. Dist., Reno, 1981—. Mem., treas. Golden Valley Homeowners Assn., Reno, 1991—99. Mem.: Back Country Horsemen Am. (treas. 1998—2000, 2001—03), Am. Guild English Handbell Ringers (Nev. regional coord. 1993—, various 1998—), Washoe County Tchrs. Assn. (Disting. Tchr. 1991, Dedicated Tchr. 2001). Democrat. Roman Catholic. Avocations: horseback riding, camping, reading. Home: 3300 Deer Foot Ln Reno NV 89506 Office: Alice Maxwell Elem Sch 2300 N Rock Blvd Sparks NV 89431

WALSH, DAWNA HAMM, art educator; b. Tuscaloosa, Ala., Aug. 11, 1947; d. Jack Hamm and Dorisnel Alexander Hamm-Sims; m. John M. Walsh, III, Aug. 21, 1971; children: Grant, Whitney, Preston, Austin. BA, Dallas Bapt. U., 1971; MA, U. North Tex., 1977; PhD, Tex. Tech. U., 1993. Chair, prof. dept. art Dallas Bapt. U., 1978—. Juror art show Richardson (Tex.) Civic Art Soc., 2003; scholarship chair Delta Kappa Gamma, Dallas, 2000—04; del. Washington Arts Task Force, Fulbright Orgn., 2003. Exhibitions include Hillcrest Gallery, 2003. Fellow, Fulbright Commn., 1970, 1975. Avocations: art, museums. Home: 4015 University Blvd Dallas TX 75205 Office: Dallas Bapt U 3000 Mountain Creek Pkwy Dallas TX 75211

WALSH, DIANA CHAPMAN, academic administrator, sociologist, educator; b. Phila., July 30, 1944; d. Robert Francis and Gwen (Jenkins) Chapman; m. Christopher Thomas Walsh, June 18, 1966; 1 child, Allison Chapman. BA in English, Wellesley Coll., 1966; MS in Journalism, Boston U. Sch. of Pub. Comm., 1971; PhD in Health Policy, Boston U., 1983; LHD (hon.), Boston U, 1994, Amer. Coll. of Greece, Athens, 1995, U. Mass., Amherst, 1999, Northeastern U., 2003. Dir. info., edn. Planned Parenthood League, Newton, Mass., 1971—74; sr. program assoc. Dept Pub. Health, Boston, 1974—76; assoc. dir. Boston U. Health Policy Inst., 1985—90; prof. Sch. Pub. Health, Sch. Medicine, Boston U., 1987—90, adj. prof. pub. health, 1990—; Florence Sprague Norman and Laura Smart Norman prof., chair dept. health and social behavior Harvard Sch. Pub. Health, 1990—93, adj. prof., 1993—; pres. Wellesley Coll., 1993—. Author: (book) Corporate Physicians, 1987; editor: Women, Work and Health: Challenges to Corporate Policy, 1980, (book series) Industry and Health Care, 1977—80; co-author: Payer, Provider, Consumer, 1977; contbr. articles to profl. jours. Bd. dirs. Planned Parenthood League of Mass., 1974—79, 1981—85, bd. overseers, 1993—94; trustee Occupl. Physicians Scholarship Fund, 1987—94, WGBH Ednl. Found., 1993—2000. Recipient Book of the Yr. award, Am. Jour. Nursing, 1980; fellow, Kellogg Nat. fellow, 1987—90. Mem.: AHA, AAAS, Consortium on Financing Higher Edn., State Street Corp., Mass. Pub. Health Assn., Soc. for the Study of Social Problems, Am. Sociol. Assn. Avocations: gender and health, social policy, writing, skiing. Office: Wellesley Coll Office of the Pres 106 Central St Wellesley MA 02481-8268*

WALSH, DIANE, pianist; b. Washington, Aug. 16, 1950; d. William Donald and Estelle Louise (Stokes) W.; m. Henry Forbes, 1969 (div. 1979); m. Richard Pollak, 1982. MusB, Juilliard Sch. Music, 1971; MusM, Mannes Coll., 1982. N.Y.C. debut Young Concert Artists Series, 1974; founding mem. Mannes Trio, 1983-94; solo appearances include: Kennedy Ctr. for Performing Arts, Washington, 1976, Met. Mus., N.Y.C., 1976, Wigmore Hall, London, 1980, Merkin Concert Hall, 1989, Miller Theatre, 1994, 96; with Mannes Trio: Lincoln Ctr.'s Alice Tully Hall, Libr. of Congress, 1987; appeared with maj. orchs. worldwide, including St. Louis Symphony, Indpls. Symphony, San Francisco Symphony, Am. Symphony, Austin (Tex.) Symphony, Bavarian Radio Symphony of Munich, Berlin Radio Symphony, Radio Symphony Frankfurt, Radio Symphony Stuttgart; has toured Europe, N.Am., S.Am., C.Am., Russia; Marlboro Festival, 1982, Bard Festival, 1990-99, Santa Fe (N.Mex.) Festival, 1995; recs. for Nonesuch Records, 1980, 82, Book-of-Month Records, 1985, Music and Arts, 1990, CRI, 1991, Koch, 1995, Biddulph Records, 1998, Stereophile, 1998, Newport Classic, 1998, Sony, 2000, Arabesque, 2004, Bridge, 2004; artistic dir. Skaneateles Festival, 1999—; mem. piano and chamber music faculty Mannes Coll. Music, 1982—. Recipient 3d prize Busoni Internat. Piano Competition, Italy, 1974, 2nd prize Mozart Internat. Piano Competition, Salzburg, Austria, 1975, 1st prize Munich Internat. Piano Competition, 1975, Naumburg Chamber Music award, 1986; NEA grantee, 1981.

WALSH, DONNA M. state legislator; b. Trenton, N.J., Jan. 28, 1943; m. Henry Walsh, Jr.; one child, Henry III. BA, U. R.I., 1971, MA, 1976. Tchr. Hope Valley Sch., R.I., 1971-88, Chariho Mid. Sch., R.I., 1998—; mem. R.I. Senate, Dist. 25, Providence, 1996—. Mem. judiciary com. R.I. State Senate, health com., edn. and welfare com. Mem. R.I. Bd. Regents for Elem. and Secondary Edn.; pres. bd. trustees Cross Mills Libr.; mem. Cross Mills Ladies Fire Co. Aux.; mem. Chariho Bus. and Profl. Women, Charlestown and Hopkinton Hist. Socs.; me. Charlestown Charter Commn., 1980; mem. Charlestown Town Coun., 1982-84; chair Charlestown Dem. Town Com., 1991-93. Mem. Nat. Sci. Tchrs. Assn., Charlestown C. of C. Democrat. Office: RI State Senate PO Box 1380 Charlestown RI 02813-0905 Address: RI State Senate State House Providence RI 02903 E-mail: sen-walsh@rilin.state.ri.us.

WALSH, ELIZABETH JAMESON, musician; b. Panhandle, Tex., Oct. 23, 1913; d. Edwin Reece and Lela (Blackshear) Jameson; m. Thomas Norris Walsh, Nov. 1, 1951 (dec. May 5, 1990); children: Thomas Edwin, Richard Malcolm, Lela Elizabeth. MusB, U. North Tex., 1941, MusM, 1942. Cert. tchr. music. Piano tchr. U. North Tex., Denton, 1940-42; music tchr. Perryton HS, Tex., 1942-43, Plainview HS, Tex., 1943-45; choir dir. Presbyn. and Disciples Ch., Plainview, 1943-45; music tchr. Dallas Pub. Sch., 1945-53; organist, choir dir. Midway Hills Ch., Dallas, 1954-60; piano tchr. Hockaday Pvt. Sch., Dallas, 1960-70; music tchr. Dallas Pub. Sch., 1970-82; organist, choir dir. Greenville Ave. Christian Ch., Dallas, 1975-82, Grace Meth. Ch., Dallas, 1982-91, St. Andrews Episcopal Ch., Farmers Branch, Tex., 1991—, Christ United Meth. Ch., 2001—. Composer (operetta) Day in Mexico, 1971, various titles for choir, 1996—; author: The Echo Tower, 1987, The House on the Hill, 1989; appeared as Cleopatra as Caesar and Cleopatra, Dallas Little Theatre, 1933, Jane in Jane Eyre, Amarillo Little Theatre, 1935, Anna in Anna and the King of Siam, Northway Ch. Players, 1971. Mem. Dallas Civic Chorus, 1960-65, Dallas Symphony Chorus, 1970-75, Farmer's Br. Women's Club, 1995—; v.p. Mus. Arts, 2003—. Recipient 2nd prize in Nat. Recording Contest, Nat. Piano Guild, 1973. Mem. Dallas Music Tchr. Assn., Dallas chpt. Am. Guild Organists, Musical Arts Club (sec. 2001-03, 1st v.p. 2003—), Daus. of Republic of Tex. (chaplain 1993-95, pres. James Butler Bonham chpt. 1997—, sec. 2003—, Mamie Wynne Cox award 1995, sec. 1995-97, 2003, chmn. yearbook), Pro Musica (pres. 1976-77, 85-86, 2001—, sec. 2003-2005, asst. sec. 2003—, treas. 1980-81, 96-97), Pi Beta Phi, Mu Phi Epsilon. Avocations: reading, travel. Home: 14339 Tanglewood Dr Farmers Branch TX 75234-3855

WALSH, JOANNE ELIZABETH, retired elementary school educator, librarian; b. Chgo., Nov. 25, 1942; d. Joseph Frank and Elizabeth Margaret (Gretz) Fiali; m. John Kerwin Walsh, July 17, 1976; 1 child, Kevin Joseph. BA in English, Mundelein Coll., Chgo., 1965; MEd Ednl. Adminstrn. and Supervision, Loyola U., Chgo., 1969. Tchr. Chgo. Pub. Schs., 1965-83, prin., 1983-89; tchr. libr. Burbank, Ill., 1990—93; tchr. art Tate Sch. of Discovery, Knoxville, Tenn., 1994-95; ret., 1995. Vol. Palos Cmty. Hosp., Palos Park, Ill., 1990, Palos Heights Libr., 1993; Rainbow facilitator, 1992-93; active St. John Neumann Cath. Ch., Knoxville Symphony League; decorating com. City of Farragut. Recipent Tchr. of Yr. award McCord Sch., 1992-93. Mem.: Knoxville Newcomers Club (pres. 2002—03), Knoxville Welcome Wagon Club (pres. 1999—2000). Avocations: reading, gardening, crafts, painting. Home: 607 Gwinhurst Rd Knoxville TN 37922 E-mail: NDISGR8@aol.com.

WALSH, KATHLEEN, lawyer; b. Madison, Wis., Apr. 16, 1951; d. William Patrick and Joan Iris (Staedtler) W.; m. Stephen Michael Glynn, Mar. 17, 1981; stepchildren: Stephen Michael Jr., Theron Benson. BS, U. Wis., La Crosse, 1973; JD, U. Wis., Madison, 1984. Bar: Wis. 1984, U.S. Dist. Ct. (ea. and we. dists.) Wis. 1984. Investigator Office State Pub. Defender, Milw., 1977-80, adminstrv. asst., 1980-81; asst. city atty. City of Milw., 1984-85; staff atty. Legal Aid Soc. Milw., Inc., 1985-92, 95—. Adj. prof. Marquette U. Law Sch., Milw., 1986-92, 99; bd. dirs. Ctr. for Pub. Representation, Madison, 1986-90; mem. faculty Supreme Ct. Wis., 1987-93, Milw. Young Lawyers Assn., 1985-92. Contbr. chpt. to book, articles to profl. publs. Coord., dir. Milw. Clinic Protection Coalition, 1992-95. Named Civil Libertarian of Yr., Wis. Civil Liberties Union, 1993. Mem. ACLU, NARAL, State Bar Wis. (bd. dirs. Individual rights and responsibilities sect. 1986—), Milw. Young Lawyers Assn. (Pro Bono Tng. Seminars), Milw. Bar Assn. (faculty 1985-92, Def. Lawyer of Yr. award 1991), NOW, Planned Parenthood Wis. (Voice for Choice award 1993), Wis. Coalition Against Death Penalty, Nature Conservancy, World Wildlife Fund. Democrat. Avocations: reading, snorkeling, biking, ceramics, sculpture. Home: 929 N Astor St Milwaukee WI 53202-7000 Office: Legal Aid Soc Milw Inc 229 E Wisconsin Ave Ste 200 Milwaukee WI 53202-4231

WALSH, LISA J. elementary school educator; b. New London, Conn., Apr. 23, 1957; d. James Russell and Patricia Grace (Gannoe) Bowdish. BA, Annhurst Coll., 1979; MAT, Sacred Heart U., 1988. Tchr. Lisbon (N.Y.) Ctrl. Sch., 1989—92; Heuvelton (N.Y.) Ctrl. Sch., 1992—; owner North Fork Bed & Breakfast, Lisbon, 2003. Organist Flackville Ch., Lisbon, 1989—2001. Grantee, Reynold's Corp., 1994. Mem.: N.Y. State Sch. Music Assn., Music Educator's Nat. Conf., St. Lawrence Valley League (sec./treas. 2002—). Home: 219 Baker Rd Lisbon NY 13658 Office: North Fork Bed and Breakfast 219 Baker Rd Lisbon NY 13658

WALSH, MARIAN C. state legislator; BA, Newton Coll. Sacred Heart, 1976, MTh, Harvard U., 1982; JD, Suffolk U., 1986. Chief adminstrv. officer, dir. fin., devel. and planning Suffolk County Dist. Atty. Office, Boston, 1979-85; asst. dir., govt. rels. legis. agt. Mass. Med. Soc., Waltham, 1985-86; practice law, Milton, 1987—; mem. Mass. Ho. of Reps., Boston, 1989-92, mem. judiciary, ethics, banks and banking coms.; mem. Mass. Senate, Boston, 1993—. Adj. prof. law Newbury Coll., 1987-88; adj. prof. ethics Fisher Coll., 1990—. Mem., bd. dirs. YMCA; active West Roxbury Hist. Soc., Neighborhood Assn., Friend of Shattuck Shelter. Home: 651 W Roxbury Pkwy Chestnut Hill MA 02467-3225 Office: Mass Ho of Reps State House Rm 405 Boston MA 02133

WALSH, MARIE LECLERC, nurse; b. Providence, Sept. 11, 1928; d. Walter Normand and Anna Mary (Ryan) Leclerc; m. John Breffni Walsh, June 18, 1955; children: George Breffni, John Leclerc, Darina Louise. Grad., Waterbury Hosp. Sch. Nursing, Conn., 1951; BS, Columbia U., 1954, MA, 1955. Team leader Hartford (Conn.) Hosp., 1951-53; pvt. duty nurse St. Luke's Hosp., N.Y.C., 1953-57; sch. nurse tchr. Agnes Russel Ctr., Tchrs. Coll. Columbia U., N.Y.C., 1955-56; clin. nursing instr. St. Luke's Hosp., N.Y.C., 1957-58; chmn. disaster nursing ARC Fairfax County, Va., 1975; course coord. occupational health nursing U. Va. Sch. Continuing Edn., Falls Church, 1975-77; mem. disaster steering com. No. Va. C.C., Annandale, 1976; adj. faculty U. Va. Sch. Continuing Edn., Falls Church, 1981; disaster svcs. nurse ARC, Wichita, Kans., 1985-90, disaster svcs. nurse Seattle-King County chpt. Seattle, 1990-96; ret. Rsch. and statis. analyst U. Va. Sch. Continuing Edn. Nursing, Falls Church, 1975; rsch. libr. Olive Garvey Ctr. for Improvement Human Functioning, Inc., Wichita, 1985. Sec. Dem. party, Cresskill, N.J., 1964-66; county committeewoman, Bergen County, N.J., 1965-66; pres., v.p., Internat. Staff Wives, NATO, Brussels, Belgium, 1978-80; election officer, supr. Election Bd., Wichita, 1987, 88; v.p. McLean Newcomers, 1997-99, pres., 1999-2000. Mem. AAAS, AAUW, N.Y. Acad. Sci., Pi Lambda Theta, Sigma Theta Tau. Avocations: travel, gardening. Home: 8800 Prestwould Pl Mc Lean VA 22102-2231

WALSH, NAN, artist, painter, sculptor, consultant; b. N.Y.C., Nov. 4, 1932; d. Joseph Edward and Mary Ellen (White) Heinl; m. Albert Anthony Walsh, July 10, 1954 (dec. Oct. 9, 2002); children: Maryellen, Nanette, Mark, Gregg (dec.). BS in Elem. Edn., Fordham U., 1954; postgrad., Nat. Acad. Sch. Fine Arts, Art Life Studio Inc., White Plains and Portchester, N.Y., 1984-94, V.K. Jonynas, L.I., N.Y., 1968-88, Art Ctr. No. N.J., 1996—2002. Fashion model Martha Clyde, N.Y.C., 1951-54; tchr. Yonkers (N.Y.) Pub. Schs., 1953-55; gallery dir. Mamaroneck Artists Guild, Larchmont, N.Y., 1988-95; fine artist, art juror, cons., 1995—. Membership juror Mamaroneck Artists Guild, Larchmont, 1982-84, membership juror chair, 1996-98, mem. adv. bd., 1996-98; mem. Ctr. for Contemporary Printmaking, 1998—. One-woman shows and juried exhbns. Westchester and N.Y.C., 1976—; works represented in corp. and pvt. collecitons. Hostess chairperson Citizens for John Lindsay, Gracie Mansion, N.Y., 1970; mem. Studio Twelve, pres., show chair, 1972-80; mem. Katonah Mus. Art. Recipient numerous 1st place awards for art. Mem. Nat. League Am. Penwomen, Nat. Mus. Women in the Arts, N.Y. Soc. Women Artists, Guild Creative Art, N.Y. Artists Equity, Mamaroneck Artists Guild (v.p. 1982, 83, membership chair 1992-95 Fordham U. Art Club (show chair 1965-80). Avocations: gardening, bridge, tennis, swimming, travel.

WALSH, PATRICIA MAACK, special education educator; b. Yokohama, Japan, Sept. 10, 1950; d. Johan Gustof and Dorothy Maack; m. Frederic Peterson Walsh, Sept. 10, 1971; children: Audra Louise Walsh Lexin, Frederic Maack. AA in Art, Weber State U., 1972, BS in Child Devel., 1973; BS in Elem. Edn., Peru State Coll., 1988; MS in Psychology, U. La Verne, 1991; MS in Spl. Edn., Calif. State U., Northridge, 1996. Clear credential in spl. edn., Calif. Tchr. spl. edn. Papillion (Nebr.)-LaVista Sch. Dist., 1988-89, Eastside Union Sch. Dist., Lancaster, Calif., 1989-96, Antelope Valley Union H.S. Dist., Lancaster. Advisor H.S. Stds. Com., Lancaster, 1997—. Exit pole worker Rep. Women's Club, Palmdale, Calif., 1996.

Mem. Coun. for Exceptional Children, Calif. Assn. Resource Specialists (cert.), Assistance League, Delta Kappa Gamma. Methodist. Avocations: art, travel, ministry with children. Office: Lancaster H S 44701 32nd St W Lancaster CA 93536-7023

WALSTON, BARBARA H. music educator; b. High Point, N.C., Apr. 11, 1966; d. Penelope C. Wadsley; m. Scott W. Walston, Aug. 3, 1991; 1 child, Andrew S. MusB, U. N.C., Greensboro, 1988, MusM, 1990. Adminstrv. asst. U. N.C. Summer Music Camp, Greensboro, 1985—; band dir. Henderson Mid. Sch., Henderson, NC, 1997—2002; tchr. Friendship Christian Sch., Raleigh, NC, 2002—. Musician Friendship Bapt. Ch., Raleigh, 2001. Recipient Tchr. Exec. Inst. Grad., Vance County Schs., 2000. Mem.: N.C. Music Educators Assn. (dist. pres. 1999—2001), Phi Delta Kappa, Mu Phi Epsilon (dist. dir. 1989—98). Baptist. Avocations: reading, fitness. Personal E-mail: bhwalstonusa@netscape.net.

WALTER, DEANA A. electronics executive, small business owner; b. Rochester, N.Y., July 31, 1953; d. Dean A. and Patricia A. Prevost; m. John S. Walter, Mar. 16, 1995 (div. Sept. 27, 2001). AA in Fashion and Interior Decorating, John Robert Powers, 1972. With advt. divsn. Dem. & Chronicle, Rochester, 1971—73; leasing adminstr. Xerox Corp., Webster, NY, 1976—; prin., owner Impressions Dating Svc., Rochester, 1996—98, Shadows of the Past, Rochester, 1996—; prin., co-owner Niagara Elec. Sales, Rochester, 1987—94. Vol. Holy Cross Ch., Rochester, 1980—96. Recipient Recognition award, Astoria, 1993. Republican. Roman Cath. Home: 385 N Lemoyn Ave Rochester NY 14612 Office: Xerox Corp 800 Salt Rd Bldg 843 Webster NY 14580 Office Phone: 585-422-6786.

WALTER, JOLENE KENDRA, music educator; b. Va., July 3, 1976; m. Daniel J. Place, June 19, 1999. B in Music Edn., Ohio State U., 1998; M in Music Edn., U. S.C., 2003. Orch. tchr. Charleston Co. Sch. Dist., SC, 1998—2002. Mem.: Music Educators Nat. Conv., Am. String Tchrs. Assn. Avocations: violist, fencing. Home: 2700 Feather Run Tr H-14 West Columbia SC 29169

WALTER, KAY J. literature educator; b. La Marque, Tex., July 21, 1961; d. James J. and Robbie Walter. BA cum laude, U. Ark., Monticello, Ark., 1984; MA, U. Ctrl. Ark.; PhD, Tex. A&M, 1996. Cert. tchr. Ark. State. Instr. U. Ctrl. Ark., Conway, 1989—90; grad. asst. tchr. Tex. A&M U., Coll. Sta., 1990—96; writing ctr. dir. Blinn Coll., Brenham, Tex., 1996—99, instr., 1996—2001; lectr. Idaho State U., Pocatello, 2001—. Faculty co-sponsor Idaho State U. English Grad. Student Assn. Co-editor: Cornish Ballads and Other Poems, 1994; contbr. various conf. papers. Chair Blinn Coll. Profl. Devel. Com., 1998—2001. Recipient Ernest Duke award, 1993. Mem.: Charles Lamb Soc., Friends of Ruskin's Brantwood (life), Royal Oak Found. (life), Sigma Kappa Delta, Iota Beta Chpt. Office: Idaho State U PO Box 8056 Pocatello ID 83209 E-mail: waltkay@isu.edu.

WALTER, LYNN M. geologist, educator; PhD in Geology, U. Miami, 1983. Prof. geol. scis. U. Mich., Ann Arbor. Recipient Disting. Svc. award Geol. Soc. Am., 1999. Achievements include research on aqueous and solid phase geochemistry of sedimentary systems. Office: U Mich 2534 CC Little Bldg 425 E University Ave Ann Arbor MI 48109-1063 Fax: 734-763-4690. E-mail: lmwalter@umich.edu.

WALTER, SANDRA social worker; b. Quincy, Ill., Apr. [illegible]; d. Merle G. and Margaret A. Walter. BA, Iowa Wesleyan Coll., 1974. Lic. Bachelor Social Worker Iowa Bd. Social Work Examiners, 1999. Program coord. Planned Parenthood S.E. Iowa, Fort Madison, 1974—82; social worker 2 Iowa Dept. Human Svcs., Burlington, 1982—82, 1983—87, social worker 3; family based counselor Iowa Children and Family Svcs., Burlington, 1982—82, family counselor, 1982—83; social worker 3 Iowa Dept. Human Svcs., Sigourney, Iowa, 2000—. Democrat. Methodist. Avocations: travel, genealogy, reading. Home: 307 West Stroup Richland IA 52585 Personal E-mail: sandyw@iowatelecom.net.

WALTER, SHERYL LYNN, lawyer; b. Morris, Ill., July 18, 1956; d. C. Frank and Margaret (Juhl) W. BA in History cum laude, Grinnell (Iowa) Coll., 1978; JD cum laude, U. Minn., 1984; MPA John F. Kennedy Sch. of Govt., Harvard U., 2003. Bar: Minn. 1984, U.S. Dist. Ct. Minn. 1987, U.S. Ct. Appeals (8th cir.) 1987, D.C. 1989, U.S. Dist. Ct. D.C. 1989, U.S. Ct. Appeals (D.C. cir.) 1989. Law clk. to presiding judge 3d Jud. Dist. of Minn., Rochester, 1984-85; law clk. to Chief Judge Donald P. Lay U.S. Ct. Appeals (8th cir.), St. Paul, 1985-87; assoc. Mayer, Brown & Platt, Washington, 1987-89; gen. counsel Nat. Security Archive, Washington, 1989-94, Assn. Records Review Bd., Washington, 1994-95, Commn. Protecting and Reducing Govt. Secrecy, Washington, 1995-97, dep. spl. counsel U.S. Senate Vets. Affairs com., 1997-98; minority staff dir., chief counsel U.S. Senate Jud. Com., Youth Violence Subcom., 1998-2000; with Office of Legis. Affairs U.S. Dept. of Justice, 2000—03, acting asst. atty. gen., 2001, chief of staff office of Intelligence & Policy Rev., 2003—. Cons. Amnesty Internat., Washington, 1988-89. Mem. ABA (vice chmn. adminstrv. law sect. govt. info. subcom. 1990-96), D.C. Bar Assn. (steering com., adminstrv. law sect. 1990-97), Am. Soc. Access Profls. (bd. dirs. 1990-98, pres. 1996-97), Brit.-Am. Security Info. Coun. (bd. dirs. 1994-2000), Lawyers Alliance for World Security (bd. dirs. 1994-2000). Office: US Dept Justice 9th and Pennsylvania Ave NW Washington DC 20530

WALTER, VIRGINIA LEE, psychologist, educator; b. Temple, Tex., Oct. 30, 1937; d. Luther Patterson and Virginia Lafayette (Wilkins) W.; m. Glen Ellis, 1958 (div.); children: Glen Edward, David Walter; m. Robert Reinehr, 1963 (div.); 1 son, Charles Allen; m. Robert Bruininks, 1975 (div.). BS, U. Tex.-Austin, 1959, M.Edn., 1967; postgrad. internship program in spl. Edn. Adminstrn., 1970; Ed.D., U. Houston, 1973. Prof. ednl. psychology dept. ednl. psychology U. Minn., Mpls., 1973-85; pres. Sch. Resource Ctr., Austin, Tex., 1985-90; tchr. Llano Pub. Schs., 1988-97; dir. Walter Resources, 1998—. Chmn. State Adv. Coun. for Inservice Tng. Regular Classroom Tchrs., 1977-79; cons. spl. ednl. various sch. dists., state depts. and agys. Editl. cons.: Jour. Ednl. Psychology, 1979, Reading Rsch. Quar., 1982; assoc. editor: Exceptional Children, 1979-84; assoc. editor Teaching Exceptional Children, 1985-89; contbr. articles to profl. jours., papers to profl. confs. Named Minn. Spl. Educator of Yr., 1978; recipient Svc. award Internat. Coun. Exceptional Children, 1978; HEW Office of Human Devel. Svcs. grantee, 1976-80; Dept. Edn. contractee, 1980-83 Mem. Coun. for Exceptional Children, Nat. Assn. Children with Learning Disabilities (dir. Minn. chpt. 1978-80), Nat. Assn. Retarded Citizens, AAUP, Assn. Supervision and Curriculum Devel. Home and Office: 7108 Running Rope Austin TX 78731

WALTERS, BARBARA ANN, television journalist; b. Boston, Mass., Sept. 25, 1931; d. Lou and Dena (Selett) Walters; m. Lee Gruber, 1963 (div. 1976); m. Merv Adelson, 1986 (div. 1992); 1 child, Jacqueline. BA in English, Sarah Lawrence Coll., 1953; LHD (hon.), Ohio State U., Marymount Coll., 1975, Wheaton Coll., 1983, Temple U., Hofstra U., Ben-Gurion U. Former producer WNBC-TV; former writer CBS News; then with Stas. WPIX and CBS-TV; writer, reporter-at-large Today Show, 1961—63, regular panel mem., 1964—74, co-host, 1974—76; moderator syndicated program Not For Women Only, 1972—76; newscaster ABC Evening News (now ABC World News Tonight), 1976—78; host The Barbara Walters Spls., 1976—; co-host ABC TV news show 20/20, 1984—99, anchor, 1999—; co-exec. prodr., co-owner, co-host The View, ABC, N.Y.C., 1997—; exec. prodr. The Iyanla Show, 2001. Contbr. NBC Radio Network. Contbr. ABC programs Issues and Answers; author: (book) How to Talk With Practically Anybody About Practically Anything, 1970; contbr. to Reader's Digest, Good Housekeeping, Family Weekly; appeared in (films) At Long Last Love, 1975, Crazy Mama, 1975, Goin' South, 1978, Rock 'n' Roll High School, 1979, In God We Trust, 1980. Named Woman Yr. Comm., 1974, Broadcaster Yr., Internat. Radio and TV Soc., 1975, Woman Yr., Theta Sigma Phi; named one of Am.'s 75 Most Important Women, Ladies' Home Jour., 1970, 200 Leaders Future, Time Mag., 1974, 10 Women Decade, Ladies' Home Jour., 1979, Most Important Women 1979, Roper Report, 1979, Women Most Admired Am. People, Gallup Poll, 1982, Am.'s 100 Most Important Women, Ladies' Home Jour., 1983, Women Most Admired Am. People, Gallup Poll, 1984; named to 100 Women of Accomplishment, Harper's Bazaar, 1967, 1971, Hall Fame, Acad. TV Arts and Scis., 1990; recipient Award Yr., Nat. Assn. TV Program Execs., 1975, Emmy award, Nat. Acad. TV Arts and Scis., 1975, 1980, 1982, 1983, Mass Media award, Am. Jewish Com. Inst. Human Relations, 1975, Barbara Walters' Coll. Scholarship in Broadcast Journalism established in her honor, Ill. Broadcasters Assn., 1975, Matrix award, N.Y. Women in Comm., 1977, Hubert H. Humphrey Freedom prize, Anti Defamation League B'nai B'rith, 1978, Pres.'s award, Overseas Press Club, 1988, Lowell Thomas award, Marist Coll., 1990, Lifetime Achievement award, Internat. Women's Media Found., 1991, saluted, Am. Mus. Moving Image, 1992, Lifetime Achievement award, Women's Project and Prodn., 1993, honored for contbn. to broadcast journalism, Mus. TV and Radio, 1996, George Foster Peabody award for her interview with actor Christopher Reeve, 1996, Muse award, NY Women in Film and TV, 1997, Lifetime Achievement award, Daytime Emmy Awards, 2000, Nat. Acad. TV Arts and Scis., 2000, Silver Satellite award, Am. Women Radio and TV. Office: 20/20 147 Columbus Ave Fl 10 New York NY 10023-5900 also: The View 320 W 66th St New York NY 10023-6304*

WALTERS, BETTE JEAN, lawyer; b. Norristown, Pa., Sept. 5, 1946; BA, U. Pitts., 1967; JD, Temple U., 1970, LLM in Taxation, 1974. Bar: Pa. 1970, U.S. Dist. Ct. (ea. dist.) Pa. 1971. Law clk., assoc. William R. Cooper, Lansdale, Pa., 1969-72; spl. asst. to pub. defender Montgomery County (Pa.), 1973; pvt. practice North Wales, Pa., 1972-73; assoc. counsel Alco Standard Corp., Valley Forge, Pa., 1973-79, group counsel mfg., 1979-83; v.p., gen. counsel, sec. Alco Industries, Inc., Valley Forge, 1983—2003. Mem. corp. sponsors com. Zool. Soc. of Phila.; adv. environ. studies program U. Pitts.; bd. visitors Temple U. Mem. ABA, DAR, Pa. Bar Assn., Montgomery County Bar Assn., Am. Corp. Counsel Assn., NACD. Republican. E-mail: b.j.walters@verizon.net.

WALTERS, DORIS LAVONNE, retired pastoral counselor, counseling services facility administrator; b. Peachland, N.C., Feb. 24, 1931; d. H. Lloyd and Mary Lou (Helms) W. AA, Gardner Webb U., 1959; BA cum laude, Carson-Newman Coll., 1961; MRE, Southwestern Bapt. Theol. Sem., 1963; MA in Pastoral Counseling, Wake Forest U., 1982; DMin in Pastoral Counseling, Southeastern Bapt. Theol. Sem., 1988. Min. of edn. and youth First Bapt. Ch., Orange, Tex., 1963-66; assoc. prof. Seinan Jo Gakuin Jr. Coll., Japan, 1968-72; dir. Fukuoka (Japan) Friendship House, 1972-88, pastoral counselor, chaplain, 1983-86; Tokyo lifeline referral counselor (in English) Hiroshima South, Fukuoka, 1983-86; supr. Japanese and Am. staff Fukuoka Friendship House, 1972-86; with chaplaincy Med. Coll. Va., Richmond, 1976; resident chaplain N.C. Bapt. Hosp., Winston-Salem, 1981-82, counselor-in-tng. pastoral care dept., 1986-88; dir. missionary counseling and support svcs. Pastoral Care Found. N.C. Bapt. Hosp., Winston-Salem, 1989-93; dir. Missionary Family Counseling Svcs., Inc., Winston-Salem, 1993—2003. Mem. Japan Bapt. Mission Exec. Com., Tokyo, 1973-76. Author: An Assessment of the Reentry Issues of the Children of Missionaries, 1991, 2d printing with title Missionary Children: Caught between Cultures, 1996; translator: The Story of the Craft Dogs, 1983. Trustee Gardner Webb U., 1999-2002. Named Alumnus of Yr. Gardner Webb U., 1993; J.M. Price scholar Southwestern Bapt. Theol. Sem., 1962; First Bapt. Ch. Blackwell grantee Southeastern Sem., 1986-88. Mem. Am. Assn. Pastoral Counselors, Am. Psychotherapy Assn. (diplomate). Democrat. Avocations: photography, travel, reading, classical music, concerts. Home: 208 Oakwood Sq Winston Salem NC 27103 E-mail: mfcs@juno.com.

WALTERS, JANE, state agency administrator; MusB, BA in Music History, Rhodes Coll.; MA in Counseling, U. Memphis; PhD in Sch. Adminstrn., Duke U. Tchr., counselor Messick H.S., Memphis, asst. prin.; asst. dir. computer svcs. Memphis City Schs.; prin. Craigmont Jr. H.S., 1974-79, Craigmont Jr. and Sr. H.S., 1979-95; 21st commr. edn. State Dept. Edn., Nashville, 1995—99; exec. dir. Ptnrs. in Pub. Edn., 1999—; prin. Grizzlies Acad., Memphis, 2003—. Adv. com. edn. depts. Rhodes Coll, Christian Brothers Com., Tenn. Arts Acad.; cons. College Bd. advanced placement program. Grant reader NEA; mem. Goals for Memphis Edn. Com.; bd. dirs. World Affairs Coun, Nat. Coun. Christians and Jews, Memphis Coun. Internat. Visitors, Memphis Youth Symphony, Am. Cancer Soc., Memphis chpt. Office: 204 North Second St Memphis TN 38103

WALTERS, MARJORIE ANNE, interior designer, consultant; b. Flushing, N.Y., Dec. 5, 1925, d. Walter Bowne Williams, Florence Clara (Bach) Williams; m. Robert Leslie Walters, Sept. 17, 1949; children: Robert Bowne(dec.), Richard James. BS, Coll. William & Mary, 1947; AA, N.Y. Sch. Interior Design, 1958. Owner, pres. M.W. Walters, Interiors, Hohokus, NJ, 1958—86; pres. N.J. Ridgwood Art Inst., 1980—86; owner, pres. M.W. Walters, Interiors, Richfield Springs, NY, 1986—. Dir. Art & Program Commn., Richfield Springs, 1993—; chmn. Baker's Beach Art & Programs Commn., Richfield Springs; exec. dir. Cooperstown N.Y. Art Assn., 1986—90. Smithy-Pioneer Gallery, Cooperstown, N.Y., 2001—. Pres. Richfield Springs Hist. Assn., 1997—; v.p. Richfield Springs Libr. Bd., 1999—; mem. zoning bd. of appeals Town of Richfield Springs, 1999—. Recipient Cmty. Svc. award, Richfield C. of C., 1994, Good Citizenship award, DAR, 1994, Good Neighbor award, WBUG AM/FM, 1994. Mem.: Lake and Valley Garden Club (pres. 1998—2000). Avocations: landscape painting, flower arranging, swimming, skiing. Home and Office: 217 Walters Way Richfield Springs NY 13439

WALTERS, NATALIE A. music educator; d. John Carl and Roberta Carmel Walters. MusB, Ithaca Coll.; MusM, New England Conservatory. Tchr. music Syracuse (N.Y.) City Schs., 1990—91; band dir. Webster (N.Y.) Jr. HS, 1991—92; choral dir. Syracuse (N.Y.) City Schs., 1992—95; band dir. Lexington (Mass.) Pub. Schs., 1997—2000, Mexico (N.Y.) Acad. and Ctrl. Schs., 2000—. High brass instr. Jordan-Elbridge (N.Y.) Marching Band, 1993—95; asst. marching band dir. Belmont (Mass.) HS Band, 1997—2000; high brass instr. Ctrl. Sq. (N.Y.) Marching Band, 2000—02. Recipient Gold medal, Mass. Instrumental and Choral Conductors Assn.; grantee, Lexington (Mass.) Edn. Found., 1999, Lexington (N.Y.) PTSA, 1999. Mem.: N.Y. State Band Dirs. Assn., Music Educators Nat. Conf., N.Y. State Schs. Music Assn., West Genesee Marching Band Alumni. Democrat. Roman Cath. Office: Mexico Academy and Ctrl Schools 3338 Main Street Mexico NY 13114

WALTERS, REBECCA RUSSELL YARBOROUGH, medical technologist; b. Lancaster, S.C., Mar. 9, 1951; d. William Peurifoy and Anna Beth (Cheatham) Yarborough; m. Thomas Edward Walters, Oct. 15, 1983; 1 child, Katherine Rebecca. BA, Winthrop Coll., 1972; postgrad. in med. tech., Palmetto Bapt. Med. Ctr., Columbia, S.C., 1974; MA, Cen. Mich. U., 1978. Diplomate in Lab. Mgmt. ASCP. Teaching asst. in biology Winthrop Coll., Rock Hill, S.C., 1972-73; microbiology technologist Palmetto Bapt. Med. Ctr., 1974-76, evening shift supr., 1976-77, asst. adminstrv. dir., 1977-97, dir. lab., 1997—. Article reviewer Med. Lab. Observer; mem. Nat. Cert. Agy. for Med. Lab. Personnel. Hycel, Inc. scholar, 1976, 77. Mem. Am. Soc. for Med. Tech. (scholar 1977), S.C. Soc. Med. Tech. (pres. 1979-80, scholar 1976), Am. Soc. Clin. Pathologists (assoc.), Clin. Lab. Mgmt. Assn., Beta Beta Beta, Alpha Mu Tau (scholar 1977). Republican. Presbyterian. Avocations: reading, aerobics, gardening. Home: 104 Turtle Pointe Ct Chapin SC 29036-7695 Office: Palmetto Health Bapt Taylor At Marion Columbia SC 29220-0001

WALTERS, RITA, councilwoman; b. Chgo., Aug. 14, 1930; children: David, Susan, Philip. BA, Shaw U., Raleigh, N.C., 1975; MBA, UCLA, 1984. Tchr. adult divsn. L.A. Sch. Dist., 1975-79; instr. Ednl. Founds. Dept. Calif. State U., L.A., 1981; pres. L.A. Bd. Edn., 1985-88; city councilwoman L.A., 1991—. Chair Arts Health and Humanities Com., Public Works, Budget & Fin. Office: City Hall Rm 508 200 N Main St Los Angeles CA 90012-4110

WALTERS, TERESA, musician, music educator, concert pianist; m. Jeffrey L. Walters. BA in Music, MA in Music, U. Nebr.; D. Mus. Arts, Johns Hopkins U. Prof. music, artist-in-residence, head music dept. Coll. St. Elizabeth, Morristown, N.J., 1986—. Rec. include The Abbé Liszt Series, 1995—; composer: (cantata) The Kingdom, (cantata) One Man, Mass for Bell Choir; performances at Villa d'Este, Rome, Liszt Soc., Seville (Spain) Universal Exposition, Boston Conservatory, Carnegie Hall, N.Y., Wigmore Hall, London, Moscow Conservatory, Palais des Beaux-Arts, Brussels, Ecole Normale de Musique, Paris, Genva Conservatory, Am. Ch., Paris, YMCA, Jerusalem, (debut) Conservatorio Monteverdi, Italy, Chgo. Cultural Art Ctr. Internat. Grad. fellow, Paris, Kathryn Sisson Phillips Nat. fellow; study grantee Ladd Found., De Wolf Found., Franck Found., Miller Found., Rotary Internat.; recipient Vreeland Award for Music, Internat. Edn. award Rotary Found. Mem. Am. Liszt Soc., ASCAP, Mortar Bd., Sigma Alpha Iota, Alpha Lambda Delta, Phi Beta Kappa. Avocations: museums, art galleries, antiques, animals, birds. Office: Coll St Elizabeth 2 Convent Rd Morristown NJ 07960-6923

WALTON, ALICE L. bank executive; b. Newport, Ark., Oct. 7, 1949; d. Sam and Helen (Robson) W. BBA, Trinity U., 1971; D of Bus. Adminstrn. (hon.), S.W. Bapt. U., 1988. Investment analyst First Commerce Corp., New Orleans, 1972-75; dir., v.p. investments Walton Enterprises, Bentonville, Ark., 1975—; retail & investment broker E.F. Hutton Co., New Orleans, 1975-79; vice chair, investment dir. Walton Bank Group, Bentonville, Ark., 1982-88; former pres., chair, CEO Llama Co./Llama Asset Mgmt. Co., Fayetteville, Ark. Dean's adv. coun. U. Ark. Coll. Bus. Adminstrn., Fayetteville, 1989-90; internat. judge Students in Free Enterprise, Springfield, Mo., 1990; bd. trustees The Asia Soc., N.Y.C., 1991. Chairperson N.W. Ark. Coun., Fayetteville, 1990—; bd. dirs. Pillar's Club-United Way, Easter Seals Soc.-Arkansan of Yr., Walton Arts Ctr. Coun., Fayetteville, Ark. Named Disting. Bus. Lectr. Cen. State U., Edmond, Okla., 1989.*

WALTON, CAROLE LORRAINE, clinical social worker; b. Harrison, Ark., Oct. 20, 1949; d. Leo Woodrow Walton and Arlette Alegra (Cohen) Armstrong. BA, Lambuth Coll., Jackson, Tenn., 1971; MA, U. Chgo., 1974. Diplomate Clin. Social Work, Acad. Cert. Social Workers; bd. cert. diplomate; lic. clin. social worker. Social worker Community Mental Health, Flint, Mich., 1971-72, clin. social worker Westchester, Ill., 1974-76; dir. self travel program Chgo. Assn. Retarded Citizens, 1973; coord. family svcs. Inner Harbors Psych. Hosp., Douglasville, Ga., 1976-83; sr. mental health clinician Northside Mental Health Ctr., Atlanta, 1983—; pvt. practice clin. social worker Atlanta, 1997—2001. Mem. NASW, Ga. Soc. for Clin. Work (pres. 1981-82, pres. 1993-95). Avocation: tennis. Office: Northside Mental Health Ctr 1140 Hammond Dr Ste J-1075 Atlanta GA 30328-7145

WALTON, FLORENCE GOODSTEIN See GOODSTEIN-SHAPIRO, FLORENCE

WALTON, MAURINE ISABEL, social worker; b. Denver, June 22; d. Roman and Julia Fass Engle; m. Earl Anderson, Nov. 5, 1943 (dec. Jan. 7, 1974); children: Rene Anderson, Erlin Anderson, Jim Anderson; m. Harris George Walton, June 15, 1985. BS, Met. State U., 1984; MSW, Denver University, 1985. Social worker Introduced independant living program for foster childern while working at Aspira, 1992. Pres. Newcomers Club, Santa Maria, Calif., 1988. Nominee Women of the Yr., S.M. Womans Network, 1991. Mem.: AAUW (treas. 1999—2000), Leota Club (pres. 1973—74), Ea. Star. Democrat. Achievements include development of indep. living program for foster children, 1992. Avocation: golf. Home: 985 Foxenwood Dr Santa Maria CA 93455

WALTON, SUZANNE W. elementary school educator; b. Clarksdale, Miss., Nov. 29, 1957; d. George Wayne and Rubie Winter; m. Gary Louis Walton, June 11, 1978; 1 child, Christy Louise. BS Edn., Delta State U., 1978, MA Elem. & Reading, 1980, MA Adminstrn., 1991. Tchr. Clarksdale Mcpl. Schs., Miss., 1978—89, title 1 supr., 1989—99, tchr., 2001—; coord. Pearl River C.C., Poplarville, 2000—01. Co-chair discipline com. Clarksdale Mcpl. Schs., 1993—94, mem. calendar com., 1995—99, mem. handbook com., 1995—99, tchr. evaluator, 1992—98. Sec., treas. Clarksdale Mcpl. Sch. Bd. Election Com., 1996. Mem.: Miss. Reading Assn., Delta Kappa Gamma (pres., treas. 1996—2000). Roman Catholic. Home: 1202 May St Clarksdale MS 38614

WALTZ, KATHLEEN M. publishing executive; b. Mar. 6, 1954; m. Bill Raffel, 1990; stepchildren: Jamie, Jenny. BA, DePaul U.; postgrad., Northwestern U. Telemarketer Chgo. Tribune, 1973, mgr. recruitment advt., 1987, dir. customer satisfaction, 1989—90, dir. classified advt., 1990—95, v.p./dir. of developing bus., 1995—97; v.p., gen. mgr. Sun-Sentinel Co., Fla., 1997—98; CEO, pres., pub. Daily Press, Newport News, Va., 1998—2000, Orlando Sentinel Comm., 2000—. Bd. dirs. United Way. of Va. Peninsula, Peninsula Allice for Econ. Devel. WHRO Found. and Greater Peninsula Now; bd. dirs., exec. com. Hampton Roads Partnership; ABC/NAA liaison com., sr. exec. resource corps. Coll. of William and Mary. Mem. So. Newspapers Pub. Assn. (diversity com.). Avocations: travel, golf, gardening. Office: Orlando Sentinel 1000 N Garland Ave Orlando FL 32801

WALTZ, KATHY, publishing executive; m. Bill Raffel; stepchildren: Jamie, Jenny. BA in Liberal Arts, DePaul U.; postgrad., Northwestern U., 1991. Dir. classified advt., dir. customer satisfaction Chgo. Tribune, 1973—97, v.p., dir. developing businesses, 1995—97; v.p., gen. mgr. Sun-Sentinel Co., Ft. Lauderdale, Fla., 1997—98; pres., pub., CEO Daily Press, Hampton Roads, Va., 1998—2000, Orlando (Fla.) Sentinel, 2000—. Avocations: gardening, golf, history, travel. Office: Orlando Sentinel Comms 633 N Orange Ave Orlando FL 32801*

WALTZ, SUSAN, international relations educator; Former chmn. Amnesty Internat., London, England, 1993-98; prof. internat. pub. policy Gerald Ford Sch. Pub. Policy U. Mich., Ann Arbor, 2001—. Bd. dirs. Am. Friends Svc. Com., 2000—. Office: Ford Sch Public Policy Michigan U 611 Tappan St Ann Arbor MI 48109

WALZ, PATRICIA JEAN, psychologist; d. Paul Dennis and Marion Frances Walz; m. Wayne R. Fiser; children: Sarah Fiser, Jessica Fiser. BA, Moorhead State U., 1981; MA, U. Houston, 1985; PhD, U. Ark., Fayetteville, 1990. Cert. psychologist Coun. for Nat. Register Health Svc. Providers, 1992, profl. qualification in psychology Assn. State and Provincial Psychology Bds., 2002. Psychologist/neuropsychologist Harbor View Therapy and Counseling, Ft. Smith, Ark., 1990—94; neuropsychologist Psychology Svcs., Fort Smith, Ark., 1994—96; owner/pres. Consulting Psychology Western Ark., Ft. Smith, Ark., 1996—. Vol. Delta Soc., Ft. Smith, Ark., 1999—. Mem.: APA, Am. Coll. Forensic Examiners in

Psychology, Ark. Psychol. Assn., We. Ark. Alzheimer's Assn. (bd. dirs. 1991—97). Avocations: dog training, travel, reading. Office: Consulting Psychology Western Ark Inc 1100 S Waldron Rd Fort Smith AR 72903

WALZER, JUDITH BORODOVKO, academic administrator, educator; b. N.Y.C., May 27, 1935; d. Isidore and Ida (Gins) Borodovko; m. Michael L. Walzer, June 17, 1956; children— Sarah, Rebecca BA, Brandeis U., 1958, MA, 1960, PhD, 1967. Dir. office women's edn. Radcliffe Coll., Cambridge, Mass., 1974-77, assoc. dean., 1976-77; Allston Burr sr. tutor, asst. dean for co-edn. Harvard Coll., Cambridge, Mass., 1977-80; asst. to the pres. Princeton U., N.J., 1980-85; provost New Sch. U., N.Y.C., 1985-98, prof. lit., 1998—. Mem. adv. com. Overseas Sch., Hebrew U. in Jerusalem, 1989—. Democrat. Jewish. Office: New Sch U 65 W 11th St New York NY 10011 E-mail: walzer@newschool.edu.

WAN, JULIA CHANG, retired science educator; b. Hong Kong, Oct. 13, 1937; d. Charles S.Y. and Lucy (Wong) Chang; m. Frederic Y.M. Wan, Sept 10, 1960. BA, Wellesley Coll., 1960, MA, 1970; EdD, Boston Coll., 1978. Mem. staff Bio Rsch. Inst., Cambridge, Mass., 1960-64; physics tchr. Watertown (Mass.) H.S., 1970-73; sci. dir. Watertown Pub. Schs., 1973-79; curriculum dir. Fed. Way Sch. Dist., Fed. Way, Wash., 1979-83; asst. supt. Bainbridge Island (Wash.) Sch. Dist., 1983-93; program dir. NSF, Washington, 1993-95; dir. Ctr. for Excellence in Sci. and Math. Edn. Calif. State U., Fullerton, 1995-2000. Mem. accreditation com. N.W. Assn. Schs. and Colls., Boise, Idaho, 1981-95; mem. edn. opportunity coun. AAAS, Washington, 1995-99; bd. dirs. Challenger Ctr., Alexandria, Va., 1997-2000. Author: Designing School Health Education Curricula, 1992, 2d edit. 1995; contbr. articles and revs. to sci. mags. Bd. dirs. NOW, 1985-88; mem. Commn. on Asian-Am. Affairs, Olympia, Wash., 1990-93; bd. trustees Girls, Inc., Orange County, Calif., 1995-2000. Recipient award profl. excellence We. Wash. U., Bellingham, 1988, exemplary program award Met. Life Found., N.Y.C., 1989; grantee: NSF (numerous), Arlington, Va., 1989-2000, Beckman Found., Irvine, Calif., 1998-2000. Mem. ASCD, Am. Ednl. Rsch. Assn., Nat. Sci. Tchrs. Assn. Office: Calif State U Fullerton PO Box 6850 Fullerton CA 92834-4565 E-mail: Jwan@fullerton.edu.

WAND, PATRICIA ANN, librarian; b. Portland, Oreg., Mar. 28, 1942; d. Ignatius Bernard and Alice Ruth (Suhr) W.; m. Francis Dean Silvernail, Dec. 20, 1966 (div. Jan. 19, 1986); children: Marjorie Lynn Silvernail, Kirk Dean Silvernail. BA, Seattle U., 1963; MAT, Antioch Grad. Sch., 1967; AMLS, U. Mich., 1972. Vol. Peace Corps, Colombia, S.Am., 1963-65; secondary tchr. Langley Jr. High Sch., Washington, 1965-66; asst. libr. Wittenberg U. Libr., Springfield, Ohio, 1967-69; secondary tchr. Caro (Mich.) High Sch., 1969-70; assoc. libr. Coll. of S.I. (N.Y.) Libr., 1972-77; head, access svcs. Columbia U. Librs., N.Y.C., 1977-82; asst. univ. libr. U. Oreg., Eugene, 1982-89; univ. libr. The Am. U., Washington, 1989—. Cons. Bloomsburg (Pa.) U. Libr., 1990, Banco Ctrl., Ecuador, 1998, Am. U. Sharjah, UAE, 1999; bd. dirs. CAPCON, ERIC Clearinghouse on Higher Edn. Adminstrn. Contbr. articles to profl. jours. Pres. West Cascade Returned Peace Corps Vols., Eugene, 1985-88; v.p. Friends of Colombia, Washington, 1990—; speaker on Peace Corps, 1965—, libr. and info. svcs., 1979—. Honors Program scholarship Seattle U., 1960-62, Peace Corps scholarship Antioch U., 1965-66; recipient Beyond War award, 1987, Fulbright Sr. Lectr. award Fulbright, 1989, Disting. Alumnus award Sch. of Info. and Libr. Studies, U. Mich., 1992. Mem. ALA (chmn. com. on legislation 1997-98), Assn. Coll. and Rsch. Librs. (chair budget and fin. bd. dirs. 1987-89, chair WHCLIS task force 1989-92, chair govt. rels. com. 1993-94, chair internat. rels. com. 1996-98), On-line Computer Librs. Ctr. (adv. com. on coll. and univ. librs. 1991-96), D.C. Libr. Assn. (bd. dirs. 1993-98, pres. 1996-97). Home: 4854 Bayard Blvd Bethesda MD 20816-1785 Office: Am Univ Libr 4400 Massachusetts Ave NW Washington DC 20016-8046

WANDEL, SHARON LEE, sculptor; b. Bemidji, Minn., Mar. 19, 1940; d. Roy J. and Bonnie (Englund) Opsahl; m. Thaddeus Ludwik Wandel, Oct. 17, 1970; children: Holly, Erika. BA, Gustavus Adolphus Coll., 1962; MSW, Columbia U., 1965; Cert. in Arts Mgmt., SUNY, Purchase, 1993. Caseworker Manhattan State Hosp., N.Y.C., 1963-64; caseworker/rschr. Cmty. Svc. Soc., N.Y.C., 1965-67; teaching asst. dept. medicine NYU Med. Ctr., N.Y.C., 1967-70. Mem. adv. bd. Lamia, Inc., N.Y.C., 1999—2003. One-person shows at Silvermine Guild of Artists, New Canaan, Conn., 1993, 97, 2000, Pen and Brush, N.Y.C., 1994, Clark Whitney Gallery, Lenox, Mass., 1994, James Cox Gallery, Woodstock, N.Y., 1994, 96, Cortland Jessup Gallery, Provincetown, Mass., 1998, N.Y.C., 2000, 02, Gallery Marya, Osaka, Japan, 1999, Laura Barton Gallery, Westport, Conn., 2000, Firehouse Gallery, Damaviscotta, Maine, 2000, Gallery Irohane, Osaka, Japan, 2001; group shows include Nat. Acad. Design, N.Y.C., 1988, 90, 92, 94, 95, 97, 98, 99, 2000, Nat. Sculpture Soc., N.Y.C., 1989, 91, 93, 94, Palazzo Mediceo in Seravezza, Italy, 1994, Knickerbocker Artists, N.Y.C., 1989, 90, 92, Art of N.E. U.S.A., New Canaan, Conn., 1989, 92, Mus. of Hudson Highlands, Cornwall, N.Y., 1990, James Cox Gallery, 1992, 93, 95, 96, N.Y. Soc. Women Artists, Cork Gallery at Lincoln Ctr., 1991, Broome St. Gallery, N.Y.C., 1991, 92, Warner Comm., 1989, Lever House, N.Y.C., 1993, 94, 96, 98, Kohn Pederson Fox Gallery, N.Y.C., 1996, Patio Azul Gallery, Sedona, Ariz., 1995, Williamsville Sculpture Garden, 1995-2002, Kimberly Greer Gall., Northport, NY, 1999, Grounds for Sculpture (Hamilton), NJ, 1999, The Firehouse Gall., Damariscotta, Maine, 1999, 2002, Gall. Between The Muse, Rockland, ME, 1999, Cavalier Gallery, Nantucket, Mass., 2001, Elaine Benson Gallery, Bridgehampton, 1996, Chapel St. Art Gallery, New Haven, 1996, 97, U. Conn., 1996, Mirage Gallery, Albuquerque, 1997, Dora House, London, 1997-98, Lever House, N.Y.C., 1998, Sakai City (Japan) Mus., 2002, Cortland Jessup Gallery, Provincetown and N.Y.C., 1998-2002, Berkshires Bot. Garden, Mass., 2001, Sundance Gallery, Bridgehampton, N.Y., 1997, 98, Castle Gallery, Coll. of New Rochelle, 1998, Gallery Brocken, Tokyo, 1999, Canyon Ranch, Lenox, Mass. 1999-2003, Internat. Sculpture Biennale, Toyamura, Japan, 1999, HBO, N.Y.C., 1999, Chesterwood, Lenox, Mass., 2000, 2001; Butler Inst. Am. Art., Youngstown, Ohio, 2000; Paesaggio Gallery, W. Hartford, Conn., 2001-04, Leighton Gallery, Blue Hill, ME, 2001-04, Munson Gallery, Chatham, Mass., 2002-03, Craven Gallery, Martha's Vineyard, Mass., 2002-04, Berta Walker Gallery, Provincetown, Mass., 2002, Elan Fine Arts, Rockland, Maine, 2003-04, Clarke Galleries, Stowe, Vt., 2003-04, Palm Beach, Fla., 2003-04, NYC, 2003-04; works in permanent collections at Art Students League, 1989, Westinghouse Corp. Collection, Pitts., 1990, Nat. Acad. Design, 1994, Housatonic Mus., CT, 1998, C. of C., Toyamura, Japan, 1999; Pfizer Corp. Collection, Armonk, NY, 2000; commns. include two 8' bronze figures for Ihilani Resort, Kapolei, Hawaii, 1993, 2 5" figures Silvermine Galleries, 1993. Mem. rsch. com. Arthritis Found., N.Y.C., 1968-69. Recipient N.Am. Sculpture Exhbn. 2d place, 1991, Three River Arts Festival (Carnegie Inst.) Purchase award, 1990, Hakone Open Air Mus. (Japan) 3d and 4th Rodin Grand Prize Exhbn. Excellent Maquettes, 1990, 92, Matrix Gallery 1st prize for sculpture, 1990, Ariel Gallery Internat. Competition Group Show award, 1989, Salmagundi Club McReynolds award, 1989, Barret Coleco award, 1988, 1st place nat. competition Sundance Gallery, Bridgehampton, N.Y., 1997; Vt. Studio Ctr. fellow, 2000; elected Nat. Academician Nat. Acad. Design, 1994. Mem. Silvermine Guild of Artists (Solo Show award 1992), N.Y. Soc. Woman Artists (past pres.), Knickerbocker Artists USA, The Pen and Brush (Meisner award 1990, Solo Show award 1993), Nat. Acad. Design (elected nat. academician 1994, Cleo Hartwig award 1990), Nat. Sculpture Soc. (Meisner award 1994, Bronze award 1991, Hexter award 1993, Meisner award 1990), Audubon Artists (Chaim Gross Found. award 1993), Sculptors Guild (bd.). Avocations: travel, cooking, reading. Studio: PO Box 314 Croton On Hudson NY 10520-0314 E-mail: wandel_s@hotmail.com.

WANG, AN-YI (ANNE) CHOU, real estate broker; b. Taipei, Taiwan, Aug. 9, 1946; arrived in U.S., 1984; d. Chin-Yung and Fei-Ying Chou; m. An Tai Wang, Apr. 14, 1971; 1 child, Stewart Sei-Yu. BA in Journalism, Nat. Cheng Chi U., 1970. Lic. broker. Analyst Ctrl. Daily News, Taipei, 1970; reporter China Daily News, Taipei, 1970—71, Taiwan Times, Kaohsiung, Taiwan, 1971—72; chief editor Gen. Instrument of Taiwan Ltd., Taipei, 1972—77; reporter, chief editor Broadcasting Co. of China, Taipei, 1977—84; reporter Ctrl. Daily News, San Francisco, 1984—86, Internat. Daily News, San Francisco, 1986—87; sales rep. Century 21-City Properties, San Francisco, 1987—94; broker, owner Evergreen Realty, San Francisco, 1995—. Author (short story): Heart of Women, 1984; author: (essay) Stories of Artist, 1980, Group Image of Journalists and Pub., 1981. Mem.: San Francisco Assn. Realtors, San Mateo County Assn. Realtors, Calif. Assn. Realtors. Avocations: photography, travel, reading. Home: 2266 34th Ave San Francisco CA 94116 Office: Evergreen Realty 2124 Taraval St San Francisco CA 94116 Office Phone: 415-682-2888.*

WANG, CONG, electrical engineer; b. Hangzhou, Zhejiang, China, Nov. 1, 1965; came to the U.S., 1989; d. Ben Zuo Wang and Xia Ren Shieh. BSEE, U. Southwestern La., 1991; MSEE, U. Tex., Dallas, 1993. Elec. engr. Tex. Instruments, Dallas, 1993—, tech. ladder, 1998—. Recipient 1st place in math contest South Region, La., 1991. Mem. Chinese Orgn. Tex. Instrument (co-chair 1998—), Tau Beta Pi. Avocations: reading, hiking, volleyball, tennis, music. Office: Tex Instruments Inc MS947 13536 N Central Expy Dallas TX 75243-1108 also: PO Box 852638 Richardson TX 75085-2638

WANG, DONNA HUI, investigative medicine director; b. Guangdong, China, Aug. 20, 1961; d. Xuanwu and Huijuan Wang; m. Eugene J. Yu; 1 child, Eunice Yu. MD, Sun Yat-Sen Med. U., Guangzhou, China, 1984; postdoc. fellow, Eastern Va. Med. Sch., Norfolk, 1990. Resident Sun Yat-Sen Ophthalmic Ctr., Sun Yat-Sen Med. U., Guangzhou, China, 1984-85; vis. scholar dept. surgery and physiology Bowman Gray Sch. Medicine, Winston-Salem, N.C., 1985-87; rsch. assoc. dept. physiology Eastern Va. Med. Sch., Norfolk, 1987-90, asst. prof. dept. physiology, 1990-93; asst. prof. dept. internal medicine U. Tex. Med. Branch, Galveston, Tex., 1993-97, assoc. prof. dept. internal medicine, 1997-99; scientist, dir. histochemical core Sealy Ctr. for Molecular Cardiology, U. Tex. Med. Sch., Galveston, 1994-99; prof. dept. medicine Michigan State U., East Lansing, 1999—. Dir. Investigative medicine, Dept. Medicine, Mich. State U., East Lansing, 1999—; mem. Pub. Com. Am. Heart Assn. Coun. for High Blood Pressure, Dallas, 1999-02. Editor: Angiotensin Protocol, Methods in Molecular Medicine, 2000; contbr. articles to profl. jours. Chair The Session of Physiology and Genetics of Angiotensin I and II Receptors, The 68th Scientific Sessions of Am. Heart Assn., Anaham, Calif., 1995, The Session of Hypertension, Am. Physiol. Soc., San Francisco, 1998; peer reviewer Am. Heart Assn-Western State Affiliates Peer Review, San Francisco, 1998-99; mem. prof. com. The Microcirculatory Soc. Inc., San Diego, 1997-01. Recipient First Ind. Rsch. Support Transition award, Nat. Inst. Health, 1993, 98, 1997 Outstanding Young Investigator Travel award, The Microcirculatory Soc., Inc., Hoechst Marion Roussel 1998 Young Scholar award, The Am. Soc. Hypertension, 1998, Established Investigator award Am. Heart Assn., 1999-03. Fellow Am. Heart Assn. Coun. for High Blood Pressure Rsxh. Pub. com. mem., 1995—, Cardiovascular sect., Am. Physiol. Soc. Woman in Physiology com. mem., 1999—; mem. The Microcirculatory Soc. Inc. Office: Dept Medicine B316 Clinical Ctr East Lansing MI 48824 Fax: 517-432-1326. E-mail: donna.wang@ht.msu.edu.

WANG, LIYAN, product design engineer; b. Guiyang, Guizhou, China, Oct. 30, 1962; came to U.S., 1990; d. Tongxing Wang and Zhirong Wu; m. Cheng Qian, Apr. 24, 1987; 1 child, Kathy Qian. BS, Northwestern Poly. U., Xian, China, 1984; MS, U. Ky., 1993, PhD, 1996. Engr. in tng. Tech. editor Nat. Def. Pub. House, Beijing, 1984-90; rsch. asst. mech. engring. dept. U. Ky., Lexington, 1991-96; rsch. assoc. Ctr. for Mfg. Sys., Lexington, 1996; project engr. Altair Engring. Inc., Allen Park, Mich., 1996-97, ICEMCFD Engring., Inc., Livonia, Mich., 1998; product design engr. Visteon Automotive Sys./An Enterprise of Ford Motor Co., Dearborn, Mich., 1998—. Project leader Computational Fluid Dynamics Simulation. Contbr. articles to jours. and papers to confs. Sect. chair Ford Yan Xin Qigong Club, Dearborn; pres. Northwestern Poly. U. Student Broadcasting Sta., Xian. Mem. ASME, Soc. Mfg. Engrs., Soc. Automotive Engrs. Avocations: table tennis, swimming, jogging, yan xin qigong. Home: 6352 Marshall St Canton MI 48187-4700 Office: Visteon Corp Cube NE62-009 6100 Mercury Dr Dearborn MI 48126-2746 Fax: (313) 621-8004. E-mail: lwang@visteon.com.

WANG, MING DE, engineer; b. Yibin, Sichuan, Peoples Republic of China, July 04; came to U.S., 1994; d. Xisheng and Shoumai (Wu) W.; m. Guoxian Zhang, Oct. 4, 1970; 1 child, Ying. BSc in Chemistry, Nankai U., Tianjin, China, 1978, MSc in Organic Chemistry, 1981; PhD in Chemistry, U. Ottawa, Ont., Can., 1993. Rsch. asst. Nankai U., Tianjin, 1978-81, lectr., 1981-87; rsch. asst. in chemistry U. Ottawa, Can., 1987-89, rsch. asst., 1989-93; postdoctoral fellow in chemistry SUNY, Albany, 1994-95, U. Ottawa, 1995-96; process engr. Hadco Santa Clara, Calif., 1996-98, Carolina Circuits, C-MAC of Am., Inc., Greenville, S.C., 1998—. Coauthor 3 chpts. to books; contbr. 16 articles to profl. jours. Cert. instr. CPR, ARC, SUNY, Albany, 1994—. Recipient scholarship Ont. Min. Edn. and Tng., 1992, Sci. and Tech. award Nat. Edn. Com. Peoples Republic of China, 1990. Mem. Am. Chem. Soc., Chem. Inst. Can., China Chem. Soc. Avocations: gospel music, classic movies, travel. Home: 107 Raleigh Ct Simpsonville SC 29681-1981 Office: Carolina Circuits C-MAC of Am Inc 200 Fairforest Way Greenville SC 29607-4609 E-mail: mwang@carolina.cmac.com., Inchrist-1@excite.com.

WANG, NINA, prosecutor; b. Taipai, Taiwan, Apr. 25, 1972; arrived in U.S., 1975; d. Chien-Shih and Hope Liao Wang; m. Douglas Robert Hargrave, June 21, 2003. AB in Econs., Washington U., St. Louis, 1994; JD, Harvard U., 1997. Bar: Ill. 1997, D.C. 1997, Calif. 2001. Assoc. Fried, Frank, Harris, Shriver & Jacobson, Washington, 1997—99; law clk. Hon. Peter J. Messitte U.S. Dist. Ct., Greenbelt, Md., 1999—2000; asst. U.S. atty. U.S. Attys. Office, Denver, 2000—. Vol. Big Bros./Big Sisters, Denver, 2000—. Avocations: travel, cooking, hiking, running.

WANG, QIN, computer engineer, researcher; b. Lishui, Zhejiang, China, Jan. 15, 1973; d. Jixu Wang and Xuewen Chen; m. Ying Hu. PhD, Iowa State U., 1998—2001. Rsch. asst. Iowa State U., Ames, Iowa, 1998—2001; sr. hardware engr. EMC, Hopkinton, Mass., 2001—. Contbr. articles to profl. jours. (Best Thesis Award, 1998). Recipient PACE, Iowa State U., 1998, ABD, 2001, Best Grad. award, Zhejiang Province, 1995, 1998, Best Thesis award, 1995, 1998, Siemens prize, Siemens Inc., 1996, Nari award, Chinese State Power, 1997, Outstanding Student award, Zhejiang Univ., 1991—94; scholar Grad. Coll. scholar, Iowa State U., 1998—2001, First Level Outstanding Student Scholarship, Zhejiang Univ., 1991—94. Mem.: IEEE, Soc. Women Engrs., Nat. Scholars Honor Soc., Delta Epsilon Iota, Tau Beta Pi, Sigma Xi. Personal E-mail: qwanghz@yahoo.com.

WANG, SUSAN S. manufacturing executive; BA in Acctg., U. Tex.; MBA, U. Conn. CPA, Calif. With Price Waterhouse & Co., N.Y.C.; various fin. and acctg. mgmt. positions Xerox Corp., Westvaco Corp.; dir. fin. Solectron Corp., Milpitas, Calif., 1984, v.p. fin., CFO, 1986, sr. v.p., 1990—, also bd. dirs. Mem. adv. bd. YWCA, Santa Clara County; chairperson Fin. Exec. Rsch. Found. Recipient Top Women in Industry award YWCA; named one of San Francisco Bay Area's most powerful corp. women. Mem. AICPA, N.Y. State Soc. CPA, Fin. Execs. Inst. Office: Solectron Corp 777 Gibraltar Dr Milpitas CA 95035-6328

WANG, VERA, fashion designer; b. Manhattan, N.Y., 1949; d. Cheng Ching Wang; m. Arthur Becker, June 22, 1989; children: Cecilia, Josephine. Grad., Sarah Lawrence Coll., New York. Sr. fashion editor Vogue, N.Y.C.; design dir. Ralph Lauren Women's Wear, N.Y.C., 1987-89; prin. Vera Wang Bridal House Ltd., N.Y.C., 1990—; expanded to ready to wear, fragrance, eyewear, footwear, fine jewelry, and a home collection. Designer for Olympic figure skaters including Nancy Kerrigan's silver medal performance at the 1994 Olympics. Author: Vera Wang on Weddings, 2001. Achievements include first to successfully fuse high style and fashion with the tradition and symbolism of the bridal industry; designing wedding and red carpet gowns for Hollywood's elite. Office: Vera Wang Bridal House 225 W 39th St Fl 10 New York NY 10018-3103*

WANG, YA-HUI, conductor; b. Taiwan; arrived in U.S., 1986; Degree in Piano Performance and Conducting, Curtis Inst. Music, Peabody Conservatory. Apprentice condr. Chgo. (Ill.) Symphony Orch., 1995—96; music dir. Fort Smith (Ark.) Symphony, 1996—97; asst. condr. Detroit (Mich.) Symphony Orch., 1997—99; music dir. Akron (Ohio) Symphony Orch., 1999—2003; vice music dir. Evergreen Symphony Orch., Taipei, Taiwan, 2004—. Music dir. Omaha Nebr. Youth Orchs.; prin. condr. Chgo. (Ill.) Encore Chamber Orch.; guest condr. in field. Recipient Tokyo (Japan) Competition prize, 1994, Dimitri Mitropoulos Competition prize, Athens, Greece, 1996, Nicolai Malko Competition prize, Copenhagen, Denmark, 1998. Office: Akron Symphony Orchestra 17 N Broadway Akron OH 44308*

WANG, YUFENG, science educator; arrived in US, 1995; d. Qiancai Wang and Jinzhu Chen. BS in Genetics, Fudan U., Shanghai, China, 1993; MS in Stats. and Genetics, Iowa State U., 1998, PhD in Bioinformatics and Computational Biology, 2001. Grad. asst. Iowa State U., Ames, 1995—2001; rsch. scientist Am. Type Culture Collection, Manassas, Va., 2001—03; asst. prof. U. of Tex., San Antonio, 2003—. Author to profl. jours. albums. Fellow James Cornette Rsch. fellowship, Iowa State U., 2001. Mem.: Am. Statis. Assn., Internat. Soc. Computational Biology, Genetics Soc. Am. Achievements include research in functional divergence and age distribution of human gene families, computational approach in drug discovery, evolutionary and population genetics of infectious diseases. Home: 12235 Vance Jackson Rd Apt 614 San Antonio TX 78230 Office: University of Texas San Antonio Dept of Biology 6900 N Loop 1604 West San Antonio TX 78249 Business E-Mail: ywang@utsa.edu.

WANGSNESS, GENNA STEAD, hotel executive, innkeeper; b. Detroit, Feb. 2, 1942; d. William Allen Stead and Genevieve Josephine Schreiber; m. Roger Carroll Wangsness, Dec. 1, 1967; children: Alison Lee Clement, Bijali Anne, Brian William. BA in Liberal Studies, Georgetown U., 1995. Vol. Peace Corps, Tehran, Iran, 1965—67; sec. Office of Pres. Georgetown U., Washington, 1984—86, coord. adminstrv. svcs. Office of Pres., 1986—89, adminstrv. officer dept. surgery, 1989—92, adminstrv. office Sch. Summer and Continuing Edn., 1992—95; exec. asst. to exec. v.p. Am. Soc. Clin. Oncology, Alexandria, Va., 1995—96; pres., innkeeper The Inn at Folkston, Ga., 1997—. Author: Folkston Then and Now 1881-2003, A Self-Guided Walking Tour of Historic Downtown, Folkston, Georgia, 2003. Mem.: Alpha Sigma Lambda. Achievements include establishment of womens studies section at Charlton Public Library. Office: The Inn at Folkston 509 W Main St Folkston GA 31537

WANJI, SUE, nurse; b. Tiko, Cameroon, July 30, 1954; came to U.S., 1980; d. Paul and Bertha (Joso) Senju; m. Ernest Nkwen-tamo, Apr. 26, 1975 (div. May 1991); children: Lynette, Ilyrich, Yvonne. Cert. in nursing, Utah Valley State Coll., 1984; BA in Journalism, Brigham Young U., 1991. LPN, Calif. Utah. Charge nurse Willowwood Care, Salt Lake City, 1994-95; float nurse Salt Lake Clinic, 1995-96; charge nurse Woodland Care Ctr., Salt Lake City, 1995—. Staff writer Brigham Young U. Daily, 1990, Springville Herald, 1991. Home: 201 E South Temple Apt 607 Salt Lake City UT 84111-5500

WANLEY, PATRICIA ANN, medical/surgical nurse; b. Cin., Sept. 24, 1948; d. Charles Henry and Georgina Helen (Masterson) W. AS, U. Indpls., 1969. RN, Ark., Ind., Md. Staff nurse Ind. U. Hosp., Indpls.; staff nurse home health Bapt. Meml. Hosp., Hardy, Ark.; staff nurse Holy Cross Hosp., Silver Spring, Md.; staff nurse to pvt. physician Chevy Chase, Md. Vol. Am. Diabetes Assn. Named Outstanding Vol. Am. Diabetes Assn.; Bus. and Profl. Women's Nursing scholar, Viva Campbell Nursing scholar. Mem. ANA, Md. Nurses Assn.

WANNAMAKER, MARY RUTH, music educator; b. Ft. Collins, Colo., July 29, 1922; d. Jerry Albert and Daisy B. (Burington) Lyman; m. William H. Anderson, June 14, 1944 (dec. 1944); m. John S. Wannamaker, Sept. 7, 1946; children: Lois Wannamaker, Daisy Wannamaker Van Valkenburg. MusB, Colo. State U., 1944; M in Musicology, U. Minn., 1949, M in Ednl. Psychology, 1969. Piano tchr. U. Minn., Mpls., 1945-46; piano tchr. Drake U., Des Moines, 1945-47; prof. piano Kletzing Coll., University Park, Iowa, 1948-49; ednl. cons. Des Moines, 1975-85. Pvt. piano tchr. Des Moines, 1950—. Composer Easter ch. svc., 1965. Vol. Iowa State Hist. Libr., Des Moines, 1990—; pres. Delta Omicron Alumnae, Des Moines, 1946-50, Profl. Women's League, Des Moines, 1974-75, Iowa Pers. & Guidance Assn., Des Moines, 1978-79; violist Des Moines Symphony Orch., 1946-65; mem. Altrusa, 1970-75. Mem. Music Techs. Nat. Assn., PEO, Phi Kappa Phi (scholarship 1944). Avocations: reading, travel, concerts. Home: 200 Buffalo Hills Ln E # 107 Brainerd MN 56401-4555

WANWIG, ANNETTE CLARE, nursing administrator; b. Hudson, S.D., Oct. 2, 1948; d. Arnold Hartvig and Estella Ellen (Sorensen) Andersen; m. John Daniel Wanwig, June 3, 1973; children: Kirstin Anne, Bjorn Erik. BS, S.D. State U., 1970. RN. Nurse Harborview Med. Ctr., Seattle, 1970-72, U of Vt. Med. Ctr. Hosps., Burlington, 1972-75, St. Joseph's Hosp., Stockton, Calif., 1975-78; nurse, office mgr. Cascade Internal Medicine, Tacoma, 1978—. Mem. AAUW, Pierce County Med. Soc. Alliance, Sigma Theta Tau. Republican. Lutheran. Avocations: genealogy, nature, skiing. Home: PO Box 1609 Gig Harbor WA 98335-3609 Office: Cascade Internal Medicine 1901 S Union A-305 Tacoma WA 98405

WANZER, MARY KATHRYN, computer company executive, consultant; b. South Bend, Ind., Sept. 12, 1942; d. Cyril Joseph and Kathryn Alice (Dumke) Tlusty; m. Boyd Eugene Wanzer, May 30, 1964; children: Adam James, Christopher James. BS, Northland Coll., 1964; student, Am. U., Washington, 1972-75. Tchr. Montgomery Co. Md. Schs., Rockville, 1964-66; mathematician Johns Hopkins U., Silver Spring, Md., 1966-68; systems analyst ITT Fed. Elec. Corp., Kennedy Space Ctr., Fla., 1968-69; computer programmer Atlantic City (N.J.) Hosp., 1969-71; project leader Fairfax Hosp. Assn., Falls Church, Va., 1971-73; sr. systems analyst Xerox Corp., Leesburg, Va., 1973-76; software engr. E-Systems, Falls Church, Va., 1982-85; pres. Atlantic Office Svcs., Ltd., Bethany Beach, Del., 1988-99. Cons. Chesapeake Utilities, Dover, Del., 1990, Intervet, Millsboro, Del., 1990—92; MIS mgr. Thompson Pub. Group, Salisbury, Md., 1992—93; sys. analyst Mountaire, Selbyville, Del., 1993—96; fin. analyst Peninsula Regional Med. Ctr., Salisbury, 1996—2002; realtor Island Palms Real Estate, Vero Beach, Fla., 2002—. Leader LaLeche League, Annandale, Va., 1980—83; v.p. No. Va. Hockey Club, Fairfax County, 1986—87. Roman Catholic. Avocation: Avocations: boating, swimming. Home: The Atrium on the Ocean 2900 N AIA Unit 9C Hutchinson Island FL 34949- E-mail: MaryWanzer@cs.com.

WAPNIR, IRENE LEONOR, medical educator; b. Buenos Aires, May 11, 1954; came to U.S., 1963; d. Raul Alberto and Elsa (Michalewicz) W.; m. Ralph Steven Greco; children: Justin Michael, Eric Matthew, Ilana Rose.

BA, Goucher Coll., Balt., 1975; MD, U. Autonoma Metropolitana, Mexico City, 1980. Diplomate Am. Bd. Surgery. Intern, resident N.Y. Med. Coll., Bronx, 1980-85; attending physician and asst. prof. surgery Lincoln Hosp.-N.Y. Med. Coll., 1985-87; asst. prof. surgery UMDNJ-Robert Wood Johnson Med. Sch., New Brunswick, 1988-95, chief divsn. comprehensive breast svcs., 1991-93, assoc. prof. clin. surgery, 1995—2000; assoc. prof. surgery Sch. Medicine Stanford (Calif.) U., 2001—. Contbr. articles to profl. jours. Komen Breast Cancer Rsch. grant, fellow UMDNJ-Robert Wood Johnson Med. Sch., 1987-88. Office: Stanford Univ Sch Medicine 300 Pasteur Drive Stanford CA 94305

WARA, DIANE, dean; BS in Biology, Standord U., 1964; MD, U. Calif., Irvine, 1969. Intern in peds. Harbor Gen. Hosp., Torrance, Calif., 1969-70; resident in peds. U. Calif., San Francisco, 1970-72; fellow immunology divsn. dept. peds. USPHS, 1974-75; asst. prof. peds. U. Calif., San Francisco, 1975-79, assoc. prof. peds., 1979-84, prof. peds., 1984—, chief divsn. ped. immunology/rheumatology, program dir. ped., 1985—, assoc. dean for minority and women's affairs sch. med., 1991—. Mem. NIH study sect. on immunological scis., 1985-87, chair, 1987-89; vice chair universitywide task force on AIDS, 1989-92; vice chair ped. core com. AIDS Clinical Trials Group, 1991-92, chair ped. core com., 1992-94; mem. AIDS rsch. adv. com. NIH, 1990-95; mem. AIDS program adv. com. NIAID, 1990-94; mem. GCRC study sect., 1993-97, chair study sect., 1996-97. Contbr. articles to profl. jours. Recipient Eleanor Roosevelt award Am. Cancer Soc., 1983, Rsch. Career Devel. award Nat. Inst. of Child Health and Human Devel., 1978-83. Mem. NAS (elected to Inst. Medicine 1998), Am. Ped. Soc., Am. Rheumatism Assn., Am. Assn. Immunology, Am. Soc. for Clin. Investigation, Soc. for Ped. Rsch., Western Soc. for Ped. Rsch. (sec.-treas. 1979-83, pres. 1990-91). Office: U Calif Childrens Med Ctr 505 Parnassus Ave # M-601 San Francisco CA 94122-2722

WARANIUS VASS, ROSALIE JEAN, artist; b. Fond du Lac, Wis., Dec. 10, 1938; d. John Stanley and Anna Francis (Jonaitis) Waranius; m. Kenneth James Vass, June 11, 1960; children: Kealie, Ross, Kenlyn, Jason. BA, Alverno Coll., 1960. Cert. art tchr., Ill. Art tchr. East Aurora (Ill.) H.S., 1979-83; dir. Doctor Scholl Art Gallery, Aurora, 1984-90; studio art tchr. Marmion Acad., Aurora, 1985-90. One-woman shows include Batavia (Ill.) Pub. Libr., 1987, The Holmstad, Ill., 1988, Bellarmine Coll., Ky., 1989, Aurora (Ill.) U., 1989, St. Charles (Ill.) Pub. Libr., 1989, Roberta Campbell Art Gallery, Ill., 1991, 95, Rolling Meadows (Ill.) Libr. Art Gallery, 1991, Alverno Coll. Art Gallery, Wis., 1991, Ill. Artisan Shop, 1992, Jesse Besser Mus., Mich., 1993, Beacon St. Gallery, Ill., 1995, Saginaw (Mich.) Art Mus., 1997, Alfons Gallery, Wis., 1998, Norris Cultural Arts Ctr., Ill., 1998, Balzekas Mus., Ill., 1999, Gallery 129, Ill., 2000; exhibited in group shows including 17th Internat. Exhbn. Water Color Soc., Houston, 1994, NWS Signature Mem. Juried Exhbn., Norwalk, Calif., 1994, Aurora U., 1994, Invitational Batavia Artists, 1994, Women Artists : A Celebration, Youngstown, Ohio, 1994, No. Art Competition, Rhinelander, Wis., 1994, Watercolor Masters: Midwest Show, Lincolnwood, Ill., 1995, Norris Cultural Arts Ctr., St. Charles, 1989-98, Yello Gallery, Chgo., 1997, Alfons Gallery, Milw., 1998, Norris Cultural Arts Ctr., St. Charles, Ill., 1998, Balzekas Mus., Ill., 1999,, Gallery 129, Ill., 2000, Art & Whimsy, The Gallery, Batavia, 2001, Scribbles: Art & Text, The Gallery, Batavia, 2002, Northwest Area Arts Coun. Members Show, Woodstock, Ill., 2003, Womens Works, 2003, Vicinity Show, St. Charles, Ill., 2003, Midwest Winter Show, Wausau, Wis., 2004, The Modern Portrait Show, Lane Allen Gallery, Batavia, Ill., 2004, others; represented in permanent collections at Art and Music Festival, Ill., Whirlpool Corp., Ill., Security Bank, Iowa, First Chgo. Bank, Glenbrook North Western Healthcare, Jesse Besser Mus., Mich., Easter Seal, Ill., St. Francis Hosp., Ill. Delnor Cmty Hosp., Geneva, Ill., others. Mem. Nat. Watercolor Soc. (signature mem., life), Nat. Mus. Women in Arts, Chgo. Artists Coalition, Art Inst. Chgo. Avocations: traveling, reading, cooking. Home: O S 888 Wenmoth Rd Batavia IL 60510-9711

WARBERG, WILLETTA, concert pianist, writer, piano educator; b. Twin Falls, Idaho, June 2, 1932; d. George William Warberg and Ethel Margaret (Sargent) Warberg-Chandler; m. David Jacob Bar-Illan, Sept. 3, 1954 (div.); children: Daniela, Jeremy Oscar. Student, Colo. Women's Coll., 1950-51, Aspen Music Camp, 1951; studied with, Rudolph Firkusny, 1951-53; BS, Mannes Coll. Music, N.Y.C., 1954. Assoc. food editor Look mag., N.Y.C., 1956-61; food editor Status mag., N.Y.C., 1961-62, Ladie's Home Jour., N.Y.C., 1964-66; photog. stylist Gourmet mag., N.Y.C., 1961-64, freelance writer, photog. stylist, 1965-75; pres., owner Willetta Enterprises, advt. agy., Twin Falls, 1976-84; food columnist, music and arts critic Times News, 1978-87; duo-piano ptnr. with Robert Starer, N.Y.C., Woodstock, 1991—2000; pvt. piano tchr., Saugerties, N.Y., 1991—. Made feasibility study of restaurant situation in Israel, U.S. Dept. State ICA Point 4 Program, Washington and Israel, 1960; artist-in-residence Holy Cross Concert Series, Kingston, N.Y., 1994—. Concert pianist, Idaho, Oreg., Utah, Wash., Colo., N.Y.C., N.Y. State, 1940—; author: Cooking from Scratch, 1976, Space Age Cookery, 1977; syndicated food columnist Willetta Says, 1978-87; contbr. food and sci. articles to Cosmopolitan, Modern Maturity, Esquire, Sun Valley, Sci. Diegest, also other mags. Bd. dirs. N.W. Opera Assn., 1984-87; pres. bd. dirs. Woodstock Lyric Theatre, 1994—; v.p. bd. dirs. Woodstock Chamber Orch., 1993—; chmn. Friends of the Maverick Concerts Inc., Woodstock, N.Y., 1999—. Winner Rocky Mountain talent search contest Salt Lake Tribune and Salt Lake Telegram, 1949. Mem. Nat. Fedn. Music Clubs, Music Tchrs. Nat. Assn. (cert.), Kingston Music Soc.. Avocations: designing and sewing clothes, painting still lifes, swimming, developing recipes, writing science fiction book.

WARD, ANGIE, radio personality; Grad., Auburn U. Sportscaster Auburn U.; radio personality WTQR 104, Greensboro, NC. Named Personality of Yr., Country Music Assn., 2000, Country Radio Broadcast, 2001. Office: WTQR 104 2B PAI Pk Greensboro NC 27409

WARD, ANNE STARR MINTON, music educator, musician; d. James Royster and Bobbie Lee (Clegg) Minton; m. Benjamin Kirby Ward, June 19, 1966; children: David Alexander, Karen Virginia. Bachelor of Music cum laude, U. N.C., Greensboro, 1965, Master of Music Edn., 1966. Orch. tchr. Dade County Schs., Miami, 1967—68, Jacksonville County Schs., Fla., 1968—69; pvt. violin tchr. Florence, SC, 1974—; mem. faculty N.C. Suzuki Inst., Greenville, 1986—2003. Violinist Florence Symphony Orch., 1974—2000; concert master Florence Symphony, 2000—; violinist Piedmont Trio, SC, 1996—2000; co-chmn. Florence Ctr. Arts, Inc., 2000—03. Lay leader Ctrl. United Meth. Ch., Florence, 1996—2003; chmn. Evangelistic awards S.C. conf. United Meth. Ch., 1997—2003; mem. Florence Downtown Devel. Bd., 2002—03; bd. dirs. Florence 2010 Com., 2001—02. Mem.: Music Educators Nat. Conf., Florence-Darlington String Assn. (co-founder 1998, pres. 1998—), Suzuki Assn. Am., AMA Alliance. Avocation: gardening.

WARD, BONNIE J. insurance company executive; b. Boston, Mass., Feb. 16, 1957; d. Marcia M. and Russell A. Ward; children: Creighton A. A., Reilly X. X. BA in Polic. Sci., U. Mass., 1978. Telecomm. mgr. City of Boston/Boston City Hall, 1979—84; sr. telecomm. analyst WANG Lab., Lowell, 1984—86; sys. integration mgr. Shawmut Nat. Corp., Boston, 1986—91; v.p. telecomm. First Data Corp., Medford, 1991—95; gen. dir. tech. ops. support John Hancock Mut. Life Co., Boston, 1995—98; v.p. telecomm. Liberty Mut. Group, Portsmouth, NH, 1998—. Vol. Yankee Homecoming, Newburyport, 1985—99. Recipient Dist. svc. award, Newburyport Lions Club, 1990. Mem.: BPOE Lodge #909. Roman Catholic. Office: Liberty Mutual Group 225 Borthwick Ave Portsmouth NH 03801 Business E-Mail: bonnie.ward.ts3@libertymutual.com.

WARD, BRENDA ROBINSON, social worker; b. Gastonia, NC, Nov. 12, 1954; d. Elvin Franklin and Annie Sue (Clemmer) Robinson; m. Robert Crawford Ward, Aug. 29, 1981; children: Lauren Clemmer, Thomas Crawford. BSW, NC State U, 1977; MSW, U. N.C., 1980. LCSW NC. Social worker I Broughton Hosp., Morganton, NC, 1977—78; social worker II Smoky Mtn. Area Mental Health, Dillsboro, NC, 1980—81, Cherry Hosp., Goldsboro, NC, 1981—83; social worker III Piedmont Behavioral Healthcare, Concord, NC, 1983—91, local mental health unit coord., 1991—97, clin. social work specialist Kannapolis, NC, 1997—2002; clin. coord. Lifeworks Oupatient Program Rowan Reg. Med. Ctr., 2002—. Mem.: Cabarus County Mental Health Assn., NASW. Office: Lifeworks Outpatient Prgm Rowan Reg MC 612 Mocksville Ave Salisbury NC 28144

WARD, CHARLOTTE LOWREY, guidance counselor; b. Ft. Smith, Ark., May 17, 1942; d. Rudolph Cley and Clovis (Baggarly) Lowrey; m. James Carl Ward, Dec. 2, 1941; children: Sonya Yvette, Craig Alan, Cary Scott. BA in Edn., LA Tech. U., 1964; MEd, Northwestern State U., Natchitoches, La., 1980, postgrad., 1988. Libr. Pub. Libr., Ruston, La., 1964-65, Houston, Tex., 1965-66; sch. libr. Houston Ind. Dist., 1966-67; tchr. kindergarten Winn Parish Schs., Sikes, La., 1974-75; sch. libr. Atlanta (La.) H.S./Winn Parish Schs., 1979—; guidance counselor Winnfield (La.) Mid. - Winn Parish Sch., 1987—. Profl. counselor, La., 1987—. Sunday sch. dir., grades five and six First Bapt. Ch., Winnfield, 1975—, dir. of girls in action missionary study, 1968-80, mem. budget com., 1992—, long-range com., 1985—. Named Woman of Yr., Winnfield Women's Club, 1980. Mem. La. Tech. Alumni, Northwestern State U. Alumni, La. Counselor's Assn., la. Sch. Counselors Assn., La. Assn. Marriages and Family Counselors, La. Mental health Counselors Assn., La. Educators Assn., NEA, Am. Counselors Assn., Nat. Peer Helpers Assn., Alpha Delta Kappa. Republican. Office: Winnfield Mid Sch PO Box 1140 Hwy 167N Winnfield LA 71483

WARD, DARLENE MARIE, retail buyer; b. Aurora, IL, May 11, 1947; d. Glenn LeRoy and Helen Susan (Soderdahl) Anderson; m. Lawrence Anselm Ward Jr., Sept. 18, 1976 (div. Jan. 1992); children: Lara Kathryn, Lawrence Anselm III. BS in Profl. Studies, Aurora U., 2001. Machine shop layout planner Caterpillar, Inc., Aurora, Ill., 1981—82, various positions prior to procurement analyst-buyer, 1982—.

WARD, DORIS M. county official; BA in Govt., MS in Edn., Ind. U.; MA in Counseling, San Francisco State U.; PhD in Edn., U. Calif., Berkeley. Tchr. Indpls. Pub. Schs., 1959-67, team leader, supr. tchg. interns, 1967-68; adviser, counselor San Francisco STEP program, 1969-70; coord. curriculum San Mateo County Office of Edn., Redwood City, Calif., 1968-89; mem. bd. govs. San Francisco C.C., 1973-79; mem. bd. suprs. City and County San Francisco, 1980-92, pres. bd. suprs., 1991-92, assessor, recorder, 1992—, elected assessor-recorder, 1996. Adj. assoc. prof. Sch. Edn. Calif. State U., 1969-70, 72-73; advisor to External Masters Degree Program, U. San Francisco, 1972-76; chief cons. Calif. Assembly on regional govt., 1989-92. Contbr. articles to ednl. and polit. jours. Bd. dirs. Nat. Dem. County Officials 1987—, pres. 1994—; mem. Dem. Nat. Com., 1992—, del. 1984, 88, 92, 96 convs. Named Woman of Yr., Zeta Phi Beta, 1984; recipient Disting. Alumni award San Francisco State U., 1993, Disting. Comty. award, U. San Francisco, 1994, Spl. Merit award Sun Reporter Newspaper and numerous other awards for comty. svc. by activist orgns; grantee: NDEA, 1967, 68, Ind. State U., Terre Haute, Ind., Lilly Found., 1967, Rockefeller Found., U. Calif., Berkeley, 1974. Mem. Bay Area Assessors Assn. (sec. 1994, v.p. 95, pres. 96), Calif. Assessors' Assn. (mem. legis. com. 1993, exec. com. 95), Nat. Assn. Counties (bd. dirs. 1989-91, chair human svcs. and edn., 1991-92), Nat. Assn. Black County Officials (bd. dirs. 1987—, regional dir. 1987—), Nat. League of Cities (bd. dirs. 1991-92, vice chair and steering com. Fed. Adminstrn. Intergovtl. Rels. 1990-91), Nat. Black Caucus of Local Elected Officials (bd. dirs. 1987-95), Pi Sigma Alpha, Pi Lambda Theta. Office: City County San Francisco Assessor Recorder Office Rm 190 1 Dr Carlton B Goodlett Pl San Francisco CA 94102-4603

WARD, ERICA ANNE, lawyer, educator; b. Okiyama, Japan, Oct. 20, 1950; d. Robert Edward and Constance Regina (Barnett) Ward; m. Ralph Joseph Gerson, May 20, 1979; children: Stephanie Claire Gerson, Madeleine Ward Gerson. BA, Stanford U., 1972; JD, U. Mich., 1975. Bar: Calif. 1975, DC 1976, US Ct. Appeals (5th and DC cir.) 1977, Temp. Emergency Ct. Appeals 1983, Mich. 1989. Assoc. Wilmer, Cutler & Pickering, Washington, 1975—77; staff counsel US Senate Ethics Com., Washington, 1977—78; exec. asst. gen. counsel Dept. Energy, Washington, 1978—79; counsellor to dep. sec., 1980; assoc. dir. energy and natural resources, domestic policy staff White House, Washington, 1980—81; counsel Skadden, Arps, Slate, Meagher & Flom., Washington, 1981—87; ptnr., 1987; adj. prof. law U. Mich., Ann Arbor, 1984—85; Editor Mich. Law Rev., 1975; commr. Mackinac Is. State Pk. Commn., Mich., 1989—95. Recipient Outstanding Svc. medal, Dept. Energy, 1981. Mem.: Women's Bar Assn. DC, ABA, U. Mich. Law Sch., Cranbrook Ednl. Cmty., Detroit Zool. Soc., Edn. of Women U. Mich. Democrat. Jewish. Office: Skadden Arps Slate Meagher Flom 1440 New York Ave NW Ste 600 Washington DC 20005-6000

WARD, JACKIE M. computer company executive; Student, Ga. State U., Ariz. State U.; completed internat. bus. fellows program, Ga. State U., The London Bus. Sch. With data processing dept. J.P. Stevens Co.; with UNIVAC div. Sperry Rand Corp.; founder, chief exec. officer Computer Generation, Inc., Atlanta, v.p., then pres., 1970. Vice chmn.-elect bd. regents Univ. System Ga., 1987—; commr. Edn. Commn. of States; pres., bd. dirs. Internat. Claim Services Ltd.; mem. Com. of 200. Office: Computer Generation Inc 5775 Peachtree Dunwoody Rd NE Atlanta GA 30342-1556

WARD, JANET LYNN, magazine editor, sports wire reporter; b. Albany, Ga., Feb. 20, 1955; d. Andrew Johnson and Dorothy Iris (Pepera) W.; m. William Thomas Hankins III, Apr. 25, 1981 (div. Feb. 1990); m. Jack Wilkinson, May 22, 1993. AB in Journalism, U. Ga., 1977; JD, Woodrow Wilson Coll. Law, 1984. Sports editor Marietta (Ga.) Daily Jour., 1977-79, North Fulton extra-Atlanta Jour. Constitution, 1979-80; asst. editor In town extra-Atlanta Jour. Constitution, 1980-84; lawyer Atlanta, 1984-89; editor Am. City & County Mag., Atlanta, 1989—. Democrat. Roman Catholic. Avocations: sports, reading. Home: 372 Oakdale Rd NE Atlanta GA 30307-2070 Office: Am City & County 6151 Powers Ferry Rd NW Atlanta GA 30339-2959 E-mail: jward@intertec.com.

WARD, JEANNETTE POOLE, retired psychologist, educator; b. Honolulu, June 19, 1932; d. Russell Masterton and Bessie Naomi (Hammett) Poole; children: John Russell Ward, Lisa Joy Ward. BA, Birmingham (Ala.) So. Coll., 1963; PhD in Psychology, Vanderbilt U., 1969. NSF summer rsch. asst. U. Iowa, Iowa City, 1962, Vanderbilt U., Nashville, 1963, NASA fellow, 1963-66, NIH postdoctoral fellow, 1966-67; spl. rsch. fellow Duke U., Durham, NC, 1970-71; asst. prof. psychology U. Memphis, 1967-72, assoc. prof., 1972-77, prof., 1977-2000; ret., 2001. Editor: Current Research in Primate Laterality, 1990, Primate Laterality, 1992; mem. editl. bd. Jour. Comparative Psychology, 1988-95, Internat. Jour. of Comparative Psychology, 1995—; contbr. chpts. to books and articles to profl. jours. Fellow APA; mem. Psychonomic Soc., Animal Behavior Soc., Am. Primatology Soc., Southeastern Psychol. Assn., Soc. for Neuroscis., Internat. Soc. for Comparative Psychology (treas. 1989-90, pres.-elect 1996-98, pres. 1998-2000), Sigma Xi (pres. Memphis State U. chpt. 1989-90, rsch. award 1985). Democrat. Avocations: dogs, reading, art, music. E-mail: jeannetteward@cs.com.

WARD, JUDITH A. elementary school educator, music educator; b. Brazil, Ind., Dec. 9, 1945; d. Stanley M. and J. Irene Cobley; m. William E. Norris, Aug. 18, 1967 (div.); 1 child, Edwin S. Norris ; m. Don N. Ward, Nov. 1980 (dec.). BS cum laude, Ind. State U., 1967, MS, 1970. Elem. music tchr. Dekalb County Ctrl. United Sch. Dist., Auburn, Ind., 1967—71, Wabash (Ind.) City Schs., 1971—. Music dir. Wabash Christian Ch., 1978—; coord. Visual Performing Arts Cooperative, Wabash, 1996—; summer theatre dir., youth choir dir. Bd. dirs., music dir. Wabash Area Cmty. Theater, 1996—; music dir., mem. planning com. Cmty. Madrigal Dinner, Honeywell Ctr., Wabash, 1997—; dir., singer Market Street Beat, Wabash, 1999—. Recipient Disting. Citizen award, Wabash C. of C., 2001. Mem.: NEA, Assn. Disciple Musicians Ind. (sec., pres.), Assn. Disciple Musicians (nat. planning coun. 2001—03, sec. 2003), Ind. Gen. Music Educators Assn. (pres. 2000—02), Ind. Music Educators Assn. (area coord. Cir. the State with Song, state elem. chair Cir. the State with Song, Outstanding Elem. Music Educator 2003), Ind. State Tchrs. Assn., Delta Kappa Gamma, Sigma Alpha Iota (Ft. Wayne alum pres. 1970—72, Beta province v.p. 1978—87). Mem. Disciples Of Christ Church. Avocations: reading, latch hooking. Home: 3254 S 100 W Wabash IN 46992 Office: OJ Neighbours Elem 1545 N Wabash St Wabash IN 46992

WARD, JUDY KITCHEN, bank executive; b. Asheville, N.C., Jan. 19, 1940; d. Jesse Ernest and Mary Daisy (Pressley) Kitchen; m. Wayne Leigh; children: Robert Wayne, Shari Leigh, Rodney Victor; m. Jerry Ellsworth Ward; 1 child, Jerry E. Jr. Student, Thomas Nelson Community Coll., Hampton, Va., 1987. Bank teller 1st City Bank, Newport News, Va., 1977-82; adminstrv. asst. Va. Nat. Bank, Newport News, 1982-84; br. mgr. 1st Am. Bank Va., Newport News, 1984-91, asst. v.p., 1991—. Treas. Alternatives/Drug Abuse, Newport News and Hampton, 1986-88, bd. dirs., 1986—; cabinet mem. United Way, Newport News, 1988; mem. ways and means com. Dem. Orgn., 1987—; sec. Denbigh Little League, 1974-76; pres. local PTA, 1972-73, Block Mother's Prevention Against Child Abuse, 1967-69; bd. dirs. Dem. City Com., 1992. Recipient cert. United, 1984-88, Mar. of Dimes, 1982-88. Mem. Am. Inst. Banking (chief consul 1986, award 1987, v.p. 1990—, bd. dirs. 1991, chmn. child abuse 1992), Exch. Club (pres. James River chpt. 1990—). Episcopalian. Avocation: collecting. Home: 193 Compton Pl Newport News VA 23606-1626 Office: 1st Am Bank Va 2901 Huntington Ave Newport News VA 23607-3917

WARD, KELSEY S. purchasing agent; b. Keene, N.H. Student, U. N.H., 1976—78. Buyer III U. Tex. at Dallas, Richardson, 1983—87; purchasing agt. Electronic Data Systems, Richardson, 1987—89, product mgr., 1989—94; owner Beauty and the Beast Ltd., Concord, NH, 1994—95; CSR/affiliate relations Vistar/Windshields Am., Bedford, NH, 1995—96; MRO buyer/expediter Rockwell Internat., Manchester, NH, 1996—97; sr. purchasing and contracts agt. County Bd. of County Commrs., Naples, Fla., 1997—. Internship program mem. Collier County Mgrs. Office, Naples, 2001. Mem.: Nat. Contract Mgmt. Assn., Gulf Coast Assn. of Govtl. Purchasing Officers (sec. 1998—99), Fla. Assn. of Pub. Purchasers, Nat. Inst. Govtl. Purchasing. Democrat. Avocations: interior decorating, historic preservation, art, aviation, auto racing. Home: PO Box 9706 Naples FL 34101 Office: Collier County Govt 3301 Tamiami Trail E Naples FL 34112 Office Phone: 239-774-8949.

WARD, LESLIE ALLYSON, journalist, editor; b. L.A., June 3, 1946; d. Harold Gordon and Marilyn Lucille (Dahlstead) W.; m. Robert L. Biggs, 1971 (div. 1977); m. Colman Robert Andrews, May 26, 1979 (div. 1988). AA, Coll. San Mateo, 1966; BA, UCLA, 1968, MJ, 1971. Reporter, researcher L.A. Bur. Life mag., 1971-72; reporter, news asst. L.A. bur. N.Y. Times, 1973-76; sr. editor New West mag., L.A., 1976-78, 79-80; L.A. bur. chief US mag., 1978-79; Sunday style editor L.A. Herald Examiner, 1981-82, editor-in-chief Sunday mags., 1982-83, Olympics editor, 1984, sports editor, 1985-86, sr. writer, 1986; sr. editor L.A. Times Mag., 1988-90; travel editor L.A. Times, 1990—. Democrat. Office: LA Times Times Mirror Sq Los Angeles CA 90053

WARD, LILLIAN HAZEL, music educator; b. Hastings, Colo., Sept. 19, 1920; d. Frank Joseph and Jane (Shields) Baker; m. Peter Joseph Ward, Sept. 12, 1942; children: Mary Jane Eickhoff, Michael George. Student, Western State Coll., 1938-42. Piano tchr., San Francisco, 1951-54, Los Altos, Calif., 1955—. Author: (composition for piano) Girl Scout Song Book, 1957. Leader brownies Girl Scouts USA, San Francisco, 1952-54, Los Altos, Calif., 1955-59; guardian coun. Jobs Daus., Los Altos, 1959-68; tchr., dir. United Meth. Ch., Los Altos, 1955-73. Mem. Nat. Music Tchrs. Assn., Calif. Assn. Profl. Music Tchrs. Avocations: gardening, reading, working with the blind, spending time with grandchildren, watercolor and oil painting. Home: 246 Alicia Way Los Altos CA 94022-2346

WARD, MARILYN BEEMAN, commissioner; b. Oakland, Calif., June 6, 1929; d. Samuel William and Alice Lee (Turner) Beeman; m. Daniel Bridges Ward, Aug. 15, 1950; children: Anne Ward Ryan, Susan Ward Potts, Daniel E. Ward. Student, U. Calif., Berkeley, 1947-49; BA, Evergreen State Coll., 1978. Founding dir., loan officer Sound Savs. & Loan, Seattle, 1981-86. Cons. Bellevue (Wash.) Pub. Schs., variety of social svc. agys., 1970s and 1980s. Chmn. Harborview Med. Ctr., Seattle, 1994, 1995, 1996; mem. Wash. State Med. Quality Assurance Commn., 1986—, chmn., 1993—94; mem. vis. com. U. Wash. Sch. Social Work, chmn., 1988; mem. vis. com. U. Wash. Sch. Pub. Health. Recipient Ralph Bunche Peace award Wash. State Bar Assn., 1985, Dorothy Bullitt Cmty. Leader award Jr. League, 1996, John H. Clark Leadership award Fedn. State Med. Bds. of U.S. Mem.: Sunset Club (pres.), City Club (co-founder 1985, pres. 1985—86). Episcopalian. Avocations: photography, gardening, golf, fishing, reading. Office: PO Box 465 Medina WA 98039-0465

WARD, NINA GILLSON, jewelry store executive; b. Boston, Dec. 19, 1950; d. Rev. John Robert and Patricia (Gillson) Baker; m. Jorge Alberto Lievanos, June 6, 1981 (div.); children: Jeremy John Baker, Wendy Mara Baker, Raoul Salvador Baker-Lievanos; m. David Ward, July 24, 1998; stepchildren: Johnna Ward, Tavi Sterling. Student, Mills Coll., 1969-70; grad. course in diamond grading, Gemology Inst. Am., 1983; student in diamondtology designation, Diamond Coun. Am., 1986—. Cert. store mgr., Jewelers Cert. Coun., Jewelers Am. Artist, tchr., Claremont, Calif., 1973-78; escrow officer Bank of Am., Claremont, 1978-81; retail salesman William Pitt Jewelers, Puente Hills, Montclair, Calif., 1981-83, asst. mgr., 1983, mgr. Santa Maria, Calif., 1983-91, corp. sales trainer, 1988-89; sales and design specialist Merksamer Jewelers, Santa Maria, 1991, mgr. San Luis Obispo, Calif., 1991-92, Santa Maria, Calif., 1992-94, diamond specialist cons., 1994-96; pres., ops. mgr. Dancer House Designs, Santa Maria, Calif., 1996; pres. primary jewelry designer Dancer House Design Fine Jewelry, Inc., Kennebunk, Maine, 1997—. Artist tapestry hanging Laguna Beach Mus. Art, 1974; exhibited in Nat. Jeweler's Design Competition, 1999. Mem. Cen. Coast Pla. Adv. Bd., 1992; mem. Rep. Bus. Majority Coun. Recipient Cert. Merit Art Bank Am., 1968, 1st pl. Best of show award for jewelry design Maine Jeweler's Assn., 1998, design award, 2000, Rep. of Yr. Award Maine, 2000, 1st place award crystal divsn. nat. design competition Mfg. Jewelers and Suppliers of Am., 2001. Mem. NAFE, Internat. Platform Assn., Maine Jewelers Assn. (bd. dirs. 1999—), Speaker's Bur., Santa Maria C. of C., Compassion Internat. Republican. Avocations: tapestry weaving, creative writing. Office: PO Box 475 Kennebunk ME 04043-0475

WARD, ROSE MARIE, education educator, researcher; d. Raymond and Mary Regan; m. John Ward, July 1, 2000. D of psychology, U. of RI, 1998—2002. Statis. cons. Pro-Change Behavior Systems, Kingston, RI, 1999—2003; asst. prof. of psychology Miami U., Oxford, Ohio, 2002—. Statis. cons. Cancer Prevention Rsch. Ctr., Kingston, RI, 1998—2003. Dir. of youth and christian edn. Oxford Ch. of God, Oxford, Ohio, 1998—2003. Mem.: Soc. of Behavioral Medicine, APA.

WARD, SANDRA JUNE, physicist, researcher, educator; b. Tadley, Hampshire, Eng., Apr. 3, 1962; d. John Leslie and Sheila Rosina (Fowles) W. BS in Physics, Royal Holloway Coll./U. London, 1983; PhD, U. London, 1986. Postdoctoral rsch. assoc., dept. physics York U., Toronto, 1986-88, U. Tenn., Knoxville, 1988-91; asst. prof. dept. physics U. North Tex., Denton, 1991-97, assoc. prof., 1997—. Contbr. articles to profl. jours. Recipient Valerie Myserscough prize U.London, 1984, 85; grantee NSF, 1992-95, U. North Tex., 1991—. Mem. Am. Phys. Soc., Inst. of Physics (assoc.), Royal Inst. of Gt. Britain, Sigma Xi. Christian. Achievements include research on the physics of electronic and atomic collisions.

WARD, SARAH M. lawyer; b. Elizabeth, N.J., 1957; AB, Princeton U., 1981; JD, Fordham U., 1986. Bar: N.Y. 1987. Ptnr. Skadden, Arps, Slate, Meagher & Flom, N.Y.C. Office: Skadden Arps Slate Meagher & Flom 4 Times Sq Fl 24 New York NY 10036-6595

WARD, SELA, actress; b. Meridian, Miss. d. Granberry Holland and Annie Kate Ward. BA, U. Ala. Appearances include: (TV series) Emerald Point, N.A.S., 1983-84, Sisters, 1991— (Emmy award for Lead Actress in Drama Series 1994), Once and Again, 1999-2002 (winner lead actress in a drama series, Emmy award 2000, winner lead actress in a drama series, Golden Globe award 2001), The Rescuers: Two Women, 1997, (TV movies) Rainbow Drive, 1990, Double Jeopardy, 1993, Almost Golden: The Jessica Savitch Story, 1995 (winner lead actress in drama movie Cableace award 1996), (films) Rustler's Rhapsody, 1985, Nothing in Common, 1986, Hello Again, 1987, The Fugitive, 1993, My Fellow Americans, 1996, The Reef, 1997, 54, 1998, Rescuers: Stories of Courage, Two Women, 1997, 54, 1998, Havana Nights, 2003; lead actress (TV series) Once and Again, 1999-00; prodr. (Lifetime cable network) documentary Changing Face of Beauty, 2000, Lifetime "Intimate Portrait", 2001. Office: 289 S Robertson Blvd Ste 469 Beverly Hills CA 90211-2834

WARD-BROWN, DENISE, sculptor, educator; BFA cum laude, Temple U., 1975; MFA summa cum laude, Howard U., 1984. Assoc. prof. U. Washington, St. Louis. One-woman shows Cinque Gallery, N.Y.C., 1984, Washington Project for the Arts, Washington, 1984, Bozeman, Mont., 1986, O St. Gallery, Washington, 1989, Montgomery Coll., Tacoma Park, Md., 1989, Fitzpatrick Gallery, Washington, 1989, U. Md., Princess Anne, Md., 1991, Pierce-Arrow Gallery, St. Louis, 1993, St. Louis Art Mus., 1995, Margaret Harwell Art Mus., Poplar Bluff, Mo., 1998; group exhbns. include Corcoran Mus. Art, Washington, 1987, George Washington U., 1987, U. Richmond, Va., 1987, Shippee Gallery, N.y.C., 1987, Strathmore Arts Ctr., Rockville, md., 1988, Rockville Arts Ctr., 1989, Notre Dame Coll., Balt., 1989, No. Va. C.C., Arlington, 1989, The Kunstrum, Washington, 1990, Montgomery Coll., Tacoma Park, Md., 1990, Smithsonian-Anacostia Mus., Washington, 1990, Art St. Louis, 1992, Lindenwood Coll., St. Louis, 1993, Murray State U. Eagle Gallery, 1993, Portfolio Gallery, St. Louis, 1994, U. Wis., Eau Claire, 1994, U. Md., College Park, 1994, St. Louis Design Ctr., 1996, Gene Pool & Assocs., N.Y.C., 1996, Smithsonian Instn., 1996, numerous others. Study grantee Penland (N.C.) Sch. Crafts, 1973, Haystack Mt. Sch. Crafts, Deer Isle, Maine, 1973, 74, Howard U./Ford Found., 1982, 83, Vt. Studio Sch., Johnson, 1986, Geog. Devel. grantee Washington D.C. Commn. on the Arts and Humanities, 1984, 85; Individual Artist grantee Washington D.C. Commn. on the Arts and Humanities, 1986, 87, 89, 91, Mbari, Ritual and Rememory, Regiona Artists' Projects grantee, 1994; Fulbright scholar African Rsch. Program, Ghana, others. Office: Dept Sculpture Sch Art Washington U Camp Box 1031 1 Brookings Dr Saint Louis MO 63130-4862 Fax: 314-935-8412. E-mail: ddwardbr@art.wustl.edu.

WARDELL, LINDY CONSTANCE, nonprofit organization administrator; b. Potsdam, N.Y., Apr. 28, 1928; d. Stewart A. and Mabel A. Henderson; m. David F. Constance, Sept. 6, 1947 (dec. Apr. 1984); children: John, Kathryn, Marie, Thomas, Richard; m. Frank M. Wardell, 1989. Student, Powellson Jr. Coll., Syracuse, N.Y., 1946-47, Ctrl. City Bus. Inst., Syracuse, 1946-47. Lic. realtor. V.p. Bicentennial Bus Co., Phila., 1974-77; assoc. cons. Constance & Wallace, Phila., 1976-84; v.p. Trade Devel. Corp., Phila., 1977-84; realtor assoc. Louis Gaev Realtors, Haverford, Pa., 1985-87; pres., chmn. bd. dirs. Darby (Pa.) Cmty. Forum, 1997—; pres., chmn. bd. Darby Borough Hist. Soc., Darby, 1998—. Chmn. Friends of Darby Meth. Meeting Cemetery, 1996—; mem. adv. bd. Delaware County Daily Times, Primos, Pa., 1998-99; bd. dirs. Darby Cmty. Project, 1991—. Author: Images of America, 2003; contbr. articles to newspapers. Pres., Coun. Rep. Women, Newtown Square, Pa., 1977-85; trustee Phila. Fairmount Pk. Hist. Sites com., 2002— Recipient Outstanding Individual Achievement award Delaware County Heritage Commn., 1999; Golden Rule Found. grantee, 1997. Mem Darby Hist. Soc. (founding mem. 1998), Delaware County Hist. Soc. (Coun. of Pres., Lee C. Brown award 2003). Republican. Avocations: genealogical research, arts and crafts, historical research. Home: 16 Winthrop Rd Darby PA 19023-1116

WARDLAW, KIM A.M. federal judge; b. San Francisco, July 2, 1954; m. William M. Wardlaw Sr., Sept. 8, 1984. Student, Santa Clara U., 1972—73, Foothill C.C., Los Altos Hills, Calif., 1973—74; AB in Comm. summa cum laude, UCLA, 1976, JD with honors, 1979. Bar: Calif., U.S. Dist. Ct. (ctrl. dist.) Calif. 1979, U.S. Dist. Ct. (so. dist.) Calif. 1982, U.S. Dist. Ct. Nev. 1985, U.S. Dist. Ct. (no. dist.) Calif. 1992, U.S. Dist. Ct. Mont. 1993, U.S. Dist. Ct. Minn. 1994, U.S. Dist. Ct. (no. dist.) Ala. 1994, U.S. Dist. Ct. (so. dist.) Miss. 1995, U.S. Supreme Ct. Law clk. U.S. Dist. Ct. Ctrl. Dist. Calif., 1979—80; assoc. O'Melveny and Myers, 1980—87, ptnr., 1987—95; cir. judge U.S. Dist. Ct. Calif., LA, 1995—98, U.S. Ct. Appeals (9th cir.), 1998—. Presdl. transition team Dept. Justice, Washington, 1993; mayoral transition team City of LA, 1995—; bd. govs. UCLA Ctr. for Comm. Policy, 1994—, vice-chair, 1994—; cons. in field. Co-author: The Encyclopedia of the American Constitution, 1986; contbr. articles to profl. jours. Pres. Women Lawyers Pub. Action Grant Found., 1986—87; founding mem. LA Chamber Orch., 1992—; active Legal Def. and Edn. Fund Calif. Leadership Coun., 1993—; active Blue Ribbon of LA Music Ctr., 1993—; del. Dem. Nat. Conv., 1992. Named one of Most Prominent Bus. Attys. in LA County, LA Bus. Jour., 1995; recipient Buddy award, NOW, 1995. Mem.: NOW, ABA, Orgn. Women Execs., Assn. Bus. Trial Lawyers (gov. 1988—), LA County Bar Assn. (trustee 1993—94), Women Lawyers Assn. LA, Calif. Women Lawyers, Mex.-Am. Bar Assn. LA County, Hollywood Womens Polit. Com., Downtown Women Ptnrs., City Club Bunker Hill, Breakfast Club, Chancery Club, Phi Beta Kappa. Mailing: US Court of Appeals 9th Circuit PO Box 193939 San Francisco CA 94119-3939 Office: US Court of Appeals 9th Circuit 95 Seventh St San Francisco CA 94119*

WARDLAW, SONYA CAROL, customer service administrator, educator; b. Detroit, Mich., Aug. 7, 1958; d. Franklin Delano George and Ernestine Lee George (nee Nimmons); m. David G Wardlaw, May 5, 1998. AA, Wayne Count C.C., 1990; B in bus. adminstrn., Detroit Coll. of Bus., 1990—94; MBA, Davenport U., 1999—2000. Document control clk. Detroit Edison Co, 1978—82, meter reader, 1982—88; field collector Detroit Edison, 1990—91; circuit analyst' Detroit Edison Co, 1993—96, consistency facilitator, 1996—99, field svc. rep., 1988—99, security investigator, 1999—2001; adj. instr. Rochester Coll., Mich., 2000—; adj. instuctor Cornerstone U., Grand Rapids, 2000—; adj. instr. Baker Coll., Auburn Hills, Mich., 2001—; supr., exception billing DTE Energy, Detroit, 2001—, Multiplicity Orgn. Devel. and Tng. Cons. Inc. Facilitator DTE Energy, Detroit, 1995—; supt. New Mt. Moriah Bapt. Ch., Pontiac, Mich., 1996—2001, leader deaf team, 1999—2003, leader leadership team, 2000—02; cons. Alma Bradley & Group, Pontiac, Mich., 2002—. Mem.: Nat. Assn. of Female Entrepreneurs (assoc.). Full Gospel Bapt. Avocation: roller skating. Personal E-mail: scwardlaw@msn.com. E-mail: wardlaws@dteenergy.com.

WARDLE, VICTORIA SARAH, business analyst; b. Montreal, Canada, Nov. 9, 1972; d. John J. and Heather R. Wardle. BA in bus. adminstrn. and environ. studies, Baylor U., 1990—95. Bid and proposal analyst Azurix Corp., Houston, 1997—99; strategic bus. planning analyst Hewlett-Packard Co., Houston, 2000—. Office: Hewlett-Packard Company 20555 Sh 249 Houston TX 77070 E-mail: victoria.wardle@hp.com.

WARE, SANDRA MARIE, minister, music educator, composer; d. Frank Ware, Sr. and Mary Lillie Ware. Degree in Ministry, Loman-Hannon Coll., 1971; BS cum laude, Ala. State U., 1980, MEd, 1998. Grad. asst., tchr. music dept. piano, music appreciation, and theory Ala. State U., Mont., 1978—80; music, choral tchr. St. Jude Cath. H.S., Mont., 1979—84; music tchr. Fews Elem. Sch., Mont., 1984—2001; pastor Varick-Star AME Zion Ch., Mont., 1996—2001; music tchr. E. D. Nixon Elem. Sch., Mont., 2001—. Composer: (songs) I'll Do My Best on the Stanford Achievement Test, 1996 (Recognition of Outstanding Music award, 1996), (various motivational songs and raps) Stanford Achievement Test, various inspirational gospel selections. Mem. Mt. Zion AME Zion Ch., Mont. Recipient Cert. of Appreciation award, Fed. Prison Camp, Maxwell AFB, 1975. Master: Montgomery Edn. Assn.; mem.: NEA, Ala. Edn. Assn., Delta Omicron Music Frat. Women (assoc.; dir. musical 1977—78). African Methodist Episcopal Zion. Avocations: singing, piano, typing, choral directing, hair braiding.

WARFEL, JILL KRISTIN, political organization worker; b. Cleve., Sept. 7, 1974; d. John Eric and Delynn Ann Warfel. BA in Politics & Govt., BA in Women's Studies, Ohio Wesleyan U., 1997. Acctg. assoc. Dem. Senatorial Campaign Com., Washington, 1997—99; exec. asst. to chief of staff Com. on Edn. & the Workforce, U.S. Ho. of Reps., 1999—2001; compliance officer Bob Graham for Pres. Campaign, Miami Lakes, Fla., 2003—. Vol. Robb for Senate Campaign, Alexandria, Va., 2000—00. Mem.: Delta Gamma Sorority (life). Avocations: reading, travel. Office: Bob Graham for Pres Campaign 6843 Main St Suite 300 Hialeah FL 33014 Home: 15721 Sonoma Dr Apt 306 Fort Myers FL 33908-7328

WARFEL, SUSAN LEIGH, editor; b. L.A., Aug. 5, 1959; Ba in Journalism, Sociology, U. So. Calif., L.A., 1981. Bus. reporter L.A. Herald Examiner, 1981-83, Investor's Bus. Daily, L.A., 1983-88, sr. editor, 1988-96, mng. editor, 1996—. Office: Investor's Bus Daily 12655 Beatrice St Los Angeles CA 90066-7303

WARG, PAULINE, artist, educator; b. Detroit, Mich., Oct. 15, 1951; d. Clifford Rudolf and Marguerite Evelyn (Kaiser) W.; m. Gary Dean Snider, Apr. 14, 1990. Student, Bowling Green State U., 1969-72, diploma, 1972-75; BA summa cum laude, U. So. Maine, 1999. Cert. Spl. Needs Vocat. Instr. Maine. Owner, pres. Warg Designs Inc., Scarborough, Maine, 1975—; instr. The Jewelry Inst., Providence, R.I., 1983-87; resident instr. Lexington Arts & Crafts Ctr., Lexington, Mass., 1987; asst. mgr. cons. J.S. Ritter Jewelers Tool & Supply Co., Portland, Maine, 1991-92; instr. Maine Coll. of Art, Portland, 1992—; owner, dir. metalsmithing program Future Builders, Inc., Scarborough, Maine, 1992-2001. Lectr. Paul Revere House Mus., Boston, 1981, juror League of N.H. Craftsmen, Concord, N.H., 1985-87, stds. com. juror League of N.H. Craftsman, Concord, 1985-87, exhbn. juror Boston Mus. Sch., Boston, 1992. Contbr. articles to profl. jours. Founding mem. Portsmouth Artisans, Portsmouth, N.H., 1975-77, founding owners, treas. Sail Loft Cmty. Arts Program, Portsmouth, 1977-79. Recipient Svc. award, Maine Coll. Art, Portland, 1997, 10 Yr. Svc. award, 2001. Mem. Soc. Am. Silversmiths (artisan mem. 1992—), Maine Crafts Assn., League of NH Craftsmen (state juried artisan). Democratic. Avocations: bicycling, canoeing, photography, gardening, travel. Office: Warg Designs Inc Pine Point Business Park 15 Holly St Ste 210 Scarborough ME 04074-8867 Office Phone: 207-727-3224. E-mail: warginc@sacoriver.net.

WARGO, ANDREA ANN, retired public health official, commissioned officer; b. Pottsville, Pa., Dec. 27, 1941; d. John Andrew and Anna Mary (Blischok) W.; m. Roger Fredrick Sies, Mar. 31, 1981. BS in Biology, Chestnut Hill Coll., 1972; PhD in Biology, Georgetown U., 1978. Educator, adminstr. Cath. Archdiocese Phila., 1961-74; tchg. asst. Georgetown U., Washington, 1974-78, postdoctoral fellow, 1978-80; acting br. chief FDA, Silver Spring, Md., 1980-86, acting chief gen. hosp. and personal use devices, 1986-88; assoc. adminstr. Agy. for Toxic Substances and Disease Registry, Washington, 1988-2001; ret., 2001. Mem. Surgeon Gen.'s Policy Adv. Coun., 1996-2001. Contbr. articles to sci. publs. Grantee NSF, 1972, 73, Kidney Found., 19790-80. Mem. Assn. Women in Sci. (treas. Washington-Balt. chpt. 1979-80), Commd. Officers Assn., Georgetown U. Alumni Assn., Toastmistress Club (pres. Bethesda chpt. 1978-79), Pub. Health Svc. (scientist profl. adv. com., exec. sec. 1984-86, vice chmn. 1986-87), Sigma Xi. Avocations: languages, computers, financial planning, handwriting analysis. Home: 17604 N Stone Haven Dr Surprise AZ 85374

WARICHA, JOAN, publishing executive; BA, Boston U., 1967; MBA, Columbia U., 1980. V.p., editor-in-chief, assoc. pub. Scholastic, Inc., 1968-83; pres. Parachute Press, 1983-96; chmn., CEO Parachute Properties, 1996—; pres. Parachute Pub., 1996—, Parachute Entertainment, 1996—, Parachute Consumer Products, 1996—. Office: Parachute Properties 156 5th Ave New York NY 10010-7002 Office Phone: 212-691-1421. E-mail: jwaricha@parachuteproperties.com.

WARING, MARY LOUISE, retired social worker; b. Pitts., Feb. 15, 1928; d. Harold R. and Edith (McCallum) W. AB, Duke U., 1949; MSS, Smith Coll., 1951; PhD, Brandeis U., 1974. Lic. clin. social worker, Tenn. Sr. supervising social worker Judge Baker Guidance Ctr., Boston, 1955-65; dir. social svc. Cambridge (Mass.) Mental Health Ctr., 1965-70; assoc. prof. Sch. Social Work Fla. State U., Tallahassee, 1974-77; prof. Grad. Sch. Social Svc. Fordham U., N.Y.C., 1977-82; cons. Dept. Human Svc., N.J., 1983-84; cons., sr. staff mem. Family Counseling Svc. Bergen County, Hackensack, N.J., 1984-86; dir. Step One Employee Assistance Program Fortwood Ctr., Inc., Chattanooga, 1986-96; part-time psychotherapist Greenleaf Svcs., Chattanooga, 1996, pvt. practice, 1997-98; ret., 1999. Mem. ethics com. Chattanooga Rehab. Hosp., 1995. Contbr. articles to profl. jours. Mem. Citizen Amb. Program Human Resource Mgmt. Delegation to Russia, 1993; active Nat. Trust for Hist. Preservation, Hunter Mus. Am. Art, Chattanooga Symphony and Opera Assn., Friends of Hamilton County Bicentennial Libr. Recipient Career Tchr. award Nat. Inst. Alchohol and Alchohol Abuse, 1972-74; traineeship NIMH, 1949-51. Mem. NASW (charter), Acad. Cert. Social Workers, Nat. Mus. Women in Arts (charter), Smithsonian Assocs., Cmty. Svcs. Club Greater Chattanooga (pres. 1995, 96, v.p. 1994, 97, membership chair 1998—).

WARNATH, MAXINE AMMER, organizational psychologist, mediator; b. N.Y.C., Dec. 3, 1928; d. Philip and Jeanette Ammer; m. Charles Frederick Warnath, Aug. 20, 1952; children: Stephen Charles, Cindy Ruth. BA, Bklyn. Coll., 1949; MA, Columbia U., 1951, EdD, 1982. Lic. psychologist Oreg. Various profl. positions Hunter Coll., U. Minn., U. Nebr., U. Oreg., 1951-62; asst. prof. psychology Oreg. Coll. Edn., Monmouth, 1962-77; assoc. prof. psychology, chmn. dept. psychology & spl. edn. Western Oreg. U., Monmouth, 1978-83, prof., 1983-96, prof. emeritus, 1996—. Dir. organizational psychology program, 1983—96; pres. Profl. Perspective Internat., Salem, Oreg., 1987—; cons., dir. Orgn. R&D, Salem, Oreg., 1983—87; seminar leader Endeavors for Excellence program. Author: (novels) Power Dynamism, 1987. Mem.: APA (com. pre-coll. psychology 1970—74), Western Psychol. Assn., Oreg. Psychol. Assn. (pres. 1980—81, pres.-elect 1979—80, legis. liaison 1977—78), Oreg. Acad. Sci., N.Y. Acad. Scis., Am. Psychol. Soc. Office: Profl Perspectives Internat PO Box 2265 Salem OR 97308-2265 Office Phone: 503-371-6451. E-mail: warnatm@wou.edu.

WARNECKE, ROSE MARY, music educator; b. Tiffin, Ohio, May 2, 1956; d. George Clarence and Loretta Rose Kuzma; m. David Joseph Warnecke, July 17, 1982; children: Meghan Rose, Jessica Anne. BS magna cum laude, Findlay Coll., 1978; MEd, Wright State U., 1999. Cert. music tchr. K-12 Ohio. Instrumental dir. Delphos (Ohio) St. John's Schs., 1978—87; tchr. Jennings Local Sch. Dist., Ft. Jennings, Ohio, 1993—. Mem. Ft. Jennings Pep Band, 1993—; dir. Putnam County Elem. Youth Choir, Ohio, 1995, Ohio, 2003. Coach S.A.Y. Putnam County, Ft. Jennings, 1995—98; mem. St. John's Folk Group St. John's Cath. Ch., Delphos, 1985—90, Ft. Jennings, 1990—94. Recipient Golden Apple Achiever award, Ashland, Inc., 1998. Mem.: Music Educators Nat. Conf., Ohio Music Educators Assn., Ft. Jennings Fdn. Assn. (bldg. rep. 1995—98). Home: PO Box 33 90 Charles St Fort Jennings OH 45844 Office: Jennings Local Sch Dist PO Box 98 Fort Jennings OH 45844 Office Phone: 419-286-2238.

WARNER, EMILY HANRAHAN HOWELL, retired pilot, writer; b. Oct. 30, 1939; m. Julius "Jay" Warner. BA in English, Souther U., Baton Rouge, La. Kindergarten and elem. sch. tchr.; flight instr. Clinton Aviation Co., 1961—67, rose to positions of chief pilot and flight sch. mgr., 1967—73; pilot Frontier Airlines, 1973—86, Continental Airlines, 1986—88, United Parcel Svc., 1988—90; aviation safety inspector FAA, 1990—2002, aircrew program mgr., 1992—2002. Bd. dirs. Internat. Air Mus., Dayton, Ohio. Author: (children's books) Lily of Watts- A Birthday Discovery, 1969, Lily Takes A Giant Step, (biography) Weaving the Winds, 2003. Co-founder Northeast Women's Ctr., Denver; active with Congress of Racial Equality, ACLU, NAACP. Named to Colo. Aviation Hall Fame, 1983, Nat. Women's Hall Fame, Seneca Falls, NY, 2001; recipient Amelia Earheart award as the Outstanding Woman in US Aviation, 1973. Mem.: Colo. Aviation Hist. Soc., Internat. Soc. Women Airline Pilots (founder), Ninety-Nines: Internat. Orgn. Women Pilots. Achievements include uniform installed in Smithsonian Inst. Air and Space Mus., 1976; first woman hired as pilot by major US airline, 1973.*

WARNER, JEAN LOLLICH, poet; b. Clinton, Iowa, June 22, 1916; d. Jens George Christenson and Dibga (Allen) L.; m. Charles Howard Warner, Mar. 26, 1959 (dec.); stepchildren: Judith, Leonard. BA in Elem. Edn., Cornell Coll., Mt. Vernon, Iowa, 1938; MA in Early Childhood Edn., Columbia U., 1945. Tchr. grades 4-6 Mt. Vernon Pub. Sch., 1938-39; tchr. kindergarten-1st grade Lyons Pub. Schs., Clinton, 1939-44; tchr. kindergarten Clinton Pub. Schs., 1945-59. Iowa state rep. Early Childhood Edn. Conf., Washington, 1958, Study Conf. of Childhood in Edn., St. Louis, 1959. Contbr. poetry to American Poetry Anthology, 1984, I Have Need of the Poets, 1984, Hearts on Fire, 1985, Impressions, 1986, Best New Poets of 1989, 1989, Best Poems of the 90's, 1990, Expressions, 1991 (award of merit), Awaken to a Dream, 1991, Poetic Voices of America, 1991, Windows of the World, 1991, Down Peaceful Paths, 1991, Language of the Soul, 1992, Best Poems of 1995, 1995 (Editor's Choice award); contbr. poetry to mags. Sponsor Foster Parents Plan, Warwick, R.I., 1986-92, Children Internat., 1987-92. Summer sch. scholar Rockefeller Found., Duke U., Durham, N.C., 1955. Mem. AAUW (charter), NEA (life), PEO (internat. chpt. sisterhood), Internat. Soc. Poets, Delta Kappa Gamma (charter). Presbyterian. Avocations: reading, china painting, playing organ, knitting, travel. Home: Sarah Harding Retirement Home 308 S Bluff Blvd Room 502 Clinton IA 52732

WARNER, JO F. mathematics educator; b. Kansas City, Kans., Nov. 22, 1949; d. William Halpin and Anna Lorene Fitzsimmons; m. Allen Robert Warner, July 22, 1978; children: Robin William, Gilbert Nathaniel, Lee Alexander. BS, Ea. Mich. U., 1971, MA, 1990; EdD, Grambling State U., 2001. Math. tchr. Ann Arbor (Mich.) Pub. Schs., 1983-86; vis. lectr. math. Washtenaw C.C., Ann Arbor, 1987—; instr. tchr., placement specialist Ea. Mich. U., Ypsilanti, 1989—. Author: Math Concepts for Algebra Prep, 1998, 3d edit., 2000; newsletter editor Mich. Devel. Edn. Cons. Mem.: AAUW, Mich. Devel. Edn. Consortium (pres.), Math. Assn. Am., Nat. Assn. for Devel. Edn. (chmn. rsch. com). Avocations: reading, walking, cross country skiing. Office: Ea Mich Univ 515 Pray-Harrold Ypsilanti MI 48197

WARNER, JUDITH (ANNE) HUSS, elementary school educator; b. Plainfield, N.J., June 15, 1936; d. Charles and Martha McMullen (Miller) Huss; m. Howard R. Warner, June 14, 1958; children: Barbara, Robert. BS in Elem. Edn., Russell Sage Coll., 1959. Elem. tchr. Pitts. Bd. Edn., 1959-60; home tchr. Napa (Calif.) Sch. Bd., 1974-77; substitute tchr. Allegheny Intermediate Unit, Pitts., 1977—94. Leader Girl Scouts U.S.A., Pitts., 1966-70; vol. Children's Hosp., Pitts., 1967-74, Jefferson Hosp., Pitts., 1977-88; pres., trustee Whitehall Libr., Pitts., 1984-92; pres., bd. dirs. Friends of Whitehall Libr., Pitts., 1969-94. Mem. AAUW, DAR. Republican. Methodist. Avocations: sailing, skiing, swimming, hiking, travel. Home: 4985 Wheaton Dr Pittsburgh PA 15236-2064

WARNER, NEARI FRANCOIS, university president; b. New Orleans, July 20, 1945; d. Cornelius and Enell (Brimmer) Francois; m. Jimmie Duel Warner Sr., June 6, 1970 (div. Sept. 1983); 1 child, Jimmie Duel Jr. BS, Grambling (La.) State U., 1967; MA, Atlanta U., 1968; PhD, La. State U., 1992. Dir. Upward Bound So. U., New Orleans, 1976-89, dean jr. divsn., 1989-94; asst. v.p. acad. affairs Grambling State U., 1994-96, v.p. student affairs, 1996-97, v.p. devel., 1997-99, acting v.p. acad. affairs, 1999, provost, v.p. acad. affairs, 1999—. Sec. Conf. La. Colls./Univs., 1999—; mem. State Funding Task Force, State of La., 1998-99; bd. dirs. La. Endowment for Humanities, 1998—; pres. La. Assn. Student Asst. Program, 1986-88. Preface writer: Interdisciplinary Approach, 1998. Mem. adv. bd. Pupil Progression Commn., New Orleans, 1989-93; mem. task force Gov.'s Tech. Prep., Baton Rouge, 1991-93, Mayor's Task Force for Edn., New Orleans, 1992, Monroe (La.) City Sch., 1995. Named Role model YWCA, New Orleans, 1992, Disting. Alumnae Nat. Assn. Equal Opportunity, Washington, 1996. Mem. AAUW, NAACP, The Links, Inc. (treas. 1999—, Unsung Hero 1993), Alpha Kappa Alpha, Kappa Delta Pi, Pi Gamma Mu Democrat. Baptist. Avocations: reading, bowling. Home: PO Box 989 Grambling LA 71245-0989 Office: Grambling State U PO Box 1170 Grambling LA 71245-1170 E-mail: nfwarner@martin.gram.edu.

WARNER, ROBERTA ARLENE, retired accountant, financial services executive; b. Binghamton, N.Y., Dec. 31, 1938; d. Murrilan Earl and Ethel Margaret (Bell) W. BA, SUNY, Binghamton, 1960; MBA, Ind. U., 1962, MHA with highest distinction, 1973. CPA, N.Y.; lic. nursing home adminstr., N.Y. Sr. acct. Arthur Young & Co., CPAs, Buffalo, 1962-66; acctg. supr. Children's Hosp., Buffalo, 1966-68; controller King Manor Nursing Homes-Ave. Bldg. Corp., Buffalo, 1968-71; asst. dir. health fin. Hosp. Assn. N.Y. State, Albany, 1973-80, dir. health fin., 1980-93, Healthcare Assn. N.Y. State, Albany, 1994-97, dir. data analysis and standards, 1997-98; pres. Roberta A. Warner Co., 1999—2003, ret. Author articles in field. Trustee Ednl. Found. of Am. Women's Soc. CPAs, Am. Soc. Women Accts., 1985-87. Fellow Healthcare Fin. Mgmt. Assn.; mem. Am. Inst. CPA's, Am. Acctg. Assn., Am. Soc. Women Accts. (pres. Buffalo chpt. 1967-68), Am. Women's Soc. CPAs, N.Y. State Soc. CPA's, Ind. U. Alumni Assn. (life), SUNY Binghamton Alumni Assn. (life), Grange. Methodist. Home: 569 NY Rte 79 Windsor NY 13865-2714

WARNER, RUTH E. art educator; b. Chgo., Apr. 7, 1920; d. John Dexter Mitchell and Nadyne Helen McClure; m. Brent Flenniker, June 3, 1944 (div. 1955); m. French Harman, Oct. 30, 1956 (div. 1968); m. Robert Lee Warner, Nov. 8, 1969. Student, Amarillo Jr. Coll., Tex. Women's editor and prodr. TV KGNC-TV, Amarillo, 1952—69; instr. art San Diego C.C., 1980—.

WARNER, SUSAN, federal agency administrator; b. Rochester, N.Y., July 20, 1956; d. Harold J. and Jeannette (Nichols) Warner; divorced; children: Jennifer Lynn, Kathryn Alice. BA, Miami U., Oxford, Ohio, 1978; postgrad., Xavier U. Loan specialist HUD, Columbus, Ohio, 1978-79, Cin., 1979-83; fin. planner IDS Fin. Services, Inc., Cin., 1983-86, Manufacturer's Hanover Mortgage Corp., 1986, Shawmut Mortgage Corp., 1986-87, U.S. Dept. HUD, St. Louis, 1987—. Housing cons., Cin., 1985—. Author: Community Land Coop. Residents' Handbook, 1986. Adv. Cin. Tech. Coll., 1984—; mem. fin. com. Community Land Coop., Cin., 1985—; exhibits chair Conf. Cin. Women, 1985, corp. patrons chair, 1986, conf. coordinator, 1987—; vol. Am. Cancer soc., 1981-84, March of Dimes, 1996-2003; leader Girl Scouts. Recipient Mercury awards IDS, Cin., 1984, award for superior performance U.S. Inspector Gen. HUD, 1990, Profl. Team 2003 Excellence in Govt. award The Greater St. Louis Fed. Exec. Bd., 2003. Republican. Roman Catholic. Avocations: reading, costume designing, making teddy bears, softball, theater. Home: 771 Seven Hills Ln Saint Charles MO 63304-1436 Office: US Dept HUD 1222 Spruce St Saint Louis MO 63103-2818

WARNKE, AMY NICHOLLE, state legislator; BA, U. N.D. Rep. Dist. 42 N.D. Ho. of Reps., mem. appropriations com., com. on corrections, chmn. budget sect. on human svcs. Devel. dir. N.D. Cmty. Found.; bd. dirs. Protection and Advocacy Project. Mem.: Kappa Alpha Theta (pres., adv. bd. chmn.). Home: PO Box 12982 Grand Forks ND 58208

WARPINSKI, TERRI L. academic administrator, artist; b. Green Bay, Wis., June 2, 1955; d. Robert J. and Lucille J. (Kehoe) W.; m. Garry B. Fritz, 2001. BA, U. Wis., 1979; MA, U. Iowa, 1982, MFA, 1983. Vis. instr. Sch. Art, U. Fla., Gainesville, 1983-84; prof. dept. arts U. Oreg., Eugene, 1984—, dir. Malheur Photography Workshop, 1984—, assoc. dean Sch. Architecture and Allied Arts, 1997—2004, vice provost for acad. affairs, 2003—. Mem. vis. faculty Arrowmont Sch. Arts and Crafts, Gatlinburg, Tenn., 1990-2000. Pub. art commns., Port of Portland, Oreg. State U., Ctrl. Oreg. C.C., Knight Sch. of Law, U. Oreg. Artist residence Ucross Found., Wyo., 2000; Fulbright fellow rsch. Arava Inst. Environ. Studies, Israel, 2000, 01; Rsch. grantee Ctr. for the Study of Women in Soc., 1996. Mem. Internat. Coun. Fine Arts Deans, Coll. Art Assn., Soc. Photographic Edn. (regional dir. 1987-92, nat. bd. dirs. 2001—, chair nat. bd. 2003—). Office: U Oreg Acad Affairs 206 Johnson Hall Eugene OR 97403 Fax: 541-346-2023. E-mail: tlw@uoregon.edu.

WARREN, ALICE LOUISE, artist; b. Springfield, Mass., May 7, 1927; d. Roland D. and Ella May (McGrath) Eaton Von Der Luncken; m. John Homer Warren, June 5, 1948 (dec. Jan. 1988); children: John David (dec.), Daniel Wayne. Student, N.Y. Sch. Writing, 1952-55, Mansion House Art Sch., 1969, 70, 71; grad., Nat. Landscape Inst., 1960, Famous Writers Sch., 1965; Cert., United UMA Sch., 1967. Home nursing cert.; cert. home health aide paramedical. Nurses aide ARC, Springfield, 1942-45; vol. nurses aid, 1942-44; [illegible] West Springfield, Mass., 1945-46; freelance columnist New England Homestead, Springfield, 1960-63, freelance columnist, editor Garden Page Woman's Circle, Horticulture mags. Author, photographer: (booklet) Evergreen Shrubs, 1964. solo art exhbns. Mercy Hosp., Arts Unltd. Gallery, 1997, Bay State Med., Spring field, Mass., 1999; featured artist Barnes and Noble Bookstore, Oct. 1999, Westfield Antheneum, 2000; on-line exhbns. MindsIsland.com, 2002, ArtRepsart.com, 2002--, Art-Exchange.com, 2003--. Recipient Bill Curtin award for watercolor, 1983. Mem. Amherst Writers & Artists Inst., Springfield Art League, Scriptures Writers, Mass. Writers Guild (treas. 1963), Tobacco Valley Artists Assn. Avocations: painting, travel, photography, reading.

WARREN, BARBARA DENISE, special education educator; d. Willie D. and Earnestine Loretta Davis; m. Charles Eric Warren, Sept. 7, 1976; children: Tasha Shalace, TuJuana, Charles Jr. Cert. in practical nursing, Albany Vocat. Tech. Sch., 1983; BS, Albany State U., 1998; MEd, Clark-Atlanta U., 2002, EdS, 2003. LPN, Ga. Para profl. Dougherty County Sch., Albany, Ga., 1992—97; tchr. Dekalb County Sch., Atlanta, 1997—. Mentor tchr. Dekalb County Schs., Atlanta, 2000. Mem.: Coun. Exceptional Children, Ga. Assn. Educators (bldg. rep. 2000—). Avocations: reading, gardening, music, cooking. Home: 345 Lori Ln Riverdale GA 30296 Office: Paul D West Mid Sch 2376 Headland Dr East Point GA 30344

WARREN, DIANE, song writer; Owner Real Songs, L.A. Author over 75 top ten pop songs including How Do I Live, I Don't Want to Miss a Thing, If You Asked Me To, Don't Turn Around, Set The Night To Music, I'll Still Love You More, Because You Loved Me, Rhythm of the Night, many others. Office: Realsongs 6363 W Sunset Blvd Fl 8 Hollywood CA 90028-7330

WARREN, ELIZABETH, law educator; BS, U. Houston, 1970; JD, Rutgers U., 1976. Robert Braucher vis. prof. law Harvard U., Cambridge, Mass., 1992-93, Leo Gottlieb prof. law, 1995—. Mem. Nat. Bankruptcy Rev. Commn. Contbr. articles to profl. jours. Named one of 50 Top Women Lawyers Nat. Law Jour., 1998. Mem. Am. Law Inst. (v.p.). Office: Harvard U Law Sch Hauser 200 Cambridge MA 02138

WARREN, ELIZABETH CURRAN, retired political science educator; b. St. Louis, Mo., Aug. 23, 1927; d. Maurice Donovan and Florence Schulte Curran; m. Geoffrey Spencer Warren, June 26, 1949; children: Kathryn Lloyd, Patricia, Michele, Deborah Perry. BA, Bryn Mawr Coll., 1949; MA, U. Kans., 1965; PhD, U. Nebr., 1970. Adj. prof. polit. sci. Loyola U. Chgo., 1977—80, asst. prof. polit. sci., 1980—87, ret., 1987. Cons. Dept. Housing, City of Chgo., 1981; cons. on subsidized housing City of Crystal Lake, Ill., 1982. Author: Legacy of Judicial Policy-Making, 1988, God, Caesar and the Freedom of Religion, 2003; co-author: Impact of Subsidized Housing on Property Values, 1983. Village pres. Village of Glencoe, Ill., 1985—93, trustee, 1974—83; organizer, sec.-treas. Sr. Housing Aid, Glencoe, 1982—2001; mem. Glencoe Garden Club, 1989—, pres., 1997—99. Mem.: Skokie Country Club. Avocations: gardening, skiing, music, swimming, writing. Home: 900 Valley Rd Glencoe IL 60022

WARREN, JANE, state representative; b. Torrington, N.Y., Sept. 8, 1950; children: Jeremy, Justin. BA, U. Wyo., 1974, MA, 1980, PhD, 1876. Supr. Youth Crisis Ctr., 1984; dir., therapist, mediator Cmty. Health Ctr., 1984—; child family therapist, 1985—90; adj. prof. U. Wyo., 2000—; state rep. dist. 13 Wyo. Ho. of Reps., Cheyenne, 2000—, mem. labor, health and social svcs., and mgmt. audit coms. Creator adolescent substance abuse prevention programs; adv. com. Albany County Detention Ctr.; founder Sexual Assault/Family Violence Edn. Ctr.; chair Cmty. Svcs. Block Grant Bd., 2000—. Mem.: United Way, Rotary. Democrat. Buddhist. Office: State Capitol Cheyenne WY 82002

WARREN, KATHERINE VIRGINIA, art gallery director; b. Balt., Aug. 10, 1948; d. Joseph Melvin and Hilda Virginia (Thiele) Heim; m. David Hardy Warren; 1 child, Gabriel Kristopher Coy; 1 stepchild, Michael Jonathan Warren. BA, U. Calif., Riverside, 1976, MA, 1980. Asst. curator Calif. Mus. Photography, Riverside, 1979-80, acting dir., 1980-81, asst. dir., curator of edn., 1981-84; dir. univ. art gallery U. Calif., Riverside, 1980—. Bd. dirs. Riverside Arts Found., 1980-89, chmn. bd., 1986-88. Marius De Brabant fellow U. Calif., 1977-79. Mem. Am. Assn. Mus., Western Mus. Conf. Office: Sweeney Art Gallery U Calif Riv Side Riverside CA 92521-0001

WARREN, MAXINE WOOD, artist, art educator; b. Ponca City, Okla., Jan. 14, 1927; d. William Roy and Helen Enrica (Huffer) Wood; m. William Guy Warren, Jr., June 1, 1949; 1 child, Alison. BFA, Okla. State U., 1948, MS, 1971; student, Santa Fe Inst. Fine Arts, 1986, student, 1992. Art tchr. McKinley Elem. Sch., Ponca City, 1950, 56-60; dir.-initiator Park Bldg. Contemporary Art Gallery Conoco, Inc., Ponca City, 1962-65; art tchr. Trout Elem., Ponca City, 1967-70; chmn. art dept. Ponca City Sr. H.S., 1971-86; studio artist paintings and monotypes Riverbluff Studio, Ponca City, 1986—. Artist cons. Native Am. Found.-Chief Standing Bear, Ponca City, 1994—; mem. art faculty Arts Adventure, Ponca City, 1993, 94; bd. dirs. Okla. Visual Arts Coalition, Oklahoma City, 1992-2001, Arts Place, Ponca City, 2003; initiator artists survival kit, 1998—, Artists-in-Residence, 1976; chmn. visual arts Marland Estate Commn., Ponca City, 1976-79. Represented in permanent collections Okla. Contemporary Art Mus., Oklahoma City, 1969; Philbrook Art Mus., Tulsa (honorable mention 1948, 66, 68). Recipient 2d prize Internat. Am. Greetings, 5th prize Internat. Ford Times Mag., 1963, 2d prize Internat. Golden Press Book illustration, 1962. Mem. Individual Artists Okla., Ponca City Art Assn., Okla. Edn. Assn., Okla. Retired Educators Assn., Living Artists Soc., Nat. Mus. Women in Arts, Okla. Art Inst., Ind. Artists Okla., Tulsa Artists Coalition, Zeta Tau Alpha. Republican. Avocations: discussion group, books, dogs. Studio: 7182 River Ridge Dr Ponca City OK 74604-9103

WARREN, PAMELA ALLYSON, psychologist; d. James Herbert Trail, Jr. and Jacqueline Joann Trail; m. Bruce Eugene Warren, Jan. 9, 1982; 1 child, Rachel Marie. B.A., MA, So. Ill. U., PhD, 1991. Lic. clin. psychologist Ill., 1993. Counselor So. Ill. U., Carbondale, 1986—89, instr., 1989—91; head psychology dept. Carle Clinic Assn., Urbana, 1991—; faculty U. Ill. Med. Sch., Dept. Psychiatry, 1994—; clin. supr. Resolutions Employee Assistance Program, Champaign, 1996—2001; faculty U. Ill., Psychology Dept., 2000—. Mem. work injury network steering com. Carle Clinic Assn., Urbana, 1999—; nat. psychol. cons. Work Injury Network, 1999—; cons. Blue Cross Blue Shield Ins., Waco, Tex., 2002—, WebilityMD.com, Wayland, Md., 2001—, CompPartners, Irvine, Calif., 2003—; mem. supported employment com. Disability Mgmt. Employer Coalitions, Eugene, Oreg., 2002—; mem. complimentary and alternative medicine steering com. Carle Clinic Assn., Urbana, 2003—; faculty SmithKline-Beecham Pharms., 1993—96; psychol. cons. Ill. State Univs. Retirement Sys., Champaign, 2001—; presenter in field. Hospice vol. Meml. Hospice, Carbondale, Ill., 1984—91. Scholar, So. Ill. U., 1983—91. Fellow: Prescribing Psychologists' Register; mem.: APA, Assn. Applied Psychophysiology and Biofeedback, Assn. Behavior Analysis, Psi Chi. Achievements include development of state-of-the-art model to assess and treat psychological concerns in order to prevent psychological disability. Avocations: travel, art, reading, sports. Office: Carle Clinic Assn 602 W Univ E-6 Urbana IL 61801

WARREN, ROSANNA, poet; b. Fairfield, Conn., July 27, 1953; d. Robert Penn Warren and Eleanor Clark; m. Stephen Scully, 1981; children: Katherine, Chiara; stepson, Benjamin. BA summa cum laude, Yale U., 1976; MA, Johns Hopkins U., 1980. Pvt. art tchr., 1977-78; clerical worker St. Martin's Parish, N.Y.C., 1977-78; asst. prof. English Vanderbilt U., Nashville, 1981-82; vis. asst. prof. Boston U., 1982-88, asst. prof. English and modern fgn. langs., 1989-95, assoc. prof. English, 1995—, Emma Mactachlan Metcalf prof. Humanities, 2000—. Poetry cons., contbg. editor Partisan Rev., 1985-98; poet-in-residence Robert Frost Farm, 1990. Author: The Joey Story, 1963, Snow Day, 1981, Each Leaf Shines Separate, 1984, Stained Glass, 1993, Departure, 2003; editor, contbr.: The Art of Translation: Voices from the Field, 1989; editor: Eugenio Montale's Cuttlefish Bones, 1993, Satura, 1998; translator (with Stephen Scully) Euripides' Suppliant Women, 1995, poetry anthologies include In Time, 1995, From This Distance, 1996, Springshine, 1998; contbr. to periodicals including Agni Rev., Am. Poetry Rev., Antioch Rev., Atlantic Monthly, Chelsea, Chgo. Rev., Georgia Rev., Nation, New Republic, New Yorker, N.Y. Times, Paris Rev., Threepenny Rev., Partisan Rev., Ploughshares, Southern Rev., Washington Post. Recipient McLaughlin English prize Yale U., 1973, Charles E. Clark award Yale U., 1976, Nat. Discovery award in poetry 92nd St. YMHA-YWCA, 1980, Newton Arts Coun. award, 1983, Lavan Younger Poets prize Acad. Am. Poets, 1992, Lamont Poetry prize Acad. Am. Poets, 1993, Lila Wallace Writers' Fund award, 1994, Witter Bynner prize in poetry Acad. Arts and Letters, 1994, May Sarton award New Eng. Poetry Club, 1995, Pushcart prize, 2003; named Scholar of House Yale U., 1975-76; Yaddo fellow, 1980; Ingram Merrill grantee, 1983, 93; Guggenheim fellow, 1985-86; Am. Coun. Learned Societies grantee, 1989-90. Fellow: Am. Acad. of Arts and Sci.; mem.: PEN, ALTA, MLA, Am. Acad. Poets (chancellor 2000), Assn. Literary Scholars and Critics (v.p. 2004). Home: 28 Tappan St Roslindale MA 02131-1621 Office: Univ Professors Program Boston Univ 745 Commonwealth Ave Boston MA 02215-1401

WARREN, SUSAN HANKE MURPHY, international marketing business development executive; b. Detroit, Nov. 26, 1949; d. Homer Graf and Catherine H. (Fly) Hanke; m. William Joseph Murphy, Sept. 14, 1974 (div. 1984); m. Philip Hamilton Warren, Nov. 12, 1989; 1 child, Catherine Jane; 1 stepchild, Sarah Kate. MA in French and Spanish Langs./History, Denison U., 1971; MA in Internat. Studies, Am. U., 1979; MBA, Harvard U., 1981. Cert. tchr., Ohio. Br. chief, Africa, Office of Academic Exch. Programs, U.S. Dept. State, Washington, 1975-79; fin. and project mgr. corp. devel. Corning (N.Y.) Inc., 1981-83; mgr. strategic planning Ciba-Corning Diagnostics, Medfield, Mass., 1983-88, new venture mgr., 1988-91, dir. customer and mktg. svcs. U.S. comml. ops., 1991-93; dir. bus. planning U.S. comml. ops. Chiron Diagnostics, Emeryville, Calif., 1993-95, dir. worldwide mktg., immunoassays, 1995-98; dir. disease focus mktg. Bayer Diagnostics, Tarrytown, N.Y., 1999-2000; v.p. mktg. and sales Mosaic Technologies, Waltham, Mass., 2000-01; v.p. mktg. Parexel, Inc., 2001—. Alumni advisor Harvard Bus. Sch., Cambridge, Mass., 1995—. Editl. adv. bd.: Clinical Lab Products. Trustee First Parish, Westwood, Mass., 1985-88; mem. project funding com. The Junior League, Washington, Elmira, N.Y., Boston, 1972-85; mem. sch. site coun. Meml. Sch., Medfield, 1998-99. Recipient The Beacon Soc. award, 1989. Mem. Biomed. Mktg. Assn., Am Assn. Clin. Chemistry, Am. Mgmt. Assn. Republican. Avocations: sailing, alpine skiing, water skiing, golf. Office: Mosaic Technologies Inc 303 Bear Hill Rd Waltham MA 02451-1016 Address: 19 Clovelly Rd Wellesley MA 02481-6135 E-mail: skh@aol.com.

WARREN-MACNAUGHT, FELICIA, music educator, musician; d. Robert Lee Warren and Gloria W. Butler; m. Kevin B. MacNaught, July 29, 1995; 1 child, John Robert MacNaught. BS in Music Edn., East Carolina U., 1984; MA in Musical Performance, U. Kent, 1996. Band dir. MacWilliams Mid. Sch., Fayetteville, NC; band dir., assoc. dir. Cape Fear High Sch.; band dir. Stedman Jr. High Sch., Dixon Jr./Sr. High Sch., Holly Ridge. 1st flutist Fayetteville Symphony Orch., 1993—2003. Recipient Band Masters award Excellence, N.C. Music Educators, 2002. Mem.: Cumberland County Band Dirs. Assn., Southeastern Dist. Bd. Dirs. Assn., N.C. Music Educators Assn. Republican. Methodist. Avocations: horseback riding, running, music. Office Phone: 910-483-8222.

WARRES, MARGIE BLACK, social work administrator, department chairman, human services manager, department chairman; b. Phila., Feb. 17, 1918; d. Harry M. and Eva (Stulbaum) Black; m. H. Leonard Warres, June 11, 1939; children: Stephen Elliot, Neil Eric. Student, Goucher Coll., 1936-38; BA magna cum laude, Bklyn. Coll., 1941; MSW, U. Pa., 1944. Cert. ACSW, LCSW. Past caseworker Pub. Welfare Office, Kent County, Del.; exec. sec. pub. welfare com. Md. Conf. Social Concern, 1947—50; exec. dir. Cen. Scholarship Bur., 1952-88. Condr. workshops for pub. sch. counselors Balt. Dept. Edn., 1967. Author: The Birth and Blossoming of a Bureau: CSB 1924-88, 1991; editor Med. Chi Alliance Md. Black Eyed Susan pub., 1996-98, co-editor, 2002-2003; contbr. articles to profl. jours. Vol. Care-Medico, Afghanistan, 1973; counc. State & Eastern regl. councilor of Southern Med. Assn. Aux.; mem. Jewish Bd. Edn., 1964—70; past bd. electors Balt. Hebrew Congregation; past mem. Parents Coun. of Balt.; asst. to pres. Eastern regl. ARZA org., 1980—85; bd. dirs. Md. Higher Edn. Loan Corp., 1986—96; past pres. Child Study Assn. of Balt. and Md., Balt. City Med. Aux., Alliance to the Med. and Chirurgical Faculty Md.; v.p. Balt. Hebrew Congregation Sisterhood, 1997—2002; spkr. Goucher Coll. scholarship luncheon, 1999; chair Uniongram Luncheon, 1998, 2002, Bernice Kramer Meml., Balt., 2002; Ea. regional chair Internat. Health Com. of AMA Aux., 1970—73, nat. chair, 1973—75; past bd. dirs. AMA Alliance; chair Ann. Interfaith Inst., 1996; Steering Com. Cir. of Giving Assoc: Jewish Cmty. Fedn., Balt., 2002—; bd. dirs. Ctl. Scholarship Bur. for Life, Med. Chi Alliance, STEP, Inc., 1991—. Recipient Harry Greenstein award, 1977; Disting. Mem. honoree Child Study's 75th Anniversary Gala, 1999. Mem. Child Study Assn. Md. Adv. Bd. Jewish. Achievements include organizing first overseas travellers charter groups for Baltimore City and Maryland Med. Chi. orgs., 1965; Established scholarships at Goucher Coll. & Central Scholarship Bureau for special needs students, 1970. Avocations: travel, theater, art, music, writing.

WARRICK, LOLA JUNE, agent; b. San Francisco, June 19, 1923; d. Sigfrid Oscar and June Vesta (Merrifield) Bjorkqvist; m. Enos A. Warrick, June 12, 1948 (dec. June 1983); children: James Daryl, Nancy Jean, Gary Elton. AA, Merrit Bus. Sch. Supr. McClellan AFB, Sacramento; spl. svcs. U.S. Govt.; owner, mgr. Burke-Warrick Theatre, Sacramento; mgr., asst. Naify Enterprises, Sacramento; asst. mgr. Fox West Coast Theatre; booking agt. Burke-Warrick Theatres. Author: Merifield A to Z, 1995. Named Citizen of Yr., North Highlands Cmty., 1999. Mem.: DAR (regent 1998—2000, State and Nat. awards 1998—2000), North Highlands Garden Club. Avocations: genealogy, computers.*

WARRICK, RUTH, actress; b. St. Joseph, Mo., June 29, 1916; d. Frederick R. Jr. and Annie L. (Scott) W.; m. Erik Rolf (div.); m. Carl Neubert (div.); m. Robert McNamara, (div.); m. L. Jarvis Cushing Jr. (div.). Student, U. Mo.; studies with Antoinette Perry, Brock Pemberton. Cons. High Sch. Drop-out Program, U.S. Dept. Labor, 1962, Job Tng. Corps., 1964-66. Actress: (stage prodns.) Bury the Dead, 1937, Dial M for Murder, 1955, The Thorntons, 1956, Miss Lonelyhearts, 1957, Anna in The King & I, 1957-58, Single Man at a Party, 1959, Take Me Along, 1960, Who's Afraid of Virginia Woolf?, 1965, Long Day's Journey into Night, 1966, The Secret Life of Walter Mitty, 1966, Any Resemblance to Persons Living or Dead, 1971, Misalliance, 1972, Conditions of Agreement, 1972, Irene, 1973-74, Roberta, 1976, Legends, 1987 Butterflies Are Free, 1988, (broadway) Irene, 1971-72, Roberta, 1980, The King and I, 1958-59; (feature films) 34 films including The Corsican Brothers, 1941, Citizen Kane, 1941, Journey into Fear, 1942, The Iron Major, 1943, Forever and a Day, 1943, The Iron Major, 1943, Guest in the House, 1944, Mr. Winkle Goes to War, 1944, China Sky, 1945, Song of the South, 1946, Daisy Kenyon, 1947, Perilous Holiday, 1946, Let's Dance, 1950, The Great Dan Patch, 1949,, Three Husbands, 1950, Ride Beyond Vengeance, 1966, How to Steal the World, 1968, The Great Bank Robbery, 1969, (TV series) Father of the Bride, 1961-62, Peyton Place, 1964-67, As The World Turns, All My Children (2 Emmy award nominations), rec. artist Phoebe Tyler Regrets, author: (autobiography) The Confessions of Phoebe Tyler, 1980. Del. Global Forum for Human Survival, Moscow, 1990; bd. dirs. Bus. and Industry for Arts in Edn.; sponsor Learning to Read Through the Arts; co-founder Operation Bootstrap Watts, Calif., 1949-52, 64; regent of Cathedral St. John the Divine, N.Y.C. Recipient Humanitarian award Midland Empire Arthritis Found. given each year in her name, 1976, Arts in Edn. award given each year in her name, 1983, Arts in Edn. award Bus. and Industry for Arts in Edn., 1983, Medal N.Y. Arts Assn., 1996; Emmy Silver Circle, 1997; named Tchr. Cities in Schs., N.Y.C. Schs., 1976, TV-Hall of Fame, 1998. Mem. Bus. and Industry for Arts in Edn. (bd. dirs.), English-Speaking Union (bd. dirs.), Juvenille Diabetes Assn. (chair). Avocations: swimming, walking, music, metaphysics. Office: c/o Anthony & Assocs 250 W 57th St Ste 1928 New York NY 10107-0001 also: ABC Press Rels 77 W 66th St Fl 5 New York NY 10023-6201

WARRIOR, PADMASREE, communications executive; BSChemE, Indian Inst. Tech.; MSChemE, CornellU. From rschr. to sr. v.p. Motorola, Inc., Schaumburg, Ill., 1984—2003, sr. v.p., 2003—, chief tech. officer, 2003—. Gen. mgr. Thoughtbeam, Inc.; mem. coun. digital economy Tex. Gov.; mem. rev. panel Tex. Higher Edn. Bd.; dir. Ferro Corp. Recipient Women Elevating Sci. and Tech. award, Working Woman Mag., 2001. Office: Motorola Inc 1303 E Algonquin Rd Schaumburg IL 60196*

WARSHAUER, IRENE C. lawyer; b. N.Y.C., May 4, 1942; m. Alan M. Warshauer, Nov. 27, 1966; 1 child, Susan. BA with distinction, U. Mich., 1963; LLB cum laude, Columbia U., 1966. Bar: N.Y. 1966, U.S. Dist. Ct. (so. and ea. dist.) N.Y. 1969, U.S. Ct. Appeals (2d cir.) 1969, U.S. Dist. Ct. (no. dist.) N.Y. 1980, U.S. Supreme Ct. 1972. With 1st Jud. Dept., N.Y. State Mental Health Info. Svc., 1966-68; assoc. Chadbourne Parke Whiteside & Wolff, 1968-75; mem. Anderson Kill & Olick, P.C., N.Y.C., 1975-99, Fried & Epstein, N.Y.C., 2000—. Mediator U.S. Dist. Ct. (so. dist.) N.Y., N.Y. State Supreme Ct.; lectr. Columbia Law Sch., Def. Rsch. Inst., Aspen Inst. Humanistic Studies, ABA, Rocky Mountain Mineral Law Found., CPR Inst. Dispute Resolution; arbitrator NASD EEOC, NYSE, Am. Arbitration Assn. Contbr. chpts. to books, articles to profl. jours. Mem. County Dem. Com., 1968—. Named to Hon. Order Ky. Cols. Mem.: ABA, N.Y. State Bar Assn. (chmn. subcom. mentally disabled and cmty. 1978—82), Assn. Bar City N.Y. (judiciary com. 1982—84, mem. alternative dispute resolution com. 2000—). Avocations: gardening, cooking, birding, theatre. Office: Fried & Epstein 1350 Broadway New York NY 10018-7702

WARSHAW, CAROLE KLEIN, education educator, consultant; d. Irving and Frieda Patlis Klein; m. Gerald Jay Warshaw, June 9, 1956; children: Ms. Jodie Sharon Arrington, Howard Gary, Dr. Joel David. BA, Hunter Coll., N.Y.C., 1957; MS in Spl. Edn., Hofstra U., 1976; Profl. Diploma-Adminstrn., St. John's U., Queens, N.Y., 1987, EdD, 1993. Cert. elem. sch. tchr. N.Y.C. Bd. Edn., 1957, asst. prin. N.Y.C. Bd. Edn., 1989, adminstrn./supr. N.Y. State Dept. Edn., 1987, clin. edn. trainer Fla. Dept. Edn., 2000. Tchr. N.Y.C. Bd. Edn., Queens, 1957—84, tchr. trainer, 1984—89, dir. testing, 1989—90; assoc. prof., coord. master's program Lynn U., Boca Raton, Fla., 1994—. Liaison to dept. of edn. Lynn U., Boca Raton, 1995—; cons. Florence Fuller Child Devel. Ctrs., Boca Raton, 1999—, Toussaint L'Ouverture H.S., Delray Beach, Fla., 2001—; clin. supervision trainer Fla. Dept. Edn., Boca Raton, 1999—. Contbr. articles to profl. jours. V.p. Coalition of Boynton Beach (Fla.) Residents, 1992—94, Temple Beth Emeth, Bklyn., 1964—65; pres. Palm Shores Homeowners Assn., Boynton Beach, 1993—94. Impact II grantee, N.Y.C. Bd. Edn., 1981. Mem.: Coun. Adminstrs. and Suprs., Coun. for Exceptional Children, Phi Delta Kappa, Kappa Delta Pi (counselor 1997—). Independent. Hebrew. Avocations: bridge, travel, music. Office: Lynn U 3601 N Military Trl Boca Raton FL 33431 E-mail: cwarshaw@lynn.edu.

WARSHAW, ROBERTA SUE, lawyer; b. Chgo., July 10, 1934; d. Charles and Frieda (Feldman) Weiner; m. Lawrence Warshaw, July 5, 1959 (div. June 1978); children: Nan R., Adam; m. Paul A. Heise, Apr. 2, 1994. Student, U. Ill., 1952-55; BFA, U. So. Calif., 1956; JD, Northwestern U., 1980. Bar: Ill. 1980. Atty., fin. specialist Housing Svcs. Ctr., Chgo., 1980-84, Chgo. Rehab. Network, 1985-91, 92-95; dir. housing State Treas., State of Ill., Chgo., 1991; sole practitioner, 1995—. Legal worker Sch. of

Law, Northwestern U. Legal Clinic, Chgo., 1977-80; real estate developer, mgr., marketer, Chgo., 1961-77; bd. dirs. Single Room Housing Assistance Corp., Lebanon County Mediation Svcs., mediator, sec., 2001; asst. dir. Lebanon Valley Coll. Program, Hania, Crete, 1998. Co-author: (manual) The Cook County Scavenger Sale Program and The City of Chicago Reactivation Program, 1991, (booklet) Fix the Worst First, 1989; co-editor: The Caring Contract, Voices of American Leaders, 1996. Alderman 9th ward City of Evanston, Ill., 1985-93, mem. planning and devel., rules com., unified budget com., chair flood and pollution control com.; pres. Sister Cities Found.; mem. cmty. and econ. devel. policy Nat. League Cities, 1990-93; mem. Dem. Nat. Com.; bd. dirs. Dem. Ctrl. Com. Evanston, 1973—; elected committeeman Evanston Twp. Dem. Com., 1994-98, dem. committeeman Mt. Gretna Borough, 2000—; del. Dem. Nat. Conv., 1996; Dem. committeeman Mt. Gretna Borough, 2000—; vol. tax preparer; tax counseling for elderly, 2000—; bd. dirs., mediator Lebanon County Mediation Svcs., 2000—, sec., 2001-03, pres., 2003—. Mem. ABA (affordable housing com.), Ill. State Bar Assn., Chgo. Bar Assn. (real estate coms.), Decalogue Soc. Lawyers, Chgo. Coun. Lawyers (housing com.), IRS Tax Counseling for the Elderly (vol. tax preparer). Avocations: politics, travel, hiking, camping, athletic activities. Home: 104 Brown Ave PO Box 537 Mount Gretna PA 17064-0537 E-mail: femdem1@narl.com.

WARWICK, DIONNE, singer; b. East Orange, N.J., Dec. 12, 1940; m. Bill Elliott (div. 1975); children: David, Damon. Ed., Hartt Coll. Music, Hartford, Conn. As teen-ager formed Gospelaires and Drinkard Singers, then sang background for rec. studio, 1966; debut, Philharmonic Hall, N.Y. Lincoln Center, 1966; appearances include London Palladium, Olympia, Paris, Lincoln Ctr. Performing Arts, N.Y.C.; records include Don't Make Me Over, 1962, Walk On By, Do You Know The Way to San José, What The World Needs Now, Message To Michael, I'll Never Fall In Love Again, I'll Never Love This Way Again, Deja Vu, Heartbreaker, That's What Friends are For; albums include Valley of the Dolls and Others, 1968, Promises, Promises, 1975, Dionne, 1979, Then Came You, Friends, 1986, Reservations for Two, 1987, Greatest Hits, 1990, Dionne Warwick Sings Cole Porter, 1990, Hidden Gems; The Best of Dionne Warwick, Vol. 2, 1992, (with Whitney Houston) Friends Can Be Lovers, 1993, Dionne Warwick and Placido Domingo, 1994, Aquarela Do Brasil, 1994, From the Vaults, 1995, Sings the Bacharach and David Songbook, 1995, Dionne Sings Dionne, 1998, I Say a Little Prayer for You, 2000; TV appearance in Sisters in the Name of Love, HBO, 1986; screen debut Slaves, 1969, No Night, So Long, also, Hot! Live and Otherwise; co-host: TV show Solid Gold; host: TV show A Gift of Music, 1981; star: TV show Dionne Warwick Spl. Founder Dionne Warwick Scholarship Fund, 1968, charity group BRAVO (Blood Revolves Around Victorious Optimism), Warwick Found. to Help Fight AIDS; spokeswoman Am. Sudden Infant Death Syndrome; participant U.S.A for Africa; Am. Amb. of Health, 1987. Recipient Grammy awards, 1969, 70, 80; NAACP Key of Life award, 1990. Address: Arista Records Inc 6 W 57th St New York NY 10019-3901

WARWICK, MARGARET ANN, health science facility administrator, consultant; b. Camden, N.J., June 7, 1931; d. Ralph Arthur and Margaret Wilson (Dilworth) W. BS, Fairleigh Dickinson U., 1955. Staff mem., med. tech. Jefferson Med. Coll. Hosp., Phila., 1955—61; clin. chemist West Jersey Health System, Camden, NJ, 1961—68, lab. supr. Voorhees, 1968—80, mgr. clin. lab. services, 1980—85, quality assurance mgr. clin. lab svcs., 1985—96; founder, pres. Clin. Lab. Cons. Services, Inc., Cherry Hill, 1985—96; ret., 1996. Mem. faculty chemist dept. Harcum Jr. Coll., Bryn Mawr, Pa., 1958-64; ednl. coordinator West Jersey Hosp. Sch. of Med. Tech., Voorhees, 1963-81. Vice pres. Wilderness Acres Civic Assn., Cherry Hill, 1980-81; chmn. com. Respond Inc. at Asbury United Meth. Ch., Camden, 1985-94, trustee, 1984-93. Mem. Am. Assn. for Clin. Chemists (secret treas. 1966-70, chmn. elect 1971-72, chmn. 1972-73 Phila chpt.), Clin. Lab Mgmt. Assn., Am. Soc. of Clin. Pathologist, Am. Soc. for Med. Tech., N.J. Soc. for Med. Tech. (bd. dirs. 1978-79). Republican. Methodist. Avocations: golf, boating.

WASHA, KIRSTEN THOMAS, mental health services professional; b. Marshfield, Mass., July 27, 1968; d. Craig Richard and Polly Baker Washa. BS in Exercise Physiology, U. Maine, 1993; MS in Counseling Psychology, Northeastern U., 1999. Lic. mental health counselor Mass. Adminstrv. asst. Reuters Am., Inc., Boston, 1993—98; mental health counselor U. Mass., Lowell, Mass., 1998—99; case mgr. Value Options, Boston, 2000—. Intern Gasnold SA Clinic, Falmouth, Mass., 2003. Vol. The Samaritans Suicide Prevention Hotline, Boston, 1996—97. Mem.: Employee Assistance Profl. Assn. Avocations: poetry, horseback riding, music, yoga, tennis. Home: 17 Mystic Street Apt 2 Charlestown MA 02129

WASHBURN, BARBARA POLK, cartographer, researcher, explorer; b. Boston, Nov. 10, 1914; m. Bradford Washburn, Apr. 27, 1940; children: Dorothy, Edward, Elizabeth. Grad., Smith Coll., 1935; DSc (hon.), U. Alaska, 1995, Boston U., 1996, Simmons Coll., 2001. Sec. Harvard Biol. Labs., 1936-38; exec. sec. Mus. of Sci., 1939-40; remedial reading tchr. Shady Hill Sch., Cambridge, Mass.; asst. to Henry Bradford Washburn Jr. First ascent of Mt. Bertha, Alaska, 1940, Mt. Hayes, Alaska, 1941; first woman to climb Mt. McKinley, Alaska, 1947; worked with husband on numerous sci. expdns., including Mt. McKinley, the Grand Canyon, Bangkok, London, Nepal, China, Alaska, Zurich, Milan, 1945—; participated in remapping the Grand Canyon for Nat. Geographic/Mus. of Sci., 1971-76; cons. to Govt. of Alaska State Parks Recreational Area in Tokositna Valley, 1980. Editor new chart of Squam Lake, 1977, new map of Presdl. Range, Squam Lake, N.H., 1989; contbr. articles to Anchorage Daily News, 1987. Bd. dirs. Boston Children's Svc. Assn.; overseer Brigham & Women's Hosp., Boston; mem. corp. Fernald Sch., 1976; mem. Cambridge LWV, 1945-50, Mt. Auburn Hosp. Aux., Cambridge, 1945-60; pres. Women's Travel Club of Boston, 1949-51; pres. Cambridge Smith Coll. Club, 1952-54; bd. svc. league Mus. of Sci., 1959-62, sec., 1961-62; chmn. personal interview program for Smith, Alumnae Fund in Boston, 1964-65. Recipient Achievement award 100th Ann. Dinner of the Girl's Latin Sch. Alumni Assn., 1978; honored by Mus. of Sci. with plaque for yrs. of work, 1974, gold medal Royal Scottish Geog. Soc. for Outstanding Contbns. to Cartographic Rsch., 1979, Smith medal for Lifetime Exploration and Mapmaking, 1980, 1st Alexander Graham Bell award of Nat. Geog. Soc., 1980, Centennial award, 1988, award of Yukon Ter. Commr., 1997. Home: 1010 Waltham St Lexington MA 02421-8044

WASHBURN, JOAN THOMAS, business owner, art gallery director; b. N.Y.C., Dec. 26, 1929; d. Frank B. and Josephine (Hartman) Thomas; m. Alan Lindsay Washburn, Sept. 26, 1953; children: Brian, Susan. BA, Middlebury (Vt.) Coll., 1951. Asst. Kraushaar Gallery, N.Y.C., 1951-53; dir. pub. rels. Wadsworth Atheneum, Hartford, Conn., 1953-55; dir. contemporary art Graham Gallery, N.Y.C., 1955-67; asst. Cordier-Ekstrom Gallery, N.Y.C., 1967-69; dir. Am. painting dept. Sotheby Parke-Bernet, N.Y.C., 1973-75; pres., dir. Washburn Gallery, N.Y.C., 1971—. Mem. Art Dealers Assn. (bd. dirs. 1989—, v.p. 1991—). Gallery: 20 W 57th St New York NY 10019-3917 Office Phone: 212-397-6780.

WASHBURN, NAN, conductor; BM in Performance with highest honors, U. Calif., Santa Barbara, 1976; MM in Performance, New England Conservatory of Music, 1979. Mem. faculty New England Conservatory, Boston, 1979-80; artistic dir. Women's Philharmonic, San Francisco, 1980-90, assoc. condr., 1988-90; mem. faculty, condr. classical ensembles Cazadero Music & Arts Ctr., 1982-87; resident condr. Am. Jazz Theater, Oakland, Calif., 1987-97; music dir., condr. Camellia Symphony Orchestra, Sacramento, 1990-96, Orchestra Sonoma (formerly the Rohnert Park Chamber Orch.), 1995—; condr. San Francisco State U. Symphony, 1996-97, Acalenes Chamber Orch., Lafayette, Calif., 1997-98, Channel Islands Symphony Orch., Thousand Oaks, Calif., 1997—. Mem. commissioning program panel Minn. Composer's Forum, 1988, music presenter's panel Calif. Arts Coun., 1992, 93, artist fellowship panel, 1995; guest condr. Antelope Valley Symphony Orch., Lancaster, Calif., 1987, Napa Valley (Calif.) Symphony Orch., 1990, Rudolf Steiner Coll., Sacramento, 1991, Sacramento Symphony Orch., 1989, 91, Women's Philharmonia, San Francisco, Oakland, 1991, Oreg. Mozart Players, Eugene, 1993, Eugene Symphony Orch., 1993, 94, Calif. All-State Honor Orch., Santa Clara, 1994, Columbus (Ohio) Women's Symphony, 1992, 94, Cumberland Valley Chamber Players, Chambersburg, Pa., 1994, Honor Festival Orch., Sacramento, 1993, 95, Berkeley (Calif.) Symphony Orch., 1995, 96, Richmond (Va.) Symphony Orch., 1996, Colo. Symphony Orch., Denver, 1997; lectr. Internat. Congress Women in Music, Atlanta, 1986, Festival New Am. Music, Sacramento, 1987, 90, Condrs. Inst., Columbia, S.C., 1988, conf. Calif. Music Educators Assn., Santa Clara, 1994. Recipient N.Y. Women Composers award, 1992, Role Model award Girl Scouts, 1996, Indy award Sonoma County Independent, 1998, 13 ASCAP awards Am. Symphony Orch. League, 1983, 85-90, 92-97. Mem. Am. Symphony Orch. League, Assn. Calif. Symphony Orchs., Condr.'s Guild, Musicians Union Local 6 (San Francisco), Pi Kappa Lambda. Office: Channel Islands Symphony Orch PO Box 7231 Thousand Oaks CA 91359-7231

WASHBURN, PATRICIA CHEYNE, retired psychologist, environmentalist, conservationist; b. Plattsburgh, N.Y., Apr. 27, 1941; d. Gerald Kenneth and Doris Rothermel Cheyne; m. Christopher Hiram Washburn, July 24, 1965; children: Diane, James. BA Psychology, Hartwick Coll., 1963; MA Counseling Psychology, Immaculata Coll., 1991. Juvenile probation officer Oneida County, Utica, NY, 1963—64; elem. sch. tchr., 1964—86; play therapist, cons. Children Unltd., Pottstown, Pa., 1991—2001; co-founder Coventry Land Trust; planning commr. North Coventry Planning, 2001—. Mem.: Nat. Mus. Am. Indian (charter mem.), Natural Lands Trust, Phila. Zoo, Nat. Trust Historic Preservation, Nature Conservancy, Assn. for Play Therapy.

WASHBURN, SANDRA PAYNTER, art educator; b. Warrenton, N.C., Oct. 23, 1952; d. Claude Jackson and Evelyn Gupton Paynter; m. Frank Elton Washburn, Jr., May 11, 1973; 1 child, Reaves Avery 1 stepchild, Frank E. III. BFA in Art Edn., U. N.C., Greensboro, 1976. CETA art resource person Guilford County Schs., Greensboro, 1976—77; art tchr. J.F. Webb H.S., Oxford, NC, 1978—81; watermedia instr. Cultural Arts Divsn.-Pks. and Recreation, Chattanooga, 1994—97, Mountain Art Guild, Signal Mountain, Tenn., 1996—; art tchr. Brainerd Bapt. Sch., Chattanooga, 2001—03, David Brainerd Christian Sch., Chattanooga, 2002—. Panel of selection juror Assn. for Visual Artists, Chattanooga, 2000—; discussion facilitator Art in Pub. Places-Mayor's Office, Chattanooga, 2002—03. Two person exhbn., Stone, Steel and Acrylics, 2002, Surface and Substance, 2002, exhibited in group shows at Gallery 1401, Chattanooga, 2003. Vol. Hospice Chattanooga, 1995—2000; participant Art for Healing Ann. Exhbn. & Auction Meml. Hosp., Chattanooga, 2001—03; participant Cancer Awareness Through the Arts Meml. Hosp. Cancer Ctr., Chattanooga, 2002—03. Recipient Art for Healing Purchase award, Cam Busch Endowment, Chattanooga, 2001. Mem.: Nat. Mus. Women in the Arts, So. Watercolor Soc. (signature, Tenn. state rep. 1998—), Nat. Watercolor Soc. (signature), Tenn. Watercolor Soc. (signature, treas., v.p., exhbn. chair 1995—, workshop instr. 2002—03, award 2000, Mabel Larson award 2002). Independent. Avocations: painting, fitness, reading, gardening, music. Home: 77 Dogwood Ln Soddy Daisy TN 37379 Office: David Brainerd Christian Sch PO Box 21927 Chattanooga TN 37424

WASHINGTON, EARLINE, healthcare executive; b. Balt., Dec. 6, 1947; d. Clifton Lee Cox and Dorothy Mae (Cooper) Ford; m. Curtis Washington, June 6, 1964; children: Curtis Jr., Kimberly. Student, Essex (Md.) C.C., 1978, Towson State U., Balt., 1985, Balt. City C.C., 1997. Nursing asst. Md. Gen. Hosp., Balt., 1965-66; optical asst. Greater Balt. Med. Ctr., optician; enrollment coord. Cmty. Family Health Ctr., Balt.; admissions dir. Elder Health Inc., Balt., 1996—. Sec. Empowerment Zone, East Harbor Village Ctr., Balt., 1994-96; mem. F.O.F. Family Support Adv., Balt., 1995-96, flaghouse Cts. Adv. Bd., Balt., 1994-96; cmty. activist Greater Balt. Med. Ctr., 1989-96; mem. Provider Network Group, Balt., 1996—; chmn. bldg. fund New Antioch Bapt. Ch., 1993-95, pres. Flower Cir., 1990-96; mentor Women Entrepreneur Bus., balt., 1993-95. Named Outstanding Cmty. Liaison, Flag House Cts., 1993; recipient Outstanding Vol. award City Springs Elem. Sch., 1993; T. Rowe Price Corp. Acad. scholar, 1994. Democrat. Baptist. Avocations: flora design, cooking, travel. Office: 1154 Sherwood Ave Baltimore MD 21239-2230

WASHINGTON, JOSEPHINE HARRIET, biologist, endocrinologist, educator; b. Demopolis, Ala., Dec. 14, 1958; d. Joseph C. and Edna (Burns) W. BS in Chemistry, Judson Coll., 1980; MS in Biology, Ala. A&M U., 1985; MEd in Biology Edn., Ala. State U., 1992; postgrad., Howard U., 1992—. Grad. rsch. asst. Ala. A&M U., Normal, 1982-85; histopathology technician VA, Biloxi, Miss., 1985-86; instr. in biology Stillman Coll., Tuscaloosa, Ala., 1986-95, asst. prof. biology, 1995—. Health career advisor Stillman Coll., 1986-95, sec. math. and sci. divsn., 1988-89, sec. profl. ethics and conduct com., 1989-90, mem. com. acad. advising, 1993-95. Grantee Dept. Edn., 1993-95, NASA, 1995. Mem. AAUW, Nat. Assn. Biology Sci. Tchrs., Alpha Zeta. Democrat. Methodist. Avocations: piano, reading.

WASHINGTON, MARIAN, women's basketball coach; b. West Chester, Pa. 1 child, Josie. B.Phys. Edn. and Health, West Chester State Coll., 1970. Tchr. phys. edn. Martin Luther King Jr. H.S., Kansas City, Mo.; grad. asst. health, phys. edn. and recreation U. Kans., Lawrence, 1972, women's athletics dir., 1974-79, head basketball coach, 1974—. Asst. coach 1996 Olympics, Atlanta; coach U.S. Select Team, 1983; mem. Kodak All-Am. selection com.; regional chair for Wade trophy. Commr. Kans. AIAW. Named 1997 Big 12 Coach of the Yr., 1996 Big Eight and Black Coaches Assn. Coach of the Yr., Black Coaches Assn. Women's Coach of the Yr., 1992, Big Eight Conf. Coach of the Yr., 1992, Kans. Basketball Coaches Assn. Women's Coach of the Yr., 1992, Outstanding Black Woman in Sports, Ebony Mag.; recipient William I, Koch Outstanding Woman of the Yr. award, Giant Steps award Ctr. for Study of Sport in Soc. at Northeastern U. and Nat. Consortium for Acads. and Sports, 1995; inductee West Chester State Women's Athletic Hall of Fame. Mem. Black Coaches Assn. (pres. 1993-94), Women's Basketball Coaches Assn. (bd. dirs.). Office: Univ of Kansas/Allen Fieldhouse Women's Athletics Dept 280 Parrott Lawrence KS 66045-0001

WASHINGTON, NANCY JANE HAYES, librarian; b. High Point, Dec. 31, 1936; d. Lester Eli and Annie Rose (Caldwell) Hayes; m. Charles D. Washington, Dec. 26, 1969 (div. June 1981). AA, Mars Hill Coll., 1957; BA, U. S.C., 1959; MA, U. West Fla., 1980; MLS, Fla. State U., 1982. Music tchr. private studio, Columbia, S.C., 1959-67; asst. dir. film libr. State Dept. Edn., Columbia, 1967-68; elem. sch. tchr. Richland County Schs., Columbia, 1969-71; serials cataloging and acquisitions asst. U. West Fla., Pensacola, 1972-83, serials acquisitions libr., reference libr., 1983-84; bibliographer humanities, arts and social scis. U. S.W. La., Lafayette, 1984-86; asst. dir. sys. libr. svcs. U. S.C., Columbia, 1986-94, dir. publs. divsn. librs. and info. sys., 1994—. Author: Univ. S.C. Regional Campuses Faculty Senate: It's First 25 Years, 1993; editor Ex Libris, 1994-2000; editor: Renovation and Restoration of the USC Horseshoe: A Memoir, 2002; contbr. articles to profl. jours. Bd. dirs. Columbia Mus. Art, 1992-94. Mem. Am. Libr. Assn., S.E. Libr. Assn., S.C. Lib. Assn., Richland Kiwanis Club (sec.), Phi Kappa Phi, Beta Phi Mu. Episcopalian. Avocations: reading, gardening, photography, attending concerts and plays, singing. Office: Thomas Cooper Libr Univ SC Greene St Columbia SC 29208-0001

WASHINGTON, TYONA, adult education educator; d. William and Juanita Washington; 1 child, Derick Reed. AAS, CUNY, Bklyn., 1983, BS, 1993, MS, 1997; MS in Supervision, Coll. of St. Rose, 2004. Tchr. Frederick Douglass Ctr.-N.Y.C. Dept. Edn., Bklyn., 1994—2002, ctr. adminstr., 2002—03; adult literacy tchr. [illegible] Bklyn., 1999—; dist. recruitment cert. specialist Dept. Human Resources/Dept. Profl. Devel., Bklyn., 2002—. Chairperson sch. leadership team Frederick Douglass Ctr., Bklyn., 2002—03. Mem.: Nat. Alliance Black Sch. Educators, N.Y. Alliance Black Sch. Educators, Assn. Black Educators N.Y., United Fedn. Tchrs. (chpt. leader 1999—2003, Ely Trachtenberg award 2002), Am. Fedn. Tchrs. (del. NY State Unified Tchrs. 2000—). Avocations: reading, travel, music. Home: 177 Kingston Ave #3B Brooklyn NY 11213 Office: NYC Dept Edn 832 Marcy Ave Brooklyn NY 11216 Office Phone: 718-636-5770.

WASHINGTON, VALORA, non-profit administrator; b. Columbus, Ohio, Dec. 16, 1953; d. Timothy Washington and Elizabeth (Jackson) Barbour; children: Omari, Kamilah. BA in Social Sci. with honors, Mich. State U., 1974; PhD, Ind. U., 1978; PhD (hon.), Bennett Coll., 1992. Assoc. instr. sch. edn. Ind. U., Bloomington, 1975-77; dir., cons. Urban League Ind., Indpls., 1977-78; substitute tchr. Indpl. Pub. Schs., 1978; dir. U. N.C., Chapel Hill, 1980-82; congrl. sci. fellow Soc. for Rsch. in Child Devel., Washington, 1981-82; prof. edn. U. N.C., Chapel Hill, 1978-83; asst. dean, assoc. prof. Howard U., Washington, 1983-86, Am. U., Washington, 1986-87; prof., v.p. Antioch Coll., Yellow Springs, Ohio, 1987-90; v.p. Kellogg Found., Battle Creek, Mich., 1990-99; exec. dir. Unitarian Universalist Svc. Com., 1999—. Cons. Ford Found., N.Y.C., 1990; project evaluator Carnegie Corp., N.Y.C., 1989-90, Ohio Bd. Regents, Columbus, 1990—. Author: (with others) Creating New Linkages for the Adoption of Black Children, 1984, Project Head Start: Past, Present and Future Trends in the Context of Family Needs, 1987, Black Children and American Institutions: An Ecological Review and Resource Guide, 1988, Affirmative Rhetoric, Negative Action: The Status of Black and Hispanic Faculty in Higher Education, 1989; contbr. articles to profl. jours; contbr. chapters to numerous books. Recipient Capital U. award, 1990, award Springfield Alliance Black Educators, 1989; named one of Ten Outstanding Young Women Am., 1980, Outstanding Young Woman N.C., 1980, one of 100 Young Women of Promise Good Housekeeping Mag., 1985, one of 25 Most Influential Working Mothers, Working Mothers Mag., 1997. Mem. Nat. Coun. Negro Women (chmn. 1982-83), Am. Assn. for Higher Edn. (sec. black caucus 1989), Soc. for Rsch. in Child Devel. (pres. black caucus 1987-89), Nat. Assn. for the Edn. of Young Children (sec. of bd. dir. 1990—), Phi Delta Kappa, Delta Kappa Gamma.

WASHINGTON-VELAZQUEZ, SARAH ELIZABETH, tax auditor; b. Roanoke, Va., Nov. 27, 1959; d. James Augustus Washington and Sarah Elizabeth Costen-Washington; 1 child, Javier Velazquez. BS in Bus. Adminstrn./Acctg. with high honors, Antillian U., Mayaguez, P.R., 1983; postgrad., Western State U., 2002—. Tchr. English Korean Lang. Inst., Seoul, 1979—80; cost acct. Safeway Foods, Sacramento, 1983—86; state tax auditor State of Calif., Riverside, 1987—. Cons. Calif. State EEO Adv. Bd., Sacramento, 1988—90. Mem.: Black Law Student Assn. (treas. 2003—04). Seventh-Day Adventist. Avocations: marathon runner, travel, photography. Office Phone: 909-961-5584. E-mail: sewvelaz@msn.com.

WASIK, BARBARA HANNA, psychologist, educator; b. Douglas, Ga., May 29, 1942; d. Frank Joseph and Josephine (Nahoom) Hanna; m. John L. Wasik, June 24, 1966; children— John Gregory, Mark Timothy, Jeffrey Joseph AB, U. Ga., 1963; MA, Fla. State U., 1965, PhD, 1967. Lic. psychologist, N.C. Postdoctoral research fellow Duke U., Durham, N.C., 1967-68; dir. research Ford Found. grant, Durham, N.C., 1968-69; from asst. prof. to assoc. prof. U. N.C., Chapel Hill, 1969-77, prof., 1977—, assoc. dean Grad. Sch., 1972-75, chmn. div. human devel. and psychol. services, 1975-77, assoc. dean Sch. Edn., 1977-83, 1988—92, sr. investigator Child Devel. Ctr., 1972—. Mem. commn. NAS, 1998—2000; co-facilitator Nat. Forum Home Visiting, 1999—. Assoc. editor Jour. Applied Behavior Analysis, 1972; mem. editorial bd. Behavioral Assessment, 1984-85; contbr. chpts. to books and articles to profl. jours. Mem. N.C. Psychological Assn. (sec. 1982-85, pres. 1988-89), Am. Psychol. Assn. (divsn. 25 sec-treas. 1983-86, coun. rep. 1994-99, bd. edn. affairs 1999-2001, chair bd edn. affairs 2001), Soc. Research in Child Development, Southeastern Psychol. Assn., Assn. Advancement Behavior Therapy. Democrat. Roman Catholic. Home: 609 Brookview Dr Chapel Hill NC 27514-1402

WASKO-FLOOD, SANDRA JEAN, artist, educator; b. N.Y.C., Mar. 12, 1943; d. Peter Edmund and Margaret Dalores (Kubek) Wasko; m. Michael Timothy Flood, June 28, 1969. BA, UCLA, 1965, postgrad., 1968-69, Calif. State U., Northridge, summer 1968; student, Otis Art Inst., L.A., 1969, Marie Kaufman, Rio de Janeiro, 1970-72, Museo de Arte Moderno, 1970-73, Foothill Coll., Los Altos, Calif., 1973-74, Claremont (Calif.) Coll., 1975, U. Wis., Janesville, 1977, Beloit (Wis.) Coll., 1977-78, U. Wis., 1977-78; grad. etching student, Warrington Colescott. Instr. printmaking Washington Women's Arts Ctr., 1983; artist-in-residence U. Md., College Park, 1985; instr. printmaking Arlington (Va.) Arts Ctr., 1984-85; prof. St. Mary's (Md.) Coll., 1985; instr. printmaking Arlington County Lee Arts Ctr., 1989-97; workshop coord. cultural affairs div. Arlington County Cultural Affairs, 1989-97; printmaking instr. Home Studio, Alexandria, Va., 1987—. One woman shows include Wisconsin Women in the Arts Gallery, Madison, 1977, Mbari Art, Washington, 1981, Miya Gallery, Washington, 1981, Slavin Gallery, Washington, 1982, Stuart Mott House, Washington, 1983, Washington Printmakers Gallery, 1986, 88, 91, St. Peter's Ch., N.Y.C., 1989, Montana Gallery, Alexandria, Va., 1991, Montpelier Cultural Arts Ctr., Laurel, Md., 1992, Gallery 10, Washington, 1994, 96, Sch. 33, Balt., 1996; mus. and internat. shows include Boston Printmakers: The 39th North Am. Print Exhbn., Framingham, Mass., Jan.-Mar., 1986, Internat. Graphic Arts Found. and Silvermine Guild Arts Ctr., New Canaan, Conn., Feb., 1988, prints: Washington, The Phillips Collection, Washington, Sept.-Oct., 1988, Contemporary Am. Graphics, Book Chamber Internat., Moscow, 1990, Gallery 10 Artists of Washington D.C. Vartai Gallery, Lithuania, 1994, Peninsula Fine Arts Ctr., Newport News, Va., 1995-96, Riva Sinistra Arte, Florence, Italy, 1997, Contemporary Art Ctr. Va., Virginia Beach, 2000, Charles Sumner Sch. Mus., Washington, D.C., 2001, numerous others; juried shows include Washington Women's Arts Ctr.: Printmakers VII show, 1985, Washington Women's Arts Ctr., 1981, 82, Seventh Ann. Faber Birren Color Show Nat. Juried Open Exhibit, Stamford, Conn., 1987, Acad. of the Arts 25th Ann. Juried Exhbn., 1989, Fla. Printmakers Nat., 1994, S.W. Tex. State U., 1995, Peninsula Fivie Arts Ctr., Newport News, Va., 1998, Washington Women Artists, Womens Caucus for Art, 2001, Rockville Art Place, Md., 2002, Internat. Photography, 2003, and numerous others; invitational shows include Office of the Mayor, Mini Art Gallery, Washington, "Glimpses: Women Printmakers", 1981, Pyramid Paperworks, Balt., 1984, Gallery 10 "Nightmare Show": Washington, D.C., 1987, The Intaglio Process, The Benedicta Art Ctr. Gallery, St. Joseph, Minn., 1988, Women's Caucus for Art, Washington Artists in Perspective, Westbeth Gallery, N.Y.C., 1990, 91, Wesley Theol. Sem., 1992, Balt. City Hall, N.Am. Print Alliance, 1993, The Five Elements Women's Caucus For Art, 1994, WPA/Corcoran Auction, 1999, Washington Theological Union, Washington, 1999, Cannon Rotunda, U.S. House of Reps., Washington, 2000, Charles Sumner Sch. Mus., Washington, 2001, Washington Women Artists Marching into the Millennium, Women's Caucus for Art, 2001 and numerous others; galleries: Slavin Gallery, Washington, D.C., 1981-83, Washington Printmakers Gallery, Washington, 1985-96, White Light Collaborative, Inc., N.Y.C., 1988-89, Montana Gallery, Alexandria, Va., 1989-91, Gallery 10, Washington, 1992-97, Charleuoix Gallery, Albuquerque, NM, 1999, and numerous others; collections include Nat. Mus. of Women in the Arts, Washington, Corcoran Gallery of Art, Washington, Museo de

Arte Moderno, Buenos Aires, Cultural Found., USSR, Coll. Notre Dame, Balt., Potomac Hosp., Woodbridge, Md.; dir. Labyrinths for Peace 2000, U.S. Capitol, 2002; featured artist Kali Guide: A Directory of Resources for Women, 2d reprint, 2002. Pres. Washington Area Printmakers, Washington, D.C., 1985-86; pub. rels. dir. Washington Women's Arts Ctr., 1980; bd. dirs. Washington Women's Arts Ctr., 1981-82; program chair D.C. chpt. Women's Caucus for Art, 1998—; founding mem. the Labyrinth Soc., 1999-2000; special projects dir. Labryinth Soc., 2000; cons. Labyrinth Making and Products. Recipient Award of Honorable Mention Nat. Gallery of Art, 1989, Best of Show, Artists Equity Exhibit, Gallery 901, Washington, 1997; grantee Friends of the Torpedo Factory Art Ctr., Alexandria, Va., 1989, D.C. Commn. on the Arts and Humanities Summer Edn. and Sports Program, 2000, 01; individual artists fellow Va. Commn. for Arts, 1994. Mem.: Arts/Sci. Collaborative, Inc. (N.Y.C.), Artists Using Sci. and Tech. (San Francisco), YLEM, The Labyrinth Soc., Washington Sculpture Group, Am. Print Alliance, Md. Printmakers, Women's Caucus for Art, So. Graphics Coun., Pyramic Atlantic, Nat. Print Orgn., Corcoran Gallery/Washington Project for the Arts. Avocations: classical music, hiking, reading. Home: 8106 Norwood Dr Alexandria VA 22309-1331 Studio: 57 N St NW Washington DC 20001-1254 E-mail: sandra@waskoart.com.

WASS, HANNELORE LINA, educational psychology educator; b. Heidelberg, Germany, Sept. 12, 1926; came to U.S., 1957, naturalized, 1963; d. Hermann and Mina (Lasch) Kraft; m. Irvin R. Wass, Nov. 24, 1959 (dec.); 1 child, Brian C.; m. Harry H. Sisler, Apr. 13, 1978. BA, Tchrs. Coll., Heidelberg, 1951; MA, U. Mich., 1960, PhD, 1968. Tchr. W. Ger. Univ. Lab. Schs., 1958-60; mem. faculty U. Mich., Ann Arbor, 1958-60, U. Chgo. Lab. Sch., 1960-61, U. Mich., 1963-64, Eastern Mich. U., 1965-69; prof. ednl. psychology U. Fla., Gainesville, 1969-92, prof. emeritus, 1992—, faculty assoc. Ctr. for Gerontol. Studies. Cons., lectr. in thanatology. Author: The Professional Education of Teachers, 1974, Dying-Facing the Facts, 1979, 2d edit., 1988, 3d edit., 1995, Death Education: An Annotated Resource Guide, 1980, vol. 2, 1985, Helping Children Cope With Death, 1982, 2d edit., 1984, Childhood and Death, 1984; founding editor (jour.) Death Studies, 1977-92; cons. editor: Ednl. Gerontology, 1977-92, (book series) Death Education, Aging and Health Care, 1980-96; contbr. approximately 200 articles to profl. jours. and chpts. in books. Mem. Am. Psychol. Assn., Gerontol. Soc., Internat. Work Group Dying, Death and Bereavement (bd. dirs.), Assn. Death Edn. and Counseling. Home: 6014 NW 54th Way Gainesville FL 32653-3265 Office: U Fla 346 Norman Hall Gainesville FL 32611-2053 E-mail: wass@nersp.nerdc.ufl.edu .

WASSENBERG, EVELYN M. medical and surgical nurse, nursing educator; b. Oct. 8, 1933; d. Patrick A. and Mary A. (Kieffer) L'Ecuyer; m. Maurice P. Wassenberg, Oct. 29, 1955; children: Sherry Ann Gaines, Laura Marie O'Neil. Diploma in nursing, Marymount Sch. Nursing, Salina, Kans., 1955; BS in Nursing, Marymount Coll. of Salina, 1982; MN, Wichita State U., 1987. Cert. nurse specialist. Dir. nursing svc. Community Meml. Hosp. Inc., Marysville, Kans., 1962-79; house supr. Luth. Hosp., Beatrice, Nebr., 1980-82; primary nurse Beatrice Cmty. Hosp., 1983; instr. Ft. Scott (Kans.) C.C., 1983-2001; nurse Girard (Kans.) Hosp., 2001; ICU nurse Nevada (Mo.) Regional Health Ctr., 2001—03. Mem. Mary Queen of Angels Cath. Ch. Named Nurse of Yr. Bourbon County Kans., 1992. Mem. Am. Nursing Assn., Kans. State Nursing Assn., Sigma Theta Tau. Address: 216 S Crawford St Fort Scott KS 66701-3231 Office: Nevada Regional Med Ctr 800 S Ash St Nevada MO 64772

WASSERHEIT, JUDITH N. social services administrator, b. N.Y.C., 1954; m. Jeffrey Harris, 1981; one child. BA cum laude, Princeton U., 1974; MD, Harvard U., 1978; MPH, Johns Hopkins U., 1989. Co-dir., co-developer Harborview Med. Ctr., U. Wash., 1982-84; infectious disease physician Internat. Ctr. for Diarrheal Disease Rsch., 1984-86; asst. chief Sexually Transmitted Disease Clin. Svcs. Balt. City Health Dept., 1986-89; chief Sexually Transmitted Disease Br. Nat. Inst. Allergy and Infectious Diseases, NIH, 1989-92; dir. Sexually Transmitted Disease Prevention Disease Ctr. for Disease Control & Prevention, HHS, 1992—. Editor: Reproductive Tract Infections: Global Impact and Priorities for Women's Health, 1992; contbr. articles to profl. jours. Recipient Spl. Recognition award Pub. Health Svc., 1990, 91, Young Profl. award Maternal-Child Health, APHA, 1991, Presdl. Meritorious Rank award, 1996; Pub. Health Leadership Inst. Scholar, 1993. Mem. Phi Beta Kappa, Sigma Xi.

WASSERMAN, HELENE WALTMAN, art dealer, artist; b. Phila., Jan. 29, 1929; d. William T. and Bertha (Brener) Waltman; m. Richard M. Wasserman, June 23, 1950 (div. 1972); children: Ann Zelver, Ellen Rubinfeld, Stephen; m. Mark C. Cooper, Jan. 22, 1988. BFA, U. Pa., 1951. Pvt. practice art dealer, 1972—. Apptd. appraiser Supreme Ct., State of N.Y., 1978. One-woman shows at Philmont Gallery, Phila., 1964, Roko Gallery, N.Y., 1965; exhibited in group shows at Phila. Mus. Art, Pa. Acad. Fine Arts, Philbrook Mus., Tulsa, Woodmere Gallery, Roko Gallery, 1953-68. Active Nassau County Art Commn., 1968-72; trustee, Sculpture Ctr., N.Y.C., bd. dirs., 1991. Mem. Pvt. Art Dealers Assn., Cosmopolitan Club, Nature Conservancy. Avocations: painting, sculpting, garden design.

WASSERMAN, KRYSTYNA, librarian, art historian; b. Lodz, Poland, Aug. 10, 1937; came to U.S., 1971; d. Henryk and Polina (Volk) Ostrowski; m. Paul Wasserman, Apr. 14, 1972. M in Journalism, U. Warsaw, Poland, 1963; MLS, Pratt Inst., 1972; MA, U. Md., 1981. Reporter Ekran-The Screen Mag., Warsaw, 1960-62; sec. edn. com. Inst. Sci., Tech. and Econ. Info., Warsaw, Poland and Internat. Fedn. for Documentation, The Hague, Netherlands, 1962-71; ind. editor reference books College Park, Md., 1972-82; libr. Nat. Mus. Women Arts, Washington, 1982—2002, curator book arts, 2002—. Curator numerous art exhbns. Contbr. articles to profl. jours.; editor: A Guide to the World Training Facilities in Documentation and Information Work, 1965, 2nd edit., 1969. ASTEF fellow Govt. of France, 1967. Avocations: photography, walking, travel, collecting socks, collecting masks. Office: Nat Mus Women in Arts 1250 New York Ave NW Washington DC 20005-3970

WASSERMAN, MARLIE P(ARKER), publisher; b. Chgo., Feb. 14, 1947; d. Theodore E. and Faye (Beller) Parker; m. Mark Wasserman, Nov. 24, 1968; children— Aaron David, Danielle Elizabeth. B.A., Duke U., 1969; M.A., Old Dominion U., 1970. Editor, U. Chgo. Press, 1970-78; sr. editor Rutgers U. Press, New Brunswick, N.J., 1978-83, asst. dir. and editor-in-chief, 1983-87, assoc. dir., editor-in-chief, 1987-94; exec. editor social sciences Routledge, N.Y.C., 1994-95; dir. Rutgers U. Press, New Brunswick, 1995—. Office: Rutgers U Press 100 Joyce Kilmer Ave Piscataway NJ 08854-8045

WASSERMAN, MURIEL, artist; b. N.Y.C., May 27, 1935; d. Max Weintraub and Mollie (Baum); m. Stanley Eli Wasserman, May 22, 1955; children: Debra, David, Mark. BA, Queen's Coll., N.Y., 1976; MA, Pratt Inst., Bklyn., 1982; postgrad, Adelphi U., Bklyn. Mus. Art Sch., Five Town Music & Arts Found., N.Y., Newark (N.J.) Sch. of Art, Bklyn. Coll., N.Y.; studied with Phillip Guston, Rudolf Nakien, Richard Bove, Arthur Coppedge, Jack Rabinowitz. Fine art instr. Valley Stream Library, L.I., 1975-78; art instr. Valley Stream Adult Edn., L.I., 1978—84, St. John's U., Queens, N.Y., 1980-94. Docent Nassau Mus. Adminstrn., L.I., 1975-76, cataloger, 1976. Columnist: Sunstorm L.I. Art Periodical, 1983-84; one-woman shows include The Gallery at the Bryant Libr., Roslyn, N.Y.; exhibited in group shows at Long Beach (N.Y.) Mus. Art (numerous shows), Isis Gallery, Port Washington, N.Y., Five Town Music & Art Found. (numerous shows), Nat. Assn. Women Artists (numerous shows), Hechscher Mus., N.Y. (numerous shows), Sarah Lawrence Coll., Bronxville, N.Y., Ark. Arts & Sci. Ctr., Pine Bluff, Schenectady (N.Y.) Mus. & Planetarium, Candada Beach Hotel Gallery, P.R., Firehouse Gallery, Nassau C.C., N.Y., Pace U. Art Gallery, Pleasantville, N.Y., Mus. of the Southwest, Midland, Tex., N.Y. Acad. Sci., Christina Rose Gallery, N.Y.C., numerous others. Recipient Painting award Town of Hempstead, Am. Artist Mag. Mem. Nat. Assn. Women Artists (numerous awards), L.I. Craft Guild. Avocation: gardening. Home: 70 Brentwood Ln Valley Stream NY 11581-2344

WASSERMAN, SUSAN VALESKY, accountant, artist, yoga instructor; b. St. Petersburg, Fla., June 5, 1956; d. Charles B. Valesky and Jeanne I. (Schulz) Morgan; m. Fred Wasserman, III, May 19, 1990; 1 child, Sara Elisabeth. BS in Merchandising, Fla. State U., 1978; BA in Acctg., U. South Fla., 1983. CPA Fla.; ChFC, cert. yoga tchr. Fla. Inst. for Integrated Yoga Studies, 2002, yoga therapist Integrated Yoga Therapy, 2004. Mgmt. trainee Burdines Dept. Stores, Miami, Fla., 1978-79; store mgr. Levi Straus Inc., San Francisco, 1979; pvt. practice acct. St. Petersburg, 1980—; acct., tax and fin. planning specialist Barber, Stowe & Co., St. Petersburg, 1997-98; owner White Egret Yoga Studio, South Pasadena, Fla., 2002—. Exhibitions include Longboat Key (Fla.) Art Ctr., 1993, Fla. Suncoast Water Color Soc., Sarasota, 1994, South Pasadena Artspring, 1998—2000 (Judges award, 1998). Mem.: Suncoast Yoga Tchrs. Assn., Yoga Alliance. Home and Studio: 7015 Grevilla Ave S Saint Petersburg FL 33707-2050 Office: 5800 4th St N Saint Petersburg FL 33703-1402 Office Phone: 727-347-7354. E-mail: yogisue@prodigy.net.

WASSERMAN-SCHULTZ, DEBBIE, state legislator; b. Forest Hills, N.Y., Sept. 27, 1955; BA in Polit. Sci., U. Fla., 1988, MA, 1990. Mem. Fla. Ho. of Reps., 1992—. Mem. Gov.'s Commn. on Edn., 1996—; mem. legis. adv. coun. So. Regional Edn. Bd., 1995—; bd. dirs. Fla. Distance Learning Network, 1994; mem. Classrooms First Task Force, 1993. Recipient award for oustanding family advocacy Dade County Psychol. Assn., 1993, Giraffe award Women's Advocacy Majority Minority, 1993, Legis. Svc. award Fla. Assn. Women Lawyers, 1993, Quality Floridian award Fla. League of Cities, 1994, AMIT Woman of Yr. award, 1994, Outstanding Legislator of Yr. award Fla. Fedn. Bus. and Profl. Women, 1994, Rosemary Barkett award Acad. Fla. Trial Lawyers, 1995, Woman of Vision award Weizmann Inst. Sci., others; named one of Six Most Unstoppable Women, South Fla. Mag., 1994. Mem. Omicron Delta Kappa. Democrat. Jewish. Avocations: bowling, golf, politics, old houses. Office: 402 S Monroe St Tallahassee FL 32399-6526 also: 2500 Weston Rd Ste 101 Weston FL 33331-3616

WASSERSTEIN, WENDY, playwright; b. Bklyn., Oct. 18, 1950; d. Morris and Lola Wasserstein. BA, Mt. Holyoke Coll., 1971; MA, CCNY, 1973; MFA, Yale Drama Sch., 1976. Author: (plays) Any Woman Can't, 1973, Happy Birthday, Montpelier Pizz-zazz, 1974, (with Christopher Durang) When Dinah Shore Ruled the Earth, 1975, Uncommon Women and Others, 1975, Isn't It Romantic, 1981, Tender Offer, 1983, The Man in a Case, Miami, 1986, The Heidi Chronicles, 1988 (Pulitzer prize for drama, 1989, Outer Critics Cir. award for best play, 1989, N.Y. Drama Critics Cir. award, 1989, Susan Smith Blackburn prize, 1989), The Sisters Rosensweig, 1991 (Outer Critics Cir. award, 1993), An American Daughter, 1997, Old Money, 2000, (screenplays) Uncommon Women and Others, 1978, The Sorrows of Gin, 1979, (with Durang) House of Husbands, Isn't It Romantic, The Heidi Chronicles, (children's book) Pamela's First Musical, 1995; actress (plays) An American Daughter, Life with Mikey; author: (essays) Bachelor Girls, 1990, Shiksa Goddess, 2003. Recipient Hale Matthews Found. award; grantee Am. Playwrights Project, 1988, Commissioning Program Phoenix Theater; Guggenheim fellow, 1983. Mem.: bd. Channel Thirteen, MacDowell Colony, WNET, British Am. Arts Assn., Dramatists Guild for Young Playwrights, artistic bd. Playwrights Horizons, Coun. Dramatists Guild. Address: c/o Phyllis Wender / Rosenstone Wender 10th Fl 38 E 29th St New York NY 10021*

WASSON, BARBARA HICKAM, music educator; b. Spencer, Ind., Feb. 12, 1918; Student, DePauw U., 1937-38; BA, Vassar Coll., 1939; MusM, Chgo. Mus. Coll., 1944; postgrad., Ind. U., 1962-63. Founder, co-dir. Wasson Piano Studios, Dayton, 1946—; instr. Cedarville (Ohio) Coll., Dayton, 1970-72; adj. prof. Wright State U., Dayton, 1973-78; asst. prof. U. Cin., 1982-87. Named Cert. Tchr. of Yr., Western Dist. of Ohio, 1998, 2001, Family of Yr., Ohio Fedn. Music Clubs, 2002; recipient Family of Yr. award Ohio Fedn. Music Clubs, 2002. Mem. Ohio Music Tchrs. Assn. (pres. 1980-82, chmn. western dist. 1976-78), Dayton Music Club (pres. 1989-91), Mu Phi Epsilon (pres. Dayton alumnae chpt. 1986-88). Home: 9620 Belfry Ct Dayton OH 45458-4157 E-mail: wassonpno@aol.com.

WASSON, LILA ELIZABETH, educational consultant; b. Bradenton, Fla., Jan. 6, 1924; d. Lawyer and Margaret Jane (Moore) Jenkins; m. Robert Paul Wasson, June 14, 1951; children: Robert Paul, Sandra Wasson Brown, Kathy Elizabeth. BS, Fla. A&M U., 1945, MS, 1968. Tchr. sci. Union Acad., Bartow, Fla., 1946; tchr. phys. edn. Rosenwald High Sch., Panama City, Fla., 1946-51; subs. tchr. Sunflower and Wilson Village Schs., Anchorage, 1960-63; elem. tchr. Hanscom Primary Sch., Hanscom AFB, Mass., 1965-87; ednl. cons. J.B. Enterprises, Bedford, Mass., 1990-91. Master tchr. MA in Teaching program Harvard U., Cambridge, Mass., 1968-71 Author: The Classroom Teacher's Guide: For the Beginning Years and Beyond, 1998. Mem. AAUW (rec. sec. 1990-91), LWV, Mass. Ret. Tchrs. Assn. Democrat. Baptist. Avocations: travel, reading, teaching and promoting children's literature. Home: 26 Gould Rd Bedford MA 01730-1248

WASSON-SHAW, CAROL R. music teacher; b. Dayton, Ohio, Feb. 8, 1951; d. Audley Jackson and Barbara (Hickam) Wasson; m. Stephen D. Shaw, Feb. 21, 1981 (div. Apr. 1998); children: Tiffany Elise, Tia Nicole. BMusic in Piano Performance, Wright State U., Fairborn, Ohio, 1978. Pvt. tchr. piano, 1965—; pvt. tchr. violin and viola, 1980—; owner, mentor to music tchrs. Shaw's Music Ctr., Centerville, Ohio, 1993—. Lectr., tcht. piano to preschoolers. Chmn. jr. philharm. Dayton Philharm. Women's Assn., 1979-80; chmn. fundraiser South Dayton Montessori, Kettering, Ohio, 1987-88. Mem. Nat. Guild Piano Tchrs. (chmn. Dayton-Wasson Audition Ctr. 1998—), Music Tchrs. Nat. Assn., Dayton Music Club (chmn. judges Dist. IIIB Jr. Festival 1994—, co-chmn. 1999-2002, chmn. 2001—), Mu Phi Epsilon, Centerville Noon Optimists. Office: Shaw's Music Ctr 35 Marco Ln Centerville OH 45458-3818

WATANABE, CORINNE KAORU AMEMIYA, judge, state official, lawyer; b. Wahiawa, Hawaii, Aug. 1, 1950; d. Keiji and Setsuko Amemiya; m. Edwin Tsugio Watanabe, Mar. 8, 1975; children: Traciann Keiko, Brad Natsuo, Lance Yoneo. BA, U. Hawaii, 1971; JD, Baylor U., 1974. Bar: Hawaii 1974. Dep. atty. gen. State of Hawaii, Honolulu, 1974-84, 1st dep. atty. gen., 1984-85, 87-92, atty. gen., 1985-87; assoc. judge Hawaii Intermediate Ct. Appeals, Honolulu, 1992—. Mem. ABA, Hawaii Bar Assn. Office: Hawaii Intermediate Ct Appeals 426 Queen St 2d Fl Honolulu HI 96813

WATANABE, NANA, photographer; b. Tokyo, Jan. 12, 1952; came to U.S., 1974; d. Kenji and Mie Watanabe; m. Julian Mark Fifer, Nov. 3, 1988; 1 child, Anais Fifer. BA in English Lit., Keio U., Tokyo, 1971. Freelance photographer, N.Y.C., Tokyo, Paris, 1980—. Named Photographer of Yr., Am. Photographer mag., 1987. Avocations: languages, tennis. Home: 1010 5th Ave New York NY 10028-0130 Office: Nana Watanabe Studio 150 W 28th St New York NY 10001-6103

WATERER, BONNIE CLAUSING, retired secondary school educator; b. Toledo, Sept. 25, 1940; d. Kermit Henry and Helen Ethel (Waggoner) Clausing; m. Louis P. Waterer, June 17, 1961; children: Ryan, Reid. BS in Home Econs. Edn., Ohio State U., 1962; MA in Home Econs. Edn., San Jose State U., 1966. Tchr. James Lick H.S., San Jose, 1963-67, 1973-76; adult edn. instr. Met. Adult Edn. Program, San Jose, 1968-75; home econs. instr. Independence H.S., San Jose, 1976-99, home econs. dept. chair, 1976-80; home econs. coord. East Side Union H.S. Dist., San Jose, 1980-99, coord. coll. and career resource ctrs., 1995-99, ret., 1999—. Child care occupations instr. Ctrl. County Occupl. Ctr., San Jose, 1989-99; child devel. instr. Evergreen Valley Coll., San Jose, 1995 Bd. dirs. NAMI Yavapai County, Ariz. Mem.: AAUW (v.p. Prescott br. 2004—), Home Econs. Tchrs. Assn. Calif. (pres. 1989—91, Outstanding Tchr. award 1987), Calif. Assn. Family and Consumer Sci. (Tchr. of Yr. award 1994), Am. Assn. Family and Consumer Sci., Phi Upsilon Omicron, Delta Kappa Gamma (sec. Prescott br. 2002—), Omicron Nu. Democrat. Methodist. Avocations: travel, computing, cooking, sewing. Home: 1052 Vantage Pt Cir Prescott AZ 86301 E-mail: bh2oer@aol.com.

WATERMAN, MIGNON REDFIELD, public relations executive, state legislator; b. Billings, Mont., Oct. 13, 1944; d. Zell Ashley and Mable Erma (Young) Redfield; m. Ronald Fredrick Waterman, Sept. 11, 1965; children: Briar, Kyle. Student, U. Mont., 1963-66. Lobbyist Mont. Assn. Chs., Helena, 1986-90; mem. Mont. Senate, Dist. 26, Helena, 1990—; with pub. rels. dept. Mont. Coun. Tchrs. Math., Helena, 1991-96. Mem. edn., pub. welfare and instns. sub-com. fin. and claims commn. Mont. Senate, rev. oversight com., 1995—, post-secondary policy & budget com., 1995—. Sch. trustee Helena (Mont.) Sch. Dist. 1, 1978-90; bd. dirs. Mont. Hunger Coalition, 1985—; pres. Mont. Sch. Bds. Assn., 1989-90; active Mont. Alliance for Mentally Ill (Mon Ami award 1991). Recipient Marvin Heintz award Mont. Sch. Bds. Assn., 1987, Friends of Edn. award Mont. Assn. Elem. and Middle Sch. Prins., 1989, Child Advocacy award Mont. PTA, 1991, award Mont. Alliance for Mentally Ill, 1991, Outstanding Adv. award Nat. Easter Seals Soc., 1997, Pres.'s award Mont. Assn. Rehab., 1997. Mem. Mont. Sch. Bds. Assn. (Marvin Heintz award 1988, pres.1989-90), Mont. Elem. Sch. Prins., Mont. Parent, Teacher, Student Assn. (child advocacy award 1991). Democrat. Methodist. Home and Office: 530 Hazelgreen Ct Helena MT 59601-5410 Office: Mt State Senate State Capitol Helena MT 59620

WATERS, ALICE, executive chef, restaurant owner, writer; b. Chatham, N.J., Apr. 28, 1944; 1 child. Grad. in French Cultural Studies, U. Calif., Berkeley, 1967; postgrad., Montessori Sch., London; degree (hon.), Mills Coll., Oakland, Calif., 1994. Exec. chef, owner Chez Panisse, Berkeley, Calif., 1971—, Chez Panisse Cafe, Berkeley, Calif., 1980—, Cafe Fanny, Berkeley, Calif., 1984—. Mem. adv. bd. U. Calif., Berkeley; active The Garden Project, San Francisco; spkr. in field of food safety and health. Author: Chez Panisse Menu Cookbook, Chez Panisse Vegetables, (storybook and cookbook for children) Fanny at Chez Panisse. Developer Martin Luther King Jr. Mid. Sch. Edible Schoolyard, Berkeley. Named Best Chef in Am., James Beard Found., 1992, Best Restaurant in Am., 1992, Humanitarian of Yr., 1997, Mother of Am. Cooking, N.Y. Times; named one of 10 Best Chefs in the World, Cuisine et Vins du France, 1986; recipient Spl. Achievement award, James Beard Found., 1985, Restaurant and Bus. Leadership award, Restaurants and Instns. Mag., 1987, Barbar Boxer Top Ten Women award, 1991, Le Tour du Monde en 80 Toques, Metziner & Varaut, 1991, Nat. Edn. Diplomate award, 1996. Office: Chez Panisse 1517 Shattuck Ave Berkeley CA 94709-1598

WATERS, BETTY LOU, newspaper reporter, writer, b. Texarkana, Tex., June 13, 1943; d. Chester Hinton and Una Erby (Walls) W. AA, Texarkana Jr. Coll., 1963; BA, East Tex. State U., 1965. Gen. assignment reporter [illegible] feature writer Ind. and Daily Mail, Anderson, S.C., 1968-69; reporter Citizen-Times newspaper, Asheville, N.C., 1969-74; edn. and med. reporter News Star World Pub. Co., Monroe, La., 1974-79; reporter, writer Delta Democrat Times, Greenville, Miss., 1980-89, staff writer Tyler (Tex.) Morning Telegraph, 1990—. Named Citizen of Yr., Sigma Sigma chpt. Omega Psi Phi, 2001, recipient 1st place award for articles, La. Press Women's Contest, 1978, 1st place for interview, 1979, news media award, N.C. Easter Seal Soc., 1973, 3d place award for feature writing, Miss. Press Assn., 1984, for gen. news, 1983, for investigative reporting, 1988, 1st place for best series of articles, 1990, award for outstanding edn. series, Tex. State Tchrs. Assn., 1998, Sch. Bell award for outstanding series, 1997, Tex. Coll. Women Changing the World award, 2000, hon. mentions, Tex. AP, 1966. Mem. Sigma Delta Chi.

WATERS, CRYSTAL, vocalist, songwriter; b. Camden, NJ; BA, Howard U., 1985. With Parole Bd., Washington; represented by Mercury Records, 1989—. Songwriter, Basement Boys, 1987; albums include Surprise, 1991, Storyteller, 1994, Crystal Waters, 1997, The Best of Crystal Waters, 1998. Office: Mercury Records 825 8th Ave New York NY 10019-7416 also: AM PM Entertainment Concepts Inc Vito Bruno 270 Lafayette St Ste 602 New York NY 10012-3327

WATERS, JENNIFER NASH, lawyer; b. Bridgeport, Conn., Dec. 21, 1951; d. Lewis William and Patricia (Cousins) W.; m. Todd David Peterson, Sept. 19, 1981; children: Elizabeth, Andrew. BA, Radcliffe, 1972; JD, Harvard, 1976. Bar: D.C. 1977, U.S. Supreme Ct. 1980. Clk. U.S. Ct. Appeals (D.C. cir.), Washington, 1976-77; assoc. Jones, Day, Reavis & Poque, Washington, 1977-79, Crowell & Moring, Washington, 1979-83, ptnr., 1983—. Mem. ABA (ho. of dels. 1997-99), Fed. Energy Bar Assn. (bd. dirs. 1988-99, v.p. 1994-95, pres. 1996-97). Office: Crowell & Moring LLP 1001 Pennsylvania Ave NW Fl 10 Washington DC 20004-2505

WATERS, LISA LYLE, airport administrator, consultant; b. Hialeah, Fla., Dec. 11, 1962; d. Richard Donald and Marthal Annette Lyle; m. Edward Carl Waters, Mar. 8, 1986; children: Valerie Nicole, Rebecca Elizabeth. BS in Aviation Agmt., AS in Flight Tech., Fla. Inst. Tech., Melbourne, 1984. Lic. comml. pilot. Airport planner Reynolds, Smith & Hills, Tampa, Fla., 1985-88; sr. airport planner LPA Group Inc., Tampa, 1988-89; noise abatement officer Palm Beach County Dept. Airports, West Palm Beach, Fla., 1990-93, mgr. noise abatement and cmty. affairs, 1994-96, dir. noise and tech. svcs., 1996—2000; owner, v.p. MEA Group Inc., West Palm Beach, 2000—. Mem. editl. bd.: Airport Noise Report, 1999—2001. Mem. bd. advisors Fla. Inst. Tech. Sch. of Aeronautics. Mem. Am. Assn. Airport Execs., Fla. Airport Mgrs. Assn., Fla. Aero Club. Avocations: children, cooking. Home: 17044 76th St West Palm Beach FL 33409 Office: MEA Group Inc 2001 Palm Beach Lakes Blvd Ste 406 West Palm Beach FL 33409

WATERS, MARY BRICE KIRTLEY, federal agency administrator; B, U. Ill.; JD, George Mason U. Bar: D.C. Sr. dir., legis. counsel ConAgra Foods, 1986—2001; asst. sec. congl. rels. USDA, Washington, 2001—; legis. asst. Rep. Larry Hopkins, Ky., 1982—86; dir. agrl. task force Rep. Rsch. Com., 1981—82. Past chair Washington Agrl. Roundtable; mem. Trade Policy Forum. Office: USDA Congl Rels 1400 Independence Ave SW Washington DC 20250

WATERS, MAXINE, congresswoman; b. St. Louis, Aug. 15, 1938; d. Remus and Velma (Moore) Carr; m. Sidney Williams, July 23, 1977; children: Edward, Karen. Grad. in sociology, Calif. State U., L.A.; hon. doctorates, Spelman Coll., N.C. Agrl. &, Tech. State U., Morgan State U. Former tchr. Head Start. Mem. Calif. Assembly from dist. 48, 1976-91, Dem. caucus chair, 1984; mem. U.S.Congress from 35th Calif. dist., 1991—; mem. Banking, Fin., Urban Affairs com., Ho. subcom. on banking, capitol subcom. on banking, employment and tng. subcom. on vets., veterans affairs com., banking and fin. svcs. com., ranking house subcom. on gen. oversight and investigations; chair Congl. Black Caucus. Mem. Dem. Nat. Com., Dem. Congl. Campaign com.; del. Dem. Nat. Conv., 1972, 76, 80, 84, 88, 92, mem. rules com. 1984; mem. Nat. Adv. Com. for Women, 1978—; bd. dirs. TransAfrica Found., Nat. Women's Polit. Caucus,

Ctr. Nat. Policy, Clara Elizabeth Jackson Carter Found. Spellman Coll., Nat. Minority AIDS Project, Women for a Meaningful Summit, Nat. Coun. Negro Women, Black Women's Agenda; founder Black Women's Forum; dep. City Councilman David Cunningham, 1973-76, chief dep. Minority Whip; mem. Congl. Children's Working Group, Congl. Progressive Caucus, Dem. Nat. Com.; chair Dem. Caucus Spl. Com. election Reform; vice chair Steering Com. Mem. Calif. Peer Counseling Assn., Nat. Com. Econ. Conversion and Disarmament; mem. bd. Ctr. Study Sport in Soc., L.A. Women's Found. Democrat. Office: US Ho Reps 2344 Rayburn HOB Washington DC 20515-0001*

WATERS, SYLVIA, dance company artistic director; BS in Dance, The Juilliard School; studied with, Antony Tudor and Martha Graham; PhD (hon.), State U. N.Y., Oswego, 1997. Prin. dance Alvin Ailey Am. Dance Theater, N.Y.C., 1968—74; artistic dir. Alvin Ailey Repertory Ensemble, N.Y.C., 1974—. Panelist Nat. Endowment for the Arts, N.Y. State Council on the Arts. Office: Alvin Ailey Repertory Ensemble 211 W 61st St Fl 3 New York NY 10023-7832*

WATERS, ZENOBIA PETTUS, retired finance educator; b. Little Rock, Mar. 4, 1927; d. Henry Augustus and Lillie Liddell (Edwards) Pettus; m. Willie Waters, Jr., Jan. 29, 1949 (div. Feb. 1955); children: Pamela E. Reed, Zenobia W. Carter. BA cum laude, Philander Smith Coll., Little Rock, 1964; MEd, U. Wash., 1968. Cert. tchr. Ark., 1966. Office mgr. United Friends of Am., Little Rock, 1946—52; sec. State Dept. Edn., Little Rock, 1958—64; lectr. bus. Philander Smith Coll., Little Rock, 1965—67, asst. prof. bus., 1968—88, assoc. prof. bus. adminstrn., 1988—92, bd. dirs., faculty rep., 1976—80; asst. prof. bus. Ark. Bapt. Coll., Little Rock, 1970—84. Asst. bus. mgr. Philander Smith Coll., Little Rock, 1970—74, dir. summer sessions, 1970—81. Mem. adv. bd.: Two Centuries of Methodism in Arkansas, 2000; contbr. articles to profl. jours. Dean West Gulf Regional Sch., 1975—77; vol. Dem. Party, Little Rock, 1986—92; contact person U.S. Presdl. Campaign, Little Rock, 1992; cert. lay spkr. United Meth. Ch., 1979—; pres. so. ctrl. juris United Meth. Women, 1984—88; bd. dirs. Gen. Bd. of Global Ministries, N.Y.C., 1984—88, Aldersgate Camp, Little Rock, 1976—79, St. Paul Sch. Theology, Kansas City, Mo., 1984—88, Mount Sequoyah, Fayetteville, Ark., 1984—88. Recipient Edn. Found. award, AAUW, 1983, Svc. award, Gen. Bd. Global Ministries/Women's Divsn., 1988; fellow, Nissan, 1989; grantee Ford Found. grantee, 1967. Mem.: AAUW, Nat. Trust for Historic Preservation, United Meth. Women (pres., recognition pins 1963—2001), Phi Delta Phi, Iota Phi Lambda. Avocations: reading, walking, writing. Home: 1701 Westpark Dr Apt 219 Little Rock AR 72204

WATKINS, ANN ESTHER, mathematics educator; b. L.A., Jan. 10, 1949; d. Rex Devere and Burnice Gordine (Duckworth) Hamilton; m. William Earl Watkins, Oct. 5, 1973; children: Mary Ann, Barbara Lee. BA, Calif. State U., Northridge, 1970, MS, 1972; PhD, UCLA, 1977. Instr. math. Los Angeles Pierce Coll., Woodland Hills, Calif., 1975-90; prof. math. Calif. State U., Northridge, 1990—. Editor: (with Albers, Rodi) New Directions in Two Year College Mathematics, 1985; co-author: (with Landwehr) Exploring Data, 1986, 2d edit., 1994, (with Landwehr, Swift) Exploring Surveys, 1987, (with Albers, Loftsgaarden, Rung) Statistical Abstract of Undergraduate Programs in the Mathematical Sciences and Computer Science, 1992 (with Scheaffer, Gnanadesikan, Witmer) Activity-Based Statistics, 1996, 2d edit., Statistics in Action, 2003; assoc. editor: American Mathematical Monthly, 1996-2000; editor Coll. Math. Jour., 1989-94; co-editor: (with Apostol, Mugler, Scott and Sterrett) A Century of Calculus, Part II, 1992; mem. editl. bd. Jour. Statis. Edn., 1992-95; mem. adv. bd. Math. Horizons mag., 1992—. Grantee NSF, 1987-90, 92-2004. Mem. Math. Assn. Am. (2d v.p. 1987-88, pres. 2001-03, chair So. Calif. sect. 1988-89, gov. So. Calif. sect. 1995—), Am. Statis. Assn., Nat. Coun. Tchrs. Math. E-mail: ann.watkins@csun.edu.

WATKINS, BRENDA L. music educator; b. Norfolk, Va., Apr. 18, 1946; d. Rosser Lee Jones and Erma Constance Norsworthy; m. Claude William Watkins, Nov. 1, 1964; 1 child, Kimberly Lynn, Cynthia Anne, Katherine Lee. Student, William & Mary Coll., 1964, Old Dominion U., 1964-68. Adminstrv. asst. Va. Nat. Bank, Norfolk, 1964-71; pre-sch. tchr. asst. Westwood Hill Bapt. Ch., Virginia Beach, 1972-74; pre-sch. music tchr. Bellamy Manor and Broad Bay Manor, Virginia Beach, 1993-96; music tchr. Court House Pre-Sch., Virginia Beach, 1994-97, Great Neck Pre-Sch., Virginia Beach, 1994-97; co-music tchr. Music and Arts Music, Chesapeake, Va., 1998—. Author, editor: Childhood Memories, 1994. Vol. info. desk Assn. for Rsch. and Enlightment, Virginia Beach, 1999. Mem. Music Tchrs. Nat. assn., Tidewater Music Tchrs. Assn., Order of Ea. Star (Kempsville chpt.), Ladies Oriental Shrine N.Am. (Zulekia Ct. #35), U.S. Amateur Ballroom Dancers Assn., Inc., Va. Dept. Game and Inland Fisheries (cert. boat safety). Lutheran. Avocations: writing, music, boating, walking. Home: 612 Cardamon Ct Virginia Beach VA 23464-1901

WATKINS, CAROL A. special education educator; b. Norfolk, Va., Dec. 7, 1954; d. Bernard Melvin and Jean Everton Dixon; m. William Stanley Watkins, Jr., July 23, 1954; children: William Stanley Watkins III, Bryce Reid. MEd, Va. Commonwealth U., 1986. Postgrad. prof. lic. Commonwealth of Va., 2003. Tchr./ spl. edn. New Kent County Pub. Schools, New Kent, 1984—95; dept. chair Hanover County Pub. Schools, Mechanicsville, Va., 1995—2002, 2003—. Fellow Grad. student tuition, Va. Commonwealth U., 1983-1984; grantee Project Unite Grant, Commonwealth of Va., 1994-1995. Avocations: volunteer- lewis ginter botanical gardens, consultant with the pampered chef*, old church community center member, ptsa faculty representative. Home: 8099 Candleberry Drive Mechanicsville VA 23111 Office: Lee-Davis HS 7052 Mechanicsville Turnpike Mechanicsville VA 23111 E-mail: cwatkins@hanover.k12.va.us.

WATKINS, CAROLE S. human resources specialist, health facility administrator; b. 1960; BA, Franklin U., Columbus, Ohio. Staff The Limited, Columbus, Ohio, 1989—96; v. p. human resources Cardinal Distribution, Columbus, Ohio, 1996—2000; sr. v.p. pharm distbn. and provider svcs. Cardinal Health, Columbus, 2000; exec. v.p. human resources Cardinal Health, Inc., Columbus, 2000—. Office: Cardinal Health 7000 Cardinal Pl Dublin OH 43017

WATKINS, DIANE LUCILLE, biology educator; b. L.A., Apr. 13, 1958; d. Walter and Carolyn (Hankins) W.; 1 child, Kevin Tracey McGee. BS, Johnson C. Smith U., 1986; BS in Metaphysics, U. Metaphysics, 1996; MEd in Ednl. Adminstrn., Calif. State U., Dominguez Hills, Calif., 2001. Master hypnotist; Silva Stress Mgmt. instr. Tchr. L.A. Unified Sch. Dist., 1986—. Master tchr. U. So. Calif., L.A., 1989-90, Teach Am., L.A., 1988-90, Nat. U., L.A., 1993-94. L.A. Ednl. Partnership grantee, 1989, Eisenhower grantee, 1994. Mem. Nat. Sci. Tchrs. Assn., Nat. Assn. Biology Tchrs., Calif. Sci. Tchrs. Assn., Nat. Guild Hypnotists, Alpha Kappa Alpha. Avocations: computers, painting, knitting. Office: Local District F 2151 N Soto St Los Angeles CA 90032

WATKINS, JENNIE SHORE, elementary school educator; b. Huntington, W.Va., Dec. 2, 1957; d. William Locke and Glenna Leah Shore; m. Ronald Lee Watkins, Feb. 25, 1989; 1 child, Caleb Lee. BS in Elem. Edn., Cumberland Coll., 1996; M in Elem. Sch. Counseling, Ea. Ky. U., 2002. Tchr. music Ctrl. Primary/South Elem. Sch., Corbin, Ky., 1997—2001; tchr. 4th grade South Elem., 2001—. Tchr. rep. Site Based Decision Making Coun. South Elem. Sch., 1999—. Nominee Disney Tchr. of Yr., Orlando, Fla., 2001. Mem.: Ky. Music Educators Assn., Ky. Reading Assn., Ky. Counseling Assn., Assn. Profl. Educators. Republican. Baptist. Avocation: singing. Home: 1130 Whippoorwill Rd Corbin KY 40701 Office: South Elem 406 W 17th St Corbin KY 40701

WATKINS, JOAN MARIE, osteopath, occupational medicine physician; b. Anderson, Ind., Mar. 9, 1943; d. Curtis David and Dorothy Ruth (Beckett) W.; m. Stanley G. Nodvik, Dec. 25, 1969 (div. Apr. 1974). BS, West Liberty State Coll., 1965; Cert. of Grad. Phys. Therapy, Ohio State U., 1966; DO, Phila. Coll. Osteo., 1972; M of Health Professions Edn., U. Ill. Chgo., 1986; MPH, U. Ill., 1989. Diplomate Osteo. Nat. Bds., Am. Bd. Preventive Medicine, Am. Bd. Occupl. and Environ. Medicine, Am. Bd. Emergency Medicine. Resident in phys. medicine and rehab. U. Pa., 1973—74; emergency osteo. physician Cooper Med. Ctr., Camden, 1974-79, Shore Meml. Hosp., Somers Point, N.J., 1979-81, St. Francis Hosp., Blue Island, Ill., 1981-82, Mercy Hosp. and Med. Ctr., Chgo., 1982-90, dir. emergency ctr., 1984-88; resident in occupl. and preventive medicine U. Ill., 1988-90; corp. med. dir. occupl. health svc. Univ. Cmty. Hosp., Tampa, 1992—. Fellow Am. Coll. Occupl. and Environ. Medicine, Am. Soc. Preventive Medicine, Fla. Assn. Occupl. and Environ. Medicine (pres. 1999-2001). Avocations: sailing, needlework, swimming. Home: 4306 Harbor House Dr Tampa FL 33615-5408 Office: U Community Hosp Occupational Health Svcs 3100 E Fletcher Ave Tampa FL 33613-4613 Office Fax: (813) 615-7711.

WATKINS, LASANDRA, science educator; d. Hartsell and Willie Mae Fields; m. Lawrence Watkins, Sr., June 26, 1971; children: LaZaundzria Denise, Lawrence Jr., LaMarr Nathaniel. BS in Biology, Alcorn A&M Coll. (now Alcorn State U.), Lorman, MS, 1970; MA, Rowan U., Glassboro, NJ, 1999, post grad., 2001. Cert. tchr. biol. sci. N.J., 1976, prin./supr. N.J., 1999. Tchr. Camden City (N.J.) Bd. of Edn., 1971—73, 1977—, Camden County Coll., Upward Bound, Blackwood, NJ, 1979—83. Mem. Nat. Hook-Up of Black Women, Camden, NJ, 2001; supporter Volunteers of Am., Camden, NJ, 1987; mem. Nat. Congress of Black Women, Washington, 1986—92. Recipient Woman of the Yr., Nat. Stop the Violence Alliance, 2001; scholar Mellon Grant, 1993. Mem.: NAACP, NEA, N.J. Edn. Assn. (union/bldg. rep. 1990), Camden Edn. Assn. (chair new mem. com. 2002, chair profl. devel. 2002, chair new mem. com. 1977, chair profl. devel. 1977), Jack and Jill of Am., Inc. (chaplain 1998—2002), Order of the Ea. Star (Prince Hall affiliate) (warder 2003, alt. star point), Alpha Epsilon Lambda (v.p. svc. 2000, pres. 2002), Alpha Kappa Alpha Sorority (Upsilon Delta Omega chpt.). Avocations: cooking, antiques, doll collecting, shopping, western movies. Home: 715 Hunter's Lane Mount Laurel NJ 08054 Office: Woodrow Wilson HS 3100 Federal Street Camden NJ 08105 Personal E-mail: lswatkins715@aol.com.

WATKINS, LINDA THERESA, educational researcher; b. York, Pa., Sept. 29, 1947; d. Nathan Franklin and Madelyn Marie (Mandl) W.; m. Hugh Jerald Silverman, June 22, 1968 (div. Apr. 1983); children: Claire Christine (Silverman) Goberman, Hugh Christopher Silverman; m. Patrick Grim. BA, Muhlenberg Coll., 1968; MA, San Jose (Calif.) State Coll., 1970; PhD, Stanford (Calif.) U., 1977; cert., Hofstra U., 1991. Rsch. asst. prof. L.I. Rsch. Inst., Stony Brook, N.Y., 1977-79; asst. prof. NYU, 1979-85; rsch. assoc. dept. psychiatry SUNY, Stony Brook, 1985-87; dir. of rsch., planning and grants mgmt. Bd. Coop. Ednl. Svcs. Eastern Suffolk, Patchogue, NY, 1987—2004. Adj. lectr. SUNY Sch. Soc. Welfare, 1994; cons. Dowling Coll., Oakdale, N.Y., 1991, Tele-Niger Evaluation Project, Paris, 1972; survey cons. Redbook Mag., N.Y., 1987; interviewer Am. Inst. for Rsch., Kensington, Md., 1973. Contbr. articles to profl. jours. Rsch. grant Ronald McDonald Children's Charities, 1988, Am. Broadcasting Co., 1978, Dissertation rsch. grant Nat. Assn. of Broadcasters, 1974; NDEA fellowship, 1972. Mem. ASCD, APA, Soc. for Rsch. in Child Devel., Am. Ednl. Rsch. Assn. Avocation: house restoration. Home: 99 Sweezey St Patchogue NY 11772-4160 Office: Bd Coop Ednl Svcs Suffolk 1 15 Andrea Rd Holbrook NY 11741 Business E-Mail: itwatkin@suffolk.lib.ny.us.

WATKINS, LISA M. financial analyst; b. Baytown, Tex., Aug. 14, 1964; d. Bob R. and Ruth (Reeder) Allen; m. Don A. Watkins, Oct. 14, 2000; children: Valerie Ann, Joe Chambers. AA in Bus. Adminstrn., Lee Coll., 1985; BBA in Gen. Bus., U. Houston, Clear Lake, 1987, BS in Finance, 1994, MS in Fin., 1998. Accounts receivable supr. D.E. Harvey Builders, Inc., Houston, 1988-89; document contbr. Halliburton, Houston, 1989-90, cost engr., 1990-94, internal auditor, 1994-95, acct., 1995-96, scheduler, 1996-2000; earned value analyst Lockheed Martin Corp., Houston, 2000—. Methodist. Avocation: cross stitch. Office: Lockheed Martin Corp PO Box 58980 Mail Code L1S Houston TX 77258 E-mail: bugsbunny@ev1.net.

WATKINS, MELYNDA, research scientist, chemist; b. Shaw AFB, S.C., Jan. 23, 1971; d. Leonard Virgil and Nancy Ruth Watkins. Student, Monash U., Melbourne, Victoria, Australia, 1992; BS in Chemistry, U. Ill., 1994. Asst. scientist Fujisawa USA, Melrose Park, Ill., 1995-96; assoc. scientist Solvay Pharms., Marietta, Ga., 1996-97; sr. rsch. scientist Triangle Pharms., Durham, N.C., 1997—. Adv. Rape Crisis Svcs., Urbana, Ill., 1993-95. Mem. Am. Chem. Soc., Pharm. Stability Discussion Group. Avocations: volleyball, exercise, travel. Home: 1508 Woodway Club Dr Apt 1031 Durham NC 27713-8316

WATKINS, SARA, musician; b. June 8, 1981; Mem. bank Nickel Creek; with Sugar Hill Records, 1998—. Musician: (recordings) Nickel Creek, 2000 (Cert. Gold, 2002, 2 Grammy nominations, 2001), This Side, 2002 (Cert. Gold, 2003, Grammy award for Contemporary Folk Album, 2003), (CD) Ten From Little Worlds, Not All Who Wander Are Lost, G.I.gantic, Faraway Land, Let it Fall, 26 Miles, More Than Words, Pickin' on ZZ Top, Philadelphia Folk Festival: 40th Anniversary, Telluride Bluegrass Festival: Reflection, Vol. 1, This is Americana, Vol 1: A View From Sugar Hill, Pickin' on the Rolling Stones, Prancer Returns, Further Down the Old Plank Road. Named Southwest Regional champions, Pizza Hut Internat. Bluegrass Music Showdown, 1994, Ariz. State Fiddle Champion, 1996, Emerging Artist of Yr., IBMA, 2000, Instrumental Group of YR., 2001; named one of Five Music Innovators for the Millennium, Time mag., 2000. Office: Q-Prime 131 S 11th St Nashville TN 37206*

WATKINS, SHERRY LYNNE, elementary school educator; b. Bloomington, Ind., Oct. 13, 1944; d. Quentin Odell and Velma Ruth W. BSEd, Ind. U., 1966, MSEd, 1968. Tchr. 4th grade North Grove Elem. Sch., Ctr. Grove Sch. Dist., Greenwood, Ind., 1966-68; tchr. 4th and 6th grades John Strange Sch., Met. Dist. of Wash. Twp., Indpls., 1968-91; tchr. 4th grade Allisonville Sch. Met. Sch. Dist. of Wash. Twp., Indpls., 1991—. Bd. dirs. ISTA Ins. Trust and Fin. Svcs. Mem. People for Ethical Treatment of Animals. Mem.: AAUW, ACLU, NEA (nat. del. 1978—), World Confedn. Orgn. of Tchg. Profls. (del. Costa Rica 1990), Washington Twp. Edn. Assn. (pres. 1986—89), Ind. Tchrs. Assn. (state del. 1966—), Alpha Omicron Pi, Delta Kappa Gamma (chpt. pres. 1992—94, chmn. coordinating coun. Indpls. area 1994—96, state legislature chair 1997—99, state profl. affairs chair 2001—03). Avocations: traveling, cultural activities. Office: Allisonville Sch 4920 E 79th St Indianapolis IN 46250-1615

WATKINS, SHIRLEY ROBINSON, agriculture department administrator; BS in Home Econs., U. Ark., Pine Bluff; MEd in Supervision, U. Memphis. Various positions with U. Ark. Ext. Svc.; dir. nutrition svcs. Memphis City Schs.; dep. under sec. Food, Nutrition and Consumer Svcs., USDA, Washington, 1993-95, dep. asst. sec. for mktg. and regulatory programs, 1995-97, under sec. agr., 1997—. Office: Food Nutrition and Consumer Svcs Dept Agr 1400 Independence Ave SW Washington DC 20250-0002

WATKINSON, PATRICIA GRIEVE, museum director; b. Merton, Surrey, Eng., Mar. 28, 1946; came to U.S., 1972; d. Thomas Wardle and Kathleen (Bredl) Grieve. BA in Art History and Langs. with honors, Bristol U., Eng., 1968. Sec. Mayfair Fine Arts and The Mayfair Gallery, London, 1969-71; adminstr. Bernard Jacobson, Print Pub., London, 1971-73; freelance exhbn. work, writer Kilkenny Design Ctr., Davis Gallery, Irish Arts Council in Dublin, Ireland, 1975-76; curator of art Mus. Art, Wash. State U., Pullman, 1978-83, dir., 1984-98; exec. dir. Ft. Wayne (Ind.) Mus. Art, 1998—. Asst. prof. art history Wash. State U., Pullman, 1978; mem. adv. bd. Exhibits USA, 1999—. Co-author, co-editor: Gaylen Hansen: The Paintings of a Decade, 1985. Mem. Assn. Am. Colls. and Univ. Mus. and Galleries (western regional rep. 1987-89), Art Mus. Assn. Am. (Wash. state rep. 1986-87), Internat. Coun. Mus. (modern art com. 1986-89), Wash. Mus. Assn. (bd. dirs. 1984-87), Am. Fedn. Arts (western region rep. 1987-89), Wash. Art Consortium (pres. 1993-95), Western Mus. Assn. (bd. dirs. 1996-98), ARTTABLE. Office: Ft Wayne Mus Art 311 E Main St Fort Wayne IN 46802-1997

WATLEY, NATASHA, softball player; b. Canoga Pk., Calif., Nov. 27, 1981; d. Edwin and Carolyn. BA in sociology, UCLA, Calif., 2003. Softball player, shortstop U.S. Nat. Team, 2001. Finalist USA Softball Nat. Player of Yr., 2002, 2003; named Shortstop First Team All-Pacific Region, 2003, First Team All-Am., Nat. Fastpitch Coaches Assn., 2000, 2001, 2002, 2003; named to First Team All-Pacific Region, 2000, 2001, 2002, First Team All-Pac 10, 2000, 2001, 2002, All-Tournament Team, Women's Coll. World Series, 2002, 2003; recipient Team Gold medal, U.S. Cup, 2001, Internat. Softball Fedn. World Championships, 2002, Pan Am. Games, 2003, Pac-10 Player of Yr., 2003. Office: US Olympic Tng Ctr 2800 Olympic Pkwy Chula Vista CA 91915*

WATNE, DARLENE CLAIRE, state legislator; b. Minot, N.D., Feb. 11, 1935; d. Charles A. and Anna Marie Widdel (Fjeld) W.; m. Clair A. Watne, Mar. 27, 1954; children: Carmen, Steven, Nancy, Matthew. Court reporting diploma, Minot (N.D.) Bus. Coll., 1975; grad., Real Estate Inst., 1991. Cert. residential real estate specialist, N.D. Exec. sec. Grand Exalted Ruler Elks, Minot, N.D., 1964-75; pres. Bus. Coll., Minot, 1974-76; ct. reporter N.W. Judicial Dist., Minot, 1976-90; real estate broker Watne Realtors Better Homes & Gardens, Minot, 1990-99; mem. N.D. Senate from 5th dist., Bismark, 1994—. Active Joint Civil Svcs. to the Poor, 1995—. Bd. dirs. ARC, Salvation Army, Red Cross; numerous state polit. interim senate coms. Named Minot Woman of Distinction in Bus. and Industry, 1993, Liberty award ND Bar Assn., 2000, named Citizen of Yr. ND Builders Assn., 2001. Republican. Avocations: reading, laking. Home: 520 28th Ave SW Minot ND 58701-7065

WATROUS, NAOMA DICKSION, retired clinical psychologist; b. Pauls Valley, Okla. d. William M. and Almeda (Cosby) Dicksion. BS, Okla. Coll. for Women, 1940; EdD, Okla. U., 1960; MS, Okla. State U., 1950; cert. in gerontology, U. Calif., Long Beach, 1993. Lic. clin. psychologist, Washington; lic. marriage, family and child counselor, gerontologist. Clin. psychologist VA Hosp., Washington, 1961-72; supervisory clin. psychologist Washington D.C. Mental Health Svc., 1972-76, clin. psychologist, 1988-96, VA Hosp. and Med. Svcs., Long Beach, Calif., 1976-88; ret., 1996. Cons. KDH Mental Health Svc., Noble, Okla., 1996-97. Amb. Noble C. of C., Okla., 1997-98; vol. Ret. Srs. Vol. Program, 2000—. Recipient Cert. of Commendation Dept. Human Svcs., Govt. of D.C., 1990, 95. Mem. APA (group psychotherapy charter mem.). Avocations: oil painting, art therapy. Home: 201 Skyridge Trl Noble OK 73068-8111 Personal E-mail: dick4139_ou@ionet.net.

WATSON, ANNE FORLAW, music educator; b. Teachey, N.C., Jan. 3, 1949; d. William Haines and Maude Stuart Forlaw; m. Ronnie Michael Watson, Dec. 20, 1970; children: Susan Yvonne Watson Leary, Marshall Glenn. B of Music Edn., Greensboro Coll., 1971; M of Music Edn., Shenandoah U., 1999. Master's lic. N.C. Bd. Edn., Nat. Bd. Cert. 2003. Music tchr. Mechanicville (N.Y.) Mid. Sch., 1973—75; part-time music tchr. East of Cooper Sch., Mt. Pleasant, SC, 1973—75; music tchr. Duplin County Schs., Rose Hill, NC, 1975—79; tchr. music, art and drama New Hanover County Schs., Wilmington, NC, 1979—81; tchr., arts coord. Pamlico County Schs., Bayboro, NC, 1984—. Co-chair Sch. Improvement Team, Bayboro, 2000—03; mentor for initial lic. tchrs. Pamlico County Schs., Bayboro, 1998—2003, arts coord., collaborator arts dept., 1982—. Organizer, dir. Ch. Praise Bd., Bayboro United Meth. Ch., 2002—; chmn. pastor-parish rels. com. Bayboro United Meth. Ch., 2001—; mem. E-Comtys. Com., Pamlico County, NC, 2002. Recipient Arts in Edn. award, N.C. Arts Coun., 1995—96. Mem.: NEA, Delta Kappa Gamma (music asst. 2002—), Music Educators Assn. Democrat. Methodist. Avocations: singing, dance, sewing. Home: 752 Alligator Loop Rd Merritt NC 28556 Office: Pamlico County HS PO Box 699 Bayboro NC 28515 E-mail: annew@pamlico.net.

WATSON, BETTY, artist; b. Passaic, N.J., Feb. 19, 1928; d. Joseph Francis and Doris Lillian (Wilcox) Rean; m. Robert Watson; children: Winthrop, Caroline Watson Keens. Student, Phoenix Sch. of Design, N.Y.C., 1946, Pa. Acad. Fine Arts, 1947, Art Students League, N.Y.C., 1947, 48, 49-51; BA, Wellesley Coll., 1949; postgrad., NYU, 1950-51; MFA, U. N.C., 1965. Asst. in art Barnard Coll., N.Y.C., 1949-51; asst. to Ferdinand Roten, Art Dealer Balt., 1952; instr. art Calif. State U., Northridge, 1968-69. One person shows include U. N.C., Greensboro, 1962, Place Gallery, Provincetown, Mass., 1966, Newsweek Gallery, N.Y.C., 1966, Gallery Saint, Norfolk, Va., 1966, Elliott U. Ctr., 1972, Morehead Gallery, 1982, GAL Gallery, Greensboro, 1993, Francis Marion U., S.C., 1995, Jackson Libr. U.N.C., Greensboro, N.C., 2000; exhibited in group shows at Nat. Acad. Design, N.Y.C., Am. Gallery, N.Y.C., A.M. Sachs Gallery, N.Y.C., Beilin Gallery, N.Y.C., Waverly Gallery, N.Y.C., N.C. Mus. of Art, Raleigh, Montclair (N.J.) Arts Mus., South Eastern Ctr. Contemporary Art, Winston-Salem, N.C., Calif. State U., Northridge, Collector's Gallery at N.C. Mus. of Art, Raleigh, Weatherspoon Mus., U. N.C., Greensboro, Corp. Art Directions, N.Y.C., 1991-95; represented in book: Betty Watson Paintings: Five Decades, 1999. Mem. Phi Beta Kappa. Home: 9 Fountain Manor Dr Apt D Greensboro NC 27405-8032

WATSON, BRENDA BENNETT, insurance company executive; b. Decatur, Ga., Aug. 26, 1940; d. Robert Joseph and Clarissa Mae (Weekes) Bennett; m. James H. Pair Jr., Apr. 4, 1969 (div. Aug. 1993); children: Richard S. Pair, Randall J. Pair, Ronald G. Pair; m. James Leigh Watson, Sept. 9, 1995. Student, DeKalb Coll., 1971. Lic. property and casualty agt., Fla., Ga., Okla., Tenn., Tex. Underwriter W. K. Stringer Co., Atlanta, 1961-65, Tharpe & Assocs., Atlanta, 1965-68; sr. v.p. Alexander - Howden, Atlanta, 1968-82; exec. v.p., ptnr. Pair Underwriting Mgrs. Inc., Atlanta, 1982-86; pres. Walkingstick-LaGere-Pair Underwriting Mgrs., Inc., Chandler, Okla., 1986-88; exec. v.p., dir. LaGere-Walkingstick Ins. Agy., Chandler, Okla., 1988—. Exec. v.p. Nat. Am. Ins. Co., Chandler, Okla., 1987—, Austin, Tex., 1999—; exec. v.p., bd. dirs. Chandler Ins. Ltd., Cayman Islands, 1985—. Dir., past pres. Gateway to Prevention and Recovery, 1994-98. Mem. Nat. Assn. Ins. Women (pres. Atlanta chpt. 1978-79, Woman of Yr. 1979-80). Republican. Episcopalian. Office: Wells Fargo Bank Bldg 2028 E Ben White Blvd Ste 200 Austin TX 78741 Home: Apt 24 6204 Waterford Blvd Oklahoma City OK 73118-1107 E-mail: bwatson@naico.com.

WATSON, CAROLINE, elementary school educator; b. Huntington, NY, July 14, 1941; d. Edwin Shepard Watson and Helen Obiedzeuski. BS, NYU, 1964; MA, CW Post, 1976. Tchr. Middle Island (NY) Sch., 1965—67; dance specialist Ward Melville HS, Setauket, NY, 1967—69; dance specialist, coord. Smithtown (NY) Sch. Dist., 1969—96. Choreographer, dir. Waldo Theatre, Waldo Boro, Maine, 1998. Choreographer (various theatre groups), 1967—80. Mem.: Smithtown Lions. Achievements include development of dance program that fulfilled a physical edn. requirement for HS. Avocation: hiking. Home: 30 Lodgowood Dr Boothbay ME 04537

WATSON, CATHERINE ELAINE, journalist; b. Mpls., Feb. 9, 1944; d. Richard Edward and LaVonne (Slater) W.; m. Al Sicherman (div.); children: Joseph Sicherman, David Sicherman. BA in Journalism, U. Minn., 1967; MA in Teaching, Coll. of St. Thomas, 1971. Reporter Mpls. Star Tribune, 1966-72; editor Picture mag., 1972-78, Travel sect., 1978—2001; editor in chief Galena (Ill.) Gazette, 1990-91. Instr. split rock arts program U. Minn., 1996-2003; sr. travel editor Star Tribune, 2001-. Author: Travel Basics, 1984. Contbr. articles to newspapers and travel mags. and books. Recipient Newspaper Mag. Picture Editor's award Pictures of Yr. Competition, 1974, 75, awards for writing and photography Soc. Am. Travel Writers, 1983-2003, Photographer of Yr. award, 1990, Alumna of Notable Achievement award U. Minn. Coll. Liberal Arts, 1994; rsch. grant Jerome Found./Gen. Mills Found., 2004; named Lowell Thomas Travel Journalist of Yr., 1990. Mem. Am. Newspaper Guild, Soc. Am. Travel Writers, Phi Beta Kappa, Alpha Omicron Pi. Office: 425 Portland Ave Minneapolis MN 55488-1511

WATSON, DIANE EDITH, congresswoman; b. L.A., Nov. 12, 1933; d. William Allen Louis and Dorothy Elizabeth (O'Neal) Watson. AA, L.A. City Coll., 1954; BA, UCLA, 1956; MS, Calif. State U., L.A.; PhD, Claremont Grad. Sch., 1987. Tchr., sch. psychologist L.A. Unified Sch. Dist., 1960-69, 73-74; assoc. prof. Calif. State U., L.A., 1969-71; health occupations specialist Bur. Indsl. Edn., Calif. Dept. Edn., 1971-73; mem. L.A. Unified Sch. Bd., 1975-78, Calif. Senate from dist. 26, 1978-98, chairperson health and human svcs. com.; U.S. amb. to Micronesia Dept. of State, 1999-2001; mem. U.S. Congress from 33d Calif. dist., 2001—, mem. govt. reform com. and internat. rels. com. Mem. Legis. Black Caucus, edn. com., budget and fiscal rev. com., criminal procedure com., housing and land use com. Calif State Sen.; del. Dem. Nat. Conv., 1972—; mem. Dem. Nat. Com.; mem. exec. com. Nat. Conf. State Legislators Author: Health Occupations Instructional Units-Secondary Schools, 1975, Planning Guide for Health Occupations, 1975; co-author: Introduction to Health Care, 1976. Recipient Mary Church Terrell award, 1976, Brotherhood Crusade award, 1981, Black Woman of Achievement award NAACP Legal Def. Fund, 1988; named Alumnus of Yr., UCLA, 1980, 82. Mem. Calif. Assn. Sch. Psychologists, L.A. Urban League, Calif. Tchrs. Assn., Calif. Commn. on Status Women. Democrat. Roman Catholic. Office: US Ho Reps 125 Cannon HOB Washington DC 20515-0533

WATSON, EASTER JEAN, psychotherapist, financial program consultant; b. Leland, Miss., U.S.A., Mar. 15, 1948; d. Tom and Louise B. Watson; m. Boisie Lee Watson, Oct. 24, 1965 (div. Apr. 1983); children: LaTonia Deonnette, Lorenzo Tomas, Derek Ondrea(dec.). MA. Social Work, Atlanta U., Georgia, 1987; B.A. Sociology/Minority Studies, U. Notre Dame, Indiana, 1974. Psycho-therapist Oak Park & River Forest Mental Health Ctr., Ill., 1991—92; program cons. child welfare program Assn. House of Chicago, Chicago, Ill., 1993—94; exec. dir. Easter Watson, MSW & Assoc., Chicago, Ill., 1994—95; child welfare admin. Kinara Com. Svcs., Chicago, Ill., 2000—01; psycho-therapist cons. Self employed, Chicago, Ill., 2001—03; asst. dir. of child welfare YMCA of Metro, Chicago, Ill., 1996—2000. Cons. alternative sch. Chgo. Pub. Sch., Mgmt. Planning Inst., Chgo., 2001—; field instr. Chgo. State U., Chgo., 2001—, Nat. Louis U., Chgo., 2001—, Roosevelt U., 2001. Coord. (parent conference) The Power of Parents, 2003. Mem. Operation PUSH, Chgo., 1996—. Grantee, U. Notre Dame, 1972. Protestant. Home: 8049 South Sacramento Ave Chicago IL 60652 Office: Holistic Comprehensive Profl Svs Inc 10630 South Western Ave Chicago IL 60642

WATSON, ELIZABETH MARION, protective services official; b. Phila., Aug. 25, 1949; d John Julian and Elizabeth Gertrude (Judge) Herrmann; m. Robert LLoyd Watson, June 18, 1976; children: Susan, Mark, David. BA in Psychology with honors, Tex. Tech. U., 1971. With Houston Police Dept., 1972-92, detective homicide, burglary and theft, 1976-81, lt. records div. northeast patrol div., 1981-84, capt. inspections div., auto theft div., 1984-87, dep. chief west patrol bur., 1987-90, police chief, 1990-92; with Austin, Tex. Police Dept., 1992—, police chief, 1992—. Mem. adv. bd. S.W. Law Enforcement Inst., Richardson,Tex., 1990—. Mem. editorial bd. Am. Jour. Police, 1991—. Mem. Internat. Assn. Chiefs of Police (mem. major cities chiefs, mem. civil rights com.), Police Exec. Rsch. Form, Tex. Police Chiefs Assn. Roman Catholic. Home: 2118 Wychwood Dr Austin TX 78746-7864

WATSON, ELLA H. principal; b. Memphis, Feb. 26, 1946; d. Kelsey Julius and Tennie Aline Hollowell; m. Vernon F. Watson, June 21, 1969; children: Angela D. Watson-McClarty, Tamara L. BS, LeMoyne-Owen Coll., 1968; MA, Memphis State U., 1970; EdS, U. Miss., Oxford, 1987; PhD, Pacific Western U., 1992. Tchr. Memphis City Schs., 1968—99, staff devel. trainer, 1984—87, prin., 1999—. Reading prof. Memphis State U., 1985; prof. life long learning Le-Moyne-Owen Coll., Memphis, 1985; faculty rep. Memphis Edn. Assn., 1983; exec. officer Memphis Prins. Assn., 1998. Developer : (video) Project Approach to Teaching, 1990. Fin. officer YMCA Greater Memphis, 1990; docent Nat. Civil Rights Mus., Memphis, 1988; bd. mem. Blue City Culture Ctr., Memphis, 1992. Named Tchr. of Yr., Newspaper in Edn., Memphis; recipient Ordinary People award. Mem.: NEA (rep.), ASCD (rep.), Nat. Assn. Elem. Sch. Prins. (pres.). Baptist. Office: Brookmeade Elem Sch 3777 Edenbury Dr Memphis TN 38127

WATSON, EMILY, actress; b. London, Jan. 14, 1967; m. Jack Waters, 1995. Motion picture and stage actress. Films include Breaking the Waves, 1996 (nominee Best Actress Oscar 1997, nominee Golden Globe award 1997, Robert award 1997, N.Y. Film Critics Circle award 1996, Nat. Soc. Film Critics award 1996, L.A. Film Critics Assn. New Generation award 1996, European Film award 1996, others), The Mill on the Floss, 1997, Metroland, 1997, The Boxer, 1997, Hilary and Jackie (nominee Best Actress Oscar 1999, nominee Golden Globe award 1999), The Cradle Will Rock, 1999, Angela's Ashes, 1999, Trixie, 2000, Gosford Park, 2001 (SAG award outstanding performance by the cast, 2002), In Search of the Assasin, 2001, Equilibrium, 2002, Punch-Drunk Love, 2002, Red Dragon, 2002. Office: c/o SAG 5757 Wilshire Blvd Los Angeles CA 90036-3635

WATSON, EVELYN EGNER, radiation scientist; b. Corbin, Ky., Dec. 15, 1928; d. Edgar Mattison and Bertha Mae (Mayfield) Egner; m. Earl Greene Watson, Nov. 10, 1953; children: Nancy Eileen, Philip Allen. AA, Cumberland Coll., 1946; student, Lincoln Meml. U., 1947-48; BA, U. Ky., 1949; postgrad., U. Tenn., 1968. Math. and sci. tchr. Lynch (Ky.) High Sch., 1949-50; office mgr. Whitley County Sch. System, Williamsburg, Ky., 1950-53; sr. lab. tech. Radiation Internal Dose Ctr. Oak Ridge (Tenn.) Assoc. Univs., 1961-71, scientist, 1971-79, program mgr., 1979-89, program dir., 1989-94; cons. internal dosimetry Tenn., 1994—. Lectr. in field; cons. USFDA, Rockville, Md., 1983-88. Assoc. editor Jour. Nuclear Medicine, 1981-86; editor newsletter Soc. Nuclear Medicine S.E. chpt., 1988-99; co-author: MIRD Primer, 1988; contbr. articles to profl., chpts. to books. Bd. dirs. Youth Haven, Oak Ridge, Tenn., 1970-74, Clinch River Home Health, Clinton, Tenn., 1988-94. Recipient Excellence in Tech. Transfer award Fed. Lab. Consortium, 1985, Lifetime Scientific Achievement award Assn. Women in Sci., 1993. Mem. Soc. Nuclear Medicine (med. internal radiation dose com. 1980—, chmn. 1994—, Marshall Brucer award for Disting. Svc. to S.E. chpt. 1999), Health Physics Soc. (Disting. Svc. award 1981, treas. 1976-77, Lifetime Achievement award 1994), European Assn. Nuclear Medicine, Nat. Coun. on Radiation Protection and Measurements (sci. com. 1986-98), Sigma Xi. Mem. Ch. of Christ. Avocations: reading, word puzzles, handicrafts. Home: 104 New Bedford Ln Oak Ridge TN 37830-8289

WATSON, GAIL H. retired librarian; b. Hattiesburg, Miss., May 12, 1941; d. Robert Elkin and Virginia Lucille (Swann) Hill; m. Tommy Gene Watson, June 4, 1963; children: James Todd, Thomas Gregory. BA, U. So. Miss., 1963; M in Librarianship, U. S.C., 1975; MEd, Tenn. State U., Nashville, 1983. Tchr. Hawkins Jr. H.S., Hattiesburg, 1963-64, Seminary (Miss.) H.S., 1965-66; libr. Bush River Elem. Sch., Newberry, S.C., 1973-74, Prosperity (S.C.) Elem. Sch., 1974-76; tchr. Franklin County H.S., Winchester, Tenn., 1977-83; libr. South/J.D. Jackson Jr. H.S., Cowan, Tenn., 1983—2003; ret., 2003. Mem. SACS rev. teams, Tenn., 1985—. Tenn. Dept. Edn. grantee, 1995. Mem. ALA, Soc. for Promotion of Christian Knowledge, Franklin County Librs. (chair 1998-2003), Delta Kappa Gamma, Kappa Delta. Democrat. Episcopalian. Avocations: reading, travel. Home: 143 S Carolina Ave Sewanee TN 37375-2405

WATSON, GEORGIANNA, librarian; b. Lock Haven, Pa., Feb. 18, 1949; d. George and Anna (Eisenhower) Rhine; children: Sharga Nicolle, George Winfield-Martin. BS in Edn., Lock Haven State U., 1971; MLS, Brigham Young U., 1978; M in Pub. Adminstrn., John Jay Coll. Criminal Justice, N.Y.C., 1986. Tchr. Mifflin County Sch. Dist., Lewistown, Pa., 1971—72; libr. Shiprock Boarding Sch. Bur. Indian Affairs, N.Mex., 1972—79, libr. Ft. Sill Indian Sch. Lawton, Okla., 1979—80; libr. U.S. Mil. Acad., West Point, 1980—83, head pub. services, libr., 1983—. Owner The Paint Pony, Walden, NY. Mem. Southeastern N.Y. Libr. Resource Coun. (continuing edn. com., govt. documents interest group), Southeastern N.Y. Reference Libr. Interest Group, Am. Quarter Horse Assn., Internat. Arabian Horse Assn., Am. Paint Horse Assn., N.Y. State Horse Coun. (Mid-Hudson dir.), Pi Alpha Alpha. Republican. Home: 8 St Michaels Ln Walden NY 12586-2466 Office: US Mil Acad Dept Army West Point NY 10996-1799 E-mail: gwatso@hvc.rr.com.

WATSON, HELEN RICHTER, educator, ceramic artist; b. Laredo, Tex., May 10, 1926; d. Horace Edward and Helen Mary (Richter) Watson. B.A., Scripps Coll., 1947; M.F.A., Claremont Grad. Sch. and U. Ctr., 1949; postgrad. Alfred U., 1966; Swedish Govt. fellow Konstfackskolan, Stockholm, 1952-53. Mem. faculty Chaffey Coll., Ontario, Calif., 1950-52; founder ceramic mus., Laredo, Tex., 2003; chmn. ceramics Mt. San Antonio Coll., Walnut, Calif., 1955-57; prof., chmn. ceramics dept. Otis Art Inst., Los Angeles, 1958-81; mem. faculty Otis-Parsons Sch. Design, 1983-88, ret. 1988; studio ceramic artist, Claremont, Calif. and Laredo, Tex., 1949—; design cons. Interpace, Glendale, Calif., 1963-64; artist-in-residence Clarement Men's Coll., 1977. Claremont Grad. Sch. fellow, 1948-49; Swedish Govt. grantee, 1952-53; recipient First Ann. Scripps Coll. Disting. Alumna award, Claremont, 1978. Address: 1906 Houston St Laredo TX 78040-7709

WATSON, IRENE, seminar and retreat facilitator, author, artist; b. Peace River, Can., June 3, 1946; arrived in USA, 1990; d. Peter and Mary (Krawchuk) Novak; m. Robert Watson, June 10, 1967; children: Juanita, Daryn. B in Liberal Studies summa cum laude, St. Edwards U., 1996; MA with honors, Regis U., 2000. Career counselor Can. Employment Ctr., Peace River, 1965—68; owner, mgr., florist Flora-Delite Flower, Peace River, 1968—78; tax collector Mcpl. Affairs, Peace River, 1978—79; adminstrn. mgr. Royal Can. Mounted Police, Edmonton, Canada, 1979—80; pvt. practice Austin, Tex., 1991—; program facilitator Nexoda Devel. Inst., Austin, 1997—. Instr. Austin CC, 1998—2001. Author: Sacred Passages: A Way to Higher State of Consciousness, 2000, Passages Through Time: Our Family, 2004, The Big Aha, 2004. Pres., v.p., treas., sec. Peace River C. of C., 1969—78; pres., v.p., treas., sec., bd. dirs. Kinette Svc. Club, 1971—81; pres., v.p., bd. dirs. Austin Pavillon Bd., 1994—2002; bd. dirs. Northern Econ. Devel., Peace River, 1978. Mem.: Assn. for Spirit at Work, [illegible] genealogy. Office: Nekoda Devel Inst 7101 Hwy 71 W #200 Austin TX 78735 Office Phone: 512-288-8555.

WATSON, KATHARINE M. state representative, b. Danville, Pa., Nov. 6, 1945; m. James Watson. BS in English, U. Pa., 1967. Formerly owner Coleraine Cons. Pub. Rels.; formerly h.s.English tchr.; former dep adminstr. County of Bucks; mem. Pa. Ho. of Reps., 2001—. Mem. Ctrl. Bucks Sch. Bd., 1985—89, Warrington Twp. Bd. Suprs., 1994—2001, vice chair, 1999—2000. Republican. Office: 159A E Wing Harrisburg PA 17120-2020 Home: 1410 W 2d St Rd Warminster PA 18974 Office Phone: 215-674-0500. E-mail: kwatson@pahousegop.com.

WATSON, KATHY, political organization administrator; b. Skowhegan, Maine; Owner Kathy Watson Co.; mem. Pittsfield Rep. Com., 1982—, Somerset County Rep. Com., 1982—; vice chmn. Maine Rep. Party, 1986-88, 94-98, chmn., 1998—. Co-chmn. Maine women for Reagan/Bush, 1984; county chair Reagan for Pres., 1988, McKernan for Gov., 1990, Snowe for Congress, 1990, 92, Cohen for U.S. Senate, 1990, Snowe for Senate, 1994; mem. Bush adv. com., 1992; del. Rep. Nat. Conv., 1988, 92, 96; mem. rules com. Rep. Nat. Com., 1992, 96. Bd. dirs. Sr. Connections/Bridges. Mem. Assoc. Gen. Contractors Am.

WATSON, LORETTA, medical/surgical nurse; d. Thomas Louis and Mary Louise Watson. LPN, Young Meml. Vocat., Morgan City, 1978; AS, RN, Prince George's C.C., Largo, Md., 2000. LPN Lakewood Hosp., Morgan City, 1978, South La. Med. Ctr., Houma, 1979—87, D.C. Gen. Hosp., Washington, 1991—2000, RN, 2001, Hunter Med., Vienna, Va., 2002, Park Plaza Hosp., Houston, 2002—, charge nurse, 2003—; RN D.C. Gen. Hosp. Deaconess Mount Olive Bapt. Ch., 1997—. Mem.: Black Nurses Assn. Democrat. Avocations: reading, collecting angels, travel, decorating. Home: 1802 Spring Green Ct Missouri City TX 77489 Office Phone: 713-527-5800.

WATSON, MARILYN FERN, writer; b. Oklahoma City, July 30, 1934; d. Charles Haddon and Mary Perle (Knotts) Rounds; m. Donald Wayne Watson, Aug. 14, 1954; 1 child, Lyndon Lee. BS in Psychology magna cum laude, Ea. N.Mex. U., 1973, postgrad., 1980-81. Apprentice technician, Sante Fe Opera, 1982. Geol. draftsman Lion Oil Co., Roswell, N.Mex., 1956-57; freelance writer, artist Roswell, N.Mex., 1960—; pvt. tutor learning disabled, gifted children, 1976-77; founder, owner Creativity Unltd., Roswell, N.Mex., 1994—. Contbr. articles to mags. and profl. jours. Ofcl. centennial historian, artist United N.Mex. Bank, Roswell, 1990; chairperson/sponsor Heritage awards Hist. Ctr. S.E. N.Mex., Roswell, 1995, found. bd., 1996-97. Recipient Writer's Digest Mag. award, 1959, Guideposts Fedn. award, 1978. Mem. Psi Chi, Phi Kappa Phi. Methodist. Avocations: gardening, hiking, reading/collecting classic literature, designing stained glass, sculpture. Home: 100 S Pennsylvania Ave Roswell NM 88203-4533 Office: Creativity Unltd 100 1/2 S Penn Ave Roswell NM 88203-4533 Other: Home: # 8 Hall St Napier Hawkes Bay New Zealand

WATSON, MARLAN, reporter; b. Haiti; Student, Spellman Coll.; BS in Music, A.M. and N. Coll. Reporter Sta. WNYW-TV, N.Y.C., 1968—. Actor: (films) Cotton Comes to Harlem, 1969; (Broadway plays) Hello Dolly, 1969; exec. prodr.: (TV series) Brown Sugar. Office: WNYW 205 E 67th St New York NY 10021

WATSON, MARY ANN, marriage and family therapist; b. Quitman, Ga., Dec. 14, 1933; d. Paul Hansel and Mary Rebecca (Bowman) Bennet; m. Edgar Lee Watson, Oct. 23, 1954; children: Edgar Lee, Rebecca Watson Stansell, Elizabeth Watson Alford. BA magna cum laude, Shorter Coll., Rome, Ga., 1954; MA, West Ga. Coll., Carrollton, 1972. Cert. employee assistance profl., substance abuse profl. Alcohol and drug counselor Floyd County Health Dept., Rome, 1971-73; psychologist Ga. Dept. Human Resources, Rome, 1972-79; counselor Harbi Clinic, Rome, 1971-80; employee assistance counselor Peachtree-Parkwood Hosp., Atlanta, 1978-81; program cons. Windwood/Floyd Hosp., Rome, 1981—; pres. Southeastern Employee Assistance Svcs., Rome, 1981—; family therapist in pvt. practice Rome, 1981—. Chmn. wellness com. Bekaert Corp., Rome, 1987—; chmn. disaster response Floyd Med. Ctr., Rome, 1992-93. Author articles; presenter, author seminars; presenter on radio talk shows. Mem. APA, Am. Assn. Marriagy and Family Therapists (clin. mem.), Employee Assistance Profls. Assn., Christian Counselors, Nat. Assn. Addiction Counselors, Rome Rotary Club, Greater Rome C. of C. (chmn. Women in Mgmt. 1989-90), Bartow County C. of C. (mem. Drugs Don't Work 1994—), Gordon C. of C. Presbyterian. Avocations: music, swimming, gardening, cooking, decorating. Home: 105 Pine Valley Rd Rome GA 30165-4339 Office: Southeastern Employee Assistance and Counseling 305 W 5th St Rome GA 30165-2818

WATSON, MARY ANN, military officer, counselor; b. Brewton, Ala., July 24, 1964; d. Charles Hall; 1 child, Dominique. Bachelors Degree, Columbia Coll., 1999; Masters Degree, Troy State U., 2003. Cadet scout leader Girl Scouts Am., Pensacola, 1991, brownie troop leader Jacksonville, 2001. Democrat.

WATSON, MARY ELIZABETH GRIDER, employment security officer, retailer; b. Stevenson, Ala., July 22, 1941; d. James William and Villie Louise Grider; m. Frank Lee Watson Jr. June 28, 1960 (div. July 1971); children: Celena, Jeff, Kim. Student, Auburn U., U. Ala. Substitute tchr. Mobile County Schs., Mobile, Ala., 1974-75; exec. sec. Corrugated Paper Mills, Stevenson, Ala., 1975-78; br. mgr. Dept. Indsl. Rels., Stevenson, 1978—; owner ReSell, Stevenson. Rep. Ala. Reunion, Stevenson, 1988; mem. adv. bd. The Daily Sentinel, Scottsboro, Ala., 1996—. Recipient award Legion of Leaders, 1985-87, Cert. of Recognition, Ala. Rehab. Assn., 1981. Mem. Jackson County C. of C., Stevenson C. of C. (vice chmn. 1986-87, bd. dirs. 1991-92). Avocations: fishing, gardening, softball, quilting, cooking. Office: Dept Indsl Rels 206 W Main St Stevenson AL 35772-3566

WATSON, MARYFRANCES ELIZABETH, management consultant, librarian; b. Chgo., Dec. 23, 1950; d. Alexander Gray and Frances (Dluzen) W. BA, Knox Coll., 1972; MALS, Rosary Coll., 1979; MA, St. Xavier Coll., 1984. Tech. svcs. libr., sr. asst. libr. St. Xavier Coll., Chgo., 1979-87; info. tech. resources mgr., lectr. libr. scis. Dominican U. (formerly Rosary Coll.), River Forest, Ill., 1989-94, asst. dean Grad. Sch. Libr. Info. Sci., 1994-95; libr. dir. In-Flight Phone Corp., Oakbrook Terrace, Ill., 1995-97; sr. cons. Global Rsch. Svcs., Chgo., 1997—. Contbr. articles to profl. jours. Mem. ALA, Ill. Libr. Assn., Special Librs. Assn. Office: Global Rsch Svcs 3477 N Broadway St Ste 121 Chicago IL 60657-2519

WATSON, PATRICIA L. library director; b. Jan. 15, 1939; m. Jack Samuel Watson, 1960; children: Bradley, Amanda. BA, Univ. Tenn., 1961, MS in Libr. and Info. Sci., 1975. Cataloging asst. tech. svcs. dept. Knoxville Pub. Libr., 1961-65; adminstrv. asst. Knoxville-Knox County Pub. Libr., 1975-78, head West Knoxville br. libr., 1978-85; dir. Knox County Pub. Libr. System, 1985—. Bd. dirs. Tanasi Girl Scout Coun., 1981-86, KORRNET (Knoxville-Oak Ridge Area Cmty. Network), 1998—; treas. Univ. Tenn. Grad. Sch. Libr. and Info. Sci. Alumni Orgn., 1983-84; elder Farragut Presbyn. Ch. Mem. ALA, Tenn. Libr. Assn. (pres. 1992-93), East Tenn. Libr. Assn. (pres. 1988-89), Rotary Internat. Office: Knox County Pub Libr System 500 W Church Ave Knoxville TN 37902-2505

WATSON, PATTY JO, anthropology educator; b. Superior, Nebr., Apr. 26, 1932; d. Ralph Clifton and Elaine Elizabeth (Lance) Andersen; m. Richard Allan Watson, July 30, 1955; 1 child, Anna Melissa. MA, U. Chgo., 1956, PhD in Anthropology, 1959. Archaeologist ethnographer Oriental Inst.-U. Chgo., 1959-60, research assoc., archaeologist, 1964-70; instr. anthropology U. So. Calif., Los Angeles, 1961, UCLA, 1961, L.A. State U., 1961; asst. prof. anthropology Washington U., St. Louis, 1969-70, assoc. prof., 1970-73, prof., 1973—, Edward Mallinckrodt disting. univ. prof., 1993—. Mem. rev. panel NSF, Washington, 1974-76; fellow Ctr. Advanced Study in Behavioral Scis., Stanford, Calif., 1981-82, 91-92. Author: The Prehistory of Salts Cave, Kentucky, 1969, Archaeological Ethnography in Western Iran, 1979; author: (with others) Man and Nature, 1969, Explanation in Archeology, 1971, Archeological Explanation, 1984, Girikihaciyan, A Halafian Site in Southeastern Turkey; author: (editor) Archeology of the Mammoth Cave Area, 1974, Prehistoric Archeology Along the Zagros Flanks, 1983; co-editor: The Origins of Agriculture, 1992, Of Caves and Shell Mounds, 1996. Recipient Arthur Holly Compton Faculty Achievement award Washington U., St. Louis, 2000, Peter H. Raven award for lifetime achievement Acad. Sci. St. Louis, 2002; grantee NSF, 1959-60, 68, 70, 72-74, 78-79, NEH, 1977-78, Nat. Geog. Soc., 1969-75. Fellow Am. Anthropol. Assn. (editor for archaeology 1973-77, Disting. Lectr. award 1994, Disting. Svc. award 1996), AAAS (chair sect. H 1991-92); mem. NAS, Cave Rsch. Found., Am. Acad. Arts and Scis., Am. Philos. Soc., Soc. Am. Archaeology (exec. com. 1974-76, 82-84, editor Am. Antiquity 1984-87, Fryxell medal 1990), Assn. Paleorient (sci. bd.), Nat. Speleological Soc. (hon. life, editorial bd. bull. 1979—, sci. award), Archaeol. Inst. Am. (Gold Medal for Disting. Archaeol. Achievement 1999). Office: Dept Anthropology CB #1114 Washington U Saint Louis MO 63130-4899 E-mail: pjwatson@artsci.wustl.edu.

WATSON, PAULA D. library administrator; b. N.Y.C., Mar. 6, 1945; d. Joseph Francis and Anna Julia (Miksza) De Simone; m. William Douglas Watson, Aug. 23, 1969; children— Lucia, Elizabeth AB, Barnard Coll., 1965; MA, Columbia U., 1966; MSL.S., Syracuse U., 1972. Reference librarian U. Ill., Urbana, 1972-77, city planning and landscape architecture librarian, 1977-79, head documents library, 1979-81; asst. dir. gen. services U. Ill. Library, Urbana, 1981-88, acting dir. gen. svcs., 1988-93, dir. ctrl. pub. svcs., 1989-93, asst. univ. libr., 1993-95, dir. electronic info. svcs., 1995—. Author: Electronic Journals: Acquisition and Management, 2003; contbr. articles to profl. jours. N.Y. State Regents fellow Columbia U., N.Y.C., 1965-66; Council on Library Resources profl. edn. and tng. for librarianship grantee, 1983 Mem. ALA (sec. univ. librs. sect. ALA-Assn. Coll. and Rsch. Librs. 1989-91, com. on instnl. coop., chair pub. svcs. dirs. group, 1997-99, mem. com. inst. coop./OCLC virtual electronic libr. steering com.), Ill. Library Assn. Avocation: gardening. Home: 715 W Delaware Ave Urbana IL 61801-4806 Office: U Ill 246 A Library 1408 W Gregory Dr Urbana IL 61801-3607 Office Phone: 217-333-0318.

WATSON, REBECCA ELAINE, human resources specialist, consultant; b. Dallas, Nov. 11, 1960; d. John Cephas and Mary Magdeline (Rhea) Bishop; m. Billy Don Wilkinson, July 31, 1982 (div.); children: Eric Tyler Wilkinson, Kristen Rhea Wilkinson; m. David John Watson, June 12, 1999; children: Laura Nicole, David John II. BEd, U. Dallas, 1982, MBA, 1995. Adminstrv. asst. IBM, Irving, Tex., 1982-85, equal opportunity coord., 1985-90, human resources data analyst Roanoke, Tex., 1990-94; sr. human resources/payroll application specialist Westinghouse Security Sys., Irving, 1994-97, team leader fin. and adminstrv. sys., 1996-97; sr. cons. Cambridge Tech. Ptnrs., 1997-98; sr. assoc. dir. Comp-U-Temp, USA, Tex., 1998-2000; v.p. WW Cons., 2000—. Mem.: NOW, NAFE, Greenpeace, Sigma Iota Epsilon. Democrat. Episcopalian. Avocations: needlepoint, rollerblading, reading, golf, bowling.

WATSON, REBECCA WUNDER, federal agency administrator, lawyer; b. Chgo., Feb. 17, 1952; d. David Hart and Shirley May (Dahlin) Wunder; m. Keith C. Thomson, Oct. 6, 1979 (div. Dec. 1989); m. Gregory B. Watson, Jan. 20, 1996. BA, U. Denver, 1974, MA in LS, 1975, JD, 1978. Bar: Bar: Wyo. 1978, Colo. 1989, D.C. 1995, Mont. 1995. Law clk. U.S. Dist. Ct. for Dist. Wyo., Cheyenne, 1978-80; assoc., then ptnr. Burgess & Davis, Sheridan, Wyo., 1980-88; pvt. practice, Denver, 1988-90; asst. gen. counsel for energy policy Dept. Energy, Washington, 1990-93; of counsel Crowell & Moring, Washington, 1993-95; ptnr. Gough Shanahan Johnson & Waterman, Helena, Mont., 1995—2002; asst. secy. land mgt. U.S. Dept Interior, Washington, 2002—. Contbr. author: ABA Natural Resource Law

Handbook, 1993; contbr. articles to law jours. Mem. ABA (chmn. natural resource com. sect. adminstrv. law 1994-97, chmn. pub. lands com. sect. natural resources, energy and environ. law 1997-99), Wyo. Bar Assn., Mont. Bar Assn., Phi Beta Kappa. Republican. Avocations: cooking, reading, travel, hunting. Home: 460 Farmington Rd W Accokeek MD 20607-9412 Office: US Dept Interior Land and Materials Mgt 1849 C St NW Washington DC 20240 Office Phone: 202-208-6734. E-mail: Rebecca_Watson@ios.doi.gov.

WATSON, RENÉE, marketing professional, special events consultant; b. San Antonio, Apr. 1, 1962; d. Clarence and Lettye Watson. BBA, U. Tex., San Antonio, 1987; MPA, CUNY, 1989. Chief staff to Councilman George Stevens, San Diego, 1991-95; dep. chief staff for Senator Rodney Ellis, Tex. Senate, Houston, 1995-97; dir. field mktg. UniverSoul Circus, Atlanta, 1997-99; cons. Watson Consulting, 1999—; program coord. planning and resource mgmt. Bexar County Courthouse, San Antonio, 2000—; program mgr. Small Minority Women Owned Bus. Enterprise. Mem. Leadership San Antonio, 1991, Leadership Calif., Pasadena, 1993, Leadership Am., N.Y.C., 1995, Leadership Tex., 2002; mem. China del. People to People Amb. Program, 1997. Fellow Nat. Urban Fellows, 1989; named 40 under 40 Rising Stars in San Antonio Bus. Jour. Democrat. Baptist. Avocations: reading, travel, walking, gardening, dance. E-mail: powernae@hotmail.com.

WATSON, RUBIE, museum director; BS in archaeology and anthropology, U. Calif., Berkeley; MS in Anthropology, Rice U.; PhD in Social Anthropology, London Sch. Econs. Assoc. prof. anthropology, acting dir. Asian Studies program U. Pitts.; assoc. curator Peabody Mus. Archeology & Ethnology, sr. lectr. dept. anthropology Harvard U., Cambridge, Mass., 1992-95, assoc. dir., then Howells dir. Peabody Mus., 1995—. Author several books including Inequality Among Brothers: Class and Kinship in South China, 1985; editor: Memory, History, and Opposition under State Socialism, 1994; co-editor: Marriage and Inequality in Chinese Society, 1990, Harmony and Counterpoint: Ritual Music in Chinese Context, 1996. Office: Peabody Mus Archeology Harvard U 11 Divinity Ave Cambridge MA 02138-2019

WATSON, SHARON GITIN, psychologist, executive; b. N.Y.C., Oct. 21, 1943; d. Louis Leonard and Miriam (Myers) Gitin; m. Eric Watson, Oct. 31, 1969; 1 child, Carrie Dunbar. BA cum laude, Cornell U., 1965; MA, U. Ill., 1968, PhD, 1971. Psychologist City N.Y. Prison Mental Health, Riker's Island, 1973-74, Youth Services Ctr., Los Angeles County Dept. Pub. Social Services, L.A., 1975-77, dir. clin. services, 1978, dir. Youth Services Ctr., 1978-80; exec. dir. Crittenton Ctr. for Young Women and Infants, L.A., 1980-89, Assn. Children's Svcs. Agys. of So. Calif., L.A., 1989-92, L.A. County Children's Planning Coun., 1992-99; cons. L.A. County Chief Adminstrv. Office, 2001—; mem. L.A. City Commn. for Children, Youth and Their Families, 2000—, L.A. County Children's Planning Coun., 2001—. Mem. L.A. delegation Pres.'s Summit for Am.'s Future, 1997. Mem. Commn. for Children's Svcs. Family Preservation and Family Support Policy Com., 1989—99, Interagy. Coun. Child Abuse and Neglect Policy Com., 1993—99, Mayor's Com. on Children, Youth and Families, 1993—95; bd. dirs. Adolescent Pregnancy Childwatch, 1985—89, L.A. Ednl. Partnership, 1999—2003, LISC Health Sector, 1996—99, L.A. Roundtable for Children, 1988—94; trustee L.A. Ednl. Alliance for Restructuring Now, 1992—99. Mem.: APA, Assn. Children's Svcs. Agys. So. Calif. (sec. 1981—83, pres. elect 1983—84, pres. 1984—85), Calif. Assn. Svcs. for Children (sec.-treas. 1983—84, pres. elect 1985—86, pres. 1986—87), U.S. Figure Skating Assn. (chmn. sanctions and eligibility 1993—96, membership com. 1996—99, strategic planning com. 2000—02, regional vice chmn. competitions com. 2000—02, sec. 2002—, bd. dirs. 1992—, mem. exec. com. 2002—, nat. competition judge), U.S. Olympics Com. (Jr. Olympics com. 1998—2000), Pasadena Figure Skating Club (pres. 1985—87, 1989—90), So. Calif. Inter-Club Assn. of Figure Skating Clubs (vice chair 1989—91, chair 1991—93). Home and Office: 4056 Camino Real Los Angeles CA 90065-3928 E-mail: sharonla12@aol.com.

WATSON, SHEILA NELSON, secondary school educator; b. Union, Miss., Jan. 15, 1954; m. Hanna J. Watson, Sept. 6, 1969; children: Mendy, Sara. BS, Miss. State U., Starkville, MS, 1981, MA, 1987. Tchr. of gifted Neshoba County Schs., Philadelphia, Miss., 1981—2002. Office: Neshoba Ctrl High School 1125 Golf Course Rd Philadelphia MS 39350-2019

WATSON, SUSAN DALE, psychologist; b. Columbia, S.C., Dec. 11, 1952; d. Luther Fred and Helen Elizabeth (Snyder) W. BA in Edn., U. S.C., 1973; MDiv, So. Sem., 1977; PhD in Psychology, LaSalle U., 1997. Pastor Portland Bridge Mission, Louisville, 1977-79; pvt. practice counselor, 1980-87; psychotherapist Campion, Barrow & Assocs., Greenwood, Ind., 1987—. Cons. Christian Missionary Fellowship, Indpls., 1988—; cons. local cts. and dept. family and children, Indpls., 1988—. Named to Outstanding Young Women in Am. Mem. ACA, Internat. Assn. for Trauma Counselors, Internat. Assn. for Marriage and Family, Assn. for Spiritual, Ethical and Religions Values in Counseling. Avocations: tennis, reading, antiques. Office: Campion Barrow & Assocs 494 S Emerson Ave Ste B Greenwood IN 46143-1953 Home: PO Box 47125 Indianapolis IN 46247-0125

WATSON, VERA K. music educator, pianist, conductor; b. Voronezh, Russia, Oct. 13, 1972; d. Stepan Efremovich and Valentina Vasilevna Kulinchenko; m. Lee Watson, Sept. 20, 1997; 1 child, Leeann. BM, South-Ukrainian State Pedagogical U., Odessa, Ukraine, 1990—95; MM, Russian Acad. of Music, Moscow, Russia, 1995—97; postgrad., Moscow State Open Pedagogical U. Cert. tchr. of music in piano MTNA . Music tchr. Odesskya Secondary Sch., Odessa, Ukraine, 1994—95; condr. children's chorus Moscow Mcpl. Choir, Russia, 1995—96; tchr. of chorus classes The Acad. of Chorus Art, Russia, 1996—97; music tchr. St. John's Gramma Sch., Jacksonville, Fla., 1997—98; condr. Palms Presbyn. Ch., Jacksonville, Fla., 1998—; chair piano dept., artist-in-residence Douglas Anderson Sch., Jacksonville, Fla., 1999—, recitalist, 2001—. Dir. of d.a. piano concerto competition Douglas Anderson Sch., Jacksonville, Fla., 1999—; judge Smta, Fsmta, Fla., 1998—; piano instr. U. of North Fla. Summer Camp, Jacksonville, Fla., 2000—. Harmony grantee for the best piano program in NE Fla., Jacksonville Symphony, 2000, Surdna Outstanding Tchr. fellow, 2003. Mem.: Nat. Guild of Piano Teachers, Jacksonville Music Teachers Assn. (scholarship chairperson 1997—2002), Federated Clubs of Am. (v.p. Jacksonville dist. 1997—).

WATSON-BOONE, REBECCA A. library and information studies researcher, educator; b. Springfield, Ohio, Mar. 7, 1946; d. Roger S. and Elizabeth Boone; m. Dennis David Ash, 1967 (div. 1975); m. Frederick Kellogg, 1979 (div. 1988); m. Peter G. Watson-Boone, May 26, 1989. Student, Earlham Coll., 1964-67; BA, Case Western Res. U., 1968; MLS, U. N.C., 1971; PhD, U. Wis., 1995. Asst. reference libr. Princeton (NJ) U., 1970-76; head cen. reference dept. U. Ariz., Tucson, 1976-83, assoc. dean Coll. Arts and Scis., 1984-89. Loaned exec. Ariz. Bd. Regents, 1988-89; pres. Ctr. for Study of Info. Profls., 1995—2002. Author: Constancy and Change in the Worklife of Research University Librarians, 1998; contbr. articles to profl. jours. Mem. ALA (div. pres. 1985-86, councilor 1988-92), Assn. for Libr. and Info. Sci. Edn., NAFE. Mem. Soc. Of Friends. Office: 7728 County Rd Y Oconto WI 54153 E-mail: rebeccawb@centurytel.net.

WATSON-BYERS, ELOISA, social worker; arrived in U.S., 1971; d. Arnold Uriah Cyrus and Maria Watson; m. Melvin Anderson Byers, Sept. 3, 1989; children: Terrence Byers, Kamaaya Byers. BA in Sociology/Social Work, Herbert H. Lehman, 1981; M in Social Work Adminstrn., Columbia U., 1997. Caseworker Child Welfare, Bklyn., 1981—85; rsch. asst. Agy. for Child Devel., Bklyn., 1985—87; quality assurance specialist Spl. Svcs. for Children, Bklyn., 1987; supr. II Child Protective Svc., Bklyn., 1988—89; adminstrv. asst. Child Welfare Adminstrn., Bklyn., 1988—89, dir. adminstrn., 1989—94; sch. social worker Bd. Edn., Bklyn., 1994—. Med. social worker Vis. Nurse Svcs., Bklyn., 1990—. Mem.: NASW. Avocations: singing, badminton, volleyball. Office: Dept Edn 601 Oceanview Ave Brooklyn NY 11235

WATSON-COLEMAN, BONNIE, state legislator; m. William E. Coleman Jr.; 1 child, William Coleman stepchildren: Troy Coleman, Jared Coleman. Grad., N.J. Thomas Edison State Coll., Leadership N.J., 1991; PhD (hon.), Richard Stockton Coll. Cert. pub. mgr. Chief bur. ho. and pub. accomodations N.J. Divsn. on Civil Rights, field rep.; mem. N.J. Gen. Assembly; chmn. Assembly Appropriations Com.; mem. Assembly Budget Com.; established Office of Civil Rights, Contract Compliance and Affirmative Action N.J. Dept. Transp., 1974—80; asst. commr. Dept. Cmty. Affairs, 1980; ret., 1994; pvt. practice, 1994; chmn. N.J. Dem. Party, 2002—. Mme. bd. trustees, bd. chmn. Richard Stockton Coll., Pamona, NJ; former chmn. N.J. State Coll. Gov. Bds. Assn., Inc. Advocate Civil Rights Children; deaconess, choir mem. Shiloh Baptist Ch. Trenton, NJ. Recipient award, Nat. Voting Rights Mus., Inst. Bridge Crossing Jubilee 2000 Appreciation award, Carver Century Club's Gerge Washington Carver Humanitarian award, New Jersey's Appreciation award, Puerto Rican Parade of Trenton, Coll. N.J.'s 12 Ann. Coll. Bound Jr. and Sr. Conf. Edl. Enhancement award, Displaced Homemakers Network of N.J., Inc. Appreciation award, Toastmasters Internat. Union Pub. Speaking Club 6520 Recognition award . Mem.: NAACP (life; Met. Trenton), Nat. Polit. Congress Black Women (Mercer/Trenton chpt.), Alpha Kappa Alpha Sorority, Inc. (Epsilon Upsilon chpt.). Democrat. Office: 150 W State St Trenton NJ 08608

WATT, LINDA E. ambassador; married; 2 children. BA, Vanderbilt U., 1973; MA, U. N.Mex., 1975. With Dept. of State, 1976—, London, San Jose, Quito, Moscow; polit. advisor U.S. So. Command, Santo Domingo; U.S. amb. to Panama U.S. Dept. State, 2002—. Office: US Embassy Panama Apo AA 34002 Office Phone: 507-207-7238.

WATTERS, CORA TULA, musician, educator; b. Portsmouth, Ohio; d. James Arthur and Nelle (Barber) W.; children: Gina Marie, Michael Earnest III, Lisa Michelle Iezzi, Patrice Annette England, Lora Diane Okwesa, James Vincent Yezzi (dec.). B in Gen. Studies cum laude, Ohio U., 1979; student, Miami U., Oxford, Ohio, LaSalle U., Rio Grande Grad. Sch., 1996; PhD in Metaphysics, Am. U., 2003. Mem. USMC Band, Quantico, Va., 1954—55; tchr. Musician Performer, 1950—; tchr. Spl. Edn. MRDD Sch., West Union, Ohio, 1983-88; dir. Shawnee Hills Sch. Fine and Performing Arts, 1983-88; tchr. Spl. Edn. West Union (Ohio) Elem. Sch., 1989-91; adjunct faculty music Southern State, Hillsboro, Ohio, 1989-92; tchr. Art West Union (Ohio) Jr. H.S., 1991-92; tchr. Music Seaman (Ohio) Elem. Sch., 1992-94; adj. faculty Am. Indian studies Antioch Coll., Yellow Springs, Ohio, 1993—; tchr. Acad. Tutor Ohio Valley Vocat. Sch., West Union, 1994-97; tchr. Ohio Valley Schs., 1999-2000; instr. vocal music North Adams H.S., Adams County, Ohio, 2000-01. Bldg. rep., state union rep., union rep., Ohio Valley Sch. Edn. Assn., 1992-96; owner Shawnee Hills Pub., 1996—; singer, dancer, profl. storyteller. Co-author: Brain Tanning-Indian Style, 1980; composer: Red, White and Blues, 1989, Watters and Daughter-At Last!, 1990, (CD) Red, White and Blues, 2000; music dir., screenwriter White Buffalo Media, Inc., 2000; author: Tales of 10 Moons, 1993, Jimmie's Place, 1996, Ohio Indians-Prehistoric to Present, 1997, Progressive Revelations of God, 1997, Progressive Revelation (Children's Workbook), 1997, Woodland Indians Children's Workbook, 1997, Digging Up Your Indian Roots, 1996, Meals from Tula's Lodge, 1997, Caproni's History and Cookbook, 1998, How Crow Lost His Feathers, 2003; From the Rocking Chair, 1999; contbr. to Encyclopedia of Appalachia, 1999-2000; columnist People's Defender, 2002—; editor/wirter Am. Indian Religious calendars, 3d edit.; profl. storyteller of Appalachian & American Indian tales; performances include VA Creative Arts Festival, Constn. Hall, Washington (Gold medal vocal solo 2000, Nat. Silver medal jazz/blues solo 2000); webmaster Am. Indians Tula List, 2000—. Chair Humane Soc., Adams County, Ohio, 1980-83; bd. mem. Adams Brown Alcohol Coun., West Union, Ohio, Adams Co. Arts Coun., 1981-83; prin. chief Shawnee Nation-Ohio Blue Creek Band; minority rep., mem. exec. com. Adams County to Ohio Valley Regional Devel. Devel. Com.; bd. dirs. Ohio Indian Affairs Commn., 2003—; ct. judge Shawnee Nation Ohio Blue Creek Band, bd. dirs. children's svcs.; bd. dirs. United Nation of Turtle Island. Cpl. USMC, 1952-55. With USMC, 1952—55. Named Outstanding Tchr. Spl. Edn. Consortium, 1987, 95, Ashland Oil Outstanding Tchr. Nominee, 1992, 95, One of 1000 Outstanding Women (Native Am.) in OYOHO, 1982, 83; recipient Holloway Human Rights award State Ohio Edn. Assn., 1993, Ohio State Commendation award for outstanding tchg., 1993, found. & chair 4 yrs. of OMEA- Music Comp. for those with spec. needs (Ohio); 5 Gold medals regional winner music/drama VA Creative Arts Competition, 2000, 1st pl., 2001, silver medal for poster art and wood sculpture, 2002; nat. gold medal for original vocal solo, silver medal for jazz solo; 1954 winner Ted Mack show N.Y.C., USMC Base, Quantico, Va.; Gold and Silver medals for vocal and jazz performance Vets. Adminstrn.. Mem. Am. Indian Inter-Tribal Alliance (leader), Ohio Shawnees Blue Creek Band (prin. chief), Am. Cancer Soc., So. Ohio Nat. Am. Substance Abuse, Native Am. Coun. of Ohio, Ohio Mental Health and Ohio Arts Coun., N.Am. Alliance Ohio, Families and Children First. Baha'i Faith. Avocations: family, religion, my tribe. Home: 696 Blacks Run Rd Lynx OH 45650-9702

WATTERS, MARY TERESA, communications executive; b. Princeton, W.Va., Aug. 12, 1954; d. Raymond L. and Ruth (Belcher) W.; m. Thomas Richard Whittington, Sept. 16, 1978 (div. 1993); children: Matthew A. Whittington, Samuel B. Whittington. BS, Concord Coll., 1976; MFA, Catholic U. Am., 1978. Wardrobe asst. Arena Stage, Washington, 1978; wardrobe mistress Folger Theatre Group, Washington, 1979-80; program asst. Nat. Exec. Search, Washington, 1980-82; chief writer The Resume Place, Washington, 1983-86; writer, editor J. Cooper & Assocs., Washington, 1987-88; dir. mktg. & promotion Blue Sky Puppet Theatre, Riverdale, Md., 1988-89; sr. writer Ullico Inc., Washington, 1989—99; sr. assoc., creative dir. Fingerhut Powers Smith & Assocs., Washington, 1999—. Author: (plays) Quilting Bee, 1977, The Rage, 1995, His Nightmare, 1995, If We Shadows Have Offended, 1996, In the Shadow of the Raven, 1998, Miranda-A Mermaid's Tale, 2001. Chair Citizens for Doyle Niemann, 1990; coord. Ams. for Harkin, 1992; chair bd. dirs. Christian Family Montessori Sch., Mt. Rainier, Md., 1985-87. Recipient Award of Excellence Life Communicators Assn., 1995, Best of Show, 1996, Silver Inkwell award of merit IBAC, Washington, 1996, 97, Svc. award Nat. Conf. of Christians and Jews, Prince George's County, 1997. Mem. Women in Comm., Potomac Writer's Group. Democrat. Avocations: songwriting, music, storytelling. Home: 4230 31st St Mount Rainier MD 20712-1732 Office: 1925 K St NW Washington DC 20006

WATTERS, SUSAN J. communications executive; b. Lafayette, Ind. m. David J. Steel; children: Colin, Andrew. BA, Bryn Mawr Coll.; MA, Tufts U.; postgrad., Fletcher Sch. Law. Staff writer Christian Sci. Monitor, Boston, Congl. Quar., Washington; bur. chief Fairchild Publs., Washington, 1979-98, Fairchild News Svc., Washington, 1998—. Adj. prof. Am. U., Washington, 1993-94. Office: 68 Observatory Cir NW Washington DC 20008-3611 Office Phone: 202-338-0863.

WATTLETON, FAYE (ALYCE FAYE WATTLETON), educational association administrator; b. St. Louis, July 8, 1943; d. George and Ozie (Garrett) Wattleton; m. Franklin Gordon (div.); 1 child, Felicia. BS in Nursing, Ohio State U., 1964; MS in Maternal and Infant Health Care, Columbia U., 1967; LHD (hon.), St. Paul's Coll., 1985, Spelman Coll., 1986; LLD (hon.), Northeastern Univ. Law Sch., 1990; LHD (hon.), Long Island Univ., 1990, Univ. of Pa., 1990, Bard Coll., 1991; HHD (hon.), Oberlin Coll., 1991; LLD (hon.), Wesleyan Univ., 1991; LHD (hon.), Hofstra U., 1992, Haverford Coll., 1992; D in Pub. Svc. (hon.), Simmons Coll., 1993; LHD (hon.), Meadville-Lombar Sem./U. Chicago. Tchr. Miami Valley Hosp. Sch. Nursing, Dayton, Ohio, 1964-66; asst. dir. Montgomery County Combined Pub. Health Dist., Dayton, 1967-70; exec. dir. Planned Parenthood, Dayton, 1970-78; pres. Planned Parenthood Fedn. Am., Inc., N.Y.C., 1978-92, Ctr. for Advancement Women, N.Y.C., 1995—. Author: How to Talk to Your Child About Sexuality, 1986, Life on the Line, 1996. Bd. dirs. Inst. for Internat. Edn., Quidel Corp., Savient Pharm., Jazz at Lincoln Ctr., Well Choice Inc.; bd. trustees Columbia U.. Recipient Am. Humanist award, 1986, John Gardner award, 1987, award of Excellence Am. Public Health Assn., 1989, Humanitarian award Congrl. Black Caucus Found., 1989, Claude Pepper Humanitarian award Internat. Platform Assn., 1990, Pioneer of Civil Rights and Human Rights award Nat. Conf. of Black Lawyers, 1990, Florina Lasker award N.Y. Civil Liberties Union Found., 1990, Whitney M. Young Jr. Service award Boy Scouts of Am., 1990, Ministry of Women award Unitarian Universalist Women's Fed., 1990, Spirit of Achievement award Albert Einstein Coll. of Med. Yeshiva Univ., 1991, 20th Anniversary Advocacy award Nat. Family Planning and Reproductive Health Assn., 1991, Women of Achievement award Women's Projects and Production, 1991, Margaret Sanger award, 1992, Jefferson Public Service award, 1992, Dean's Distinguished Service award Columbia Sch. of Public Health, 1992; named one of Best Mgrs. of Non-Profit Orgns. in Am., Bus. Week, Outstanding Mother Nat. Mother's Day Com., 1997; inducted to Nat. Women's Hall of Fame, 1993. Office: Ctr for Advancement Women 25 W 43d St Ste # 1120 New York NY 10036

WATTLEWORTH, ROBERTA ANN, physician, medical educator; b. Sioux City, Iowa, Dec. 26, 1955; d. Roland Joseph and Elizabeth Ann (Ahart) Eickholt; m. John Wade Wattleworth, Nov. 7, 1984; children: Adam, Ashley. BS, Morningside Coll., Sioux City, 1978; D of Osteopathy, Coll. Osteo. Medicine/Surgery, Des Moines, 1981; M.Healthcare Adminstrn., U. Osteo. Med. & Health Scis., Des Moines, 1999. Intern Richmond Heights (Ohio) Gen. Hosp., 1981-82, resident in anesthesiology, 1982-84; anesthesiologist Doctor's Gen. Hosp., Plantation, Fla., 1984-85; resident in family practice J.F. Kennedy Hosp., Stratford, N.J., 1985-87; educator family practice U. Osteo. Medicine and Health Scis., Des Moines, 1987-89; family practitioner McFarland Clinic, P.C., Jewell, Iowa, 1989-94; lectr. family practice Osteopath. Med. Ctr., Des Moines U., 1999—. Med. dir. nursing home Bethany Manor, Story City, Iowa, 1990-99, Jewell Vol. Fire and Rescue Squad, 1990-99. Bd. dirs. Heartland Sr. Svcs., 1995—99, Iowa Rural Health Assn. Named Nat. Outstanding Osteo. Educator of Yr., Nat. Student Osteo. Med. Assn., 2001—02. Fellow Am. Coll. of Osteo. Family Physicians; mem. Am. Osteo. Assn., Am. Med. Dirs. Assn. (sec.-treas. Iowa chpt. 1997-99), Am. Geriatric Assn., Am. Coll. Osteo. Family Physicians (pres. Iowa chpt. 1995-96), Iowa Osteo. Med. Assn. (trustee 1995-99, v.p. 1999—, pres.-elect, 2000-01, pres. 2001-2002). Lutheran. Avocations: gardening, cooking, painting. Office: 3200 Grand Ave Des Moines IA 50312-4104 E-mail: Roberta.Wattleworth@dmu.edu.

WATTS, ALICE L. nurse; b. Kremlin, Mt., Dec. 15, 1920; d. Joseph Martin and Lucia Marie (Meyr) Mangels; m. Everett Bowen Watts, Jan. 25, 1946; children: James Everett, Donald Elton, Sheila Ann, Sandra Elaine. LPN. Nurse/lpn Phillips Co Hosp., Malta, Mont., PCH-Home Health, Malta. Leader Brownie Scouts, Malta, Mont., 1963-64, 4-H club, 1966-68; deaconess Congregational Ch., 1989-99. Named Sr. Citizen of Yr., Phillips County, Mont., 2003. Mem.: Order Eastern Star. Avocations: knitting, crocheting. Home: PO Box 924 Malta MT 59538-0924 Office: Phillips Co Hosp Health Malta MT 59538

WATTS, BEVERLY L. civil rights executive; b. Nashville, Feb. 4, 1948; d. Willliam E. and Evelyn L. (Bender) Lindsley; 1 child, Lauren. BS in Sociology, Tenn. State U., 1969; MS in Cmty. Devel., So. Ill. U., 1973. Mgr., exec. sec. State of Ill. Minority and Female Bus. Enterprise Program, Chgo.; equal opportunity specialist U.S. Dept. of Health, Edn., and Welfare, Chgo.; reginal dir., civil rights/equal employment opportunity USDA, Chgo.; dir. mgmt. and adv. svcs. Ralph G. Moore and Assocs., Chgo.; exec. dir. Ky. Commn. Human Rights, 1992—. Grad. Harvard U. John F. Kennedy Sch. Govt. State and Local Execs. Program, Leadership Louisville, 1994, Leadership Ky., 1995, Duke U. Strategic Leadership for State Execs., John F. Kennedy Sch. exec. program, Harvard U., 1998; pres. Internat. Assn. Ofcl. Human Rights Agys.; mem. long term planning commn. Ky. Health Policy Bd.; mem. Ohio Valley March of Dimes; mem. equal opportunity com. Ky. Coun. on Postsecondary Edn., Louisville Met. Housing Coalition; mem. Ky. housing adv. com. Leadership Louisville Found. Bd., Bus. & Profl. Women Rover City Bd.; bd. dirs. Metro United Way. Recipient Chgo. Forum Gavel award, BEEP Gold Seal award, NAHRW Individual Human Rights award, So. Women in Pub. Svc. Pacesetter award, River City Woman of Achievement award Bus. and Profl. Women, Ky. Charles W. Anderson Laureate award. Mem. Nat. Urban Affairs Coun., Nat. Coun. Negro Women, Ky. Women's Leadership Network, Chgo. Forum, Affirmative Action Assn., Chgo. Urban Affairs Coun. (pres.), Coalition 100 Black Women, Nat. Coun. Negro Women. Office: Ky Commn on Human Rights 322 W Broadway Fl 7 Louisville KY 40202-2106

WATTS, EMILY STIPES, English language educator; b. Urbana, Ill., Mar. 16, 1936; d. Royal Arthur and Virginia Louise (Schenck) Stipes; m. Robert Allan Watts, Aug. 30, 1958; children: Benjamin, Edward, Thomas. Student, Smith Coll., 1954-56; AB, U. Ill., 1958, MA (Woodrow Wilson Nat. fellow), 1959, PhD, 1963. Instr. English U. Ill., Urbana, 1963-67, asst. prof., 1967-73, assoc. prof., 1973-77, prof., dir. grad. studies dept. English, 1977—; bd. dirs. U. Ill. Athletic Assn., chmn., 1981-83; mem. faculty adv. com. Ill. Bd. Higher Edn., 1984—, vice chmn., 1986-87, chmn., 1987-88. Author: Ernest Hemingway and The Arts, 1971, The Poetry of American Women from 1632 to 1945, 1977, The Businessman in American Literature, 1982; contbg. editor: English Women Writers from the Middle Ages to the Present, 1990; contbr. articles on Jonathan Edwards, Anne Bradstreet to lit. jours. John Simon Guggenheim Meml. Found. fellow, 1973-74 Mem. AAUP, Midwest MLA, Am. Inst. Archaeology, Assn. Lit. Scholars Critics, Authors Guild, Ill. Hist. Soc., The Phila. Soc., Phi Beta Kappa, Phi Kappa Phi. Presbyterian. Home: 1009 W University Ave Champaign IL 61821-3317 Office: U Ill 208 English Bldg 608 S Wright St Urbana IL 61801

WATTS, GINNY (VIRGINIA C. WATTS), artist; b. Chester, Pa., Jan. 24, 1931; d. Edwin Swoope Craig and Ruth Irene Tonge; m. Lynch S. Watts, Jr., July 21, 1951 (wid.); children: L. Kenneth, Karen Elizabeth Watts Dick, Monica Faye Watts Malandruccolo, Dawn Ellen Watts Eller; m. Alfred E. Meeds, May 5, 1948 (div. Nov. 1950); children: Brenda Joyce Meeds Parker, Edwin Lewis, Michael Alfred. Student, Del. Tech. and C.C., Georgetown, 1998-99. County coord. Easter Seals, Wilmington, Del., 1985-86; resident advisor Dept. Mental Retardation Kencrest Svcs., Dover, 1986-87, program mgr., 1987-90; fine arts instr. Del. Tech. and C.C., Georgetown, 1998—, 2002—. Instr. workshops Millsboro Art League, Del., 1998—. One person shows include Millsboro Art Gallery, 2000; exhibited in group shows at Del. Art Ctr., 1942—, Del. Tech. and C.C., 1997—, Millsboro Art League and Gallery, Del., 1997—, Fine Arts Event, Rehoboth Beach, Del., 2000, Geyers Art Gallery, Milford, Del., 2000, 01, 2002, others; artist oil, graphite and watercolor paintings, 1942—; group mural: wall of Art Gallery/Del. Tech. C.C., 1998; mural for lobby of Presentations, 2000; fine art work exhibited in offices of U.S. Sen. from Del.; contbr. articles to area newspapers. Vice-pres. Adult Art League, Del. Tech. C.C., 1997—; bd. dirs. Millsboro Art League, 1998—, pres., 2001—; mem. Sussex County Arts Coun., 1997—, Nat. Mus. Women in the Arts; bd.

advisors Del. Tech. adult plus program Del. Tech. and C.C.; pres. Adult PLUS Art League, 1998—; pres. Millsboro Art League, 2001-. Recipient Excellence of Artistic Achievement award DAPA and Del. Tech. C.C. Avocations: fitness swimming, hiking, biking, camping, gardening.

WATTS, HELENA ROSELLE, military analyst; b. East Lynne, Mo., May 29, 1921; d. Elmer Wayne and Nellie Irene (Barrington) Long; m. Henry Millard Watts, June 14, 1940; children: Helena Roselle Watts Scott, Patricia Marie Watts Foble. BA, Johns Hopkins U., 1952, postgrad., 1952-53. Assoc. engr. Westinghouse Corp., Balt., 1965-67; sr. analyst Merck, Sharp & Dohme, Westpoint, Pa., 1967-69; sr. engr. Bendix Radio divsn. Bendix Corp., Balt., 1970-72; sr. scientist Sci. Applications Internat. Corp., McLean, Va., 1975-84; mem. tech. staff The MITRE Corp., McLean, 1985-94; ret., 1994. Adj. prof. Def. Intelligence Coll., Washington, 1984-85. Contbr. articles to profl. jours. Mem. IEEE, AAAS, AIAA, Nat. Mil. Intelligence Assn., U.S. Naval Inst., Navy League U.S., Air Force Assn., Assn. Former Intelligence Officers, Assn. Old Crows, Mensa, N.Y. Acad. Sci. Republican. Roman Catholic. Avocations: photography, reading. Home: 6541 Franconia Rd # 108 Springfield VA 22150

WATTS, SARA KATHRYN, musician, educator; b. Oklahoma City, Nov. 26, 1948; d. Ann Rorem - Brown, Robert Wilson Brown (Stepfather). MusB, Va. Commonwealth U., 1973; MusM, Manhattan Sch. of Music, 1978. Violinist Richmond (Va.) Symphony, 1971—73, Galliard String Quartet, N.Y.C., 1979—80; freelance violinist Comml. Recs., Chamber Music, N.Y.C., 1976—89; violinist NJ State Opera, Newark, 1980—89, Orch. Sinfonica de Minera, Mexico City, 1980; instr. violin and chamber music Manhattan Sch. of Music Preparatory and Ext. Divsns., N.Y.C., 1982—89, Geroge Fox U., Newberg, Oreg., 1993—96. Grantee, Conte Found. Trust, 1977. Mem.: Music Educators Nat. Conf., Am. Fedn. Musicians, Nat. Music Edn. Assn. Avocation: bicycling. Home: 3701 SE Kelly St Portland OR 97202

WATTS, SONJA MARIE, assistant principal, educational consultant; d. James Matthew and Frances Johnson Watts; m. Lonnie Thomas Barnes, III, Jan. 2, 1975 (div. June 1986); children: Antoine Lateef Barnes, Duane Antonio Barnes, Lonnie Thomas Barnes IV. BA, Norfolk State U., 1976; MA, George Washington U., Washington, 1986. English tchr. Norfolk (Va.) Pub. Schs. Sys., 1977—97, instrnl. leader, 1997—2000; ednl. cons. Watts Works Comm., Alexandria, Va., 1998—; asst. prin. Fairfax (Va.) County Pub. Schs., 2001—. Owner, ednl. cons. Watts Works Comm., Alexandria, Va., 1998—; pub. rels. dir., conf. coord. Azusa Fellowship Internat., Norfolk, 1999—2000; cons. Stedman Graham's Leadership Inst., Chgo., 2001—; east coast developer, contact Teens Can Make It Happen Program, Alexandria, 2001—. Prodr., talk show host (radiotalk show) Keeping It Real; editor: Hamton Rds. Happenings Newspaper; singer: (TV series) Rock Church Proclaims; dir. diversity and leadership program Working Woman Mag. Dir. United Way S. Hampton Rds., Norfolk, 1998—2001; regional prdr., coord. Coll. Fund., Va., 1999—2001; chairperson Excel Awards Hampton Rds. Black media Profls., Norfolk, 2000—01; project coord. Fathers and Families Fest, Chesapeake, Va., 2000—01; honoree, spl. project coord. Fathers in Tng.; dir. gospel choir Maury HS; pub. rels. dir., conf. coord. Azusa Fellowship Internat., Norfolk, 1999—2000. Named Woman of the Month, Hampton Roads Minute; recipient Mace award, City of Norfolk, 1992, Living the Legacy, Celebrating the 150th Anniversary of Women's Rights Movement, 1998, Keeping the Flame of Creativity Alive in the 21st Century, 2000. Mem.: NAFE, Nat. Assn. Secondary Schs. Prins., Va. Assn. Secondary Schs. Prins., Mt. Vernon Rep. Women's Com., Delta Sigman Theta. Avocations: speaking, travel, writing. Home: 5980 Richmond Hwy Ste 603 Alexandria VA 22303 Office: West Potomac HS 6500 Quander Rd Alexandria VA 22307 Personal E-mail: smwatts@vzavenue.net. Business E-Mail: sonja.watts@fcps.edu.

WATTS, SUSAN HELENE, theater educator; d. Howard Harold and Madelyn Rebecca (Moore) Watts. BA, Mich. State U., 1963; MS, U. Kans., 1984. Tchr. Douglas County Schs., Castle Rock, Colo., 1964—74; owner/mgr. Old Bank Cafe, Oskaloosa, Kans., 1976—80; tchr. Valley Falls H.S., 1984—86; instr. Highland C.C., 1986—89; tchr. Oskaloosa H.S., 1986—89; communication coord./actor Omaha Magic Theatre, 1989—90; instr./divsn. chair McCook C.C., 1990—. Charter mem. Leadership McCook, 1990—; bd. mem. S.W. Nebr. Cmty. Theater Assn., 1990—2001; del. Nebr. Transfer Initiative, 1995—; chair local integrity subcom. North Ctrl. Accreditation Com., 1998—2001; adv. bd. Bright Beginnings, 1997—2001; mem. Campus Pres.'s Adv. Coun., 1993—97. Actor: (plays) Marvin's Room, Pools Paradise, Morning's At Seven, (stand up comedy) An Evening with Cassandra; author: (humor column) Dear Cassandra; dir.: (over sixty plays and musicals) (Outstanding Kans. Theatre Tchr., 1983). Banquet com. writer/performer McCook C. of C., 1998—2002; mem. goal setting task force McCook City Coun., 1998—98; mem. McCook Humane Soc., McCook, 1995—2003; bd. dirs. SpringFest, 1998—2000. Named Outstanding Kans. Theatre Tchr., Assn. Kans. Theatre, 1983. Mem.: NEA, Soc. Stage Dir. Choregraphers, Mid-Plains Edn. Assn., Nebr. State Edn. Assn., Kiwanis, Alpha Delta Kappa, Delta Kappa Gamma. Avocations: golf, gardening. Office: McCook Cmty Coll 1205 E Third Mc Cook NE 69001

WATTS, WENDY HAZEL, wine consultant; b. York, Pa., Oct. 9, 1952; d. Alphonso Irving and Daphne Jean (Gainsford) Watts; m. Frederic Joseph Bonnie, (div. 1986); m. Kenneth Scott Herron, Feb. 14, 1987 (div. Jan. 1992). BS, U. Cin., 1975. Store mgr. The Grapevine, Inc., Birmingham, Ala., 1978-81; sales rep. Supreme Beverage Co., Birmingham, 1981-84, Internat. Wines Co., Birmingham, 1984-90; nat. sales exec. Kermit Lynch Wine Mcht., Berkeley, Calif., 1990-91; on-premise mgr., fine wine mgr. Premier Beverage Co., Birmingham, 1991-94; key accounts mgr. Ala. Crown Distbg. Co., Birmingham, 1994-95; dir. of wine Mountain Brooke location Western Supermarkets, 1995—2001; dist. mgr. Winebow Italian Imports, 2001—. Instr. ednl. wine tasting classes, 1996—; spkr., instr. various groups, Birmingham; co-chmn. Sonoma Wine Tour of Birmingham, 1987-88, chmn., 1989-90; chmn. Wine Tour of France, Birmingham, 1988-89; mem. exec. com. Taste of the Nation, 1992—. Wine columnist Black and White, 1992—93; wine radio show host, 1992—. Co-chmn. Multiple Sclerosis Wine Auction, 1992—93, mem. exec. com., 1997—; co-chair Share Our Strengths Taste of the Nation, Birmingham, 1996-98; mem. bd. Magic City Harvest, 1999-2004, 2004-. Democrat. Avocations: wine and food tasting, designing, bicycling, film, hiking.

WAVLE, ELIZABETH MARGARET, college official; b. Homer, N.Y., Jan. 18, 1957; d. John Andrew Jr. and Louise Hayford (Estey) W. BMus, SUNY, Potsdam, 1979; AM in Libr. Sci., U. Mich., 1980; MS in Edn., Elmira Coll., 1990. Sr. libr. asst. U. Mich., Ann Arbor, 1979-80; pub. svcs. libr. Elmira (N.Y.) Coll., 1980-84, instr. music, 1981-97, head tech. svcs., 1984-97, coord. women's studies, 1992, 96-97; assoc. dir. Ithaca (N.Y.) Coll., 1998—. Mem. South Ctrl. Rsch. Libr. Coun. Interlibr. Loan Adv. Com., Ithaca, N.Y., 1991-93; mem. regional automation com. South Ctrl. Rsch. Libr. Coun., Ithaca, 1994-95, resource sharing com., 1996-97, mem. pers. com., 2000—, trustee, 2003—. Contbr. revs., essays to profl. publs. Mem.: First Unitarian Soc. Ithaca. Democrat. Avocations: music, reading, antiques. Home: 30 Washington St Trumansburg NY 14886-1008 Office: 1201 Gannett Ctr Ithaca Coll Ithaca NY 14850 E-mail: ewavle@aol.com.

WAWREJKO COCHRAN, DIANE, performing arts association administrator; BA in Classical Ballet, Mercyhurst Coll., 1978; MFA in Performance & Choreography, Ariz. State U.; student in Dance, U. Surrey. Resident, workshop artist Urban Gateways, Chgo.; prof., dance program dir. U. Tex.-Pan Am.; exec. dir. Nat. Dance Assn. Dancer Ctrl. Ballet of China, first U.S. tour, Laurie Eisenhower and Dances, Repertory Dance Theatre, PBS; contbr. articles to profl. jours. Office: NDA c/o AAHPERD 1900 Association Drive Reston VA 20191-1598

WAX, NADINE VIRGINIA, retired bank executive; b. Van Horne, Iowa, Dec. 7, 1927; d. Laurel Lloyd and Viola Henrietta (Schrader) Bobzien; divorced; 1 child, Sharlyn K. Wax Munns. Student, U. Iowa, 1970-71; grad. Nat. Sch. Real Estate and Fin., Ohio State U., 1980-81. Jr. acct. McGladrey, Hansen, Dunn (now McGladrey-Pullen Co., CPAs), Cedar Rapids, Iowa, 1944-47; office mgr. Iowa Securities Co. (now Wells Fargo Mortgage Co.), Cedar Rapids, 1954-55; asst. cashier Mchts. Nat. Bank (now U.S. Bancorp.), Cedar Rapids, 1956-75; asst. v.p. Mchts. Nat. Bank (now U.S. Bancorp), Cedar Rapids, 1976-78, v.p., 1979-90; ret., 1990. Vol. St. Luke's Hosp. Aux., Cedar Rapids, 1981—85, SCORE, 1999—2004; bd. dirs., v.p. Kirkwood C.C. Facilities Found., 1970—2004; bd. dirs., treas. Kirkwood C.C., 1984—91; trustee Indian Creek Nature Ctr., Cedar Rapids, 1974—2004, pres., 1980—81; mem. Linn County Regional Planning Commn., 1982—92, Cedar Rapids-Marion Fine Arts Coun., 1994—97; bd. suprs. Compensation Commn. for Condemnation, 1987—92; bd. dirs. Am. Heart Assn., Cedar Rapids, 1983—94; mem. Iowa Employment and Tng. Coun., Des Moines, 1982—83. Recipient Outstanding Woman award, Cedar Rapids Tribute to Women and Industry, 1984. Mem. Fin. Women Internat. (state edn. chmn. 1982-83), Am. Inst. Banking (bd. dirs. 1968-70), Soc. Real Estate Appraisers (treas. 1978-80), Linn County Bankers Assn. (pres. 1979-80), Cedar Rapids Bd. Realtors, Cedar Rapids C. of C. (bus.-edn. com. 1986-91), Cedar Rapids Country Club. Lutheran. Avocations: travel, reading, walking. Home: 147 Ashcombe SE Cedar Rapids IA 52403-1700

WAXBERG, EMILY STEINHARDT, educator; b. N.Y.C., Nov. 19, 1918; d. Samuel M. and Leonora Steinhardt; m. Ira L. Waxberg; children: Ronald, Drew, Kelton. BA in Art, Empire State U., 1974; MS, C.W. Post, 1975; MA, PhD, Nova U., 1976—79. Lic. spl. edn. tchr. N.Y. Tchr. Bd. Edn., N.Y., 1980. Tchr. Bd. Edn., N.Y.; cons. Wartburg Day Health Care Ctr., Bklyn.; recreation therapist, supr. Pilgrim State Hosp., Brentwood, N.Y.; subs. tchr. BOCES, L.I. Past pres. Town of Oyster Bay (N.Y.) Arts Coun., Suburban Art League, L.I. Docent Nassau County Art Mus., Roslyn, N.Y., 1990—, Coe Mansion, Oyster Bay, 1990—; ombondsman United Presbyn. Home, Syosset, N.Y., 1996—. Grantee, N.Y. State, 1995; named Woman of Yr. in Arts in 2001, Town of Oyster Bay, L.I., Woman of Distinction in Arts, 2002. Mem.: Ind. Art Soc., BACCA Ind. Art League, L.I. Arts Coun., Art League Nassau County, Nat. League Am. Pen Women. Avocations: music, reading, travel, art. Home: 37 Fox Pl Hicksville NY 11801-5752

WAXLER, BEVERLY JEAN, anesthesiologist, physician; b. Chgo., Apr. 11, 1949; d. Isadore and Ada Belle (Gross) Marcus; m. Richard Norman Waxler, Dec. 24, 1972; 1 child, Adam R. BS in Biology, No. Ill. U., 1971; MD, U. Ill., Chgo., 1975. Diplomate Am. Bd. Anesthesiology, Am. Bd. Pathology. Intern dept. pathology Northwestern U., Chgo., 1975-76, resident, 1976-79; instr. Rush Presbyn. St. Luke's Med. Ctr., Chgo., 1979-81; asst. prof. pathology Loyola U., Maywood, Ill., 1981-84; resident dept. anesthesiology Stroger Hosp. Cook County (formerly Cook County Hosp.), Chgo., 1984-87, attending anesthesiologist, 1987—; divsn. chair PACU Stroger Hosp. of Cook County, Chgo., 2004—; clin. asst. prof. U. Ill., Chgo., 1988-05; asst. prof. Rush Med. Coll., Chgo., 1996— . Contbr. articles to profl. jours. Grantee, Varlen Corp., 1982; Nat. Rsch. Svc. fellow, Nat. Cancer Inst., 1980. Mem.: AAAS, Ill. Soc. Anesthesiologists, Chgo. Soc. Anesthesiologists, Am. Soc. Anesthesiologists, Internat. Anesthesia Rsch. Soc. (B. B. Sankey Anesthesia Advancement award 1989), Sigma Xi. Office: Stroger Hosp Cook County Chicago IL 60612

WAXMAN, ANITA, producer; Prodr. (plays) Mrs. Klein, Below the Belt, Wild Honey (Drama Desk award nomination), The Foreigner; co-prodr. (plays) Present Laughter (Tony award nomination), Breaking the Code, Circle & Bravo, Long Day's Journey Into Night, Annie get Your Gun, Mr. & Mrs. Nobody. Office: care Longacre Theatre 220 W 48th St New York NY 10036-1424

WAY, BARBARA HAIGHT, dermatologist; b. Franklin, N.J., Dec. 27, 1941; d. Charles Padley and Alice Barbara (Haight) Shoemaker; m. Anthony Biden Way; children: Matthew Shoemaker Way, Sarah Shoemaker Way. AB in Music cum laude, Bryn Mawr Coll., 1962, postgrad., 1963-64; MD, U. Pa., 1968. Diplomate Am. Bd. Dermatology. Systems engr. IBM, Balt., 1962-63; mem. dean's staff Bryn Mawr (Pa.) Coll., 1963-64; med. intern U. Wis. Hosps., Madison, 1968-69, resident in dermatology, 1969-72; physician emergency rm. St. Francis Hosp., La Crosse, Wis., 1969-72, founder dept. dermatology, 1972; asst. prof. dept. dermatology Tex. Tech U. Sch. Medicine, Lubbock, 1972-73, from asst. clin. to assoc. clin. prof., 1973-74, asst. prof., assoc. chair, 1974-76, assoc. prof., chair, 1976-81, assoc. clin. prof., 1981-92; clin. prof. Tex. Tech. U. Health Scis. Ctr., Lubbock, 1995—, founder, dir. dermatology residency tng. program, 1978-81, pvt. practice, 1973-74, 81—; acting dir. Lubbock City Health Dept., 1982-83. Courtesy staff Covenant Hosp., Lubbock, subsect. chief, 1992, 94; courtesy staff Covenant Lakeside Hosp., Lubbock, mem. credentials com., 1990, 92, 94, 95, founding dir. phototherapy unit, 1990-91, 93, mem. exec. com., 1991, 93, 98, chief dermatology sect., 1991, 93, 98. Alumna admissions rep. Bryn Mawr Coll., 1972-75, 87-96; mem. selection com. outstanding physician Lubbock chpt. Am. Cancer Soc., 1991-94, chmn., 1991; bd. dirs. Tex. Tech. U. Med. Found., 1987-89, Double T. Connection, 1988-90. Fellow Am. Acad. Dermatology (reviewer jour.); mem. Tex. Dermatol. Soc. (chmn. roster com. 1980), Tex. Med. Assn. (mem. sexually transmitted diseases com. 1986-90, mem. coun. pub. health 1990-92, vice councillor dist. III 1992-98, councillor dist. III 1998-2000, chmn. reference com. fin. and orgnl. affairs ann. session 1992), Lubbock County-Garza County Med. Soc. (mem. various coms. 1980-2000, chmn. sch. and pub. health com. 1983, mem. bd. censors 1983-85, chair 1985, sec. 1986, v.p. 1987, liaison with Tex. Tech. U. Health Scis. Ctr. com. 1988-91, co-chmn. pub. rels. com. 1988-89, alt. Tex. Med. Assn. del. 1988-89, del. 1990-95, 98-2000, pres.-elect 1989, pres. 1990, chmn. ad hoc bylaws com. 1991-94, chmn. Hippocratic award 1991), Women's Dermatologic Soc. (founding sec.). Office: 4102 24th St Ste 201 Lubbock TX 79410-1801 Fax: 806 797-1102.

WAYBURN, PEGGY (CORNELIA ELLIOTT WAYBURN), writer, editor; b. N.Y.C., Sept. 2, 1917; d. Thomas Ketchin and Cornelia (Ligon) E.; m. Edgar Wayburn Sept. 12, 1947; children: Cynthia, William, Diana, Laurie. BA cum laude, Barnard, 1942. Copywriter Vogue Mag., N.Y.C., 1943-45, J. Walter Thompson, San Francisco, 1945-47; self employed freelance writer, San Francisco, from 1948. Author: Adventuring in the San Francisco Bay Area, Adventuring in Alaska; (prize-winning audio visual series) Circle of Life; contbr. articles to mags. and profl. jours. Bd. advisors Am. Youth Hostels; past trustee Sierra Club Found. Recipient Annual award Calif. Conservation Assn., 1966. Mem. Sierra Club (hon. v.p., Spl. Svc. award 1967, Women's award 1989), Phi Beta Kappa. Avocations: traveling, hiking, river-running. Home: San Francisco, Calif. Deceased.

WAYLONIS, JEAN LYNNETTE, elementary school educator; b. Brookville, Pa., Mar. 9, 1953; d. Leslie Edwin Gray and Lillian Wanita Bryant; m. Anthony John Waylonis, June 16, 1973; children: Anthony James, Ellen Claire. BS in child devel. and early childhood edn., Pa. State U., 1971—75; MA in early childhood spl. edn., George Wash. U., 1997—99. Postgraduate Professional License Va. Dept. of Edn., 2000. Pre-kindergarten tchr. Norfolk Pub. Schools, Norfolk, Va., 1976—78; dir. Subic Bay Naval Base Nursery Sch. Assn., Philippines, 1979—81; family adv. Family Advocacy Ctr., Subic Bay Naval Base, Philippines, 1981—82; multi-age inclusion tchr. FCPS - Belvedere Elem., Falls Church, Va., 1989—. Mentor Fairfax County Pub. Schools, Falls Ch., Va., 1992—99; trainer Project Realign, Washington, 1995—98; cons./trainer/presenter Collaborative Inclusion Project Team, Washington, 1992—99; presenter Fairfax County Pub. Schools, Fairfax, Va., 1992—. Composer: (song) Five Little Bunnies; contbr. article George Mason U. TAC Newsletter. Presenter Child Day Care Coun., Richmond, Va., 1997. Recipient Outstanding Leader award, Girl Scout Coun. Nation's Capital, 1996, Exceptional Inclusion Tchr., Va. Divsn. of Early Childhood, 1995; grant, Coun. for Exceptional Children, 1995. Mem.: AAUW (assoc.), NEA (assoc.), Nat. Assn. for Educators of Young Children (assoc.). Catholic. Avocations: sewing, travel. Home: 7201 Galgate Dr Springfield VA 22153 Office: FCPS - Belvedere Elementary School 6540 Columbia Pike Falls Church VA 22041 Personal E-mail: waylonis@erols.com. E-mail: jean.waylonis@fcps.edu.

WAYNE, ELSIE ELEANORE, Canadian parliament member; b. Shediac, N.B., Can., Apr. 20, 1932; d. Paxton Lee Fairweather and Ada (Catherine) Cook; m. Richard Seymour Wayne, July 4, 1968; children: Daniel Allan, Stephen Paxton. LLD (hon.), St. Thomas U., Fredericton, N.B., Can., 1988; D in Pub. Adminstrn. (hon.), Husson Coll.; LittD (hon.), U. N.B. Mem. St. John (N.B., Can.) Common Coun., 1977-83; mayor City of St. John, 1983-93; mem. parliament, 1993—. Commr. Atlantic Region, Citizen's Forum on Cans. Future, 1991; mem. Econ. Devel. Adv. Bd., Parliament Saint John, 1993-97, 97—; appointed dep. leader, nat. caucus chair, critic for veterans affairs, 1997—; bd. dirs. Market Sq. Corp. Chairwoman Red Shield Campaign Salvation Army, mem.; hon. chairwoman St. John Coun. Women, YMCA/YWCA Fund Raising Campaign, 1986, Big Bros./Big Sisters Campaign, 1987; hon. v.p. Canadian Red Cross; past mem. Exec. Com. Family Svcs, 2d Bn. Delancey's Brigade; past commr., ex-officio mem. St. John Transit Commn., planning adv. coun. City of St. John; mem. St. John Boys and Girls Club Endowment Fund; bd. dirs. St. John Non-Profit Housing, United Way Greater St. John, St. John Found., St. John Port and Devel. Commn., Youth Enterprise Ctr.; past bd. dirs. Gertrude Aarela Sheltered Workshop Physically Handicapped, Centracare Hosp.; bd. govs. U. N.B., Jr. Achievement; former dir. Gertrude Aarela Sheltered Workshop, St. John. Recipient Transportation of Yr. award, 1991, Cans. Literacy Vol. award, 1991, YM-YWCA Red Triangle award, 1992, Can. 125 Commemorative medal, 1992, Toastmasters Internat. Communicator Achievement award, The Orange Prize, 1993, Can. Achiever's award; named hon. gunner The Loyal Co., 1993, one of fifty most influential people in Atlantic Can. Atlantic Lifestyles Bus. Mag., 1993. Mem. Fedn. Canadian Mcpls. (nat. bd. dirs., mem. transp. com.), Cities of N.B. Assn. (past pres.), Carleton and York Regtl. Assn. (assoc., hon.), St. George's Soc. (hon.), Royal Canadian Legion (hon. local br.), Royal NB Rifle Assn., Inc. (hon. v.p.), Quota Club (hon. v.p.), Hon. Order of Ky. Colonels (hon. col.). Office: Ste 711 Justice Bldg House of Commons Ottawa ON Canada K1A 0A6 also: House of Commons Rm 466 W Block Ottawa ON Canada K1A 0A6

WAYNE, JEANETTE MARIE, auditor; b. Mt. Clemens, Mich., Apr. 17, 1965; d. Robert Thomas W. and Sharon Elaine (Mominee) Nole; m. Ronald Edward Klicki, Sept. 14, 1985 (div. Oct. 1989). Asst. mgr. Little Caesars, Mt. Clemens, Mich., 1981-83, Cheese & Co., Birmingham, Mich., 1984; courier Chevrolet, Detroit, 1984; libr. EDS Chevorlet, Detroit, 1985-86, migration specialist, 1987; software support EDS Saturn, Troy, 1988-89, ops tech, 1990-93; ops tech cons EDS Tech Architecture, Plano, Tex., 1993-2000; sr. auditor EDS Corp. Audit, Plano, Tex., 1997-2000, program mgr., 2000—. Program mgr. Bus. Process Leadership SAP Deployment. Republican. Office: EDS 5400 Legacy Dr Plano TX 75024-3199

WEARE, SALLY SPIEGEL, art educator, artist; b. Chgo., Dec. 11, 1942; d. Manuel and Janice (Gottlieb) Spiegel; m. Shane Weare, June 7, 1964; children: Tobias, Kate. BA, U. Iowa, 1964; postgrad., St. Martin's Sch. of Art, 1966-67; MFA in Painting, Mills Coll., 1977. Lectr. Calif. Coll. of Arts and Crafts, Oakland, 1979; vis. artist Art Inst. of Chgo.; instr. Vista Coll., Berkeley, 1980, 87-90, Ctr. for Exptl./Interdisciplinary Art San Francisco State U., 1979-84. Leader round table discussion U.S. Embassy, Belgrade, Serbia, 1996. Exhibited works in solo show at Chaos Gallery, Belgrade, Yugoslavia, 1996; group shows at Berkeley (Calif.) Art Ctr., Sonoma County Mus. Visual Art, Santa Rosa, Calif., 1997, 98. Mem. Women's Caucus for Art Coll. Art Assn., 1979-83; bd. dir. Women Environ. Artists Directory. Va. Ctr. for the Arts fellow, 1991, Millay Colony fellow, N.Y., 1992. Studio: 2663 Bennett Ridge Rd Santa Rosa CA 95404 E-mail: sallyweare@hotmail.com.

WEATHERFORD, SHARON DAVIS, music educator; b. Ozark, Ala., Oct. 31, 1953; d. James Leon and Jean Nelson Davis; m. Ron W. Weatherford, Apr. 29, 1983; 1 child, Tiffany Anne. MusB, Ga. So. U., 1975, MusM, 1978, M in mid. grades, 1980, Ednl. Specialist in mid. Grades, 1987, Ednl. Specialist in music, 1992, M in ednl. leadership, 2001. Cert. tchr. support sys. Ga. Dept. Edn., 2003. Tchr. Adrian (Ga.) Sch., 1975—83, David Emanuel Acad., Stillmore, Ga., 1975, Swainsboro (Ga.) HS, 1983—2003. Asst. band dir. Swainsboro HS, 1986—2003, choral dir., 1983—2003. Dir.:. Dir. Emanuel Arts Coun. Prod., Swainsboro, 1983—95; foster parent Dept. Family and Children's Svcs., Swainsboro, 1999—2002; presenter Ga. Dept. of Edn., Jekyll Island, Ga., 1995; active Hawhammock Bapt. Ch. Mem.: ASCD, Music Educators NC, Phi Beta Kappa. Baptist. Achievements include development of staff devel. unit, P.L.A.N., 1999. Avocations: needlecrafts, reading, fast pitch softball supporter, computer design. Home: 196 Forest Creek Dr Swainsboro GA 30401

WEATHERLY-MCWATERS, BARBARA CANNON, artist; b. Savannah, Ga., Mar. 27, 1927; d. John Respess and Irma Elizabeth (Murray) Cannon; m. William Earl Weatherly, Nov. 11, 1950 (dec. Jan. 1990); children: William Craig, Barbara Page; m. Roy McWaters, May 1, 1993. Student, U. Ga., 1946-48, High Mus. Sch. of Art, 1948-50, Continuing Art Edn. Workshops, 1960—. Mem. Gallery 209, Savannah, Ga., 1975, pres., 1986-87, 94-95. Scenery chief Cmty. Children's Theatre, Savannah, 1964-65; treas. Huntingdon Jr. Woman's Club, Savannah, 1964-65. Recipient First award Ga. Fedn. of Women's Clubs. Mem. DAR. Home: 929 N Hills Dr Dandridge TN 37725-4686

WEATHERSPOON, JACKIE K. state legislator; b. N.Y.C., Oct. 12, 1951; m. Russell D. Weatherspoon; 4 children. BS, SUNY, Brockport, 1973; MPA, Harvard U., 1991. Mem. N.H. Ho. of Reps. (dist. 20), Concord, 1996—; mem. election law com. N.H. Ho. of Reps., Concord, 1996—. UN observer, 1994—; sub. tchr., assoc. dean. Cellist Phillips Exeter Acad. Orch.; mem. Ch. Women United. Episcopalian. Office: NH State Legis State House Concord NH 03301

WEATHERSPOON, TERESA GAYE, professional basketball player; b. Jasper, Tex., Dec. 8, 1965; Grad., La. Tech. Inst., 1988. Guard Blusto, Italy, 1988—89, 1990—93, Magenta, Italy, 1989—90, Como, Italy, 1996—97, CSKA, Russia, 1993—95, WNBA - N.Y. Liberty, N.Y.C., 1997—2003, L.A. Sparks, 2004—. Named, NCAA Women's Basketball Team Decade, 1980, La. State Player of Yr., 1988, Kodak All-Am., 1987, 1988, WNBA defensive player of yr., 1997, 1998, WNBA All-Star, 1999—2002; named to All-WNBA 2nd team, 1997—2000; recipient Gold medals, World Championship, 1986, Goodwill Games, 1986, World Univ. Games, 1987, Broderick Cup, Wade Trophy. Achievements include first player in WNBA history to record 1,000 career assists. Office: c/o Los Angeles Sparks 555 N Nash St El Segundo CA 90245

WEATHERUP, WENDY GAINES, graphic designer, writer; b. Oct. 20, 1952; d. William Hughes and Janet Ruth (Neptune) Gaines; m. Roy Garfield Weatherup, Sept. 10, 1977; children: Jennifer, Christine. BA, U. So. Calif., 1974. Lic. ins. agt. Freelance graphic designer, desktop pub., Northridge, Calif. Mem. NAFE, U. So. Calif. Alumni Assn., Alpha Gamma Delta. Republican. Methodist. Avocations: photography, travel, writing novels, computers. Home: 17260 Rayen St Northridge CA 91325-2919 E-mail: weatherw@aol.com.

WEAVER, BARBARA FRANCES, librarian, consultant; b. Boston, Aug. 29, 1927; d. Leo Francis and Nina Margaret (Durham) Weisse; m. George B. Weaver, June 6, 1951; 1 dau., Valerie S. Clark. BA, Radcliffe Coll., 1949; MLS., U. R.I., 1968; EdM, Boston U., 1978. Head libr. Thompson (Conn.) Pub. Libr., 1961-69; dir. Conn. State Libr. Svc. Ctr., Willimantic, 1969-72; regional adminstr. Cen. Mass. Regional Libr. System, Worcester, 1972-78; asst. commr. of edn., state libr. State of N.J., Trenton, 1978-91; dir. R.I. Dept. State Libr. Svcs., Providence, 1991-96; chief info. officer State of RI, 1996—2001; govt. cons. in tech. mgmt., orgnl. devel. and libr. adminstrn., 2001—. Lectr. Simmons Coll., Boston, 1976-78 Mem. Conn. Libr. Assn. E-mail: barbaraw829@charter.net.

WEAVER, BARBARA HORNING, social worker; b. Blue Ball, Pa., Oct. 6, 1942; d. Titus Horst Horning and Grace Herr Nissly; m. Paul E. Weaver, June 6, 1964 (div. Mar. 1986); children: Ann, Leigh, Zachary. BS, Lebanon Valley coll., 1983; MA in bilingual studies, LaSalle U., 1987; MSW, U. Denver, 1990. Social worker Bur. of Children's Svcs., Lancaster, Pa., 1983—88; marriage family therapist pvt. practice, Denver, 1990—92; probation off. 20th Jud. Dist., State of Colo., 1991—; lic. clin. social worker State Bd of Examiners, Colo., 1991—; drug alcohol evaluator 20th Jud. Dist., State of Colo., Boulder, 1991—93; social worker Chinese Children Adoption Internat., Denver, 1993—; exe. dir. Adoption Journey, Longmont, Colo., 2001—. Juvenile placement review Bolder County Adv. Bd., Longmont, 1994—96. Scholar, Rotary Internat., Bangladesh, 1997—98. Mem.: Nat. Assoc. Social Workers. Avocations: internat. travel, cultural themes, languages. Home: 5612 N 71st St Longmont CO 80503 Office: Adoption Journey 5612 No 71st St Longmont CO 80503 E-mail: ajourney2001@aol.com.

WEAVER, CONSTANCE, communications executive; Various mgmt. positions in product mgmt., mktg. and corp. planning McGraw Hill; exec. dir. unit Bus. Week; leadership positions with responsibility for investor rels. and fin. comms. Microsoft Corp., MCI Comms.; v.p. investor rels. AT&T Corp., Bedminster, NJ, 1996—2002, exec. v.p. pub. rels., mktg. comms. and brand, 2002—. Bd. dirs. Applied Digital Solutions, Inc.; former dir. PrimarkCorp. Bd. dirs. Somerset Hills YMCA, N.J. Performing Arts Ctr. Mem.: Nat. Investor Rels. Inst. (former dir.), NJ300, Fin. Women's Assn., Arthur W. Page Soc., The Wisemen. Office: AT&T Corp 1 AT&T Way Bedminster NJ 07921*

WEAVER, DIANE CELESTE, music educator; b. Peoria, Ill., May 31, 1947; d. Harlan Richard and Frances Lucille Berger; m. Roger William Weaver, June 19, 1977; children: Noah Star, Benjamin Brooks, David Morgan. BA, Lawrence U., Appleton, Wis., 1969. Cert. tchr. Wash., 1989. French tchr. Crystal Falls Sch. Dist., Mich., 1969—70; builder-owner-mgr. Mountain Song Restaurant, Marblemount, Wash., 1974—86; substitute tchr. Darrington Sch. Dist., Wash., 1979—98; music specialist Sedro-Woolley Sch. Dist., Wash., 1989—; creator and dir. Sedro-Woolley Youth Orch., Wash., 1999—. Musician (concertmistress) Skagit Valley Symphony Orch. Many positions, including dist. tng. chmn. Boy Scouts of Am., Skagit Valley, Wash., 1987—97; elder Mt. Baker Presbyn. Ch., Concrete, Wash., 1995—98; mem. and bd. mem. Marblemount Presch., Wash., 1980—90. Named Scouting Family of the Yr., Boy Scouts of Am., 1995; recipient Dist. Award of Merit, 1994, nominee for profl. exch. to South Africa, People to People Ambs., 2003. Mem.: Music Educators Nat. Conf., Am. String Tchrs. Assn., Nat. Kodaly Educators Assn., Wash. Edn. Assn. Protestant. Avocations: being a loving mom to 3 sons who are valedictorians and eagle scouts, French, travel, reading, hosting exchange students. Home: 1216 Independence Blvd Sedro-Woolley WA 98284 Office: Sedro-Woolley Schl Dist 801 Trail Rd Sedro-Woolley WA 98284 Office Phone: 360-855-3500. Personal E-mail: weaver@sos.net.

WEAVER, DIANNE JAY, lawyer; b. Kansas City, Mo., June 28, 1944; d. Thomas G. and Anna Jeanette Jay; m. Benjamin J. Weaver, Sept. 16, 1970; children: Jay, Jennifer, Scott, Elizabeth. BS, U. Kans., 1965; JD, Ind. U., 1970. Bar: Ind., Fla., Colo.; bd. cert. trial lawyer. Former ptnr. Weaver & Weaver, P.A., Ft. Lauderdale, Fla.; former of counsel Krupnick Campbell Malone Roselli Buser Slama & Hancock P.A., Ft. Lauderdale; ptnr. Harrell & Johnson, P.A., Jacksonville, 2002—. Speaker in field. Contbr. articles to profl. jours. Trustee Civil Justice Found.; bd. dirs. Trial Lawyers for Pub. Justice; chmn. publicity com. Civil Justice Found. Fellow Roscoe Pound Found. (life); mem. ATLA (bd. govs., sec.), Acad. Fla. Trial Lawyers (bd. dirs.), So. Trial Lawyers Assn. (bd. govs.), Fla. Bar Assn. (chair trial advocacy com.),. Fed. Bar Assn., Broward County Women Lawyers Assn. (founding pres.). Office: Harrell & Johnson PA 4735 Sunbeam Rd Jacksonville FL 32257*

WEAVER, DONNA L. engraver; Grad. in Fine Arts, Art Acad. Cin., 1966. Sculptor Kenner Toys, 1966—80; sculptor, engraver US Mint, 2000—. Avocation: bas-relief. Office: 801 9th St NW Washington DC 20220

WEAVER, DONNA RAE, company executive; b. Chgo., Oct. 15, 1945; d. Albert Louis and Gloria Elaine (Graffis) Florence; m. Clifford L. Weaver, Aug. 20, 1966; 1 child, Megan Rae. BS in Edn., No. Ill. U., 1966, EdD, 1977; MEd, De Paul U., 1974. Tchr. H.L. Richards High Sch., Oak Lawn, Ill., 1966-71, Sawyer Coll. Bus., Evanston, Ill., 1971-72; asst. prof. Oakton Community Coll., Morton Grove, Ill., 1972-75; vis. prof. U. Ill., Chgo., 1977-78; dir. devel. Mallinckrodt Coll., Wilmette, Ill., 1978-80, dean, 1980-83; campus dir. Nat.-Louis U., Chgo., 1983-90, dean div. applied behavioral scis., 1985-89; dean Coll. Mgmt. and Bus., 1989-90; pres. The Oliver Group, Inc., Kenilworth, Ill., 1993-97; mng. ptnr. Le Miccine, Gaiole-in-Chianti, Tuscany, Italy, 1996—. Cons. Nancy Lovely and Assocs., Wilmette, 1981-84, North Ctrl. Assn., Chgo., 1982-90. Contbr. articles to Am. Vocat. Jour., Ill. Bus. Edn. Assn. Monograph, Nat. Coll. Edn.'s ABS Rev., Nat. View. Mem. Ill. Quality of Work Life Coun., 1987-90, New Trier Twp. Health and Human Svcs. Adv. Bd., Winnetka, Ill., 1985-88; bd. dirs. Open Lands Project, 1985-87, Kenilworth (Ill.) Village House, 1986-87. Recipient Achievement award Women in Mgmt., 1981; Am. Bd. Master Educators charter disting. fellow, 1986. Mem. Nat. Bus. Edn. Assn., Delta Pi Epsilon (past pres.). Avocations: reading, traveling, decorating. Office: 505 N Lake Shore Dr Apt 4010 Chicago IL 60611-3619 Address: Azienda Agricola Le Miccine S Traversa Chiantigiana 53013 Gaiole in Chianti Italy

WEAVER, ELIZABETH A. state supreme court justice; b. New Orleans; d. Louis and Mary Weaver. BA, Newcomb Coll.; JD, Tulane U. Elem. tchr. Glen Lake Cmty. Sch., Maple City, Mich.; French tchr. Leelanau Sch., Glen Arbor, Mich.; pvt. practice Glen Arbor, Mich.; law clk. Civil Dist. Ct., New Orleans; atty. Coleman, Dutrey & Thomson, New Orleans; atty., title specialist Chevron Oil Co., New Orleans; probate and juvenile judge Leelanau County, Mich., 1975—86; judge Mich. Ct. of Appeals, 1987—94; justice Mich. Supreme Ct., Lansing, 1995—. Chief justice Mich. Supreme Ct., 1999—2000; instr. edn. dept. Ctr. Mich. U.; mem. Mich. Com. on Juvenile Justice, Nat. Conv. State Adv. Groups on Juvenile Justice for U.S.; chair Gov.'s Task Force on Children's Justice, Trial Ct. Assessment Commn., Office Juvenile Justice and Delinquency Prevention; jud. adv. bd. mem. Law and Orgnl. Econs. Ctr. U. Kans.; treas. Children's Charter of Cts. of Mich. Chairperson Western Mich. U. CLE Adv. Bd.; mem. steering com. Grand Traverse/Leelanau Commn. on Youth; mem. Glen Arbor Twp. Zoning Bd.; mem. charter arts north Leelanau County; mem. citizen's adv. coun. Arnell Engstrom Children's Ctr.; mem. cmty. adv. com. Pathfinder Sch. Treaty Law Demonstration Project; active Grand Traverse/Leelanau Mental Health Found. Named Jurist of Yr., Police Officers Assn. of Mich.; named one of five Outstanding Young Women in Mich., Mich. Jaycees; recipient Eastern award, Warren Easton Hall of Fame, Lifetime Dedication to Children award, Mich. Champions in Childhood Injury Prevention, 2000, Recognition award for outstanding svc. to Mich. children and families, Gov. Engler and Family Independence Agy., 2000, Profls. award, Mich. Assn. Drug Cts., 2002, Mary S. Coleman award, Ctr. for Civic Edn. Through Law, 2002. Fellow: Mich. State Bar Found.; mem.: ABA, Antrim County Bar Assn., Leelanau County Bar Assn., Grand Traverse County Bar Assn., La. Bar Assn., Nat. Coun. Juvenile and Family Judges, Mich. Bar Assn. (chair CLE adv. bd., chair crime prevention ctr., chair juvenile law com.), Delta Kappa Gamma (hon.). Office: Mich Supreme Ct 3300 Grandview Plz 10850 E Traverse Hwy Traverse City MI 49684-1364

WEAVER, F. LOUISE BEAZLEY, curator, director; b. Jacksonville, Fla., Apr. 26, 1953; d. Donald William Beazley and Frances Ann Weaver; 1 child, Elizabeth. BA in Humanities, Am. Coll. Switzerland, 1975; BA in Art History, U. Ariz., 1979; MA in Art History, U. Va., 1982. Co-curator Nat. Mus. Am. Art, Washington, 1983—84; assoc. dir. Konglomerati Book Art, St. Petersburg, Fla., 1985—86; dir., curator Derby Lane, St. Petersburg, 1991—. Comnr. Pub. Arts for the City, St. Petersburg, 1994—2001; adv. bd. Fla. Gulf Coast Art Mus., Largo, Fla., 1997—2001. Contbr. articles Greyhound Review, 2001—02. Mem. bd. Fla. Orch. Symphony, Tampa, Fla., 2000—. Mem.: Soc. Am. Archivists, Am. Assn. Mus. Office: Derby Lane 10490 Gandy Blvd Saint Petersburg FL 33702 E-mail: history@derbylane.com.

WEAVER, JACQUELYN KUNKEL IVEY, artist, educator; b. Richmond, Ky., Mar. 14, 1931; d. Marion David and Margaret Tabitha (Brandenburg) Kunkel; m. George Thomas IveySr., 1951 (dec. 1989); children: George Thomas Ivey Jr., David Richard Ivey; m. Harrell Fuller Weaver, 1991. BFA, Wesleyan Coll., 1987. Owner J. K. Ivey Art, Macon, Ga., 1974-91, J.K. Ivey Bookkeeping and Tax Svc., Macon, Ga., 1976-84, Ivey-Weaver Art Studio, Macon, 1991—. Tchr. drawing, painting and sculpture, 1991—. Exhibitions include Mid. Ga. Art Assn. Gallery, Macon, 1980—, Mus. Arts and Scis., 1987, 1991, 1994, 1996, 1998, 2002, Attaway Cottage, 1990—, AAPL Salmugundi Club, N.Y.C., 1992, Frames and Art Gallery, Macon, 1995—, CLWAC Nat. Arts Club, NYC, 1995, Stofko-Dixon Fine Arts, Bolingbroke, Ga., 1996—2001, Hilton Head Island (SC) Art League, Self Family Art Ctr., 1997, 2001, Christopher Gallery, Cohasset, Mass., 1997—98, Parthenon Centennial Park, Nashville, 1998, Lowndes/Valdosta Cult. Arts Ctr., Valdosta, Ga., 1992, 1994, 1998, Brazier Art Gallery, Richmond, Va., 2002, Gallery 51, Forsyth, Ga., 2003, 2004, Roundtree Gallery, Seaside, Fla., 2003—04. Bd. dirs., treas. Mid. Ga. Art Assn., Macon, 1981-84, 92, publicity chmn., 1988-89, chmn. nominating com., 1997, mem. fin. com., 1998-99, audit com., 1998. Mem.: Hilton Head Island Art League, Oil Painters of Am., Portrait Painters Am., Inc., Mid. Ga. Art Assn., Catherine Lorillard Wolf Art Club, Mus. Arts and Scis., Wesleyan Coll. Alumnae Assn., Nat. Mus. Women in Arts (charter). Presbyterian. Avocations: ballroom dancing, reading, walking, music. Office: Ivey-Weaver Art Studio 6183 Hwy 87 Macon GA 31210 Fax: 478-744-0983. Office Phone: 478-477-1385. E-mail: jweave550@bellsouth.net.

WEAVER, JANET S. newspaper editor; m. Mark Weaver; children: Sam, Rachel. Grad., U. Mo., 1984. Reporter, asst. city editor Stuart (Fla.) News, 1986—89; from reporter to dep. mng. editor/features and sports Virginian-Pilot, Norfolk, Va., 1989—94; mng. editor The Wichita (Kans.) Eagle, 1994—97, Sarasota (Fla.) Herald-Tribune, 1997—99, exed. editor, 1999—2003; dean faculty Poynter Inst., St. Petersburg, Fla., 2003—. Mem.: Am. Soc. Newspaper Editors (bd. dirs.). Office: The Poynter Institute 801 Third Street South Saint Petersburg FL 33701*

WEAVER, JENNEFER JEAN, musician, educator; b. Greenville, Sc, Feb. 27, 1959; d. James Neville Jean and Ensign Joy Wilson; m. Keith Lamar Weaver, Sept. 17, 1983; children: Joshua, Jeremiah, Josiah, James, Jerusha, Joy. BS, James Madison U., Harrisonburg, VA, 1982. Dental asst. Dr. Owen Graves, Harrisonburg, Va., 1982—86; piano accompanist JMU, Harrisonburg, Va., 1999—; piano instr. Harrisonburg, Va., 1987—. Pres. Piano Teachers Forum, Harrisonburg, Va., 1999—2000, vice-president, 1997—99, reception coord., 2000—. Membership chmn. Alpha Gamma Delta, Harrisonburg, Va., 1978—79, ho. mgr., 1979—80, rush chmn., 1980—81. Fellow Gamma Gamma Greek Honor Soc., JMU Panhellenic Coun., 1982. Mem.: NGPT, VMTA, MTNA. R-Consevative. Presbyterian. Avocations: soccer mom, band booster, choral booster, choir accompanist, pta member. Home: 276 Franklin Street Harrisonburg VA 22801 Office: Piano Studio of Jennefer Weaver 276 Franklin Street Harrisonburg VA 22801 Personal E-mail: jenneweaver@msn.com.

WEAVER, JOYCE R. hypnotherapist; b. Mineola, N.Y., Aug. 11, 1938; d. Samuel H. and Anne (Feinberg) Rosnel; m. Paul G. Weaver, June 5, 1960; children: Caryn L. Weaver Sutherland, Greg G. BA, SUNY, Albany, 1960, MA, 1965; MS, L.I. Univ., 1978; PhD, LaSalle U., 1995. Cert. secondary educator, N.Y.; advanced clin. hypnotherapy instr.; ordained min. spiritual healing Loving Touch Ctr., 1992. Tchr. English Washingtonville (N.Y.) Pub. Schs., 1960-61, Valley Ctrl. Pub. Schs., Montgomery, N.Y., 1961-63; hotline coord. Town of Islip (N.Y.) Drug & Alcohol Counseling Ctr., 1973-78; sr. counselor Smithhaven Ministries Seabury Barn, Stony Brook, N.Y., 1979; adminstr. I Suffolk County Dept. Social Svcs., Hauppauge, N.Y., 1980-91; pvt. practice hypnotherapy Tranquility, East Islip, N.Y., 1991—. Workshop leader Assn. for Past-Life Rsch. & Therapies, Riverside, Calif., 1995-98; spkr. in field. Pres. Islip Dist. PTA, 1971-72; bd. dirs. Great South Bay YMCA, Bay Shore, N.Y., 1974-76; chaplain's asst. Southside Hosp., Bay Shore, 1977-80; clk. of ministry & counsel, Conscience Bay Friends Monthly Mtg., Rel. Soc. of Friends (Quaker) 1999—, co-clk. mtg., 2002—. Mem. Nat. Guild Hypnotists (trainer 1993—), Kappa Delta. Avocations: genealogy, needlework, walking, hiking. Office: Tranquility PO Box 14 East Islip NY 11730-0014

WEAVER, KITRA K. sales and marketing executive; b. Tawas City, Mich., Apr. 12, 1957; d. James Elmer Jr. and Glenda Kay (Ray) Weaver; m. Mark William Goldstein, Apr. 20, 1985 (div. Mar. 1989). Grad. h.s., Houston, 1975. Contract sales rep. Gen. Office Outfitters, Dallas, 1982-85; v.p. Money Saver Advertiser, Dallas, 1985-88; dir. mktg. One Hour Motophoto, Dallas, 1985-88; br. mgr. Meta Gram Am., Dallas, 1988-90; sales rep. Rollins Protective Svc., Atlanta, 1990-92; regional sales mgr. The Marlin Co., North Haven, Conn., 1992—. Mentor The Marlin Co., Orlando, Fla., 1993-98. Chair ticket com. SOS/Taste of the Nation, Orlando, 1991-2000; chair ticket sales UCP.Ctrl. Fla. Chili Cookoff, Orlando, 1990-93; co-founder Bus. Womens Network, 2000—. Republican. Methodist. Avocations: cooking, reading, sports, fundraising, the arts. Office: The Marlin Co 100 Kenna Dr North Haven CT 06473-2516

WEAVER, KITTY DUNLAP, author; b. Frankfort, Ky., Sept. 24, 1910; d. Arch Robertson and Rebecca (Johnson) Dunlap; m. Henry Byrne Weaver, June 29, 1933. Student, Sorbonne, Paris, summer 1930; AB, William and Mary Coll., 1932; MA, George Washington U., 1933; BS, U. Md., 1947; postgrad., Georgetown U., U. Pa., George Washington U., 1964-67, Moscow U., 1983; studied with Alfred Adler, Vienna, 1932. Jr. H.S. tchr., 1931-32; poultry farmer, 1947-55; author, 1970—. Author: Lenin's Grandchildren, 1971, Russia's Future, 1981, Bushels of Rubles, 1992. Mem. Sulgrave (Washington) Club, Aldie Hort. Soc., Chevy Chase (Md.) Club, Met. Club (Washington), Garden Club Am., Fauquier Loudoun Garden Club. Home: 40820 John Mosby Hwy Aldie VA 20105-2820

WEAVER, LAURA FISHER, financial planner; b. Memphis, Tenn., July 25, 1969; d. Landon C. and Nettie Jean Fisher; m. Thomas J. Weaver III, June 8, 1991; 1 child, Hannah Nöel. AA in Bus., Itawamba C.C., Tupelo, Miss., 1994; postgrad., U. Miss. Cert. office adminstr. V.p. Washington Mut. Bank, Tupelo, 1995—2002; fin. planner Am. Internat. Group, Inc., Tupelo, 2003—. Coord. Am. Cultural Exch. Svc., Inc., Seattle, 2003—; notary pub. State of Miss., 1995—. Author: Whisper, 2001; author: (essay) A Bridge Between Two Worlds, 2001, Daddy's Girl, 2001. Chair, pres. Tupelo Police Wives Aux., Inc., 1993—95. Mem.: Mystery Writers Am. Republican. Baptist. Avocations: ceramics, writing, reading, singing, interior decorating. Home: PO Box 2672 Tupelo MS 38803 Office: Am Internat Group Inc Am Gen 1600 N Gloster Tupelo MS 38804*

WEAVER, LYN ANN SIMMONS, psychologist; b. Harrisonburg, Va., Oct. 27, 1944; d. Sidney Linwood and Annye Mae Simmons; m. Norris Elwood Weaver, May 27, 1967; 1 child, Tonya Lyn Bowers. BS, James Madison U., 1967, MS, 1973; EdD, U. Va., 1986. Lic. psychologist, sch. psychologist. Psychologist Woodrow Wilson Rehab. Ctr., Fisherville, Va., 1973-74; asst. to supt. Highland County Schs., Monterey, Va., 1974-81; owner NorLyn Enterprises, Dayton, Va., 1983-89; psychologist Mecklenburg County Schs., Boydton, Va., 1989-90, asst. prin. high sch., 1990-92; instr. psychology Southeastern C.C., Whiteville, N.C., 1992; psychologist Columbus County Schs., Whiteville, N.C., 1992-99, Brunswick County Schs., Bolivia, N.C., 1999—, pvt. practice, Chadbourn, N.C., 1993-99, Ocean Isle, N.C., 1999—. Psychologist, mgmt. First Mental Health EPA's, HMO, N.C., 1996—; psychologist Dept. Human Resources, Raleigh, N.C., 1999. Author: The Virginia Principal, 1990. Mem. ERA Summit, N.C. Equity, Women's Activist. Mem. AAUW, APA, N.C. Sch. Psychologist Assn., Bus. and Profl. Women (com. mem. 1999—, pres. 2000-01). Avocations: reading, travel, music. Office: Mgmt Solutions PO Box 6275 Shallotte NC 28470-6275 E-mail: lynw@2khiway.net.

WEAVER, MOLLIE LITTLE, lawyer; b. Alma, Ga., Mar. 11; d. Alfred Ross and Annis Mae (Bowles) Little; m. Jack Delano Nelson, Sept. 12, 1953 (div. May 1970); 1 dau., Cynthia Ann; m. 2d, Hobart Ayres Weaver, June 10, 1970; stepchildren: Hobart Jr., Mary Essa, Robert. BA in History, U. Richmond, 1978; JD, Wake Forest U., 1981. Bar: N.C. 1982, Fla. 1983; Cert. profl. sec.; cert. adminstrv. mgr. Supr., Western Electric Co., Richmond, Va., 1952-75; cons., owner Cert. Mgmt. Assocs., Richmond, 1975-76; sole practice, Ft. Lauderdale, Fla., 1982-86, Emerald Isle, N.C., 1986-89, Richmond, 1989—. Author: Secretary's Reference Manual, 1973. Mem. adv. coun. to Bus. and Office Edn., Greensboro, N.C., 1970-73, adv. com. to bus. edn. Va. Commonwealth U., Richmond, 1977. Recipient Key to City of Winston-Salem, N.C., 1963; Epps award for scholarship, 1978. Mem. ABA, N.C. Bar Assn., Fla. Bar Assn., Word Processing Assn. (v.p., founder Richmond 1973-75), Adminstrv. Mgmt. Soc. (com. chmn. Richmond, 1973-75), Phi Beta Kappa, Eta Sigma Phi, Phi Alpha Theta. Republican. E-mail: legal311@aol.com. Home: 12301 Renwick Pl Glen Allen VA 23059-6959

WEAVER, PAMELA ANN, hospitality research professional; b. Little Falls, N.Y., July 7, 1947; d. Floyd Aron Weaver and Norma May (Putnam) Hoyer; m. Ken Ward McCleary, Mar. 2, 1947; children: Brian Wilson, Blake McCleary, Ryan McCleary. AA, Fulton Montgomery C.C., Amsterdam, NY, 1968; BA, SUNY, 1970; MA, U. South Fla., 1973; PhD, Mich. State U., East Lansing, 1978. Mem. math. dept. Riviera Jr. H.S., Miami, Fla., 1970-72; grad. asst. Office Med., Edn. R & D Mich. State U., East Lansing, 1973-74, grad. asst. dept. mktg., 1974-75, instr. mktg.; asst. prof. mktg., hospitality svcs. adminstrn. Ctrl. Mich. State U., Mt. Pleasant, 1978-79, 1982-86, chair acad. senate, 1985-86, prof. mktg., hospitality svcs. adminstrn., 1986-89; prof. dept. hospitality and tourism mgmt. Va. Poly. Inst. and State U., Blacksburg, 1989—. Contbr. over 100 articles to profl. jours. Mem. Coun. on Hotel, Restaurant and Instl. Edn. (John Wiley & Sons, Inc. award for Litetime Achievement to Hospitality Industry 1994). Office: Va Poly Inst and State U Wallace Hall Blacksburg VA 24061-0429 E-mail: weaver@vt.edu.

WEAVER, PEGGY (MARGUERITE MCKINNIE WEAVER), plantation owner; b. Jackson, Tenn., June 7, 1925; d. Franklin Allen and Mary Alice (Caradine) McKinnie; children: Elizabeth Lynn, Thomas Jackson III, Franklin A. McKinnie. Student, U. Colo., 1943-45, Am. Acad. Dramatic Arts, 1945-46, S. Meisner's Profl. Classes, 1949, Oxford U., 1990, 91. Actress, 1946-52; mem. staff Mus. Modern Art, N.Y.C., 1949-50; woman's editor radio sta. WTJS-AM-FM, Jackson, Tenn., 1952-55; editor, radio/TV Jackson Sun Newspaper, 1952-55; columnist Bolivar (Tenn.) Bulletin-Times, 1986—2000; chmn. Ho. of Reps. of Old Line Dist., Hardeman County, Tenn., 1985-91, 94-97. Pres. Hardeman County chpt. Assn. Preservation of Tenn. Antiquities, 1991—95; charter mem. adv. bd. Tenn. Arts Commn., Nashville, 1967—74, Tenn. Performing Arts Ctr., Nashville, 1972—; chmn. trustees br. Tenn. Libr. Assn., Nashville, 1973—74; Henry County regional chmn. Opera Memphis, 1979—91; mem. nat. coun. Met. Opera, N.Y.C., 1980—92, Tenn. Bicentennial Com., Hardeman County, 1993—96; bd. sec. Memphis Brooks Mus. League, 1997—98; founder Paris-Henry County (Tenn.) Arts Coun., 1965. Mem. DAR, Nat. Soc. Colonial Dames Am. (chmn. Memphis Town com. 2002-), Oxford Alumni Assn. N.Y., English Speaking Union (London chpt.), Crescent Club, Summit Dilettantes. Methodist. Avocations: horseback riding, travel, theatre. Office: 402 Heritage Plantation Hickory Valley TN 38042 Office Phone: 731-764-6009.

WEAVER, SIGOURNEY (SUSAN ALEXANDRA WEAVER), actress; b. N.Y.C., Oct. 8, 1949; d. Sylvester (Pat) Weaver and Elizabeth Inglish; m. James Simpson, 1984; 1 child, Charlotte. BA in English, Stanford U., 1971; MA in Drama, Yale U., 1974. Actress: (theatre): The Constant Wife, 1974, The Merchant of Venice, 1986, The Guys, 2002, The Mercy Seat, 2002; co-writer, actress (theater) Radio Days, 1979; films include: Annie Hall, 1977, Madman, 1978, Alien, 1979, Eyewitness, 1981, The Year of Living Dangerously, 1982, Deal of the Century, 1983, Ghostbusters, 1984, Une femme ou deux, 1985, Aliens, 1986 (Acad. award nomination for best actress), Half Moon Street, 1986, Working Girl, 1988 (Golden Globe Best Supporting Actress 1989), Gorillas in the Mist, 1988 (Golden Globe award 1989), Ghostbusters II, 1989, 1492: Conquest of Paradise, 1992, Dave, 1993, Death and the Maiden, 1994, Jeffrey, 1995, Copycat, 1995, Snow White: A Tale of Terror, 1997, The Ice Storm, 1997 (BAFTA Film award 1998), A Map of the World, 1999, Galaxy Quest, 1999, Airframe, 1999, Company Man, 2000, Speak Truth to Power, 2000, Heartbreakers, 2001, (voice) Big Bad Love, 2001, Tadpole, 2002, The Guys, 2002, Holes, 2003; co-prodr., actress: (films) Alien 3, 1992, Alien: Resurrection, 1997; actress: (TV series) Somerset, 1970-76, (TV miniseries) The Best of Families, 1977, (TV movies) 3 by Cheever: The Sorrows of Gin, 1979, 3 by Cheever: O Youth and Beauty!, 1979. Recipient Lifetime Achievement award, Chicago Internat. Film Festival, 2001. Achievements include speaks fluent French and German. Office: ICM 8942 Wilshire Blvd Beverly Hills CA 90211-1934*

WEAVER, VICTORIA ANN, nursing researcher; b. Bethlehem, Pa., Oct. 5, 1955; d. Earl Elton Weaver and Helen Etta Mae Zlomsowitch. BSN, U. Kans., 1991, MSN, 1995. RN Pa., cert. enterostomal therapy nurse, clin. rsch. assoc. Home health enterostomal therapy nurse Clinicare Family Health Svcs., Kansas City, Kans., 1982—86; enterostomal therapy nurse, cert. nurse specialist U. Kans. Med. Ctr., Kansas City, 1986—97; med. info. specialist Convatec, Skillman, NJ, 1997—2000, sr. clin. rsch. assoc., 2000—. Regional and nat. youth rally leadership WOCN, Cin., 1986—2003; med. chmn. Nat. United Ostomy Assn., Irvine, Calif., 2003—. Contbr. chapters to books, articles to profl. jours. Named Enterostoma Therapy Nurse of Yr., Kans, Mo., Iowa, Nebr., Ill., 1988. Mem.: Wound Ostomy Continence Nursing Soc., Assn. Clin. Rsch. Profls.

WEAVER-STROH, JOANNE MATEER, education educator, consultant; b. May 21, 1930; d. Kenneth Hall and Jean (Weakley) Mateer; children: Karen, Mark, Laurie. BS in Edn., U. Pa., 1952, elem. and secondary prin. cert., 1979; MS in Psychology Reading, Temple U., 1968. Tchr. Paoli (Pa.) Sch., 1952-53, Somerville Sch., Ridgewood, N.J., 1953-55, Bryn Mawr (Pa.) Sch., 1955-57, Erdenheim Sch., Springfield, Pa., 1957-58; reading specialist Abington (Pa.) Sch. Dist., 1966-67, curriculum specialist, 1967-73, coord. human rels. programs, 1973-80; prin. Rydal Elem. Sch., Abington, 1980-88, Willow Hill Elem. Sch., 1988-96; ret., 1996. Cons., tchr. Marywood Coll., Scranton, Pa., 1972—; coord. drug and alcohol abuse program Abington Sch. Dist., 1989-96; cons. Conflict Resolution, 1996—. Chmn. Abington Human Rels. Adv. Coun., 1973-88; chmn. Cmty. Rels. Com. Abington Twp., 1978—; mem. Ea. Montgomery County Human Rels. Adv. Coun., 1981-83; chmn. No Place for Hate project Abington Twp., 2003-; mediator Abington Twp.; leader Stephen Ministry program Abington Presbyn. Ch. Named Citizen of the Week Times Chronicle Newspaper, 1976; recipient award Four Chaplains Temple U., 1979, Disting. Citizens award Roslyn Jr. C. of C., 1981, Citizens for Progress Humanitarian award, 1982, Cmty. award Abington YMCA, 1987, Dr. Martin Luther King Jr. award Abington Twp., 1989, East Montgomery County/Pa. State Human Rels. Interfaith award, 2000, Citizens That Care award, Abington Cmty. Taskforce award, 2003, Disting. Cmty. Svc. award Intersvc. Clubs of Glenside, 2003. Mem. ASCD, NASEP, Internat. Coop. Learning Assn., Pa. Assn. Elem. Prins., Phi Delta Kappa, Delta Kappa Gamma. Republican. Home: 109 Durham Ct Maple Glen PA 19002-2854 E-mail: rwstroh@att.net.

WEBB, CAROL E, school system administrator; b. Ottawa, Kans., July 14, 1947; d. Laura Jean Floyd and John Richard Baker; m. Marvin C Webb, July 27, 1969; children: Brian Justin, Karen Emily. BS in edn., Emporia State U., 1965—68, MS, 1968—71; PhD, The U. of Iowa, 1991—2003. Permanent Professional Teaching License Dept. of Edn./Iowa, 1979. Classroom tchr. Coun. Grove Unified Sch. Dist., Kans., 1968—70, Osage City Unified Sch. Dist., Kans., 1970—72; dir. Mobile Meals of Topeka, Inc., 1972—74; instr. in elem. edn. Ill. State U. Tchr. Edn. Ctr., 1978—79; elem. tchr. Davenport Cmty. Sch. Dist., 1980—88, reading specialist, 1989—93, coord. for learning and curriculum, 1993—2000; asst. supt. Bettendorf Cmty. Sch. Dist., Iowa, 2000—. Mem.: Nat. Staff Devel. Coun., Sch. Administrators of Iowa, Pi Lambda Theta (chpt. pres. 1989—90), Nat. Coun. for the Social Studies, Iowa Coun. for the Social Studies (exec. coun. regional treas. 1997—99), Internat. Reading Assn., Assn. for Supervision and Curriculum Develoopment, Iowa Reading Assn. (state treas. 1997—2002, president-elect 2004 2002—). United Methodist. Avocations: reading, researching, teaching. Office: Bettendorf Community School District 3311 Central Ave Bettendorf IA 52722

WEBB, DONNA LOUISE, academic director, educator; b. Yakima, Wash., Aug. 12, 1929; d. Manuel Lawrence and Rena May (Sewell) Matson; (div.); children: Marlene Park, Ed Webb III. AA in Vocat. Edn., Portland (Oreg.) Community Coll., 1976; BA in Psychology, Warner Pacific Coll., 1980; MEd in Career and Vocat. Edn., Oreg. State U., Corvallis, 1980, EdD in Career and Vocat. Edn., 1983. Dir. placement Andrews U., Mich., 1969-74, dir. career edn. and coop. work experience Portland, 1976-78; coord. youth program Fed. Experiment/Chronically Unemployed Youth, Vancouver, Wash., 1979; dir. career counseling Clark Coll., Vancouver, 1979; tchr. coop. edn. project Multnomah County ESD, Portland, 1981; pvt. practice counselor Portland, 1982-84; dir. career devel. & coop. edn. Walla Walla (Wash.) Coll., 1984-87; assoc. dir. Ctr. for Lifelong Learning Loma Linda (Calif.) U., 1987-91; corp. trainer Pacific Inst., Seattle, 1991-94, account mgr. consulting and rsch., 1994—. Home decorator Frederick & Nelson; payroll and computerized bookkeeper Hilo Care Ctr.; with pers. office Flour-Utah Mining; employment counselor Snelling & Snelling Employment Agy.; tchr. bus. edn. Portland Adventist Acad. Contbr. articles to profl. jours. Mem. ASTD, Assn. Per. Adminstr. (columnist San Bernardino Sun newspaper), Coun. for Adult and Exptl. Learning, Calif. Assn. for Counseling and Devel., Coop. Edn. Assn., Nat. Commn. for Coop. Edn., Phi Delta Kappa. Office: 4501 W Powell Blvd Apt 72 Gresham OR 97030-5070

WEBB, DORIS MCINTOSH, human resources specialist; b. Aliquippa, Pa., May 26, 1930; d. Hayward Victor and Elaine Eloise (Kiernan) McIntosh; m. Alan D. Webb Sr. JD, Aug. 15, 1953 (dec. Sept. 1979); children: Alan D. Jr., Amy E. Webb-Burke. Student, Western Coll. for Women, 1949-51; BS in Bus. Adminstrn., Geneva Coll., 1953, tchr. cert., 1968; MEd, U. Pitts., 1972. Mgr. Crestmont Home Supply Co., Aliquippa, 1953-57; real estate mgr. McIntosh Constrn. Co., Aliquippa, 1957-62; tchr. bus. Rochester (Pa.) H.S., 1968-78; bus. tchr. adult edn. Alleghney C.C., Pitts., 1972-75, Draughon's Jr. Bus. Coll., Knoxville, Tenn., 1979—81, Hartford C.C., Bel Air, Md., 1981—85; corp. sec. McIntosh & Webb Inc., Cockeysville, Md., 1981-88; exec. dir., CEO housing authority City of Havre de Grace, Md., 1989-98; v.p. human resources, tng., devel. McIntosh and Webb Assocs., Charlottesville, Va., 1999—. Chmn. North Boroughs, WQED, Pitts., 1964-68; mem. fin. com. Housing Authority Risk Retention Corp. of Housing Authority Ins. Co., Cheshire, Conn., 1995-97, mem. fin. com. Housing Authority Ins. Co., 1995-97; housing cons. for pub. housing and modernization programs, 1989-97; Sect. 8 Fed. Housing insp., 1996—; owner Ebenezer House bed and breakfast, Rochelle, Va., 2003—. Recipient Geneva Coll. Alumni Disting. Svc. award, 1993. Mem.: ASTD, NAFE, AAUW, The Profl. Woman Network, Profl. Woman Spkrs. Bur., Colonial Williamsburg Found. Republican. Lutheran. Avocations: fox hunting, beagling, traveling, remodeling homes, decorating. Personal E-mail: dmwebb@cstone.net.

WEBB, ELIZABETH LOUISE, real estate broker, artist; b. South Bend, Ind., Apr. 5, 1958; d. Carl J. and Loretta H. (Niedbalski) Kot; m. William Roger Young (div. Jan. 1986); m. Martyn Webb, June 2002. BA, Ft. Lewis Coll., 1992. Mgr. Wendy's Hallmark, Show Low, Ariz., 1980-83; br. ops. specialist First Interstate Bank, 1985-89; mgr. Oak Ridge Sports Ctr., Pagosa Springs, Colo., 1989-90; teller supr. Norwest Bank, Durango, Colo., 1994-98; ptnr., co-owner Navajo Trails Car Wash, Pagosa Springs, Colo., 1998—2001, Mr. Kad Kar Wash, Pagosa Springs, Colo., 1998—2001; real estate broker Durango, 2000—. Bd. dirs. Habitat for Humanity of LaPlata, Colo., 2002—. Mem. Nat. Assn. Realtors, Colo. Assn. Realtors, Durango Area Assn. Realtors. Avocations: landscaping, bicycling, aerobics, skiing. Home: 706 Fantango Rd Durango CO 81301-9203 Office Phone: 970-375-7027. E-mail: lyoung@frontier.net.

WEBB, EMILY, retired plant morphologist; b. Charleston, S.C., Apr. 10, 1924; d. Malcolm Syfan and Emily Kirk (Moore) W.; m. John James Rosemond, Apr. 23, 1942 (div. 1953); 1 child, John Kirk; m. Julius Goldberg, Sept. 9, 1954; children: Michael, Judith. Student, Coll. Charleston, 1951—54; AB in Liberal Arts and Sci. with honors, U. Ill., Chgo., 1968, MS in Biol. Scis., 1972, PhD in Biol. Scis., 1985. Undergrad. fellow in bacteriology Med. Coll. S.C., Charleston, 1952-54; teaching asst. U. Ill., Chgo., 1969-72, 77-84, rsch. asst., 1977; teaching fellow W.Va. U., Morgantown, 1974, instr., 1974-75. Rsch. in N.Am. bot. needlework art, 1986—. Author: Studies in Several North American Species of Ophioglossum, 1986; translator Nat. Transl. Ctr., Chgo., 1976; contbr. articles to profl. jours. James scholar U. Ill., 1968-69. Mem. DAR, ACLU. Democrat. Episcopalian. Avocations: garden design, writing, money management. Home and Office: 1356 Mandel Ave Westchester IL 60154-3433

WEBB, EVELYN DUNBAR, elementary school educator; b. New Haven, Conn., Apr. 6, 1954; d. Marshall Nelson Dunbar and Evelyn Louise Clinton; m. John Henry Webb, Aug. 9, 1986; children: Jenianne Elisabethe Zimmerman, Heather Merri. AAS, Ctrl. Va. C.C., Lynchburg, 2000; BA in English, Randolph-Macon Woman's Coll., Lynchburg, Va., 2002. Dir. of fiscal svcs. The Valley RR Co., Essex, Conn., 1993—96; client acctg. specialist First Step, Inc., New London, Conn., 1996—97; asst. office mgr. Old Va. Candle Co., Lynchburg, Va., 1997—99; tchr., tutor New Vistas Sch., Lynchburg, Va., 2002—03; writing workshop instr. Lynchburg Fine Arts Ctr., Va., 2003—; tchr. James River Day Sch., Lynchburg, 2003—; co-owner, v.p. Gremlin Systems, Ltd., Old Lyme, Conn., 1985—96. Poet coord. Valley View Retirement Cmty., Lynchburg, 2002—; founder and coord. Prime Time Writers' Forum, Lynchburg, Va., 2000—02. Author: (short fiction) The Word Collector (Margaret I. Raynal Fiction Award, 2000), (poetry) Aunt Maude's Window (Margaret Walker Meml. Poetry Prize, 2002), (short fiction) The Gift (San Gabriel Writers' League Writing for Children Award, 2003), (poetry) The Gihon River Review Literary Journal, Cairn Literary Journal, (poetry, short fiction & plays) Hail, Muse! etc. Literary Journal, (essay) Alice Joins the Lobster Quadrille (Helen Calvert Award for Ekphrasis, 2001); contbr. articles to profl. jours. Grantee Jessie Ball DuPont Summer Rsch. grantee, Randolph-Macon Woman's Coll., 2001—02, Edn. grantee, Finch Coll. Alumnae Assn., 2003; scholar CVCC Honor scholar, Randolph-Macon Woman's Coll., 2000—02, David K. Cornelius scholar, 2001. Mem.: Soc. for Children's Book Writers & Illustrators, Poetry Soc. of Va. (membership chairperson 2001—02), AAUW, Phi Beta Kappa, Omicron Delta Kappa, Alpha Sigma Lambda, Phi Theta Kappa. Independent. Avocations: yoga, reading, bicycling. Home: 403-F Kerry Ln Lynchburg VA 24502-5727 Office: James River Day School 5039 Boonsboro Rd Lynchburg VA 24503-1801 Personal E-mail: motherworld2002@yahoo.com.

WEBB, KARRIE, professional golfer; b. Ayr, Queensland, Australia, Dec. 21, 1974; Profl. golfer LPGA, 1995—. Won Weetabix Women's Brit. Open, 1995, 97, Healthsouth Inaugural, 1996, Sprint Titleholders Championship, 1996, SAFECO Classic, 1996, 97, ITT LPGA Tour Championship, 1996, Susan G. Koman Internat., 1997, Australian Ladies Masters, 1998, City of Hope: Myrtle Beach Classic, 1998, Wegman's Rochester Internat., 1999, Mercury Title-holders Championships, 1999, Standard Register PING, 1999, Australian Ladies Masters, 1999, 2000, The Office Depot, 1999, 2000, ier Classic, 1999, Nabisco Championship, 2000, Take Fuji Classic, 2000; recipient Vare Trophy LPGA, 1997; named Rolex Rookie of Yr., LPGA, 1996. Office: care LPGA 100 International Golf Dr Daytona Beach FL 32124-1082

WEBB, LUCY JANE, actress, film producer, consultant; d. Phillip Carlen and Marcia Jane Webb; m. Kevin Pollak, Dec. 19, 1995. BA, U. Tenn.; student, New Sch. Social Rsch. Lydon Baines Johnson intern Joe Evans Congressman, Tenn.; Congl. intern Albert Gore, Jr. Congressman, Tenn.; pres. Calm Down Prodns., Inc., LA; prodr. Warner Bros. TV, CBS. V.p. spl. events Women in Film, LA. Actor: (TV series) Private Benjamin, Laughtrax, Not Necessarily the News; prodr.: (plays) All Grown Up and No Place to Go. Chmn. AIDS charity Angel Women at Risk. Recipient ACE award, Cable ACE Assn., 1985, 1986, 1987, 1988, 1990. Mem.: Beverly Hills Country Club. Democrat. Roman Catholic. Avocations: piano, antiques, travel, films. Office Phone: 323-650-4027.

WEBB, LYNNE MCGOVERN, communication scholar, consultant; b. Shamokin, Pa., Mar. 20, 1951; d. Charles Ralph (dec.) and Ethel Elizabeth (Harris) McGovern; m. Ronald E. Webb, Sept. 28, 1974 (div. June 1981); m. Robert Blakely Moberly, Apr. 6, 1984; children: Laura Ellen, Richard Edward, Reed JoeMinGee (dec.). BS, Pa. State U., 1972; MS, U. Oreg., 1975, PhD, 1980. Field rep. East Ctrl. Ill. Area Agy. on Aging, Campaign, Ill., 1972-74; grad. tchg. asst. U. Oreg., Eugene, 1974-78; instr. Berea (Ky.) Coll., 1978-80; asst. prof. U. Fla., Gainesville, 1980-86, assoc. prof., 1986-90; vis. assoc. prof. U. Hawaii, Honolulu, 1990-91; assoc. prof. U. Memphis, 1991-99; prof., assoc. dept. chair U. Ark., Fayetteville, 1999—. Cons. Fla. Farm Bur., Gainesville, 1981, Clay County Electric Coop., Keystone Heights, Fla., 1987, Retirement Rsch. Found., Chgo., 1988. Mem. Am. Comm. Assn. (bd. dirs. 1999-2000), Fla. Speech Comm. Assn. (v.p. 1986-87), So. States Comm. Assn. (chair applied comm. divsn. 1989-90, chair gender studies divsn. 1992-93, chair membership 1993, v.p. 1994, pres. 1995), Nat. Comm. Assn. (chair com. on comm. and aging 1982-83, legis. coun. 1989-92, 93-96, chair applied comm. sect. 1994-95, resolutions com. 1996, chair women's caucus 1998-99, mem. affirmative action com. 2000-01, nominating com. 2001). Democrat. Methodist. Avocation: gourmet cooking. Office: Univ Ark Dept Comm 417 Kimpel Hall Fayetteville AR 72701

WEBB, MARGOT, writer; b. Halle, Germany, Aug. 28, 1927; d. Egmont and Ilse Lewin; widowed; children: Robert Dave, Peter Dave, Sandy Kyte; m. Ezra C. Levy. B, Calif. State U., 1960, M, 1964; PhD, U. So. Calif. Tchr. 6th grade L.A. Unified Sch. Dist., 1958-88. Lectr. in field. Author: Shadows at Noon, 1992, Coping With Street Gangs. Jewish. Avocations: classical music, Scrabble, walking, travel. Home: Pvt Mail Box 805 25852 Mcbean Pkwy Valencia CA 91355-2004

WEBB, MARTHA JEANNE, author, speaker, film producer; b. Grinnell, Iowa, Oct. 26, 1947; d. Frederick Winfield and Helen (Potter) W.; m. Bruce A. Clark; children: Marjorie, Paula, David. Student, St. Cloud State U., 1965-67, U. Minn., 1967-69, Coll. of St. Catherine, 1979-81. Personnel, pub. relations, drug abuse edn. NIH, 1967-77; account services Doremus & Co., Mpls., 1977-79; v.p. adminstrn. Webb Enterprises, Inc., Mpls., 1979-81; v.p. Russell-Manning Prodns., Mpls., 1981-86; pres. Clark Webb, Inc., Mpls., 1986-92. Pres. Minn. Film Bd., 1986-87, BCW Corp., 1988—. Author: Dress Your House for Success, 1997, Finding Home, 1998; co-prodr. Hubert H. Humphrey: A Passion for Justice, Whitney Mus., 1998. Recipient Summit awards, 1999, Distinction Communicator awards, 1998, Silver award Internat. Film and TV Festival of N.Y., 1983, 84, 85, 86, 87, Golden Eagle award CINE Festival, 1985, Gold award Telly Awards, 1987.

WEBB, MARTY FOX, principal; b. Des Moines, July 15, 1942; d. Joseph John and Jean (Way) Fox; m. Andrew H. Rudolph, Aug. 17, 1963 (div. Jan. 1988); children: Kristen Ann, Kevin Andrew; m. Eugene J. Webb, Nov. 23, 1991. BS, U. Mich., 1964; MEd, Houston Bapt. U., 1982; EdD, U. San Francisco, 1993. Cert. adminstr., Tex., elem. and spl. edn. educator, Mich., Tex. Tchr. spl. edn. Hawthorn Ctr., Northville, Mich., 1964-70; tchr. Bellaire (Tex.) Sch. for Children, 1977-80; prin. Corpus Christi Sch., Houston, 1980-97; founding head The Monarch Sch., Houston, 1997—. Spkr. in field. Bd. dirs. DeBusk Found. Recipient Elem. Sch. Recognition award U.S. Dept. Edn., 1989-90, Blue Ribbon Sch. award, 1990, Outstanding Doctoral Student award, 1994. Mem. ASCD, U. Mich. Alumni Assn. Avocations: reading, flyfishing, camping, hiking, bodybuilding. Home: 3531 Sun Valley Dr Houston TX 77025-4148 Office: The Monarch Sch 1231 Wirt Rd Houston TX 77055-6852 Office Phone: 713-479-0800. Business E-Mail: mwebb@monarchschool.org.

WEBB, MARY GREENWALD, cardiovascular clinical specialist, educator; b. Tecumseh, Mich., Jan. 15, 1945; m. William R. Webb, Sept. 9, 1967; children: Adam, Stephanie. Diploma, Toledo Hosp. Sch. Nursing, 1966; BS, U. South Fla., 1986, MS, 1988; PhD, U. Fla., 1993. Instr. Pasco Hernando C.C., New Port Richey, Fla., 1993-95; assoc. prof. nursing U. South Fla., Tampa, 1995—. Recipient Mentors Sci. Rsch. award, NIH; fellow, Kellogg Found. Mem. Sigma Theta Tau (Excellence in Nursing Edn. award, 1999), Phi Kappa Phi. Home: 6422 Wisteria Loop Land O Lakes FL 34639-3116

WEBB, VERONICA, fashion model, journalist; b. Detroit, Feb. 25, 1965; d. Leonard Douglas and Marion (Stewart) W. Student, New Sch. Social Rsch., 1983; signed with, Ford Models, Inc., N.Y.C., 1992—. Contbg. editor, columnist Paper Mag., 1989—; contbg. editor features column Interview Mag., 1990—; spokesmodel Revlon, 1992-96. First featured on cover of Vogue, 1988; appearances incluce (films) Jungle Fever, 1991, Malcolm X, 1992, For Love or Money, 1993, Catwalk, 1995, 54, 1998, Holy Man, 1998, In Too Deep, 1999, The Big Tease, 1999. First African-Am. to receive exclusive cosmetics contract. Mem. Lifebeat (bd. dirs. 1994—). Office: United Talent Agy 9560 Wilshire Blvd Ste 500 Beverly Hills CA 90212

WEBBER, HELEN, artist, designer; b. NYC; d. David and Frieda (Berlin) Ross; children: Joel Benjamin (dec.), Daniel Saul, Rachel Frieda. BA, Queens Coll., 1951; postgrad., Columbia U., 1953; MA, RISD, 1963. Site specific artist/designer, product designer toys, books; tchr. in design dept. Calif. Coll. Arts and Crafts, Santa Cruz, Calif., 1982, 1984, 1987; lectr. U. Calif. Keynote spkr. ASID, San Diego and Kansas City, 1983, Nat. Home Furnishings League, San Ferancisco, 1980, Chgo., 1982; lectr., exhibitor Internat. Congress Women Architects, Paris, 1983, U. Calif., Santa Cruz, 1987, Commnwealth Club, San Francisco, 1989, guest lectr. RISD Alumni Conf., 1996; instr. Hussian Coll. Art, Phila., 2003. Author, illustrator: Good-Night, Night, The Sea Is My Blanket, 1963, My Kite it the Magic Me, Summer Sun; prin. commissions in 5 media tapestry, clay, glass, metal and wood for 6 Carnival Cruise Line ships; Festival, Tropical Fantasy, Holiday, Celebration, Destiny, Pittsburg Calif. Civic Ctr., Metro Commerce Bank, San Francisco, Statendam/Holland Am. Cruise Lines, VA Med. Ctr., Cleve., Ohio, Vets. Cemetery, Riverside, Calif., VA Hosp., Lyons, N.J., East Tex. Med. Ctr., Tyler, St. Patrick's Hosp., Lake Charles, La., Gatwick Penta Hotel, London, Jewish Home for the Aged, Houston, Jewish Home for Aging, Riverdale, N.Y., Betty Ford Pavilion, Palm Springs, Fla., Sphohn Hosp., Corpus Christi, Tex., St. Agnes Hosp., Fresno, Calif., Chevron Corp., San Ramon, Calif., Merck & Co., Rahway, N.J., Kodak, Kingsport, Tenn., Kaiser Permanente, Bristol Hosp., Conn., Sacramento and San Jose, Calif., Quail Lodge Resort, Carmel Valley, Calif., Episcopal Homes Found., San Francisco, Menorah Manor, Dunedin, Fla., Hyatt Regency, Phoenix, Ariz., 1st United Meth. Ch., Wichita Falls, Tex., Cen. Maine Hosp., Lewiston, Maine; designer, artist textile, wallpaper, sheets, towels, children's games for Collins & Aikman, Burlington, Covington, Peerage of Eng., Edward Fields, Pastime Industries. Mem. Design Internat. (pres., co-founder San Francisco 1984-85), Women -in-Design Internat. (founder, pres. 1977-83, Outstanding Contbn. to Design award 1980), Urban Art Internat. (bd. dirs.). Studio: 103 S Village Ave Exton PA 19341 E-mail: helenwebber@comcast.com.

WEBBER, LINDA JUDITH RITZ, interior designer; b. Bronx, N.Y. d. Murray and Marilyn Ritz; children: Ronald Alan, Amy Beth. BFA, Boston U., 1964; MEd, U. Hartford, 1967. Lic. interior designer, Conn. Elem. art supr., Winthrop, Mass., 1964-65; jr. high sch. art tchr. Wethersfield, Conn., 1965-66; freelance artist various bus. and industries; interior designer A. J. Skenderian, West Hartford, Conn., 1975-77, John LaFalce Inc., Canton, Conn., 1978-97; art tchr. Avon Mid. Sch., 1995-96; art curator U. Conn. Health Ctr., 2001. Art career counsellor Bloomfield (Conn.) Mid. Sch., 1979-81; lectr. in found. studies and interior design Paier Coll. of Art, 1988-89. One-woman shows include Reno Gallery, Hartford, Conn., 1971, Represented in permanent collections U. Conn. Health Ctr., Farmington, created mural, Forces of Life, Ctr. for Women's Health at U. Conn. Health Ctr. Mem. adv. com. for fine arts Bloomfield Bd. Edn., 1975-78; mem. title VII com.,, 1978-81; mem. bd. for student publs. Boston U., 1962-64; curator Weyerhauser and Musser Mansions, Historic Homes on Miss., 1997; cons. art. adv. com. U. Conn. Health Ctr., 1998—. Recipient Graphic Artist award West Hartford Art League, 1975, Carriage House prize Art League of New Britain, 1996, 99, Color Explorations painting prize West Hartford Art League, 1996. Mem. Conn. Women Artists, Clinton Art Soc. (merit award 1971), Wintonbury Art League (pres. 1991-93, Leonard Waller Meml. award 1981, Pritchett prize, Freidman Floor Covering award for a watercolor 1988, Honorable Mention award Essex 1989), Conn. Watercolor Soc. Avocation: ballroom dancing. E-mail: webberbydesign@attbi.com.

WEBBER, PAMELA D. information technology executive; Sr. mgr. applications devel. eCommerce Arrow Electronics, Inc., Melville, NY. Mem.: The Computer Tech. Industry Assn. (bd. mem. electronics industry data exch. leadership 2003—). Office: Arrow Electronics 50 Marcus Dr Melville NY 11747

WEBER, ADELHEID LISA, former nurse, chemist; b. Cottbus, Germany, June 1, 1934; came to the U.S., 1958; d. Johannes Gustav Paul and Johanna Katinka (Askevold) Haertwig; m. Joseph Cotrell Weber (dec. 1986), Oct. 25, 1957; children: Robert Andreas, Miriam Lisa. RN, Stadtisches Hosp., Dortmund, Germany, 1956; BS in Distributive Sci., Am. U., 1983; MBA, U. Md., 1991; postgrad., New Eng. Acupuncture Sch., 2000—. RN. Nurse Krankenhaus, Wuppertal, Germany, 1956-57; pvt. nurse Wellesley, Mass., 1969-74; lab. tech. Microbiol. Assoc., Bethesda, Md., 1979-84; switchboard operator Best Products Co., Bethesda, 1983-87; lab. tech. Uniformed Svcs. U. Health Scis., Bethesda, 1984-90; info. rsch. tech. Info. Rsch. Internat. Inc., Bethesda, 1987; chemist USDA, Beltsville, Md., 1990-93, ret., 1993; distbr. Morinda Health Product-Noni Juice, 1999—. Vol. Sibley Meml. Hosp., Washington, 1991. Recipient Cert. award County of Montgomery, Md., 1988, Whitman Walker Clinic, 1987. Mem. NAFE, Soc. for Rsch. Adminstrs., Am. Chem. Soc., Nat. Assn. for Amputees, Soc. for Applied Spectroscopy, Nat. Trust for Historic Preservation, Hemlock Soc. Nat. Capital Area, Nat. Mus. for Women in Arts, Wash. Performing Arts Soc. Avocations: stained glass, pottery, gardening, needlework, reading. Home: 23 Sunset Ln Osterville MA 02655-2036

WEBER, ALOIS HUGHES, principal; b. Clay County, Mo., Dec. 19, 1910; d. William Swan and Nora Mildred (Elam) Hughes; m. Frank Thomas Ewing Weber, May 28, 1934 (dec. 1980); children: Patricia Katherine Weber Brusuelas, Susan Weber Mills. BA, William Jewell Coll., Liberty, Mo., 1932; MA, U. Mo., Kansas City, 1971. Elem. prin. Linden (Mo.) Sch. Dist. #72, 1931-34; elem. tchr. Eugene (Mo.) Sch. Dist., 1935-38, Sycamore Sch., Boone County, Mo., 1938-41; reserve tchr. Kansas City (Mo.) Schs., 1941-55, contract tchr., 1955-63; head tchr. Allen Sch., Kansas City, 1963-67; remedial reading tchr. Benjamin Franklin Sch., Kansas City, 1967-69; reading cons. Div. Urban Edn., Kansas City, 1969-73; coord. Title I Elem. Reading and Compensatory Edn., Kansas City, 1974-79; ret. Instr., trainer ARC, Am. Assn. Ret. Persons, Staying Healthy After Fifty, State of N.Mex., 1987-89, Growing Old with Health and Wisdom, 1989-95; tutor Literacy Vols. of Am., Inc., Rio Rancho, N.Mex., 1990-93; spkr. AARP Health Care Reform, Health Care Am., 1992—, Lovelace Sr. Adv. Group, 1993-98. Vol. Corrales Libr., 1980-88; bd. dirs. Read West, Literacy Vols. Am., Rio Rancho, 1989-92; bd. dirs. Adobe Comty. Theatre, Corrales, 1989-90; lectr. in field; mem. State of N.Mex. steering com. Growing Old with Health and Wisdom, 1989-95; asst. state coord. Am. Assn. Ret. Persons, Health Advocacy Svcs., N.Mex., 1995-98; pres. adv. bd. Meadowlark Sr. Ctr., Rio Rancho, 1997-2003. Recipient Area Cmty. Svc. award AARP, Nat. award for HAS Outstanding Project Achievement, 1993; Area Cmty. Svc. award State of N.Mex., 1988, Cert. of Appreciation, ARC, 1988, Cert. of Appreciation for outstanding cmty. svc. N.Mex. Legislature, State Senate, 1997, Cert. of Appreciation Rio Rancho, N.Mex. Dept. Pub. Safety Srs. and Law Enforcement Together, 1997; NSF grantee, 1973. Mem. AAUW, N.Mex. Assn. Edn. Retirees (exec. com. 1987-89), Albuquerque Assn. Edn. Retirees (exec. sec., bd. dirs. 1990-95), PEO (chpt. BD chaplain, 1990-94), West Mesa Assn. Ednl. Retirees (membership chmn. 1991, v.p. 1993, pres. 1994), Grad. Club Albuquerque. Democrat. Baptist. Avocations: bridge, reading, travel. Home: 3321 Esplanade Cir SE Rio Rancho NM 87124-2198

WEBER, BECKY, state legislator; b. Sept. 24, 1954; Restaurant developer; ins. agt.; mem. Wis. State Assembly, Madison, 2002—, mem. budget rev. com., vice chair aging and long-term care com., mem. govt. ops. and spending limitations com., mem. ins. com., mem. rural affairs com., mem. small bus. com. Republican. Office: State Capitol Bldg Rm 115W PO Box 8953 Madison WI 53708 Address: 2811 Antier Trail Green Bay WI 54313

WEBER, GAIL MARY, lawyer; b. Austin, Minn., Dec. 7, 1954; d. Clemence Peter and Aryls Marion (Mulick) W.; m. Thomas Jeffrey Miller, Sept. 24, 1983; 1 child, Paula Suzanne. AA, Austin C.C., 1975; BA in Psychology and English with high scholastic honors, St. Cloud State U.,

1978; JD, Hamline U., 1983. Bar: Minn. 1983, U.S. Supreme Ct. Minn. 1983, U.S. Dist. Ct. Minn. 1984. Child care specialist Gerard Schs., Austin, 1978-80; legal intern St. Paul Dept. Edn., 1981-82; law clk. Alton, Severson, Sovis & Groves, Apple Valley, Minn., 1982, Heuer Madden & Gruesner, Mpls., 1983, assoc., 1983-85, Heuer Weber & Assocs., Mpls., 1986-88, Robbins & Rashke, Mpls., 1986-93; ptnr. Robbins Rashke & Weber, Edina, 1993—; pvt. practice Edina, Minn., 1985-93. Coach high sch. mock trial program, Mpls., 1986-94, vol. Chrysalis, Mpls., 1986—; co-chmn. Legis. Action Com., Minn. Women Lawyers, 1987-89. Mem. ACLU, 1990, Minn. Civil Liberties Union, 1990, Big Sisters, St. Paul, 1980-82, Greenpeace; Sunday sch. tchr., 1995-98; co-leader Daisy Scouts, 1996-97. Recipient Appreciation award Chrysalis Ctr. for Women, 1989-97. Mem. Minn. Trial Lawyers Assn., Nat. Employment Lawyers Assn. (Minn. chpt.), Fed. Bar Assn., Minn. Soc. Criminal Justice (sec. 1988, v.p. 1989, bd. dirs.), Minn. Women Lawyers (bd. dirs. 1989-91), Minn. Trial Lawyers Assn., LWV (asst. editor newsletter 1987-89, bd. dirs., chair edn. study 1994-95), Delta Theta Phi. Democrat. Roman Catholic. Avocations: reading, theater, Karate, opera, golf. Office: 7600 Parklawn Ave Ste 410 Edina MN 55435-5130

WEBER, GLORIA RICHIE, retired minister, retired state legislator; married; 4 children. BA, Washington U., St. Louis; MA, MDiv, Eden Theol. Sem., Webster Groves, Mo. Ordained to ministry Evang. Luth. Ch. Am., 1974. Family life educator Luth. Family and Children's Svcs. Mo.; mem. Mo. Ho. of Reps., 1993-94. Mo. state organizer, dir. comm. Mainstream Voters C.A.R.E., 1995. Editor: Interfaith Voices for Peace and Justice, 1996—. Exec. dir. Older Women's League, 1990—95. Named Woman of the Yr., Variety Club, 1978, Woman of Worth, Older Women's League, 1993; recipient Woman of Achievement award, St. Louis Globe-Dem., 1977, Unselfish Cmty. Svc. award, St. Louis Sentinel Newspaper, 1985, Faith in Action award, Luth. Svcs. St. Louis, 1994. Mem.: Assn. Lutheran Older Adults (mem. nat. bd. 2004—), N.Am. Interfaith Network (bd. dirs. 1993—2003), Nat. Assn. Luth. Older Adults (bd. dirs. 2004—), Phi Beta Kappa. Democrat. Office Phone: 314-892-1192. E-mail: gloriaweber9@aol.com.

WEBER, GRACE T. school system administrator; b. Buffalo, Apr. 25, 1940; d. Leslie F. and Wanda A. Weber. BA, Valparaiso U., 1962; MA in Tchg., St. Louis U., 1966. Cert. tchr., Mo. Tchr. L.I. Luth. High Sch., Brookville, N.Y., 1962-65, Pattonville Sch. Dist., St. Louis, 1966-96, curriculum coord., 1996—. Mem. steering com. Mo. Geog. Alliance, St. Louis, 1998—; participant Fulbright Summer Seminar, U.S. Dept. Edn., India, 1990, Egypt and Zimbabwe, 1995. Mem. Cmty. Leadership for Tchrs., Focus St. Louis, 1991-92. Recipient Springboard to Learning Travel award, 1986. Mem. NEA, Mo. Edn. Assn., Nat. Assn. Gifted Educators, Nat. Assn. Geog. Educators, Nat. Coun. Social Studies, Delta Kappa Gamma (rec. sec. Delta state orgn. 2001—, 1st and 2d v.p. Pi chpt. 1990-94, pres. Pi chpt. 1994-98). Avocations: travel, reading, walking.

WEBER, JANICE ANN, library director, grant writer; b. Baytown, Tex., Aug. 28, 1952; d. James Thelmer Jr. and Doris Geraldine (Bush) Foster; m. Louis Haldane Weber, Feb. 1, 1983. BS, Tex. Women's U., Denton, 1982, MLS, 1985. Libr. dir. Dimmit County Libr., Carrilo Springs, Tex., 1985-86, Val Verde County Libr., Del Rio, Tex., 1986-89, Laredo (Tex.) Pub. Libr., 1989—. Sec., bd. dirs. Literary Vol. of Am., Laredo, 1989-95, bd. dirs. Webb County Heritage Found., Laredo, 1990-94; chmn. Webb County Hist. Commn., 1989-94; mem. Tuesday Music & Lit., Laredo, 1997—. Grantee numerous orgns., 1990—. Mem. Nonprofit Mgmt. Assn., Tex. Libr. Assn., Tex. Mcpl. Libr. Dirs. Assn. Avocations: gourmet cooking, weaving. Office: Laredo Pub Libr 1120 E Calton Rd Laredo TX 78041-7328

WEBER, LISA M. insurance company executive; BA in Psychology, SUNY. With Painewebber, 1988—98; sr. v.p. human resources Metlife, Inc., N.Y.C., 1998—2001, sr. exec. v.p., chief adminstrv. officer, 2001—. Bd. dirs. New Eng. Fin., Gt. Am. Fin.; bd. dirs. benefits com. Metlife, Inc.; mem. social responsibility com. Metlife Found. Bd. Mem.: Phi Beta Kappa. Office: Metlife Inc 1 Madison Ave New York NY 10010

WEBER, LYNN, sociology educator; BA in Sociology, Memphis State U., 1971, MA in Sociology, 1973; PhD in Sociology, U. Ill., Urbana, 1976. Asst. prof. Dept. Sociology and Social Work Memphis State U., 1976-81, assoc. prof. Dept. Sociology and Social Work, 1981-86, assoc. dir., co-founder Ctr. Rsch. on Women, 1982-88, prof. Dept. Sociology and Social Work, 1986—96; dir. Ctr. Rsch. on Women U. Memphis, 1988—96; dir. Women's Studies Program U. S.C., 1996—. Faculty devel. assignment Memphis State U., 1987-88; vis. scholar Dept. Health Edn. Temple U., 1987; faculty devel. assignment U. Memphis, 1994-95; disting. vis. prof. gender studies Dept. Sociology and Criminal Justice U. Del., 1994; mem. program com. Assn. for General and Liberal Studies, Memphis, 1993, Soc. for Applied Anthropology, 1992; coord. faculty rsch. seminar on race, class and gender MSU, 1988-90; cons. various founds. and orgns. Co-author: The American Perception of Class, 1987, Women of Color and Southern Women: A Bibliography of Social Research, 1988, 89, 91, 92, (on-line bibliographic database) Research Clearinghouse on Women of Color and Southern Women; adv. editor: The Sociological Quarterly, 1980-85, Gender & Society, 1991-94; reviewer: various scientific publs. including Social Science Quarterly, Am. Sociological Review, Social Problems, Signs: A Jour. of Women in Culture and Society, others; contbr. articles to profl. jours. Recipient numerous grants and fellowships including, NSF, 1988-91, 1995—, NIH, 1989-93, others. Mem. Am. Sociological Assn. (coun. sect. on racial and ethnic minorities 1987-90, dissertation award com. sect. on sex and gender 1990-92, chair 1992, com. on coms. 1991-93, Disting. Contbns. to Tchg. award 1993, Jessie Bernard award 1993), So. Sociological Soc. (program com. 1995), Sociologists for Women in Soc., Society for the Study of Social Problems, Alpha Kappa Delta. Home: 200 Windsor Point Rd Columbia SC 29223-1823 Office: Univ SC Womens Studies WOST Office 201 flinn Hall 1324 Pendleton St Columbia SC 29208

WEBER, MARIE FLORENCE MORANO, music educator; b. Red Bank, N.J., Nov. 2, 1956; d. Philip Joseph and Mildred Antoinette Morano; m. Timothy Michael Weber, June 24, 1988. MusB, Heidelberg Coll., 1979; MA, Regent U., 1994. Music tchr. Carteret Bd. Edn., Carteret, NJ, 1979—89, Portsmouth Pub. Sch., Portsmouth, Va., 1989—. Music dir. St. Luke Cath. Ch., Va. Beach, Va., 2001—. Mem.: NEA, Am. Fedn. Musicians Local 125, Portsmouth Edn. Assn., Va. Edn. Assn., Music Educators Nat. Conf., Va. Music Educators Assn. (dist. rep. 1998—2003), Fellows Club. Roman Catholic. Avocations: music, crafts, sewing, reading. Home: 1800 John Brown Lane Virginia Beach VA 23464 Office: Portsmouth City Pub Schools Crawford Pkwy Portsmouth VA 23705

WEBER, MARY ELLEN, astronaut; b. Cleve., Aug. 24, 1962; d. Andrew Jr. and Joan W.; m. Jerome Elkind. BS in Chem. Engring., Purdue U., 1984; PhD in Physical Chemistry, U. Calif., Berkeley, 1988. With Tex. Instruments, with SEMATECH; astronaut NASA, Houston, 1992—, with crew on STS-70 on space shuttle Discovery, 1995, with cres on STS-101 on space shuttle Atlantis, 2000. Patentee in field; legis. affairs liaison NASA Hdqs., Washington, chmn. procurement bd. for Biotech. Program contractor. Contbr. articles to profl. jours. Avocations: scuba diving, flying, sky diving, golf. Office: Astronaut Office/CB NASA Lyndon B Johnson Space Ctr Houston TX 77058

WEBER, MARY ELLEN HEALY, economist; b. San Francisco, May 28, 1943; d. Ignatius Bernard and Grace Marie (Hogan) Healy; m. Stephen Francis Weber, Dec. 21, 1971. BA, Dominican Coll., 1965; postgrad., Nat. U. Mex., 1967; vis. scholar, Stanford U., 1969-70; postgrad., Cath. U. Chile, 1970-71, U. Chile, 1971-72; PhD, U. Utah, 1974. Tchg. fellow U. Utah, 1965-68; asst. prof. Smith Coll., 1972-75; country economist World Bank, IBRD, 1975-76; sr. economist Internat. Rsch. & Tech. Corp., McLean, Va., 1976-78; dir. regulatory analysis, chief economist OSHA, U.S. Dept. Labor, Washington, 1979-84; pres. Weber Software Enterprises, 1984-86, Web-Wolf Data Systems, Inc., 1986-90; dir. econs., exposure and tech. divsn. Office of Pollution Prevention & Toxics US EPA, Washington, 1990—, acting dep. dir., 2000—. Social Sci. Rsch. Coun. fgn. area fellow, 1969-71. Mem. Sr. Execs. Assn., Exec. Women in Govt. Roman Catholic.

WEBER, MELISSA MURPHY, state representative; b. N.J., Sept. 26, 1969; m. Bob Weber. Dir. Montgomery County Weed and Seed Program; criminal justice task force Am. Legisl. Exch. Coun.; mem. Brehon Law Soc., Denison U. Alumni Recruiting Team. Mem.: Brehon Law Soc., Montgomery Bar Assn., Pa. Bar Assn., Montgomery County Commn. on Women and Families, Phila. Alumnae Chpt., Delta Gamma Nat. Soc. Republican. Roman Catholic. Office: 6 E Wing Harrisburg PA 17120-2020

WEBER, MOLLY ANNE, actor; d. Patricia Downey. Student, Carnegie Mellon U. Actor: (TV series) CSI, Angel, The Guarian, Time of Your Life, Stark Raving Mad; (films) Cultural Wars, Living in a Question, Sign of the Cross, The Demolitionist. Mem.: AFTRA, SAG. Office: Badgley/Connor 9229 Sunset Blvd #311 Berkeley CA 90069

WEBER, NANCY WALKER, charitable trust administrator; b. Adrian, W.Va., Aug. 26, 1936; d. James Everett and Wanna Virginia (Alderman) Walker; m. J. Raymond Jacob, Jr., June 12, 1955 (div. 1967); children: Paul M., Sharon J. Kazdin; m. George Harry Weber, Apr. 27, 1983 (dec. Mar. 1995). Student, Peabody Prep. Mus., 1946-53. Asst. buyer cosmetics Hutzler's Dept. Store, Balt., 1967-69; exec. sec. to exec. v.p. Martin Marietta Corp., Bethesda, Md., 1969-75; asst. exec. to exec. dir. hosp. U. Utah, Salt Lake City, 1976-80; dir. program adminstrn. Lucille P. Markey Charitable Trust, Miami, Fla., 1983-97; evaluation adminstr. for Markey Programs NRC, Balt., 1997—. Pianist, organist Middle River Bapt. Ch., Balt., 1953-61; vol. Keswick Multicare Ctr. Named Mrs. Del. in Mrs. Del./Am. Pagent, 1967. Baptist. Avocations: piano, organ. Home and Office: 3824 Michael S Landing Cir E Jacksonville FL 32224-8677 E-mail: hamletnww@aol.com.

WEBER, SHARI, state legislator; b. Owatonna, Minn., July 1, 1953; m. Marvin E. Weber. Student, St. John;s Acad. and Coll., Moorhead State U. Dir. downtown devel. Herington (Kans.) Main St. Program, Herington, Kans., 1993-97; rep. Dist. 68 Kans. State Ho. of Reps., Topeka, 1995—2003. Henry Toll fellow, 2000. Address: 405 E Lewerenz Herington KS 67449 Office Phone: 785-271-1404. E-mail: sjweber@kansas.net.

WEBER, SUSAN A. lawyer; b. 1958; BA, Drake U., 1984; JD, MBA, SUNY, Buffalo, 1989. Bar: Pa. 1990, D.C. 1992, Ill. 1993, U.S. Ct. Appeals (4th cir.) 1990, U.S. Ct. Appeals (3d cir.) 1991, U.S. Ct. Appeals (7th cir.) 1992. Clk. to Justice Byron White U.S. Supreme Ct.; clk. to Judge James Sprouse U.S. Ct. Appeals (4th cir.); with Sidley Austin Brown & Wood, Chgo., 1993—, ptnr., 1997—. Office: Sidley Austin Brown and Wood One Bank Plz 10 S Dearborn St Chicago IL 60603*

WEBER-JAVERS, FLORENCE R. nurse; b. Milw., Mar. 29, 1953; d. Frank A. and E. Mae (Brown) Weber; m. Lawrence P. Wittig, Aug. 17, 1974 (div. Jan. 1983); children: Jodi, Drew; m. Russell L. Weber-Javers, Sept. 9, 1983; stepchildren: Andrea K. Javers Notaro, Jennifer L. Javers Long, John R. Javers. ADN, Milw. Area Tech. Coll., 1978; Diploma in Enterostomal Therapy Edn., Jewish Hosp./Washington U., St. Louis, 1980. RN. RN St. Michael Hosp., Milw., 1978-80; cert. orthopedic fitter Knueppel's, Milw., 1974-84; enterostomal therapy nurse Stein Med., Milw., 1984-86; home health enterostomal therapy Nurse Case Mgr., Las Vegas, 1986-88; enterostomal therapy nurse Home Care/Olsten Kimberly, Las Vegas, 1988—2002, various home health agys., HMOs, med. facilities and acute care hosps., Las Vegas, 1988—. Pressure reduction mattress sales cons., Pegasus, Fla., 1985; clin. trial cons. Convatec (Squibb), N.J., 1982-86, Hollister, Inc., Libertyville, Ill., 1982-84. Vol. Am. Cancer Soc., 1980—. 1st lt. U.S. Army Nurse Corps Res., 1984-89. Recipient scholarship Am. Cancer Soc., Milw., 1980; named Comty. Nurse of the Yr., March of Dimes, Las Vegas, 1995. Mem. Wound, Ostomy and Continence Nurses Soc., United Ostomy Assn. of So. Nev. (advisor 1986—), Assn. for Advancement of Wound Care. Avocations: boating, reading, swimming, skiing. Home: 4525 N Valadez St Las Vegas NV 89129-5353 E-mail: javerss@aol.com.

WEBSTER, BARBARA SHEPPARD, art association administrator; b. Atlantic City, N.J., Apr. 25, 1936; d. Edward Francis and Rita Joan (Gargale) Sheppard; m. Russell Thomas Webster, Sept. 7, 1957 (dec. Sept. 1976); children: Russell Todd, Catherine Sheppard. BA, Douglass Coll., 1957; MEd, Rutgers U., 1965. Asst. field dir. Pub. Opinion Surveys, Princeton, N.J., 1957-60; tchr., counselor Bound Brook (N.J.) H.S., 1960-62; tchr., performer, choreographer divsn. continuing edn. Westport (Conn.) Pub. Summer Sch., Staples H.S., 1968-86; mng. dir. Levitt Pavilion for Performing Arts, Westport, Conn., 1983-85; exec. dir. Stamford (Conn.) Cmty. Arts Coun., 1985-87, Artspace, Inc., New Haven, 1987—97; gen. mgr. Conn. Dance Sch., Inc., Fairfield, 1997—; career counselor Bunnell H.S., Stratford, 1999—. Mentor Inner City Cultural Devel. Conn. Commn. Arts, Bridgeport, 1992-93, Hartford, 1993-94, New Haven, 1994—97; participant Alliance N.Y. State Arts Couns., Greenwich, Conn., 1986, Yale Sch. Orgn. and Mgmt., 1987; founding dir. Media Arts Ctr., New Haven, 1991-95; founder Summer Arts for Youth-SAY!, 1994—. Choreographer opening ceremonies 28th gen. assembly Unitarian Universalists, New Haven, 1989. Mem. Arts and Bus. Roundtable, New Haven, 1995-97, Arts! Artists! Athletes! Spl. Olympics World Games, New Haven, 1994-95; participant Vision Project Gtr. New Haven, 1994. Mem. AAUW (Norwalk-Westport chpt. 1994-96, Bound Brook (N.J.) chpt. 1960-63), New Haven Rotary (Outstanding Com. Chair 1994-96, dir. vocat. svc. 1996-97, Rotarian of Yr. 1997, Paul Harris fellow 1997—). Mem. Unitarian Universalist Ch. Avocations: travel, dance, yoga, tai-chi, fashion design. Home: 13 Reimer Rd Westport CT 06880-2733 Office: Conn Dance Sch 42 Halley Ct Fairfield CT 06825 Office Phone: 203-384-2492. E-mail: barweb@aol.com.

WEBSTER, COLLEEN MICHAEL, English language educator; b. Sunnyvale, Calif., Sept. 21, 1965; d. E. Patrick and Patricia Colleen (Medlar) W. BA in English, Coll. of Notre Dame of Md., 1987; MA in English, U. Del., 1989, ABD, 1992. Adj. faculty Coll. of Notre Dame, Balt., 1990-94, Harford C.C., Bel Air, Md., 1991-94, assoc. prof., 1994—; adj. faculty Goucher Coll., Balt., 1992-93, Towson State U., Balt., 1992-93. Organizer/moderator book club Coll. of Notre Dame, Balt., 1994-95, moderator book club Pikesville C.C., 1994-95, moderator Bel Air book club, 2000—; poetry reading coord. Steppingstone Mus., Havre de Grace, Md., 1993-98; spkr. Md. Humanities Coun., 2000—. Pres. Md. Jr. Coll. Women's LaCrosse League; lacrosse coach Hartford C.C. Recipient Judson Jerome Poetry scholar Antioch Writer's Conf., 1995; named Coach of Yr. Am. Juco Assn., 1996, 97; nominated Pushcart prize, 2002. Democrat. Avocations: running, mountain biking, kayaking, marathons. Office: Harford Cmty Coll 401 Thomas Run Rd Bel Air MD 21015-1627

WEBSTER, JOLENE DENISE, music educator; b. Richmond, Ind., Oct. 7, 1959; d. John Raleigh Webster and Lois Elvina Cramer; children: Emily Naples, Johnny Naples, Bethany Narvaez. B.Sacred Music, Clear Creek Coll., Pineville, Ky., 1985; B.Religious Edn., Clear Creek Coll., 1985; MusM, Southwestern U., Ft. Worth, Tex., 1988; postgrad., Tex. Christian U., 1988—89. Cert. tchr. K-12 music Tex. Dir. seconary choral music Coppell H.S., Tex., 1989—; minister of music Rejoice Luth. Ch., Coppell, 1993—. Condr. (performance) Carnegie Hall, N.Y.C., 1999, St. Peter's Basilica, Rome, 2001, Canterbury Cathedral, Eng., 2003, Que., London, tenberg, Germany, Munich, Prague, Salzburg and Vienna, Austria, Paris. Chair Music in Our Schs., Tex., 1999—2000; assoc. in ministry, minister of music Evang. Luth. Ch. Am. Scholar Pres.'s scholar, Southwestern U., 1988. Mem.: Tex. Music Educators Assn., Tex. Choral Dirs. Assn., Am. Choral Dirs. Assn. Lutheran. Home: 902 W Glade Rd Hurst TX 76054 Office: Coppell High Sch 185 W Parkway Blvd Coppell TX 75019

WEBSTER, LESLEY DANIELS, bank executive; married; 2 children. PhD in Econs., Stanford U. Asst. prof. Wash. U., 1977-83; with Chase Securities, 1983—90; mng. dir., head arbitrage trading group Union Bank Switzerland, N.Y.C., 1990-94; exec. v.p. market risk mgmt. Chase Manhattan Corp. (now JPMorganChase), N.Y.C., 1994—. Bd. dirs. United Way of N.Y.C., chair Women United in Philanthropy for N.Y.C. Named one of 25 Women to Watch, US Banker Mag., 2003. Mem.: Securities Industry Assn. (risk mgmt. com.). Office: Chase Manhattan Corp 270 Park Ave Fl 12 New York NY 10017-2036*

WEBSTER, LINDA JANE, clinical social worker, consultant; b. Whitinsville, Mass., Mar. 23, 1948; d. David and Erva Viola (Chesley) Longmuir; m. Barry Ward Webster, Dec. 16, 1988; 1 child, Jeffrey. BS magna cum laude, Springfield (Mass.) Coll., 1969; MEd, U. Hartford, 1971; M. in Social Work, U. Utah, 1981, PhD, 1997. Lic. clin. social worker Utah; diplomate Am. Bd. Examiners and Nat. Assn. Social Workers. Sch. psychologist Bd. Edn., New Britain, Conn., 1969-77; dir. Project React Capital Region Edn. Coun., Bloomfield, Conn., 1977-79; coord. acute and intensive treatment Valley West Mental Health Ctr., Salt Lake City, Utah, 1981-86; program dir. Western Inst. NeuroPsychiatry, Salt Lake City, 1986-88; social worker pvt. practice Murray, Utah, 1988—. Cons. Episcopal Social and Pastoral Ministries, Salt Lake City, 1986-88; adj. faculty U. Utah, Grad. Sch. Social Work, Salt Lake City, 1986-93. Vol. Episcopalian Ch., Salt Lake City, 1980—; mentor Murray (Utah) H.S., 1997. Mem. Nat. Assn. Social Workers (sec. Utah chpt. 1986-88), Alumni Assn. U. Utah Grad Sch. Social Workers, (pres. 1986-89), Phi Kappa Phi. Avocations: skiing, tennis, basketball, teddy bears, crafts. Office: PhD LCSW 111 E 5600 S Ste 314 Murray UT 84107-8167

WEBSTER, LINDA JEAN, communications educator, media consultant; b. LA, July 16, 1948; d. Stanley Stewart and Irene M. (Sabo) W. BS, So. Conn. State U., New Haven, 1981, MA, 1983; PhD, La. State U., Baton Rouge, 1987; BA, St. Gregory U., 2002. CEO CBE Enterprises, Inc., Baton Rouge, 1984-89; rsch. fellow La. State U., Baton Rouge, 1983-87; instr. speech Southeastern La. U., Hammond, 1984-89, Hancock Coll., Santa Maria, Calif., 1989; curator of edn. Lompoc (Calif.) Mus., 1989; asst. prof. speech U. Ark., Monticello, 1990-95, assoc. prof. speech, dir. honors program, 1995-2000, prof. speech and journalism, 2000—, chmn. faculty senate, 2003—. Faculty advisor student newspaper The Weevil and student yearbook The Boll Weevil, U. Ark., Monticello, yearbook dir. journalism program; exec. dir. Drew County Hist. Mus., Monticello, 1992-95; media dir. Oasis Resources-Homeless Shelter, Warren, Ark., 1991-99, chair bd. dirs., 1998-99; bur. chief Pine Bluff (Ark.) Comml., 1992-94; media consulting WZXS-FM, Holly Ridge, NC, 1995-97; apptd. State Ark. Mus. Svcs. Rev. Panel, 1997-98, re-apptd., 1999-2000, elected chair panel, 1999; chair Drew County Salvation Army, 1999-2000; faculty exec. MBA program U. Chgo., 2001-, chair faculty assembly, 2003—. Editor Jour. Comm. Studies, 1997-2000, on-line version, 2001—; assoc. editor; asst. Popular Measurement, 1998—; S.E. regional corr. Ark. Cath., 1999-2000, columnist, 2003—; contbr. chpts. to books and articles to profl. jours. Vol. Boys/Girls Club, Monticello, 1992—93, Therapy Animal; campaign dir. Gloria Wright Election, Monticello, 1995, dir. re-election campaign, 2000; campaign media dir. Ken Harper Election-Dist. 82, 1996; sec. Drew County Rep. Conv., 1998—2000; vice chair St. Mark Parish Coun., 2001—02; chair Migrant Worker Ministry to S.E. Ark.; diocesan comns. on adult faith formation Catechist Tng. Faculty; faculty Diocesan Theology Program. Recipient Noel Ross Strader award Coll. Media Advisors, Inc., 1991, Coll. Tchr. of the Yr. award Ark. State Commn. Assn., 1993, Alpha Chi Tchr. of Yr. award, 1999, Faculty Excellence Gold award, 1999; Master fellow Ark. Distance Learning Acad., 2000-01. Mem. AAUW, AAUP, Assn. for Edn. in Journalism and Mass Comm., Nat. Women's Studies Assn., Am. Soc. for History of Rhetoric, Ark. Press Women (state pres. 1993-95, Communicator of Achievement award 1991), Ark. State Comm. Assn. (1st v.p.-elect 1997-98, 1st v.p. 1998-99, pres. 1999-2000, Stds. Bearer 1997—), So. State Comm. Assn. (chair honors session 1995, constitutio com. 1997-2000), Internat. Comm. Assn., Oral History Assn., Speech Comm. Assn. (commn. chair 1993-96), Nat. Comm. Assn. (sec. sr. coll. and univ. sect. 1997-99), Edn. Comm. Assn. (campus Cath. minister 1999—), Assn. Edn. Journalism and Mass Comm. Roman Catholic. Avocations: historic preservation, gardening. Office: U Ark-Arts & Humanities Monticello AR 71656 E-mail: webster@uamont.edu.

WEBSTER, LOIS SHAND, association executive; b. Springfield, Ill., Sept. 25, 1929; d. Richings James and C. Odell (Gilbert) S.; m. Terrance Ellis Webster, Feb. 12, 1954 (dec. July 1985); children: Terrance Richings, Bruce Douglas, Andrew Michael. BA, Millikin U., 1951; cert. in libr. tech., Coll. Du Page County, Glen Ellyn, Ill., 1974; postgrad. libr. sci., No. Ill. U., 1977-82. Exec. asst. Am. Nuclear Soc., La Grange Park, Ill., 1973—. Contbr. articles and book chpts. to profl. publs. Field dir. Springfield coun. Girl Scouts U.S., 1951-54; libr. advisor Du Page County coun. Girl Scouts U.S., 1973-74. Recipient Octave J. Du Temple award Am. Nuclear Soc., 1989. Mem. Spl. Librs. Assn. (divsn. chmn. 1984-85, chmn. by-laws com. 1987-89, bd. dirs. 1989-92, sec. 1990-91, visioning com. 1992—), Coun. Engring. and Sci. Soc. Execs., Am. Soc. Assn. Execs., Met. Chgo. Libr. Assembly (bd. dirs. 1982-85). Avocations: travel, genealogy. Home: 5383 Newport St Lisle IL 60532-4126 Office: Am Nuclear Soc 555 N Kensington Ave La Grange Park IL 60526-5535

WECHSLER, JESSICA See JOSELL, JESSICA

WECHSLER, MARY HEYRMAN, lawyer; b. Green Bay, Wis., Jan. 8, 1948; d. Donald Hubert and Helen (Polcyn) Heyrman; m. Roger Wechsler, Aug. 1971 (div. 1977); 1 child, Risa Heyrman; m. David Jay Sellinger, Aug. 15, 1981; 1 stepchild, Kirk Benjamin; 1 child, Michael Paul. Student, U. Chgo., 1966-67, 68-69; BA, U. Wash., 1971; JD cum laude, U. Puget Sound, 1979. Bar: Wash. 1979. Assoc. Law Offices Ann Johnson, Seattle, 1979-81; ptnr. Johnson, Wechsler, Thompson, Seattle, 1981-83; pvt. practice Seattle, 1984-87; ptnr. Mussehl, Rosenberg et al, Seattle, 1987-88, Wechsler, Becker LLP, Seattle, 1988—. Mem. Bd. Ct. Edn., 1998—2003, sec., 2003—04; bd. dirs. U. Wash. Law Sch. Child Advocacy Clinic, 1996—99; mem. Wash. State Commn. on Jud. Selection, 1995—96, Wash. State Commn. on Domestic Rels., 1996—97, 1999—2003; chair edn. com. Access to Justice Bd., 1996—99, mem. pub. trust and confidence com., 2000—04; presenter in field. Author: Family Law in Washington, 1987, rev. edit., 1988, Marriage and Separation, Divorce and Your Rights, 1994; contbr. articles to legal publs. Mem. Wash. State Ethics Adv. Com., 1992-95; bd. dirs. Seattle LWV, 1991-92. Named one of Seattle's Top Lawyers, Seattle Mag., 2003. Fellow Am. Acad. Matrimonial Lawyers (Wash. state chpt., sec.-treas. 1996, v.p. 1997-98, pres. 1999-2000, nat. arbitration com. 1999-2000, nat. interdisciplinary com. 1999-2000, nat. admissions procedure com. 2000-02, nat. long range planning com. 2003, chair 2003—); mem. ABA (chmn. membership Wash. state 1987-88), Wash. State Bar Assn. (exec. com. family law sect. 1985-91, chair family law sect. 1988-89), profl. devel. com. 2002-03, media project com. 2001, ct. improvement com. 1998-2000, legs. com. 1991-96, Outstanding Atty. of Yr. family law sect. 1988, comms. com. 1997-98, disciplinary hearing officer 1998—), Wash. Women Lawyers, King County Bar Assn. (legis. com. 1985-2000, vice-chair 1990-91, chair family law sect. 1986-87, chair domestic violence com. 1986-87, trustee 1988-90, policy planning com. 1991-92, 2d v.p. 1992-93, 1st v.p. 1993-94, pres. 1994-95, long-range planning com. 1998-99, awards com. 1997-99, nominations com. 2003, co-chair Bench-Bar Conf. 2003, Outstanding Atty. award 1999), Nat. Conf. of Bar Pres., King County Bar Found. (trustee 1997-2000), Am. Judicature Soc. (v.p. Washington chpt. 2000-03, pres. 2003—). Office: Wechsler Becker LLP Ste 4550 701 5th Ave Seattle WA 98104-7097 Office Phone: 206-624-4900.

WECHSLER, SUSAN LINDA, research and development software manager; b. Burbank, Calif., Oct. 7, 1956; d. Robert Edward and Sharron Ilene Wechsler; m. Gary Daniel Grove, Aug. 24, 1975 (dec. Dec. 1980); m. Dane Bruce Rogers, Feb. 28, 1987; children: Shayna Marneen Rogers, Ayla Corinne Rogers. BA in Math., Calif. State U., Long Beach, 1979. R&D software design engr. Hewlett-Packard Co., Corvallis, Oreg., 1980-97, R&D project mgr. sys. integration team for laptops, 1997—2002, software project mgr. internet svcs. team, 2002—. Presenter at confs. Contbr. articles to profl. publs.; co-developer nine calculators and handheld computers; patentee in field; co-designer HP 200LX Palmtop PC/Organizer, 1994; writer user interface DMI and BIOS software for laptop computers, 1994-97. Pres. Gifts for a Better World, Corvallis, Oreg., 1994, bd. dirs. 1990-1995. Democrat. Avocations: sewing, raising orchids, reading. Office: Hewlett-Packard Mail Stop 123E 1000 NE Circle Blvd Corvallis OR 97330-4291 E-mail: susan@hp.com.

WECHTER, CLARI ANN, paint manufacturing company executive; b. Chgo., June 1, 1953; d. Norman Robert and Harriet Beverly (Golub) W.; m. Gordon Jay Siegel, Feb. 10, 1980; 1 child, Alix Jessica. BA, U. Ariz., 1975; BE, Loyola U., Chgo., 1977. Cert. tchr., Ill. Saleswoman, v.p. sales Federated Paint Mfg. Co., Chgo., 1979—. Republican. Jewish. Avocation: travel. Home: 25 E Cedar St Chicago IL 60611-1109 Office: Federated Paint and Pioneer Powder Mfg Co 1521 N 31st Ave Melrose Park IL 60160

WECK, KRISTIN WILLA, bank executive; b. Elgin, Ill., Nov. 5, 1959; d. John Francis and Florence Elaine (Ebel) W. BBA, Augustana Coll., Rock Island, Ill., 1981. Lic. real estate broker, Ill., life/health ins. producer; registered securities rep. (series 7 and series 24); registered uniform investment advisor series 65. Intern with investment banking group First Chgo. Bank, London, 1980; intern Prudential-Bache Co., Ft. Lauderdale, Fla., 1981; residential appraiser Fox Valley Appraisal Counselors, Ltd., West Dundee, Ill., 1982-84; asst. real estate loan officer First Nat. Bank, Barrington, Ill., 1982-84; savs. and loan field examiner III Office of Thrift Supervision, Chgo., 1984-90; mng. agt. Resolution Trust Corp., Elk Grove Village, Ill., 1990-91; pres., treas., bd. dirs. Cardunal Savs. Bank, West Dundee, Ill., 1991—; dir. Prairie State Bank, Marengo, Ill., 1998—2002. Project Bus. cons. Jr. Achievement, 1992-96; literacy tutor Vols. of Am., 1998-99; dist. chmn. Found. Ednl. Excellence, 2003-04. Recipient Outstanding Achievement award Fed. Home Loan Bank Bd., 1985, Leading Us In Commerce and Industry award for fin. svcs., 1998, Sam Walton Bus. Cmty. Leader award, 1999. Mem. Nat. Assn. Securities Dealers (registered rep., registered prin.), Rotary Club Dundee Twp. (pres. 2001-02, Rotarian of Yr. 1997-98, Disting. Pres. 2002). Republican. Lutheran. Avocations: scuba diving, golfing, walking, reading. Home: PO Box 930 Dundee IL 60118-0930 Office: Cardunal Savs Bank 704 W Main St # 97 Dundee IL 60118-2028 Personal E-mail: kweck@cardunal.net.

WECK, MARY KATHERINE, special education educator; b. Portsmouth, Va., Feb. 5, 1962; d. Harry Eugene Baum Sr. and Mary Ellen Dempsey; children: Donald Richard, Lindsey MaryAnn. A in Applied Bus., Lima Tech. Coll., 1992; BS in Criminal Justice, Defiance Coll., 1996; tchg. cert. spl. edn., Norfolk State U., 1999. Spl. edn. tchg. cert. Va. Legal sec. Myers & Myers Law Office, Celina, Ohio, 1992—93; investigator Child Protective Svcs., Van Wert, Ohio, 1995—96; tchr. asst. Virginia Beach (Va.) City Pub. Schs., 1997—99, spl. edn. tchr., 1999—2002. Tchr. Prins. Adv. Com., Virginia Beach, 2000—02. Voter registrar Van Wert County, 1992. Recipient Am. Scholar Collegiate award, 1995. Presbyterian. Avocations: ballroom dancing, beaches, books. Office: Kempsville HS Virginia Beach VA 23462

WECKESSER, SUSAN ONEACRE, lawyer; b. Akron, Ohio, July 23, 1938; d. Leland E. and Maryethel (Parsons) Oneacre; m. John V. Rhinehart, Mar. 28, 1958 (div. 1971); children: Kirk Andrew Rhinehart, Kristin Rhinehart; m. John C. Weckesser, Aug. 19, 1972 (div. 1997). BEd, Ohio U., 1959; MA, CUNY, 1974; JD, U. N.Mex., 1983. Bar: N.Mex. 1983, U.S. Dist. Ct. (N.Mex.) 1984, U.S. Ct. Appeals (10th cir.) 1987. Dir. publs. N.Mex. Mcpl. League, Santa Fe, 1972-83; assoc. Patrick A. Casey, Santa Fe, 1983-86; pvt. practice Santa Fe, 1986-98; mem. legal bur. N. Mex. Risk Mgmt. Divsn., Santa Fe, 1998—2003; pvt. practice, 2003—. Bd. dirs. St. Elizabeth Shelter, Santa Fe, 1996—. Mem.: N.Mex. Trial Lawyers Assn. (bd. dirs. 1996—98). Democrat. Office: PO Box 4819 Santa Fe NM 87502-4819

WEDDINGTON, ELIZABETH GARDNER (LIZ GARDNER), actress; b. N.Y.C., Oct. 13, 1932; d. A. Adolph and Anne Mary (Gardner) Blank; m. George Lee Weddington, Jr., Oct. 23, 1965; 1 child, Georgiana Marie. Student, Moravian Sem. for Girls. Actress TV, radio, telephone, N.Y./Calif, 1957—; editor comml. scripts N.Y., 1969—; freelance writer N.Y. City Tribune, various other publs., N.Y., 1984—. Columnist polit. commentary, 1984—; appeared in over 300 TV commls., also TV and radio voice-overs. Mem. County Com., Conservative Party, N.Y.C., 1988-90, 94-96, 17th Precinct Comty. Coun., N.Y.C., 1974-96; rep. Yorkville Area Cath. Coun., N.Y.C., 1986-93. Recipient Mayor's Vol. Action Ctr. award, N.Y.C., 1981-82, Cert. Recognition N.Y.C. Dept. Police Dep. Commr. Community Affairs, 1981. Mem.: Nat. League Am. Pen Women, Am. Fedn. Radio and TV Artists, Screen Actors Guild, Friends of Va. Archives, N.Y. State Soc. Children Am. Revolution (sr. historian 1988—90, sr. 2d v.p. 1990—92), Colonial Dames Am. (N.Y. claims com. 1993—96, chpt. XXIX N.C. 1999—, courtesy mem. parent chpt.), Daus. Colonial Wars, United Daus. of Confederacy (pres. N.Y. divsn. 1988—90, nat. chmn. revision of gen. bylaws com. 1989—91, McMath Scholar gen. com. 1991—92, nat. chmn. gen. bylaws com. 1992—96, gen. chmn. radio and TV com. 1998—2000, mem. Mrs. Simon Baruch Univ. award com. 2000—02, chmn. chpt. bylaws com. 2002—), N.Y. State Soc. Dames of Ct. of Honor (pres. 1984—88), N.Y. State Soc. Daus. 1812, Nat. Soc. U.S. Daus. of 1812 (organizing pres. Pres. James Madison chpt. 360 1988—98), Nat. Soc. Children and Am. Revolutin - Fraunces Tavern Soc. (sr. pres. 1985—89), Nat. Soc. DAR (assoc.; corr. sec. 1992—94, Washington colonial chpt. 1996—, Mary Washington Colonial chpt. 1996—, mem. Warren chpt. 1996—, treas. 2001—, chmn. nat. def. com. 2001—, Warren chpt., chmn. com. Mary Washington Colonial chpt.). Republican. Roman Catholic. Avocations: genealogy, military, english, constitutional and religious history, opera, antiques, porcelains. Home and Office: 316 N Main St Warrenton NC 27589-1826 E-mail: betsy1013@vance.net.

WEDDINGTON, SUSAN, political party official; m. Bob Weddington; 1 child, Sean. BA in Comms. with honors, Trinity U. Tchr. photojournalism; owner three small bus.; dir. media rels. Tex. Conservative Coalition, rsch. analyst; legis. asst. Rep. state rep.; vice chmn. Rep. Party Tex., 1994, 96, state chmn., 1997—. Del. four State Rep. Convs.; Tex. del. Rep. Nat. Conv., San Diego, 1996, Tex. rep. Nat. Rules Com.; worked 76 in 96 Polit. Action Com.; RPT liaison Campaign for Rep. Leadership Polit. Action Com. Active Drug Stop, San Antonio Citizens Against Pornography, crisis pregnancy ctrs.; bd. dirs. Pray Tex.; mem. Castle Hills First Bapt. Ch., San Antonio; dir. comms., rsch. Tex. Pub. Policy Found. Mem. Nat. Coun. Women Advisors to Congress (charter), Bexar County Rep. Women's Forum, Daus. of Liberty Rep. Club, Bexar County Hispanic Rep. Women's Club. Office: Rep Party of Tex 900 Congress Ave, Ste 300 Austin TX 78701-3218

WEDEL-COWGILL, MILLIE REDMOND, secondary school educator, performing arts educator, communications educator; b. Harrisburg, Pa., Aug. 18, 1939; d. Clair L. and Florence (Heiges) Aungst; m. T.S. Redmond, 1956 (div. 1967); children: T.S. Redmond II; m. Frederick L. Wedel, Jr., 1974 (div. 1986); m. Paul R. Cowgill, May 19, 2001. BA, Alaska Meth. U., 1966; MEd, U. Alaska, Anchorage, 1972; postgrad. in comm., Stanford U., 1975-76. Lic. third class broadcasting, FCC. Profl. actress Charming Models & Models Guild of Phila., 1954-61; asst. dir. devel. in charge pub. rels. Alaska Meth. U., Anchorage, 1966, part-time lectr., 1966, 73; comm. tchr. Anchorage Sch. Dist., 1967-96; owner Wedel Prodns., Anchorage, 1976-86; cons. comms., media and edn., owner Cowgill Cons., 2003—. Pub. rels. staff Alaska Purchase Centennial Exhibit, U.S. Dept. Commerce, 1967; writer gubernatorial campaign, 1971; instr. Chapman Coll., 1990-93; adj. instr. U. Alaska, Anchorage, 1972, 77-79, 89-2001; cons. Cook Inlet Native Assn., 1978, No. Inst., 1979; judge Ark. Press Women's Writing Contest, 1990-91; sec. exec. bd. Alaska Dept. Edn. Profl. Tchg. Practices Commn., 1993-94. Bd. dirs. Sta. KAKM, Alaska Pub. TV, membership chmn., 1978-80, nat. lay rep. to Pub. Broadcasting Svc. and Nat. Assn. Pub. TV Stas., 1979; bd. dirs. Ednl. Telecom. Consortium for Alaska, 1979, Mid-Hillside Cmty. Coun., Municipality of Anchorage, 1979-80, 83-88, Hillside East Cmty. Coun., 1984-88, pres., 1984-85; rsch. writer, legal asst. Vinson & Elkins, Houston, 1981; v.p., bd. dirs. Inlet View ASD Cmty. Sch., 1994-95, pres., 1995-97; mem. Valley Forge Freedoms Found., Murdoch Scholarships; bd. dirs. Rev. Richard Gay Trust, Alaska and Pa., 1992-2000. Recipient awards for newspapers, lit. mags.; award Nat. Scholastic Press Assn., 1981, 82, 83, 84; Alaska Coun. Econs., 1982, Merits award Alaska Dept. Edn., 1982-93, Legis. commendation State of Alaska, Nat. Blue Ribbon Outstanding Sch. award, 1993. Mem. NEA (AEA bldg. rep., state del. 70s, 80s, 94-95), Assn. Pub. Broadcasting (charter mem., nat. lay del. 1980), Indsl. TV Assn. (San Francisco and Houston 1975-81), Alaska Press Club (chmn. high sch. journalism workshops, 1968-69, 73, awards for sch. newspapers 1972, 74, 77), Alaska Fedn. Press Women (dir. 1978-86, 94-95, pres. 1995-96, h.s. journalism competition youth projects dir., award for brochures 1978, chair youth writing contest 1994-95), Internat. Platform Assn., World Affairs Coun., Chugach Electric (chair 1990, nomination com. for bd. dirs. 1988-90), Stanford U. Alumni Club (Alaska pres. 1982-84, 90-92, 99-2000, v.p. 1998-99, cowgill cons. 2003—), Naples Downtown Rotary, Imperial Golf Course Country Club, Club at Pelican Bay, Naples (Fla.) Philharm. League, Naples Players Theatre Guild, Pelican Bay Women's League, Delta Kappa Gamma. Presbyterian. Office: PO Box 111489 Anchorage AK 99511-1489 also: PO Box 770662 Naples FL 34107-0662

WEDGE, BARBARA JANE, women's health nurse; b. Springfield, Ill., June 24, 1940; d. Allan Thomas and Susannah Alice (Barnes) Goodwin; children: John Thomas, Michelle Louise. AS, Forest Pk. C.C., St. Louis, Mo., 1968; BSN, Webster U., 1990. RN Mo., 1968. Clin. nursing supr. Ob-Gyn Clinic Barnes-Jewish Hosp., St. Louis, 1972—90, clin. nurse mgr. Women's Wellness Ctr., 1990—2002; ret. Cons. BJC-Home Health Profl. Adv. Bd., St. Louis, 1995—2002. Contbr. articles clinical rsch. to profl. jour. Hostess & mentor World Affairs Coun. of St. Louis, St. Louis, 1994—98; mem. Internat. Sister Cities-Stuttgardt, St. Louis; mem. chairperson Friends of Thomas Dunn Meml. Adult Edn., St. Louis, 2002—03. D-Conservative. Roman Cath. Achievements include development of and implemented advanced practice nurse collaborative practice with Wash. Univ.faculty; teen pregnancy ctr. for an underserved population. Personal E-mail: rquito@aol.com.

WEDGE, CAROLE C. architectural firm executive; B in Environ. Design, U. Colo.; BArch, Boston Archtl. Ctr. Joined Sheple Bulfinch Richardson & Abbott, Boston, 1986, prin., 2000, pres., 2004—. Lectr. in field. Mem.: ALA, AIA, Soc. Coll. and Univ. Planners, Assn. Coll. and Rsch. Librs. Office: Shepley Bulfinch Richardson & Abbott 40 Broad St Boston MA 02109-4306

WEDGEWORTH, ANN, actress; b. Abilene, Tex., Jan. 21, 1935; m. Rip Torn (div.); 1 child, Danae ; m. Ernest Martin; 1 child, Dianna. Attended, U. Tex.; BA in Drama, So. Methodist U. Broadway debut in Make A Million, 1958; other Broadway appearances Chapter Two (Tony award), Thieves, Blues for Mr. Charlie, The Last Analysis; off-Broadway appearances Line, Chapparal, The Crucible, Days and Nights of Beebee Fenstermaker, Ludlow Fair, The Honest to God Shnozzola, A Lie of the Mind, Elba, The Aunts, The Debutante's Ball; premiers of In the Moonlight Eddie at Pasadena Playhouse, Natural Affection in Pheonix, The Dream in Phila.; toured with nat. cos. of The Sign in Sidney Brustein's Window and Kennedy's Children; appeared in TV series Three's Company, The Edge of Night, Another World, Somerset, Filthy Rich, Evening Shade; other TV appearances All That Glitters, The Equalizer, Roseanne, Bronk, Evening Shade, Twilight Zone, Trapper John, M.D.; TV film The War Between the Tates, Right to Kill, Cooperstown, Fight for Justice: The Nancy Conn Story, Bogie, A Stranger Waits; movies Handle With Care (Nat. Soc. Film Critics award), Thieves, Bang the Drum Slowly, Scarecrow, Catamount Killing, Law and Disorder, One Summer Love, Dragon-Fly, Birch Intervals, Soggy Bottom, USA, No Small Affair, Sweet Dreams, Mens Club, A Tiger's Tale, Made in Heaven, Far North, Miss Firecracker, Green Card, Steel Magnolias, Love and a 45, The Whole Wide World, The Hunter's Moon, Hard Promises, Andy, My Science Project; TV host Evening at the Improv, A&E. Address: 70 Riverside Dr Apt 6E New York NY 10024-5716

WEDGWOOD, RUTH, law educator, international affairs expert; b. N.Y.C. d. Morris P. and Anne (Williams) Glushien; m. Josiah Francis Wedgwood; May 29, 1982; 1 child, Josiah Ruskin Wedgwood. BA magna cum laude, Harvard U., 1972; fellow, London Sch. Econs., 1972-73; JD, Yale U., 1976. Bar: D.C., N.Y., U.S. Supreme Ct. Law clk. to judge Henry Friendly U.S. Ct. Appeals (2d cir.), N.Y.C., 1976-77; law clk. to justice Harry Blackmun U.S. Supreme Ct., Washington, 1977-78; spl. asst. to asst. atty. gen. U.S. Dept. Justice, Washington, 1978-80; asst. U.S. atty. U.S. Dist. Ct. (so. dist.) N.Y., N.Y.C., 1980-86; prof. law Yale U., New Haven, 1986—2002, fellow Inst. for Social and Policy Studies, 1989—; fellow Berkeley Coll., Yale U., 1989—; Edward B. Burling prof. internat. law and diplomacy Nitze Sch. Advanced Internat. Studies Johns Hopkins U., Washington, 2001—. Mem. Sec. of State's Adv. Com. Internat. Law, 1993—; sr. fellow for internat orgns. and law Coun. Fgn. Rels., 1994—; Charles Stockton prof. internat. law U.S. Naval War Coll., Newport, RI, 1998—99; mem. Hart-Rudman Commn. on Nat. Security in the 21st Century, Nat. Sec. Study Group, Dept. Def. Adv. Comm., 1999—2001; mem. acad. adv. com. to spl. rep. UN Sec.-Gen. for Children and Armed Conflict, 1999—; dir. studies Am. Soc. Internat. Law, 2000—; guest scholar U.S. Inst. Peace, 2001—02; dir. studies Hague Acad. Internat. Law, 2001—02; elected U.S. mem. UN Human Rights Com., Geneva, 2002—; mem. Hist. Rev. Panel, adv. to dir. CIA, 2002—; mem. Def. Policy Bd., advisor to U.S. Sec. Def., 2002—. Exec. editor Yale Law Jour., 1975-76; author: The Revolutionary Martyrdom of Jonathan Robbins, 1990, The Use of Force in International Affairs, 1992, American National Interest and the United Nations, 1996, Toward an International Criminal Court?, 1999, After Dayton: Lessons of the Bosnian Peace Process, 1999; mem. bd. editors Yale Jour. Law and Humanities, 1988-98, Am. Jour. Internat. Law, 1998-, World Policy Jour. (New Sch. Social Rsch.), 2001-; contbr. articles to profl jours. and popular publs. including N.Y. Times, Washington Post, Christian Sci. Monitor, Internat. Herald Tribune, Wall St. Jour., Washington Times, Fin. Times, L.A. Times, Die Zeit, Fgn. Affairs, Fgn. Policy, Nat. Interest, Time mag.; commentator for CNN, PBS, Fox, Nat. Pub. Radio, MSNBC, BBC, Lehrer News Hour, PBS. Prin. rapporteur U.S. Atty. Gen.'s Guidelines on FBI Undercover Ops., Informant Use and Racketeering and Gen. Crime Investigations, 1980; bd. dirs. Lawyers Com. for Human Rights, N.Y.C., 1988-94; mem. policy adv. com. UN Assn. U.S.A., 1998—; bd. dirs. Lawyers Alliance for World Security, 1999-, Freedom House, 2003-. Recipient Israel Peres prize, 1976, Disting. Contbn. to Internat. Law award N.Y. State Bar Assn., 2000; Ford Found. Rsch. grantee; Rockefeller Found. fellow. Mem. ABA (standing com. on law and nat. security 2002-, coun. Internat. Law sect. 2003-), Am. Law Inst., Am. Soc. Internat. Law (exec. com. 1995-98), Internat. Law Assn. (v.p. 1994-, program chmn. Am. br. 1992), Assn. Am. Law Sch. (chmn. sect. internat. law 1995-96), Assn. Bar City N.Y. (arms control and internat. security affairs com., chmn. 1989-92, chmn. internat. affairs coun. 1992-95, exec. com. 1995-99), Union Internationale des Avocats, U.S.A. (chpt. bd. govs. 1993-98), Coun. on Fgn. Rels., Internat. Inst. for Strategic Studies, Elizabethan Club, Mory's Assn., Yale Club (N.Y.C.). also: Coun on Fgn Rels 58 E 68th St New York NY 10021-5953 Office: Johns Hopkins Sch Advanced Internat Studies 1619 Massachusetts Ave NW Washington DC 20036 E-mail: rwedgwood@jhu.edu.

WEE, CHRISTINE DIJOS, elementary school educator; b. Honolulu, Jan. 8, 1968; d. Cosme Wayne and Victoria Amparo Dijos; m. Phillip Ying Kin Wee, July 15, 2000; 1 child, Deanna Rae Patacsil. BEd, U. Hawaii, Manoa, 1991. Cert. tchr. Hawaii, prof. diploma in elem. edn. Univ. Hawaii, 1992. Kindergarten tchr. Island Paradise Sch., Honolulu, 1992—93, Pauoa Elem. Sch., Honolulu, 1993—94, choral dir., 1997—2002, 6th grade tchr., 1994—2002, choral dir., 2003—, 5th grade tchr., 2003—; spl. edn. summer sch. aide Wailupe Valley Elem. Sch., Honolulu; Challenger Ctr.-trained educator, NASA program Barber's Point Elem. Sch., Kapolei, Hawaii, 1996—2002. Regional conf. del. Sch.-to-Work, Honolulu, 1998; cadre mem. Roosevelt Complex Writing Inst., Honolulu, 1999; mem. music action rsch. team Hawaii State Dept. Edn., 1999—2001. Mem. coun. Sch. Cmty.-Based Mgmt. Coun., Pauoa Elem. Sch., 2001—03; vol., chmn. Honolulu Dist. Choral Festival, 1994—2002; mem. ch. choir; mem. Sweet Adelines Internat.; bd. dirs. Pauoa Elem. Sch. PTA, 1996—97. Mem.: Hawaii Music Educators Assn. (3d v.p. 2000—02, chmn. 2001—02), Hawaii state tchr. assoc. (union rep. 1995—96, 2000—01, student svcs. coord. 2002—03). Avocations: walking, collecting keychains and unicorns/Pegasuses. Home: 823 9th Ave Honolulu HI 96816 Office: Pauoa Elem Sch 2301 Pauoa Rd Honolulu HI 96813 E-mail: unipeg823@hotmail.com.

WEEDN, TRISH, state legislator; b. Oklahoma City, May 10, 1950; d. Carl R. and Teddeline (Morrell) Throckmorton; m. James A. Weedn; children: Marnie, Mindy. Assessor McClain County, Okla., 1979-88; mem. Okla. State Senate, 1989—. Former chmn. McClain County Dem. Com; sect./treas. Purcell Pentacostal Holiness Ch. Mem. Okla. Assn. Assessing Officers, S.W. Coll. Ministry. Democrat. Pentecostal. Office: Okla State Senate State Capitol Oklahoma City OK 73105

WEEKES, WANDA L. information technology manager; d. Garvin M. and Jennifer M. Weekes. BS in Acctg., U. Conn., 1995. Info. tech. cons. Costello & Assocs., Inc., Norwalk, Conn., 1996—97; sr. bus. analyst Oxford Splty. Mgmt., Norwalk, 1997—98, Internat. Masters Pubs., Stamford, Conn., 1998—99, data arch., 1999—2001, dir. bus. sys. N.Y.C., 2001—03, v.p. bus. sys., 2003—. E-mail: wanda.weekes@imp-usa.com.

WEEKS, BRIGITTE, publishing executive; b. Whitchurch, Hants, Eng., Aug. 28, 1943; came to U.S., 1965; d. Jack and Margery May (Millett) W.; m. Edward A. Herscher, Sept. 6, 1969; children— Hilary, Charlotte, Daniel. Student, Univ. Coll. of North Wales, Bangor, 1962-65. Asst. editor Boston Mag., 1966-70; editor Kodansha Internat., Tokyo, 1969-72, Resources for the Future, 1973-74; asst. editor The Washington Post Book World, 1974-78, editor, 1978-88; sr. v.p., editor-in-chief Book-of-the-Month Club, N.Y.C., 1988-94; editor-in-chief Guideposts Books, N.Y.C., 1994—2002, Crossings Book Club, N.Y.C., 2002—. Pres. Nat. Book Critics Circle, 1990. Office: Bookspan 1271 Ave of the Americas New York NY 10020-9991

WEEKS, HELEN BALLARD, retail executive; CEO Ballard Designs, Inc., Atlanta, Ga., 1982—. Office: Ballard Designs Inc 1670 Defoor Ave NW Atlanta GA 30318-7562

WEEKS, SKYLA GAY, music educator; b. Kansas City, Mo., Jan. 16, 1963; d. Milfred Dale and Willo Dean (Vest) Hammerbacher; m. Russell Dwaine Weeks, June 8, 1990; 1 child, Tyler Blair. B Music Edn., U. Mo., 1985. K-12 vocal music tchr. Malcolm Pub. Schs., Nebr., 1986—87, Sheldon Sch., Mo., 1993—94; K-8 vocal music tchr Westview Sch., Neosho, Mo., 1993—94; entertainer Bur. Lecturers & Concert Artists, Lawrence, Kans., 1995—96; K-12 music tchr. Hermitage R-IV, Mo., 1998—2002, Macks Creek R-V, 2003—. Author: (songs) All I Need, 2001. Recipient tchr. appreciation award, Mo. Scholars Acad., 2001. Mem.: Mo. Music Educators Conf. Office Phone: 573-363-5911.

WEEKS, TRESI LEA, lawyer; b. Brownwood, Tex., Dec. 3, 1961; d. Dean Moore and Patsy Ruth (Evans) Adams; m. Kevin Weeks, Oct. 26, 1998. BA in Fgn. Svc., BA in French, Baylor U., 1984, JD, 1987. Bar: Tex. 1987, U.S. Dist. Ct. (no. dist.) Tex. 1988, U.S. Ct. Appeals (5th cir.) 1989. Atty. Richard Jackson & Assocs., Dallas, 1987-91, Amis, Bell & Moore, Arlington, Tex., 1992-98; sole practitioner Plano, Tex., 1999—. Vol. Legal Svcs. of North Tex., Dallas, 1988-97, Dallas Com. for Fgn. Visitors, 1989-92; bd. dirs. Plano Internat. Presch., 1995-96. Recipient Pro Bono Svc. award Legal Svcs. of North Tex., 1989, 90, 91. Mem. AAUW (pub. policy dir. Plano, Tex. br. 1992, 93-94, v.p. 1994-95), State Bar Tex. (mem. mentor program for lawyers com. 1994-98, mem. local bar svcs. com. 1994-96), Dallas Bar Assn., Dallas Women Lawyers Assn. (bd. dirs. 1989-90, v.p. 1992, pres. 1993). Avocations: scuba diving, reading, hiking, growing herbs, writing. Office: 555 Republic Dr Ste 200 Plano TX 75074

WEEMS, CARRIE MAE, photographer; BA, Calif. Inst. Arts, Valencia, 1981; MFA, U. Calif., San Diego, 1984; postgrad., U. Calif., Berkeley, 1984-87. Asst. prof. Hampshire Coll., Amherst, Mass., 1987-91, Calif. Coll. Arts and Crafts, Oakland, 1991-95; artist, prof. Harvard U., 1995—. Vis. prof. Hunter Coll., N.Y., 1988-89, Williams Coll., 2000, Harvard U., 2001. One-person shows include Inst. Contemporary Art, 1991, Trustman Gallery, Simmons Coll., Boston, 1991, The New Mus. Contemporary Art, N.Y., 1991, Matrix Gallery, Wadsworth Atheneum, Hartford, Conn., 1991, Albright Coll., Reading, Pa., 1991, Greenville County Mus. Art, S.C., 1992, San Francisco Art Inst., 1992, Linda Carthcart Gallery, Santa Monica, Calif., 1993, Rhonda Hoffman Gallery, Chgo., 1993, New Langton Arts, San Francisco, 1993, Hood Mus. Art, Dartmouth Coll., N.H., 1994, Mus. Modern Art, N.Y., 1995, The Bunting Inst., 1996, Contemporary Arts Mus., Houston, 1996, Everson Art Mus., Syracuse, N.Y., 1998, High Mus. Art, Atlanta, 2000, Internat. Ctr. Photography N.Y., 2000, Parrish Art Mus., 2001; group shows include Reframing the Family Artists Space, 1991, Whitney Mus. Am. Art, 1991, Mus. Modern Art, 1992, Randy Alexander, 1992, Artists of Conscience: 16 Years of Social and Polit. Commentary, Alt. Mus. N.Y., 1991-92, Through the Kitchen Door, NAME, 1991-92, Disclosing the Myth of Family, Art Inst. Chgo., The Betty Rymer Gallery, Chgo., 1992, The Theater of Refusal: Black Art and the Mainstream Criticism (traveling), 1993-94, States of Loss: Migration, Displacement, Colonialism and Power, Jersey City Mus., N.J., 1993-94, Gesture and Pose, Mus. Modern Art, N.Y., 1994, Bad Girls, Part 1, New Mus. Contemporary Art, N.Y., 1994, Who's Looking at the Family? Barbican Art Gallery, London, 1994, Equal Rights and Justice, High Mus. Art and Nat. Black Arts Fest, Atlanta, 1994, Imaging Families: Images and Voices, Smithsonian Instn., 1994-95, Black Male, Representations of Masculinity in Contemporary Am. Art, Whitney Mus. Am. Art, N.Y., 1994-95, Embedded Metaphor, Ringling Mus. Art, Sarasota, 1996, Alternate Cultures, Johannesberg Biennial, Africa, 1997, Changing Spaces, Detroit Inst. Art, 1998, Bearing Witness,

Polk Mus. Art, 1998, Art Worlds in Dialog, Mus. Ludwig, Cologne, Germany, 1999, Paradise Now, Exit Art, N.Y., 2000, Collection in Context, Studio Mus. Harlem, N.Y., 2001. Office: c/o PPOW 476 Broome St Fl 3 New York NY 10013-2237

WEEMS, HELEN RACHEL, piano teacher, accompanist; b. Morgantown, W.Va., Dec. 12, 1962; d. David Burnola and Charys (Ford) Weems; m. Robert Raymond Provine, June 8, 1996. BA, Sch. of the Ozarks, Point Lookout, Mo., 1986; MM, Peabody Conservatory of Music, Balt., 1991; MA, U. Md. Baltimore County, Balt., 1996. Cert. piano tchr. Music Tchrs. Nat. Assn., 2004. Radio host Sta. KSOZ, Point Lookout, 1985-86, Sta. WJHU, Balt., 1994-96; freelance pianist, tchr., singer, 1975—. Balinese dancer UMBC Gamelan, Balt., 1993—96; coord. Harper's Glen Watch, Columbia, 1998—; Choir dir. St. Luke's Episcopal Ch., Brookeville, Md., 1997—. Neighborhood improvement grantee, Gov.'s Office of Crime Control and Prevention, 1999—2002. Mem.: Greater Columbia Music Tchrs. Assn. (v.p. 1997—2000), Howard County Music Tchrs. Assn. (pres. 1996—2003, concert mgr. 2002—). Democrat. Episcopalian. Avocations: running, gardening. Office: Helen R Weems Piano Studio 5473 Green Dory Ln Columbia MD 21044-1912

WEERTMAN, JULIA RANDALL, materials science and engineering educator; b. Muskegon, Mich., Feb. 10, 1926; BS in Physics, Carnegie-Mellon U., 1946, MS in Physics, 1947, DSc in Physics, 1951. Physicist U.S. Naval Rsch. Lab., Washington, 1952-58; vis. asst. prof. dept. materials sci. and engring. Northwestern U., Evanston, Ill., 1972-73, asst. prof., 1973-78, from asst. prof. to assoc. prof., 1973-82, prof., 1982-99, Walter P. Murphy prof., 1989, chmn. dept., 1987-92, asst. to dean grad. studies and rsch. Tech. Inst., 1973-76, Walter P. Murphy prof. emeritus, 1999—. Mem. various NRC coms. and panels. Co-author: Elementary Dislocation Theory, 1964, 1992, also pub. in French, Japanese and Polish; contbr. numerous articles to profl. jours. Mem. Evanston Environ. Control Bd., 1972-79. Recipient Creativity award NSF, 1981, 86; Guggenheim Found. fellow, 1986-87. Fellow Am. Soc. Metals Internat., Minerals, Metals and Materials Soc. (leadership award 1997); mem. NAE, Am. Acad. Arts and Scis., Am. Phys. Soc., Materials Rsch. Soc. (Von Hippel award 2003), Soc. Women Engrs. (disting. engring. educator award 1989, achievement award 1991). Home: 834 Lincoln St Evanston IL 60201-2405 Office: Northwestern U Dept Material Sci & Engring 2220 Campus Dr Evanston IL 60208-0876 E-mail: jrweertman@northwestern.edu.

WEESE, CYNTHIA ROGERS, architect, educator; b. Des Moines, June 23, 1940; d. Gilbert Taylor and Catharine (Wingard) Rogers; m. Benjamin H. Weese, July 5, 1963; children: Daniel Peter, Catharine Mohr. BSA.S., Washington U., St. Louis, 1962; B.Arch., Washington U., 1965. Registered architect, Ill. Pvt. practice architecture, Chgo., 1965-72, 74-77; draftsperson, designer Harry Weese & Assocs., Chgo., 1972-74; prin. Weese Langley Weese Ltd., Chgo., 1977—; design critic Ball State U., Muncie, Ind., Miami U., Oxford, Ohio, 1979, U. Wis.-Milw., 1980, U. Ill.-Chgo., 1981, 85, Iowa State U., Ames, 1982, Washington U., St. Louis, 1984, U. Ill., Champaign, 1987-92, Kans. State U., 1992; dean sch. architecture Washington U., St. Louis, 1993—. Bd. regents Am. Architecture Found., 1990-93; bd. mem. Landmarks Commn. St. Louis.; mem. Mayor's Task Force Downtown Now, St. Louis, 1997—. Recipient Alpha Rho Chi award Washington U., 1965, Met. Chgo. YWCA Outstanding Achievement award, 1990. Mem. AIA (bd. dirs. Chgo. chpt. 1980-83, v.p. 1983-85, 1st v.p. 1986-87, pres. 1987-88, regional dir. 1990-92, Disting. Bldg. awards 1977, 81-83, 86, 91, 95, Interior Architecture award 1981, 90, 92, nat. v.p. 1993, chmn. urban design task force St. Louis 2004 1997—), AIA/ACSA Coun. on Archtl. Rsch. (chair 1991-92), AIA Found. (pres. Chgo. chpt. 1988-89), Soc. Archtl. Historians (bd. dirs. 1992-94), Chgo. Women in Architecture, Chgo. Network, Nat. Inst. Archtl. Edn. (bd. dirs. 1988-90), Chgo. Archtl. Club (pres. 1988-89), Washington U. Sch. Architecture Alumni (nat. coun. 1988-93), Lambda Alpha. Clubs: Arts, Chgo. Archtl. Democrat. Office: Washington U Sch Architecture PO Box 1079 Saint Louis MO 63188-1079

WEESE, MIRANDA, dancer; b. San Bernardino, Calif. Student, Sch. Am. Ballet, 1990. Apprentice N.Y.C. Ballet, 1991—93, mem. corps de ballet, 1993—94, soloist, 1994—95, prin., 1996—. Dancer (ballets) Apollo, Concerto Barocco, Divertimento No. 15, The Four Temperaments, Romeo and Juliet, Chiaroscuro, The Sleeping Beauty, others, PBS TV spl. Martins' Swan Lake Live from Lincoln Ctr. Fellow USA Dance fellow, Princess Grace Found., 1995—96. Office: NYC Ballet NY State Theatre 20 Lincoln Ctr Plz New York NY 10023-6913

WEESS, PAMELA R. financial services representative; b. Mineola, N.Y., June 12, 1958; d. Fritz and Brunhilde Weess. BS in Health Scis., Long Island U., N.Y., 1980; MPA, Long Island U., 1985. Data liaison specialist Med. Soc. State of N.Y., Lake Success, 1986—88, mgr. dept. physician records divsn membership, 1988—90; mgr. membership/mktg. dept. Am. Phys. Soc., N.Y.C., 1991—92; dir. membership svc. dept. N.Y. Merc. Exch., N.Y.C., 1992—94; corp. sales exec. N.Y. Sports Clubs, N.Y.C., 1994—99; mgr. mktg. and advt. dept. Illuminating Engring. Soc. N. Am., N.Y.C., 1999—2001; fin. svcs. rep. Garden City Fin. Group MetLife Fin. Svcs., Garden City, NY, 2001—. Co-dir. blood drive Greater Long Island Running Club, Plainview, NY, 1993—; mem. Last Hope Animal Rescue, Syosset, NY, 1997—. Mem.: Am. Soc. Assn. Execs. (cert.), N.Y. Soc. Assn. Execs., Am. Coun. on Exercise (cert. fitness instr.). Avocations: running, skiing, tennis. Office: MetLife Fin Svcs 1205 Franklin Ave Ste 150 Garden City NY 11530 E-mail: pweess@metlife.com.

WEFALD, SUSAN, state commissioner; m. Robert O. Wefald; children: Sarah, Kathryn, Tom. BA, U. Mich., 1969; postgrad., U. N.D. Licensed social worker; cert. consumer credit counselor. Elected mem. Bismarck Pub. Sch. Bd., pres.; commr. N.D. Pub. Svc. Commn. Mem. Energy Conservation Com., Com. Consumer Affairs Nat. Assn. Regulatory Utility Commrs.; sec. Mid Am. Regulatory Comm. Violinist, charter mem. Bismarck-Mandan Symphony Orch.; pres. Sakakawea Girl Scout Coun.; bd. dirs. Mo. Slope United Way. Office: ND Pub Svc Commn 600 E Boulevard Ave Bismarck ND 58505-0660 Fax: 701-328-2410.

WEGENAST, JUDY H. elementary school educator, consultant; b. Grafton, N.D., Aug. 4, 1944; d. Donald M. and Donna (Ramsey) Matter; m. Jerry G. Wegenast, May 28, 1966; children: Kim. L. Albrecht, Elisa D. Wegenast. EdB, Valley City State U., 1966; MS, N.D. State U., 1982. Tchr. St. John's, Wahpeton, N.D., 1967; remedial reading Wahpeton (N.D.) Indian Sch., 1968; tchr. West Fargo (N.D.) Pub. Sch., 1968-70, Fargo (N.D.) Pub. Schs., 1970-91, peer coach, 1991—. Instr. N.D. State U. Fargo, Grand Forks, N.D., 1986—; cons. SW Enterprises, fargo, N.D., 1985—. Bd. dirs. Yunder Farm Childrens Mus., Fargo, N.D., 1992—. Named Tchr. of Month, Fargo (N.D.) C. of C., 1989, Tchr. of Yr., IBM/Tech. and Learning, Fargo, N.D., 1992, Fargo Tchr. of Yr., 1992, N.D. Tchr. of Yr., 1992. Mem. Valley Reading Assn., N.D. Edn. Assn., Fargo Edn. Assn. NEA, ASCD, Alpha Delta Kappa. Avocations: painting, gardening, golf, reading, wood working. Office: Centennial Elem 4201 25th St S Fargo ND 58104-6800

WEGNER, DARLENE JOY, civic worker, event coordinator; b. Pasadena, Calif., May 2, 1953; d. Glenn Raymond and Evelyn Pryor (Ingram) Thornton; m. Robert Culbertson, July 25, 1975 (div. May 1977); m. Karl James, June 21, 1986; 1 child, Heather Joy. Student, East L.A. Jr. Coll., 1971-72, Chaffey Coll., Rancho Cucamonga, Calif., 1995. Exec. sec. Wells Fargo Bank, Rosemead, Calif., 1972-76; adminstrv. sec. Ford Aerospace, Pasadena, 1977-78; sales sec. A&F Sales Engring., Pasadena, 1979-84; sr. sec. Xerox Med., Pasadena, 1984-89; cmty. activist Ontario (Calif.) City Hall, 1991-92; vice chmn. Concerned Citizens Commn. on Pornography and Obscenity, Ontario, 1992-93; project dir. Inland Empire Prayer Gathering Nat. Day of Prayer, Ontario, 1993-94; office adminstr. Prayer Command Post, Ontario, 1995-96; adminstrv. svcs. dir. Inland Empire Secretarial Svcs., Ontario, 1996-98; adminstrv. asst. Somebody Cares-Inland Empire, 1998-99, Inland Empire, 2000—. Author: Beauty Instead of Ashes, 1994; freelance writer, 1997-98. Republican. Mem. Community Ch. Avocations: doll making, gardening, crafts, writing, reading.

WEGNER, JUDITH WELCH, law educator, former dean; b. Hartford, Conn., Feb. 14, 1950; d. John Raymond and Ruth (Thulen) Welch; m. Warren W. Wegner, Oct. 13, 1972. BA with honors, U. Wis., 1972; JD, UCLA, 1976. Bar: Calif. 1976, D.C. 1977, N.C. 1988, U.S. Supreme Ct. 1980, U.S. Ct. Appeals. Law clk. to Judge Warren Ferguson, U.S. Dist. Ct. for So. Dist. Calif., L.A., 1976-77; atty. Office Legal Counsel and Land & Natural Resources Divsn. U.S. Dept. Justice, Washington, 1977-79; spl. asst. to sec. U.S. Dept. Edn., Washington, 1979-80; vis. assoc. prof. U. Iowa Coll. Law, Iowa City, 1981; asst. prof. U. N.C. Sch. Law, Chapel Hill, 1981-84, assoc. prof., 1984-88, prof., 1988—, assoc. dean, 1986-88, dean, 1989-99; sr. scholar Carnegie Found. for Advancement of Tchg., 1999—2001; chmn. UNC Faculty, 2003—. Spkr. in field. Chief comment editor UCLA Law Rev., 1975-76; contbr. articles to legal publs. Mem. ABA (chmn. planning com. African Law Sch. Initiative 1994, co-chmn. planning com. 1994 mid-yr. deans meeting sect. on legal edn. and admission to bar), N.C. Assn. Women Attys. (Gweneth Davis award 1989), N.C. State Bar Assn., Assn. Am. Law Schs. (mem. exec. com. sect. on law & edn. 1985-88, mem. exec. com. sect. on local govt. law 1989-92, mem. accreditation com. 1986-88, chmn. 1989-91, program chmn. 1992 ann. meeting, program chmn. 1994 ann. meeting, mem. exec. com. 1992-96, pres. 1995), Soc. Am. Law Tchrs., Nat. League Cities (coun.-mentor program 1989-91), Women's Internat. Forum, Order of Coif (nat. exec. com. 1989-91), Phi Beta Kappa. Democrat. Office: U NC Sch Law Van Hecke Wettach Hall Campus Box 3380 Chapel Hill NC 27599-3380 Office Phone: 919-962-1671. E-mail: judith_wegner@unc.edu.

WEHMEIER, SARAH E. secondary school educator, director, music educator; b. St. Louis, Oct. 22, 1973; d. Paul Kenneth Wehmeier and Shirley Ann Wittlief Wehmeier. MusB, U. Wis., Whitewater, 1996; MA in Edn., Marian Coll., 2003. Tchr. music Herman Consolidated Sch., Wis., 1997, Wauwatosa Pub. Schs., 1997—98, Waukesha Pub. Schs., 1998—99; dir. bands Waukesha South High Sch., 1999—. Mem. adminstrv. coun. Waukesha South High Sch., 2001—, mem. sch. day task force, 2001—, writing com., 2001—. Musician Waukesha Park Band, 2002—. Mem.: Nat. Band Assn., Music Educators Nat. Conf. Office: Waukesha Sch Dist 401 E Roberta Ave Waukesha WI 53186 E-mail: weh22@hotmail.com.

WEHNER, KAY Y. poet; b. Brill, Wis., July 26, 1922; d. Burritt C. and Olivia P. Leonard; children: Kurt Thomas, Todd Craig. BA, U. Wis., 1945; postgrad., U. Calif., Berkeley, 1958-59. Author: (poetry) Granite and Kettle Moraine, 1980, Far Falcons, 1980, Incantations from Heron Lake, 1988, Spirit of Tallinn, 1991, Under the Rain, 1995, Torn Horizons, 2000. Home: 650 Hilldale Ave Berkeley CA 94708-1316

WEHOFER, DONNA LYNN, music educator; b. Cin., May 28, 1961; d. Donald Richard and Carol Ann Caldwell; m. Steven Samuel Wehofer, July 2, 1988; children: Christopher Samuel, Michael Richard. B of Music Edn., U. Cin., 1983. Music educator West Clermont Sch. Dist., Cin., 1983—91; early childhood music educator First Meth. Presch. and First Presbyn. Presch., Murfreesboro, Tenn., 1995—98; elem. music educator Murfreesboro City Sch. Dist., Tenn., 1998—; dir. children's choirs First Presbyn. Ch., Murfreesboro, Tenn., 1996—99, 2002—. Flute judicator Ohio Music Edn. Assn., Cin., 1984—89; flutist Murfreesboro Philharmonic Symphony Orch., Tenn., 1993—. Editor (adapted scripts for children's concerts): Peter and the Wolf and other mus. stories, 1989—93; author (mus. guides): Murfreesboro Philharmonic Children's Concert Series, 1996—98; dir.(children's concerts): Mid. Tenn. Woodwind Quintet, 1996—2001. Co-chair edn. com. Murfreesboro Philharmonic Orch., Tenn., 1995—98; publicity chmn. Jr. League Murfreesboro, Tenn., 1996—99; bd. dirs. Murfreesboro Youth Orch., Tenn., 1997—99. Recipient Disting. Classroom Educator award, Tenn. Edn. Assn., 2001; Tech. in Literacy grant, Tenn., 2000. Mem.: Murfreesboro Edn. Assn. (exec. bd. dirs. 2000—02, Disting. Classroom Educator award 2001), Francis Bohannon Music Club (chair nominating com. 2002—04), Delta Kappa Gamma. Presbyterian. Avocations: music, gardening, reading, travel, skiing. Home: 2902 Standing Bear Way Murfreesboro TN 37127 Office: Reeves Rogers Elem Sch 1807 Greenland Dr Murfreesboro TN 37130

WEHRMAN, NATALIE ANN, retired music educator; b. Springfield, Mo., Apr. 11, 1928; d. William Herman Seboldt and Isabel Johanna Browser; m. Harlan Henry Wehrman, June 22, 1952; children: Marcel Alyce, Nathan Scott, Stephanie Ann, Brian Lee, Denise Kay. BS, So. Mo. State Tchrs. Coll., 1950; postgrad., U. Mo., 1951, Concordia Coll., Seward, Nebr., 1951—52. Bus. and music tchr. Concordia HS, Seward, Mo., 1951—52; bus. tchr. Lockwood (Mo.) Sch., 1952—54; pvt. music instr., piano, organ and voice Lockwood, 1953—88; ret., 1988. Music coord., head organist, adult choir Immanuel Luth. Ch., Lockwood, 1967—. Mem.: Assn. Luth. Ch. Musicians, Assn. Guild Organists, Bus. and Profl. Women (officer 1952—80, Woman of Yr. 1955), Nat. Music Tchrs. Assn., Luth. Women's Missing League, Mo. Music Tchrs. Assn., Am. Legion Aux. Lutheran. Avocations: quilting, travel. Home: Rte 2 Box 19 Lockwood MO 65682

WEIDEMANN, CELIA JEAN, social scientist, management consultant, financial consultant; b. Denver, Dec. 6, 1942; d. John Clement and Hazel (Van Tuyl) Kirlin; m. Wesley Clark Weidemann, July 1, 1972; 1 child, Stephanie Jean. BS, Iowa State U., 1964; MS, U. Wis., Madison, 1970, PhD, 1973; post grad., U. So. Calif., 1983. Advisor UN FAO, Ibadan, Nigeria, 1973—77; ind. rschr. Asia and Near East, 1977—78; program coord., asst. prof., rsch. assoc. U. Wis., Madison, Wis., 1979—81; chief inst. and human resources US AID, Washington, 1982—85; team leader, cons. Sumatra, Indonesia, 1984; dir. fed. econ. program Midwest Rsch. Inst., Washington, 1985—86; founder, pres. emeritus Weidemann Assoc., Arlington, Va., 1986—2000; pres. Weidemann Found., Arlington, Va., 2000—. Cons. U.S. Congress, Aspen Inst., Ford Found., World Bank, Egypt, Nigeria, Gambia, Pakistan, Indonesia, AID, Thailand, Jamaica, Panama, Philippines, Sierra Leone, Kenya, Jordon, Poland, India, Egypt, Russia, Finnish Internat. Devel. Agy., Namibia, pvt. client Estonia, Lativa, Russia, Japan, Internat. Ctr. Rsch. on Women, Zaire, UN FAO, Ghana, Internat. Statis. Inst., The Netherlands, Global Exch., 1986-87, Asian Devel. Bank, Mongolia, Nepal, Vietnam, Bangladesh, Indonesia, Philippines; mem. bd. visitors Sch. Human Ecology, U. Wis., 2002—; peer reviewer NRC, NAS. Author: (book) Planning Home Economics Curriculum for Social and Econ. Develop., Agrl. Ext. for Women Farmers in Africa, 1990, Fin. Services for Women, 1992, Egyptian Women and Micro.: The Invisible Entrepreneurs, 1992, Small Enterprise Development in Poland: Does Gender Matter?, 1994, Micro. and Gender in India, 1995, Supporting Women's Livelihoods: Micro Fin. That Works for the Majority, 2002; contbr. chapters to books and articles to profl. journals. Am. Home Econ. Assn. Fellow, 1969-73; grantee Ford Found., 1987-89. Mem. Soc. Internat. Devel., Am. Sociol. Assn., Assn. for Women in Devel. (pres. 1989, founder, bd. dirs.), Women in Devel. (steering com.), Coalition for Women's Econ. Devel. and Global Equality, Internat. Devel. Conf. (bd. dirs., exec. com.), Internat. Platform Assn., Pi Lambda Theta, Omicron Nu. Avocations: mountain trekking, piano and pipe organ, canoeing, photography, poetry. Office: Weidemann Assoc, Inc 933 N Kenmore St Ste 405 Arlington VA 22201-2236 Office Phone: 703-599-5906. E-mail: jweidemann@aol.com.

WEIDENFELD, SHEILA RABB, television producer, author; b. Cambridge, Mass., Sept. 7, 1943; d. Maxwell M. and Ruth (Cryden) Rabb; m. Edward L. Weidenfeld, Aug. 11, 1968; children: Nicholas Rabb, Daniel Rabb. BA, Brandeis U., 1965. Assoc. prodr. Metromedia, Inc., Sta. WNEW-TV, N.Y.C., 1965-68; talent coord. That Show with Joan Rivers, NBC, N.Y.C., 1968-71; coord. NBC network game programs, N.Y.C., 1969-71; prodr. Metromedia, Inc., Sta. WTTG-TV, Washington, 1971-73, creator/prodr. Take It From Here, NBC (WBC-TV), Washington, 1973-74; press sec. to first lady Betty Ford, spl. asst. to Pres. Gerald R. Ford, 1974-77; mem. Pres.'s Adv. Commn. on Hist. Preservation, 1977-81; TV prodr., moderator On the Record, NBC-TV, Sta. WRC-TV, Washington, 1978-79; pres. D.C. Prodns., Ltd., 1978; prodr., host Your Personal Decorator, 1987; mem. Sec. State's Adv. Commn. on Fgn. Svc. Inst., 1972-74; founding mem. Project Censured Panel of Judges, 1976—. Bd. dirs. First Star. Author: First Lady's Lady, 1979. Mem. U.S. Holocaust Meml. Coun., 1987-97; corporator Dana Hall Sch., Wellesley, Mass.; bd. dirs. Wolf Trap Found., Women's Campaign Fund, 1978-79; bd. dirs. D.C. Contemporary Dance Theatre, 1986-88, D.C. Rep. Ctrl. Com., 1984—, D.C. Preservation League, 1987-90; chmn. C&O Canal Nat. Hist. Park Commn., 1988—; bd. dirs. Am. Univ. Rome, 1988—, Friends of the Scuola San Rocco, 2002—. Recipient awards for outstanding achievement in the media AAUW, 1973, 74, Silver Screen award A Campaign to Remember for the U.S. Holocaust Meml. Coun., 1989, Bronze medal Internat. Film and Video Festival N.Y., 1990; named hon. consul gen. of Republic of San Marino to Washington; knighted by Order of St. Agatha, Republic of San Marino, 1986. Mem. NATAS (Emmy award 1972), Washington Press Club, Am. Newspaper Women's Club, Am. Women in Radio and TV, Cosmos Club, Consular Corps, Sigma Delta Chi. Home: 3059 Q St NW Washington DC 20007-3081

WEIDMAN, SHEILA, marketing professional; b. Bradenton, Fla., July 11, 1961; BS in Sci., Journalism and Comms., U. Fla., 1983. Comms. mgr. ASHRAE, 1983—88; mgr. corp. comms. Georgia-Pacific Corp., 1988—90, dir. external comms. and corp. advt., 1990—98, dir., spl. asst. to chmn. and CEO, 1998—2000, sr. dir. corp. mktg. and sales excellence, 2000—01, v.p. corp. mktg., 2001—02, v.p. corp. comms. and mktg., 2002—. Com. mem. Am. Heart Assn., Atlanta Hist. Soc.; mem. Leadership Atlanta, Class of 2004. Recipient Women of Achievement awards, YWCA, 1995. Mem.: Atlanta Sports Coun. (bd. dirs., chmn. mktg. com.), Atlanta CMO Roundtable, CMO Group of N.Am., Ga. Press Assn., Ga. State CMO Roundtable, Met. Atlanta C. of C. (vice chair chmn.'s campaign 2003), Mktg. Leadership Coun. (vice chair chmn.'s campaign 2004), Pub. Rels. Soc. Am., Sales and Mktg. Execs., Atlanta Press Club. Office: Georgia-Pacific Corp 133 Peachtree St NE Atlanta GA 30303*

WEIERMILLER, KATHY, publishing executive; V.p., CFO Orange County Register, Santa Ana, Calif. Office: The Orange County Register 625 N Grand Ave Santa Ana CA 92701-4347

WEIFENBACH, TERRI LYNN, photographer, printer; b. N.Y.C., Jan. 4, 1957; d. William Lester and Phyllis Marjorie W.; m. John R. Gossage, Aug. 21, 1992. BA, U. Md., 1979. Author: In Your Dreams, 1997, Hunter Green, 2000, Lana, 2002; author: (with John Gossage) Snake Eyes, 2002; one-woman shows include Jackson Fine Arts, Atlanta, 1999, Verso Photo Gallery, Tokyo, 2000, Addison Ripley Fine Art, Washington, 2001, Robert Klein Gallery, Boston, 2001, exhibited in group shows at Ctr. for Creative Photography, Tucson, 1999, U. Md. Art Gallery, 1979, High Mus., Atlanta, 2000, Noorderlicht, Groningen, The Netherlands, 2001; photographer (group shows) Daiter Contemporary, Chgo., 2003, Photoeye Gallery, Santa Fe, 2003; Represented in permanent collections Mus. Ludwig, Cologne, Germany, Ctr. Creative Photography, Ariz., Santa Barbara (Calif.) Mus. Art, Sprengel Mus. Hanover (Germany), Mus. Photographic Art, San Diego. Home: # 502 2070 Belmont Rd NW Washington DC 20009

WEIGHTMAN, ESTHER LYNN, emergency trauma nurse; b. Tawas City, Mich., June 13, 1966; d. Garrie Lee and Naomi Ruth (Atwood) Schneller; m. Robert Thomas Weightman, Dec. 31, 1996; children: Erin Elizabeth, Kaili Marie. BS in Christian Secondary Edn., Ozark Bible Inst. & Coll., Neosho, Mo., 1988; BSN, Ind. Wesleyan U., Marion, 1991; MS in Cmty. Health Nursing, U. Colo. Health Scis. Ctr., Denver, 1995. RN, Colo.; cert. ACLS, pediatric advanced life support, trauma nurse core course; Profl. Spl. Svcs. licensee Colo. Dept. Edn. Staff nurse emergency dept. Marion Gen. Hosp., 1991-92, Penrose-St. Francis Healthcare Sys., Colorado Springs, Colo., 1992-95; staff nurse registry QS Nurses Corp., Colorado Springs, 1992-2001; staff devel. nurse 302d ASTS-USAFR, Peterson AFB, Colo., 1994-2001; staff nurse emergency dept. Med. Ctr. of Aurora, Colo., 1997-2001; staff nurse ICU St. Peter's Hosp., Helena, Mont., 2001—02, VA Mont. Healthcare Sys., Ft. Harrison, Mont., 2002—; staff devel. nurse Mont. Air N.G., Great Falls, 2003—. Mentor various healthcare instrnl. facilities, 1991—; vol. tchr. health classes Knowledge is Power, Red Cross Shelter, Colorado Springs, 1995-96. Mem.: Emergency Nurses Assn., Res. Officers Assn., Sigma Theta Tau. Avocations: cooking, orchestra (trumpet).

WEIGLE, PEGGY, information technology executive; BA in philosophy cum laude, U. Mass. V.p. N. Am. sales Arbor Software, 1996; v.p. worldwide field operations Hyperion (merged with Arbor Software), v.p., gen. mgr. performance mgmt. divsn.; CEO Perfecto Tech. (now Sanctum, Inc.), 1999—. Chmn. application sub-com. BENS Silicon Valley Cyber Security Working Group; mem. tech. sub-com. Silicon Valley Blue Ribbon Task Force on Aviation Security and Tech. Named one of 50 Most Powerful Women in Networking, Network World mag., 2003. Office: Sanctum Inc 2901 Tasmand Dr Ste 205 Santa Clara CA 95054*

WEIHMULLER, PATRICIA A, retired minister, artist; m. Fred H. Weihmuller, Aug. 31, 1957; children: Fredric, Susan Smith, Steven, Amy Kovanda. Secretarial Diploma, Blair Bus.Coll., Colorado Springs, 1955; Mgmt. Cert., William Rainey Harper Coll., Palatine, Ill., 1992; leadership diploma, Stephen Ministries, St. Louis, 1993; cert., William Rainey Harper Coll., 1983. Cert. profl. sec. Profl. Secs. Internat., 1983. Exec. sec. State Farm Ins. Co., Dearborn, Mich., 1959—60; exec. sec. Unocal, Schaumburg, Ill., 1971—92, Motorola (temp.), Schaumburg, Ill., 1993—94; Stephen ministry leader Prince of Peace Luth. Ch., Schaumburg, Ill., 1993—98, Stephen min., 1991—2004; oil painter Hoffman Estates, Ill., 1996—2004. Mem. Star (Rep. orgn.), Schaumburg Township, 1967—2004; election judge Cook County Bd. of Elections, Schaumburg Twp., 1995—2004; exec. sec. Parish Planning Coun. Prince of Peace Luth. Ch., Ill., 1989—92, bible study leader; mem. Naomi Cir. Prince of Peace Luth. Ch., Schaumburg, 1967—2004. Avocations: bridge, painting, reading, sewing, travel. Personal E-mail: fpweih@aol.com.

WEIKEL, SANDRA G. music educator; b. Hamilton, Ohio, Apr. 1, 1955; d. Heather P. Gilbert; 1 child, Derek Vaughn. B in Music Edn., U. Louisville, 1978. Cert. Tchr. N.Mex., 1984, Ky., 1979, S.D., 1980. Band dir. Roswell Ind. Sch. Dist., N.Mex., 1986—, Hagerman H.S., N.Mex., 1984—86, Viborg H.S., 1982—83, South Shore H.S., SD, 1980—82. French horn player SW Symphony, Hobbs, N.Mex., 1986—, Roswell Symphony, 1986—94; trumpet player Nacho Average Jazz Band, 1990—97; horn player ENMUR Cmty. Band, 2002—, Pecos Valley Brass, 1988—. Dir.(orch.): The Music Man. Rec. sec. Delta Kappa Gamma Soc., Roswell, 1992—2003. Mem.: SE N.Mex. Music Assn. (licentiate). Democrat-Npl. Methodist. Avocations: softball, travel, piano, music box collector, tennis. Home: 3411 Highland Rd Roswell NM 88201 Office: Berrendo Middle School 800 Marion Richards Rd Roswell NM 88203 Personal E-mail: sgweikel@wmconnect.com. E-mail: sweikel@risd.k12.nm.us.

WEIKSNER, SANDRA S. lawyer; b. D.C., Nov. 9, 1945; d. Donald B. and Dick (Cutter) Smiley; m. George B. Weiksner, Aug. 19, 1969; children: Michael, Nicholas. BA in Psychology, Stanford U., 1966, JD, 1969. Teaching fellow Stanford U., Calif., 1969-70; assoc. Cleary, Gottlieb, Steen & Hamilton, N.Y.C., 1970-77, ptnr., 1978—2003, sr. counsel, 2003—. Vis. lectr. Yale Law Sch., 1991-92. Bd. dirs. N.Y. Law Sch.; mem. Union Theol. Sem. Fellow Am. Bar Found., Am. Coll. Trusts and Estates Counsel, Internat. Acad. Estate and Trust Law; mem. ABA, N.Y. State Bar Assn., Assn. Bar of City of N.Y., Conn. Bar Assn. Democrat. Unitarian Universalist. Home: 164 E 81st St New York NY 10028-1804 Office: Cleary Gottlieb Steen & Hamilton 1 Liberty Plz Fl 43 New York NY 10006-1404

WEILER, ANGELA M. librarian, writer; b. Cortland, N.Y., Feb. 23, 1952; d. Nicola S. and Gloria Maria Stefano; 1 child, Briana. BA, Syracuse U., 1974, MLS, 1997. Reference libr. Cazenovia (N.Y.) Coll., 1996—97; circulation coord., instrn. coord. SUNY-Morrisville Coll. Libr., 1997—. State libr. contract adv. team SUNY, Albany, 2000—. Author short stories; contbr. articles to jours. Grantee Applied Rsch. grant, SUNY Morrisville Alumni Assn., 1998; scholar Regents scholar, N.Y. State Bd. Regents, 1970. Mem.: Ea. N.Y. Assn. Coll. and Rsch. Librs., SUNY Librs. Assn. (chair instrn. com. 2002—), Beta Phi Mu. Avocations: literature, music, art, theater, cinema. Office: Morrisville State Coll Eaton St Morrisville NY 13408 Business E-Mail: weileram@morrisville.edu. E-mail: weileram@yahoo.com.

WEIL-GARRIS BRANDT, KATHLEEN (KATHLEEN BRANDT), art historian; b. Surrey, Eng. d. Kurt Hermann and Charlotte (Garris) Weil; m. Werner Brandt (dec. 1983). BA with honors, Vassar Coll., 1956; postgrad., U. Bonn, Germany, 1956-57; MA, Radcliffe U., 1958; PhD, Harvard, 1966; MA, Oxford U., 1998. Asst. prof. NYU, N.Y.C., 1963-67, assoc. prof., 1967-72, prof., 1973—; asst. prof. NYU Inst. Fine Arts, N.Y.C., 1966-67, assoc. prof., 1967-72, prof., 1973—; vis. prof. Harvard U., Cambridge, Mass., 1980; editor in chief The Art Bulletin, N.Y.C., 1977-81; Slade prof. Oxford U., 1998. Cons. on Renaissance art Vatican Mus., 1987—; vis. fellow Bibliotheca Hertziana (Max-Planck Inst.) Rome. Author: Leonardo and Central Italian Art, 1974, Problems In Cinquecento Sculpture, 1977; author: (with J. d'Amico) The Renaissance Cardinal's Ideal Palace, 1981, (with C. d'Acidini, J. Draper, N. Penny) Giovinezza di Michelangelo, 1999-2000; contbr. numerous articles to profl. jours.; editor: Michelangelo: la Cappella Sistina: documentazione e interpretazione, vol. III, 1996. Mem. Am. com. Medici Archive Project, 1996—; bd. dirs. Raccolta Vinciana, 1997—. Decorated officer Order of Merit (Italy); recipient rsch. award Humboldt Found., 1985, Disting. Tchg. award Lindback Found., 1967, Golden Dozen Tchr. award NYU, 1993, Alumni Great Tchr. award, 1996; Guggenheim fellow, 1976; grantee Henkel Found., 1987, Samuel H. Kress Found., 1999. Mem. Coll. Art Assn. (bd. dirs. 1973-74, 77-81), Renaissance Soc. Am. (editl. bd. 1992—), Soc. Archtl. Historians, N.Y. Acad. Scis., Phi Beta Kappa (pres. NYU chpt. 1979-81). Avocations: art films, conservation, music, dance. Office: NYU Inst Fine Arts 1 E 78th St New York NY 10021-0119

WEIMER, JESSICA R. music educator; b. Grand Junction, Colo., July 10, 1979; d. Harold S. Weimer and Juy A. Maki. BA in Music Edn. cum laude, Mesa State Coll., Grand Junction, 2002. Pvt. violin tchr., Grand Junction, 2000—; mem. Grand Junction Symphony Orch., 2002—; music seller Borders, Grand Junction, 2003—. Head counselor, tchr. Colo. ASTA String Camp, Rangely, 1997—. Author: (novels) Work in Progress. Vol. Western Colo. Bot. Soc., Grand Junction, 1998—2000. Recipient Gold award, Girl Scouts Chipeta Coun., 1997; grantee, Mesa State Found., 1998—2002; scholar, 1998—2002. Mem.: Suzuki Assn. Ams. (assoc.), Colo. Am. String Tchrs. Assn. (assoc.; pres. Collegiate chpt. 2001—02), Music Educators Assn. (assoc.; pres. 2000—01). Avocations: violin player, reading, hiking, frisbee dog owner, concerts.

WEINBERG, DALE GLASER, technical writer, consultant, trainer; b. N.Y.C., Oct. 21, 1948; d. Milton and Joyce I. (Litsky) Glaser; m. Howard Weinberg, June 20, 1971 (separated); 1 child, Tracy J. BS in English Edn., NYU, 1971; MS in English Edn., Iona Coll., New Rochelle, N.Y., 1975. Lic. secondary tchr. English, N.Y. Programmer, documentation adminstr. ITT Continental Baking, Rye, N.Y., 1971-78; owner, pres. Techically Write, Eastchester, N.Y., 1978—. Cons., course leader, tchr. writing seminars throughout U.S., Am. Mgmt. Assn., N.Y.C., 1980; designer, tchr. bus. writing Am. Mgmt. Assn.-Operation Enterprise, Hamilton, N.Y., 1998; ind. tech. writing and tng. cons., 1978—. Editor: Money Smarts, 1982, A Funny Thing Happened on the Way to the Interview, 1995; designer, editor, prodr. 3 major publs. Eastchester (N.Y.) Mid. Sch., 1993—; assoc. editor Calif. Ride Reporter, 1993—. Recipient Spl. Svc. award/citation for publs. Eastchester Mid. Sch., 1994. Mem. IEEE Profl. Comm. Soc. (assoc.), Soc. Tech. Comm. (sr.), Assn. Computing Machinery. Avocations: scuba diving, yoga, skiing, theater, reading, travel. Office: Technically Write 19 Soundview Dr Eastchester NY 10709-1526

WEINBERG, ELISABETH H. physical therapist, health facility administrator; b. Chgo., Jan. 18, 1934; d. Hermann Heckel and Alice Matilda Lodoen; m. Elliott Weinberg, Nov. 1956; children: Pamela, Arthur, Rachel. Student, Coll. of Wooster, 1952-54; BS, Med. Coll. Va., 1954-56. Staff therapist Med. Coll. Va., Richmond, 1956-57; dir. phys. therapy Soc. Crippled Children and Adults, Balt., 1957-67; cons. Health Care Agy., Cin., 1975-84; v.p. Weinberg Rehab., Inc., Cin., 1984-96, adminstr., advisor, 1996-97, ret., 1997. Cons. Health Dept. Ohio, Columbus, 1984-96. Sec.-treas. Nat. Coun. Jewish Women, Frederick, Md., 1957-67; active Nat. Rep. Party, Cin., 1990-99, State Rep. Women, Columbus, 1998-99; mem. sisterhood Beth de Filloh Temple, Brunswick, Ga., 1998-99. Mem. AAUP. Home: 101 Enclave Ln Saint Simons Island GA 31522-5293

WEINBERG, H. BARBARA, art historian, educator, curator paintings and sculpture; b. N.Y.C., Jan. 23, 1942; d. Max and Evelyn Kallman; m. Michael B. Weinberg, Aug. 30, 1964. AB, Barnard Coll., 1962; MA, Columbia U., N.Y.C., 1964, PhD, 1972. From asst. prof. to prof. art history Queens Coll. and Grad. Sch., CUNY, 1972-94; curator Am. paintings and sculpture Met. Mus. Art., N.Y.C., 1990-98; Alice Pratt Brown curator Am. paintings and sculpture Met. Mus. Art, N.Y.C., 1998—. Author: The Decorative Work of John La Farge, 1977, The American Pupils of Jean-Léon Gérome, 1984, The Lure of Paris: Nineteenth-Century American Painters and Their French Teachers, 1991, Thomas Eakins and the Metropolitan Museum of Art, 1994; co-author: American Impressionism and Realism: The Painting of Modern Life, 1885-1915, 1994, Am. Drawings and Watercolors in The Metropolitan Mus. of Art: John Singer Sargent, 2000, John Singer Sargent in The Metropolitan Mus. Art, 2000, Childe Hassam, American Impressionist, 2004; mem. editl. bd. Am. Art Jour., 1984—. Mem.: Phi Beta Kappa. Office: Met Mus Art 1000 5th Ave New York NY 10028-0113

WEINBERG, LILA SHAFFER, writer, editor; d. Sam and Blanche (Hyman) Shaffer; m. Arthur Weinberg, Jan. 25, 1953; children: Hedy Merrill Cornfield, Anita Michelle Miller, Wendy Clare Rothman. Editor Ziff-Davis Pub. Co., 1944—53; assoc. chief manuscript editor jours. U. Chgo. Press, 1966—80, sr. manuscript editor books, 1980—98; mem. faculty Sch. for New Learning DePaul U., Chgo., 1973—89. Vis. faculty continuing edn. programs U. Chgo., 1984-92. Author: (with A. Weinberg) The Muckrakers, 1961 (selected for White House Library 1963), Verdicts Out of Court, 1963, Instead of Violence, 1963, Passport to Utopia, 1968, Some Dissenting Voices, 1970, Clarence Darrow: A Sentimental Rebel, 1980; contbr. articles and revs. to various publs. Bd. dirs. Hillel Found. U. Chgo., 1988-96. Recipient Friends of Lit. award Chgo. Found. Lit., 1980, Social Justice award Darrow Community Ctr., 1980, Disting. Body of Work award Friends of Midwest Authors, 1987, John Peter Altgeld Freedom of Speech award, 2001. Mem. Soc. Midland Authors (dir. 1977-83, pres. 1983-85, Best Biography award 1980), ACLU, Clarence Darrow Commemorative Com., YIVO, Authors' League, Work in Progress. Home: 5421 S Cornell Ave Chicago IL 60615-5646 E-mail: lilawein@aol.com.

WEINBERG, LORETTA, state legislator; b. N.Y.C., Feb. 6, 1935; d. Murray Isaacs and Raya Hamilton; m. Irwin S. Weinberg, July 25, 1960 (dec. Feb. 1999); children: Daniel J., Francine S. BA, UCLA, 1956. Former aide N.J. Assemblyman D. Bennett Mazur, Trenton; mem. N.J. Assembly, Trenton, 1992—. Mem. Teaneck Coun., 1990-94. Recipient Legis. Leadership award No. N.J. Chiropractic Assn., 1992, Woman of Achievement award Bus. and Profl. Women's Club of East Bergen, 1993, Carrie Chapman Catt award No. N.J. NOW, 1997, Ethical Recognition award Ethical Culture Soc. of Bergen County, 1998; named Citizen of Yr. N.J. Jewish War Vets., Legislator of Yr., 2000. Mem. Nat. Coun. Jewish Women (life mem., Hannah G. Solomon award 1995, Disting. Achievement award Women's Commn.). Democrat. Jewish. Office: State of NJ 545 Cedar Ln Teaneck NJ 07666-1740

WEINBERG, LOUISE, law educator, author; b. N.Y.C. m. Steven Weinberg; 1 child, Elizabeth. AB summa cum laude, Cornell U.; JD, Harvard U., 1969, LLM, 1974. Bar: Mass. Sr. law clk. Hon. Chas. E. Wyzanski, Jr., Boston, 1971-72; assoc. in law Bingham, Dana & Gould, Boston, 1969-72; teaching fellow Harvard Law Sch., Boston, 1972-74; lectr. law Brandeis U., Waltham, Mass., 1974; assoc. prof. law Suffolk U., Boston, 1974-76, prof., 1977-80; vis. assoc. prof. law Stanford U., Palo Alto, Calif., 1976-77; vis. prof. law U. Tex., Austin, 1979; prof. law Sch. Law, U. Tex., Austin, 1980-84, Thompson prof. law, 1984-90, Andrews and Kurth prof. law, 1990-92; Fulbright and Jaworski regents rsch. prof. U. Tex., Austin, 1991-92, Angus G. Wynne, Sr. prof. civil jurisprudence, 1992-97, Fondren chair faculty excellence, 1995—, Eugene R. Smith Centennial rsch. prof. law, 1993-97, holder William B. Bates chair adminstrn. justice, 1997—. Vis. scholar Hebrew U., Jerusalem, 1989; Forum fellow World Econ. Forum, Davos, Switzerland, 1995—; pub. spkr., lectr. in field. Author: Federal Courts: Judicial Federalism and Judicial Power, 1994, and ann. supplements; co-author: Conflict of Laws, 1990, 2d edit., 2002; contbr. chpts. to books, articles to profl. jours. Bd. dirs. Ballet Austin, 1986-88, Austin Coun. on Fgn. Affairs, 1985—, Austin Civil War Round Table, 1998—. Recipient Disting. Educator award Tex. Exes Assn., 1996. Mem.: Supreme Ct. Hist. Soc., Am. Constn. Soc., Maritime Law Assn., Tex. Asian C. of C., Assn. Am. Law Schs. (chair sect. on conflict laws 1991—93, exec. com. sect. on fed. cts. 2001—02, program chair 2002—03, chair 2003—04, treas. sect. on admiralty 2004—, acting chair 2004—), The Philos. Soc. Tex., Am. Law Inst. (consultative com. complex litigation 1989—93, consultative com. enterprise liability 1990—95, adv. group fed. judicial code revision project 1996—2001, mems.' consultative group, intellectual property 2004—, adv. group internat. jurisdiction and judgements 2004—), Phi Kappa Phi, Phi Beta Kappa. Office: U Tex Sch Law 727 Dean Keeton St Austin TX 78705-3224 E-mail: lweinberg@mail.law.utexas.edu.

WEINBERG, MYRL, medical association administrator; Exec. Assn. for Retarded Citizens, Joseph P. Kennedy, Jr. Found., Am. Diabetes Assn.; pres. Nat. Health Coun. Office: Nat Health Coun 1730 M St NW Ste 500 Washington DC 20036

WEINBERG, RUTHMARIE LOUISE, special education educator, researcher; b. Woodbury, N.J., Feb. 9, 1953; d. Louis Albert Schopfer, Sr. and Ruth Marie (Bilse) Schopfer; m. Robert Weinberg, June 26, 1982. AS Human Svcs., Camden County Coll., 1973; BA Tchr. of the Handicapped, Glassboro State Coll., 1975; MA Sch. Adminstrn., Rowan U., 1998. Cert. tchr. of the handicapped 1975, supr. 1998, prin./supr. 1998. Supr. of cottage life, tchr. and supr. of mentally retarded Am. Inst. Mental Studies, Vineland, NJ, 1975—79; spl. edn. tchr. Haddon Heights (N.J.) H.S., 1979—. Girl Scout leader for clients Am. Inst. Mental Studies, Vineland, NJ, 1975—79, supr. summer recreation program, 1975—79. Recipient Gov.'s award for excellence in tchg., Gov. Florio and Commr. John Ellis, N.J., 1991. Mem.: Haddon Heights Ednl. Assn., N.J. Ednl. Assn., Nat. Ednl. Assn. Avocations: music, dance, sports, nature walks, exploring new horizons. Home: 422 Austin Ave Barrington NJ 08007 Office: Haddon Heights Jr & Sr HS 301 2nd Ave Haddon Heights NJ 08035-1407

WEINBERG, SYDNEY STAHL, historian; b. N.Y.C., Oct. 2, 1938; d. David Leslie and Berenice (Jarvis) Stahl; divorced; children: Deborah Sara, Elisa Rachel; m. Gerald Tenenbaum, Mar. 23, 1996. BA, Barnard Coll., 1960, Columbia U., 1964, PhD, 1969. Instr. history N.J. Inst. Tech., 1967-69, asst. prof., 1969-72; assoc. prof. history Ramapo Coll. N.J., Mahwah, 1972-74, prof., 1974—, dir. MA program in liberal studies, 1994—. Dir. Garden State Immigration History Consortium, 1987-89. Author: The World of Our Mothers: The Lives of Jewish Immigrant Women, 1988; contbr. articles to profl. jours. Sec.-treas. Berkshire Conf. Women Historians, 1994-97. NEH fellow, 1977-78. Mem. Am. Hist. Assn., Orgn. Am. Historians, Am. Studies Assn., Jewish Studies Assn., Assn. Grad. Liberal Studies Programs. Home: 80 La Salle St Apt 19F New York NY 10027-4716 Office: Ramapo Coll MA Liberal Studies Program Office Mahwah NJ 07430

WEINBERGER, ADRIENNE, artist, appraiser; b. Washington, Apr. 28, 1948; d. Samuel Aaron and Marta (Barta) W.; m. Edward Herschel Egelman, Mar. 21, 1980; children: Serge Maurice, Liana Dora. BA, Goucher Coll., 1970; MEd, Johns Hopkins U., 1973; MA, Northwestern U., 1974; postgrad., Sch. of Mus. of Fine Arts, 1979-82. Lectr. Art Inst. Chgo., 1973-75; lectr., docent trainer Mus. of Fine Arts, Boston, 1978-82; mus. educator Yale Ctr. Brit. Art, Yale Art Gallery, New Haven, 1984-86; instr., coord. alumni coll. Albertus Magnus Coll., New Haven, 1987-89; instr. Mpls. C.C., 1989-94; propr. Studio 95, Edina, Minn., 1995-99, Charlottesville, Va., 1999—. Panelist New England Regional Confs., Am. Assn. Muss., Mass., Conn., 1976-77; mem., workshop leader New Haven Green Found., New Haven 350 Com., 1987-88; pres. Cmty. Art Fund., 2000—. Author, illustrator, pub.: New Haven Coloring Book, 1987, CulchaMan Visits New York City, 1988, CulchaMan Visits Washinton, D.C., 1988. Participant Edina Futures Forum, 1990; dir. Edina-Woodhill Assn., 1997—98; active State Affirmative Action Commn., 1996—98; del. chair, mem. nominating com. Dem. State Conv., St. Paul, 1994, del., chair Rochester, 1996, St. Cloud, 1998, del. Norfolk, 2000; active Dem. State Exec. Com., 1997—99; sec. Dem.-Farmer Labor Party, Edina, Eden Prairie, 1990—94, chair, 1994—96, treas. 3d Congl. Dist., 1996—99; mem. Dem. State Cen. Com., 1994—99; adv. bd. gifted edn. svcs. Edina Pub. Schs., 1993—96; bd. dirs. Consortium for Advancement of Arts, 2001—03, Leadership Charlottesville, 2002, Northwestern U. Alumni Club, 2003—, Northwestern U. Club Va. Recipient Juror's award Berkshire Mus., Pittsfield, Mass., 1981, New Haven Brush & Palette Club, 1985, Edina Art Ctr., 1991. Mem. Am. Soc. Appraisers (accredited sr. appraiser; sec. Twin Cities chpt. 1997-99, pres. Richmond chpt. 2000-01, 3d v.p. Richmond chpt. 2001—), Charlottesville C. of C. (Amb. Corps. 2000, legis. action com., founder, pres. cmty. art fund 2000—), U. Va. Art Mus.(vol. bd. 2003-), Leadership Charlottesville, Northwestern U. Alumni Club (bd. dirs. 2003—). Avocations: travel, reading, politics, advising on education. Office: Studio 95 3100 Waverly Dr Charlottesville VA 22901-9576 E-mail: studio95@ganotronic.com.

WEINBERGER, DIANE, motivation and image consultant; b. Chgo., Feb. 9, 1948; d. James Charles and Alice Valestin; married Oct. 9, 1976. BA in Drawing and Design, U. Mo. Sr. sec./salesperson IBM, St. Louis, 1970-81; model St. Louis, 1981-82; artist, 1970—; ind. dir. Color Me Beautiful, Rancho Palos Verdes, Calif., 1995—. Mem New Neighbors of Palos Verdes Peninsula (past v.p. ways and means com.), Leads Club (past dir.), Greater St. Louis Artists (past pres. 1985-86), Seaview HOA (pres. 1995-), Pet Protectors League (pres. 2000-). Avocations: rescuing and rehabilitating abandoned cats, drawing and design.

WEINBERGER, JANE DALTON, retired nurse, volunteer; b. Maine, Mar. 29, 1919; m. Caspar Willard Weinberger, Aug. 16, 1942; children: Caspar Willard and Arlin Weinberger. Student, U. Maine, 1936-38, student, 1938-41; BSN, Somerville Hosp. Sch. Nursing, 1940; postgrad., Boston U., 1941. Reg. nurse Calif. Vol. St. Luke's Hosp., San Francisco, 1947-77; owner, editor, author Windswept House Pubs., Mt. Desert, Maine, 1984—; ret., 1999—. Author: (Children's Books) The Little Ones, Lemon Drop, Tabitha Jones, Wee Peter Puffin, Fanny and Sarah, Cory the Cormorant, That's What Counts, VIM: A Very Important Mouse, Mrs. Witherspoon's Eagles; (adult biography): As Ever, Canned Plums and Other Vissitudes of Life. Bd. Trustees Nat. Symphony Assn., 1970—, Capitol Children's Mus., 1970-85; bd. dirs. Folger Shakespeare Libr., 1970—, chmn. 1981-86; founding mem. New Globe Theatre, London, 1999; bd. vols. D.C. Gen. Hosp., 1970-75, hon. bd. mem. 1975—; bd. dirs. Jackson Lab. (Cancer Rsch. Inst.), 1984—, mem. Internat. Coun. Jackson Lab., 1990—; mem. women's com. Washington Performing Arts Soc., 1970—; sponsor The Internat. Hospitality Soc., Washington, 1970-85, other vol. orgns.; Rep. coms. campaign mgr., San Francisco, 1964-68. 2nd lt. U.S. Army Nurse Corps, 1942-43, PTO. Recipient Svc. to Humanity award, Alpha chpt. Chi Eta Phi, 1974, Deborah Morton award, Westbrook (Maine) Coll., 1992. Mem. Maine Media Women, Nat. News Women, Maine Writers and Pubs. Alliance, Jr. Army Navy Guild (hon.), Soc of Sponsors USN, The Century Club of Calif., Congressional Club (Washington), Pal's Club, (Sacramento,Calif.). Episcopalian. Avocations: cooking, gardening, swimming, boating, collecting glass paperweights, minature porcelain boxes. Office: Windswept House PO Box 159 Mount Desert ME 04660-0159

WEINER, ANNE LEE, social worker; b. Chelsea-Malden, Mass., Nov. 2, 1932; d. Nathan and Edith E. (Sigel) Varnick; m. Paul J. Weiner, Jan. 25, 1959; children: Berdine R., Ronald M. Diploma in med. sec., Chandler Sch. for Women, 1952; AA in Social Work, Middelsex C.C., 1974; BSW, Salem Coll., 1987. Med. sec. New Eng. Med. - Boston U. Hosp., Boston, 1952-1960; social worker Lynn-Union Hosp., Lynn, Mass., 1968-1982; home care social worker Mass. Elder Care, Peabody, 1982-1987; nursing home social worker Logan Homes, Wingate Homes, Hill Haven Homes, Mass., 1987-99. Mem. region bd. Hadassah steering com. social work, Hadassah, Boston and Fla. Atlantic region, pres. Chessed, 2003—; active Hist. Soc. Peabody; organizer social work support groups, North Shore, Mass. Office: Lakes Delray # 114 Watersedge J Delray Beach FL 33484 Personal E-mail: lighthousealw@bellsouth.net.

WEINER, CLAIRE MURIEL, freelance writer; b. Bronx, N.Y., Dec. 18, 1951; d. David and Norma (Berry) W. BA, U. Miami, Coral Gables, Fla., 1973; MA, U. Md., 1980. Pub. rels. specialist Hialeah Recreation Div., Hialeah, Fla., 1974-77; freelance writer North Miami Beach, 1977-78, Germantown, Md., 1989—, Montgomery County, Md., 1981—. Govt. affairs liaison for new ednl. data base co. being formed, Montgomery County, 1982—; acting comm. dir. Ednl. Info. Svcs., 1996—. Contbr. articles to local newspapers; contbr. travel articles to profl. jours, mags. Active membership com. newsletter Greater Miami Jewish Fedn., 1974-77; [illegible] B'nai B'rith Women, Washington, 1985-89. Named Hon. Citizen of Historic Williamsburg. Life fellow Am. Biog. Inst. Rsch. Assn., World Lit. Acad.; mem. NAFE, Internat. Platform Assn., Nat. Trust for Hist. Preservation. Jewish. Home: 18828 Sky Blue Cir Germantown MD 20874-5398

WEINER, FERNE, psychologist; b. N.Y.C., June 14, 1928; d. Irving Kapp and Peggy (Finkelstein) Hessberg; m. Howard Weiner, July 20, 1948; children: Irving Kenneth, Laurie. BA, Skidmore Coll., 1965; MA, Sarah Lawrence Coll., 1971; PhD, U. Hawaii, 1975. Lic. psychologist, Calif., Hawaii. Asst. prof. West Oahu Coll. U. Hawaii, Honolulu, 1975-77; staff psychologist Cmty. Guidance Clinic, Manchester, Conn., 1978-83; chief cons. psychologist Consultation and Evaluation Ctr., Meriden, Conn., 1984-85; psychologist cons. Disability Determination Svcs., Hartford, Conn., 1986-87, Honolulu, 1988—; police psychologist Honolulu Police Dept., 1988. Pvt. practice, Greenwich, Conn., 1983-87, Honolulu, 1988—; cons. Adopt-A-Sch. Project, Honolulu, 1991-94; interviewer, therapist Sexual Abuse Treatment Team, Manchester, 1979-83; cons., trainer Conn. schs., day care, ch. groups, 1979-87. Contbr. articles to profl. jours. Active Disaster Assistance Mgmt. Team, Hawaii, 1994-95; v.p., sec. Queens Court at Kapiolani Bd., Honolulu, 1992-95; admissions rep. Hawaii Sarah Lawrence Coll., Honolulu, 1970-80; cons. to adoptees search Orphan Voyage, Conn., 1980-87; mentor Girl Scout Coun. Am., Oahu, 1993-94. Mem. Am. Psychol. Assn. (clin. psychotherapy and neuropsychology divsn.), Hawaii Psychol. Assn., Nat. Registry Health Svcs. Providers, Outrigger Canoe Club, Honolulu Club. Democrat. Jewish. Avocations: aerobics, interior design, property renovation, gourmet cooking, travel. Address: 9776 Claiborne Sq La Jolla CA 92037-1158 E-mail: wferne1@san.rr.com.

WEINER, KAREN COLBY (KAREN LYNN COLBY), psychologist, lawyer; b. Oak Park, Ill., Oct. 28, 1943; d. Leonard L. and Mildred Irene (Berman) Colby; m. J. Laevin Weiner, July 26, 1964; children: Joel Laevin, Doren Robin, Anthony Justin. BA, Mich. State U., East Lansing, 1964; JD, U. Detroit, 1977, MA, 1986, PhD, 1988. Bar: Mich. 1977, D.C. 1978. Speech therapist Oak Park Sch. Dist., 1965-68; law clk. justice G. Mennen Williams Mich. Supreme Ct., Lansing, 1977-79; assoc. Dickinson, Wright, Moon, Van Dusen & Freeman, Detroit, 1979-83; intern in psychology Detroit Psychiat. Inst., 1986-88; psychologist Northland Clinic, Southfield, Mich., 1987-88, Counseling Assocs., Southfield, 1988—; postdoctoral intern Wyandotte (Mich.) Hosp. and Health Ctr., 1988-90; dir. psychol. svcs., quality assurance coord. Counseling Assocs., Southfield, 1991-99. Mem. ethics and stds. com., Internat. Coaching Fedn.; hearing panelist Atty. Discipline Bd., Detroit, 1982-95; hearing referee Mich. Civil Rights Commn., Detroit, 1983-91; mem. Mich. Bd. Psychology, 1999—, vice chair, 2004—; adj. prof. U. Detroit Mercy, 2001-03; mem. ethics com. Internat. Coaching Fedn., 2003—; mem. Inst. Life Coach Tng., 2004. Contbr. articles to profl. jours. Mem. adv. bd. Mich. chpt. Anti-Defamation League, 1981-90. Fellow Mich. Psychol. Assn. (mem. ethics com. 1992—, chmn. legis. com. 1993, chmn. ethics com. 1997-99); mem. APA, Internat. Coaching Fedn. (ethics and stds. com.), Mich. Soc. for Psychoanalytic Psychology (pres. 1995-97, sec. 1991-92, treas. 1992-94), Women Lawyers Assn. Mich. (pres. 1981-82, pres. Found. 1982-83), Mich. Bar Assn. (chmn. spl. com. for expansion under represented groups in law 1980-83). Jewish. Home: 2501 Long Lake Rd West Bloomfield MI 48323 Office: 29260 Franklin Rd Ste 115 Southfield MI 48034-1144 E-mail: drkcw@comcast.net.

WEINER, MARCIA MYRA, judge; b. Apr. 12, 1934; BA, St. Mary's U., San Antonio, 1965, JD, 1970. Bar: Tex. 1971. Atty-advisor HUD, San Antonio, 1971—84, chief counsel, 1984—97; elected justice of the peace Precinct 2 Pl., Bexar County, Tex., 2000—. Recipient Spl. Achievement awards, HUD, 1972, 1975, 1977, Hub Fed. Women's Program award, Leigh Curry award, Fed. Women's Program Coun. Mgmt. award, Outstanding Bus. Woman of Yr., 2000. Mem.: Coll. State Bar Tex., San Antonio Bar Assn., Bexar County Women's Bar Assn., Fed. Bar Assn., Tex. Bar Assn., Greyhound Pets of Am., Tex. Wanderers, Randolph Roadrunners, Alamo Unit #2 of Am. Legion Aux. Jewish. Office: Justice Ct Precinct 2 6715 Bandera Rd San Antonio TX 78238

WEINER, MINA RIEUR, museum consultant, civic worker; b. N.Y.C., Oct. 20, 1936; d. Charles Isaac and Gertrude (Levinson) Rieur; m. Stephen A. Weiner, Sept. 1, 1958; children: Karen Lessall Goss, Paul Rieur (dec.),

James Rieur. BA, Cornell U., 1957; MA, NYU, 1987. Life mem. Cornell Univ. Coun., Ithaca, NY, 1958—; guest curator N.Y. Hist. Soc., 1995-96, 99, [illegible] dir. N.Y. City Fire Mus., 1996-98; [illegible] Rockwell Mus., 1995-97; guest curator Mus. City of N.Y., 1988-94, spl. projects coord., 1990-95; guest curator South St. Seaport Mus., 1989. Mem. exec. bd. dirs. LWV, Port Washington, N.Y., 1970-73; trustee Sands Point Civic Assn., N.Y., 1975-79; creator, coord. Vols. in Port Schs., Port Washington, 1976-78; mem. Sands Point Planning Bd., 1977-81; bd. dirs. Port Washington Pub. Schs., 1979-85, v.p., 1979-81, pres., 1981-85; mem. State Legis. Network, N.Y. State Sch. Bds. Assn., 1980-85; founder Port Washington Youth Coun.; mem. adv. bd. dirs. Mediation Alternative Project, Edn. Assistance Ctr., Port Washington, 1981-86; collections cons. Cow Neck Peninsula Hist. Soc., 1987-92. Editor: Survey on Port Washington Pub. Schs., 1972-73; contbr. articles to profl. jours. Avocations: reading, tennis. Home: 190 Harbor Rd Port Washington NY 11050-2636

WEINER, RUTH EILEEN BLOWER KASSEWITZ, retired public relations executive; b. Columbus, Ohio, May 15, 1928; d. E. Wallett and Helen (Daub) Blower; m. Jack Kassewitz, July 28, 1962 (dec.); m. Morton D. Weiner, Dec. 22, 2002. BS in Journalism-Mgmt., Ohio State U., 1951. Copywriter Ohio Fuel Gas Co., Columbus, 1951-55, Merritt Owens Advt. Agy., Kansas City, 1955-56; account exec. Grant Advt., Inc., Miami, 1956-59; account supr. Venn/Cole & Assocs., Miami, 1959-67; dir. comms. Ferendino/Grafton/Candela/Spillis Archs. & Engrs., Miami, 1967-69, Dade County dept. Housing and Urban Devel., Miami, 1969-72, Met. Dade County Govt., County Mgrs. Office, 1972-78; adminstr. pub. rels. U. Miami/Jackson Meml. Med. Ctr., 1978-90, ret., 1990. Bd. dirs. Girl Scouts USA, Tropical, Fla., 1974—76, 1981—83, Lung Assn. Dade-Monroe Counties, 1976—87, Met. YMCA, 1996—2003; exec. com. Miami-Dade C.C. Found., 1984—99; pres. Mental Health Assn. Dade County, 1982; mem. City of Miami Ecol. and Beautification Com. (now TREEmendous Miami, Ind.), 1978—2000; 1st vice-chmn., 1996—98; bd. govs. Barry U., Miami, 1981—83; trustee Nat. Humanities Faculty, 1981—83; treas., past chmn. Health, Edn., Promotion Coun., Inc.; adv. bd. Miami's For Me, 1987—88; mem. Coral Gables Cable TV Bd., 1983—86; cmty. adv. bd. Jr. League Greater Miami, Inc., 1989—92; founding mem. Nat. Honor Roll, Women in Pub. Rels., No. Ill. U., 1993; trustee emeritus United Protestant Appeal, 1992—99; ch. moderator Plymouth Congl. Ch., 1986—88, trustee, 1995—99, co-pres. Women's Fellowship, 2001—02. Recipient Disting. Svc. award Plymouth Congl. Ch., Miami, 1979; Ann Stover award, 1983; Golden Image award Fla. Pub. Rels. Assn., 1987; named Woman of Yr. Plymouth Congl. Ch., U. Miami Med. Sch., 1991, Humanitarian of Yr. YMCA of Gtr. Miami, 1998; honoree Fla. Women of Achievement. Fellow Pub. Rels. Soc. Am. (pres. South Fla. chpt. 1969-70, nat. chmn. govt. sect. 1973-74, nat. dir. 1974-76; cont. edn. coun. 1981-83; Silver anvil award 1973, del Assembly 1970-73, 86-89, Paul M. Lund Pub. Svc. award 1993, Miami chpt. Lifetime Achievement award 1995); mem. Women in Comms. (pres. Gtr. Miami chpt. 1962-63; Clarion awards 1973, 75, Cmty. Headliner 1985), Miami Internat. Press Club (bd. dirs. 1986-87, treas. 1992), 200 Club Greater Miami (v.p. 1999-2000), Rotary Club of Miami (bd. dirs. 1988-97, pres. 1993-94, Disting. Rotarian of Yr. 1996, Rotarian of Yr. internat. dist. # 6990 1999), Delta Delta Delta (pres. Miami alumnae chpt. 1997-99). Home: 335 Costanera Rd Coral Gables FL 33143

WEINER, SANDRA JOAN, computer catalog reseller company executive; b. N.Y.C., Oct. 27, 1951; d. Louis and Rose (Rosansky) Kornbluth; m. Gerald Weiner, Feb. 14, 1992. BA magna cum laude, Queens Coll., 1973; MA in Romance Langs., Princeton U., 1975. Instr. French lang. Princeton (N.J.) U., 1973-77; mgr. cargo tariffs Air France, N.Y.C., 1977-82; mgr. internat. pricing Emery Worldwide, Wilton, Conn., 1982-86, dir. pricing, 1986-89; pres. Riverview Traffic Group, Trumbull, Conn., 1989-90; mgr. strategic sourcing, program mgr. Pitney Bowes, Shelton, Conn., 1990-94; mgr. quality and adminstrn. Entex Info. Svcs., Rye Brook, N.Y., 1994-95; group dir. prodn. and mktg., purchasing, v.p. merchandising Micro Warehouse Inc., Norwalk, Conn., 1995—2001. Mem. adv. bd. Cargo Rate Svcs., Miami, Fla., 1984—90. Bd. dirs. Literacy Vols. Greater Norwalk, 1987. Fullbright-Hayes scholar, 1973. Avocations: gardening, bridge. Office: Micro Warehouse Inc 535 Connecticut Ave Ste 104A Norwalk CT 06854-1738

WEINER, SANDRA SAMUEL, critical care nurse, nursing consultant; b. N.Y.C., Jan. 12, 1947; d. Herbert A. and Ruth (Wallerstein) Samuel; m. Neil D. Weiner, June 15, 1969 (div. June 1980); 1 child, Jaime Michelle. BS in Nursing, SUNY, Buffalo, 1968; cert. in critical care, Golden West Coll., 1982; postgrad., UCLA, U. West L.A. Sch. Law, 1992. RN, Pa., Calif. Staff nurse N.Y. Hosp.-Cornell Med. Ctr., 1968-69; head nurse med.-surg. nursing Abington (Pa.) Hosp., 1969; assoc. prof. Sch. Nursing, U. Pa., Phila., 1970; instr. nursing Coll. Med. Assts., Long Beach, Calif., 1971-72; surg. staff nurse Med. Ctr. of Tarzana, Calif., 1978-79, Cedars-Sinai Med. Ctr., L.A., 1979-81; supr. recovery rm. Beverly Hills Med. Ctr., L.A., 1981-92; post anesthesia care unit nurse Westside Hosp., 1992-96, Midway Hosp., Beverly Hills, Calif., 1996-99, Encino (Calif.) - Tarzana Med. Ctr., 1996—. Med. cons. RJA & Assocs., Beverly Hills, Calif., 1984-92; instr. CPR, L.A., 1986-95. Mem. women's aux. Ctr. Theater Group Vols., L.A., 1986-94, Maple Ctr., Beverly HIlls, 1987-96. Mem. ANA, Am. Soc. Post-Anesthesia Nursing, Am. Assn. Critical Care Nurses, Heart and Lung Assn., Post Anesthesia Nurses Assn., U.S. Ski Assn. Democrat. Jewish. Avocations: skiing, aerobics, travel, theater, ballet. Home: 12633 Moorpark St Studio City CA 91604-4537

WEINER, SHARON ROSE, public relations executive; d. Mike and Elaine (Feinberg) W.; m. William H. Stryker. BA, Northwestern U., 1965; MBA, U. Hawaii, 1975. Sales rsch. asst. WBBM-TV, Chgo., 1965-66; acct. exec. Pub. Relations Bd., Chgo., 1966-67; pub. relations mgr. Levi Strauss & Co., San Francisco, 1967-73, C. Brewer Co., Honolulu, 1975-76; v.p. Fawcett McDermott Cavanagh Inc., Honolulu, 1976-79; pres., chief exec. officer Stryker Weiner Co., Honolulu, 1979—. Bd. dirs. Hawaii Vis. Bur., Honolulu; v.p. bd. dirs. Aloha coun. Boy Scouts Am. Aloha United Way, Honolulu, Honolulu Symphony. Mem. Pub. Relations Soc. Am. (Gregg W. Perry award 1988), Soc. Am. Travel Writers, Pacific Area Travel Assn., Oahu Country Club, Pacific Club.

WEINER, WENDY L. elementary school educator, writer; b. Milw., Jan. 2, 1961; d. Kenneth J. and Jessie M. Weiner. AA, U. Wis. Washington County, West Bend; BS, MS, U. Wis., U. Wis., Milw., 1993; prin. lic., Marian Coll. Cert. nat. cert. early childhood edn. NBPT, tchr. Wis. Tchr. Milw. Pub. Schs. Contbr. articles to profl. jours. Mem. Milw. Pub. Mus. Tchr. Adv. Coun., TV and Tech. Com., Vision and Tech. Com., Learning Mag.'s Student Best Adv. Coun. Recipient Presdl. Award in Sci. Tchg. Excellence, AT&T Recognition in Sci. Tchg. Excellence, Wis. Aerospace Educator of Yr., Milw. Tchr. of Yr., Grad. Last Decade award U. Wis. Milw. Alumni Assn., Warner Cable-Tchg. Creativity with Cable award, Excellence in Sci. Tchg. award. Wis. Elem. Sci. Tchrs. Assn., Nat. Urban Tech. in Edn. award Coun. Great City Schs., Sen. Herb Kohl Tchr. Achievement award, Ameritech-Wis. Bell Gold Tchr. Recognition award, 1992, Presdl. award for elem. sci. tchg. excellence; grantee Greater Mil. Edn. Trust, Wis. Space Grant Consortium/NASA, NSF. Mem. PTA, Wis. Aerospace Edn. Assn. (instr. mag. adviser 1996-2000, Sam's Club Tchr. of Yr. 2002), YMCA-Young Astronauts, Nat. Arbor Day Assn., NSTA, Wis. Elem. Tchrs. Assn., Milw. Kindergarten Assn., Wis. Secondary Sci. Assn., Wis. Assn. Sch. Adminstrs., Milw. Reading Assn., Midwest Devel. Corp., Assn. Presdl. Awardees in Sci., Soc. for Elem. Presdl. Awardees, Coun. Elem. Sci. Internat., Civil Air Patrol (sr. officer). Avocations: crafts, walking. Office: Parkview Sch 4966 N 91st St Milwaukee WI 53225-4127

WEINER-HEUSCHKEL, SYDELL, theater educator; b. N.Y.C., Feb. 18, 1947; d. Milton A. and Janet (Kay) Horowitz; children: Jason, Emily; m. Ron Heuschkel, Sept. 5, 1992. BA, SUNY, Binghamton, 1968; MA, Calif. State U., L.A., 1974; postgrad., Yale U., 1968-70; PhD, NYU, 1986; MS, Calif. State U., Dominguez Hills, 1996. Lic. marriage and family therapist. Prof. theater arts, chmn. dept., dir. honors program Calif. State U. Dominguez Hills, Carson, 1984—. Guest lectr. Calif. Inst. Arts, 1988. Appeared in play Vikings, Grove Shakespeare Festival, 1988; dir. Plaza Suite, Brea (Calif.) Civic Theatre, 1982, Gypsy, Carson Civic Light Opera, 1990, Same Time Next Year, Muckehthaler, 1987, Slow Dance on the Killing Ground, Alternative Repertory Theatre, 1989; co-author: School and Community Theater Problems: A Handbook for Survival, 1978, (software) Public Speaking, 1991; contbr. Am. Jour. Psychotherapy, 1997, Jour. Clin. Psychology, 1998. Yale U. fellow, 1969; recipient Lyle Gibson Disting. Tchr. award, 1989. Mem. Screen Actors Guild, Am. Fedn. TV and Radio Artists, Calif. State U. Women's Coun. (treas. 1989-91), Phi Kappa Phi. E-mail: sweiner@csudh.edu.

WEINGAND, DARLENE ERNA, librarian educator, consultant; b. Oak Park, Ill., Aug. 13, 1937; d. Edward Emil and Erna (Heidenway) W.,; m. Wayne Anthony Weston, Sept. 7, 1957 (div. June 1976); children: Kathleen Mary, Lynda Anne, Judith Diane, Barbara Jeanne; m. James Elberling, May 1977 (div. 1980); m. Roger Paul Couture, Apr. 7, 1984. BA in History and English, Elmhurst Coll., 1972; MALS, Rosary Coll., 1973; PhD in Adult Edn./Libr. Sci., U. Minn., 1980. Asst. prof. U. Wis., Madison, 1981-86, assoc. prof., 1986-92, prof., 1992-99, prof. emerita, 1999—, SLIS acting dir., 1991, summer 86, SLIS asst. dir., 1990-94, adminstr. SLIS Continuing Edn. Svcs., 1981-99. Cons. in mktg., continuing edn., libr. futures, info. issues, and mgmt., 1980—; invited mentor Snowbird Leadership Inst., 1990, 92; vis. fellow Curtin U. Tech. Perth, Australia, 1990; Fulbright lectr. U. Iceland, 1988; lectr. 2d World Conf. on Continuing Edn. for Libr. and Info. Sci., Barcelona, 1993, Internat. Fedn. Libr. Assn.; adj. prof. U. Hawaii Manoa, 1999—. Author: Customer Svc. Excellence: A Concise Guide for Librarians, 1997, Future Driven Library Marketing, 1998, Marketing/Planning Library and Information Services, 1999, 4th edit., 2001, Administration of the Small Public Library, 4th edit., 2001, Budgeting and the political Process in Libraries, Simulation Games, 1992 (with others), Connections: Literacy and Cultural Heritage: Lessons from Iceland, 1992, Managing Today's Public Library: Blueprint for Change, 1994, author (with others) Continuing Professional Education and Internat. Fed. of Libr. Assoc.: Past, Present, and a Vision for the Future, 1992; contbr. articles to profl. jours. Recipient excellence award Nat. Univ. Continuing Edn. Assn., 1989, Econ. and Cmty. Devel. award, 1989, outanding achievement in audio applications award Internat. Teleconferencing Assn., 1991, LITA/Libr. Hi-Tech award, 1996, disting. alumna award Dominican U., 1998. Mem. ALA, Internat. Fedn. Libr. Assns. (ALA rep.), Assn. for Libr. and Info. Sci. Edn. (bd. dirs. 1990-93, rsch. grantee 1992, Russia project fellow 1994), Hawaii Libr. Assn., Wis. Assn. for Adult and Continuing Edn., Phi Delta Kappa, Beta Phi Mu. Office: U Hawaii-Manoa 4Q Hamilton Libr Honolulu HI 96815 E-mail: weingand@lava.net.

WEINGARTEN, RHONDA, lawyer; b. N.Y.C., Dec. 18, 1957; d. Gabriel and Edith (Appelbaum) W. BS, Cornell U., 1980; JD cum laude, Benjamin N. Cardozo Sch. Law, 1983. Bar: N.Y. 1984, U.S. Dist. Ct. (so. and ea. dists.) N.Y. 1984. Legis. asst. Labor Com. N.Y. State Senate, Albany, 1979-80; assoc. Stroock, Stroock and Lavan, N.Y.C., 1983-86; counsel to pres. United Fedn. Tchrs., N.Y.C., 1986—98; tchr. Clara Barton HS, Brooklyn, 1991—97; asst. sec. United Fedn. Teachers, N.Y.C., 1995, treas., 1997, pres., 1998—; v.p. Am. Fedn. Teachers. Bd. dirs. N.Y. State United Teachers; adj. instr. Cardozo Sch. Law, N.Y.C., 1986; mem. Mayor Bloomberg's transition com., N.Y.C., 2001. Mediator Bklyn. Mediation Ctr. Victim Services Agy., 1981-82 (outstanding achievement award, 1981); mem. N.Y. Com. Safety and Health, 1986, Park Slope Safe Homes Project, 1984—, Dem. Nat. Com.; bd. dirs. Justice Resource Ctr., Coun. for Unity, N.Y. Com. on Occupational Safety and Health, N.Y. Region Anti-Defamation League, United Way Greater N.Y., Internat. Rescue Com. Mem. ABA (labor and employment sect.), N.Y. State Bar Assn., Women's Bar Assn., Council N.Y. Law Assocs., Cardozo Sch. Law Alumni Assn. (treas., bd. dirs. 1983—). Democrat. Jewish. Office: United Fedn Tchrs 260 Park Ave S New York NY 10010-7214*

WEINHOLD, LINDA LILLIAN, psychologist, researcher; b. Reading, Pa., Nov. 9, 1948; d. Aaron Zerbe Weinhold and Nancy Louise (Spotts) Weikel; m. Jack Wayne Prisk, Jan. 21, 1967 (div. 1969). Lic. practical nurse, AVTS, 1970; BS, Penn State U., 1975; MS, C.W. Post Ctr., 1982; PhD, Fordham U., 1986. LPN; cert. profl. counselor. Instr., asst. prof. Gettysburg (Pa.) Coll., 1985-86; post doc. fellow John Hopkins U., Balt., 1986-88; staff fellow NIH NIDA Addiction Rsch. Ctr., Balt., 1988-93; cons. NIH NIDA Medications Devel., Rockville, Md., 1993-94; soc. sci. program coord. Med. Ctr. NIDA Rsch., Washington, 1994-95; cons. The Clin. Cons. Group Antech, Inc., Balt., 1995; substance abuse counselor Hope Village, Inc., Washington, 1996—. Various presentations. Mem. Am. Psychological Assn., Phi Kappa Phi, Sigma Xi. Democrat. Avocations: singing, dance, painting, photography, reading. Home: 2611 Bowen Rd SE Apt 203 Washington DC 20020-6623 Office: Hope Village Inc 2840 Langston Pl SE Washington DC 20020-3241

WEINHOLD, VIRGINIA BEAMER, interior designer; b. Elizabeth, N.J., June 21, 1932; d. Clayton Mitchell and Rosemary (Behrend) Beamer; divorced; children: Thomas Craig, Robert Scott, Amy Linette. BA, Cornell U., 1955; BFA summa cum laude, Ohio State U., 1969; MA in Design Mgmt., Ohio State U., 1982. Freelance interior designer, 1969-72; interior designer, dir. interior design Karlsberger and Assocs. Inc., Columbus, Ohio, 1972-82; assoc. prof. dept. design Ohio State U., 1982—, grad. studies chairperson, 1986-89, 1995-96; lectr. indsl. design Ohio State U., 1972, 79-80. Trustee Found. for Interior Design Edn. and Rsch., 1991-97. Mem. Inst. Bus. Designers (chpt. treas. 1977-79, nat. trustee 1979-81, nat. chmn. contract documents com. 1979-84, chpt. pres. 1981-83), Constrn. Specifications Inst., Interior Design Educator's Coun. (nat. treas. 1989-93), Interior Design Educator's Coun. Found. (nat. treas. 1992-94), Illuminating Engring. Soc. (chpt. v.p. 1997-98), AIA (assoc.), Internat. Interior Design Assn. (nat. dir. 1994-97). Prin. works include Grands Rapids (Mich.) Osteo. Hosp., Melrose (Mass.) Wakefield Hosp., Christopher Inn, Columbus, John W. Galbreath Hdqrs., Columbus, Guernsey Meml. Hosp., Cambridge, Ohio, Trinity Epis. Ch. and Parish House, Columbus, Hale Hosp., Haverhill, Mass., Ohio State U. Dept. Indsl. Design Lighting Lab., others. Author: IBD Forms and Documents Manual, Interior Finish Materials for Health Care Facilities, Subjective Impressions: Lighting Hotels and Resturants, 1989, Effects of Lighting on The Perception of Interior Spaces, 1993. Home: 112 Glen Dr Columbus OH 43085-4010 Office: Ohio State U Dept Design 128 N Oval Mall Columbus OH 43210-1318

WEINKAUF, MARY LOUISE STANLEY, clergywoman; b. Eau Claire, Wis., Sept. 22, 1938; d. Joseph Michael and Marie Barbara (Holzinger) Stanley; m. Alan D. Weinkauf, Oct. 12, 1962 (dec. Nov. 2000); children: Stephen, Xanti. BA, Wis. State U., 1961; MA, U. Tenn., 1962, PhD, 1966; MDiv, Luth. Sch. Theology, Chgo., 1993. Grad. asst., instr. U. Tenn., 1961-66; asst. prof. English Adrian Coll., 1966-69; prof., head dept. English Dakota Wesleyan U., Mitchell, S.D., 1969-89; instr. Columbia Coll., 1989-91. Pastor Calvary Evang. Luth. Ch., Siloa Luth. Ch., Ontonagon Faith, White Pine, Mich., Gowrie, Iowa. Author: Hard-Boiled Heretic, 1994, Sermons in Science Fiction, 1994, Murder Most Poetic, 1996. Trustee The Ednl. Found., 1986-90; bd. dirs. Ontonagon County Habitat for Humanity, 1995-97; mem. bd. Luth. Campus Ministry for Wis. and Upper Mich., 1996—2002, Fortune Lake Bible Camp, 2003—. Mem. AAUW (divsn. pres. 1978-80), Nat. Coun. Tchrs. English, S.D. Coun. Tchrs. English, Sci. Fiction Rsch. Assn., Popular Culture Assn., Milton Soc., S.D. Poetry Soc. (pres. 1982-83), Delta Kappa Gamma (pres. local chpt., mem. state bd. 1972-89, state v.p. 1979-83, state pres. 1983-85), Sigma Tau Delta, Pi Kappa Delta, Phi Kappa Phi. E-mail: woodwork@nnex.net.

WEINSHENKER, NAOMI JOYCE, clinical psychiatrist, educator, researcher; b. Ridgewood, N.J., Mar. 28, 1961; d. Theodore and Anne Betty (Jaffe) W. BA summa cum laude, Yale U., 1983; MD, U. Pa., 1989. Diplomate Am. Bd. Psychiatry and Neurology. Rotating intern Overlook Hosp., Summit, N.J., 1989-90; resident in adult psychiatry Mass. Mental Health Ctr., Harvard U. Med. Sch., Boston, 1990-92, fellow in child and adolescent psychiatry, 1992-93, Boston Children's Hosp., Harvard U. Med. Sch., 1993-94; staff psychiatrist Choate Health Systems, Woburn, Mass., 1994-96; asst. prof. clin. psychiatry U. Medicine and Dentistry of N.J., Newark, 1996-2000; asst. prof. clin. psychiatry Sch. Medicine NYU, 2000—. Staff psychiatrist Univ. Behavioral HealthCare, Newark, 1996—97; asst.dir. Univ.Hosp. Psychiat. Outpatient Ctr., 1998—2000; mem. faculty NYU Child Study Ctr., 2000—; cons. child outpatient svcs. Tri-City Mental Health and Retardation Ctr., Inc., Medford, Mass., 1996. Contbr. articles to profl. jours.; editl. asst. Emergency Medicine mag., 1983-84. Vol. psychiatry unit, coord. psychiatry vols., Yale-New Haven Hosp., 1979-83; vol. recruitment coord. Phila. Adult Spl. Olympics, 1985. Mem. Am. Psychiat. Assn., Am. Acad. Child/Adolescent Psychiatry, N.J. Psychiat. Assn. (Essex County rep. Tri-County chpt. 1997-98, treas. 1998-99, sec. 1999-00, v.p. 2000-2001, pres.-elect 2001-02), N.J. Coun. Child/Adolescent Psychiatry, Phi Beta Kappa, Sigma Xi. Democrat. Jewish. Avocations: singing, viola, musical theatre, nutrition and vegetarianism, weight training and aerobics. Office: NYU Child Study Ctr 577 First Ave New York NY 10016

WEINSHIENK, ZITA LEESON, federal judge; b. St. Paul, Apr. 3, 1933; d. Louis and Ada (Dubov) Leeson; m. Hubert Troy Weinshienk, July 8, 1956 (dec. 1983); children: Edith Blair, Kay Anne, Darcy Jill; m. James N. Schaffner, Nov. 15, 1986. Student, U. Colo., 1952-53; BA magna cum laude, U. Ariz., 1955; JD cum laude, Harvard U., 1958; Fulbright grantee, U. Copenhagen, Denmark, 1959; LHD (hon.), Loretto Heights Coll., 1985; LLD (hon.), U. Denver, 1990. Bar: Colo. 1959. Probation counselor, legal adviser, referee Denver Juvenile Ct., 1959-64; judge Denver Mcpl. Ct., 1964-65, Denver County Ct., 1965-71, Denver Dist. Ct., 1972-79, U.S. Dist. Ct. Colo., Denver, 1979—, sr. judge, 1998—. Precinct committeewoman Denver Democratic Com., 1963-64; bd. dirs. Crime Stoppers. Named one of 100 Women in Touch with Our Time Harper's Bazaar Mag., 1971, Woman of Yr., Denver Bus. and Profl. Women, 1969; recipient Women Helping Women award Soroptimist Internat. of Denver, 1983, Hanna G. Solomon award Nat. Coun. Jewish Women, Denver, 1986, Soaring Eagle award Colo. Womne's Leadership Conf., 1997; inducted into Colo. Women's Hall of Fame, 2000. Fellow Colo. Bar Found., Am. Bar Found.; mem. ABA, Denver Bar Assn., U. Ariz. Alumni Assn. (Disting. Citizen's award 1994), Colo. Bar Assn., Nat. Conf. Fed. Trial Judges (exec. com., past chair), Dist. Judges' Assn. of 10th Cir. (past pres.), Colo. Women's Bar Assn. (Mary Lathrop award 1995), Fed. Judges Assn., Denver Crime Stoppers Inc. (bd.dirs.), Denver LWV, Women's Forum Colo., Harvard Law Sch. Assn., Phi Beta Kappa, Phi Kappa Phi, Order of Coif (hon. Colo. chpt.). Office: US Dist Ct US Courthouse Rm 4-841 901 19th St Denver CO 80294-2500 Office Phone: 303-844-2784.

WEINSTEIN, ELLEN, performing company executive; BFA in Dance, SUNY. Dancer Garden State Ballet, Savannah Ballet; tchr., choreographer Nat. Dance Inst., N.Y.C., 1985—89, assoc. artistic dir., 1989—94, artistic dir., 1995—. Cons. Nat. Dance Inst. Nat. Outreach Program. Choreographer (films) Disney, Polaroid's 50th Anniversary Celebration, Radio City Music Hall. Office: National Dance Institute 594 Broadway Rm 805 New York NY 10012

WEINSTEIN, HELENE E. state legislator; b. N.Y.C., Sept. 6, 1952; BA, Am. Univ., 1973; JD, New Eng. Sch. Law, 1976. Assemblywoman dist. 41 N.Y. State Assembly, 1981—, chair standing assembly com. on judiciary, 1993—. Chair task force on women's issues N.Y. State Assembly, 1987-92, task force on food, farm & nutrition, 1987-88, ethics, ways and means, aging com., codes com., jud. com.; mem. facilities rev. bd. N.Y. State Ct. Mem. Legis. Women's Caucus, Bklyn. Women's Polit. Caucus, Jewish Women's Leadership Caucus. Mem. B'nai B'rith, Bklyn. Bar Assn. Home: 3520 Nostrand Ave Brooklyn NY 11229-5203 Office: NY State Capitol State Capital Albany NY 12207

WEINSTEIN, JOYCE, artist; b. June 7, 1931; d. Sidney and Rose (Bier) W.; m. Stanley Boxer, Nov. 28, 1952. Student, CCNY, 1948-50, Art Students League, 1948-52. Exec. coord. Women in Arts Found., Inc., 1975-79, 81-82, coord. bd., 1983-87. One-person shows include Perdalma Gallery, N.Y.C., 1953-56, L.I. U., Bklyn., 1969, U. Calif.-Santa Cruz, 1969, T. Bortolazzo Gallery, Santa Barbara, Calif., 1972, Dorsky Gallery, N.Y.C., 1972, 74, Galerie Ariadne, N.Y.C., 1975, Gloria Cortella Gallery, N.Y.C., 1976, Meredith Long Contemporary Gallery, N.Y.C., 1978, 79, 88-90, Martin Gerard Gallery, Edmonton, Alta., Can., 1981, 82, 84, Galerie Wentzel, Cologne, Fed. Republic of Germany, 1982, 87, Haber Theodore Gallery, N.Y.C., 1983, 95, Gallery One, Toronto, Ont., Can., 1983, 2002, Paul Kuhn Gallery, Calgary, 1985, Eva Cohn Gallery, Highland Park, Ill., 1985, Meredith Long & Co., Houston, 1988, 90, Alena Adlung Gallery, N.Y.C., 1989, Flanders Art Gallery, Mpls., 1999 Harmon-Meek Gallery, Naples, Fla., 2000, Gallery One, Toronto, 2002; exhibited in group shows at Marlborough Gallery, N.Y.C., 1968, Bula Mus. Art, Calcutta, India, 1970, Phoenix Gallery, N.Y.C., 1988, Provident Nat. Bank, 1988, Alena Adlung Gallery, 1989, 90, Edmonton Art Mus., 1975, 77, 83, 85, 89, Rose Fried Gallery, N.Y.C., 1970, Hudson River Mus., 1971, Dorsky Gallery, 1972, 94, Suffolk Mus., Stony Brook, N.Y., 1972, N.Y. Cultural Ctr., 1973, Stamford (Conn.) Mus., 1973, Landmark Gallery, N.Y.C., 1974, Women's Interart Ctr., N.Y.C., 1974, 75, 78, New Sch. Social Rsch., N.Y.C., 1975, Bklyn. Mus., 1975, Galerie Ariadne, 1975, Mus. of Modern Art, N.Y.C., 1981, The Queens Mus. N.Y., 1984, The Centre de Creacio Contemporania, Barcelona, Spain, 1987, Fairleigh Dickinson U., Hackensack, N.J., 1976, Gloria Cortella, Inc., 1976, Northeastern U., Boston, 1977, Lehigh (Pa.) U., 1977, Meredith Long Contemporary Gallery, 1977, 78, 79, 80, Galerie Wentzel, 1981-85, Martin Gerard Gallery, 1981-84, Gallery One, 1983, 84, Haber Theodore Gallery, 1982-85, Jerald Melberg Gallery, Charlotte, N.C., 1984, Richard Green Gallery, N.Y.C., 1986, Rosel Art Fair, Basel Switzerland, 1986, Meredith Long & Co., 1988-90, Broome St. Gallery, N.Y.C., 1991, 97, Andre Zarre Gallery, N.Y.C., 1990, Cork Gallery, N.Y.C., 1990, Chgo. Internat. Art Exbn., 1990, Queens Coll., N.Y.C., 1991, Miami Art Fair, 1993, Bklyn. Botanic Gardens, 1994, Dorothy Blau Gallery, Bay Harbor Islands, Fla., 1997-98, Harmon-Meek Gallery, Naples, Fla., 1998-99, Flanders Contemporary Art, Mpls., 1999, Hubert Gallery, N.Y.C., 2003; represented in permanent collections: Pa. Acad. Fine Arts, N.J. State Mus., Ciba-Geigy Corp., New Sch. Social Rsch., Bula Mus. Art, U. Calif., Mus. Modern Art, N.Y.C., McMullen Gallery, Edmonton, Ga., De Spisset Mus., U. Santa Clara, Edmonton Art Gallery Mus., The Hines Collection, Boston, others; represented by Smith Anderson Gallery, Palo Alto, Calif., Flanders Art Gallery, Harmon-Meek Gallery, Naples, Fla., Flanders Contemporary Art, Mpls., Dorothy Blau Gallery, Bay Harbor Island, Fla., Gallery One, Toronto. Recipient Lambert Fund award Pa. Acad. Fine Arts, 1955, Susan B. Anthony award NOW, 1983. Home: 46 Fox Hill Rd Ancramdale NY 12503-5311

WEINSTEIN, LORI JILL, social worker; b. Washington, Apr. 17, 1958; d. Richard and Lila (Edison) Barth; m. Stuart Harris Weinstein, Oct. 1, 1988; children: Joshua David, Shoshanna Lynn. BA, U. Md., 1980; MSW, Cath. U., Washington, 1983. Lic. cert. social worker-clin. Geriat. social worker The Roosevelt for Sr. Citizens, Washington, 1984-85; resident counselor Housing Opportunities Commn., Kensington, Md., 1985-88; lead adoption social worker Dept. Health and Human Svcs., Rockville, Md., 1988—. Field instr. Cath. U., 1990-91, Sch. Social Work, U. Md., Balt., 1996-97; trainer Montgomery County Dept. Health and Human Svcs., Rockville, 1991—. Designer/developer adoption tracking sys. V.p. Nat. Jewish Musical Arts Found., Rockville, 1986—; bd. dirs. Women of Reform Judaism, Chevy Chase, Md., 1988—; mem. Am. Med. Ctr. Cancer Rsch., Olney, Md., 1993-95; vol. Hospitality and Info. Svc., Washington, 1993—. Recipient Field Placement grant Cath. U., 1982. Mem. NASW. Democrat. Avocations: needlework, gardening.

WEINSTEIN, MARIE PASTORE, psychologist; b. N.Y.C., Oct. 3, 1940; d. Edward and Sarah (Mancuso) Pastore; children: Arielle Rebecca Dorros, Damon Alexander. BA in Polit. Sci. and Lit., Ind. U.; MS in Psychology, L.I. U.; PhD in Ednl. Psychology, CCNY, 1986. Cert. sch. psychologist; lic. psychologist, N.Y. Pvt. practice, 1978—; dir., adminstr. learning ctr. Guidance Ctr. Flatbush, Bklyn., 1978—82; clin. team coord./psychologist Lorge Upper and Lower Sch., N.Y.C., 1982—85; psychologist devel. disabilities ctr. Roosevelt Hosp., N.Y.C., 1985—87; chief psychologist Blueberry Treatment Ctrs., Bklyn., 1987—89; cons. psychologist Safe Space, N.Y.C., 1989—2003; law guardian Panel of Forensic Psychologists, 1994—. Cons. psychologist United Cerebral Palsy Hearst Presch., Bklyn., 1988-89, Charles Drew Day Ctr., Queens Village, N.Y., 1982-85, Warbasse Nursery Sch., Bklyn., 1981-85, YWCA Montessori Sch., 1993-94; adj. asst. prof. Baruch Coll. CUNY, 1989; pvt. practice, Bklyn.; rsch. cons. Children's TV Workshop, N.Y.C., 1979; clin. cons. Bedford Stuyvesant Mental Health Ctr., Bklyn., 1990, Youth Counseling League, N.Y.C., 1993; cons. dist. 2 N.Y.C. Bd. Edn., 1988; guest lectr. Met. Hosp. Dept. Psychiatry, N.Y.C., 1988, Dist. 3 Bd. Edn., 1993; edn. cons. Lit. Vols. N.Y., 1974-76. Contbg. author to children's ency., 1970. Fellow Am. Orthopsychiat. Assn. (program com. 1990—); mem. APA, Internat. Congress on Child Abuse and Neglect, Manhattan Fedn. Child and Adolescent Svcs. Office: 26 Court St Ste 2112 Brooklyn NY 11242-1121

WEINSTEIN, MARTA, packaging services company executive; Founder iLogistix (formerly Logistix), Fremont, Calif., 1984—, co-chair, 1998—. Office: iLogistix 48301 Lakeview Blvd Fremont CA 94538-6533

WEINSTEIN, RUTH JOSEPH, lawyer; b. N.Y.C., Mar. 26, 1933; d. David Arthur and Toby (Landau) J.; m. Marvin Walter Weinstein, June 3, 1962; children: Rosalyn S., Steven M., Barbara E. AB magna cum laude, Radcliffe Coll., 1954; LLB, Harvard U., 1957. Bar: N.Y. 1957, D.C. 1966. Assoc. Hale Russell & Gray and predecessor firms, N.Y.C., 1957-66, ptnr., 1966-85, Winthrop Stimson Putnam & Roberts, N.Y.C., 1985-98, sr. counsel, 1999-2000, Pillsbury Winthrop, N.Y.C., 2000—. Chairperson Practising Law Inst. Forum, N.Y.C., 1978. Mem. sch. bd. Union Free Sch. Dist. 5, Rye Town, N.Y., 1976-79, pres., 1978-79; mem. The Friends of Crawford Park. Mem. ABA, Assn. of Bar of City of N.Y. (com. on Aeronautics Assn. 1987-90), Harvard Radcliffe Club of Westchester. Avocations: boating, skiing. Home: 21 Meadowlark Rd Rye Brook NY 10573-1209 Office: Pillsbury Winthrop 1 Battery Park Plz New York NY 10004-1490

WEINSTEIN, SHARON SCHLEIN, corporate communications executive, educator; b. Newark, Apr. 15, 1942; d. Louis Charles and Ruth Margaret (Franzblau) Schlein; m. Elliott Henry Weinstein, May 7, 1978. BA, U. Pa., 1964; MA, New Sch. for Social Rsch., N.Y.C., 1985. Sr. editor Merrill Lynch, N.Y.C., 1972-74; pub. rels. officer Chase Manhattan Bank, N.Y.C., 1974-79; mgr. corp. communication Sanford C. Berstein & Co., N.Y.C., 1980-83; v.p. corp. affairs Nat. Westminster Bancorp, N.Y.C., 1983-95; dir. corp. comms. Nat. Securities Cleaning Corp., N.Y.C., 1995-98; asst. v.p. corp. comm. Guardian Life Ins. Co., N.Y.C., 1998—2002; comms. mgr. Zurich N.Am., N.Y.C., 2002—. Adj. asst. prof. NYU, 1988—. Home: 161 W 15th St New York NY 10011-6720

WEINSTOCK RAD, KATHERYN LOUISE, music educator; d. Henry Robert and Jeanallan Joyce Weinstock; m. Jalal Rad, Aug. 23, 1993. Aux. music study, U. Birmingham, England, 1983—84, U. Keele, Staffordshire/Newcastle, 1983—84; MusB, U. Tulsa, 1985, MusM, 1988. Cert. Okla. Tchr. Cert. State of Okla., 1988. Cellist Signature Symphony Okla. Sinfonia, Tulsa, 1982—, Tulsa (Okla.) Philharm., 1982—; adj. cello instr. Northeastern State U, Tahlequah, Okla., 1988—90; music tchr. Tulsa Pub. Sch., 1989—96; dir. of strings, tchr. Broken Arrow (Okla.) Pub. Sch., 1996—99; music curriclum coord. Tulsa Pub. Sch., 1999—2002; music coord. Tulsa Cmty. Music Sch., 2003; adj. cello instr. Performing Arts Ctr. Edn. Tulsa C.C., 2000—; fine arts coord. Cent. High Sch. Acad. Arts, 2003—. Mem. bd. fine arts task force Tulsa Pub. Sch., 1996—; adv. Barthelmes Conservatory, 2000—02; bd. mem. Chamber Music Tulsa(Okla.), 2001—; performer cellist Tulsa Philharmonic, Tulsa Signature Symphony, Okla. City Philharmnic; prin. cellist Light Opera Orchestra of Okla.; performer has performed with many classical, pop/rock, jazz and blues artists, including a live performance on NPR. Grandstand, judge Vet. Day Parade, Tulsa, 1999—2002; mem. Tulsa Now Task Force - Mayor Bill Fortune, 2002—; fundraiser raised over one half million dollars music programs Tulsa Pub. Schs. Recipient Tchr. Touching Tomorrow Award, Tulsa Pub. Sch., 1996, Superior Civilian Svc. Award, Dept. of the U.S. Army, 1999—2000; grantee VH-1 save the Music Grant, VH-1, 2001, U.S. Dept. Edn., 2002. Mem.: Hyetchka, Am. Federation of Musicians. Avocations: playing cello in variety of genres, cooking, exercise. Home: 630 Pioneer Rd Sapulpa OK 74066

WEINTRAUB, ELLEN L. commissioner; b. 1957; m. Bill Dauster; 3 children. BA cum laude, Yale Coll.; JD, Harvard Law Sch. Bar: NY, DC and Supreme Court. Chair Fed. Election Commn., Washington, 2002—03, vice chair, 2004—; of counsel Perkins Coie, Political Law Group; litigator Cahill Gordon & Reindel; counsel Com. on Stds. of Ofcl. Conduct for U.S. Ho. Reps. Office: 999 E St NW Washington DC 20463

WEIR, ANNE, writer; b. Boston, Feb. 9, 1942; d. John Weir and Martha (Kingman) Perry; children: Emily Weir, Sarah Noel, Katherine Joy. BA, Swarthmore Coll., 1964; MEd, U. Maine, 1984. Cert. elem. and secondary edn. tchr. Editor: Marlowe: Being In the Life of the Mind, 1996, A Book of Certainties, 1998, The Color Book, 1998, Marlowe, corrected and augmented, 1999, Christopher's Journey, Acts & Scenes, News, The Bird's Eye, 1996-2000, A Native Woman poems, 1999, American City, 2000, A Codebook for the Plays, 2000, Waking, An Academic Celebration, 2001, A Teacher's Holiday, "Streamlines" A Study in Bibliography, New Songs, 2001, The Reincarnation of Love, 2002, Literary Picture Notebooks, And in Aftertimes, 2003. Office: Marlowe Books PO Box 10364 Portland ME 04104-0364

WEIR, DAME GILLIAN CONSTANCE, concert organist, harpsichordist; b. Martinborough, New Zealand, Jan. 17, 1941; d. Cecil Alexander and Clarice M. Foy (Bignell) W. Grad., Royal Coll. Music, London, 1965; Mus D (hon.), U. Victoria of Wellington, New Zealand, 1983; DLitt (hon.), Huddersfield U., 1997; Mus D (hon.), Hull U., 1999, Exeter U., 2001; Doctorate (hon.), U. Ctrl. Eng., 2001; Mus D (hon.), Leicester Univ., 2003. Artist in residence numerous univs. including Yale U, Washington U., St. Louis, U. Western Australia, others; vis. lectr. Royal No. Coll. Music, Manchester, Eng., 1974-89; vis. prof. organ Royal Acad. Music, London, 1997-98; Prince Consort prof. Royal Coll. of Music, London, 1999—; spkr. BBC programs on music and performance; subject of Melvyn Bragg's TV documentary South Bank Show, 2000. Concert appearances with leading Brit. Orchs. and Boston Orch., Seattle Orch., Australian ABC Orch., Wurttemberg Chamber and other fgn. orch.; appeared in major internat. festivals including Edinburgh, Flanders, Aldeburgh, Bath, Proms, Europalia; appeared at concert halls including Royal Festival Hall, Royal Albert Hall, Lincoln Ctr., NY, Sydney Opera House; numerous radio and TV appearances in Brit. and world-wide including Royal Festival Hall Jubilee; organ cons.; adjudicator internat. competitions; contbr. The Messiaen Companion, 1995; contbr. articles to profl. jour.; recs. include complete organ works of Olivier Messiaen, others; TV documentary film on career, 1982, BBC TV programs The King of Instruments, 1989. Decorated comdr., dame comdr. Order Brit. Empire; recipient Turnovsky award 1985, Evening Std. award for outstanding solo performance, 1998-99, winner (1st prize)St. Albans Internat. Organ Competition, 1964. Fellow Royal Coll. Organists (hon., mem. coun. 1977—, mem. exec. 1981-85, pres. 1994-96, 1st Woman pres.), Royal Can. Coll. Organists (hon.), Royal Coll. Music (hon.); mem. Royal Acad. Music (hon.), Inc. Soc. Musicians (1st woman pres. 1992-93), Albert Schweitzer Assn. (Silver medal 1998), Soloists' Ensemble (pres. 1997). Office: care Karen McFarlane Artists 2385 Fenwood Rd Cleveland OH 44118-3803

WEIR, LINDA WOODRUFF, insurance broker, theater director; b. San Antonio, Tex., Nov. 3, 1948; d. Elsie Lawyer and Marion Bower Woodruff; 1 child, Jennifer Camille Harvey. AA, CZ Coll., 1966—68. Broker Swett & Crawford, Los Angeles, 1982—95, Clearwater, Fla., 1995—97, Knott Ltd., Clearwater, 1997—2002, Strickland Gen. Agy. of FL, Inc., Clearwater, 2002—. Dir., prodr.: (plays) The Rainmaker, (Lary award favorite dir. of a drama, 2002), Carousel (Lary award favorite musical, 2002); actor: The Lion in Winter (Lary award favorite actress drama, 2000), The Sisters Rosenzweig (Lary award favorite supporting actress comedy, 1998). Bd. mem. Eight O'Clock Theatre, Largo, Fla., 1999—2003. Mem.: Profl. Liability Underwriting Soc., West Coast Players, Eight O'Clock Theatre (bd. mem. 1999—2003). Avocations: theater, singing.

WEIR, SONJA ANN, artist; b. Hazleton, Pennsylvania, Oct. 12, 1934; d. Stephen and Anna (Prehatny) Tatusko; m. Richard Clayton Weir, Jan. 14, 1956; children: Robert, Carl, Donna, Lisa, and Nancy. Studied with Mary Ellen Silkotch, 1963—83; student, Art Students League, N.Y.C., 1985—87. Artist Knickerbocker Toy Co., Middlesex, NJ, 1980; represented by Agora Gallery, Soho, NY, 1999. Tchg. adult art edn. in Jointure, NJ., 2001-03; guest spkr. career day Bridgewater H.S., 1993-94. One-woman shows include Johnson and Johnson, Piscataway, N.J., 1992, Stillman, N.J., 2003, (Meml. Award), Somerset County Libr., Bridgewater, N.J., 1992-94, Manville, N.J. Pub. Libr., 1994-99; exhibited in group shows at Raritan Valley Art Assn., 1982-83, 95, 98 (Best in Show Award 1983, 2d prize 1995, 1st place for oil 1998), Ariel Gallery, N.Y.C., 1991, Am. Artists Profl. League, 1991, 94, Barren Art Ctr., Woodbridge, N.J., 1993, Agora Gallery, Soho, N.Y., 1995-99, Somerset County Libr., 1998-99, Am. Artists Profl. League, 1999, Atrium Gallery, Morristown, N.J., 2001, Agora Gallery, N.Y.C., 2001, Somerset County Cultural and Heritage Gallery, 2003, Johnson and Johnson, Stillman, N.J., 2003, Children's Specialized Hosp., N.J., 2003, Barrons Art Ctr., Woodbridge, N.J., 2003, Art Extraordinaire, Bernardsville, N.J.,2004; featured in Artis Apectrum mag., vol. 11/6, 1999, Star Ledger, 2000, 03, Agora Gallery, N.Y.C., 2001, Chronicle, Bound Brook, N.J., 2003; represented in permanent collections N.W.B. Bank of South Bound Brook, N.J., Summit Bank. Recipient Peter Matulavage Award Salmagundi Club, Meml. Award Am. Artists Profl. League, N.Y.C., Samual Lightment Meml. Award Salmagundi Club, 2003; featured in Artis Spectrum mag., 1999, Star Ledger, 2003. Fellow: Nat. Am. Artists Profl. League (v.p. N.J. chpt. 1988—91, publicity com. 1988—91, show chmn. 1989—91, pres. N.J. chpt. 1992—95, editor newsletter 1992—99, nat. exec. bd. 1998—2000, show chmn. 2001—03, nat. pres. 2001—04); mem.: Miniature Art Soc. Fla., Raritan Valley Arts Assn. (pres. 1982—84), Nat. Miniature Assn. (assoc.), Nat. Mus. Women in the Arts. Home: 25 Madison St South Bound Brook NJ 08880-1244

WEIS, JUDITH SHULMAN, biology educator; b. N.Y.C., May 29, 1941; d. Saul B. and Pearl (Cooper) Shulman; m. Peddrick Weis; children: Jennifer, Eric. BA, Cornell U., 1962; MS, NYU, 1964, PhD, 1967. Lectr. CUNY, 1964-67; asst. prof. Rutgers U., Newark, 1967-71, assoc. prof., 1971-76, prof., 1976—. Congl. sci. fellow U.S. Senate, Washington, 1983—84; mem. grante rev. panel NSF, Washington, 1976—82, program dir., 1988—90; mem. rev. panel EPA, 1984—92; mem. NOAA Nat. Sea Grant Rev. Panel, 1997—; vis. scientist EPA Lab., Gulf Breeze, Fla., 1992. Mem. marine bd. NAS, 1991—94. Grantee NOAA, 1977—, N.J. EPA Rsch., 1978-79, 81-83, N.J. Marine Scis. Consortium Rsch., 1987—; NSF fellow, 1962-64, U.S. Geol. Survey, 1996—, NSF, 1998—. Mem.: NOW (pres. Essex County 1972), AAAS (chair biology sect. 1999), Assn. Women in Sci. (councilor 2002—), Ecol. Soc. Am., Estuarine Rsch. Fedn., Soc. Environ. Toxicology and Chemistry (bd. dirs. 1990—93), Am. Inst. Biol. Scis. (bd. dirs. 1986—88, 1989—91, 1997—99, pres.-elect 2000—01, pres. 2001), Sierra Club (bd. dirs. N.J. chpt. 1986—88). Avocations: choral singing, swimming, light opera. Office: Rutgers U Dept Biol Scis Newark NJ 07102 Business E-Mail: jweis@andromeda.rutgers.edu.

WEIS, MARGARET EDITH, writer, editor; b. Independence, Mo., Mar. 16, 1948, d. George Edward and Francis Irene (Reed) W.; m. Robert William Baldwin, Aug. 22, 1970 (div. 1981); children: David William (dec.), Elizabeth Lynn; m. Donald Bayne Stewart Perrin, 1996 (div. 2003). BA in Creative Writing, U. Mo., 1966-70. Proofreader Herald Pub. House, Independence, Mo., 1970-73, advt. dir., 1973-82; dir. div. Independence (Mo.) Press, 1977-82; editor TSR Inc, Lake Geneva, Wis., 1982-86. Freelance writer; co-owner Sovereign Press, Williams Bay, Wis., margaret-weis.com. Author: (short story) The Test of the Twins, 1984, (books) The Endless Catacombs, 1984, Tower of Midnight Dreams, 1984, (with Tracy Hickman) The Dragonlance Chronicles, Vols. 1-3, 1984, 85, Dragonlance Legends, Vols. 1-3, 1985, 86, The Darksword Trilogy, Vols. 1-3, 1987, (with Roger Moore) Riddle of The Griffon, 1985, (under Margaret Baldwin) The Boys Who Saved The Children, 1982, Kisses of Death, 1983, (with Pat O'Brien) Wanted: Frank and Jesse James, The Real Story, 1981, (with Janet Pack) Children of The Holocaust, 1986, My First Thanksgiving, 1983, (with Gary Pack) Computer Graphics, 1984, Robots and Robotics, 1984, (short story) The Thirty Nine Buttons, 1987, (novella) (with Tracy Hickman) The Legacy, 1987, Wanna Bet?, 1987; editor: The Art of Dungeons and Dragons, 1985, Leaves of the Inn of the Last Home, 1987, The Art of Dragonlance, 1987, Dragonlance Tales, vol. 1, 2, 3, 1987, (with Tracy Hickman) The Rose of the Prophet, 1989, (with Tracy Hickman) Death's Gate, vol. 1, 1990, vols. 2, 3, 4, 5, 6, 7, Star of the Guardian, vol. 1, The Lost King, 1990, King's Test vol. 2, 1991, King's Sacrifice Vol. 3, 1991, Ghost Legion Vol. 4, 1991, Dragons of Summer Flame, 1996, (with Don Perrin), Doom Brigade, 1997, Mag Force 7 novels, 3 vols., The Soulforge, 1998, Brothers in Arms, 1999, (with Tracy Hickman) Starshield, Vols. 1-3, 1997, Legacy of the Darksword, 1997, War of Souls, 3 vols., 2000; editor: Kender, Gully Dwarves and Gnomes, 1989, Love and War, 1991, Reign of Istar, 1993, Dragons of War, 1996, Dragons of Chaos, 1997, Relics and Omens, 1998, Sovereign Stone Role-Playing Games, 1999, Sovereign Stone novels, (with Tracy Hickman) vol. 1, Well of Darkness, 2000, vol. 2, Guardians of the Lost, 2001, Journey Into the Void, vol. 3, 2003, Mistress of Dragons, 2003, Draconian Measures, 2000, Dragon's Son, 2004, Ashes and Amber, 2004. Named to Writer's Hall of Fame, 2002, Adventure Gaming Hall of Fame, 2002; recipient Origins award, 2001. Avocations: role-playing games, flyball, agility.

WEISBART, JENNIFER RACHEL, mathematician, educator; b. Canoga Park, Calif., July 16, 1970; d. Monica Berit Stellert-Weisbart and Marvin Weisbart, Carolyn Weisbart (Stepmother). BA, U. Wash., 1994; tchr. credential, Ctrl. Wash. U., 1997; MEd (hon.), U. Wash., 2003. Cert. tchr. math, spl. edn., & elem. Wash., 1997, math. tchr. Calif., 2001, edn.specialist mild/moderate disabilities instruction Calif., 2001. 9-12 math, 3rd grade tchr. Chabad Cheder K-12 Sch., Seattle, 1998—99; 7-8 math and sci., 10-12 spl. edn. tchr. Northshore Sch. Dist., Bothell, Wash., 1999—2001; 9-12 math and sci., spl. edn. tchr. Oxnard (Calif.) Union H.S. Dist., 2001—02; 9-12 math. spl. edn. tchr. Walnut (Calif.) Valley Unified Sch. Dist., 2003; devel. math prof. Mt. San Antonio Coll., 2004—. Presenter in field. Mem.: ASCD, Am. Math. Assn. 2 Yr. Colls., Nat. Coun. Tchrs. Math., Kappa Delta Pi, Pi Lambda Theta. Avocation: dance. Office: Mt San Antonio Coll LAC 1100 N Grand Ave Walnut CA 91789 E-mail: teacherweisbart@webtv.net.

WEISBERG, LOIS, arts administrator, city official; Commr. Chgo. Dept. Cultural Affairs, 1989—. Office: Chicago Cultural Center 78 E Washington St Chicago IL 60602-4816

WEISBERGER, BARBARA, artistic director, educator, choreographer; b. Bklyn., Feb. 28, 1926; d. Herman and Sally (Goldstein) Linshes; m. Sol Spiller, Sept. 3, 1945 (div. 1948); m. Ernest Weisberger, Nov. 15, 1949; children: Wendy, Steven. BS in Edn., Psychology, Pa. State U., 1945; L.H.D. (hon.), Swarthmore Coll., 1970; D.F.A. (hon.), Temple U., 1973, Kings Coll., 1978, Villanova U., 1978, U. New England, 1996. Founder, dir., tchr. Wilkes-Barre (Pa.) Ballet Theater, 1953-63; founder, dir. Pa. Ballet, Phila., 1962-82, Carlisle (Pa.) Project, 1984—; artistic advisor Peabody Dance, Balt., 2001—. Vice chmn. dance panel Nat. Endowment for the Arts, Washington, 1975-79. Performed with Met. Opera Ballet, N.Y.C., 1937, 38, Mary Binney Montgomery Co., Phila., 1940-42, ballet mistress, choreographer, Ballet Co. of Phila. Lyric Opera, 1961-62; choreographic works include Italian Concerto, Bach, Symphonic Variations, Franck; also operas for, Phila. Lyric Opera Co. Named Disting. Dau. of Pa., 1972, Disting. Alumna, Pa. State U., 1972; recipient 46th ann. Gimbel Phila. award, 1978. Mem. Psi Chi. Home and Office: 571 Charles Ave Kingston PA 18704-4711

WEISBLATT, BARBARA ANN, secondary school educator; b. New Brunswick, N.J., Mar. 21, 1958; d. Stanley Herman and Clara Armel Friedelbaum; m. Alan Joel Weisblatt, Dec. 27, 1992. BA in French/Spanish, Rutgers U., 1979, MAT in French, 1986, supr. cert., 1991. Cert. French, Spanish tchr. K-12 N.J. Tchr. Somerville (N.J.) HS, 1980—; supr. Somerville Pub. Schs., 1993—94. Mem. Holocaust HS and Dist. Coms., Somerville, 1995—, Mid. States Steering Com., Somerville, 2000—02, HS Renaissance Com., Somerville, 2000—, HS Quality Coun., Somerville, 2002—. Author: (test) French Placement Test for Middle School Students, 1995. Mem. Hebrew HS bd. edn. Temple Sholom, Bridgewater, NJ, 1995—. Recipient Tchr. Recognition award, Gov. State of N.J., 2001; NEH grantee, Figaro Inst., 1991. Mem.: NEA, Assn. for Supervision and Cirriculum Devel., Fgn. Lang. Educators N.J., Am. Assn. Tchrs. French, Somerville Edn. Assn., N.J. Edn. Assn. Avocations: reading, photography, travel, exercise. Home: 85 Perrine Pike Hillsborough NJ 08844 Office: Somerville HS 222 Davenport St Somerville NJ 08876 Office Phone: 908-218-4157.

WEISBURGER, ELIZABETH KREISER, retired chemist; b. Greenlane, Pa., Apr. 9, 1924; d. Raymond Samuel and Amy Elizabeth (Snavely) Kreiser; m. John H. Weisburger, Apr. 7, 1947 (div. May 1974); children: William Raymond, Diane Susan, Andrew John. BS, Lebanon Valley Coll., 1944, DSc (hon.), 1989; PhD, U. Cin., 1947, DSc (hon.), 1981. Rsch. assoc. U. Cin., 1947-49; col. USPHS, 1951-89; postdoctoral fellow Nat. Cancer Inst., Bethesda, Md., 1949-51, chemist, 1951-73, chief carcinogen metabolism and toxicology br., 1972-75, chief Lab. Carcinogen Metabolism, 1975-81, asst. dir. chem. carcinogenesis, 1981-89, ret. Cons. in field; lectr. Found. for Advanced Edn. in Scis., Bethesda, 1980-95; adj. prof. Am. U., Washington, 1982-83. Asst. editor-in-chief Jour. Nat. Cancer Inst., 1971-87; mem. editl. adv. bd. Chem. Health and Safety, 1994-99, Jour. Applied Toxicology, 1996—; contbr. articles to profl. jours. Trustee Lebanon Valley Coll., 1970—, pres. bd. trustees, 1985-89. Recipient Meritorious Svc. medal USPHS, 1973, Disting. Svc. medal, 1985; Hillebrand prize Chem. Soc. Washington, 1981, Charles Gordon award, 1999. Fellow AAAS (nominating com. 1978-81); mem. Am. Chem. Soc. (Garvan medal 1981, Tillmanns-Skolnick award divsn. chem. health and safety 2001), Am. Assn. Cancer Rsch., Soc. Toxicology, Am. Soc. Biochem. and Molecular Biology, Royal Soc. Chemistry, Am. Conf. Govtl. Indsl. Hygienists (Herbert Stokinger award 1996, William Wagner award 2003), Grad. Women in Sci. (hon.), Iota Sigma Pi. Lutheran. Office Fax: 301-309-0078.

WEISENBECK, SHARON M. healthcare regulatory administrator; b. Durand, Wis., Mar. 18, 1941; d. William E. and Margaret Mary (Weiss) W. BS, Coll. St. Teresa, 1966; MS, U. Mich., 1970. Asst. prof. Coll. St. Teresa, Winona, Minn.; asst. chmn. dept. nursing East Cen. U., Ada, Okla.; edn. supr. State of Wis., Madison; exec. dir. Ky. Bd. Nursing, Louisville. Office: 312 Whittington Pky Ste 300 Louisville KY 40222-4925

WEISENTHAL, REBECCA G. clinical psychologist; b. Detroit, Dec. 23, 1965; d. Lee Avery and Fredrika Phyllis Weisenthal; m. Michael Anthony Cataldo, Sept. 5, 1995. BA, Oberlin Coll., 1988; EdM, Harvard U., 1989; PsyD, Ill. Sch. Profl. Psychology, Chgo., 1994. Lic. clin. psychologist, Ill., Calif. Youth counselor MaComb County Youht Interim Care Facility, Warren, Mich., 1989-90; psychology intern U. Chgo., 1991-92, Women's Health Resources, Chgo., 1992-93, U. Calif., Berkeley, 1993-94; postdoctoral fellow Kaiser Permanente, Martinez, Calif., 1994-95; psychologist No. Ill. U., Dekalb, 1995—. Author: Group Therapy for Learning Disabilities, 1997. Chair, bd. dirs. social programs Congregation Beth Shalom, Dekalb, 1999—; vol. Friends We Care Network, Dekalb, 1999. Mem. APA, Calif. Psychol. Assn. Democrat. Jewish. Avocations: running, swimming, travel, reading, film. Office: No Ill U Counseling & Student Ctr 200 Campus Life Bldg Dekalb IL 60115 Home: 4700 Clear Stream Ct Charlotte NC 28269-0301

WEISERT, MARY CAROL, language educator; b. Quincy, Ill., Oct. 9, 1947; d. John Alphonsus and Ruth Margaret (Sullivan) Mayerle; m. John Steven Weisert, Nov. 27, 1971; children: Michael John, Lisa Ann. BS, U. Minn., 1969, MA, 1973. Spanish instr. North Harris County Coll., Houston, 1979—86, St. Luke Catholic Sch., Indpls., 1987—88, St. Monica Cath. Sch., Indpls., 1988—90; subs. tchr. Eagle-Union Schs., Zionsville, Ind., 1990—95; instr. tchg. Eng. second lang. Ivy Tech. State Coll., Indpls., 2001—. Vol. Conner Prairie Mus., Fishers, Ind., 1999—, Julian Ctr., Indpls., 1996—, Ind. Transportation Mus., Noblesville, 1996—.

WEISS, BARBARA G. artist; b. Phila., Mar. 14, 1917; d. Carl Jacob Greenspan, Nellie Ellen Moyed; m. Victor Hugo Jr., May 6, 1942 (div. Dec. 1945); m. John Weiss, Nov. 10, 1946; children: Warren P., Willard Eric. Student, Calif. Art Ctr., Los Angeles, 1962—64. Owner, creator Balema Hugo Studio, Phila., 1942—49; interior designer L.A., 1953—63. Organizer workshops Charles Reid and other Artists of note, Thousand Oaks, 1994—96; creator gallery City of Thousand Oaks Civic Arts Plaza, 1996; creator mo. art show Umbrella Artists, Westlake Village, 1997—. Represented in permanent collections, L.A., Tucson, San Francisco, Paris, Rome; dir.(show): (art) The Gallery/Bernscat Municpal Art Gallery, 1993—95, Heritage Gallery/Ventura County Adminstrn. Bldg., 1994—96; Exhibited in group shows at Viva Gallery, Los Angeles, 1996—97, collections, Still life, Corina/M. & Mme René BoeuF (Chagal collectors), A Cap Martin Morning on Santarini, Anne Murphy (Collects Calif. Arts), geometrics, Dr. Francoise Farneti, Rome, Le Lac, Pamela Peterson Gallery Dir., Rythmns, A LeMarché, Le Petit Pont, Mme Monique Salvie, Tuscon, Ar. Social chmn. San Fernando Valley for John F. Kennedy campaign, Pierre Salinger Senatorial Campaign; pres. Westlake Village Art Guild, Calif., 1994—96, program dir., 1993—2001; art show dir. Caruso Holdings Ltd., Westlake Village, Calabasas, Calif., 1997—. Recipient 1st prize, Westlake Village Art Guild, 1996, Best of Show, Dr. Winefrid Higgins, Judge, U. Calif./San Diego, 1998, 1st prize, Westlake Village Art Guild, 2000. Mem.: Valley Watercolor Soc. Home: 31756 Bedfordhurst Ct Westlake Village CA 91361

WEISS, ELINOR, elementary school educator; b. Bronx, Aug. 7, 1946; d. Alex and Molly Forman; m. Joel Howard Weiss; children: Sandra, Robin. B in Edn., SUNY, Buffalo, 1968, MEd in Reading, 1971. Tchr. Buffalo Bd. Edn., 1968—. Co-owner Adventure Unltd. Day Camp, Williamsville, N.Y., 1974-86. Com. Amherst Dem. Party; del. Citizens to Save the Librs.; chair Pfohl Bros. Landfill Cleanup Com.; candidate N.Y. State Assembly, 1992. Recipient Hannah G. Solomon woman of yr. award Nat. Coun. Jewish Women, Buffalo, 1991. Mem. NEA, Handgun Control, Inc., Environ. Advocates. Democrat. Jewish. Avocations: swimming, reading. Home: 6177 Ranch View Dr N East Amherst NY 14051-2093

WEISS, EVA, retired bridge commissioner; b. Warsaw, Oct. 3, 1919; d. Rafal and Sarah (Sarpinsky) Schechtman; m. Samuel Weiss, Dec. 24, 1940; children: Renny, Michal. Bridge commr., Burlington County, N.J., 1978-90. Jewish. Avocations: oil painting, bowling, sewing, traveling. Home: 8 Greenvale Rd Moorestown NJ 08057-2235

WEISS, GAIL ELLEN, legislative staff director; b. N.Y.C., Apr. 11, 1946; d. Joseph and Elaine (Klein) W.; m. John A. Kelly. BA, U. Md., 1967. Staff asst. U.S. Office Econ. Opportunity/Job Corps, Washington, 1967-69; legis. asst. Hon. William L. Clay, Mem. Congress, Washington, 1969-72; rsch. asst. Rt. Hon. Roy Hattersley, Mem. Parliament, London, 1972-73; legis. asst. various coms. U.S. Ho. of Reps., Washington, 1973-90, staff dir. Com. on P.O. and Civil Svc., 1991-94, Dem. staff dir. Com. on Econ. and Ednl. Opportunities, 1995&. Mem. working group Pres.'s Task Force on Nat. Health Reform, 1993. Democrat. Jewish. Office: Com on Edn and the Workforce 2101 Rayburn Ho Office Bldg Washington DC 20515-0001

WEISS, JUDITH ANN, music educator; d. Robert and Florence Weiss; m. Richard Rubin, Aug. 31, 1983; children: Robert, Jonathan. BA in Edn., U. Hartford, 1977; MS in Edn., CUNY81. Cert. music tchr. N.Y., N.J. Vocal music tchr. Meml. Jr. HS, Huntington Sta., NY, 1977—80, Rocky Point (N.Y.) Jr.-Sr. HS, 1980—83, South Side HS, Rockville Ctr., NY, 1983—84; music tchr. Meml. Elem.. Sch., East Brunswick, NJ, 1984—86, Farmingdale (N.J.) Sch., 1987—90, Ctrl. Elem. Sch., East Brunswick, 1994—. Condr. elem. divsn. Dist. Wide Vocal Music Festival, East Brunswick, 2003—04, co-founder, 2003, co-dir., 04. Prodr.(dir.): (musicals), 1977—99; dir.: (plays), 1977—79; author: Elementary Music Curriculum, 1985; dir.: (musical prodns.) Meml. Jr. H.S., 1977—80, Rocky Point (N.Y.) Jr.-Sr. H.S., 1980-83, South Side H.S., Rockville Ctr., 1984, Meml. Elem. Sch., 1994, Ctrl. Elem. Sch., 1994—98. Recipient Tchg. Recognition award, State of N.J., 2001; grantee Blue Ribbon grant tchg. mentor, East Brunswick (N.J.) Edn. Found., 1999—2000, 2003—04. Mem.: N.J. Music Educators Assn., Music Educator's Nat. Conf., East Brunswick Edn. Assn. Avocations: gardening, reading, crafts, home improvement, music. Office: Central Elementary School 371 Cranbury Rd East Brunswick NJ 08816

WEISS, JULIE, costume designer; Costume designer: (stage) The Elephant Man, 1979 (Tony award nomination best costume design 1979); (films) I'm Dancing as Fast as I Can, 1982, Independence Day, 1983, Second Thoughts, 1983, Spacehunter: Adventures in the Forbidden Zone, 1983, Testament, 1983, The Mean Season, 1985, Creator, 1985, F/X, 1986, Cherry 2000, 1987, Masters of the Universe, 1987, The Whales of August, 1987, 1969, 1988, Tequila Sunrise, 1988, Steel Magnolias, 1989, Wicked Stepmother, 1989, The Freshman, 1990, Married to It, 1991, Honeymoon in Vegas, 1992, House of Cards, 1993, Searching for Bobby Fischer, 1993, Naked in New York, 1993, It Could Happen to You, 1994, 12 Monkeys, 1995 (Acad. award nominee for best costume design 1996), Marvin's Room, 1996, The Edge, 1997, Touch, 1997, A Simple Plan, 1998, Finding Graceland, 1998, Fear and Loathing in Las Vegas, 1998, Isn't She Great, 1999, American Beauty, 1999; (TV movies) The Gangster Chronicles, 1981, The Elephant Man, 1982 (Emmy award nominee for best costume design 1982), Little Gloria...Happy at Last, 1982 (Emmy award nominee for best costume design 1983), The Dollmaker, 1984 (Emmy award for best costume design 1984), Do You Remember Love?, 1985, Evergreen, 1985 (Emmy award nominee for best costume design 1985), Conspiracy of Love, 1987, A Woman of Independent Means, 1994 (Emmy award for best costume design), Love She Sought, 1990, The Portrait, 1993. Office: c/o Costume Designers Guild 13949 Ventura Blvd Ste 309 Sherman Oaks CA 91423-3570

WEISS, LYNNE S. pediatrician, educator; MD, Hahnemann Med. Coll., Phila., 1974. Diplomate Pediatrics Am. Bd. Pediatrics, 1979, Pediatric Nephrology Am. Bd. Pediatrics, 1982. Intern in Pediatrics Michael Reese Hosp., Chgo., 1974—75, resident in Pediatrics, 1975—77, fellow in Nephrology (pediatric), 1977—79; physician divsn. Nephrology dept. Pediatrics Robert Wood Johnson Univ. Med. Group, New Brunswick, NJ, 1985—. Prof. Pediatrics Robert Wood Johnson Univ. Hosp., New Brunswick, NJ, 1987—, dir. Pediatric Nephrology Ctr., 1987—. Office: Clin Acad Bldg Ste 6140 125 Paterson St New Brunswick NJ 08901-1977

WEISS, MARCIA ANN, special education educator; b. Pitts., June 23, 1950; d. Donald Burton and Mary (Sidey) Riblet; m. Howard L. Weiss, Oct. 27, 1974; children: Joseph, Miriam, Deborah. BA, Northeastern Ill. U., 1974, MEd, 1992. Spl. edn. educator Keshet, Northbrook, Ill., 1991—92; program dir., tchr. Archdiocese of Chgo., 1992—93; learning disabilities specialist Chgo. Pub. Schs., 1993—94; clin. supr. learning disabilities clinic Northwestern U., Evanston, Ill., 1994—96; ednl. cons. St. Juliana Sch., Chgo., 1996—98; tutor, ednl. therapist pvt. practice, Skokie, Ill., 1984—. Mem.: Coun. for Exceptional Children, Internat. Dyslexia Assn., Profls. in Learning Disabilities. Home: 8537 Crawford Ave Skokie IL 60076

WEISS, MILI DUNN, artist, educator; b. Phila., July 15, 1920; d. Max Dunn and Rebecca Rubin; m. Emanuel Gordon Weiss, June 21, 1942; children: Randall Dunn, Linda Weiss Levitsky. BFA, Tyler Sch. of Art, Temple Univ., Phila., 1942; BS in Practical Arts, Boston Univ., Mass., 1943; post graduate study, Mus. Sch., Boston, Mass., 1945. Tchr., painting and related media Cheltenham Ctr. for the Arts, Cheltenham, Pa., 1957—95; lectr., Looking at Art Mus. Galleries, Phila., 1980—90; dir. edn. Cheltenham Ctr. for the Arts, Cheltenham, Pa., 1985—95. Exhibitions include Eng., France, Holland, China U.S. Mus., Pa. Acad. of Fine Arts, Butler Inst. of Am. Art, Nat. Acad. of Design, N.Y., numerous permanent collections; contbr. articles to profl. jour.; prints reproduced, Making Art Safely, drawings reproduced, Voices of Marshall St. Recipient Outstanding Artist Educator, Cheltenham Twp., 1985, Outstanding Aquisitions Exhibit, Biliotheque Nat., 1992, Phila. Treasures, Mayor Edward Rendell, 1998. Mem.: Cheltenham Ctr. for the Arts (bd. mem., pres.), Phila. Water Color Soc. (bd. mem.), Artists Equity (sec.). Avocations: shell collecting, raising orchids, gardening, poetry. Home: 411 Randall Rd Wyncote PA 19095

WEISS, MYRNA GRACE, financial planner; b. N.Y.C., June 22, 1939; d. Herman and Blanche (Stiftel) Ziegler; m. Arthur H. Weiss; children: Debra Anne Huddleston, Louise Esther Pennington. BA, Barnard Coll., 1958; MA, Hunter Coll., 1968; MPA, NYU, 1978; cert. in Mktg., U. Pa. Tchr., N.Y.C. and Vallejo, Calif., 1959-68; dir. admissions Columbia Prep. Sch., N.Y.C., 1969-72; dir. PREP counselling NYU, N.Y.C., 1973-74; dept. head Hewitt Sch., N.Y.C., 1974-79; mgr. Met. Ins. Co., N.Y.C., 1979-84; mktg. exec. Rothschild, Inc., N.Y.C., 1984-85; pres. First Mktg. Capital Group Ltd., N.Y.C., 1985—; mng. dir. Wrap Co. Internat. N.V., 1992-97; advisor Lared Group, N.Y.C., 1987-97; CEO, pres., bd. dirs. Ibnet, 1998—2002. Advisor Gov.'s Hwy. Safety Com., N.Y.C., 1985-88; pres. Fin. Women's Assn. N.Y., 1984-85. Bd. dirs. 92nd Y, N.Y.C., 1972-90, ARC, N.Y.C., 1989-96, 97—, asst. treas., 1993-96, 97—. Mem. Internat. Women's Forum (bd. dirs. 1990-92), Econ. Club N.Y., Women's Econ. Roundtable (bd. dirs. 1988-90). Office: 1st Mktg Capital Group Ltd 1056 5th Ave New York NY 10028-0112 E-mail: mzweiss@nyc.rr.com.

WEISS, NANCY P. artist; b. Chgo., June 12, 1938; d. Manny and Helen (Spero) Passman; m. Lenard Garsen Weiss, Aug. 30, 1958; children: Pamela Lee, Elizabeth Susan. Student, U. Colo., 1956-57, U. Calif., Berkeley, from 1958, CCAC, Oakland, Calif., 1980-81, San Francisco Art Inst., 1984-85. Artist, 1950—. Exhibited in shows at Bolinas (Calif.) Mus., 1992-2002, Galleria Le Logge, Assisi, Italy, 1997, 98, 99; contbr. to The Calif. Art Rev., 1990. Chair Berkeley Civic Arts Commn. City of Berkeley, 1980-85; mem. adv. bd. No. Calif. chpt. Nat. Mus. Women in the Arts; bd. dirs. Eureka Theatre Co., San Francisco. Democrat. Jewish. Avocations: walking, yoga, tennis. Fax: (415) 362-3110.

WEISS, RENÉE KAROL, editor, musician; b. Allentown, Pa., Sept. 11, 1923; d. Abraham S. and Elizabeth (Levitt) Karol; m. Theodore Weiss. BA, Bard Coll., 1951; student, Conn. Sch. Dance; studied violin with, Sascha Jacobinoff, Boris Koutzen, Emile Hauser, Ivan Galamian. Mem. Miami U. Symphony Orch., 1941, N.C. State Sympnony, 1942-45, Oxford U. Symphony, Opera Orchs., Eng., 1953-54, Woodstock String Quartet, 1956-60, Bard Coll. Chamber Ensemble, 1950-66, Hudson Valley Philharmonic, 1960-66, Hudson Valley String Quartet, 1965, Princeton Chamber Orch., 1980-93; orchestral, chamber work, 1966—. Participant Theodore and Renée Weiss poetry writing workshops Princeton U., 1985, Hofstra Coll., 1985, modern poetry workshop Cooper Union, 1988, Princeton Adult Edn.; tchr. modern dance to children Bard Coll., Kindergarten Tivoli, N.Y. Pub. Sch., 1955-58. Author: (children's books) To Win A Race, 1966, A Paper Zoo, 1968 (best books for children N.Y. Times, Book World 1968, N.J. Author's award 1968, 70, 88), The Bird From the Sea, 1970, Biography: David Schubert: Works and Days, 1984; co-editor, mgr. Quar. Rev. Lit., 1945—; author of poetry: (with Theodore Weiss) The Always Present Present, 2004; poetry readings (with Theodore Weiss) at various colls. in U.S. and abroad, including China. Mem. PEN (Nora Magid Lifetime Achievement award with Theodore Weiss 1997). Office: Q R L Poetry Series Princeton U 185 Nassau St Princeton NJ 08540-4914 E-mail: QRL@princeton.edu.

WEISS, RITA SANDRA, transportation executive, educator; b. Phila., May 24, 1935; d. Jack J. and Cecelia (Alper) Brown; m. Irvin J. Weiss, Oct. 29, 1955; children: Brett David, Judith Weiss Bohn. BS in Edn., Temple U., 1955; MA in Edn., U. Md., 1976. Cert. elem. tchr., Md. Tchr. Solis-Cohen Elem. Sch., Phila., 1955-59, Geneva Nursery Sch., Rockville, Md., 1966-71; dir. Har Shalom Nursery Sch., Potomac, Md., 1971-78; ednl. cons. Am. Automobile Assn., Falls Church, Va., 1978-88; program analyst Nat. Hwy. Traffic Safety Adminstrn. U.S. Dept. Transp., Washington, 1988-93, divsn. chief Nat. Hwy. Traffic Safety Adminstrn. State and Cmty. Svcs., 1993-97; tchr. presch. Washington Hebrew Early Childhood Ctr, Potomac, Md., 1997—. Author numerous traffic safety publs. Dept. Transp. fellow, 1993-94; recipient Disting. Svc. to Safety award Nat. Safety Coun., 1994. Mem. NHTSA Profl. Women's Assn. (rec. sec., area rep.), Nat. Safety Coun. (bd. dirs., chmn. edn. resources div., chmn. community agys. sect.), Md. Community Assn. for Edn. Young Children (pres., newsletter editor, historian), Childhood Edn. Internat. (assoc.), U. Md. Alumni Assn., Women's Transp. Seminar. Avocations: needlework, reading, hiking, theater. Address: 803 Gaither Rd Rockville MD 20850 Office Phone: 301-279-7505. E-mail: action19@comcast.net.

WEISS, SARA C. religious organization administrator; Dir. of devel. The Long Island Coun. of Churches, Hempstead, NY. Created and devel. anthropology curriculum and libr. acquisitions for first anthropology dept., Miami-Dade C.C., South Miami, Fla. Office: The Long Island Council of Churches 1644 Denton Green Hempstead NY 11550

WEISS, SUSAN, newspaper editor; Managing editor Life Section, USA Today, Arlington, Va. Office: USA Today 1000 Wilson Blvd Ste 600 Arlington VA 22209-3905

WEISS, SUSAN F. accountant; b. Providence, Mar. 9, 1965; d. Frank and Maria (Felsner) Weiss. BS in Acctg., R.I. Coll., 1988; postgrad., Bryant Coll., 2000—. Cert. mgmt. acct. Acctg. intern Ann & Hope Svc. Corp., Cumberland, R.I., 1986-88; sr. cost acct. Quebecor Printing, Inc., Providence, 1988-98; cost acct., material requirements project mgr. Union Industries, Inc., Providence, 1998; cost acctg. mgr. AAI.Fostergrant, Smithfield, R.I., 1999—. Mem. Am. Soc. Women Accts. (pres. R.I. chpt. 2001-02), Inst. Mgmt. Accts. Avocation: ballet. Home: 86 Meadowcrest Dr Cumberland RI 02864-6434 Office: 500 George Washington Hwy Smithfield RI 02917-1926 E-mail: sweiss@aaifgg.com.

WEISS, SUSETTE MARÉ, technical and photographic consultant, mass communications and media relations specialist, investor; b. New Orleans, June 14, 1959; d. Stanley and Dorothy Lee (Cambre) Weiss. AA in Photojournalism, La. State U., Monroe, 1977; PhD in Comparative Religion, Universal Life Coll., Modesto, Calif., 1990. Cert. retinal angiographer; cert. ophthalmic asst. Prodn. supr., lab. mgr. Colorpix Custom Photogs., Inc., New Orleans, 1978-84; ophthalmic photographer Ochsner Clinic, New Orleans, 1984-85; dir. ophthalmic photography Omni/Medivision, Metairie, La., 1986-87; audiovisual meeting planner, technician and cons. New Orleans, 1988-89; tech. and photographic supr. Retina and Vitreous Assocs. of Ala., Mobile, 1989; dir. photography Dauphin West Eye, Ear, Nose and Throat Specialists, Mobile, 1989-91; tech. sales rep., tech. specialist Nikon, Inc., Melville, N.Y., 1992-95; contractual cons. Simply Susette, Inc., New Orleans, 1995—, pvt. investor, 2001—. Mass comm. specialist with emphasis in photographic imaging and media rels. Inventor stereo-imaging calibrator and quantitative stereopsis technique; author: Redefining the Wheel: Stereo-Photomicroscopy and Ophthalmology, 150 Years of Advancement; contbr. photography to Inc. Mag., Mademoiselle, Good Housekeeping, Income Opportunities, Mari Times, 1998-99; videographer Chrysler Corp. comml.; Rep. Conv. speech coverage aired by ABC, CBS, NBC, C-SPAN, 1998; exclusive media coverage and photos for New Orleans Mus. of Art's Famous Native-Am. Painting Acquistion, Times Picayune Newspaper, 1998; nat. test trial photos selected to demonstrate the tech. advancements in Neopan 400 film, Fuji Film, Photokina 1990 World News Conf. Recipient Best of Show photography award Biol. Photographers' Assn., 1991, 1st pl. gen. photography award Biol. Photographers' Assn., 1991. Mem. Ophthalmic Photographers' Soc. (audio-visual chair 1991, audio-vusial co-chair 1992 nat. edn. meeting), Am. Soc. Mag. Photographers, Profl. Photographers Am., Biol. Photographers Assn., Lakeview Civic Assn. Achievements include ongoing rsch. and devel. in new techniques and applications of teletronic comms. and imaging for the med. and comml. field. Home and Office: 14031 W Hyde Park Dr # 101 Fort Myers FL 33912 E-mail: ssusette@bellsouth.net., et=parley@comcast.net.

WEISS, TAMMY LEE, information technology manager; b. Scranton, Pa., Sept. 25, 1969; d. Terrance and Evelyn Weiss. BS in Computer Info. Systems, Franciscan U. Steubenville, Ohio, 1991; MBA, Marywood U., 1996. Cert. webmaster 2000. Computer programmer Metlife, Clarks Summit, Pa., 1991—99, info. tech. project mgr., 1999—. Mem.: ASPCA, Humane Soc. U.S., Alpha Epsilon Lambda, Sigma Phi. Roman Catholic. Avocations: travel, animals. Home: 312 S Abington Rd Clarks Green PA 18411 Office: Metlife 1028 Morgan Hwy Clarks Summit PA Personal E-mail: tweiss@metlife.com.

WEISS-CORNWELL, AMY, interior designer; b. Mpls, Minn, Dec. 8, 1950; d. August Carl and Margaret Amelia (Wittman) Weiss; m. Dan Cornwell, July 31, 1995; 1 child, Emma Cornwell. AA in Home Econs., Cerritos Coll.; student, Long Beach State U., Santa Ana Jr. Coll. Asst. to interior designer Bobbi Hart at Pati Pfahler Designs, Canoga Pk., Calif., 1974-75; interior designer B.A. Interiors, Fullerton, Calif., 1976-78, Birns Co., Rancho Mirage, Calif., 1978-79; staff interior designer Assoc. Design Studios, Costa Mesa, Calif., 1979-81; interior designer Carole Eichen Interiors, Fullerton, 1981, Sears, Roebuck and Co., Alhambra, Calif., 1982-84; sr. corp. designer, mgr. design studio Barratt Am., Irvine, Calif., 1984-88; owner, retail designer Amy Weiss Designs, Coronado, Calif., 1988—; office, yacht designer, 1997—. Designer in residence San Diego Design Ctr., 1990—92; participant Pacific Design Ctr.; Designer on Call program, 1994—95. Prin. works include interior designs for residences, yachts; comml. interiors including lobbies and offices. Mem. Am. Soc. Interior Designers (Globe-Guilders steering com. 1989-92, chmn. Christmas party, co-chmn. Christmas on Prado 1989, 89, designer for ASID showcase house 1992, 93), Bldg. Industry Assn. (sales and mktg. coun. awards com. 1993, mem. sales and mktg. coun. 1986-88, mem. home builders coun. 1994, 2d place M.A.M.E. award 1987, 1st place M.A.M.E. award 1986, 2d place S.A.M. award 1987), Building Industry Assn. Remodeler's Coun., Nat. Kitchen and Bath Assn., Coronado C. of C., Coronado Cays Yacht Club. Office: Amy Weiss Designs 1123 Marysville Ave Chula Vista CA 91913 Office Phone: 619-216-6002. Fax: 619-482-0438. E-mail: amyweissdesigns@cox.net.

WEISSLER, FRAN, theatrical producer; Co-prodr. plays Othello, Medea, Zorba, My One and Only, Cabaret, Cat on a Hot Tin Roof, Gypsy, Fiddler on the Roof, Bye Bye Birdie, My Fair Lady, Falsettos, Chicago, Full Gallop; prodr. (play) Chicago. Co-recipient 3 Tony awards. Office: Shubert Theatre 225 W 44th St New York NY 10036-3991

WEISSMAN, ANN PALEY, art educator, artist, consultant; b. N.Y.C., Aug. 20, 1931; d. Bernard and Sylvia Paley; m. Arthur Weissman, Jan. 27, 1951; children: Nili, Kenneth, Margot. BA in Psychology and Sociology, Hunter Coll., 1952; student, fine and applied art, Broome C.C., 1983—. Social worker Learning Ctr., Binghamton, NY, 1968—70; dir. Hope Lodge (Am. Cancer Soc.), 1970—73; consumer advisor, cons. Cuisinarts, Greenwich, Conn., 1970—85; designer, owner Arbor Art, Binghamton, 1998—; tchr., cons. Discovery Ctr., Binghamton, 2000—. Archtl. guide Preservation Assn. S Tier, Binghamton, NY, 1981—; fin. advisor, tchr. Broome C.C. and Office for Aging, Binghamton, 1989—; fin. advisor Discovery Ctr., Binghamton, 1985—. 1850 Christmas, 2001; inventor flower collars and tree masks. Bd. mem. Commn. of Arch. and Urban Design, Binghamton, NY, 1998—; v.p. bd. Preservation Assn. of Binghamton, 1991—; docent So. Tier Roberson Meml. Mus., Binghamton, 1962—69; cons. Binghamton Planning Commn., 2000—. Mem.: Madrigal Choir of Binghamton (mem. bd. pub. rels. 1985—). Avocations: gardening, ceramics, music, cooking, decorating. Home: 5 Vincent St Binghamton NY 13905

WEISSMAN, SHARON THERESA, speech language pathologist; b. Chgo., July 28, 1975; d. Sidney Herman and Julie Ellen Weissman. BS, Vanderbilt U., 1997; MS, So. Ill. U., 2000. Cert. clin. competence Am. Speech Lang. Hearing Assn. Speech lang. pathologist Chgo. Pub. Schs., 2000—, Comm. Therapy Svcs., Schaumburg, Ill., 2001—. Mem.: Am. Speech Lang. Hearing Assn., Ill. Speech Lang. Hearing Assn. Avocations: tap dancing, figure skating, clarinet. Home: Apt 2E 4437 N Greenview Chicago IL 60640 Office: Chgo Pub Schs 125 S Clark Chicago IL 60640 E-mail: la_sharona75@hotmail.com.

WEISSMANN, HEIDI SEITELBLUM, radiologist, educator; b. N.Y.C., Feb. 4, 1951; d. Louis and June (Joseph) Seitel Bloom; m. Murray H. Weissmann, June 16, 1973; 1 dau., Lauren Erica BS in Chemistry magna cum laude, Bklyn. Coll., CUNY, 1970; MD, Mt. Sinai Sch. Medicine, N.Y.C., 1974. Diplomate Nat. Bd. Med. Examiners. Intern Montefiore Med. Ctr. Bronx, N.Y., 1974-75, resident in diagnostic radiology, 1975-78; fellow in computerized transaxial tomography and ultrasonography N.Y. Hosp.-Cornell U. Med. Ctr., N.Y.C., N.Y., 1978-79; instr. in radiology and nuclear medicine Albert Einstein Coll. Medicine, Montefiore Med. Ctr., Bronx, N.Y., 1979-80; asst. prof. radiology and nuclear medicine Albert Einstein Coll. Medicine and Montefiore Med. Ctr., Bronx, N.Y., 1980-84, assoc. prof. nuclear medicine, 1984-94, assoc. prof. radiology, 1986-94; dir. Ctr. for Women, Medicine and Healthcare, Washington, 1994—. Adj. attending physician Montefiore Med. Ctr., 1979-87; chmn. Nuclear Medicine Grand Rounds: Greater N.Y., 1980-87; physician coord. Nuclear Medicine Technologist In-Service Tng. Program, 1982-86; cons. NIH, 1984-86, NIH Diagnostic Radiology, 1985-86 Assoc. editor Nuclear Medicine Ann., 5 vols., 1979-84, editor, 5 vols., 1985— ; contbr. chpts. to books, articles to jours.; editor Jour. Sci. and Engring. Ethics, 1994—; reviewer Jour. of Radiology, 1981—, mem. editl. adv. bd., 1985-86, assoc. editor, 1986— ; reviewer. Jour. of Nuclear Medicine, 1981—, Am. Jour. of Roentgenology, 1986—, Gastroenterology, 1986—, Western Jour. of Medicine, 1985—; contbr. audiovisual programs and films Recipient Saul Horowitz, Jr., Meml. award (Disting. Alumnus award), Mt. Sinai Sch. Medicine, 1980, Pres.' award, Am. Roentgen Ray Soc., 1979, Berta Rubinstein, M.D., Resident award, 1978, Cavallo award for moral courage, 1993, others. Mem. Radiol. Soc. N.Am. (mem. subcom. for nuclear medicine of program com., 1981, 82, 83, chmn. 1984, 85, 86), Soc. Nuclear Medicine (trustee 1983-87, 88—, sec.-treas. Correlative Imaging Council 1979-82, exec. bd. 1982-84, pres. 1984-86, exec. bd. 1986—, mem. acad. council 1980—, task force on interrelationship between nuclear medicine and nuclear magnetic resonance 1983-85, gov. Greater N.Y. chpt. 1983-85, treas., 1985-86, 86-87, 2d ann. Tetalman award of Edn. and Research Found. 1982, mem., vice chmn. coms. and subcoms.), Soc. Gastrointestinal Radiologists, Am. Inst. Ultrasound in Medicine, N.Y. Acad. Scis., Assoc. Alumni Mt. Sinai Med. Ctr., Nuclear Radiology Club (chmn. 1983—). Phi Beta Kappa. Home and Office: 14 Powder Hill Rd Saddle River NJ 07458-3215

WEIS-TAYLOR, CARRIE LYNN, curator, artist; b. Big Rapids, Mich., June 3, 1967; d. Gerald Francis Weis and Constance Marie Gregory; m. Joseph William Willette (div.); children: Kala Catherine Willette, Bradley Joseph Willette; m. James Michael Taylor, June 10. B Integrated Studies in Fine Art and Art History, Ferris State U., 2003; postgrad., Kendall Coll. Art and Design, 2004—. Bus. mgr. Design Implementation, Grand Haven, Mich., 1994—98; custom framer Carlyn Gallery, Grand Haven, 1998—99; gallery curator Ferris State U., Big Rapids, Mich., 1999—. Bd. mem. Renascence Com., Big Rapids, Card Wildlife Edn. Ctr., Big Rapids; owner Malynn's Fine Art and Framing, Big Rapids, 2003—; founder, bd. mem. Artworks Art Gallery, Mich., 2000; juror Scholastic Art Awards, Grand Rapids, 2000, Grand Rapids, 01; mem. Flite art task group Ferris State U., 2001—02, mem., pres. A&S art task group, 2003. Exhibitions include Muskegon Mus. Fine Art, Rankin Art Gallery, others. Recipient 2nd Pl., Lakeland Painters, 1998, 1st Pl., 1999, 5th Pl., Muskegon (Mich.) Fine Art Guild, 1998. Avocations: gardening, bicycling, hiking, tennis. Home: 20600 18 Mile Rd Big Rapids MI 49307 Office: Ferris State Univ 820 Campus Dr Big Rapids MI 49307

WEISZ, RACHEL, actress; b. London, Mar. 7, 1971; BA, U. Cambridge, England. Motion picture and T.V. actress. Films include Chain Reaction, 1996, Going All the Way, 1997, Amy Foster, 1997, Land Girls, 1998, I Want You, 1998, The Mummy, 1999, Sunshine, 1999, Beautiful Creatures, 2000, Enemy at the Gates, 2001, The Mummy Returns, 2001, About a Boy, 2002, The Shape of Things, 2003 (also prodr.), Confidence, 2003, Runaway Jury, 2003, She Died on Canvas, 2003, others; (TV film) My Summer with Des, 1998. Office: c/o CAA 9830 Wilshire Blvd Beverly Hills CA 90212*

WEITZ, JEANNE STEWART, artist, educator; b. Warren, Ohio, Apr. 30, 1920; d. William McKinley and Ruth (Stewart) Kohlmorgan; m. Loyal Wilbur Weitz, Aug. 1, 1940 (dec. 1986); children: Gail, Judith, John, Marc. BS in Art and English, Youngstown U., 1944; MEd in Art, U. Tex., El Paso, 1964; postgrad., Tex. Tech U., 1976. Indsl. engr. Republic Iron & Steel, Youngstown, Ohio, 1942-43; art tchr. pub. schs., Bessemer, Pa., 1943-44, El Paso (Tex.) Independent Sch. Dist., 1944-50, 54-78, art. cons., 1978-87; art tchr. Hermosa Beach (Calif.) Independent Sch. Dist., 1950-53, El Paso Mus. Art, 1960-65; lectr. in art U. Tex., El Paso, 1963-66; instr. El Paso Community Coll., 1970-78; free-lance artist, lectr. El Paso, 1987-91; supr. student tchr. U. Tex., El Paso, 1989-91; mgr. Sunland Art Gallery, 1994-95. Represented in group exhibitions at Sun CarnivalExhbn., 1961, El Paso Mus. Art, 1962; author highsch. curriculum guide; exhibited at LVAA Shows, 1990 (5 First Places), Westside Art Guild, 1992, LVAA, 1992 (1st in Watercolor). Coordinator art edn. El Paso Civic Planning Coun., 1985-86; chmn. art edn., art resources dept. City of El Paso, 1982-83. Recipient Purchase award El Paso Art Assn. Spring Show, 1995, 1st pl. award KCOS (PBS), 1996, 1st pl. award Westside Art Guild, 1996, 2d pl. El Paso Art Assoc., 1998, 1st pl. award West Side Art Guild, 1998, 99, H.M. El Paso Pastel Soc. Show, 1998. Mem.: Pastel Soc. N.Mex. (v.p. 2001, pres. 2003), Rio Grande Art Assn., N.Mex. Watercolor Soc. (signature mem. 2004), Pastel Soc. El Paso (v.p. 1999—2000), Rio Bravo Watercolorists (sec. 1998), Nat. Soc. Am. Pen Women, Westside Art Guild (pres. 1993—95), Nat. Art Edn. Assn. (sec. 1988—93, two 1st place award LVAA shows 1989), Lower Valley Art Assn. (Hon. Mention award 1988), El Paso Mus. Art Guild, Nat. Soc. Arts and Letters (sec. El Paso chpt. 1988—), Tex. Art Edn. Assn. (local orgn. 1981, conf. planner, Hon. Mention award 1972). Republican. Presbyterian. Avocations: printmaking, travel. Home: 22 Canon Escondito Sandia Park NM 87047 E-mail: jweitz@prodigy.net.

WEIZMANN, MARIA PIA, ESL educator; b. Oslo, June 3, 1968; d. Liv Vigdis and Antonio Manchinu. AA, No. Virgina C.C., 1992; BS Criminal Justice, Fla. Met. U., 2000; BA French, U. of South Fla., 2002; MBA, Fla. Met. U., 2002; MS, Shenandoah U., 2002; PhD in Edn., Capella U., 2002. Real estate sales agt. Shannon & Luchs, Springfield, Va., 1987—89; exec. asst. to the pres. Consensus Builders, Inc., Tampa, Fla., 1999—2000; receptionist & translator Marine Tech. Corp., Hampton, Va., 1989—94; receptionist/administrative asst. Khalsa Chiropractic/Boston Orthopedics, Cambridge, Mass., 1994—95; dir. of ops. and human resources Khalsa Chiropractic/Boston Orthopedics, Cambridge, Mass., 1995—97; billing & collections analyst Neurology Associates, Tampa, 1997—99; instr. ESL Fla. Met. U., Tampa, 2000—. Program chmn. Fla. Met. U., 2000—. Author: (textbook) The Grammar Reference: American English, 2002; editor: (history & recipe book) 101 Recipes: Escargots!, 2002. Vol., petitioner The Humane Soc., Tampa and Washington, D.C., 1996—2002; asst. to case mgrs. Hillsborough County Comprehensive Sanctions Ctr., Tampa, 2000—00; vol. academic tutor Northside Mental Health Ctr. (for related juveniles), Tampa, 1999—99. Mem.: Phi Sigma Iota - Internat. Fgn. Lang. Honor Soc. Avocation: dancing, swimming, researching and writing. Office: Florida Metropolitan University 3319 West Hillsborough Avenue Tampa FL 33614

WEJCMAN, LINDA, state legislator; b. Dec. 1939; m. Jim. Student, Iowa State U. Minn. State rep. Dist. 61B, 1991—; cons. Mem. local govt and met. affairs com., energy, health and human svcs., housing and judiciary coms. Home: 3203 5th Ave S Minneapolis MN 55408-3248 Office: Minn Ho of Reps 203 State Capital Bldg Saint Paul MN 55155-0001

WEJMAN, JANET P. information technology executive, air transportation executive; BS, Northwestern U., Evanston, Ill. Programmer United Airlines; dir. sys. devel. Covia Technologies, 1988—92; with Chgo. & Pronunciation? Airlines, Inc., Houston, 1996—. Office: Continental Airlines PO Box 4607 Houston TX 77210-4607*

WELBORN, CARYL BARTELMAN, lawyer; b. Phila., Jan. 29, 1951; d. Raymond C. and Helen Ann (Roach) Bartelman; m. Lucien Ruby, Apr. 11, 1987. AB, Stanford U., 1972; JD, UCLA, 1976. Bar: Ill. 1976, Calif. 1978. Assoc. Isham Lincoln & Beale, Chgo., 1976—78; from assoc. to ptnr. Morrison & Foerster, San Francisco and L.A., 1978—95; prin. Law Office of Caryl Welborn, 1995—2004; ptnr. Piper Rudnick LLP, San Francisco, 2004—. Lectr. real property law. Named Best Lawyers in America. Mem. ABA (chmn. com. on partnerships, real property sect. 1989-93), Am. Coll. Real Estate Lawyers (bd. govs. 1994-2002, pres. 2001). Office: Piper Rudnick LLP 333 Market St 32nd Fl San Francisco CA 94105-2150 E-mail: caryl.welborn@piperrudnick.com.

WELBURN, BRENDA LILIENTHAL, professional society administrator; Grad., Howard U.; postgrad., U. Pa. Social worker, Phila.; rsch. analyst U.S. Ho. Reps. Select Com. on Assassinations; legis. asst. to Senator Paul Tsongas Mass.; dir. govtl. affairs Nat. Assn. State Bds. Edn., Alexandria, Va., 1984—88, dep. exec. dir., 1988—93, exec. dir., 1993—. Presenter in field. Author: The American Tapestry: Educating a Nation; contbr. articles to profl. jours. Office: Nat Assn State Bds Edn 277 S Washington St Alexandria VA 22314

WELCH, CAROL MAE, lawyer; b. Oct. 23, 1947; d. Leonard John and LaVerna Helen (Ang) Nyberg; m. Donald Peter Welch, Nov. 23, 1968 (dec. Sept. 1976). BA in Spanish, Wheaton Coll., 1968; JD, U. Denver, 1976. Bar: Colo. 1977, U.S. Dist. Ct. Colo. 1977, U.S. Ct. Appeals (10th cir.) 1977, U.S. Supreme Ct. 1981. Tchr. State Hosp., Dixon, Ill., 1969, Polo Cmty. Schs., Ill., 1969-70; registrar Sch. Nursing Hosp. of U. Pa., Phila., 1970; assoc. Hall & Evans, Denver, 1977-81, ptnr., 1981-92, spec. counsel, 1993-94; mem. Miller & Welch, L.L.C., Denver, 1995—. Mem. Colo. Supreme Ct. Jury Inst., Denver, 1982—; vice chmn. com. on conduct U.S Dist. Ct., Denver, 1982-83, chmn., 1983-84; lectr. in field. Past pres. Family Tree, Inc. Named to Order St. Ives, U. Denver Coll. Law, 1977. Mem. ABA, Am. Coll. Trial Lawyers (state com.), Internat. Soc. Barristers, Internat. Assn. Def. Counsel, Am. Bd. Trial Advs. (treas. Colo. chpt. 1991-92, pres. 1992-93), Colo. Def. Lawyers Assn. (treas. 1982-83, v.p. 1983-84, pres. 1984-85), Denver Bar Assn., Colo. Bar Assn. (mem. litigation sect. coun. 1987-90), Colo. Bar Found. (trustee 1992—, pres. 1995-97), Def. Rsch. Inst. (chmn. Colo. chpt. 1987-90, regional v.p. 1990-93, bd. dirs. 1993-96), William E. Doyle Inn, The Hundred Club. Office: Miller & Welch LLC 730 17th St Ste 925 Denver CO 80202-3598

WELCH, JEANIE MAXINE, librarian; b. L.A., Jan. 22, 1946; d. Howard Carlton and Roberta Jean (Dunsmuir) W. BA, U. Denver, 1967, MA, 1968; M of Internat. Mgmt., Am. Grad. Sch. Internat. Mgmt., 1981. Asst. libr. Am. Grad. Sch. Internat. Mgmt., Glendale, Ariz., 1968-83; reference libr. Lamar U., Beaumont, Tex., 1983-85, head reference, 1985-87; reference unit head U. N.C., Charlotte, 1988-98, asst. coord. reference svcs., 1998-2000, bus. ref. libr., 2000—. Author: The Spice Trade, 1994, The Tokyo Trial, 2002; contbr. articles to profl. jours. Chpt. pres. NOW, Beaumont, 1985-87, state sec., Tex., 1986; exec. bd. Ariz. State Libr. Assn., 1976-80. Rsch. grantee Tex. Libr. Assn., 1986; recipient Best Bibliographies in History, 2003; named Dun & Bradstreet Info. Svcs. Online Champion of Yr., 1996; recipient Highly Commended award Literati Club, 2000 Mem.: ALA, N.C. Libr. Assn., Phi Beta Delta. Democrat. Methodist. Office: U NC Atkins Libr Charlotte NC 28223 E-mail: jmwelch@email.uncc.edu.

WELCH, J(OAN) KATHLEEN, entrepreneur; b. Pensacola, Fla., Jan. 28, 1950; d. Leslie Peter and Frances Louise (Hughes) Morales. Assoc. Occupl. Studies in Massage Therapy, Boulder Coll. Massage Therapy, 2000; advanced degree in Tuina (Chinese Massage), China Acad. Traditional Chinese Medicine, Beijing, China, 2001. Cert. advanced clin. hypnotist 1997, massage therapist 1998, canine massage therapist 2000, equine massage therapist 2000. Salesperson Arthur Murray Dance Studio, Colo., 1970—81; sales rep. Warner-Lambert Co., Morris Plains, NJ, 1981—83; supr., mgr. Dance Club Internat., Chatham, NJ, 1983—90; dist. rep. Nat. Fedn. Ind. Bus., 1990—95; pres. I Am Consulting, 1993—; radio sales rep. Fress Media, 1995—96; acct. exec. Atlantic Lucent Techs., 1997; computer programmer Mailcraft, Inc., 1997—98. Developer sales program Dance

Club Internat.; judge Nat. Dance Coun. Am., 1977—90, dance coach 1975—90; coach winners U.S. Ballroom Championships Hustle divsn., 1978, choreographer, 1971—90, competitor, 1972—81; condr. New Age lectrs., seminars and workshops, 1994—; Kofutu Touch Healing practitioner, 1994—; Reiki II practitioner, 1995—; Kinesiology practitioner, 1995—; Regenesis practitioner, 1996—; tchr. meditation, yoga, Tai Chi, Chee Gung (Qigong), 1995—. Co-prodr., promoter, talent scout for TV program: Astrology Today (formerly It's in the Stars), 1989-94; performed on nat. TV with leading personalities including George Raft, Donald O'Connor, and Mike Douglas. Recipient awards Arthur Murray Studio, 1971-81, 1st place counselor award Arthur Murray All Star Tournament, 1977, 1st place Supr. award Dance Club Internat., 1st place Registrar award Dance Club Internat. in the Tournament of Champions, 1984; ranked No. 1 rep. in Profls. Corner, N.Y. div. Nat. Fedn. Ind. Bus., 1991, ranked No. 2 rep., 1992; named Internat. Woman of Yr., 1993. Mem. Imperial Soc. Tchrs. of Dancing (assoc. Ballroom br., Latin-Am. br.), Am. Dance Tchrs. Assn. Mem. Unity Ch. Avocations: travel, metaphysics and new age studies, horse training and showing, Kung Fu. Home and Office: PO Box 181277 Denver CO 80218 E-mail: jkathleenwelch@hotmail.com.

WELCH, JOAN MINDE, elementary school educator; b. Auburn, N.Y., May 25, 1940; d. Arland E. and Alice (Stoker) Minde; m. Richard J. Welch (div. Oct. 1989); children: Mindy Aileen, James Edward. Student, Merrill Palmer Inst., Detroit, 1960-61; BS magna cum laude, SUNY, Buffalo, 1962; postgrad., Syracuse (N.Y.) U., 1970-71, SUNY, Cortland, 1973-74. Cert. tchr. home econs. N-6, N.Y. 4-H agt. N.Y. State Coop. Ext., Cortland, 1961-62; tchr. spl. edn. Cayuga Internat. BOCES, Auburn, N.Y., 1969-72; instr. YMCA-Women's Ednl. and Indsl. Union, Auburn, 1997—; elem. tchr. Moravia (N.Y.) Ctrl. Schs., 1980—. 4-H evaluator N.Y. State Coop. Ext., Ithaca, 1990—; mgr., tchr. Responsive Classroom, Moravia, 1995—. Co-leader Auburn Divorced, Separated, Widowed Group, 1985-92. Mem. Am. Fedn. Tchrs., N.Y. State United Tchrs., Nat. Soc. DAR (Children of Am. Revolution chair Owasco chpt. 1974—), N.Y. State DAR, Delta Kappa Gamma (v.p. 1996—), Phi Upsilon Omicron (chaplain 1961—). Roman Catholic. Avocations: genealogical research, historical collections. Office: M Fillmore Elem Sch 24 S Main St Moravia NY 13118-2307

WELCH, KATHRYN ANNE, music educator; b. South Bend, Wash., Nov. 8, 1963; d. Robert Dean and Donna Dale Welch. BA in Music Edn., Wash. State U., 1987. Music dir. White Pass Sch. Dist., Randle, Wash., 1987—91, Kalama (Wash.) Sch. Dist., 1991—2003, Toledo (Wash.) Sch. Dist., 2003—. Class advisor Kalama Sch. Dist., 1995—2002. Mem.: Music Educators Nat. Conf. (assoc.). Baptist. Office: Toledo High School PO Box 820 Toledo WA 98591 Personal E-mail: bandgoob@aol.com.

WELCH, KATHY JANE, information technology executive; b. San Antonio, Aug. 5, 1952; d. John Dee and Pauline Ann (Overstreet) W.; m. John Thomas Unger, Jan. 8, 1977. BAS in Computer Sci., So. Meth. U., 1974; MBA in Fin., U. Houston, 1978. Programmer, analyst Tex. Instruments, Houston, 1974-76, project leader, 1976-78, br. mgr., 1978-81; mgr. systems and programming Global Marine, Houston, 1981-84, mgr. office automation, 1984-85, mgr. user systems, 1985-88; dir. MIS Advanced Tech. divsn. Browning-Ferris Industries, Houston, 1988-89; dir. Telecom. and Computer Svcs., 1989-93, v.p. info. tech. Talent Tree Svcs., Inc., Houston, 1993-96; info. tech. cons. Tech Ptnrs., Inc., Houston, 1996—2000, project dir., 2000—03, v.p. info. tech., 2003—. Mem. Mensa, Beta Gamma Sigma. Office: Tech Ptnrs Inc Ste 200 10055 Grogans Mill Rd The Woodlands TX 77380 E-mail: kathy.welch@tpi.net.

WELCH, KELLI CARRUTH, secondary school counselor; d. Roy Cornell and Sue Ramsey Carruth; m. Harry E. Welch, Jr., June 22, 1991; children: Kelsie, Ashley, Haley. BS, Northwestern State U., 1991, MEd, 1998, 30 completed cert. in sch. adminstrn. and student tchr. supervision, 2003. Cert. tchr., counselor La. PE tchr. Alexandria (La.) Sr. High, 1992—97, coach 1992—97, secondary counselor, 1997—. Ednl. adv. bd. Renaissance for Youth, Alexandria, 2001—02. Named La. Secondary Counselor of Yr., La. Counselor Assoc., 2002, Woman of the Century, Alexandria Town Talk, 2002. Mem.: La. Counselor Assoc., Rapides Parish Counselor Assoc., Delta Kappa Gamma-Beta XI. Methodist. Avocations: family activies, coaching, working with less fortunate children. Office: Alexandria Sr HS 800 Ola Ln Alexandria LA 71303

WELCH, LYNNE BRODIE, nursing school dean; b. Norwalk, Conn., Oct. 19, 1941; d. John and Jeannette Brodie; m. C. William Welch, Aug. 1965 (div. Dec. 1980); children: John, Andrew. BS, U. Conn., 1963; MSN, Cath. U. Am., 1968; EdD, Columbia U., 1979. From staff nurse to instr. Sch. of Nursing Stamford (Conn.) Hosp., 1963-65; staff nurse, instr. Children's Hosp. Ctr., Washington, 1965-66; staff nurse CCU Washington Hosp. Ctr., 1966-67; staff nurse ICU/CCU Danbury (Conn.) Hosp., 1968-69; asst. prof. Western Conn. State U., Danbury, 1970-79; assoc. prof., chairperson Pace U., Pleasantville, N.Y., 1979-82; prof., dean Sch. Nursing So. Conn. State U., New Haven, 1982-86; prof., dean Coll. of Nursing and Allied Health U. Tex., El Paso, 1986-89; statewide dir. S.C. Area Health Edn. Consortium Med. U. of S.C., Charleston, 1989-91; prof., dean Sch. of Nursing Marshall U., Huntington, W.Va., 1991—98, dean Coll. Nursing & Health Professions, 1998—. Mem. joint bd. Kellogg Community Partnership, Morgantown, W.Va., 1991—; mem. bd. W.Va. Ptnrs. of the Americas, Charleston, 1992—; chairperson W.Va. Health Care Planning Commn. Task Force, Charleston, 1992—. Editor: Women in Higher Education: Changes and Challenges, 1990, Minority Women in Higher Education, 1992, Roles of Nursing Faculty in Higher Education, 1992, Strategies for Promoting Pluralism in Education and the Work Place, 1997. Mem. Leadership Tri State, Ashland, Ky., 1992, Leadership W.Va., 1993, Leadership El Paso, Class 10, 1988. Mem. ANA, Nat. League for Nursing, Am. Assn. Acad. Administrs. (state commr. 1979-92), Sigma Theta Tau, Phi Kappa Phi. Republican. Presbyterian. Avocations: gardening, cooking, travel. Home: 3200 Orchard Dr Huntington WV 25701-9534 Office: Marshall U Pritchard Hall 426 1 John Marshall Dr Huntington WV 25755-0003

WELCH, MARTHA GRACE, physician, researcher; b. Buffalo, N.Y., June 21, 1944; d. Thomas Harris and Jane Elizabeth (Todd) W.; m. Anthony H. Horan, July 11, 1970 (div. May 1985); 1 child, Thomas Bramwell Welch Horan. BA, N.Y.U., 1966; MD, Columbia U., 1971. Diplomate Am. Bd. Psychiatry and Neurology. Intern Greenwich (Conn.) Hosp. Assn., 1971-72; resident Albert Einstein Coll. Med., Bronx, N.Y., 1972-74, fellow, 1974-77, instr., 1977-79; dir., founder The Mothering Ctr., Greenwich, 1978—; asst. clin. prof. psychiatry Columbia U., N.Y.C., 1997—. Author: Holding Time, 1989, (with others) Autistic Children, 1983; contbr. articles to profl. jours. Pres. alumni coun. Columbia U. Coll. Physicians and Surgeons, 2001-2002 Recipient Alumni Achievement award Middlebury (Vt.) Coll., 1995. Mem. Am. Psychiat. Assn., Internat. Soc. for Devel. Psychobiology, Soc. for Neuroscience. Avocations: reading, skiing, tennis, sewing, biking, music. Office: 15 E 91st St New York NY 10128-0648

WELCH, PATRICIA, retired nursing educator, association executive; b. Middlesboro, Ky., Oct. 10, 1922; d. Charles William and Charlotte Paulina (Willis) W. Diploma in nursing U. Tenn., Knoxville, 1944. RN, Ky. Commd. ens. USN, 1944, advanced through grades to lt. comdr., with nurse corps, 1944-70, ret., 1970; nursing educator Appalachian Regional Healthcare, Middlesboro, 1970-88; exec. dir. United Way, Middlesboro, 1995—. City councilor City of Middlesboro, 1992—, mem. hist. commn., 1990—. mem. adv. bd. Salvation Army, Middlesboro, 1972—, Boys' Group Home, Middlesboro, 1985—. Mem. Bell County C. of C. (bd. dirs. 1997—), Middlesboro Garden Club (pres. 1994), Bus. and Profl. Women's Club

(pres. 1972-99, Woman of Yr., Woman of Achievement), Kiwanis. Republican. Baptist. Avocations: community service, travel, reading. Home: 504 Gloucester Ave Middlesboro KY 40965-2040 E-mail: www.unitedway@ctuw.org.

WELCH, PEGGY, state representative; b. Fulton, Miss., Oct. 13, 1955; BS in Social Studies and Edn., Miss. Coll., 1977; ASN, Ivy Tech. State Coll., 1995; student, Ind. U., 1992—94. Substitute tchr. Monroe County Cmty. Sch. Corp., 1981—82, 1991; dir., probation officer Monroe County Cmty. Corrections Program, 1983—90; cert. childbirth educator Lamaze of Bloomington, Inc., 1983—94; grad. sec., dept. theater and drama Ind. U., Bloomington, 1991—94; RN, oncology Bloomington Hosp. CCU and Cancer Care Units, 1995—; state rep. dist. 60 Ind. Ho. of Reps., Indpls., 1998—, mem. human affairs, tech. R & D, and ways and means coms. Chair, nursing programs adv. bd. Ivy Tech. State Coll., Bloomington; adv. bd. Ind. U. Sch. Nursing. Named Ind. C. of C. Small Bus. Champion, 2003; recipient Heart of Ind. award, Am. Heart Assn., 2003, Child Safety Advocate award, Ind. Safe Kids Coalition, 2002, Legis. Leadership award, Ind. United Sr. Action, 2001, Meritorious Svc. award, Ind. Assn. Homes and Svcs. for the Aging, Inc., 2001, numerous other awards. Mem.: Ind. State Nurses Assn., Children's Organ Transplant Assn. (bd. dirs.), Fraternal Order of Police, NAACP, Women in Govt., Bloomfield C. of C., Greater Bloomington C. of C., Brown County C. of C., Local Coun. of Women, Ind. U. Theater Circle, RN Club, Monroe County Dem. Women's Club. Democrat. Office: Ind Ho of Reps 200 W Washington St Indianapolis IN 46204-2786

WELCH, RAQUEL, actress; b. Chgo., Sept. 5, 1940; d. Arm and Josepha (Hall) Tejada; m. James Westley Welch, May 8, 1959 (div.); children: Damon, Tahnee; m. Patrick Curtis (div.); m. Andre Weinfeld, July 1980 (div.). Actress: (films) including Fantastic Voyage, 1966, One Million B.C., 1967, The Biggest Bundle of Them All, 1968, Fathom, 1967, The Queens, 1967, 100 Rifles, 1969, Magic Christian, 1970, Bedazzled, 1971, Fuzz, 1972, Bluebeard, 1972, Hannie Caulder, 1972, Kansas City Bomber, 1972, Myra Breckinridge, 1970, The Last of Sheila, 1973, The Three Musketeers, 1974 (Golden Globe award for best actress), The Wild Party, 1975, The Four Musketeers, 1975, Mother, Jugs and Speed, 1976, Crossed Swords, 1978, L'Animal, 1979, Chairman of the Board, 1998, (TV movies) The Legend of Walks Far Woman, 1982, Right to Die, 1987, Scandal in a Small Town, 1988, Trouble in Paradise, 1989, Torch Song, 1993, Naked Gun 33 1/3, 1993, Folle d'elle, 1998; (Broadway debut) Woman of the Year, 1982; star Victor/Victoria (on Broadway), 1997; (TV series) Central Park West, 1995; author: The Raquel Welch Total Beauty and Fitness Program, 1984. Address: Innovative Artists 1999 Ave Of Stars Ste 2830 Los Angeles CA 90067-4612

WELCH, RHEA JO, special education educator; b. Jacksonville, Ill., Jan. 26, 1957; d. James Daniel and Bobbye Jo (Weatherford) W.; 1 child, James Alexander. BA, William Woods U., Fulton, Mo., 1980; cert., U. Ill., Springfield, 1981; postgrad., MacMurray Coll., 1985, 86, 88, So. Ill. U., 1990, 91. Cert. 6-12 tchr., spl. edn., Ill. Tchr. recreational skills Ill. Sch. for Visually Impaired, Jacksonville, 1984; cross categorical tchr. Sangamon Area Spl. Edn. Dist., Springfield, 1988-89; tchr.'s aid Four Rivers Spl. Edn. Dist., Jacksonville, 1981, substitute tchr. spl. edn., 1982-86, tchr. learning disabled, 1987; substitute tchr. with severe behavioral disorders, 1989 Mem. human rights com. Jacksonville Devel. Ctr., 1992—; pub. speaker; project dir. for community svc. programs Garrison Sch., Ill. Adv. Coun. on Voluntary Action-Serve Ill.; originator Class Time Community Svc. Voluneerism Four Rivers Spl. Edn. Dist.; coord. Spl. Olympice Ivan K. Garrison Sch., 1992-93; speaker Ill. Coun. Children With Behavior Disorders, 1997. Vol. ARC, instr. HIV-AIDS, CPR, First Aid. Named Staff Mem. of Month, Ivan K. Garrison Alternative Sch., 1992, 2001; recipient 2 Disting. Svc. citations, 1992; grantee, Kraft Food Co., 1991—92. Mem. Coun. for Exceptional Children, Nat. Soc. for Experiential Edn. Episcopalian. Office: Four Rivers Spl Edn Dist 936 W Michigan Ave Jacksonville IL 62650-3113

WELCH, SHARON I. customer service representative, artist; b. St. Paul, July 23, 1951; d. James Elroy Scovill and Frances Theresa Hargrove; m. Warren E. Welch, Oct. 15, 1983. Student, Mt. Mary Coll., S.D. Artist Network. Dir. Signature Art Gallery, treas. Dir. Signature Gallery, Watertown, SD. Author: Where Sin Used to Dwell Grace Now Abounds, 2000. Spkr. at women's retreats; instr. Jr. Achievement. Recipient 1st place watercolor award, Brookings (SD) Art Coun., 1997, 1st place mixed media award, Granery, Groton, SD, 1998, 1st place watercolor award, Broadway Gallery, Watertown, 1999, 3rd Pl. Mixed Media, Brookings, S.D. Art Coun., 2003. Avocations: kayaking, camping, reading, travel. Home: 9 8th Ave NE Watertown SD 57201 Office Phone: 605-753-5040.

WELCH DICKERMAN, TANYA L. speech pathology/audiology services professional, consultant, small business owner; d. Charles E. and Eliza Welch; m. Robert K. Dickerman. BA in Elem. Edn., Lindenwood Coll., 1992; MS in Comm. Disorders/Speech-Lang. Pathology, Fontbonne Coll., 1994. Cert. clin. competence in speech-lang. pathology Am. Speech-Lang.-Hearing Assn., 1995. Speech-lang. pathologist Farmington (Mo.) R-7 Sch. Dist., 1994—, Farmington Sports and Rehab. Ctr., 1994—2002; speech-lang. pathologist (pm) Nat. Health Care, Desloge, Mo., 1994—99; co-owner B&D Auto Parts, Inc., Bonne Terre, Mo., 2000—. Mem.: Mo. State Tchrs. Assn., Mo. Speech-Lang.-Hearing Assn., Am. Speech-Lang.-Hearing Assn. Office: Farmington R-7 School Dist Farmington MO 63640 E-mail: twelch@farmington.k12.mo.us.

WELCOME, PATRICIA, lawyer; b. St. Christopher, W.I., July 4, 1958; BA, U. V.I., 1987; JD cum laude, Tex. So. U., 1990. Bar: V.I. 1991, U.S. Ct. Appeals (3d cir.) 1993. Law clk. to Hon. Eileen Petersen Territorial Ct. V.I., 1990-92; asst. legal counsel Legis. of V.I., St. Croix, 1992; assoc. Douglas L. Capdeville, St. Croix, 1999; pvt. practice St. Croix, 1999—. Recipient Am. Jurisprudence award for Bus. Assn., 1989, award for Consumer Protection, 1989. Mem. ABA, V.I. Bar Assn. (scholarship 1988-90, pres. elect. 1997-98, pres. 1998-99, chair young lawyers com. 1992-93, bar ethics coms. 1994—). Office: Phoenix Ct Carriage House 27 and 28 King Cross St Christiansted VI 00820

WELD, ALISON GORDON, artist; b. Ft. Knox, Ky., June 10, 1953; d. Paul Woodbury and Mary Jean (Cameron) W.; m. Charles Robert Russell, July 1, 1990. Student, Wolverhampton (Eng.) Poly., 1974-75; BFA, Alfred U., 1975; MFA, Art Inst. Chgo., 1979. Curatorial asst. Am. Mus. Natural History, N.Y.C., 1980-83; curator Robeson Gallery, Rutgers U., Newark, N.J., 1983-88; asst. curator fine art N.J. State Mus., Trenton, 1988-99. Solo exhbns. E.L. Stark Gallery, N.Y.C., Morris Mus., Morristown, N.J., Susan Schreiber Gallery, N.Y.C. U. Bridgeport, Conn., 1996, Ednl. Alliance, N.Y.C., 1991, Aljira, Newark, 1997, Hunterdon Mus. Art, 1998, Pacifico Fine Art, N.Y.C., 2001, Molley Coll. Art Gallery, 2002, Robert Steele Gallery, N.Y.C., 2003, Ben Shahn Gallery, William Patterson U., Wayne, N.J., 2003; curator: Dream Singers, Story Tellers: An African American Presence, Fukui Fine Arts Mus., Japan, N.J. State Mus., 1992-94, (show of self-taught and mainstream artists) A Density of Passions, N.J. State Mus., 1989, Art by African Americans in the Collection of the N.J. State Mus., 1998. Artist grantee N.J. State Coun. Arts, 1983-84, artist Rutgers Ctr. for Innovative Printmaking, 1994.

WELDEN, ALICIA GALAZ-VIVAR, foreign language educator; b. Valparaiso, Chile, Dec. 4, 1937; came to U.S., 1976; d. Pedro and Juanita (Vivar) Galaz; m. Oliver Welden, May 2, 1973; children: Arnold, Jacqueline, Cinthya, Jonathan. Grad., U. Chile, Santiago, 1955; PhD, U. Ala., Tuscaloosa, 1980. Prof. U. Chile, 1966-76; lectr. Appalachian State U.,

N.C., 1982-89; assoc. prof. U. Tenn., Martin, 1989—. Dept. chair U. Chile, Antofagasta, 1966-68; founder, editor Tebaida Lit. Rev., Chile, 1968-70. Author: Antologia de Gongora, 1962, Jaula Gruesa, 1972, Oficio de Madurez, 1987, Alta Marea, 1989, Sonia Baramco, 1996. Regional pres. Pablo Neruda's Presidential Candidacy, Chile, 1969-70. Mem. MLA, Am. Coun. Tchrs. Fgn. Langs., Tenn. Philol. Assn., Soc. Chilean Writers, Ctr. Poetical Hispanic Studies, Phi Kappa Phi. Roman Catholic. Office: Univ Tenn Modern Fgn Langs Martin TN 38238-0001

WELDON, VIRGINIA V. retired corporate executive, pediatrician; b. Toronto, Sept. 8, 1935; came to U.S., 1937; d. John Edward and Carolyn Edith (Swift) Verral; children: Ann Weldon Doyle, Susan Weldon Mohart. AB cum laude, Smith Coll., 1957; MD, SUNY-Buffalo, 1962; LHD (hon.), Rush U., 1985. Diplomate Am. Bd. Pediat., Am. Bd. Pediatric Endocrinology and Metabolism, Nat. Bd. Med. Examiners (bd. dirs. 1987-89). Intern Johns Hopkins Hosp., Balt., 1962-63, resident in pediatrics, 1963-64; fellow pediatric endocrinology Johns Hopkins U., Balt., 1964-67, instr. pediatrics, 1967-68, Washington U., St. Louis, 1968-69, asst. prof., 1969-73, assoc. prof., 1973-79, prof., 1979-89, v.p. Med. Ctr., 1980-89, dep. vice chancellor med. affairs, 1983-89; v.p. sci. affairs Monsanto Co., St. Louis, 1989, v.p. pub. policy, 1989-93, sr. v.p. pub. policy, 1993-98; dir. Ctr. for Study Am. Bus., Washington U., 1998-99. Mem. gen. clin. rsch. ctrs. adv. com. NIH, Bethesda, Md., 1976—80, mem. rsch. resoruces adv. coun., 1980—84; bd. dirs. CPI Corp., 2002—04; advisor Monsanto Co., 1989—98. Contbr. articles to sci. jours. Mem. risk assessment mgmt. commn. EPA, 1992—97; commr. St. Louis Zool. Park, 1983—92; mem. Pres.'s Com. of Advisors on Sci. and Tech., 1994—2000; trustee Calif. Inst. Tech., 1996—, Whitaker Found., 1997—99, St. Louis Sci. Ctr.; bd. dirs., vice chmn., chmn. St. Louis Symphony Orch.; bd. dirs. United Way Greater St. Louis, 1978—90, St. Louis Regional Health Care Corp., 1985—91; mem. adv. com. on agrl. biotech. USDA, 2000—01. Fellow: AAAS, Am. Acad. Pediat.; mem.: St. Louis Med. Soc., Soc. Pediat. Rsch., Endocrine Soc., Am. Pediat. Soc., Assn. Am. Med. Colls. (disting. svc. mem., del., chmn. coun. acad. socs. 1984—85, chmn. assembly 1985—86), Nat. Acads. (nat. assoc.), Inst. Medicine, Knights of Malta, Equestrian Order of Holy Sepulchre, Alpha Omega Alpha, Sigma Xi. Roman Catholic. Home: 242 Carlyle Lake Dr Saint Louis MO 63141-7544

WELDY, LANA GAIL, secondary school educator; b. Colorado Springs, Colo., Dec. 16, 1973; d. Bill Little and Lee Luetje; m. Steve Matthew Weldy; children: Joshua Matthew, Jonathan Micheal. M in Curriculum and Instrn., Coll. of the S.W., Hobbs, N.Mex., 2003. Tchr. English Hobbs (N.Mex.) Mcpl. Schs., 1999—. Sponsor Nat. Jr. Honor Soc. Hobbs H.S., 2002—. Home: 7420 Valdez Hobbs NM 88240 Office: Hobbs Mcpl Schs Jefferson Hobbs NM 88240 Personal E-mail: weldyl@hobbsschools.net.

WELLER, ELIZABETH BOGHOSSIAN, child and adolescent psychiatrist; b. Aug. 7, 1949; m. Ronald A. Weller, Feb. 18, 1978; children: Andrew, Christine. BS, Am. U., Beirut, Lebanon, 1971, MD, 1975. Lic. psychiatrist, Lebanon, Mo., Ohio, Pa. Intern Am. U. of Beirut, 1974-75; resident Renard Hosp./Washington U., St. Louis, 1975-78; fellow U. Kans. Med. Ctr., Kansas City, 1978-79; asst. prof. psychiatry U. Kans. Med. Sch., Kansas City, 1979-85; chief child/adolescent psychiatry Ohio State U., Columbus, 1985-94, assoc. chair dept. psychiatry, 1994-96; prof. psychiatry and pediat. U. Pa., 1996—, chair dept. psychiatry child and adolescent psychiatry, 1996-99, vice chair dept. psychiatry, prof. psychiatry/pediatrics, 1996—. Fred Allen chair dept. psychiatry Children's Hosp. of Phila., med. dir. Child Guidance Ctr., 1996-99; pres. Am. Bd. Psychiatry and Neurology, 2004. Co-author: Psychiatric Disorders in Child/Adolescent, 1990, Current Perspectives on Major Depressive Disorders in Children, 1984, Children's Interview for Psychiatric Syndromes, 1999. Fellow APA, Am. Acad. Child/Adolescent Psychiatry; mem. AMA, ACP, World Fedn. for Mental Health, Soc. Biol. Psychiatry, Pa. Psychiat. Assn. (pres. 1995). Office: 34th St and Civic Ctr Blvd Philadelphia PA 19104-4399 Office Phone: 215-590-7573. E-mail: weller@email.chop.edu.

WELLER, ROBIN LEA, elementary school educator, secondary school educator; b. Jacksonville, Ill., Aug. 9, 1955; d. James Robert and Lois Lea Ford; m. Michael Lewis Weller, June 22, 1975; children: Christopher Lewis, Robert Michael, Morgan Lea. B in Elem. Edn., U. Ill., Springfield, 1985. Owner Robin's Nest Flower Shop, Greenfield, Ill., 1976—81; lang. arts instr., counselor Greenfield Elem. Sch., 1985—; GED instr. Greene County Ill. Inpact Incarceration Program, Roodhouse, Ill., 1993—. Methodist. Avocations: painting, gardening, music. Home: 302 Walnut St Greenfield IL 62044 Office: Greenfield Elem Sch 115 Prairie St Greenfield IL 62044 E-mail: rweller1955@yahoo.com.

WELLER, TRUDY A. psychotherapist; b. Lancaster, Pa., Feb. 14, 1948; d. Stearns H. Kline and Ruth N. (Kantner) Boyer; 1 child, Iris E. BS, Kutztown U., 1996, MA, 2000. Trainer Threshold, Reading, Pa., 1978—83; tchr. Headstart, Reading, 1983—89; counselor, foster care dir. Luth. Home, Topton, Pa., 1997—2001; clin. counseling supr. Cath. Social Agy., Reading, 2001—. Mobile therapist Alpha Counseling, Reading, 2000—. Mem.: Am. Kite Flyers Assn., Am. Counseling Assn. Democrat. Achievements include development of therapeutic approach called Nature, Nurture, Network. Avocations: hiking, collecting irises, ice skating, gardening, kite flying. Home: 604 Main St Oley PA 19547

WELLES, FERNE BINGHAM MALCOLM, retired archivist; b. Fayetteville, Ark., June 2, 1921; d. William Thomas and Nellie E. (Coffey) Bingham; m. Eugene Glenn Malcolm, Sept. 5, 1940 (dec. 1975); children: Rebecca Malcolm Schubert, Rachel Malcolm Woods, Eugene Glenn Jr.; m. Edward Randolph Welles II, Nov. 2, 1984 (dec. 1991). AA, Penn Valley Coll., Kansas City, Mo., 1977; BA in Am. Culture, U. Mo., Kansas City, 1981, MA in History, 1986. Archival intern Regional Br. Nat. Archives, Kansas City, Mo., 1976; historian, archivist, hist. writer St. Luke's Hosp. Kansas City, 1975-85; archivist, historiographer, researcher Episc. Diocese West Mo., Kansas City, 1974-85; historian, archivist, writer Grace and Holy Trinity Cathedral, Kansas City, 1972-79, 86-87. Supr. grad students Emporia (Kans.) State U., 1983; presenter paper at history conf. Contbr. to numerous hist. publs. Pres. Kansas City Bus. and Profl. Women's Guild, 1982-83; mem. Women's C. of C., Kansas City, 1980-83; vestry mem. Grace and Holy Trinity Cathedral, 1982-84. Mem. AAUW (chmn. ednl. found. program 1989-92), Kansas City Area Archivists (edn. com.), Woman's City Club, Nat. Episc. Historians Assn., Phi Alpha Theta. Democrat. Episcopalian. Avocations: hiking, photography. Home: 4545 Wornall Rd Apt 1002 Kansas City MO 64111-3232

WELLES, JUDITH, public affairs executive; b. N.Y.C., Jan. 15, 1946; d. John and Millicent (Richman) Welles; m. Alan M. Bekelman, 1966 (div. 1994); children: David Bekelman, Justin Bekelman; m. Timothy P. Shank, Apr. 18, 1998; 1 child, Jenica Shank. BA, Vassar Coll., 1963. Speechwriter, editor U.S. Dept. Interior, Washington, 1965-66; asst. to dir. VISTA, Washington, 1967-70; speechwriter to sec. HHS, Washington, 1971-76, mgr. pub. affairs, 1977-86; dir. comm. and pub. affairs Pension Benefit Guaranty Corp., Washington, 1987-2000; worklife editor, sr. reporter PlanetGov.com, Fairfax, Va., 2000—. Commr. County Health Planning Commn., Md., 1986-88. Recipient 1st place ann. report competition Fin. World, 1991, 92. Mem. Nat. Assn. Govt. Communicators (Gold Screen award 1992, award of Excellence 1994). Office: PlanetGov dot com Ste 190 11781 Lee Jackson Hwy Fairfax VA 22033-3309 E-mail: Jwelles@planetgov.com.

WELLING, MARY ANN, secondary school educator; b. Moline, Ill., Oct. 24, 1925; d. Camiel Joseph DeWitte and Margaret Carton De Witte; m. Vern Anthony Welling (dec.); children: John Joseph, James Anthony, Mary Lisa Faust. BA, Western Ill. U., 1977, MSc, 1980. Cert. ednl. specialist in edn. adminstrn. Western Ill. U., 1983, tchr. physical edn. State of Ill., 1977, tchr. elem. and sec. edn. State of Ill., 1980, ednl. adminstrn. State of Ill., 1983. Sec. Moline Pub. Hosp., Moline, Ill., 1943—60, tchr., athletic dir. St. Anne Sch., 1961—83; tchr., dept. head Rock Island H.S., 1983—95. Pres. Rock Is./Milan Fedn. of Teachers (Divsn. of Am. Fedn. of Teachers), 1985—95; sec. Peoria Diocese Commn. on Edn., 1985—. Past pres., bd. dirs. Assn. for Retarded Citizens, Rock Is., Ill., 1986—90; trustee Wilber L. Burress Endowment Found. Assn. for Retarded Citizens, Rock Is., Ill., 1991—; past v.p. Am. Cancer Soc. (NW region), 1986—2002; fund distbn. panel mem. United Way of the Quad Cities, 2000—02; v.p. Diocesan coun. of Cath. Women, Peoria, Ill., 2002—; pres. Sacred Heart Ch., Altar and Rosary Soc., Moline, Ill., 2001—; lay min. Sacred Heart Ch., 1975—. Recipient Evelyn Colbert ARC award for service (first recipient), 1988, Master Tchr. award, Rock Is./Milan Sch. Dist., 1995. Mem.: Ill. Ret. Teachers Assn., Quad City Bot. Ctr., Phi Delta Kappa. Roman Cath. Avocations: sewing, sports, church, politics. Home: 1143 45th St Rock Island IL 61201

WELLINGTON, JEAN SUSORNEY, librarian; b. East Chicago, Ind., Oct. 23, 1945; d. Carl Matthew and Theresa Ann Susorney; m. Donald Clifford Wellington, June 12, 1976; 1 child, Evelin Patricia. BA, Purdue U., 1967; MA in LS, Dominican U., River Forest, Ill., 1969; MA, U. Cin., 1976. Head Burnam Classical Libr. U. Cin., 1970—. Compiler Dictionary of Bibliographic Abbreviations Found in the Scholarship of Classical Studies and Related Disciplines, 1983, 2d edit., 2002, revised and expanded edit., 2003. Mem. Art. Librs. Soc. N.Am. (chair Ohio br. 1984-85). Office: U Cin Classics Libr PO Box 210191 Cincinnati OH 45221-0191

WELLS, ANNIE, photographer; b. 1954; B in Sci. Writing, U. Calif., Santa Cruz; postgrad., San Francisco State U. Past photographer Herald Jour., Logan, Utah, Greeley (Colo.) Tribune, Associated Press, San Francisco; photographer Press Dem., Santa Rosa, Calif., 1989—97, L.A. Times, 1997—. Photographer (permanent collections) Nat. Mus. Women Arts, Washington. Recipient Pulitzer Prize spot news photography, 1997. Office: LA Times 202 West First St Los Angeles CA 90012 E-mail: annie.wells@latimes.com.

WELLS, CAROL MCCONNELL, genealogist, retired archivist; b. Phila., Feb. 21, 1918; d. William Hugh McConnell and Edith Mary Lower; m. Tom Henderson Wells, Dec. 31, 1943 (dec.); children: Lucy, Sarah, Tom, Christopher, Julia, Peter. BA, Pa. State Coll., 1939; MA, Northwestern State U., 1973. Archivist Northwestern State U., Natchitoches, La., 1974-88; editor So. Studies, Natchitoches, 1982-88. Spkr. in field. Author: Williamson County, Tennessee: A Genealogical Abstract of the County Court Minutes, 1800-1804, 1987, 88, Davidson County, Tennessee, County Court Mnutes 1783-1792, 1990, Davidson County, Tennessee, County Court Minutes, 1792-1799, 1991, Davidson County, Tennessee, County Court Minutes 1799-1803, 1991, many others. Mem. Natchitoches Hist. Found., 1994—. Lt. (j.g.) USNR, 1942-44. Named Woman of Yr. C. of C., 1975; recipient Clio award Phi Alpha Theta, 1988. Mem. DAR, PEO Sisterhood, Phi Mu, Phi Beta Kappa, Phi Kappa Phi. Republican. Anglican Catholic. Avocation: gardening. Home: 607 Williams Ave Natchitoches LA 71457 E-mail: granny@cp-tel.net.

WELLS, FAY GILLIS, writer, lecturer, broadcaster, aviation historian; b. Mpls., Oct. 15, 1908; d. Julius Howells and Minnie Irene (Shafer) Gillis; m. Linton Wells, Apr. 1, 1935 (dec. 1976); 1 child, Linton Wells II. Student, Mich. State Coll., 1925-28. Freelance corr. in USSR N.Y. Herald Tribune and AP, 1930-34, aviation mags., 1930-36; fgn. corr. Italy-Ethiopian War N.Y. Herald Tribune, 1935-36, spl. Hollywood corr., 1937-38; contbr. book revs. Saturday Rev., 1939-42; dep. chief of mission U.S. Comml. Co., Portuguese West Africa, 1942-46; syndicated boating columnist, 1960-62; White Ho. corr. Storer Broadcasting Co., 1964-77. Aircraft pilot, 1929; designer yacht interiors Alta Grant Samuels, 1958-62; now co-chmn. Internat. Forest of Friendship; hon. co-chmn. Nat. Air Heritage Coun.; mem. com. to select 1st journalist in space, 1985—; judge of trophy winners Nat. Air Space Mus., 1988—. Recipient Sherman Fairchild Internat. Air Safety Writing award, 1965, Amelia Earhart medal, 1967, Golden Age of Flight award Nat. Air and Space Mus.-Dept. Transp., 1984, Elder Statesman of Aviation, 1984, award Internat. Conf. Women Engrs. and Scientists, 1984, Lifetime Achievement award Women in Aerospace Scis., 1996, Achievements award San Diego Aerospace Mus., 1997, Disting. Alumni award Elizabeth N.J. Edn. Coun., 1997, Pres.'s Personal award of excellence, 1997, Inspiration award Internat. Orgn. Women Pilots, 1997, Honors award Women in Aviation, 1990; named to Hall of Fame, Women in Aviation Pioneers, 1992; asteroid # 4820 named in her honor, 1995. Mem. NAFE, DAR, Aviation/Space Writers Assn., Am. Women in Radio and TV (pres. Washington chpt. 1968-69, CBS Charlotte Friel award 1972, Ester Tufty Meml. award 1998, Woman of Yr. award 2001), White Ho. Corrs. Assn. (hon. life), Aircraft Owners and Pilots Assn., The Ninety-Nines (founding mem., Most Valuable Pilot, Washington chpt. 1975, Spirit of Inspiration award 1996), OX5 Aviation Pioneers (Outstanding Woman of Yr. award 1972), Internat. Soc. Woman Geographers, Broadcast Pioneers, Zonta Internat. (life hon.), Nat. Aero. Assn. (named elder statesman 1984, Katherine Wright award 2001, Amelia Earhart Festival award 2002), Overseas Press Club (founding mem. 1939), Nat. Press Club, Internat. Forest Friendship (founding mem., co-gen. chmn. 1976—, Fay Gillis Wells Gazebo dedicated 1991). Home: Alexandria, Va. Died Dec. 2, 2002.

WELLS, GLADYSANN, library director; MLS, SUNY, Albany. Legis. session rsch. aide N.Y. State Legislature, 1972—73; legis. reference libr. N.Y. State Libr., Albany, 1973—78; with Sen. Rsch. Svc., 1978—80; Sen. Libr., 1980; dir. Ariz. State Libr., 1997—. Editor several books on the economy of the northeast; contbr. articles to profl. jours. Avocations: cross country skiing, hiking, snow shoeing. Office: Ariz State Libr 1700 W Washington Ste 200 Phoenix AZ 85007-2896

WELLS, JULIA ELIZABETH See DAME ANDREWS, JULIE

WELLS, KAREN KAY, medical librarian; b. Petaluma, Calif., Jan. 9, 1956; d. Albert Lee and Miyoko (Kay) W.; m. John Edward Guth, Aug. 4, 1979 (div. 1986). BS with honors, U. Colo., 1977; MEd with honors, U. Ill., 1980, MS with honors, 1982. Cert. tchr., Colo., Ill. Grad. asst. grad. libr. U. Ill., Urbana, 1981-82; asst. prof. med. libr. svcs. sch. medicine Mercer U., Macon, Ga., 1982-83; libr., head dept. Presbyn.-St. Luke's Med. Ctr., Presbyn.-Denver Hosp., 1983-84; libr., dept. head AMI-St. Luke's Hosp. Health Scis. Libr., Denver, 1984-88, instr., cons. dialog pharm. database, 1985-87; head libr. Manville Health, Safety and Environ. Libr., Denver, 1988-89; info. cons. Wells Info. Svc., Denver, 1989—91, sr. admistrv. assessor, 1996—98; med. libr. Exemple Luth. Med. Ctr., Wheat Ridge, Colo., 2000—. Coord. Westend Consumer Health Info. Libr., 2000—. Mem. ALA, Med. Libr. Assn., Colo. Coun. Med. Librs. (cons. med.-sci. databases 1984—), U. Colo. Alumni Assn., U. Ill. Alumni Assn., Beta Phi Mu, Kappa Delta Pi. Democrat. Presbyterian. Avocations: racquetball, diving. Office: Exempla Luth Med Ctr 8300 W 38th Ave Wheat Ridge CO 80033

WELLS, KIMBERLY K. not-for-profit organization executive; BA in Psychology, MA in Counseling Psychology. Dir. youth svcs., dir. program svcs., assoc. exec. dir. Home Sweet Home Mission, 1987—97; exec. dir. Corp. Alliance to End Prtnr. Violence, 1997—. Mem. Workplace Com. Nat. Task Force to End Sexual and Domestic Violence Against Women; chair Promotion Com., State of Ill.; mem. Gov.'s Commn. on Status of Women in Ill. Violence Reduction Group, Ill. Corp. Citizenship Initiative; mem. steering com. Ill. Family Violence Coordinating Coun.; mem. 11th Jud. Cir. Family Violence Coordinating Coun. Planning Com.; co-chair McLean County Domestic Violence Task Force Youth and Children Work Group; treas., bd. dirs. Ill. Ctr. for Violence Prevention; grad. Leadership Am. Am. Issues Forum, 1999; guest lectr. Ill. State U., Heartland C.C. Office: 2416 E Washington St Ste E Bloomington IL 61704-4472

WELLS, KITTY (MURIEL DEASON WRIGHT), country western singer; b. Nashville, Aug. 30, 1919; d. Charles Carey and Murtle Bell (Street) Deason; m. Johnnie Robert Wright, Oct. 30, 1937; children: Ruby Jean Wright Taylor, Bobby Wright, Carol Sue Wright-Sturdivant. Grad. high sch. Country music singer; sang gospel in chs. as a child; performed on radio, early 1930s; with John and Jack and the Tenn. Mountain Boys, late 1930's-early 1940's, regular on Grand Ole Opry, from 1952, now with Johnny Wright, Bobby Wright and the Tennessee Mountain Boys; songs include: Release Me, It Wasn't God Who Made Honky Tonk Angels, Making Believe; albums include Kitty Wells & Roy Drusky, Vol. 1 & 2, Back to Back Patsy Kline, 1995, (with Red Foley, Webb Pierce, others) Ducts, 1995; author: Kitty Wells Cookbook. Bd. dirs. Nashville Meml. Hosp. Recipient award as number 1 female singer Cashbox Mag., 1953-62, Billboard 1954-65, award of yr. for top female country vocalist Record World mag. 1965, award for highest artistic achievement in rec. arts 1964, various awards Downbeat mag., award as all-time queen of country music Music Bus. mag. 1964, Woman of Yr. award 1974, named Top Female Artist of Decade, Record World mag. 1974, named to Country Music Hall of Fame 1976. Mem. Country Music Assn., Nat. Assn. Rec. Arts and Scis. Mem. Ch. of Christ. Achievements include being the first woman to hit No. 1 on the country charts with "It Wasn't God Who Made Honky Tonk Angels.".

WELLS, LESLEY, federal judge; b. Muskegon, Mich., Oct. 6, 1937; d. James Franklin and Inez Simpson Wells; m. Charles F. Clarke, Nov. 13, 1998; children: Lauren Elizabeth, Caryn Alison, Anne Kristin, Thomas Eliot. BA, Chatham Coll., 1959; JD cum laude, Cleve. State U., 1974; cert., Nat. Jud. Coll., 1983, 85, 87, cert., 89. Bar: Ohio 1975, U.S. Dist. Ct. (no. dist.) Ohio 1975, U.S. Supreme Ct. 1989. Pvt. practice, Cleve., 1975; ptnr. Brooks & Moffet, Cleve., 1975—78; dir., atty. ABAR Litigation Ctr., Cleve., 1979-80; assoc. Schneider, Smeltz, Huston & Ranney, Cleve., 1980-83; judge Ct. of Common Pleas, Cleve., 1983-94, U.S. Dist. Ct. (no. dist.) Ohio 6th Cir., Cleve., 1994—. Adj. prof. law and urban policy Cleve. State U., 1980-83, 90-93. Editor, author: Litigation Manual, 1980. Past pres. Cleve. Legal Aid Soc.; legal chmn. Nat. Women's Polit. Caucus, 1981-82; chmn. Gov.'s Task Force on Family Violence, Ohio, 1983-87; mem. biomed. ethics com. Case Western Res. U. Med. Sch., 1985-94; mem. N.W. Ordinance U.S. Constn. Commn., Ohio, 1986-88; master William K. Thomas Inn of Ct., 1989—, counselor, 1993, pres., 1998-99; trustee Rosemary Ctr., 1986-92, Miami U., 1988-92, Urban League Cleve., 1989-90, Chatham Coll., 1989-94. Recipient Superior Jud. award Supreme Ct. Ohio, 1983, J. Irwin award Womenspace, Ohio, 1984, award Womens City Club, 1985, Disting. Alumna award Chatham Coll., 1988, Alumni Civic Achievement award Cleve. State U., 1992, Golden Gavel award Ohio Judges Assn., 1994, Outstanding Alumni award Cleve. Marshall Law Alumni Assn., 1994, Greater Cleve. Achievement award YWCA, 1995. Mem. ABA (coun. litigation sect. 1996-99), Am. Law Inst., Ohio Bar Assn., Ohio Womens Bar Assn., Cleve. Bar Assn. (Merit Svc. award 1983), Cuyahoga County Bar Assn., Nat. Assn. Women Judges, Philos. Club Cleve. Office: 18-A US Court House 801 W Superior Ave Cleveland OH 44113-1836

WELLS, LINDA ANN, editor-in-chief; b. N.Y.C., Aug. 9, 1958; d. H. Wayne and Jean (Burchell) W.; m. Charles King Thompson, Nov., 1993. BA in English, Trinity Coll., 1980. Edit. asst. Vogue Mag., N.Y.C., 1980-83, assoc. editor beauty, 1983-85; style reporter New York Times, N.Y.C., 1985, beauty editor, food editor, 1985-90; founding editor, editor-in-chief Allure Mag., N.Y.C., 1990—. Spkr. Am. Womens' Econ. Devel., N.Y., 1988-89, Brand Futures Group, N.Y., 1999. Contbr. numerous articles to N.Y. Times Mag., Allure Mag., 1985—. Chmn. N.Y. Shakespeare Festival, 1993, 94; bd. fellows Trinity Coll., 1998—; bd. visitors Mary Inst. Country Day Sch., St. Louis. Recipient Fragrance Found. award 1991, 99, 2000, 2001, Nat. Mag. Design award, 1994, Legal Def. and Edn. Fund Equal Opportunity award NOW, 1994, Trinith Coll. Alumni Achievement award, 2000, Cosmetic Exec. Women Achiever award, 2001. Mem. Am. Soc. Mag. Editors (bd. dirs. 1993-97). Office: Allure Mag Conde Nast Publs 4 Times Sq Fl 10 New York NY 10036-6522

WELLS, MARY ELIZABETH THOMPSON, minister; b. Dallas, Oct. 9, 1936; d. Owen Perry and Ruth Marie (Baker) Thompson; children: Todd Whitney, Britony Ruth. BA in Sociology, Syracuse (N.Y.) U., 1958; MA in Child Devel., Tufts U., 1964, MEd in Counseling Psychology, 1974; postgrad. in theology, St. Vincent de Paul Sem., 1996—. Asst. dir. pub. relations Inst. for Crippled and Disabled, N.Y.C., 1958-59; head tchr. Eliot-Pearson Children's Sch., Tufts U., Medford, Mass., 1964-66; psychotherapist Mental Health Ctr. of Greater Cape Ann, Gloucester, Mass., 1974-89; deacon, chaplain, spiritual dir. St. Paul's Episcopal Ch., Delray Beach, Fla., 1998—. Mem. Am. Psychol. Assn., Am. Orthopsychiat. Assn., Gulfstream Bath & Tennis Club, Assn. Clinical Pastoral Educators, Assn. Profl. Chaplains, Spiritual Dirs. Internat. Home: 1183 Canoe Point Delray Beach FL 33444 Office: St Paul's Episcopal Ch 188 S Swinton Ave Delray Beach FL 33444-3698

WELLS, MELISSA FOELSCH, foreign service officer; b. Tallinn, Estonia, Nov. 18, 1932; emigrated to U.S., 1936, naturalized, 1941; d. Kuno Georg and Miliza (Korjus) Foelsch; m. Alfred Washburn Wells, 1960; children: Christopher, Gregory. BS in Fgn. Service, Georgetown U., 1956. Fgn. svc. officer Dept. State, Washington, 1958-61, consular officer, 1961-64; econ. officer mission OECD, Paris, 1964-66; econ. officer London, 1966-71; internat. economist, 1971-73; dep. dir. maj. export projects Dept. Commerce, 1973-75; comml. counselor Brazil, 1975-76; amb. to Guinea-Bissau and Cape Verde Dept. of State, 1976-77; U.S. rep. ECOSOC, UN, N.Y.C., 1977-79; resident rep. UNDP, Kampala, Uganda, 1979-81, dir. IMPACT program Geneva, 1982-86; amb. to Mozambique, 1987-90; amb. to Zaire, Kinshasa, 1991-93; under-sec. gen. for adminstrn. and mgmt. UN, N.Y., 1993-94; consul gen. Sao Paulo, Brazil, 1995-97; amb. to Republic of Estonia Dept. of State, 1998—2001. Bd. dirs. U.S.-Baltic Found. Mem. Am. Fgn. Service Assn. Office: Casa Wells Plz Leoncio Bento 7 38830 Agulo Gomera Canary Islands Spain

WELLS, PATRICIA TRENT, retail marketing executive; b. N.Y.C., June 29, 1943; d. Ralph Harold and Lorraine Mary (Parker) Trent; m. Peter Scoville Wells, Dec. 8, 1973. BA in History, Marymount Manhattan Coll., N.Y.C., 1992; MA in Folk Art Studies, NYU, 1999. Ops. mgr. customer svc. Bell Atlantic, N.Y.C., 1970-84, mktg. mgr., 1984-90, assoc. dir. internal auditing, 1990—, supervising sr. auditor, 1990—2000; sr. specialist retail markets Verizon Corp., N.Y.C., 2001—. Pres. Marymount Manhattan Coll. Adv., Bd. Mem. Sovereign Mil. Order of Temple of Jerusalem, N.Y. Jr. League, Inst. of Internal Auditors. Home: 449 E 78th St New York NY 10021-1649 Office: Verizon Corp 1095 Ave Americas New York NY 10036

WELLS, TONI LYNN, accountant; b. Lexington, Ky., June 24, 1959; d. George Andrew and Noreta Florence (Collins) W. AA, Hinds Jr. Coll., 1979; BSBA in Fin., U. So. Miss., 1982, M in Profl. Acctancy, 1984. Internal auditor First Nat. Bank Co., New Orleans, 1984; staff auditor Touche Ross & Co., Jackson, Miss., 1984-85, semi-sr., 1985-87; staff auditor Occidental Petroleum Corp., L.A., 1987-88, sr. auditor, 1988, audit supr., 1988-92, gen. acctg. supr. Corpus Christi, Tex., 1992-95, regional accounts payable supr. Houston, 1995-96, sr. ops. analyst, 1996-97; contr. Laurel Industries (subs. of Occidental Petroleum Corp.), Cleve., 1997-98; fin. planning and analysis, fin. mgr. Dallas, 1998—. Vol. jr. achievement Calallen H.S., Spl. Olympics; alt. del. West Tex. Diocese, Episcopal. Ch. Coun., 1995. Mem. Am. Soc.

Women Accts., U. So. Miss. Alumni Assn., U. So. Miss. Golden Eagles, Corpus Christi Plant Recreation Club (sec. bd. dirs.), Internat. Order of St. Luke, Scottish Heritage Soc. (advisor to treas. 1994-95). Episcopalian. Avocations: hiking, bicycling, antiques, travel.

WELLS, WENDY, art educator; b. Quonset Point Naval Air Station, R.I., Jan. 10, 1950; d. John Bartlett and Barbara (Sanderson) Wells; m. Donald Walter Jamieson, Oct. 8, 1977 (div. Dec. 1985); children: Megan Wells-Jamieson, Jessica Wells-Jamieson; m. Stephen Charles Waldo, Sept. 23, 1989; 1 child, Ethan Charles Waldo. BA in Studio Art, Johnson (Vt.) State Coll., 1973. Cert. tchr. art, K-12 Vt. Activity therapist Washington County Mental Health, Montpelier, Vt.; presch. art tchr. Downings Nursery Sch., Montpelier, Vt.; program dir. Turtle Island Children's Ctr., Montpelier, Vt.; prevention educator Washington County Youth Svcs., Montpelier, Vt.; art tchr., K-12 Bethel (Vt.) Schs. Vol. coord. Ret. Sr. Vol. Program, Montpelier. Recipient Presdl. Educator award, Nat. Merit, Washington, D.C., 1996. Mem.: East Branch Edn. Assn. (pres. 2002—03), Nat. Art Edn. Assn. Office: Whitcomb Jr/Sr High Sch 273 Pleasant St Bethel VT 05032 Home: 3135 E Bethel Rd Randolph Center VT 05061 E-mail: wwells@bethelschools.org.

WELLS-MAXWELL, VIOLET, writer, artist; b. Redkey, Ind., Aug. 3, 1927; d. James William Philebaum and Etta Catherine Hunt; m. Paul Eugene Wells, Sept. 5, 1947 (dec. May 1975); children: Carol Parrott, Randy Wells, Joy Wells; m. Rudolph Neff Maxwell, Sept. 22, 1990 (dec. Aug. 2002). BBA, Olivet Nazarene U., 1949. Sec. Olivet Nazarene U., Kankakee, Ill., 1947-49; receptionist Speech Clinic Ohio State U., 1950-54; art and music instr. Ea. Nazarene Coll., Boston, 1955-69; art tchr., 1960-99; receptionist Office for Fin. Aid to Students Mt. Vernon (Ohio) Nazarene Coll., 1970-73; realtor assoc. Gtr. Ohio Realty, Mt. Vernon, 1974-76; real estate assoc. Century 21 Dalbec, Willsboro, N.Y., 1976-82; nutrition supr. Shaklee Products, Mt. Vernon, Ohio, 1990—2002. Exhbns. include Dixie Days Street Fair, Mt. Vernon, 1997, Dan Emmett Festival, 1994-96, Mt. Vernon (Ohio) News, 1988, Lake Holm Ch. Gallery, Mt. Vernon, 1988, Heritage Hall Gallery, Mt. Vernon, 1996-98. Mem. ch. choir, Mt. Vernon, 1970-75; active Celebration of the Arts high sch., middle sch., Mt. Vernon, 1992-99. Mem. Poetry Appreciation, Mt. Vernon Pub. Libr. Avocations: Mark Twain, poetry, singing, restoring art work. Studio: 500 N Gay St Mount Vernon OH 43050-1708 Personal E-mail: vwm76@earthlink.net.

WELNA, CECILIA, retired mathematics educator; b. New Britain, Conn., July 15, 1927; d. Joseph and Sophie (Roman) W. BS, St. Joseph Coll., 1949; MA, U. Conn., 1952, PhD, 1960. Instr. Mt. St. Joseph Acad., 1949-50; asst. instr. U. Conn., 1950-55; instr. U. Mass., Amherst, 1955-56; prof., chmn. dept. math. and physics U. Hartford, 1957-82, dean Coll. Edn., Nursing and Health Professions, 1982-91, prof. math., 1991—2004. Mem. Math. Assn. Am., Nat. Council Tchrs. Math., Assn. Tchrs. Math. Conn., Sigma Xi. E-mail: seawell31@aol.com.

WELSH, DIANE M. federal judge; BA in Polit. Sci. magna cum laude, Villanova U., 1976, JD, 1979. Bar: Pa. 1979, U.S. Dist. Ct. (ea. dist.) Pa. 1981, U.S. Ct. Appeals (3rd cir.) 1984, U.S. Supreme Ct. 1985. Legal counsel Pa. Senate Judiciary Com., 1980-81; dep. dist. atty. Bucks County Dist. Atty.'s Office, Pa., 1981-84; ptnr. Gold-Bikin Welsh & Assocs., 1984-94; magistrate judge U.S. Dist. Ct. (ea. dist.) Pa., Phila., 1994—. Spkr. in field. Contbr. articles to legal jours. Trustee Manor Jr. Coll., 1981-83, Norristown State Hosp., 1987-90. Mem. ABA, Fed. Bar Assn., Fed. Magistrate Judge Assn., Nat. Assn. Women Judges, Pa. Bar Assn., Montgomery County Bar Assn., Phila. Bar Assn., Brehon Law Soc. Office: US Courthouse 3029 US Courthouse 601 Market St Philadelphia PA 19106-1713

WELSH, JUDITH SCHENCK, communications educator; b. Patchogue, L.I., N.Y., Feb. 5, 1939; d. Frank W. and Muriel (Whitman) Schenck; m. Robert C. Welsh, Sept. 16, 1961; children: Derek Francis, Christopher Lord (dec.). BEd, U. Miami (Fla.), 1961, MA in English, 1968. Co-organizer Cataract Surg. Congress med. meetings, 1963-76; grad. asst. instr. Dale Carnegie Courses Internat., 1967; adminstr. Office Admissions, Bauder Fashio Coll., Miami, 1976-77, instr. comms., 1977—, also pub. coll. monthly paper. Freelance writer regional and nat. publs.; guest spkr. Optifair Internat., N.Y.C., 1980, Fla. Freelance Writers Assn. ann. conf., Ft. Lauderdale, 1991, Suncoast Writers' Conf., Tampa, Fla., 2000, Book Island Festival, Fernandina, Fla., 2000; guest spkr., mem. seminar faculty Optifair West, Anaheim, Calif., 1980, Optifair Midwest, St. Louis, 1980, Face to Face, Kansas City, Mo., 1981; conf. dir. So. Fla. Writers Conf., Nat. Writers Assn./U. Miami, 1997—98, 1999—2000; guest spkr. So. Fla. Writers Conf., Fla., 2002—03. Co-editor: The New Report on Cataract Surgery, 1969, Second Report on Cataract Surgery, 1974; editor: Surgidev's Cataract Surgery N.O.W., 1982—; contbr. Miami Today, 1985, Ft. Lauderdale Sun/Sentinel, 1986, Prime Times, Club Life, Gainesville Sun, The Oklahoman, South Fla. mag., Miami Herald; staff writer (internet cos.): AOS, Press-Release-Writing.Com; author: (book) How to Write Powerful Press Releases, 2003. Mem. NAFE, Fla. Freelance Writers Assn., Nat. Writers Club (award), Nat. Writers Assn. (conf. dir. 1997-2000), Coral Reef Yacht Club, Riviera Country Club, Rotary Internat. (Paul Harris award), Delta Gamma. Congregationalist. Home and Office: 1600 Onaway Dr Miami FL 33133-2516

WELSH, MELINDA ANN, editor; b. L.A., Sept. 3, 1956; d. Martin G. and Patricia (Corkill) W.; m. Dave Webb, Apr. 3, 1982. BS, U. Calif., Davis, 1981. Journalist, 1982—; editor Sacramento News & Rev., 1989—2001; exec. editor 3 newspapers News & Rev., Sacramento, Chico, Reno, 1995—2001; editor at large News and Rev., 2001—. Bd. officer (sec.) Inst. for Alternative Journalism, San Francisco; bd. dirs., v.p. Chico Cmty. Pub. Inc.; adj. prof. journalism Sacramento (Calif.) City Coll., 2001—. Recipient 28 1st and 2d place awards Calif. Newspaper Pubs. Assn., 1990-97, 5 awards for newspaper excellence Nat. Newspaper Assn., 1993, 96. Mem. Soc. for Profl. Journalists (award for excellence), First Amendment Coalition, Assn. of Alternative Newsweeklies. Democrat. Home: 1224 Elk Pl Davis CA 95616-5709 Office: Sacramento News & Review 1015 20th St Sacramento CA 95814-4202

WELSH, SARA LOUISE, retired secondary school educator; b. Chanute, Kans., Apr. 27, 1910; d. William Jasper Welsh and Sara Hattie Robinson. MA, U. Okla., 1932. Cert. Life tchg. cert. Tchr. Seminole (Okla.) H.S., 1932—64, Seminole H.S. and Seminole Jr. Coll., 1941—64; asst. prof. of history U. Okla., Norman, 1964—87. Adv. for social studies majors U. Okla., Norman, 1964—77, chair social studies edn. com. Co-author: History of the Greater Seminole Oil Field, 1981. Named to Seminole Hall of Fame, Seminole C. of C., 1978. Mem.: AAUW (pres., sec.), Okla. Hist. Soc., So. Hist. Assn., Delta Kappa Gamma. Presbyterian. Avocations: gardening, reading, cooking.

WELSHIMER, GWEN R. state legislator, real estate broker, appraiser; b. Poughkeepsie, N.Y., Nov. 5, 1935; d. Freanor Ralph and Beulah M. (Reedy) Grant; m. Billy L. Blake (div. 1979); children: Donald E., Jerry A.; m. Robert E. Welshimer (dec. 1996). Student, Kans. State U., 1953-54; cert., Jones Real Estate Coll., Colorado Springs, Colo., 1975. Cert. real estate appraiser, 1993. Exec. sec. Coll. Bd. Trustees, Bellevue, Wash., 1967-69; exec. sec. to chmn. bd. dirs. Garvey Industries, Wichita, Kans., 1969-73, adminstrv. asst. pers. and pub. affairs, 1969-73; copywriter Walter Drake & Sons, Colorado Springs, 1973-75; real estate agt. UTE Realty, Colorado Springs, 1975-76; newspaper pub., owner Black Forrest News, Colorado Springs, 1976-79; real estate broker, appraiser Gwen Welshimer Real Estate, Wichita, 1979—; coord. Epic Real Estate Sch., Wichita, 1988—; legislator Kans. Ho. of Reps., Topeka, 1990—; mem. bus., commerce and labor, ethics and elections, health and human svcs., new economy nat. conf. state legislatures cultural and econ. devel. com., 2001—; mem joint health care reform legis. oversight com., 2001—. Dem. precinct committeewoman, Wichita; bd. dirs. United Meth. Urban Ministries, Wichita, 1990—, Counseling & Mediation Ctr., Wichita, Great Plains Comprehensive Agriculture & Med. Inst. Mem.: Women Dems., Lions Club Internat. Democrat. Methodist. Home: 6103 Castle Dr Wichita KS 67218-3601 Office: Kans Ho of Reps State Capitol Topeka KS 66612

WELSOME, EILEEN, journalist; b. N.Y.C., Mar. 12, 1951; d. Richard H. and Jane M. (Garity) Welsome; m. James R. Martin, Aug. 3, 1983. BJ with honors, U. Tex., 1980. Reporter Beaumont (Tex.) Enterprise, 1980—82, San Antonio Light, 1982—83, San Antonio Express-News, 1983—86, Albuquerque Tribune, 1987—94, Westword Newspaper, Denver, 2000—01. Author: The Plutonium Files, 1999. Recipient Clarion award, 1989, News Reporting award, Nat. Headliners, 1989, John Hancock award, 1991, Mng. Editors Pub. Svc. award, AP, 1991, 1994, Roy Howard award, 1994, James Aronson award, 1994, Gold Medal award, Investigative Reporters and Editors, 1994, Sigma Delta Chi award, 1994, Investigative Reporting award, Nat. Headliners, 1994, Selden Ring award, 1994, Heywood Broun award, 1994, George Polk award, 1994, Sidney Hillman Found. award, 1994, Pulitzer Prize for nat. reporting, 1994, PEN/Martha Albrand award for first nonfiction, 2000, PEN/West Literary award for rsch. nonfiction, PEN, 2000, John S. Knight fellow, Stanford U., 1991—92. E-mail: ewelsome@att.net.

WEMHOENER, DOLORES LUCILLE, cultural organization administrator, entertainer; b. Quincy, Ill., Aug. 20, 1929; d. George Joseph and Lillian Ella-Mae Mating; m. Gerald Junior Wemhoener, June 3, 1951 (dec. Dec. 1990); children: Theodore Jay, Pamela Diane, Jeffrey Stuart. Degree in music, Quincy Conservatory of Music, 1950. Accompanist dancing sch., Quincy, 1945—50; sec. loan dept. Broadway Bank, Quincy, 1949—51; alumni sec. Franklin Coll, Ind., 1951—52; legal sec. Judge Robert Hunter, Quincy, 1952; tchr. piano Quincy Conservatory, Ill., 1955—, sec., 1965—70, v.p., 1975—80, pres., 1980—85. Accompanist ch. svc. Salem United Ch. of Christ, Quincy, Ill., 1991—. Home: 2130 State St Quincy IL 62301

WEN, GWEN GUOYAO, music educator; b. Nanjing, China, Nov. 3, 1947; arrived in U.S., 1986, naturalized, 1999; 1 child, Wen Shen. Diploma in Piano Performance, Cen. Conservatory of Music, Beijing, 1967; M in Piano Performance, St. Louis Conservatory of Music, 1990. Orchestra pianist Cen. Ballet, Beijing, 1973—86; accompanist Cen. Conservatory of Music, Beijing, 1976—86; soloist/accompanist Internat. Recording Co., Beijing, 1973—86; accompanist St. Louis Conservatory of Music, 1987—90, State Ballet Mo./Ballet Conservatory in St. Louis, 1990—95; piano instr. Beverly Milder's Musical Arts, St. Louis, 1990—99; ind. piano instr. Gwen Wen's Piano Studio, St. Louis, 1990—. Mem.: Piano Tchrs. Roundtable (v.p. programs 2003—), Nat. Fedn. Music Clubs (festival judge 1998, co-chmn. keyboard merit 2003), Music Tchrs. Nat. Assn.

WEN, SHEREE, computer company executive; BS in Physics, Natural Tsiug Hua U, Taiwan; PhD, U. Calif., Berkeley, 1979. Rsch. divsn. staff IBM, 1979-81, dept. mgr. Materials, Characterization and Analysis, 1981-84, program mgr. Tech., 1981-86, [illegible] to sr. v.p.; pres. WenLab USA Inc., N.Y.C. Patentee in field; Contbr. articles to profl. jours. Recipient John E. Dom Achievement award Am. Soc. for Metal, 1978, Outstanding tech. Achievement award, IBM, 1986, invention Achievement award, IBM, 1987, The Robert Lansing Hardy gold Metal The Metals, Materials & Minerals Soc. (TMS-AIME); the AIME as the most promising young Materials Scientist in Am., 1979 Mem. TMS-AIME's Process Monitor & Control Com. (chmn.), Materials Design & Mfg. Divsn. Award Com.; Indsl. Liaison for U. Calif. at Berkeley's ctr. for Materials. Office: WEN Tech Corp 999 Central Park Ave Yonkers NY 10704-1088 Fax: 914-376-7092.

WENDEL, JOAN AUDREY, music educator; b. N.Y.C., Dec. 1, 1931; d. Adam and Edna Sophia Wohlfart; m. Ralph Aurel Wendel, July 21, 1962 (dec. May 1998); 1 child, Tracy Lynn. BA summa cum laude, Dowling Coll., 1969; MA, Adelphi U., 1971. Cert. elem. tchr., N.Y. Sec. A.C. Edwards Inc., Sayville, N.Y., 1950-53; office mgr. John V. Potter Ins., East Islip, N.Y., 1953-59, Pilger Agy., Patchogue, N.Y., 1959-66; tchr. Connetquot CSD of Islip, Bohemia, N.Y., 1969-91; pvt. music tchr. Bohemia, 1979—; music dir. Christ Luth. Ch., Cape Coral, Fla., 1996—, Sounds of Fla., Cape Coral, 1999—2003. Mem. Music Tchrs. Nat. Assn., Music Educators Nat. Conf., Assn. Luth. Ch. Musicians, Ft. Myers Music Tchrs. Assn. (v.p. 1999), Order Eastern Star (worthy matron 1964, assoc. grand marshal 1973, grand musician 1987). Republican. Lutheran. Avocations: walking, golf, music, reading. Home: 2218 SE 10th Ter Cape Coral FL 33990-6217 Office: Christ Luth Ch 2911 Del Prado Blvd S Cape Coral FL 33904-7297

WENDEL, SHIRLEY ANNE, college dean; Diploma, St. Mary's Hosp. Sch. Nursing, 1970; AA, Penn Valley Cmty. Coll., 1972; BSN, Avila Coll., 1974; MN, U. Kans., 1980; PhD, Kansas State U., 1998, U. Kans., 1999. Staff nurse St. Mary's Hosp., Kans. City, Kans., 1970-74, Unity Hosp., Fridley, Minn., 1974-76; nursing instr. Kans. City Kans. Cmty. Coll., 1976-80, dean nursing edn., 1980-98, dean of nursing and allied health, 1998—. Mem. adv. com. Johnson County Cmty. Coll. nursing program, Avila Coll. nursing program, Mid Am. Nazarene Coll. nursing program; asst. Den Mother Cub Scouts, 1985-87; active Annual Health Fair. Mem. Nat. League Nursing, Kans. Assoc. Degree Nursing Educators, Collegiate Nurse Educators Greater Kans. City, Sigma Theta Tau. Home: 12100 W 141st St Shawnee Mission KS 66221-2902 Office: Kansas City Kansas Community College 7250 State Ave Kansas City KS 66112-3003 E-mail: swendel@toto.net.

WENDELBURG, NORMA RUTH, composer, pianist, educator; b. Stafford, Kans. d. Henry and Anna Louise (Moeckel) W. MusB, Bethany Coll., 1943; MusM, U. Mich., 1947, Eastman Sch. Music, 1951, postgrad., 1964-65, 66-67, PhD in Composition, 1969; postgrad., Mozarteum, 1953-54, Vienna Acad. Music, 1955. Tchr. music edn., piano Wayne (Nebr.) State Coll., 1947-50; asst. prof. Bethany Coll., Lindsborg, Kans., 1952-53, U. Iowa, 1956-58; asst. prof. composition, theory, piano Hardin-Simmons U., Abilene, Tex., 1958-66, chmn. grad. com. Sch. Music, 1960-66, founder, chmn. ann. univ. festival contemporary music, 1959—; assoc. prof. music Dallas Bapt. Coll., 1973-75; rsch. asst. to dir. grad. studies Eastman Sch. Music, 1966-67; assoc. prof., chmn. dept. theory and composition S.W. Tex. State U., 1969-72; mem. faculty Friends Bible Coll., Haviland, Kans., 1977-83. Guest composer colls. including U. Ottawa, 1984; performed in Eng. and Prague; performed Am. Conservatory Mus., Charles Ives Ctr. for Am. Music, 1990—; various solo recitals and festivals. Composer: Symphony, 1967, Suite for Violin and Piano, 1965, Song Cycle for Soprano, flutes, Piano, 1974, Music for Two Pianos, 1985, Affirmation, 1982, Interlacings (organ), 1983, (recorded) Suite No. 2 for Violin and Piano, 1989, Fantasy for Trumpet and Piano, 1990, Sonata for Clarinet and Piano, Sinfonietta, 1994, Concerto for Clarinet and Orch.; performances Mosaic, Smetana Hall, Prague, 1999, Symphony Orch. of Prague, 1999, Symphony Hall, Boston, 1998, Concertino for Oboe and String Orch., Alice Tully Hall Lincoln Ctr., N.Y.C., 1999, Warsaw Rhapsody, Warsaw Philharm. Orch., Lutoslawski Hall, 1999, performed Warsaw Rhapsody, Warsaw, 1999, CD Mosaic, 2001. Recipient Meet the Composer award N.Y. State Coun. Arts, 1979; named Kans. Composer of Yr., Kans. Fed. Music Clubs, 2000; Composition scholar Composers' Conf. Middlebury (Vt.), 1950, Berkshire Ctr., 1953; Fulbright awardee, 1953-55; Resident fellow Huntington Hartford Found., 1955-56, 58, 61; MacDowell Colony fellow, 1958, 60, 70; Nat. Festival Performing Arts fellow, 1989. Mem. ASCAP (Composition awards 1988-2001), Music Tchrs. Nat. Conf., Am. Soc. Univ. Composers, Minn. Composers Forum, Am. Women Composers, Music Club (Hutchinson), Sigma Alpha Iota. Republican. Avocations: travel, photography, gardening. Address: 2206 N Van Buren St Hutchinson KS 67502-3738

WENDELL, BARBARA TAYLOR, retired real estate agent; b. Ames, Iowa, Jan. 30, 1920; d. Harvey Nelson and Ruby (Britten) Taylor; m. Donald Thomas Davidson Sr., May 22, 1942 (dec. Oct. 1962); children: Donald Thomas Jr., John Taylor, Ann Elizabeth Davidson Costanzo; m. Connell S. Wendell, Oct. 10, 1992 (dec. Sept. 1995). BS in Home Econs. Sci., Iowa State U., 1943. Assoc. tchr. Ames (Iowa) Pub. Schs., 1970-73; retail mgr. Gen. Nutrition Ctr., Ames, 1974-77; sales assoc. Century 21 Real Estate, Ames, 1978-82, Friedrich Realty, Ames, 1982-89. Pres. Ames City PTA Coun., 1950; leader, advisor Boy Scouts Am., Ames, 1952-58; chmn. Campfire Leaders' Assn., Ames, 1959-61; sec. bd. dirs. Campfire Girls, Ames, 1964-66; property com. United Meth. Ch., Ames, 1964-67; vol. Para-Legal Svcs. for Elderly; active Octagon for the Arts, Brunier Gallery, Med. Ctr. Aux., Art Gallery Com.; vol. at Med. Ctr., 1962—. Mem. Nat. Home Econs. in Homemaking (chmn. fgn. student rels. com.), Internat. Orch. Assn., Iowa State U. Meml. Union (life), Iowa State U. Alumni Assn. (life), Ames Community Arts Coun. Republican. Avocations: floriculture, wildlife and forest conservation, indian culture, fitness and nutrition, gerontology. Home: 1110 Johnson St Ames IA 50010-4206

WENDELN, DARLENE DORIS, English language educator; b. Indpls., July 18, 1956; d. Robert Edward and Doris Mae (Brabender) W. BS, U. Indpls., 1978; MS, Ind. U., 1986. Lic. tchr., Ind. Secondary English tchr., coach Centerville (Ind.)-Abington Sch. Corp., 1978—. Coach girls' tennis regional and sectional championships. Mem. NEA, Nat. Coun. Tchrs. English, Ind. H.S. Tennis Coaches Assn., U.S. Tennis Assn. Lutheran. Avocations: bicycling, tennis, golf, reading. Office: Centerville High Sch Willow Grove Rd Centerville IN 47330

WENDER, PHYLLIS BELLOWS, literary agent; m. Ira Tensard Wender; children: Justin Bellows, Sarah Tensard. BA, Wells Coll., 1956. Publicity dir. Grove Press, N.Y.C., 1958-61, Dell Pub. Co., N.Y.C., 1961-63; theatrical agt. Artists Agy. Inc., N.Y.C., 1963-68; agt. Wender & Assocs., N.Y.C., 1968-81; prin., agent, ptnr. Rosenstone/Wender, N.Y.C., 1981—. Bd. dirs. Just Women Inc., Bklyn., 1982, mem. adv. com., 1983-87; bd. dirs. Fortune Soc., N.Y.C., 1977-80; trustee Wells Coll., Aurora, N.Y., 1981-90. Mem. Women's Media Group (dir. 1988-90), Cosmopolitan Club. Office: Rosenstone Wender 38 East 29th St 10th Flr New York NY 10016

WENDLING, LOUISE, wholesale distribution executive; Sr. v.p., gen. mgr. ea. Can. region Costco Wholesale, Issaquah, Wash. Sr. v.p., country mgr. Costco Wholesale Can. Ltd., Ottawa, Ont., Canada. Office: 415 W Hunt Club Rd Ottawa ON Canada K2E IC5

WENDT, LINDA M. educational association administrator; b. Garmisch Partenkirchen, Germany; m. Martin J. Wendt (dec.); 1 child, Angelica. BS, Western Mich. U., 1967. Cert. fund raising exec., Va. Tchr. Mich. (Tex.) Pub. Schs., 1968-80, small bus. owner Battle Creek, Mich., 1980-85; supr. Allied Stores, Battle Creek, Mich., 1985-86; pres. Wendt Assoc., LLC, Battle Creek, Mich., 1986—. Steering com. Ctr. for Workforce Excellence, [illegible] 1991—; v.p. Volunteerism in Action, Battle Creek, 1988-91; chair Oper. GRAD Oversight, Battle Creek, 1995—. Com. chair Cereal Fest, Battle Creek, 1986-91; campaign divsn. chair United Arts Coun., Battle Creek, 1990, campaign vol. United Way, Battle Creek, 1986—; bd. dirs. Thornapple Arts Coun.; nat. leadership coun. Jr. Achievement; bd. dirs. Rotary Dist. Found., 2000—, Battle Creek Rotary Club Found., 1998—; trustee Miller Coll., 2003; regional v.p. Jr. Achievement, Inc., 2000—; sch. bd. Endeavor Charter Acad. Fellow, U.S.-China Ednl. Inst., 1995. Mem. AAUW, Rotary (com chair 1993—, bd. dirs.), Battle Creek C. of C. Avocations: tennis, boating. Office: Wendt Assoc LLC 4941 Walnut Ridge Battle Creek MI 49017

WENGER, NANETTE KASS, cardiology educator, cardiologist, researcher; b. N.Y.C., Sept. 3, 1930; d. Aaron Zelig and Edith (Malkin) Kass; m. Julius Wenger; children: Deborah, Judith, Beth. BA summa cum laude, Hunter Coll., 1951; MD, Harvard U., 1954. Intern Mt. Sinai Hosp., N.Y.C., 1954-55, chief resident in cardiology, 1956-57; sr. resident in medicine Grady Meml. Hosp., Atlanta, 1958; fellow in cardiology Sch. Medicine, Emory U., 1958-59; instr. medicine Schs. Medicine and Dentistry, Emory U., Atlanta, 1959-62, assoc. in medicine, 1962-64, asst. prof. cardiology, 1964-68, assoc. prof., 1968-71, prof., 1971—; mem. med. staff Crawford W. Long Hosp., Atlanta, 1977—. Dir. cardiac clinics Grady Meml. Hosp., 1960—, chief cardiology, 1998—; cons. cardiology VA Med. Ctr., Atlanta, 1988—; participant numerous profl. symposiums and confs.; mem. cardiovas. and renal drugs adv. com. U.S. FDA, 1978-82; co-chair nat. plan for cardiac rehab. com. Div. Vocat. Rehab., Social and Rehab. Svcs., HEW, 1973-90; mem. Internat. Task Force for Prevention of Coronary Heart Disease, 1989—; founding fellow Soc. Geriatric Cardiology, 1986, bd. dirs., 1987—, pres., 1994-95. Mem. editl. bd. various profl. publs. including Cardiac Rehab. Quar., 1974-79, Primary Care, 1975-79, Internat. Jour. Sports Cardiology, 1983—, Med. Month, 1983-84, Jour. Cardiovasc. and Pulmonary Medicine, 1983—, Geriatric Cardiology, 1986—, Nutrition, Metabolism and Cardiovasc. Disease, 1989—; reviewer publs. including Am. Jour. Medicine, 1972—, Am. Jour. Cardiology, 1979—, Am. Heart Jour., 1975—, European Heart Jour., 1983—; editor Am. Jour. Geriatric Cardiology, 1992—. Active Ga. affiliate Am. Heart Assn., 1960—, chair Heart Sunday program, 1968-69, program chair Fulton County Heart Unit, 1969-71, bd. dirs., 1969-79, 80-82, pres., 1977-78; fellow coun. clin. cardiology, Am. Heart Assn., 1970, chair rehab. com., 1972-75, chair artherosclerosis task force, 1973-74, program v.p., 1975-76, pres., 1977-78, bd. dirs., 1975-79, mem./past mem. numerous other coms.; mem. med. adv. and cardiovasc. health coms. Butler St. YMCA, 1980-82. Recipient Myrtle Wreath award Atlanta Hadassah, 1967, award of Achievement, Nat. Ctr. for Vol. Action, 1978, Bronze Disting. Svc. medallion Ga. affiliate Am. Heart Assn., 1970-71, Silver Disting. Svc. medallion, 1978, Gold Disting. Svc. medallion, 1979, Disting. Achievement award, Scientific Councils Am. Heart Assn. and Women in Cardiol. Mentoring award, 1999, Juha P. Kokko award for Excellence in Cardiovascular Lecturing and Edu., Dept. Med. Housestaff, Emory Univ. Sch. Med., 1999-2000, James D. Bruce Meml. award for Disting. Contbn in Preventative Medicine, Am. Coll. Physicians/Am. Soc. of Internal Med., 2000, Atlanta Women in Law and Medicine Shining Star award, 2000, R. Bruce Logue award for Excellence in Medicine, Am. Heart Assn., 2001, Disting. Fellow award, Soc. Geriatric Cardiology, 2002; honoree Women of Yr. issue Time Mag., 1976; named Joseph B. Wolff Mem. Lectr., Am. Coll. Sports Medicine, 2001. Fellow ACP, Am. Coll. Cardiology (gov. for Ga. 1983-86, trustee 1987-89, mem. various coms.); mem. AMA, WHO (mem. expert adv. panel on cardiovasc. disease 1989—), Am. Assn. Cardiovasc. and Pulmonary Rehab. (trustee 1985-88, chairperson ethics com. 1985—, 2nd Ann. Lecture award 1987), Nat. Heart, Lung and Blood Inst., Internat. Soc. and Fedn. Cardiology (pres. sci. coun. on rehab. of cardiac patients 1984-88), Soc. German Cardiologists (officer, pres. 1994-95), Med. Assn. Ga., Med. Assn. Atlanta, Atlanta Clin. Soc.(emeritis), Soc. for Prevention of Heart Disease and Rehab. (hon.), Soc. Women's Health (bd. dirs. 2000—, vice chair 2002—), Philippine Heart Assn. (hon.), Philippine Coll. Cardiology (hon.), Omicron Delta Kappa. Office: Emory Univ Sch Medicine 49 Jesse Hill Jr Dr SE Atlanta GA 30303-3033 Office Phone: 404-616-4420.

WENGER, SHARON LOUISE, pediatrics educator, researcher, cytogeneticist; b. Washington, Sept. 25, 1949; d. William Fred and Lois Helen (Compton) W.; m. George E. Fromlak Jr., Jan. 10, 1976; children: Nicholas Edward, Holly Louise, Andrea Lee. BA in Biology, Thiel Coll., 1971; MS in Human Genetics, U. Pitts., 1973, PhD in Human Genetics, 1976. Asst. prof. Sch. of Medicine U. Pitts., 1980-89, assoc. prof. Sch. of Medicine, 1989—. Contbr. articles to profl. jours. Mem. Am. Soc. Human Genetics, Midwest Soc. for Pediatric Rsch. Achievements include research in association of sister chromatid exchange with rare fragile site Xq27 and support for imprinting in Fragile X syndrome by late DNA synthesis at Xq27 area. Office: Children's Hosp Pitts 3705 5th Ave Pittsburgh PA 15213-2524

WENIG, MARY MOERS, law educator; b. N.Y.C. d. Robert and Celia Lewis (Kauffman) Moers; m. Jerome Wenig, Dec. 19, 1946 (dec. Oct. 1994); children: Margaret Moers Wenig, Michael M. Wenig. BA, Vassar Coll., 1946; JD, Columbia U., 1951. Bar: N.Y. 1952, U.S. Ct. Appeals (2d cir.) 1954, U.S. Dist. Ct. (so. dist.) N.Y. 1956, Conn. 1977. Assoc. Cahill, Gordon, Reindel & Ohl, N.Y.C., 1951-57; assoc. Greenbaum, Wolff & Ernst, N.Y.C., 1957-60, Skadden, Arps, Slate, Meagher & Flom, N.Y.C., 1960-71; asst. prof. sch. law St. John's U., N.Y.C., 1971-75, assoc. prof. sch. law, 1975-78; rsch. affiliate Yale Law Sch., New Haven, 1978-79; prof. sch. law U. Bridgeport, Conn., 1978-82, Charles A. Dana prof. law, 1982-92; prof. sch. law Quinnipiac U., Bridgeport, 1992-95, Hamden, 1995—. Cons. The Merrill Anderson Co., Stratford, Conn., 1982—, Conn. Permanent Commn. on Status of Women, 1978-79; vis. prof. sch. law Pace U., White Plains, N.Y., 1979; commr. State of Conn. Permanent Commn. on Status of Women, 1985-91; mem. Conn. Gen. Assembly's Adv. Commn. to Study the Uniform Marital Property Act., 1985-86; bd. dirs. Tax Analysts. Author: Tax Management Portfolio on Disclaimer, 1992; editor: PLI Tax Handbooks, 1978-86; co-editor: Bittker, Fundamentals of Federal Income Taxation, student edit., 1983; co-author: (with Douthwaite) Unmarried Couples and the Law, 1979; contbr. tax, estate planning, trust and estates and marital property articles to profl. jours.; editorial adv. bd. Estate Planning for the Elderly & Disabled, 1987-90, Community Property Jour., 1986-88, Estate Planning, 1975—, Estates, Gifts & Trusts Jour., 1976—; assoc. editor: Encyclopedia of Marriage and the Family, 1996. Mem. probate com. Conn. Law Revision Commn., 1985—, com. to study the probate system Conn. Probate Assembly, 1988-91, task force on the legal rights of women in marriage NOW, 1987-91; 2nd cir. rep. Fedn. of Women Lawyers Jud. Screening Panel, 1979; bd. govs. Radcliffe Club N.Y., 1975-77; mem. 1st selectman's com. on taxation relief for the elderly Town of Westport, 1974-75; pres. bd. dirs. Conn. Women's Ednl. and Legal Fund, Inc., 1975-79, bd. dirs., 1973-79. Named Salute to Women honoree Outstanding Women of Conn., Greater Bridgeport YWCA, 1990, Women in Leadership honoree New Haven YWCA, 1979, honoree U. Bridgeport Sch. Law Women's Law Assn., 1990; Harlan Fiske Stone scholar Columbia U. Sch. Law, 1949; recipient Award for Equality United Nations Assn.-USA of Conn., 1987; Summer Stipend grantee NEH, 1984, rsch. grantee Conn. Bar Found., 1980. Fellow Am. Coll. Trust & Estate Counsel (bd. regents 1985-91); mem. ABA (advisor to NCCUSL 1980-84, sect. coun. mem. 1970-72), Internat. Acad. Estates & Trust Law (exec. coun. 1992-94), Conn. Bar Assn. (sects.' exec. coun., Disting. Svc. commendation 1977), Assn. Am. Law Schs., Assn. of Bar of City of N.Y., N.Y. State Bar Assn., Am. Law Inst., Am. Coll. Tax Counsel. Democrat. Jewish. Office: Quinnipiac U Sch Law 275 Mount Carmel Ave New Haven CT 06518-1961 Home: 198 Saint James Pl Brooklyn NY 11238-2302

WENIGER-PHELPS, NANCY ANN, media specialist, photographer; b. Kingman, Kans., Sept. 4, 1948; d. Watson and Reva Jo (Schlup) W. BA in Phys. Edn., Ottawa (Kans.) U., 1970; MA in LS, U. Denver, 1980. Cert. K-12 media specialist, secondary phys. edn. tchr., Ariz. Phys. edn. tchr. Grand Junction (Colo.) Sch. Dist., 1970-73; dist. mgr. World Book Ency., 1973-74; personal sec. Younger Bail Bond Svc., Grand Junction, 1974-76; media specialist K-12, phys. edn. tchr. Kingman (Kans.) Unified Sch. Dist., 1976-78, Ovid (Colo.) Sch. Dist., 1980-82, Sargeant Sch. Dist., Monte Vista, Colo., 1982-84, Antonito Sch. Dist., Ovid, Colo., 1984-85; photographer's asst. Bill Westenberg Photography, Alamosa, Colo., 1985-86; sch. media specialist Window Rick (Ariz.) Unified Sch. Dist., 1986-96. Profl. photographer; trainer adult and student storytellers; head dist. lib. computer program. Author: Photographic Uses in the Library; exhibited in group shows Gallup (N.Mex.) Gallery, 1989, Window Rock Elem. Sch., 1989, Sunflower Shop, Wichita, Kans. 1989-90, 96-98, also Alamosa, Colo., 1985-87, 1st Nat. Bank, Kingman (Kans.), Fernley (Nev.) Phys. Therapy, 1993, Greatest Little Art Show in Reno, Nev., 2003, Moms Arts and Crafts Show, Reno, Nev., 2003; photo consignment Trout Creek Nursery, Trucker, Calif., 2003. Mem. Washoe County Friends of Libr., Reno, Nev., vol. book sorter, vol. book sale. Mem. AAHPERD, ALA, Am. Fedn. Tchrs., Internat. Platform Assn., Ariz. Fedn. Tchrs., Window Rock Fedn. Tchrs., Ariz. Edn. Media Assn., Assoc. Photographers Internat. Ariz. Edn. Assn., Alpha Delta Kappa. Home and Office: 5255 Tyrone Rd Reno NV 89502

WENNER, JUDITH WILLS, secondary school educator; b. Boston, May 7, 1948; d. Fred Willis and Jane Thurston Wills; m. Richard Davis Wenner, Aug. 24, 1968; children: Elisabeth Jeanne, Edward Thurston, Richard Wills. Student, Bucknell U., 1966—68; BA, Montclair (N.J.) State U., 1970; EdM, East Stroudsburg (Pa.) U., 1991. Cert. secondary level tchr. of Spanish N.J. Tchr. Randolph (N.J.) H.S., 1970—73, 1985—88, Hackettstown (N.J.) H.S., 1978—83, Lenape Valley H.S., Stanhope, NJ, 1983—85; tchr., dept. chair, Fernando Marcial chair Blair Acad., Blairstown, NJ, 1988—. Tchr., active youth work, women's ministries, choir Knowlton Presbyn. Ch., Columbia, NJ, 1974—2003. Mem.: Am. Coun. Tchrs. Fgn. Language, Nat. Assn. Coll. Admission Counseling. Republican. Presbyterian. Avocations: church activities, outdoor activities, travel. Office: Blair Acad 2 Park St PO Box 600 Blairstown NJ 07825

WENTS, DORIS ROBERTA, psychologist; b. L.A., Aug. 26, 1944; d. John Henry and Julia (Cole) W. BA, UCLA, 1966; MA, San Francisco State U., 1968; postgrad., Calif. State U., L.A., 1989-90, Claremont (Calif.) Grad. U, 1990—. Lic. ednl. psychologist, credentialed sch. psychologist, Calif. Sch. psychologist Diagnostic Sch. for Neurologically Handicapped Children, L.A., 1969-86; pvt. practice Monterey Park, Calif., 1986—. Instr. Calif. State U., L.A., 1977. Co-author: Southern California Ordinal Scales of Development, 1977. Mem. Western Psychol. Assn., L.A. World Affairs Coun., L.A. Conservancy, Zeta Tau Alpha (officer Santa Monica alumnae chpt. 1970—, Cert. of Merit 1979), Sigma Xi. Avocations: travel, watersports, theatre, bridge, photography. Office: Claremont Grad U Dept Psychology Claremont CA 91711 E-mail: Dori.Wents@cgu.edu.

WENTWORTH, BETTE WILSON, artist, educator; b. Paducah, Tex., Aug. 14, 1938; d. Herbert Woodrow and Mertice (Foster) Wilson; m. Nicholas Noyes Wentworth, Apr. 25, 1964; children: Mark Benning, Alan Hunter. BA, U. Tex., 1961; postgrad., Sch. Social Work Smith Coll., 1961-62, Glassell Sch. of Art, Houston, 1976-80. Social caseworker De Pelchin Faith Home, Houston, 1962-66; artist Houston, 1968-97, Austin, 1997-99; art tchr. continuing edn. Spring Br. Independent Sch. Dist., Houston, 1980-91. Juror Tenneco Internat. Children's Exhibit, 1983, Scholastic Art awards Houston Independent Sch. Dist., 1984. Exhibited in solo show at North Fourth Cafe, Albuquerque, 1997, group shows at The Art League of Houston, 1982 (2d place), 83, Watercolor Art Soc., Houston, 1983, 84, 85, 87 (1st place), 88, Jewish Cmty. Ctr. 1983, Galveston Art League, 1983, Town and Country Gallery, 1987, Aries Gallery, 1989, Aquamedia, Wash., 1988, Waterloo Watercolor Group Spring Show, 1997. Pres. Bunkerhill West Civic Club, 1988; vol. Trinity Hosp. Aux., 1999; pres. Brenham Fine Arts League, 2001—03; bd. dirs. Altharetta Yeargin Art Mus., Seton Hosp. Vol. Aux., vol. Mem. Watercolor Art Soc. Houston (chmn. 13th nat. exhibition), The Art League Houston, Waterloo Watercolor Group. Episcopalian. Avocations: walking, reading. Home and Office: 491 Oak Forest Rd Bellville TX 77418-9617

WENTWORTH, LYNN A. telecommunications industry executive; BSBA, Babson Coll.; MS in Taxation, Bentley Coll.; MBA Ga. State U. Various positions with numerous depts. including handling tax, strategic planning, investor rels. and finl. planning Bellsouth Corp., 1985—2003, v.p., treas., 2003—. Tutor C.W. Hill Elem. Sch., Atlanta. Mem.: AICPA, Ga. Soc. CPA's. Office: Bellsouth Corp 1155 Peachtree St NE Atlanta GA 30301-3610

WERB, ZENA, cell biologist, educator; BSc in Biochemistry, U. Toronto, 1966; PhD in Cell Biology, Rockefeller U., 1971. Postdoctoral fellow in protein chemistry Strangeways Rsch. Lab., Cambridge, Eng., 1971-73, rsch. scientist, 1973-75; vis. asst. prof. medicine Dartmouth Med. Sch., Hanover, N.H., 1975-76; asst. prof. radiobiology and radiology U. Calif., San Francisco, 1976-80, asst. prof. anatomy, 1979-80, asst. prof. anatomy and radiology, 1980-83, prof. anatomy, 1983—. Vis. prof. Sir William Dunn Sch. Pathology, U. Oxford, Eng., 1985-86. Mem. editl. bd. Jour. Cell Biology, 1982-85, Am. Jour. Physiology, 1982-87, Neoplasia, 1999—, Jour. Cell Scis., 1999—; adv. editor Jour. Exptl. medicine, 1985—; bd. reviewing editors Sci., 1990—; assoc. editor Matrix Biology, 1999—; contbr. numerous articles to profl. jours. Recipient Excellence in Sci. award Am. Soc. Exptl. Biology, Women's Excellence in Scis. award Fdn. Am. Socs. Exptl. Biology, 1996; U. Toronto scholar, 1963-66; John Simon Gugenheim Found. fellow, 1985-86, other grants and awards. Mem. AAAS, ASCB, ASIP, ASBMB, ISMB. Office: U Calif Dept Anatomy HSW 1320 513 Parnassus Ave San Francisco CA 94143-0001

WERDEGAR, KATHRYN MICKLE, state supreme court justice; b. San Francisco; d. Benjamin Christie and Kathryn Marie (Clark) Mickle; m. David Werdegar; children: Maurice Clark, Matthew Mickle. Student, Wellesley Coll., 1954—55; AB with honors, U. Calif., Berkeley, 1957; JD with highest distinction, George Washington U., 1962; JD, U. Calif., Berkeley, 1990. Bar: Calif. 1964, U.S. Dist. Ct. (no. dist.) Calif. 1964, U.S. Ct. Appeals (9th cir.) 1964, Calif. Supreme Ct. 1964. Legal asst. civil rights divsn. U.S. Dept. Justice, Washington, 1962—63; rsch. atty., author Calif. State Study Commn. on Mental Retardation, 1963—64; assoc. U. Calif. Ctr. for Study of Law and Soc., Berkeley, 1965—67; spl. cons. State Dept. Mental Health, 1967—68; cons., author Calif. Coll. Trial Judges, 1968—71; dir. criminal law divsn. Calif. Continuing Edn. of Bar, 1971—78; assoc. dean acad. and student affairs, assoc. prof. Sch. Law, U. San Francisco, 1978—81; sr. staff atty. Calif. 1st Dist. Ct. Appeal, 1981—85, Calif. Supreme Ct., 1985—91; assoc. justice Calif. 1st Dist. Ct. Appeal, 1991—94, Calif. Supreme Ct., San Francisco, 1994—. Regents' lectr. U. Calif., Berkeley, 2000. Author: Benchbook: Misdemeanor Procedure, 1971, Misdemeanor Procedure Benchbook rev., 1975, Misdemeanor Procedure Benchbook, 1983; contbr. California Continuing Education of the Bar books; editor: California Criminal Law Practice series, Discovery, 1975, California Uninsured Motorist Practice, 1973, I California Civil Procedure Before Trial, 1977. Recipient Charles Glover award, George Washington U., 1962, J. William Fulbright award for disting. pub. svc., George Washington U. Law Sch. Alumni Assn., 1996, excellence in achievement award, Calif. Alumni Assn., 1996, Roger J. Traynor Appellate Justice of Yr. award, 1996, Justice of Yr. award, Consumer Attys. of Calif., 1998, Citation award, Boalt Hall Sch. Law U. Calif., Berkeley, 2002, also 5 Am. Jurisprudence awards, 1960—62. Mem.: Am. Law Inst., Nev./Calif. Women Judges Assn., Calif. Judges Assn., Nat. Assn. Women Judges, Calif. Supreme Ct. Hist. Soc. (bd. dir.), Order of the Coif. Office: Calif Supreme Court 350 McAllister St San Francisco CA 94102-4797

WERESH, THELMA FAYE, sculptor, artist; b. Baca County, Colo., Mar. 15, 1919; d. William Lee Cotton and Myrtle Mae (Quiet) Cotton-Winston; m. Andrew Anthony Weresh, Jan. 28, 1939; children: Charlotte Maria, Catherine Ann. BA, Coll. St. Mary, 1967. Art tchr. Ralston (Nebr.) Pub. Schs., 1967-73, Father Flanagan's Boys Home, Boys Town, Nebr., 1973-75. Bd. dirs. Alliance of Arts Coun., Lincoln, Nebr., 1975; chmn. Visual Arts Commn., Loveland, Colo., 1990-91. One person exhibn. includes Ariel Gallery, N.Y., 1991; featured in Artist's Profile KRMA TV, 1995. Recipient SOHO Internat. 1st Place, 1990, 1st Place United Coun., 1990, 2nd Place, 1991, 1st Place George Lewis, 1991, 1st Place Southwest Art, 1992, 1st Place Women Artists, 1992, Spl. award Mus. N.W., 1992, First Annual Hall of Fame award Revue mag., 1996. Mem. Allied Artists Am., Loveland (Colo.) Sculpture Group. Home: 2009 Lakewood Dr Loveland CO 80538-3423

WERKMAN, ROSEMARIE ANNE, former public relations professional, civic worker; b. Washingtonville, N.Y., Apr. 21, 1926; d. Alexander and Michelina (Russo) Di Benedetto; m. Henry J. Werkman, June 29, 1947; children: Elizabeth, Kristine, Hendrik. Student, U. Miami, Fla. Billing clk. Stern's Dept. Store, N.Y.C., 1945; clk., typist Doubleday-Doran Book Pub., N.Y.C., 1945-46; receptionist Moser & Cotins Advt. Agy., Utica, N.Y., 1947-48, Washingtonville Sch., N.Y., 1960-75. Author: (biography/autobiography) Love, War and Remembrance, 1992; author short stories; poetry pub. in several anthologies. Mem. Dem. Com., Blooming Grove; bd. dirs. Blooming Grove Hist. Assn.; mem. com. Update: Blooming Grove Master Plan; mem. Orange County Coun. Disabled; bd. dirs. Rehab. Support Svcs; charter mem. Orange County Citizens Found.; mem. steering com. Blooming Grove (N.Y.) BiCentennial Celebration, 1999; participant restorations Habitat for Humanity, 2001—; mem. steering com. Hist. Brotherhood Winery, Inc., 2003—. Named Poet of Merit, Am. Poetry Assn., 1989, Poet Laureate Orange County, N.Y., 2002; recipient Notable Civic Contbns. award Blooming Grove/Washingtonville C. of C., 1996, Rose award, 1996. Mem. Blooming Grove C. of C. (v.p.), Orange County Classic Choral Soc., Clearwater (Fla.) Chorus. Democrat. Roman Catholic. Avocations: reading, gardening, furniture refinishing, singing.

WERMUTH, MARY LOUELLA, secondary school educator; b. Oakland County, Mich., May 2, 1943; d. Burt and Ila A. (Cole) W.; m. David J. Kohne, Dec. 28, 1975; 1 child, John B. BA, Oakland U., 1965, MA, 1969, 81. Tchr. Rochester Cmty. Schs., Rochester Hills, Mich., 1965-96; instr., counselor Internat. Acad., Bloomfield Hills, Mich., 1996—. Farmer, 1964—; presenter in field; bd. dirs. Mich. Future Problem Solving; exchange tchr. New South Wales, Australia, 1996; ptnr. Old Indian Enterprises, 1982—; faculty Internat. Acad., dean humanities, 1996-2000; mem. adv. coun. Honors Coll., Oakland U., 2002—; ednl. travel cons. Author: Images of Michigan, 1981, Michigan Centennial Farm History, 1986. Pres. Horizons Residential Ctrs., Inc., New Baltimore, Mich., 1984—; artistic dir. Phoenix Theater Co., 1997—2001, prodr.; ptnr. Rediscovery Ctr., Holly, Mich., 2000—; bd. dirs. Honors Coll. Oakland U., 2002—; bd. dirs. Amerris Ind. Schs., 2000—. Recipient Disting. Alumni award Oakland U., 1976. Mem. NEA, Rochestern Edn. Assn., Mich. Edn. Assn., Mich. Coun. Tchrs. English (coms. 1985, 87), Oakland U. Alumni Assn. (pres. 1971-73), Mich. Centennial Farm Assn. (bd. dirs. 1979—), Mich. Assn. Gifted Edn. (v.p. 1991-93), Oakland County Tchrs. English (coms. 1985-93, editor profl. writing ad copy). Office: Internat Acad 1020 E Square Lake Rd Bloomfield Hills MI 48304-1957

WERNER, ELIZABETH HELEN, librarian, language educator; d. Fielding and Lucy Elizabeth McDearmon; m. Michael Andrew Werner, Aug. 21, 1976. BA, Mills Coll., 1966; MA, Ind. U., 1968; MLS, U. Md., 1973. Instr. Spanish McDaniel Coll., Westminster, Md., 1968—72; libr., assoc. prof. Clearwater (Fla.) Christian Coll., 1975—; chmn. Sunline Libr. Users Group Tampa Bay Libr. Consortium, 2003—. Sec. Sunline Libr. users group Tampa Bay Libr. Consortium, Tampa, Fla., 1993—94, 1998—2000, 2002—03, chmn., 2003—. Contbr. book revs. to profl. jours. Com. mem. Upper Pinellas County Post Office Customers' Adv. Coun., Clearwater, 1992—2000. Mem.: Am. Assn. Tchrs. Spanish and Portuguese, Fla. Assn. Christian Librs. (sec. 1987—90, 1995—98, 2000—, pres. 1991—94), Assn. Christian Librs. (Christian libr. consortium team coord. 1998—), Fla. Libr. Assn., Friends of Clearwater Libr. Avocations: reading, choir, travel, language study, genealogy. Office: Clearwater Christian Coll 3400 Gulf-to-Bay Blvd Clearwater FL 33759

WERNER, GLORIA S. librarian; b. Seattle, Dec. 12, 1940; d. Irving L. and Eva H. Stolzoff; m. Newton Davis Werner, June 30, 1963; 1 child, Adam Davis. BA, Oberlin Coll., 1961; ML, U. Wash., 1962; postgrad., UCLA, 1962—63. Reference libr. UCLA Biomed. Libr., 1963—64, asst. head pub. svcs. dept., 1964—66, head pub. svcs. dept., head reference divsn., 1966—72, asst. biomed. libr. pub. svcs., 1972—77, assoc. biomed. libr., 1977—78, biomed. libr., assoc. univ. libr., dir. Pacific SW regional Med. Libr. Svc., 1979—83; asst. dean libr. svcs. UCLA Sch. Medicine, 1980—83, assoc. univ. libr. for tech. svcs., 1983—89, dir. librs., acting univ. libr., 1989—90, univ. libr., 1990—2002. Adj. lectr. UCLA Grad. Sch. Libr. and Info. Sci., 1977—83; mem. accrediting commn. Western Assn. Schs. and Colls., N.W. Assn. Schs. and Colls. Editor: Bull. Med. Libr. Assn., 1979—82; assoc. editor Bull. Med. Libr. Assn., 1974—79, mem. editl. bd. Ann. Stats. Med. Sch. Librs. U.S. and Can., 1980—83. Mem.: ALA, Assn. Rsch. Librs. (bd. dirs. 1993—98, v.p./pres.-elect 1995—96, pres. 1996—97, past pres. 1997—98). Office: UCLA Rsch Libr Adminstrv Office 405 Hilgard Ave Los Angeles CA 90095-9000

WERNER, JANE, museum administrator; m. Robert Rutkowski; 2 children. B. Synaesthetic Edn., Syracuse U. With Buhl Sci. Ctr., Franklin Inst. and Sci. Mus.; dep. dir. Pitts. Children's Mus., exec. dir. Carnegie-Mellon U./Studio for Creative Inquiry fellow. Office: Pittsburgh Childrens Mus Allegheny Sq North Side 10 Childrens Way Pittsburgh PA 15212

WERNER, KAREN ELAINE, music educator; b. Mexico, Mo., July 14, 1953; d. Leroy Herbert and Myrtle Marie Sperry; children: Kristina, Angela. BS in Music Edn., Southwest Mo. State U., 1975; MA in Music History, U. Mo., 1980. Cert. music tchr. Mo. Music tchr. Niangua (Mo.) Pub. Schs., 1975—76; dir. choirs Ava (Mo.) Jr. and Sr. H.S., 1977—81; head choral dept. McEvoy Music, San Diego, 1984—89; music tchr. La Jolla (Calif.) Elem., 1989—94; assoc. prof., dir. MACC singers Moberly (Mo.) Area C.C., 1994—. Music dir. La Jolla Children's Theater Workshop, 1990—94; music workshop leader Choral Condrs. Guild, San Diego, 1991—94; clinician, adjudicator area high schs. music contests and festivals, 1994—; vis. instr. Christ Ch. U. Coll., Canterbury, Kent, England, 1999; presenter Global Edn. Conf., Kansas City, 2001. Bd. dirs. Moberly Area Coun. of Arts, 1997—2002; music dir. Palisades Presbyn. Ch., San Diego, 1991—94. Recipient Gov.'s award for Tchg. Excellence, 2003. Mem.: Mo. C.C. Assn. (chair salary com.), Am. Choral Dirs. Assn. (chair state repertoire and stds. 1999—2003), Mo. Assn. Depts. and Schs. Music (bd. dirs. 2001—04), Music Educator's Nat. Conf. (dist. choral v.p. 1981—84). Methodist. Avocations: running, gardening, travel. Office: Moberly Area Cmty Coll 101 College Ave Moberly MO 65270 Office Phone: 660-263-4110. Business E-Mail: karenw@macc.edu.

WERNER, MARY ANN, lawyer; b. Latrobe, Pa., July 11, 1954; BA in English, Coll. of charleston, 1982; JD with highest honors, george Washington U., 1987. Bar: Pa. 1988, D.C. 1990, U.S. Ct. Appeals (D.c. cir.) 1990, Va. 1991, U.S. Dist. Ct. D.C. 1991. Law clk. to Hon. Spottswood W. Robinson III U.S. Ct. Appeals (D.C. cir.), 1987-88; v.p., counsel Washington Post, 1988—. Adj. prof. George Washington Nat. Law Ctr., 1990-92; mem. exec. com. Libel Def. Resource Ctr. Editor-in-chief George Washington Law Rev., 1986-87. Mem. ABA (1st amendment and media litigation coms.), D.C. Bar (publs. com., bd. editors Washington Lawyer), Newspaper Assn. Am. (legal affairs com.), Order of Coif. Office: Washington Post 1150 15th St NW Washington DC 20071-0002

WERNER, PATRICE (PATRICIA ANN WERNER), dean; b. Jersey City, May 31, 1937; d. Louis and Ella Blanche (Smith) W. BA in French, Caldwell Coll., 1966; MA in French, McGill U., 1970; PhD in French, NYU, 1976; postgrad. Inst. Ednl. Mgmt., Harvard U., 1991. Joined Dominican Sisters of Caldwell, 1954. Sch. tchr. Archdiocesan Sch. Systems, N.J., Ala., 1954-62; tchr. French, Latin Jersey City, Caldwell, NJ, 1962-72; instr. French Caldwell (NJ) Coll., 1973-76, dir. continuing edn., 1976-79, chair dept. fgn. langs., assoc. prof. French, 1979-85, acad. dean, prof. French, 1985-94, pres., 1994—. Trustee Caldwell Coll.; mem. corp., trustee Providence Coll.; coll. bd. Dominican Higher Edn. Coun. Recipient Excellence in Edn., N. Essex C. of C. Found., 2003, Outstanding Woman in Am. History, DAR Maj. Joseph Bloomfield Chpt., The Archbishop T.E. McCarrick award for Disting. Svc. to the Ch., 2000, Cmty. Woman of Achievement, West Caldwell Hist. Soc. and West Essex Women's Club, 2000, Woman of Achievement award, N. N.J. Coun. of Boy Scouts of Am., 1999; scholar AATF Summer Grant. Master: Assn. Cath. Coll. and U.; mem.: N.J. C. of C., Dominican Higher Edn. Coun., Coll. Bd., Assn. Growing Bd. U. and Coll., Am. Assn. Higher Edn., Neylan Commn. (bd. dirs., sec.- treas.), Nat. Assn. Ind. Coll. and U. (bd. dirs., com. policy analysis and pub. relations), Coun. Ind. Coll. (bd. dirs., pub. info. com.), Ind. Coll. Fund. N.J. (bd. trustees, vice chmn. exec. com.), Assn. Ind. Coll. and U. in N.J. (vice. chmn. bd. dirs.), N.J. Pres. Coun. (treas. exec. bd.). Avocations: tennis, reading, avid sports fan, travel. Office: Caldwell Coll 9 Ryerson Ave Caldwell NJ 07006-6195 Office Phone: 973-618-3217. E-mail: spwerner@caldwell.edu.

WERNER DENADAI, MARY, architectural firm executive; Prin. John Miller Archs., Chadds Ford, Pa., 1977—. Bd. trustees Nat. Trust for Hist. Preservation; bd. dirs. Preservation Action, Cliveden, Preservation Pa.; v.p., mem. Hist. Preservation Bd. of Commonwealth of Pa. Recipient F. Otto Haas award, Pa., 1999; fellow, Am. Inst. of Archs., 2003. Office: John Miller Architects 104 Lakeview Dr Chadds Ford PA 19317

WERNER-JACOBSEN, EMMY ELISABETH, developmental psychologist; b. Eltville, Germany, May 26, 1929; came to U.S., 1952, naturalized, 1962; d. Peter Josef and Liesel (Kunz) W. BS, Johannes Gutenberg U., Germany, 1950; MA, U. Nebr., 1952, PhD, 1955; postgrad., U. Calif., Berkeley, 1953-54. Research asso. Inst. Child Welfare, U. Minn., 1956-59; vis. scientist NIH, 1959-62; asst. prof. to prof. human devel., rsch. child psychologist U. Calif., Davis, 1962-94, rsch. prof., 1995—. Sr. author: The Children of Kauai, 1971, Kauai's Children Come of Age, 1977; author: Cross-Cultural Child Development: A View from the Planet Earth, 1979, Vulnerable, but Invincible, 1982, 3d edit., 1998, Child Care: Kith, Kin and Hired Hands, 1984, Overcoming the Odds, 1992, Pioneer Children on the Journey West, 1995, Reluctant Witnesses: Children's Voices From the Civil War, 1998, Through the Eyes of Innocents: Children Witness World War II, 2000, Unschuldige Zeugen, 2001, Journeys From Childhood to Mid Life: Risk, Resilience and Recovery, 2001, A Conspiracy of Decency: The Rescue of the Danish Jews in World War II, 2002; contbr. articles to profl. jours. Fellow Am. Psychol. Soc., German Acad. Social Pediats. (hon.), Soc. for Rsch. in Child Devel.

WERNETTE, KAREN MARIE, veterinarian; b. Eaton Rapids, Mich., Apr. 24, 1954; d. Victor Joseph and Pauline R. (Strong) W.; m. David John Cushman, Apr. 9, 1988; children: Alex David Cushman, Kevin Andrew Cushman. BS in Zoology, U. Mich., 1975; BS in Animal Husbandry, Mich. State U., 1977, DVM, 1982. Assoc. vet. Animal Health Clinic & Hosp., Waukegan, Ill., 1982; emergency veterinarian A-Northshore Emergency Vet. Ctr., Northfield, Ill., 1983, 94-95; anesthesiology resident Ohio State U. Coll. Vet. Medicine, Columbus, 1983-84; assoc. veterinarian Noyes Animal Hosp., Barrington, Ill., 1995-96; dir. membership AVMA, Schaumburg, Ill., 1996—2000; assoc. veterinarian Orphans of the Storm Animal Clinic, Vernon Hills, Ill., 2001—. Bd. dirs. Nat. Mastitis Coun., Madison, Wis., 1992-95; mem. PTO. Mem. AVMA, Ill. State Vet. Med. Assn., Mich. Vet.

Med. Assn., Chgo. Vet. Med. Assn. United Methodist. Home: 511 N Country Ridge Ct Lake Zurich IL 60047-2824 Office: AVMA 1931 N Meacham Rd Schaumburg IL 60173-4364

WERNICK, SANDRA MARGOT, advertising and public relations executive; b. Tampa, Fla., Sept. 13, 1944; d. Nathan and Sylvia (Bienstock) Rothstein. BA in English, U. Fla., 1966. Tchr. English Miami Beach (Fla.) Sr. H.S., 1967; adminstrv. asst. pub. rels. Bozell & Jacobs, Inc., N.Y.C., 1968-69; asst. to dir. pub. rels. Waldorf-Astoria, N.Y.C., 1969-70; dir. advt. and pub. rels. Hyatt on Union Sq., San Francisco, 1974-82; pres. Wernick Mktg. Group, San Francisco, 1982—; exec. dir. Sales and Mktg. Execs. of the Bay Area, 1995-2000; mng. ptnr. The Stanford Group, 1998-99; pres. Auction Magic, San Francisco, 2003—. Bd. dirs. Nat. Kidney Assn., San Francisco, 1985-87; advisor Swords to Plowshares, San Francisco, 1988-89; mem. mktg. com. to bd. Boy Scouts of Greater East Bay, 1995-2000. Recipient Award of Merit, San Francisco Advt. and Cable Car Awards, 1979, Award of Excellence, San Francisco Art Dirs. 1978, Disting. Mktg. award Sales and Mktg. Internat., 1997, awards Am. Hotel and Motel Assn., 1981, 82. Mem. NAFE, Women in Comms. (bd. dirs. 1987-89), Am. Women in Radio and TV (bd. dirs. 1989-90), Pub. Rels. Soc. Am., San Francisco Publicity Club (pres. 1989, awards of excellence 1990, 94, 95-98), Variety Club, Profl. Bus. Women's Assn., Calif. Pacific Med. Ctr. (aux. 1988-95). Democrat. Jewish. Office: 1690 Broadway Ste 705 San Francisco CA 94109-2107 E-mail: sandie@wernickmarketinggroup.com.

WERRONEN, BETSY WARREN, political organization administrator; BA in Polit. Sci., Newton Coll. Sacred Heart, 1965. Legis. asst. to Sen. Thruston B. Morton, 1966-68; exec. asst. to Sen. Edward W. Brooke, 1968-75; dir. legis. nuclear energy and taxes Edison Electric Inst., 1979-81, chief lobbyist on nuclear power issues, 1979-81; acting asst. sec. of state for legis. affairs Dept. of State, Washington, 1981-85, prin. dep. asst. sec. of state for legis. affairs, 1987-89; prin. dep. asst. sec. for congl., intergovtl., pub. affairs Dept. of Energy, Washington, 1985-86; founder, pres. Warren and Co., 1989—; fin. chmn. Rep. Com. DC Rep. Party, Washington, 1998-2000, chmn. Rep. Com., 2000—. Mem. nat. steering com., congl. steering com. Women for Bush/Quayle, 1992; co-chair Ward 2, 1996-98; alternate del. Rep. Nat. Conv., 1996, 2000. Apptd. U.S. election observer, El Salvador, 1988; bd. dirs. Fgn. Student Coun., 1993-97. Mem. League of Rep. Women (1st v.p. 1997-99, pres. 1999—). Office: DC Rep Party 1275 K St, NW, Ste 102 Washington DC 20005

WERT, BARBARA J. YINGLING, special education consultant; b. Hanover, Pa., May 18, 1953; d. Richard Bruce and Jacqueline Louise (Myers) Yingling; m. Barry Thomas Wert, Aug. 23, 1975; children: Jennifer Allison, Jason Frederick. BS in Elem. Edn., Kutztown (Pa.) U., 1975; MS in Spl. Edn., Bloomsburg (Pa.) U., 1990; PhD, Pa. State U., 2002. Cert. in elem. edn., spl. edn., Pa., cert. early childhood, Pa. Dir. children's program Coun. for United Ch. Ministries of Reading, Reading, Pa., 1975-76; instr. Berks County Vo-Tech., Oley Valley, Pa., 1976-77; asst. tchr. Ostrander Elem. Sch., Wallkill, N.Y., 1982-85; spl. needs surp., instrnl. support tchr., cons. Danville (Pa.) Child Devel. Ctr., 1986—; dir. Little Learners Pre-Sch., Northumberland, Pa., 1991-94, ednl. cons., 1991—. Pvt. cons. Families with Spl. Needs, Northumberland, 1991—; adj. prof. spl. edn., Bloomsburg U., 1995, 97, 98, 99, 00. Recipient Parent Profl. Partnership award 1993. Mem. A.C.D., Coun. for Exceptional [illegible] early childhood 1991—, sec. 1991-93, newsletter editor, v.p. 1993-94, pres. 1995-96), Nat. Assn. for Edn. Young Children (v.p. Pa. divsn. for early childhood 1993—, tchr. edn. divsn., coun. for behavior disorders divsn., learning disabilities divsn.), Local Autism Support and Advocacy Group. Avocations: photography, needlework, hiking, reading. : 230 Evergreen Dr Winfield PA 17889-9170 Office Phone: 570-389-4110. E-mail: bwert@bloomu.edu.

WERTHEIM, MARY DANIELLE, elementary education coordinator; b. N.Y.C. d. Daniel Leo and Helen Loretta (Sudimick) Conroy; m. Stanley Claude Wertheim, Mar. 9, 1963. BA in English with honors, CCNY, 1960, MA, 1979. Coord. English and lang. arts Horace Mann Lower Sch., Riverdale, N.Y., 1969—. Pvt. investor Wertheim Trust, N.Y.C., 1985—; pres. winner's cir. Horace Mann Investment Club, Riverdale, 1989—. Founder, advisor Horace Mann Lower Sch. Cmty. Svc. Group, Riverdale, 1980—; active Rep. nat. Com., 1980—. Mem.: ASCD, Nat. Assn. Investors Corp., The Internat. Netsuke Soc. (sec. N.Y. chapter), Priory Scholars, Am. Firm, Mensa, The Grolier Club. Avocations: desk top publishing, manuscript collecting, frogs, sherlock holmes. Home: 180 Cabrini Blvd New York NY 10033-1138 Office: Horace Mann Lower Sch 4440 Tibbett Ave Bronx NY 10471-3416 E-mail: herbieboo@aol.com.

WERTHEIM, MITZI MALLINA, technology company executive; b. N.Y.C. d. Rudolf and Myrtle B. (McGraw) Mallina; m. Ronald P. Wertheim, Feb. 25, 1965 (div. July 1988); children: Carter, Tiana. BA, U. Mich., 1960. Asst. dir. div. research Peace Corps, Washington, 1961-66; sr. program officer Cafritz Found., Washington, 1970-76; dep. undersec. navy, 1977-81; with Fed. Sector Div. IBM, 1981-94; v.p. enterprise solutions SRA Corp., 1994-98, CNA Corp., 1998—. Woodrow Wilson vis. fellow, 1979, 80 Bd. dirs. Nat. Coalition Sci. and Tech., 1983—86; mem. vis. com. MIT, 1983—89; bd. dirs. Youth Policy Inst., 1986—91, VITA, 1990—2000, Cebrowski Inst., Naval Post Grad. Sch.; founder MIT Seminar XXI, 1985—. Recipient Federally Employed Women award Def. Dept., 1980; Disting. Pub. Svc. medal Navy Dept., 1981; fellow Maxwell Sch. Syracuse U., 1996-97. Mem.: Naval Studies Bd., Coun. on Fgn. Rels. Episcopalian. Home: 3113 38th St NW Washington DC 20016-3726

WERTHEIM, SALLY HARRIS, academic administrator, dean, education educator, consultant; b. Cleve., Nov. 1, 1931; d. Arthur I. and Anne (Manheim) Harris; m. Stanley E. Wertheim, Aug. 6, 1950; children: Kathryn, Susan B., Carole J. BS, Flora Stone Mather Coll., 1953; MA, Case Western Res. U., 1967, PhD, 1970. Cert. elem. and secondary edn. tchr., Ohio. Social worker U. Hosps., Cleve., 1953-54; tchr. Fairmount Temple Religious Sch., Cleve., 1957-72; mem. faculty John Carroll U., Cleve., 1969—, chair dept. edn., 1979—86, dean Grad. Sch., 1986—99, dir. planning and assessment, 1999—. Cons. in field; cons. Jennings Found., Cleve.; chmn. sch. com. Cleve. Commn. on Higher Edn., 1987-99. Contbr. articles to profl. jours. Sec. Cuyahoga County Mental Health Bd., Cleve., 1978—82; pres. Montefiore Home for Aged, Cleve., 1987—90; bd. dirs. Mt. Sinai Med. Ctr., Cleve., 1984—93, Cleve. Edn. Fund, 1992—94; chair edn. com. Cleve. Found. Commn. on Poverty, 1988—93, Cleve. Cmty. Bldg. Initiative, 1993—95, United Way Svcs., 1994—2001; trustee Mt. Sinai Health Care Found., 1998, Gerson Found., 1998, Miller Found., 1998, Begun Found., 2001, Mandel Found., 2001; pres. Jewish Family Svc. Assn., Cleve., 1974—77; v.p. Jewish Cmty. Fedn., 1988—91, pres., 1994—97, trustee, 1975, life trustee, 1997—. Named One of 100 Most Influential Women, Cleve. mag., 1983, One of 29 Most Influential Women, Cleve. Mag., 1997; recipient award John Carroll U., Curtis Miles award for cmty. svc., 1997; grantee Jennings Found., 1984-87, Cleve. and Gund Found., 1987-90, Lilly Found., 1988; S.H. Wertheim scholarship and edn. excellence award established John Carroll U., 1997. Mem. Am. Assn. Colls. for Tchrs. Edn. (bd. dirs. 1982-85), Ohio Assn. Colls. for Tchrs. Edn. (pres. 1981-83), Coun. of Grad. Schs. Avocations: flower arranging, travel, antiques. Office: John Carroll U Planning & Assessment Cleveland OH 44118

WERTHEIMER, MARILYN LOU, school librarian, educator; b. Pueblo, Colo., Dec. 1, 1928; d. Louis Robert and Alice Erdine Schuman; m. Y. Ernest Satow, Jan. 4, 1953 (div. Oct. 1958); m. Michael M. Wertheimer, Sept. 12, 1970; stepchildren: Karen Anne, Mark David, John Benjamin. BA, Stanford U., 1950; MA, Columbia U., 1953; postgrad., U. Calif., Berkeley, 1961—62; MLS, U. Calif., L.A., 1967. Sec., proofreader various publ. firms, N.Y.C., 1953—56; sec. Rockefeller Brs. Fund, 1956—57; personal staff, sec. Nelson A. Rockefeller, 1957—58; sec. Gen. Dynamics Corp., San Diego, 1959—64; cataloguer U. Calif., 1965—68; reference libr. U. Colo., Boulder, 1968—93, prof. honors sem., 1972—91, prof. emeritus, 1993—. Mem. libr. del. U.S. Exch. China, 1985, U.S. Exch. Russia, 1988; cons. Archives of History Am. Psychology, Akron, Ohio, 1980. Co-author: Sources of Information in the Social Sciences, 1986; co-editor: History of Psychology: A Guide, 1979. Mem. del. vis. Tibet, Boulder-Lhasa Sister Cities Program, 1988; vol. Christian Sci. Ch., 1986—; bd. dirs. U. Club, U. Colo., Boulder, 1976—79. Recipient First prize, Internat. Libr. Photography, Owings Mills, Md., 1999—2000. Mem.: ALA. Democrat. Home: 546 Geneva Ave Boulder CO 80302 Office: Norlin Libr U Colo Campus Box 184 Boulder CO 80309-0184 E-mail: wert@psych.colorado.edu.

WESELY, ELAINE GALE, purchasing manager; b. Portland, Oreg., Oct. 28, 1945; d. Lester Persinger and Rosene (Griffith) Pecht; children: John David, Chauni Elizabeth Alexander, Rachel Ann Parks. Grad., South Salem H.S., 1963. Cert. purchasing mgr. Exec. asst. to dir. of commerce Oreg. Dept. Commerce, Salem, 1976-79; adminstr. Oreg. Contractors' Bd., Salem, 1979-83; dep. adminstr. Oreg. Purchasing Divsn., Salem, 1983-88; purchasing mgr. ST Microwave Corp., Sunnyvale, Calif., 1988-92; purchasing officer City of Sunnyvale, 1992—. Mem. Calif. Assn. Pub. Purchasing Officers, Nat. Assn. Purchasing Mgrs., Nat. Assn. Accounts Payable Profls. Republican. Avocations: travel, reading, gardening. Office: City of Sunnyvale 650 W Olive Ave Sunnyvale CA 94086-7637

WESELY, MARISSA CELESTE, lawyer; b. N.Y.C., Apr. 25, 1955; d. Edwin Joseph and Yolanda Teresa (Pyles) W.; m. Frederick Hamerman; 1 child, Emma Elizabeth Wesely Allen. BA magna cum laude, Williams Coll., 1976; JD cum laude, Harvard U., 1980. Bar: N.Y. 1981. Assoc. Simpson Thacher & Bartlett, N.Y.C., 1980-82, 84-88, ptnr., 1989—, assoc. London, 1982-84. Lectr., cons. Harvard Inst. Internat. Devel., Beijing, 1981, Jakarta, Indonesia, 1982; guest lectr. Yale Law Sch., New Haven, 1991; spkr. Am. Conf. Inst., Practicing Law Inst., Bankers Assn. for Fgn. Trade, N.Y. State Bar Assn. confs., 1993—. Bd. dirs. City Lore, N.Y.C. Mem. N.Y.C. Bar Assn., N.Y. State Bar Assn. (mem. exec. com. sect. internat. law and practice), Internat. Bar Assn., Phi Beta Kappa.

WESEMAN, VICKI LYNNE, elementary school educator; b. Hastings, Nebr., Oct. 29, 1954; d. Virgil John and Vera Lillie (Berg) Kennedy; m. Creighton Lee Weseman, May 28, 1988 (div. Oct. 1999); 1 child, Jason K. BS, U. Nebr., 1977, MA, 1988. Cert. elem. tchr. Nebr., profl. tchr. Nebr. Elem. tchr. Hanover Elem. Sch., Glenvil, Nebr., 1977—2003, Lincoln Elem. Sch., Grand Isle., Nebr., 2003—. Pres. Adams County Edn. Assn., Hastings, Nebr., 1996—97; team leader stds. Adams County Schs., Hastings, 2000—01. Oregon Trail rodeo pageant coord. Adams County Agrl. Soc., Hastings, 1992—. Named Miss Rodeo, Nebr., 1977, Com. Person of Yr., Oregon Trail Rodeo, Hastings, 1999. Mem.: Nebr. Edn. Assn. (mem. selection com. 2000), Women's Profl. Rodeo Assn. Democrat. Lutheran. Avocation: barrel racing in rodeo. Home: 835 Briggs Ave Hastings NE 68901 Office: Lincoln Elem 805 Beal St Grand Island NE 68801

WESKAMP, KELLEY S. loan account manager, real estate company executive; b. Boulder City, Nev., Jan. 9, 1964; d. Dale P. and Phyllis J. (Cooper) W. BA in English Lang. Lit. with distinction, [illegible] Coll., 1985. Cons. Ely Leadership Mgmt., Lakewood, Colo., 1985-88; budget asst. Bureau Reclamation, Denver, 1988-90; real estate owned technician FDIC, Denver, 1990-93; real estate specialist Westfall and Co., Westminster, 1993-95, account mgr., 1995-97, Castle Advisors subs. Chgo. Title, 1998-99; sr. account mgr. Litton Loan Servicing, Houston, 1999—. Participant Bench Mark Study, Pete Marwick Assocs., 1997. Contbr. article to mag. Democrat. Roman Catholic. Avocations: weaving, reading, travel, cooking. Home: 12080 W Mexico Ave Lakewood CO 80228-3909

WESLEY, IRMA R. art historian, educator; b. Bklyn., June 8, 1926; d. Benjamin B. and Sallie (Sarah) E. Wesley; 1 child, Susan Rose Hallett. BA, Hofstra U., 1947; MA in Edn., Queens Coll., 1955. Docent Bowne Ho., Flushing, NY, 1981—99, Onderdonk Ho., Ridgewood, NY, 1988—94; tour guide Wyckoff Ho., Bklyn., 1988—92; docent Queens Mus. Art, Flushing, 1996—; lectr. Kew Gardens (N.Y.) Cmty. Ctr., 1999—. Lectr. in field; lectr. Roslyn Sr. Adult Edn. Dept., NY, 2000—, Atria Retirement Home, Kew Gardens, NY, 2003—. Mem. adv. bd. Kew Gardens Cmty. Ctr., 2001; lectr. Queens Historical Soc., Hallmark Retirement Home-Manhattan, N.Y.C., 2003—; bd. dirs. Greater Ridgewood Hist. Soc., 1990—94. Mem.: United Fedn. Tchrs. (lectr. sr. divsn.). Home: 83-83 118th St Apt 2G Kew Gardens NY 11415

WESLEY, LATONYA RASHAWN, legislative assistant; b. Detroit, Oct. 22, 1974; Student, Spelman Coll., 1992-94; BA in Polit. Sci., Mich. State U., 1997; postgrad., U. Balt., 2002—. Legis. corrd. U.S. Senate, Washington, 1998-99; adminstrv. asst. APA, Washington, 1999-2000, legis. asst., 2000—. Contbr. to Psychol. Sci. Agenda. Legis. intern Mich. State Senate, Lansing, 1997; vol. Atlanta Project, 1993, Econ. Crisis Ctr., East Lansing, Mich., 1996, Debbie Stabenow Campaign for U.S. Ho. of Reps., East Lansing, 1996, Make a Difference Day, Ft. Meade, Md., 1998-99, AIDS Walk, Washington, Walk for Wellness-Am. Heart Assn., Balt., 1999, ARC, East Lansing, 1997; mentor, tutor Cornerstone Charter Sch., Washington, 1998; telefundraiser Am. Cancer Soc., East Lansing, 1997; mentor Brent Elem. Sch., Washington, 1998. Mem. Mich. State U. Alumni Assn., Zeta Phi Beta (grammateus 2000-02, Md. del. Rho Eta Zeta chpt. 2001, 2d anti-basileus, 2002—, fundraising chmn., 2001-02, fundraising co-chmn., 2002—), LEST Club. Office: APA 750 1st St NE Washington DC 20002 Home: 6537 Penn Ave #102 Forestville MD 20747 Fax: 202-336-6063. E-mail: lwesley@apa.org., rashawn74@netstorm.net.

WESLEY, RUBY LAVERNE, nursing educator, administrator, researcher; b. Detroit, Nov. 25, 1949; d. David Williams and Leatrice (Gragg) Williams; 1 child, Nathaniel Rogers Wesley III. Diploma, Providence Hosp. Sch. Nursing, Southfield, Mich., 1971; BS in Nursing, Wayne State U., Detroit, 1974, MEd, 1977; PhD, U. Md., Balt., 1987. Clin. instr. U. Tenn. Sch. Nursing, 1978-79; community health nursing instr. U. Md., Balt., 1984-85; assoc. prof. Bowie State U., 1985-89; asst. dean Coppin State Coll., Balt., 1989-90; asst. prof. Wayne State U., 1991—; nurse researcher Rehab. Inst. Mich., 1992, dir. nursing practice, 1992-93, dir. nursing, 1993-96; asst. v.p. med./surg. rehab. nursing Sinai Hosp., Detroit, 1996—98; chief oper. officer Detroit Inst. for Children, 1998—99; pres., CEO Big Bros./Big Sisters of Metro Detroit, 2000—02; v.p. programs Detroit Urban League, 2002—03; exec. dir. Wayne County Patient Care Mgmt. Sys., 2003—. Henry C. Welcome fellow, 1986-87; Nat. Inst. Disability and Rehab. rsch. fellow, 1991-92. Home: 2422 Sheridan St Detroit MI 48214-1723

WESNER, JENNIFER ISLA, music educator; b. Raleigh, N.C., Oct. 6, 1977; d. Antoni Thomas and Isla Kathleen (Hill) Wesner. MusB, U. N.C., 2000. Tchr. West Lee Mid. Sch., Sanford, NC, 2000—, band dir., 2000—. Mem.: S.E. Band Dirs. Assn. (adjudicator 2000—). Home: 2775 Mallard Cove Rd Sanford NC 27330 Office: West Lee Middle School 3301 Wicker St Sanford NC 27330

WESSELKAMPER, SUE, academic administrator; m. Tom Wesselkamper; 2 children. BA History, Govt., Edgecliff Coll.; M Social Work, U. Mich.; PhD Social Welfare, CUNY. Head cmty., social svs. program New River Cmty. Coll.; dir. social work field instrn. program Radford U., Va.; dean sch. arts and scis., assoc. prof. social work Coll. New Rochelle, NY; pres. Chaminade U. Honolulu, 1995—. Author: Enhancing Ethnic Identity Through Cross-Cultural Interaction, An Intercultural Approach to Contemporary Ethnicity, Issues in Implementing Cultural Diversity Content, Role of the Social Worker in Health Planning. Chmn. bd. dirs. Family Svcs. Westchester County, NY; mem. adv. com. Pew Charitable Trust 3d Black Colls. Project on Student Retention; mem. Hawaii Cath. Conf., Hawaii State Network of Am. Coun. on Edn.'s Women Leaders in Higher Edn. Avocations: reading, movies, hiking, travel. Office: Chaminade U of Honolulu 3140 Waialae Ave Honolulu HI 96816

WESSLER, MARY HRAHA, real estate company executive; b. Des Moines, Nov. 4, 1961; d. Francis M. and Shirley A. (Malone) Hraha; 1 child, Nick. BA in Mass Comm., Iowa State U., 1984; postgrad., U. Denver, 1990. Dir. mktg. Real Estate Mgmt. Corp., Scottsdale, Ariz., 1984-87; v.p. Great West Mgmt. and Realty, Ltd., Denver, 1987-97; reg. v.p. AIMCO, Denver, 1997-98; v.p. JPI, Denver, 1999—2001, Omni Properties, Inc., Denver, 2001—. Instr. Multi-Housing World Nat. Apt. Assn., Inst. of Real Estate Mgmt.; spkr. in field. Mem.: Apt. Assn. Metro Denver (past bd. dirs.), Colo. Apt. Assn. (bd. dirs. 1990—2003), Nat. Apt. Assn. (v.p. Region 8 2000—03, bd. dirs. 2000—03). Home: 4185 S Granby Cir Aurora CO 80014 Office Phone: 303-692-0451 ext. 175. Personal E-mail: mjwessler@cs.com. E-mail: mwessler@omniprop.com.

WESSNER, DEBORAH MARIE, telecommunications executive, information systems consultant; b. St. Louis, Aug. 15, 1950; m. Brian Paul Wessner, Sept. 15, 1972; children: Krystin, David. BA in Math. and Chemistry, St. Louis U., 1972; M Computer Info. Sci., U. New Haven, 1980. Statistitian Armstrong Rubber Co., New Haven, 1972-74; programmer analyst Sikorsky div. United Techs., Stratford, Conn., 1974-77; project engr. GE, Bridgeport, Conn., 1977-79, software mgr. Arlington, Va., 1979-81; mgr. software ops. Satellite Bus. Systems, McLean, Va., 1981-83; v.p. ops. DAMA Telecommunications, Rockville, Md., 1983-87; dir. network ops. and adminstrn. Data Gen. Network Svcs., Rockville, 1987-91; dir. bus. ops. Sprint Internat., Reston, Va., 1991-92; v.p. network adminstrn. Citicorp, Washington, 1992-93, v.p. telecomm. product mgmt. Reston, Va., 1994-95, v.p. product mgmt., 1996-97, v.p., dir. Yr. 2000 program, 1997-99; v.p. global procurement C&W, 2000—01; v.p. contracts SAIC, 2003—. Assoc., cons. KDB Assocs., Columbia, Md., 1986—. Mem. exec. bd. Howard County PTA. Mem.: NAFE, Am. Bus. Women's Assn. Avocations: sailing, windsurfing, tennis.

WEST, ALEXANDRA (ANNIE WEST), artist, creative director; b. Chgo., Dec. 10, 1963; Degree, U. Provence, Aix-Marseilles, France, 1984; BA in French Studies, U. Mich., 1986; MFA, Sch. Art Inst. Chgo., 1992. Studio artist Whitney Mus. Am. Art, N.Y.C., 1993; creative dir. The Hub/New Line Cinema, N.Y.C., 1996—. Artist resident Banff (Can.) Ctr. for Arts, 1994, Sculpture Space, Utica, N.Y., 1995, Ucross Found., Wyo., 1996; vis. artist Temistocles 44, Mexico City, 1994; panelist San Francisco Camera Work, San Francisco, 1995, Conn. Tchrs. Conf., 1996; guest curator Digital Film Festival, N.Y.C., 1998. Exhibited in shows at Beacon St. Gallery, Chgo., 1989, Chgo. Gallery, 1990, Gallery II, Chgo., 1991, [illegible] Gallery, N.Y., 1993, Whitney Mus. Am. Art, N.Y., 1993, Hyde Park Art Ctr., Chgo., 1994, Miranushi/Lederman Prodns., Amsterdam, 1994, Temistocles 44, 1994, Cheap Art, Hamburg, 1994, Randolph St. Gallery, Chgo., 1991, 94, San Francisco Camera Work, 1995, Gallery 450, N.Y., 1995, Washington Project for Arts, Washington, 1995, Aldrich Mus. of Contemporary Art, Conn., 1995, [illegible] Gallery, N.Y., 1995, P.P.O.W. Gallery, N.Y., 1995, ATA Gallery, San Francisco, 1996, Exit Art, N.Y.C., 1997; included in Joan Flasch Artists' Book Collection, Art Inst. Chgo., MOMA/Franklin Furnace Archive. Fellow Ernst Haas Photography, 1995, Nat. Endowment for Arts, 1995-96; Art Matters grantee, 1994.

WEST, BETSY, broadcast executive; m. Oren Jacoby. Grad., Brown U.; MS, Syracuse U. Reporter WHEN Radio, Syracuse, N.Y., 1974; writer, editor ABC Radio, 1975; writer ABC News World News Tonight, Chgo., 1978-82; sr. prodr. ABC News Nightline, 1983-89; sr. broadcast prodr. ABC News Turning Point, 1989-98; exec. prodr. ABC News; v.p. primetime news CBS, N.Y.C., 1998—. Recepient 19 Emmy awards, Christopher award, duPont-Columbia award. Mem. Phi Beta Kappa (trustee). Office: CBS News 524 W 57th St New York NY 10019-2924

WEST, CAROLYN MARIE, psychologist, educator, writer; b. St. Louis, Mo., Jan. 14, 1964; d. Georgia Mae West. PhD, U. Mo., St. Louis, 1994. Predoctoral intern U. Notre Dame Counseling Ctr., South Bend, Ind., 1993—94; postdoctoral clin. and tchg. fellowship Ill. State U. Counseling Ctr./Psychology Dept., Normal, Ill., 1994—95; postdoctoral rsch. fellow U. N.H. Family Rsch. Lab., Durham, NH, 1995—97; assoc. prof., psychology U. Wash., Tacoma, 1997—. Author (editor): (book) Violence in the Lives of Black Women: Battered Black and Blue, 2002 (Nat. Inst. on Alcohol Abuse and Alcoholism Rsch. Supplement ($63, 443), 2003), essay. Rschr. Gov. Domestic Violence Action Group, Seattle, 2001—02; steering com. mem. Pierce County Commn. Against Domestic Violence, Tacoma, 2000—03. Recipient Outstanding Young Women of Am. Award, 1997, Outstanding Rsch. Award in the Field of Domestic Violence in the African Am. Cmty., U. of Minn., 2000. Mem.: APA, Psychology for Women in Psychology (governing bd. mem. 1993—96). Achievements include research in University of Washington, Tacoma Founder's Endowment Grant, 1998 ($5, 000). Office: Univ Wash Tacoma IAS Box 358436 1900 Commerce St Tacoma WA 98402

WEST, DOE, bioethicist, social justice activist, researcher; b. Tucson, July 14, 1951; d. George Oliver and Dorothy Marie (Watson) W. AA, Dutchess C.C., 1975; BS, SUNY, New Paltz, 1977; BA, Logos Bible Coll., 1986, MDiv, 1993; MS, Boston U., 1980; PhD, Northeastern U., 2001. Dir. 504/compliance officer dept. health and hosp. City of Boston, 1979-81, commr. handicap affairs, 1981-84; pres. Myth Breakers, Inc., 1984—. Project coord. task force on human subject rsch. Fernald State Sch., 1994; sr. rsch. assoc. N.E. Family Study, Harvard Sch. Pub. Health, 2002-. Postdoctoral fellow Ctr. for Psychol. Rehab. Boston U., 1999-2002. Home: PO Box 985 Framingham MA 01701 E-mail: doewest@aol.com.

WEST, EILEEN M. caseworker; b. Somerset, Pa. d. Casimir M. and Beatrice T. Stanis; m. Richard E. West (div. 1981); children: Theodore, Cynthia, Michael. BA, Pa. State U., 1970. Cert. FACTS program leader, Pa. Caseworker Susquehanna County Bd. Assistance, Montrose, Pa., 1970-73, Cumberland County Children & Youth Agy., Carlisle, Pa., 1988-89, ChildLine, Harrisburg, Pa., 1989—. Pa. Dept. Pub. Welfare liaison to Pa. Coalition Against Rape, Harrisburg, 1993-95. Chief shop stewart Svc. Employees Internat. Union 668, 1991—, alt. mem. statewide grievance appeal com., 1992-93, chair, 1993—, mem. statewide mobilization com. 1992-93, chpt. mobilizer, 1992-93, mem. statewide budget and fin. com., 1993, chpt. treas., 1993, chpt. v.p., 1994, area contract mobilizer, 1995—, del. Ea. Regional Women's Conf., Boston, 1995; mem. Molly Pitcher Stitchers Embroiderers' Guild Am., 1993—, publicity chairperson Susquehanna chpt., 1992-94, mem. Wyoming Valley chpt. 1995—, program chairperson Susquehanna chpt. 1996—, pres., 1996—; mem. 146 Knights of Lithuania Coun., 1991, v.p., 1992, pres., 1993, ritual chair, 1994—; tchr. Polyclinic Needlework Show, Harrisburg, 1993, 95. Republican. Roman Catholic. Avocations: needlework, reading, herb gardening. Home: 410 Norman Rd Camp Hill PA 17011-6130 Office: Commonwealth of Pa DPW ChildLine PO Box 2675 Harrisburg PA 17105-2675

WEST, FRANCES LEE, retired doll artist, freelance writer; b. Groves, Tex., Jan. 31, 1934; d. Henry Brewer Crittenden and Nora Josephine Billiot Showalter; m. Ronald Bruce West, May 14, 1955; children: Berry Jo Carter, Melissa Alyce Nelson. Student, Credit Burs. Am., Houston, 1957. Owner

Dälzenstuff, Flower Mound, Tex., 1992-98. Mem. The Crafter's Network, Artists' Breakfast Club. Democrat. Avocations: listening to opera, reading, sewing, houseboating, writing. Home: 3708 Spring Meadow Ln Flower Mound TX 75028-1221

WEST, GAIL BERRY, lawyer; b. Cin. d. Theodore Moody and Johnnie Mae (Newton) B.; m. Togo D. West, Jr., June 18, 1966; children: Tiffany Berry, Hilary Carter. BA magna cum laude, Fisk U., 1964; MA, U. Cin., 1965; JD, Howard U., 1968. Bar: D.C. 1969, U.S. Supreme Ct. 1978. Staff atty. IBM, 1969-76; spl. asst. to sec. HUD, 1977-78; staff asst. to spl. asst. to Pres., Washington, 1978-80; dep. asst. sec. for manpower res. affairs installations Dept. Air Force, 1980-81; atty. AT&T, Washington, 1983-84; exec. dir. govt. affairs Bell Comm. Rsch. Inc., Washington, 1984-95; dir. govt. rels. Armstrong World Industries, Inc., Washington, 1995—2003, cons., 2003—. Mem. exec. com. ARC, Washington, 1974-85; bd. dirs. Family and Child Svcs., Washington, 1974-87; trustee Corcoran Gallery Art, 1983-2000, Arena Stage, 1992-99, Decatur House, 1994—, WETA, 1995-2001, Fisher House Found., Inc.; bd. dirs. Meridian House, 1994-2000; mem. D.C. Commn. Fine Arts, 2003-; mem. cathedral chpt. Nat. Cathedral. Ford Found. fellow, 1965-68. Mem. ABA, D.C. Bar Assn., Unified Bar D.C. Democrat. Episcopalian. Home: 4934 Rockwood Pkwy NW Washington DC 20016-3211

WEST, KAREN MARIE, music educator, musician; d. Mario J. and Albertine C. Arduino; m. Billy Ray West, June 21, 1997; children: Billy Jr., Edward, Deborah Manna, Julia Harmelin, Nora Harmelin. B in Music Edn., Temple U., 1967. String tchr. Phila. Pub. Schs., 1968—72; violinist Colo. Philharm., Evergreen, Colo., 1968; orch. dir. Winslow Pub. Schs., Winslow Twp., NJ, 1985—; violinst Melodia Trio, Cedarbrook, NJ, 1990—. Adjudicator, mgr. All-South Jersey Orch., NJ, 1985—; adjudicator All-State Orch., NJ, 1985—; mem. Gifted and Talented Adv. Com., Winslow Twp., 2001—02. Mem.: South Jersey Band and Orch. Dirs. Assn., N.J. Edn. Assn., Music Educators Nat. Conf., Internat. Soc. Violin Bottle Collectors.

WEST, MARIA MCDONALD, social worker; b. Faunsdale, Ala., Aug. 16, 1923; d. John W. and Maria Newill (Brown) McDonald; m. Herbert B. West, Nov. 29, 1946; children: Newill, Herbert, McDonald, Selden, Jane. BA, Judson Coll., 1945; MSW, Yeshiva U., 1975. Bd. cert. diplomate, Cert. Ind. Social Worker. Caseworker Family and Children's Aid, Norwalk, Conn., 1974-81; family counselor Epsic. Social Svc., Bridgeport, Conn., 1981-82; pvt. practice Darien, Conn., 1980—. Mem. NRHCPCSW, NASW, Conn. Soc. Clin. Soc. Work. Home: 28 Driftway Ln Darien CT 06820-6130

WEST, MARY BETH, federal agency administrator; b. Wis., Nov. 20, 1944; BA with honors, U. Mich., 1966; JD, Stanford U., 1972. Bar: Calif. 1973, D.C. 1974. With Office Legal Adviser Dept. State, 1973-75, 82-88, 92-96; with Am. Indian Lawyer Tng. Program, 1975-78; with Office of Gen. Counsel NOAA, 1978-82; dep. asst. sec. of state for oceans, fisheries and space Bur. Oceans & Internat. Environ. and Sci. Affairs Dept.State, Washington, 1995—2003; prof., state dept. chair Indsl. Coll. of Armed Forces, 2003—. Vis. prof. U. N.Mex. Sch. Law, 1988-92. Contbr. articles to profl. jours. Bd. dirs., bd. visitors Stanford Law Sch., 1989-91; bd. dirs. Trinity Forum, 1989-92, N.Mex. Mediation Assn., 1991-92, Coun. on Ocean Law, 1992-96, Am. Soc. internat. Law Com. on State Responsibility, 1992-97; adv. bd. Univ. Va. Ctr., 2001-. Office: Indsl Coll of Armed Forcess 408 4th Ave SW Washington DC 20319-5062

WEST, MOLLY MARIE, music educator; b. Denver, May 14, 1963; d. Gerald D. and Margaret M. Malone; children: Robert T., Elizabeth M., David G. MusB in Edn., Benedictine Coll., 1985; MEd, Lesley Coll., 1994. Cert. Orff Schulwerk level I Colo. State U., 1995, Orff Shulwerk level II Colo. State U., 1998. Elem. music tchr. Jefferson County Pub. Schs., Golden, Colo., 1987—97, mid. sch. vocal music and drama tchr., 1997—. Choral dir. Evergreen (Colo.) Children's Choral, 1996—. Mem.: Am. Choral Directors Assn. (assoc.). Home: 12004 Bear Park Rd Conifer CO 80433 Office: West Jefferson Middle School 9449 S Barnes Ave Conifer CO 80433

WEST, NANCY LEE, music educator, performance artist, entertainer; b. Evansville, Ind., Dec. 5, 1929; d. Harold Addison and Helen Beatrice (Roland) Hill; m. Owen L. West, Aug. 2, 1952; children: Gail Ann, Janet Lee, Robert Owen. BFA, Wesleyan U., Ill., 1952. Pvt. practice, Gibson City, Ill., 1952-57, Urbana, Ill., 1957-59, Buckhannon, W.Va., 1959-68, Eureka, Ill., 1968—; music tchr. Elliott (Ill.) Elem. Sch., 1953-54; piano soloist various events. hotels, restaurants in W.Va. and Ill., 1953—; dance orch. leader various parties, clubs, benefits, Ill., 1985—; piano accompanist various musical prodns., performances in W.Va. and Ill., 1953—. Cello player Symphony Orch., Bloomington, Ill., 1950-52. Mem. adv. bd. Ctrl. Ill. Youth Symphony, Peoria, 1969-78; mem. women's bd. Eureka Coll. Recipient Purchase award Walnut Grove Fine Arts Assn., Eureka, 1978, Best of Show award, Clarksburg, W.Va., 1966, One Person Show award Volkwein Music, Pitts., 1967; winner Grand prize Salem Coll., W.Va., 1965. Mem. Am. Coll. Musicians, Music Tchrs. Nat. Assn., Am. Fedn. Musicians, AAUW, Peoria Area Music Tchrs. Assn. Mem. Christian Ch. Avocations: sewing, crafts, reading, dance. Home and Office: 810 N Main St Eureka IL 61530-9412

WEST, NATALIE ELSA, lawyer; b. Greenwich, Conn., Mar. 11, 1947; AB, Smith Coll., 1968; JD, U. Calif., Berkeley, 1973. Bar: Calif. 1974. Counsel Calif. Fair Polit. Practices Commn., Sacramento, 1975-79; city atty. City of Berkeley, Calif., 1980-85, City of Novato, Calif., 1985-92, City of Brentwood, Calif., 1994-99; gen. counsel Livermore-Amador Valley Water Mgmt. Agy., 1996—2001; shareholder McDonough, Holland & Allen, Oakland, Calif., 1991—. Lectr. law U. Calif., Berkeley, 2000-01. Pres. city attys. dept. League of Calif. Cities, 1986-87, bd. dirs., 1995-97. Mem. State Bar Calif., Alameda County Bar Assn. Office: McDonough Holland & Allen 9th Fl 1901 Harrison St Oakland CA 94612-3582

WEST, NETTIE J.R. music educator; b. Schoharie, N.Y., Oct. 12, 1925; d. Everett C. and Christina M. Maria (Youngs) Ruland; m. J. Russell Langwig, Sept. 11, 1948 (div. 1976); children: J. Russell, John Everett, Christina; m. Robert L. West, Oct. 8, 1983; stepchildren: Elizabeth Ann, Kathleen Suzanne, Laurel Marie. BS, BM cum laude, Skidmore Coll., 1947; MA, U. Buffalo, 1968; cert. Suzuki tchg., Sch. for Strings, N.Y.C., 1983, Ithaca Coll., 1978-79. Music instr. Suzuki Sounds Violin Sch., Lagrangeville, N.Y., 1984—; orch. tchr. Hyde Park (N.Y.) H.S., 1983-84; Suzuki violin tchr. The Music Box, Poughkeepsie, 1997-99, Hudson Valley Philharm. Music Sch., Poughkeepsie, 1979-80; sub. tchr. Arlington Sch., Wappingers Dist., 1976-80; violinist Woodstock (N.Y.) Chamber Orch., 1983—. Attendee internat. confs. Suzuki Method, Matsumoto, Japan, 1983, 89, 99, Alberta Canada, 1985, Berlin, Germany, 1987, Adelaide, Australia, 1991, Dublin, Ireland, 1995; instr. Dutchess C.C., 2003—. Mem. Religious Soc. Friends, Bulls-Head Oswego Meeting, 1980—, mem. worship group Green Haven Corr. Fac., 1980—; facilitator Alternatives to Violence Project, 1980—, coord. 1986-89; mem. Martha's Vineyard Hist. Assn. Mem. Suzuki Assn. Am., Inc., Music Educators Nat. Conf., N.Y. State Sch. Music Assn., Lagoon Pond Assn. Inc. of Martha's Vineyard. Avocations: swimming, skiing, bird watching, reading, attending concerts.

WEST, ROBERTA BERTHA, writer; b. Saline County, Mo, Sept. 7, 1904; d. Robert and Amanda Melvina (Driver) Baur; m. Harold Clinton West, Aug. 27, 1932; children: Arle Faith W. Lohof, Lydia Ann (Lyda) F H. Hyde, Danna Rose F H. Burns. AB, William Jewell Coll., 1928; AM, U. Mo., 1930. Cert. tchr., Mo., Mont. Elem. and secondary sch. tchr. Mo. and Mont. Sch., 1922-47; supt. sch. Hogeland Sch., Mont., 1947-48, 55; prof. fgn. lang. Will Mayfield Coll., Marble Hill, Mo., 1930; columnist Quad County Star, Viburnum, Mo., 1982—; writer and rschr. ch. history, 1964-91. Cons. hist. com. Yellowstone Conf. Meth. Ch., 1971-84; compiler Mont. list of Meth. Mins. 1784-1984. Author: Northern Montana Methodist History, 3 vols., 1974, Faith, Hope and Love in the West, 1971; editor: Brother Van by Those Who Knew Him, 1975, reprinted, 1989,; also contbr. articles. Recipient 1st John M. Templeton prize, 1959, Wedgwood Jasper Plate 70th Anniversary of Class of 1927 Wm. Jewell Coll., 1997. Mem. Alpha Zeta Pi. Democrat. Achievements include first to At age 98, still writing weekly for the Star. Avocation: crocheting. Home: PO Box 583 Viburnum MO 65566-0583 Office: Quad County Star Viburnum MO 65566

WEST, SUSAN D. lawyer; b. Jackson, Miss., July 17, 1952; d. William Lloyd Smith, Jr. and Betty Jo Connolly; m. Thomas Mellen West, II, Feb. 26, 1994. BS in Anthropology, U. Tulsa, 1978, JD, 1981. Pvt. practice, Tulsa, 1981—84; title examiner, asst. counsel Hexter Fair Title Co., Dallas, 1984—89; asst. counsel Chgo. Title Ins. Co., Dallas, 1989—99; comml. underwriting counsel Ticor Title Co., Dallas, 1999—2000, Commerce Title Co., Dallas, 2000—. Mem.: Dallas Bar Assn., Okla. Bar Assn., Tex. Bar Assn. Home: 6831 E Grand Ave Dallas TX 75223 Office: Commerce Title Co 4th Fl 2728 N Harwood Dallas TX 75201

WEST, SYNTHA JANE TRAUGHBER, mental health services professional; b. Gladewater, Tex., Oct. 22, 1938; d. Jimmy J. and Virginia Lavon (Wood) Traughber; m. Royce Glen West; children: Rock David, Royal Jim. BA, Baylor U., 1961; MEd, Tex. A&M U. Commerce, 1965, PhD, 1971. Lic. profl. counselor, marriage and family therapist, cert. counselor, expert in traumatic stress and bereavement trauma. Adj. asst. prof. East Tex. State U., Commerce, 1975—76; lead H.S. counselor Longview (Tex.) Ind. Sch. Dist., 1975—77; head H.S. counselor Marshall (Tex.) Ind. Sch. Dist., 1977—80; counselor Tyler Jr. Coll., Tex., 1992; Mid. and H.S. counselor Winona (Tex.) Ind. Sch. Dist., 1980—97; mental health therapist Walker & Assocs., Tyler, 1997—98, Andrews Ctr., Tyler, 1998—99. Dir. guidance Brewer H.S., White Settlement, Tex., 1971—75, Kerens (Tex.) Ind. Sch. Dist., Kerens, 1966—69, Rains Ind. Schs. Dist., Emory, Tex., 1966; spkr. in field. Author: Today's Dreams, Tomorrow's Realities, 2001, (poetry) Poetry Gems 2000, 2001, America at the Millennium, 2000. Pianist, asst. First Bapt. Ch., Owentown, Tex., 2000—; bd. dirs. Gladewater (Tex.) Former Students, 1997—. Nominee Tex. Women's Hall of Fame, 1999, 2000; named Ms. Congeniality, Ms. Tex. Sr. Pageant, 2000, Ms. Tex. Sr., 2001. Mem.: Tex. Ret. Sch. Pers., Piney Woods Counseling Assn., Tex. Counseling Assn., Sheriff's Assn. Tex. Avocations: dancing, twirling batons, patriotic flag routine, piano. Home: 12446 Chapman Rd Tyler TX 75708-3210

WESTBERG, POLLY PEMBROOKE, art educator; b. New Orleans, Oct. 1, 1951; d. William Baxter Hutto and Lillian Fay Hutto-Black; m. David Ray Westberg, 1973 (div. 1982); 1 child, Leif Eric. BS in Edn., U. Ala., 1979. Tchr. Fultondale High Sch., Ala., 1981—83, Gresham Jr. High Sch., Hoover, 1983—88, Bragg Jr. High Sch., Gardendale, 1989—93, Gardendale High Sch., 1994—99, Leeds High Sch., Leeds, 2000—03. Dir. after sch. art program City Ctr. Art, Birmingham, Ala., 1992—94; dir., owner ARt Connexion, 1995—97. Advisor Gardendale Arts Coun., 1998. Mem.: Ala. Art Casting, Birmingham Art Assn. (bd. dirs., v.p. 1999—2001), Ala. Edn. Assn. Methodist. Avocations: art, painting, drawing, sculpting. Home: 3294-A Warringwood Dr Birmingham AL 35216 Office: Leeds High Sch 602 Whitmore St Leeds AL 35094 E-mail: pollywestberg@earthlink.net.

WESTBIE, BARBARA JANE, retired graphics designer; b. Little Rock, Nov. 3, 1946; d. Freeman Bryant Davis and Virginia Lee Thompson; children: Suzanne Michelle, Derrek Christopher. Grad. in graphic design, U. Calif., Davis, 1992; student, Miramar Coll., San Diego, 1976, Chabot Coll., Hayward, Calif., 1974. Exec. dir. Ambiance, Danville, Calif., 1980—84; dir. Lake Gallery, Tahoe City, Calif., 1985—87; art cons. Reed Gallery, Tahoe City, 1988—90; ret., 1990. Art dir., creative cons. Associated Students Re-Entry Ctr. Chico State U., Calif., 2001—03. Inventor Fat Fuzzy/Iknonotrisc Family, 1981, artist (poster/logo) Project Mana Fund-raising Event, 1988, (brochure/media kit) Chocolate Festival, 1989. Vol. crisis intervention counselor CIS/Tahoe Women's Svcs., Kings Beach, 1989—91; lead counselor Emotions Anonymous 12-Step Program, North Lake Tahoe Area, 1990—93; vol. pk. svc. Washoe Lake State Pk., Carson City, Nev., 1993—94; coord. new vols. ARC, Chico, 2000—01, vol. Butte County, 2000—, Emergency Animal Rescue Svcs., 2002—. Named Vol. of Yr., Tahoe Women's Svcs., 1989; recipient Disting. Svc. award, CIS/Tahoe Women's Svcs., 1989—90. Mem.: Smithsonian Instn. (assoc.). Protestant. Avocations: skiing, reading, gardening, writing, painting.

WESTBROOK, DEBORAH KAY, music educator; b. Kingwood, W.Va., July 15, 1961; d. Kenneth W. and Wilma S. Poling; m. Richard Burton Westbrook, Aug. 7, 1982. BA Music Edn., Fairmont State Coll., 1984. Band dir. Rowlesburg/Aurora Sch. Dist., W.Va.; band, choir dir. West Preston High Sch., Masontown, 1985—91, Preston High Sch., Kingwood. Dir. Valley Ministeral Assn. Cantata, Masontown, 1991—; adj. prof. Fairmont State U., 2003—. Musician: Take Note-ice. Ch. musician Cath. Ch. Preston County, Kingwood, 1996—. Mem.: NEA, Band Master Assn., W.Va. Music Educators Assn., Delta Kappa Gamma. Roman Catholic. Avocation: reading.

WESTBROOK, REBECCA VOLLMER, secondary school educator; b. Hagerstown, Md., Jan. 12, 1943; d. Harry Frederick and Margaret Caldwell (Jack) Vollmer; m. John William Westbrook Jr., Apr. 4, 1972; children: Margaret Rebecca, John Willliam III. BA in French and Spanish cum laude, Thiel Coll., 1964; MAT in French and Spanish, Emory U., 1965; cert. in French studies, Inst. Am. U., Aiv-en-Provence, France, 1963. Cert. tchr. Ga., 1966, Fla., 1985. Tchr. French and Spanish Henry Grady H.S., Atlanta, 1966—70, Northside H.S., Atlanta, 1970—76, Forest H.S., Ocala, Fla., 1985—; instr. French and Spanish Jefferson C.C., Louisville, 1980—82. Cons. Itinerant Tutors, Louisville, 1983—84. Active Girl Scouts Am.; mem. Ocala Women's Club, 1989—92. Mem.: NEA, Alpha Delta Kappa, Phi Sigma Iota. Avocations: travel, antiques, reading. Home: 2630 SE 14th St Ocala FL 34471 Office: Forest HS 1614 Fort King St Ocala FL 34471

WESTCOTT, JOAN CLARK, poet; b. Union City, Pa., Feb. 8, 1919; d. William Clyde and Marjorie (Clark) W. BA, Vassar Coll., 1941; grad., Katherine Gibbs Sec. Sch., Boston, 1942. Clk. Boston Port Embarkation, 1942—43; sec. Harvard U., Cambridge, Mass., 1943-45, Players Theater, Sarasota, Fla., 1947-49, AEC, UCLA, 1950-52; sec. to John Loveton L.A., 1953-54; sec. to J. West Arch., Sarasota, 1955-60. Author: (poetry) Fragments of Stained Glass, 1967, More Fragments of Stained Glass, 1968, Bits of Chaff, 1970, Taffeta and Lace, 1976, Ribbon of Light, 1980, Fragments of Stained Glass III, 1988, Homeward Bound, 1997. Poetry books plus papers in Rare Books and Spl. Collections Libr., U. Fla., Gainesville. Mem. Planetary Soc., Habitat Nat. Wildlife Fedn., Women in the Arts, Union of Concerned Scientists. Avocations: gardening, reading, needlepoint, working on autobiography from diaries. Home: 4100 E Fletcher Ave Tampa FL 33613-4863

WESTEBBE, BARBARA LIEBST, writer, sculptor; b. Newton, Kans., Dec. 8, 1925; d. Harold Charles and Marie Josiphine (Whitcomb) Liebst; m. Richard Manning Westebbe, Dec. 18, 1947; children: Mark, Shelly, Bruce, Susy. Student, Kans. State Tchrs. Coll., 1945; grad., Utrecht (Holland) U., 1954; postgrad., George Washington U., 1955, 56, 57. Tchr. 8th grade Deerhead Sch., Medicine Lodge, Kans., 1945; illustrator, engr. Culver Aircraft Corp., Wichita, Kans., 1946; mem. Sen. Arthur Capper staff U.S. Senate, Washington, 1946-47; asst. to chmn. Nat. Assn. Motor Bus Operators, Washington, 1947-48; office mgr. to Dr. R. McFarland Human Engrng. Dept. Sch. Pub. Health, Harvard U., Cambridge, Mass., 1949-51; prin. Am. H.S., Den Haag, Holland, 1953-54; editor of Den Haag transls. of Den Ramp series Am. Acad. Scis., Den Haag, Holland, 1954-56; writer weekly column Athens (Greece) Post Newspaper, 1961-65; founder, dir. Life Conservation, Inc., Fredricksburg, Va., 1973—. Exhibited in group exhbns. at Pierce Coll., Athens, 1966; editor (poems under pseudonym Colleen Cody) Fed. Poet, 1967-70; author poems; writer quar. column Downs Syndrome Mag., 1990-94. Bd. dirs. Nat. Womens Party, 1946-66; mem. archtl. review bd. Stafford County Svcs., Falmouth, Va., 1989—; mem. Fredricksburg Ctr. Creative Arts, 1990—. Recipient Citizen of Yr. award Am. Legion. Mem. Nat. Edn. Soc., Alpha Zigma Tau. Avocations: gardening, teaching special artists, pets, sculpting. Home and Office: 807 Holly Corner Rd Fredericksburg VA 22406-5360

WESTERBERG, MARY L. retired secondary school educator; b. Ironwood, Mich., Nov. 17, 1942; d. Rudolph Henry and Gertrude Ethel (Saari) W. BA, Mich. State U., 1964, MA in Teaching, 1969; postgrad., U. Minn., Duluth, U. N.H. Cert. life English, history and French tchr., Minn. Tchr. Alpena (Mich.) High Sch.; tchr. English and French, Anoka (Minn.) Sr. High Sch., also chmn. Bldg. Leadership Team; ret. Organizer, co-developer workshops for parents; mem. com. on religion in pub. schs. Bd. dirs., rec. sec., program com. Finn Fest '02 Minn. Alumni disting. scholar. Mem. NEA (del. rep. assembly), Nat. Coun. Tchrs. English, Mich. Coun. Tchrs. English (legis. liaison com., censorship com., resolutions chmn., rep. to Minn. Coalition against Censorship), Minn. Edn. Assn. (IPD state coun., exec. bd., chmn. profl. growth, conf. presenter, Univ. IPD award), AHEA (v.p., chmn. settlement task force, chmn. IPD), Midwestern River Project (cons., tchr., curriculum developer), Delta Kappa Gamma (local pres., v.p.).

WESTERHAUS, CATHERINE K. social worker; b. Corydon, Ind., Oct. 13, 1910; d. Anthony Joseph and Permelia Ann (Mathes) Kannapel; m. George Henry Westerhaus, Apr. 15, 1950. BEd in Music, Kans. U., 1934; MSW, Loyola U., Chgo., 1949. Cert. Acad. Cert. Social Workers. Clin. social worker Friendly Acres Home of Aged, Newton, Kans.; county welfare dir., state adult svcs. supr. Newton-Harvey County, State of Kans.; vol. cert. social worker Newton. Project dir.: Memories of War Years, 1995, The War Years Including Veterans of Harvey County, Kansas, 1995; contbr. articles to profl. jours. Vol. to veterans, home-bound and disabled people, residents in nursing homes, patients in hospitals. With USNR, 1945-46. Named Kans. Social Worker of Yr., 1975, Kans. 5th Dist. Legionnaire of Yr., 1998. Mem. NASW (cert.), Kans. Soc. Cert. Social Work, Am. Legion (comdr. Wayne G. Austin post 1981-82, del Nat. Conv. 1997, Legionnaire of Yr. Dept. Kans. 1998). Home: 20215 SE 30th Ave Pratt KS 67124-8371

WESTERLUND, FREZIL DANIEL-ELLIS, pastor; b. Seneca, SC, Jan. 3, 1947; d. Helan Maclain and Mary Frezil (Daniel) Ellis; m. Douglas Webb Westerlund, May 27, 1980; children: Ragin Maclain, Felicia Jean. BA art history, U. of Ark., Little Rock, Ark., 1975—81; MA counseling, Luth. Theol. So. Sem., Columbia, SC, 1984—86, MDiv, 1986—88. Cert. Ordained Min. Evang. Luth. Ch. in Am., 1988. Pastor East and West St. Olaf churches, Byron, Minn., 1992—, St. Johns Ridgley, Scribner, Nebr., 1988—92. Chaplain, lt. col. Civil Air Patrol aux USAF, St. Paul, 1991—. Decorated Comdr. Commendations Neb. Wing, No. Ctrl. Region Civil Air Patrol, Gen. E. W. Rawings award for Exceptional Svc. Air Force Assn., Comdr. Commendations Minn. Wing, Civil Air Patrol, Meritorious Svc. award No. Ctrl. Region Civil Air Patrol. R-Consevative. Luth. Avocations: Am. Indian, dogs, painting, travel. Office: East and West Staint Olaf Lutheran Churc 6200 County Road #3 South West Byron MN 55920 Personal E-mail: dan-web-west@msn.com.

WESTERMAN, LIANE MARIE, research scientist executive; b. Long Branch, NJ, June 20, 1949; d. Charles Wilson and Edith Doris (Johnson) Case; m. S. Thomas Westerman; children: David Aaron, Charles Paul. BA in Psychology, Monmouth U., West Long Branch, N.J., 1972; MA in Teaching, Coll. of N.J., 1979. Cert. tchr. of handicapped, N.J. Tchr. spl. edn., dir. afternoon program S.E.A.R.C.H., Ocean, N.J., 1972-74; tchr. spl. edn. Jackson (N.J.) Twp. Sch. System, 1974-79; exec. dir. Otologic Edn., Inc., Shrewsbury, N.J., 1980-88; dir. clin. rsch. Nat. Patent Analytical Systems, Inc., Roslyn Heights, N.Y., 1983-86, v.p. rsch., 1986-88; pres. Westerman Rsch. Assocs., Inc., Shrewsbury, N.J., 1988—. Participant numerous convs., profl. organs. and spl. interest groups, U.S.A., Israel and The Netherlands, 1974—; software devel. expert to knowledge engr. for Visual Perceptual System, 1984—; v.p. Otologic Edn., Inc., Shrewsbury, 1988—. Co-contbr. articles and chpts. to profl. publs.; U.S. and Can. patentee computer-aided drug-abuse detection. Fundraiser Am. Heart Assn., 1991; active MADD; activist Nat. Audubon Soc. Mem. Am. Acad. Otolaryngology, Head and Neck Surgery (assoc.), Internat. Regulatory Affairs Profls. Soc., Nat. Graphic Soc., Assn. Clin. Pharmacologists, Regulatory Affairs Profls. Soc., Monmouth County Assn. Children with Learning Disabilities, Psi Chi, Sigma Xi. Avocations: travel, classical music, creative writing. Office: Westerman Rsch Assocs Inc 170 Ave at the Common Ste 6 Shrewsbury NJ 07702-4003

WESTERMANN-CICIO, MARY LOUISE, academic administrator, library studies educator; b. N.Y.C., Mar. 11, 1953; d. A. Louis and Anne U. (Skelly) Morse; m. Edward L. Cicio, June 20, 1998. BS in Biology, L.I. U., 1975, MS in Libr. Sci., 1976, MPA in Health Care Adminstrn., 1986; MA in History, SUNY, Stony Brook, 1992, PhD, 2001. Con. med. libr. Nassau-Suffolk Health Systems Agy., Melville, N.Y., 1976-77; dir. John N. Shell Libr. Nassau Acad. Medicine, Garden City, NY, 1977—88; instr. L.I. U., Greenvale, N.Y., 1977-88, adj. prof., 1983-88; assoc. prof. Palmer Grad. Libr. Sch., 1988-95, asst. dean, 1995—. Trustee L.I. Libr. Resources Coun., 1986-91; mem. adv. bd. Sr. Connections Program, Adelphi U., 1987-92; bd. dirs. Nassau County coun. Girl Scouts, 2002—. Recipient E. Hugh Behymer award L.I. U., 1976, Disting. Alumni award Palmer Sch. L.I. U., 1993, Jackson Turner Maid award SUNY at Stony Brook, 1993. Mem. ALA, Med. Libr. Assn. (sec. med. socs. sect. 1981-82, instr. continuing edn. 1982, chmn. med. soc. sect. 1986-87; cert. health scis. librianship, Murry E. Gottlieb award 1998), Acad. Health Info. Professions, Spl. Librs. Assn. (sec. L.I. chpt. 1978-80, bd. dirs. 1982-84, pres. elect 1988, pres. 1989-90), Cath. Libr. Assn. (instr. workshop, Libr. of Yr. award 1992), Suffolk-Nassau on-Line Retrievers (chmn. 1981), Med. and Sci. Librs. of L.I. (pres. 1980-81), Nassau County Libr. Assn. (chmn. health svcs. com. 1978-81, 83-93, bd. dirs. 1990-92), Beta Beta Beta, Beta Phi Mu (bd. dirs. Beta Mu chpt. 1987-89, Golden Anniversary award 1999), Pi Alpha Alpha. Office: LI Univ CW Post Campus Palmer Sch Libr and Info Scis Greenvale NY 11548 E-mail: westerma@liu.edu.

WESTFIELD, MARGARET ANN HOYERT, architect; b. Cheverly, Md., July 31, 1959; d. Robert Scott and Frances Keefauver Hoyert; m. Michael Matthew Westfield, Sept. 3, 1983; children: Marina Michelle, Emily Elizabeth. BArch, U. Md., 1982; MA Preservation Studies, Boston U., 1985. Registered Pa., 1986, N.J., 1988. Ptnr. Westfield Architects & Preservation Cons., Haddon Heights, NJ, 1988—; historic architect State of N.J., Trenton, 1998—2000. Adj. lectr. Drew U., Madison, NJ, 1999—; adj. prof. Burlington County Coll., Pemberton, 2000—. Mem.: Haddon Heights Hist. Soc. (pres. 1999—2001), Assn. Preservation Tech. (chair Delaware Valley chpt. 1996—2000), Preservation N.J. (dir. 2001). Office: Westfield Architects 425 White Horse Pike Haddon Heights NJ 08035-1706

WESTHEIMER, RUTH SIEGEL (KAROLA WESTHEIMER), psychologist, television personality; b. Frankfurt, Fed. Republic Germany; came to U.S., 1956; m. Manfred Westheimer; children: Miriam, Joel. Grad. psychology, U. Paris Sorbonne; Master's degree, New Sch. for Social Research, N.Y.C., 1959; EdD, Columbia U., 1970. Research asst. Columbia U. Sch. Pub. Health, N.Y.C., 1967-70; assoc. prof. Lehman Coll., Bronx, N.Y., 1970-77; with Bklyn. Coll., West Point Milit. Acad.; counsellor, radio talk show hostess Sexually Speaking Sta. WYNY-FM, N.Y.C., 1980-90; hostess TV series Good Sex, Dr. Ruth Show, Ask Dr. Ruth, 1987-92; pvt. practice, 1976—. Adj. assoc. prof. NYU; leader seminars for residents and interns in pediats. on adolescent sexuality Brookdale Hosp. Author: Dr. Ruth's Guide to Good Sex, 1983, First Love: A Young People's Guide to Sexual Information, 1985, Dr. Ruth's Guide for Married Lovers, 1986, (autobiography) All In a Lifetime, 1987, Sex and Morality: Who is Teaching Out Sex Standards?, 1988, Dr. Ruth's Guide to Erotic and Sensuous Pleasures, 1991, Dr. Ruth's Guide to Safer Sex, 1992, Dr. Ruth Talks to Kids, 1993, The Art of Arousal, 1993, Dr. Ruth's Encyclopedia of Sex, 1994, Heavenly Sex, 1995, Sex for Dummies, 1995, The Value of Family, 1996; co-author: (with Steven Kaplan) Surviving Salvation; contbr. articles to mags.; appeared in film A Woman or Two, 1986; appeared on TV show Quantum Leap, 1993, Play Boy Making Love Series (video), 1996, All New Dr. Ruth Show (nominated 5 times by Ace awards, Ace award for excellence in cable TV, 1988), What's Up, Dr. Ruth (gold medal Internat. Film and TV Festival for excellence in ednl. TV), You're on the Air with Dr. Ruth, Never Too Late, 1992—, Dr. Ruth's House, (calendar) Dr. Ruth's Good Sex Night-to-Night Calendar, 1993, 94, (boardgame) Dr. Ruth's Game of Good Sex; exec. prodr. documentary on Ethiopian Jews Surviving Salvation, 1991; columnist Ask Dr. Ruth. Pres. YMHA, Washington Heights. Recipient Mother of Yr. award Nat. Mother's Day Com., Liberty medal City of N.Y. Fellow N.Y. Acad. Medicine. Office: Pierre A Lehu Comms Connection 145 W 45th St Ste 1009 New York NY 10036-4008

WESTMAN, JUDITH ANN, clinical geneticist; b. Columbus, Ohio, Nov. 7, 1957; d. Paul Marshall and Anna Marie (Stahly) Whetstone; m. David Arthur Westman, Apr. 12, 1980; children: Matthew, Joel, Rachel, Deborah. BA, Ohio No. U., 1978; MD, Ohio State U., 1981, MS, 1987. Diplomate Am. Bd. Pediatrics, Am. Bd. Med. Genetics. Resident in pediatrics Children's Hosp. Ohio State U., Columbus, 1981-84, chief resident, 1984-85, fellow clin. genetics, 1985-87, clin. asst. prof., 1987-95, clin. assoc. prof., 1995—, assoc. dean admissions and student affairs, 1996-99, assoc. dean student and med. edn., 1999—. Chair admissions com. Ohio State U. Coll. Medicine, 1990-96. Contbr. articles to profl. jours. Mem. adv. bd. Coll. Arts and Scis., Ohio No. U., Ada, 1988-97, trustee, 1997—; trustee Malone Coll., Canton, Ohio, 1988-94. Grantee FDA, 1987, NCI, 2001. Fellow Am. Acad. Pediatrics, Am. Soc. Human Genetics. Republican. Mem. Ch. of God (Anderson). Avocations: music, church activities. Office: 260 Meiling Hall 370 W 9th Ave Columbus OH 43210-1238

WESTMORELAND, BARBARA FENN, neurologist, electroencephalographer, educator; b. 1940; BS in Chemistry, Mary Washington Coll., 1961; MD, U. Va., 1965. Diplomate in neurology and clin. neurophysiology Am. Bd. Psychiatry and Neurology. Intern Vanderbilt Hosp., Nashville, 1965-66; resident in neurology U. Va. Hosp., Charlottesville, 1966-70; fellow in electroencephalography Mayo Clinic, Rochester, Minn., 1970-71, assoc. cons. neurology, 1971-73; asst. prof. neurology Mayo Med. Sch., Rochester, 1973-78, assoc. prof., 1978-85, prof., 1985—. Vice chair exam. com. cert. clin. neurophysiology Am. Bd. Psychiatry and Neurology, 1998—2003, chair exam. com. cert. clin. neurophysiology, 2003—. Co-author: Medical Neurosciences, 1978, rev. edit., 1986, first author 3d edit., 1994. Mem.: Mayo History Medicine Soc. (pres. 1990—91), Am. Acad. Neurology (chair sect. clin. neurophysiology 2000—02, A.B. Baker award for lifetime achievement in edn. 2002), Ctrl. Assn. [illegible] treas. 1976—78, pres. 1979—80, chair neurology resident in-svc. tng. exam 1994—99), Am. EEG Soc. (sec. 1985—87, pres. 1991—92), Am. Epilepsy Soc. (treas. 1978—80, pres. 1987—88), Sigma Xi (pres. chpt. 1987—88).

WESTON, DAWN THOMPSON, artist, researcher; b. Joliet, Ill., Apr. 15, 1919; d. Cyril C. and Vivian Grace Thompson; m. Arthur Walter Weston, Sept. 10, 1940; children: Roger Lance, Randall Kent, Cynthia Brooke. Student (scholar), Penn Hall Jr. Coll., Chambersburg, Pa., 1937—38; BS, Northwestern U., 1942, postgrad. in reading and speech pathology, 1960—61, MA in Ednl. Adminstrn., 1970; postgrad., U. Ill., 1964; student, Art Inst. Chgo., 1954, Pestalozzi-Froebel, Chgo., 1955, Phila. Inst. for Achievement Human Potential, 1963. Cert. tchr./adminstr. Ill. Therapist USN Hosp., Gt. Lakes, Ill., 1940—45; tchr. Holy Child and Waukegan (Ill.) High Schs., 1946—54, Lake Forest H.S., 1966—69; elem. and jr. high art dir. Lake Bluff (Ill.) Schs., 1954—58; pioneer ednl. dir. Grove Sch. for Brain-Injured, Lake Forest, 1958—66, now life mem., treas. corp., chmn. bd., 1982—. Ind. rschr., lectr. on shifting visual imagery due to trauma, 1982—99; rschr. on uneven growth, 1969—. One-woman shows include Evanston Woman's Club, Northwestern U., Deerpath Gallery, Lake Forest, The Hein Co., Waukegan, numerous group shows, 1939—76, Represented in permanent collections ARC, Victory Meml. Hosp., Waukegan, Sierra Assocs., Chgo., numerous pvt. collections U.S., Can., Japan, Africa, works include:, Poisonous Plants of Midwest set of etchings for Country Gentleman mag., 1956, Clouds mural, 1981. Mem. 1st found. bd. for srs. in Lake Forest, Ill., 1999; chair Grove Sch. Inc., 1996—; chmn. July 4th parade 100th Anniversary Child-Serve Greater Chgo., 1994; mem. Presdl. Gold Chain, Trinity Coll., 1979; mem. alumni bd. leadership com. Northwestern U., 2003; del. ann. conf. Meth. Ch., 1982—90; lay leader Grace United Meth. Ch., Lake Bluff, 1990—93. Named Citizen of Yr., Grove Sch., 1978, rm. at sch. named in her honor, 1982. Mem.: Deerpath Art League (bd. dirs.), Penn Hall Alumni Assn. (Chgo. pres. 1938—40), Art Inst. Chgo., Pi Lambda Theta. Home and Office: 349 E Hilldale Pl Lake Forest IL 60045-3031

WESTON, FRANCINE EVANS, secondary school educator; b. Mt. Vernon, N.Y., Oct. 8, 1946; d. John Joseph and Frances (Fantino) Pisaniello. BA, Hunter Coll., 1968; MA, Lehman Coll., 1973; cert., Am. Acad. Dramatic Arts, N.Y.C., 1976; PhD, NYU, 1991. Cert. elem., secondary tchr., N.Y. Tchr. Yonkers (N.Y.) Bd. Edn., 1968—; aquatic dir. Woodlane Day Camp, Irvington-on-Hudson, N.Y., 1967-70, Yonkers Jewish Community Ctr., 1971-75. Creative drama tchr. John Burroughs Jr. H.S., Yonkers, 1971-77; stage lighting designer Iona Summer Theatre Festival, New Rochelle, N.Y., 1980-81, Yonkers Male Glee Club, 1981-89, Roosevelt H.S., 1980-97; freelance, 1998—; rsch. specialist Scholarship Locating Svc., 1992-94, Yonkers Civil Def. Police Aux., 1994—; master electrician NYU Summer Mus. Theatre, 1979-80; appointed program developer for Cadet Acad. of Police & Fire Scis., Pub. Safety Magnet, Roosevelt H.S., 2001. Actress in numerous cmty. theater plays including A Touch of the Poet, 1979; dir. stage prodns. including I Remember Mama, 1973, The Man Who Came to Dinner, 1975; author: A Descriptive Comparison of Computerized Stage Lighting Memory Systems With Non-Computerized Systems, 1991, (short stories) A Hat for Louise, 1984, Old Memories: Beautiful and Otherwise, 1984; lit. editor: (story and poetry collection) Beautifully Old, 1984; editor: Command Post Dispatch quar., 1997—. Mem. Yonkers Civil Def. Police Aux., 1994—, adminstrv. asst. to commanding officer, 1996—, lt., capt. adminstrn., 2002—; steering com. chairperson Roosevelt H.S.-Middle States Assn. of Schs. and Colls. Self-Evaluation, 1985—88. Named Tchr. of Excellence, N.Y. State English Coun., 1990, 95, 2000; recipient Monetary award for Teaching Excellence, Carter-Wallace Products, 1992; named to Arrid Tchrs. Honor Roll, 1992. Republican. Roman Catholic. Avocations: swimming, animal related activities, anything theatrical. Office: Roosevelt High Sch Tuckahoe Rd Yonkers NY 10710

WESTON, JANE SARA, plastic surgeon, educator; b. Oceanside, N.Y., May 21, 1952; m. Jan K. Horn; children: Jonathan Spencer Horn, Jennifer Danielle Horn. MD, Stanford U., 1975-79. Diplomate Am. Bd. Plastic Surgery. Resident gen. surgery Sch. Medicine Stanford (Calif.) U., 1979-82, resident plastic surgery Sch. Medicine, 1982-83; fellow craniofacial surgery Hopital des Enfants Malades, Paris, 1983-84; plastic surgeon Kaiser Permanente Med. Group, San Jose, Calif., 1985-90; pvt. practice Palo Alto, Calif., 1990—. Mem. faculty Stanford U. Med. Sch., 1994-95. Active Leadership Palo Alto, 1993. Fellow ACS; mem. Am. Soc. Plastic and Reconstructive Surgeons (chair women plastic surgeons com. 1993-96, chair ethics com. 1998-99). Avocation: harp. Office: Ste 201 3351 El Camino Real Atherton CA 94027-3802

WESTON, JOAN SPENCER, editorial and production director, communications executive; b. Barton, Vt., Aug. 11, 1943; d. Rolfe Weston and Dorothy Lena (Spencer) Schoppe. BA magna cum laude, U. Mass., 1965. Tchr. high sch. Gorham (Maine) Schs., 1965-66; tchr. Sherwood Hall Sch., Mansfield, Eng., 1966-67; tchr. middle sch. Meden Sch., Warsop, Eng., 1967-68; dept. head high sch. Goffstown (N.H.) Schs., 1968-82; dir. circulation T.H.E. Jour., Acton, Mass., 1982-83; prodn. mgr. The Robb Report, Acton, 1983-87, prodn. dir., 1988; prodn. cons. Spencer Weston Assocs., Portland, Maine, 1988-93; prodn. dir. New Age Pub. Inc., Watertown, Mass., 1993-96; dir. editl. and prodn. Pvt. Colls. and Univs., Inc., Westford, Mass., 1996—. Mem. Boston Prodn. Mgrs. Group (charter), Phi Beta Kappa. Avocations: travel, music, psychology, antiques. Office: Pvt Colls and Univs 2 LAN Dr Ste 100 Westford MA 01886-3547 E-mail: jsweston@privatecolleges.com.

WESTON, MICHELE J. apparel executive, consultant; b. Detroit, Mich., Oct. 5, 1961; d. Robert E. and Susan M. Weinstock. BA, Western Mich. U., 1979—85; Cert. Degree in Performance, Drama Studio in London, 1985—86; Cert. Degree, NY U. Sch. of Continuing Edn., 1988—90. Co-owner Selling Style Inc., NYC, 2002—; media style expert MJW Style Media, NYC, 2000—03; fashion & style dir. Mode Mag./Modestyle.com, NYC, 1996—2000; sr. fashion editor Mademoiselle Mag., CondeNast Publications, NYC, 1989—91. Adv. bd. mem. Dress for Success NY, 1997—2003. Author: (book) Learning Curves: Living Your Life in Full & With Style. Ednl. role model, spkr. PENCIL, NYC, 1996—2003. Recipient Outstanding Alumni award, Western Mich. U., Coll. of Fine Arts, 2003, Woman of Size award, PLUS USA Women, 2001, Costume Design Asst. scholarship, Western Mich. U., 1982, 1985; Mem. of Intern Second Acting Co., Milw. Repertory Theatre, WI, 1983—84, Costume Design Asst. scholarship, Western Mich. U., 1980, 1981. D-Liberal. Jewish. Achievements include 1st inducted Outstanding Alumni nominated for the WMU School of Fine Arts 2001. Avocations: travel, cooking, bicycling, singing. Office: MJWStyle Media/Selling Style Inc 320 East 52nd St Ste E3 New York NY 10022 E-mail: www.sellingstyle.com.

WESTON, PEGGY HUTSON, artist, art educator; d. Lucius Arthur and Jean Elizabeth (Howell) Hutson; m. Charles Philip Weston, Sept. 29, 1973; children: Charles Matthew, Gregory Philip, Lindsey Greer. Student, U. N.C., Greensboro, 1968—71; BA in Art Edn., U. N.C., Charlotte, 1972. Cert. art tchr. grades K-12 N.C., non-profit mgmt. Duke U. Illustrator Duke Power Co., Charlotte, 1973—74; art tchr. West Mecklenburg H.S., Charlotte, 1974—77; coord. Scholastic Art, Charlotte, 1985—95; art instr. Queens U. Continuing Edn., Charlotte, 1989—96; curator corp. collection Baucom, Claytor, Benton, P.A., Charlotte, 1994—2003; art tchr. Providence H.S., Charlotte, 1996—2001; artist, CEO Artists' Atelier Carolina, Charlotte, 2000—. Artist, instr. Artists Tng. Inst., Charlotte, 1993—94; fine arts adv. team Charlotte Country Day Sch., 2002; coord., content specialist ArtsTeach, Charlotte, 2002—. Represented in permanent collections McColl Ctr., AAA Carolina, Charlotte, Bowater Co., S.C., Celanese Corp., Charlotte/Douglas Internat. Airport, Duke U., 1st Union Internat. Banking Corp., NY, Interstate Securities, Wachovia, Winston-Salem, N.C., exhibitions include Mint Mus. Art, 2003, Queens U., 2003, McColl Ctr. Visual Arts, Charlotte, 2002, Meredith Coll., Raleigh, N.C., 2002, Florence Mus. Art, S.C., 2001, Carillon Bldg., Charlotte, 2001, The Park Hotel, 2001, numerous others. Landscape designer Harding Univ. H.S., Charlotte, 1992; mem. pub. art com. Friends of Fourth Ward, Charlotte, 2002; bd. mem. Charlotte Art League, Inc., 1981—99. Recipient Outstanding Tchr. award, Scholastic Art Awards, Charlotte, 1999; Arts in Edn. grantee, Arts and Sci. Coun., Charlotte, 1994, 1995, 1996. Mem.: McColl Ctr. for Visual Art (artists' steering com. 2003). Avocation: gardening.

WESTON, PRISCILLA ATWOOD, library director; b. May 6, 1925; BA, U. N.H., 1947, cert. in libr. techniques, 1974. Libr. dir. Mansfield Libr., Temple, N.H., 1964—. Co-author: A History of Temple, N.H. 1768-1976; co-author: (with Wilton, Temple, and Lyndeborough) Images of America. Curator Temple Hist. Soc., 1964—; mem., sec. Temple Conservation Commn., 1978-88; mem. Temple Sch. Bd., 1952-55, ch. historian; dir. Hillsboro County Farm Bur., 1964-65. Mem. Greenville Woman's Club, Miller Grange (master 1964-65). Avocations: reading, gardening, genealogy, choir. Office: Mansfield Libr PO Box 210 Temple NH 03084-0210

WESTON, REBECCA LYNN, forensic educator; b. Waren, Pa., Aug. 22, 1949; BS in Criminology, 1995. Sgt. Union Co. prosecutor office, Elizabeth, NJ, 1981—2000; instr. Warren Co. Cmty. Coll., Washington, NJ, 1996—.

WESTOVER, DIANA KAY, interior designer, recruitment company executive; b. Clovis, N.Mex., Aug. 24, 1953; d. Martin B. and Mary Catherine (Eberwein) Goodwin; m. Dn Oliver Westover, June 14, 1975; children: Jacqueline Diona, Daniele Leigh. Student, Ea. N.Mex. U., 1971-73; Interior Design diploma, LaSalle U., 1973; BFA in Interior Design, N.Y. Sch. Interior Design, 1977. Cert. pers. cons. Mem. sales staff The Popular, El Paso, Tex., 1979-81; various sales and design positions Hollon's, Lubbock, Tex., 1981-82, Spears, Lubbock, 1982-84; instr. interior design N.Mex. Jr. Coll., Hobbs, 1986—; owner, mgr. EnerTech Research, mgmt. and tech. recruiting firm, Houston, 1991—. Interior designer, buyer Callaway's Hobbs, 1985-86; interior designer Designers II, Hobbs, 1986—; set designer Miss N.Mex. Pageant, Hobbs, 1984-85. Program chmn. Les County Rep. Women; bd. dirs. S.W. Symphony; active Christian Women, Hobbs, Altar Soc., Hobbs, St. Joseph's Circle, Hobbs, Rep. Women, Hobbs; v.p. Spring (Tex.) Rep. Women, 1992, bd. dirs., 1997; mem. fin. com. St. Ignatius Loyola Cath. Ch., 1993. Named Clovis Young Rep. of Yr., 1974; recipient Top Recuiter award CUF, 1997. Mem. Tex. Assn. Pers. Cons. Avocations: tennis, reading, bicycling, golf. Home: 9211 Godstone Ln Spring TX 77379-6508 also: Diana's 2400 N Grimes St Ste 6 Hobbs NM 88240-2131

WESTRICK, HEIDI LYNN, medical/surgical nurse; b. Johnstown, Pa., Dec. 15, 1966; d. Thomas and Karol Anne (Kirchner) Zwiener; m. Daniel D. Westrick, Sept. 4, 1999. Diploma, Conemaugh Valley Meml. Hosp., Johnstown, 1987; BSN, U. Pitts., Johnstown, 1993. RN Pa., cert. trauma nurse, in peritoneal dialysis, in cardiac monitoring, med. surg. nursing, acute head injuries/trauma care of acute rehab. patients. Nurse Conemaugh Valley Meml. Hosp., Johnstown, Pa., 1987—; admissions coord. Conemaugh Rehab. Unit, Crichton Ctr. Advanced Rehab., Johnstown, Pa., 1996—. Mem. Conemaugh Valley Meml. Alumni (sec. peer rev. com.), Alumni of U. Pitts. at Johnstown. Office Fax: 814-948-4261. Personal E-mail: daniel@forspeed.com.

WESTROPE, MARTHA RANDOLPH, psychologist, consultant; b. Gaffney, S.C., May 19, 1922; d. Gordon Robert and Hannah (Brown) W.; 1 adopted child, Ashley Randolph. BS, Winthrop Coll., 1942; MA, U. N.C., 1944; PhD, State U. of Iowa, Iowa City, 1952. Lic. psychologist, S.C. Pvt. practice, Greenville, S.C., 1960—; part-time pvt. practice, 1987-96; part-time staff mem. Spartanburg (S.C.) Mental Health Clinic, 1971-73, Greenville Mental Health Ctr., 1974-85, Patrick B. Harris Psychiat. Hosp., Anderson, S.C., 1985-87; med. cons. S.C. Vocat. Rehab. Dept., Greenville, 1987-91, part-time med. cons., 1993-99. Cons. S.C. Parole Bd. for Psychol. Evaluation, S.C. Dept. Corrections, 1983-87. Mem. Am. Psychol. Assn., Southeastern Psychol. Assn., S.C. Psychol. Assn., Am. Assn. for Advancement of Psychology, Greenville County Mental Health Assn., Am. Group Psychotherapy Assn., Coun. for the Nat. Register of Health Svc. Providers in Psychology. Democrat. Presbyterian. Avocations: wildlife preservation, fine arts, collecting dolls, stamps. Home: 11 Darien Way Greenville SC 29615-3236

WETHERBY, IVOR LOIS, retired librarian; b. Louisville, May 22, 1924; d. Luther Silas and Clara Marders (Hite) W.; m. Herbert Charles Howard, July 4, 1947; children: Ivor Jane, Elizabeth Wetherby, John Allen, Luther Hite, Ann Dell. AB, Ky. Wesleyan Coll., 1944; MS in Library Sci., Fla. State U. 1965; SEd, Fla. Atlantic U., 1984; EdD Fla. Internat. U., 1992. Various clerical and secretarial positions, 1944-50; tchr. Our Lady of Mercy Acad., Louisville, 1963-64; librarian Palm Beach Jr. Coll., Lake Worth, Fla., 1966-78; head librarian Sebring (Fla.) Pub. Library, 1978; health scis. reference librarian Miami (Fla.)-Dade CC, Med. Ctr. Campus, 1978-87; librarian med. library Moncrief Army Cmty. Hosp., Ft. Jackson, S.C., 1987-89; ref. libr. Fla. Internat. U., 1992, ret., 1992. Active New Life Alliance Ch., West Palm Beach, Fla., Pleasant Grove Bapt. Ch., Louisville. Mem. DAR, Palm Beach County Geneal. Soc., Daus. of Founders and Patriots of Am., Nat. Soc. Colonial Dames XVII Century, Nat. Soc. of U.S. Daus. of 1812, Holland Soc. NY, Nat. Huguenot Soc., Nat. Soc. Daus. Union 1861-65. Home: 232 Orange Tree Dr Lantana FL 33462-1130

WETTER, VIRGINIA FORWOOD PATE, broadcast executive; b. Havre De Grace, Md., Aug. 10, 1919; BA, Coll. of William and Mary, 1940. Pub. rels. Std. Oil Co. of Pa., 1940, Irwin and Leighton Contractor, 1941; pres., gen. mgr. WASA and WHDG radio Havre de Grace, MD, 1960—85; chmn. bd. Chesapeake Broadcasting Corp., 1985—. Trustee Harford CC Bd. of Trustees, 1959—69, chmn., 1966—69; pres. Md. Assn. Bds. of Edn., 1963—64, Md. Dist. of Columbia Del. Broadcaster's Assn., 1965—66; mem. Harford County Bd. Edn., 1959—69, pres., 1966—69; mem. radio code bd. Nat. Assn. of Broadcasters, 1966—71; libr. bd. Broadcast Pioneers, 1980—. Dir. Harford County Heart Assn. and Cancer Soc., Susquehanna Coun. of Girl Scouts; county chmn. Pres.'s Com. to Promote Employment of Physically Handicapped; plans bd. United Way; dir. Blood Bank of Md.; vol. Harford Meml. Hosp. Aux.; vestry St. John's Episcopal Ch., chair 50th anniversary celebration, co-chair bldg. com. Recipient Am. Broadcast Pioneer award, Broadcasters' Found., 2001, Disting. Svc. to Broadcasting award, Broadcast Pioneers of Washington Area, 2001. Mem.: Am. Women in Radio and Television (life; nat. pres. 1970—71, Bd. Dirs. award 1991, Radio Leadership award 2000), Md. Congress of Parents and Tchrs. (life), Delta Kappa Gamma (hon.). Home: 1000 Chesapeake Dr Havre de Grace MD 21078

WETTERGREN, SANDRA MARIE, personnel consultant; b. Detroit, June 1, 1950; d. Romano and Catherine (Pessenda) Previdi; m. Frank Walter Wettergren, June 14, 1969 (div. Nov. 1988); children: Amanda, Matthew. AA, Macomb C.C., 1986. Cert. pers. cons. Nat. Assn. Pers. Svcs. Recruiter Henry Labus Pers., Detroit, 1985-93; office mgr. TempStaff, Inc., Birmingham, Mich., 1993-94; area mgr., staffing specialist Contemporary Svcs., Inc., Troy, Mich., 1994—. Mem. Macomb chpt. Dem. Nat. Party, 1992—. Mem. NOW, Am. Profl. Women in Mortgages (edn. com. 1995-96), Mich. Mortgage Banker Assn. (membership com. 1995-96), Mich. Assn. Pers. Svcs. (3 sales awards 1995, Cons. of Yr. 1996), Mich. Mortgage Brokers Assn. Office: Contemporary Svcs Inc 2690 Crooks Rd Ste 111 Troy MI [illegible]

WETZEL, BETTY PREAT, writer; b. Roundup, Mont., Nov. 7, 1915; d. Alfred William and Rachel Preat (Johnston) Eiselein; m. Winston Warren Wetzel, June 5, 1940; children: Susan Hinman, Kurt, Gretchen Grafin von Rittberg, Rebecca. BA in Journalism, U. Mont., 1937. Columnist, reporter Roundup (Mont.) Rec.-Tribune, 1938-46; sec. SEATO Cholera Rsch. Lab. and Hosp., Dacca, Bangladesh, 1965-67; adminstrv. asst. to v.p. Wellesley (Mass.) U., 1969-73; dir. pub. rels. Oxfam-Am., Boston, 1973-77; book rev. editor Mont. Mag., Helena, 1989-91. Author: The Making of a Montanan, 1986, Missoula, The Town and The People, 1988, After You, Mark Twain, 1990; co-author: Older Women in the Outdoors, 1996. Bd. dirs. Flathead Lake Biol. Sta., Bigfork, Mont., 1980-86. Democrat. Avocations: mountain hiking, tennis, reading, politics, family. Home: 189 Pierce Ln PO Box 693 Bigfork MT 59911-0693

WETZEL, JODI (JOY LYNN WETZEL), history and women's studies educator; b. Salt Lake City, Apr. 5, 1943; d. Richard Coulam and Margaret Elaine (Openshaw) Wood; m. David Nevin Wetzel, June 12, 1967; children: Meredith (dec.), Richard Rawlins. BA in English, U. Utah, 1965, MA in English, 1967; PhD in Am. Studies, U. Minn., 1977. Instr. Am. studies and family social sci. U. Minn., 1973-77, asst. prof. Am. studies and women's studies, 1977-79, asst. to dir. Minn. Women's Ctr., 1973-75, asst. dir., 1975-79; dir. Women's Resource Ctrs. U. Denver, 1980-84, mem. adj. faculty history, 1981-84, dir. Am. studies program, dir. Women's Inst., 1983-84; dir. Women in Curriculum U. Maine, 1985-86, mem. coop. faculty sociology, social work and human devel., 1986; dir. Inst. Women's Studies and Svcs. Met. State Coll. Denver, 1986—, assoc. prof. history, 1986-89, prof. history, 1990—. Speaker, presenter, cons. in field; vis. prof. Am. studies U. Colo., 1985; mem. judges panel nominations rev. Nat. Women's Hall of Fame, Seneca Falls, N.Y., 2002, 03, 04. Co-author: Women's Studies: Thinking Women, 1993; co-editor: Readings Toward Composition, 2d edit., 1969; contbr. articles to profl. publs. Del. at-large Nat. Women's Meeting, Houston, 1977; bd. dirs. Rocky Mountain Women's Inst., 1981-84; treas. Colo. Women's Agenda, 1987-91; mem. judges panel, nominations reviewer Nat. Women's Hall of Fame, Seneca Falls, N.Y., 2002. U. Utah Dept. English fellow, 1967; U. Minn. fellow, 1978-79; grantee NEH, 1973, NSF, 1981-83, Carnegie Corp., 1988; named to Outstanding Young Women of Am., 1979. Mem. Am. Hist. Assn., Nat. Assn. Women in Edn. (Hilda A. Davis Ednl. Leadership award 1996, Sr. Scholar 1996), Am. Assn. for Higher Edn., Am. Studies Assn., Nat. Women's Studies Assn., Golden Key Nat. Honor Soc. (hon.), Alpha Lambda Delta, Phi Kappa Phi. Office: Met State Coll Den Campus Box 36 PO Box 173362 Denver CO 80217-3362 Office Phone: 303-556-8441. Business E-Mail: wetzelj@mscd.edu.

WETZEL, MARLENE REED, freelance/self-employed writer; b. Jordan, Mont., Apr. 5, 1937; d. Frederick Edward and Alma Jane (Flippin) Reed; m. John Hall Wetzel, May 14, 1960; 1 child, Kurt. BA magna cum laude, U. Tulsa, 1987. Govt. affairs rschr. Arabian Am. Oil Co., Dhahran, Saudi Arabia, 1979, 1980—82; asst. to dir. The Philbrook Mus., Tulsa, Okla., 1987; freelance writer, editor, 1988—98; author, 1998—. Recipient award, PEN/Amazon.com, 2000. Avocations: tennis, skiing. Home: 11950 S Mingo Rd Bixby OK 74008

WETZEL-WILLIAMS, KIMBERLY, lawyer; b. Ulysses, Kans., Jan. 27, 1958; d. Herbert O. and Manetta V. Wetzel; m. Robert E. Williams; 1 child, Matthew Williams. BS in Bus. Adminstrn., U. Kans., 1979, JD, 1982. Bar: Kans. 1982. Assoc. Mustaine & Newman, Kansas City, Kans., 1982—83; staff atty. Hyatt Legal Svcs., Kansas City, 1983—85; asst. dist. atty. Wyandotte County, Kansas City, 1985—2002; pvt. practice, 2002—. Adv. to youth officers Wyandotte County 4-H Coun., Kansas City, 2001—02; cmty. club leader Brauer Beavers 4-H Club, Kansas City, 2000—; chmn. Wyandotte County Ext. Coun., Kansas City, 2000—02; bd. dirs. Kans. State Ext. Adv. Coun., Manhattan, 2001—. Mem.: Kansas Bar Assn., Wyandotte County Bar Assn. Roman Catholic. Avocations: photography, gardening, gourmet cooking, working with youth. E-mail: kimwetzelwilliams@yahoo.com.

WEXLER, ANNE, government relations and public affairs consultant; b. N.Y.C., Feb. 10, 1930; d. Leon R. and Edith R. (Rau) Levy; m. Joseph Duffey, Sept. 17, 1974; children by previous marriage: David Wexler,

Daniel Wexler. BA, Skidmore Coll., 1951, LLD (hon.), 1978; DSc in Bus. (hon.), Bryant Coll., 1978. Assoc. pub. Rolling Stone mag., 1974-76; personnel adviser Carter-Mondale transition planning group, 1976-77; dep. undersec. regional affairs Dept. Commerce, 1977-78; asst. to Pres. of U.S., Washington, 1978-81; pres. Wexler and Assocs., Washington, 1981-82; govt. relations and pub. affairs cons., chmn. Wexler, Reynolds, Harrison & Schule, Inc., Washington, 1981-90; vice chmn. Hill and Knowlton PA Worldwide, Washington, 1990-92; chmn. The Wexler Group, 1992—. Bd. dirs. Methanex, Comcast Corp., Dreyfus Index Funds, Wilshire Mut. Funds, Dreyfus Family of Funds. Bd. dirs. Nat. Park Found., Washington Econ. Club; chmn. bd. dirs. WETA. Named Outstanding Alumna Skidmore Coll., 1972, recipient most disting. alumni award, 1984, Bryce Harlow award, 1989. Mem. Coun. on Fgn. Rels., Nat. Women's Forum. Jewish. Office: Wexler Group 1317 F St NW Ste 600 Washington DC 20004-1157

WEXLER, JOAN G. dean; b. N.Y.C., Nov. 25, 1946; m. Marvin Wexler, June 16, 1968 (div.); children: Matthew Eric, Laura Page. BS (hons. and distinction), Cornell U., 1968; MA in tchg., Harvard U., 1970; JD, Yale, 1974. Bar: N.Y. 1976. Jud. law clk. for Judge Jack B. Weinstein U.S. Dist. Ct. (ea. dist.), NY, 1974-75; assoc. Debevoise & Plimpton, N.Y.C., 1975-77; asst. prof. law NYU Sch. Law, 1978-81, assoc. prof. law, 1981-85; prof. law Bklyn. Law Sch., 1985—87, assoc. dean acad. affairs, prof. law, 1987-94, acting dean, prof. law, 1994, dean, pres. and prof. law, 1994—. Spkr. in field; evaluator trust adminstrn. and estate adminstrn. courses N.Y. State Banking Assn., 1993; mem. planning com. Bench and Bar Conf. Fed. Bar Coun., 1995, 2003, chair Winter Bench and Bar Conf., Feb. 2002, bd. dirs. Fed. Bar Coun. Found.; mem. planning com. Workshop on Family and Juvenile Law Am. Assn. Law Schs., Washington, 1993; atty. mem. Jud. Conf. of State of N.Y., 2000—; with Bklyn. Legal Svcs. Corp. (mem. adv. com. 1994-). Contbr. articles to profl. jours. Bd. dirs. Downtown Bklyn. Devel. Assn., 1992-96, Fund for Modern Cts., 1994—, Assn. of the Bar of the City of N.Y. Fund, 1994-96; active Commn. on Alcohol and Substance abuse in the Profession, 1999—; mem. Commn. on Univ. Relations, Cornell U., 2001—. Recipient Spl. Recognition award, N.Y. Women's Bar Assn., 1996, Pres. Spl. award, 2002, award, Greater Boy Scout Soc. N.Y., 1999, William Schoenfeld award, Soc. Adolescent Psychiatry, 1999. Fellow Am. Bar Found.; mem. ABA (mem. continuing legal edn. com. 1997-98, 99-2001, ind. law schs. com. 1996-97, 2000-, sect. legal edn. and admissions to bar, new deans seminar planning com. 2001—), Am. Law Inst. (mem. mem's. consultative group-law family dissolution, spl. com. inst. size 1998-2000), Fed. Bar Coun. (pres.-elect 2002-, v.p. 2001-2002, chair Winter Bench and Bar Conf. 2001-2002, planning com. 2002-2003, pres. Fed. Bar Found. 1998-99, chair, Fed. Bar Coun. and Found. nominating com. 1998), N.Y. State Bar Assn. (mem. com. on children and law 1993-97, com. legal edn. and admission 1994—), N.Y. Women's Bar Assn. (v.p. 1987-88, 92-93, bd. dirs. 1998-91, Pres.'s Spl. award 2002, Spl. Recognition award 1996), Greater Boy Scouts Coun. N.Y. (William Schoenfeld award 1999), Soc. Adolescent Psychiatry (William Schoenfeld award 1999), Jud. Conf. State N.Y. (atty. 2000-2002), Downtown Bklyn. Coun. (mem. exec. com. 2000-), State N.Y. Office of Ct. Adminstrn. (commn. on alcohol and substance abuse in profession 1999-), Practicing Law Inst. (mem. com. on programs and pubs. 1998, alt. mem., exec. com. 2001-), Fund Moderate Cts. (mem. bd. dirs., task force ct. facilities 2001), Downtown Bklyn. Devel. Assn., Assn. Bar City N.Y. Fund Inc. (v.p. 1996-97, mem. nominating com. 92-93, 1999, chair com. on honors 1997-2000, mem. com. on honors 1994-97, com. matrimonial law 1985-89, 92-95, long range planning com. 1992-95, com. on family ct. and family law, 1989-92, ad hoc com. on AIDS 1987-88, ad hoc com. surrogate parenting 1986-88), Pres.'s Coun. of Cornell Women (com. on univ. rels. 2001-), Com. to Restore Thurgood Marshall Landmark Courthouse, Bklyn. Legal Svs. Corp. A (mem adv. com. 1994-), Cornell U. (mem. Cornell Coun. 2002-, pres.'s coun. Cornell Women 1995-, mem. com. on u. rels. 2001), Second Cir. Task Force on Gender, Racial and Ethnic Fairness in Cts., N.Y. State Supreme Ct.(adv. com. 18-B family ct. panel, appellate divsn. first dept.), Jud. Conf. Second Cir. (planning and programming com. 1999-2002), Am. Assn. Law Schs. Workshop on Family and Juvenile Law, Downtown Bklyn. Coun. Exec. Com.; trustee Practising Law Inst. (mem. com. on programs and pubs., 1998-, alt. mem. exec. com., 2001-). Home: 1045 Nine Acres Ln Mamaroneck NY 10543-4706 Office: Bklyn Law Sch 250 Joralemon St Brooklyn NY 11201-3700 Business E-Mail: joan.wexler@brooklaw.edu.

WEXLER, NANCY SABIN, clinical neuropsychology educator; b. Washington, July 19, 1945; d. Milton and Leonore Wexler. AB cum laude, Radcliffe Coll., 1967; PhD in Clin. Psychology, U. Mich., 1974; DHL (hon.), N.Y. Med. Coll., 1991; DSc (hon.), U. Mich., 1991. Lic. psychologist, N.Y. Psychol. intern, teaching fellow U. Mich., 1968-74; asst. prof. psychology grad. faculty New Sch. Social Rsch., N.Y.C., 1974-76; pvt. practice psychology N.Y.C., 1974-76; health sci. adminstr. Nat. Inst. Neurol., Comm. Disorders and Stroke, NIH, 1978-83; pres. Hereditary Disease Found., Santa Monica, Calif., 1983—; prof. neuropsychology Coll. Phys. and Surgeons, Columbia U., N.Y.C., 1985-92, prof. clin. neuropsychology, 1992—. Mem. Ctr. for Brain and Behavior Coll. Phys. and Surgeons of Columbia U., 1985; mem. adv. com. Human Genome Ctr., Lawrence Berkeley Labs. and U. Calif., 1988—; mem. external adv. com. Ctr. for Human Genome Studies, Los Alamos Nat. Labs., 1990—; co-chairperson ethical, legal and social issues com. Human Genome Orgn., 1991—, mem. dir. search Nat. Ctr. for Human Genome Rsch., NIH, 1992; chairperson Joint NIH/Dept. of Energy Ethical, Legal, Social Issues Working Group on Human Genome, 1989—. Contbr. articles to profl. jours. Trustee Nat. Huntington's Disease Assn., 1983-85, Marine Biol. Lab., 1984-86, Eleanor Roosevelt Inst. Cancer Rsch., 1985-91, Found. for Care and Cure of Huntington's Disease, 1988—. Fulbright scholar U. West Indies, Jamaica, 1967-68; fellow The Hastings Ctr., 1990—; recipient award Robert J. and Claire Pasarow Found., 1987, Living Legacy award Women's Internat. Soc., 1988, Alumnae Athena award Alumnae Coun. U. Mich., 1989, award Gov.'s Office, Zulia, Venezuela, 1989, Venezuelan Presdl. award, 1990, Legis. Commendation N.Y. State, 1990, Disting. Svc. award Nat. Assn. Biology Tchrs., 1993, Nat. Med. Rsch. award Nat. Health Coun., 1993, Albert Lasker Pub. Svc. award, 1993. Mem. AAAS (bd. dirs. 1993—), APA, Am. Soc. Law and Medicine, Soc. Neurosci. (chairperson social issues com. 1988-90, organizing com. Neurobiology of Human Diesease Workshop 1980—), Am. Psychol. Soc., Am. Soc. Human Genetics, World Fedn. Neurology, Rsch. Group on Huntington's Disease, Am. Neurol. Assn. Office: Columbia U Coll Phys & Surg NY State Psychiat Inst 1051 Riverside Dr Unit 6 New York NY 10032-1013 also: Ste 511 2444 Wilshire Blvd Santa Monica CA 90403-5826

WEYEL, PEGGY ANN, secondary school educator; b. San Antonio, Mar. 23, 1946; d. Jesse Columbus and June Edith Pike James; m. Robert Edward Weyel, Jr., June 28, 1969. AA, San Antonio Coll., 1966; BA, Incarnate Word Coll., 1968; MA, U. Tex., San Antonio, 1992; EdD, Tex. A&M U., 1998. Cert. profl. supt. PK-12 Tex., 1996, profl., supr. PK-12 Tex., 1992, provisional, social studies-composite grades 6-12 Tex., 1968, profl., mid-mgmt. Tex., 1994. Tchr. Theodore Roosevelt HS, San Antonio, 1968—73, tchr. social studies 9-12 grade, 1983—2003. Pres. North East Alamo Area Coun. Social Studies, San Antonio, 1986—87; tchr. leader People to People - Initiative for Understanding - Soviet Union, San Antonio, 1988—91; program chair Tex. Alliance for Geog. Edn., San Antonio, 1990—91, tchr. cons., 1998—; steering com. for curriculum restructuring North East Ind. Sch. Dist., San Antonio, 1994; co-chair NEISD Social Studies Curriculum Restructuring, San Antonio, 1994—96. Editor, writer: newsletter THEIA Newsletter (Tex. Hunter Edn. Instr. Assn.). Pres. South Ctrl. Tex. Hunter Edn. Instrs., Inc, San Antonio, 2001—03, sec.-treas., 1988—2001; treas. Tex. Hunter Edn. Instrs., Inc, Austin, 1998—2001; area chief hunter edn. Tex. Parks and Wildlife, Austin, 1998—2003; master naturalist Alamo Area Master Naturalists, San Antonio, 2001—03. Named Educator of the Yr., Bexar County Am. Legion, 1999—2000; recipient Tex. Stars award for geography, Tex. Edn. Agy. Clearing Ho. on Promising Ednl. Programs, 1989, Award for Ednl. Excellence for School-Within-A-School, Tex. State Bd. Edn., 1995. Mem.: NRA, ASCD, North East Fedn. Tchrs., Tex. Fedn. Tchrs., Internat. Hunter Edn. Assn., Am. Fedn. Tchrs., Tex. Alliance for Geog. Edn., Tex. Coun. for the Social Studies, Nat. Coun. Social Studies, South Ctrl. Tex. Hunter Edn. Instrs. Assn, Inc (pres. 2001—03), Women's Shooting Sports Assn., Tex. State Rifle Assn., Tex. Hunter Edn. Instr. Assn., Inc. (treas. 1997—2000), Phi Delta Kappa. Achievements include research in teacher behaviors in a restructuring high school. Avocations: hunting, fishing, birding, drawing, ethnobotany. Home: 13502 Syracuse San Antonio TX 78249 Personal E-mail: pweyel@sbcglobal.net.

WEYER, DIANNE SUE, health facility administrator; b. Anchorage, Aug. 15, 1954; d. Vernon H. and Myrtle M. Larson; m. Merlin D. Weyer; 1 child, Alison. BSW magna cum laude, Augustana Coll., Sioux Falls, S.D., 1976; MPA, U. S.D., Vermillion, 1989. LCSW 1996. Program dir. Threshold, Sioux Falls, SD, 1976—78; policy analyst S.D. Divsn. Law Enforcement Assistance, Pierre, SD; youth projects coord. Mountain Plains Youth Svcs. Coalition, Pierre, SD, 1980—82; social worker S.D. Dept. Social Svcs., Pierre, SD, 1983—85; child and adolescent program specialist S.D. Divsn. Mental Health, Pierre, SD, 1985—96; Social Services Manager St. Mary's Healthcare Ctr., Pierre, SD, 1996—2000, outreach dir., 2002—. Social work adv. bd., adj. faculty Augustana Coll., Sioux Falls, SD, 1977—79; interagy. coord. coun., state bd. mem. S.D. Dept. Edn., Pierre, SD, 1989—96; state rep. for children and youth Nat. Assn. State Mental Health Program Dirs., Washington, 1985—96; chair S.D. Interagy. Coordination Network Coun., Pierre, SD, 1991—96; social work adv. bd. Presentation Coll., Aberdeen, SD; adj. faculty Capital U., Pierre, SD, 2000—01; exec. bd., past pres. S.D. Social Work Leaders in Health Care, Sioux Falls, SD, 1999—2001. Healthcare com. Pierre C. of C., 1999—2003; tchr., confirmation guide Luth. Meml. Ch., Pierre, 1985—2001; bd. dirs. Missouri Shores Resource Ctr., Pierre, 1980—82; exec. bd. Healthy Cmtys./Healthy Youth, Pierre, 1999—. Recipient Spl. Recognition award, Capitol Area Counseling Svc., 2001, S.D. Family-Based Svcs. Assn., 1994, Outstanding svc. award, S.D. Corrections Assn., 1990; grantee S.D. CASSP-Local Infrastructure Demonstration, Ctr. Mental Health Svcs., 1993—96, Rural Mental Health Demonstration, NIH, 1987—89, HHS Adminstrn. Children, Youth and Family Svcs., 1987—90. Mem.: NASW, S.D. Alliance for the Mentally Ill, S.D. Social Work Leadership in Healthcare (sec., v.p., pres. 1998—2001, Spl. Recognition award 0196), Nat. Social Work Leadership in Healthcare. Home: 1217 Hilgers Dr Pierre SD 57501 Office: St Mary's Healthcare Ctr 800 E Dakota Pierre SD 57501 Personal E-mail: MWDW1234@aol.com. Business E-Mail: dianneweyer@chi-midwest.org.

WEYMOUTH, ELIZABETH MORRIS GRAHAM (LALLY WEYMOUTH), editor, columnist; b. July 7, 1943; d. Philip L. and Katharine (Meyer) Graham; m. Yann Weymouth (div.); children: Katharine Scully, Pamela. BA in Am. History and Lit. with honors, Harvard U. Worker for Senator Robert F. Kennedy Bedford Stuyvesant Restoration Corp., 1968—69; freelance journalist, contbg. editor numerous publs. including NY Times Mag., Esquire, Atlantic Monthly, Parade, LA Times, New York, 1977—83; contbg. editor LA Times, 1983—86; fgn. affairs columnist Washington Post, 1986—; contbg. editor Newsweek, 1998—, sr. editor, spl. diplomatic corr., 2001—. Author: America in 1876, The Way We Were, 1976; editor, compiler Thomas Jefferson: The Man, His World, His Influence, 1973. Office: Washington Post 1150 15th St NW Washington DC 20071-0002*

WEYMOUTH, TONI, social worker, writer, educator; b. L.A., May 17, 1945; d. William Morgan and Grace Lucille Allen; m. Ira Mark Smith, Jan. 15, 1972 (div. Jan. 1975); children: Jeffery Paul Smith, Jennifer Suzanne Smith; m. Donald Leroy Weymouth, Oct. 25, 1990. BA in Psychology, Calif. State U., Fresno, 1993, MSW, 1989; EdD in Sexology, Inst. Advanced Study of Human Sexuality, 1994. Social worker Big Bros./Big Sisters, Fresno, Calif., 1980-86, Fresno Mental Health Dept., 1989-91. Therapist, activist Parents of Prisoners Support Group, Fresno, 1995—; instr. Fresno Unified Sch. Dist., 1999—. Author: Outsiders Looking In: How to Keep from Going Crazy When Someone You Love Goes to Jail, 1998, Maiden Voyage: The Art of Romance, 1999. Activist, writer Amnesty Internat., Fresno, 1995—, Death Penalty Focus, Fresno, 1995—. Mem. NOW (v.p. 1981-83). Home: 4732 E Michigan Ave Fresno CA 93703-1653 Office: OLinc Pub PO Box 6012 Fresno CA 93703-6012

WHALEN, DENISE LASCO, family therapist; b. Pottsville, Pa., Jan. 14, 1968; d. Philip John and Carol Ann (Kachelries) Lasco; m. Walter William Whalen, May 15, 1993. AAS in Bus. Adminstrn., Penn State U., 1987, B in Behavioral Sci., 1989; MA in Counseling Psychol., Kutztown U., 1994. Homeless svc. coord. Econ. Opportunity Cab., Pottsville, Pa., 1989; caseworker Sch. City Children & Youth, Pottsville, 1989-91; family therapist Turning Point, Pottsville, 1991-97; therapist Family Life Svcs., Topton, Pa., 1995—; clin. mental health counselor Pottsville Hosp., 1997—99; therapist Psych. Assocs., 1999—. Mem. ACA, Internat. Assn. Marriage & Family Counselors. Republican. Lutheran. Avocations: painting, stained glass, reading. Home: 215 Arlene St Minersville PA 17954-2101 Office: Psychological Associates Claude A Lord Blvd Pottsville PA 17901

WHALEN, LORETTA THERESA, religious educational administrator; b. Bklyn., May 21, 1940; d. William Michael and Loretta Margaret (Malone) Whalen; children: Ann Lindsay, Margaret Force. RN, St. Vincent's Hosp., N.Y.C., 1960; BSN, U. Pa., 1965; MA in Edn., Fordham U., 1971; cert. in sociology religion, Louvain U., Belgium, 1974; PhD in Global Edn., The Union Grad. Sch., 1994. Staff nurse Holy Family Hosp., Atlanta, 1967-69; Latin Am. communication dir. Med. Mission Sisters, Maracaibo, Venezuela, 1969-71; intensive care nurse St. Vincent's Hosp., N.Y.C., 1971-72; mem. ministry team Med. Mission Sisters, various locations, 1972-74, dir. communications Phila., 1974-77; asst. to exec. Interreligious Peace Colloquium, Washington, 1977; freelance writing, photography Ch. World Svc., N.Y.C., 1978-79; dir. Office Global Edn. Nat. Council Chs., N.Y.C., 1980-99. Co-author: Make a World of Difference: Creative Activities for Global Learning, 1990, Tales of the Heart: Affective Approaches to Global Education, 1991; mem. editorial bd., rev. editor Connections Mag., 1984-87; contbr. articles to profl. jours. Mem. Peace and Justice Commn., Archdiocese of Balt., 1985-89. Mem. Amnesty Internat., Bread for the World, NOW, World Wildlife Fund, Greenpeace, Sigma Theta Tau. Democrat. Roman Catholic. Avocations: photography, writing, racquetball, interior design, travel.

WHALEN, LUCILLE, retired academic administrator; b. Los Angeles, July 26, 1925; d. Edward Cleveland and Mary Lucille (Perrault) W. BA in English, Immaculate Heart Coll., Los Angeles, 1949; MSLS, Catholic U. Am., 1955; DLS, Columbia U., 1965. Tchr. elem. and secondary parochial schs., L.A., Calif., 1945—52; tchr., libr. Conaty Meml. H.S., L.A., 1950—52; reference/serials librarian, instr. in library sci. Immaculate Heart Coll., 1955-58; dean Immaculate Heart Coll. (Sch. Library Sci.), 1958-60, 65-70; assoc. dean, prof. SUNY, Albany, 1971-78, 84-87, prof. Sch. Info. Sci. and Policy, 1979-87; dean grad. programs, libr. Immaculate Heart Coll. Ctr., Los Angeles, 1987-90; ref. libr. (part-time) Glendale Community Coll., 1990—. Dir. U.S. Office Edn. Instn. Author, editor (with others): Reference Services in Archives, 1986, author, editor (with Nina Redman): (with Nina Redman), 2nd edit., 1998; author (with Nina Redman): Human Rights: A Reference Handbook, 1989, 2d edit., 1998. Mem. ACLU, Common Cause, Amnesty Internat. Democrat. Roman Catholic. Home: 320 S Gramercy Pl Apt 101 Los Angeles CA 90020-4542 Office: Glendale CC 1500 N Verdugo Rd Glendale CA 91208-2809 E-mail: lucillew@aol.com.

WHALEN, NORMA JEAN, special education educator; b. Albuquerque, N. Mex., Nov. 26, 1936; d. Ervin O'dell and Louise (Harcrow) Betts; m. Thomas Leo Whalen; children: Timothy, Patrick, Anna, Emily Wells, Kevin. BEd, Carson-Newman Coll., Jefferson City, Tenn., 1959. Cert. Tchr Secondary Edn. Fla., 1959, Tchr. - History Fla., 1959. Sec. sch. tchr. La Puente Jr. HS, La Puente, Calif., 1959—62; tchr. Umatilla (Fla.) Elem. Sch., 1969—70; substitute tchr. Lake County Schs., Leesburg, 1969—70, 1975—79; tchr., evening class Lee Adult H.S., Leesburg, Fla., 1979—80; elem. sch. tchr. St. Paul's Cath. Ch., Leesburg, Fla., 1980—81; spl. edn. tchr. Lee Opportunity Ctr. Lifestream Behavioral Ctr., Leeburg, Fla., 1990—2003. Cons. curriculum devel. St. Paul's Cath. Ch., Leesburg, 1986—89, tchr. 1st communion and confession classes, 1986—2003. Dir. learning resource ctr. St. Paul Cath. Ch., Leesbug, 1986—89; Bd. dirs. Melon Patch Theater, Leesburg, Fla., 1976—81. Recipient Best Supporting actress award, Melon Patch Theater, 1979, Disting. Svc. award, 1980, Svc. award, Lake County Bd. Edn., 1999, Nat. Assn. Mentally Ill Parents Org., 2000. Mem.: NEA, Leesburg Edn. Assn. Roman Catholic. Avocations: crocheting, reading, swimming, cooking, travel. Home: 2904 Pecan Avenue Leesburg FL 34748 Office: Lee EdnOpportunity Ctr 207 Lee St Leesburg FL 34748-4914

WHALEN, PATRICIA THERESE, marketing and public relations educator, consultant; b. Columbus, Ohio, June 26, 1955; d. Daniel Edward and Rose Eileen Whalen. BA in English, Ohio State U., 1977; MS in Bus. Adminstrn., Ind. U., 1981; PhD, Mich. State U., 1999. Sales promotion specialist Clark Components Div., Buchanan, Mich., 1978-81, supr., advt. and pub. rels., 1981-82; mgr. corp. comm. Clark Equipment Co., Buchanan, Mich., 1982-84, dir. govt. affairs South Bend, Ind., 1984-86; dir. pub. rels. COMSAT World Systems Div., Clarksburg, Md., 1986-87, dir. mktg. communications Washington, 1987-90; dir. mktg. COMSAT Mobile Comm., Washington, 1990-94; instr. dept. advt. Mich. State U., 1995—; asst. prof. integrated mktg. comms. Northwestern U., Madill Sch. Journalism, 1999—2001; dir. prof. devel. Internat. Advt. Assocs., 2001—. Seminar speaker in field. Contbr. articles to profl. jours. Bd. dirs. Jr. Achievement, Niles, Mich., South Bend, Ind., 1982-86, Tri-county Pvt. Industry Coun., St. Joseph County, Mich., 1983-85. Mem. Pub. Rels. Soc. Am. (tech. com. 1982—, Silver Anvil award 1982), Soc. Satellite Profls. (bd. dirs. 1990-93). Roman Catholic. Avocations: golf, snow skiing, tennis, internat. travel, pub. speaking. Home: 5307 Davis St Skokie IL 60077-1536 E-mail: p_whalen@northwestern.edu.

WHALEN, SARAH EVE, professional soccer player; b. Greenlawn, N.Y., Apr. 28, 1976; Student in psychology, U. Conn. Mem. U.S. Nat. Women's Soccer Team, 1996—, including Nike Victory Tour, 1995, U.S. Women's Cup, 97. Named 1997 Soccer Am. Player of Yr. Achievements include holder U.Conn. career record for games played (99). Office: US Soccer Fedn 1801-1811 S Prairie Ave Chicago IL 60616

WHAM, DOROTHY STONECIPHER, retired state legislator; b. Centralia, Ill., Jan. 5, 1925; d. Ernest Joseph and Vera Thelma (Shafer) Stonecipher; m. Robert S. Wham, Jan. 26, 1947; children: Nancy S. Wham Mitchell, Jeanne Wham Ryan, Robert S. II. BA, MacMurray Coll., 1946; MA, U. Ill., 1949; D of Pub. Adminstrn. (hon.), MacMurray Coll., 1992. Counsellor Student Counselling Bur. U. Ill., Urbana, 1946-49; state dir. ACTION program, Colo./Wyo. U.S. Govt., Denver, 1972-82; mem. Colo. Ho. of Reps., 1986-87, Colo. Senate, 1987-2000, chair jud. com., 1988-2000; ret., 2000. With capital devel. com., health, environ., welfare, instns., legal svcs. Mem. Civil Rights Commn. Denver, 1972-80; bd. dirs. Denver Com. on Mental Health, 1985-88, Denver Symphony, 1985-88. Mem. APA, AAUW, LWV, Colo. Mental Health Assn. (bd. dirs. 1986-88), Civitan. Republican. Avocations: travel, furniture refinishing. Home: 3430 S Race St Englewood CO 80110

WHARE, WANDA SNYDER, lawyer; b. Columbia, Pa., Nov. 5, 1959; d. William Sylvester and Dorothy Jacqueline (Luttman) W.; m. James Robert Snyder, Nov. 14, 1987; 1 child, Eric James. BA, Franklin & Marshall Coll., 1981; JD, Dickinson Sch. Law, 1984. Bar: Pa. 1984. Asst. counsel Pa. Dept. Labor and Industry, Harrisburg, 1984-87; assoc. Gibbel, Kraybill & Hess, Lancaster, Pa., 1987-89; corp. counsel Irex Corp., Lancaster, 1990-98, chmn. awareness subcom., 1995-97, mem. continuous improvement coun., 1995-97; corp. counsel Specialty Products & Insulation Co., Lancaster, 1998—2001; v.p., sec. Specialty Products Investments, Inc., Wilmington, Del., 1998—2001; asst. sec. Specialty Products Insulation Co., Wilmington, Del., 2000—01; assoc. Nikolaus & Hohenadel LLP, 2001—. Class agt. Franklin and Marshall Coll., 2002—; parish-staff rels. com. First Meth. Ch., Lancaster, 1987—92, com. on status and role of women, 1989—95, chmn., 1992—95, adminstrv. team, 2001—, chair lit. prodn. com., 2003—; chmn. com. on status and role of women Ea. Pa. Conf. of United Meth. Ch., 1996—98. Office: Nikolaus & Hohenadel LLP 212 N Queen St Lancaster PA 17603 Office Phone: 717-299-3726. E-mail: wwhare@comcast.net., wwhare@nikolaushohenadel.com.

WHARTON, MARGARET MARY, nun, education educator; b. San Diego, Calif., Sept. 2, 1948; d. John Philip Wharton and Mary Elizabeth Roundtree. BA in Math., Salve Regina Univ., Newport, R.I., 1976; MA in Math., Appalachian Univ., 1997. Cert. tchg. math/secondary N.C, 1994, R.I., 1982. Tchr. St. Anthony Sch., Guam, 1969—72, Cathedral Grade Sch., Guam, 1972—74, 1978—82, vice prin., 1973—74, Santa Barbara Sch., Guam, 1983—84, tchr., 1982—85; sub. tchr. Gaston/Charlotte-Mecklenburg Sch., 1990; tchr. St. Michael's Sch., Gastonia, NC, 1990—94, Acad. of Our Lady, Guam, 1976—78, 1985—88; tchrs. aide Appalachian State Univ., 1996; prof. Southern W.Va. Cmty. & Tech. Coll., 1998—2000, Marshall Univ., 2000—01, Shenandoah Univ., 2001—. Contbr. scientific papers. Mem.: Coll. Reading & Learning Assn., N.C. Coun. of Tchrs. of Math., Math. Assn. of Am., Nat. Assn. of Devel. Educators, Va. Assn. of Devel. Educators, Nat. Coun. of Tchrs. of Math. Democrat. Roman Cath. Avocations: astronomy, research, medicine.

WHEALEY, LOIS DEIMEL, humanities scholar; b. N.Y.C., June 20, 1932; d. Edgar Bertram Deimel and Lois Elizabeth (Hatch) Washburn; m. Robert Howard Whealey, July 2, 1954; children: Richard William, David John, Alice Ann. BA in History, Stanford U., 1951; MA in Edn., U. Mich., 1955; MA in Polit. Sci., Ohio U., 1975. Tchr. 5th grade Swayne Sch., Owyhee, Nev., 1952-53; tchr. 7th grade Ft. Knox (Ky.) Dependent's Sch., 1955-56; tchr. adult basic edn. USAF, Oxford, 1956-57; tchr. 6th grade Amerman Sch., Northville, Mich., 1957-58; tchr. 8th grade English, social studies Slauson Jr. High Sch., Ann Arbor, Mich., 1958-59; adminstrv. asst. humanities conf. Ohio U., Athens, 1974-76, 83. Part-time instr. Ohio U., Athens, 1966-68, 75, VISTA with Rural Action, 1996-98. Contbr. articles to profl. jours. Mem. Athens County Regional Planning Commn., 1974—78, treas., 1976—78; mem. Ohio coord. com. Internat. Women's Yr., 1977; v.p. Black Diamond Girl Scout Coun., 1980—86; chair New Day for Equal Rights Amendment, 1982; mem. Athens City Bd. Edn., 1984—90, v.p., 1984, pres., 1985; mem. Tri-County Vocat. Sch. Bd., Nelsonville, Ohio, 1984—90, v.p., 1988—89; mem. adv. com. Ohio River Valley Water Sanitation Commn., 1986—95; Ohio outreach liaison Nat. Town Meeting for Sustainable Am., 1999; bd. dirs. Ohio Environ. Coun., 1984—90, sec., 1986—90; bd. dirs. Ohio Alliance for Environ., 1994—98, v.p., 1998; bd. dirs. Organize Ohio, 1999—, bd. pres., 2001—; bd. dirs. Ohio Women, Inc., 1995—, sec., 1997—; bd. dirs. Unitarian Universalist Svc. Com., 2001—03, Ohio Meadville Dist. Unitarian-Universalist Assn., 1975—81; co-chair nat. vol. network Unitarian Universalist Svc. Com., 2003—. Recipient Unsung Unitarian Universalist award Ohio-Meadville Dist. Unitarian Universalist Assn., 1984, Thanks badge Black Diamond Girl Scout Coun., 1986, How-to award Ednl. Press Assn. Am., 1990, Donna Chen Women's Equity award Ohio U., 1994, Cmty. Svc. award Athens County Cmty. Svcs. Coun., 1998, award for an individual contbn. over a lifetime Ohio Alliance for Environment, 2002; named Woman of Achievement, Black Diamond Girl Scout Coun., 1987, Peacemaker Appalachian Peace and Justice Network, 1998, Outstanding Feminist, Athens Herstory Celebration, 2002. Mem. AAUW (pres. Athens br. 1969-70, 89-90, 93-2001, AAUW/Ohio bd. 1995—), LWV (pres. 1975-77), Phi Lambda Theta (life). Democrat. Avocations: classical music, genealogy. Home: 14 Oak St Athens OH 45701-2605

WHEATLEY, DEBORAH A. music educator; b. Mt. Clemens, Mich., Oct. 28, 1954; d. Ernest William Wheatley and Joanne Smith. AA with honors, Miami (Fla.)-Dade C.C., 1975; BA magna cum laude, U. Ctrl. Fla., 1978; grad., U.S. Army Element Sch. Music, Norfolk, Va. Music tchr. Lecanto (Fla.) Primary, 1978—81; band dir. Lecanto Mid. Sch., 1981—83, fine arts tchr., 1986—96, band dir., 1996—; with signal corps band U.S. Army Elem. Sch. Music, Ft. Gordon, Ga., 1984; summer duty U.S. Army, 1986—92. Recipient U.S. Army Commendation medal, 1986. Republican. Avocations: running, promoting healthy lifestyle to middle school students. Home: 1801 Silverwood St Inverness FL 34453 Office: Lecanto Mid Sch 3800 W Educational Path Lecanto FL 34461 Office Phone: 352-746-2050. E-mail: debwheat@mailstation.com.

WHEATLEY, LYNN MARIE, humanities educator; d. Charles and Ginnie Charbonneau; m. Timothy Wheatley, July 12, 1999. BS in English/Secondary Edn., Bethel Coll., 1996. Cert. English tchr. Dept. Edn., Tenn., 1996, Spanish tchr. Dept. Edn., Tenn., 1999. Tchr. Weakley County Bd. Edn., Dresden, Tenn., 1997—99, Marion County Dept. Edn., Jasper, Tenn., 1999—. Track/cross country coach Marion County Dept. Edn., Jasper, Tenn., 2000—. With USAR. Mem.: NEA, Am. Legion. Republican. Roman Catholic. Personal E-mail: lynn_wheatley@yahoo.com.

WHEATON, MARILYN, music educator, pianist, organist; b. Warren, Ohio, Feb. 1, 1933; d. Russell and Donabelle Irene Donehue; m. Warren Randall Wheaton, June 20, 1953; 1 child, Janean Renee Vaupel-Wilson. BS in Music Edn. cum laude, Kent State U., 1955. Cert. Yamaha music instr. Pvt. piano and organ tchr., Ohio and Ariz., 1950—; profl. pianist, organist, accompanist, 1946—; elem. music supr. Austintown Pub. Schs., Youngstown, Ohio, 1955-61. Founder, dir. Potter's Clay Christian singing group, Phoenix, 1981-85; choir dir., organist, pianist at various chs., Ohio and Ariz., 1942—; rep. for elem. music texts and programs Mahoning County Schs., Youngstown, 1959-60; tchr., organizer student trips to numerous concerts; tchr., dir. choirs and soloists for dist. and state competitions, 1955—. Composer (poems to music) Seven Last Words of Christ, also anthems, introits, reponses; arranges music for beginning and handicapped students. Dir., accompanist Terry's Variety Show, Austintown, 1951, Potter's Clay, 1980-85. Kent State U. and Youngstown U. scholar, 1951-55. Mem. Music Tchrs. Nat. Assn., Delta Omicron (life, charter mem., pres. Delta Upsilon chpt.). Avocations: travel, camping, reading, walking. Home and Office: 3245 W Yucca St Phoenix AZ 85029-4133

WHEELAN, BELLE S. state agency administrator; 1 child, Reginald. BA in Psychology and Sociology, Trinity U.; MA in Devel./Ednl. Psychology, La. State U.; D in Ednl. Adminstrn., U. Tex., 1984. Asst. prof. psychology, dir. devel. edn., dir. acad. support svcs. San Antonio Coll., 1977—87; dean student svcs. Thomas Nelson C.C., Hampton, Va., 1987—89; provost Tidewater C.C., Portsmouth, Va., 1989—92; pres. Ctrl. Va. C.C., 1992, No. Va. C.C., 1998—2001; sec. of edn. Commonwealth of Va., Richmond, 2002—. Mem. Jobs for Va. Grads. Bd., Am. Coll. Testing Bd., Nat. Commn. on NAEP 12th Grade Assessment and Reporting, 2003—. Recipient Outstanding Alumnus award, Trinity U., 2002, Strong Men and Women award, 2003. Mem.: Nat. Coun. on Black Am. Affairs (mem. pres. roundtable). Office: Sec of Edn Ninth St Office Bldg 5th Fl 202 N 9th St Richmond VA 23219 also: PO Box 1475 Richmond VA 23218 Office Phone: 804-786-1151.

WHEELER, BARBARA J. management consultant; b. Coral Gables, Fla., June 1, 1960; d. Robert Henry and Mary Jean (Seiler) W. BA, Miami U., 1982. Commd. 2nd lt. USAF, 1984, advanced through grades to capt., 1988, chief command control comm., def. sect., XIDB project mgr., intelligence agency; resigned, 1992; prin. cons. Litton-PRC, McLean, Va., 1994-97; dir. TRW Mgmt. Cons., Reston, Va., 1998-2000; strategic and program mgmt. counsulting, writer Montgomery Village, Md., 2000—. Mem. NAFE, Am. Prodn. and Inventory Control Soc., Project Mgmt. Inst. (cert.), Am. Legion. Avocations: reading, lecturing, travel, ice skating. E-mail: bjwheeler@comcast.net.

WHEELER, BARBARA MONICA, lawyer; b. Chgo., Mar. 20, 1947; d. John Benjamin and Elizabeth (Keife) Wheeler. BA, St. Dominic Coll., 1969, cert. Lewis U. Sch. Paraprofl. Studies, 1976; JD, DePaul U., 1980. Bar: Ill. 1980. Gen. supt. Md. Manor Devel. Co., Chgo., 1970-74; v.p. Omega Constrn. Co., Chgo., 1974-78; asst. state's atty. Cook County, Ill. Mem. Bd. Edn., Community High Sch. Dist. 99, DuPage County, 1974-76, pres., 1976—; mem. Ill. Assn. Sch. Bds., dir.-at-large Tri County div., 1976-77, dir. DuPage div., 1977-78, state dir., 1982-85, v.p., 1985-87, mem. exec. com., 1984-87; bd. dirs. Sch. Mgmt. Found. Ill., 1983; mem. task force on purposes of edn. in eighties Nat. Sch. Bds. Assn. Mem. ABA, Ill. Bar Assn., Chgo. Bar Assn., Am. Mgmt. Assn., Phi Alpha Delta. Roman Catholic. Office: Nat Bd Professional Teaching Standards 1525 Wilson Blvd Ste 500 Arlington VA 22209-3276

WHEELER, CATHY JO, federal agency administrator; b. Birmingham, Ala., Feb. 14, 1954; d. Charles Edwin and Hazel Josephine Wheeler; m. David Arthur Tate, 1994. BA, U. Montevallo, 1975; postgrad., U. Ala., 1982-84. With Social Security Adminstrn., Birmingham, 1975—, sr. employment devel. specialist, 1983-85, mgr. tech. tng. dept., 1985-91, mgmt. analyst, 1991—2000, staff advisor to asst. regional commr. Process Ctr. Ops., 2000-01, fin mgmt specialist, 2001—. V.p. Fed. Women's Program, Birmingham, 1984—85; treas., charter mem. Federally Employed Women, Birmingham, 1984—88. Mem. Art Alumni Adv. Bd., 1997—2001, v.p., 1998—2000; bd. dirs. U. Montevallo Found., 2002—. Mem.: ASTD (treas. 1987—88, pres. elect 1989, pres. 1990, asst. regional dir. 1991—92), Ala. Designer-Craftsmen, Soc. Govt. Meeting Planners (v.p. 1989—90, sec. 1990—91), U. Montevallo Nat. Alumni Assn. (bd. dirs. 1991—94, v.p. fin. 1994—98, pres.-elect 1998—2000, pres. 2000—02, parliamentarian 2002—04), Riverchase Women's Club, Jaycees (v.p. mgmt. devel. Hoover Ala. chpt. 1988—89), Chi Omega Alumni Assn. (treas. 1991, advisor 1991—). Avocations: photography, reading, travel. Home: 4001 Fairchase Ln Birmingham AL 35244-1300 Office: Social Security Adminstrn 2001 12th Ave N Birmingham AL 35285 E-mail: cathyjowheeler@bellsouth.net.

WHEELER, DOLORES, food products executive; married. Pres., CEO Gossner Foods, Logan, Utah. Bd. dir. Bus. and Econ. Delvel., Logan, Utah. Office: Gossner Foods 1051 N 1000 W Logan UT 84321-6852 Fax: 435-752-3147.

WHEELER, ELIZABETH DARRACOTT, volunteer; b. Richmond, Va., July 14, 1917; d. Clements Cawvin and Dorothy Hartung Darracott; m. Charles Horatio Wheeler, III, July 9, 1940 (dec. Sept. 16, 2000); children: Charles Horatio IV, Anne Wheeler Stratton, William Darracott. BA, U. Richmond, 1938. Cert. tchr. 1938. Instr., Varina, Va., 1938—40. Author: (book) Sir John Dodderidge, Celebrated Barrister of Britain, 1555-1628, 1992, Ten Remarkable Women of the Tudor Courts and Their Influence in Founding the New World, 1530-1630, 2000. Pres., sr. bd. mem. Va. Home, Richmond, 1961—62, pres., jr. bd. dirs., 1946—56; residential col. Richmond Area Cmty. Campaign, Richmond, 1957—57; tchr., mem. Grace Covenant Presbyn. Ch., Richmond, 1918—2002; mem., patriotic svc. com. Colonial Dames of Am., Richmond, 1944—64. Mem.: The Tuckahoe Woman's Club, The Woman's Club.

WHEELER, GERALDINE HARTSHORN, historian, writer; b. Pomona, Calif., Feb. 5, 1919; d. Albion True and Beatrice Osa (Barnes) Hartshorn; m. Lloyd Franklyn Wheeler, Dec. 2, 1938 (dec. Mar. 1996); children: Russell Lloyd, Robert Gerald. AA, Santa Barbara (Calif.) C.C., 1950's. Co-owner Atheling's, Santa Barbara, Calif., 1971-76, Pomona, 1976-90; chmn. bd. trustees Atheling Heritage Trust, Claremont, Calif., 1994—. Pub., editor: mag. Athling's, 1974—75, newsletter Grand Priory of America Order of St. Lazarus, 1974—86; editor: St. Margaret's Jour., 1975—; author: (essays) A World Full in 1891, 1975—, President John Adams - A Profile, 1975—, Ralph Waldo Emerson--A Profile, 1975, The Many Masks of Communism, 1975, A Tale of St. Nicholas, 1995, Post Cards and Postal Cards, 1996, Pocahontas Kinships, 1996. Vol. PTA, Fontana and Santa Barbara, 1945-60; active Hist. Soc. Pomona Valley, 1950—; mem. various coms. and choir First Congl. Ch., Santa Barbara, 1952-72; leader Cub Scouts Am., Santa Barbara, 1953-56; grey lady unit chmn. Santa Barbara chpt.-ARC, 1958-62; women's project bd. v.p., activities chmn., active various coms. Santa Barbara Hist. Soc., 1960-74; exec. sec. 1960 Nixon for Pres. Campaign, Santa Barbara, 1960; mem. spkrs. bur. Nixon for Gov. Campaign, Santa Barbara, 1962; mem. Rep. state ctrl. com. State of Calif., 1962-64; blitz chmn. Rockefeller for Pres. Campaign, Santa Barbara, 1964; coord. vol. svcs. Office of Civil Def., City of Santa Barbara, 1965-76; coord. tv series on earthquakes Sta. KEYT, Office of Civil Def., Santa Barbara, 1968; bd. dirs. Calif. Ctrl. Coast Area, U.S.O., 1968-76, treas. bd., 1970-76; supporter Vis. Nurses and Hospice Assn., 1994—; others. Decorated Dame of Grace, Mil. and Hospitaller Order of St. Lazarus of Jerusalem, Cert. of Merit, 1973, The Alan Weaver Hazelton award; recipient Cert. of Merit, Santa Barbara Jr. Coll., 1954-55, Medal of Appreciation SAR, 1972, Cert. of Award Nat. Soc. Daus. of Founders and Patriots of Am., 1977. Mem. Calif. Hist. Soc., New Eng. Hist. and Geneal. Soc., The Pomona Ebell (pres. 1998-2000), Wilson Ctr. Assocs., Smithsonian Assocs., Nat. Trust for Hist. Preservation, Am. Farmland Trust, Nat. Woman's History Mus., Nat. Mus. Women in the Arts, Nat. Arbor Day Found. Republican. Avocations: book collecting, reading, genealogy, classical music, needlework. Home: 1047 E Baseline Rd Claremont CA 91711-1577

WHEELER, GWEN, medical, surgical, and critical care nurse; b. Bogalusa, La., Oct. 5, 1949; d. John David and Marie (Taylor) Easterling; m. Thomas D. Wheeler, July 20, 1968; children: Thomas D. Jr., Daniel Blair. AD, S.W. Miss. Jr. Coll., Summit, 1986; student, St. Josephs Coll., 1990—95, U. So. Miss., 1995—98; M in Nursing Sci., Southeastern La. U., 2000. Cert. critical care nurse, ACLS, advance trauma life support system, RN, cert. adult nurse practitioner. Emergency rm. staff nurse Riverside Med. Ctr., Franklinton, La., 1992, nursing supr., 1992-94, staff nurse emergency room, 1998—2001; ICU staff nurse Bogalusa (La.) Cmty. Med. Ctr., Franklinton, La., 1994—98; adult nurse practitioner Franklinton Rural Health Clinic, 2001—. Mem. AACN, La. Nursing Assn., Emergency Nurses Assn. Office: FRHC 2004 S Marvin Magee Dr Franklinton LA 70438 Office Phone: 985-839-3555.

WHEELER, KATHRYN S. editor; b. Grosse Ile, Mich. d. Emich Duane and Anna K. Solms; m. William Donald Wheeler, Sept. 23, 1969. BA, Hope Coll., 1976; student, U. Mont., 1981. Editor Herman Miller Inc., Zeeland, Mich., 1977-80; copywriter Exclamation Point Advertising, Billings, Mont., 1981-84; sr. copywriter Aves Advertising, Grand Rapids, Mich., 1985-89; staff writer David Perkins & Assocs., Grand Rapids, 1990-94; editor School Zone Publishing, Grand Rapids, 1994-95; sr. editor Instructional Fair Group (now McGraw-Hill Children's Pub.), Grand Rapids, 1998—. Cons. in ednl. writing, 1994—, adj. prof. Grand Valley State U., 1986-90. Editor: ednl. CD and book series; author: Tunnel 2000, 1999, The Suspicious Stranger, 1999, No Room for Neighbors, 1999, Finders Keepers, 2000, Patty Saves the Day, 2001, Patriotic Traditions, 2002. Advertising cons. Sara Smolenski Campaign, 1996, bd. mem. Carol Irons Com., 1989. Grantee Mich. Coun. for the Arts, 1988. Mem. Soc. Children's Book Writers and Illustrators. Democrat. Episcopalian. Office: McGraw Hill Childrens Pub 3195 Wilson Ave Grand Rapids MI 49544

WHEELER, SUSIE WEEMS, retired educator; b. Cassville, Ga., Feb. 24, 1917; d. Percy Weems and Cora (Smith) Weems-Canty; m. Dan W. Wheeler Sr., June 7, 1941; 1 child, Dan Jr. BS, Fort Valley (Ga.) State U., 1945; MEd, Atlanta U., 1947, EdD, 1978; postgrad., U. Ky., 1959-60; EdS, U. Ga., 1977. Tchr. Bartow County Schs., Cartersville (Ga.) City Schs., 1938-44, Jeanes supr., 1946-58; supr., curriculum dir. Paulding Sch. Sys.-Stephens Sch., Calhoun City, 1958-64; summer sch. tchr. Atlanta U., 1961-63; curriculum dir. Bartow County Schs., 1963-79; ret., 1979. Pres., co-owner Wheeler-Morris Svc. Ctr., 1990—; mem. Ga. Commn. on Student Fin., 1985-95. Coord. Noble Hill-Wheeler Meml. Ctr. Project, 1983—. Recipient Oscar W. Canty Cmty. Svc. award, 1991, Woman in History award Fedn. Bus. and Profl. Women, 1995, New Frontiers Cmty. Svc. award, 1997, Outstanding Achievement for Preserving Georgia Hist., 2000; recognized for dedicated svc. on behalf of Bartow County Citizens Comm. Clarence Brown, 2003; named one of Women of Excellence, Star of the Past Bartow Women at Work, 2003. Mem. AAUW (v.p. membership 1989-91, Ga. Achievement award 1993, Edn. Found. award Cartersville-Bartow br.), Ga. Assn. Curriculum and Supervision (pres.-elect 1973-74, pres. 1974-75, Johnnye V. Cox award 1975), Delta Sigma Theta (pres. Rome alumnae chpt. 1978-80, mem. nat. bd. 1984, planning com. 1988—, Dynamic Delta award 1967, 78, Grand Chpt. cert. recognition 2002, recognition 50 plus years, Delta Sigma Theta Sorority, Inc., 2002), Ga. Jeanes Assn. (pres. 1968-70). Home: 105 Fite St Cartersville GA 30120-3410

WHEELER-HAPP, DARRA ANNE, secondary school educator; b. Bklyn., Apr. 5, 1961; d. Dennis Francis and Florence Elizabeth Wheeler; m. Gary Happ, Feb. 5, 1994; children: Jackson, Garrett. BS in Edn., SUNY, Cortland, 1983; M in Edn., SUNY, New Paltz, 1991. Tchr. lang. arts grades 7-8 Circleville (N.Y.) Mid. Sch., 1986—87; tchr. English grade 7 Shaker Jr. H.S., Latham, NY, 1986—87; tchr. grade 5 Roe-Jan Elem., Hillsdale, NY, 1991—98; compensatory edn. educator Taconic Hills Sch. Dist., Hillsdale, 1998—. Author: (newspaper column) Answers from the Teacher, 1999—. Mem.: NEA. Avocations: singing and playing guitar, bicycling, kayaking, walking.

WHEELOCK, PAM, financial executive; BA in History, Coll. St. Catherine; MA in Applied Econs., Marquette U. Exec. budget officer Minn. Dept. Fin., 1988—92; budget dir. City of St. Paul, 1992—94, dep. mayor, 1994—96, dir. dept. planning and econ. devel., 1996—99; commr. Minn. Dept. Fin., 1999—2002; sr. v.p., CFO Minn. Sports and Entertainment, 2002—. Office: Minn Wild 317 Washington St Saint Paul MN 55102*

WHELAN, ELIZABETH ANN MURPHY, epidemiologist; b. N.Y.C., Dec. 4, 1943; d. Joseph and Marion (Barrett) Murphy; m. Stephen T. Whelan, Apr. 3, 1971; 1 child, Christine B. BA, Conn. Coll., 1965; MPH, Yale U., 1967; MS, Harvard U., 1968, ScD, 1971. Coordinator County study Planned Parenthood, 1971-72; research assoc. Harvard Sch. Pub. Health, Boston, 1975-80; exec. dir. Am. Council Sci. and Health, N.Y.C., 1980-92, pres., 1992—. Mem. com. on pesticides and toxics EPA; mem. U.S. Com. of Vital Stats., HHS; mem. Nat. Adv. Com. on Meat and Poultry Inspection USDA; guest lectr. Queen Elizabeth 2 (Cunard Line). Author: Sex and Sensibility, 1973, Making Sense Out of Sex, 1974, Panic in the Pantry, 1975, 92, A Baby?...Maybe, 1975, Boy or Girl?, 1976, The Pregnancy Experience, 1977, Preventing Cancer, 1978, The Nutrition Hoax, 1983, A Smoking Gun, 1984, Toxic Terror, 1984, 86, 93, Balanced Nutrition, 1988; contbr. articles to profl. jours. and consumer publs. Bd. dirs. Food and Drug Law Inst., Nat. Agrl. Legal Fund, Media Inst., N.Y. divsn. Am. Cancer Soc. Recipient Disting. Achievement medal Conn. Coll., 1979, award Am. Pub. Health Assn. Environ., 1992, Disting. Alumnus award Yale U., 1994-95, Ethics award Am. Inst. Chemists, 1996. Mem. APHA (Early Career award 1982, Homer Calver award 1992), Am. Inst. Nutrition, Am. Med. Writers Assn. (Walter Alvarez award 1986), U.S. Com. Vital Stats. Office: Am Council Sci and Health 1995 Broadway Fl 2 New York NY 10023-5882 E-mail: whelan@acsh.org.

WHELAN, MARY JANE, accountant, writer, photographer; b. Canton, Ohio; d. William D. Rank and Marie E. Strahl; m. Thomas Whelan, Jan. 16, 1963; children: Thomas J., Michaela M. Rogers. Cert. tax cons. Acctg. and tax cons., Lawrenceville, Ga., 1984—2003; writer Royal Reign Publs., White City, Oreg., 1995—. Author: Accounting and Tax Consulting; author: (photographer) (poetry) Tides of Love, 2003. Nominee Bus. Woman of Yr., Atlanta, 1986; recipient 5 Editors Choice awards, Poet of Merit trophy. Avocations: travel, writing, singing, racquetball, hiking. Home: P O Box 2328 White City OR 97503 Office Phone: 541-601-9307. Personal E-mail: royalreignpub@aol.com.

WHELAN, SUSAN, member of parliament; b. Windsor, Ont., Can., May 5, 1963; d. Elizabeth and Eugene Whelan. Degree in commerce, U. Windsor, B in Laws, 1988; JD, U. Detroit. Bar: Ont. 1990. Assoc. Yuffy, Roberts, Goldstein, Manzocco, Windsor, 1988-93; M.P. for Essex-Windsor House of Commons, 1993—, parliamentary sec. to Min. Nat. Revenue, 1993-96, mem. standing com. pub. accouts, 1994-96, assoc. mem. standing com. on fin., 1994-96, vice chair fin. com., 1996-97, mem. justice subcom. on draft regulations on firearms, 1996-97, mem. subcom. on rev. of spl. import measures act, 1996, chair industry com., 1997—2002, min. internal cooperation, 2002—03. Former dir. Essex Region Conservation Found., Alzheimer Soc. Windsor and Essex County. Named "Hon. Susan E. Whelan", Minister for Internat. Coop., 2002. Mem. Law Soc. Upper Can., Can. Bar Assn., Essex County Law Assn. Office: 46 Fox St N8M2S2 Essex ON Canada*

WHELCHEL, BETTY ANNE, lawyer; b. Augusta, Ga., Dec. 22, 1956; d. John Davis and Charnell (Ramsey) W.; m. Douglas Charles Kruse, June 20, 1987. AB, U. Ga., 1978; JD, Harvard U., 1981. Bar: D.C. 1981, N.Y. 1984, gaikokuho-jimu-bengoshi (fgn. lawyer) Japan, 1988-89. Atty.-advisor U.S. Dept. Treasury, Washington, 1981-84; assoc. Shearman & Sterling, N.Y.C., 1984-87, 89-90, Tokyo, 1987-89; dep. gen. counsel Deutsche Bank N.Am., N.Y., 1990—99; global gen. counsel Deutsche Bank Asset Mgmt., 1999—. Lectr., NAS, 2003; staff atty. Depository Instns. Deregulation Com., Washington, 1983-84. Mem. Assn. of the Bar of the City of N.Y. (com. on diversity, com. on fgn. and comparative law 1992-97, chmn. 1996-99, com. on internat. affairs 1996-99). Office: Deutsche Asset Mgmt 345 Park Ave New York NY 10154 E-mail: betty.a.whelchel@db.com.

WHELCHEL, SANDRA JANE, writer; b. Denver, May 31, 1944; d. Ralph Earl and Janette Isabelle (March) Everitt; m. Andrew Jackson Whelchel, June 27, 1965; children: Andrew Jackson, Anita Earlyn. BA in Elem. Edn., U. No. Colo., 1966; postgrad., Pepperdine Coll., 1971, UCLA, 1971. Elem. tchr. Douglas County Schs., Castle Rock, Colo., 1966-68, El Monte (Calif.) schs., 1968-72; br. libr. Douglas County Librs., Parker, Colo., 1973-78; zone writer Denver Post, 1979-81; reporter The Express newspaper, Parker, Colo., 1979-81; history columnist Parker Trail newspapers, 1985-93; columnist Authorship Mag., 1991—, Gothic Jour., 1994; writing tchr. Aurora Parks and Recreation, 1985-91; writing instr. Arapahoe C.C., 1991-2000; exec. dir. Nat. Writers Assn., 1991—. Lectr. on writing and history Durango Writer's Workshop, 1996-97, Estes Park Writer's Retreat, 1996-97, Pikes Peak Writer's Workshop, 1997, Sinipee Writer's Workshop, 1998, Oasis for Seniors, 2000, Denver Women's Press Club, 1999, Rocky Mountain Gold Conf., 1999, Colo. Writers Fellowship, 2000, Colo. Ind. Publishers, 2000; spkr. Internat. Olympiad of Mind, Paris, 2000, Art Cafe, 2003; motivational spkr. various Optomist groups in Denver area. Editor Authorship mag., 1992-98; lit. agent NWLA, 1996-99; contbr. short stories and articles to various publs. including: The Writer, Writer's Open Forum, Writer's Jour., Reunions, Fresno Bee, Ancestry Newsletter, Calif. Horse Rev., Host mag., Jack and Jill, Child Life, Children's Digest, Peak to Peak mag.; author (non-fiction books): Your Air Force Academy, 1982, A Guide to the U.S. Air Force Acad., 1990, Parker, Colorado: A Folk History, 1990, The Beginning Writer's Writing Book, 1996, A Folk History of Parker and Hilltop, 1996, (treatment writer documentary) Wild Blue, 2003; co-author: The Writer's Office, 1998, The Register, 1989, (coloring books) A Day at the Cave, 1985, A Day in Blue, 1984, Pro Rodeo Hall of Champions and Museum of the American Cowboy, 1985, Pikes Peak Country, 1986, Mile High Denver, 1987. Mem.: Nat. Writers Assn. (pres. 1990, 1991, 2003—04), Colo. Author's League (awards com. 1999—2000, who's who com. 2001), Parker Area Hist. Soc. (pres. 1987—89), Nat. Writer's Club (treas. Denver Metro chpt. 1985—86, v.p. membership 1987, sec, 1990, bd. dirs., pres. 1990—91, v.p. programs 1992, v.p. membership 2002, bd. dirs., pres. 2003).

WHETSTONE, CHARLOTTE ANDREWS, principal; b. N.Y.C., Apr. 11, 1952; d. Jeanelle Andrews; m. W. Mabrey Whetstone, Jan. 15, 1977; children: Whitney Elizabeth, Briana Elise. BSc, U. Fla., 1973; MEd, Auburn U., 1978. Cert. supr./adminstr. Ala. Prin. Coosada Elem. Sch., Millbrook, Ala., 1998—; asst. prin. Robinson Springs Elem. Sch., Millbrook, Ala., 1997—98; tchr. Wetumpka Elem. Sch., Wetumpka, Ala., 1988—97, Brewbaker Elem. Sch., Montgomery, Ala., 1978—88. Actor: (cmty. theater) Rumors. Quality assurance com. mem. Elmore County Dept. of Human Resources, Wetumpka, Ala., 2000—03; comprehensive sys. of pers. devel. com. mem. State Dept. of Edn., Montgomery, Ala., 2000—02; chair of future growth com. First United Meth. Ch., Wetumpka, Ala., 1998—2000. Recipient Master Educator, Renaissance Learning, 2002—04. Mem.: NAESP, Nat. Edn. Assn., Coun. for Exceptional Children (life). Methodist. Avocations: reading, travel, community theater. Home: 450 Holiday Dr Titus AL 36080 Office: Coosada Elementary School 5260 Airport Rd Millbrook AL 36054 Personal E-mail: cwhetst450@aol.com.

WHICHELLO, CAROL, political scientist, educator, writer; b. Newton, N.J., Mar. 29, 1945; d. Arthur Frederick Whichello and M. W. Niper. BA, Salem Internat. U., 1967; MEd, Coll. N.J., 1978. Cert. tchr. N.J., Fla. Tchr. Freehold Twp. (N.J.) Bd. Edn., 1967—97; adj. prof. polit. sci. Indian River C.C., 1998—; sub. tchr. Martin County Sch. Bd., Fla., 2001—. Past exed. bd. dirs., legis. chairperson Freehold Twp. Edn. Assn. Mem. Stuart (Fla.) Heritage Mus., 1998—, bd. mem., 2002—. Recipient N.J. Mid. Sch.Tchr. of Yr. in Social Studies, N.J. Social Studies Tchrs., 1989. Democrat. Baptist. Avocations: writing, editing historical works. Home: 1668 SW Crossing Cir Palm City FL 34990-2460

WHILDIN, LEONORA PORRECA, retired nursing educator; b. Boston, Mass., Dec. 7, 1926; d. John and Anna (Annunziata) Porreca; m. William Miller Whildin; children: Susan Lee, Robert Miller, Walter Thomas. BS, Boston U., 1954; MS, Columbia U., 1971. RN, Mass., N.Y., N.J.; cert. nurse midwife, N.Y. Cadet nurse corps. Boston City Hosp., 1943-46, staff, asst. head nurse neurology, neurosurgery, 1946-48, scrub nurse neurosurgery, 1948-50; civilian nurse Dept. of Army, Bremerhaven, Germany, 1948; pub. health nurse Bklyn. Vis. Nurse Assn., 1954-56; instr. Helene Fulde Sch. of Practical Nursing, N.Y.C., 1956-57; pub. health nurse V.N.A. Morris Co., Morristown, N.J., 1967; instr. All Souls Hosp. Sch. of Nursing, Morristown, N.J., 1968-69; guest lectr. Seton Hall U., South Orange, N.J., 1978. Del. Am. Nurses Assn, Mass., 1954; By-Laws Com. Am. Coll. Nurse Midwives, N.Y., 1972, By-Laws Com. Am. Coll. Nurse Midwives (N.J. chpt.), 1980; bd. mem. V.N.A. Morris Co., Morristown, N.J., 1977-78; v.p. bd. health, Randolph Twp., Randolph, N.J., 1972-74. Coun. woman Randolph Twp., 1972-78; mayor (1st woman mayor) Randolph Twp., 1977; Dem. party county com., Morris Co., Morristown, N.J., 1972-96; Dem. party state com., N.J., 1992-98; vol. United Way of Morris County. Mem. APHA, ANA, LWV, Mass., N.Y., N.J. (bd. mem. 1964-66), Sigma Theta Tau. Democrat. Avocations: ice skating, knitting, crafts, hiking. [illegible] Radtke Rd Randolph NJ 07869-3815

WHILEY, JULIA HELEN, writer, actor; b. Miami, Feb. 20, 1951; d. Maceo and Sherah Jones; m. Leroy Eugene Whiley, Oct. 26, 1990; m. Morgan Eugene Thomas, Aug. 8, 1982 (div. Oct. 20, 1990); children: Ayana Sheba Sanders, Aliscia Leala, Latasha Lanae. BA in Comm., Old Dominian U., 2002. Lic. message therapist Fla. Dept Profl. Regulations, 1995. Sec. Fla. Dept. Rehab. Svcs.- Vocat. Rehab., Miami, 1973—76; cert. worker II Fla. Dept. Health and Rehab. Svcs.- Food Stamps Office, 1976—80; veneral disease investigator Dade County Healt Dept., 1980—86; commd. USN, 1983, ret. petty officer, 1996. Actress, playwright, screenwriter, poet Norfolk Playwright Forum, Va., 2002—. Author of poems, (short stories) Love On The Fang Side Of The Moon, (screenplays) Detective Story, (plays) A lovely Day, One More Try; actor: (plays) Ti-jean, The Great Dismale Swamp, Everyman, Antigone, Abolishian Museum, African Kings and Queens; dir.: True West. Decorated Sailor Of The Month. Mem.: Dramatist Guild Am., Am. Screen Writers Assn. Liberal. Avocations: acting, writing. Personal E-mail: juliawhi51@aol.com.

WHIPKEY-LOUDEN, HARRIET BEULAH, fine arts and theatre productions executive; b. Willmar, Minn., Mar. 9, 1932; d. Frank Leroy and Annetta Cecelia (Cafferty) Whipkey; m. James William Louden, Aug. 20, 1956; children: Liza Katherin, Cheryl Anne. BS, St. Cloud State U., 1954; MA, Montclair State Coll., 1978. English-speech tchr. Minn. Dept. Edn., Verndale, Sauk Centre, Sauk Rapids, Minn., 1954-57, Bd. of Edn., Marquette, Mich., 1958-62, Slinger, Wis., 1963-67; drama dept. chair Bd. Edn., Pattonville High, St. Louis, 1967-69; speech and theatre dept. chair Bd. of Edn., Westfield, N.J., 1969-85; v.p. Louden Enterprises, Phoenix, 1990—. Dir.-producer The Scholarship Show, Marquette, Mich., 1960; drama cons. New Faces of Charleston, Charleston, N.C., 1986-89, Internat. Models Talent Competition, Scottsdale, Ariz., 1986-89; edn. cons. Nat. Assn. Restaurant Mgrs., Scottsdale, 1988. Co-founder, chair 1st All Upper Peninsula Art Show, 1960; founder, pres. Ariz. State U. Theatre Assn., 1985-88; creator, dir. Children's Touring Theatre, St. Louis, 1968, Westfield, N.J., 1971, Summer Theatre Workshop, Pine-Strawberry, Ariz., 1990; founding bd. mem. N.J. Theatre Forum, 1979; TV talk show host Channel 9 Cable, Scottsdale, 1986-88; bd. mem. Phoenix East Valley Social Svcs.; founder Youth Theatre, Pine, Ariz., 1995. Grantee N.J. Dept. Edn., 1978; recipient Gov.'s Citation, State of Mich., 1960. Mem. AAUW (pres. Marquette chpt. 1960), Ariz. Arts Commn., Ariz. for Cultural Devel., Ariz. Theatre Edn. Assn., Ariz. State U. Toastmasters, Friends of Ariz. State U. Art Mus. Avocations: theatre, art, travel, mountain living. Home and Office: 5836 E Angela Dr Tempe AZ 85284-3460

WHIPPLE, JUDITH ROY, editor; b. N.Y.C., May 14, 1935; d. Edwin Paul and Elizabeth (Levis) Roy; m. William Whipple, Oct. 26, 1963. AB, Mount Holyoke Coll., 1957. Head libr. Am. Sch. Lima (Peru), S.A., 1957-59; asst. editor children's books G.P. Putnam's Sons, N.Y.C., 1959-62; assoc. editor W.W. Norton & Co., Inc., N.Y.C., 1962-68; editor Four Winds Press, 1968-75; editor-in-chief Scholastic Gen. Book Divsn., 1975-77; pub. Four Winds Press subs. Scholastic Inc., N.Y.C., 1977-82; pub., v.p. Macmillan Pub. Co., N.Y.C., 1982-89, exec. editor, 1989-94; editl. dir. Cavendish Children's Books, Tarrytown, NY, 1994—2002. Mem. PEN, Children's Book Coun. (pres. 1977, bd. dirs. 1970-79), Women's Nat. Book Assn., Soc. Children's Book Writers and Illustrators. Avocations: gardening, swimming, piano, travel. E-mail: jrwhipple@stny.rr.com.

WHIPPLE, MARY MARGARET, state legislator; b. Watsela, Ill., May 26, 1940; BA, Am. U.; MA, George Washington U. Mem. Va. State Senate, 1996—, mem. agrl., conservation & natural resources comm., mem. local govt. com., mem. privileges & elections com., mem. transp. com. Democrat. Presbyterian. Office: Gen Assembly Bldg 910 Capitol St Rm 430 Richmond VA 23219-3400

WHISENHUNT, LIVIA L. marketing executive; b. Auburn, Ala., Oct. 15, 1958; d. Jack McKee and Fabiola (Tirado Plata) Whisenhunt; m. Dewey W. Johnson, Oct. 6, 1990. Grad. high sch. Proprietor Covington Gas & Grocery, Atlanta, 1980-81; gen. mgr. Petroleum Mktg. Co. of Ga., Atlanta, 1981-84; v.p. Ballenger-Hunt Investment Corp., Atlanta, 1984-86; pres. Petroleum Source & Systems Group, Atlanta, 1986—. Mem. Assn. Energy Engrs., Nat. Minority Purchasing Coun. Republican. Roman Catholic. Avocations: golf, tennis, orienteering, fishing, bird hunting.

WHISLER, ELIZABETH ANNE, government agency administrator; d. Radm Glenn Edward Whisler Jr. and Elizabeth Louise Flannery. BA in English, Villanova U., 1996; MA in Irish Lit., U. Ulster, Ireland, 1999. Pub. rels. Newport Harbor Corp., RI, 1996—97; writer and editor Fodor's Travel Guides, Dublin, 1999—, Belfast, Ireland, 1999—; island ops. U.S. Dept. of State, Dublin, 1999—2002, Belfast, 1999—2002; congl. liaison U.S. Pentagon, Washington, 2002—. Mem. Nat. Mus. Women in the Arts, 2002—03, Dem. Nat. Com., 2003. Recipient Bronze medals for paddle-boarding, R.I. State Lifeguard Tournament, 1998, Newport Invitational Lifeguard Tournament, 1999. Mem.: Villanova Univ. Alumni Assn., Am. Friends Univ. Ulster. Roman Catholic. E-mail: elizabeth.whisler@pentagon.af.mil.

WHITACRE, CAROLINE CLEMENT, immunologist, researcher; b. Cin., Nov. 4, 1949; d. Richard Soteldo and Rosalyn (Wilson) W.; m. Michael Francis Para, June 28, 1975: 1 child, Alexander. BA, Ohio State U., 1971, PhD, 1975. Postdoctoral fellow Northwestern U., Chgo., 1975-78, instr., 1978-81; asst. prof. Ohio State U., Columbus, 1981-87, assoc. prof., 1987-92, prof. of microbiology and immunology, 1992—, interim chair, 1992-94, chair, 1994—. Mem. com. on fellowship awards Nat. Multiple Sclerosis Soc., 1992-97, com. air, 1995-97, chair com. on gender and autoimmunity, 1997-99. Contbr. articles to profl. pubs. Nat. Insts. for Allergy and Infectious Diseases grantee, 1987—, NIH-Nat. Insts. for Neurol. Disorders and Stroke grantee, 1991—, Nat. Multiple Sclerosis grantee, 1991—. Mem. AAAS, NIH (spl. study sect. 1987-91, neurol. disorders com. 1991-95), Am. Assn. Immunologists, N.Y. Acad. Scis. Presbyterian. Achievements include discovery that experimental autoimmune encephalomyelitis can be suppressed by the oral administration of myelin basic protein due to the anergy or deletion of myelin basic protein specific T lymphocytes; research on multiple sclerosis and the animal model, experimental autoimmune encephalomyelitis,sex differences in autoimmune diseases, and effects of stress on immune function. Office: Ohio State U 2078 Graves Hall 333 W 10th Ave Columbus OH 43210-1239 E-mail: whitacre.3@osu.edu.

WHITAKER, DIANA MARIE, medical/surgical nurse; b. Utica, N.Y. d. Wendell Wolfred Witaker and Gail Ita Glenson. EMS tech. AS degree, Indian River C.C., 1995, ADN, 1999. RN, Fla.; nat. registered paramedic. Firefighter, rescue EMT Griffiss AFB, Rome, N.Y., 1993; paramedic Marint Meml. Hosp., Stuart, Fla., 1995-99, Indian River Meml. Hosp., Vero Beach, Fla.; RN Holmes Regional Med., Melbourne, Fla., 1999—. EMT course coord., instr. City Coll. of Chgo., 1990-91. Team capt. Relay for Life-ACS, Stuart, Fla., 1998; coord. Crop Walk, Stuart, 1998-99; mem. Women in Mil. Svcs. Meml. Found., 1998-99. Staff sgt. USAF, 1982-90. Mem. Nursing Student Assn. (project in touch recruiter, pub. rels. officer, runner ho. of dels. 1998, Cmty. Svc. award 1999), Am. Cancer Soc. (coord., leader 1998-99). Avocations: helping the homeless, bicycling, weight lifting, college. Home: #10R 4589 Whispering Pines Ln Fort Pierce FL 34982-6967

WHITAKER, EILEEN MONAGHAN (EILEEN MONAGHAN), artist; b. Holyoke, Mass., Nov. 22, 1911; d. Thomas F. and Mary (Doona) Monaghan; m. Frederic Whitaker. Ed., Mass. Coll. Art, Boston. Annual [illegible] in natl. and regional juried shows; represented in permanent collections, Frye Mus., Seattle, NA, Hispanic Soc., N.Y.C., High Mus. Art, Atlanta, U. Mass., Norfolk (Va.) Mus., Springfield (Mass.) Mus. Art, Reading (Pa.) Art Mus., Nat. Acad., U. Mass., Okla. Mus. Art, St. Lawrence U., Wichita State U., San Diego Mus. Art, Retrospective show, Founders Gallery U. San Diego, 1988, invitational one-person show Frye Art Mus., 1990; included in pvt. collections; featured in cover article of American Artist mag., Mar. 1987, in article Art of Calif. mag., July 1991; invitational Am. Realism Exhbn. Cir. Gallery, San Diego, 1992; author: Eileen Monaghan Whitaker Paints San Diego, 1986. Recipient numerous major awards, including Allied Artists Am., Am. Watercolor Soc., 1st prize Providence Water Color Club, Wong award Calif. Watercolor Soc., De Young award Soc. Western Artists, 1st award Springville (Utah) Mus., Ranger Fund purchase prize, Orbrig prize NA, Walter Biggs Meml. award, 1987; silver medal Am. Watercolor Soc., Watercolor West; fellow Huntington Hartford Found., 1964. Mem. Nat. Acad. Design (Academician NA, William P. and Gertrude Schweitzer prize for excellence in watercolor 171st Annual Exbhn. 1996); mem. Am. Watercolor Soc. (Dolphin fellow), Watercolor West (hon.), San Diego Watercolor Soc. (hon.), Providence Watercolor Club (award), Phila. Watercolor Club. Home: 1579 Alta La Jolla Dr La Jolla CA 92037-7101 E-mail: fandemwhitaker@aol.com.

WHITAKER, ELIZABETH, lawyer; b. Washington, Feb. 20, 1953; BA magna cum laude, Wehaton Coll., 1975; JD with honors, So. Meth. U., 1980. Bar: Tex. 1980. Fellow: Dallas Bar Found., Tex. Bar Found.; mem.: Order of Coif, Coll. of State Bar Tex., State Bar Tex. (chair continuing legal edn. com. 1996—97, bd. dirs. 1996—99, chair bd. dirs. 1998—99). Office: Hankinson & Whitaker LLP 2305 Cedar Springs Ste 230 Dallas TX 75201

WHITAKER, FREDA N. trust company executive; BS, U. Mo., Kansas City. With Patrons Bank (now NationsBank), Olathe, Kans., Johnson County Bank (now Firstar); exec. v.p. The Midwest Trust Co., Overland Park, Kans. Mem.: Ea. Kans. Estate Planning Coun., Estate Planning Soc. Kansas City (past pres.). Office: The Midwest Trust Co 10740 Nall Ave Ste 100 Overland Park KS 66211

WHITAKER, RUTH M. newswriter, photographer, horse breeder; b. Jacksonville, Fla., Feb. 18, 1935; d. Clifford Orville Bailey and Margaret Agnes Carlton Bailey Walden; m. Ray Gene Whitaker, Sept. 1, 1951; children: Raymond Eugene, Charles David, Frank Robert, Cynthia Ann, Wayne Douglas, Linda Ruth, Margaret Lee. Student, Palmer Inst, San Antonio Coll. Real Estate. Sales Lee Schwartz Shop, Uvalde, Tex., 1949—50; sales, window decorator Julian's, 1950—51, Levine's Dept. Store, San Angelo, 1951—52; asst. photographer Joske's Portrait Studio, 1952—54; photographer Studer's Aztec Theatre Bldg, 1954—55; reporter, photographer Hondo Anvil Herald, Hondo, 1960—62; reporter, photographer, columnist Medina Valley Times, Deville, 1970—84, Devine News, Devine, 1984—97, 2000—. Horse breeder Am. Quar. Horses, 1960—2002; owner dog kennel. Mem.: Biry Hermann Sons (sec.-treas. 1995—). Republican. Methodist. Avocations: hand tooled leatherwork, painting, genealogy. Office: The Devine News 216 S Bright Devine TX 78016 E-mail: rmw@devtex.net.

WHITAKER, RUTH REED, state legislator, retired newspaper editor; b. Blytheville, Ark., Dec. 13, 1936; d. Lawrence Neill and Ruth Shipton (Weidemeyer) Reed; m. Thomas Jefferson Whitaker, dec. 29, 1961; children: Steven Bryan, Alicia Morrow. BA, Hendrix Coll., 1958. Copywriter, weather person KTVE TV, El Dorado, Ark., 1958-59; nat. bridal cons. Treasure House, El Dorado, 1959; bridal cons. Pfeifers of Ark., Little Rock, 1959-60; dir. of continuity S. M. Brooks Advt. Agy., Little Rock, 1960-61; layout artist C. V. Mosby Co., St. Louis, 1961-62; editor, owner Razorback Am. Newspaper, Ft. Smith, Ark., 1979-81; ret., 1981; mem. from dist. 3 Ark. State Senate, 2000—. Host Crawford Conversations TV show; contbr. author indsl. catalog, 1979 (Addy award). State sec. Rep. Party of Ark., 1992-94, mem. Ark. Electoral Coll., 1996, del. Rep. Nat. Conv., 1996; ; mem. Ben Geren Regional Park Commn., Sebastian County, Ark., 1984-89, pres., 1990; past pres. Jr. Civic League; mem. Ft. Smith Orchid Com.; mem. com. of 21 United Way; publicity chmn. Sebastian County Rep. Com., 1983-84; state press officer Reagan-Bush Campaign, 1984; exec. dir. Ark. Dole for Pres., 1995-96; pres. Women's Aux. Sebastian County Med. Soc., 1974; mem. Razorback Scholarship Fund; class agt. alumni fund Hendrix Coll., 1990, 91, 92; mem. Sparks Woman's Bd.; 1st vice chmn. 3d Dist. Rep. Party; state committeewoman Rep. Party Ark.; chmn. Crawford County Rep. Com.; apptd. by Gov. of Ark. to Commr. Ark. Ednl. TV Network Commn., sec. 1998-99; mem. city coun. City of Cedarville, Ark., 1998; dist. panelist NOW in Bux., 2003. Recipient Disting. Vol. Leadership award Nat. Found. March of Dimes, 1973, Appreciation award Ft. Smith Advt. Fedn., 1977, 78, Recognition award United Cerebral Palsy, 1980, Hon. Parents of Yr. award U. Ark., 1984, Firekeeper award Sparks Hosp. Women's Ctr., 2003. Mem. AAUW, Alden Soc. Am. (life), Ft. Smith C. of C., Ark. Nature Conservancy, Am. Legion Aux., Frontier Rschrs. Soc. (pres. 1995-96), Daus. Union Vets. Presbyterian. Avocations: philanthropy, genealogy, writing, photography, ornithology. Home: PO Box 349 Cedarville AR 72932-0349

WHITAKER, SHIRLEY ANN, telecommunications company marketing executive; b. Asmara, Eritea, Ethiopia, Oct. 13, 1955; (parents Am. citizens); d. Calvin Randall and Ruth (Ganeles) Peck; m. John Marshall Whitaker, June 16, 1973; 1 child, Kathryn Ann. AA, Tacoma Community Coll., 1974; BA, Wash. State U., 1977, MBA, 1978. Planning adminstr. for econ. rsch. GTE NW, Everett, Wash., 1978-80; specialist in demand analysis western region GTE Svc. Corp., Los Gatos, Calif., 1980-81, fin. analyst Stamford, Conn., 1981-83, staff specialist demand analysis and forecasting, 1983-84; group mgr. for rate devel. Nat. Exch. Carrier Assn., Whippany, N.J., 1984-87; mgr. pricing strategy and migration GTE Calif., Thousand Oaks, 1987-88; mgr. market forecasting GTE Telephone Ops. Hdqrs., Irving, Tex., 1989-90, dir. revenue analysis, 1990-92, dir. market rsch., 1992-93, dir. process re-engring., 1993-94, dir. network and resource mgmt., 1994-97; gen. sales mgr. customer contact GTE Network Svcs., Victorville, Calif., 1997-2000; dir. employee devel. Verizon Comm., N.Y.C., 2000—01, dir. support and response ctrs. Trenton, NJ, 2001—. Mem. Am. Mktg. Assn. (mem. chair 1984), Beta Gamma Sigma, Phi Kappa Phi, Rotary (sec. 2000). Avocation: sailing.

WHITAKER, SUSANNE KANIS, veterinary medical librarian; b. Clinton, Mass., Sept. 10, 1947; AB in Biology, Clark U., 1969; MS in Library Sci., Case Western Res. U., 1970. Regional reference librarian Yale Med. Library, New Haven, 1970-72; med. librarian Hartford Hosp., Conn., 1972-77; asst. librarian Cornell U., Ithaca, N.Y., 1977-78; vet. med. librarian Coll. Vet. Medicine, Cornell U., 1978-98, vet. pub. svcs. libr., 1998—. Mem. Med. Libr. Assn. (sec.-treas. vet. med. librs. sect. 1983-84, chmn. 1984-85, chmn. pub. rels. com. 2000—), Med. Libr. Assn. (upstate N.Y. and Ont. chpt.), Acad. Health Info. Profls. Home: 23 Wedgewood Dr Ithaca NY 14850-1064 Office: Cornell U Coll Vet Medicine Flower-Sprecher Libr Ithaca NY 14853-6401 Office Phone: 607-253-3499. Business E-Mail: skw2@cornell.edu.

WHITAKER, WILMA NEUMAN, retired mathematics instructor; b. Chgo., Aug. 18, 1937; d. August P. and Wilma M. (Kaiser) Neuman; m. G.D. Whitaker, Mar. 28, 1970; children: Brett Allan Karlsen, Karen J. Whitaker Laflin, Mark D. Whitaker, David R. Whitaker. BA in Math., DePauw U., 1959; MEd in Math., Francis Marion Coll., 1988. Cert. secondary tchr., Ill., Mich., S.C.; cert. realtor Mich. High sch. math tchr. Dist. 209, Hillside, Ill., 1959-61, Dist. 214, Mt. Prospect, Ill., 1961-65; apprentice pharmacist Karlsen Pharmacy, Mt. Prospect, 1961-67; realtor Durbin Co., Clarkston, Mich., 1977-81; sub. tchr. Clarkston (Mich.) Cmty. Schs., 1979-80; [illegible] Florence (S.C.)-Darlington Tech. Coll., 1981-85, math dept. head, 1985-87, dean arts and scis., 1987-95, instr. math., 1995-99, ret., 1999. Stephen min. St. Lukes Luth. Ch., Florence, 1991—, coun., 1989-92, tchr., 1981-98; founder, organizer Spring Cmty. Walk Along Rotary Beauty Trail, Florence, 1988, 89, 91. Named Faculty Mem. of Yr., Florence-Darlington Tech. Coll., 1987, Adminstr. of Yr., 1992, Exec. of Yr., Florence chpt. Profl. Secs. Internat., 1993. Mem. Optimist Club of Florence (v.p. 1991-92, pres. 1992-93), Optimist Internat. (lt. gov. Zone 6 S.C. 1993-94, 95-96, gov.-elect S.C. dist. 1994-95, gov. 1995-96, lt. gov. Zone 8 1996-97), Theta Sigma Phi, Delta Zeta. Avocations: antiques, bible study, travel, needlework.

WHITE, ALICE ELIZABETH, physicist, researcher; b. Glen Ridge, N.J., Apr. 5, 1954; d. Alan David and Elizabeth Joyce (Jones) W.; m. Donald Paul Monroe, Oct. 13, 1990; children: Ellen Elizabeth White Monroe, Janet Clare White Monroe. BA in Physics, Middlebury (Vt.) Coll., 1976; MA in Physics, Harvard U., 1978, PhD in Physics, 1982. Postdoctoral mem. tech. staff AT&T Bell Labs., Murray Hill, N.J., 1982-84, mem. tech. staff, 1984-88; dir. Bell Labs Lucent Technologies, Murray Hill, N.J., 1988—. Contbr. over 100 articles to profl. pubs.; patentee in field. Recipient Alumni Achievement award Middlebury Coll., 1994; Bell Labs. fellow, 2001. Fellow Am. Phys. Soc. (Maria Goeppert-Mayer award 1991); mem. IEEE, Optical Soc. of Am., Phi Beta Kappa. Office: Bell Labs Lucent Technol Rm 1D-339 PO Box 636 New Providence NJ 07974-0636

WHITE, ANNETTE IRENE, marketing professional; b. L.A., Oct. 28, 1970; d. Fleming Leonard White and Jessica Frances Chavez-White. BBA, ASU, Tempe, Ariz., 1999; student Leadership Mgmt., ASU Leadership Inst., Tempe, Ariz., 2000—. V.p. mktg. mgr. Chicanos Por La Causa, Phoenix, 1994—. Pres. ASU Downtown Alumni Bd., Phoenix, 2003—, pres. elect., 2001—03; mem. at large DeColores Domestic Viol Shelter, Phoenix, 2001—; rep. Environ.-Comm. Action Coun., Phoenix, 2003—. Mem.: Amnestiy Internat., Nat. Coun. of La Raza, Am. Legion Post 41. Democrat. Cath. Avocations: music, interior decorating, research. Office: Chicanos Por La Causa 1112 E Buckeye Rd Phoenix AZ 85034

WHITE, BARBARA ANN, physical science technician; b. Beckley, W.Va., June 28, 1963; d. Robert Diehl and Jo Ann (Watson) Rhodes; m. Randy Dale White, Aug. 31, 1985 (div. Oct. 1999); 1 child, Julia Ann-Marie. BS in Zoology, Marshall U., 1985. Asst. mgr. Rt. 16 Gift Shop, Beckley, 1981-85; biol. scis. technician VA Med. Ctr., Huntington, W.V., 1986, 89-92; data entry clk. Navy Fed. Credit Union, Vienna, Va., 1987; med. technologist Nat. Health Labs., Vienna, 1987-89; phys. sci. technician Appalachian Farming Sys. Rsch. Ctr., USDA, Beaver, W.Va., 1992—, mem. chem. response team, 1993-95, chmn. ednl. outreach, 1996-97. Troop leader, recruiter Black Diamond coun. Girl Scouts U.S.A., 1992—, spl. event coord., 1993—; Career Day spkr. Raleigh County Bd. Edn., Beckley, 1993—; coord. children's ministry Mabscott (W.Va.) United Meth. Ch., 1995-98. Recipient honor award Beckley Area Fedn. Assn. Mem. AAUW (br. pres. 1995-97, W.Va. program v.p. 1999-01, organizer sister to sister summit 1999-00), Am. Chem. Soc. (technician affiliate group). Democrat. Office: USDA ARS Appalachian Farming Sys Rsch Ctr 1224 Airport Rd Beaver WV 25813-9423 Home: 2282 Robert C Byrd Dr Beckley WV 25801-8789 E-mail: bawhite@citynet.net.

WHITE, BETTY, actress, comedienne; b. Oak Park, Ill., Jan. 17, 1922; m. Allen Ludden, 1963 (dec.). Student pub. schs., Beverly Hills, Calif. Appearances on radio shows This Is Your FBI, Blondie, The Great Gildersleeve; actress: (TV series) including Hollywood on Television, The Betty White Show, 1954-58, Life With Elizabeth, 1953-55, A Date With The Angels, 1957-58, The Pet Set, 1971, Mary Tyler Moore Show, 1974-77, The Betty White Show, 1977, The Golden Girls, 1985-92 (Emmy award for best actress 1986), The Golden Palace, 1992-93, Maybe This Time, 1995—, The Story of Santa Claus, 1996, A Weekend in the Country, 1996; (TV miniseries) The Best Place to be, 1979, The Gossip Columnist, 1980, (films) Advise and Consent, 1962, Dennis the Menace 2, 1998, Hard Rain, 1998 ; guest appearances on other programs; summer stock appearances Guys and Dolls, Take Me Along, The King and I, Who Was That Lady?, Critic's Choice, Bells are Ringing. Recipient Emmy award NATAS, 1975, 76, 86; L.A. Area Emmy award, 1952. Mem. AFTRA, Am. Humane Assn., Greater L.A. Zoo Assn. (dir.). Office: c/o William Morris Agy Betty Fanning 151 S El Camino Dr Beverly Hills CA 90212-2704

WHITE, BEVERLY JANE, cytogeneticist; b. Seattle, Oct. 9, 1938; Grad., U. Wash., 1959, MD, 1963. Diplomate Nat. Bd. Med. Examiners, Am. Bd. Pediatrics, Am. Bd. Med. Genetics; lic physician and surgeon, Wash., N.J., Calif. Rsch. trainee dept. anatomy Sch. Medicine U. Wash., Seattle, 1960-62, pediatric resident dept. pediatrics, 1967-69; rotating intern Phila. Gen. Hosp., 1963-64; rsch. fellow med. ob-gyn. unit Cardiovascular Rsch. Inst. U. Calif. Med. Ctr., San Francisco, 1964-65; staff fellow lab. biomed. scis. Nat. Inst. Child Health and Human Devel. NIH, Bethesda, Md., 1965-67, sr. staff fellow, attending physician lab. exptl. pathology Nat. Inst. Arthritis, Metabolism and Digestive Diseases, 1969-74, acting chief sect. cytogenetics, 1975-76, rsch. med. officer, attending physician sect. cytogenetics lab. cellular biology and genetics, 1974-86, dir. cytogenetics unit, interinstitute med. genetics program clin. ctr., 1987-95; dir. cytogenetics Corning Clin. Labs., Teterboro, N.J., 1995-96; assoc. med. dir. cytogenetics Nichols Inst.-Quest Diagnostics, San Juan Capistrano, Calif., 1996-97, med. dir. cytogenetics, 1998—2000, med. dir. genetics divsn., 2000—02, med. dir. cytogenetics and genetic counseling, 2002—. Vis. scientist dept. pediat. divsn. genetics U. Wash. Sch. Medicine, 1983-84; intramural cons. NIH, 1975-95; cons. to assoc. editor Jour. Nat. Cancer Inst., 1976; cons. dept. ob-gyn. Naval Hosp., Bethesda, 1988-89; lectr., presenter in field. Recipient Mosby Book award, 1963, Women of Excellence award U. Wash. and Seattle Profl. chpt. Women in Comm., 1959, Reuben award Am. Soc. for Study Sterility, 1963. Fellow Am. Coll. Med. Genetics (founding), Am. Acad. Pediatrics; mem. AMA. Am. Soc. Human Genetics, Assn. Genetic Technologists (program com. 1989). Home: 14 Toulon Laguna Niguel CA 92677 Office: Nichols Inst Quest Diagnostics Inc Dept Cytogenetics San Juan Capistrano CA 92690-6130 E-mail: bjwsur@aol.com.

WHITE, BONNIE YVONNE, management consultant, retired educator; b. Long Beach, Calif., Sept. 4, 1940; d. William Albert and Helen Iris (Harbaugh) W. BS, Brigham Young U., 1962, MS, 1965, EdD in Ednl. Adminstrn., 1976; postgrad., Harvard U., 1987. Tchr. Wilson High Sch., Long Beach, Calif., 1962-63; grad. asst. Brigham Young U., Provo, Utah, 1963-65; instr., dir. West Valley Coll., Saratoga, Calif., 1965-76; instr., evening adminstr. Mission Coll., Santa Clara, Calif., 1976-80; dean gen. edn. Mendocino Coll., Ukiah, Calif., 1980-85; dean instrn. Porterville (Calif.) Coll., 1985-89, dean adminstrv. svc., 1989-93. Rsch. assoc. SAGE Rsch. Internat., Orem, Utah, 1975-99. Mem. AAUW, Faculty Assn. Calif., Cmty. Colls., Calif., Coun. Fine Arts Deans, Assn. Calif. C.C. Adminstrs., Assn. Calif. C.C. Adminstrs. Liberal Arts, Zonta (intern), Soroptimists (intern). Republican. Mem. Lds Ch.

WHITE, CAROLYN LOUISE, music educator; b. LaCrosse, Wis., Sept. 5, 1939; d. Julius Elmer and Nora Marie Forde; m. Ronald Glenn White, Aug. 18, 1962; children: Elizabeth, Sara, Andrea. BA, Luther Coll., 1961. Tchr. Madison (Wis.) Pub. Schs., 1961—67; piano tchr. pvt. lessons, Madison, 1965—; substitute tchr. Verona Area Schs., Wis., 1970—85. Dir. music camp Bethel Horizons, Madison; sec., pres. Fitchrona EMS, Verona, 1978—83; accompanist children's choir Bethel Luth. Ch., Madison, Wis. Mem.: Verona Area Performing Arts Series (pres. 1998—2003), Madison Symphony Orch., Madison Symphony Orch. League (pres. 2000), Madison Area Piano Tchrs. Assn. (pres. 1992), Attic Angel Assn., Madison Civics

Club (pres. 1998). Achievements include development of Verona Area Performing Arts Series. Avocations: gardening, travel, reading. Home: 6871 Sunset Dr Verona WI 53593

WHITE, CONSTANCE BURNHAM, state official; b. Odgen, Utah, July 2, 1954; d. Owen W. and Colleen (Redd) Burnham; m. Wesley Robert White, Mar. 18, 1977. BA in English magna cum laude, U. Utah, 1976, postgrad., 1977, Boston Coll., 1979; JD, Loyola U., 1981. Law clerk Kruse, Landa, Zimmerman & Maycock, Salt Lake City, 1979; law clerk legal dept. Bell & Howell, Lincolnwood, Ill., 1980; clerk, assoc. Parsons, Behle & Latimer, Salt Lake City, 1981-82; assoc. Reynolds, Vance, Deason & Smith, Salt Lake City, 1982-83; chief enforcement sect. Utah Securities Divsn., Salt Lake City, 1984-87, chief licensing sect., 1988, asst. dir., 1989-90; legal counsel Utah Dept. Commerce, Salt Lake City, 1990-92, exec. dir., 1993-95, commr. pub. svc. div., 1995. Mem. Gov.'s Securities Fraud Task Force, 1984; spl. asst. atty. gen., 1986-88; spl. asst. U.S. atty., 1986—. Mem. North Am. Securities Adminstrs. Assn. (vice chair market manipulation com. 1988-89, penny stock/telecom. fraud com. 1989-90, chair uniform examinations com. 1990-92, chair forms revision com. 1992), Utah State Bar (securities adv. com. 1991—, task force on community-based mediation 1991—, chair securities sect. 1992-93). Office: Utah Pub Svc Commn 160 East 300 South Salt Lake City UT 84111

WHITE, DARLENE MCDONALD, school system administrator, consultant; b. Phoenix, Nov. 22, 1951; d. Harold and Mable Oates McDonald; m. Clarence White, Oct. 26, 1988; children: Cassaundra, Calicia, Christopher; children: Davida Sharpe, Darnetta Sharpe. EdB, Ariz. State U., 1973, MEd, 1975; EdD, No. Ariz. U., 1993. Cert. supt. Ariz., 1996, Colo., 1997, Va., 2000. Elem. prin. Roosevelt Sch. Dist., 1984—94, dir. spl. edn., 1994—98; dir. elem. edn. Harrison Sch. Dist., Colo. Springs, Colo., 1998—2000; sch. supt. Va. Sch. Deaf, Blind and Multi-Disabled, Hampton, Va., 2000—.

WHITE, EVELYN, human resources administrator; With U.S. Postal Svc. Corp., Dept. of Energy, Office of Personnel Mgmt.; asst. and dep. dir. personnel USDA, dir. human resources, 1994; dep. asst. sec. human resources Office of Human Resources, Washington, 1997—. Chair Sec.'s Welfare to Work and Office of Sec. Quality of Work Life Initiatives. Named to Washington Carver Hall of Fame. Office: Office of Human Resources 200 Independence Ave SW Washington DC 20201-0004

WHITE, FLORENCE MAY, learning disabilities specialist; b. Ottawa, Kans., Sept. 1, 1936; d. O.C. Robert and Effie Lynne (Walker) Arnold; m. Donald L. White, June 1, 1958 (dec. Jan. 1996); children: Tab Vincent, Jacque Sue, Michelle May. BA, Ottawa U., 1958; MS, Kans. U., 1974; postgrad., Kans. U. Med. Ctr., 1975-76. Cert. reading specialist, learning disabilities specialist; cert. elem. and mid. sch. edn.: lang. arts, social studies, elem. curriculum. Classroom tchr. 2d grade Wellsville (Kans.) Elem., 1958-59; learning disabilities tchr. Olatha (Kans.) Spl. Edn. Coop., 1971-74; learning disabilities specialist, tchr. 7-9 Ottawa Mid. Sch., 1974-77; learning disabilities specialist, tchr. Paola Spl. Edn. Coop., Richmond, Kans., 1980-95; tchr. learning disabilities classes elem. level Ctrl. Heights Elem. Sch., Richmond, Kans., 2001—02. [illegible] on learning disabilities to civic groups and local orgns., 1972-75. Den mother Boy Scouts Am. and Brownies, Ottawa, 1968-70; chair state GOP women's polit. activities Rep. State Party, Topeka, 1964-67; chair scholarship contest DAR, Ottawa dist., 1984-96, Sunday sch. tchr. Meth. Ch., Ottawa; crafts tchr. local 4-H, Ottawa; mem. Central Heights PTA (projects com. 1980-95); mem. Ottawa Arts Coun. State of Kans. scholar State Spl. Edn. Dept., 1976. Mem. Internat. Reading Assn., Kans. Reading Assn., Franklin County Reading Coun. (exec. bd. 1993-94, v.p., pres.-elect 1989-91, pres. 1991-92), PEO, Alpha Delta Kappa (projects com. 1988—, environment com., hospitality com.). Roman Catholic. Avocations: oil painting, reading, travel, music, flower arranging.

WHITE, FRANCES LAVONNE, academic administrator; b. Houston, Oct. 15, 1947; d. John Wesley Jr. and Irma Johnetta (Porter) Williams; m. Harley Sr. White, Dec. 22, 1971; 1 child, Ivan Whitney. AA in Edn., Merritt Coll., 1968; BS in Psychology, Calif. State U., Hayward, 1970, MS in Counseling and Psychology, 1972; PhD in Edn., U. Calif., Berkeley, 1990. Instr. psychology Peralta Colls., Oakland, Calif., 1980—90, dir. staff devel., 1990—91; dean social scis., arts, phys. edn. Laney Coll., Oakland, 1991—94, Evergreen Valley Coll., San Jose, Calif., 1994—96; interim chancellor San Jose/Evergreen Colls., 1996; exec. vice chancellor City Coll., San Francisco, 1996—99; pres. Skyline Coll., San Bruno, Calif., 1999—. Mem. Oakland Citizen's Adv. Bd., 1986—88; pres., bd. dirs. Adminstrs. Calif. C.C. Assn., Sacramento, 1994—2000; chmn. bd. dirs. Families on Track, South San Francisco, Calif., 1999—; mem. leadership com. United Way, San Mateo County, Calif., 2000—01; mem. cmty. adv. bd. Seton Med. Ctr., Daly City, Calif., 1999—; bd. dirs. C.C. League Calif., Sacramento, 1999—2000. Named Educator of Yr., Iota Phi Lambda, 2001; recipient Tom Lakin Leadership award, Calif. C.C. Africa American Trustees, 1997. Mem.: AAUW, San Bruno Rotary (bd. dirs. 1999—, Mem. of Yr. 2001). Avocations: reading, bicycling, singing, walking, meditation. Office: Skyline Coll 3300 College Ave San Bruno CA 94066 Home: PO Box 56954 Hayward CA 94545-6954

WHITE, GAYE LEE, elementary school educator; d. Raymond Emil and Muriel Lillian Rosenbaum; m. Randy Ervin White, Apr. 30, 1988; children: Joshua Allen, Kaycee Raye. Assocs. in Bus., Lake Mich. Coll., 1979; BS, Ea. Mich. U., 1987; MA, Mich. State U., 2001. Conf. coord. Ea. Mich. U., Ypsilanti, Mich., 1984—87; tchr. Arkay, Inc., Lincoln Park, Mich., 1987—88, Warren (Mich.) Woods Pub. Schs., 1988—. Mem. curriculum coordinating com. Warren Woods Pub. Schs., 1999—, grade level chairperson, 2000—, social studies olympiad coach, 2002—. Vol. FOP Lodge, St. Joseph, 1992—2002, Blossomtime Parade Com., St. Joseph, 1992—2004; leader Cub Scouts, Warren, 2002—03; asst. treas. Brownie Troop 731, 2002—03; educator, leader Earth Explore, 2004; choir mem. Heritage Presbyn. Ch., St. Clair Shores, Mich., 2000—. Named Tchr. of the Yr., WDIV-Newsweek, 1999. Avocations: travel, camping, hiking, scrapbooks. Home: 22717 Carolina Saint Clair Shores MI 48080 Office: Warren Woods Pub Schs 11999 Martin Warren MI 48093 Office Phone: 586-436-4406.

WHITE, GLADYS HOPE FRANKLIN, reading specialist; b. Elizabeth City, N.C., Mar. 22; d. Elbert and Pearl (Smithwick) Franklin; m. Frank Hollowell White, Apr. 12, 1941; children: Johnese Armelda, Sharon Faye. BS, Hampton Inst. U., 1939; MA, Columbia U., 1949; EdD, U. Sarasota, 1978. Elem. tchr. and music Brawley H.S., Scotland Neck, N.C., 1939-41; elem. critic tchr. Elizabeth City Pub. Schs., elem. tchr., music tchr. P.W. Moore H.S.; coll. edn. reading specialist Tex. Coll., Tyler; Jeanes supr. Currituck/Camden Pub. Schs., elem. supr., Wake County Pub. Schs., Raleigh, N.C.; assoc. prof. edn. and reading N.C. Agrl. and Tech. U., Greensboro, N.C., 1962-82; founder, dir. project CARE Episcopal Ch. of the Redeemer, Greensboro, 1983—. Dir. tchr. tng. inst. Nat. Def. Edn. Inst., Greensboro, 1965-68; tech. asst. reading lang. U.S. Right to Read Program, U.S. Edn. Dept., Wilmington, Del.; cons., workshop founder. Project Care exec. bd. Episcopal Ch. of Redeemer, Greensboro, N.C., 1982—; mem. Pres. Clinton's Exec. Coun. com., 1996-98; mem. Dem. Congrl. Campaign com., Washington, 1998; mem. Friends Chavis Learning Libr., Greensboro, 1982—. Mem. Internat. Reading Assn. (life, chair paraprofls., reading com.), Nat. Assn. of Bus. Profl. Womens Clubs (corr. sec., chair archives, chair scholarship com. 1960-92), Hampton U. Alumni Assn. (pres. emeritus 1990—, Greensboro chpt. past pres., Trendsetter award 1995), Lady Sertoma (life), Delta Sigma Theta (Delta Diamond award 1988, Leadership award 1991), Kappa Delta Phi. Democrat. Episcopalian. Avocations: tutoring, mentoring, sewing, crafts, reading. Home: 1206 E Side Dr Greensboro NC 27406-2149 Office: Episcopal Ch of the Redeeemer 901 E Friendly Ave Greensboro NC 27401-3103

WHITE, GWENDOLYN A. recreational facility executive; b. Detroit, Sept. 14, 1955; d. Charles E. Hunter and Margaret J. Hannold; children: Stevan H., Cathleen G. Cert. pvt. pilot, alcohol misuse prevention program. Horse breeder, trainer Pers. Bus./Paso Fino Horse Assn., Edinburg, Va., 1979—92; unit sec. Shenandoah Co. Meml. Hosp., Woodstock, Va., 1980—91; sec., mgr. Pioneer Lodge, Inc., Willow, Alaska, 1992—2001; CEO BAL, Inc. dba Willow Air Svc., 1997—. Mem.: Women in Aviation Internat., Aircraft Owners & Pilots Assn., Willow C. of C. Methodist. Avocations: photography, writing, snow machining, cross country skiing, horseback riding. Office: BAL Inc dba Willow Air Svc PO Box 42 Willow AK 99688

WHITE, HELEN LOU, school nurse practitioner; b. Caldwell, Kans., Aug. 24, 1936; d. Orville George and Mildred Estelle (Garrison) Fauchier; m. Wayne Lee White, Sept. 1, 1957; children: Michelle Lee, Dana Lynn, Jacki Lou. Diploma, St. Francis Sch. Nursing, Wichita, Kans., 1957; cert. sch. nurse, Pittsburg State U., Kans., 1983. RN Kans., nat. cert. sch. nurse. Staff nurse St. Francis Hosp., Wichita, Kans., 1957—60, St. Lukes Hosp., Wellington, Kans., 1961—63, Wellington Hosp. and Clinic, 1971—74; sch. nurse and dir. health svcs. Unified Sch. Dist. # 353, Wellington, 1974—94; ret., 1994. Mem.: Am. Nurses Assn., Nat. Assn. Sch. Nurses (Kans. dir. bd. dirs. 1985—89), Kans. Sch. Nurse Orgn. (pres.-elect 1981—83, pres. 1983—85, Kans. Sch. Nurse of Yr. 1991, legis. co-chair 2000—), Kappa Kappa Iota. Democrat. Methodist. Avocations: acting, theater directing, piano, singing, travel. Home: 438 E 20th St N Wellington KS 67152

WHITE, HELENE R. sociologist, educator; b. Paterson, NJ, July 11, 1949; d. Sidney and Madeleine Beck Raskin; m. Larry H. White, June 18, 1972. BA, Douglass Coll., 1971; MPhil, Rutgers U., 1975, PhD, 1976. From asst. prof. to prof. Rutgers U., New Brunswick, 1975—. Co-prin. investigator Nat. Inst. Drug Abuse, Washington, 1978—; grant reviewer NIH, Washington, 1992—; prin. investigator Alcoholic Beverage Med. Rsch. Found., Balt., 1992—2002; behavioral and social adv. coun. Alcoholic Beverage Med. Rsch. Found., Balt., 1997—2003; prin. investigator Robert Wood Johnson Found., Princeton, NJ, 1997—. Editor: Alcohol, Science and Society, 1982, Society, Culture and Drinking Patterns Reexaminned, 1991; guest editor (journ.) Journal of Drug Issues, 1996; contbr. articles to profl. jours., chapters to books. Recipient Pub. Svc. Award, Criminal Justice Alcoholism Coalition. Mem.: Am. Soc. Criminology, Discovery Inst. (bd. dirs., v.p.), Am. Sociol. Assn. (chair info. alcohol and drugs sect. 1991—92, chair alcohol and drugs sect. 2002—03). Avocations: golf, cooking, exercise. Office: Rutgers U Ctr Alcohol Studies 607 Alison Rd Piscataway NJ 08854-8001 Business E-Mail: hcwhite@rci.rutgers.edu.

WHITE, IRENE, insurance professional; b. Taumuning, Guam, Jan. 3, 1961; d. Antonio Gill and Irma Magdalena (Idrogo) Gill; m. William Paul Franck, Aug. 4, 1979 (div. July 1984); m. Richard Nelson White, May 12, 1989 (div. Dec. 1993); 1 child, Karen Elizabeth. Cert. ins. adjuster, Tex., assoc. in claims; chartered property casualty underwriter, 1997. Ins. adjuster Gen. Accident Group, San Antonio, 1983-85, Crum & Forster Ins., San Antonio, 1985-89, Aetna Life & Casualty, San Antonio, 1979-83, adjuster, analyst, cons., complex case mgr. Dallas, 1989-96; sr. account exec., regional mgr. Travelers, Dallas, 1996—. Big sister Big Bros. and Sisters, San Antonio, 1987-89; vol. counselor March of Dimes, San Antonio, 1988-89; catechist St. Mark the Evangelist Cath. Ch., Plano, Tex., 1999—. Republican. Avocation: gardening. Office: Ste 200 1301 E Collins Blvd Richardson TX 75081 E-mail: irene.white@travelers.com.

WHITE, JEANETTE K. state senator, health facility administrator; b. Thief River Falls, Minn., May 2, 1943; m. William White; 2 children. BS in Polit. Sci. and Sociology, U. Iowa, 1965; MS in Cmty Develop., So. Ill. U., 1972; postgrad., U. Bt. Health adminstr. Sojourns Cmty. Health Clinic, Westminister, Vt.; senator State of Vt., 2003—. Mem. Putney Selectboard, United Way, Leadership S.E. Vt., Vt. Cmty. Develop. Bd., So. Vt. Area Health Edn. Ctr. Office: 35A Old Depot Rd Putney VT 05346

WHITE, JEANNETTE LEE, information technology executive; BA in econ. with honors, George Wash. U.; exec. edn., Dartmouth; YPO/MIT Pres. Seminar on eBusiness, MIT, Cambridge. Sys. mgr. Employee Benefit Rsch. Inst., Wash. DC; regulatory analysis staff Office Mgmt. and Budget, Exec. Office of the Pres.; founder, CEO Sytel, Inc., 1987—. Bd. trustees George Mason U. Found.; bd. vis. U. Md. Sch. Pub. Affairs; chpt. officer Young Pres. Orgn.; chairwoman Montgomery United Way; served on Gov. apptd. bd. Md. Tech. Devel. Corp. (Tedco); bd. dirs. High Tech Coun. Md. Named Exec. Yr., High Tech Coun. Md., 1998; named one of 100 Most Powerful Women in Wash., Washingtonian mag., 2001; recipient Nat. Entrepreneur award in innovative bus. strategies category, Working Woman mag., 2000. Office: Sytel Inc 6430 Rockledge Dr Ste 400 Bethesda MD 20817 Office Phone: 301-530-1000. Office Fax: 301-530-1032.*

WHITE, JENNIFER PHELPS, counselor; b. Palo Alto, Calif., Aug. 31, 1943; d. Delmer Frank and Luella Elizabeth (McHugh) Phelps; m. Charles Evan White, Oct. 29, 1965; children: George Kevin, Colleen Elizabeth. AA in Liberal Arts, Foothill Jr. Coll., 1964; BA in Sociology & Anthropology, U. N.Mex., 1967, MPA, 1987. Lic. profl. mental health counselor N.Mex. Counseling and Therapy Bd. Sales clk. Barron Park Pharmacy, Palo Alto, 1960-64; caseworker State of N.Mex., Albuquerque, 1968-70; info. sys. coord. City of Albuquerque, 1971-75; rsch. specialist Pub. Interest Rsch. Group, 1976-77; interviewer Sandia Market Rsch., 1980-81; acad. adviser, counselor U. N.Mex., 1981-88; rehab. specialist Intracorps, 1988-89; dir. career svcs. ctr. YWCA, 1989-96; athletic advisor U. N.Mex., Albuquerque, 1996—. Mem. women in transition Planning Commn. State of N.Mex., Albuquerque, 1990—; mem. career guidance project adv. com. Commn. on Status of Women, Albuquerque, 1993-95; employment cons. Genesis Project, Albuquerque, 1989-91; mem. steering com. United Staff U. N.Mex., 1996—, staff coun., 2000—. Chair women's affirmative action coun. City of Albuquerque, 1976-82; mem. steering com. Choice Pac, Albuquerque, 1984—; mem. Human Rights Coalition, 1995—. Named Outstanding N.Mex. Women, Office of Gov., State of N.Mex., 1994; recipient Grassroots Accomplishment award Nat. Coun. Negro Women, Las Mujeres de Lulac, 1994, Human Rights award City of Albuquerque, 1995. Mem. NOW (mem. Albuquerque and N.Mex. chpts., bd. dirs., pres., coord. 1975—, lobbyist N.Mex. State Legislature 1978-87), Nat. Abortion Rights Action League/Right to Choose (bd. dirs. 1980-93), Career Devel. Assn., Women Work! Nat. Network (Svc. awards 1994-95), Women's Housing Coalition (bd. dirs., pres., v.p. 1989—, project change bd. dirs. 1996—). Democrat. Avocations: political activist, pre-columbian anthropology, sewing. Home: 416 Montclaire Dr SE Albuquerque NM 87108-2630 Office: Univ NMex Athletic Dept Main Campus Albuquerque NM 87131-0001

WHITE, JILL CAROLYN, lawyer; b. Santa Barbara, Calif., Mar. 20, 1934; d. Douglas Cameron and Gladys Louise (Ashley) W.; m. Walter Otto Weyrauch, Mar. 17, 1973. BA, Occidental Coll., L.A., 1955; JD, U. Calif., Berkeley, 1972. Bar: Fla. 1974, Calif. 1975, U.S. Dist. Ct. (no. and mid. dists.) Fla., U.S. Ct. Appeals (5th and 11th cirs.), U.S. Supreme Ct. Staff mem. U.S. Dept. State, Am. Embassy, Rio de Janeiro, 1956-58; with psychol. rsch. units Inst. Human Devel., Inst. Personality Assessment and Rsch., U. Calif., Berkeley, 1961-68; adj. prof. criminal justice program U. Fla., Gainesville, Fla., 1976-78; pvt. practice immigration and nationality law, Gainesville, 1976—2002. Contbr. articles to profl. jours. Mem.: Fla. Bar (immigration and nationality law cert. com. 1994—99, chmn. cert. com. 1997—98, cert. in immigration and nationality law 1995—), Bar Assn. 8th Jud. Cir. Fla., Am. Immigration Lawyers Assn. (bd. dirs. Ctrl. Fla. chpt. 1985—94, 1995—96, 1997—2000, chmn. Ctrl. Fla. chpt. 1988—89, co-chmn. so. regional liaison com. 1990—92, nat. bd. dirs. 1988—89), Altrusa. Democrat. Office Phone: 352-380-9122. E-mail: jwhite49@earthlink.net.

WHITE, JOY KATHRYN, retired claims consultant, artist; b. Pawnee, Okla., Jan. 12, 1941; d. Stephen G. Gover, Vera Fay Gover; m. Bob Al White, Aug. 10, 1962; children: Stephen, Robert. H.S. diploma, Weatherford H.S., 1959. Ins. filing clk. Jane Phillips Med. Ctr., Bartlesville, Okla., 1986—; Am. Indian Beadworker The Silver Quail, Dewey, Okla., 1972—, ret., 2003—. Artist Am. Indian Beadwork Indian Colors, 1989 (2d Pl., 1989), Eagle Woman, 1996 (1st Pl., 1996), Justice?, 1992 (1st Pl., 1992), Blue Cut Glass Beaded Staff, 1994 (1st Pl., 1994), Buckskin Dress, 1993 (1st Pl., 1993), Magistic, 2000 (1st Pl., 2000), Unnamed- Green Cut Glass Medallion, 1998 (1st Pl., 1998), Unnamed- White Cut Glass Bolo, 2001 (1st Pl., 2001, 2002, 2nd Pl., 2002, 3d Pl., 2002, Honorable Mention, 2003), Cut Glass Beaded Cane, 2002 (1st Pl., 2002), Beaded Turtle Medallion, 2002 (1st Pl., 2003), Beaded Bolo, 2002 (2d Pl., 2002), Beaded Fan, 2000 (2d Pl., 2003). Tribal mem. Pawnee Nation; pres. Pilot Club of Dewey, 1986—87; mem., adv. Indian Summer Art Festival Com., Bartlesville, 1990—. Mem.: Am. Women in Arts, Pani Art Assn., Osage Gem and Mineral Soc., Bartlesville Indian Women's Club (pres. 1998—2000). Democrat. Baptist. Avocations: canning, cooking, sewing, gardening, art. Home: 505 E Third Dewey OK 74029

WHITE, JOYCE LOUISE, librarian; b. Phila., June 7, 1927; d. George William and Louisa (Adams) W. BA, U. Pa., 1949; MLS, Drexel U., 1963; MA in Religion, Episc. Sem. S.W., 1978. Head libr. Penniman Libr. Edn. U. Pa., Phila., 1960-76; archivist St. Francis Boys' Home, Salina, Kans., 1982-84; libr. Brown Mackie Coll., Salina, 1983-86; libr., dir. St. Thomas Theol. Sem., Denver, 1986-95; libr., dir. Archbishop Vehr Theol. Libr. Archdiocese of Denver, 1995-96. Author: Biographical and Historial Yarnall Library, 1979, Colorado Episcopal Clergy in the 19th Century: A Biographical Register, 2003; asst. editor: Women Religious History Sources, 1983; contbr. articles to profl. jours. and chpts. to books. Vol. libr. St. John's Cath., Denver, 1993—. Mem. Ch. and Synagogue Libr. Assn. (life, founding, pres. 1969-70, exec. sec. 1970-72, exec. bd. 1967-76, ann. conf. chair 1996). Avocations: gardening, cats, church libraries. Office: St John's Cathedral Libr 1350 Washington St Denver CO 80203-2008

WHITE, JUDITH LOUISE, social worker, counselor; b. Lodi, Ohio, Feb. 27, 1939; d. Henry and Charlotte Virginia (Spahr) Schmelzer; m. Downer Dale White, Sept. 4, 1959; children: Mark, Kelly, Kristy, David. AA, Northland Pioneer Coll., 1980; postgrad., No. Ariz. U., 1984—, Ariz. State U., 1985—; BS in Human Svcs., Prescott Coll., 1992. Tchr. White Mountain Apache Heart Start Program, Whiteriver, Ariz., 1976-80, child svcs. coord., 1976-80; cons. Nat. Indian Head Start, 1980—; family svcs. coord. Whiteriver Elem. Sch., 1987—. Trainer Indian Child & Family Conf., Phoenix and Albuquerque, 1982-86, Fetal Alcohol Syndrome-Indian Health Services, Whiteriver, 1984—; cons. White Mountain Apache Head Start Resource Access Project, 1984—; assoc. tchr. Northland Pioneer Jr. Coll., Holbrook, Ariz., 1985—; trainer pilot parent program; coord. Whiteriver Pilot Parents. [illegible] Children, Phoenix, 1985—, White Mt. Apache Child Protective Team, Kinishba Coun. Prevent Child Abuse. Mem. NASW (presenter conf. 1990), Coun. Exceptional Children, Nat. Assn. Edn. Young Children, White Mt. Assn. Edn. Young Children. Avocations: music, reading, theater, art. Home and Office: 660 N Spring Creek Trail Cornville AZ 86325

WHITE, JUNE MILLER, mathematics educator, educational consultant; b. E. Bernstadt, Ky., June 13, 1938; d. James Fulton and Ida Mae (Hansel) Miller; m. Richard Allen White, Aug. 27, 1960; children: Jennifer Lynn, Richard Allen Jr. BS with high honors, Denison U., 1960; MA, U. Rochester, 1969; PhD, Bryn Mawr Coll., 1980. Engring. asst. AT&T, Kansas City, Mo., 1960-61; math. tchr. William Chrisman H.S., Independence Pub. Schs., Independence, Mo., 1961-62, Brighton (N.Y.) H.S., 1962-69, Conestoga H.S., Tredyffrin-Easttown Pub. Schs., Berwyn, Pa., 1970-72; chair math. dept. Hill Top Prep. Sch., Rosemont, Pa., 1972-76, curriculum coord., 1976-81; instr. math. St. Petersburg Jr. Coll., Clearwater, Fla., 1982-84, dir. math. program, 1984—2002, prof. math. edn., 2002—. Presenter at various confs. Author: A Collection of Mathematics Applications for College Students, 1989; editor SPECTRUM, 1983-95; contbr. articles to profl. jours. Elder Northwood Presbyn. Ch., Clearwater, 1986-90; chmn. blood drive ARC, King of Prussia, Pa., 1973-74; chmn. citizens adv. com. Upper Merion Pub. Schs., King of Prussia, 1975-76. Mem. Am. Math. Assn. of Two Yr. Colls., Math. Assn. Am. (v.p. Fla. and Caribbean sect. 1988-91, sec. 1994-99, pres.-elect 1999, pres. 2000), Nat. Coun. Tchrs. Math., Fla. Assn. Cmty. Colls., Rsch. Coun. for Diagnostic and Prescriptive Math., Pinellas County Assn. for Children and Adults with Learning Disabilties (bd. dirs. 1987-88), Phi Beta Kappa. Avocations: camping, sailing, travel. Home: 4951 Bacopa Ln S Unit 103 Saint Petersburg FL 33715-2617 E-mail: whitejune@spjc.edu.

WHITE, KAREN RUTH JONES, information systems executive; b. Ft. Meade, Md., Oct. 8, 1953; d. Frank L. Jones and Inge H. Lesser; m. M. Timothy Heath, Apr. 23, 1973 (div. Aug. 1976); m. Carl W. White, May 30, 1993. AS in Electronic Data Processing, N.H. Tech. Inst., Concord, 1977; BS in MIS with high honors, Northeastern U., Boston, 1984, MS in Info. Sys., 1997. Profect mgmt. prof. Project Mgmt. Inst., 2001. Programmer Chubb Life Ins. Co., Concord, N.H., 1977-79, Retailers Electronics Account Processing, Woburn, Mass., 1979-82; sr. programmer, analyst N.H. Ins. Group, Manchester, 1982-84; prin. systems analyst Wang Labs., Inc., Lowell, Mass., 1984-89; project mgr. TASC, Inc., Reading, Mass., 1989-2000; dir. consulting svcs. PM Solutions, Havertown, Pa., 2000—. Bd. dirs. Brandywyne Common Assn., Derry, N.H., 1991-94; mem. St. Paul's Sch. Advanced Studies Pgm Alumni Assn., Concord, N.H. With U.S. Army Res., 1974-84. Decorated Army Commendation medal, 1980. Mem.: NAFE, IEEE (program chair 5th reengring. forum 1996, mem. exec. adv. bd. 1996—99, dep. conf. chair 6th reengring. forum 1998, computer soc., tech. com. in software engring.), Project Mgmt. Inst. (Mass. Bay chpt. program dir. 1992—93, project chair PMI '96 1994—96, dir. seminars/symposium 1996—98, PMI 2000 adv. group 1999—2000, ethics rev. com. 2000—02, awards rev. com. 2001—03, chair ethics rev. com. 2003—), Sigma Epsilon Rho. Home: 50 Merrill Rd Weare NH 03281-4708 Office: PM Solutions 50 Merrill Rd Weare NH 03281-4708 Office Phone: 603-529-5849.

WHITE, KATE, editor-in-chief; m. Brad Holbrooke; 2 children. BA, Union Coll. Editor Child mag., 1988—89; editor-in-chief Working Woman mag., N.Y.C., 1989—91, McCall's mag., N.Y.C., 1991—94, Redbook, N.Y.C., 1994—98, Cosmopolitan mag., 1998—. Author: Why Good Girls Don't Get Ahead and Gutsy Girls Do, Nine Secrets of Women Who Get Everything They Want, If Looks Could Kill, 2002, A Body to Die For, 2003. Recipient Matrix award, Women in Comms., 2003—. Office: Cosmopolitan Hearst Magazines 224 W 57th St New York NY 10019-3299

WHITE, KATHARINE STONE, museum administrator; b. Lexington, Mass., Nov. 5, 1914; d. Edward Carleton and Katharine (Brooke) Stone; m. John Warren White, Dec. 20, 1941; children: Susan White West, Patience H., John F. (dec.). BA, Vassar Coll., 1936. Rschr. film libr. Mus. Modern Art, N.Y.C., 1938-41; film programmer DeCordova Mus., Lincoln, Mass., 1962-63; film programmer dept. edn. Boston Mus. Fine Arts, 1970-74; trustee Mus. Fine Arts, Boston, 1974-90, hon. trustee, 1990—. Editor, chair trustee handbook com. Assn. Am. Mus., 1982. Chmn. Planning Bd., Lincoln, 1955-60; pres. Lincoln Hist. Soc., 1963-65.

WHITE, KATHERINE E. law educator; BSE elec. engring. and computer sci., Princeton U., 1988; JD, U. Wash., 1991; LLM in Intellectual Property, George Washington U., 1996. Bar: Mich. 1996, U.S. Supreme Ct, U.S. Ct. Appeals (fed. cir.), U.S. Ct. Appeals [illegible] Ill. Rev., U.S. Patent and Trademark Office, Wash. 1992. Intellectual property counsel U.S. Army Corps Engrs., Washington, 1992—95; jud. law clk. for Hon. Randall Rader U.S. Ct. Appeals (fed. cir.), 1995—96; assoc. prof. Wayne State U. Law Sch., Detroit, 1996—. Adj. prof. George Washington U. Law Ctr., Washington, 1994—96; regent U. Mich., Ann Arbor, 1999—; mem. patent pub. adv. com. U.S. Patent and Trademark Office, 2000—02. Actor: Intellectual Property Litigation, Pretrial Practice Guide, 1999; co-author (with Eric Dobrusin): Intellectual Property Litigation, Pretrial Practice Guide, 1999; contbr. articles to profl. publs. CPT JAG U.S. Army, 1992—95, maj. JAG USAR, 1995—. Recipient Fulbright Sr. Scholar award, Max-Planck Inst. for Fgn. Internat. Patent, Copyright and Competition Law, 1999—2000; grantee, Max-Planck-Inst. for Fgn. Internat. Patent, Copyright and Competition Law, 2000; scholar, ROTC, Washington Law Found., 1988—91; Shaw fellow, 1994—96, White House Fellow, special coun. to the sec. of agr., 2001—02. Mem.: AAUP, ABA, Wolverine Bar Assn., Wash. State Bar Assn., Nat. Bar Assn., Mich. Patent Lawyer's Assn., Am. Intellectual Property Law Assn., Am. Assn. Law Schs., State Bar Mich. (mem. coun. intellectual property law sec., co-chmn. student liaison com., co-chmn. com. pattent issues in legislation), Princeton Club Mich. Office: Wayne U Law Sch 471 W Palmer Detroit MI 48202

WHITE, KATHLEEN, director; b. St. Louis, July 10, 1959; d. Thomas Ray Halterman and Nancy Corine (Dexheimer) Rutsaert. BS in Edn., Ill. State U., 1984; MA in Edn., Chapman U., 1996; MA in Ednl. Adminstrn., Calif. State U., Bakersfield, 2002. Elem. tchr. St. Mary's Sch., Cheyenne, Wyo., 1984-89, Earlimart (Calif.) Sch. Dist., 1989—. Peer coach for pre-interns, new tchr. mentor, leadership team, BTSA support provider. Recipient Anna Keaton scholarship Assn. Residence Halls, Ill. State U., 1984. Mem.: Assn. Calif. Sch. Adminstrs. Democrat. Roman Catholic. Avocations: reading, music, crafts, traveling, competition silhouette rifle. Office: Earlimart Sch Dist PO Box 11970 Earlimart CA 93219-1970

WHITE, KATHY BRITTAIN, medical association executive; BS, MS, Ark. State U.; PhD in Mgmt., U. Memphis. Various sr. positions with AlliedSignal Corp., Guilford Mills, Inc.; chief info. officer Baxter Internat., 1995-96; chief info. officer, sr. v.p. Allegian Corp. (now merged with Cardinal Health), 1996-99; exec. v.p., chief info. officer Cardinal Health, Dublin, Ohio, 1999—. Bd. dirs. MECON, Inc., San Ramon, Calif., Children's Meml. Med. Ctr./Children's Meml. Hosp., Children's Meml. Found., Chgo.; former assoc. prof. info. technology U. N.C., Greensboro. Bd. dirs. Lake Forest Grad. Sch., Ill. Mem. ACHE. Office: Cardinal Health 7000 Cardinal Pl Dublin OH 43017-1091

WHITE, LANI NYLA, real estate developer; d. Fleet Russell and Nyla Marie White. BA in Art, Mills Coll.; MFA in Art, U. Calif., Irvine; MA in Drama, U. Calif., Santa Barbara. Cert. real estate broker, Colo. Owner/broker Lani White & Assoc., Aspen, Colo.; pres., owner Aspen Polo Club. Horse trainer, polo sch. Mem. Colo. Assn. Realtors, Nat. Assn. Realtors, Music Assocs. Aspen, Aspen Hist. Soc., Aspen Soc. for Animal Rights (co-dir), U.S. Polo Assn. (del.), Maroon Creek Country Club, El Dorado Polo Club. Avocations: polo, skiing, tennis, animal rights. E-mail: apsenrealestate@aol.com.

WHITE, LIBBY KRAMER, librarian; b. Boston, Sept. 30, 1934; d. Samuel and Ida (Drucker) Kramer; m. Gerald Milton White, June 6, 1956; children: Charles, Andrew, Judith White Cuttler, Abigail White D'Costa. BS in Social Sci., Simmons Coll., Boston, 1956; MLS, SUNY, Albany, 1972; MALS, SUNY, 1998. Librarian Temple Israel, Albany, N.Y., 1966-73; bookmobile librarian Schenectady County Pub. Library, 1973, br. librarian, 1973-76, ref./YA librarian, 1976-85, ref./ethnic culture librarian, 1985—; libr. Jewish Vocat. Svc. Balt., 1998—, Beth Israel Congregation, Owings Mills, Md., 1998—. Chmn. Nat. Library Wk., Schenectady, 1985, 96; resident advisor Summer Seminars in Judaic Studies, Skidmore Coll., Saratoga Springs, N.Y., 1987-95. Book reviewer Sch. Libr. Jour., 1980—, Libr. Jour., 1989, Assn. Jewish Librs. Newsletter, 1994—; cons. various encys., mags.; contbr. articles profl. jours. Trustee Beth Israel Synagogue, Schenectady, 1986-94, 95-98. Mem. Md. Libr. Assn., Assn. Jewish Librs. (mem. Sydney Taylor awards com. 1999—). Jewish. Avocations: reading, writing short stories, travel. Home: PO Box 319 Easton MD 21601 Office: Jewish Vocat Svc 1515 Reisterstown Rd Baltimore MD 21208-4333 also: Beth Israel Congregation 3706 Crondall Ln Owings Mills MD 21117-2205 E-mail: white_libby@juno.com., lwhite@jvsbaltimore.org., llibbylib@aol.com.

WHITE, LILLIAS, actress; Appeared in Broadway plays Titanic, Cats, Once on This Island, Dreamgirls, Rock 'n' Roll: The First 5000 Years, Barnum, How to Succeed in Business..., The Life (Tony award 1997); (off-Broadway) Waiting for Godot, The Princess and The Black-eyed Pea, Antigone Africanus, Romance in Hard Times (Obie award); (nat. and internat. tour) Ain't Misbehavin', The Wiz, Tintypes, Dreamgirls (Drama-Logue award); (TV series) Sesame Street (Emmy award), Law & Order, NYPD Blue; (film) (voice) Hercules; concert appearance include Carnegie Hall, Lincoln Ctr., The White House. Office: Don Buchwald & Assocs 10 E 44th St Fl 2 New York NY 10017-3654

WHITE, LORAY BETTY, TV talk show host, writer, television producer, vocalist, actress, television director; b. Houston, Nov. 27, 1934; d. Harold White and Joyce Mae (Jenkins) Mills; m. Sammy Davis Jr., 1957 (div. 1958); 1 child, Deborah R. DeHart. Student, UCLA extension, 1948-50, 90-91, Nichiren Shoshu Acad., 1988-92; AA in Bus., Sayer Bus. Sch., 1970; study divsn. mem. dept. L.A., Calif. Study Group of Japan, 1970-86. Editor, entertainment writer L.A. Community New, 1970-81; exec. sec. guest rels. KNBC Prodns., Burbank, Calif., 1969-75; security specialist Xerox X10 Think Tank, L.A., 1975-80; exec. asst. Ralph Powell & Assocs., L.A., 1980-82; pres., owner, producer LBW & Assocs. Pub. Rels., L.A., 1980—; owner, producer, writer, host TV prodn. co. Pub. Pub. Rels., L.A., 1987—. Dir., producer L.B.W. Prodn. "Yesterday, Today, Tomorrow, L.A., 1981—; with CBS news dept./Bogey's Corner, The Vol. Brigade Corps, KCBS News, 1999. Actor: (films) Ten Commandments, 1956; singer: (films) The Jazz Review, 1960—65; headline singer Radio City Music Hall, N.Y.C., 1961, Can Can Cafe Concert in Mex., 1967—75, feature singer Hilton Hotel Mex., featured singer Hotel Maria Isabel, Acapulco, Disneyland, Calif.; singer: TV, 1981—, (Broadway plays) Joy Ride; appearances in the following (endorsements) Budweiser Beer, Old Gold Cigarettes, Salem Cigarettes, TV comml s. including Cheer, Puffs Tissue, Coca Cola, Buffern, others, entertainment editor (newspaper) L.A. Community News, 1970—73, writer (column) Balance News, 1980—82. Vol. ARC, 1995, L.B.W. & Assocs., Ltd. Ann. Prodn. of Mother and Daughter of the Yr. Tribute, 1999, L.B.W. & Assocs., United Peace and Cultural Exch. Dinner and Awards Show, 1999; mem. Habitat for Humanity Internat, Nat. Com. Preserve Soc. Sec. and Medicare, 1998-99, Nat. Black Network Assn., AARP, So. Calif. Com. Sr. Citizens, re-elect Scott Wildmen Rep. campaign; mem. resident adv. bd. Burbank Housing Authority, HUD, 2002—; mem. Com. to Reelect Ted McConkey to Burbank City Coun., 1999; bd. dirs. Chamblee Found. of Calif., 1998-; apptd. area coord. San Fernando Valley area; exec. prodr. The Fifth L.B.W. and Assocs. Internat. Ann. Achievement Awards Show, 1999. The Sixth L.B.W. and Assocs. Internat. Ann. Achievement Awards Show, 2000. Recipient Cert. of Honor, ARC, 1984, Internat. Orgn. Soka Gakkai Internat. of Japan, Cmty. Vols. of Am. award, 1994, Mother and Daughter of Yr. Tribune, 2000-01, 6th Internat. Achievement award L.B.W. and Assoc.; named Performer of Yr. Cardella Demillo, 1976-77. Mem. ARC (planning, mktg., prodn. event com. 1995), UCLA Alumni Assn., Lupus Found. Am. (So. Calif. chpt.), Nat. Fedn. Blind, Myohoji-Hokkeko Internat.as a mem. of the USA, 2002. Attended Tozon Internat. with 56 countries, 300,000 mem. participated in "The 750th Anniv. of Nichiren Shoshu Head Temple Taisekiji" in Japan. Libr. of Congress [illegible] (charter). Buddhist. Avocations: singing, acting, tv writing and producing. Office Phone: 818-955-7728. Office Fax: 818-955-7728. Personal E-mail: lbwbootsie@aol.com.

WHITE, MARGIT TRISKA, financial advisor; b. Greenport, N.Y. d. Joseph A. and Esther M. (Olstad) Triska; m. Robert Lamar Cannon (div. 1971); children: Catherine Margit, Sandra Leigh, Robert Milchrist II. BA, Duke U. CFP. Adminstr. Washington Opportunities for Women, 1971-80; account exec. Merrill Lynch, Bethesda, Md., 1980-82; v.p. investments, fin. planner Prudential Securities, Washington, 1982-94, Morgan Stanley Dean Witter, Washington, 1994—. Mem. fin. adv. bd. Bus. Women Internat., Women of Washington. Mem. Internat. Assn. Fin. Planning, Inst. Cert. Fin. Planners, Women in Housing and Fin., Fin. Women's Assn., The Internat. Alliance, Zeta Tau Alpha. Office: Morgan Stanley Dean Witter 1775 Eye St NW Ste 200 Washington DC 20006-2409

WHITE, MARILYN DOMAS, information science educator; b. Franklin, La., Aug. 16, 1940; d. George Julian and Norma Domas; m. Roger Stuart White, Aug. 31, 1968; 1 child, Joshua Stuart. BA, Our Lady of the Lake Coll., San Antonio, 1962; MS, U. Wis., 1963; PhD, U. Ill., 1971. Dir. Commerce Libr. U. Wis., Madison, 1963-65; head Social Sci./Bus. Libr. So. Ill. U., Edwardsville, 1965-67; cons. So. Ill. U./U.S. AID Adv. Team, South Vietnam, 1967; asst. prof. SUNY, Buffalo, 1972-74; lectr., vis. asst. prof. U. Md., College Park, 1976-77, asst. prof. info sci., 1977-82, assoc. prof. info. sci., 1982—. Cons. USIA, Washington and abroad, 1977-83, Inst. for Def. Analyses, Bowie, Md.,Supercomputing Rsch. Ctr., 1990-91, Am. Health Care Assn., Washington, 1990-92, Am. Coun. on Edn., 1995. Contbr. articles to Libr. Quar., Libr. & Info. Sci. Rsch., to Jour. Documentation, Jour. Am. Soc. for Info. Sci., others; editor (rev. editor): (Jours.) Libr.& Info. Sci. Rsch. James Lyman Whitney grantee ALA, 1983, Spl. Libr. Assn. rsch. grantee, 1993-94, Coun. Libr. Resources grantee, 1995-96, Info. Sci. Abstracts grantee, 1997-98. Mem. Am. Soc. for Info. Sci., Spl. Libr. Assn. Office: U Md Coll Info Studies Hornbake 4117F South Wing College Park MD 20742-0001 Office Phone: 301-405-2047. E-mail: whitemd@umd.edu.

WHITE, MARTHA VETTER, allergy and immunology physician, researcher; b. Richmond, Va., Oct. 23, 1951; d. Robert Joseph and Miriam Ernestine (Thomas) Vetter; m. Frederick Joseph Kozub, Oct. 11, 1975 (div. June 1982); m. John Irving White, Feb. 18, 1984; children: Josh, Christie. Student, Vanderbilt U., Nashville, 1969-71; BA, U. Richmond, 1973; MD, Va. Commonwealth U., Richmond, 1978. Cert. m. Bd. Pediatrics, Am. Bd. Allergy and Immunology. Pediatric intern and resident Va. Commonwealth U., Richmond, 1978-81; locum tenans Pub. Health, Richmond, Va., 1981-82; fellow Allergy and Immunology U. Southern Calif., L.A., 1983-84, Georgetown U., 1983-84; sr. staff fellow Food and Drug Adminstrn., Bethesda, Md., 1984-85; NSRA fellow Nat. Inst. Allergy and Infectious Diseases, Bethesda, Md., 1985-88; sr. staff fellow, 1988-93; rsch. dir. Inst. for Asthma and Allergy, Wheaton, Md., 1993—. Cons. Sandoz Pharms., Marion Merrell Dow, Glaxo, Boehringer Ingleheim, Ciba-Geigy, Miles Genentech; rschr. Glaxo, Abbott, Pfizer, Marion Merrell Dow, Miles, Rhône Poulenc Rhoen, Sanofi, Adams, Astra, Merck, Neurbiol. Techs., 3M, Zeneca, Wyeth, Smith-Kline Beecham; bd. dirs. Allery & Asthma Network/Mothers of Asthmatics, 1987—; med. editor MA Report, 1986—; assoc. editor Allergy, Asthma and Immunology Guide, 1989-90. Contbr. numerous scientific papers, abstracts, chpts. and reviews in field. Recipient Norwich Eaton Rsch. award, 1987; Merrell Dow scholar in allergy, 1989; Geigy fellow, 1984. Mem.: Soc. Prin. Investigators (pres. 2002—03), Am. Thoracic Soc., Am. Coll. Allergy and Immunology, Adm. Acad. Allergy and Immunology, Am. Acad. Pediat., Am. Assn. Immunologists, Gamma Sigma Epsilon, Psi Chi, Beta Beta Beta. Office: Inst Asthma and Allergy 11160 Viers Mill Rd # 414 Wheaton MD 20902

WHITE, MARY ANN, bank executive; b. Blackey, Ky., June 21, 1932; d. William Bradley and Audrey Ison; divorced; 1 child, William R. Student, Cannon Trust Sch., Charlotte, N.C., 1974; grad. Nat. Grad Trust Sch., Northwestern U., Evanston, Ill., 1978. With 1st Nat. Bank and Trust Co., Georgetown, Ky., 1953—, asst. trust officer, 1962-64, asst. cashier, 1964-74, asst. trust officer, asst. v.p., 1974-76, v.p., trust officer, 1976—. Treas. Sr. Citizens Exec. Bd., Georgetown; bd. dirs. Urban Renewal and Cmty. Devel. Agy. Bd., Georgetown, C. of C., Georgetown; pres. Scott County Bus. Women's Club, Georgetown. Mem. Fin. Women Internat. (sec., treas., v.p.). Avocations: flower gardening, cooking, travel. Office: 1st Nat Bank and Trust Co 101 W Main St Georgetown KY 40324-1320

WHITE, MARY BETH, guidance counselor, adult education educator; b. Nashville, Aug. 10, 1951; d. Roy William and Myra Kathryn (De Cleene) Huffman; m. Frank White, Feb. 21, 1976 (div. Aug. 1997); children: Andrew Huffman, Leigh Ann. BA in Psychology, Quincy U., 1973; MS in Edn., Vanderbilt U., 1977; cert. guidance and counseling, Tenn. State U., 1997. Tchr. Wilson County Devel. Ctr., Lebanon, Tenn., 1977-79, Mt. Juliet (Tenn.) Jr. High, 1979-80; guidance counselor Holy Rosary Acad., Nashville, 1992-97; instr. Vol. State C.C., Gallatin, Tenn., 1999—; owner Hermitage Learning Ctr., 2000—. Roman Catholic. Avocations: tennis, travel. Office: Hermitage Learning Ctr 3441 Lebanon Pike Hermitage TN 37076-2097 Home: 423 Jaywood Ln Mount Juliet TN 37122-3756

WHITE, MARY JO, former prosecutor, lawyer; b. Kansas City, Mo., Dec. 27, 1947; d. Carl and Ruth King Monk; m. John W. White, Jan. 24, 1970. BA, Coll. William and Mary, 1970; MA in Psychology, New Sch. for Social Rsch., 1971; JD, Columbia U., 1974. Bar: NY 1975. Law clk. to Hon. Marvin E. Frankel, So. Dist. N.Y., NY, 1975—76; assoc. Debevoise & Plimpton, 1976—78, litig. ptnr., 1983—90, ptnr., chair of litig., 2002—; asst. U.S. atty. So. Dist. N.Y., chief appellate atty. of criminal div., 1978—81; instr. in profl. responsibility and ethics Columbia Law Sch., 1981—; chief asst., acting U.S. Atty. Ea. Dist. N.Y., Bklyn., 1990—93; U.S. Atty. So. Dist. N.Y., Manhattan, 1993—2002. Chair Atty. Gen. Janet Reno's Adv. Com. of U.S. Attys., 1993—94. Recipient "Magnificent 7" award, Bus. & Profl. Women USA, Law Enforcement Person of the Year award, Soc. of Profl. Investigators, Human Relations Award, Anti-Defamation League Lawyer's Div., 1996, Edward Weinfeld award for disting. contbn. to Admin. of Justice, N.Y. County Lawyers' Assn., 1998, Nat. Law Jour. 2002 list of Top Women Litigators, John P. O'Neill Pillar of Justice award, Respect for Law Alliance, 2002, Sandra Day O'Connor award for Distinction in Public Svc., 2002, dir. of FBI's Jefferson Cup award for contbn. to Rule of Law in the fight against terrorism and crime, 2002, George H. W. Bush award for excellence in counter-terrorism and the Agency Seal Medallion, CIA, 2002, Women of Power and Influence award, NOW. Fellow: Am. Coll. Trial Lawyers; mem.: ABA, N.Y. State Bar Assn., Assn. Bar City of N.Y. Achievements include First women to serve as U.S Atty. for So. Dist. of N.Y; first chairperson of Atty. Gen. Janet Reno's Advisory Com.of U.S. Attys. Office: Debevoise & Plimpton 919 Third Ave 47th Fl New York NY 10022

WHITE, MARY JO, state legislator, lawyer; b. Chgo., Dec. 27, 1941; d. Joseph and Patricia White; m. H. William White, Mar. 6, 1966; children: H. William III, David, Alison. BA, Quincy U., 1963; JD, U. Pitts. Mem. Pa. Senate, Dist. 21, Harrisburg, 1996—; vice chmn. comms. and tech. com. Pa. Senate, Harrisburg, mem. aging and youth com., mem. appropriations com., mem. cmty. and econ. devel. com., mem. intergovtl. affairs com., mem. jud. com., mem. pub. health and welfare com.; former defender Venango County Pub. Defender's Office, 1974-76; past v.p. environ. govtl. affairs Quaker State Corp. Past chmn. Am. Petroleum Inst.'s Used Oil Workshop Gruop; bd. dirs. N.W. Regional Planning and Devel. Corp., Pa. Environ. Coun.; mem. Venango County Assn. for the Blind, Venango Cmty. Found.; chair nursing adv. com. Clarion U.; mem. Barrow Civic Theatre Found., Cmty Health Action Team. Office: Pa State Senate Senate Box 203021 168 Capitol Bldg Harrisburg PA 17120-3021 [illegible] Rd Butler PA 16001-2561

WHITE, MEG (MEGAN MARTHA WHITE), musician, vocalist; b. Grosse Pointe, Mich., 1974; m. John Gillis, 1996 (div. 2000). Drummer, vocalist The White Stripes, 1997—; toured with Pavement and Sleater-Kinney, 1999, 2000. Performer: (albums) The White Stripes, 1999, De Stijl, 2000, White Blood Cells, 2001, Maximum, 2002, Elephant, 2003. Mailing: Monotone Inc 8932 Keith Ave Los Angeles CA 90069*

WHITE, MICHELLE JO, economics educator; b. Washington, 1945; d. Harry L. and Irene Rich; m. Roger Hall Gordon, July 25, 1982. AB, Harvard U., 1967; MSc in Econs., London Sch. Econs., 1968; PhD, Princeton U., 1973. Asst. prof. U. Pa., Phila., 1973-78; from assoc. prof. to prof. NYU, N.Y.C., 1978-83; prof. econs. U. Mich., Ann Arbor, 1984—2001, dir. PhD program in econs., 1992—94, 1998—99; prof. econs. U. Calif., San Diego, 2000—. Vis. asst. prof. Yale U., New Haven, 1978; vis. prof. People's U., Beijing, 1986, U. Warsaw, 1990, U. Wis., Madison, 1991, U. Munich, Germany, 1992, 2002, Tilburg U., The Netherlands, 1993, 95, U. Chgo., 1993, Copenhagen Bus. Sch., 1995, Uppsala U., Sweden, 1997, Hebrew U., Israel, 1997, U. Calif. Law Sch. Berkeley, 1999; rsch. assoc. Nat. Bur. Econ. Rsch., 2002--; cons. Pension Benefit Guaranty Corp., Washington, 1987, World Bank, 1999; chmn. adv. com. dept. econs. Princeton U., 1988-90. Editor: The Non-profit Sector in a Three Sector Economy, 1981, Financial Distress and Bankruptcy: Economic Issues, 1997; contbr. numerous articles to profl. jours. Bd. dirs. Com. on Status of Women in Econs. Profession, 1984-86. Resources for Future fellow, 1972-73; grantee NSF, 1979, 82, 88, 91, 93, 96, 2002, Sloan Found., 1984, Fund for Rsch. in Dispute Resolution, 1989; Fulbright scholar, Poland, 1990. Mem. Am. Econ. Assn., Am. Law and Econ. Assn. (bd. dirs. 1991-92, 2001-04, chair nominating com. 2002), Am. Real Estate and Urban Econs. Assn. (bd. dirs. 1992-95), Social Scis. Rsch. Coun. (bd. dirs. 1994-2000, treas. 1996-2000), Midwest Econs. Assn. (1st v.p. 1996-97). Office: U California-San Diego Dept Economics 9500 Gilman Dr La Jolla CA 92093-0508

WHITE, OTHELL, interior designer; b. Valley Head, Ala., Dec. 30, 1942; d. Charles Ray and Lily Cleo (Couch) White; children: Thomas Gregory Owens, Steven Craig Adams, Pamela Gayle Adams. Student, McKenzie Coll., Chattanooga, 1961, Delgado Coll., New Orleans, 1977-79. Interior designer Smartt Cabinets, Chattanooga, 1981-83; decorator cons. J.C. Penney, Chattanooga, 1983-85; owner, interior designer Pizzazz, Chattanooga, 1985-88; freelance interior designer Chattanooga, Boca Raton, Fla., 1988-89; interior designer Concepts in Kitchens, DelRay Beach, Fla., 1990-91, Othell Interior Design, Chattanooga, 1993—. Mem. Am. Soc. Interior Design, Interior Design Soc. Republican. Roman Catholic. Avocations: walking on beach, writing, reading, painting.

WHITE, PAMELA JANICE, lawyer; b. Elizabeth, NJ, July 13, 1952; d. Emmet Talmadge and June (Howlett) W. BA, Mary Washington Coll., 1974; JD, Washington and Lee U., 1977. Bar: Md. 1977, U.S. Dist. Ct. Md. 1978, D.C. 1979, U.S. Dist. Ct. D.C. 1979, U.S. Ct. Appeals (4th cir.) 1979, U.S. Ct. Appeals (D.C. cir.) 1981, U.S. Ct. Claims 1981, U.S. Ct. Appeals (2d cir.) 1983, N.Y. 1983, U.S. Dist. Ct. (so. dist.) N.Y. 1983, U.S. Ct. Appeals (9th cir.) 1988, U.S. Supreme Ct. 1981. Assoc. Ober, Grimes & Shriver, Balt., 1977-84; prin. Ober, Kaler, Grimes & Shriver, Balt., 1985—. Chair Employment Group, 1994—; mem. Md. Bd. Law Examiners, 1986-94, Md. Judiciary Pub. Trust and Confidence Com., 2001-04; select com. on Gender Equality, 1989-2000, chair, 1997-99, spl. com. on ethics 2002-04; mem. fed. dist. ct. adv. group Civil Justice Reform Act, 1990; exec. com. Md. Inst. for Continuing Profl. Edn. Lawyers, 2000-02; adv. bd. Md. Mediation and Conflict Resolution Ctr., 2001-02; equal justice coun. Legal Aid Bur., 2000—. Note and comment editor Washington and Lee Law Rev. 1976-77, Washington and Lee Law Council 1983-87, pres. 1991-92. Mem. Fed. Ct. Bicentennial Com., 1988-90; vol. Profl. Gov.'s Drug-Free Workplace Initiative, 1990-93; bd. trustees Washington and Lee U., 1995—. Named Disting. Alumna, Washington and Lee U., 1994, Disting. Alumna, Mary Washington Coll., 2001; named among Md. Top 100 Women, 2004. Fellow Am. Bar Found., Md. Bar Found. (award for excellence 1996, bd. dirs. 2000-02); mem. ABA (chair tort and ins. practice employer/employee rels. com. 1999-2000, del. 2000-02), Am. Arbitration Assn. (arbitrator, mediator employment and comml. panels), Balt. Bar Found. (bd. dirs. 2003—), Fed. Bar Assn., Md. Bar Assn. (coun. legal edn. sect. 1987-96, chmn. 1992-93, labor sect. coun. 1992-96, professionalism com. 1991—, chmn. 1994-97, bd. govs. 1993-95, 1998-2003, exec. com. 1994-95, 99-2001, pres. 2001-02, immediate past pres. 2002-03, task force on professionalism chair 1996-97), D.C. Bar Assn., Balt. City Bar Assn. (exec. coun. 1995-96, 1997-98), Women's Bar Assn. Md. (treas. 1986-87, v.p. 1987-88, pres.-elect 1988-89, pres. 1989-90, bd. dirs. 1984-86, Rita C. Davidson award 2000), Md. Assn. Def. Counsel, Pro Bono Resource Ctr. (exec. com. 2000-02, bd. trustees 2002-03, Leaders of Equal Justice award 2002), Order of Coif, Phi Beta Kappa. Presbyterian. Avocation: baseball. Office: Ober Kaler Grimes & Shriver 120 E Baltimore St Ste 800 Baltimore MD 21202-1643 Office Phone: 410-347-7323. E-mail: pjwhite@ober.com.

WHITE, PATRICIA DENISE, dean; b. Syracuse, N.Y., July 8, 1949; d. Theodore C. and Kathleen (Cowles) Denise; m. Nicholas P. White, Feb. 20, 1971 (div. 1997); children: Olivia Lawrence, Alexander Cowles. BA, U. Mich., 1971, MA, JD, 1974. Bar: D.C. 1975, Mich. 1988, Utah 1995. Assoc. Steptoe & Johnson, Washington, 1975-76; vis. asst. prof. Coll. of Law U. Toledo, 1976-77; assoc. Caplin & Drysdale, Washington, 1977-79; asst. prof. Law Ctr. Georgetown U., 1979-84, assoc. prof. Law Ctr., 1985-88; vis. prof. Law Sch. U. Mich., Ann Arbor, 1988-94; prof. U. Utah, Salt Lake City, 1994-98; counsel Parsons, Behle and Latimer, Salt Lake City, 1995—98; dean, prof. Ariz. State U. Coll. Law, 1999—. Counsel Bodman, Longley and Dahling, Detroit, Ann Arbor, 1990-95. Contbr. articles to profl. jours. Office: Ariz State U Coll Law McAllister & Orange Sts PO Box 877906 Tempe AZ 85287-7906 Office Phone: 480-965-6188.

WHITE, PAULINE M. interior decorator; b. Kansas City, Mo., Oct. 2, 1933; d. George Francis and Anna Elizabeth (Schnase) Adams; m. Norman Edgar White, Aug. 7, 1952; children: Donna Jean, Norman Alan. BA, Kansas City U., 1951; cert., Elizabeth Bolden Sch. Design, 1952. With Southwestern Bell Telephone Co., Kansas City, 1950-52; supr. AT&T Telephone Co., Kansas City, 1957-61; with med. records divsn. Shawnee Mission Hosp., Overland Park, Kans., 1961-70; tchr. ceramics and crafts Donahues Plastics, Gladstone, Mo., 1970-72; recreation leader, tchr. City of Columbia, Mo., 1980-88; decorator, interior planner for home J.C. Penney, 1988—. Tchr. Broadway Christian Ch., 1973-96; vol. tchr., counselor Ctrl. Mo. Regional Ctr. for Developmentally Disabled, Columbia, 1980—. Mem. Ryan Club (pres. 1980). Republican. Avocation: work for learning impaired.

WHITE, REBECCA E. advocate; b. Washington, Nov. 17, 1945; d. Edward and Anna Pendleton White. BS, D.C. Tchrs. Coll., 1971; postgrad., Pepperdine U., 1993, Calif. State U., 2003—. Cert. tchr., D.C., Calif. Tchr. English D.C. Pub. Schs., Washington, 1971-73; paralegal specialist U.S. Dept. Justice, Washington, 1973-81; adminstr. U.S. Dept. Vet. Affairs VA Med. Ctr., L.A., 1982-89, 94-96, Sepulveda, Calif., 1992-94; patient/employee advocate U.S. Dept. Vet. Affairs, L.A., 1982-89, 92-96; tchr. English L.A. Unified Sch. Dist., 1989-91, children's advocate, 1989—; tchr. English Inglewood (Calif.) Unified Sch. Dist., 1996-97, children's advocate, 1996-98; tchr. spl. edn. Gladstone St. Elem. Sch., Azusa, Calif., 2003—. Cmty. advocate Baldwin Hills Cmty., L.A., 1983—; children's advocate L.A. County Schs., 1999—; mem. L.A. World Affairs Coun., 1999—. Mem. NEA, Calif. Tchrs. Assn. Avocations: writing, hiking, entertaining, reading. Office: Gladstone St Elem Sch 1040 E Gladstone St Azusa CA 91702

WHITE, RHEA AMELIA, information scientist, consciousness researcher; b. Utica, NY, May 6, 1931; d. John Raymond and Rhea Jane (Parry) White. BA, Pa. State U., 1953; MLS, Pratt Inst., Bklyn., 1965; postgrad., SUNY, Stony Brook, 1990-92. Rsch. fellow Parapsychology Lab. Duke U., Durham, N.C., 1954-58; editor Jour. Am. Soc. Psychical Rsch., N.Y.C., 1959-62, 84-00, editor-in-chief, 2001—; libr. dept. psychiatry Maimonides Med. Ctr., Bklyn., 1965-67; dir. info. Am. Soc. Psychical Rsch., N.Y.C., 1965-80; reference libr. East Meadow (N.Y.) Pub. Libr., 1965-95; founder, dir. Parapsychology Sources of Info. Ctr., Dix Hills, N.Y., 1981-90; editor Rsch. in Parapsychology, Metuchen, N.J., 1981-85, Theta, Durham, N.C., 1981-86; founder, editor Parapsychology Abstracts Internat., Dix Hills, 1983-89, Exceptional Human Experience, Dix Hills, 1990—; founder, producer PsiLine Database, Dix Hills, 1983—; mng. editor Advances in Parapsychol. Rsch., N.Y.C., 1977; founder, dir. Exceptional Human Experience Network, New Bern, 1990-94, 95—; with Exceptional Human Experience News, 1994—2002. Rsch. fellow Menninger Found., Topeka, 1963-65; abstractor Psychol. Abstracts, Washington, 1967-91; cons. Scarecrow Press, Metuchen, NJ, 1980-85; referee Jour. Parapsychology, Durham, 1981-85; sr. rsch. cons. Ctr. Sci. Anomalies Rsch., 1981—; chmn., keynote spkr. conf. on women and parapsychology Parapsychology Found., Dublin, Ireland, 1991; keynote speaker Acad. Religion and Psychical Rsch. Conf., 1992; founder, editor EHE News, Dix Hills, 1994, New Bern, 1995—; instr. exceptional human experience course Portland (Oreg.) State U., 1999. Author: Parapsychology: Sources of Information, 1973, Surveys in Parapsychology, 1975, Parapsychology: New Sources of Information, 1990; (with M. Murphy) The Psychic Side of Sports, 1978; parapsychology book reviewer Libr. Jour., NYC, 1974-86, Reprint Bull., 1974-79, (with Michael Murphy) In the Zone, 1995; regional editor European Jour. Parapsychology, 1975-90; mem. editl. bd. Advances in Parapsychol. Rsch., 1980-85, Archaeus, 1985-93, 3 books on key aspects of the transformative potential of non-ordinary exceptional hum. experiences; contbr. over 100 articles to profl. jours. Recipient Hans Peter Luhn award Am. Soc. Info. Sci., N.Y.C. chpt., 1965; Coll. Human Scis. hon. fellow Internat. Inst. Integral Human Scis. Mem.: Soc. Psychical. Rsch., Am. Anthrop. Assn., Soc. Sci. Study of Religion, Assn. Near-Death Studies, Acad. Religion and Psychical Rsch. (mem. bd. 1982—84, publs. com. 1982—97), Parapsychology Assn. (mem. coun. 1958, 1962—63, 1982—85, pres. 1984, dir. 1986, Lifetime Outstanding Rsch. award 1992, conf. spkr. 1993), Ctr. for Psychology and Social Change, Spiritual Frontiers Fellowship, Internat., Internat. Assn. Religion and Parapsychology, Found for Shamanic Studies, Internat. Soc. for Study Subtle Energies and Energy Medicine, Inst. Noetic Scis., Soc. for Anthropology of Consciousness, Penn State Alumni Assn. Coll. Liberal Arts. Avocations: hiking, gardening, animals, reading, listening to music. Home and Office: 414 Rockledge Rd New Bern NC 28562-9553 E-mail: ehenwhite@cox.net.

WHITE, ROSLYN R. music educator; b. Charlotte, NC, Sept. 3, 1974; d. Charles E. and Marina K. White. BA in instrumental performance, Elizabeth City State U., 1996; MusM in violin performance, U. NC, 1998. Cert. Suzuki. Violin tchr. Albemarle After Sch. Program, Elizabeth City, NC, 1994—95; pvt. violin tchr. Charlotte, NC, 1994; violin tchr. Greensboro (NC) Music Acad., 1997—2000; symphony musician Winston Salem (NC) Symphony, 2000—; violin tchr. Greensboro (NC) Day Sch., 2000—03, Simply Strings Violin Studio, Greensboro, 2000—; symphony musician Greensboro (NC) Symphony, 2001—02, Charlotte (N.C.) Philharmonic Orch., 2003—. Ch. musician Grace and Love Fellow., Kernersville, NC, 2003, Mt. Zion Bapt. Ch., Greensboro, 2000—01. Mem.: Music Educators of NC, Suzuki Assn. Am. Republican. Achievements include first to solo debut violin, Mitchell Cmty. Coll., NC 2001. Avocations: travel, movies, swimming.

WHITE, SALLIE SNOW WILBER, retired elementary school educator; b. Providence, Mar. 26, 1917; d. Bayard Frances and Mildred May (Armour) Snow; m. William J. Wilber, July 15, 1939 (dec. Dec. 1978); children: Drew B., William J., Harold B., Sallie B.; m. Jesse Freeman White, June 23, 1979 (dec. 1991). Grad. Sargent Coll., Boston U., 1938. Tchr. swimming and archery Sargent Summer Camp, Peterboro, N.H., 1937-38, counselor, 1939; tchr. sci. and math. Torsfield (Mass.) Elem. Sch., 1956-77, advisor to student tchrs., 1960-77; homemaker Naples, Fla., 1977—. Republican. Baptist. Avocations: gardening, knitting, painting, needlepoint, fishing. Home: 69 Pleasant St Manchester MA 01944-1104

WHITE, SARAH JOWILLIARD, retired counselor; b. Oxford, N.C., Sept. 1, 1921; d. John Hiriam and Emma (Redfern) Isham; m. Hamilton B. Carson, Sept. 20, 1945 (div. 1968); 1 child, Lynne Denise. Student, Bennett Coll., 1939-42, Cornell U., 1979-82; BA, CCNY, 1973. Clk. N.Y. Dept. Law, N.Y.C., 1948—53; auditor U.S. Fed. Govt. Svc., N.Y.C., 1955—62; postal clk. U.S. Govt., Mt. Vernon, NY, 1963—66; prin. N.Y. State Dept. Labor, N.Y.C., 1966—88, ret., 1988; youth organizer N.Y. State Careerists Soc., Inc., N.Y.C., 1989—. Youth and employment counselor Women in Community Svc., Nat. Coun. Negro Women, Manhattan sect., N.Y.C., 1983—. Vol. Advanced Vocation Edn. Day, Albany, N.Y., 1988; vol., coord. Decade of the Youth, N.Y.C., 1989-90; corres. sec. Lower East Side United Neighbors, N.Y.C., 1989. Recipient Youth award, 1987, Recognition award, 1987, Internat. Assn. Pers. Employees Youth award, Plaque for Women in Cmty. Svcs., Outstanding Vol. Svc. award Gov. Mario Cuomo, 1994, Outstanding Vol. award, 1991-92, Outstanding Vol. award Women in Cmty. Svc., 1994, Cert. Appreciation, 1995, Appreciation award South Bronx Job Alumni chpt., 1995, Nat. Coun. Negro Women Recognition award, 1996; named one of N.Y.'s Finest Vols. Women in Cmty. Svcs. Mag., 1994, Woman on the Move, Cable TV, 1994, Outstanding Recognition award Women in Cmty. Svcs., 1996, Joint Action in Cmty. Svc. award, 1996, Nat. N.E. Regional award Women in Cmty. Svcs., 1997, Youth Recognition award Yale U., New Haven, 1997, award Joint Action in Cmty. Svc., 1997, N.E. Regional Pres. Vol. award, 1998, JAC Recognition award, 1998, Horthers Regional award, 1998, Nat. Coun. Negro Women Pres.'s award, 1998, 99, Cert., Women in Cmty. Svc. Northeast Regional Pres. award, 1998, Nat. Coun. Negro Women Pres. award, 1998, Joint Action Cmty. Svc. award, 1998, 99, Nat. Pres.'s award Women in Cmty. Svc., 1999, Samuel and May Rudin Cmty. Svc. award NYU, 1999. Mem.: NAFE, Internat. Assn. Pers. Employees, Nat. Coun. Negro Women (chairperson, Achievement award 1988—90, Cmty. Svc. award 2001, Legacy award 2002), Assn. U.S. Govt. Job Corps (Alumni Recognition award 1995), N.Y. Careerists Soc. (sec., Merit award 1988), Black Alumni CCNY (pub. rels. com., Outstanding award 1989). Democrat. 7th Day Sabbath Keeper House of God. Avocations: reading, writing, music.

WHITE, SHANON KATHLEEN, accountant, consultant; b. Hackensack, NJ, July 25, 1953; d. Patrick William Carr, Trudy McFarland; m. Chester Haines White, II; 1 child, Tiffany. Associate of Arts in Accounting, Community College of Aurora, Aurora, Colorado, 1982—84. Acct. Denver Cascade, Inc, Denver, 1984—86, MDC, Inc, Denver, 1986—86; owner Jacqueline, Too, Denver, 1986—86; contr. Michael's Constrn. Co., Kans. City, Kans., 1987—87; acctg. mgr., sys. mgr. Walton Constrn. Co, Inc, Kans. City, Mo., 1987—93; owner Profit Enhancement Profls., Olathe, Kans., 1993—98; acctg. mgr. Mark One Electric Co, Inc, Kans. City, Mo., 1998—99; owner Shanon White Cons., Kans. City, Mo., 1999—2002. Selection Com. Kans. City Fairness in Constrn. Bd., Kans. City, 1991—92; Bd. Pres. Greater Kans. City NAWIC Scholarship Found., Kans. City, 1992—95. Treas. Romanelli West Homes Assoc., Kans. City, 1999—2002. Mem.: Nat. Assn. of Women in Constrn. (pres. 1991—92), Greater Kansas City Timberline Users Group (organizer, local coord. 2001—03). Avocation: Traveling, Dining, Reading. Office: Shanon White Consulting 10500 Meadow Ln Leawood KS 66206 Business E-Mail: scarrwhite@earthlink.net.

WHITE, SHELBY KATHRYN, music educator; b. Little Rock, Aug. 5, 1975; d. David Larry and Beverly Louise Joyner Staggs; m. James David White, Dec. 15, 1994. B Music Edn, Harding U., 1996, MEd, 2000. Cert. tchr. Ark., 1996. Choral dir. Bryant H.S., Ark., 2000—. Supr./mentor tchr. Bryant Pub. Schs., Ark., 2000—, choral music dept. chairperson, 2003—. Soprano Ark. Chamber Singers, Little Rock, 2002—, Coram Deo Music Ministries, North Little Rock, 1998—; v.p. for choral music Ark. Music Educators Assn., 2002—. Mem.: Am. Choral Dirs.' Assn. (assoc.), Music Educators Nat. Conf. (assoc.). Church Of Christ. Avocations: interior design, reading.

WHITE, SUSAN ROCHELLE, psychologist, investor; b. Highland Park, Mich., Jan. 23, 1957; d. John Tyree and Jayne Rochelle White. BA, U. Mich., 1979; MS, Ea. Mich. U., 1990. Lic. psychologist Mich. Disability examiner State of Mich. - Dept. Social Svcs., Southfield, 1980-88, group leader Whitmore Lake, 1988-92; case mgr. State of Mich. - Dept. Mental Health, Mt. Clements, 1992-93; group leader State of Mich. Family Ind. Agy., Whitmore Lake, 1993-94, psychologist, 1994—2002, youth residential dir., 2002—. Rschr. Aggression Replacement Tng., 1998. Mem.: APA (assoc.), Mich. Women Psychologists. Avocations: guitar, racquetball, bicycling, animal training, rental property renovation. Office: Family Ind Agy PO Box 349 Whitmore Lake MI 48189-0349 E-mail: whites@michigan.gov.

WHITE, SUSIE MAE, school psychologist; b. Madison, Fla., Mar. 5, 1914; d. John Anderson and Lucy (Crawford) Williams; m. Daniel Elijah White, Oct. 20, 1958 (dec. Sept. 29, 1968). BS, Fla. Meml. Coll., St. Augustine, 1948; MEd, U. Md., 1953; postgrad., Mich. State U., 1955, Santa Fe Community Coll., 1988; Cert. Child Care Supervision, W.T. Loften Edn. Ctr., Gainesville, Fla., 1994. Elem. tchr. Grove Park (Fla.) Elem. Sch., 1943; tchr. Douglas High Sch., High Springs, Fla., 1944-55; sch. psychologist Alachua County Sch. Bd., Gainesville, Fla., 1956-69, coord. social svcs., 1970; owner, dir. Mother Dear's Child Care Ctr., Gainesville, 1988—. Author: Determined--in spite of...Autobiography of Susie Mae Williams White, 1998, Lord, Fix Me Inspirational Poems, 2000. Del. Bapt. World Alliance, Bapt. Conv. Fla., Tokyo, 1970; state dir. leadership Fla. Bapt. Gen. Conv., 1971-85. Recipient Cert. of Appreciation, Fla. State Dept. Edn., 1971, Appreciation for Disting. Svc. award, Fla. Gen. Bapt. Conv., 1979, Hall of Fame award, Martin Luther King Jr. Hall of Fame, 1994, Cert. Appreciation for Outstanding Svc. & Leadership, Mt. Sinai Woman's Conv., 1997, The Susie Mae White scholarship fund established, Mt. Sinai Congress Christian Edn., 1995, Cert. Appreciation, Friendship Bapt. Ch., 2000, Deloris Keith Meml. Good Neighbor award, East Gainesville Devel. Task Force, Inc., 1999, Trophy for Being Inspiration to Young Women, Alachua Pratical Academic Cultural Edn. Ctr. for Girls, Inc., 2001, Plaque for Appreciation of 60 Yrs. of Svc., Friendship Baptist Ch., 2001, Plaque for Appreciation of Leadership & Dedication to Cmty., Faith Tabernacle of Praise Mins., Inc., 2001. Mem. Nat. Ret. Tchrs. Assn., Alachua County Tchrs. Assn., Fla. Meml. Coll. Nat. Alumni Assn., AAUW, Heroines of Jerico, Masons. Democrat. Avocations: gardening, speaking, working with police on crime prevention. Office: Child Care Ctr 811 NW 4th Pl Gainesville FL 32601-5049

WHITE, TOMMI A. human resources firm executive; Grad., Oakland U. Dir. sys. Ryder; asst. v.p., project dir. br. automotion Nat. Bank Detroit; divsn. v.p. Automated Data Processing, N.J.; exec. v.p., chief adminstrn. & technology officer Kelly Svcs., Inc., Troy, Mich., 1998—. Office: Kelly Svcs 999 W Big Beaver Rd Troy MI 48084-4716

WHITEHAWK, ANN, secondary school educator; b. Sioux Falls, S.D., Aug. 9, 1951; d. A. Shirley Christensen and Eunice Elthea Ugland; m. Ronald Mario Whitehawk, Jan. 29, 1971; children: Jenine Nicole, Michael Christopher. BA in Comms., U. Tex., Arlington, Tex., 1973. Tchr. St. George Cath. Sch., Fort Worth, Tex., 1973—75; mus. dir. Republic Rio Grande, Laredo, Tex., 1984—85; tchr. United HS, Laredo, Tex., 1987—. Sponsor Laredo (Tex.) Youth Coun., 1985—87; mem. dist. edn. improvement com. United Ind. Sch. Dist., Laredo, 1992—98; mem. site base decision making com. United High, Laredo, 1991—98; mem. liaison and ins. com. United Ind. Sch. Dist., Laredo, 1988—2002. Founder El Paso (Tex.) Lupus Assn., 1979; co-founder Laredo (Tex.) Youth Coun., 1985—87. Named Woman of Yr., El Paso (Tex.) Lupus Assn., 1983. Mem.: Tex. Comm. Assn., Tex. Forensic Assn., Nat. Forensic League. Democrat. Roman Cath. Avocations: painting, furniture refinishing. Home: 323 Farrell Rd Laredo TX 78045-2322 Office: United High School 8800 McPherson Laredo TX 78045

WHITEHEAD, JENIFER BARRON, corporate communications specialist, consultant; b. Collierville, Ind., July 1, 1970; d. Douglas Lloyd and Frances Diane (Parnell) Barron; m. James Davis Whitehead, Mar. 24; children: Corbin Daniel, Hayden James, Cole Alexander, Elijah Reid. BA in Journalism, U. Memphis, 1995. Adminstrv. asst., pub. rels. specialist Fellowship Christian Athletes, Memphis, 1995—97; pub. rels. acct. mgr. O'Connor Kenny Ptnrs., Inc., Memphis, 1997—2000; freelance writer, interactive cons. Memphis, 2000—01; comms. mgr. Svc. U Corp., Germantown, Tenn., 2001—02; comms. advisor FedEx Corp., Memphis, 2002—, comms., interactive cons., 2002—. Author: poem, story. Attendee Young Reps., Memphis, 2002—; counselor, spkr. LifeChoices, Memphis, 1995—2000; mem. Young Alumni Coun. U. Memphis, 2000—01; writer, comms. cons., participant Agape Mex. Missions, Memphis and Playa del Carmen, Mexico, 2003. Mem.: Pub. Rels. Soc. Am. (profl. devel. 2000—01, numerous awards 1997—2001). Republican. Avocations: writing, speaking, volunteering, coaching, art. Office: FedEx Corp 942 S Shady Grove Rd Memphis TN 38120

WHITEHILL, ANGELA ELIZABETH, artistic director; b. Leeds, Yorkshire, Eng., Oct. 21, 1938; came to U.S., 1952, naturalized, 1995; d. Donald Paul and Audrey May (Clayforth) Warner; m. Norman James Whitehill, Dec. 23, 1959; children: Norman James III, Pamela Elizabeth; m. William Parker Noble, Dec. 27, 1998. Student, Arts Ednl. Sch., London, 1955-59. With corps de ballet Ballet Paris, 1958-59; dir. London Sch. Ballet, St. Thomas, V.I., 1960-63; asst. dir. Ocean County Ballet Co., Toms River, N.J., 1965-68; founder, dir. Shore Ballet Sch., Toms River, 1968-76; artistic dir. Shore Ballet Co., Toms River, 1971-76; artist in residence Castleton State Coll., Rutland, Vt., 1977-79; founder, artistic dir. Burklyn Ballet Theatre, Johnson, Vt., 1977—; dir. Ballet Umbrella, Dance Coun., Burklyn Designs, 2003—. Vis. prof. Colby Sawyer Coll., New London, N.H., 1978-79; resident designer Atlanta Ballet Co., 1982-83; designer, pub. relations N.J. Ballet Co., Orange, 1983-85; artistic dir. Vt. Ballet Theatre, Burlington, 1985-94; master tchr. 1st Congress Internat. de Ballet Classico Contemporaneo, Mex., 2000. Choreographer Aransky Dances, 1983, A Deux, 1984, 4 Plus 2, 1986, Twins From A Time Gone By, 1987, Heart of the Island, 2002; co-author: Parent's Book of Ballet, 1988, 2d edit., 2003, The Young Professional's Book of Ballet, 1990, The Dancer's Book of Ballet, 2000, Ballet Magic, The Burklyn Story, 2001, Nutcracker Backstage, 2004. Dir. Vt. Ballet Theatre Found., Calledonia County, 1993-96. Recipient Francis Hopkins award Ocean County, N.J., 1976, Woman of Achievement award Vt. Woman, 1989, Author's award N.J. Inst. Tech., 1989. Mem. Vt. Council on the Arts, Regional Dance Am. Mem. Soc. Of Friends. Home: 218 Ocean Ave Island Heights NJ 08732 Home (Winter): PO Box 907 Island Heights NJ 08732-0907 Office: Burklyn Ballet Theatre PO Box 302 Johnson VT 05656-0302 E-mail: awhitehill@aol.com.

WHITEHURST, MARY TARR, artist, poet, writer; b. Norfolk, Va., Nov. 20, 1923; d. Henry Bennitt and Martha Ida Tarr; m. Jerry Rutter Whitehurst, Dec. 24, 1943; children: Henry Armistead, Jeffrey Tarr, Martha W. Bryant. Student, Coll. William & Mary, 1940-42, Wytheville C.C., 1968, Sullins Coll., 1976-80, Va. Western C.C., 1988. Docent Mus. Fine Arts, Roanoke, Va., 1973-75. Dir., endowing mem. Fine Arts Ctr. of New River Valley, Pulaski, Va., 1980-93; charter, endowing mem. Bristol Mus. Fine Arts, Va./Tenn., 1975-80; benefactor, mem. Arts Found. Radford U., Va., 1991—. One-woman shows include Mus. Fine Arts, Roanoke, Va., 1977, Emory & Henry Coll., Emory, Va., 1982, Radford U. Art Gallery, Va., 1991, Ashland Area Art Galery, Ky., 1993, Va. Polytech. Inst. & State U., Blacksburg, 1985—, New River C.C. Found., 1985—, Coll. William & Mary, Williamsburg, 1995; endowment Poly. Inst. & State U., Blacksburg, Va., 1998; author: (poetry) Silent As Birds, 1997. Endowing mem. Va. Polytech. Inst. & State U., Blacksburg, 1985—, New River C.C. Found., 1985—, Coll. William & Mary, Williamsburg, 1995; mem. Va. Polytech. Found., Blacksburg, Va. Recipient Clement Gueenberg award of distinction Mus. Fine Arts, Roanoke, 1976, Grumbacher Gold medal Soc. Water Color Artists, 1995; art dept. named in honor New River C.C., Dublin, Va., 1994. Mem. Catharine Lorillard Wolfe Art Club (Joyce Williams water color award 1985), Midwest Transparent Water Color Soc. (signature mem.), Va. Water Color Soc. (dir. 1994), Ala. Water Color Soc., Blacksburg Regional Artists Assn., Allied Artists (assoc.), So. Water Color Soc. (two awards 1997, Blue Ribbon winner 2000). Avocations: travel abroad, art collection, history, philanthropy. Home: Painters Wood 2492 Forest Hill Dr Draper VA 24324-3224

WHITELAW, DOLORES FAHEY, artist; b. Bklyn., June 12, 1941; d. John Michael and Irene Marie (Bulger) Fahey; m. Bruce David Whitelaw, June 23, 1962; children: Erin Carolyn, Casey Bruce. Student, Newark Sch Fine & Indsl. Arts, 1959, 60, Art Student League, 1962, 63. One woman shows include E3 Gallery, N.Y.C., 1996, Les Malamut Art Gallery, Union, N.J., 1998; exhibited in group shows at Carole Franklin Gallery, Emerson, N.J., 1997, JCB Internat., N.Y.C., 1997, La MaMa La Galleria, N.Y.C., 1998, Westbeth Gallery, N.Y.C., 1998. Mem. Orgn. Ind. Artists, City Without Walls. Home: 362 Forest Dr Union NJ 07083-7942

WHITELEY, ROSE MARIE, city clerk, treasurer; b. Benkelman, Nebr., Mar. 26, 1942; d. Alvin James and Grace Rebecca (Alsbury) W. BS, Nebr. State U., Kearney, 1963; MS, Colo. State U., 1968. Cert. home cons./bus. secondary tchr. Home econs. instr. Deuel County H.S., Chappell, Nebr., 1963-66; adult ednl. cons. McCalls Patterns, N.Y.C., 1967-70; exec. dir. Nebr./Iowa chpt. Nat. Multiple Sclerosis Soc., Omaha, 1971-78; grant writer, fundraising dir. Omaha Theatre, 1978-94; city clk., treas. City of Benkelman, 1994—. Cons. Fundraising/Grantwriting, Omaha, 1987-94, 94—. Contbr.: The Harvest Gardener, 1992. Treas. Prevention Policy Bd., 1994—, Dundy County Resource Ctr., 1994-2001, pres., 2001—; mem. Benkelman Tree Bd., 1994—. Mem. S.W. Clks. Assn. (pres.), Nebr. Mcpl. Clks. Assn., Internat. Inst. of Mcpl. Clks., Kappa Omicron Phi. Avocations: gardening, gourmet cooking. Home: HC 61 Box 58 Benkelman NE 69021-9156 Office: City of Benkelman PO Box 347 Benkelman NE 69021-0347

WHITEMAN, MARTHA JOYCE, retired elementary school educator; b. Muncie, Ind., July 17, 1939; d. Doyt Randall and Susan (Straley) Whiteman; m. Jerry Spencer, July 3, 1960 (div. 1967); children: Jay Dee Spencer, Todd Alan Spencer. BA, Ball State U., 1970, MA, 1975; postgrad., Mich. State U., U. Mich. Cert. tchr. Mich. Tchr. Bennett Elem. Sch., Marion, Ind., 1965-67; tchr. elem. sch. Grand Rapids (Mich.) Pub. Schs., 1970-77, reading cons., 1977-87, tchr. compensatory edn., 1987-96, itinerant tchr. Title I, 1996-2001. Presenter Compensatory Edn. Parent Orgn., Grand Rapids, 1980—89, Jefferson Sch. Family Math Program, Grand Rapids, 1992; tchr. Summer Success Acad., 1991—95; mem. Mich. Math. Inservice Project, 1991—92, 1992—93; math. svc. trainer Compensatory Edn. Tchrs. and Paraprofessionals, 1991—93; in-svc. MEAP trainer Grand Rapids Pub. Sch. Tchrs., 1995—2001. Mem.: NEA (life), Mich. Coun. Tchrs. Math., Mich. Reading Assn., Grand Rapids Edn. Assn. (rep. 1985—90, sch. bd. contact 1986—88), Mich. Edn. Assn. (life). United Ch. Of Christ. Avocations: sewing, crafts, cooking. Home: 6211 Woodwater Ave NE Belmont MI 49306-9255

WHITENER, CAROLYN RAYE, artist; b. Corpus Christi, Texas, Feb. 2, 1941; d. Rayburn N. and Alice G. Hamilton; m. Howard Dwain Whitener; children: Mark Dwain, Rynn Rayna. Student, U. Sci. and Arts Okla., 1981-85. Co-owner Honk'n'Holler's, Stillwater, Okla., 1962-75; owner Clynn's Designs, Okla. City, 1969—; co-owner W&W Cattle Ranch, Okla., 1973—; comml. artist, co-owner Colorvision, Inc., Okla. and Tex., 1979—. Cons. Tele-Weight, Buena Vista, Colo., 1985-92, Craig Versus Boren, 1972-76; comml. design cons. for one and two dimensional rendering drawings Rynn's Lawncare & Landscaping, Oklahoma City, 1997—. Active Grady County Environ. Coalition, 1991-92; adv. mem. Gov.'s Okla. Commn. on Status of Women, 2000. Recipient Outstanding Cmty. Svc. award, 1992, One Person Who Made a Difference LWVOK, 1997, Pres. Prestigious award Okla. State U., 1996, First Adv. award Okla. Commn. on Status of Women, 2001, Gov. Commendation award Gov. Frank Keating, 2001, State of Okla. Citation award Rep. Richard Phillips and Sen. Mike Fair, 2001; named Woman of Yr. Okla. City Coun. of Beta Sigma Phi, 1997-98. Mem. Okla. Assn. Family Cmty. and Edn., Grady County Ext. Homemakers, Oklahoma City Newcomer's Club, Beta Sigma Phi (Woman of Yr. award 1997-98, Outstanding Svc. award 1992, Evening Lions Homecoming Window Design awards, 1966-68). mem. adv. coun., Status of Okla. Women, 2001-. Democrat. Methodist. Avocations: art, sewing, cooking, travel, meeting new people. Home: 5300 W Memorial Rd Apt 7K Oklahoma City OK 73142-2036 E-mail: CrWhitener@aol.com.

WHITESIDE, CAROL GORDON, foundation executive; b. Chgo., Dec. 15, 1942; d. Paul George and Helen Louise (Barre) G.; m. John Gregory Whiteside, Aug. 15, 1964; children: Brian Paul, Derek James. BA, U. Calif., Davis, 1964. Pers. mgr. Emporium Capwell Co., Santa Rosa, 1964-67; pers. asst. Levi Strauss & Co., San Francisco, 1967-69; project leader Interdatum, San Francisco, 1983-88; with City Coun. Modesto, 1983-87; mayor City of Modesto, 1987-91; asst. sec. for intergovtl. rels. The Resources Agy., State of Calif., Sacramento, 1991-93; dir. intergovtl. affairs Gov.'s Office, Sacramento, 1993-97; pres. Great Valley Ctr., Modesto, Calif., 1997—. Trustee Modesto City Schs., 1979-83; nat. pres. Rep. Mayors and Local Ofcls., 1990. Recipient Lifetime Achievement award League of Calif. Cities, 2002; named Outstanding Woman of Yr. Women's Commn., Stanislaus County, Calif., 1988, Woman of Yr., 27th Assembly Dist., 1991; Toll fellow Coun. of State Govts., 1996. Republican. Lutheran. Office: Great Valley Ctr 201 Needham St Modesto CA 95354-0903 E-mail: carol@greatvalley.org.

WHITESIDE, DORA ANN, social studies educator; d. Odessa Whiteside-McCray and Dobbie Ray Whiteside; 1 child, Daireeous Raychard. BS, U. of North Ala., 1996—98; MEd (hon.), Tex. So. U., 2001—03. Teacher Tex., 1999. Counselor/social studies tchr. Aldine Ind. Sch. Dist., Houston, Tex., 1999—. Dir.(also writer, prodr.): (school prodns.) Moments in African American History. Ch. trustee/bd. mem. Magnolia Missionary Bapt. Ch., Houston, Tex., 2001—03. Mem.: Profl. Educators (assoc.).

WHITESIDE, DOROTHY JEAN, education educator; d. Lee Omar Waters and Anna May Waters McDonald; m. B. Kenneth Whiteside, July 12, 1963; children: Kristi, Dana, Michelle. BS, S.E. Mo. State U., 1965, MAT, 1980. Cert. tchr. Mo., Ark. Tchr. Qulin Pub. Schs., Mo., 1965—68, Malden R-1 Schs., Mo., 1974—92; adj. instr. Three Rivers C.C., Poplar Bluff, Mo., 1984—92, Ark. State U., Beebe, 1992—94; v.p. continuing edn. Foothills Tech. Inst. (now Ark. State U.), Searcy, 1994—. V.p. then pres.

SEMO Tchrs. Orgn., Cape Girardeau, Mo., 1980—88; pres. New and Related Div., Little Rock, 1999—2001. Mem.: Ark. Assn. Career and Tech. Edn. (membership chair 2001—, bd. dirs. 1999—, Regional Educator of Yr. 2001), Searcy C. of C. (edn. chair 2002—). [illegible] Office: Ark State U Searcy PO Box 909 1800 E Moore Searcy AR 72145 Office Phone: 501-207-4050. E-mail: dwhiteside@searcy.asub.edu.

WHITESIDE, JENNIE SUSAN, elementary school educator, secondary school educator; b. Kansas City, Mo., Nov. 21, 1950; d. Robert Nichols and Nola Mae Dischman; m. Morey Bruce Sullivan, Sept. 1, 1972 (div. 1975); m. Leslie Lowell Whiteside, May 1978; children: Jacob, James. BS in Edn., Ctrl. Mo. State U., 1973. Art instr. Archie (Mo.) Cass R-V Sch. Dist., 1973—; freelance designer On the Whiteside, Archie, 2003—. Dir. Western Mo. Conf. Art Competition, Cass/Bates County, 1978—; dist. judge Odyssey of the Mind Competition, Kansas City, Mo., 1990—94. Author: Mo. Jaycee Women's Prayer, 1981; actor: Amuse You Theatre Group, 1994; costume designer, choreographer U. Mo. Kansas City Performing Arts Ctr., 2002; Exhibited in group shows at Mo. Art Educators Exhibit, 1994; designer stained glass windows Archie United Meth. Ch., 2003. Tiger cub and webelo leader Cub Scout Troop 242, Archie, 1989—95; scoutmaster Boy Scout Troop 242, Archie, 1995—2001, asst. scoutmaster, 2002—; youth leader, puppet dir. Archie United Meth. Ch., 1985—2001. Named Chpt. Sweetheart, Beta Sigma Phi, 1990, Cass County Art Tchr. of Yr., Harrisonville (Mo.) Fine Arts Assn., 1993, 1996, 2002, Honored Woman, Boy Scout Tribe of Mic-O-Say, 1997; recipient Boy Scout Leaders Tng. award, 1998. Mem.: Archie PTO, Cmty. Tchrs. Assn., Archie Jaycees, Delta Kappa Gamma (State Golden Anniversary Com. 1987—2003, initiated tchr.'s scholarship Show Me Coun. 1992, creator You Showed Us Award for outstanding chpt. mems. in Show Me Cou 1992—, finalist Delta State Achievement award 2002, v.p., pres. Mu chpt.). Avocations: drawing, painting, sculpting, sewing, floral design. Office: Archie Cass R-V Sch Dist PO Box 106 Archie MO 64725

WHITESIDE, PATRICIA LEE, fine art antique and personal property appraiser; b. Keokuk, Iowa, Dec. 29, 1957; d. Francis Lee and Ruby Elaine (Higbee) W. AA, Merced Coll., 1980; Cert. Appraisal Studies, NYU, 1997, 99. Proprietor estate specialist Lexington Ave. Antiques, Magnolia, Mass., 1984-88; pub., editor, dir. The Art and Antique Tour Guide, 1988—; art advisor, pres. Fine Art and Antique Tour Assocs., 1988—; estate specialist East Coast region, 1981—, New Eng. Appraisers Assn., Palm Beach, Fla., 1988—. Contbr. articles to profl. publs. and newspapers. Active Palm Beach Civic Assn., 1995—, Palm Beach C. of C., 1990—, Children's Mus., Boca Raton, Fla., others. Recipient award Mass. Hist. Assn., Harvard U., 1987, others. Mem. New Eng. Appraisers Assn. (S. Fla. regional dir.), Soc. for the Preservation of New Eng. Antiquities, Compass Inc. Charities, Palm Beach Hist. Soc., Epilepsy Assn., Nat. Assn. Profl. Appraisers, others. Democrat. Avocations: painting, hist. preservation, writing children's books, sailing, travel. Office: PO Box 2101 Palm Beach FL 33480-2101 Office Phone: 561-820-0100.

WHITE-WALKER, ROXANA, elementary school educator; b. Beckley, W.Va., Sept. 13, 1947; d. George S. and Rosetta D. (Duey) White; m. Aug. 22, 1970; children: Joyce D., Walter W., Yalena A. BS in Edn., Lincoln U., Jefferson City, Mo., 1971; MEd, U. Louisville, 1989. Dir. presch. USAF, Eileson AFB, Alaska; elem. tchr. Wichita (Kans.) Pub. Schs.; tchr. kindergarten Westphalia (Mo.) Sch. Dist.; elem. tchr. Jefferson County Pub. Schs., Louisville. Former unit dir. Head Start, Phoenix. Treas. King Elem. Sch. PTA; rep. Jefferson County Pub. Sch. Mem. Ky. Edn. Assn. (rep. Jefferson County), Black Tchr. Caucus, Golden Key. Home: 316 Shawnee Dr Louisville KY 40212-2649

WHITE-WHITFIELD, LISA DENISE, social worker, grant writer; b. L.A., June 11, 1968; d. Charles L. White and Martha Jackson, Burrell Jackson (Stepfather); m. Ervin L. Whitfield, Apr. 25, 1992 (div. Oct. 1, 1995); 1 child, Alexis Ximara. BS in Bus. Adminstrn., Calif. State U., Long Beach, 1992; postgrad., Calif. State U., Carson, 2000. Tchg. credential Calif. Bank teller Wells Fargo Bank, Lakewood, Calif., 1987—88; proof operator Bank of Am., Long Beach, 1988—89; spl. edn. tchrs. asst. Inglewood (Calif.) Unifield Sch. Dist., 1989—91; adminstrv. asst. Remax Realtors, Carson, 1991—92; substitute tchr. Compton (Calif.) Unified Sch. Dist., 1992—93; acctg. clk. United Airlines, El Segundo, Calif., 1993—94; social worker LA County Dept. Pub. Social Svcs., 1994—. Mentor Welfare-to-Work Career Mentor Program, El Monte, CALIF., 2002—. Vol. March of Dimes, L.A., 1994—2000; vol., bd. mem. The Dance Connection Dance Acad., L.A., 2002; vol. Redeemer Christian Acad., L.A., 1999, West Angeles Ch. of God in Christ, L.A., 1996—2002. Scholar, Calif. Regional Purchasing Com., 1986. Mem.: ASPA, Dominguez Pub. Adminstrn. Assn., Assn. County Administrs., Calif. State U. Long Beach Alumni Assn. Avocations: marathon running, social research, volunteering, travel, hiking. Office: Los Angeles County Dept Social Svcs 10728 S Central Ave Los Angeles CA 90059

WHITE-WINTERS, JILL MARY, nursing educator; b. Milw., June 30, 1955; d. John Paul Gabor and Ann Lorraine (Ladish) Gordy; m. Jack Mark Winters; children: Jeffrey, Eric, David, Michael. BSN, U. Wis., Milw., 1978; MS in Nursing, Marquette U., 1991; PhD, U. Wis., 1996. Nurse various hosps., Milw., 1978—85, Peck Foods Corp., Milw., 1985-88; prof. U. Wis., Milw., 1996—2001, Marquette U., Milw., 2001—. Contbr. chpts. to books, articles to profl. jours. Grantee, Nat. Inst. Nursing Rsch., Wis. Women's Health Found., Nat. Inst. Disability and Rehab. Rsch. Mem. AACCN (grantee 1997), ANA, Midwest Nursing Rsch. Soc., Sigma Theta Tau (v.p. local chpt. 1997-99). Roman Catholic. Avocation: golf. Home: 10320 N Provence Ct Mequon WI 53092-5228 Office: Marquette U Coll Nursing PO Box 1881 Milwaukee WI 53201-1881 Office Phone: 414-288-3848.

WHITFIELD, PATRICIA ANN RAINWATER, education educator; b. Atlanta, July 20, 1945; d. George Ernest and Annie M. (Barrett) Rainwater; m. William Nicholls Whitfield, July 17, 1965; 1 child, Ann Nicholls Whitfield Carter. BS, U. Richmond, 1967, MEd, 1984; PhD, U. Va., 1987. Asst. then assoc. prof. Longwood U., Farmville, Va., 1992—2003, assoc. dean coll. edn., 1997—2003, dir. grad. studies, 1999—2002, dir. tchr. edn., 2002—03; assoc. prof. Va. Union U., Richmond, 2003—. Bd. examiners Nat. Coun. AccreditationTchr. Edn., Washington, 2001—. Contbg. editor: Intervention, 1990—. Bd. dirs. Bahari Found., Richmond, Va., 1997—. Mem.: Assn. Tchr. Educators Va. (pres.-elect 2003—), Coun. Exceptional Children, Phi Delta Kappa. Baptist. Avocations: singing, handbell ringing, travel. Office: Va Union Univ 1500 N Lombardy St Richmond VA 23220

WHITING, CAROL LOUISE, pastor; d. Donald Floyd Kieffer and Adele Inez; m. Malcolm Merrill Whiting, Jr., Feb. 24, 1968; children: Scott Michael, Todd Merrill. AS, Corning C.C., 1965; BS in Med. Tech., U. Buffalo, 1967; MDiv, Asbury Theol. Sem., 1998. ASCP. Med. technologist Arnot Ogden Hosp., Elmira, NY, 1967—73, St. Joseph's Hosp., Elmira, 1973—74, Streator (Ill.) Medicare Clinic, Streator, 1975—80, St. Mary's Hosp., Streator, 1980—89, St. Elizabeth Hosp., Edgewood, Ky., 1989—98; pastor Olivet United Meth. Ch., Maysville, Ky., 1998—2000, Benson/Curry United Meth. Ch., Cynthiana, Ky., 2000—. United Methodist.

WHITING, SUSAN D. marketing professional; BA in Econs. cum laude, Denison U. Mgmt. devel. program Neilsen Media Rsch., Dunedin, Fla., 1979-86, v.p. Nielsen Homevideo Index, 1986-87, mktg. mgr., 1987-93, sr. v.p., dir. mktg., 1993-97, gen. mgr. nat. svcs. & emerging markets, 1997—. Mem. Cable Television Adminstrv. and Mktg. Assn., Women in Cable & Telecomm., Conn. Women's Forum (v.p.), N.Y. Radio and TV Rsch. Coun. (past pres.). Office: Nielsen Media Rsch 375 Patricia Ave Dunedin FL [illegible]-0190

WHITING DOBSON, LISA LORRAINE, video production educator, producer, director; b. Lansing, Mich., July 22, 1959; d. Lowell Stanton and Ruth Lorraine (Gregory) Whiting. BS in Psychology, Mich. State U., 1981, BA in Telecomm. cum laude, 1984, MA in Telecomm., 1988; AA in Dance magna cum laude, Lansing C.C., 1984. Prodr., dir. Cath. Diocese Lansing, 1984—; video instr., prodr., dir. dept. telecomm., internat. studies and media Mich. State U., East Lansing, Mich., 1987—; instr. media tech. Lansing C.C., 1999—. Dance instr. Synergy, 2002—. Mem. Jr. League of Lansing. Office: Mich State U Dept Telecom 409 Communication Arts Bldg East Lansing MI 48824-1212 E-mail: whiting3@msu.edu.

WHITLEY, ANGELA JANE, social worker; b. Ashland, Ky., Sept. 7, 1962; d. George Richard and Rearl Y. Coleman; m. Raymond Russel Whitley, Mar. 20, 1982; children: Raymond Todd, Rachael Elizabeth. BSW, Morehead State U., 1993. Lic. social worker W.Va. Dir. Social Svcs. Woodland Oaks, Ashland, Ky., 1994; Parent Coord. Appalachian Family First, Ironton, Ohio, 1994—95; Coord. Healthy Families/New Steps Team for W.Va. Children, Huntington, W.Va., 1996—. Chairperson Partners in Cmty. Outreach, Huntington, W.Va., 2000. Treas. Boyd (Ky.) County Softball Boosters, 2000—01, Boyd (Ky.) County Academic Boosters, 2002—, Boyd (Ky.) County AABC, 1996—98. Democrat. Office: Team for W Va Children 625 4th Ave Huntington WV 25701

WHITLOCK, BETTY, retired secondary school educator; b. Somerset, Ky., Mar. 17, 1942; d. Rual Robert and Hazel Ellen (Biers) Wilson; m. L. Craig Whitlock, June 12, 1962 (dec. 2002); children: Michael Craig, Jeffrey Robert, Katherine Elizabeth. BA, Georgetown Coll., 1964; MA, Miss. Coll., 1980, EdS, 1982; postgrad., U. So. Miss., 1986. Nat. bd. cert. tchr. Adolescence and Young Adulthood/English Lang. Arts. Tchr. kindegarten First Bapt. Ch. Kindergarten, Clinton, Miss., 1970-72, Northside Bapt. Ch. Kindegarten, Clinton, Miss., 1972-73; tchr. high sch. Miss. Bapt. H.S., Jackson, 1973-75, Clinton H.S., 1975—. Bd. dirs. Miss. Youth Congress, 1985—; chmn. com. Lit. Map of Miss., 1985—; cons. Miss. H.S. Activities Assn., 1991—. Co-author: Mississippi Writers: An Anthology, 1987, Mississippi Writers: Reflections on Childhood and Youth, 1988, (textbook) Dramatic Interpretation, 1994. Tchr. Sunday sch. First Bapt. Ch., Clinton, 1969—. Mem. Nat. Coun. Tchrs. English, Nat. Forensic League, Miss. Coun. Tchrs. English (chmn. maps 1975—, Outstanding Tchr. award 1992), Miss. Speech Communication Assn. (dir. congress 1973—), Miss. Profl. Educators, Miss. Forensic League (chmn. 1988-99), Jackson Cath. Forensic League (moderator 1991-93), Miss. Coll. Faculty Wives, Phi Delta Kappa. Republican. Baptist. Avocation: writing. Home: 100 Hannah Dr Clinton MS 39056-5107 Office: Clinton High Sch 401 Arrow Dr Clinton MS 39056-3108 Office Phone: 601-924-5656. E-mail: nanawhit@aol.com.

WHITLOCK, VERONICA P. interior designer, educator; b. N.Y.C., Sept. 29, 1961; d. Emmet and Gloria Welch Whitlock; children: Alexander M. Laughlin, III, Julia W. Laughlin. BA in Studio Art and Art History cum laude, Duke U., 1983; BFA in Interior Design with distinction, N.Y. Sch. Interior Design, 1989. Cert. Nat. Coun. Interior Design Qualification, lic. interior designer Conn., cert. N.Y. Adminstrv. asst. William Doyle Galleries, N.Y.C., 1984—86; assoc. Timmins-Munn, Inc., N.Y.C., 1987—98; interior designer V.W. Interiors, Greenwich, Conn., 1994—; tchr. N.Y. Sch. Interior Design, N.Y.C., 2001—. Vol. Jr. League, Greenwich, 1999—. Mem.: Interior Designers for Licensing N.Y. (bd. mem. 0001), Am. Soc. Interior Designers (profl.), Decorators Club. Home and Office: 25 Halsey Dr Old Greenwich CT 06870

WHITMAN, CHRISTINE TODD, former governor; b. Sept. 26, 1946; d. Webster Bray and Eleanor Schley Todd; m. John Whitman, 1974; children: Kate, Taylor. BA in Govt., Wheaton Coll., 1968. Former freeholder Somerset County, N.J.; former pres. State Bd. Pub. Utilities; host radio talk show Sta. WKXW, Trenton, N.J.; gov. State of N.J., 1994-2001; adminstr. EPA, Washington, 2001—03. Chmn. Com. for an Affordable N.J.; bd. dirs. Texas Instruments Columnist newspapers. Bd. freeholders Somerset County, N.J., 1982-87; bd. pub. utilities, 1988-89; Rep. candidate for senator State of N.J., 1990. Republican. Achievements include first female governor in N.J.; delivered Republican response to President Clinton's 1995 State of the Union address.*

WHITMAN, MARGARET C. (MEG WHITMAN), internet company executive; b. N.Y., 1957; m. Griffith R. Harsh IV; children: Griff, Will. B in Econs., Princeton U., 1977; MBA, Harvard U., 1979. Brand asst. Procter & Gamble, 1979—81; v.p. Bain & Co., 1982—89; with Walt Disney Co. most recently as sr. v.p. mktg. consumer products divsn., 1989—92; with Stride Rite Corp., 1992—95, corp. v.p. strategic planning, 1992—93, exec. v.p. Keds divsn., pres. Stride Rite Divsn.; pres., CEO Florists' Transworld Delivery (FTD), 1995—97; gen. mgr. preschool divsn. Hasbro, 1997—98; pres., CEO eBay, Inc., San Jose, Calif., 1998—. Dir. Procter & Gamble. Bd. trustees Princeton U. Office: eBay Inc 2145 Hamilton Ave San Jose CA 95125*

WHITMAN, MARINA VON NEUMANN, economist, educator; b. N.Y.C., Mar. 6, 1935; d. John and Mariette (Kovesi) von Neumann; m. Robert Freeman Whitman, June 23, 1956; children: Malcolm Russell, Laura Mariette. BA summa cum laude, Radcliffe Coll., 1956; MA, Columbia U., 1959, PhD, 1962; LHD (hon.), Russell Sage Coll., 1972; LLD (hon.), Cedar Crest Coll., 1973, Hobart and William Smith Coll., 1973; LHD (hon.), U. Mass., 1975, N.Y. Poly. Inst., 1975; LLD (hon.), Coe Coll., 1975, Marietta Coll., 1976. Mem. faculty U. Pitts., 1962-79, prof. econs., 1971-73, disting. pub. svc. prof. econs., 1973-79; v.p., chief economist Gen. Motors Corp., N.Y.C., 1979-85, group v.p. pub. affairs, 1985-92; disting. vis. prof. bus. adminstrn., pub. policy U. Mich., Ann Arbor, 1992-94, prof. bus. adminstrn., pub. policy, 1994—. Bd. dirs. Unocal; mem. Trilateral Commn., 1973-84, 88-95; mem. Pres. Adv. Com. on Trade Policy and Negotiations, 1987-93; mem. tech. assessment adv. coun. U.S. Congress Office of Tech. Assessment, 1990-95; mem. Consultative Group on Internat. Econs. and Monetary Affairs, 1979—; mem. U.S. Price Commn., 1971-72, Coun. Econ. Advisers, Exec. Office of Pres., 1972-73. Author: Government Risk-Sharing in Foreign Investment, 1965, International and Interregional Payments Adjustment, 1967, Economic Goals and Policy Instruments, 1970, Reflections of Interdependence: Issues for Economic Theory and U.S. Policy, 1979, New World, New Rules: The Changing Role of the American Corporation, 1999; bd. editors: Am. Econ. Rev., 1974-77; mem. editl. bd. Fgn. Policy; contbr. articles to profl. jours. Trustee Nat. Bur. Econ. Rsch., 1993—, Princeton U., 1980-90, Inst. Advanced Study, 1999—; bd. dirs. Inst. for Internat. Econs., 1986—, Salzburg Seminar, 1994—, Eurasia Found., 1992-95; bd. overseers Harvard U., 1972-78, mem. vis. com. Kennedy Sch., 1992-98. Fellow Earhart Found., 1959-60, AAUW, 1960-61, NSF, 1968-70, Social Security Rsch. Coun.; recipient Columbia medal for excellence, 1973, George Washington award Am. Hungarian Found., 1975. Mem. Am. Econ. Assn. (exec. com. 1977-80), Am. Acad. Arts and Scis., Coun. Fgn. Rels. (dir. 1977-87), Phi Beta Kappa. Office: U Mich Gerald Ford Sch Pub Policy 411 Lorch Hall Ann Arbor MI 48109-1220 Office Phone: 734-763-4173. E-mail: marinaw@umich.edu.

WHITMAN, SHARON MAY, music educator; d. Cora M. and Edward E. Wright; m. Dennis Dwayne Whitman, Oct. 18, 1947; children: Jason G., Jeffrey A. BS in Music Edn., Lamar U., Beaumont, Tex., 1971; MEd in Counseling, Northwestern State U., Natchitoches, La., 2000. Cert. sch. counselor Northwestern State U., 2000, vocal and band music tchr. Lamar U., 1971. Exec. sec. Tex. Am. Bancshares, Fort Worth, 1972—77; choral dir. DeRidder H.S. and Mid. Sch., La., 1984—86; vocal music tchr. [illegible], La., [illegible]—92, Allen Parish Pub. Schs., Oakdale, La., 1991—2000; choral dir. New Kent H.S. and Mid. Sch., Va., 2000—. French horn player Beaumont Symphony Orch., Tex., 1966—71; mem. chorus Ft. Worth Opera Co., Tex., 1972—77; gifted performing arts instr. New Kent H.S., Va., 2000—, color guard instr., 2000—03. Singer various broadway musicals. Fund raiser Artists Civic Theatre and Studio, Lake Charles, La., 1985—92. Grantee Jazz Outreach, La. Arts and Humanities Coun., 1999. Mem.: Music Educators Nat. Conf., Am Choral Dir. Assn. (assoc.). Conservative. Southern Baptist. Achievements include development of vocal music curriculum. Avocations: antique/depression glass collecting, reading, educational research, travel. Office: New Kent HS 7501 Egypt Rd New Kent VA 23124

WHITMER, AMANDA JANE, elementary school educator; b. Bowling Green, Ohio, July 3, 1974; d. Ned Allen and Jane Phyllis Whitmer. BA, Cedarville U., 1996. Kindergarten tchr. Cridersville Elem. Sch., Cridersville, Ohio, 1996—97; tchr. 3rd grade Rogers Heights Elem. Sch., Bladensburg, Md., 1999—. Founder wellness com. Rogers Heights Elem. Sch., 2000—01. Mem.: NEA, Prince Georges County Educators Assn.

WHITMORE, MENANDRA M. librarian; b. Ancash, Peru; d. Rafael and Jacinta (Moreno) Mosquera; m. Jacob L. Whitmore III, Jan. 7, 1965; children: Jacqueline Grace, Michelle Jacinta. Degree in social work, U. Catolica del Peru, 1967; MLS, U. P.R., 1974, Catholic U. Am., 1984. Social worker Cornell U., Vicos, Peru, 1960-62, Servicio de Extension Agricola del Peru, 1962-63, Am. Friends Svc. Com., Mex. and Peru, 1963-65; libr. Colegio Maria Auxiliadora, P.R., 1971, Country Day Sch., San Jose, Costa Rica, 1974-76, Colegio San Ignacio, P.R., 1976-77; dir. libs. Am. Coll. P.R., 1977-80; libr. Lib. Gov. Printing Office, 1981-84; chief acquisitions sect., mgr. Hispanic employment program Pentagon Libr., Washington, 1984-99, chief tech. and stds. divsn., 1999—2002, acting dir., 2002—03, dir., 2003—. Author: (all pub. under name Menandra Mosquera) Bibliography on Hypsipyla, 1976, Bibliography of Forestry of Puerto Rico, 1984, Useful Trees of Tropical North America, 1998. Recipient commendation Dept. Def., 1987-98. Mem. ALA, Soc. for Acquisition Latin Am. Libr. Materials, Reforma (treas. Washington chpt. 1988, pres. 1989-91, 95-99, nat. ways and means chair 1991-92).

WHITNEY, JANE, foreign service officer; b. July 15, 1941; d. Robert F. and Mussette (Cary) W. BA, Beloit Coll., 1963; CD, U. Aix, Marseille, France, 1962. Joined Fgn. Svc., U.S. Dept. State, 1965; vice consul Saigon, Vietnam, 1966—68; career counselor, 1968—70; spl. asst. Office of Dir. Gen., 1970—72; consul Stuttgart, Fed. Rep. Germany, 1972-74, Ankara, Turkey, 1974—76; spl. asst. Office of Asst. Sec. for Consular Affairs, 1976—77; mem. Bd. Examiners Fgn. Svc., 1977—78, 1979—81; consul Munich, 1978—79, Buenos Aires, 1981—82; ethics officer Office of Legal Adviser, 1982—85; advisor Office of Asst. Sec. for Diplomatic Security, 1985—86; dep. prin. officer, consul Stuttgart, 1986—90; prin. officer, consul gen. Perth, Australia, 1990—91. Mem. Presbyterian Ch. Recipient awards U.S. Dept. State, 1968, 70, 81, 85, 87, 90.

WHITNEY, LORI ANN, legislative staff member; b. Rhinelander, Wis, Feb. 20, 1968; d. Larry R. and Mary E. (Gaffney) Whitney. BA in Spanish/Polit. Sci. cum laude, U. Wis., Eau Claire, 1990. Messenger Wis. State Assembly, Madison, 1991—95; postal clk. Assembly Post Office Wis. State Assembly, Madison, 1995—2003; postmistress Assembly Postoffice Wis. State Assembly, 2003—. Fundraiser State Employees Combined Campaign, Madison, 1992—, mem. state coordinating com., 1996—; fundraiser Multiple Sclerosis Soc., 1993—; mem. Amnesty Internat., 1991—; fundraiser, vol. Am. Diabetes Assn.; monthly donor Planned Parenthood Nat. Leadership Coun.; vol., donor Planned Parenthood Advocates of Wis.; mem., donor YWCA; blood donor ARC; vol. Prevent Child Abuse Wis., 1994—; mem., donor So. Poverty Law Ctr., 1994—, People for the Am. Way, 1996—, Wis. Coalition Against the Death Penalty, 1993—; campaign vol. David Clarenbach and Tammy Baldwin, Madison, 1992, State Rep. Tammy Baldwin, 1994, 1996, 1998, Fred Risser, 1996, Russ Feingold, 1998, Tammy Baldwin and Al Gore, 2000, Tammy Baldwin, Jim Doyle, Kathleen Falk, Barbara Lawton, 2002. Recipient Hopebuilder Habitat for Humanity award, 1995, 9 SECC Fundraising awards, Cmty. Vol. award, United Way, 2002, Hannah Needham Rogers award, Planned Parenthood Advocates of Wis., 2002. Mem.: NOW. Democrat. Avocations: reading, sports, rock music, movies (comedy), travel. Home: 15 N Hancock St Apt 102 Madison WI 53703-2839

WHITNEY, MARILYN BETH, music educator; b. Grand Island, Nebr., June 21, 1949; d. Daniel Webster and Edna L. Fore; m. Roland Carl Whitney; children: Daniel Carl, Beth Ann. BFA, Kearney State Coll., 1971. Vocal music tchr. Elm Creek (Nebr.) Pub. Sch., 1971—. Mem.: Eagles Aux. (assoc.; regional pres. 1987—88, sec. 1995—2003, Tchr. of the Yr. 1976). Home: 303 E 26th St Kearney NE 68847 Office: Elm Creek Pub Sch 230 Calkins Elm Creek NE 68836 Business E-Mail: mwhitney@esu10.org.

WHITNEY, PHYLLIS AYAME, author; b. Yokohama, Japan, Sept. 9, 1903; d. Charles J. and Lillian (Mandeville) W.; m. George A. Garner, July 2, 1925 (div. 1945); m. Lovell F. Jahnke, 1950 (dec. 1973). Grad., McKinley High Sch., Chgo., 1924. Instr. dancing, San Antonio, 1 yr; tchr. juvenile fiction writing Northwestern U., 1945; children's book editor Chgo. Sun, 1942-46, Phila. Inquirer, 1947, 48; instr. juvenile fiction writing N.Y.U., 1947-58; leader juvenile fiction workshop Writers Conf., U. Colo., 1952, 54, 56. Pres. exec. bd. 5th Ann. Writers Conf., Northwestern U., 1944. Author: A Place for Ann, 1941, A Star for Ginny, 1942, (vocat. fiction for teenage girls) A Window for Julie, 1943, (mystery novel for adults) Red Is for Murder, 1943, The Silver Inkwell, 1945, Willow Hill, 1947, Writing Juvenile Fiction, 1947, Ever After, 1948, Mystery of the Gulls, 1949, Linda's Homecoming, 1950, The Island of Dark Woods, 1951, Love Me, Love Me Not, 1952, Step to the Music, 1953, A Long Time Coming, 1954, Mystery of the Black Diamonds, 1954, The Quicksilver Pool, 1955, Mystery on the Isle of Skye, 1955, The Fire and The Gold (Jr. Lit. Guild), 1956, The Highest Dream (Jr. Lit. Guild), The Trembling Hills (Peoples Book Club), 1956, Skye Cameron, 1957, Mystery of the Green Cat (Jr. Lit. Guild), 1957, Secret of the Samurai Sword (Jr. Lit. Guild), 1958, The Moonflower, 1958, Creole Holiday, 1959, Thunder Heights, 1960, Blue Fire, 1961, Mystery of the Haunted Pool, 1961 (Edgar award Mystery Writers Am.), Secret of the Tiger's Eye, 1961, Window on the Square, 1962, Mystery of the Golden Horn, 1962, Seven Tears for Apollo, 1963, Mystery of the Hidden Hand, 1963 (Edgar award Mystery Writers Am. 1964), Black Amber, 1964, Secret of the Emerald Star, 1964, Sea Jade, 1965, Mystery of the Angry Idol, 1965, Columbella, 1966, Secret of the Spotted Shell, 1967, Mystery of the Strange Traveler, 1967, Silverhill, 1967, Hunter's Green, 1968, Secret of Goblin Glen, 1968, Mystery of the Crimson Ghost, 1969, Winter People, 1969, Secret of the Missing Footprint, 1970, Lost Island, 1970, The Vanishing Scarecrow, 1971, Listen for the Whisperer, 1971, Nobody Likes Trina, 1972, Snowfire, 1973, Mystery of the Scowling Boy, 1973, The Turquoise Mask, 1974, Spindrift, 1975, Secret of Haunted Mesa, 1975, The Golden Unicorn, 1976, Secret of the Stone Face, 1977, The Stone Bull, 1977, The Glass Flame, 1978, Domino, 1979, Poinciana, 1980, Vermilion, 1981, Guide to Fiction Writing, 1982, Emerald, 1983, Rainsong, 1984, Dream of Orchids, 1985, Flaming Tree, 1986, Silversword, 1987, Feather on the Moon, 1988, Rainbow in the Mist, 1989, The Singing Stones, 1990, Woman Without a Past, 1991, The Ebony Swan, 1992, Star Flight, 1993, Daughter of the Stars, 1994, Amethyst Dreams, 1997; sold first story to Chgo. Daily News; later wrote for pulp mags., became specialist in juvenile writing, now writing entirely in adult field. Spent first 15 years of life in Japan, China and P.I. (father in shipping and hotel bus.). Recipient Friends of Lit. award for contbns. to children's lit., 1974; Reynal and

Hitchcock prize in Youth Today contest for book Willow Hill; Today's Woman award Coun. Cerebral Palsy Auxs., 1983, Agatha award Malice Domestic, 1990, Rita award Romance Writers Am., 1990, Lifetime award Romance Writers Am., 1990, Midland Authors award for a lifetime of literary achievement, 1995. Mem. Mystery Writers Am. (pres. 1975, Grandmaster award for lifetime achievement 1988), Am. Crime Writers League, Sisters in Crime, Authors League of Am., Authors Round Table (pres. 1943-44). Address: care McIntosh and Otis 353 Lexington Ave New York NY 10016-0941

WHITSELL, HELEN JO, lumber executive; b. Portland, Oreg., July 20, 1938; d. Joseph William and Helen (Cornwell) Copeland; m. William A. Whitsell, Sept. 2, 1960; 2 children. BA, U. So. Calif., 1960. With Copeland Lumber Yard Inc., Portland, 1960—, pres., chief exec. officer, 1973-84, chmn., chief exec. officer, 1984—. Office: Copeland Lumber Yards Inc PO Box 80769 Portland OR 97280-1769

WHITSITT, MARJORIE RAE, artist, educator; b. Superior, Wis., Dec. 3, 1922; d. Roy James and Emma Martha Emerson; m. William Harwood Whitsitt, Dec. 28, 1942 (div. 1962); children: William Harwood, Richard LeRoy, Lynne Marie. BS, U. Wis., Superior, 1964, MS in Tchg., 1966; PhD, U. Wis., Madison, 1975. Art tchr. Denfeld H.S., Duluth, Minn., 1964-66; art supr. McCaskill Lab. sch., instr. art edn. U. Wis., Superior, 1966-71, coord. art therapy program, prof. art, 1973-87, prof. emeritus, 1987—. Workshop leader Art Therapy - Creativity in Superior, 1977-87, Panama City, Fla., 1990-98; instr., lectr. Capstone House, 1990—. One-woman shows include Warwick Hotel Gallery, Trans-Atlantic Gallery, Houston, Tex., A Room of One's Own Gallery, Madison, Wis., Lakehead U., Thunder Bay, Can., Beijing Art Acad., Hangzhou, China, Visual Arts Ctr. N.W. Fla., Panama City, Fla.; exhbns. include: Nat. Watercolor Exhbns./Visual Arts Ctr. of N.W. Fla., Panama City, 1991-94, 96-99, Lake Superior Watercolor Soc., Tweed Gallery, U. Minn., Duluth, 1984-88, Beaux Arts Gallery, Pinellas Park, Fla., Cape May N.J. Art Ctr., St. Louis Mus., Duluth. Coord. Ann. Arts for Handicapped People U. Wis., Superior, 1980-87; vol. Visual Arts Ctr., Panama City, 1988—. Faculty Devel. and Rsch. grantee U. Wis., 1974, 80. Mem. Am. Assn. Artist-Therapists, Nature Conservancy, Nat. Mus. of Women in the Arts. Avocations: reading, swimming, traveling, psychic studies, painting. Home: 2454 Pretty Bayou Blvd Panama City FL 32405-1747

WHITSON, BARBARA LEE, psychologist, consultant; b. Marietta, Ohio, Aug. 15, 1943; d. Richard Howard and Jean Elizabeth (Fox) Sullivan; m. Lish Whitson, Sept. 16, 1965; children: Lish Richard, Kimberly Shawn. BA, Swarthmore (Pa.) Coll., 1965; MEd, U. Wash., Seattle, 1971, PhD, 1981. Nat. cert. sch. psychologist. Part time teaching asst. U. Wash., Seattle, 1971-74; sch. psychologist Seattle Pub. Sch., Mercer Island, Wash., 1973-75; instr. Seattle Pacific U., 1974, 81, 82, Seattle U., 1975, 77, U. Wash., Seattle, 1976; program specialist gifted and talented U.S. Office Edn., Seattle, 1976-77; program specialist gifted Edmonds Sch. Dist., Lynnwood, Wash., 1977-79; sch. psychologist Shoreline Sch. Dist., Seattle, 1984-90, 91—, program specialist, 1986-94. Profl. edn. adv. bd. sch. psychology U. Wash., 1995—. Mem. title IV adv. coun. Wash. Spt. Pub. Instrn. Olympia, 1979-82, U.S. Office of Edn. fellow, 1976-77. Mem. Wash. State Assn. Sch. Psychologists, [illegible] Gifted Child Assn., Wash. Athletic Club, Women's Univ. Club. Office: Shoreline Pub Schs 18560 1st Ave NE Seattle WA 98155-2148

WHITSON, ELIZABETH TEMPLE, graphics designer; b. Washington, D.C., Oct. 1, 1959; d. Norman Burkey Musselman, Elizabeth Temple (Henry) Musselman; m. William Stuart Whitson, Dec. 21, 1985; 1 child, Ian Alexander. BA, Va. Tech. U., 1982. Artist, office asst. Artisan Graphics, Alexandria, Va., 1983—84; graphic artist, office asst. Gestalt Assocs., Alexandria, 1984—86; graphic artist, sales rep., prodn. mgr. Gestalt Prodns., Herndon, Va., 1986—89, ImageMatrix, Inc., Falls Church, Va., 1989—91; graphic designer, publ. dept. head CompuSlides, Vienna, Va., 1991—94, New Media Comms., Vienna, 1994—95; graphic designer, owner Port City Prodns., Inc., Alexandria, 1993—. Editor (illustrator): "Highlights of the Alexandria Com.", 1988—. Mem. Brookville/Seminary Valley Civic Assn., Alexandria, 1988—2002; vol. Torpedo Factory Art Ctr.; active mem. The Alexandria Libr. Co.; com. vol., tchr., mem. Old Presbyn. Meeting House. Mem.: DAR (corr. sec. 1995—98, chmn. two coms. Mt. Vernon chpt.), The Old Presbyterian Meeting House (worship com. 1995—97, childcare com. 2000—03, childhood edn. com. 2003—), Friends of Gunston Hall, The Alexandria Assembly, Nat. Soc. Colonial Dames of Am. (rec. sec. 1999—2002, directory chmn. 2002—). Presbyterian. Avocations: remodeling, gardening, painting, illustration, piano. Home and Office: 1701 Sherwood Hall Ln Alexandria VA 22306

WHITSON, SANDRA JOYCE, antiques dealer; b. Balt., Apr. 4, 1948; d. Frank Gilson and Frances (Moore) W.; m. Ronald Edward Van Anda, Jan. 9, 1986. BA in Theology, Loyola Coll., Balt., 1980. Legal sec. Fedder & Garten, P.A., Balt., 1967-78; antiques dealer, Lititz, Pa., 1980—. Author: Figural Napkin Rings, 1995. Mem. Antique Toy Collectors Assn. Democrat. Presbyterian. Avocation: collecting figural napkin rings. Home: PO Box 272 Lititz PA 17543-0272

WHITTAKER, JEANNE EVANS, former newspaper columnist; b. Detroit, Jan. 1, 1934; d. Alfred Heacock and Margaret (Evans) W.; m. Charles Martin Hines Jr., Sept. 29, 1962 (div. Feb. 1970); children: Charles M. Hines III, Margaret Helen Whittaker Zimmerman. Student, Northwestern U., 1952-53; BS in History, U. Mich., 1956. Clubmobile worker UN forces ARC, Republic of Korea, 1956—58; staff programmer ARC France, Chaumont, 1958—61; dir. Bexar County chpt. youth ARC, San Antonio, 1961—62; staff writer/columnist Detroit Free Press, 1970—75; editor Mich. Social Register, 1975—77; Lifestyle editor Observer and Eccentric newspapers, Birmingham, Mich., 1977—87; staff writer, columnist Detroit News, 1987—91; cons. in field, 1992—. Bd. dirs. Wayne State U. Press. Contbr. articles to mags. Bd. dirs. Detroit chpt. ARC, 1989-92; Mem. Univ.-Liggett Sch. Aumni Bd., 2003—; mem. adv. bd. Greenfield Village Antiques Show, 2000—. Recipient Penney-Mo. award U. Mo., 1984; 1st place lifestyles/Family award Mich. Press Assn., 1982, 84, Gen. Excellence award 1982, 86; Gen. Excellence award Suburban Newspaper Assn., 1979. Mem. Detroit Hist. Soc. (bd. dirs. 1986-91), Detroit Inst. Arts Women's Assn. Episcopalian. Avocations: writing, reading, travel. Home: 552 Cadieux Rd Grosse Pointe MI 48230-1508 E-mail: jeannewhittaker@aol.com.

WHITTAKER, JUDITH ANN CAMERON, lawyer; b. N.Y.C., June 12, 1938; d. Thomas Macdonald and Mindel (Wallman) Cameron; m. Kent E. Whittaker, Jan. 30, 1960; children: Charles Evans II, Catherine Cameron. BA, Brown U., 1959; JD, U. Mo., 1963. Bar: Mo. 1963, U.S. Dist. Ct. (we. dist.) Mo. 1963, U.S. Ct. Appeals (8th cir.) 1965, U.S. Supreme Ct. 1980, D.C. 1987. Assoc. and ptnr. Sheffrey, Ryder & Skeer, Kansas City, Mo., 1963-72; asst. and assoc. gen. coun., exec. v.p. gen. coun. Hallmark Cards, Inc., Kansas City, 1972—; dir., v.p., gen. coun. Univision Holdings, Inc., Kansas City, 1988-92; sec., bd. dirs. Crown Media Holdings, Inc., 2000—; of counsel Shook, Hardy & Bacon, Kansas City, Mo., 2994—. Bd. dirs. Am. Arbitration Assn., 1997—. Trustee Brown U. Providence, 1977-83, U. Mo. Law Found., Kansas City, 1977-90; dir. Kansas City (Mo.) Indsl. Devel. Authority, 1981-84, Legal Aid Kansas City, 1971-77, De La Salle Sch. Episcopalian. Avocations: reading, skiing, hiking, piano, golf. Office: Shook Hardy & Bacon 2555 Grand Blvd Kansas City MO 64198-2613

WHITTEMORE, ALICE, biostatistician; b. N.Y.C., July 5, 1936; BS, Marymount Manhattan Coll., 1958; MA, Hunter Coll., 1964; PhD in Mathematics, CUNY, 1967. From asst. prof. to assoc. prof. math. Hunter Coll., N.Y.C., 1967-74; adj. assoc. prof. environ. med. N.Y.U., 1974-76, mem. faculty dept. statistics, 1976-87; prof. epidemiology dept. health rsch. and policy Stanford U., Palo Alto, Calif., 1987—. Recipient Sloan Found. rsch. grant, Soc. Ind. and Applied Math. Inst. Math and Soc., 1974-76, Rockefeller Found rsch. grant 1976-77. Mem. NAS Inst. Medicine, AAAS, Soc. Indsl. and Applied Math, Am. Math Soc., Math Assn. Am., Sigma Xi Office: Stanford U Sch Medicine Dept Health Rsch and Policy HBP Redwood Bldg Stanford CA 94305-5092

WHITTEMORE, JOAN M. music educator; b. St. Louis, Mo., May 12, 1944; d. Raymond Ralph and Mary Ann Whittemore. MusB in Music Edn., Fontbonne Coll., Clayton, Mo., 1967; MusM, U. Ill., Urbana-Champaign, 1980, D in Musical Arts, 1986. Sister of St. Joseph of Carondelet; cert. Vocal and Instrumental Music K-12 Mo., 1967. Founder and dir. Carondelet Children's Chorus, Webster Groves, Mo., 1999—, Carondelet Women's Chorus, Webster Groves. Venetian scholar, rschr. music of Venetian Composers; music faculty Webster U. Composer: (choral music for treble voices) Scarecrow Poems; editor: (choral /orchestral composition) Beatus vir of Antonio Vivaldi, Nunc Dimittis of Baldassare Galuppi, Magnifical of Nicola Porpora; contbr. articles to profl. jours. Recipient Gladis Krieble Delmas award, 1986; grantee Regional Arts Commn., St. Louis, 2002—; Melodious Accord fellow, Alice Parker, 1997, 2001. Mem.: Coll. Music Soc., Music Educators Nat. Conf., Am. Choral Directors Assn. (assoc.; rsch. and publs. com. 1993—). Roman Catholic. Achievements include publication of Revision Repertoire of the Ospedali Veneziani. Home and Studio: 1315 Belton Ave Webster Groves MO 63119 E-mail: maestra6@earthlink.net.

WHITTEN, LAURA A. secondary school educator; b. Lakewood, N.J., Sept. 23, 1964; AA in Gen. Studies, Southwestern Coll., Chula Vista, Calif., 1985; BA in Drama, San Diego State U., 1988; MS in Edn1. Tech., Nat. U., San Diego, 1997. English lang. tchr. Orange Glen H.S., Escondido, Calif., 1989-93; English lang. and drama tchr. Valley H.S., Escondido, Calif., 1993-98, Valley Center (Calif.) H.S., 1998—. Test preparation instr. Britannica Learning Ctr., Bonita, Calif., 1989-94, Hit Any Key Computer Learning Ctr., San Diego, 1996—. Scholarship coord. Dollars for Scholars San Diego County Office Edn., 1998. Recipient Excellence in Lang. Arts Instrn. award Old Globe Theatre, 1992, 93. Mem. NCTE, Calif. Assn. Tchrs. English, We. Assn. Schs. and Colls. (vis. com. mem. 1998), Kappa Delta Pi. Avocations: reading, baseball, computers, shopping. Home: 1230 Sybil Ct Escondido CA 92026-2129 Office: Valley Center HS Cole Grade Rd Valley Center CA 92082 E-mail: laurart@home.com.

WHITTEN, MARY LOU, nursing educator; b. Vandalia, Ill., Apr. 8, 1946; d. Otto M. and Lucille (Mattes) Elam; m. Dennis L. Whitten, Aug. 27, 1966; children: Michael, Christopher, Andrew. BSN, Baylor U., 1968; MS in Nursing, So. Ill. U., 1990. RN, Ill. Instr. health occupations Okaw Vocat. Sch., Vandalia, Ill.; head nurse med.-surg. Fayette County Hosp., Vandalia; DON Kaskaskia Coll., Centralia, Ill. CPR instr. Am. Heart Assn. Vol. ARC. Mem. Am. Assn. of Women in C.C. Ill., Ill. Coun. Dirs. of Nursing, Phi Kappa Phi. Home: RR 3 Box 848 Vandalia IL 62471-9204 Office: Kaskaskia Coll 27210 College Rd Centralia IL 62801-7800 Office Phone: [illegible]

WHITTEN, NANCY BIMMERMAN, clinical social worker, marriage therapist; b. Wilmington, Del., Oct. 17, 1934; d. Harry Gordon and Marian Bimmerman; m. Robert Hunt Whitten, Jan. 2, 1960 (div. 1982); 1 child, Barbara Louise Whitten Debnam. BS in Biology, Bucknell U., 1956; postgrad., Stanford U., 1956-57, U. Del., 1957-59; M Social Svcs., Bryn Mawr Coll., 1995. Lic. clin. social worker, Del., Md. V.p. Robert Hunt Whitten Inc, Wilmington, 1960-81; br. mgr. Chase Manhattan Bank, Wilmington, 1985-88; realtor Patterson Schwartz Real Estate, Wilmington, 1988-95; clin. intern Penn Coun. for Relationships, Phila., 1995-96; med. social worker Chester River Home Care and Hospice, Chestertown, Md., 1997; clin. social worker S.O.A.R., Inc. (Survivors of Abuse in Recovery), Milford, Del., 1998—, bd. dirs., 1994-98; psychotherapist Nancy B. Whitten, LCSW, Easton, Md., 1997—. Crisis counselor Crime Victims Ctr., West Chester, Pa., 1992-95; condr. marriage seminars Mental Health Assn. Talbot County, Easton, Md., 1997-98, bd. dirs. 1996-99, pres.-elect 1998-99, pres., 2000—. Elks scholar Stanford U., 1956. Mem. NASW, Am. Assn. for Marriage and Family Therapy (clin. mem., cert.), Mortar Bd., Psi Chi, Phi Sigma. Unitarian Universalist. Avocations: sailing, fishing, tennis. Home and Office: 9660 Leeds Landing Cir Easton MD 21601-5562

WHITTEN-FRICKEY, WENDY ELISE, entertainer; b. Silver Spring, Md., Mar. 15, 1963; d. Ray Sloan and Elsie Helen (Calderone) Whitten; m. Keith James Frickey, Nov. 24, 1990. BS in Agr. and Life Sci., U. Md., 1985. Mktg. and promotion asst. Pimlico and Laurel Racetracks, Balt., 1987-89; co-owner mktg. and advt. San Carlos Park Animal Hosp., Fort Myers, Fla., 1990-94; owner, pres. Ion Imagination Entertainment, Inc., Nashville, 1994—. Food technologist quality control Unilever USA-Shedds, Balt., 1987-88, dairy flavors applications-Quest, 1989-90. Author, songwriter, singer, narrator: (book and tape) The Adventures of Flumpa and Friends, Someday...Someday, Book 1, 1994 (Parents Choice award 1996, Nat. Parenting Ctr. award 1997); songwriter, prodr., singer: (CD/tape) Flumpa's World...Frogs, Rain Forests and Other Fun Facts, 1998 (Parents' Choice award 1998, others), Flumpa's World-Out of This World, 2000 (Film Adv. Bd. award 2000, Parent's Guide to Children's Media award 2000, Dr. Toy 100 Best award 2000, others), Flumpa's World--Water, Water Everywhere, 2003; entertainer with Flumpa and Friends Live!; performer White House, various festivals, schs. and zoos. Recipient Certificate of Merit Printing Industries Am., 1996. Mem. AFTRA, BMI, Pub. Mktg. Assn., Coun. for Agrl. Sci. and Tech., Inst. of Food Technologists, Small Pub. Assn. of N.Am., Nat. Sci. Tchrs. Assn., Nat. Acad. Rec. Arts and Scis. Avocations: photography, travel. Office: Ion Imagination Entertainment Inc PO Box 210943 Nashville TN 37221-0943 E-mail: flumpa@aol.com.

WHITTIER, SANDRA M. nursing services administrator; b. Lynn, Mass., Mar. 28, 1950; d. Charles Harlow and Barbara Janet (Nealey) Bickford; m. Stephen Martin (dec. 1980), m. Douglas Whittier, 1985. Diploma, Beverly (Mass.) Hosp. Sch., 1971; BSN cum laude, Salem State Coll., 1989, MSN, 1998. Cert. home health nurse, adminstrn. nurse ANA. Staff/charge nurse ICU Beverly Hosp., 1971-72, staff/charge nurse acute/chronic hemodialysis, 1972-75; ICU staff nurse Lynn Hosp., 1975-78, head nurse, 1978-81; staff Vis. Nurse Assn. Greater Lynn, Mass., 1982-85; staff nurse Anne Arundel Gen. Hosp. Home Care & Hospice, 1985-86; dir. nursing and social svc. Vis. Nurses Ea. Mass., Somerville, 1987-91; dir. nursing Am. Home Care, Lynnfield, Mass., 1991-92; clin. coord. nursing and rehab. Whidden Home Care & Hospice, Everett, Mass., 1992—99; case mgr. Marblehead/Swampscott VNA, 1999—. Mem. adv. bd. Home Care Provider, Mosby Pub., 2000—. Contbg. author: Nurse Manager Survival Guide, 1993, 2d edit., 1997; co-author: Home Health Aide: Guidelines for Care, 1995. Mem. Home Health Nursing Assn. (founding), Sigma Theta Tau.

WHITTINGHILL, ELIZABETH JANE, speech pathology/audiology services professional; b. London, Jan. 28, 1955; arrived in U.S.A., 1971; d. John C.K. and Cecily A. Buckley; m. Dexter Conwell Whittinghill III; children: Kyle Ann, Leigh Jane, Sarah Beth. BA, Middlebury Coll., 1976; MA, U. Denver, 1978. Lic. speech lang. pathologist Am. Speech Lang. and Hearing Assn. Speech therapist Logansport (Ind.) Pub. Schs., 1978—82, Griffiths Larabee, Augusta, Maine, 1990—96; speech lang. specialist SalemCounty Spl. Svcs. Schs., Woodstown, NJ, 1997—. Mem. profl. tour People to People, 2000. Mem. vestry St. Marles Ch., Waterville, Maine, 1994—96, Holy Trinity Ch., Wenonah, NJ, 2003—. Mem.: Salem County Speech Therapists (organizer 2000—), Phi Beta Kappa. Episcopalian. Avocations: reading, sewing, gardening, swimming. Office: Salem County Special Services Sch Dist 328B N Broadway Pennsville NJ 08070

WHITTINGTON, CATHY DEE, chemist; b. Upland, Pa., Oct. 29, 1955; d. Frank Adam and Virginia Helen (Keil) W. AA in biology, Widenen Univ., 1984, BA, 1996. Asst. mgr. McDonald's, Brookhaven, Pa., 1973-75; blood lab. tech. CCMC, Chester, Pa., 1976-77; environmental tech. Scott Paper Internat., Chester, Pa., 1979-83; paramedic V AmbulCare Ambulance, Phila., 1984-96; sr. rsch. assoc. Scott Paper Corp. R&D, Phila., 1996-97; rsch. cons. Kimberly Clark Corp., Chester, Pa., 1997; process specialist HIA Cons., Chester, 1997-99; chemist Novell Inc., Provo, Utah, 1999—. Network engr. Novell, Inc., Provo, Utah, Scott Paper House of Quality, team orgn. Scott Paper R&D. Amb. lt. Parkside Vol. Fire Co., Parkside, Pa., 1977—. Recipient Military History Excellence award Daughter's of Founders & Patriots of Am., 1977, tech. excellence award, 1987-91. Mem. Tech. Orgn. of Pulp & Paper Ins., Nat. Archieves (assoc.). Republican. Baptist. Avocations: walking, hiking, reading. Home: 139 W Roland Rd Brookhaven PA 19015-3217 Office: Novell Inc 301 W Germantown Pike Bldg 1 Norristown PA 19403-4227

WHITTLESEY, JUDITH HOLLOWAY, public relations executive; b. Bartlesville, Okla., Dec. 28, 1942; d. Harry Haynes and Suzanne (Arnote) Holloway; m. Dennis Jeffrey Whittlesey, Aug. 3, 1968; children: Kristin Arnote, Kevin Jeffrey. BA, U. Okla., 1964; postgrad., Tulsa U., 1965, U. Va., 1971-72. Staff aide Office of the V.P. of U.S., Washington, 1979-81, Com. for Future of Am., Washington, 1981-82; dep. dir. scheduling and advance Mondale-Ferraro Campaign, Washington, 1982-84; dir. media rels. Susan Davis Internat., Washington, 1986-87, v.p., 1987-88, exec. v.p., 1988—. Bd. dir. Cultural Alliance of Greater Washington, 1983-93, Washington Project for the Arts, 1987-93, Levine Sch. Music, 1993-98, Food Rsch. and Action Ctr., 1993—; bd. dir. Decatur House, Suited For Change. Chevy Chase Presbyn. Ch., Washington, Leadership Washington, 2004. Avocation: art/contemporary. Office: Susan Davis Internat 1000 Vermont Ave NW Washington DC 20005-4903 Office Phone: 202-408-0808. E-mail: jwhittlesey@susandavis.com.

WHITWORTH, CAMILLE, newscaster; b. Houston; BA in Mass Comm., Hampton U., 1993. Reporter WAVE 3 TV, Louisville; gen. assignment reporter NBC 17, Raleigh, NC. Creator, co-host WAVE 3 Step Awards; reporter Winter Olympics for NBC 17, 2002. Vol. Nat. Assn. Black Journalists, NAACP, ARC; active Louisville Ballet. Nominee Spot News coverage, Ohio Valley Regional Emmy Award; recipient numerous awards, AP, award for excellence in reporting, Ky. chpt. Nat. Press Photographers Assn. Office: NBC 17 Studios 1205 Front St Raleigh NC 27609

WHITWORTH, KATHRYNNE ANN, professional golfer; b. Monahans, Tex., Sept. 27, 1939; d. Morris Clark and Dama Ann (Robinson) W. Student, Odessa (Tex.) Jr. Coll., 1958. Joined tour Ladies Profl. Golf Assn., 1959—. Mem. adv. Square Two Golf Co. Named to Hall of Fame Ladies Profl. Golf Assn., Tex. Sports Hall of Fame, Tex. Golf Hall of Fame, World Golf Hall of Fame; Capt. of Solhiem Cup, 1990-92. Mem. Ladies Profl. Golf Assn. (sec. 1962-63, v.p. 1965, 73, 88, pres. 1967, 68, 71, 89, 1st mem. to win over $1,000,000). Office: care Ladies Profl Golf Assn 2570 Volusia Ave [illegible]

WHITWORTH, WENDY WALKER, cable network executive; b. Bronxville, N.Y. m. Ralph Whitworth; children: Amaya, Walker. BA, LLD (hon.), Hollins Coll. TV prodr. White House CNN, 1980-93, sr. v.p., sr. exec. prodr. Larry King Live (TV), 1993—. Sr. event prodr. super-power summits CNN, 1984, 88, 92, presdl. inaugurations, 1989, 93. Recipient Houston Internat. Film Festival award, 1988, Best Talk Show Series award CableAce, 1993; named one of 20 Most Fascinating Women in Politics by George Mag., Named One of the Most Influential People, Brills Content, 1999. Office: One CNN Ctr 1 Cnn Ctr NW Atlanta GA 30303-2762

WHOBREY, VIRGINIA JEAN, retired director; b. Dorset, Ohio, May 21, 1931; d. Rufus Lowery and Ruth Emma Spencer; m. Anthony Herbert Whobrey, Mar. 13, 1960 (dec. 1989); children: Everett Brett, Raymond Henry, Gene Lowery, Antoinette Michele Pfenning. BA, Hiram (Ohio) Coll., 1953; postgrad. in Counseling, Miami U. Oxford, Ohio, 1958—59, East Tenn. U., Johnson City, 1964—65; student, Lake Erie Coll., 1969. Lic. profl. counselor Ohio, 1988, Qualified Mental Retardation Profl. Ohio, 1980, cert. lifetime tchr. Ohio, 1979. Tchr. home econs./dramatics Maple Heights (Ohio) City Schs., 1953—58; tchr., slow learners Middletown (Ohio) City Schs., 1958—59; counselor BVR/State Hosp., Burlington, Vt., 1959—60; tchr. Marion (Ohio) City Schs., 1958—59; guidance dir. Haines City (Fla.) Jr. HS, 1965—66; dir. guidance, coord. spl. svcs. Union County Schs., Lake Butler, Fla., 1966—69; tchr. EDMR Jefferson (Ohio) City Schs., 1969—79; tchr. MI/Mental Retardation Dayton Mental Health Ctr., Dayton, Ohio, 1979—84, vocation evaluator-civil and forensic hosp. team leader, 1984—88; dir. - set up pilot program Mentally Ill/Mental Retardation Montgomery Co MRDD-County Mental Health Bd., Dayton, Ohio, 1998—99; dir. of ICF/Mental Retardation unit Dayton (Ohio) Mental Health Ctr., 1988—91; dir. new dimensions state operated svcs. Dayton Mental Health Ctr./Mental Health Bd., 1991—98. Bd. dirs. Miami Valley Housing Opportunities, Dayton, Ohio; bd. dirs. Pathways mental health, substance abuse, devel. disabilities svs. Gaston, Lincoln, Cleve. Counties, NC. Avocations: painting, crafts, reading, travel. Home: 125 Mark Twain Ct Mount Holly NC 28120 Personal E-mail: btwho647@aol.com.

WHOULEY, KATE, book industry consultant, writer; b. Key West, Fla., Oct. 10, 1958; d. Paul Francis and Anne Marie (Ford) W. BA magna cum laude in Philosophy, Lit. and Music, Baldwin Wallace Coll., 1980. Bookseller, asst. mgr., store mgr. Waldenbooks, Newport, R.I., Needham, Mass., 1980-83; book buyer, mgr. gen. books Boston U. Bookstore, 1983-86; mdse. and mktg. dir. Garland & Grace/dba Booksmith Music-smith, West Barnstable, Mass., 1986-88; founder, owner, cons. Books in Common, Centerville, Mass., 1988—. V.p. Booksellers Pub. Inc. subs. Am. Bookseller Assn., Tarrytown, N.Y., 1994-98. Author: Customers and Service, 1997; series editor Open Learning Study Series, 1997—2000; tech. editor Bookselling for Dummies, 2003; editor, co-author: Manual on Bookselling, 5th edit., 1996; author: Cottage for Sale, Must Be Moved, 2004. Prin. flute Cape Cod Conservatory Concert Band, 1993—. Recipient Grover award Baldwin Wallace Coll., 1980. Mem. Am. Booksellers Assn., New Eng. Booksellers Assn., AAUW, Coop. Am. Avocations: music, gardening, reading, holistic studies, middle eastern dance.

WHYTE, BETTINA MARSHALL, financial crisis manager; b. L.A., Apr. 4, 1949; d. William Robert and Inez E. Marshall. BS in Indsl. Econs., Purdue U., 1971; MBA in Fin. and Acctg., Northwestern U., 1974. Cert. Insolvency and Restructuring Acct. Lending officer Harris Trust & Savings Bank, Chgo., 1971-74; v.p. Continental Bank Chgo., 1974-82; pres. KRW & Assocs., Inc., Houston, 1982-88; ptnr. Peterson & Co. Cons., Houston, 1988-90, Price Waterhouse, Houston, 1990-97, nat. dir. of bus. turnaround svcs.; prin. Jay Alix & Associates, New York, NY, 1997—. Bd. dirs. Washington Group Internat. Inc., 2002—, Amerisure Mut. Ins. Co. Contbg. editor: "Turnaround Topics" column, Am. Bankruptcy Inst. Jour. Mem. Am. Assn. Bankruptcy Trustees, Am. Bankruptcy Inst. (exec. bd., 1998-, pres.-elect, 2002-03, pres., 2003-), Assn. Insolvency Accountants, Phi Beta Kappa, Beta Gamma Sigma, Phi Kappa Phi. Avocation: showing and breeding Irish Setters. Fax: 212-4901344.*

WHYTE, NANCY GOOCH, microbiologist, chemist; b. Oak Hill, W Va., July 15, 1936; d. Benjamin Adair and Martha (Baker) Gooch; children: James, Nancy, David. BA, W. Va. Univ., Morgantown, W.Va., 1954—58; M

Gen. Admin., U. Md., 1982. Registered Microbiologist, 1976. Supr., microbiology Alexandria Hosp. (Inova), Alexandria, Va., 1971—95; microbiologist US Environ. Protection Agy., Arlington, Va., 1998—. Assoc. prof. (adj.) Prince Georges Cmty. Coll., Largo, Md., 1996—2001. [illegible] bytery Commr. Presbyn. Ch., NY Ave. Office: US Environ Protection Agy 1921 Jefferson Davis Hwy 3rd Fl Arlington VA 22202 Home: 2802 Lumar Dr Fort Washington MD 20744-2037 E-mail: whyte.nancy@epa.gov.

WHYTE, NANCY MARIE, performing arts educator; b. Myrtlepoint, Oreg., Mar. 12, 1948; d. Lawrence Edward and Carol Elizabeth (Johnson) Guderian; m. Anthony John Whyte, Aug. 7, 1967 (div. Sept. 1968); 1 child, Charles Lawrence; m. Douglas Brian Graff, June 27, 1971 (div. Oct. 1974); m. Lawrence Hanson, Mar. 12, 1976 (div. Aug. 1984); m. Joseph Paul Deacon, Aug. 10, 1985; 1 child, Nina Alexandra. Student, U. Wash., 1969-72, Am. Sch. Dance, 1972; BA, Evergreen State Coll., 1987. Owner, dir. Nancy Whyte Sch. Ballet, Bellingham, Wash., 1969—; artistic dir. Garden Street Dance Players, Bellingham, 1969-72, MT Baker Ballet, Bellingham, 1975—, Alpha nd Omega Worship Dancers, 2003—; co-dir. Exptl. Performance Workshop, Bellingham, 1975-77; instr. creative dance St. Paul's Primary Sch., Bellingham, 1993-97; facilitator dance workshop Allied Arts/Whatcom Co., Bellingham, 1995—. Guest lectr. Western Wash. U., Bellingham, 1976—83, Bellingham, 1996—; guest faculty Dance Theatre N.W., Tacoma, 1995—; liturgical dance cons. Assumption Cath. Sch., 2001—; artistic dir. Alpha and Omega Worship Dancers, 2003—. Author: Memoirs of a Child of Theatre Street, 1993; soloist Raduga Folk Ballet/N.Y. Character Ballet, N.Y.C., 1978-79; choreographer numerous ballets, 1972—. Mem. Nat. Dance Assn., Dancers Over 40, Sacred Dance Guild, Vancouver Ballet Soc. Democrat. Avocations: voice, writing. Office: MT Baker Ballet 1412 Cornwall Ave PO Box 2393 Bellingham WA 98227-2393 Office Phone: 360-734-9141.

WHYTE, RACHEL L. child abuse prevention specialist, social worker; b. Mesa, Ariz., June 23, 1943; d. Barney W. and Dorothy Loomis Appleby; m. Michael N. Whyte, Nov. 6, 1993; m. Gary K. Fadely, Jan. 12, 1963 (div. 1971); children: Rebecca W. Halstead, Carolyn M. Sonmor. BSW, Ariz. State U., 1978, MSW, 1988. Cert. ind. social worker Ariz. Bd. of Behavioral Health Examiners. Med. social worker Hosp., Home Care and Long-Term Care Settings, Phoenix, 1978—86; hunger program specialist Cmty. Svcs. Adminstrn., Ariz. Dept. of Econ. Security, Phoenix, 1989—92; social work cons. Children's Rehabilitative Svcs., /Ariz. Dept. of Health Svcs., Phoenix, 1992—94, Office of Women's and Children's Health, Ariz. Dept. of Health Svcs., Phoenix, 1994—95; statewide coord. Office of Prevention and Family Support, Ariz. Dept. of Econ. Security, Healthy Families Ariz., Phoenix, 1995—. Program cons. Healthy Families Ariz. Steering Com., Phoenix, 1995—; rep. from Ariz. Dept. Econ. Security Maricopa County Pub. Health Dept. Maternal and Child Health Adv. Bd., Phoenix, 1997—; rep. from Ariz. Dept. Health Svcs. Ariz. Dept. of Econ. Security Family Support/Family Preservation Adv. Com., Phoenix, 1994—95; program facilitator Ariz. Perinatal Social Work Network, Phoenix and Tucson, 1994—95; parents adv. coun. coord. Children's Rehabilitative Svcs. Parent Adv. Coun., Phoenix, Tucson, Yuma, Flagstaff, Ariz., 1992—94; program rep. Gov.'s Adv. Coun. on Hunger, Phoenix, 1989—92. Mentor Big Bros./Big Sisters, Phoenix, 1991—95; cmty. vol. Urban League of Am., Phoenix, 1965—70; campaign worker Phoenix, 1964—2003. Recipient Gov.'s Award for Pub. Svc., Gov.'s Office, State of Ariz., 1991. Mem.: NASW (pres. Ariz. chpt. 2002—, various positions 1981—, Social Worker of Yr. Ariz. chpt. br. 1 1991, 2004), Dollars Up Investment Club (sec. 1999—2003). Avocations: exercise, travel, family photo albums, writing, grandchildren. Home: 1801 E Harmont Dr Phoenix AZ 85020 Personal E-mail: rlwhyte@aol.com.

WIANT, SARAH KIRSTEN, law library administrator, educator, director; b. Waverly, Iowa, Nov. 20, 1946; d. James Allen and Eva (Jorgensen) W.; m. Robert E. Akins. BA, Western State Coll., 1968; MLS, U. North Tex., 1970; JD, Washington & Lee U., 1978. Asst. law libr. Tex. Tech. U., 1970-72, 020, Washington & Lee U., Lexington, Va., 1972—, dir., 1978—, asst. prof. law, 1978-83, assoc. prof. law, 1984-92, prof. law, 1993—. Participant Conf. on Fair Use, NII, 1995-98. Co-author: Copyright Handbook, 1984, Libraries and Copyright: A Guide to Copyright Law in the 1990s, 1994, Legal Research in the District of Columbia, Maryland and Virginia, 1995, 3d edit., 2004, UCITA Encyclopedia of Lib. and Information Science, 2d edit., 2003; contbr. chapters to books; mem. adv. bd. Westlaw, 1988—93, 2003—. Mem.: ABA (com. on librs. 1987—93), U.S. Trademark Assn., Maritime Law Assn., Spl. Librs. Assn. (chair copyright com. 1990—96, John Cotton Dana award 1997), Am. Assn. Law Sch. (chmn. sec. on librs. 1990—92, accreditation com. 1991—94), Am. Assn. Law Librs. (mem. exec. bd. 1981—84, mem. copyright com. 1990—94, chmn. 2003—, copyright office rep., Pres.' award 2001, Spl. Dist. Svc. award Southeastern chpt. 1997). Office: Washington & Lee U Law Libr Lewis Hall Lexington VA 24450 Office Phone: 540-458-8540. E-mail: wiants@wlu.edu.

WIBKER, SUSAN GAYLE, lawyer; b. Shreveport, La., Apr. 8, 1952; d. Robert William and Audrey (Hill) W. BS, Northwestern State U., Natchitoches, La., 1974, MS, 1979; JD, U. Mich., 1991. Bar: Alaska 1992, D.C. 1993. Mental health counselor, Washington and Alaska, 1979-88; asst. dist. atty. Dist. Atty.'s Office, Anchorage, 1991-96; asst. atty. gen. Atty. Gen.'s Office, Anchorage, 1996. Office: Atty Gen's Office 1031 W 4th Ave Ste 200 Anchorage AK 99501-5903

WICK, LAURIE CLARE, director, consultant; b. Seattle, May 13, 1948; d. Andrew Palmer and Marion Richardson Wick; m. Robert Neill Weiss, Jan. 25, 2002; m. Charles Robertson Jr. Ross, May 20, 1974 (div. Jan. 1990); 1 child, Carrie Marin. BEd, U. of Pacific, Stockton, Calif., 1970; MEd, U. Wash., 1983. Tchg. credential Wash., pre-primary cert. Am. Montessori Soc. Asst. tchr. Sun Valley (Idaho) Playsch., 1974, Lake Hills Montessori, Bellevue, Wash., 1975—76; tchr. Fountainhead Montessori, Orinda, Calif., 1976—78; tchr., dir. The Learning Tree Montessori, Seattle, 1979—. Pres. Learning Tree Montessori Bd., Seattle, 1979—. Editor: (book) Is Mother Nature God's Wife, 1992. Vol. Dem., Wash., 1980—2003. Mem.: Childcare Dirs. Assn. (sec. 1998—2002), Pacific NW Montessori Assn. (treas. 1991—). Unitarian Universalist. Avocations: skiing, hiking, gardening. Office: The Learning Tree Montessori 1721 15th Ave Seattle WA 98122 E-mail: seatree@aol.com.

WICK, SISTER MARGARET, former college administrator; b. Sibley, Iowa, June 30, 1942; BA in Sociology, Briar Cliff Coll., 1965; MA in Sociology, Loyola U., Chgo., 1971; PhD in Higher Edn., U. Denver, 1976. Instr. sociology Briar Cliff Coll., Sioux City, Iowa, 1966-71, dir. academic advising, 1971-72, v.p., acad. dean, 1972-74, 76-84, pres., 1987-99, Colls. of Mid-Am., 1985-87. Mem. adv. bd. Nations Bank, Sioux City. Bd. dirs. Mary J. Treglia Cmty. House, 1976-84, Marian Health Ctr., 1987-97, Iowa Pub. TV, 1987-95. Mem. North Ctrl. Edn. Assn. (cons.-evaluator for accrediting teams 1980-84, 89—), Siouxland Initiative (adv. bd.), Quota Internat., Rotary. Home: 3390 Windsor Ave Dubuque IA 52001-1326 Office: Briar Cliff Coll Office of the President 3303 Rebecca St Sioux City IA 51104-2324

WICKHAM, DIANNE, nursing administrator; b. Dillon, Mont., Feb. 26, 1952; d. William Byron Wickham and Margaret Dewalt (Lovell) Starkweather. ADN, No. Mont. Coll., 1974; BSN, Mont. State U., 1978, MSN, 1980. RN, Mont. Clin. dir. St. Patrick Hosp., Missoula, Mont., 1980-81; asst. prof. Lewis Clark State Coll., Lewiston, Idaho, 1981-83, Mont. State U., Bozeman, Mont., 1983-86; home health nurse West Mont. Home Health, Helena, 1986-87, dir. clin. svcs., 1987-90; critical care nurse St. James Hosp., Butte, Mont., 1986-87; exec. dir. Mont. State Bd. of Nursing, Helena, 1990—. Mem. long term care com. Gov. Task Force on Aging, Helene, Mont., 1993-95, mem. task force to devel. investigator tng. Nat. Com. of State Bds. Nursing, Chgo., 1993—, mem. adj. faculty Mont. State U., Bozeman, 1993—, cons. in field, 1994—. Judge Soroptomists scholarship award, 1993, JC Penneys Golden Rule award, Helena, 1995. [illegible] State award for excellence Am. Acad. Nurses Practitioners, 1994. Office: Mont State Bd Nursing 111 N Jackson St Helena MT 59601-4140

WICKHAM, KATHLEEN WOODRUFF, education educator; b. Wilson Boro, Pa., May 31, 1949; d. Ralph E. and Ann Mary (Korp) Woodruff; m. Peter Kuntz Wickham Jr., Sept. 30, 1978; children: Matthew Peter, Timothy Kuntz. BA, Glassboro State Coll., 1971; MA, Memphis State U., 1987; EdD, U. Memphis, 1999. Reporter The Daily Advance, Dover, N.J., 1971-75, The Press, Atlantic City, N.J., 1975-77, The Star-Ledger, Newark, 1977-81; instr. U. Memphis, 1983—99; asst. prof. U. Miss., 1999—; reporter Jannett News Svc., 1999. Presenter in field. Author Math. Tools for Journalists, 2002; contbr. articles to newspapers, mags. and jours.; acad. editor Perspectives: Online Journalism, 1998. Fellow, Am. Soc. Newspaper Editors, 1999. Mem. Nat. Headliner Club, Autism Soc. Am. (Memphis chpt. pres. 1988-89, conf. co-chair 1989, 92, 95, Tenn. state soc. pres. 1989-90), Soc. Profl. Journalists (v.p. local chpt., pres. 1999-2000—), Investigative Reporters and Editors, Kappa Tau Alpha. Avocations: reading, computer technology. Office: U Miss Farley Hall Oxford MS 38677

WICKIZER, CINDY LOUISE, retired elementary school educator; b. Pitts., Dec. 12, 1946; d. Charles and Gloria Geraldine (Cassidy) Zimmerman Sr.; m. Leon Leonard Wickizer, Mar. 20, 1971 (div. Oct. 2003); 1 child, Charlyn Michelle. BS, Oreg. State U., 1968. Tchr. Enumclaw (Wash.) Sch. Dist., 1968-99, ret., 1999. Mem. Wash. State Ret. Tchrs. Assn., Am. Rabbit Breeders Assn. (judge, chmn. scholarship found. 1986-87, pres. 1988-94, 96-98, dist. dir. 1994-96, 2003—, Disting. Svc. award 1987, Hall of Fame 1998), Wash. State Rabbit Breeders Assn. (life, Pres.'s award 1983, 94, sec., dir., v.p. 1995-97), Vancouver Island Rabbit Breeders Assn., Wash. State Rabbit and Cavy Shows Inc. (sec. 1994—), Evergreen Rabbit Assn. (sec., v.p., pres.), Alpha Gamma Delta, Women of Vision (bd. dir. 2004-), Sons/Daughters Pearl Harbor Survivors. Home: 20825 Star Rte 410 E PMB 196 Sumner WA 98390 E-mail: CindyWick@aol.com.

WICKIZER, MARY ALICE See BURGESS, MARY ALICE

WICKLINE, MARIAN ELIZABETH, former corporate librarian; b. St. Louis, Feb. 18, 1915; d. William Anderson and Grace B. (Gooding) W. BA, Mills Coll., 1935; postgrad., U. Calif., Berkeley, 1935-37. Tech. files asst. Shell Devel. Co., San Francisco, 1938-45; libr. western div. Dow Chem. Co., Pitts. and Walnut Creek, Calif., 1945-75; ret., 1975. Mem. Planning Commn., Danville, Calif., 1982—86, El Dorado County Libr. Commn., Placerville, Calif., 1989—92, mem. policy adv. com. gen. plan, 1989—92, mem. commn. on aging, 2000—02; bd. dirs. Greenstone Country Cmty. Svcs. Dist., 1994—98. Named Woman of Yr. San Ramon Valley C. of C., Danville, Calif., 1983. Mem. AAUW (Gift Honoree 1982, 84), Am. Chem. Soc., Spl. Libr. Assn. (pres. San Francisco Bay region chpt. 1973-74, chair chemistry divsn. 1970-71). Avocation: gardening. Home: 5474 Comstock Rd Placerville CA 95667-8712

WICKMAN, PATRICIA ANN, retired social worker; b. San Diego, Calif., Nov. 18, 1928; d. Charles King Warrington and Sylvia Elisabeth Howard; m. Glenn A. Wickman, June 30, 1951; 1 child, Stacy Ann. BSc with distinction, U. Minn., 1951; MA, Coll. Idaho, 1971; student in History, Boise State U., 1988—91. Social worker Settlement House Mpls. Dept. Welfare, Mpls., 1948—49; social worker State Dept. Pub. Assistance, Idaho, 1950—55; tchr. Eng., drama, speech Meridan Sch. Dist., Meridan, Idaho, 1955—57, libr., 1958; substitute tchr. Boise Sch. Dist., Boise, 1958—60, pilot counseling program elem. sch., 1969—70. Lectr. in field; workshop leader in field. Author: History of Environmental Movements in the United States, 1972, Militarizing America, Reagan years, 1982, (plays) Fashion, Folly and Feminism, 1982, History of the Boise Branch, AAUW, 2001; editor: Des Arab Newsletter, 1973—74; contbr. articles to newspapers; guest : (TV series). Vol. counselor State of Idaho Corrections Program Dist. IV, 1970—73; pres. Ada County Citizens Crisis Coalition, Ada County, Idaho, 1984—86; leader 4-H, 1967—77; pres., chmn. Collister Sewer Bond Drive, 1968—72; mem. Ada County Adv. Com. Planning, 1978—82; bd. dirs. League of Women Voters, 1960—67; vol. AdaCo Spl. Olympics, 1972—82; precinct leader Ada County, Idaho; Sunday sch. tchr. Luth. & Unitarian Ch.; bd. dir. Ada County Citizens Crisis Coalition, 1983—88. Unitarian Universalist. Home: 1178 E Beacon Lt Rd Eagle ID 83616

WICK-PELLETIER, JOAN, academic administrator, mathematician; b. Northampton, Mass., Nov. 13, 1942; children: Maurice Pelletier, Emile Pelletier. AB, Smith Coll., 1964; MSc, McGill U., 1967, PhD, 1970. Asst. prof. math. Concordia U., Montreal, Canada, 1970—72, York U., Toronto, 1972—76, assoc. prof. math., 1977—81, prof. math., 1981—2002; dean Coll. Arts and Sci. SUNY, Albany, NY, 2002—. Assoc. v.p. rsch. York U., 1990—94; v.p. Internat. Math. Olympiad, 1995. Bd. dirs. Albany (N.Y.) Symphony Orch., 2003—. Mem.: Women in Higher Edn., Am. Women in Math., Am. Math. Soc., Canadian Math. Soc. (v.p. 1987—89). Office: SUNY 1400 Washington Ave Albany NY 12222

WICKWIRE, PATRICIA JOANNE NELLOR, psychologist, educator; d. William McKinley and Clara Rose (Pautsch) Nellor; m. Robert James Wickwire, Sept. 7, 1957; 1 child, William James. BA cum laude, U. No. Iowa, 1951; MA, U. Iowa, 1959; PhD, U. Tex., Austin, 1971; postgrad., U. So. Calif., 1951-66, UCLA, 1951-66, Calif. State U., Long Beach, 1951-66. Lic. ednl. psychologist, marriage, family and child counselor, Calif. Tchr. Ricketts Ind. Schs., Iowa, 1946-48; tchr., counselor Waverly-Shell Rock Ind. Schs., Iowa, 1951-55; reading cons., head dormitory counselor U. Iowa, Iowa City, 1955-57; tchr., sch. psychologist, adminstr. S. Bay Union H.S. Dist., Redondo Beach, Calif., 1962-82, dir. student svcs. and spl. edn. Cons. mgmt. and edn.; pres. Nellor Wickwire Group, 1981—; mem. exec. bd. Calif. Interagy. Mental Health Coun., 1968-72, Beach Cities Symphony Assn., 1970-82; chmn. Friends of Dominguez Hills, Calif., 1981-85. Contbr. articles in field to profl. jours. Pres. Calif. Women's Caucus, 1993-95, 2003—. Mem. APA, AAUW (exec. bd., chpt. pres. 1962-72), Nat. Career Devel. Assn. (media chair 1992-98), Am. Assn. Career Edn. (pres. 1991—), L.A. County Dirs. Pupil Svcs. (chmn. 1974-79), L.A. County Pers. and Guidance Assn. (pres. 1977-78), Assn. Calif. Sch. Adminstrs. (dir. 1977-81), L.A. County SW Bd. Dist. Adminstrs. for Spl. Edn. (chmn. 1976-81), Calif. Assn. Sch. Psychologists (bd. dirs. 1981-83), Am. Assn. Sch. Adminstrs., Calif. Assn. for Measurement and Evaluation in Guidance (dir. 1981, pres. 1984-85, 98-2000), ACA (chmn. Coun. Newsletter Editors 1989-91, mem. com. on women 1989-92, mem. com. on rsch. and knowledge 1994—, chmn. 1995—, mem. and chmn. bylaws com. 1998-2001, rep. to joint com. on testing practices 2001—), Assn. Measurement and Eval. in Guidance (Western regional editor 1985-87, conv. chair 1986, editor 1987-90, exec. bd. dirs. 1987-91), Calif. Assn. Counseling and Devel. (exec. bd. 1984—, pres. 1988-89, jour. editor 1990—), Nat. Assn. for Ind.-Edn. Coop. (bd. dirs. 2002—), Internat. Career Assn. Network (chair 1985—), Pi Lambda Theta, Alpha Phi Gamma, Psi Chi, Kappa Delta Pi, Sigma Alpha Iota. Office: The Nellor Wickwire Group 2900 Amby Pl Hermosa Beach CA 90254-2216

WIDEMAN, CAROL M. accountant, consultant; b. York, AL, July 7, 1949; d. Coleman and Martha J. W.; 1 child, Tangiera L. Loftis. BA in Acctg., Suffolk U., 1978; MA in Mgmt., Cambridge Coll., 1985. Auditor Dept. of Revenue, Boston, 1978-79; acct./analyst Mass. Port Authority, Boston, 1979-86; town acct. Town of Canton, Mass., 1986-96, Town of Littleton, Mass., 1996-99. Legis. com. Mass. Mcpl. Auditors/Accts. Assn., Boston, 1994—; fin. cons. Blue Hill Ave. Coalition, 1995-98. Mem. Meeting House Hill Assn., Dorchester, Mass., 1998—; chairperson, liaison Metco Parent Group, Roxbury, Mass., 1982-84. Recipient Foster Parent [illegible] (Mass.) Svcs. for Children, 1998. Mem. Mass. Mcpl. Assn., Mass., Mcpl. Auditors & Accts. Assn., Eastern Mass. Mcpl. Auditors and Accts. Assn., Assn. Gov. Accts. Home: 39 Mount Everett St # 3 Dorchester MA 02125-2437

WIDENER, PERI ANN, business development executive; b. Wichita, Kans., May 1, 1956; d. Wayne Robert and LuAnne (Harris) W. BS, Wichita State U., 1978; MBA, Fla. Tech., 1992. Advt. intern Associated Advt., Wichita, 1978; pub. rels. asst. Fourth Nat. Bank, Wichita, 1978-79; mktg. communications rep. Boeing Co., Wichita, 1979-83, pub. rels. rep. Huntsville, Ala., 1983-85, pub. rels. mgr., 1985-92; sr. pub. rels. mgr. Boeing Mil. Airplanes, Seattle, 1992-95; bus. devel. mgr. Boeing Defense & Space Group, Washington, D.C., 1995-97, mem. exec. devel. program, 1993—, dir. Airborne Laser activities, 1997—; dir. bus. devel. The Boeing Co., Washington, 1998—, Info. Space and Def. Sys., Washington; dir. Lasers & ElectroOptics, Washington Office, 1998. Preston Huston scholar, Wichita State U., 1978; recipient Best Electronic Ad award Def. Electronics mag., 1982, Best Total Pub. Rels. Program award Huntsville Press Club, 1985, Huntsville Media awards, 1986, 87, 88, 89, 90, 91, Huntsville Advt. Fedn. Addys, 1988. Mem. Pub. Rels. Soc. Am. (Seattle chpt.), Women in Communications, Pub. Rels. Coun. Ala. (bd. dirs. 1985-92, state pres. 1992, officer Huntsville chpt. 1984-91, pres. No. Ala. chpt. 1989, Excellence award 1986-91, Achievement award 1986-91, Pres.'s award Huntsville chpt. 1985, State Practitioner of Yr., 1989, PRCA Medallion award excellence, numerous others), Internat. Assn. Bus. Communicators (D2 Silver Quills award 1985, 91, D6 Silver Quills 1993, 94), Pub. Rels. Soc. Am. (accredited 1989—), So. Pub. Rels. Fedn. (practitioner of yr. 1991, Excellence award 1986-91, Lantern award 1991), Huntsville-Madison County C. of C. (pub. rels. adv. com. 1987-92), Huntsville Press Club (bd. dirs. 1989-92), Sigma Delta Chi (pres.'s award 1991). Office: The Boeing Co 1200 Wilson Blvd Arlington VA 22209-2305

WIDGOFF, MILDRED, physicist, researcher; b. Buffalo, Aug. 24, 1924; d. Leo Widgoff and Rebecca Shulimson; children— Eve Widgoff Shapiro, Jonathan Bernard Widgoff Shapiro. BA, U. Buffalo, 1944; PhD, Cornell U., 1952. Rsch. assoc. Brookhaven Nat. Lab., Yaphank, N.Y., 1952-54; rsch. fellow Harvard U., Cambridge, Mass., 1955-58; asst. prof. rsch. Brown U., Providence, 1959-66, assoc. prof. rsch., 1966-74, prof. physics, 1974-95; prof. rsch., 1995—. Fellow Am. Phys. Soc.; mem. Sigma Xi, Phi Beta Kappa, Phi Kappa Phi. Office: Brown U Dept Physics PO Box 1843 Providence RI 02912-1843

WIDNALL, SHEILA EVANS, aeronautical educator, former secretary of the airforce, former university official; b. Tacoma, July 13, 1938; d. Rolland John and Genievieve Alice (Krause) Evans; m. William Soule Widnall, June 11, 1960; children: William, Ann. BS in Aero. and Astronautics, MIT, 1960, MS in Aero. and Astronautics, 1961, DSc, 1964; PhD (hon.), New Eng. Coll., 1975, Lawrence U., 1987, Cedar Crest Coll., 1988, Smith Coll., 1990, Mt. Holyoke Coll., 1991, Ill. Inst. Tech., 1991, Columbia U., 1994, Simmons Coll., 1994, Suffolk U., 1994, Princeton U., 1994. Asst. prof. aeros. and astronautics MIT, Cambridge, 1964-70, assoc. prof., 1970-74, prof., 1974-93, head divsn. fluid mechanics, 1975-79; dir. Fluid Dynamics Rsch. Lab., MIT, Cambridge, 1979-90; chmn. faculty MIT, Cambridge, 1979-80, chair com. on acad. responsibility, 1991-92, assoc. provost, 1992-93; sec. USAF, 1993-97; Inst. prof. MIT, Cambridge, 1997—. Trustee Sloan Found., 1998—; bd. dirs. Gen. Corp., Chemfab Inc., Bennington, Vt., Aerospace Corp., L.A., Draper Labs., Cambridge, Gencorp; past trustee Carnegie Corp., 1984-92, Charles Stark Draper Lab. Inc.; mem. Carnegie Commn. Sci., Tech. and Govt. Contbr. articles to profl. jours.; patentee in field; assoc. editor AIAA Jour. Aircraft, 1972-75, Physics of Fluids, 1981-88, Jour. Applied Mechanics, 1983-87; mem. editorial bd. Sci., 1984-86. Bd. visitors USAF Acad., Colorado Springs, Colo., 1978-84, bd. chair, 1980-82; trustee Boston Mus. Sci., 1989-93. Recipient Washburn award Boston Mus. Sci., 1987. Fellow AAAS (bd. dirs. 1982-89, pres. 1987-88, chmn. 1988-89), AIAA (bd. dirs. 1975-77, Lawrence Sperry award 1972, Durand Lectureship for Pub. Svc. award 1996, pres. 2000-01), Am. Phys. Soc. (exec. com. 1979-82); mem. ASME (Applied Mechs. award 1995, Pres. award 1999), NAE (coun. 1992-93, v.p. 1998—), NAS (panel on sci. responsibility), Am. Acad. Arts and Scis., Soc. Women Engrs. (Outstanding Achievement award 1975), Internat. Acad. Astronautics, Seattle Mountaineers. Office: MIT Bldg 33-411 77 Massachussetts Ave Cambridge MA 02139

WIDYOLAR, SHEILA GAYLE, dermatologist; b. Vancouver, B.C., Can., June 11, 1939; d. Walter Herbert and Olive Louise (O'Neal) Roberts; Kithi K. Widyolar, 1960 (dv. 1979); 1 child, Keith. BS, Loma Linda U., 1962; MD, Howard U., 1972. Resident U. Calif., Irvine, 1973-76; dermatologist pvt. practice, Laguna Hills, Calif., 1976—. Clin. instr. U. Calif. Sch. Medicine, 1978-86. Chmn. bd. dirs. Opera Pacific, Costa Mesa, Calif., 1996-97. Fellow Am. Acad. Dermatology, Am. Soc. Dermatophthology; mem. AMA, Calif. Med. Assn., Dermatological Soc. Orange County (pres. 1983), Alpha Omega Alpha. Avocations: music, travel. Office: Ste 403 23911 Calle de Mag Dalena Laguna Hills CA 92653 Office Phone: 949-452-3814.

WIE, MICHELLE SUNG, amateur golfer; b. Honolulu, Haw., Oct. 11, 1989; d. Byung-Wook and Hyun-Kyong Sung Wie. Played in major LPGA Tournaments US Women's Open, 2003, Kraft Nabisco Championship, 2003, 2004; winner Jennie K. Wilson Invitational, 2001, Haw. State Women's Stroke Play Championship, 2001, USGA Women's Amateur Pub. Links Championship, 2003. Mem.: Haw. State Jr. Golf Assn. Achievements include youngest player to win Haw. State Women's Stroke Play Championship, Jennie K. Wilson Internat., and US Amateur Pub. Links Championship; youngest player to make an LPGA cut, playing in the Kraft Nabisco Championship. Avocations: reading, drawing, computers. Office: 100 Internat Golf Dr Daytona Beach FL 32124-1092*

WIEBE, KIMBERLY P. music educator; b. Binghamton, N.Y., Oct. 3, 1967; d. James Russell and Patricia Anne Phelps; m. Keith DeWayne Wiebe, July 26, 1997. BA in Christian Missions, Bob Jones U., 1990. Pvt. piano instr., Binghamton, 1990—97, Huntington, W.Va., 1997—. Mem. Jr. Music League Huntington, 1999; dir. music Calvary Bapt. Ch., Binghamton, 1993—97. Mem.: Music Tchrs. Nat. Assn., Nat. Guild Piano Tchrs. Republican. Baptist. Avocation: tennis. Home: 16 Persimmon Ln Huntington WV 25701 E-mail: kimwiebepiano@aol.com.

WIEBENSON, DORA LOUISE, architectural historian, editor, author; b. Cleve., July 29, 1926; d. Edward Ralph and Jeannette (Rodier) W. BA, Vassar Coll., 1946; MArch, Harvard U., 1951; MA, NYU, 1958, PhD, 1964. Architect, N.Y., 1951-66; lectr. Columbia U., 1966-68; assoc. prof. U. Md., 1968-72, prof., 1972-77; vis. prof. Cornell U., 1974; prof. U. Va., Charlottesville, 1977-92, prof. emeritus, 1992—, chmn. div. archtl. history, 1977-79, assoc. fellow U. Va. Ctr. Advanced Studies, 1982-83; pres. Archtl. Publs., N.Y.C., 1982—; editor-in-chief Centropa, 2000—. Editor: Marsyas XI: 1962-64, 1965, Essays in Honor of Walter Friedlaender, 1965; Architectural Theory and Practice from Alberti to Ledoux, 1982, rev., 1983, Spanish transl., 1988; Guide to Graduate Degree Programs in Architectural History, 1982, rev., 1984, 86, 88, 90; co-editor: The Architecture of Historic Hungary, 1998, Hungarian transl., 1998; author: Sources of Greek Revival Architecture, 1969, Tony Garnier: The Cité Industrielle, 1969, Japanese transl., 1983, The Picturesque Garden in France, 1978, Mark J. Millard Architectural Collection, Vol. I: French Books: Sixteenth through Nineteenth Centuries, 1993; contbr. articles to profl. jours. Student fellow Inst. Fine Arts, 1961-62, 62-63; grantee Am. Philos. Soc., 1964-65, 70, Samuel H. Kress Found., 1966, 72-73, 98, Gen. Rsch. Fund, U. Md., 1969, 74, 76,

NEH, 1972-73, Am. Coun. Learned Socs., 1976, 81, 85, Ctr. Advanced Studies, U. Va., 1980, 81, 97, Graham Found. Advanced Studies Fine Arts, 1982, 93, Archtl. History Found., 1996; fellow Yale Ctr. Brit. Art, 1983; sr. rsch. fellow NEH, 1986-87. Mem. Soc. Archtl. Historians (bd. dirs. 1974-77, 80-83, chair edn. com. 1976-90), Coll. Art Assn., Am. Soc. Eighteenth Century (mem. exec. bd. 1991-94).

WIECEK, BARBARA HARRIET, advertising executive; b. Chgo., Mar. 30, 1956; d. Stanley Joseph and Irene (Zagajewski) W. AA, Am. Acad. of Art, Chgo., 1977. Illustrator Clinton E. Frank Advt., Chgo., 1977-78, art dir., 1978-80, assoc. creative dir., 1980-84, v.p.; instr. Am. Acad. of Art, Chgo., 1977-80; assoc. creative dir. Tatham, Laird & Kudner, 1984—, ptnr., 1986—, creative dir., 1987—, sr. ptnr., 1995—, exec. creative dir., 1996. Recipient Silver Awd. Internat. Film Festival of N.Y., 1981, Gold Awd. Internat. Film Festival of N.Y., 1981. Roman Catholic. Avocations: painting, writing, gardening, remodeling, cycling. Office: Tatham Euro RSCG 36 E Grand Ave Chicago IL 60611-3506

WIEDEMANN, RAMONA DIANE, occupational therapist; b. Topeka, Kans., Oct. 1, 1962; d. John Daniel Fay and Sue Ann Strotman; m. William Newell Wiedemann, Aug. 9, 1986; children: William Jr., Meaghan, Nathaniel, Emily, Daniel, Madeleine. BS in Occupl. Therapy, Tex. Woman's U., 1988. Occupl. therapist Healthcare Staff Resources, Dallas, 1988-91, Associated Rehab. Svcs., Greenville, Tex., 1991-96, 97-99, 1st Rehab., Ft. Worth, 1996, Cmty. Rehab. Svcs., Dallas, 1996-97. Mem. Am. Occupl. Therapy Assn. Republican. Methodist. Avocations: reading, travel, bicycling. Home: 1001 Caledonia Paris TN 38242-1114

WIEDERHOLT, ANGELA MARIE, special education educator; b. Maryville, Mo., Mar. 9, 1977; d. Steven Eugene and Linda Marie Wiederholt. BS in Elem. Edn. and Mentally Handicapped, N.W. Mo. State U., 1999. Spl. edn. tchr. Millard Pub. Schs., Omaha, 1999—. Team mem. Millard Transition Team, Omaha, 2001—03. Mem.: Coun. for Exceptional Children. Republican. Roman Catholic. Avocations: reading, writing, crocheting.

WIEDOWER, SISTER M. VERONIQUE, religious organization administrator; b. San Diego, Dec. 5, 1947; d. Joseph Willie Wiedower and Odelia Francies Muller-Wiedower. MusB, St. Mary's Coll., Notre Dame, Ind., 1970; Master's degree, U. Notre Dame, 1979. Mem. theology and music faculty Holy Cross H.S., Mountain View, Calif., 1970—72, St. Francis H.S., Mountain View, 1972—76, Bishop Kelly H.S., Boise, Idaho, 1979—82; mem. theology faculty St. Joseph's Coll. Sem., Mountain View, 1979—85; dir. formation Sisters of the Holy Cross, Notre Dame, 1985—92, leadership team, 1994—; pastoral assoc. St. Brendan Ch., San Francisco, 1992—94 Bd. trustees Mt. Carmel Health Sys., Columbus, Ohio, 1996—98, St. Mary's Coll., Notre Dame, 1995—, St. Alphonsus Regional Med. Ctr., Boise, 1998—. Roman Catholic. Avocations: music, handcrafts. Office: Sisters of the Holy Cross 301 Bertrand Hall St Mary's Notre Dame IN 46556-5000 E-mail: veronique@cscsisters.org.

WIEGAND, SYLVIA MARGARET, mathematician, educator; b. Cape Town, South Africa, Mar. 8, 1945; came to U.S., 1949; d. Laurence Chisholm and Joan Elizabeth (Dunnett) Young; m. Roger Allan Wiegand, Aug. 27, 1966; children: David Chisholm, Andrea Elizabeth. AB, Bryn Mawr Coll., 1966; MA, U. Wash., 1967; PhD, U. Wis., Madison, 1972. Mem. faculty U. Nebr., Lincoln, 1967—, now prof. math.; program dir. Nat. Sci. Found., 2002—03. Vis. assoc. prof. U. Conn., Storrs, 1978-79, U. Wis., Madison, 1985-86; vis. prof. Purdue U., 1992-93, Spring 1998, Mich. State U., Fall 1997. Editor Communications in Math., 1990—, Rocky Mountain Jour. Math., 1991—; contbr. rsch. articles to profl. jours. Troop leader Lincoln area Girl Scouts U.S., 1988-92. Grantee NSF, 1985-88, 90-93, 94-96, 97—; Vis. Professorship for Women, 1992, Nat. Security Agy., 1995-97. Mem. AAUP, Assn. Women in Math (pres.-elect 1995-96, pres. 1997-99), London Math. Soc., Math. Assn. Am., Am. Math. Soc. (mem. coun. 1994-96, chmn. policy com. on meetings and confs. 1994-96, mem. nominating com. 1997—), Can. Math. Soc. (bd. mem. at large 1997—). Avocations: running, family activities. Office: U Nebr Dept Math Lincoln NE 68588-0323 E-mail: swiegand@math.unl.edu.

WIEMERS, KATHY LYN, chemist; b. Kearney, Nebr., Jan. 24, 1969; d. Lesley LaVerne and Janice Rae (Merrick) Wiemers; m. Bernard Robert Oleksa, Jr., Feb. 14, 1992 (div. June 1994); 1 child, Philip M. BJ, U. Nebr., 1991; BS, U. Nebr., Kearney, 1995; PhD, U. Mo., 2001. Teaching asst. in chemistry U. Mo., Columbia, 1995-96, rsch. asst., 1996—; process engr. Novellus, 2000—01; v.p. sci. and tech. IPG, 2002—. Editor Nebr. Blueprint, 1987-90; contbr. articles to Daily Nebraskan, 1990-91. Sr. Enhancement Fellow in Chemistry, U. Mo., 1995. Mem. Am. Chem. Soc., Am. Women in Sci., Chemistry Graduate Student Assn. (pres. 1997).

WIENER, CHERYL RENEE, music educator, musician; b. Long Island City, N.Y., June 5, 1951; d. Abraham Holtzman Wiener and Marcella Engleman Warner. MusB, Hartt Sch., U. Hartford, 1975; MusM, Yale Sch. Music, 1978. Cert. provisional educator. Adj. music tchr. Ctrl. Conn. State U., New Britain, Conn., 1978—79; percussion tchr. Rubin Acad., Jerusalem, 1979—81; music tchr. Betsy Ross Arts Magnet Sch., New Haven, 1987—89; percussion tchr. Neighborhood Music Sch., New Haven, 1987—89; adj. music tchr. Newtown H.S., Conn., 1990—92, Holyoke C.C., Mass., 1998—2000; music tchr. Cmty. Music Sch., Springfield, 1998—2000; tchr. instrumental music Future Musicians Inc., Portland, Conn., 1999—2000, Regional Sch. Dist. 13, Durham, Middlefield, Conn., 2000—. Percussionist Hartford Symphony Orch., Conn., 1974—89, 1997—2003, New Haven Symphony Orch., New Haven, 1982—91, 1999—; percussionist/asst. tympanist Jerusalem Symphony Orch., Jerusalem, 1979—81; percussionist Israel Philharmonic Orch., Tel Aviv, 1980—81, Greater Bridgeport Symphony Orch., Bridgeport, Conn., 1983—89; tympanist Waterbury Symphony Orch., Waterbury, Conn., 1983—89, New Britain Symphony Orch., New Britain, Conn., 1984—89; tchr. pvt. percussion music Wiener Percussion Studio, Conn., 1991—. Adv. chemically sensitive Ecol. Health Orgn., Hebron, Conn., 1993—96. Scholar, Yale Summer Sch. Music and Art, Norfolk, Conn.; Aspen Sch. Music sch., Aspen Music Festival. Mem.: Conn. Educators Assn., Am. Fedn. Musicians.

WIER, PATRICIA ANN, publishing executive, consultant; b. Coal Hill, Ark., Nov. 10, 1937; d. Horace L. and Bridget B. (McMahon) Norton; m. Richard A. Wier, Feb. 24, 1962; 1 child, Rebecca Ann. BA, U. Mo., Kansas City, 1964; MBA, U. Chgo., 1978. Computer programmer AT&T, 1960-62; lead programmer City of Kansas City, Mo., 1963-65; with Playboy Enterprises, Chgo., 1965-71, mgr. systems and programming, 1971; with Ency. Britannica, Inc., Chgo., 1971—; v.p. mgmt. svcs. Ency. Britannica USA, 1975-83, exec. v.p. adminstrn., 1983-84; v.p. planning and devel. Ency. Britannica, Inc., 1985, pres. Compton's Learning Co. divsn., 1985; pres. Ency. Britannica (USA), 1986-91, Ency. Britannica N.A., 1991-92; exec. v.p. Ency. Britannica, Inc., 1986-94; pres. Ency. Britannica N.Am., 1991-94; mgmt. cons. pvt. practice, Chgo., 1994—. Cons. pvt. practice, Chgo., 1994—; bd. dirs. NICOR, Inc., Mannatech, Inc., Alcas Corp.; mem. coun. Northwestern U. Assocs. Life mem. coun. Grad. Sch. Bus., U. Chgo.; mem. bd. regents Lewis U.; chmn. bd. dirs. San Miguel Sch. Mem. Direct Selling Assn. (bd. dirs. 1984-93, chmn. 1987-88, named to Hall of Fame 1991), Women's Coun. U. Mo. Kansas City (hon. life) Com. 200, The Chgo. Network. Roman Catholic. Office: Patricia A Wier Inc 175 E Delaware Pl Apt 8305 Chicago IL 60611-7748

WIES, BARBARA, editor, publisher; b. Dec. 5, 1939; BA, U. Conn., 1961; student, New Sch. for Social Rsch., 1961-62. Product devel. Fearn Soya, Melrose Park, Ill., 1973-75; product devel. Modern Products, Milw., 1973-75; editor, pub. Bestways Mag., Carson City, Nev., 1977-89; pub. The Healthy Gourmet Newsletter, 1989-91, Fine Wine-Good Food Newsletter, 1991—; publicity dir. Nev. Artists Assn., 1994—; owner Gualala (Calif.) Galleries, 1989-90; assoc. pub., mgr. Edn. Range Mag., 1998—. Owner, operator cooking sch. Greensboro N.C. 1969-73; instr. Very Spl. Arts Nev., 1997. Author: Natural Cooking, 1968, Wok and Tempura, 1969, Japanese Home Cooking, 1970, The Wok, 1971, Super Soy, 1973, The Health Gourmet, 1981, International Healthy Gourmet, 1982; one-woman show paintings Dolphin Gallery, Gualala, Calif., 1990, River Gallery, Reno, 1994; 2 women show 1992, 94, 96, Dolphin Gallery, Calif., 1994, solo exhbn. Nev. Artists Assn. Gallery, 1993, 95, 96, 97; featured artist Nev. State Libr., 1996, Silver State Gallery, Reno, 1998, West Nev. C.C., 1996, art show judge, 1997; restaurant critic Reno Gazette Jour., 1995-2001. Performer Nev. Arts sponsored Tumblewords, 2000—; del. Nev. Episcopal Diocese Convention, 2002, Vestry St. Peter's Episcopal Ch., 2003—. Grantee Nev. Arts Coun., 2002; recipient First Place adult fiction Nev. State Lit. Co., 1995, First Place fiction State Lit. Comp., 1998, 2d Place fiction Writers Block; Nev. Arts Coun. fellow, 1999-2000. Mem. Nat. League Am. Pen Women (chair 1st and 2d ann. lit. competition Reno br., chairperson 1st Nat. Lit. award), Inst. Food Technologists, Pastel Soc. of the West Coast, Inst. Am. Culinary Profls.

WIESE, DENISE KAY, music educator; d. Bruce James and Janice Anita Smith; m. Paul Raymond Wiese, Dec. 14, 1991; 1 child, James Paul. BS in Music Edn., N.D. State U., 1984; MusM, U. St. Thomas, St. Paul, Minn., 1996. Tchr. music Chokio Alta. Pub. schools, Alberta, Minn., 1984—89, Fergus Falls Pub. Schs., Minn., 1989—. Recipient Heritage award, N.D. Gov., 1982. Mem.: NEA, Minn. Band Directors Assn, Minn. Music Edn. Assn.

WIESE, NEVA, critical care nurse; b. Hunter, Kans., July 23, 1940; d. Amil H. and Minnie (Zemke) W. Diploma, Grace Hosp. Sch. Nursing, Hutchinson, Kans., 1962; BA in Social Sci., U. Denver, 1971; BSN, Met. State Coll., 1975; MS in Nursing, U. Colo., Denvr, 1978; postgrad., U. N.Mex., 1986; PhD, Kennedy Western U., 1999. RN, N.Mex.; CCRN. Cardiac ICU nurse U. N.Mex. Hosp., Albuquerque; coord. critical care edn. St. Vincent Hosp., Santa Fe, charge nurse CCU, clin. nurse III intensive and cardiac care, part-time rsch. asst. Recipient Mary Atherton Meml. award for clin. excellence St. Vincent Hosp., 1986. Mem. ANA (cert. med. surg. nurse), AACN (past pres., sec. N.Mex. chpt., Clin. Excellence award 1991, Lifetime Achievement award 1997), N.Mex. League Nursing (past v.p., bd. dirs., sec., membership com. 1992-97). Home: 849 Rio Vista St Santa Fe NM 87501-1549

WIESEL-LEARY, MARCIA L. school psychologist; b. Ottumwa, Iowa, Sept. 14, 1951; d. Richard J. and Marie E. (Courts) Wiesel; m. James D. Leary, July 17, 1976; 1 child, Richard J. BS, U. Wis., Superior, 1973, MS in Edn., 1976; D in Psychology, So. Calif. U., 2003. Psychologist Courage House, Aitkin, Minn., 1976-78; sch. psychologist Des Moines Pub. Schs., 1978—95; psychologist Alachua County Schs., Gainesville, Fla., 1995—. Adj. instr. sch. psychology program U. Fla., 2001—02. Pres. Luther Meml. Ch., Des Moines, 1987-89; advisor Spl. Care Parents, Des Moines, 1988—; chair Des Moines Youth Symphony, 1990—. Recipient Outstanding Leadership award Area Ednl. Agy., Johnston, Iowa, 1991. Mem. Coun. for Exceptional Children (pres. elect Gatorland chpt. 2003-2004, state positive behavior support trainer 1999-), Nat. Assn. Sch. Psychologists, Fla. Assn. Sch. Psychologist. Avocations: biking, running, reading.

WIESENBERG, JACQUELINE LEONARDI, social sciences educator; b. West Haven, Conn., May 04; d. Curzio and Filomena Olga (Turrinziani) Leonardi; m. Russel John Wiesenberg, Nov. 23; children: James Wynne, Deborann Donna. BA, SUNY, Buffalo, 1970; postgrad., 1970-73, 80—. Interviewer, examiner U.S. Dept. Labor, New Haven, 1948-52; sec. W.I. Clark Co., Hamden, Conn., 1952-55; acct. VA Hosp., West Haven, 1956-60; acct.-commissary USAF Missle Site, Niagara Falls, N.Y., 1961-62; tchr. Buffalo City Schs., 1970-73, 79; acct. Erie County Social Svcs., Buffalo, 1971-73; lectr., 1973—. Contbr. articles to CAP, USAF mag. Capt., Nat. Found. March of Dimes, 1969—, com. mem. telethon, 1983-86; vol. VA, 1973—; den mother Boy Scouts Am., 1961-68; chmn. Meals on Wheels, Town of Amherst, 1975-76; leader, travel chmn. Girl Scouts U.S., 1968-77; mem. Nat. Congress Parents and Tchrs., 1957—; heart fund vol. Heart Assn., 1960-86; rep. Am. Diabetes Assn., 1994—, vol. diabetes collection, 1994-95; mem. Humane Soc. U.S., ASPCA, N.Y. Srs. Coalition. Mem. AAUW, NAFE, Internat. Platform Assn., Nat. Pks. and Conservation Assn., Am. Astrol. Assn., Nat. Arbor Day Found., Western N.Y. Conf. Aging, Nat. Geog. Soc., Wilderness Soc., Nat. Wildlife Fedn., Nat. Trust for Hist. Preservation, Nature Conservancy, Ctr. for Marine Conservation, Internat. Funds Animal Welfare, North Shore Animal League, The Nature Conservancy, The Libr. Congress, U. Buffalo Found., Pvt. Land Conservancy-Nat. Park Trust, U. Buffalo Alumni Assn., Epsilon Delta Chi, Alpha Iota. Home: 14 Norman Pl Amherst NY 14226-4233

WIESENFELD, BESS G. interior designer; b. Elizabeth, N.J., May 6, 1915; d. Morris and Rebecca (Sokolov) Gazevitz; m. Benjamin Wiesenfeld, Oct. 23, 1938 (dec.); children: Myra Judith Wiesenfeld Lewis, Elaine Phyllis Wiesenfeld Livingston, Ira Bertram (dec.), Sarah Ann Wiesenfeld Wasserman. BFA, N.Y. Sch. Interior Design, 1982. Pres. Anasarca Corp., 1958—; real estate devel. Colonia, N.J., 1961—; pres. Carolier Lns., Inc., 1986—, BGW LLC, Bess & Co. Patron Met. Opera; sustaining mem. N.J. Symphony Orch. Mem.: AAUW, Am. Soc. Interior Designers (allied mem.), Friends of Music at Princeton, Friends of Art Mus. of Princeton, N.J., Mus. Modern Art, Met. Mus. Art. Jewish. Home: 374 New Dover Rd Colonia NJ 07067-2713 also: 2600 S Ocean Blvd Palm Beach FL 33480-5484

WIESNER, CAROL A. financial services company executive; BS in Bus. Adminstrn., Pa. State U., 1960. CPA, Calif. Sr. auditor Price Waterhouse & Co., 1960-67; various positions Litton Industries, Inc., Woodland Hills, Calif., 1967-88, v.p., treas., 1988-94, v.p., controller, 1994—2000; ret. Mem. AICPA, Calif. Soc. CPA. Office: 21240 Burbank Blvd Woodland Hills CA 91367-6675

WIEST, DIANNE, actress; b. Kansas City, Mo., Mar. 28, 1948; Student, U. Md. Appeared in numerous plays including Ashes (off-Broadway), 1976, Leave It to Beaver is Dead, The Art of Dining (Obie award, 1979, Theatre World award 1983), Bonjour La Bonjour, Three Sisters, Serenading Louie (Obie award, 1983), Othello, After the Fall, Heartbreak House, Our Town, and Hunting Cockroaches, 1987, In the Summer House, 1993, Blue Light, 1994; appeared in films including It's My Turn, 1980, I'm Dancing as Fast as I Can, 1982, Independence Day, 1982, Footloose, 1984, Falling in Love, 1984, The Purple Rose of Cairo, 1985, Hannah and Her Sisters, 1986 (Acad. award for Best Supporting Actress 1987), Radio Days, 1987, Lost Boys, 1987, September, 1987, Bright Lights, Big City, 1988, Parenthood, 1989 (Acad. award nominee), Cookie, 1989, Edward Scissorhands, 1990, Little Man Tate, 1991, Cops and Robbersons, 1994, The Scout, 1994, Bullets Over Broadway, 1994 (Golden Globe award Best Supporting Actress-Drama 1995, Acad. award for Best Supporting Actress 1995), Drunks, 1995, The Birdcage, 1996, The Associate, 1996, Practical Magic, 1998, The Horse Whisperer, 1998, Portofino, 1999; TV appearances include The Wall, 1982, The Face of Rage, 1983, Simple Life of Noah Dearborn, 1999, The 10th Kingdom, 2000.

WIGFIED-PHILLIP, RUTH GENIVEA, genealogist, author, researcher; b. Couer d' Alene, Idaho, Dec. 1, 1918; d. Arthur and Jenivea Caroline (Crisp) Wigfield; m. Milton Fred Phillip, May 14, 1942 (dec. Nov., 1984); children: Rochelle Ruth, Gloria Genivea, Nancy Lenore, Douglas Fred, Andrea Arleen. BA, U. Montana, Missoula, 1939; registered genealogist, Augustine Genealogy Sch., Torrance, Calif., 1985, Desc. of William the Conquerer, Desc. of Companion of William Conquerer, Augustine Genealogy Sch., Torrance, Calif., 1997. Med. technician Deaconess Hosp., Great Falls, Mont., 1939-42; social worker Mont. State Welfare Dept., Helena, 1944-46; musical instr. Mont. Music Tchrs. Assn., Great Falls, 1947-62, Missoula, 1962-72; genealogy rschr. Phillip Heritage House, Missoula, 1962-66, writer, author, 1972—. Author, editor: (5 newsletters on genealogy) Wigfield Genealogy, 1972—, Crisp Genealogy, 1981—, Lipscomb Genealogy, 1981, Martin Genealogy, 1981, New Race, 1985—. Mem. Immanuel Luth. Ch., Sunday sch. supt., 1965-72; sec. Mont. State Music Tchrs. Union, 1969-71. Recipient music scholarship Harlowtown Music Dept., Harlowtown, Mont., 1932-35. Mem. DAR (regent Bitterroot chpt. 1973-75, state Indian chmn. 1976-90, 25 yr. h on. award Bitterroot chpt. 1997), Guild of St. Margaret of Scotland (grand dame Mont., 1986—), Eastern Star (organist), Rebecca Lodge (organist). Avocations: bridge, garden club, travel, fishing, golf. Home and Office: Phillip Genealogy Heritage House 605 Benton Ave Missoula MT 59801-8633

WIGFIELD, RITA L. elementary school educator; b. Mpls., Dec. 14, 1945; d. Willard Ernest and Bernice Eleanor (Peterson) Ahlquist; m. Vernon Carter Wigfield, Oct. 9, 1982. BS, U. Minn., 1967; grad., St. Thomas Coll.; postgrad., Hamlin U. Cert. elem. educator, Minn. Tchr. Alice Smith Sch., Hopkins, Minn., 1967-80, Meadowbrook Sch., Hopkins, 1980-86, Gatewood Sch., Hopkins, 1986—. Owner Swede Country, Minnetonka, Minn., 1983—; elem. team leader Prin.'s Adv. Bd.; chmn. bldg. tech. com. Hopkins Sch. Dist., past supr. bldg. sch. patrol; coop. tchrs. Gustavus Adolphus Coll.; cons. and presenter in field. Author: We Love Literature, 1991 (Grand Prize Scholastic Inc., 1991). Mem. Wooddale Choir Evang. Christian Ch., decorating com., Mission commn., organizer fellowship dinners; mem. Loaves and Fishes, Minn. Landscape Arboretum. Recipient Hon. Mention Learning Mag., 1990, Nat. Coun Econ. edn./Internat. Paper Col. Found., 1992, 2d pl. Minn. Coun. Econ. Edn., 1992, Ashland Oil award, 1994; named Minn. Tchr. of Yr., 1992. Mem. ASCD, Nat. Assn. Miniature Enthusiasts, Am. Quilting Soc., Internat. Reading Assn., Minn. Edn. Assn., Hopins Edn. Assn. (bldg. rep., treas.), Delta Kappa Gamma (pres. Beta Beta chpt.), Kappa Delta Pi. Avocations: miniatures, quilting, flowers, cross-stitch, antiques. Home: 4719 Diane Dr Hopkins MN 55343-8785 Office: Gatewood Elem Sch 14900 Gatewood Dr Minnetonka MN 55345-6731

WIGGERLY, DEBORAH JEAN, speech pathology/audiology services professional, educator; d. Thomas Eugene and Peggy (Chafin) Wood; m. Kerry Allen Wiggerly, May 31, 1975; children: Kyle Andrew, Kate Alayne, Keith Aaron. MA, Ball State U., 1978, BS, 1977. Adminstrv. Lic., Dir. Spl. Edn. Ind. Profl. Stds. Bd., 2002. Tchr. Salem Cmty. Schs., Daleville, Ind., 1982—83, Muncie Cmty. Schs., Ind., 1979—82, 1984—. Tech. trainer/facilitator Muncie Cmty. Schools, 2001—; web master North View Elem. Sch., Muncie, 2000—, Speech and Hearing Area Educators, Ind., 2001—. Mem.: ASCD, NEA, Muncie Tchrs. Assn., Speech and Hearing Area Educators, Coun. for Exceptional Children, Ind. Speech and Hearing Assn., Ind. State Tchrs. Assn., Pi Lambda Theta. Avocations: gardening, jogging, walking. [illegible] E-mail: [illegible]@comcast.net. E-mail: dwiggerly@muncie.k12.in.us.

WIGGERS, CHARLOTTE SUZANNE WARD, magazine editor; b. Cleve., Dec. 14, 1943, d. Raymond Paul and Irene Mary (Knapp) W.; m. John Houston Black, Feb. 1975 (div. 1980). AB, Smith Coll., 1966. Asst. editor The Hudson Rev., N.Y.C., 1966-76; assoc. editor The Print Collector's Newsletter, N.Y.C., 1977-79; copy editor Electronics mag., McGraw-Hill, N.Y.C., 1979-81; sr. copy editor Spectrum mag., N.Y.C., 1981-85; mng. editor Essence mag., N.Y.C., 1985—. Active St. Thomas Ch. Fifth Ave. Avocations: swimming, writing, photography, tennis. Home: 50 W 85th St Apt 5 New York NY 10024-4572 Office: Essence Magazine 1500 Broadway Ste 600 New York NY 10036-4015

WIGGINS, CELESTINE K. state legislator; b. Newport, N.H., Nov. 29, 1929; m. Frank Wiggins; 4 children. Student, U. N.H., 1947-48, Keene State Coll., 1967-71, Vt. State Coll., 1982-83. Postmaster U.S. Postal Svc., ret., 1992; mem. dist. 4 N.H. Ho. of Reps., Concord, 1996—, mem. criminal justice and pub. safety com., 1996—. Clk. Newport (N.H.) Sch. Dist.; chmn. Sullivan County Dem. Orgn., 1996—; chmn. Newport Revitalization Commn., 1994-96; bd. dirs. Sullivan County chpt. United Way, 1993—. Mem. Nat. League Postmasters (vice chmn. nat. legis. com. 1984-91). Roman Catholic. Office: NH State Legis State House Concord NH 03301

WIGGINS, DOROTHY L. retired primary school educator; b. Auburn, N.Y., Sept. 6, 1935; d. Kenneth Howard and Frances Emma Lefavor; m. Richard James Wiggins; children: Richard Jr., Robin, Marc. BA, SUNY, Brockport, 1956; M in Elem. Edn., SUNY, Oswego, 1976. Kindergarten tchr. Red Creek (N.Y.) Ctrl. Sch., 1956—94; ret., 1994. Bd. dirs., Literacy Vols., NY, 1999. Named Tchr. of the Yr., Wayne County Tchrs. Assn. Mem.: Lioness Club (past pres.), Delta Kappa Gamma (past pres.). Avocations: reading, playing piano and organ, crossword puzzles, jigsaw puzzles. Home: 4885 Butler Center Rd Wolcott NY 14590

WIGGINS, GLORIA, nonprofit organization administrator, television producer; b. N.Y.C., Jan. 17, 1933; d. John and Gladys (Jones) Pruden; m. Albert Wiggins, Jan. 15, 1954 (dec. Aug. 1982); children: Michael, Teresa. BA, Richmons Coll., Staten Island, N.Y.; MA, SUNY, Albany. Project dir. Suffolk County Black History Assn., Smithtown, N.Y., 1982; pres., chair, founder Zamanii Internat. Devel. Corp., Central Islip, N.Y., 1983—; chair, founder Ikeda Mandela Uhuru Cultural Ctr., Inc., Central Islip, 1991—. Chair Univ. Sons & Daughters of Ethiopia, Deer Park, N.Y., 1990-91. Producer, artist: (pub. access TV) Celebration of Kwanzaa, 1993 (grant 1993); prodr.: (pub. access TV) Living Arts, 1994 (grant 1994), (exhibit) Adventure to the Homeland, 1995 (grant 1995), African Women/African Art, 1992 (grant 1992), 2d Roots Internat. Homecoming Festival, 1998, Women Achievers of 1998, Black History Celebration Senegal, 1999, We Sing America, 2000, International Poets, 2000, Postive Images, 2000, African American Couples in the Arts, 2000, Public Library Exhibits, 2000, TV Public Access, 2001, African Americans in West Africa, Celebration of Black History Month, 2001, (TV pub. access program of Senegalese in N.Y.) A Naming Ceremony, (pub. access TV) 10th Birthday Celebration Pow Wow, 2002, TV Pub. Access programs 100th Birthday Celebration, 2002, African Immigrants in Harlem, 2003, Smithtown Art Exhibit, Sr. Citizen Art Exhibit, Nigerian Art Exhibit, 2003, West African Photography Exhibit, Ikeda Mandela Uhoru Cultural Ctr., 2003; author (poem) Man of Two Worlds (prize 2001). Pres. Mariners Harbor Tenant Assn., Staten Island, 1968-70; vol. Peace Corps, 1980, Peace Corps, 1979. Recipient Internat. Libr. Photography editors choice award, 1998, Poet of the Yr. medallion and the Diamond Homer trophy Famous Poets Soc., 1999, Internat. Poet Merit award Internat Soc. Poets African Woman, 2002, Famous Poets Soc. award Proud to Belong, 2004; grantee Chase Manhattan Bank, 1986, NY Decentralization Coun. on the Arts, 1987-93, Suffolk County Office of Cultural Affairs, 1987-88, 2002. Avocations: art, television production, swimming, writing, community service. Home: 248 Tree Ave Central Islip NY 11722-2745 Office Phone: 631-234-2533. E-mail: fatal14@juno.com.

WIGGINS, IDA SILVER, elementary school educator; b. Bklyn., Apr. 23; d. Joseph C. and Alice V. (Carter) Silver; m. G. Franklin Wiggins, Dec. 27, 1955; children: Bryan Franklin, Sharon-Amy. BS, NYU, 1955, MA, 1966; D Christian Letters (hon.), Shaw Divinity Sch., Raleigh, N.C., 1988. Cert.

tchr., N.Y. Tchr. Durham (N.C.) County Pub. Sch., 1955-56, Johnston County Pub. Sch., Clayton, N.C., 1956-60; ednl. cons. Child Care Ctr., N.Y., 1960-61; tchr. Lakeland Cen. Schs., Shrub Oak, N.Y., 1961-91, Hudson Valley Christian Acad., Mahopac Falls, N.Y., 1991—. Tchr. adv. panel Silver Burdett Pub. Co., Morristown, N.J., 1987-88; mem. lang. arts task force, elem. math com., social studies curriculum com. Lakeland Cen Schs., 1989—; bd. dirs. Tutorial Program, Peekskill, 1986—. Writer: (choral reading) Martin Luther King, Jr., 1970. Life mem. Peekskill Hosp. Aux., 1980; former bd. mem. Peekskill YWCA, 1982, Peekskill Mus., 1988; life mem. NAACP, Peekskill, 1989; trustee Shaw U., Raleigh, N.C.; former bd. dirs. Hudson Valley Hosp. Found. Mem. AAUW, Am. Fedn. Tchrs., N.Y. State United Tchrs., Lakeland Fedn. Tchrs., Nat. Black Child Devel. Inst., Nat. Coun. Negro Women, Blacks in Govt. (life W. Point chpt.), The Links, Inc., Delta Kappa Gamma, Alpha Kappa Alpha. Baptist. Home: 1282 Maple Ave Peekskill NY 10566-4853

WIGGINS, KAREN SUE, education educator, counselor; b. Houston, Tex., June 30, 1953; d. Jack Myrl Townsend and Elsie Jane Townsend (Head); m. Kenneth Lyle Wiggins, Dec. 30, 1994; children: Townsend Cade Norris, Adam Ryan. BSc in elem. edn., SW Tex. State U., 1971—77; MSc in edn., U. of Houston Clear Lake, 1982—84; PhD in human services, Capella U., 1997—2001. Cert. Tex. Sch. Counselor State Bd. for Educator, 2001, Reading Specialist State Bd. for Educator Cert., Tex., 1984, Generic Spl. Edn. Classroom Tchr. State Bd. for Educator Cert., Tex., 2000, Elem. Tchr. State Bd. for Educator Cert., Tex., 1977, Basic CRT Cert. Nat. Orgn. of Victims Assistance, Wash. DC, 2003, cert. Irlen Screener Irlen Scotopic Sensitivity Screening, Calif., 2003. Tchr. Aldine Ind. Sch. Dist., Houston, 1977—80, Dallas Ind. Sch. Dist., 1980—81, Pasadena Ind. Sch. Dist., Tex., 1982—86, Big Bend C.C., Grafenwhoer, Germany, 1986—88, Pasadena Ind. Sch. Dist., Tex., 1988—91, Clear Creek Ind. Sch. Dist., League City, Tex., 1991—99; sch. counselor Galveston Ind. Sch. Dist., Tex., 1999—; adj. prof. dept. of edn. U. of St. Thomas, Houston, 2002—; adj. prof. LeTourneau U., Houston, 2003—. Mem.: ACA, Nat. Orgn. of Victims Assistance, Tex. Sch. Counselor Assn., Am. Sch. Counselor Assn., Tex. Counseling Assn.

WIGGINS, KELLEY J.K. music educator; b. Nashville, Tenn., Aug. 12, 1977; d. Paul Marshall and Mary Josephine (Kerrigan) Krech; m. Franklin Campsey Wiggins, Dec. 18, 1999; 1 child, Parker Krech. MusB, David Lipscomb U., Nashville, Tenn., 1995—99. Cert. Vocal Music Edn. David Lipscomb U./Tenn., 1999. Music specialist DuPont Elem. Sch., Old Hickory, Tenn., 1999—2000; choral dir. Portland HS, Portland, Tenn., 2000—. Songwriter, Gallatin, Tenn., 1992—; mem. SACS com.: DuPont Elem. Sch., Old Hickory, Tenn., 1999—2000; singer RSVP Band, Nashville, 2002—; choir mem. Gallatin Ch. of Christ, Gallatin, Tenn., 2002—; co-chair SACS Com. for Portland HS, Portland, Tenn., 2002—; co-sponsor Forensics Team: Portland HS, Portland, Tenn., 2002—. Entertainer Chamber of Commerce, Gallatin, Tenn., 2002—03, Portland, Tenn., 2003—. Recipient Tchr. of the Month, DuPont Elem. Sch., 2000. Mem.: Profl. Educator's Assn. (assoc.), Tenn. Music Edn. Assn. (assoc.), The Nat. Assn. for Music Edn. (assoc.). Church Of Christ. Avocations: singing, landscaping, travel. Home: 202 Putter Point Dr Gallatin TN 37066 Office: Portland High School 600 College St Portland TN 37148 E-mail: wigginskjk@yahoo.com.

WIGGINS, MARGARET REYNOLDS, elementary school educator; b. Augusta, Ga., Oct. 17, 1948; d. Aaron Estes and Myrtle Powell Reynolds; m. Arles Wayne Wiggins, Apr. 16, 1972; children: Mark, Anna Kay, Mary Beth. BA in Music, Augusta Coll., 1970; M of Music Edn., U. Ga., 1973. Cert. nat. cert. tchr. 2002. Music tchr. K-12 Richmond County Bd. Edn., Augusta, 1970—76, music tchr. K-5, 1988—89, Columbia County Bd. Edn., Evans, Ga., 1989—. Substitute organist, piano tchr. various chs., Augusta. Recipient Proclamation for Dedicated Svc., State Rep. Ben Harbin, State of Ga., 2003. Mem.: Alpha Delta Kappa (sec., v.p., pres. 1973—). Republican. Baptist. Avocation: decorating. Office: Columbia County Bd Edn Blue Ridge Elem Sch 550 Blue Ridge Dr Evans GA 30809

WIGGINS, MARIANNE, writer; b. Lancaster, Pa., 1947; m. Salman Rushdie, 1988 (div. 1993); 1 child. Author: (novels) Babe, 1975, Went South, 1980, Separate Checks, 1984, Herself in Love and Other Stories, 1987, John Dollar, 1989, Bet They'll Miss Us when We're Gone: Stories, 1991, Eveless Eden, 1995 (nominee Orange prize, 1991), Almost Heaven, 1998, Evidence of Things Unseen (nominee for Nat. Book award, 2003). Recipient Whiting award, Nat. Endowment for the Arts Grant, Janet Heidinger Kafka prize. Home: P O Box 461597 Los Angeles CA 90046-9597

WIGGINS, NANCY BOWEN, real estate broker, market research consultant; b. Richmond, Va., Oct. 9, 1948; d. William Roy and Mary Virginia (Colson) Bowen; m. Samuel Spence Saunders, Aug. 16, 1969 (div. 1977); m. Edwin Lindsey Wiggins, Jr., Apr. 16, 1983 (div. 1999); children: Neal Bowen, Mark Edwin. AA, St. Mary's Coll., Raleigh, N.C., 1968; postgrad., Trinity U., 1968-69; BA, U.S. Internat. U., San Diego, 1970; MA, U. Tex., Arlington, 1975; postgrad., Tulane U., 1976-77. Cert. comml. investment mem. Bank teller Bank of Am., San Diego, 1971-72; lectr. U. Tex., Arlington, 1974-76; instr. Johnson C. Smith U., Charlotte, N.C., 1977-78; human svcs. planner Centralina Coun. of Govt., Charlotte, 1978-80; mktg. rsch. analyst First Union Nat. Bank, Charlotte, 1980-81; mktg. rep. Burroughs Corp., Charlotte, 1981-83; ptnr., mktg. researcher George Selden & Assocs., Charlotte, 1983-84; pres., broker Bowen Wiggins Co., Charlotte, 1984-92; pres. WRB, Inc. (merger Bowen Wiggins Co. and W. Roy Bowen Co., Inc.), Charlotte, 1992-96; mgr., prin. Nancy Wiggins, LLC, Charlotte, 1996—; ptnr. Buster & Wiggins Internat., Myrtle Beach, S.C. Instr. U. N.C., Charlotte, 1984-85, 87-90, Winthrop U., Rock Hill, S.C., 1985-86, 91-92; bd. dirs. Roy Bowen, Inc., Frogmore, S.C., v.p., sec., 1990. Contbr. articles to profl. jours. Vice chmn. United Cerebral Palsy Coun., Charlotte, 1984; chmn. bd. dirs. Carriage House Condominium Assn., Charlotte, 1980-82; mem. Charlotte Mayor's Budget Adv. Com., 1980-81, Charlotte-Mecklenburg Planning Commn., 1994-99, mem. planning com., 1994-95, zoning com., 1995-97, vice-chmn. zoning com., 1997, planning com. 1998, vice chmn. planning com. 1998—, exec. com., 1997—; pres. Mecklenburg Dem. Women's Club, 1990; mem. state exec. com. N.C. Dem. Party, 1991-95, 99-2000; mem. Mecklenburg County Solid Waste Adv. Bd., 1991-92, chmn. recycling com., 1991-94, 95-96; mem. Comml. Investment Real Estate Inst., 1997-98, bd. dirs. N.C. chpg., 1999. Mem. AAUW, Charlotte Region Comml. Bd. Realtors, N.C. Assn. Appraisers (bd. dirs., pres. 1989-90), Internat. Coun. Shopping Ctrs., Internat. Real Estate Fedn. (Paris, U.S. del. Retail Conf. at World Congress 1998, U.S. vice chair trade missions, sec.-gen. exch. com. 1999-2000), Am. Planning Assn., Charlotte C. of C. (bd. advisors 1997), Multimillion Dollar Club, Tournament Players Club Piper Glen, Rose Soc., Good Friends, Nat. Assn. Realtors, FIABCI, Paris, Internat. Trade Mission Com. (sec. gen. internat. exch. com.), N.C. Citizens for Bus. and Industry, NAR Charlotte (region comml. bd.), CCIM (N.C. chpt. bd. dirs.), Pi Sigma Alpha. Democrat. Episcopalian. Avocations: gardening, art collecting. Home: 6919 Seton House Ln Charlotte NC 28277-4517 Office: Ste 300 501 N Church St Charlotte NC 28202-2207

WIGGINS, PATRICIA ANN, computer systems analyst, state legislator; b. Pasadena, Calif., Apr. 19, 1940; d. Ralph Curtis and Grace Lucille (Alpeter) W.; m. Yosef Pilch, Aug. 10, 1971 (div. July 1977); m. Guy Reed Conner, Mar. 13, 1983; stepchildren: Stephen Silverman, James Silverman. BA in English, UCLA, 1977. Bookkeeper Europa Motors Ltd., Studio City, Calif., 1959-62, Volvo Imports, North Hollywood, Calif., 1962-64, George Pope Assets, San Francisco, 1964-69; client rels. coord. Property Rsch. Corp., L.A., 1969-72; computer systems analyst Sys. Devel. Corp., Santa Monica, Calif., 1977-83, Fireman's Fund Ins., San Rafael, Calif., 1984; computer systems analyst, ptnr. Peer Protocols, Ltd., Costa Mesa, Calif., 1984-89; campaign mgr. Sen. Mike Thompson, Napa, Calif., 1990; field rep. Assemblywoman Valerie Brown, Santa Rosa, Calif., 1992-94; coun. mem. City of Santa Rosa, Calif., 1994 [illegible] Santa Rosa, 1990—. Mem. Calif. State Assembly, 1998—. Recipient Vol. Recognition, County of Sonoma, 1996. Mem. NOW, Bus. & Profl. Women, Nat. Women's Polit. Caucus (v.p. 1996), Sonoma Land Trust (bd. mem. 1993-97). Democrat. Avocations: reading, walking. Home: 315 Carrillo St Santa Rosa CA 95401-5111

WIGGINS-ROTHWELL, JEANINE ELLEN, artist; b. Jacksonville, Fla., Apr. 15, 1967; d. Otis K. Wiggins and Minnie Lois (Odem) Martin; m. John Joseph Rothwell, Jan. 2, 1993. Student, Fla. C.C., 1984, 85, U. Ga., 1985; BFA in Painting, U. Fla., 1995. Freelance illustrator Earth Art, Inc., Gainesville, Fla., 1990—; airbrush artist Shade Tree Creations, Inc., Gainesville, 1995, Cain Studios, Inc., Gainesville, 1994; artist, art dir. Themeworks, Inc., High Springs, Fla., 1997-98. Illustrator covers Horizons, 1995, Salamander, 1994, (Best in the West 1st pl. award 1984); painter set design Spunk, 1994. Donator art works and graphic illustrations Dance Alive, Gainesville, 1994, 95, Artitorium Coop. Gallery, Gainesville, 1988, 89, Greens of Alachua's Celebration of Diversity, Gainesville, 1994; artist, rep. of women's issues NOW, 1996. Recipient first pl. Sunday Afternoon With the Artist, Flagler County Art League, 2001, Spring Art Show, Millenium Art Guild, 2002; coll. scholar Lions Club, 1984. Democrat. Avocations: swimming, canoeing, dance, camping, writing. Home: 44 Bracken Ln Palm Coast FL 32137-8770

WIGGLEWORTH, MARGARET, property manager; b. Potomac, Md. Student, U. Md. Staff mem. judiciary com. and govtl. affairs com. Senator Charles McC. Mathias, Jr., Md., 1980—85; asst. dir. nat. affairs NPR, 1985—87; exec. dir. U.S. Coalition Svc. Industries, Inc., 1987—98; pres., CEO Colliers Internat. Property Consultants USA Inc., Boston, 1998—. Office: Colliers Internat Property Consultants USA Inc 20th Fl 50 Milk St Boston MA 02109

WIGHT, JULIA HELEN, secondary school educator; b. Rochford, England, May 19, 1945; arrived in US, 1965; d. Sigmund and Marion St. Bride Kohn; m. Richard Gordon Wight, June 8, 1968. BA in Art History, U. Wash., 1974, EdM, 1976. Cert. tchr. Montessori, 1965. Tchr. N.W. Montessori Sch., Seattle, 1966—74, asst. prin., 1976—79, prin., 1979—85, tchr., 1985—87; tutor Seattle, 1987—90; tchr. Eton Sch., Bellevue, Wash., 1985—3198; pres. Who's New Internat. Women's Club, Panama City, Panama, 1995—98. Cons., lectr. in field. Mem.: Pacific N.W. Montessori Tchrs. Assn. (pres.). Democrat. Episcopalian. Avocations: walking, languages, watercolors. Home: 4163 Beach Dr SW # 301 Seattle WA 98116

WIGHTMAN, ANN, lawyer; b. Dayton, Ohio, July 29, 1958; d. William L. and Mary Ann (Lamb) W. AB, Ohio U., 1980; JD, Case Western Res. U., 1984. Bar: Ohio 1984, U.S. Dist. Ct. (so. dist.) Ohio 1984, U.S. Ct. Appeals (6th cir.) 1991, U.S. Ct. Appeals (7th cir.) 1992, U.S. Supreme Ct. 1993. Assoc. Smith & Schnacke, Dayton, 1984-89; sr. assoc. Faruki Gilliam & Ireland, Dayton, 1989-91, ptnr., 1991—. Adj. prof. U. Dayton Sch. Law, 1988-93; chmn. Artemis House, Inc., Dayton, 1988-90, bd. dirs., 1985-95; arbitrator Am. Arbitration Assn.; mem., bd. dirs. Legal Aid Soc. Dayton, Inc., 1996—; bd. dirs. Impact Weekly. Mem. Vol. Lawyer's Project, Dayton, 1988-96; mem. Challenge 95 Task Force, Dayton, 1989-90, Up and Comer, Dayton, 1990; vol. arbitrator Montgomery County Common Pleas Ct., 1989—; bd. dirs. ACLU of Ohio Found., 1991-94; mem. Leadership, Dayton, 1992. Mem. ABA (trial and environ. sects.), Ohio Bar Assn., Phi Beta Kappa. Home: 240 W Dixon Ave Dayton OH 45419-2902 Office: Faruki Gilliam & Ireland 10 N Ludlow Shl Ste 500 Dayton OH 45402-1854

WIGINTON, CHRISTINE SHERRILL, elementary school educator; b. Odessa, Tex., Nov. 25, 1968; d. Virginia and Ronnie Henderson; m. Jeff Keith Wiginton, Nov. 22, 1971. BS, WTSU, Canyon, 1994. Cert. elem. math. tchr. Tex., 1994. 4th grade tchr. Greenwood Ind. Sch. Dist., Midland, Tex., 1994—96, 5th grade math and sci. tchr., 1996—97, 4th grade tchr., 1997—. Sunday sch. tchr. First Bapt. Ch., Midland, Tex., 2002—03. Mem.: Delta Kappa Gamma (life; pres. 2002—). Baptist. Avocations: reading, scrapbooking, gardening.

WIIEST, JOAN ELOISE, secondary school educator; b. Curtis, Nebr., Nov. 26, 1944; d. Edgar William and Muriel Elsie (Wells) Harbert; m. Ronald Lorraine Wiiest; children: William Andrew, Michael Adrian, Charles Arthur, Kenneth Arlynn, Stephen August, Loraine Aloise, Matthew Anders. Grad., McCook (Nebr.) Jr. Coll., 1964; BS, U. Nebr., 1971. Elem. sch. tchr., Utica, Nebr., 1964—75; K-6 tchr. country sch., Moorefield, Nebr., 1975—85; K-6 resource tchr. Curtis, Nebr., 1985—90; K-12 resource tchr., 1990—98; 7-12 resource tchr., 1998—. Organizational coord. Stockville (Nebr.) Little League, 1993—2003; foster parent, 2001—; fellowship chmn. St. John's Ch., Curtis, 1993—2003. Avocations: gardening, sewing, sports with kids, band events. Office: Medicine Valley Jr Sr High Sch PO Box 9 Curtis NE 69025

WIJNBERG, SANDRA S. professional services company executive; BA English, UCLA; MBA, U. So. Calif., L.A. With Morgan Stanley & Co. Inc.; joined PepsiCo as v.p., treas., 1994; sr. v.p., CFO KFC Corp. Divsn.; sr. v.p., treas. Tricon Global Restaurants Inc, 1997—2000; sr. v.p., CFO Marsh & McLennan Cos., N.Y.C., 2000—. Bd. dirs. Pvt. Sector Coun., 2001—, Tyco Internat. Ltd., 2003—. Corp. adv. bd. N.Y.C. Ballet. Office: Marsh & McLennan Co 1166 6th Ave New York NY 10036*

WILAMOWSKI, DORIS, psychotherapist; b. N.Y.C., Aug. 18, 1950; d. Samuel and Fay (Kesner) W.; children: Stephanie, Jacquelyn. BA magna cum laude, U. Conn., 1972; MSW, Columbia U., 1974. Cert. social worker, N.Y. Clin. social worker Manhattan VAMC, N.Y.C., 1974—86; pvt. practice N.Y.C., 1977—; critical care cons. Estee Lauder, N.Y.C., 2001—, Clear Channel, N.Y.C., 2001—. Cons. Ctr. Law and Social Work, N.Y.C., 1977-78, U. Coll. Hosp., London, 1981; group leader, advisor Galsworthy House, London, 1981; seminar leader Hadassah, Short Hills-Millburn, N.J., 1982; adj. prof. N.Y.U. Sch. Social Work, N.Y.C., 1986-87; psychotherapist Mental Health Consultation Ctr., N.Y.C., Theodore Reik Consultation Ctr., N.Y.C. Advisor Murray Hill Mental Health Adv. Com., N.Y.C., 1979-86, Psychology Today, The 2004 Handbook of Therapists, Am.'s Best Therapists. Mem. NASW, Phi Beta Kappa, Phi Kappa Phi. Avocation: violin. E-mail: violinist@optonline.net.

WILBANKS, JANICE PEGGY, special education educator; b. Boaz, Ala., Oct. 20, 1962; d. Olen Toliver and Evelyne Ziddie Brown; m. Charles Ray Ledon Wilbanks Sr., Nov. 4, 1978; 1 child, Charles Ray Ledon Jr. AS cum laude, N.E. State Coll., 1992; BSc in Edn., Athens State Coll., 1994; MA, U. Ala., 1997. Spl. edn. tchr. State of Ga., Atlanta, 1994—, State of Ala., Montgomery, Ala., 1994—. EBD tchr. Pennville Elem., Summerville, Ga., 1999—2000. Mem.: Ga. Assn. Edn. Baptist. Avocations: reading, gardening, swimming, painting. Home: 1801 Adamsburg Rd E Fort Payne AL 35967

WILBER, CLARE MARIE, musician, educator; b. Denver, Mar. 21, 1928; d. Thomas A. and Kathleen M. (Brennan) O'Keefe; m. Charles Grady Wilber, June 14, 1952 (dec. 1998); children: Maureen, Charles, Michael, Thomas (dec.), Kathleen, Aileen, John Joseph. AB, Loretto Heights Coll., 1948; MS, Fordham U., 1950; MM, Colo. State U., 1972. Instr. biology and music various colls. and univs., 1951-83; mgr. Ft. Collins (Colo.) Symphony, 1969-81, exec. dir., 1981-85, exec. dir. emerita, 1985—; pvt. music instr. Ft. Collins, 1973—. Trustee Ft. Collins Symphony, 1986-95, mem. young artist competition com., 1985—. Composer Fantasie Romantique, 1972, Mass in D, 1980, Seascapes for Suzanne, 1988, Panoramas for Polly, 1990, Journeys for Jennifer, 1994, Augustine's Lament, 1996, Collage for Cynthia, 1997, Daydreams for Drew, 2001. Mem. adv. coun. Ft. Collins [illegible], 1972—74, mem. adv. bd. Children's Sch. of Sci., Woods Hole, Mass., 1965—95. Recipient AT&T Crystal Clef award, 1982, Clare Wilber award named in her honor, Ft, Collins Symphony, 1992. Mem. Ft. Collins Music Tchrs. Assn. (treas. 1984-90), Colo. State Music Tchrs. Assn., Music Tchrs. Nat. Assn. (cert. music tchr. 1978—), Marine Biol. Lab. Assocs., Cosmos Club (assoc.), Sigma Xi (assoc.), Delta Omicron (local chpt. pres. 1970-72, sec. 1988—, Spl. Svc. award 1974, Star of Delta Omicron award 1995). Republican. Roman Catholic. Home and Office: 900 Edwards St Fort Collins CO 80524-3824

WILBUR, JANIS A. financial consultant, sales professional; b. Canadian, Tex., June 18, 1940; d. Harry Samuel Jr. and Margaret Hervey Wilbur; m. Martin Alfred Wasserman, Oct. 18, 1969 (div. Dec. 1981); 1 child, Paul Scott Wasserman. Student, U. Hawaii, 1958; BS in Commerce, Tex. Christian U., 1962. Cert. sr. advisor. Exec. asst. First Nat. Bank, Dallas, 1962-65, So. Union Gas, Dallas, 1965-69; adminstrv. sec. IBM, Armonk, N.Y., 1969-72; owner Leisure Sports Sys., Dallas, 1972-79; sec. to econometrics prof. So. Meth. U., Dallas, 1989-95; part time sales assoc. Neiman Marcus, Dallas, 1989—; registered rep., cert. sr. advisor First Dallas Securities, Dallas, 2003—, 2003—. Pub. (quarterly newsletter) The Fin. News RE-View, 1999. Vol. Am. Cancer Soc., Am. Diabetes Assn., Dallas Crippled Children Soc., Am. Heart Assn., Dallas Ct. Apptd. Spl. Advs., bd. planned giving program, 2002—; mem. women's coun. Dallas Arboretum and Bot. Garden, 2000; organizer ann. golf tournament benefiting Parkinson Disease; vol. Buckner Orphans Home, 2000—01. Mem.: DAR (nat. com. chmn. on Americanism and manual for citizenship 1999, Literacy Challenge chmn. 2001—02, chaplain 2002—, vice regent 2003, regent 2004, Michael Stoner chpt.), NAFE, Internat. Exec. Guild, First Dallas Alumni Club (charter), Park Cities Bapt. Ch. Women's Bible Study, Water Skiing Club, Dallas Skiing Club, Kappa Alpha Theta Alumni (v.p. 1989—99, pres. 2000—01, advisor 2002—, treas. 2003—04). Republican. Baptist. Avocations: tennis, bridge, snow skiing, cooking, water rafting, hiking. Home: 9563 Windy Knoll Dr Dallas TX 75243-7561 Office: First Dallas Securities 2905 Maple Ave Dallas TX 75201 Office Phone: 214-954-1177. Personal E-mail: janiswilbur@sbcglobal.net.

WILBUR, KATHLEEN, state agency administrator; m. Tom Wilbur; children: Thomas, William, Samuel, Raymond. BA, Mich. State U. Chief staff State Senator William Sederburg, Lansing, 1983-90; dir. Mich. Dept. Licensing, Regulation, Lansing, 1991, Mich. Dept. Occupational Profl. Regulation, Lansing, 1991-95; deputy dir. Mich. Dept. Commerce, Lansing, 1991-95, acting dir., 1995-96, dir., 1996, Mich. Dept. Consumer Industry Svcs., Lansing, 1996—. Chmn. MERRA Bd. Trustees, 1996—; mem. Mich. Investment Advisory Com, 1996—; bd. dirs. Mich. State Housing Authority, Mich. Municipal Bond Authority, Mich. State Fair, Women's Caring Program, Mich. Festival. Mem. Mich. State U. Alumni Assn., East Lansing Area Zonta Club. Office: Michigan Dept Consumer & Industry Services PO Box 30004 Lansing MI 48909-7504

WILCOX, DIANE MARIE, educational psychologist, software designer; b. Cin., June 26, 1957; d. Herbert Arthur and Doris Ann Beard; m. Thomas Minshull Wilcox, Sept. 18, 1982; children: Alexandra Frances, Annika Marie. BBA in Bus. Mgmt., Coll. William and Mary, 1979; MA in Ednl. Psychology, U. N.C., 1994, PhD in Ednl. Psychology, 1997. Sales and tech. support corr. Tax Mgmt., Inc., Washington, 1980-82; dist. rep. Bur. Nat. Affairs, Inc., Washington, 1982-86; freelance computer graphic designer, editor Diane Wilcox & Assocs., San Rafael, Calif., 1986-91; instr. psychology King's Coll., Charlotte, N.C., 1995; pres. Mindforge, Inc., Burlington, N.C., 1996-98, Wilcox Instrnl. Media, LLC, Hillsborough, N.C., 1998—; instnl. design mgr. Autodesk, Inc., San Rafael, 2000—. Designer ednl. CD-ROM Mindforge Fractions, 1998. Cons. for gifted and talented programs River Mill Charter Sch., Saxapahaw, N.C., 1999-2000; vol. art instr. Grady Brown ELem. Sch., Hillsborough, N.C., 1997-98. Mem. APA, Am. Ednl. Rsch. Assn., Internat. Soc. for Performance Improvement. Avocations: art, music, dance. E-mail: drwilcox@wilcoxmedia.com.

WILCOX, HELENA MARGUERITA (RITA), music educator; b. Manhattan, Kans., Feb. 16, 1930; d. Virgil Otis Jones and Helena Mary Viers-Jones; children: Charles E., Marguerita E., Patricia A. MusB, State U. Iowa, 1952, MA, 1959. Cert. music tchr. Ariz., 1959, Calif., 1967, Jr. Coll. Calif., 1972. Pvt. kindergarten, Springerville, Ariz., 1959—60; art supr. Yuma (Ariz.) Elem. Sch. Dist., 1960—67; violin tchr. Ariz. Western Cmty. Coll., Yuma, 1965—67; string instrument tchr. Stockton (Calif.) Unified Sch. Dist., 1967—2002; Suzuki violin tchr. San Joaquin Delta Coll., Stockton, 1972—; orch. Stockton (Calif.) Symphony Assn., 1967—; tchr. summer arts Stockton (Calif.) Arts Commn.; organ. Symphony Orch., Yuma, 1962—67. Production grant, Stockton Unified Sch. Dist., 1980. Mem.: Calif. Tchrs. Assn., Suzuki Assn. of the Am., Music Tchrs. Assn., Stockton Br. (pres. 2003), Am. String Tchrs. Assn. (pres. 1975). Democrat. Unitarian. Home: 2348 W Alpine Ave Stockton CA 95204

WILCOX, MAUD, editor; b. N.Y.C., Feb. 14, 1923; d. Thor Fredrik and Gerda (Ysberg) Eckert; m. Edward T. Wilcox, Feb. 9, 1944; children: Thor (dec.), Bruce, Eric, Karen. AB summa cum laude, Smith Coll., 1944; A.M., Harvard U., 1945. Teaching fellow Harvard U., 1945-46, 48-51; instr. English Smith Coll., Northampton, Mass., 1947-48, Wellesley Coll., Mass., 1951-52; exec. editor Harvard U. Press, 1958-66, humanities editor, 1966-73, editor-in-chief, 1973—89; freelance editorial cons. Cambridge, 1989—; ret. Cons., panelist NEH, Washington, 1974-76, 82-84; cons. Radcliffe Pub. Course, 1991. Mem. MLA (com. scholarly edits. 1982-86), Assn. Am. Univ. Presses (chair com. admissions and standards 1976-77, v.p. 1978-79, chair program com. 1981-82), Phi Beta Kappa. Democrat. Episcopalian. Home and Office: 63 Francis Ave Cambridge MA 02138-1911 E-mail: maudwilcox@post.harvard.edu.

WILCOX, SHIRLEY JEAN LANGDON, genealogist; b. Arcata, Calif., Dec. 10, 1942; d. Elmore Harold and Alberta May (Starkey) Langdon; m. Wayne Kent Wilcox, June 22, 1963; 1 child, Harold Bonner. BS, U. Md., 1964. Cert. Bd. for Certification of Genealogists. Tchr. Prince George's County (Md.) Sch. System, 1964-67, substitute tchr., 1968-73; profl. genealogist Lanham, Md., Arlington, Va., 1973—; genealogy tchr. Fairfax County Pub. Schs., 1995-99. Level II coord. Mid-Atlantic Genealogy and History Inst., George Mason U., Fairfax, Va., 1986; trustee bd. for Certification of Genealogists, 2000—. Editor: A Bibliography of Published Genealogical Source Records, Prince George's County, Maryland, 1975, Prince George's County Land Records, Vol. A, 1696-1702, 1976, 1850 Census Prince George's County, Maryland, 1978, 1828 Tax List Prince George's County, Maryland, 1985. Elder Presbyn. Ch., 1970-73, 95-98. Fellow Nat. Geneal. Soc. (chmn. conf. program subcom. 1990, 2d v.p. 1990-94, councilor 1994-96, pres. 1996-2000); mem. DAR (libr. Belle Air chpt. 1985—, Outstanding Jr. Mem. award 1979), Assn. Profl. Genealogists (pres. 1991-93, pres. Nat. Capital area chpt. 1994-96, Grahame Thomas Smallwood Jr. award of merit 1995), Va. Geneal. Soc. (gov. 2001—), Prince George's County Geneal. Soc. (pres. 1973, 75-76, book rev. editor 1976-96, Jane Roush McCafferty award of excellence 1985), Fairfax Geneal. Soc. (pres. 1986-89), Soc. Mayflower Descs. in D.C., Paperweight Collectors Assn. (pres. Md.-D.C.-Va. chpt. 1988-90), Clay Family Soc. (dir. 2002—), numerous others. Avocation: collecting paperweights. Home: 1500 23rd St S Arlington VA 22202-1523

WILCOXSON, CAROL ANN, piano teacher; b. Greenville, S.C., Feb. 15, 1943; d. Carroll Raleigh and Dorothy Ann (Brunson) Greene; children: Danielle Elise, Paul Edwin. BS, East Tex. State U., 1965; MLA, So. Meth. U., 1996. Cert. Music Tchr.'s Nat. Assn., Am. Nat. Coll. Musicians' judge (piano). Caseworker Buckner Children's Home, Dallas, 1965-66; caseworker, supr. Dept. Human Resources, Dallas, El Paso, Tex., 1967-74; pvt. practice piano tchr. Dallas, 1981—; pianist Old San Francisco Steak House, Dallas, 1995—. Vol., interviewer White Rock Ctr. of Hope-Food Pantry & Short-Term Help, Dallas, 1989-93. Mem. Am. Coll. Musicians (piano guild judge 1989—), ADHD Parent Support (bd. dirs 1990-95), Dallas Music Tchr. Assn. (bd. dirs. 1996-2000), Mesquite (Tex.) Area Music Tchrs. (pres., v.p. 1998). Methodist. Avocations: hiking, reading, research study, creative writing, travel. Home and Office: 11108-B Valley Dale Dallas TX 75230

WILCOXSON, KATHLEEN LOUISE, state legislator, educator; b. Lawton, Okla., Jan. 2, 1948; d. Lloyd and Susan McCullough; m. Lunden Wilcoxson; 1 child, Stacy. BS in Elem. Edn., MS in Spl. Edn., EdD in Curriculum and Instrn. Former tchr.; mem. Okla. State Senate, 1997—, mem. Edn. Com., Fin. Com., Tourism Com., Vets. Affairs Com. Mem. C. of C., Am. Bus. Women's Assn., Rep. Women's Club. Avocations: gardening, reading. Office: State Capitol Bldg 2300 N Lincoln Blvd Rm 533 Oklahoma City OK 73105-4805

WILDASIN, ELIZABETH SEWELL, band director; b. Easton, Md., July 22, 1950; m. Newton Edward Wildasin, June 25, 1972; children: Lelia Marie, John Edward. BA, Western Md. Coll., Westminster, 1972; MEd, Salisbury U., Md., 1976. Advanced profl. cert. Md. State Dept. of Edn., 1972. Orch./gen. music tchr. Perry Hall Jr. H.S., Md., 1972—73; band/gen. music tchr. Riverview Mid. Sch., Denton, Md., 1973—76; music dir. Easton Ch. of the Brethren, Easton, Md., 1980—85; lead tchr., 3-year-olds Presbyn. Nursery Sch., Easton, Md., 1982—85; computer lab coord. Easton Mid. Sch., Md., 1985—86; band/vocal/gen. music tchr. Chapel Dist. Elem. Sch., Cordova, Md., 1986—96, instrnl. facilitator, 1996—2002; band dir. St. Michaels Mid./H.S., Saint Michaels, Md., 2002—. Music tchr. team leader Talbot County Pub. Sch., Easton, Md., 1994—96; county liaison Md. Music Educators Assn., 2002—; adv. com. mem. Cmty. Alliance for the Performing Arts, Easton, Md., 2002—. Music com. chair, choir mem., children's choir accompanist St. Mark's United Meth. Ch., Easton, Md., 1985—2003. Named Outstanding Arts Educator, Talbot County Arts Coun., 2003; recipient Extra Mile award, Talbot County Pub. Schs., 1989. Mem.: Music Educators Nat. Conf., Md. Music Educators Assn. (county liaison 2002—03), NEA, Md. State Tchrs.' Assn., Talbot County Edn. Assn., Delta Omicron (life). Avocations: walking, reading. Office: Saint Michaels Middle/High School 200 Seymour Ave Saint Michaels MD 21663 Office Phone: 410-745-2852.

WILDE, MARY, secondary school educator; BS, Concordia Tchrs. Coll.; MS, U. Mo.; specialist degree, West Ga. Coll. Elem. tchr.; mid. sch. tchr. Booth Mid. Sch., Peachtree City, Ga., 1983—. Coach team Sci. Olympiad. Named Outstanding Earth Sci. Tchr., 1992. Mem. Ga. Sci. Tchrs. Assn. (pres.-elect). Office: Booth Mid Sch 250 Peachtree PkySouth Peachtree City GA 30269-1740

WILDE, PATRICIA, retired artistic director; b. Ottawa, Ont., Can., July 16, 1928; m. George Bardyguine; children: Anya Bardyguine, Youri Bardyguine. Dancer Am. Concert Ballet, Marquis de Cuevas Ballet Internat., N.Y.C., 1944-45, Ballet Russe de Monte Carlo, N.Y.C., 1945-49, Roland Petit's Ballet Paris, Met. Ballet Britain, London, 1949-50; prin. ballerina N.Y.C. Ballet, 1950-65; dir. Harkness Sch. Ballet, N.Y.C., 1965-67; ballet mistress, tchr. Am. Ballet Theatre, N.Y.C., 1969-77, dir. Am. Ballet Theatre Sch., N.Y.C., 1977-82; artistic dir. Pitts. Ballet Theatre, 1982-97, artistic adviser, master tchr., 1997—. Tchr. Am. Ballet Theatre, 1969—77, Joffrey scholarship program, N.Y.C. Ballet, 1968—69; established Sch. of Grand Theatre of Geneva, 1968—69; adjudicator Regional Ballet in Am. S.E. and S.W., 1969—82; choreographer N.Y. Philharmonic; guest tchr. various ballet cos. and colls.; trustee Dance U.S.A.; panelist Nat. Choreographic Project. Recipient Leadership award in Arts and Letters YWCA, 1990, Pitts. Woman of Yr. in Arts award, 1993, Cultural award for outstanding contbns. to cultural climate of region Pitts. Ctr. for Arts, 1997, History Makers award in arts and letters Sen. John Heinz History Ctr. and the Hist. Soc. Western Pa., 1999. Office: Pitts Ballet Theatre 2900 Liberty Ave Pittsburgh PA 15201-1511

WILDEISEN, REBECCA ALYSSA, psychologist, educator; b. St. Louis, Mo., June 17, 1970; d. Joseph William Wildeisen and Helene Marilyn Meyer. BA, U. Mo., St. Louis, 1993; PsyD, Ill. Sch. Profl Psychology, 2000. Lic. clin. psychologist Ill., cert. alcohol and drug counselor Ill. Counselor, advocate St. Marthas Hall Battered Women's Shelter, St. Louis, 1990—94; psychiat. aide Hawthorn Children's Psychiat. Hosp., St. Louis, 1992—94; domestic violence-substance abuse facilitator Pillars Comty. Mental Health Ctr., Summit, Ill., 2000—01; mental health counselor Women's Treatment Ctr., Chgo., 2001—02; therapist Alexian Bros. Behavioral Health Hosp., Hoffman Estates, Ill.; clin. psychologist Clarus Ctr., Naperville, Ill., 2001—. Adj. prof. Nat.-Louis U., Wheaton, Ill., 2001—03; co-chair domestic violence-substance abuse com. DuPage County Family Violence Coord. Counsel, Wheaton, 2002—03. Mem.: APA, Ill. Group Psychotherapy Soc. Jewish. Avocations: martial arts, dance, singing. Office: Clarus Ctr Ste 205 1220 Iroquois Chicago IL 60653

WILDER, DOROTHY MAY, artist, educator, librarian; b. Castalia, N.C. d. David Lee and Leila Pleasant (May) W.; m. Frederick Howell Fornoff (div.). BA, U. N.C., 1981; MFA, Carnegie Mellon U., 1983; MLS, SUNY, Albany, 1997; ArtsD, NYU, N.Y.C., 2001. Lectr. in art, dir. ceramics studio U. Pitts., Johnstown, Pa., 1975-79; asst. prof. art Rensselaer Poly. Inst., Troy, N.Y., 1983-90; assoc. prof. art Ea. Wash. U., Cheney, 1991-95, Hartwick Coll., Oneonta, N.Y., 1995; adj. faculty art The New Sch./Parsons Sch. Design, N.Y.C., 1995-98; mus. libr. 20th Century Art Libr. Met. Mus. Art, N.Y.C., 1997-98; libr. Louisburg (N.C.) Pub. Libr., 2001, Franklin County (NC) Libr., 2002—. Archival/artistic cons. Nat. Mus. Dance, Saratoga Springs, N.Y., 1997-98; lectr., presenter in field. One woman shows at U. Pitts., Johnstown, 1985, 86, 88, Rensselaer County Coun. Arts, Troy, N.Y., 1985, Shelnutt Gallery, Troy, 1986, Louisburg (N.C.) Coll. Fine Arts Ctr. Gallery, 1987, Chatham Coll., Pitts., 1990, SOHO 20, N.Y.C., 2002; installation at Cedar Rock, N.C., 1995, Fulton St. Gallery, Troy, 1998; exhibited at numerous group exhbns., including Greene Gallery, Rensselaer Poly. Inst., Troy, 1985, Albany (N.Y.) Inst. History and Art, 1986, Russell Sage Coll. Gallery, Troy, 1987, Green Gables Mountain Playhouse, Jennerstown, Pa., 1988, Cooperstown (N.Y.) Art Assn. Exhbn., 1988, U. N.C., Chapel Hill, 1989, Three-Rivers Arts Festivals, Pitts., 1979, 81, 82, 85, 88, 89, Rice Gallery, Albany Inst. History and Art, 1989, 91, Schenectady (N.Y.) Mus., 1990, Campo San Giacomo dell'Orio, Venice, Italy, 1990, 92, 93, Ea. Wash. U., Cheney, 1992, Casa Italiana Zerelli-Marimó, N.Y.C., 1995, Carolina Club at George Watts Alumni Ctr., U. N.C., 1995, Parson's Sch. Design, N.Y.C., 1998, FultonSt. Gallery, Troy, 1998, others. Recipient Paul Beer Trust mini grant Rensselaer Poly. Inst., Troy, 1985, 86, 87; Faculty Rsch. grantee Ea. Wash. U., Cheney, 1993. Avocations: tree farming, gardening. Home: 5568 NC 56 Hwy East Castalia NC 27816

WILDER, ELAINE KATHRYN, university official; b. N.Y.C., Apr. 2, 1942; d. Edward Z. and Kathryn A. (Katsaras) Pichler; m. Edward H. Wilder, Jr., June 18, 1983; children: Kathryn Walker Norris, Audrey Walker, David Walker, Frank Scott Wilder II, Edward H. Wilder III, Lynn Wilder-Mullin. Grad. in respiratory therapy, Kennebec Valley Tech. Coll., Fairfield, Maine, 1983; AS in Gen. Studies, U. Maine, Augusta, 1995. Nat. cert. respiratory therapy technician. Physician and clinic asst. ARC, various locations, 1965-77; coord. archives Waterville (Maine) Pub. Libr., 1981; faculty asst., coord. tutoring svcs., tutor U. Maine, Augusta, 1984—. Bd. dirs. Augusta Area Food Bank,1986—; mem. U. Maine Sys. Disabilities Network, Orono, 1994—; workshop presenter in field. Bd. dirs. St. Mark's Home, Augusta, 1984—, Belgrade Regional Health Ctr., Belgrade Lakes, Maine, 1995—; mem. planning bd. St. Mark's Home for Women, Augusta, 1994—; vol., mediator Consumer Fraud divsn. Atty. Gen.'s Office, State of Maine. Mem. Am. Assn. for Respiratory Care, Learning Disabilities Assn. Maine, Phi Theta Kappa. Office: U Maine 46 University Dr Augusta ME 04330-9488

WILDER, ELEANOR MARIE (NORA ROBERTS WILDER), writer; b. Washington, Oct. 10, 1950; d. Bernard Edward Robertson and Eleanor Margaret Harris; m. Ronald Eugene Aufdem-Brinke, Aug. 17, 1968 (div. 1985); children: Daniel, Jason; m. Bruce Allen Wilder, July 6, 1985. Grad. high sch., Silver Spring, Md.; writer, 1979—. Author: Homeport, 1998, The Reef, 1998, River's End, 1999, Carolina Moon, 2000, others; (writing as J.D. Robb) Judgement in Death, 1990, Conspiracy in Death, 1999, Witness in Death, 2000. First inductee Romance Writers of Am. Hall of Fame, 1986; recipient Waldenbooks award, 1985, 86, 88, 91, 92, 94, B. Dalton award, 1990, 91, 92, Centennial award, Waldenbooks Lifetime Achievement award. Mem. Washington Romance Writers, Romance Writers Am. (Lifetime Achievement award), Mystery Writers Am. Democrat. Roman Catholic. Avocations: dancing, reading, films.

WILDER, EUNICE, city official; BA, Howard U., 1959. Treas. Office of Treas., City of Richmond, Va. Office: City of Richmond Office of the Treas Rm 107 900 E Broad St City Hall Richmond VA 23219 also: PO Box 26505 Richmond VA 23261-6505 E-mail: ewilder@ci.richmond.va.us.

WILDER, GINGER, newscaster; B in Broadcast News, U. Ga. Intern Fitzgerald Herald Leader; achor, reporter CNN Affiliate, Athens, Ga.; edn. reporter Channel 4-Cables News, Cumming Ga.; reporter WSAV-TV, Savannah, Ga., 2000—. Avocations: reading, travel, family, pets. Office: WSAV-TV3 1430 E Victory Dr Savannah GA 31404

WILDEROTTER, MARY AGNES, cable television executive; b. Neptune, N.J., Feb. 9, 1955; d. Dennis James and Constance Rosemary (Shields) Sullivan; m. Philip Jay Wilderotter; children: Christopher, Daniel. BA in Econs., Holy Cross Coll., 1977. Accts. receivable supr. CableData, Sacramento, 1979-80, mgr. acctg. svcs., 1980-82, mgr. reg. support, 1982, mktg. mgr., 1982-83, dir. mktg., 1983, dir. nat. accts., 1983-85, v.p., 1985—. Bd. dirs. Phoenix Cable Ptnrs., San Rafael, Calif., 1988—, Satellite Video Ctr., Rancho Cordova, Calif., 1988—, CAbleData Europe Ltd., Leeds, Eng., 1989—. Mem. Nat. Cable TV Assn. (bd. dirs. 1987—), Women in Cable (exec. mem.), Cable TV Adminstrn. & Mktg. Soc., Calif. Cable TV Assn., Nat. Acad. Cable Programming. Republican. Roman Catholic. Office: CableData 11020 Sun Center Dr Rancho Cordova CA 95670-6184

WILDING, DIANE, marketing, financial and information systems executive; b. Chicago Heights, Ill., Nov. 7, 1942; d. Michael Edward and Katherine Surian; m. Manfred Georg Wilding, May 7, 1975 (div. 1980). BSBA in Acctg. magna cum laude, No. Ill. U., 1963; postgrad., U. Chgo., 1972-74; cert. in German lang., Goethe Inst., Rothenburg, Germany, 1984; cert. in internat. bus. German, Goethe Inst., Atlanta, 1994; cert. in Web page design, Kennesaw State U., 2000. Lic. cosmetologist. Systems engr. IBM, Chgo., 1963-68; data processing mgr. Am. Res. Corp., Chgo., 1969-72; system R & D project mgr. Continental Bank, Chgo., 1972-75; fin. industry mktg. rep. IBM Can., Ltd., Toronto, Ont., 1976-79; regional telecom. mktg. exec. Control Data Corp., Atlanta, 1980-84; gen. mgr. The Plant Plant, [illegible] 1986-93; SAP cons., IBM, Atlanta, 1993—. Pioneer installer on-line Automatic Teller Machines, Pos Equipment. Author: The Canadian Payment System: An International Perspective, 1977. Mem. Chgo. Coun. on Fgn. Rels.; bd. dirs. Easter House Adoption Agy., Chgo., 1974-76. Mem. Internat. Brass Soc., Goethe Inst., Mensa. Clubs: Ponte Verde (Fla.); Royal Ont. Yacht, Libertyville Racquet. Avocations: travel, gourmet cooking, foreign languages, antiques. Home: PO Box 723055 Atlanta GA 31139-0055 Office: IBM 1600 Riveredge Pkwy NW Atlanta GA 30328-4697 E-mail: wilding@usa.com.

WILDS, KAREN R. housing authority executive; b. Newport News, Va. BS Govtl. Adminstrn., Christopher Newport U., 1976; M of Urban Studies, Old Dominion U., 1983. Cmty. devel. dir. Newport News (Va.) Redevel. and Housing Authority, 1985—99, exec. dir., 1999—. Mem. VA Gen. Assembly Housing Study Commn. Com. on Eminent Domain, Richmond, 1999—. Vice dhmn., bd. dirs. Office of Human Affairs, Newport News, 2000—02. Mem.: Nat. Assn. Housing and Cmty. Devel. Ofcls. (mem. cmty. revitalization and devel. com. 2001—).

WILDT, JANETH KAE, small business owner; b. Bath, Mich., July 15, 1950; d. Gareth Macey and Mary Elizabeth (Shipley) Harte; children: Kimberly Kae, Larry Micheal. Student, Lansing C.C. Owner Ceramics By George, Bath, Mich., owner, caretaker; truck driver RJ Trucking, Inc., Auburndale, Mich., ETV Trucking, Inc., Grand Rapids, Mich. Avocations: cooking, yardwork, ceramics. Home and Office: Ceramics by George 13367 Center Rd Bath MI 48808

WILE, DAWN M. protective services official; d. James F. and Dolores A. Wile. BS in Biology, Coll. New Rochelle, 1984; student, U. New Haven, 1997—2004, student in Forensic Sci. and Criminology, 2002. Cert. fire/arson investigation U. New Haven, 2002, fire sci./tech. U. New Haven, 2000, fire marshal/inspector Office of the State Fire Marshal, Conn., 1998. Paramedic Profl. Ambulance Svc., West Hartford, Conn., 1885—1992; firefighter, paramedic East Hartford (Conn.) Fire Dept., 1989—98; dep. fire marshal East Hartford Fire Dept., 1998—. Recipient Cert. Acad. Achievement, Office Of The State Fire Marshal, 1998; Grad. fellow, U. New Haven, 1999—2000. Mem.: Capitol Region Fire Marshal's Assn., Conn. Fire Marshal's Assn., Internat. Assn. Arson Investigators (Conn. chpt.), New Eng. Assn. Fire Marshals, Beta Beta Beta (sec. 1982—83, v.p. 1983—84, Theta Epsilon chpt.), Alpha Phi Sigma (Alpha Tau chpt.). Independent. Achievements include research in effects of interferon on schistosoma mansoni infections in mice. Avocations: greyhound rescue, Karate (black belt), photography, martial arts, scuba diving. Office: East Hartford Fire Dept 758 Main St East Hartford CT 06108

WILENSKY, GAIL ROGGIN, economist, researcher; b. Detroit, June 14, 1943; d. Albert Alan and Sophia (Blitz) Roggin; m. Robert Joel Wilensky, Aug. 4, 1963; children: Peter Benjamin, Sara Elizabeth. AB with honors, U. Mich., 1964, MA in Econs., 1965, PhD in Econs., 1968; hon. degree, Hahnemann U., 1993, Rush U., 1997, U. of Scis., Phila., 2002. Economist President's Commn. on Income Maintenance Programs; exec. dir. Md. Coun. of Econ. Advs., 1969-71; sr. rschr. Urban Inst., Washington, 1971-73; assoc. rsch. scientist, pub. policy and pub. health U. Mich., Ann Arbor, 1973-75, vis. asst. prof. econs., 1973-75; sr. rsch. mgr. Nat Ctr. for Health Svcs. Rsch., Hyattsville, Md., 1975-83; assoc. profl. lectr. George Washington U., 1976-78; v.p. div. health affairs Project HOPE, Millwood, Va., 1983-90; adminstr. Health Care Fin. Adminstrn., Washington, 1990-92; dep. asst. to the pres. for policy devel. White House, 1992-93; sr. fellow Project HOPE, Bethesda, Md., 1993—, chair phys. payment rev. com., 1995-97; chmn. Medicare Payment Adv. Commn., 1997—2001; co-chair Pres.'s Task Force to Improve Healthcare Delivery for Vets., 2001—03. Contbr. 100 articles in field to profl. jours. Vol. Am. Heart Assn., 1980-85, bd. dirs., 2002—; mem. health adv. com. Compt. Gen. U.S., 1987-90; bd. dirs. United Healthcare Corp., Cephalon, ManorCare, Gentiva Health Svcs., Inc., Quest Diagnostics; mem. vis. com. med. sch. U. Mich., 1993-97; trustee United Mine Workers Am. Retirement Fund, 1993—. Flinn Found. disting. scholar, 1985; recipient Dean Conley award Am. Coll. Healthcare Execs., 1989. Mem. NAS (mem. inst. medicine 1989—), Am. Econ. Assn. (women's com. 1982-84), Fedn. Orgn. of Profl. Women (chmn. econ. task force 1981-83), Am. Statis. Assn., Nat. Tax Assn., Washington Women Economists, Assn. Health Svc. Rsch. (dir. 1984-87), Found. Health Svc. Rsch. (bd. dir. 1987-90), Acad. Health (chair bd. dir. 2000—, Cosmos Club (Washington). Home: 2807 Battery Pl NW Washington DC 20016-3439

WILEY, DIANNE, aeronautical engineer; PhD in Applied Mechanics, UCLA; student, Def. Systems Mgmt. Coll., 1996. With Northrop Grumman, mgr. airframe tech., sr. tech. specialist on B-2 program; program mgr. Boeing Phantom Wks., Seal Beach, Calif. Office: Boeing Phantom Works PO Box 2515 Seal Beach CA 90740

WILFERT, CATHERINE M. medical association administrator, medical educator; Asst. prof. pediatrics Duke U., 1969-80, prof. pediatrics and microbiology, chief pediatric infectious diseases, 1980-98, prof. emeritus; sci. dir. Elizabeth Glaser Pediat. AIDS Found., Santa Monica, Calif., 1997—. Mem. Inst. Medicine. Office: Elizabeth Glaser Pediatric AIDS Found 2950 31st St Ste 125 Santa Monica CA 90405-3092

WILHELM, GRETCHEN, retired secondary school educator, volunteer; b. Ames, Iowa, Sept. 30, 1938; d. Harley Almey Wilhelm and Orpha Elizabeth Lutton. BS in Math., Iowa State U., 1960; MS in Math., Oreg. State U., 1969. Permanent profl. endorsement for math. grades 7-12 and gen. sci. Iowa, life endorsement math. grades 7-12 and all scis. grades 7-12 Minn. Math. tchr. Shenandoah (Iowa) H.S., 1960—63, Robbinsdale (Minn.) Sr. H.S., 1963—68; jr. mathematician on faculty Inst. Atomic Rsch. Iowa State U., Ames (Iowa) Lab. U.S. Atomic Energy Commn., 1969; math. tchr. Robbinsdale Cooper Sr. High, New Hope, Minn., 1969—94, math. dept. chmn., 1974—76; ret., 1994. Dist. math. curriculum devel. com. Robbinsdale Sch. Dist., New Hope, 1984—89. Election judge, New Hope, 1994, 1996, 1998, 2000; charter mem. Plymouth (Minn.) Creek Christian Ch., 1978, bd. mem., 1978—79, 1982—84, 1989—91, 1997—2001. Recipient NSF Math. Inst. stipend, Oreg. State U., Corvallis, 1962, 1963, 1964, 1965. Mem.: AAUW (life; Mpls. br. bd. dirs., edn. rep. 1997—98), NEA (life), Minn. Geneal. Soc., Iowa Geneal. Soc., Women Descs. Ancient and Hon. Arty. Co., US Daus. War of 1812, Thomas Stanton Soc., Thomas Minor Soc., New Eng. Women Descs., Dau. Am. Colonists, Colonial Dames the XVII Century, Colonial Dames Am., Nat. Soc. DAR (life; chpt. 2nd vice regent 1987—88, chpt. registrar 1988—94, State constn. week chmn. 1991—95, chpt. 1st vice regent 1994—96, state registrar 1995—97, state officers club v.p., chaplain 1995—97, chpt. chaplain 1996—98, state DAR good citizen chmn. 1997—99, chpt. regent 1998—2000, state regent 2001—03, nat. bd. mgmt. 2001—03, charter mem. State Regents Club 2001—, Nat. Officers Club 2001—, hon. state regent 2003—, state membership chmn. 2003—). Republican. Mem. Christian Ch. (Disciples Of Christ). Avocation: geneaology. Home: 3925 Winnetka Ave N Minneapolis MN 55427

WILHELM, KATE (KATY GERTRUDE), author; b. Toledo, June 8, 1920; d. Jesse Thomas and Ann (McDowell) Meredith; m. Joseph B. Wilhelm, May 24, 1947 (div. 1962); children: Douglas, Richard; m. Damon Knight, Feb. 23, 1963; 1 child, Jonathan. PhD in Humanities (hon.), Mich. State U., 1996. Writer, 1956—. Co-dir. Milford Sci. Fiction Writers Conf., 1963-76; lectr. Clarion Fantasy Workshop Mich. State U., 1968-94. Author: More Bitter Than Death, 1962; (with Theodore L. Thomas) The Clone, 1965, The Nevermore Affair, 1966, The Killer Thing, 1967, Let the Fire Fall, 1969, The Year of the Cloud, 1970, Abyss: Two Novellas, 1971, Margaret and I, 1971, City of Cain, 1971, The Clewiston Test, 1976, Where Late the Sweet Birds Sang, 1976, Fault Lines, 1976, Somerset Dreams and Other Fictions, 1978, Juniper Time, 1979; (with Damon Knight) Better Than One, 1980, A Sense of Shadow, 1981, Listen, Listen, 1981, Oh! Susannah, 1982, Welcome Chaos, 1983, Huysman's Pets, 1986, (with Richard Wilhelm) The Hills Are Dancing, 1986, The Hamlet Trap, 1987, Crazy Time, 1988, Dark Door, 1988, Smart House, 1989, Children of the Wind: Five Novellas, 1989, Cambio Bay, 1990, Sweet, Sweet Poison, 1990, Death Qualified, 1991, And the Angels Sing, 1992, Seven Kinds of Death, 1992, Naming the Flowers, 1992, Justice for Some, 1993, The Best Defense, 1994, A Flush of Shadows, 1995, Malice Prepense, 1996, The Good Children, 1998, Defense for the Devil, 1999, No Defense, 2000, The Deepest Water, 2000, Desperate Measures, 2001, Skeletons, 2002, Clear and Convincing Proof, 2003; (multimedia space fantasy) Axoltl, U. Oreg. Art Mus., 1979, (radio play) The Hindenburg Effect, 1985; editor: Nebula Award Stories #9, 1974, Clarion SF, 1976; contbr. articles to popular mags., profl. jours. Mem. Nat. Writers Union, Mystery Writers Am., Authors Guild. Address: 1645 Horn Ln Eugene OR 97404-2957 E-mail: kate@katewilhelm.com.

WILHELMI, CYNTHIA JOY, information technology professional, consultant; Student, Iowa State U., 1964—66, BA in Art and Edn., 1966; MA in Comm., U. Nebr., Omaha, 1996. Master Artist-in-Residence Nebr. Arts Coun., Omaha, 1985—91; grad. tchg. asst., tchg. fellow U. Nebr., Omaha, 1993—95; Family Friends of Eastern Nebr. program coord. Vis. Nurse Assn., Omaha, 1996—97; instr. Midland Luth. Coll., Fremont, Nebr., 1997—99; info. tech. cons., project mgr., test engr., bus. analyst Bass & Assocs., Omaha, 1999—2000; info. tech. cons. Robert Half Internat. Cons., 2000, Maxim Group/TEKSystems, 2000—02, Client Resources Inc., 2003; data mgr. TEKsystems, 2003—; govt. proposal coord. NuGenSof cons. co., 2000—; farmer, 2000—; data mgr. Raytheon, 2003—. Bus. analyst, sr. test engr., project mgmt., third party vendor interface mgmt., CD installation testing, tech. documentation IT data mgr.; govt. info. tech. proposal coord. Editor, pub., contbg. author Salaam mag., 1985-86. Mem. adv. coun. Foster Grandparents, Omaha, 1999—; bd. dirs., pub. rels./publicity chair U. Nebr. Friends of Art, Omaha, 1997-99; bd. dirs. Nebr. SIDS Found., 2002—03. Named Outstanding Grad. Tchg. Asst., U. Nebr., Omaha, 1995, Adm. in the Gt. Navy of Nebr., 1990. Mem. AAUW, Am. Meteor. Soc., Soc. for Tech. Comm. (bd. dirs., chair pub. rels. 1999), Nebr. Adms. Assn., Soc. for Collegiate Journalists (hon.), Phi Delta Gamma, Mensa (Nebr., Western Iowa exec. com. 2003-, SIGHT coord. 2003—, mem. nat. nominating com. 2004). Republican. Address: 13516 Redwood St Omaha NE 68138-6205 E-mail: cwi813@earthlink.net., wilhelmi_c@yahoo.com.

WILHELMI, MARY CHARLOTTE, education educator, college official; b. Williamsburg, Iowa, Oct. 2, 1928; d. Charles E. and Loretto (Judge) Harris; m. Sylvester Lee Wilhelmi, May 26, 1951; children: Theresa Ann, Sylvia Marie, Thomas Lee, Kathryn Lyn, Nancy Louise. BS, Iowa State U., 1950; MA in Edn., Va. Poly. Inst. and State U., 1973, cert. advanced grad. studies, 1978. Edn. coord. Nova Ctr. U. Va., Falls Church, 1969-73; asst. adminstr. Consortium for Continuing Higher Edn. George Mason U., Fairfax, Va., 1973-78, adminstr., asst. prof., 1978-83; dir. coll. mktg., pub. affairs, assoc. prof. No. Va. C.C., Annandale, 1983—. Bd. dirs. No. Va. C.C. Ednl. Found., Inc., No. Va. C.C. Real Estate Found.; v.p. audience devel. Fairfax (Va.) Symphony, 1995—; chmn. Health Systems Agy. No. Va., Fairfax, Va.; mem. George Mason U. Inst. for Ednl. Transformation. Mem. Editl. bd. Va. Forum, 1990-93; contbr. articles to profl. jours. Bd. dirs. Fairfax County chpt. ARC, 1981-86, Va. Inst. Polit. Leadership, 1995—, Fairfax Com. of 100, 1986-88, 90—, Arts Coun. Fairfax County, 1989—, Fairfax Spotlight on the Arts, Inc., 2002—; bd. dirs. Hospice No. Va., 1983-88, devel. bd., 1997-2000; steering com. Hurrah for Hospice Gala, 1999, Nat. Capital Region Hospices Gala, 2002, 2003, No. Va. Mental Health Inst., Fairfax County, 1978-81, Fairfax Profl. Women's Network, 1981; vice chair Va. Commonwealth U. Ctr. on Aging, Richmond, 1978—; supt.'s adv. coun. Fairfax County Pub. Schs., 1974-86, No. Va. Press Club, 1978—; mktg. chair, exec. com. Internat. Childrens Festival, 1997—; pres. Fairfax Ext. Leadership Coun., 1995; mem. Leadership Fairfax Class of 1992, Commonwealth Va. Combined campaign, State Adv. Coun., 1999-2003. Named Woman of Distinction, Soroptimists, Fairfax, 1988, Bus. Woman of Yr., Falls Church Bus. and Profl. Women's Group, 1993; fellow Va. Inst. Polit. Leadership, 1995. Mem. State Coun. Higher Edn. Va. (pub. affairs adv. com. 1985—), Greater Washington Bd. Trade, Fairfax County C. of C. (legis. affairs com. 1984—, millenium steering com. 1999) Va. Women Lobbyists, 1991—, No. Va. Bus. Roundtable, Internat. Platform Assn., Phi Delta Kappa (20-Yr. Continuous Svc. award 2001), Kappa Delta Alumni No. Va., Psi Chi, Phi Kappa Phi. Roman Catholic. Avocations: piano, organ, reading, hiking. Home: 4902 Ravensworth Rd Annandale VA 22003-5552 Office: NVCC 4001 Wakefield Chapel Rd Annandale VA 22003-3796 Office Phone: 703-323-3753. E-mail: mcwilhelmi@nvcc.edu.

WILHELMS, PATRICIA SUE, choral director; b. Canton, Ill., June 22, 1946; d. Roscoe Wilson Parrott, Gladys Susan Sophia Schmidt; m. David Wayne Wilhelms. MusB, Millikin U., 1968. Cert. profl. edn. Wash. Asst. choral dir. Richwoods H.S., Peoria, Ill., 1968—69; elem. tchr. St. Mary's Sch., Aberdeen, Wash., 1975—85; dir. choral activities Aberdeen H.S., 1985—. Choir screening chair N.W. divsn. Music Educator's Nat. Conf., Reston, Va., 1997; chmn. music dept. Aberdeen H.S., 2001—. Named to Outstanding Young Women Am., 1972, 1974; recipient Svc. Above Self award, Rotary Internat., 1990, Wash. award for Excellence in Edn., State of Wash., 1990. Mem.: Internat. Assn. Jazz Educators, Nat. Choral Dirs. Assn., Wash. Interscholastic Activities Assn. (music rep. dist. 4 exec. bd. 1995—), Wash. Music Edn. Assn. (regional pres. 1998—2000), Wash. Music Educator's Assn. (regional pres.-elect 1996—98, all-state choir screening chair 1999). Avocations: antiques, genealogy, travel. Home: 628 Essex Ave Aberdeen WA 98520 Office: Aberdeen HS 414 No I St Aberdeen WA 98520 Office Fax: 360-538-2046.

WILHITE, NANCY JANE, evangelist; b. Knoxville, Tenn., Oct. 7, 1944; d. Melvin Bertrand Wilhite and Laura Brownlee Rogers. BS in Elem. Edn., U. Tenn., 1965; MDiv, Emory U., 1992. Cert. elders order (ordination) 1994, evangelist. Tchr. Knoxville City Schs., 1966, 1969—71; recreation dir. and social worker ARC mil. base hosp., 1966—68; tchr. Birmingham City Schs., Ala., 1968—69; field dir. Tanasi Girl Scout Coun., Knoxville, 1971—76; owner and dir. Kaleidoscope Pre-Sch., Gatlinburg, Tenn., 1981—86; exec. housekeeper Holiday Inn, Gatlinburg, 1986—87; pastor Holston Conf. United Meth. Ch., Harriman, Tenn., 1991—94; evangelist Kaleidoscope Ministries, Inc., Knoxville, 1994—, preacher, dramatist, tchr. Author: (book) The Rev. William Hurd Rogers and His Descendants, 2004. Mem.: Nat. Assn. United Meth. Evangelists (v.p. 2000—03). Avocation: genealogy. Office: Kaleidoscope Ministries Inc PO Box 52307 Knoxville TN 37950-2307 E-mail: ladymin@earthlink.ne.

WILHOIT, TRISHA C. elementary school educator; b. Greeneville, Tenn., June 20, 1976; d. Everette Kenneth and Mary DiAnn (Brown) Casteel; m. Christopher Norman Wilhoit, May 29, 1999; 1 child, Kenly Kate. BFA, Converse Coll., 1998; EdM, U. Tenn., 2001. Elem. art tchr. Farragut Primary, Knoxville, Tenn., 2000—01; art tchr. Maryville (Tenn.) H.S., 2000—01, Roosevelt Elem., Kingsport, Tenn., 2001—. Planning coun. chair Roosevelt Elem., Knoxville, 2003—. Named Miss Fairest of the Fair, Greene County, Tenn., 1992; scholar, J. Clayton Arnold, 2001, Charles F. Whiteside, 2001; Leadership scholar, Converse Coll., 1994—98. Mem.: Tenn. Art Edn. Assn., Nat. Art Edn. Assn. Republican. Avocations: horseback riding, cooking. Home: 218 Wilhoit Rd Chuckey TN 37641 Office: Theodore Roosevelt Elem 1051 Lake St Kingsport TN 37660

WILJANEN, LYNN M. social sciences educator; b. Duluth, Minn., Mar. 4, 1962; m. Thomas Moskios, Aug. 12, 2000. Ph.D. Counseling Psychology, U. of Wis., Madison, 1987—95. Asst. prof., social sci. Wor-Wic C.C., Salisbury, Md., 2002—; dir., career services Frostburg State U., Frostburg, Md., 1998—2000; asst. dir., career ctr. Colo. State U., Fort Collins, Colo., 1995—98. Adj. prof. Colo. State U., Fort Collins, Colo., 1995—98. Author: (paper presentation) First-Generation College Students: Bridging the Gap Between Home and School, Rural First-Generation College Students: A Sense of Place and Career Choices, (career program) Career Development for First-Generation College Women. Vol. Am. Cancer Soc. Relay for Life, Salisbury, Md., 2001—03. Grantee Careers for First-Generation Coll. Women, U. of Minn., 1994. Mem.: Soc. for the Tchg. of Psychology, Soc. of Counseling Psychology, Soc. for the Psychology of Women. Achievements include research in Presenter, First-Generation College Students As Pioneers, National and Regional presentations 1995-2003. Avocations: salt water fishing, sailing, gardening. Office: Wor-Wic Community College 32000 Campus Drive Salisbury MD 21804 E-mail: lwiljanen@worwic.edu.

WILKE, CONSTANCE REGINA, elementary school educator; b. Camden, N.J., Mar. 20, 1944; d. Matthew Stanley Sr. and Regina Rita (Przeradzki) Wojtkowiak; m. Alvin Frank Wilke Jr., Apr. 20, 1968; children: Joseph Alvin, Suzanne Renee. BA in Elem. Edn., Glassboro State U., 1967, MA in Reading and Supervision, 1979. Cert. tchr. and reading speicalist, N.J. Tchr. 5th grade Bellmawr (N.J.) Bd. Edn., 1967-70; tchr. 2d grade Ethel M. Burke Sch., Bellmawr, N.J., 1970-97; tchr. 5th grade Bell Oaks Sch., Bellmawr, 1997—. Author: Wojtkowiak Family History, 1992. Vol. Gloucester (N.J.) City Libr., 1972-75, Vet.'s Standdown, Meals on Wheels, Cathedral Soup Kitchen; contact reassurance vol. Am. Heart Assn. Walk; sec. E.M. Burke Sch. PTA, Bellmawr, 1973-78, publicity person, 1980-85, pres., 1982-85, author and editor publicity book, 1980-83, rec. sec., 1995-97; advisor Cmty. Edn. Bd., Gloucester City, 1973-74; eucharistic minister St. Mary's Ch., Gloucester City, 1990—, 150 yr. Jubilee com., renew com., lector, parish coun.; dir., founder of Internat. Day at E.M. Burke Sch., dir. and founder Vet.'s Day Program, MS Read-a-thon, Jump Rope for Heart, Book It programs, Reading is the Ticket program. Named Citizen of Yr., Polish-Am. Congress, 1983, N.J. VFW Citizenship Tchr. of Yr., 2002. Mem. NEA, N.J. Epilepsy Found., N.J. Edn. Assn., West Jersey Reading Assn., Bellmawr Edn. Assn. (faculty rep.), Asthma Assn. Roman Catholic. Achievements include being instrumental in having Veteran Memorial built honoring Bellmawr veterans. Office: Bell Oaks Sch 256 Anderson Ave Bellmawr NJ 08031-1199

WILKEN, CLAUDIA, judge; b. Mpls., Aug. 17, 1949; BA with honors, Stanford U., 1971; JD, U. Calif., Berkeley, 1975. Bar: Calif. 1975, U.S. Dist. Ct. (no. dist.) Calif. 1975, U.S. Ct. Appeals (9th cir.) 1976, U.S. Supreme Ct. 1981. Asst. fed. pub. defender U.S. Dist. Ct. (no. dist.) Calif., San Francisco, 1975-78, U.S. magistrate judge, 1983-93, dist. judge, 1993—; ptnr. Wilken & Leverett, Berkeley, Calif., 1978-84. Adj. prof. U. Calif., Berkeley, 1978-84; prof. New Coll. Sch. Law, 1980-85; mem. jud. br. com. Jud. Conf. U.S.; past mem. edn. com. Fed. Jud. Ctr.; chair 9th cir. Magistrates Conf., 1987-88. Mem. ABA (mem. jud. adminstrn. divsn.), Alameda County Bar Assn. (judge's membership), Nat. Assn. Women Judges, Order of Coif, Phi Beta Kappa. Office: US Dist Ct No Dist 1301 Clay St # 2 Oakland CA 94612-5217

WILKENING, LAUREL LYNN, academic administrator, planetary scientist; b. Richland, Wash., Nov. 23, 1944; d. Marvin Hubert and Ruby Alma Wilkening; m. Godfrey Theodore Sill, May 18, 1974 BA, Reed Coll., Portland, Oreg., 1966; PhD, U. Calif., San Diego, 1970; DSc (hon.), U. Ariz., 1996. From asst. prof. to assoc. prof. U. Ariz., Tucson, 1973—80, dir. Lunar and Planetary Lab., head planetary scis., 1981—83, vice provost, prof. planetary scis., 1983—85, v.p. rsch., dean Grad. Coll., 1985—88; divsn. scientist NASA Hdqrs., Washington, 1980; prof. geol scis., adj. prof. astronomy, provost U. Washington, Seattle, 1988—93; prof. earth system sci., chancellor U. Calif., Irvine, 1993—98. Dir. Rsch. Corp., 1991-2003, Seagate Tech., Inc., 1993-2000, Empire Ranch Found., 1998-2003; vice chmn. Nat. Commn. on Space, Washington, 1984-86, Adv. Com. on the Future of U.S. Space Program, 1990-91; chair Space Policy Adv. Bd., Nat. Space Coun., 1991-92; co-chmn. primitive bodies mission study team NASA/European Space Agy., 1984-85; chmn. com. rendezvous sci. working group NASA, 1983-85; mem. panel on internat. cooperation and competition in space Congl. Office Tech. Assessment, 1982-83; trustee NASULGC, 1994-97, UCAR, 1988-89, 97-98, Reed Coll., 1992-2002. Editor: Comets, 1982. U. Calif. Regents fellow, 1966-67; NASA trainee, 1967-70. Fellow Meteoritical Soc. (councilor 1976-80), Am. Assn. Advanced Sci.; mem. Am. Astron. Soc. (chmn. div. planetary scis. 1984-85), Am. Geophys. Union, AAAS, Planetary Soc. (dir. 1994-2000, v.p. 1997-2000), Phi Beta Kappa, Democrat. Avocations: gardening, camping, swimming.

WILKERSON, DIANNE, state legislator; BS in public admin., Amer. Intl. Coll.; JD, Boston Coll. Law Sch., 1981. Partner Roche, Carens, & DeGiacomo; mem. Mass. Senate, Boston, 1993—. Mem.: Boston College Law School Alumni Assoc., Delta Sigma Theta. Office: Mass State Senate Rm 312C State House Boston MA 02133

WILKERSON, LUANN, dean, medical educator; BA magna cum laude, Baylor U., 1969; MA in English, U. Tex., 1972; EdD, U. Mass., 1977. Tchg. asst. dept. English U. Tex., Austin, 1970-72; tchr. grade 8 lang. arts Quabbin Regional H.S., Barre, Mass., 1974-75; rsch. asst. Clinic to Improve Univ. Tchg. U. Mass., Amherst, 1974-76, staff assoc., 1976-77; dir. tchg. and media resource ctr., asst. prof. speech and theatre Murray (Ky.) State U., 1977-80; acting dir., coord. faculty devel. office ednl. devel. and resources Coll. Osteopathic Medicine Ohio U., Athens, 1980-81; assoc. dir. office curricular affairs, asst. prof. family medicine Med. Coll. Wis., Milw., 1981-83; ednl. specialist ednl. devel. unit Michael Reese Hosp. and Med. Ctr., Chgo., 1983-84; dir. faculty devel. office ednl. devel. Harvard Med. Sch., Boston, 1984-91, lectr. in med. edn., 1988-91; dir. Ctr. for Ednl. Devel. and Rsch. UCLA Sch. Medicine, 1992-99, asst. dean med. edn., 1992-94, assoc. prof. medicine, 1992-95, prof. medicine, 1996—, assoc. dean med. edn., 1995-97, sr. assoc. dean med. edn., 1998—. Mem. editl. bd. Advances in Health Scis. Edn., 1995—, Med. Edn., 1995—, Acad. Medicine, 2001—; reviewer: Acad. Medicine, 1989—, Tchg. and Learning in Medicine, 1990—, Jour. Gen. Internal Medicine, 1988—, Am. Ednl. Rsch. Assn., 1987—, Rsch. Med.Edn. Ann. Conf., 1988—; contbr. articles to profl. jours. and chpts. to books; lectr. in field. Recipient Clinician Tchr. award Calif. Regional Soc. Gen. Internal Medicine, 1995, Excellence in Edn. award UCLA Sch. Medicine, 1998. Mem. Am. Assn. Med. Colls. (mem. rsch. med. edn. com. 1990-93, western chair group on ednl. affairs 1995-97, co-dir. fellowship in med. edn. rsch. 1995-97, convenor spl. interest group on faculty devel. 1997-98, chair group on ednl. affairs 1997—), Am. Ednl. Rsch. Assn., Profl. and Orgnl. Devel. Network (mem. nat. core com. 1977-80, 84-86, exec. dir. 1984-85), Phi Beta Kappa. Office: UCLA Sch Medicine Ctr Ednl Devel & Rsch PO Box 951722 Los Angeles CA 90095-1722 E-mail: lwilkerson@mednet.ucla.edu.

WILKERSON, PATRICIA HELEN, director; b. Victoria, Tex., Aug. 2, 1936; d. Milo Andrew and Gertrude H. (Nichols) Beeman; children: Cheryl Lynn, Susan Leigh, Debra Ann, Jon Craig. Student, U. Corpus Christi, 1954-56, Del Mar Coll., 1970-71-86-88. Tax clk. Nueces County Tax Assessor, Corpus Christi, Tex., 1956—57; corr. sec. Boy Scouts of Am. Gulf Coast Coun., Corpus Christi, 1957—58; elem. dir, nursery sch. coord. First Bapt. Ch., Corpus Christi, 1972—73, pre-K tchr., sec., 1975—85; dir. child devel. ctr. 2d Bapt. Ch., Corpus Christi, 1985—99, Northway Bapt. Ch., Dallas, 1999—. ASSIST pre-sch. leader Corpus Christi Bapt. Assn., 1967-99; conf. leader, cons. Bapt. Gen. Conv., Dallas, 1967—; mem. early childhood adv. bd., Del Mar Coll., Corpus Christi, 1981-86; mem. adv. com. Tex. Bapt. Weekday Assn., Dallas, 1995-98, Gulf Coast Tng. coalition. Writer Presch. Sunday Sch. Curriculum, 1992-99, Southern Bapt. Conv. Sunday sch. tchr., various Tex. Bapt. Chs., 1959—; presch. divsn. dir. Second Bapt. Ch., Corpus Christi, 1986-98, dir. child devel. ctr., 1985-99; dir. Child Devel. Ctr., Northway Bapt. Ch., Dallas, 1999-2003; conf. leader Dallas Bapt. Assn., 2000-02, Northway (Tex.) child devel. ctr., 1999-2003. Mem. Bay Area Assn. Edn. Young Children (sec. 1981-82, co-chair conf. 1991, Week of the Young Child chair 1995-96). Avocations: reading, sewing, cats, nature study. Home: 3841 N Belt Line Rd Apt 1305 Irving TX 75038-5774 Office: Northway Bapt ChCtr 3877 Walnut Hill Ln Dallas TX 75229

WILKERSON, PINKIE CAROLYN, state legislator, lawyer; b. L.A., Feb. 8, 1948; d. Calvin and Dora (Garner) W.; 1 child, John David Barabin Jr. BA cum laude, Grambling (La.) State U., 1968; MA with honors, Ohio U., 1971; JD with honors, So. U., 1979; LLM, Tulane U., 1989. Bar: La., N.Y., U.S. Tax Ct., U.S. Supreme Ct. Asst. dist. counsel IRS, L.A.; asst. prof. law So. U. Sch. Law, Baton Rouge; asst. atty. gen. La. Dept. Justice, Baton Rouge; with Merrill Lynch, Pierce, Fenner & Smith, N.Y.C.; asst. dist. atty. for Lincoln and Union Parishes, 3d Jud. Dist., La.; pvt. practice, Grambling; mem. La. Ho. of Reps., Baton Rouge, 1992—. Mem. So. U. Law Rev., 1978-79. Mem. adv. bd. Grambling State U.; bd. dirs. Phillips Sch. Theology, Atlanta; past pres. United League Voters; past v.p. Ruston-Grambling LWV. Named to Hall of Fame, Grambling State U., 1993; recipient Significant Achievement award Ohio U., 1994. Mem. Nat. Bar Assn. (bd. dirs. 1985-89), La. Bar, N.Y. State Bar Assn., Grambling State U. Alumni Assn. (life), So. U. Alumni Assn. (life), Delta Sigma Theta. Democrat. Methodist. Home: 611 E Grand Ave Grambling LA 71245-2305 Office: 302 College Ave Grambling LA 71245-2626

WILKERSON, RITA LYNN, special education educator, consultant; b. Crescent, Okla., Apr. 22; BA, Cen. State U., Edmond, Okla., 1963; MEd, Cen. State U., 1969; postgrad., U. Okla., 1975, Kans. State U. Elem. tchr. music Hillsdale (Okla.) Pub. Sch., 1963-64; jr. high sch. music and spl. edn. Okarche (Okla.) Pub. Sch., 1965-71; cons. Title III Project, Woodward, Okla., 1971-72; dir. Regional Edn. Svc. Ctr., Guymon, Okla., 1972-81; dir., psychologist Project W.O.R.K., Guymon, 1981-90; tchr. behavioral disorders Unified Sch. Dist. 480, Liberal, Kans., 1990—; sch. psychologist Hardesty (Okla.) Schs., 1994. Cons. Optima (Okla.) Pub. Schs., 1990, Felt (Okla.) Pub. Schs., 1990, Texhoma (Okla.) Schs., 1994, Balko (Okla.) Pub. Schs., 1996; spl. edn. cons. Optima Pub. Schs., 1992—, Goodwell (Okla.) Pub. Schs., 1992—; diagnostician Tyrone, Okla. Pub. Schs., 1992-95; home svcs. provider Dept. Human Svcs., Guymon, 1990; active Kans. Dept. Social and Rehab. Svcs., 1993—; adj. tchr. Seward County C.C., 1994—. Grantee Cen. State U., 1968-69, Oklahoma City Dept. Edn., 1988-89. Mem. ASCD, NAFE, NEA (liberal Kans. chpt.), AAUW, Coun. Exceptional Children, Okla. Assn. Retarded Citizens, Okla. Assn. for Children with Learning Disabilities, Phi Delta Kappa. Republican. Avocation: crafts. Home: 616 N Crumley St Guymon OK 73942-4341 Office: Unified Sch Dist 480 7th And Western Liberal KS 67901

WILKES, N. TIFFANY, social studies educator; b. West Palm Beach, Fla., Feb. 15, 1974; d. Ronald Elson and Nancy Wilkes. BS, Fla. State U., 1997. Tchr. social studies Palm Beach (Fla.) Gardens H.S., 1997—. Coach cheerleading Palm Beach Gardens (Fla.) HS, coach flag football. Named to All Star Team, Internat. Womens Flag Football Assn., 2000—02; recipient Cheerleading Nat. Champion award, Jupiter HS, 1992. Mem.: Cert. Teachers Assn. (life). Democrat. Avocations: running, flag football, education. Office: Palm Beach Gardens High School 4245 Holly Drive Palm Beach Gardens FL 33410

WILKEY, ELMIRA SMITH, illustrator, artist, publisher, writer, educator; b. Kankakee, Ill., Dec. 13, 1936; d. Edmond Anthony Dorothy Agnes (Schilling) Smith; m. Lowell Gene Wilkey; children: A. Shelley, Eric, Martin, Barry, Tad, Jeremy. BA cum laude, Loretto Heights Coll. (now Regis U.), 1958. Mgr. Duncan Assocs., Champaign, Ill., 1960-61; English/drama speech tchr. Kankakee Sch. Dist., 1958-60; substitute tchr. Kankakee County, 1965-80; art instr. Kankakee C.C., 1988, 2000; behavior couns. Nutri-Sys., Bourbonnais, Ill., 1987-91; English tchr. Bishop McNamara H.S., Kankakee, 1994-2000; founder, co-owner, printer Studio Sans Serif Divsn., Bronte Press Ltd. Edits., Manteno, Kankakee, Bourbonnais, 1977—. Textbook art cons. DSP, Boston, 1965-74; art adj. Olivet Coll., Bourbonnais, 1993-94; writer, art presenter W.C. Workshops Olivet Coll., Kankakee Art League, 1980-90; lectr. in field. Illustrator: Come Spring, History of Rockville, Hoofbeats, 2001; with Children's Book Program, cable TV, Manteno, Ill., 1996-99, ten books including classic, historical prose, poetry, folklore, herbal subjects, and 2 children's books; columnist Pat's Meanders, 1992—; one woman shows include Galesburg Civic Art Ctr., 1984, Tall Grass Art Assn., ONU Brandenberg Gallery, 1994; exhibited in solo shows at Prairie State Coll., 1980, Western Mich. U.; group shows include Ill. Women in the Arts Invitation, Prairie State Coll., 1980, Copley Soc., Boston, 1986, Tall Grass Art Assn., 2001, Xavier U., 2004. Cmty. arts. coun. Kankakee; cmty. art adv. bd. Kankakee C.C.; donated artwork Hospice, Catholic Charities, United Way. Recipient numerous awards in art; Straw Series Signature art technique, V.I.P. Mem. Nat. League Am. Penwomen (Ill. state pres, Chgo. br. v.p. 1979—, treas. 2002—), Ill. State Poetry Soc. (charter), Midwest Watercolor Soc., Nat. Mus. Women in Arts, Great Books (charter, pres. 1980-85), Miniature Book Soc., Christians in Visual Arts. Republican. Roman Catholic. Avocations: walking, herb/plant identification, singing, piano, camping. Home and Office: Studio Sans Serif Divsn The Bronte Press 4136 W 6940N Rd Bourbonnais IL 60914-4208 Fax: 815-936-9913. Personal E-mail: miraswilkey@yahoo.com.

WILKEY, MARY HUFF, investor, writer, publisher; b. Dayton, Ohio, Sept. 30, 1940; d. Charles Joseph and Frances Rose (Wintersteen) Huff; divorced; children: Christopher Tyson, Charles Cory, Jennifer Jo. Student, Sinclair C.C., Dayton, 1979—85. Pvt. sec. Dare, Inc., Troy, Ohio, 1962-63; legal sec. Smith & Schnacke, Dayton, 1963-68; adminstrv. asst. U.S. Magistrate, Dayton, 1971-74; legal technician Coolidge, Wall, Womsley & Lombard Co., L.P.A., Dayton, 1968-75, 81-85, Lair & Owen, Dayton, 1979-81; owner, operator Village Mill Country Store, Tipp City, Ohio, 1987-88; owner, mgr. Happy Days Residence, Franklin, Ohio, 1989—. Author, pub. (directory) Your Personal Guide, 1988, 89, 'elf Expressions Ezine, 2001—. Phone support vol. Operation Golden Ring, Dayton, 1984-85; vol. Sta. WPTD Pub. TV, Dayton, 1983-85. Mem. NAFE, Mensa, Internat. Platform Assn., Greater Dayton Real Estate Investor Assn. Avocations: Bible study, creative writing, natural health, real estate, internet marketing. E-mail: elfbutter@earthlink.net.

WILKIE, EDITH B. foundation administrator; BA, Vassar Coll., 1968; degree in french language studies, Monterey Inst. Internat. Study, 1995. Jr. staffer thru adminstrv. asst. Rep. Ogden R. Reid, 1968-75; exec. dir. arms control/foreign policy caucus U.S. Congress, 1978-95; pres./cons. Peace Through Law Edn. Fund, 1995—. Legislative asst. foreign and defense policy/chief of staff, Rep. Fortney Stark, Calif.; bd. dirs. Ploughshares Fund, PEACE-PAC, Coun. for a Livable World, Demilitarization for Democracy. Office: Council for Livable World 322 4th St NE Washington DC 20002-5824

WILKINS, AMY P. publishing executive; Assoc. pub., advt. dir. Health Mag., 1994—95, pub., 1995—97; pres. Petersen Youth Group1, 1997—98; pub. Biography Mag., 1998—2000, Smithsonian, Smithsonian Air & Space Mag., 2000—. Office: Smithsonian Mag 420 Lexington Ave Ste 2335 New York NY 10170

WILKINS, ARLENE, social worker; b. Balt., Oct. 20, 1936; d. Joseph Martin and Alice Gertrude (Mickey) Martin Patterson; m. E.J. Wilkins, Jan. 15, 1963; children: Del, Deirdre, Justin, Patrick. BA, Wilkes Coll., 1959; MA, U. Pa., 1962. Lic. social worker. Social worker Children's Svc. Inc., Phila., 1960-62, Western Psychiat. Inst. and Clinic, Pitts., 1966-67, Bethesda United Presbyn. Ch., Pitts., 1967-70; clin. social worker Allegheny Gen. Hosp., Northview Heights Health Ctr., Pitts., 1986-99, ret., 1999; pvt. practice Pitts., 1999—. Program chmn. St. Andrew United Presbyn. Ch., Sewickley, Pa., 1981-83, elder, 1999-00; bd. dirs., sec., Cmtys. Outreach Ministry, 1995-00; past bd. dirs. Open Door Crafton Cmty. Agy. Mem. NASW, MSW (bd. cert. diplomate). Republican. Home: 416 College Park Dr Coraopolis PA 15108-2311

WILKINS, CAROLINE HANKE, consumer agency administrator, political worker; b. Corpus Christi, Tex., May 12, 1937; d. Louis Allen and Jean Guckian Hanke; m. B. Hughel Wilkins, 1957; 1 child, Brian Hughel. Student, Tex. Coll. Arts and Industries, 1956—57, Tex. Tech. U., 1957—58; BA, U. Tex., 1961; MA magna cum laude, U. Ams., 1964. Instr. history Oreg. State U., 1967-68; adminstr. Consumer Svcs. divsn. State of Oreg., 1977-80, Wilkins Assoc., 1980—. Mem. PFMC Salmon Adv. subpanel, 1982-86. Author: (with B. H. Wilkins) Implications of the U.S.-Mexican Water Treaty for Interregional Water Transfer, 1968. Dem. precinct committeewoman, Benton County, Oreg., 1964-90; publicity chmn. Benton County Gen. Election, 1964; chmn. Get-Out-the-Vote Com., Benton County, 1966; vice chmn. Benton County Dem. Ctrl. Com., 1966-70; vice chmn. 1st Congl. Dist., Oreg., 1966-67, chmn., 1967-68; vice chmn. Dem. Party of Oreg., 1968-69, chmn., 1969-74; mem. exec. com. Western States Dem. Conf., 1970-72; vice chmn. Dem. Nat. Com., 1972-77, mem. arrangements com., 1972, 76, mem. Dem. Charter Commn., 1973-74; mem. Dem. Nat. Com., 1972-77, 85-89, mem. size and composition com., 1987-89, rules com., 1988; mem. Oreg. Govt. Ethics Commn., 1974-76; del., mem. rules com. Dem. Nat. Conv., 1988; 1st v.p. Nat. Fedn. Dem. Women, 1983-85, pres., 1985-87, parliamentarian, 1993-95, 99-2001, chair Pres.'s coun., 2001-2003, chair by-laws com., 2003—; mem. Kerr Libr. bd. Oreg. State U., 1989-95, pres., 1994-95; mem. Corvallis-Benton County Libr. Found., 1991-2001, sec., 1993, v.p., 1994, pres., 1995, mission and goals com. chair 2000-01; bd. dirs. Oreg. chpt. U.S. Lighthouse Soc., pres., 1997-98; bd. dirs. Oreg. State U.-Corvallis Symphony, 1998-2001, v.p. 1999-2000, resources com.; pres. Oreg. Fedn. Dem. Women, 1997-2001, Oreg. State-Corvallis chpt., UNIFEM, 1998-2002; bd. dirs. Oreg. State U. Acad. Lifelong Learning, 2003—; mem. Women and Philanthropy, Oreg. State U. Giving Cir., 2003-. Named Outstanding Mem. Nat. Fedn. Dem. Women, 1992, Woman of Achievement, Oreg. State U. Women's Ctr., 1998. Mem.: Soc. Consumer Affairs Profls., Nat. Assn. Consumer Agy. Adminstrs., Oreg. State U. Folk Club (pres. faculty wives 1989—90, scholarship chair 2000—01, grants com. 2002—03), Zonta Internat. (vice area bd. dirs. dist. 8 1992—94, bd. dist. 8 1994—96, by laws and resolutions chair 1997—98, internat. rels. coord. dist. 8 2000—02, dist. 8 nominating com. 2003—). Office: 3311 NW Roosevelt Dr Corvallis OR 97330-1169

WILKINS, CAROLYN ANN, music educator; b. Durant, Okla., Apr. 25, 1946; d. Billy Ray and Eunice Gertrude Mitchell; children: Joli Jorgenson, Joshua. BA in Music Edn., Southeastern State U., 1968; MA in Edn., Tex. A&M, 1976. Lifetime cert. in edn. Tex., std. cert. in edn. Okla. Tchr. vocal music McKinney I.S.D., Tex., 1968—71, Durant I.S.D., Okla., 1971—73, 1981—, Plano I.S.D., Tex., 1973—77, Hugo I.S.D., Okla., 1980—81. Tchr. upward bound program S.O.S.U., Durant, Okla., 1990—93; music min. First Christian Ch., Durant, 1993—. Dir. cmty. choir S. Ea. State U., Durant, 1997—2000; performer Summer Theater S.O.S.U., Durant, 2000. Mem.: NEA, Okla. Music Educators Assn. (2000 Hall of Fame), Music Educators Nat. Conv. (state vocal v.p., chmn. all state choir, Dir. of Distinction 1998), Okla. Choral Dirs. Assn., Durant C. of C. (mem. magnolia ct. 2002). Baptist. Avocations: antiques, piano, collecting carolers. Home: 115 Lynn Haven Dr Durant OK 74701 Office: Durant Mid Sch 401 N 6th Durant OK 74701

WILKINS, RITA DENISE, product development, research and technology director; b. Detroit, June 21, 1951; d. William H. and Alice L. (Hayes) Smith. Student, George Peabody Coll., 1969-70, Cleveland (Tenn.) State C.C., 1973-75. Mgmt. coord., legal coord. Arlen Realty and Devel. Corp., Chattanooga, 1973-76; asst. v.p., office mgr. Newburger Andes & Co., Atlanta, 1976-78, asst. v.p., project mgr., 1978-79; acquisition devel. mgmt. rep. Cardinal Industries, Inc., Atlanta, 1983-86; pres., sr. cons. CPC/Foresite, Charleston, SC, 1986—96; dir. info. Sys., rsch. Charleston, 1996—2000; dir. product. devel. tech. Advantage West, Asheville, NC, 2000—01; info. architect, tech. cons. DataTech Resources, Hendersonville,

NC, 2001—. Guest lectr. Ga. State U. Contbr. articles to profl. jours. E-mail: rita.robinette@datatechresources.com.

WILKINS, SHEILA SCANLON, management consultant; b. Oakland, Calif., Sept. 23, 1936; d. Michael Joseph and Joan (Daly) Scanlon; m. Thomas Wayne Wilkins, Aug. 14, 1965; children: Mary, John, Kathleen. BMusic, AB Liberal Arts maxima cum laude, Holy Names Coll., Oakland, 1958, MA in Music, 1972; MA in Ednl. Adminstrn., St. Mary's Coll., Moraga, Calif., 1983. Cert. tchr., Calif.; cert. in human resources mgmt., human resources tng. and devel. Tchr., dir. student activities Vallejo (Calif.) Unified Sch. Dist., 1962-63; tchr. Berkeley (Calif.) Unified Sch. Dist., 1963-66; pub. rels. asst. Alta Bates Hosp., Berkeley, 1973-74; tchr. Walnut Creek (Calif.) Sch. Dist., 1974-80; dist. tchg. Moraga Sch. Dist., 1980-83; tech. tng. adminstr. Crocker Nat. Bank, Walnut Creek, Calif., 1984-85; tng. officer Wells Fargo Bank, Concord, Calif., 1985-86; tng. mgr. Fab 3 Intel Corp, Livermore, Calif., 1986-91, orgn. cons. CIS ops. Folsom, Calif., 1991-92, mgr. profl. devel. corp. edn. Santa Clara, Calif., 1992-94; prin. The Wilkins Group, Walnut Creek, Calif., 1994—. Contbr. articles to profl. jours. Chair parent com. Boy Scouts Am., Concord, 1977-80; pres. Parents Club of St. Francis Sch., Concord, 1978-79; v.p. Parents Club of Carondelet High Sch., Concord, 1983-84. Mem. Internat. Soc. for Performance Improvement (cert. performance technologist, v.p. fin. 1988-89, pres. 1989-91 Bay area chpt.), Internat. Fedn. Tng. and Devel. Orgns. Home: 2182 Gill Port Ln Walnut Creek CA 94598-1150 Office: 2182 Gill Port Ln Walnut Creek CA 94598-1150

WILKINSON, BARBARA J. physician, medical educator; b. Mitcham, Surrey, Eng., June 5, 1946; came to U.S., 1954, naturalized, 1963. d. Arthur Frederick and Elizabeth (Law) Wilkinson. BA in Zoology with highest distinction, U. Maine, 1969; MD, Boston U., 1973. Diplomate Am. Bd. Pediatrics. Pediatric intern Boston City Hosp., 1973-74; fellow in neonatology U. Rochester/Strong Meml. Hosp., Rochester Gen. Hosp., Rochester, N.Y., 1976-78; resident in pediatrics Maine Med. Ctr., Portland, 1974-76, assoc. neonatologist, outreach educator, 1979-83, lectr. for pediatric med. students, 1983—2003; clin. instr. of pediatrics U. Vt. Coll. Medicine/Maine Med. Ctr., Portland, 1980-83, clin. asst. prof. of pediatrics, 1983. Participant at emergency and family practice grand rounds on bereavement Maine Med. Ctr., early 1990s, co-facilitator Sudden Infant Death Support Group, 1980-2004; adj. faculty in allied health scis. So. Maine Vocat. Tech. Inst., South Portland, 1984-86; adj. faculty pathophysiology courses So. Maine Tech. Coll., South Portland, 1998-2000. Mem. Maine SIDS Found.; mem., contact person Maine Children's Meml. Libr. for Bereaved Parents, 1990s-; precinct ward clk. Elections, Portland, 1990's-2001. Fellow Am. Acad. Pediatrics; mem. AAUW (life), Am. Acad. Pediat., Altrusa Internat., Nat. Honor Soc., Phi Beta Kappa, Phi Kappa Phi. Avocations: watercolor painting, silk screening, photography, reading. Home: 56 Garrison St Portland ME 04102-1933

WILKINSON, DORIS, medical sociology educator; b. Lexington, Ky., June 13, 1936; d. Howard Thomas and Regina Wilkinson. BA, U. Ky., 1958; MA, Case Western Res. U., 1960, PhD, 1968; MPH, Johns Hopkins U., 1985; postgrad., Harvard U., summer 1991. Asst. prof. U. Ky., Lexington, 1968-70; assoc. prof., then prof. Macalester Coll., St. Paul, 1970-77; [illegible] Am. Social Assn., Washington, 1977-80; prof. med. sociology Howard U., Washington, 1980-84; vis. prof. U. Va., 1984-85; prof. sociology U. Ky., Lexington, 1985—. Chmn. panel women in sci. program NSF, Washington, 1976; rev. panelist Nat. Inst. Drug Abuse, Washington, 1978—79; mem. bd. sci. counselors Nat. Cancer Inst., Bethesda, Md., 1980—84; vis. scholar Harvard U., Cambridge, Mass., 1989—90, vis. prof. (summers), 1992, 93, 94, 97; Rapoport vis. prof. social theory (summers) Smith Coll., 1995, 96; bd. dirs. Nat. Conf. for Cmty. Justice, 1992—96; dir. Heritage Project, 2000—. Author: Workbook for Introductory Sociology, 1968; editor: Black Revolt: Strategies of Protest, 1969; co-editor: The Black Male in America, 1977, Alternative Health Maintenance and Healing Systems, 1987, Race, Gender and the Life Cycle, 1991, Race, Class and Gender, 1996; social history photographic exhbn. "The African American Presence in Medicine" Harvard Med. Libr., 1991, Pearson Mus.- So. Ill. U. Med. Sch., 1992, N.J. Coll. Medicine and Dentistry, 1993, Louisville Mus. History and Sci., 1994, U. Cin. Med. Sch. Libr., 1994, Albert Einstein Coll. of Medicine, 1995, Midway Coll., 1996; contbr. articles to profl. jours. Bd. overseers Case Western Res. U., Cleve., 1982-87; apptd. Ky. Commn. on Women, 1993-96. Recipient Pub. Humanities award U. Ky., 1990, Midway Coll. Women's History Month award, 1991, Gt. Tchr. award Nat. Alumni Assn. U. Ky., 1992, Disting. Scholar award Assn. Black Sociologists, 1993; inducted into Hall of Disting. Alumni, U. Ky., 1989; fellow Woodrow Wilson Found., 1959-61, Ford Found., 1989-90; grantee Social Sci. Rsch. Coun., 1975, Nat. Inst. Edn., 1978-80, Nat. Cancer Inst., 1986-88, Ky. Humanities Coun., 1988, 2001, Am. Coun. Learned Soc., 1989-90, NEH, 1991; Disting. Prof. in Coll. Arts and Scis., U. Ky., 1992-93, Coll. of Social Work Hall of Fame, U. Ky., 1999; Disting. Professorship named in hon., 2000. Mem.: Ea. Sociol. Soc. (v.p. 1983—84, pres. 1992—93, I. Peter Gellman award 1987), Soc. for Study of Social Problems (v.p. 1984—85, pres. 1987—88), D.C. Sociol. Soc. (pres. 1982—83), So. Sociol. Soc. (honors com. 1993—94), Am. Sociol. Assn. (exec. assoc. 1977—80, budget com. 1985—88, v.p. 1991—92, mem. coun. 1994—97, elected History of Sociology sect. 2003, Dubois-Johnson-Frazier award 1988), Phi Beta Kappa.

WILKINSON, FRANCES CATHERINE, librarian, educator; b. Lake Charles, La., July 20, 1955; d. Derrell Fred and Catherine Frances (O'Toole) W.; div.; 1 child, Katrina Frances. BA in Communication with distinction, U. N.Mex., 1982, MPA, 1987; MLS, U. Ariz., 1990. Mktg. rsch. auditor Mktg. Rsch. N.Mex., Albuquerque, 1973-78; freelance photographer, 1974-75; from libr. supr. gen. libr. to assoc. dean libr. svcs. U. N.Mex., Albuquerque, 1978—2001, interim dean libr. svcs., 2001—02, assoc. dean, 2002—. Cons., trainer ergonomics univs. and govt. agys. across U.S., 1986—; bd. dirs. Friends of U. N.Mex. Librs., Aubuquerque, 1991-94; mediator Mediation Alliance, 1991-94, U. N.Mex. Faculty Dispute Resolution, 1999—; mediation coach U. N.Mex., 1999-2000. Author, editor books; editor jour. columns; contbr. articles to profl. jours. Counselor, advocate Albuquerque Rape Crisis Ctr., 1981-84. Recipient James Fulton Zimmerman award for adminstrv. excellence, Friends of U. N.Mex. Librs., Inc. Mem.: ALA (com. mem. 1990—2000, 2003—, Leadership in Libr. Acquisitions award 2000), N.Mex. Assn. Rsch. Librs., N.Mex. Preservation Alliance (vice chair 1995—96), N.Mex. Libr. Assn., N.Am. Serials Interest Group (mem. exec. bd. 1997—2001, com. mem. 1994—97, 2001—03), Pi Alpha Alpha, Phi Kappa Phi (chpt. treas. 1991—92, chpt. pres. 1992—94). Home: PO Box 8102 Albuquerque NM 87198-8102 Office: U N Mex Gen Libr MSC 05 3020 1 University of New Mex Albuquerque NM 87131-0001 E-mail: fwilkins@unm.edu.

WILKINSON, JEANNE CAROL, artist, educator; b. Duluth, Minn., Sept. 27, 1949; d. Gordon Eugene and Shirley Jean (Anderson) W.; m. Richard Earl Yonda, June 29, 1975 (div. April 1985); children: Aaron Mark, Andrew John; m. Frank Oscar Lind III, Mar. 24, 1993. Attended, U. Minn., Mpls., 1968-70; BA in Painting and Art Edn., U. Wis.-Stout, 1986; MFA in Painting, Pratt Inst., Bklyn., 1989. Organizer rural coop. truck farm Winding Rd. Farm, Boyceville, Wis., 1972-74; dairy farmer Nat. Farm Orgn., Boyceville, 1974-82; freelance artist Wis., 1981-86; exhbns. preparator NY Pub. Library, NYC, 1990-91; adminstrv. asst. Anita Shapolsky Gallery, NYC, 1991-92; art history lectr. Kingsborough Cmty. Coll., CUNY, Bklyn., 1992—; adminstrv. asst. Estate of Artist Margery Edwards, NYC, 1992—; art reviewer Cover Mag., NYC, 1993—, Review mag., NYC, 1996—, d'Art Internat., NYC, 1998—, Tribeca Tribune, NYC, 1999—. Represented in numerous exhbns. including NY County Lawyer's Assn., 1995, Dealer's Choice Art Initiatives, NYC, 1995, Janos Gat Gallery, NYC, 1994, Judith Klein Gallery, 1997-99, Lower Manhattan Cultural Coun., 1997, Muhlenberg Coll. Exhbn., 1999, The Painting Ctr., NYC, 2004; e-novel "The Meetings of WEarth" at www.environmentalfiction.com. Democrat. Studio: 224 Livingston St Brooklyn NY 11201-5812

WILKINSON, LAURA, Olympic athlete; b. Houston, Dec. 17, 1977; d. Ed and Linda Wilkinson; m. Eriek Hulseman. Student, U. Tex.; BS in pub. rels., U. Tex. at Austin. Placed 5th World Championships, 1998; winner platform Gold Medal Goodwill Games, 1998; winner nat. title summer nats., 1999; winner Gold Medal 10 meter platform, 2000. Pub. spkr. Office: US Diving Inc 201 S Capitol Ave Ste 430 Indianapolis IN 46225

WILKINSON, LOUISE CHERRY, psychology educator, dean; b. Phila., May 15, 1948; BA magna cum laude with honors, Oberlin Coll., 1970; EdM, EdD, Harvard U., 1974. Prof., chmn. dept. ednl. psychology U. Wis., Madison, 1976-85; prof., exec. officer Grad. Sch. PhD Program CUNY, N.Y.C., 1984-86; disting. prof., dean Grad. Sch. Edn. Rutgers U., 1986—2003; dean Sch. Edn., disting. prof. edn., psychology and comm. scis. Syracuse (NY) U., 2003—. Chairperson ednl. strategic planning Rutgers U.; mem. nat. rev. bd. Nat. Inst. Edn., 1977, 85, 87; cons. Nat. Ctr. for Bilingual Rsch., 1982, 84, U.S. Dept. Edn., 1995-96; adv. bd. Nat. Reading Rsch. Ctr., 1992-98. Co-author: Communicating for Learning, 1991; editor: Communicating in Classroom, 1982, Social Context of Instruction, 1984, Gender Influences in the Classroom, 2002; co-editor: Literacy and Language Learning, 2004; mem. editl. bds.: ; contbr. articles to profl. jours. Fellow: APA, Am. Assn. for Applied and Preventive Psychology, Am. Psychol. Soc.; mem.: NJ Coun. Acad. Policy Advisors, Am. Ednl. Rsch. Assn. (v.p. 1990—92, program chair 1997). Home: 303 Sedgwick Dr Syracuse NY 13203-1314

WILKINSON, ROSEMARY REGINA CHALLONER, poet, writer; b. New Orleans, Feb. 21, 1924; d. William Lindsay Challoner Jr. and Julia Regina (Sellen) Challoner/Schillo; m. Henry Bertram Wilkinson, Oct. 15, 1949; children: Denis James, Marian Regina, Paul Francis, Richard Challoner. Lifetime credential to teach poetry, San Francisco State U., 1978; LHD (hon.), Livre U., Pakistan, 1975; DLitt (hon.), World Acad. Arts & Culture, Rep. of China, 1981. Lectr./reader of poetry. Author: (poetry) A Girl's Will, 1973, California Poet, 1976, Earth's Compromise, 1977, It Happened to Me, 1978, I Am Earth Woman, 1979, The Poet and the Painter, 1981, Poetry and Arte, 1982, Gems Within, 1984, Nature's Guest, 1984, In the Pines, 1985, Longing for You, 1986, Purify the Earth, 1988, Sacred in Nature, 1988, Earth's Children, 1990, New Seed, 1991, Angels and Poetry, 1992, Cambrian Zephyr, 1993, Collected Poems, 1994, Poetry: Nature, 1996, Poetry: Spiritual, 1997, Poetry Calendar 2000, 1999, A Song in the Wind with Love, 2001, My Plea, 2001, Selected Verses, 2001, Blessing of Poetry, 2002, others, (epic) An Historical Epic, 1974. Founder Poetry-Fine Arts Divsn. of San Mateo (Calif.) County Fair, 1977, Dr. Williams Poetry Workshop, Burlingame H.S., 1985; sec.-gen. World Acad. Arts and Culture-USA, San Francisco, 1985—95, pres., 1994—. Mem.: Authors League Am., The Authors Guild, Acad. Am. Poets, Poetry Soc. of Am., Nat. League Am. Pen Women Inc. (Washington 4th and 5th v.p. 1986—90, Berkeley, Calif. pres. 1988—90, Lake Tahoe br. 1988—), World Acad. of Arts and Culture/World Congress of Poets, World Congress of Poets (Taipei, Taiwan [illegible] 1991, [illegible] 1985—95, pres. 1995—2003), Soroptomist Internat. (hon.). Democrat. Roman Catholic. Avocations: reading, research, brush painting, lecturing. Home: 3146 Buckeye Ct Placerville CA 95667-8334

WILKINSON, SHARON P. department of state official, former ambassador; b. Buffalo, Jan. 26, 1947; Grad., Brown U., U. Chgo. Vice consul Dept. State, San Paulo, Brazil, consul Accra, Ghana, program officer for Africa Bur. Cultural Affairs, staff asst. to asst. sec. inter-am. affairs, desk officer for Portugal, mgmt. analyst Office Mgmt. Ops.; dir. Face-to-Face Program Carnegie Endowment for Internat. Peace; dep. prin. officer Tijuana, Mexico; dir. Office of Diplomatic, pub. liaison Bur. Consular Affair Dept. State, consul gen., dep. chief mission Lisbon, Portugal, U.S. amb. to Burkina Faso, 1996—99; dir. Office West African Affairs, 1999—2000; U.S. amb. Mozambique, 2000—03; Dept. State Diplomat in residence Coll. of Liberal Arts & Scis., Ariz. State U., 2003—04. Achievements include career mem. of the Sr. Foreign Service, Class of Minister Counselor; speaks Portuguese, Spanish and French. Office: Dept State Wash DC 2330 Maputo Place Washington DC 20521-2330

WILKINSON, SIGNE, cartoonist; b. Wichita Falls, Tex. married. BA in English, 1972; student, Pa. Acad. Fine Arts. Reporter West Chester (Pa.) Daily Local News, Academy of Natural Scis., Phila.; freelance cartoonist Phila. and N.Y. publs.; cartoonist San Jose (Calif.) Mercury News, 1982-85, Phila. Daily News, 1985—. Illustrator: Abortion Cartoons in Demand, 1992, You Bet Your Tomatoes, 2002, How to Grow the $735 Tomato, 1999; contbr. to Univ. Barge Club News, various mags. Bd. dirs. Fair Hill Burial Ground. Recipient Pulitzer Prize for editl. cartooning, 1992, Overseas Press Club award, 1997, 2001, Robert F. Kennedy award, 2002. Mem. Assn. Am. Editl. Cartoonists (pres. 1994-95). Avocations: gardening, rowing. Office: Phila Daily News PO Box 7788 400 N Broad St Philadelphia PA 19130-4015 Business E-Mail: wilkins@phillynews.com.

WILL, KATHERINE HALEY, academic administrator; m. Oscar Henry Will, III; 4 children. Student, Carleton Coll., 1970-73; BA in English, Tufts U., 1974; MA in English, U. Ill., Urbana, 1975, PhD in English, 1986. Instr. English Augustana Coll., Sioux Falls, S.D., 1977-86, asst. prof. English, 1986-90, faculty dir. new student seminar program, 1987-91, assoc. prof. English, 1990-96, dean grad. study, dir. gen. edn., 1991—96; provost, prof. English Kenyon Coll., Gambier, Ohio, 1996-99; pres. Whittier Coll., Whittier, Calif., 1999—. Participant Mgmt. Devel. Seminar for Higher Edn. Adminstrs., Harvard U., summer 1992; cons. and presenter in field. Contbr. articles to profl. jours. Bd. dirs. United Way Great L.A. NEH fellow Summer Seminar in Romanticism and Gender, UCLA, 1989. Mem.: Found. for Ind. Higher Edn. (bd. dirs.), Assn. for Ind. Calif. Colls. and Univs. (exec. com.), Nat. Assn. Ind. Colls. and Univs. (pub. policy com.), Am. Coun. Edn. (mem. Commn. on Govt. and Pub. Affairs). Office: Whittier Coll Office Pres PO Box 634 13406 E Philadelphia Whittier CA 90608-4413 E-mail: willk@kenyon.edu.*

WILL, SANDRA GAIL, controller; b. Windber, Pa., July 26, 1963; d. Gerald Ray and Dorothy Jane (Zimmerman) Mock; m. Robert Douglas Will, Jan. 26, 1985; children: Zachary Douglas, Laura Elizabeth, Jeffrey Daniel. BS in Fin., Pa. State U., 1984; MBA, U. Pitts., 2000. Fin. trainee Alcoa, Newburgh, Ind., 1985, project acct., 1985-87, product acct., 1988, sr. product acct., 1988-90, product acctg. supr., 1990-93, controller Ft. Meade, Fla., 1993-95, Leetsdale, Pa., 1995-96, Pitts., 1997—2000, Cleve., 2000—. Mem. Inst. Mgmt. Accts. Avocations: reading, boating, gardening. Office: Alcoa 1600 Harvard Ave Cleveland OH 44105-5404

WILLANS, JEAN STONE, bishop, religious organization executive; b. Hillsboro, Ohio, Oct. 3, 1924; d. Homer and Ella (Keys) Hammond; m. Richard James Willans, Mar. 28, 1966; 1 dau., Suzanne Jeanne. Student, San Diego Jr. Coll.; DD (hon.), Am. Coll. Sems., 1996. Ordained archdeacon, 1996, ordained priest 1997, consecrated bishop 1998, Ch. of the East. Asst. to v.p. Family Loan Co., Miami, Fla., 1946-49; civilian supr. USAF, Washington, 1953-55; founder, dir. Blessed Trinity Soc.; editor Trinity mag., L.A., 1960-66; co-founder, exec. v.p., dir. Soc. of Stephen, Altadena, Calif., 1967—; exec. dir. Hong Kong, 1975-81. Lectr. in field. Author: The Acts of the Green Apples, 1974, rev. edit. 1995; co-editor: Charisma in Hong Kong, 1970, Spiritual Songs, 1970, The People Who Walked in Darkness, 1977, The People Who Walked in Darkness II, 1992, 2d edit., 2000. Recipient Achievement award Nat. Assn. Pentecostal Women, 1964; monument erected in her honor Kowloon Walled City Park, Hong Kong Govt., 1996. Republican. Office: Soc of Stephen PO Box 6225 Altadena CA 91003-6225

WILLARD, GARCIA LOU, artist; b. Huntington, W.Va., Apr. 15, 1943; d. Harry Lee and Laura Lillian (Riley) Hall; m. Victor Percy Young, Sept. 2, 1972 (dec. Mar. 1980); m. Roger Lee Willard, Aug. 22, 1988. Student, Marshall U., 1978-83, W.Va. U., 1993, U. N.D., 1994-95. Owner, pres. Young's Fine Art, Huntington, 1975-85, Dyna Line, Wheeling, W.Va., 1980-85; instr. pastel and drawing Oglebay Mus.'s Stifel Fine Art Ctr., Wheeling, 1984-87; instr. pastel and portraiture Ohio U., Athens, 1987; owner, operator Outlines, Phoenix, Ariz., 1988-91; contbg. artist Sonoran Gallery, Phoenix, 1993—. Mem. adv. bd. Profl. Art League, St. Clairsville, Ohio, 1984-85; lectr. and exhbn. juror various art orgns., Ohio, W.Va., Pa., 1987-88; art cons. Journey's End Designs, Wheeling, 1987. One woman shows include: Delf-Norona Mus., Moundsville, W. Va., Ariel Gallery, N.Y.C., Sonoran Gallery, Phoenix; Group shows include: Pen & Brush Club, N.Y.C., 1988, Hermitage Found. Mus., Va., 1988; contbr., illustrator: (book) Dr. Horton on African Art, 1985. Advisor Ariz. Fine Arts Commn., Phoenix, 1989-92. Recipient Best of Show award Delf-Norona Mus., 1985, Molly Guion award for graphics Catharine Lorillard Wolfe Art Club, 1988, Douglas Pickering Carnegie Mellon award, 1986. Fellow Am. Artists Profl. League (Pastel award 1988); mem. Pastel Soc. Am. (signature mem. artist mem., A & M design award, 1988), Acad. Artists Assn. (artist mem., award for pastel portrait 1989), Degas Pastel Soc. (artist mem., M. Grumbacher award for pastel excellence 1988), Nat. Drawing Assn., Art Assn. Harrisburg (artist mem.), Signature Mem. Pastel Soc. Am., N.Y.C. Republican. Avocations: archeology, astronomy, paper-making, attending symphonies, traveling. Office: Sonoran Gallery 8819 W Corrine Dr Peoria AZ 85381-8166 Office Phone: 623-773-1958. Personal E-mail: rlwillard1@msn.com.

WILLARD, NANCY MARGARET, writer, educator; b. Ann Arbor, Mich. d. Hobart Hurd and Margaret (Sheppard) W.; m. Eric Lindbloom, Aug. 15, 1964; 1 child, James Anatole. BA, U. Mich., 1958, PhD, 1963; MA, Stanford U., 1960. Lectr. English Vassar Coll., Poughkeepsie, NY, 1965—. Author: (poems) In His Country: Poems, 1966; Skin of Grace, 1967; A New Herball: Poems, 1968, Testimony of the Invisible Man: William Carlos Williams, Francis Ponge, Rainer Maria Rilke, Pablo Neruda, 1970, Nineteen Masks for the Naked Poet: Poems, 1971, The Carpenter of the Sun: Poems, 1974, A Visit to William Blake's Inn: Poems for Innocent and Experienced Travelers, 1981 (Newbery Medal 1982), Household Tales of Moon and Water, 1983, Water Walker, 1989, The Ballad of Biddy Early, 1989; (short stories) The Lively Anatomy of God, 1968, Childhood of the Magician, 1973; (juveniles) Sailing to Cythera and Other Anatole Stories, 1974, All on a May Morning, 1975, The Snow Rabbit, 1975, Shoes Without Leather, 1976, T0e Well-Mannered Balloon, 1976, Night Story, 1986, Simple Pictures are Best, 1977, Stranger's Bread, 1977, The Highest Hit, 1978, Papa's Panda, 1979, The Island of the Grass King, 1979, The Marzipan Moon 1981, Uncle Terrible, 1982, (adult) Angel in the Parlor: Five Stories and Eight Essays, 1983, The Nightgown of the Sullen Moon, 1983, Night Story, 1986, The Voyage of the Ludgate Hill, 1987, The Mountains of Quilt, 1987, Firebrat, 1988; (novel) Things Invisible To See, 1984, Sister Water, 1993; (play) East of the Sun, West of the Moon, 1989, The High Rise Glorious Skittle Skat Roarious Sky Pie Angel Food Cake, 1991, A Nancy Willard Reader, 1991, Pish Posh said Hieronymus Bosch, 1991, Beauty and the Beast, 1992; illustrator: The Letter of John to James, Another Letter of John to James, 1982, The Octopus Who Wanted to Juggle (Robert Pack), 1990, (novel) Sister Water, 1993, (essays) Telling Time, 1993, (juvenile) A Starlit Somersault Downhill, 1993, (juvenile) The Sorcerer's Apprentice, 1993; author, illustrator: An Alphabet of Angels, 1994; (juvenile) Gutenberg's Gift, 1995, The Good Night Blessing Book, 1996, Cracked Corn and Snow Ice Cream, 1997, The Tortilla Cat, 1998; (poems, with Jane Yolen) Among Angels, 1995, Swimming Lessons, 1996, The Magic Cornfield, 1997; editor: (anthology of poems) Step Lightly: Poems for the Journey, 1998, The Tale I Told Sasha, 1999, (juvenile) Shadow Story, 1999, (juvenile) The Moon and Riddles Diner and the Sunny Side Cafe, 2001, (juvenile) The Mouse, the Cat and Grandmother's Hat, 2003, (scholastic) Cinderella's Dress, 2003. Recipient Hopwood award, 1958, Devins Meml. award, 1967, John Newbery award, 1981, Empire State award, 1996; Woodrow Wilson fellow, 1960; NEA grantee, 1987. Mem. The Lewis Carroll Soc. Office: Vassar Coll Dept English Raymond Ave Poughkeepsie NY 12604-0001

WILLARD, SHIRLEY FAY, management executive; b. San Francisco, Nov. 7, 1933; d. James Lynn and Blanche Bernice (Miller) Cooper; m. Robert Edgar Willard, May 29, 1954; children: Laura Marie, John Judson. Student, Wash. State U., 1951-54; BA in Bus., Calif. State U., 1973. Mgmt. trainee Emporium, San Francisco, 1954-55; asst. buyer Filene's, Boston, 1955-58; pres. Calif. Legal Forms Svcs., Newport Beach, 1985—. Treas. Releaf Costa Mesa, Calif., 1994—. Office: Calif Legal Forms Svc Inc 2973 Harbor Blvd Ste 104 Costa Mesa CA 92626 E-mail: sfwillard@dslextreme.com.

WILLARD-JONES, DONNA C. lawyer; b. Calgary, Alberta, Can., Jan. 19, 1944; m. Douglas E. Jones. BA with honors, U. B.C., 1965, student, 1965-66; JD, U. Oreg., 1970. Bar: Ak. 1970, U.S. Dist. Ct. Ak. 1970, U.S. Ct. Appeals (9th cir.) 1971, U.S. Customs Ct. 1972, U.S. Tax Ct. 1975, U.S. Supreme Ct. 1981. Assoc. Boyko & Walton, 1970-71, Walton & Willard, 1971-73; ptnr. Gruenberg & Willard, 1974, Gruenberg, Willard & Smith, 1974-75, Richmond, Willoughby & Willard, 1976-81, Willoughby & Willard, 1981-89; pvt. practice Anchorage, 1990—. Chmn. fed. adv. group Implementation of Civil Justice Reform Act of 1990, 1991-92; lawyer rep. 9th Cir. Jud. Conf., 1979-80; mem. spl. com. on contempt Ak. Supreme Ct., 1991-92; chmn. Bankruptcy Judge Merit Screening com., 1979; mem. Am. Judicature Soc., 1973-92, Am. Trial Lawyers Assn., 1981-92; bd. dirs. Ak. Legal Svcs. Corp., 1979-80; spkr. in field. Mem. U. B.C. Law Rev.; assoc. editor Oreg. Law Rev.; copy editor Ak. Bar Rag, 1979-84, contbg. editor, 1979-92; annual reviser Probate Counsel, 1972-88. Mem. Anchorage Port Commn., 1987-93, chmn., 1990-93; chmn. Ak. State Officers Compensation Commn., 1986-92; mem. Anchorage Transp. Commn., 1983-87, chmn., 1986-87; vice-chmn. Ak. Code Revision Commn., 1976-78; bd. trustees Ak. Indian Arts, Inc., 1970-92; mem. Chilkat Dancer Ak., 1965—. Recipient Rikli Solo Lifetime Achievement. award, ABA Gen. Pract., 1998. Fellow Am. Bar Found. (life); mem. ABA (ho. dels. 1980-84, 86-96, bd. govs. 1992-96, sec. 1995-96), Nat. Conf. Bar Pres. (exec. coun. 1985-88), Nat. Conf. Bar Founds. (bd. trustees 1983-90), Am. Arbitration Assn., We. States Bar Conf. (pres. 1983-84), Ak. Bar Assn. (Bd. Govs. Disting. Svc. award 1991, bd. govs. 1977-80, pres. 1979-80, pres. 1979-80, numerous coms.), Am. Law Inst. Presbyterian. Office: 124 E 7th Ave Anchorage AK 99501-3608 also: Am Bar Assn 750 N Lake Shore Dr Chicago IL 60611-4403 Fax: 907-278-0449.

WILLE, KARIN L. lawyer; b. Northfield, Minn., Dec. 14, 1949; d. James Virginia Wille. BA summa cum laude, Macalester Coll., 1971; JD cum laude, U. Minn., 1974. Bar: Minn. 1974, U.S. Dist. Ct. Minn. 1974. Atty. Dresselhuis & Assoc., Mpls., 1974-75; assoc. Dorsey & Whitney, Mpls., 1975-76; atty. Dayton-Hudson Corp., Mpls., 1976-84; gen. counsel B. Dalton Booksellers, Edina, Minn., 1985-87; assoc. Briggs & Morgan, Mpls., 1987-88; shareholder Briggs and Briggs, Mpls., 1988—. Co-chair Upper Midwest Employment Law Inst., 1983—. Named Leading Minn. Atty., Super Lawyer, Mpls.-St. Paul Mag., Twin Cities Bus. Monthly and Minn. Law and Politics; named one of Best Lawyers in Am. Mem. ABA, Minn. State Bar Assn. (labor and employment sect., corp. counsel sect., dir. 1989-91), Hennepin County Bar Assn. (labor and employment sect.), Minn. Women Lawyers, Phi Beta Kappa. Office: Briggs & Morgan 80 S 8th St Ste 2200 Minneapolis MN 55402-2157 E-mail: kwille@briggs.com.

WILLE, LOIS JEAN, retired newspaper editor; b. Chgo., Sept. 19, 1931; d. Walter and Adele S. (Taege) Kroeber; m. Wayne M. Wille, June 6, 1954. BS, Northwestern U., 1953, MS, 1954; Litt.D. (hon.), Columbia Coll., Chgo., 1999; H.D. (hon.), Marquette U., 1338; Rosary Coll., 1990. Reporter Chgo. Daily News, 1958-74, nat. corr., 1975-76, assoc. editor charge editorial page, 1977; assoc. editor charge editorial and opinion pages Chgo. Sun-Times, 1978-83; assoc. editor editorial page Chgo. Tribune, 1984-87, editor editorial page, 1987-91, ret., 1991. Author: Forever Open, Clear and Free: the Historic Struggle for Chicago's Lakefront, 1972, At Home in the Loop: How Clout and Community Built Chicago's Dearborn Park, 1997. Recipient Pulitzer prize for public svc., 1963, Pulitzer prize for editorial writing, 1989, William Allen White Found. award for excellence in editorial writing, 1978, numerous awards Chgo. Newspaper Guild, numerous awards Chgo. Headline Club, numerous awards Nat. Assn. Edn. Writers, numerous awards Ill. AP, numerous awards Ill. UPI. Home: 1530 S State St Apt 1011 Chicago IL 60605 E-mail: lowille@aol.com.

WILLE, ROSANNE LOUISE, higher education administrator; b. Hackensack, N.J., Aug. 4, 1941; d. Albert Wille and Rose Marie (Rock) Eberhardt; m. George B. Jacobs, Mar. 12, 1980; children: Leigh, Steven, Alexander, Jeffrey. M Pub. Adminstrn., Rutgers U., 1986; PhD, N.Y.U., 1980. Dept. chair Rutgers U., Newark, N.J., 1978-84, Lehman Coll., Bronx, NY, 1984-87, dean, 1987-92, provost, sr. v.p., 1992—2002; cons. for higher edn., 2002—. Contr. articles to profl. jours. Bd. dirs. Family Support Svcs., Bronx, N.Y., 1994—, bd. dirs. South Bronx Overall Economic Devel., Inc., Bronx, 1991—. Recipient Vision award Family Support Svcs., Bronx, 1996, Thousand Points of Light award Pres. George Bush, Washington, 1991. Mem. N.Y. Acad. Scis., N.Y. Acad. Medicine, Am. Assn. Higher Edn. Avocations: aviation, golf. Address: PO Box 4148 South Hackensack NJ 07606-4148 E-mail: rlwille@earthlink.net.

WILLEFORD, PAMELA P. ambassador; m. George Willeford III; children: Emily Ann, Nancy Kathryn. BA in English and Spanish, U. Tex. Former tchr., Dallas; former dir. devel., coord. Tex. Capitol Rededication Tex. State Preservation Bd.; mem. Tex. Higher Edn. Coordinating Bd., Austin, 1995—, chair, 1998—2003; ptnr., pres. Pico Drilling Ltd., Breckenridge, Tex.; U.S. Amb. to Switzerland, 2003—. Office: Dept of State 5110 Bern Pl Washington DC 20521-5110*

WILLEM, KAREN J. business software company financial executive; BA in Biology, Bucknell U.; MBA in Fin., U. Pitts. V.p., corp. contr. Network Gen., v.p. worldwide sales ops.; exec. v.p. fin. and ops., CFO, Brio Tech., Palo Alto, Calif. Office: Brio Tech 3460 W Bayshore Rd Palo Alto CA 94303-4227

WILLEMS, CONSTANCE CHARLES, lawyer; b. Zuilen, Utrecht, The Netherlands, Oct. 31, 1942; came to U.S., 1967, naturalized, 1977; d. Anton Henri and Maria (Van der Meys) Charles; m. Cornelis Franciscus Willems, May 25, 1965; 1 son, Maurice. BA in Sociology magna cum laude, U. New Orleans, 1974; JD with honors, Tulane U., 1977. Bar: La. 1977, U.S. Dist. Ct. (ea. dist.) La. 1977, U.S. Ct. Appeals (5th cir.) 1977, U.S. Dist. Ct. (mid. dist.) La. 1979, U.S. Supreme Ct. 1983, U.S. Dist. Ct. (we. dist.) La. 1997. Assoc. McGlinchey, Stafford, Mintz, Cellini and Lang, New Orleans, 1977-81, ptnr., 1982—, now McGlinchey Stafford, New Orleans. Instr. law office mgmt. Loyola U. Sch. Law, 1986—90; instr. European law Tulane U. Sch. Law, New Orleans, 1994, New Orleans, 96, New Orleans, 98; bd. mem. World Trade Ctr. New Orleans, 2001. Mem. task force on municipalization; hon. consul for The Netherlands, 1989—; sec.-treas. Consular Corps.; bd. visitors Coll. Liberal Arts, U. New Orleans, 1995—, pres., 1999—; bd. dirs. United Way Gtr. New Orleans, 1987—91, Coun. Internat. Visitors, 1992—94, Com. of 21, 1994—, New Orleans Opera Assn., 1995—. Recipient Disting. alumni award U. New Orleans, 1989. Mem. ABA, La. Assn. Women Attys. (pres. 1983-85, 86-87), La. State Bar Assn. (mem. ho. dels. 1984-85, chair internat. law sect. 1994—), Dutch-Am. Bus. Coun. (founder), New Orleans Ballet Assn. (sec. 2000—). Office: McGlinchey Stafford 643 Magazine St New Orleans LA 70130-3477

WILLENBRINK, ROSE ANN, lawyer; b. Louisville, Ky., Apr. 20, 1950; d. J.L. Jr. and Mary Margaret (Williams) W.; m. William I. Cornett Jr. Student, U. Chgo., 1968-70; BA in Anthropology with highest honors, U. Louisville, 1973, JD, 1975. Bar: Ky. 1976, Ind. 1976, U.S. Dist. Ct. (we. dist.) Ky. 1976, Ohio 1999. Atty. Mapother & Mapother, Louisville, 1976-79; v.p., counsel Nat. City Bank, Louisville, 1980-99, v.p., sr. atty. Cleve., 1999—2004, Louisville, 2004—. Mem. ABA, Ohio Bar Assn., Ky. Bar Assn., Louisville Bar Assn., Conf. on Consumer Fin. Law, Corp. House Counsel Assn., Phi Kappa Phi. Home: 6803 Chadworth Pl Prospect KY 40059 Office: Nat City Bank 101 S 5th St Louisville KY 40202 Office Phone: 502-581-7640. E-mail: Rose.Ann.Willenbrink@nationalcity.com

WILLENZ, JUNE ADELE, writer, public affairs executive, playwright, screenwriter; BS, U. Mich., 1945, MA, 1947; ABD, New Sch. for Social Rsch., 1951. Instr. English Montgomery Coll., Md. Exec. dir. Am. Vets. Com., 1965—2002; chair standing com. on women World Vet. Fedn., 1983—; conf. organizer Women In and After War, Bellagio, Italy, Rape in Armed Conflicts, Istanbul; lectr. USIA; radio and TV guest appearances; del. White House Conf. on Youth, White House Conf. Aging; planning com. 5th and 6th legis. confs. World Vets. Fedn.; scholar in residence Am. U., 1997—; rep. for U.S. Internat. Seminar on Peace Keeping, Baeria, Norway, 2001; lectr., spkr., presenter in field; presenter Internat. Red Cross Conf. on Humanitarian Law, Sondvolden, Norway, 2001. Author: Women Veterans: America's Forgotten Heroines, 1983; co-author: Gender Differences, 1991; editor, author: Dialogue on the Draft, 1967, Human Rights of the Man in Uniform, 1969; editor: AVC Bull.; presenter Am. Hist. Assn., Am. Polit. Sci. Assn.; columnist Stars and Stripes; advisor, commentator (documentary film) The GI Bill: The Law That Changed America, 1997; contbr. articles to profl. jours. Exec. com. 1st VA Adv. Com. Womens Vets., 1983—86, First Lady's Women's Conf. Cir., 1995; mem. UN Decade for Women, head of working group on refugee women and women in armed conflict; accredited non-govtl. orgn. rep. UN; organizer Workshops on Refugee Women, Armed Conflict, Gender Justice, and other issues at UN, N.Y.C. and Geneva; pub. mem. 19th Fgn. Officer Selection Bd. USIA; testified before congl. coms.; exec. agys., chair Task Force on Vets. and Mil. Affairs for Leadership Com. on Civil Rights; spkr. Nat. Urban League, Ctr. for Policy Rsch., NAACP, Nat. League of Cities Vets. Program; advisor; co-chair Coordinating Com. on Voluntary Nat. Svc.; organizer nat. conf. Dialogue on Nat. Svc., 1989, The Draft, 1966, Human Rights of Man in Uniform, 1968, 1970; spkr. Ednl. Problems of Vietnam Vets., 1972; chair subcom. on disabled vets. Pres. Com. Employment of People with Disabilities, 1995—96; active Inter-Univ. Seminar Armed Forces & Soc.; adviser Vets. Brain Trust Conf., 1997. Recipient La Médaille de la Ville de Paris, Mayor of Paris, 2000, Human Rights award, UNA Nat. Capital, 2001, honored by Congl. Black Caucus, 1997, honored for outstanding leadership on behalf of disabled vets., U.S. Dept. Labor, 2002. Mem. Non-Govtl. Orgn. Com. on Status of Women (convener task force on women in armed conflict, convener working group on refugee women), Authors Guild.

WILLERT, SISTER ST. JOAN, health care corporation executive; b. Wheeling, W.Va., June 13, 1924; d. Arthur Edgar and Viola (Fitzsimmons) W. BA, Mt. St. Mary's Coll., 1946; human relations cert., Loyola U., L.A., 1951; MS, Mt. St. Mary's Coll., 1953; health care adminstrn., St. Louis U., 1975. Cert. health care adminstrn., elem. sch. adminstrn., secondary sch. adminstrn. Elem. sch. tchr. Diocese of San Francisco, L.A., and Fresno, 1945-54; elem. sch. prin. several cities, 1954-65; secondary sch. prin. Queen of the Valley Acad., Fresno, Calif., 1965-67, Salpointe Catholic High Sch., Tucson, 1967-70; regional superior Sisters of St. Joseph, L.A., 1970-74, Washington, Md. 1974-77; with health care adminstrn. Daniel Freeman Hosp., Inglewood, Calif., 1977-79; pres., chief exec. officer Health Care Corp. Ariz., Tucson, 1979—. Bd. dirs. Freeman Health Ventures, St. John of God, L.A.; bd. sec. Downtown Devel. Corp., Tucson, 1986—; bd. pres. Our Lady of Lourdes Health Ctr., Pasco, Wash. 1975-81, 85—; bd. chairperson Health Care Corp., St. Louis, 1986—. Contbr. articles to MSMC, 1966, Health Progress, 1982. Chairperson state campaign Arizonans to Protect Quality Health Care, Phoenix, Tucson, 1984-85. Named for Outstanding Svc. to Community Una Noche Plateada, Tucson, 1982; honoree Tucson Diocesan Found. Mem. Ariz. Hosp. Assn. (bd. dirs. 1979—, sec. 1988, chairperson-elect 1989-90, Salisbury Leadership award 1985), Cath. Health Assn. (bylaws com. 1985-86, nominating com. 1984-85), Health Care Corp. Sisters of St. Joseph (chairperson 1985—). Democrat. Roman Catholic. Avocations: reading, tennis, writing. Office: Carondelet St Marys Hosp 1601 W Saint Marys Rd Tucson AZ 85745-2623

WILLETT, ANNA HART, composer, painter; b. Bartlesville, Okla., June 18, 1931; d. Thomas Kellogg Willett and Mary Kathryn (Feist) Willett Dalferes; m. Roger Garland Horn, Aug. 1956 (div. June 1962). B in Music Edn., Southwestern La. Inst., 1954; studied with H. Gunderson, 1955—64; MA, La. State U., 1964, postgrad. in piano, voice majors, 1976-87; studied with K. B. Klaus, Jr., studied with D. Constanides, 1976—87. Lifetime tchr. cert. La. Pub. sch. vocal music tchr. Iberville Parish, Plaquemine, La., 1954-55, Orleans Parish, New Orleans, 1966-71; elem. music pedagogy tchr. St. Mary's Dominican Coll., New Orleans, 1972. Post-grad. rsch. history life scholar in late Medieval English Crown changes LSU. Composer: Dances for Solo Violin, 1981, Weaving Song, 1982, Entertainer's Song (from the opera Omar), 1983, Hercules Piano Variations, 1986, En Ivrez Solo Song, 1989, Solo Songson Poems of Alfieri, 1996, 2000, Variations on a Southern Folk Hymn for piano, Memories of New Orleans, variations for piano, voice Recital at Fest for All, (Operas) How to Murder Mother, 1982, Who Murdered Mother, 1982, Omar, 1984, Caught, 1986, Benedetto Cellini the Opera, 1997, Lines on Wine, 1987, Druid Installation, 1992, Seven Gables, 1998, The Icey Road, 1999; exhibitions include La. State Archives, Baton Rouge, Zeigler Gallery, Jennings, La., Old Bogan Fire Sta., Baton Rouge, Represented in permanent collections David S. Adler, MD; author: The Math. of History, 2000. Mem. ch. choir St. Albans Episc. chapel, 1976—. Scholar, Loyola U. South, New Orleans, 1972—73. Mem.: AAUW, Sigma Alpha Iota, Alpha Sigma Alpha. Avocations: gardening, bridge, local archeology. Home: 2244 Ferndale Ave Baton Rouge LA 70808-2830

WILLETT, LAURA R. internist; MD, U. Calif., San Francisco, 1983. Diplomate Am. Bd. Internal Medicine. Intern Beth Israel Hosp., Boston, 1983—84, resident in internal medicine, 1984—86; physician divsn. gen. internal medicine Robert Wood Johnson U. Med. Group. Office: Robert Wood Johnson Med Group Clinical Acad Bldg 125 Paterson St Ste 5100 A New Brunswick NJ 08901-1977

WILLETT, ROSLYN LEONORE, public relations executive, food service consultant, writer; d. Edward and Celia (Stickler) Sternberg; m. Edward Willett (div.); 1 child, Jonathan Stanley. BA, Hunter Coll., N.Y.C.; postgrad., Columbia U., CUNY, NYU, New Sch. Dietitian YWCA, N.Y.C.; tech. and patents libr., food technologist in charge tech. svcs. and devel. Stein Hall & Co. N.Y.C.; editor McGraw-Hill, Inc., N.Y.C., Harcourt Brace Jovanovich, Inc., N.Y.C.; pub. rels. writer Farley Manning Assocs., N.Y.C.; cons. pub. rels. and food svc. Roslyn Willett Assocs., Inc., N.Y.C., 1959—. Adj. prof. Hunter Coll., Poly U., Columbia U. Sch. Pub. Health; dir. West End Writers Workshop, 1998—2002; seminar presenter in field. Author: The Woman Executive in Woman in Sexist Society, 1971, short stories, essays; assoc. editor Timber Creek Rev., Words of Wisdom, 2001—. V.p. North Shore Ams. for Dem. Action; ofcl. rapporteur Post-Assembly Tech. Sessions, WHO; juror Am. Film Festival, Arts and Scis., 1962—88; chmn. Women's Polit. Caucus, Inc. NY, NJ, Conn, 1971—73; v.p. Mid Hudson Arts and Sci. Ctr., Poughkeepsie, NY; apptd. to regional adv. coun. Fed. SBA, 1976—78; bd. dirs. Small Bus. Task Force, Assn. for Small Bus. and Professions, 1981—85, Rhinebeck Chamber Music Soc., 1985—86, Will Inst., New Paltz, 1980—2001, Women Studies Abstracts, 1971—81; mem. Hunns Lake Assn., 1999—2001. Mem. Pub. Rels. Soc. Am. (accredited), Food Svc. Cons. Soc. Internat. (bd. dirs. 1978-80), N.Y. Acad. Scis., Inst. Food Technologists, Juilliard Assn., Ukiyo-E Soc., Alliance Française, Paris Club, N.Y. Print Club. Avocations: writing, dance, art collecting, hiking, swimming. Home: 97 W Hunns Lake Rd Stanfordville NY 12581-5606 Office: 441 West End Ave New York NY 10024-5328

WILLETT, TERI KAY, art educator; b. Jefferson City, Mo., May 15, 1953; d. Robert Jewell and Esther Mane Cunningham; m. Roger Gregory Willett, Aug. 7, 1976; children: Sarah Ellen Willett-Otto, Jesse Timothy, Anthony Carter. BA, St. Mary Coll., 1975; M in Religious Edn., Loyola U. New Orleans, 1987; MA, Ctrl. Mo. State U., 1997. PC-III Tchg. Cert. Mo., 1998. Educator Holy Family Sch., Independence, Mo., 1985—87, Nativity of Mary Sch., Independence, Mo., 1986—87, St. Mary's H.S., Independence, Mo., 1987—. Workshop presenter Mo. Art Edn. Assn., 1996—. Watercolor paintings, Self Portrait: Me and the Girls (Grand Prize of Show, 1999). Merit badge counselor Boy Scouts Am., Kansas City, Mo., 1993—2003. Recipient Secondary Tchr. of Yr., Nat. Cath. Educators Assn., 1994, Teacher's Honor Award, Nelson/Atkins Mus. of Art, 1996. Mem.: Kans. Watercolor Soc. (assoc.), Mo. Watercolor Soc. (assoc. Signature Status 2002), Mo. Art Edn. Assn. (assoc.; dist. #3 rep. 1993—2003). Achievements include 2 International Shows of Art, 2 National Shows of Art, 4 One woman Show, and several Invitational Art shows. Home: 3602 N Osage Independence MO 64050 Office: St Mary's High School 622 N Main Independence MO 64050 Personal E-mail: terikay@comcast.net. E-mail: twillett@stmhs.org.

WILLETT BIRD, SUSAN, public and motivational speaker; m. John R. Campbell. Law degree, Stanford Law Sch. Practiced law Pillsbury, Madison & Sutro, San Francisco; sr. officer Grubb & Ellis Co.; founder, CEO, chief futurist Wf360, LLC (founded as Women.Future), 1999—. Past. pres. Am. Mediation Coun.; spkr. in field. Co-prodr.: (Broadway plays) Jelly's Last Jam. Mem. Women's Leadership bd. Kennedy Sch. Govt., Harvard U.; mem. internat. coun. Kilby Internat. Awards. Recipient NY Bus. award for success and leadership in bus., Crain, Life of City award, NY Woman mag. Mem.: Internat. Women's Forum, Com. of 200 (founding mem., former chair), Law Review. Achievements include facilitated the MainEvent Middle East RoadShow in Dubai, Cairo, and Amman and the Asia/Pacific RoadShow in Japan, China, Singapore, and Australia. Office: Wf360 1345 Ave Americas 18th Fl New York NY 10105 Office Phone: 917-452-0290.*

WILLETTS, ELIZABETH M. humanities lecturer, actress; b. Toms River, N.J., Nov. 19, 1969; d. Ronald John Edwin and Virginia Ethel Willetts. BA, Rutgers U., 1992; MA, Montclair State U., 1994; postgrad., Drew U. Lectr. in humanities Ocean County Coll., Toms River, 1995—, coord. of recruitment, 1999—; actress N.J. and N.Y.; choreographer, 1992—. Spkr. Ocean County Spkrs. Bur., 1998—; vocalist First United Meth. Ch., Toms River, 1990—. Author poetry. Named Most Promising Actress, Newark Star Ledger, 1994. Mem. NOW, AAUW, Ocean County Pers. and Guidance Assn., Circle K. (advisor 1998—). Avocations: writing, singing, dance, travel. Office: Ocean County Coll College Dr Toms River NJ 08754-2001

WILLEY, FRIEDA ANDERS, adult education educator; b. Independence, VA, Aug. 17, 1936; d. David Alex Anders and Dixie Alice Snow; m. Edward Lake Willey, June 16, 1962; 1 child, Betsy Eden Hawthorne. AA, Bluefield Coll., 1958; BS in Elem. Edn., Salisburg U., 1977, MA, 1978. Elem. sch. tchr. Cecil City Bd. of Edn., Elkton, Md., 1958—62, Dorchester City Bd. of Edn., Cambridge, Md., 1962—84; jr. high sch. tchr. Wythe City Bd. of Edn., Wytheville, Va., 1984—85, Harrington (Del.) Sch. Dist., 1985—86; secondary spl. edn. tchr. Orange County Bd. of Edn., Orange, Va.,
1986—2003, adult educator, 1995—; interpreter Montpelier Found., Montpelier Station, Va., 1999—. Methodist. Avocation: reading, hist. places, writing fiction.

WILLIAMS, ALICE NOEL TUCKERMAN, retired foundation administrator; b. Bethesda, Md., Dec. 21, 1918; d. Walter Rupert and Edith (Abercrombie-Miller) Tuckerman; m. Robert Hugh Williams, June 21, 1939 (dec. 1983); children: Sarah Fenno Williams Lord, Edith Tuckerman Williams Ward. Mem. ladies bd. St. John's Child Devel. Ctr., Washington, 1960—69; pres. ladies bd. St. John's Devel. Ctr., Washington, 1969-72, v.p., trustee, 1970-72. Bd. dirs. Recording For The Blind and Dyslectic, Washington, 1990—94. Mem. Colonial Dames Am. (pres. Washington chpt. 1970-74), Sulgrave Club, The Investment Group (co-founder, pres. 2004). Episcopalian. Avocations: volunteer work, reading.

WILLIAMS, ANASTASIA P. state legislator; b. Panama, May 6, 1957; children: Lisa, Dianne, Jonnathon, Eddy. Grad., Bishop Keough Regional H.S., 1976. Mem. R.I. Ho. of Dels. Mem. West Elmhood Devel. Corp., R.I. Housing & Mortgage, Hartford Cmty. Park. Democrat. Office: RI Ho of Reps State Capitol Providence RI 02903

WILLIAMS, ANN CLAIRE, federal judge; b. Detroit, Aug. 16, 1949; m. David J. Stewart. BS, Wayne State U., 1970; MA, U. Mich., 1972; JD, U. Notre Dame, 1975; hon. degree, Lake Forest Coll., 1987, U. Portland, 1993, U. Notre Dame, 1997. Law clk. to Hon. Robert A. Sprecher, 1975-76; asst. U.S. atty. U.S. Dist. Ct. (no. dist.) Ill., Chgo., 1976-85; faculty Nat. Inst. for Trial Advocacy, 1979—, also bd. dirs.; adj. prof., lectr. Northwestern U. Law Sch., 1979—, John Marshall Law Sch., 1979—; judge U.S. Dist. Ct. (no. dist.) Ill., 1985-99, U.S. Ct. Appeals (7th cir.), Chgo., 1999—. Chief Organized Crime Drug Enforcement Task Force for North Ctrl. Region, 1983-85; mem. ct. adminstrn. and case mgmt. com. Jud. Conf. U.S., 1990-97, chair, 1993-97. Sec. bd. trustees U. Notre Dame; founder Minority Legal Resources, Inc. Recipient Earl Burns Dickerson award, Chgo. Bar Assn., 1997, Tradition of Excellence award, Minority Legal Resources, Inc., 1997, Thurgood Marshall Jurist of Year, Legal Ministry of Second Baptist Church, 1997, Alumni of Year, Black Law Students Assn, U. Notre Dame, 1997. Mem. FBA, Fed. Judges Assn., Ill. State Bar Assn., Ill. Jud. Coun., Cook County Bar Asn., Women's Bar Assn. Ill., Black Women's Lawyers Assn. Greater Chgo. Office: US Ct Appeals 7th Circuit 219 S Dearborn St Ste 2612 Chicago IL 60604-1803*

WILLIAMS, ANN MEAGHER, retired hospital administrator; b. Hull, Mass., May 28, 1929; d. James Francis Meagher and Dorothy Frances (Meagher) Mullins; m. Joseph Arthur Williams, May 15, 1954; children: James G., Mara A., A. Scott (dec.), Gordon M., Mark J., Antoinette M., Andrea M. BS, Chestnut Hill Coll., 1950; MS, Boston Coll., 1952. Radioisotope biologist Air Force Cambridge Rsch. Ctr., Bedford, Mass., 1952-55; asst. mgr. Roxbury Businessmen's Exch., Boston, 1956-66; owner, operator Chatterlane, Osterville, Mass., 1961-66; realtor James E. Murphy Inc., Hyannis, Mass., 1968-77; dir. cmty. affairs Cape Cod Hosp., Hyannis, 1977-95; realtor James E. Murphy, Inc., Osterville, 1995—. Bd. dirs. Cmty. Coun., Mid Cape, Mass., 1977-88, Cape Cod Mental Health Assn., 1977-82, Ctr. for Individual and Family Svcs., Mid Cape, 1982-87, Am. Cancer Soc., Mid Cape, 1981-96, Cape Cod C.C. Ednl. Found., 1997—, exec. com., 1999—; mem. sch. com. Cape Cod Regional Tech. High Sch., 1978—, exec. com., 1983—; mem. United Way of Cape Cod, 1988-89; chmn. fin. com. City of Barnstable, Mass., 1969-77. Named Woman of Yr. Bus./Profl. Women's Club, 1982; recipient cert. of appreciation Am. Cancer Soc., 1983, 88, Pres. Recognition award United Way Cape Cod, 1989. Life Achievement award Mass. Assn. Hosp. Dir., Cons. 2000. Mem.: Nat. Assn. Hosp. Devel., SE Mass. Hosp. Mktg. & Pub. Rels., New Eng. Hosp. Mktg. & Pub. Rels., Am. Soc. Hosp. Mktg. & Pub. Rels., Chestnut Hill Coll. Alumnae Assn., Rotary Leadership Inst. (regional vice chmn. 2003—), Rotary Internat. (gov. 2002—03), Rotary (bd. dir. Osterville 1993—98, pres. 1996—97, asst. gov. dist. 7950 1998—99, area rep. 1999—2000, gov. 2002—03), Hyannis Area C. of C. (bd. dir. 1993—98, ga 2002—03). Roman Catholic. Avocation: community theater. Home: 25 Wedgewood Dr Centerville MA 02632-3162 Office: Linda Hiller & Co 8 W Bay Rd Osterville MA 02655 E-mail: amwms@capecod.net.

WILLIAMS, ANNA M. social worker; b. Fort Meade, Md., Sept. 5, 1956; d. William Arthur and Jacqueline Rae (Hull) W. BA in African Studies, BA in Social Work, U. Md., Balt. County, 1978; MSW, U. Pitts. 1981. Lic., cert. social worker. Investigator child abuse Dept. Social Svcs., Balt., 1978-80; counselor, program coord., supr. girls unit Ward Home for Children, Pitts., 1981-86; mental health therapist Pace Sch., Pitts., 1986-89; program coord. Justice Resources Inc., Balt., 1989-94; therapist Union Meml. Hosp., Balt., 1993-94; v.p. resdl. svcs. Children's Home Wyoming Conf., Binghamton, N.Y., 1994-95; dir. Casey Family Svcs., Balt., 1995—; bus. owner Basket Magic, 1993—; ptnr. Dynamic Families LLC, 2003—. Cons. Youth Advocacy Program, Balt., 1992-94. Bd. dirs. Ward Home for Children, Pitts., 1986-88, South Balt. Youth Ctr., 1993-94, Florence Crittenton, Balt., 1996—, v.p. bd. program, 2001-06, 2002-03; spkr. Meth. Women; adv. bd. WSKG Pub. Broadcasting, 1994-96; cmty. adv. bd. Johns Hopkins Sch. Pub. Health, 1998—; active New Psalmist Bapt. Ch. Mem. NASW, Nat. Girls Caucus (charter), Md. Assn. Resources for Family and Youth (bd. mem. 1997-2002, treas. 1999-2000), Kiwanis Internat., Alpha Kappa Alpha. Democrat. Avocations: reading, cooking, gardening, interior decorating. Office: Casey Family Svcs 25 N Caroline St Baltimore MD 21231 Office Phone: 410-342-7554.

WILLIAMS, ANNETTE POLLY, state legislator; b. Belzoni, Miss., Jan. 10, 1937; Student, Milw. Area Tech. Coll.; BS, U. Wis. Mem. Wis. State Assembly, Milw., 1980—. Attendee African-Am. Leadership summit, New Orleans; organizer Com. 21, 1985, Black Ribbon Commn. to study forced busing, Milw., 1989; panelist Nat. Conf. State Legislators, 1989; active parental sch. choice legislation; lectr. numerous colls. and univs. T.V. appearances include 60 Minutes, ABC World News, This Week with David Brinkley, McNeil Lehrer Report, The British Broadcasting Company, Great Lakes Watch on Washington, CBS This Morning, Both Sides with Rev. Jesse Jackson, CNN News; contbr. articles to profl. jours. Dem. adminstrv. and exec. com.; state chairperson Wis. Jesse Jackson for Pres. campaign; del. Nat. Dem. Conv., 1984, 88; mem. Nat. Dem. Platform Com., 1984; bd. dirs. Rainbow Coalition; founder, chmn. bd. dirs. Milw. Parental Assistance Ctr. Recipient Carrie Chapman Catt award as Nat. Women's Bus. Advocate of Yr., Outstanding Leadership award Dem. party Wis., Harambee Martin Luther King Jr. award for Outstanding Accomplishment and Svc. Am. Legis. Exchange Coun., 1991, Nat. Human Rights award Nat. Cath. Ednl. Assn., 1992, Seton award Career Youth Devel., 1992, Image award for Excellence in Community Svc. and Love of Youth Gamma Phi Delta, 1992, Community Leadership award Libertarian Party Wis., 1992, Liberty award, 1993, Martin Luther King Jr. Community Svc. award Lydell Comm., 1994; named Legislator of Yr. Freedom Mag., 1992; vis. fellow Auckland (New Zealand) Inst. Tech., 1993. Mem. Nat. Black Caucus State Legislators (bd. dirs.). Home: 3927 N 16th St Milwaukee WI 53206-2918 Office: Wis State Assembly State Capitol PO Box 8953 Madison WI 53708-8953

WILLIAMS, ARDITH JEAN, gifted and talented educator; b. Afton, Wyo., Mar. 28, 1950; d. Williams Arthur and LaRue (Edwards) Wilmot; m. Tim C Williams, May 6, 1977; children: Dustin Joseph, (TJ) Timothy Jacque, Jacob Arthur. BS, U. of Idaho, 1976. Cert. Advanced EMT-A Idaho Emergency Med. Svc., 1990; standard exceptional child K to 12 Idaho, 2001, early childhood spl. edn. Idaho, 2001, elem. tchr. Colo., 1977. Law enforcement ranger Nat. Pk. Svc.- Craters of the Moon, Arco, Idaho, 1976; office mgr. Idaho N.G., Pocatello, Idaho, 1977; elem. tchr. grades 3-5 and phys. edn. Moffat County Sch. Dist., Maybell, Colo., 1977—78; spl. edn. tchr. k-12 Butte County Sch. Dist., Arco, Idaho, 1981—; 911 dispatcher

Butte County Sheriff, Arco, Idaho, 1993—99; sixth grade social studies and wellness tchr. Butte County Sch. Dist. 111, Arco, Idaho, 2000—01; presch. tchr. Butte County Sch. Dist. #111, Arco, Idaho, 2001—02. Drug free/healthy lifestyles com. Butte County, Arco, Idaho, 1998—; graduation requirements com. Butte County Sch. Dist. #111, Arco, Idaho, 1999—; spl. edn. rep. Arco/Howe Elem. Sch. Improvement Team, Arco, Idaho, 2002—; Idaho paraprofl. trainer Dept. of Edn., Boise, Idaho, 2003—. 4-H camp nurse Bingham County 4-H, Blackfoot, Idaho, 1993—2003; mem. Idaho Search and Rescue, Arco, Idaho, 1990—99; volunteer-advanced EMT-A Lost River EMT's, Arco, 1990—2003; vol. dispatcher Arco Fire Dept., 1988—93; food chmn. Fun Run, Arco, 2000—03; cub scout leader Boy Scouts of Am., Arco, 1996—2003, merit badge advisor, 2000—03. Specialist fifth class WAC, 1968—71, i. Recipient Tchr. of the Yr. for Dist. 111, Post Register's Newspaper in Edn. Tchr. of the Yr. contest, 2001, Cert. of Achievement, Dept. of the Army, 1971, Svc. Plaque, Idaho N.G., 1977. Mem.: Idaho Edn. Assn. (assoc.), Butte Edn. Assn. (assoc.; negotiator 1993—95), Coun. of Exceptional Children (assoc.). Democrat-Npl. Latter Day Saint. Avocations: watching fireworks and setting up firework displays, steelhead fishing. Office: Arco Elementary PO Box 675 Arco ID 83213

WILLIAMS, BARBARA ANNE, retired academic administrator; b. Camden, N.J., Oct. 14, 1938; d. Frank and Laura Dorothy (Szweda) W. BA cum laude, Georgian Ct. U., 1963; MLS, Rutgers U., 1965; MA, Manhattan Coll., 1973; postgrad., NYU, 1976—81, postgrad., 1993—. Cert. English tchr., N.J.; joined Sisters of Mercy, 1957. Sec. Camden Cath. H.S., 1956-57; registrar Georgian Ct. U., Lakewood, NJ, 1960-66, dir. libr. svcs., 1966-74, dean acad. affairs, 1974-80, pres., 1980-2000, sci. and math. libr., 2000—, pres. emerita, 2000—, archivist, 2003—. Bd. dirs. N.J. Natural Gas Co., 1986-91. Mem. editl. bd. N.J. Woman mag. Bd. dirs., mem. ednl. adv. coun. Diocese of Trenton, N.J., 1983-90; mem. adv. bd. Ocean County Ctr. for Arts, Lakewood, N.J., 1983-91; mem. Ocean County Pvt. Industry Coun., 1983-92; bd. dirs. Monmouth/Ocean Devel. Coun., 1981-84; mem. State of N.J. Student Assistance Bd., 1995-99; mem. Ocean County School-to-Career Com., 1996-2000; mem. art adv. coun. Nat. Mus. Cath. Art and History, 2000—. Named Outstanding Woman N.J. Assn. Women Bus. Owners, 1983; recipient Humanitarian award Monmouth/Ocean Devel. Coun., 1985, Salute to Policymakers award Exec. Women N.J., 1986, Woman in Leadership award Monmouth Coun. Girl Scouts, 1987, Citizen of Yr. Alcoholism & Drug Abuse Coun. Ocean County, 1993, Brotherhood/Sisterhood award Monmouth/Ocean County chpts. NCCJ, 1994, Friend of Scouting award Boy Scouts Am. Jersey Shore Coun., 1999, Leadership award Mercy Higher Edn. Colloquium, 2000. Mem. Assn. of Mercy Colls. (pres. 1981-83, sec. 1996-98), Mercy Higher Edn. Colloquium (mem. exec. com. 1980-87), Ocean County Bus. Assn. (trustee 1982-84), Nat. Assn. Inc. Colls. and Univs. (secretariat 1981-83, 87-91), NAIA (coun. of pres. 1997 2000). Home and Office: Georgian Ct U 900 Lakewood Ave Lakewood NJ 08701-2600 E-mail: williamssb@georgian.edu.

WILLIAMS, BARBARA KITTY, nursing educator; b. Kingsport, Tenn., July 14, 1944; d. Charles H. Penley and Ada Ruth Baldwin; m. Emerson Williams, Dec. 23, 1961. RN, Johnston Meml. Hosp. Sch. Nursing, Abingdon, Va., 1970; BS in Profl. Arts, St. Joseph's Coll., North Windom, Maine, 1981; BSN, East Tenn. State U., 1986; MSN, U. Va., 1991. RN Tenn., Va., clin. nurse specialist, Am. Nurses Credentialing Ctr., 1993. Critical care nurse Holston Valley Cmty. Hosp., Kingsport, 1971—74; faculty Kingsport Sch. Practical Nursing, 1974—76; asst. nursing dir. Johnson County Hosp., Mountain City, Tenn., 1976—78; dir. med. surg. svcs. Bristol (Tenn.) Regional Med. Ctr., 1978—85; asst. prof. nursing Virginia Highlands C.C., Abingdon, Va., 1988—. Adv. bd. YWCA, Bristol, Tenn., 1996—98; mem. bd. Shots for Tots, Rotary Club, Bristol, Tenn., 1995. Mem.: AAUP (award), Bristol Art Guild (pres. 1995—97), Pastel Soc. Am., Assn. Depot Artist, Bristol C. of C. (amb. 1995), Bristol Toastmasters (pres. 1982), Sigma Theta Tau. Methodist. Avocations: painting, travel. Office: Va Highlands Cmty Coll Box 828 Abingdon VA 24212

WILLIAMS, BARBARA STAMBAUGH, editor; b. Jenkins, Ky., Nov. 22, 1937; d. James Cosby and Jessie Kate (Bise) Stambaugh; m. Manning Williams, Sept. 11, 1963. BS in Journalism, U. Tenn., 1959. Polit. reporter News and Courier, Charleston, S.C., 1961-63, 67-76, asst. mng. editor, 1976-81; city hall reporter Camden (N.J.) Courier Post, 1963-67; editor The Evening Post, Charleston, S.C., 1981-90, The Evening Post and News Courier, Charleston, S.C., 1990-91, The Post and Courier, Charleston, S.C., 1991—. Pres. Nat. Conf. Editl. Writers, Rockville, Md., 1992. Bd. dirs. Charleston Sci. and Cultural Edn. Fund. Named Outstanding Newspaper Woman in S.C., S.C. Press Assn., 1962. Mem. Sigma Delta Chi (ByLiner award 1973). Office: The Post & Courier 134 Columbus St Charleston SC 29403-4800 E-mail: barbara@postandcourier.com.

WILLIAMS, BETTY, peace activist; b. Belfast, Northern Ireland, May 22, 1943; m. Ralph Williams, 1961 (div.); 2 children; m. James T. Perkins, 1983. LL.D. (hon.), Yale U.; L.H.D. (hon.), Coll. Siena Heights, 1977. Co-organizer (with Mairead Corrigan) of movement Women for Peace (now Community of Peace People), Belfast, 1976-80. Co-founder (with Mairead Corrigan) mag. Peace by Peace. Co-recipient Nobel Prize for Peace for 1976 (awarded 1977), Norwegian People's Peace Prize, 1976, Carl von Ossietzky prize German Fed. Republic, 1976. Roman Catholic. Address: 208 Camelia St Gulf Breeze FL 32561-4228 also: PO Box 725 Valparaiso FL 32580-0725

WILLIAMS, BETTYE JEAN, English educator; b. Pine Bluff, Ark., July 2, 1946; d. Eunice and Dorothy (Willingham) W. BA in English, Agrl. Meth. and Normal Coll., 1968; M of English, Pittsburg State U., 1970; PhD in Am. Lit., Ind. U. Pa., 1993. Prof. English U. Ark., Pine Bluff, 1968-96, Ind. U. Pa., 1990-93, Pines Tech. Coll., Pine Bluff, 1995. NEH fellow, 1992-93. Mem. NAUW (pres. 1989-90), Nat. Assn. Advancement of Coll. People, Nat. Urban League, Nat. Lang. Assn., Coll. Lang. Assn., Sigma Tau Delta, Delta Sigma Theta. Democrat. Baptist. Avocation: needlepoint. Home: 3402 W 36th St Pine Bluff AR 71603

WILLIAMS, BOBBRETTA M. educational company executive; b. Des Moines, Dec. 11, 1948; d. Robert and Margaret (Preston) Elliston; m. Cecil H. Brewton, Jr.; 1 child, Ayana Michelle. BSE, N.E. Mo. State, 1971; MSE, Drake U., 1975, EdS, 1978, EdD, 1981; BA, Upper Iowa U., 1991. Cert. adminstr., supr., tchr. Tchr. Des Moines (Iowa) Pub. Schs., 1971—90; pres. ABC Diversified, ednl. communications tng. and consultation, Des Moines, 1990—93; coord. Hiatt Jr. High Sch., Des Moines; cons. Voluntary Transfer, Des Moines; elem. prin. Longfellow Sch., Des Moines; dir. Children and Families of Iowa, 1993—2000; cons. Exec. Resources Assistance, 2000—01; dir. The Outreach Project, 2001—.

WILLIAMS, BONNIE LEE, city official; b. Ogdensburg, N.Y., May 30, 1947; d. James Rodger and Violet (Robinson) Cuthbert; m. Earl Williams, Sept. 27, 1997; 1 child, Bonnie-Marie. AA, St. Petersburg Jr. Coll., 1967. Cert. mcpl. clk. Sec. bldg. and pub. works City of Treasure Island, Fla., 1967-73, bd. coord., 1974-78, dep. city clk., 1978—. Mem. Sunset Beach Civic Assn., Treasure Island, 1967-89. Mem. Internat. Inst. Mcpl. Clks., Fla. Assn. City Clks., Treasure Island Hist. Soc. Inc. (pres. 1989-91), Pinellas County Clks. Assn. Republican. Congregationalist. Avocations: writing, bicycling, swimming, computers, reading. Office: City of Treasure Island 120 108th Ave Treasure Island FL 33706-4702

WILLIAMS, CAMILLA, soprano, voice educator; b. Danville, Va. d. Booker and Fannie (Cary) W.; m. Charles T. Beavers, Aug. 28, 1950. BS, Va. State Coll., 1941; postgrad., U. Pa., 1942; studies with, Mme. Marian Szekely-Freschl, 1943-44, 1952, Berkowitz and Cesare Sodero, 1944-46, Rose Dirman, 1948-52, Sergius Kagen, 1958-62; MusD (hon.), Va. State U., 1986, D. (hon.), 1985. Prof. voice Bronx Coll., N.Y.C., 1970, Bklyn. Coll., 1970-73, Queens Coll., N.Y.C., 1974, Ind. U., Bloomington, 1977—, prof. emeritus voice. 1st black prof. voice Cen. Conservatory Music, Beijing, People's Republic China, 1983. Created role of Madame Butterfly as 1st black contract singer, N.Y.C. Ctr., 1946, 1st Aida, 1948; 1st N.Y. performance of Mozart's Idomeneo with Little Orch. Soc., 1950; 1st Viennese performance Menotti's Saint of Bleecker Street, 1955; 1st N.Y. performance of Handel's Orlando, 1971; other roles include Nedda in Pagliacci, Mimi in La Boheme, Marguerite in Faust; major tours include Alaska, 1950, London, 1954, Am. Festival in Belgium, 1955, tour of 14 African countries for U.S. Dept. State, 1958-59, Israel, 1959, concert for Crown Prince of Japan as guest of Gen. Eisenhower, 1960, tour of Formosa, Australia, New Zealand, Korea, Japan, Philippines, Laos, South Vietnam, 1971, Poland, 1974; appearances with orchs. including Royal Philharm., Vienna Symphony, Berlin Philharm., Chgo. Symphony, Phila. Orch., BBC Orch., Stuttgart Orch., many others; contract with RCA Victor as exclusive Victor Red Seal rec. artist, 1944—. Recipient Marian Anderson award (1st winner), 1943, 44, Newspaper Guild award as First Lady of Am. Opera, 1947, Va. State Coll. 75th anniv. cert. of merit, 1957, NYU Presdl. Citation, 1959, Gold medal Emperor of Ethiopia and Key to City of Taiwan during Pres. Johnson's Cultural Exchange Program, 1962, Art, Culture and Civic Guild award, 1962, Negro Musician's Assn. plaque, 1963, Harlem Opera and World Fellowship Soc. award, 1963; named Disting. Virginian Gov. of Va., 1972; inducted Danville (Va.) Mus. Fine Arts and History Hall of Fame, 1974; Camilla Williams Park designated in her honor, Danville, 1974; honored by Ind. U. Sch. Music Black Music Students' Orgn., 1979; named to Hon. Order Ky. Cols., 1979; honored by Phila. Pro Arte Soc., 1982; Disting. award of Ctr. for Leadership and Devel., 1983; Taylor-Williams student residence hall at Va. State U. named in Billy Taylor's and her honor, 1985, hon. by New York Philharmonic, 1998, hon. by Amistad Rsch. Ctr., Tulane Univ., for Outstanding Contbn. to the Arts, 1998. Mem. NAACP (hon. life), Internat. Platform Assn., Alpha Kappa Alpha. Office: Ind U Sch Music Bloomington IN 47401

WILLIAMS, CAROL ANN, state legislator; b. Cambridge, Mass., Feb. 2, 1937; widowed; 4 children. Student, San Jose State U., 1969; grad., N.H. Coll., 1995. Adminstr. Santa Clara County, ret.; mem. N.H. Ho. of Reps. (dist. 39), Concord, 1996—; mem. resources, recreation and devel. coms. N.H. Ho. of Reps., Concord, 1996—. Mem. Gov.'s Commn. on Disabilities, 1994—; bd. dirs. Granite State Ind. Living, 1996—. Roman Catholic. Home: 127 Prout Ave # 1 Manchester NH 03103-2840 Office: NH State Legis State House Concord NH 03301

WILLIAMS, CAROL H. advertising executive; b. Chgo. d. Clarence Earl Williams and Betty Jane Norment-Williams; m. Tipkins Hood; 1 child. Student, Northwestern U. Copywriter Leo Burnett Agy., Chgo., 1969—80; creative dir., sr. v.p. Foote-Cone & Belding, San Francisco, 1980—85; prin., owner Carol H. Williams Advt., Inc., Oakland, Calif., 1986—. Active US Dream Acad. Recipient Outstanding Women in Mktg. and Comm. award, Ebony Mag., 2001. Office: Carol H Williams Advertising Inc 555 12th St Ste 1700 Oakland CA 94607-4058*

WILLIAMS, CAROL JORGENSEN, social work educator; b. New Brunswick, NJ, Aug. 12, 1944; d. Einar Arthur and Mildred Estelle (Clayton) Jorgensen; m. Oneal Alexander Williams, July 4, 1980. BA, Douglass Coll., 1966; MS in Computer Sci., Stevens Inst. Tech., 1986; MSW, Rutgers U., 1971, PhD in Social Policy, 1981. Child welfare worker Bur. Children's Svcs., Jersey City, 1966-67, Outagamie County Dept. Social Svcs., Appleton, Wis., 1967-69; supr. WIN N.J. Divsn. Youth and Family Svcs., New Brunswick, 1969-70; coord. Outreach Plainfield (N.J.) Pub. Libr., 1972-76; rsch. project dir. County and Mcpl. Govt. Study Commn., N.J. State Legislature, 1976-79; prof. social work Kean U., Union, 1979—, assessment liaison social work program, 1987-2000, dir. MSW program, 1995-2000. Chmn. faculty senate gen. edn. com. Kean U., N.J., 1990-94, chmn. faculty senate ad hoc com. for 5-yr. review of gen. edn. program, 1991-93, retention and tenure com. Sch. of Liberal Arts, 1988-94, vice chmn., 1992-94; cons. N.J. div. Youth and Family Svcs., 1979-93, Assn. for Children N.J., 1985-88; cons., evaluator Thomas A. Edison Coll., 1977—, N.J. Dept. Human Svcs., 2003; cons. advanced generalist practice La. State U. Grad. Sch. Social Work, 2002. Adv. coun. Outdoor World, 2000-03. Named Grad. Tchr. of Yr., Kean U. social work grad. students, 2001. Mem.: NASW (chpt. com. on nominating and leadership identification 1990—92, co-chmn. 1991—92), NOW, Nat. Network Social Work Mgrs., Kean U. Fedn. Tchrs., Assn. Baccalaureate Program Dirs. (com. on info tech. and distance edn. 1995—, assoc. editor of BPQ Update 2000—, mem. editl. bd. Jour. Baccalaureate Social Work), Coun. on Social Work Edn. (dir. APM Med. Tech. Ctr. 1999—2002, chair subcom. on abstract rev. 2000—02, commn. on confs. and faculty devel. 2000—02, chair electronic poster session 2002—, bd. dirs. 2003—, pers. com. 2003—, investment com. 2003—), Outdoor World (adv. coun. 2000—02), Good Sam Club. Democrat. Home: 32 Halstead Rd New Brunswick NJ 08901 1619 Office: Kean U Social Work Program Morris Ave Union NJ 07083-7117 E-mail: caroljwilliams@worldnet.att.net.

WILLIAMS, CAROL MARIE, retired secondary school educator; b. Kansas City, Kans., June 10, 1939; d. Leonard Cropley and Minnie Marie (Wass) Nicholson; m. Howard Dean Williams, Dec. 29, 1961; children: Jeffrey Allen, Gregory Scott AA, Kansas City (Mo.) Jr. Coll., 1959; BS in Edn., Ctrl. Mo. State U., 1962. English tchr. Raytown (Mo.) H.S., 1961-62; English tchr., coord. dist. lang. arts Ruskin H.S., Kansas City, Mo., 1964-66; English tchr. Hickman Mills H.S., Kansas City, 1969-70; tchr. English, debate, history, leadership comms., student govt. Andover (Kans.) H.S., 1982-95, dist. lang. arts coord., dept. chair, 1982-95; English tchr. Olathe South (Kans.) H.S., 1996—2003. Coord., debate and forensics coach Andover Sch. Dist., 1982-85, chair North Ctrl. Accreditation, 1983-84, supt., prin. adv. couns., 1983-95, dist. curriculum coun., 1983-95; coord. AP Lang. Exam. Prep. Workshop; new tchr. mentor; sr. connector tchr. Publicity editor The Lamp mag., 1969 (Nat. Recognition award 1969); contbg. editor Topeka mag., 1977-79; co-editor Andover Rsch. jour., 1993. Recipient Outstanding Tchr. and Mentor Recognition award U. Kans., Outstanding H.S. Edn. Recognition award Kans. Newman Coll., Golden Apple award Andover Sch. Dist. 385, 1992. Mem. NEA, Kans. Olathe-NEA, Nat. Coun. Tchrs. of English, Kans. Assn. Tchrs. of English. Republican. Episcopalian. Avocations: reading, music, tennis, travel, writing. Home: 1204 W 63d St Kansas City MO 64113 Office: Olathe South HS 1640 E 151st St Olathe KS 66062-2851

WILLIAMS, CAROLE ANN, retired cytotechnologist; b. Duquesne, Pa., Apr. 14, 1934; d. Theodore Wylie and Dorothy Belle (Mehrmann) Williams. BS, Chatham Coll., 1956; postgrad., Case-Western Res. U., 1956-57; MS, Calif. State U., 1989. Cytotechnologist Clin. Path. Lab. of Paul Gross, Pitts., 1957-59; chief cytotechnologist, tchg. supr. Presbyn. U. Hosp., Pitts., 1959-63; staff Pathology Lab. of Drs. Armanini & Wegner, Stockton, Calif., 1964; chief cytotechnologist, tchg. supr. Hosp. of Good Samaritan, L.A., 1964-89; dir. cytotechnology tng. program UCLA Med. Ctr., 1989-99. Condr. workshops in field. Mem. Am. Soc. Clin. Pathologists (cytotech exam. com. bd. registry 1978-84, mem. bd. govs. 1990-95), Calif. Assn. Cytotechnologists (pres. 1967-68, 72-73), Internat. Acad. Cytology, Am. Soc. Cytopathology (Technologist of Yr. award 1981, Excellence in Edn. award 1998). Democrat. Presbyterian. Home: 2460 Stoner Ave Los Angeles CA 90064-1326 Office: Unilab Pathology Inst 448 N Bedford Beverly Hills CA 90210 E-mail: cwilly@ucla.edu.

WILLIAMS, CAROLYN, school counselor; b. Barnwell, S.C., Nov. 17, 1949; d. Jessie Ashley and Harriett (Holmes) Odom; m. Melvin Lee Williams; children: Tarla, Melanie, Harriett. BS in Edn., Paine Coll., 1972; MEd, Augusta Coll., 1979, MEd in Counseling, 1992; EdS in Counseling, Ga. So. U., 2000. Cert. sch. counselor, Ga.; lic. profl. counselor, Ga.; nat. cert. counselor. Tchr. Richmond County Bd. Edn., Augusta, Ga., 1973-94; counselor Columbia County Bd. Edn., Martinez, Ga., 1994—. Assessor tchr. performance Ga. Dept. Edn., Augusta, 1983-90; mem. bias com. Ga. Assessment Divsn., Atlanta, 1993—. Chair Stevens Creek Guidance Com., 1994-96. Recipient 3d Pl. Coach award Math. Count Competitions, 1988, 89, Honors Tchrs. award NASA, 1988. Mem. Am. Sch. Counselor Assn., Ga. Sch. Counselors Assn., Columbia County Sch. Counselor Assn., Ga. Educators Assn., Nat. Assn. Educators. Avocations: speaking to church groups, reading, presenting workshops on stress relief, travel. Home: 3308 Sugar Mill Rd Augusta GA 30907-3627

WILLIAMS, CAROLYN, secondary school educator; Resource specialist, tchr. spl. needs students Bernardo Heights Middle Sch., San Diego. Past bd. mem. Internat. Dyslexia Soc. Mem.: Nat. Bd. for Profl. Tchg. Stds. (bd. mem.). Office: Bernardo Heights Middle Sch 12990 Paseo Lucido San Diego CA 92128

WILLIAMS, CAROLYN ANTONIDES, university dean; b. Louisville, Oct. 27, 1939; d. John Dwight and Dorothy Ida Marie (Hoffman) Antonides; m. Frank Canon Williams, Dec. 26, 1961. BS with honors in Nursing, Tex. Woman's U., 1961; MS in Pub. Health Nursing Edn., U. N.C., 1965, PhD in Epidemiology, 1969. Asst. prof. nursing Emory U., Atlanta, 1968, assoc. prof., 1969, prof., dir. grad. programs and rsch., 1969-71; assoc. prof. nursing, asst. prof. epidemiology U. N.C., Chapel Hill, 1971-81, assoc. prof. nursing, rsch. assoc. Health Svcs. Rsch. Ctr., from 1971, assoc. prof. epidemiology, 1981-84; dean Coll. Nursing, prof. U. Ky., Lexington, 1984—. Mem. Pres.'s Commn. Study of Ethical Problems in Medicine and Biomed. and Behavioral Rsch., 1980-82; chair rsch. adv. com. Am. Nurses Found., 1979-81; mem. planning com. study of nursing and nursing edn. Inst. Medicine of NAS, 1980; cons. WHO in S.Am. Mem. editorial bd. Family and Community Health, 1977-90, Advances in Nursing Sci., 1979-88, Internat. Jour. Nursing Studies, 1981—; also articles, chpts. to books. USPHS fellow U. N.C., 1969. Fellow APHA (publs. bd., Young Practitioner award 1973), Am. Acad. Nursing (pres. 1983-85); mem. ANA (chair commn. nursing rsch. 1980-82), Coun. Nurse Rschrs., Soc. Epidemiol. Rsch., Am. Assn. Colls. Nursing (pres. 2000—), Delta Omega, Sigma Theta Tau (bd. dirs.). Democrat. Baptist. Office: U Ky Coll Nursing 315 Con Hslc Bldg Lexington KY 40536-0001

WILLIAMS, CAROLYN ELIZABETH, manufacturing executive; b. L.A., Jan. 24, 1943; d. George Kissam and Mary Eloise (Chamberlain) W.; m. Richard Terrill White, Apr. 9, 1972; children: Sarah Anne, William Daniel. BS, Ga. Inst. Tech., 1969; MM, Northwestern U., 1988. Saleswoman Ea. Airlines, Atlanta, Montreal (Can.) and Seattle, 1964-69; job analyst Allied Products Corp., Atlanta, 1969-70, mgr. Frankfort, Mich., 1970-71, planning analyst, sr. planning analyst Chgo., 1972-74, dir. planning, 1974-76, staff v.p. planning, 1976-79, v.p. planning and bus. research, 1979-86, v.p. corp. devel., chief planning officer, 1986-93; pres. White, Williams & Daniels, 1993—. Mem. adv. bd. Ga. Inst. Tech.; bd. dirs. United Way. Mem. Winnteka Yacht Club.

WILLIAMS, CECELIA PEAY, retired psychologist; b. Boston, Sept. 29, 1924; d. Moses and Rosa Ophelia Peay; 1 child, Rona. Grad., Boston Clerical Sch., 1944; BA, Calif. State U., L.A., 1966, MS, 1970. Legal secretary private practice Attorney's Office, Boston, Ma, 1944—45; sec. Washington D.C. Vet's Adminstrn., John Hay Whitney Found., N.Y.C., Crippled Children's Soc., L.A.; adminstrv. sec. Galton Inst., L.A., 1965—68; bus. tchr. L.A. Unified Sch. Dist., 1969—72, sch. psychologist, 1973—98, adminstrv. cons., 2000—. Oral commr. Bd. Behavioral Sci. Mem. Baldwin Hills Neighborhood Assn., L.A., 1988—. Mem.: L.A. Assn. Sch. Psychologists (pres. 1980—81), Delta Kappa Gamma Beta Xi (pres. 1993—94), Chi State Delta Kappa Gamma.

WILLIAMS, CECILIA LEE PURSEL, optometrist; b. Lewisburg, Pa., Nov. 15, 1948; d. Lee LaVerne and Geraldine May (Steininger) Pursel; m. Richard Lee Williams, May 17, 1975; 1 son, Kent Lec. Student, Lycoming Coll., 1966-68; BS, Pa. Coll. Optometry, 1970, OD, 1972. Lic. and/or cert. optometrist, D.C., Pa., N.Y., N.J., Va. Rsch. optometrist in soft lens materials Gumpelmayer Optik, Vienna, Austria, 1973; optometrist Sterling Optical Co. Contact Lens Ctr., Washington, 1974-79; pvt. practice optometry Springfield, Va., 1980—. Recipient Clin. Efficiency award Pa. Coll. Optometry, 1972; Women's Aux. of Pa. Optometrists scholar, 1968-70, 70-72; Pa. State grantee, 1968-70, 70-72. Mem. Optometric Ctr. of Nation's Capital (dir. 1977-80), Am. Optometric Assn., Va. Optometric Assn., No. Va. Optometric Soc., Nat. Honor Soc. for Optometry, Omega Delta. Home: 3600 Wilton Hall Ct Alexandria VA 22310-2176 Office: 7241 Commerce St Springfield VA 22150-3411

WILLIAMS, CHARLOTTE EDWINA, secondary school educator, real estate manager; b. Phila., Jan. 5, 1945; d. Charles Edward and Elaine Frances Lydia (Scott) Williams; m. Charles Ross, III, Jan. 19, 1971 (div. June 1985); 1 child, Amber Charlotte. BS, Cheyney (Pa.) State U., 1968; MEd, U. So. Miss., 1989; postgrad., Temple U., 1996—. Tchr. Phila. Pub. Schs., 1968—69, adminstr., 1968—69, tchr., 1972—, adminstr., 1972—. Majority inspector Election Bd., Phila., 1982-90; treas. West Ctrl. Germantown Neighbors, Phila., 1995—; sec. Jack and Jill of Am., Inc., Phila., 1980-82. Mem. Phi Delta Kappa, Alpha Kappa Alpha. Avocations: photography, real estate remodeling.

WILLIAMS, CHERYL A. secondary school educator; b. Neosho, Mo., July 7, 1957; d. Travestine Williams. BS in Math., Tex A&M U., 1978, postgrad., 1978-79, Rose State Coll., 1980-81, Sheppard Tech. Tng. Ctr., 1980-81; MS in Math., U. Tex., 1997. Computer scientist Tinker AFB, Oklahoma City, 1980-81, Defense Comm. Agy., Washington, 1986; tchr. Parent Child Inc., San Antonio, 1989; asst. sec. Antioch Bapt. Ch., San Antonio, 1989-92; substitute tchr. San Antonio Ind. Sch. Dist., 1990-93; instrnl. asst. Northside Ind. Sch. Dist., San Antonio, 1995-96, asst. tchr., 1994-95, North East Ind. Sch. Dist., San Antonio, 1996—2001; rep. West Telemarketing, 1998-99; math. tutor Alamo C.C. Dist., 1998—99, instr. math., 1998—, St. Philips Coll., 1998—2001; math. tutor Trave and G.G.'s Tutorial Svc., 1999—; instr. math. Guardian Angel Performing Arts Acad., 2002—. Asst. mgr. Fashion Pl., San Antonio, 1994—95; tax preparer H&R Block, 1994—95; distbr. Avon, 1999—2001; indep. beauty cons. Mary Kay Cosmetics, 1999—; scorer Harcourt Brace Corp., 2001, Randstad, 2001; rep. Express Svcs., 2001; cons. Prepaid Legal Svcs., Inc., 2003. Counselor YMCA, San Antonio, 1989-91; active Girl Scouts U.S., 1964-86; mem. choir, asst. sec. area ch., 1972, tutor, 1970—, tchr. Sunday Sch., 1973-86, asst. sec. Sunday Sch., 1973-86, 88—, asst. ch. sec., 1988-91; mem. Dorcas Circle, Lupus Found. Am., Biomed. Rsch. U. Tex., 1995—; mem. Epilepsy Found. Am., Tex. Head Injury Assn., Nat. Head Injury Assn., Smithsonian Instn. Mem. NEA, Tex. Edn. Assn., Mu. Alpha Theta. Avocations: jigsaw puzzles, bowling. Office: 1606 E McKinney #4212 Denton TX 76209

WILLIAMS, COLLEEN, newscaster; b. Winston-Salem, NC; married; 1 child. BS in edn., Creighton U., U. Nebr. Drive-time anchor, gen. assignment reporter WOW Radio, Omaha, 1977; anchor WOWT_TV, Omaha, 1978—81, KPIX-TV, San Francisco, 1981—83, KCBS-TV, Los Angeles, 1983—86; weekend anchor NBC4, Los Angeles, 1986—93, anchor, Channel 4 News at 5pm, 1993—, anchor, Channel 4 News at 11pm, 1997—. Recipient Local Emmy Awards, Los Angeles, Best Daily Newscast (60 min.), 1995, Outstanding contbn. to "OJ Simpson: The Trial" news series, 1995, AP Trophy for best news mini-series, "Kids Who Kill", 1987. Office: NBC4 3000 W Alameda Ave Burbank CA 91523*

WILLIAMS, CONSTANCE, state senator; b. June 27, 1944; m. Sankey V. Williams; 2 children. BA, Barnard Coll., 1966; MBA, U. Pa., 1980. Rep. Pa. House of Reps., 1996—2001; Pa. state senator, 2001—. Democrat. Jewish. Office: 352 Capitol Bldg Senate Box 203017 Harrisburg PA 17120-2020 E-mail: cwilliams@pasenate.com.

WILLIAMS, CYNTHIA ANN, small business owner, pediatrics nurse; b. Portsmouth, Va., Dec. 8, 1959; d. Kenneth Leroy Miller and Connie Lee Miller (Joyner); life ptnr. Ivan Joseph Williams; m. John Leonard Bibbins; m. Sidney Small III; children: Sidney Lekenny Small, Joshua Tadarrell Small; m. Ashton Mcgregor Smith Jr.; children: Ebony Ashtone Smith, Ashley Mahogany Smith. Diploma in med. specialist, Acad. Health Sci., Fort Sam Houston, Tex., 1982, diploma for lic. practical nurse, 1986; AAS, U. Md., 1994; BSN, George Mason U., 2004; BA in Theology, Christian Life Sch. Theology, 2004—. Cert. Basic Cardiac Life Support, 1982, Neonatal Advanced Life Support, 1986, lic. Practical Nurse, 1986, cert. Emergency Medical Technician Basic, 2001; Ordained Minister Victory New Testament Fellowship, 2000; foster parent Va. Enlisted US Army, 1981, advanced through ranks to staff sgt., ret., 2001; wardmaster mother baby unit Dewitt Army Cmty. Hosp., US Army, Fort Belvoir, Va., 1995—96; North Atlantic regional command retention Dewitt Army Cmty. Hosp., North Atlantic Regional Med. Command/US Army, Fort Belvoir, Va., 1996—98, in charge of ob-gyn clinic and well woman clinic, 1998—2000, in charge of ob-gyn clinic Seoul, Republic of Korea, 2000—01; in charge first replacement med. detachment,anthrax coord. 121st Gen. Hosp., 18th Med. Command, Seoul, Republic of Korea, 2001; pvt. duty in- home pediat. nurse Unique Nursing, Annandale, Va., 2003—; mgr. Anchor of Hope Bookstore, Woodbridge, Va., 2003—; owner, founder record label Eternal Life Prodns.; owner, founder clothing line One of Those Women. Combat lifesaver instr. US Army, Taegu, 1987—2000, customer svc. sch. excellence instr., Seoul, 2000—01; EMT, 2001—02. Author: One Of Those Women, 2001, Marriage: Not Just A Simple "I Do", 2001. Dir., founder FreeWill Fellowship Ministry, Woodbridge, 2000—; min. Hope Aglow Christian Ctr., Woodbridge, 2002—; ptnr. in many ministries. Mem.: NonCommissioned Officer Assn., Mighty Warrior Intercessor Prayer Team, U.S. Official Presdnl. Prayer Team. Avocations: writing, gardening, art, crafts, foster parenting. Office: Free-Will Fellowship Ministry 12600 Westport Ln Woodbridge VA 22192 E-mail: oneofthosewomen@yahoo.com.

WILLIAMS, DARCEL PATRICE, writer, editor; b. Houston, Nov. 23, 1958; d. Leroy and Estelle Forch Williams; m. Jason LaRue Williams, Sr., May 26, 1979 (div. Sept. 0, 1985); 1 child, Jason LaRue II. Student, Tex. So. U., 1977—81, U. Houston, 1985—88. Lic. massage therapist City of Tulsa, 1993. Acctg. Taft Broadcasting, Houston, 1981—85; office mgr. DeColores Prodns., Houston, 1989—90; cmty. ctr. dir. Helping Hands - Riverview Pk., Tulsa, 1995; author Am. Book Pub. Group, Salt Lake City, 1999—, sr. editor, 1999—2003. Creative adviser/cons. Various Ind. Entrepreneurial Enterprises, Tulsa, 1989—2003. Author: (novels) Soaring On Clipped Wings (Book of Month, 2004), (screenplays) Fighting to Love; senior editor: novels Cryer's Valley, Have No Mercy; web designer, writer (web site) www.DarcelWilliams.com;, author poetry. Named Humanitarian of Month, 2003. Mem.: Younity Revs. Guild Worldwide, Disilgold Lit. Network Assn., Nat. Writers Union, Authors Den Forum (life). Achievements include design of safety design product for use in vehicular transportation of children; product for walking in hazardous environmental conditions. Avocations: singing, music, sewing and design, swimming, reading.

WILLIAMS, DEEANNA MAXINE, secondary school educator; d. Max Leffingwell and Phyllis Elaine (Evans) Gaines; children: Jon Simpson, Samantha Ayla, Sarah Jon. BS Secondary Math. Edn., Ea. Mont. Coll., Billings, 1986. 5-12 Math Teacher Mont., 1986. Coll. math instr. Ea. Mont. Coll., Billings, 1991—92; jr. high math tchr. Lodge Grass (Mont.) Jr. High, 1992—96; homework helpline math tchr. CESA/Ameritech, Eau Claire, Wis., 1996—97; mid. sch. math tchr. Lovell Mid. Sch., Lovell, Wyo., 1997—99; h.s. math tchr. Lame Deer H.S., Lame Deer, Mont., 1999—2003; alternative ed.math instuctor Lame Deer Alternative Edn., Lame Deer, Mont., 2003—. Adv. bd. mem. TCUP, Lame Deer, Mont., 2003—. Adv. coun. mem. Head Start Program, Lame Deer, Mont., 2001—02. Mem.: Phi Delta Kappa. Home: PO Box 1371 Lame Deer MT 59043 Office: Lame Deer Alternative Edn Cheyenne Ave Lame Deer MT 59043 Personal E-mail: tia@rangeweb.net. E-mail: deeannawilliams@lamedeer.k12.mt.us.

WILLIAMS, DELETA, state legislator; BS, Ctrl. Mo. State U. Mem. Mo. Ho. of Reps. from 121st dist., 1993—. Mem. Citizens for Drug Free Environment, Inc. Mem. Bus. and Profl. Women, C. of C., Women's Dem. Club, Mo. Fedn. Dem. Women's Club. Address: 110 E Hale Lake Rd Warrensburg MO 64093-3015 Office: Mo Ho of Reps State Capitol Building Jefferson City MO 65101-1556

WILLIAMS, DIANA, news anchor, reporter, journalist; BA in Econs., Duke U. Gen. assignment reporter WSOC-TV, Charlotte, N.C.; 6 and 11 PM news anchor, reporter WBTV, Charlotte, N.C.; gen. assignment reporter, noon anchor, 5 o'clock news anchor reporter WNEV-TV, Boston; gen. assignment reporter WABC-TV/ABC Inc., N.Y.C., 1991—92, reporter, anchor Eyewitness News, 1992—, host Eyewitness News Up Close. Reporter N.Y.C. Dem. Nat. Conv., 1992, San Diego Rep. Conv., 1996, Phila. Rep. Conv, 2000; trustee Nat. Academy for Television Arts and Sciences. Recipient Headliner award, New York Associated Press award. Mem.: The Duke Library Advisory Bd.*

WILLIAMS, DIANE, writer, editor; b. Chgo., Jan. 16, 1946; d. William Maurice and Mary Rosen Swartz; m. Paul Casey Williams, June 28, 1970 (div. 1993); children: Jacob, Alexander. BA in English Lit., U. Pa., 1968. Asst. editor J. G. Ferguson divsn. Doubleday, N.Y.C., 1969—71, Scott, Foresman Co., Glenview, Ill., 1971—73; assoc. editor Sci. Rsch. Assoc., Chgo., 1973—76; co-editor StoryQuarterly, Glenview, 1985—97; founding editor NOON, N.Y.C., 2000—. Vis. asst. prof. Syracuse (N.Y.) U., 1999; vis. assoc. prof. Bard Coll., Annandale-on-Hudson, NY, 2001. Co-editor: (anthology) The American Story: The Best of StoryQuarterly, 1990; author: (stories) This Is About the Body, the Mind, the Soul, the World, Time, and Fate, 1990, Some Sexual Success Stories Plus Other Stories in Which God Might Choose to Appear, 1992, (stories and novella) The Stupefaction, 1996, Excitability: Selected Stories, 1998, Romancer Erector, 2001; contbr. stories to jours.;, author short stories, novellas. Recipient Pushcart prize, 1991, 1992, 2000. Office: NOON PMB 298 1369 Madison Ave New York NY 10128

WILLIAMS, DIANE ELIZABETH, architectural historian, photographer; b. Glendale, Calif., July 9, 1948; BA, Calif. State U., L.A., 1973; MA, UCLA, 1988. Cert. elem. tchr., Calif. Tchr. L.A. area schs., 1975-78; editorial asst. L.A. Times, 1978-80, copyeditor, feature writer, 1980-83; preservation planning cons. Sierra Madre, Calif., 1983-94; assoc. planner Environ. Planning Assocs., L.A., 1989; asst. planner City of Burbank, Calif., 1989-90; assoc. planner City of Claremont, Calif., 1990-91; planner City of Glendale, Calif., 1991-94; sr. archtl. historian Hardy Heck Moore & Assocs., Austin, Tex., 1994, ptnr., 1995; preservation planning cons. Austin, 1996—. Instr. Cerritos Community Coll., Norwalk, Calif., 1990-94. Bd. dirs. Pasadena Heritage, 1984-90, sec., 1985-86; mem. steering com. Pasadena Residents in Def. of the Environment, 1988-90; reader Henry E. Huntington Libr. and Art Gallery, 1985—; commr. Cultural Heritage Commn., City of Pasadena, 1990-93; mem. state bd. of rev. Tex. Hist. Commn., 1999—, vice chmn., 2003-04, chmn. 2004—. Recipient Cecilia Steinfeldt fellowship for Rsch. in the Arts and Material Cutlure, 2002. Mem. Soc. Archtl. Historians (bd. dirs. So. Calif. chpt. 1989-94, v.p. 1991-92, bd. dirs. Tex. chpt. 1997—, founding editor SPECS 1997). Avocations: hiking, travel, study of Native Am. cultures, photography. Office: Diane E Williams & Assocs PO Box 49921 Austin TX 78765-0921 Office Phone: 512-458-2367. E-mail: texashistory@juno.com.

WILLIAMS, DONNA LEE H. state agency administrator; b. Wilmington, Del., Nov. 13, 1960; d. Ronald Lee and Loretta M. (Simonson) H.; m. John R. Williams, Oct. 8, 1988. AA, Wesley Coll., 1979; BA in Govt., Coll. William and Mary, 1981; JD, Widener U., 1984. Atty. Prickett, Jones, Elliott, Kristol & Shnee, Dover, Del., 1983-87, Bayard Handelman & Murdock, Dover, 1987-92; ins. commr. State Del., Dover, 1993—. Mem. Nat. Assn. Ins. Commrs., Del. Bar Assn., Kent County Bar Assn. (past pres.), Women Bus. Leaders, Women's Rep. Club Dover (pres. 1985-87). Methodist. Avocations: travel, sewing, english handsmocking, golf. Office: Del Dept Ins 841 Silver Lake Blvd Dover DE 19904-2465

WILLIAMS, DOROTHY S. consultant nurse; b. New Orleans, La., July 17, 1951; d. Daniel Joseph and Bertha Ella Smith; children: Dwaine LeRoi Smith, Andre' LaRay. BS, Coll. Bibl. Studies, 2003. RN Bd.Nurse Examiners, Tex., 1981; Ordained minister Hope of Glory Ministry, Houston, 2001. Nurse Kelsey-Seybold Clinic, Houston, 1997—. Author: (book) Let Go & Let God, 2002. Chaplain intern St. Lukes Episcopal Hosp., Houston, 1999—2000; vol. Kelsey-Rsch. Found., Houston, 2002, Susan G. Komen Breast Cancer Found., Houston, 1999. Office: Hope Of Glory Ministry POBox 451307 Houston TX 77245 Personal E-mail: nursedsw@aol.com. E-mail: hogministry@aol.com.

WILLIAMS, DOROTHY STANDRIDGE, soft drink company official, civic worker; b. Powder Springs, Ga. d. Robert Anderson and Bertie Mae (Elsberry) Standridge; m. Harold Thomas Barfield (div.); 1 child, H. Gregory; m. J. Arden Williams (div.). Student, DeKalb Coll., Atlanta, 1982—83, U. Que., 1997, U. Laval, Que., 1998, U. Paris-Sorbonne, 2000. Assoc. promotion mgr., promotion coord. Coca-Cola USA, Atlanta, 1978-83, promotions mgr., 1983-86; mgr. internat. promotion svcs. The Coca-Cola Co., Atlanta, 1986-90, mgr. global promotion svcs., 1990-94. Cons., judge Point-of-Purchase Advt. Inst., 1995. Attaché Atlanta Conv. and Visitors Bur., 1992—; vol. Welcome South Ctr., Atlanta, 1995—; bd. advisors Life Coll. for Knowledge and Tng., 1995—; chmn. cmty. rels. com. Life Coll., 1995-96, vice chmn. bd. adv. Knowledge and Tng. program, 1997-98, chmn. bd. advisors Knowledge and Tng. program, 1998-99. Mem. Ga. Trust for Hist. Preservation, Atlanta High Mus. Art, Atlanta Bot. Garden, Alliance Francaise, Smyrna Hist. Soc. Avocations: travel, french studies, interior design, hiking, bridge.

WILLIAMS, EDNA ALETA THEADORA JOHNSTON, journalist; b. Halifax, N.S., Can., Sept. 19, 1923; d. Clarence Harvey and Edna May (Lewis) Johnston; m. Albert Murray Williams, Apr. 16, 1949 (dec.); children: Murleta, Norma, Martin, Charla, Kerrick, Renwick, Julia. Student, Maritime Bus. Coll., 1943. Typist Dept. Treas. (Navy), Halifax, 1944-49; with Bedford (N.S.) Mag., Halifax br., 1954-55, Presbyn. Office, New Glasgow, N.S., 1965-67, Thomas and Sutherland, New Glasgow, 1967-69; family editor, columnist, reporter New Glasgow Evening News, 1969-88, ret., 1988; soc. corr. Evening News, 1997—. Mem. Glasgow Bapt. rep. Pictou County Coun. of Chs., 1978-82, sec., 1980-82; pres. ch. aux. 2d United Bapt. Ch., 1979-83, organist, 1970—, chorus dir. Men's Choir, 1980—, hon. mem. ch. aux., v.p., 1993—, treas. Ch.'s Men's Brotherhood, 1995—; organist St. James Anglican Ch., 1983-85, provincial organist, 1994—, 2nd Baptist Ch., 2003—; organist St. Bee's Anglican Ch., 1996—; provincial pres. Women's Inst. of African United Bapt. Assn., 1983-86; mem. coun. Halifax YMCA; founding mem. Pictou County YM-YWCA, 1966—, bd. dirs., 1967-77, corr. sec., v.p., 1974-75, 75-77; past pres., past provincial dir. Home and Sch. provincial sec. African United Bapt. Assn. of N.S., 1988-90; sec. area IV Atlantic United Bapt. Conv., 1989-93; past officer local interracial com.; bd. dirs. Big Bros./Big Sisters, 1984-86, Pictou County United Way, 1983-96, Palliative Care Aberdeen Hosp., 1985—, Black United Front; ref. person media and religion Black History Month; chair Pictou County Srs. Festival, 1999—. Recipient Hon. award United Way, 1993, Grot award Black Cultural Centre N.S., 1999; honored by Pictou County Music Festival, 1994, 2d United Bapt. Ch., 1997. Mem. N.S. Sr. Secretate, Can. Press Assn., Black Journalists Assn. N.S. Home: 230 Reservoir St New Glasgow NS Canada B2H 4K4 Office: Evening News 352 East River Rd Glasgow NS Canada B2H 5E2

WILLIAMS, ELEANOR CLAFLIN (CLAFFY WILLIAMS), artist; b. Brookline, Mass., Jan. 31, 1916; d. Thomas Mack and Alice Morton (Osborn) Claflin; m. Thomas Blake Williams, Jan. 26, 1940; children: Thomas B. Jr., Susan Williams Dickie, Eleanor Williams Wright, Sandra M. Williams Weiss. Student, Sweet Briar Coll. Art tchr.; lectr. on contemporary art. One woman shows include Pual Platt Libr., Cohasset, Mass., 1998, Cohasset Paul Pratt Meml. Libr., 1999; exhibited in various art shows including Copley Soc., Boston, 1974, 77, 98, 99, 2000, Chinese Cultural Inst., Boston, 1992, 98, 2000, South Shore Art Ctr., Cohasset, 1996, 97, 98, 2000, Modern Art D'unet, Tonniens, 1993, Chinese Cultural Inst., Boston, 1992, 96, Ariel Gallery, Soho, N.Y., 1990, Art Complex, Duxbury, Mass., 1982, 97; 3 paintings in book The Best in Acrylic Painting, 1996, Artexpo in N.Y.C. promoted by ARTREPS, 1998; 3 paintings in Creative Inspirations, 1997. Pres. bd. dirs. South Shore Art Ctr., Cohasset, Mass., 1985-87, mem. adv. bd., 1987—; dir. Prison Art Project, Boston, 1973-76; bd. dirs. Copley Soc., Boston, 1975-79. Recipient 1st prize for graphics North River Art Assn., Marshfield, Mass. Avocations: skiing, tennis, walking, reading, travel.

WILLIAMS, ELEANOR JOYCE, retired government air traffic control specialist; b. College Station, Tex., Dec. 21, 1936; d. Robert Ira and Viola (Ford) Toliver; m. Tollie Williams, Dec. 30, 1955 (div. July 1978); children: Rodrick, Viola Williams Smith, Darryl, Eric, Dana Williams Robinson, Sheila Williams Watkins, Kenneth. Student, Prairie View A&M Coll., 1955-56, Anchorage Community Coll., 1964-65, U. Alaska-Anchorage, 1976. Clk./stenographer FAA, Anchorage, 1965-66, adminstrv. clk., 1966-67, pers. staffing asst., 1967-68, air traffic control specialist, 1968-79, air traffic control supr. San Juan, P.R., 1979-80, Anchorage, 1983-85, airspace specialist Atlanta, 1980-83, with Washington, 1985-87; area mgr. Kansas City Air Rt. Traffic Control Ctr., Olathe, Kans., 1987-89, asst. mgr. Quality Assurance, 1989-91, supr. traffic mgmt., 1991, supr. system effectiveness section, 1991-93, asst. air traffic mgr., 1993-94; air traffic mgr. Cleve. Air Route Traffic Control Ctr., Oberlin, Ohio, 1994-97; acting mgr. sys. mgmt. br. Des Plains, Ill., 1995-96; mem. human resource reform team task force Washington, 1996—; acting regional exec. mgr. Great Lakes Region Des Plaines, Ill., 1996-97. Proprietor Williams Apts., Anchorage. Sec. Fairview Neighborhood Coun., Anchorage, 1967-69; mem. Anchorage Bicentennial Commn., 1975-76; bd. dirs. Mt. Patmos Youth Dept., Decatur, Ga., 1981-82; mem. NAACP; del. to USSR Women in Mgmt., 1990; v.p. A&M Consol. Lincoln H.S. Alumni Assn., 2000—; mem. citizens amb. program People to People Internat.; mem. adv. bd. Lincoln Recreation Ctr. Recipient Mary K. Goddard award Anchorage Fed. Exec. Assn. and Fed. Women's Program, 1985, Sec.'s award Dept. Transp., 1985, Pres. VIP award, 1988, C. Alfred Anderson award, 1991, Disting. Svc. award Nat. Black Coalition of Fed. Aviation Employees, 1991, Paul K. Bohr award FAA, 1994, Nat. Performance Rev. Hammer award from V.P. Al Gore, 1996, Regional Adminstrs. award for meritorious svc. Gt. Lakes Regional Adminstrn., 1997, Top Flight award for outstanding svc. FAA, 1997; A salute to Her Name in the Congl. Record 104th Congress, 1995, Execs. in Profile award for exemplary career performance Region Ten Blacks in Govt., 1998, Pres.'s award for outstanding svc. Lincoln Former Students Assn.; named Disting. Alumnus Lincoln H.S., 2000; named Youth Advocate Cmty. Champion State of Tex., Tex. Commn. Alcohol & Drug Abuse, 2001; inducted into Black Aviation Hall fame, 2001. Mem.: Women in Mgmt. (del. Soviet Union), Internat. Platform Assn., Fed. Mgrs. Assn., Air Traffic Contrs. Assn., Profl. Women Contrs. Orgn., Nat. Black Coalition of Fed. Aviation Employees (pres. cen. region chpt. 1987—92, Over Achievers award 1987, Disting. Svc. award 1988, Sojourner Truth award Great Lakes region 1997), Blacks in Govt., Nat. Assn. Negro Bus. and Profl. Women USA Inc. (North to the Future club, charter pres. 1975—76), Gamma Phi Delta. Democrat. Baptist. Avocations: singing, sewing. Home: 7931 Old Seward Hwy Apt 8 Anchorage AK 99518-3265 E-mail: ejw4atc@aol.com., ejtwmsent@msn.com.

WILLIAMS, ELIZABETH A. financial planner, business consultant; b. San Francisco, Jan. 16, 1948; d. John and Myrtle Mary (Thierry) W.; children: Brian, Jonathan. Cert. in bus., U. Calif., 1979. Cert. computers loan processing. Manpower coord., fed. programs U.S. Govt., San Francisco; patient svc. rep. Health Care Svc., Oakland, Calif.; ins. and real estate cons.; pres. Investments Unlimited, Oakland, EWJ & Assocs. Mktg. Firm; leisure svcs. commr. City of Pitts.; CEO Ultimate Vacations Inc. Mem. NAACP, Contra Costa County Womens Commn.; bd. dirs. Coun. on Child Abuse. Recipient Pub. Speaking award; European Investment fellow. Mem. AAUW, NAFE, Nat. Real Estate Owners Assn., Nat. Notary Assn., Order Ea. Star, Heroines Jericho, Daus. Isis, Soroptimist Inc., Toastmistress Club, Beta Phi Sigma. Home: PO Box 523 Pittsburg CA 94565-0052

WILLIAMS, ELIZABETH A.W. foundation administrator; B, Smith Coll.; M, Northwestern U. City editor, edn. reporter, features writer Phila. Evening Bulletin, 1972-77; various editl. positions Phila. Inquirer, 1977-87, assoc. mng. editor, 1988-92; dir. ops. & spl. projects The Pew Charitable Trusts, Phila., 1998—. Office: Pew Charitable Trusts 2005 Market St Ste 1700 Philadelphia PA 19103-7017

WILLIAMS, ELIZABETH EVENSON, writer; b. Sioux Falls, S.D., Sept. 25, 1940; d. A. Duane and Eleanor (Kelton) Evenson; m. Louis P. Williams Jr., Aug. 31, 1968; 1 child, Katherine. BS, S.D. State U., 1962; MA, U. Wis., 1964; postgrad., U. Minn., 1969-70; MA, S.D. State U., 1983, PhD, 1997. Dir. pubs. No. State Coll., Aberdeen, S.D., 1965-68; instr. journalism S.D. State U., Brookings, 1968—69, 1985—89; asst. editor Journalism Quar., Mpls., 1969-70; pub. info. specialist S.D. Com. on Humanities, Brookings, 1975-78; asst. and instr. speech dept. S.D. State U., Brookings, 1981-92, adj. journalism faculty, 1989—; part-time dir. Women's Ctr., Brookings, 1988-90; reading series coord. S.D. Com. on Humanities, Brookings, 1986-91. Adj. sociology faculty S.W. State U., Marshall, Minn., 1998—99, Marshall, 2000—01, Augustana Coll., Sioux Falls, SD, 2001, S.D. State U., Brookings, 2001—. Author: Emil Loriks: Builder of a New Economic Order, 1987, More Reflections of a Prairie Daughter, 1993, Free to Speak His Mind: W.R. Ronald, Prairie Editor and an AAA Architect, 1999; weekly columnist Brookings Daily Register, 1985-92, RFD News, 1992-95; contbr. articles to profl. jours. Vestry mem. St. Paul's Ch., Brookings, 1975-76, 84-86, 92-97, sr. warden, 1995-97, 2003-; pres. LWV of S.D., 1985-89, treas., 1990-92, 99—; trustee Brookings Pub. Libr., 1994—. S.D. Humanities Com. grantee, 1984, 87, 90. Mem. Nat. Fedn. Press Women (1st place nat. writing contest 1977), Phi Kappa Phi, Pi Kappa Delta, Alpha Kappa Delta. Episcopalian. Avocations: golf, photography, travel. Home: 1103 3rd St Brookings SD 57006-2230 E-mail: lizerly@brookings.net.

WILLIAMS, ELIZABETH YAHN, writer, lecturer, lawyer; b. Columbus, Ohio, July 20, 1942; d. Wilbert Henry and Elizabeth Dulson (Brophy) Yahn. BA cum laude, Loyola Marymount U., 1964; secondary tchg. credential, UCLA, 1965; JD, Loyola U., 1971. Cert. tchr. h.s. and jr. coll. English and history. Writer, West Covina, Calif., 1964—; designer, 1966-68; tchr. jr./sr. h.s. L.A. City Schs., Santa Monica, Calif., 1964-65, La Puente (Calif.) H.S. Dist., 1965-67; legal intern, lawyer Garvey, Ingram, Baker & Uhler, Covina, Calif., 1969-72; lawyer, corp. counsel Avco Fin. Svcs., Inc., Newport Beach, Calif., 1972-74; pvt. practice Santa Ana, Calif., 1974—87; writing scholar Episcopal Diocese of L.A., 1999. Mem. faculty continuing edn. State Bar of Calif., 1979; adj. prof. Western State U. Sch. Law, Fullerton, Calif., 1980; mem. fed. cts. com. Calif. State Bar, San Francisco, 1977-80. Author: (1-act plays) Acting-Out Acts, 1990, Grading Graciela, 1992, Boundaries in the Dirt, 1993; author: (lyricist) Peter and the Worry Wrens, 1995; author: (lyricist, narrator) Love in Our Midst, 2000; author: (poetry chapbook) A Medley of Cherry, 2000, Verses for Violins, 2001, Joy: Moments for Reflection, 2002; editor: The Music of Poetry, 1997, 1998; contbr. articles to profl. jours.; panelist (TV show) Action Now, 1971, interviewee Women, 1987; scriptwriter, dir.: TV show Four/Four, 1994; author: (3-act adaptation) Saved in Sedona, 1995, (play, screenplay) Showtunes, 2004; scriptwriter, prodr., host: TV show Guildelights to Success, 1996; developer board game Go With Your Goals!. Mem. alumni bd. Loyola-Marymount Coll., L.A., 1980-84; mem. adv. bd. Rancho Santiago Coll., Santa Ana, 1983-84; spkr. Commn. on Status on Women, Santa Ana, 1979. Grantee, Ford Found., 1964—65; French scholar, Ohio State U., 1959, acad. scholar, Loyola-Marymount U., 1960—64, Book Expo 2000 scholar, Pubs. Mktg. Assn.-San Diego Pubs. Alliance Pub Mktg. U., 2000, Writer's grantee, Vt. Ctr. Studio, 2003. Mem.: Nat. League Am. Pen Women, Magee Park Poets, Orange County Bar Assn. (chmn. human and individual rights com. 1974—75, comml. law and bankruptcy com. 1978—79, corp. and bus. law sect. 1980—81, faculty Orange County Coll. Trial Advocacy 1982), Calif. Women Lawyers (life; bd. dirs. 1975—76, co-founder), Phi Theta Kappa (life most disting. hon.). Avocation: directing and producing ensemble and liturgical dramas and musicals. Address: PO Box 233 San Luis Rey CA 92068-0233 Office Phone: 760-439-5168. E-mail: dreywilliams@hotmail.com.

WILLIAMS, ELLEN C. political party official; m. Greg Williams; children: Sam, Joey. Grad., U. Ky. Staff asst. Congressman Larry Hopkins. Cons. Lexington/Bluegrass Bd. of Realtors; active Anderson County United Way Bd., Ch. of Lawrenceburg. Polit. dir. Dole/Kemp Ky.; dep. campaign mgr. Larry Forgy campaign for Gov.; exec. dir. Rep. Party of Ky., 1990-92; regional polit. dir. Nat. Rep. Com.; chmn. Ky. Republican Party, 1999-; exec. asst. Senator Bob Kasten; mem. Regan/Bush '84; exec. dir. Young Rep. Fedn., 1983. Office: Rep Party of Ky PO Box 1068 Frankfort KY 40602 E-mail: chair@rpk.org.

WILLIAMS, ELYNOR A. public affairs specialist; b. Baton Rouge, Oct. 27, 1946; d. Albert Berry and Naomi Theresa (Douglas) W. BS, Spelman Coll., 1966; MS, Cornell U., 1973. Tchr. home econs. Eugene Butler Jr.-Sr. H.S., Jacksonville, Fla., 1966-68; publicist, pkg. editor, copy editoir Gen. Foods Corp., White Plains, N.Y., 1968-71; writer, rschr. expanded nutrition edn. program Cornell U., summer 1972, tutor, com. on spl. edn. projects, 1972-73; comm. specialist N.C. agrl. ext. svc., A & T State U. Greensboro & N.C. State U., Raleigh, 1973-77; sr. pub. rels. specialist Western Elec., Greensboro, 1977-83; dir. corp. affairs Hanes Group, Winston-Salem, N.C., 1983-86; dir. pub. affairs Sara Lee Corp., Chgo., 1985-90, v.p. pub. responsibility, 1990—. Bd. dirs. Greensboro Drug Addiction Coun., 1977-83, v.p., 1983; mem. Carolina Theatre Commn., 1977-81; mem. steering com. Guilford County Women's Coalition, 1978; agy. bd. mem. solicitor United Way Campaign, 1977-82; issues chmn. Triad Coun. Girl Scouts Am., 1979-82; mem. Mayor's Energy Conservation Commn., 1977-78; vice chmn. adv. com. dept. comm. arts Cornell U., 1978-79; bd. dirs. Leadership Greensboro Alumni Assn., 1980-81, Women's Aid, 1980, Guilford Tech. Coll., 1981-84; pres. Guilford County Women's Polit. Caucus, 1980-81, Friends of Greensboro Coll. Adv. Com., 1980-82, Greensboro Symphony's Audience Devel. Adv. Com., 1980-82; candidate N.C. Ho. of Reps., 1980; mem. adv. bd. Greensboro Daily News Summer Journalism Inst., 1981; vice chmn. 6th Congrl. Black Leadership Caucus, 1980-81; mem. pub. rels. adv. bd. YWCA, 1980-81; trustee U. N.C. 2000, 1982; mem. Nat. Women's Polit. Caucus; mem. policy coun., N.C. Women's Polit. Caucus, 1982; chmn. Employment Task Force, Gov.'s Assembly on Women and the Economy, 1981; deacon Chgo. United Ch., 1986—; bd. dirs. Hayes-Taylor

YMCA, 1983-84, YMCA, Winston-Salem/Forsyth County, 1984-86; mem. adv. coun. Office of Women in Econ. Devel., N.C. Dept. Commerce, 1985; mem. exec. com. Nat. Women's Econ. Alliance, 1985—; mem. nat. tech. adv. com. OICs of Am., Inc., 1995—; mem. Greensboro Dialogue Task Force, 1983. Recipient Outstanding Svc. award Nat. Coun. Negro Women, 1988, Black and Hispanic Achievers Industry award, 1989, Silver Trumpet award Publicity Club Chgo., 1990, Lifetime Achievement award Dollar and Sense mag., 1991; named to Black Women's Hall of Fame, 1988, Top Black Women in Corp. Am., Essence mag., 1989, One of 15 women Who Make a Difference Minorities and Women in Bus. mag., 1989, One of 100 Best and Brightest Black Women in Corp. Am. Ebony mag., 1990, a Nat. Headliners Women in Communications, 1992, one of 50 Top Black Execs. in Corp. Am. Ebony mag., 1992; United Negro Coll. Fund scholar, 1962-66; Cornell U. Grad. Sch. fellow, 1972-73; regional finalist White House fellowship program, 1981-82. Mem. LWV, NOW (mem. corp. adv. bd. legal def. and edn. fund), NAACP (Unsung Heroine award 1989), Exec. Leadership Coun. (founder, bd. dirs. 1986), Internat. Assn. Bus. Communicators, Pub. Rels. Soc. Am., Cosmopolitan C. of C. (bd. dirs. 1988-89), Alpha Kappa Alpha. Democrat. Methodist. Office: Sara Lee Corp 3 1st Nat Plz Fl 46 Chicago IL 60602

WILLIAMS, EMMA, management executive; b. Cleveland, Ark., Feb. 8, 1928; d. James and Frazier (Byers) Wallace; m. Augusta Griggs, Mar. 20, 1954 (dec.); children: Judy A., Terri V.; m. John Williams. Grad. H.S., Chgo. Pres., CEO Burlington No. Inc., Inglewood, Calif., 1986—. Republican. Avocations: reading, gardening, housekeeping. Office: Burlington No Corp 2nd Fl 2650 Lou Menk Dr Fort Worth TX 76131-2830 E-mail: judygr7@aol.com.

WILLIAMS, FREDA BERRY, administrative assistant; b. Petersburg, Va., June 9, 1956; d. William Lewis and Estella Virginia (Bouldin) Berry; m. LaMar Williams, Sr., Sept. 9, 1980 (div. Nov. 1992); children: LaMar Jr., Keana Trahearn, Genique Renee. Student, John Tyler C.C., Chester, Va., 1973-80; Diploma, United Truck Master, Clearwater, Fla., 1988. Lic. tractor trailer driver, reupholsterer, drafting technologist. Reupholstery worker Berry's Sewing Shop, Colonial Heights, Va., 1969-75; office asst. John Tyler C.C., 1975-76; domestic worker Ramada Inn, Richmond, Va., 1977-78; engr., drafter C.C. Towns & Assocs., Colonial Heights, 1979; owner, operator Williams Ind. and Assocs., Colonial Heights, 1981-88; sewing machine operator Crawford Mfg., Richmond, 1982-88; tractor trailer driver Capital Dist., Ashland, Va., 1988-91; transp. clk. Golden Capital Dist., Ashland, 1991, transp. adminstrv. asst., 1991-95. Network mgr. Pegasus Female Execs., 1985—88; cons. Williams Enterprises and Assocs--Cyberspace and Catalog Svc., 2000—. County exec. Women's Congl. Congress 4th Dist., Richmond, 1988—89; spokesperson Safety Coun. Transp. Dept., 1991—94; mem. policy coun. Chesterfield Head Start, 1998—, treas., 1998—99, mem. sch. yr. health adv. com., 1990 2000, merchandiser, 1996 ; head of women's fellowship ministry Pavilion of Joy, 2001—, primary Sunday sch. tchr., 2001—. Mem. Newbridge Book Club, NAFE. Baptist. Avocations: drawing, painting, arts and crafts.

WILLIAMS, GALE CADY, secondary school educator; b. Newark, Ohio, Jan. 9, 1950; d. Paul Clifford and Betty Cady; m. Joseph Alan Williams, Jr., July 10, 1992; children: Nicholas Paul, Brian Gabriel, Rachel Elizabeth. BS, Ohio State U., 1973. Ohio secondary edn. grades 7-12 [illegible] English cert. English instr. Licking County Joint Vocat. Sch., Newark, 1973-77; ind. craftswoman Newark, 1985-90; reporter The Advocate, Newark, 1990-93; educator Newark Sr. H.S., Newark, Ohio, 1993—2000; editl. asst. Bus. First Newspaper, Columbus, Ohio, 2000—; freelance journalist Newark, 2000—. Adviser, editor Newark H.S. The Paper, 1993—2000; judge annual publs. competion Ohio Sch. Bds. Assn., 1997; spkr. in field. Edn. reporter The Adv., 1991-93, writer weekly column on edn., 1992-93; feature writer The Legend Mag., 1993-94; coord. newspaper in edn. The Newark Advocate, 1990-92. Pres. City of Newark Litter Prevention Adv. Bd., 1990—; mem. City of Newark Historic Hudson Lighting Assessment Bd., 1995; active Second Presbyn. Ch. Recipient First Pl. Cmty. Svc. award, The Associated Press, 1993. Mem. NOW, Nat. Coun. Tchrs. English, Nat. Dem. Party, Newark Tchrs. Assn. Avocations: writing, music and concerts, reading periodicals, antique shopping, family activities. Office: Newark Sr HS 314 Granville St Newark OH 43055-4483

WILLIAMS, GLADYS TUCKER, elementary school principal; d. Lee William and Cora Lena (Barksdale) Tucker; m. John Thomas Williams; children: Jon Trevor, Jamia Tiffani. BS, D.C. Tchrs. Coll., 1971; MA, George Washington U., 1981, EdD, 2003. From speech/lang. pathologist to prin. Prince Georges County Schs., Upper Marlboro, Md., 1971—. Mem. Nat. Assn. Elem. Prins. & Adminstrs., Assn. Sch.-Based Adminstrs. & Supervisors, Md. State Tchrs. Assn., Alpha Delta Kappa, Delta Kappa Gamma (v.p. 1994-95). Office: Lewisdale Elem 2400 Banning Pl Hyattsville MD 20783-2799

WILLIAMS, GRETCHEN MINYARD, food store executive; b. Dallas, Dec. 18, 1956; d. Marvin Tipton and Clarine (Cooper) Minyard; m. Joseph Larry Williams, June 10, 1978. BBA, Tex. Christian U., 1978. Dir. employee rels. Minyard Food Stores, Inc., Coppell, Tex., 1978-80, v.p. employee rels., 1980-83, v.p. corp. rel., 1983-85, vice chmn. of bd. dirs., 1985-88, co-chmn. bd. dirs., 1988-98, co-CEO, co-chmn. bd. dirs., 1998—. Bd. dirs. Cullen/Frost Bank, N.A., Dallas. Adv. bd. mktg. edn. Dallas Ind. Sch. Dist., Dallas, 1981—; campaign mem. Old City Park, Dallas, 1988, Tex. Christian U. Fund Drive, Ft. Worth, 1987-88; adv. bd. Dallas Bapt. U., 1985—. Mem. Dallas/Ft. Worth Retail Grocers Assn. (chmn. bd. 1988—, avt. com.), AGAPE Social Svcs. Inc. (bd. dirs. 1987—), Baylor Health Care System (bd. dirs. 1989—), Zeta Tau Alpha (pres 1986-87). Avocations: reading, traveling. Office: Minyard Food Stores Inc PO Box 518 777 Freeport Pky Coppell TX 75019-4411

WILLIAMS, GWENDOLYN SUE, principal, educator; b. Teague, Tex., July 6, 1944; d. Vernon and Mae Etta Levels; m. Theodore Williams, July 21, 1970; children: Terrence Verone, Gerrick Tyrone. BS, Prairie View A&M U., 1966; MS, Nova U., 1976, EdS, 1981. Cert. tchr. Tex., N.C., prin. Fla., N.C. Tchr. sch. Dade County, Miami, 1970—85; tchr. Ft. Worth (Tex.) Ind. Sch., 1966—70; tchr. sch. Riyadh, Saudi Arabia, 1985—89, Dade County, Miami, 1989—93, Guilford County, Greensboro, NC, 1993—95; asst. prin. Asheboro (N.C.) City Schs., 1995—2002, prin., 2002—. Mem. funding com. United Way, Asheboro, 1999—2001; mem. adv. bd. YMCA After Sch. Program, Asheboro, 2003—; dir. Asheboro Day Care, 1999—. Mem.: ASCD, Delta Phi Upsilon. Democrat. United Methodist. Avocations: gardening, shopping, mentoring, volunteering, home decorating. Home: 1312 Plantation Cir Asheboro NC 27205 Office: Asheboro City Sch South Asheboro Mid Sch 523 W Walker Ave Asheboro NC 27203

WILLIAMS, HARRIET CLARKE, retired academic administrator; b. Bklyn., Sept. 5, 1922; d. Herbert Edward and Emma Clarke (Gibbs) W. AA, Bklyn. Coll., 1958; student, Art Career Sch., N.Y.C., 1960; cert., Hunter Coll., 1965, CPU Inst. Data Processing, 1967; student, Chineses Cultural Ctr., N.Y.C., 1973; hon. certs., St. Labre Sch./St. Joseph's, Ind. Sch., Mont., 1990. Adminstr. Baruch Coll., N.Y.C., 1959-85. Mktg. researcher 1st Presbyn. Arts and Crafts Shop, Jamaica, N.Y., 1986-96; tutor in art St. John's U., Jamaica, 1986-96; founder, curator Internat. Art Gallery, Queens, N.Y., 1991—. Exhibited in group shows at Union Carbide Art Exhibit, N.Y.C., 1975, Queens Day Exhbn., N.Y.C., 1980, 1st Presbyn. Arts and Crafts Shop, N.Y.C., 1986, others; contbr. articles to profl. publs. Vol. reading tchr. Mabel Dean Vocat. High Sch., N.Y.C., 1965-67; mem. polit. action com. dist. council 37, N.Y.C., 1973-77; mem. negotiating team adminstrv. contracts, N.Y.C., 1975-78; mem. Com. To Save CCNY, 1976-77, Statue Liberty Ellis Island Found., Woodrow Wilson Internat. Ctr. Scholars, Wilson Ctr. Assocs., Washington, St. Labre Indian Sch., Ashland, Mont. Appreciation award Dist. Coun. 37, 1979; recipient Plaque Appreciation Svcs., Baruch Coll., Key award St. Joseph's Indian Sch., 1990, Key award in Edn. and Art, 1990, others. Mem. NAFE, AAUW, Women in Mil. Svc., Assn. Am. Indian Affairs, Nat. Mus. of Am. Indian, Artist Equity Assn. N.Y., Am. Indian Edn. Found., Lakota Devel. Coun., Am. Film Inst., Bklyn. Coll. Alumni, Nat. Geographic Soc., Nat. Mus. Woman in the Arts, Statue of Liberty Ellis Island Found., Inc., Alliance of Queens Artists, U.S. Naval Inst., El Museo Del Barrio, Am. Mus. Natural History, Internat. Ctr. for Scholars-Wilson Ctr. Assocs., Arrow Club-St. Labre Indian Sch., Mus. of Television and Radio, Women in Mil. Meml. Found., Nat. Mus. of Am. Indian, U.S. Holocaust Mus., Navy Meml. (adv. coun.), U.S. Golf Assn. Roman Catholic. Avocations: aerobics, vol. work, world travel, music. Office: Baruch Coll 17 Lexington Ave New York NY 10010-5518

WILLIAMS, HATTIE, educational consultant; b. New Llano, La., Nov. 16, 1976; d. Albert Lee and Huae Yi Williams. BA in Sociology, BA in Psychology, BA in Philosophy, U. Mo., 1999; MS in Instrnl. Design & Tech., Emporia State U., 2001. Intern Mo. State Probation and Parole, Kansas City, 1997—97; grad. tchg. asst. Emporia State U., Kans., 1999—2000; ind. contractor John Wiley & Sons Pub. Co., Hoboken, NJ, 2000—00; grant work Dr. Nancy Smith Emporia State U., 2000—01; ednl. cons. Sprint PCS, Overland Park, 2001—. Author: (poetry) Butterflies (Pub. by The Poetry Guild, 1997), Friendship (Pub. by Blue Mountain Arts, 1998), Inside the Cocoon (pub. by The Internat. Libr. of Poetry, 1997). Vol. developer Youth Friends, 2003—03, mentor, 2002—03; mem. Rotaract, 1997—99; youth leader Gaia Cmty., Overland Park, 2000—03; pres., founder Athens in Kanssd City, 2002—03. Recipient Chancellor's award, U. Mo., Kans. City, 1995—99; scholar, Nat. Jewish Women's Assn., 1995—99. Mem.: NAFE, ASTD (newsletter editor 2002—), Alpha Kappa Delta. Unitarian Universalist.

WILLIAMS, HELEN MARGARET, retired accountant; b. Fresno, Calif., Mar. 16, 1947; d. James Ray Jr. and Barbara (LaRue) Franklin; m. Phillip Dean Bangs, Apr. 16, 1977; children: Aluvia, Adevia, Rodney. AA in Home Economics, Sacramento City Coll., 1969, AA in Acctg., 1971; BS in Acctg. and Fin. cum laude, Calif. State U., Sacramento, 1988. Acct. tech. Sacramento Regional Transit Dist., 1974-87, revenue rm. contr., 1987-88, acct. I, 1988, acct. II, 1988-97. Editor employee newsletter Sacramento Regional Transit Dist., 1986-90. Past mother and worthy adv. Rainbow for Girls; past host parent Am. Field Svc., past chair host family selection com. Mem. Am. Soc. Women Accts. (chair scholarship com. 1992-94, chair pub. com. 1993-94, bd. dirs. 1993-96, 2000—, sec. 1994-95, 99-2000, 2002—, chair roster com. 1995-96, chair hospitality com. 1996-98, 2001-2002, chair publicity com. 1998-99, treas. 2000-02), Calif. State U.-Sacramento Alumni Assn., Capital Investors Investment Club (fin. ptnr., recording ptnr. 1998—), Order Ea. Star, Precious Moments Collectors Club (newsletter editor 1992—, treas. 1993—). Avocations: sewing, interior design, needlework, collectibles, geneology.

WILLIAMS, HOLLY THOMAS, retired business executive; b. Pitts., Dec. 24, 1931; d. Andrew Matthew and Elizabeth (Kuklinca) Thomas; m. Donald Evan Williams, May 14, 1961. AA cum laude, Keystone Jr. Coll., LaPlume, Pa., 1978; BS magna cum laude, U. Scranton, 1981. Dancer Arthur Murray Studios, Pitts., 1953-60, franchise owner Scranton, Pa., 1960-80, mgr. [illegible] 1984-85, franchise owner, 1985-2001. Fund raiser United Cerebral Palsy of Lackawanna County, Scranton, 1970-79, St. Joseph's Children's Hosp., Scranton, 1962-76; exec. sec. Foxhowe Assn., Buck Hill Falls, Pa., 1984-85. Mem. AAUW (bd. dirs. 1985-86, 94-2001, br. pres. 1999 2001), Scranton Club. Republican. Christian. Avocations: reading, golf, bridge, dance, travel. Home: 213 Karen Dr Scranton PA 18505-2207 also: PO Box 151 Buck Hill Falls PA 18323-0151

WILLIAMS, IDA JONES, consumer and home economics educator, writer; b. Coatesville, Pa., Dec. 1, 1911; d. William Oscar and Ida Ella (Ruth) Jones; m. Charles Nathaniel Williams, Mar. 17, 1940 (dec. July 1971). BS, Hampton Inst., 1935; MA, U. Conn., 1965. Cert. high sch. tchr., English, sci., home econs., Va., Pa. Sci. and home econs. tchr. Richmond County H.S., Ivondale, Va., 1935-36; English and home econs. tchr. Northampton County H.S., Chesapeake, Va., 1936-40, consumer and home econs. tchr. Machipongo, Va., 1940—70, Northampton Jr. H.S., Machipongo, 1970—76. Author: Starting Anew After Seventy, 1980 (plaque 1980), News and Views of Northampton County High Principals and Alumni, 1981, Great Grandmother, Leah's Legacy-Remember You're Free, 2000; co-author: The History of Virginia State Federation of Colored Women's Clubs, Inc., 1996; editor: Fifty Year Book 1935-1985 - Hampton Institute Class, 1985, Favorite Recipes of Ruth Family & Friends, 1986. V.p. Ea. Lit. Coun., Melfa, Va., 1987-89; mem. Ea. Shore Coll. Found., Inc., Melfa, 1988-2000; mem. Gov.'s Adv. Bd. on Aging, Richmond, Va., 1992-94; instr. Ladies Community Bible Class, 1976-80 (Plaque 1980); sec., treas., v.p. Hospice Support of Ea. Shore, 1980-94; mem. Northampton/Accomack Adv. Coun., 1992-94; marshall 28th anniv. commencement Ea. Shore C.C., 1996; bd. dirs. Ea. Shore C.C. Found., 1998-2000. Named Home Econs. Tchr. of Yr., Am. Home Econs. Assn. and Family Cir., 1975, Woman of Yr., Prog. Women of E.S., 1997, Ida J. Williams scholarship fund named in her honor, Keller Ch. Christ, 1999; recipient Nat. Sojourner Truth Meritorious Svc. award, Negro Bus. and Profl. Women's Clubs, Gavel Ea. Shore Ret. Tchrs. Assn., 1994, Jefferson award, Am. Inst. Pub. Svc., Wavy-TV-Bell Atlantic and Mattress Discounters, 1991, Gov.'s award for vol. excellence, 1994, Contribution to Edn. award, Ea. Shore Coll. Found., 1997, Leadership award, 2001, trophy for outstanding and dedicated svc., 2001, plaque, Southeastern Assn. Colored Women's Clubs, Inc., 2001, award for dedicated svc., Nat. Assn. Colored Women's Club, Inc., 1998, E.S. C.C. Found., Inc. Svc. award, 2000, Exemplary Svc. award, Nat. Assn. Colored Women's Club, 2001, Black Achievement award, Ebenezer A.M.E. Ch., 2003, Achievement award, Chester County Hist. Soc. of Pa., 2003, Ednl. Achievement award for commitment to edn., Northampton County H.S. Alumni Assn., 2003, plaque 1st Black Northampton County, Ea. Shore Va. C. of C. outstanding contbns. ea. shore cmty., 2002. Mem. AARP (Citation award 1996, Mem. of Yr. 1997, v.p. Northampton chpt. 1998-2000), Progressive Women of Ea. Shore (pres. 1985-93, Gold Necklace 1993, Woman of Yr. 1997), C. of C., Univ. Women (v.p. Portsmouth br. 1985-87), Ea. Shore Ret. Tchrs. (pres. 1977-84), Dist. L Ret. Tchrs. (pres. 1989-91, chmn. legis. com. 1998, 99, 2001, Dedicated and Outstanding Svc. award 2003), Va. State Fedn. Colored Women's Club (pres. 1990-94, editor history com. 1994-96), Am. Assn. Ret. Persons (Va. state legis. com. 1995-2001). Mem. Ch. of Christ. Avocations: crafts, travel, writing, lecturing. Home and Office: PO Box 236 14213 Lankford Hwy Eastville VA 23347-0236

WILLIAMS, JANE CROUCH, mental health counselor, social worker; b. Knoxville, Tenn., Apr. 23, 1931; d. Brockway and Elsie Irene (Wayland) Crouch; m. James Bowers Bell, June 27, 1950 (div. Sept. 1971); children: Steven Easterly Bell, Sharon Irene Bell Mann Trotter, Joseph Brockway Bell, Robert Wayland Bell; m. Don Roy Williams, Mar. 28, 1989 (dec. Jan. 25, 2003). Student, U. Cin., 1949-50, Ft. Sanders Hosp. Sch. Nursing, 1950; BS in Social Work, U. Tenn., 1985. Office nurse Knoxville Surg. Group, 1955-82; therapist Overlook Health Ctr., Sevierville, Tenn., 1985-89; therapist, counselor Seymour (Tenn.) Family Physicians, 1985-89; coord. mental health day treatment Ridgeview Psychiat., Campbell County, Tenn., 1989-94, 2003—; mental health counselor Wynn-Habersham Health, Campbell County, 1995 97, ret., 1997; rschr. Mountain Heritage Rsch., La Follette, Tenn., 1993-98. Rsch. cons. for family historians, 1955—. Author: Descendants of William Goddard of Sullivan County, Tennessee, 1994, 2nd edit., 1997. Christian counselor Presbyn. Ch., La Follette, 1993—; elder 1st Presbyn. Ch., La Follette, 1993—; mem. divsn. reconciliation and compassion East Tenn. Presbytery, Knoxville, 1995-2000; life mem. East Tenn. Hist. Soc., Knoxville, 1955—, Meml. Found. Germanna Colonies of Va., Culpeper, Va., 1981—. Mem. NSW, Nat. Geneal. Soc., Phi Kappa Phi, Phi Beta Kappa. Republican. Avocations: genealogy, oil painting, spending time with grandchildren. Home: 200 Ellison Rd Ste 1 La Follette TN 37766-3042 Office: First Presbyn Ch PO Box 408 La Follette TN 37766-0408 E-mail: wayland@jellico.net.

WILLIAMS, JEANETTE K. association executive; b. Seattle, Wash., June 11, 1914; d. Louis Herman and Olga Nilovna (Kerlov) Klemptner; m. David Houston Williams, Aug. 8, 1942 (dec.); children: Patricia Ellen Kraniotis, George Frederick Williams. BA in Interior Design, U. Wash., 1934; MusB, Am. Conservatory Music, Chgo., 1938, MusM in Violin, 1939, MusM in Composition, 1940. Performing musician Solo All Girls Band, Chgo., 1936-40; vice chair., county chair King County Dem. Ctrl. Com., Seattle, 1962-69; mem. Seattle City Coun., 1970-90; mayor apptd. chmn. Sand Pt. Cmty. Liaison Com., Seattle, 1991—; bd. appointed pres. Citizens Sand Point Planning Assn., Seattle, 1993—. Mem. Nat. Task Force Ride Share, U.S. Dept. Transp., Washington, 1979-80, sponsor legis. to establish greenbelts in Seattle, 1979; del., chmn. human resources nat. assns., regional couns., 1981-84; initiated agreement & fin. package for W. Seattle bridge, 1980-84. Author: (legis.) women's rights, fair housing, fair employment, etc., 1970-90, Women's Commissions & Office of Rights, 1971— (Women's Caucus award 1975). Sponsor, del. Seattle-Chonggung, China Sister City, 1980, 85; pres. Seattle City Coun., 1980-82; chmn. Sand Point Cmty. Liaison Com., Seattle, 1991—; pres. Citizens Sand Point Planning Assn., Seattle, 1993—. Recipient woman in politics award Womens' Polit. Caucus, Wash., 1975, Woman of achievement award Matrix Table, Seattle, 1980, outstanding official in pub. svc. award Mcpl. League, Seattle, King County, 1982, achievement award Women in Transp., Wash., 1984. Democrat. Avocations: concerts, exhibits, travel, avid mariner baseball fan. Home: 7132 58th Ave NE Seattle WA 98115-6253 Office: Citizens Sand Point Planning Assn PO Box 15580 Seattle WA 98115-0580

WILLIAMS, JEANNE ELIZABETH, music educator; b. Greensboro, N.C., Aug. 23, 1950; d. James Henry and Mary Jessye Long Williams. BS in Music Edn., Winston-Salem State U., 1974. Cert. K-12 music N.C., kinder musick N.J. Reading tutor grade 3 Winston-Salem/Forsyth County Schs., NC, 2000—01, tchr. music, 2001—. Organist St. Phillips Moravian Ch. Mem. Watchfulnetwork Bus. Orgn.; performed with Maya Angelou Mt. Zion Bapt. Ch., 1984—87, mem. chancel choir, 2003; mem. Carver Sch. Rd. Adv. Libr. Bd.; organist Mt. Zion Bapt. Ch.; performerd with Robert Shaw Chorale Westminster Choir Coll., 1982. Recipient Cert. of Achievement in music, Appalachian State U., 2003. Mem.: N.C. Assn. Educators, Music Educators Nat. Conf., Nat. Assn. Music Edn., N.C. Music Educators, Nat. Women Achievement, Order Ea. Star, Zeta Phi Beta (mem. Rho Zeta chpt.). Avocations: reading, organ, dance, volleyball, traveling to the Caribbean.

WILLIAMS, JENNIFER LYNNE, writer; b. Mountain View, Calif., Sept. 25, 1971; d. Juan (Stepfather) and Linda Ann Candelaria; m. Christian Richard Williams, Dec. 10, 1998. B in Mktg., San Jose State U., 1994; diploma in med. transcription, Med. Careers Inst., Newport News, Va., 2003. Mktg. dir. Sparlling Industries, Mountain View, 1993 95; mktg. adminstr. Wells Fargo Bank, San Jose, 1995—96; tech. writer JLR Consulting, San Jose, Calif., 1996—99; revision editor MR&D, Virginia Beach, Va., 2000 [illegible] of the Soul (Poet of the Yr. Internat. Soc. Poetry, 2001); author: Eternal Portraits (Poet of the Yr. Internat. Soc. Poetry, 2002). Mem. mayor's youth com. San Jose Mayor's Office, 1988—90; event planner various religious orgns., Calif., 1990—98. Named Grand Champion, Calif. State Talent Competition, 1993. Mem.: NVTHS (life). Personal E-mail: jenlynnerw@aol.com.

WILLIAMS, JOAN ELAINE, podiatric surgeon, educator; b. La Mesa, Calif. d. William E. and Dottie B. Williams; m. Edward Homewood Miller, 1987; children: Carol Martins, William Baerg, Michael Baerg. BS, Calif. Coll. Podiatric Med., 1978, D of Podiatric Medicine, 1981; MS, Pepperdine U., 1979. Diplomate Am. Bd. Podiatric Surgery, Am. Bd. Podiatric Orthopedics and Primary Podiatric Medicine. Chief podiatric medicine and surgery dept. vets. affairs Puget Sound Health Care System, Seattle, 1982—; clin. asst. prof. podiatric medicine Calif. Coll. Podiatric Medicine, San Francisco, 1982—, U. Osteo. Medicine and Health Sci., Des Moines, Iowa, 1982-90; clin. assoc. prof. U. Osteo. Medicine and Health Scis., Des Moines, Iowa, 1990—. Oral bd. examiner Am. Bd. Podiatric Orthopedics, Chgo., 1988; reviewer merit rev. grant Vets. Affairs Ctrl. Office, Washington, 1989; lic. exam reviewer Nat. Bd. Podiatric Med. Examiners, State College, Pa., 1993—. Editor: Preferred Practice Guidelines, 1992-94; contbr. articles to profl. jours. County del. Wash. State Rep. Party, Seattle, 1994. Recipient Acad. scholarship Pepperdine U., 1979. Fellow Am. Coll. Foot and Ankle Surgeons, Am. Coll. Foot and Ankle Orthopedics. Presbyterian. Avocations: classical music, playing cello. Office: Puget Sound Health Care Sys Dept Vets Affairs 1660 S Columbian Way Seattle WA 98108-1532

WILLIAMS, JODY, political organization administrator; b. Rutland, Vt., Oct. 9, 1950; BA, U. Vt.; MA, Sch. Internat. Tng., Johns Hopkins Sch.; PhD (hon.), Briar Cliff Coll., Marlboro Coll., U. of Vermont, Williams Coll. Past English tchr., Washington, Mex.; former coord. Nicaragua-Honduras Edn. Project, Washington; assoc. dir. Children's Project Med. Aid El Salvador, L.A./El Salvador, 1986—92; founder Internat. Campaign to Ban Landmines Vietnam Vet. Found. Am., Washington, 1991—; amb. Internat. Campaign to Ban Landmines, Alexandria, Va., 1997—; founder Sponsor a Mine-Detection Dog program, 1998—. Spkr. in field. Contbr. articles to profl. jours, co-authored After the Guns Fall: The Enduring Legacy of Landmines. Past vol. El Salvadoran rescue group. Recipient Distinguished Peace Leadership award, Nuclear Age Peace Found., Fiat Lux award, Clark U., Nobel Peace Prize, 1997, Hollywood Humanitarian award, 2002. Office: ICBL 110 Maryland Ave NE # 6 Washington DC 20002-5626

WILLIAMS, JUANITA (TUDIE WILLIAMS), home health care nurse, administrator; b. Springfield, Mo., June 3, 1954; d. Clay Caldwell Deeds and Martaun LaVeda Smith; m. Phillip E. Williams, June 21, 1996; 1 child, Megan E. Deeds. BSN, U. of State N.Y., Albany, 1990. Cert. med.-surg. nurse. Staff nurse St. John's Regional Health Ctr., Springfield, 1975-78; head nurse cardiac Cox Med. Ctr., Springfield, 1978-92; dir. continuous quality improvement/edn. svcs., dir. clin. svcs. Cmty. Home Health Care, Springfield, 1992—. Mem. adv. bd. Columbia Health Ctr., Springfield, 1992—; coord. quality assurance bd. Cmty. Home Health, Springfield, 1992-96; mem. cardiac adv. bd. Cox Med. Ctr., Springfield, 1985. Contbr. articles to profl. jours. Mem. Mo. State Nurses Assn. Republican. Roman Catholic. Avocation: photography. Home: 7674 W Farm Road 128 Springfield MO 65802-9172 Office: Cmty Home Health 2828 N National Ave Springfield MO 65803-4306

WILLIAMS, JUANITA ROSALIE, artist; b. Zanesville, Ohio, Aug. 7, 1933; d. Joseph Russell and Gladys Lucille (Worden) Somers; m. Roy George Williams, Feb. 16, 1952 (div. 2002); children: Karin Sue Williams Brandi, Kenneth Roy. Grad. high sch., Zanesville. Juror Bexley (Ohio) Art Guild, Capital U., 1984. One-woman shows include Collector's Gallery Columbus Mus. Fine Art, Ohio, 1972, Pomerene Fine Arts Ctr., 1991, McDonough Gallery, Marietta Coll., 1991, Blue Sky Gallery, Columbus, 1992, exhibited in group shows at Zanesville Art Ctr., 1981, 1990, Franklin U., Columbus, Ohio, 1985, Marietta (Ohio) Coll., 1991, Pomerene Fine Arts Ctr., Coshocton, Ohio, 1991, No. Ariz. U., 1992, French Art Colony, Gallipolis, Ohio, 1992, Soc. Layerists in Multi-Media, San Miguel Allende, Mex., 1996, Marlborough, Eng., 1997, Sirius Gallery, Santa Fe, 2001, Represented in permanent collections Zanesville Art Ctr., Ohio, Soc. Bank Cleve., Edward Cherry Corp., Columbus, Nat. WaterColor Soc. Bd. dirs.

Zanesville Art Ctr., 1986-90. 92-95. Recipient 1st award Rocky Mountain Nat., 1984, Elsie and David Wu-Ject Key award Am. Watercolor Soc., 1989, 4th award San Diego Watercolor Soc., 1993. Mem. Nat. Watercolor Soc., Soc. Layerists in Multi-Media, Ohio Watercolor Soc. (Gold Buckeye award 1986), Southeastern Ohio Watercolor Soc. (co-founder, 1st pres. 1978-79). Avocations: gardening, interior decorating, reading, metaphyics, travel. Mailing: #1 Sandia Trail S Corrales NM 87048

WILLIAMS, JUDITH ELLEN, educational administrator; b. Oakland, Nebr., Jan. 9, 1953; d. Alva Charles and Helen Lanore (Bader) Tracy; m. Rudolph Edward Williams, Dec. 26, 1992; children: Stephanie, Ashley. BA, Antioch U., L.A., 1985. Tng. specialist St. Luke Med. Ctr., Pasadena, Calif., 1983-88; program dir. mental health unit Glendale (Calif.) Meml. Hosp., 1988-91; program dir. Psychiat. Mgmt. Resources, San Diego, 1991-93; dir. psychiatry program U. So. Calif., L.A., 1993-96; rsch. coord. Alzheimer Disease Ctr., Ind. U. Sch. Medicine, Indpls., 1996-99, dir. ops., 1999—. Avocations: reading, jet skiing, travel. Office: Ind U Sch Med 550 University Blvd # 3124 Indianapolis IN 46202-5149 E-mail: jwillia2@iupui.edu.

WILLIAMS, JULIE FORD, mutual fund officer; b. Long Beach, Calif., Aug. 7, 1948; d. Julious Hunter and Bessie May (Wood) Ford; m. Walter Edward Williams, Oct. 20, 1984; 1 child, Andrew Ford. BA in Econs., Occidental Coll., 1970. Legal sec. Kadison, Pfaelzer, Woodard, Quinn & Rossi, L.A., 1970-71, 74-77; legal sec. Fried, Frank, Harris, Shriver & Jacobson, N.Y.C., 1971-72, Pallot, Poppell, Goodman & Shapo, Miami, Fla., 1973-74; adminstrv. asst. Capital Research-Mgmt., Los Angeles, 1978-82; corp. officer Cash Mgmt. Trust Am., 1982—, Bond Fund Am., 1982—, Tax-Exempt Bond Fund Am., 1982—, AMCAP Fund, 1984-98, 2000—, Am. Funds Income Series, 1985—, Am. Funds Tax-Exempt Series II, 1986—, Capital World Bond Fund, 1987—, Am. High-Income Trust, 1987—, Intermediate Bond Fund Am., 1987—, Tax-Exempt Money Fund Am., 1989—, U.S. Treasury Money Fund Am., 1991—, Fundamental Investors, 1992-2000, Ltd. Term Tax-Exempt Bond Fund Am., 1993—, Am. High-Income Mcpl. Bond Fund, 1994—; v.p. fund bus. mgmt. group Capital Rsch. Mgmt., 1986—; sec. Growth Fund of Am., 1998-2000; Am. Mutual Fund, 2000—. Pres. Alumni Bd. Govs. Occidental Coll., 1997-98; bd. trustees Occidental Coll., 1999-2003. Democrat. Episcopalian. Office: Capital Rsch & Mgmt Co 333 S Hope St 55th Floor Los Angeles CA 90071-1452

WILLIAMS, JULIE LLOYD, lawyer; b. Washington, May 24, 1950; d. Walter Herbert and Jean (Grabill) W.; m. Don Scroggin, May 9, 1981; 1 child, Patrick Conner. BA, Goddard Coll., 1971; JD, Antioch Sch. Law, 1975. Bar: Va. 1975, D.C. 1976. Assoc. Fried, Frank, Harris, Shriver, Washington, 1975-83; assoc. gen. counsel Fed. Home Loan Bank Bd., Washington, 1983-86, dep. gen. counsel, 1986-89; dep. chief counsel Office of Thrift Supervision, Washington, 1989-91, sr. dep. chief counsel, 1991-93; dep. chief counsel Comptr. of the Currency, Washington, 1993-94, chief counsel, 1994-98, acting comptr., 1998-99, 1st sr. dep. comptr., chief counsel, 1999—. Co-author: (handbook) How to Incorporate: A Handbook for Entrepreneurs & Professionals, 1987; author: Savings Institutions: Mergers, Acquisitions & Conversions, 1988. Mem. ABA (banking law com.), Women in Housing and Fin. Home: 3064 Q St NW Washington DC 20007-3080 Office: Office Comptroller Currency 250 E St SW Washington DC 20024-3208

WILLIAMS, KAREN HASTIE, lawyer; b. Washington, Sept. 30, 1944; d. William Henry and Beryl (Lockhart) Hastie; m. Wesley S. Williams, Jr.; children: Amanda Pedersen, Wesley Hastie, Bailey Lockhart. Cert., U. Neuchatel, Switzerland, 1965; BA, Bates Coll., 1966; MA, Tufts U., 1967; JD, Cath. U. Am., 1973. Bar: D.C. 1973. Staff asst. internat. gov. relations dept. Mobil Oil Corp., N.Y.C., 1967-69; staff asst. com. Dist. Columbia U.S. Senate, 1970, chief counsel com. on the budget, 1977-80; law clk. to judge Spottswood Robinson III U.S. Ct. Appeals (D.C. Cir.), Washington, 1973-74; law clk. to assoc. justice Thurgood Marshall U.S. Supreme Ct., Washington, 1974-75; assoc. Fried, Frank, Harris, Shriver & Kampelman, Washington, 1975-77, 1975-77; adminstr. Office Mgmt. and Budget, Washington, 1980-81; of counsel Crowell & Moring, Washington, 1982, ptnr., 1982—. Bd. dirs. Chubb Corp., Gannett Co., Inc., Sun Trust Bank, Inc., Washington Gas Light Co., Continental Airlines. Trustee Greater Washington Research Ctr., chair. Mem. ABA (pub. contract law sect., past chair), Nat. Bar Assn., Washington Bar Assn., Nat. Contract Mgmt. Assn., NAACP (legal def. fund, bd. dirs.). Office: Crowell & Moring Ste 1200W 1001 Pennsylvania Ave NW Washington DC 20004-2595

WILLIAMS, KAREN JOHNSON, federal judge; b. Orangeburg, S.C., Aug. 4, 1951; d. James G. Johnson and Marcia Johnson (Reynolds) Dantzler; m. Charles H. Williams, Dec. 27, 1968; children: Marian, Ashley, Charlie, David. BA, Columbia Coll., 1972; postgrad., U. S.C., 1973, JD cum laude, 1980. Bar: S.C. 1980, U.S. Dist. Ct. S.C. 1980, U.S. Ct. Appeals (4th cir.) 1981. Tchr. Irmo (S.C.) Mid. Sch., 1972—74, O-W H.S., Orangeburg, 1974—76; assoc. Charles H. Williams PA, Orangeburg, 1980—92; judge U.S. Ct. Appeals (4th cir.), 1992—. Exec. bd. grievance commn. S.C. Supreme Ct., Columbia, 1983—92. Child devel. bd. First Bapt. Ch., Orangeburg; bd. dirs. Orangeburg County Mental Retardation Bd., 1986—94, Orangeburg-Calhoun Hosp. Found., Columbia Coll., 1988—92, Reg. Med. Ctr. Hosp. Found., 1988—92; adv. bd. Orangeburg-Calhoun Tech. Coll., SC, 1987—92. Mem.: ABA, Bus. and profl. Women Assn., S.C. Trial Lawyers Assn., Orangeburg County Bar Assn. (co-chair Law Day 1981), S.C. Bar Assn., Fed. Judges Assn., Am. Judicature Soc., Rotary, Order of Coif, Order of Wig and Robe. Home: 2503 Five Chop Rd Orangeburg SC 29115-8185 Office: Lewis F Powell Jr US Cthse Annex 1100 E Main St Ste 617 Richmond VA 23219-3517*

WILLIAMS, KATHRYN BLAKE, retired librarian; b. Lancaster, Pa., Mar. 20, 1923; d. Harry Leslie and Mary Kauffman (Strine) Blake; m. William George Williams Sr., June 1, 1945; children: Leslie Williams Aronson, William George Jr. BS in Edn., U. Pa., 1944; elem. cert., Shippensburg U., 1969, MLS, 1973. Home economist Pa. State Extension Svc., Carlisle, 1944-46; kindergarten tchr. Blind Assn. Harrisburg, Pa., 1955; asst. elem. tchr. Sweeney Day Sch., Harrisburg, 1955-57; week-day kindergarten tchr. Presbyn. Ch., Camp Hill, Pa., 1961-63; 1st grade tchr. West Shore Sch. System, Lemoyne, Pa., 1965-71; dir. Ralpho Twp. Pub. Libr., Elysburg, Pa., 1973-75; libr. Bloomsburg (Pa.) Univ. of Pa., 1979-80, Bloomsburg Hosp., 1980-81. Mem. adv. coun. North Cen. Region Job Tng. of Pa., Ridgeway, 1991-96; organizing dir. DuBois office, vista vol. Mid-State Literacy Coun., State College, Pa., 1987-88. Leader, day camp dir. Girl Scouts U.S., Harrisburg, 1957; field svc. coord. Am. Field Svc., Camp Hill, 1963-65; weekly radio panelist United Coun. of Chs., Harrisburg, 1963-65; vol. libr. DuBois (Pa.) Regional Med. Ctr., 1990—; story teller Bloomsburg Pub. Libr., 1974-83; commr. to gen. assembly Presbyn. Ch., 1983, elder, 1973—, deacon, 1994—, sec. of deacons, 1994-97; sec. Presbyn. Women Huntington, 1998—; grandparent vol. pub. sch. Mem. AAUW (v.p. 1987-89), Pa. State Edn. Assn. (life), Friends of DuBois Pub. Libr. (pres. 1984-86), Presbyn. Women (resource coord. 1975-85, mission coord. 1992-97). Avocations: golf, sewing, reading, quilting, public speaking. Home: 377 Treasure Lk Du Bois PA 15801-9008

WILLIAMS, LAVERNE CARMEN, performance artist, poet, musician; b. Queens, Sept. 10, 1965; d. Joseph Edward and Blanche Valaria Williams. BA in Comms., Marist Coll., N.Y. Editl. asst. West Pub. Co., 1987—89; asst. editor Matthew Bender Co., 1989—91; freelance editor, 1991—94; staff writer African Am. Weekly, 1994—95; tchg. asst. Amityville Schs., 1995—96. Creator, editor (anthology) Rising to the dawn: A Rape Survivor's Journey into Healing, 1998; publ.: mag. Survivor Mag., 1999— (Woman award, 2000); Artist Against Domestic Violence in our Community, Fayetteville, N.C., 2003. Vol. Rape Crisis Ctr., Fayetteville, NC, 2001. Avocations: poetry, gardening, guitar, keyboards. Home: 5323 Ahoskie Dr Hope Mills NC 28348 E-mail: ladytunda65@aol.com.

WILLIAMS, LENA, sportswriter; BA cum laude in English, Howard U.; MS in Journalism, Columbia U. Assoc. editor Black Sports Mag.; from clk. Sports Dept. to sports writer N.Y. Times, N.Y.C., 1974, sports writer. Author: It's the Little Things: The Everyday Interactions That Get Under the Skin of Blacks and Whites, 2000. Named one of Outstanding Women in Mktg. and Comms., Ebony Mag., 2001; recipient Excellence award, Nat. Assn. Black Journalism, 1997, Black Achievers award, Young Men's Christian Assn. Office: New York Times 229 W 43d St New York NY 10036*

WILLIAMS, LENA HARDING, educational administrator; b. Portsmouth, Va., June 12, 1947; d. Arthur McKinley and Mildred (Smith) Harding; m. Leroy Stephen Williams, July 8, 1966; children: Michael LaMar, Darryl LaVon, Stephen LaSean. AB in English Edn. and Speech, Norfolk State U., 1969; postgrad., U. Va., 1972-73, Norfolk State U., 1987, Old Dominion U., 1973-88, MS in Ednl. Administrn., 1993. Cert. 7-12 English and speech tchr., mid. sch. and h.s. prin., postgrad. cert., Va.; cert. Nat. Bd. for Profl. Tchg. Stds. Tchr. English S.H. Clarke Sch. Portsmouth Schs., 1969-70, tchr. English W.E. Waters Sch., 1970-71, tchr. English Churchland Mid. Sch., 1971-74, chmn. English dept., 1974-86, 88-99, cons. coll. bd. English vertical teaming, 1997, adminstrv. intern in curriculum and instrn., 1999; asst. prin. Hunt-Mapp Mid. Sch., Portsmouth, 1999—. Fieldtester Va. Standards of Learning Lang. Arts; tchr./trainer Portsmouth Schs., 1986-88, lead mentor tchr., 1990—, cons. coll. bd.; presenter SAT prep. workshop, New-Tchr. Insvc., Writing Across the Curriculum, Reading to Learn, Technology in the Classroom. Active Hodges Manor Civic League, Portsmouth, 1985—, PTA; dir. Christian edn., summer camp youth adv., coord. vol. tutorial svc., mem. sr. choir, usher, coord. youth activities, mem. ch. coun., bd. dirs. kindergarten, Edna Hyke Corbett Achievement Award Found.; coord. Multiple Sclerosis Read-a-Thon, Back to Sch. Seminar; community campaign vol. Mother's March, Am. Cancer Soc., Muscular Dystrophy, Am. Heart Assn.; co-sponsor Cavalier Manor Deep Doubles Tennis Tournament. Named State Tchr. of Yr., State Bd. Edn., Richmond, Va., 1992, Outstanding Young Educator, Portsmouth Jaycees, 1978, Va. Secondary Reading Tchr. of Yr., Secondary Reading Coun. Va., 1999; recipient 25 svc. and honor awards from local orgns. Fellow Hampton Rds. Inst. for Advanced Study of Tchg.; mem. ASCD, NEA, NAACP, Va. Edn. Assn., Nat. State Tchrs. of Yr. Assn., Nat. Coun. Tchrs. of English, Internat. Reading Assn., Va. State Secondary Reading Assn., Va. Congress English Teachers, Va. Assn. Tchrs. of English (Foster B. Gresham award 1994), Portsmouth Edn. Assn., Portsmouth Reading Coun., Tidewater Assn. Tchrs. English, Delta Sigma Theta. Democrat. Avocations: singing, speaking, reading, collecting dolls. Home: 801 Nottingham Rd Portsmouth VA 23701-2118 Office: Hunt-Mapp Mid Sch 3701 Willett Dr Portsmouth VA 23707-1295 E-mail: LLWMS2@aol.com.

WILLIAMS, LILLIAN SERECE, educator; BA, U. Buffalo, 1966, MA, 1973, PhD, 1979. Tchr. Buffalo (N.Y.) Bd. Edn., 1966—69; asst. prof. U. Buffalo, 1972—76, vis. asst. prof., 1985—87, assoc. prof., dept. chair, 2002—; asst. prof. Howard U., Washington, 1976—85; from asst. to assoc. prof. U. Albany, NY, 1987—2002. Historian NAACP, Balt., 1992—93, Girl Scouts of the U.S.A., N.Y.C., 1995—97, N.Y. State Mus., Albany, 1997—98; dir. Inst. for Rsch. on Women U. Albany, 1998—2002. Author: Strangers in the Land of Paradise, 1999; editor: (documentary) Records of the National Association of Colored Women, 1993, 1994. Recipient Nuala McGann Drescher award, United Univ. Profls., Lifetime Achievement award, Niagara County Black Achievers, Niagara Falls, N.Y., 2000; State Farm Ins. fellow, Nat. African Am. Women Leadership Inst., 2001. Mem.: Afro-Am. Hist. Assn.the Niagara Frontier, Orgn. Am. History, Delta Sigma Theta. Avocations: reading, art, interior decorating. Office: SUNY Buffalo African Amer Studies Dept 732 Clemens Hall Buffalo NY 14260

WILLIAMS, LINDA HUNT, not-for-profit developer, consultant; b. New Orleans, Aug. 12, 1948; d. Abram Davis and May (Botsay) Hunt; m. W. Patrick Williams, Oct. 7, 1983; 1 child, Erica Bailey. BBA in Mgmt., Loyola U., New Orleans, 1986; MPA with honors, U. N.C., Charlotte, 1996. Mem. adj. faculty Ctrl. Piedmont C.C., Charlotte, N.C., 1988-94; staff dir. Charlotte Area Ednl. Consortium, N.C., 1994-96; mem. staff U.S. Senate, Charlotte, 1997-99; exec. dir. Children's Scholarship Fund-Charlotte, 1999—2001, ret., 2003; mem.-at-large Wake County Commn. on Women, 2003. Treas. exec. bd. Mecklenburg County Republican Party, 1997-99, vice chmn. exec. bd., 1999-2001; mem. at large N.C. Exec. Com., 1997-2001, N.C. Mecklenburg County Exec. Com., 1997-2001, N.C. 9th Congl. Dist. Exec. Com., 1997—2001, N.C. State Exec. Com., 1999-2001; alt. del. Rep. Conv., 2000; 2d v.p. exec. bd. Substance Abuse Prevention Svcs. of the Carolinas, 1997-98. With USN, 1967-72. Fellow, Inst. of Polit. Leadership, UNC-W, 2002. Mem. Am. Soc. Pub. Adminstrs., Pi Alpha Alpha (v.p. 1996-97, pres. 1997-98), Rotary, Kiwanis (pres.-elect Holly Springs chpt.), Sunset Ridge Homeowners Assn. (v.p.). Roman Catholic. Avocations: family, reading, camping, fishing.

WILLIAMS, LISA ROCHELLE, logistics and transportation educator; b. Toledo, Feb. 11, 1964; d. Lionel and Mary Moore; divorced; 1 child, Matthew Malik. BS, Wright State U., 1985, MBA, 1988; MA, PhD, Ohio State U., 1992. Prof. Ctrl. State U., Wilberforce, Ohio, 1988-89, Pa. State U., University Park, 1992—; prof., Oren Harris chair in logistics U. Ark. Cons. CLSA, University Park, 1992—; owner, operator Collage, State College, Pa., 1994-96. Author: Evolution, Status and Future of the Corporate Transportation function, 1991; contbr. articles to profl. jours. Mem. Coun. of Logistics Mgmt. (chmn. com. 1997—), Am. Soc. Logistics and Transp., World Conf. on Transport Rsch. (chmn. track com. 1997-98), Alpha Kappa Alpha. Home: 3525 Del Mar Heights Rd #205 San Diego CA 92130-2122

WILLIAMS, LUCINDA, country musician; b. Lake Charles, La., 1953; d. Miller W.; m. Greg Sowders (div.). Albums include: Ramblin' On My Mind, 1979, Happy Woman Blues, 1980, Lucinda Williams, 1988, Passionate Kisses, 1989 (Grammy award Best Country Song 1994), Sweet Old World, 1992, Car Wheels on a Gravel Road, 1998 (Grammy award for best contemp. folk album, 1999), Essence, 2002 (Grammy award for best female rock vocal); contbr. songs to: Sweet Relief, 1993, Born to Choose, 1993. Office: c/o Universal Music Group 1755 Broadway New York NY 10019

WILLIAMS, LYNN STENSTROM, small business owner; b. Urbana, Ill., Mar. 5, 1959; d. Ralph Hubert and Patricia (Fitzgerald) Stenstrom; m. Randy West Williams; children: Sarah, Mary. BA in Urban Planning, U. Ill., Urbana/Champaign, 1981; MPA, Ind.U., Bloomington, 1983. Adminstrv. asst. Owen Healthcare, Inc., Houston, 1984—87; Owner Lynn's Texas Fibers, Pearland, Tex., 1994—. Recipient First Place, Handknitting Category, Victoria Cultural Council - Fabric of our Cultures, 1998, Honorable Mention, Victoria Cultural Coun.l - Fabric of our Cultures, 1997. Mem.: Contemporary Handweavers of Houston (Publicity Chairman 1997—99), Contemporary Handweavers of Tex. (Best in Show 50th Anniversary award 1999, First Place Hand Woven Daytime Fashion 2001, 2nd Place Handspun Work 2001), Pi Alpha Alpha. Roman Catholic. Home: 3007 Rothbury Dr Pearland TX 77584 Office: Lynn's Texas Fibers 3007 Rothbury Dr Pearland TX 77584

WILLIAMS, MAMIE ALETHIA, minister; b. Sumter, S.C., Aug. 13, 1950; BA BA in Religion, Philosophy and Social Sci., Claflin U., 1972; MDiv, Wesley Theol. Sem., Washington, 1978. Ordained deacon United Meth. Ch., 1979. Clergy Calvary United Meth. Ch., Washington, 1977—82, Centennial-Caroline Street United Meth. Ch., Baltimore, 1982—88, Hughes United Meth. Ch., Washington, 1988—98; dist. supt. Balt.-Washington Conf. United Meth. Ch., Columbia, Md., 1998—. Preacher Nat. Hist. Convocation, 1978, N.E. Jurisdictional Laity Convocation, 1985, Eighth Annual Session, Zimbabwe Annual Conf., 1987; acting pres. So. Chrisitian Leadership Conf., Balt.; pastoral counselor Johns Hopkins Hosp., Balt. Pres. Wash. Inner City Self-Help, Washington; chair Nat. Coun. Negro Women Interfaith Breakfast, Washington, Annapolis City Pub. Housing Transition Team, Annapolis, Md.; 3d v.p. NAACP, Balt.; del. World Conf. on Peace and Freedom, 1979, Nat. Youth/Young Adult Consultation, 1972; mem. Shalom Zone Mission to Zimbabwe, 1998—99; chair, Ecumenical Prayer Breakfast Nat. Black Family Reunion, 1996—. Recipient Freedom award, Anne Arundel County Br. of NAACP, 1996. Home: 233 Mill Church Rd Arnold MD 21012-1066 Office: Baltimore-Washington Conf 9720 Patuxent Woods Dr Ste 100 Columbia MD 21046-1526 Personal E-mail: maw813@aol.com. E-mail: maw813@aol.com.

WILLIAMS, MARCIA PUTNAM, human resources specialist; b. Ossining, N.Y., July 3, 1948; d. Charles Samuel and Lois Barbara (Putnam) W. BA, U. Denver, 1970, MA, 1972. Warehouse person, truck driver Strear Foods/United Food Svc., Denver, 1977-79; truck driver Beverage Distributors Corp., Aurora, Colo., 1979-84; tour guide for morale, welfare, and recreation USN, Sigonella, Sicily, 1984-85; reservations sales agt. Western/Delta/United Airlines, Denver, 1986-88; unemployment ins. rep. Dept. Labor and Employment State of Colo., Denver, 1988-90; site mgr., sr. outplacement counselor Army Career and Alumni Program, Ft. Carson, Colo., 1990-91; labor and employment specialist Dept. Labor and Employment State of Colo., Denver, 1991—. Guidance counselor Mesa County Sch. Dist. 51, Grand Junction, Colo., 1976-77, Douglas County Sch. Dist., Castle Rock, Colo., 1975-76, Adams County Sch. Dist., North Glenn, Colo., 1974-75; world history tchr. Ithaca (N.Y.). City Sch. Dist., 1972-74. Author: National Job Hotline Directory, 1995-2000. Mem. Internat. Assn. Pers. in Employment Security (legis. chair 1997-98). Avocations: photography, travel, sports, cooking, motorcycles. Home: PO Box 211113 Denver CO 80221-0396

WILLIAMS, MARCIA R. social services administrator; d. Olevia Thomas; m. Nathaniel T. Williams; 1 child, Regina N. BS, Elmhurst Coll., Elmhurst, Ill., 1980; MA Social Work, George Williams Coll. at Aurora U., Aurora, Ill., 1998. Cert. Child Protection Investigator Ill. Dept. of Children and Family Svc., 1990, Trainer Ill. Dept. of Children and Family Svcs., 1999, lic. Child Welfare Ill. Dept. of Children and Family Svcs., 2000, cert. Peer Reviewer Counsel of Accreditation, 1998. Cook county correctional officer Cook County Dept. of Corrections, Chgo., 1982—86; child welfare worker Vol. of Am., Chgo., 1986—90; child welfare specialist Ill. Dept. of Children and Family Svcs., Chgo., 1989—90, child protection investigator, 1990—93, child protection supr., 1993—2000, child protection mgr., 2002—. Sec. U. Ill. Upward Bound Parent Adv. Bd., Chgo., 2000—03; v.p. 8300 South Dante Block Club, Chgo., 1998—2001. Mem.: Alpha Kappa Alpha. Avocations: reading, cooking, party planning, playing cards, crocheting. Personal E-mail: marciar929@hotmail.com.

WILLIAMS, MARILYN, state legislator; Mem. Mo. Ho. of Reps. from 159th dist., 1993—. Democrat. Address: RR 1 Box 98 Dudley MO 63936-9719 Office: Mo Ho of Reps State Capitol Building Jefferson City MO 65101-1556

WILLIAMS, MARSHA KAY, data processing executive; b. Norman, Okla., Oct. 26, 1963; d. Charles Michael and Marilyn Louise (Bauman) Williams; m. Dale Lee Carabetta, Dec. 13, 1981. BS in Computer Mgmt. and Sci., Met. State Coll., Denver, 1996; M Tech. Mgmt., U. Denver, 2001. Data processing supr. Rose Mfg. Co., Englewood, Colo., 1981-84, Mile High Equip. Co., Denver, 1984-88; mgr. info. tech. Ohmeda Monitoring Sys., Louisville, Colo., 1988-97; v.p., chief info. officer Cobe Cardiovasc., Inc., Arvada, Colo., 1997—2002, The Sorin Group, Inc., 2002—. Mem. info. tech. adv. bd. Warren Tech. Sch., 1994—98, chairperson, 1996—98; mem. adv. bd. U. Denver, 2001—04. Mem.: Bus. and Profl. Women's Assn. (Young Careerist 1991, Woman of Yr. 2002). Home: 4700 Yates Ct Broomfield CO 80020-5622 Office: Sorin Group 14401 W 65th Way Arvada CO 80004-3524 E-mail: marsha.williams@cobecv.com.

WILLIAMS, MARTHA, consumer products company executive, entrepreneur; b. 1953; Founder, CEO, pres. StyleMaster, Chgo., 1991—. Office: StyleMaster 1330 W 43rd St Chicago IL 60609

WILLIAMS, MARTHA ETHELYN, information science educator; b. Chgo., Sept. 21, 1934; d. Harold Milton and Alice Rosemond (Fox) W. BA, Barat Coll., 1955; MA, Loyola U., 1957. With IIT Rsch. Inst., Chgo., 1957-72, mgr. info. scis., 1962-72, mgr. computer search ctr., 1968-72; adj. assoc. prof. sci. info. Ill. Inst. Tech., Chgo., 1965-73, lectr. chemistry dept., 1968-70; rsch. prof. info. sci., coordinated sci. lab. Coll. Engring. U. Ill., Urbana, also dir. info. retrieval rsch. lab., 1972—, prof. info. sci. grad. sch. of libr. info. sci., 1974—, affiliate, computer sci. dept., 1979—. Chair large data base conf. Nat. Acad. Sci./NRC, 1974, mem. ad hoc panel on info. storage and retrieval, 1977, numerical data adv. bd., 1979-82, computer sci. and tech. bd., nat. rsch. network rev. com., 1987-88, chair utility subcom., 1987-88, subcom. promoting access to sci. and tech. data for pub. interest; task force on sci. info. activities NSF, 1977; U.S. rep. review com. for project on broad system of ordering, UNESCO, Hague, Netherlands, 1974; vice-chair Gordon Rshc. Conf. on Sci. Info. Problems in Rsch., 1978, chair, 1980; mem. panel on intellectual property rights in age of electronics and info. U.S. Congress, Office of Tech. Assessment; program chmn. Nat. Online Meeting, 1980-2001; founder, pres. Info. Market Indicators, Inc., 1982-; cons. in field; invited lectr. Commn. European Communities, Industrial R&D adv. com., Brussels, 1992. Editor-in-chief: Computer-Readable Databases Directory and Data Sourcebook, 1976—89, founding editor:, 1989—; editor: Ann. Rev. Info. Sci. and Tech., 1976—2001, Online Rev., 1979—92, Online and CD-ROM Rev., 1993—2000; mem. editl. adv. bd.: Database, 1978—88, mem. editl. bd.: Info. Processing and Mgmt., 1982—89, The Reference Libr., founding editor: Online Info. Rev., 2000—; contbr. articles to profl. jours. Trustee Engirng. Info., Inc., 1974-87, bd. dirs., 1976-91, chmn. bd. dirs., 1982-91, v.p., 1978-79, pres., 1980-81; regent Nat. Libr. Medicine, 1978-82, chmn. bd. regents, 1981; mem. task force on sci. info. activities NSF, 1977-78; mem. nat. adv. com. ACCESS ERIC, 1989-91. Recipient best paper of year award H. W. Wilson Co., 1975; Travel grantee NSF, Luxembourg, 1972, Honolulu, 1973, Tokyo, 1973, Mexico City, 1975, Scotland, 1976 Fellow: AAAS (mem. nominating com. 1983, 1985), Nat. Fedn. Abstracting and Info. Svcs. (hon.), Inst. Info. Scis. (hon.); mem.: NAS (mem. joint com. with NRC on chem. info. 1971—73), Internat. Fedn. for Documentation (U.S. nat. com.), Assn. Sci. Info. Dissemination Ctrs. (v.p. 1971—73, pres. 1975—77), Assn. Computing Machinery (pub. bd. 1972—76), Am. Soc. Info. Sci. (councilor 1971—72, mem. publs. com. 1974—, pres. 1987—88, councilor 1987—89, contbg. editor bull. column 1974—78, Award of Merit 1984, Pioneer Info. Sci. award 1987, Watson Davis award 1995), Am. Chem. Soc. Home: 2134 Sandra Ln Monticello IL 61856-8036 Office: U Ill 1308 W Main St Urbana IL 61801-2307 E-mail: m-will13@uiuc.edu.

WILLIAMS, MARTHA GARRISON, lawyer; b. Greenville, S.C., July 3, 1942; d. William Theodore and Edith (Roberts) G.; m. Ray R. Williams Jr.; 1 child, Ray R. III. BA, Randolph-Macon Coll., 1964; JD, U. S.C., 1967. Bar: S.C. 1967, U.S. Dist. Ct. S.C. 1967, U.S. Ct. Appeals 1970. Atty. regulatory div. U.S. Dspt. Agr., Washington, 1967-68; atty. Liberty Corp., Greenville, S.C., 1971-72, asst. v.p., asst. sec., 1972-82, counsel, 1980-82, v.p., gen. counsel, sec., 1982—; atty. investment div. Liberty Life Ins. Co., Greenville, 1968-72, asst. sec., 1972-82, asst. v.p., 1976-79, v.p., 1979—, counsel, 1980-82, gen. counsel, sec., 1982—, also bd. dirs. Bd. dirs. ARC,

Greenville, 1981-86, S.C. Dept. Health and Environ. Control, Greenville, 1985—. Mem. ABA, S.C. Bar Assn., Greenville County Bar Assn., Assn. Life Ins. Council, Am. Soc. Life Ins. Council, Am. Soc. Corp. Secs., Fedn. Ins. Counsel, Am. Corp. Counsel Assn., Am. Council Life Ins., Life Insurers Conf. Office: Liberty Corp 2000 Wade Hampton Blvd Greenville SC 29615-1037

WILLIAMS, MARY, state legislator; b. July 8, 1949; m. Al Williams. Grad., U. Wis., Stevens Point, 1974. Former tchr.; restaurant owner; mem. Wis. State Assembly, Madison, 2002—, vice chair agr. com., vice chair rural affairs com., mem. forestry com., mem. natural resources com., mem. small bus. com., mem. tourism com. Republican. Office: State Capitol Bldg Rm 18 W PO Box 8953 Madison WI 53708 Address: 542 Billings Ave Medford WI 54451

WILLIAMS, MARY ANN, musical instrument executive, music educator; b. Muscatine, Iowa, Oct. 3, 1937; d. Paul Lavern and Marie S. Rockstad; children: Anne, Bradley, Margaret. B in Music Edn., U. Ill., 1959; M in Edn., Southwestern Okla. State U., 1980. Tchr. Surrattaville Jr. H.S., Clinton, Md., 1960—63; presch. tchr. Weatherford, Okla., 1975—77; piano tchr. Southwestern Okla. State U., Weatherford, 1981—93; keyboard mgr. and sales Penders' Music, Oklahoma City, 1993—. Organist 1st United Meth. Ch., Weatherford, 1975—84, Placentia (Calif.) Presbyn. Ch., 1985—88, Crown Heights Christian Ch., Oklahoma City, 1988—. Mem.: Sigma Alpha Iota (pres. coll. chpt. 1955, Ruby Sword of Honor 1955), Music Tchrs. Nat. Assn., Pi Kappa Lambda, Am. Guild of Organists (bd. mem. 1988—90). Home: 4711 Hemlock Ln Oklahoma City OK 73162 Office: Penders Music Co 4401 NW 63rd Oklahoma City OK 73116 E-mail: mwilliams@penders.com.

WILLIAMS, MARY ELLEN COSTER, judge; b. 1953; married; 2 children. BA in Latin and Greek (summa cum laude), MA in Latin, Cath. U., 1974; JD, Duke U., 1977. Assoc. Fulbright and Jaworski, Washington, 1977—79, Schnader, Harrison, Segal and Lewis, Washington, 1979—83; asst. U.S. atty. civil divsn. Washington, 1983—87; ptnr. Janis, Schuelke and Weschler Law Firm, Washington, 1987—89; adminstrv. judge Gen. Svcs. Adminstrn. Bd. of Contract Appeals, Washington, 1989—2003; judge U.S. Ct. of Fed. Claims, Washington, 2003—. Fellow: Am. Bar Found. (life); mem.: D.C. Bar (sec.), D.C. Young Lawyers Sect. (chair), Bar Assn. of D.C. (found. pres., trustee, bd. dirs.), ABA (section rep. com. of ethics and professionalism 1998—2000, commn. on evaluation of rules of profl. conduct 1998—2000, pres. task force on govt. lawyers 2000—01, chair sect. pub. contract law 2002—, chair elect, vice chair, sec.). Office: US Ct of Fed Claims 717 Madison Pl NW Washington DC 20005*

WILLIAMS, MARY PEARL, judge; b. Brownsville, Tex., Jan. 12, 1928; d. Marvin Redman and Theo Mae (Kethley) Hall; m. Jerre Stockton Williams, May 28, 1950; children: Jerre Stockton, Shelley Wiliams Austin, Stephanie Williams Laden. BA, U. Tex., 1948, JD, 1949. Bar: Tex. 1949, U.S. Supreme Ct. 1955, U.S. Dist. Ct. (we. dist.) Tex. 1987. Asst. atty. gen. State of Tex., Austin, 1949-50; relief judge Mcpl. Ct., Austin, 1964; asst. instr. dept. govt. U. Tex., Austin, 1966-67; atty. Office of Emergency Preparedness, Exec. Office of Pres., Washington, [illegible] mem. arbitration panel Am. Arbitration Assn., 1972-73; judge County Ct. Law 2, Travis County, Tex., 1973-80, 53d Jud. Dist. Ct., Austin, 1981-2000, sr. judge, 2000—, Cons. HEW, 1966—67. Mem. adv. com. Juvenile Bd. Travis County, 1964—67; trustee United Way, 1974—78. Named Outstanding Woman, Austin Am.-Statesman, 1974, Austin Citizen, 1978, Woman of the Yr., Austin Dist. Bus. and Profl. Women, 1977; named to Austin HS Hall of Fame, 1996. Fellow: ABA, Am. Bar Found.; mem.: Inst. Jud. Adminstrn., Am. Judicature Soc., Am. Law Inst., Travis County Bar Assn., Coll. State Bar Tex., State Bar Tex., Jr. League Austin, Kappa Alpha Theta, Delta Kappa Gamma (hon.). Democrat. Methodist. Home: 3503 Mt Barker Dr Austin TX 78731-5101 Office: Travis County Courthouse PO Box 1748 Austin TX 78767-1748 E-mail: marypw@mindspring.com.

WILLIAMS, MINNIE CALDWELL, retired educator; b. Chapel Hill, N.C., Feb. 25, 1917; d. Bruce and Minnie (Stroud) Caldwell; m. Peter Currington Williams Sr., July 25, 1938; children— Peter Jr., Bruce, James, Jacqueline, Charles. B.S. in English, N.C. Central U., 1938, M.A. in Elem. Edn., 1942; postgrad. U. Ill., 1962, U. South Fla., 1965, Fla. State U., 1967. Cert. elem. tchr., N.C.; cert. spl. edn., Fla. Tchr. Weldon pub. schs., N.C., 1940-60, Pinellas County Sch., St. Petersburg, Fla., 1961-80, reading specialist, 1961-80, spl. edn. tchr., 1961-80. Exec. Democratic committeeman, Pinellas County, Fla., 1983-85, local campaign and poll worker; co-chairperson United Way Com; bd. mem. St. Petersburg YWCA. Recipient Ret. Tchrs. award Dixie Hollins High Sch., 1984; Ret. Tchrs. award NAACP, 1980; Panhellenic Service award Greek Orgn., 1980. Mem. Nat. Assn. Ret. Tchrs., Am. Bus. Women Assn., Profl. Bus. Women, Garden Club of St. Petersburg, Delta Sigma Theta (NAACP rep.), Kappa Delta Pi. Baptist. Avocations: Travel; reading; gardening; arts; bowling. Home: 1726 28th Ave S Saint Petersburg FL 33712-3830

WILLIAMS, MONICA BERNARDETTE ELLEN, jewelry designer; b. Port Jefferson, N.Y., July 5, 1980; d. Bernard Gerard Williams and Monica Ellen Donnelly. BA summa cum laude, SUNY, Stony Brook, 2003. Jewelry designer, costume jewelry dealer Grandma's Top Drawer Jewelry Boutique, Port Jefferson, 1998—. Mem.: Vintage Fashion and Costume Jewelry, Welcome Inn Soup Kitchen, Sigma Beta, Golden Key, Phi Beta Kappa. Roman Catholic. Personal E-mail: liquidsilver9@att.net.

WILLIAMS, NANCY CAROLE, nursing researcher; b. Conover, N.C., Dec. 22, 1953; d. Howard G. and Edith (Hager) W. Diploma nursing, Gaston Coll., Dallas, N.C., 1981; student, U. N.C., 1990—. Charge nurse critical care unit Lincoln County Hosp., Lincolnton, N.C., 1981-83; primary charge nurse N.C. Meml. Hosp., Chapel Hill, N.C., 1983-85; charge nurse U. N.C. Clin. Rsch., Chapel Hill, 1985—. Mem. Nat. Assn. Rsch. Nurses and Dietitians, Am. Nurses Assn., N.C. Nurses Assn. Home: 202 6th St SW Conover NC 28613-2720

WILLIAMS, NATALIE, professional basketball player, restaurant executive; b. Utah, Nov. 30, 1970; d. Nate Williams; 1 adopted child, Sydney 1 child, Turasi. Profl. basketball player Portland Power ABL, 1997—99, Long Beach StringRays, 1998, Utah Starzz, 2000—; mem. U.S. Women's gold-medal winning basketball team, Sydney, Australia, 2000; owner Natalie's, Salt Lake City, 2002—. Named Female Athlete of Yr., USA Basketball, 1999, Winter Championship Team, 2002, Utah's Female Athlete of Century, 2nd Greatest Athlete Utah, Sports Illustrated . Office: 301 W South Temple Salt Lake City UT 84101

WILLIAMS, NELLIE JAMES BATT, secondary education educator; b. Nashville; d. Ivan C. and Lottie B. (Phillips) James; A.B., Stowe Coll., 1942; MS, U. Ill., 1945; postgrad. Ill. Inst. Tech., 1959, 64, Oberlin Coll., 1965, St. Louis U., 1962, 63, 67, 68, Rockhurst Coll., 1972, Webster Coll., 1984, 85, U. Mass, 1990; m. Napoleon Williams, July 21, 1973 (dec. 1989); 1 child by previous marriage, Charles W. Batt, Jr. Tchr. Sumner High Sch., St. Louis, 1949-54, Handly High Sch., 1954-63; tchr., head mathematics dept. Northwest High Sch., St. Louis, 1963-76; instr., dept. head, Acad. Math. and Sci., St. Louis, 1976-92; instr., head dept. Harris Teacher Coll., Forest Park C.C. Active NAACP, YWCA. NSF grantee, 1959, 62-65, 67, 72. Mem. Math. Club Greater St. Louis, Top Ladies of Distinction, Math. Assn. Am., Assn. Women in Math., Delta Sigma Theta Sorority (edn. com.). Methodist. Home: 7584 Amherst Ave Saint Louis MO 63130-2803

WILLIAMS, PAMELA SUE, music educator; b. Willard, Ohio, Nov. 18, 1954; d. Thomas Albert and Kathleen West; 1 child, Sheena Marie. Bachelor of Music, Heidelberg Coll., 1976. Vocal music dir. Eastwood Schs., Luckey, Ohio, 1977—83, Perrysburg Schs., Ohio, 1983—. Bd. dirs. Perrysburg Arts Coun., 1997. Mem.: NEA, Ohio Music Edn. Assn. (conv. chmn. 1998), Am. Choral Dirs. Assn. Avocations: piano, musical theater. Home: 214 Three Meadows Ct Perrysburg OH 43551 Office: Perrysburg HS 13385 Roacton Rd Perrysburg OH 43551

WILLIAMS, PAT L. military officer; b. Sumner, Miss., May 19, 1961; d. Otha M. and Vera N. Williams; m. Not Married. BA in Comms., Miss. State U., 1982; MA in Nat. Security Affairs Western Hemisphere, Naval Postgrad. Sch., 1995; MA in Nat. Security and Strategic Studies, Naval War Coll., 2001. Joint profl. mil. edn. phase 1. Commd. 2d lt., 1984; advanced through grades to lt. comdr., 1984; yeoman Fleet Logistics Support Squadron 30, Naval Air Sta., N. Island, Calif., 1984—89; officer candidate Officer Candidate Sch., Newport, RI, 1989; adminstrv. budget and supply officer Pers. Support Activity New London, Groton, Conn., 1989—91; head message ctr. Naval Computer and Telecomms. Sta., Mauritius, 1991—92; officer in charge pers. support detachment Naval Hosp. Long Beach, 1992—94; br. head, program mgr. Bur. Naval Pers., Arlington, Va., 1996—97; flag aide Comdr. Navy Recruiting Command, Arlington, 1997—98; assignments officer Comdr. Naval Pers. Command, Millington, Tenn., 1998—2000; commdg. officer Mil. Entrance Processing Sta., San Antonio, 2002—. Mil. social aide The White House, Washington, 1997—98. Named Navy Marksman (Pistol), USN, 1991; recipient Achievement medal with two gold stars, 1991—92, Nat. Def. Svc. medal, 1991, Mil. Outstanding Vol. medal, 1996—98, Commendation medal with three gold stars, 1998—2000. Mem.: Nat. Naval Officers Assn. (life; Secretary 1993—94, None). Avocations: running, reading, travel. Office: Naval War Coll 1950 Stanley Rd Ste 103 Fort Sam Houston TX 78234 Home: 4411 River Brook Dr San Antonio TX 78244-2819 Personal E-mail: plaquinn@msn.com. E-mail: sntcdr@mepcom.army.mil.

WILLIAMS, PATRICIA ANNE, philosopher, writer; b. Alexanderia, Va., May 26, 1944; d. Samuel Leonard and Kay Cloaninger Williams. BA, Coll.of William and Mary, Williamsburg, Va., 1966; MA in English, U. Va., 1967, MA Philosophy, 1985; PhD, U. of Guelph, Ont., Can., 1989. Lectr. La Trobe U., Melbourne, Australia, 1968—71; asst. prof. Virginia State U., Petersburg, 1990—95. Del. Citizen Amb. People to People Program, China, 1993. Author: (book) Doing without Adam and Eve: Sociobiology and Original Sin, 2001 (Outstanding Acad. Title award Choice Mag., 2002), Where Christianity Went Wrong, When, and What You Can Do About It, 2001; editor: Evolution and Human Values, 1995; contbr. jours., encys. including Zygon: Jour. of Religion and Sci., Biology and Philosophy, Quar. Rev. of Biology, Encyclo. Ethics. Mem. ACLU, 1973—; charter mem. U.S. Holocaust Meml. Mus., Washington, 1993—; mem. So. Poverty Law Ctr. Wall of Toleration, Montgomery, Fellow NEH fellow, 1989. Mem.: Inst. on Religion in an Age of Sci., Internat. Soc. for History, Philosophy, and Social Studies of Biology (program chmn. 1992—93), Philosophy of Sci. Assn., Am. Philos. Assn. Mem. Soc. Of Friends. Avocations: travel, hiking. Home: PO Box 69 Covesville VA 22931 Personal E-mail: theologyauthor@aol.com.

WILLIAMS, PATRICIA C. federal judge; [illegible] dist. U.S. Dist. Ct. Wash., 1997. Office: 904 W Riverside Ave Ste 304 Spokane WA 99201-1011 Fax: 509-454-5636.

WILLIAMS, PEARL See GOOD, EDITH

WILLIAMS, PEGGY RYAN, academic administrator; b. Montreal, Que., Can., May 27, 1947; d. Fred Smith and Carol (Kennedy) Ryan; m. David A. Williams, May 30, 1970. BA psychology, U. Toronto, St. Michael's Coll., Can., 1968; MEd, U. Vt., 1976; EdD, Harvard U., 1983. Caseworker children's svcs. Monroe County Dept. Social Svcs., Rochester, NY, 1968-72; med. social worker Med. Ctr. Hosp. of Vt., Burlington, 1972; coord. instrn, academic advisor CC of Vt., Lamoille County, 1973—75, project dir. Northwestern Vt., 1975—76, regional dir. Montpelier, 1976-82; part-time instr. C.C. Vt., 1978—85; asst. to the pres. Johnson (Vt.) State Coll., summer 1981; tchg. fellow Harvard U., 1981; dir. ednl. and pers. svcs., office of chancellor Vt. State Colleges, Waterbury, 1982-85; assoc. prof. Trinity Coll., Burlington, 1985—89, chair, dept. bus & economics, 1985-88, assoc. acad. dean, 1988-89; pres. Lyndon State Coll., Lyndonville, Vt., 1989-97, Ithaca (N.Y.) Coll., 1997—. Adj. faculty Johnson State Coll., 1984—86; mem. policy adv. group for outcomes and assessment and instnl. effectiveness N.Y. State Edn. Dept., 1998—; external advisor SUNY Adv. Coun. on Tchr. Edn., 2000—. Bd. mem. Tompkins Trust Co., 1999—; active The Ithaca Downtown Partnership Cmty. Adv. Bd.; com. mem. Cornell U. Johnson Mus. Art Cmty. Adv. Coun.; bd. mem. Sacred Heart Sch. Montreal; mem. adv. bd. Tompkins County Soc. for the Prevention Cruelty to Animals, 1999—; mem. adv. coun. Finger Lakes Land Trust, 2000—. Recipient Jackie M. Gibbons Leadership award, Am. Coun. Edn./Nat. Identification Program, 1984, Margaret R. Williams Emerging Profl. award. Mem. Am. Assn. Higher Edn., 1973-, Am. Coun. on Edn., 1981- (bd. dirs. 2000-), Nat. Assn. Women in Edn., 1985-, Office: Ithaca Coll Job Hall Ithaca NY 14850*

WILLIAMS, PENNY, state legislator; b. N.Y.C., May 6, 1937; d. Peter and Polly Sheffield Potter Baldwin; children: Joseph Hill Jr., Peter Baldwin, James Chestnut. Student, Sarah Lawrence Coll., U. Tulsa. Mem. Okla. Ho. of Reps., Okla. City, 1981-89, Okla. Senate from 33rd dist., Okla. City, 1989—. Trustee St. Gregory's Coll.; mem. Tulsa Com. on Fgn. Rels. Mem. LWV, Tulsa C. of C. Democrat. Episcopalian. Home: 1366 E 25th St Tulsa OK 74114-2702

WILLIAMS, PHYLLIS CUTFORTH, retired realtor; b. Moreland, Idaho, June 6, 1917; d. William Claude and Kathleen Jessie (Jenkins) Cutforth; m. Joseph Marsden Williams, Jan. 21, 1938 (dec. 1986); children: Joseph Marlis, Bonnie Lou Williams Thompson, Nancy Kay Williams Stewart, Marjorie Williams Karren, Douglas Claude, Thomas Marsden, Wendy Kathleen Williams Clark, Shannon Irene Williams Ostler. Grad., Ricks Coll., 1935. Tchr. Grace (Idaho) Elem. Sch., 1935-38; realtor Williams Realty, Idaho Falls, Idaho, 1972-77; mem. Idaho Senate, Boise, 1977. Owner, mgr. river property. Compiler: Idaho Legisladies Cookbook, Cookin' Together, 1981. With MicroFilm Ctr., LDS Ch. Mission, Salt Lake City, 1989-90; former block chmn., vol. Cancer Drive; active Idaho State Legisladies Club, 1966-84, v.p., 1982-84; mem. Bonneville County (Idaho) Rep. Women. Republican. Avocations: genealogy, cooking, music, politics, photography, travel.

WILLIAMS, PHYLLIS S. education educator, religious organization administrator; b. Bessemer, Ala., Mar. 2, 1953; d. Charles and Lela Williams. Bachelors, Oberlin Coll., Ohio, 1975; PhD, Auburn U., Ala., 1996; postgrad., Johns Hopkins U. Sch. of Medicine, Balt., 1996—97. Cert. gifted K-12 tchr. Ala., 2003, learning disabilities K-12 tchr. Ala., 2003, psychometrist Ala., 2003. Post doctoral fellow Johns Hopkins Dept. of Pediat.-The Kennedy Krieger Inst., Balt., 1996—97; psychometrist Bessemer City Sch. Sys., Ala., 1997—2000; prof. edn. Birmingham-So. Coll., Ala., 2000—. Stewardship dir. 1st Adamsville SDA Ch., Ala., 1997—; founder, CEO, Holy Grounds, Inc., Brookwood, Ala., 1998—; chmn. coord. collaborative edn. program Birmingham-So. Coll., Ala., 2000—. Dir.: Christian Home School Collaboration; spkr. (commencement) Becoming Like Christ in the 21st Century. Grantee, Oberlin Coll., 1971-1975, Auburn U., 1994-1996, Kennedy Krieger Inst., 1996-1997. Mem.: Am. Psychol. Soc., Coun. of Exceptional Children. Seventh Day Adventist. Achievements include Founded a non-profit organization for the cognitive and social development of children with special needs in an inclusive Christian learning environment. Avocations: foster parent, mentoring/tutoring, travel. Office: Birmingham-Southern Coll 900 Arkadelphia Rf Birmingham AL 35444 E-mail: pwilliam@bsc.edu.

WILLIAMS, REBA WHITE, financial executive, writer; m. Dave H. Williams. BA in Enlgish, Duke U.; MBA, Harvard U.; MA in Art History, Hunter Coll.; MA in Philosophy, PhD in Art History, CUNY. Former rschr. McKinsey & Co., Inc.; securities analyst Mitchell Hutchins, Inc. Dir. spl. projects, mem. bd. dir. Alliance Capital Mgmt.; vice chmn. White Williams Holdings, Ltd., 2001—. Mem. editl. bd. Print Quar.; contbr. articles to Am. Artist, Bus. and Soc., Instl. Investor Chgo. Daily News, Fin. Analysts Jour., others; author catalog essays. Mem. Manhattan Cmty. Bd. 8, 1999-2000; mem. Art Commn. City NY, 1995-98, pres., 1997-98; mem. NY State Coun. on the Arts, 1996-99, vice chmn., 1999; hon. keeper of Am. prints The Fitzwilliam Mus., Cambridge, Eng. Decorated Polish Order of Merit, cavalier of grand cross Order of Poland 1st class; recipient Pacesetter award NY City Coun., 1999, Disting. Cultural Leadership award NY Rep. County Com., 1999, Augustus Graham medal Bklyn. Mus., 1998, others. Mem. Cosmopolitan Club. Office: White Williams Holdings 41 W 57th St 4th Fl New York NY 10019 Office Phone: 212-725-1705. E-mail: reba@rebawhitewilliaams.com.

WILLIAMS, RITA CARROLL, language educator, poet; b. Norfolk, Va., Jan. 11, 1962; d. William Henry Carroll Jr. and Joyce Riddick Carroll; m. Stafford Clayton Williams Jr., Dec. 2, 1985; 1 child, Thaddeus Clayton. BA in English, BS in Geology, Elizabeth City State U., 1985; student in mid. grades lang. arts, 2002. Author: (poetry) Daily Inspirations: Daily Living With God, 2002, Daily Inspirations: One More Day's Journey on the Way to Heaven, 2003, Book 2, 2003, (poetry recorded on Cd and cassette) The Sound of Poetry, (poetry featured in poetry anthologies) Our Forgotten Graces and Patterns. Recipient Outstanding Achievement in Poetry award, Famous Poets Soc., 1999, Editor's Choice award, Internat. Libr. Poetry, 1999, 2003, Outstanding Poetry award, 2003. Mem.: NEA, Internat. Soc. Poets, N.C. Assn. Educators, Alpha Kappa Mu (Cert. of Merit). Avocations: writing poetry, stamp collecting, coin collecting, sports card collecting. Home: 1468 Lambs Grove Rd Elizabeth City NC 27909-7502

WILLIAMS, ROBERTA GAY, pediatric cardiologist, educator; b. Rocky Mount, N.C., Oct. 23, 1941; BS, Duke U., 1963; MD, U. N.C., 1968. Diplomate Am. Bd. Pediats. (mem. com. ofcl. examiners 1985—, bd. dirs. and rep. sub-bd. chmn. com. 1992—, mem. exec. com. 1993—), Am. Bd. Pediat. Cardiology (chmn. 1991-92, cons. 1993). Med.-pediat. intern N.C. Meml. Hosp., Chapel Hill, 1968-69; pediat. resident Columbia Presbyn. Med. Ctr., N.Y., 1969-70; fellow in cardiology Children's Hosp. Med. Ctr., Boston, 1970-73, from asst. in cardiology to assoc. in cardiology, 1973-75, sr. assoc. in cardiology, 1976-82; from instr. pediats. to asst. prof. pediats. Harvard Med. Sch.-Children's Hosp., Boston, 1973-82; assoc. prof. pediats. UCLA Med. Ctr., 1982-86, chief divsn. pediat. cardiology, 1982-95, prof. pediats., 1986-95; chmn. pediat. U. N.C. Sch. Medicine, Chapel Hill, 1995-2000, U. So. Calif., L.A., 2000—; v.p. pediat. and acad. affairs Children's Hosp. L.A., 2000—. Attending physician Cardiac Med. Svcs., Children's Hosp. Med. Ctr., Boston, 1974, cardiology cons. Cardiothoracic Surgery Svc., 1974, med. dir. Cardiovasc. Surgery ICU, 1974-79, dir. Cardiac Graphic Lab. and Cost Ctr., 1977-82, mem. com. neonatal ICU, [illegible] cardiac svcs. subcom. N.Y. State Cardiac Adv. Com., 1996—; mem. adv. coun. Nat. Heart, Lung and Blood Inst., 1999—2003; chair pediatric cardiac svcs. com., cardiac adv. com. N.Y. State Dept. Health, 1995—, mem. exec. com. cardiac adv. com., 1995—; seminar leader in field. Mem. editl. bd.: Pediat. Cardiology, 1979, Circulation, 1983-91, Am. Jour. Cardiology, 1984-91, Jour. Applied Cardiology, 1985, Clin. Cardiology, 1988, Internat. Jour. Cardiology, 1992-95, Archives of Pediats. and Adolescent Medicine, 1994—; editl. cons. Jour. of Am. Coll. of Cardiology, 1992-94. Mem. exec. coun. cardiovasc. disease in the young Am. Heart Assn., 1979-85, mem. subcom. congenital cardiac defects, 1980-82, subcom. nominating com., 1982-83; mem. Am. Heart Assn.-Greater L.A. affiliate, 1983—, exec. com. and rsch. com., 1984—, judge young investigator competition, 1984, mem. program com., 1986-90, v.p. med.-exec. com., 1991-92, pres.-elect, 1992-93, and numerous other coms.. Fellow Am. Coll. Cardiology (allied health profls. com. 1984-87, mem. physician workforce adv. com. 1988-94, mem. manpower adv. com. 1988—, mem. extramural continuing edn. com. Heart House 1990—, co-chmn. Bethesda conf. 1993, gov. So. Calif. chpt. 1994—, pres. Calif. chpt. 1994—, govt. rels. com., 1998—, trustee 2000—), Am. Acad. Pediats. (sec. exec. com. sect., mem. com. on fetus and newborn 1985-88, mem. exec. com. sect. on cardiology 1985—, chmn. program com. 1988-89, mem. subcom. Am. Heart Assn. task force on assessment of diagnosis and therapeutic cardiovasc. procedures 1989, chair sect. cardiology 1989, mem. mem. coun. on sects. mgmt. com. 1995—); mem. Soc. for Pediat. Rsch., Am. Pediat. Soc. (dept. chair 1995, exec. com. 1997), Am. Soc. Echocardiography (mem. exec. com. 1975-78, com. on guidelines for technician tng. 1975-78, bd. dirs. 1976-80, treas. exec. coun. com. 1981-83, steering com. Future of Pediatric Edn. Task Force, 1996-99, chmn. Future of Pediatric Subsplty. Workgroup, 1996-99, co-chair Bethesda conf. #32 2000). Avocations: photography, hiking. Office: Childrens Hosp LA MS 71 4650 Sunset Blvd Los Angeles CA 90029-2106 E-mail: rwilliams@chla.usc.edu.

WILLIAMS, ROSLYN PATRICE, marketing executive; b. Hollywood, Fla., Nov. 8, 1957; d. Charlie Thomas and Christine (Brown) W.; 1 child, Kristina Latrice. BA, Hampton U., 1979. Newsroom asst. The Miami (Fla.) Herald, 1980-81; multi-line adjuster Allstate Ins. Co., Coconut Creek, Fla., 1982-83; asst. program and promotions mgr. WDZL TV, Hollywood, Fla., 1983-86; media buyer/planner Gigi Advt., Miami, 1986-87; acct. exec. WRBD-AM Radio, Ft. Lauderdale, Fla., 1987-90, WEDR-FM Radio, Miami, 1990-97; exec. dir. South Fla. Black Film Festival, Ft. Lauderdale, 1996—. Cons. Minority Media and Telecomms. Coun., 1998—; cons. Urban World Film Festival Coll. Tour, 1999; officer/sec., bd. dirs. South Fla. Black Film Festival, 1989-91; talk show host "Bus. in the Black", Miami Dade Chamber/WMBM-AM, 1989-90; co-founder, organizer Black Bridal Expo, South Fla., 1992-94; mem. adv. bd. For Women Only Expo, Ft. Lauderdale, 1993-94. Avocations: golf, reading, hiking, roller blading. Office: South Fla Black Film Festival PO Box 833722 Hollywood FL 33083-3722

WILLIAMS, RUBY JO, retired principal; b. Marshall, Tex., Sept. 26, 1936; d. Henry Clay and Luberta Smith; m. Q.D. Williams (dec. Apr. 1998). BA, Wiley Coll., Marshall, Tex., 1959; M in Edn., U. N. Tex., 1972; postgrad. in Mid-Mgmt., Tex. Woman's U., 1987. Cert. elem., secondary sch. educator, mid-mgr., Tex. Tchr. Gainesville (Tex.) Sch. Dist., 1962-69, Sherman (Tex.) Sch. Dist., 1969-86, appraiser, 1986-87, prin., 1987-96, Edison coord., 1996-98. Mem., past chmn. Grayson Coll. Trustees, Grayson County, 1992—, Cmty. Block Grant, Sherman, Tex.; mem Hosp. Metraplex Bd., Sherman. Named Outstanding Citizen, City of Sherman, 1979. Mem. NAACP (life), AAUW (pres., v.p., Woman of Yr., Woman of Achievement, Outstanding Woman Educator 1978-79), Nat. Alliance of Black Sch. Educators, Tex. Elem. Prins. Assn., Goals for Sherman (multicultural chmn.) Mem. Ch. of Christ. Avocations: reading, travel, cooking, sewing. Home: 2015 E Alma Ave Sherman TX 75090-4006

WILLIAMS, RUTH LEE, clinical social worker; b. Dallas, June 24, 1944; d. Carl Woodley and Nancy Ruth (Gardner) W. BA, So. Meth. U., 1966; M Sci.in Social Work, U. Tex., Austin, 1969. Milieu coordinator Starr Commonwealth, Albion, Mich., 1969-73; clin. social worker Katherine Hamilton Mental Health Care, Terre Haute, Ind., 1973-74; clin. social worker, supr. Pikes Peak Mental Health Ctr., Colorado Springs, Colo., 1974—2000; pvt. practice social work Colorado Springs, 1978—2000;

pres. Hearthstone Inn, Inc., Colorado Springs, 1978—; practitioner Jin Shin Jyutsu, Colorado Springs, 1978—2000; dir. cmty. rels. Walker Wear, 2001—. Pres., v.p. bd. dirs. Premier Care (formerly Colorado Springs Mental Health Care Providers Inc.), 1986-87, chmn. quality [illegible] 1987-89, v.p. bd. dirs., 1992-93; bd. dirs. Beth Haven, Inc., JAC Svcs. Author, editor: From the Kitchen of The Hearthstone Inn, 1981, 2d rev. edit., 1986, 3d rev. edit., 1992. Mem. Am. Bd. Examiners in Clin. Social Work (charter mem., cert.), Colo. Soc. Clin. Social Work (editor 1976), Nat. Assn. Soc. Workers (diplomate), Nat. Bd. Social Work Examiners (cert.), Nat. Assn. Ind. Innkeepers, So. Meth. U. Alumni Assn. (life). Avocations: gardening, hiking, sailing. Office: 11555 Howells Rd Colorado Springs CO 80908-3735

WILLIAMS, RUTH RUSSELL, artist; b. Townsville, NC, Mar. 16, 1932; d. Sandy Terry and Virginia Dabney; m. Samuel Williams, Dec. 25, 1971; m. Odell Russell, 1946 (div.); children: Rick Russell, Matthew Russell, Robin Russell, Paula Russell Evans. Student, Henderson Inst., NC, Apex Beauty Coll., Richmond, Va. Cosmetologist Ruth's Beauty World, Richmond, Va., Henderson, NC, 1951—2001; folk artist, 1977—. Artist (calendar) Neighbors (The Am. Folk Art of Ruth Russell Williams), 2002. Recipient Key to the City, Office of Mayor, Woodlawn, Ohio, 1993, plaque, Nat. Coalition of 100 Black Women, Phila., 1999. Mem.: N.C. Mus. Art Assn. (artist), Sigma Gamma Rho (hon. medallion 1998). Presbyterian. Avocations: painting, cooking, reading, traveling, music. Home: 45 Williams Ln Henderson NC 27537

WILLIAMS, RYNN MOBLEY, community health nurse; b. Georgetown, S.C., Aug. 2, 1950; d. Ralph Edward and Pearl (Hill) Mobley; m. C. Rogers Jr., July 3, 1971 (div. Mar. 1992); 1 child, Julie Pearl; m. L. Benton Williams, May 2, 1998. Student, Georgetown County Sch. Nursing, 1970; AS, SUNY, Albany, 1982; AS in Criminal Justice, Georgetown Tech. Coll., 1992; BS in Health Adminstrn., Calif. Coll. Health Scis., 1999; BSN, U. S.C., 2002. Cert. community nurse, med. asst., gerontology Am. Nurses Credentialing Ctr. Mem. staff Georgetown Meml. Hosp., 1969-71; office nurse Dr. L. Benton Williams, Georgetown, 1971—; jail nurse Georgetown County Detention Ctr., 1991-92; staff devel. nurse Prince George Village, 1992—98, Winyah Convalescent Ctr., Georgetown, 2002—. Mem. ANA, Am. Assn. Office Nurses, Nat. Assn. Physicians Nurses, S.C. Nurses Assn., Order Ea. Star. Baptist. Avocations: crafts, cross stitch, photography, fabric painting, wedding photography. Home: 2221 Pringle Ferry Rd Georgetown SC 29440-6086 Office: 1743 N Fraser St Georgetown SC 29440-6407 also: Winyah Convalescent Ctr 2715 S Island Rd Georgetown SC 29440

WILLIAMS, SERENA, professional tennis player; b. Saginaw, Mich., Sept. 26, 1981; Singles semifinalist, Chgo., 1998; singles titles include U.S. Open, 1999, 2001, 2002, Grand Slam Cup, 1999, Paris Indoors, 1999, L.A., 1999, Indian Wells, 1999, 2001, Sanex Championship, 2001, French Open, 2002, Wimbledon, 2002, State Farm Women's Tennis Classic, 2002, Nasdaq-100 Open, 2002, Italian Open, 2002, Princess Cup, 2002, Sparkassen Cup, 2002, Australian Open, 2003; doubles titles include Oklahoma City, 1998, French Open (with Venus Williams), 1999, Hannover Open (with Venus Williams), 1999, Olympics, Sydney, 2000, Wimbledon, 2000, 2002, Australian Open, 2001, 2003. Ranked #27 on WTA Tour, 1998; #6 in 1999. Recipient Espy award for Best Female Athlete, ESPN, 2003, Espy award for Best Female Tennis Player, 2003. Office: c/o USTA 70 W Red Oak Ln White Plains NY 10604-3602 also: ATP Tour 201 Atp Tour Blvd Ponte Vedra Beach FL 32082-3211*

WILLIAMS, SHEILA A.T. elementary education educator, consultant; b. Columbus, Miss., Dec. 30, 1963; d. James Thurman and Lillian Augusta Thomas; divorced; children: Phillip James Thomas, Kristin Nicole Sims. BA in English, U. Miss., Oxford, 1986. Cert. in elem. edn. K-8, Miss. Tchr. Oxford City Schs., 1986-88; flight attendant Eastern Airlines, Miami, Fla., 1988-89; photographer Sears, Columbus, Miss., 1989-90; tchr. Cumberland County Schs., Fayetteville, N.C., 1994-95, Oktibbeha County Schs., Crawford, Miss., 1995-98, Lowndes County Schs., Columbus, 1990-94, 98—. Pres., founder S.H.A.K.E.R./Flight Buddies Aviation Program, Columbus, 1994—. Coord. Promote the Vote mock election, Crawford, 1996. Recipient Excellence in Tchg. award Nat. Coun. Negro Women, 1999; named Tchr. of Yr., Southview Mid. Sch., 1995. Fellow U.S. Space Found.; mem. AAUW, Air Force Assn. (Christa McAuliffe award 1998), Tuskegee Airmen (v.p. 1999—), Nat. Historic Preservation Soc. Democrat. Baptist. Avocations: flying, writing, swimming, hiking, reading. Mailing: 1374 Tara Rd Jonesboro GA 30238-6502

WILLIAMS, SUE, artist; b. Chicago Heights, Ill., 1954; Student, Cooper Union, 1973; BFA, Calif. Inst. Arts, 1976. One-woman shows include Laughelton Gallery, N.Y.C., 1989, Amy Lipton Gallery, 1991, Stuart Regen Gallery, L.A., 1992, Gallery 210, St. Louis, 1992, 303 Gallery, 1992, 1994, 1996, 1998, San Francisco Art Inst., 1993, Vera Vitagioia, Naples, 1993, Galerie Rizzo, Paris, 1993, Galerie Walcheturm, Zurich, 1994, Modulo, Lisbon, Portugal, 1994, 1996, Galleria Il Capricorno, Venice, Italy, 1994, 1997, Jack Hanley Gallery, San Francisco, 1995, Galerie Metropol, Vienna, Austria, 1995, Regen Projects, L.A., 1996, Jean Bernier Gallery, Athens, Greece, 1996, 1998, Galerie Ghislaine Hussenot, Paris, 1996, Johnen & Schottle, Cologne, Germany, 1997, Ctr. d'Art Contemporain, Geneva, 1997, Sadie Coles, London, 1998, Neue Galerie un Landesmus. Joanneum, Graz, Austria, 1998, exhibited in group shows at Adam Baumgold Fine Art and Simon Capstick-Dale Fine Art, N.Y.C., 1996, Friedrich Petzel Gallery, 1996, Galerie Andreas Binder, 1996, Spiral Wacoal Art Ctr., Tokyo, 1996, Weatherspoon Art Gallery, Greensboro, N.C., 1997, Elizabeth Harris Gallery, 1997, Fine Arts and Lehmann Maupin, N.Y.C., 1997, Mus. d'Art Contemporani Barcelona, 1997, Whitney Mus. Am. Art, 1997, Emory U., 1998, The Aldrich Mus. Contemporary Art, Ridgefield, Conn., 1998, Pat Hearn and Mattehw Marks Gallery, N.Y.C., 1998, Landesgalerie Oberosterreich, Linz, Austria, 1998, Kunsthalle Krems, Austria, 1998, numerous others, Represented in permanent collections; performer The New Mus., N.Y.C., 1986, contbr. articles to profl. jours., reviewer in field. Office: care 303 Gallery 525 West 22d St New York NY 10011

WILLIAMS, SUE DARDEN, library director; b. Miami, Fla., Aug. 13, 1943; d. Archie Yelverton and Bobbie (Jones) Eagles; m. Richard Williams, Sept. 30, 1989. BA, Barton Coll., Wilson, N.C., 1965; M.L.S., U. Tex., Austin, 1970. Cert. librarian, N.C., Va. Instr. Chowan Coll., Murfreesboro, N.C., 1966-68; libr.'s asst. Albemarle Regional Libr., Winston, N.C., 1968-69; br. libr. Multnomah County Pub. Libr., Portland, Oreg., 1971-72; asst. dir. Stanly County Pub. Libr., Albemarle, N.C., 1973-76, dir., 1976-80; asst. dir. Norfolk (Va.) Pub. Libr., 1980-83, dir., 1983-94, Rockingham County Pub. Libr., Eden, N.C., 1996—. Mem. ALA (coun. 1987-91, orientation com. 1990-92, chair 1991), Libr. Adminstrv. and Mgmt. Assn. (pub. rels. sec. 1985-87bd. dirs. 2004—), Southeastern Libr. Assn. (staff devel. com. 1986-88, Rothrock award com. 1984-86, sec. pub. libr. sect. 1982-84), Va. Libr. Assn. (SELA rep. 1993-96, coun. 1984, 88-91, 93-96, ad hoc conf. guidelines com. 1985-86, chmn. conf. program 1984, awards and recognition com. 1983, mem. SELA outstanding libr. program award com. 2002), Pub. Libr. Assn. (bd. dirs.-at-large Met. area 1986-89), Va. State Libr. (coop edn. com. 88-89), N.C. Libr. Assn. (scholarship com. 1999—, chair 2001—), LAMS. Home: 109 Chowan Rd Murfreesboro NC 27855 Office: Albermarle Regional Libr PO Box 68 303 W Tryon St Winton NC 27986 Office Phone: 252-358-7832. E-mail: swilliams_arl@yahoo.com.

WILLIAMS, SUNITA L. astronaut; b. Euclid, Ohio, Sept. 19, 1965; d. Deepak N. and Ursaline B. Pandya; m. Michael J. Williams. BS in Physical Sci., U.S. Naval Acad., 1987; MS in Engring. Mgmt., Fla. Inst. Tech., 1995. Commn. ensign USN, 1987, advanced through grades to lt. comdr., various assignments, 1987—89, overseas combat, 1989—92; officer in charge Hurrican Andrew Relief Ops. USS Sylvania, 1992—93; various assignments USN, 1993—95; served on USS Saipan, Norfolk, Va., 1995—98; astronaut NASA, Houston, 1998—. Decorated Commendation medal USN, Achievement medal USN & USMC, Humanitarian Svc. medal USN. Mem.: Soc. Flight Test Engrs., Soc. Exptl. Test Pilots, Am. Helicopter Assn. Office: Astronaut Office CB NASA Johnson Space Center Houston TX 77058

WILLIAMS, SUSAN MARIE, music educator; b. Indpls., July 19, 1958; d. John Stanley and Kathleen Ann Slamkowski; m. Stuart Clifford Williams, June 27, 1981; children: Zachary, Benjamin. BS, Clarke Coll., 1980; MA in Liberal Studies, Valparaiso U., Ind., 1987. Musc tchr. Union Twp. Sch., Wheeler, Ind., 1981—85; music tchr. elem., high sch. LaCrosse (Ind.) Sch., 1985—87; music tchr. elem., middle and high sch. Morgan Twp. (Ind.) Sch., 1987—88; elem. music. Portage (Ind.) Twp. Schs., 1988—2001, dept. chair. Choir dir. Ctrl. Elem., Portage, 1988—; rep. area I curriculum/assessment guide Ind. Acad. Stds. for Music, 2000. Facilitator Compassionate Friends, 1995—. Grantee Ind. Portfolio grant, Ind. Dept. Edn., 1999—2001. Mem.: Music Educators Nat.Conf., Ind. Music Educators. Avocations: running, water-skiing, skiing, bicycling, travel. Office: Ctrl Elem Sch 2825 Russell Portage IN 46368 Office Phone: 219-764-6553. E-mail: swilliams@portage.k12.in.us.

WILLIAMS, SUZANNE, state representative; b. Oklahoma City, Feb. 3, 1945; m. Ed Williams; 2 children. BA in Edn., Baylor U.; MA in Spl. Edn., U. Colo. Educator; state rep. dist. 41 Colo. Ho. of Reps., Denver, 1996—, mem. edn. and transp. and energy coms. Recipient Insider award, Aurora Sentinel, 1994, Gov.'s award for curriculum innovation, 1985, Gov.'s Action Plan award, 2000. Mem.: AAUW, Women in Govt., Aurora Sister Cities Internat., Delta Kappa Gamma. Democrat. Avocations: reading, music, exercising. Office: State Capitol # 271 200 E Colfax Ave Denver CO 80203

WILLIAMS, TAMBOR, state representative; b. Washington, D.C., Mar. 28, 1941; m. Jim Eckersley; 2 children. BA in English and Philosophy, CUNY; MA in Counseling, Western State U.; JD, U. Colo. Atty.; state rep. dist. 50 Colo. Ho. of Reps., Denver, 1996—, mem. appropriations and edn. coms., and joint com. on legis. audit, chair bus. affairs and labor com. Mem.: Colo. Bar Assn., No. Colo. Latino C. of C., Evans C. of C., Greeley/Weld C. of C. Republican. Congregationalist. Avocations: travel, reading, hiking, cooking. Office: State Capitol # 223 200 E Colfax Ave Denver CO 80203

WILLIAMS, TANYA DAWN, art appraiser, consultant; b. Spokane, Wash., June 17, 1967; d. Stanley T. and Tessa M.D. Williams. AAS, Fashion Inst. Tech., N.Y.C., 1987; BA, NYU, N.Y.C., 1989. Cert. in appraisal studies, fine and decorative arts NYU, 2002, registered notary public Fla., 2003. Lang. specialist-consular asst. Immigration & Naturalization Svc. - U.S. Embassy, Moscow, 1992—93, overseas immigration specialist Rome, 1993—99; propr. Tanya Williams Estate & Fine Art Appraisals, Sarasota, Fla., 2002—. Cons. The Complete Player Inst., Boca Raton, Fla., 1999—2000. Mem.: Appraisers Assn. Am., Inc., Longboat Key C. of C. Avocations: tennis, travel, performing arts, internat. rels., vol. humane soc.. Office: Tanya Williams Estate & Fine Art Appraisals PO Box 2275 Sarasota FL 34230

WILLIAMS, TERRIE MICHELLE, publicity agency executive; b. Mt. Vernon, N.Y., May 12, 1954; MA, BA cum laude, Brandeis U., 1975; MS, Columbia U., 1977. Exec. dir. World Inst. of Black Community, N.Y.C., 1982; dir. pub. rels. Essence Communications Inc., N.Y.C., 1982-86, v.p., dir., 1986-88; pres. The Terrie Williams Agy., N.Y.C., 1988—. Med. soc. worker N.Y. Hosp., N.Y.C., 1977-80; program adminstr. Black Filmmaker Found., N.Y.C., 1980-81; exec. dir. Black Owned Communications Alliance, N.Y.C., 1981-82. Author: The Personal Touch, 1995. Recipient Entrepeneur of the Yr. award Nat. Assn. Market Developers, 1990, Flo Kennedy Media award, 1990, Matrix award N.Y. Women in Communications, 1991. Mem. Women in Communications, NOW, Brandeis U. Alumni Assn. (bd. dirs.), N.Y. TV Acad. Arts and Scis., Pub. Rels. Soc. Am. (D. Parke Gibson award 1981). Office: The Terrie Williams Agy 1500 Broadway Ste 502 New York NY 10036-4015

WILLIAMS, THERESA ANN ALESHIRE, poet, writer, educator; b. Twentynine Palms, Calif., Jan. 24, 1956; d. Waldo Jackson Aleshire and Thelma Vesta Hollingsworth; m. Charles Allen Williams, June 15, 1974; children: Dale, Allen, Brian. BA in English/Art cum laude, E. Carolina U., 1985, MA in English, 1987; MFA in Fiction Writing, Bowling Green State U., 1989. Lectr. English Bowling Green (Ohio) State U., 1999—, assoc. faculty creative writing, 2003. Author: (novels) The Secret of Hurricanes, 2002 (Paterson Fiction prize finalist, 2003), (short stories) Easy Street, 2003, Jane, 2004. Finalist Allen Ginsberg Poetry award, 1996. Mem.: Associated Writing Program, Phi Kappa Phi. Office: Bowling Green State U Dept English Bowling Green OH 43403 Business E-Mail: terria@bgnet.bgsu.edu.

WILLIAMS, TONDA, entrepreneur, consultant; b. N.Y.C., Nov. 21, 1949; d. William and Juanita (Rainey) W.; 1 child, Tywana. Student, Collegiate Inst., N.Y.C., 1975-78, C.W. Post Coll., 1981-83; BA in Bus. Mgmt., Am. Nat. U., Phoenix, 1983; grad., L.I. Bus. Inst., 1996. Notary pub. N.Y. Asst. controller Acad. Ednl. Devel., N.Y.C., 1971-81; mgr. office Chapman-Apex Constrn. Co., Bayshore, N.Y., 1982-84; specialist computer RGM Liquid Waste Removal, Deerpark, N.Y., 1985-87; contr. LaMar Lighting Co., Freeport, N.Y., 1987—; owner, pres. Omni-Star, Bklyn., 1981—; pres. Omni-Data Tech., Bayshore, N.Y., 1996—. Author: Tonda's Songs in Poetry, 1978, The Magic of Life, 1991; co-author: Computer Management of Liquid Waste Industry, 1986. Recipient Golden Poet award World of Poetry, 1992. Mem. Am. Mus. Natural History, Am. Soc. Notary Pubs. Avocations: bowling, chess, singing. Home: 74 Cedar Dr Bay Shore NY 11706-2419 Fax: 631-968-1016. E-mail: tonda@omnidatatech.com.

WILLIAMS, UNA JOYCE, psychiatric social worker; b. Youngstown, Ohio, June 24, 1934; d. Samuel Wilfred and Frances Josephine (Woods) Ellis; children: Wendy Louise, Christopher Ellis, Sharon Elizabeth. BA, U. Ala., 1957; MSW, Adelphi U., 1963. Diplomate in profl. counseling Internat. Acad. Behavioral Medicine, Counseling and Psychotherapy. Dir. Huntington Program for Sr. Citizens; psychiat. social worker-supr. N.Y. State Dept. Mental Hygiene, Suffolk Psychiat. Hosp., Central Islip; info.-referral counselor Mental Health Assn. Nassau County, Hempstead, N.Y.; therapist Madonna Heights Family Clinic, Dix Hills, N.Y.; med. and psychiat. social worker Northport (N.Y.) VA Med. Ctr., psychiat. social worker acute psychiat. treatment svs.; med. social worker dialysis svcs. Northport (N.Y.) Va. Med. Ctr. Cons. on programs for aging Luth. Social Svcs. met. N.Y., 1959, sr. citizens programs, Bd. Edn. Port Jefferson, N.Y., 1963. Chmn. Huntington Twp. Com. Human Rels., 1970; sec. bd. trustees Unitarian Universalist Fellowship Huntington, 1984. Mem. NASW (diplomate in social work), Am. Assn. Family Counselors and Mediators,Germany Philatelic Soc. (pres. chpt. 30, 1990, Mem. of Yr. 1987). Avocations: oil painting, stamp collecting, music (voice & piano), family genealogy. Home: 316 Lenox Rd Huntington Station NY 11746-2640

WILLIAMS, VANESSA, recording artist, actress; b. Millwood, N.Y., Mar. 18, 1963; d. Milton and Helen; m. Ramon Hervey II, 1988 (div. 1997); children: Melanie, Jillian, Devin; m. Rick Fox, 1999; 1 child. Recording artist, 1988—. Stage appearances include: (Broadway) Kiss of the Spider Woman, 1994-95; film appearances include Pick-up Artist, 1987, Under the Gun, 1989, Another You, 1991, Harley Davidson and the Marlboro Man, 1991, Eraser, 1996, Hoodlum, 1997, Soul Food, 1997, Dance with Me, 1999, Light It Up, 1999; (TV films) Full Exposure: The Sex Tapes Scandal, 1989, Perry Mason: The Case of the Silenced Singer, 1990, Stompin' at the Savoy, 1992, Jacksons: An American Dream, 1992, Bye Bye Birdie, 1995, Futuresport, 1998, Courage to Love, 2000 (prodr.), Don Quixote, 2000, Keep the Faith, [illegible], A Diva's Christmas Carol, 2000, (TV mini series) Nothing Lasts Forever, 1995, The Odyssey, 1997; (TV guest appearance) The Fresh Prince of Bel-Air, 1990, Vanessa Williams and Friends: Christmas in N.Y., 1996, Star Trek: Deep Space Nine, 1996, The Odyssey, 1997; albums: The Right Stuff, 1988, The Comfort Zone, 1991, The Sweetest Days, 1994, Star Bright, 1996, Next, 1997, Alfie, the Best of Vanessa, 1998, Dance with Me, 1998; # 1 hit single Save the Best for Last; vocalist: (films) Adventures of Priscilla, Queen of the Desert, 1994, Pocahontas, 1995. Recipient 8 Grammy award nominations; named one of 50 Most Beautiful People, People Mag. Achievements include being the first Black to be named Miss America, 1983 (resigned title 1983). Office: Mercury Records care Dawn Bridges 825 8th Ave New York NY 10019-7416 also: Mercury Records 11150 Santa Monica Blvd Los Angeles CA 90025-3380 Address: William Morris Agy 151 El Camino Dr Beverly Hills CA 90212

WILLIAMS, VENUS, professional tennis player; b. Lynwood, Calif., June 17, 1980; d. Richard and Oracene Williams. Profl. debut Bank of West Classic, Oakland, Calif., 1994; owner V Starr Interiors; designer Venus Williams Collection Wilson's Leather Co. Mem. U.S. Fed Cup Team, 1995, 99, 2003. Recipient ESPY award for outstanding women's tennis player, 2001, Espy award for Best Female Tennis Player, 2001, Espy award for Best Female Athlete, 2002; named Most Impressive Network Newcomer award, 1997, TENNIS Mag. Most Improved Player, WTA Tour, 1998; winner mixed doubles (with Gimelstob) Australian Open, 1998, Roland Garros, 1998, doubles (with Serena Williams) French Open, 1999, U.S. Open, 1999, Australian Open, 2001, 03, Wimbledon, 2002, singles and doubles gold medal winner, Sydney Olympics, 2000, singles U.S. Open, 2000, 01, Wimbledon, 2000, 2001; winner 28 Career Singles Titles and 9 Career Doubles Titles, WTA Tour. Mem.: WTA Tour Players' Coun. Jehovah'S Witness. Avocations: interior decorating, fashion design. Office: US Tennis Assn 70 W Red Oak Ln White Plains NY 10604-3602

WILLIAMS, VERONICA MYRES, psychotherapist, social worker; b. Shreveport, La., May 11, 1947; d. McEura and Margie Virgina (Reagan) Myres; divorced; children: Nicole Leann, Jennifer Lyn, Erica Maria. BA, La. Tech. U., Ruston, 1969; MSW, U. Mich., Ann Arbor, 1977; PhD, So. Calif. U., 2001. Diplomate Am. Bd. Clin. Social Workers, Am. Psychotherapy Assn.; cert. social worker, Mich. Probation counselor Citizens Probation Authority, Flint, Mich., 1970-72; unit dir., therapist Svcs. to Overcome Drug Abuse Among Teenagers, Flint, 1972-74; psychiat. therapist Psycho-Therapeutic Treatment Clin., P.C., Flint, 1974-77; psychiat. social worker Hurley Med. Ctr., Flint, 1977-79; field instr. Sch. Social Work U. Mich., Ann Arbor, 1978-79, 86—; psychiat. social worker Inst. Mental Health, Flint, 1979-81, Psychotherapeutic Treatment Clinic, 1981-83; clin. social worker Flint Bd. Edn., 1979-83; pupil apprasial spl. edn. Caddo Parish Sch. Bd., Shreveport, La., 1983-85. Developer dropout prevention program Flint Bd. Edn., 1986-98; Beecher Sch. Dist., 1998—; psychiat. therapist Mott Children's Health Ctr., 1986-92, Oakland Psychol. Clinic, P.C., 1991-92; owner, dir. V. Williams, PhD, MSW, ACSW, BCD, PC, 1992—. Bd. dirs. Boys & Girls Club. Mem. NASW, ACSW, NEA, Mich. Edn. Assn. Democrat. Office: 225 E 5th St Ste 110 Flint MI 48502 Office Phone: 810-232-0018. E-mail: vwilliams000@ameritech.net.

WILLIAMS, VERONICA ANN, marketing professional, consultant, information technology executive; b. Washington, Feb. 8, 1956; d. Vernon and Shirley Ann (Felton) Williams. BA in Econs. with honors, Brandeis U., 1977; MBA, Northwestern U., 1979. Systems mktg. rep. Control Data Corp., Chgo., 1979-81, mktg. rep., 1981-82; staff mgr. AT&T, Basking Ridge, N.J., 1982-84, nat. account exec. N.Y.C., 1984-86, mgr. bus. planning Berkeley Heights, N.J., 1986-87, product mgr. Morristown, N.J., 1987-88; dist. mgr. Unisoft Corp., N.Y.C., 1988-89; acct. mgr. Lotus Devel. Corp., N.Y.C., 1989-90; dir. bus. devel., 1990-91, Software Corp. of Am., Stamford, Conn., 1990-91; founder, prin., mng. dir. ACT, Inc., South Orange, NJ, 1993—. Adv. bd. Fall COMDEX, 1994—96, 1999, COMDEX/SCIB, 1996—; founder and creator COMDEX/DISCOVER IT Wireless & Mobile Computing Showcase, Healthcare Forum, 1996—, Expo Commn., 1998, Consumer Electronics Show ExpoComm, 1998—; developer, presenter, moderator Enterprise Computing Solutions Conf., 1994—95, Wireless Datacomm, 1994—95, Mobile World, 1994—95, PDA Forum, 1996, Networld & Interop, 1996, Network World Unplugged, 1996; judge Windows World Open Contest spring COMDEX, 1996, 97, Apple Enterprise Awards PCEXPO, 1995; featured guest TV Computer Chronicles, 1996, Chgo. Tomorrow, 2001; strategic mktg. and wireless computing advisor; spkr. in field. Author: Wireless Computing Primer: A Comprehensive Guide to Wireless and Mobile Computing, 1996, Personal Computing Made Simple, 2002, Turning Tech. Into Value: It's Not Just Sales and Promotion, 2004; contbr. over 40 articles to profl. jours. Mem. South Orange Planning Bd., 1985-87, South Orange Citizens Budget Adv. Com., 1983-87; spkr. Nat. Assn. Broadcasters Ann. Conf., 2003. Named BMBA Alumni of Yr., Kellogg Grad. Sch. Bus., 2000; named one of Women Who Mean Bus., 1999. Mem. Nat. Black MBA Assn. (fin. chmn. Chgo. br. 1979-81, Performance award 1981), Rotary Internat.(2003), Nat. Assn. Broadcasters (spkr. 2003). Avocations: swimming, scuba diving, skiing, music. Home: 541 Scotland Rd South Orange NJ 07079-3009 Office: ACT Inc PO Box 978 71 S Orange Ave Ste 440 South Orange NJ 07079 Office Phone: 973-761-1860. E-mail: info@act-it.com.

WILLIAMS, VICKY ANN, music educator, musician; b. Columbia, Tenn., Mar. 19, 1966; d. Donald Lee and Martha Jane Williams. MusB, Mid. Tenn. State U., 1988. Cert. Profl. Tchr. Tenn., 1988. Band dir. Mt. Juliet Mid. Sch., Tenn., 1992—; asst. band dir. Mt. Juliet H.S., 1992—. Prin. French horn Tenn. Valley Winds, Murfreesboro, Tenn., 1985—. Mem. Mid. Tenn. Band Orch. Assn., Nashville, 1988. Mem.: Tenn. Music Educator's Assn. (mem.). Home: 611 N Greenwood Ext Lebanon TN 37087 Office: Mt Juliet Middle School 1003 Woodridge Pl Mount Juliet TN 37122 E-mail: williamsv@wcschools.com.

WILLIAMS, VIDA VERONICA, guidance counselor; b. Charleston, S.C., May 4, 1956; d. Timothy and Dotlee (Pendarvis) W. BA, Fisk U., 1978; MS in Edn., Queens Coll., 1986, postgrad., 1994-95, profl. diploma in adminstrn./supervision, 2001. Cert. sch. counselor, spl. edn. tchr., N.Y. Job counselor Trident Work Experience, Charleston, 1980; spl. edn. tchr. Jr. High Sch. 158, Bayside, N.Y., 1983-86, Pub. Sch. 214, Bklyn., 1986-90; guidance counselor I.S. 171, 364, Pub. Sch. 214, Bklyn., 1990-95, I.S. 302, Bklyn., 1995—; dir. Springfield Garden Meth. After Sch. Tutorial Program, Jamaica, N.Y. Co-dir. I.S. 302 Gospel Chorus, 1994-95; counselor Dist. 19 Bereavement, Bklyn., 1991-95; bd. dirs. Alpha Kappa Alpha Day Care Ctr., St. Albans, N.Y., 1992-94; dir. Springfield Gardens Meml. Ch. After-Sch. Tutorial Program, 1997-98. Vol. Voter Registration, Jamaica, 1992, Increase the Peace Corps, N.Y.C., 1992, Feeding of 5,000, Jamaica, 1993, Victim Svcs., Bklyn., 1994-95; chair activities Harlem Dowling Foster Care, Jamaica, N.Y., 1995; active Allen A.M.E. Ch. Gospel Choir, 1994-95, Voices of Victory, 1994-95. Named one of Outstanding Young Women Am., 1980, Am. Registry Outstanding Profs., 2003, Woman Yr., 2004. Mem. Alpha Kappa Alpha. Avocations: reading, singing, sewing, arts and crafts. Home: 11240 205th St Jamaica NY 11412-2214 Office: Gifted and Talented Acad IS 59 132-55 Ridgedale St Springfield Gardens NY 11413 Office Phone: 718-527-3801. E-mail: wvida1@aol.com.

WILLIAMS, VIVIAN LEWIE, retired counseling administrator; b. Columbia, SC, Jan. 23, 1923; d. Lemuel Arthur Sr. and Ophelia V. (McDaniel) Lewie; m. Charles Warren Williams, Apr. 4, 1947 (div. 1967); children: Pamela Ann Williams-Coote, Charles Warren Jr. (dec.). BA, Allen U., 1942; MA in Psychology, U. Mich., 1946, postgrad., 1946, 48; MS, U. So. Calif.,

1971, postgrad., 1971-72. Cert. marriage and family therapist, Calif.; cert. Calif. C.C. counselor. Asst. prof. psychology Tenn. State Agrl. and Indsl. U., Nashville, 1946-47; asst. prof. edn. Winston-Salem (N.C.) State U., 1947-50; asst. prof. edn., dir. tchr. edn. Allen U., Columbia, SC, 1951-53; specialist reading, coord. lang. arts Charlotte (N.C.) Mecklenburg Schs., 1963-67, cons. comprehensive sch. improvement project, 1967-69; asst. prof. edn., psychology Johnson C. Smith U., Charlotte, 1967-69; counselor team leader Centennial, U. So. Calif. Tchr. Corps, L.A., 1970-73; counselor Compton (Calif.) C.C., 1973—2003, adv. fgn. student, 1975-85; ret., 2003. Co-developer Hyde Park Estates and The Moors, Charlotte, N.C., 1960-63. Pres. bd. dirs. Charlotte Day Nursery, 1956-59; bd. dirs. Taylor St. USO, Columbia, S.C., 1951-53; sec. southwest region Nat. Alliance Family Life, 1973-74; sec. bd. dirs. NCCJ, Charlotte, 1959-62. Recipient Faculty Audit Program award Ford/Carnegie Found., Harvard U., Cambridge, Mass., 1968, Pub. Svc. Achievement award WSOC Broadcasting Co.; fellow U. Mich., 1946. Mem. NAACP (life, Golden Heritage mem. 1992), AAUW (life), NEA (life), Am. Fedn. Tchrs., Faculty Assn. Calif. C.C., Nat. Acad. Counselors and Family Therapists (life, clin. mem., pres. S.W. region 1989), C.C. Counselors Assn., The Links, Inc. (Harbor area chpt. historian 1985-87, chaplain 1990-94, 96-98), Jack and Jill Am. (charter mem., organizer Charlotte chpt., pres. 1954-56), Women on Target, Calif. Tchrs. Assn., Delta Sigma Theta, Alpha Gamma Sigma (Golden Apple award 1981). Democrat. Methodist. Avocations: sewing, crafts, photography. Home: 6621 Caro St Paramount CA 90723-4755

WILLIAMS, WENDY, civil engineer; b. Mobile, Ala., Mar. 8, 1965; d. George Marshall Jr. and Celia H. Marshall; m. Michael A. Williams, July 15, 1985; children: Michael A. II, Maurice D. BSCE, U. Ala., 1997; M in Econ. Fin., Clark Atlanta U. Pres, For Your Convenience, Prichard, Ala., 1997—. CEO NAACP, Mobile, 1997—. Author: The Morals of Conduct, 1998, In the Presence of my Enemies. Mem.: Am. Chem. Soc., Alpha Kappa Alpha. Republican. Baptist. Avocations: basketball, volleyball, track. Office: For Your Convenience 2015 W Station St Prichard AL 36670 E-mail: LoveKnowledge7@aol.com.*

WILLIAMSEN, DANNYE SUE, personal development educator, health facility administrator; b. Memphis, Mar. 26, 1949; d. Roy Fauntly and Arliss Wyleen Goodroe; m. Jon Charles Beckum, Dec. 23, 1969 (div. Mar. 1972); m. John Dean Williamsen, Dec. 24, 1986. BA cum laude, U. Memphis, 1995. Adminstr. Security Investments, Inc., Memphis, 1972-75; nightclub owner, investor Memphis, 1976-78; internat. tech. analyst ContiCommodity, Inc., Memphis, 1977-80; owner, tech. analyst Commodity Cons., Inc., Memphis, 1981; project mgr. B&P Devel. Co., Austin, Tex., 1982-84; asst. to pres. Memphis C. of C., 1984-86; owner, dental technician Williamsen Dental Lab., Memphis and Prophetstown, Ill., 1986—; ptnr., editor Personal Edn. Network, Prophetstown, Ill., 2001—; owner Networx Pub., Prophetstown, Ill., 2002—. Bd. dirs. Heartland Equine Assisted Therapeutic Ctr., Rock Falls, Ill., 2000—01. Author: Illusions, 1998, IT'S YOUR MOVE! Transform Your Dreams from Wishful Thinking to Reality, 2004; editor: Creative Living-an evolving approach to bus. life, 2001—, (e-newsletter) Metaphysical Minute, 2003—. Mem. AAUW (pres. 1998-99), APA, NOW, NAFE, Am. Bus. Women's Assn., Assn. for Humanistic Psychology, Small Pubs. Assn. N.Am., Pubs. Mktg. Assn., Psi Chi, Chi Beta [illegible] 16th St Moline IL 61265 Office Phone: 815-537-2959. Personal E-mail: wmsen@essex1.com. Business E-Mail: dannyew@networxpublishing.com.

WILLIAMS GIFFORD, SUSAN, state legislator; m. Mark Williams Gifford. BA, Western Mich. U. Bd. of selectmen Warcham, 1999—2002; state rep. Mass. House, 2003—. Republican. Office: Rm 540 State House Boston MA 02133

WILLIAMS-LOCKETT, LOLITA MONIQUE, accountant; BBA in Orgnl. Mgmt. and Leadership, Edward Waters Coll., 1998; MBA in Acctg., U. Phoenix, 2003. Asst. dir. adminstrv. svcs. Fla. CC, Jacksonville, 1993—; adj. prof. acctg. & bus. Office Phone: 904-633-8359. E-mail: lmlockett1@aol.com.

WILLIAMSON, DIANA JEAN, nurse; b. Portland, Oreg., Dec. 21, 1956; d. Gerald George and Jean Elizabeth Musson; m. Bradley Alan Williamson, Dec. 12, 1981. Grad., Good Samaritan Hosp./Med. Ctr., 1977. RN, Oreg.; cert. psychiat. and mental health nurse. Staff nurse Western Lane Hosp., Florence, Oreg., 1977-79; asst. head nurse Providence Portland Med. Ctr., Portland, 1979-99, staff nurse, 1999—. Activist Oreg. Wildlife Fedn./Witness Against Lawless Logging, Portland and Rhododendron, Oreg., 1996. Mem. ANA, Am. Inst. Archaeology, Oreg. Nurses Assn. (unit rep.), Oreg. Wildlife Fedn., Defenders of Wildlife. Democrat. Avocations: reading, music, wine. Home: PO Box 239 Rhododendron OR 97049-0239

WILLIAMSON, DONNA C. E. investment company executive; ScB in Applied Math., Brown U.; MS in Mgmt., MIT. Corp. v.p. Baxter Internat.; founding officer, corp. sr. v.p. Caremark Internat., Inc.; mng. dir., sr. v.p. ABN AMRO Pvt. Equity, Chgo., 1999—, also bd. dirs. Bd. dirs. PSS World Med., Inc., A.G. Edwards, Inc., Gulf South Med. Supply, Inc., Haemonetics Corp. Bd. d. Greater Chgo. chpt. ARC. Office: ABN AMRO Pvt Equity 208 S La Salle St Lbby 10 Chicago IL 60604-1004

WILLIAMSON, DONNA MARIA, pastoral counselor; b. Oswego, N.Y., Feb. 26, 1944; d. Donald Carl and Helen Mary (Saber) Townsley; m. Patrick H. Williamson, July 7, 1962; children: Kevin Patrick, Michael Brian, Timothy Daniel. Grad. pub. schs., Fulton, N.Y. Cert. in clin. pastoral edn., pastoral care, Onondaga Pastoral Counseling Ctr.; weight loss counselor. Chaplain Loretto Geriatric Ctr., Syracuse, 1981-82; hosp. chaplain St. Rose of Lima Parish, Syracuse, 1982-84, pastoral counselor, 1984—. Weight loss counselor Nutri-System, Syracuse, 1988-91. Founding mem. Fulton Community Nursery Sch., 1967, Commn. on Women in Ch. and Society, Syracuse, 1984; mem. Alethea, Ctr. on Death and Dying, Inc., Syracuse, 1978, Syracuse Area Domestic Violence Coalition's Religious Task Force, 1994—; chair Syracuse Diocesan Commn. on Women in Ch. and Soc., 1997-98, 98-99. Mem. Charles F. Menninger Soc. Roman Catholic. Avocations: flower arranging, vocalist. Office: St Rose of Lima Parish 409 S Main St North Syracuse NY 13212-2811 Fax: 315-458-1290.

WILLIAMSON, (EULAH) ELAINE, elementary school educator; b. N.Y.C., July 27, 1945; d. Eddie Lee and Eulah Genola (Hardie) Riley; m. George Lesile Williamson, Feb. 17, 1973; children: George Todd, Michelle Elaine, Heather Dawn. BA, Hampton U., 1967; MA in Urban Edn., Jersey City State Coll., 1998. Cert. elem. tchr. K-8, N.J. Tchr. elem. Englewood (N.J.) Pub. Schs., 1967-78, Irvington (N.J.) Pub. Schs., 1988-97; tchr. math. Hackensack (N.J.) Mid. Sch., 1997—. Mem. NEA, Nat. Black Child Devel. Inst., N.J. Edn. Assn., Hackensack Edn. Assn., Phi Delta Kappa. Democrat. African Methodist. Avocations: photography, football, horseback riding. Office: Hackensack Mid Sch 360 Union St Hackensack NJ 07601-4394

WILLIAMSON, GLORIA, state legislator; b. Philadelphia, Miss. m. Edward Williamson; children: Sherry Toler, Wendy Sparks. Student, East Ctrl. Jr. Coll. Mem. Miss. Senate from 18th dist., Jackson, 2000—. Vice chair agrl. com. Dem. chair, Miss. Mem. GFWC, MFWC, Futura Club, Jr. Auxiliary, Women's Polit. Network. Methodist. Office: 521 Holland Ave Philadelphia MS 39350

WILLIAMSON, JO ANN, psychologist; b. Wichita, Kans., Feb. 12, 1951; d. Howard T. Murray and Ferryl Arlene (Rumsey) Fleming; m. James Wallace Johnson, Apr. 5, 1984 (div. 1984); m. Michael R. Williamson, Dec. 21, 1990; children: Wesley, Wade. BA, U. Kans., 1973; MA in Psychology, U. Mo., 1974; PhD in Psychology, Auburn U., 1979. Lic. psychologist, Kans. Clin. asst. prof. Ohio State U., Columbus, 1979-80; asst. prof. Chgo. Med. Sch., 1980-81; psychologist U. Mo., Kansas City, 1981-82; psychologist II Rainbow Mental Health Ctr., Kansas City, 1982-83; pvt. practice Wichita, 1983-86; pres. Jo Ann Murray, Ph.D., P.A., Wichita, 1986-90; psychologist Iowa Meth. Hosp., Des Moines, 1989, Hutchinson (Kans.) Correctional Facility, 1990, Cedarvale, Wichita, 1991; cons., psychologist, clin. dir. Cowley County Mental Health, Winfield, Kans., 1990-96; assoc. Affiliated Family Counselors, Wichita, 1996—2003; pvt. practice, 2003—. Contbr. articles to profl. jours. Mem. APA (div. clin. psychology).

WILLIAMSON, MARILYN LAMMERT, English educator, university administrator; b. Chgo., Sept. 6, 1927; d. Raymond Ferdinand and Edith Louise (Eisenbies) Lammert; m. Robert M. Williamson, Oct. 28, 1950 (div. Apr. 1973); 1 child, Timothy L.; m. James H. McKay, Aug. 15, 1974. BA, Vassar Coll., 1949; MA, U. Wis., 1950; PhD, Duke U., 1956. Lectr. Duke U., Durham, N.C., 1955-56, 58-59, N.C. State U., Raleigh, 1957-58, 61-62; asst. prof. Oakland U., Rochester, Mich., 1965-68, assoc. prof., 1968-72; prof. English Wayne State U., Detroit, 1972-90, Disting. prof. English, 1990-97, Disting. prof. emerita, 1997—, chmn. dept. English, 1972-74, 81-83, assoc. dean Coll. Liberal Arts, 1974-79, dir. women's studies, 1976-87, dep. provost, 1987-91, sr. v.p. for acad. affairs, provost, 1991-95, 98-200. Pres. Assn. Depts. English, 1976-77. Author: Infinite Variety, 1974, Patriarchy of Shakespeare's Comedies, 1986, British Women Writers 1650-1750, 1990; editor: Renaissance Studies, 1972, Female Poets of Great Britain, 1981, Shakespeare Studies: Middle Comedies, 2003; contbr. articles to profl. jours. Pres. LWV, Rochester, 1963-65. Recipient Detroit Disting. Svc. award, 1986, Faculty Recognition award Bd. Govs., Wayne State U., 1991; Bunting Inst. fellow, 1969-70, AAUW fellow, 1982-83, J.N. Keal fellow, 1985-86. Mem.: MLA (exec. coun. 1977—80, mem. editl. bd. 1992—94), Fed. State Humanities Coun. (bd. dirs. 1994—2001, chair 1997—99), Mich. Coun. Humanities (bd. dirs. 1988—2001, chair 1991—93), Shakespeare Assn. Am., Mich. Acad. (pres. 1978—79), Coll. English Assn., Renaissance Soc. Am. Democrat. Home: 2275 Oakway Dr West Bloomfield MI 48324-1855

WILLIAMSON, MARVEL, dean, nursing administrator, sexologist, educator, writer; b. Holton, Kans., Nov. 4, 1953; d. Thomas Arthur and Lois M. (Ihrig) Ansley; m. Paul Williamson, May 12, 1973; children: Marcus W., Sean W. BS in Nursing, Wichita State U., 1976; MS in Nursing, U. Ky., 1978; PhD, U. Iowa, 1987. Cert. sex educator. Prof. U. Iowa, Iowa City, 1980-89; dir. patient svcs. Ransom Meml. Hosp., Ottawa, Kans., 1989-91; dir. schs. nursing at Rolla, Sikeston and Kansas City Park Coll., Parkville, Mo., 1991-97; prof. Albany (Ga.) State U., 1997-99; sexologist Silver Spring, Md., 1999—2001; dean Kramer Sch. Nursing, Oklahoma City U., 2001—. Contbr. articles to profl. jours. Mem. ANA, Am. Assn. Sex Educators, Counselors and Therapists, Sigma Theta Tau. Home and Office: 3141 NW 18th St Oklahoma City OK 73107 Office: Oklahoma City U 2501 N Blackwelder Oklahoma City OK 73106

WILLIAMSON, PHILEMONA, artist; b. N.Y.C. BA, Bennington Coll., 1973; MA, NYU, 1979. Various positions Harlem Sch. Arts, 1978—83; vis. artist Norfolk (Va.) State U., 1982; artist Met. Mus. Art, 1983; artist, tchr. workshops Arts [illegible] Prince, Haiti, 1987; artist-in-residence Very Spl. Arts, 1987—88; supr. student tchrs. dept. post-baccalaureate edn. Sch. Visual Arts, 1988—89; adj. faculty R.I. Sch. Design, 1989—90; painting faculty Bard Coll. Milton Avery Grad. Sch. Arts, 1991; adj. faculty Parsons Sch. Design, 1991—92, vis. artist MFA program, 1994. Mem. adv. bd. Getty Ctr. Edn. in Arts, 1989—98; panelist in field; artist-in-residence Millay Colony for Arts, Austerlitz, NY, 1983. One-woman shows include The Queens (N.Y.) Mus. Art, 1988, Wenger Gallery, L.A., 1989, Fine Arts Gallery, Southampton (N.Y.) Coll. L.I. U., 1990, June Kelly Gallery, N.Y.C., 1990, 1992, 1995, 1998, African Am. Mus., Hempstead, N.Y., 1991, Powers Art Gallery, East Stroudsburg U., Pa., 1992, Pa. State U., University Park, 1993, Flushing Coun. on Culture and Arts, N.Y.C., 1993, John Michael Kohler Arts Str., Sheboygan, Wis., 1999, exhibited in group shows at The Mint Mus. Art, Charlotte, N.C., 1991, U. Wis. at Milw. Fine Arts Gallery, 1992, Lehman Coll. Art Gallery and Krasdale Foods Arts Gallery, Bronx, 1994, Anderson Gallery, Buffalo, 1994, Kingsborough C.C. Art Gallery of CUNY, Bklyn., 1996, Pratt Manhattan Gallery, N.Y.C., 1996, Rubelle and Norman Schafler Gallery, Pratt Inst., Bklyn., 1996, Spelman Coll. Mus. Fine Art, Atlanta, 1996, numerous others, Represented in permanent collections pub. and corp. collections. Recipient Arts in Transit Poster Commn., Union Sq. Sta., N.Y., 1992, Joan Mitchell Found. award in painting, 1997; fellow Fellow in painting, NEA, 1987—88, fellow in painting, N.Y. Found. Arts, 1991; grantee exhbn. grantee, Artist Space, 1988; Pollock-Krasner Found. grantee, 1989—90, Ludwig Vogelstein grantee, 1993—94. Office: care June Kelly Gallery 591 Broadway New York NY 10012-3232

WILLIAMSON, RAMONA DIANE, special education educator; b. Baton Rouge, Apr. 20, 1962; d. John Thomas and Virginia (Harmeyer) W. BA, Nicholls State U., 1983; MEd, U. New Orleans, 1994, postgrad., 1994, 2000. Mid/moderate spl. edn. tchr. St. Bernard Parish Pub. Schs., Chalmette, La., 1988-96; grad. asst. U. New Orleans, 1996-97. Mem. vis. com. So. Assn. Colls. and Schs., La., 1994-98; new tchr. mentor St. Bernard Parish Pub. Schs., 1997—; presenter internat. profl. confs., U.S., Australia. Contbr. articles to profl. jours. Vol. Algiers Point Assn., New Orleans, 1987—; guide Preservation Resource Ctr./Live in a Landmark Program, New Orleans, 1990-98; vol., neighborhood coord., runner, liaison Christmas in October, New Orleans, 1993—. Recipient Tchr. of Yr. award Wal-Mart Found., 1999; La. State Dept. Edn. grantee, 1991-2001, La. Fedn. Coun. Exceptional Children grantee. Mem. La. Fedn. Coun. for Exceptional Children, St. Bernard Coun. Internat. Reading Assn., Kappa Delta Pi. Republican. Presbyterian. Avocations: travel, gardening, cooking, reading. Office: CF Rowley Elem Sch 49 Madison Ave Chalmette LA 70043-4429 Home: 8408 Prince Dr Chalmette LA 70043-1036 E-mail: ramonaw413@aol.com.

WILLIAMSON, SANDRA KAYE, education educator; b. Greenville, Ohio, Aug. 28, 1951; d. James Sherman and Dortha Maria (Mikesell) Clapp; m. John Leslie Williamson, July 5, 1975; children: Bradley, Laura. BS, Ea. Ky. U., 1973, MEd, 1979; PhD, Kent State U., 1999. Cert. tchr., home economist. Educator West Clermont Schs., Amelia, Ohio, 1973—75, Fayette County Schs., Lexington, Ky., 1975—83, U. Akron, Akron, Ohio, 1990—93; tchg. fellow Kent State U., Kent, Ohio, 1993—95; instructional technologist Neumann Coll., Aston, Pa., 1996—97; asst. prof. U. Del., Newark, Del., 1997—99, Lincoln U., Lincoln U., Pa., 2000—01, Wilmington (Del.) Coll., 2001—. Editor: Am. Assn. Family & Consumer Sci., Districts, 1990—93; author: Orientation to Professional Studies: Home Economics, 1992, Nutrition for Healthy Living, 1997, (on line chat rooms) Treehouses, 2000. Chmn. PTA, Medina, Ohio, 1986—89; mem. AHEA reaccreditation U. Akron, Akron, 1992—93. Mem.: Am. Ednl. Rsch. Assn., Assn. Ednl. Comm. & Tech., Am. Assn. Family & Consumer Scis., Kappa Delta Pi. Avocations: computer technology, emerging technologies. Home: 126 Soltner Dr Kennett Square PA 19348-1445 Office: 320 DuPont Hwy New Castle DE 19720 E-mail: swill@wilmcoll.edu.

WILLIAMSON, SUSAN, mathematician, educator; b. Boston, Mass., Dec. 29, 1936; d. Richard Phillip and Mary Elizabeth Williamson. AB, Radcliffe Coll., Cambridge, Mass., 1958; MA, PhD, Brandeis U., Waltham, Mass., 1963. Instr. Cardinal Cushing Coll., Brookline, Mass., 1962—63; asst. prof. Boston Coll., Chestnut Hill, Mass., 1963—64, Regis Coll., Weston, Mass., 1965—67, assoc. prof., 1967—71, acad. dean, 1973—75, prof., 1971—2002, prof. emerita, 2002—. Reviewer Math. Revs., Ann Arbor, 1968—. Contbr. articles to profl. jours. Mem.: AAUP, Math. Assn. Am., Am. Math. Soc. Avocation: Landscape drawing. Home: 37 Hagen Rd Newton Centre MA 02459 Personal E-mail: susanwilliamson@compuserve.com.

WILLIAMS-WENNELL, KATHI, human resources specialist; b. Danville, Pa., Sept. 22, 1955; d. Raymond Gerald and Julia Dolores (Higgins) Williams; m. Mark Kevin Wennell, Apr. 3, 1982; children: Ryan Christopher Wennell, Lauren Ashley Wennell. BA, Immaculata Coll., 1977; MEd, Pa. State U., 1978. Cert. rehab. counselor Pa., profl. human resources. From project dir. to coord. devel. activities Cmty. Interactions, Blue Bell, Pa., 1978-83; from mgmt. trainee to coord. coll. recruiting and rels. Meridian Bancorp, Inc., Reading, Pa., 1983-86, mgmt. recruiter, 1986-88, compensation analyst, 1989-93, recruiter, spl. projects, 1993-96; cons. Chet Mosteller & Assocs., Reading, Pa., 1996—. Cons. Norristown (Pa.) Life Ctr., 1981; instr. Immaculata (Pa.) Coll., 1981—83, Alvernia Coll., Reading, 1988—89. Meridian campaign coord. United Way Berks County, Reading, 1985. Named Recruiter of the Yr., LaSalle U., Phila., 1986; recipient Excellence in Programming award, Nat. Assn. Bank Women, Pa., 1986. Mem.: Soc. Human Resources Mgmt. Republican. Roman Catholic. Avocations: walking, golf, tennis, piano, reading. Home: 69 S Hampton Dr Wyomissing PA 19610-3108 Office Phone: 610-779-3870. Personal E-mail: kwennell@aol.com.

WILLIMAN, PAULINE, shorthand reporter, farm foundation administrator; b. Albany County, N.Y., Jan. 11, 1926; d. Harrison and Alta Allen (Hallenbeck) Salisbury; m. Raymond Williman, Jan. 11, 1947 (div. Oct. 1951). Grad., Albany Stenotype Secretarial, 1941-42. Cert. shorthand reporter. Staff reporter Empire Stenographers, Albany, 1942-46; exec. sec. Res. Officers Assn., Dept. of N.Y., Albany, 1947-49; ofcl. reporter N.Y. State Supreme Ct./Third Jud. Dist., Albany, 1958-64; ofcl. stenographer N.Y. State Senate, Albany, 1979-98; profl. shorthand reporter self employed, Albany, N.Y., 1949—. Mem. Cert. Shorthand Reporter Licensure Bd., Albany, 1992—; specialized in reporting tech. engring. rev. procs. involving water supply and waste water treatment facilities throughout N.Y. state, 1952-94; mem. edn. and small bus. coms. Bus. Coun. N.Y. State, 1985-2000. Contbr. articles to profl. jours. Mem. RNSC Inner Circle, Washington, 1980-97; mem. Senatorial Bus. Adv. Bd., Washington, 1982-86. Recipient recognition and commendation for svc. N.Y. State Senate, 1998. Mem. Am. Water Works ASsn. (life), Nat. Ct. Reporters Assn., N.Y. State Ct. Reporters Assn., Kiwanis Internat. (club pres. 1997-99, award of excellence 1999). Republican. Mem. Dutch Reformed Ch. Avocations: golf, gardening, fitness, reading, music. Office: 447 Loudonville Rd Albany NY 12211-1499

WILLING, KATHERINE, former state legislator; m. Donald Willing. BS, Purdue U. Formerly tchr.; mem. from 39th dist. Ind. Ho. of Reps., 1992-97, mem. aged and aging, agr., edn., ways and means coms. Mem. Boone County Coun., 1988-92; bd. govs. Boone County Jr. Achievement; v.p. Boone County Leadership; bd. dirs., formerly treas. Witham Meml. Hosp. Found. Recipient Richard G. Lugar Excellence in Svc. award. Mem. Boone County Rep. Women's Club (pres.), Boone County and Carmel Clay County C. of C., Farm Bur., Zonta, Tri Kappa, Alpha Chi Omega. Home: [illegible]

WILLINGER, RHONDA ZWERN, optometrist; b. Bklyn., Apr. 26, 1962; d. Jerome Max and Jeanette (Zwern) Willinger; m. Wayne Ken Chan, Aug. 26, 1990; children: Jamie S. Chan, Jared Max. BS, U. Miami, 1983, OD with honors, New Eng. Coll. Optometry, 1987. Resident in optometry VA Med. Ctr., Bedford, Mass., 1987-88; pvt. practice, Burlington, Mass., 1988-89; pvt. practice specializing in contact lenses Framingham, Mass., 1989—. Scholar New Coll., U. South Fla., 1979-81; honors scholarship U. Miami, 1981-83. Mem. Am. Optometric Assn. (contact lens sect.), Mass. Soc. Optometrists. Avocation: violin. Home: 228 Lowell Ave Newton MA 02460-1830 Office: 659 Worcester Rd Framingham MA 01701-5204

WILLINGHAM, JEANNE MAGGART, dance educator, ballet company executive; b. Fresno, Calif., May 8, 1923; d. Harold F. and Gladys (Ellis) Maggart. Student, Tex. Woman's U., 1942; student profl. dancing schs. worldwide. Tchr. dance Beaux Arts Dance Studio, Pampa, Tex., 1948—; artistic dir. Pampa Civic Ballet, 1972—. Mem. Tex. Arts and Humanities Coun. Mem. Tex. Arts Alliance, Pampa C. of C. (fine arts com.), Pampa Fine Arts Assn. Office: Pampa Civic Ballet Beaux Arts Dance Studio 315 N Nelson St Pampa TX 79065-6013 Office Phone: 806-669-6361.

WILLINGHAM, MARY MAXINE, fashion retailer; b. Childress, Tex., Sept. 12, 1928; d. Charles Bryan and Mary (Bohannon) McCollum; m. Welborn Kiefer Willingham, Aug. 14, 1950; children: Sharon, Douglas, Sheila. BA, Tex. Tech U., 1949. Interviewer Univ. Placement Svc., Tex. Tech U., Lubbock, 1964-69; owner, mgr. buyer Maxine's Accent, Lubbock, 1969—. Speaker in field. Leader Campfire Girls, Lubbock, 1964-65; sec. Cmty. Theatre, Lubbock, 1962-64. Recipient Golden Sun award Dallas Market, 1985, Woman of Excellence award in Bus., YWCA, 2001; named Outstanding Mcht., Fashion Retailer Mag., 1971, also Outstanding Retailer. Mem. Lubbock Symphony Guild, Ranch and Heritage Ctr., Faculty Women's Club. Office: 16 Briercroft Shopping Ctr Lubbock TX 79412-3022

WILLIS, ANNA L. commissioner; b. Winchester, Ky., Jan. 11, 1941; d. Walter Jerome and Mary Frances Newell; m. Norman Lee Willis, Mar. 5, 1969; children: Mia Teresa Pugh, Angela Lee. BA in Sociology, Ky. State U., 1964; postgrad., U. Ill., 1975, cert. gerontology, 1996; MS in Mgmt., Nat. Louis U., 1981. Dir. social svcs. Columbus Hosp., Chgo., 1974-78; dir. Evanston (Ill.) Twp. Gen. Assistance, 1978-89; dep. commr. Chgo. Dept. on Aging, 1990-98, commr., 1998—. Adv. coun., bd. mem. Northwestern U. Ctr. for Gerontology, 1998—; created frozen meals program for seniors; created and implemented depts. response to city wide emergency. Mem. Ill. Alliance for Aging, Unity Fin. Network (pres. 1998), Chgo. Fund on Aging (bd. dirs. 1998), Zonta Internat. Democrat. Avocation: reading. Office: Chgo Dept on Aging 30 N Lasalle St Ste 2320 Chicago IL 60602-2504 Fax: 312-742-0699.

WILLIS, BEVERLY ANN, architect; b. Tulsa, Feb. 17, 1928; d. Ralph William and Margaret Amanda (Porter) W. BFA, U. Hawaii, 1954; PhD in Fine Arts (hon.), Mt. Holyoke Coll., 1983. Registered architect, Calif. Prin. Willis Atelier, Honolulu, 1954-58, Willis & Assocs., Inc., San Francisco, 1958-88, Beverly Willis Architects, N.Y.C., 1988—. Pres., dir. Architecture Rsch. Inst., Inc., N.Y.C., 1993—; co-chair Rebuild Downtown Our Town Coalition, 2002; lectr. Internat. Women's U., Kassel, Germany, 2000. Author: Invisible Images: The Silent Language of Architecture, 1997; contbg. author: Creating Sustainable Urban Environments: Future Forms for City Living, 2002; prin. works include Union St. Stores (merit award San Francisco AIA, award of distinction State of Calif.), Nob Hill Cts. (merit award AIA), 1970, Margaret Hayward Park (grand and merit awards Pacific Coast Bldg. Con., Honor award Design Internat.), 1983, San Francisco Ballet Bldg., 1984, Manhattan Village Acad. H.S., N.Y.C., 1995; contbr. articles to profl. jours., chpts. to books. Founding trustee Nat. Bldg. Mus., Washington, 1976—; bldng. rsch. adv. bd. Nat. Acad. Sci., 1971-79, chair Fed. Construction Coun., 1976-79. Recipient Phoebe Hearst Gold Medal award, 1969. Fellow AIA (v.p. Calif. coun. 1979, pres. 1980); mem. Achievement Rewards for Coll. Scientists, Internat. Women's Forum, Villa Taverna Club, Lambda Alpha (pres. San Francisco chpt. 1981-82). Clubs: Villa Taverna (San Francisco). Avocations: poetry, sketching, tennis, walking. Office: 29 Broadway Rm 1100 New York NY 10006-3255 E-mail: bevwillis@architect.org.

WILLIS, CINDY DAWSON, school system administrator; b. Gassaway, WVa, Nov. 15, 1958; d. James G. and Dorothy Joan Dawson; m. Richard Willis; 1 child, Michael Lewis. Biology Diploma, W.Va. Inst. Technology, 1981; Diploma in Edn. Administrn., 1987. Tchr. Clay County (W.Va.) H.S., 1981—99; prin. Lizemore (W.Va.) Sch., 1999; asst. prin. Clay County H.S., 1999—2001, prin., 2001—03; adminstrv. asst. Clay County Bd. Edn., 2003—.

WILLIS, CONNIE (CONSTANCE E. WILLIS), author; b. 1945; Tchr. elem. and jr. H.S., Branford, Conn., 1967-69. Author: (novels) Letter from the Clearys (Nebula award, 1982, Hugo award, 1983), Lincoln's Dreams, 1987, Doomsday Book (Nebula award, 1992, Hugo award, 1993), Impossible Things, 1993, Unchartered Territory, 1994, Even the Queen (Nebula award, 1992, Hugo award, 1993), Fire Watch (Nebula award, 1982, Hugo award, 1983), The Last of the Winnebagos (Nebula award, 1988, Hugo award, 1989), Death on the Nile (Hugo award, 1994), The Soul Selects (Hugo award, 1997), Uncharted Territory, 1994, Remake, 1995, Bellwether, 1996, To Say Nothing of the Dog (Hugo award, 1999), Miracle, 1999, Water Witch, 1982, Light Raid, 1989, Promised Land, 1997, Miracle and other Christmas Stories, 1999, The Winds of Marble Arch (Hugo award, 2000), Passage, 2001 (Locus award). Named Best Sci. Fiction/Fantasy Author of Nineties Locus Mag. Address: 1716 13th Ave Greeley CO 80631-5418 E-mail: conniewillis@juno.com.

WILLIS, DAWN LOUISE, legal assistant, small business owner; b. Johnstown, Pa., Sept. 11, 1959; d. Kenneth William and Dawn Louise (Joseph) Hagins; m. Marc Anthony Ross, Nov. 30, 1984 (div.); m. Jerry Wayne Willis, Dec. 16, 1989 (div.). Grad. high sch., Sacramento, Calif. Legal sec. Wilcoxen & Callahan, Sacramento, 1979-87, paralegal, 1987-88; legal adminstr. Law Office Jack Vetter, 1989-99; owner, mgr. Your Girl Friday Secretarial and Legal Support Svcs., 1991—; legal asst. Foley & Lardner, 1999-2001; case mgr. Larry Lockshin, Esq. Law Corp., 2001—02; legal asst. Hunter, Richey, Di Benedetto & Eisenbeis, 2002—03; legal sec. Downey Brand LLP, 2003—. Vol ARC, 1985, Spec Olympics, 1997—. Mem.: Sacramento Legal Secys Asn. Democrat. Avocations: water sports, camping, reading, cooking. Office: Downey Brand LLP 555 Capitol Mall Sacramento CA 95814 E-mail: doe9121@cwnet.com.

WILLIS, ELEANOR LAWSON, not-for-profit developer; b. Nashville, Sept. 15, 1936; d. Harry Alfred Jr. and Helen Russell (Howse) Lawson; m. Alvis Rux Rochelle, Aug. 25, 1956 (div. Mar. 1961); m. William Reese Willis Jr., Mar. 7, 1964 (div. June 1994); children: Alfred Russell Willis, William Reese III, Brent Lawson. BA cum laude, Vanderbilt U., 1957. Host children's syndicated TV show Sta. WSIX-TV, Nashville, 1961-64; tchr. head start program Metro Pub. Sch., Nashville, 1965-67; co-investigator cognitive edn. curriculum project Peabody Coll., Nashville, 1979-81; dir., founder Heads Up Child Devel. Ctr., Inc., Nashville, 1973-87; dir. Tenn. Vols. for Gore for Pres. Campaign, Nashville, 1987-88; dir. devel. Vanderbilt Inst. Pub. Policy Studies, Vanderbilt U., Nashville, 1988—. Bd. dirs. Vanderbilt Child Devel. Ctr. Author: (with others) I Really Like Myself, 1973, I Wonder Where I Came From, 1973. Pres. Nashville Bar Aux., 1967-68, Nashville Symphony Guild, 1984-85, W.O. Smith Nashville Community Music Sch., 1987-03; founder, bd. dirs. Rochelle Ctr., Nashville, 1968-03; vice-chmn. Century III Com., Nashville, 1978-80; Homecoming 1986 Steering Com., Nashville, 1985-86; mem. Cheekwood Fine Arts Ctr., Nashville City Ballet, Nashville Symphony Assn., Dem. Women of Davidson County; appointed Metro Arts Commn., 1992, Metro Ednl. Access Corp.; exec. dir. Friends of Warner Park, 1994; leadership coun. John F. Kennedy Ctr., 1995—; founder Nashville Tree Found.; bd. dirs. Cumberland Region Tomorrow, 2001. Recipient Leadership Nashville award, 1982; Seven Leading Ladies award Nashville Mag., 1984; Eleanor Willis Day proclaimed by City of Nashville, 1987; named to Acad. for Women of Achievement, 2003. Mem. Exchange Club of Nashville, Vanderbilt Alumni Assn. Presbyterian. Avocations: reading, camping, running. Office: 50 Vaughn Rd Nashville TN 37221-3706

WILLIS, GERRI, news correspondent; Knight-Bagehot fellow, Columbia Bus. Sch., 1991—92. Sr. fin. corr. Smart Money mag.; personal fin. editor CNN Bus. News, 2003—; co-host CNNfn's The Flipside. Author: The SmartMoney Guide to Real Estate Investing, 2003. Recipient Excellence in Retirement Savings Reporting award, Am. U. Sch. Comm. and Investment Co. Inst. Edn. Found., 2001. Office: CNN 5 Penn Plz Fl 20 New York NY 10001-1810 Office Phone: 212-714-7800.*

WILLIS, JUDY ANN, lawyer; b. Hartford, Conn., July 7, 1949; d. Durward Joseph and Angeline Raphael (Riccardo) Willis. BA, Ctrl. Conn. State U., 1971; postgrad., U. Conn. Law Sch., 1976—77; JD, Boston Coll., 1979. Bar: Mass. 1979, U.S. Dist. Ct. Mass. 1980, Calif. 1990. Sr. atty. H.P. Hood Inc., Charleston, Mass., 1979-83; v.p. law Parker Bros., Beverly, Mass., 1983-89; sr. v.p. bus. affairs Mattel, Inc., El Segundo, Calif., 1989—. Office: Mattel Inc M1-0920 333 Continental Blvd El Segundo CA 90245-5012 E-mail: judy.willis@Mattel.com.

WILLIS, SHANDRA DENISE, music educator; b. Gadsden, Ala., June 3, 1968; d. Roger J. Willis and Judy C. Richardson. BSE, Jacksonville State U., 1991. Band dir. Anniston (Ala.) City Schs., 1994—, music dept. head, 1997—99. Coach Jacksonville Parks and Recreation, 1992—94. Mem.: Music Educators Nat. Conf., Ala. Bandmasters Assn., Delta Omicron. Republican. Meth. Avocations: reading, dogs, outdoor activities. Office: PO Box 6222 Anniston AL 36204

WILLIS, TRICIA LEE, special education educator; d. Harold Lee and Belinda Lee Gibb; m. Don Edward Willis, Dec. 29, 2001; 1 child, Brandon Gibb. BA in History, Calif. State U., San Marcos, 1996; MBS, Southeastern U., 1999. Tchr. Atoka (Okla.)-Coal Alternative Sch., 1997—98, Coalgate (Okla.) Pub. Schs., 1998—. Grantee, Rural Okla. Cmty. Found., 2000, 2001. Mem.: Coun. for Exceptional Children. Achievements include development of program for emotionally disturbed students. Avocations: reading, travel, sports. Office: Coalgate Pub Schs 2 West Cedar Coalgate OK 74538 Office Phone: 580-927-2338.

WILLISCROFT-BARCUS, BEVERLY RUTH, lawyer; b. Conrad, Mont., Feb. 24, 1945; d. Paul A. and Gladys L. (Buck) W.; m. Kent J. Barcus, Oct. 1984. BA in Music, So. Calif. Coll., 1967; JD, John F. Kennedy U., 1977. Bar: Calif. 1977. Elem. tchr., Sunnyvale, Calif., 1968-72; legal sec., legal asst. various law firms, 1972-77; assoc. Neil D. Reid, Inc., San Francisco, 1977-79; sole practice Concord, Calif., 1979—. Exam. grader Calif. Bar, 1979—; real estate broker, 1980-88; tchr. real estate King Coll., Concord, 1979-80; judge pro-tem Mcpl. Ct., 1981-93; mem. Stage Right Drama Group, Concord, Calif., 1999—; lectr. in adoption law. Co-author: Adoption Law in California, Adoption Practice, Procedure and Pitfalls in California; lectr. in field. Bd. dirs. Contra Costa Musical Theatre, Inc., 1978-82, v.p. adminstrn., 1980-81, v.p. prodn., 1981-82; mem. community devel. adv. com. City of Concord, 1981-83, vice chmn., 1982-83, mem. status of women com., 1980-81, mem. redevel. adv. com., 1984-86, planning commnr. 1986-92, chmn., 1990; mem. exec. bd. Mt. Diablo coun. Boy Scouts Am., 1981-85; bd. dirs. Pregnancy Ctrs. Contra Costa County, 1991-2001, chmn., 1993-2000 Mem. Concord C. of C. (bd. dirs., chmn. govt. affairs com. 1981-83, v.p. 1985-87, pres. 1988-89, Bus. Person of Yr. 1986), Calif. State Bar (chmn. adoptions subcom. north, 1994), Contra Costa County Bar Assn., Christian Legal Soc., Todos Santos Bus. and Profl. Women (co-founder, pres. 1983-84, pub. rels. chmn. 1982-83, Woman of Achievement 1980, 81), Soroptimists (fin. sec. 1980-81). Office: PO Box 981 Pittsburg CA 94565-0098 Personal E-mail: Beverlybarcus@hotmail.com.

WILLMORE, LEANNA, music educator; b. Ogden, Utah, Sept. 11, 1943; d. Don Norman and Velma Beasley Read; children: Trent B. Florence, West Kenneth. BS in Music Edn., Weber State U., Ogden, Utah, 1971, M.Music Edn., U. Utah, 1983. Choir tchr. Valley Jr. H.S., Huntsville, Utah, 1971—73, Bonneville H.S., Ogden, Utah, 1973—90, Bingham H.S., South Jordan, Utah, 1990—99, Riverton High Sch., Utah, 1999—. Bd. dirs. WestEd, San Francisco. Named Dist. Tchr. of the Yr., Jordan Sch. Dist., 1998, Music Educator of the Yr. award, Nat. Fedn. of H.S. sect. 7, 2000; recipient State Music Educator of the Yr. award, Utah H.S. Activities Assn., 1999, Music Educator of the Yr. award, Nat. Fedn. of H.S., 2002. Mem.: Music Educators Nat. Conf. (state pres. 1991—93, western divsn. pres. 1998—2000), Delta Kappa Gamma (state pres. 1989—91). Avocation: gardening. Home: 256 Sterling Dr Bountiful UT 84010 Office: Riverton High Sch 12476 S 2700 W Riverton UT 84065

WILLNER, ANN RUTH, political scientist, educator; b. N.Y.C., Sept. 2, 1924; d. Norbert and Bella (Richman) W. BA cum laude, Hunter Coll., 1945; MA, Yale U., 1946; PhD, U. Chgo., 1961. Lectr. U. Chgo., 1946-47, rsch. assoc. Ctr. for Econ. Devel. and Cultural Change, 1954-56, 61-62; advisor on orgn. and tng. Indonesian Ministry for Fgn. Affairs, Jakarta, 1952-53; expert for small scale indsl. planning Indonesian Nat. Planning Bur., Jakarta, 1953-54; fgn. affairs analyst Congl. Reference Svc., Libr. of Congress, 1960; asst. prof. polit. sci. Harpur Coll., Binghamton, NY, 1962-63; postdoctoral fellow polit. sci. and Southeast Asian studies Yale U., New Haven, 1963-64; rsch. assoc. Ctr. Internat. Studies, Princeton U., 1964-69; assoc. prof. polit. sci. U. Kans., Lawrence, 1969-70, prof., 1970-98. Vis. prof. polit. sci. CUNY, 1975; cons. govt. agys. and pvt. industry Polit. sci. editor: Ency. of the Social Scis., 1961; mem. editl. bd. Econ. Devel. and Cultural Change, 1954-57, Jour. Comparative Adminstrn., 1969-74, Comparative Politics, 1977— ; author: The Neotraditional Accomodation to Political Independence, 1966, Charismatic Political Leadership: A Theory, 1968, The Spellbinders, 1984; also monographs, jour. articles, book chpts., newspaper columns. Grantee Rockefeller Found., 1965, Social Sci. Rsch. and Am. Coun. Learned Socs., 1966. Mem. Am. Polit. Sci. Assn. (gov. coun. 1979-81), Nat. Press Club. Home: 560 N St SW # N405 Washington DC 20024-4605 Office Phone: 202-484-2092.

WILLNER, DOROTHY, anthropologist, educator; b. N.Y.C., Aug. 26, 1927; d. Norbert and Bella (Richman) W. Ph.B., U. Chgo., 1947, MA, 1953, PhD, 1961; postgrad., Ecole Pratique des Hautes Etudes, U. Paris, France, 1953-54. Anthropologist Jewish Agy., Israel, 1955-58; tech. asst., adminstrn. expert in community devel. UN, Mexico, 1958; asst. prof. dept. sociology and anthropology U. Iowa, Iowa City, 1959-60; research assoc. U. Chgo., 1961-62; asst. prof. dept. sociology and anthropology U. N.C., Chapel Hill, 1962-63, Hunter Coll., N.Y.C., 1964-65; assoc. prof. dept. anthropology U. Kans., Lawrence, 1967-70, prof., 1970-90; professorial lectr. Johns Hopkins U. Sch. Advanced Internat. Studies, 1992. Author: Community Leadership, 1960, Nation-Building and Community in Israel, 1969. Contbr. numerous articles to profl. publs. Fellow Am. Anthrop. Assn., Soc. Applied Anthropology, Royal Anthrop. Inst.; mem. Cen. States Anthrop. Soc. (past pres.), Assn. Polit. and Legal Anthropology (past pres.). Home: # N 407 560 N St SW Washington DC 20024-4605

WILLOUGHBY, ANNE, health facility administrator, researcher, educator; Rschr. NICHD, 1984, leader pediat., adolescent, and maternal AIDS, educator HIV/AIDS in mothers and children; dir. Rsch. Mothers and Children's Ctr., 2002—. Office: 6100 Executive Bldg Rm 4B11 Bethesda MD 20892

WILLOUGHBY, JUDITH ANNE, conductor, music educator; d. Rupert Alexander and Betty Jean Willoughby; m. Horatio Cabrere Miller, Aug. 11, 1973 (div. June 1999); 1 child, Allison Elizabeth Miller. BM, Northwestern U., 1971; MM, Temple U., 1973. Prof. music and dir. cultural affairs Montgomery County C.C., Blue Bell, Pa., 1973—2001; music dir. Temple U., Phila., 1992—2002; assoc. prof. Northwestern U., Evanston, Ill., 2001—. Pres. Pa. Presenters, 1997—99; panelist in field. Guest condr. numerous honor choirs, profl. choirs and orchs. Mem.: Coll. Music Soc., Collegiate Choral Assn. (pres. 1986—88), Music Educators Nat. Conf., Internat. Fedn. Choral Music, Am. Choral Dirs. Assn. (life; pres. 1988—90, guest condr. nat. women's honor choir 2003), Chorus Am. (bd. dirs. 1996—, sec. 1997—99). Avocations: travel, reading, gardening, sewing. Office: Northwestern U Sch Music 711 Elgin Rd Evanston IL 60208-1200

WILLOUGHBY, SARAH-MARGARET C. chemist, educator, chemical engineer, consultant; b. Bowling Green, KY, Oct. 15, 1917; d. Austin Burrell Claypool and Minerva Dallas Renfrow-Claypool; m. John Richard Evans, II, Aug. 30, 1938 (dec. Dec. 1942); 1 child, Richard Claypool Evans ; m. Olief Glenn Willoughby, June 18, 1948 (dec.); children: Sarah, Stephen(dec.). BS, Western Ky. U., 1938; PhD, Purdue U., 1950. Registered profl. engr., Ind., Tex. Chemist Devoe-Reynolds, Inc., Louisville, 1941—42; jr. engr. chem. lab. div. Curtiss-Wright Corp., Louisville, 1942—44; tech. asst. Purdue U., West Lafayette, Ind., 1944—46, fellow, 1946—50; rsch. chemist, coatings divsn. Monsanto Chem. Co., Boston, 1950—52; assoc. prof. of chemistry U. Tex., Arlington, 1954—84, co-dir. Ctr. for Microcrystalline Polymer Rsch. Studies, 1978—82, prof. emeritus chemistry, 1984. Cons. Albert H. Halff Assocs., Dallas, 1980—86. Nominee Dallas-Ft. Worth Trailblazer award, 1996; named to Hall of Disting. Alumni, Western Ky. U., 1994; recipient Outstanding Chem. Engr. award, Purdue U., 1996. Fellow: Am. Inst. Chemists; mem.: N.Y. Acad. Sci., Soc. Women Engrs. (sr.), Am. Chem. Soc. (emeritus mem.), Nat. Soc. Daughters of Founders and Patriots (v.p. N.E. Tex. chpt. 1997—), Friends of St. George, Plantagenet Soc., Colonial Dames Am., Nat. Soc. Colonial Dames of XVII Century (chpt. regent 1980—82), Nat. Soc. DAR (chpt. regent 1967—69, nat. bicentennial com. mem. 1975—76), Nat. Soc. Children of Am. Revolution (Tex. sr. state pres. 1968—70), Nat. Soc. Magna Carta Dames (Tex. state pres. 1986—88), Colonial Order of the Crown, Soc. Descendants of Knights of the Most Noble Order of the Garter, Sovereign Colonial Soc. Ams. of Royal Descent, Order Ky. Cols., Sigma Xi (emeritus mem.), Alpha Chi Omega (Lambda Epsilon chapt.). Home: 1630 Pecan Park Dr Arlington TX 76012

WILLS, CONNIE SUE, special education educator; b. Summersville, W.Va., Jan. 11, 1960; d. Wallace Wayne and Norma Halstead; m. Lloyd Richard Wills; children: Kenneth Cooper, Amanda, Andrea. Reading Specialist K-12, Marshall Grad. Coll., Charleston, W. Va. Title I grades 3 and 4 Beaver (W. Va.) Elem. Sch., 1997—2000; reading tchr. Mabscott (W. Va.) Elem. Sch., 2000—. Mem.: Internat. Reading Assn., W. Va. Reading Assn. Baptist. Avocations: crafts, reading, travel. Home: 400 College Ave Beckley WV 25801 Office: Raleigh County Bd of Edn Adair St Beckley WV 25801

WILLS, KATHERINE V. TSIOPOS, English language educator; b. St. Louis, Sept. 30, 1957; d. Vasilios and Kalliope (Stratos) Tsiopos. BA, Washington U., 1979; MA, Ind. U., 1990. Rsch. dir. U. Chgo. Gynecology, 1980-82, Northwestern U., Chgo., 1982-86; pres. Port of Nashville (Ind.) Inc., retailer of nautical items and antiques, 1986—. Vis. lectr. English dept. Ind. U. Purdue U., Indpls., 1991—; vol. Women's Writers' Conf. Contbr. articles and poetry to jours. Recipient essay award Scholastic Mag., Inc., 1973, award for acad. excellence and community svc. Am. Hellenic Progessvie and Ednl. Assn., A poetry award Wednesday Club of St. Louis, Mo., 1977, Roger Conant Hatch hon. mention for writing, Washington U., 1977. Greek Orthodox. Home: 7772 Bellsville Pike Nashville IN 47448-8995

WILLS, LOIS ELAINE, art gallery owner, religious education educator; b. Dayton, Ohio, Feb. 26, 1939; d. Harold Otto and Marjorie Elizabeth (Schmidt) Wallen; m. David P. Wills, Sept. 26, 1960 (dec.); children: Marianne, Melody, Michele. Degree, Coll. of Mount St. Joseph, Cin.; BFA, Coll. of Mt. St. Joseph, 2000, MA, 2004. Cert. catechist. Educator, substitute various schs., 1985-90; gallery dir. Studio San Giuseppe, Cin., 1987-90; curator Murdock Art and Antiques, Cin., 1990-92; mgr. Cin. Antique Mall, 1992-93; dir. religious edn. St. John the Bapt., Dover, Ind., 1993-96, Blessed Sacrament, Ft. Mitchell, Ky., 1996—2002; owner Fine Arts Gallery, Ga., 2002—. Group exhibits include Clermont County Libr., Batavia, Ohio, 1990, Murdock Gallery, Cin., 1990, Studio San Giusseppe, Mount St. Joseph Coll., Cin., 1990, Milford Libr., Cin., 1991, Cathedral Fresh Art Exhibit, Covington, Ky., 1998 (1st pl.); Coll. Mt. St. Joseph Studio San Guiseppi, Ga. State Fair, Ga., 2003; represented in pvt. collections. Mem. Youth Encouragement Svcs., Aurora, Ind., 1985—; active Dearborn Highland Arts Coun., Lawrenceburg, Ind., 1990-95; mem. Rev. Club, Lawrenceburg, 1985-2002; dir. religious edn. Blessed Sacrament Parish, Ft. Mitchell, Ky., 1996-2002. Mem. Martin Gardener Houston Country Club. Avocations: art, reading, traveling, gardening, swimming. Office: 203 River Valley Trl Kathleen GA 31047-2135

WILLS, PATRICIA MARY, controller; b. Evergreen Park, Ill., May 27, 1960; d. Thomas James and Patricia Ann (Sheehan) W. BA, Chgo. State U., 1992. Acct. R R Donnelley & Sons, Chgo., 1985-93; acctg. supr. Barton Printing, Chgo., 1993-95, estimator, 1995-97, contr., 1997—. Mem. strategic planning com. Barton Printing, 1993-95, mem. std. precedure com., 1993-94, mem. mgr.'s com., 1997, mem. ISO 9000 team, 1997. Team leader United Way, Chgo., 1993. Mem. NAFE. Democrat. Roman Catholic. Avocations: reading, camping. Home: 12643 S Kostner Ave Alsip IL 60803-2627 Office: Barton Printing Ste 520 5750 Old Orchard Rd Skokie IL 60077-1081

WILLS, SHERIAN ATKINS, editor, writer; b. Roanoke, Va., Sept. 17, 1943; d. Lynwood Elmore and Virginia Louise (Bushnell) Bayne; m. Hubert O. Wills, May 5, 1987 (div.); m. Larry LeRoy Atkins, Sr., June 10, 1960 (dec. Jan. 8, 1987); children: Larry L. Jr., Cavin W., Maria E. Diploma in Writing, Writers Digest Sch., 1986, Writers Digest Sch., 87, Writers Digest Sch., 1993, Inst. Childrens Lit., 1994, diploma in Writing, 2001. Freelance writer, Bedford, Va., 1987—. Contbr. articles, short stories and poems to mags.; editor: The Smith Mt. Lake Herald, 2002—. Mem.: Dayton (Ohio) Christian Scribes, Valley Writer's Club, Va. Writer's Club. Avocations: writing, reading, crocheting, crafts, sewing. Home: 6266 Dickerson Mill Rd Bedford VA 24523-6341

WILLSIE, SANDRA K. dean, internist, educator; BS in Med. Tech., Pittsburg (Kans.) State U., 1975; DO, U. Health Sci.-Coll. Osteo., Kansas City, Mo., 1983. Diplomate in internal medicine, pulmonary disease and critical care medicine Am. Bd. Internal Medicine. Rotating intern Univ. Hosp., Kansas City, Mo., 1983-84; resident in internal medicine U. Mo.-Kansas City Affiliated Hosps., 1984-87; fellow in pulmonary diseases Truman Med. Ctr.-West, Kansas City, Mo., 1987-89; instr. medicine U. Mo.-Kansas City Sch. Medicine, 1984-89; med. dir. pulmonary clinic Truman Med. Ctr., 1991-2000; asst. prof. medicine U. Mo. Kansas City Sch. Medicine, 1989-94, assoc. prof. medicine, 1994-99, dep. asst. dean, 1994—97, asst. dean, 1997-2000, prof. medicine, 1999-2000, U. Health Scis., Kansas City, Mo., 2000—, vice dean acad. affairs, adminstrn., med. affairs, 2000—02, v.p. acad. affairs, dean, 2002—. Contbr. articles to profl. jours. Fellow ACP, Am. Coll. Chest Physicians; mem. Am. Thoracic Soc., Mo. Thoracic Soc., Soc. Critical Care Medicine, Met. Med. Soc., Am. Osteo. Assn. Office: Univ of Health Scis 1750 Independence Ave Kansas City MO 64106-1453

WILLSON, MARY FRANCES, ecology researcher, educator; b. Madison, Wis., July 28, 1938; d. Gordon L. and Sarah (Loomans) W.; m. R.A. von Neumann, May 29, 1972 (dec.). BA with honors, Grinnell Coll., 1960; PhD, U. Wash., 1964. Asst. prof. U. Ill., Urbana, 1965-71, assoc. prof., 1971-76, prof. ecology, 1976-90; rsch. ecologist Forestry Scis. Lab., Juneau, Alaska, 1989-99; sci. dir. Great Lakes program Nature Conservancy, 1999-2000. Prin. rsch. scientist, affiliate prof. biology, Inst. Arctic Biology and Sch. Fisheries and Ocean Scis., U. Alaska, Fairbanks-Juneau. Author: Plant Reproductive Ecology, 1983, Vertebrate Natural History, 1984; co-author: Mate Choice in Plants, 1983. Fellow Am. Ornithologists Union; mem. Brit. Ornithologists Union, Soc. for Study Evolution, Am. Soc. Naturalists (hon. mem.), Ecol. Soc. Am., Brit. Ecol. Soc. E-mail: mwillson@gci.net.

WILMER, ANN, public relations executive; b. Waynesboro, Pa., Oct. 18, 1952; d. Vaughn Edward and Frances Laura (Hudson) W. BS in Journalism cum laude, cert. of East Asian studies, U. Fla., 1975; EdM, Salisbury State Coll., 1979. Pub. rels. dir. Delmarva Adv. Coun., Salisbury, Md., 1975-77; advt. mgr. Ahtes & Hanna Ptnrs., Inc., Salisbury, 1979-80; substitute tchr. Wicomico County Sch. Bd., Salisbury, 1979-82; instr. Wor Wic Tech. C.C., 1982-85; pub. affairs officer Md. Dept. State Planning, Balt., 1985-87; publs. adminstr. Md. Dept. Housing and Cmty. Devel., 1988; pub. affairs officer Md. Dept. Natural Resources, 1988-97; pres. Capital Letters, Salisbury, Md., 1997—. Lectr. comm. Salisbury U., 1998—; freelance editor, religion writer and pub. rels. cons. Active Md. State Dem. Com., 1982-86; nat. committeewoman Young Dems. of Am., Md., 1984-86; mem. Preservation Trust of Wicomico, Inc., 1990-96, pres., 1991-95; trustee Salisbury Area Property Owners Assn., 1991-92; founder Green Ribbon Campaign for Open Records, 2000. Named Outstanding Young Woman of the Yr., Salisbury Jaycees, 1982. Mem. Soc. Profl. Journalists (v.p. U. Fla. chpt. 1973-74, Pres. award 1975). Avocations: opera, needle arts, genealogy. Office: Capital Letters 408 N Division St Ste A Salisbury MD 21801-4274

WILMER, MARY CHARLES, artist; b. Atlanta, Aug. 25, 1930; d. William Knox and Harriott Creighton (Thomas) Fitzpatrick; m. John Grant Wilmer, Dec. 28, 1950; children: John Grant, Knox Randolph, Charles Inman, Mary Catherine; m. Olin Grigsby Shivers, May 18, 1982. AB, Agnes Scott Coll., 1970; BFA, Coll. of Art, 1974. Co-pres. St. Elizabeth's Guild, Cathedral of Saint Philip. Exhibited in one-woman shows at Image South Gallery, 1974, Aronson Gallery, 1977, 79, Heath Gallery, 1982-, Coach House Gallery, 1983, 89; two-person show (with daughter Catherine Wilmer) Swan Coach House Gallery, Atlanta, 2003; group shows include Colony Square, 1975, Coach House Gallery, 1999; portrait painter, 1974—. Bd. dirs. Hillside Cottages, 1963-65, Atlanta Child Svcs., 1965-68, Atlanta Coll. Art, 1965-85, Atlanta Puppetry Arts, 1982-87, Atlanta Med. Heritage, 1999-2000; co-chmn. Ga. Commn. Nat. Mus. of Women in the Arts, (pres.) 1985-87. Mem. Piedmont Driving Club, Jr. League, Piedmont Garden Club. Episcopalian. Address: 1 Vernon Rd NW Atlanta GA 30305-2964

WILMER, PAMELA SUE, music educator; d. Herbert Marc and Ramona Lee Gottlieb; m. Mark Bradford Wilmer, Aug. 6, 1988; children: Corinne Michelle, Lauren Rae. BS in Elem. Edn., Ball State U., 1982; MusM Edn., U. Houston, 1988. Cert. tchr. Ind., Tex., Alaska, N.Mex Depts. Edn. Elem. tchr. Houston Ind. Sch. Dist., 1982—85; elem./music tchr. Cypress-Fairbanks Ind. Sch. Dist., Houston, 1985—92; music specialist Anchorage (Alaska) Schs., 1993—99, Farmington (N.Mex.) Mcpl. Schs., 1999—. Preschool music coord. Pvt. Anchorage PreSchools, 1994—99. Musician (singer/performer): Polaris Mother Singers (PMS). Mem.: Music Educators Nat. Conf., N.Mex Music Educator's Assn. Home: 4004 Skyline Dr Farmington NM 87401 E-mail: pwilmer@fms.k12.nm.us.

WILMOT, LOUISE C. charitable organization executive, retired career officer; b. Wayne, N.J., Dec. 31, 1942; d. W.J. Currie and Dorothy Murphy; m. James E. Wilmot. BA in History, Coll. St. Elizabeth, Convent Sta., N.J., 1964; student, Naval War Coll., Newport, R.I., 1977; M in Legis. Affairs, George Washington U., 1978. Commd. ensign USN, 1964; advanced through grades to rear adm., 1991; comm. watch officer, registered publs. custodian, women's barracks officer Naval Air Sta., Pensacola, Fla.; with NATO staff Allied Forces, So. Europe, 1966-68; officer recruiter Recruiting Area Seven, Dallas; Naval Senate liaison officer Office Legis. Affairs, Washington; head women's equal opportunity br. Bur. Naval Pers., 1974-76; exec. officer Navy Recruiting Dist., Montgomery, Ala., 1977-79, command of Omaha, 1979-82; dep. dir accession policy Asst. Sec. Def. for Manpower, Installations, and Logistics, Washington, 1982-85; comdr. Navy Recruiting Area Five, Gt. Lakes, Ill., 1985-87; exec. asst., Naval aide Asst. Sec. Navy for Manpower and Reserve Affairs, Washington, 1987-89; comdr. Naval Tng. Ctr., Orlando, Fla., 1989-91; vice chief Naval Edn. and Tng., Pensacola, 1991-93; comdr. Naval Base, Phila., 1993-94; ret. U.S. Navy, 1994; dep. exec. dir. Cath. Relief Svcs., Balt., 1994—. Decorated DSM, Def. Superior Svc. medal, Legion of Merit with 3 gold stars. Office: Cath Relief Svcs 209 W Fayette St Baltimore MD 21201-3403

WILMOTH, JENNIFER LYNN, music educator; b. Richmond, Va., Dec. 15, 1975; BA in Music, East Carolina U., 1997. Intern Richmond Symphony, 1997, youth orch. mgr., 1997, edn. coord., 1997—2000; music min. St. Michael's Cath. Ch., Richmond, 1999—; music tchr. Woodlake Child Devel. Ctr., Richmond, 2000—01, St. Bridgets Sch., Richmond, 2001—. Mem.: Va. Music Educators Assn.

WILMS, ANNE M. information technology executive; Grad., Trinity Coll., Dublin, Ireland, 1979, U. Chgo., 1993. Dir. info. sys. Wis. Power and Light, Madison; with Oracle Corp., Redwood City, Calif.; mgr. info. tech. So. Nat. Gas Co. Sonat, Inc., 1995, v.p. info. tech. Sonat Svcs., 1996, v.p., CIO Sonat Svcs., 1998; v.p., CIO Rohm and Haas Co., Phila., 1999—. Bd. dirs. Elemica, CIDX. Mem. bd. councillors Hist. Soc. Pa.; bd. mem. Red Cross S.E. Pa.; mem. CIO adv. coun. Villanova U. Office: Rohm and Haas Co 100 Independence Hall West Philadelphia PA 19106-2399

WILNER, LOIS ANNETTE, retired speech and language pathologist; b. Newark, Jan. 15, 1935; d. Benjamin and Ida (Schwam) Friedman; m. Sherman Wilner, July 6, 1957 (dec. Apr. 1996); children: Bonnie Joy, Robert Steven. BS, Newark State Tchrs. Coll., 1953-57; MA, Newark State Coll., 1969-73. Tchr. 5th grade Maplewood South Orange Bd. Edn., South Orange, N.J., 1957-58; permanent substitute Parsippany (N.J.)-Troy Hills Bd. Edn., 1967-68, speech and language pathologist, 1968-95, ret., 1995. Cons., speech and lang. pathologist Ctr. for Communication Disorders, Livingston, N.J., 1987-89. Contbr. newsletter Condo Seabreeze Assn., 1995-97, asst. sec., 1996-97; program v.p. Palm Isles Singles Club, 1996-97. Mem. AAUW, NEA, N.J. Edn. Assn., N.J. Ret. Educators Assn. South Fla. (pres. 2002-03, co-pres. 2003-04), Morris County Edn. Assn., N.J. Speech-Hearing Assn., Morris County Speech-Hearing Assn. (libr. 1987-90), Palm Isles Art Club (sec. 1995-96, sec./reservations chmn. 1996-97, pres. 1998-2000), B'nai B'rith Women (Roseland, Livingston and [illegible] 1995-00), Alpha Delta Kappa (pres. Mu chpt. 1990-92, N.J. state scholarship chmn. 1992-94). Home: 7609 Island Breeze Ter Boynton Beach FL 33437-5405

WILS, MADELYN, film company executive; b. Queens, NY, 1955; Owner, prodr. Bread and Butter TV; pres., CEO Tribeca Film Inst., NYC, 2004—. Trustee Alliance Downtown NY, Inc., Conservancy Hist. Battery Pk., Gateway Sch. NY; dir. Hudson River Park Trust; bd. mem. Lower Manhattan Devel. Corp., NYC, 2001—. Office: Tribeca Film Inst 375 Greenwich St New York NY 10013*

WILSON, ALEXANDRA M. communications executive; B in Comm. summa cum laude, M in Comm., JD, U. Pa. Bar: D.C. 1984. Assoc. Crowell & Moring, Wiley, Rein & Fielding; chief cable svcs. bur. FCC, 1990—94; v.p. pub. policy Cox Enterprises, Atlanta, 1994—. Faculty mem. ann. conf. on cable TV law Practising Law Inst.; co-chair conf. on local cable and tel. competition Strategic Rsch. Inst.; spkr. in field. Mem.: Fed. Comm. Bar Assn. (pres.-elect 2002—03, sec., asst. sec., co-chair various coms., mem. exec. com.). Office: Cox Enterprises Inc 1400 Lake Hearn Dr Atlanta GA 30319

WILSON, ANNE GAWTHROP, artist, educator; b. Detroit, Apr. 16, 1949; d. Gerald Shepard and Nancy Craighead (Gawthrop) Wilson; m. Michael Andreas Nagelbach. Student, U. Mich. Sch. of Art, 1967-69; BFA, Cranbrook Acad. Art, Bloomfield Hills, Mich., 1972; MFA, Calif. Coll. Arts and Crafts, 1976. Prof. Dept. Fiber & Materials Studies Sch. of the Art Inst., Chgo., 1979—. Panelist Nat. Endowment for Arts, Washington, 1986, Western States Arts Fedn./Nat. Endowment for Arts Regional Fellowships for Visual Artists, Santa Fe, 1995; co-curator Artemisia Gallery, Chgo., 1988; co-moderator Women's Caucus for Art, Chgo., 1992; panelist workshop instr. Internat. Symposium '92, Toyama, Japan, 1992; panelist The Textile Mus., Washington, 1994; bd. trustees Haystack Sch., Deer Isle, Maine, 1990-95; lectr. Kansas City Art Inst., 1996, Australian Nat. U. Canberra Sch. Art, 1996, Textile Conservation Ctr./Courtauld Inst. Art, London, 1995, others; represented by Roy Boyd Gallery, Chgo., Revolution, Detroit and N.Y. One person shows include Chgo. Cultural Ctr., 1988, Halsey Gallery, Sch. Arts, Coll. Charleston, S.C., 1992, Madison (Wis.) Art Ctr., 1993-94, Roy Boyd Gallery, Chgo., 1994, 96, Ill. Wesleyan U., Sch. Art, Bloomington, 1995, Revolution, Detroit, 1998, Revolution, N.Y.C., 1998, Mus. for Textiles Contemporary Gallery, Toronto, Can., 1999, Mus. Contemporary Art, Chgo., 2000; exhibited in group shows Netherlands Textile Mus., 1989, Musee Cantonal des Beaux-Arts, Palais de Rumine, Lausanne, Switzerland, 1989, John Michael Kohler Arts Ctr., Sheboygan, Wis., 1992-93, 95, Mus. Contemporary Art, Chgo., 1996, 97, Ariz. State U. Art Mus., Tempe, 1997-98, Bowdoin Coll. Mus. Art, Brunswick, Maine, 1998, TBA Exhbn. Space, Chgo., 1999, Angel Row Gallery, Halifax, 1999-2000, Boulder (Colo.) Mus. Contemporary Art, 2000, Gallery 400 Sch. Art and Design Coll. Arch. and the Arts, U. Ill., Chgo., 2000, Asheville (N.C.) Mus. Art, 2000, Chgo. Cultural Ctr., 2000, Memphis Coll. Art, 2001, U. Calif. San Diego, La Jolla, 2001; represented in permanent collections Art Inst. Chgo., Met. Mus. Art, N.Y., Mus. of Contemporary Art, Chgo., Calif. Poly. State U., San Luis Obispo, Calif., M. H. De Young Meml. Mus., San Francisco, Art Inst. Chgo., Cranbrook Acad. Art Mus., Bloomfield Hills; contbr. articles and revs. to profl. jours. Recipient Louis Comfort Tiffany Found. award, 1989; Nat. Endowment for Arts curatorial fellow in decorative arts and mus. edn. Fine Arts Mus. San Francisco, 1978; Nat. Endowment for Arts Visual Artists Fellowship grantee, 1982, 88, Chgo. Artists Abroad grantee, 1988, 89, Ill. Arts Coun. Individual Artist grantee, 1983, 84, 87, 93, 99, Chgo. Artists Internat. Program grantee, 1996. Mem. Coll. Art Assn. (regional co-chair annual conf. 2001). Office: Sch of the Art Inst Fiber Dept 37 S Wabash Ave Chicago IL 60603-3002

WILSON, ANNETTE SIGRID, elementary school educator; b. Harlan, Iowa, Jan. 30, 1953; d. Anker Christian and Ruth Edith Eastergard; m. John Roger Wilson, Dec. 21, 1974; children: Elicia Ruth, Elizabeth Annette. BS, Bob Jones U., 1975; MAE, U. No. Iowa, 2001; diploma, Nancy Bounds Modeling and Finishing Sch., 1999. Educator Arlington Bapt. Sch., Baltimore, Md., 1976—78, Calvary Bapt. Sch., Normal, Ill., 1978—80, Walnut (Iowa) Pub. Sch., 1986—2000, Council Bluffs (Iowa) Cmty. Schs., 2000—04; trainer Area Edn. Agy., Council Bluffs, 1994—98. Homebound spl. edn. instr.1984, 1983—84. Recipient Optimist Award for Outstanding Tchr., 1992, 1996, Leadership award, Area XIII, 1998. Mem.: Phi Delta Kappa Internat. Home: 902 Baldwin St Harlan IA 51537

WILSON, AVON W. state representative; b. Wichita Falls, Tex., Sept. 24, 1929; m. Bill Wilson. BA, N. Tex. State U., 1949; MED, Ea. N.Mex. U., 1996. Tchr. Fort Stockton and Big Spring Schs., Tex., 1949—55, Roswell Ind. Sch. Dist., N.Mex., 1955—80; owner Gift Shop, Roswell, 1976—86; dir. Adult Basic Edn. Ea. N.Mex. U., Roswell, 1986—; state rep. dist. 59 N.Mex. State Legis., Santa Fe, 2001—. Mem. Edn. com. N.Mex. State Legis., Santa Fe, mem. Human Resources/Labor com. Mem.: Altrusa Internat. Roswell (v.p./pres. 1992—). Republican. Methodist. Home: PO Box 381 Roswell NM 88202-0381 Office: New Mexico State Capitol Rm 202A Santa Fe NM 87501

WILSON, BETH A. college official; BA, Calif. State Coll., Sonoma; MBA, Nat. U. Asst. dir. Am. Bus. Coll., 1976-81; scholarship adminstr. Nat. U., 1982-84; v.p. br. ops. Nat. Coll., 1990-91; from exec. dir. bus. sch., group mgr. to v.p. adminstrn. United Edn. and Sofware, 1984-90; exec. dir. Capital Hill campus, then area ops. mgr. Nat. Edn. Ctrs., Inc., 1991-95; ops. dir., regional ops. dir. Corinthian Schs., Inc., Santa Ana, Calif., 1995-97, regional ops. dir. coll. region of Rhodes Colls. divsn., 1997-98, v.p. ops. parent co., 1998—. Office: Corinthian Colls Inc 6 Hutton Centre Dr Ste 400 Santa Ana CA 92707-5764

WILSON, BLENDA JACQUELINE, foundation administrator; b. Woodbridge, N.J., Jan. 28, 1941; d. Horace and Margaret (Brogsdale) Wilson; m. Louis Fair Jr. AB, Cedar Crest Coll., 1962; AM, Seton Hall U., 1965; PhD, Boston Coll., 1979; DHL (hon.), Cedar Crest Coll., 1987, Loretto Heights Coll., 1988, Colo. Tech. Coll., 1988, U. Detroit, 1989; LLD (hon.), Rutgers U., 1989, Ea. Mich. U., 1990, Cambridge Coll., 1991, Schoolcraft Coll., 1992; DHL (hon.), Cambridge Coll., 2001, Antioch U., 1999, Salve Regina U., 2002; DPublic Svc. (hon.), U. Mass., 2002; DHL (hon.), Merrimack Coll., 2001. Tchr. Woodbridge Twp. Pub. Schs., 1962-66; exec. dir. Middlesex County Econ. Opportunity Corp., New Brunswick, N.J., 1966-69; exec. asst. to pres. Rutgers U., New Brunswick, N.J., 1969-72; sr. assoc. dean Grad. Sch. Edn. Harvard U., Cambridge, Mass., 1972-82; v.p. effective sector mgmt. Ind. Sector, Washington, 1982-84; exec. dir. Colo. Commn. Higher Edn., Denver, 1984-88; chancellor and prof. pub. adminstrn. & edn. U. Mich., Dearborn, 1988-92; pres. Calif. State U., Northridge, 1992-99, Nellie Mae Found., Braintree, Mass., 1999—. Am. del. U.S./U.K. Dialogue About Quality Judgments in Higher Edn.; adv. bd. Mich. Consolidated Gas Co., Stanford Inst. Higher Edn. Rsch., U. So. Col. Dist. 60 Nat. Alliance, Nat. Ctr. for Rsch. to Improve Postsecondary Teaching and Learning, 1988-90; bd. dirs. Alpha Capital Mgmt.; mem. higher edn. colloquium Am. Coun. Edn., vis. com. Divsn. Continuing Edn. in Faculty of Arts & Scis., Harvard Coll., Pew Forum on K-12 Edn. Reform in U.S., The Coll. Bd., Federated Dorchester Neighborhood Ho., Fed. Res. Bank of Boston. Dir. U. Detroit Jesuit High Sch., Northridge Hosp. Med. Ctr., 1993-99, Arab Cmty. Ctr. for Econ. and Social Svcs., Union Bank, J. Paul Getty Trust, James Irvine Found., 1996-99, Internat. Found. Edn. and Self-Help, Achievement Coun., L.A.; dir., vice chair Met. Affairs Corp.; exec. bd. Detroit area coun. Boy Scouts Am.; bd. dirs. Commonwealth Fund, Henry Ford Hosp.-Fairlane Ctr., Henry Ford Health System, Met. Ctr. for High Tech., United Way Southeastern Mich.; mem. Nat. Coalition 100 Black Women, Detroit, Race Rels. Coun. Met. Detroit, Women & Founds., Greater Detroit Interfaith Round Table NCCJ, Adv. Bd. Valley Cultural Ctr., Woodland Hills; trustee assoc. Boston Coll.; trustee emeritus Cambridge Coll.; trustee emeritus bd. dirs. Found. Ctr.; trustee Henry Ford Mus. & Greenfield Village, Sammy Davis Jr. Nat. Liver Inst. Mem. AAUW, Assn. Governing Bds. (adv. coun. of pres.'s), Edn. Commn. of the States (student minority task force), Am. Assn. Higher Edn. (chair-elect), Am. Assn. State Colls. & Univs. (com. on policies & purposes, acad. leadership fellows selection com.), Assn. Black Profls. and Adminstrs., Assn. Black Women in Higher Edn., Women Execs. State Govt., Internat. Women's Forum, Mich. Women's Forum, Women's Econ. Club Detroit, Econ. Club, Rotary. Office: Nellie Mae Edn Found 1250 Hancock St 205N Quincy MA 02169-4331

WILSON, BONNIE JEAN, lawyer, educator, investor; b. Alameda County, Calif. d. August and Violet Adeline (Lockard) Ritzenthaler; m. Allan Nicholas Wilson (dec.); children: Albert Clyde, Bruce Allan. BA, cert. in elem. tchg., U. Calif., Berkeley; JD, Thomas Jefferson SOL, 1981. Bar: Calif.; cert. tchr., Calif. Elem. sch. tchr. Contra Costa and San Diego Counties; intern San Diego County Dist. Atty. Office, 1981; pvt. practice La Jolla, Calif., 1982—. Mem. La Jolla Presbyn. Ch., San Diego Symphony Assn., Friends of the La Jolla Libr.; adv. dir. San Diego Opera Assn.; edn. activist, 1972-76. Mem. Calif. State Bar Assn., San Diego County Bar Assn., La Jolla Newcomer's Club (bd. dirs. 1968-69), U. Calif. Berkeley Alumni Club (bd. dirs. San Diego chpt. 1961-62), Am. Assn. Ind. Investors (bd. dirs. 1991-97), Pi Lambda Theta Lambda, La Jolla Beach and Tennis Club. Presbyterian. Home: 2235 Bahia Dr La Jolla CA 92037-7007

WILSON, CAROL ANN, retired business manager; b. Hardtner, Kans., Dec. 29, 1942; d. Elmer C. and Dorothy B. (Joachims) Hartwig; m. Robert Carlisle Wilson; children: Kimberly Skinner, Stacey Hedges. BSEd, Northwestern Okla. State U., Alva, 1963; MS Sch Adminstrn., Ft. Hays (Kans.) State U., 1991. Cert. Kans. Sec. Northwestern Okla. State U., 1963-66; tchr. Unified Sch. Dist. # 507, Satanta, Kans., 1966-67, sec., 1967-81, clerk of bd., 1981-91; legal sec. Neubauer, Sharp, Liberal, Kans., 1991; ednl. fin. cons. Porter & Kreie, CPA, Ulysses, Kans., 1991-92; bus. mgr. Unified Sch. Dist. 214, Ulysses, Kans., 1992—98; ret., 1998. Field rep. KPERS, Topeka; ednl. cons. Unified Sch. Dist. 214, Ulysses, 1991—92; liaison, cons. Satanta Rec. Com. Mem. bd. dirs. Satanta Recreation Commn.; mem. Youth Orgn. Club Civic Group, Satanta, Satanta C. of C., Satanta Arts Coun. Mem. AAUW, Kans. Assn. Sch. Bus. Officials, Assn. Sch. Bus. Officials. Republican. Lutheran. Avocations: reading, sewing, traveling. Home: PO Box 655 Satanta KS 67870-0655 Office: KPERS 611 N Kansas Ave Topeka KS 66603

WILSON, CAROLYN CAMPBELL, art historian; b. Bryn Mawr, Pa., Dec. 1, 1946; d. Robert North and Ruth (Spurlock) W.; m. Michael Ede Newmark, Aug. 28, 1976; children: Georgina Newmark, Serena Newmark, Diana Newmark. BA, Wellesley Coll., 1968; MA, NYU, 1970, PhD, 1977. Lectr. Index of Christian Art Princeton (N.J.) U., 1975; lectr. U. Md., College Park, 1976-77; asst. curator of sculpture Nat. Gallery of Art, Washington, 1978-83; rsch. curator for Renaissance art Mus. Fine Arts, Houston, 1983-93; ind. scholar, 1994—. Mem. com. Barr award, 2001—. Author: Small Bronze Sculpture at the National Gallery of Art, 1983, Italian Paintings...Museum of Fine Arts, 1996, St. Joseph in Italian Renaissance Society and Art, 2001. Grantee Ford Found., 1970-73, Kress Found., 1990, Getty Grants Program, 1988, Gladys Krieble Delmas Found., 1995; Kness fellowship 2001, Mildred A. Mascoli fellow Folger Libr., 2003; recipient Vasari award, Bainton Book prize; finalist Barr award. Mem. Coll. Art Assn., Renaissance Soc. Am., Midwest Art History Assn., Assn. Ind. Historians of Art, News on the Rialto, Wellesley Coll. Friends of Art. Home: 2222 Goldsmith St Houston TX 77030-1119

WILSON, CAROLYN ROSS, retired school system administrator; b. Lake Charles, La., June 25, 1941; d. Charles Wesley and Lucille Gertrude (Payne) Ross; m. James David Wilson, Apr. 10, 1971; 1 child, Charlise. BS in Music Edn. cum laude, Xavier U., 1962; MMus in Music Edn., Cath. U., Washington, 1968; postgrad., U. D.C., 1985-86, George Washington U., 1987-88, Harvard U., 1989. Tchr. Xavier U. Jr. Sch. Music, New Orleans, 1960-61, Orleans Parish Schs., New Orleans, 1962-63, D.C. Pub. Schs., Washington, 1964-87, curriculum writer, summer 1984, 85, adminstrv. intern Ea. High Sch., 1987-88, asst. prin. Cardozo High Sch., 1988-89, asst. prin. Duke Ellington Sch. of Arts, 1989-93; prin. Duke Ellington Sch. Arts, Washington, 1993-97—; proposal reader U.S. Dept. Edn., 1998, 98, 99. Curriculum writer music dept. D.C. Pub. Schs., Washington, 1984-85, dir. All City High Sch. Chorus, 1973. Composer: A Dedication to Federal City Alumnae Chapter of Delta, Sigma Theta Sorority, Inc., 1973. Lector Immaculate Conception Ch., Washington, 1986—; named D.C. Tchr. of Yr., 1987. Recipient Cert. of Merit-Outstanding Tchr. and Prin. award D.C. Govt., 1994; U.S. Dept. Edn. Effective Schs. grantee, Washington, 1992. Mem. ASCD, Instn. for Devel. Ednl. Activities (6th yr. fellow, session chair 1988, seminar leader 1991, 92, 93, 94), Delta Sigma Theta (Federal City Alumnae chpt.). Roman Catholic. Avocations: reading, travel, bowling, musical arranging, playing the piano.

WILSON, CAROLYN TAYLOR, librarian; b. Cookeville, Tenn., June 10, 1936; d. Herman Wilson and Flo (Donaldson) Taylor; m. Larry Kittrell Wilson, June 14, 1957 (dec.); children: Jennifer Wilson Rust, Elissa Anne Wilson. BA, David Lipscomb Coll., 1957; MLS, George Peabody Coll., 1976. Tchr. English Fulton County Sch. System, Atlanta, 1957-59; serials cataloger Vanderbilt U. Libr., Nashville, 1974-77; asst. libr. United Meth. Pub. House, Nashville, 1978-80; collection devel. libr. David Lipscomb U., Nashville, 1980—, acting dir. Beaman Libr., 1998, dir. Beaman Libr., 1999—. Cons. and rschr. in field; project dir. Tenn.'s Lit. Legacy for Tenn. Humanities Coun., 1994—, ALA grant, Frontier in Am. Culture, 1996-98; project dir. Tenn. Humanities Coun. grant, 1998—; rep. Tenn. Avd. Coun. Librs., Acad. Librs., 1999—. Rsch. asst. Handbook of Tennessee Labor History, 1987-89. Adv. bd. So. Festival of Books, Nashville, 1988-90, 90—, vol. coord., 1989, 90—; project dir. Women's Words (summer grant program) for Tenn. Humanities Coun., Tenn.'s Literary Legacy (summer grant program), 1994-96, Growing Up Southern (summer grant), 1996—, ALA grant The Frontier in Am. Culture, 1996—. Recipient Nat. Honor Soc. award Phi Alpha Theta, 1956, Internat. Honor Soc. award Beta Phi Mu, 1980, Frances Neel Cheney award Tenn. Libr. Assn., 1992; nominee Athena award, 1992; Growing Up Southern summer grantee, 1996—. Mem. ALA, Tenn. Hist. Soc., Tenn. Libr. Assn. (Frances Neel Cheney award 1992), Southeastern Libr. Assn. (chmn. outstanding S.E. author award com. 1991-92, chmn. So. Books competition 1992-94, sec. exec. bd. 1997—), Women's Nat. Book Assn. (pres., v.p., treas., awards chmn. 1980—), Disciples of Christ Hist. Soc. (bd. dirs. 2002—), Tenn. Writers Alliance (bd. dirs. 1995—). Democrat. Avocations: reading, cooking, jogging, sailing. Office: David Lipscomb U Beaman Libr # 310 Nashville TN 37204 E-mail: carolyn.wilson@lipscomb.edu.

WILSON, CARRIE LYNN, technologist; b. Balt., Dec. 31, 1977; d. Joyce Ann Wilson. AAS in Radiol. Tech., Anne Arundel C.C., Arnold, Md., 1999; cert. in diagnostic med. sonography, U. Md., Baltimore County, 2000. Cert. RT(R) ARRT, RDMS ARDMS. Radiol. technologist U. Md. Med. Sys., Balt., 1999—2000; ultrasonographer/radiol. technologist Kent and Queen Anne's Hosp., Chestertown, Md., 2000—02; ultrasonographer North Arundel Hosp., Glen Burnie, Md., 2000—. Instr. Anne Arundel C.C., Arnold, Md., 2001—02. Mem.: Md. Soc. Radiol. Technologists, Soc. Diagnostic Med. Sonographers. Democrat. Avocations: running, hiking, boating.

WILSON, CASSANDRA, singer; b. Jackson, Miss., 1955; Albums include Point of View, 1986, Blue Skies, 1988, Days Aweigh, 1987, Jumpworld, 1990, She Who Weeps, 1991, Cassandra Wilson Live, 1992, Blue Light 'Till Dawn, 1993, Dance to the Drums Again, 1993, After the Beginning Again, 1994, New Moon Daughter, 1996, Travelling Miles, 1999, Belly of the Sun, 2002, Glamoured, 2003. Office: Blue Note Records 150 5th Ave New York NY 10011-4311

WILSON, CHERYL LEE, special education educator; b. Great Lakes, Ill., Feb. 6, 1956; d. Donn William and Jean Elizabeth Hoyer; m. Robert Henry Wilson; children: Michael, Joshua. BS in Edn., U. Ctrl. Ark., 1978, MS in Edn., 1984. Learning disabilities tchr. Harrison (Ark.) Pub. Schs., 1978—78, secondary learning disabilities tchr., 1979—80, elem. moderately handicapped tchr., 1980—87, elem. learning disabilities tchr., 1987—88; learning disabilities tchr. N. Little Rock Pub. Schs., 1978; secondary mildly handicapped tchr. N.W. Ark. Alternative Sch., Bentonville, 1979; instnl. instr. level 1 Conway (Ark.) Human Devel. Ctr., 1989; elem. moderately handicapped tchr. Conway Pub. Schs., 1989—93. Named Vol. of Yr., Nat. Multiple Sclerosis Soc., Ark. chpt., 1995, 1998, Multiple Sclerosis Ark. Mother of Yr., 1996. Mem.: AAUW (pres. 1999—2004, Mavis Standefer Scholarship named honoree Conway br. 1994), NEA, Ark. Edn. Assn. (life), Kappa Kappa Iota. Methodist. Avocations: reading, travel, scrapbooks. Home: 4600 Palm Springs Cir #1 Conway AR 72034 Personal E-mail: cwilson72@yahoo.com.

WILSON, CHERYL YVONNE, elementary school educator, secondary school educator; b. Dayton, Ohio, Sept. 25, 1958; d. Samuel Wesley Wilson Sr. and Hazel Oneida Wilson; m. Henry Heard Cofield Jr., July 27, 1985. Student, Ohio State U., 1976—81; AA, Miami U., 1987. Legal sec. Raymond W. O'Neal, Sr. Atty. at Law, Middletown, Ohio, 1982—83; reorder buyer Dason's Hardware Ctr., 1984—85; Writer's Digest Novel Writing Workship Middletown City Sch. Dist., 1986—87; deputy clk. Butler County Clk. Cts., Hamilton, 1990—91; mail room clk. Butler County Printing Co., 1992—95; mail courier, security officer Johnson Controls Svcs., Inc., 1998—2000. Pres., CEO Ohio Writer's Pub. Co., Middletown, 1987—, 1991—. Mem. U.S. Bicentennial Commn., 2003—, curator, exec. dir., 2003. Nominee 87th Spingarn medal award, NAACP, 1998, 2001, Coretta Scott King book award, 2002, Oprah Winfrey Angel Network Use Your Life award, 2003. Mem.: NAACP (life Bronze Plaque award 2002), Internat. African Am. Genealogy Rsch. Pub. Assn. (curator 2003—, exec. dir. 2003—), Middletown Hist. Soc. (life). Republican. Mem. Lds Ch. Avocations: writing, reading, photography.

WILSON, CLEO FRANCINE, entertainment company executive; b. Chgo., May 7, 1943; d. Cleo Antonio Chancey and Frances (Page) Watson; divorced; children: SuLyn Silbar. BA in English with distinction, U. Ill., 1976. Supr. Playboy Enterprises, Inc., Chgo., 1980-82; grants mgr. Playboy Found., Chgo., 1982-84, exec. dir., 1984—, v.p. pub. affairs, 2001—. Pres. Intuit: The Ctr. for Intuitive and Outsider Art, 1996—, 2000—. Pres. AIDS Found. Chgo., 1990-93; v.p. Donors Forum Chgo., 1986-88; sec. Chgo. Women in Philanthropy, 1986-87; advisor Chgo. Dept. Cultural Affairs, 1988-90. Recipient Kizzy Image award Black Woman Hall of Fame, 1984; named one of Chgo's. Up and Coming by Dollars & Sense mag., 1985, Phenomenal Woman award An Expo for Today's Black Woman, 1997. Home: 6571 N Glenwood Ave Chicago IL 60626-5121 Office: Playboy Enterprises Inc 680 N Lake Shore Dr Fl 15 Chicago IL 60611-4455

WILSON, CONSTANCE KRAMER, bank officer; b. Dayton, Ohio, Aug. 9, 1959; d. Michael Carl and Mona Louise (Miller) Kramer; m. Thomas Singleton Wilson, July 27, 1985; stepchildren: Thomas Douglas, Kirsten Lea, Heather Elizabeth, Ashley Paige. BS in Finance, Ind. U., 1981. Sr. credit analyst NCNB Nat. Bank, Charlotte, 1982-83, commercial loan officer, 1983-86, stockbroker, 1987-88, trust officer, 1988—; investment advisor Planned Mgmt. Co., Charlotte, 1986-87; mem. N.C. State Senate, 1989-90. Mem. Gov.'s Infant Mortality Commn., N.C. State House, 1992—, emerging polit. leader program U. Va., 1993, Gov.'s Commn. on Literacy; del. Rep. Party County Dist. State, 1988-89; vice chmn. Mecklenburg Young Reps., Charlotte, 1989; mem. exec. com. Rep. County and State, 1989. N.C. Inst. fellow, Wilmington, 1989. Republican. Home: 726 Lansdowne Rd Charlotte NC 28270-5902 Office: NCNB Nat Bank 1 Ncnb Pla To9 1 Charlotte NC 28255-0001

WILSON, DEBORA J. broadcast executive; m. Larry Wilson; 1 stepchild, Kevin ; 1 child, Christine. BS in Fin. and Bus. Adminstrn., George Mason U. With Bell Atlantic Network Svcs.; joined The Weather Channel, 1994, sr. v.p. new bus. devel., exec. v.p., gen. mgr. online svcs.; pres., CEO The Weather Channel Interactive, 1999—2003; COO The Weather Channel Network and The Weather Channel Interactive, 2003—04; pres. The

Weather Channel Cos., 2004—. Recipient Tami Award, 2000. Mem.: Interactive Adv. Bureau, Cable & Telecom. Assoc., National Cable Television Assoc., bd. of dir. Lightbridge, Inc. Office: 300 Interstate North Pkwy SE Atlanta GA 30339-2403

WILSON, DEBORAH GRIM, music educator; b. Reading, Pa., Jan. 24, 1955; d. Robert Frederick and Jean (LeMay) Grim; m. Michael Louis Wilson, Dec. 27, 1975; children: Michelle Josephine, Stephanie Nicole. BS in Music Edn., Indiana U. Pa., 1976; MA, Western State Coll., 1984. Cert. tchr. early adolescent and young adult music/band, board cert. tchr. 2003. Tchr. elem. music W. End Sch. Dist., Nucla, Colo., 1978—80, Clifton Elem. Sch., Grand Junction, Colo., 1980—81; elem. band dir. Sch. Dist. #51, Grand Junction, 1981—84; jr. high. band dir. Orchard Mesa Mid. Sch., Grand Junction, 1984—89; elem. music tchr. Wingate Sch., Grand Junction, 1989—98; mid. sch. band. dir. Grand Mesa Mid. Sch., Grand Junction, 1998—. Mem.: Colo. Band Masters Assn., Colo. Music Educators Assn., Am. Sch. Band Dirs. Assn. Home: 711 Jasmine Ln Grand Junction CO 81506

WILSON, DEBORAH LYNN, secondary school educator, music educator; b. Shelbyville, Ky., June 10, 1957; d. Virgil Thomas Wilson and Mavis Adams Billings. BS in Music Edn., Austin Peay State U., 1979; MS, Murray State U., 1989. Instr. Murray State U., Ft. Campbell, Ky., 1983—90; music tchr. Greenwood Mid. Sch., Clarksville, Tenn., 1990—93; vocal-choral instr. N.E. H.S., Clarksville, 1993—. Music dir. various theatres, Tenn., 1979—; dir., co-founder Vocal Express Children's Chorus, Clarksville, 1985—91; music dir. Holland Am. Cruise Line, Seattle, 1990—93, St. Bethlehem United Meth. Ch., Clarksville, 1996—; dir. Adult Pop Piano, Clarksville, 1997—. Composer: (plays) The Dastrdly Dr. Deaveroux, 1990; performer: (recs./CDs) Four Hands Down, 2001, Grace, 2001, Happy Holidays, 2001. Organizer project Nicaragua Holland Am. Cruise Line; active Save the Children, Nicaragua; exec. asst. Symposium 2000-World Peace Conf., Nashville, 2000. Mem.: Tchr. Edn. Assn., Music Educators Nat. Conf., Mid. Tenn. Vocal Assn. Avocations: playing honky tonk piano, travel, swimming, visiting friends, composing. Home: 2141 Memorial Drive Clarksville TN 37043 Office: Northeast High School 3701 Trenton Rd Clarksville TN 37040

WILSON, DEBORRAH, physical education educator; b. Tachikowa, Japan, Aug. 18, 1950; BS in Phys. Edn. and Health, U. Del., 1972; MEd, Wilmington Coll., 2000. Elem. phys. edn. tchr. Downes Elem. Sch.; instr. of programs, teen dir. YWCA, 1972—78; phys. edn. specialist Christina Sch. Dist., 1978—. Recipient Outstanding Alumni award U. Del., 1993, Disting. Svc. award Maclary PTA, 1993, Del. Congress Parents and Tchrs. Inc.; named Ea. Region Elem. Sch. Phys. Edn. Tchr. of Yr., Nat. Assn. Sport and Phys. Edn., 1993, Elem. Phys. Edn. Tchr. of Yr., State of Del., 1993, Tchr. of Yr. Elem. Sch., 2000. Home: 731 Art Ln Newark DE 19713-1208

WILSON, DIANE E. music educator; d. Richard Lorraine Finley and Ella Hulda Dohrmann; m. Wayne Everett Wilson, Nov. 18, 1950; children: Matthew, Marc, Luke, Bethany. AA, Rochester C.C., Minn., 1968; BS, Concordia Coll., 1970. Cert. mid. sch. tchr. Minn. Music tchr. grades K-12 Herman Pub. Schs., Minn., 1970—71; music tchr. grades K-6 Frazee Pub. Schs., Minn., 1971—73; music tchr. grades K-8 St. Mary's Grade Sch., Caledonia, Minn., 1986—89; tchr. instrumental music Caledonia Pub. Schs., 1989—2001; tchr. vocal music grades 6-12 Stewartville Pub. Schs., Minn., 2001—. Dir. ch. choir, Caledonia, 1980—2000; mem. cmty. band Zymbrota, Minn., 2003; chair Comprehensive Arts Planning Program, Caledonia, 1992—97. Mem.: NEA, Minn. Edn. Assn., Minn. Music Educators Assn. Lutheran. Avocations: quilting, cross stitch, cross country skiing. Home: 433 Beverly St East Wanamingo MN 55983 Office: Stewartville Mid Sch 500 Fourth St SW Stewartville MN 55976

WILSON, DONNA MAE, dean, language educator; b. Columbus, Ohio, Feb. 25, 1947; d. Everett John and Hazel Margaret (Bruck) Palmer; m. Steven L. Wilson, Nov. 16, 1968. BA, Ohio State U., 1973, MA, 1976; postgrad studies, U. Wash., Seattle Pacific U., U. Mass., 1980—93; cert., U. Salamanca, Spain, 1985; PhD in Higher Edn., U. Mass., 2003. Tchg. assoc. Ohio State U., Columbus, 1974-76; lectr. U. Wash., Seattle, 1977-78; grants officer Seattle U., 1978-82; adj. prof. Shoreline Coll., Seattle, 1982-84; coord. fgn. langs., prof. Spanish Bellevue (Wash.) Coll., 1984-87; prof. Spanish Highline Coll., Des Moines, Wash., 1987-98, chair fgn. lang. dept., 1990-94, chair arts and humanities, 1994-98; assoc. dean acad. affairs Greenfield (Mass.) Coll., 1998—2002. Spkr. at lang. orgns., confs. regional and nat., 1985—. Editor: (book) Fronteras: En Contacto, 1992-93; (jours.) Modern Lang. Jour., 1991, 92, 94, 96, 97, 98, 2001, Hispania, 1993, 95; text editor D. C. Heath and Co., Harcourt, Brace and Jovanovich, Houghton Mifflin, Prentice Hall; contbr. articles to profl. jours., chpt. to English of Science and Technology Learning, 2000. Mem. Mass. Bd. Higher Edn. Exit Assessment, 1999-2000; pres. Mass. Coun. Acad. Deans, 2000-2001; assoc. deans think tank New England Resource Ctr. Higher Edn., 2000-02. Recipient cert. of excellence Phi Theta Kappa, 1990, Pathfinder award Phi Beta Kappa, 1995; fellowshp grant Coun. Internat. Edn. Exchange, Santiago, Chile, 1992. Mem. Nat. Coun. Instr. Adminstrs., Am. Assn. Tchrs. of Spanish (v.p. Wash.), Am. Coun. Tchrs. of Fgn. Langs. (cert. oral proficiency), Assn. Dept of Fgn. Langs. (exec. bd. 1994-97), Pacific N.W. Coun. Fgn. Langs., 1986-98, Nat. Assn. Fgn. Lang. Suprs., Sigma Delta Mu. (nat. exec. sec. 1992-98), Nat. Assn. of Women in Higher Edn. Avocations: travel, assessment rsch. on 2d lang., outdoors. E-mail: donna123@educ.umass.edu.

WILSON, ELEANOR MCELROY, county official; b. Lancaster, Pa., Sept. 10, 1938; d. Hartford Ford and Jane Ann McElroy; m. Frank Eugene Wilson, July 17, 1976 (dec. Jan. 1980). AA, Monterey Peninsula Jr. Coll., Monterey, Calif., 1959; BA in Edn., San Jose State U., 1963; MA in Bus. /Mgmt., Webster U., St. Louis, 1981; MA in Internat. Rels., Salve Regina Coll., Newport, R.I., 1990; MA in Nat. Security/Strategic Studies, Naval War Coll., Newport, 1991. Sec. Geo. Dovolis Real Estate, Monterey, 1957-59; legal sec. Thompson & Thompson Attys., Monterey, 1959-61; legal asst., supr. Thomson J. Hudson, Atty., Monterey, 1963-68, legal asst., 1972-74. Mem. Orange County Grand Jury Superior Ct., Santa Ana, Calif., 1982—83; citizen mem. Orange County Parole Bd., Santa Ana, 1993—96, 1999—2001; mem. Orange County Juvenile Justice Commn., Orange, 1992—2000, chair, 1995; nat. adv. coun., bd. advisors Flying Leatherneck Hist. Found., 2000—. Col. USMCR, 1968—98. Decorated Legion of Merit. Mem.: Sloan Found. (bd. dirs. 1996—98), Marine Corps Aviation Assn. (bd. dirs. 1980—94, bd. advisers 1994—), Marine Corps Heritage Found. (bd. dirs. 1992—98). Avocations: reading, golf, tennis, travel.

WILSON, F. JILL, real estate executive, Internet consultant; b. Dallas, Dec. 9, 1944; d. Earl Kenneth Wilson and Dorothy Ruth Bowers; m. David Holcomb, Sept. 1969 (div. Mar. 1971); m. Donald Lee McRee, Mar. 20, 1983. BBA, So. Meth. U., 1966; MBA, St. Mary's U., 1973. Cert. property mgr., comml. investment mem. Pres., owner Wilson Schanzer Inc., San Antonio, 1978-93; pres. Security Capital Group Realty Svcs., San Antonio, 1993-95; ptnr. Wilson-McRee Cons., San Antonio and Vail, Colo., 1992—; CEO ApartmentWorld.com, San Antonio, 1999—2000; mng. dir. RentPort, Inc., NY, 2000—01; strategy dir. Epekeia Inc., 2002—. Mem. exec. bd. dirs. St. Mary's U. Sch. Bus., San Antonio, 1990—; mem. adv. bd. Via Transit, San Antonio, 1998; sec. fin. bd. Health and Med. Facilities, San Antonio, 1986-92; mem. adv. bd. Housing Fin. Bd., San Antonio, 1984-89. Recipient Corp. award Tex. Coun. of Family Violence, 1992; named Bus. Woman of Yr., San Antonio Express News, 1992, Entrepreneur of Yr. Inc. Mag./Ernst & Young, 1991. Mem. Tex. Apt. Assn. (pres. 1991), Bus. and Profl. Women (pres. 1989), Internat. Women's Forum (Women and Corp. Who Make a Difference 1991), Tex. Women's Forum, Colo. Forum, North San Antonio C. of C. (vice chmn. 1990). Avocations: skiing, hiking, mountain climbing. Home: 3487 River Way San Antonio TX 78230

WILSON, FAYE, retail executive; Exec. v.p. Bank Am. Corp., San Diego; sr. v.p. value initiatives Home Depot, Atlanta. Office: Home Depot Inc 2455 Paces Ferry Rd SE Atlanta GA 30339-4024

WILSON, FRANCES C. career military officer; BS, Mich. State U.; MEd, Pepperdine U.; MA in Psychology, U. No. Colo.; MS in Bus. Mgmt., Salve Regina Coll.; PhD in Edn., U. So. Calif. Commd. 2d lt. USMC, 1972, advanced through grades to maj. gen.; air traffic control officer Marine Corps Air Sta., Yuma, Ariz., Kaneohe, Hawaii, 1975; tchr. instrnl. mgmt. Marine Corps Devel. & Edn. Ctr., Quantico, Va.; staff sec. 3d Marine Divsn., Okinawa, Japan, 1980-81; asst. prof., co. officer brigade of midshipmen U.S. Naval Acad., Annapolis, Md.; mgmt. analyst HQ USMC, Washington; spl. asst. for gen. and flag officer matters Joint Staff, Pentagon, exec. asst. to vice dir., 1987; comdr. 4th Recruit Tng. Battalion, Parris Island, S.C., 1988-90, Camp H.M. Smith, Svc. Battalion Marine Corps Pacific; sec. Joint Staff, until 1997; commanding gen. Marine Corps Base, Quantico, 1997-99, Third Force Svc. Support Group, Okinawa, Japan, 1999—2001; dir. pers. mgmt. divsn. M&RA Hdqrs. Marine Corps, 2001; comdt. Indsl. Coll. Armed Forces, Nat. Def. U., Ft. McNair, DC. Decorated Def. Superior Svc. medal, Def. Meritorious Svc. medal, Meritorious Svc. medal, Navy Commendation medal, Navy Achievement medal.

WILSON, FRANCES EDNA, protective services official; b. Keokuk, Iowa, Aug. 4, 1955; d. David Eugene and Anna Bell (Hootman) W. BA, St. Ambrose Coll., 1982; MA, Western Ill., 1990; cert. massage therapist, Shocks Ctr. Edn., Moline, Ill., 1993. Lic. massage therapist, Iowa; cert. Rape Aggression Def. Systems instr.; 2d degree black belt Tai Ho Jujitsu. Trainer, defensive tactics Davenport (Iowa) Police, 1990—, police corporal, 1985-94, police sgt., 1994—; apptd. recs. bur. comdr. Iowa Assn. Women Police, Davenport, 1996-98, pres., 1989-92, patrol supr., coord. comm. training operator, 1998—2001, CTO coord., 1999—2001, sr. sgt. day shift patrol, 2001—02, adminstrv. sgt. day shift, 2003—; adj. instr. Kaplan Coll., 2003—. Cons., def. tactics Scott C.C., Bettendorf, Iowa, 1993—; owner Wilson Enterprises Ltd., Davenport, 1995—; spkr. workshops; guest spkr. Genesis Employee Assistance Program, 1996—; training com. Davenport Police Dept., 1996-2001, recruitment com., 2001—; rape aggression def. instr., 1997—; instr. Rape Aggression Def. Kids, 1999—; with Davenport Cmty. Adult Edn., 2002; mem. Family Connection bd., 1996-2002. Bd. dirs. Scott County Family YMCA, Davenport, 1990-95, instr., 1989—, The Family Connection, Ltd., West Family YMCA, 2003-; instr. Davenport Cmty. Adult Edn., 1991-94; mem. Iowa SAFE KIDS Coalition, 1992—; mem. First Presbyn. Ch., Davenport, 1986—, bd. deacons, 1995; vol. asst. Davenport Police Dept.'s Sgts. Planning Com. on Tng., 1991, K-9 Unit, 1990-94; apptd. adminstv. sgt. 2nd sr. sgt., 2001; instr., bd. dirs. Scott H Co. Family YMCA, 2003-2004. Recipient Law Enforcement award Davenport Optimist Club, 1997. Mem. NOW, Am. Soc. Law Enforcement Trainers, Law Enforcement Alliance Am., Am. Women Self Def. Assn., Nat. Ctr. for Women and Policing, Iowa Assn. Women Police (pres. 1989-92, Officer of Yr. 1995), Iowa State Police Assn., Iowa Assn. Chiefs of Police and Peace Officers, Internat. Assn. Women Police, So. Poverty Law Ctr. Avocations: photography, reading, education, massage therapy, enjoying life. Office: Davenport Police Dept 420 N Harrison St Davenport IA 52801-1304 Office Phone: 319-326-6125. E-mail: frankie_wilson@juno.com.

WILSON, GAYLE ANN, civic worker; b. Phoenix, Nov. 24, 1942; d. Clarence Arthur and Charlotte Evelyn (Davison) Edlund; m. Theodore William Graham, Sept. 14, 1963 (div. May 1983); children: Todd Chandler, Philip Edlund; m. Pete Wilson, May 29, 1983. BA, Stanford U., 1965; postgrad., U. San Diego, 1982. First lady State of Calif., Sacramento, 1991-99; bd. directors ARCO, Los Angeles, CA, 1999—. Adv. for early childhood health and improved math. and sci. edn.; bd. dirs. Ctr. for Excellence in Edn., McLean, Va., 1985—, also former chmn.; mem. Jr. League San Diego, 1968—, also past pres.; bd. dirs. Calif. Inst. Tech., Pasadena, 1995—, Children's Inst. Internat., Phoenix House; former spokesperson Access for Infants and Mothers (AIM), Calif. Breast Cancer Initiative, Never Shake a Baby Campaign, Partnership for Responsible Parenting; mem. Calif. Sesquicentennial Commn.; hon. chmn. Calif. Sci. Fair, Calif. 4-H Found., Calif. Perinatal Outreach-BabyCal, Calif. Commn. on Improving Life Through Svc., Keep Calif. Beautiful; hon. co-chmn. Calif. Mentor Initiative; mem. adv. coun. Ct. Apptd. Spl. Advs.; mem. adv. coun. computers in schs. program Detweiler Found.; hon. chmn. bd. dirs. Leland Stanford Mansion Restoration Found.; founding mem. Achievement Rewards for Coll. Scientists; mem. San Diego Park and Recreation Commn., 1980-83; regent Children's Hosp. L.A. Found., 1998—; bd. dirs. Center Theatre Group, L.A., 1998—, ARCO. Recipient Guardian Angel award L.A. ChildShare, 1995, lifetime achievemecnt award Jr. League L.A., 1996. Mem. Phi Beta Kappa. Republican. Avocations: lyric writing, singing, performing, watercolors. Office: 2132 Century Park Ln Apt 301 Los Angeles CA 90067-3320

WILSON, HEATHER ANN, congresswoman; b. Keene, N.H., Dec. 30, 1960; d. George Douglas Wilson and Martha Lou Wilson-Kernozicky. m. Jay Hone; 3 children. BS, USAF Acad., 1982; M. Philosophy, Oxford U., 1984, PhD, 1985. U.S. mission NATO, Brussels, 1987-89, Nat. Security Coun., Washington, 1989-91; pres. Keystone Internat., Inc., Albuquerque, 1991-95; cabinet sec. N.Mex. Dept. Children, Youth and Families, Santa Fe, 1995-98; mem. U.S. Congress from 1st N.Mex. Dist., Washington, 1998—; mem. armes svcs. com., energy and commerce com. Adj. prof. U. N.Mex.; mem. Def. Adv. Com. on Women in the Svcs. Contbr. articles to profl. jours. Capt. USAF, 1982-89. Rhodes scholar, 1982. Republican. Avocations: parenting, hiking, skiing. Office: 318 Cannon House Office Blg Washington DC 20515-3101 E-mail: ask.heather@mail.house.gov.

WILSON, JANE, artist; b. Seymour, Iowa, Apr. 29, 1924; d. Wayne and Cleone (Marquis) W.; m. John Gruen, Mar. 28, 1948; 1 child, Julia. BA, U. Iowa, 1945, MA, 1947. Mem. fine arts faculty Parsons Sch. Design, 1973-83, 89-90. Vis. artist U. Iowa, 1974; adj. assoc. prof. painting and drawing Columbia U., 1975-85, assoc. prof., 1985-86, prof., 1986-88, acting chair, 1986-88; Andrew Mellon vis. prof. painting Cooper Union, 1977-78. One-woman shows include Hansa Gallery, N.Y.C., 1953, 55, 57, Stuttman Gallery, N.Y.C., 1958, 59, Tibor de Nagy Gallery, N.Y.C., annually, 1960-66, Graham Gallery, N.Y.C., 1968, 69, 71, 73, 75, Fischbach Gallery, N.Y.C., 1978, 81, 84, 88, 90, 91, 93, 95, 97, D.C. Moore Gallery, N.Y.C., 1999, 2001, 03, Munson-Williams-Proctor Inst., Utica, N.Y., 1980, Cornell U., Ithaca, N.Y., 1982, Compass Rose Gallery, Chgo, 1988, Am. U., Washington, 1989, U. Richmond, Va., 1990, Earl McGrath Gallery, L.A., 1990-91, 93, Dartmouth Coll., Hanover, N.H., 1991, Arnot Mus., Elmira, N.Y., 1993-94, Parrish Mus., Southampton, N.Y., 1996, Glenn Horowitz Gallery, East Hampton, N.Y., 1996, Heckscher Mus., Huntington, N.Y., 2001, McKinney Ave. Contemporary, Dallas, 2003; represented in permanent collections Met. Mus., Mus. Modern Art, Whitney Mus., Wadsworth Athenaeum, Heron Art Mus., NYU Rockefeller Inst., Vassar Coll., Pa. Acad. Fine Arts, Hirsch Horn Mus., Washington, Nelson-Atkins Mus., Kansas City, Mo., San Francisco Mus. Modern Art, Heckscher Mus., L.I. Mus., Stony Brook, others. Recipient Purchase prize Childe Hassam Fund, 1971, 73, 81, Ranger Fund Purchase prize 1977; Ingram-Merrill grantee, 1963, Louis Comfort Tiffany grantee, 1967, Eloise Spaeth award The Guild Hall, East Hampton, N.Y., 1988. Lifetime Achievement award The Guild Hall, 2001. Mem. Am. Acad. Arts and Letters (Award in Art 1985), Nat. Acad. Design (pres. 1992-94), Phi Beta Kappa.

WILSON, JANIE MENCHACA, nursing educator, researcher; b. Lytle, Tex., Mar. 15, 1936; 1 child, Kathryn Lynn Kohlleppel. BSN, Incarnate Word Coll., San Antonio, 1958; MSN, U. Tex., San Antonio, 1973; PhD in Nursing, U. Tex., Austin, 1978. RN. Oper. rm. nurse Santa Rosa Hosp., San Antonio, 1958-59; instr. [illegible] Hosp. [illegible] Nursing, Austin, [illegible]-66; staff nurse Med. Coll. Ga., Augusta, 1967-68; instr. dept. nursing San Antonio Coll., 1968-72, prof. dept. nursing edn., 1976—; counselor Project GAIN Tex. Nurses Assn., Austin, 1973-76. Rsch. assoc. Ctr. for Health Care Rsch. and Evaluation, U. Tex. System, Austin, 1974-75; cons. Nurse Aide Competency Evaluation Program, San Antonio, 1989—; mem. manuscript rev. panel Nursing Rsch., N.Y.C., 1989-91. Contbr. chpts. to books, articles to profl. jours. Bd. dirs. Ctr. for Health Policy Devel., San Antonio, 1988-92; mem. Nat. Adv. Coun. on Nurse Edn. and Practice, 1995—. 1st lt. USAF, 1960-63. Mem. AAUP, ANA (coun. nurse rschrs., coun. cultural diversity, fellow program for ethnic minorities 1975-77), Am. Acad. Nursing, Nat. League Nursing, Nat. Assn. Hispanic Nurses, Sigma Theta Tau. Roman Catholic. Avocations: music, reading, fishing, dance, sewing. Office: San Antonio Coll 1300 San Pedro Ave San Antonio TX 78212-4201 Home: 78 Gleneden Avenue Oakland CA 94611 E-mail: jwilson@accd.edu.

WILSON, JEAN L. retired state legislator; b. Phila., June 13, 1928; d. Horace and Catherine (Lennox) Terry; m. Benjamin H. Wilson (dec.); children: Sheryl J. Gordon, Denise T. Munn. BS in Edn., Pa. State U., 1949. Tchr. Columbia Inst., Phila., 1949-50, Wilkes Coll., Wilkes Barre, Pa., 1950-51; office mgr., exec. sec. Camden Fibre Mills, Warminster, Pa., 1969-82; mem. Pa. Ho. of Reps., 1988-92. Legis. chmn. Doylestown V.I.A.; active Benj. H. Wilson Sr. Ctr., Ctr. for Learning in Retirement, Del. Valley Coll.; former mem. bd. Bucks County Opportunity Coun.; treas. Bucks County chpt. Fox Chase Cancer Ctr. Avocations: duplicate bridge, golf. Home: 12 Far View Rd Chalfont PA 18914-2511

WILSON, JENNIFER, psychologist; b. Bklyn., Aug. 3, 1967; d. Herbert T. Blomquist and Teresa M. Leone; m. Jason Wilson, July 6, 2001; 1 child, Gabrielle R. BA in English Lit., St. Mary's Coll., Moraga, Calif.; MA in Psychology, St. Mary's Coll., Berkeley, Calif.; PhD in Psychology, Wright Inst. Pvt. psychologist, Alamogordo, N.Mex., 2002—. Capt. USAF, 1999—2002. Decorated Achievement medal USAF. Mem.: APA. Republican. Roman Catholic. Home: 2373 Saguaro Loop Alamogordo NM 88310 Office: 916 N White Sands Blvd Alamogordo NM 88310

WILSON, JILL MARIE, early childhood educator; b. St. Louis, Nov. 29, 1953; d. Arthur Walter and Mary Katherine (Heitzler) Buback; m. Gary Wayne Wilson, July 22, 1972 (div. Sept. 1997); children: Christopher, Patricia. AAS, East Ctrl. Coll., 1988; degree in spl. edn., U. Mo., 1990—. Advt. artist Christian Bd. Publ., St. Louis, 1972-77; paraprofl. Franklin County Spl. Edn. Coop., St. Clair, Mo., 1988-90; early childhood tchr., dir. Meramec Valley R-3 Early Childhood Ctr., Pacific, Mo., 1990—. Freelance artist, 1977—. Treas. Oak Hill Elem. PTO, St. Louis, 1984-85; mem., coach, mgr., treas. Union Girls Softball Assn., 1990-96; elem. sch. program facilitator Jr. Achievement, St. Louis, 1999. Mem. Assn. for Childhood Edn. Internat., Mo. Nat. Edn. Assn., Early Childhood Tchr.'s Club, Mo. Coun. for Exceptional Children, Phi Theta Kappa. Avocations: decorative painting, reading, computers, canoeing, walking. Office: Meramec Valley R-3 Early Childhood Ctr 2001 W Osage St Pacific MO 63069-1126 Home: 3891 Highway 50 Beaufort MO 63013-1400

WILSON, JOANNE, federal agency administrator; BA, MA, Iowa State U. Tchr. grades 2 and 4, Ames, Iowa; continuing edn. instr. Braille and mobility for blind students La. Tech. U.; founder, dir. La. Ctr. Blind; commr. rehab. svcs. adminstrn. Dept. Edn., Washington, 2001—. Cons. Conn. Bd. Edn. and Svcs. for the Blind, N.J. Orientation and Adjustment Ctr. for the Blind, N.Y. Commn. for the Blind; founder, chair La. Rehab. Svcs. Coun. Office: Dept Edn Rehab Svcs Adminstrn 300 C St SW Washington DC 20202-2531

WILSON, JUDY ROBINSON, language educator, writer; d. Jack Calvin and Jewel Robinson; m. Bryon Dewayne Wilson, Aug. 9, 1984; children: Jamie Rose Richards, Jason Ray Young, Tiffany Marie, Bryon Dewayne Wilson, Jr. PhD, U. So. Miss., 2000. Editl. asst. Pub. Miss. Philol Assn., Hattiesburg, 1994—96, editor, 1997; vis. writer pub. sch. program U. So. Miss., Hattiesburg, 1997—98; dir. Ala. Ctr. for Lit. Arts, Monroeville, 2001—02; asst. prof. Eng. and creative writing S.W. Minn. State U., Marshall, 2002—, dir. creative writing. Submissions reader, screener prize issues Mis. Rev., Hattiesburg, 1995—96; asst. fiction editor Georgetown Rev., Hattiesburg, 1997; ESL tutor U. So. Miss., Hattiesburg, 1995—97. Author: (short stories) Driven, Drive the Slivers Deep, Silk, Crossings, Portrait (So. Lit. Festival award for Best Short Fiction, 1995), Whales, A Different Kind of Neverending (German Translation), Garbage Truck Man, A Different Kind of Neverending, Cicada, Playing Trondalette, Peacekeeper, (poem) Compatibility. Cmty. support Leadership Now, C. of C., Monroeville, Ala., 2001—02; writer local history Arco (Minn.) Centennial Com., 2003—03. Recipient Joan Johnson Writing award for Fiction, 1997, Henfield Found. Transatlantic Rev. award for Fiction, 1997; Truman Capote fellow, 1999. Avocations: writing, reading, travel. Office: Southwest Minn State Univ 1501 State St Marshall MN 56258 E-mail: wilsonj@southwestmsu.edu.

WILSON, KAREN LEE, researcher; b. Somerville, N.J., Apr. 2, 1949; d. Jon Milton and Laura Virginia (Van Dyke) W.; m. Paul Ernest Walker, 1980; 1 child, Jeremy Nathaniel. AB, Harvard U., 1971; MA, NYU, 1973, PhD, 1985. Rsch. assoc., dir. excavation at Mendes, Egypt Inst. Fine Arts, NYU, 1979-81; coord. exhbn. The Jewish Mus., N.Y.C., 1981-82, adminstrv. cataloguer, 1982-83, coord. curatorial affairs, 1984-86; curator Oriental Inst. Mus. U. Chgo., 1988-96, mus. dir., 1996—2003. Author, editor: Mendes, 1982; contbr. articles to profl. jours. Mem.: Coll. Art Assn., Am. Oriental Soc. E-mail: k_wilson@uchicago.edu.

WILSON, LAURA ANN, newspaper editor; b. Otis AFB, Mass., Oct. 3, 1967; d. Robert Carl Laidacker, Emmett Adkins, Jr. and Wanda June (Laidacker); m. Charles John Wilson, Dec. 12, 1992; children: Brendan, Emily. Cert., Lucas Travel Sch., 1988; AA, Pierce Coll., 1993; BS, U. So. Fla., 1997. Intern The Tampa Tribune, Fla., 1996, bus. clerk, 1996; mgn. editor The Pinellas News, St. Petersburg, Fla., 96-98; cmty. editor The Star Democrat, Easton, Md., 1998-2000, spl. sects. editor, 2000—03; editl. specialist Shore Health System, 2003. Spkr. Career Day, Clearview Elem. Sch., St. Petersburg, Fla., 1997, Easton Middle Sch., Md., 1998: guest spkr. Md. Nonprofits, Balt., 1999; student mentor, Talbot Mentors, Easton, 1999—. Mem. The Writers Guild (v.p. USF chpt. 1994), Soc. Profl. Journalists (pres. USF chpt. 1996). Avocations: bowling, walking, reading, travel, movies. Office: Shore Health Sys 219 S Wash St Easton MD 21601 E-mail: lwilson@chespub.com.

WILSON, LAURA ELEANOR, landscape architect; b. Columbus, Ohio, July 9, 1930; d. Russell Brown and Geraldine Gertrude (Rang) W. BS in Landscape Architecture, Iowa State U., 1953. Landscape arch. Rose Greely Landscape Arch., Washington, 1953-55, Prentiss French Landscape Arch., San Francisco, 1955-57, Nat. Park Svc., San Francisco, 1957-72, Santa Fe, 1972-83; sculptor pvt. practice, Santa Fe, 1983—. Landscape architecture: designer and team capt. Visitor Ctr. Cabrillo Nat. Monument, 1969, (Garden Club award 1972), Lehman Caves New Mex., 1966, Redwoods NewMex., Visitor's Ctr., 1971; sculptor: solo exhibitions include Cadmium Gallery, San Francisco, 1962, Art Assocs. W. San Francisco, 1969, 71. St.John's Coll. Santa Fe, New Mex., 1972-1998, Concepts Gallery, Santa Fe, 1984, 86, 88, 90, 92, Santa Fe Contemporary Art, 1995; group show: New Mex. Sculptor's Guild Fuller Lodge Art Ctr., Los Alamos, 1992; invitational, juried incl. 1987's New Mexico Selections Coll. of Santa Fe, invitation to outdoor sculpture Coll. Santa Fe, 1991-2003, Friends of Contemporary Art, 2000, N.Mex. Sculptor's Guild, 2002, Gov.'s Gallery, N.Mex. State Capitol,

2002. Recipient Trailblazer award, State of New Mex. Commn., 1998, Muchas Gracias award, City of Santa Fe, 1998, Santa Fe Living Treasure award, 2003. Mem. emeritus Am. Soc. Landscape Architects, Don Diego Neighborhood Assn. (pres. 1995-2001, Santa Fe, New Mex.) Home: 1107 Don Cubero Ave Santa Fe NM 87505-1620

WILSON, LAVERNE, nursing administrator; b. Fontaine, Ark., July 27, 1931; d. James Gordon and Sophronia (Scott) Nutt; m. John Bruce Wilson, June 30, 1950 (div. 1971); children: Deborah French, Emily Wilson-Godinet, Valerie Keating, John B. Jr., B.G. Scott Wilson. AA, Ark. State U., 1974. Cert. health facility surveyor. Charge nurse Ark. Methodist Hosp., Paragould, 1975-78; instr. Delta Vo-Tech, Marked Tree, Ark., 1978-81; clin. nurse educator VA Hosp., North Little Rock, 1981-83; adminstrv. coordi. Ark. Methodist Hosp., Paragould, 1983—, in-svc. coord., 1983-88; coord. inspection of care rev. Ark. Found. for Med. Care, Ft. Smith, 1988-90; nursing home insp. and utilization rev. nurse Office of Long Term Care, Dept. Human Svcs., State of Ark., 1990—; pres. J.G.N., Inc. Mem. Ark. Bus. and Profl. Women's Orgn., Alpha Gamma Delta. Democrat. Baptist. Avocations: travel, boating. Home: 4905 Burrow Dr North Little Rock AR 72116-7019

WILSON, LINDA, librarian; b. Rochester, Minn., Nov. 17, 1945; d. Eunice Gloria Irene Wilson. BA, U. Minn., Morris, 1967; MA, U. Minn., 1968. Libr. rsch. svcs. U. Calif., Riverside, 1968-69, head dept. phys. scis. catalog, 1969-71; city libr. Belle Glade (Fla). Mcpl. Libr., 1972-74; instr. part-time Palm Beach Jr. Coll., Belle Glade, 1973; head adult-young adult ext. Kern County Libr. Sys., Bakersfield, Calif., 1974-80; dir. dist. libr. Lake Agassiz Regional Libr. System, Crookston, Minn., 1980-85; supervising libr. San Diego County Libr., 1985-87; county libr. Merced (Calif.) County Libr., 1987-93; learning network mgr. Merced Coll., 1994-95; city libr. Monterey Park (Calif.) Bruggemeyer Meml. Libr., 1995—. Mem. Leadership Merced, 1987-88, East Site Based Coordinating Coun., Merced, 1990-92, Merced Gen. Plan Citizens Adv. Com., 1992-95, Sister City Com., Merced, 1992-95. Recipient Libr. award Eagles Aux., 1984, Woman of Achievement award Commn. on the Status of Women, 1990, Libr. award Calif. Libr. Trustees and Commrs., 1990, Woman of Yr. award Merced Bus. and Profl. Women, 1990, People Who Make a Difference award Monterey Pk. United Dems., 2003, Woman of Yr. award 29th Congl. Dist., 2004. Mem. ALA (sec. pub. libr. sys. sect. 1988-89), Met. Coop. Library Sys. (pres. 1999-2000), Calif. Libr. Assn. (sec. govt. rels. com. 1991-92, continuing edn. com. 1993-96, pub. rels. 1997-2000, nominations com. 2000-01), Minn. Libr. Assn. (pres. pub. libr. divsn. 1985), Merced County Mgmt. Coun. (pres. 1989), Merced Bus. and Profl. Women (Woman of Yr. 1987, pres. 1988-89), East L.A.-Montebello Bus. and Profl. Women (v.p. 1998-2002, pres. 2002-), Rotary (pres. Monterey Park chpt. 1999-2000). Democrat. Lutheran. Avocations: travel, walking, reading, swimming, stamp collecting. Home: 1000 E Newmark Ave Apt 22 Monterey Park CA 91755-3129 Office Phone: 626-307-1418. Business E-Mail: lwilson@montereypark.ca.gov. E-mail: lindalwilson@juno.com.

WILSON, LINDA B. education specialist, medical association administrator; b. Kingston, Pa., Apr. 15, 1962. MSN in Critical Care and Trauma, Thomas Jefferson U., 1985. RN, Pa., N.J.; cert. ambulatory perianesthesia nurse, post anesthesia nurse, nursing continuing and staff devel. Resident N.J./Bermuda Perianesthesia [illegible] Thomas Jefferson U. Hosp., Phila., 1998—, ASPAN, 1999—. Cert. post anesthesia nurse, ambulatory perianesthesia nurse, nursing continuing edn. and staff devel. Mem. Am. Soc. Perianesthesia Nurses (co-chair nat. conf. 1998). Home: Po Box 1969 Philadelphia PA 19105-1969

WILSON, LINDA LEE, finance company executive; b. Lakewood, Ohio, Nov. 9, 1943; d. Jon E. and Virginia L. (Weaver) Brown; m. Curtis Wilson, July 30, 1983 (div. 1991); children: Catherine, Laura. BA in English, UCLA, 1970. Lic. ins. agt. Pres. Americorp Fin. Group, Inc., Bellevue, Wash., 1984—. Co-founder panel discussion Women in Transition. Mem. AAUW (bd. dirs.), Internat. Assn. Fin. Planners (bd. dirs. Wash. chpt.), Soroptimist Internat., Toastmasters Internat. Avocation: equestrian.

WILSON, LINDA SMITH, academic administrator; b. Washington, Nov. 10, 1936; d. Fred M. and Virginia D. (Thompson) Smith; m. Malcolm C. Whatley, June 29, 1957 (div. 1969); 1 child, Helen K. Whatley ; m. Paul A. Wilson, Jan. 22, 1970; 1 stepchild, Beth A. BA, Tulane U., 1957, HLD (hon.), 1993; PhD, U. Wis., 1962; DLitt (hon.), U. Md., 1993. Rsch. assoc. U. Md., College Park, 1962—64, rsch. asst. prof., 1964—67; vis. asst. prof. U. Mo., St. Louis, 1967—68; asst. to vice chancellor for rsch., asst. vice chancellor for rsch., assoc. vice chancellor for rsch. Washington U., St. Louis, 1968—75; assoc. vice chancellor for rsch. U. Ill., Urbana, 1975—85; assoc. dean U. Ill. Grad. Coll., Urbana, 1978—85; v.p. for rsch. U. Mich., Ann Arbor, 1985—89; pres. Radcliffe Coll., Cambridge, Mass., 1989—99, pres. emeritus, 1999; sr. lectr. Harvard Grad. Sch. Edn., 1989—2003; bd. dirs. Myriad Genetics, Tulane U., Tulane Murphy Found., Friends of DaPonte String Quartet, 2003—. Rsch. resources adv. coun. NIH, Bethesda, Mass., 1978—82; mem. Nat. Commn. on Rsch., Washington, 1978—80; dir.'s adv. coun. NSF, Washington, 1980—89; com. on govt.-univ. relationships NAS, 1981—83, govt.-univ.-industry rsch. roundtable, 1984—89, coord. coun. for edn., 1991—93; energy rsch. adv. bd. Dept. of Energy, 1987—90; chmn. adv. com. office sci. and engring. pers. NRC, 1990—96; adv. com. edn. and human resources NSF, Washington, 1990—95; sci., tech. and states task force Carnegie Commn. on Sci., Tech. and Govt., 1991—92; overser Mus. Sci., Boston, 1992—2001; trustee Mass. Gen. Hosp., 1992—99, hon. trustee, 1999—2002; trustee Com. on Econ. Devel., 1995—; bd. dirs. Inacom, Inc., 1997—2003, Citizens Fin. Group, Inc., 1997—2000, Value Line, Inc., 1998—2000; bd. vis. Coll. Letters and Sci. U. Wis., 1999—; dean's adv. coun. Newcomb Coll., 1999—. Contbr. articles to profl. jours. and book chpts. Adv. bd. Nat. Coalition for Sci. and Tech., Washington, 1983—87; bd. govs. YMCA, Champaign, Ill., 1980—83. Named One of 100 Emerging Leaders, Am. Coun. Edn. and Change, 1978; recipient Centennial award, Newcomb Coll., 1986, Disting. Alumni award, U. Wis., 1997, Radcliffe medal, 1999. Fellow: AAAS (bd. dirs. 1984—88); mem.: Am. Coun. Edn. (commn. on women in higher edn. 1991—93, chair 1993), Inst. Medicine (coun. mem. 1986—89, com. on setting NIH priorities, com. on govt.-industry collaboration in biomed. edn. and rsch.), Assn. for Biomed. Rsch. (bd. dirs. 1983—86), Nat. Coun. Univ. Rsch. Adminstrs., Soc. Rsch. Adminstrs. (Disting. Contbn. to Rsch. Adminstrn. award 1984), Am. Chem. Soc. (bd. coun. com. on chemistry and pub. affairs 1978—80), Phi Kappa Phi, Phi Delta Kappa, Alpha Lambda Delta, Sigma Xi, Phi Beta Kappa. Home: 47 Keene Neck Rd Bremen ME 04551

WILSON, LOIS M. minister; b. Winnipeg, Man., Can., Apr. 8, 1927; d. Edwin Gardiner Dunn and Ada Minnie (Davis) Freeman; m. Roy F. Wilson, June 9, 1950; children: Ruth, Jean, Neil, Bruce BA, United Coll., Winnipeg, 1947, BDiv, 1969; Diploma in TV prodn., Ryerson Tech. Inst., 1974; DDiv (hon.), Victoria U., Toronto, 1978, United Theol. Coll., Montreal, 1978, Wycliff Coll., 1983, Queens U., Kingston, 1984, U. Winnipeg, 1986, Mt. Allison U., 1988; LLD (hon.), LLD (hon.), Dalhousie U., 1989, Ripon Coll., Wis., 1992; DCL (hon.), Acadia U., 1984; DHuml (hon.), Mt. St. Vincent, Halifax, 1984. Ordained to ministry United Church of Can., 1965. Minister, Thunder Bay, 1965-69, Hamilton, 1969-78, Kingston, 1978-80; moderator United Church of Can., Kingston, 1980-82, McGeachy sr. scholar, 1989-91; pres. Can. Council of Chs., Toronto, Ont., 1976-79; co-dir. Ecumenical Forum Can., Toronto, Ont., 1983-89; pres. World Council of Chs., Geneva, 1983-91; chancellor Lakehead U., Thurder Bay, Ont., 1990-2000; chmn. contemporary theology Lafayette-Orinda (Calif.) Presbyn. Ch., 1995; ind. senator Senate of Can., 1998—2002. Mem. adv. coun. internt. devel. studies U. Toronto, 1987-93, Fair Oto Can., Across Boundries Multifaith Inst., Mining Watch Can.; spokesperson Project Ploughshares, 1st and 2d UN Conf. on Disarmament, N.Y.C., 1978-82; officer Human Rights Commn., Ont., 1973; mem. bd. regents Victoria U., 1990—; chief Can. Fact finding Mission to Sri Lanka, 1992; team mem. Ctrl. Am. Monitoring Group to El Salvador and Guatemala, 1993; spl. envoy of Can. to The Sudan, 1999—; lectr. in field. Author: Like a Mighty River, 1980, Turning the World Upside Down, 1989, Miriam, Mary and Me, 1992, Telling Her Story, 1992, Stories Seldom Told, 1997, Nuclear Waste, 2000; mem. adv. bd.: Can. Woman Studies Jour., York U., 1993—; contbr. articles to profl. publs. Apptd. Can. Senator, 1998; pres. Social Planning Coun., Thunder Bay, 1967—68, Can. Com. for Scientists and Scholars, Toronto, 1982; mem. Refugee Status Adv. Com., 1985—89; chmn. Urban Rural Mission, Can., 1990—96; mem. environ. assessment panel Can. Nuclear Fuel Waste Mgmt. and Disposal Concept, 1989—96; bd. dirs. Elizabeth Fry Soc., Hamilton, 1976—79, Amnesty Internat., 1978—90, Can. Inst. for Internat. Peace and Security, 1984—88, Energy Probe, 1981—86, Internat. Ctr. Human Rights and Dem. Devel., 1997—98, Can. Univ. Svc. Overseas, 1983—85; trustee Nelson Mandela Fund, 1990—92. Decorated Order of Can., Order of Ont., Companion of Order of Can.; recipient Queens Jubilee medal, Commemorative medal for 125th Anniversary of Confederation of Can., 1992, World Federalist Peace award, 1985, Pearson Peace medal UN Assn. of Can., 1985; named hon. pres. Student Christian Movement of Can., Toronto, 1976. Mem. DPR Korea Assoc., Canada (chmn. 2002-), Women, Peace and Security (co-chair 2001-), CAW (pub. rev. bd. 1986—), Can. Assn. Adult Edn. (bd. dirs. 1986-90), Friends Can. Broadcasting (bd. dirs. 1986—, v.p.), Civil Liberties Assn. (v.p. 1986—), UNIFEM (nat. v.p. 1993-95, mem. CCIC team to monitor El Salvador election 1994), World Federalists (pres. Can. chpt. 1996-2000, v.p. World Federalist Movement 1998—), Parliament of World's Religions (del. 1993), Christian-Jewish Dialogue Jerusalem (keynote speaker 1994). Mem. United Ch. Of Can.

WILSON, MABLE JEAN, paralegal; b. Pine Bluff, Ark. d. James Arthur and Ruthia Mae (Dansby) Watson; children: Dana Eileen, Dana Kent, Carlos Alexander Fuller. BS, cert. in paralegal studies, U. So. Calif., 1982-86. Dep. sheriff L.A. County, 1971-80; ind. paralegal Wilson's Divorce Clinic, L.A., 1980—. Participant Dist. Atty. Victim Witness Program, L.A., 1991; active Brotherhood Crusade, L.A., 1992; mem. adv. bd. West L.A. Coll.-Paralegal Studies. Recipient Merit award L.A. County Bar Assn., 1993, Merit cert. City of L.A., County of L.A., Calif. Senate, U.S. Congress, Gov. State of Calif. Mem. Assn. Family and Conciliation Cts., Folk Power Inc. (bd. dirs. 1993—), Alpha Svc. Co. (v.p. 1993—, profl. women's adv. bd., Women's Inner Circle of Achievement), adv. bd on Paralegal Studies, W. L.A. Coll. Avocations: interior decorating, making stained glass windows, ceramics, painting, writing poetry. Office: 3860 Crenshaw Blvd Ste 201 Los Angeles CA 90008-1816

WILSON, MAGGIE ISABELLE LOVELL, art educator, English educator; b. Branchville, Ala., Jan. 26; d. Winston Porter and Ruth Kate (Buckner) Lovell. AB, Samford U., Birmingham, Ala., 1971; MA, EdS, U. Ala., 1978; MFA, Loyola U., 1979; PhD, Sussex (Eng.) U., 1981. Cert. elem./secondary tchr. Tchr. English Birmingham Pub. Schs., 1972-92; tchr. English secondary edn. Terrell County Schs., Dawson, Ga., 1992-93. Author, illustrator: Carousel of Creative Communication, 1976, Leeds, Her Story, 1979; author: Creative Expressions, 1980, Into Our Third [illegible] 1984, From Brush Arbor Days to the Twentieth Century, 1992. Historian Leeds (Ala.) First United Meth. Ch., 1990-99; docent Birmingham Mus. Art, 1970-80. Recipient numerous awards Ala. Watercolor Soc., Birmingham, 1970—, Pres. award Kappa Pi, Samford U., Birmingham, 1971, Art of Distinction Salon Des Nations, Paris, 1984. Mem. AAUW, Internat. Biog. Assn., Ala. Coun. Tchrs. English (bd. mem. 1976—), Leeds Art Coun., Leeds Hist. Soc., Birmingham Art Assn., Internat. Soc. Artists, Leeds Bus. and Profl. Women (pres. 1971-76, 86, 88—, Woman of Yr. 1996-97), Leeds United Meth. Women (pres. 1972-76, 84—), La. Watercolor Soc. (awards 1986-99), So. Watercolor Soc., Kappa Delta Epsilon, Phi Gamma Mu. Home: 610 Montevallo Rd SW Leeds AL 35094-1926

WILSON, MARCIA SANDMEYER, artist; b. Rochester, Ny, Feb. 6, 1937; d. Earl Cranston and Katharine Margaret (Hubler) Sandmeyer; children: Diana Slote, Thomas, Rebecca. AB, Vassar, Poughkeepsie, N.Y., 1958. Exhibitions include painting, woodcarving, etching, collage Woodcarvings, 1982 (fellowship woodcarving, N.J. State Coun. Arts, 1982), exhibitions include two person exhibit Stories and Dreams, Noyes Mus., 2002. Home: 259 Leonia Ave Leonia NJ 07605 E-mail: marciawilson@earthlink.net.

WILSON, MARGARET BUSH, lawyer; b. St. Louis, Jan. 30, 1919; married; 1 child, Robert Edmund. BA cum laude, Talladega Coll., 1940; LL.B., Lincoln U., 1943. Ptnr. Wilson & Wilson, St. Louis, 1947-65; now with firm Wilson & Assocs. Asst. dir. St. Louis Lawyers for Housing, 1969-72; asst. atty. gen. Mo., 1961-62; atty. Rural Electrification Adminstrn., Dept. Agr., St. Louis, 1943-45; instr. civil procedure St. Louis U. Sch. Law, 1971; chmn. St. Louis Land Reutilization Authority, 1975-76; mem. Mo. Coun. Criminal Justice, 1972—; chmn. Intergroup Corp., 1985-87; bd. dirs. Mut. of N.Y. Mem. gen. adv. com. ACDA, 1978-81; trustee emeritus Washington U., St. Louis; chmn. bd. trustees Talladega Coll., Ala., 1988-92; nat. bd. dirs. ARC, 1975-81, United Way, 1978-84, Police Found., 1976-93; treas. NAACP Nat. Housing Corp., 1971-84, chmn. nat. bd., 1975-84; dep. dir./acting dir. St. Louis Model City Agy., 1968-69; adminstr. Mo. Commn. Svc. and Continuing Edn., 1967-68. Recipient Bishop's award Episcopal Diocese Mo., 1962; Juliette Derricotte fellow, 1939-40, Disting. Lawyer award Bar Assn. Metro St. Louis, 1997. Mem. ABA (chmn. youth edn. for citizenship 1991-94, chmn. Nat. Law Day 1998-2000), Nat. Bar Assn., Mo. Bar Assn., Mound City Bar Assn., St. Louis Bar Assn., Alpha Kappa Alpha. Office: Wilson & Assocs 4054 Lindell Blvd Saint Louis MO 63108-3202

WILSON, MARGARET SULLIVAN, retired executive dean, consultant; b. Norwich, Conn., Mar. 21, 1924; d. John Joseph and Margaret Ellen (Connelly) Sullivan; BS, Eastern Conn. State U., 1944; MA, U. Conn., 1949; m. William Robert Wilson, July 20, 1950 (dec.); children: Margaret Ellen, William Robert. Reading cons. Greenwich (Conn.) Pub. Schs., 1948-50; asst. prof. early childhood, chmn. dept. early childhood Eastern Conn. State U., Willimantic, 1967-77, exec. asst. to pres., 1977-78, v.p. adminstrv. affairs, 1978-80, exec. dean, 1980-89, emeritus dean, 1989—; commr. Nat. Commn. Prevention Infant Mortality, 1986-93, chair Norwich Econ. Devel. Commn., 1988-91, Southeastern Connecticut regional Planning Comm., 1999-2001(mem. 1993—); dir. Rose City Community Land Trust Housing, Com. on City Plan, 1992—; del. White House Conf. on Children, 1970, 80, White House Conf. on Travel and Tourism, 1995; corporator Chelsea Groton Savs. Bank, Norwich, Conn. Mem. Conn. Mental Health Bd., 1979-83; mem. adv. bd. Norwich Hosp.; chmn. rev. com. Conn. Health Coordinating Council; mem. Eastern Regional Mental Health Bd., 1976-83, chmn., 1979-81; mem. Norwich Bd. Edn., 1954-69, 80-83, adv. coun. head start and day care programs, 1986-91; mem. Conn. Dem. Cen. Com., 1966-82, Dem. Town Com., 1964-82, 86-90; chmn. Blue Ribbon Commn. To Establish Goals for U. Conn. Health Ctr., 1975-76; sr. warden Ch. of Resurrection, Norwich., 1988-91, Dio Com on Ministry Higher Edn. Named Citizen of Yr., C. of C., 1970; recipient Disting. Alumni award Eastern Conn. State U., 1972, Mental Health Bell award Conn. Mental Health Assn., 1972, Valiant Women award Council Ch. Women, 1976, Woman of Yr. award Bus. and Profl. Women, 1978, Jefferson award Inst. Pub. Service, 1982, pres. Norwich Mus. Trust, Inc., 1992—; mem., vice chair Southeastern Conn. Regional Planning Commn., 1993—; dir. Family Svc. Southeastern Conn., 1995—, Southeastern Conn. Enterprise Region, Norwich Comm. and Tech. Learning Ctr.; past-pres. Eastern Conn. Cmty. Found.; del. White House Conf. on Aging, 1995. Mem. Norwich Area C. of C. (dir. 1979-81), Greater Willimantic C. of C. (edn. com. 1980-88), United Ch. Women Conn. (bd. dirs.). Democrat. Office: 83 Windham St Willimantic CT 06226-2211 Home: Apt 65 206 Washington St Norwich CT 06360-3553

WILSON, MARIE C. foundation administrator; b. Ga. 5 children. D in Cmty. Svc.(hon.), Drake U. Dir. women's programs Drake U.; mem. DesMoines City Coun.; pres. Ms. Found. for Women, N.Y.C., 1984—. Co-creator Take Our Daus. To Work Day, 1993—; U.S. govt. del. UN Fourth World Conf. on Women, Beijing, 1995; co-founder, pres. The White House Project, 1998—. Co-author: Mother Daughter Revolution, 1993; author: Closing the Leadership Gap: Why Women Can and Must Help Run the World, 2004. Recipient Robert W. Scrivner award for creative grantmaking, Leadership for Equity and Diversity award, Women & Philanthropy. Office: Ms Found for Women 120 Wall St 33rd fl New York NY 10005*

WILSON, MARY ALICE, violinist, music teacher; b. Nov. 2, 1939; MusB, Northwestern U., 1961. Orch. band dir., pvt. tchr. Luth. Schs., Deerfield Pub. Schs., 1961-64; pvt. tchr. violin and piano Cleve., 1964-77; dir. Suzuki Program, violin tchr. W.Va. U., 1977—; founder, leader Seneca String Quartet, Morgantown, W.Va., 1986—. Accompanist. Ch. vol. Tchg. and Music, Cleve., Chgo., Morgantown, 1960—. Mem.: Am. String Tchrs. Assn. (co-developer, chmn. 5th yr. state solo competition), W.Va. Music Tchrs. Assn. (dist. chmn. of strings 1977—, state officer pub. 1989—, State Outstanding Tchr. Yr. 1996), Music Tchrs. Nat. Assn. (state office of composition contest 1989—). Home: 237 Poplar Dr Morgantown WV 26505-2519 E-mail: cbwilson@mail.wvu.edu.

WILSON, MARY CHRISTINA, history educator; b. Lakewood, Ohio, Aug. 15, 1950; d. William Draughn and Norma (Nelson) W.; m. Philip S. Khoury, Aug. 28, 1980. Student, Am. U. Beirut, Lebanon, 1970-71; AB, Oberlin Coll., 1972; PhD, Oxford U., 1983. Instr. history Wellesley (Mass.) Coll., 1982-83; vis. asst. prof. history NYU, N.Y.C., 1984-88; asst. prof. history U. Mass., Amherst, 1988-91, assoc. prof. history, 1991-96, prof. history, 1996—, dir. Middle Eastern Studies Program, 1992-96, dir. grad. program dept. history, 1993-96, chmn. dept. history, 1997—2000. Cons. MacArthur Found., Chgo., NEH, Washington, Social Sci. Rsch. Coun., N.Y.C.; trustee Am. Ctr. Oriental Rsch., 2000—. Author: King Abdullah, Britain and the Making of Jordan, 1987; co-editor: The Modern Middle East, 1993, 2d edit., 2003. Alumni fellow Oberlin Coll., 1982-83; Social Sci. Rsch. Coun. fellow, N.Y.C., 1984-85; fellow Bunting Inst., Radcliffe Coll., Cambridge, 1988-89, NEH, Washington, 1988-89, Inst. for Advanced Study of Humanities, U. Mass., Amherst, 1990. Mem. Am. Hist. Assn., Brit. Soc. for Middle Ea. Studies, Middle East Studies Assn. (nominating com. 1987, mem. editl. bd. bull. 1987-94, book rev. editor 1987-95, bd. dirs. 1999-2002). Avocations: reading, gardening. Office: History Dept Herter Hall U Mass Amherst MA 01003

WILSON, MARY ELIZABETH, epidemiologist, educator; b. Indpls., Nov. 19, 1942; d. Ralph Richard and Catheryn Rebecca (Kurtz) Lausch; m. Harvey Vernon Fineberg, May 16, 1975. AB, Ind. U., 1963; MD, U. Wis., 1971. Diplomate Am. Bd. Internal Medicine, Am. Bd. Infectious Diseases. Tchr. of French and English Marquette Sch., Madison, Wis., 1963-66; intern in medicine Beth Israel Hosp., Boston, 1971-72, resident in medicine, 1972-73, fellow in infectious diseases, [illegible] weitzer Hosp., Deschapelles, Haiti, 1974-75, Harvard Health Svcs., Cambridge, Mass., 1974-75; asst. physician Cambridge Hosp., 1975-78; hosp. epidemiologist Mt. Auburn Hosp., Cambridge, 1975-79, chief of infectious diseases, 1978—2002, dir. Travel Resource Ctr., 1996—2002. Adv. com. immunization practices CDC, Atlanta, 1988-92; acad. adv. com. Nat. Inst. Pub. Health, Mex., 1989-91; cons. Ford Found., 1988; site dir. GeoSentinel network, 1999-2002, spl. cons., 2002--; instr. in medicine Harvard Med. Sch., Boston, 1975-93, asst. clin. prof., 1994-99, assoc. prof. medicine, 1999—, assoc. Ctr. Health & Global Environ., 1996-2000; asst. prof. depts. epidemiology and population and internat. health Harvard Sch. Pub. Health, 1994-99, assoc. prof. population and internat. health, 1999—; lectr. Sultan Qaboos U., Oman, 1991; chair Woods Hole Workshop, Emerging Infectious Diseases, 1993. Author: A World Guide to Infections: Diseases, Distribution, Diagnosis, 1991; co-editor: (with Richard Levins and Andrew Spielman) Disease in Evolution: Global Changes and Emergence of Infectious Diseases, 1994; mem. editl. bd. Current Issues in Pub. Health, Emerging Infectious Diseases, Global Change and Human Health; sect. editor, travel medicine and tropical diseases, editl. bd. Infectious Diseases in Clin. Practice; assoc. editor Jour. Watch Infectious Diseases; editl. adv. bd. Clinical Infectious Diseases. Mem. Cambridge Task Force on AIDS, 1987-90, Earthwatch, Watertown, Mass., Cultural Survival, Inc., Cambridge; bd. dirs. Horizon Communications, West Cornwall, Conn., 1990-97. Recipient Lewis E. and Edith Phillips award U. Wis. Med. Sch., 1969, Cora M. and Edward Van Liere award, 1971, Mosby Scholarship Book award, 1971, Leo Blacklow teaching award, 1999; scholar in residence Bellagio (Italy) Study Ctr., Rockefeller Found., 1996; fellow Ctr. for Advanced Study in the Behavioral Scis., Stanford, 2002. Fellow: ACP, Royal Soc. Tropical Medicine and Hygiene, Infectious Diseases Soc. Am.; mem.: Soc. for Epidemiol. Rsch., Internat. Union Against Tuberculosis and Lung Disease, Soc. for Vector Ecology, Wilderness Med. Soc., Internat. Soc. Travel Medicine, Peabody Soc., Mass. Infectious Diseases Soc., Am. Soc. Tropical Medicine and Hygiene, N.Y. Acad. Scis., Am. Soc. Microbiology, Aesculapian Club, Alpha Omega Alpha, Phi Sigma Iota, Sigma Sigma. Avocations: playing the flute, hiking, reading, travel.

WILSON, MARY ELIZABETH, priest; b. Luling, Tex., Nov. 5, 1951; d. Thomas Wilson III and Nell Hall Wilson; m. Paul Morgan Hervey (div. Dec. 27, 1970); children: Stephanie Dee Bamberger, Robert Thomas Hervey. BBA, Univ. Tex., Austin, Tex., 1990; MDiv, Protestant Episcopal Theol. Seminary, Alexandria, Va., 1994—97. Advt. clk. Martha White Foods, 1978—80; asst. office mgr. Hematronix, 1982—84; telebanking assoc. Bank One, 1992; exec. asst. to v.p. of regulatory affairs EduCare, Austin, Tex., 1992—95; asst. priest, deacon Christ Episcopal Ch., Tyler, Tex., 1997—2000; rector St. John's Episcopal Ch., Silsbee, Tex., 2000—. Dean S.E. Convocation, Tex., 2003—04. Recipient Vera Gang Scott Scholarship. Mem.: Diocese Mission Funding (mem. 2003), Bishop Coadjutor Election Task Force (mem. 2002), Walkabout for Bishop Suffrogan Election (leader 2003), Exec. Bd. Diocese of Tex. & Fin. Com. (mem. 2001—03), Ubi Caritas Bd. Dir., Task Force Bishop Suffragan Election (mem. 2003), Ecclesiastical Trial Court (mem. 2003), Task Force Com. for Diocesan Representation to Council (mem. 2003), Crime Com. Victims Ctr. (mem. 2002—03), Kiwanis (mem. 2002—03), Nat. Hon. Fraternity, Phi Theta Kappa. Episc. Avocations: exercise, appreciation, reading, cooking, hiking. Home: 103 Magnolia Lane Silsbee TX 77656 Office: St Johns Episcopal Church 1305 Roosevelt Drive Silsbee TX 77656 E-mail: StJohn.Silsbee@aol.com.

WILSON, MARY ELLEN, retired project administrator; b. L.A., Aug. 7, 1927; d. Nels Efraim and Ellen (Matson) Lovemark; m. Richard Spencer Dyer, Mar. 6, 1952 (dec. July 1960); children: Robert Alan, Terry Ann; m. Edward LeRoy Wilson, Jan. 21, 1961 (dec. Jan. 1992); 1 child, Pamela Susan; stepchildren: Scott Stanton, Jefferey Kevin Wilson. Expediter C F Braun & Co., Alhambra, Calif., 1947-53; project expediter The Ralph M. Parsons Co., Pasadena, Calif., 1977-79, project coord., 1979-83, project adminstr., 1984-89. Docent Scott Gallery, Huntington Libr., Pasadena, 1992—, Huntington Gallery; publicity profl. Pasadena Rep. Women's Club, 1960s; pres. Pasadena Charity for Calif. Pediat. Ctr., L.A., 1955-60; First Lady, Pasadena Tournament of Roses, 1973-74; mem. L.A. World Affairs Coun., 1997—. Mem. Annandale Golf Club. Republican. Avocations: golf, tennis, bridge, traveling. Home: 727 S Orange Grove Blvd Apt 5 Pasadena CA 91105-1726

WILSON, MARY FLYNN, writer, educator; b. Bklyn., Nov. 15, 1938; d. Edwin Anthony and Ann Rita (Eckart) Flynn; children: Mary Kate, Colin, Daniel. BA in English Lit. magna cum laude, Merrimack Coll., 1960. Cert. initial educator, Conn.; cert. minister. Edit. asst. [illegible] 1960-61; journalist Reporter-Dispatch, White Plains, N.Y., 1961-67; adminstrv. asst. Immaculate Conception Parish, New Hartford, Conn., 1981-86; exec. sec. to CEO Petroleum Meter & Pump, Avon, Conn., 1986-87; copy editor The Hartford (Conn.) Courant, 1987-96; adj. faculty N.W. Conn. C.C., Winsted, 1994—. Admissions rep. Merrimack Coll., North Andover, Mass., 1960-68, fund-raiser, 1990—. Author: Trinita at 75, 1999, (newspaper series) Reporter Dispatch, 1963; editor: Producing Patient-Centered Health Care, 1999, Hoist Your Sails...Attaining Life and Job Happiness, 1999. Campaign mgr. Dem. Party, New Hartford, 1970, 72; town co-chair United Way, Barkhamsted, Conn., 1974-75; group leader 4-H, Barkhamsted, 1978-82; lay min. Immaculate Conception Parish, New Hartford, Conn., 1978-88; vol. musician Valerie Manor Health Care, Torrington, Conn., 1995—; adv. bd. mem. Trinita Retreat Ctr., New Hartford, 1998—. Recipient Commendation, Sigma Delta Chi-N.Y. state chpt., 1963, Cmty. Svc. award N.Y. State Pubs. Assn., 1963, commendation Conn. Bd. Higher Edn., 1995. Mem. Congress Conn. C.C., Fedn. Christian Ministries, Merrimack Coll. Alumni Coun., Cancer Survivors Group. Roman Catholic. Avocations: water sports, art, handwork, opera, carpentry. Home: 26 Center Hill Rd Pleasant Valley CT 06063-4100 Office: NW Conn Cmty Tech Coll Park Pl East Winsted CT 06063 E-mail: MaryflynnWilson@yahoo.com.

WILSON, MELANIE D, rancher; d. Jerry David and Bonnie June Wilson. A of occupl. studies in electronic engring., ITT Tech. Inst., 1991—93. Electronic technician Tex. Instruments, Richardson, Tex., 1992—93; test technician CPC Vending - Rowe Internat., Rockwall, Tex., 1993—94; billing mgr. A-1 Nursing, Inc., Terrell and Dallas, Tex., 1994—95; acctg. Pascal Enterprises, Inc., Dallas, 1995—99; safety mgr./trainer Sun Gro Horticulture, Inc., Terrell, 1999—2002; v.p. ops. Jerry Wilson Trucking, L.L.C., Terrell, 2002—. Consulting Jerry Wilson Trucking, L.L.C., Terrell, 2002—, Sun Gro Horticulture, Inc., Terrell, 1999—2002. Avocations: travel, ranching, farming, gardening, movies. Home: 15358 County Rd 355 Terrell TX 75161 Office: Jerry Wilson Trucking LLC 1132 South Hwy 34 Terrell TX 75160 Personal E-mail: onrybrat@aol.com. E-mail: little_wheel@sbcglobal.net.

WILSON, MICHELINE, small business owner; b. Villotte-Sur-Aire, Meuse, France, Dec. 7, 1945; came to U.S., 1967; d. Jean Roger Clausse and Mauricette Marie Bohin; m. Steven Owen Wilson, June 1, 1976 (div. 1984). Bachelor's, Lycee de Jeunes Filles, Metz, Moselle, France, 1964. Lic. cosmetology. Hairstylist Mr. John's Beauty Salon, Augusta, Ga., 1968-70, Laurens, S.C., 1970-72; hairstylist, owner Micheline Hair Salon, Lakeland, Fla., 1973—. One-woman show Burdines, 1996. Recipient awards Lakeland Art Guild, 1990, 92, 95, Ridge Art Assn., Winterhaven, Fla., 1994, Fla. Strawberry Festival, Plant City, 1993, Chgo. Cosmetologists, 2000, Small Bus. award Lakeland Area C. of C., 2001; named one of Top 200 Fastest Growing Salons in the Nation Three Yrs. in a Row, Best Philanthropic Program for Salons of Its Size in the Nation; nominated Global Salon Bus. award Salon Today Mag., 2003. Mem. The Salon Assn., Nat. Assn. Women Bus. Owners. Avocations: painting, world beat music, yoga, dance, nutrition. Office: Micheline Salonspa 5035 S Lakeland Dr Lakeland FL 33813-2558

WILSON, MILLIE L. artist, educator; b. Hot Springs, Ark., Nov. 26, 1948; d. Wilson Barto and Betty Jane Bearden. Cert., Yale Summer Sch. Music and Art, 1970; BFA, U. Tex., Austin, 1971; MFA, U. Houston, 1983. NFA, BFA. Sr. faculty art Calif. Inst. of Arts, Valencia, 1985—2003; resident artist Sch. of the Art Inst. of Chgo., 1998; panelist, artist Nat. Photographers Gallery, London, 1994, Molteplici Culture, Rome, 1994; spkr., artist Seattle Art Mus., 1994; resident artist Calif. Coll. of Arts and Crafts, Oakland, 1995—96, San Francisco State U., 1996; lectr. visual art U. Rochester, 1997. Mem. adv. bd. Silver Lake Film Festival, L.A., 2000; dir. program in art Calif. Inst. of Arts, Valencia, 1988—93. Exhibitions include Matthew Marks Gallery, N.Y.C., 1998, Ruth Bloom Gallery, Santa Monica, Calif., 1995, Serralvej Found., Oporto, Portugal, 1995. Active in feminist and progressive orgns., L.A., 1975—2003. Recipient Calif. Cultural Affairs grant, City of L.A., 1998; fellow, NEA, 1993; grantee, Pollock-Krasner Found., 1996. Mem.: Coll. Art Assn. Democrat. Avocations: investigation, research, reading, flea markets, writing. Office: Calif Inst of Arts 24700 Valencia CA 91355 E-mail: milwilson@earthlink.net.

WILSON, MIRIAM GEISENDORFER, retired physician, educator; b. Yakima, Wash., Dec. 3, 1922; d. Emil and Frances Geisendorfer; m. Howard G. Wilson, June 21, 1947; children— Claire, Paula, Geoffrey, Nicola, Marla. BS, U. Wash., Seattle, 1944, MS, 1945; MD, U. Calif., San Francisco, 1950. Mem. faculty U. So. Calif. Sch. Medicine, L.A., 1965—, prof. pediatrics, 1969—. Office: U So Calif Med Ctr 1129 N State St Rm 1g24 Los Angeles CA 90033-1044

WILSON, NANCY JEANNE, laboratory consultant, medical technologist; b. Neptune, N.J., Apr. 17, 1951; d. Harry E. Sr. and Kathryn E. (O'Shea) W. BS, Monmouth Coll., 1975; MPA, Fairleigh Dickinson U., 1988. Clin. intern med. tech., staff med. technologist Riverview Med. Ctr., 1975; staff med. technologist Rush Clin. Labs., Red Bank, NJ, 1976, Kimball Med. Ctr., Lakewood, NJ, 1977—78, clin. lab. supr., 1978—86; infection control practice Jersey Shore Med. Ctr., Neptune, N.J., 1990; dir. lab. and diagnostic svcs. Carrier Clinic, Belle Mead, NJ, 1990—2002, lab. and infection control cons., 2002—. Mem. Am. Soc. Clin. Pathologists (diplomate lab. mgmt.), Am. Assn. Clin. Chemistry, Am. Soc. Microbiology, Clin. Lab. Mgmt. Assn., Am. Soc. Clinics Lab. Sci., Pi Alpha Alpha. Avocations: golf, walking, relaxing. Home: 42 Monument St Freehold NJ 07728-1721

WILSON, NANCY LAFARRA, elementary school educator, art educator, artist; b. Dermott, Ark., July 18, 1958; d. William Earl and Verle Methvin LaFarra; m. Stephen Anthony Wilson, Oct. 26, 1979 (div. Apr. 1997); children: Jonathan, Adrienne. BA in Art, U. Ark., Monticello, 1980. Cert. in K-12 art, secondary biology, mid. sch. sci., 1-6 elem. edn. U. Ark. Activities dir. Sr. Citizen Ctr., McGehee, Ark., 1980—82; sci. and art tchr. Delta H.S., Rohwer, Ark., 1984—86; kindergarten tchr. Delta Elem. Sch., Rohwer, 1987—88, 1st grade tchr., 1988—93; K-6th elem. art tchr. McGehee Elem. Sch., 1993—. Panelist The Praxis Series: Profl. Assessments for Beginning Tchrs., 1995; mem. Barrett Hamilton Adv. Com., 1995. Exhibitions include Grand Prairie Festival of Arts, Stuttgart, Ark., 1976—2003, Ark. Artists Registry Gallery, Little Rock, 2000, Fort Smith Art Ctr., 2000, 2002—03, Arts and Sci. Ctr., Pine Bluff, 2001, Senator Blanche Lincoln's office, Washington, 2003—, Kans. City Artists Coalition, Kans. City, 2003, numerous others. Mem.: Monticello Art League, Ark. Art Educators Assn. (regional dir. S.E. 2002—04, Elem. Art Tchr. of the Yr. 1997), Nat. Art Educators Assn. Baptist. Avocations: painting, camping, photography. Home: 7 Mangum St Mc Gehee AR 71654 Office: McGehee Elem Sch 409 Oak St Mc Gehee AR 71654

WILSON, NANCY LINDA, religious organization administrator; b. Mineola, N.Y., July 13, 1950; Grad., Allegheny Coll.; student, Boston U.; MDiv, SS, Cyril and Methodius Sem. Ordained to ministry Universal Fellowship of Met. Cmty. Chs. Dist. coord. N.E. dist. Universal Fellowship of Met. Cmty. Chs., clk. bd. of elders Fellowship hdqrs., 1979-86, sr. pastor Met. Comty. Ch., 1986—; vice-moderator UFMCC, L.A., 1993—. Bd. trustees Samaritan Inst. Religious Studies; founder, chief ecumenical officer Ecumenical Witness and Ministry; vice chair Progressive Religious Alliance. Author: Our Tribe: Queer Folks, God, Jesus and the Bible, 1995; co-author: Amazing Grace; prodr.: (brochure) Our Story Too. Rockefeller scholar. Office: Met Cmty Ch 8714 Santa Monica Blvd West Hollywood CA 90069-4000

WILSON, PAMELA, microbiologist, educator; b. Crockett, Tex., Nov. 25, 1948; d. Francis Corley Wilson and Gladys DeZelle; m. Robert Dale Alexander, Apr. 6, 1976 (div. Aug. 1987); children: Matthew Robert Alexander, Shane Gregory Alexander. BA in Microbiology, U. Tex., 1971. Cert. med. tech. Am. Assn. Clin. Pathologists. Adj. faculty Wenatchee (Wash.) Valley Coll., 1984—2003; microbiologist Ctrl. Wash. Hosp., 1987—2000; adj. faculty microbiology and chemistry N. Seattle C.C., 2004—. Pres. Wenatchee Jr. Hosp. Guild, 1994; vol. AIDS patients Multifaith Care Teams, Seattle, 2000—03; docent Burke Mus., Seattle, 2002—03. Mem.: DAR. Home and Office: 4549 18th Ave NE Seattle WA 98105

WILSON, PAMELA AIRD, physician; b. Milw., May 13, 1947; d. Rushen Arnold and Marianna (Dickie) W.; m. Paul Quin, June 20, 1981. BS in Zoology, U. Md., 1969; MS in Physiology, U. Wis., 1971; MD, U. Md., Balt., 1976. Diplomate Am. Bd. Internal Medicine. Asst. prof. U. Wis., Madison, 1984-91, assoc. prof., 1991—. Bd. dirs. Wis. chpt. Am. Lung Assn. past pres. ; exec. com. Wis. Thoracic Soc., past pres.; mem. Gov.'s Coun. on Phys. Disabilities, 1990—. Office: U Wis Hosps & Clinics 600 Highland Ave # H6380 Madison WI 53792-0001

WILSON, PAMELA K. corporate financial executive; BS, U. Ill.; MBA, NYU. With J.P. Morgan, 1980—2000; sr. v.p. WL Ross & Co. LLC, N.Y., 2000—. Office: WL Ross & Co LLC Manhattan Tower 19th Fl 101 East 52nd St New York NY 10022

WILSON, PATRICIA POTTER, library science and reading educator, educational and library consultant; b. Jennings, La., May 3, 1946; d. Ralph Harold and Wilda Ruth (Smith) Potter; m. Wendell Merlin Wilson, Aug. 24, 1968. BS, La. State U., 1967; MS, U. Houston-Clear Lake, 1979; EdD, U. Houston, 1985. Cert. tchr., learning resources specialist (libr.), Tex. Tchr. England AFB (La.) Elem. Sch., 1967-68, Edward White Elem. Sch./Clear Creek Ind. Schs., Seabrook, Tex., 1972-77; libr. C.D. Landolt Elem. Sch., Friendswood, Tex., 1979-81; instr./lectr. children's lit. U. Houston, 1983-86; with U. Houston/Clear Lake, 1984-87, asst. prof. libr. sci. and reading, 1988-94, assoc. prof. learning resources and reading edn., 1994—2001, assoc. prof. emeritus, 2001—, faculty devel. com. chair, 1995-97, mem faculty senate, 1992-93, reading search com. chair, tchg. task force, 1997-98, reading and libr. sci. program chair, 1997-98, mem. Piper award com., 1996—98, U. Faculty award com., 1997, U. learning assessment task force, 1997-98, promotion and tenure com. chair, 1999. Cons. Hermann Hosp., Baywood Hosp., 1986-87, Bedford Meadows Hosp., 1989-90, Wetcher Clinic, 1989; co-owner, v.p. Potter Farms, Inc., 1994—. Editor: A Review Sampler, 1985—86, 1989—90; author: Happenings: Developing Successful Programs for School Libraries, 1987, The Professional Collection for Elementary Educators, 1996, Premiere Events: Library Programs That Inspire Elementary Patrons, 2001, Leadership for Today's School Library, 2001, Igniting the Spark: Library Programs that Inspire High School Patrons, 2001, Center Stage: Library Programs That Inspire Middle School Patrons, 2002; contbg. editor: Tex. Libr. Jour., 1988—94; contbr. articles to profl. jours. Trustee Freeman Meml. Libr., Houston, 1982—87, v.p., 1985—86, pres., 1986—87; trustee Evelyn Meador Libr., 1993—94, adv. bd., 1994—; mem. Bay Area Houston Symphony League, Assistance League of the Bay Area, 1997—, Clear Lake Area Panhellic Assn., 2002—, Bay Area Houston Econ. Partnership, 2002—, Banquet Com.; founder Friends of Neumann Libr., 1998; chmn. hospitality com. Lunar Rendevous Festival, 1998—2001; gen. chmn. Lunar Rendezvous Festival, 2002, mem. adv. bd., 2002—; vice chmn. Clear Lake Met. Ballet, 2003—; co-chmn. Kickoff Reception, 2003; mem. adv. bd. Bay Area Soc. Prevention Cruelty Animals, 1994—98, Bay Area Turning Point, 1998—; bd. dirs. Sta. KUHT-TV, 1984—87, Friends of Neumann Libr., 1998—99; vice chair bd. dirs. Bay Area Houston Ballet and Theatre, 2003—; dir. Learning Resources Book Rev. Ctr., 1989—90; bd. dirs. UHCL Alumni Assn., 1988—2001, v.p. adminstrn., 2000, anniversary hon. com., 1999—2000, mem. 25th anniversary com., 1999, alumni ball com., 1999; mem. Armand Bayou Nature Ctr., Houston, 1980, bd. dirs., 1989—94. Named Outstanding Vol. of Yr., Houston's Nat. Philanthropy Day, 1999; named one of 10 Men and Women of Heart, Bay Area Turning Point, 2001; recipient Rsch. award, Tex. State Reading Assn., 1993, Pres. award, Tex. Coun. Tchrs. English, Disting. Tchg. award, Enron Corp., 1996, Disting. Alumni award, U. Houston-Clear Lake, 1998, Disting. Alumna award, U. Houston-Main Campus, Coll. Edn., 2002; grantee, Tex. Libr. Assn., 1993. Mem. ALA, Am. Assn. Sch. Librs., Internat. Reading Assn., Nat. Coun. Tchrs. English (Books for You rev. com. 1985-88, 97-98, Your Reading rev. com. 1993-96), Tex. Coun. Tchrs. English, Antarctican Soc., Alumni Assn. U. Houston-Clear Lake (bd. dirs. 1998-2001, v.p. adminstrn. 2000, anniversary hon. com. 1999-2000, 25th anniversary com. 1999, alumni ball com. 1999), Bay Oaks Country Club, Clear Lake Panhellenic, Phi Delta Kappa, Phi Kappa Phi (sec. 1997-98, pres. 1998-99), Lakewood Yacht Club. Methodist.

WILSON, PATTI L. psychologist, educator; b. Memphis, May 21, 1974; d. Charles W. and Linda Fay Wilson; life ptnr. Dustin T. Gault. BA, Christian Bros. U., 1995; MS, PhD, U. Memphis, 2000. Cert. psychologist, health svc. provider Tenn., Health Related Boards, Bd. of Examiners in Psychology, 2002, apprentice spl. group State Tenn. Dept. Edn., 2001. Assoc. prof. Austin Peay State U., Clarksville, Tenn., 2000—; sch. psychologist Houston County Schs., Erin, Tenn., 2001—. Contbr. articles to profl. jours. Mem.: APA, NASP (nat. cert. sch. psychologist), Tenn. Assn. Sch. Psychologists (bd. mem. 2002—03), Psi Chi, Alpha Chi. Home: 2830 Scenic Dr Clarksville TN 37043 Office: Austin Peay State Univ 601 College Street Box 4537 Clarksville TN 37044 Personal E-mail: wilsonp@apsu.edu. E-mail: wilsonp@apsu.edu.

WILSON, PAULETTE ADASSA, language educator, writer; b. St. Thomas, Jamaica, Dec. 15, 1954; came to U.S., 1986; d. Robert Ashton and Inez Celestine (Grant) W. Diploma, Shortwood Tchrs. Col., Kingston, Jamaica, 1978; BA, U. West Indies, Kingston, Jamaica, 1984; MA, Rutgers U., 1993, PhD, 1996. Tchr. St. Hugh's H.S., Kingston, Jamaica, 1977-78, Morant Bay H.S., St. Thomas, Jamaica, 1978-81, Kingston Coll., Jamaica, 1984-86; lectr. spanish & portuguese dept. Rutgers U., New Brunswick, N.J., 1991-95; visiting prof. langs. dept. Clemson U., Clemson, S.C., 1995-96, asst. prof., 1996—. Advisor Sigma Delta Pi, Clemson (S.C.) U., 1995—, African/Caribbean Students Assn., Clemson U., 1995-96. Mem. MLA, Am. Assn. Tchrs. Spanish & Portuguese. Avocations: travel, basketball, gardening, writing. Office: Clemson U PO Box 341515 Clemson SC 29634-0001 Home: Apt 9C 95 Cedar Ln Florence NJ 08518-2903

WILSON, PEGGY, state representative, registered nurse; b. Anamosa, Iowa, Sept. 18, 1945; m. Woody Wilson; 3 children. A in Registered Nursing, Kirkwood C.C., 1970; cert. in EMT tng., U. Alaska. Past gen. mgr. life ins. co.; past dairy farmer; past state rep. N.C. House of Rep.; state rep. State of Alaska, 2001—. EMT Tok Area Emergency Mgmt. Svc. Mem.: Rotary, Pilot Internat. (past v.p.). Avocations: reading, travel, hunting, boating, shooting. Office: State Capitol Rm 104 Juneau AK 99801-1182

WILSON, REBECCA ANN, retired English and special education educator; b. Balt., Md., Feb. 21, 1945; d. Bertram Bradford and Nancy Ann Wiley; m. David Lloyd Wilson, July 29, 1967; children: Laura Beth, Amy Lynn. BA in Secondary Edn., Shepherd Coll., 1967; postgrad., W.Va. U. Cert. Spl. Edn. Tchr. W.Va., 1968. Tchr. Jefferson County Schs., Charles Town, W.Va., 1967—72, substitute tchr., 1975—79. Vol. Jefferson County Spl. Olympics, Charles Town, W.Va., 1986—97; judge Jefferson County Fair, 1968—; adv. com. Jefferson County Bd. Edn., Charles Town, W.Va., 1990; chmn. W.Va. Adv. Coun. for Edn. Exceptional Children, Charleston, 1986—92; mem. Gov. Sch. Adv. Coun., Charleston, 2001—; mem. bd. edn. Jefferson County, Charles Town, W.Va., 1994—98; mem. bd. dirs. Shepherdstown Day Care Ctr., Regional Edn. Svc. Agy. Mem.: AAUW (life), Internat. Assn. Jazz Edn., Homakers Club, Shepherdstown Women's Club (pres. 2000—), Md. 4-H All Stars (life), Order of Ea. Star. Democrat. Episcopalian. Avocations: travel, attending national conventions, reading, cooking. Home: 103 Prospect Ave PO Box 624 Shepherdstown WV 25443

WILSON, REBECCA JO, dean, education educator; b. Wabash, Ind., July 8, 1949; d. DeVon A. and Marcella Jean Wilson; adopted children: Abbi Kim, Amanda Faye. BS in Edn., Taylor U., 1972; MS in Edn., U. So. Calif., L.A., 1985; EdD, Ball State U., 1991. Life tchg. cert., Ind. Tchr. grade 4 Fayette County Schs., Connersville (Ind.) Sch., 1972; tchr. grade 1 Lancaster (Ohio) City Schs., 1972-81; tchr. grade 1 and 2 Seoul (Korea) Fgn. Sch., 1981-89; dir. student tchg., prof. edn. Bethel Coll., Mishawaka, Ind., 1991-96, assoc. dean instrn., 1996—. Adj. prof. Ind. Wesleyan U., Marion; spkr. in field. Author: Middle School English, 1988. Bd. dirs. Adoptions Alternative, South Bend, Ind., Harris Prairie Ch. of Christ Pre-sch.; orphan escort Holt Adoption Agy., Seoul, 1983, 84. Jennings scholar Martha Holden Jennings Found., Lancaster, 1976; doctoral fellow Ball State U., Muncie, Ind., 1989-90. Mem. ASCD, Internat. Reading Assn., Assn. Tchr. Educators, Ind. Assn. for Tchr. Educators, Ind. Assn. for Colls. Tchr. Edn., Ind. Reading Assn. (St. Joseph Valley Coun. v.p.-elect 1992-93, v.p. 1993-94, pres. 1994-95, past pres. 1995-96), Ind. Reading Profs., Phi Delta Kappa. Avocations: racquetball, reading, sewing, traveling. Office: Bethel Coll 1001 W Mckinley Ave Mishawaka IN 46545-5509 E-mail: WilsonR@Bethel-IN.edu.

WILSON, RENEE LAYNE, protective services official, personal trainer; b. Honolulu, Nov. 24, 1959; d. Maxine Joyce Wilson; 1 child, Bradon Tyler. Student, Aims Coll., 1978—81; degree in criminal justice. Police officers std. tng.: Calif. 2001, basic law tng.: Colo. 1980. Police officer City of Livermore, Calif., 2000—02, Dept. Pub. Safety, Hayward, Calif., 2002—. Named World Record Holder, World Assn. of Bench Press and Deadlift, 1998, 1999, 2000, Nat. Record Holder, United States Powerlifting Fedn., 1998, 1999, 2000, Multiple State record holder, State of Wash., Oreg. and Calif., 1998, 1999, 2000, 2001; recipient Trainer award, Women in Leadership, 2000, Olympic Gold medal, Calif. Police and Fire Games, 2003. Mem.: GBPOA (Golden Bears Police Officers Assn.), WPOA (Womens Police Officers Assn.), LAMBDA (life). Methodist. Achievements include Law Enforcement World Record Bench Press, 2004. Avocations: weightlifting, swimming, softball, painting. Home: 363 Diablo Rd #41 Danville CA 94526 Office: Dept Public Safety 25800 Carlos Bee Blvd Hayward CA 94542 Office Phone: 510-885-3791. Personal E-mail: pow203@aol.com. E-mail: rwilson@csuhayward.edu.

WILSON, RITA, actress; b. LA, Oct. 26, 1958; m. Tom Hanks; 2 children. Actor: (films) The Day It Came to Earth, 1979, Cheech & Chong's Next Movie, 1980, Volunteers, 1985, The Bonfire of the Vanities, 1990, Sleepless in Seattle, 1993, Mixed Nuts, 1994, Now and Then, 1995, That Thing You Do!, 1996, Jingle All the Way, 1996, No Dogs Allowed, 1996, Psycho, 1998, Runaway Bride, 1999, The Story of Us, 1999, Perfume, 2001, Auto Focus, 2002; (TV films) Barbarians at the Gate, 1993, If These Walls Could Talk, 1996, From the Earth to the Moon, 1998, Invisible Child, 1999; prodr.: (films) My Big Fat Greek Wedding, 2002, Connie and Carla, 2004; (TV series) My Big Fat Greek Life, 2003. Mailing: 2600 Malibu Rd Malibu CA 90265*

WILSON, RITA P. insurance company executive; Sr. v.p. corp. rels. Allstate Ins. Co., Northbrook, Ill., 1990-94, 96—, pres. Allstate Indemnity, 1994-96; sr. v.p. corp. rels. Ameritech, Chgo., 1994-96. Office: Allstate Ins Co 2775 Sanders Rd Ste F8 Northbrook IL 60062-6127

WILSON, ROBERTA (BOBBI) GAIL, performing arts educator; d. Robert Wallace and Ruth Lorraine (Bayne) Wilson; m. Thomas D. Bachenberg, June 2, 1975 (div. Jan. 6, 1978). BA in Music Edn., U. No. Colo., 1975; student in voice, choral conducting, U. Nev., 1981—82; student in Shakespeare and Directing, U. So. Oreg., 1996; student in Theatre, Union Inst. and Univ., 1999—. Tchr. vocal music Lewis-Palmer Schs., Monument, Colo., 1975—79, Sheridan (Colo.) HS, Sheridan, Colo., 1975—79; singer, dancer, actor MGM Grand Hotel, Reno, 1980—82, Nev. Opera and Ballet, Reno, 1980—82; freelance singer, dancer, actor, dir. LA, 1982—93; performing arts dir., vocal music Inst. Music and Drama, Christian Bros. HS, Sacramento, 1993—97; dir. Arts Acad. Cotter HS and Jr. HS Acad. Performing Arts, Winona, Minn., 1997—2000; dir. music and drama Studio Acad. HS for Arts, Rochester, Minn., 2001—02; coord. Dist. Arts Fountain (Colo.) Ft. Carson Sch. Dist. 8, 2002—. Performer Colo. Opera Festival, Colo. Springs, 1976—78; dir., choreographer Ctrl. Minn. Children's Theatre, St. Cloud, Minn., 2001. Vol. Dem. Party, LA, 1992. Named Tchr. of Month, Kiwanis Club, 1993. Mem.: Ednl. Theatre Assn., Music Educators Nat. Conf. Democrat. Meth. Office: Fountain Fort Carson School Dist 425 W Alabama St Fountain CO 80817

WILSON, S. LIANE, bank executive; Sr. v.p. info. systems Wash. Mut. Inc., Seattle, exec. v.p. corp. comm., 1995-2000, vice-chmn., 2000—01, cons., 2001—02; bd. dirs. Network Assoc., 2002—.

WILSON, SAL, systems analyst; b. Cedar Rapids, Iowa, May 9, 1947; d. Joseph John and Alma (Klouda) Nemec; m. Robert Foster Wilson, Oct. 1982. BS in Computer Sci., Mt. Mercy Coll., 1985. Cert. netware engr., info. tech. specialist IV. Systems analyst State of Iowa Dept. Human Rights, Des Moines, 1987-97; exec. v.p. Lawyer Forms Inc., Cedar Rapids, Iowa, 1992—; client/server developer State of Iowa Dept. Human Svcs., Des Moines, 1997—. Home: 2179 Blake Blvd SE Cedar Rapids IA 52403- Office: State of Iowa Dept Human Svcs Hoover Bldg 1st St Fl N Des Moines IA 50319-0001 E-mail: mrspkhead@hotmail.com.

WILSON, SHARON ROSE, literature educator, researcher; b. Denver, May 13, 1941; d. John William Wilson and Rose Schlagel; m. Roger Lloyd Brown, May 5, 1973 (div. 1998); 1 child, Stephen Roger Wilson-Brown. BA, Colo. State Coll., 1963; MA, Purdue U., 1967; PhD in Eng., U. Wis., 1976. Cert. secondary edn., Colo. Teaching asst. Purdue U., West Lafayette, Ind., 1963-65, U. Wis., Madison, 1965-70; instr. U. Northern Colo., Greeley, 1970-73, asst. prof., 1974-78, assoc. prof., 1978-84, prof. eng., women's studies, 1985—. Vis. humanist Boulder County Women's Resources Ctr., 1980; speaker and lectr. in field. Author: Margaret Atwood's Fairy-Tale Sexual Politics, 1993, The Self-Conscious Narrator and His Twentieth-Century Faces, 1976; co-editor: Approaches to Teaching Atwood's The Handmaid's Tale and Other Works, 1996; editor: Margaret Atwood's Textual Assasinations; contbr. articles to profl. jours. Founding mem. local Nat. Orgn. for Women, 1982; women's issues chairperson League of Women Voters, Longmont, 1978-85; founding co-pres. Margaret Atwood Soc., 1983-88. Recipient numerous rsch. grants. Mem. MLA (organizer of spl. sessions 1980, 85, 88), Colo. Seminars (adv. bd. 1980—, coord. of program), Colo. Women's Studies Assn. (conf. coord. 1977), Margaret Laurence Soc., Samuel Beckett Soc. (charter), Doris Lessing Soc. (v.p. 2002-2005), Internat. Assn. Fantastic in the Arts, Assn. for Canadian Studies in the U.S., Popular Culture Assn., Pacific Ctrl. Canadian Studies Network, Western Canadian Studies Assn., Rocky Mountain MLA. Avocations: swimming, reading, attending theatre and film performances, art. Office: U Northern Colo Eng Dept Greeley CO 80639-0001

WILSON, SONJA MARY, retired secondary school educator, poet; b. Lake Charles, La., Mar. 28, 1938; d. Albert Ronald and Annelia (DeVille) Molless; m. Willie McKinley Williams, Apr. 28, 1956 (div. May 1969); children: William P., Dwayne L., Rachelle A., Devon A., Lisa M., Ricardo Soto; m. Howard Brooks Wilson, Nov. 12, 1982 (div. Dec. 1999); stepchildren: Howard N. Wilson, Yvonne Wilson. AA in Social and Behavioral Scis., Mt. St. Jacinto Coll., 1992; designated subjects credential, U. Calif., San Bernardino, 1983; student, Calif. State Poly. U., 1986; M in Adminstrn., Laverne U., 1985; BS in Edn. Methodologies, So. Ill. U., 1995; postgrad., Riverside (Calif.) City Coll., 1988—89, postgrad., 1994. Prin.'s sec. Elsinore (Calif.) H.S., Elsinore Jr. H.S., 1974-83, tchr. bus. and adult vocat. edn. coord., 1979-88, class adviser, 1983-88; ret., 1988. Long-term substitute tchr. Perris H.S. Dist., 1991—94; spkr. in field. Judge Lake Elsinore Unified Sch. Dist. Bd., 1986—, clk., 1988, pres., 1988, 98, 2002, clk., 2004; active Lake Elsinore Elem. Sch. Bd., 1976-88; pres., sec.-treas., v.p. Riverside County Sch. Bds. Assn., 1979-98; assoc. sponsor, advisor Black Student Union/Future Leaders of Am., 1984-90; svc. unit rep., leader Girl Scouts U.S.A., bd. dirs. San Gorgonio coun., 1995-2003, nominating com., 1998—; den leader Boy Scouts Am.; active Ctrl. Dem. Com., 1989-91; del. PTSA, 1991-93; mem. Econ. Devel. Com., Elsinore, Resurrection Choir, 1996-; vol. dir. United Way, 2003—; mentor Riverside CC, 1998-2004. Tribute in her honor Black Student Union/Future Leaders Am., 1989, Wall of Tolerance, 2003; recipient Excellence in Edn. award Hilltop Community Ctr. Club, 1989, Leadership award Black Art and Social Club, 1989, Svc. award Sojourner Truth Media Network, 1989, Proclamation award City of Elsinore, 1989, County of Riverside, 1984, Golden Leaf award PTSA, Honor Our Own award, LANBEA. Mem.: NAACP (life; treas. 1998—2000, pres. 2000—02, charter, historian Lake Elsinore chpt. 2004, plaque), Calif. Ret. Tchrs. Assn. (resource rep. 2001—04, pres. 2004), Calif. Sch. Employees Assn. (pres., treas., regional rep. asst., conf. del., state negotiation com.), Calif. Elected Women Ofcls. Assn., Calif. Sch. Bds. Assn. (legis. com. 1981—97, nominations com. 1988, regional dir. 1988—92, conf. planning com. 1989, Fed. Rels. Network del. 1992, audit com. 1993, dir./del. trainer 1993, media com., dir. at large black 1993—95, alt. del., sgt. at arms 1994—95, Fed. Rels. Network del. 1995), Calif. Coalition Black Sch. Bd. Mems. (v.p., program liaison 1989, pres. 1990), Internat. Soc. Poets, Nat. Coun. Negro Women (life; charter, Willa Mae Taylor sect.), Lake Elsinore C. of C. (Palkman award 2004), Hilltop Cmty. Club (plaque), Lake Elsinore Black Art Culture Club (charter, treas. 1997—, RTA com.), Black Art and Social Club (founder), Eta Phi Beta (charter, Gamma Alpha chpt. pres. 1992—94, western region dir. 1997—2001, nat. chaplain 2002—, cmty. rev. team 2003—, Vol. of Yr. award 1999—2000). Avocations: travel, writing poetry, gardening, child-care, dance. Home: 30402 Jernigan St Lake Elsinore CA 92530-5045 E-mail: sonjawilson@msn.com., Sonja.Wilson@leusd.k12.ca.us.

WILSON, SUE, state legislator; b. Albuquerque; BA, So. Meth. U. Mem. N.Mex. Senate, Dist. 19, Santa Fe, 1996—; mem. fin. com. N.Mex. Senate, mem. Indian and cultural affairs com. Republican. Home: 1516 Gray Rock Pl NE Albuquerque NM 87112-6639

WILSON, SUSAN ELIZABETH, lawyer; b. Charlottesville, Va., Aug. 17, 1957; d. Colon Hayes Jr. and Patricia Ann (Webb) W. AA, Emory U., 1977, BA, 1979; MA in Journalism, U. Ga., 1984, JD, 1991. Bar: Ga. 1991, N.C. 1992, U.S. Dist. Ct. [illegible] Supreme Ct. Ga. Atlanta, 1989; summer clk., summer assoc. B.J. Rounds & Assocs., Athens, Ga., 1990, 91; vol., ind. contractor Pisaah Legal Svcs., Asheville, N.C., 1991-92; ptnr. Wilson & Rudolph, Black Mountain, N.C., 1992; atty. Buncombe County Dept. Social Svcs., Asheville, 1992—. Mem. adv. bd. Buncombe County Teen Ct., 1994—, chair adv. bd., 1996—; mem. adv. bd. Buncombe Alternatives, Inc., 1995—, vice-chair, 1998—; mem. adv. bd. Earn and Learn, 1997—. Mem. Phi Sigma Tau. Episcopalian. Avocations: reading, hiking, music. Home: 6 Squirrel Ridge Dr Weaverville NC 28787-8316 Office: Buncombe County IV-D 40 Coxe Ave Asheville NC 28801-3307

WILSON, SYLVIA ALYCE, musician, educator; b. Mpls., June 19, 1950; d. Robert Leighton and Doris Mae Butts; m. Dennis Charles Wilson, Sept. 12, 1970; children: Ryan Bradley, Virginia Anne Cooper. BS in Music Edn. with high distinction, U. Minn., 1972, MA in Music Edn., 1987. Orch. tchr. Anoka-Hennepin Sch. Dist. No. 11, Coon Rapids, Minn., 1972—77, music tchr., 1986—89, 1992—; substitute music tchr. St. Louis Park (Minn.) Sch. Dist. No. 283, 1978—85; orch. tchr. Wayzata (Minn.) Sch. Dist. #284, 1985—86; orch./choir tchr. Roseville (Minn.) Area Pub. Schs. #623, 1989—90. Musician Lake String Quartet, Mpls., 1982—85; piano tuner, pvt. music tchr., 1982—86; preschool music tchr. West Bank Sch. Music, Mpls., 1983—85; judge Minn. State HS League, St. Paul, 2003—; presenter in field. Contbr. articles to profl. jours. Violinist, violist Mpls. Civic Orch., 1970—, Cantati Evangelica, Mpls., 1995—2001; VBS tchr. First Bapt. Ch. Mpls., 1990—94, choir dir., bell choir dir., 1992—2000. Named Outstanding Sr., Am. Legion, 1972; recipient Meritorious Orch. Program award, Minn. String Tchrs. Assn., 1987, 2002; grantee, Anoka-Hennepin Ednl. Found., 1999—2001; scholar, U. Minn., 1968. Mem.: NEA, Anoka-Hennepin Edn. Minn. (bldg. rep. 2000—), Am. String Tchrs. Assn., Music Educators Nat. Conf., Pi Kappa Lambda, Sigma Alpha Iota (pres., vice-president, treas., corr. sec. 1970—, co-chair benefit music scholarships, Music scholar 1970, Sword of Honor 1971). Home: 2700 Joppa Ave S Saint Louis Park MN 55416 Office: Northdale Mid Sch 11301 Dogwood St Coon Rapids MN 55448

WILSON, TINA MARIE, special education educator; b. Jersey City, N.J., Mar. 5, 1957; d. Lemuel Steven and Elizabeth (Oglesbey) Wilson. Cert. Computers, Electronic Computer Programming Inst., Jersey City, 1977; BSBA, Jersey City State Coll., 1981; MA, N.J. City U., 2004. Tchr. bus. Am. Bus. Inst., Bklyn.; instr. Urban League of Hudson County, Jersey City; personal asst. Flip Wilson's Prodns., Malibu, Calif.; tchr. spl. edn. Jersey City Pub. Schs., NJ City U., 2004—. Mem.: Nat. Black Caucus Spl. Edn., Coun. Exceptional Children, Order Ea. Star. Avocations: swimming, golf, flying, bicycling, tennis. Home: 2 Hague St Apt 37 Jersey City NJ 07307*

WILSON, TRISHA, interior architectural designer; b. Augusta, Ga. d. Lemuel Edward Wilson and Doris (Howard) Gray. BS in Interior Archtl. Design, U. Tex., 1969. Interior designer Titche-Goettinger Allied Stores, Dallas, 1969-72; ptnr. Merrill/Wilson and Assocs., Dallas, 1972-75; chmn., chief exec. officer Wilson and Assocs., Dallas, N.Y.C., L.A., Singapore and Johannesburg, South Africa, 1975—. Bd. dirs. Shelby Williams Industries, Exec. Travel Svc., SPCA of Tex.; mem. found. adv. coun. U. Tex. Sch. Architecture; devel. bd. U. Tex. Adv. dir. Susan G. Komen Found.; bd. dirs. State Fair of Tex., Dallas; mem. Rep. Nat. Com., Friend of Kennedy Ctr. Found. Dallas Assembly; past chmn. bd. dirs. Tex. bus. Hall Fame Found., corp. com. Dallas Mus. Art; trustee Dallas Mus. Art; past adv. bd. dept. home econs. U. Tex., Austin; founder, chmn. Wilson Edn. Found. Named to Design Hall of Fame, Interior Design Mag., 1993. Mem. Am. Soc. Interior Designers (state chpt. bd. dirs. 1978-80), Ins. bus. Designers, Tex. Women's Forum, Dallas Women's Found., Internat. Women's Forum, Soc. Partially Sighted, U. Tex. Ex-Students' Assn. (adv. bd., at-large rep. exec. council), Young Pres. Orgn. Avocations: travel, fine art and antiques. Office: Wilson and Assocs 3811 Turtle Creek Blvd Fl 15 Dallas TX 75219-4461 also: Wilson and Assocs 415 E 54th St Ste 15D New York NY 10022-5101 also: 8342 1/2 Melrose Ave Los Angeles CA 90069-5420

WILSON, VICTORIA JANE SIMPSON, farmer, nurse; b. Floresville, Tex., Nov. 30, 1952; d. Joseph Eugene and Eva Gertrude (Ferguson) Simpson; m. Richard Royce Wilson, May 15, 1976; children: Sarah Beth, Nathan Lawrence. BSN, U. Cen. Ark., 1977; MS in Nursing, Northwestern State U., 1981. Charge nurse surg. St. Vincent Infirmary, Little Rock; staff nurse ICU La. State U. Med. Ctr., Shreveport, La.; patient edn. coord. White River Med. Ctr., Batesville, Ark.; co-owner, CEO Health Plus, Stuttgart, Ark.; co-owner Wilson Enterprises, Humphrey, Ark., 1992—99; staff nurse St. Vincent Health Sys., 2000—01; mem. faculty Southeast Ark. Coll., 2000; Level I coord. faculty Jefferson Sch. Nursing, Pine Bluff, Ark., 2001—. Mem.: ANA, Ark. Nurses Assn., Sigma Theta Tau. Home: 51 Wilson Ln Humphrey AR 72073-9097 E-mail: wilsonv@jrmc.org.

WILSON, WANDA MAE FRENCH, animal association administrator; b. Cin., Nov. 20, 1936; d. William Reily French and Grace Mae Walker; m. David William Jordan; children: Melinda, Wendy, Sandra. Student, Nat. Coll., Kans. City, Mo., 1954—55, Shippensburg U., Cumberland County, Pa., 1972—73, Harisburg Area C.C., Harrisburg, Pa., 1973—75. Employment Interviewer Pa. Dept. Labor and Industry, Harrisburg, Pa., 1970—76, emplyer rels. rep. Lebanon, Pa., 1976—94; founder Little Mouse Club of the Western Hemisphere, New Cumberland, Pa., 1994—. Founder, partner designer custom Jewelery and repair Wilson Jordan Enterprises, Harrisburg, Pa., 1973—. Contbr. articles to profl. jours. and mags. Pres. women's assn. Unitarian-Universalist Womens Group, Harrisburg, 1979—80; sch. tchr. Unitarian Churches, Indpls., Detroit, Cin., Harrisburg, 1962—74; bd. dirs., edn. com. Unitarian Ch., Harrisburg, Pa., 1969—72; charter member National Mus. for Women in the Arts, Washington, 1987—pres; charter mem. Nat. Women's History Mus.; Co organizer, finance committee officer First Feminist Credit Union, Harrisburg, 1973—74; organizer, founder Harrisburg chpt.NOW, Harrisburg, 1972—75; leader Girl Scouts of Am., Indianapolis, Detroit, Cincinnati, 1962—69; union chpt. treas., shop steward Svc. Employee Internat. Union, Harrisburg. Mem.: Unitarian Universalist Women's Assn., Harrisbug Astron. Soc. (trustee 1975—81, v.p. 1980), Mensa (editor 1980—85), N.Am. Rat and Mouse Club Internat. (editor 1994—97, Named Most Valuable mem. 1994), Little Mouse Club (head facilitator, chief info. officer 1997—). Unitarian. Avocations: total solar eclipse chasing, reading, dollhouses, minatures, archaeology. Home: 603 Brandt Ave New Cumberland PA 17070 Personal E-mail: wwmice@att.net.

WILSON-ALLEN, TAWANA BELINDA, community and political organizer, consultant; b. Mooresville, N.C., Dec. 16, 1949; d. Jehu Nivens and Ruby (Henderson) Alexander; m. Emmanuel Allen; children: Niki, Bruce, Tamia. BA in Sociology, N.C. Ctrl. U., 1972; postgrad. in Urban Adminstrn., U. N.C., Charlotte, 1979-81; Cert. Profl. Orgn., Midwest Acad., Chgo., 1984; Cert. in Polit. Campaign Mgmt., Kent State U., 1985. Tchr., dir. pre-kindergarten Pub. Schs./Dept. Human Resources, Prince George County, Md., 1972-77; organizer Coun. Sr. Citizens, Mecklenburg County, N.C., 1983-85; exec. dir. North Carolinians for Effective Citizenship, Charlotte, 1983-86; assoc. dir. Carolina Cmty. Project, Charlotte, 1986-90; devel. dir. Rural Advancement Fund, Charlotte, 1989-90; congl. liaison U.S. Rep. Melvin Watt, 12th Dist., Charlotte, 1993—. Founder, pres. Inst. Cmty. Resources, Charlotte, 1990-92; trainer leadership devel. Charlotte Presbytery, 1990—; regional field dir. Harvey Gantt for U.S. Senate Campaign, Charlotte, 1990, Mel Watt for Congress Campaign, Charlotte, 1992. Founder/trainer Electoral Skills Program Cmty. Based Campaigns, 1990—; program design/trainer leadership devel. program Miss/Mr. Black Teenage World, 1986-92, Leadership Coalition of So. Black Youth, 1986-92. Mem. Nat. Dem. Com., Washington, 1996; 1st v.p. Black Polit. Caucus, Charlotte-Mecklenburg, 1996—; mem. Black Women's Caucus, Charlotte-Mecklenburg, 1995—; coord. Mecklenburg Voter Coalition, [illegible] 1996—; mem. Emily's List, Washington, 1996—; bd. dirs. Charlotte Sister Cities, Com., 1996; session mem., elder Eastfield Presbyn. Ch., 1996; mem. Presbyn. Women; organizer Charlotte/Kumasi, Ghana Sister Cities Com., 1994—. Recipient Bd. Dirs. Svc. award Cmty. Rels. Com., Charlotte, 1995. Mem. Focus on Leadership (v.p. program chair 1991-95, trainer 1996, Svc. awards 1989-95, Pres.'s award 1995, v.p. emeritus 1995), Delta Sigma Theta. Avocations: piano, flute, water color art, african art and artifacts collector. Home: 6921 Folger Dr Charlotte NC 28270-5947 Office: Congressman Melvin Watt 324 N College St Charlotte NC 28202-2150

WILSON-FELLOWS, SUZANNE, motion picture producer; b. Washington, Oct. 13, 1953; d. Howard Karbel and Margaret Irene (Heath) Wilson; m. James Stewart Fellows, Feb. 25, 1976 (div. June 1988); 1 child, James S. BA in Theater, BA in Psychology, UCLA, 1972. Actress, 1958-75; exec. prodn. coord. Walt Disney Pictures & TV, Burbank, Calif., 1987-89; asst. to prodr. Sleeping with the Enemy, Fox, L.A., 1989-90; animation specialist DreamWorks, SKG, Universal City, Calif., 1995-97. Assoc. prodr. Boxer and the Blonde, Homeward Bound 1, 1990-92, Fatherhood, 1992-93. Mem. AAUW, Women In Film, Ind. Feature Project. Democrat. Jewish. Office: DownHome Prodns LLC 626 Santa Monica Blvd Santa Monica CA 90401-2502

WILSON-JONES, LINDA, guidance counselor; b. Hattiesburg, Miss., Apr. 11, 1955; d. Herman and Mary (Chapman) W.; m. James L. Jones, Jr., Aug 12, 1972 (div. Dec. 1986); children: Rhoda Grechelle Jones, James LeMontrell Jones III. BA, Miss. State U., 1995, MS, 1997, Ednl. Splst., 1998. Cert. guidance counselor Miss., La. Substitute tchr., adminstrv. asst. Meridian (Miss.) Pub. Schs., 1990-95; day treatment splst., mental health counselor Weems Mental Health, Meridian, 1995-96; counselor, facilitator, educator Choctaw Housing Authority, Phila., 1996-98; counselor, program supr., transition program coord. Youth Excitement Team, Inc., Meridian, 1998—; guidance counselor, sch. drug coord., test coord. Rankin County Schs., Brandon, Miss., 1999—. Cons. profl. devel., pres. JoLin Cons. Group, Meridian, 1998—, How to Plan a Workshop demonstration, 1998; counselor Classroom Guidance Lessons, 1999. Mem. task force, facilitator, cons. Miss. Coalition Against Domestic Violence, 1998; facilitator Sem. on Male Perspective about Domestic Violence, Green, Yellow and Red. Know the Signs, 1998; event coord. Meridian's Martin Luther King Parade and Celebration. Mem. Miss. Counseling Assn. (mem. exec. bd. 1997—), Miss. Assn. Multi-Cultural Counseling and Devel. (pres.) Doct. Student Assn. (sec.), Miss. Assn. Multi-Cultural Counseling and Devel. (conf. coord. 1997-99), Order of Ea. Star (grand sec. Bathsheba grand chpt. Miss. jurisdiciton 1997-99), Zeta Phi Beta, Inc. Democrat. Methodist. Avocations: reading motivational articles, travel, meeting new people, interacting with positive people. Office: 5108 Druid Ln Meridian MS 39307-4169 also: JoLin Cons Group 5108 Druid Ln Meridian MS 39307-4169

WILSON-PLEINESS, CHRISTINE JOYCE, writer, poet, columnist, real estate investor; b. Chgo., July 27, 1951; d. Peter Joseph Thelen and Edna (Milewski) Dombrowski; m. Douglas A. Wilson, July 7, 1973 (div. Oct. 1986); children: Amy Kathleen, Lauri Ellyn; m. Glenn B. Pleiness, Dec. 5, 1998. BS in Edn., No. Ill. U., 1973; MFAW, Spalding U., 2003. Asst. store mgr. County Seat Co., Joliet, Ill., 1981-83; cash applicator Aurora (Ill.) Pump Co., 1984-85, accounts payable clk., 1986-89; accounts payable technician Horizon Sportswear, Inc., Madison Heights, Mich., 1989-90; accounts payable rep. Crain Comm., Inc., Detroit, 1990-95; accounts payable specialist Philip Svcs. Corp., Detroit, 1995-96, ORACLE project team, 1996, accounts payable team leader, 1996-97; accounts payable and expense supr. Superior Cons. Co., Inc., Southfield, Mich., 1997-98; accounts payable auditor The Profit Recovery Group Internat. Inc., Clawson, Mich., 1998-99; accounts payable supr. ACN Inc., Farmington Hills, Mich., 1999-2000, Roush Industries, Livonia, Mich., 2000—02; accounts payable coord. The Oakland Press, Pontiac, Mich., 2002—. Mem., bd. dirs. Somerset Square Condominium Assn., Sterling Heights, 1996, 97; rec. sec. Troy Cmty. Chorus, 1999-2000. Recipient Tchr. Edn. scholarship State of Ill., 1969. Mem. Parents Without Ptnrs. (treas. chpt. 761, 1996-98, Appreciation award 1997, 98, 99), Monday Night Writing Group (founding, facilitator 1997-2002), Beta Sigma Phi (Woman of Yr. award 1989, 98, Order of the Rose 2000). Avocations: writing, reading, dance, attending the theatre, singing. Home: 50074 N Jimmy Ct Chesterfield MI 48047 E-mail: tinaw51@yahoo.com.

WILSON-STEWART, MARILYN LUCILLE, retired human resources director; b. Lima, Ohio, Feb. 6, 1933; d. Russell A. and Ruth Alma Parcher; m. Billy A. Stewart, May 15, 1965 (div. Apr. 1991); m. Bobbie H. Wilson, Nov. 7, 1953 (div. Feb. 4, 1960); children: Bobbie Craig Wilson, Keith Russell Wilson. Exec. sec. specialized human resources program, Baker Bus. U., Flint, Mich., 1953. Stenographer, statistician Flint Child Guidance Clinic, 1953—64; human resources tng. Gen. Motors Corp., Marion, Ind., 1964—95; ret., 1995. Pres. bd. dirs. Marion (Ind.) Urban League, 1973, YWCA, Marion; pres. Women's Ministry; 1st v.p. Ch. Women United Grant County. Recipient GM award for Excellance in Cmty. Svc., 1973, Pres. award, NAACP, local br., 1991. Mem.: Order Ea. Star (past worthy matron). Democrat. Baptist. Avocations: reading, Bible teacher, crafts, cooking.

WILSON-WEBB, NANCY LOU, education administration consultant, director; b. Maypearl, Tex, Jan. 20, 1932; d. Madison Grady Wise and Mary Nancy Pearson-Bedford (Haney) Wilson; m. John Crawford Webb, July 29, 1972. BS magna cum laude, Abilene Christian U., Tex., 1953; EdM (hon.), Tex. Christian U., 1985. Cert. tchr., mid-mgmt., sch. adminstr., Tex. Tchr. elem. grades Ft. Worth Ind. Sch. Dist., 1953-67, adult edn. tchr., 1967-73; dir. adult edn. consortium for 38 sch. dists. Tex. Edn. Agy., 1973-2000. Pres. Nat. Commn. on Adult Basic Edn., "Most Outstanding adult ed. Admin. in US" by AAAC; 1994-95; pres. Tex. Adult Edn. Adminstrn., 1994; apptd. mem. Tex. State Literacy Coun., 1987-94, Tex. State Sch. Bd. Commn., 1994-99; exec. bd. Tex. Coun. Co-op Dir., 1989-2001, Bd. Nat. Assn. of AAACE, 1988; pres., 1994—; apptd. to Gov. Ann Richard's Task Force for Edn.; ranch owner, mgr., 1998-2003. Cons. to textbooks, 1994-98; editor textbooks, 1999. Pres. Jr. Womans Club, Ft. Worth, 1969, Fine Arts Guild, Tex. Christian U., Ft. Worth, 1970-72, Ft. Worth Womens Civic Club Coun., 1970, pres. Aquarius Women's Club; active Exec. Libr. Bd., Ft. Worth, 1990-2003, Jewel Charity Ball, 1988-2003; bd. dirs. Literacy Plus in North Tex., 1988-99, pres., 2001—; bd. dirs. Greater Ft. Worth Literacy Coun., 1976-88, 2002—, pres., 2001-03; commr. Ed-16 Task Forces Tex. Edn. Agy., 1985-94; literacy bd. dir. Friends of Libr., 1967-2002, Opera Guild Bd. Ft. Worth, 1965-85, Ft. Worth Ballet Guild, Johnson County (Tex.) Corr. Bd., 1990-2000; bd. dirs. Salvation Army, Ft. Worth, 1996-2003, Ft. Worth Libr.; active Tarrant County Bd. on Aging, 1997-98, Commn. Status of Women, Ft. Worth, 1973-99, Southside Ch. of Christ. Recipient Bevy award Jr. Womans Club, 1968, Proclamation Commr. Ct. Outstanding 43 Yr. Literacy Svc. to Tarrant County Com. Ctr., 1994, Tarrant County Woman of Yr. award, Fort Worth Star Telegram, 1995, Outstanding Leadership award Ft. Worth ISD Sch. Bd., 1985, 95, Mayor's Proclamation of Nancy Webb Week, 1996; named one of Most Outstanding Educators in U.S. Nat. Assn. Adult Edn., 1983, Most Outstanding Woman Edn., City of Ft. Worth, 1991, others; nominated to Tex. Hall of Fame for Women, 1991; named to Ft. Worth Hall of Fame, 1992; scholar Germany, 1983. Mem. NEA, DAR (Mary Isham Keith chpt. 1985-2002, Nat. Literacy award 1992, Leadership Literacy award 1985-87, 89, 94, Nat. Educators award 2003), AAUW, Am. Assn. Adult and Continuing Edn. (v.p. 1987-89, chair 1993 internat. conv. 1992, Nat. Adminstr. of Yr. in Adult Edn. 1998, Most Outstanding Adminstr. Adult Edn. in US 1999), Tex. Assn. Adult and Cont. Edn. (pres. 1985-86, Most Outstanding Adult Adminstr. in Tex. 1984), Tex. Coun. Adult Edn. Dirs. (pres. nat. com. on edn., Nat. Dept. Labor award 1992), Coun. World Affairs (bd. dir. 1980-2002), Am. Bus. Women's Assn., Ft. Worth C. of C., Lecture Found., Internat. Reading Assn. (Literacy Challenge award 1991), Ft. Worth Adminstrv. Assn., Southwest Cattle Raisers Assn., Ligon Assn., Zonta, Tanglewood Garden Club, Ft. Worth Garden Club (exec. bd. dirs. 2000-03), Woman's Club, Ft. Worth Petroleum Club, Carousel Dance Club, Met. Dinner Dance Club, Ridglea Country Club, Girls Svc. League, Aquarius (pres. 2001-02), Crescent Club (Dallas), Alpha Delta Kappa (Nat. Literacy award 1992), Greater Ft. Worth Literacy Coun. (pres. 2000-03), Phi Delta Kappa, Mary Isham Keith DAR (Nat. award 1993, Nat. Found. award 2003). Democrat. Mem. Lds Ch. Home: 3716 Fox Hollow St Fort Worth TX 76109-2616

WILT, MAUREEN MOFFITT, social worker, educator; b. St. Louis, Mo., May 1, 1950; d. William A. Moffitt, Jr. and Dolores Finan Moffitt; children: John Christopher II, Robert Westley Finan. BS, SE Mo. State U., Cape Girardeau, Mo., 1972; MSW in Social Welfare, U. Kans., Lawrence, 1987. LMSW Kans., 1987, LCSW Mo., 1991. Clin. social worker Independence Regional Health Ctr., Mo., 1986—98; clin. social worker, p.r.n. Two Rivers Hosp., Kans. City, 1992—; hospice clin. social worker, p.r.n. Carondelet Hospice, Blue Springs, Mo., 1999—2001, Kans. City Hospice, Mo., 1999—; grief therapist Pvt. Practice, Kans. City, Mo., 1993—; field liaison U. Kans., Lawrence, 1996—98; asst. prof. of social work Ctrl. Mo. State U., Warrensburg, Mo., 1998—. Vice-chair Internat. Affairs Com. at Ctrl. Mo. State U., Warrensburg, 2002—; faculty advisor Social Work Grad. Orgn., Ctrl. Mo. State U., Warrensburg, Mo., 2000—; com. mem. Student Wellness Adv. Com., Ctrl. Mo. State U., Warrensburg, Mo., 2002—. Interviewer (holocaust visual history project) Steven Spielberg's Survivor of the Shoah Project, Midwest Center of Holocaust Education's Witness to the Holocaust; contbr. articles to news pubs. including Social Work Today, 2003. White rose essay contest judge Midwest Ctr. for Holocaust Edn., Overland Pk., Kans., 2000—03; judge for Blue Springs family of the yr. award Blue Springs Family of the Yr. Com., Blue Springs, Mo., 2001—03; pres. alumni assn. and chairperson of the ann. llama run benefit RHS Cross Country Alumni, Raytown, Mo., 2001—; mem. bd. dirs. Take Back Your Time Day. Recipient Martin Luther King, Jr., Humanitarian Award, Ctrl. Mo. State U. and the Warrensburg C. of C., 2003, Martin Luther King, Jr., Group Leadership Award-Bridgebuilders, Ctrl. Mo. State U. and the Warrensburg Chamber of Commerce, 2003, Phi Alpha Nat. Social Work Honor Soc., Beta Theta Chpt. of Phi Alpha at Ctrl. Mo. State U., 2001. Mem.: Union Concerned Scientists, Mo. Assn. Social Welfare, Assn. Baccalaureate Social Work Program Dirs. (presenter Fostering Cmty. Connection Conf. proceedings 21st ann. conf.), Physicians for Social Responsibility, Nat. Assn. Social Workers (western unit chairperson for the mo. chpt. 2000—01), Midwest Ctr. Holocaust Edn., Mo. Consortium Social Work Educators, Coun. On Social Work Edn., Bridgebuilders, Friends Falun Gong, Amnesty Internat., Tchg. Tolerance, Sierra Club. Avocations: photography, family, friends, students, peace and environmental issues. E-mail: wilt@cmsu1.cmsu.edu.

WILTROUT, ANN ELIZABETH, foreign language educator; b. Elkhart, Ind., Aug. 3, 1939; d. F. LeRoy and Margaret Elizabeth (Williams) W. BA, Hanover Coll., 1961; MA, Ind. U., 1964, PhD, 1968. Vis. asst. prof. Ind. U., Bloomington, 1968-69; asst. prof. Miss. State U., Mississippi State, 1969-71, assoc. prof., 1971-87, prof., 1987—2002, prof. emerita fgn. lang., 2002—. NEH fellow in residence Duke U., 1977-78. Author: A Patron and a Playwright in Renaissance Spain, 1987; contbr. articles to profl. publs. Recipient Disting. Svc. cert. Inst. Internat. Edn., 1986; named Humanities Tchr. of Yr., 1998. Mem. MLA (life; del. to assembly 1975-78), Am. Assn. Tchrs. of Spanish and Portuguese (life), Soc. Scholars in Arts and Scis., Soc. Mayflower Descs. (life), Phi Kappa Phi, Sigma Delta Pi. Avocations: Shakespeare, travel, reading, roses. Office: Miss State U Dept Fgn Langs Drawer FL Mississippi State MS 39762 E-mail: wiltrout@ra.msstate.edu.

WILTSEY, SUSAN A. secondary school educator, priest; b. Richmond, Va., July 16, 1945; d. John M. and Marjorie G. Allman; 1 child from previous marriage, Katherine. AB, Randolph-Macon Coll., 1967; MA, U. Calif., Santa Barbara, 1977. Tchr. Dos Pueblos H.S., Goleta, Calif., 1971—91, Millcreek H.S., St. George, Utah, 1991—. Democrat. Episcopalian. Home: 40 W Shinava Dr Ivins UT 84738 Office: Millcreek H S 2410 Riverside Dr Saint George UT 84790

WIMBERG, LINDA B. elementary school educator, school librarian; b. Atlantic City, May 1, 1960; d. Thomas and Shirley (Slick) Blankenship; m. John M. Wimberg, June 27, 1987. BA, Upsala Coll., 1982; MA, Rowan U.,

1995. Cert. elem. and English edn. Tchr., grade 5 Galloway Twp. Bd. Edn., Galloway. Drama club instr., math. and sci. curriculum coms. Recipient the Golden U award. Mem. NJ Libr. Assn., Ednl. Media Ssn. NJ, Galloway Twp. Edn. Assn.

WIMBERLY, LINDA ROBERTS, music educator, artist; b. Lincoln, Nebr., Sept. 26, 1945; d. Arthur Thomas Roberts and Dorothy Mae Moore; m. Charles Augustus Wimberly, July 2, 1966 (div. Aug. 1985); children: Susan Lynn, Sheri Beth. Student, North Ga. Coll., 1963—64, Shorter Coll., 1964—67; BA, U. Ala., 1995. Pvt. music instr., Marietta, 1965—; entertainer, vocalist The Fireside Restaurant, Marietta, 1973—76; vocalist, contralto soloist N.W. Presbyn. Ch., Atlanta, 1988—96, dir. music, 1991—96; composer vocal, piano, choral works, 1995—; guitar instr. continuing edn. Kennesaw (Ga.) State U., 1996—2003; pres., owner Artist L'Inc Corp., Marietta, 2000—. Edn. ptnr. Ga. Wildlife Fedn., Atlanta, 2000—. One-woman shows include South Trust Bank, Mableton, 2001, Imagine Sta., Lehigh Valley, Pa., 2003, exhibitions include Period Gallery, Omaha, 2001, 2002, Upstream People Gallery, 2002, exhibited in group shows at N.W. Presbyn. Ch., Atlanta, 1995, Mable House Artfest, Mableton, Ga., 2000, Mon-Dak Heritage Ctr., Sidney, Mont., 2000, 2001, Marietta/Cobb Mus. Art, 2002, 2004, many others, Represented in permanent collections;, author articles, poetry and essays. Recipient Writing residency, Vt. Studio Ctr., 1997. Mem.: ASCAP, Acad. Am. Poets, Music Tchrs. Nat. Assn., Golden Key (life). Avocations: environment, nutrition, organic lifestyle, fitness. Office: Artist L Inc Corp PO Box 4833 Marietta GA 30060

WIMMER, KATHRYN, retired elementary school educator; b. St. Louis, May 8, 1929; d. Arthur Jordan and Louise Clara Sykes; m. Harry William Wimmer, Aug. 4, 1951; children: Robert William, Richard Jordan. BS in Edn., U. Mo., 1951; postgrad., U. South Fla., 1971—72. Cert. tchr. Mo., Fla. Tchr. Affton (Mo.) Sch., 1951—52, Heege Sch., Affton, 1965—67, Gulf Gate Sch., Sarasota, Fla., 1967—72; piano tchr. Crestwood, Mo., 1963—65. Artist, musician. V.p. Southgate Cmty., Sarasota, 1989—90; pres. bd. dirs. Assoc. Women's Club, Sarasota, 1990—91, bd. dirs., 1986—93; vol. Gulf Gate Libr., Sarasota, 1993—. Recipient tennis trophy, Bath and Racquet Tennis Club, Sarasota, 1979, swimming trophy, Southgate Cmty. Assn., 1987, 1988, Wall of Honor cert., Roosevelt H.S., St. Louis, 2003. Mem.: Mysterium High IQ Soc., Delta Gamma (scholarship chmn., treas., rush chmn., social chmn.). Democrat. Presbyterian. Avocations: sewing, literature, cards, dance, travel.

WINANS, ANNA JANE, dietician; b. Freeport, Ill., June 13, 1939; d. Leo Dale and Gwendolyn Jane White; m. Roger Eugene Winans, Aug. 26, 1967; children: Robert, Jonathan. BS in Dietetics, Iowa State U., 1962. Registered dietitian. Clin. dietitian VA Hosp., Madison, Wis., 1963-67; coord. U. Wis. Hosp., Madison, 1967-69; instr. nutrition Madison Gen. Hosp., 1969-75, Madison Area Coll., 1976-81; nutritionist Women, Infants and Children Nutrition Program, USDA, Fremont, Nebr., 1981—. Nutrition cons. area health care facilities, Wis., 1976-81, Nebr., 1985—. Sec. Chapel Hill Pool Bd., Elkhorn, Nebr., 1987-89; bd. dirs. Homeowner's Assn., Elkhorn, 1989-93; active Elkhorn Woman's Club, 1982—, Elkhorn Libr. Found., 1999-2000; mem. Elkhorn Libr. Bd., 1985—, pres., 1989-91, 94. Mem. Am. Dietetic Assn. (registered), Nebr. Dietetic Assn., Omaha Dietetic Assn., PEO (pres. 1999), Omicron Nu, Psi Chi. Methodist. Avocations: travel, reading, nature activities. Home: 910 S 218th St Elkhorn NE 68022-1952 Office: WIC 230 W 22d St Fremont NE 68025-5054

WINBLAD, ANN, investment company executive; BA in Math. and Bus. Adminstrn., MA in Internat. Econs. and Edn., U. St. Thomas, St. Paul, Minn. Programmer; co-founder Open Sys, Inc., 1976-83; strategic planning cons., IBM, Microsoft, Price Waterhouse, and many start-ups; ptnr. Hummer Winblad Venture Ptnrs., San Francisco, 1989—. Bd. dirs. Dean & Deluca, Intacct, Market Wire, The Knot, Voltage Security. Co-author: Object-Oriented Software, 1990. Trustee U. St. Thomas, St. Paul, Mich. Office: Hummer Winblad Venture Ptnrs 2 S Park St 2d Fl San Francisco CA 94107-1807

WINCHELL, KRISTINA ANNE, psychologist, school system administrator; b. Glens Falls, N.Y., Nov. 6, 1970; d. Robert Harvey Winchell and Lee Anne Simpkins. PhD in Sch. Psychology, Temple U., 2002. Cert. sch. psychologist, supr. N.Y., N.J.., Pa. State Psychology Bds. Child study team chairperson, sch. psychologist Greater Egg Harbor Bd. of Edn., Absecon, NJ, 1999—2000; supr. spl. svcs., sch. psychologist Egg Harbor City (N.J.) Bd. Edn., 2000—. Ednl. rschr. Temple U., Phila., 1994—. Editor: Preventing School Violence: The Teacher Variance Approach. Mem.: APA, N.J. Assn. Sch. Psychologists, Pa. Psychol. Assn., Nat. Assn. Sch. Psychologists. Home: 301 Park Ave New York NY 10022 Personal E-mail: kawinchell@aol.com.

WINCHELL, MARGARET J. realtor; b. Clinton, Tenn., Jan. 26, 1923; d. Robert Love Webster and Mayme Jane Warwick; m. Charles M. Winchell, June 7, 1941; children: David Alan(dec.), Margaret Winchell Boyle; m. Robert George Sterrett, July 15, 1977 (dec. 1982). Student, Denison U., 1940, Miami U., Oxford, Ohio, 1947, 48. Saleswoman Fred K.A. Schmidt & Shirmer Real Estate, Cin., 1960-66, Cline Realtors, Cin., 1966-70; owner, broker Winchell's Showplace Realtors, Cin., 1972—; ins. agt. United Liberty Life Ins. Co., Cin., 1966—, dist. mgr., 1967-70, 77-82, regional mgr., 1982—; stockbroker Waddell & Reed, Columbis, Ohio, 1972—, Security Counselors. Annuity and ins. specialist Fin. Cons., 1982—, dir., 1984, 85, 86, 87, owner; instr. evening coll. Treas., v.p. Parents Without Ptnrs., 1969, sec., 1968; pres. PTA, Hamilton Fairfield Singles; vol. leader, sr. dance leader Sycamore Sr. Str., 1990—2000; nat. spkr. Child Evangelism Fellowship and Nat. Sunday Sch. Convs., 1955—57; dir. Child Evangelism Cin.; pres. Christian Solos, 1974; chaplain Bethesda N. Hosp.; leader singles group Hyde Park Cmty. United Meth. Ch.; ordained Stephen min. Montgomery Comm. Bapt. Ch., 1990—2003. Mem.: Womens Coun. Real Estate Bd. (treas.), Nat. Assn. Real Estate Bds. West Schell Realtors (v.p.), Hamilton Singles Club (pres.), Guys and Gals Singles Club (founder, 1st pres.), Travel Go Go Club, Alfonta Club. Home and Office: 8221 Margaret Ln Cincinnati OH 45242-5309 E-mail: peg&dave6789@aol.com.

WINCHESTER, SUSAN, human resources specialist, state representative; b. Chickasha, Okla., Mar. 24, 1950; m. James R. Winchester; 1 child, Davis. BS, U. Okla., Norman, 1972; MHR in Human Resource Devel., U. Okla., 1994. Co-owner Am. Dusting Co., 1974—89; adult tng. and devel. coord. Canadian Valley Vo-Tech., 1987—92; owner Winchester Group, Chickasha, Okla., 1992—; rep. Ho. of Reps. State of Okla., Okla. City, 1999—. Vice chair ins. com. Okla. Ho. of Reps., Okla. City, 1999—, mem. appropriations and budget com. (subcom. on edn.), banking and fin., pub. health coms., 1999—. Mem. Leadership Chickasha; selection com. Okla. Found. for Excellence; bd. dirs. Leadership Okla., Okla. 4H Found. Mem.: Am. Legislative Exchange Coun., Mustang C. of C., Tuttle C. of C., Chickasha C. of C., Am. Soc. Tng. and Devel. Republican. Office: 2300 N Lincoln Blvd Rm 539 Oklahoma City OK 73105 Home and Office: PO Box 2162 Chickasha OK 73023

WINCKLER, CINDY, state representative; b. DesMoines, May 27, 1950; Educator Davenport Cmty. Sch. Dist., Pleasant Valley Sch. Dist., Calamus Sch. Dist., Davis County Sch. Dist.; mem. Iowa Ho. Reps., DesMoines, 2001—, mem. econ. devel. com., mem. appropriations com., mem. edn. com., mem. labor and indsl. rels. com., mem. ways and means com. Past nat. pres. Bus. and Profl. Women USA. Democrat. Office: State Capitol East 12th and Grand Des Moines IA 50319 also: 6 Thode Ct Davenport IA 52802

WINDELS, SUE, state senator; b. Nampa, Idaho, July 11, 1946; m. Carl Windels; children: Derek, Daniel. BA, Ea. Wash. U., 1967, MA, 1973. Vol. Peace Corps, 1967-69; tchr., 1969—; Dem. rep. dist. 27 Colo. Ho. of Reps. 1999-2000; Dem. senator dist. 19 Colo. State Senate, 2000—. Mem. edn., state, vets. and mil. affairs and stat audit com. Colo. Ho. of Reps.; mem. edn., judiciary and capitol devel. coms. Colo. State Senate. Founder (legis. newsletter) Voter's Voice, 1996-98. Mem. Interfaith Alliance; legis. dir. Jefferson County PTA, 1996-98; dir. pub. policy Colo. PTA, 1997. Mem. AAUW. LWV, Kiwanis. Office: Colo State Senate State Capitol 200 E Colfax Rm 307 Denver CO 80203 also: 13925 W 73d Ave Arvada CO 80005 E-mail: windels@sni.net., suewindels@aol.com.

WINDERS, GLENDA, publishing executive; Editl. dir. Copley News Svc., San Diego, 1997—. Office: Copley News Svc PO Box 120190 San Diego CA 92112-0190

WINDHAM, MELBA B. real estate broker; b. Royston, Ga., Jan. 15, 1947; d. Teasley Barton Burns and Willie Pauline Craft; m. Gene H. Windham, Dec. 31, 1969 (div.); 1 child, Charlee W. Alvarez. BA in Journalism, U. Ga., 1969. Lic. real estate broker S.C., 1986, Ga., 1986. With ins. sales Carswell of Carolina, Hilton Head Island, SC, 1991—98; broker in charge Del Webb Cmtys., Inc., Bluffton, SC, 1998—. Author: (weekly columns) Island Packet, 1993—98; contbr. articles to mags. Chmn. Relay for life American Cancer Soc.; bd. dirs. Low Country Players, Hilton Head Island, 1994, American Cancer Soc., Hilton Head Island, 1995—2003. Mem.: Hilton Head Island (S.C.) Assn. Realtors (bd. dir. 2002—), S.C. Assn. Realtors (state dir. 2003), Nat. Assn. Realtors. Democrat. Presbyn. Avocations: golf, writing. Home: P22 Acorn Ln Hilton Head Island SC 29928 Office: Del Webb Cmtys Sun City Hilton Head 127 Sun City Blvd Bluffton SC 29909

WINDSOR, HARRIET SMITH, state official; m. Richard L. Windsor; children: James A. Smith Jr., Julia A. Smith. BA, Juniata Coll.; PhD, MA, U. Del. Cert. lay spkr. Peninsula Conf. Former English tchr. Seaford Sr. HS; dean instrn., dept. English Chmn. Del. Tech. and Cmty. Coll. Owens Campus; mem., dir. State Personnel Gov. Thomas R. Carper's Cabinet, 1993—2001; Sec. of State State of Del., 2001—. Writer, spkr. numerous local, state and nat. bds. Serves Dist. Com. Ordained Ministry; mem., choir dir., organist, ch. sch. tchr., supt., adminstrv. bd. chmn., chmn. Pastor Parish Rels. Com. Millsboro Grace United Meth. Ch., lay leader, 2002—. Named Del. Mother of Yr., 1999, Woman of Yr., Sussex Ctrl. Jr. HS students; named to Del.'s Hall of Fame, 1997. Office: 401 Federal St Ste 3 Dover DE 19901 Mailing: Townsend Bldg PO Box 898 Dover DE 19903*

WINDSOR, JOAN RUTH, author, professional counselor; b. Rahway, N.J., Dec. 26, 1934; d. Thomas Clifford and Ruth L. (Labar) Laurent; m. James Clayton Windsor, June 22, 1957; children: James Laurent, Robin Joan Windsor Rice. BA in French, Coll. William and Mary, 1956, MEd in Counseling and Guidance, 1969. Lic. profl. counselor, Va. Tchr. 4th grade Rahway (N.J.) Sch. System, 1956-57, Rochester (N.Y.) Sch. System, 1957-58; edn. diagnostician Coll. William and Mary, Williamsburg, Va., 1968-70, Child Devel. Clinic, Hampton, Va., 1968-72; learning devel. counselor Personal Devel. Inst., Newport News, Va., 1972-75, personal devel. counselor, 1975-88, owner mgr., counselor Williamsburg, Va., 1988—. Continuing edn. instr. Coll. William & Mary, Williamsburg, 1994-95; presenter med. rsch. Jungian Analysts, Memphis, Tenn., 1995, Internat. Parapsychol. Assn., Durham, N.C., 1995. Author: (books) The Inner Eye, 1986, Dreams and Healing, 1988, Passages of Light, 1991; also articles. Grantee: Pvt. Grant, Williamsburg, Va., 1992. Mem. ACA. Avocations: swimming, reading. Office: Personal Devel Inst PO Box 1056 Williamsburg VA 23187-1056 Office Phone: 757-229-4873.

WINDSOR, PATRICIA (KATONAH SUMMERTREE, PERRIN WINTERS), author, educator, lecturer; b. NYC, Sept. 21, 1938; d. Bernhard Edward and Antoinette (Gaus) Seelinger; m. Laurence Charles Windsor, Jr., Apr. 3, 1959 (div. 1978); children: Patience Wells, Laurence Edward; m. Stephen E. Altman, Sept. 21, 1986 (div. 1989). Student, Bennington Coll., 1956-58, Westchester Community Coll.; AA, NYU. V.p. Windsor-Morehead Assoc., NYC, 1960—63; info. mgr. Family Planning Assn., London, 1974-76; faculty mem. Inst. Children's Lit., Redding Ridge, Conn., 1976-94, 99—; editor-in-chief AT&T, Washington, 1978-80; instr. U. Md. Writers Inst., Open Univ., Washington, 1980-82; creative developer, faculty mem. Long Ridge Writer's Group, Danbury, Conn., 1988-2000; dir. Summertree Studios, Savannah, Ga., 1992—. Dir. Wordspring Lit. Cons., 1989—, Wordworks Writing Cons., 1999—, Born Author Lit. Cons., 2003-; dir. Devel. Writing Workshops, Katonah, NY, 1976-78; judge Internat. Assn. Bus. Communicators, Washington, 1979, 89; lectr. LI U., Jersey City State Coll., Skidmore Coll., others, 1987—; instr. Coastal Ga. Ctr. for Continuing Edn., 1996—, Armstrong Atlantic U. Continuing Edn., 1997-2000, Anne Arundel (Md.) C.C., 2000—, workshop coord., 2000—; dir., founder Born Author Consultants, 2002—; designer Windsomethings Art & Design, 2003—. Author: The Summer Before, 1973 (ALA Best Book award 1973, transl. 1980 Austrian State prize 1980, also Brit., Norwegian, German edits.), Something's Waiting for You, Baker D, 1974 (starred selection Libr. Jour., Brit., Japanese edits.), Home Is Where Your Feet Are Standing, 1975, Diving for Roses, 1976 (NY Times Outstanding Book for Young Adults award, starred selection Libr. Jour.), Mad Martin, 1976, Killing Time, 1980, Demon Tree, 1983 (pen name Colin Daniel), The Sandman's Eyes, 1985 (Edgar Allan Poe Best Juvenile Mystery award Mystery Writers Am.), How a Weirdo and a Ghost Can Change Your Life, 1986, The Hero, 1988 (highest rating Voice of Youth Advocate), Just Like the Movies, 1990, The Christmas Killer, 1991 (Edgar nominee, Brit., Danish, French edits.), Two Weirdos and a Ghost, 1991, A Weird and Moogly Christmas, 1991, The Blooding, 1996 (YALSA pick for reluctant readers), The House of Death, 1996; columnist The Blood Rev., 1990-92, Savannah Parent, 1990-92; columnist Coastal Senior, 1997-99; also short stories in anthologies and mags.; actress: The Haunting of Hill House, City Lights Theatre Co., 1991. Mem. City Lights Theatre Co., Savannah, Ga., 1991. Mem. Horror Writers Am., Internat. Women's Writing Guild, Children's Book Guild, Authors Guild, Poetry Soc. Ga., Savannah Storytellers. Avocations: skiing, painting, modern dance. Office: Born Author Dot Com PO Box 799 Severna Park MD 21146

WINDWARD, SHIRLEY, secondary school educator, poet; b. Washington, Jan. 10, 1919; d. Albert Carl Weimar and Della Jost; m. Erwin Windward, Aug. 8, 1942; children: Stephen, Rolfe. BA in Edn., U. Wis., 1940; MA in English, UCLA, 1964. Cert. tchr. Calif. Tchr. Ctrl. H.S., Sheboygan, Wis., 1940—42, L.A. Valley Schs., Northridge, Calif., 1955—60; tchr., adminstr. Paul Revere Sch., L.A., 1960—68; tchr., adminstr., founder Windward Sch., Santa Monica, 1971—76, L.A., 1977—2004. Author: Midwife Chronicles, 1998; author: (with Audrey Hargreaves) Slipping Honey In, Two Kisses; contbr. poetry to profl. jours. Buddhist. Avocations: choral music, travel, ceramics, public readings.

WINE-BANKS, JILL SUSAN, lawyer; b. Chgo., May 5, 1943; d. Bert S. and Sylvia Dawn (Simon) Wine; m. Ian David Volner, Aug. 21, 1965; m. Michael A. Banks, Jan. 12, 1980. BS, U. Ill., Champaign, Urbana, 1964; JD, Columbia U., 1968; LLD (hon.), Hood Coll., 1975. Bar: N.Y. 1969, U.S. Ct. Appeals (2d, 4th, 5th, 6th, 7th and 9th cirs.), U.S. Supreme Ct. 1974, D.C. 1976, Ill. 1980. Asst. press. and pub. rels. dir. Assembly of Captive European Nations, N.Y.C., 1965-66; trial atty. criminal divsn. organized crime & racketeering U.S. Dept. Justice, 1969-73; asst. spl. prosecutor Watergate Spl. Prosecutor's Office, 1973-75; lectr. law sem. in trial practice Columbia U. Sch. Law, N.Y.C., 1975-77; assoc. Fried, Frank, Harris, Shriver & Kampelman, Washington, 1975-77; gen. counsel Dept. Army, Pentagon, Washington, 1977-79; ptnr. Jenner & Block, Chgo., 1980-84; solicitor gen. State of Ill. Office of Atty. Gen., 1984-86, dep. atty. gen., 1986-87; exec. v.p., chief oper., officer ABA, Chgo., 1987-90; atty. pvt. practice, 1990-92; v.p., dir. transaction and govt. rels. Motorola Internat. Network Ventures, 1990-97; dir. strategic alliances Motorola Cellular Infrastructure Group, 1997—99; v.p. alliance mgmt. Maytag Corp., 1999-2001; CEO Winning Workplaces, Evanston, Ill., 2001—03; chief officer Chgo. Pub. Schs. Edn. to Careers, 2003—. Mem. EEC disting. vis. program European Parliament, 1987; chmn. bd. dirs. St. Petersburg Telecom., Russia, 1994-97, Omni Capital Ptnrs., Inc., 1994-97. Recipient Spl. Achievement award U.S. Dept. Justice, 1972, Meritorious award, 1973, Cert. Outstanding Svc., 1975; decorated Disting. Civilian Svc. Dept. Army, 1979; named Disting. Vis. to European Econ. Cmty. Mem.: The Chgo. Network, Internat. Women's Forum, Exec. Club (bd. dirs. 1999—2001), Econ. Club. Address: 155 N Harbor Dr #701 Chicago IL 60601 E-mail: jwine_banks@cps.k12.il.us.

WINEBRENNER, SUSAN KAY, writer, consultant; b. Milw., Mar. 11, 1939; d. Samuel Bernard and Lillian (Ginsberg) Schuckit; m. Neil T. Winebrenner, Feb. 11, 1981 (dec.); children: Stacy Lynne Naimon, Kari Beth Naimon. BS, U. Wis., 1956, MS, U. Wis., Milw., 1979. Cert. tchr., Ill., Wis. Tchr. Shorewood (Wis.) Pub. Sch., 1961—81, River Forest (Ill.) Sch. Dist. 90, 1981—83; gifted coord. Forest Park (Ill.) Sch. Dist. 91, Ill., 1983—86; cons. Self-Edn. Cons. Svcs., San Marcos, Calif., 1986—. Author: Super Sentences Activity Book, 1987, Teaching Gifted Kids in the Regular Classroom, 2nd edit., 2000, Teaching Kids with Learning Difficulties in the Regular Classroom, 1996, Cluster Grouping Fact Sheet, 2001; contbr. numerous atricles on differentiating instruction for atypical learners. Recipient Outstanding Tchr. award Joint Coun. on Econ. Edn., Wis., 1979. Mem. ASCD (presenter), Nat. Assn. Gifted Children (presenter). Home and Office: 1450 La Loma Dr San Marcos CA 92069-4737 E-mail: susan.winebrenner@adelphia.net.

WINFIELD, KAREN ANN, art educator, artist, small business owner; b. St. Louis, Nov. 3, 1951; d. Victor Arthur and Norma Mae Silber; m. Scott Buckner Winfield, June 29, 1974; children: Leslie Winfield Ballentine, Eric Buckner, Elizabeth Lauren. BS in Edn., U. Mo., 1973. Lic. profl. tchr. Colo. Asst. libr. F.L. Schlagle H.S., Kansas City, Kans.; art tchr. Hickman Mills H.S., Kansas City, Mo., 1975—80; fine arts coord., art tchr. Johnson County Pk. and Recreation Dist., Shawnee Mission, Kans., 1981—85; libr. Notre Dame de Sion, Kansas City, Mo., 1988—91; owner Heart and Hand Dolls, 1991—97; art tchr. Falcon (Colo.) Sch. Dist. 49, 1994—95, Acad. Sch. Dist. 20, Colorado Springs, 1995—; owner Truly Victorian Mercantile, 1995—. Mem. Bridge Gallery, Colorado Springs; freelance calligrapher, 1980—91. Exhibited in group shows at Art in the Woods Exhibit, 1990 (Kans. City Star Purchase award, 1990), Wearable Art Exhbn., 2000—01, Colo. Art Educators Exhibit, 2003 (Best Photog., 2003), Body Packaging III: Identity Crisis, 2003, Bus. of Art Ctr., Manitou Springs, 2003. Pres. Faith Luth. Ch. Women, Prairie Village, Kans., 1982—83. Mem.: ArtSource Colo., Tri-Lakes Ctr. for the Arts, Bus. of Art Ctr., Colo. Art Edn. Assn. (ArtSource rep. 2002—03), Nat. Art Edn. Assn. Avocations: fiber arts, aerobic training. Office: Liberty HS 8720 Scarborough Dr Colorado Springs CO 80920 E-mail: kwinfie@d20.co.edu.

WINFREY, OPRAH, television talk show host, actress, producer; b. Kosciusko, Miss., Jan. 29, 1954; d. Vernon Winfrey and Vernita Lee. BA in Speech and Drama, Tenn. State U. News reporter Sta. WVOL Radio, Nashville, 1971-72; reporter, news anchorperson Sta. WTVF-TV, Nashville, 1973-76; news anchorperson Sta. WJZ-TV, Balt., 1976-77, host morning talk show People Are Talking, 1977-83; host talk show A.M. Chgo. Sta. WLS-TV, 1984; host The Oprah Winfrey Show, Chgo., 1985—; nationally syndicated, 1986—; host series of celebrity interview spls. Oprah: Behind the Scenes, 1992—; owner, prodr., chmn., CEO Harpo Prodns., 1986—. Ptnr. in Oxygen Media, an Internet and cable TV co., 2000—; founder, editl. dir. O. The Oprah Magazine in conjunction with Hearst Mags., 2000—. Appeared in films The Color Purple, 1985 (nominated Acad. award and Golden Globe award), Native Son, 1986, Beloved, 1998 (exec. prodr.); About Us: The Dignity of Children, 1997 (TV), Before Women Had Wings, 1997 (TV; also exec. prodr. ABC series Oprah Winfrey presents); prodr. Dr. Phil (TV series), 2002—; Listen Up: The Lives of Quincy Jones (TV spl.), 1990, prodr., actress ABC-TV mini-series The Women of Brewster Place, 1989, also series Brewster Place, 1990, movie There Are No Children Here, 1993; exec. prodr. (ABC Movie of the Week) Overexposed, 1992; host, supervising prodr. celebrity interview series Oprah: Behind the Scenes, 1992, ABC Aftersch. Spls., 1991-93; host, exec. prodr. Michael Jackson Talks...to Oprah-90 Prime-Time Minutes with the King of Pop, 1993; exec. prodr. miniseries: Oprah Winfrey Presents: The Wedding, 1998, Oprah Winfrey Presents: David and Lisa, 1998, Oprah Winfrey Presents: Tuesdays with Morrie, 1999 (TV), Oprah Winfrey Presents: Amy and Isabelle, 2001 Recipient Woman of Achievement award NOW, 1986, Emmy award for Best Daytime Talk Show Host, 1987, 91, 92, 94, 95, 97, Nat. Book Found's 50th Anniversary gold medal, 1999, America's Hope award, 1990, Industry Achievement award Broadcast Promotion Mktg. Execs./Broadcast Design Assn., 1991, Image awards NAACP, 1989, 91, 92, 94, Entertainer of the Yr. award NAACP, 1989, CEBA awards, 1989, 90, 91, George Foster Peabody's Individual Achievement award, 1996, Gold Medal award IRTS, 1996, Lifetime Achievement award NATAS, 1998, People's Choice award, 1997, 98, Horatio Alger award, 1993; named Broadcaster of Yr. Internat. Radio and TV Soc., 1988; recognized as one of America's 25 Most Influential People, Time mag.; inducted to Television Hall of Fame, 1994, Bob Hope Humanitarian Award, 2002. Office: Harpo Prodns 110 N Carpenter St Chicago IL 60607-2145*

WING, ADRIEN KATHERINE, law educator; b. Aug. 7, 1956; d. John Ellison and Katherine (Pruitt) Wing; children: Che-Cabral, Nolan Felipe. AB magna cum laude, Princeton U., 1978; MA, UCLA, 1979; JD, Stanford, 1982. Bar: N.Y. 1983, U.S. Dist. Ct. (so. and ea. dists.) N.Y. 1983, U.S. Ct. Appeals (5th and 9th cirs.). Assoc. Curtis, Mallet-Prevost, Colt & Mosle, N.Y.C., 1982-86, Rabinowitz, Boudin, Standard, Krinsky & Lieberman, 1986-87; assoc. prof. law U. Iowa, Iowa City, 1987-93, prof., 1993—, disting. prof. law, 2001—. Mem. alumni council Princeton U., 1983-85, 96-2000, mem. exec. com., 2002—, trustee Class of '78 Alumni Found., 1984-87, 93—, v.p. Princeton Class of 1978 Alumni, 1993-98, trustee Princeton U. 1995; mem. bd. visitors Stanford Law Sch., 1993-96; vis. prof. U. Mich., 2002. Mem. bd. editors Am. J. Comp. Law, 1993—. Mem. Iowa Commn. on African Ams. in Prisons, 1999—. Mem.: ABA (exec. com. young lawyers sect. 1985—87, law sch. site inspector 2002—), U.S. Assn. Constl. Law (bd. dir.), Am. Assn. of Law Schs. (minority sect. bd. 1996—, chair 2002), Am. Friends Svc. Com. (bd. dirs. Mid. East 1998—), Am. Soc. Internat. Law (exec. coun. 1986—89, exec. com. 1988—99, nominating com. 1991, 1993, group chair S. Africa 1993—95, membership com. 1994—95, exec. coun. 1996—99), Internat. Assn. Dem. Lawyers (UN rep. 1984—87), Nat. Conf. Black Lawyers (chmn. internat. affairs sect. 1982—95, UN rep.), Internat. Third World Legal Studies Assn. (bd. dirs. 1996—, nominating trustee Princeton com. 1997—2000), Coun. on Fgn. Rels., Iowa Peace Inst. (bd. dirs. 1993—95), Iowa City Fgn. Rels. Coun. (bd. dirs. 1989—94), Transafrica Scholars Forum Coun. (bd. dirs. 1993—95), Black Alumni of Princeton U. (bd. dirs. 1982—87). Democrat. Avocations: photography, writing, poetry. Office: U Iowa Sch Law Boyd Law Bldg Iowa City IA 52242 E-mail: adrien-wing@uiowa.edu.

WING, ELIZABETH SCHWARZ, museum curator, educator; b. Cambridge, Mass., Mar. 5, 1932; d. Henry F. and Maria Lisa Schwarz; m. James E. Wing, Apr. 18, 1957; children: Mary Elizabeth Wing-Berman, Stephen R. BA, Mt. Holyoke Coll., 1955; MS, U. Fla., 1957, PhD, 1962. Interim asst. curator Fla. Mus. Natural History, U. Fla., Gainesville, 1961-69, asst. curator, 1969-73, assoc. curator, 1973-78, curator, 1978—; U. Fla., Fla. Mus. Natural History, Gainesville, 1990-92. U.S. rep. Internat. Congress Archaeozoology, 1981—. Author: (with A.B. Brown) Paleonutrition, 1979, (with E.J. Reitz) Zooarcheology, 1999; editor (with J.C. Wheeler) Economic Prehistory of the Central Andes, 1988; contbr. articles to profl. jours. Recipient Fryxell award Soc. Am. Archaeology, 1996; NSF grantee, 1961-64, 68-73, 79-80, 84-85, 89-91, 95-96. Mem. Soc. Ethnobiology (pres. 1989-91). Office: U Fla Dickenson HALL/Fla Mus Natural History PO Box 117800 Gainesville FL 32611-7800

WING, JENNIFER MARY, literature educator; d. Marcia Carol and Steve Mosher Wing. BA, U. Ga., Athens, 1996; MA, Ga. State U., 2000, postgrad., 2001—. Mgr. of clothing line The Pilates Studio, N.Y.C., NY, 1997—98; pharmacy technician CVS, Lithia Springs, Ga., 1998—2000; prof. Ga. State U., Atlanta, 2000—. Rsch. asst. Ga. State U., Atlanta, 2000—, tutor in writing ctr., 1999—2000, regent's test grader, 2000—, mentor to new tchrs., 2002—03. Contbr. articles to profl. jours. and encys., chapters to books. Mem. Amnesty Internat., N.Y.C., NY, 2002, World Wildlife Fund, N.Y.C., NY, 1992. Mem.: MLA (assoc.), Planning Com. for GEA New Voices Conf. (assoc.; mktg. divsn. 2003), Profl. Devel. Com. (assoc.; mktg. divsn. 2002). Avocations: acting, writing poetry, playing string bass, singing, cooking. Office: Georgia State U University Plaza Atlanta GA 30303

WINGATE, BETTYE FAYE, librarian, educator; b. Hillsboro, Tex., Oct. 31, 1950; d. Warren Randolph and Faye (Gilmore) W. BA summa cum laude, Baylor U., 1971, MA, 1975; MLS, Tex. Womans U., 1985. Cert. prov. sec., learning resources endorsement. English tchr. Mexia HS, Tex.; reading tchr. Connally Ind. Sch. Dist., Waco, Tex.; reading tchr., libr. Grapevine-Colleyville Ind. Sch. Dist., Grapevine, Tex.; libr., ret., May 02 Crockett Mid. Sch., Irving, Tex. Mem. librs. coms., Campus Action Planning Com., 1989-93, Irving Ind. Sch. Dist. Site Based Decision-Making Com., 1992-94, mem. staff devel. coun., 1994-96, chair media fair com., 1996-2001; rev. Linworth Pub.; spkr., presenter in field. Founding sponsor Challenger Ctr., Air Force Meml. Found. Recipient Tex. Media awards, 1988, 89, 94. Mem. ALA, NEA, Am. Assn. Sch. Libr. (vol. libr. Kids Connect), Tex. State Tchr. Assn. (assn. rep.), Tex. Libr. Assn. (chmn. state media awards com. 1989-91), Tex. Assn. Edn. Tech., Tex. Computer Edn. and Tech., Assn. Ednl. Comm. and Tech., Planetary Soc., Nat. Space Soc., Nat. Parks & Conservation Assn., Baylor Alumni Assn. (life), Wilderness Soc., Sierra Club, Beta Phi Mu, Delta Kappa Gamma (scholar 1985). E-mail: bettye.winate@yahoo.com.

WINGATE, CONSTANCE BLANDY, librarian; b. Woodbury, N.J., Mar. 7, 1935; d. John Chase and Josephine Spond (Black) Blandy; m. Len B. Cooke Jr., 1978 (div. 1987); m. John B. Wingate, Mar. 12, 1999. BA, U. Pa., 1956; MA, U. Denver, 1957. Adult cons. Onondaga Library System, Syracuse, N.Y., 1965-66; asst. dir. Mt. Vernon (N.Y.) Public Library, 1966-75; dep. dir. Queens Borough Public Library, Jamaica, N.Y., 1975-79, dir., 1980-94. Founder pres. Literacy Vols. Mt. Vernon, 1972-74. Trustee METRO, 1980-91, v.p., 1985-88, pres., 1988-91; mem. N.Y. State Libr. Svcs. and Constrn. Act Adv. Coun., 1982-88, chmn., 1986-87; bd. dirs. Queens Coun. on the Arts, 1988-94, v.p., 1989-93; bd. dirs. Queens Mus. of Art, 1988-98, v.p., 1994-96, pres. 1996-98; bd. dirs. Queens Libr. Found., 1996-2003. Mem.: ALA, Circumnavigators Club (Internat. sec. 2002—). Republican. Episcopalian. Home: Apt 10D 166-25 Powells Cove Blvd Beechhurst NY 11357

WINGATE, TANYA WILLIAMS, school disciplinarian; b. Norfolk, Va., Oct. 8, 1963; d. Joseph H. and Joan C. Williams. BS, Old Dominion U., Norfolk, Va., 1987; MEd, Regent U., Virginia Beach, Va., 1997; postgrad., Nova Southeastern U., Ft. Lauderdale, Fla. Cert. tchr. Va. Note ops. adminstr. Crestar Bank, Norfolk, 1985—95; tchr. Norfolk Pub. Schs., 1995—2001, orientation coord., 2001—02, safe schs. coord., 2002—03, dean of students, 2003—. Pres. Enoch Youth Assn., Norfolk, 2001—. Mem.: VASSAP, Norfolk Fedn. Tchrs., Ednl. Leader Assn. Democrat. Baptist. Avocations: reading, sewing, singing. Office: Norfolk Pub Schs Lafayette Winona Middle Sch 1701 Alsace Ave Norfolk VA 23509

WINGERT, HANNELORE CHRISTIANE, real estate agent, chemical company executive; b. Karlsbad, Czechoslavakia; came to U.S., 1962, naturalized, 1967; d. Andreas and Gisela Maria (Ciharz) Zwickel; m. Rudolf Wingert, Feb. 9, 1963; children: Angela Helene, Christopher Rudolf. I.BA, Stadt. Berufsschule, Germany, 1961; postgrad. in mgmt., Bergen Community Coll., 1983. Lic. real estate, N.J., Calif. Clk. various cos., N.J., 1963, bilingual sec., 1963-78; exec. sec., adminstrv. asst. Lurgi Corp., Hasbrouck Heights, N.J., 1978-81; sr. exec. sec. Degussa Corp., Teterboro, N.J., 1981-83, asst. product mgr. silica, 1983-85, asst. product mgr. H202, 1985-87, sales promotion coord., 1987; sales assoc. Schlott Realtors, Kinnelon, N.J., 1987-90, Coldwell Banker, 1990—2001, Hanson/McMillin Realty, Escondido, Calif., 2002—. Author real estate newsletter, 1992—, community newsletter, 1977-79. Mem. Garden State Multiple Listing Svc.; chmn. master planning com. High Crest Lake, West Milford, N.J., 1974-75; advisor Jr. Woman's Club Kinnelon-Butler (N.J.), 1973-74; techr. computer classes Bd. Realtors, Passaic County, 1989-92. Mem. Nat. Assn. Realtors, Calif. Assn. Realtors, No. San Diego County Assn. Realtors, NJ, 2002-, Fed. of Woman's Clubs (past pres.), High Crest Lake Woman's Club (pres. 1972-73) (West Milford, NJ). Republican. Roman Catholic. Home: 743 Atwood Pl San Marcos CA 92069 Office Phone: 760-233-5320. E-mail: HCWingert@cox.net.

WINICK, BERNYCE ALPERT, artist, photographer; b. N.Y.C. Student, Bklyn. Mus. Art Sch., 1938—41; BA in Fine Arts and Music, NYU; pvt. studies with, Mario Cooper, N.Y.C., 1969—86; student, Traphagen Sch. Fashion, 1958—61, Art Students League N.Y., 1961—64, Nat. Acad. Design Sch. Fine Arts, 1968—72. Artist, Woodmere, L.I., N.Y., 1969—. Designer, fashion artist, fashion con. in field. One-woman shows include Hewlett-Woodmere Pub. Libr., L.I., 1969, Galerie Internat., N.Y., 1977, Salmagundi Club, Thomas Moran (First prize Nat. Acad. Sch., 1972, Salmagundi Club 1981, 87, 90, Nat. Arts Club, 1985, Nat. Acad. Sch., 1972, First Prize Meml. award 2002), Gallery Internat. 57, N.Y., 1989, Discovery Art Gallery, Sea Cliff, L.I., 1989, 96, 98, Glen Cove, N.Y., 1993-94, Chelsea Ctr., East Norwich, N.Y., 1993, 96, 98, 2000, 2002, Z Gallery, SoHo, N.Y., 1994, County Exec. Bldg., 1997, Fine Arts Mus. L.I., 1997, Town Hall, Hempstead, N.Y., 2000, Winners Exhibn. Nat. Arts Club., N.Y. 2002; exhibited in group shows at Discovery Art Gallery, Glen Cove, N.Y., 1988, 91-93, Nat. Acad. Sch. Fine Arts, N.Y., 1972, Long Beach Mus., L.I., 1979, 81-85, 89 (2d prize 1989), Chen Chung Gallery of St. John's U., N.Y., 1980, Salmagundi Club, N.Y., 1980-81, Am. Watercolor Soc., N.Y., 1982, 85, 88, 92, Fine Arts Mus. L.I., N.Y., 1983, 88-89, 91-92, 96 (2d prize), The Nat. Arts Club, N.Y., 1985-86, 88-89, 2002, Nassau County Mus., L.I., 1985-86, 88, Nat. Assn. Women Artists, N.Y., 1986, 88, 91-93, C.W. Post Coll., L.I., N.Y., (Hon. mention 1985), L.I. Arts Coun. Freeport, 1995-96 (Hon. mention), Chelsea Cultural Ctr., N.Y., 1995, 2001, (Suburban Art League award), Rockville Ctr. Guild for the Arts, N.Y., 1995 (Hon. mention), 97 (Best in Show for photography), Chelsea Ctr. (Peacock Showcase award, First prize 2000), (Merit award 2001), East Norwich, N.Y., Discovery Art Gallery, Glen Cove, N.Y., 1996, 2000, 2002, Fine Arts Mus. L.I., N.Y., 1997, Discovery Art Gallery, Sea Cliff, N.Y., 1998, L.I. Arts Coun. Freeport, N.Y. (Hon. mention 1996, First prize in black and white photography 99), Canton Art Inst. Ohio, Galerie Internat., Gallery Internat. 57, Z Gallery, Salle Augustin-Chenier, Quebec, Can., Town Hall, Town of Hempstead, N.Y., 2000, N.Y. Inst. Tech., Wisser Meml. Libr., 2001, Nat. Arts Club (First photography prize 2002), Heckscher Mus., Huntington, N.Y., 2003 (hon. mention), Salmagandi Club, N.Y., 2002 (Thomas Moran Meml. award, First prize), Mills Pond House, St. James, N.Y., 2002 (hon. mention), Nat. Arts Club, N.Y., 2001 (First prize), others; work included in U.S. Dept. State Art in Embassies program, many pvt. and corp. collections; invitationals include Chelsea Cultural Ctr., L.I.; photographs in numerous publications including South Shore Record, 1995, The Encyclopedia of Watercolour Landscape Techniques, 1996, Popular Photography, 1996, 97, 99, 2000, 04, Photography on America Online, 1997, 99, 2000, New York: Sterling Publishing Co., Inc., 1998, Watercolor Planning and Painting, 1998, Abstracts in Watercolor, 1996, New York Times, 1999, 2001; photography in (books) Capturing the Seen and Unseen in Photographs, 2001, Thirty Nine Musical Photographs, 2003, Town and Country Mag.; photographs exhibited in Mill Pond House, Salmagundi Club, NYU, Nat. Assn. Women Artists, and Artists Unlimited, Tampa, Fla. (various photography awards). Fellow Royal Soc. Encouragment Arts Manufactures and Commerce (London); mem. Am. Watercolor Soc., Nat. Assn. Women Artists, Discovery Gallery, Tri County Artists, Long Beach Art League, Nat. Arts Club. Avocation: pianist. Home and Office: 923 Beth Ln Woodmere NY 11598-1507

WINIK, JOANNE, broadcast executive; BA, Racine Coll. Pres., gen. mgr. KLRN-TV, San Antonio, 1988—. Board of directors PBS, 1999—. Office: KLRN-TV PO Box 9 San Antonio TX 78291-0009

WINKER, MARGARET A. editor; MD, U. Ill. Resident in internal medicine U. Chgo., fellowship in geriatric medicine; clin. asst. prof. geriatrics sect. U. Ill. Med. Ctr.; sr. editor Jour. of AMA. Contbr. articles to profl. jours. Mem. Am. Geriatrics Soc. (chair pub. edn. com. 1997). Office: U Chgo Graham Sch Gen Studies 5835 S Kimbark Ave Chicago IL 60637-1635 Fax: 773-702-6814.

WINKIE, DUSTI KAI, test scoring director; b. Marengo, Iowa, Aug. 2, 1957; d. Wallace Benjamin and Beverly Mae Winkie. BA, U. of Iowa, Iowa City, Iowa, 1979—81, MA, 1983—86. Sec. Ctrl. States Theater Corp., Des Moines, 1975—76; spotwelder Amana Refrigeration, Amana, Iowa, 1976—77; nurse's aide Beverly Manor Convalescent Ctr., Belle Plaine, Iowa, 1978—80; rsch. asst. U. of Iowa, Iowa City, 1981—81; interviewer for 65+ rural health study U. Hospitals, Iowa City, 1981—82; substitute tchr. Dept. of Def. Dependents Schools, Idar-Oberstein, Germany, 1983—83, Darmstadt, Germany, 1986—88; reading, comm., and math. instr. US Army, Darmstadt, Germany, 1987—90; german instr. Kirkwood C.C. Continuing Edn., Belle Plaine, Iowa, 1991; scorer NCS, Iowa City, 1993—97; scoring dir. Pearson Ednl. Measurement, Iowa City, 1997—. German tutor pvt., Belle Plaine, Iowa, 1991—93. Mem. Am. Legion Aux., Belle Plaine, Iowa, 1993—2003; vol. in elem. sch. lang. arts instrn. Belle Plaine Cmty. Schools, Belle Plaine, Iowa, 1976—79, Dept. of Def. Dependents Schools, Idar-Oberstein, Germany, 1982—83, Darmstadt, Germany, 1986—89, Belle Plaine Cmty. Schools, Belle Plaine, Iowa, 1991—93. Recipient Graduation With Highest Distinction And Honors In Psychology, U. of Iowa, 1981, elected to Phi Beta Kappa, Phi Beta Kappa, 1981. Achievements include development of Children's Loneliness Scale; Online Scoring Training. Avocations: studying germanic languages, translating letters and documents, restoring antique furniture, travel.

WINKLEBY, MARILYN A. medical researcher; BA in Social Sci., Calif. State U., Sacramento, 1968, MA in. Clin. Psychology, 1974; MPH in Epidemiology/Biostat, U. Calif., Berkeley, 1983, PhD in Epidemiology, 1986. Project dir. cervical cancer screening study UCLA Sch. Pub. Health, 1974-77; co-prin. investigator Calif. Ctr. Sudden Infant Death Syndrome Risk Factor Study, Sch. Medicine, Dept. Cmty. Health U. Calif., Davis, 1977-81, co-investigator cmty. cardiovascular surveillance program, adj lectr. Sch. Medicine, Dept. Cmty. Health, 1981-82, project coord. epidemiology unit, stress and hypertension study Dept. Epidemiology Berkeley, 1983-87, rsch. epidemiologist Dept. Behavioral and Devel. Pediat. San Francisco, 1986-91; sr. rsch. scientist/prin. investigator Stanford Ctr. Rsch. in Disease Prevention, Stanford U. Sch. of Medicine, Palo Alto, Calif., 1987—. Epidemiology cons. SIDS Info. and Counseling Project, Dept. Health, State of Calif., Berkeley, 1980-83; founder, dir. Stanford Med. Youth Sci. Program, 1988—; lectr. divsn. health rsch. and policy, dept. medicine Stanford U., 1989—. Contbr. articles to profl. jours. Bd. dirs. Loaves and Fishes Family Kitchen, San Jose, Calif., 1988-92, Mountain View Cmty. Health Clinic, 1992-95. Fellow Am. Heart Assn. (coun. epidemiology 1989, Established Investigator award 1996). Office: Stanford Ctr Rsch in Disease Prevention 1000 Welch Rd Ste 302 Palo Alto CA 94304-1808

WINKLER, AGNIESZKA M. marketing and software executive; b. Rome, Feb. 22, 1946; came to U.S., 1953; naturalized, 1959; d. Wojciech A. and Halina Z. (Owsiany) W.; children from previous marriage: children: Renata G. Ritcheson, Dana C Sworakowski; m. Arthur K. Lund. BA, Coll. Holy Name, 1967; MA, San Jose State U., 1971; MBA, U. Santa Clara, 1981. Tchg. asst. San Jose State U., 1968-70; cons. to Ea. European bus. Palo Alto, Calif., 1970-72; pres./founder Commart Communications, Palo Alto, 1973-84; pres./founder, chmn. bd. Winkler Advt., Santa Clara, Calif., 1984—; chmn. bd. SuperCuts, Inc.; chmn., founder TeamToolz, 2000—01, Value Storm, 2002—. Bd. dirs. Reno Air, Lifeguard, Lifeguard Life Ins. Author: Warp Speed Branding, 1999. Trustee Santa Clara U., 1991—; trustee O'Connor Found., 1987-93, mem. exec. com., 1988—, mem. Capital Campaign steering com., 1989; mem. nat. adv. bd. Comprehensive Health Enhancement Support System, 1991—; mem. mgmt. west com. A.A.A.A. Agy., 1991—, vice chair no. Calif. coun., 1996—; project dir. Poland Free Enterprise Plan, 1989-92; mem. adv. bd. Normandy France Bus. Devel., 1989-92; mem. bd. regents Holy Names Coll., 1987—; bd. dirs. San Jose Mus. Art, 1987; mem. San Jose Symphony, Gold Baton, 1986; mem. nat. adv. com. Chess, 1991—; dir. Bay Area Coun., 1994—. Recipient CLIO award in Advt., Addy award and numerous others; named to 100 Best Women in Advt., Ad Age, 1988, Best Woman in Advt., AdWeek and McCall's Mag., 1993, one of 100 Best and Brightest Women in Mktg. & Advt., Nat. Assn. Women Bus. Owners, 1996. Mem. Family Svc. Assn. (trustee 1980-82), Am. Assn. Advt. Agys. (agy. mgmt. west com. 1991), Bus. Profl. Advt. Assn., Polish Am. Congress, San Jose Advt. Club, San Francisco Ad Club, Beta Gamma Sigma (hon.), Pi Gamma Mu, Pi Delta Phi (Lester-Tinneman award 1966, Bill Raskob Found. grantee 1965). Office: AMW Consulting 633 Post # 515 San Francisco CA 94109

WINKLER, CHERYL J. state legislator; m. Ralph Winkler; children: Robert C., Ralph E. Student, U. Cin. Clk. Green Twp., 1984-85, trustee, 1986-90; former rep. Ohio State Ho. Reps. Dist. 20; rep. Ohio State Ho. Reps. Dist. 34, 1993—, mem. interstate coop. com., children and youth com., mem. reference, edn. and state govt. com., mem. select com. on tech., mem. joint com. on juvenile corrections & overcrowding. Mem. Cin. Bar Assn. Aux., Green Twp. and Bridgetown Civic Clubs, Western Hamilton County Econ. Coun. Home: 5355 Boomer Rd Cincinnati OH 45247-7926 Office: Ohio Ho of Reps State House Columbus OH 43215

WINKLER, DOLORES EUGENIA, retired health facility administrator; b. Milw., Aug. 10, 1929; d. Charles Peter and Eugenia Anne (Zamka) Kowalski; m. Donald James Winkler, Aug. 18, 1951; 1 child, David John. Grad., Milw. Bus. Inst., 1949. Acct. Curative Rehab. Ctr., Milw., 1949-60; staff acct. West Allis (Wis.) Meml. Hosp., 1968-70, chief acct., 1970-78, reimbursement analyst, 1978-85, dir. budgets and reimbursement, 1985-95; ret., 1995. Mem. adv. coun., fin. com. Tau Home Health Care Agy., Milw., 1981—83. Mem.: Inst. Mgmt. Accts. (pres. 1983—84, nat. dir. 1986—88, pres. Mid Am. Regional Coun. 1988—89, award of excellence 1989), Healthcare Fin. Mgmt. Assn. (pres. 1989—90, Follmer Bronze award 1980, Reeves Silver award 1986, Muncie Gold award 1989, medal of honor 1993), Beta Chi Rho (pres. 1948). Avocations: travel, photography, golf. Home: 12805 W Honey Ln New Berlin WI 53151-2652

WINKLER, GAIL CASKEY, design historian, writer, educator; b. Chgo., Aug. 5, 1942; d. Robert E. and Ethel (Barquist) Caskey; m. Robert H. Winkler, Jan. 22, 1964 (div. 1976); m. Roger W. Moss, July 19, 1981. BA, Beloit (Wis.) Coll., 1964; MA, U. Wis., 1971, MS, 1977, PhD, 1988. Instr. U. Wis., Madison, 1976-81; sr. ptnr. LCA Assocs., Phila., 1982—; adj. faculty U. Pa., Phila., 1986—; asst. prof. U. Del., 1991-93. Author: Victorian Interior Decoration, 1986, Victorian Exterior Decoration, 1987, Floor Coverings for Historic Buildings, 1988, The Well-Appointed Bath, 1989, An Analysis of Drapery, 1993; (museum installations include), William Conner House, Conner Prairie, Fishers, Ind., Lanier Mansion, Madison, Ind., Tudor Hall in Pamplin Park, Petersburg, Va., Fairlawn Mansion, Superior, Wis., Adams House Mus., Deadwood, S.D., Villa Louis, Prairie du Chien, Wis., Hixon House, LaCrosse, Wis., Campbell House Mus., St. Louis, Dr. Richard Eells House, Quincy, Ill., (projects include) studies of the historic finishes and furnishings of the U.S. Senate and House, Chambers, Va. State Capitol, Richmond, City Hall, Phila., Capitol of the Commonwealth Pa., Rutherford B. Hayes house, Fremont, Ohio, Buchanan house, U.S. Naval Acad., Anderson Cottage (summer White House Abraham Lincoln), Washington, D.C., Wright Bros.' Printing Shop, Dayton, Ohio, Capitol of State of Va. Fellow Am. Soc. Interior Designers (bd. dirs. Pa. East chap. 1983-88, 2001—, Athena award 1989, Medallist award 1995), Found. Interior Design Edn. and Rsch. (rsch. com. 1986-96). Office: 604 S Washington Sq Philadelphia PA 19106-4118 Office Phone: 215-925-8367.

WINKLER, MARY BERNICE, special education educator; b. Hamilton, Ohio, Sept. 24, 1946; d. William Frederick and Bernadette Elizabeth Vogel; m. Harold Winkler, Dec. 30, 1966; children: James Robert, Wade Charles. BS in edn., Miami U., 1968; EdM in spl. edn., U. NC, Charlotte, 2003. Cert. tchr. Nat. Bd., NC State Improvement Project. Tchr., Ohio; spl. edn. tchr.; staff devel. tchr. Coord. Cabarrus County NCSIP, Concord, NC, 2002—. Vol. Cmty. Free Clinic, Concord, 1995—98. Mem.: Coun. of Exceptional Children, Internat. Dyslexia Assoc. Home: 5465 Ddr Run Ct Davidson NC 28036

WINKLEY-PIKES, SANDRA KAY, special education educator; b. Dallas, Tex., Jan. 17, 1959; d. Leon and Lillie Bell Steward; m. Clyde Pikes, Jr., July 20, 2002; children: Crysta LaDawn Pikes, Clyde Pikes III, Caleb Anthony Pikes; 1 child, Derek LaRussell Winkley II. EdB, Tex. A&M U., 1979; EdM, Tex. A&M Universtiy, 1987. Cert. tchr. Tex. Bd. of Certification, 1979. Spl. edn. tchr. W.W. Samuell HS, Dallas, 1980—, spl. edn. liaison, 2000—03. Named Outstanding Young Women of Am., Outstanding Young Women of Am., 1981; recipient Tchr. of the Yr. Finalist, Dallas Roatary Club, 2001, Unsung Hero award, WB33 TV, Dallas, Tex., 2002. Mem.: Alpha Kappa Alpha. Democrat. Baptist. Avocations: reading, movies, travel, gardening, volunteering at church. Home: 1313 Devonshire Lane Mesquite TX 75150 Office: WW Samuell High School 8928 Palisade Drive Dallas TX

WINN, JANICE GAIL, food products administrator; b. Springfield, Mass., Nov. 2, 1951; d. Ross Eleanor (Droskovich) W. BA, Western New Eng. Coll., 1976. Gen. mdse. mgr. Mott's Shop-Rite, East Hartford, Conn., 1979-84; sr. merchandiser Imperial Distbrs., Auburn, Mass., 1984-85; dir. of gen. mdse. Waldbaums Food Mart, Holyoke, Mass., 1985-91; dir. health, beauty care and gen. mdse. Big Y Foods, Inc., Springfield, 1991—. Republican. Avocations: travel, spending time with partner and family. Office: Big Y Foods Inc 2145 Roosevelt Ave Springfield MA 01104-1650

WINN, KATHLEEN ANN, bank officer, real estate broker; b. Buffalo, Aug. 22, 1958; d. Francis Joseph and Jane Marie (Barrett) Ginnett; m. John H. Westberg, Aug. 7, 1988 (div. Aug. 27, 1998); children: Melissa G. Proctor, Kimberlee M. Proctor, Barrett Westberg, Paige L. Westberg; m. Albert Leroy Winn, Aug. 29, 1999; stepchildren: Christopher A., Ashley E., Arianne K. BA, U. Ariz. Cert. Real Estate Inst., real estate specialist. Loan officer Chase Manhattan, Phoenix, 1993—99; mortgage loan officer Miner Kennedy, Scotsdale, 1999—2000; mortgage broker Optimum Fin., Scotsdale, 2000—. Bd. dirs., founder Shalom Ho., Tucson, 1986—88; chmn. RAPAC, Tucson, 1984—86, Phoenix, 1988. Mem.: Cert. Real Estate Specialists. Republican. Home: 3803 E Flossmoor Cir Mesa AZ 85206

WINN, STEPHENIE, special education program specialist; b. Albany, N.Y., Apr. 8, 1970; d. Stephen Allen and Sharon Lynn Jenkins Winn. BA in Art with honors, U. LaVerne, 1992; MS in Spl. Edn. magna cum laude, Nat. U., L.A., 1995, MS in Instnl. Leadership summa cum laude, 1996; postgrad., U. So. Calif., L.A., 1997—. Calif. multiple subject tchg. credential, Calif. specialist tchg. credentials learning handicapped and severely handicapped. Tchg. asst. art dept. U. LaVerne, Calif., 1991-92; tchr. L.A. County Office Edn., Downey, 1993-99, sr. program specialist, 1999—. Mem.: Internat. Order of the Rainbow for Girls (past grand rep. Okla. in Calif. 1989—90, Grand Cross 1989, PMA of Doric Star Assembly), Sierra Club, Phi Delta Kappa (USC chpt.). Avocations: the arts, dance, sailing, scuba diving.

WINN, VALDENIA C. state representative; b. Kansas City, Kans., Dec. 7, 1950; BS, U. Kans., 1972, MA, 1975, PhD, 1993. Prof. Kansas City C.C., 1972—; mem. Kans. Ho. of Reps., 2000—, mem. Com. on Edn., Com. on Higher Edn., Com. on Transp., Com. on Econ. Devel., Joint Com. on Econ. Devel., Joint Select Com. on Sch. Fin. Treas. N.E. Coop. Coun., 1987—; project dir. Fulbright-Hayes Groups Projects Abroad to Senegal, 1999, Title III Planning Grant Adminstr., 2000. Chair Kans. Territorial Sesquicentennial Dinner, Kans. Hist. Mus., 2004—; active BILLD Legis. Leadership Program. Democrat. Office: 284-W State Capitol 300 SW 10th Ave Topeka KS 66612 Address: 1044 Washington Blvd Kansas City KS 66102

WINNECKE, JOYCELYN, editor; m. Bill Adee. Degree, U. So. Ind. Writer obituaries Evansville (Ind.) Courier and Press, 1977; reporter Wash. bur. Scripps Howard; city editor Indpls. Star; dep. metro editor, then metro news editor Chgo. Sun-Times, 1994—99; mng. editor Chgo. Sun Times, 1999—2002, Chgo. Tribune, 2002—. Office: Chgo Tribune 435 N Michigan Ave Chicago IL 60611*

WINNER, KARIN E. editor; Editor San Diego Union-Tribune, 1995—. Office: San Diego Union-Tribune Pub Co 350 Camino De La Reina San Diego CA 92112-0191 E-mail: Karin.winner@uniontrib.com.

WINNIE, GLENNA BARBARA, pediatric pulmonologist; b. Lansing, Mich., Oct. 14; d. Robert John and Irene (Fetchik) W.; m. Jeffrey Alan Cooper, Mar. 17, 1990; children: Robert Jefferson Cooper, David Jamison Cooper. BS, Mich. State U., 1973; MD, Vanderbilt U., 1977. Diplomate Am. Bd. Pediatrics, Am. Bd. Pediatric Pumonology. Resident in pediatrics Case Western Res. U./Babies and Childrens Hosp., Cleve., 1977-79, fellow in pediatric pulmonology, 1979-82; asst. prof. pediatrics Albany (N.Y.) Med. Coll., 1982-90, assoc. prof. pediatrcis, 1990-95, head pediatric pulmonology sect., 1982-95; adminstrv. dir. pulmonary divsn., co-dir. cystic fibrosis U. Pitts., 1995—. Dir. Albany Pediat. Pulmonary and Cystic Fibrosis Ctr., 1982—95; adminstrv. dir. pulmonary divsn. Children's Hosp. of Pitts., 1995—99; co-dir. Cystic Fibrosis Ctr., 1995—, dir. pulmonary divsn., 1999—, dir. pediatric sleep lab., 2001—, Children's Hosp. of Pitts., 2001—. Contbr. articles to profl. jours. Bd. dirs. Albany Ronald McDonald Ho., 1986-88, Cystic Fibrosis Found.-Western Pa. chpt., 1996—. Rsch. grantee Nat. Cystic Fibrosis Found., 1984-86, 88-90, 99-01, NIH, 1987-93. Mem.: Soc. Pediat. Rsch., Am. Acad. Sleep Medicine, Capital Dist. Pediatric Soc. (treas. 1985—90, pres. 1990—91), Am. Coll. Physician Execs., Am. Thoracic Soc. (rsch. fellowship review com. 1989—92), Am. Acad. Pediatrics (exec. com. chest sect. 1996—2001). Episcopalian. Achievements include description of role of Epstein Barr virus in pulmonary exacerbations in cystic fibrosis. Office: Childrens Nat Med Ctr 111 Michigan Ave NW Washington DC 20010-2970

WINNINGHAM, MARE, actress; b. Phoenix, May 16, 1959; m. A Martinez (div. 1981); m. William Maple, 1983; children: Riley, Paddy, Jack, Calla. Appeared in (TV movies and miniseries): The Thorn Birds, 1983, Special Olympics/A Special Kind of Love, 1978, Amber Waves, 1980 (Emmy award 1980), The Women's Room, 1980, Off the Minnesota Strip, 1980, A Few Days in Weasel Creek, 1981, Freedom, 1981, Missing Children: A Mother's Story, 1982, Helen Keller: The Miracle Continues, 1984, Single Bars, Single Women, 1984, Love is Never Silent, 1985 (Emmy award nomination 1986), Who Is Julia?, 1986, A Winner Never Quits, 1986, Eye on the Sparrow, 1991, God Bless the Child, 1988, Turner & Hooch, 1989, Love and Lies, Crossing to Freedom, Fatal Exposure, 1991, She Stood Alone, Those Secrets, Intruders, 1992, Better Off Dead, 1994, The Boys Next Door, 1996, Betrayed by Love, 1994, Letter to My Killer, 1995, George Wallace, 1997, Little Girl Fly Away, 1998, Everything That Rises, 1998, Too Rich: The Secret Life of Doris Duke, 1999, (miniseries) Sally Hemings: An American Scandal, 2000, (TV appearances) Six Feed Under, 2002, Touched by a Angel, 2002; appeared in (films): One Trick Pony, 1980, Threshold, 1983, St. Elmo's Fire, 1985, Nobody's Fool, 1986, Shy People, 1987, Made in Heaven, 1987, Miracle Mile, 1988, Turner and Hooch, 1989, Hard Promises, 1992, Teresa's Tattoo, Wyatt Earp, 1994, Georgia, 1995 (Acad. award nomination best supporting actress 1995), Bad Day On The Block, 1997, The Adventures of Ociee Nash, 2003, Dandelion, 2003; sang title song in (film) Freedom, 1981; singer (solo album) What Might Be, 1992, Red and Brown, 1996. Office: care William Morris Agy 151 El Camino Dr Beverly Hills CA 90212-2704 also: IFA Talent Agy 8730 W Sunset Blvd Ste 490 Los Angeles CA 90069

WINOGRAD, AUDREY LESSER, retired advertising executive; b. N.Y.C., Oct. 6, 1933; d. Jack J. and Theresa Lorraine (Elkind) Lesser; m. Melvin H. Winograd, Apr. 29, 1956; 1 child, Hope Elise. BA, U. Conn., 1953. Asst. advt. mgr. T. Baumritter Co., Inc., N.Y.C., 1953-54; asst. dir. pub. rels. and creative merchandising Kirby, Block & Co., Inc., N.Y.C., 1954-56; divsn. mdse. mgr., dir. advt. and sales promotion Winograd's Dept. Store, Inc., Point Pleasant, N.J., 1956-73, v.p., 1960-73, exec. v.p., 1973-86; pres., CEO AMW Assocs., Atlanta, 1976—2002, ret., 2002—. Editor bus. newsletters. Bd. dirs. Temple Beth Am, Lakewood, N.J., 1970-72, Temple Emanuel, Atlanta, 1999-2001. Mem. NAFE, Jersey Pub. Rels. and Advt. Assn. (pres. 1982-83, bd. dirs.), Retail Advt. and Mktg. Assn. Internat., Monmouth Ocean Devel. Coun., Monmouth County Bus. Assn. (bd. dirs. 1985-97, pres. 1988-90, Woman of Yr. 1992-93, Person of Yr. 1995), N.J. Assn. Women Bus. Owners, Am. Soc. Advt. and Promotion, Ocean C. of C. (bd. dirs. 1994-97, award 1993, 94), Retail Advt. Conf. (Career Achievements and Contbns. to Soc. award 1993), Soc. Prevention Cruelty to Animals, Animal Protection Inst. Am., Human Soc., Internat. Fund Animal Welfare, World Wildlife Fund, Friends of Animals, Defenders of Wildlife, Nat. Humane Edn. Soc., In Defense of Animals, Atlanta Humane Soc., Sierra Club, Peta, Natural Resources Def. Coun. Avocations: collecting animal collectibles, gourmet cooking, environmental protection, exercise. Office: AMW Assocs 5304 Vernon Lake Dr Atlanta GA 30338-3527

WINOKUR, MARISSA JARET, actress; b. NYC, Feb. 2, 1973; Studied at, Am. Musical and Dramatic Acad. Actor: (plays, Broadway) Grease, 1995, Hairspray, 2002 (Tony award for best actress, 2003); (plays) Guys and Dolls, Peter Pan, Little Shop of Horrors, Romeo and Juliet, Nunsense II, Grandma Sylvia's Funeral, Hair, Happy Days; (films) Demo Real, 1998, Why Love Doesn't Work, 1999, Never Been Kissed, 1999, American Beauty, 1999, Sleep Easy, Hutch Rimes, 2000, Scary Movie, 2000, Amy's Orgasm, 2001, On Edge, 2001, Now You Know, 2002; (TV films) Beautiful Girl, 2003; co-exec. prodr. (TV films) Beautiful Girl, 2003; actor(guest appearances): (TV series) The Steve Harvey Show, 1998, Felicity, 1999, Dharma & Greg, 1999, 2000, Moesha, 2000, Curb Your Enthusiasm, 2000, Just Shoot Me, 2000, The Ellen Show, 2001, Boston Public, 2001. Office: McKeon-Valeo Mgmt 9107 Wilshire Blvd Ste 321 Beverly Hills CA 90210 Office Phone: 310-288-5888. Office Fax: 310-288-5868.*

WINOKUR, PAULA COLTON, artist, educator; d. Samuel A. and Elizabeth Lillian Colton; m. Robert M. Winokur, Aug. 31, 1958; children: Stephan Todd, Michael David. BFA, BS, Temple U. Tyler Sch. Art, 1958. Prof. Arcadia U., Glenside, Pa., 1973—2003. One-woman shows include ceramic sculpture Earth Shift, various mus. and galleries, U.S. and abroad, Represented in permanent collections, Pa. Conv. Ctr. Trustee Watershed Ctr. Ceramic Arts, Newcastle, Maine; mem. program bd. Nat. Coun. Ceramic Arts, 1979—82; mem. adv. bd. Clay Studio, Phila., 1992—2003. Individual Artist fellow, Nat. Endowment Arts, 1976, 1988, Craftsmen's fellow, Pa. Coun. Arts, 1986.

WINSLETT, STONER, artistic director; b. Jacksonville, Fla., Aug. 17, 1958; m. Donald Paulding Irwin; children: Louise Gray Irwin, Elizabeth Irwin, Alexander Pankoff, Caroline Irwin. Student, Am. Ballet Theatre Sch., N.C. Sch. of the Arts; grad. summa cum laude, Smith Coll., 1980. Artistic dir. Richmond Ballet. Pres. John Butler Found. Mem.: Phi Beta Kappa. Office: Richmond Ballet 407 E Canal St Richmond VA 23219-3811

WINSLEY, SHIRLEY J. state legislator, insurance agent; b. Fosston, Minn., June 9, 1934; d. Nordin Marvel Miller and Helga Christine Sorby; m. Gordon Perry Winsley, July 19, 1952; children: Alan, Nancy. ABS, Tacoma C.C., 1970; BA, Pacific Luth., 1971. Mem. legis. staff Wash. Senate, Olympia, 1971-75; appraiser Pierce County Assessor, Tacoma, 1971-75; mem. Wash. Ho. of Reps., Olympia, 1974, 77-92; exec. dir. Lakewood (Wash.) Chamber, 1975-76; mem. Wash. Senate, Dist. 28, Olympia, 1993—; ins. agent, family counselor New Tacoma Cemetary & Funeral Home, 1996—; pres. Wash. Senate, Dist. 28, 2003—. Mem., Wash. St. Advisory Council Accrditation of Vocational-Technical Institutes, Wash. St. Historical Soc., Lakewood Sr. Ctr., LEAP. Republican. Lutheran. Home: 1109 Garden Cir Tacoma WA 98466-6218 Office: PO Box 40428 Olympia WA 98504-0428

WINSLOW, ANNE BRANAN, artist; b. Waynesboro, Ga., July 28, 1920; d. Walter Augustus and Rubie (Griffin) Branan; m. James Addison Winslow Jr., May 8, 1943; children: Lu Anne, Jan Renee. BS in Fine Art, Queens Coll., Charlotte, N.C., 1941; postgrad., U. South Fla., 1974-75. One-woman shows include Dunedin (Fla.) Art Ctr., 1980, Tampa (Fla.) Originals Gallery, 1982, Pub. Libr., St. Petersburg, Fla., 1982, Lee Scarfone Gallery, 1983, 84, Studio 1212, Clearwater, Fla., 1983, 87, 90, Gallery 600, Largo, Fla., 1986, Gallery of State Capitol, Tallahassee, 1987, Berghoff Gallery, Clearwater, 1988, 92, Anderson-Marsh Gallery, St. Petersburg, 1989, 92, Loveland (Colo.) Mus., 1990, Gallery at City Hall of Tampa, 1990, Lawrence Charles Gallery, Tampa, 1993, Gallery Contemporanea, Jacksonville, Fla., 1994; painting, oil painting, Fla. Series II, Images II, 1980, Amagedon, 1974, Eastern Series III, 1984, original handpulled serigraphs, 1991, 92. Mem. Studio 1212, Fla. Artist Group, Mus. Women in Arts, Fla. Printmakers Soc., Generator Gallery (founding). Republican. Avocations: world travel, reading, gardening. Home: 3750 Peachtree Rd NE Apt 901 Atlanta GA 30919-1322 E-mail: annewinslow@canterburycourt.org.

WINSLOW, BETTE KILLINGSWORTH, dance studio owner; b. Springfield, Mo., Dec. 10, 1919; d. Troy Kenwood andWinifred Elizabeth (Reed) Killingsworth; m. Kenelm Crawford Winslow, Sept. 5, 1947; children: Katherine, Jeanette, Kenelm, Elizabeth, Priscilla. Student, Christian Coll., 1937-39, Perry Mansfield Theater Arts Camp, summer 1938; studied with, George Balanchine, 1939-41, Pierre Vladimiroff, Anatole O'Boukhoff, Anatole Vilzak, Ludmila Shollar, Muriel Stuart, Jack Stanley, Jose Fernandez, Doris Humphrey, Jose Limon, Martha Graham, Nimura. Dancer Vogue Ballet, Rodeo, Vincent Youman Concert Revue, Met. Opera Ballet, N.Y.C., Boston and Can., 1939-44; program dir. overseas clubs ARC, New Guinea, Philippines and Korea, 1944-47; owner dance studios, pvt. tchr. dance Hermon, N.Y., Ishpeming, Mich., and Taos, N.Mex., 1947—. Dir. Dance Taos summer workshops, 1986-92. Choreographer numerous dance prodns., original ballets. Recipient Disting. Alumni award Columbia Coll., 1996, Taos Living Treasure award, 1998; special honor, Taos Dance, 2000. Avocation: sewing. Home: PO Box 927 El Prado NM 87529-0927 Office: PO Box 425 Taos NM 87571-0425

WINSLOW, EMILY B. psychologist, researcher; b. Indpls., July 25, 1968; d. Charles H. Winslow and Miriam A. Vessels; m. Stanley Guy Davis, Sept. 30, 1994; 1 child, Austin Winslow Davis. PhD, U. Pitts., 2001, MS, 1995; BS, Ind. U., 1990. Rsch. project coord. Ind. U., Bloomington, 1990—91; grad. student rschr. U. Pitts., 1991—2001; clin. psychology intern Duke U. Med. Ctr., Durham, NC, 1998—99; faculty rsch. asst. Ariz. State U., Tempe, 2002—. Contbr. chpt. in book, articles to profl. jours. Rsch. Grant, NIMH, 1998—2000, Postdoctoral Fellowship, 2002—. Mem.: Soc. for Rsch. in Child Devel., Phi Beta Kappa. Office Phone: 480-727-6158.

WINSTEAD, ANTOINETTE FAY, performing arts educator; b. Colorado Springs, Colo., Dec. 25, 1964; d. James R. and Jo A. Winstead. AA, San Antonio Coll., 1985; BFA, NYU, 1987; MA, Our Lady of the Lake U., San Antonio, 1995; MFA, Columbia U., N.Y.C., 1989. English lectr. Our Lady of the Lake U., San Antonio, 1994—95, asst. prof., 1995—2000, assoc. prof., 2000—. Artistic chair The Renaissance Theater Guild, San Antonio, 2002—; book reviewer Choice Rev./ALA, Middletown, Conn., 2002—. Author (dramatic reading): (novel excerpt) God Done Blessed You; dramatic reading (novel excerpt) Their Eyes Were Watching God; actor: (play) Mother Knows Best, Black Lily/White Lily; dir.: Innocent Thoughts, A Fool of Passion, Family Portrait, All the World's a Stage, Our Town, In the Blood, (choreographer) (musical) Forever Free; costume coord. (play) Bee-Luther- Hatchee; author: (poetry) A Garland of Poems: A Collection from Ten Female Poets, Poetic Voices of America, (short stories) The Thing Itself, (play) Too Long Coming, The Meeting; author: (director) One Drink Too Many; contbr. poetry ot profl. pubs. Co-chair Ad Hoc U.C. Libr. Fundraising Com., Universal City, Tex., 1999—2000; grant reviewer Tex. Commn. on the Arts Grant Rev. Panel, Austin, 1997—98; sec. Universal City Pub. Libr. Adv. Commn., 1996—2000, co-chair, 2002—03; sec. Universal City Pub. Libr. Found., Universal City, Tex., 1999—2002; pres. San Antonio Poets Assn., San Antonio, 2002—. Recipient Supt.'s Tchg. award, Judson Ind. Sch. Dist., 1993; scholar Honor sholar, NYU, 1987. Mem.: SAT Playwrights, The Internat. Women's Writing Guild, Sigma Tau Delta (life). Office: Our Lady of the Lake University 411 SW 24th St San Antonio TX 78207 Personal E-mail: winsa@lake.ollusa.edu.

WINSTEAD, ELISABETH WEAVER, poet, writer, English language educator; b. Nashville, July 31, 1926; d. Charles Preston and Carrie Lawrence (Hadley) Weaver; m. George Alvis Winstead, July 18, 1942. BA, Vanderbilt U., 1946; MA, Peabody Coll. Vanderbilt U., 1947; postgrad., Vanderbilt U., 1980-83, Trevecca Nazarene, 1975-79. Cert. tchr. of lang. arts, bus. edn., social sci., English, Tenn., Va., Ind., Idaho, Ariz. Head bus. edn. dept. La Crosse (Ind.) High Sch., 1947-48, Franklin (Tenn.) High Sch., 1952-54, Belmont Coll., Nashville, 1954-56; with English dept. Boise (Idaho) High Sch., 1948-49; critical analyst Dept. Commerce, Washington, 1949-50; with bus. edn. dept. Averitt Coll., Danville, Va., 1950-52; elem. and high sch. tchr. Met. Nashville Schs., 1956-85. Cons. Model Tchr. Program, Nashville Met. Sch., 1958-68, mem. faculty adv. coun., 1970-79, mem. profl. devel. coun., 1980-84. Author: Social Studies Curriculum Guide, 1970, Metro Beautiful Programs, 1976, Metro PTA School History, 1980; contbr. poetry to anthologies and popular mags., including Ideals, New Hope Books, The Vanderbilt Review. Chmn. TB Seal Drive, Franklin, 1956-60, March of Dimes Fund Drive, Nashville, 1982-84, Red Cross Blood Drive, Nashville, 1984-86; capt. Heart Fund Drive, Nashville, 1979-81. Recipient Tchr. Appreciation awrd Sta. WKDA, 1970, Galaxy of Stars award Nashville Met. Schs., 1982, Ednl. Appreciation award City of Nashville, 1983, Commendation for pub. svc. Tenn. Legislature, 1994; named to Honorable Order of Ky. Cols., 1988. Mem. NEA, Am. Childhood Edn. Internat., Tenn. Hist. Soc., Wisdom Soc., Kappa Delta Pi (hon.), Pi Omega Pi (hon.), Pi Gamma Mu (hon.). Baptist. Avocations: camping, boating, gardening, reading, creative writing. Home: 3819 Gallatin Rd Nashville TN 37216-2609

WINSTON, FLAURA K. engineering researcher; Ph. D., Univ. of Penn. School of Medicine. Asst. physician Children's Hosp. of Phila., 1994—; founder, dir. TraumaLink. Recipient Melville medal ASME, 1995. Fellow: Bloomberg School of Public Health, John's Hopkins Univ. Office: The Children's Hosp of Phila 3535 TraumaLink 10th Fl 34th St and Civic Ctr Blvd Philadelphia PA 19104

WINSTON, JANE KAY, secondary education educator, artist; b. Omaha, July 5, 1947; d. Paul Henry and Jean (Irwin) Kupfer; 1 child, Daniel. BFA in Edn., U. Nebr., Lincoln, 1969; student, Midland Luth. Coll., Fremont, Nebr., 1965-67. Art tchr. Beveridge Jr. High, Omaha, 1969-73, Idaho Falls (Idaho) H.S., 1975-80, Skyline H.S., Idaho Falls, Idaho, 1987—. Mem. Idaho Falls Snowfest Com., 1991. Named Idaho Secondary Art Educator of Yr., 1996; Idaho Falls Edn. Found. grantee, 1992. Mem. Idaho Falls Art Guild, Idaho Art Edn. Assn., Nat. Art Edn. Assn., Eagle Rock Art Guild (life), Delta Kappa Gamma. Avocations: reading, playing board and card games, travel. Home: 5845 S Holmes Ave Idaho Falls ID 83404-7619 Office: Skyline High School 1767 Blue Sky Dr Idaho Falls ID 83402-4802

WINSTON, JANET MARGARET, real estate agent, civic volunteer; b. Binghamton, N.Y., Sept. 30, 1937; d. Cornelius Adrian and Vera Helene (Strohman) Salie; m. Edmund Joseph Winston, Nov. 29, 1958 (dec. July 1981); children: Mark Edmund, Deborah Ann. Student, SUNY, 1955-57, Bliss Coll., 1978. Sales assoc. HER Realtors, Worthington, Ohio, 1979—. Dist. chair women's divsn. Cmty. Chest ARC, Kalamazoo, 1970; docent Indpls. Mus. Art, 1975, Columbus (Ohio) Mus. Art, 1976—, beaux art mem., 1976—87; docent Chinese Son of Heaven Exhibit, 1989, mus. fund drive, 1986—87, 1989—95; trustee Worthington Resource Ctr., 1979—84, v.p., 1984, chair youth employment svcs., 1980—83; trustee, sec. Worthington Hills Civil Assn., 1986—89. Recipient Nat. Sales award The Dozen, 1996, TopHER award, 1980—. Mem.: Ohio Assn. Realtors, Nat. Assn. Realtors, Columbus Bd. Realtors (pub. rels. com. 1980, 1983, 1986, sales adv. com. 1987, pub. rels. com. 1988, svcs. task force 1989, 10 Million Dollar Club award), Sessions Soc. (bd. dirs. 2001—03), Worthington C. of C., Worthington Women's Club, Worthington Hills Garden Club (bd. dirs. 1989), Worthington Hills Women's Club. Republican. Episcopalian. Avocations: art, music, golf. Home: 8036 Golfview Ct Columbus OH 43235-1230 Office: HER Realtors 6902 N High St Worthington OH 43085-2555 Office Phone: 614-825-8852.

WINSTON, JUDITH ANN, lawyer; b. Atlantic City, Nov. 23, 1943; d. Edward Carlton and Margaret Ann (Goodman) Marianno; m. Michael Russell Winston, Aug. 10, 1963; children: Lisa Marie, Cynthia Eileen. BA magna cum laude, Howard U., Washington, 1966; JD, Georgetown U., 1977. Bar: DC 1977, US Supreme Ct. Dir. EEO project Coun. Great City Schs., Washington, 1971-74; legal asst. Lawyers Com. for Civil Rights Under Law, Washington, 1975-77; spl. asst. to dir. Office for Civil Rights, HEW, Washington, 1977-79; exec. asst., legal counsel to chair U.S. EEO Commn., Washington, 1979-80; asst. gen. counsel U.S. Dept. Edn., 1980-86; dep. dir. Lawyers Com. for Civil Rights Under Law, 1986-88; dep. dir. pub. policy Women's Legal Def. Fund, Washington, 1988-90, chair employment discrimination com., 1979-88, ednl. cons., 1974-77; asst. prof. law Washington Coll. Law of Am. U., 1990-93, assoc. prof. law, 1993-95; gen. counsel U.S. Dept. Edn., Washington, 1993-2001; exec. dir. Pres.'s Initiative on Race, 1997-98; undersec. U.S. Dept. Edn., 2000-01; rsch. prof law Washington Coll. Law Am. U., Washington, 2001—02; prin. Winston Withers & Assocs., LLC, Washington, 2002—. Author: (book) Desegregating Schools in the Great Cities: Philadelphia, 1970, Chronicle of a Decade 1961-70, 1970, Desegregating Urban Schools: Educational Equality/Quality, 1970; contbr. articles to profl jours. Pres. bd. dirs. Higher Achievement Program; bd. dirs. Ptnrs. for Dem. Change, Nat. Pub. Radio, So. Edn. Found.; Nat. Law Ctr. on Poverty and Homelessness. Named Woman Lawyer of the Yr, Women's Bar Asn, 1997; recipient Margaret Brent, Am Bar Asn Comn Women in the Profession, 1998, Thurgood Marshall award, DC Bar, 1999. Fellow: ABA Found; mem.: ACLU, Lawyers Comt Civil Rights Under Law, Nat Bar Asn, Washington Bar Asn, Washington Coun Lawyers, DC Bar Asn, Fed Bar Asn, Links Inc, Phi Beta Kappa, Delta Theta Phi, Alpha Kappa Alpha. Democrat. Episcopalian. Home: 1371 Kalmia Rd NW Washington DC 20012-1444 Office: Winston Withers & Assocs 2120 L St NW # 510 Washington DC 20037 Office Phone: 202-478-6135. Business E-Mail: jwinston@winwithassocs.com.

WINSTON, KRISHNA, foreign language professional; b. Greenfield, Mass., June 7, 1944; d. Richard and Clara (Brussel) W.; 1 child, Danielle Billingsley. BA, Smith Coll., 1965; MPhil, Yale U., 1969, PhD, 1974. Instr. Wesleyan U., Middletown, Conn., 1970-74, asst. prof., 1974-77, assoc. prof., 1977-84, prof., 1984—, acting dean, 1993-94. Coord. Mellon Mays Undergrad. Fellowship, 1993—. Author: O v. Horváth: Close Readings of Six Plays, 1975; translator: O. Schlemmer, Letters and Diaries, 1972, S. Lenz, The Heritage, 1981, G. Grass, Two States, One Nation, 1990, C. Hein, The Distant Lover, 1989, G. Mann, Reminiscences and Reflections, 1990, J. W. V. Goethe, Wilhelm Meister's Journeyman Years, 1989, C. v. Krockow, The Hour of the Women, 1991, E. Heller, With the Next Man Everything Will be Different, 1992, R. W. Fassbinder, The Anarchy of the Imagination, 1992, G. Reuth, Goebbels, 1994, E. Lappin; editor: Jewish Voices, German Words, 1994, P. Handke, Essay on the Jukebox, 1994, P. Handke, My Year in the No-Man's-Bay, 1998, G. Grass, Too Far Afield, 2000, P. Handke, On a Dark Night I Left My Silent House, 2000, G. Grass, Crabwalk, 2003. Vol. Planned Parenthood, Middletown, 1972-77; mem. Recycling Task Force, Middletown, 1986-87; chmn. Resource Recycling Adv. Coun., Middletown, 1989—; trustee Ind. Day Sch., Middlefield, Conn., 1989—. Recipient Schlegel-Tieck prize for translation, 1994, 2001, Helen and Kurt Wolff prize for transl., 2001; German Acad. Exch. Svc. fellow, Kahn fellow Smith Coll., 2000-01. Mem. MLA, ALTA, Soc. for Exile Studies, Am. Assn. Tchrs. German, PEN, Phi Beta Kappa (pres. Wesleyan chpt. 1987-90). Home: 655 Bow Ln Middletown CT 06457-4808 Office: Wesleyan Univ German Studies Dept Middletown CT 06459-0040 E-mail: kwinston@wesleyan.edu.

WINSTON, MARY A. publishing executive; BS in Acctg. and Info. Sys., U. Wis.; MBA, Northwestern U. Sr. auditor Arthur Andersen & Co., 1983—87; various positions Ameritech, 1987—91; dir. bus. devel. and strategy Biotech Divsn. Baxter Internat., 1991—95; sr. mgmt. positions Warner-Lambert, 1995—2002; v.p. Visteon Corp., 2002—04, treas., 2002—03, controller, 2003—04; exec. v.p. Scholastic Corp., N.Y., 2004—, CFO, 2004—. Office: Scholastic Corp 557 Broadway New York NY 10012

WINSTON, SANDRA, health sciences administrator; b. Kansas City, Mo., Apr. 16, 1962; d. Roosevelt and Delilah Winston. BSBA, U. Ark., Fayetteville, 1984. Pharm. sales person Bristol-Myers Squibb, Little Rock, 1989-94; with legis. affairs divsn. Office of Lt. Gov. Huckabee, Little Rock, 1994-95; asst. for internat. office Family Life, Little Rock, 1995-96; health and human svcs. liaison Office of Gov. Huckabee, Little Rock, 1996-99; dir. Health Svcs. Agy., Little Rock, 1999—. Mem. Conway C. of C. (bd. dirs.). Office: Ark Health Svcs Agy 5800 W 10th St Ste 805 Little Rock AR 72204-1763

WINTER, JANE, medical educator; b. N.Y.C., 1952; MD, U. Pa., 1977; intern, U. Chgo., 1977-78, resident int. medicine, 1978-80. Fellow in hematology and oncology Columbia P&S, N.Y.C., 1980-81, Northwestern U., 1981-83, prof., 1983—. Mem.: Ea. Coop. Oncology Group, Am. Soc. for Blood and Marrow Transplantation, Am. Assn. Cancer Rsch., Am. Fedn. for Clin. Rsch., Am. Soc. Clin. Oncology, Am. Soc. Hematology. Office: Divsn Hematology/Oncology 676 N St Clair St Ste 850 Chicago IL 60611-2978 E-mail: j-winter@northwestern.edu.

WINTER, KAREN KNIGHT ALICE, special education educator; b. Oxford, Miss., July 13, 1955; d. Will D. and Emma Gene Winter. BS, U. Miss., 1979; BA, Harding U., Searcy, Ark., 1986; MEd, U. Miss., 1992, MEd, 2000. Pharm. rsch. technician U. Miss., University, 1979—83; tchr., humanitarian aid worker Coll. Ch.-Searcy, various locations Africa, Asia, East Europe, 1986—94; spl. edn. tchr. North Miss. Regional Ctr., Oxford, 1994—. Humanitarian aid worker Namwianga Christian Schs., Zambia, 1987—92, Helping Hands, Romania, 1992—94. Author: New Guinea Run, 2001; contbr. articles to profl. jours. Scholar Presdl. scholar, Harding U., 1983. Republican. Ch. Of Christ. Home: 207 McLaurin Dr Oxford MS 38655 Office: North Mississippi Regional Ctr 967 Regional Dr Oxford MS 38655

WINTER, KATHRYN, music educator, writer; arrived in U.S., 1946; d. Sigmund and Alice. MusB, Manhattan Sch. Music, 1956, MusM, 1957. Piano tchr. "Y" 92d St., N.Y.C., 1958—62, Rubin Conservatory of Music, Jerusalem, 1968—81; piano and music tchr. young musicians program U. Calif., Berkeley, 1982—; residency as writer Millay Colony for Arts, Steepletop, NY, 1997. Author: (short stories) Madison Review, Stories, Across the Generations, (novel) Katarina (translated to French, German, Chinese and Slovak), 1998. Avocations: dance, singing, walking.

WINTER, MARNA K. special education educator; b. Raleigh, N.C. d. Dr. Stephan Alan and Molly VanCouten Kiefer; m. Kenneth W Winter. BA in Elem. Edn., Elon (N.C.) Coll., 1998, postgrad., 1998—2002; MSupport Early Childhood Intervention, U. N.C., 2003. Cert. tchr. N.C., 1994. Tchr., grades 3-5 Cmty. Charter Sch., Charlotte, NC, 1999—2000; classroom and 5th at risk inclusion edn. Pub. Sch. Sys., Burlington, NC, 2000—03; pvt. tutor Burlington, NC, 2000—. At risk morning homework club facilator Pub. Sch. Sys., Burlington, NC, 2000—03; co-writer of curriculum Burlington Police, Burlington, NC, 2003. Vol. Frank Porter Graham Child Devel. Inst., Chapel Hill, 2003—; calendar com. mem. Alamance Burlington Sch. Sys., Burlington, NC, 2000—01. Mem.: Alamance Burlington Educators, Coun. Exceptional Children, N.C. Assn. Educator. Avocations: running, cooking, reading.

WINTER, MILDRED M. educational administrator; BA summa cum laude, Harris Tchrs. Coll.; MEd, U. Mo.; postgrad., Harvard U., U. Cin. Exec. dir. Parents As Tchrs. Nat. Ctr. Inc., St. Louis. Tchr., cons., Mo., 1962-68; developer, dir. Ferguson-Florissant Parent-Child Early Edn. Program, Mo., 1969-72; first dir. early childhood edn. Mo. Dept. Elem. and Secondary Edn., 1972-84; sr. lectr. dept. elem. and early childhood edn. U. Mo., St. Louis; cons. in field. Contbr. articles to profl. jours. Named Outstanding Leader in Field of Edn., Mo. House of Reps., 1982, Outstanding Educator and Adv. for Young Children, Mo. Gov. Christopher S. Bond, 1984, Pioneer in Edn., State Bd. Edn., Mo. Dept. Edn., 1991, St. Louis Woman of Achievement in Edn., 1992; cited for Pioneering Leadership in Edn. Resolution, Mo. Senate, 1995; recipient Outstanding Svc. award Assn. Edn. of Young Children, 1984, Vol. Accreditation Leadership award, 1993, Spl. award Nat. Soc. Behavioral Pediat., 1992, Charles A. Dana Pioneering Achievements Health and Edn. Inst. Medicine award NAS, 1995. Office: Parents As Tchrs Nat Ctr Inc Ste 230 10176 Corporate Square Dr Saint Louis MO 63132-2924

WINTER, MIRIAM THERESE (GLORIA FRANCES WINTER), nun, religious education educator; b. Passaic, N.J., June 14, 1938; d. Mathias William and Irene Theresa (Marton) W. BMus, Cath. U. Am., 1964; M in

Religious Edn., McMaster Divinity Coll., Hamilton, Ont., Can., 1976; PhD in Liturgical Studies, Princeton Theol. Sem., 1983; LHD (hon.), Albertus Magnus Coll., 1991, St. Joseph Coll., 1993. Joined Med. Mission Sisters, Roman Cath. Ch., 1955. Dir. liturgy and liturgical music Med. Mission Sisters, Phila., 1960-76, pub. rels. dir., coord., 1963-72; assoc. prof. liturgy, worship and spirituality Hartford (Conn.) Sem., 1980-85, prof., 1985—; prof. liturgy, worship, spirituality, and feminist studies, 1994—. Mem. faculty St. Therese's Inst., Phila., 1964-68, acad. dir., 1968-72; Immaculate Conception Sem. Summer Program, Mo., 1969, Cath. U. Summer Grad. Program, Washington, 1970, Hope Ecumenical Inst., Jerusalem, summer 1974, 75, 76, McMaster Divinity Coll. Grad. Program, 1976, Continuing Edn. Program, 1976, N.Y. Archdiocesan Sch. Liturgical Music, summer 1980, 82, Vancouver Sch. Theology, summer 1982, USN Chaplains through Auburn Theol. Sem., 1990; mem. adj. faculty Union Inst., Cin., 1992-94; with emergency relief work Internat. Rescue Com., Cambodia, 1979-80, Malteser-Hilfsdienst Auslandsdienst, Germany, 1984, Med. Mission Sisters, Ethiopia, 1985; lectr. instr., performer, worship leader, song leader for various groups by invitation, nat. and internat., 1967—. Author: Preparing the Way of the Lord, 1978, God-With-Us: Resources for Prayer and Praise, 1979, An Anthology of Scripture Songs, 1982, Why Sing? Toward a Theology of Catholic Church Music, 1984, WomanPrayer, Woman Song: Resources for Ritual, 1987, WomanWord: A Feminist Lectionary and Psalter, 1990, WomanWisdom: A Feminist Lectionary and Psalter, Women of the Hebrew Scriptures, Part I, 1992 (1st pl. award for books on liturgy Cath. Press Assn., 1992), WomanWitness: A Feminist Lectionary and Psalter, Women of the Hebrew Scriptures, Part II, 1992 (1st pl. award for books on liturgy Cath. Press Assn., 1993), The Gospel According to Mary: A New Testament for Women, 1993; co-author: Defecting in Place: Women Claiming Responsibility for Their Own Spiritual Lives, 1994 (2d pl. award for books on gender studies Cath. Press Assn., 1995), The Chronicles of Noah and Her Sisters: Genesis and Exodus According to Women, 1995 (2d pl. award for books on gender studies Cath. Press Assn., 1996), Songlines: Hymns, Songs, Rounds and Refrains, 1996, The Singer and the Song: An Autobiography of the Spirit, 1999, Out of the Depths, The Story of Ludmila Javorova, Ordained Roman Catholic Priest, 2001 (1st pl. award for books on popular presentation of the Cath. faith Cath. Press Assn., 2002); author: numerous songs included in albums Keepsake, Hymns-ReImagined, SpiritSong, EarthSong, WomanSong, Remember Me, Sandstone, Songs of Promise, RSVP: Let Us Pray, Gold, Incense and Myrrh, In Love, Seasons (Christian Oscar award Nat. Evang. Film Found., 1971), Knock, Knock, Praise the Lord in Many Voices (live rec. of Mass of a Pilgrim People premiered at Carnegie Hall), 1967, I Know the Secret, Joy is Like the Rain (Gold album in USA and Australia); contbr. articles to profl. jours. Bd. dirs. Capitol Region Conf. Chs., 1984-91, v.p., 1986-88. pres. bd. dirs., 1988-90, past pres., 1990-91, Archdiocesan Office Urban Affairs, 1986-95; mem. Christian Conf. ann. event WINFEST, 1986, 87; mem. small christian communities design team Archdiocese of Hartford, 1987-91, mem. major events design team RENEW, 1986; commn. chair Archdiocesan Office of Synod, 1991; mem. New Eng. team Ministry of Money, 1984-90, 93; mem. The New Century Hymnal editl. com. United Ch. of Christ, 1993-95; active Ho. of Bread, Pediats, AIDS Unit Yale-New Haven Hosp., Covenant to Care, Voices of Joy Gospel Choir women imprisioned at Niantic. Grantee Lilly Endowment, 1989-90, 91-93; recipient Ho. of Reps. citation Commn. of Dn. 1068 Women in Leadership Edn. award YWCA Conn., 1989, Convenant to Care award for ministry to children, 1990, McMaster U. Alumni Gallery, 1982, Celebration of 120 Women in Leadership, 1987, Bayley-Ellard H.S. Hall of Fame, 1993, Conn. Women's Hall of Fame, 2002. Mem. ASCAP (Popular Awards list 1968—), AAUW (Excellence in Equity award Conn. chpt. 1995), Nat. Assn. Pastoral Musicians, N.Am. Acad. of Liturgy, Societas Liturgica. Avocations: photography, calligraphy. Office: Hartford Sem 77 Sherman St Hartford CT 06105-2260 E-mail: mtwinter@hartsem.edu.

WINTER, NANCY FITZ, media and public relations executive; b. Farmville, Va., Dec. 8, 1949; d. James Herbert Fitz Sr. and Hazel Virginia Adams; m. Louis Eugene Winter Jr., Feb. 3, 1973 (div. Nov. 1986); 1 child, Ross Monroe; m. Robert William Olney, June 8, 1991 (div. Dec. 2001). BS, Va. Commonwealth U., 1972; MA, Am. U., 1976. Asst. editor of publs. Life Ins. Co. of Va., Richmond, 1972-75; reporter, photographer Hanover Herald Progress, Ashland, Va., 1975; reporter Sta. WTVR-TV, Richmond, 1976-77; CEO Media Dynamics, Richmond, 1977-80; morning anchor, reporter Sta. WWBT-TV, Richmond, 1978-80; field prodr. Newsweek Broadcasting, N.Y.C., 1977-80, Sta. WUSA-TV, Washington, 1977-80; polit. reporter Sta. WTVR-TV, Richmond, 1980-81; dir. devel. Richmond Meml. Hosp., 1982-84; v.p. mktg. and comm. Am. Heart Assn. Va., 1984-97; cons. in field Richmond, 1997-99; pub. rels. profl. Commonwealth of Va., Dept. Health, Richmond, 1999—2003. Recipient awards, Va. Soc. Hosp. Mktg. and Pub. Rels. Mem.: Pub. Rels. Soc. Am., Nat. Pub. Health Info. Coalition, Richmond Pub. Rels. Assn. Episcopalian. Avocations: antiques, travel, reading, painting, genealogy.

WINTER, RUTH GROSMAN (MRS. ARTHUR WINTER), journalist; b. Newark, May 29, 1930; d. Robert Delmas and Rose (Rich) Grosman; m. Arthur Winter, June 16, 1955; children: Robin, Craig, Grant. BA, Upsala Coll., 1951; MS, Pace U., 1989. With Houston Press, 1955-56; gen. assignment Newark Star Ledger, 1951-55, sci. editor, 1956-69; columnist L.A. Times Syndicate, 1973-78, Register and Tribune, syndicate, 1981-85, isyndicate.com, 1999-2001. Columnist myskinMD.com, 2000-01; contbr. to consumer mags.; instr. St. Peters Coll., Jersey City.; vis. lectr. mag. writing Rutgers U. Author: Poisons in Your Food, rev. edits., 1971, 91, 99, 2004, How to Reduce Your Medical Bills, 1970, A Consumer's Dictionary of Food Additives, 1972, rev. edit., 2004, Vitamin E, The Miracle Worker, 1972, So You Have Sinus Trouble, 1973, Ageless Aging, 1973, So You Have a Pain in the Neck, 1974, rev. edit., 2000, A Consumer's Dictionary of Cosmetic Ingredients, 1974, 4th rev. edit., 1994, 5th rev. edit., 1999, Don't Panic, 1975, The Fragile Bond: Marriage in the 70's, 1976, Triumph Over Tension, 1976 (N.J. Press Women's Book award), Scent Talks Among Animals, 1977, Cancer Causing Agents: A Preventive Guide, 1979, The Great Self-Improvement Sourcebook, 1980, The Scientific Case Against Smoking, 1980, People's Guide to Allergies and Allergens, 1984, A Consumer's Guide to Medicines in Food, 1995; co-author: The Lean Line One Month Lighter Program, 1985, Thin Kids Program, 1985, Build Your Brain Power, 1986, Eat Right: Be Bright, 1988, A Consumer's Dictionary of Medicines: Prescription, Over-the-Counter and Herbal, 1994, 97, Super Soy.: The Miracle Bean, 1996, rev. edit., 2000, Pain in the Neck, 1997, rev. edit., 2000, Anti Aging Hormones, 1997, Brain Workout, 1997, 2003, Vitamin E: Your Protection Against Exercise Fatigue, Weakened Immunity, Heart Disease, Cancer, Aging, Diabetic Damage, Environmental Toxins, 1998, Smart Food, 1999, The Female Athlete's Body Book: Preventing and Treating Sports Injuries in Women and Girls, 2003. Recipient award of merit ADA, 1966, Cecil award Arthritis Found., 1967, Am. Soc. Anesthesiologists award, 1969, Arthritis Found. award, 1978; named Alumnus of Year Upsala Coll., 1971, Woman of Year N.J. Daily Newspaper Women, 1971, Woman of Achievement Millburn Short Hills Profl. and Bus. Women's Assn., 1991, Golden Triangle award Am. Dermatol. Assn., 1998. Mem. Soc. Mag. Writers, Authors League, Nat. Assn. Sci. Writers, Am. Med. Writers Assn. (Eric Martin Meml. award), N.J. Daily Newspaper Women (awards news series 1958, 70, named Woman of Achievement 1971, 83), Am. Soc. Journalists and Authors (pres. 1977-78, spl. service award 1983, Lifetime Achievement award 2004), N.J. Press Women (pres. 1982-84) Home and Office: 44 Holly Dr Short Hills NJ 07078-1318

WINTERER, BARBARA JEAN, designer, author; b. Manchester, N.H., Apr. 1, 1938; d. John Edward and Elizabeth Virginia Grace; m. Allen George Winterer, Mar. 30, 1959 (div. 1977); children: Audrey Lyn Winterer-Chavez, Amy Jo Winterer DeNoble. AA, Mesa (Ariz.) C.C., 1980; BS summa cum laude, U. Md., Heidelberg, Germany, 1996. Art designer

Morningstar Art Design Studio, Pagosa Springs, Colo., 1988—. Interpreter Colo. State Park; U.S. rail ranger Durango-Silverton R.R.; master gardener Colo. State U.; bd. dirs. Southwest Cmty. Resources; health care provider Archuleta County Sch. Dist., Pagosa Springs, Colo.; farm medic. Contbr. articles to newspapers and jours. Ofcl. U.S. reporter at World Eskimo Indian Olympics, Faribanks, Alaska, 1994; asst. dir. Ariz. Myasthenia Gravis Found., 1977-80; mem. ARC Disaster Response Team, Pagosa Springs, ARC Durango chpt.; bd. mem., chmn. pub. rels. com. Habitat for Humanity, Pagosa Springs, Colo; interpreter Chimney Rock Hist. Archeol. Site.; docent and vol. Bur. of Land mgmt., Anasazi Heritage Ctr. Mus.; mem. Friends of Libr., Dolores, Colo. Recipient Humanitarian award Phila. Inst. Human Potential, 1972, Chancellor of Germany award for acad. achievement, 1986, Citation of Meritorious Achievement award in the arts and humanitarianism Internat. Biograph. Ctr., 1997. Mem. AAUW, Libr. of Congress (assoc.), Cortez Garden Club, Alpha Sigma Lambda, Phi Theta Kappa. Avocations: gardening, gourmet cooking. Office: Morningstar Art Design Studio PO box 388 Dolores CO E-mail: inuit@pagosa.net.

WINTERHALTER, DOLORES AUGUST (DEE WINTERHALTER), art educator; b. Pitts., Mar. 22, 1928; d. Joseph Peter and Helen August; m. Paul Joseph Winterhalter, June 21, 1947 (dec.); children: Noreen, Audrey, Mark. Student, Yokohama, Japan, 1963-64; Paris, 1968-70, La Romita Sch. Art, Terni, Italy, 2001. Cert. tchr. Japanese Flower Arranging, Kamakuri Wood Carving. Tchr. YWCA, Greenwich, Conn., 1978-84, Friends of the Arts and Scis., Sarasota, Fla., 1992—; tchr./lectr. classes and workshops, 2004; tchr. workshops Venice Art Ctr. and Home Studios, 2004—. Lectr. Sarasota Art Assn., 1984—; tchr., workshop presenter, Bangkok, 1971; mem. staff Hilton Leech Art Studio and Gallery, Sarasota; events chmn. State of Fla. Watercolor Exhbn., Sarasota, 1995; cultural exch. tchr. univs., fine arts acads., China; mem., tchr. Venice Art Ctr., Sarasota, 1996—2003, Art Ctr., Sarasota, 1999—2002; Hilton Leech Tchr., Sarasota, 1996—99; mem. Women's Caucus of Arts in Am., 1996—98; selected demonstrator Fine Arts of Sarasota, 1995—98; paper cons. D'Arches Watercolor Paper Co., Paris, 1983—2000; tchr., lectr., judge Sumie Inks; demonstrator Fla. Watercolor Conv., Ocala, 2000; workshop instr. Venice (Fla.) Watercolor/Monoprint and Sumi-e, 2003—; tchr. home studio. Exhbns. Xiam, China, 1994, Creators Tour of Fine Arts Soc. Sarasota, 1994-2001; numerous works in watercolor, ink, oriental brushwork; paintings in numerous corp. collections. Pres., Am. Women's Club, Genoa, Italy, 1962; participant to help raise money for scholarships Collectors and Creators Tour of Fine Arts Soc. of Sarasota, 1994. Recipient numerous awards Old Greenwich (Conn.) Art Assn., 1971-84, Sarasota, 1985, Collectors and Creators Tour award Fine Arts Soc. Sarasota, 1994, Pat Buckman award, 2000; named Artist of Yr., Fine Arts Soc. Sarasota, 1994, Venice Art Ctr., 2000. Mem. Suncoast Fla. Watercolor Soc. (life), Fla. Watercolor Soc., Long Boat Key Art Assn., Sarasota Art Assn., Sumi-e Soc. Am., Nat. League Am. PEN Women (pres. 1994-96, scholarship bd. 1996-98), Internat. Soc. Marine Painters, Venice Art Ctr., Art Sarasota, Womens Contemporary Arts Soc. (tchr.). Democrat. Roman Catholic. Avocations: wood carving, travel, bridge, creative design in crochet and fashion. Home and Office: 4027 Westbourne Cir Sarasota FL 34238-3249

WINTER-NEIGHBORS, GWEN CAROLE, special education educator, art educator, consultant; b. Greenville, SC, July 14, 1938; d. James Edward (dec. Feb. 1980); children: Robin Carole Winter, Charles O. McClen, Dustin Winter TeBrugge; m. Thomas Frederick Neighbors, Mar. 24, 1989. BA in Edn. and Art, Furman U., 1960, MA in Psychology, 1967; cert. in guidance/pers., Clemson U., 1981; EdD in Youth and Mid. Childhood Edn., Nova Southeastern U., 1988; postgrad., U.S.C. Spartanburg, 1981-89; cert. clear specialist instrn. with honors, Calif. State U., Northridge, 1991; art edn. cert., Calif. State U., L.A., 1991; JD, Glendale U., 1999. Cert. tchr. art, elem. edn., psychology, secondary guidance, S.C. Tchr. 7th grade Greenville Jr. H.S., 1960-63; art tchr. Wade Hampton H.S., Greenville, 1963-67; prin. adult edn. Woodmont H.S., Piedmont, S.C., 1983-85, Mauldin H.S., Greenville and Mauldin, S.C., 1981; tchr. edn. psychology edn. dept. Allen U., Columbia, S.C., 1969; activity therapist edn. dept. S.C. Dept. of Corrections, Columbia, 1973-76; art specialist gifted edn. Westcliffe Elem. Sch., Greenville, 1976-89; tchr. self-contained spl. day class Elysian Heights Elem. Sch., Echo Park and L.A., Calif., 1989-91; art tchr. med. drawing Sch. Dist. Greenville County Blue Ridge Mid. Sch., Greer, 1991-95; tchr./asst. head edn. dept. N. Creenville Coll., 2001—02. Participant nat. conf. U.S. Dept. Edn./So. Bell, Columbia, 1989; com. mem. nat. exec. com. Nova Southeastern U., 1988—89; asst. chmn., tchr. edn. dept. North Greenville coll., 2001; adm., staff North Greenville Coll., 2001, U. S.C., Spartanburg; adj., student tchr., supr. U. SC, 2002; adv. bd. S.C. Gov. Sch. for Arts & Humanities; parent/tchr. adv. bd. Spl. Edn.; adj. prof U. SC Univ. Ctr., Greenville, 2002—03; ind. rep. Primerica Fin. Svs., 2003—04. Mozart Book, 1988; author: (drama) Let's Sing a Song About America, 1988 (1st pl. Nat. Music award, 1990); contbr. The International Library of Poetry Ode to Stardust', 2002. Life mem. Rep. Presdl. Task Force, 1970—; mem. voter registration com. Lexington County Rep. Party, 1970—80; grand jury participant 13th Jud. Ct. Sys., Greenville, 1986—88, guardian ad litem, 1988—2004; mem. arts educators adv. task force S.C. Gov. Sch. Arts and Humanities, 2002—; mem. spl. edn. parent adv. bd. representing Sue Cleveland Elem. Sch. Greenville Co. Sch. Dist., Spl. Edn. Topics and Trends, 2001—02; poll manager Greenville Co. Tchr. Incentive grantee Sch. Dist. Greenville County, 1986-88, Project Earth grantee Bell South, 1988-89, 94-95, Edn. Improvement Act/Nat. Dissimination Network grantee S.C. State Dept. Edn., 1987-88, Targett 2,000 arts in Curricular grantee S.C. Dept. Edn., 1994-95, Alliance grantee Bus. Cmty. Greenville, 1992-95, Greer Art Rsch. grantee, 1993-94, S.C. Govs. Sch. Study grantee, 1994, Edn. Improvement Act Competitive Tchr. grantee S.C. Dept. Edn., 1994-95, Alliance Grand grant, 1995-96; recipient Am. Jurisprudence Bancroft-Whitney award Glendale U. Sch. Law, 1997, 98, Excellence Recognition in Real Property award Glendale Law Faculty, 1997, Excellence in Art of Appellate Advocacy, Glendale U. Sch. Law, 1998, Am. Jurisprudence Bancroft-Whitney award Constl. Law I, 1998. Mem.: ABA, Palmetto State Tchr. Assn., S.C. Art Edn. Assn., S.C. Arts Alliance, Nat. Mus. Women in Arts, Nat. Art Edn. Assn., Phi Delta Kappa. Baptist. Avocations: computers, art, writing, music composition, law. Home: 26 Charterhouse Ave Piedmont SC 29673-9139

WINTERS, BARBARA JO, musician; b. Salt Lake City; d. Louis McClain and Gwendolyn (Bradley) W. AB cum laude, UCLA, 1960, postgrad., 1961, Yale, 1960. Mem. oboe sect. L.A Philharm., 1961-94, prin. oboist, 1972-94; ret. Clinician oboe, English horn, Oboe d'amore. Recs. movie, TV sound tracks. Avocation: painting in oils and mixed media. Home: 3529 Coldwater Canyon Ave Studio City CA 91604-4060 Office: 135 N Grand Ave Los Angeles CA 90012-3013

WINTERS, DARCY LAFOUNTAIN, medical management company executive; b. Middletown, N.J., Aug. 27, 1955; d. Donald Mark LaFountain and Suzanne (Gilman) LaFountain Westergard; m. Leland Monte McNabb, July 4, 1981 (div. Feb. 1989); 1 child, Leland Monte Jr.; m. Stephen H. Winters, May 30, 1997. BBA in Internat. Fin. cum laude, U. Miami, 1977. Real estate agent, Grad. Realtor's Inst. Market rsch. asst. Burger King Corp., Miami, Fla., 1975-77, regional mktg. supr. Huntington Beach, Calif., 1977-78; mgr., restaurant planning Holiday Inns, Inc., Memphis, 1978-79, mgr., nat. promotions, 1979-83; dir., lodging and travel planning Holiday Corp., Memphis, 1983-86; affiliate broker The Hobson Co., Realtors, Memphis, 1986-88, Crye Leike, Memphis, 1988-92; sr. v.p. comm. and planning Medshares Mgmt. Group, Inc., Memphis, 1991-2000. Founder, Lunch for Two, LLC, 2001—. Active Friends Pink Palace Mus., Memphis, 1987-91, Family Link/Runaway, Memphis, 1980-88; chmn. Foster Care Rev. Bd., Memphis, 1988-98; bd. dirs. Bethany Home, Memphis, 1989—, pres., 1995, treas., 1998; bd. dirs. Am. Cancer Soc., 1994—, v.p. 2000,

Univ. Club of Memphis, 2000—; mktg. com. Health Industry Coun., 1994-95. Named Profl. Vol. of Yr., Friends of Pink Palace Mus., Memphis, 1989, 93, U.S. Masters Swimming All-Am., 1993, 94; grad. Leadership Memphis, 1995; named Cmty. Hero for Olympic Torch Relay, 1996, named One of Fifty Women Who Make a Differnce in 1998, Women's News, Mertie Buckman Empowerment award, 1999. Mem. Le Bonheur Club, Memphis Runners Track Club, Univ. Club (bd. dirs. 2000—). Republican. Episcopalian. Avocations: competitive long distance running, tennis, swimming. Home: 1004 Murray Hill Ln Memphis TN 38120-2674 Office: Lunch for Two LLC 4745 Poplar Ave #303 Memphis TN 38117

WINTERS, JACKIE F. small business owner, foundation administrator; b. Topeka, Kans., Apr. 19, 1937; m. Marc Winters; 4 children. Student in intergovtl. rels., Oreg. State U.; Oreg. State U.; Policy Alts. Flemming fellow. Clerk typist Oreg. Health Sci. Ctr., 1959—69; supr. Econ. Opportunity Office Gov. Tom McCall, 1969—79; asst. Gov. Vic Atiyeh, 1979—85; owner Jackie's Ribs, 1985—; ombudsman Oreg.; mem. Oreg. Ho. of Reps., 1998—2002, Oreg. Senate, 2003—. Pres., campaign chmn. United Way MArion/Polk Counties; creator Oreg. Food Share Program; supporter local activities Scouts, YMCA, battered women's shelters; candidate Oreg. Ho. of Reps., 1996. Recipient Disting. Svc. award, City of Salem. Republican. Office: 900 Court St North East H212 Salem OR 97301 Office Phone: 503-986-1710.

WINTERS, JANICE JOYNER, accountant; b. Reform, Ala., Dec. 1, 1969; d. Floyd Harold and Ruby Ann (Gore) J.; m. Ronnie D. Winters. ASBA, Brewer State Jr. Coll., Fayette, Ala., 1990; BS in Acctg., U. Ala., 1992. CPA. Staff acct. Pickens County Med. Ctr., Carrollton, Ala., 1992-93, asst. comptr., 1993—2003, controller, 2003—. Charter mem. Leadership Pickens, Pickens County, Ala., 1993-94. Mem. Ala. Soc. CPAs. Office: Pickens County Medical Ctr PO Box 478 Carrollton AL 35447-0478

WINTERS, SHELLEY (SHIRLEY SCHRIFT), actress; b. St. Louis, Aug. 18, 1922; m. Vittorio Gassman (div.); 1 child, Vittoria; m. Anthony Franciosa, 1957 (div. Nov. 1960). Student, Wayne U. Began acting career in vaudeville, later played roles on legitimate stage; motion pictures include The Diary of Anne Frank, 1958 (Acad. award best supporting actress), Odds Against Tomorrow, Let No Man Write My Epitaph, Matter of Convictions, Lolita, 1962, Wives and Lovers, 1963, The Balcony, 1964, A House Is Not a Home, 1964, Patch of Blue, 1966 (Acad. award best supporting actress), Time of Indifference, 1965, Alfie, 1965, The Moving Target, 1965, Harper, 1966, Enter Laughing, 1967, The Scalp Hunters, 1968, Buona Sera Mrs. Campbell, 1968, Wild in the Streets, 1968, The Mad Room, 1969, How Do I Love Thee, 1971, What's the Matter with Helen, 1971, The Poseidon Adventure, 1972, Blume in Love, 1973, Cleopatra Jones, 1973, Something to Hide, 1973, Diamonds, 1975, Next Stop Greenwich Village, 1976, The Tenant, 1976, An Average Man, 1977, Tentacles, 1977, Pete's Dragon, 1977, King of the Gypsies, 1978, The Visitor, 1980, Looping, 1981, S.O.B., 1981, My Mother, My Daughter, 1981, Over the Brooklyn Bridge, Ellie, Déjà vu, 1983, The Delta Force, 1986, Marilyn Monroe: Beyond the Legend, 1987, Purple People Eater, 1988, An Unremarkable Life, 1989, Touch of a Stranger, 1990, Stepping Out, 1991, The Pickle, 1993, Raging Angels, 1995, Mrs. Munck, 1995, Jury Duty, 1995, Heavy, 1995, Backfire, 1995, The Portrait of a Lady, 1996, Gideon's Webb, 1998, La Bamba, 1999; appeared in: TV films Revenge!, 1971, The Devil's Daughter, 1973, Double Indemnity, 1974, The Sun Symbol 1974, Elvis 1978, Alice in Wonderland, plays A Hatfull of Rain, 1955, Girls of Summer, 1957, Night of the Iguana, Cages, Who's Afraid of Virginia Wolf?, Minnie's Boys, Marlon Brando: The Wild One, 1996; TV miniseries The French Atlantic Affair, 1979; Author: play One Night Stands of a Noisy Passenger, 1971; autobiography Shelley: Also Known As Shirley, 1980, Shelley II: The Middle of My Century, 1989. Recipient Emmy award Best Actress, 1964, Monte Carlo Golden Nymph award, 1964, Internat. TV award as best actress Cannes Festival, 1965 Address: ICM care Jack Gilliardi 8942 Wilshire Blvd Beverly Hills CA 90211-1934

WINTER-SWITZ, CHERYL DONNA, travel company executive; b. Jacksonville, Fla., Dec. 6, 1947; d. Jacqueline Marie (Carroll) Winter; m. Frank C. Snedaker, June 24, 1974 (div. May 1976); m. Robert William Switz, July 1, 1981. AA, City Coll. of San Francisco, 1986; BS, Golden Gate U., 1990, MBA, 1992. Bookkeeper, agt. McQuade Tours, Ft. Lauderdale, Fla., 1967-69; mgr. Boca Raton (Fla.) Travel, 1969-76; owner, mgr. Ocean Travel, Boca Raton, 1976-79; ind. contractor Far Horizons Travel, Boca Raton, 1979-80; mgr. Tara/BPF Travel, San Francisco, 1981-84; mgr. travel. dept. Ernst & Whinney/Lifeco Travel, San Francisco, 1984-86; travel cons. Golden Gate U., San Francisco, 1986-99, Siemer & Hand Travel, San Francisco, 1989-99, Ravenel Travel, Charleston, SC, 1999-2000, Carlson Carolina Travel, Mt. Pleasant, SC, 2000—02, Sato/Navigant Travel, 2003—. Instr. Golden Gate U., 1986-99, U. San Francisco. Mem. Amateur Trapshooting Assn., Hotel and Restaurant Mgmt. Club. Republican. Episcopalian. Avocations: trap shooting, gardening, cooking, travelling, reading. Home: 1189 W Park View Pl Mount Pleasant SC 29466-7910 Office: Carlson Carolina Travel 806 Johnnie Dodds Blvd Mount Pleasant SC 29464

WINTHROP, EMILIE See CUTHBERT, EMILIE

WINTON, LINDA, corporate financial executive; b. Phila. BA in Secondary Edn. & Spanish, La Salle Coll., Phila., 1971—75; MA in Spanish Lang. & Lit., NYU, Madrid, 1978—79; MS in Adult Edn. & Human Resource Tng. and Devel., U. of So. Maine, Gorham, 1990—91. Cert. Tchr. of Spanish Pa. Dept. Edn., 1975, N.J. Dept. Edn., 1975, Tchr. of French N.J. Dept. Edn., 1977, Exhbn. Mgr. Internat. Assn. for Exhbn. Mgmt., 2003. Spanish & French tchr. Willingboro H.S., NJ, 1975—77; ESL instr. Camden Learning Ctr., NJ, 1975—77, Shell Oil Co., Madrid, 1977—79, Inst. Internat. Madrid, Madrid, 1977—79; esl instr. Iberia Airlines, Madrid, 1977—79; export sales Wheatland Tube Co., EMSI, Pa., 1979—81; Spanish and French tchr. Haddonfield H.S., 1981—82; Spanish instr. U. Ky., 1982—84; dir. Gorham Adult and Cmty. Edn., Maine, 1989—93; prin. Tng. Assocs. Maine, 1990—91; sales rep., account mgr. Diversified Expositions, Maine, 1994—97; pres., CEO New Markets Internat. LLC, Falmouth, Maine, 1997—. Programmer Tampa Bay Coun. for Internat. Visitors, Fla., 1986—87; sr. programmer Maine Coun. for Internat. Visitors, 2000—. Recipient, Ofines Award for Study of Linguistics, 1978; fellow, Nat. Endowment for the Humanities, 1984. Mem.: Meeting Profls. Internat. (internat. devel. com. 2000—01, fin. com. 2001—02, global issues adv. group 2001—02, membership com. 2002—, internat. membership com. 2002—03, new eng. chpt. liaison to the multicultural initiative 2003—), Internat. Assn. for Exhbn. Mgmt. (dept. commerce liaison com. 2001—03), Maine Internat. Trade Ctr., Profl. Conv. Mgmt. Assn., World Affairs Coun. of Maine. Office: New Markets Internat LLC 12 Arbor Rd Falmouth ME 04105 E-mail: nmi@maine.rr.com

WINTOUR, ANNA, editor; b. London, Nov. 3, 1949; arrived in U.S., 1976; d. Charles and Elinor Wintour; m. David Shaffer, Sept. 1984; children: Charles, Kate. Student, Queens Coll., 1963—67. Deputy fashion editor Harper's and Queen Mag., London, 1970—76; fashion editor Harper's Bazaar, NY, 1976—77; fashion and beauty editor Viva Mag., NY, 1977—78; contbg. editor fashion and style Savvy Mag., NY, 1980—81; sr. editor N.Y. Mag., 1981—83; creative dir. U.S. Vogue, NY, 1983—86; editor-in-chief British Vogue, London, 1986—87, House and Garden, NY, 1987—88, Vogue, NY, 1988—. Office: Vogue 4 Times Sq New York NY 10036*

WINZER, P.J. lawyer; b. Shreveport, La., June 7, 1947; d. C.W. Winzer and Pearlene Hall Winzer Tobin. BA in Polit. Sci., So. U., Baton Rouge, 1968; JD, UCLA, 1971. Bar: Bar: Calif. 1972, U.S. Supreme Ct. 1986. Staff atty. Office of Gen. Counsel, US HEW, Washington, 1971-80; asst. spl.

counsel U.S. Office of Spl. Counsel Merit Systems Protection Bd., Dallas, 1980-82; regional dir. U.S. Merit Systems Protection Bd., Alexandria, Va., 1982—. Mem. Calif. Bar Assn., Fed. Cir. Bar Assn., Delta Sigma Theta. Office: US Merit System Protection 1800 Diag. L.D.J. Ste. 902 Alexandria VA 22314-2840

WIRTH, KELLEY K. state representative; b. Panorama City, Calif., Aug. 2, 1965; m. Thomas Wirth; children: Kennedy, Meghan. BS, Oreg. State U., 1989; MS, U. So. Calif., 1992. State rep., dist. 16 Oreg. House Rep., Salem, 2001—; sys. analyst, planning commr. City of Corvallis, Oreg., 1996—; sys. analyst Asst. to 3d Infantry Divsn. Chief of Staff, 1993—99. Adj. computer tech. faculty City Colls. Chgo.-Europe, 1992; bd. mem. Land Devel. Hearings Bd. City of Corvallis, 1998—, mem. Neighborhood Tech. Rev. Group, 1997—. Mem.: Corvallis LWV. Democrat. Episcopalian. Office: 900 Court St NE H-479 Salem OR 97301

WIRTH, MELISSA KAY, medical/surgical nurse, rehabilitation nurse; b. Chgo., May 3, 1950; d. Herbert Ralph and Beatrice Louise Wirth; m. Milton Rafael Ayala, Aug. 24, 1974 (div. Jan. 4, 1984); 1 child, Rafael. BA in Sociology, Ill. Wesleyan U., 1972; BSN, Columbia U., 1980. RN Fla. Nurse Columbia Presbyn. Hosp., N.Y., 1980—84, USAF Hosp., Laughlin AFB, Tex., 1984—87, Healthcare Staffing Agys., Orlando, Fla., 1988—91, Fla. Hosp., Orlando, 1992—. 1st lt. USAF, 1984—87. Mem.: Conchologists of Am., Fla. Lighthouse Assn., Ctrl. Fla. Shell Club. Republican. Avocations: guitar, piano, bicycling, swimming, shells. Office: Florida Hospital 601 E Rollins Orlando FL 32803

WIRTH, SANDRA LEE, real estate company owner; b. Buffalo, June 8, 1945; d. Dominic A. and Santina (Lopez) Liberatore; 1 child, H. William III. Prin. Metro Sandra Lee Wirth Robshaw Gallery of Homes, Tonawanda, N.Y.; regional mgr. Paul Robshaw Galler of Homes, Tonawanda, N.Y., mgr. line Cheektowaga, N.Y.; broker assoc. B.W. Morris and Son Realtors, Buffalo; owner Metro Sandra Lee Wirth, Real Estate; mem. N.Y. Assembly, Dist. 148, Albany, 1994—. Chmn., past pres. West Seneca Druga Abuse Prevention Coun.; sponsor Call Home Free Program, Nat. Crime Prevention Coun.'s Nat. Night Out. Named Realtor of the Yr., Elma Bus. Person of the Yr. Mem. Nat. Assn. Realtors (cert.), N.Y. Assn. Realtors (state dir.), Greater Buffalo Bd. Realtors (1st v.p. 1988, treas. 1989, pres. elect 1990), Greater Buffalo Assn. Realtors (pres.), Buffalo and West Seneca C. of C. Office: 1500 Union Rd West Seneca NY 14224-2171

WIRTSCHAFTER, IRENE NEROVE, tax specialist, consultant; b. Elgin, Ill., Aug. 05; d. David A. and Ethel G. Nerove; m. Burton Wirtschafter, June 2, 1945 (dec. 1966). BCS, Columbus U., 1942. Cert. tax profl., enrolled agt., IRS. Commd. ensign Supply Corps, USN, 1944, advanced through grades to capt., 1975; comdg. officer Res. Supply Unit, 1974-75; ret., 1976; agt. Office Internat. Ops. IRS, 1967-75; internat. banking specialist; real estate profl., appraiser, 1976-80; pvt. practice tax cons. Sr. intern program U.S. Senate, 1981; mem. Sec. Navy's Adv. Com. Ret. Pers., 1984—86, VA Adv. Com. Women Vets., 1987—90. Past troop leader Girl Scouts U.S.A.; lt. col. and mission pilot CAP, 21 air races; comml. instrument pilot land and sea; Navy liaison officer Commd.'s Retiree Coun., Patrick AFB, 1985—89; mem. Nat. Com. Internat. Forest of Friendship, Atchison, Kans., 1976—; elected silver rep. Nat. Silver Haired Congress, 1977—2001; elected rep. Silver Haired Legis., 1984, Silver Haired Senate, 1988—; trustee Internat. Women's Air and Space Mus., 1993—, bd. dirs., 1999—; state rep. Nat. Coun. to Preserve Social Security and Medicare, 1999; bd. dirs., treas. Honor Am., 2001—04; sec. Navy League, 2000; cons. Jr. Achievement, 1989—94; founder sr. action com. Brevard County, 1981; chmn. College Park Airport Johnny Horizon Day, 1975; elected dir. Fla. Space Coast Philharm., 1985—, treas., 1986—92, bd. dirs., adv. mgr. Cocoa Beach Citizen's League, 1990—92; co-chmn. Internat. Women's Yr. Take Off Dinner, Washington, 1976; 1st v.p. Friends of Cocoa Beach Libr., 1988—90, pres., 1990—92, bd. dirs., 1993—; apptd. to Cocoa Beach Libr. Br., 1996—; mem. Cocoa Beach Bus. Improvement Coun.; elected senator Silver Haired Legislature, Fla., 1985—; vol., founding mem. Brevard Zoo; chmn. Cocoa Beach Code Enforcement Bd., 1989—96; co-chmn. sr. adv. com. Cape Canaveral Hosp., 1994—; trustee Assn. Naval Aviation 1988—. Named Hon. Citizen, Winnipeg, Man., Can., 1966, Atchison, 1989, New Orleans, 1988, Hon. Dep. State Fire Marshal, Fla., 1987, Ky. Col., La. Col.; recipient cert. of appreciation, Cocoa Beach Women's Club, 2000, Svc. Above Self award, Rotary, 1998. Mem.: RMGS, TROA, AAUW, Navy League (sec. 2001), WAVES Nat. (bd. dirs. chpt. 75 1989—, founder), Cocoa Beach Area C. of C., Assn. Enrolled Agts., Banana River Squadron (founder, comptr. 1984—), Assn. Naval Aviation (nat. trustee 1988—), Naval Order U.S. (treas. nat. capitol commandry), Naval Res. Assn. (nat. treas. 1975—77, nat. adv. com. 1985—), Naval Award of Merit 1992), Internat. Platform Assn. (life), Ninety Nines (past chpt. sect. and nat. officer, 99 achievement awards), Jazz Soc. Brevard, Patrick Women's Golf Assn. (treas. 1996—97), Silver Wings (nat. sec. 1986, bd. dirs. 1990—, nat. v.p. 2001, Woman of Yr. award 1985), Tailhook Assn. (life), Rotary. Avocations: aviation, golf, music. Home: 1825 Minutemen Cswy Apt 301 Cocoa Beach FL 32931-2033 Fax: 321-783-4899. E-mail: irenwirt@juno.com.

WIRTZ, DORIS W. secondary school educator; b. Portland, Oreg., May 14, 1947; d. Walter Arthur Galer and Taza Flora Register; m. James C. Bowen, June 6, 1969 (div. 1971); m. Robert Edwin Wirtz, June 5, 1976; children: Robert Jr., Lynn Wallace, Craig, Kiley McKenna. BA in English, Portland State U., 1983, MA in English, 1986, postgrad. Cert. tchr. Sales staff Jantzen, Inc., Portland, 1971—77; adj. faculty Portland State U., 1981—86, Portland C.C., 1986—90; secondary tchr. Lake Oswego (Oreg.) H.S., 1995—. Mem.: DAR, NEA, Women in Comm., Oreg. Ednl. Assn., Smithsonian Inst., Oreg. Shakespearean Assn., Women in the Arts, Amnesty Internat, Phi Kappa Phi. Lutheran. Avocations: gardening, reading, travel, history, Renaissance studies. Home: 3015 Royce Way Lake Oswego OR 97034 Office: Oswego Sch Dist PO Box 70 Lake Oswego OR 97034

WIRTZ, DOROTHY MARIE, retired language educator; b. Keokuk, Iowa, Mar. 9, 1915; d. John and Alma Adelaide (Schard) Wirtz. BA, U. Iowa, 1939; MA, U. Wis., 1940, PhD, 1944. Tchg. asst. U. Wis., 1939—44; asst. prof. French U. Minn., , 1944—50; dir., French House U. Wis., 1945; sec. Ariz. Tax Commn., Phoenix, 1952—58; dep. state treas. of Ariz., 1956—58; prof., French Ariz. State U., 1958—73; ret., 1973. Sec. to Dem. whip Ariz. H. of Reps., Phoenix, 1950—52. Contbr. articles to profl. pub. and poetry magazines; author: (poetry) Evolution, 2003. Pres. Ariz. Fgn. Lang. Soc., Phoenix, 1968. Mem.: AAUW (cultural chmn.), Phi Beta Kappa (pres., Phoenix Chap., 1974). Democrat. Mem. United Ch. Of Christ. Avocations: art, music, literature, travel. Home: 1711 W State Ave Phoenix AZ 85021

WISCHMEIER, ELAINE ALICE, music educator; d. Lester Raymond and Adeline Mae Neiman; m. Richard Edwin Wischmeier, Aug. 16, 1964; children: Eric Alan, Brian Edward. MusB in Edn., Taylor U., 1961; student, Ind. U., 1962—63, U. Nebr., Kearney, 1985, student, 1986, student, 1988. Cert. tchr. Nebr., 1964. Music tchr. Grace U., Omaha, 1961—64, Nebr. Christian Schs., Ctrl. City, Nebr., 1964—66, Shawnee Mission Pub. Sch., Overland Pk., Kans., 1967—69; prof. music Inst. Biblico Portugues, Antão do Tojal, Portugal, 1976—78; music tchr. Nebr. Christian Schs., 1978—79, Venango (Nebr.) Pub. Sch., 1984—87, Nebr. Christian Schs., 1988—, tchr. English, 1988—. Counselor Mid-Am. Jr. HS Music Camp, Omaha, 1991—2001, 1994—2001. Mem.: Nat. Fedn. State HS Assns., Nebr. Music Educators Assn., Music Educators Nat. Conv. Republican. Evangelical. Home: 2115 17th Ave Central City NE 68826 Office: Nebr Christian Schs 1847 Inskip Ave Central City NE 68826

WISE, HELENA SUNNY, lawyer; b. Ridgecrest, Calif., Dec. 3, 1954; d. Strother Eldon and Mary Helen (Harinek) W.; children: Marie Evelyn, Shawnie Helene. BA with honors, UCLA, 1976; JD with highest honors, Loyola Marymount U., 1979. Bar: Calif. 1979, Nev. 1992, U.S. Dist. Ct. (ctrl. dist.) Calif. 1980, U.S. Dist. Ct. (ea. dist.) Calif. 2001, U.S. Dist. Ct. Ariz. 1992, U.S. Ct. Appeals (9th cir.) 1980, U.S. Supreme Ct. 2000. Ptnr. Geffner & Satzman, Los Angeles, 1980-87; pvt. practice Burbank, Calif., 1987—. Arbitrator talent agy. disputes SAG. Columnist Los Angeles Lawyer mag., 1985-86. Chmn. founder Barristers Child Abuse Com., L.A. 1982-86; mem. exec. bd. Vols. in Parole, L.A., 1983-90; mem. Dem. Chair's Circle, L.A., 1985; mem. adv. bd. Over Easy Found., 1987—; vol. Love is Feeding Everyone. Fellow ABA (exec. coun. labor and employment law 1986-89, liaison young lawyers sect., bd. dirs. young lawyers divsn. 1986-88, mem. MSN team Nat. Com. on Child Abuse, del., teller Ho. of Dels. 1978-79), L.A. County Bar Assn. (v.p. sr. bar 1984-86, pres. young lawyers sect.), State Bar Calif. (bd. dirs. Calif. Young Lawyers Assn., labor law ad hoc com. on wrongful discharge, mem. juv. law com.), UCLA alumni rep., USAC 1992-94, student rels. com. 1992-94), Am. Legion Women's Auz. Avocations: photography, skiing, playing organ. Office: 3111 W Burbank Blvd Ste 101 Burbank CA 91505-2350 Fax: 818 843-7958.

WISE, JOANNE HERBERT, art director; b. Bryn Mawr, Pa., Aug. 11, 1943; d. Charles Nugent and Carolyn (Le Maistre) Herbert; m. Douglas Wise, Nov. 26, 1976. Student, Acad. Fine Arts, Phila. Sec. to corp. v.p. Fawcett Publs., N.Y.C., 1964-66; sec. to promotion dir. Weightman Advt., Phila., 1966-70; assoc. media mgr. Scott Paper Co., Phila., 1970-75; promotion dir. Jimmy Carters Nat. Campaign, Atlanta, 1976; dir. The Wise Collection, Tokyo, Houston and N.Y.C., 1980—. Curator Japan Hands, N.Y.C., 1987-89; coord. screen project Sculptor Jiro Okura, Roanoke, Va., 1990-91; moderator, presenter Shaker/Japanese North Country Studio Conf., 1993, exec. dir., 1995—. Pub.: newsletter Current Influences in Contemporary Art, 1986—95. Pres. Tokyo/Am. Club, 1980; founder Tex. Print Alliance, Houston, 1982; exec. dir. North Country Studio Conf., 1995—. Avocations: skiing, cooking, travel, art collecting, racquet sports. Office: The Wise Collection PO Box 286 Lyme NH 03768-0286

WISE, KITTY, writer, composer; b. Plaindealing, La., June 26, 1947; d. Warren G. Wise. BA in English, U. Wyo., 1992. Cert. educator, Wyo. CEO, sec., v.p. Precision Well Svc., Inc., Gillette, Wyo., 1982-89; founder, CEO, sec.-treas. WiseWords Pub., Inc., Gillette, 1997—. Author: A Lost Soul, 1990, Somewhere Beyond Tomorrow, 1997, (trilogy) The Wind In My Hair, 1992, Listen To The Wind, 1996, Anywhere The Wind Blows, 1997; co-author, editor, artist (work book) The Empowered Exec's Handbook for Life The Labyrinth A Journey Into Your Personal Power, 1997, Teaching Parents to be Good Teachers: First, Do No Harm, 1999; author of short stories; composer various songs. Recipient Svc. award Gillette Jaycees, 1976-77, Am. Legion, Gillette, 1997. Office: Wisewords Pub PO Box 2878 Gillette WY 82717-2878 Home: 2152 Century Blvd #303 Rock Springs WY 82901

WISE, PATRICIA, opera singer and educator; b. Wichita, Kans. d. Melvin R. and Genevieve F. (Dotson) W.; 1 child, Jennifer. B. Music Edn., U. Kans., Lawrence, 1966. Prof. voice Ind. U. Sch. Music, Bloomington, 1995—; tchr. master classes San Francisco, Vienna Conservatory, Salzburg (Austria) Mozarteum; voice tchr. Domingo Young Artist program Washington Opera. Debut as Susanna in Marriage of Figaro, Kansas City, 1966; prin. roles include Lucia, Gilda, Micaela, Juliette, Zerbinetta, Pamina, Musetta, Lulu, Violetta, Nedda, others; appeared with leading Am. opera cos. including, Chgo., Santa Fe, N.Y.C., San Francisco, Houston, San Diego, Miami, Balt., Phila., Pitts.; European appearances, 1971-76, London Royal Opera, Glyndebourne Festival, Vienna Volksoper, Geneva Opera; guest artist with Vienna, Hamburg, Munich, Cologne, Frankfurt, and Berlin State Operas; guest appearances in Madrid, Barcelona, Rome, La Scala Milan, Nice, Paris Chatelet, Zurich, Dresden, Salzburg Festival, Theatro Colon, Buenos Aires; appeared with orchs. including, Chgo. Symphony Orch., Los Angeles Symphony Orch., N.Y. Handel Soc., Israel Philharm. Orch., Vienna Philharm. Orch., N.Y. Philharm., Cleve. Orch., Berlin Symphonic Orch., BBC Orch., Nat. Orch. France; Angel Recordings; internat. TV, film appearances. Recipient Morton Baum award N.Y.C. Ctr., 1971, Dealey Meml. award Dallas Symphony, 1966, Naftzger young Artist award Wichita Symphony, 1966, Midland Young Artist award Midland (Tex.) Symphony Orch., 1966; M.B. Rockefeller Fund grantee, 1967-70; Sullivan Found. grantee, 1967-68; named Kammersänger Vienna Staatsoper, 1989. E-mail: patwise@indiana.edu.

WISE, SANDRA CASBER, lawyer; BA, Macalester Coll., 1969; JD, U. Minn., 1972. Bar: Minn. 1972, D.C., 1986, W.Va., 1987. Legis asst. to Rep. Martha Keys, Washington, 1977-78; asst. to asst. to the pres. for women's issues Sara Weddington, The White Ho., Washington, 1979; staff sub-com. on pub. assistance Ho. Com. on Ways and Means, Washington, 1980, staff sub-com. on health, 1981-85; atty. White, Fine and Verville, 1986; staff dir. sub-com. on social security Ho. Com. on Ways and Means, Washington, 1987-94, minority counsel subcom. on social security, 1995-2000; first lady State of W.Va., 2001—.

WISE, SUSAN TAMSBERG, management and communications consultant, speaker; b. Memphis, Nov. 16, 1945; d. Joseph Lane and Mable Rosa (Koth) Tamsberg; m. Roy Thomas Wise, June 29, 1968; children: Kristin Rebecca, Mary Catherine. BA in Math., Columbia (S.C.) Coll., 1967; M in Edn., Ga. State U., Atlanta, 1986. Tchr. high sch. math. various pub. schs., N.C., S.C., and Ga., 1967-73; instr. Cen. Piedmont Community Coll., Charlotte, N.C., 1979; devel. dir. Classique, Inc., Kannapolis, N.C., 1979-81; asst. v.p. First Nat. Bank of Atlanta, 1981-87; Ga. dir. The Exec. Speaker, Inc., Atlanta, 1987-90; pres. TrimTime, Inc., Atlanta, 1988—, Wise Consulting Inc., Atlanta, 1990—. Speaker Girl Scouts USA, Jr. League, numerous med. assns., Atlanta and S.E. area, 1985—; affiliate Exec. Coaching Network, Inc. Tng. cons. Jr. League of Atlanta, 1988-89; bd. dirs. Incarnation Luth. Ch., Atlanta, 1984; mem. ch. coun., bd. dirs. Luth. Ch. of the Redeemer, 1994. Mem. ASTD (v.p., bd. dirs., Leadership award 1987), Kappa Delta Pi. Republican. Avocations: international traveling, antiques, needlework.

WISEHART, MARY RUTH, retired religious organization administrator; b. Myrtle, Mo., Nov. 2, 1932; d. William Henry and Ora (Harbison) W. BA, Free Will Bapt. Bible Coll., 1955, George Peabody Coll. Tchrs., 1959, MA, 1960, PhD, 1976. Free Will Bapt. Bible Coll., Nashville, 1956-60, chmn. English dept., 1961-85; exec. sec.-treas. Free Will Bapt. Women Nat. Active for Christ, 1985-98. Author: Sparks Into Flame, 1985, Beyond the Gate, 1998; contbr. poetry to jours. Mem. Nat. Coun. Tchrs. English, Scribbler's Club. Free Will Baptist. Avocations: photography, music, drama. E-mail: wisemrw@aol.com.

WISEMAN, CYNTHIA SUE, language educator; b. New Albany, Miss., Sept. 8, 1952; d. Paul W. and Betty J. (Gore) W.; m. Ivan A. Tardio, Jan. 25, 1983 (div. Dec. 1997); children: E. Alexandra, Robert Paul. BA in English Lit., U. Miss., 1974; postgrad., La Sorbonne, Paris, 1978-79; MA in Tchg., Sch. for Internat. Tng., 1982; postgrad., Columbia U. With Peace Corps, Senegal, 1975-77; editor Guita Rev., N.Y., 1991-92; adj. instr. ESL Am. lang. program Hunter Coll., CUNY, N.Y.C., 1992-95; dir. Queensborough Adult Learning Ctr., CUNY, N.Y.C., 1991-92; adj. instr. ESL, lang. program Columbia U., N.Y.C., 1989-91; adj. instr. ESL, LaGuardia C.C., CUNY, 1987—; adj. prof. dept. culture and comm. NYU, N.Y.C., 1995—. Adj. prof. John Jay Coll. Criminal Justice, CUNY, 1995-98, instr. Internat. English Lang. Inst., 1989—. co-chmn. part-timers caucus TESOL, Alexandria, Va., 1996-99, mem.-at-large HEIS, TESOL, 1999—; chair signage TESOL, 1999; mem. exec. bd. CUNY ESL Coun., 1997-99. Active AIDS orgns., N.Y.C., 1990—. Mem. N.Y. State Tchs. English to Speakers of Other

langs. (pres. 2001, v.p. 2000, exec. bd., chmn. sociopolit. com. 1995-97). Democrat. Avocations: cycling, rollerblading. Home: 300 Cathedral Pky Apt 1F New York U STM 10028 1631 Office: CUNY Hunter Coll 10th Fl East Bldg 695 Park Ave New York NY 10021-5024

WISEMAN, GRETCHEN RENEE, personal care industry executive; d. Richard Earl and Sandra Lee Wiseman. BA, Buena Vista U., Storm Lake, Iowa, 1996. Cert. tchr. Ohio, 2003. Camp counselor Easter Seals, Des Moines, Iowa, 1994—98; k-8 multicategorical resource rm. tchr. Rockwell-Swaledale CSD, Rockwell, Iowa, 1996—98; residential specialist Sunshine Inc, of NW Ohio, Maumee, Ohio, 1998—; spl. educaiton tchr./tech. coord. The Aurora Acad., Toledo, Ohio, 2000—03; intervention specialist George A. Phillips Acad., Toledo, Ohio, 2003—. Home: 27695 Tracy Rd Lot 248 Walbridge OH 43465 Personal E-mail: unicorn_gw@yahoo.com.

WISEMAN, MARY BITTNER, philosopher, educator; b. Philadelphia, PA, Aug. 21, 1936; d. Leo Joseph and Helen Crooks Bittner; m. John O'Connor, 1960 (div. 1968); 1 child, Emily ; m. Charles Wiseman, Aug. 21, 1970 (div. 1989); m. Harvey Goldstein, Jan. 9, 1989. AB St. John's Coll., Annapolis, Md., 1959; AM Harvard U., 1964; PhD Columbia U., 1974. Prof. philosophy Bklyn. Coll./CUNY, 1972—98; prof. philosophy, comparative lit. Grad. Sch. CUNY, 1983—98. Lectr. in field. Author: The Ecstasies of Roland Barthes, 1989; contbr. articles to profl. jours. Recipient Alumni award of merit, St. John's Coll., 1989; NEH fellow, 1980, E.R. Wolfe fellow, 1996—97. Mem.: Coll. Art Assn., Am. Philos. Assn., Am. Soc. for Aesthetics.

WISHARD, DELLA MAE, former newspaper editor; b. Bison, S.D., Oct. 21, 1934; d. Ervin E. and Alma J. (Albertson) Preszler; m. Glenn L. Wishard, Oct. 18, 1953; children: Glenda Lee, Pamela A., Glen Ervin. Grad. high sch., Bison. Mem. S.D. Ho. of Reps., Pierre, 1984-96; pub., editor Bison (S.D.) Courier, 1996-2000. Columnist County Farm Bur., 1970-96. Committeewoman state Rep. Cen. Com., Perkins County, S.D., 1980-84, 98-01. Mem. Am. Legis. Exch. Coun. (state coord. 1985-91, state chmn. 1991-96), Fed. Rep. Women (chmn. Perkins County chpt. 1978-84), S.D. Farm Bur. (state officer 1982), Perkins County Rep. (chmn. 2000-03). Lutheran. Avocations: writing, gardening. Home: 1510 Canyon St Spearfish SD 57783

WISHERT, JO ANN CHAPPELL, music educator, elementary and secondary education educator; b. Carroll County, Va., July 10, 1951; d. Joseph Lenox and Helen Alata (Wagoner) Chappell; m. Clarence Hinnant Wishert, Jr., June 10, 1987; 1 child, Kelly Marie. BA, Oral Roberts U., 1974; MS, Radford U., 1977; degree in advanced postgrad studies, Va. Poly. Inst. and State U., 1981; postgrad., U. S.C., Spartanburg, 1990, U. S.C., Columbia, 1995, The Citadel, 1996, Winthrop U., 1995, 96, postgrad., 2003. Cert. elem. music supr., Va., elem. and secondary music tchr., S.C., music tchr., ednl. specialist, N.C. Head start tchr. Rooftop of Va., Galax, 1975; elem. music tchr. Carroll County Pub. Schs., Hillsville, 1975-78; grad. asst., supr., course advisor Coll. Edn., Va. Poly. Inst. and State U., Blacksburg, 1975-81, pregrad. interviewer placement svcs., 1981-83; music dir. Heritage Acad., Charlotte, N.C., 1984-85, fine arts specialist, 1985-86; choral dir. Chester County Schs., Chester, 1986—2002; music tchr. Old Pointe Elem./Rock Hill Sch. Dist. #3, 2002—. Fine arts chair Chester H.S., 1995-2002, adept evaluator, 1996—; guest condr. workshop Patrick County Schs., Stuart, Va., 1980; liaison for Chester County Schs. to S.C. Gov.'s Sch. for Arts, 1990-91; faculty mem., sponsor Tri-M Music Honor Soc., Curriculum Leadership Acad., 2003. Soloist PTL TV Network, Charlotte, 1984-85. Guest spkr. on battered women and marital abuse to chs. and workshops; entertainer; co-dir. Chester City Schs. Choral Festival; active Arts Coun. Chester County, 1988—, S.C. Arts Alliance and Arts Advocacy, Winthrop Consortium for the Arts, Rock Hill Sch. Dist. Tchr. Forum, 2003—; sponsor Beta Club. Named Tchr. of the Yr., Chester Sr. H.S., 1989, Chester County Schs., 1991, Old Pointe Elem. Sch., 2003-04, Educator of Yr., Chester County C. of C., 1992, Tchr. of the Week, The Herald, 1995, Rock Hill Sch. Dist. Educator of the Day, 2002, 2003. Mem. ASCD, AAUW (mem. bylaws com. Chester br. 1987-93, sec. 1988-89, fine arts chmn. 1995-2002), Music Educators Nat. Conf., S.C. Music Educators Assn. (del. pub. rels. network Chester County Schs. 1991), S.C. Edn. Assn., Palmetto State Tchrs. Assn., Am. Ednl. Rsch. Assn., Am. Assn. Choral Dirs., Chester County Edn. Assn., Nat. Assn. Secondary Music Edn. (team evaluator divsn. tchr. edn. cert. 1989, 91-2002), S.C. State Coun. Internat. Reading Assn., S.C. Reading Assn., State So. Assn. Schs. and Colls. (mem. evaluation team, mem. steering com.), All U.S.A. Chorus Student Group (alumni), Tri-M Music Honor Soc. (sponsor), 4-H Club (life), Phi Delta Kappa., Old Pointe Elem. (spl. areas dept. chair, 2003-2004). Republican. Baptist. Avocations: reading, cross stitch, needlepoint, music. Home: 1122 Virginia Dare Dr Rock Hill SC 29730-9669 E-mail: jwishert@rock-hill.k12.sc.us.

WISHNICK, MARCIA MARGOLIS, pediatrician, geneticist, educator; b. N.Y.C., Oct. 10, 1938; d. Hyman and Tillie (Stoller) Margolis; m. Stanley Wishnick, June 12, 1960; 1 child, Elizabeth Anne. BA, Barnard Coll., 1960; PhD, NYU, 1970, MD, 1974. Diplomate Am. Bd. Pediatrics, Nat. Bd. Med. Examiners. Rsch. technician Lederle Labs./Am. Cyanamid, Pearl River, N.Y., 1960-66; postdoctoral fellow N.Y. Pub. Health Lab., N.Y.C., 1970-71; resident in pediatrics NYU-Bellevue Med. Ctr., N.Y.C., 1974-77, asst. prof. pediatrics, 1977-82; clin. assoc. prof. pediatrics Bellevue Med. Ctr. NYU Med. Ctr., N.Y.C., 1982-87; clin. prof. pediatrics NYU-Bellevue Med. Ctr., N.Y.C., 1987—; pvt. practice, 1977—2003. Contbr. articles to profl. jours. Fellow Am. Acad. Pediatrics; mem. AMA, N.Y. Pediatric Soc., N.Y. Med. Soc. Office Phone: 808-937-0312.

WISMER, PATRICIA ANN, retired secondary school educator; b. York, Pa., Mar. 23, 1936; d. John Bernhardt and Frances Elizabeth Loreen Marie (Fry) Feiser; m. Lawrence Howard Wismer, Aug. 4, 1961. BA in English, Mt. Holyoke Coll., 1958; MA in Speech/Drama, U. Wis., 1960; postgrad., U. Oreg., 1962, Calif. State U., Chico, 1963-64, U. So. Calif., 1973-74. Tchr., co-dir. drama program William Penn Sr. High Sch., York, 1960-61; instr. English, dir. drama York Jr. Coll., 1961-62; assoc. church editor San Francisco Examiner, 1962-63; reporter, publicist News Bur. Calif. State U. Chico, 1963-64; chmn. English Dept. Chico Sr. H.S., 1966-96; mentor tchr. Chico Sr. High Sch., Chico Unified Sch. Dist., 1983-93. Judge writing awards Nat. Coun. Tchr. English, 1970—; cons. No. Calif. Writing Project, 1977—; curriculum cons., freelance writer and photographer, 1996—. Author: My Life with Vanessa: A Journal of the Plagued Years, 1998, 40 Year Photo Retrospective, 2002; newsletter editor Chico Cat Coalition, 1999—. Mem. Educators for Social Responsibility, Planetary Soc., Upper Calif. Coun. Tchrs. English (bd. dirs. 1966-85, pres. 1970-71), Calif. Assn. Tchrs. English, Nat. Coun. Tchrs. English, NEA, Calif. Tchrs. Assn., Chico Unified Tchrs. Assn. American. Democrat. Lutheran. Avocations: photography, play prodn., video prodn. Home: 623 Arcadian Ave Chico CA 95926-4504 Office: PO Box 1250 Cannon Beach OR 97110-1250 E-mail: pwismer@aol.com.

WISNER, PAMELA L. social worker; b. Stevensville, Newfoundland, Can., Dec. 4, 1958; d. John R. Wisner, Leslie S. Wisner. BA in Psychology and Sociology, U. Mobile, 1980; M in Counseling, La. Bapt. U., 1998. LCSW Ala. Bd. Social Work Examiners, 1995, cert. Cognitive Behavioral Therapist 1999, Forensic Counselor 1999, Addictions specialist, Domestic Violence Counselor endorsement 1999. Dir. cmty. svc. RAPHA, Mobile, Ala., 1995—96; coord., counselor Charter of Mobile, 1996—2000; therapist, family cons. Gulf Coast Therapeutic Program, Inc., Mobile, 2000—. Mem.: Nat. Bd. Cognitive Behavioral Therapists, Am. Psychotherapy Assn. (diplomate 1999). Avocation: Avocations: travel, reading, cats, crafts, cooking. Home: 5405 Forest Park Dr Mobile AL 36618 Office: Therapeutic Programs Inc 601 Bel Air Blvd Ste 410 Mobile AL 36618

WISNIEWSKI, MARY JOSEPHINE, art educator, religious organization administrator; b. Milw., June 6, 1957; d. Thaddeus Louis and Rita Marie Wisniewski. BFA in Inter-Arts, U. Wis., Milw., 1981; MA in Curriculum Instrn. Arts Edn., U. Tex., San Antonio, 1997. Cert. elem. tchr. Tex. Supr. dance and art program div. recreation Milw. Pub. Schs., 1981—83; day care tchr. Milw., 1983—84; tchr. kindergarten Vols. Edn. and Social Svc., San Antonio, 1984—85; tchr. pre-kindergarten Houston Ind. Sch. Dist., 1985—87; art tchr. Northside Ind. Sch. Dist., San Antonio, 1987—91; dir. mission awareness Archdiocese San Antonio, 1991—. Founding mem. and mem. leadership team Tex. Mission Coun., San Antonio, 1992—; coord. San Antonio Mission Coun., 1992—; mem. adv. bd. Incarnate Word Missionaries, San Antonio, 2002—. Prodr.: (documentaries) Mending A Broken World, 1993—, Children: Our Future, Our Hope, 1998. Rep. for poor div. cmty. action City Coun. Adv. Group, San Antonio, 2000—02; coord. Tex./Honduras Partnership Team, 1999—2002. Edn. grantee, Archbishop Floros Charity Fund, 1984, Houston Educators grantee, Houston Bus., 1986, The Call grantee, Lilly Found., 2003. Roman Catholic. Avocations: swimming, dance, sailing, music. Office: Archdiocese of San Antonio 2718 W Woodlawn San Antonio TX 78228 E-mail: mwisniewski@archdiocese.org.

WISS, MARCIA A. lawyer; b. Columbus, Ohio, May 15, 1947; d. John William and Margaret Ann (Cook) W.; children: Christopher C. Wiss, Joan Merle. BS in Fgn. Svc., Georgetown U., 1969, JD, 1972. Bar: D.C. 1972. Econ. analyst World Bank, Washington, 1969; atty. U.S. Dept. Justice, Washington, 1972-73; atty. office gen. counsel Overseas Pvt. Investment Corp., Washington, 1973-78; gen counsel-designate Inst. for Sci. and Tech. Cooperation, Washington, 1979; ptnr. Kaplan Russin & Vecchi, Washington, 1987-92, Whitman & Ransom, 1992-93, Whitman, Breed, Abbott & Morgan, Washington, 1993-96, Wilmer, Cutler & Pickering, Washington, 1996-2000, Hogan & Hartson, Washington, 2000—. Gen. counsel Washington chpt., Soc. Internat. Devel., 1980-2001; gen. counsel, Assn. for Women in Devel., 1982—; bd. advisers, Procedural Aspects of Internat. Law Inst., 1985—; gen. counsel internat. policy coun. agr., adj. prof. of law Georgetown U. Law Ctr., 1984—, Johns Hopkins Sch. of Advanced Internat. Studies, 2001—. Editor Georgetown Law Ctr. Jour. Law and Policy in Internat. Bus., 1971-72. Chair Holy Trinity Parish Coun., Washington, 1976. Mem. Am. Fedn. Govt. Employees (chmn. 1975-76), D.C. Bar (steering com. divsn. 12, 1985-88, co-chmn. fin. and banking com. 1985), Am. Soc. Internat. Law (v.p. 1991-94, coun. 1987-90), Washington Fgn. Law Soc. (pres. 1983-84). Roman Catholic. Office: Hogan & Hartson 555 13th St NW Washington DC 20004

WISSLER-THOMAS, CARRIE, professional society administrator, artist; b. Ephrata, Pa., Nov. 2, 1946; d. Robert Uibel and Grace Urbane (Nicholas) Wissler; m. James Richard Gamber, June 12, 1968 (div. 1972); m. Scott Kerry Thomas, Mar. 3, 1972; 1 child, Dylan Crayton Llewellyn. BA, Hood Coll., 1968; MS, Temple U., 1986. Copywriter WGSA Radio, Ephrata, Pa., 1970-71, William Assocs., Harrisburg, Pa., 1977; correspondent Art Matters of Phila., Harrisburg, 1984-86; art columnist Pennsylvania Beacon, Harrisburg, 1983-85; writer Strictly Business, Harrisburg, 1985-86; painting instr. Art Assn. of Harrisburg, 1980-86; freelance artist Harrisburg, 1968—; exec. dir., pres. Art Assn. of Harrisburg, 1986—. Exhbn. panel Harrisburg City Govt. Ctr., 1983-89; art adv. panel Harrisburg [illegible] Ctr. at Harrisburg, 1988-95; chmn. Easter Seals Art Show by Disabled Artists, Harrisburg, 1983-86; trustee Pa. Coll. Art and Design, 1989—; mem. Harrisburg Multi-Cultural Coalition, 1992-94; chmn. Harrisburg Gallery Walk, 1989—; bd. dirs. Historic Harrisburg Assn., Better Bus. Bur.; pres. Allied Arts Affiliates Coun., 1993-95; mem. Dauphin Co. commn. on status of women, 2000-01. Prin. work includes Broadway Babies oil painting, 1982 (Grumbacher Gold Medallion 1982); over 30 solo exhibitions. Mem. Hist. Soc. Cocalico Valley, Ephrata, 1982—, Dauphin County Hist. Soc., Harrisburg, 1986—; minority inspector Paxtang Election Bd., Harrisburg, 1977-79; mem. ACLU, Pa., 1988-91; bd. dirs. Hist. Harrisburg Assn., 1992-98. Recipient Women Who Work award Communications and the Arts Pomeroy's, 1985, Disting. Svc. to Arts award Harrisburg Community Theatre, 1991. Mem. Am. Coun. on Arts, Art Assn. Harrisburg (pres. 1980-84), Rotary. Democrat. Anglican. Avocations: reading, biographies, visiting museums/galleries, gardening. Home: 2721 N 2nd St Harrisburg PA 17110-1205 Office: Art Assn of Harrisburg 21 N Front St Harrisburg PA 17101-1606 Office Phone: 717-236-1432.

WISSMANN, CAROL RENEÉ, sales executive; b. Berkeley, Calif., July 9, 1946; d. Conrad Clayton and Carol Elizabeth (Ward) W. BA, Whittier Coll., 1968; Montessori Diploma, Coll. Notre Dame, Belmont, 1970. Dist. mgr. U.S. C. of C., Washington; divsn. mgr. Classified Yellow Pages Inc., Cookeville, Tenn., 1986; pres. The BelleMann Corp., Gig Harbor, Wash., 1988—. Cons., writer, spkr. in field. Mem.: Seattle Free Lances (pres.). Republican. Avocations: horseback riding, ballroom dancing. Home and Office: PMB 305 5114-E Point Fosdick Dr NW Gig Harbor WA 98335-1733 E-mail: BelleMann@hotmail.com.

WITBECK, GLENDA M. poet; b. Ingram, Ark., July 4, 1948; d. Joseph Siegel and Violet Marie Flanigan; m. Leander J. Johnson (div.); m. Arthur M. Witbeck, Apr. 4, 1980; 1 child, David J. Grad. h.s., St. Louis, 1966. Typist U. Kans., Lawrence, 1966—69, office mgr., 1969—71; office asst. Lawrence Leiter, Kansas City, Mo., 1971—73; word processor Honeywell, Seattle, 1977—80, word processing supr., 1980—83. Author numerous poems. Mem.: Internat. Poetry Soc. Avocations: needlecrafts, crafts, reading. Home: 120 Brookside Ln Oceanside CA 92056-4835

WITCHER, PHYLLIS HERRMANN, secondary school educator; b. Wilmington, Del., Feb. 23, 1938; d. Carl Victor and Ruth Naomi (Ice) Herrmann; m. Murray H. Witcher, Apr. 8, 1961 (div. 1992); children: David, Stephanie Witcher Stewart. BS, U. Del., 1960; MEd, West Chester U., 1982. Cert. secondary tchr., Pa. Tchr. pub. schs., Pa., Tenn., Del., 1974—; textile analyst Sears Roebuck Labs., Chgo., 1977-79; ind. admissions counselor Coll. Selection Svcs., Chadds Ford, Pa., 1983—. Bd. dirs. Unionville-Chadds Ford Sch. Dist., 1986-91, Chester County Intermediate Unit, Exton, Pa., 1988-91; instr. family law policy U. Del. Acad. Lifelong Learning, 2003. Author, speaker, legis. witness No-Fault Div., 1996. Bd. dirs. Mental Health Assn. in Del., Wilmington, 1985-93; past pres. Del. Symphony League, Wilmington, 1985; founder, pres. Protecting Marriage, Inc., Chadds Ford, 1991. Recipient Giraffe Project Nat. Commendation, 1994. Republican. Roman Catholic. Avocations: sewing, tennis, public speaking. Home: 2304 Riddle Ave Apt 2C Wilmington DE 19806-2163 Office: Protecting Marriage Inc PO Box 7436 Wilmington DE 19803-0436 E-mail: phyllaw@comcast.net.

WITEK, KATE, state senator, trucking company executive; b. Detroit, Oct. 22, 1954; m. Charles Wite, 1974; children: Thomas Charles, Kimberly Rose. Student, Ea. Mich. U. Owner, mgr. Witek Trucking Co.; mem. Nebr. Senate, Lincoln, 1992-98; Auditor of Pub. Accounts NE, Lincoln, 1999—. Mem. commerce and ins. com., govt., mil. and vet. affairs com. Mem. Nat. Small Bus. United, Nebr. Motor Carriers, Millard Jaycees. Republican. Home: 5179 S 147th St Omaha NE 68137-1439 Office: Auditor of Public Accounts State Capitol Suite 2303 PO Box 98917 Lincoln NE 68509-8917

WITHEE, DIANA KEERAN, art historian, art dealer, educator; d. Royal Victor and Johanna Polterock Keeran; m. Gregory Wallace Withee, June 8, 1968 (div. 2004); children: Christopher Edward, Jefftrey Wallace, Brett Andrew. BA in Art History cum laude, Pomona Coll., Claremont, CA, 1969; MA in Art History, Tulane U., 1976; ABD in Art History, U. Md., College Park, 1994. Rsch. & prodn. asst., art documentaries Nat. Mus. of Am. Art, Washington, 1980—83; art history instr. Montgomery Coll., Rockville, Md., 1984—85; art history instr. & cons. Montgomery County Pub. Schs., Rockville, Md., 1986—87; curatorial asst., manuscripts and rare books Walters Art Gallery, Baltimore, Md., 1988—90; mus. educator Nat. Gallery of Art, Washington, 1990—93; guide supr., mus. educator Hillwood Mus., Washington, 1993—98; art dealer Sumner and Dene Gallery, San Diego, 1999—2002, Whitt-Krauss Objects of Fine Art, San Diego, 1999; art instr. Ctrl. Tex. Coll., San Diego, 2001—; art dealer Susan St. Fine Art Gallery, Solana Beach, Calif., 2002—. Cons. Time-Life Books, Alexandria, Va., 1992; bd. dirs. San Diego State U. Arts Coun. Prodn. asst. (videotape) Anni Albers, William H. Johnson, Reuben Nakian, Jacob Kainen:Five Decades as an Artist, asst. prodr. Americans in Brittany and Normandy, curator (art exhibition) More than a Miniature: Works of Art in Medieval Manuscripts, (exhibition) The Power of the Press: Revolution & Communications 1450-1600; author: (mag. articles) The Walters Art Gallery Bulletin, (contributing author) Culture et Revolution: The French Revolution and Its Aftermath, (instructor's manual) The Inquiring Eye: The European Renaissance, (book) Teacher Programs in Art Museums: A Directory; contributing author (magazine) The Post, presenter (symposium paper) Intimate Portrayals of Napoleon's Family, (scholarly conference paper) Anatomical Observations of Women's Life Stages in the Frescoes of Thera, (scholarly conference presentation) An Altar in the Miniature Fresco at Thera and Its Implications, lecturer (scholarly lecture) Timeless Cycles: Youth, Beauty and Ag in the Bronze Age Frescoes of Thera, scholarly presenter (scholarly conference presentation) The Boxing Boys and Fishermen Frescoes at Thera: An Analysis of their Physical Ages and Its Implications, Physical Growth and Aging Characteristics Depicted in the Theran Frescoes at Thera, conference presenter (conference presentations) Developing Good Relationships Between Guides and Security, lecturer (museum lecture series) C.W.Post and the Breakfast Cereal Revolution, The Gilded Age: The Newport Mansions; editor: (newsletter) COVA Newsletter. Recipient Letter of Commendation, Nat. Gallery of Art, 1991, Cash Bonus award, 1992; scholar Grad. assistantship, U. Md., 1986-1988; Mus. fellowship, U. of Md., 1988-89, Travel fellowship, Wash. Chpt., Am. Inst. of Archaeology, 1991. Mem.: Phi Kappa Phi. Achievements include development of new methodology of deciphering Aegean Bronze Age art; ran numerous national programs in museum education for National Gallery of Art; re-organization of entire Hillwood guide program; volunteered to teach Navy & Marine personnel aboard the aircraft carrier John C. Stennis on its deployment to participate in war in Afghanistan two months after 9/11. Home: 850 State St #128 San Diego CA 92101 Office: Susan Street Fine Art Gallery 415 Cedros Ave Solana Beach CA 92075 Personal E-mail: dwithee@msn.com. E-mail: gallery@susanstreetfineart.com.

WITHERELL, MARY, editor; Degree, Barnard Coll., 1983. Former acting mng. editor Cosmo Girl; mng. editor Ladies' Home Jour., N.Y.C., 2002—. Office: Ladies' Home Jour 125 Park Ave 20th Fl New York NY 10017-5516*

WITHERS, HEATHER NOWELL, minister; b. Liverpool, Eng., Sept. 9, 1938; d. Richard William Wilkinson and Sylvia Nowell Dormer; m. Donald Mead Withers, Mar. 16, 1984. BA in social sci., U. Liverpool, 1960; MA in sociology, Carleton U., 1964; PhD in sociology, U. Ore., 1970. Ordination Assn. of Unity Churches, 1989, cert. in gerontology U. of Neb. at Omaha, 1980; in pub. adminstrn. U. Liverpool, 1961. Asst. prof. Coll. of St. Mary, Omaha, 1970—72; coord. of rsch. planning and evaluation Neb. Dept. on Aging, Lincoln, 1981—83, acting dir., 1981—83; min. Unity Ch. of Practical Christianity, St. Joseph, Miss., 1989—[illegible] Lincoln, Nebr., 1993—98; dir. Good Neighbor Emergency Assistance Inc., Ames, Iowa, 2000—01; min. Unity Ch. of Ames, Iowa, 2001—. Com. chair, human rels. U.N. Assn., Lincoln, Nebr., 1998—2000; adv. bd. Beyond Welfare, Ames, Iowa, 2001—02; bd. mem. Statewide Health Coordinating Coun., Lincoln, Nebr., 1978—82; pres. Nebr. Network Total Health, Lincoln, 1984—86, Women's Career Network, St. Joseph, Miss., 1992—93. Recipient Cmty. Svc. award, Good Neighbor Emergency Assistance, 2002, Comprehensive Scholarship award, Unity Sch. of Christianity, 1988; Fellowship award, Province of Ont., 1963. Mem.: South Ctr. Unity Churches Assn. (bd. mem. 1997—99), Assn. of Unity Churches, Ames Ministerial Assn. (pres. 2003—). Democrat. Unity. Avocations: reading, walking, travel, theater. Home: 1226 Ridgewood Ave Ames IA 50010 Office Phone: 515-233-1613. E-mail: myrddin@isunet.net.

WITHERSPOON, CAROLYN BRACK, lawyer; b. Little Rock, Mar. 29, 1950; d. Gordon Paisley and Mildred Louise (Lemon) Brack; m. Joseph Roger Armbrust, July 25, 1970 (div. 1976); 1 child, Catherine Paisley Armbrust ; m. John Leslie Witherspoon, June 15, 1979. Student, U. Ark., 1968-70, So. Meth. U., 1970; BA, U. Ark., 1974, JD with honors, 1978. Bar: Ark. 1978, U.S. Dist. Ct. (ea. and we. dists.) Ark. 1978, U.S. Ct. Appeals (8th cir.) 1979, U.S. Supreme Ct. 1981. Asst. atty. City of Little Rock, 1978, chief dep. atty., acting city atty., 1984-85; assoc. House, Wallace & Jewell, Little Rock, 1985-87, ptnr., 1987-90; dir. McGlinchey Stafford Lang, Little Rock, 1990-97, Cross, Gunter, Witherspoon & Galchus, Little Rock, 1997—. Mem. com. Fed. Ct. Practice, 1988—91; mem. civil practice com. Ark. Supreme Ct., 1989—97, mem. continuing legal edn. bd., 1998—2001; chair adv. com. Civil Justice Reform Act, 1993—95; mem. State Bd. Bar Examiners, 2001—. Contbr. articles to profl. jours. Commr. Ark. Real Estate Commn., 1978—81; past chmn. Little Rock Housing Authority Bd. Commn.; past pres., bd. dirs. Advs. Battered Women; past. bd. dirs., pub. rels. chmn. LWV; past pres. Ark. Women's History Inst. Recipient Labor Law award, Am. Jurisprudence, 1977. Fellow: Coll. Labor and Employment Lawyers, Am. Bar Found. (Ark. Fellows chair); mem.: ABA (EEO com., ho. dels. 1997—), William R. Overton Inn of Ct. (pres. 1992—93), Nat. Inst. Mcpl. Law Officers (state chmn. 1985—87, v.p. 1987—89), Pulaski County Bar Assn. (pres. 1989—90), Ark. Assn. Women Lawyers (pres. 1982—83), Ark. Bar Assn. (pres. 1995—96, Golden Gavel award 1989, 1993, Ark. Inst. Cont. Legal Edn. award 1991), Transp. Lawyers Assn. (mem. exec. com. 1997—99), Nat. Conf. Bar Pres. (mem. exec. coun. 1996—99), Am. Jur Soc., Am. Law Inst. Avocations: hunting, fishing, reading, traveling. Office: Cross Gunter Witherspoon and Galchus 500 President Clinton Ave Ste 200 Little Rock AR 72201-1747 Office Phone: 501-371-9999. E-mail: cspoon@cgwg.com.

WITHERSPOON, REESE (LAURA JEAN WITHERSPOON), actress; b. Nashville, Tenn., Mar. 22, 1976; m. Ryan Phillippe, 1999; 2 children. Motion picture and T.V. actress. Film appearances include The Man in the Moon, 1991, Jack the Bear, 1993, Freeway, 1996, Pleasantville, 1998, Twilight, 1998, Best Laid Plans, 1999, Cruel Intentions, 1999, Election, 1999, Am. Psycho, 2000, Little Nicky, 2000, Legally Blonde, 2001, The Importance of Being Earnest, 2002, Sweet Home Alabama, 2002, Legally Blonde 2: Red, White & Blonde, 2003 (also exec. prodr.), Vanity Fair, 2004, others; appeared in TV series Friends, 2000, (T.V. films) Wildflower, 1991, Desperate Choices: To Save My Child, 1992. Recipient Catalan Internat. Film Festival Award Best Actress, 1997, Movieline Young Hollywood Award for Breakthrough Performance (Female), 1999, Online Film Critics Soc. Award for Best Actress, 1999, National Soc. of Film Critics Award for Best Actress, 1999. Office: c/o Steve Dontanville William Morris 151 El Camino Dr Beverly Hills CA 90212-2412 also: c/o Blymel O'Neill 8912 Burton Way Beverly Hills CA 90211-1707

WITHERSPOON, SOPHIA, professional basketball player; b. July 6, 1969; BA in Recreation, U. Fla., 1991. Guard Nyon, Switzerland, 1991-92, Rouen, France, 1994-95, Ferencvarosi, Hungary, 1995-96, Alcamo, Italy, 1996-97, N.Y. Liberty, N.Y.C., 1997-99, Portland Fire, 1999—. Named Italian All-Star, 1996-97, WNBA Player of the Wk., 1997. Office: Portland Fire 1 Center Ct Ste 150 Portland OR 97227-2104

WITHROW, LUCILLE MONNOT, nursing home administrator; b. Alliance, Ohio, July 28, 1923; d. Charles Edward Monnot and Freda Aldine (Guy) Monnot Cameron; m. Alvin Robert Withrow, June 6, 1945 (dec. 1984); children: Cindi Withrow Johnson, Nancy Withrow Townley, Sharon Withrow Hodgkins (dec.), Wendel Alvin. AA in Health Adminstrn., Eastfield Coll., 1976. Lic. nursing home adminstr., Tex.; cert. nursing home ombudsman. Held various clerical positions, Dallas, 1950-72; office mgr., asst. adminstr. Christian Care Ctr. Nursing Home, Mesquite, Tex., 1972-76; head adminstr. Christian Care Ctr. Nursing Home and Retirement Complex, Mesquite, 1976-91; nursing home ombudsman Tex. Dept. Aging and Tex. Dept. Health, Dallas, 1991-93; legal asst. Law Offices of Wendel A. Withrow, Carrollton, Tex., 1993—. Mem. con. on geriatric curriculum devel. Eastfield Coll., Mesquite, 1979, 87; mem. ombudsman adv. com. Sr. Citizens Greater Dallas; nursing home cons.; notary pub., 1995—. Vol. Dallas Arboretum and Bot. Soc.; mem. Ombudsman adv. com. Sr. Citizens of Greater Dallas; charter mem. Stage Show Prodns. Recipient Volunteerism award, Tex. Atty. Gen., 1987, Tex. Gov., 1992. Mem. Tex. Assn. Homes for Aging, Am. Assn. Homes for Aging, Health Svcs. Speakers Bur., White Rock Kiwanis. Mem. Ch. of Christ. Avocations: reading, travel, theater. Home: 11344 Lippitt Ave Dallas TX 75218-1922 Office: Law Office of W A Withrow 1120 Metrocrest Dr Ste 200 Carrollton TX 75006-5872

WITHROW, MARY ELLEN, federal agency administrator; b. Marion, Ohio, Oct. 2, 1930; d. Clyde Welsh and Mildred (Stump) Hinamon; m. Norman David Withrow, Sept. 4, 1948; children: Linda Rizzo, Leslie Legge, Norma, Rebecca Gooding. Mem. Elgin Local Bd. Edn., Marion, Ohio, 1969-73, pres., 1972; safety programs dir. ARC, Marion, 1968-72; dep. registrar State of Ohio, Marion, 1972-75; dep. county auditor Marion County, Ohio, 1975-77, county treas., 1977-83; treas. State of Ohio, Columbus, 1983-94; treas. of the U.S. Dept. Treasury, Washington, 1994—. Chmn. Ohio Bd. Deposits, 1983—. Mem. exec. com. Ohio Dem. Com., mem. exec. com. women's caucus; mem. Dem. Nat. Com.; mem. Met. Women's Ctr.; pres. Marion County Dem. Club, 1976; participant Harvard U. Strategic Leadership Conf., 1990.; mem. Dem. Leadership Coun. Recipient Donald L. Scantlebury Meml. award, 1991, Women of Achievement award YWCA of Met. Columbus, 1993, Outstanding Govt. Svc. award Am. Numis. Assn., 1995; inducted Ohio Women's Hall of Fame, 1986; named Outstanding Elected Dem. Woman Holding Pub. Office, Nat. Fedn. Dem. Women, 1987, Advocate of Yr., SBA, 1988, Most Valuable State Pub. Ofcl., City and State newspaper, 1990; Women Execs. in State Govt. fellow Harvard U., 1987. Mem. LWV (dem. leadership coun.), State Assn. County Treas. (legis. com. 1979-83, treas. 1982), Nat. Assn. State Treas. (pres. 1992, Jesse Unruh award 1993, chair long range planning com., mem. exec. com.), Nat. Assn. State Auditors Comptrs. and Treas. (pres. 1990, strategic planning com., intergov. rels. com., chair state and mcpl. bonds com.), Coun. State Govts. (exec. com., internat. affairs com., orgnl. planning and coord. com., strategic planning task force), Women Execs. in State Govt. (chair fund devel. com.), Altrusa Bus. and Profl. Women's Club (hon.), Delta Kappa Gamma (hon.), Delta Sigma Pi (hon.). Clubs: Bus. and Profl. Women's. Office: Dept Treasury 1500 Pennsylvania Ave NW Washington DC 20220 0002

WITHROW, SHERRIE ANNE, financial specialist; b. Sacramento, Mar. 10, 1960; d. Jim and Ilene (James) Withrow. Student, Diablo Valley C.C., Pleasant Hill, Calif., 1977-81, Tarrant County Jr. Coll., Ft. Worth, 1982-83, Coll. of Marin, Kentfield, Calif., 1988, Merritt Coll., Oakland, Calif., 1990; [illegible] Florissant, Mo., 1981. Internal cashier AAA Automobile Club Mo., St. Louis, 1977-79; receiving clk. Dayton-Hudson Target Stores, Florissant and Ft. Worth, 1979-81; supr. credit and collection World Svc. Life Ins. Co., Ft. Worth, 1982-83; bank br. balancer, data processing divsn. Tex. Am. Bank Svcs., Inc., Ft. Worth, 1984-85; asst. to contr. Positive Video-Post Prodn., Orinda, Calif., 1985-87; with contractor's desk adminstrn. dept. Shell Oil Co., Martinez, Calif., 1987-88; asst. to CFO J.T. Thorpe & Son, Inc., Richmond, Calif., 1988-89; founder, gen. ptnr. HomeVisions Constrn. Svcs., El Sobrante, Calif., 1989-99, AudioVisions Sound and Lighting Co., El Sobrante, 1990-2000; corp. acctg. and investments Liquidity Fund Mgmt., Inc., 1990-92; founder, gen. ptnr. AV Electric, El Sobrante, 1994-2000; tax and payroll benefits specialist, founder Roll 'em!, El Sobrante, 2001—. Audio engr., cons. and project fin. cons. Contbr. (poetry) The Brilliance of Night, Internat. Libr. of Poetry Compilation, 2000, The Best Poems and Poets of 2001, 2001, The Silence Within, 2001, Nature's Echoes, 2001, Internat. Libr. poetry; audio recs.: The Sound of Poetry, 2001. Fundraiser Sr. Citizen Subsidized Housing Complex, Martinez, 1987-88. David L. Underwood scholar Florissant Valley (St. Louis) C.C., 1980-81. Mem.: Internat. Platform Assn., Phi Theta Kappa. Democrat. Office: Roll 'em! PO Box 20368 El Sobrante CA 94820-0368 also: 3776 Raap Ave Martinez CA 94553-3817 E-mail: sher@sherbear.com.

WITKIN, EVELYN MAISEL, retired geneticist; b. N.Y.C., Mar. 9, 1921; d. Joseph and Mary (Levin) Maisel; m. Herman A. Witkin, July 9, 1943 (dec. July 1979); children— Joseph, Andrew. AB, NYU, 1941; MA, Columbia U., 1943, PhD, 1947; DSc honoris causa, N.Y. Med. Coll., 1978, Rutgers U., 1995. Mem. staff genetics dept. Carnegie Inst., Washington, 1950-55; mem. faculty State U. N.Y. Downstate Med. Center, Bklyn., 1955-71, prof. medicine, 1968-71; prof. biol. scis. Douglass Coll., Rutgers U., 1971-79, Barbara McClintock prof. genetics, 1979-83, Waksman Inst. Microbiology, 1983-91; Barbara McClintock prof. emerita Waksman Inst. Microbiology, Rutgers U., 1991—. Author articles; mem. editorial bds. profl. jours. Postdoctoral fellow Am. Cancer Soc., 1947-49; fellow Carnegie Instn., 1957; Selman A. Waksman lectr., 1960; Phi Beta Kappa vis. scholar, 1980-81; grantee NIH, 1956-89; recipient Prix Charles Leopold Mayer French Acad. Scis., 1977, Lindback award, 1979, Nat. Medal of Science award, 2002. Fellow AAAS, Am. Acad. Microbiology; mem. NAS, Am. Acad. Arts and Scis., Environ. Mutagen Soc., Am. Genetics Soc. (Thomas Hunt Morgan medal, 2000), Am. Soc. Microbiology. Home: 1 Firestone Ct Princeton NJ 08540-5220 E-mail: ewitkin@aol.com.

WITMAN, LAURA KATHLEEN, writer, security professional; b. Pottstown, Pa., Mar. 4, 1957; d. William Tedford and Kathleen (Nieman) W. Student, San Bernardino Valley Coll., 1976-79; Degree in Actg. magna cum laude, Adelphi Bus. Coll., San Bernardino, Calif., 1985. Cert. acctg. bookkeeper. Silent alarm monitor, payroll acct. Comml. Security Alliance, San Bernardino, Calif., 1985—87. Author: The Sun, 1994; (poetry) World of Poetry, 1990, National Library of Poetry, 1992, 94, 95, 96, 98, Sparrowgrass, 1993; (short story) Antivivesection Soc., 1993, Animal Voice, 1994, Paws Newsletter, 1993, 94, 96, A Dogs Day Newsletter, 1994, House Rabbit Soc., 1994, 95, songs. Mem. Gay and Lesbian Ctr. Inland Empire, Heartland Christian Fellowship Met. Cmty. Ch., Inland Empire Pride Coun. Mem. People for Ethical Treatment of Animals, House Rabbit Soc. Democrat. Home: 7877 Willow Ave Riverside CA 92504-2624

WITSELL, ETHEL HOLDEN HOWARD, artist; b. Columbus, Ga., Jan. 3, 1941; d. William and Ethel (Holden) Howard; m. Edward Leigh Witsell, Nov. 1, 1963; children: William, Alice. BA, Columbus Coll. Exhibits include: Rankin Exec. Gallery, Columbus, 1990—, Columbus Coll. Fine Art Hall, 1980—, 3d Army Headquarters War Room, Atlanta; pvt. collections. Mem. Nat. League Am. Pen Women, Jr. League Columbus. Republican. Episcopal. Home: 3201 Turkey Ln Phenix City AL 36869-3326

WITT, BETH M. music educator; b. Port Clinton, Ohio, Nov. 17, 1952; d. Frederick Wiliam and Mary Kathryn Windisch; m. David L. Witt, July 13, 1973; children: Keith M., Karen M. MusB in Edn., U. Toledo (Ohio), 1973; MusM in Edn., Bowling Green (Ohio) State U., 1998. Music educator grades 7-12 Benton-Carroll-Salem Schs., Oak Harbor, Ohio, 1973—75, music educator grades K-5, 1981—99, music educator grades 4-6, 1985—2000, music educator grades 5-12, 2000—. Choir dir., organist St.

Paul UCC, Oak Harbor, Ohio, 1972—2000. Mem.: Ohio Music Educators Assn. Avocations: needlecrafts, golf, rollerblading, swimming. Home: 2639 Morrison Rd Fremont OH 43420 Office: Benton Carroll Salem Schs 11681 WSR 163 Oak Harbor OH 43449

WITT, CATHERINE LEWIS, neonatal nurse practitioner, writer; b. Burlington, Iowa, Nov. 21, 1957; d. Rodney Darrell and Neola Ann (Wharton) Lewis; m. John Robert Witt, Mar. 31, 1984; children: Jeffrey Lewis, Jennifer Diane. BSN, U. No. Colo., 1980; MSN, U. Colo., 1987. Cert. neonatal nurse practitioner. Staff nurse St. Joseph's Hosp., Denver, 1980-85; neonatal nurse practitioner Denver Children's Hosp., 1986-88; coord. neonatal nurse practitioner and neonatal transport Presbyn.-St. Luke's Med. Ctr., Denver, 1988—2002; neotal nurse practitioner NNP Svcs. of Colo., 2003—. Contbr. chapters to books, articles to profl. jours. Troop leader Girl Scouts US; children's Bible tchr., altar guild Episcopal Ch. Mem. Nat. Assn. Neonatal Nurses (co-chair program com. 1992-94, bd. dir.-at-large 1997-99, sec. 1999-2000, pres. 2003--), Nat. Cert. Corp. (test. com. 1994-96, nominations com. 2004). Democrat. Episcopalian. Avocations: altar guild, reading, sewing, dance. Home: 17586 E Dickenson Pl Aurora CO 80013-4180 Office: Presbyn-St Luke's Med Ctr 1719 E 19th Ave Denver CO 80218-1235 E-mail: clwitt@comcast.net.

WITT, DOREEN MARIE, business executive; b. Dubuque, Iowa, Apr. 28, 1960; d. John Dale and Janet Louise (Chunat) Kenkel; m. Carey Michael Witt, Oct. 4, 1986; children: Zachariah Harding, Cody Michael, Greyson Jacob. Student, Loras Coll., 1979; BS in Mktg., Iowa State U., 1983. Asst. mgr. Sanger Harris, Dallas, 1983, sales mgr., 1983, area mgr., 1983-85; product devel. specialist County Seat Stores, Dallas, 1985; S.W. account exec. Perry Ellis Sportswear, Dallas, 1985-86; account exec. Radio Stas. KOKE, KKMJ, Austin, Tex., 1986-90, 93-98; sr. acct. exec. Radio Sta. KKMJ, Austin, 1990-93; dir. sales tng. Radio Stas. KKMJ, KFGI, KJCE, Austin, 1993-96, key acct. mgr., 1996-97, Radio Stas. KKMJ, KFGI, KJCE, nontraditional revenue devel., Austin, 1998—. Vol. Volente (Tex.) Vol. Fire Dept., 1986—; voter registrar Williamson County, Leander, Tex., 1987; lay reader, sunday sch. tchr. St Lukes on the Lake Episcopal Ch. 1986—. Mem. Am. Mktg. Assn., Austin Bus. Forum (sec. 1987-88, v.p. membership 1988-90, 92—), Am. Women in Radio and TV (v.p. membership 1986-88, membership co-chair 1992—, v.p. scholarship 1988-91, del. 1988, 90, Appreciation award 1986, 87-88, 89-91). Republican. Avocations: water skiing, snow skiing, jogging, travel, bible study. Home: 7328 Reed Dr Leander TX 78641-9147 Office: KKMJ MAJIC 95 5 FM 4301 Westbank Dr Ste 350B Austin TX 78746-4453

WITT, NANCY CAMDEN, artist; b. Richmond, Va., Oct. 24, 1930; d. Roland Parker and Lucy Catherine (Haydon) Riddick; m. Robert Roy Camden, 1951 (div. 1960); children: John Bradley, Matthew David; m. John Temple Witt, Apr. 2, 1966 (div. June 1990); 1 child, Jeremy Temple. BA, Old Dominion U., 1965; MFA, Va. Commonwealth U., 1967; DFA (hon.), Randolph-Macon Coll., 1997. Comml. artist, 1952-60; chmn. art dept. Richard Bland Coll., Petersburg, Va., 1960-63; studio artist Ashland, Va., 1965—; owner Cross Mill Gallery, Ashland. One woman shows include Sharon Bennett Gallery, Atlanta, 1973, Asheville (NC) Mus. Fine Arts, 1976, Longwood Coll., Farmville, Va., 1974, 77, Randolph-Macon Woman's Coll., Lynchburg, Va., 1974, 79, Phillip Morris Inc., Richmond, 1978, VMI, Lexington, 1965, 79, Touchstone Gallery, NYC., 1974, Roanoke Coll., Salem, 1979, 20th Century Gallery, Williamsburg, Va. 1974, 82, 93, Randolph-Macon Coll., Ashland, Va., 1974, 79, 84, SECCA, Winston-Salem, 1980, U. Ill., Chgo., 1989, Portsmouth (Va.) Mus., 1984, Cudahy's, Richmond, Va., 1990, 92, 94, 96, 98, 2000, 2002, Between the Muse Gallery, Camden, Maine, 1996, Nancy Moore Fine Art, NYC., 1996, 98, Élan Fine Arts, Rockport, Maine, 2003, Rentz Gallery, Richmond, 2004, others; exhibited in group shows at Valentine Mus. Biennial, Richmond, 1962, Mint Mus., Charlotte, 1971, Miss. Mus. Art, 1979, Chrysler Mus., Norfolk, 1983, Touchstone Gallery, NYC., 1986, Huntington (W.Va.) Mus. Art, 1992, Ridderhof Martin Gallery, Mary Washington Coll, Fredericksburg, Va., 2001; represented in permanent collections Markel Corp., Richmond, David Rockefeller Collection, Phillip Morris Co., Fed. Res. Bank, U. Va., Charlottesville, Va., Norfolk, Ethyl Corp., Richmond, CSX Corp., Richmond, Wheat First, Richmond, others; author: On Alternate Days: The Paintings of Nancy Witt, 1995, (film) Vanishing Point, 1973. Named Va. Artist of Yr., Woman's Caucus for Art, Va., 1993. Mem. Jungian Venture (co-founder, convener 1984-86). E-mail: wittn@rcn.com.

WITTE, MARLYS HEARST, internist, educator; b. N.Y.C., 1934; MD, NYU Sch. Medicine, 1960. Intern N.C. Meml. Hosp., Chapel Hill, 1960-61; resident Bellevue Hosp. Ctr., N.Y.C., 1961-63; fellow NYU Hosp., St. Louis, 1965-69; instr. Washington U., St. Louis, 1965-69; prof. surgery U. Ariz., 1969—; attending internist Ariz. Health Sci. Ctr., Tucson, 1965-69, 69—. Mem. AAAS, AMA, Alpha Omega Alpha. Office: U Ariz Coll Medicine PO Box 245063 1501 N Campbell Ave Tucson AZ 85724-0001

WITTE, PEGGY, metal products executive; m. Bill Witte. Chair, CEO, pres. Royal Oak Mines, Inc., Kirkland, Wash. Office: Royal Oak Mines Inc 501 Lakeview Dr Kirkland WA 98033

WITTENBERG, RACHEL ANNE, special education educator; b. Oswego, N.Y., Dec. 24, 1972; d. Robert Harris and Deborah Anne Wittenberg. BS in Elem. Edn./Spanish, SUNY, Oswego, 1996; MA in Spl. Edn., U. Ariz., 2000. Ednl. enrichment coord. Big Bros. Big Sisters, Tucson, 1997—98; inclusion specialist Los Amigos Sch., Tucson, 2000—01; learning disabilities math specialist Sierra Mid. Sch., Tucson, 2001—02, learning disabilities reading specialist, 2002—. Tutor Casey Family Program, Tucson, 1998—2000. AmeriCorps VISTA vol. Big Bros. Big Sisters, Tucson, 1997—98; AmeriCorps campus rep. U. Ariz., Tucson, 1998—99. Mem.: Phi Sigma Iota. Avocations: reading, writing, travel, hiking, swimming. Home: Apt 4 835 N 6th Ave Tucson AZ 85705 Office: Sierra Mid Sch 5801 S Del Moral Blvd Tucson AZ 85706 Office Phone: 520-545-4827. E-mail: rachelwz@susd12.org.

WITTMANN, JANE GORDON, volunteer; b. Salinas, Calif., Aug. 5, 1946; d. Walter Max and Harriet Loveland Gordon; m. William Walter Wittmann, June 29, 1968; children: Emily Harriet Wittmann Gaskill, Gordon Thomas. BA in English, U. Calif., Davis, 1968. Mem. Shasta County Devel. Std. Com, Redding, Calif., 1978—81, Shasta County-Wide Planning Adv. Com., Redding, Calif., 1981—82; forewoman Shasta County Grand Jury, Redding, Calif., 1983—84, chair pub. works com., 1984—85; Brownie leader Sierra Cascade Coun. Girl Scouts USA, 1978—80, jr. leader, 1980—83, cadette leader, 1983—86, sr. leader, 1986—90, svc. unit treas., 1982—90, Day Camp co.- coord., 1986—87, coun. bd. dirs., 1990—91, 1st v.p. coun. bd. dirs., 1991—92, pres. coun. bd. dirs., 1992—97, chair self-evaluation task group, 1991—92, chair performance assessment task force, 1997—98; sec. Pacheco Elem. Sch. Home and Sch. Assn., 1985—87; assoc. mem. bd. dirs. Shasta Cmty. Concert Assn., 1993—95, bd. dirs., 1995—2000, pres., 2000—; ch. sch. coord. 1st Presbyn. Ch., Redding, 1988—91, elder on session, 1991—93, elder, 1991—. Mem.: AAUW (bull. editor 1973—74, membership treas. 1974—75, rec. sec. 1975—76, pres.-elect 1976—77, pres. 1977—78, historian 1978—79, legis. chair 1979—84, cmty. area rep. 1984—85, audit com./newsletter ads 1997—98, audit com. 1998—99). Presbyterian. Avocations: family activities, handbell choir, singing. Home: 6396 Vista del Sierra Dr Anderson CA 96007

WITTNER-KAUFMAN, MICHELE SUSAN, psychologist; d. Faith and Harold Samuel Wittner; m. Wayne Ross Kaufman. D of psychology, NovaSoutheastern U., 1991—97. Lic. Psychologist State Edn. Dept. of NY, 1998. Staff psychologist NYC Police Dept. -Psychol. Services, Corona, NY, 1997—2001; sr. psychologist Behavioral Associates, NYC, 1999—; psychologist Harlem United, NYC, 2001—02; clin. psychologist, faculty mem. Child Protection Ctr., The Children's Hosp. at Montefiore, Bronx, NY, [illegible] Manhattan Psychol. Assn., NY State Psychol. Assn. Office: Behavioral Associates 114 East 90th St New York NY 10128-1550

WITTY, CHRISTINE (CHRIS WITTY), speed skater; b. West Allis, Wis., June 23, 1975; Student, Carroll Coll. Speed skater, 1985—. Mem. U.S. nat. team, 1988—. Recipient 1000 meter Silver medal Olympic Games, Nagano, Japan, 1998, 1500 meter Bronze medal, 1998; finished 2nd U.S. Olympic Team Trials, 2000. Avocations: cycling, movies, mountain biking. Home: PO Box 564 Park City UT 84060-0564

WIZEN, SARABETH MARGOLIS, financial consultant; b. Ypsilanti, Mich., May 11, 1950; d. Isidor and Ada (Eglovitch) Margolis; m. Sidney K. Wizen, July 27, 1975. BA, Mich. State U., 1972; MA, Eastern Mich. U., 1974. Adminstr. Faulkner Dawkins & Sullivan, N.Y.C., 1976-77, Dean Witter Reynolds, N.Y.C., 1977-79; adminstrv. salesman Cowen & Co., N.Y.C., 1979; v.p., dir. ops. Brookehill Equities, Inc., N.Y.C., 1979-87; pres., bd. dirs. Brookehill Ptnrs., Inc., N.Y.C., 1987-99; sr. fin. advisor First Union Securities, Westport, Conn., 2000—. Apptd. to NASD Bd. Arbitrators, 1996. Named to Willow Run H.S. Hall of Fame, 1998. Mem. Fin. Women's Assn. N.Y. (bd. dirs. 1989-95, 97-98, 2000—), Met. Mus. Art, Mich. State U. Alumni Assn., Eastern Mich. U. Alumni Assn., Alpha Epsilon Phi Alumni Assn. Office: First Union Securities One Penn Plaza New York NY 10119 E-mail: sarabethmw@aol.com.

WIZENBERG, CHANAH LIORA, language educator, poet; b. Newton, Mass., Apr. 9, 1960; life ptnr. Renee Simone, Nov. 19, 1965; children: Jacob James-Michael, Aaron Michael-James, Briana Cloutier, Collin Cloutier. Student, Johnson & Wales U., 1984; BA, Hunter Coll., 1994; postgrad., Goddard Coll., 2004—. Cert. tchr. NY, NC, Mass. Mem. Gender Equity Team of N.Y. State, N.Y.C., 1994—95; tchr. English Greenfield H.S., Mass., 2000—02, JFK Mid. Sch., Northampton, Mass., 2000; tchr. h.s. English New Leadership Charter Sch., Springfield, Mass., 2003—. Mem. Selection Com. for Consortium Grantees, 2004. Contbr. poetry to Poder Mag. and Returning Woman Mag. Mem. Congregation B'nai Israel, Northampton, 2000—. Grantee, Consortium, 2003. Mem.: Mass. Tchrs. Assn. Democrat. Jewish. Achievements include development of Improvisation and Choreography for children; Creative Writing Club for Literary Journal. Avocations: poetry, reading, chess, bicycling, swimming. Personal E-mail: plodinalong@msn.com.

WOERNER, LOUISE, management consultant; b. Jackson, Tenn., June 2, 1942; d. Victor I. and Leland (Horner) W. m. Don Kollmorgen, July 2, 1987. BS cum laude, Trinity U., San Antonio, 1964; MBA, U. Chgo., 1965. Pres. Wheels, Inc., Key West, Fla., 1975-87, L. Woerner, Inc. dba HCR, Rochester, N.Y., and Washington, 1978—, L. Woerner Co., Inc., Washington, 1978— ; exec. v.p. J.A. Reyes Assocs., Inc., Washington, 1971-79; mem. trade mission U.S. Dept. Commerce, Japan, 1986; dir. communications Memphis Area C. of C., 1968-69; mgr. new bus., dir. pub. relations Allied Stores, Inc., Dallas, 1967-68; sr. assoc. D.R. Fagin & Assocs., Inc., Dallas, 1965-67; exec. dir. Home Care Research Rochester, 1978—; mem. panel of community leaders Buffalo dist. FRS, 1984-87, econ. analyst mem. small bus. and agrl. adv. council Fed. Res. Bank, N.Y.C., 1985-86; econ. analyst exec. office of Pres. U.S., 1970-71; mem. adv. council SBA, 1984; mem. N.Y. State Tax Council, 1984; mem. Chase/Lincoln First Bank Met. Adv. Bd., 1985—, Chase/Lincoln First Bank Health Adv. Bd., 1986—, Pvt. Industry Council of Rochester/Monroe County, 1983-86, N.Y. State Assembly Speaker's Small Bus. Adv. Group, 1984, mem. com., 1987—; mem. long-term health care planning program Monroe Community Coll. Author: Scheduling Home Health Care Personnel, 1988; contbr. numerous articles to profl. jours. Small Bus. Innovation Research award, phase I and phase II grantee; Gannett Found. grantee; recipient citation of appreciation Am. Bus. Women's Assn., 1983, Presdl. award for Entrepreneurial Excellence, White House Conf. Small Bus., 1986, Small Bus. award Office Systems '88, 1988, achievement award Wall St. Jour.; named Outstanding Young Career Woman of Tex., 1968, Small Bus. Person of Yr., SBA, 1983, Bus. Adv. of Yr. Small Bus. Adminstn. for Upstate N.Y., 1983. Mem. Bus. and Profl. Women's Club Dallas (Dist. 15 Woman of Yr. 1980, cert. of appreciation 1974), Rochester C. of C., Rochester Women's Network, Univ. Chgo. Grad. Sch. Bus. Alumni Cabinet (bd. dirs. 1984-87, award)., Am. Mgmt. Assn., Washington Forum (treas. 1987). Club: Zonta (dir. 1983-85) (Washington).

WOERTZ, PATRICIA A. petroleum industry executive; b. Pitts., Mar. 1953; B in Acctg., Pa. State U., 1974; grad. Internat. Exec. Devel. Program, Columbia U., 1994. Acct. Ernst & Young, Pitts., 1974; with Gulf Oil Corp., Pitts., 1977-81, Houston, 1981-85; with debt. reduction process, merger of Gulf and Chevron, 1985-87; fin. mgr. Chevron Info. Tech. Co., 1989-91, strategic planning mgr., 1991-93; pres. Chevron Can. Ltd., Vancouver, B.C., 1993-96, Chevron Internat. Oil Co., 1996-98; v.p. logistics and trading Chevron Products Co., Chevron Corp., 1996-98; pres. Chevron Products Co., 1998—2001; v.p. Chevron Corp., 1998—2001; exec. v.p. Global Downstream Chevron Texaco Corp., San Francisco, 2001—, mem. exec. com. Mem.: Calif. C. of C. (bd. mem. 1999—), Am. Petroleum Inst. (bd. dirs.). Office: 6001 Bollinger Canyon Rd San Ramon CA 94583-2324*

WOGAMAN, DIERDRE E. retired pipeline operator, real estate agent; b. Fort Belvoir, Va., July 8, 1953; d. Robert W. Atkinson and Pamela Perkins Frederick; m. Donald R. Wogaman, May 13, 1995. AA, Bucks County C. C., 1973. Owner Ran Dea Trucking, New Hope, Pa., 1973-78; truck driver Matlack, Inc., Pensauken, N.J., 1978-79, Shell Oil Co., Willow Grove, Pa., 1979-81; pipeline operator Shell Pipe Line Corp., Columbus, Ohio, 1981-94, BP Oil Pipeline Co., Columbus, Ohio, 1994—99; owner ASP Properties, Columbus, Ohio, 1985—; real estate agent Century 21, Dublin, Ohio, 1990—2001, ret., 2003. Ind. assoc. PrePaid Legal, 1997—. Mem. Guild RSZ First Cmty. Ch., vol. Franklin County Children's Svcs. Mem. Am. Horse Show Assn., Ohio Horseman's Coun., Ctrl. Ohio Combined Training Assn., Mid Ohio Dressage Assn., Columbus Bd. of Realtors. Avocations: horseback riding, sailing, scuba diving, traveling, reading. Address: 1178 Monroe Rd Littleton NH 03561-3013

WOGEN, CATHY LYNN, academic director; b. Farmington, Minn., Aug. 5, 1957; d. Normand Ernest and Betty Ann (Cline) deVaudreuil; m. David Lee Wogen, June 13, 1981; children: Carlene, Elizabeth, Glen. BS in Computer Sci., St. Cloud State U., 1980; student, Alnwick (Eng.) Tchrs. Acad., 1976-77. Cons. MCOS, St. Cloud, Minn., 1985-89; evening computer instr. St. Cloud Bus. Coll., 1983-90, evening dir., 1990-92, acad. dir., 1992—. Post/secondary rep. Bus./Edn. Partnership, St. Cloud, 1993; mem. at large Parochial Sch. Bd., 2000-2002, sec., 2002-03, chmn. diversity enhancement com., 1998-2003. Mem. St. Cloud C. of C. Democratic. Lutheran.

WOHLEBER, LYNNE FARR, archivist, librarian; b. Pitts., Mar. 16, 1939; d. Donald Elmer and Helen Rose (Lula) F.; m. David Louis Wohleber, Oct. 14, 1972 (div. Sept. 1989); 1 child, Jeffrey David. AB, Allegheny, 1961; MLS, U. Pitts., 1991. Comms. sec. Aluminum Co. of Am., Pitts., 1968-73; shop mgr. The Thread Shed, Pitts., 1986-90; libr. Coun. Am. Embroiderer's Libr., Carnegie, Pa., 1985-93; archivist Episcopal Diocese of Pitts., 1989—. Cons. Calvary Episcopal Ch. Archives, Pitts., 1992—93, Bapt. Home Libr., Mt. Lebanon, Pa., 1994, First United Meth. Ch. Archives, Pitts., 1995, Episcopal Diocese of Albany, 2000; archival cons. Christ Ch., New Brighton, 2001, Old St. Luke's, Scott Twp., 2002; bldg. archives workshop instr., 1995, 2000—; presenter in field. Libr. com., bd. deacons, rec. sec. Bower Hill Cmty. Ch., 1996-99, nominating com. 1998-99, elder, 2003—; contemporary svc. task force, 2002—; coord. presch. program Am. Lung Assn., Pitts., 1977-87; capt., ward chair Am. Cancer Soc., Pitts., 1978-84; newsletter editor Mendelssohn Choir of Pitts., 1973-87; den leader Boy Scouts Am., Mt. Lebanon, Pa., 1983-84. Mem. [illegible] (planning com. 1999 Pitts. conf.), Mid-Atlantic Regional Archives Conf. (co-chair spl. events 1992, publs. com. 1996-2001, panelist 1999 spring conf., conf. local arrangements com. 2003—), Nat. Episcopal Historians and Archivists (Pitts. coord. for 1997 Episcopal Tri-History Conf., bd. dirs. 1996-2004, treas. 1999-2004), Hist. Soc. Episcopal Ch., Curators, Archivists and Record Profls. We. Pa. (co-chair Archives Week 1999 com.), Women's Episcopal History Project, Episcopal Diocesan and Nat. Archivists, Beta Phi Mu. Republican. Presbyterian and Episcopalian. Home: 110 Skylark Cir Pittsburgh PA 15234-1018 Office: Episcopal Diocese of Pitts 900 Oliver Bldg 535 Smithfield St Pittsburgh PA 15222-2403 E-mail: wohleber@pgh.anglican.org.

WOHLER, MARJORIE LYNN COULTER, medical and surgical nurse, health facility administrator; b. Gilmer, Tex., Mar. 6, 1948; d. Cleo Sr. and Ima Neola (Dean) Coulter; m. Robert Frederick Jr., Mar. 9, 1979. Diploma, Bapt. Hosp. Sch. Nursing, 1970; BSN, McNeese State U., 1975; MS in Nursing, Tex. Woman's U., 1978; postgrad., Baylor Coll., 1981-82. Cert. breast self-examination. Dir. nursing svc. Beaumont (Tex.) Remedial Clinic; staff nurse/charge Bapt. Hosp., Beaumont; asst. prof. Lamar U., Beaumont; nurse mgr. St. Elizabeth Hosp., Beaumont. Mem. Health Profl. Edn. Forum, Sigma Theta Tau. Home: 5655 Margaret Ln Beaumont TX 77708-2921

WOHLGELERNTER, BETH, organization executive; b. N.Y.C., Jan. 30, 1956; d. Maurice Nathaniel and Esther Rachel (Feinerman) W. BA, Barnard Coll., 1977. Exec. aide to pres. Barnard Coll., N.Y.C., 1977-80; spl. asst. to pres. The Commonwealth Fund, N.Y.C., 1980-81; asst. to chief exec. officer/pres. Mary McFadden, Inc., N.Y.C., 1981-84; exec. adminstr. The Donna Karan Co., N.Y.C., 1984-90; nat. exec. dir. Hadassah, The Women's Zionist Orgn. Am., Inc., N.Y.C., 1990-97; v.p. trade svcs. Trade Finance Svcs., N.Y.C., 1998—. Comm. adv. coun. AT&T, 1992—. Bd. dirs., v.p. N.Am. Conf. on Ethiopian Jewry, N.Y.C., 1981-85, 98—, bd. advisors, 1985-98; bd. govs. Lincoln Sq. Synagogue, N.Y.C., 1988-94, bd. trustees, 1994—; bd. trustees United Israel Appeal, 1991—.

WOHLTMANN, HULDA JUSTINE, pediatric endocrinologist, diabetologist; b. Charleston, S.C., Apr. 10, 1923; d. John Diedrich and Emma Lucia (Mohrmann) W. BS, Coll. Charleston, 1944; MD, Med. U. S.C., 1949. Diplomate Am. Bd. Pediatrics. Intern Louisville Gen. Hosp., 1949-50; resident in pediatrics St. Louis Children's Hosp., 1950-53, 1953-65, instr., 1953-58, asst. prof., 1958-65, postdoctoral fellow biochemistry, 1961-63; assoc. prof. pediatrics, head pediatric endocrinology Med. U. S.C., Charleston, 1965-70, prof., 1970-90, prof. emeritus, 1999—. Bd. dirs. Franke Home, Charleston, 1975-97, treas., 1989-91; mem. adv. bd. for ethics ctr. Newberry (S.C.) Coll., 1989—; trustee Luth. Theol. So. Sem., 1991-97. Contbr. articles to sci. jours. Mem. Am. Pediatric Soc., Ambulatory Pediatric Assn., Endocrine Soc., Am. Diabetes Assn., Am. Acad. Pediatrics, Midwest Soc. Pediatric Rsch., So. Soc. Pediatric Rsch., S.C. Diabetes Assn. (bd. dirs. 1970-86, pres. 1970-73, 84-85, v.p. 1982-83, Profl. Svc. award 1977), Lawson Wilkins Endocrine Soc., Sugar Club; fell. Am. Acad. Pediatrics. Lutheran. Home: 3 46th Ave Isle Of Palms SC 29451-2607

WOIKE, LYNNE ANN, computer scientist; b. Torrance, Calif., Oct. 20, 1960; d. Stephen J. and Virginia (Ursich) Shane; m. Thomas W. Woike, Feb. 13, 1988; 1 child, Karla. BSc in Computer Sci. cum laude, Calif. State U., Dominguez Hills, 1994. Computer cons. Unocal Oil Co., Wilmington, Calif., 1992-94; x-window/motif software developer Logican Inc., San Pedro, Calif., 1994-95; reticle engr. TRW, Inc., Redondo Beach, Calif., 1982-88, sr. mem. tech. staff product data mgmt. database adminstr., 1995-98, chmn. product data mgmt. change control bd., 1995—98, sr. Unix/NT system adminstr., 1999; tech. lead, subscriber database DIRECTV, Inc., El Segundo, Calif., 1999—2002; computer and network mgr. Northrop Grumman Mission Systems, Redondo Beach, Calif., 2002—. Mem. IEEE, IEEE Computer Sci., Assn. for Computing Machinery (chmn. student chpt. 1993-94), Calif. State U. Sci. Soc. (computer sci. rep. 1993-95). Office: Northrop Grumman Mission Sys One Space Park R5/B180 Redondo Beach CA 90278 Office Phone: 310-813-3360. Personal E-mail: woike@pacbell.net.

WOJAHN, R. LORRAINE, retired state senator; b. Tacoma, Washington, Sept. 17, 1920; m. Gilbert M. Wojahn (dec.); children: Mark C., Gilbert M. Jr. (dec.). Student, U. Washington, 1938—39. Mem. Wash. State Ho. of Reps., Olympia, 1969-76, Wash. State Senate, Olympia, 1977—2001, ret., 2001. Pres. pro tempore; vice chmn. rules, health and human svcs. com.; mem. labor and commerce, ways and means coms. Bd. dirs. Allenmore Hosp.; trustee Consumer Credit Counseling Svcs., Inc., Tacoma-Pierce County; active, past pres. Eastside Boys and Girls Club, Tacoma-Pierce County; active Wash. State Hist. Soc. Democrat.

WOJCICKI, ESTHER DENISE, journalist, educator; d. Philip and Rebecca Hochmann; m. Stanley G Wojcicki, Nov. 17, 1961; children: Susan, Janet, Anne. BA, U. of Calif., 1958—61, M.J., 1962—63, Gen. Secondary, 1961—62; Advanced Degree, Sorbonne, 1964—66; M.A., San Jose State U., 1988—90, Ednl. Adminstrn. Credential, 1988—89. Cert. Nat. Bd. for Profl. Tchg. Standards, 2000. Secondary tchr. Pacific H.S., San Leandro, Calif., 1962—63; english-journalism tchr. San Carlos H.S., Calif., 1966—68; reporter LA Times, Calif., 1956—58; stringer/writer Time Mag., New York, 1961—63; journalism dept.chair &tchr. Palo Alto H.S., Palo Alto, Calif., 1984—. Ednl. cons. Stanford Learning Systems, Calif., 1990—. Editor (also writer): (manual) Using Technology in the Classroom; (manual) Writing Center; contbr. booklet & video Assignment Rescue. Dir. of edn. Varian Fry Found., Menlo Park, Calif., 1998—2003; chair of evaluation com. Mid-Peninsula Jewish Cmty. Day Sch., Palo Alto, Calif., 1999—2003; chair Stanford Campus Homeowners, Stanford, Calif., 1969—73; pres. Stanford Campus Recreation Assn., Stanford, Calif., 1978—80. Recipient Excellence in Scholastic Journalism, Soc. of Profl. Journalists, 2001, Thinkquest Internat. First Pl. Coach, Thinkquest, 2000; Carnegie Found. scholar, Carnegie Found., 2000—02. Mem.: Calif. Teachers Assn. (assoc.), Journalism Educators of Am. (assoc.). Avocations: travel, jogging, hiking. Office: Palo Alto High School 50 Embarcadero Rd Palo Alto CA 94301 Personal E-mail: wojcicki@stanford.edu. E-mail: ewojcicki@pausd.palo-alto.ca.us.

WOJCIK, KATHLEEN LOUISE, state representative; b. Chgo., July 15, 1936; d. George Frederick and Anna Marie (Nowak) Zorger; m. Norbert Robert Wojcik Sr., Aug. 25, 1956; children: Norbert Robert Jr., Noreen Wojcik Gallagher. Student, William Rainey Harper Coll. Exec. sec. E.L. Reibold Sales Promotion Agy., Chgo., 1956-60; twp. clk., mgr. office Schaumburg Twp., Hoffman Estates, 1968-83; broker Quinlin & Tyson Realty, Schaumburg, Ill., 1970-75; owner, broker Kathleen L. Wojcik Realty, Schaumburg, 1976—; state rep. Ill. Gen. Assembly, Springfield, 1983—. Active Republican Orgn. Schaumbrug Twp., 1960—; twp. coordinator Women for Reagan, Women for Percy, Schaumburg, 1984; co-chmn. Small Businessmen for Reagan/Bush, Cook and DuPage Counties, Ill, 1984. Named Best Legislator of Yr. Ill Small Bus. Adminstrn., 1985, Legislator of Yr. Ill Assn. Homes for the Aging, 1985; recipient Superior Rating Taxpayers' Fedn. Ill, 1985, Cert. Appreciation Chgo. Bar Assn., 1986, Meritorious and Distg. Service award VFW, 1987. Mem. DAR, VFW, Am. Legion, Nat. Conf. State Legislators, Am. Legis. Exchange Council (membership co-chair 1983), NW Suburban Assn. Commerce and Industry, Ill. Realtors Assn. (legis. chmn.), Twp. Clks. Assn. Ill. (pres. 1979), Twp.

Clks. Assn. Cook County (bd. dirs. 1973-82, past pres.). Lodges: Moose. Avocation: golf. Home: 411 Redwood Ln Schaumburg IL 60193-2747 Office: 514 W Wise Rd Schaumburg IL 60193-3815

WOLAHAN, CARYLE GOLDSACK, nursing educator; b. Somerville, N.J., July 27, 1942; d. Wilbur Wood and Jane (Hadley) Goldsack; m. Thomas Warren Hussey, June 26, 1965 (dec. Oct. 1970); 1 child, Timothy Stephen; m. William Kevin Wolahan, Sept. 30, 1983 (dec. Jan. 2001). BS, Wagner Coll., 1964; MEd, Columbia U., 1973, EdD, 1979. Sch. nurse, tchr. Malverne (N.Y.) Pub. Schs., 1966-67, Dover-Wingdale Pub. Schs., Dover Plains, N.Y., 1967-68; head nurse Harlem Valley State Hosp., Wingdale, N.Y., 1968-69; asst. prof., acting dir. div. nursing Trenton (N.J.) State Coll., 1973-77; assoc. prof., acting dir. Felician Coll., Lodi, N.J., 1979-80, dir. div. nursing, 1982-87; dir. nursing program Stern Coll., Yeshiva U., N.Y.C., 1980-82; assoc. dean Coll. Nursing SUNY Health Sci. Ctr., Bklyn., 1987-91, acting dean Coll. Nursing, 1991-92; dean sch. nursing Adelphi U., 1992-2000; prof. nursing Adelphi U. Sch. Nursing, 2000—. Contbr. articles to profl. jours., chpts. to books; editor Topics in Clin. Nursing, 1983. Trustee Cath. Med. Ctrs. Bklyn. and Queens, 1989-2000, chair continuous quality improvement com., 1998-2000; regional bd. St. Vincent's Cath. Med. Ctrs. Recipient NEAA award, Disting. Trustee award United Hosp. Fund, 2000; Named Woman of Achievement Alpha Omicron Pi; named to Nursing Hall of Fame Tchrs. Coll. Columbia U., 1999. Mem. ANA (del. 1978-87), N.J. State Nurses Assn. (coun. on edn. 1976-82, chmn. com. on ednl. preparation 1984-88), N.Y. State Nurses Assn. (chair pub. rels. com. 1990-92, spkrs. bur., recruitment com. Dist. 14, 1990, chair coun. on edn.), Nat. League for Nursing (accreditation com. 1985-90, site visitor 1984-98), Am. Acad. Nursing, Nursing Edn. Alumni Assn. Tchrs. Coll. (pres. 1990-94. v.p. 2003—), Lake Hopatcong Yacht Club (fleet surgeon 2004—), Sigma Theta Tau. Episcopalian. Avocations: boating, reading, theater, hand crafts. Home: 13 Ford Rd Landing NJ 07850 Office Phone: 516-877-4557. E-mail: wolahan@adelphi.edu.

WOLANER, ROBIN PEGGY, internet and magazine publisher; b. Queens, N.Y., May 6, 1954; d. David H. and Harriet (Radlow) W.; children: Terry David, Bonnie Lee. BS in Indsl. and Labor Rels., Cornell U., 1975. Sr. editor Viva Mag., N.Y.C., 1975-76; editor Impact Mag., N.Y.C., 1976-77; circulation mgr. Runner's World Mag., Mountain View, Calif., 1977-79; cons. Ladd Assocs., San Francisco, 1979-80; gen. mgr. Mother Jones Mag., San Francisco, 1980-81, pub., 1981-85; founder, pub. Parenting Mag., San Francisco, 1985-91, pres., 1991-92; v.p. Time Pub. Ventures, 1990-96; pres., CEO Sunset Pub. Corp., 1992-95; exec. v.p. CNET, 1997—2002. Bd. dirs. Working Assets, Tides Found. Jewish. E-mail: robinw@cnet.com.

WOLANIN, BARBARA ANN BOESE, art curator, art historian; b. Dayton, Ohio, Dec. 12, 1943; d. William Carl and Elisabeth Cassell (Barnard) Boese; m. Thomas R. Wolanin, 1966 (div. 1980); children: Peter, Andrew; m. Phillip F. Brown, 2001. AB, Oberlin Coll., 1966, AM, 1969; MAT, Harvard U., 1967; PhD, U. Wis., 1981. Art tchr. Newton (Mass.) Pub. Schs., 1969-71; asst. prof. art history Trinity Coll., Washington, 1978-83, James Madison U., Harrisonburg, Va., 1983-85; curator U.S. Capitol, Architect of the Capitol, Washington, 1985—. Author: (exhbn. catalog) [illegible] Constantino Brumidi, 1998; contbr. articles to profl. jours. Woodrow Wilson fellow, 1967, Kress fellow U. Wis., 1974, Smithsonian fellow, 1976; recipient Faculty Devel. award James Madison U., 1985. Mem. Women's Caucus for Art (pres. D.C. chpt. 1998-2001, nat. bd. 2002), Art Table (bd. D.C. chpt. 2003-), Coll. Art Assn., Am. Inst. Conservation, Phi Beta Kappa (pres. Trinity Coll. 1982-83). Home: 7807 Hamilton Spring Rd Bethesda MD 20817 Office: US Capitol Office Architect Washington DC 20515-0001 E-mail: bwolanin@aoc.gov.

WOLCOTT, NANCY BOOKOUT, music director; b. Rochester, N.Y., Sept. 20, 1932; d. Raymond and Esther Anna (Mohr) Bookout; m. Vernon Wolcott, July 6, 1956; children: Deborah Nan, David Miles. MusB, U. Rochester, 1954; Sacred Music Master, Union Theol. Sem., 1956. Music dir., organist St. Mark's Luth. Ch., Balt., 1957-58; soprano soloist Franklin St. Presbyn. Ch., Balt., 1959-62; youth choir dir. First United Meth. Ch., Bowling Green, Ohio, 1963-70; music dir. Ashland Ave. Bapt. Ch., Toledo, 1971-85, First Presbyn. Ch., Bowling Green, 1986—. Festival coord. Adult Choir Festival, Toledo, 1974, 85, Chorister's Guild Youth Choirs, Toledo, 1976, 84; staff tchr. creative arts Bowling Green State U., 1977-94; workshop leader Am. Guild Organists, Toledo, 1981, Choristers Guild, Toledo, 1981, 83, 85, 87. Editor (Renaissance Madrigal show) Music and Drama of Elizabethan England, 1969, (children's day pageant) An American Heritage, 1972. Mem. Am. Guild Organists (sec. 1983-84), N.W. Ohio Sigma Alpha Iota (pres. 1985-87, Sword of Honor Alumnae chpt. 1983). Democrat. Presbyterian. Avocations: reading, theater, traveling. Home: 1056 Fort Dr Bowling Green OH 43402-1205

WOLD, KIMBERLY G. legislative staff member; Grad., Brigham Young U. Pub. affairs program mgr. Phoenix Met. C. of C., 1982-86; asst. dist. dir. U.S. Congressman Jon Kyl, 1987-93, dist. dir., 1993-95; dep. campaign mgr. John Kyl Campaign for U.S. Senate, 1994; dep. state dir. U.S. Sen. John Kyl, 1995-98, state dir., 1998—. Bd. dirs. Drugs Don't Work in Ariz., Maricopa County Victim Compensation Bd.; mem. Gov.'s Commn. on Violence Against Women. Home: 2560 N Lindsay Rd Apt 46 Mesa AZ 85213-1521 Office: Office of Sen Jon Kyl 2200 E Camelback Rd Ste 120 Phoenix AZ 85016-3455

WOLD, VERA O'BRYAN, retired medical/surgical nurse; b. S.D., Dec. 10, 1926; d. Boyd Marselus and Theodoshia Forrest (Eastin) O'Bryan; m. Clifford Eugene Wold, Sept. 9, 1927; children: Rosmary, Bryan, Leo, Jerry. Diploma, St. Mary's Hosp., Pierre, S.D., 1947. Night nurse, supr. Winner (S.D.) Gen., 1947—48; night nurse Naeve Hosp., Albertlea, Minn., 1948; flr. supr. St. Olaf, Austin, Minn., 1948—49, surg. nurse, 1953; flr. nurse, supr. Mercy Hosp., Milw., 1950—51; flr. nurse St. John's, Fargo, ND, 1951—52; night nurse Drs. Hosp., Pinole, Calif., 1982—88; ret., 1988. With cadet corp., 1944—47. Democrat. Avocation: needlepoint, sewing and quilting. Home: 1229 Mcdonald Dr Pinole CA 94564-2503

WOLENSKY, JOAN, occupational therapist, interfaith minister; b. Wilkes Barre, Pa., Mar. 4, 1954; d. Paul and Anna (Havrilla) W.; children: Maurisa Ann Fela, Jennifer Andrea Fela. BS, Coll. Misericordia, Dallas, Pa., 1985; DDiv (hon.), New Theol. Sem., N.Y.C., 1992. Cert. interfaith minister; cert. minister Order of Melchizedek, 1992; ordained minister Order of Holy Spirit, 1998; Reiki master, USUI and Karuna Sys.; cert. nat. and internat. spiritual response therapy counselor/tchr.; cert. master tchr. magnified healing. Founder, adminstr. N.E. Pa. Interfaith Ministries/Celestial Pathways Ctr., Harveys Lake, Pa., 1988; founder, dir., adminstr. Occupational Therapy Cons. Svcs., Harveys Lake, 1989; traveling occupational therapist. Dean, mem. adv. bd. Sage Inst., Shokan, N.Y.; mem. adv. bd. and quality assurance bd. At Home Health Care, Wilkes-Barre; mem. Am. Bd. Disability Analysts, 2003; mem., spkr. Am. Congress Rehab. Medicine, 1995. Contbr. articles to profl. jours. Recipient Supr.'s award City of Richmond Nursing Home, 1989; Mary K. Minglin scholar Am. Occupational Therapy Assn., 1984. Mem. Assn. for Interfaith Mins., Holistic Consortium of N.E. Pa., Inst. for Higher Healing/Wellness, Spiritual Response Assn., Universal Holistic Healers Assn., N.E. Native Am. Assn. Avocations: martial arts, yoga, angels, guitar. Home: PO Box 197 Harveys Lake PA 18618-0197

WOLF, ALICE K. state legislator, former mayor; b. Vienna, Dec. 24, 1933; d. Frederick Koerner and Renee (Engel) K.; m. Robert A. Wolf, 1955; children: Eric Jeffrey, Adam Nathaniel. BS, Simmons Coll., 1955; MPA, Harvard U., 1978; EdD (hon.), Wheelock Coll., 2001. Residence staff MIT, Lincoln Lab, 1955-62, Computer Corp Am., 1967-71, pers. dir., 1971-76; mem. Cambridge Sch. Com., 1974-81, vicechairwoman, 1976-77, 80-81; chairwoman Ward 7 Dem. Com., 1976-85; committeewoman Mass. State Dem. Com.; former vice mayor City of Cambridge, Mass., mayor, 1990-91; mem. dist. 25 Middlesex Mass. Ho. of Reps., Boston. Del. Dem. Nat. Conv., 1980, 88, 92, State Conv., 1979, 81, 83, 85, 87, 89. Mem. NOW, Mass. Women's Polit. Caucus Cambridge Mental Health Assn., Am. for Dem. Action, Nat. Orgn. Women Am. Civil Liberties Union, Nat. Office: Mass Ho of Reps State House Rm 238 Boston MA 02133 Home: 48 Huron Ave Cambridge MA 02138-6706 E-mail: rep.alicewolf@hou.state.ma.us.

WOLF, CYNTHIA TRIBELHORN, librarian, library educator; b. Denver, Dec. 12, 1945; adopted d. John Baltazar and Margaret (Kern) Tribelhorn (dec.); m. H.Y. Rassam, Mar. 2l, l969 (div. Jan. l988); children: Najma Christine, Yousuf John; adopted children: Leonard Joseph Lucero, Lakota E. Rassam-Lucero, McKinley William Osborn, Kevin Trey, Jackson Andrew Lee, Rachel A.; m. Walter Larry Peck, June 21, 1965 (div. Feb. 1967). BA, Colo. State U., l970; MLS, U. Denver, l985. Cert. permanent profl. librarian, N.Mex. Elem. tchr. Sacred Heart Sch., Farmington, N.Mex., l973-78; asst. prof. libr. sci. edn. U. N.Mex., Albuquerque, 1985-91, dir. libr. sci. edn. divsn., 1989-91; pres. Info. Acquisitions, Albuquerque, 1990-99; libr. dir. Southwestern Coll., Santa Fe, 1992-94; mem. youth resources Rio Grande Valley Libr. Sys., Albuquerque, 1994-95, adult reference svc., 1995-98; with Albuquerque Pub. Schs., 1998—, coach nat. sch. reform policy, 2000—; instr. U. N.Mex., 1998-99. Fine arts resource person for gifted edn. Farmington Pub. Schs., 1979-83; speaker Unofficial Mentorships and Market Rsch., 1992-98. Mem. Farmington Planning and Zoning Commn., l980-8l; bd. dirs. Farmington Mus. Assn., l983-84; pres. Farmington Symphony League, l978. Mem. ALA, N.Mex. Library Assn., LWV (bd. dirs. Farmington, 1972-74, 75, pres.). Avocations: mixed media graphics design, market research, creative approaches to personal journals, board game design.

WOLF, EDITH MALETZ, retired educator; b. Warsaw, Nov. 12, 1922; came to U.S., 1923; d. Michael and Sonia Chai (Ingerov) Maletz; m. Jordan Melvin Wolf, July 7, 1946; 1 child, David Richard (dec.). BS, U. Wis., 1944, MS, 1968. Cert. tchr. Wis. Tchr. Milw. Pub. Schs., 1945-85, acting vice prin., 1980-81, ret., 1985. Author: The Magic Dreydle, 1962, The New Governess, 1970, (play) The Dream. Mem. Saturday Arts, Milw., 1970-80, Wis. Painters and Sculptors, Milw., 1944—. Scholarship Dudley Krafts Watson, 1944. Mem. AAUW, Hadassah (sec. 1980-81, pres. emeritus, donor chair, program chair), Nat. Mus. Women in the Arts, Florentine Opera Club (founding mem.), U. Wisc. Alumni Assn., Cousteau Soc. Avocations: reading, writing fiction, plays, painting, gardening.

WOLF, ELLEN C. water company executive; BA, Duke U.; MBA in Acctg. and Fin., U. Pa. With Bell Atlantic Corp. and subs. cos.; CFO Bell Atlantic Mobile; exec. dir. strategic planning and bus. devel. Bell Atlantic Enterprises Internat., v.p., treas., officer, 1995-99; CFO Am. Water Works Co., Inc., Voorhees, N.J., 1999—. Office: Am Water Works Co Inc 1025 Laurel Oak Rd Kirkwood Voorhees NJ 08043

WOLF, IRNA LYNN, psychologist; b. Dunottar, South Africa, Aug. 30, 1949; came to U.S., 1977; d. John and Tolsa W.; m. Raymond Frank Shamos, Feb. 22, 1970; children: [illegible] Troy Joseph. MFA cum laude, U. Witwatersrand, 1976; MA, U. Rochester, 1983; PhD, Ariz. State U., 1991, postgrad., 1997. Lic. psychologist, Ariz., diplomate Am. Bd. Psychology; cert. sch. psychologist. Rsch., tchg. asst. Ariz. State U., Tempe, 1984-89; ind. rsch., 1989-97, pvt. practice, 1997 . Lectr. in field; cons. Human Info. Processing, 1997—. Contbr. articles to profl. jours. Recipient Certificate of Appreciation Paradise Valley Police Dept., 1992. Mem. APA, Am. Psychol. Soc., Nat. Assn. Sch. Psychologists, We. Psychol. Assn., Ariz. Psychol. Assn., Phi Kappa Phi. Republican. Avocations: painting, drawing, hiking, swimming. Home: 4516 E Onyx Ave Phoenix AZ 85028-4200

WOLF, JEAN D. educational consultant, writer; b. Norfolk, Va., Oct. 19, 1947; d. James Charles and Jean Audrey (Emanuel) Dempsey; m. Donald Marshall Wolf, Oct. 2, 1971; children: James; Andrew, Katharine, Jeffrey and John (quads). AB in Polit. Sci., Smith Coll., 1969; MEd, Harvard U., 1977. Analyst, edn. and pub. welfare divsn. Congl. Rsch. Svc./Libr. of Congress, Washington, 1969-73; cons. ABT, Cambridge, Mass., 1973-74, Dunbar Assocs., Washington, 1999—. Chmn. Phillips coun. The Phillips Collection, Washington, 1996-98; chmn. Washington docents Nat. Gallery of Art, 1988-90; bd. dirs., bd. of lady visitors Children's Hosp., Washington, 1994—. Roman Catholic. Avocations: writing, travel. Home: 1 E Kirke St Chevy Chase MD 20815-4216 also: 6 Rue Chanoinesse Paris 75004 France

WOLF, KATIE LOUISE, state legislator; b. Wolcott, Ind., July 9, 1925; d. John H. and Helen Munsterman; m. Charles W. Wolf, 1945; children: Mark, Marcia. Grad., Ind. Bus. Coll., 1944. Registration officer County of White, Ind., 1960, mgr. lic. bur., 1960-68; clk. 39th Jud. Cir. Ct., 1968-78; mem. Ind. Ho. of Reps., 1985-86, Ind. State Senate, 1987—. Mem. Dem. Nat. Com., 1968-90; del. Dem. nat. convs., 1972, 76, 80, 84. Recipient Athens award, 1987; named Woman of Yr. Bus. and Profl. Women's Club, 1984, Outstanding Freshman Legislator, 1985. Lutheran. Office: Ind Senate Dist 7 200 W Washington St Indianapolis IN 46204-2728

WOLF, LINDA S. advertising executive; Grad., Ohio Wesleyan U. Asst. account exec. Leo Burnett Group, Chgo., 1978; exec. v.p. new bus., dir. worldwide, group pres. N.Am. Leo Burnett Co., Inc., Chgo., 1978-2000; CEO Leo Burnett USA, Chgo., 2000—. Office: Leo Burnett Co Inc 35 W Wacker Dr Ste 3710 Chicago IL 60601-1648*

WOLF, MARGERY JONES, social sciences educator, writer, researcher; b. Santa Rosa, Calif., Sept. 9, 1933; d. Alvia Makee and Alvie Nathan Jones; m. Keith Mac Marshall. AA, Santa Rosa Jr. Coll., Calif., 1952. Vis. assoc. prof. Duke U., Durham, NC, 1984—85; prof. U. Iowa, Iowa City, 1985—2001. Assoc. editor Signs: Jour. of Women in Culture and Soc., Chgo., 1981—86; chair women's studies program U. Iowa, Iowa City, 1985—91, exec. com., Coll. of Liberal Arts, 1990—93; assoc. editor Sex Roles: A Jour. of Rsch., 1988—91; exec. bd. mem. Assn. of Feminist Anthropologists, Arlington, Va., 1992—95; pres. Am. Ethnol. Soc., Arlington, Va., 1995—97; exec. bd. mem. Am. Anthrop. Assn., Arlington, Va., 1995—97, sec. (corp.), 2000—03. Author: (book) The House of Lim, Women and the Family in Rural Taiwan; editor (author): Women in Chinese Society; author: Revolution Postponed:Women in Contemporary China, A Thrice Told Tale:Feminism, Postmodernism, and Ethnographic Responsibility; mem. editl. bd.: Am. Anthropologist, 1989—94. Commr. Commn. on the Status of Women, Santa Rosa, Calif., 2002—03; mem. of bd. Nat. Women' History Project, Santa Rosa, Calif., 2002—03. Named Lewis Henry Morgan lectr., U. Rochester, 1983; recipient Regents Award for Faculty Excellence, State Bd. of Regents, Iowa, 1998, Rsch. grant, Com. on Scholarly Communication with the People's Republic of China, NAS, 1980-1981; fellow, Ctr. for Advanced Study in the Behavioral Scis., 1981-1982, Nat. Humanities Ctr., N.C., 1994-1995; grantee Rockefeller Residency Program in the Humanities, Rockefeller Found., 1987-1993. Mem.: Am. Anthrop. Assn. Achievements include field research in Taiwan, 1958-1971, China, 1980-81.

WOLF, MICHELE SUE, poet, writer, editor; b. Denville, N.J., June 21, 1954; d. Sheldon Wolf and Dorothy Joyce Yospe; m. Sanford Michael Herzon, Aug. 5, 2001. BS in Pub. Comm., Boston U., 1976; MS in Journalism, Columbia U., 1978. Publicist Boston Ballet, 1976—77; assoc. copy editor Charles Scribner's Sons, N.Y.C., 1979—81; copy editor Simon & Schuster, Inc., N.Y.C., 1981—84; assoc. editor Harper's Bazaar, N.Y.C., 1985—87; freelance writer and editor, 1987—; dir. comms. The Writer's Ctr., Bethesda, Md., 2002—03. Author: (poetry books) The Keeper of Light, 1995 (winner Painted Bride Quar. poetry chapbook series, 1995), Conversations During Sleep, 1998 (Anhinga prize for poetry, 1997); contbr. poetry to jours., anthologies. Recipient Nat. Mag. award for personal svc., Am. Soc. Mag. Editors, 1993, Nat. Media award, Am. Speech-Lang.-Hearing Assn., 1994; residency fellow, Va. Ctr. for the Creative Arts, 1987, 1988, Edward F. Albee Found., 1989, Corp. of Yaddo, Saratoga Springs, N.Y., 1990. Mem.: Assn. Writers and Writing Programs, Poetry Soc. Am., Nat. Writers Union, Am. Soc. Journalists and Authors, PEN Am. Ctr. Office: 4615 N Park Ave # 810 Chevy Chase MD 20815-4514 E-mail: michelewolf@juno.com.

WOLF, MURIEL HEBERT, soprano, performing company executive, music educator; b. Boston, Nov. 15, 1925; d. Joseph Aurel and Gertrude May (Schellenger) Hebert; m. Anton Wolf, Feb. 5, 1949 (dec. Jan. 1989); m. Albert Paul Steger, Feb. 14, 1991. BMus in Voice with Distinction, New Eng. Conservatory of Music, 1949, MMus in Musical Rsch., 1950; Artist's Diploma with Highest Honors, Acad. of Music, Vienna, Austria, 1955; Postgrad. in Musicology, Brandeis U., 1956-57; Postgrad. in Opera, Ind. U., 1962-64. Instr. in music and theatre Verde Valley Sch., Sedona, Ariz., 1957-62; coord. of voice SUNY, Buffalo, 1979-84, prodr., dir. of opera, 1966-79, instr. of music, 1965-68, asst. prof. of music, 1968-71, assoc. prof. of music, 1971-84, prof. of music, 1984-93, prof. emeritus, 1993—. Guest lectr., dir. opera U. No. Ariz., Flagstaff, 1961—62; lectr., recitals Am. Psychiat. Assn., N.Y.C., Dallas, Montreal, 1979—88; co-chair Ctrl. Opera Svc. Nat. Conf. Met. Opera Auditions; founder Musictheater Advocates, Inc., Buffalo, 1974. Contbg. editor: Opera Quar., 1981—87; contbr. Internat. Dictionary of Opera, 1993. Founder, pres. The Anton and Muriel Wolf Found., Inc., 1999—. Grantee, N.Y. State Coun. of Arts, Buffalo, 1973, 1975, 1977, Cameron Baird Found., 1976, Polonia Cultural Inst., 1979; scholar Fulbright, Vienna and Salzburg, Austria, 1953—55. Mem.: Nat. Assn. Tchrs. Singing (conf. panelist, moderator and lectr.), Met. Opera Assn., Nat. Opera Assn. (conf. panelist, moderator and lectr., assoc. editor jour. 1962—82). Avocation: travel. E-mail: mhwolf@adelphia.net.

WOLF, SHARON ANN, psychotherapist; b. Dallas, May 13, 1951; d. Frank Allan and Ursula (Mohnblatt) W.; 1 child, Allan. BA in Psychology, New Eng. Coll., 1973; MA in Counseling Psychology, Antioch Grad. Sch., 1976; PhD in Clin. Psychology, Union Grad. Sch., 1989. Cert. Mental Health Counselor, 1997. Behavioral spl. ednl. planner Philbrook Children's Learning Ctr., Concord, N.H., 1972; asst. to spl. edn. cons. N.H. Hosp., Concord, 1972-73; spl. edn. planner Rochester (N.H.) Child Devel. Ctr., 1973; counseling practicum Morrill Sch., Concord, N.H., 1973, Contoocook Valley Mental Health Ctr., Henniker, N.H., 1973-74, counseling psychology intern, 1974-76; lab. instr. New Eng. Coll., Henniker, 1973; ednl. and guidance counselor asst. Hillsboro (N.H.)-Deering Sch. Dist., 1973-74; pediatric psychology intern parent-infant devel. program Ctrl. N.H. C.M.H. Ctr., Concord, 1986-87; assoc. psychologist Easter Seal Rehab. Ctr., Manchester, N.H., 1976-80, Ctrl. N.H. Community Mental Health Svcs., Concord, 1980-88; intern forensic psychology Concord Dist. Ct., 1987-88; pvt. practice Northfield, N.H., 1988—. Psychol. cons. children and youth program Twin Rivers Counselling Ctr., Franklin, N.H. 1980-83, therapist, 1984-86; therapist Ctrl. N.H. Comm. Mental Health Ctr., 1980-83, Parent-Infant Devel. Program, Concord, N.H., 1983-88. Fellow Am. Orthopsychiat. Assn.; mem. [illegible] Counseling and Devel., New England Coun. on Crime and Delinquency, N.H. Assn. of the Deaf, N.H. Registry of Interpreters for the Deaf. Avocations: rug hooking, music, spending time with son. Office: PO Box 253 Tilton NH 03276-0253

WOLFE, BARBARA L. economics educator, researcher; b. Phila., Feb. 15, 1943; d. Manfred and Edith (Heimann) Kingshoff; m. Stanley R. Wolfe, Mar. 20, 1965 (div. Mar. 1978); m. Robert H. Haveman, July 29, 1983; children: Jennifer Ann Wolfe, Ari Michael Wolfe. BA, Cornell U., Ithaca, N.Y., 1965; MA, U. Pa., 1971; PhD, U Pa., 1973. Asst. prof. Bryn Mawr (Pa.) Coll., 1973-76; rsch. assoc. Inst. Rsch. on Poverty, Madison, Wis., 1976-77, dir., 1994—2000; from asst. prof. to assoc. prof. U. Wis., Madison, 1977-88, prof., 1988—. Adj. prof. Australian Nat. U., 2002-; resident scholar NIAS, Wassenear, Netherlands, 1984-85, 96-97; vis. scholar Russell Sage Found., N.Y., 1991-92. Co-author: Succeeding Generations, 1994; editor: (book) Role of Budgetary Policy in Demographic Transitions, 1994, contbr. articles to profl. jours. Active Commn. on Children with Disabilities, Washington 1994-95, Tech. Adv. Panel Social Security, Washington, 1994-95. Recipient Best Article of Yr. award Rev. Income and Wealth, 1992, Fulbright award Coun. Internat. Exch. of Scholars, 1984. Mem.: Assn. Pub. Policy Mgmt. (policy coun. 2001—), Internat. Inst. Pub. Fin. (bd. mgmt. 1994—2000, v.p. 2000—03), Am. Econ. Assn. (bd. com. 1989—92, exec. bd. 1996—99). Office: U Wis Inst Rsch on Poverty 1180 Observatory Dr Madison WI 53706-1320 Office Phone: 608-262-0662. E-mail: wolfe@LaFollette.wisc.edu., bwolfe@wisc.edu.

WOLFE, DEBORAH CANNON PARTRIDGE, government education consultant, educator, minister; b. Cranford, N.J. d. David Wadsworth and Gertrude (Moody) Cannon; 1 son, H. Roy Partridge. BS, N.J. City U.; MA, EdD, Tchrs. Coll., Columbia U.; postgrad., Vassar Coll., U. Pa., Union Theol. Sem., Jewish Sem. Am.; hon. doctorates, Seton Hall U., 1963, Coll. New Rochelle, 1963, Morris Brown U., 1964, Glassboro/Rowan Coll., 1965, Bloomfield Coll., 1988, Monmouth Coll., 1988, William Paterson Coll., 1988; LLD (hon.), Kean Coll., 1981; LHD (hon.), Stockton State Coll., 1982; LLD (hon.), Jersey City State Coll., 1987, Centenary Coll., William Paterson Coll., 1989, Tuskegee U., 1989, Glassboro State Coll., 1985, Tuskegee U., 1989, St. Peter's Coll., 1989, Rider Coll., 1989, Georgian Court Coll., 1990; DSc (hon.), Stevens Inst. Tech., 1991; LLD (hon.), Rutgers U., 1992, Thomas Edison Coll., 1992; DSc, U. Med. and Dentistry N.J., 1989, CUNY, 2001, LHD (hon.), 2001. Former prin., tchr. pub. schs., Cranford, also Tuskegee, Ala.; faculty Tuskegee Inst., Grambling Coll., NYU, Fordham U., U. Mich., Tex. Coll., Columbia U.; supervision and adminstrn. curriculum devel., social studies U. Ill., summers; prof. edn., affirmative action officer Queens Coll., officer; prof. edn. and children's lit. Wayne State U.; edn. chief U.S. Ho. of Reps. Com. on Edn. and Labor, 1962—. Fulbright prof. Am. lit. NYU; U.S. rep. 1st World Conf. on Women in Politics; chair non-govtl. reps. to UN (NGO/DPI exec. com.), 1983—; editl. cons. Macmillan Pub. Co.; cons. Ency. Brit.; adv. bd. Ednl. Testing Svc.; mem. State Bd. Edn., 1964-94; chairperson N.J. Bd. Higher Edn., 1967-94; mem. nat. adv. panel on vocat. edn. HEW; mem. citizen's adv. com. to Bd. Edn., Cranford; mem. Citizen's Adv. Com. on Youth Fitness, Pres.'s Adv. Com. on Youth Fitness, White House Conf. Edn., 1955, White House Conf. Aging, 1960, White House Conf. Civil Rights, 1966, White House Conf. on Children, 1970, Adv. Coun. for Innovations in Edn.; v.p. Nat. Alliance for Safer Cities; cons. Vista Corps, OEO; vis. scholar Princeton Theol. Sem., 1989—; chairperson Human Rels. Coun., N.J., 1994—; vis. prof. U. Ill., U. N.C., Wayne State U.; theologian-in-residence Duke U.; mem. trustee bd. Sci. Svc.; mem. N.J. Commn. on Holocaust Edn., 1996. Contbr. articles to ednl. publs. Bd. dirs. Cranford Welfare Assn., Cmty. Ctr., 1st Bapt. Ch., Cranford Cmty. Ctr. Migratory Laborers, Hurlock, Md.; trustee Sci. Svc., Seton Hall U., bd. regents; mem. Pub. Broadcasting Authority, N.J. Commn. on Holocaust Edn., 1996—, Tuskegee U. Alumni, 1995; mem. N.J. Conv. of Progressive Baptists, 1995, v.p., 1996—, pres., 1999-2001; parliamentarian Progressive nat. Bapt. Conv.; sec. Kappa Delta Pi Ednl. Found., nat. bd. dirs., 2001—, laureate rep.; mem. adv. com. Elizabeth and Arthur Schlesinger Libr., Radcliffe Coll., trustee Edn. Devel. Ctr., 1965—; assoc. min. 1st Bapt. Ch.; chair Human Rels. Commn., Monroe, 1995; v.p., then pres. N.J. Conv. Progressive Bapt., 1996—; parliamentarian Progressive Nat. Baptist Conv.; mem. exec. com. Nat. Coun. Agrl. Rsch., Ext. and Teaching, 1997—; mem. N.J. Holocaust Commn., 1996— Named N.J. Educator of Yr., 2003; named to, NABSE

Hall of Fame; recipient Woman of Yr. award, Delta Beta Zeta, Morgan State Coll., Medal of Honor, DAR, 1990, Disting. Svc. medal, Nat. Top Ladies of Distinction, 1991, Disting. Svc. award, Nat. Assn. State Bds. Edn., 1992, 1994, Disting. Svc. to Edn. award, N.J. Commn. on Status of Women, 1993, Svc. to Children award, N.J. Assn. Sch. Psychologists, 1993, Disting. Medal award, U. Medicine and Dentistry N.J., Union Coll., citation, N.J. State Coun. on Vacat. Edn., 1994, N.J. State Bd. Edn., 1994, Svc. award for 50 Yrs., Cranford Bd. Edn., 1995, Women Who Count award, Zonta Internat., 1996, Minister's Appreciation award, Progressive Nat. Bapt. Conv., 1996, Edn. award, Tuskegee U. Alumni, 1996, Women Who Make a Difference award, Zonta Internat., 1995, Dr. George Washington Carver award, Pa. Acad. Sci., 1998, Lifetime Svc. award, William Patterson U., 1999, Triumph award, N.J. Dept. State, 2001. Mem.: NAACP (Medal of Honor 1994), AAUP, AAUW (nat. edn. chmn.), NCCJ, NEA (life), ASCD (rev. coun.), AAAS (chmn. tchr. edn. com.), LWV, N.J. Conv. of Progressive Bapts. (1st woman elected pres. 1999), Alliance Black Clergywomen (pres.), Nat. Assn. State Univs. and Colls. and Land Grant Colls. (mem. exec. bd. 1996, mem. coun. on agr. ext. and tchg.), Ch. Women United (UN rep., mem. exec. com.), Internat. Platform Assn., Am. Coun. Edn. (mem. commn. fed. rels.), Nat. Soc. Study Edn., Internat. Assn. Childhood Edn., Am. Acad. Polit. and Social Sci., Comparative Edn. Soc., Internat. Reading Assn., Fellowship So. Churchmen, Am. Tchrs. Assn., N.Y. Tchrs. Assn., Nat. Assn. Black Educators (pres.), Nat. Assn. Negro Bus. and Profl. Women (chmn. spkrs. bur., Nat. Achievement award 1958), Nat. Panhellenic Coun. (dir.), Am. Coun. Human Rights (v.p.), Coun. Nat. Orgns. Children and Youth, N.J. Commn. Holocaust Edn., N.J. Holocaust Commn., N.J. Fedn. Colored Women's Clubs, UN Assn.-USA (mem. exec. com.). Home: 4102 Monroe Village Monroe Township NJ 08831

WOLFE, ETHYLE RENEE (MRS. COLEMAN HAMILTON BENEDICT), college administrator; b. Burlington, Vt., Mar. 14, 1919; d. Max M. and Rose (Saiger) Wolfe; m. Coleman Hamilton Benedict, Dec. 4, 1954. BA, U. Vt., 1940, MA, 1942; postgrad., Bryn Mawr Coll., 1942—43; PhD, NYU, 1950; LHD (hon.), CUNY, 1989; LittD (hon.), Iona Coll., 1989. Tchg. fellow U. Vt., 1940—42; rsch. fellow Latin Bryn Mawr (Pa.) Coll., 1942—43; instr. classics Bklyn. Coll., 1947—49, instr. classical langs., 1949—54, asst. prof., 1954—59, assoc. prof., 1960—68, prof., 1968—, acting chmn. dept. classics and comparative lit., 1962—63, chmn. dept., 1967—72; dean Bklyn. Coll. Sch. Humanities, 1971—78; exec. officer Bklyn. Coll. Humanities Inst., 1980—89; provost and v.p. for acad. affairs Bklyn. Coll., 1982—88, provost emeritus, 1989. Exec. com., chmn. com. on undergrad. affairs, com. on univ.-wide programs CUNY; study group AAAS, 1987—89, pub., 1987—89; dir. Nat. Core Visitors Programs, 1985—89, Fund for Improvement of Postsecondary Edn.-funded Ctr. for Core Studies, 1987—88; co-chair senate report Chancellor's Coll. Prep. Initiative, 1991; exec. com The Liberal Art of Sci.: Agenda for Action. Mem. editl. bd.: Classical World, 1965—71; co-editor: The Am. Classical Rev., 1971—76; contbr. articles to profl. jours. Named Ethyle R. Wolfe Inst. for the Humanities Bklyn. Coll. in her honor, 1989; named to Hall of Honor, U. Vt., 1991, Disting. U. Faculty Sen. Emeritus, CUNY, 1992; recipient Kirby Flower Smith award, 1939, Goethe prize, U. Vt., 1940, Alumni Achievement award, 1985, Nat. Presdl. medal, NEH, Charles Frankel prize, 1990; grantee, 1971, 1982—84, Mellon Found., 1982—85, 1986—89, Exxon, 1986—89, Josiah Macy, 1986—90. Mem.: Am. Soc. Papyrologists, Classical Assn. Atlantic States (exec. com.), Vergilian Soc. Am., Archeol. Inst. Am., Am. Philol. Assn., N.Y. Classical Club (past pres., exec. com.), Phi Beta Kappa (pres. 1988—90, past pres. Rho of N.Y. chpt., Spl. Citation of Honor on Sesquicentennial U. Vt. 1998). Home: 360 W 22nd St New York NY 10011-2600 Office: care Ethyle R Wolfe Inst Humanities Bklyn Coll Bedford Ave # H Brooklyn NY 11222

WOLFE, GERALDINE, administrator; b. Monticello, Ark., Mar. 29, 1944; d. John Wesley and Hazeline (Daniels) Fisher; 1 child, Arin. BA, Keuka Coll., 1965; MA, Mt. Holyoke Coll., 1967; MSEd, Elmira Coll., 1981; cert. ednl. adminstrn. SUNY-Brockport, 1985; PhD Cornell U., 1988. Tchr. biology and health Corning Sch. Dist., N.Y., 1967-90; asst. prof. SUNY, Plattsburgh, 1990-93; adminstr. Saranac Lake Ctrl. Sch. Dist., 1993-96; asst. supt. Schenectady City Sch. Dist., 1996-99; supt. Catskill (N.Y.) Ctrl. Sch. Dist., 1999—. Mem. Mid. States Evaluation Team, 1985; chmn. bd. trustees Friendship Bapt. Ch., Corning, 1984-90; bd. dirs. Hamilton Hill Arts Ctr., 1996-99, Oslo scholar U. Oslo, 1964, Coop. Ext., Common Ground of Catkill, Workforce Investment Act, Youth Coun., Grene County Collubirative Community Partnership for Youth; Mem. N.Y. State Profl. Health Educators Assn., Women in Ednl. Adminstrn., LWV, Sigma Xi, Sigma Lambda Sigma. Club: Cosmopolitan (officer 1979-81) (Elmira). Mem. allocations com. United Way, 1982-90; mem. edn. com. Planned Parenthood, 1984-90. Mem. NAACP, ASCD, Nat. Assn. Sec. Sch. Prins., Am. Assn. Sch. Adminstrs., Nat. Alliance Black Sch. Educators, N.Y.S. Assn. for Computers and Technologies in Edn., N.Y.S. Assn. Compensatory Educators, N.Y. State Coun. Sch. Supts., Cornell Edn. Soc., Jr. League of Elmira, Rotary Club of Catskill, Capital District Assn. of Women Adminstrs., Delta Kappa Gamma, Phi Delta Kappa. Avocations: tennis, cross countryskiing; travel; piano; reading. Home: 7 Forest Hills Dr Elmira NY 14905-1141 Office: Catskill Ctrl Sch Dist 343 W Main St Catskill NY 12414-1621

WOLFE, HARRIET MUNRETT, lawyer; b. Mt. Vernon, N.Y., Aug. 18, 1953; d. Lester John Francis Jr. and Olga Harriet (Miller) Munrett; m. Charles Briant Wolfe, Sept. 10, 1983. BA, U. Conn., 1975; postgrad., Oxford (Eng.) U., 1976; JD, Pepperdine U., 1978. Bar: Conn. 1979. Assoc. legal counsel, asst. sec. Citytrust, Bridgeport, Conn., 1979-90; v.p., sr. counsel, asst. sec. legal dept. Shawmut Bank Conn., N.A., Hartford, 1990-96, pvt. practice, 1996-97; exec. v.p., gen. counsel, sec. Webster Fin. Corp., Waterbury, Conn., 1997—. Govt. rels. com. Electronic Funds Transfer Assn., Washington, 1983—. Mem. ABA, Conn. Bar Assn. (mem. legis. com. banking law sect.), Conn. Bankers Assn. (trust legis.com.), Guilford Flotilla Coast Guard Aux., U.S. Sailing Assn., Phi Alpha Delta Internat. (Frank E. Gray award 1978, Shepherd chpt. Outstanding Student award 1977-78). Home: 621 Northwood Dr Guilford CT 06437-1124 Office: Webster Fin Corp Webster Plaza Waterbury CT 06702 E-mail: hwolfe@websterbank.com.

WOLFE, JENNIFER NAN, special education educator, consultant; b. Dubuque, Iowa, Nov. 10, 1976; d. Charles James and Barbara Dean Wolfe. BS in Edn., U. Conn., Storrs, 1999, MA in Edn., 2000. Cert. spl. edn. tchr. Conn., 2000, coach Conn., 2001. Spl. edn. tchr. East Hampton Mid. Sch., Conn., 2000—02, Odyssey Cmty. Sch., Manchester, Conn., 2002—03; emotional inelligence and spl. needs cons. Charles J. Wolfe Assocs., Simsbury, Conn., 2003—. Mem.: Coun. for Exceptional Children. Office: Charles J Wolfe Assocs 59 Winterset Ln Simsbury CT 06070 Personal E-mail: jennifernan1976@hotmail.com.

WOLFE, JOAN LUEDDERS, non-profit organizations consultant; b. Detroit, May 2, 1929; d. William R. and Mary Lucinda (Deane) Luedders; m. Willard Wolfe, June 26, 1953; children: John Roberts, Peter Harper (dec.). BA in Econ., U. Mich., 1951; Dr. Pub. Svc. (hon.), Western Mich. U., 1973. Founder, chmn. West Mich. Environ. Action Coun., exec. dir., 1971-73; 1st woman mem. Mich. Natural Resources Commn., 1973-82, chair, 1977. Bd. dirs. Mich. League Conservation Voters. Author: Making Things Happen: The Guide for Members of Volunteer Organizations, 1981, Making Things Happen: How to Be an Effective Volunteer, 1991. Named Conservationist of Yr. Mich. United Conservation Clubs, 1971, Funep 500 Environ. Achiever Friends of UN Environ. Program, one of Mich. 50 Hist. Women to Know, Mich. History Mag., 2002; inducted Mich. Women's Hall of Fame, 1996; recipient Women of Achievement and Courage award Mich. Women's Found., 1998, Environ. Quality award Mich. Soc. Internal Medicine, 1970, Conservation award Am. Motors Corp., 1973, others. Mem. Nat. Audubon Soc. (nat. bd. dirs. 1982-87).

WOLFE, LINDA, writer; b. N.Y.C., Nov. 15, 1932; d. Harry M. Friedman and Mina Romanoff Kaufman; m. Max Pollack; 1 child, Jessica Wolfe Bernstein. MA, NYU, 1958. Editl. asst. Oxford U. Press, N.Y.C., 1955—60, Partisan Rev., N.Y.C., NY, 1958—60; writer, rschr. Time, Inc., N.Y.C., 1960—71; contbg. editor N.Y. Mag., N.Y.C., 1971—96; consulting editor Woman Mag. (Conde Nast), N.Y.C., 1990—90. Author: (book) The Literary Gourmet, 1962, The Cooking of the Caribbean Islands, 1970, Playing Around: Women and Adultery, 1975, The Cosmo Report: Women and Sex in the Nineteen-Eighties, 1981, Private Practices (a novel), 1981, The Professor and the Prostitute and Other True Tales of Murder and Madness, 1986, Wasted: The Preppie Murder, 1989 (Notable Book of Yr., N.Y. Times, 1989), Double Life: The Shattering Affair Between New York's Chief Judge Sol Wachtler & Socialite Joy Silverman, 1994, Love Me To Death: A Journalist's Memoir of the Hunt for her Friend's Killer, 1998, The Murder of Dr. Chapman: The Legendary Trials of Lucretia Chapman and Her Lover, 2004. Recipient Edgar Allan Poe award nominee, Mystery Writers of Am., 1989. Mem.: PEN (exec. bd. dirs. 1994—95), Nat. Book Critics Circle (v.p. 1997—2002). Avocations: 18th-century English dance, travel.

WOLFE, MARGARET RIPLEY, historian, educator, consultant; b. Kingsport, Tenn., Feb. 3, 1947; d. Clarence Estill and Gertrude Blessing Ripley; m. David Earley Wolfe, Dec. 17, 1966; 1 child, Stephanie Ripley. BS magna cum laude, East Tenn. State U., 1967, MA, 1969; PhD, U. Ky., 1974. Instr. history East Tenn. State U., 1969-73, asst. prof., 1973-77, assoc. prof., 1977-80, prof., 1980—, sr. rsch. prof. history, 1999—. Author: Lucius Polk Brown and Progressive Food and Drug Control, Tennessee and New York City, 1908-1920, 1978, An Industrial History of Hawkins County, Tennessee, 1983, Kingsport, Tennessee: A Planned American City, 1987, Daughters of Canaan: A Saga of Southern Women, 1995; gen. editor: Women in Southern Culture Series; contbg. author to books, also introductions to books; contbr. articles to profl. jours. Mem. Tenn. Com. for Humanities, 1985-85, exec. coun. mem., 1984-85; mem. Women's Symphony Com., Kingsport, 1990-95; exec. com. Tenn. Commemorative Woman's Suffrage Commn., 1994-95; mem. state rev. bd. Tenn. Hist. Commn., 1995—. Haggin fellow U. Ky., 1972-73; recipient Disting. Faculty award East Tenn. State U., 1977, East Tenn. State U. Found. rsch. award, 1979, Alumni cert. merit, 1984. Mem. AAUP, ACLU (exec. com. Tenn. 1991-92), NOW, Tenn. State Employees Assn., Am. Studies Assn. (John Hope Franklin Prize com. 1992), Am. Hist. Assn., Orgn. Am. Historians, So. Assn. Women Historians (pres. 1983-84, exec. com. 1984-86), So. Hist. Assn. (com. on status of women 1987, program com. 1988, interim chair program com. 1988, mem. com. 1993, 94, 95, nominating com. 1994, chair nominating com. 1995, chmn. mem. com. 1997, exec. coun. 1998-2000), Smithsonian Assocs, Tenn. Hist Commn. (state rev. bd. 1995—), Tenn. Hist. Soc. (editl. bd. 1995—), Coordinating Com. for Women in History, East Tenn. Hist. Soc. (mem. editl. bd. Jour. East Tenn. History), St. George Tucker Soc., Phi Kappa Phi. Office: ETSU at Kingsport Kingsport TN 37660 also: East Tenn State U Dept History Johnson City TN 37614 E-mail: wolfem@etsu.edu.

WOLFE, MILDRED NUNGESTER, artist; b. Celina, Ohio, Aug. 23, 1912; d. Roy Clifford and Augusta Wilhelmina (Hoenie) Nungester; widowed; children: Karl Michael, Elizabeth Hoenie. AB, U. Monte Vallo, 1932; MA, Colo. Coll., 1944. Tchr. Decatur (Ala.) City Schs., 1933-42; tchr. art and art history Millsaps Coll., Jackson, Miss., 1960-70; artist Wolfe Fine Art Studio, Jackson, 1945—. Artist 4 lithographs of So. scene, 1940s, lithographs displayed in Montgomery Mus. of Art, 1940, Libr. of Congress, London, Warsaw, Coventry, 1944; oil portrait of Eudora Welty, Nat. Portrait Gallery, Washington, 1989; represented in permanent collections at Miss. Mus. Art, Huntsville Mus. Art, Ga. Mus. Art. Recipient 1st prize oil painting, Ala. Art League, Montgomery, 1935, 1st prize watercolor Miss. Art League, Jackson, 1949, award of merit Grumbacher Internat., Lakeland, Fla., 1952, Visual Arts award Miss. Inst. Arts and Letters, Jackson, 1989. Mem. Miss. Mus. of Art, Miss. Watercolor Soc. Office: Wolfe Fine Art Studio 4308 Old Canton Rd Jackson MS 39211-5920

WOLFE, PAMELA KLINE, history educator; b. Richmond, Va., Dec. 14, 1957; d. Paul Miller and Betty (Halterman) Kline; m. Robert Edward Wolfe, Apr. 5, 1980; children: Matthew Chambers, Hannah Elizabeth. BA French/Secondary Edn. summa cum laude, Bridgewater (Va.) Coll., 1979; postgrad., U. Strasbourg, France, 1978; MA, U. Md., 1983. Cert. in French and history edn. Tchr. French Yeshiva of Greater Washington, Silver Spring, Md., 1980—, tchr. history, 1983—, chmn. social studies dept., 1987—. Secular coord. LEAP program for gifted and talented students, testing coord., 2002—; judge Nat. Peace Essay Contest, Nat. Inst. Peace, Washington, 1992—; grader AP test Coll. Bds./AP, Princeton, N.J., 1996—, table leader 2003—; coach geography bee Yeshiva Team, Silver spring, 1993—, coach citizen bee, 1993-95. Dist. organizer Neighborhood Watch, Silver Spring, 1994-95; mem. Piney Br. Elem. Sch. PTA, 1992-98, Eastern Mid. Sch. PTA, 1995-2000, Montgomery Blair H.S. PTA, 1996-2000, Albert Einstein H.S. PTA, 2001——. George C. Marshall fellow, 1976. Mem. Phi Alpha Theta. Democrat. Avocations: reading, animals, fencing, yoga, skiing. Office: Yeshiva of Greater Wash 12721 Goodhill Rd Silver Spring MD 20906

WOLFE, SHEILA A. journalist; b. Chgo. d. Leonard M. and Rena (Karn) W. BA, Drake U. Reporter Chgo. Tribune, 1956-73, asst. city editor, 1973-75; day city editor Chgo. Tribune, 1975-79; city editor Chgo. Tribune, 1979-81, met. coordinator, 1981-83, adminstrv. asst. to mng. editor, 1983-2000. Pres. City News Bur. Chgo. 1986-88, 94-96. Recipient Beck award for outstanding profl. performance Chgo. Tribune, 1979; recipient Disting. Service award Drake U., 1982 Mem. Phi Beta Kappa. Home: 71 E Division St Chicago IL 60610-8307 E-mail: chicagoshe@aol.com.

WOLFF, CATHERINE ELIZABETH, opera company executive; b. Evanston, Ill., June 11, 1957; AB with honors, Vassar Coll., 1979; MA in Performing Arts Mgmt., Am. U., 1982. Adminstrv. asst. Opera Am., 1982-85; artistic adminstr. Pitts. Opera, 1985-94; exec. dir. Del. Symphony Orch., Wilmington, 1994-95; gen. dir. Syracuse (N.Y.) Opera Co., 1996—. Music panelist N.Y. State Coun. Arts, 2000—02, co-chair music panel, 2003. McGuire fellow Vassar Coll., 1979. Mem. Opera Am., Am. Symphony Orch. League, Phi Beta Kappa. Office: Syracuse Opera Co PO Box 1223 Syracuse NY 13201-1223

WOLFF, CYNTHIA GRIFFIN, humanities educator, author; b. St. Louis, Aug. 20, 1936; d. James Thomas and Eunice (Heyn) Griffin; m. Robert Paul Wolff, June 9, 1962 (div. 1986); children— Patrick Gideon, Tobias Barrington; m. Nicholas J. White, May 21, 1988. BA, Radcliffe Coll., 1958; PhD, Harvard U., 1965. Asst. prof. English Manhattanville Coll., Purchase, N.Y., 1968-70; asst. prof. English U. Mass., Amherst, 1971-74, assoc. prof., 1974-76, prof., 1976-80; prof. humanities MIT, Cambridge, 1980-85, Class of 1922 prof. lit. and writing, 1985—. Exec. com. for Am. lit. MLA, 1979-81; mem. selection bd. Literary Classics Am., 1981—; exec. bd. for fgn. grants Am. Council Learned Socs., 1981-84. Author: (literary criticism) Samuel Richardson, 1972, (literary biography) A Feast of Words: The Triumph of Edith Wharton, 1977, 2d edit., 1995, Emily Dickinson, 1986; bd. editors Am. Quar., 1979-84. Grantee AAUW, 1964-65, NEH, 1975-76, 1983-84, 97-98; Am. Council Learned Socs., 1984-85, Guggenheim, 1998—. Mem. Am. Studies Assn.

WOLFF, DIANE PATRICIA, writer, film producer; b. N.Y.C., Oct. 12, 1945; d. Irving Mark and Catherine Halkett (Grossman); m. Wallace Gorell (div.). BS, Columbia U., 1968; postgrad., U. Calif., Berkeley, 1977-78, Stanford U., 1978-79; student, Interuniv. Ctr., Tokyo. Prodr. Sta. KRON-TV, San Francisco, 1983-87; prodr. ind. films, 1990-92; prodr. CD-ROM Exec. Prodrs., 1994-96; contbg. editor New Asia Pacific Review, Westport, Conn., 1996-98. Journalist Nat. Interest, N.Y. Times, San Francisco Chronicle, San Jose Mercury News, Orlando Sentinel Author: Chinese Writing: An Introduction, 1975, Ghenghis Khan: A Memoir, 2003, Khubilai Khan: A Memoir, 2003, Gone with the Gator, 2001; project editor: A Sun-Herald Serial Novel, Sack of Baghdad and Other Stories of Muslims and Mongols, Pitless Measurement of History: China and Tibet. Nat. def. fgn. lang. fellow Columbia U., 1967; recipient Most Notable Book award Am. Libr. Assn., 1975. Mem. Author's Guild, Am. Soc. Journalists & Authors, Assn. For Asian Studies, Asia Soc. Avocations: sailing, swimming, fitness, cooking. Home: 1184 Green Oak Trail Port Charlotte FL 33948 E-mail: wuwolff@msn.com.

WOLFF, ELEANOR BLUNK, actress; b. Bklyn., July 10, 1931; d. Sol and Bessie (Schultz) Blunk; m. William Howard Wolff, June 19, 1955; children: Ellen Jill, Rebecca Louise. BA in Edn., Speech and Theatre, Bklyn. Coll., 1972, MS in Spl. Edn., 1975; postgrad., Adelphi U., 1980-81. Cert. tchr., N.Y. Fashion model Garment Ctr., N.Y.C., 1949—50; sec. to v.p. out-of-town/export sales Liebmann Breweries Inc., Bklyn., 1950—58; tchr. N.Y.C. Bd. Edn., Bklyn., 1971-76; sec. to dir. environ. programs, pub. affairs officers, speakers bur. project leader Power Authority State of N.Y., N.Y.C., 1976-85; tchr. Hewlett-Woodmere (N.Y.) Sch. Dist., 1986-89; instr. adult edn. County of Nassau, N.Y., 1986-97. Actress/model, N.Y.C., 1992—; mem. Love Creek Prodns. V.P. program devel. for youth ctr. Wavecrest Gardens Community Assn., Far Rockaway, N.Y., 1959-63; teen leader Far Rockaway Jewish Ctr. Youth Coun., 1965-68; pres. Parents Assn. P.S. 215Q, Far Rockaway, 1966-67; tutor N.Y. C. Bd. Edn. Sch. Vol. Program, Far Rockaway, 1969-71; chair civic affairs Dem. Club, Far Rockaway, 1961-63; vol. program presenter Child Abuse Prevention Svcs., Roslyn, N.Y., 2003-; committeewoman Dem. Ctrl. Com., Queens County, N.Y., 1963-64; v.p. membership, mem. constn. com. Nassau County Dem. Women's Caucus, 1988, 89; awards com. Bklyn. Coll., 1993-97, chair theatre arts affiliate, 1990-94, 2001-; mem. comm. adv. com. Hewlett-Woodmere Sch. Dist. 14, 1996-97; committeewoman Nassau County Dem. Party, 1998—; press/media steward vol. Goodwill Games, 1998. Named Mother of Yr. Congregation Shaaray Tefila, Far Rockaway, 1968; recipient Merit award Wavecrest Gardens Cmty. Assn., 1960, Theater Arts Trophy for disting. svc. Bklyn. Coll. Alumni, 1992. Mem.: SAG (awards nominating com. 2000—01), AFTRA, Actors Equity Assn., Alumni Assn. Bklyn. Coll. (life), Cmty. Garden Club of North Woodmere Park (corr. sec. 2001—03). Avocations: painting, piano, gardening. Office: 1344 Broadway Ste 110 Hewlett NY 11557-1353 Business E-Mail: eleanorwolff@cs.com.

WOLFF, GRACE SUSAN, pediatrician, pediatric cardiologist; b. Rome, N.Y. BS, Le Moyne Coll., 1961; MD, Med. Coll. Wis., 1965. Diplomate Am. Bd. Pediatrics, Pediatric Cardiology. Intern St. Vincents Hosp., N.Y.C., 1965-66; pediat. resident Babies Hosp.-Columbia Presbyn., 1967-69; fellow in pediat. cardiology Childrens Hosp., Boston, 1969-71; pediatrician, pediatric cardiologist U. Miami (Fla.) -Jackson Meml. Hosp., 1977—; chief divsn. pediat. cardiology, 1995—; prof. U. Miami. Mem. Am. Acad. Pediats., Am. Bd. Pediats., NASPE, Am. Acad. Pediat., Am. Coll. Cardiology, Am. Heart Assn. Office: U Miami-Jackson Meml Hosp PO Box 016960-R76 Miami FL 33101 Office Phone: 305-585-6683. E-mail: gwolff@med.miami.edu.

WOLFF, JEAN WALTON, writer; b. San Rafael, Calif., Apr. 12, 1955; d. Warren and Alice Eleanor (Broadbent) W. BA with honors, U. Calif., Santa Cruz, 1978; MPH, U. Calif., Berkeley, 1987. Sr. account rep. Preferred Health Network, Emeryville, Calif., 1989-90; writer U. Calif., Berkeley, 1990-91, Aptos, Calif., 1987—. Editor: Long Baptisms, 1997; author: (play) Love Radio; contbr. articles to San Francisco Chroicle, San Jose Mercurty News.contbr.; creator In Your Dreams greeting cards. Vol. Janus Recovery Ctr., Santa Cruz, 1979, Santa Cruz County Fair, 1991, In Celebration of Muse, Santa Cruz, 1998, 2001. Recipient Poetry award Santa Cruz County Fair, 1991, 93, 94; Regents fellow, 1986. Mem. Nat. Writers Union, Santa Cruz Art League. Avocations: painting, collages. Office: In Your Dreams Prodns PO Box 851 Capitola CA 95010

WOLFF, MARGARET LOUISE, lawyer; b. Rochester, N.Y., Jan. 27, 1955; d. Harvey A. and Miriam W. (Weinstein) W. BA cum laude, Mt. Holyoke Coll., 1976; JD, Case Western Res. U., 1979. Bar: N.Y. 1980. Assoc. Skadden, Arps, Slate, Meagher & Flom, N.Y.C., 1979-87, ptnr., 1987—. Editor Case Western Res. U. Law Rev. Home: 114 E 90th St New York NY 10128-1550 Office: Skadden Arps Slate Meagher & Flom 919 3rd Ave New York NY 10022-3902

WOLFF, SIDNEY CARNE, astronomer, observatory administrator; b. Sioux City, Iowa, June 6, 1941; d. George Albert and Ethel (Smith) Carne; m. Richard J. Wolff, Aug. 29, 1962 BA, Carleton Coll., 1962, DSc (hon.), 1985; PhD, U. Calif., Berkeley, 1966. Postgrad. research fellow Lick Obs, Santa Cruz, Calif., 1969; asst. astronomer U. Hawaii, Honolulu, 1967-71, assoc. astronomer, 1971-76; astronomer, assoc. dir. Inst. Astronomy, Honolulu, 1976-83, acting dir., 1983-84; dir. Kitt Peak Nat. Obs., Tucson, 1984-87, Nat. Optical Astronomy Observatories, 1987-2001; dir. Gemini Project Gemini 8-Meter Telescopes Project, 1992-94; astronomer, project scientist Large Synoptic Survey Telescope, 2001—. Pres. SOAR Inc., 1999-2003; project scientist Large Synoptic Survey Telescope, 2002—. Author: The A-Type Stars--Problems and Perspectives, 1983, (with others) Exploration of the Universe, 1987, Realm of the Universe, 1988, Frontiers of Astronomy, 1990, Voyages Through the Universe, 1996, 2nd edit., 2003, Voyages to the Planets, 1999, 2nd edit., 2003, Voyages to the Stars and Galaxies, 1999, 2nd edit., 2003; founding editor: Astronomy Edn. Rev., 2002; contbr. articles to profl. jours. Trustee Carleton Coll., 1989—, chair acad. affairs com., 1995—. Rsch. fellow Lick Obs. Santa Cruz, Calif., 1967; recipient Nat. Meritorious Svc. award NSF, 1994. Fellow Royal Astronical Soc.; mem. Astron. Soc. Pacific (pres. 1984-86, bd. dirs. 1979-85), Am. Astron. Soc. (coun. 1983-86, pres.-elect 1991, pres. 1992-94). Office: Nat Optical Astronomy Obs PO Box 26732 950 N Cherry Ave Tucson AZ 85719-4933

WOLFF, VIRGINIA EUWER, writer; b. Portland, Oreg., Aug. 25, 1937; d. Eugene Courtney and Florence Evelyn (Craven) Euwer; m. Art Wolff, July 19, 1959 (div. July 1976); children: Anthony Richard, Juliet Dianne. AB, Smith Coll., 1959; postgrad., Goddard Coll., Warren Wilson Coll., L.I. U., Portland State U., Lewis & Clark Coll. Cert. tchr., Oreg. Tchr. The Miquon Sch., Phila., 1968-72, The Fiedel Sch., Glen Cove, N.Y., 1972-75, Hood River Valley (Oreg.) H.S., 1976-86, Mt. Hood Acad., Govt. Camp, Oreg., 1986-98. 2d violinist Quartet con brio, Portland, 1989-94, Parnassius Quintet, Portland, 1996—. Author: Probably Still Nick Swansen, 1988, The Mozart Season, 1991, Make Lemonade, 1993, Bat 6, 1998, True Believer (Nat. Book award, Michael L. Printz honor, Pacific N.W. Booksellers Assn. award, Jane Addams Book honor, 2002), 2001, represented US, honor book, Internat. Board on Books for Young People, 2004. Violinist Mid-Columbia Sinfonietta, Hood River, 1976—, Oreg. Sinfonietta, Portland, 1988—, Parnassius Chamber Ensemble, 2000-. Recipient Young Adult Book award Internat. Reading Assn., 1989, PEN U.S.A. Ctr. West, 1989, Best Young Adult Book of Yr. award Mich. Libr. Assn., 1993, Child Study Children's Book award Bank Street Coll., 1994, Oreg. Book award Oreg. Lit. Arts, 1994, 2001, Jane Addams Children's Book award Jane Addams Peace Assn. and the Women's Internat. League for Peace and Freedom, 1999, Nat. Book award, 2001, Printz Honor Book award, 2002, Jane Addams Honor Plaque, 2002; named to Carnegie medal Shortlist, ALA, 2002. Mem. Soc. Children's Book Writers/Illustrators (Golden Kite 1994, 2002), Chamber Music Soc. Oreg. Avocations: chamber music, swimming, hiking, playing violin, gardening. Office: Curtis Brown Ltd care Elizabeth Harding 10 Astor Pl Fl 3 New York NY 10003-6982

WOLFGANG, BONNIE ARLENE, musician, bassoonist; b. Caribou, Maine, Sept. 29, 1944; d. Ralph Edison and Arlene Alta (Obetz) W.; m. Eugene Alexander Pridonoff, July 3, 1965 (div. Sept. 1977); children: George Randall, Anton Alexander, Stephan Eugene. MusB, Curtis Inst. Music, Phila., 1967. Soloist Phila. Orch., 1966; soloist with various orchs. U.S., Cen. Am., 1966-75; prin. bassoonist Phoenix Symphony, 1976—, with Woodwind Quintet, 1986—. Home: 9448 N 106th St Scottsdale AZ 85258-6056

WOLFINGER, AUDREY JANE, retired librarian; b. Mt. Penn, Pa., June 21, 1933; d. Harry Charles and Eva (Trace-Eckenroth) W. BS in Edn., Kutztown State Tchrs. Coll., 1955; tchrs. cert., Temple U., 1956; MS in Libr. Sci., Fla. State U., 1970. Mem. adminstrv. libr. staff Neshaminy Sch. Dist., Langhorne, Pa., 1955-84; libr., audio visual coord. Neshaminy Jr. High, Langhorne, 1955-76; libr. Neshaminy H.S., Langhorne, 1976-84; ret., 1984. Editor Wolfinger Family Newsletter, 1988—. Bd. dirs. Neshaminy Valley Music Theatre, Langhorne, 1964-65. Mem. Nat. Soc. DAR, Nat. Soc. Daus. of the Am. Colonists, Nat. Geneal. Soc., Geneal. Soc. Pa., Bucks County Geneal. Soc. (v.p. 1990-94, pres. 1994-98; resource ctr. dir. 1998, pres. protem 2001—), Kutztown U. Alumni Assn., Fla. State U. Alumni Assn. Avocations: piano baroque music, reading british mysteries, researching family history. Home: 14 Brook Dr Furlong PA 18925-1037 Office: Bucks County Geneal Soc PO Box 1092 Doylestown PA 18901-0020 E-mail: a.j.wolfinger@rcn.com.

WOLFKILL-HOFF, RAMONA LEA, music educator; d. Allan Meredith and Erika Wolfkill; m. Shannon Lloyd Hoff, Nov. 17, 2001. BA in Edn., Ctrl. Wash. U., Ellensburg, 1988; MA in Edn., Antioch U., Seattle, 2000. Cert. tchr. Wash. K-5th grade music educator Palo Verde Unified Sch. Dist., Blythe, Calif., 1990—91; kindergarten tchr. Heritage Christian Sch., Bothell, Wash., 1991—93. K-6th grade music educator Northshore Sch. Dist., Bothell, Wash., 1999—2001, kindergarten tchr. 2000—01; k-5th grade music educator Marysville Sch. Dist., Wash., 2001—. Mem.: NEA, Music Educators Nat. Conf., Wash. Edn. Assn. Office: Allen Creek Elem 6505 60th Dr NE Marysville WA 98270

WOLFMAN, BRUNETTA REID, education educator; b. Clarksdale, Miss., Sept. 4, 1931; d. Willie Orlando and Belle Victoria (Allen) Reid Griffin; m. Burton Wolfman, Oct. 4, 1952; children: Andrea, Jeffrey. BA, U. Calif., Berkeley, 1957, MA, 1968, PhD, 1991; DHL (hon.), Boston U., 1983, DP (hon.), Northeastern U., 1983; DL (hon.) Regis Coll., 1984, Stonehill Coll., 1985; DHL, Suffolk U., 1985; DET (hon.), Wentworth Inst., 1987; AA (hon.), Roxbury Community Coll., 1988. Asst. dean faculty Dartmouth Coll., Hanover, N.H., 1972-74; asst. v.p. acad. affairs U. Mass., Boston, 1974-76; acad. dean Wheelock Coll., Boston, 1976-78; cons. Arthur D. Little, Cambridge, Mass., 1978; dir. policy planning Dept. Edn. Boston, 1978-82; pres. Roxbury C.C., Boston, 1983-88, ACE sr. assoc., 1988-94, NAWE sr. assoc., 1994-98; assoc. v.p. acad. affairs George Washington U., Washington, 1994-96, assoc. v.p. and acting provost emeritus, 1996—. Mem. Accrediting Commn. on Edn. on Health Svcs. Administr.; pres. bd. dirs. Literacy Vols. of Capitol Region; mem. comment. com. bd., pub. rels. com. LVA, Inc.; bd. dirs. Am. Coun. Edn., Harvard Cmty. Health Plan. Author: Roles, 1983; contbr. articles to profl. jours. Mem. bd. overseers Wellesley Coll., 1981, Boston Symphony Orch.; trustee Mus. Fine Arts, Boston; mem. Coun. on Edn. for Pub. Health; chair Provincetown bd. Coun. on Aging, 1999—; bd. dirs. Boston-Fenway Program, 1977, Freedom House, Boston, 1983, Boston Pvt. Industry Coun., 1983; bd. dirs., co-chmn. NCCJ, Boston, 1983; bd. dirs. Elder Svcs. Cape Cod and the Islands, 2003. Named Wolfman Courtyard in their honor, Evergreen Ctr., 2000; recipient Freedom award, NAACP No.Calif., 1971, Amelia Earhart award, Women's Edn. and Indsl. Union, Boston, 1983; scholar Nat. Assn. Women in Edn. Mem. AAUW, Am. Sociol. Assn., Assn. Black Women in Higher Edn., Greater Boston C. of C. (edn. com. 1982), Sierra Club, Mass. Audubon Soc., Cosmos Club (Washington), Provincetown Art Assn. (sec. bd. trustees, mus. sch. com.), Alpha Kappa Alpha (Humanitarian award 1984), Phi Delta Kappa. Home: 657 Commercial St Provincetown MA 02657-1759 E-mail: bruburt2@comcast.net.

WOLFORD, KATHRYN FRANCES, religious organization executive; b. Reading, Pa., Dec. 12, 1957; d. Howard Francis Wolford and Katherine Eva (Auker) Carbaugh. BA in History, Gettysburg Coll., 1979; MA in Religious Studies, U. Chgo. Divinity Sch., 1980; MA in Pub. Policy, U. Chgo., 1981; PhD (hon.), Gettysburg Coll., 1995; PhD (hon.), Muhlenberg Coll., 2003. Country program rep. Ch. World Svc., Dominican Republic, 1983-85; regional rep. Nat. Coun. Chs., U.S.A., N.Y.C., 1985-90; program dir. for L.Am., Luth. World Relief, Balt., 1991-93, pres., 1993—. Named Md. Top 100 Women, 2002. Mem.: Amnesty Internat., Phi Beta Kappa. Democrat. Lutheran. Avocation: sailing

WOLFRAM, SUZANNE G. minister, educator, dean; b. Denver, May 13, 1950; d. Donald J. and Phyllis (Hoffman) Wolfram; m. David M. Larue, July 16, 1977; children: Justin Larue, Jennifer Larue. BA, U. Colo., Denver, 1970, MA, 1976; MA in Edn., U. Calif., Santa Barbara, 1973; diploma in Christian ministry, Belleview Bible Sem., Westminster, Colo., 2003. Ordained min. Pillar of Fire Ch., 1976; cert. tchr. Colo., Utah. Min. Pillar of Fire Ch., Denver, 1976—; elder, 2001—; dean Belleview Christian Coll., Westminster, 1995—, also bd. dirs. Mem. com. edn. Pillar of Fire Ch., Denver. Contbr. articles to profl. jours. and websites. Bd. dirs. Colo. Homeschool Arts, Denver, 2002—03. Mem.: Math. Assn. Am., Nat. Coun. Tchrs. Math. Republican. Avocation: piano. Office: Belleview Christian Coll 3455 W 83d Ave Westminster CO 80031 Office Phone: 303-427-5461. Business E-Mail: sgw@belleview-college.org.

WOLFSKILL, MARY MARGARET, archivist; b. Ft. Benning, Ga., June 10, 1946; d. Clifford Lawrence and Margaret W. BS in History, Radford Coll., 1968; MA in Mgmt., Ctrl. Mich. U., 1979; MS in Women's Studies, George Washington U., 1980. Cert. archivist. Reference libr. Manuscript Divsn. Libr. of Congress, Washington, 1968-70, archivist, prestdl. papers, 1970-71, archives specialist preparation sect., 1971-84, asst. head reference libr., 1984-88, head reference svcs., 1988—. Mem. Soc. Am. Archivists, Mid-Atlantic Regional Archives Conf. Democrat. Roman Catholic. Office: Libr Congress Manuscript Divsn Washington DC 20540-0001

WOLFSON, BARBARA LIBENSPERGER, guidance counselor; b. Mar. 9, 1949; BS in Elem. Edn., Trenton State Coll., 1971, M in Student Pers. Svcs. Guidance, 1983. Elem. sch. tchr. Trenton (N.J.) Bd. Edn., 1971-83, guidance counselor, 1983—. Chmn. Raritan Township (N.J.) Zoning Bd. 1988-92; mem. Raritan Township Recreation Bd., 1992-93, Cable TV Bd., 1993-94, County com., 1986-2000. Mem. Daus. Am. Revolution, Order of Ea. Star (Ashler chpt.), Trenton Edn Assn. (chief del.), Cedar Mar. Yacht Club. Avocations: skiing, sailing, animal rights advocate. Home: 15 Blackwell Rd Flemington NJ 08822-1955

WOLFSON, MARSHA, internist, nephrologist; b. Bklyn., Feb. 14, 1944; d. Murray and Rose (Cohen) W. Student, Boston U., 1961-63; BS, Fairleigh Dickinson U., 1965; MD, Med. Coll. Pa., 1970. Diplomate Am. Bd. Internal Medicine, Am. Bd. Nephrology. Staff physician NIH, Bethesda, Md., 1975-77; clinic instr. Georgetown U. Sch. Medicine, Washington, 1975-77; asst. prof. medicine Oreg. Health Scis. U., Portland, 1977-82; attending physician VA Hosp., Portland, 1983-87, chief nephrology, 1977-95; assoc. prof. medicine Oreg. Health Scis. U., Portland, 1982-95, clin. prof., 1995—;

med. dir. nutrition support svc. VA Hosp., Portland, 1987-95; med. dir. global clin. affairs Baxter Healthcare Corp., McGaw Park, Ill., 1995—2003; sr. med. dir. Nephrology Aremia Therapeutic Area U.S. Med. Affairs, Amgen Inc., 2003—. Cons. in field. Co-author: The Science and Practice of Clinical Medicine, 1980, Clinical Dialysis, 1984, 90, Current Nephrology, 1984, Progress in Clinical Kidney Disease and Hypertension, 1985, Dialysis Therapy Handbook, 1986, Clinical and Physiological Applications of Vitamin B6, 1986, Acute Renal Failure: Diagnosis, Treatment, and Prevention, 1989; contbr. numerous articles to profl. jours. Bd. dirs. Kidney Assn. Oreg., Portland. Lt. comdr. USPHS, 1975-77. Mem. ACP, Women in Nephrology (pres. 1988), Multnomah County Med. Soc., Oreg. Med. Assn., Am. Soc. Parenteral and Enteral Nutrition, Am. Soc. Artificial Internal Organs, Am. Soc. Clin. Nutrition, Am. Inst. Nutrition, Am. Fedn. for Clin. Rsch., Internat. Soc. Nephrology, Am. Soc. Nephrology, Alpha Omega Alpha. Office: Amgen Inc One Amgen Dr Mailstop 27 5 C Thousand Oaks CA 91320

WOLFZAHN, ANNABELLE FORSMITH, psychologist; b. N.Y.C., Jan. 23, 1932; d. Paul Phillip and Addie (Samuelson) Forsmith; m. Herbert Eytan Wolfzahn, Feb. 4, 1956; children: Risa, Felice, Orna. BA, Hunter Coll., 1953; MA in Counseling Psychology, Manhattan Coll., 1971; PhD in Clin. and Community Psychology, Union Inst., 1979. Cert. sch. psychologist, sch. counselor, N.Y. Counselor for handicapped children Bklyn. Tuberculosis Assn., 1952; social worker Child Placement Svcs., 1953-58; fellow in social and community psychiatry Albert Einstein Coll. Medicine, 1977-79; intern Bronx (N.Y.) Devel. Svcs., 1977-79; intern head trauma program Rusk Inst., NYU Med. Ctr., 1979; psychologist Creedmore Psychiat. Ctr., 1980-82, Harlem Valley Psychiat. Ctr., 1982-87; clin. coord. of group homes Green Chimneys Children's Svcs., 1987-88; with Ulpan Akiva and Assaf Harofeh Med. Ctr., Tel Aviv U., Israel, 1988-89; nursing home cons., psychotherapist Bklyn. Ctr. for Psychotherapy, 1989-91; pres., coord. Westchester chpt. Vols. for Israel, 1992—; pres. Westchester region Zionist Orgn. Am., 2003—; freelance psychologist, counselor, 1994—; retired, 2001—. Mem. workshops in field; mem. staff Mother-Child Home Program of White Plains, N.Y., 1975-76; mem. curriculum com. Learning in Retirement Iona Coll. (LIRIC), 1994—; counselor with multiple sclerosis victims and their families. Group shows include Wuchinich Gallery, Mt. Kisco Libr., 1998, Somers Gallery, Somers Libr., 1998, Greenberg Gallery, Greenberg Libr., 1998, Gallery at New Rochelle Libr., 1998, Woods Gallery, Burke Ctr., White Plains, N.Y., 1998, Levine Art Gallery, Putnam Arts coun., 1998, Mid-Rockland Arts Festival, 1998, The Bendheim Performing Arts Ctr., 1999, Reflection of Westchester Exhibit, 1999, Art on Main St., 1999, Open Studios, 2000, Westchester Arts Coun., 2000, Oresman Art Exhibit, Oresman Gallery, Larchmont, N.Y., 2002, Visions of Israel, 2003, Westchester Land Trust, 2004, others; contbr. articles to profl. jours. Vol. Vols. for Israel, 1988, 91 92, 2003—, founder, pres., coord. Westchester Region chpt., 1993—; mem. archaeol. dig Bet Shaan, Israel; arts amb. White Plains Arts Coun., 2000—; active Westchester Arts Coun., SHARE Project. Recipient Vol. award White Plains Hosp., 1974-76, John C. Klein Meml. Writing award Newspaper Inst. Am., 1965; Alvin Johnson scholar, 1953. Mem. APA (life), Westchester County Psychol. Assn., N.Y. Neuropsychology Assn., Am. Mental Health Affiliates of Israel, N.Y. Acad. Scin. Nat. Coun. Jewish Women Am. Orthopsychiat. Assn. Avocations: oil painting, lap swimming, writing, travel, photography. Home: 10 Hillerest Springdale Rd Scarsdale NY 10583-7329

WOLLERSHEIM, JANET PUCCINELLI, psychology educator; b. Anaconda, Mont., July 24, 1936; d. Nello J. and Inez Marie (Ungaretti) Puccinelli; m. David E. Wollersheim, Aug. 1, 1959 (div. June 1972); children: Danette Marie, Tod Neil; m. Daniel J. Smith, July 17, 1976. AB, Gonzaga U., 1958; MA, St. Louis U., 1960; PhD, U. Ill., 1968. Lic. psychologist, Mont. Asst. prof. psychology, asst. dir. testing/counseling ctr. U. Mo., 1968-71; prof. psychology U. Mont., Missoula, 1971—, dir. clin. psychology, 1980-87; chair Mont. Bd. Psychologists, 1977-78; cons. Mont. State Prison, 1971-85, Trapper Creek Job Corps, 1973—2003; pvt. practice Missoula, 1971—. Author numerous rsch. articles. Bd. dirs. Crisis Ctr., Missoula, 1972-73; mem. profl. adv. bd. Head Start, Missoula, 1972-79. Recipient Disting. scholar award U. Mont., 1991. Fellow Am. Psychol. Assn. (bd. dirs. div. clin. psychology 1990-92); mem. Rocky Mountain Psychol. Assn. (pres. 1983-84), Nat. Coun. Univ. Dirs. Clin. Psychology (bd. dirs. 1982-88). Home and Office: 105 Greenwood Ln Missoula MT 59803-2401 Office Phone: 406-543-6946. E-mail: jpwoller2000@yahoo.com.

WOLOVITZ, VIVIAN TOBY, fine arts educator, artist; b. Phila., Dec. 24, 1950; d. Harry and Ann Muriel (Blank) W.; m. Michael Slotznick, Feb. 23, 1986; children: Molly, William. BFA, Tyler Sch. of Art, 1972; MFA, Md. Inst. Coll. of Art, 1978. Vis. asst. prof., artist-in-residence Grand Valley State Coll., Allendale, Mich., 1978-79; assoc. prof. fine arts Moore Coll. of Art and Design, Phila., 1980—. Numerous acad. related activities Moore Coll. of Art, 1980—, chair dept. fine arts, 1996-2001. Exhibited in solo and groups shows nat. and abroad including Stephen Haller Gallery, N.Y.C., Albers Gallery, Memphis, Jessica Berwind Gallery, Phila., Balchik, Bulgaria; vis. artist U. Guanajuato, Mexico. Recipient Ind. Artist grant Pa. Coun. for Arts, 1995. Avocation: traveling to foreign countries. Home: 1020 Little Shiloh Rd West Chester PA 19382-7664 Office: Moore Coll Art and Design 20th And Race St Philadelphia PA 19103-1178

WOLPE, MARCY SHEAR, artist, art educator; b. Iowa City, Feb. 14, 1949; d. Louis John and Selma (Lang) Shear; m. Robert Neil Wolpe, Oct. 1, 1971. BA in Speech Pathology, U. Md., 1970; postgrad. in speech pathology, U. Pitts., 1972; MFA in Printmaking, Design, George Washington U., 1982. Part-time lectr. dept. art George Washington U., Washington, 1981-83; artist, painter, printmaker, 1982—; part-time faculty dept. art Montgomery Coll., Rockville, Md., 1984; workshop instr. Acad. Arts, Easton, Md., 1992; part-time instr. dept. art Salisbury (Md.) State U., 1993-96. V.p. bd. dirs. Washington Printmakers' Gallery, 1987-89; editor WPG News, Washington, 1992-96. One-woman shows include Acad. Arts, Easton, Md., 1991; group exhbns. include George Washington U., 1982, Dimock Gallery, Washington, 1982, Washington Women's Arts Ctr., 1982, 83, 84, Va. Intermont Coll., Bristol, Va., 1983, Fairfax County Coun. Arts, Arlington, Va., 1983, Springville (Utah) Mus. Art, 1983, 86, Acad. Artists' Soc., Springfield, Mass., 1984, 86, Arts Club Washington, 1984, 85, Nat. Arts Club, N.Y., 1984, 86, A.A.O. Gallery, Buffalo, 1984, 85, 87, North Miami (Fla.) Mus. and Art Ctr., 1984, Yale U., 1984, Auburn (Ill.) Arts Assn., 1985, Hunterdon Art Ctr., Clinton, N.J., 1985, Rose Art Mus., Waltham, Mass., 1985, Montpelier Cultural Arts Ctr., Laurel, Md., 1985, Artists' Welfare Fund, Inc., N.Y.C., 1986, Weinberg Ctr. for Arts, Frederick, Md., 1986, Mt. St. Mary's Coll. Fine Arts Gallery, Santa Monica, Calif. 1986, Galerie Triangle, Washington, 1986, Dulin Gallery Art, Knoxville, Tenn., 1986, Columbia Fine Arts Gallery and Mus. Art and Arch., 1986, Abington Art Ctr., Jenkintown, Pa., 1986, Springville (Utah) Mus. Art, 1987, Art Barn, Washington, 1987, Silvermine Guild Galleries, New Canaan, Conn., 1987, 88, Montpelier Cultural Arts Ctr., 1987, Midtown Gallery, Washington, 1987, Germanow Gallery, Rochester, N.Y., 1987, Washington Printmakers' Gallery, 1987, 89, Parkersburg (W.Va.) Art Ctr., 1988, Knoxville Mus. Art, 1988, Hunterdon Art Ctr., Clinton, N.J. 1988, Trenton (N.J.) State Coll., 1988, Internat. Monetary Fund Art Soc. Gallery, Washington, 1988, Boston Printmakers', Brockton, Mass., 1988, Woodmere Art Mus., Phila., 1988, Washington Printmakers' Gallery, Washington, 1992, The Pushkin Mus., Moscow, 1992, Miriam Periman Gallery, Chgo., 1992, Atrium Gallery, Salisbury, Md., 1993, Balcony Gallery, Berlin, Md., 1993, Trenton State Coll., 1993, Erector Sq. Gallery, 1994, The Baltimore Life Gallery, 1995, Hunterdon Art Ctr., 1996, Nabisco Headquarters, East Hanover, N.J., 1997, Yale U., 1997, various others. Bd. dirs. Am. Cancer

Soc., Silver Spring, Md., 1976-80. Mem. Soc. Am. Graphic Artists, Md. Printmakers, Boston Printmakers, Phila. Print Club. Avocations: writing, walking. Office: 8 Ocean E Marathon FL 33050-2508 E-mail: mswolpe@aol.com.

WOLPERT-DEFILIPPES, MARY K. science administrator; BS in Pharmacy cum laude, Creighton U., 1963; MS in Pharmacology, U. Mich., 1966, PhD in Pharmacology, 1969; postdoctoral student, Yale U., 1969—. Rsch. assoc. in pharmacology Yale U., New Haven, 1970-71; staff fellow lab. chem. pharmacology NIH, Bethesda, Md., 1971-75, pharmacologist drug evaluation br., 1976-81, supervisory pharmacologist drug evaluation br., 1981-82, dep. chief drug evaluation br., 1982-85, pharmacologist Office of Assoc. Dir., 1985-88, program dir. Grants and Contracts Ops. Br., 1988-97, chief Grants and Contracts Ops. Br., 1997—. Contbr. articles to profl. jours.; patentee in field. Mem. Gamma Pi Epsilon, Rho Chi. Office: Nat Cancer Inst Divsn Cancer Treatment and Diagnosis Rm 8153 Exec Pla N Bethesda MD 20892

WOLPERT RICHARD, CHAVA, artist; b. Frankfurt, Germany, Feb. 26, 1933; arrived in Palestine, 1934,arrived in U.S., 1958; d. Ludwig Y. and Else (Ahrens) Wolpert; m. Henry A. Richard, 1959 (dec. Jan. 1971). Student, Bezalel Acad. Arts and Crafts, Jerusalem, 1954-56. Artist-in-residence The Jewish Mus., N.Y.C., 1958—88. Painter, designer/creator of contemporary style ceremonial Judaica such as candelabra, Passover sets, Torah ornaments, decorative Judaica in enamel, silver, other metals, glass, porcelain, wood, acrylics, fabrics and oil painting; represented in 10 mus. collections in U.S., Australia, Europe, Israel. Pvt. Israeli Army, 1951—53. Recipient 2 Merit awards Interfaith Forum on Religion, Art and Arch., 1980, 83, Jurors' Choice award Liturgical Art Guild, 1991, Best in Judaica award Liturgical Art Guild, 1997. Mem. Judaic Art Guild, Liturgical Art Guild. Avocation: reflexology.

WOLSIFFER, PATRICIA RAE, retired insurance company executive; b. Indpls., Aug. 15, 1933; d. Charles L. and Dorothy M. (Smith) Bohlsen; m. Edward C. Wolsiffer, Oct. 5, 1956; children: John M., Anderson, Sherry L. Anderson Cooney, Edward J. Wolsiffer. Student, Ind. Central U., 1974-75. Various secretarial positions, 1964-71; with Blue Cross/Blue Shield Ind. (Associated Ins. Cos., Inc.), Indpls., 1971-88, supr. personnel, 1973-76, exec. asst. to pres., 1976-79, corp. sec., 1979-85, exec. asst. to chmn. bd., chief exec. officer, 1985-88; ret. Vol. Hancock Meml. Hosp. Guild. Mem.: Daus. of the Nile, Order Eastern Star. Republican. Home: 5550 E 100 N Greenfield IN 46140-9445 Office: 120 Monument Cir Indianapolis IN 46204-4906

WOLTER, VIRGINIA LYNN, librarian; b. Flint, Mich., Nov. 5, 1962; d. James Herbert and Elizabeth Jane (Yeatter) W. BA in Anthropology, U. Mich., Flint, 1988; M Info. and Libr. Studies, U. Mich., Ann Arbor, 1990. Libr./vol. Art Danforth Coop Libr., Ann Arbor, 1990; ref. libr. Toledo-Lucas County Pub. Libr., Toledo, 1991—. Mem. Database for Libr. Sys. Toledo, 1995—; mem. People for the Am. Way, 1995—, Rails to Trails Conservation, 1996—. Mem. ACLU, Nature Conservancy, Soc. for Creative Anachronisms, Ohio Libr. Coun. (intellectual freedom com. 1992-94). Unitarian Universalist. Avocations: needlework, illumination, reading. Office: Toledo-Lucas Cty Pub Libr West Toledo Branch 1320 W Sylvania Ave Toledo OH 43613-3073

WOLTZ, MARY LYNN MONACO, management consultant; b. Columbus, Ohio, Mar. 11, 1951; d. Frank Guy and Mary Catherine (Montenaro) Monaco, m. James David Woltz, June 19, 1971; children: Joseph David, Bethany Anne. Student, Ohio State U., 1969-71. Tchr. Career Acad., Columbus, Ohio, 1971-72; mgr. Battelle Meml. Inst., Columbus, Ohio, 1973—. Pub. spkr. schs., bus., clubs. and profl. orgns., Ohio, 1981; dir. mktg. The General's Books. Amb. Assn. World Affairs, Columbus, 1968; co-chmn. United Way, Columbus, 1976; committeewoman Ohio Crime Prevention Assn., Columbus, 1988; mem. founding bd. Ohio Crime Prevention Found., Columbus, 1989—; founding mem., pres. Parents Support Group, 1990-94; cons. Lao Mai Assn., Columbus, 1981-85. Named Ohio Crime Practitioner of the Yr., 1988; recipient Nat. Crime Prevention award Nat. Crime Prevention Coalition, Washington, 1988, Spotlight award Nat. Crime Prevention Coalition and Am. Dist. Telegraph, 1993. Mem. Am. Soc. Indsl. Security (sec. 1992-93, mem. exec. bd. 1993-94). Roman Catholic. Avocations: singing, exercise physiology. Office: Battelle Meml Inst 505 King Ave Columbus OH 43201-2681

WOMMACK, JANICE MARIE, insurance company executive; b. Springfield, Mo., Aug. 5, 1939; d. Karl William and Mary Ida (Cotter) Engelking; m. Lewis Rick Stephenson, Oct. 23, 1964 (div. 1988); children: Lara G. Stephenson Cunningham, Lewis Arn; m. Francis L. Wommack, Dec. 26, 1988; stepchild, Jon Wommack. Dental asst. Dr. Pete Emily, Denver, 1960-64; claims sec. State Farm Mutual Auto Ins. Co., Tulsa, 1965-71, exec. sec. Springfield, 1971-73; with Am. Nat. Property & Casualty Co., Springfield, 1973—, liability supr., 1982-88, dir. divisional support, 1988-99, ret., 1999, part-time, 1999—. Mem. Springfield Claims Assn., Springfield C. of C. (pres. women's div. 1985), Greater Ozark Bus. and Profl. Women's Assn. (pres. elect. 1988—), Alliance, St. John's Health Styles. Avocations: reading, travel, walking. Home: 78 Drury Ln Blue Eye MO 65611-7209 Office: Am Nat Property & Casualty 1949 E Sunshine St Springfield MO 65899-0001 Home: Winter 10719 WhiteHNN Rd Sun City AZ 85351-1536

WON, CYNTHIA JANE, secondary school educator; b. San Francisco, Apr. 6, 1942; d. John and Alice Mar Won. BA French, San Francisco State U, 1967; MA in Mandarin, San Francisco State U., 1969; EDD Multicultural Edn., U. San Francisco, 1987. Tchr. Galileo High Sch., San Francisco, 1969—80, Lowell High Sch., 1980—81, Washington High Sch., 1981—; mem. SATII Mandarin pioneer com. Ednl. Testing Svc., 1991—92. Recipient Singapore Chinese Am. Heritage award, 1973, French award, Que., Can., 1985; Taiwan Mandarin scholar, 1978, Rockefeller scholar, Beijing Long Inst., Beijing, 1988, Mandarin scholar, U. Mar., 1992, Beijing Lang. Inst., 1993. Office: George Washington High Sch 600 32d Ave San Francisco CA 94121

WONG, CARRIE, public relations executive; BS in Cellular & Molecular Biology, U. Wash. Ptnr. Niehaus Ryan Wong, South San Francisco. Avocation: bug collecting. Office: 601 Gateway Blvd Ste 900 South San Francisco CA 94080-7006

WONG, DIANA SHUI IU, artist; Student, Chinese U., Hong Kong; BA, Acad. Fine Arts, Rome; postgrad., Royal Sch. Arts, London. Artist, Santa Monica, Calif., 1960—. Guest on CNBC-TV News Hong Kong, 1997. One-women shows include Galleria Fontanella, Rome, 1960, City Hall Gallery, Hong Kong, 1962, Chatham Galleries, Kowloon, Hong Kong, 1964, Nat. Mus. History, Taipei, Taiwan, 1969, L.A. Mission Coll., San Fernando, Calif, 1976, M.M. Shinno Gallery, L.A., 1977, 82, 85-87, Pacific Asia Mus., Pasadena, Calif, 1983, Silpakom U. Art Gallery, Bangkok, 1987, Alison Fine Arts Gallery, 1988, Gallery Q # 1, Tokyo, 1989, Filippin Gallery, Milan, 1992, LA Artcore Gallery, L.A., 1992, Seibu Art Gallery, Hong Kong, 1992, Merging One Gallery, Santa Monica, Calif., 1993, 96, Nat. Gallery, Beijing, 1994, Galleria Spazio Prospectiva, Milan, 1995, Trigram Gallery, Hong Kong, 1997, Robert V. Fullerton Art Mus., San Bernardino, Calif., 1997, Galleria Mazzocchi, Parama, Italy, 1998, L.A.A. Artcore Brewery, 1999, 456 Gallery, N.Y.C., 2000; exhibited in group shows includeBrand Libr. Art Galleries, Glendale, Calif., 1976, UCLA Group Invitational, 1978, L.A. County Mus. Art, 1982, LA Artcore Gallery, 1984, U. Hilo, Hawaii, 1986, Howard Salon, Taiwan, 1987, LA Artcore, Glendale, 1989, Korean Cultural Svcs., L.A., 1989, Johnson-Humrick House Mus.,

Ohio, 1990, Art LA, L.A., 1992, LaLit Kala Acad., New Dehli, 1996, David Lawrence Gallery, Beverly Hills, Calif., 1997, Alisan Fine Arts, Hong Kong, 1997, Pyong Tack (Korea) Internat. Art Festival, 1997, 98, Pao Galleries, Hong Kong, 1997, Gallery of the Rim, San Francisco, 1997, L.A. Internat. Art Festival, 1997, Merging One Gallery, Santa Monica, 1998, Gallery Blu, 1998, RTKL, Architects Gallery, L.A., 1998, Space One Gallery, Izu, Japan, 2001, Hong Kong Cultural Ctr., 2002; represented in permanent collections Hong Kong Mus. Art, The Walker Art Collection, others. Recipient Black and White Composition award, Internat. Young Artists Competition, Gubbio, Italy, 1960, 6th Annual Juried Show, 3rd prize, N.J., 1970, 66th Nat. Orange Festival, 2nd place, San Bernardino, 1981. Mem. Am. I-Ching Soc. (pres.), Chinese Hist. Soc. So. Calif. (life). Home and Office: 1518 15th St Santa Monica CA 90404-3305

WONG, FAYE LING, public health service officer; BS in Dietetics, U. Wash., 1972; MPH, U. Calif.-Berkeley, 1973. Registered dietitian, lic. Ga. Relief dietary supr. Va. Mason Hosp., Seattle, 1968—72; chief Bur. of Nutrition Coconino County Dept. Pub. Health, Flagstaff, Ariz., 1974—76; nutrition cons. Office of Cmty. Health Svcs., Oreg. State Health Divsn., Portland, 1976—81; dir. Sentinel Site project Detroit Health Dept., 1981—83; pub. health nutritionist field svcs. br. Ctr. for Health Promotion and Edn. CDC, Atlanta, 1983—89, program analyst Ctr. for Chronic Disease Prevention and Health Promotion, 1988—89, chief field svcs. br. divsn. nutrition, 1989—92, chief program ops., program svcs. br., 1992—94, asst. chief divsn. cancer prevention and control, 1994—95, asst. chief policy and devel., 1995—96, assoc. dir. diabetes edn., dir. nat. diabetes edn. program, 1996—2000, dir. Youth Media Campaign, 2001—. Contbr. numerous articles, abstracts to profl. jours., to resource manuals. Recipient Award for Disting. Svc., Dept. Health and Human Svcs., 2000, Questar Internat. award, 2000, Thoth award., Pub. Rels. Assn. Am., 2000, Aesculapius Awards for Excellence, Nat. Diabetes Edn. Program, 1999, 1998, Award for Excellence in recognition of outstanding leaderhsip and dedicated svc., Assn. of State and Territorial Pub. Health Nutrition Dirs., 1991. Mem.: Am. Diabetes Assn. (mem. health profls. sect. 1996—), Am. Assn. Diabetes Educators (mem. pub. health specialty practice group 1996—), Am. Dietetic Assn. (mem. nominating com. 1999—, mem. diabetes care and edn. practice group 1996—), APHA (pres. 2001—, co-chair task force on aging 2001—, chair, exec. dir. search com. 2001—, chair editl. bd. Am. Jour. Pub. Health 1997—2000, mem. exec. bd. pub. policy rev. and devel. com. 1995—, mem. food and nutrition sect. 1975—, Apple award 1991). Office: CDC 1081 N Hills Dr Decatur GA 30033

WONG, YOKE CHENG, food scientist, musician; b. Seremban, Malaysia, Dec. 5, 1971; arrived in U.S., 1990; d. Nien Long Wong and Kin Soon Kok; m. Qian Zhang, Dec. 22, 1995; children: Emily Wong Zhang, Daniel Wong Zhong. BS, Kans. State U., 1993, MS, 1995. Rsch. asst. Kans. State U., Manhattan, 1994—95; quality assurance profl. Sunshine Biscuit, Kansas City, Kans., 1995—96; food technologist Ajinomoto, Kuala Lumpur, Malaysia, 1997; project leader ConAgra Frozen Foods, Omaha, 1998—2001, Season of Hope, 2002. Composer: (CD) The Fountain of Life, 2000. Mem.: Music Tchr. Nat. Assn. Home: 15711 Lafayette Ave Omaha NE 68118 E-mail: yokejohn@hotmail.com.

WONG-STAAL, FLOSSIE, geneticist, medical educator; BA, UCLA, 1968, PhD, 1972. Tchg. asst. UCLA, 1969-70, rsch. asst., 1970-72; post-doctoral fellow U. Calif., San Diego, 1972-73; Fogarty fellow Nat. Cancer Inst., Bethesda, Md., 1973-75, vis. assoc., 1975-76, cancer expert, 1976-78, sr. investigator, 1978-81, chief molecular genetics of hematopoietic cells sect., 1982-89; Florence Seeley Riford chair in AIDS rsch., prof. medicine U. Calif. San Diego, La Jolla, 1990—. Vis. prof. Inst. Gen. Pathology, First U. Rome, Italy, 1985. Mem. editl. bd. Gene Analysis Techniques, 1984—, Cancer Letters, 1984-94, Leukemia, 1987—, Cancer Rsch., 1987, AIDS Rsch. and Human Retroviruses (sect. editor), 1987—, DNA and Cell Biology (sect. editor), 1987—, Microbial Pathogenesis, 1987-90, AIDS: An Internat. Jour., 1987—, Internat. Jour. Acquired Immunodeficiency Syndrome, 1988—, Oncogene, 1988—, Jour. Virology, 1990—; contbr. articles to profl. jours. Recipient Outstanding Sci. award Chinese Med. and Health Assn., 1987, The Excellence 2000 award U.S. Pan Asian Am. C. of C. and the Orgn. of Chinese Am. Women, 1991. Mem. Am. Soc. for Virology (charter), Phi Beta Kappa. Office: U Calif San Diego Dept Med 0665 9500 Gilman Dr La Jolla CA 92093-5003

WONSEWITZ, POM CHA, artist, horticulturist; b. Hong-Sung, Korea, June 15, 1944; arrived in U.S., 1971; d. Moo-Youg Pyon and Yun-Soon Kim; m. Raymond Dwight Wonsewitz, July 16, 1971; children: Paul E., David R. AA, Yuba Coll., 1972; BA cum laude, Cameron U., 1996. Mgr. Flowerama Inc., Palmer, Alaska, 1984—87; instr. arts and crafts Ft. Sill (Okla.) Mil. Installation, 1990—91; substitute tchr. Lawton (Okla.) Pub. Schs., 1999—2000; assn. mgr. Homeland Corp., Oklahoma City, 2000—02; freelance artist PC1Sewitz Art Studio, Lawton, 2002—. One-woman shows include Carnegie Libr. Hall, Lawton, 1994, Pride Gallery, 1995, Higher Edn. Ctr., Ducan, Okla., 1996. Chair, vice chair ARC, Lawton-Ft. Sill, 1981—84; chair ARC Dentac, Ft. Sill, 1982—83; vice chair ARC Reynold Army Hosp., Ft. Sill, 1981—82; vol. floral designer Hospice of Lawton Area, 1998—99; vol. ESL instr. Lawton-Ft. Sill Outreach, 1983—84. Nominee First Lady of Lawton, 1983; recipient Molly Pitcher award, Ft. Sill Mil., 1983; scholar, McMahon Found., 1991, 1992, 1993, Leslie Powell Found., 1994—95. Mem.: Sierra Pastel Soc. Home and Office: PC1Sewitz Arts 15 SW 50th St Lawton OK 73505 E-mail: pomcha@swb.net.

WOO, CATHY M. artist; b. Oakland, Calif., May 20, 1949; d. Robert F. and Mary Barber; m. Daniel D. Woo, Apr. 25, 1971; children: Elliott S., Travis D. BA in Psychology, U. Calif., Berkeley, 1971; JD, Seattle U., 1978. Exhibited in group shows at Kindred Gallery, Seattle, 1982, Mercer Island Visual Arts League, Wash., 1982, Edmonds Arts Festival, 1982, 6th Ann. Eastside Assn. Fine Arts Show, Peter Kirk Gallery, Kirkland, Wash., 1982 (3rd prize award), 42nd Ann. Exhbn. Northwest Watercolors, Bellevue Art Mus., Wash., 1982, Edmonds Art Festival, 1983, 7th Ann. Eastside Assn. Fine Arts Show, Peter Kirk Gallery, 1983, Fergus-Jean Gallery, Harbor Springs, Mich., 1983, exhibitions include 43rd Ann. Exhbn. Northwest Watercolors, Bellevue Art Mus., Wash., 1983, exhibited in group shows at Northwest Watercolor Soc. and Safeco Ins. Co., Seattle, 1984, Puget Sound Country Show, Louise Matzke Gallery, 1984, 8th Ann. Eastside Assn. Fine Arts Show, Peter Kirk Gallery, Kirkland, Wash., 1984 (Hon. Mention), Edmonds Art Festival, Wash., 1984 (cash prize award), Fergus-Jean Gallery, Harbor Springs, Mich., 1984, Mont. Inst. Arts, 1984 (Best of Show awar), exhibitions include 44th Ann. Exhbn. Northwest Watercolors, Bellevue Art Mus., Wash., 1984 (First prize best transparent watercolor), exhibited in group shows at Women Painters of Wash., Seattle, 1985, exhibitions include Pacific Marine Ins. Corp., 1985, exhibited in group shows at Allied Arts Group Show, 1985, Sander Gallery, 1985, Gallery Mack, 1985, 9th Ann. Eastside Assn. Fine Arts Show, Peter Kirk Gallery, Kirkland, Wash., 1985, exhibitions include 45th Ann. Exhbn. Northwest Watercolors, Bellevue Art Mus., Wash., 1985, 46th Ann. Exhbn. Northwest Watercolors, Bellevue Art Mus., 1987, Woodin Gallery and Chateau Ste. Michelle Winery, Woodinville, Wash., 1987, exhibited in group shows at Pacific Northwest Art Exposition, Seattle, 1987, one-woman shows include Northwest Art Exchg., Gaches Mansion, La Connor, Wash., 1987, exhibitions include 29th Ann. Puget Sound Area Exhbn., Frye Art Mus., Seattle, 1987, exhibited in group shows at Matzke-Runnings Gallery, 1987, 11th Ann. Eastside Assn. Fine Arts Show, Gallery Dubois, Bellevue, 1987, Mercer Island Visual Arts League, Wash., 1987 (Hon. Mention), 2d Pacific Northwest Art Exposition, Seattle, 1987, exhibitions include 47th Ann. Exhbn. Northwest Watercolors, Bellevue Art Mus., Wash., 1987, exhibited in group shows at Puget Sound Country Show, Stillwater Gallery, Inc., Seattle, 1987, exhibitions include Northwest Watercolor Soc. 51st Ann. Open Exhbn., Howard/Mandville Gallery, Kirkland, 1991 (Seattle Art/Schminchke award), exhibited in group shows at Peter Kirk Gallery, 1993 (Northwest Watercolor Soc. award), Chuck Webster 1st Ann. Invitational Art Show, Kirkland, 1995, Backstreet Frame and Art, Bellevue, 1995 (Best of Show award), Waterworks 95, Tolles Gallery, Mercer Island, 1995, exhibitions include A Celebration of Watercolor, Meydenbauer Conv. Ctr., Bellevue, 1996, exhibited in group shows at Images of Women, ArtsWest Gallery, Seattle, 1996, Heartworks, Whatcom Mus. of History and Art, Bellingham, Wash., 1996, Soundings South: An Exploration of Water Media on Paper, Wash. Ctr. Performing Arts, Olympia, 1996, Reaching for the Light, Blue Horse Gallery, Bellingham, 1996, Moss Bay Gallery, Kirkland, 1996, exhibitions include Northwest Watercolor Soc. 56th Ann. Open Exhbn., Howard/Mandville Gallery, 1996 (Dakota Art Store Merchandise award), exhibited in group shows at Waterworks 96, Tolles Gallery, Mercer Island, 1996 (Northwest Watercolor Soc. merit award), exhibitions include Nat. Watercolor Soc. 76th Ann. Exhbn., Muckenthaler Cultural Ctr., Fullerton, Calif., 1996, A Celebration of Watercolor, Maydenbauer Conv. Ctr., Bellevue, 1997, exhibited in group shows at Heartworks, Whatcom Mus. History and Art, Bellingham, 1997, Moss Bay Gallery, Kirkland, 1997, Waterworks 97, Tolles Gallery, Mercer Island, 1997 (Northwest Watercolor Soc. merit award), exhibitions include Intimate Views of Women, Janet Laurel-A Woman's Gallery, Seattle, 1998, exhibited in group shows at Heartworks, Whatcom Mus. History and Art, Bellingham, 1998, exhibitions include Watercolor Messages, Meydenbauer Conv. Ctr., Bellevue, 1998, exhibited in group shows at Waterworks 98, Tolles Gallery, Mercer Island, 1998 (NBBJ Architects award), Mus. Northwest Art Auction 99, La Conner, 1999, one-woman shows include Alki Bathhouse Art Studio, Seattle, 1999, exhibited in group shows at Fresh Air, Issaquah Gallery, Wash., 1999 (Eastside Assn. Fine Arts award), Mus. Northwest Art Auction 2000, La Conner, 2000, Millennium Images, Wash. State Conv. & Trade Ctr., Seattle, 2000, Beyond Beginnings, Edmonds C.C. Art Gallery, Lynnwood, Wash., 2000, exhibitions include Evergreen State Coll., Olympia, Wash., 2000 (F&W Pub. Merchandise award), exhibited in group shows at Frye Art Mus., Seattle, 2000, exhibitions include Nat. Watercolor Soc. 80th Ann. Exhbn., Muckenthaler Cultural Ctr., Fullerton, 2000 (Purchase award, 2000), exhibited in group shows at Mus. Northwest Art Auction 2001, La Connor, 2001, Starbucks Coffee House on Alki, Seattle, 2001, The Runnings Gallery, 2001, exhibitions include Nat. Watercolor Soc. 81st Ann. Exhbn., Brea, Calif., 2001. Mem.: Women Painters of Wash., Northwest Watercolor Soc. (pres., bd. dirs. 1997—98, Best Transparent Watercolor award 1984), Nat. Watercolor Soc. (Purchase award 2000). Home: 3328 59th Ave SW Seattle WA 98116 Office Phone: 206-250-9123. Personal E-mail: cmwoo@msn.com.

WOO, SHARON Y. healthcare organization executive; b. Honolulu; BA in Music and Math., Mills Coll.; secondary tchg. credential, San Francisco State U. Bd. dirs. Sutter Health Inc., Sacramemto. Trustee Gateway H.S., Golden Gate nat. Parks Assn., Multicultural Alliance, San francisco Ballet, numerous others; chmn. adv. coun. San Francisco Sch. Vols. Office: Sutter Health Inc 2200 River Plaza Dr Sacramento CA 95833-4134

WOOD, ANDRÉE ROBITAILLE, archaeologist, researcher; b. Chgo., Feb. 10, 1929; d. Andrew George and Alice Marie (Fortier) Robitaille; m. Richard Lawrence Wood, Jan. 14, 1956; children: Mary Wood Molo, Matthew William Wood, Melissa Irene Wood, Elizabeth Wood Wesel, John Andrew Wood. BA, No. Ill. Univ., DeKalb, 1977, MA, 1982. Freelance archaeologist, 1981-84; rsch. asst. Prehistoric Project Oriental Inst., Univ. Chgo., Ill., 1984—. Rsch., discovery, removal, analysis and identification of ancient blood residues on lithic material excavated at ten millenium old site, Çayönü in Ergani, Turkey. Contbr. articles to profl. jours. Avocations: writing poetry, boating, tennis, golf. Home: 356 Old Sutton Rd Barrington IL 60010-9113 also: 8735 Midnight Pass Rd Apt 604B Sarasota FL 34242-2892

WOOD, APRIL CARTHENA, judge; b. Mission Viejo, Calif., Aug. 10, 1973; d. James Daniel and Tara Holt Wood; m. Jeffrey John Berg, May 8, 1999; children: Alexis Grace Berg, Alexander John Berg. BA in prelaw, Pensacola Christian Coll., 1994; JD, Regent U. Sch. of Law, 1997. Bar: NC 1997, cert.: NC (mediator) 2001. Atty. Pvt. Practice, Thomasville, NC, 1997—2002; dist. ct. judge 22nd Jud. Dist. of NC, Lexington, 2002—. Adj. prof. Davidson County Cmty. Coll., Lexington, 1999—2001. Adv. bd. Davidson County Day Reporting Ctr., Lexington, 2003. Recipient missions award, Robertson Sch. of Govt., 2003. Mem.: Lexington Christian Women's Assoc., Marine Corps League, Thomasville Woman's, Thomasville Lions. Republican. Baptist. Office: Dist Ct Judges' Chambers 110 West Ctr St Lexington NC 27292

WOOD, BETTY JEAN, conceptual artist, art educator; b. Pitts., Mar. 2, 1942; d. Ralph Alphas and Mary Cordis Blanton; m. John E. Ayers, Aug. 25, 1963 (div. May 1987); children: Mark Ayers, Kristin Ayers Torres; m. Frederick Harrison Wood, Jr., Nov. 28, 1987 (dec. Jan. 2002); children: Andrew, Christopher. BA with honors, Pa. State U., 1984; MFA, U. Okla., 1992. Artist-in-residence Okla. Arts Coun., 1993—; adj. prof. U. Okla., Norman, 1997—98; asst. instr. Okla. Arts Inst., Okla. State U., Stillwater, 1998; guest lectr. Southwestern State U., Weatherford, Okla., 2001; instr. Oklahoma City Mus. of Art., 2002—; guest lectr. Goddard Art Ctr., Ardmore, Okla., 2003. Spl. project asst. ConservArt Assoc., Culver City, Calif., 1991—93; asst. preparator Fred Jones, Jr. Mus. of Art, U. Okla., 1992—, installation asst., 1992; co-coord. SummerWind Arts Festival, Norman, 1994—96; coord. SummerWind Arts Festival, Children's Events, 1995—; art cons. Dept. Edn., San Juan, 1986, bd. dirs. Children's Art Network, Norman, 1996—2001; coord./curator spl. exhbn. Ctrl. Pa. Festival of the Arts, State College, 1987. Author: (book reviews) Museologist, 1986—87, Community Based Art Education, 1995; one-woman shows include Bricktown Fin. Inst., Okla., numerous others, exhibited in group shows at 50th Anniversary Nat. Art Exhibit, Wind River Valley Artist's Guild, Wyo., Leslie Powell Gallery, Okla., IAO Gallery, Gallery on the Sq., Ky., Period Gallery, Nebr., Kirkpatrick Galleries of Omniplex, Okla., Goddard Art Ctr., numerous others, East Ctrl. U., Purdue U., West Lafayette, Ind., Lamar U., Beaumont, Tex., Soho Art Dist., N.Y.C., others, Represented in permanent collections Sch. of Visual Arts, Pa. State U., Sch. of Art, U. Okla., Okla., Fred Jones, Jr. Mus. of Art, Okla. City Art Mus., Okla. Sch. of Arts and Scis., pvt. collections U.S. and abroad. Recipient numerous awards for art. Mem.: U. Okla. Art Alumni Assn. (pres. 1993), Beta Sigma Phi Sorority (pres. 1983—84). Democrat. Avocations: guest lectr., children's workshops, reading, antiques, exhibit my artwork. Home: 3316 Riviera Dr Norman OK 73072-7613 Office Phone: 405-364-1064. E-mail: fredwood@ou.edu.

WOOD, BRENDA JEAN, pastor, evangelist; b. Patrick AFB, Fla., Sept. 24, 1961; d. Terry Robert Hubbard and Cherry Ann Redwine, James William Redwine (Stepfather); m. Ross Landan Wood, Apr. 11, 1981; children: Jared Ross, Dwight Adam Myers, Christopher Wayne Pitts, Leslie Anne. AA, Weatherford Coll., Weatherford, Texas, 1981; BA Psychology, Calif. State U., San Bernardino, Calif., 1995; MS Marriage & Family Therapy, Fuller Theol. Sem., Pasadena, Calif., 1999, MA in Theology, 2002. Ordained Min. Assemblies of God, Calif., 2001, lic. Min. Assemblies of God, Calif., 1999. Youth pastor Full Gospel Assembly of God, Norco, Calif., 1995—97; intern counselor Turning Point Counseling, Diamond Bar, Calif., 1997—99; christian edn. dir. New Life Christian Fellowship, Riverside, Calif., 1998—98, youth pastor, 1998—98, sr. pastor, 1998—. Spkr. Religious and Civic Functions, 1995—; evangelist New Life Christian Fellowship, Mexico, 2002—, Nigeria, 2003, pastoral counselor, Calif., 1995—; parenting educator Safe Haven Program, Riverside, Calif., 2002—03. Chaplain Calif. Dept. of Forestry, Riverside, Calif., 2001—04; mem. Cops and Clergy, Riverside, Calif., 2002, bd. mem., 2002; mem. Jurupa C. of C., Riverside, Calif., 2003, Pastors Prayer Fellowship, Riverside, Calif., 2001. Scholar Music, Weatherford Coll., 1979. Mem.: Gen. Coun. Assemblies of God, So. Calif. Dist. Coun. Assemblies of God, Inland Empire Women In Ministry, Credentialed Women Ministers Assemblies of God. Assemblies Of God. Avocations: spending time with my family, gardening, travel. Home: 1804 Noah Dr Corona CA 92880 Office: New Life Christian Fellowship 9010 Limonite Ave Riverside CA 92509

WOOD, CHRISTIE ANN, artist; b. Texas City, Tex., Dec. 6, 1955; d. Clarence Jefferson and Mary Ellen (Standley) W. BME, U. North Tex., 1978. Asst. ops. mgr. North Tex. State U. Computer Ctr., Denton, 1980-81, programmer, 1981; computer sci. tchr. La. Sch. Professions, Shreveport, 1981-82; computer analyst Bossier Parrish Sch. Bd., Bossier City, La., 1982-84; sr. mktg. support Unisys Corp., Dallas, 1984-87; mktg. mgr. Unisys Corp. WHQ, Blue Bell, Pa., 1987-91; product devel. mgr. Unisys Corp., Blue Bell, Pa., 1991-93; software devel. project leader Paramount Packaging, Chalfont, Pa., 1993-96; owner, artist stained glass Art Glass Ensembles, Denton, Tex., 1996—; exec. dir. Internat. Guild Glass Artists, 1999—2000. Awards chmn. Data Processing Mgmt. Assn., Dallas, 1985. Editor: The LINC Systems Appraoch, 1989, The LINC Systems Approach 3.0, 1992, The LINC Systems Approach 4.0, 1995; composer cantata. Flutist Shreveport Symphony Orch., 1981-84, Canterbury Chamber Consort, 1989-91, Ensemble Pro Musica, 1991—; bd. dirs. Voces Novae et Antiquae, 1995-2001, Nehemiah' Way, 1992-93, Dallas Symphony Chorus, 2001—, The Helios Ensemble, 2003—; chmn. St. Peter's Evang. Luth. Ch., 1993-95. Recipient Exemplary Action award Burroughs Corp., 1985. Mem. Ensemble Pro Musica, Internat. Guild Glass Artists (bd. dirs. 1995-99), Stained Glass Assn. Am. Democrat. Avocations: flutist, computer science, illustrations.

WOOD, CORINNE, former lieutenant governor; b. Barrington, Ill., May 28, 1954; m. Paul R. Wood; children: Ashley, Brandon, Courtney. BS, U. Ill.; JD, Loyola U. Bar: Ill. 1979. Pvt. practice; counsel Ill. Savs. and Residential Fin. Bd.; atty. Hopkins & Sutter, Chgo.; gen. counsel Ill. Commr. of Banks and trusts; state rep. 59th dist. 90th Ill. Gen. Assembly, Springfield; rep. State of Ill., 1997—99, former lt. gov., 1999—2003. Appointed spec. asst., Ill. Atty. Gen. Former co-capt. Shields Twp. Rep. Precinct; Lake Forest chmn. John E. Porter for Congress, 1994, 96; adv. mem. Coun. of Women Advisors to U.S. Congress; past 1st v.p., bd. dirs. Women's Rep. Club, past pres., bd. mem. 10th Congl. Dist. of Lake Forest/Lake Bluff chpt.; past pres. (fin. chmn.), mem. bd. govs. Lake County Rep. Fedn.; bd. dirs. Allendale Shelter Club, Allendale Assn.; adv. bd. A Safe Place; transition bd. dirs. Anne M. Kiley Ctr. for the Developmentally Disabled; mem. LWV of Lake Forest/Lake Bluff; mem. Lake Forest Open Lands Assn.; former Lake Forest chmn., sustaining mem. Jr. League of Chgo.; former new mems. chair, membership com., Sunday sch. tchr. First Presbyn. Ch. of Lake Forest; den leader Pack 43, Boy Scouts Am.; plan commr. City of Lake Forest, 1993-97, sr. housing commr., 1993-97, ad hoc com. on sr. housing bd. mem. Recipient City of Lake Forest Spl. Recognition of Pub. Svc.. award. Mem. ABA, Ill. Bar Assn., Lake County Bar Assn., Chgo. Bar Assn., House Financial Insts. Comm., Comm. on Aging, Edn. Appropriations Comm., Labor and Commerce Comm., appointed mem., Legislative Rsch. Bureau, bd. mem. Republican.

WOOD, DEBRA LYNN, music educator; b. Kansas City, Mo., July 31, 1958; d. Dale Leonard and Mary Ann Coble; m. Karl Keith Kreeger, Jr., June 21, 1980 (div. Nov. 23, 1994); children: Nicholas Kreeger, Alexander Kreeger, Benjamin Kreeger; m. Steven A. Wood, Dec. 23, 1995. BS in Music Edn., William Jewell Coll., 1980; MEd in Curriculum and Instrn., Lesley U., 2001. Cert. tchr. Mo. Music tchr. Osborn (Mo.) R-O Schs., 1982—84, Kearney (Mo.) R-I Schs., 1991—95, music specialist, 1995—. Mem. at risk students team Kearney R-I Schs., 1998—, mem. profl. devel. com., 2001—. Excellence in Edn. grantee, Mo. Dept. Edn., 2000. Mem.: Am. Orff Assn., Mo. Music Educators Assn. Mem. Disciples Of Christ. Avocations: genealogy, reading, needlepoint, gardening. Office: Kearney R I Sch Dist 1005 S Jefferson Kearney MO 64060 Personal E-mail: iteachmusic@uniteone.net.

WOOD, DIANE PAMELA, judge; b. Plainfield, N.J., July 4, 1950; d. Kenneth Reed and Lucille (Padmore) Wood; m. Dennis James Hutchinson, Sept. 2, 1978 (div. May 1998); children: Kathryn Hutchinson, David Hutchinson, Jane Hutchinson. BA, U. Tex., 1971, JD, 1975, Georgetown U., 2003. Bar: Tex. 1975, D.C. 1978, Ill. 1993. Law clk. U.S. Ct. Appeals (5th cir.), 1975—76, U.S. Supreme Ct., 1976—77; atty.-advisor U.S. Dept. State, Washington, 1977—78; assoc. Covington & Burling, Washington, 1978—80; asst. prof. law Georgetown U. Law Ctr., Washington, 1980—81, U. Chgo., 1981—88, prof. law, 1988—95, assoc. dean, 1989—92, Harold J. and Marion F. Green prof. internat. legal studies, 1990—95, sr. lectr. law, 1995—; spl. cons. antitrust divsn. internat. guide U.S. Dept. Justice, 1986—87, dep. asst. atty. gen. antitrust divsn., 1993—95; judge U.S. Ct. Appeals (7th cir.), 1995—. Contbr. articles to profl. jours.; bd. editors: Am. Jour. Internat. Law. Bd. dirs. Hyde Park-Kenwood Cmty. Health Ctr., 1983—85. Mem.: Am. Law Inst. (elected coun. mem. 2003), Am. Soc. Internat. Law, Phi Alpha Delta. Democrat.

WOOD, EMILY CHURCHILL, special education educator, social studies educator, consultant; b. Summit, N.J., Apr. 11, 1925; d. Arthur Burdett and Ruth Vail (Pierson) Churchill; m. Philip Warren Wood, June 22, 1946; children: Martha, Arthur, Warren, Benjamin. BA, Smith Coll., 1946; MA in Teaching, Manhattanville Coll., 1971; postgrad., U. Tulsa, 1974-79, Langston U., 1990-92. Cert. tchr. social studies, learning disabilities, elem. edn., econs., Am. history, world history. Tchr. Miss Fines Sch., Princeton, N.J., 1946-47, Hallen Ctr. for Edn., Portchester, N.Y., 1973-74, Town and Country Sch., Tulsa, Okla., 1974-79, Tulsa Pub. Schs., 1979-97, Heritage Acad., Tulsa, 1998—; adj. instr. Tulsa C.C., Tulsa, 1998—. Ednl. cons. Tulsa, 1997—; leader colloquia Bill of Rights Arts and Humanities Coun., Tulsa, 1989; mem. literacy task force Tulsa 2000 Edn. Com., 1990-92; chmn. internat. student exch. Eisenhower Internat. Sch., Tulsa, 1992-97. Author: (with others) Visual Arts in China, 1988, Applauding Our Constitution, 1989, The Bill of Rights: Who Guarantees What, 1993; contbr. articles to profl. jours. Leader, founder Am. Field Svc., Tulsa, 1982—84; pres., v.p. Booker T. Washington H.S. PTA, Tulsa, 1985; campaign mgr. auditors race Dem. Party, Tulsa, 1988, 1992, 1994; bd. dirs. Smith Coll. Alumnae, Northampton, Mass., 1956—59, Sister Cities Internat., Tulsa, 1992—2001, nominations chair, 1999—2001; bd. dirs. Tulsa Global Alliance; trustee Okla. Found. for Excellence, 2000—. Named Tulsa Tchr. of Yr. Tulsa Classroom Tchrs. Assn., 1988, Nat. Elem. Tchr. of Yr., Nat. Bar Aux., 1992, Outstanding Elem. Social Studies Tchr., Nat. Cound. or Social Studies, 1999; recipient Elem. Medal of Excellence, Okla. Found. for Excellence, 1990, Valley Forge Tchrs. medal Freedoms Found., 1992, Paragon award Tulsa Commn. on Status of Women, 1996, Pinnacle award Mayor's Commn. on Status of Women, 1998, Liberty Bell award Tulsa Bar Assn., 1998, Global Vision award Tulsa Global Alliance, 2002. Mem. UN Assn. Ea. Okla. (pres. 2000—), Nat. Coun. Social Studies (religion program com. 1984—, bd. dirs. 1997—), DAR, Okla. Edn. Assn., Okla. Coun. Social Studies (pres. 1995, tchr. of yr. 1984), Okla. Bar Assn. (law related com. 1988—, tchr. of yr. 1990), Okla. Coun. Econ. Edn. (state and nat. awards 1981, 89, 92), Kent Place Alumnae Assn. (disting. alumna award 1992). Avocations: reading, swimming, travel, walking. Home: 3622 S Yorktown Pl Tulsa OK 74105-3452 E-mail: emily_wood46@hotmail.com.

WOOD, EVAN RACHEL, actress; b. Raleigh, NC, Sept. 7, 1987; Actor: (films) Digging to China, 1998, Practical Magic, 1998, Detour, 1999, Little Secrets, 2001, S1m0ne, 2002, Thirteen, 2003, The Missing, 2003; (TV films) In the Best of Families: Marriage, Pride & Madness, 1994, Search for Grace, 1994, A Father for Charlie, 1995, Death in Small Doses, 1995, Get to the Heart: The Barbara Mandrell Story, 1997, Down Will Come Baby, 1999; (TV series) Profiler, 1998—99, Once and Again, 1999—2002, (guest appearances) American Gothic, 1995—98, Touched by an Angel, 2000, The West Wing, 2002, CSI: Crime Scene Investigation, 2003. Office: Agy for Performing Arts 9000 Sunset Blvd Ste 1200 Sherman Oaks CA 91403*

WOOD, FRANCES DIANE, medical secretary, artist; b. Caddo, Okla., Mar. 7, 1950; d. Clovis Lynn and Hilda Dee (Guthrie) Wood; m. Samuel Dante Wolfe, Aug. 20, 1990 (div. Mar. 1992). BA, Southeastern Okla. State U., 1972; postgrad., Grayson County Coll., 1984—87, Rose State Coll., 2001—02, U. Ctrl. Okla., 2003—. Ins. clk. Sherman Cmty. Hosp., Tex., 1973-74; med. sec. Essin Clinic, Sherman, Tex., 1980-83; med. transcriptionist Texoma Med. Ctr., Denison, Tex., 1983-88, Wilson N. Jones Meml. Hosp., Sherman, Tex., 1989-95; CEO Designs by Diane, Caddo, Okla., 1995—. Conv. del. Blue Cross-Blue Shield Tex., Dallas, 1980—83; v.p. Jett Transcription, Denison, Tex., 1988. Exhibitions include paintings in cmty. art shows, Represented in permanent collections Shamrock Bank, Caddo, Okla., Indian Terr. Mus., Caddo. Charter mem. Caddo Edn. Found., Okla., 1993-95; sponsor Save the Children, Philippines, 1995. Mem. Am. Soc. Prevention Cruelty to Animals, Friends of Internat. Fellowship of Christians and Jews, Physicians Com. for Responsible Medicine, Nat. Trust Historic Preservation, Okla. Sheriffs Assn. (hon.), Arts Coun. Co-op (life), Nat. Arbor Day Found., Sierra Club, Sacred Heart Auto League, People for the Ethical Treatment of Animals, Urban League Greater Oklahoma City. Democrat. Avocations: pet care, interior decorating, astronomy, folk medicine, gardening.

WOOD, HEIDI, commissioner; BA with honors, Brown U., 1987. Analyst SG Cowen; fin. cons. Shearson Lehman Hutton, Wedbush Morgan; from v.p., sr. analyst to exec. dir. Morgan Stanley, 1999—; commr. aerospace investment Aerospace Commn., Arlington, Va. Mem.: N.Y. Aerospace Analyst Soc. (treas.). Office: Aerospace Commn Crystal Gateway One Ste 940 1235 Jefferson Davis Hwy Arlington VA 22202-3283

WOOD, HELEN CHAMBLEE, accountant; b. Varnado, La., June 29, 1920; d. Joseph Russ Fornea and Linnio Rebecca Stallings; m. Karl David Wood. Recipient invitation to Washington, U.S. Dept. Interior, 1972, 1975, invitation to inaugural ceremonies gov., Jackson, Miss., 1971. Mem.: Smithsonian Instn., Libr. of Congress. Avocations: painting, gardening, reading, community service. Home: Bogalusa, La. Died Jan. 11, 2003.

WOOD, JANE ROBERTS, writer; m. Dub Wood. Author: The Train to Estelline, 1987, A Place Called Sweet Shrub, 1990, Dance a Little Longer, 1993, Grace, 2001, Roseborough, 2003, Mocha, 2004. Recipient Tex. Inst. Letters award for best short story, 1998; fellow NEA, NEH. Office: c/o U North Texas Press PO Box 311336 Denton TX 76203-1336

WOOD, JANE SEMPLE, editor, writer; b. Easton, Pa., June 23, 1940; d. Royer Daniel and Wilhelmina Annette (Welchel) Semple; m. James MacPherson Wood, Sept. 8, 1961; children: James MacPherson Jr., Robert Semple. BA in Journalism, U. Calif., Berkeley, 1961. Reporter San Jose (Calif.) Mercury News, 1962, asst. dir. pub. rels. Nat. Symphony Orch., Washington, 1963-65; free-lance writer and editor Adoption Listing Svc. of Ohio, Cleve., 1976; freelance writer and editor AIA, Cleve., 1977; free-lance writer and editor City of Bedford Heights, Ohio, 1980-81, City of Shaker Heights, Ohio, 1979-80, pub. info. officer, dir. publs., 1980-85, 92-99; founding editor Shaker mag., Shaker Heights, Ohio, 1983—2003; free-lance writer Exec. Living, Cleve., 1990-91; contbg. editor Corp. Cleve., 1991-92; editor e-letter This Week in Shaker, 2003—; columnist Sun Press, 2003—. Pub. rels. cons. Cable TV Com., Shaker Heights, 1978-85, Oak Park Exch. Congress, Shaker Heights, 1981. Vol. editor, columnist Friends of Shaker Sq., Cleve., 1979-82; vol. pub. rels. com. Cleve. Ballet, 1980, Cleve. Orch., 1983; vol. contbg. editor Univ. Hosps., Cleve., 1990-92; mem. Calif. Ann. Fund Adv. Coun., 2000. Recipient Grand award City Hall Digest, 1983, 85, 87, Excellence in Journalism award Soc. Profl. Journalists, 1988, 92, 95, Woman of Profl. Excellence award Cleve. YWCA, 1986, Ace award of Merit, 1991, Hon. mention Blue Pencil Competition of Nat. Assn. Govt. Communicators, 1993, Ohioana James P. Barry Editl. Excellence award, 1999; Jane Wood Excellence in Journalism award named in her honor, 2003. Mem.: U. Calif. Alumni Assn. (permanent class sec. 1961). Avocations: cooking, swimming, reading, traveling, concerts.

WOOD, JEANNE CLARKE, charitable organization executive; b. Pitts., Dec. 21, 1916; d. Joseph Calvitt and Helen Caroline (Mattson) Clarke; m. Herman Eugene Wood, Jr., May 6, 1936 (dec.); children: Helen Hamilton (Mrs. John Harry Mortenson), Herman Eugene III. Student, Collegiate Sch. for Girls, Richmond, Va., 1932-33. Asst. to Dr. and Mrs. J. Calvitt Clarke, Christian Children's Fund, Inc., Richmond, 1938-64; founder Children, Inc., Richmond, 1964, pres., internat. dir., 1964—. Author: (with Helen C. Clarke) In Appreciation: A Story in Pictures of the World Wide Family of Christian Children's Fund, Inc, 1958, Children's Christmastime Around the World, 1962, Children-Hope of the World-Their Needs, 1965, Children-Hope of the World-Their Friends, 1966; Editor: CI News, 1964. Recipient citation Eastern Council Navajo Tribe, 1970, citations Mayor of Pusan (Korea), 1971, citations Mayor of Seoul, 1971, citations Gov. of Kanagawa Prefecture (Japan), 1972, commendation Pres. of U.S., 1972, citation Stephen Philibosian Found., 1975, citation Santa Ana (El Salvador) Dept. Edn., 1975, citation Nat. Sch. for Blind, Dominican Republic, 1982, citation Navajo Tribal Council of Navajo Nation, Window Rock, Ariz., 1982 Home and Office: Children Inc PO Box 5381 1000 Westover Rd Richmond VA 23220-6624

WOOD, JOAN E. state representative; b. Milo, Idaho, June 3, 1934; m. Thomas D. Wood; 5 children. Grad., Ririe (Idaho) H.S. Ptnr. ranch/farm/trucking corp.; state rep. dist. 35A Idaho Ho. of Reps., Boise, 1996—, vice chair resources and conservation com., chair transp. and def. com., mem. revenue and taxation com.; mem. drug and alcohol rehab. caucus com. Mem.: Multistate Hwy. Transp. Agreement Com., Am. Legis. Exch. Coun., Outdoors Unltd. Multiple Use Resource Orgn., Ctr. Constnl. Studies, Upper Valley Rep. Women, Jefferson County Rep. Women (past pres.). Republican. Lds Ch. Office: State Capitol PO Box 83720 Boise ID 83720-0038

WOOD, JULIE M. educational consultant; b. Lawrence, Mass., Mar. 5, 1949; d. Frederick Paul and Eileen Mary Laffey; m. John Armstead Wood, Jr., Sept. 9, 1989; stepchildren: Crispin, Georgia. BS in Elem. Edn. cum laude, U. Conn., 1971, MA in Reading Instrn. cum laude, 1972; EdM in Tech. in Edn., Harvard U., 1992, EdD in Human Devel. and Psychology, 1999. Tchg. fellow Harvard Grad. Sch. Edn., Cambridge, Mass., 1994—95, instr., 1997—98, dir. Jeanne S. Chall Reading Lab., 1999—2000, lectr., 1999—. Founder, owner, dir. The Reading Loft, Amherst, NH, 1975—83; co-founder, co-dir. Literacy Inst., Dorchester, Mass., 1997; non-resident tutor Adams House Harvard U., Cambridge, 1993—; dir. tng. Am. Reads MIT, Cambridge, 1998—2001; writer, designer Edn. Devel. Ctr., Newton, Mass., 2000—01; ednl. cons. Disney Interactive, Burbank, Calif., 2001; cons. Blues Clues Nickelodeon, N.Y.C., 2001; writer, web expert Scholastic, Inc., N.Y.C., 2001—02; dir. rsch. Soliloquy Learning, Needham, Mass., 2002—03; spkr. in field. Author: (children's software) Bookbytes: Reading and Responding to Literature, 1994; columnist: Scholastic, 2000; contbr. articles to profl. jours. Recipient Rsch. Fellowship award, Action for Children's TV, 1995, 1996; Advanced Doctoral grantee, Harvard U., 1997—98, Tchg., Curriculum, Innovation grantee, 2000. Mem.: Women in Tech. (co-founder 1993), Am. Edn. Rsch. Assn., Internat. Reading Assn. Avocations: jazz, writing, photography. Home and Office: 71 Langdon St Cambridge MA 02138

WOOD, KIMBA M. judge; b. Port Townsend, Wash., Jan. 2, 1944. BA cum laude, Conn. Coll., 1965; MSc, London Sch. Econs., 1966; JD, Harvard U., 1969. Bar: U.S. Dist. Ct. D.C. 1969, U.S. Ct. Appeals D.C. 1969, N.Y. 1972, U.S. Dist. Ct. (ea. and so. dists.) N.Y. 1974, U.S. Ct. Appeals (2d cir.) 1975, U.S. Supreme Ct. 1980, U.S. Dist. Ct. (we. dist.) N.Y. 1981. Assoc. Steptoe & Johnson, Washington, 1969-70; with Office Spl. Counsel, OEO Legal Svcs., Washington, 1970-71; assoc., then ptnr. LeBoeuf, Lamb, Leiby & MacRae, N.Y.C., 1971-88; judge, U.S. Dist. Ct. (so. dist.) N.Y., N.Y.C., 1988—. Mem. ABA (chmn. civil practice, procedure com. 1982-85, mem. coun. 1985-88, jud. rep. 1989-91), N.Y. State Bar Assn. (chmn. antitrust sect. 1983-84), Fed. Bar Coun. (trustee from 1978, v.p., 1984-85), Am. Law Inst. Office: US Dist Ct US Courthouse 500 Pearl St New York NY 10007-1316

WOOD, LARRY (MARY LAIRD), journalist, writer, public relations executive, educator, environmental consultant; b. Sandpoint, Idaho; d. Edward Hayes and Alice (McNeel) Small; children: Mary, Marcia, Barry. BA summa cum laude, U. Wash., 1939, MA summa cum laude, with highest honors, 1940; postgrad., Stanford U., 1940-43, U. Calif., Berkeley, 1946-47, cert. in photography, 1971; postgrad. journalism, U. Wis., 1971-72, U. Minn., 1971-72, U. Ga., 1972-73; postgrad. in art, architecture and marine biology, U. Calif., Santa Cruz, 1974-76, Stanford Hopkins Marine Sta., 1977-80. Lifetime secondary and jr. coll. teaching cert., Wash., Calif. Feature writer and columnist Oakland Tribune and San Francisco Chronicle, Calif., 1939—; archtl. and environ. feature and travel writer and columnist San Jose (Calif.) Mercury News (Knight Ridder), 1972-90; teaching fellow Stanford U., 1940-43; dir. pub. rels. 2-counties, 56-park East Bay Regional Park Dist., No. Calif., 1948-68; pres. Larry Wood Pub. Rels., 1946—; pub. rels. dir. Calif. Children's Home Soc., 1947-58. Prof. pub. rels., mag. writing, journalism, investigative reporting San Diego State U., 1974-75; disting. vis. prof. journalism San Jose State U., 1976; assoc. prof. journalism Calif. State U., Hayward, 1978; prof. sci. and environ. journalism U. Calif. Berkeley Ext. grad. divsn., 1979—; press del. nat. convs. Am. Geophys. Union Internat. Conf., 1986—, AAAS, 1989—, Nat. Park Svc. VIP Press Tour, Yellowstone after the fire, 1989—, Nat. Assn. Sci. Writers, 1989—, George Washington U./Am. Assn. Neurol. Surgeons Sci. Writers Conf., 1990, Am. Inst. Biol. Scis. Conf., 1990, Nat. Conf. Sci. Writers, Am. Heart Assn., 1995, Internat. Cardiologists Symposium for Med./Sci. Writers, 1995, Annenberg Program Electronic Media Symposium, Washington, 1995; EPA del. to USSR and Ea. Europe; expert witness on edn., pub. rels., journalism and copyright; cons. sci. writers interne project Stanford U., 1989—; spl. media guest Sigma Xi, 1990—; mem. numerous spl. press corps; selected White House Spl. Media, 1993—; selected mem. Duke U. 14th Ann. Sci. Reporters Conf., 1995; internat. press guest Can. Consulate Gen. Dateline Can., 1995—, French Govt. Tourist Office, 1996—, Ministerio delle Risorse Agricole Alimentari e Forestali and Assocs. Conf., 1995; appeared in TV documentary Larry Wood Covers Visit of Queen Elizabeth II Contbr. over 5,500 articles to newspapers, nat. mags., nat. and internat. newspaper syndicates including L.A. Times-Mirror Syndicate, Knight-Ridder Syndicate, Washington Post, Phila. Inquirer, Chgo. Tribune, Miami Herald, Oakland Tribune, Seattle Times, San Francisco Chronicle, Parade, San Jose Mercury News (Nat. Headliner award), Christian Sci. Monitor, L.A. Times/Christian Sci. Monitor Worldwide News Syndicate, Washington Post, Phila. Inquirer, Hawaiian Airlines In Paradise and other in-flight mags., MonitoRadio, Donnelly Family Circle, Ill. Life, Mechanix Illus., Popular Mechanics, Parents (contbg. editor), House Beautiful, Am. Home (awards 1988-89), Archl. Digest, Better Homes and Gardens, Sunset, Architectural Digest, National Geographic World, Travel & Leisure, Chevron USA/Odyssey (Calif. Pub.'s award 1984), Xerox Edn. Publs., Europe's Linguapress, PSA Mag., Off Duty, Oceans, Sea Frontiers, AAA Westways, AAA Via, Travelin', others; home and garden columnist and editor, 5-part series Pacific Coast Ports, 5-part series Railroads of the West, series Immigration, Youth Gangs, Endangered Species, Calif. Lighthouse Chain, Lighthouses of the World, Pacific Coast Wetlands, Elkhorn Slough Nat. Estuarine Res., Ebey's Landing Nat. Hist. Island Res., Calif. Water Wars, BLM's Adopt a Horse Program, Mt. St. Helen's Eruption, Oreg's Covered Bridges, Loma Prieta Earthquake, Oakland Firestorm, Missing Children, Calif. Prison Reform, Columbia-Alaska's Receding Glacier, Calif. Underwater Parks, and many others; author: Wonderful U.S.A.: A State-by-State Guide to Its Natural Resources, 1989; co-author: McGraw-Hill English for Social Living, 1944, Fawcett Boating Books, 1956-66, Fodor's San Francisco, Fodor's California, 1982-89, Bell and Howell/Charles Merrill Focus on Life Science, Focus on Physical Science, Focus on Earth Science, 1983, 2d edit, 1987, State of California's Golden State Travel Guide, 1998; contbr. Earth Science 1987; 8 works selected for use by Europe's Woltors-Nordoff-Longman English Language Texts, U.K., Netherlands, 1988; author: (with others) anthology West Winds, 1989; reviewer Charles Merrill texts, 1983-84; book reviewer Profl. Communicator, 1987—; selected writings in permanent collections Oakland Pub. Libr., U. Wash. Main Libr.; environ. works included in Dept. Edn. State of Md. textbook; contbr., author Journalism Quar.; author script PBS/AAA America series, 1992; contbg. editor. Parents, Fashion Showcase, Spokane Mag. Nat. chmn. travel writing contest for U.S. univ. journalism students Assn. for Edn. in Journalism and Mass Communication/Soc. Am. Travel Writers, 1979-83; judge writing contest for Nat. Assn. Real Estate Editors, 1982—; cons. S. Carolina Dept. Parks, Recreation and Tourism, 1999—; press del. 1st Internat. Symposium Volcanism and Aviation Safety, 1991, Coun. for Advancement of Sci. Writing, 1977—, Rockefeller Media Seminar Feeding the World-Protecting the Earth, 1992, Global Conf. on Mercury as Pollutant, 1992, Earth Summit Global Forum, Rio de Janeiro, 1992; invited Nat. Park Svc. Nat. Conf. Sci. Writers, 1985, Postmaster Gen.'s 1992 Stamps, 1991, Internat. Geophys. Union Conf., 1982—, The Conf. Bd., 1995—, Corp. Comm. Conf., Calif. Inst. Tech.'s Media and Sci. Seminar, 1995—, Medical Writers Delegation to Russia and Estonia, 1997, N.Y. Times Opinion Rsch. Co. Corp. Image Conf., 1999, EPA and Dept. Energy Tech. Conf., 1992, Am. Soc. Photogrammetry and Remote Sensing Internat. Conv. Mapping Global Change, 1992, U.S. Conf. on Oceans, 1998, N.Y. Mus. Modern Art Matisse Retrospective Press Rev. and all media previews, 1992—, celebration 150th anniversary Oreg. Trail, 1993, Nat. Coun. Advancement Sci. Writing, 1977-2003, Sigma Xi Nat. Conf., 1988-2003, Nat. Sci. Writers Confs., 1977-2003, PRSA Travel and Tourism Conf., 1993—, Internat. Conf. Environment, 1994, 95, Quality Life Europe, Prague, 1994, Calif. Sesquicentennial, 1996, 14th Ann. Sci. Writers Conf., 1996, Picasso Retrospective, 1996, others; mem. Gov.'s Conf. Tourism N.C., 1993-2002, Calif., 1976—, Fla., 1987—, N.C. Govs. conf. on tourism and film, 2000-, U.C. Irvine Calif. Computer Sci. Symposium, 2000, Sea Grant's conf. on sci. in the news, 2000, N.Y. conf. bd. conf. on environ. journalism, 2000, on economics, 2001; press guest 14 U.S. states and 12 fgn. countries' Depts. Tourism, 1986—. Named to Broadway Hall of Fame, U. Wash., 1984; recipient Broadway Disting. Alumnus award, 1995; citations for environ. writing Nat. Park Svc., U.S. Forest Svc., Bur. Land Mgmt., Oakland Mus. Assn., Oakland C. of C., Chevron USA, USN plaque and citation, Best Mag. articles citation Calif. Pubs. Assn., 1984, U.S. Treasury award, 1946; co-recipient award for best Sunday newspaper mag. Nat. Headliners, citation for archtl. features Oakland Mus., 1983; honoree for achievements in journalism Nat. Mortar Bd., 1988, 89; named one of 10 V.I.P. press for Yellowstone Nat. Park field trip on "Let Burn" rsch., 1989, Calif.'s top 40 Contemporary Authors for writings on Calif. underwater parks, 1989, nat. honoree Social Issues Resources Series, 1987, Gov.'s Calif. Women of Achievement award, 1988-90; invited V.I.P. press, spl. press guest . Mem. AAAS, Am. Bd. Forensic Examiners, Calif. Acad. Scis., San Francisco Press Club, Nat. Press Club, Pub. Rels. Soc. Am. (charter mem. travel, tourism, environment and edn. divs.), Nat. Sch. Pub. Rels. Assn., Environ. Cons. N.Am., Am. Assn. Edn. in Journalism and Comm. (exec. bd. nat. mag. div. 1978, panel chmn. 1979, 80, author Journalism Quar. jour.), Women in Comm. (nat. bd. officer 1975-77, book reviewer Prof. Communicator), Soc. Profl. Journalists (nat. bd. for hist. sites 1980—), Nat. Press Photographers Assn. (hon. life, cons. Bay Area interne project 1989—, honoree 1995), Investigative Reporters and Editors (charter), Bay Area Advt. and Mktg. Assn., Nat. Assn. Sci. Writers, Calif. Writers Club (state bd., Berkeley bd. 1989—, honoree ann. conv. Asilomar, Calif. 1990), Am. Assn. Med. Writers, Internat. Assn. Bus. Communicators, Soc. Environ. Journalists (charter), Am. Film Inst., Am. Heritage Found. (citation 1986, 87, 88), Soc. Am. Travel Writers, Internat. Oceanographic Found., Oceanic Soc., Calif. Acad. Environ. News Writers, Seattle Advt. and Sales Club (former officer), Nature Conservancy, Smithsonian Audubon Soc., Nat. Wildlife Fedn., Nat. Parks and Conservation Assn., Calif. State Parks Found., Calif. Environ. Leadership Roundtable (trustee), Fine Arts Mus., San Francisco, Seattle Jr. Advt. Club (charter), U. Wash. Comm. Alumni (Sch. Comm. alumni, life, charter mem. ocean scis. alumni, Disting. Alumni 1987), U. Calif., Berkeley Alumni (life, v.p., scholarship chmn. 1975-81), Stanford Alumni (life), Mortar Board Alumnae Assn. (life, honoree 1988-89), Am. Mgmt. Assn., Nat. Soc. Environ. Journalists (charter), Calif. Environ. Leadership Roundtable, Phi Beta Kappa (v.p., bd. dirs. Calif. Alumni Assn., statewide chmn. scholarship awards 1975-81), Purple and Gold Soc. (planning com., charter, 1995—), Pi Lambda Theta, Theta Sigma Phi. Home: Piedmont Pines 6161 Castle Dr Oakland CA 94611-2737

WOOD, LESLIE ANN, retail administrator; b. Chgo., Apr. 9, 1957; d. Howard Arnold and Anita Eleanor (Andler) W. AA, Harper Coll., 1977; BS in Comm. Scis., Ill. State U., 1979; MBA, Olivet Nazarene U., 1998. Advt. asst. Harry Alter Co., Chgo., 1979-80; clk. typist Career Guild, Evanston, Ill., 1980-81; reporter Aparacor, Evanston, Ill., 1981-82; sales mgmt. trainee Prudential Ins. Co. Am., Millburn, NJ, 1983-84; fin. cons. Summit Fin. Resources, Livingston, NJ, 1984; mgr. Chgo. area Renault Inc. divsn. AMC/Jeep/Renault, Elk Grove Village, Ill., 1985-87; customer rels. specialist Chrysler Motors, Lisle, Ill., 1987-88; dist. svc. and parts mgr. Chrysler, Lisle; dist. parts mgr. Subaru of Am., Addison, Ill., 1989-91, dist. fixed ops. mgr., 1992-95; univ. rep. Olivet Nazarene U., Schaumburg, Ill., 1996-97; mktg. cons. WZSR STAR 105.5, Crystal Lake, Ill., 1997-99; parts cons. Am. Isuzu Motors, Cerritos, Calif., 1999—2001; parts and svc. mgr. Hyundai Motor Am., Aurora, Ill., 2002—, dist. parts svc. mgr., 2002—. Mem. ch. choir, rainbows coord. Stephens Min. Avocations: aerobics, circuit weight training, sewing, stained glass crafts. Home and Office: PO Box 517 O Fallon MO 63366-0517

WOOD, LINDA DEE, psychologist; b. Cleve., Ohio, May 16, 1944; d. Mildred Louise Lorber (Cohn) and Henry Hunt Cohn; m. Stephen Alan Wood, May 27, 1985; m. Donald Hugh Schreiber, May 18, 1963 (div. June 5, 1972); m. Jay Richard Baker, Feb. 17, 1976 (div. Mar. 4, 1981); children: Gary Harris Schreiber, Matthew Edward Schreiber, David Robert Schreiber. BA, Nova U., 1986—86; BS, Fla. Atlantic U., 1996; MS, Nova Southeastern U., 1997, D in Psychology, 2001. Lic. contractor Fla. Dept. Profl. Regulation, 1986, prin. broker dealer Fla. Dept. Profl. Regulation, 1987, real estate Fla. Dept. Profl. Regulation, 1987. Comptroller Preterm, Cleve. Inc., 1977—80; dep. fin. dir. City of Tamarac, Fla., 1981—84; dir. fin. City of Pompano Beach, Fla., 1981—86; v.p. Investors Fed. Savs. and Loan, Deerfield Beach, Fla., 1986—90; dir. housing Miami Beach (Fla.) Devel. Corp., 1991—93; psychology intern N.E. Ohio U. Coll. Medicine, Rootstown, 2000—01; psychology resident Ctr. Group Counseling, Boca Raton, Fla., 2002—03; pvt. practice Boca Raton, 2003—. Pres. Hillsboro Securites Inc., Deerfield Beach, Fla., 1986—89, Investors Miami Beach Develop Corp., 1986—89. Treas. Cloister Del Mar, Boca Raton, Fla., 1994—97. Mem.: APA. Avocations: travel, quilting, painting. Home: 1905 N Ocean Blvd Apt 12A Fort Lauderdale FL 33305-3707

WOOD, LINDA MAY, librarian; b. Ft. Dodge, Iowa, Nov. 6, 1942; d. John Albert and Beth Ida (Riggs) Wiley; m. C. James Wood, Sept. 15, 1964 (div. Oct. 1984). BA, Portland State U., 1964; M in Librarianship, U. Wash., 1965. Reference libr. Multnomah County Libr., Portland, Oreg., 1965-67, br. libr., 1967-72, adminstrv. asst. to libr., 1972-73, asst. libr., asst. dir., 1973-77; asst. city libr. L.A. Pub. Libr., 1977-80; libr. dir. Riverside (Calif.) City and County Pub. Libr., 1980-91; county libr. Alameda County Libr., Fremont, Calif., 1991—. Adminstrv. coun. mem. Bay Area Libr. and Info. Svcs., Oakland, Calif., 1991—. Chair combined charities campaign County of Alameda, Oakland, Calif., 1992; bd. dirs. Inland AIDS project, Riverside, 1990-91; vol. United Way of Inland Valleys, Riverside, 1986-87, Bicentennial Competition on the Constitution, 36th Congl. Dist., Colton, Calif., 1988-90. Mem. ALA (CLA chpt. councilor 1992-95), Calif. Libr. Assn. (pres. 1985, exec. com., ALA chpt. councilor 1992-95), Calif. County Librs. Assn. (pres. 1984), League of Calif. Cities (cmty. svcs. policy com. 1985-90), OCLC Users Coun. (Pacific Network del. 1986-89). Democrat. Avocations: folk dancing, opera, reading. Office: Alameda County Libr 2450 Stevenson Blvd Fremont CA 94538-2326 Office Phone: 510-745-1536. E-mail: lwood@aclibrary.org.

WOOD, MARGARET, performing company executive; Entertainment and spl. events dir. Stratton Mountain Resort, Stratton, Va.; gen. mgr. Broward Ctr. for the Performing Arts, Ft. Lauderdale, Fla.; interim gen. dir. Anchorage Opera; gen. dir. Dance Conneticut, 2000—. Co-founder Performing Artservices Inc., NY; founder Dance Umbrella, 1975. Office: Dance Conneticut 224 Farmington Ave Hartford CT 06105

WOOD, MARIAN STARR, publishing company executive; b. N.Y.C., Mar. 30, 1938; d. Edward James and Betty (Starr) Markow; m. Anthony Stuart Wood, Mar. 21, 1963. BA, Barnard Coll., 1959; postgrad., Columbia U., 1959—64. Tchg. asst., lectr. Columbia U., N.Y.C., 1960-64; editor Praeger Pubs., N.Y.C., 1965-71; sr. editor Henry Holt & Co., N.Y.C., 1972-81, exec. editor, 1981-96, assoc. pub., assoc. pub. Marian Wood Books, 1996-99; v.p. Marian Wood Books at G.P. Putnam's Sons, N.Y.C., 1999—. Recipient Roger Klein Found. award for career achievement, 2001. E-mail: marian.wood@us.penguingroup.com.

WOOD, MARY ELIZABETH, retired physician assistant; b. Leaksville, N.C., Dec. 20, 1934; d. William Clayton and Irma Simpson Crews; m. Donald Leon Moore, Feb. 6, 1954 (dec. Nov. 1983); children: Donald Leon Moore, Jr., Patricia Lynn Moore Stewart, Mary Elizabeth Moore Mooney; m. William Zeno Wood, May 30, 1987 (dec. Feb. 1989); stepchildren: William Zeno Wood, Jr., Marty Wood Lesher, John. BA in Edn., U. N.C., 1956; cert., Wake Forest U., 1992. Cert. physician asst. 1992. Physician asst. in orthopedic surgery Wake Forest U. Med. Ctr., Winston-Salem, NC, 1992—98. Mem.: Piedmont Assn. Physician Assts. (Director 1992—94), Associated Artists of Winston-Salem. Home: 156 Muirfield Dr Winston Salem NC 27104

WOOD, MYRA LINDEN FRANK, consultant; b. Richmond, Va., Oct. 26, 1950; d. J. C. and Myra Teresa (Lanzarone) Frank; m. Timothy Franklin Long (div. Jan. 1981); m. Robert Andrew Hudson (div. 1994); m. Frederick W. Wood, Sept. 25, 1999. BA, Erskine Coll., 1972; student, Inst. Fin. Edn., 1982-88. Chief activities therapist S.C. Dept. Corrections, Columbia, 1973-75, acting prin., 1975-77, coll. coord., 1977-78; owner, operator Carolina Coast Seafood, Aiken and Beaufort, S.C., 1978-80; from teller to savs. counselor Security Fed. Savs. & Loan, Aiken, 1981-83; customer svc. rep. Bankers 1st Savs. & Loans, Augusta, Ga., 1983-84, mgr. br. adminstrn., 1984-85; coord. automated teller machines, banking officer 1st Fed. Savs. Bank, Brunswick, Ga., 1985-88; ptnr., cons. electronic banking/software devel. RAH Systems, Brunswick, 1988-93; ptnr. specific application computer programming, software tng. Details & More, Greenville, S.C., 1989-90, ptnr. event planning, various mfg. positions and mktg./sales, 1989-91; cons. office and computer svcs. Mauldin, S.C., 1992-93. Lectr. S.C. Edn. Tchrs. Assn., Columbia, 1974, S.C. Assn. Social Workers, Columbia, 1975, Bus. and Profl. Women's Club, Columbia, 1978; small bus. owner, distbr. Nuskin product line, 1987—90; ind. mktg. rep. Network 2000/U.S. Spring, 1988—92; computer specialist Top Food Svcs. Carolina,

Inc., Duncan, SC, 1989—90; admintrv./sales mgr. Cusom Catering, Duncan, 1990; cons. Contract Office/Computer Svcs., Greenville, 1992—; Shaklee ind. distbr., 1998—; dir., sec.-treas., CFO FMW Holdings, Inc., 2000—. Book rev. writer A Class Act, Greenville, 1996—; appeared with Aiken Cmty. Theatre, 1981. Bd. dirs. Quest Soc., Greenville, 1992-95; mem. hospice com. Am. Cancer Soc., Augusta, 1981; lectr. St. John's United Meth. Ch., 1981-82, A Class Act, 1998; registrar, treas. Sugar Creek Soccer Club, Greenville, 1996-97. Mem. A Creative Gathering Writers Group, Writer's Roundtable. Democrat. Avocations: writing, reading, travel, study/research exploring the internet. Home and Office: PO Box 333 Mauldin SC 29662-0333 E-mail: cobfrank@charter.net.

WOOD, NANCY ELIZABETH, psychologist, educator; d. Donald Sterret and Orne Louise (Erwin) W. BS, Ohio U., 1943, MA, 1947; PhD, Northwestern U., Evanston, Ill., 1952. Prof. Case Western Res. U., Cleve., 1952-60; specialist, expert HEW, Washington, 1960-62; chief rsch. USPHS, Washington, 1962-64; prof. U. So. Calif., L.A., 1965—. Learning disabilities cons., 1960-70; assoc. dir. Cleve. Hearing and Speech Ctr., 1952-60; dir. licensing program Brit. Nat. Trust, London. Author: Language Disorders, 1964, Language Development, 1970, Verbal Learning, 1975 (monograph) Auditory Disorders, 1978, Levity, 1980, Stoneskipping, 1989, Bird Cage, 1994, Out of Control, 1999. Pres. faculty senate U. So. Calif., 1987-88. Recipient Outstanding Faculty award Trojan Fourth Estate, 1982, Pres.' Svc. award U. So. Calif., 1992. Fellow APA (cert.), AAAS, Am. Speech and Hearing Assn. (legis. coun. 1965-68); mem. Internat. Assn. Scientists. Republican. Methodist. Office: U So Calif University Park Los Angeles CA 90089-0001

WOOD, PAULA DAVIDSON, lawyer; b. Oklahoma City, Dec. 20, 1952; d. Paul James and Anna Mae (Ferrero) Davidson; m. Andrew E. Wood; children: Michael Paul, John Roland. BS, Okla. State U., 1976; JD, Oklahoma City U., 1982. Bar: Okla. 1983, U.S. Dist. Ct. (we. dist.) Okla. 1983, U.S. Supreme Ct. 1995; cert. pub. mgr. Pvt. practice, Oklahoma City, 1984-85; ptnr. Davidson & Wood, Oklahoma City, 1985-87; child support enforcement counsel Okla. Dept. Human Svcs., Oklahoma City, 1987-92, child support adminstr. (IV-D dir.), 1992-96; pvt. practice Oklahoma City, 1997—2004; atty. Legal iad Svcs. Okla., Inc., Oklahoma City, 2004—. Adj. instr. Tech. Inst. Okla. State U., Oklahoma City, 1985. Articles editor Oklahoma City U. Law Rev., 1982. Bd. dirs. Okla. Youth Symphony, 2000-01. Mem. Okla. Bar Assn. (sec. family law sect. 1987, Golden Gavel award 1987, Artist of the Yr. 1999), Nat. Child Support Enforcement Assn. (bd. dirs. 1995, sec. 1997), Okla. Child Support Enforcement Assn. (pres. 1992), S.W. Regional Child Assn. (pres. 1996), Western Interstate Child Support Enforcement Coun. (sec. 1995). Republican. Roman Catholic. Home: 3020 Shadybrook Dr Midwest City OK 73110-4133 Office: Legal Aid Svcs Okla Inc 2901 Classen Blvd Ste 112 Oklahoma City OK 73106 Office Phone: 405-521-1302. Personal E-mail: pwoodatty@aol.com.

WOOD, PHOEBE A. food products executive; Grad., Smith Coll.; MBA, UCLA. With Atlantic Richfield Co.; v.p. CFO Propel, Inc. divsn. Motorola, Inc.; exec. v.p., CFO Brown-Forman Corp., Louisville, 2002—. Office: Brown-Forman Corp 850 Dixie Hwy Louisville KY 40210

WOOD, ROBERTA SUSAN, retired foreign service officer; b. Clarksdale, Miss., Oct. 4, 1948; d. Robert Larkin and Dorothy Eloise (Shelton) Wood. BA with distinction, Rhodes Coll., Memphis, 1970; postgrad., Nat. U. Cuyo, Mendoza, Argentina, 1970-71; MPA, Harvard U., 1980. Joined U.S. Fgn. Svc., 1972; svc. in Manila, Philippines, Naples and Turin, Italy, and Port-au-Prince, Haiti; mgmt. analyst Dept. State, Washington, 1980-84; U.S. consul gen. Jakarta, Indonesia, 1984-87, NATO Def. Coll., Rome, 1987-88, Marseilles, France, 1988-91, Montreal, Que., Can., 1991-94; min., dep. chief of mission Am. Embassy, Quito, Ecuador, 1994-95; U.S. consul gen. Moscow, 1997-98; dep. asst. sec. state wstn. hemisphere affairs Washington, 1998—2001.

WOOD, ROSEMARY RUSTON, environmental health scientist, consultant; b. Auckland, New Zealand, Oct. 20, 1952; d. Agnes Rosetta Eady and Edward Phillip Wood; life ptnr. Diane Marie Reilly, Mar. 28, 1997. MD, U. of Auckland, 1971—79; Cert. of Proficiency with distinction, Inst. of Classical Homoeopathy, 1994—98. Risk assessment scientist Harding Lawson Associates, Novato, Calif., 1991; prin. risk assessment scientist SLR Internat. Corp, Concord, Calif., 2001—. Instr. Inst. of Classical Homoeopathy, San Francisco, 1997—98. Mem. New Zealand Green Party, Wellington, New Zealand, 2002—. Mem.: Society for Risk Analysis (councilor, no. calif. br. 2001—02). Siddha Yoga. Avocations: homoeopathic medicine, writing poetry, child and animal welfare, hiking, gardening. Office: SLR International Corp 1430 Willow Pass Rd Ste 230 Concord CA 94520 E-mail: rrwood@slrcorp.com.

WOOD, RUTH LUNDGREN WILLIAMSON See LUNDGREN, RUTH WILLIAMSON WOOD

WOOD, SIGRID LYNN, art educator; b. Bad Axe, Mich., Feb. 24, 1947; d. Roy Nelson Wood and Irene Elizabeth Albro. BS in Edn., Ctrl. Mich. U., Mt. Pleasant, 1970, MA, 1980. Art tchr. Swartz Creek Schs., Mich., 1970—71, Jefferson Schs., Monroe, Mich., 1971—73; dir. sales and mktg. Holiday Inn, Mt. Pleasant, Mich., 1974—2000; art tchr. Mt. Pleasant Schs., Mich., 2000—. Recipient Best of Show in fibers, Mt. Pleasant Art Assn., 1st pl. award in fibers; grantee, Saginaw Chippewa Tribe, 2000—. Mem.: Mich. Art Edn. Assn. (region 12 liason). Methodist. Avocations: porcelain dollmaker, stained glass maker, hot glass bead maker, weaver, pottery. Home: 417 N Franklin Mount Pleasant MI 48858

WOOD, SUSAN, applied technology center executive; Honours BS in Physics, Victoria U., Manchester, Eng., 1969; MS in Metall. Engring., U. Pitts., 1973, PhD in Materials Engring., 1976. Rsch. mgmt. positions to gen. mgr. materials tech. divsn. Westinghouse Sci. and Tech. Ctr., Pitts.; various positions to mgr. mfg. tech. dept. Westinghouse Electronic Sys., Balt.; v.p., dir. Savannah River Tech. Ctr., Westinghouse Savannah River Co., Aiken, S.C., 1994—. Presenter, spkr. at nat. and internat. confs.; former mem. Def. Sci. Bd.; mem. nuclear materials tech. divsn. rev. com. Los Alamos (N.Mex.) Nat. Lab. Contbr. articles to profl. jours. Bd. Dirs. Women in Engring. Program Advs. Network, United Way Aiken County, 1997; bd. dirs., advisor univs. throughout U.S. Named Disting. Alumnus, U. Pitts. Sch. Engring., 1997. Achievements include patents in materials engineering. Office: Westinghouse Savannah River Savannah River Tech Ctr Aiken SC 29808-0001

WOOD, SUSAN, poet, literature educator; b. Commerce, Tex., 1946; BA, East Tex. State U., 1968; MA, U. Tex., Arlington, 1970; postgrad., Rice U., 1973—76. H.S. tchr., 1970—73; prof. English., chmn. dept. Rice U., Houston, 1981—. Presenter in field; book editor Houston Chronicle, 1975—76; editor, writer Washington Post, 1977—81. Editor: newspaper and mag.; author: Bazaar, 1981, Campo Santo, 1991 (Lamont Poetry Selection, 1991), Asunder, 2001; contbr. poems to jours. Guggenheim fellow, 1998. Office: Rice Univ 6100 Main Houston TX 77005

WOOD, VALERIE J. public information officer, writer; d. Alfred Standell Williams, Sr. and Mary Jane Mabee; m. Ralph Wilson Wood, Jr., Apr. 17, 1982. Student, Western Md. Coll., 1976, Catonsville C.C., 1977—79. Ordained reverend Universal Life Ch., 2002; grad. introductory auditor tng. Insp. Gen.s' Auditor Tng. Inst. Pub. affairs specialist Office of the Insp. Gen., Social Security Adminstrn., Balt., 1998—. Editor nat. bi-weekly publ. Eye on OIG Office of the Insp. Gen., Social Security Adminstrn., Balt., 2001—, visual info. and arts specialist for publs, 2001—. Author: (novels) Enforcer; contbr. sports commentary to editl. column www.teamracin.com; photographs, interviews, articles in monthly sports mag., Hockey Ink!. Mem.: Am. Cat Fanciers Assn. (life). Republican. Avocations: genealogy, writing, photography/graphic arts, gardening, culinary.

WOOD, VIVIAN POATES, mezzo soprano, educator, writer; b. Washington, Aug. 19, 1923; d. Harold Poates and Mildred Georgette (Patterson) W. Studies with Walter Anderson, Antioch Coll., 1953-55; Denise Restout, Saint-Leu-A-Fôret, France and Lakeville, Conn., 1960-62, 64-70; Paul A. Pisk, 1968-71; Paul Ulanowsky, N.Y.C., 1958-68; Elemer Nagy, 1965-68, Vyautas Marijosius, 1967-68; MusB, Hartt Coll. Music, 1968; postgrad. (fellow), Yale U., 1968; MusM (fellow), Washington U., St. Louis, 1971, PhD (fellow), 1973. Debut in recital series Internat. Jeunesse Musicals Arts Festival, 1953; solo fellowship Boston Symphony Orch., Berkshire Music Ctr., Tanglewood, 1964, St. Louis Symphony Orch., 1969, Washington Orch., 1949, Bach Cantata Series Berkshire Chamber Orch., 1964, Yale Symphony Orch., 1968. Appearances in U.S. and European recitals, oratorios, operas, radio and TV, 1953-68; soloist Landowska Ctr., Lakeville, 1969, Internat. Harpsichord Festival, Westminister Choir Coll., Princeton, N.J., 1973; prof. voice, head voice area Sch. of Music, U. So. Miss., Hattiesburg, 1971-2000, ret. 2000, prof. emerita, 2000—; asst. dean Coll. Fine Arts, 1974-76, acting dean, 1976-77; guest prof. Hochschüle für Musik, Munich, 1978-79; prof. Italian Internat. Studies Program, Rome, 1986; Miss. coord. Alliance for Arts Edn., Kennedy Ctr. Performing Arts, 1974—; mem. Miss. Gov.'s Adv. Panel for Gifted and Talented Children, 1974—, 1st Miss. Gov.'s Conf. on the Arts, 1974—. Author: Polenc's Songs: An Analysis of Style, 1971. Recipient Young Am. Artists Concert award N.Y.C., 1955; Wanda Landowska fellow 1961-68. Mem. Miss. Music Tchrs. Assn., Nat. Assn. Tchrs. of Singing, Music Tchrs. Nat. Assn., Am. Musicology Soc., Golden Key, Mu Phi Epsilon, Delta Kappa Gamma, Tau Beta Kappa (hon.), Pi Kappa Lambda. Democrat. Episcopalian.

WOODALL, SUSAN ELAINE, minister; b. Toledo, Ohio, Oct. 22, 1958; d. James Alva and Helen Marie Tipton; m. Larry Lee Woodall, June 5, 1999. BA in polit. sci., sociology, Adrian Coll., 1980; M in div., Methodist Theo. Sch., 1984, MA in alcoholism drug abuse min., 1986. Ordained United Church of Christ. Outpatient counselor Maryhaven, Inc., Columbus, Ohio, 1982—84; pastor Lyme Congl. UCC, Bellevue, Ohio, 1985—94; mental health therapist Bellevue Area Counseling Svcs., 1989—94; pastor First Congl. Ch., Rootstown, Ohio, 1994—. Author various poetry publications. Bd. mem. Fish and Loaves Food Pantry, Bellevue, 1987—93, Christian Cupboard Food Pantry, Bellevue, 1999—; vol. County Clothing Ctr., Ravenna, Ohio, 2000—. Mem.: Ministerial Assoc., Ravenna Area (pres. 1999—2000), Ministerial Assoc., SW Portage County (pres. 2003—04). Democrat. Avocations: singing, guitar and clarinet, writing poetry, swimming, reading. Home: 3053 Hartville Rd Rootstown OH 44272 Office: First Congl Ch UCC 4022 St Rt 44 PO Box 127 Rootstown OH 44272

WOODARD, ALFRE, actress; b. Tulsa, Nov. 8, 1953; m. Roderick Spencer; 2 children. Student, Boston U. Appeared in (films) Remember My Name, 1976, Health, Cross Creek, 1983 (Acad. award nomination), Extremities, 1986, Scrooged, 1988, Mandela, 1988, Miss Firecracker, 1989, Grand Canyon, 1991, The Gun in Betty Lou's Handbag, 1992, Passion Fish, 1992, Heart and Souls, 1993, Rich in Love, 1993, Bopha!, 1993, Blue Chips, 1994, Crooklyn, 1994, How to Make an American Quilt, 1995, (TV series) Tucker's Witch, 1982-83, Sara, 1985, St. Elsewhere, 1985-87, Hill Street Blues (Emmy award for guest appearance in drama series 1984), L.A. Law (Emmy award for guest appearance in drama series 1987), (TV spls.) For Colored Girls Who Have Considered Suicide/When the Rainbow is Enuf, Trial of the Moke, Words by Heart, (TV films) A Mother's Courage: The Mary Thomas Story, Child Saver, Ambush Murder, Freedom Road, 1979, Sophisticated Gents, 1981, The Killing Floor, Unnatural Causes, 1986, Mandela, 1987, The Child Saver, Sweet Revenge, 1990, Blue Bayou, 1990, Bopho, 1993, Race to Freedom: The Underground Railroad, 1994, Blue Chips, 1994, Crooklyn, 1994, Wizard of Oz in Concert, 1995, Statistically speaking, 1995, The Piano Lesson, 1995, How to Make an American Quilt, 1995, Journey to Mars, 1996, Gulliver's Travels, 1996, Primal Fear, 1996, A Step Toward Tomorrow, 1996, Star Trek: First Contact, 1996, Member of the Wedding, 1997, Miss Evers' Boys, 1997, Follow Me Home, 1997, Cadillac Desert (mini series), 1997, Down in the Delta, 1998, Brown Sugar, 1998, Funny Valentines, (tv) 1999, Mumford, 1999, others,(plays) For Colored Girls Who Have Considered Suicide, When the Rainbow is Enuf, (off-Broadway plays) A Map of the World, 1985, A Winter's Tale 1989, So Nice They Named Twice, Horatio, What's Cookin', 2000, Love and Basketball, 2000, Dinosaur, 2000. Recipient Emmy awards for guest appearance in drama series.*

WOODARD, BETH STUCKEY, librarian, educator; b. Fairbury, Ill., Oct. 25, 1956; d. James Dale and Helenjean (Lauterbach) Stuckey; m. Billy Dean Woodard, July 14, 1979 (div. June 1993); children: Rebecca Lindsay, Sarah Lauren; m. Gregory Allen Wolfe, Oct. 21, 1995. BA, Ill. Wesleyan U., 1978; MS, U. Ill., 1979. Reference libr. U. S.C., Columbia, 1979-82; reference libr., ast. prof. libr. adminstrn. U. Ill., Urbana, 1983-85, cen. info. svcs. libr., 1985-99, 2001—, assoc. prof., 1990—, acting head of reference, 1993-94, 97, 2002—03, interim commerce librarian, 1999-2001, staff devel. and tng. coord., 2002—. Cons. Oberlin (Ohio) Coll., 1996, Ea. Ill. U., 1999, So. Ill. U., Edwardsville, 1999, U. Toronto, 2001, Lincoln Christian Coll., 2003, U. Chgo., 2004. Contbr. book chpts. to Reference and Information Services, 1991, 95, 2001; editor: (spl. jour. issue) Ill. Librs., 1991, U. Chgo., 2004; contbr. articles to profl. jours. Chair fund raising com. Oakwood (Ill.) Twp. Pub. Libr., 1997-98, trustee, 2001—, v.p., 2003—. Mem. ALA, Reference and User Svcs. Assn. (evaluation of reference and adult svcs. com. 1990-92, chair 1992-94, bd. dirs. 1994-2001, editor newsletter 1997-2001, Isadore Gilbert Mudge/ R.R. Bowker award 1998), Assn. Coll. and Rsch. Librs. (mem. continuing edn. com. 1988-90, chair 1990-92, chair guidelines for bibliographic instrn. programs 1994-96, sec. instrn. sect. 1992-93, chair comms. com. 1993-94, vice-chair instrn. sect. 2000-01, chair instrn. sect. 2001-2002, chair Dudley awards com. 2002-03, chair nominating com. 2003-04), Phi Kappa Phi, Beta Phi Mu, Alpha Lambda Delta. Office: U of Ill 1408 W Gregory Dr Urbana IL 61801-3607 E-mail: bswoodar@uiuc.edu.

WOODARD, CAROL JANE, educational consultant; b. Buffalo, Jan. 19, 1929; d. Harold August and Violet Maybelle (Landsittel) Young; m. Ralph Arthur Woodard, Aug. 19, 1950; children: Camaron Jane, Carsen Jane, Cooper Ralph. BA, Hartwick Coll., 1950; MA, Syracuse U., 1952; PhD, SUNY, Buffalo, 1972; LHD (hon.), Hartwick Coll., 1991; postgrad., Bank St. Coll., Harvard U. Cert. tchr., NY State. Tchr., Orchard Park, NY, 1950-51, Danville, Ind., 1951-52, Akron, NY, 1952-54; dir. Garden Nursery Sch., Williamsville, NY, 1955-65; tchr. Amherst Coop. Nursery Sch., NY, 1967-69; asst. prof. early childhood edn. SUNY, Buffalo, 1969-72, lab. demonstration tchr. and student teaching supr., 1969-76, assoc. prof., 1972-79, prof., 1979-88, prof. emeritus, 1988—; dir. Consultants in Early Childhood, 1988—. Cons. Lutheran Ch. Am., Villa Maria Coll., Buffalo Pub. Sch., Buffalo Mus. Sci., Headstart Tng. Programs, Erie Cmty. Coll., NY State Dept. Edn., numerous workshops.; cons. sch. systems, indsl. firms, pub., civic orgns. in child devel.; vis. prof. The Netherlands and East China Univ., Shanghai, People's Republic of China; sci. trainer The Wright Group, 1995. Author 7 books for young children, 2 textbooks in field; co-author: Physical Science in Early Childhood, 1987; co-author nat. curriculum for ch. sch. for 3-yr.-olds; author: (booklet) You Can Help Your Baby Learn; author/coord. TAKE CARE child protection project, 1987; contbr. chpt. to books, articles to profl. jour. Trustee Hartwick Coll., Oneonta, NY, 1978-87; cons. EPIC Birth to Three Program, 1992; design cons. indoor playground Noah's Ark Jewish Ctr., Buffalo, 1992; Sites Project coord., cons. Let's Talk project Buffalo Pub. Sch., 1994—; student tchg. supr. SUNY, Fredonia, 1994—. Mem. Nat. Assn. Edn. Young Children, Early Childhood Edn. Council Western NY, Assn. Childhood Edn. Internat., Phi Delta Kappa, Pi Lambda Theta. Home: 85 Ruskin Road East Aurora NY 14052-3028

WOODARD, CLAUDETTE J. state representative, retired educational association administrator; b. 1945; married; 2 children. MEd in Curriculum and Instr. School improvement facilitator; ret.; rep. Ohio State Ho. Reps., Columbus, 2000—. Mem. edn. com. Ohio State Ho. Reps., mem. fed. grant review and edn. oversight subcom., mem. fin. and appropriations com., mem. primary and secondary edn. subcom., mem. ins. com.; adv. bd. Case Western Res. Mental Devel. Ctr. Chmn. spl. needs com. Boy Scouts Am. Spl. Projects; mem. Nat. Coun. Negro Women; treas. Coun. Exceptional Children; pres. Black Women's Polit. Action Com.; co-chmn. Women in Appt. Office Project; bd. dirs. Heights Cmty. Congress; mem. Cleve. Heights-Univ. Heights Bd. Edn., 1991—99. Mem.: Sch. Union Assn., Alpha Kappa Alpha (Meritorious Svc. award 1996). Democrat. Office: Ohio State House Reps 77 South High Street 10th Floor Columbus OH 43215-6111

WOODARD, NINA ELIZABETH, banker; b. L.A., Apr. 3, 1947; d. Alexander Rhodes and Harriette Jane (Powers) Matthews; divorced; children: Regina M., James. D. Grad., Pacific Coast Banking Sch., 1987; BS in Mgmt., Calif. Coast U., 1993; postgrad., Ctr. for Creative Leadership, 1994. Lifetime cert. sr. profl. in human resources. Dental asst. Donald R. Shire DDS, L.A., 1965-66; with Security Pacific Nat. Bank, Marina Del Rey, Calif., 1968-69, First Interstate Bank, Casper, Wyo., 1971—, adminstr. asst. pers., 1975-78, asst. v.p., asst. mgr. pers., 1978-82, v.p., dir. mktg. and pers., 1982-84, v.p., mgr. human resources, 1984-88; v.p., mgr. employee rels. First Interstate Bank Ltd., L.A., 1988-93; v.p., mgr. employee rels. Ams. region Standard Chartered Bank, 1993-95, sr. v.p. human resources, 1995-99, sr. v.p. advisor cultural integration and employee comm., 1999-2000, sr. v.p. mgmt. cultural integration, 2000—. Instr. mktg. Am. Inst. Banking, 1983, Casper Coll., 1982; mng. dir. Aradhana Human Resources Consulting Pvt. Ltd., India, 2002-2003; dir. Western Region Performance Consulting Internat. India, 2003. Mem. Civil Svc. Commn., City of Casper, 1983-88; bd. dirs. YMCA, 1984-87, Downtown Devel. Assn.; pres. Downtown Casper Assn.; instr. St. Patrick's Parish Religious Edn., 1991-92, mem. parish coun., 1993-94; advisor to the parish coun. Parish of the Resurrection, Jersey City, 1999. Named Bus. Woman of Yr., Bus. and Profl. Women, 198, Young Career Woman, 1975. Mem. Nat. Assn. Bank Women, Bus. and Profl. Women (dist. dir.), Am. Soc. Pers. Adminstrn. (regional v.p., state coun. Wyo. 1987-88), Pers. and Indsl. Rels. Assn. (chmn. govt. affairs com. 1989-90, Fast Track award 1991, Pres.'s Achievement award 1993, conf. chmn. 1991, 92, dist. chair 1993, 2d v.p. 1994), Fin. Women Internat. (Wyo. state chair 1986, regional edn. and tng. chair 1987, dist. coord. L.A. 1993, L.A. group chair 1994, nat. bd. dirs.), Soc. Human Resource Mgmt. (area I v.p. 1996-99, N.Y. chpt., NEHRA chpt.), Am. Alumni Assn. India, Bombay Mgmt. Assn., Bombay Midtown Rotary Club. Republican. Roman Catholic. Office: Standard Chartered Bank 2d Fl 23-25 MG Rd Fort Mumbai Mumbai India

WOODBRIDGE, NORMA JEAN, registered nurse, writer; b. Flushing, N.Y., Apr. 21, 1931; d. Charles Jahleel Woodbridge and Ruth Eyman Dunning. BS in Nursing Edn., Temple U., 1958; RN, U. Pa., 1952; LittD, World Congress Poets, Cairo, 1990. RN, Fla. Sr. RN, forensic State of Fla. Dept. Corrections, 1992-95; staff nurse Pines Village, North Ft. Myers, Fla., 1995—97; staff RN Lee Convalescent Ctr., Ft. Myers, Fla., 1997-98; unit mgr. Tandem Health Care, Norht Ft. Myers, 1998-99; nurse Cape Coral (Fla.) Gen. Staff Rehab., 1999—. Author-in-residence Highland Pk. (N.J.) Sch. Sys., 1988-90. Author: African Realities and Dreams, 1987, Resting Places, 1988, Meditations of a Modern Pilgrim, 1990; contbr. Christmas Blessings, 2002; composer (jazz album) Watercolor Dreams, 1982; playwright Switch: Switch, 1998; poetry reading on NPR, 2001. Recipient Poet of the Millenium award, Internat. Poets Acad., 2000; fellow, Yaddo Writing Colony, 1988. Mem.: ASCAP, N.J. Poetry Soc. (v.p. 1987—88), Soc. Am. Poets, Peace River (Fla.) Writers Group. Avocations: travel, fishing, gourmet cooking, hiking, theatre. Home: 2606 Zoysia Ln Fort Myers FL 33917-2476

WOODBURY, MARDA LIGGETT, librarian, writer; b. N.Y.C., Sept. 20, 1925; d. Walter W. and Edith E. (Fleischer) Liggett; m. Philip J. Evans, Sept. 1948 (div. 1950); 1 child, Mark W. Evans; m. Mark Lee Woodbury, 1956 (div. 1969); children: Brian, Heather. Student, Bklyn. Coll., 1942-44; BA in Chemistry and Polit. Sci., Bard Coll., 1946; BS in L.S., Columbia U., 1948; postgrad., U. Calif., Berkeley, 1955-56, 60-61, MJ, 1995. Cert. tchr. Libr. various spl., med. and pub. librs., San Francisco, 1946-60, Coll. Pk. High Sch., Mt. Diablo, Calif., 1962-67; elem. sch. libr. Oakland and Berkeley, Calif., 1967-69; libr. dir. Far West Lab. Ednl. Rsch. & Devel., San Francisco, 1969-73; libr., editor Gifted Resource Ctr., San Mateo, Calif., 1973-75; libr. cons. Rsch. Ventures, Berkeley, Calif., 1975—2003; libr. dir. Life Chiropractic Coll., San Lorenzo, Calif., 1980-95. Author: A Guide to Sources of Educational Information, 1976, 2d edit., 1982, Selecting Instructional Materials, 1978, Selecting Materials for Instruction, Vol. I: Issues and Policies, 1979, Vol. II: Media and the Curriculum, 1980, Vol. III: Subject Areas and Implementation, 1980, Childhood Information Resources, 1985 (Outstanding Ref. Work, Assn. Ref. Librs. 1985), Youth Information Resources, 1987, Stopping the Presses: The Murder of Walter W. Liggett, 1998; mem. editorial bd. Ref. Libr., 1980-95. Home: 145 Monte Cresta Ave Apt 402 Oakland CA 94611-4809 Office Phone: 510-653-5876. E-mail: MardaWoodbury@msn.com.

WOODCOCK, JANET, federal official; b. Washington, Pa., Aug. 29, 1948; d. John and Frances (Crocker) W.; m. Roger Henry Miller, Nov. 16, 1981; children: Kathleen Miller, Susanne Miller. BS cum laude, Bucknell U., 1970; MD, Northwestern U., Chgo., 1977. Diplomate Am. Bd. Internal Medicine. Intern Hershey Med. Ctr./Pa. State U., 1977-78, resident in internal medicine, 1978-80, chief resident in medicine, 1980-81; fellow in rheumatology U. Calif./VA Med. Ctr., San Francisco, 1982-84; instr. medicine divsn. rheumatology and immunology VA Med. Ctr., San Francisco, 1984-85; med. officer divsn. biol. investigational new drugs Ctr. for Biologics Evaluation and Rsch./FDA, Rockville, Md., 1986-87, group leader divsn. biol. investigational new drugs, 1987-88, dep. dir. divsn. biol. investigational new drugs, 1988, dir. divsn. biol. investigational new drugs, 1988-90; dir. Ctr. for Drug Evaluation and Rsch./FDA, Rockville, Md., 1994—; acting dep. dir. Ctr. for Biologics Evaluation and Rsch., FDA, Rockville, Md., 1990-92, dir. office of therapeutics rsch. and rev., 1992-94; dir. Ctr. for Drug Evaluation and Rsch., FDA, Rockville, 1994—. Instr. medicine, asst. prof. divsn. gen. internal medicine Hershey Med. Ctr./Pa. State U., 1981; analytical chemist rsch. divsn. A.B. Dick Co., Niles, Ill., 1971-73. Nat. Merit scholar Bucknell U., 1966, Pa. State scholar, 1966; Rsch. fellow Am. Rheumatism Assn.; VA Investigator grantee, 1985. Mem. Alpha Omega Alpha, Alpha Lambda Delta. Office: Ctr Drug Evaluation & Rsch US Food & Drug Admin 5600 Fishers Lane Rockville MD 20857*

WOODFORD, ANN MARGUERITE, social services administrator, social worker; b. Bklyn., Mar. 12, 1954; d. Nicholas Gonzaga and Lilly Marguerite (Nielson) W. BS cum laude, CUNY, Bklyn., 1976; MA, Fordham U., 1979, MSW, 1990. Cert. secondary edn. educator. Youth dir. tchr. Cath. Diocese Bklyn., 1976-88; therapist, social worker Angel Guardian Home, Bklyn., 1988-90; program coord. Talbot Perkins Childrens Svcs., N.Y.C., 1990-92; supr. Angel Guardian Home Intensive Med. Mgmt. Program, Bklyn., 1992-96; program coord., supr. Cardinal McCloskey Svcs., Therapeutic Foster Boarding Home, Bronx, N.Y., 1996-97; exec. dir. Amethyst House, S.I., N.Y., 1997—. Resident vol. staff Providence House, Bklyn., 1981-96, Women Helping Women, Flushing, N.Y., 1984-85; cons. Providence House, Bklyn., 1981-97, Angel Guardian Home, Bklyn., 1996—. Mem. Sisters of Charity, Halifax, 1977—; bd. dirs. Advs. for Svcs.

for the Blind Multihandicapped, 1994—, S.I. Com. on Alcoholism and Substance Abuse, 1997, co-chair, 1999—; leader Girl Scouts Am., 1994—. Named Outstanding Leader, Girl Scouts Am., Greater N.Y. Coun., 1996. Mem. NASW. Democrat. Roman Catholic. Avocations: gardening, cooking, camping, arts and crafts, singing. Office: Amethyst House Inc 75 Vanderbilt Ave Staten Island NY 10304-2604

WOODHAM, PATRICIA H. accounting and business consultant; b. Dothan, Ala., June 7, 1950; d. Ralph and Willie Frances (Hodges) Harrison; m. Jerry Frank Parmer, July 12, 1968 (dec. June 1995); children: Latricia Lynne, Jerry Wayne; m. James Edward Woodham, June 27, 1998. Student, Broward C.C., Pompano Beach, Fla., 1988-89. Contr. Atlantic Oil Co., Fayette, Ala., 1974-78; personnel dir. Fayco, Fayette, 1978-80; controller SAC Cons., Birmingham, 1980-82, Yarborough Co., High Point, N.C., 1982-84, S.E. Med. Cons., Tucker, Ga., 1984-86, Golnick Advtsg., Ft. Lauderdale, Fla., 1986-87; paraprofl. Ernst & Young, Ft. Lauderdale, 1987-91, Eric Young CPA, Norcross, Ga., 1991-95, Tim Couch CPA, Lawrenceville, Ga., 1995-96; bus. cons. McDaniel & Assoc. P.C., Dothan, Ala., 1996—. Pres. Women's Aux., Fayette, 1976-80; acct. Republican Woemn, Dothan, 1998; mem. Flower PAC, Thomasville, Ga., 1970-95. Mem. Inst. Mgmt. Accts. (dir. 1999—). Republican. Baptist. Avocations: fishing, hiking, football, reading, gardening. Home: RR 2 Box 135 Headland AL 36345-9431

WOODHOUSE, ELIZABETH C. retired government agency administrator; b. Cin., Nov. 10, 1911; d. John Michael Hughes and Katherine Martha Berger; m. Elton Lee Woodhouse, Mar. 25, 1932 (dec. Feb. 8, 1970); children: Allan, Jerry, Carolyn, Margaret. BS, Urbana (Ohio) U., 1979; Masters Degree, Cath. Distance U., 2002. Dir. Child Care Ctr., Springfield, Ohio, 1953—82, Mental Health Soc., Springfield, Ohio, 1955—70, USDA Food Svc., Columbus, Ohio, 1977—97. Author: Beginnings, 1987, Johnny Appleseed Poems, 2001. Pres. Child Care Assn., Springfield, 1960—65, Mental Health Assn., Springfield, 1966—70; county chair Ohioana Libr. Assn., Columbus, 1980—; pres. Friends of the Libr. Clark County Pub. Libr., Springfield, Ohio, 2001; pres. Springfield Symphony Orch., 1997—99; pres., sec., treas. Altrusa Internat., 1970, Federated Women's Clubs, 1945—2001. Recipient 3 awards, Clark County and Ohio State Mental Health Assns., Elizabeth Woodhouse award named in her honor, Wittenberg U., Springfield, 1997. Roman Catholic. Avocations: doll collecting, collecting teapots. Home: 508 Latimer Dr Springfield OH 45503 E-mail: equote@aol.com.

WOODHOUSE, GAY VANDERPOEL, former state attorney general, lawyer; b. Torrington, Wyo., Jan. 8, 1950; d. Wayne Gaylord and Sally (Rouse) Vanderpoel; m. Randy Woodhouse, Nov. 26, 1983; children: Dustin, Houston. BA with honors, U. Wyo., 1972, JD, 1977. Bar: Wyo. 1978, U.S. Dist. Ct. Wyo., U.S. Supreme Ct. Dir. student Legal Svcs., Laramie, Wyo., 1976—77; assoc. Donald Jones Law Offices, Torrington, 1977—78; asst. atty. gen. State of Wyo., Cheyenne, 1978—84, sr. asst. atty. gen., 1984—89, spl. U.S. atty., 1987—89, asst. U.S. atty., 1990—95, chief dept. atty. gen., 1995—98, atty. gen., 1998—2000. Chmn. Wyo. Tel. Consumer Panel, Casper, 1982—86; advisor Cheyenne Halfway House, 1984—93; chmn. Wyo. Silent Witness Initiative Zero Domestic Violence by 2010, 1997, Wyo. Domestic [illegible] Commn., 1999—2001; mem. State Bar Commn. First Dist., 2002—05; spl. projects cons. N.Am. Securities Adminstrs. Assn., 1987—89; Chmn. bd. Pathfinder, 1987; S.E. Wyo. Mental Health. Mem.: Federalist Soc. for Law and Pub.Policy Studies (v.p., Wyo. chpt. 2003—04), Prevent Child Abuse Wyo., Laramie County Bar Assn., Cheyenne (Wyo.) C. of C., Toastmasters, Rotary. Republican. Avocations: inline speed skating, stained glass. Address: 211 W 19th St Ste 308 Cheyenne WY 82001 Office: 123 Capitol Bldg Cheyenne WY 82002-0001 Office Phone: 307-432-9399. Personal E-mail: gaywoodhouselaw@aol.com. Business E-Mail: gay@woodhouselawoffice.com.

WOODRUFF, DEBRA A. occupational health nurse; b. Salem, Ill., Dec. 22, 1952; d. Merle D. and Georgia Lee (Johnson) Anderson; m. Thomas E. Howarth, June 16, 1973 (div. Sept. 1979); 1 child, Michael T. Diploma in Practical Nursing, Vo-Tech Teche Area, New Iberia, La., 1972; ADN, Miss. Delta Jr. Coll., Moorhead, 1975. LPN, La.; cert. occupl. health nurse. LPN in ICU Iberia Gen. Hosp., New Iberia, 1972-73, head nurse ICU, 1979-81; charge nurse infection control Bolivar County Hosp., Cleveland, Miss., 1973-79, dir. long-term care, 1981-89; sr. indsl. nurse Baxter Healthcare Corp., Cleveland, 1989-96, Tampa, Fla., 1996—. Mem. Am. Assn. Occupl. Health Nurses, Miss. Assn. Occupl. Health Nurses. Republican. Baptist. Avocations: reading, singing, cross-stitch, exercise. Office: Baxter Healthcare Corp 7511 114th Ave Largo FL 33773-5129

WOODRUFF, DIANE CAREY, college president; b. San Jose, Calif., Dec. 5, 1942; d. Evan Dennis and Dorothy Elizabeth Jelcick; m. D. Thomas Woodruff, July 11, 1998. BA, U. Calif. Berkeley, 1964, EdD, 1979, postgrad. fellow, U. Calif. L.A., 1979. Asst. supt. State Dept. Edn., Sacramento, 1983; dean Sacramento City Coll., 1983-85; dir. comms. and edn. devel. Los Rios Dist., Sacramento, 1985-88; v.p. Napa Valley Coll., Napa, Calif., 1988-92, supt./pres., 1992—. Author: Motivating and Dissatisfying Factors in a Group Profl. Educators, 1979. Recipient Woman of Yr. award, Calif. legis., 1996; leadership award, Napa Valley Peace Table, 1999; named Woman of Distinction in Wine Country, 2000. Mem. Rotary Napa. Office: Napa Valley Coll 2277 Napa Vallejo Hwy Napa CA 94558-6236 E-mail: dwoodruff@campus.nvc.cc.ca.us.

WOODRUFF, FAY, paleoceanographer, geological researcher; b. Boston, Jan. 23, 1944; d. Lorande Mitchell and Anne (Fay) W.; m. Alexander Whitehill Clowes, May 20, 1972 (div. Oct. 1974); m. Robert G. Douglas, Jan. 27, 1980; children: Ellen, Katerina. RN, Mass. Gen. Hosp. Sch. Nursing, Boston, 1966; BA, Boston U., 1971; MS, U. So. Calif., 1979. Rsch. assoc. U. So. Calif., L.A., 1978-81, rsch. faculty, 1981-96. Keynote spkr. 4th Internat. Symposium on Benthic Foraminifera, Sendai, Japan, 1990. Contbg. author: Geological Society of America Memoir, 1985; contbr. articles to profl. jours. Life mem. The Nature Conservancy, Washington, 1992; bd. dirs. Friends of Friendship Park, Inc., 1995-2001; co-founder, v.p. Resources Families Adopted Ea. European Children, Inc., L.A., 1996-2000. NSF grantee, 1986-94. Mem. Am. Geophys. Union, Geol. Soc. Am., Internat. Union Geol. Scis. (internat. commn. on stratigraphy, subcommn. on Neogene stratigraphy 1991-99), Soc. Woman Geographers (sec. So. Calif. chpt. 1990-96), Soc. Econ. Paleontologists and Mineralogists (sec., editor N.Am. Micropaleontology sect. 1988-90), Sigma Xi. Office: U So Calif Earth Scis Los Angeles CA 90089-0001

WOODRUFF, JANE, sales executive; b. Derby, Eng., July 20, 1945; d. George John Schwaegerman and Joyce (Robinson) Turnock; m. Charles Walter Woodruff, Aug. 1, 1964 (div. 1976); 1 child, Jon Bradley. BA, Purdue U., 1967, MS, 1968, MA, 1970. Tchr. Kansas City (Mo.) Schs., 1970-73; asst. dir. communicatons Skyline Corp., Elkart, Ind., 1974-77; market analyst Motor Wheel Corp. subs. Goodyear Tire and Rubber Co., Lansing, Mich., 1977-80, mgr. planning and research, 1980-82, mgr. car and light truck mktg., 1982-84; account exec. Motor Wheel Corp., Farmington Hills, Mich., 1984-96; acct. exec. Enkei Internat., Madison Heights, Mich., 1996-98, asst. dept. mgr., O.E.S., 1998—. Chmn. Motor Wheel Savs. Bond Drive, Lansing, 1980; fundraiser Capital Area United Way, Lansing, 1981; cons. bus. projects Jr. Achievement, Lansing, 1981-82. NDEA scholar U.S. Dept. Edn., 1967-68; teaching fellow Purdue U., 1968-70; recipient Cert. Achievement YWCA, Lansing, 1980. Mem. Indsl. Mktg. Group Am. Mktg. Assn. (treas.), Automotive Market Research Council, Soc. Automotive Engrs. Office: Enkei Internat 32400 Industrial Dr Madison Heights MI 48071-1527

WOODRUFF, JUDY CARLINE, broadcast journalist; b. Tulsa, Nov. 20, 1946; d. William Henry and Anna Lee (Payne) W.; m. Albert R. Hunt, Jr., Apr. 5, 1980; children: Jeffrey Woodruff, Benjamin Woodruff, Lauren Ann Lee. Student, Meredith Coll., 1964-66; BA, Duke U., 1968. News announcer, reporter Sta. WAGA-TV, Atlanta, 1970-75; news corr. NBC News, Atlanta, 1975-76, White House corr. Washington, 1977-83; anchor Frontline, PBS documentary series, 1983-90; corr. MacNeil-Lehrer News Hour, PBS, Washington, 1983-93; anchor, sr. corr. CNN, Washington, 1993—, prime anchor, sr. coord. Bd. advisors Henry Grady Sch. Journalism, U. Ga., 1979-82, Benton Fellowship in Broadcast Journalism, U. Chgo., 1984-90, Knight Fellowship in Journalism, Stanford U., 1985—; bd. visitors Wake Forest U., 1982-89; trustee Duke U., 1985—; founding bd. dirs. Internat. Women's Media Found. Author: This is Judy Woodruff at the White House, 1982. Active Commn. on Women's Health, The Commonwealth Fund. Recipient award Leadership Atlanta, Class of 1974, Atlanta chpt. Women in Comms., 1975, Edward Weintal award for excellence in fgn. policy reporting, 1987, Joan Shorenstein Barone award for series on def. issues, 1987, Helen Bernstein award for excellence in journalism N.Y. Pub. Libr., 1989, Pres.'s award Nat. Women's Hall of Fame, 1994, CableAce award for best newscaster, 1995, Allen H. Neuharth award for excellence in journalism, 1995. Mem. NATAS (Atlanta chpt. Emmy award 1975), White House Corrs. Assn. Office: Cable News Network 820 1st St NE Washington DC 20002-4243

WOODRUFF, KATHRYN ELAINE, English language educator; b. Ft. Stockton, Tex., Oct. 12, 1940; d. James Arthur and Catherine H. (Stevens) Borron; m. Thomas Charles Woodruff, May 18, 1969; children: Robert Borron, David Borron. BA, Our Lady of the Lake U., San Antonio, 1963; MFA, U. Alaska, 1969; PhD, U. Denver, 1987. Cert. tchr., Tex., Colo. English and journalism tchr. Owensboro (Ky.) Cath. High Sch., 1963-64, Grand Junction (Colo.) Dist. 12, 1964-66; English tchr. Monroe High Sch., Fairbanks, Alaska, 1966-67; teaching asst. U. Alaska, Fairbanks, 1967-69, instr., 1969-70, U. Colo., Boulder, 1979, Denver, 1988-89, Regis Coll., Denver, 1987-89; asst. prof. Econs. Inst., Boulder, 1989-92; assoc. prof. English Colo. Christian U., Lakewood, 1993—. Tchr. Upward Bound, Fairbanks, 1968; instr. ethnic and women writers course U. Colo., Denver, 1988-93; mem. Assoc. Writing Programs; soprano Boulder Chorale, Cantabile Singers, St. John's Cathedral Choir, Augustana Chamber Choir; mem. Women's Studies Delegation to South Africa, 1998; active in missionary work in Ecuador, 1998, European Singing Tour with Augustana Arts, 1998, 2000. Author: (poetry) Before the Burning, 1994; poetry readings in Colo., Tex. and Paris; poems publ. in Denver Quarterly, The Incliner, Southwestern Am. Lit. Friend Chautauqua Music Festival, Boulder, 1985—; dir. 12th Annual Arts Festival, Fairbanks, 1969; active Augustana Chamber Chorus, St. John's Cathedral Choir; bd. mem. Denver Bach Soc. Recipient Poet's Choice award Internat. Soc. Poetry, 1997; named one of Outstanding Young Women Am., 1966; nominated for Poet Laureate of Colo., 1996; NEH grantee, 1996. Mem. AAUW, MLA, Am. Assn. Univ. Professors, Assoc. Writing Programs, Soc. Internat. Devel. UN Assn., Nat. Women's Hall of Fame, Acad. of Am. Poets, Denver Bach Soc. (bd. dirs. 2003), Internat. Women's Writing Guild. Democrat. Mem. Christian Ch. Avocations: singing, tennis, skiing, volleyball, travel. Office: Colo Christian U 180 S Garrison St Lakewood CO 80226-1053

WOODRUFF, KAY HERRIN, pathologist, educator; b. Charlotte, N.C., Sept. 22, 1942; d. Herman Keith and Helen Thelma (Tucker) Herrin; m. John T. Lyman, May 3, 1980; children: Robert, Geoffry, Carolyn. BA in Chemistry, Duke U., 1964; MD, Emory U., 1968. Diplomate Am. Bd. Pathology (trustee 1993—, sec. 1998-2000, v.p. 2000-2001, pres. 2001—). Medicine and pediat. intern U. N.C., Chapel Hill, 1968-69, resident in anatomic pathology, 1969-70; chief resident in anatomic pathology, instr. U. Okla., Oklahoma City, 1970-71, fellow in electron microscopy-pulmonary pathology, instr., 1971-72; chief resident in clin. pathology U. Calif., San Francisco, 1972-74, asst. clin. prof. dept. anatomic pathology, 1974-91, assoc. clin. prof., 1991—; chief electron microscopy VA Hosp., San Francisco, 1974-75; pvt. practice, San Pablo, Calif., 1981—. Pres. med. staff Brookside Hosp., San Pablo, 1994, med. dir. Regional Cancer Ctr., 1995-98 ; assoc. pathologist Children's Hosp., San Francisco, 1979-81, St. Joseph's Hosp., San Francisco, 1977-79; cons. pathologist Lawrence Berkeley (Calif.) Lab., 1974-93; med. dir. Bay Area Tumor Inst. Tissue Network, San Pablo, 1989—; asst. clin. prof. pathology health and med. scis. program U. Calif., Berkeley and U. Calif., San Francisco Joint Med. Program, 1985-91, assoc. clin. prof., 1991—, others. Contbr. articles and abstracts to med. jours. Mem. exec. bd. Richmond (Calif.) Quits Smoking, 1986-90, Bay Area Tumor Inst., Oakland, Calif., 1987—; mem. exec. bd. Contra Costa unit Am. Cancer Soc., Walanut Creek, Calif., 1985-87, mem. profl. edn. com., 1985-90, mem. pub. edn. com., 1985-86, mem. task force on breast health Calif. div., 1992-93; mem. transfusion adv. com. Irwin Meml. Blood Bank, San Francisco, 1977-83; chmn. transfusion adv. com. Alameda Contra County Blood Bank, 1989-92; commr. Calif. Bd. Med. Quality Assurance, 1978-80; pres. Brookside Found., San Pablo, Calif., 1998-2000 Recipient young investigator award Am. Lung Assn., 1975-77; Outstanding Svc. awards Am. Cancer Soc., 1986, 87, Disting. Svc. award, 1988; Disting. Clin. Tchg. award U. Calif., San Francisco and Berkeley Joint Med. Program, 1987, Outstanding Tchg. award, 1988, Excellence in Basic Sci. Instrn. award, 1990, Excellence in Tchr. Clin. Scis. award, 1993; cert. of recognition Cmty. Svc. Richmond, 1989. Mem. AMA, Coll. Am. Pathologists (editl. bd. CAP Today 1986-90, bd. govs. 1990-96, chmn. coun. on practice mgmt. 1994, William Kuhn award for outstanding comm. 1996, Presdl. Medal of Honor 1995, 96), Am. Med. Women's Assn. (exec. bd. 1984-87, regional bd. govs. 1984-87), No. Calif. Women's Med. Assn. (pres. 1982-84), Calif. Soc. Pathologists (bd. dirs. 1988-90), No. Calif. Oncology Group, South Bay Pathology Soc. (pres. 1987), Am. Assn. Blood Banks, Calif. Med. Assn., Alameda-Contra Costa County Med. Soc., Am. Soc. Clin. Pathology, Calif. Pathology Soc. Avocation: classical piano. Office: Doctors Med Ctr 2000 Vale Rd San Pablo CA 94806-3808

WOODRUFF, MARY BRENNAN, elementary school educator, educator; d. John L. and Josephine (Martino) Brennan; m. Paul R. Woodruff; children: Christopher, Jeffery. BS, SUNY, Brockport; MS, SUNY, Buffalo, 1987. Cert. elem. tchr. N.Y., 1968. Third grade tchr. Middleport (N.Y.) Elem., fifth grade tchr., 1979—2003, math specialist K-6, 2003—. Sch. improvement presenter, mem., dist. curriculum guide, facilitator Social Studies curriculum, Royalton-Hartland Cen. Sch., Middleport, NY, 1989—, co-author mentor program for Royalton-Hartland District, Project "Deep" Elem. Econ. faciliator Contributing author Royalton-Hartland Curriculum Guide 1989; designer of spelling program 5th grade. Campaign mgr. Rep. Legislator, Orleans County, 1979-87. Mem.: ASCD, Royalton-Hartford Tchrs. Assn. (v.p., pres. 1998—, chmn. grievance com.), N.Y State United Tchrs. (v.p. exec. coun., Leadership award 1997, 2004), Delta Kappa Gamma, Delta Xi. Avocations: political action, writing, reading.

WOODRUFF, VALERIE, secretary of education; m. Frank Woodruff; 1 child, Scott 1 stepchild, Sheri. BEd in Secondary Edn., Alderson Broaddus Coll., W. Va.; MA in guidance and counseling, U. Del.; postgrad. studies in vocat. edn. and curriculum devel., Temple U., 1999—. From tchr. to prin. New Castle County, Del., Cecil County Md.; assoc. sec. for curriculum and instructional improvement Del. Dept. Edn., Dover, Del., 1992—99, acting sec., 1999—2000, sec, 2000—. Office: Del Dept Edn Townsend Bldg #279 401 Federal St Ste 2 Dover DE 19903-1402

WOODRUFF, VIRGINIA, broadcast journalist, writer; b. Morrisville, Pa. d. Edwin Nichols and Louise (Meredith) W.; m. Raymond F. Beagle Jr. (div.); m. Albert Plaut II (div.); 1 child, Elise Meredith. Student, Rutgers U. News corr. Sta. WNEW-TV Metromedia, N.Y.C., 1967; nat., internat. critic-at-large Mut. Broadcasting System, 1968-75; lectr. Leigh Bur., 1969-71; byline columnist N.Y. Daily Mirror, N.Y.C., 1970-71; first Arts critic Teleprompter and Group W Cable TV, 1977-84; host/producer The First Nighter N.Y. Times primetime cable highlight program, 1977-84; pres., chief exec. officer Starpower, Inc., 1984-91; affiliate news corr. ABC Radio Network, N.Y.C., 1984-86; pres. Promarket People Inc., 1991-93; S.W. contbg. corr. Am. in the Morning, First Light, Mut. Broadcasting System, 1992; S.W. freelance corr. Voice of Am., USIA, 1992—. Perennial critic Off-Off Broadway Short Play Festival, N.Y.C., 1984—; was 1st Woman on 10 O'Clock News, WNEW-TV, 1967. Contbg. feature writer Vis a Vis mag., 1988-91. Mem. celebrity panel Arthritis Telethon, N.Y.C., 1976. Selected episodes of First Nighter program in archives N.Y. Pub. Libr., Billy Rose Theatre Collection, Rodgers and Hammerstein Collection, Performing Arts Rsch.Ctr. Mem. Drama Desk. Clubs: National Arts, Dutch Treat. Presbyterian.

WOODRUM, PATRICIA ANN, librarian; b. Hutchinson, Kans., Oct. 11, 1941; d. Donald Jewell and Ruby Pauline (Shuman) Hoffman; m. Clayton Eugene Woodrum, Mar. 31, 1962; 1 child, Clayton Eugene, II. BA, Kans. State Coll., Pittsburg, 1963; MLS, U. Okla., 1966. Br. libr. Tulsa City-County Libr. System, 1964-65, head brs., 1965-66, head reference dept., 1966-67, chief extension, chief pub. svc., 1967-73, asst. dir., 1973-76, exec. dir., 1976-96; owner Paradigm Mgmt. Cons. Svcs., 1997—. Active Leadership Tulsa Alumni; mem. Ct. Apptd. Spl. Advocates Bd.; chmn. bd. Bot. Garden/Edn. and Rsch. Ctr.; adv. bd. chair Ctr. for Edn. and Counseling; pres. Tulsa Garden Ctr.; bd. dirs. Oasis. Recipient Disting. Libr. award Okla. Libr. Assn., 1982, Leadership Tulsa Paragon award, 1987, Women in Comm. Newsmaker award, 1989, Outstanding Alumnus award U. Okla. Sch. Libr. Info. Studies, 1989, Headliner award Tulsa Press Club, 1996, Disting. Alumnus Coll. Arts and Scis., U. Okla., 2000; inducted into Tulsa City-County Libr. Hall of Fame, 1989, Okla. Womens Hall of Fame, 1993. Mem. ALA, Pub. Libr. Assn. (pres. 1993-94), Okla. Libr. Assn. (pres. 1978-79, Disting. Libr. award 1982, Meritorious Svc. award 1996), Tulsa Press Club. Democrat. Episcopalian. Avocations: swimming, gardening. E-mail: pwoodrum@tulsa.connect.com.

WOODS, ABBI JOHNSON, music educator; b. Charleston, W.Va., Sept. 7, 1957; d. Bob C. and Helen S. Johnson; m. Kevin Glenn Woods, Sept. 5, 1987; 1 child, Jonathan Taylor. BA, Marshall U., 1979. Chorus dir. 7-12 Wahama H.S., Mason, W.Va., 1979—87; music tchr. K-8 Gilmore Elem. Sch., Sandyville, W.Va., 1987—89; music tchr. K-5 Ripley (W.Va.) Elem. Sch., 1989—99; chorus dir. 6-8 Ravenswood (W.Va.) Mid. Sch., 1999—. Music dir. (summers) Agapé Missions, Haiti, 1987, 88. Children's dir. 1st Bapt., Ravenswood, 1997—2003, adult choir dir., 1983—2003, youth choir dir., 2003. Avocations: horseback riding, running, piano. Home: 612 Fitzhugh St Ravenswood WV 26164 Office: Ravenswood Mid Sch 409 Sycamore St Ravenswood WV 26164 E-mail: awoods@wirefire.com.

WOODS, BERNICE IRENE, graphics specialist, small business owner; b. Bristol, Tenn., Feb. 15, 1956; d. Walter Edward Jr. and Mary Jane (Fleenor) Quinn; m. Robert Millard Morton, June 9, 1977 (div. Aug. 1985); m. Onzie Gene Woods, Oct. 4, 1990; 1 child, Stacey Renée Woods. AS in Legal Secretarial, Bristol Comml. Coll., 1977; BS in Bus. Adminstrn. cum laude, Bristol Coll., 1984. Legal sec. Penn, Stuart, Eskridge & Jones, Abingdon, Va., 1976; office mgr., legal sec. Jim Bates, Esq., Blountville, Tenn., 1977-78; graphics specialist Eastman Chem. Co., Kingsport, Tenn., 1978—2001; owner Enchanted Woods, Kingsport, Tenn., 1995—; acctg. tech. Eastman Chem. Co., Kingsport, Ind., 2001—. Designer [illegible] displays, brochures Northeast Tenn. chpt. Am. Chem. Soc., Kingsport, 1993-96; contbr. articles to profl. jours. Vol. United Way Greater Kingsport, 1988-89, Johnson City (Tenn.) Suzuki Assn., 1994—, Am. Heart Assn., 1996; bd. dirs., entertainment dir. Sonrise Emmaus Cmty, Kingsport, 1994-95; mem. Miller-Perry PTA, 1996-2002; Art Fair Com. mem., 1996—; chairperson Suzuki Sch. Music Fundraising com., 1996-98; chair new beginnings cir. United Meth. Ch., 2002; decorating com. Fall festival, 2002-03. Mem. Profl. Picture Framers Assn., Crossings Golf Assn., Suzuki Assn. Am., United Meth. Women. Avocations: acrylic painting, travel, bicycling, golf. Home: 405 Heatherview Ct Kingsport TN 37663-2967 Office: Eastman Chem Co PO Box 1972 Kingsport TN 37662-1972

WOODS, ELEANOR C. music educator; b. Stamford, Conn., Oct. 30, 1939; d. Richard and Anna Marie (Feldtmose) Cunliffe; m. David R. Woods, Aug. 18, 1962; children: Richard, Laurie. BA, Smith Coll., 1961; MAT, Yale U., 1962. String tchr., music tchr. Kariat Jr. High Sch., Spring Valley, N.Y., 1962-65; musich tchr. Flint Hill Sch., Fairfax, Va., 1966-68; violin tchr. Am. U. Prep, Washington, 1972; pvt. instr. Washington, 1972—; violin tchr. Nat. Cathedral Sch., St. Albans, Washington, 1988—. Chmn. Washington Internat. Competition, 2001—. Named Tchr. of Yr., Am. String Tchrs. Assn. of Md., 1993. Mem. Md. State Music Tchrs. Assn. (chmn., judge of competitions 1976—), Wash. Music Tchrs. Assn. (judge of competitions 1976—), Suzuki Assn. Am., Suzuki Assn. Greater Washington Area.

WOODS, HARRIETT RUTH, retired political organization president; b. Cleve., June 2, 1927; d. Armin and Ruth (Wise) Friedman; m. James B. Woods, Jan. 2, 1953; children: Christopher, Peter, Andrew. Student, U. Chgo., 1945; BA, U. Mich., 1949; LLD (hon.), Webster U., 1988, U. Missouri, 2003. Reporter Chgo. Herald-Am., 1948, St. Louis Globe-Democrat, 1949-51; prodr. Star, KPLR-TV, St. Louis, 1964-74; moderator, writer Sta. KETC-TC, St. Louis, 1962-64; council mem. University City, Mo., 1967-74; mem. Mo. Hwy. Commn., 1974, Mo. Transp. Commn., 1974-76, Mo. Senate, 1976-84; lt. gov. State of Mo., 1985-89; pres. Inst. for Policy Leadership, U. Mo., St. Louis, 1989-91, lectr., 1995—. Pres. Nat. Women's Polit. Caucus, 1991-95; fellow inst. politics J.F. Kennedy Sch. Govt., Harvard U., 1988; adj. prof. U. Mo., St. Louis, 1995—, Hunter Coll., N.Y.C., 2004—. Author: Stepping Up to Power: The Political Journey of American Women, 2000. Bd. dirs. LWV of Mo., 1963, Nat. League of Cities, 1972-74; Dem. nominee for U.S. Senate, 1982, 86; commr. St. Louis Regional Conf. and Sports Complex Authority, 2000—. Jewish.

WOODS, JACQUELINE F. telecommunications industry executive; B.A., Univ. of Calif. (Davis); M.A., Univ. of Southern Calif. Pres. Ameritech Ohio subs. Ameritech Corp., Cleve., Ameritech Ill., Cleve.; v.p. of licensing and pricing Oracle Corp. Office: 500 Oracle Pwky Redwood City CA 94065 Fax: 312-207-1601.

WOODS, JANE HAYCOCK, state legislator; b. Bethesda, Md., Oct. 10, 1946; d. Stephen Pineo and Ruth (Yanovsky) Haycock; m. James Richard Fitzalan Woods, July 14, 1973. BA in Edn., Am. U., 1968. Tchr. Fairfax (Va.) County Pub. Sch., 1968-74, 76-87; co-mgr. Comml. Real Estate, Fairfax, 1982-91; mem. Va. Ho. of Dels., Fairfax, 1988-92, Va. Senate, 1992-2000. Chair City of Fairfax (Va.) Rep. Com., 1983-88, 11th Congl. Rep. Dist. Com., 1992; bd. mem. Va. Fedn. Rep. Women, 1986—. Named Outstanding Woman, City of Fairfax Commn. on Women, 1987. Mem. Nat. Assn. Parliamentarians (Outstanding Tchr. 1990), Va. Girls State (bd. mem.), Annandale C. of C. (Citizen of Yr. 1990), Fairfax C. of C. (Outstanding Woman 1989), Am. Legion Aux., Phi Delta Kappa. Methodist. Avocations: gardening, reading. Office: 3932 Old Lee Hwy # B Fairfax VA 22030-2417

WOODS, JEAN FRAHM, science educator; b. Boise, Idaho, Oct. 24, 1931; d. Theodore Roosevelt and Bonnie Mae (Gross) Frahm; m. Lonnie Lee Woods, June 24, 1951 (dec. May 7, 1977); children: Jeffrey Lee, Nicholaus Lon, Karl Eugene. BS in Sci. Edn., Home Econs., U. Idaho, Moscow, 1954; MS in Zoology, U. Wis., 1960. Tchr. 4th grade Rapid City (S.D.) Schs., 1954-55; tchr. 7th and 8th grades Lovelock (Nev.) Schs., 1956-57; tchr. biology, chemistry, home econs. Richfield (Idaho) H.S., 1957-59; dietitian U. Idaho, Moscow, 1961-62; tchr. sci., home econs. Eagle

(Idaho) Jr. H.S., 1962-63; sci. tchr. 7th grade Meridian (Idaho) Schs., 1981-97. Tchr. of Yr. Meridian Schs., 1987. Mem. AAUW, Nat. Sci. Tchrs. Assn., Idaho Sci. Tchrs. Assn., Boise Home Economists (treas. 1968, pres. 1969), Native Daus. of Idaho, Delta Kappa Gamma (1st v.p.) 2001-03. Avocations: reading, biking, bird watching. Home: 3518 Catalina Rd Boise ID 83705-4604

WOODS, KRYSTYNA JANINA, artist, pharmacist; b. Warwick, Queensland, Australia, Jan. 28, 1961; arrived in U.S., 1998; d. Jan and Janina Dzierzanowski; m. Ross Maxwell Woods, Aug. 28, 1993; children: Harrison George Maxwell, Jack Henry Alexander. BPharm, U. Queensland, Brisbane, 1980. Registered pharmacist Pharmacy Bd. Queensland. Preregistration pharmacist, asst. mgr. Payless Chemists, Brisbane, 1980—81; pharmacist, mgr. Benowa Pharmacy, Gold Coast, Australia, 1981—83; chief pharmacist, asst. mgr. Sorrento Pharmacy, Gold Coast, Australia, 1983—85; chief pharmacist, mgr. Moses Edward St. Pharmacy, Brisbane, 1986—88; chief pharmacist, part-time mgr. Aspley Day & Night Pharmacy, Brisbane, 1988—93; locum pharmacist mgr. Auchenflower Pharmacy, Brisbane, 1993—95, Terry White Pharmacy, Brisbane, 1993—95, Transit Ctr. Pharmacy, Brisbane, 1993—95; owner, mgr., chief pharmacist Indooroopilly Day & Night Pharmacy, Brisbane, 1995—2000. Model, actress Viviens Model Agy., Brisbane and Sydney, 1985—93; actress, model print, TV, radio and stage Margo Mott/Buckinghams, Gold Coast, 1985—93, Queensland Theatre Co., Brisbane, 1985—93, Javeenbah Little Theatre, Gold Coast, 1985—93, Gold Coast Little Theatre, 1982—84; mentor Young Australian Profls. in Am., N.Y.C., 2003; lectr. Mt. Gravatt Tech. Coll. Further Edn., Brisbane, 1989; interviewed by mags. N.J. Monthly, 2001, Australian House and Garden Mag., 1999, Sunday Mail Mag., 1998. One-woman shows include Natura Gallery Heritage Hotel, Brisbane, 1995—97, Brisbane Herbsfest, 1995—97, one-woman shows and exhbns., Wentworth Gallery, Palm Beach, 1995—96, White Plains, 1995—96, Boston, 1995—96, Chgo., 1995—96, one-woman shows include Madison Studio Gallery, 2001, The Show Gallery, Chatham, 2002—03, Internat. Art Expo, N.Y.C., 2003, Solange Rabello Art Gallery, Miami, 2003, Australian Consulate, N.Y.C., 2003, Natural Gallery, exhibitions include Village Gallery, Laguna Beach, 2003. Rep. city for state visit by Queen Elizabeth II; asst. to pres. in presentation to MP regarding protection of pharmacy ownership Queensland Pharmacy Guild, Brisbane, 1997. Recipient Award of Merit for Outstanding Achievement, Manhattan Arts Internat., 1999, Art Show awards, city couns. and art assns., 1977—89, Adjudicator's Choice award, Warana Drama Festival and Arts, 1982. Mem.: Arts Coun. of Morris Area (invited spkr. art promotion 2002), Nat. Mus. Women in Arts, Catharine Lorillard Wolfe Art Club (assoc.). Roman Catholic. Avocations: tennis, golf, interior decorating, reading, travel. Office: Krysia D Designs 422 Walton Rd Maplewood NJ 07040 Office Phone: 973-313-1137. E-mail: krysiadart@aol.com.

WOODS, NANCY FUGATE, dean, women's health nurse, educator; BS, Wis. State U., 1968; MSN, U. Wash., 1969; PhD, U. N.C., 1978. Staff nurse Sacred Heart Hosp., Wis., 1968, Univ. Hosp., Wis., 1969-70, St. Francis Cabrini Hosp., 1970; nurse clinician Yale-New Haven Hosp., 1970-71; instr. nursing Duke U., Durham, N.C., 1971-72, from instr. to assoc. prof., 1972-78; assoc. prof. physiology U. Wash., Seattle, 1978-82, prof. physiology, 1982-84, chairperson dept. parent and child nursing, 1984-90, prof. dept. parent and child nursing, 1990—, dean Sch. Nursing, 1998—; dir. Ctr. Women's Health Rsch., U. Wash., Seattle, 1989—. Pres. scholar U. Calif., San Francisco, 1985-86. Contbr. articles to profl. jours. Fellow ANA, Am. Acad. Nursing, Inst. Medicare, N.A.S.; mem. AAUP, APHA, Am. Coll. Epidemiology, Soc. Menstrual Cycle Rsch. (v.p. 1981-82, pres. 1983-85), Soc. Advancement Women's Health Rsch. Office: U Wash Sch Nursing PO Box 357260 Seattle WA 98195-7260

WOODS, NIKKI, radio personality; Former 5th grade tchr.; morning radio host, entertainment reporter Sta. WGCI-FM, Chgo. Vol. Big Sister, Little Sister Program, Chgo. Rape Crisis Ctr., Walter S. Christopher Sch. for Children. Office: WGCI 332 S Michigan Ave Ste 600 Chicago IL 60604

WOODS, PHYLLIS MICHALIK, librarian; b. New Orleans, Sept. 12, 1937; d. Philip John and Thelma Alice (Carey) Michalik; 1 child, Tara Lynn Woods. BA, Southea. La. U., 1967. Cert. speech and English tchr., libr. sci., La. Tchr. speech, English and drama St. Charles Parish Pub. Schs., Luling, La., elem. tchr., secondary tchr. remedial reading, Chpt. I reading specialist, Wicat tchr. coord., elem. sch. libr.; media specialist Jefferson Parish Pub. Sch. System. Tchr. cons. St. Charles parish writing project La. State U. Writing Project. Author: Egbert, the Egret, Egbert's Picnic, Egbert Visits Sammy, Angel Without Wings, The Necklace and Egbert's Calf, The Hurricane, The Cleanup Day, The Rainbow, The Fair, The Tornado; songwriter; musical compositions include The Fruits of the Spirit, Father's Day Song, Mother's Day Song; contbr. articles and poems to River Parish Guide, St. Charles Herald. Sch. rep. United Fund, St. Charles Parish Reading Assn.; parish com. mem. Young Authors, Tchrs. Who Write; active 4-H leader; bd. trustees Michalik Scholarship Trust. Mem. ASCD, Internat. Platform Assn., Internat. Reading Assn., Am. Fedn. Tchrs., St. Charles Parish Reading Coun., Newspaper in Edn. (chmn., historian), La. Assn. Newspapers in Edn. (state com.), Jefferson Parish Libr. Assn., Jefferson Parish Reading Assn., Jefferson Parish Tchrs. Union.

WOODS, ROSE MARY, former presidential assistant, consultant; b. Sebring, Ohio, Dec. 26, 1917; d. Thomas M. and Mary (Maley) W. Ed. high sch.; L.D.H., Pfeiffer Coll., 1971. With Royal China, Inc., Sebring, 1935-43, Office Censorship, 1943-45, Internat. Tng. Adminstrn., 1945-47, Herter Com. Fgn. Aid, 1947, Fgn. Service Ednl. Found., 1947-51; sec. to senator, then v.p. Nixon, 1951-61; asst. Mr. Nixon with firm Adams, Duque & Hazeltine, Los Angeles, 1961-63, firm Nixon, Mudge, Rose, Guthrie, Alexander & Mitchell, N.Y.C., 1963-68; exec. asst. to former Pres. Nixon, 1969-75. Now consultant. Named 1 of 10 Women of Year Los Angeles Times, 1961, 1 of 75 Most Important Women in Am. Ladies Home Jour., 1971 Home: 3700 S Union Ave Alliance OH 44601-9446

WOODS, SANDRA KAY, real estate executive; b. Loveland, Colo., Oct. 11, 1944; d. Ivan H. and florence L. (Betz) Harris; m. Gary A. Woods, June 11, 1967; children: Stephanie Michelle, Michael Harris. BA, U. Colo., 1966, MA, 1967. Personnel mgmt. specialist CSC, Denver, 1967; asst. to regional dir. HEW, Denver, 1968-69; urban renewal rep. HUD, Denver, 1970-73, dir. program analysis, 1974-75, asst. regional dir. cmty. planning and devel., 1976-77, regional dir. fair housing, 1978-79; mgr. ea. facility project Adolph Coors Co., Golden, Colo., 1980, dir. real estate, 1981, v.p. chief environ. health and safety officer, 1982-96, v.p. strategic selling initiatives, 1996—2000; pres. Woods Properties LLP, Golden, 2000—. Mem. Exec. Exch., The White House, 1980. Bd. dirs. Golden Local Devel. Corp., 1981-82; fundraising dir. Coll. Arts and Scis., U. Colo., boulder, 1982-89, U. Colo.found.; mem. exec. bd. NCCJ, Denver, 1982-94; v.p. women in bus. Inc., Denver, 1982-83; mem. steering com. 1984 Yr. for All Denver Women, 1983-84; mem. 10th dist. Denver br. Fed. Res. Bd., 1990-96, chmn. bd., 1995-96; bd. dirs. Nat. Jewish Hosp., 1994—; chmn. Greater Denver Corp., 1991—. Named one of Outstanding Young Women Am., U.S. Jaycees, 1974, 78, Fifty Women to Watch, Businessweek, 1987, 92, Woman of Achievement YWCA, 1988. Mem. Indsl. Devel. Resources Coun. (bd. dirs. 1986-89), Am. Mgmt. Assn., Denver C. of C. (bd. dirs. 1988-96, Disting. Young Exec. award 1974, mem. Leadership Denver, 1976-77), Colo. Women's Forum, Nat. Assn. Office and Indsl. Park Developers (sec. 1988, treas. 1989), Committee of 200 (v.p. 1994-95), Phi Beta Kappa, Pi Alpha Alpha, PEO Club (Loveland). Republican. Presbyterian. E-mail: sandrawoods@qwest.net.

WOODS, SARAH LYNN, advertising executive; BA in commn., advt., U. Oreg., 1996. Acct. coord. to sr. acct. coord. Bernard Hodes Advt., San Diego, 1996—98; acct. exec. TMP Advt. Monster.com, San Diego, 1998—2000; acct. handler Bernard Hodes Advt., London, 2001; market rsch. interviewer Transport for London, London, 2001; market rsch. UK Census 2001, London, 2001; nat. acct. exec. Ariz. Republic Newspaper Gannett, Phoenix, 2001—03; classified advt. mgr. recruitment Tribune Newspapers, Mesa, Ariz., 2004—. Vol. Soc. for Human Resources Mgmt., Las Vegas, 2000. Avocations: travel, sailing, skiing, piano, volunteering. Office: Tribune Newspapers 120 W First Ave Mesa AZ 85210 Office Phone: 480-898-6465.

WOODS, SHARHONDA MICHELE, military officer; b. Jacksonville, NC, Aug. 22, 1976; d. Richard Cecil and Linda Joyce Berry; m. David Lawrence Woods, Dec. 18, 1998. BA in Criminal Justice, U. Ala., 1998. Dir. Cmty. Svc. Ctr., U. Ala., Tuscaloosa, 1997—98; commd. USAF, 1998, advanced through grades to capt., 1998; chief logistics plans 55th Logistics Support Squadron, Offutt AFB, Nebr., 2000; installation deployment officer 42d Air Base Wing, Maxwell AFB, Ala., 2000—02; exec. officer 42d Logistics Group, Maxwell AFB, 2001—02; chief plans and programs 12AF Davis-Monthan AFB, Ariz., 2002—03; chief transportation 12AF, Davis-Monthan AFB, Ariz., 2003—. Facilitator Dorothy I. Height Leadership Inst., Washington, 1998—2003; trainer Faith Cmtys. Adv. Bd./Ala. Coalition Against Domestic Violence, Montgomery, Ala., 2001—02. Vice chair Nat. Coun. Negro Women, Washington, 1999—2003; judge Shell Oil Excellence in Tchg. Award, 2001; bd. dirs. Brewster Ctr. Domestic Violence Shelter, 2003—; adv. bd. Girls First Inc., 2003—; co-chair Black Youth Vote!, Washington, 2002—; adv. bd. Rap the Vote, 2002. Mem.: Delta Sigma Theta, Inc. Avocations: reading, travel, volunteer work, fencing. Office: 12AF Transportation 2915 S 12th Air Force Dr Davis Monthan Afb AZ 85707 E-mail: ladywoods2003@yahoo.com.

WOODS, STEPHANIE, television producer, reporter; BA in Comm., George Mason U. Prodr. The Insiders with Jack Anderson, Fin. News Network; prodr. CNBC, Ft. Lee, N.J.; sr. prodr., reporter Nightly Bus. Report, Washington. Office: NBR 1325 G St NW Ste 1005 Washington DC 20005-3126

WOODS, SUSANNE, academic administrator, educator; b. Honolulu, Hawaii, May 12, 1943; d. Samuel Ernest and Gertrude (Cullom) W. BA in Polit. Sci., UCLA, 1964, MA in English, 1965; PhD in English and Comparative Lit., Columbia U., 1970; MA (hon.), Brown U., 1978. Institute of Educational Management Harvard U., 1993. Staff Senator Daniel K. Inouye, 1963; asst. editor Rand Corp., Calif., 1963-65; instr. Ventura Coll., Calif., 1965-66; lectr. CUNY, 1967-69; asst. prof. U. Hawaii, 1969-72; asst. prof. English Brown U., Providence, 1972-77, assoc. prof., 1977-83, prof., 1983-93, dir. grad. studies, 1986-88, assoc. dean faculty, 1987-90; v.p., dean Franklin and Marshall Coll., Lancaster, Pa., 1991-95, prof. English, 1991—99; provost, prof. English Wheaton Coll., Norton, Mass., 1999—. Vis. assoc. prof. U. Calif., 1981-82; chair exec. bd. NEH-Brown Women Writers Project, 1988—. Author: Natural Emphasis, 1984; gen. editor: Women Writers in English, 1350-1850, 1992—; editor: The Poetry of Aemilia Lanyer, 1993; contbr. numerous articles to profl. jours. and scholarly books; reviewer for various profl. jours., including Renaissance Quar., Jour. of English and Germanic Philology; reader for PMLA Jour., SEL Jour., also others; editorial bd. Hunting Libr. Quar., 1987-90, Ben Jonson Jour., Duquesne U. Press. Pres. Cultural Coun. of Lancaster County, 1993-95, bd. dirs., 1990-95; bd. dirs. Lancaster Gen. Hosp. Found., 1992-95; active various polit. campaigns, 1960-64, 68-76, 84, 92. Bronson fellow, 1976, Huntington Library, 1979-80, 81, Clark Library, 1981, Huntington-NEH, 1984-85, Woodrow Wilson Found., 1968-70 Mem. Am. Council Edn. (R.I. women's coord. 1988-90), MLA (chmn. div. 17th Century English lit. 1982), N.E. MLA (chmn. English Renaissance sect. 1978, Milton sect. 1983), Am. Assn. Higher Edn., Nat. Women's Studies Assn., Renaissance Soc. Am., Milton Soc. (exec. com. 1987-89), Lyrica Soc. (pres. 1987-90), Alpha Gamma Delta. Democrat. Episcopalian. Episcopalian. Achievements include Founding Director, Brown University Women Writers Project (literary recovery and text encoding). Avocations: music, travel, boating, scuba. Office: Wheaton Coll Office of Provost 26 E Main St Norton MA

WOODS COGGINS, ALMA, artist; b. Canton, Pa., May 24, 1924; d. Fred and Essica Ortha (Manahan) Woods; m. Jack B. Coggins, Jan. 15, 1948. Grad. h.s., New Albany, Pa., 1941. Exhibited in shows at Wyomissing Inst. Fine Arts, Reading Mus., Yellow Springs Art Show, Valley Forge Small Paintings Exhbn., Pa. State Delawre County Cmapus, MainlineArt Ctr. Ann. Exhbn., Chester County Art Assn. Shows, Small Paintings Nat. Exhbn./Ky. Highlands Mus., Pa. State U., Harrisburg, numerous others. Sec. zoning hearing bd. Zoning Commn., Pike Twp., 1965-99. Recipient awards for art. Mem. Berks Art Alliance, Chester County Art Assn., Pen and Brush. Avocation: gardening. Home: PO Box 57 Boyertown PA 19512-0057

WOODSIDE, LISA NICOLE, humanities educator; b. Portland, Oreg., Sept. 7, 1944; d. Lee and Emma (Wenstrom) W. Student, Reed Coll., 1962-65; MA, U. Chgo., 1968; PhD, Bryn Mawr Coll., 1972; cert., Harvard U. Inst. Ednl. Mgmt., 1979; MA, West Chester U., 1994. Cert. tchr. ecstatic trance postures Cuyamungue Inst., New Mex., 2003, wellness counseling, creative energy options. Mem. dean's staff Bryn Mawr Coll., 1970-72; asst. prof. Widener U., Chester, Pa., 1972-77, assoc. prof. humanities, 1978-83, asst. dean student svcs., 1972-76, assoc. dean, 1976-79, dean, 1979-83; acad. dean, prof. humanities Holy Family Coll., Phila., 1983—, v.p., dean acad. affairs, prof. humanities, 1990-98, prof. humanities, 1998—. Cons. State N.J. Edn. Dept., 1990; accreditor Commn. on Higher Edn., Middle States Assn., 1977-83, 94; reader for test of spoken English, Ednl. Testing Svc., 2002-03. Co-author: New Age Spirituality: An Assessment. City commr. for cmty. rels., Chester, 1980-83; mem. Adult Edn. Coun. Phila. Recipient Crasilneck award for best paper Am. Soc. Clin. Hypnosis; Am. Assn. Papyrology grantee Bryn Mawr Coll., also S. Maude Kaemmerling fellow. Mem.: MLA, AAUW (univ. rep. 1975—83), APA, Pa. Coll. Tchrs. Assn., Mid. States Classics Assn., Am. Philol. Assn., Audubon Soc., Psi Chi, Alpha Sigma Lambda, Phi Eta Sigma. Home: 360 Saybrook Ln # A Media PA 19086-6761 Office: Humanities Dept Holy Family Univ Torresdale Philadelphia PA 19114

WOODSON, GAYLE ELLEN, otolaryngologist; b. Galveston, Tex., June 9, 1950; d. Clinton Eldon and Nancy Jean (Stephens) W.; m. Kevin Thomas Robbins; children: Nicholas, Gregory, Sarah. BA, Rice U., 1972; MD, Baylor Coll. Medicine, 1975. Diplomate Am. Bd. Otolaryngology (bd. dirs., residency rev. com. for otolaryngology, exam. chair). Fellow Baylor Coll. Medicine, Houston, 1976, Inst. Laryngology & Otology, London, 1981-82; asst. prof. Baylor Coll. Medicine, 1982-87; asst. attending Harris County Hosp. Dist., Houston, 1982-86; with courtesy staff Saint Luke's Episcopal Hosp., Houston, 1982-87; assoc. attending The Methodist Hosp., Houston, 1982-87; asst. prof. U. Calif. Med. Sch., San Diego, 1987-89; chief otolaryngology VA Med. Ctr., San Diego, 1987-92; assoc. prof. U. Calif. Sch. Med., San Diego, 1989-92; prof. otolaryngology U. Tenn., Memphis, 1993—2000, So. Ill. U., 2003—. Numerous presentations and lectures in field. Contbr. numerous articles and abstracts to med. jours., also videotapes. Recipient deRoldes award, Am. Layrngol. Assn., 2003. Fellow ACS (bd. govs.), Royal Coll. Surgeons, Soc. Univ. Otolaryngologists (past pres.), Am. Soc. Head and Neck Surgery, Am. Laryngol. Assn. (historian, de Roaldes award, 2003), Triological Soc.; mem. AMA, Am. Acad. Otolaryngology-Head and Neck Surgery (bd. dirs. 1993-96), Am. Med. Women's Assn. (past pres. Memphis br.), Soc. Head and Neck Oncologists Eng., Am. Physiol. Soc., Assn. Women Surgeons, Am. Soc. Head and Neck Surgeons, Johns Hopkins Soc. Scholars, Collegium OtoRhinolaryngolcum Amicus Sacrum. Office: Southern Illinois Univ PO Box 19662 Springfield IL 62794-9662 E-mail: gwoodson@siumed.edu.

WOODSON, JACQUELINE, writer; b. Columbus, Ohio, Feb. 12, 1964; 1 child. Fellow MacDowell Colony and the Fine Arts Work Ctr., Provincetown, Mass. Author: (book) Last Summer With Maizon, 1990, Martin Luther King Jr., and His Birthday, 1990, The Dear One, 1991, Maizon at Blue Hill, 1992, I Hadn't Meant to Tell You This, 1994, Between Madison and Palmetto, 1995, Autobiography of a Family Photo, 1995, From the Notebooks of Melanin Sun, 1995, A Way Out of No Way, 1996, The House You Pass on the Way, 1997, We Had a Picnic this Past Sunday, 1997, If You Come Softly, 1998, Lena, 1998, Miracle's Boys, 2000, Sweet, Sweet Memory, 2000; (book) The Other Side, 2001; author: (book) Hush, 2002, Our Gracie Aunt, 2002, Visiting Day, 2002, Locomotion, 2003 (Nat. book award nominee, 2003). Recipient Coretta Scott King Honors, 2001, Kenyon Review award for lit. excellence in fiction, 3 Am. Libr. Assn. awards, 2 Jane Adams Peace award honors, 3 Lambda Lit. awards.*

WOODSON-HOWARD, MARLENE ERDLEY, former state legislator; b. Ford City, Pa., Mar. 8, 1937; d. James and Susie (Lettrich) Erdley; m. Francis M. Howard; children: George Woodson, Bert Woodson, Robert Woodson, Daniel Woodson, David Woodson. BS, Ind. U. of Pa., 1958; MA, U. South Fla., 1968; EdD, Nova U., 1981. Prof. math. Manatee Community Coll., 1970-82, dir., Inst. Advancement, 1982-86; exec. dir. Manatee Community Coll. Foundation, 1982-86; pres. Pegasus Enterprises, Inc., 1986—; state senator Fla., 1986-90. Candidate for gov. of Fla., 1990; past pres. New Coll. Libr. Assn.; past pres. Manatee Symphony; bd. dirs. Manatee Red Cross; bd. dirs. Manatee Players, Inc., v.p.; trustee Fla. Kiwanis Found. Mem. Manatee C. of C., Sarasota C. of C., Sarasota Kiwanis (bd. dirs., v.p., pres.). Republican. Roman Catholic. Home: 12 Tidy Island Blvd Bradenton FL 34210-3301 E-mail: marlenewhoward@aol.com.

WOODSWORTH, ANNE, university administrator, librarian; came to U.S., 1983; d. Thorvald Ernst and Roma Yrsa Lindner; 1 child, Yrsa Anne. BFA, U. Man., Can., 1962; BLS, U. Toronto, Ont., Can., 1964, MLS, 1969; PhD, U. Pitts., 1987. Edn. libr. U. Man., 1964—65; reference libr. Winnipeg Pub. Libr., 1965—67; reference libr. sci. and medicine dept. U. Toronto, 1967—68; med. libr. Toronto We. Hosp., 1969—70; rsch. asst. to chief libr. U. Toronto, 1970—71, head reference dept., 1971—74; pers. dir. Toronto Pub. Libr., 1975—78; dir. librs. York U., Toronto, 1978—83; assoc. provost for librs. U. Pitts., 1983—88, assoc. prof., 1988—91; dean Palmer Sch. Libr. and Info. Sci., L.I. U., 1991—98; dean Sch. Edn. Dowling Coll., Oakdale, NY, 1999—2000; dean sch. info. and libr. sci. Pratt Inst., Bklyn., 2000—02, acting provost, 2002—03; provost Katherine Gibbs Sch., Melville, NY, 2003; learning sys. advisor Bklyn. Pub. Libr., 2004—. Pres. Anne Lindner Ltd., 1974-83; rsch. libraries adv. coun. OCLC, 1984-87. Author: The Alternative Press in Canada, 1972, Leadership and Research Libraries, 1988, Patterns and Options for Managing Information Technology on Campus, 1990, Library Cooperation and Networks, 1991, Managing the Economics of Leasing and Contracting Out Information Services, 1993, Reinvesting in the Information Job Family, 1993, The Future of Education for Librarianship: Looking Forward from the Past, 1994. Sec., mem. bd. trustees Katharine Gibbs Sch., L.I., 2003-; dir. Sr. Fellows Inst., 1995-98; trustee L.I. Librs. Resources Coun., 1993-96; bd. dirs. Population Rsch. Found., Toronto, 1980-83. Grantee Can. Coun., 1974, Ont. Arts Coun., 1974, Coun. on Libr. Resources, 1986, 88, 91, 93; UCLA sr. fellow, 1985. Mem. ALA (com. on accreditation 1990-94, councillor 1993-97), Can. Assn. Rsch. Librs. (pres. 1981-83), Assn. Rsch. Librs. (bd. dirs. 1981-84, v.p. 1984-85, pres. 1985-86), Assn. Coll. and Rsch. Librs. (chair K.G. Saur award com. 1991-93), Assn. for Libr. and Info. Sci. Edn. (chair honors and awards com. 1995, bd. dirs. 1998-99, v.p. 1998-99), Am. Soc. Higher Edn., Internet Soc., Am. Soc. Info. Sci. (convenor 1999-2000), Archons of Colophon.

WOODWARD, DEBBIE CAROL, special education educator; b. Lufkin, Tex., Mar. 1, 1953; d. Robert Charles and Peggy Jean Beddingfield; m. Allen Wiley, Aug. 15, 1975 (div. Aug. 1984); 1 child, Richard Charles Wiley ; m. Lee George Woodward, July 24, 1998. BS, Stephen F. Austin State U., Nacogdoches, Tex., 1995. Tchr. 5th grade Lufkin Ind. Sch. Dist., Tex.; owner Wiley's Wee Wons Nursery, Bryan, Tex., Wiley's Wee Wons Day Sch. and Nursery, Lufkin; faculty Ctr. for Retarded, Houston; spl. edn. tchr. Galena Park Ind. Sch. , Houston, Channelview Ind. Sch. Dist., Tex. Homebound spl. svcs. provider and cons. Galena Park Ind. Sch. Dist., Houston, Channelview Ind. sch. Dist.; salesperson Avon Products. Active Cystic Fybrosis Found., Susan G. Komen Breast Cancer Found., Shriners Hosps., Inc.; pvt. cons. for families and schs. of terminally children in Galena Park and Channelview. Mem.: Coun. for Exceptional Children, Order Ea. Star.

WOODWARD, ISABEL AVILA, educational writer, foreign language educator; b. Key West, Fla., Mar. 14, 1906; d. Alfredo and Isabel (Lopez) Avila; m. Clyde B. Woodward, June 6, 1944 (dec.); children: Joy Avis Ball, Greer Isabel, Woodward Sucke. Student, Fla. State Coll. for Women, 1925, AB in Edn., 1938; cert. in tchg. Spanish, U. Miami, 1961; summer study, U. Fla., Eckerd Coll.; postgrad., St. Lawrence U., U. Miami. Tchr., Key West, 1927-42; remedial reading cons., 1941-42; reading tchr., asst. reading lab. and clinic St. Lawrence U., summer 1941; Spanish translator U.S. Office of Censorship, Miami Beach, 1943; tchr. Central Beach Elem. Sch., Miami Beach, 1943-44, Silver Bluff Elem. Sch., 1943-50, Henry West Lab. Sch., Coral Gables, Fla., 1955-57, Dade Demonstration Sch., Miami, 1957-61. Author 125 sch. radio lessons for tchg. Spanish Workshop for Fla.; spkr. poetry and short story writing, 1977; guest lectr. on writing the short story Fla. Inst. Tech., Jensen Beach, 1981; guest lectr. Cicle Bay Yacht Club, Stuart, Fla., 1995. Freelance writer; contbr. to Listen Mag., Sunshine Mag., Lookout Mag., Christian Sci. Monitor, Miami Herald, Three/Four, Child Life, Wee Wisdom, Fla. Wildlife, Young World: sponsor Port St. Lucie Jr. Woman's Club, 1983. Recipient Honoris Causa award Alpha Delta Kappa, 1972-74, award Contra Costa Times, Calif., 1985, 1st prize for short story in nat. Ark. writers conf. contest, 1992; named one of 5 Outstanding Fla. Tchrs. 1972-74. Mem. Nat. League Am. Pen Women (1st v.p. Greater Miami br. 1974-76, historian 1978—, librarian 1978—, awards for writing 1973, 74, 77, 1st and 3d pl. state writing awards for adult and juvenile fiction 1983, state 1st prize short story 1985), AAUW, Alpha Delta Kappa, Psi Psi Psi. Address: 1950 SW Palm City Rd Apt 5104 Stuart FL 34994-4304

WOODWARD, JOANNE GIGNILLIAT, actress; b. Thomasville, Ga., Feb. 27, 1930; d. Wade and Elinor (Trimmier) W.; m. Paul Newman, Jan. 29, 1958; children: Elinor Terese, Melissa Stewart, Clea Olivia. Student, La. State U., 1947-49; grad., Neighborhood Playhouse Dramatic Sch., N.Y.C. First TV appearance in Penny, Robert Montgomery Presents, 1952; understudy broadway play Picnic, 1953; appeared in plays Baby Want a Kiss, 1964, Candida, 1982, The Glass Menagerie, Williamstown Theatre Festival, 1985, Sweet Bird of Youth, Toronto, 1988; motion pictures include Three Faces of Eve, 1957 (Acad. award Best Actress, Nat. Bd. Rev. award, Fgn. Press award), Count Three and Pray, 1955, Long Hot Summer, 1958, No Down Payment, 1957, Sound and the Fury, 1959, A Kiss Before Dying, 1956, Rally Round the Flag Boys, 1958, The Fugitive Kind, 1960, Paris Blues, 1961, The Stripper, 1963, A New Kind of Love, 1963, A Big Hand for the Little Lady, 1965, A Fine Madness, 1965, Rachel, Rachel, 1968, Winning, 1969, WUSA, 1970, They Might Be Giants, 1971, The Effect of Gamma Rays on Man-in-the-Moon Marigolds, 1972 (Cannes Film Festival award), Summer Wishes, Winter Dreams, 1973 (N.Y. Film Critics award), The Drowning Pool, 1975, The End, 1978, Harry and Son, 1984, Glass Menagerie, 1987, Mr. & Mrs. Bridge, 1990, Philadelphia, 1993, The Age of Innocence (voice), 1993, My Knees Were Jumping: Remembering the Kindertransports, (voice) 1998; TV appearances include All the Way Home; TV-film appearances in Sybil, 1976, Come Back, Little Sheba, 1977, See How She Runs, 1978 (Emmy award), Streets of L.A., 1979, The Shadow Box, 1980, Crisis at Central High, 1981, Do You Remember Love?, 1985

(Emmy award), Blind Spot, 1993 (Emmy nomination, Lead Actress - Miniseries, 1993), Breathing Lessons, 1994 (Emmy nomination, Lead Actress - Special, 1994, Golden Globe award, Best Actress), James Dean: A Portrait, 1996; narrator film documentary Angel Dust, TV documentary on Group Theatre, 1989. Co-recipient (with Paul Newman) Kennedy Ctr. Honors for Lifetime Achievement in the Performing Arts. Democrat. Episcopalian. Office: ICM 40 W 57th St Fl 16 New York NY 10019-4098*

WOODWARD, MARY LOU, retired elementary education educator; b. Vandalia, Mo., Sept. 9, 1931; d. Carl Wesley and Katy Jane (Williams) Lovelace; m. A. Leon Woodward, Aug. 17, 1954; children: Charles Leon, Paul Louis, Robert Lee, William Lawrence. BA, N.E. Mo. U., 1954; MA, Washington U., St. Louis, 1980. Lifetime tchg. cert. in elem. and secondary edn. Tchr. elem. edn. Vandalia Pub. Schs., 1950-52, Berkeley (Mo.) Pub. Schs., 1954-55, St. Louis Pub. Schs., 1959-95. Mem. St. Louis tchrs. ret. com., ad hoc com. St. Louis Pub. Schs. Retirement Sys., 1988-95; cons. affective domain, presenter workshops for Title I Ctr., Insvc. Ctr., 1976-79; cons. spl. projects St. Louis Pub. Schs., 1979-82. Mem. Grand Oak Hill Neighborhood Assn., 1959—, pub. newsletter, 1960-75; block co-chmn. Operation Brightside, 1970-95; mem., spokesperson Mo. State Found., Columbia, 1990-1997; mem. Concerned Citizens Against Govt. Waste, Nat. Right to Work, Mo. Bot. Gardens, St. Louis Art Mus., St. Louis Zoo, Mo. Hist. Soc., St. Louis Sci. Ctr., St. Louis Geneal. Soc. Leader caregiver support group Oak Hill Presbyn. Ch., 1998—; pub. Caregiver Corner, 1999—. Mem. Mo. State Tchrs. Assn. (state exec. bd. 1984-90, pres. local chpt. 1992-94, pres.-elect local chpt. 1990-92, pub. newsletter 1972-92, Outstanding Educator of Yr. 1994), Ret. Tchrs. St. Louis, Am. Assn. Ret. Persons. Avocations: reading, travel, word puzzles, drama, research, computers. Home: 4158 Arsenal St Saint Louis MO 63116-3923

WOODY, CAROL CLAYMAN, data processing executive; b. Bristol, Va., May 20, 1949; d. George Neal and Ida Mae Clayman; m. Robert William Woody, Aug. 19, 1972. BS in Math., Coll. William and Mary, Williamsburg, Va., 1971; MBA with distinction, Wake Forest U., 1979. Programmer trainee GSA, 1971-72; systems engr. Citizens Fidelity Bank & Trust Co., Louisville, 1972-75; programmer/analyst-tng. coord. Blue Bell, Inc., Greensboro, N.C., 1975-79; supr. programming and tech. svcs. J.E. Baker Co., York, Pa., 1979-82; fin. design supr. bus. systems Lycoming divsn. AVCO, Stratford, Conn., 1982-83; project mgr. Yale U., New Haven, 1984-97; cons. ImageWork Technologies Corp., 1998-2001; co-owner Sign of the Sycamore, antiques; product developer Software Engring. Inst. Carnegie Mellon U., 2001—. Mem. Data Processing Standards Bd., 1977, CICS/VS Adv. Council, 1975; speaker Nat. Fuse Conf., 1989, Aion expert systems nat. conf., 1990, bus. sch. Coll. William & Mary, 1994. Author various manuals; contbr. articles to profl. jours. IBM Corp. fellow, 1978; Stephen Bufton Meml. Ednl. Found. grantee, 1978-79. Mem. Am. Bus. Woman's Assn. (chpt. v.p. 1978-79, Merit award 1978), NAFE (founder shoreline network 1993), Assn. for System Mgmt., Assn. for Image Info. Mgmt., Project Mgmt. Inst., Network Inc. of Conn. (treas. 1996-97), Delta Omicron (alumni pres. 1973-75, regional chmn. 1979-82). Republican. Presbyterian. Home: PO Box 1450 Guilford CT 06437-0550

WOOFTER, VIVIEN PERRINE, interior designer, consultant; d. Orie Ray and Hazel Lucille (Bostic) Perrine; m. Perry Wilson Woofter, Oct. 5, 1952; children: [illegible] BS in Home Econ., W.Va. U., 1952, LHD (hon.), 1998. Lic. interior designer Va., 2003. Interior designer GSA, Washington, 1968—76; head interior design The White Ho., 1976—77, U.S. Dept. Health & Human Services, 1977—81; sr. interior designer U.S. Dept. of State, 1981—88; dir. interiors & furnishings divsn. Overseas Buildings Ops., U.S. Dept. of State, 1988—. Mem. W.Va. U. Alumni Bd., Morgantown, 1994—, vol. mem. designer renovation W.Va. U. President's Ho. Com., 1996—2003; mem. W.Va. U. Found. Bd., 1999—; pres. Coll. Creative Arts Vis. Com., 2001—. Author: Develop. Furniture Standards- Phys. Handicap (Written up in Congl. Record, 1977); interior design Interior Design Hdqs. Bldg. for HHS (Fed. Design Coun. of Excellence, 1979), Riyadh Embassy, Paris, Buenos Aires - (Meritorius Honor & Superior Honor, 1988). Restoration work Met. Theater, Morgantown, 2003. Mem.: Internat. Interior Design Assoc. Achievements include development of Art Programs for all new embassies, Culturally Significan Program for US State Dept. Overseas Ident; a Maintenance Manual for US State Dept. Culturally Significant Buildingsofp; Featured in Articles, in Architectural Digest, Southern Accents, Paris Match, Chicago Tribune, other newspapersnchi. Home: 4856 N 35th Rd Arlington VA 22207 Office: Interiors & Furnishings Div Overseas Buildings Ops US Dept State Washington DC 20520 Personal E-mail: vivienwoofter@erols.com. E-mail: woofterv@state.gov.

WOOLARD, CONNIE WARD, artist, retired art gallery manager; b. Wilkes-Barre, Pa., Mar. 25, 1931; d. Harold Walton and Betty Bertha (Mandeville) Ward; m. Maurice Emmett Woolard, Oct. 25, 1952; children: Karin Elise Woolard Snoots. Student, U. Md., 1949-50, Abbott Art Sch., 1951-52. Comml. artist Rex Engraving Co., Silver Spring, Md., 1953-60, art dir., 1959-60; mgr. Town Ctr. Gallery, Rockville, Md., 1978—90, Bethesda, Md., 1990—99, ret., 1999. Freelance artist, fine artist, 1965—. One-woman shows include Town Ctr. Gallery, 1984, 1986, 1989, 1991, 1993, 1996, Art Contemporary, Bethesda, 1982, Sugar & Frichtl Gallery, 1993. Recipient Salmagundi Non-Member award Salmagundi Club, N.Y.C., 1983, Judges Choice award Nat. League Am. Penwomen, 1996, Juror's award Miniature Painters Sculptors and Gravers Washington, 1997, Grumbacher award 2d pl. and 3d pl. pencil drawing, 2002, award Cider Painters Am., Arthur M. Wagman awrd Peerless Rockville Historic Preservaton Ltd., 2003, Mid Atlantic Regional award, Balt. Watercolor Soc., 1985, others. Mem.: Potomac Valley Watercolorists, Miniature Painters, Sculptors & Engravers Soc. Washington, Nat. League Am. Penwomen (past sec., pres., named Women Yr. 1984), So. Watercolor Soc. (signature mem.), Phila. Watercolor Soc. (Cert. of Merit), Washington Watercolor Assn. (past pres.), Rockville Art League (past pres.), Salmagundi Club (Maria Szerti Meml. award 2001, Nat. Soc. Painters in Casein and Acrylic award). Avocations: gardening, reading, photography. Home: 3922 Havard St Silver Spring MD 20906-4311

WOOLDRIDGE, PATRICE MARIE, marketing professional, martial arts and meditation educator; b. Chgo., June 3, 1954; d. Charles E. and Marlys E. Reardon; m. Patrick Wooldridge, June 27, 1981. AS, Moraine Valley Coll., 1974; BA, Govs. State U., 1976, MA, 1977; MBA, Loyola U., Chgo., 1983. Community prof. Govs. State U., University Park, Ill., 1977-78; counselor, social worker Bloom Twp. High Sch., Chicago Heights, Ill., 1977-78; market analyst Dr. Scholl Footcare, Chgo., 1978-79; supr. consumer rsch. Unocal, Schaumburg, Ill., 1979-84; group rsch. dir. Tatham-Laird & Kudner, Chgo., 1984-87; v.p., assoc. dir. strategic planning & rsch. Bayer Bess Vanderwarker Advt., Chgo., 1987-90; v.p. dir. qualitative svcs. Goldring/MIL Rsch., 1990-91; pres. Wooldridge Assocs., Inc., Chgo., 1991—. Instr. dancing, 1969-89; instr. T'ai Chi the Sch. of Q'ai Chi Chuan N.Y.C./T'ai Chi Found., 1986—; instr. Arica the Arica Inst., N.Y.C., 1978—. Performer The Anawim Players, Chgo., 1985-97; treas. Karma Thegsum Choling, Chgo., 1987-97; bd. dirs. Illustrated Theatre Co., Chgo., 1987, The Human Process, Chgo., 1992—; bd. dirs. T'ai Chi Found., Inc., 1994-97, 2003-05, pres. bd., 2003-2004; adv. bd. N.W. Suburban Boy Scouts, Schaumburg, 1984; participant White House Conf. on Small Bus., 1996. Recipient Gold Medallion 2000 Ogilvy Awards. Mem. Am. Mktg. Assn., Qualitative Rsch. Cons. Assn., Union of Concerned Scientists, The Planetary Soc. Home and Office: 1717 W Rascher Ave Chicago IL 60640-1117

WOOLEVER, GAIL WALUK, elementary school educator, artist, secondary school educator; b. Auburn, Ind., Apr. 26, 1952; d. Edward and Dorothy Mae (Rieke) Waluk; m. Stephen J. Woolever, July 18, 1981; 1 child, Zachary. BA, Valparaiso U., 1974; MS, Ind. U., 1979. Cert. permanent tchr., Ind. Art tchr. Kankakee Valley Sch. Corp., Wheatfield, Ind., 1974—. One-woman show includes Munce Art Ctr., 1988; group show includes studio show, 1990, PAC Show, 2000; designer 8 sets of stained glass windows, 1993-95, logo design for sch., 1992; stained glass window designer and constn. with two other tchrs. for intermediate sch., 2001; owner Heart to Hand Art Studio; coord. and designer, fused glass window Wheatfield Elem. Sch., 2003, Grace Fellowship, 2003. Den leader Cub Scouts, DeMotte, Ind., 1989-94; Sunday sch. tchr. jr. high Demotte United Meth., 1993-97, jr. high youth leader, 1995-96; sec. Little League, Wheatfield, Ind., 1994-95. Eli Lilly Grant, 2000, Grace Fellowship, Sr. High S. Sch., 2003—04. Mem. NEA, Nat. Art Edn. Assn., Ind. State Tchrs. Assn., Prairie Arts Coun., Hobart Arts League, Delta Kappa Gamma. Avocations: artist, reading, gardening, cooking, sewing. Home: 3219 W 1700 N Wheatfield IN 46392-8935 Office: Wheatfield Elem Sch PO Box 158 Wheatfield IN 46392-0158

WOOLEVER, NAOMI LOUISE, retired editor-in-chief; b. Williamsport, Pa., Sept. 17, 1922; d. Samuel Bruce and Kathryn Elizabeth (Schmidt) W. BS, Pa. State U., 1944, MA, 1966, postgrad., 1974-76. Reporter, women's editor Gazette & Bulletin, Williamsport, 1944-53; women's editor Sun-Gazette, Williamsport, 1953-72, assoc. city editor, 1972-74; prof. journalism Williamsport Area Community Coll., 1974-76; nat. editor, mng. editor Grit Pub. Co., Williamsport, 1976-81, editor in chief, 1981-88. Career cons. high sch. and coll. journalism classes, Pa. Contbr. articles to profl. jours. Named Woman of Yr., Williamsport Univ. Women, 1967. Mem. Pa. Women's Press Assn. (pres. 1960-62, Pa. Newswoman of Yr. 1958), Nat. Fedn. Press Women (bd. dirs. 1960-62), Soroptimist Club (pres. Williamsport chpt. 1958-60), Univ. Women's Club (pres. 1961-63), Friends of James V. Brown Libr., Williamsport Country Club, Williamsport Woman's Club, Lycoming County Hist. Soc., Gen. John Burrow's Hist. Soc. (bd. dirs.), Clio Club (pres. 1991-93), Pa. State Alumni Assn. (life mem.), Phi Kappa Phi, Kappa Tau Alpha, Zeta Tau Alpha. Republican. Mem. United Methodist Ch. Avocations: music, duplicate bridge, photography, sports. Home: 326 N Montour St Montoursville PA 17754-1832

WOOLEY, GERALDINE HAMILTON, poet, writer; b. Idlewild, Mich., Feb. 15, 1942; d. Charles Loren and Alice (Smith) Hamilton; m. David Wooley, June 11, 1961 (div. 1983); children: Vickie Wooley Houston, Monica Wooley Roberts, Deborah Wooley Williams. GED, Flint, Mich. Cosmetologist pvt. practice, Flint, Mich., 1967-70; tchr's. aide Flint Cmty. Schs., 1969-71; nurse's aide Clara Barton Home, Flint, 1972; factory worker GM AC Plant, Flint, 1973-76; child care worker Beecher Cmty. Schs., Flint, 1987-89, poet, songwriter Flint, 1994—. Songwriter Hilltop Records, Hollywood, Calif., 1996—. Author: (poems) Between The Raindrops, 1995 (Editor's Choice 1995), At Water's Edge, 1995 (Editor's Choice 1995), Tapestry, 1996 (Editor's Choice 1996), Memories of Tomorrow, 1996 (Editor's Choice 1996), (poems) A Treasury of Famous Poets, 1997 (Editor's Choice award 1997). Mem. PTA Flint Sch. Dist., 1969-70. Named to Internat. Poetry Hall of Fame, 1996. Mem. Internat. Soc. Of Poets, Nat. Writers Assn., Internat. Black Writers. Democrat. Avocations: camping, playing organ, exploring old houses, writing. E-mail: LadyKnight77@webtv.net.

WOOLF, AMY KASPAR, librarian, storyteller; b. Peoria, Ill., June 7, 1954; d. Edgar Armand and Gwendolyn Eleanor (Mackenzie) Kaspar; m. William Randolph Woolf, Oct. 7, 1978; children: Katherine Michele, Sarah Elizabeth. BA magna cum laude, Bradley U., 1976; MS in LS, U. Ill., 1977. Children's libr. Wichita (Kans.) Pub. Libr., 1978—86; head libr. Botanica, The Wichita Gardens, 1987—2002; artist, storyteller Arts Ptnrs., Wichita, Kans., 2002—. Storyteller Wichita Pub. Schs., 1986-98. Chmn. Children's Libr. Assn., 1984—; mem. William Allan Colite Children's Book Award Selection Com., 1985—. Mem.: Wichita Area Libr. Assn. Avocations: quilting, gardening. Office: Arts Ptnrs 201 N Water Ste 300 Wichita KS 67202

WOOLLEY, CATHERINE (JANE THAYER), writer; b. Chgo., Aug. 11, 1904; d. Edward Mott and Anna L. (Thayer) W. AB, UCLA, 1927. Advt. copywriter Am. Radiator Co., N.Y.C., 1927-31; freelance writer, 1931-33; copywriter, editor house organ Am. Radiator & Standard San. Corp., N.Y.C., 1933-40; desk editor Archtl. Record, 1940-42; prodn. editor SAE Jour., N.Y.C., 1942-43; pub. relations writer NAM, N.Y.C., 1943-47. Condr. workshop on juvenile writing Truro Ctr. for Arts, 1977, 78, 92, Cape Cod Writers Conf., 1990, 91, 92; instr. writing for juveniles Cape Cod Writers Conf., 1965, 66, 92. Author: juvenile books (under name Catherine Woolley) I Like Trains, 1944, rev., 1965, Two Hundred Pennies, 1947, Ginnie and Geneva, 1948, paperback edit., 1988, David's Railroad, 1949, Schoolroom Zoo, 1950, Railroad Cowboy, 1951, Ginnie Joins In, 1951, David's Hundred Dollars, 1952, Lunch for Lennie, 1952 (pub. as L'Incontentabile Gigi in Italy), The Little Car That Wanted a Garage, 1952, The Animal Train and Other Stories, 1953, Holiday on Wheels, 1953, Ginnie and the New Girl, 1954, Ellie's Problem Dog, 1955, A Room for Cathy, 1956, Ginnie and the Mystery House, 1957, Miss Cathy Leonard, 1958, David's Campaign Buttons, 1959, Ginnie and the Mystery Doll, 1960, Cathy Leonard Calling, 1961, paperback edit., 1988, Look Alive, Libby!, 1962, Ginnie and Her Juniors, 1963, Cathy's Little Sister, 1964, paperback edit., 1988, Libby Looks for a Spy, 1965, The Shiny Red Rubber Boots, 1965, Ginnie and the Cooking Contest, 1966, paperback 1979, Ginnie and the Wedding Bells, 1967, Chris in Trouble, 1968, Ginnie and the Mystery Cat, 1969, Libby's Uninvited Guest, 1970, Cathy and the Beautiful People, 1971, Cathy Uncovers a Secret, 1972, Ginnie and the Mystery Light, 1973, Libby Shadows a Lady, 1974, Ginnie and Geneva Cookbook, 1975, adult book Writing for Children, 1990, paperback, 1990; (under name Jane Thayer) The Horse with the Easter Bonnet, 1953, The Popcorn Dragon, 1953, rev. edit. 1989, Korean edit., 1999, Where's Andy?, 1954, Mrs. Perrywinkle's Pets, 1955, Sandy and the Seventeen Balloons, 1955, The Chicken in the Tunnel, 1956, The Outside Cat, 1957, English edit., 1958, 83, Charley and the New Car, 1957, Funny Stories To Read Aloud, 1958, Andy Wouldn't Talk, 1958, The Puppy Who Wanted a Boy, 1958, rev., 1986, paperback edition, 1988, French translation Le Petit Chien Qui Voulait Un Garcon, 1991, Korean translation, 1998, The Second-Story Giraffe, 1959, Little Monkey, 1959, Andy and His Fine Friends, 1960, The Pussy Who Went To the Moon, 1960, English edit., 1961, A Little Dog Called Kitty, 1961, English edit., 1962, 75, The Blueberry Pie Elf, 1961, English edit., 1962, revised edit., 1994, Spanish edit., 1995, Andy's Square Blue Animal, 1962, Gus Was a Friendly Ghost, 1962, English edit., 1971, Japanese edit., 1982, A Drink for Little Red Diker, 1963, Andy and the Runaway Horse, 1963, A House for Mrs. Hopper; the Cat that Wanted to Go Home, 1963, Quiet on Account of Dinosaur, 1964, English edit., 1965, 74, paperback edit., 1988, Emerald Enjoyed the Moonlight, 1964, English edit., 1965, The Bunny in the Honeysuckle Patch, 1965, English edit., 1966, Part-Time Dog, 1965, English edit. 1966, The Light Hearted Wolf, 1966, What's a Ghost Going to Do?, 1966, English edit. 1972, Japanese edit., 1982, The Cat that Joined the Club, 1967, English edit. 1968, Rockets Don't Go To Chicago, Andy, 1967, A Contrary Little Quail, 1968, Little Mr. Greenthumb, 1968, English edit., 1969, Andy and Mr. Cunningham, 1969, Curious, Furious Chipmunk, 1969, I'm Not a Cat, Said Emerald, 1970, English edit. 1971, Gus Was A Christmas Ghost, 1970, English edit. 1973, Japanese edit., 1982, Mr. Turtle's Magic Glasses, 1971, Timothy And Madam Mouse, 1971, English edit., 1972, Gus And The Baby Ghost, 1972, English edit. 1973, Japanese edit., 1982, The Little House, 1972, Andy and the Wild Worm, 1973, Gus Was a Mexican Ghost, 1974, English edit. 1975, Japanese edit., 1982, I Don't Believe in Elves, 1975, The Mouse on the Fourteenth Floor, 1977, Gus Was a Gorgeous Ghost, 1978, English edit., 1979, Where Is Squirrel?, 1979, Try Your Hand, 1980, Applebaums Have a Robot, 1980, Clever Raccoon, 1981, Gus Was a Real Dumb Ghost, 1982, Gus Loved His Happy Home, 1989; contbr. stories to juvenile anthologies in U.S., Great Britain, France, Germany, and Holland, sch. readers, juvenile mags. Trustee Truro Pub. Libraries, 1974-84; Mem. Passaic (N.J.) Bd. Edn., 1953-56, Passaic Redevel. Agy., 1952-53; pres. Passaic LWV, 1949-52. Named mem. N.J. Literary Hall of Fame, 1987; recipient Phantom Friends Lifetime Achievement award, 1992; dedication of Catherine Woolley Children's Rm. in Truro Pub. Libr., 1999. Mem. Authors League Am., Friends of Truro Libr., Truro Hist. Soc., Amnesty Internat. U.S.A., Kenilworth Soc. Democrat. Home: PO Box 71 Truro MA 02666-0071

WOOLLEY, DONNA PEARL, lumber company executive; b. Drain, Oreg., Jan. 3, 1926; d. Chester A. and Mona B. (Cheever) Rydell; m. Harold Woolley, Dec. 27, 1952 (dec. Sept. 1970); children: Daniel, Debra, Donald. Diploma, Drain High Sch. Sec. No. Life Ins. Co., Eugene, Oreg., 1943-44; sec., bookkeeper D & W Lumber Co., Sutherlin, Oreg., 1944, Woolley Logging Co. & Earl Harris Lumber Co., Drain, 1944-70; pres. Woolley Logging Co., 1970—, Smith River Lumber Co., 1970—, Mt. Baldy Mill, 1970-81, Drain Plywood Co., 1970-81, Woolley Enterprises, Inc., Drain, 1973—, Eagle's View Mgmt. Co., Inc., Eugene, 1981—. Bd. dirs. Wildlife Safari, Winston, 1991, Oreg. Cmty. Found., Portland, 1990-99, chair, 1997-99; bd. trustees Linfield Coll., McMinnville, U. Oreg. Found., 1980-99; bd. dirs. Oreg. Trl. coun. Boy Scouts Am., 1980—, World Forestry Ctr., Portland, 1990, Umpqua C.C. Fedn., 2001. Recipient Pioneer award, U. Oreg., 1982, Econ. and Social Devel. award, Soroptimist Club, 1991, First Citizen of Eugene award, 2000, Aubrey Watzek award, Lewis & Clark Coll., Howard Vollum award, Associated Fund Raisers in Philanthropy Oreg. chpt., 2001, Pioneer award, Umpqua C.C., 2003, Hart Pioneer award, Wildlife Safari, 2003. Mem. Oreg. Women's Forum, Pacific Internat. Trapshooting Assn., Amateur Trapshooting Assn., Eugene C. of C. (bd. dirs. 1989-92), Arlington Club, Town Club (bd. dirs., pres.), Sunnydale Grange, Cottage Grove/Eugene Rod & Gun Club. Republican. Avocations: golf, travel. Office: Eagle's View Mgmt Co Inc 1399 Franklin Blvd Eugene OR 97403-1979

WOOLLEY, MARGARET ANNE (MARGOT WOOLLEY), architect; b. Bangor, Maine, Feb. 4, 1946; d. George Walter and Anne Geneva (Collins) W.; m. Gerard F. Vasisko, June 22, 1985. BA, Vassar Coll., 1969; MArch, Columbia U., 1974. Registered arch. N.Y. Urban designer Mayor's Office Lower Manhattan Devel., 1974-76, Mayor's Office Devel., N.Y.C., 1976-78; project mgr. Office Econ. Devel., N.Y.C., 1978-81, dep. dir. design and engring., 1981-83; dep. dir. design. N.Y.C. Pub. Devel. Corp., 1983-85, asst. v.p. design, 1985—86; v.p. design N.Y.C. Econ. Devel. Corp., 1986—94; dep. program dir. corrections program unit N.Y.C. Dept. Design and Constrn., 1996-97, program dir. cts. and juvenile justice units, 1997—2001, asst. commr. architecture and engring., 2001—. Mem. N.Y. State Licensing Bd. Architecture, 1994—2004; mem. archtl. registration exam. com. Nat. Coun. Archtl. Registration Bds., 1995—99, mem. practice analysis steering com., 1999—2001; mem. archtl. registration exam. devel. task force, 2001—; chair archtl. registration exam. specifications task force, 2000—01. Mem. assoc. bd. of regents L.I. Coll. Hosp., Bklyn., 1982—93, mem. planning and devel. com., 1983—93, pres. assoc. bd. of regents, 1988—89. William Kinne Fellows scholar, 1973. Mem. AIA (bd. dirs. N.Y.C. chpt. 1988-90, nat. pub. archs. steering com. 1993-95) N.Y. State Assn. Archs. (bd. dirs. 1990-92), Heights Casino Club, Vassar Club, Jr. League. Home: 135 Willow St Brooklyn NY 11201-2255

WOOLLEY, MARY ELIZABETH, research administrator; b. Chgo., Mar. 16, 1947; John Joseph and Ellen Louise (Bakke) McEnerney; m. John Stuart Woolley, Dec. 6, 1969 (div. 1985); children: George Newsom, Nora Ellen; m. Michael Howland Campbell, Jan. 1, 1989. BS, Stanford U., 1969; MA, San Francisco State U., 1972; postgrad., U. Calif., San Francisco and Berkeley, 1974-75. Assoc. dir. Inst. Epidemiology and Behavioral Medicine, San Francisco, 1979-81; adminstr. Med. Rsch. Inst. of San Francisco, 1981-82, v.p., adminstr., 1982-86, v.p., exec. dir., 1986-90; pres. Research! Am., Alexandria, Va., 1990—. Cons. in fin. and mgmt. NIH, Bethesda, Md., 1984—92; adj. faculty U. Calif. Sch. Pub. Health, Berkeley, 1983—92, mem. Dean's adv. coun., 1995—2002; founding mem. Whitehead Inst. Bd. Assocs., 1995—; bd. dirs. Lovelace Inst., Respiratory Rsch. Inst., vice chmn., 1999—; bd. dirs. Children's Rsch. Inst., Washington, 2003—; lectr. to profl. assns.; mem. bd. visitors Harvard U. Sch. Pub. Health, Cambridge, 2002—; mem. Johns Hopkins Sch. of Nursing Dean's Coun., 2002—. Editor Jour. of Soc. Rsch. Adminstrs., 1986-89, mem. editl. rev. bd., 1989-95; mem. editl. bd. Jour. Women's Health, 1992—, Sci. Comm., 1994—; contbr. articles and editls. to profl. jours. Bd. dirs. Kensington (Calif.) Edn. Found., 1986-89, Enterprise for H.S. Students, 1990-92; mem. capital campaign com. Calif. Shakespeare Festival, 1989-91, v.p. Med. Rsch. Assns. Am., 1993-95; bd. advisors Friends of Cancer Rsch., 1996—; bd. dirs. Nat. Patient Safety Found., 1998-2000, Friends of Nat. Inst. of Nursing Rsch., 2001—. Recipient Silver Touchstone award Am. Hosp. Assn., 1994, Disting. Svc. award Columbia Coll. Physicians and Surgeons, 1994, Advocacy award Fedn. Am. Socs. Exptl. Biology, 1998, Advocacy award Friends Nat. Inst. Nursing Rsch., 1999, Leadership award Coun. Scientific Soc. Pres.'s, 1999, Advocacy award Friends of Dental Rsch., 2002. Fellow AAAS; mem. Assn. Ind. Rsch. Insts. (pres.-elect 1987-89, pres. 1989-90), Inst. Medicine (elected), Soc. Rsch. Adminstrs. (bd. dirs. 1986-90, bd. advisors 1990-93, Hartford-Nicholson Svc. award 1990, Disting. Contbn. to Rsch. Adminstrn. award, 1993), Calif. Biomed. Rsch. Assn,. (bd. govs. 1986-90), Md. Gov.'s Commn. on Women's Health, 1993-96. Democrat. Office: Research! Am 908 King St Ste 400E Alexandria VA 22314-3067

WOOLLS, ESTHER BLANCHE, library science educator; b. Louisville, Mar. 30, 1935; d. Arthur William and Esther Lennie (Smith) Sutton; m. Donald Paul Woolls, Oct. 21, 1953 (div. Nov. 1982); 1 son, Arthur Paul AB in Fine Arts, Ind. U., 1958, MA in Libr. Sci., 1962, PhD in Libr. Sci., 1973. Elem. libr. Hammond (Ind.) Pub. Schs., 1958-65, libr. coord., 1965-67, Roswell (N.Mex.) Ind. Schs., 1967-70; prof. libr. sci. U. Pitts., 1973-97; prof., dir. Sch. Lib. and Info Sci. San Jose (Calif.) State U., 1997—. Exec. dir. Beta Phi Mu, 1981-95. Author: The School Library Media Manager, 1995, 2d edit., 1999, So You're Going to Run a Library, 1995, Ideas for School Library Media Centers, 1996; co-author: Information Literacy, 1999; editor: Continuing Professional Education and IFLA: Past, Present, and a Vision for the Future, 1993, Delivering Lifelong Continuing Professional Education Across Space and Time, 2001. Fulbright scholar, 1995-96; recipient Disting. Svc. award Pa. Sch. Librs. Assn., 1993. Mem. ALA (mem. coun. 1985-89, 95—), Am. Assn. Sch. Librs. (bd. dirs. 1983-88, pres. 1993-94, Disting. Svc. award 1997), Pa. Learning Resources Assn. (pres. 1984-85), Internat. Assn. Sch. Librs. (pres. 1998-2001), Internat. Fedn. Libr. Assns. (mem. standing com. sch. librs. sect. 1991-99, sec. Continuing Profl. Edn. Round Table 2000—). Home: 130 E San Fernando St #403 San Jose CA 95112-3600 Office: San Jose State U Sch Lib & Info Sci 1 Washington Sq San Jose CA 95192-0029

WOOLSEY, LYNN, congresswoman; b. Seattle, Nov. 3, 1937; BS, U. San Francisco, 1981. Mgr. human resources Harris Digital Telephone, 1969—80; owner Woolsey Personnel Svs., 1980—92; mem. U.S. Congress from 6th Calif. dist., 1993—, ranking mem. edn. reform subcom. ho. com. edn. and the workforce. Mem. Petaluma City Coun., 1984-92 Democrat. Office: US Ho Reps 2263 Rayburn Ho Office Bldg Washington DC 20515-0506 Address: 1101 College Ave St 200 Santa Rosa CA 95404 also: 1050 Northgate Dr St 140 San Rafael CA 94903

WOOLSTON-CATLIN, MARIAN, psychiatrist; b. Seattle, Jan. 20, 1931; d. Howard Brown and Katharine Nichols (Dally) Woolston; m. Randolph Catlin Jr., July 5, 1959; children: Laura Louise, Jennifer Woolston, Randolph III. BA cum laude, Vassar Coll., 1951; MD, Harvard U., 1955. Diplomate Nat. Bd. Med. Examiners. Intern in pediat. medicine Children's Hosp., Boston, 1956, asst. resident in pediat. medicine, 1956; resident in psychiatry Mass. Mental Health Ctr., Boston, 1957-59; fellow in child psychiatry Tavistock Clin., London, 1960; Commonwealth fellow in child psychiatry Harvard U. at Gaebler Children's Unit, Waltham, Mass., 1975-78, clin. instr. psychiatry, 1978-79; pvt. practice Wellesley Hills, Mass., 1978-91, Medfield, Mass., 1991—. Clin. instr. psychiatry Harvard U. at Mass. Mental Health Ctr., Boston, 1957-59, 78-82, Tufts U. at Mass. Mental Health Ctr., 1957-59; mem. exec. bd. Parents' and Children's Svcs., Boston, 1983-86. Designer H.H. Hunnewell Meml. Garden for New Eng. Flower Show Mass. Hort. Soc., 1975 (Ames Cup award). Mem. exec. bd. Ext. Divsn. New Eng. Conservatory Music, 1972-75; charter mem. reuse com. Medfield State Hosp., 1992—. Fellow Am. Acad. Child and Adolescent Psychiatry; mem. AMA, Am. Psychiat. Assn. (life), Mass. Psychiat. Assn., Mass. Med. Soc., Boston Vassar Club (exec. bd. 1963-75), Hills Garden Club Wellesley (exec. bd. and design chief 1973-75). Episcopalian. Avocations: landscape design, sculpting. Home and Office: 314 North St Medfield MA 02052-1204

WOOLWORTH, SUSAN VALK, primary school educator; b. Toledo, Ohio, Apr. 24, 1954; d. Robert Earl and Alice (Melick) Valk; children: Alison Valk, Andrew Baker. BA, Pine Manor Jr. Coll., Chestnut Hill, Mass., 1974; BS, Boston U., 1976. Tchr. kindergarten Lancaster (Pa.) Country Day Sch., 1986—. Bd. dirs. Fulton Opera House; past bd. dirs. Planned Parenthood, Vis. Nurse Assn., Hands-On House. Mem.: Jr. League (sustainer), Sigma Gamma. Republican. Episcopalian. Avocations: walking, gardening, tennis, decorating.

WOOTEN, CAROL CAMPBELL, academic administrator; d. James Fredrick Campbell and Ruth Caroline Pectol; m. Ronald Lee Wooten, June 22, 1968 (div. Dec. 31, 1998); children: Robert, Caroline; m. Edward Tomlinson, Oct. 5, 2002. BS, Emory and Henry Coll., 1968; MA, Memphis State U., 1972; EdD, U. Pitts., 1993. Cert. secondary prin. Pa., supr. curriculum and instrn. Pa., supt.'s letter Pa. Rschr. U. Pitts., 1988—91; h.s. prin. Riverview Sch. Dist., Oakmont, Pa., 1992—93; mid. sch. prin. Southside Sch. Dist., Hookstown, Pa., 1993—94, asst. supt., 1994—99, supt., 1999—2003; chief acad. officer Propel Charter Schs., Pitts., 2003—. Bd. dirs. Pitts. Habitat for Humanity, 1998—. Recipient tech. grants, state and fed. govt., 1995—2003. Mem.: Forum for Western Pa. Sch. Supts., Edn. Policy and Issues Ctr. (leadership com. 2001—03), Pa. Assn. for Supervision and Curriculum Devel. (exec. bd. 1993—96). Avocations: theater, rock music, opera, symphonic music. Home: 112 Highpointe Dr Pittsburgh PA 15220 Office: Propel Charter Schs 700 River Ave Pittsburgh PA 15212 Office Phone: 412-323-1201. E-mail: carolwooten@comcast.net.

WOOTEN, CAROL G. conductor, music educator; MusB in Edn., Gordon Coll., 1987; student, Gordon-Conwell Theol. Sem., 1999. Cert. tchr. Mass. Music dir. Danvers Pub. Schs., Danvers, Mass., 1988—92; dir. of music Orange UMC, Chapel Hill, NC, 1992—96; dir. worship and arts ministry Epworth United Meth. Ch., Durham, NC, 2000—; founder and condr. Triangle Youth Music Chorus, Durham and Chapel Hill, NC, 2000. Instr. pvt. lessons, 1976—96; adjudicator, 1998—; dir. various workshops, 1998—. Founding dir. Arts Ministry, Inc., Durham and Chapel Hill, 2002—. Recipient First Pl. award, Jubilate Choral Soc., 1987. Mem.: Fellowship of United Meths. in the Arts, Am. Choral Dirs. Assn. (life), Chorister's Guild (chpt. pres. 1994—96), Worship List (advisor and chaplain 1998—2003). Independent. Avocations: outdoors, reading, travel.

WOOTEN, JOAN HEDRICH, minister; b. Washington, Jan. 4, 1953; d. Albert Louis and Maxine Keller Hedrich; m. David Randall Wooten, Jan. 11, 1983; children: Michael, Sarah. BA, Coll. William and Mary, 1975; MA, Bryn Mawr Coll., 1978; MDiv, Gordon-Conwell Theol. Sem., 1981; ThM, Duke U. Div. Sch., 1987. Ordained 1982. Chaplain U.S. Navy, Oak Harbor, Wash., 1982—84, Yokosuka, Japan, 1984—86, Norfolk, Va., 1987—90, res. chaplain, 1990—, capt.; pastoral counselor Episcopal Diocese of So. Va., Norfolk, 1990—93; campus min. Presbytery of Ea. Va., Portsmouth, 1993—2001; interim and stated supply pastor Presbytery Fla., 2003—. Doctoral fellow Union Theol. Sem., Richmond, 2001—. Singer Va. Symphony Chorus, Norfolk, 1992—2001. Decorated Commendation medal U.S. Navy. Presbyterian. Avocations: music, languages, cooking.

WORBY, RACHEL, conductor; b. Nyack, N.Y. m. David Obst (div.); m. Gaston Caperton (div.); 1 child, Diana. MusB in Piano Performance, SUNY; MA in Musicology, Ind. U.; PhD in Musicology, Brandeis U. Dir., condr. Youth Concerts Carnegie Hall, N.Y.C., 1984; condr. Youth Concerts LA (Calif.) Philharm., 1985—86; music dir. Wheeling (W.Va.) Symphony Orch., 1986—2002, Pasadena (Calif.) POPS Orch., 1999—. Guest condr. Barcelona (Spain) Symphony Orch., Irish Chamber Orch., Transylvania Philharm., London (Eng.) Philharm. Orch., Adelaide Symphony Orch., Queensland Symphony, Ojai Festival; mem. Nat. Coun. Arts, 1994—98. Founder Am. Music Festival, Cluj, Romania. Nominee ACE award, 1990; grantee, Martha Baird Rockefeller Fund, 1982. Office: The Pasadena Pops Orchestra 81 North Raymond Ave Ste 500 Pasadena CA 91103*

WORDEN, KATHARINE COLE, sculptor; b. N.Y.C., May 4, 1925; d. Philip Gillette and Katharine (Pyle) Cole; m. Frederic G. Worden, Jan. 8, 1944; children: Fred, Dwight, Philip, Barbara, Katharine. Student, Potters Ch., Tucson, 1940-42, Sarah Lawrence Coll., 1942-44. Exhibited in group shows at Royce Galleries, Galerie Francoise Besnard, Paris, Cooling Gallery, London, Galerie Schumacher, Munich, Selected Artists Gallery, N.Y.C., Art Inst. Boston, Reid Gallery, Nashville, Weiner Gallery, N.Y.C., Boston Athanaeum, House of Humor and Satire, Gabrovo, Bulgaria, 1983, Newport Bay Club, 1984; pvt. collections Grand Palais, Paris, Dakar and Bathurst, Africa. Dir. Stride Rite Corp., 1980-85; occpl. therapist psychopathic ward L.A. County Gen. Hosp., 1953-57; Headstart vol., Watts, Calif., 1965-67; tchr. sculpture Watts Towers Art Ctr., 1967-69; participant White House Women Doers Luncheon meeting, 1968; dir. Cambridgeport Problem Ctr., Cambridge, Mass., 1969-71; mem. Jud. Nominating Commn., 1976-79; bd. overseers Boston Mus. Fine Arts, 1980-83; bd. govs. Newport Seamens Ch. Inst., 1989-91; tustee Comm. Rsch., Miami, Fla., 1960-69, chmn. bd., 1966-69; trustee Newport Art Mus., 1984-86, 92-94, Jamestown Cmty. Theatre, 1994-97, 99—, Newport Health Found., 1986-91, Hawthorne Sea Fund, 1990-93; bd. dirs. Boston Ctr. for Arts, 1976-80, Child and Family Svcs. of Newport County, 1983-97, 99—. Mem. Common Cause (Mass adv. bd. 1971-72, dir. 1974-75), Mass. Civil Liberties Union (exec. bd. 1973-74, dir. 1976-77). Home: 24 Fort Wetherill Rd Jamestown RI 02835-2908

WORDEN, MARNY, artist, musician; b. Williamsport, Pa., Sept. 23, 1926; d. Harold Ernest and Marion Francis (Tillinghast) W.; m. Richard Dean Blair, Sept. 9, 1949 (div. 1957); 1 child, Brian Eric; m. John Riley Olson, Dec. 19, 1957. BA, U. Toledo, 1946; MAT, Ind. U., 1968. English tchr. Tex. Sch. for Deaf, Austin, 1954-62, Ind. Sch. for Deaf, Indpls., 1962-65; French, Spanish tchr. Indpls. City Schs., 1965-70; curriculum projects dir. Ind. Sch. for the Deaf, Indpls., 1970-71, tchr. English, Latin, 1972-79. Symphony musician and pvt. tchr. flute, piccolo, 1942—; dir. Tillinghast Early Music Consort; adjudicator Ind. Sch. Music Competitions. Author: (textbooks) 1,2,3 Language Series, 1970, (adaptations for the deaf) Beowulf, 1973, Song of Roland, 1974. Recipient of craftsman's rating in lapidary work, silversmithing; stone sculptures. Mem. Internat. Porcelain Artists & Tchrs., Inc. Avocations: oil paintings, watercolors, porcelain painting, performing. Address: 5504 Nordic Ln Richmond VA 23237-3807

WORDEN, MICHELE MARIE, speech pathology/audiology services professional; b. Chgo., July 12, 1960; d. Joseph Patrick and Natalie Marie McNulty; m. Scott B. Worden, Mar. 11, 2000. BA, U. St. Francis, 1982; Master's in Speech and Hearing, Bradley U., 1984. Speech lang. pathologist AERO Spl. Edn. Coop., Burbank, Ill., 1984—85, ECHO Spl. Edn. Coop., S. Holland, Ill., 1985—, Wee Care Therapy Ltd., Dyer, Ind., 1997—99. Active Ill. Spl. Olympics, 1988—98, 2001, 2003. Mem.: Ill. Speech Lang. Hearing Assn., Am. Speech Lang. Hearing Assn. Avocations: art, crafts, sewing, travel. Home: 12601 Haas Dr Palos Park IL 60464 Office: ECHO Spl Edn Coop 350 W 154th St South Holland IL 60473-1229

WORELL, JUDITH P. psychologist, educator; b. N.Y.C. d. Moses and Dorothy Goldfarb; m. Leonard Worell, Aug. 11, 1947 (div.); children: Amy, Beth, Wendy; m. H.A. Smith, Mar. 23, 1985 BS magna cum laude, Queens Coll., 1950; MA, Ohio State U., 1952, PhD in Clin. Psychology, 1954; DHL (hon.), Colby-Sawyer Coll., 1993. Research assoc. Iowa Psychopathic Hosp., Iowa City, 1957-59; research assoc. Okla. State U., 1960-66; asst. prof. U. Ky., Lexington, 1969-71, assoc. prof., 1971-75, prof. ednl. and counseling psychology, 1976—, dir. counseling psychology tng. program, 1980-93, chairperson dept. ednl. and counseling psychology, 1993-97, prof. emerita, 1999—. Author: (with C.M. Nelson) Managing Instructional Problems, 1974; (with W.E. Stilwell) Psychology for Teachers and Students, 1981; Psychological Development in the Elementary Years, 1982; (with Fred Danner) The Adolescent as Decision-maker: Applications to Development and Education, 1989; (with Pam Remer) Feminist Perspectives in Therapy: An Empowerment Model for Women, 1992; (with N. Johnson) Shaping the Future of Feminist Psychology: Education, Research, and Practice, 1997, (with Norine Johnson & Michael Roberts) Beyond Appearance: A New Look at Adolescent Girls, 1999, Encyclopedia of Women and Gender: Sex Similarities and Differences and the Impact of Society on Gender, 2001, (with Pam Remer) Feminist Perspectives in Therapy: Empowering Diverse Women, 2002; assoc. editor Jour. Cons. and Clin. Psychology, 1976-79, mem. editl. bd., 1984-89; assoc. editor Psychol. Women Quar., 1984-89, editor, 1989-95; mem. editorial bd. Sex Roles, 1984-2000, Psychol. Assessment, 1991-97, Clin. Psychology Rev., 1991-97, Women and Therapy, 1992-2000; cons., reviewer 10 jours.; contbr. articles to profl. jours. Named U. Ky. Campus Woman of Yr., 1976, Outstanding Univ. Grad. prof., 1991, Disting. Ky. psychologist, 1990; USPHS fellow, 1953; NIMH rsch. grantee, 1962-69. Fellow APA (pres. Clin. Psychology of Women 1986-88, chmn. com. state assn. rels. 1982-83, fellow selection divsn. 35 com. 1983-84, policy and planning bd. 1989-92, publs. and comm. bd. 1992-99, chair 1996-98, chair jours. com., pres. divsn. psychology of women 1997-98, Disting. Leader for Women in Psychology 1990, Carolyn Wood Sherif award, 2001, coun. rep. 2000-02), Ky. Psychol. Assn. (pres. 1981-82, rep. at large 1995-97), Southeastern Psychol. Assn. (exec. coun. mem.-at-large, pres.-elect 1993-94 pres. 1994-95), Am. Women in Psychology, Phi Beta Kappa. Home: 3892 Gloucester Dr Lexington KY 40510-9729 Office: U Ky Dept Ednl and Counseling Psychology 245 Dickey Hl Lexington KY 40506-0017 E-mail: jpwphd@aol.com.

WORK, JANE MAGRUDER, retired professional society administrator; b. Owensboro, Ky., Mar. 30, 1927; d. Orion Noel and Willie May (Stallings) Magruder; m. William Work, Nov. 26, 1960; children: Paul MacGregor, Jeffrey William. BA, Furman U., 1947; MA, U. Wis., 1948; PhD, Ohio State U., 1959. Dir. radio U. South Miss., Hattisburg, 1948-51; pub. rels. assoc. Ohio Fuel Gas Co./Columbia Gas, Columbus, 1952-62; adj. prof. comm. Pace U., N.Y.C., 1963-75; dir. speechmodule ERIC, Washington, 1975-76; mgr. orgn. liaison, dir. legis. analysis Nat. Assn. Mfgs., Washington, 1977-84, asst. v.p. legis. analysis, 1984-87, v.p. legis. analysis, 1987-93, v.p. mem. comm., 1993-2001, ret., 2001. Adv. bd. pub. affairs NYU Grad. Bus. Sch., 1983-87; adv. bd. Prodn. Mag., 1984-87; cons. IBM, Xerox, 1963-77. Contbr. articles to profl. jours. Mem. transition team Consumer Product Safety Commn., Washington, 1979—80; chair No. Va. Pvt. Industry Coun., Fairfax County, 1979—85; co-chair Va. Gov.'s Employment & Tng. Task Force, Richmond, 1983; bd. dirs. Alzheimer's Assn. Nat. Capital Area, 2002—. Named to Acad. Women Achievers YWCA, 1987. Mem.: World Future Soc. (steering network 1993 Gen. Assembly), The Planning Forum (bd. dirs. Capital chpt. 1990—93), Speech Comm. Assn. (sect. chmn. 1980—82), Am. Soc. Assn. Execs. (rsch. adv. com. 1989—97), Nat. Assn. Industry-Edn. Coop. (bd. dirs. 1983—2001), Issue Mgmt. Assn. (bd. dirs. 1985—88), Future Homemakers of Am. (bd. dirs. 1985—88), Pi Kappa Delta (hon.), Alpha Psi Omega (hon.). Republican. Unitarian Universalist. Avocations: gardening, volunteering. Home: 6245 Cheryl Dr Falls Church VA 22044-1809

WORK, JANICE RENÉ, pediatric dentist; b. Porterville, Calif., Aug. 22, 1944; d. Weldon and Vivian May (Campbell) W. AA, Porterville Jr. Coll., 1964; BA, Brigham Young U., 1967, MFA, 1978; DDS, Georgetown U., 1984; pediatric cert., U. Nebr. Med. Ctr., 1991. Diplomate Am. Bd. Pediatric Dentists, 1998. Dentist Dedicated Dental Svcs., Media, Pa., 1985, Lehigh Dental Assocs., Bethlehem, Pa., 1985-86, Grenfell Regional Health Svcs., Forteau, Labrador, Canada, 1986-88, Temporary Dental Help, Manhattan Beach, Calif., 1991, Dr. Randall G. Turner, Torrance, Calif., 1991, United Health Ctr. San Juaquim Valley, Inc., Huron, Calif., 1991; pediatric dentist Sacramento, 1992—. Mem. cleft palate panel The Sutter Hosp., 1992—. Chair Prevent Abuse and Neglect through Dental Awareness (PANDA) com., Sacramento; mem. bd. Sacramento Dist. Dental Found., 1993-98, Sacramento Dist. Midwinter Com., 1994-98, Sacramento Dist. Health Com., 1995-98. Fellow Acad. Gen. Dentistry, Acad. Dentistry Internat. Avocations: scuba diving, skiing, biking, camping. Home: PO Box 293690 Sacramento CA 95829-3690 Office: Dr Jan s Dentistry for Children 7260 E Southgate Dr Ste A Sacramento CA 95823-2609

WORKMAN, KAYLEEN MARIE, special education and adult education educator; b. Paola, Kans., Aug. 25, 1947; d. Ralph I. and Pearl Marie (Shults) Platz; m. John Edward Workman, Aug. 10, 1980; children: Andrew Ray, Craig Michael. BS in Edn., Emporia State U., 1969, MS in Edn., 1983. Tchr. English/speech Lincoln (Kans.) High Sch., 1969-70, substitute tchr., 1970-71, Hudson (Wis.) Sch. Dist., 1971-72; tchrs. aide learning disabilities Park Forest South (Ill) Jr. High Sch., 1978—97; learning disabilities/English instr. George York Sch., Osawatomie, Kans., 1978-97, instr. math and sci., spl. edn., 2003—; adult edn. instr. Adult Edn. Ctr., Osawatomie State Hosp., 1997-2000; spl. edn. tchr. Ottawa (Kans.) H.S., 2000—02; math. and sci. tchr. spl. edn. George York Cmty. Sch., Osawatomie, Kans., 2003—. Supr. Loose Ends Clown Troop, 1988-91; instr. Alphapointe Ctr. Blindness, Kans. City, Mo., 2004—; presenter in field. Author of poems. Com. mem., sec. Cub Scouts, Osawatomie, 1987-88, com. mem. Boy Scouts Am., 1988-91, sec., 1990-91; forensics judge Osawatomie H.S. Forensics Team, 1991-92; hunter's safety instr. Osawatomie Sportsman's Club, 1982-86; mem. Osawatomie Cmty. Band, 1990-92. Mem. Osawatomie-NEA (v.p. 1982-83, 93-94, pres. 1983-84, 94-95, sec. 1986), Kans.-NEA (Sunflower uniserv adminstrv. bd. 1985, Sunflower uniserv coord. coun.), Learning Disabilities Assn., Delta Kappa Gamma. Avocations: hunting, fishing, collecting santa clauses, writing poetry, shopping.

WORKMAN, MARGARET LEE, lawyer; b. May 22, 1947; d. Frank Eugene and Mary Emma (Thomas) W.; m. Edward T. Gardner III; children: Lindsay Elizabeth, Christopher Workman, Edward Earnshaw. AB in Polit. Sci., W.Va. U., 1969, JD, 1974. Bar: W.Va. 1974. Asst. counsel to majority, pub. works com. U.S. Senate, Washington, 1974-75; law clk. 13th jud. cir., W.Va. Ct., Charleston, 1975-76, judge, 1981-88; pvt. practice Charleston, 1976-81, 99—; justice W.Va. Supreme Ct. Appeals, Charleston, 1989-99, chief justice, 1993, 97. Advance person for Rosalyn Carter, Carter Presdl. Campaign, Atlanta, 1976. Democrat. Episcopalian.

WORLEY, DEBERE, educational consultant; b. Toledo, Apr. 22, 1953; d. Thomas Daniel and Dorothy Mae Worley. BS in Edn., Bowling Green State U., 1976; MS in Edn., U. Toledo, 1990. Cert. tchr., Ohio. Tchr. Toledo Pub. Schs., 1977—; rehab. technician Lucas County, Toledo, summers 83-85; ednl. cons. State Tchrs. Ret. Sys., Columbus, Ohio, 96-98, 99—; mem. pres.'s coun. Avon Products, Inc., Atlanta, 1997-98. Grad. asst. U. Toledo, 1988-89, Bowling Green State U., 1995-96. Author poetry: Dreams Really Do Come True, 1999. Recipient scholarships U. Toledo, 1988-89, Bowling Green State U., 1995-96. Avocations: crafts, home decorating, gardening, home repair, collecting collectibles and restoring antiques. Office: St Jude Parish Family 3650 Victory Ave Toledo OH 43607-2564

WORLEY, KAREN BOYD, psychologist; b. Hot Springs, Ark., Apr. 23, 1952; d. Wayne Johnson and Lou (Hull) Boyd; m. Timothy Riker, Sept. 22, 1979; children: Travis, Tyler, Kaitlin, Kelsey. BA, Okla. State U., 1974; PhD, Tex. Tech. U., 1983. Lic. psychologist, Ark. Rsch. asst. Rsch. and Tng. Ctr. for Mentally Retarded Tex. Tech. U., Lubbock, 1974-77, teaching asst., 1977-78; psychology intern Kansas City (Mo.) VA Med. Ctr., 1978-79; psychologist Johnson County Mental Health Ctr., Shawnee Mission, Kans., 1979-81; pvt. practice Pleasant Valley Clinic, Little Rock, 1982-97; asst. prof. dept. pediatrics U. of Ark. for Med. Sci., 1912—2001, assoc. prof., 2002, dir. family treatment program, 1991—. Mem. Gov.'s Task Force on Child Abuse in Arks., 1983—85, Gov.'s Task Force on Youth Violence, 1998—99, Atty. Gen.'s Youth Violence Adv. Coun., 1998—99, Pulaski County Child Abuse Task Force, 1985, Pulaski County Family Svcs. Rev. Com., 1986—87, Com. to Rev. Investigation Procedures Ark. Children and Family Svcs., 1986, Child Sexual Abuse Network, 1988—93, Atty. Gen.'s Crime Victim Adv. Bd., 1999—, Angela R. Oversight Com., 1999—2003; bd. dirs. Ark. Child Sexual Abuse Edn. Commn., 1985—91, Suspected Child Abuse and Neglect, 1986—92, co-chair, 1998—; bd. dirs. Ark. Commn. on Child Abuse, Rape and Domestic Violence, 1991—, Victims of Crime Act Bd., 1992—97; cons. Mother's Support Group, Parent Ctr., Little Rock, 1983—92, Atty. Gen's Victims Adv. Bd., 1999—2000; chmn. Ark. Commn. on Child Abuse, Rape, and Domestic Violence, 2003—. Contbr. articles to profl. publs. Recipient Commr.'s award Office on Child Abuse and Neglect, 2001. Mem.: APA, Assn. for Treatment of Sexual Abusers (pres. 2000—), Am. Profl. Soc. on Abuse of Children, Nat. Register Health Svc. Providers in Psychology (coun.), Ark. Psychol. Assn., Phi Kappa Phi. Methodist. Office: Family Treatment Program 1120 Marshall St Little Rock AR 72202-4610

WORLEY, NANCY L. secretary of state; b. Madison County, Ala., Nov. 7, 1951; d. Leonard O. and Lillian (Smith) W. BA magna cum laude, U. Montevallo, Ala., 1973; MA, Jacksonville (Ala.) State U., 1974; postgrad., U. Ala., Tuscaloosa and Huntsville, 1974, U. Edinburgh, Scotland, 1975. Cert. English, speech and Latin tchr., Ala. Instr. English, NE State Jr. Coll., Rainsville, Ala., Calhoun Community Coll., Decatur, Ala.; tchr. lang. arts Decatur City Schs.; sec. of state State of Ala., Montgomery, 2003—. Contbr. articles to profl. jours. Named Ala.'s Outstanding Young Educator, Dist. Tchr. of Yr., Decatur City Schs.; grantee grantee UN. Mem. NEA, Ala. Edn. Assn. (pres., 1983-84, 95-97, legis. com.), Ala. Fgn. Lang. Tchrs. Assn. (past pres.), Ala. Classroom Tchrs. Assn. (past pres., bd. dirs.), Sigma Tau Delta, Kappa Delta Pi, Lambda Sigma Chi, Omicron Delta Kappa. Office: Office of the Sec of State PO Box 5616 Montgomery AL 36103-5616*

WORLEY, VIRGINIA KING, microbiologist; b. Pitts., Apr. 15, 1925; d. Wilbert Frederick and Helena Anna (Blotter) King; m. Carl Milton Worley, Apr. 14, 1945 (div. Dec. 1963); children: Mark, Seth, Paul, Marianne. BS in Microbiology, U. Pitts., 1946; M in Music Edn., Duquesne U., 1991. Part-time organist, choir dir. various chs., Pitts., 1944-85; environ. health sanitarian Allegheny County Health Dept., Pitts., 1969-87; music min. St. Peter Roman Catholic Ch., Pitts., 1985-94; dir. therapeutic music programs various schs. and chs., Pitts., 1990—; gen. music. tchr., 1990—; music min. Good Shepherd Luth. Ch., Pitts., 1994-98, Allegheny United Meth. Ch., 1999—2001, St. Luke Luth. Ch., 2001—, Allegheny United Ch. Christ, 2001—. Pvt. tutor piano and pipe organ, 1955—. Bd. dirs. Freedom House Enterprises, 1979—; founder Greater Pitts. Women's Ctr. and Shelter, 1975, Greater Pitts. Cmty. Food Bank, 1980; mem. Ctrl. Northside Citizen's Coun., Pitts., 1993—, Manchester Citizens' Corp., Pitts., 1983—; bd. dirs. Phoenix Youth Orch. Grantee various founds., 1990—. Mem. AAUW, Am. Guild Organists (bd. dirs. 1994-95), Nat. Orgn. Parish Musicians, Nat. Mus. Women Arts, Pitts. Assn. Arts Edn. and Therapy, Choristers Guild, Pi Kappa Lambda. Democrat. Avocations: camping, hiking, nature study. Home: 1413 Faulsey Way Pittsburgh PA 15233-1909

WORMACK, KAREN ELISE, small business owner, poet; b. Newark, Sept. 6, 1962; d. John Wesley Wormack Jr. and Gloria Marlena (Erwin) Wormack-Davis. BA in English/Comms., Kean Coll., 1985; MPA, Marywood U., Scranton, Pa., 2000. Cert. hypnotherapist 1998, lic. real estate salesperson SEC, N.J., SEC, Pa., life ins. investment rep. SEC, Series 6, 1987, SEC, Series 53, 1990. Customer svc. agt. Piedmont Airlines, Newark, 1986-87; investment rep., life ins. rep. Investment Rop. First Investor's Corp., Piscataway, NJ, 1987-90; sales assoc. Weichert Realtors, Morristown, NJ, 1991-93; real estate salesperson Shawnee Resort, Shawnee-on-Delaware, Pa., 1995-96; owner The Pocono Love Basket, 1995—; clin. hypnotherapist The Hypnosis Inst. N.Y., 1998; quality assurance coord. Cmty. Access Unltd., Human Svc. Agy. for Devel. Disabled, Elizabeth, NJ, 1999-2000; team leader Home Based Waiver Program Servicing Children and Adults with devel. disability, Step-By-Step, Inc., 2000—; therapeutic staff support Colonial Intermediate Unit 20, Easton, Pa., 2001, Youth Advocate Program, 2001—02; owner The Fancy Cone, Stroudsburg, Pa., 2001—, Ho. Guilded Scribe, Stroudsburg, Pa., 2003; referral agt. Weichert Realtors, Morristown, 1996—. Sec., counselor Hugh O'Brian Youth Found., North Brunswick, NJ, 1988—89. Author: A Voice Crying in the Wilderness, 1990, The Adventures of Prissy and Missy, 1993, Enchanted Seraphim!, 1999, Emmanuel's Accolades!, 2000, A Good Teacher's Love, 2003; Lyricist: songs My Name is in the Book of Life, 2001, Where You Are We Want to Be, 2001, The Manners Song, 2002, Worship Him, 2004. Mem. Pocono Mt. C of C, 2003. Recipient Outstanding Poet award, World of Poetry, 1990, Clearance C. and Elizabeth Walton Medal of Honor for Excellence in Pub. Adminstrn., Marywood U., 2000. Mem.: Nat. Bd. Realtors, Assn. for the Severely Handicapped, Support Your Local Poet=Hooray (chairperson Strindsburg, Pa. 2004—), Pocono Mountain C. of C., Alpha Epsilon Lambda, Pi Alpha Alpha. Avocations: poetry, song writing, modeling, philanthropy, exploring caves. Home: 503 Thomas St Stroudsburg PA 18360-2104 E-mail: kewormack@aol.com.

WORONOV, MARY PETER, actress; b. Bklyn., Dec. 8, 1946; d. Victor D. and Carol W.; m. Ted Gershuny, 1969 (div.); m. Ted Whitehead, 1979. Student, Cornell Univ. Actress (films) The Chelsea Girls, 1967, Death Race 2000, 1975, Rock 'n' Roll High School, 1979, Eating Raoul, 1982, Black Widow, 1987, Warlock, 1989, Good Girls Don't, 1995, The Munster's Scary Little Christmas, 1996, Invisible Mom II, 1999, (TV series) Logan's Run, 1977, Sledge Hammer!, 1987, (TV movie) Challenge of a Lifetime, 1985, (TV special) Cheech and Chong's Get Out of My Room, 1985, (stage prodns.) Kitchenette, 1968, Boom Boom Room, 1974; author: Wake for the Angels: Paintings and Stories, 1994, Swimming Underground: My Years in the Warhol Factory, 1995. Avocation: painting.

WORRELL, ANNE EVERETTE ROWELL, newspaper publisher; b. Surry, Va., Mar. 7, 1920; d. Charles Gray and Ethel (Roache) Rowell; m. Thomas Eugene Worrell, Sept. 12, 1941; 1 child, Thomas Eugene. Student, Va. Intermont Coll., 1939, LittD (hon.), 1991; student, U. Richmond, 1965. Founding stockholder Worrell Newspapers Inc., 1949, v.p., dir., 1969-73; v.p., sec. Worrell Investment Co., Charlottesville, Va.; pres. The Genan Co. (formerly Bristol Newspapers). Pres. Bristol Jr. League, 1959; bd. dirs. The Corp. for Thomas Jefferson's Poplar Forest Found., Va. Hist. Soc., Va. Intermont Coll., Antiquities; active Bayly Mus., Monticello Cabinet. Named Outstanding Alumna, Va. Intermont Coll., 1981. Mem.: DAR

(Shadwell chpt.), Nat. Trust for Hist. Preservation, Greencroft Club, Farmington Country Club, Contemporary Club. Episcopalian. Home: Seven Sunset Circle Farmington Charlottesville VA 22901 Office: Pantops PO Box 5386 Charlottesville VA 22905-5386

WORRELL, CYNTHIA LEE, bank executive; b. Moncton, N.B., Can., May 27, 1957; came to U.S., 1979; d. Ronald William and Audrey Helen (Crothers) Jones; m. Geoffrey H. Worrell, Sept. 1, 1979; children: Lindsay Andrea, Geoffrey Andrew, Ashley Taylor. Student, U. New Brunswick, Fredericton, 1979. Lic. real estate broker, Mass., Pa., Calif. Instr. New Brunswick C.C., Fredericton, N.B., Can., 1978-79, Massasoit C.C., Brockton, Mass., 1981-82, Brockton Cmty. Schs., 1981-82; regional mgr. and instr. Worldwide Ednl. Svcs., Clifton, N.J., program dir. Taunton, Mass., 1995; procedures and documentation analyst Capital Blue Cross, Harrisburg, Pa., 1985; v.p., br. mgr. Comfed Mortgage Co., Inc., Mass., 1985-90; sr. residential loan officer Bank of Am., Santa Clara, Calif., 1990-92; regional sales mgr., asst. v.p. Shearson Lehman Mortgage, San Jose, Calif., 1992-93; br. mgr. Cypress Fin., San Jose, 1993-94, PNC Mortgage Corp. Am., San Jose, 1994—; program dir. worldwide Ednl. Svcs., Taunton, Mass., 1995; area prodn. mgr. Plymouth Mortgage Co., Foxborough, Mass., 1995-96, Ameriquest Mortgage, Hingham, Mass., 1996-97; br. mgr. Bank United of Tex. Commonwealth United Mortgage, West Bridgewater, Mass., 1996—; br. mgr. Nat. City Mortgage-Commonwealth United Mortgage, 1997-98, Family Choice Mortgage, West Bridgewater, 1998—2000, Orchard Mortgage, Raynham, Mass., 2000—. Guest spkr. numerous trade shows, real estate bd. seminars, cmty. workshops, stress mgmt. personal profiles, motivational speaking and workshops; instr. mortgage banking Calif. State U., Hayward, 1994—; mem. adv. bd., instr., outside cons. Calif. State U. Ext. divsn., 1993-95; cert. trainer Carlson Learning Co., 1993—; trainer in diversity, conflict resolution, sexual harassment, and time mgmt.; cmty. trainer WCR, BPW, Old Colony Vocat. Sch., Wareham H.S., Wareham Mid. and Elem. Schs., Wareham Supts. Office, Fall River Sch. Dist., Old Rochester Jr. and Sr. H.S., Bristol County Tng. Consortium, and Transitional Assistance, Bridgewater Cmty., Wareham Foster Parents, Wareham Decas Sch., 1996—. Mem. editl. bd. Mortgage Originator, 1995; contbr. articles to profl. jours. Vol. Handi Kids, Bridgewater, Mass., 1985—90, Fremont/Newark YMCA youth basketball and soccer; active Forest Park PTA, Self-Def. Inst. Tau Kwon Do Club; donor Berwick Boys Club; mem. adv. com. Wareham H.S., mem. coun.; alumni dir. U. New Brunswick, 1998—; bd. dirs. Wareham Childcare; trustee Le Lycee Internat. de la Nouvelle Angleterre, Inc., Boston, 1997; trustee, chair Tabor Acad., Marion, Mass. Named to IBC 200 Women of Achievement, 1991-92, ABI 2000 Notable Women, 1991-92,ABI Personalities of Am., 1992, Internat. Order of Merit, 1992, The World Found. of Successful Women, 1992, Outstanding Young Women in Am., 1984, 88. Mem. NAFE, Mass. Mortgage Bankers Assn., Data Entry Mgmt. Assn., Middleboro C. of C., Chief Exec. Club Boston, Wareham Bus. and Profl. Women's Club (v.p. program dir.), Taunton Area C. of C., Toastmasters, Plymouth Bd. Realtors, Bristol County Bd. Realtors, Women's Coun. of Realtors, Bristol County C. of C. Republican. Avocations: swimming, golf, horseback riding, curling. Home: 2 Peter Cooper Dr Wareham MA 02571-2209 Office: Orchard Mortgage 473 South St W Raynham MA 02767-5306

WORRELL, MARY THORA, loan officer; b. Montreal, Quebec, Can., [illegible] Henry G. Worrell, July 18, 1953 (div. Aug. 1974), children: Deborah, Geoffrey, John. BA, Sir George Williams U., Montreal, 1957. Lic. real estate agt., Mass. Lectr. Sir George Williams U., Montreal, Canada, 1963—74, rsch. Pvt. Stock, Palo Alto, Calif., 1979-90; loan officer Gt. We. Bank, Dublin, Calif., 1990-91, San Francisco Fed. Savs. Bank, 1991-92; residential loan specialist Eureka Bank, Foster City, Calif., 1992-93; residential loan officer First Interstate Bank, Oakland, Calif., 1993-94; loan officer First Nationwide Bank, Walnut Creek, Calif., 1994-95, Chase Manhattan Mortgage, San Francisco, 1995-96; sr. loan officer Pacific Bay Bank, San Pablo, Calif., 1996-97, Wausau Mortgage Corp., Pleasanton, Calif., 1997—. Speaker, mem. panel nat. prayer breakfast Ho. Commons, Ottawa, Can., 1972; speaker Wharton Sch. Human Resources, Phila., 1976; group leader Nat. Sci. Found. and George Washington U., 1976-77; mem. prison visitation com. Antioch Missionary Bapt. Ch., Oakland, Calif., 1992-98. Recipient Outstanding Svc. Conf. Speaker Pub. Rels. Student Soc. Am., 1976. Avocations: american jurisprudence, prison fellowship, eagle watching, golf, ballroom dancing. E-mail: mthora@yahoo.com.

WORSHAM, CHRISTINE BEHRENS, healthcare administrator; b. Portsmouth, Ohio, June 29, 1958; d. Carl William Behrens and Karin Rita (Roeder) Behrens-Ellis; m. Willis Scott Worsham, Oct. 7, 2000. AS in Sci., Brunswick Coll., 1979, AS in Nursing, 1981; BA in Econs., George Mason U., 1987; M in Healthcare Adminstrn., Xavier U., 1989. CCRN. Staff nurse Bath County Community Hosp., Hot Springs, Va., 1981-82; critical care nurse U. Va. Med. Ctr., Charlottesville, Va., 1982-85; med. paralegal Donahue, Ehrmantraut, Montedonico, Washington, 1986; adminstrv. intern U. Va. Med. Ctr., Charlottesville, 1987; adminstrv. resident Alleghany Regional Hosp., Lowmoor, Va., 1989-95; exec.v.p. Odin Co., 1995—. Bd. dirs. Odin Co.; v.p. comms. Odin Sys. Internat. Mem. aux. Safe Harbor, St. Simons, Ga., 1991; active Med. Assistance Program, Brunswick, 1990, Rep. Women's Orgn., St. Simons, 1990; mem. found. bd. S.E. Ga. Regional Med. Ctr. Mem. AACCN, Am. Hosp. Assn., Am. Coll. Healthcare Execs., Golden Isles Investment Club St. Simons (pres. 1994), Omicron Delta Epsilon Theta. Presbyterian. Home: 1335 Hilltop Rd Charlottesville VA 22903

WORTH, LYNN HARRIS, writer; b. Flushing, N.Y., Sept. 21, 1934; d. Andrew Lamar Harris and Jean Hofmann; m. Chauncey Merrill Smith, Jr., June 20, 1992. AA in Journalism, Vt. Coll., 1954; degree in Interior Design, NY Sch. Interior Design, 1971. Editl. asst. Time Mag., N.Y.C., 1954—56; pub. rels. asst. Silver Hill Found., New Canaan, Conn., 1958—61. Ptnr. Chameleon Interiors, Westport, Conn., 1972—84. Editor and pub.: Va. Gamebird Jour., editor, pub.: Magyar Vizsla News, mem. editl. staff: AKC Perspectives; contbr. articles to mags. Publicity dir. Westport Young Woman's League, 1967—68; publicity/pub. rels. Girl Scouts Am., Dist. 2, Fairfield County, 1967—69, LWV, Westport; founding mem. Lake Country SPCA; pres. Vizsla Club of Am. Welfare Found.; publicity/pub. rels. polit. campaign for Gov. Tom Meskill, Conn. Mem.: Magyar Vizsla Soc. (founding mem.), numerous regional dog clubs, Vizsla Club of Am. (Am. Kennel Club del., v.p., sec. 1980—). Home: PO Box 1755 Clarksville VA 23927

WORTHAM, ANNE ESTELLE, education educator; b. Jackson, Tenn., Nov. 26, 1941; d. Johnny and Bernice Wortham. BS, Tuskegee Inst., 1959—63; PhD, Boston Coll., 1977—82. Rschr., asst. editor Esquire Mag., NYC, 1965—67; rsch. asst. Huntley-Brinkley Report, NBC News, NYC, 1967—69; rsch. libr. ABC Radio News, NYC, 1970—71; freelance writer-rschr. Ford Found., IBM World Trade Corp., NYC, 1971—72; rsch. assoc. Ednl. Policy Ctr., NYC, 1972—74; rsch. libr. King Features Syndicate, NYC, 1974—77; adj. asst. prof. of sociology Wellesley Coll., Mass., 1982—83; asst. prof. of pub. policy Harvard U., 1983—86; asst. prof. of sociology Wash. and Lee U., Lexington, Va., 1989—91; assoc. prof. of sociology Ill. State U., 1991—. Cons. Nat. Endowment for the Humanities, Washington, 1985—92; vis. scholar Hoover Instn., Stanford, Calif., 1986—89; cons. Mass. Dept. of Edn., 1996, US Dept. of Edn., Washington, 1987, Nat. Endowment for the Humanities, Washington, 1991—92. Author: The Other Side of Racism: A Philosophical Study of Black Race Consciousness; contbr. chapters to books The Libertarian Alternative:Essays in Social and Political Philosophy, 1975, American Sociological Association Presidential Volume on Public Policy, 1990, Civil Wrongs: What Went Wrong with Affirmative Action, 1994, Opposing Viewpoints: Interracial America, 1998, Character and Identity: Sociological Foundations of Literary and Historical Perspectives, 2000, articles to jours. Student participant Operation Crossroads Africa, Ethiopia, 1962; vol. US Peace Corps, Tanzania, 1963—65. Inst. for Humane Studies fellowship, Inst. for Humane Studies, 1977—78, Earhart Grad. fellowship, Earhart Found., 1978, Danforth Grad. fellowship, Danforth Found., 1979—81, Seifert Grad. fellowship, The Found. for Econ. Edn., 1979—81, Ludwig von Mises Humanities fellowship, Ctr. for Libertarian Studies, 1982—83, Earhart Post-Graduate fellow, Earhart Found., 1983—84, John M. Olin Faculty fellowship, John M. Olin Found., 1985—86, Earhart Found. Rsch. grant, Earhart Found., 2000. Mem.: Am. Sociol. Assn. Office: Illinois State University Campus Box 4660 Normal IL 61790

WORTHING, CAROL MARIE, minister; b. Duluth, Minn., Dec. 27, 1934; d. Truman James and Helga Maria (Bolander) W.; children: Gregory Alan Beatty, Graydon Ernest Beatty. BS, U. Minn., 1965; MDiv, Northwestern Theol. Seminary, 1982; DMin, Grad. Theol. Found., Notre Dame, Ind., 1988; MBA in Ch. Mgmt., Grad. Theol. Found., Donaldson, Ind., 1993; cert., Austin Presbyn. Theol. Sem., 2001; PhD, Grad. Theol. Found., 2002. Cert. Episcopal Diocese of Tex., 2003. Secondary educator Ind. (Minn.) Sch. Dist., 1965-78; teaching fellow U. Minn., 1968-70; contract counselor Luth. Social Svc., Duluth, 1976-78; media cons. Luth. Media Svcs., St. Paul, 1978-80; asst. pastor Messiah Luth. Ch., Fargo, N.D., 1982-83, vice pastor, 1983-84; assoc. editor Luth. Ch. Am. Ptnrs., Phila., 1982-84; editorial assoc. Luth. Ptnrs. Evang. Luth. Ch. Am., Phila. and Mpls., 1984—; parish pastor Resurrection Luth. Ch., Pierre, S.D., 1984-89; assoc. pastor Bethlehem Luth. Ch., Cedar Falls, Iowa, 1989-90; exec. dir. Ill. Conf. Chs., Springfield, 1990-96, Tex. Conf. of Chs., 1996—. Mem. pub. rels. and interpretation com. Red River Valley Synod, Fargo, 1984-86, mem. ch. devel., Pierre, 1986-87; mem. mgmt. com. office comm. Luth. Ch. in Am., N.Y.C., Phila., 1984-88; mem. mission ptnrs. S.D. Synod, 1988, chmn. assembly resolutions com., 1988; mem. pre-assembly planning com., ecumenics com., chmn. resolutions com. N.E. Iowa Synod, 1989-90; mem. ch. and society com., 1990-96; ecumenical com., 1995-96; Luth. Ecumenical Rep. Network, 1995—; mem. Cen. and So. Ill. Synod, 1996; mem. S.W. Tex. Synod, 1996—, mem. ecumenical com., 1998-2001; nat. edn. cons. Am. Film Inst., Washington, 1967-70; chaplain state legis. bodies, Pierre, 1984-89; mem. exec. bd. Luth. Ecumenical Rep. Network for Region 4, Evang. Luth. Ch. in Am., 2002—. Author: Cinematics and English, 1967, Peer Counseling, 1977, Tischrede Lexegete, 1986, 88, 90, Way of the Cross, Way of Justice Walk, 1987, Introducing Collaboration as a Leadership Stance and Style in an Established Statewide Conference of Churches, 1993, The Anointing of Jesus--A Christological Necessity, 2001. Co-facilitator Parents of Retarded Children, 1985; bd. dirs. Countryside Hospice, 1985; cons. to adminstrv. bd. Mo. Shores Women's Ctr., 1986. Named John Macquarrie fellow, Grad. Theol. Found., 2002. Mem. NAFE, Nat. Assn. Ecumenical Staff (chair of site selection com. 1991-92, chair of scholarship com. 1993-94, mem. profl. devel. com. 1993-94, chair program planning com. 1996, bd. dirs. 1995-96), Pierre-Ft. Pierre Ministerium (v.p. 1986-87, pres. 1987-88). Democrat. Avocations: writing prose and poetry, concerts, theater, art, photography. Home: Ste 2B4 40 N I H 35 Austin TX 78701-4339 Office: Tex Confs Chs Ste 125 1033 La Posada Dr Austin TX 78752-3830 E-mail: cworthing@txconfchurches.org.

WORTHING, MARCIA LYNN, cosmetics company executive; b. Columbus, Ohio, Jan. 8, 1943; d. Ford Buxton and Dorothy Jean (Leonard) W.; m. Ronald Martin Foster, Jr., Dec. 15, 1973; children: Christopher Worthing, Geoffrey Worthing. BA, San Francisco [illegible] Francisco, 1966-67; editorial asst. Am. Mgmt. Assn., N.Y.C., 1967-69; publs. editor Merrill Lynch Pierce Fenner & Smith, N.Y.C., 1969-72; publs. editor Avon Products, Inc., N.Y.C., 1972-73, supr. pers., 1973-74, mgr. employment, 1974-76, mgr. tng., 1976-78, dir. pers., 1978-81, gen. mgr. hqrs., 1981-82, v.p. adminstrn., 1982-84, v.p. human resources, from 1984, sr. v.p., 1994-98, vice chair and exec. v.p. Mullin & Assocs. Ltd., N.Y.; bd. dirs. United Water Resources; chmn. N.Y. Bd. Trade; serves as a memeber on the bd. of several nonprofit organizations, including: The Am. Women's Econ. Devel. Corp., The Inst. for Women's Policy Rsch., The Inst. for Global Ethics and Play for Living. Office: Mullin & Associates Ltd 2 Grand Central Tower 23rd Floor 140 East 45th Street New York NY 10017-3144

WORTHINGTON, CAROL PEARCE, writer, editor; b. Dubuque, Iowa, Dec. 25, 1947; d. Wallace Harry Pearce and Edna Louisa (Williams) Meyer; m. Robert Theodore Worthington, June 23, 1984. BA, Clarke Coll., 1972; MFA, Villanova U., 1974. Sr. editor Show Magazine, N.Y.C., 1975-77; assoc. editor Backstage Newspaper, N.Y.C., 1977-78; sr, editor Weight Watchers Magazine, N.Y.C., 1978-82. Featured poetry reader at various readings, N.Y.C., 1995-96. Author: Amelia Earhart, A Biography, 1988, Career Chic, 1990; co-author (with J. Francois Eid, M.D.) Making Love Again, 1992; contbr. articles to mags. and pocket books, 1981-91, short stories to Quar. West, Oregon East, Greensboro Rev., Caribbean Writer and other lit. mags.; poetry published in Small Pond, Anemone, Dell Love Poems, Julien's Journal, N.Am. Mentor, Princeton Arts Rev. Recipient Langston Hughes Poetry award YM-YWCA, N.Y.C., 1982, Annual Poetry award Poetry Soc. Am., 1985, Deer Valley Fiction award U. Utah, 1986; creative writing fellowships to Wesleyan U., Columbia U., Bennington Coll.; poetry and watercolors selected for Cornell Med. Libr. Tri-institutional Art Show, 1994-2003; named artist in residence Millay Colony for the Arts. Mem. AMWA, Princeton Club.

WORTHINGTON, CAROLE YARD LYNCH, lawyer; b. Knoxville, Tenn., Aug. 29, 1951; d. Charles R. and Alma (Allred) Yard; m. Robert F. Worthington Jr., Sept. 14, 1996; 1 child, Cassandra Kathleen. BA, U. Tenn., 1972, JD, 1977. Bar: Tenn. 1977, Ga. 1982. Assoc. Thomas, Leitner, Mann, Warner & Owens, Chattanooga, 1977-78, Thomas, Mann & Gossett, Chattanooga, 1978-81, ptnr., v.p., 1981-86; ptnr. Grant, Konvalinka & Harrison, P.C., Chattanooga, 1987-96, Carole Lynch Worthington, Atty. at Law, Knoxville, 1996—. Sec. Nat. Transp. Rsch. Ctr., Inc. Author: Estate Planning Tennessee Practice, 1992; asst. editor Tenn. Law Rev., 1976-77. Vice chmn. allocations United Way of Chattanooga, 1985, pilot campaign, 1986; active Jr. League of Chattanooga, 1981-92; mem. alumnae adv. coun. U. Tenn. Coll. Law, 1983-92, dean's cir., 1989—; bd. dirs. Mental Health Assn. Chattanooga Inc., 1986-92, 1st v.p., 1988-89, sec., 1989-92; trustee St. Nicholas Sch., 1992-95, East Tenn. Opera Guild, 2001—. Recipient Alumni Leadership award U. Tenn. Coll. Law, 1988, 92. Fellow Am. Bar Found., Tenn. Bar Found., Chattanooga Bar Found.; mem. ABA (del. at large 1991-97, 98-2001), com. on legal aid and indigent defendants 1994-95, select com. of house 1994-96, standing com. on charter and by laws 1999-2000, standing com. on credentials and admissions 1999-2000, standing com. on credentials and admissions 1999-2000, com. on client rels. 2000-2002), Chattanooga Bar Assn. (bd. govs. 1982-89, sec.-treas. 1985-86, pres. 1987-88), Knoxville Bar Assn. (chair pro bono com. 2002), Tenn. Bar Assn. (vice chair comml. law, banking and bankruptcy 1988-90, unified bar study com. 1990-91, chair bar leadership conf. 1990, editl. bd. Tenn. Bar Jour. 1991-94, Tenn. Bar Assn. long range planning com. 1992-95, 97-99, bd. govs. 1994-96, chair long range planning com. 1995-96, future of bar com. 1998-2001), Ga. Bar Assn., Nat. Conf. Lawyers and Realtors (ABA del. 1990-92), Nat. Conf. Bar Pres.'s (exec. coun. 1989-92, treas. 1992-93, sec. 1993-94, pres.-elect 1994-95, pres. 1995-96), Tenn. Bd. Profl. Responsibility, Phi Alpha Delta, East Tenn. Opera Guild Bd., 2001-02. Home: First Tennessee Plaza Ste 1950 800 S Gay St Knoxville TN 37929 E-mail: carole@clw-law.com.

WORTHINGTON, JANET EVANS, retired academic dean, English language educator; b. Springfield, Ill., Jan. 30, 1942; d. Orville Ray and Helen May (Tuxhorn) Evans; m. Gary H. Worthington; children: Rachael Allene, Evan Edmund, Adam Nicholas Karl. Student, Blackburn Coll., 1960-62; BA in English Lang. and Lit., U. Chgo., 1965; MA in English, U. Iowa, 1969; PhD in English Edn., Fla. State U., 1977; postgrad., W. Va. Inst. Tech., 1981-82, Rensselaer Poly. Inst., 1984. Teaching. fellow Fla. State U., Tallahassee, 1971-72, grad. assistant, 1972-73; coord. lang. arts rsch. Piedmont Schs. Project, Greer, S.C., 1973-76; English instr. Woodrow Wilson High Sch., Beckley, W.Va., 1976-77; Reading specialist, adj. instr. in English W. Va. Inst. Tech., Montgomery, W.Va., 1977-78; asst. prof. W.Va. Inst. Tech., Montgomery, 1979-82, assoc. prof., 1983-87, prof. English, 1987-88, dir. Oak Hill, 1988-90, tech. writing program coord. Community and Tech. Coll. Montgomery, 1983-88; dir. continuing edn. Nicholls State U., Thibodaux, La., 1990-97; dean Ctr. for Lifelong Learning, Plattsburgh (N.Y.) State U., 1997—2003. Tech. writing cons., various bus., 1986—, Dept. of Mines, State of W.Va., 1980-81; reading cons. Dept of Mines, 1980-81, Mt. Hope (W.Va.) High Sch., 1980-81, Reading Tchrs. Study Group, Kanawha County, W.Va., 1981-83; project mgr. Dept. of Mines, State of W.Va., 1981-83, Dept. of Nat. Resources, State of W.Va., 1984-85; involved in curriculum devel. for various depts., W.Va. Inst. Tech., 1973-90, Raleigh County Schs., Beckley, W.Va., Piedmont Schs. Project, Greer, S.C., English and reading instr. Upward Bound Program, W.Va. Inst. Tech., 1980-85; adj. instr. W.Va. Coll. Grad. Studies, 1979, 81, 83. Author (with William Burns): Practical Robotics: Systems, Interfacing, and Applications, 1986, (with A.B. Somers): Candles and Mirrors: Response Guides for Teaching Novels and Plays in Grades Six through Twelve, 1984, Response Guides for Teaching Children's Books, 1979; editorial bd.: W.Va. Community Coll. Jour.; reviewer: Macmillan Pub. Co. texts, 1985; editor: Diamond Shamrock, 1985; co-producer, host (TV series): About the Author; contbr. numerous articles to profl. jours.; participated in numerous presentations. Mem. W.Va. Community Coll. Assn.; bd.dirs., Curtain Callers, 1979-89, Fayette Fine Arts Coun., 1986-87; promotions chair, W.Va. Children's Book award com., 1984-85. Mem. AAUW (recording sec. 1983-85, pres. 1985—), Assn. for Tchrs. of Tech. Writing, Nat. Assn. for Devel. Edn., Soc. for Tech. Comm. Home: 4 Pinewood Dr Peru NY 12972-4638 Office: Plattsburgh State U of NY Ctr for Lifelong Learning 101 Broad St Plattsburgh NY 12901-2637

WORTHY, PATRICIA MORRIS, law educator, lawyer; b. Fort Benning, Ga., May 28, 1944; d. Walter and Ruby Mae (Lovett) Morris. AA, Queensborough C.C., 1964; BA, Bklyn. Coll., 1966; JD, Howard U., 1969. Bar: DC 1971. Trial atty. NLRB, Washington, 1969-71; dep. gen. counsel ACTION, Washington, 1971-74; assoc. Dolphin, Branton, Stafford & Webber, Washington, 1974 77; dep. asst. sec. for regulatory functions HUD, Washington, 1977-80; adj. prof. Howard U. Sch. Law, 1979-92; chmn. D.C. Pub. Svc. Commn., 1980-91, Washington Met. Area Transit Commn., 1980-91; chief of staff Office of Mayor Sharon Pratt Kelly, Washington, 1991-92; prof. law Howard U., Washington, 1992—2001; dean acad. affairs Howard U. Law Sch., Washington, 2001—02, 2003—, interim dean, 2002—03. Chmn. D.C. Jud. Nomination Commn. Bd. dirs. Nat. Black Child Devel. Inst., 1975 80, Anacostia Econ. Devel. Corp., 1970-74; chmn. Occupl. Safety and Health Bd., Washington, 1979-80; trustee WETA-TV Channel 26, 1984-94. Mem. ABA, Nat. Conf. Black Lawyers, Nat. Conf. Bar Examiners (multistate profl. responsibility com. 1986-89), World Peace Through Law (chairperson young lawyers sect. 1973-75). Office: Howard U Sch Law Van Ness & Connecticut Ave NW Washington DC 20001

WOS, CAROL ELAINE, small business owner; b. Bremerton, Wash., Apr. 21, 1957; d. Standley Ralph and Janet Estele (Galber) Stocker; m. George Joseph Wos; children: Samuel Harrison, Bridget Monique. BS in Chem., Wash. State U., 1979. Mfg. engr. Internat. Bus. Machines, E. Fishkill, NY, [illegible] Corp., Eagan, Minn., 1980—83; sr. process devel. engr. Cray Rsch. Inc., Chippewa Falls, Wis., [illegible]—90, mem. cleanroom design and constrn. team, 1991—92, bump/tab process engr., 1993—94; owner, mgr. The Nature of Things, Eau Claire, 1995—99; program asst. Camp Fire USA, Lewiston, Idaho, 1999—; nursing asst. Good Samaritan Village, Moscow, Idaho. Bd. dirs. Eau Claire Regional Arts Coun., 1991 97; vol. Jr. Achievement.

WOSK, MIRIAM, artist; b. Vancouver, B.C., Can., Aug. 17, 1947; d. Morris J. and Dena W.; 1 child, Adam. Student, U. B.C., Can., 1966; AAS, Fashion Inst. Tech., N.Y.C., 1969; postgrad., Sch. Visual Arts, New Sch. Social Rsch., N.Y.C., 1969-74. Freelance illustrator 1st cover of Ms. mag., 30th ann. cover Ms. mag., Mademoiselle, N.Y. Times, Esquire, Vogue, N.Y. Mag., Viva, McCalls, Saturday Rev., Sesame St., New West, Psychology Today, 1969—79; curator group show The Inner Lives of Women: Psyche, Spirit and Soul Spring St. Gallery, L.A., 1996. One woman shows include Transam. Ctr., L.A., 1983, West Beach, L.A., 1988, Wilshire Pacific Bldg., L.A., 1991, 2001, Robert Berman Gallery, Santa Monica, Calif., 1991, 2001, Drago, Santa Monica, 1992, Jazz, Pacific Design Ctr., West Hollywood, Calif., 1995; exhibited in group shows at Harkness House Gallery, N.Y.C., 1979-80, Dist. 1199 Cultural Ctr. Inc., N.Y., 1981, Smithsonian Inst., Washington, 1981; Transam. Pyramid, San Francisco, 1983, Barnsdall Art Gallery, L.A., 1983, Functional Art Gallery, L.A., 1985, One Market Plaza, San Francisco, 1986, Laforet Mus., Tokyo, 1986, Art et Industrie Gallery, N.Y.C., 1986, Otis Parsons Sch. Design, L.A 1987, B1 Gallery, Santa Monica, 1987, Katharina Rich Perlow Gallery, N.Y.C., 1988, Sam Francis Studio, Santa Monica, 1988, Gallery Functional Art, Santa Monica, 1989, 91, Santa Monica Mus. Art, 1990, 99, 2000, Getty Mus., Malibu, Calif., 1990, James Corcoran Gallery, Santa Monica, 1990, Joan Robey Gallery, Denver, 1992, Cultural Ctr., Eureka, Calif., Calif. State U., Long Beach, 1992, Pacific Design Ctr., L.A., 1992, U. Art Mus., Long Beach, 1992, L.A. County Mus. Art, 1992, 96, Helander Gallery, Palm Beach, Fla., 1993, Spring Street Gallery, L.A., 1994, 96, Anderson Ranch Art Ctr., Aspen, Colo., 1995, Park Ave. Armory, N.Y.C., 1997, 98, 2000, Adam Baumgold Gallery, N.Y.C., 1997, Pub. Corp. Arts, Long Beach Arts, 1998, Boritzer Gray Hamano, Santa Monica, 1999, Santa Monica Fine Arts Studio, 1999, Jan Baum Gallery, L.A., 2000, Ricco/Maresca Gallery, N.Y.C., 2003, Rosamund Felsen Gallery, Santa Monica, 2003; pub. in nat. and internat. mags., books and newspapers including The Golden Age of Magazine Illustration: The Sixties and Seventies. New Feminist Criticism-Art-Identity Action, Los Angeles Times, Washington Post, Casa Vogue, L'Express Paris and Idea Internat. (Japan). Recipient Merit award Art Dirs. Club N.Y., cert. of merit Soc. Illustrators, cert. excellence Am. Inst. Graphic Artists; named guest editor Maedmoiselle Mag. Studio: 436 Adelaide Dr Santa Monica CA 90402

WOSTREL, REBEKAH A. artist, educator; b. Gloucester, Mass., June 26, 1969; d. Herbert John Wostrel and Mary Lillian Meader; m. Edward John Coffey III, Sept. 21, 2002. BA in Anthropology, Smith Coll., Northampton, Mass., 1991; MFA in Ceramics, Pa. State U., State College, 1997. Curatorial asst. Peabody Mus. Archaeology and Ethnology, Cambridge, Mass., 1992—95; ceramic instr. U. Calif., Berkeley, 1999, The Clay Studio, Phila., 1999—2001; ceramic lectr. U. Pa., Phila., 2001—; adj. prof. St. Joseph's U., Phila., 2001—; ceramic lectr. Princeton U., NJ, 2002—; ceramic instr. Harvard U., Cambridge, Mass., 2003. Vis. scholar Friends World Coll., Machakos, Kenya, 1989—90; presenter in field. One-woman shows include The Clay Studio, 2001, Princeton Arts Coun., 2002, Ubud Bali, 2002, Represented in permanent collections Pa. State U. and pvt. residences. Founding mem. The Saturnalian Croquet League, 1998—. Mem.: Nat. Coun. on Edn. for Ceramic Arts, Am. Coun. for So. Asian Art, Coll. Art Assn. Democrat. Avocations: yoga, knitting, reading, writing, gardening.

WOTEKI, CATHERINE ELLEN, nutritionist; b. Fort Leavenworth, Kans., Oct. 7, 1947; d. Joseph Jeremiah and Catherine (Costello) O'Connor; m. Thomas Henry Woteki, June 7, 1969. BS, Mary Washington Coll., 1969; MS, Va. Poly. Inst. and State U., 1971, PhD, 1973. Registered dietitian. Asst. prof. Drexel U., Phila., 1975-77; project dir. Congl. Office of Tech. Assessment, Washington, 1977-80; group leader USDA, Washington, 1980-83; dep. dir. Nat. Ctr. for Health Statis., Washington, 1983-90; dir. Food and Nutrition Bd., Washington, 1990-93; dep. assoc. dir. for sci. Office of Sci. and Tech. Policy, Washington, 1994-95; undersec. food safety USDA

Office of Food Safety, Washington, 1996—. Contbr. over 43 articles to profl. jours. Named Outstanding alumna Va. Poly. Inst. and State U., 1987; recipient Elijah White award Nat. Ctr. for Health Statis., 1987, Spl. Recognition award USPHS, 1987, Staff Achievement award Inst. of Medicine, 1991. Mem. Am. Inst. Nutrition, Am. Dietetic Assn. Coun. on Rsch., Inst. Food Technologists, Am. Pub. Health Assn. Office: USDA Office Food Safety 1400 Independence Ave SW Washington DC 20250-0002

WOTIPKA, CHRISTINE MIN, education educator; BA in Internat. Rels. and French with highest honors, U. Minn., Twin Cities, 1993; MA in Sociology, Stanford U., 1999, PhD in Internat. Comparative Edn., 2001. Vol. U.S. Peace Corps, Thailand, 1993—95; econ. rschr., English editor 1st Econ. Rsch. Inst., 1995—96; rsch. asst. Comparative Sociology Workshop, 1996—2001; cons. MentorNet, 2001; asst. prof. edn., dir. master's program in internat. and comparative edn. Stanford (Calif.) U., 2001—. Faculty affiliate Expansion and Impact of World Human Rights Regime project, 2002—; MacArthur Consortium affiliate Ctr. for Internat. Security and Coop., 2000—; mem. adv. bd. sci. and tech. TV Digital Turbulence, 2002—. Office: Stanford U Sch Edn 485 Lasuen Mall Stanford CA 94305-3096

WOTRING, MELANIE JEAN See HASTINGS, MELANIE

WOYSKI, MARGARET SKILLMAN, retired geology educator; b. West Chester, Pa., July 26, 1921; d. Willis Rowland and Clara Louise (Howson) Skillman; m. Mark M. Woyski, June 19, 1948; children: Nancy Elizabeth, William Bruno, Ronald David, Wendelin Jane. BA in Chemistry, Wellesley (Mass.) Coll., 1943; MS in Geology, U. Minn., 1945, PhD in Geology, 1946. Geologist Mo. Geol. Survey and Water Resources, Rolla, 1946-48; instr. U. Wis., Madison, 1948-52; lectr. Calif. State U., Long Beach, 1963-67, lectr. to prof. Fullerton, 1966-91, assoc. dean Sch. Natural Sci. and Math., 1981-91, emeritus prof., 1991—. Contbr. articles to profl. jours.; author lab. manuals; editor guidebooks. Fellow Geol. Soc. Am. (program chmn. 1982); mem. South Coast Geol. Soc. (hon. pres. 1974), Mineral Soc. Am. Home: 880 Morningside Dr Apt M-320 Fullerton CA 92835-3577

WOZNIAK, JOYCE MARIE, sales executive; b. Detroit, Aug. 3, 1955; d. Edmund Frank and Bernice (Liske) W. BA, Mich. State U., 1976; MA, Nat. U., San Diego, 1988; postgrad., U.S. Internat. U., 1989-90. Probation officer San Diego County Probation, 1979-81; prodn. engr. Tuesday Prodns., Inc., San Diego, 1981-85; nat. sales mgr. Advance Rec. Products, San Diego, 1986-88; acct. exec. Joyce Enterprises, San Diego, 1986-95; sales exec. Audio-Video Supply Inc., San Diego, 1988-98; account exec. M.C.S.I. (formerly Consol. Media Sys., Inc.), San Diego, 2000—02; sys. integration specialist TV Magic, Inc., San Diego, 2002—03; sys. sales engr. Opticomm Corp., San Diego, 2003—. Producer (video) Loving Yourself, 1987, southwest cable access program, 1986-95; registered marriage, family and child counselor-intern, Calif., 1989. Active Zool. Soc. San Diego. Mem.: Internat. TV Assn. (treas. San Diego chpt. 1990—91), NAFE, NATAS, Calif. Assn. Marriage and Family Therapists, Art Glass Assn. So. Calif., Nat. Assn. Broadcasters. Office: 6827 Nancy Ridge Dr San Diego CA 92121 E-mail: joycewozniak@hotmail.com.

WRAY, BETTY BEASLEY, allergist, immunologist, pediatrician; b. Ga., 1935; MD, Med Coll. Ga., 1960. Diplomate Am. Bd. Allergy and Immunology, Am. Bd. Clin. Lab. Immunology. Intern Talmadge Meml. Hosp., Augusta, Ga., 1960-61, resident in pediatrics, 1962, 64-65, fellow in pediatric allergy, 1966-68; staff mem. Med. Coll. Ga., Augusta, 1979—, prof. pediat. medicine, interim dean Sch. Medicine, v.p. clin. activities, 2000—02, prof. emeritus, 2002—. Mem.: Am. Coll. Allergy, Asthma and Immunology, Am. Acad. Pediat., Am. Acad. Allergy and Immunology, Am. Pediatric Soc. Office: Med Coll Georgia BG 1009 Augusta GA 30912 E-mail: bettyw@mail.mcg.edu.

WRAY, GERALDINE SMITHERMAN (JERRY WRAY), artist; b. Shreveport, La., Dec. 15, 1925; d. David Ewart and Mary Virginia (Hoss) Smitherman; m. George Downing Wray, June 24, 1947; children: Mary Virginia Hill, Deanie Galloway, George D. Wray III, Nancy Armistead. BFA with honors, Newcomb Art Sch., Tulane U., 1946. Tchr. children's art. One woman shows include Don Batman Gallery, Kansas City, Mo., 1982, Gallery II, Baton Rouge, 1985, McNeese Coll., Lake Charles, La., 1987, Dragonfly Gallery, Shreveport, La., 1987, Barnwell Garden and Art Ctr., Shreveport, 1988, 95, Southdown Mus., Houma, La., 1989, La. State U., Shreveport, 1991, WTN Radio Station, Shreveport, 1993, The Cambridge Club, Shreveport, 1993, Centenary Coll., 1993, Northwestern State U., Natchitoches, La., 1995, Goddard Mus., Ardmore, Okla., 1996, Art Buyers Caravan, Atlanta, 1996, Lockhaven (Pa.) U., 1996, Billingsley Gallery, Pensacola, Fla., 1996, Casa D'Arte, Shreveport, La., 1996, N.E. State U., Monroe, La., 1997, Art Expo, N.Y.C., 1997, Palmer Gallery, Hot Springs Ark., 1998, Tower Art Gallery, Shreveport, La., 1999, Meadows Mus. Retrospective, Shreveport, 2003, Schumpert Hosp. Integrated Medicine, Shreveport, 2003, Midwestern Tex. U., 2003, Wichita Falls, Tex., 2003; group shows include Watercolor USA Springfield, Mo., 1988, Waddell's Gallery, Shreveport, 1988, 91, Water Works Gallery, Dallas, 1990, Southwestern Watercolor Show, 1991 (D'Arches award, Creative Artist award 1997), Masur Mus. Exhbn. (honorable mention 91, 92), Bossier Art Ctr., Bossier City, La., 1992, Irving Art Assn. (honorable mention), 1992, Leon Loard Gallery, Montgomery, Ala., 1993, Ward-Nasse Gallery, N.Y.C., 1993, 97, Soc. Experimental Artists Internat. (1st. place, honorable mention), 1993, Palmer Gallery, Hot Springs, Ark., 1994, Nat. Watercolor Soc. Ann., 1994-96, 98, 2003, Art Expo, N.Y.C., 1996, Casa D'Arte, Shreveport, 1996, Art Buyers Caravan, Atlanta, 1996, Off The Wall Gallery, Savannah, Ga., 1997, Art Effects Gallery, Merian, Pa., Boulevard Art Gallery, Macon, Ga., 1997, Visual Inspirations, Newton, N.J., 1997, Mossey Brake Gallery, Tex., 1997, Barnwell Ctr. (with children & grandchildren), Shreveport LA, 1998, Manhattan Arts Mag. Showcase Award, Nat. Assn. Women Artist Traveling Show, Meadows Mus., Shreveport, La., 2003, Integrated Medicine, 2003, Northwestern U., La., 2004; permanent collections include NAWA, Zimmerli Mus., Rutgers Univ., N.J.-Meir Mus., Lynchburg, Va., Goddard Mus. Ardmore, Okla., Bibl. Arts Ctr., Dallas, La. State Capitol Bldg., Lockhaven Univ. Penn., LSUS Med. Ctr., Shreveport, LA., Shacknow Mus., Plantation, Fla., Meadows Mus., Shreveport, La., 2003, Integrated Medicine Schompert Wellness Ctr., Shreveport, 2003, Northwestern U., Natchitoches, La., 2004, Midwestern U., Tex., 2003. Art chmn. Jr. League, Shreveport, 1955-60; bd. dirs. Holiday-in-Dixie Cotillion, Shreveport, 1974-76. Inducted into Visual Artists Hall of Fame, Shreveport, La., 1998. Mem. Nat. Assn. Women Artists, Nat. Watercolor Soc. (signature mem. 1994, 96), Southwestern Watercolor Soc. (signature mem. 1991), La. Watercolor Soc. (signature mem. 1990), La. Artists Inc. (elected mem.), Internat. Soc. Exptl. Artists (signature mem.), Western Fedn. Soc. Artists (signature mem.), Watercolor Soc. Houston (signature mem.). Episcopalian. Avocation: tennis. Home: 573 Spring Lake Dr Shreveport LA 71106-4603 E-mail: jwray@softdisk.com.

WRAY, NELDA P. medical association administrator; MD with honors, Baylor Coll. Medicine; MPH, U. Tex. Sch. Pub. Health. Prof. medicine & med. ethics Baylor Coll. Medicine; dir. Houston Ctr. Quality Care & Utilization Studies. Adj. assoc. prof. U. Tex. Sch. Pub. Health; chief gen. medicine sect. Houston VA Med. Ctr. Mem. editl. rev. bd. Jou. Gen. Internal Medicine. Apptd. chair Tex. Health Info. Coun., 1995. Robert Wood Johnson Health Policy fellow, Washington. Office: Houston Ctr Quality Care & Utilization Studies VA Med Ctr (152) 2002 Holcombe Blvd Houston TX 77030-4211

WREGE, JULIA BOUCHELLE, tennis professional, physics educator; b. Charleston, W.Va., Apr. 11, 1944; d. Dallas Payne and Mary Louise (Hagan) Bouchelle; m. Douglas Ewart Wrege, July 13, 1968; children: Dallas Ewart, Shannon Bouchelle. BS in Physics, Ga. Inst. Tech., 1965, MS in Physics, 1967. Systems analyst GE Apollo Systems, Daytona Beach, Fla., 1967-68; med. scientist Space Instruments Research, Atlanta, 1968-70; head tennis profl. Riverside Tennis Club, Atlanta, 1971-72, Am. Adventures, Roswell, Ga., 1972-75, Hampton Farms Tennis Club, Marietta, Ga., 1975-79; head women's tennis coach Ga. Inst. Tech., Atlanta, Ga., 1979-86, 91-92; v.p. Sirius Software, Inc., 1988—. Instr. physics So. Coll. Tech., 1990-98; stadium chmn., umpire, referee USTA, Atlanta, 1977—; sec. Tennis Techs., Inc., 1997—. Author: Tournament Manual, 1977, 3d edit., 1989; co-developer software TMS Tennis Tournament, 1989. Pres. Dickerson Mid. Sch. Parent-Tchr.-Student Assn., Marietta, Ga., 1982-85. Named Umpire of Yr., Ga. Tennis Assn., 1978, So. Tennis Assn., 1978; Ga. Tennis Coach of Yr., Assn. Intercollegiate Athletics for Women-Ga. Tennis Coaches Assn., 1981, 82, 83; named to Ga. Tech. Athletic Hall of Fame, 1997. Mem. U.S. Profl. Tennis Assn. (pres. 1980), U.S. Tennis Assn. (mem. tennis rules com. 1999—), Intercollegiate Tennis Coaches Assn., Ga. Tennis Assn. (pres. 1976-81, 94-96, v.p. 1974-76, 91-92), Atlanta Lawn Tennis Assn., Atlanta Profl. Tennis Assn., Alpha Xi Delta, Sigma Pi Sigma. Republican. Episcopalian. Home: 1366 Little Willeo Rd Marietta GA 30068-2135

WRIGHT, B. ANN, academic administrator; d. Leroy Dale Hines and Dorothy Probst Griffith; m. Willard Alan Wright; children: Randy Alan, Rebecca Ann Murphy. BS, U. of Rochester, 1958—63, MA, 1963—66, PhD, 1970—77. Secondary School English NY State, 1963. English tchr. Geneseo H.S., Geneseo, NY, 1971—77; dir. of admission U. of Rochester, NY, 1984—91; dean of enrollment mgmt. Smith Coll., Northampton, Mass., 1991—99; v.p. for enrollment Rice U., Houston, 1999—. Cons. Columbia U., U. of Oreg., Hobart/William Smith, Haverford, 1984—; pres. NY State Assn. of Coll. Admission Counselors, Albany, NY, 1984—86; trustee The Coll. Bd., NYC, 2000—; chair U.S. News Adv. Com., Washington. Trustee The Harley Sch., Rochester, NY, 1988—91. Recipient Disting. Svc. award, NY State Assn. of Coll. Admission Counselors, 1989, John B. Muir Editor's award, Nat. Assn. of Coll. Admission Counseling, 1991. Mem.: The Coll. Bd. (life; trustee 2000—), Nat. Assn. of Coll. Admission Counselors (life; regional pres.). Independent-Republican. Protestant. Avocations: physical fitness, travel, sports, reading. Office: Rice University 6100 Main St MS 7 Houston TX

WRIGHT, BARBARA WINCKLHOFER, nursing educator; b. Cranbury, N.J., Aug. 3, 1933; BS, Boston Coll.; EdD, Rutgers U.; MA, PhD, NYU. RN. Dep. mayor, then mayor Plainsboro Twp., 1977-85; assemblywoman dist. 14 N.J. State Assembly, 1992-2000, dep. spkr., 1998-99; assoc. dean, assoc. prof. Seton Hall U. Coll. Nursing, South Orange, N.J., 2000—. Mem. N.J. Soc. for Assn. Execs. (assn. exec. of yr. 1989). Office: Seton Hall U 400 S Orange Ave South Orange NJ 07079-2697

WRIGHT, BETTY REN, children's book writer; b. Wakefield, Mich., June 15, 1927; d. William and Revena Evelyn (Trezise) W.; m. George Albert Frederiksen, Oct. 9, 1976. BA, Milw.-Downer Coll., 1949. With Western Pub. Co., Inc., 1949-78, mng. editor Racine Editl., 1967-78. Author numerous juv. and jr. novels, including The Doll House Murders, 1983, Christina's Ghost, 1985, The Summer of Mrs. MacGregor, 1986, A Ghost in the Window, 1987, The Pike River Phantom, 1988, Rosie and the Dance of the Dinosaurs, 1989, The Ghost of Ernie P., 1990, A Ghost in the House, 1991, The Scariest Night, 1991, The Ghosts of Mercy Manor, The Ghost of Popcorn Hill, 1993, The Ghost Witch, 1993, A Ghost Comes Calling, 1994, Out of the Dark, 1995, Haunted Summer, 1996, Too Many Secrets, 1997, The Ghost in Room 11, 1998, A Ghost in the Family, 1998, The Moonlight Man, 2000, The Wish Master, 2000, Crandalls' Castle, 2003; also numerous picture and ednl. books including Pet Detectives, 1999, The Blizzard, 2003; contbr. fiction to mags. Recipient Alumni Svc. award Lawrence U., 1973, Lynde and Harry Bradley Maj. Achievement award, 1997, numerous awards for books including Mo. Mark Twain award, 1986, 96, Tex. Bluebonnet award, 1986, 88, Young Readers award Pacific N.W. Libr. Assn., 1986, Reviewer's Choice Booklist, Ala. Young Readers award, 1987, Ga. Children's Choice award, 1988, Ind. Young Hoosier Book award, 1989, 96, Children's Choice Book/Internat. Reading Assn.—CBC, 1984, S.C. Children's Choice award, 1995, Okla. Sequoyah Children's Choice award, 1988, 95, award Fla. Sunshine State, 2001. Mem.: Coun. Wis. Authors (Juvenile Book award 1985, 1996), Allied Authors, Phi Beta Kappa. Avocations: reading, travel. Home and Office: 6223 Hilltop Dr Racine WI 53406-3479

WRIGHT, CATHIE, state legislator; b. Old Forge, Pa., May 18, 1929; 1 child, Victoria. AA in Acctg., Lackawanna Jr. Coll.; student, U. Scranton. Former mayor and city councilwoman City of Simi Valley; mem. Calif. State Assembly, 1980-92, Calif. State Senate, 1992—. Chair Simi Valley Cmty. Devel. Com., Simi Valley Drug Abuse Program; former mem. transp., adv. planning, criminal justice planning bd., animal control com. for Ventura County. Named Woman of Yr., Simi Valley C. of C., 1979, Am. Mothers' Legis. Mother of the Yr., 1985, Outstanding Woman of the Yr., Zonta-Santa Clarita Valley, 1986. Mem. VFW, Las Manitas Aux. Republican. Office: State Capitol Rm 5052 Sacramento CA 95814 E-mail: senator.wright@sen.ca.gov.

WRIGHT, CECILIA POWERS, gifted and talented educator; b. Phila., Sept. 30, 1946; d. Robert Francis and Rosemary (Redditt) Powers. BS, West Chester (Pa.) U., 1968; MS, Pa. State U., 1972; MA, Gratz Coll., Melrose Park, Pa., 1996. Tchr. Haverford Twp. Sch. Dist., Havertown, Pa., 1968—73; author/editor and instr. McGraw Hill, Paoli, Pa., 1973—78; tchr. Lower Merion Sch. Dist., Wynnewood, Pa., 1987—90; tchr. of gifted West Chester Area Sch. Dist., 1990—. Instr., cons. Regional Tng. Ctr., Gratz Coll., Randolph, NJ, 1996—; seminar presenter Coll. of N.J., Trenton, 1998—2000. Author (and editor): Careers: A Multicultural View, 1977 (Excellence award, 1977). Leader Girl Scouts U.S., Havertown, 1983—87; chairperson good citizens DAR, Chester County, Pa., 1996—. Named to Leaders in Am. Elem. Edn., Haverford Twp. Sch. Dist., 1971; recipient award, Nat. Band Assn., 2000—01. Mem.: NEA, Band and Orch. Assn. (pres. 2000), Pa. State Edn. Assn. (rep. 1998—). Avocations: watercolor, travel, biking. Home: 15 E Wilmot Ave Havertown PA 19083

WRIGHT, CHERYL DIANE, marketing professional; b. San Jose, Calif., Oct. 1954; d. Edward James Wright, Uva Estelle Wright. BS in Animal Sci., Calif. Poly. State U., San Luis Obispo, 1975; MS in Mass. Comm., San Jose State U., 1978. V.p. Bank of Am., San Francisco, 1985—87; sr. mgr. Deloitte & Touche, San Francisco, 1987—92; mgr. info. resource audit Sun Microsystems, Inc., Palo Alto, Calif., 1992—94, strategic mktg. mgr., 1994—96, bus. devel. mgr., 1999—2001; prin. Cheryl Wright Mktg. Consulting, Incline Village, Nev., 2001—02; v.p. mktg. MuseGlobal, Salt Lake City, 2002—. Instr. info. tech. Golden Gate U., San Francisco, 1987—88. Contbr. chapters to books, articles to profl. jours. Vol. Tahoe Women's Svcs., Incline Village, 2001—01. Mem.: AAUW. Avocations: skiing, hiking, rock climbing, kayaking. Personal E-mail: cheryl@cherylwright.net.

WRIGHT, CLIFFLORA L. social worker, educator, alcohol/drug abuse services professional, consultant; b. Cleve., June 16, 1946; d. Oliver Windell (Stepfather) and Addie Lee (Estmus) Holmes; m. Emmett Wright Jr., June 21, 1967 (div. 1974); children: Emmett Lee, Damon Jason; m. Oliver Person. Student, Spelman Coll., 1964—67; BA, Cleve. State U., 1969; MS in Social Adminstrn., Case Western Res. U., 1982. Lic. ind. social worker Ohio, 1986, cert. chem. dependency counselor Ohio, 1984, criminal justice specialist Am. Coll. Cert. Forensic Counselors, 1995. Social worker Ohio Dept. Youth Svcs., Cleve., 1969—86; adminstrv. social worker supr., grant & proposal writer Augustine Soc. Group Home, 1986—91; clin. coord. Cuyahoga County, Dept. Justice Affairs, Youth Devel. Ctr., 1986—2000; social worker Ctr. Interpersonal Devel., Lakewood, 2000—; pres. Wright Decisions and Assocs., Cleve., 2000—; adjuct prof. Mandel Sch. of Applied Social Sciences, Case Western Res. U. (CWRU/MSSASS), Cleveland, Ohio, 1996—96, Mandel sch. of Applied Social Sciences, Case Western Res. U. (CWRU/MSASS), Cleveland, Ohio, 1998—98, David N. Meyers Coll., Cleveland, Ohio, 1999—99, John Carroll U., Dept. of Sociology and Human Resources, University Heights, Ohio, 1999—99, 2000—00, Mandel sch. of applied Social Sciences, Case Western Res. U. (CWRU/MSASS), Cleveland, Ohio, 2000—00, Cuyahoga C.C., Cleveland, Ohio, 2001—02, John Carroll U., Dept. of Sociology and Human Resources, University Heights, Ohio, 1995—95. Adj. prof. John Carroll U., University Heights., Ohio, 1995, 99, 2000, Case Western Res. U., Cleve., 1996, 98, 2000, David N. Meyers Coll., 1999, Cuyahoga C.C., 2001—02. Mem.: NASW. Liberal. Baptist. Avocations: reading, swimming, music, travel, crocheting, walking, camping. Office: Wright Decisions & Assocs 4812 E 174th St Cleveland OH 44128-3926

WRIGHT, DANA JACE, retired emergency nurse practitioner; b. Cleve., Apr. 20, 1952; d. William James and Murl Jean (White) Ewing; m. David Alan Samball, June 22, 1968 (div. Apr. 1971); 1 child, David; m. David M. Wright, July 11, 1981; children: William James, Karen Marie. Assoc. in Nursing, AA, Valencia Community Coll., 1973; BS in Respiratory Therapy, U. Cen. Fla., 1975; MEd, Auburn U., 1979; D in Nursing, Case Western Res. U., 1982. RN, Fla., Ohio, N.Y., Ga.; cert. emergency med. technician; cert. and registered respiratory therapist; cert. med.-surg. nurse; lic. real estate agt., N.Y. Nursing asst. Holiday Hosp., Orlando, Fla., 1970-71, staff nurse critical care unit, intensive care unit, 1973; pvt. duty nurse Med. Personnel Pool, Orlando, 1973-74; nurse critical care burn team Upjohn, Inc., Augusta, Ga., 1976-77; ednl. dir. dept. respiratory therapy U. Hosp., Augusta, 1975-76; mem. staff respiratory therapy VA Hosp., Augusta, 1976-77; clin. instr. respiratory therapy Med. Coll. Ga., Augusta, 1976-77, Columbus Coll., 1977-78; ednl. dir. respiratory therapy Med. Ctr. Hosp., Columbus, 1977-79; staff nurse, relief supr. Kelly Health Care, Beachwood, Ohio, 1979-81; staff nurse Med. Staff, Inc., Cleve., 1981-83; dir. nursing S.R.T. Med. Staff Inc., Cleve., 1983; pres. Wright Properties, Buffalo, 1987-94, Med. Ctr. Vending, 1994-97; ret. nurse, 1994. Part-time nurse Millard Fillmore Suburban Hosp., 1990-91. Treas. Ch. Women's Assn., Snyder, N.Y., 1985-86; mem. nursing resources panel North Ohio Lung Assn., 1981-82; mem. Profl. Parent Network, Buffalo, 1987—, Erie Co. Commn. on the Status of Women, 2000-, vol. Food Shuttle, 1996-; rep. of McLain found. to grantmakers, 2000-. Mem. ANA (alt. del. 1993-94), Am. Assn. Nurses Practicing Independently (assoc.), Nat. Nurses Bus., N.Y. State Nurses Assn. (nurse rsch. cons. 1991-92, 94, chair nurse entrepreneurs 1992-94, WNY regional review team 1992-94), Women's Dental Guild, Internat. FEdn. of u. Woman, AAUW (mem. at large 2003-) Republican. Home and Office: 49 Colony Ct Buffalo NY 14226-3507

WRIGHT, DIANE, procurement manager; b. St. Louis, Jan. 11, 1956; d. Henderson and Ernestine Brady; m. Kevin Wright; children: Deidre Terrell, Samuel Terrell. BA in Mgmt., Webster U., St. Louis, MO, 1997. Dir. bus. affairs Harris-Stowe State Coll., St. Louis, 1998; mgr. procurement Bi-State Devel. Agy., St. Louis, 1998—. Recruiter vote registration St. Louis Job Corps Center, St. Louis, 1987—95. Recipient Silver Spike award, Bi-State Devel. Agy., 2000 and 2001. Mem.: Nat. Inst. Govt. Purchasing. Avocations: sewing, travel. Office: Bi-State Devel Agy 707 North First St Saint Louis MO 63102-2552 Office Fax: 314982-1558. Business E-Mail: dwright@bsda.org.

WRIGHT, DIXIE LEE, special needs persons consultant; b. Winslow, Ind. d. Edward Franklin and Ann Berenece Corne; m. Lendon L. Wright; children: Kevin, LeeAnn, Michael. BS in Edn., Ind. U.; postgrad., U. No. Colo., 1980. Self employed workshop developer for schs. and agys.; career coord. postsecondary sch.; ind. contractor Colo. State Rehab. and other govtl. and ind. agys. working with spl. needs persons. Cons., job assessor for special need persons, Colo.; presenter in field. Author: Know How is the Key, 1997, Job Survival: How to Adjust and Keep Your Job, 2000, Stuff You Need to Know to Teach Job Retention, 2000, Job Smarts, 2004. Bd. dirs. Littleton C. of C. Mem.: AARP (state coord. works program), Bus. Profl. Women (adv. bd., pres.). Avocations: art, drawing, public speaking.

WRIGHT, ELEASE, insurance company executive; Sr. v.p. human resources Aetna Inc., Hartford, Conn., 1999—. Office: 151 Farmington Ave Hartford CT 06156-0001

WRIGHT, EVELYN LOUISE, artist; b. Odessa, Mo., Aug. 2, 1913; d. Elmer Clarence and Anna Bell (Ford) Adams; m. Douglas P. Wright, July 19, 1934 (dec. Dec. 27, 1986); children: Annetta Louise, Judith Elaine, Duane Douglas. Student, Stockton Coll., Calif., 1958—60, U. of Pacific, Stockton, 1960—61, Merced Coll., Calif., 1962—64, Columbia Coll., 1962—64. Graphic artist, Independence, Mo., 1928—34; asst. mgr., bookkeeper Wrights, Stockton, 1945—86; owner, instr. Evelyn's Art Classes and Workshops, Stockton, 1980—; instr. Stockton Sch. Sys., 1945—, Ripona Sch., Calif., 1992—94. Recipient Best of Show award, Richard Yip Art Co., 1980, award, Sonora Nat. Festival, 1982, 1984, Lodi Grape Festival, 1986. Avocation: travel. Home and Studio: 508 W Morada Ln Stockton CA 95210

WRIGHT, FAITH-DORIAN, artist; b. Bklyn., Feb. 9, 1934; d. Abraham and Molly (Janoff) J.; children: Jordan Merritt, Igrid-beth. BS, NYU, 1955, MA, 1958; postgrad., Pratt and Parsons Sch. of Design. Works exhibited in Kathryn Markel Gallery, N.Y.C., 1981, 92, Cumberland Gallery, Nashville, 1981, 92, Barbara Gillman Gallery, Miami, 1982, Hand and Hand Gallery, 1985, 86, Suzanne Gross, Phila., 1986, 87, Gallery Four, Alexandria, Va., 1986, 87, 88, Henri Gallery, Washington, 1986, 87, 88, 89. 90. 91. 92. 93. 94, Benton Gallery, Southampton, 1986, 87, 88, 89, 91, 92, 93, King Stephen Mus., Hungary, 1987, Nat. Gallery Women in the Arts, 1987, 88, 90, 91, 92, Ruth Volid Gallery, Chgo., 1990, James Gallery, Pitts., 1990, Aart Vark Gallery, Phila., 1990, Merrill Chase Gallery, Chgo., 1990, 91, 92, Guild Hall Mus., East Hampton, N.Y., 1991, Joy Berman Gallery, Phila., 1992, Ctr. for Book Arts, N.Y.C., 1992, Barnard-Biederman Fine Arts, N.Y.C., 1994, Arlene Bujese Gallery, East Hampton, 1994, 95, 96, Stoney Brook U., 1994, Harper Collins Exhbn. Space, 1995, Ctr. for Book Arts, 1996, arlene bujese, 1997, Galerie Cargo, Paris, 1997, N.Y. State Mus., Albany, 1997, U. Mont., Missoula, 2002, Nat. Mus. Women in Arts, Washington, 2002, Arlene Bupene, East Hampton, N.Y., 1997-03, Seton Hall U., NJ, 2003, Arlene Bujese Gallery, East Hampton, N.Y. 2003—, Gayle Wilson Gallery, Southampton, N.Y., 2003—; permanent collections Nat. Postal Art Mus., Ottawa, Can., Nat. Inst. Design, Ahmedabad, India, Fine Arts Acad., New Delhi, India, Mus. Modern Art, N.Y.C., Nat. Mus. Women in the Arts, Washington, D.C., Israel Mus., Jerusalem, Brenau Coll., Grainsville, Ga. Blue Cross, Blue Shield, Phila., Mc Donald's, Oakbrook, Ill., The Hyatt Collection, Chgo., Guild Hall Mus., Saul, Ewing, Reineck & Saul, Phila., Shevick, Ravich, Koster, Tobin, Clark, N.J., Sidley & Austin, L.A., Catalano & Sparber, N.Y., Islip (N.Y.) Mus. of Art, NY Pet Rescue Orgn., Larchmont, Islip (NY) Mus.; contbr. critical essays to various periodicals. Mem. Women in Arts, Women's Caucus for Arts, Artists Equity, Visitation Bd. of Met. Mus.-Rockefeller Connection. Address: 300 E 74th St New York NY 10021-3712

WRIGHT, FAYE See DAYA MATA, SRI

WRIGHT, GLADYS STONE, music educator, composer, writer; b. Wasco, Oreg., Mar. 8, 1925; d. Murvel Stuart and Daisy Violet (Warren) Stone; m. Alfred George Wright, June 28, 1953. BS, U. Oreg., 1948, MS, 1953. Dir. bands Elmira (Oreg.) U-4 High Sch., 1948-53, Otterbein (Ind.)

High Sch., 1954-61, Klondike High Sch., West Lafayette, Ind., 1962-70, Harrison High Sch., West Lafayette, 1970-84. Organizer, condr. Musical Friendship Tours, Cen. Am., 1967-79; v.p., condr. U.S. Collegiate Wind Band, 1975—; bd. dirs. John Philip Sousa Found. 1984—; chmn. Sudler Cup, 1986—, Sudler Flag, 1982; pres. Internat. Music Tours, 1984—, Key to the City, Taxco, Mex., 1975. Editor: Woman Conductor, 1986—; composer: marches Big Bowl and Trumpets and Tabards, 1987; contbg. editor: Informusica (Spain). Bd. dirs. N. Am. Wildlife Park, Battleground, Ind. 1985. Recipient Medal of the order John Philip Sousa Found., 1988, Star of Order, 1991, Internat. Contbrn. to Music award Phi Beta Mu, 2000; 1st woman guest condr. U.S. Navy Band, Washington D.C., 1961, Goldman Band, N.Y.C., 1958, Kneller Hall Band, London, 1975, Tri-State Music Festival Massed Orch., Band, Choir, 1985; elected to Women Bd. Dirs. Hall of Fame of Disting. Women Condr., 1994; inductee Hall of Fame Disting. Condrs., Nat. Band Assn., 1999. Mem. Am. Bandmasters Assn. (bd. dirs. 1993, 1st woman mem.), Women Band Dirs. Nat. Assn. (founding pres. 1967, sec. 1985, recipient Silver Baton 1974, Golden Rose 1990, Hall of Fame 1995), Am. Sch. Band Dirs. Assn., Nat. Band Assn. (Citation excellence 1970), Tippecanoe Arts Fedn. (bd. dirs. 1986-90), Tippecanoe Fife and Drum Corps. (bd. dirs. 1984), Daughters of Am. Revolution, Col. Dames-Pre Quitanen Chpt., New England Women, Tau Beta Sigma (Outstanding Svc. to Music award 1970), Phi Beta Mu (1st hon. women mem. 1972), North Am. Wildlife Park (bd dirs, 1990—). Avocations: historic preservation, environ. activities.

WRIGHT, GWENDOLYN, art center director, writer, educator; b. Chgo., May 14, 1946; d. William Kemp and Mary Ruth (Brown) W.; m. Paul Rabinow, Nov. 18, 1980 (div. 1982); m. Thomas Bender, Jan. 14, 1984; children: David, Sophia. BA, NYU, 1969; MArch, U. Calif., Berkeley, 1974, PhD, 1980. Assoc. prof. Columbia U., N.Y.C., 1983-87, prof., 1988—; dir. Buell Ctr. for Study Am. Architecture, N.Y.C., 1988-92. Cons. Fulbright Scholars, Coun. Internat. Exch. Scholars, Washington, 1988-91, ArchNet, 1999--, Nat. Bldg. Mus., Washington, 2001--. Author: Building the Dream: A Social History of Housing in America, 1980, Moralism and the Model Home, 1981, The History of History in American Schools of Architecture, 1990, The Politics of Design in French Colonial Urbanism, 1991; writer N.Y. Times, 1999; presenter PBS TV series History Detectives, 2003—. Fellow Ford Found., 1979-80, Stanford Inst. for Humanities, 1982-83, Mich. Inst. for Humanities, 1991, Getty Ctr. for History of Art and the Humanities, 1992-93, Guggenheim Found., 2004—. Fellow Soc. Am. Historians, N.Y. Inst. for Humanities; mem. Soc. Archtl. Historians, Coll. Art Assn., Am. Hist. Assn., Orgn. Am. Historians. Democrat. Home: 54 Washington Mews New York NY 10003-6608 Office: Columbia U Avery Hall New York NY 10027 Office Phone: 212-854-1587.

WRIGHT, HELEN KENNEDY, retired professional association administrator, publisher, editor, librarian; b. Indpls., Sept. 23, 1927, d. William Henry and Ida Louise (Crosby) Kennedy; m. Samuel A. Wright, Sept. 5, 1970 (dec. 1998); 1 child, Carl F. Prince II (dec.). BA, Butler U., 1945, MS, 1950; MSLS, Columbia U., 1952. Reference libr. N.Y. Pub. Libr., N.Y.C., 1952 53, Bklyn. Pub. Libr., 1953-54; reference libr., cataloger U. Utah, 1954-57; libr. Chgo. Pub. Libr.; asst. dir. pub. svcs. ALA, Chgo., 1958-62, editor Reference Books Bull., 1962—85, asst. dir. for new product [illegible] 1985 80, dir. office for libr. outreach svcs., 1987—88, mng. editor yearbook, 1988-89. Contbr. to Ency. of Careers, [illegible] and Info. Sci., New Book of Knowledge Ency., Bull. of Bibliography, New Golden Book Ency. Recipient Louis Shores/Oryx award, 1991. Mem. Phi Kappa Phi, Kappa Delta Pi, Sigma Gamma Rho. Roman Catholic. Home: 1138 W 111th St Chicago IL 60643-4508

WRIGHT, HELEN PATTON, professional society administrator; b. Washington, Jan. 15, 1919; d. Raymond Stanton and Virginia (Mitchell) Patton; m. James Skelly Wright, Feb. 1, 1945 (dec. 1988); 1 son, James Skelly; m. John H. Pickering, Feb. 3, 1990. Student, Sweet Briar Coll., 1936-38; grad., Washington Sch. Secretaries, 1939, Am. U., 1989. Tchr. Washington Sch. Secs., N.Y.C., 1939-40; sec. The White House, 1941-43, Am. Embassy, London, 1943-45; asst. to exec. dir. Senate Atomic Energy Com., 1946-47. Bd. dirs. Constitution Project, 2001—. Author: My Journey Recollections of the First Seventy Years, 1995. V.p., mem. budget and admissions com. United Fund New Orleans, 1960-62; chmn. met. divsn., campaign; v.p. Dept. Pub. Welfare, Orleans Parish and City New Orleans, 1960-62, Milne Asylum for Destitute Orphan Boys, New Orleans, 1958-62; mem. bd. New Orleans Social Welfare Planning Coun., 1954-62, New Orleans Cancer Soc., 1958-60; v.p. Juvenile Ct. Adv. Com. New Orleans, 1961; successively sec., v.p., pres. Parents' Assn. Metairie Park Country Day Sch., 1956-59; v.p. La. Assn. Mental Health, 1960-62; del. dir. to Nat. Assn. Mental Health, 1960-62; bd. mem. Washington Health and Welfare Coun., 1962-64, Hillcrest Children's Ctr., Washington, 1963-69, D.C. Mental Health Assn., 1962-72, 73-76; bd. dirs. Hospice Care of D.C., 1981-88, 90-96, pres., 1986-88; mem. adv. bd. civil commitment project Nat. Ctr. for State Cts., 1981; bd. dirs. Nat. Assn. Mental Health, 1960-66, 67-74, sec., 1968-70, pres.-elect, 1970-71, pres., 1972-73, cons. on assn. film, 1972; mem. commn. on mentally disabled ABA, 1973-80, commn. on legal problems of elderly, 1997; mem. adv. bd. Alzheimer's Assn. Greater Washington chpt., 1996, bd. dirs. Constn. Project; chmn. altar guild Christ Ch. Cathedral, New Orleans, 1960, Little Sanctuary of St. Albans Sch., Washington, 1965; pres. Altar Guild, St. Alban's Ch., 1976, 77; chmn. Washington com. Nat. Cathedral Assn., 1976-79, trustee, 1976-90, sec., 1977, v.p., 1980-83, trustee emeritae, 1997; bd. dirs. Nat. Ctr. Voluntary Action; mem. task panel Mental Health Problems, Scope and Boundaries, Pres.'s Commn. Mental Health, 1977; mem. tech. rev. com. Md. Psychiat. Rsch. Ctr., 1979-81. Mem. ABA (commn. on legal problems of the elderly 1997-99). Address: Apt 1007 8100 Connecticut Ave Chevy Chase MD 20815

WRIGHT, JANE COOKE, oncologist, educator, consultant; b. N.Y.C., Nov. 30, 1919; d. Louis T. and Corinne (Cooke) W.; m. David D. Jones. AB, Smith Coll., 1942; MD with honors, N.Y. Med. Coll., 1945; D in Med. Scis., Women's Med. Coll. Pa., 1965; ScD, Denison U., 1971. Intern Bellevue Hosp., N.Y.C., 1945-46, resident, 1946, mem. staff, 1955-67; resident Harlem Hosp., 1947, chief resident, 1948; clin. Cancer Rsch. Found., Harlem Hosp., 1949-52; dir., 1952-55; mem. staff Harlem Hosp., 1949-55; practice medicine specializing in clin. cancer chemotherapy N.Y.C.; mem. faculty dept. surgery Med. Ctr., N.Y. U., N.Y.C., 1955-67, adj. assoc. prof., 1961-67, also dir. cancer chemotherapy services research, 1955-67; prof. surgery N.Y. Med. Coll., N.Y.C., 1967-87, prof. surgery emeritus, 1987—, assoc. dean, 1967-75; mem. staff Manhattan VA Hosp., 1955-67, Midtown, Met., Bird S. Color, Flower-Fifth Ave. Hosps., all N.Y.C., 1967-79, Westchester County Med. Center, Valhalla, N.Y., 1971-87, Lincoln Hosp., Bronx, N.Y., 1979-87. Cons. Health Ins. Plan of Greater N.Y., 1962-94; cons. Blvd. Hosp., 1963—, St. Luke's Hosp., Newburgh, N.Y., 1964—; pelvic malignancy rev. com. N.Y. Gynecol. Soc., 1965-66, St. Vincent's Hosp., N.Y.C., 1966—, Dept. Health, Edn. and Welfare, 1968-70, Wyckoff Heights Hosp., N.Y.C., 1969—, NIH, 1971—, others; adv. bd. Skin Cancer Found. Contbr. articles to profl. jours. Mem. Manhattan coun. State Commn. Human Rights, 1949—, Pres.'s Commn. Heart Disease, Cancer and Stroke, 1964-65, Nat. Adv. Cancer Coun. NIH, 1966-70, N.Y. State Women's Coun., 1970-72; bd. dirs. Medico-CARE, Health Svcs. Improvement Fund Inc.; trustee Smith Coll., Northampton, Mass., 1970-80. Recipient numerous awards, including; Mademoiselle mag. award, 1952; Lady Year award Harriet Beecher Stowe Jr. High Sch., 1958; Spirit Achievement award Albert Einstein Sch. Medicine, 1965, certificate Honor award George Gershwin Jr. High Sch., 1967; Myrtle Wreath award Hadassah, 1967; Smith medal Smith Coll., 1968; Outstanding Am. Women award Am. Mothers Com. Inc., 1970; Golden Plate award Am. Acad. Achievement, 1971; Exceptional Black Scientists Poster Ciba Geigy, 1980 Fellow N.Y. Acad. Medicine; mem. Nat. Med. Assn. (edit. bd. jours.), Manhattan Ctrl. Med. Soc., N.Y. County Med. Soc. (nominating com.), AMA, AAAS, Am. Assn. Cancer Rsch. (dir. Rsch. Salute 1971-74), N.Y. Acad. Scis., N.Y. Cancer Soc., Internat. Med. and Rsch. Found. (v.p.), Am. Cancer Soc. (dir. div.), N.Y. Cancer Soc. (pres. 1970-71), Am. Soc. Clin. Oncology (sec. treas. 1964-67), Contin Soc., Sigma Xi, Lambda Kappa Mu, Alpha Omega Alpha. Clubs: The 400 (N.Y. Med. Coll.). Address: 7002 Kennedy Blvd East Apt 9C Guttenberg NJ 07093

WRIGHT, JO ANNE, Episcopal priest; b. Wichita, Kans., May 31, 1935; d. Everett Joseph and Agnes Josephine (Ketcham) Steinheimer; m. John Cook Wright, June 25, 1955 (div. June 1976); children: Elizabeth, Jennifer, Melanie, Kennedy Weston. AB, Oberlin Coll., 1955; MDiv, Ch. Divinity Sch. of Pacific, Berkeley, Calif., 1987. Ordained deacon Episcopal Ch., 1987, ordained priest, 1987. Pre-sch. tchr. Children's Hour Headstart, Lawrence, Kans., 1977-79; reference libr. Lawrence (Kans.) Pub. Libr., 1979-84; rector St. Luke's Episcopal Ch., Wamego, Kans., 1987-98, St. John's Episcopal Ch., Vinita, Okla., 1999—; mem. diocesan coun. Diocese of Okla., 2000—01, dean NE region, 2001—. Youth officer Diocese of Kans., Topeka, 1987-92, rural missioner, 1992-98, mem. standing com., mem. diocesan coun., 1997-98; pres. Vinita Minsterial Alliance, 2001, sec., 2003. Writer monthly column Plenteous Harvest, 1987-92. Chair Wamego Coun. Chs., 1998, CROP walk organizer, 1988, 92, 95; tour leader Ednl. Opportunities, Israel, 1998. Roanridge grantee Episcopal Ch. U.S.A., 1995. Mem. Phi Beta Kappa. Democrat. Avocations: reading, travel. Home: 221 S Bell St Vinita OK 74301-3408 Office: St John's Episcopal Ch 522 W Canadian Ave Vinita OK 74301-3612 E-mail: jowright@junct.com.

WRIGHT, JUDITH MARGARET, law librarian, educator, dean; b. Jackson, Tenn., Aug. 16, 1944; d. Joseph Clarence and Mary Catherine (Key) Wright; m. Mark A. Johnson, Apr. 17, 1976; children— Paul, Michael BS, U. Memphis, 1966; MA, U. Chgo., 1971; JD, DePaul U., 1980. Bar: Ill. 1980. Librarian Oceanway Sch., Jacksonville, Fla., 1966-67; program dir. ARC, South Vietnam, 1967-68; documents and reference librarian D'Angelo Law Library, U. Chgo., 1970-74, reference librarian, 1974-77, dir., lectr. in law, 1980-99, assoc. dean for libr. and info. svcs., lectr. in law, 1999—. Mem. adv. bd. Legal Reference Svcs. Quar., 1981—. Mem. ABA, Am. Assn. Law Libraries, Chgo. Assn. Law Libraries. Democrat. Methodist. Office: U Chgo Law Sch D'Angelo Law Libr 1121 E 60th St Chicago IL 60637-2745 Fax: 773-702-2889. E-mail: jm-wright@uchicago.edu.

WRIGHT, JUDITH RAE, retired accountant; b. Paoli, Ind., Feb. 16, 1929; d. Samuel Earl and Bernice Louise (Lomax) Hudelson; m. James Edward Walters, July 11, 1947 (div. June 1971); children: Jamie Jo, Jennifer Rae; m. George Ralph Wright, Feb. 20, 1972 (dec. Apr. 1977). Student, Northwood Inst., West Baden, Ind., 1968-69, Ind. U.-Purdue U., Indpls., 1972-77. Acct. Ind. Hwy. Commn., Indpls., 1969—72, Ind. Dept. Correction, Indpls., 1972-76, Ind. Dept. Pub. Welfare, Indpls., 1976-78, Ind. Office Social Svcs., Indpls., 1978-79; acct. supr. Ind. Dept. Pub. Welfare, Indpls., 1979-92, ret., 1992. Mem. First Christian Ch. Recipient Gov.'s Spl. Achievement award, 1992. Mem. Assn. Govt. Accts., Am. Legion Aux., Order of Eastern Star, Kappa Kappa Kappa. Republican.

WRIGHT, KATHY DIANE, secondary school educator; b. Warner Robins, Ga., Sept. 23, 1961; d. Thomas Neal and Mary Rose Wright. BS, [illegible] 1997. Tchr. Colquitt County Bd. Edn., Moultrie, Ga., 1983—93, Decatur County Bd. Edn., Bainbridge, Ga., 1993—94, Colquitt County H.S., Moultrie, 1994—. Mem.: Am. Choral Dirs. Assn. (Ga. pres. 2001—03), Music Educators Nat. Conf. (dist. chair 1985—90, 2002). Home: 833 Georgia Hwy 111 Moultrie GA 31768 Office: Colquitt County High Sch 1800 Park Ave Moultrie GA 31768

WRIGHT, KATIE HARPER, educational administrator, journalist; b. Crawfordsville, Ark., Oct. 5, 1923; d. James Hale and Connie Mary (Locke) Harper; m. Marvin Wright, Mar. 21, 1952; 1 child, Virginia K. Jordan. BA, U. Ill., 1944, MEd, 1959; EdD, St. Louis U., 1979. Elem. and spl. edn. tchr. East St. Louis (Ill.) Pub. Schs., 1944-65, dir. Dist. 189 Instrnl. Materials Program, 1965-71, dir. spl. edn. Dists. 188, 189, 1971-77, asst. supt. programs, 1977-79; interim supt. East St. Louis Sch. Dist. 189, 1993-94. Adj. faculty Harris/Stowe State Coll., 1980, adj. prof. edn. emeritus; mem. staff St. Louis U., 1989—; interim supt. Dist. 189 Schs., 1994—; mem. Pres.'s Commn. on Excellence in Spl. Edn. Author: Delta Sigma Theta/East St. Louis Chapter History, 1992; contbr. articles to profl. jours.; feature writer St. Louis Argus Newspaper, 1979—. Mem. Ill. Commn. on Children, 1973-85, East St. Louis Bd. Election Comms., East St. Louis Fin. Adv. Authority, 1999—; pres. bd. dirs. St. Clair County Mental Health Ctr., 1970-72, 87—; bd. dirs. River Bluff coun. Girl Scouts USA, 1979—, nat. bd. dirs., 1981-84; bd. dirs. Jackie Joyner-Kersee Youth Ctr. Found., 1991—, United Way, 1979—, Urban League, 1979—, Provident Counseling Ctr., 1995-98; pres. bd. trustees East St. Louis Pub. Libr., 1972-77; pres., bd. dirs. St. Clair County Mental Health Ctrs., 1987; mem. adv. bd. Magna Bank; charter mem. Coalition of 100 Black Women; mem. coord. coun. ethnic affairs Synod of Mid-Am., Presbyn. Ch. U.S.A.; mem. Ill. Dept. Corrections Sch. Bd., 1995—; charter mem. Metro East Links Group, Gateway chpt. The Links, Inc.; mem. Ill. Minority/Female Bus. Coun., 1991—; mem. Pres.'s Commn. on Excellence in Spl. Edn., 2001--. Recipient of more than 150 awards including Lamp of Learning award East St. Louis Jr. Wednesday Club, 1965, Outstanding Working Woman award Downtown St. Louis, Inc., 1967, Ill. State citation for ednl. document Love is Not Enough, 1974, Delta Sigma Theta citation for document Good Works, 1979, Girl Scout Thanks badge, 1982, award Nat. Coun. Negro Women, 1983, Cmty. Svc. award Met. East Bar Assn., 1983, Journalist award Sigma Gamma Rho, Spelman Coll. Alumni award, 1990, A World of Difference award, 1990, 92, Edn. award St. Louis, YWCA, 1991, SIU-E-Kimmel award, 1991, St. Clair County Mental Health award, 1992, Gateway East Met. Ministry Dr. M.L. King award, 1993, Nat. Coun. Negro Women Black Leader of Yr., 1995, Disting. Alumni award U. Ill., 1996, Pioneer award Mosque 28B, 2000, Tri Del Globe award, 2001, Urban League Merit award, 2002, Ill. Office of Edn. award, 2002, Eugene B. Redmond Writers Club award, 2002; named Woman of Achievement, St. Louis Globe Democrat, 1974, Outstanding Adminstr. So. region III Office Edn., 1975, Woman of Yr. in Edn. St. Clair County YWCA, 1987, Nat. Top Lady of Yr., 1988, Disting. Alumnus U. Ill., 1996, Vashon H.S. Hall of Fame, 1989, Citizen Amb., South Africa, 1996, Sr. Illinoisan Hall of Fame, 1997. Mem. Am. Librs. Trustees Assn. (regional v.p. 1978-79, 92, nat. sec. 1979-80), Ill. Commn. on Children, Mensa, Coun. for Exceptional Children (mem. pres.'s commn. excellence spl. edn.), Top Ladies of Distinction (pres. 1987-91, nat. editor 1991—, Journalism award 1992, Media award 1992), Delta Sigma Theta (chpt. pres. 1960-62, Letters award 2000), Kappa Delta Pi (pres. So. Ill. U. chpt. 1973-74), Phi Delta Kappa (Svc. Key award 1984, chpt. pres. 1984-85), Iota Phi Lambda, Phi Lambda Theta (chpt. pres. 1985-87), East St. Louis Women's Club (pres. 1973-75). Republican. Home: 733 N 40th St East Saint Louis IL 62205-2138

WRIGHT, LILYAN BOYD, physical education educator; b. Upland, Pa., May 11, 1920; d. Albert Verlenden and Mabel (Warburton) Boyd; m. Richard P. Wright, Oct. 23, 1942; 1 child, Nicki Wright Vanek. BS, Temple U., 1942, MEd, 1946; EdD, Rutgers U., 1972. Tchr. health and phys. edn. Woodbury (N.J.) High Sch., 1942-43, Glen-Nor High Sch., Glenolden, Pa., 1944-46, Chester (Pa.) High Sch., 1946-54; chmn. women's dept. health and phys. edn. Union (N.J.) High Sch., 1954-61; with Trenton State Coll., 1961-90, head women's program health and phys. edn., 1967-77, chmn. dept. health, phys. edn. and recreation, 1977-86, adj. faculty mem., 1990-92, prof. emeritus, 1991—. Mem. N.J. State Coun. Div. Girls and Women's Sports, 1958-80; chmn. New Atlantic Field Hockey Sectional Umpiring, 1981-85; chmn. New Atlantic Field Hockey Assn., 1985-90; with recreation after sch. program Newport Counseling Ctrl., 1992-93; vol. coach field hockey Goshen-Lempster Coop. Sch., 1995—. Active Chester United Fund; water safety, first aid instr.; vestry Ch. Epiphany, Newport, N.H., 1992—, sr. warden, 1995-99; vestry St. Luke's Episcopal Ch., 1988-91, clk. of the vestry, 2000—; trustee Olive Pettis Libr., Goshen, 1992—, chair of trustees, 1998—, Goshen budget com., 1999—; dist. ednl. improvement team for Goshen-Lempster Sch. Dist., 1995—, mem. sch. bd., 2001—. Recipient U.S. Field Hockey Assn. award, 1989; ARC Scholarship in her honor N.J. Athletic Assn. Girls, 1971; named to Hall of Fame, Temple U., 1976; named Nat. Honorary and Emeritus Field Hockey Umpire. Mem. AAHPERD (chmn. Ea. Dist. Assn. Div. Girls and Women's Sports, sec. to coun. for svcs. Ea. Dist. Assn. 1979-80, chmn. 1980-81, chmn. com. on aging and adult devel. of ea. dist. 1993-97, 2001—, N.J. rep. to council for convs. 1984-85, Honor Fellow award 1986), N.J. AHPER (pres. 1974-75, past pres. 1975-76, v.p. phys. edn. div., parliamentarian 1990—, Disting. Service and Leadership award 1969, 93, Honor Fellow award 1977, Presdl. Citation award 1993, 95, 96, 97, 98, 99, Disting. Leadership award 1994), N.J. Women's Lacrosse Assn. (umpiring chmn. 1972-76), Nat. Assn. Phys. Edn. in Higher Edn., Eastern Assn. Phys. Edn. Coll. Women, North Jersey, Ctrl. Jersey bds. women's ofcls., Am., Pa. (v.p. 1953-54), Chester (pres. 1949-54) fedns. tchrs., U.S. Field Hockey Assn. (exec. com., chair honorary umpire award com. 1992), North Jersey Field Hockey Assn. (past pres.), N.H. Field Hockey Umpires' Assn., No. New Eng. Lacrosse Officials Bd., U.S. Women's Lacrosse Assn. (Honorary and Emeritus Umpiring Rating award), Kappa Delta Epsilon, Delta Psi Kappa (past pres. Phila. alumni chpt.), Kappa Delta Pi. Home: PO Box 239 Goshen NH 03752-0239

WRIGHT, LINDA JEAN, manufacturing executive; b. Chgo., Dec. 14, 1949; d. Eugene F. and Rosemary Margaret (Kiley) Kemph; m. Kelly W. Wright, Jr., Feb. 1979 (div. 1984); m. Samuel Neuwirth Klewans, Aug. 28, 1986 (div. 1991). Student, Loretto Heights Coll., 1967-69, U. Ill., 1970-71. Asst. to v.p. Busey 1st Nat. Bank, Urbana, Ill., 1969-72; spa mgr., supr. sales tng. Venus and Apollo Health Club, San Antonio, 1973-76; owner Plant Shop, San Antonio, 1976-77; with Enterprise Bank, Falls Church, Va., 1977-84, comml. lending officer, 1978-84, sr. v.p., 1979-84, corp. sec. of bd. dirs., 1980-84; pes., CEO Fairfax Savs. Bank, 1984-87, Bankstar, N.A. (formerly Bank 2000 of Reston, N.A.), 1988-90; v.p. Ryan-McGinn Inc., Arlington, Va., 1991-95, Bethlehem Corp., 1995—. Bd. dirs. INOVA Inst. Rsch. and Edn., 1990-94. Apptd. pub. ofcl., chmn. Va. Small Bus. Fin. Authority, Richmond, 1984-88; trustee Inova Health System, 1992-95; mem. exec. com. Fairfax-Falls Church United Way, United Way Capital Area, Washington, 1984-85; mem. Fairfax County Spl. Task Force, 1986; bd. dirs. Fairfax Com. of 100, 1993095; mem., bd. dirs. Hospice No. Va., Arlington, 1985-86, chmn. No. Va. Local Devel. Corp., 1986; mem. ops. bd. Fairfax Hosp., 1987-94; pres. No. Va. Transp. Alliance, 1987-92; bd. dirs. Va. Found. for Rsch. and Econ. Edn., 1989-91, No. Va. coun. Am. Heart Assn., 1989-94. Mem. Fairfax County C. of C. (dir., v.p., pres. 1987-88), Nat. Assn. Bank Women (chmn. No. Va. group 1980-81), Fairfax Hunt Club, Tower Club (bd. govs. 1989-95). Roman Catholic. Avocations: aviation, fox hunting.

WRIGHT, MARGARET HAGEN, computer scientist, administrator; b. San Francisco, 1952; m. 1965; 1 child. BS, Stanford U., 1964, MS, 1965, PhD in Computer Sci., 1976. Devel. engr. Sylvania Electronic System, 1965-71, sr. rsch. assoc. Stanford U., Palo Alto, Calif., 1976-88; mem. tech. staff Bell Labs. now Lucent Techs., Murray Hill, N.J., 1988—; head sci. computer rsch. dept. Lucent Techs., Murray Hill, 1999—. Assoc. editor [illegible] Programming. Mem. NAE, Assn. Computing Machinery (bd. dirs. numerical analysis assn. spl. interest group), Soc. Indsl. and Applied Math., Math. Programming Soc. Achievements include research contributing to enlarged knowledge of methods for nonlinear programming, particularly unconstrained; linearly constrained and nonlinearly constrained optimization; mathematical software, numerical linear algebra; software library development. Office: AT&T Bell Labs Lucent Tech Rm 2C 462 600 Mountain Ave New Providence NJ 07974-2008

WRIGHT, MARIE ANNE, management information systems educator; b. Albany, N.Y., Oct. 21, 1953; d. Arthur Irving and Ethel (Knickerbocker) W. BS, U. Mass., Boston, 1981; MBA, Clarkson U., 1984; PhD, U. Mass., Amherst, 1989. Grad. asst. Clarkson U., Potsdam, N.Y., 1982; sys. analyst St. Lawrence U., Canton, N.Y., 1983-84; instr. Bentley Coll., Waltham, Mass., 1984-85; tchg. asst. U. Mass., 1985, rsch. asst., 1986; computer cons. Amherst (Mass.) Police Dept., 1986-88; asst. prof. Elms Coll., Chicopee, Mass., 1986-89; assoc. prof. Western Conn. State U., Danbury, Conn., 1990—2002, prof., 2002—. Cons. Ctr. for Human Devel., Springfield, Mass., 1986-87, Early Childhood Ctr., 1986-87. Contbr. articles to profl. jours. and mags. Recipient MIS award U. Mass., 1981. Mem. AAUW, IEEE, Assn. Computing Machinery, Internat. Computer Security Assn., Info. Sys. Security Assn., Am. Soc. Indsl. Security, Computer Security Inst., Assn. Info. Sys., Am. Coll. Forensic Examiners Internat., Beta Gamma Sigma. Democrat. Avocations: cross-country skiing, swimming, reading. Office: Western Conn State U MIS Dept Danbury CT 06810

WRIGHT, MARIE BEULAH BATTEY, retired advertising executive; b. Cordell, Okla., Jan. 12, 1917; d. John William and Mary (Yoder) Battey; m. Joseph Barney Gifford, Sept. 3, 1948 (dec. 1960); m. Harold Arthur Wright, May 18, 1979. BFA, U. Okla., 1937; posTgrad., Oklahoma City Symphony, 1939—40; postgrad., Baylor U., 1943-44. Host 15-minute daily piano show U. Okla. Radio Sta., 1935; supt. music Woodward (Okla.) Pub. Schs., 1937-38; sales and promotion mgr. KOME, Tulsa, 1940-43; instr. Sch. Radio Baylor U., Waco, Tex., 1943-45; asst. program mgr. KWKH, Shreveport, La., 1945-47; salesman KTBS Radio, Shreveport, 1947-55; comml. mgr. KTBS-TV, Shreveport, 1955-57, KEEL Radio, Shreveport, 1957-62, v.p., gen. mgr., 1963-75; v.p. Lin Broadcasting, Shreveport, 1963-75; gen. mgr. KEEL/AM and KMBQ/FM, Shreveport, 1968-80; v.p. Multimedia Broadcasting, Shreveport, 1975-80. Freelance mus. in arrangements Okla. City radio stas., 1938-39; editl. writer radio stas.; author: The Killing of the Presidency, 1974 (RTNDA Best Editl. 1973). Mem. publicity com. United Fund, 1955-62, exec. com. Shreveport Symphony, 1976-82, Strand Theatre of Shreveport Corp., 1977-94; bd. dirs. Downtown Devel. Corp., 1975-81; La. rep. So. Growth Policies Bd., 1985-96; mem. La. State Arts Coun., 1992-96; bd dirs. Caddo-Bossier Cmty. Action, 1969-71; mem. housing com. Caddo Parish, Shreveport, 1969; mem. City Charter Com., Shreveport, 1970; bd. dirs. Amb. Club, Shreveport, 1971-74; bd. dirs. David Raines Assn., Shreveport, 1969; mem. Com. of 500 March of Dimes, Shreveport, 1969; exec. asst. Shreveport Summer Theatre, 1950-60. Named Broadcaster of Yr., La. Assn. Broadcasters, Shreveport, 1970, Women Who Have Made a Differnce, YWCA, Shreveport, 1988; recipient Humanitarian award Shreveport Negro C. of C., 1969, Humanitarian award for outstanding contbn. to the arts, 1995. Mem. Shreveport C. of C. (bd. dirs. 1968-71, 1st woman mem.). Democrat. Avocations: theatre, symphony, reading, politics. Home: 701 Livingston Ave Shreveport LA 71107-3914

WRIGHT, MARY E. (MARY E. GUEN), clinical psychologist; b. Rochester, Minn., Jan. 3, 1951; d. Robert George and Rosemarie Celine (Nowicki) Tompkins; m. Scotty Kane Wright, Mar. 17, 1977 (div. May 1984); children: Drew Robert, Rosemary Elizabeth. BA, U. South Ala., 1985; MA, U. Mo., 1989, PhD, 1993. Lic. psychologist, Calif., Ark. Family therapist Boone County Juvenile Ct. Svcs., Columbia, Mo., 1986—87; psychology extern, adolescent dept. Charter Hosp. of Columbia, Columbia, 1987; psychology clk. Psychology Clinic, Columbia, 1987—88, Mid-Mo. Mental Health Ctr., Columbia, 1988—89, Biggs Forensic Ctr./Fulton (Mo.) State Hosp. Sex Offender Program, 1989—90; psychology intern Atascadero (Calif) State Hosp., 1990—91; psychologist, program coord., team leader Fulton State Forensic Hosp. Sex Offender Program, 1991—93; primary therapist coord. Boone County Juvenile Sex Offender Project, Columbia, 1992—93; staff psychologist Atascadero State Hosp., 1993—96; staff adolescent psychologist team leader Wyo. State Hosp., Evanston, 1996—97, forensic psychologist, forensic examiner, 1996—98, core faculty psychologist, 1998—99; clin. psychologist, dir. psychol. svcs. Cornerstone Med. Group, Van Buren, Ark., 1999—2000; pvt. practice Ft. Smith, Ark., 1999—; clin. dir. RSVP program Ark. Dept. Corrections, 2002—. Author publs.; presenter in field. Mem. Crawford County Child Sexual Abuse Task Force, 1999-2002. Recipient awrds and grants. Mem. APA, Nat. Alliance for Mentally Ill, Ark. Psychol. Assn., Children and Adults with Attention Deficit. Democrat. Roman Catholic. Avocations: horticulture, books, historic preservation, human rights, outdoors. Home: 414 E Purdon St England AR 72046-1860 E-mail: cheekypin@aol.com.

WRIGHT, MARY ELLEN, theater educator; b. Commerce, Tex. d. Joseph Perry and Ora Berniece Gentry; m. James Hatfield; children: Christopher Collin, Sarah Allison Wright Metzger. BA summa cum laude, U. Tex., Tyler, 1988, MAIS, 1991—91; PhD, Tex. Tech U., Lubbock, 2001. Lectr. U. Tex. at Tyler, 1994—95, 1996—2001, asst. prof., 2002—. Adjudicator Tex. U. Interscholastic League, 1993—, St. Gregory's Sch., Tyler, 1999—; conf. planner Assn. for Theatre in Higher Edn., 1994—98; presenter in field. Costume designer (musical) Annie, (play) The Mandrake; dir.: (play) A Small Family Business, Eleemosynary; costume designer (play) Oleanna (Citation for Excellence in Costume Design, 1992); author: (play) Maggie and Mac; author: (presenter) (workshop) Creative Drama in the Classroom; costume designer (play) Othello; dir.: (play) The King Stag; costume designer (musical) The Fantasticks; dir.: (play) Art; costume designer (musical) Sound of Music, (play) Comic Potential (Citation of Excellence for Costume Design, 2001); dir.: (play) Beauty Queen of Leenane, Pygmalion; contbr. articles to profl. publs. Recipient award, Assn. for Theatre in Higher Edn., 2002, Citation of Excellence for Festival Hosting, Kennedy Ctr./Am. Coll. Theatre Festival, 1999—2000; grantee Adrian Hall Del. Project, Tex. Commn. on the Arts, 2003. Mem.: Tex. Ednl. Theatre Assn., Assn. for Theatre in Higher Edn. (conf. planner 1994—98), Alpha Chi, Phi Kappa Phi, Alpha Psi Omega (advisor 1996—2003), Gamma Phi Beta (life). Home: 5404 Briar Cove Dr Tyler TX 75703 Office: U Tex at Tyler 3900 University Blvd Tyler TX 75799 E-mail: mwright@mail.uttyl.edu.

WRIGHT, MATTIE PEARL, civic worker; b. St. Petersburg, Sept. 22, 1938; d. Willie and Mattie Watkins; m. Ernest Rayfield Wright, July 26, 1958; children: Patricia, Vincent, Kimberly. Student, St. Petersburg Jr. Coll., 1986, Lakewood C.C., St. Petersburg, 1993, U. South Fla., 1995. Tchr. pvt. sch., 1986-90. Owner, mgr. 17 house rental properties. Contbr. poems to anthologies. Coord. Crime Watch, South St. Petersburg, 1984—; pres. Neighborhood Assn., South St. Petersburg, 1985—; vol. Pinellas County Sch. Sys., Exch. Ctr. for Prevention Child Abuse, North St. Pe6ersburg, 1995—. Republican. Baptist. Home: 3634 2nd Ave S Saint Petersburg FL 33711-1312

WRIGHT, MILDRED ANNE (MILLY WRIGHT), conservator, researcher; b. Athens, Ala., Sept. 9, 1939; d. Thomas Howard and Anne Louise (Ashworth) Speegle; m. William Paul Wright, Nov. 20, 1965; children: Paul Howard, William Neal. BS in Physics, U. Ala., Tuscaloosa, 1963. Rschr. in acoustics Wyle Labs., Huntsville, Ala., 1963-64; tchr. physics, English Huntsville H.S., 1964-67; ptnr. Flying Carpet Oriental Rugs, Florence, Ala., 1974—. Adj. mem. faculty U. North Ala., Florence, 1988, lectr. Inst. for Learning in Retirement, 1991—. Columnist Times Daily, 1992—; photojournalist, writer River Views Mag., 1993—1997; contbr. articles to profl. jours. (1st pl. award 1986, 87). Pianist, organist Edgemont Meth. Ch., Florence, 1987-90 (Outstanding Svc. award 1990); mem. steering com. Melton Hollow Nature Ctr., Florence, Design Ala., Florence, 1991, River Heritage Discovery Camp, 1993-95; mem. River Heritage Com., Florence, 1991—; accompanist Shoals Boy Choir, Muscle Shoals, Ala., 1992-93; bd. dirs. Heritage Preservation, Inc., Capital award, 1992, pres., 1990-92, 96-97, treas., 1995-96, Tenn. Valley Hist. Soc., pres., 1991-95, Ala. Preservation Alliance, treas., 1992-97, Florence Main Street program, 1992-94, Maud Lindsay Free Kindergarten, Frank Lloyd Wright Rosenbaum House Found., Inc., 1992-98, Gen. Joseph Wheeler Home Found., 1994-98, treas. 1995-97, newsletter editor, 1995-97; mem. adv. bd. Friends of the Ala. Archives, 1995-98, sec., 1996-98; mem. adv. coun. Human Environ. Scis. Dept., 1992-98; mem. Coby Hall steering com. U. North Ala., 1992-98, Kennedy-Douglas Ctr. Arts; adv. bd. Old Cahawba of Ala., 1996-97; adv. bd. Waterloo Mus., 1995—, Florence Children's Mus., 1995-96; mem. bd. Friends of the Florence-Lauderdale Pub. Libr., 2002—, newsletter editor, 2002—. Recipient Disting. Svc. award Ala. Hist. Commn., 1991, Merit award Ala. Preservation Alliance, 1995, Gen. Joseph Wheeler Home Found. Merit award, 1996. Mem. Ala. Writers' Conclave (Creative Works award 1986, 87), Ala. Hist. Assn., Ala. Archeol. Soc., Natchez Trace Geneal. Soc., Colbert County Hist. Landmarks Found., Nat. Trust for Hist. Preservation, Tennessee Valley Art Assn. (Florence film com. vice chmn. 2003-2004), La Grange Living History Assn., Trail of Tears Assn., Florence Film Com. (v.p. 2003-04), Firenze Club, Florence Study Club, Optimist Club, Sigma Pi Sigma. Avocations: bridge, photography, travel, discovering old buildings, gardening. Home: PO Box 279 Florence AL 35631-0279

WRIGHT, MURIEL DEASON See WELLS, KITTY

WRIGHT, NANCY HOWELL, interior designer; b. Sept. 6, 1932; d. David Austin and Catherine Howell; m. Hastings Kemper Wright, June 19, 1954; children: Mark, Barbara; children: Kenneth, Donald. BFA, Ohio Wesleyan U.; student, Parsons Sch. Design, 1977. Interior decorator Country Manor of Branford (Conn.), 1971-75; design mgr., 1976-97; pres., owner Nancy Wright Interiors, 1997—. Sec. Branford Art League, 1977; bd. dirs. Harrison House Hist. House, Branford, Conn., 1983-84; mem. Rep Town Com., Branford, 1990-92; recording sec. Branford Garden Club, 1991—. Mem. Am. Soc. Interior Designers (award for best Conn. retail store design, 1980, Conn. Coalition), Branford Garden Club (rec. sec. 1990-94, membership chmn. 1995, v.p. 1997-99, pres. 1999-2000, Ronald McDonald chair 2002, design chair 2003—), Delta Phi Delta. Republican. Episcopalian. Home and Office: 35 Wood Rd Branford CT 06405-4935

WRIGHT, PEGGY SUE ESPY, elementary school educator; b. Chattanooga, Dec. 27, 1929; d. Lavada Pilgrim Espy Newell; m. John Lawton Wright, Nov. 27, 1959; children: John Lawton III, Stephen Martin. BA, U. Chattanooga, 1951, MEd, 1976; spl. cert., Emory U., 1957. Cert. elem. tchr., K-12 reading tchr., adminstrv., supr., music tchr., Tenn. Tchr. Bright Sch., Chattanooga; tchr. summer reading program McCallie Sch., Chattanooga; tchr. Chpt. I reading Chattanooga Pub. Schs. Adj. prof. Chattanooga State Tech. C.C.; workshop leader; presenter in field. Violinist Chattanooga Symphony; active local ch.; pres. Chattanooga Sister City Assn.; chmn. Tenn. Literacy Com. Mem. NEA, Internat. Reading Assn., Tenn. Reading Assn. (pres.), Tenn. Edn. Assn., Chattanooga Edn. Assn., MCCAC (past pres.), Delta Kappa Gamma, Alpha Xi. Presbyterian.

WRIGHT, RACHEL, curator; b. Spokane, Wash., Feb. 23, 1972; d. J. Lawrence and Mary Wright; m. Kevin Price, Sept. 1, 2001. BA cum laude, Santa Clara (Calif.) U., 1994; MA in Art History, U. Tex., 1998. Photo rschr. Corbis, Seattle, 1999—2000, sr. rschr., fine art specialist, 2000—01, fine art product editor, 2001—02, curator, collections specialist, 2002—03, corp. curator, 2003—. Mem.: Pi Sigma Alpha. Office: Corbis 710 2d Ave Ste 200 Seattle WA 98104

WRIGHT, ROMONA XYLENA, music educator; b. Binghamton, NY, Feb. 18, 1976; d. Johnny L. and Maggie F. Wright. MusB, Columbus State U., 1995—98. Cert. Teacher (T-4) - Music - P-12 GA, 1995. Min. of music New Providence Missionary Bapt. Ch., Columbus, Ga., 1995—2001; elem. music tchr./choral dir. Fulton County Schools, Atlanta, Ga., 1998—2000; pvt. piano instr. Mars Music Ctr., Lawrenceville, Ga., 2000—02; mid. sch. choral dir. Cobb County Sch. Dist., Marietta, Ga., 2001—02; pvt. piano/voice instr. Music & Arts Ctr., Marietta, Ga., 2002—. Asst. sponsor Tri-Cities H.S. Drill Team/Flag Corps, East Point, Ga., 1998—2000; accompanist Cobb County Mid. Sch. Treble Honors Chorus, Smyrna, Ga., 2002—02; mem. Elizabeth Bapt. Ch. Inspirational Voices, Atlanta, 2003—. Feature dancer Super Bowl XXXIV Pregame Show, Atlanta, GA, 2000. Recipient Outstanding Svc. award, New Providence Missionary Bapt. Ch., 2001. Mem.: Music Educators' Nat. Conf., GA Music Educators' Assn. Avocations: piano, singing, reading, shopping, travel. Personal E-mail: momo_0417@yahoo.com.

WRIGHT, SANDRA, science administrator; B in Acctg., Calif. State U., Long Beach. V.p., contr. Aerojet; with Litton; corp. v.p., contr. Northrop Grumman Corp., LA, 2001—. Office: Northrop Grumman Corp 1840 Century Park E Los Angeles CA 90067-2199

WRIGHT, SHARON, reporter; BA Broadcast Journalism, Mich. State U. Gen. assignment and state capitol reporter, weekend anchor Sta. WBRE-TV, Wilkes Barre, Pa., 1976—79; gen. assignment reporter, investigative reporter Sta. KMGH-TV, Denver, 1979—81; consumer investigative reporter Sta. WBZ-TV, Boston, 1981—86; gen. assignment reporter, consumer investigative reporter NBC 5, Chgo., 1986—. Recipient Outstanding Alumna award, Mich. State U., 1986, 10 Emmys. Office: NBC 5 454 N Colmbus Dr Chicago IL 60611

WRIGHT, SUSAN WEBBER, judge; b. Texarkana, Ark., Aug. 22, 1948; d. Thomas Edward and Betty Jane (Gary) Webber; m. Robert Ross Wright, III, May 21, 1983; 1 child, Robin Elizabeth. BA, Randolph-Macon Woman's Coll., 1970; MPA, U. Ark., 1972, JD with high honors, 1975. Bar: Ark. 1975. Law clk. U.S. Ct. Appeals (8th Cir.), 1975-76; from asst. prof. to assoc. prof. law U. Ark., Little Rock, 1976—83, prof., 1983-90, asst. dean, 1976-78; dist. judge U.S. Dist. Ct. (ea. dist.) Ark., Little Rock, 1990—, chief judge, 1998—. Vis. assoc. prof. Ohio State U., Columbus, 1981, La. State U., Baton Rouge, 1982—83; mem. adv. com. U.S. Ct. Appeals (8th cir.), St. Louis, 1983—88. Author (with R. Wright): (book) Land Use in a Nutshell, 1978, Land Use in a Nutshell, 2d edit., 1985; editor-in-chief: Ark. Law Rev., 1975; contbr. articles to profl. jours. Mem.: Ark. Assn. Women Lawyers (v.p. 1977—78), Am. Law Inst., Pulaski County Bar Assn., Ark. Bar Assn., Am. Judicature Soc., Ark. Women's Forum. Episcopalian. Office: US District Court 600 W Capitol Ave Ste 522 Little Rock AR 72201-3329 Office Phone: 501-604-5100. Business E-Mail: susan_wright@ared.uscourts.gov.

WRIGHT, SUSIE FLORA, medical/surgical nurse; b. Jerome, Ark., Aug. 25, 1946; d. Nathan and Linard Nelson; m. Walter Lee Wright (dec. Aug. 17, 1973); children: Sandra Faye Brown, Yolanda Kenyata, Adrienne Carmel, Andr'E Jamaal. ADN, Blackhawk Coll., Moline, Ill., 1975. Nurse/burn unit Trinity Health Sys., Rock Island, Ill., 1975—80, nurse post anesthesia care unit Rock Island/ Moline, Ill., 1980—96, lead nurse post anesthesia care unit Moline, Ill., 1996—. Mem.: Ill. Soc. Post Anesthesia Nurses, Am. Soc. Post Anesthesia Nurses (assoc.). Home: 540 23d Ave Rock Island IL 61201 Office: Trinity Health Sys 7th St Campus 500-700 John Deere Rd Moline IL 61265 Personal E-mail: writeone1@prodigy.net.

WRIGHT, SYLVIA, government agency administrator; b. Balt. BA, Temple U., 1963, MA, 1965. Group leader Sch. Improvement Program Office U.S. Dept. Edn., Washington, dir. Sch. Support and Tech. Programs, 2001—. Office: US Dept Edn FB6 Rm 3E121 400 Maryland Ave SW Washington DC 20202

WRIGHT, TIFFANY ERIN, secondary school educator; b. Plainfield, NJ, Oct. 16, 1974; d. Charles O. and Juliette G. Wright. BA in English, Gettysburg Coll., 1993—97; M in edn., Millersville U., 2000—02. Cert. Secondary English Edn. Pa., 1997, Emergency Secondary Math Edn. Pa., 1998. English instr. York County Sch. of Tech., Pa., 2002—, softball coach, 2003—; edn. outreach coord. and summer camp dir. Penn Laurel Girl Scout Coun., Lancaster, Pa., 2001—02; ednl. supr./english instr./math instr. Cornell Abraxas, South Mountain, Pa., 1997—2000; softball coach Littlestown Area H.S., Littlestown, Pa., 1998—2000. Presenter Emerging Practices: Creating Learning Communities for the 21st Century, Tchr. Edn. Assembly, Grantville, Pa., 1997; mem. Assessment Com. of York County Sch. of Tech., Pa., 2002—; powder puff football coach York County Sch. of Tech., Pa., 2002; accreditation team mem. Mid. States and Coun. of Occupl. Edn., Altoona, Pa., 2003; mem. student assistance program York County Sch. of Tech., Pa., 2002—, vice chairperson, Renaissance Program, 2003—. Chorus mem. Ctrl. Pa. Women's Chorus, Harrisburg, 2002—03, Unitarian Universalist Ch. of York. Recipient Fred D. Grist award, Adams County Literacy Coun., 2000; Meml. scholarship, Millersville U., 2002—03. Mem.: Pa. State Educators Assn. (assoc.), Assn. for Supervision and Curriculum Devel. (assoc.). Democrat. Unitarian Universalist. Avocations: travel, exercise, reading, outdoor activities. Home: 361 E Market St Apt 3 York PA 17403 Office: York County School of Technology 2179 South Queen St York PA 17402 Personal E-mail: tewright27@hotmail.com. E-mail: twright@ycstech.org.

WRIGHT CARRIER, J. T. business owner; b. McKenzie, Tenn., July 31, 1952; d. Gilbert M. and Mildred B. Wright; m. William W. Carrier III, July 28, 1973; 1 child, Morgan Bailey. BA in Psychology cum laude, Memphis State U., 1974, MA in Ednl. Counseling, Pers. Svcs., 1976, PhD, 1992. Sales rep. API Inc., Memphis, 1980—; casting dir. Theatrics Etc., Memphis, 1980—. Profl. model; casting dir., crew svcs. staff for nat. feature and advt. accts. including Warner Bros., Disney, Phillips 66, Exxon, KC Masterpiece BBQ Sauce, Northwest Airlines; scriptwriter for corp. videos, including Fed. Express, Memphis Bus. Jour.; developer Careers 2000 ednl. video series for adolescents. Pub. Crisis Intervention Studies for Memphis Police Dept.; crew svcs. for U.S. Def. Dept. tng. videos. Co-founder Memphis and Shelby County Film, Tape and Music Commn. Named Miss Memphis, 1972, Top Casting Co. Adweek Mag., 1986. Mem. Nat. Career Devel. Assn. Avocations: environmentalism, ballet, modern dance, theatre. Office: Theatrics Etc PO Box 11862 Memphis TN 38111-0862

WRIGHT SAPONE, TANYA D, director; b. St. Louis, Mo., Apr. 14, 1972; d. Raymond Edward and Marie Ellen Wright; m. Brian Sapone, Nov. 11, 2000; 1 child, Merrick Paolo Sapone. BS in Edn., U. of Nebr., Omaha, 1994, MS in Spl. Edn., 1999, MS in Ednl. Adminstrn., 2003. Cert. tchg. Nebr., 1995. Dir. of spl. edn. Girls and Boys Town, Boys Town, Nebr., 2000—; tchr. Heartland Sch., Omaha, 1997—2000. Mem. Metro Spl. Edn. Dirs., Omaha, 2000—. Mem.: Coun. for Exceptional Children. Office: Girls and Boys Town 13803 Flanagan Blvd Boys Town NE 68010 Personal E-mail: wrightt@boystown.org.

WRIGHT-WHITE, KIMBERLY ZENORA, vice principal; b. Newark, May 1, 1969; d. Rhonie Lee and Opal Pocohontas Wright; m. Michael Elton White, Dec. 18, 1993; children: Alexa White, Ashley White, Ariel White. BJ, Howard U., 1991; MEd, St. Peter's Coll., Jersey City, 1997. Cert. elem. tchr., ednl. supr., ednl. adminstr. Youth coord. Mayor's Office City of Newark, 1991—95; tchr. Newark Pub. Schs., 1995—98, vice prin., 1998—. Mem. adv. com. Mid. Sch. Forum, Newark, 1997—98; chair Bragaw Ave. Elem. Sch. Mgmt. Team, Newark, 1997—98. Elder Clinton Ave Presbyn. Ch., Newark, 1998—. Mem.: Nat. Art Edn. Assn. Democrat. Office: George Washington Carver Elem Sch 333 Clinton Pl Newark NJ 07112 Business E-Mail: kwhite@nps.k12.nj.us.

WRIGLEY, CLAUDIA STEPHENS, gifted and talented educator; b. Atlanta, Dec. 12, 1952; d. Ray and Fannie P. Stephens; m. Greg R. Wrigley, June 30, 1974; children: Sarah Elizabeth, Stephanie Elaine. MusB, Shorter Coll., 1974; MEd, Ga. So. U., 1984. Cert. music tchr. Fla., elem. tchr. Fla. Tchr. Berry Acad., Mt. Berry, Ga., 1974—77, Assembly of God Day Sch., Ft. Worth, 1977—78, Temple Christian Sch., Ft. Worth, 1978—80; tchr. gifted Montgomery County Schs., Mt. Vernon, Ga., 1980—84; tchr. music Trion City Schs., Ga., 1984—86; tchr. gifted Chickamauga Schs., Ga., 1986—89; tchr. gifted, drama, chorus Clay County Sch. Sys., Green Cove Springs, Fla., 1993—. Accompanist Dorter's Inlet Bapt. Ch., Orange Park, Fla., 2003—. Gifted Challenge Grant, Fla. Dept. Edn., 1997. Mem.: Music Educators Nat. Conf., Phi Kappa Phi, Delta Kappa Gamma. Avocations: walking, collecting cows, drama. Home: 4986 Canary Ct Orange Park FL 32003 Office: Green Cove Springs Jr HS 1220 Bonaventure Ave Green Cove Springs FL 32043*

WRISTON, KATHRYN DINEEN, lawyer, financial consultant; b. Syracuse, N.Y. d. Robert Emmet and Carolyn (Bareham) Dineen; m. Walter B. Wriston, Mar. 14, 1968; 1 stepchild. Student, U. Geneva, 1958-59; BA cum laude, Smith Coll., 1960; LLB, U. Mich., 1963. Bar: N.Y.1964, U.S. Ct. Appeals (2d cir.) 1964, U.S. Supreme Ct. 1968. Assoc. Shearman & Sterling, N.Y.C., 1963-68. Audit com., corp. responsibility com., fin. com., 2003. Goodyear Tire and Rubber Co., 2002-03, mem. fin. com., 2003; bd. dirs. Northwestern Mut. Life Ins. Co., mem. ins. products and mktg. com., 1986-89, audit com., 1989—, chmn. audit com., 2001—, investment and fin. policy com., 1989-95; dir. Santa Fe Snyder Corp., 1990-2000, mem. audit com. 1990-93, 95-2000, nominating com., 1990-99, compensation com., 1998-99, conceptual framework task force Indep. Standards Bd., 1998-2000, dir. 1990-2000; trustee Fin. Acctg. Found., 1992-97, selection com., 1992-97, audit com., 1992-96, chair, 1993-96, chair devel. com., 1996-97, fin. com., 1994-97. exec. com., 1996-97; task force on timely fin. reporting guidanace Fin. Acctg. Stds. Bd., 1982-83, mem. bd. agenda adv. com., 1981-85, process and structure com., 1981-85, chair, 1983-85, adv. coun., 1981-85; exec. com. CPR Inst. for Dispute Resolution, 1994-99; dir. The Stanley Works, 1996—, mem. corp. governance, 1996—, mem. fin. and pension coms., 1996-97, 2002—, chair audit com., 1997-2002, exec. com., 1997—. Vis. com. U. Mich. Law Sch., 1973—; trustee Fordham U., Bronx, N.Y., 1971-81, vice-chair bd. trustees, 1980-81, student affairs com., 1971-77, chair, 1974-77, faculty affairs com., com. on law sch., 1978-81, grievance com., 1971-81; ea. region selection panel Pres. Commn. on White House Fellowships, 1981-83, chair, 1982-83; bus. com. Nat. Ctr. for State Cts., 1982-88; bd. overseers Rand Inst. for Civil Justice, 1985-93; trustee John A. Hartford Found., 1991—, pres., 2002—, grant com., 1991—, vice-chair, 1992—, chair evaluation com., 1998—, audit com., 1992—, chair, 1993—, sec., 1996-02; mem. Gov. Wilson's N.Y. Little Hoover Commn., 1974; bd. trustees CAth. Health Care Sys., N.Y.C., 1999—. Mem. ABA, Nat. Assn. Accts., Practicing Law Inst. (exec. 1976—, programs and publs. com., chair 1979—, membership com. 1976-79, chair 1977-79, nominating com. 1978, 81-85, v.p., 1985—, mem. bar rev. courses 1978-79, fin. com. 1989—, mem. Am. Law Inst./ABA subcom. on Am. law network 1989-91), Fin. Women's Assn. N.Y., N.Y. County Lawyers Assn. (legal aid com. 1972-76), N.Y. State Bar Assn., Assn. of Bar of City of N.Y.

WRITER, SHARON LISLE, secondary school educator; b. L.A., Aug. 29, 1939; d. Harlan Lawerance and Emma Mae (Cordery) Lisle; m. Robert Vincent Writer, Dec. 30, 1961; children: Martin Carl, Cynthia Louise, Brian Robert, Scott Andrew. BS, Mt. St. Marys Coll., 1961; MS in Sci. Edn., Calif. State U., Fullerton, 1989; postgrad., U. Calif., Irvine, 1987, Colo. Sch. Mines, 1994. Cert. secondary tchr., Calif. Tchr. St. Mary's Acad., L.A., 1961-62, Escambia High Sch., Pensacola, Fla., 1962-63; rsch. asst. U. So. Calif., L.A., 1964-65, U. Calif., Irvine, 1965-66; tchr. aide Cerro Villa Jr. High Sch., Villa Park, Calif., 1975-76, tchr., 1976-88, Villa Park High Sch., 1988—98, mentor tchr., 1990—97; lectr. Calif. State Univ., Long Beach, 1999—; CA Dir. of Sci. Olympiad, Southern Section, 2000—. Tchr. of yr. com. Orange (Calif.) Unified Sch. Dist., 1992, supt. adv. coun., 1990-1998, curriculum sci. com., 1991-1997. Active Villa Park Womens League, 1975—, Assistance League of Orange, 1991—; project leader, county coord. Orange County 4-H Assn., Anaheim, Calif., 1975-84; bd. sec. Orange County Sci. Fair, 1986-91, awards chmn., 1991-94, pres., 1994—; mem. judging policy adv. com. Calif. State Sci. Fair, 1996-2001. Recipient Outstanding Sci. Tchr. award Orange County Sci. Tchrs. Assn., 1993; named Tchr. of Yr. Villa Park High Sch., 1990, 94, Outstanding Coach Orange County Sci. Olympiad, 1990, 92, 94, 96, Calif. State Sci. Olympiad, 1987. Mem. NSTA (conv. hospitality com. 1989, 90, hospitality co-chair 1994 nat. conv.), Am. Chem. Soc., Calif. Sci. Tchr. Assn., Orange County Sci. Educators Assn. (Disting. Sci. Tchr. award 1993). Roman Catholic. Avocations: tennis, swimming, water skiing, needlepoint. Home: 18082 Rosanne Cir Villa Park CA 92861-6431 Office: CSULB Dept Sci Edn 1250 Bellflower Blvd Long Beach CA 90840-4501

WROBLE, LISA ANN, writer, educator; b. Dearborn, Mich., June 17, 1963; d. Robert Frank and Ruth Marie (Schiller) W. Diploma, Inst. Children's Lit., 1983; BA cum laude, Ea. Mich. U., Ypsilanti, 1985. Cert. ESL tchr., ltd. profl. class B, Libr. Mich. Asst. editor cmty. rels. Vets. Adminstrn., Ann Arbor, Mich., 1983-85; prodn. coord. Cmty. Crier Newspaper/COMMA Graphics, Plymouth, Mich., 1985-86; proofreader Valassis Inserts, Livonia, Mich., 1986-89; tech. writer Nat. TechTeam, Dearborn, Mich., 1989-90; freelance writer Plymouth, 1990—; libr. asst. Redford (Mich.) Dist. Libr., 1996—2002. Publicist Garden City (Mich.) Osteo. Hosp., 1990-91; creative writing instr. Cmty. Edn. Plymouth (Mich.)-Canton Schs., 1992-93, 97-2002, Collier County (Fla.) Schs., 2003—; instr. Inst. of Children's Lit., 2000—. Author: (12 book series) Kids Throughout History, 1997, 98, The Oceans, 1998, How Things Work, Childcraft, vol. 9, 2000, The New Deal in American History, 2002, Danger on Ice, 2003, Nature Recovers, 2003, Firefighters!, 2003; contbg. editor Metroparent, 1991-93; contbg. tech. writer Cleaner Times, 1992-95, Facilities Planning News, 1993-96, FM Data Monthly, 1997-2000, Mich. Learning, 1998—, Wonder Years, Partnership for Learning, 2000—; book rev. editor Parenting Today's Teens, 1998-2001; columnist Christian Libr. Jour., 1999-2002; book reviewer BookPage Promotions, 1997—, The ALAN Rev., 1993—, Christian Libr. Jour., 1997—, The Wonder Years, 2001—; software reviewer Compute Publs., 1989-92, Falsoft Inc., 1991-94; contbr. articles, essays and sects. to reference books, multi-media CD ROMs and textbooks; contbg. writer Eye on the Web, 1998, Bridges CX, 1999-2000, Career Explorer, 1999-2000, Teach-Michigan Found., 1998-2000, Partnership for Learning, 2000—. Tutor Cmty. Literacy Coun., Plymouth, 1989-93; vol. spkr. in schs. Recipient Reading Tutor award Cmty. Literacy Coun., 1991-93. Mem. Soc. Childrens Book Writers and Illustrators (adv. com. mich. chpt. 1993-94, 98-2003, workshop facilitator 1990, 97—, mentorship coord. 2000-03), Internat. Reading Assn., Nat. Writers Assn. (vol. critiquer 1989-93), Fla. Freelance Writers Assn., Childrens Lit. Assn., Mich. Reading Assn., Womens Nat. Book Assn., Text and Acad. Authors Assn., Peninsula Writers, Livonia Writers Group. Republican. Roman Catholic. Avocations: swimming, photography, crafting, cooking, rollerblading. Home and Office: 2614 Fountain View Cir #102 Naples FL 34109-1705 E-mail: lisawtoo@yahoo.com.

WROBLESKI, JEANNE PAULINE, lawyer; b. Phila., Feb. 14, 1942; d. Edward Joseph and Pauline (Popelak) Wrobleski; m. Robert J. Klein, Dec. 3, 1979. BA, Immaculata Coll., 1964; MA, U. Pa., 1966; JD, Temple U., 1975. Bar: Pa. 1975. Pvt. practice law, Phila., 1975—; pres., shareholder Jeanne Wrobleski & Assocs., LLC, Phila., 1999—. Lectr. Bus. Law Wharton Sch., Phila.; mem. Commn. on Women and the Legal Profession, 1986—89; v.p. Center City Residents' Assn.; Eisenhower Citizen Amb. del. Soviet Union; judge Pro Tem Phila. Ct. Common Pleas; bd. dirs. Charlotte Cushman Found. Bd. dirs., mem. exec. com. Temple Law Alumni; del. Moscow Conf. on Law and Econ. Coop., 1990; del. to jud. conf. 3d Cir. U.S. Ct. Appeals, 1991; mediator U.S. Dist. Ct. (ea. dist.) Pa., 1996; bd. trustees Phila. Prisons; Bd. dirs. South St. Dance Co., Women in Transition; bd. dirs., vice chair The Wilma Theater. Rhea Liebman scholar, 1974.

Mem.: ABA, AAUW, Jagiellonian Law Soc. (exec. com.), Am. Judicature Soc., Phila. Bar Assn. (chmn. women's rights com. 1986, com. on jud. selection and retention 1986—87, chmn. appellate cts. com. 1992, bus. cts. task force, com. on bus. litigation), Pa. Bar Assn., Phila. Art Alliance, Nat. Mus. Women in the Arts, Pa. Acad. Fine Arts, Penn Club, Lawyers Club, Founders Club, The Cosmopolitan Club, Lambda Iota Tau, Alpha Psi Omega. Democrat. Office: Jeanne Wrobleski & Assocs LLC 1845 Walnut St Fl 24 Philadelphia PA 19103-4708 Office Phone: 215-814-9320. E-mail: jwrobleski@wwdlaw.com.

WROBLOWA, HALINA STEFANIA, electrochemist; b. Gdansk, Poland, July 5, 1925; came to U.S., 1958, naturalized, 1970; 1 child: Krystyna Wrobel-Knight, grandson Christopher E. Knight. MSc, U. Lodz, Poland, 1949; PhD, Warsaw Inst. Tech., 1958. Chmn. dept. prep. studies U. Lodz, 1950-53; adj. Inst. for Phys., Chemistry Acad. Scis., Warsaw, Poland, 1958-60; dept. dir. electrochemistry lab. energy inst. U. Pa., Phila., 1960-67; dir. electrochemistry lab., 1968-75; prin. research scientist Ford Motor Co., Dearborn, Mich., 1976-91; pvt. practice cons., 1991. Chmn. Gordon Rsch. Conf. on Electrochemistry, 1983. Contbr. chpts. to books, articles to profl. jours., patent lit. Served with Polish Undeground Army, 1943-45, decorated Mil. Silver Cross of Merit with Swords. Mem. Electrochem. Soc., Internat. Electrochem. Soc., Mensa, Sigma Xi. E-mail: chris777@voicenet.com.

WRUBEL, BARBARA, lawyer, educator, former editor; b. N.Y.C., Aug. 16, 1942; d. Harold and Rose (Friedberg) Kolsky; m. Peter Stefan Wrubel, July 30, 1966; 1 dau., Dana. B.A. cum laude, Queens Coll., N.Y.C., 1964; postgrad. U. Calif.-Berkeley, 1964-65; J.D., Fordham U., 1981. Bar: N.Y. 1982, U.S. Dist. Ct. (so. dist.) N.Y. 1982, U.S. Dist. Ct. (ea. dist.) N.Y. 1983. Atty., Skadden, Arps, Slate, Meagher & Flom, N.Y.C., 1981; adj. assoc. prof. law NYU, N.Y.C., 1982—, Fordham U. Sch. Law, N.Y.C., 1981— ; lectr. Am. Law Inst., Practising Law Inst., ABA, 1982— ; editor edn. books, N.Y.C., 1965-78; freelance photographer. Author: (with Leon J. Saul) Psychodynamics of Hostility, 1976; columnist (with Sheila L. Birnbaum) on products liability Nat. Law Jour., 1981— ; contbr. articles to law publs.; editor Law Rev. Fordham U., 1980-81. Mem. Assn. Bar City N.Y., ABA, N.Y. Bar Assn., Fed. Bar Council, Women's Bar Assn. State N.Y. Home: 351 E 84th St New York NY 10028-4423 Office: Skadden Arps Slate Meagher & Flom 4 Times Sq Fl 24 New York NY 10036-6595

WU, SUSAN YING CHU LIN (YING-CHU LIN), engineering company executive, engineer; b. Beijing, June 23, 1932; came to U.S., 1957; d. Chi-yu and K.C. (Kung) Lin; m. Jain-Ming Wu, June 13, 1959; children: Ernest H., Albert H., Karen H. BSME, Nat. Taiwan U., 1955; MS in Aero. Engring., Ohio State U., 1959; PhD in Aeros., Calif. Inst. Tech., 1963. Sr. engr. Elecro-Optical Systems, Inc., Pasadena, Calif., 1963-65; asst. prof. aero. engring. U. Tenn. Space Inst., Tullahoma, 1965-67, assoc. prof., 1967-73, prof., 1973-88; adminstr. Energy Conversion R&D Programs, Tullahoma, 1981-88; pres., chief exec. officer ERC, Inc., Huntsville, Ala., 1987-2000, chmn., 2000—. Presdl. appointee adv. bd. Nat. Air and Space Mus., Smithsonian Inst., 1993-2000. Contbr. over 90 articles to profl. jours. Mem. Better Sch. Task Force, Tullahoma, 1985-86; founding mem. Tullahoma Edn. Found. for Excellence, trustee Rochester Inst. Tech., 1992-94; mem. adv. com. NASA Aeronautics and Space Transp. Tech., 1994-2000. Recipient Chancellor's Rsch. award U. Tenn., 1978, Outstanding Educator of Am. [illegible] 1959, 60, 62, Plasmadynamics and Lasers award AIAA, 1994, Faraday Meml. medal Internat. Liaison Group for MHD Pow Generation, 1999. Fellow ASME, AIAA (assoc.); mem. Soc. Women Engrs. (hon., life; achievement award 1985), Sigma Xi. Office: ERC Inc 555 Sparkman Dr NW Ste 1622 Huntsville AL 35816-3431 E-mail: swu@erc-incorporated.com.

WU-CHU, STELLA CHWENYEA, nutritionist, consultant; b. Kaohsiung, Taiwan, Sept. 22, 1952; came to U.S., 1976; d. Jin-Shoui and Sue-Tuan (Ling) Wu; children: Christine, Whitney. BS, Fu-Jen Cath. U., Taiwan, 1974; MA, San Francisco State U., 1979. Registered dietitian. Intership U. Calif., Berkeley, 1978; food svc. supr. Calif. Surgery Hosp., Oakland, 1979—80; nutritionist, cons. Solano Napa Agy. on Aging, Vallejo, Calif., 1980—; nutrition cons. Marin County Div. of Aging, San Rafael, Calif., 1981—; nutritionist San Francisco Commn. on Aging, 1990—, nutrition cons. Contra Costa Office on Aging, 1995—. Mem. adv. bd. Staying Health project Am. Soc. on Aging, 1999—2000; nutritional advisor Veggie Life Mag., Walnut Creek, Calif., 1993, Salt Free Cooking Made Easy. Chief editor quar. publ. Taiwanese Assn. publ., 1991-94. Cmty. liaison East Bay Taiwanese Assn., Walnut Creek, 1992-93; v.p. No. Calif. Formosan Fedn., 1993; dist. supportive com. chair United Meth. Women, 1995-97, Bayview dist. social actions mission coord., 1997-98; adv. bd. Overseas Chinese Inst. on Aging, 2000—, Am. Soc. Aging, 2000. Mem. Am. Dietetic Assn., Am. Pub. Health Assn., Jacob Inst. of Women's Health, Nat. Assn. Nutrition and Aging Svcs., Formosan Assn. for Pub. Affairs, Am. Assn. of Meals on Wheels. Avocations: reading, concerts, dance, creative writing (in chinese). Home: 70 Seabreeze Dr Richmond CA 94804-7410 Office: San Francisco Commn Aging 25 Van Ness Ave Ste 650 San Francisco CA 94102 6057 E-mail: stellawc@aol.com.

WUDUNN, SHERYL, journalist, correspondent; b. N.Y.C., Nov. 16, 1959; d. David and Alice (Mark) WuDunn; m. Nicholas D. Kristof, Oct. 8, 1988. BA, Cornell U., Ithaca, N.Y., 1981; MBA, Harvard U., 1986; MPA, Princeton U., 1988. Lending officer Bankers Trust Co., N.Y.C., 1981—84; intern reporter Wall St. Jour., L.A., 1986; bus. reporter South China Morning Post, Hong Kong, 1987; corr. N.Y. Times, Beijing, 1989—93, Tokyo, 1995—99, exec. dir. Nexgen group N.Y.C., 1999—. Co-author: China Wakes, 1994, Thunder From the East, 2000. Recipient Pulitzer Prize for fgn. reporting, 1990, George Polk award, L.I. U., N.Y., 1990, Hal Boyle award, Overseas Press Club, 1990. Avocations: aerobics, singing. Office: Nexgen Group The New York Times 229 W 43rd St New York NY 10036

WUETIG, JOYCE LINDA, realtor; b. Little Rock, Feb. 11, 1938; d. John Clifford and Viva Emily (Summerhill) Dilbeck; m. James Russell McKinney, Aug. 30, 1958 (div. Sept. 1981); children: Melissa Ellen, James Blake; m. Frederick Lewis Wuetig, June 1, 1985. BA, Hendrix Coll., 1959; postgrad., Incarnate Word Coll., 1970-072. Cert. residential specialist; lic. real estate broker, Tex., Ark. Tchr. Little Rock Sch. Dist., 1959-62; fashion cons. Doncaster, Inc., San Antonio, 1975-83; tchr. Edgewood Ind. Sch. Dist., San Antonio, 1982-83; sales assoc. Dijon Plaza Realtors, San Antonio, 1978-83; relocation specialist HEB Grocery Co., San Antonio, 1981-82; asst. v.p. Independence Fed. Bank, Little Rock, 1984-85; sales assoc. Agar Realtors, Little Rock, 1986-89; broker assoc., cert. residential specialist McKay & Co. Residential Realtors, Little Rock, 1989-98; accredited buyer rep. Ebby Halliday Realtors, Colleyville and Southlake, Tex., 1998—. Mem. com. Southwest Found. Forum, San Antonio, 1975-81; chmn. San Antonio Kitchen Tour, 1977-80; host mother, area activities chmn. Am. Field Svc., San Antonio, 1975-76, 77-78; life mem. Tex. PTA. Mem.: DAR, AAUW, Southlake C. of C. (leadership ambassador com.), Ebby Halliday Realtors Platinum Plateau, Little Rock Realtors Assn., N.E. Tarrant County Bd. Realtors, Tex. Realtors Assn., Ark. Realtors Assn., Nat. Assn. Realtors, Little Rock Realtors Million Dollar Club (licentiate). Methodist. Home: 1310 Regency Ct Southlake TX 76092-9516 Office Phone: 817-410-9990. Personal E-mail: jfwuetig@earthlink.net.

WUGHALTER, EMILY HOPE, physical education educator; b. Bklyn., Nov. 24, 1954; d. Milton and Leah (Isaacs) W. BA in Phys. Edn. and Teaching, CUNY, 1977; MS in Phys. Edn. and Motor Learning, Univ. Colo., 1978; EdD, U. Ga., 1981. Tchr. math. COMPASS House, N.Y.C.; tchr. phys. edn. St. Pius. High Sch., Bronx, Hebrew Acad. of West Queens, 1976-77; instr. Boulder City Parks and Recreation, 1977; grad. asst. Univ. Ga., 1978-81; assoc. prof. NYU, 1981-91; prof. San Jose Univ., 1991—. Measurement, design, and evaluation cons. N.Y. Alliance for the Pub. Schs.; phys. fitness evaluator N.Y.C. Affiliate Am. Heart Assn.; exercise science trainer Young Women's Christian Assn. Author: (with A.L. Rothstein) Basic Stuff Series I- Motor Learning, 1987; contbr. articles to profl. jours. Recipient Recognition award N.Y.C., 1989 and 1990, Mable Lee award, 1992; Curricular Change grantee N.Y.U., 1987, 91, Spencer Found. Young Scholars Rsch. award grantee, 1982-83, and numerous others. Mem. Am. Alliance of Health, Phys. Edn., Recreation, and Dance, Am. Coll. of Sports Medicine, Am. Edn. Rsch. Assn., Nat. Assn. for Phys. Edn. in Higher Edn., Nat. Women's Studies Assn., Western Soc. for Phys. Edn. Coll. Women, No. Am. Soc. for the Study of Psychol. of Sport and Phys. Activity, Calif. Assn. of Health, Phys. Edn. Recreation and Dance. Home: 358 Hihn St Felton CA 95018-9201 Address: San Jose Univ Dept of Human Performance 1 Washington Sq San Jose CA 95192-0001

WULF, SHARON ANN, management consultant; b. New Bedford, Mass., Aug. 23, 1954; d. Daniel Thomas and Norma Dorothy (McCabe) Vieira; m. Stanley A. Wulf, 1983. BS in Acctg. cum laude, Providence Coll., 1976; MBA, Northeastern U., 1977; PhD, Columbia Pacific U., 1984. Staff acct., intern Laventhol & Horwath, Providence, 1977; jr. fin. analyst Polaroid Corp., Waltham, Mass., 1977-78, fin. analyst Freetown, Mass., 1978-79, Cambridge, Mass., 1979-81; sr. fin. cons., mktg. strategic planner Digital Equipment Corp., Stow, Mass., 1981-82, Maynard, Mass., 1982-83, mgr. fin. devel. program, 1983-84, strategic fin. cons. engring. divsn., 1984-86, group mgr. planning & strategic ops. Hudson, Mass., 1986-87, group mgr. strategic bus. planning, 1987-89; mktg. planning mgr. Diigital Equipment Corp., Marlboro, Mass., 1989-90, new ventures bus. devel. mgr., 1990-92; pres. Enterprise Sytems, Framingham, Mass., 1993—; sr. instr. Cambridge Coll., 1997—, prof., 1998—. Lectr. fin. acctg. Southeastern Mass. U., 1979—81; adj. prof. acctg., mgmt. & fin., knowledge mgmt. strategies Northeastern U., Boston, 1980—; instr. Nat. Tech. U ., 1991—95; instr., vis. asst. prof. mgmt. Framingham State Coll., 1999—; exec. com. enterprise forum MIT, 1987—92, lectr. network leadership workshop, 2003; prin. Work Sys. Assocs., Inc., Marlborough, Mass., 1992—93; bd. advisors Spaceball Tech., Inc., Lowell, Mass., Terasys., Inc.; sr. faculty advisor healthcare master's degree program Mass. Gen. Hosp., 2000—02; cons. in field; keynote spkr. CRMA, 2003, FLMI, 2003, IFMA, 2004. Author: Building Performance Values, 1996, Customer Service Action Plans, 1997, Leadership in Action: The Way It Is Cersus The Way It Should Be, 1997. Chair pub. support and fund raising ARC, New Bedford, 1974-84; bd. dirs. Vets. Outreach Ctr., Metrowest, Framingham, 1989-93; v.p. MIT Leadership Found., Cambridge, 1991-93; mem. exec. com. MIT Enterprise Forum, also co-chair stant up clinics, 1986-92. Mem. Black Alumni of MIT (bd. advisors 1989-92), Univ. Coll. Faculty Soc., Phi Sigma Tau. Home: 902 Salem End Rd Framingham MA 01702-5532 Office: Enterprise Systems 1257 Worcester Rd Ste 301 Framingham MA 01701-5217 Fax: 508-626-9038. E-mail: sharonw@enters.com.

WULFF, JULIE BADER, purchasing agent; b. St. Louis, May 17, 1963; d. Frederick Raymond and Eileen Elizabeth (Thompson) Bader; m. Robert Joseph Wulff, Nov. 11, 1995. BSChemE, U. Mo., 1985; MBA, U. Mo., St. Louis, 1996. Process engr. Procter & Gamble Paper Co., Cape Girardeau, Mo., 1985-89; making prodn. mgr. Procter & Gamble Mfg. Co., St. Louis, 1989-91, reliability dept. mgr., 1991-94, quality dept. mgr., 1994—98, plant purchasing mgr., 1998—. Tutor St. Louis Literary Coun., 1991-93; bd. dirs. Jr. C. of C., St. Louis, 1994-95. Recipient [illegible] award, 1996; Enterprise Leasing scholar, U. Mo., St. Louis, 1995. Mem. Inst. for Supply Mgmt., Phi Kappa Phi, Beta Gamma Sigma, Alpha Mu Alpha. Avocations: snow skiing, reading, step aerobics, traveling.

WULFF, VIRGINIA MCMILLAN, association executive; b. Glendale, Calif., May 27, 1958; d. Reginald Joseph and Virginia Ellen (Cavett) McMillan; m. Robert Reid Wulff, June 20, 1981; children: Kellyn Melissa, Katharine Cooper, Kyle Reid. BA in English with honors, Stanford U., 1980. Prodn. mgr. Addison Wesley/Benjamin Cummings Pub., Menlo Park, Calif., 1980-82; ways and means chair Oak Elem. PTA, Los Altos, Calif., 1988-89, pres., 1990-91, Los Altos/Mountain View PTA Coun., Los Altos, 1992-93; v.p. coms. Sixth Dist. PTA, San Jose, Calif., 1995-99, editor The Bell, 1995-99. Sec., mem. exec. bd. Peninsula Youth Theatre, Mountain View, Calif., 1994—; pres. San Juan Sensations Team, Los Altos, 1995—. Editor: The Bell, 1995-98. Oak chair Measure A Com., Los Altos, 1993, 95, 97; mem. parcel taxes bond measure coms. Los Altos Elem.; mem. Mountain View/Los Altos H.S. Dist. Bond Com., 1996, 97; lead parent rep. Castilleja Sch., 1998—; legislation chair Blach PTA, 1999—, Sixth Dist. PTA, San Jose, CA, 1995-98. Mem. AAUW. Home: 136 Waverly Pl Mountain View CA 94040-4573

WULKE, JOY, artist; b. San Bernardino, Calif., May 23, 1948; d. Harold and Minnie-Lou (Sisson) W.; m. David Connell, Sept. 11, 1983; 1 child, Gioia Montana. BA in Architecture, Wash. State U., 1970; M Environ. Design, Yale U., 1974. Owner, mgr. Old Mole Art Coop., Pullman, Wash., 1970-71; owner, designer, artist Fiberworks, 1972-76, Joy Wulke Studio Art & Design, Stony Creek, Conn., 1976—. Seminar instr. Yale U. New Haven, 1974; product designer Dansk, Armonk, N.Y., 1975-79, GEAR & Schumacher, N.Y.C., 1978-80; assoc. prof. Mont. State U., Bozeman, 1981-83; mem. adj. faculty RISD, Providence, 1983-85; mem. guest faculty Glastgow (Scotland) Sch. Art, 1988; founding dir. Projects for New Millennium, Stony Creek, 1993—; environ. and space cons. Tchr. Ctr., Inc., New Haven, 1973-98; mem. adv. coun. Wash. State U. Sch. Architecture, Pullman, 1995—; cons. on pub. art Conn. Commn. on Arts, Hartford, 1980—. Group exhbns. include Wadsworth Atheneaum Gallery of the Senses, Hartford, Conn., 1981, NYU, 1992, Lyman Allyn Museum, New London, Conn., 1992, San Bernardino County Museum, 1993, Delaware Ctr. for Contemporary Art, Wilmington, 1995, Urban Glass, Bklyn., 1996, Rockville (Md.) Arts Place, 1999, Discovery Museum, Bridgeport, 2000; commd. works include La. World's Fair, New Orleans, 1984, Lincoln Ctr. Film forum, N.Y.C., 1991, Middlesex Hosp., Middletown, conn., 1994, Mont. State U., Missoula, 1996, Cermack Plaza, Chgo., 1998, So. Conn. State U., New haven, 2000. Bd. dirs. David Bermant Found., Santa Barbara, Calif., 1989-98; mem. cultural planning coun. Greater N.H. Arts Coun., New Haven, 1997—. Grantee Conn. Commn. on Arts, 1986—, Comm. Found. Greater New Haven, 1996, New Eng. Found. for Arts, 1994. Avocations: travel, photography, installations in abandoned buildings using light and reflection. Home: 26 Prospect Hill Rd Branford CT 06405-5711

WULTICH, DONNA MARIE, sales professional; b. Washington, Oct. 11, 1958; d. Nicholas and Helen Catherine (Kenny) W. BS in Comm., James Madison U., 1982. Sales staff Western Union, Washington and McLean, Va., 1982-84, ITT, Washington, 1984-88, Software AG, Reston, Va., 1989-94, sales mgr., 1994—. Mem. Wolftrap Found. (vol., curtain raiser), Washington Ski Club, Ashlburn Singles Club (founder). Avocations: whitewater rafting, hiking, biking, camping. Home: 44062 Parliamentary Sq Ashburn VA 20147-4927 Office: Software AG Americas 11190 Sunrise Valley Dr Reston VA 20191-5453

WUNDER, HAROLDENE FOWLER, taxation educator; b. Greenville, S.C., Nov. 16, 1944; d. Harold Eugene Fowler and Sarah Ann (Chaffin) Crooks. BS, U. Md., 1971; M Acctg., U. S.C., 1975, PhD, 1978. Vis. asst. prof. U. S.C., Columbia, 1977-78; asst. prof. U. Pa., Phila., 1978-81; vis. asst. prof. U. N.C., Chapel Hill, 1981-82; asst. prof. U. Mass., Boston, 1982-86; vis. assoc. prof. Suffolk U., Boston, 1986-87; assoc. prof. U. Toledo, 1987—93; prof. Calif. State U., Sacramento, 1993—. Contbr. articles to profl. and acad. jours. Fellow George Olson fellowship, 1975. Mem.: AICPA, Nat. Tax Assn., Am. Taxation Assn., Am. Acctg. Assn., Calif. Soc. CPAs, Beta Gamma Sigma. Avocation: reading. Office: Calif State U Sch Bus Adminstrn Sacramento CA 95819-6088 Business E-Mail: wunderh@csus.edu.

WUNDERMAN, JAN DARCOURT, artist; b. Winnipeg, Man., Can., Jan. 22, 1921; d. Rene Paul and Georgette Marie (Guionet) Darcourt; m. Frank Joseph Malina, 1938 (div. 1945); m. Lester Wunderman (div. 1967); children: Marc, Geroge, Karen Renee. BFA, Otis Art Inst., L.A., 1942. One man shows include Easthampton Guild Hall, L.I., 1977, Denise Bibro Fine Art Gallery, N.Y.C., 1996-98, 2002, Roko Gallery, 1963, 66, 68, 71, 73, 76; represented in numerous permanent pub., corp. and pvt. collections including Zimmerli Mus., NYU Loeb Collection, Norfolk Mus., Alfred Kouri Collection, Skidmore Coll. Print Collection, Nat. Assn. of Women Artists, Rutgers U., 1994, Albright Knox Mus., 1998-99, Daimler Chrysler Coll., Germany, 2002, abstract-nonrepresentational. Recipient Ohashi award Pan Pacific Exhbn., Tokyo and Osaka, 1962, Emily Lowe award 1965, J.J. Akston Found. prize, 1965, Canaday Meml. prize, 1979, Marian De Solo Mendes prize, 1981, Charles Horman Meml. prize, 1983, Amelia Peabody award Nat. Assn. Women, 1991, Grumbacher Gold medal of honor, 1992, Doris Kreindler award 1992. Mem. Nat. Assn. Women Artists (medal of honor 1966, Marcia Brady Tucker award 1965, E. Holzinger prize 1966, Jane C. Stanley prize 1977, Marge Greenblatt award 1990, Amelia Peabody award 1991, Solveig Stomsoe Palmer prize 1997), Am. Soc. Contemporary Artists (corr. sec. 1977-78, Bocour award 1980, Elizabeth Erlanger Meml. award 1990, Kreindler award 1992, N. Ransom award 2002), Contemporary Artists Guild (rep. by Denise Bibro Fine Art N.Y.C., Irwin Zlowe Meml. award 1998). Avocations: history, travel. Studio: 41 Union Sq W Rm 516 New York NY 10003-3208 Office Phone: 212-989-9197.

WUNNICKE, BROOKE, lawyer; b. Dallas, May 9, 1918; d. Rudolph von Falkenstein and Lulu Lenore Brooke; m. James M. Wunnicke, Apr. 11, 1940; (dec. 1977); 1 child, Diane B. BA, Stanford U., 1939; JD, U. Colo., 1945. Bar: Wyo. 1946, Colo. 1969, U.S. Dist. Ct. Wyo. 1947, U.S. Dist. Ct. Colo. 1970, U.S. Supreme Ct. 1958, U.S. Ct. Appeals (10th cir.) 1958. Pvt. practice law, 1946-56; ptnr. Williams & Wunnicke, Cheyenne, Wyo., 1956-69; of counsel Calkins, Kramer, Grimshaw & Harring, Denver, 1969-73; chief appellate dep. atty. Dist. Atty's Office, Denver, 1973-86; of counsel Hall & Evans L.L.C., Denver, 1986—. Adj. prof. law U. Denver Coll. of Law, 1978-97; lectr. Internat. Practicum Inst. Denver, 1978-2003. Author: (book) Ethics Compliance for Business Lawyers, 1987; co-author: Standby Letters of Credit, 1989, Corporate Financial Risk Management, 1992, Legal Opinion Letters Formbook, 2002, 2004, UCP 500 and Standby Letters of Credit-Special Report, 1994, Standby and Commercial Letters of Credit, 1996, 2000, 2004; contbr. articles. Pres. Laramie County Bar Assn., Cheyenne, Wy., 1967-68; Dir. Cheyenne C. of C., Cheyenne, Wy., 1965-68. Named 1st Frank H. Ricketson Jr. Adj. Prof., U. Denver Coll. Law, 1997; recipient awards for outstanding svc., Colo. Dist. Attys. Coun., 1979, 1982, 1986, Disting. Alumni award, U. Colo. Sch. of Law, 1986, 1993, Lathrop Trailblazer award, Colo. Women's Bar Assn., 1992, William Lee Knous award, U. Colo. Sch. Law, 1997, Eleanor P. Williams award for disting. svc. to legal profession, 1997, Potter Lifetime Profl. Svc. award, 1999, Def. Rsch. Inst. Nat. award, 1999, Law Star award, U. Denver Coll. Law, 2003. Fellow Colo. Bar Found. (hon.); mem. ABA, Wyo. State Bar, Denver Bar Assn. (hon. life; trustee 1977-80, award of merit), Colo. Bar Assn. (hon., life, Award of Merit 1999), Am. Arbitration Assn. (nat. panel, regional panel), William E. Doyle Inn of Ct. (hon.), Order of Coif, Phi Beta Kappa. Republican. Avocations: reading, writing, teaching, lecturing. Office: Hall & Evans LLC 1125 17th St Ste 600 Denver CO 80202-2037

WUNSCH, KATHRYN SUTHERLAND, retired lawyer; b. Tipton, Mo., Jan. 30, 1935; d. Lewis Benjamin and Norene Marie (Wolf) Sutherland; m. Charles Martin Wunsch, Dec. 22, 1956 (div. May 1988); children: Debra Kay Wolff, Laura Ellen Stubberud. AB, Ind. U., 1958, JD summa cum laude, 1977; postgrad., Stanford (Calif.) U., 1977. Founder Wunsch and George, San Francisco, 1989-93, Kathryn Wunsch and Assoc. Counsel, San Francisco, 1993-99; ret., 1999. Articles editor Ind. U. Law Rev., 1975-76. Trustee Minuteman Found., 2002—03; founder, pres. Sun City Anthem Lifelong Learning Ctr., 2004—. Mem. Sun City Anthem Garden Club (founder, pres. 2001—), Phi Beta Kappa. Republican. Avocations: collecting fine art and antiques, theater, opera, gardening, hiking.

WURTH, PATSY ANN, geographic information systems specialist; b. Paducah, Ky., Dec. 5, 1947; d. James Edward and Olean Barbara (Sirls) W.; m. Jerry Leon Scarbrough, Aug. 7, 1965 (div. 1985); children: Tracy Ann, Ashli Michele, Scott Jeremy; m. Robert W. Luther, Feb. 25, 1995 (div. 1998). BS magna cum laude, Murray (Ky.) State U., 1988, MS, 1991. Cert. EMT. Instr. Ky. Cabinet for Human Resources, Frankfort, 1983-93, Vocat. Edn. Region I, Paducah, Ky., 1983-91, Murray State U., 1983-91, Calloway County Red Cross, Murray, 1985-89; exec. dir. Marshall County Red Cross, Benton, Ky., 1985-88; profl. intern Johnson Controls, Cadiz, Ky., 1986; grad. asst. Murray State U., 1988-91; fellow U.S. Dept. Energy/Oak Ridge (Tenn.) Nat. Lab., 1989-90; rsch. fellow U.S. Army Corps Engrs. Constrn. Engring. Rsch. Lab., Champaign, Ill., 1991-92, acting team leader spatial techs. support team, 1992-93; GIS facility mgr. environ. scis. divsn. Oak Ridge (Tenn.) Nat. Lab., 1993-95; mgr. GIS svcs. Solutions to Environ. Problems, Inc., Oak Ridge, 1995-96, Aegis Svcs. Corp., Clinton, Tenn., 1996-97; GIS program coord. Roane State C.C., Oak Ridge, 1996—; GIS program mgr. Sci. Applications Internat. Corp., Oak Ridge, Tenn., 1998—2001. Exec. dir. Marshall County Red Cross, Benton, Ky., 1985-88; first aid attendant Ohio River Steel, Calvert City, Ky., 1985-86. Troop leader Kentuckiana Girl Scouts, Benton, 1973-84, fund drive chair, 1973-84. Mem. LWV, Am. Soc. Safety Engrs., Ky. EMT Instrs. Assn. (instr.), Western Ky. EMT Assn., Am. Soc. Photogrametry and Remote Sensing (Western Great Lake region sec.-treas. 1992), Nat. Safety Coun. (cmty. health and emergency svcs. com.), Assn. Women in Sci., Women in Tech. and Sci. (chmn. 1997-98), Tenn. Geog. Info. Coun. (bd. dirs. 1997-2000), S.E. Regional ESRI Users Group (chair 1995), Nat. Assn. Environ. Profls., Oak Ridge Area ESRI Users Group (chmn. 1996-2000), Epsilon Pi Tau, Alpha Chi. Democrat. Roman Catholic. Home: 330 Melton Hill Dr Clinton TN 37716-7106 Office: Roane State CC 701 Briarcliff Ave Oak Ridge TN 37830

WURTMAN, JUDITH JOY, research scientist; b. Bklyn., Aug. 4, 1939; d. Alexander Mordecai and Jeanette Teicher Hirschhorn; m. Richard Jay Wurtman; children: Rachael, David. BA, Wellesely (Mass.) Coll., 1959; MA in Biology Edn., Harvard U., 1960; PhD, George Washington U., 1973. Tchr. Malden Sch. System, 1959-60; rsch. asst. Microbiol. Assocs., Bethesda, Md., 1962-67; exhibit researcher Boston Mus. Sci., 1973-74; asst. prof. Newton (Mass.) Coll., 1974-76; postdoctoral fellow dept. nutrition MIT, Cambridge, 1976-78, rsch. scientist dept. nutrition, dept. brain and cognitive sci., 1987—2002; program dir. Triad Weight Mgmt. Ctr., McLean Hosp., 1998—2002; dir. women's health program MIT Clin. Rsch. Ctr., 2002—; founder Adara Ctr. Weight Control, 2002—; dir. women's health program MIT Clin. Rsch. Ctr., Cambridge. Mem. sci. adv. bd. NutriSystem, Phila., 1988-89, Interneuron Pharms., Boston, 1989-98; bd. dirs. Walden Labs; scientific advisor Internutria, Framingham, 1994—; founder Adara Weight Loss Ctr., 2001. Author: Eating Your Way Through Life, 1979, The Carbohydrate Craver's Diet, 1983, The Carbohydrate Craver's Diet Cookbook, 1984, Managing Your Mind and Mood Through Food, 1987; editor: Nutrition and the Brain (8 vols.), 1983—, The Serotonin Solution, 1996; columnist efit.com, 2000—. Mem. bd. overseers Boston Lyric Opera, 1996-2002; bd. dirs. Women's Indsl. and Ednl. Union, 2001--, Temple Beth Zion, 2001--; bd. visitors Hebrew Coll., 1996—. Mem. Am. Inst. Nutrition, Am. Dietitic Assn., Am. Soc. for Clin. Nutrition, Boston Soc. Psychiatry and Neurology, Soc. for Light Treatment and Biol. Rhythms, Sigma Xi. Office: MIT Dept of Brain and Cognitive Scis E25-604 Cambridge MA 02139 also: Adara Weight Mgmt Ctr 20 Park Plz Boston MA 02116 E-mail: frieda@mit.edu.

WURTZ, MARGARET JOHNSTON, artist, calligrapher; b. Yonkers, N.Y., Feb. 19, 1930; d. James and Leontine (Orbanes) Johnston; m. Elmer S. Wurtz, May 5, 1951; children: Marguerite, Raymond, Eileen, James, Jeanette. BA, Molloy U., 1973; MA/LS, SUNY Stonybrook, 1985. Art [illegible] St. Joseph, Babylon, N.Y., 1963-80; freelance artist and calligrapher Babylon, 1980—; propr. Marline Designer Shirts, Bolton Landing, NY, 1986-90. Student workshops Soc. of Scribes, N.Y.C., 1984—; active artist/exhibitor Wet Paints, Sayville, N.Y., 1994—. Artist fabric collage, 1985, pastel painting, 1998-2003. Vol. L.I. Maritime Mus., 1998—, St. Lawrence Soup Kitchen, Sayville, N.Y., 1998—, St. Patrick Soup Kitchen, Bay Shore, N.Y., 1995-2002, Cabinet for Sick, Sayville, 2003—. Mem. Sumpwams Garden Club (various awards 1985-2003). Roman Catholic. Avocations: gardening, piano, golf, bicycling, boating. Home: 15 Poplar St Sayville NY 11782-3116

WURZBACH, LINDA, educational consultant; b. San Antonio, Jan. 21, 1954; d. Delmar Earl Wurzbach, Dorothy Lang Wurzbach; m. Mark Allison Tatom. BS, U. Tex., 1975, MEd, 1978. Lic. tchr. Tex. Tchr. Austin Indep. Sch. Dist., Austin, Tex., 1976—81; project mgr. Tex. Sch. for the Blind and Visually Impaired, Austin, 1981—82, tchr., 1982—89; project dir. The Psychol. Corp., San Antonio, 1989—90; planner Tex. Edn. Agy., Austin, 1990—96; sr. project assoc. Coun. Chief State Sch. Officers, Washington, 1996—98; pres. Resources for Learning, Austin, 1998—. Cons. Tex. Edn. Agy., Austin, 1998—, Region 20 Edn. Svc. Ctr., San Antonio, 1998—, State Bd. Educator Cert., Austin, 1998—, Calif. Comm. Tchr. Credentialing, Sacramento, 1998—2000, Alain Locke Charter Acad., Chgo., 1998—99, Ill. State Bd. Edn., Springfield, Ill., 1998—99, Ky. Profl. Standards Bd., Frankfort, 1999—2000, Region 13 Edn. Svc. Ctr., Austin, 2000—, Region 18 Edn. Svc. Ctr., Midland, 2002—03, Chgo. Children's Choir, 2000—00, Parks and Recreation Dept., Austin, 2001—02, Charles A. Dana Ctr., U. Tex., Austin, 2001, Inner-City Tchg. Corps, Chgo., S.W. Ednl. Devel. Lab., 2002—, Okla. Commn. Tchr. Preparation, 2003—, La. State Dept. Edn., 2003—, N.Mex. State Dept. Edn. and U. Mex., 2003—. Editor: TxBESS Activity Profile, 2001, Fine Arts Curriculum Frameworks, 2000; author: Works in Progress, 1997, Portfolio Assessment for Beginning Teachers, 1999, Performance Assessment System, 2000; prodr.: (video) If You Love It, Teach It., 2000, Express Yourself, 2001, Fine Arts for All Students, 2003, Beginning Teacher Induction Toolkit: A Systems Approach, 2004; contbr. articles to profl. jous. Mem.: U.S. Women's C. of C., Internat. Game Developers Assn., Nat. Coun. Measurement in Edn., Am. Ednl. Rsch. Assn., Nat. Staff Devel. Coun., Assn. Supervision and Curriculum Develop. Home: 4504 Moose Dr Austin TX 78749 Office: Resources for Learning Bldg A Ste 103 206 Wild Basin Rd Austin TX 78746 Office Phone: 512-327-8576. Office Fax: 512-327-8577. Business E-Mail: lindaw@resourcesforlearning.net.

WUTHRICK, EILEEN B. special education educator; b. Salem, Ohio, Aug. 29, 1949; d. Frederick Christian and Effie Marie Wuthrick. BA, Mt. Union Coll., 1973; EdM, Kent State U., 1996, Ednl. Specialist degree, 2003. Cert. tchg. Dept. Edn., Ohio, edn. handicapped K-12, learning disabled K-12, severe behavior handicapped K-12, reading K-12, visual art K-12, elem. 1-8, adminstrv. specialist. Art tchr. Carrollton (Ohio) Exempted Village Sch., 1975—77, West Br. Local Schs., Beloit, Ohio, 1977—78; spl. edn. tchr. Alliance (Ohio) City Schs., 1978—86, Marlington Local Schs., Alliance, 1986—. Spkr. in field. Contbr. articles to profl. jours. Grantee, Martha Holden Jennings Found., 2001—02; Bank One Ednl. grantee, 2001—02. Mem.: Coun. for Exceptional Children, NEA, Ohio Edn. Assn., Phi Delta Kappa. Avocations: painting, drawing, music, gardening, skiing.

WYATT, JENNIFER LYNNE, director; b. Ft. Belvoir, Va., Dec. 17, 1966; d. Lonnie W. Wyatt, Jr. and Evelyn H. Wyatt; children: Savannah Leigh Parris, Carolina Paige Parris. BA, U. N.C., Asheville, 1988; MS, Western Carolina U., 1999; postgrad., N.C. State U., 2001—. Nat. cert. counselor Nat. Bd. Cert. Counselors, 1999. Basic skills instr. Asheville-Buncombe Tech. C.C., 1995—96, assessment/retention specialist, 1996—99; dean acad. affairs South Coll., Asheville, 1999—2002; dir. undergraduate acad. svcs. Appalachian State U., Boone, NC, 2003—. Mem.: ACA, Nat. Acad. Advising Assn. Avocation: reading. Office: Appalachian State Univ CAS 100 IG Greer Hall Boone NC 28608 E-mail: wyattjl@appstate.edu.

WYATT, JUDITH LOIS, psychotherapist, consultant; b. Chgo., June 9, 1946; d. Joseph and Anne Wyatt; m. David Alan Henderson, Dec. 24, 1967 (div. Mar. 1979); m. Chauncey Ross Hare, Sept. 17, 1989. BA, U. Chgo., 1969; MS in Counseling, San Francisco State U., 1983. Cert. MFT BBS CA 1984. Peer counselor Changes, Chgo., 1973—74; pvt. workshop leader San Francisco, 1974—77, 2001—02; counselor, psychotherapy Fort Help Counseling Ctr., San Francisco, 1977—84; pvt. practice marriage and family therapy San Francisco, 1983—; orgn. cons. Fort Help Counseling Ctr., San Francisco, 1984; trainer HUD, Social Sec., Forest Svc., San Francisco, 1986. Author: Understanding Work Abuse, 1989; co-author: Work Abuse: How to Recognize, 1997. Mem.: Calif. Assn. Marriage and Family Therapy, Internat. Bioenergetic Assn., Internat. Soc. Study Dissociation, Phi Beta Kappa. Avocations: writing, poetry, dance.

WYATT, LENORE, civic worker; b. N.Y.C., June 12, 1929; d. Benedict S. Rosenfeld and Ora (Copel) Kanner; m. Bernard D. Copeland, May 17, 1953 (dec. March 1968); children: Harry (dec.), Robert (dec.); m. C. Wyatt Unger, Mar. 26, 1969 (dec. Feb. 1992); 1 child, Amy Unger; m. F. Lowry Wyatt, Sept. 12, 1992 (dec. Nov. 1996). Student, Mills Coll., 1946-48; BA, Stanford U., 1950, MA, 1952; postgrad., NYU, 1952-53. Instr. Stanford U., Palo Alto, Calif., 1952, Hunter Coll., N.Y.C., 1952-53, Calif. State U., Sacramento, 1956-60, U. Calif., Davis, 1965-69; property mgr. Unger, Demas & Markakis, Sacramento, 1974-83. Former actress and model; fin. com. Charles Wright Acad.; fin. mgr. several trusts. Pres. Sacramento Opera Assn., 1972—73; treas. Sacramento Children's Home, 1990—92, v.p., 1992—; former mem. bd. dirs. Sutter Hosp. Aux., Sutter Hosp. Med. Rsch. Found., Sacramento Symphony League, Temple B'nai Israel Sisterhood, Sacramento chpt. Hadassah, Sacramento Children's Home Guild; formerly active Sacramento Opera Assn., Crocker Soc. of Crocker Art Gallery, Sacramento Symphony Assn., Sacramento Reportory Theater Assn.; founding mem. Tacoma Cmtys. Art Sch.; past mem. bd. dirs. Charles Wright Acad.; past mem., bd. dirs. Tacoma Art Mus. Mem.: Stanford U. Alumni Assn. (past bd. dirs. Sacramento), Sacramento Pioneer Assn., Am. Contract Bridge League, Del Paso Country Club (past capt. women's golf group, Sacramento), Thunderbird Country Club, Tacoma Club, Wash. Athletic Club, Maui Country Club, Tacoma Country and Golf Club, Sutter Club. Republican. Jewish. Avocations: golf, duplicate bridge. Home: 70551 Placerville Rd Rancho Mirage CA 92270

WYATT, MARCIA JEAN, fine arts educator, administrative assistant; b. Petersburg, Va., Nov. 2, 1959; d. Andrew Ezekiel and Lillian (Bonner) Wyatt; m. Nicholas Charles Cooper-Lewter, Nov. 29, 1986 (div. 1998). BS in Elem. Edn., Va. State U., Ettrick, 1984; MEd in Spl. Edn., 1993; Degree in Adminstrv. Ednl. Leadership, St. Mary's U., Mpls., 2000. Lic. minister, 1987; ordained to clergy, 1990. Tchr. Marion (Ind.) Community Schs., 1985-86, Inglewood (Calif.) Unified Schs., 1986-87; office mgr. C.R.A.V.E. Christ Counseling, Tustin, Calif., 1986—; asst. minister New Garden of Gethsemane B.C., L.A., 1987-90; assoc. minister New Hope Bapt. Ch., St. Paul, 1990—; assoc. pastor New Garden of Gethsemane B.C., L.A., 1990—; assoc. minister New Hope Bapt. Ch., 1990—, pulpit coord., 2002; pres. C.R.A.V.E. Christ Singers, L.A., 1987-90; adminstr. asst. Eldorado Bank, Orange, Calif., 1988-90; tchr. fine arts Broadway Cmty. Sch., Mpls., 1996—, Mpls. Sch. Dist., 1990—; assessment coord. Broadway Cmty. Sch., Mpls., 1999—; with Wyatt Consulting, Shoreview, Minn., 1986—; 4th grade tchr. Hall Cmty. Sch., Mpls. Founder, dir. Diversity in Motion program for A.A. students, 1992—; stage dir. Babu's Magic with dancer Chuck Davis, 1994; cons. Everyday Learning Corp., 1996—; assessment coord., curriculum writer Mpls. Pub. Schs., 1999—; 4th/5th grade curriculum instrn. assessment team lead Elizabeth Hall Elem. Sch., extended day coord., 2003. Nominated to Pres.'s Commn. White House Fellowships [illegible] Christ Ministries (Relax in Christ, Affirm with Christ, Visualize Christ, Experience Christ); pulpit coord. New Hope Bapt. Ch. Imagination grantee Star Tribune, 1994, 95-96, Fulbright grantee, Namibia, 1996, African studies grantee U. Wis., 1995-96, FASSE grantee U. Minn., 1996. Mem. NAFE, Alpha Kappa Alpha. Avocations: reading, music, fish breeding. Office Phone: 763-668-2650., 651-772-4080. E-mail: mwyatt@mpls.k12.mn.us.

WYCHOCK, KAREN MARIE, principal, set designer, craftsman; b. Wilkes-Barre, Pa., Apr. 24, 1955; d. Carl and Mary Wychock. BS in Art Edn., Kutztown U., 1977; MS in Art Edn., Pa. State U., 1982; MS in Ednl. Adminstrn., Gwynedd-Mercy Coll., 1999. Cert. secondary adminstrn. Pa., 2002. Elem. art tchr. Neshaminy Sch. Dist., Langhorne, Pa., 1977—90, secondary art tchr., 1990—99, lead art tchr., 1996—99, asst. prin. Neshaminy Mid. Sch., 1999—2002, prin. Neshaminy Mid. Sch., 2002—; owner Times Gone By, Levittown, Pa., 1994—. Regional rep. Pa. Art Edn. Assn., Harrisburg, 1990—97. Named Outstanding Regional Rep., Pa. Art Edn. Assn., 1993; recipient Mid. Sch. Art Tchr. of the Yr. in Pa., 1992. Mem.: ASCD, Nat. Assn. Secondary Sch. Prins. (Pa. Asst. Prin. of the Yr. 2002), Bucks County Guild Craftsmen, Pa. Guild Craftsmen, Pa.-Jersey Basketry Guild (pres. 2000—02, v.p. 2002—03). Avocations: basketry, gardening, travel, photography, art. Office: Neshaminy Middle School 1200 Newtown-Langhorne Rd Langhorne PA 19047 Personal E-mail: kwychock@neshaminy.k12.pa.us.

WYCKOFF, LYDIA LLOYD, art curator; b. Washington, Nov. 16, 1937; d. Edward Lester Lloyd and Martha Althea Hall; m. David Willard Wyckoff, June 1, 1963 (div. July 1990); children: Barbara, Christopher. MFA, U. Lausanne, Switzerland, 1955; MA, Wesleyan U., 1975; MPhil, Yale U., 1980, PhD, 1985. Lectr. U. Miami, 1962-67; rsch. assoc. Mus. of Am. Indian-Heye Found., N.Y.C., 1967-79; postdoctoral fellow Yale U., New Haven, 1985-87; curator, dir. Native Am. and non-western art Philbrook Mus. Art, Tulsa, 1991—2001. Cons. Housatonic Adolescent Hosp., Newtown, Conn., 1985; bd. dirs. Osage Tribal Mus., Pawhuska, Okla., The Trust for Pub. Land; guest curator Yale U., 1993—; adj. assoc. prof. U. New Haven, 1967-77; vis. asst. prof. Bard Coll., 1983-84; adj. asst. prof. Fairfield (Conn.) U., 1986-90, U. Tulsa, 1990—. Author, editor: Hopis, Tewas and American Road, 1983 (Choice award 1983); author: Designs and Factions, 1990, (jours.) New Scholar, 1986, Am. Anthropology, 1991; author, editor: Visions and Voices, 1996 (Okla. Book award), Woven Worlds, 2001; contbr. articles and revs. to profl. publs. Rsch. grantee Mus. of Am. Indian, 1960s, Ctr. for Inter-Am. Studies, 1960s, Yale Ctr. for Native Am. Art and Anthropology, 1979, NEA, 1993, 96, 99, 2000. Fellow Am. Anthropol. Assn.; mem. AAUP, Coun. for Mus. Anthropology. Office: Philbrook Mus Art 2727 S Rockford Rd Tulsa OK 74114-4104 Home: 8004 Maple Ave Takoma Park MD 20912-6319

WYERS, GISELLE ELEANOR, music educator, conductor; d. Jan Gerbrand and Judy Eleanor Wyers; m. Jeff Rice, July 16, 2000. Mus D, U. of Ariz., Tucson, Ariz., 1998—2000; MusM conducting, Westminster Choir Coll., Princeton, NJ, 1994—96; MusB, U. of Calif., Santa Cruz, Calif., 1987—91. Prof., choral conducting Boise State U., Boise, Idaho, 2000—; grad. tchg. asst. U. of Ariz., Tucson, Ariz., 1998—2000; prof., choral conducting Lewis and Clark Coll., Portland, Oreg., 1996—98, Mt. Hood C.C., Gresham, Oreg., 1996—98; asst. condr. Greater Princeton Youth Orch., Princeton, NJ, 1994—96; dir. of music Fremont United Meth. Ch., Portland, Oreg., 1992—94; artistic dir./condr. San Lorenzo Valley Cmty. Chorus, Boulder Creek, Calif., 1991—92. Nat. chair of student concerns com. Coll. Music Soc., 2003—; N.W. regional chair of youth and student activities Am. Choral Directors Assn., 2001—. Composer: (choral composition) Ave Maria (Winner, Cambridge Madrigal Singers Internat. Choral Composition Competition, 2003); author: (scholarly article) Am. Choral Rev., (doctoral dissertation) The Third Art: The Embodiment of Meaning through Texture in the Choral Works of Robert Kyr, (presentation) Coll. Music Soc. Nat. Conf., Feminist Theory and Music 6 Internat. Conf.; singer: (backup singer for CD) A Merry Little Christmas, Linda Ronstadt. Vol. Idaho Humane Soc., Boise, Idaho, 2002—03, Ruth Melichar Bird Ctr., Boise, Idaho, 2001—03. Recipient Medici Scholar Award, U. of Ariz., 1999, Guest Condr., Idaho Br. of Am. Choral Directors Assn., 2002, Idaho Music Educators All-State Conf., 2002; fellow Elsie Hilliard Hillman Conducting Fellowship, Elsie Hilliard Hillman, 1994-1996, Ainslee Cox Fellowship for Excellence in Conducting, Ainslee Cox, 1995, U. of Ariz. Tchg. Fellowship, U. of Ariz., 1998-2000. Mem.: Music Educators Nat. Conf., Coll. Music Soc. (nat. chair of student concerns com. 2003), Am. Choral Directors Assn. (nw regional chair of youth and student activities 2001—03), Internat. Fedn. of Choral Music, Phi Beta Kappa. Office: Boise State University 1910 University Drive Boise ID 83725 Personal E-mail: gwyers@boisestate.edu. E-mail: gwyers@boisestate.edu.

WYKES, MARY MAUSHAK, real estate agent; b. Elgin, Ill., May 13, 1925; d. William Frederick and Grace Stoxen Maushak; m. Arthur Albert Wykes, Oct. 13, 1956 (dec. Mar. 17, 2001); children: Pamela Wykes Armstrong, Paul Arthur. BS, U. Ill., Champaign, 1946; postgrad., Northwestern U., Chgo., 1950—52. Cert. tchr. Ill., realtor Md. Asst. office mgr. IBM Corp., Chgo., 1946—52; personnel asst. Internat. Minerals and Chem. Corp., Chgo., 1952—57; exec. asst. Hewitt Assocs., Libertyville, Ill., 1958—60; ch. sec. Deerfield Presbyn Ch., Ill., 1961—62; employee devel. specialist Nat. Bur. Stds., Gaithersburg, Md., 1970—87; realtor Shannon, Luchs & Weichert Realtors, Gaithersburg, Md., 1978—2003; adult evening sch. tchr. Montgomery County Schs. and Montgomery Coll., Gaithersburg, Md., 1970—85. Mem. Grace United Meth. Ch., 1968—2003. Mem.: AAUW (program chmn. 2003—, morar bd. alumni assn. D.C. chpt.), Stds. Alumni Assn., Rockville-US Power Squadron (mem.-at-large 2002—03). Home: 18900 Diary Rd Montgomery Village MD 20886 Office: Weichert Realtors 19238 Montgomery Village Ave Montgomery Village MD 20886

WYKLE, MAY L. dean, educator, researcher; BSN, Case Western Res. U., 1956, MSN Psychiat. Nursing, PhD Edn., Case Western Res. U. Dean, Cellar prof. gerontological nursing Frances Payne Bolton Sch. Nursing, Ohio, 1988—; dean, dir. u. ctr. aging and health Case Western Res. U. Established ednl. programs, Europe, Africa, Asia; vis. prof. U. Mich., U. Tex.-Houston, U. Zimbabwe-Africa; del., served on planning com. White Ho. Conf. on Aging, 1993. Contbr. articles, chapters to books; author: Decision Making in Long-Term Care, Practicing Rehabilitation with Geriatric Clients, Stress and Health Among the Elderly, Family Caregiving Across the Lifespan, Service Minority Elders in the 21st Century (AJN Book of Yr. award, 2000). Dir. Robert Wood Johnson Tchg. Nursing Home Project; project dir. several tng. grants; cons. nursing homes, psychiat. hosps.; mem. bd. dirs. numerous cmty. orgns., nursing homes, profl. assns. Named first Pope Eminent scholar, Rosalynn Carter Inst. Human Devel. Southwestern State U., Americus, Ga., Outstanding Rschr. in State of Ohio, Ohio Rsch. Coun. on Aging, Ohio Network Edn. Cons. in field of Aging, 1992; recipient Humanitarian award, Outstanding Contbns. to Nursing Profession, 1999, Acad. award, NIMH Geriatric Mental Health, Merit award, Cleve. Coun. Black Nurses, Gerontological Doris Schwartz Nursing Rsch. award, Gerontological Soc. Am., Belle Sherwin award, Cleve. Vis. Nurse Assn., Leadership award excellence in geriatric care, Midwest Alliance in Nursing, Disting. nurse-scholar lectr. award, Nat. Coun. Nursing Rsch., Nursing Educator award, New Cleve. Woman mag. . Fellow: Gerontological Soc. Am., Am. Acad. Nursing; mem.: NIA, NIMH, NINR, Vets Adminstrn. (geriatric/gerontology adv. com.), Sigma Theta Tau Internat. (pres.-elect 1999). Office: 10900 Euclid Ave Cleveland OH 44106

WYLAN, BARBARA, artist; b. Providence, 1933; divorced; children: Andrea, Brock. BFA, R.I. Sch. of Design, Providence, 1955; studied with Donald Stoltenberg, [illegible], Charles Movalli, Dong Kingman. Tchr. watercolor workshops; juror various exhbns. One-woman shows include: Barbara Wylan at The Spectrum, The Spectrum of Am. Artists and Craftsmen, Brewster, Mass., 1983, 84, 86, 87, 88, 90, 92, 93, 95, 2000, 03, Two Islands: Nantucket and New Zealand, 1985; One-woman shows Watercolors by Barbara Wylan, Sturgis Libr., Mass., 1974, Color Landscapes, 1977, Recent Watercolors, Falmouth Artists' Guild, Mass., 1977, Outdoors on Cape Cod, Skylight Gallery, Colo., 1979, Recent Paintings, Market Barn Gallery, Falmouth, Mass., 1981, Watercolors of Italy, Dom's Restaurant, Mass., 1981, Pastels of China, Sturgis Libr., 1983, China, Cape Cod Conservatory, 1984, Favorite Photographs of Barnstable, Cape Cod Conservatory, Mass., 1986, Personal Responses to the Earth, Cape Cod Mus. Nat. History, Brewster, Mass., 1987, Small Abstracts by Barbara Wylan, Market Barn Gallery, Falmouth, Mass., 1989, Recent Watercolors by Barbara Wylan, 1991, Paintings of Animals, Old Selectmens' Gallery,W. Barnstable, Mass., 1995, Dawn and Dusk, Cahoon Mus. of Am. Art, Cotuit, Mass., 1998; exhibited in over 100 group shows including Watercolor USA (Springfield award 1982), Nat. Soc. Painters in Casein and Acrylic 38th Ann., Nat. Arts club, N.Y.C. (Dr. David Soloway award 1991); represented in permanent collections, pvt., corp. and instnl. collectors including Mobile (Ala.) Mus. Art, Cahoon Mus. Am. Art, Cotuit, Mass., Cape Mus. Fine Arts, Dennis, Mass.; represented by The Spectrum of Am. Artists and Craftsmen, Brewster, Hyannis, Nantucket, Mass., Palm Beach Gardens, Fla., North Conway, N.H., Woods Hole (Mass.) Art Gallery. Mem. Nat. Soc. Painters in Casein and Acrylic, Watercolor USA Honor Soc., New Eng. Watercolor Soc., Copley Soc. Boston, and Twenty-one in Truro.

WYLDE, KATHRYN S. not-for-profit developer; BA, St. Olaf Coll., 1968. Pres., CEO NYC Housing Partnership, 1982—96; founding pres. and CEO NYC Investment Fund, 1996—; pres., CEO Partnership for NYC and C. of C., 2000—. Mem. adv. bd. Met. Ctr. Brookings Instn., Ctr. Urban Future, Ctr. New Economy, PR, Rep. Com. City Jour. Mem. bd. Biomedical Rsch. Alliance NY, TeleMedia Accelerator, Manhattan Inst., Rsch. Found., City U. NY. Recipient HBSCNY Bus. Statesman award. Office: Partnership for NYC One Battery Pk Plz 5th Fl New York NY 10004*

WYLIE, JOAN BLOUT, real estate rehabilitator, designer, ceramist; b. Montgomery, Ala., Jan. 29, 1920; d. Jack Jonas and Ida (Lewis) Dreyfus; m. Elkan Rogers Blout, Aug. 27, 1939 (div. June 1981); children: James E. Blout, Susan B. Merry Lausch, William Blout; m. Laurence Wylie, Dec. 26, 1987 (dec. 1995). Student, Skidmore Coll., 1938-39; BA in Design, Finch Coll., N.Y.C., 1940. Owner, pres. YaYa Designs, Cambridge, Mass., 1977—; entrepreneur purchasing and revitalizing properties, Cambridge, 1978—; owner, mgr. rental housing, Cambridge, 1978—. Exhibited fountain, sculptures, tableware at University Place, Cambridge, 1991. Bd. dirs. Cambridge Cmty. Ctr., 1952-99; bd. dirs., treas. Riverside/Cambridgeport Cmty. Assn., 1983-93. Mem. Cambridge Art Assn. (bd. dirs. 1998—), Cambridge Boat Club, Cambridge Hist. Soc., Soc. Arts and Crafts, French Libr. and Cultural Ctr. Mem. Soc. Of Friends. Home: 1010 Memorial Dr Cambridge MA 02138-4866

WYLIE, QUINETA G. BEAGLE, state political party executive; b. Higgins, Tex., July 5, 1948; d. Quinten Howare and Gerri Stimson Beagle; m. Allan George Wylie, 1969; children: Trevor McClean, Allan Stimson. BS, Okla. State U., 1973; MBA, U. No. Colo., 1978. Vice chmn. Okla. State Rep. Party, 1993-95, chmn., 1995—. Former adminstrn. Alaska Flying Club. Rep. chmn. Logan County, Okla., 1988; former Rep. chmn. Okla. County; mem. exec. com. Rep. Nat. Com. Mem. Freedoms Found. at Valley Forge, Okla. Hist. Soc., Okla. Fedn. Rep. Women (bd. dirs. 1990-93, chmn. 1st Ladies 1990-92), Oklahomans for Integrity in Govt. (adv. bd. 1992-93). Home: 5701 Parkhurst Rd Edmond OK 73034-9233

WYLLY, BARBARA BENTLEY, performing arts association administrator; b. Bala-Cynwyd, Pa., June 10, 1924; d. William Henry and Virginia (Barclay) Bentley; m. William Beck Wylly, Apr. 26, 1947; children: Virginia Wylly Johnson, Barbara Wylly Klausman, Thomas C. II. A, Briarcliff Jr. Coll., 1943. Pres. bd. dirs. Hillside Hosp. Inc., Atlanta, 1982, mem. adv. coun., 1982—; pres. Atlanta Symphony Assocs., 1975-76, mem. adv. bd., 1976—; chmn. bd. dirs. Ctr. for Puppetry Arts, Atlanta, 1988—2003. Bd. dirs. Mountain Conservation Trust, Atlanta Opera Guild, 1999—, bd. sponsors Georgian Chamber Players Bd., 2000-. Republican. Episcopalian. Avocations: walking, reading, music. Home: 940 Foxcroft Rd NW Atlanta GA 30327-2622 Office: Ctr Puppetry Arts 1404 Spring St NW Atlanta GA 30309-2820

WYMAN, L. PILAR, indexer; b. Beirut, Nov. 14, 1964; d. Samuel Haynes and Laura Pilar (Garzon) W.; m. Peter John McMenamin, Nov. 4, 1991; children: Leith Maria, Hugh Haynes. BA, St. John's Coll., 1986. Typist Editl. Svcs., Annapolis, Md., 1983-86, assoc. indexer, 1989-93; chief indexer Wyman Indexing, Annapolis, 1990—. Instr. Basic Indexing and Applied Indexing USDA Grad. Sch., 1996—. Author: (booklet) Indexing FAQ, 1994; contbr. articles, letters, and indexes to profl. pubs.; editor: Key Words, bull. of Am. Soc. Indexers, 2000—, Indexing Specialties: Medicine, 1999. Minority grad. fellow NSF, 1987. Mem. Soc. for Tech. Comm., Am. Med. Writers Assn., Am. Soc. Indexers (chair Washington chpt. 1995-96). Democrat. Episcopalian. Avocations: sailing, reading, parenting, travel. Address: TA Wyman Indexing 1223 Mount Pleasant Dr Annapolis MD 21401-5237

WYMAN, NANCY S. state legislator; b. Bklyn., Apr. 21, 1946; d. Arthur and Ann (Rosenzweig) Schmukler; m. Ronald Michael Wyman, Sept. 11, 1966; children: Stacey, Meryl. Student, L.I. Coll. Hosp., 1966. X-ray technician Bapt. Hosp., Miami, Fla., 1966-67, Baird Orthopedics, Miami, 1967-70, Rockville (Conn.) Orthopedics, 1975-83; legis. aide State of Conn., Hartford, 1983-87, state rep., 1987-94; state comptroller, 1995—. Named Legislator of Yr., Nat. Abortion Rights Reproductive Rights Action League, 1990, Arts Commn., 1992, Coun. Small Towns, 1992; recipient Friend of Edn. award Conn. Edn. Assn., 1990. Democrat. Jewish. Home: 18 Pilgrim Dr Tolland CT 06084-2906

WYMAN, VIOLA BOUSQUET, elementary school educator; b. Woonsocket, R.I., Dec. 6, 1923; d. Philias and Lela (Ladouceur) Bousquet; m. James Vernon Wyman, June 24, 1950; children: J. Vernon, Douglas Philip, Carolyn Wyman Blumenkrantz. B of Edn, R.I. Coll., 1945. Elem. tchr. Mansfield (Mass.) Sch. Dept., 1945-46, Woonsocket (R.I.) Sch. Dept., 1946-50, Needham (Mass.) Sch. Dist., 1950-52, Swansea (Mass.) Sch. Dept., 1952-53, Cumberland (R.I.) Sch. Dept., 1961-90. Mem. R.I. Supreme Ct. Disciplinary Coun., Providence, 1996—2001; jud. evaluation com. R.I. Supreme Ct., Providence, 1997—99; chmn. of bd. R.I. Supreme Ct., Providence, 2001—. Mem. NEA, AAUW. Avocations: photography, tennis, reading.

WYNDEWICKE, KIONNE ANNETTE (ANNETTE JOHNSON MOORER), reading educator; b. Preston, Miss. d. Clifton Thomas and Missouria (Jackson) Johnson; m. Eugene C. Moorer, Sept. 23, 1961 (div.). BS, Ill. State U., 1961; postgrad., Williams Coll., 1972, Columbia Coll., 1972; MEd, Nat. Coll. Edn., 1982. Social worker Cook County Dept. Pub. Aid, 1961; tchr. reading Chgo. Bd. Edn., 1961—; asst. to news dir. Sta. WCIU-TV, 1972-74; asst. women's editor Chgo. Defender, 1970-72; social sec. Dr. William R. Clarke, 1972—. Part-time photog. model, fashion commentator, pub. relations cons., pub. spkr. Contbr. articles to local newspapers. Co-chmn. installation Profl. Womens Aux., Provident Hosp., 1961, corr. sec., 1969, publicity chmn., 1969-72, 74-77. Selected as one of

13 persons in U.S. to attend Innovative Tchr. Tng. Seminar, funded by Henry Luce Found. at Williams Coll., 1972, Woman of the Day, WAIT Radio, 1978; one of 25 Black Women of Chgo. at receive Kizzy award, 1977; recipient Outstanding Cmty. Svc. award Beatrice Caffrey Youth Svc., Inc., 1978, 83, 85. Mem. Ill. Speech and Theatre Assn., Speech Comm. Assn. Am., Ret. Tchrs. Assn. Chgo., Internat. Platform Assn., Art Inst. Chgo., YWCA. Lutheran. Home: 2901 S King Dr Apt 1514 Chicago IL 60616-3314

WYNN, KARLA WRAY, artist, agricultural products company executive; b. Idaho Falls, Idaho, Oct. 1, 1943; d. Wiliam and Elma (McCowin) Lott; m. Russell D. Wynn, June 7, 1963 (div. 1996); children: Joseph, Jeffrey, Andrea. Student, Coll. of Holy Names, 1962-63, Providence Coll. Nursing, 1962-63; BFA, Idaho State U., 1989; postgrad., Alfred U., 1993. Co-owner R.D. Wynn Farms, American Falls, Idaho, 1963-96, office mgr., 1975-84; co-owner Redi-Gro Fertilizer Co., American Falls, 1970-96, office mgr., 1980-84; pres. Lakeside Farms, Inc. (name now Redi-Gro Fertilizer Inc.), American Falls, 1975—96; artist, 1990—. Owner Blue Heron, Pocatello, Idaho, 1991-96. Watercolors, oil paintings and ceramic clay sculptures exhibited at various art shows and galleries. Buddhist.

WYNN, NAN L. historic site administrator; b. Rock Island, Ill., Dec. 4, 1953; BA, Western Ill. U., 1975. Spl. events coord. Ill. Dept. Conservation, Springfield, 1975-77; mus. dir. Blackhawk State Hist. Site, Rock Island, 1977-81; site dir. Old State Capital Hist. Site, Vandalia, Ill., 1981-87; site mgr. Lincoln Tomb State Hist. Site, Springfield, 1986—. Office: Lincoln Tomb State Hist Site Oak Ridge Cemetery 1500 Monument Ave Springfield IL 62702-2500

WYNN, SUSAN RUDD, physician; BS, Tex. A&M U., 1979, MD, 1981; postgrad., Mayo Grad. Sch. Medicine, 1981-84, 84-86. Diplomate Am. Bd. Pediatrics, Am. Bd. Allergy and Immunology; lic. Tex. Assoc. cons. dept. pediatrics Mayo Clinic, Rochester, Minn., 1987; pvt. practice, allergy and clin. immunology Fort Worth (Tex.) Allergy and Asthma Assocs., 1988—. Instr. in pediatrics, Mayo Med. Sch., 1986-87; presenter in field. Mem. editl. bd. Annals Allergy, Asthma and Immunology, 1997—; contbr. articles to profl. jours. Bd. visitors Scott and White Clinic, 1994—; adv. bd. M. D. Anderson Physicians, 1992-94; bd. regents Tex. A&M U. Sys., 1999-2005. Recipient Residents' award Northwest Pediatric Soc., 1984, Leon Unger award Am. Coll. Allergists, 1985, Geigy fellow, 1987, travel grantsee, dist. fellow Am. Coll. Allergy, Asthma & Immunology, 1998. Mem. AMA (chmn. med. student sect. 1980-81, chmn. com. on women in medicine 1987-89), Mayo Assn. of Fellows (treas. 1984-85), Mayo Alumni Assn. (exec. com. 1983-87, 1995-2002), The Mayo Alumnus (adv. bd. 1983-87), Tarrant County Med. Soc. (bd. dirs. 1990—, v.p. 1994-95, pres.-elect 1995-96, pres. 1996-97, trustee 1998—), Minn. Med. Assn. (trustee 1984-85), Tex. Med. Assn. (vice spkr. 1997-2001, spkr. 2001—, various coms.), Am. Acad. Pediats., Am. Coll. Allergy and Immunology (bd. regents 1994-97), Alpha Omega Alpha, Alpha Zeta, others. Office: 5929 Lovell Ave Fort Worth TX 76107-5029

WYSCHOGROD, EDITH, philosophy educator; b. N.Y.C. d. Morris and Selma Shurer; m. Michael Wyschogrod, Mar. 6, 1955; children: Daniel, Tamar. AB, Hunter Coll., [illegible]; PhD, Columbia U., 1970. Prof. philosophy Queens Coll., Flushing, N.Y., 1967-92; J. Newton Rayzor prof. philosophy and religious thought Rice U., Houston, 1992—2003, emerita, 2003—. Author: Emmanuel Levinas: The Problem of Ethical Metaphysics, 1974, 2d edit., 2000, Spirit in Ashes, 1985, Saints and Postmodernism, 1990, An Ethics of Remembering: History, Heterology and the Nameless Others; co-editor: Lacan and Theological Discourse, 1989, The Enigma of Gift and Sacrifice, 2002, The Ethical, 2003. Nat. Humanities Ctr. fellow, 1981, Woodrow Wilson Ctr. fellow, 1987-88, Guggenheim fellow, 1995-96. Fellow Am. Acad. Arts and Scis.; mem. Am. Acad. Religion (pres. 1992-93). Home: 522 West End Ave New York NY 10024 E-mail: stedith@rice.edu.

WYSE, KAREN ANN, artist; b. Newark, N.J., May 16, 1944; BA, N.Y. Sch. for the Arts. Owner Bizarre Bazaar, Oakland, Calif. Invited artist Contra Costa County Colls., 2002, 03.

WYSE, LOIS, advertising executive; b. Cleve. d. Roy B. Wohlgemuth and Rose (Schwartz) Weisman; m. Marc Wyse (div. 1980); m. Lee Guber (dec. 1988). Pres. Wyse Advt. Inc., 1951—, Media and Mktg./Health Expo, 2004—. Author: 60 books; syndicated columnist: Wyse Words; contbg. editor: (mag.) Good Housekeeping, 1983—98. Mem. bd. overseers Beth Israel Med. Ctr. Ctr. for Communications, N.Y.C. Mem. Woman's Forum, PEN, Author's Guild, League of Profl. Theater Women. Office: 18 E 41st St New York NY 10017 Office Phone: 212-689-8787. E-mail: lolowy@fastmail.fm.

WYSKOWSKI, BARBARA JEAN, lawyer; b. Jersey City, Feb. 20, 1967; d. Robert Louis and Barbara Joan (Dabrowski) W. BA, Rutgers U., New Brunswick, N.J., 1988; JD, Rutgers U., Camden, 1992; postgrad., Sch. Nursing, Muhlenberg Regional Med. Ctr., Plainfield, N.J. Bar: N.J., 1993, U.S. Dist. Ct. N.J., 1993. Law clk. Kevin William Kelly, Esq., Brick, N.J., 1989, Monke & Marriot, Sea Girt, N.J., 1990, Ann Segal, Esq., Voorhees, N.J., 1991; rsch. asst. Sch. Law Rutgers U., Camden, 1991-92; pro bono atty. Ocean-Monmouth Legal Svcs., Toms River, N.J., 1993-94; pvt. practice Manasquan, N.J., 1993—. Cons. in field; lectr. in field. Advocate Women Against Abuse, Phila., 1989-90; pres. Amnesty Internat., 1989-92. Mem. ABA, Am. Bankruptcy Inst., Nat. Assn. Consumer Bankruptcy Attys., IWIRC, INSOL Internat., N.J. State Bar Assn. (mem. lawyer to lawyer cons. network 1993-95), Ocean County Bar Assn., So. Monmouth Bd. Realtors. Avocations: surfing, running, skating. Home: 105 New England Ave G4 Summit NJ 07901 Office: Mellinger Sandels & Kartzman 101 Gibraltar Dr Morris Plains NJ 07950

WYSOCKY, KAREN ANN, music educator; b. Milw., Jan. 2, 1959; d. Richard Edward and Clarice Brigitta Wysocky. BA in Music Edn., U. Wis., Milw., 1982; MusM in Piano Pedagogy, So. Meth. U., Dallas, 1984. Choral dir. Ozaukee Mid. H.S., Fredonia, Wis., 1984—86, West Bend H.S., Wis., 1986—. Named One of Outstanding Young Women in Am., 1987. Mem.: Wis. Sch. Music. Assn. (membership chair 1986), Am. Choral Dirs. Avocations: reading, gardening, knitting, figure skating. Home: 1815 S Indiana Ave West Bend WI 53095 Office: West Bend High Sch 1305 E Decorah Rd West Bend WI 53095 Office Phone: 262-335-5650.

WYSS-TREADWELL, MARY JOSEPHINE, music educator, consultant; b. Indpls., Dec. 28, 1954; d. John Edward and Helene Josephine (Fischer) Wyss; m. Steven A. Treadwell. BA in Music Edn. and Music Therapy, Coll.Mount St. Joseph, Cin., 1976. Registered music therapist 1978, cert. Orff Schulwerk Level I 1992, lic. Kindermusik Internat. educator 1996, cert. Orff Schulwerk Level II 1999. Music specialist Indpls. Pub. Schs., 1977—; early childhood music specialist Indpls. Children's Choir, Kindermusik of Indpls., 1996—. Co-Founder Kindermusik of Indpls., 1996—. Grantee VH-1 Save the Music grant, VH-1 Save the Music Found., 2000. Mem.: Ind. Profl. Educators, Inc., Kindermusik Educators Assn., Ind. Orff Schulwerk Assn. (hospitality chair 2000—), Ind. Orff Schulwerk Assn. (v.p. 1998—2000), Ind. Orff Schulwerk Assn. (sec., treas. 1994—98), Am. Orff Schulwerk Assn., Music Educators Nat. Conf. (nat. registered music educator 1991, nat. cert. music educator 1993), Ind. Music Educators Assn. (regional rep., bd.mem. 1990—92, Outstanding Elem. Music Educator of the Year 2002). Roman Catholic. Avocation: folk dancing. Home: 6185 Orinoco Ave Indianapolis IN 46227-4895 Office: Indpls Pub Sch #20 1849 E Pleasant Run Parkway S Dr Indianapolis IN 46203 Personal E-mail: wyssj@mail.ips.k12.in.us. Business E-Mail: wyssj@mail.ips.k12.in.us.

WYSZYNSKI, TORI LIN, psychologist, consultant; b. New York City, NY, Sept. 13, 1957; d. Vincent Licata and Wilhemina Buscher; m. Gregory Anthony Wyszynski, Oct. 4, 1985; 1 child, Cory Patrick. PhD Orgnl. Psychology, The Calif. Sch. of Profl. Psychology, Alhambra, Calif., 1998, MSW Orgnl. Psychology; BA Psychology, Calif. State U. Northridge, Northridge California, 1992. Lean Manufacturing Principle & Practices, MIT, 2000; Behavioral Assessment & Counseling Techniques LA, Calif., 1997; Project Management Internat. Inst. For Learning, 1999. Career counselor The Work Source Ctr. of Calif., Los Angeles, Calif., 2002—; orgnl. devel. specialist The Boeing Co., Long Beach, Calif., 1997—2001. Compensation & benefits specialist Nash Co. & Associates, Palos Verdes, Calif., 1998—2001. Author (lecture/speaker): (international center for quality) Performance Measurements for the 21st Century (Quality Pride Award, 1999); author: (book) The Recruiter's Handbook, Designing Metrics for Complex Work Envioronments. Mem. The Ctr. for the Study of Work Teams, U. of N. Tex., 1997—2001. Mem.: APA (assoc.). R-Consevative. Roman Catholic. Achievements include research in Emphasis on organizational diagnostic instruments for complex work environments. Avocations: hiking, pianist, writer. Home: 3928 North Oleander Court Calabasas CA 91302 Personal E-mail: drwyszynski@aol.com.

XU, FRAN FENG, financial researcher; b. Shanghai, Jan. 6, 1964; d. Kexiao Xu, Lirong Zheng; m. James Jianbo Shi; children: Jarren Shi children: Jaysen Shi. MA, Ind. U., 1995. Options specialist Charles Schwab & Co. Inc., Fishers, Ind., 1997—99; sr. rsch. analyst Charles Schwab & Co. Inc., San Francisco, 1999—2003; credit analyst III Providian Fin. Corp., San Francisco, 2003—. Contbr. articles to fin. jours. Mem.: Assn. for Investment Mgmt. and Rsch. Avocation: painting, reading. Office: 123 Mission St San Francisco CA 94105 Office Phone: 415-644-2519. Business E-Mail: fran_xu@providian.com.

YABLONSKI, JANICE BETH, museum administrator, publishing executive; b. Cooperstown, N.Y., July 20, 1967; d. Edward Stanley Yablonski and Matilda Ann Lenk. BA in Am. History, Barnard Coll., 1989; MA in Am. Studies, Columbia U., 1992; Cert. in Arts Adminstrn., NYU, 1997. Asst. to mgr. spl. publs. dept. The Met. Mus. Art, N.Y.C., 1989-91, asst. mgr. adminstrn., spl. publs. dept., 1993-96, assoc. mgr. adminstrn., spl. publs. dept., 1996—98, sales mgr. spl. pubs. dept., 1998—99, mgr. e-commerce, mktg. and publicity dept., 1999—. Mem. Am. Assn. Mus. Office: The Met Mus Art Mktg and Publicity Dept 6 E 82nd St New York NY 10028-0304

YACOBIAN, SONIA SIMONE, metals company executive; b. Cairo, Egypt, Feb. 13, 1943; came to U.S., 1966, naturalized, 1971; d. Simon and Lucy (Guendimian) Samsonian; divorced; children: Tatiana, Richard. BS, Lycee of Cairo, 1962; BBA, U. Cairo, Egypt, 1965; student Pace U., 1978-80. Asst. mgr. new accounts Lincoln Savs. & Loan, Los Angeles, 1973-77; sr. acct. U.S. Industries, N.Y.C., 1977-81; dep. mgr. French C. of C., N.Y.C., 1981-82; mgr. mktg. Samancor Metals, New Rochelle, N.Y., 1982-84; pres. NIDDAM Inc., Huntington Sta., N.Y., 1984—; sales agency for Delachaux, France. Republican. Orthodox Christian. Home: 37 Wintergreen Dr Melville NY 11747-1812 Office: NIDDAM Inc 315 Walt Whitman Rd Ste 207 Huntington Station NY 11746-4112

YACOUB, ALLISON, music educator; b. South Miami, Fla., Oct. 28, 1975; d. Austin and Ronda Bridges; m. David Yacoub, June 23, 2001. BS in Music Edn. magna cum laude, Towson (Md.) U., 1998; MS in Music Edn., Towson (Md.) U., 2003. Cert. tchr. Md. Music tchr. Baltimore County Pub. Schs., Balt., 1998—2001; band/orch. dir. Park Sch. of Balt., Brooklandville, Md., 2002—03; summer camp music tchr. Friends Sch. of Balt., 2003—; band and strings dir. Howard County Pub. Schs., 2003—. Grad. asst. music dept. Towson U., 2003; clinician All Junior-Senior Honor Band/Towson U., Towson, Md., 2002—03; clinician honor band and orch. Baltimore County Pub. Schs., 1999—2001. Recipient 1st prize, Peggy-Friedman Gordon Music Competition, 1996. Mem.: Md. Music Educators Assn., Music Educators Nat. Conf. Republican. Avocations: travel, performing in musical venues, church ministry.

YAEGER, THERESE FRANCIS, management professional; b. Chgo., 1955; d. Walter W. and Eileen O'Brien Bronson; m. Paul Alan Yaeger, 1975; children: Colleen Rose, Elizabeth Marie, Anne Therese, Julia Eileen. BA in Lit. and Comm. magna cum laude, Benedictine U., 1995, MS in Mgmt. and Orgnl. Behavior, 1996, PhD in Orgn. Devel., 2001. Gen. mgr. Bestway Carpeting Inc., Naperville, Ill., 1976—; assoc. dir. PhD dept. Orgn. Devel. Benedictine U., Lisle, 1995—. Mem. presenter Midwest Acad. Mgmt., 1996—, Orgn. Devel. Network, 1995—, Acad. Mgmt., 1996—, APA, Divsn. 13, 2001; adj. faculty Mgmt. & Orgnl. Behavior Benedictine U., 1996—; exec. bd. Midwest Acad. Mgmt. Author: (with others) Appreciative Inquiry: Rethinking Human Organization Toward a Positive Theory of Change, 1999, Appreciative Inquiry: An Emerging Direction for Organization Development, 2001, Global and International Organization Development, 2001, Organization Behavior and Change: Managing Human Resources, 2002; editor (mag.) DuPage Arts Life, 1995, 96; asst. editor (newsletter) rsch. O.D. Inst. OD Jour., 1996—; columnist Chgo. ASTD's Tng. Today, 1997—. Mem. ASTD., Chgo. Orgn. Devel. Inst. Chpt., Soc. Profl. Journalists, Nat. Acad. Mgmt. (exec. bd. mgmt. cons. divsn. 2003—). Roman Catholic.

YAES, JOYCE, musician, artist, educator; b. N.Y.C., July 18, 1944; m. Robert Yaes, Nov. 16, 1986. BA, Bklyn. Coll., 1966, MA, 1972; postgrad., Juilliard Sch., 1971-75, Mannes Coll., 1975, Manhattan Sch. Music, 1974-75, U. Neuchatel, Switzerland, 1967, U. San Miguel, Mex., 1969. Cert. tchr., N.Y., Ky. Tchr. art and music, N.Y.C., 1966-86; tchr. music Emerson Sch., N.Y.C., 1976-80; agt. ins. N.Y.C., 1982-87; tchr. Living Arts and Sci. Ctr., Lexington, Ky., 1987—. Pvt. tchr. music; violinist various orchs., N.Y., Ky.; dir. various art shows. Author: Humanities and Arts Perspectives, Microphishe Education Perspectives; one-woman show U. Ky. Ctr. for Arts, Arts Club Washington, 1994; 2-woman show Lexington Art League; exhibited in group shows Paula Insel Gallery, Harrison Gallery, N.Y.C., Aspen (Colo.) Gallery, Bklyn. Mus., Lincoln Ctr. Cork Gallery, Tchr. Group Show, N.Y.C., Lexington Art League, ArtsPlace, Lexington, Monserrat Gallery, N.Y.C., Accents Gallery, Lexington, Guild Hall, East Hampton, N.Y., West Hampton (N.Y.) Gallery, also others. Mem. United Fedn. Tchrs., Music Tchrs. Assn. (mem. exec. com.), Music Educators Nat. Conf., Port Educators Assn., Nat. Assn. Female Execs., Lexington Art League, Federated Music Club, U. Ky. Woman's Club. Avocations: horseback riding, ice skating, painting, travel, bicycle riding.

YAFFE, BARBARA MARLENE, journalist; b. Montreal, Que., Can., Mar. 4, 1953; d. Allan and Anne (Freedman) Y.; m. Wilson E. Russell, Aug. 30, 1985. Student, McGill U., 1970-73; BA, U. Toronto, 1974; B in Journalism, Carleton U., 1974. Reporter Montreal Gazette, 1975-76, Toronto Globe and Mail, 1976-79, reporter, columnist, 1979-81; chief nat. TV news bur. CBC, St. Johns, Canada, 1981-84, Edmonton, Canada, 1983; reporter Toronto Globe and Mail, St. John's, 1984-86; editor Sunday Express, St. John's, 1987-88, Vancouver Sun, 1988-93, columnist, 1993—. Recipient Gov. Gen.'s award Roland Michener Found., 1977. Office: c/o Vancouver Sun 200 Granville St Vancouver BC Canada V6C 3N3 E-mail: byaffe@png.canwest.com.

YAITES, LILLIANN, minister; b. Kansas City, Kans., Mar. 30, 1951; d. Irvin and Gladys Lovie Cushon; m. James Roy Yaites; children: James Brewer, Reginald Brewer, James, Natosha. AA in Bus. Adminstrn., Kansas City Cmty. Jr. Coll., 1971; BSBA, Emporia State U., 1973; postgrad., St. Paul Sch. Theology, 2004—. Mgr. info. tech. Sabre Inc., Ft. Worth, 1984—2000, GetThere Inc., Dallas, 2000—01; min., treas. Campus Dr. United Meth. Ch., Fort Worth, 2002—. Counselor Campus Dr. United Meth. Ch., Ft. Worth, 2000—; with life connections programs Fed. Bur. Prisons. Author: (book) I'm Saved, Now What?, 2001 (Book of the Month for Oct. Black Book Worm, 2001). Avocations: singing, writing. Office: Yaites Ministries PO Box 163674 Fort Worth TX 76161-3674 Business E-Mail: gimlmak@sbcglobal.net.

YAKLIN, LORI STILLWAGON, government agency administrator; BBA, U. Mich.; M in Adminstrn., Ctrl. Mich. U. Founding exec. dir. Mich. Sch. Bd. Leaders Assn.; dir. Sch. Choice Office of the Under Sec. U.S. Dept. Edn., sr. advisor on family ednl. rights Office of Innovation and Improvement. Spkr. in field. Office: US Dept Edn FOB-6 Rm 7E306 400 Maryland Ave Washington DC 20202

YALMAN, ANN, judge, lawyer; b. Boston, June 9, 1948; d. Richard George and Joan (Osterman) Y. BA, Antioch Coll., 1970; JD, NYU, 1973. Trial atty. Fla. Rural Legal Svcs., Immokalee, Fla., 1973-74; staff atty. EEO, Atlanta, 1974-76; pvt. practice Santa Fe, N.Mex., 1976—; probate judge Santa Fe County, 1999—. Part time U.S. magistrate, N. Mex., 1988-96. Commr. Met. Water Bd., Santa Fe, 1986-88. Mem. N.Mex. Bar Assn. (commr. Santa Fe chpt. 1983-86). Home: 441 Calle La Paz Santa Fe NM 87505-2821 Office: 304 Catron St Santa Fe NM 87501-1806

YALOW, ROSALYN SUSSMAN, nobel laureate, biophysicist; b. N.Y.C., N.Y., July 19, 1921; d. Simon and Clara (Zipper) Sussman; m. Aaron Yalow, June 6, 1943; children: Benjamin, Elanna. AB, Hunter Coll., 1941; MS, U. Ill., Urbana, 1942, PhD, 1945; DSc (hon.), U. Ill., Chgo., 1974, Phila. Coll. Pharmacy and Sci., 1976, N.Y. Med. Coll., 1976, Med. Coll. Wis., Milw., 1977, Yeshiva U., 1977, Southampton (N.Y.) Coll., 1978, Bucknell U., 1978, Princeton U., 1978, Jersey City State Coll., 1979, Med. Coll. Pa., 1979, Manhattan Coll., 1979, U. Vt., 1980, U. Hartford, 1980, Rutgers U., 1980, Rensselaer Poly. Inst., 1980, Colgate U., 1981, U. So. Calif., 1981, Clarkson Coll., 1982, U. Miami, 1983, Washington U., St. Louis, 1983, Adelphi U., 1983, U. Alta. (Can.), 1983, SUNY, 1984, Tel Aviv U., 1985, Claremont (Calif.) U., 1986, Mills Coll., Oakland, Calif., 1986, Cedar Crest Coll., Allentown, Pa., 1988, Drew U., Madison, N.J., 1988, Lehigh U., 1988; LHD (hon.), Hunter Coll., 1978; DSc (hon.), San Francisco State U., 1989, Technion-Israel Inst. Tech., Haifa, 1989, Med. Coll. Ohio Toledo, 1991; LHD (hon.), Sacred Heart U., Conn., 1978, St. Michael's Coll., Winooski Park, Vt., 1979, Johns Hopkins U., 1979, Coll. St. Rose, 1988, Spertus Coll. Judaica, Chgo., 1988; DHC (hon.), U. Rosario, Argentina, 1980, U. Ghent, Belgium, 1984; D. Humanities and Letters (hon.), Columbia U., 1984; DSc (hon.), Fairleigh Dickinson U., 1992, Conn. Coll., 1992, Smith Coll., Northampton, Mass., 1994, Union Coll., Schenectady, 1994. Diplomate Am. Bd. Scis. Lectr., asst. prof. physics Hunter Coll., 1946-50; physicist, asst. chief radioisotope service VA Medical Ctr., Bronx, NY, 1950-70, chief nuclear medicine, 1970-80, acting chief radioisotope service, 1968-70, sr. med. investigator emeritus; research prof. Mt. Sinai Sch. Medicine, CUNY, 1968-74, Disting. Service prof., 1974-79, Solomon A. Berson Disting. prof.-at-large, 1986—; Disting. prof.-at-large Albert Einstein Coll. Medicine, Yeshiva U., 1979-85, prof. emeritus, 1986, chmn. dept. clin. scis. Montefiore Med. Ctr., Bronx, 1980-85. Cons. Lenox Hill Hosp., N.Y.C., 1956—62, WHO, Bombay, 1978; sec. U.S. Nat. Com. on Med. Physics, 1963—67, mem. nat. com. Radiation Protection, subcom. 13, 1957, Pres.'s Study Group on Careers for Women, 1966—72; sr. med. investigator VA, 1972—92, sr. med. investigator emeritus, 1992—. Co-editor: Hormone and Metabolic Research, 1970—79, [illegible] Diabetologica Latina, 1975—77, Ency. Universalis, 1978—, editl. bd. Mt. Sinai Jour. Medicine, 1976—79, Diabetes, 1976, Endocrinology, 1967—72, contbr. numerous articles to profl. jours. Bd. dirs. N.Y. Diabetes Assn., 1974. Recipient VA William S. Middleton Med. Rsch. award, 1960, Eli Lilly award, Am. Diabetes Assn., 1961, Van Slyke award, N.Y. met. sect. Am. Assn. Clin. Chemists, 1968, award, ACP, 1971, Dickson prize, U. Pitts., 1971, Howard Taylor Ricketts award, U. Chgo., 1971, Gairdner Found. Internat. award, 1971, Commemorative medallion, Am. Diabetes Assn., 1972, Bernstein award, Med. Soc. State N.Y., 1974, Boehringer-Mannheim Corp. award, Am. Assn. Clin. Chemists, 1975, Sci. achievement award, AMA, 1975, Exceptional Svc. award, VA, 1975, A. Cressy Morrison award, N.Y. Acad. Scis., 1975, sustaining membership award, Assn. Mil. Surgeons, 1975, Disting. Achievement award, Modern Medicine, 1976, Albert Lasker Basic Med. Rsch. award, 1976, La Madonnina Internat. prize, Milan, 1977, Golden Plate award, Am. Acad. Achievement, 1977, Nobel prize for Physiology/Medicine, 1977, citation of esteem, St. John's U., 1979, G. von Hevesy medal, 1978, Rosalyn S. Yalow R&D award established, Am. Diabetes Assn., 1978, Banting medal, 1978, Torch of Learning award, Am. Friends Hebrew U., 1978, Virchow Gold medal, Virchow-Pirquet Med. Soc., 1978, Gratum Genus Humanum Gold medal, World Fedn. Nuc. Medicine or Biology, 1978, Jacobi medallion, Assoc. Alumni Mt. Sinai Sch. Medicine, 1978, Jubilee medal, Coll. of New Rochelle, 1978, VA Exceptional Svc. award, 1978, Fed. Woman's award, 1961, Harvey lectr., 1966, Am. Gastroenterol. Assn. Meml. lectr., 1972, Joslin lectr., New Eng. Diabetes Assn., 1972, 1st Hagedorn Meml. lectr., Acta Endocrinologica Congress, 1973, Franklin I. Harris Meml. lectr., 1973, Sarasota Med. award for achievement and excellence, 1979, Gold medal, Phi Lambda Kappa, 1980, Achievement in Life award, Ency. Britannica, 1980, Theobald Smith award, 1982, Pres.'s Cabinet award, U. Detroit, 1982, John and Samuel Bard award in medicine and sci., Bard Coll., 1982, Disting. Rsch. award, Dallas Assn. Retarded Citizens, 1982, Nat. medal of Sci., 1988, Abram L. Sachar Silver medallion, Brandeis U., 1989, Disting. Scientist of Yr. award, ARCS, N.Y.C., 1989, Golden Scroll award, The Jewish Advocate, Boston, 1989, spl. award, Clin. Ligand Assay Soc., Washington, 1988, numerous others. Fellow: Clin. Soc. N.Y. Diabetes Assn., Am. Coll. Radiology (assoc. in physics), N.Y. Acad. Scis. (chmn. biophysics divsn. 1964—65); mem.: NAS, Am. Physiol. Soc., Endocrine Soc. (pres. 1978, Koch award 1972), Soc. Nuc. Medicine, Soc. Nuc. Medicine (hon.), Am. Gastroenterol. Assn. (hon.), Am. Coll. Nuc. Physicians (hon.), Harvey soc. (hon.), Med. Assn. Argentina (hon.), Diabetes Soc. Argentina (hon.), The N.Y. Acad. Medicine (hon.), N.Y. Roentgen Soc. (hon.), Biophys. Soc., Am. Assn. Physicists in Medicine, Radiation Rsch. Soc., Am. Phys. Soc., Am. Acad. Arts and Scis., Tau Beta Pi, Sigma Delta Epsilon, Pi Mu Epsilon, Sigma Pi Sigma, Sigma Xi, Phi Beta Kappa. Office: Vet Affairs Med Ctr 130 W Kingsbridge Rd Bronx NY 10468-3904*

YAMAGUCHI, COLLEEN S. lawyer; BBA, U. Hawaii, 1982, MBA, 1985; JD, Georgetown U., 1986. Bar: Wash. 1986. Law firm, Seattle, from 1986; ptnr. Sidley & Austin, L.A., 1998—. Assoc. editor Tax Lawyer, 1995-86. Former mem. steering com. Women in Leadership, Wash. Mem. Exec. Devel. Inst., Japanese Am. C. of C. Office: Sidley & Austin 555 W 5th St Los Angeles CA 90013-1010 Fax: 213-896-6600. E-mail: cyamaguc@sidley.com.

YAMAGUCHI, KRISTI TSUYA, ice skater; b. Hayward, Calif., July 12, 1971; d. Jim and Carole (Doi) Y.; m. Bret Hedican, July 8, 2000. Gold medalist, Figure Skating Albertville Olympic Games, 1992; U.S. Skating champion, 1992; World Skating champion, 1991, 1992; World Junior champion, 1988; world profl. figure skating champion, 1994. Founder Always Dream Found., 1996—; goodwill amb. Winter Olympics, Salt Lake City, 2002. Named Skater of the Yr., 1996, Favorite Female Athlete, Nickelodeon's Kid's Choice Awards, 1996—98, Athlete of the Yr. for figure skating, US Olympic Com., 1989; named to World Figure Skating Hall of Fame, 1999, US Figure Skating Hall of Fame, 1998; recipient Women First award, YWCA, 1993, Make a Wish grantor recognition for the yr. award, 1999. Avocations: tennis, rollerblading, reading, dance.

YAMAGUCHI, YURIKO FUJITA, artist; b. Japan, Jan. 25, 1948; came to the U.S., 1971; d. Alexander and Michi (Hirose) Fujita; m. Hiroyuki Yamaguchi, Mar. 25, 1975; children: Seiji, Mariko. BA, U. Calif., Berkeley, 1975; MFA, U. Md., 1979. Instr. U. Md., College Park, 1988—97; adj.

faculty Corcoran Sch. Art, Washington, 1988-97, George Washington U., 2003—. Vis. artist Md. Inst. Art, Balt., 1991, Balt., 95, Mass. Coll. Art, Boston, 1994; adj. faculty George Washington U., 2002—; artist in residence Oberpfälzer Kunstllerhaus. Exhibited in group shows at Hirshhorn Mus., 1984, L.A. County Mus., 1987, Koplin Gallery, L.A., 1991, 1994, 1996, 1999, 2002, Gallery Emon, Japan, 1997, 2000, Numark Gallery, 1999, 2003, Hand Workshop Art Ctr., 2000, Howard Scott Gallery, Columbia U., 2003, Del. Ctr. for Contemporary Arts, 2001, Suyama Space, Seattle, 2002, one-woman shows include Penine Hart Gallery, N.Y., 1989, 1994, Columbia U., NY, commd. wall mural, Atlanta Internat. Airport, 1998, Represented in permanent collections Hirshhorn Mus., Nat. Mus. Women in Arts, Nat. Mus. Am. Art, Smith Coll. Art Mus., exhibited in group shows at Kanagawa Modern Art Mus., Japan, 2004, Represented in permanent collections Corcoran Gallery of Art. Va. Mus. Fine Arts fellow, 1988, 85, 2001; Mid-Atlantic Found. fellow, 1995; Va. Commn. Arts grantee, 1994, 2000, Salzburg Kunstlerhaus Residency grantee, 1993. E-mail: yuriko414@aol.com. Home: 1517 Snughill Ct Vienna VA 22182-1724

YAMAUCHI, GLORIA, aerospace engineer; married, 1988. Aerospace engr. NASA. Avocations: fishing, golf, basketball, softball. Office: NASA Ames Rsch Ctr Bldg T12B Rm 104 Moffett Field CA 94035

YAN, HAIPING, theatre and comparative literature educator; b. Shanghai, July 4, 1959; d. Ciqing and Xionlan (Chen) Y.; m. Zhigang Yang, Aug. 26, 1961. BA, Fudan U., Shanghai, 1982; MA, Cornell U., 1987, PhD, 1990. Instr., artistic dir. Shanghai Yang-pu Children's Performing Arts Ctr., 1973-78; asst. prof. Chinese Lit. Fudan U., 1982-84; tchg. asst. modern langs. and linguistics Cornell U., Ithaca, N.Y., 1984-85, tchg. asst. Asian studies, 1988-89, vis. prof. East Asian studies, 1990-91; vis. asst. prof. theatre and East Asian studies Oberlin (Ohio) Coll., 1991—92, vis. asst. prof. theatre and comparative lit., 1992-94; asst. prof., theatre U. Colo., Boulder, 1994—2001, prof., drama and performance studies, 2001—. Lectr. in field; Zijiang chair prof., humanistic studies E. China Women U., Shanghai, 2001—; sr. scholar-in-residence Ctr. for World Performance Studies, U. Mich., Ann Arbor, 2002—03; prof., drama and performance studies UCLA. Contbr. articles to profl. jours. Recipient 1st prize for excellence in drama Soc. Chinese Dramatists and Ministry of Culture of People's Republic of China, 1980-81, Sage scholarship Cornell U., 1983-84, Martin M. McVoy, Jr. Trust scholarship Cornell U., 1984-85, 85-86, 86-87, 87-88, Larry E. Gubb scholarship Cornell U., 1988, Cornell U. China-Japan Mellon grant, 1988, Rsch. grant U. Colo., 1994, Rsch. Travel award U. Colo., 1995, grant U. Colo., 1995. Mem. MLA, Assn. of Theatre in Higher Edn., Assn. Asian Studies, Chinese Dramatists' Assn. (China), Chinese Writers' Assn. (China), Telluride Assn. (student 1985-86, 86-87, 87-88, faculty 1989-90). Avocations: singing, traveling, gardening. Office: Univ Colo Boulder Dept Theatre and Dance PO Box 261 Boulder CO 80309-0261 Home: 47078 Bing Dr Canton MI 48187-4680 Address: 2337 Macgowan Hall Dept Theatre UCLA 102 E Melonitz Box 95622 Los Angeles CA 90095-1622

YANCEY, ELIZABETH STILPHEN, political scientist; b. Hempsted, N.Y., Nov. 22, 1945; d. Norris Williams and Gladys (Howgate) Stilphen; m. Thomas Erwin Yancey, July 31, 1971; children: Linda Siti, David Arthur, Karen Elaine. BA in Biology, Earth Sci., Marietta (Ohio) Coll., 1968; MA in Paleontology, U. Calif., Berkeley, 1971; postgrad., Blinn Coll., Bryan, Tex., 1999. Cert. secondary sch. tchr., Ohio, Idaho, Tex. Rsch. technician dept. bacteriology Harvard Med. Sch., Boston, 1968-69; tchg. lab. asst. paleontology dept. U. Calif., Berkeley, 1970-71; tchg. lab. asst. geology dept. U. Malaysia, Kuala Lumpur, 1971; substitute tchr. Pocatello (Idaho) pub. schs., 1976-77; lectr. night sch. Idaho State U., Pocatello, 1978; aliener AMI Computers, Pocatello, 1979; lab. technician Tex. A&M U., 1981-82; presch. tchr. A&M Meth. Nursery Sch., College Station, Tex., 1982-83; substitute tchr. College Sta. Ind. Sch. Dist., 1983-87; clk. Bur. Census U.S. Govt., College Station, 1990; interviewer Pub. Policy Rsch. Inst., Tex. A&M U., College Station, 1998—. Girl Scout leader Blue Bonnet coun. Peace Luth. Ch., 1984-85; Sunday Sch. tchr. Meth. Ch., 1979-83, Our Savior's Luth. Ch., 1984-85, Peace Luth. Ch., 1986-87. Lutheran. Avocations: crocheting lace, raising dogs, cavies and cats.

YANCEY, VICTORIA FRANCINE, education educator; d. Harold and Margaret Covington Ward; 1 child, Raina Ivy. BA, Pa. State U., 1972; MEd, Antioch U., 1976; ABD, Temple U., Phila., 1980; EdD, Fielding Grad. Inst., 2002. Cert. counselor Pa., thought field therapist Calif., Pa., mediator Pa., therapist Pa. Tchr. Sch. Dist. of Phila., 1972, counselor, 1976, adminstr., 2001, coord., 2003; therapist Inst. for Learning, Phila., 1987; park ranger Dept. of Interior, U.S. Govt., 1996; instr. U. Phoenix, 2003—. Presenter Assn. for Thought Field Therapy, San Diego, 2002—. Author: (book) Thought Field Therapy in Educational Settings, poems in religious publs. Mem. Women Making a Difference, Habitat for Humanity, Phila.; pres. TWIGS, Inc. Grantee Scholarship pageant, Internat. Woman, 2000, Rsch. grant, Fielding Grad. Inst., 2001. Mem.: Women's Heritage Soc., Nat. Assn. Univ. Women, Delta Sigma Theta (Svc. award 2003). Presbyterian. Avocations: travel, reading, dance, writing, public speaking.

YANCY, DOROTHY COWSER, college president; 1 child. BA in History and Social Sci., Johnson C. Smith U.; MA in History, U. Mass.; PhD in Polit. Sci., Atlanta U. Cert. MNGT, Harvard U. Tchr. Albany State Coll., Hampton U., Evanston (Ill.) Twp. H.S.; dir. Afro-Am. studies program Barat Coll., Lake Forest, Ill.; prof. Sch. History, Sch. Mgmt. Ga. Inst. Tech., Atlanta, 1972-94. Lectr. Acad. Pub. Adminstrn. and Social Studies of Small Hural and Ulan Bator, Mongolia, 1991; apptd. spl. master Fla. Pub. Employee Rels. Commn.; mem. labor del. to Soviet Union and Europe, 1988, 90; cons. to govt. agys., unions and cos., including GM, AT&T Bell Labs; arbitrator fed. mediation and conciliation svs. Am. Arbitration Assn. Contbr. over 40 articles to profl. jours. Bd. advisors USAR Historically Black Colls. and Univs./Minority Instn.; bd. dirs. College Fund/UNCF; past mem. N.C. Post-Secondary Eligibility Commn.; former bd. dirs. Opera Carolina, Charlotte Urban League, Charlotte C. of C. Fulbright scholar; named one of Six Best Tchrs. in U.S., Newsweek on Campus, 1988. Mem. Assn. Social and Behavioral Scientists (past pres., Torchbearer award, Belle Ringer Image award), Indsl. Rels. Rsch. Assn. (past pres. Atlanta chpt.), Ctrl. Intercollegiate Athletic Assn. (past pres.), Links, Inc. (past mem. exec coun.), Coun. Ind. Colls. (former mem. governing bd.), Assn. for Study of African-Am. Life and History (exec. coun.), Omega Psi Phi, Phi Kappa Phi, Alpha Kappa Mu, Sigma Rho Sigma, Omicron Delta Kappa, Phi Beta Kappa (mem. Delta Ga. chpt.). Episcopalian. Office: 100 Beatties Ford Rd Charlotte NC 28216-5302 E-mail: dcyancy@jcsu.edu.

YANDA, CATHY L. counselor, illustrator; d. Ronald K. Vaughan and Betty J. Freshour; 1 child, Micah Topping. AA in Liberal Arts, Chapman Coll., 1987; BS in Psychology, Wright State U., 1989. Sr. instr. USMC, 29 Palms, Calif., 1979—87; disease intervention specialist Combined Health Dist. of Montgomery County, Dayton, Ohio, 1990—, hiv educator/counselor, 1989—90; owner Sati, Dayton, 1998—2002; ho. mgr. Victoria Theatre, Dayton, Ohio, 2002—. Cons. Children's Med. Ctr., Dayton, 2001—. Contbg. illustrator Nuts & Bolts and Magic Wands: Children's Writing from the Bottom Up, 2001; contbg. author and pub.: newsletter Canal St. Tavern News, 2002. Bd. dirs. AIDS Found. Miami Valley, Dayton, 1993—95. Buddhist.

YANDELL, CATHY MARLEEN, language educator; b. Anadarko, Okla., Dec. 27, 1949; d. Lloyd O. and Maurine (Dunn) Y.; m. Mark S. McNeil, Sept. 7, 1974; children: Elizabeth Yandell McNeil, Laura Yandell McNeil. Diplôme d'études, Inst. des Professeurs de Français à l'Etranger, Sorbonne, Paris, 1970; BA, U. N.Mex., 1971; MA, U. Calif., Berkeley, 1973, PhD, 1977. Tchg. asst. U. Calif., Berkeley, 1971-75, acting instr., 1976-77; asst. prof. Carleton Coll., Northfield, Minn., 1977-83, assoc. prof., 1983-89, prof. French, 1989—. Chair commn. on the status of women Carleton Coll., Northfield, 1983-85, ednl. policy com., 1985-86, 96-97, romance langs. and lit., 1988-91, chair faculty affairs com., 2000-02, pres. of faculty, 1991-94, Bryn-Jones disting. tchg. prof. humanities, 1996-99, mentor to jr. faculty, 1996—, W.I. and Hulda F. Daniell prof. French lit., lang. and culture, 1999—; dir. Paris French Studies Program, 1998, 2004. Author: Carpe Corpus: Time and Gender in Early Modern France, 2000; co-author: Vagabondages: Initiation ā la litt. d'expression française, 1996; contbr. to Art & Argumentation: The Sixteenth Century Dialogue, 1993, French Texts/American Contexts: French Women Writers, 1994, Montaigne: A Collection of Essays, Vol. 4, Language and Meaning, 1995, Reflexivity in Women Writers of the Ancien Régime, 1998, High Anxiety, 2002, Ronsard, figure de la variété, 2002, Lectrices d'Ancien Régime, 2003; editor: Pontus de Tyard's Solitaire Second, ou prose de la musique, 1980; contbr. articles to profl. jours. Active exec. com., then mem. Amnesty Internat., Northfield, 1980—. Regents' Travelling fellow, U. Calif. at Berkeley, 1975—76, Faculty Devel. grantee, Carleton Coll., 1988, 1991, NEH Rsch. fellow., 1994—95, Mellon Faculty fellow, 2003. Mem. MLA (del. 1989-92, exec. com. French 16th century lit., 2001—, 16th century studies coun. 2001—). Democrat. Home: 514 5th St E Northfield MN 55057-2220 Office: Carleton College 1 N College St Northfield MN 55057-4044 Office Phone: 507-646-4245. E-mail: cyandell@carleton.edu.

YANDELL, RUTH B. music educator; b. Cebu, Philippines; d. Alfredo A. and Susana L. Buot; m. David Palmer Yandell, June 29, 1966; children: Scott B., Eric L. BA, Silliman U., Dumaguete, Philippines, 1957; BA in Music, Philippine Womens U., Manila, 1962; MA in Music, Western Mich. U., 1966. Cert. Nat. Music. Tchrs. Assn. Mem. faculty Silliman U., 1962-64; music dir./accompanist Ariz. State U. Lyric Opera Theatre, Tempe, 1968-71; faculty/piano dept. coord. Mesa (Ariz.) C.C., 1971—. 2nd v.p. Young Artist com., Az., 1998-99. Author: (textbook) Introduction to Music Theory, 1995, Keyboard Technique, Level I, 1996, Keyboard Technique, Level II, 1997. Pres. Maricopa C.C. Dist. Asian Pacific Islander Assn., 2001—; scholarship chmn. Asian Pacific Islander Assn., 1999. Fulbright grantee, 1964-66; Western Mich. U. fellow, 1964-66; Aspen Music Festival scholar, 1965. Mem. Ariz. State Music Tchrs. Assn., Nat. Music Tchrs. Assn. Office: Mesa Cmty Coll 1833 W Southern Ave Mesa AZ 85202-4822 E-mail: ruth.yandell@mcmail.maricopa.edu.

YANG, DEBRA W. lawyer; b. L.A. Grad., Boston Coll. Lawyer; judge L.A. Mcpl. and Superior Cts.; fed. prosecutor; U.S. atty., 2002—. Adj. prof. U. So. Calif. Law Sch. Office: Ctrl Dist Calif US Courthouse Rm 1200 312 N Spring St Los Angeles CA 90012

YANG, SUSAN XIA, business consultant, massage therapist; b. Chuang De, China, Sept. 1, 1964; arrived in USA, 1989; d. Ming-Qi Yang and Chung-Zhen Cheng; m. Shide Hao, Jan. 5, 1988 (div. Apr. 1996); 1 child, Annie P. BA in Econs., Beijing Normal U., 1985; Diploma in Massage Therapy, Swedish Massage Inst., N.Y.C., 1998. Lic. massage therapist, N.Y., 1998. Rsch. asst. Econ. Rsch. Inst., State Planning Commn., Beijing, 1985—89; lobby asst., canvasser Conn. Citizen Action Group, West Hartford, Conn., 1989—92; export asst. Colt Mercantile Internat., N.Y.C., 1993—96; owner, dir. Miracle Touch Massage Therapy, P.C., Fresh Meadows, NY, 1998—; bus. cons. DermaRite Industries NJ, 2003—. Coach for women Alley Pond Strider Running Club, Queens Village, NY, 2001—; race dir. PS Q 178 Fun Run, Jamaica Estates, NY, 2002. Rep. in police dept. Utopia Civic Assn., Fresh Meadows, NY, 2001—. Recipient 5th place, female, Rocket City Marathon, Alabama, 1998, 1st place, female, Atlantic City Marathon, N.J., 1998, Treadmill Marathon, N.Y., 1995, N.Y.C. Marathon, 1996—97, Boston Marathon, 1997. Mem.: Am. Massage Coun., Am. Massage Therapy Assn., N.Y. Road Runners Club. Avocation: running, tennis, ping-pong, skiing, martial arts. Office: Miracle Touch Massage Therapy 75-20 188th St Fresh Meadows NY 11366 Office Phone: 718-454-6868.

YANNUZZI, ELAINE VICTORIA, food and home products executive; b. Summit, N.J. d. Emil and Alice (Vance) Y. BA, Seton Hall U., 1968. Pres. Expression Unltd., Warren, N.J., 1971-89; pvt. practice cons. pub. industry and bus. Bedminster, N.J., 1989—. Presenter seminar N.Y. Food and Wine Show, Splty. Food Show; lectr. NYU, Rutgers U.; moderator Am. Women's Econ. Devel., N.Y.C., 1985-87; spkr. Women Bus. Owners N.J., Princeton, 1986. Author: Gift Wrapping Food, 1985; editorial advisor Fancy Food mag., 1985—; editorial cons. Family Circle Gt. Ideas mag., 1987-89. Named Entrepreneur of Yr. N.J. Living mag., 1983, Woman of Yr. NYU, 1986. Mem. Roundtable for Women (bd. dirs. 1986-89, Pacesetter award 1985), Nat. Assn. for Splty. Food Trade (steering com. 1986). Home and Office: 612 Timberbrooke Dr Bedminster NJ 07921-2106 Office Phone: 908-781-5558.

YANTA, KRISTIN, publishing executive; d. Robert and Jeanne Zaske; m. Bradley Yanta, Aug. 18, 2001. BA in Psychology, Concordia Coll., 1996; MS in Sch. Psychology, EdS in Sch. Psychology, U. Wis., 2000. Cert. sch. psychologist 2001, lic. Minn. Dept. Children, Families and Learning, 1999. Sch. psychologist Austin Ind. Sch. Dist., Minn., 1999—2000, Anoka-Hennepin Ind. Sch. Dist., Coon Rapids, 2000—02; assoc. dir. product devel. AGS Pub., Circle Pines, 2002—; ind. demonstrator Stampin' Up!, Andover, 2003—. Contbr. resource book Group Reading Assessment Can and Should Lead to Instructional Changes. Mem.: APA, NASP, Internat. Dyslexia Assn., Learning Disabilities Assn. Am., Internat. Reading Assn., Minn. Sch. Psychologists Assn. (tech. com. 2002—). Avocations: stamping/scrapbooking, music, reading, travel. Office: AGS Pub 4201 Woodland Rd Circle Pines MN 55014

YAO, HILDA MARIA HSIANG, banker, strategic planner; b. Honolulu, Sept. 11, 1956; d. Hsin-Nung and Dorothy Wen (Wu) Y. BA cum laude, U. Pacific, 1975; MA, U. Wis., 1976. Ops. analyst Visa Internat., San Mateo, Calif., 1977-80; sr. product mgr. Bank of Am., San Francisco, 1980-81, asst. v.p., strategic planner Calif. electronic banking div., 1981-84, v.p., div. strategic planner U.S. wholesale svcs. world banking div., 1984-85, v.p., head dealer corp. svcs., 1985-89, v.p., dir. retail banking adminstrn., 1989-90, v.p., CFO internat. pvt. banking divsn., 1990-92, v.p., dir., deputy mgr. internat. investment svcs., 1992-93, v.p., head fiduciary policy, 1993-95, sr. v.p., dir. pvt. banking, trust and investment mgmt., 1995-97, sr. v.p., dep. mng. dir. internat. pvt. banking, 1997—. Bd. regents U. Pacific, Stockton, Calif., 1984-85, 91—; treas. pres.'s jr. adv. coun. Bank of Am., 1982-83; active exec. com. Campaign for Wis., 1991—; bd. dirs. U. Wis. Found., 1995—; bd. visitors Coll. of Letters and Sci. U. Wis., Madison, 1995—; mem. adv. bd. program in medicine and philosophy Calif. Pacific Med. Ctr., San Francisco, 1993—; mem. Pacific Coun. on Internat. Policy, 1996—; mem. China study group Pacific Coun. on Internat. Policy and Rand Corp., 1996—; hon. advisor China Soc. for People's Friendship Studies, 1992—. U. Wis. fellow, 1975-76, alumni fellow U. Pacific, 1983, Outstanding Young Alumna award U. Pacific, 1989. Mem. Nat. Vehicle Leasing Assn. (treas. 1988-89), World Affairs Counc., Calif. Acad. Scis., Commonwealth Club Calif., Bank Am. Club, Bankers Club San Francisco, World Trade Club, Univ. Club, The Mus. Soc., Calif. Legion of Honor, Bascom Hill Soc. U. Wis., President's Circle U. Pacific, Nat. Soc. Hist. Preservation, 1841 Club-Punahou Sch., Odyssey Club. Avocations: shakespeare, opera, languages, swimming, golf. Home: Gramercy Towers 1177 California St San Francisco CA 94108-2212 Office: Bank of Am 50 California St Ste 233 San Francisco CA 94111-4624

YAO, JIANHUA, chemist, researcher; b. Suzhou, People's Republic of China, Feb. 26, 1962; d. Dawu Yao and Xiuzhen Lu; m. Youlu Yu, Mar. 21, 1987. BSc, Nanjing (China) U., 1982, MSc, 1985; PhD, Concordia U., Montreal, Can., 1992. Mem. tchg. and rsch. staff Nanjing U., 1985-87; postdoctoral fellow Concordia U., 1992-93; rsch. assoc. Nat. Rsch. Coun. Can., Ottawa, 1993-95; rsch. chemist Phillips Petroleum Co., Bartlesville, Okla., 1995—. Contbr. [illegible] articles to profl. jours., patentee in field. Mem. ACS. Home: 1532 Whitney Ln Bartlesville OK 74006-6037 Office: Phillips Petroleum Co 332 Pl Rsch Ctr Bartlesville OK 74004-0001

YARBOROUGH, NELLIE CONSTANCE, principal, minister; b. Cedar Groove, N.C. d. Anderson and Bessie Y.. BA, Ea. Nazarene Coll., Quincy, Mass., 1978; MA, Antioch U./Cambridge (Mass.) Coll., 1979. Co-founder, exec. sec. Mt. Calvary Holy Ch., Boston, 1944—92, nat. youth pres., 1948—88, state sec. and treas., 1962—95; nat. missionary pres. Mt. Calvary Ch., Boston, 1960—90; founder, prin. Dr. Brumfield Johnson Acad., Boston, 1992—; founder, dean NCY Bible Inst., Boston, 1992—. Editor: (manual) YPHA Book, 1944; asst. editor: Jesus the Son of God, 1968, Spiritual Voice, 1948—72. Mem. adv. bd. Vision New Eng., Acton, Mass., 1998—; bd. dirs. Roxbury (Mass.) Multi-Svc. Ctr., 1970—85, Consumer's Credit, Boston, 1978—85, Project Right, Boston, 1991—, Blue Hill Task Force, Boston, 1995—. Named Pastor of the Yr., Vision New Eng., 1995, Woman of the Yr., Urban League of Ea. Mass., 1996; recipient Sojourner Truth award, Boston Profl. League, 1993. Democrat. Pentecostal. Avocations: reading, exercise, travel, motivational speaking. Home: 250 Seaver St Boston MA 02121 Office: Mt Calvary Holy Ch Am 9-19 Otisfield St Boston MA 02121

YARBROUGH, ALLYSON DEBRA, electrical engineer; b. Peterborough, England, Feb. 14, 1958; d. Freddy Dekhoma and Rosalind Mavis Y.; m. John Russell Scarpulla, May. 8, 1990. BSEE, N.Mex. State U., 1979; MSEE, Cornell U., 1985, PhD in Elec. Engring., 1988. Rsch. asst. Nat. Atmospheric and Ionospheric Ctr., Arecibo, P.R., 1979; microwave applications engr. Hewlett-Packard Co., Santa Rosa, Calif., 1979-82; assoc. prof. Calif. State U., L.A., 1988-89; tech. staff Aerospace Corp., El Segundo, Calif., 1989-93, sect. mgr., 1993-99, dept. dir., 1999—. Mem. IEEE, Microwave Theory and Techniques Soc., Alpha Kappa Alpha, Eta Kappa Nu. Democrat. Roman Catholic. Avocations: woodworking, sewing, collecting vintage radios. Home: 26821 Grays Lake Rd Palos Verdes Estates CA 90275

YARBROUGH, ISABEL MILES, dentist, educator; b. Columbus, Ga., May 24, 1956; d. Wiley and Lillie Miles; m. David E. Yarbrough; children: Davida Elizabeth, David Earl Jr. BS in Zoology, Ala. A&M U., 1978; DDS, Loyola U., 1982. Instr. endodontics Howard U. Sch. Dentistry, Washington, 1989-91; asst. prof. biology Ala. A&M U., Normal, 1991-94; dentist Drs. David and Isabel Yarbrough, Huntsville, Ala., 1993—. Mem. NAACP, Huntsville, 1996. Capt. U.S. Army, 1986-89. Mem. North Ala. Med. Assn., Huntsville-Madison Dental Soc., Delta Sigma Theta, Psi Omega. Avocations: reading, swimming, jogging. Home: 204 Cheswick Dr Madison AL 35757-8720 Office: 4530 Bonnell Dr NW Ste A Huntsville AL 35816-2002

YARBROUGH, KAREN A. state representative; b. Wash., DC, Aug. 22, 1950; m. Henderson Yarbrough; children: Tami, Vicki, Carmen, Sara, Marcus, Henderson Jr. BA Bus. Admin., Chgo. State Univ., Chgo., Ill, 1993; MA Inner city Studies, NE Ill. Univ., Ill., 1996. Chief Exec. Officer Hathaway Ins. Agy., 1975—; Rep., Dist. 7 State House of Rep., 2000—. Candidate House of Rep., Dist. 7, Ill., 1998. Mem.: Juvenile Justice Reform, Ins. (Vice Chair), Appropriations - pub. safety, Maywood Chamber of Comm. (past pres. 1989—92, 1994—96), United Way of Suburban Chgo. (bd. exec. 1998—), Proviso Area United Way (v.p. 1987—2000), Profl. Indep. Ins. Agents (bd. mem. 1997—), Oak Park Young Men's Christian Assoc. (bd. mem. 1998), Elem. & Sec. Ed., Maywood Youth Mentoring Program (mem.), Maywood Live Theater (founder). Democrat. Bapt. Office: 292-S Straton Office Bldg Springfield IL 62706 also: 1030 South 17th Maywood IL 60153

YARBROUGH, KATHRYN DAVIS, public health nurse; b. Montrose, Colo., Aug. 31, 1947; d. L.O. and V. Jean (Dunn) Davis; m. James H. Yarbrough, Aug. 8, 1970; children: James, Jason. Diploma, Good Samaritan Hosp. Sch. Nursing, Phoenix, 1971; BSN, Kennesaw State Coll., 1996. RN, Ga.; cert. NAACOG. Supr. Cherokee County Health Dept., Canton, Ga., 1976-97. Den mother Boy Scouts Am., Canton, 1986-87; bd. dirs. Cancer soc., Canton, 1987—, Cherokee County Violence Ctr., 1990, First Steps Bd., 1993-97, Cherokee County Advocacy Ctr., 1994-97; HIV cons. ARC, Canton, 1988—, disaster vol., Cherokee County, 1993-99; co-chair Early Intervention Coun., Canton, 1991-93; mem. Leadership Cherokee, 1994, Interagy Coun., 1994; mem. Blue Ridge Jud. Cir. Domestic Violence Task Force, 1995. Mem.: ANA, Ga. Nurses Assn., Svc. League Cherokee County (hon.). Methodist. E-mail: Kyarbro216@aol.com.

YARBROUGH, MARTHA CORNELIA, music educator; b. Waycross, Ga., Feb. 8, 1940; d. Henry Elliott and Jessie (Sirmans) Y. BME, Stetson U., 1962; MME, Fla. State U., 1968, PhD, 1973. Choral dir. Ware County H.S., Waycross, 1962-64, Glynn Acad., Brunswick, Ga., 1964—70; asst. choral dir. Fla. State U., 1970-72; cons. in music Muscogee County Sch. Dist., Columbus, Ga., 1972-73; cons. in tchr. edn. Psycho-Edno. Cons., Inc., Tallahassee, 1972-73; asst. prof. music edn., dir. choruses and oratorio socs. Syracuse (NY) U., 1973-76; assoc. prof. music edn. Syracuse U., 1976-83, prof., 1983-86, acting asst. dean Coll. Visual and Performing Arts, 1980-82, acting dir. Sch. Music, 1980-82, chmn. music edn., 1982-86; prof. music La. State U., Baton Rouge, 1986—, coord. music edn., 1986—2000, Haymon prof. of music, 1995—. Artist-in-residence Sch. Music U. Ala., Tuscaloosa, 1989-90, 98, 2002; chair exec. com. Music Edn. Rsch. Coun., 1992-94. Co-author: Competency-Based Music Education, 1980; mem. editl. com.: Jour. Rsch. in Music Edn., editor-in-chief:, 2000—; contbr. chapters to books, articles to profl. jours. Mem. Music Educators Nat. Conf. (Sr. Rschr. award 1996), La. State Music Assn., Am. Ednl. Rsch. Assn., Soc. Rsch. Music Edn. (mem. exec. com. 1988-90, program chair 1990-92, chair 1992-94), AAUP, Coll. Music Soc., Pi Kappa Lambda, Phi Beta, Kappa Delta Pi. Office: Sch Music La State U Baton Rouge LA 70803-2504 E-mail: cyarbro@lsu.edu.

YARD, MOLLY, social activist; b. China; d. James Maxon and Mabelle Merriam (Hickcox) Y.; m. Sylvester Garrett; 3 children. AB, Swarthmore Coll., 1933, Hon. LLD, 1988. Chmn. Am. Student Union; active in Dem. party politics, Pa. and Calif., 1940s and 50s; active in civil rights movement, Pa., 1960s and 70s; staff mem. VISTA, 1960s; active NOW, from 1970s, polit. dir., 1985-87, pres., 1987-91.

YARD, SHERRY, chef; b. Bklyn. Pastry chef Spago, Beverly Hills, Calif. Recipient pastry chef of yr. award, So. Calif. Restaurant Writers Assn. Office: Spago 176 N Canon Dr Beverly Hills CA 90210

YARED, LINDA S. mechanical engineer; b. East Grand Rapids, Mich., July 31, 1952; d. Fozee S. and Penny (Bassler) Y. BS in Mech. Engring., U. Md., 1987. Sr. tech. rep. Xerox Corp., Rosslyn, Va., 1979-84; sr. engr. Mack Trucks, Allentown, Pa., 1987-90, Allied Signal Braking Systems, South Bend, Ind., 1990-95; project engr. Tri/Mark Corp., New Hampton, Iowa, 1995-99, Up and Running Inc, Granger, Ind., 1999—. Patentee in field. Mem. ASME, NOW (treas. 1994), Soc. Automotive Engrs. (sec. 1988-90), Soc. Women Engrs. Avocation: dog obedience training. Office: Up and Running Inc 227 E Cleveland Rd Ste 6 Granger IN 46530-7098

YARMO, FANNY F. not-for-profit fundraiser; b. Kansas City, Mo., Dec. 25, 1910; d. Sol and Della Fox; m. Al Yarmo (dec. Feb. 19, 1987); 1 child, Robert L. ; m. Leo Sofnas, 1936 (div. 1950). BS in Bus. summa cum laude, U. Kans., 1931. Ins. sec. Norman Hobart, Kansas City, 1931—32; Spanish translator Ismert Hincke Milling, Kansas City, 1932—35; pres. Fan-Ro Corp., Kansas City, 1954—75; regional treas. Sisterhood, Kansas City,

1989—90. Hon. fellow Truman Libr. Sch. for Democracy, Kansas City, 1992—, patron Truman Libr. Independence, Mo., 1999; patron vis. artists Kemper Art Mus., Kansas City, 1999—; charter patron Spencer Libr.-- Nelson-Atkins Mus., Kansas City, 1999; TZDA art patron Jewish Cmty. Ctr., Overland Park, Kans., 1999—; life mem. Hadassah Menorah Hosp., 1945—; mem. Kansas City Historic Found., 1999—; charter patron Kemper Mus. Art; vol. Friends of O.P. Arts, Congregation Hesed Com.; mem. Nat. Wildlife Pres, Friends of DAV; vice chmn. then life mem. chmn. NCJW, Kansas City; life mem. chmn. Brandeis U. Women, Kansas City, 1960; spl. gifts chmn. Fedn., Kansas City, 1965; mem. pres. coun. Art Inst., 1980—87; mem. nat. com. Kemper Art Mus., Kansas City, 2001—03; mem. univ. assocs. U. Mo., Kansas City, 1995—. Mem.: AAUW, Symphony Women's Assn., Mo. Reperatory Theatre Patron, Smithsonian Inst., Oakwood C.C. (life), Native Sons of Kansas City, Jewish War Vets Assn., Phi Chi Theta. Jewish. Avocations: bridge, Mah Jongg, Bible study, computers. Home: 102 E woodbridge Ln Kansas City MO 64145

YARNO, WENDY, pharmaceutical executive; BA, Portland State U., 1982; MBA, Temple U., 1988. Profl. rep. U.S. Human Health, 1983—85, mktg. analyst, 1985—87, product mgr. pediatric vaccines, 1988, assoc. dir. econ. affaris, 1989, sr. dir. mktg. planning, 1990—91, nat. account exec., 1991, sr. dir. managed health care affairs, 1992, project leader for U.S. Health Care Reform, 1992—93; v.p. ctrl. region Merck-Medco, 1994; v.p. hypertension and heart failure therapeutic bus. group U.S. Human Health, 1994—97; v.p. Ortho McNeil Pharm., Johnson & Johnson, 1997—98; v.p. worldwide human health Merck & Co., Inc., Whitehouse Station, NJ, 1999, v.p. human resources, 1999, sr. v.p. human resources, 2000—. Named Hon. Chairperson for Dinner of Hope, Somerset Hills Handicapped Riding Ctr. Office: Merck and Co Inc One Merck Dr Whitehouse Station NJ 08889-0100

YARRINGTON, PATRICIA, oil industry executive; b. Apr. 1956; B Polit. Sci., Pomona Coll., 1977; MBA, Northwestern U. With Chevron Corp., 1980—; sr. fin. analyst Chevron U.S.A. Inc., 1984—86, mgr. investor relations, 1986; various supervisory positions Chevron Products Co., Chevron U.S.A. Prodn. Co., Chevron Rsch. and Tech. Co.; mgr. credit card enterprises Chevron Products Co., 1995—97, comptr., 1997—98; pres. Chevron Can. Ltd., Vancouver, Canada, 1998—2000; v.p. strategic planning Chevron Corp., 2000—01; v.p. pub. and govt. affairs ChevronTexaco Corp., San Ramon, Calif., 2002—. Bd. dirs. Chevron Phillips Chem. Co. Bd. dirs. ChevronTexaco Found. Office: ChevronTexaco Corp 6001 Bollinger Canyon Rd San Ramon CA 94583-2324

YARYAN, RUBY BELL, psychologist; b. Toledo, Apr. 28, 1938; d. John Sturges and Susan (Bell) Y.; m. John Frederick Buenz, Jr., Dec. 15, 1962 (div. 1968). AB, Stanford U., 1960; PhD, U. London, 1968. Lic. clin. psychologist; diplomate Am. Bd. Psychology, Am. Acad. Experts in Traumatic Stess. Rsch. dir., univ. radio and TV, U. Calif., San Francisco, 1968-70; dir. delinquency coun. U.S. Dept. Justice, Washington, 1970-73; evaluation dir. Office Criminal Justice Planning, Sacramento, Calif., 1973-76; CAO project mgr. San Diego County, 1977-92; dir. devel. svcs. Childhelp USA, Woodland Hills, Calif., 1992-94; rsch. coord. Neuropsychiat. Inst. and Hosp., UCLA, 1986-87; exec. dir. Centinela Child Guidance Clinic, Inglewood, Calif., [illegible] Nat. Found. Emotionally Handicapped, North Hills, Calif., 1990-93; pvt. practice, Beverly Hills, Calif., 1973—; supr. psychologist Los Angeles County Dept. Mental Health, 1998—. Psychologist Sr. Psychology Svcs., North L.A. County, 1994-98; cons. White House Conf. Children, Washington, 1970; mem. Nat. Adv. Com. Criminal Justice Standards and Goals, Washington, 1973; clin. affiliation UCLA Med. Ctr. Contbr. articles to profl. jours.; chpts. to books and monographs in field. Chair Human Svcs. Commn., City of West Hollywood, Calif., 1986; first vice-chair United Way/Western Region, L.A., 1988; mem. planning-allocations-rsch. coun. United Way, San Diego, 1980-82. Grantee numerous fed., state and local govt. orgns. Mem. Am. Psychol. Assn., Western Psychol. Assn., Calif. Psychol. Assn., Am. Orthopsychiat. Assn., Am. Profl. Soc. on Abuse of Children, Phi Beta Kappa. Episcopalian. Avocations: painting, music, theatre, writing, reading. Office: 337 S Beverly Dr Ste 107 Beverly Hills CA 90212-4307 Office Phone: 310-271-3921.

YATES, ALLISON A. scientific organization administrator; BS, MS, Univ. of Calif.; PhD, Univ. of Calif. at Berkley, 1974. Dean Univ. of Southern Miss., 1988—97; dir. food and nutrition bd. Inst. of Medicine, the Nat. Acads., 1994-1996, 1997—. Office: Inst Medicine, the Nat Acads 500 5th St NW Washington DC 20001

YATES, CHERYL ANN, home economist, educator; b. Cheyenne, Wyo., Oct. 11, 1945; d. Robert Watson and Harriette Julia (Oberg) Yates. BS, U. Wyo., 1968; MA, Ariz. State U., No. Ariz. U. Cert. home econ. tchr. Ariz. Tchr. Carson Jr. HS, Mesa, Ariz., 1968—69; tchr., chmn. home econs. dept. Powell Jr. HS, Mesa, 1970—80; tchr. Mountain View HS, Mesa, 1980—81, Dobson HS, Mesa, 1981—, dept. chair, 1981—. Contbr. articles to mags. in field. Active Friends of Channel 8. Mem.: NEA, Mesa Edn. Assn., Ariz. Edn. Assn. Republican. Office: 1502 W Guadalupe Rd Mesa AZ 85202

YATES, ELLA GAINES, library consultant; b. Atlanta, June 14, 1927; d. Fred Douglas and Laura (Moore) Gaines; m. Joseph L. Sydnor (dec.); 1 child, Jerri Gaines Sydnor Lee; m. Clayton R. Yates (dec.). AB, Spelman Coll., Atlanta, 1949; MS in L.S, Atlanta U., 1951; JD, Atlanta Law Sch., 1979. 1954Asst. br. librarian Bklyn. Pub. Library, 1951; head children's dept. Orange (N.J.) Pub. Library, 1956—59; br. librarian East Orange (N.J.) Pub. Library, 1960—69; med. librarian Orange Meml. Hosp., 1967—69; asst. dir. Montclair (N.J.) Pub. Library, 1970—72, Atlanta-Fulton Pub. Library, 1972—76, dir., 1976—81; dir. learning resource ctr. Seattle Opportunities Industrialization Ctr., 1982—84; asst. dir. adminstrn. Friendship Force, Atlanta, 1984—86; state librarian Commonwealth of Va., 1986—90; library cons. Price Waterhouse, 1991; adv. bd. Library of Congress Center for the Book, 1977—85; interim dir. Atlanta-Fulton Pub. Libr., 1998—99; cons., dir. Woodruff Libr., Atlanta, 2000—02. Cons. in field; vis. lectr. U. Wash., Seattle, 1981-83; mem. Va. Records Adv. Bd., 1986-90; mem. Nagara Exec. Bd., 1987-91. Contbr. to profl. jours. Vice chmn. N.J. Women's Coun. on Human Rels., 1957-59; chmn. Friends Fulton County Jail, 1973-81; bd. dirs. United Cerebral Palsy Greater Atlanta, Inc., 1979-81 Coalition Against Censorship, Washington, 1981-84, YMCA Met. Atlanta, 1979-81, Exec. Women's Network, 1979-82, Freedom To Read Found., 1979-85, Va. Black History Mus., Richmond, 1990-91; sec., exec. dir. Va. Libr. Found. Bd., 1986-90. Recipient meritorious svc. award Atlanta U., 1977, Phoenix award City of Atlanta, 1980, Serwa award Nat. Coalition 100 Black Women, 1989, Black Caucus award, 1989, disting. svc. award Clark-Atlanta U., 1991, ednl. support svc. award Tuskegee Airmen, 1993, Alumnae Achievement award Spelman Coll., 1998, Annie McPheters award Atlanta-Fulton Pub. Libr., 1998, Disting. Alumnae award Clark Atlanta U., 2001; named profl. woman of yr. NAACP N.J., 1972, outstanding chum of yr., 1976; named outstanding alumni Spelman Coll., 1977, named to alumni hall of fame, 1995. Mem. ALA (exec. bd. 1977-83, commn. freedom of access to info.), NAACP, Southeastern Libr. Assn., Nat. Assn. Govt. Archives and Records Adminstrs. (exec. bd. 1987-91), Delta Sigma Theta (Pinnacle leadership award 2001). Baptist. Home and Office: 1171 Oriole Dr SW Atlanta GA 30311-2424

YATES, KIMBERLY NICOLE, school psychologist; b. St. Louis, Sept. 26, 1971; d. Clarenc and Odelia Yates. BA, Ala. A&M U., 1993; MEd, Howard U., 1995; EdD, Nova Southeastern U., 1999. Sch. psychologist Nat. Assn. Sch. Psychologists, 1994—. Mem. Alpha Kappa Alpha, Kappa Delta Pi. Democrat. Pentecostal. Avocations: aerobics, swimming. E-mail: kny11@aol.com.

YATES, LINDA SNOW, financial services marketing executive, real estate; b. St. Louis, July 20, 1938; d. Robert Anthony Jerrue and June Alberta (Crowder) Armstrong; m. Charles Russell Snow, Nov. 26, 1958 (div. 1979); children: Cathryn Louise, Christopher Armstrong, Heather Highstone, Sean Webster; m. Alan Porter Yates, July 22, 1983. BBA, Auburn U., 1973, MEd, 1975, EdD, 1998. Cert. profl. sec. Div. head placement div. Solutions Group, Atlanta, 1981-83; employment coord. Fulton Fed. Savs., Atlanta, 1983-84; owner, recruiter Data One, Inc., Atlanta, 1984-85; ops. mgr. Talent Tree Temporaries, Atlanta, 1985-87; legal asst., sec. Rice & Keene, Atlanta, 1987-90; legal word processing asst. Kilpatrick & Cody, Atlanta, 1990-94; pres., owner Power Comm., Cashiers, N.C., 1994-98; regional coord. S.E. region, regional mktg. rep. WorldConnect Comms., Tulsa; dir. mktg. electronic collection divsn. Am. Fin. and Credit Svcs., Inc.; area v.p., loan agent Enterprise Lenders, LLC; bd. dirs., corp. sec. The Hilltop Assocs. Inc., 1999—; real estate sales Apex Realty, Inc. Adj. instr. DeKalb Coll., Atlanta, 1980-84, Mercer U., Atlanta, 1981-82; instr. bus. So. Union State Jr. Coll., Valley, Ala., 1974-75; legal sec. Swift, Currie, McGhee & Hiers, Atlanta, 1979-80, Samford, Torbert, Denson & Horsley, Opelika, Ala., 1969-71; dir. acad. planning, chmn. edn. divsn., mem. part-time faculty in ednl. adminstrn. CEU Grad. Coll., Nuevo Leon, Mex. Columnist Neon News Flash, 1995. Mem. Paralegal Assn. Beaufort County (charter mem., sec. 1993-94), Women Bus. Owners, Nat. Assn. Pers. Cons., Internat. Soc. Poets (Disting. mem., Internat. Poet of Merit 1996, Internat. Poetry Hall of Fame 1996), Cashiers Writers Group, Phi Delta Kappa, Alpha Xi Delta. Republican. Episcopalian. Avocations: golf, writing, international travel. Office: 1 Wade Hampton Dr Ladys Island SC 29907

YATES, MARY CARLIN, ambassador; b. Portland, Oreg., Dec. 1946; m. John Melvin Yates. BA in English, Oreg. State U.; M in Comparative East West Humanities, postgrad., NYU. Joined fgn. svc., 1980; press attaché for Amb. Pamela Harriman Dept. of State, sr. cultural attaché Am. Embassy, U.S. amb. to Burundi Washington, 1999—. Office: DOS Amb 2100 Bujumbura Pl Washington DC 20521

YATES, MILDRED CAMPBELL, retired literature educator; b. Beaumont, Tex., Jan. 1, 1920; d. William Holland and Eula Mildred (Owens) Campbell; m. Reed Henry Yates, Jr., May 17, 1944; children: Reed Henry III, Mary Campbell Yates Kirkpatrick. BFA, U. Ga., 1940; MA in English, Lamar U., 1962. Cert. tchr. grades 5-12, Tex. Tchr. elem. lang. arts and music Beaumont (Tex.) Ind. Sch. Dist., 1953-67; asst. prof. elem. lang. arts edn. Lamar U., Beaumont, 1968-70; tchr. Am. lit. and world civilization French H.S., Beaumont, 1970-79. Bd. dirs. Mental Health Assn., Austin, Tex., 1972-76; commr. Beaumont Landmark Corp., 1980-84; dir. of bd. Arts Related Curriculum, Beaumont, 1982-89; docent French Hist. House, Beaumont, 1979—. Co-author: (devel. reader) Images, 1971, Keystone, 1975; co-author, co-editor: With a Dome More Vast, 1986 (Kate Warnick award 1986); author. (essay) Beaumont Women, A Memoir, 1992. Pres. Beaumont Heritage Soc., 1980-82; genealogist Tex. Gulf Hist. Soc., Beaumont, 1986—; pres., sec. Tyrrell Hist. Libr. Assn., Beaumont, 1987—; tchr. adult classes First United Meth. Ch., Beaumont, 1998—; bd. dirs. Beaumont Music Commn., 1988—, chmn. Speaker's Bur., Jefferson Theatre Restoration, 1998—. Nominee for Jefferson award Beaumont Enterprise, 1996; recipient Preservation award Main St. Project, Beaumont, 1997. Mem. Art Mus. of Tex., Pi Beta Phi (sec.). Methodist. Avocations: reading, travel, hist. preservation, [illegible]

YATSONSKY, JOAN MARIE, nursing educator; b. Honesdale, Pa., June 16, 1952; d. William Vincent and Mary Jeanne Yatsonsky; children: Aaron Micheal Tregaskis(dec.), Summer Anne Tregaskis(dec.). AS in Nursing, Luzerne County C.C., 1993; BSN, Pa. State U., 2002; student, Duke U., 2003—. RN Pa., 1993, cert. nurse operating room, Cert. Bd. Peri-Operative Nursing, 1996, RN N.J., 1997, Fla., 1997, cert. registered nurse first asst., Certification Bd. Peri-operative Nursing, 2000. Nurse operating rm. Mercy Hosp., Scranton, Pa., 1983—; prin., owner RNFA Associates, Waymart, Pa., 1997—; nurse educator, patient care specialist Lehigh Valley Hosp. Muhlenberg, Bethlehem, Pa., 2003—. Neurosurgical coord. Mercy Hosp., Scranton, 2001—, cardiothoracic surgery coord., 1994—95. Chmn. rally for a cure Susan G. Komen Found., Waymart, Pa., 2002—03; liaison Certification Bd. Perioperative Nursing, Scranton Area, 2002—03. Recipient Citizenship Award, 1954; scholar Grace Keen Nursing scholarship, Pa. State U., Worthington Campus, Dunmore Pa, 2001. Mem.: Penn State Alumni Assn., Assn. Peri-Operative Nurses (chpt. pres. 2003—), Am. Assn. Neuroscience Nurses, Phi Kappa Phi, Sigma Theta Tau. Republican. Roman Catholic. Avocations: travel, photography, golf, writing. Home: RD 2 Box 2916 Owego Turnpike Waymart PA 18472 Office: Lehigh Valley Hospital Muhlenberg 2545 Schoenersville Road Bethlehem PA 18017 Personal E-mail: trigger@socantel.net.

YAX, ELLEN MARIE, photography finisher; b. Boonton, N.J., Nov. 26, 1962; d. Bernard Joseph and Theresa Lorretta (Evans) Merchak; m. Thomas Alan Yax, Sept. 24, 1988. Cert. achievement, Gemini Sch. Art and Design, 1987. Driver Hertz-Rent-a-Car, Romulus, Mich., 1981-89; sign painter Sign Specialties, Allen Park, Mich., 1988; photography finisher N.Am. Photo, Livonia, Mich., 1989—. Vol. St. Hilary's Ch., Redford, Mich., 1992—; mem. St. Hilary's Rosary Altar Soc., 1994—, sec., 1997. Roman Catholic. Avocations: art, traveling. Office: 27451 Schoolcraft Rd Livonia MI 48150-2201

YAZDI, MAHVASH, utilities executive; BS in Indsl. Mgmt., Poly. U., Pomona; MBA, U. So. Calif.; grad. mgmt. info. tech. program, Harvard U. CIO Hughes Aircraft; joined Edison Internat., 1997, sr. v.p. bus. integration, CIO So. Calif. Edison subs., sr. v.p. bus. integration, CIO. Bd. dirs. Claremont U. Consortium, Ptnrs. in Care Found., Columbus Newport Corp.; adv. dir. Lotus Corp., IBM Corp.; mem. So. Calif. Forum of the Trusteeship of the Internat. Women's Forum, 2003. Office: Edison Internat 2244 Walnut Grove Ave Rosemead CA 91770

YDE, JACQULYN RAE, interior designer, architectural colorist; b. Freeport, Ill. d. John Harrison and Ethlyn Roberta (Puckett) Groves; children: Michael, Michelle, Mark, Matthew, Gregory; m. Al Alschuler, 2000. Student, Harper C.C., Palatine, Ill., Chgo. Architecture Found.; degree, Harrington Inst. Interior Design, 1975. Lic. interior designer, NCIDQ cer. 1980-. Ptnr. Swedroe/Yde Design Assocs., Miami Beach, Fla., 1983—88; pres. Jacqulyn Yde Design, Inc., Miami, Fla., 1988—. Color design City of Miami Beach, 1986, South Beach hotels, 1987-, Fisher Island (original models) 1982-83, Suzanne's in the Grove Club and restaurant, 1986; mem. interior design adv. bd. Art Inst. Ft. Lauderdale, Fla., 1990-; public speaker, color/light/healing environ. Prin. works include North Shore Historic Homes, Miami Beach, 1988. Color designer North Miami Sr. H.S., 1987, Miami-Dade County Auditorium, Crescent and Sagamore Hotels, South Beach, Fla., Island Pointe Condominium, Bay Harbor, Fla. Named Designer of Yr., Art Deco Socs., Miami Style. Mem. Am. Soc. Interior Designers (bd. dirs. 2001—), The Color Assn. U.S. Avocations: writing, travel, reading, theatre, opera. E-mail: jycolordesign@aol.com.

YEAGER, BERNICE WHITTAKER, elementary and secondary school educator; b. Bethany, W.Va., June 26, 1915; d. Robert Helsabeck and Louise (McGraw) Whittaker; m. Roy Harold Yeager (dec. 1967). AB, Concord Coll., W.Va., 1934; MS, U. Tenn., 1937. Tchr./prin. Mercer County Schs., Princeton, W.Va., 1934-45, supr. instrn., 1945-47; asst. prof., supervising tchr. Winthrop Tng. Sch.-Winthrop Coll., Rock Hill, S.C., 1948-64; coordinator reading Lancaster (S.C.) City Schs., 1964-70, Lancaster County Schs., 1970-75; tchr. Catawba Acad., Rock Hill, S.C., 1975-82; substitute tchr. Charlotte-Mecklenburg Schs., Charlotte, N.C., 1983—. Cons. in field. Chmn. youth activities ARC, Rock Hill, 1970-75. Named Woman of the Yr., Rock Hill Bus. and Profl. Women, 1977, others. Mem. NEA, S.C. Edn. Assn., AAUW, S.C. Ret. Tchrs. Assn., Phi Kappa Phi, Delta Kappa Gamma. Lutheran. Address: 862 Mary Knoll Ct Rock Hill SC 29730-3727

YEAGER, CAROLINE HALE, radiologist, consultant; b. Little Rock, Sept. 5, 1946; d. George Glenn and Crenor Burnelle (Hale) Y.; m. William Berg Singer, July 8, 1978; children: Adina Atkinson Singer, Sarah Rose Singer. BA, Ind. U., Bloomington, 1968; MD, Ind. U., Indpls., 1971. Diplomate Am. Bd. Radiology; med. lic. State of Calif. Intern Good Samaritan Hosp., Los Angeles, 1971-72; resident in radiology King Drew Med. Ctr. UCLA, Los Angeles, 1972-76; dir. radiology Hubert Humphrey Health Ctr., Los Angeles, 1976-77; asst. prof. radiology UCLA, Los Angeles, 1977-84, King Drew Med. Ctr. UCLA, Los Angeles, 1977-85, dir. ultrasound, 1977-84; ptnr. pvt. practice Beverly Breast Ctr., Beverly Hills, Calif., 1984-87; cons. Clarity Communications, Pasadena, Calif., 1981—; pvt. practice radiology Claude Humphrey Health Ctr., 1991-93; dir. sonograms and mammograms Rancho Los Amigos Med. Ctr., 1993-94. Trustee Assn. Teaching Physicians, L.A., 1976-81; cons. King Drew Med. Ctr., 1984, Gibraltar Savs., 1987, Cal Fed. Inc., 1986, Medical Faculty At Home Professions, 1989—, Mobil Diagnostics, 1991-92, Xerox Corp., 1990-91, Frozen Leopard, Inc., 1990-91. Author: (with others) Infectious Disease, 1978, Anatomy and Physiology for Medical Transcriptionists, 1992; contbr. articles to profl. jours. Trustee U. Synagogue, Los Angeles, 1975-79; mem. Friends of Pasadena Playhouse, 1987-90. Grantee for innovative tng. Nat. Fund for Med. Edn., 1980-81. Mem. Am. Inst. Ultrasound in Medicine, L.A. Radiology Soc. (ultrasound sect.), Nat. Soc. Performance and Instrn. (chmn. conf. Database 1991, publs. L.A. chpt. 1990, info. systems L.A. chpt. 1991, dir. adminstrn. L.A. chpt. 1992, Outstanding Achievement in Performance Improvement award L.A. chpt. 1990, bd. dirs. 1990-93, Pres. award for Outstanding Chpt. 1992, v.p. programs 1993), Stanford Profl. Women L.A. Jewish. Avocations: writing, humor, design. Home and Office: 3520 Yorkshire Rd Pasadena CA 91107-5440

YEAGER, DEBRA LYN, science educator; b. St. Paul, Mar. 20, 1957; d. Lyle Milton and Grace Jeanette (Mitchell) Yeager, Wilma Mitchell; life ptnr. Christopher Charles Pfannes. AS in Computer Sci., Mesa C.C., Ariz., 1982; student, Scottsdale C.C., Ariz., 1979—80. Ordained minister Order of Melchizedek, 1991. Investigator - profiler Elk River Sheriff's Dept., Minn., 1992—94; sensor sci. tchr. Open U. of Minn., Mpls., 1994—99; sensory sci. tchr. Yeager Consulting / Into the Mystic, Minnetonka, Minn., 1998—, Wis. Indianhead Tech. Coll., New Richmond, 2003—, West Ctrl. Cancer Symposium, Willmar, Minn., 2003, U. Alaska-Sitka, 2003—, U. Manitoba, 2004—, U. Coll. Dublin, Ireland, 2004—, Queens U.-Belfast, Ireland, 2004—; on the air talent, lectr. Kare 11 - NBC TV Mpls, 2002—03, WCCO 4 - CB3 TV Mpls., 2002, NW Mag. Cable Show, New Hope, Minn., 1996, Criminologist and profiler Crema Law Offices, Mpls., 1999—. Author: (novel) Encounters with the Sixth Dimension (Book in print), Intervention across time, Medium, Rare - the Bio of Debra Yeager, Karman from MU. Mem.: Delta Zeta (hon.). Achievements include research in Metaphysical Studies, development of Programs of Metaphysical Studies. Avocations: motorcycling, designing jewelry, horse training, running, travel. Home and Office: PO Box 315 Taylors Falls MN 55084-0315 Personal E-mail: century30@aol.com.

YEAGER, RUTH, lawyer; Asst. U.S. Atty., Dept. Justice, Tyler, Tex., chief civil divsn., 1988—2002; U.S. Atty. Ea. Dist. Tex., 1993—94. Office: US Attys Office 110 N College Ave Ste 700 Tyler TX 75702-0204 E-mail: ruth.yeager@usdoj.gov.

YEAGLEY, JOAN HOWERTON, writer; b. Denver, Colo., Jan. 25, 1930; d. Harold Emery Howerton and Jeannette Louise Boule; m. Harold Arthur Yeagley, Apr. 14, 1951; children: Jan, Donn, Jeff, Jeanne. BSc in Edn., Kans. State U., 1984. Cons. N.E. Kans. Libr. Sys.; tchr. creative writing Mo. Southern State Coll., Joplin, Crowder Coll.; workshop leader in field. Author: Four Bookmark Poets, The Studs of McDonald County, 1987; contbr. articles and stories to mags. Great books coord. Kans. City Pub. Libr./Great Books Found., Chgo. Recipient Kans. City Star award, Kans. City Star, 1965—67, Gold Quill award, Crowder Coll., 1988, Sager Creek Arts Ctr. award, John Brown U., 1995—96. Home: 61 Tiffany Ln Stella MO 64867 E-mail: jnyeagley@leru.net.

YEARGIN-ALLSOPP, MARSHALYN, medical epidemiologist, pediatrician; b. Greenville, S.C., May 17, 1948; d. Grady Andrew and Willie Mae (Blocker) Yeargin; m. Ralph Norman Allsopp, Apr. 5, 1975; children: Timothy Chandler, Whitney Marisha. Student Bennett Coll., 1964-66; BA, Sweet Briar Coll., 1968; MD, Emory U., 1972. Diplomate Am. Bd. Pediatrics. Intern Montefiore Hosp., Bronx, N.Y., 1972-73, resident, 1973-75; instr. pediatrics Albert Einstein Coll. Medicine, Bronx, 1975-77, asst. prof. pediatrics, 1977-78, 80-81; pediatrician Montefiore-Morrisania Comprehensive Health Care Ctr., Bronx, 1975-78, Louise Wise Adoption Agy., N.Y.C., 1975-80, Children's Evaluation and Rehab. Ctr., Rose F. Kennedy Ctr., Bronx, 1980-81; officer USPHS, 1981—, comdr., 1983—; epidemiologic intelligence surveillance officer birth defects br. Ctrs. for Disease Control, Atlanta, 1981-83, preventive medicine resident, 1982-84, med. epidemiologist, 1984—; pediatric cons. Clayton County Early Intervention Program, Jonesboro, Ga., 1983—; med. dir. Easter Seal Presch. Program, Atlanta, 1981-83; physician Com. on Handicapped, N.Y.C., 1979-81, United Cerebral Palsy Program, Bronx, 1980-81. Bd. overseers Sweet Briar Coll., 1981-89; bd. dirs. Neighborhood Arts Ctr., Atlanta, 1984-87; mem. prevention edn. com. Retarded Citizens, Atlanta, 1984-96; mem. fundraising campaign Greater Atlanta YWCA, 1985; bd. trustees Pace Acad., 1986—; co-chmn. Minority Atlanta Families in Ind. Schs., Inc., 1986—; chair, bd. dirs. profl. adv. com. Cerebral Palsey Ctr., REACH, Inc., Atlanta, 1988—; mem. State of Ga. Interagy. Coun. for Edn. of the Handicapped Act., 1988-96; mem. sci. adv. bd. Nat. Alliance for Autism Rsch. Recipient Disting. Alumna award, Sweet Briar Coll., 1992. Fellow Am. Acad. Pediatrics, Am. Acad. Cerebral Palsy and Devel. Medicine; mem. AMA, Atlanta Med. Assn., Jack and Jill of Am., Phi Beta Kappa, Delta Sigma Theta. Office: Ctrs for Disease Control 4770 Buford Hwy NE Atlanta GA 30341-3717

YEARWOOD, TRISHA, country music singer, songwriter; b. Monticello, Ga., 1964; m. Chris Latham (div.); m. Robert Reynolds, May 21, 1994 (div.). Degree in Music Bus., Belmont U. Intern MTM Records, demo singer, commercial jingles singer; recording artist MCA Records. Albums include Trisha Yearwood, 1991 (double platinum), Hearts in Armor, 1992 (Grammy nomination: Best Country Female Vocal, 1994 for "Walkaway Joe"), The Song Remembers When, 1993, Thinkin' About You, 1995, Everybody Knows, 1996, (songbook) A Collection of Hits, 1997, Where Your Road Leads, 1998, Real Live Woman, 2000; back-up vocalist Garth Brooks albums; opening act Garth Brooks Tour, 1991; TV appearances on TNN American Music Shop, The Tonight Show, Late Night with David Letterman, Good Morning America, A&E Live By Request, 1998 Academy Awards, 1996 Summer Olympic Closing Ceremonies. Named Best New Country Artist by Am. Music Awards, 1992, Top New Female Vocalist by Acad. Country Music, 1992, Top Female Vocalist of Yr., 1998; Top Female Vocalist of Yr., Country Mus. Assn., 1997, 98; first female in country music history to have debut single reach #1 on charts with She's in Love with the Love, 1991; recipient Grammy awards for best female country vocal, 1998, best country vocal collaboration (with Aaron Neville) 1994, (with Garth Brooks), 1998.

YEATTS, DOROTHY ELIZABETH FREEMAN, nurse, educator, retired county official; b. Richmond, Va., Jan. 19, 1925; d. Robert Franklin and Elizabeth Bell (Wiggins) Freeman; m. Roy Earl Yeatts, Nov. 27, 1948; children: Martha Jane Yeatts Couch, Robert Patrick. Diploma in nursing, Stuart Circle Hosp., Richmond, Va., 1947; BS in Nursing, Coll. William and

Mary, 1947; cert. pub. health nursing supr., U. N.C., 1974. RN, Va., N.C. Vis. nurse Instructive Vis. Nurses Assn., Richmond, 1947-49; maternity nurse N.C. Bapt. Hosp., Winston-Salem, 1969-71; pub. health nurse I, Forsyth County Health Dept., Winston-Salem, 1971-72, pub. health nurse coord., 1972-74, pub. health nurse supr., 1974-78. Sunday sch. tchr. Tuckahoe Presbyn. Ch., Richmond, 1954-57, Trinity Presbyn Ch., Winston-Salem, 1960-84; pres. Buckingham Park Garden Club, Richmond, 1956-58, Women of Trinity Presbyn. Ch., 1963-64; elder Trinity Presbyn. Ch., 1978-81, circle bible moderator, 1984-97; bd. dirs. Forsyth Cancer Soc., Winston-Salem, 1980-86; instr. ARC, Winston-Salem, 1978-97, vol., 1993-97. Republican. Avocations: arts and crafts, fishing, stamp collecting, woodcarving, sewing. Home: 310 Coventry Park Ln Winston Salem NC 27104-3676 E-mail: ryeatts@triad.rr.com.

YEAZELL, RUTH BERNARD, English language educator; b. N.Y.C., Apr. 4, 1947; d. Walter and Annabelle (Reich) Bernard; m. Stephen C. Yeazell, Aug. 14, 1969 (div. 1980). BA with high honors, Swarthmore Coll., 1967; MPhil, Yale U., 1970, PhD, 1971. Asst. prof. English Boston U., 1971-74, UCLA, 1975-77, assoc. prof., 1977-80, prof., 1980-91, Yale U., 1991—, dir. grad. studies, 1993-98, Chace family prof., 1995—, chair, 2000—. Author: Language and Knowledge in the Late Novels of Henry James, 1976, Death and Letters of Alice James, 1981, Fictions of Modesty: Women and Courtship in the English Novel, 1991, Harems of the Mind: Passages of Western Art and Literature, 2000; assoc. editor Nineteenth-Century Fiction, 1977-80; editor: Sex, Politics and Science in the 19th Century Novel, 1986, Henry James: A Collection of Critical Essays, 1994. Dir. Lewis Walpole Libr., 1996—. Woodrow Wilson fellow, 1967-68, Guggenheim fellow, 1979-80, NEH fellow, 1988-89, Pres.'s rsch. fellow U. Calif., 1988-89. Mem. MLA (exec. coun. 1985-88), English Inst. (supervising com. 1983-86). Office: Yale U Dept English New Haven CT 06520-8302

YECKE, CHERI PEARSON, education agency administrator, columnist, author; b. St. Paul, Feb. 5, 1955; d. Leo Sylvester and Marceline Mae (Intihar) Pierson; m. Dennis Joseph Yecke, Dec. 22, 1973; children: Anastasia, Tiffany. BA, U. Hawaii, 1975; MST, U. Wis., River Falls, 1984; postgrad., U. Va. Apptd. mem. State Bd. Edn., 1995—98, dep. sec. edn., 1998—2001, sec. edn., 2001—02; dir. tchr. quality and pub. sch. choice US Dept. Edn., 2002—03; sr. adv. to White House on USA Freedom Corps., 2003; commr. edn. State of Minn., 2003—. Author: The War Against Excellence: The Rising Tide of Mediocrity in America's Middle Schools, 2003. Mem.: Edn. Leaders Coun. Republican. Home: 2106 Arnold Palmer Dr Blaine MN 55449

YECKEL, ANITA T. state legislator; b. Salt Lake City, Nov. 12, 1942; m. Robert Yeckel; 2 children. BS in Polit. Sci., postgrad., U. Mo., St. Louis. With 1st Nat. Bank, St. Louis, 1960-68, Am. Home Savs. & Loans Assn., 1982-92; mem. Lindebergh Sch. Dist. Bd. Edn., 1990—, Mo. Senate from 1st dist., Jefferson City, 1996—. Mem. Kiwanis. Republican. Roman Catholic. Office: 8819 Gladlea Saint Louis MO 63127 Fax: 314-843-7542. E-mail: ayeckel@services.state.mo.us.

YEE, AMY SUMEI, science educator; b. San Francisco, Sept. 22, 1958; d. Robert Shee Hong and Sim Kuen (Wong) Y.; m. K. Eric Paulson, July 7, 1984; 1 child, Christopher. AB in Biochemistry, U. Calif., Berkeley, 1980; PhD in Biochemistry, U. Calif., Davis, 1985. Postdoctoral fellowship molecular cell biology Rockefeller U., 1986-89; assoc. Howard Hughes Med. Inst., 1989; asst. prof. Tufts U. Sch. Medicine, Boston, 1990—. Guest investigator Rockefeller U., 1989; NIH reviewer, 1994. Contbr. articles to profl. jours. Recipient Alumni scholarship U. Calif., Berkeley, 1976-78, Jastro-Shields Grad. fellowship U. Calif., Davis, 1981-83, 84-85, NIH Tng. grant U. Calif., Davis, 1982-83, Michael Swackhammer Rsch. fellowship U. Calif., Davis, 1984, Am. Cancer Soc. Postdoctoral fellowship Rockefeller U., 1986-89; recipient Am. Cancer Soc. Jr. Faculty Rsch. award Tufts U., 1991-94, Established Investigator award Am. Heart Assn., 1996. Mem. Am. Soc. Biochemistry and Molecular Biology. Office: Tufts Univ Sch Medicine Dept of Biochemistry 136 Harrison Ave Boston MA 02111-1800

YEE, JANICE, dentist; b. N.Y.C., July 20, 1963; d. Jimmy and Yuen-Hing (Chin) Y. BS, Fordham U., 1985; DMD, Tufts U., 1989. Assoc. dentist Dr. Robert Guen, Brookline, Mass., 1989-92; sr. dentist Pub. Health Svc.-ZUNI, N.Mex., 1992-94; clin. prof. Sch. Dental Medicine Tufts U., Boston, 1990-92; clin. prof. N.Y.U. Dental Sch., N.Y.C., 1993; pvt. practice East Patchogue, N.Y., 1994—. Bd. dirs. YMCA, Boston, 1992. Lt. USPHS, 1993-94. Mem. ADA. Avocations: travel, reading, movies, needlepoint. Office: 250 Patchogue-Yaphank Rd Ste 4 Patchogue NY 11772-4862

YEE, NANCY W. travel consultant; b. Honolulu, Nov. 6, 1917; d. Sai Ho and Ah Oi Sen Wong; m. Ken Yee, Dec. 2, 1941; children: Roy Jensen, Sylvia Mei-ling McCaffrey, Carolyn Mei-en Lee, Susan Mei-jen. BA in Edn. Music and Dance, U. Hawaii, 1941. Sr. translator U.S. Postal Censorship, Honolulu, 1941-45; pvt. tchr. English and civics Honolulu, 1945-50; radio announcer Chinese KGMB Radio/TV, Honolulu, 1946-56; ptnr. Ken's Electric Motor Svc., Honolulu, 1949-65; travel cons. Royal Adventure/Quality, Honolulu, 1957—; sec., officer mgr. KEMS Inc., Honolulu, 1965-85. Radio announcer Chinese, KAHU, Honolulu, 1956; chmn. Small Bus. Adminstrn. Adv. Bd., Honolulu, 1967-68; advisor Jr. Achievement, Honolulu, 1970-71; pres. Women's Propeller Club U.S., Honolulu, 1977-78. Den mother Cub Scouts, 1948-50; mem., choir mem. First Chinese Ch. of Christ, 1950-99; chmn. fund raiser, den mother Pacific Girl Scouts Am., 1958-68; mem. Honolulu Youth Symphony, 1967-71; sec. Ctrl. Dist. PTA, Honolulu, 1968; vol. Hawaii Heart Assn., Honolulu, 1970-73; vol. tchr. Chinese song and dance Mun Lun Sch., 1970; mem., pres. Mun Lun Sch. PTA, 1970, Palolo Home Aux, Honolulu, 1977-78, Associated Chinese U. Women, 1978. Named Chinese Model Mother of the Yr., United Chinese Soc., Honolulu, 1986, Hawaii Chinese Living Treasure, Chinese Youth Hawaii, Honolulu, 1995. Avocations: playing chinese butterfly harp, singing chinese operas, traveling, cruising, volunteer work.

YEH, HSIAO YEN C. artist; b. Chung-Qing, China, Mar. 4, 1942; arrived in U.S., 1963; d. Chien-Chung Chen and Gin-Ger Fan; m. Raymond W.H. Yeh, Sept. 16, 1967; children: Bryant P.Y., Clement C.Y., Emily S.Y. BA, U. Oreg., 1967; MEd, U. Minn., 1969. Owner, artist Art Inc., Oklahoma City, Honolulu, 1984—. Art instr. Firehouse Art Sta., Norman, Okla., Ctrl. State U., Edmond, Okla., 1989-91; art specialist U. Hawaii, Honolulu, 1993-95. Mem. AAUW (bd. mem.), Assn. Chinese U. Women (bd. mem. 1997-99), Nat. Assn. Art Educators. Home: 1821 Kumakani Pl Honolulu HI 96821-1327

YELLEN, JANET LOUISE, government official, economics educator; b. Bklyn., Aug. 13, 1946; d. Julius and Anna Ruth (Blumenthal) Y.; m. George Arthur Akerlof, July 8, 1978; 1 child, Robert Joseph. BA in Econs. summa cum laude, Brown U., 1967; PhD, Yale U., 1971. Asst. prof. econs. Harvard U., Cambridge, Mass., 1971-76; lectr. London Sch. Econs. and Polit. Sci., Washington, 1978-80; asst. prof. econs. Sch. Bus. Adminstrn., U. Calif., Berkeley, 1980-82, assoc. prof., 1982-85, prof. Haas Sch. Bus., 1985—, Bernard T. Rocca Jr. prof. internat. bus. and trade, 1992—99, Eugene E. and Catherine M. Trefethem prof. bus., 1999—; cons. div. internat. fin., Bd. Govs. of FRS, Washington, 1974-75, economist trade and fin. studies sect., 1977-78, mem., 1994-97; chair coun. econ. advisers The Cabinet, Washington, 1997-99. Rsch. fellow MIT, Cambridge, 1974; cons. Congl. Budget Office, 1975-76, mem. panel econ. advisers, 1993—; rsch. affiliate Yale U., New Haven, 1976; mem. adv. panel in econs. NSF, 1977-78, 91-92; mem. Brookings Panel on Econ. Activity, 1987-88, 90-91, sr. adviser, 1989—; Yrjö Jahnsson Found. lectr. on macroecon. theory, Helsinki, 1977-78; mem. Coun. on Fgn. Rels., 1976-81. Author: (monograph) (with Arrow and Shavell) The Limits of the Market in Resource Allocation, 1977; assoc. editor Jour. Econ. Perspectives, 1987-91; contbr. articles to profl. jours. Hon. Woodrow Wilson fellow, 1967, grad. fellow NSF, 1967-71, Guggenheim fellow, 1986-87; grantee NSF, 1975-77, 90-94. Mem. Am. Econ. Assn. (adv. com. to Pres. 1986-87, nominating com. 1988-90), Phi Beta Kappa. Address: Hass Sch Bus U Calif Berkeley CA 94720-1900

YELLIN, JUDITH, small business owner; b. Balt., Feb. 21; d. Jack and Sarah (Grebow) Levin; m. Sidney Yellin, Jan. 1; children: David, Paul, Tamar. Student, U. Md., Catonsville C.C. Mgr. credit dept. Lincoln Co., Balt.; office mgr. Seaview Constrn. Co.; owner, operator Yellin Telephone Soliciting Agy.; mgr. Liberty Antique Shop; owner, mgr. Judith Yellin Electrology, 1973—. Creator jewelry; chief examiner Md. State Bd. Electrology, 1978-81; designer jewelry. Contbr. poetry: New American Poetry Anthology, 1988, Great Poems of the Western World, Vol. II, 1990. Mem. Am. Electrolysis Assn., Md. Assn. Profl. Electrologists. Avocations: writing, travel, collecting Haitian art, art deco art, art nouveau, antique jewelry. Home: 6232 Blackstone Ave Baltimore MD 21209-3909 Office: Judith Yellin Electrology 1401 Reisterstown Rd Baltimore MD 21208-6502

YENCHKO, SUZANNE, research and development company executive; b. Hazleton, Pa., Aug. 5, 1946; d. Joseph and Anna (Mital) Yenchko; m. Edward Jules Weintraub, Aug. 2, 1975 (div. Sept. 1993); stepchildren: Jessica Anne Lawrence, Morris Harry Weintraub. BA in English Lit., Susquehanna U., 1968; MBA, Mt. St. Mary's Coll., 1981. Legis. liaison Pa. Dept. Commerce, Harrisburg, 1969-71; asst. exec. dir. Pa. Assn. Retarded Children, Harrisburg, 1971-73; exec. dir. Pa. Joint Coun. Criminal Justice Sys., Harrisburg, 1973-76; dir. Adams County Office Aging, Gettysburg, Pa., 1976-83; dir. house consumer affairs com. Pa. Ho. of Reps., Harrisburg, 1983-85; dir. environ. resources Pa. Chamber Bus. and Industry, Harrisburg, 1985-95; dir. state govt. rels. AMP Inc., Harrisburg, 1995-99; regional pub. affairs mgr. Internat. Paper, Camp Hill, 1999—2002; v.p. Delta Devel. Group Inc., Mechanicsburg, Pa., 2003—. Mem. steering com. White Ho. Conf. Aging, Harrisburg, 1980—81; com. mem. Capitol Region Econ. Devel. Com., Harrisburg, 1990—97, bd. dirs., 2001—. Bd. dirs. Ctrl. Pa. Youth Ballet, Carlisle, 1994—2000, Theatre Harrisburg, 1995—2001, Whitaker Ctr. Sci. and Arts, 2001—; chair Pa. Commn. Women, Harrisburg, 1995—2001; chair lit. ho. tour West Shore Pub. Libr., Camp Hill, 1998; bd. dirs. Ctrl. Pa. Tech. Coun., chair govt. affairs com.; environ. com. chair Pa. Bus. Roundtable, 1999—2002. Named to Best Women in Bus. in Pa., 1999. Mem.: Soc. Women Environ. Profls., Women Pa. Govt. Rels., N.C. Citizens Bus. and Industry (com. 1996—99), Harrisburg Young Profls., Susquehanna U. Bd. (bd. dirs. 2002—). Republican. Lutheran. Avocations: photography, historic preservation, gardening, skiing, architecture. Home: 3625 N 2nd St Harrisburg PA 17110-1502 Office Phone: 717-441-9030. E-mail: syench@aol.com.

YEO, KIM ENG, artist; b. Singapore, Apr. 24, 1947; came to U.S., 1978; d. Cheng Chye and Seok Kim (Chew) Lee; m. Bock Cheng Yeo; children: Beng Lin, Beng Jene. Student, Nanyang Acad. Fine Arts, Singapore, 1963; BSc with honors, U. Singapore, 1968. Watercolor demonstrator Flushing Art League, N.Y.C., 1980-84; art instr. Poppenhusen Inst., N.Y.C., 1984; substitute art tchr. UN Internat. Sch., N.Y.C., 1984-85; freelance paper product designer, 1981-87; textile designer J. Brown Designs, N.Y.C., 1987-91; tchg. artist Flushing (N.Y.) Town Hall, 1995—2002; artist-in-residence Pub. Sch. 214, 165, Francis Lewis H.S., Flushing, 1997-2001. Art cons. Corp. Art Directions, N.Y.C.; visual arts panelist, Flushing Coun., 1985-87, Queen's Coun., 1998-99, 2001-04. One person shows at Alliance Francais, 1975-77, Bhirasri Inst. Modern Art, Bangkok, Thailand, 1975-77, Flushing Coun. on Arts, 1995, 2000; exhibited Mallette Gallery, L.I., N.Y., 1998, 99, Artfolio Gallery, Singapore, 2000; exhibited in group shows at Womanart Gallery, N.Y.C., 1979-80, Nat. Art League, Douglastown, N.Y., 1979-86, Flushing Coun. on Arts, 1984-88, 96-2004, Postcrypt Art Gallery, N.Y.C., 1997, Singapore Watercolor Soc., 1997-99, 2001-03; represented in corp. and pvt. collections; artist greeting cards UNICEF, 1997-98; featured on QPATV Artists Series, 1993, QPTV Queens Jour., 2000. Benefit show UN Devel. Fund for Women Singapore, 1999. Mem. Flushing Art League (bd. dirs., treas. 1979-85, award 1986), Flushing Coun. on Arts. Buddhist. Avocations: gardening, bookmaking. Home: 16202 77th Ave Flushing NY 11366-1022 Fax: (718) 591-8483. E-mail: artist@kimengyeo.com.

YEOMANS, KATIE MORSE, writer; b. Ft. Collins, Colo. d. Charles W. Morse, III and Rea Elaine Morse; m. Robert John Yeomans, Sept. 6, 1996; 1 child, Robert John Jr. BA in English/Journalism cum laude, U. N.H., 1995; MFA in Creative Nonfiction, Goucher Coll., 1999. Boat capt. Coastal Discoveries, Newburyport, Mass., 1995—; assoc. editor Offshore Mag., Boston, 1995—99; sr. editor Nat. Fisherman, Portland, Maine, 1999—2000; freelance author, 2000—. Author: Dead Men Tapping, 2003. Recipient Writing award, Internat. Regional Mags. Assn., 2001, 2002. Mem.: Investigative Reporters and Editors (Writing awards 2001), Boating Writers Internat. (Writing awards 1998, 2000, 2002). Episcopalian. Avocations: boating, fishing, reading, travel, snowboarding. Home: PO Box 1024 Newburyport MA 01950

YERKES, SUSAN GAMBLE, newspaper columnist; b. Evanston, Ill., Sept. 5, 1959; d. Charles Tyson Yerkes and Darthea (Campbell) Higgins. BA in Liberal Arts (hon.), U. Austin, 1974; MA in Mass Comms., Wichita State U., 1976. Pub. affairs dir. anchor KAKE-TV, Wichita, Kans., 1977-81; freelance writer pub. rels. YS Comms. Global, 1981-84; metro columnist San Antonio Light, 1986-93; lifestyle columnist S.A. Express News, San Antonio, 1993—. Radio TV host WOAI-AM, San Antonio, 1993—; nat. assn. broadcast editls., Boston, 1978-81. Recipient 1st Place Column Writing Nat. Press Women, 1988, Tex. AP Mng. Editors, 1995, 97, Vivian Castelberry award Assn. for Women in Journalism, 1997. Mem. Internat. Women's Forum, Women in Comm., Pub. Rel. Soc. Am., Rotary, Phi Beta Kappa. Episcopalian. Avocations: Argentine tango, horseback riding, travel, reading, friends, the Internet. E-mail: syerkesexpress-news.net. Home: 68 Granburg Cir San Antonio TX 78218-3011 Office Phone: 210-287-7326. E-mail: syerkes@espress-news.net.

YERKOVICH, GLORIA, social service administrator; b. 1942; Founder CHILD FIND, 1981.

YERXA, JANE ANNE, artist; b. Wichita, Kans., July 3, 1933; d. Laurence Alan and Mary Jane (Nation) Figge; m. Jay Allen Yerxa, June 23, 1956; children: Jeffrey Todd, James Jay, Jonathan Alan. BA in Fine Arts and Comml. Arts, U. Kans., 1955. Fashion artist Wichita (Kans.) Beacon, 1955-56; freelance fashion artist Fall River, Mass., 1956-57; freelance artist agrl. extension dept. Wash. State U., Pullman, 1959; pub. rels. coord. Spokane (Wash.) Symphony, 1972. Docent Expo '76 Gallery, Spokane. Represented in pvt. collections in Kans., Tex., N.Mex., Ariz., Calif., Utah, and Wash. Vol. Spokane Art Sch., 1973-83, Corbin Art Ctr., Spokane, 1989-90. Mem. DAR, Spokane (Wash.) Watercolor Soc., Riverridge Fine Arts Assn. (v.p. 1994-95, pres. 1984, 85, 1st place watercolors 1986, Best of Show award 2002)), Stanek House Art Ctr. (charter mem.), Bible Study Fellowship, Gamma Alpha Chi, Alpha Delta Pi. Avocations: reading, cloth doll making, sewing, watching old movies.

YESLOW, ROSEMARIE, real estate professional; b. Detroit; d. Karl E. and Madeline E. (Paret) Norberg; widowed; children: Bradford (dec.), Tod, Eric (dec.), Mark. Student, U. Miami, 1947-49; AA in Journalism, Broward Jr. Coll., 1972; student, Fla. Atlantic U., 1973-75. Grad. Real Estate Inst., 1995. Ins. agt. Wittenstein Ins. Agy., Hollywood, Fla., 1965-75; owner, operator The Karl Motel/Apartments, Hallandale, Fla., 1980-95; realtor/assoc. The Keyes Co., Hollywood, 1990-93; realtor, assoc. Ebby Halliday Real Estate, Dallas, 1993—. Real estate investor, Hollywood, 1960—. Contbr. articles to profl. jours. Edn. v.p. Nat. Coun. Jewish Women, Hollywood, 1960-66; unit and dept. chmn. LWV, Ft. Lauderdale, Fla., 1960-72; edn. chmn. Dem. Exec. Com., Broward County, Fla., 1976-78; mem. planning and zoning bd. City of Hallandale, 1988-92. Mem. Nat. Assn. Realtors, Tex. Real Estate Assn., Greater Dallas Assn. Realtors, Hallandale Adult Cmty. Ctr. (adv. com., Cert. of Appreciation 1989), Hallandale Citizens United, Hallandale C. of C. (bd. dirs. 1987-92, Small Bus. Person of Yr. award 1990), Sierra Club. Democrat. Jewish. Avocations: camping, reading, hiking, swimming. Home: 4247 Throckmorton St Dallas TX 75219-2206 Office: Ebby Halliday Real Estate 8333 Douglas Ave Ste 100 Dallas TX 75225-5892 Office Phone: 214-692-0000.

YESS, DENISE ANNE, speech pathology/audiology services professional, educator; b. NYC, Dec. 14, 1948; d. James and Jeanne A. Mahon; children: Desiree(dec.), James P. Yess Jr. MS, Boston U., 1980. Cert. Orton-Gillingham trained provider. Speech lang. pathologist Cohasset Pub. Schs., Cohasset, Mass., 1980—; pvt. practice Scituate, Mass., 1980—. Adj. prof. Newbury Coll., Brookline, Mass., 1993; guest lectr. Emerson Coll., Boston, 1999—2000; pvt. practitioner Area Lang./Lit., Scituate, 1980—; cons. speech/lang. Vis. Nurse Assn., Scituate, 1980—94; adj. prof. Bridgewater State Coll., Bridgewater, Mass., 1992—93. Big sister Big Sister Orgn., Boston, 1999—2000. Recipient Tchr. of Yr. award, Parent/Sch. Orgn., 2001. Mem.: Am. Speech and Hearing Assn. (steering com. 2000—, facilitator for profl. e-mail listserve, guest lectr., cert. clin. competency 1981, elected position). Avocations: writing, reading, art, music. Office: Cohasset Pub Schs-Joseph Osgood 210 Sohier St Cohasset MA 02025 Personal E-mail: yess@comcast.net.

YETERIAN, ISABELLE M.C. lawyer; b. Dallas, Nov. 24, 1974; d. Charles F. Yeterian and Francoise Perdreau, Maria Sabina Parisi (Stepmother). LLB, U. London, 1998; maitrise droit des affaires, U. Sorbonne, 1998. Bar: N.Y. 2000. Assoc. Shearman & Sterling, N.Y.C., 1998—2002, Mayer, Brown, Rowe & Maw LLP, N.Y.C., 2002—. Pro bono atty. for asylum seekers, 1998—. Mem.: ABA, N.Y. State Bar Assn.

YETMAN, LEITH ELEANOR, academic administrator; b. Kellits, Clarendon, Jamaica, West Indies; came to U.S., 1967; d. 2nd child of 12 children of Percival Augustus and Grace Elizabeth (Anderson) Y.; m. Noel W. Miller, Apr. 8, 1961 (div. 1977); children: Donovan, Jo-Ann, Kirk, Lori-Anne; adopted children: LaFara, Samantha, Brandon Ryan. Attended, Bethlehem Teachers Coll., St. Elizabeth, Jamaica, 1960; BSC, Baruch Coll., 1976; MA, Columbia U., 1979. Cert. tchr., N.Y.; accredited Grace Inst. Bus. Tech., Bklyn., 1998. Legal sec. various law firms, N.Y.C., 1969-76; instr. Taylor Bus. Inst., N.Y.C., 1977-79; founder, pres., dir. N.Y. Inst. English and Bus. (formerly N.Y. Inst. Bus. Tech., N.Y.C., 1981—; founder Grace Inst. Bus. Tech., Bklyn., 1996. Founder Grace Inst. Bus. Tech., Bklyn., 1996. Recipient Outstanding Achievement award Baruch Coll. Alumni Assn., 1989, Outstanding Achievement award Baruch Coll. Alumni Assn., citations Hon. Virginia Fields, Gov. N.Y. State, Hon. George E. Pataki, letters of recognition and praise Ex-First Ladies Barbara Bush, Hillary Clinton, Ex-Pres. Bill Clinton, Senator Charles Rangel, Ex-Mayor David Dinkins, others; Leith E. Yetman Day proclaimed June 1, 1994 by Manhattan Borough Pres. Office: NY Inst English and Bus 248 W 35th St New York NY 10001 Personal E-mail: myiebo2@aol.com.

YETT, SALLY PUGH, elementary school educator, gifted and talented educator; b. St. Louis, Feb. 15, 1935; d. John D. and Esther Ruth Pugh; m. Donald Edward Yett, June 19, 1964; children: Stephen Edward, John Harold. BFA, Washington U., St. Louis, 1956; tchg. credential, Calif. State U., L.A., 1989. Cert. gen. clear multiple subject and art supplementary Calif. Dept. Edn. Recreation therapist ARC, San Antonio, 1956-58; dir. recreation therapy dept. Jewish Hosp., St. Louis, 1958-64; tchr. art-gifted class Juan Cabrillo Elem., Malibu, Calif., 1975-78; educator prekindergarten Malibu Meth. Pre-Sch., 1979-81; educator grades 9-12 Santa Monica (Calif.) Sch. Dist., 1981-89; spl. edn. educator grades 1-6 art L.A. Unified Sch. Dist.-Visual and Performing Arts Magnet, 1990—; resource tchr., art edn. advisor Calif. State U., L.A., 2001—, master tchr. Dominguez Hills, 2003—. Judge Making History, L.A., 1998—; participant UCLA Tchrs. and Scholars Symposium, 1999—2003; cons. edn. dept. Calif. State U., L.A.; state judge History Day in Calif., 2003. Exhibitions include Malibu Art Festival, 1976 (3rd place award), Malibu Art Assn. Show, 1984 (3rd place award), Roberts Art Gallery, 1989, CAEA State Conv.-Calif. State Bakersfield Exhibit, 2001; contbr. articles to profl. jours. PTA pres. Juan Cabrillo Elem., Malibu, 1976—78, Malibu Park Jr. HS; pres. Santa Monica Jr. Programs, 1979—81; 2d, 3d, and 4th v.p. Santa Monica/Malibu PTA Coun., 1982—85; pres. Malibu Art Assn., 1992—93. Nominee Tchr. of Yr., Walt Disney Co.; recipient Honoree Bravo award, L.A. Music Ctr.; grantee, Calif. Cmty. Found., 2003. Mem.: Internat. Studies Overseas Program, East West Players Orgn., Calif. Alliance Arts Edn., Ams. for the Arts, Smithsonian Inst., Huntington Mus., Gene Autrey Mus., Nat. Mus. Women, Mus. Natural History, Calif. Art Edn. Assn., Calif. Coun. Social Studies, Soc. Calligraphy (bd. dirs., pub. rels. 1987—91), Tchrs. and Writers Collaborative, Nat. Art Edn. Assn., L.A. Conservancy, Pacific Asia Mus., Craft and Folk Mus., UCLA Fowler Mus. Cultural History, L.A. County Art Mus., S.W. Mus., Mus. Contemporary Art, Shakespeare Festival/L.A., Metro. Mus. Art, People to People Internat. (Indigenous Art del. to New Zealand, Australia 1998), Art Mus. Long Beach, Smithsonian Nat. Mus. Am. Indian, Mus. L.Am. Art, UCLA Book Club, Kappa Alpha Theta. Avocations: travel, reading, calligraphy, hiking, gardening. Home: 2042 Hanscom Dr South Pasadena CA 91030-4012

YGLESIAS, HELEN BASSINE, author, educator; b. N.Y.C., Mar. 29, 1915; d. Solomon and Kate (Goldstein) Bassine; m. Bernard Cole, 1938 (div. 1950); children: Tamar Cole, Lewis Cole; m. Jose Yglesias, Aug. 19, 1950 (div. 1992); 1 child, Rafael. Student pub. schs.; LHD (hon.), U. Maine, 1996. Literary editor Nation Mag., 1965-70; adj. assoc. prof. writing Columbia Sch. Arts, N.Y.C., 1973—. Vis. prof. creative writing Writers Workshop, U. Iowa, Iowa City, 1980. Author: (novels) How She Died (Houghton Mifflin award), 1972, Family Feeling, 1976, Sweetsir, 1981, The Saviors, 1987, The Girls, 1999, (non-fiction) Starting: Early, Anew, Over and Late, 1978, Isabel Bishop, 1989. Home: Apt 1303 1261 5th Ave New York NY 10029-3866

YI, JENNY KISUK, public health educator; b. Korea, Sept. 8, 1958; came to U.S., 1973; d. Moon Se and Kyong Suk (Yim) Y. BS in Biology, U. Wash., 1982; BS in Nutrition, U. Minn., 1986, MPH, 1987; PhD in Pub. Health, U. Mass., 1992. Pub. health nutritionist Minn. Health Dept., Mpls., 1986-87; sr. pub. health nutritionist Cape Cod WIC Program, Hyannis, Mass., 1987-88; acad. advisor U. Mass., Amherst, 1990-92; asst. prof. U. Houston, 1992—. Bd. dirs. Asian Am. Health Coalition, Houston; mem. adv. bd. Baylor Coll. Medicine Breast Cancer Edn. Project, Houston, 1995—. Contbr. articles to profl. jours. Recipient Cert. of Appreciation, Everywoman's Ctr., U. Mass., 1991. Fellow Okura Health Leadership Found.; mem. APA, Nat. Women's Health Network, Asian Am. Psychol. Assn. Avocations: travel, playing piano, gardening, reading mystery novels. Office: Univ Houston 3855 Holman St Houston TX 77004-4710

YIH, ANN, writer, journalist; d. Roy Y. and Madeline Wu Yih. BA, Duke U., 1985; MS, Columbia U. Grad. Sch. of Journalism, 1987. Pub. rels. coord. Foote, Cone & Belding Advt., NYC, 1985—86; prodr./writer WCVB-TV, Boston, 1987—90; prodr. WCBS-TV, NYC, 1990—96; sr. prodr. CBS News Off Tenth, NYC, 1996—97; sr. broadcast prodr. CBS News Saturday Early Show, NYC, 1997—2002. Recipient Emmy award: Outstanding Single Newscast, NY Emmy Awards, 1994—95. Home: PO Box 547 Palisades NY 10964 Office Phone: 845-638-2898. Personal E-mail: annyih@aol.com.

YIH, MAE DUNN, state legislator; b. Shanghai, May 24, 1928; d. Chung Woo and Fung Wen (Feng) Dunn; m. Stephen W.H. Yih, 1953; children: Donald, Daniel. BA, Barnard Coll., 1951; postgrad., Columbia U., 1951-52. Asst. to bursar Barnard Coll., N.Y.C., 1952-54; mem. Oreg. Ho. Reps. from 36th dist., 1977-83, Oreg. Senate from 19th dist., 1983—. Mem. Clover Ridge Elem. Sch. Bd., Albany, Oreg., 1969-78, Albany Union H.S. Bd., 1975-79; mem. Joint Legis. Ways and Means Com., Senate Transp. Com., 1999, Senate pres. pro-temore, 1993. Episcopalian. Home: 34465 Yih Ln NE Albany OR 97321-9557 Office: Oreg Senate S 307 State Capitol Salem OR 97310-0001

YIN, BEATRICE WEI-TZE, medical researcher; b. Taipei, Taiwan, Mar. 9, 1959; came to U.S., 1970; d. Chuan Keun and Ming Hsien (Huang) Y. BS, CUNY, Flushing, 1982, MS, 1988. Rsch. asst. Meml. Sloan-Kettering Cancer Ctr., N.Y.C., 1982—. Inventor Monoclonal antibodies to human gastrointestinal cancers, 1992. Avocations: readings, travel, gardening. Office: Meml Sloan Kettering Cancer Ctr 1275 York Ave New York NY 10021-6094

YING, JACKIE, chemical engineer, educator; Prof. MIT, Cambridge, 1992—. Exec. dir. Inst. Bioengring. and Nanotech., Singapore, 2003—. Mem. editl. bd. Advances in Chem. Engring., Jour. Metastable and Nanostructured Materials, Nanoparticle Sci. and Tech., Jour. of Electroceramics, Jour. of Porous Materials, Applied Catalysis A. David and Lucile Packard fellow, 1995; recipient Exxon Solid-State Chemistry Fellowship award Am. Chem. Soc., 1997, Camille Dreyfus Tchr.-Scholar award, 1996, Colburn award Am. Inst. Chem. Engrs., 2000. E-mail: jyying@mit.edu.

YITTS, ROSE MARIE, nursery school executive; b. Bridgeport, Conn., Apr. 29, 1942; m. Richard Francis Yitts, Dec. 28, 1963; children: Anthony Michael, Jennifer Lisa, Heather Michelle. BS, So. Conn. State Coll., 1963; MS, So. Conn. State U., 1983. Tchr. Trumbull Bd. Edn., Conn., 1963-69; substitute tchr. Seymour and Oxford Bd. Edn., Conn., 1970-79; tchr. aide spl. edn. Oxford Bd. Edn., 1979-82; dir., founding ptnr., pres. and treas. Strawberry Tyme Nursery Sch. and Day Care Ctr. Ltd., Seymour, 1983—. Den leader, com. chmn. Boy Scouts Am., Seymour, 1973-77; troop leader Girl Scouts U.S., Seymour, 1978-80; chair fundraisers, coach George J. Hummel Little League, Seymour, 1982-86, 1st woman pres., 1987-88, player agt., 1990; tchr., spl. edn. curriculum developer Ch. of Good Shepherd, mem. parish coun., 1984-86; elected mem., corr. sec. Seymour Libr., bd. dirs., 1983-89; elected mem. Republican Town Com., 1996-, mem. exec. bd., 2000, GOP 5 State, 1998—2002, elected mem. Seymour Bd. Edn., 1999—, corr. sec., 2003—; bd. dirs. Seymour Hist. Soc., 2003. Recipient award of merit, honorable mention, Golden Poet award, World of Poetry, 1987, Editor's Choice award, Nat. Libr. Poetry, 1994, 1995, Joseph Gido award, Seymour Rep. Town. Com., 2001. Mem. Nat. Assn. for Edn. of Young Children, Oxford Bus. Assn. (membership com. 1993-95), Seymour Hist. Soc. (life mem.). Republican. Office Phone: 203-881-2055. E-mail: michmax2@aol.com.

YIU, FANG, structural engineer, researcher; b. Shanghai, Apr. 21, 1972; d. Boxian Yiu and Jingfang Hua. BS, Shanghai Inst. Ry. Tech., 1993; MS, Tongji U., Shanghai, 1995; PhD, Cornell U., 2003. Cost evaluation cert., cert. fundamental engr. Structural engr. Shanghai Posts & Telecoms. Design Inst., 1993-95; rsch. asst. dept. civil and environ. engring. Cornell U., Ithaca, NY, 1998—2002; sr. staff tech. profl. Mustang Engring., L.P., 2002—. Asst. engring. mgr. Shanghai Designing INst. Telecomms., Shanghai, 1993—95; peer advisor dept. civil and environ. engring. Cornell U., Ithaca, 1999—2000, engring. grad. student assn. rep., 2000—02. Referee: for profl. jours. Mem. civil engring. del. People to People Amb., Spokane, Wash., 2000—; treas. Chinese Students and Scholars Assn., Ithaca, 1998—99. Mem.: ASCE, Soc. Woman Engrs., Earthquake Engring. Rsch. Inst. (treas. 2000—). Mailing: Apt 714 Timber Creek Pl Dr Houston TX 77084 Office: 16001 Park Ten Pl Houston TX 77084 E-mail: fy16@cornell.edu.

YNDA, MARY LOU, artist, educator; b. Los Angeles, Apr. 4, 1936; d. Ernest Pastor Ynda and Mary Estella (Ruiz) Zapotocky, m. Gary Lynn Coleman, Sept. 1, 1956 (div. Feb. 1983); children: Debra Lynn, Lisa Annette, David Gary; m. Miles Ciletti, May 25, 1991. Student, Immaculate Heart Coll., Los Angeles, 1973-79; AA in Fine Arts, Los Angeles City Coll., 1976; BA, Calif. State U., L.A., 1993. Instr. Fashion Inst. Design, L.A., 1980-81; tchr. art to disabled First St. Gallery, Claremont, Calif., 1991-94; tchr. art Tierra Del Sol Found., Sunland, Calif., 1995-96. Exhibited in group shows at Double Rocking G Gallery, L.A., 1983, Improv Theater West, West Hollywood, Calif., 1983, Exposition Gallery Calif. State U., L.A., 1983, L.A. Art Core Gallery, 1985, Poly. Tech. Sch., Pasadena, Calif., 1986, Bad Eye Gallery, L.A., 1987, Art in the Hall VI West Hollywood City Hall, 1989, Echo Park Gallery, L.A., 1991, Art N Barbee Gallery, 1992, A Celebration of City Life, 1993, DADA Show-Downtown Lives, L.A., 1994, 96, Spirit Exhbn. for Women's Caucus for Art, Santa Ana, Calif., 1995; designer Spoken Word CD Long Days and Monster Nights, 1994; contbg. author poetry Spoken Word Voices of the Angels, 1982; book rev. Yesterday and Tomorrow: California Women Artists, 1989. Archetypes and Contemporary Images in The Hispanic World. The City of Lancaster Mus./Art Gallery, Lancaster Calif. Mem. Women's Caucus for Art. Democrat. Avocations: mask making, fetish art, study of animal behavior.

YNTEMA, MARY KATHERINE, retired mathematics educator; b. Urbana, Ill., Jan. 20, 1928; d. Leonard Francis and M. Jean (Busey) Y. BA in Math., Swarthmore Coll., 1950; MA in Math., U. Ill., 1961, PhD in Math., 1965. Tchr., secondary math. Am. Coll. for Girls, Istanbul, Turkey, 1950-54, Columbus (Ohio) Sch. for Girls, 1954-57; computer programmer MIT Lincoln Lab., Lexington, Mass., 1957-58; tchr., secondary math Roundup (Mont.) High Sch., 1959-60; asst. prof. math U. Ill., Chgo., 1965-67; asst. prof. computer sci. Pa. State U., University Park, 1967-71; assoc. prof. to prof. math. Sangamon State U., Springfield, Ill., 1971-91; ret., 1991. Avocation: enjoyment of nature.

YOCHEM, BARBARA JUNE (RUNYAN), sales executive, lecturer; b. Knox, Ind., Aug. 22, 1945; d. Harley Albert and Rosie (King) Runyan; m. Donald A. Yochem (div. 1979); 1 child, Morgan Lee; m. Don Heard, Dec. 12, 1987 (div. 1998). Grad. high school, Knox, Ind., 1963. Sales rep. Hunter Woodworks, Carson, Calif., 1979-84, sales mgr., 1984-87; sales rep. Comml. Lumber and Pallet, Industry, Calif., 1987-92; mgr. Desert Shadows Apts., Herperia, Calif., 1998—, Hesperia, Calif., 1998; real estate agt. Marina Properties, Victorville, Spring Valley Lake, 2000—01, Coldwell Banker Home Real Estate, 2001—. Owner By By Prodns., Glendora, Calif., 1976—. Author: Barbara Yochem's Inner Shooting; contbr. articles to profl. jours. Head coach NRA Jr. Olympic Shooting Camp, 1989-94. Recipient U.S. Bronze medal U.S. Olympic Com., 1976, World Bronze medal U.S. Olympic Com., 1980; inductee Calif. Trapshooting Hall of Fame, 1998. Avocation: reading. Address: 9936 SVL Box Victorville CA 92392-5144 Office Phone: 760-245-2227. E-mail: BYochem@hotmail.com.

YOCUM, CAROL COSENS, minister; b. Lansing, Mich., Jan. 9, 1949; d. Dennis E. and Emajean Cosens; m. Dennis E. Yocum, May 1, 1976; children: Julianne S., Elizabeth D., Karalee C. BA, Adrian Coll., 1971; MDiv, Wesley Theol. Sem., 1975. Pastor Harpers Ferry Parish, W.Va., 1973—77; pastor then sr. pastor Wellers/Deerfield UMC's, Thurmont, Md., 1977—86; assoc. then sr. pastor Calvary United Meth. Ch., Mt. Airy, Md., 1986—. Bd. govs. Wesley Theol. Sem., Washington, 1977—88; relocating refugees Ch. World Svcs., New Windsor, Md., 1994—. Avocations: music, gardening, reading, walking. Home: 109 Troon Cir Mount Airy MD 21771 Office: Calvary United Methodist Ch 403 S Main St Mount Airy MD 21771

YODER, ANNA A. elementary school educator; b. Beach City, Ohio, Sept. 5, 1934; d. Abram J. and Barbara D. (Miller) Y. BS, Ea. Mennonite Coll., 1966; MEd, Frostburg State Coll., 1974. Cert. elem. tchr., Ohio, recreational leader. Tchr. Garrett County Schs., Oakland, Md., 1966-70, prin. elem. sch., 1970-74; tchr. E. Holmes Local Schs., Berlin, Ohio, 1974-98, ret., 1998. Chairperson edn. com. German Culture Mus., Berlin, Ohio, 1987-90; cons. bilingual edn. E. Holmes Local Schs., Berlin, Ohio, 1982-98, ret., 1998. Supporting mem. German Culture Mus., Berlin, Ohio, 1983—; mem. Killbuck (Ohio) Valley mus., 1988—, Holmes County Hist. Soc., Millersburg, Ohio, 1989—; life mem. Mennonite Info. Ctr., Berlin, Ohio, 1985—; sustaining mem. The Wilderness Ctr., Wilmot, Ohio, 1974—. Jennings scholar Martha Holden Jennings Found., 1983-84; Silver Poet award World of Poetry, 1986. Mem. AAUW (v.p. Holmes County chpt. 1994), Creative Arts Soc. (sec.-treas. 1987-89), Delta Kappa Gamma (sec. Beta Iota chpt. 1987-90, pres. 1990-92, pres. 1998-2000, chpt. v.p. 2002-). Mennonite. Avocations: nature studies-birds and flowers, handcrafts. Home: 5229 State Route 39 Millersburg OH 44654-8408

YODER, ELIZABETH JANE, neuroscience researcher; b. Champaign, Ill., Jan. 23, 1968; d. Chris and Donnalee (Blair) Y. BS in Biomechanics and Exercise Sci., Ariz. State U., 1990; MS in Neurosci., U. Calif., San Diego, 1992, PhD in Neurosci., 1996. Lab. asst. in zoology Ariz. State U., Tempe, 1989-90; summer rsch. fellow Barrow Neurol. Inst., Phoenix, 1990; grad. student rschr. Sch. of Medicine U. Calif., San Diego, 1990-96; postgrad. rschr. in neurology Sch. of Medicine UCLA, 1996—98; rschr. in physics U. Calif., San Diego, 1998—2001, rschr. in radiology Sch. Medicine, 2001—03, rsch. faculty in radiology Sch. Medicine, 2003—. Democrat. Avocations: running, jazz, poetry, museums, hiking.

YODER, MARY JANE WARWICK, psychotherapist; b. Corryton, Tenn., Nov. 20, 1933; d. Harry Alonzo and Mary Luzelle (Furches) Warwick; m. Edwin Milton Yoder, Jr., Nov. 1, 1958; children: Anne Daphne, Edwin Warwick. BA, U. N.C., Chapel Hill, 1956; MFA, U. N.C., Greensboro, 1969; MSW, Va. Commonwealth U., 1987; cert. individual psychotherapy, Smith Coll., 1991. Lic. ind. clin. social worker, D.C.; lic. clin. social worker, Va. Editorial asst. Harper & Bros., N.Y.C., 1956-57; flight attendant Pan Am. Airlines, N.Y.C., 1957-59; adj. faculty mem. in ballet Guilford Coll., Greensboro, 1961-64; ballet tchr., adminstr. Jane Yoder Sch. of Ballet, Greensboro, 1964-75; homilitics listener Va. Theol. Sem., Alexandria, 1978-80; social worker, dance therapist Woodbine Nursing Ctr., Alexandria, 1983-87; staff psychotherapist D.C. Inst. Mental Health, 1987-92; pvt. practice Capitol Hill Ctr. Individual and Family Therapy, 1992—. Ballet and book critic Greensboro Daily News, 1961-73. Dancer, choreographer Greensboro Civic Ballet, 1961-75. Mem. Nat. Assn. Social Workers, Greater Washington Soc. for Clin. Social Work, Inc., Washington Sch. Psychiatry, Washington Soc. for Jungian Psychology, Jungian Venture, Army Navy Country Club, Phi Beta Kappa. Episcopalian. Avocations: ballet, modern dance, horseback riding, swimming, reading. Office: Capitol Hill Ctr Individual and Family Therapy 530 7th St SE Washington DC 20003-2768 E-mail: janeyoder@worldnet.att.net.

YODER, PATRICIA DOHERTY, public relations executive; b. Pitts., Oct. 30, 1939; d. John Addison and Camella Grace (Conti) Doherty; children: Shari Lynn, Wendy Ann; m. James Ronald Wolfe, Oct. 30, 1999. BA, Duquesne U., 1961. Press sec. U.S. Ho. of Reps., 1965-69; dir. Office of Pub. Info., City of Ft. Wayne, 1973-76; asst. mgr. pub. and corp. comm. Mellon Bank N.A., Pitts., 1977-79; v.p. pub. affairs Am. Waterways Operators Inc., Washington, 1980-83, sr. v.p., gen. mgr., 1983-86, exec. v.p., dir. banking, 1989-91; exec. v.p., dir. internat. banking Hill and Knowlton Inc., Pitts.; sr. v.p. corp. and pub. affairs PNC Fin. Svcs. Group, Pitts., 1987-89; v.p., mgr. corp. pub. rels. and advt. GE Capital Svcs. Corp., Stamford, Conn., 1991-95; corp. v.p. pub. affairs and comm. GTE Corp., Stamford, 1995-96; sr. v.p. corp. comm. Avis Group Holdings, Garden City, N.Y., 1996-99; prin. PDY Assocs., 1999—. Trustee Shadyside Hosp., Pressley Ridge Sch., Pitts., Ellis Sch.; bd. dirs. Children's Mus., Civic Light Opera, Pitts. Ballet Theatre, Jr. League of City of N.Y. Recipient Outstanding Woman Bus. and Industry, 1988, Disting. Alumni award Duquesne U., 1996. Mem. Pitts. Field Club, Duquesne Club, Indian Harbor Yacht Club, Boca Raton (Fla.) Resort Country Club. Roman Catholic. Home and Office: 500 SE 5th Ave Apt 601 Boca Raton FL 33432-5510 also: 535 E 86th St Apt 16E New York NY 10028-7533 E-mail: pdyoder@att.net.

YODER-GAGNON, PAMALA S. retired orthopedic nurse; b. Portage, Mich., Aug. 7, 1952; d. Jacob L. and Florence M. (Van Dommelen) Yoder; m. Georges Gagnon, July 3, 1982; children: Brianna Kay Marie, Garrett Patrick Antoine, Cameron Michael André. AAS, Kalamazoo Valley C.C., 1974, AAS in Nursing, 1975; BSN magna cum laude, Nazareth Coll., 1991. Staff nurse Borgess Med. Ctr., Kalamazoo, 1976-77, dept. dir. orthopedic/trauma unit, 1977-97, dept. dir. renal transplant, med. surgery unit, 1992-94, dir. and program coord. orthopedics, 1997-98, compiler HCFA orthopedic demonstration project, 1997-98; ret., 1998. Mem. Nat. Assn. Orthopedic Nurses (v.p. local chpt. 1986-89, pres.-elect 1990-91, pres. 1991-92). Home: 8362 Morning Dove Ln Kalamazoo MI 49009-0806

YODER-WISE, PATRICIA SNYDER, education educator; b. Wadsworth, Ohio, July 2, 1941; d. Belford Grant and Leona Cora (Mohler) Snyder; m. Robert Thomas Wise, Feb. 17, 1973; children: Doreen Ellen, Deborah Ann. BSN, Ohio State U., 1963; MSN, Wayne State U., 1968; EdD, Tex. Tech. U., 1984. RN, Tex. Interim dir. nursing ctr. Tex. Tech. U. Health Sci. Ctr. Sch. Nursing, Lubbock, 1988-89, interim assoc. dean practice program, 1989-90, interim dean, prof., 1991-93, dean and prof., 1993-2000, prof., 2000—; clin. prof. U. Tex. Health Sci. Ctr., San Antonio, 1993—2000. Mem. rev. panel Nursing Outlook, 1993—; mem. adv. com. GlaxoWellcome, 1996-2000; v.p. ANCC, 2000-03, sec. 2003-04; mem. Nat. Quality Forum Provider Panel, 2001-04. Author (editor): Leading and Managing in Nursing, 1994 (Book of Yr. award, 1996, 1999, 2003); peer reviewer: Jour. Profl. Nursing, 1984—2003, mem. editl. bd.: Jour. Continuing Edn. in Nursing, 1978—; editor, 1988—. Participant Leadership Tex.-Found. for Women's Resources, 1997-98; mem. Leadership Tex., 1998-99, Leadership Am., 1999-2000. Recipient of Woman of Excellence in Medicine, YWCA, Lubbock, 1996. Fellow: Am. Acad. Nursing (chair Inst. for Nursing Leadership 1999—2002, mem. planning com. 2004); mem.: ANA (del. 1995—2000, chair constituent assembly 1998—2000, sec. 2000—02, 1st v.p. 2002—), Tex. Nurses Assn. (pres. 1995—99). Office: Texas Tech Univ HSC Sch Nursing 7309 93rd St Lubbock TX 79424-4939

YOGEV, SARA, psychologist; b. Tel Aviv, May 23, 1946; came to U.S., 1975; d. Israel and Cila (Fink) Frankel; m. Ram Yogev, Oct. 2, 1967; children: Eldad, Shelly, Tomer. BA, Hebrew U., 1965-69, MA, 1970-73; PhD, Northwestern U., Evanston, Ill., 1976-79. Cert. clin. psychologist, Ill. Clin. experience dist. sch. psychologist Office Edn. and Culture, Jerusalem, Israel, 1968-71; intern. Beer Yaakov Psychiatric Hosp., Israel, 1971-72; asst. dir. Dept. Psychology, Hebrew U., Jerusalem, Israel, 1972-73; psychotherapist Mental Health Ctr., Hebrew U., Jerusalem, Israel; clin. psychologist Inst. Psychoanalysis, Jerusalem, Israel, 1973-75; psychotherapist, supr. Youth and Family Services, Ill., 1977-80; pvt. practice psychology Skokie and Chicago, Ill., 1981—. Academic experience instr. counseling psychology, 1977-79, asst. prof., Northwestern U., 1979-82, research psychologist at the rank asst. prof., 1983-86, visiting scholar, Ctr. Urban Affairs and Policy Research, 1987. Author: For Better or Worse But Not for Lunch: Making Your Marriage Work in Retirement, 2001; contbr. articles to profl. jours. and books. Mem. American Assn. for Marriage and Family Therapy, American Psyhological Assn., Nat. Register Health Service. Jewish. Office: # 32 5225 Old Orchard Rd Skokie IL 60077-1027 also: 500 1 East Superior St Chicago IL 60611 Office Phone: 847-470-1925.

YOKOUCHI, KATHY, nursing administrator; Exec. officer Hawaii Bd. Nursing, Honolulu. Office: Hawaii Bd Nursing PO Box 3469 Honolulu HI 96801-3469

YOKUM, JANE, music educator; b. Harrisonburg, Va., Oct. 8, 1954; d. George William and Mary Virginia Anderson; m. Jack Randall Yokum, June 12, 1976; children: Jonathan, Daniel. BA in Music Edn., Shepherd Coll., 1976; MA in Comm. Studies, W.Va. U., 2002. Tchr. music Grant County Schs., Petersburg, W.Va., 1976—86, Pendleton County Schs., Franklin, W.Va., 1990—91, Hardy County Schs., Moorefield, W.Va., 1991—. Music dir. Christ Ctrl. Cmty. Ch., Upper Tract, W.Va. Mem.: W.Va. Profl. Educators, W.Va. Music Educators Assn., Nat. Assn. Music Educators.

YOLEN, JANE, author; b. N.Y.C., Feb. 11, 1939; d. Will Hyatt and Isabelle (Berlin) Y.; m. David Wilber Stemple, Sept. 2, 1962; children: Heidi Elisabet, Adam Douglas, Jason Frederic. BA, Smith Coll., 1960; EdM, U. Mass., 1978; LLD (hon.), Coll. of Our Lady of the Elms, 1980. Asst. editor This Week mag., 1960; mem. staff Saturday Rev., 1960; asst. editor Gold Medal Books, 1961, Rutledge Press, 1961-63; asst. juvenile editor A.A. Knopf, Inc., 1963-65; freelance writer, 1965—; lectr. dept. edn. Smith Coll., 1979-84; editor Jane Yolen books, imprint Harcourt Brace Jovanovich, 1988-97. Tchr. writers confs. Centrum, Cape Cod Writers Conf., Soc. Children's Book Writers, U. Mass.; mem. Mass. Coun. on Arts, 1974. Author: Pirates in Petticoats, 1963, The Witch Who Wasn't, 1964, The Emperor and the Kite, 1968, Writing Books for Children, 1973, The Girl Who Cried Flowers, 1974, The Hundredth Dove, 1978, The Dream Weaver, 1979, Commander Toad in Space, 1980, The Gift of Sarah Barker, 1981, Touch Magic, 1981, Dragon's Blood, 1982, Tales of Wonder, 1983, Heart's Blood, 1984, Cards of Grief, 1984, Dragonfield, 1985, Merlin's Booke, 1986, The Lullabye Songbook, 1986, Ring of Earth, 1986, Favorite Folktales From Around the World, 1986, Piggins, 1987, Owl Moon, 1987, Three Bears, 1987, A Sending of Dragons, 1987, The Devil's Arithmetic, 1988, Sister Light/Sister Dark, 1988, White Jenna, 1989, Dove Isabeau, 1989, Baby Bear's Bedtime Book, 1990, Tam Lin, 1990, Bird Watch, 1990, Sky Dogs, 1990, Wizard's Hall, 1991, All those Secrets of the World, 1991, Wings, 1991, Hark! A Christmas Sampler, 1991, Encounter, 1992, Briar Rose, 1992, Letting Swift River Go, 1992, What Rhymes with Moon, 1993, Welcome to the Greenhouse, 1993, Honkers, 1993, Here There Be Dragons, 1993, Grandad Bill's Song, 1994, Good Griselle, 1994, The Girl in the Golden Bower, 1994, Old Dame Counterpane, 1994, Old Macdonald's Songbook, 1994, Here There Be Unicorns, 1994, Beneath the Ghost Moon, 1994, The Wild Hunt, 1995, Ballad of the Pirate Queens, 1995, And Twelve Chinese Acrobats, 1995, Water Music, 1995, Among Angels, 1995, Here They Be Witches, 1995, O. Jerusalem, 1996, Welcome to the Sea of Sand, 1996, Passager, 1996, Hobby, 1996, Sacred Places, 1996, Here There Be Angels, 1996, Milk and Honey, 1996, Meet The Monsters, 1996, Once Upon Ice, 1997, Merlin, 1997, Child of Faerie, 1997, Twelve Impossible Things Before Breakfast, 1997, Miz Berlin Walks, 1997, Nocturne, 1997, Armageddon Summer, 1998, House/House, 1998, Prince of Egypt, 1998, Raising Yoder's Barn, 1998, The Wizard's Map, 1999, The Pictish Child, 1999, The Fairies' Ring, 1999, Moonball, 1999, Gray Heroes: Elder Tales From Around the World, 1999, How Does a Dinosaur Say Goodnight, 2000, Off We Go, 2000, Queen's Own Fool, 2000, Not One Damsel in Distress, 2000, Mirror/Mirror, 2000, Color Me a Rhyme, 2000, Welcome to the River of Grass, 2001, The Fish Prince and Other Merman Stories, 2001, Odysseus in the Serpent's Maze, 2001, Dear Mother/Dear Daughter, 2001, Hippolyta and the Curse of the Amazons, 2002, Wild Wings, 2002, Firebird, 2002, Horizons, 2002, Animal Train, 2002, Harvest Home, 2002, Girl in a Cage, 2002, Sword of the Rightful King, 2003, How Do Dinosaurs Get Well Soon, 2003, Take Joy, 2003, My Brothers' Flying Machine, 2003, Hoptoad, 2003, Mightier than the Sword, 2003, The Radiation Sonnets, 2003, The Flying Witch, 2003, Jason and the Gorgon's Blood, 2004, How Do Dinosaurs Clean their Rooms?, 2004, The Barefoot Book of Ballet Stories, 2004, Prince Across the Water, 2004, over 200 others. Mass. del. Dem. Nat. Conv., 1972; town coord. Robert Drinan's campaign, 1970; chmn. bd. trustees Hatfield (Mass.) Libr., 1978-83. Mem. Soc. Children's Book Writers (bd. dirs. 1974—), Children's Lit. Assn. (bd. dirs. 1977-79), Sci. Fiction Writers Am. (pres. 1986-88), Mystery Writers Am., Authors Guild. Democrat. Jewish/Quaker. Home: PO Box 27 Hatfield MA 01038-0027

YONTS-SHEPARD, SUSAN, forest service administrator; BA in History and Polit. Sci., Transylvania U.; grad. sr. exec. fellow program, Kennedy Sch. Govt., Harvard U. Pub. affairs positions Washington and Idaho Panhandle Nat. Forest; with Washington Office in Land Mgmt. Planning, Legis. Affairs; program mgr. Nat. Appeals and Litigation; dep. dir. for strategic planning and resource assessment USDA Forest Svc., Washington, assoc. dep. chief for programs and litigation, 2002—. Mem. working group Columbia River Basin Team, No. Spotted Owl Team; agy. rep. to exec. office Pres., Coun. on Environ. Quality. Office: USDA Forest Svc PO Box 96090 Washington DC 20090-6090

YOO, GRACE, legal association administrator; Exec. dir. Nat. Asian Pacific Am. Bar Assn., Washington. Office: Nat Asian Pacific Am Bar Assn Ste 315 733 15th St NW Washington DC 20005

YORK, ALEXANDRA, writer, lecturer; m. Barrett Randell. BA in Comm. Arts, Teaching Degree in Speech Edn., Mich. State U. Cert. speech, English, French educator, Mich. Writer, prodr., reporter bi-weekly feature Sta. WPIX-TV, N.Y.C., 1968; host two interview/talk shows on contemporary art scene ABC Radio Network, 1968; free-lance writer, 1968—; prin. actress radio and TV commls., including nat. Clairol TV spokesperson, 1970-82; pres. Promethena Artist Rep. Co., 1989—; editor Art Ideas mag., 1994-2000. Founding pres. Am. Renaissance for 21st Century Art, 1992—; lectr. in field. Author three books on self-help 1973, 77, 81, From the Fountainhead to the Future and Other Essays on Art and Excellence, 2000, Crosspoints: A Novel of Choice, 2004; editor, pub. Imprint of ART, Silver Rose Press, 2000-, Promethena Press, 2003-; series editor: Silver Rose Anthology: Award-Winning Short Stories, 2001; prodr. and curator major art exhibits Romantic Realism: Visions of Values, 1992, The Legacy Lives: The World at its Most Beautiful and Man and Woman at Their Best, 1996, 97; contbr. articles to newspapers and mags. including Reader's Digest, Vogue, USA Today, Vital Speeches; featured guest TV shows including The Today Show, Larry King Live, ABC's Eyewitness News. Recipient Whiting Meml. award for outstanding svc. to cultural world from the Internat. Soc. for Philos. Enquiry, 1997. Mem. Authors Guild, Nat. Arts Club (literary com. 1993—), Rolls-Royce Owners' Club (v.p. comm., editor 1991-94, McFarlane award 1992), Classic Car Club Am., Urasenke Internat. Tea Ceremony Soc. Avocations: travel, sports, cars, food/wines, ceremonial japanese tea, opera. Office: FDR Sta PO Box 8379 New York NY 10150-1919 Fax: (212) 759-1922.

YORK, CANDACE A. marketing professional, writer; b. Lubbock, Tex., Mar. 7, 1954; d. Billy John and Francis Ann York; m. James R. Callahan, Feb. 23, 1947. BFA in Art History, U. Tex., 1976. Archival asst. S.W. collection Tex. Tech. U., Lubbock, 1976—77; claims analyst Met. Life, Austin, Tex., 1977—78; mktg. software engr., info. devel. IBM Corp., Austin, Tex., 1978—. Author: 155 Tips to Protect Your Home and Wealth From Fire, 2003, numerous poems, short stories; contbr. articles to profl. jours. Vol. Austin (Tex.) Cmty. Gardens, 2003—04, Tex. Sch. Blind, 2003. Named Internat. Poet of Merit, Internat. Libr. Poetry, 2001; recipient Excellence award, Soc. Tech. Comm., 1980, Honorable Mention award, Iliad Press, 2001, 1st pl. poetry in motion competition, 2001, 2nd place, Sol poet laureate competition, 2002. Mem.: Assn. Interactive Media, Pub. Rels. Soc. Am. (programs com. Austin chpt. 2003), Acad. Am. Poets, Internat. High IQ Soc. Avocations: poetry, photography, guitar, painting, tai chi. Home: 8210 Bent Tree Rd #213 Austin TX 78759 E-mail: canyork@aol.com.

YORK, CYNTHIA A. retail executive; b. Anderson, Ind., Feb. 8, 1952; d. Andrew Pierce and Nancy Howard Upchurch; m. David M. York, Sept. 5, 1980 (dec. Nov. 1994); 1 child, David M. York II. BS, Western Ky. U., 1974. Sr. merchandising mgr. J.C. Penny, Anderson, Ind., 1974—91; retail mgr. Cracker Barrel, 1991—2001, Bloomington, 2001—. Mem.: AAUW. Office: Cracker Barrel Old Country Store 380 N Jacob Dr Bloomington IN 47404

YORK, GLADYS DOUGHTY, minister; b. Fall River, Mass., May 30, 1911; d. Wilbert Howe and Nellie Mae (Alexander) Doughty; m. Neal Farwell York, June 18, 1939 (dec. Jan. 1974); 1 child, Ruth Edna. BA, Jackson Coll., 1932; BD, Andover Newton Theological Sc., 1935. Ordained to ministry United Ch. of Christ, 1935. Min. First Congl. Ch., North Yarmouth, Maine, 1935-67, Danville (Maine) Union Ch., 1950-58, Princeton, Waite-Talmage, and Grand Lake Stream Chs., 1967-76, Highland Lake Congl. Ch., Westbrook, Maine, 1976-81, East Windham (Maine) Union Ch., 1977—. Author: GDNFY: Both a License Number and a Statement of Faith, 1990. Recipient Disting. Ministry award Alumni Assn. Andover Newton Theological Sch., 1986. Mem. New Eng. Mins. Assn., Internat. Assn. Women Mins. Home and Office: 80 Gray Rd North Yarmouth ME 04097-6007

YORK, JANET BREWSTER, nurse, family and sex therapist, artist; b. N.Y.C., Mar. 5, 1941; d. Edward Cox and Janet Stone Brewster; m. Albert Thompson York, Mar. 31, 1962 (dec.); children: Clifton Gaston, Torrance Brewster, 1 adopted child, Justin Brigham. AA with honors, Briarcliff Coll., 1961; RN with highest honors, U. Iowa, 1965; BA summa cum laude, Marymount Manhattan Coll., 1975; MA with honors, NYU, 1978. Nurse Manhattan Eye, Ear and Throat Hosp., N.Y.C., 1966-74; nurse, counselor Washington Free Clinic, 1969-71; family therapist Ackerman Family Inst., N.Y.C., 1976-80; sex therapist N.Y. Med. Coll., Flower Fifth Ave. Hosp., N.Y.C., 1976-80; pvt. practice pvt. practice, N.Y.C., 1978—. Supervisory staff grad. edn. program in human sexuality N.Y.U. Med. Ctr., 1982-89, sculptor, 1988—, operator Piccadil Kennel, breeder Cavalier King Charles Spaniels and Chinese Cresteds; bd. dirs. Animal Med. Ctr. Represented in permanent collection The Dog Mus. of Am., St. Louis; author: Corneel the Cavalier, Corneel at the Plaza; contbr. articles to profl. jours; author: (videotape) Death as a Part of Life. Named Vita fellow Internat. Coun. Sex Edn. and Parenthood, Am. U., 1981; recipient Evelyn Monte Sculpture award, 1988, 94, Ellsworth Howell Art Sculpture award Pen & Brush Club, 1991, 93, 96, 99, 2000, 02, Dog Fanciers Club, 1999. Mem. Nat. Assn. Women Artists, Am. Medallic Soc., Nantucket Art Assn., Walker Art Ctr., Nat. Sculpture Soc., Am. Kennel Club (art adv. com.), Nat. Mus. Women in Arts, Lawrence Beach Club, Rockaway Hunting Club, Millbrook Club, Progressive Dog Club/L.I. Kennel Club (bd. dirs.). Home: 155 E 72nd St New York NY 10021-4371 E-mail: Piccadiljy@aol.com.

YORK, KAREN KAY, accountant, farmer; b. Cedar Falls, Iowa, Jan. 30, 1950; d. Richard Arthur and Betty Lenore Wittren; m. Edward Louis York, June 28, 1969; 1 child, David Christian. AAS, McHenry C.C., Crystal Lake, Ill., 1978. Layout artist Black Dot Publ. Co., Crystal Lake, 1972-74; sch. bus. driver Sch. Dists. 47, 155, Crystal Lake, 1975-83; gen. acct., office mgr. Yornell Tool & Mold, Crystal Lake, 1976-87; staff acct. Scot Forge Co., Spring Grove, Ill., 1987—. Advisor and edml. dir. Scot Forge Employee Ownership Coun., 1981—; spkr. in field. Contbr. articles to co. newsletter. Trustee Employee Ownership Found., 1998-99. Named Employee Owner of Yr. Employee Stock Ownership Assn., 1998, Ill. Employee Owner of Yr. Ill. Employee Ownership Assn., 1998. Mem. Nat. Employee Ownership (at-large bd. govs. 1992—). Avocations: raising and training horses, scuba diving, gardening, motorcycling. Office: Scot Forge Co 8001 Winn Rd # 8 Spring Grove IL 60081-9687

YORK, KAREN SUE, artist, art historian; b. Wichita, Kans., Sept. 19, 1955; d. Jack Shannon and Pat Sue (Sittel) Compton; m. Kevin Blaine Hardin, June 1977 (div. 1981); 1 child, Kate; m. Robert Sterling York, Sept. 19, 1981. BFA, Tex. Woman's U., 1995; MA, Ind. U., 1998, PhD, 2003. Jr. art dir. Ackerman, Inc., Tulsa, Okla., 1975-77, Fred Davis & Assocs., Tulsa, 1977-78; graphic designer Tulsa, 1978-82; art dir. Advantage Advt., Tulsa, 1982-83; entertainment mgr. Tulsa, Houston, Denton, Tex., 1983-95. Art dir. Internat. Jugglers Assn., 1982-84. One-woman show includes Tex. Woman's U., 1995. Recipient Ben Keith award North Tex. Art League, 1995; fellow Ind. Art Mus., 2000-03. Mem. Phi Kappa Phi (Acad. Excellence award 1994, 95), Gamma Beta Phi, Alpha Chi, Ind. Univ. Art History Assn. (pres. 1998-99). Avocations: metalsmith, rockhound, scuba diver, golfer. Home: 3534 Burks Ct Bloomington IN 47401-8465

YORK, LINDA KAY, real estate appraiser, real estate company executive; b. Peru, Ind., Feb. 4, 1944; d. Robert W. and Evelyn J. (Hurd) Kollmeyer; m. Carl D. York, Oct. 7, 1977; children: Carl, Michelle, Cynthia, Erick, Ronda, Jennifer, Todd, Taya. Student, St. John's Coll., 1962-63, Fairmont State Coll., 1983-84. State cert. gen. real estate appraiser, W.Va.; ind. fee appraiser; lic. appraisal tchr., W.Va. Appraiser Petroplus & Assoc., Morgantown, W.Va., 1983-86; ptnr. Puccio & York, Fairmont, W.Va., 1986—. Instr. Fairmont State Coll., 1995—, United Tech. Sch., Gore, W.Va., 1993—. Life mem. Monongalia Gen. Hosp. Aux., Morgantown, 1990. Mem. Nat. Assn. Ind. Fee Appraisers (pres. Morgantown chpt. 1990-94), W.Va. U. Alumni Assn. (life). Democrat. Baptist. Avocations: reading, international travel. Home: 1035 Bakers Ridge Rd Morgantown WV 26508-1442 Office: Puccio & York 617 Locust Ave Fairmont WV 26554-4721

YORK, STAR LIANA, sculptor; b. Washington, Apr. 14, 1952; d. Robert Erastus and Adele York Northam; m. Rodney James Barker. Student, Prince Georges C.C.; BFA, U. Md.; postgrad., Balt. Inst. Art. Tchr., artist in residence CETA Program, Md., 1974-76. Subject of book and mag. articles; exhibited in group shows at Prince Georges Com Coll., 1970-72, U. of Md., 1972-74, Balt. Inst. Art, 1975, Artist in Residence at Prince Georges Com Coll, CETA, Medicine Man Gallery: Leading The West, 1997, Southwest Art Mag. traveling exhibit of all mag. cover artist, 1998; one person show at Gilcrease Mus., Tulsa, Okla., 1998; group mus. shows at Tuscon Fine Art, 1991, 92, 93, 94, Beninington Fie Art, Vermont, 1997, Wildlite Fine Art, Jackson, Wyo., 1997, Albuquerque Fine Art, N.M., 1992; AWA group shows at Total Arts Gallery, Taos, N.M., 1999, Trailside Gallery, Scottsdale, Ariz., 1998; one and two person shows at Zaplin Lampert, Sante Fe, N.M. 1994, 95, 98, 99, Dewey Gallery, Sante Fe, 1992, 93, Meyer Gallery, Scottsdale, Ariz., 1992, 93, Mountain Trails Gallery, Jackson, Wyo., 1997, Shriver Gallery, Taos, N.M., 1983, 84, 85, 86, 87, 88, 89, 90, 91, 92, 93, 94, 95, 96, 97, 98, 99, Pendragon Gallery, Annapolis, Md., 1980, 81, 82, 83, Squashblossom Gallery, Aspen, Colo., 1984, 85, 86, 87, 88, Cogswell Gallery, Vail, Colo., 1986, 87, 88, Dakota Gallery, Boca Raton, Fla., 1985, 86, 87, 88, 89, 90, Ton Atim Gallery, Durango, Colo., 1992, 94, 96, 98, Silverado Skies Gallery, Miami, 1989, 1990, Christi Lee Gallery, Basalt, Colo., 1997, Hawthorn Gallery, Branson, Mo., 1990. Recipient first place Lance Internat. award Nat. Sculpture Soc., N.Y.C., 1978-80, first place sculpture Catherine Lorillard Soc., N.Y.C. Mem. Am. Women Artists Assn. (chairperson 1996—), Am. Polocrosse Assn., Am. Quarter Horse Assn. Avocation: polocrosse. Home: 533 Onate Pl Santa Fe NM 87501-3676 Office: Am Women Artists 533 Onate Pl Santa Fe NM 87501-3676

YORK, VERMELLE CARDWELL, real estate broker and developer; b. Evergreen, Ala., Jan. 30, 1925; d. Frederick Lofton and Emmie Mildred (Pitts) Cardwell; m. E. Travis York, Jr., Dec. 26, 1946; children: Lisa, Travis. BS, Auburn U., 1946. Pres. Tralisa Corp., Gainesville, Fla., 1966—87, sec., treas., 1988—94, Caret Corp., Gainesville, Fla., 1979—86, pres., 1987—. Mem. devel. com. Harn Mus., Gainesville, 1990-96, Hospice House, Gainesville, 1992-96; co-chair March of Dimes, Gainesville, 1995, Red Ribbon Campaign, 1989, 90; bd. dirs. Keep Alachua County Beautiful, Phillips Ctr. Performing Arts U. Fla. Recipient President's Medallion, U. Fla., 1980; named Woman of Distinction Santa Fe C. C., 1988. Mem. Gainesville Builders Assn. (bd. dirs. 1997—), The Heritage Club (mem. amb. com. 1991-96), P.E.O. (pres. 1989-90), Surfside N. Club, (dir. 1988-91), Gainesville Women's Forum (membership chair 1994-96), Altrusa, Rotary, DAR, Phi Kappa Phi. Avocation: genealogy. Office: Caret Corp 4020 SW 78th St Gainesville FL 32608-3608

YORKE, MARIANNE, lawyer, real estate executive; b. Nov. 4, 1948; d. Joseph George and Catherine Veronica (Friel) Y. BA, West Chester U., 1971; JD, Temple U., 1980; MS in Ognl. Dynamics summa cum laude, U. Pa., 1987; M in Corp. Real Estate, Internat. Assn. Corp. Real Estate Execs., 1996. Bar: Pa. 1981, N.Y. 1992. Mgr. CIGNA Corp., Phila., 1982-85, asst. dir., 1985-90; v.p. Chase Manhattan Bank, N.Y.C., 1990-92; real estate dir. Johnson & Johnson, 1992—. Real estate atty. Garfinkel & Volpicelli, Phila., 1980-82; prin., mng. ptnr. Yorke/Eisenman, Real Estate, Phila., 1976-89, prin., mng. ptnr. Yorke/Mac Lachlin Real Estate, Phila., 1989-2002; lectr. Women in the Arts, 1982-90; guest spkr. Wharton Sch. Class of 1989, U. Pa., grad. sch. arts and sci. Class of 1988; asst. prof. bus. law Rider U. Grad Sch., 2002 (eve.), asst. prof. legal environ., Rutgers U. 2003— (eve.) Contbr. articles to profl. jours. Solicitor Pa. Ballet, Phila., 1983-90, United Way, Phila., 1983-90; mem. steering com. U. Pa., 1986-90, dir. alumni assn., 1987-90; mem. adv. com. for econ. devel. Luth. Settlement House Adv., 1986-88; mem. Ctr. Adv. Bd., 2000—; bd. dirs. Hamilton Townhouse Assn., Phila., 1988-90, chmn. ins. com., 1989-90, 718 Broadway Inc., N.Y.C., 1990-94, Johnson Health Care Svcs. Recipient Live for Life Mgmt., Johnson Health Mgmt., 1995, Pres. Quality Process Excellence award, EthiconEndo Surgery, 2000, Process Excellence award, Ethicon, Inc., 2001. Mem. ABA (forum on constrn. 1982-90), Pa. Bar Assn. (condominium and zoning com. 1982-90), Assn. of Bar of City of NY (sects. on internat. law and real property law 1992-94), Phila. Bar Assn., Phila. Women Real Estate Atty., Nat. Assn. Corp. Real Estate Exec. (internat. coun. 1984—, comml. coun. 1984—), Internat. Atty., Roundtable, Women's Law Caucus, Phi Alpha Delta. Independent. Roman Catholic. Home: The Admiralty 55 Ocean Ave Monmouth Beach NJ 07750-1366 Office: Johnson & Johnson W H 7135 1 Johnson & Johnson Plz New Brunswick NJ 08933-0002

YORKMAN, MARQUETTA MARCYE BODINE, financial professional; b. Balt., Sept. 13, 1970; d. Bodine Coline and Mark Anthony Yorkman. BFA, Am. InterContinental U., Atlanta, 1998. Investor rels. rep. Chapman Online, Balt., 2000—01; mktg. cons. and para-planner My Plan Mgmt. Group, Balt., 2001—02; asset mgmt. specialist Citicorp Trust Bank, Hanover, Md., 2002—03; fin. profl. The MONY Group, Timonium, Md., 2003—. Fashion stylist, image cons. Marcye Bodine Styling Co. Contbr. articles to profl. jours. Vol./ walker Multiple Sclerosis Soc., Balt., 2000—02; mentor Big Bros. and Big Sisters, Balt., 2001—02; spkr. Women's Housing Coalition, Balt., 2003. Grantee, State of Ga. grantee, 1996—98; scholar, Md. State scholar, 1989. Baptist. Office: The MONY Group 1954 Greenspring Dr Ste 510 Timonium MD 21093 Office Phone: 888-208-0168. Personal E-mail: marcyestylingis@hotmail.com. E-mail: myorkman@mony.com.

YOSHIKI-KOVINICK, MARIAN TSUGIE, author; b. L.A., Feb. 17, 1941; d. Eddie Junichi and Teruko Ruth Yoshiki; m. Philip Peter Kovinick, June 17, 1973. BA, U. So. Calif., 1963; MA, Azusa Pacific U., 1980. Tchr. Pasadena (Calif.) Unified Sch. Dist., 1964-66, Centinela Valley Union H.S. Dist., Lawndale, Calif., 1966-83; freelance writer, rschr. L.A., 1983—; archivist/reference specialist Archives of Am. Art Smithsonian Instn., 1996—. Rsch. supr. NEH project Calif. Asian Am. Artists Biog. Survey, 1999—, Huntington Libr. Reader, The Getty Rsch. Inst. Extended Reader. Rschr., cons. for various exhbns., including The Woman Artist in the American West, 1976, California Light, 1990, rschr. for books Elsie Palmer Payne, 1990, Guy Rose, American Impressionist, 1995, American Scene Painting, 1991, In Living Color: The Art of Hideo Date, 2001; co-author: An Encyclopedia of Women Artists of the American West, 1998, Publications in Southern California Art, vol. 6, 1999; contbr. Grove's Ency. of American Art Before 1914, 1999, Southwest Art, 1998, The Neville-Strass Collection: American Women Artists, 1819-1947, 2003. Recipient Western Heritage award, 1999; Hist. Soc. So. Calif./Haynes Found. rsch. grantee, 2002. Mem. Huntington Corral of Westerners, Art Librs. Soc. Democrat. Avocations: calligraphy, crocheting, needlepoint, gardening, photography. Home and Office: 4735 Don Ricardo Dr Los Angeles CA 90008-2812

YOSHIUCHI, ELLEN HAVEN, health educator, clinical counselor; b. Newark, Apr. 15, 1949; d. Michael Joseph and Adeline V. (Lindblom) Haven; m. Takeshi Yoshiuchi, Dec. 1, 1973; children: Teri Takumi, Niki Noboru. BA summa cum laude, CUNY, 1980; M Profl. Studies in Human Rels., N.Y. Inst. Tech., 1991. Cert. bereavement svcs. counselor, cert. kidney early evaluation program. Pvt. practice childbirth edn., 1983—89; program asst. parent/family edn. St. Luke's/Roosevelt Hosp. Ctr., N.Y.C., 1989—93, mem. faculty parent/family edn. program, 1990—2002; mem. faculty Family Ctr. at Riverdale Neighborhood House, Bronx, 1991—96; faculty mem. The Greater N.Y. March of Dimes, N.Y.C., 1996—2001; mgr. patient svcs. N.Y.C. chpt. The Leukemia and Lymphoma Soc., 1998—2004; program dir. Nat. Kidney Found. of Greater N.Y., 2004—. Mem. perinatal bereavement com. St. Luke's/Roosevelt Hosp. Ctr., N.Y.C., 1989-95. Editor ASPO/N.Y.C. News, 1983-86; contbr. articles to profl. jours. Trustee Pan Asian Repertory Theatre, N.Y.C., 1996-2001. Fellow: Am. Coll. Childbirth Educators; mem.: Coun. Nephrology Social Workers, C.G. Jung Found. for Analytical Psychology, Lamaze Internat. (cert. tchr., pres. N.Y.C. chpt. 1987—91, nominating com. 1991—93, dir. ednl. program 1991—93), N.Y. State Perinatal Assn. Office: 475 Park Ave S New York NY 10016-6901

YOST, BERNICE, detective agency owner; b. Houston; d. Kenneth Wayne and Georgia (Sampson) Cox; m. Matthew Yost. Student, L.A. Trade Tech, 1968-70, Compton Coll., 1974-76, Ariz. State U., 1983-85. Staff acct. Moultrie, Liggens, Terrel CPA's, L.A., 1969-71; spl. agt. IRS, L.A., 1972-79, supervisory spl. agt. Phoenix, 1979-91, Washington, 1991-93; owner, operator Yost Detective Agy., Silver Spring, Md., 1995-2000, Culver City, Calif., 1998—2001, Beverly Hills, Calif., 2001—. Recipient Albert Gallatin award for merit, 1993. Mem. Nat. Orgn. of Black Law Enforcement Execs. Democrat. Baptist. Avocations: tennis, jogging, sewing. Home: 369 S Doheny Dr #309 Beverly Hills CA 90211-3577 E-mail: berniceyost@aol.com.

YOST, JEAN MARIE, administrative assistant; b. Washington, Aug. 8, 1928; d. John Joseph and Violet Jessica (Cusick) Werres; m. Meredith Loy Yost, June 11, 1955; children: Jean Marie Samuels, John Paul. Student, Loretto Hts. Coll., Denver, 1946-48. Sec. Marshal of the Supreme Ct. of U.S., Washington, 1946-58; exec. sec. Marriott Corp., Bethesda, Md., 1987-89, Bechtel Power Corp., Gaithersburg, Md., 1979-81; adminstrv. asst. Nat. Elec. Mfrs. Assn., Washington, 1989-95; legal sec. Glinsmann & Glinsmann, Gaithersburg, MD, 1995-96; profl. staff asst. York Internat., 1996-99; profl. staff asst. Dept. Juvenile Justice Washington County, Hagerstown, Md., 2000—. Contbr. (poetry) A Flood of Contentment Theater of The Mind, Today's Famous Poems, 2003, Letters from the Soul, 2003, The Colors of Life, 2003, CD reading listening, The Colors of Life, 2003. Pres. YWCA-Y Wives of Damascus, Md., 1976; sec. PTA, Damascus, 1976; 4-H leader, Damascus; active CCD, Silver Spring, Md., 1969. Mem.: AAUW, NAFE, Nat. Assn. Adminstrv. Assts. and Execs., Internat. Assn. Adminstrv. Profls. (sec. Toll Gate chpt.), Internat. Soc. Poets. Avocations: music, photography, travel, needlework, plays and musicals. Office: Dept Juvenile Justice Washington County Hagerstown MD 21740

YOST, KELLY LOU, pianist; b. Boise, Idaho, Aug. 10, 1940; d. Roy Daniel and Helen Roberta (Kingsbury) Frizzelle; m. Nicholas Peter Bond, Dec. 27, 1961 (div. 1973); 1 child, Brook Bernard; m. Samuel Joseph Yost, June 16, 1984. B.A. music, U. Idaho, 1962; postgrad., U. So. Calif., 1966-68. Pvt. tchr. classical piano, Twin Falls, Idaho, 1962-88; rec. artist, owner ind. record label Channel Prodns., Twin Falls, 1986—. Soloist U. Idaho Symphony Orch., Moscow, 1962; pianist, keyboardist Magic Valley Symphony Orch., Twin Falls, 1985, 86; touring guest piano soloist Vandaleer Concert Choir, Moscow, 1961. Recorded record albums: Piano Reflection (excerpts included in Simple Abundance by Sarah Ban Breathnach), 1987, (selection synchronized with Japanese film Gaia Symphony #4), 2001, Quiet Colors, 1991, Roses and Solitude, 1996, Still...Still...Still, 1998, Brand New Feel (in Japan), 2002; recorded record albums Dreams, Japan, 2003. Mem. NARAS, Assn. Ind. Music, Music Tchrs. Nat. Assn., Idaho Music Tchrs. Assn. (sec. 1981-82), Magic Valley Cmty. Concert Assn. (bd. dirs. 1964-87), Phi Beta Kappa, Kappa Kappa Gamma (Alumnae Achievement award 1996). Avocations: snow skiing, hiking, philosophy. Office: Channel Prodns PO Box 454 Twin Falls ID 83303-0454

YOST, NANCY RUNYON, artist, small business owner; b. Eaton, Ohio, July 16, 1933; d. Stanley Everett and Treva (Geeting) Runyon; m. Kenneth John Yost, Aug. 17, 1952 (div. Dec. 1962); 1 child, Debra Colleen Yost Mayne. BS in Art Edn., Miami U., Oxford, Ohio, 1966, MEd in Art, 1970. Cert. profl. permanent tchr., Ohio. Sec. N.Am. Aircraft, Columbus, Ohio, 1957, Miami U., Oxford, 1957-61, textile instr., 1978, Living Arts Ctr., Dayton, Ohio, 1972-73; coord. art, music and phys. edn. Stewart Jr. High Sch., Oxford, 1981-86; art instr. Talawanda Sch. System, Oxford, 1965-90, dist. coord., 1986-90; owner, creator Allegro Adornments Bus., 1988—. Postgrad. Sem. Charles Jeffrey, Cleve., Inst. Art, Miami U., 1973, David Van Dommelen Penn State at U. Tenn., 1975, Bill Helwig, N.Y., 1975, Nik Krevitsky, N.Y., 1976, Tom Shafer, Columbus, Ohio, 1982; mem. curriculum coun. Talawanda Sch. Dist., 1982—; rep. Amway Corp., 1980-81, World Book Co., Chgo., 1986-88; lectr. Miami U., 1986; invited workshop speaker, presenter Nat. Art Edn. Assn. Conv., Phoenix, 1992. One-woman shows include Creative Fibers Studio, Buffalo, 1974, Fitton Ctr. for the Creative Arts, Hamilton, Ohio, 2003, one-woman retrospective, Preble County Art Ctr., 1998, exhibited in group shows at Dayton Art Inst., Invitational Fiber Artists Am., Ball State U., 1974, Christkindl Markt, Canton Art Inst., 1994 (hon. mention), Art All Over, Oxford, Ohio, 2002. Supr. Community Artworks, 1986; mem. adv. bd. Miami U. Summer Theatre, 1991-93; mem. spl. events planning com. Miami U. Art Mus., 1993—. Recipient Winner Most Creative Costume Ohio Mart, 1992, 93, First Pl. awards Community Photo Contest, 3d Pl. and Hon. Mention award Oxford Audubon Photo Show, 1994, 1st Pl. 3D Design, Greater Hamilton Art Exhibit at Fitton Ctr, 1995, Cash award ribbon and Purchase award Wyo. Art Show, 1996, Cash award ribbon Minnetrista Arts Fair, 1996, Best in Show Preble Co. Arts Assn. Juried Show, 1997, First Pl. Sculpture, 1997, 2d Pl Ribbon cash award Christ Kindl Markt, Canton Art Inst., 1999, 1st Pl. 3D Design award, Greater Hamilton Art Exhibit, 2000. Mem. Southwestern Art Edn. Assn., Ohio Art Edn. Assn., Ohio Edn. Assn., Talawanda Edn. Assn., Ohio Designer Craftsmen, Ohio Arts and Crafts Guild, Oxford Arts Club, Kappa Delta Pi. Avocations: commissioned artwork, sculpture, wearable art, fabric, metal collages, limited edition prints, painted wood furniture. Home: 6674 Fairfield Rd Oxford OH 45056-8813

YOTHER, MICHELE, publisher; b. Atlanta, Aug. 25, 1965; d. Carole (Spence) Marsh; m. Michael B. Yother, Mar. 17, 1990; children: Christina Michele, Grant Michael. BA in acctg. cum laude, Ga. State U., 1990. Asst. v.p. Bank Am., Atlanta, 1986-90; pres. Gallopade Internat. Inc., Atlanta, 1990—. Pres. Carole Marsh Family Interactive Multimedia, 1993—. Pub. over 10000 children's books, computer disks and activities. Equifax Bus. scholar Ga. State U., 1989. Mem. Women's Nat. Book Assn. (bd. dirs. 1994-95), Bank Am. Club (pres. 1989), Golden Key. Methodist. Home: 502 Rose Down Trce N Peachtree City GA 30269-3718 Office: Gallopade Internat Inc Ste 600 665 Highway 74 S Peachtree City GA 30269-3003

YOTSUKURA, LINDSAY AMTHOR, language educator; b. Sept. 11, 1962; BA cum laude, Williams Coll., Williamstown, Mass., 1980—84; EdM, Harvard Grad. Sch. Edn., Cambridge, Mass., 1986—87; MA, Ohio State U., Columbus, 1989—91, PhD, 1991—97. Mombusho English fellow Ministry of Edn., Akita Prefecture, Japan, 1984—86; Japanese instr. Kalamazoo Coll., 1987—89; Japanese lectr. U. Md., College Park, 1996—97, asst. prof., Japanese, 1997—. Author: (book) Negotiating Moves: Problem Presentation and Resolution in Japanese Business Discourse, 2003; contbr. chapters to books, articles to profl. jours. Grantee, Assn. for Asian Studies, 2001, Japan Found., 2001, Cheng & Tsui Publishers, 2003; Fulbright scholar, 1994—95. Mem.: Assn. Tchrs. Japanese (mem. bd. dirs.), Am. Assn. of U. Suprs., Coords., Dirs. of Fgn. Lang. Programs, Assn. of Japanese Bus. Studies, Assn. for Asian Studies, Am. Assn. of Applied Linguistics, Internat. Pragmatics Assn. Office: Univ Md 3215 Jimenez Hall Sch Langs College Park MD 20742

YOUMANS, JOYCE M. curator, researcher; d. Jasper D. and Karen S. Youmans. BA, U. Mo., Kansas City, 1995; MA in Art History, U. Kans., 2002. Rsch. asst. The Nelson-Atkins Mus. of Art, Kansas City, Mo., 1994—99, curatorial asst., 1999—2002, asst. curator African art, 2002—03; lectr. Kans. City (Mo.) Art Inst., 2003—. Lectr. U. Kans., Lawrence, 2002—03; rschr., Shawnee Mission, Kans., 1995—. Contbr. articles to profl. jours. Office: The Nelson-Atkins Mus of Art 4525 Oak St Kansas City MO 64111-1873

YOUNATHAN, MARGARET TIMS, nutritionist, educator; b. Clinton, Miss., Apr. 25, 1926; d. Peter Asbury and Eula Lee (Tatum) Tims; m. Ezzat S. Younathan, Aug. 11, 1958; children: Janet Nadya, Carol Miriam. BA, U. So. Miss., 1946, BS, 1950; MS, U. Tenn., 1951; PhD, Fla. State U., 1958. Instr. food and nutrition Oreg. State U., 1951-55; postdoctoral rsch. assoc. Fla. State U., 1958-59; sr. nutritional cons. Ark. Dept. Health, Little Rock, 1962-68; instr. pediat. U. Ark. Sch. Medicine, Little Rock, 1962-65, asst. prof. pediat., 1965-68; assoc. prof. food and nutrition Sch. Human Ecology La. State U., 1971-79, prof., 1979-94; ret., 1994. Internat. nutrition work in Sierra Leone, 1984, Jamaica, 1987. Contbr. articles on food and nutrition rsch. to profl. jours. Summer faculty grantee La. State U. Coun. on Rsch., 1980, rsch. grantee Lou Ana Foods, Inc., 1987. Mem. Inst. Food Technologists, Am. Soc. for Nutritional Scis., Am. Dietetic Assn., Am. Assn. Family and Consumer Sci., La. Assn. Family and Consumer Sci. (pres. dist. D 1981-82, Disting. Home Economist award 1988), Sigma Xi, Phi Kappa Phi, Gamma Sigma Delta, Omicron Nu, Phi Upsilon Omicron. Mem. Christian Ch. (Disciples Of Christ). Home: 1048 Castle Kirk Dr Baton Rouge LA 70808-6023 Office: Sch Human Ecology La State U Baton Rouge LA 70803-4300 E-mail: eyounat@aol.com.

YOUNG, ALICE, lawyer; b. Washington, Apr. 7, 1950; d. John and Elizabeth (Jen) Y.; m. Thomas L. Shortall, Sept. 22, 1984; children: Amanda, Stephen. AB magna cum laude, Yale U., 1971; JD, Harvard U., 1974. Bar: N.Y. 1975. Assoc. Coudert Bros., NYC, 1974-81; mng. ptnr. Graham & James, NYC, 1981-87; ptnr. Milbank, Tweed, Hadley & McCloy, NYC, 1987-93; ptnr., chair Asia Pacific Practice Kaye, Scholer LLP, NYC, 1994—. Bd. dirs. Mizuho Trust and Banking Co., mem. exec. com., 2003—; spkr. Traphager Distinguished Alumni Speakers Forum, Harvard Law Sch., 2004. Contbr. articles to profl. jours. Bus. com. Nat. Com. on U.S.-China Rels., 1993—, U.S.-China Bus. Coun., 1993—, Com. of 100, 1993—, vice-chmn., 1999—; bd. overseers visitation com. to Law Sch. Harvard U., 1994—99, chair subcomm. on grad. program, 1996; trustee Lingnan Found., NYC, 1984—91, Pan-Asian Repertory Theatre, NYC, 1987—90, Aspen Inst., Colo., 1988—, Am. Assembly, 2000—; bus. com. Met. Mus. Art, NYC, 1989—94; active Coun. on Fgn. Rels., 1977—, Chmn.'s Forum, 2000—; trustee Asia Found., 2002—. Named one of Top 100 Minority Leaders, 1998, one of 40 Under 40 Crain's Bus., NYC, 1989; Bates fellow Yale U., 1970, NDFL fellow Harvard U., 1967-68; recipient

Star award NY Women's Agenda, 1992, Justice in Action Award, Asia Am. Legal Defense and Edu. Fund, 2004. Mem. ABA, NY State Bar Assn. (fgn. investment com.), Assn. Bar City NY (spl. com. on rels. with Japanese bar, Union Internat. des Avocats), Nat. Asian Pacific Am. Bar Assn., Asian Am. Bar Assn. NY, Harvard Law Sch. Assn. NYC (trustee 1990-94), Japan Soc. (sec. 1989-97), Asia Soc. (pres.'s coun. 1984-2002). Office: Kaye Scholer LLP 425 Park Ave New York NY 10022-3506 E-mail: ayoung@kayescholer.com.

YOUNG, ANN ELIZABETH O'QUINN, historian, educator; b. Waycross, Ga. d. James Foster and Pearl Elizabeth (Sasser) O'Quinn; m. Robert William Young, Aug. 18, 1968; children: Abigail Ann, Leslie Lynn. Student, Shorter Coll.; BA, MA, U. Ga., PhD, 1965. Asst. prof. history Kearney (Nebr.) State Coll. (name changed U. Nebr.-Kearney), 1965-69, assoc. prof., 1969-72, prof., 1972-00, prof. emeritus, 2000—. Participant Inst. on Islam, Middle East and World Politics, U. Mich., summer 1984, Coun. on Internat. Ednl. Exch., London, 1990, NEH Seminar NYU, 1993, faculty senate mem., 1985—, sec. 1993-94, pres., 1995-96. Conbg. author Dictionary of Georgia Biography; contbr. articles to profl. revs. Mem. NEA, PEO, Phi Alpha Theta, Delta Kappa Gamma (chpt. pres. 1978-79), Phi Mu. Republican. Presbyterian. Office: U Nebr at Kearney Dept History Kearney NE 68849-0001

YOUNG, ANNE B. neurologist, educator; AB, Vassar Coll., 1969; MD, Johns Hopkins U., 1973, PhD in Pharmacology, 1974. From asst. prof. to prof. chemistry Dept. Neurology, U. Mich., 1978-91; Julieanne Dorn prof. neurology Harvard Med. Sch., 1991—; chief neurology Mass. Gen. Hosp., 1991—. Fellow Scottish Rite Found., Lexington, 1973; med. intern Mt. Zion Hosp. & Med. Ctr., San Francisco; neurological resident Dept. Neurology U. Calif., San Francisco.; David Segal vis. prof. Columbia U., 1996; presdl. lectr. Am. Acad. Neurology, 1996. Contbr. numerous articles to profl. jours. Recipient Tchr./Investor Devel. award NIH, 1979-84, Facility Devel. award Merck, 1987-89, Milton Wexler award for Huntington's Rsch. Huntington's Dis. Soc. Am., 1989, Weinstein-Goldenson award United Cerebral Palsy Assn., Inc., 1990. Mem. Inst. Medicine-Nat. Acad. Science. Office: Dept Neurology Mass Gen 15 Parkman St Ste 835 Boston MA 02114-3117

YOUNG, ANNETTE D. state representative; b. Miss., June 25, 1952; d. Terry W. and Alice R. Douglas; m. Roger Allen Young (dec.); children: Robert, Kristina. Pres. Young Enterprises; mem. SC Ho. of Reps., 1991—; ho. majority leader, 1995. Mem. Givhans Sch. Improvement Coun., 1990, bd. dirs. YMCA; del. Rep. Nat. Conv., 1988; chmn. Dorchester Rep. Party, 1988—90; chmn. legis. del. Dorchester County, 1991—94. Named Rep. of Yr., Dorchester County, 1986—87; recipient, Archdale Women's Club, [illegible]. Mem., Summerville C. of C. Republican. Office: State Capitol 308 C Blatt Bldg Columbia SC 29211

YOUNG, BARBARA, psychiatrist, psychoanalyst, psychiatry educator, photographer; b. Chgo., Oct. 27, 1920; d. William Harvey and Blanche (DeBra) Y. AB, Knox Coll., 1942; MD, Johns Hopkins U., 1945; grad., Balt. [illegible] Inst., 1955. Intern Univ. Hosps., Iowa City, Iowa, 1945-46, asst. resident in neurology, 1945-47; asst. resident in psychiatry Phipps Clinic, Johns Hopkins U. Hosp., Balt., 1947-49; staff psychiatrist Perry Point (Md.) VA Hosp., 1949-51; practice medicine specializing in psychiatry/psychoanalysis Balt., 1951—; instr. Johns Hopkins U., 1953-69, asst. prof. psychiatry, 1969—, prof. emeritus, 1997—; freelance photographer, 1958—. Lectr. dept. psychiatry Johns Hopkins U.; lectr. Lucy Daniels Found., Carey, N.C., dept. humanities Yale U. Med. Sch., Boston Inst. for Psychotherapy, local psychiat. and social orgns. Works represented in Mus. Modern Art, N.Y.C., Balt. Mus. Art, Santa Barbara (Calif.) Mus. Art, Eastman House, Rochester, N.Y., Yale U. Gallery of Art; photographer: The Plop-A-Lop Tree, 1995, Tales of Courage: Recovering LIfe After Catastrophe, 2003; contbr. articles to profl. jours. Mem. Am. Psychoanlytic Assn., Am. Psychiat. Assn., Balt.-Washington Soc. for Psychoanalysis. Democrat. Address: 5307 Herring Run Dr Baltimore MD 21214-1937

YOUNG, BRENDA ANN, nurse; b. Lancaster, Pa., June 26, 1969; d. Glenn and Jean (Iverson) Martin; m. Greg L. Young, Oct. 26, 1991. Diploma, Lancaster (Pa.) Gen. Hosp., 1990; BSN, Millersville U., 1995; postgrad., U. Del., 1996—. RN, Pa. Critical care nurse, telemetry staff nurse Lancaster Gen. Hosp., 1990—. EMT Rothsville (Pa.) Vol. Ambulance Corps., 1991—; mem. Rothsville Vol. Fire Co., 1991—; activities asst. Sertoma Burncamp, Lancaster, 1996. Mem. Am. Assn. Critical Care Nurses, Am. Acad. Nurse Practitioners, Lancaster Gen. Hosp. Alumni Assn. Republican. Methodist. Avocations: running, exercise, playing piano. Home: 11 Village Dr Lititz PA 17543-7407 Office: Lancaster Gen Hosp 555 N Duke St Lancaster PA 17602-2207

YOUNG, CANDACE C. educational consultant, researcher; b. Sante Fe; d. Robert S. and Helen V. Cartwright; m. Larry D. Young; children: Zachary C., Sydney C. BA in History and Govt., Columbia (Mo.) Coll., 1973; MA in Polit. Sci., U. Mo., 1973, PhD in Polit. Sci., 1982. Tchg. and rsch. asst. U. Mo., 1974—80; asst. prof. polit. sci. Truman State U., Kirksville, Mo., 1980—87, assoc. prof. polit. sci., 1987—95, prof. polit. sci., 1995—. Dir. Truman Inst. Policy Studies, Kirksville, Mo., 2000—; academic resource adv. com. Mo. Commn. of Future of Higher Edn., Jefferson City, Mo., 2003—. Recipient Gov.'s award for excellence in tchg., Gov. Carnahan, 1995. Mem.: Mo. Assn. Faculty Senates (adv. bd. 2003—, pres. 2001—02).

YOUNG, CAROL ANN (CASEY YOUNG), information systems consultant; b. Teaneck, N.J., Aug. 7, 1951; d. Stephen John and Mildred Olga (Weideman) Martin; m. Chester Frederick D'Elia, May 10, 1980 (div. 1983); 1 child, Antonio Preston; m. Stanley Warren Young, Jr., June 10, 1985 (div. 1999); 1 child, Jesse Stephen; m. Kenneth Allen Dawes, Aug. 16, 2003. BA in Theatre, Montclair State U., 1973; MA in Theatre, U. Mich., 1975. Assoc. instr. Eastern Mont. Coll., Billings, 1975-76; tchr. English Browning (Mont.) Jr. High, 1976-79; project adminstr. ITT, N.Y.C., 1980-82; info. ctr. adminstr. Selective Ins., Branchville, N.J., 1982-86; data base adminstr. AT&T, Parsippany, N.J., 1986-90, United Parcel Svc., Mahwah, N.J., 1991-94; prin. cons. RYC, Inc., Key Biscayne, Fla., 1994—98; mgr. IBM, San Jose, Calif., 1998—; prin., owner Mountain Vines Pub., 2003—. Author: Exploring IBM e-business Software, 2001; contbr. articles to profl. jours. Leader, den mother, com. mem. Cub Scouts, Milford, Pa., 1989—96 Mem. Internat. DB2 Users Group (v.p. bd. dirs. 1994—96, chairperson planning 1995-96, pres. 1996-98, Best User Spkr. 1992). Democrat. Episcopal. Avocations: inline skating, reading, crafts, writing. Address: 108 Cardiff Ct Santa Cruz CA 95060-2434

YOUNG, CAROL J. editor; Grad., Syracuse U. Reporter Providence Jour.-Bull., 1965—80, asst. city editor, then state editor, 1980—84, met. editor, 1987, assoc. exec. editor, 1995—. Office: Providence Jour 75 Fountain St Providence RI 02902*

YOUNG, CATHARINE M. state legislator; m. Dick Young; 3 children. BS magna cum laude in Mass Comm., SUNY, Fredonia. News reporter; state rep. State of N.Y., 1998—. Highest ranking Rep. mem. Govtl. Opers. Com.; standing com. assignments include Aging, Health and Sml. Bus. Coms.; appt. Task Force on Ednl. Stds.; regional whip on issues of sexual assault reform; mem. Energy, Envrion. and Agr. Task Force/Am. Legis. Exch. Coun. (ALEC). Dir. comms. and devel. Rehab. Ctr. Named Rep. Woman of Yr., 2000, Cattaraugus County Rep. Woman of yr.; recipient Bus. First's 40 Under Forty award, N.Y. Republican. Office: 700 Westgate Plaza West State St Olean NY 14760

YOUNG, CHRISTINE E, writer, journalist, private investigator; d. Raymond J and Joan Collyer Young; m. John P Pertel, Aug. 29, 1992; children: Allie Lynn, Katelynn Elizabeth, Anna Jordan, Noah John. BA, cum laude, U. of So. Maine, Portland, Maine, 1994—95. Licensed Private Investigator Maine, 2002. Prin., owner Access Investigative Services, Augusta, Maine, 2004—; investigative journalist WMTW, ABC News, Portland, Maine, 1992—2003; writer, news editor AOL/Time Warner, Dulles, Va., 1999—2002. Investigative journalist Sun Jour., Lewiston, Maine, 1992—96; tv and print model Burger King, Old Spice. Procter & Gamble, Ford Motors, Fla. Orange Juice, Red Lobster Restaurants, New York, NY, 1979—89. Spkr., lectr. Various citizen groups, Portland, Maine, 2001—03. Recipient Nat. Headliner Award, Press Club of Atlantic City, 1996, Enterprise reporting, AP, 1997, Nat. Clarion Award for Investigative Reporting, Assn. for Women in Comm., 1999, Alfred I duPont Columbia U. Journalism Award, Columbia U., 2000, Pub. svc. reporting, AP, 1999, Edward R.Murrow Award for Investigative Reporting, Radio and TV News Directors Assn., 2000, Enterprise reporting, AP, 2002; fellow Poynter Inst. for Media Studies, Poynter Inst., 1998. Fellow: Investigative Reporters and Editors. Achievements include First televised exposure of inhumane, dangerous working conditions of migrants at DeCoster Egg Farm in Turner, Maine, which was ultimately fined 3.8 million dollars by federal government in 1997; Exposed illegal election practices of Christian Civic League of Maine, leading to hearings and fines by Maine Ethics Commission. Avocations: films, books, theater, real estate, investing. Personal E-mail: cyoung207@hotmail.com.

YOUNG, CYNTHIA MYERS, artist; b. Ravenna, Ohio, May 20, 1933; d. Robert Glen Myers and Edith Freeman (Myers) Schultz; m. Alfred Avery Young, Nov. 26, 1955; 1 child, Meredith Coe Young Barritz. Student, RISD, 1954; BA, Conn. Coll. for Women, 1955; postgrad., U. Hawaii, 1963; MFA, George Washington U., 1979. Adj. faculty North Va. C.C., Alexandria, 1980-94, Annandale, 1993-95, Merrymount Coll., McLean, Va., 1989; bd. mem. D.C. chpt. Artists' Equity, 1989—, Touchstone Gallery, D.C., 1990—, Eye Wash Artists Newsletter, D.C., 1992-93; juror Potomac (Md.) Watercolor Soc., The Art Ctr., Springfield, Va., Falls Ch. (Va.) Cmty. Ctr., McLean Art Guild; artist-in-residence Nat. Pk. Svc., Washington, Art Found., La Napoule, France, Ctr. for Internat. Studies, Collegio Colombo, Viareggio, Italy, Va. Ctr. for the Creative Arts, Lynchburg, Va. One-person shows Touchstone Gallery, Washington, 1995, 98, 2000, Emerson Gallery, McLean, Va., 1999. Chairperson Cmty. for Creative Non-Violence Shelter for the Homeless (Mitch Snyder), collected 50 artworks for homeless shelter, Washington, 1989. Recipient David Lloyd Kreeger Painting award George Washington U., Washington, Graphics award Art Inst., San Diego, Saul Alexander award Found. Purchase award, Charleston, Dudley B Cooper award, Norfolk; fellow Va. Ctr. for the Creative Arts. Home: 6903 Southridge Dr Mc Lean VA 22101-5463

YOUNG, DEBORAH (DEBORAH AYLING YANOWITZ), social worker, librarian; b. Syracuse, N.Y., June 27, 1930; d. David and Joan (AyLing) Y. Student, Pa. State U., Wilkes-Barre and Altoona; postgrad., Pa. State U., Wilkes-Barre, 1988; BA magna cum laude, Wilmington Coll., 1972; MSW, Western Mich. U., 1979; postgrad., Elmira Coll, 1983-84; MLS, U. Pitts., 1994. Cert. social worker, Mich., Pa., NY, Va.; cert. pub. libr., NY, Va., Pa., Mich.; cert. homemaker-home health aide Found. Hospice and [illegible] Kalamazoo Pub. Schs., 1974-76; group leader, project coord. Kalamazoo Parks-Recreation Dept.-Youth Conservation Corps, 1977, 78; dir. summer camp Huntington Family Ctrs., Inc., Syracuse, 1980-82; agy. dir. Schuyler Head Start-Day Care, Inc., Watkins Glen, Montour Falls, N.Y., 1982-87; pvt. practice child and elder care, N.Y., 1988-90; social worker, discharge planner VA Med. Ctr., Altoona, Pa., 1990-91; libr. worker U. Pitts. Sch. Libr. and Info. Scis., 1993-94; vocat. worker Laurelton (Pa.) Ctr., 1994-95; children-young adult svcs. coord., reference libr. Petersburg (Va.) Pub. Libr., 1996-97; libr. dir. Berwick (Pa.) Pub. Libr., 1997-98, Hollidaysburg (Pa.) Free Pub. Libr., 1999—2002. Vol. ARC, NY, 1965—, 1965—, 1965—; ref. and children's vol. helper Altoona Area Pub. Libr., 1992—96; caregiver Babysitter Heaven Referral Svc., Altoona, 1995—96; mem. Blair County Health and Welfare Coun., Altoona, 1990—95; help-line tel. worker Contact, Altoona, 1992; mem. choir Blessed Sacrament Cathedral, Altoona, 1991—2001; mem., rotating chmn. Watkins Glen Human Svcs. Com., 1982—87; bd. dirs. Mental Health Assn. Human Svcs. Coalition, Columbia and Montour counties, Pa., 1997, 1998; mem., past camp staffer Cir. Pines Ctr., Delton, Mich., 1967—. Scholar Wilmington Coll., 1968-72, Office Vocat. Rehab., Pa. Dept. Labor and Industry, 1993-94; grad. fellow Western Mich. U., 1976. Mem. NASW, ALA, Religious Soc. Friends and Brethren in Christ, Green Key Honor Soc. Democrat. Roman Catholic. Avocations: swimming, travel, cooking, reading, writing.

YOUNG, DEBORAH ELSPETH, industrial hygienist, educator; b. Allentown, Pa., Aug. 7, 1964; d. Lawrence Henry and Sue Crowley Young. B, Va. Tech U., Blacksburg, 1986; postgrad. in PhD program, Va. Tech. U., Blacksburg, 2002—; MS, N.C. State U., Raleigh, 1989. Cert. indsl. hygienist Am. Bd. of Indsl. Hygiene, 2001, safety profl. Bd. of Cert. Safety Professionals, 2003. Co-dir. Va. Tech Environ., Health and Safety Svcs., Blacksburg, Va., 1997—; instr. Va. Tech. Grade Dept. Indsl. and Systems Engring., Blacksburg, Va., 1998—. Faculty advisor Am. Soc. Safety Engrs., Va. Tech Student Sect., Blacksburg, Va., 1999—. Mem.: Am. Conf. Govtl. Indsl. Hygienists, Am. Indsl. Hygiene Assn. Democrat. Avocations: bicycling, running, horse farming, real estate investment, art. Home: 3200 Mathews Lane Blacksburg VA 24060 Office: Virginia Tech U 459 Tech Center Dr Blacksburg VA 24061 E-mail: dyoung@vt.edu.

YOUNG, DONA DAVIS GAGLIANO, lawyer, insurance executive; b. Bklyn., Jan. 8, 1954; d. Vincent Joseph and Shirley Elizabeth (Davis) Gagliano; m. Roland F. Young III, Aug. 18, 1979; children: Meghan Davis, Wesley Davis, Taylor Davis. BA and MA in Polit. Sci., Drew U., 1976; JD, U. Conn., 1980. Bar: Conn. 1980, U.S. Dist. Ct. Conn. 1980. Joined Phoenix Home Life Mut. Ins. Co., Hartford, Conn., 1980, asst. counsel, 1981—83, assoc. counsel, 1983, dir. reinsurance adminstrn., 1983—84, asst. v.p. reinsurance adminstrn., 1984—85, 2nd v.p., ins. counsel, 1985-87, v.p., asst. gen. counsel, 1987-89, sr. v.p. individual sales and mktg., gen. counsel, 1989-94, exec. v.p. individual sales and mktg., gen. counsel, 1994—2000; pres. The Phoenix Cos., Hartford, Conn., 2000—01, pres., COO, 2001—03, pres., CEO, chmn., 2003—. Bd. dirs. Wachovia Corp., 2000—, Sonoco Products Co., 1995—, Foot Locker Inc. Chair United Way Capital Area Cmty. Campaign, 2003; bd. dirs. Hartford Hosp.; bd. trustees Goodspeed Opera House Found. Inc. Named Laura A. Johnson Woman of Yr., Hartford Coll. for Women, 2002; recipient Leadership Award for Women in Bus., New England Coun., 1994, Antoinette Bascetta Women's Career Devel. Award, Trust House, Hartford, Conn., 2000, Outstanding Alumni Award, Drew U., 2001, Disting. Grad. Award, U. Conn. Sch. Law, 2002, Human Rels. Award, Nat. Conf. Cmty. and Justice, 2002. Mem. ABA, Am. Coun. of Life Ins., Am. Soc. Corp. Secs., Assn. Life Ins. Counsel (bd. govs.), Hartford County Bar Assn., Conn. Bar Assn., N.Y. Bar Assn. Republican. Congregationalist. Office: The Phoenix Cos 1 American Row Hartford CT 06102-5056

YOUNG, ELIZABETH, minister; AA in bibl. studies, Trinity Luth. Coll., 1980; BA in Christian edn., Puget Sound Christian Coll.; MA in bibl. studies, Northwest Baptist Seminary; MDiv in Christian counseling summa cum laude, Faith Luth. Seminary, 2000; D in Christian edn. (hon.), Christian Missions New Wine Ministries Sch. Bible. Editor: SignPost, 1987—94, Smoke Signals, 1982—99. Adv. coun. Puget Sound Christian Coll., Mountlake Terrace, 1993—97; alumni com. Trinity Luth. Coll., Issaquah, Wash., 1987—89; leader 4-H Club, Troy, Idaho, 1956—60, Auburn, Wash., 2002—04; overseer Seattle Native Am. Christian Ch., 1989—. Recipient Christian Svc. award, Faith Evang. Luth. Sem., 2002; established scholarship, Puget Sound Christian Coll., 1994—2003. Mem.: Am. Asn. Christian Counselors (dir. NW Indian mission). Home and Office: Seattle Native Am Christian Ch PO Box 18005 Seattle WA 98118

YOUNG, ELIZABETH BELL, consultant; b. Franklinton, N.C., July 2, 1929; d. Joseph H. and Eulalia V. Bell; m. Charles A. Young, Nov. 27, 1964. BA, N.C. Cen. U., 1948, MA, 1950; PhD, Ohio State U., 1959. Cert. speech pathologist; cert. audiologist. Chairperson dept. English Barber Scotia Coll., Concord, N.C., 1949-52; dir. speech area, prof. Talladega (Ala.) Coll., 1954-56; dir. speech clinic, prof. Va. State U., Petersburg, 1956-57; prof. Fla. A&M U., Tallahassee, 1959; chmn. dept. English Fayetteville (N.C.) State U., 1959-63; speech pathologist, rsch. assoc. Howard U. Sch. Dentistry, Washington, 1963-64; prof., chairperson dept. English U. Md.-East Shore, Princess Anne, Md., 1965-66; prof., supr. Speech Clinic Cath. U. Am., Washington, 1966-79; congl. staff aide U.S. Ho. of Reps., Washington, 1981-82, 88-90; prof. speech U. D.C., Washington, 1983-84; cons. nat. and local orgns. Washington, 1985-88, 90—. Lectr. over 250 speeches, seminars and workshops; speechwriter, cons. Nat. Assn. Equal Opportunity in Higher Edn., Washington, 1990. Contbr. articles to profl. jours. Fundraiser, pub. rels. polit. candidates, 1963-90; bd. dirs. United Negro Coll. Fund, 1970-80, D.C. Gen. Hosp. Handicapped Intervention Program, 1970-91. Recipient Citations and Certs. of Achievement community and nat. orgns., 1959-90. Fellow Am. Speech-Lang.-Hearing Assn.; mem. Pub. Mems. Assn. (bd. mem. 1980-91, 97—), Ohio State U. Alumni Assn., N.C. Cen. U. Alumni Assn. Democrat. Baptist. Avocations: reading, collecting sculpture of foreign countries, travel, writing, public speaking.

YOUNG, EMILY ELIZABETH, religious studies educator; b. Portland, Oreg., Aug. 2, 1942; d. Earl Ishmeal and Emily Elizabeth (Rogers) Dixson; m. Frank Burl LaQua, June 14, 1965 (dec. Jan. 1983); children: Franklin Imile(dec.), Emily Elizabeth(dec.), Geraldine Louise; m. John Charles Young, June 2, 1984. Grad., Moscow Beauty Coll., 1965; AA in Biblical Studies, Trinity Luth. Coll., 1980; BA in Christian Edn., Puget Sound Christian Coll., 1986; MA in Bibl. Studies, Northwest Bapt. Sem., 1993; MDiv, Faith Luth. Sem., 2000; D of Ministry, Northwest Bapt. Coll., 2000, PhD (hon.) in Christian Mission and Christian Edn., 2003. Hairdresser various nursing homes, Seattle, 1981—87; real estate mgr. Young's Property, 1982—2002; missionary, tchr. Puget Sound Christian Indian Mission, Tacoma, 1982—95; missionary, pastor Seattle Native Am. Christian Ch., 1989—.

YOUNG, ESTELLE IRENE, dermatologist, educator; b. N.Y.C., Nov. 2, 1945; d. Sidney D. and Blanche (Krosney) Young. BA magna cum laude, Mt. Holyoke Coll., 1967; MD, Downstate Med. Ctr., 1971. Intern Lenox Hill Hosp., N.Y.C., 1971-72, resident in medicine, 1972-73; resident in dermatology Columbia Presbyn. Hosp., N.Y.C., 1973—74, NYU Hosp., 1974—75, Boston U. Hosp., 1975-76; asst. dermatologist Harvard U. Health Svcs., Cambridge, Mass., 1975-76; assoc. staff mem. dermatology Boston U. Med. Ctr., 1976-77; practice medicine specializing in dermatology Petersburg, Va., 1976-97; mem. staff Poplar Springs Hosp., 1976—2002, Southside Regional Med. Ctr. (formerly Petersburg Gen. Hosp.), 1976—2002, Ctrl. State Hosp., 1976—. Clin. instr. dept. dermatology Med. Coll. Va., 1976-2002, asst. clinic prof., 1988-94, assoc. clin. prof., 1994-2002; sec. med. staff Petersburg Gen. Hosp., 1982. Contbr. articles to [illegible] Am. Acad. Dermatology; mem. Va. Med. Soc., Va. Dermatology Soc., Tidewater Dermatology Soc. (pres. 1982-83), Physicians for Social Responsibility Soc., Tidewater Physicians for Social Responsibility (pres. 1990), Internat. Physicians for Prevention of Nuclear War, Southside Va. Med. Soc., Sigma Xi. Home and Office: PO Box 20182 New York NY 10021-0063 Fax: (212) 249-5948. E-mail: eiy112@aol.com.

YOUNG, FREDDIE GILLIAM, principal, educator; b. Miami, Fla., Nov. 1, 1939; d. Thomas and Myrtle (Gibson) Gilliam. BS, Fla. A&M U., 1961; MS, Hunter Coll., 1970; postgrad., U. Ghana, 1970; EdD, Nova U., 1990. Cert. in supervision and adminstrn., African studies, elem. and jr. coll.; cert. asst. prin. Tchr. Collier County Pub. Schs., Naples, Fla., N.Y.C. Pub. Schs., Bronx, N.Y., Dade County Pub. Schs., Miami, prin.; adj. lead prof. Nova U. Presenter Am. Assn. Ethnic Studies Conf., Fla. Atlantic U., 1991, Assn. Carribean Studies Cairo, 1993, Georgetown, Guyana, 1994, Nat. Assn. African Am. Studies, Houston, 2000, Nat. Commn. on Educating the Black Child, others. Del. 19th congl. dist. Dem. conv., 1988; mem. Am. Jewish Com., African Am. Summitt, London, South Africa, Zimbabwe, West Africa, First Emancipation Independence Day, Ghanna, West Africa, 1998. Named Most Outstanding Black Woman, S. Fla., Women's C. of C., Educator of Yr. Zeta Phi Beta; recipient 50 outstanding svc. awards Prin. Ctr. Harvard U. Sch. Edn., 1989, Metro Dade County commendation for dedicated svc., Ida B. Wells Awd., Nat. Alliance of Black Sch. Educators; finalist for Adminstr. of Yr., 1991, DCSHA. Mem. AAUW, ASCD, Am. Jewish Com., Nat. Alliance Black Educators, S. Fla. Exec. Educators, Leadership Miami, Miami Alliance Black Educators, Nat. Black Women's Polit. Caucus, Dade County Adminstrs. Assn. (chair), Fla. Reading Assn., Dade Reading Coun., Fla. A&M U. Alumni Assn. (pres. Miami-Dade chpt.), Nova U. Alumni Assn. (sec. Miami chpt.), Phi Delta Kappa. Home: 12390 SW 144th Ter Miami FL 33186-7419

YOUNG, GENEVIEVE LEMAN, publishing executive, editor; b. Geneva, Sept. 25, 1930; came to U.S., 1945, naturalized, 1968; d. Clarence Kuangson and Juliana Helen (Yen) Y.; m. Cedric Sun, 1955 (div. 1972); m. Gordon Parks, Aug. 26, 1973 (div. 1979). BA (Wellesley Coll. scholar), Wellesley Coll., 1952. Asst. editor Harper & Row (pubs.), N.Y.C., 1960-62, editor, 1962-64, asst. mng. editor, 1964-66, mng. editor, 1966-70; exec. editor J.B. Lippincott Co., N.Y.C., 1970-77, v.p., 1972-77; sr. editor Little, Brown & Co., N.Y.C., 1977-85; editor-in-chief Lit. Guild Am., N.Y.C., 1985-88; v.p., editorial dir. Bantam Books, N.Y.C., 1988-92. Alumna trustee Phillips Acad., Andover, Mass., 1975-78, class agt., 1979-85; mem. Wellesley Bus. Leadership Coun., 1989-98; mem. Youth Counseling League, 1986-98, pres., 1989-96, mem. com. of 100, 1991-93; mem. Literacy Ptnrs., Inc., N.Y.C., 1992-2001, sec., 1996-2001; mem. Andover Devel. Bd., 1993-98; trustee Jewish Bd. Family and Children's Svcs., 1996-98. Recipient Alumna Achievement award Wellesley Coll., 1982, Matrix award, 1988. Mem. Assn. Am. Pubs. (exec. coun. gen. pub. div. 1975-78, 85-87, freedom to read com. 1972-75), Women's Media Group (pres. 1981-82, 2d v.p. 1994-95), Century Assn. Home: 30 Park Ave New York NY 10016-3801

YOUNG, GLADYS, business owner; m. H. Timothy Kuhn; 3 children. Pres. Young Pontiac Cadillac Dealership, Escondido, Calif. Dir. Downtown Escondido Redevel., Palomar Coll. Pres.'s Assn.; contbr. St. Clare's Home, The North County Interfaith Crisis Ctr., Palomar Pomerado Hosp. Health Found., EYE Counseling and Crisis Ctr., Calif. Ctr. Arts. Recipient Quality Dealer award Time Mag., 1996. Mem. New Car Dealers Assn. (San Diego county chpt. award), Escondido Auto Park Assn. (pres.), Escondido C. of C. (dir.). Office: Young Pontiac Cadillac Dealership 1515 Auto Park Way N Escondido CA 92029-2098

YOUNG, GRACE MAY-EN, pediatrician, educator; b. Pitts. AB, Harvard U., 1977; MD, Columbia U., 1981. Diplomate Am. Bd. Pediat. Emergency Medicine, Am. Bd. Pediat. From intern to resident in pediat. Children's Nat. Med. Ctr., Washington, 1981-84, fellow in pediat. emergency medicine, 1986-87; asst. prof. pediat. George Washington U. Sch. Medicine, Washington, 1986-90, NYU Sch. Medicine, N.Y.C., 1990-93; assoc. prof. pediat. U. Md. Sch. Medicine, Balt., 1993—.

YOUNG, GWYNNE A. lawyer; b. Durham, N.C., 1950; AB, Duke U., 1971; JD, U. Fla., 1974. Bar: Fla. 1974. Asst. state atty. 13th Judicial Cir., Fla.; mem. Carlton, Fields, Ward, Emmanuel, Smith & Cutler P.A., Tampa,

Fla. Instr. U. Fla. Coll. Law, 1974. Exec. editor U. Fla. Law Review, 1973-74. Pres. Jr. League Tampa, Inc., 1985-86; bd. dirs. Assn. Jr. Leagues, Inc., 1987-89, Duke U. Nat. Alumni Assn., 1993—, pres., 1999-2000; trustee Duke U., 1999—. Fellow Am. Bar Found.; mem. ABA., Office: Carlton Fields Ward Emmanuel Smith & Cutler PA 1 Harbour Pl 777 S Harbour Island Blvd Tampa FL 33602-5729

YOUNG, JACQUELINE EURN HAI, former state legislator, consultant; b. Honolulu, May 20, 1934; d. Paul Bai and Martha (Cho) Y.; m. Harry Valentine Daniels, Dec. 25, 1954 (div. 1978); children: Paula, Harry, Nani, Laura; m. Daniel Anderson, Sept. 25, 1978 (div. 1984); m. Everett Kleinjans, Sept. 4, 1988 (div. 1998). BS in Speech Pathology, Audiology, U. Hawaii, 1969; MS in Edn., Spl. Edn., Old Dominion U., 1972; advanced cert., Loyola Coll., 1977; PhD in Communication, Women's Studies, Union Inst., 1989. Dir. dept. speech and hearing Md. Sch. for the Blind, Balt., 1975-77; dir. deaf-blind project Easter Seal Soc. Oahu, Hawaii, 1977-78; project dir. equal ednl. opportunity programs Hawaii State Dept. Edn., Honolulu, 1978-85, state ednl. specialist, 1978-90; state rep. dist. 20 Hawaii State Legislature, Honolulu, 1990-92, state rep. dist. 51, 1992-94; vice-speaker Hawaii Ho. of Reps., Honolulu. Apptd. to U.S. Dept. Def. Adv. Commn. on Women in the Svc.; cons. spl. edn. U.S. Dept. Edn., dept. edn. Guam, Am. Samoa, Ponape, Palau, Marshall Islands, 1977-85; cons. to orgns. on issues relating to workplace diversity; adj. prof. commn., anthropology, mgmt. Hawaii Pacific U.; dir. mktg. Am. Cancer Soc. Hawaii Pacific, 1985—, dir. mktg., 1999—. TV writer, host, producer, 1992—. 1st v.p. Nat. Women's Polit. Caucus, 1988-90; chair Hawaii Women's Polit. Caucus, 1987-89; bd. dirs. YWCA Oahu, Kalihi Palama Immigrant Svc. Ctr., Hawaii Dem. Movement, Family Peace Ctr.; appointee Honolulu County Com. on the Status of Women, 1986-87; founding bd. mem. Windward Spouse Abuse Shelter, 1993—; campaign dir. Protect Our Constn., 1998; trustee St. Louis Sch., 1997-99; mem. nat. adv. coun. ACLU. Recipient Outstanding Woman Leader award YWCA of Oahu, 1994, Pres.'s award Union Inst., 1993, Fellow of the Pacific award Hawaii-Pacific U., 1993, Headliner award Honolulu chpt. Women in Commn., 1993, Korean Am. Alliance Washington Spl. Recognition award, 1998, Hawaii Women Lawyers Disting. Svc. award, 1999, Disting. Equity Adv. award Hawaii chpt. Nat. Coalition for Sex Equity in Edn., 1998, NEA Mary Hatwood Futrell for advancing women's rights award, 1999, Friend of Social Work award Hawaii chpt. NASW, 1998, Allan Saunders award Hawaii chpt. ACLU, 1999; named one of Extraordinary Women Hawaii, Found. Hawaii Women's History, 2001. Home: 212 Luika Pl Kailua HI 96734-3237

YOUNG, JANET CHERYL, electrical engineer; b. Roanoke, Va., Oct. 3, 1960; d. Don Gordon and Barbara Hill (Mumpower) Y. BS in Physics, U. Tenn., Chattanooga, 1982; MSEE, Va. Tech. Inst., 1991. Engr. Sci. Applications Internat. Corp., Springfield, Va., 1982—91, United Telecom Coun., Washington, 1991—93, LCC, Internat., McLean, Va., 1993—2002, Nextel Comm., Reston, Va., 2002—. Active in World Peace Mission Foundry United Meth. Ch., Washington, 1984, Community Band, Vienna, Va., 1985; vol. Shakespeare Theatre Co., 1996-97. Mem. IEEE (mem. Electromagnetic Compatibility Soc. 1987-91, Comm. Soc. 1992—). Methodist. Avocations: gardening, travel, genealogical research. Home: 4044 Chetham Way Woodbridge VA 22192 Office: Nextel Comm 2003 Edmund Halley Dr Reston VA 20191

YOUNG, JAYNE, recording industry executive; b. Houston, Dec. 6, 1961; d. James Nesbitt and Mary Frances Young. Student, Stephen F. Austin U., 1981-82, Belmont U., 1983-86. Mgr. prodn. MCA Records, Nashville, 1983-85, dir. mktg., 1985-90; pub. rels. dir. Hard Rock Cafe, Internat., N.Y.C., 1992-93; dir. product devel. RCA Records, Nashville, 1990-91; v.p. of artist repitorie W.& R. Group (divsn. Sony), N.Y.C., 1993—. Author: (series) What's a Girl to Do?; creator: (record series) Live at the Grand Old Opry, 1986—. Mem. transfer com. Jr. League Nashville, 1985-92, Jr. League N.Y., 1993—; bd. dirs. Arthritis Found., Nashville; mem. young com. N.Y. Hist. Soc., N.Y.C., 1995-97. Mem. NARAS. Republican. Baptist. Avocations: traveling, collecting antiques, auctions, yoga, tennis. Home: 1061 Madison Ave Apt 2B New York NY 10028-0239 Office: W&R Group Inc 1600 Broadway Ste 512 New York NY 10019-7413

YOUNG, JEANETTE COCHRAN, corporate planner, reporter, analyst; b. Franklin, Ind., Mar. 12, 1953; d. Charles Morris and Marjorie Elizabeth (Rohrbaugh) Cochran; m. William Alan Young, Aug. 18, 1979 (div. 1994); children: Kathryn Elizabeth, Stephen Robert. BA, De Pauw U., 1975; MBA, U. Pa., 1977. Fin. analyst Eli Lilly & Co., Indpls., 1977-79; sr. fin. analyst Samsonite, Denver, 1980, Honeywell Test Instruments divsn., Denver, 1980-82; prin. analyst Fluor Corp., Sugar Land, Tex., 1982-86; sr. fin. analyst Caterpillar, Joliet, Ill., 1989-90, Texaco Chem. Co., Houston, 1990-93; coord. planning, budget Texaco, Inc., Houston, 1993-98; asst. to pres. Texaco USA, Houston, 1996; sr. coord. budget and analysis Equilon Enterprises, LLC, Houston, 1998—2002, Shell Oil Products US, Houston, 2002—. Mem. ARC, Arapahoe County, Colo., 1982; vol. United Way of Tex. Gulf Coast, 1996—. Mem. NAFE. Methodist. Avocations: travel, reading. Office: Shell Oil Products US PO Box 2463 910 Louisiana St Houston TX 77002-5227

YOUNG, JEANNETTE ROSE, music educator; b. Columbus, Nebr., Feb. 19, 1949; d. Vladimir Joseph Hamata and Rose Elizabeth Stava; m. David Russell Young; 1 child, Angela Kroeger. MusM, U. Nebr., 1992, B in Music Edn., 1971; PhD in Adminstrn., U. Neb., 2002. Cert. Kodály method. Instr. vocal music Schuyler Ctrl. HS, Schuyler, Nebr., 1976—79; tchr. vocal music K - 9 Papillion-LaVista Sch. Dist., Papillion, Nebr., 1979—98; asst. prof. music Nebr. Wesleyan U., Lincoln, Nebr., 1998—. Dir. Kodály cert. program Nebr. Wesleyan U., Lincoln, 1998—. Recipient Kodaly cert., 1991. Mem.: Nebr. Music Educators Assn., Music Educators Nat. Conf., Nebraska Choral Dirs. Assn., Am. Choral Dirs. Assn., Coll. Music Soc., Plains States Kodály Orgn. (pres. 1989—91), Orgn. Am. Kodály Educators, Internat. Kodaly Soc., Delta Kappa Gamma (Bernita Minkwitz Internat. scholarship 1997, Rho state scholarship, Alpha Alpha chpt. scholarship). Presbyterian. Avocations: birdwatching, architecture, gardening. Home: 8138 Wemsha St Lincoln NE 68507-3377 Office: Nebr Wesleyan U 5000 St Paul Ave Lincoln NE 68504-2794 Home Fax: (402) 465-2179; Office Fax: (402) 465-2179. Personal E-mail: jry@NebrWesleyan.edu. Business E-mail: jry@NebrWesleyan.edu.

YOUNG, JENNIFER B. federal agency administrator; b. Bellevue, Ohio; m. J. T. Young. Exec. asst. Ohio Human Svcs. Dept.; dir. health legis. Nat. Govs. Assn.; exec. dir. pub. programs Am. Assn. Health Plans; sr. health policy advisor House Com. on Ways and Means, Senate Fin. Com.; dep. aasst. sec. for health legis. U.S. Dept. Health and Human Svcs., Washington, asst. sec. for legis., 2003—. Office: US Dept HHS Asst Sec for Legis 200 Independence Ave SW Washington DC 20201

YOUNG, JOAN CRAWFORD, advertising executive; b. Hobbs, N.Mex., July 30, 1931; d. William Bill and Ora Maydelle (Boone) Crawford; m. Herchelle B. Young, Nov. 23, 1971 (div.). BA, Hardin Simmons U., 1952; postgrad., Tex. Tech. U., 1953-54. Reporter Lubbock (Tex.) Avalanche-Jour., 1952-54; promotion dir. Sta. KCBD-TV, Lubbock, 1954-62; account exec. Ward Hicks Advt., Albuquerque, 1962-70; v.p. Mellekas & Assocs. Advt., Albuquerque, 1970-78; pres. J. Young Advt., Albuquerque, 1978—; dir. advt. So. Therapy, Austin, Tex., 1999—. Author: (with Louise Allen and Audre Lipscomb) Radio and TV Continuity Writing, 1962. Bd. dirs. N.Mex. Symphony Orch., 1970-73, United Way of Greater Albuquerque, 1985-89; bd. trustees N.Mex. Children's Found., 1994-96. Recipient Silver medal N.Mex. Advt. Fedn., 1977. Mem. N.Mex. Advt. Fedn. (bd. dirs. 1975-76), Am. Advt. Fedn., Greater Albuquerque C. of C. (bd. dirs. 1984), Albuquerque Petroleum Club (membership chmn. 1992-93, bd. dirs. 1993—, sec. 1994-95, v.p. 1995-97, pres. 1997-99). Republican. Office: 6009 Belfast Dr Austin TX 78723-1832

YOUNG, JUDITH ANNE, animal conservationist; b. L.A., Feb. 11, 1953; d. John Mahlstedt Young and Cynthia Sheilds Tunnicciff. Grad. h.s., L.A. CEO Otter Conservation Ctr., Statesboro, Ga., 1983—. Copyright U.S. Govt., 1995. Avocations: animal keeping, water gardens, agriculture. Personal E-mail: judy@g-net.net.

YOUNG, LAURA, dance educator, choreographer; b. Boston, Aug. 5, 1947; d. James Vincent and Adelaide Janet Young; m. Anthony Charles Catanzaro, Sept. 26, 1970 (div. Nov. 1981); m. Christopher Edward Mehl, Aug. 23, 1987. Grad. H.S., Cohasset, Mass. Dancer Met. Opera Ballet, N.Y.C., 1971-73, Boston Ballet Co., 1963-65, prin. dancer, 1965-71, 73-89, ballet mistress, 1989-91. Guest tchr. Dance Tchrs. Club Boston, 1978—82, Dance Masters Assn., 1979, 90, 92, 93, Walnut Hill Sch., Natick, Mass., 1984—87, Natick, 1990—91, Granite State Ballet, 1993, Portland Ballet, Maine, Nat. Dance Theatre Bermuda, 1993, Worcester Performing Arts Sch., Mass., 1994, Alwin Sch. Dance Summer Intensive, Albuquerque, 1994—95, Ashland Youth Ballet, Ky., 1995, N.E. Regional Festival, 1996, Okla. Summer Arts Inst., 2000, Pitts. Ballet Theater Summer Program, 2000; asst. dir. Boston Ballet II, 1984—86, tchr., dir., 1986—96, dir. Summer Dance Program, 1986—94; dir. DanceLab, 2001—; 1st hon. mem. Dance Masters Assn., Chpt. 5, 1992; mem. faculty Boston Conservatory, 1990—94; prin. Boston Ballet Sch., 1993—. Choreographer (ballets) Occasional Waltzes, 1984, Albinoni Suite, 1986, Champ Dances, 1987, A Place of Sound and Mind, 1988, Deadlock, 1989, Rumpelstiltskin, 1989. Recipient Leadership award Greater Boston C. of C., 1987; named Disting. Bostonian, Boston's 350th Jubilee Com., 1980. Mem. Am. Guild Mus. Artists, Dance Masters Am. (hon.). Office: Boston Ballet Co 19 Clarendon St Boston MA 02116-6100 Office Phone: 617-456-6261. E-mail: lyoung@bostonballet.com.

YOUNG, LAURA ELIZABETH, artist; b. Glen Ridge, N.J., Apr. 1, 1941; d. Thomas Edward and Charlotte Elizabeth (Post) Y.; m. James Andrew Murphy, Jun. 15, 1963 (div. 1985); children: Kevin Thomas, Timothy James.; m. Thomas Raymond Aprile, May 20, 1995. BA, Skidmore Coll., 1963; MA, Montclair State Coll., 1978; MFA, Rutgers U., 1983. Cert. Fine Arts and English, K-12 tchr., N.J. Adj. faculty Fine Arts Dept. Kean Coll., Union, N.J., 1983-84, Montclair (N.J.) State Coll., 1983-92, Long Island U., Bklyn., 1994; cons., workshop leader The Lincoln Ctr. Inst., N.Y.C., 1983—96. Lectr. Mus. Modern Art, N.Y.C., 1990-96; visual arts cons., workshop leader The Nashville Inst. for the Arts, 1992-98—, Lincoln Ctr. Inst.; adj. faculty Fine Arts Dept. U. Iowa, 1996—. One person shows include: Interior Space Design, N.Y.C., 1991, Manhattenville Coll., N.Y., 1993, Cedar Rapids (Iowa) Mus. Art, 1998, Monmouth (Ill.) Coll., 2001; group shows Colgate U., Hamilton, N.Y., 1995, Vincennes (Ind.) U., 2003. Grantee fellow in painting N.J. State Coun. on the Arts, Trenton, 1985, Iowa Arts Coun., 1997, 2001, Va. Ctr. Creative Arts, Sweet Briar, Va., 1985, 86, 2001, 2002-03, Intermedia Performance grantee Sch. Fine and Performing Arts, Montclair, 1992, Pollock Krasner Found. grantee, 1994. Democrat. Avocations: photography, sailing, nature walks. Home: 50 Lakeview Pl NE Iowa City IA 52240-9162

YOUNG, LAUREN SUE JONES, education educator; b. San Diego, July 21, 1947; d. Warren Calvin and Lola Esther Jones; 1 child, Forest McRay Young. AB, Occidental Coll., 1969; MS, San Diego State U., 1971; EdM, Harvard U., 1979, EdD, 1984. Adminstrv. asst. Child Devel. Research Unit, Nairobi, Kenya, 1969-70; asst. prof. San Diego State U., 1974—78, assoc. dir. Tchr. Corps., 1971—78; co-chmn. and mem. Harvard Ednl. Review, Cambridge, Mass., 1979-81; research assoc. The Huron Inst., Cambridge, 1980-82, Atari Cambridge Research Lab., Cambridge, 1982-84; policy analyst N.Y. State Dept. Social Services, Albany, 1984-85, spl. asst. to commr., 1985-87; assoc. prof. Mich. State U., East Lansing, 1987-2001; sr. program officer, dir. The Spencer Found., Chgo., 1998—. Cons. Am. Insts. for Rsch., Cambridge, 1980, Tchr. Corps, Boston area, 1978-80, instr., Pago Pago, Am. Samoa, 1979; rsch. assoc. A Study of H.S.'s, Cambridge, 1980-82; disting. visitor John D. and Catherine T. MacArthur Found., 1995-96. Co-editor: Too Little, Too Late, 1988; mem. editorial bd. Evaluation Rev. Jour., L.A., 1984-88, Jour. Negro Edn. Team mem. Operation Crossroads Africa, Morogoro, Tanzania, 1968; mem. program adv. bd. Spencer Found., 1992. Recipient Danforth Found. fellow, St. Louis, 1978-84, tchr. scholar award, M.S.U., 1993. Mem. Am. Ednl. Research Assn. Office: The Spender Found 875 N Michigan Ave Ste 3930 Chicago IL 60611-1803

YOUNG, LINDA DIANE, speech pathology/audiology services professional; b. Mt. Vernon, Ill., Sept. 4, 1949; d. Ramona Reed and John W. Davis (Deceased); 1 child, Brian Young. BS in Elem. Edn., Murray State U., 1971, MS in Comm. Disorders, 1977. Cert. early childhood edn., elem. edn., H.S. edn., early intervention specialist, lic. speech/lang. pathologist. Second grade tchr. Pinellas County Pub. Schs., St. Petersburg, Fla., 1971—74; speech/lang. pathologist Orange County Pub. Schs., Orlando, Fla., 1978—80; parent educator Valencia C.C., Orlando, 1978—80; sales rep. Kleinhenn Fund Raising Co., Anderson, Ind., 1983—86; speech/lang. pathologist Ea. Ill. Area Spl. Edn., Mattoon, 1986—87, Trico Cmty. Unit Sch. Dist., Campbell Hill, Ill., 1988—89, Cmty. Unit Sch. Dist. #186, Murphysboro, Ill., 1989—, Sullivan Cmty. Unit Sch. Dist., Sullivan, Ill. Game creator, author The Bee Safe or Bee Sorry Game, 1985; author: The Bee Safe or Bee Sorry Game, revised, 1999, (book and activities for children) The Adventures of Buzzie and Stinger, 2000. Mem. Govs. Coun. for the State of Ill. for the Dept. Children and Family Svcs., Springfield, 2002—; fundraising com., Carbondale coord. Perry Jackson County child Advocacy Ctr. Recipient Benefactor award, The Amy Schulz Child Advocacy Ctr., Mt. Vernon, Cert. Appreciation, The Amy Schulz Child Advocacy Ctr., 1999, 2000, 2001. Mem.: So. Ill. Speech/Lang./Hearing Orgn., Philanthropic Ednl. Orgn. (asst. chairperson scholar awards 1999), Rotary (breakfast club). Home: 1500 West Tripoli St Carbondale IL 62901 Office: Murphysboro CUSD #186 - Carruthers Elem 80 Candy Ln Murphysboro IL 62966

YOUNG, LORETTA ANN, auditor; b. Reading, Pa., Dec. 2, 1962; d. Milton and Delois Jean (Ridley) Y. BS, Towson U., 1985. CPA, cert. fin. svcs. auditor, internal auditor. Auditor Irving Burton Assocs., Inc., Washington, 1984-88; tax technician Gen. Bus. Svcs., Germantown, Md., 1989; auditor Montgomery County Govt., Rockville, Md., 1989-90; dir. membership devel. Nat. Forum for Black Pub. Adminstrs., Washington, 1990-91; sr. acct.-analyst Cox & Assocs. CPAs, P.C., Hyattsville, Md., 1992; mgr. ops. LKA Computer Cons., Inc., Hyattsville, 1992-94; supervisory auditor Office Specialists, Inc., Washington, 1994-97; sr. auditor Amtrak, Washington, 1997-2000; mgr. Deloitte & Touche, 2000—. Mem. AICPA, Inst. Internal Auditors, Md. Assn. CPAs., Assn. Govt. Accts. Home: PO Box 479 Germantown MD 20875-0479 Office: 1750 Tysons Blvd Mc Lean VA 22102-4219 Office Phone: 202-378-5208. E-mail: lyoung@deloitte.com.

YOUNG, LUCY CLEAVER, physician; b. Aug. 8, 1943; d. Oliver B. and Ada (Smith) Cleaver; m. Lynn H. Young, Feb. 4, 1968 (div. 1977); m. Lynn H. Young, Apr. 2, 1986; 1 child, Clinton Oliver. BS in Chemistry, Wheaton (Ill.) Coll., 1965; MD, Ohio State U., 1969. Diplomate Am. Bd. Family Practice, Bd. Ins. Medicine. Rotating intern Riverside Meth. Hosp., Columbus, Ohio, 1969-70; resident Trumbull Meml. Hosp., Warren, Ohio, 1970-71; practice medicine specializing in family practice West Chicago, Ill., 1971-73, Paw Paw and Mendota, Ill., 1973-78; co-founder, med. dir. Wholistic Health Ctr. of Mendota, 1976-78; asst. med. dir. Gt. Lakes head office Met. Life Ins. Co., Aurora, Ill., 1979-80; med. dir. Commonwealth Life Ins. Co., Louisville, 1980-85; locum tenens family practice Kron Med. Corp. of Chapel Hill, NC, 1986-89; physician Red Bird Mission & Med. Ctr., Beverly, Ky., 1989-90; family practice floater Ochsner Clinic satellites, New Orleans, 1990—. Assoc. prof. U. Ill. Abraham Lincoln Sch. Medicine, 1976-79; faculty monitor MacNeal Meml. Hosp. Family Practice Ctr. (Ill.), 1979-80; faculty preceptor U. Louisville Family Practice Dept., 1981-85; clin. faculty preceptor La. State U. Sch. Medicine, 1992—; mem. staffs Ctrl. DuPage Hosp., Winfield, Ill., 1971-73, Mendota Cmty. Hosp., 1973-80, Ochsner Found. Hosp., New Orleans, 1991—. Vol. Red Bird Med. Ctr., 1985—; part-time worship coord. Hosanna Luth. Ch., Mandeville, La., 1996-97; musician, lay preacher, nursing home visitor, 1990—. Fellow Am. Acad. Family Practice; mem. Christian Med. and Dental Assns. (del. to Ho. 1995-2000). Lutheran. Home: PO Box 0730 Madisonville LA 70447-0730 Office: Ochsner Clinic 2810 E Causeway Approach Mandeville LA 70448

YOUNG, MARGARET LABASH, librarian, information consultant, editor; b. Bridgeport, Conn., Aug. 17, 1926; d. George and Mary (Feltovic) Labash; m. Harold Chester Young, June 7, 1958 (div. July 1991); children: Jeffery Avery, Amy Margaret. BA, Cornell U., 1948; AMLS, U. Mich., 1959. Mktg. grader Harvard Bus. Sch., Boston, 1949-52; ops. rsch. sales asst. Arthur D. Little, Inc., Boston, 1953-57; reference libr. U. Mich., Dearborn, 1959-62; editor Gale Rsch., Detroit, 1964-74, Mpls., 1977-88; libr. Salzburg (Austria) Seminar, 1981-83; editor, info. cons. self employed, Hopkins, Minn., 1989—. Tax libr. cons. KPMG Peat Marwick, LLP, Mpls., 1991—; indexer Small Bus. Innovation Rsch., Minn. Project Innovation, Mpls., 1990-97. Co-editor: Directory of Special Libraries and Information Centers, edits. 3-6, 1974-81, Life Sciences Organizations and Agencies Directory, 1988; editor: Scientific and Technical Organizations and Agencies Directory, 1985, 2d edit., 1987. Host family Am. Field Svcs., 1979-80, 80-81; mem. steering com. Twin Cities Internat. Citizens Award, 1996-99. Mem. Spl. Librs. Assn. (internat. rels. chair Minn. chpt. 1994—2003, Quality in Action award, Minn. Chpt. Spl. Librs. Assn., 2003, Fannie Simon award Pub. divsn. 1989), Am. Soc. Indexers, Beta Phi Mu. Democrat. Episcopalian. Avocations: travel, gardening, classical music, dance, aerobics. Home: 313 Farmdale Rd W Hopkins MN 55343-7111

YOUNG, MARLENE ANNETTE, lawyer; b. Portland, Oreg., Mar. 3, 1946; d. Hardy Shelby and Eunice Jean (Gregory) Y.; m. Abdullah Samir Rifai, June 3, 1973 (div. May 1981); m. John Hollister Stein, Jan. 1, 1986. BS, Portland State U., 1967; PhD, Georgetown U., 1973; JD, Willamette U., 1975. Bar: Oreg. 1975. Dir. research Multnomah County Sheriff's Office, Portland, 1975-77; sole practice Wilsonville, Oreg., 1975-81; exec. dir. Applied Systems Research & Data, Wilsonville, 1976-81, Nat. Orgn. Victim Assistance, Washington, 1981—. Instr. Essex Community Coll., 1971-73, U. Utah, 1976-78, Portland State U., 1979; cons. U. Research Corp., Washington, 1979-83, ABT Assocs., Boston, 1984—. Author: Victim Service System, 1983; (manuals) Patrol Officers and Crime Victims, 1984, Prosecutors: Attorneys for the People, Advocates for the Victims, 1984; editor: Justice and Older Americans, 1977; contbr. articles to profl. jours. Mem. Ways and Means Com., Wilsonville City, 1977-79, planning commn., 1979-81; Bd. visitors Willamette Coll. Law, Salem, Oreg., 1981-83; bd. dirs. Chemeketa Community Coll., Salem, 1979. Recipient Presdl. award Nat. Orgn. Victim Assistance, Washington, 1981, 92, Pub.Policy award World Fedn. Mental Health, Washington, 1983, Found. for Improvementof Justice award, 1988. Mem. ABA (criminal justice sect., adv. bd. 1981-90), Am. Profl. Soc. Abuse of Children (bd. dirs. 1986—), Soc. Traumatic Stress Studies (bd. dirs. 1985—, treas.), World Soc. Victimology (adv. bd. 1979—, exec. com. 1986—, v.p., Hans Von Hentig award 1985). Democrat. Methodist. Avocations: piano, running, gardening, pets. Office: Nat Orgn Victim Assistance 1757 Park Rd NW Washington DC 20010-2101

YOUNG, MARY ANN, lawyer; b. Alton, Ill., May 1, 1952; d. William Jerome and Barbara Ann (Blocher) Y. Student, St. Mary of the Plains Coll., 1970-71; BA in Econs., Washburn (Kans.) U., 1974; JD, U. Mo., 1976. Bar: Mo. 1977. Pvt. practice, Holden, Mo., 1977-84, Warrensburg, Mo., 1984—. Atty. City of Holden, 1978-80; asst. prosecutor Johnson County, Mo., 1978-80, 83-88; bd. dirs. Indsl. Svc. Contactors Sheltered Workshop, Warrensburg. Mem. Rep. Women, Johnson County, 1988-89, CLIMB, Johnson County, 1989—, Task Force for Drug Free Mo., Johnson County, 1989—; 2d. v.p. Johnson County Rep. Women, 1989—. Mem. Mo. Bar Assn., Johnson County Bar Assn., Johnson County C. of C., Mo. Farm Bur. Roman Catholic. Avocations: antique collecting, gardening. Office: 307 N Holden St Warrensburg MO 64093-1705

YOUNG, MARY ELIZABETH, history educator; b. Utica, N.Y., Dec. 16, 1929; d. Clarence Whitford and Mary Tippit Y. BA, Oberlin Coll., 1950; PhD, Cornell U., 1955. Instr. dept. history Ohio State U., Columbus, 1955-58, asst. prof., 1958-63, assoc. prof., 1963-69, prof., 1969-73; prof. history U. Rochester, NY, 1973—2000, prof. emeritus, 2000—. Cons. in field. Author: Redskins, Ruffleshirts, and Rednecks: Indian Allotments in Alabama and Mississippi, 1830-1860, 1961; co-editor, contbr.: The Frontier in American Development: Essays in Honor of Paul Wallace Gates, 1969. Recipient Pelzer award Miss. Valley Hist. Assn., 1955, award Am. Studies Assn., 1982, Ray A. Billington award, 1982; Shalkenbach Found. grantee, 1951-55, Social Sci. Rsch. Coun. grantee, 1968-69; Ezra Cornell fellow Cornell U., 1951-55. Mem. Am. Hist. Assn., Orgn. Am. Historians, Soc. for Historians of the Early Am. Republic, Am. Antiquarian Soc. Home: 2230 Clover St Rochester NY 14618-4124 Office: U Rochester Dept History Rochester NY 14627 Office Phone: 585-275-2054. E-mail: yngm@mail.rochester.edu.

YOUNG, MARY KATHRYN, vocalist, educator; b. Osmond, Nebr., Jan. 11, 1972; d. Roger Dean and Donna Elaine Young. BA in Music Edn. K-12, Midland Luth. Coll., 1996. Cert. K-12 vocal music endorsement. Vocal music tchr. Marrs Acad. Omaha Pub. Schs., 1996—. Fellow: NEA, Omaha Edn. Assn., Nebr. Music Educators Assn., Music Educators Nat. Conf. Avocations: travel, golf, theater, music. Office: RM Marrs Academy 5617 S 19th St Omaha NE 68107

YOUNG, NANCY MAYER, retired secondary school educator, artist; b. Pensacola, Fla., May 24, 1933; d. Mark Bodenheimer Mayer and Elsie Nobles; m. Richard S. Young, June 7, 1955 (dec. Oct. 1996); children: Deeann, Sandra, Mark. BS, Fla. State U., 1955. Tchr. pub. schs., Athens, Ala., 1955—56; artist Sunnyvale, Calif., 1961—67; tchr. pub. schs., Arlington, Va., 1968—70; piano tchr. McLean, Va., 1968—75; salesperson art and pottery McLean and Annapolis, Md., 1975—81; salesperson Dee Real Estate, Bronxville, NY, 1981—83; travel agt. Travco, McLean, 1984—87. Mem. Beautification Bd., Cape Canaveral, Fla., 1989—96, Libr. Bd., Cape Canaveral, 1984—96. Avocation: watercolor painting. Home: 673 Heatherstone Dr Merritt Island FL 32953

YOUNG, NORA JANE, actuary, consultant; b. Fargo, N.D., June 18, 1966; d. David Allan and Elaine Emily Young. BA in Math., Whitman Coll., Walla Walla, Wash., 1987. Cert. profl. ins. woman. Actuarial intern United Pacific Ins. Co., Federal Way, Wash., 1986, actuarial student, 1987, Milliman & Robertson, Seattle, 1988-89; actuarial cons., v.p. Marsh USA Inc., Seattle, 1989—. Mem. Ins. Profls. South King County (sec. 1995-97, v.p. 1997-98, pres. 1998-99, Most Valuable Mem. 1997, Rookie of Yr. 1996), Ins. Profls. of South King County, Casualty Actuarial Soc. (assoc.), Am. Acad. Actuaries, Casualty Actuaries of the Northwest, Ins. Inst. of Am. (assoc. in risk mgmt.), Nat. Assn. Ins. Women (cert. profl.) Avocations: music, art, physical fitness. Office: Marsh USA Inc 1215 4th Ave Ste 2300 Seattle WA 98161-1086 E-mail: nora.young@marshmc.com.

YOUNG, OLIVIA KNOWLES, retired librarian; b. Benton, Ark., Sept. 3, 1922; d. Wesley Taylor and Med Belle (Crawford) Knowles; m. Calvin B. Young, Oct. 6, 1951; 1 child, Brigham Taylor. BA, Tenn. Tech. U., 1942, BS in Libr. Sci., 1946. Head periodicals and documents dept. Peabody Coll. Library, Nashville, 1946-49; area libr. U.S. Army, Austria, 1949-51; libr. Cairo Pub. Libr., Ga., 1955-57, Caney Fork Regional Libr., Sparta, Tenn., 1957-58; chief libr. Ft. Stewart (Ga.) U.S. Army, 1959-63; dir. Watauga Regional Libr., Johnson City, Tenn., 1963-70; dir. devel. and extension Tenn. State Libr. and Archives, Nashville, 1971-82, state libr. and archivist, 1982-85; ret., 1985. Mem. Tenn. Library Assn. (treas. 1970, Honor award 1985), Southeastern Library Assn., ALA, Boone Tree Library Assn. (pres. 1968), Altrusa Club (sec. 1967). Methodist. Home: 203 E Everett St Sparta TN 38583

YOUNG, PATRICIA JANEAN, speech pathologist; b. San Diego, Nov. 30, 1953; d. Bernarr E. and Janean Romig Young. AA, Palomar C.C., San Marcos, Calif., 1976; BA, Calif. State U., Chico, 1978; MA, Calif. State U., Long Beach, 1981. Cert. clin. competence Am. Speech-Lang.-Hearing Assn., lic. speech pathologist Calif., cert. tchr. Calif. Mgmt. trainee Robinson's Dept. Store, L.A., 1976—78; speech and hearing screening coord. Riverview Hearing, Speech, Lang. Ctrs., Long Beach, 1978—81, speech pathologist, 1981—84; speech pathologist, dir. Speech Pathology Svcs., Carlsbad and Temecula, Calif., 1984—; speech pathologist, augmentative comm. coord. Lake Elsinore (Calif.) Unified Sch. Dist., 1998—. Prodr. TV shows on comm. disorders Long Beach Cable TV, 1983; coord. pub. svc. announcement and interviewee for Disabilities Awareness Week ABC TV, San Diego, 1986, San Diego, 88. Contbr. poetry to lit. publs.; author: (game) Match This!, 1995. Named to Outstanding Young Women Am. Mem.: Calif. Speech-Lang-Hearing Assn. (region rep., Outstanding Achievement award 1987), Am. Speech-Lang-Hearing Assn., Zeta Tau Alpha. Avocations: writing, theater, decorating. Home: 31935 Calle Espinoza Temecula CA 92592 Office: Lake Elsinore Unified Sch Dist 545 Chaney St Lake Elsinore CA 92530 Office Phone: 909-253-7000 5390.

YOUNG, PAULA EVA, city official, journalist, writer; b. Caracas, Venezuela, May 11, 1958; came to U.S., 1962; d. James Francis and Fulvia (Guzzaloni) Y.; 1 child, Jonas Borra. Cert., Am. Acad. Dramatic Arts, N.Y.C., 1979; BA, CUNY, 1997. Lobbyist, facilitator East Bronx Coun. on Aging, N.Y.C., 1989-90; journalist N.Y. Newsday, N.Y.C., 1990-94; mng. editor, journalist City News, N.Y.C., 1994-95; dir. Office Comm. N.Y.C. Dept. Citywide Adminstrv. Svcs., 1995-98; asst. commr. pub. affairs N.Y.C. Dept. Sanitation, 1998—. Democrat. Avocations: wildlife and animal rescue, volunteer work with senior citizens, painting, gardening. Home: 2916 Barkley Ave Bronx NY 10465-2126 Office: 125 Worth St Rm 714 New York NY 10013-4006

YOUNG, REBECCA MARY CONRAD, retired state legislator; b. Clairton, Pa., Feb. 28, 1934; d. Walter Emerson and Harriet Averill (Colcord) Conrad; m. Merwin Crawford Young, Aug. 17, 1957; children: Eve, Louise, Estelle, Emily. BA, U. Mich., 1955; MA in Teaching, Harvard U., 1963; JD, U. Wis., 1983. Bar: Wis. 1983. Commr. State Hwy. Commn., Madison, Wis., 1974-76; dep. sec. Wis. Dept. of Adminstrn., Madison, 1976-77; assoc. Wadsack, Julian & Lawton, Madison, 1983-84; elected rep. Wis. State Assembly, Madison, 1985-99. Translator: Katanga Secession, [illegible] Madison, 1970-74; mem. Madison Sch. Bd., 1979-85. Recipient Wis. NOW Feminist of Yr. award, 1996, Eunice Zoghlin Edgar Lifetime Achievement award ACLU, 1997, Outstanding Legislator award Wis. Counties Assn., 1998, Voice for Choice award Planned Parenthood Wis., 1998, Luan Gilbert award for outstanding activities in domestic violence intervention and prevention Domestic Violence Intervention Svc., 1998. Mem. LWV. Democrat. Avocations: board games, hiking. Home: 639 Crandall St Madison WI 53711-1836

YOUNG, REBECCA PAYNE, secondary school educator; b. Mar. 26, 1944; d. William Nye and Marlie Josephine (Quinn) Payne; m. Robert Stephens Young, Dec. 18, 1969 (dec.); 1 child, Rachel Suzanne Young Jones. BA in German, Carson-Newman Coll., Jefferson City, Tenn., 1966; MA in German, Vanderbilt U., Nashville, 1968, MAT in German, 1976; MusM in Vocal Performance, Austin Peay State U., Clarksville, Tenn., 2000. Tchr. German S.W. Bapt. Coll., Bolivar, Mo., 1968—69; tchr. German, English, fine arts, choir Father Ryan H.S., Nashville, 1971—. Mem.: Am. Choral Dirs. Assn., Tenn. Music Educators Conf., Middle Tenn. Vocal Assn. (bd. dirs.), Music Educators Nat. Conf. Presbyterian. Avocations: dance, gardening, reading, singing. Home: 104 W Catalina Ct Hermitage TN 37076 Office: Father Ryan HS 700 Norwood Dr Nashville TN 37204

YOUNG, ROMA SKEEN, lawyer; b. Vancouver, Wash., Feb. 21, 1950; d. Carroll Hallam and Dorothy Elizabeth (Miller) Skeen; m. Robert Hugh Young, Jr., May 20,1978; children: Matthew Hallam, Brian Robert. BA, Sweetbriar Coll., 1971; JD, Georgetown U., 1978. Bar: Pa. 1978. Mem. staff U.S. Senate Energy Com., Washington, 1972-75; lobbyist Marathon Oil Co., Washington, 1975-78; assoc. Pepper, Hamilton & Scheetz, Phila., 1978-84, Wolf, Block, Schorr and Solis-Cohen, Phila., 1984-89, ptnr., 1989—. Office: Wolf Block Schorr and Solis-Cohen 15th And Chestnut St Fl 12 Philadelphia PA 19102-2625

YOUNG, RUBY WALLER, medical/surgical nurse, writer, poet; b. Nashville, Dec. 6, 1934; d. Homer Lee and Louise Comer Waller; m. Altamont M. Young, June 25, 1966; children: Sherry A., Larry A. BS, Tenn. State U., 1956; RN, Meharry Med. Coll., 1959; cert., Calif. State Coll., Long Beach, 1970, Pasadena City Coll., 1986. RN CAlif. Head nurse Morningside Hosp., Inglewood, Calif., 1960—64; staff nurse St. Francis Hosp., Lynwood, Calif., 1964—65, asst. head nurse, 1965—69; sch. nurse Compton Unified Sch. Dist., Calif., 1969—71; head svcs. adminstr. Women Job Corps, L.A., 1971—73; assoc. prof. pediat. nursing U. So. Calif., L.A., 1973—75; staff nurse Bapt. Hosp., Nashville, 1976—79; supr. pediat. nursing G.W. Hubbard Hosp., Nashville, 1979—83; dir. nursing svcs. C&M Home Health Agy., Nashville, 1983—86; owner, CEO Unique Consultations, Perris, Calif., 1987—94; dir. health care svcs. Interim Health Care, San Bernardino, Calif., 1994—99; dir. clin. svcs. Tender Loving Care Home Health Care, Riverside, Calif., 1999—2002. Author: (novels) The Impression, 1972, poetry. Mem.: Am. Bus. Womens Assn., Riverside Writers Guild, Nat. Authors Registry. Home: 22825 Cottonwood Ave Moreno Valley CA 92553-8660

YOUNG, SARAH MOSKOWITZ, educational and computer consultant, journalist; b. Galveston, Tex., June 10, 1947; d. Irving Leonard and Joyce (Schreiber) Moskowitz; children: Clement Clarke III, Leonard Arthur. B Tech. Edn., postgrad., Nat. U., San Diego, 1984; EdD, Calif. Coast U., San Diego, 1989, postgrad. Adult edn. and community coll. credentials, cert. vision and hearing tech., pers. cons., Calif.; cert. first aid and CPR instr. trainer. Tchr. Vista High Sch., San Diego, 1980-81; project dir. Robert Harrow Co., San Diego, 1981-82; instr. North County Coll., Eldorado Coll., San Diego County, 1982-84, Bangkok U., Kasesart U., 1985-86; assoc. dean, chmn. dept. edn. Phillips Coll., New Orleans, 1988-89; instr., radio performer Am. Lang. Tng., Jakarta, Indonesia, 1989-90; ednl. cons., journalist various mags. and newspapers, 1980—. Seminar speaker Sci. Rsch. Assocs., 1980; tng. officer Naval Sea Cadets, Monterey, Calif., 1988-89; mem. nat. curriculum com. Am. Assn. Med. Transcriptionists, 1978-88; med. instr. Kelsey-Jenney Coll., San Diego, 1990-91; founder Disabled Individuals Suggesting Computer Solutions. Mem., bd. dirs. Mira Mesa Town Coun., San Diego, 1980-84, sec., 1983-84; bd. dirs. Mira Mesa Community Coun., 1982-84; precinct chmn. San Diego Mayoral Election Com., 1982-84. Scholar Nat. U., 1984. Mem. NAFE, Leadership Edn. Awareness and Devel., San Diego Computer Soc., Mensa (chmn. mayor's adv. com. San Diego 1982-84, career day 1983), San Diego Press Club, Tetra Soc. San Diego (founder), Delta Omicron Epsilon. Avocations: artist, musician, world culture, languages, animals. Home and Office: 10257 Trails End Cir San Diego CA 92126-3517

YOUNG, SHARON WISDOM, retired music educator; b. Newton, Iowa, Feb. 21, 1934; d. Albert Leslie Wisdom and Eudora Bishop McKee; m. Melvin Neely Young, Apr. 9, 1983; m. Glenn Allen Butler, July 30, 1960 (div. Apr. 15, 1981); 1 child, Kirsten Butler Sanderford. BA, Hanover Coll., Hanover, Ind., 1956; MA, St. Francis Coll., Ft. Wayne, Ind., 1966. Tchr. Dep. Grade Sch., Ind., 1956—57, Lone Tree Cmty. Sch., Iowa, 1957—58; sec. Allen Sharp Atty. at Law, Williamsport, Ind., 1958—59, Ransburg Electro-Capping Corp., Indpls., 1959—60; tchr. Ft. Wayne Cmty Sch., Ft. Wayne, Ind., 1960—66, Des Plains Consol. Sch., Des Plains, Ill., 1966—69, Chesterfield County Sch., Chesterfield, Va., 1970—95; ret. Mentor program Chesterfield County Sch., Chesterfield, Va., 1995—99; cons. music Tuckahoe Elem. Sch., Henrico, Va., 2002—03; dir. music Bethel Bapt. Ch., Chesterfield, Va., 1980—83. Contbr. articles to profl. jour. Vol. mentor-breast cancer survivor Reach to Recovery, Richmond, Va., 1995—; del. Rep. Nat. Conv., Richmond, Va., 2001; worship com. chmn. Seventh St. Christian Ch., Richmond, Va., 1998—2000, choir; chmn. of dist. III Va. Music Educators Assn.; pres. Elem. Section of the Va. Music Educators Assn.; dir. Fine Arts Festival, Chesterfield and Henrico Counties, workshops on math and music. Mem.: Alpha Delta Pi, Alpha Delta Kappa (pres. Va. Fipelis Gamma Chptr.). Republican. Protestant. Avocations: grandchildren, beach, bridge, interior decorating. Home: 4411 W Grace St Richmond VA 23280

YOUNG, SONIA WINER, public relations executive, educator; b. Aug. 20, 1934; d. Meyer D. and Rose (Demby) Winer; m. Melvin A. Young, Feb. 24, 1957; 1 child, Melanie Anne. BA, Sophie Newcomb Coll., 1956; M in Ednl. Psychology, U. Tenn.-Chattanooga, 1966. Cert. speech and hearing specialist Am. Speech and Hearing Assn. Speech therapist Chattanooga-Hamilton County Speech and Hearing Ctr., 1961-66, ednl. psychology, 1966-78; staff psychologist Chattanooga Testing and Counseling Svcs., 1978-80; ins. rep. Mut. Benefit Life Ins. Co., Chattanooga, 1980-84; columnist Chattanooga Times, 1982-84; comty. affairs reporter Sta. WRCB-TV, Chattanooga, 1983-84; pub. rels. and promotions dir. Purple Ladies, Inc., Chattanooga, 1984—. Cons. psychology Ga. Dept. Human Resources, also Cheerhaven Sch., Dalton, 1970-78; adj. prof. psychology U. Tenn.-Chattanooga, 1971-80, adj. prof. dept. theatre and speech, 1988—; pres. Speak Out; bd. dirs. M. Young Comm., Vol. Ctr., 1995—, Arthritis Found., 1995-98; spl. projects dir. Chattanooga State Tech. C.C., 1995—; bd. dirs. M. Young Comm.; bd. dirs. Purple Lady, Inc. Author (columnist): (jour.) Lookout Mountain Mirror, Signal Mountain Mirror; contbg. editor: Chattanooga Life and Leisure Mag. Pres. Chattanooga Opera Guild, 1973-74, Chattanooga Opera Assn., 1979-80; bd. dirs., sec. Chattanooga-Hamilton County Bicentennial Libr., 1977-79, pres. Little Theatre of Chattanooga, 1984-90, bd. dirs., 1974—; v.p. Girls Club, Chattanooga, 1979-80; bd. dirs. March of Dimes, 1988, Chattanooga Symphony Guild, Mizpah Congregation, Chattanooga Area Literacy Coun., Chattanooga Cares, 1993—, Tourist Devel. Agy., 1990—; mem. alumni coun. U. Tenn.-Chattanooga; mem. selection com. Leadership Chattanooga, 1984-86; sec. Allied Arts Greater Chattanooga, 1978-80, residential campaign chmn., 1985; bd. dirs. Chattanooga Ctr. for the Dance, Ptnrs. for Acad. Excellence, 1987—, Chattanooga Mental Health Assn., [illegible] chmn. March of Dimes Mother's March, 1988, One of a Kind-the Arts Against AIDS-Chattanooga Cares, 1993, 94; co-chair Am. Heart Assn. Gala, 1994, chmn., 1995; chair Little Theatre Capital Campaign, 1995; chmn. Galactic Gala fundraiser Chattanooga State Coll., 1996, Chattanooga Theatre Ctr. Endowment Campaign, 1998-99, April in Paris fundraiser, Chattanooga St. Coll., 1997, Chattanooga H.S. Ctr. for the Creative Arts fundraising, 1999, chmn. Broadway Lights Broadway Nights, 1999; adv. coun. Hamilton County Magnet Schs., 1999; bd. dirs. Chattanooga Symphony Opera Assn., 1999, 2000, fundraiser Evening in Provence, 2000, 2001, fundraiser Evening in Tuscany, 2001, Evening in New Orleans, 2003; bd. dirs. Chattanooga Ballet, 2000—, Chattanooga Theatre Ctr., 2002—, AIM Ctr., 2002—, Chattanooga Cares, 2002, Chattanooga Zoo, 2002—. Recipient Disting. Citizens award City of Chattanooga, 1975, Steakley award Little Theatre Chattanooga, 1982, Pres. award, 1991, 92, Vol. of Yr., 1995, Woman of Distinction award Am. Lung Assn., 1995, Vol. of Yr. award, 1995, Penney's Golden Rule award Chattanooga Cares, 1994, Vol. of Yr., 1995, Best Actress award Chattanooga Theatre Ctr., 2000. Mem. Phi Beta Kappa (pers. Chattanooga chpt. 1978-79). Jewish. Home: 1025 River Hills Cir Chattanooga TN 37415-5611 Office: U Tenn Theatre & Speech Dept 615 Mccallie Ave Chattanooga TN 37403-2504 E-mail: purplesoni@aol.com.

YOUNG, SUSAN BABSON, retired library director; b. Boston, June 22, 1939; d. David Leaveau and Katherine Lockhart (Allen) Babson; m. Thomas Herbert Young III, June 17, 1961; children: Thomas Herbert IV, Nathaniel Allen. BA, Vassar Coll., 1961; MLS, SUNY, Albany, 1983. Cert. sch. media specialist, Mass. English and history tchr. St. Anthony's H.S., Long Beach, Calif., 1962-63; asst. dir. Geier Libr. Berkshire Sch., Sheffield, Mass., 1968-72, dir., 1972-95. Contbr. articles to profl. jours. Chair Friends of the Bushnell-Sage Meml. Libr. Capital Fund, Sheffield, Mass., 1995—, trustee, 1994—; mem. Arts Coun., Sheffield, 1983-90, 95-2000; mem. So. Berkshire Regional Sch. Com., 1998—. Mem. Am. Needlepoint Guild (1st pl. Nat. Exhibit award 1980, 85, 2d Internat. Exhibit award 1982), Embroiders Guild Am., Sheffield Garden Club (pres. 1996-98), Phi Beta Mu. Republican. Home: 321 Boardman St Sheffield MA 01257-9515 E-mail: syoung@campram.com.

YOUNG, TERESA GAIL HILGER, retired adult education educator; b. Modesto, Calif., Mar. 4, 1948; d. Richard George and Jessie Dennie (Dennis) Long; m. Charles Ray Young, June 22, 1974; 1 child, Gregory Paul. BS in Edn., Abilene (Tex.) Christian U., 1970; MEd in Curriculum, Tarleton State U., Stephenville, Tex., 1976; postgrad., Tex. Tech U., 1990-92. Cert. supr., mid-mgmt., supt., Tex. Tchr. sci. Tex. Youth Coun., Gatesville, 1970-73, Gatesville Ind. Sch. Dist., 1973-81; coord. Edn. and Tng. Ctr., Cen. Tex. Coll., Gatesville, 1983; tchr. Tex. Dept. of Criminal Justice-ID, 1984—2002; ret., 2003. Conf. presenter. Trustee Jonesboro (Tex.) Ind. Sch. Dist., 1988-96. Teacher of the Year for Region II of Tex. Dept. of Criminal Justice, 1997-98. Mem. Am. Fedn. Tchrs., Assn. Tex. Profl. Educators. E-mail: tyoung@htcomp.net.

YOUNG, TERI ANN BUTLER, pharmacist; b. Littlefield, Tex., Aug. 22, 1958; d. Doyle Wayne and Bettie May (Lair) Butler; m. James Oren Young, Aug. 1, 1981; children: Andrew Wayne, Aaron Lee. BS in Pharmacy, Southwestern Okla. State U., 1981; Pharm D, Okla. State U., 2004. Staff pharmacist St. Mary of Plains Hosp., Lubbock, Tex., 1981-84, West Tex. Hosp., Lubbock, 1984-85, asst. dir. pharmacy, 1985-86; pharmacist cons. for nursing homes Billy D. Davis & Assocs., Lubbock, 1986—; relief pharmacist Prescription Lab., Med. Pharmacy and Foster Infusion Care, Lubbock, 1987-89; staff pharmacist Univ. Med. Ctr., 1990-96, diabetic teaching pharmacist, 1995-99; pharmacist Joe Arrington Cancer Ctr., 2000—. Pharmacist Home Health Preferred Infusion, Lubbock, 1994-98, now Covenant Home Infusion, 1998-2000, Covenent Health Care Sys., Joe Arrington Cancer Ctr. Pharmacy; relief pharmacist West Tex. Hosp., 1986-91, Highland Hosp., 1990-94, Med. Infusion Technology, 1992-94. Mem. Lubbock Area Soc. of Hosp. Pharmacists (sec., treas. 1982-83), Lubbock Area Pharm. Assn., West Tex. Pharm. Assn., Am. Soc. Hosp. Pharmacists, Pilot Internat., Lubbock Genealogical Soc. Lodges: Eastern Star. Republican. Baptist. Avocations: needlework, reading, swimming, aerobics. Home: 7410 Toledo Ave Lubbock TX 79424-2214 Office: Joe Arrington Cancer Ctr Covenant Health Care Sys 4101 22nd Place Lubbock TX 79410-1130 E-mail: teayoung30@hotmail.com.

YOUNG, TERRI L. ophthalmologist; b. Sacramento, 1959; AB in Biochemistry and Sociology, Bowdoin Coll., Brunswick, Maine, 1981; MD in Medicine, Harvard U., 1986. Postdoctoral in pediat. Children's Hosp. Boston, 1986—87; resident in ophthalmology U. Ill., Chgo., 1987—90; clin. instr. ophthalmology U. Ill. Sch. Medicine, Chgo., 1989—90; extern in strabismus and adult motility disorders U. Iowa, 1991; fellow in pediatric ophthalmology, strabismus and adult motility disorders U. Pa. and Children's Hosp. Phila., 1990—92; clin. instr. opthalmology U. Pa., 1990—92; instr. neurobiology and ophthalmology Harvard Med. Sch., 1992—94; asst. prof. ophthalmology U. Minn., 1994—2000, asst. prof. pediat., 1998—2000, assoc. prof. pediat., 2000; dir.Ophthalmic Genetics Rsch. Ctr., Children's Hosp. Phila., 2000—; assoc. prof. ophthalmology and pediat. U. Pa., 2001—. Recipient Surdna Undergrad. Rsch. fellowship, Bowdoin Coll., 1980—81, Stanley J. Sarnoff Soc. Cardiovascular Rsch. award and fellowship, Harvard Med. Sch., 1983—84, Commonwealth Fund Rsch. fellowship, 1985, George and Mary Knox Harvaard Med. Grad. award, 1984, Grad. Kaiser Merit award, Nat. Med. Fellowship, 1986, Keeshin Prize Rsch. award, Inst. Medicine Chgo., 1990, Honor award, Am. Acad. Ophthalmology, 1998, Robert Wood Johnson Faculty Devel. award, 1992—97, Honor award, Am. Acad. Ophthalmology, 1998, Am. Assn. Pediatric Ophthalmology and Strabismus, 2002; selected as part of, NIH's "Changing the Face of Medicine" exhbn., 2003. Office: Childrens Hosp of Phila 34th St and Civic Ctr Blvd Philadelphia PA 19104-4399*

YOUNG, THERESA ELIZABETH JENNIFER, music educator; b. Sewickly, Pa., May 13, 1978; d. Paul William and Judith Marie Young. MusB, Baldwin-Wallace Coll. Consevartory of Music, Berea, Ohio, 2000. Music tchr. Hamilton City Sch., Ohio, 2000—. Music tchr. Girl Scouts-Great River Coun., Cin., 2001—. CSA adult adv. GRGSC, Cin., 2001—, low ropes facilitator, 2002—. Recipient Girl Scout Gold award, 1996, Girl Scout Silver award. Mem.: Omicron Delta Kappa, Mu Pho Eplison.

YOUNG, TOMMIE MORTON, social psychology educator, writer; b. Nashville; BA cum laude, Tenn. State U., 1951; MA, Vanderbilt U., 1955; PhD, Duke U., 1977; postgrad., U. Okla., 1967, U. Nebr., 1968. Coord. Young Adult Program Lucy Thurman br. YWCA, 1951-52; instr. edn. Tenn. State U., Nashville, 1956-59; instr. coord. media program Prairie View Coll. (Tex.), 1959-61; asst. prof. edn., assoc. prof. English, dir. IMC Ctr. U. Ark., Pine Bluff, 1965-69; asst. prof. English and edn., dir. learning lab N.C. Central U., Durham, 1969-74; prof., dir./chairperson libr. /dir. Afro-Am. Family Project, prof. philosophy sociol. found. N.C. Agrl. and Tech. State U., Greensboro, 1975—92; adj. prof. langs., lit. and philosophy, dir. schs. history project Tenn. State U., Nashville, 1994—. Dir. workshops, grants; pres., dir. Ednl. Cons. Svcs.; owner Historic Black Nashville Tours. Co author: Afro-Am. Genealogy Sourcebook, 1987, Oral Histories of Former All-Black Public Schs., 1991, After School Program for At-Risk Youth and Their Families, 1997, Sable Scenes, 1996, Genealogist's Guide to Discovering Your African Ancestors, 1997, A Sister Speaks, 1998, Nashville, Tennessee, 2000; contbr. poem to Poetry: American Heritage; contbr. rsch. papers, articles to profl. jours. Nat. chmn. Com. to Re-Elect the Pres.; past sec. Fedn. Colored Women's Clubs; bd. dirs. Southwestern div. ARC, Nashville area, 1994—, dir. Volun-Teens; chairperson schs. div. Durham County Unit Am. Cancer Soc.; past mem. adv. bd., bd. dirs. YMCA, Atlanta; chair Guilford County Commn. on Needs of Children; bd. advisors NIH, N.C. Coun. of the Arts; mem. Guilford County Involvement Coun.; chmn. N.C. adv. com. U.S. Civil Rights Com.; mem. exec. planning com. Greensboro, hon. staff mem. [illegible] Davidson County Dem. Women, 2003—; rep. dist. I exec. com. Davidson County Dem. Party; chair resolutions com. Nat. Fedn. Dem. Women. Recipient awards ARC, 1968, 73, NAACP, 1973, HEW, 1978, U.S. Commn. on Civil Rights, 1982, cert. of Accomplishement Contributing to Youth Devel. Bus. and Profl. Women, 2000; named Disting. Alumni Tenn. State U., 1994. Mem. AAUW (honor award 1983, pres. Greensboro br., chairperson internat. rels. com.), ALA (divsn. coll. and rsch. librs., past chair), NAACP (life, 1st v.p. Durahm br., exec. bd. Greensboro br. dir. parent edn./child advocacy program, Woman of Yr. 1992), NEA, LWV (bd. dirs. Nashville), Assn. Childhood Edn. Internat., Comperative and Internat. Edn. Assn., Archives Assoc., Internat. Platform Assn., Nat. Hist. Soc., Greenboro Jr. League (community adv. bd. 1991—), African Am. Gen. Soc. Tenn. (founder 1994), Zeta Phi Beta (chairperson polit. action com. eastern region, nat. grammateus, Polit. and Civic Svc. award 1974, Outstanding Social-Polit. Svc. award 1982, Woman of Yr. 1977), Comm. on Status of Women (Woman of Achievement 1991), Phi Kappa Phi (Disting. Alumni award Tenn. State U. 1994, Disting. Alumni NAFEO award, 1995, Carl Rowan-Oprah Winfrey lectr. Tenn. State U., 1995, Excellence in Journlism award SPJ, 1995, Tenn. Outstanding Achievement award, 1997), 100 Black Women, Steering Com., Tenn. Trust for Historic Preservation, 1999 (named Woman of Distinction Top Ladies, 2001). Home: PO Box 281613 Nashville TN 37228-8506

YOUNG, VICTORIA E. occupational health nurse, lawyer; b. Concord, Mich., Apr. 20, 1933; d. Arthur Raymond and Edith Louise (Hands) Y. Diploma, Mercy Sch. Nursing, Jackson, Mich., 1954; JD, U. West Los Angeles, Culver City, Calif., 1973; BSN, UCLA, 1960, MPH in Adminstrn., 1966. Bar: Calif., U.S. Dist. Ct., Calif.; RN, Calif.; cert. pub. health nurse, pediatric nurse practitioner. Pub. health nurse L.A. City and Los Angeles County Health Dept.; exec. dir. Santa Monica (Calif.) Vis. Nurse Assn.; sch. nurse practitioner L.A. Unified Schs.; relief nurse L.A. Times. Vol. Moorpark City Hall, Moorpark Sr. Ctr; mem. Disaster Assistance Response Team, Moorpark. Ret. capt. USNR, Desert Storm. Mem. Nat. Assn. Pediatric Nurse Assocs. and Practitioners, Calif. Bar Assn., Fleet Res. Assn., Moorpark Woman's Fortnightly Club (treas. 1998-99). Home: 4359 Brookdale Ln Moorpark CA 93021-2302

YOUNG, VIRGINIA MCLAIN, information technology consulting executive; b. St. Louis, Jan. 31, 1954; d. John Robert and Virginia Elizabeth (Hauk) McL.; m. Gary Young, June 3, 1972; children: Justin, Jennifer, Julie. BA in Mgmt., Webster U., 1988, postgrad., 1988—. Dir. pub. rels. Sta. KWK, St. Louis, 1980-83; regional adminstr. CAP Gemini Am., St. Louis, 1983-86, profl. staffing specialist, 1987-89, regional mgr. staffing, 1989-91; pres. InTeCon, Inc., St. Louis, 1991-93; br. mgr. Programming Mgmt. Sys. Inc., 1993-98; reg. dir. Howard Sys. Internat. Inc., 1998; pres. G. Young and Assocs. Inc., 1998—. Mgr. campaign State Rep. 97th Dist., Webster Groves, Mo., 1990. Mem. Met. St. Louis Real Estate Bd., NAFE. Republican. Roman Catholic. Office: G Young and Assocs Inc 8816 Manchester Rd Ste 321 Saint Louis MO 63144-2602 Home: # R 122 E Lockwood Ave Saint Louis MO 63119-3003

YOUNG, YVONNE DELEASE, elementary school educator; b. Welch, W.Va., Sept. 19, 1939; d. Albert Neal Sr. and Sylvia Claudine (Brooks) Baker; m. Thomas G. Young, June 9, 1973; 1 child, Tajauna D. Tims. BS in Edn., Wilberforce U., 1964; MEd in Adminstrn., Miami U., Oxford, Ohio, 1977. Tchr. Dayton (Ohio) Pub. Schs., 1964-95; retired, 1995. Coord. Careers in Schs., Dayton. Bd. dirs. Youth Engaged for Success, Dayton, 1973-88; vol tutor Right-to-Read, Dayton, 1970-73; vol. Feeding the Homeless, Dayton; pres. OptiMrs., Dayton, 1974—; nat. pres. Carrousels, Inc., 1999-2001. Jennings scholar U. Dayton, 1974-75. Mem. Carrousel's, Inc. (nat. pres.), Delta Sigma Theta, Phi Delta Kappa, Phi Delta Kappa. Avocations: reading, travel, dance, crossword puzzles, entertaining family. Home: 4224 Caylor Rd Dayton OH 45418-2406

YOUNGBLOOD, BETTY J. academic administrator; b. Detroit; m. Ralph P. Youngblood; 1 child. BA in Political Sci., Oakland U., Rochester, Mich.; MA in South Asian Studies, PhD in Political Sci., U. Minn. Formerly mem. faculty State U. West Ga., Tex. Tech. U.; various adminstrv. positions Kennesaw State U., Marietta, Ga.; v.p. acad. affairs MacMurray Coll., Jacksonville, Ill., Wesley Coll., Dover, Del.; vice chancellor acad. affairs, dean faculty, prof. polit. sci. U. Wis.-Superior, 1990-91, acting chancellor, 1991-92, chancellor, 1992—95; pres. We. Oreg. U., 1995—2002, Lake Superior State U., Mich., 2002—. Cons., evaluator North Ctrl. Assn. Colls. and Schs. Contbr. articles to profl. jours. Bd. dirs. United Way, Sault Ste. Marie. Rsch. grantee for study in N.W. India. Mem. Sault Ste. Marie C. of C., War Meml. Hosp., Rotary. Office: Lake Superior State Univ 650 W Easterday Ave Sault Sainte Marie MI 49783

YOUNGBLOOD, DAISY, ceramist; b. Asheville, NC; Student, Va. Commonwealth U., 1963—66. Exhibitions include, N.Y.C., San Francisco, Calif., Milian, Italy, Represented in permanent collections, Toledo Mus. of Art. Grantee fellow, MacArthur Found., 2003.

YOUNGBLOOD, DEBORAH SUE, lawyer, speech pathology/audiology services professional; b. Fairview, Okla., July 29, 1954; d. G. Dean and Beatrice J. (Hiebert) White. BS with honors, Okla. State U., 1976, MA with honors, 1979; JD cum laude, Boston Coll. Law Sch., 1991; MPH in Health Care Mgmt., Harvard U., 1992. Bar: Colo., U.S. Ct. Appeals (10th cir.). Jud. law clk. Colo. Supreme Ct., 1992-94; assoc. atty. Patton Boggs, L.L.P., Denver, 1994—97; sr. assoc. atty. Vaglica & Meinhold, L.L.C., Colorado Springs, 1997-99; pvt. practice speech-lang. pathologist North Conway, NH, 1999—2001, Sun Valley, Idaho, 2001—. Mem. leadership coun. Harvard Sch. Pub. Health, 2003—. Mem. leadership coun. Harvard Sch. Pub. Health, 2003—. Recipient LEXIS Legal Rsch. and Writing Award, Boston Coll. Law Sch. Mem.: Harvard Sch. Pub. Health Leadership (coun. 2003—), Minoru Yasui Am. Inns of Ct. (exec. coun. 1995—97), Colo. Bar Assn., Sun Valley Edn. Found. (bd. dirs.), Phi Kappa Phi. Office: 118 W Bullion St Hailey ID 83333 E-mail: youngblood@peoplepc.com.

YOUNGER, JUDITH TESS, law educator; b. N.Y.C., Dec. 20, 1933; d. Sidney and Kate (Greenbaum) Weintraub; m. Irving Younger, Jan. 21, 1955; children: Rebecca, Abigail M. BS, Cornell U., 1954; JD, NYU, 1958; LLD (hon.), Hofstra U., 1974. Bar: N.Y. 1958, U.S. Supreme Ct 1962, D.C. 1983, Minn. 1985. Law clk. to judge U.S. Dist. Ct., 1958-60; asso. firm Chadbourne, Parke, Whiteside & Wolff, N.Y.C., 1960-62; mem. firm Younger and Younger, and (successors), 1962-67; adj. asst. prof. NYU Sch. Law, 1967-69; asst. atty. gen. State of N.Y., 1969-70; assoc. prof. Hofstra U. Sch. Law, 1970-72, prof., assoc. dean, 1972-74; dean, prof. Syracuse Coll. Law, 1974-75; dep. dean, prof. law Cornell Law Sch., 1975-78, prof. law, 1975-85; vis. prof. U. Minn. Law Sch., Mpls., 1984-85, prof., 1985-91, Joseph E. Wargo Anoka County Bar Assn. prof. family law, 1991—. Of counsel Popham, Haik, Schnobrich & Kaufman, Ltd., Mpls., 1989-95; cons. NOW, 1972-74, Suffolk County for Revision of Its Real Property Tax Act, 1972-73; mem. N.Y. Gov.'s Panel To Screen Candidates of Ct. of Claims Judges, 1973-74; mem. Minn. Lawyers' Profl. Responsibility Bd., 1991-93. Contbr. articles to profl. jours. Trustee Cornell U., 1973-78. Mem.: AAUP (v.p. Cornell U. chpt. 1978—79), ABA (council legal edn. 1975—79), Minn. Bar Assn., Assn. of Bar of City of N.Y., Am. Law Inst. (adv. restatement property 1982—84). Home: 3520 W Calhoun Pkwy Minneapolis MN 55416-4657 Office: U Minn Law Sch Minneapolis MN 55455 E-mail: young001@umn.edu.

YOUNGER, LAURIE, broadcast executive; B in Comm., Queens Coll.; MBA, UCLA. Former dir. bus. affairs 20th Century Fox; dir. bus. affairs network TV divsn. The Walt Disney Co., 1985—86, v.p. bus. affairs, 1986—90; sr. v.p. bus. affairs and adminstrn. Walt Disney TV and Telecomm.; sr. v.p. ABC, Inc., 1996—98, sr. v.p., CFO, 1998—2003, exec. v.p., CFO, 2003—; exec. v.p. ABC TV Distbn., 2000—03; pres. Buena Vista Worldwide TV Distbn., 2003—. Named one of 100 Most Powerful Women in Hollywood, Hollywood Reporter, 2003. Office: ABC Inc 500 S Buena Vista St Burbank CA 91521-4551*

YOUNG-POHLMAN, COLETTE LISA, music educator; b. Honolulu, July 20, 1952; d. Richard Ah On and Winifred Oi Chin Chang Young; m. Kurt I. Pohlman, Oct. 5, 1985; 1 child, Vinson Sterling Pohlman. EdB, U. Hawaii-Manoa, Honolulu, 1974, postgrad., 1975. Part-time tchr. dept. edn. Kalani High, Honolulu, 1978—79; chpt. 1 reading tchr. McKinley High, Honolulu, 1979—80, basic skills tchr., 1980—81; part-time tchg. asst. pvt. preschs., Honolulu, 1981—82; part-time tchr. dept. edn., chpt. 1 reading Ala Wai Elem. and Palolo Elem., 1982—83; classroom tchr. Heeia Elem., Kaneohe, Hawaii, 1990; part-time tchr. dept. edn. Wailupe Valley Elem., Honolulu, 1990—91; instrnl. resource augmentation tchr. Maemae Elem., Honolulu, 1991—92; project tchr. Title I reading Washington Intermediate, Honolulu, 1992—94; instrnl. resource augmentation tchr. Accelerated Gifted & Talented Performing Arts, Kailua, Hawaii, 1994—97; classroom tchr. Mokapu Elem., Kailua, 1997—2002, instrnl. resource augmentation music tchr., 2002—. Mem., tchr. Boy Scouts Am. Troop 113, 1999—. Mem.: Hawaii State Tchrs. Assn., Hawaii Music Educators Assn., Hawaii Orff Schulwerk Assn., Am. Orff Schulwerk Assn., Music Educators Nat. Conf., Nat. Tchr. Assn. Avocations: composing songs, writing poetry, singing, keyboard, storytelling. Home: 45-427 Loli'i St Kaneohe HI 96744-5911

YOUNGREN, VIRGINIA ROTAN, psychologist; b. Houston, Mar. 21, 1946; d. Edward and Virginia Douglas Rotan; m. William H. Youngren; children: Austin, Erica, Valerie. BA, Smith Coll., 1949; PhD, Rutgers U., New Brunswick, N.J., 1977, Boston Coll., Chestnut Hill, Mass., 1992. Dir. clin. team Family Counseling, Newton, Mass., 1988—92; staff psychologist outpatient dept. McLean Hosp., 1993—98; clin. instr. dept. psychiatry Harvard Med. Sch., Cambridge, Mass., 1998—; pvt. practice Cambridge, Mass., 1998—. Editor (newsletter): Focus, 2000—; assoc. editor (newsletter): Mass. Psychol. Assn., —. Mem.: Boston Psychoanalytic Soc. and Inst., Am. Psychoanalytic Assn., Internat. Psychoanalytic Assn. (v.p. studies orgn. 2000—). Office: Ste 1-C 1105 Massachusetts Ave Cambridge MA 02138

YOUNG-STEVENS, KATHERINE TRATEBAS, occupational health nurse; b. Valparaiso, Ind., Aug. 31, 1962; d. Russell Lewis and Edith May (Downs) Tratebas; m. Jeffrey Alan Young, Oct. 22, 1988 (div. July 1994); m. Jeffrey Francis Stevens, Oct. 23, 1999. Diploma, St. Elizabeth's Hosp., 1984; BSN, Ind. U., 1987; MS in Occupational/Safety Mgmt., Ind. State U., 1996. RN Ind. Nurse II adult burn care Wishard Meml. HOsp., Indpls., 1984-88; occupl. health nurse Meth. Occupl. Health Ctrs., Indpls., 1988-92, Cmty. Occupl. Health Ctrs., Indpls., 1992-93; from occupl. health nurse to dir. health and safety Delta Faucet Co., Greensburg, Ind., 1993—2001; regional clinical mgr. Total Health Advocacy Ptnrs., Emeryville, Calif., 2001—. Named Medique Pharms. Unique Leader, State of Ind., 1994. Mem. Am. Assn. Occupl. Health Nurses, Ind. Assn. Occupl. Health Nurses (program chair 1988-92, corr. sec. 1990-94, membership sec. 1994-98, pres. 1998-2001), Ind. Acad. Occupl. Health Nurses, Mid-Ind. Assn. Occupl. Health Nursing (pres. 1995-99, chair bylaws policies and procedures 1999-2001), Calif. Assn. Occupl. Health Nurses, 2001-, Am. Soc. Safety Engr., 1997-.

YOUNT, GWENDOLYN AUDREY, humanities educator; b. Indpls., July 24, 1957; d. August de Alba and Hena Yount; 1 child, Clark. AA, L.A. City Coll., 1977; BA, UCLA, 1979, MA, 1982, Candidate in Philosophy, 1987. Cert. C.C. lifetime credential Calif., bilingual cert. competence. Ednl. aide Alexander Hamilton H.S., Los Angeles, 1975—76; tchg. fellow UCLA, 1981—88; instr. L.A. Unified Sch. Dist., 1982—90; prof. Institut Franco-Americain de Mgmt., Paris, 1983—84; instr. Santa Monica (Calif.) Coll., 1987—88; lectr. U. of Calif., Riverside, 1988—91; instr. Beverly Hills (Calif.) Adult Sch., 1986—88; assoc. prof. Riverside (Calif.) C.C., 1990—. Dir. RCC Study Abroad Program in Spain, Salamanca, Spain, 1998—2002, RCC Study Abroad Program in Costa Rica, San Jose, Costa Rica, 1993, UCLA Spanish Program in Mex., Guadalajara, Mexico, 1987. Dancer (ballet performance) Celebrate Dance, 2000; actor: (mus. theater) La Cage Aux Folles, 1998; singer: (vocal performance) Montreux Jazz Festival, 1993. Adminstr. G. Yount scholarship Riverside County Found., 1998—2003; sen. Acad. Senate, Riverside, 1997—2003; mem. Spanish lang. steering com. Riverside Pub. Libr., 1989—91; charter mem. Mus. of Tolerance, L.A., 1994—2003. Named Most Influential Instr., RCC Disabled Student Svcs., 1993, 1998, Tchr. of Distinction, LDS Ch., 1998, 2000, 2001, 2002, Tchr. of the Yr., Riverside C.C., 1999—2000, 2000—01, 2002—03; grantee Univ. grantee for grad. study, UCLA, 1979. Mem.: Philol Soc. of the Pacific Coast, Assn. for Tchrs. of Spanish, Sigma Tau Sigma, Alpha Mu Gamma (pres. 1977—78), Sigma Delta Pi (v.p. 1985—86). Liberal. Avocations: travel, reading, studying. Office: Riverside C C 4800 Magnolia Ave Riverside CA 92506 Business E-Mail: gwen.yount@rcc.edu..

YOURISON, KAROLA MARIA, librarian services professional; b. Berlin, June 30, 1937; came to U.S., 1962; m. James E. Yourison, Feb. 29, 1992. BA, U. Pitts., 1974, MLS, 1976. Libr. mgr. Siemens Rsch. & Tech. Lab., Princeton, N.J., 1983-85; mgr. libr. svcs. Software Engring. Inst., Carnegie Mellon U., Pitts., 1986—. Mem. IEEE, Spl. Librs. Assn. (chair duplicates exch. com. 1992-94, chair sci.-tech. divsn. 1994-95, past chair sci.-tech. divsn. 1995-96), Assn. Computing Machinery. Office: Software Engring Inst 5000 Forbes Ave Pittsburgh PA 15213-3815 E-mail: kky@sei.cmu.edu.

YOUSEF, MONA LEE, psychotherapist; BS in Human Devel. and Family Studies, Cornell U., 1986; MSW, NYU, 1991. Cert. social worker, HIV counselor N.Y.; credentialed alcoholism and substance abuse counselor N.Y., cert. master addictions counselor. Coord. People with AIDS buddy program Home Care Am., N.Y.C., 1987—88; rsch. asst. Gay Men's Health Crisis, N.Y.C., 1988; caseworker AIDS assessment program Gouverneur Hosp., N.Y.C., 1989; support group facilitator Body Positive, N.Y.C., 1989—92; clin. social worker mental health clinic Lower Eastside Svc. Ctr., N.Y.C., 1991—93; clin. social worker alcoholism outpatient dept. Project Renewal, Inc., N.Y.C., 1993—95; psychotherapist Counseling Ctr., Morris Heights Health Ctr., Bronx, NY, 1995—2000. Pvt. practice psychoanalytic psychotherapy, N.Y.C., 1993—. Contbg. writer PWA Coalition Newsline. Mem. NASW, Nat. Assn. Alcoholism and Drug Abuse Counselors-Assn. for Addiction Profls., Acad. Cert. Social Workers, Assn. Addiction Profls. of N.Y., Nat. Coun. Sexual Addiction and Compulsivity, N.Y. State Soc. for Clin. Social Work, Stuyvesant H.S. Alumni Assn., Psi Chi (life). Democrat. Avocations: dance, writing, going to the beach, fitness, restaurants/cuisine. Office: 19 W 34th St Penthouse New York NY 10001

YOVANOF, SILVANA, physician; b. Lubojno, Macedonia, Jan. 14, 1956; came to U.S., 1961; d. Peter and Nuna Yovanof. BS in Biology and Psychology, Loyola U., Chgo., 1978; MS, U. Ill., 1982; MD, Am. U. Caribbean, Montserrat, 1985. Diplomate Am. Bd. Internal Medicine. Intern Deaconess Hosp., St. Louis, 1986-87; resident in internal medicine St. Joseph Mercy Hosp., Pontiac, Mich., 1987-89, chief resident in medicine, 1989-90; fellow U. Ill. Med. Ctr., Chgo., 1990-92; chief dept. medicine Monongahela Valley Hosp., 2002—. Mem. adv. panel Internal Medicine for the Specialist, 1988—; affiliated with hosps. Jefferson Hosp., Pitts., 1991, MonValley Hosp., Monongahela, Pa., 1993, Mercy Hosp., Pitts., 1995, Monsour Hosp., Jeannette, Pa., 1997. Contbr. articles to profl. jours. including Neurosci. Letters. Mem.: ACP, Am. Assn. Clin. Endocrinologists, Allegheny County Med. Soc. (med. legal com. 1996—), Pa. State Med. Soc., Am. Diabetes Assn., Am. Soc. Internal Medicine. Office: Med and Endocrinology Assoc 420 W Main St Monongahela PA 15063-2552

YOWELL, NANCY T. photographer, retired elementary educator; b. Compton, Calif., Apr. 30, 1934; d. Stanley Lawrence and Violet Beatrice Taufman; m. Don Arthur Yowell (dec. Mar. 1996); children: Paul Alan Yowell, Jack Leland Yowell. BA, Calif. State U., Fullerton, 1963; MA, Azusa Pacific U., 1975. Tchr. Rowland Unified Sch. Dist., Rowland Heights, Calif., 1963-80, Redlands (Calif.) Unified Sch. Dist., 1980-94; supr. interns Calif. State U., San Bernardino, 1994—. Exhibited photos in shows including Multi Media Mini show San Bernardino County Mus., 1996, 98, City of Redlands show, 1997, Redlands Camera Club Mus. Exhibit, 1998, others. Recipient awards for photos. Mem AAUW (pres. 1983-85), Redlands Camera Club, Redlands Arts Assn., Redlands Camera Club (pres. 1997-99), Delta Kappa Gamma (treas. 1992-94, pres. 1994-96, 97-98).

YU, BIN, statistician, educator; b. Harbin, China, Mar. 18, 1963; arrived in U.S., 1985; d. Dibei Yu, Xiaomin Yu; m. Ke-ning Shen, June 15, 1987; children: Maya Yu Shen, Matthew Yan Shen. BS in Math, Peking U., 1984; MA in Stats., U. Calif. Berkeley, 1987, PhD of Stats., 1990. Asst. prof. U. Wis. Madison, 1990—92; asst. prof., assoc. prof. U. Calif. Berkeley, 1993—2000, prof., 2001—. Postdoctoral fellow MSRI, Berkeley, 1991; vis. asst. prof. Yale U., New Haven, 1993; mem. tech. staff Bell Labs. Lucent, Murray Hill, NJ, 1997—2000. Contbr. articles to profl. jours. Grantee, ARO, 1991, 1994, 1998, NSF, 1994, 1998, 2001. Fellow: IEEE, Inst. Math. Stats.; mem.: Am. Stats. Assn. Achievements include patents for lossless coding and data network tomography. Avocations: reading, walking, swimming, movies. Office: Univ Calif Berkeley 367 Evans Hall #3860 Berkeley CA 94720

YU, JESSICA, director, producer, writer, editor; b. 1966; BA in English with honors, Yale U. Bd. dirs. Internat. Documentary Assn. Prodr.(dir.): Home Base: A Chinatown Callen Heinlenville, Sour Death Balls, 1992, Breathing Lessons: The Life and Work of Mark O'Brien, 1996 (Acad. award for best documentary short subject, 1997), Better Late, 1997; (TV films) Men of Re-enaction, 1998; dir.: (documentaries, feature) The Living Museum, 1998; contbr. articles. Recipient Edward R. Murrow award, Skeptics Soc., 1995, 24 film festival awards. Fellow: Yaddo, MacDowell Colony; mem.: Phi Beta Kappa.

YU, KATHERINE KIT, internist; b. Beijing, Jan. 19, 1960; came to the U.S., 1974; BS, UCLA, 1983; MD, U. Calif., San Francisco, 1987. Intern and resident UCLA-San Fernando Valley Program, 1987-90; cons. specialist Olive-View-UCLA Med. Ctr., Sylmar, 1990-91; Kenamar fellow UCLA, 1991; physician specialist Olive-View-UCLA Med. Ctr., Sylmar, 1991—; asst. dir. prof. Sch. Medicine UCLA, 1991-98, assoc. clin. prof. Sch. Medicine, 1998—. Mem. ACP. Avocations: travel, biking, tennis, music. Office: Olive View UCLA Med Ctr 14445 Olive View Dr Sylmar CA 91342-1437

YU, LINDA, newswoman, television anchorwoman; b. Xian, China, Dec. 1, 1946; BA in Journalism, U. So. Calif., 1968. With Sta. KTLA-TV, Los Angeles, Sta. KABC-TV, Los Angeles; news anchor, reporter Sta. KATU-TV, Portland, Oreg.; gen. assignment reporter Sta. KGO-TV, San Francisco; with Sta. WMAQ-TV, Chgo., 1979-84, gen. assignment reporter, weekend anchor, 1979-80, co-anchor Monday-Friday edit. NEWSCENTERS, 4:30 PM, 1980-81, co-anchor NEWSCENTER5, 10:00 PM, 1981-84; co-anchor Eyewitness News, WLS-TV, Chgo., 1984—; spl.: Linda Yu in China, 1980; anchor WLS-TV, Chgo., 1984—. Recipient Chgo. Emmy award, 1981, 82, 87. Office: Sta WLS-TV 190 N State St Chicago IL 60601-3302

YU, PAULINE RUTH, former dean, educational association administrator; b. Rochester, N.Y., Mar. 5, 1949; d. Paul N. and Iling (Tang) Y.; m. Theodore D. Huters, Aug. 23, 1975 (div. Feb. 2000); children: Emily Elizabeth, Matthew Charles, Alexander David. BA in History and Lit. magna cum laude, Harvard U., 1971; MA in Comparative Lit., Stanford U., 1973, PhD in Comparative Lit., 1976. Asst. prof., then assoc. prof. U. Minn., Mpls., 1976-85; assoc. prof., then prof. Columbia U., N.Y.C., 1985-89; prof., founding chair dept. East Asian langs. and lit. U. Calif., Irvine, 1989-94; dean humanities UCLA, 1994—2003, prof. East Asian langs. and culture, 1994—2003; pres. Am. Coun. Learned Socs., N.Y.C., 2003—. Author: The Poetry of Wang Wei, 1980, The Reading of Imagery in the Chinese Poetic Tradition, 1987; editor and contbg. author: Voices of the Song Lyric in China, 1994, Culture and State in Chinese History: Conventions, Accommodations, and Critiques, 1997, Ways with Words: Writing about Reading Texts from Early China, 2000; editor, contbr.: The Longman Anthology; mem. editl. bd. Tang Studies, Chinese Lit., Comparative Lit. Studies, 1993—. Bd. trustees Nat. Humanities Ctr., 2000; bd. dirs. The Teagle Found., 2003—; mem. adv. coun. Dept. East Asian Studies, Princeton U., 2003—; bd. overseers Harvard U., 2003—. Guggenheim fellow, 1983-84, ACLS fellow, 1983-84, World Lit. fellow Am. Acad. Arts and Scis., 1998-; recipient Profl. Achievement award U. Calif. at Irvine Alumni Assn., 1993. Mem. MLA, ACLS (bd. dirs. 1998-), Assn. Asian Studies (mem. China and Inner Asia coun. 1982-85), Am. Comparative Lit. Assn., Am. Oriental Soc., Phi Beta Kappa Soc. (senator 1997-). Office: Am Coun Learned Societies 633 Third Ave New York NY 10017-6795 E-mail: paulineyu@acls.org.

YUAN, JUNYING, medical educator, researcher; b. Shanghai; BS, Fudan U., Shanghai, 1982; PhD in Neuroscience, Harvard U., 1989. Postdoctoral trainee in devel. biology MIT, 1989—90; instr. medicine Harvard U., 1990—91, asst. prof. medicine and program in neuroscience, 1992—96, asst. prof. cell biology and program in neuroscience, 1996—; asst. geneticist Cardiovasc. Rsch. Ctr. Mass. Gen. Hosp., 1990—96. Mem. editl. bd.: Current Biology, 1996, ad hoc reviewer: NIH Human Embryology and Devel. 2 Study Sect., 1995, regular reviewer:, 1996—; patentee in field, —; contbr. articles to profl. jours.; presenter in field, —. Recipient Wilson S. Stone Meml. award, MD Anderson Cancer Ctr. U. Tex., 1994, Established Investigator award, Am. Heart Assn., 1996—; fellow Ryan, Harvard Med. Sch., 1985—89. Office: Harvard Med Sch Dept Cell Biology 240 Longwood Ave Boston MA 02115-5701

YUE, AGNES KAU-WAH, otolaryngologist; b. Shanghai, Peoples Republic China, Dec. 1, 1947; came to U.S., 1967; d. Chen Kia and Nee Yuan (Ying0 ; m. Gerald Kumata, Sept. 25, 1982; children: Julie, Allison Benjamin. BA, Wellesley Coll., 1970; MD, Med. Coll. Pa., 1974; postgrad., Yale U., 1974-78. Intern Yale-New Haven Hosp., 1974-75, resident, 1975-78; fellow U. Tex. M.D. Anderson Cancer Ctr., Houston, 1978-79; asst. prof. U. Wash., Seattle, 1979-82; physician Pacific Med. Ctr., Seattle, 1979-90; pvt. practice Seattle, 1991—. Fellow Am. Acad. Otolaryngology; mem. Northwest Acad. Otolaryngology. Avocations: sailing, opera, cooking. Office: 1801 NW Market St Ste 410 Seattle WA 98107-3909

YUKI, GODA, science educator; PhD Biochemistry, Stanford U. Asst. prof. biology U. Calif., La Jolla. Recipient young investigator award, Nat. Alliance Rsch. Schizophrenia & Depression; fellow, Sloan Found. Office: 9500 Gilman Dr 1123 A Pac Hall La Jolla CA 92093

YUND, MARY ALICE, biotechnology consultant; b. Xenia, Ohio, Feb. 12, 1943; d. John Edward and Ethel Louise Stallard; m. E. William Yund, June 11, 1966. BA, Knox Coll., 1965; PhD, Harvard U., 1970. Asst. rsch. geneticist U. Calif., Berkeley, 1975-88; pvt. practice cons. Berkeley, 1988-97; biotech. cons. Tech. Forecasters, Inc., Alameda, Calif., 1997—. Mem. devel. biology adv. panel NSF, Washington, 1983-87; vis. scientist NSF/ CSIRO U.S./ Australia Coop. Sci. Progam, North Ryde, Australia, 1980; co-chair women in Biosci. Conf., Stanford, Calif., 1993; organizer sci. seminar series and confs. in field. Contbr. articles, revs. to profl. jours., chpts. to books. Cons., counselor Bay Area Biosci. Ctr., Oakland, Calif., 1992—. Rsch. grantee NSF, NIH, 1975-86. Mem. AAAS, Genetics Soc. Am., Soc. for Developmental Biology, Am. Soc. Zoologists, Assn. for Women in Sci. (chpt. officer 1991—), Phi Beta Kappa, Sigma Xi. Achievements include first identification and characterization of ecdysteroid receptors. Office: 723 Woodhaven Rd Berkeley CA 94708-1540

YUNGMEYER OLSON, JANE ELIZABETH, conservationist; b. Henrietta, Okla., Feb. 27, 1957; d. Harold Ross and Sally C. (Sumpter) Yungmeyer; m. James S. Olson, Oct. 21, 1994; children: Iris Mary, Sonia Rose. BS with honors, U. Wyo., 1984; cert. in Group Fitness, Boise (Idaho) State U., 1997. Pesticide applicators cert., Wyo. Bartender Fireside Lounge, Gallery Saloon, Conner Lounge, Laramie, Wyo., 1977-82; laborer, saw operator Big Horn Lumber Co., Laramie, 1978-79; lead forestry technician USDA Forest Svc., Douglas, Wyo., summer 1984, range technician Laramie, summer 1985, summer 1986, summer 1987; rsch. technician zoology dept. U. Wyo., Cody, winters 1986-87; soil conservationist USDA Soil Conservation Svc., Pinedale, Wyo., 1987-88, wetland coord. Greybull, Wyo., 1989-90, dist. conservationist Sandpoint, Idaho, 1990-91, Lander, Wyo., 1991-94. Com. mem. Equal Opportunity Com., Soil Conservation Svc., Casper, Wyo., 1989-90. Mem. NOW, Soc. for Range Mgmt. Avocations: belly dancing, aerobics, reading, gardening. Home: 2615 Woodland Ave Missoula MT 59802-3139

YURCHENCO, HENRIETTA WEISS, ethnomusicologist, writer; b. New Haven, Mar. 22, 1916; d. Edward and Rebecca (Bernblum) Weiss; m. Basil Yurchenco, June 1936 (div. 1955); 1 child, Peter; m. Irving Levine, 1965 (div. 1979). Student, Yale U., 1935-36; student piano scholarship, Mannes Coll. Music, 1936-38. Radio producer WNYC, WBAI, others, 1939-69; writer, critic, tchr., folk music editor Am. Record Guide and Musical Am., 1959-70. Prof. music CCNY, 1962-86, Bklyn. Coll., 1966-69, New Sch. for Social Rsch., 1961-68; co-dir. project for study of women in music, Grad. Ctr. CUNY; mem. exec. com. Panamerican Musical Rsch. Arts. Author: A Fiesta of Folk Songs From Spain and Latin America, 1967, A Mighty Hard Road: A Biography of Woody Guthrie, 1970, !Hablamos! Puerto Ricans Speak, 1971, Around the World in 80 Years: A Memoir, 2003, in Spanish, 2004; contbr. articles to profl. jours.; 15 field recs. from Mexico, P.R., John's Island, S.C., Guatemala, Ecuador, Morocco, issued by Libr. Congress, Folkways, Nonesuch, Folkways/Smithsonian, Global Village, Rounder Records; collections in Libr. Congress, Discoteca Hebrew U., Jerusalem, Arias Montana Inst., Madrid, Inst. Nacional Indigenista, Mexico City; collections in Am. Sephardic Found. Recipient award Nat. Inst. Fine Arts, Mex., 2003, grants-in-aid Am. Philos. Soc., 1954, 56, 57, 65, 67, 89, grants-in-aid CUNY Faculty Rsch. Fund, 1970, 83, 87; NEH grantee, 1984. Mem. Internat. Council Traditional Music (com. on women's studies), Soc. Ethnomusicology, Soc. Asian Music, Sonneck Soc., Internat. Assn. Study of Popular Music, Am. Musicologists Soc. Achievements include research in folk, tribal and popular music for Library of Congress, Mexico, Guatemala, P.R., Spain, Morocco, Balearic Islands, John's Island, S.C., Ireland, 1941-83. Home: 360 W 22d St New York NY 10011-2600 Office: 139th St And Convent Ave New York NY 10031 E-mail: hyurchenco@aol.com.

YURTH, HELENE LOUISE, librarian; b. Cleve., May 21, 1953; d. Joseph Alexander and Helen (Hegedus) Y.; m. William David Birskovich, June 14, 1975. BA in Botany, Kent State U., 1975; MS in Libr. Sci., Clarion U. Pa., 1998. Dir. Bemus Point (N.Y.) Libr., 1988-90, Smith Meml. Libr. at Chautauqua (N.Y.) Instn., 1991—. Avocations: gardening, pets, birds and nature, vegetarianism, reading. Office: Smith Meml Libr 21 Miller Ave Chautauqua NY 14722 Fax: 716-357-3657. E-mail: hyurth@hotmail.com.

YUSPEH-HIDALGO, DENISE ANNE, juvenile writer, editor; b. N.Y.C., Apr. 29, 1959; d. Michel H. and Sonia E. (Nejame) Yuspeh; children: Ariel S. Hidalgo, Jason D. Hidalgo. Internat. baccalaureate, UN Internat. Sch., N.Y.C., 1977; BA, Yale U., 1981. Editor-in-chief Kids Mag. and Children's Express Mag., N.Y.C., 1974-77; personal asst. John Guare, N.Y.C., 1978-79; stage mgr. Little Theatre, L.A., 1979-80; author, co-lyricist Sweet Pickles, N.Y.C., 1981-82; activity book author Scholastic, Marvel Books, N.Y.C., 1983-84; textbook author MacMillan, Prentice-Hall, N.Y.C., 1985-87; co. adminstr. Deja Vu/Barry Martin, N.Y.C., 1988-90; personal asst.

Marvin Hamlisch, N.Y.C., 1991—98; script supr. Disney/ABC, N.Y.C., 1994—98. Script reader Learning Corp. of Am., N.Y.C., 1981-82. Author, editor; Sweet Pickles 16 vol. dictionary, 1982; author: (sch. activity packages) Health is Harmony, 1992-93, Tales to Tell, Going Places, 1991-92, Poetry & Rhyme Time, Lots of Laughs, 1990-91, Summer Starters, Following Directions, 1985-86; co-author, lyricist: (albums) Loving Lion Looks at Love, 1983, also several musical albums; asst. prodr. Secondari Prodns., Ltd., N.Y.C., 1981-82; singer for N.Y. Renaissance Festival, Sterling Forest, N.Y., 1987, French Conservatory Choir of Carnegie Hall, 1995—1998, Cathedral Choir St. John the Divine, 1997—2000, Riverside Choral Soc. 2001-. Author, editor: Sweet Pickles, 16 vol. dictionary, 1982; author: (sch. activity packages) Health is Harmony, 1992-93, Tales to Tell, Going Places, 1991-92, Poetry and Rhyme Time, Lots of Laughs, 1990-91, Summer Starters, Following Directions, 1985-86; co-author, lyricist: (albums) Loving Lion Looks at Love, 1983, also several musical albums; asst. prodr. Secondary Prodns., Ltd., N.Y.C., 1981-82; singer for N.Y. Renaissance Festival, Sterling Forest, N.Y., 1987, French Conservatory Choir of Carnegie Hall, 1995—, Cathedral Choir of St. John the Divine, 1997—. Recipient hon. mention Nat. Arts Club Pastel show, N.Y.C., 1975. Mem. ASCAP, NAFE, Dramatists' Guild. Avocations: tae kwon do (blue belt), computers, piano and voice, traveling with children, reading. Home and Office: 66 Overlook Ter Apt 5E New York NY 10040-3827 E-mail: deniseh277@aol.com.

YUSTER-FREEMAN, LEIGH CAROL, broadcast executive; b. Trenton, N.J., July 23, 1949; d. Leon Carl and Helen Loretta (Wisniewski) Markiewicz; m. Charles Yuster (div. Apr. 1985); stepchildren: Sarah, Elizabeth, Jared, Alexandra; m. Richard N. Freeman; 1 child, Jessica Lee Freeman. Profl. dancer, 1967—71; editor R.R. Bowker, N.Y.C., 1971—72, from ISBN agy. editl. coord. to dir. prod. devel., 1972—89, dir. product devel., pub. Ulrich's Database, 1989—90, assoc. pub. Bowker Bus. Rsch., A&I Pub. New Providence, NJ, 1990—91, also pub. Ulrich's Database, 1990—91, pub. Broadcasting & Cable Yearbook, 1991—97; mng. dir. Reed Reference Pub., New Providence, 1992—94, v.p. bibliographies, 1994—96, v.p. directories, 1996; v.p. Database Pub. R.R. Bowker, New Providence, 1996—99, sr. mng. dir. prodn., 1999—2000; project mgr. workforce devel. NJN Pub. TV, Trenton, NJ, 2000—. Ptnr. Eagle Bakery, Trenton, NJ, 1991—92. Recipient Climate of Excellence award, Cahners Pub. Co., Newton, Mass., 1987, cert. of Appreciation, Consortium of Univ. Film Ctrs., Kent, Ohio, 1986. Mem.: Actors Equity Assn. Jewish. Avocations: gardening, dance, music, children and children's issues, community services. Home: 19 Theodora Dr Hillsborough NJ 08844-4723 E-mail: lfreeman@njn.org.

ZABEL, DIANE MARION, school librarian; b. Antigo, Wis., Mar. 20, 1957; d. Frank and Nina Wilcenski; m. Craig Robert Zabel, May 17, 1980; 1 child, Zachary. BS, U. Wis., 1978; M, U. Ill., Urbana-Champaign, 1980, MS, 1982. Libr., dir. Fluvanna County Libr., Palmyra, Va., 1983—84; cataloger Bosler Free Libr., Carlisle, Pa., 1984—85; asst. libr. Pa. State U., Univeristy Park, 1985—86, social sci. ref. libr., 1986—98, bus. libr., 1998—2000, endowed libr. for bus., 2001—. Co-editor: Bridging the Gap: Examining Polarity in America, 1995, The Quality Management Sourcebook, 1994, The Flexible Workplace: A Sourcebook of Information and Research, 2001. Mem.: ALA (chair collection devel. and evaluation sect. 1999—2000), Internat. Coun. Hotel, Restaurant and Internat. Edn., Assn. Coll. and Rsch. Librs. (sec. instrn. sect. 1995—96). Avocations: reading, travel. Office: Schreyer Bus Libr Pa State Univ 309 Paterno Libr University Park PA 16802-1810

ZABEL, VIVIAN ELLOUISE, secondary school educator; b. Randolph AFB, Tex., July 28, 1943; d. Raymond Louis and Dolly Veneta (Lyles) Gilbert; m. Robert Lee Zabel, Feb. 18, 1962; children: René Lynne, Robert Lee Jr., Randel Louis, Regina Louise. BA in English and Speech, Panhandle State U., 1977; postgrad., U. Ctrl. Okla., 1987-92. Cert. tchr., Okla. Tchr. English, drama, speech, debate Buffalo (Okla.) H.S., 1977-79; tchr. English, drama, speech Schulter (Okla.) H.S., 1979-80; tchr. English Morris (Okla.) H.S., 1980-81; tchr. speech, drama, debate Okla. Christian Schs., Edmond, 1981-82; tchr. English, drama, debate, speech/debate coach Braman (Okla.) H.S., 1982-83; debate coach Pawhuska (Okla.) H.S., 1983-84; tchr. English, French, drama, speech and debate coach Luther (Okla.) H.S., 1984-95; tchr. debate, forensics, yearbook, newspaper, mag., creative writing, competitive speech Deer Creek H.S., Edmond, Okla., 1995—2001; ret., 2001. Dir. drama Nazarene Youth Impact Team, Collinsville, Okla., 1979-81; tchr. h.s. Sun. sch. class Edmond Ch. of Nazarene, 1991-94; mem. cmty.-sch. rels. com. Luther Pub. Schs., 1991-92, supt.'s adv. com., 1992-94. Editor: Potpourri mag., 1975—77; author (under name Vivian Gilbert Zabel): Reflected Images; author: poetry, short stories, novels. Adult supr. Texas County 4-H, Adams, Okla., 1975-77; double diamond coach NFL; adjudicator and tournament dir. qualifying OSSAA tournaments. Recipient Disting. Svc. award NFL, 1994, Editor's Choice award for poetry, 1997, 1998, 1999, Tchr. of Excellence, 1996, Outstanding Poet award, 1997, 1998, 1999, 2001. Mem. Nat. Debate Coaches Assn., Nat. Fedn. Interscholastic Speech and Debate Assn., Okla. Speech Theatre Comms. Assn., Okla. Tchrs. English, Internat. Soc. Poets. Republican. Nazarene. Home: 2912 Rankin Ter Edmond OK 73013-5344 E-mail: vzabel@juno.com.

ZABLOCKI, ELAINE, writer; b. Bklyn., June 13, 1942; d. Harry and Anne Finkelstein; m. Benjamin D. Zablocki; 1 child, Abraham M. BA with honors, Swarthmore Coll., 1963. Adminstr. Takilma (Oreg.) Clinic, 1973-80; freelance writer, polit. cons. Oreg., 1981-82; asst. com. adminstr. Oreg. Senate Com. on Human Svcs. and Aging, Salem, 1983; newsletter mgr. New Options, Inc., Washington, 1983-85; writer Craver, Mathews, Smith & Co., Falls Church, Va., 1985-86; freelance writer specializing in healthcare Corona Comms., Arlington, Va., 1986-98, Eugene, Oreg., 1999—. Reporter WebMD, 2000—01. Author: Changing Physician Practice Patterns, 1995—; editor Physician Mgr. Newsletter, 1994-95; contbg. editor The Quality Letter for Healthcare Leaders, 1994—; editor Alternative Medicine Business News, 1999; mng. editor CHRF News Files, 2002—; contbr. numerous articles to profl. publs.

ZABRISKIE, SHERRY LAFOLLETTE, filmmaker, author, actress; b. Madison, Wis., Feb. 22, 1936; d. Philip Fox and Isabel (Bacon) LaFollette; m. George Albert Zabriskie, feb. 10, 1962; children: Oliver LaFollette, Tavia LaFollette. Student, Bennington (Vt.) Coll., 1958, Stella Adler, N.Y.C., 1959, Uta Hagen, 1959. Filmmaker Zabriskie Prodns., N.Y.C., 1962—; profl. chef Sherry's Specialties, Sharon, Conn., 1978—. Actress in Tall Story, Broadway, N.Y.C., 1959, various summer stock, 1953-62, Late Night with Conar O'Brian, N.Y.C., 1998—; Voice of Cheer opposite Alfred Drake as Voice of Gloom in Exxon's Great Energy Answer Hunt, 1975; co-author: (book) Belle Biography of Belle Case LaFollette, 1984, (screenplay) Summerdog, 1977, (cookbooks) Empanandas, 1982, Pancakes, 1983. Justice of the Peace, State of Conn., Salisbury, 1977-82; active fundraising various polit. campaigns. Recipient Golden Eagle award Coun. of Internat. Events, Washington, 1964, Silver Spoon award Woman's Day, 1978; Josephine Bay/Michael Paul Found. grantee, 1988. Mem. Actors Equity, Screen Actors Guild, Am. Fedn. Radio and TV Artists, The Authors Guild. Democrat. Avocations: travel, food, wine, gardening, walking, theater. Home: 14 Schermerhorn St Brooklyn NY 11201-4803 Office: Zabriskie Productions PO Box 21524 Brooklyn NY 11202-1524

ZACCHINO, NARDA, newspaper editor; b. San Diego, 1947; BA in english lit., UCLA. Assoc. editor L.A. Times, Calif. Office: Los Angeles Times Times Mirror Sq Los Angeles CA 90053

ZACCONE, SUZANNE MARIA, sales executive; b. Chgo., Oct. 23, 1957; d. Dominic Robert and Lorretta F. (Urban) Zaccone. Grad. high sch., Downers Grove, Ill. Sales sec. Brookeridge Realty, Downers Grove, 1975-76; sales cons. Kafka Estates Inc., Downers Grove, 1975-76; adminstrv. asst. Chem. Dist., Inc., Oak Brook, Ill., 1976-77; sales rep., mgr. Anographics Corp., Burr Ridge, Ill., 1977-85; pres., owner Graphic Solutions, Inc., Burr Ridge, 1985—. Bd. dirs. Di Trolio Flexigraphic Inst. Curriculum adv. bd. mem. Sch. Dist. 99, 1997, 1998, 1999, 2000, 2001; bd. dirs. Ditrolio Flexographic Inst. Named Supplier of Yr. Through Preferred Supplied, Gen. Binding Corp., 1988—99; recipient Supplier Mem. award, Internat. Bottled Water Assn., 1987—88, Supplier award for excellence U.S., SBA, 1990, Eugene Singer award for best managed co. in sml. bus. category, Graphic Solutions, 1992, Eugene Singer award for best managed co. in medium bus. category, 2001, Eugene Singer award for best managed co. in mid range bus. category, 2002—03, 2003, Top Performer Supplier award, Cutler Hammer Westinghouse Divsn., 1993, 1994, 1995, 1996, 1997, 1998, 1999, Blue Chip Enterprise Initiative award, 1994. Mem.: NAFE, Ditrolio Flexographic Inst. (bd. dirs.), World Label Assn. (1st pl. in World Championship 1994, 1995, 1996, 2002), Women in Packaging (exec. bd.), Inst. Packaging Profls., Women Entrepreneurs DuPage County (past pres.), Tag and Label Mfrs. Inst. (chmn. pub. rels. and mktg. com., bd. dirs., pres. 1998—2000, Best Managed Co. award 1992, 1st place award in U.S. for Screen Printing 1994, 1995, 1996, 1997, 1999, 2000, 2001, Best Managed Co. award 2001, 2002, 2003). Avocation: Avocations: reading, sailing, cooking, needlepoint, scuba diving. Office: Graphic Solutions Inc 311 Shore Dr Burr Ridge IL 60521-5859 Office Phone: 630-325-8181.

ZACH, GRACE REBECCA, retired secondary school educator; b. Rockyford, Colo., Sept. 9, 1928; d. Fredrick William Hemphill and Gladys Leanora Follin; m. George Leo Dischinger, Jr., Sept. 24, 2000; stepchildren: Susan, George III, Thomas, John; m. Robert Eugene Zach, Aug. 26, 1951 (dec. Nov. 1995); children: Randy, Diane. BA, U. No. Colo., 1950; MA in Tchg., Colo. State U., 1973. Tchr. Ft. Collins (Colo.) H.S., 1950—56, 1962—64, Poudre H.S., Ft. Collins, 1965—83, chair dept. English, 1973—83; ret., 1983. Author: Roads of Crystal Lakes, 1985. Vol. tchr. tai chi Sr. Living Ctr., Worthington, Colo., 1999—; pres. Crystal Lake Rd. Recreation Assn., Red Feather Lakes, Colo., 1997—2002. Scholar, Colo. State Coll. Edn., 1946—50. Democrat. Avocations: painting, writing, watercolors.

ZACHARY, JEAN, workforce development specialist; b. Atlanta, Nov. 7, 1945; d. Foye Mason and Cosma (Stacks) Zachary; m. James Robert Sturdevant, July 1966 (div. Aug. 1976); children: John Zachary Sturdevant, Richard Thomas Sturdevant. Student, U. Tex., 1963-66; BA, U. Houston, 1967; postgrad., Houston Bapt. U., 1976-78. Tchr. Johnston Jr. H.S./Houston Ind. Sch. Dist., 1967-71, 76-81; adminstrv. asst. Llano County Appraisal Dist., Llano, Tex., 1991-95; asst. treas. Llano County, 1995-97, grant coord., 1997-99; workforce specialist Lockheed Martin IMS, Johnson City, Tex., 1999—, Llano, 1999—. Mem. Blanco County Interagy. Coun., Johnson City, 1999—; mem. Capital Area TRACS, Austin, Tex., 1999; mem. CAPCO Criminal Justice Com., Austin, 1997-99. Author/developer seminars. Mem. Appraisal Rev. Bd., Llano County 1989-91, chair, 1990-91; mem. Hill Country RC&D, Mason County, Tex., 1997-99; project SOS!2000, Llano, 1999; team mem. Hill Country Wellness Cu., sec., 1998-99. Recipient Team Spirit award Easy Access, Inc., 1994., Mem. Preservation Tex. Inc. Avocations: reading, gardening, computers, historic preservation. Home: 106 Marschall Dr Llano TX 78643 Office: Tex Workforce Ctr for Llano County 119 W Main St Llano TX 78643-1931

ZACHERT, MARTHA JANE, retired librarian; b. York, Pa., Feb. 7, 1920; d. Paul Rodes and Elizabeth Agnes (Lau) Koontz; m. Edward G. Zachert, Aug. 25, 1946; 1 child, Lillian Elizabeth. AB, Lebanon Valley Coll., 1941; MLS, Emory U., 1953; DLS, Columbia U., 1968. Asst. Enoch Pratt Free Library, Balt., 1941-46; head librarian Wood Research Inst., Atlanta, 1947; sch. librarian DeKalb (Ga.) County Schs., 1950-52; head librarian, prof. history of pharmacy So. Coll. Pharmacy, Mercer U., Atlanta, 1952-63; instr. Ga. State Coll., 1962-63, Emory U., summers 1955-59, 1956-57, 59-60; mem. faculty Library Sch., Fla. State U., 1963-78, prof., 1973-78, Coll. Librarianship U. S.C., Columbia, 1973-74, 78-84. Vis. fellow Brit. Library, 1980; cons. So. Regional Med. Library, Emory U., 1976-77, Nat. Library Medicine, 1977, others. Author: Fine Painting in Georgia, 1950s-1960, 1994; assoc. editor Jour. Libr. History, 1966-71, 73-76; mng. editor, 1971-73; cons. editor Jour. Libr. Adminstrn., 1979-86; contbr. numerous articles to profl. jours. Fellow Med. Libr. Assn. (named among 100 Most Notables 1998); mem. ALA, Spl. Librs. Assn. (past pres. Fla. chpt., spl. citation 1977, Hall of Fame 1985), Am. Printing History Assn., Beta Phi Mu (pres. 1974-75). Home and Office: 4436 Meandering Way #108G Tallahassee FL 32308-8705

ZACHERT, VIRGINIA, psychologist, educator; b. Jacksonville, Ala., Mar. 1, 1920; d. R.E. and Cora H. (Massee) Z. Student, Norman Jr. Coll., 1937; AB, Ga. State Woman's Coll., 1940; MA, Emory U., 1947; PhD, Purdue U., 1949. Diplomate: Am. Bd. Profl. Psychologists. Statistician Davison-Paxon Co., Atlanta, 1941-44; research psychologist Mil. Contracts, Auburn Research Found., Ala. Poly. Inst.; indsl. and research psychologist Sturm & O'Brien (cons. engrs.), 1958-59; research project dir. Western Design, Biloxi, Miss., 1960-61; self-employed cons. psychologist Norman Park, Ga., 1961-71, Good Hope, Ga., 1971-99. Rsch. assoc. med. edn. Med. Coll. Ga., Augusta, 1963-65, assoc. prof., 1965-70, rsch. prof., 1970-84, rsch. prof. emeritus, 1984—, chief learning materials divsn., 1973-84, faculty senate, 1976-84, acad. coun., 1976-82, pres. acad. coun., 1983, sec., 1978; mem. Ga. Bd. Examiners Psychologists, 1974-79, v.p., 1977, pres. 1978; adv. bd. Comdr. Gen. ATC USAF, 1967-70; cons. Ga. Silver Haired Legislature, 1980-86, senator, 1987-93, pres. protem, 1987-88, pres., 1989-93, rep., spkr. protem, 1993-96, spkr., 1997-98, Nat. Silver-Haired Congress rep., 1995—, spkr. 1997-99; govs. appointee White House Conf. on Aging, 1971, 96, Ga. Coun. on Aging, 1988-96; U.S. Senate mem. Fed. Coun. on the Aging, 1990-93; senator appointee White House Conf. on Aging, 1995; Ga. Health Decision's appointee to Ga. Coalition for Health, 1996-98. Author: (with P.L. Wilds) Essentials of Gynecology-Oncology, 1967, Applications of Gynecology-Oncology, 1967. Del. White House Conf. on Aging, 1981, 95. Served as aerologist USN, 1944-46;aviation psychologist USAF, 1949-54. Recipient Jane Kennedy Excellence Aging award, 1999. Fellow AAAS, Am. Psychol. Assn.; mem. AAUP (chpt. pres. 1977-80), Sigma Xi. (chpt. pres. 1980-81) Baptist. Home: 4275 Owens Rd # 403 Evans GA 30809

ZACHMAN, KATHLEEN E. gifted and talented educator, music educator; b. Denver, Feb. 15, 1945; BA U. No. Colo., 1967; MA, U. No. Colo., 1969. Elem. music tchr. Jefferson Co. Pub. Schs., Golden, Colo., 1988—2001, Gateway assessment observer, 2001—. Home: 13182 W Jewell Cir Lakewood CO 80228

ZAFFIRINI, JUDITH, state legislator, small business owner; b. Laredo, Tex., Feb. 13, 1946; d. George and Nieves Pappas; m. Carlos Zaffirini, 1965; 1 child, Carlos Jr. BS, U. Tex., 1967, MA, 1970, PhD, 1978. Committeewoman Tex. State Dem. Exec. Com., 1978-84; mem. Tex. State Senate, 1987—, pres. pro tempore, 1997; owner Zaffirini Comms., Laredo, 1998—. Del. Dem. Nat. Conv., 1980, 84. Recipient Medal of Excellence Nat. League United Latin Am. Citizens, 1987, Jose Maria Morelos y Pavon Medal of Merit for leadership in strengthening U.S.-Mex. rels., 1987; named Woman of Achievement Tex. Press Women, 1980, Gov. of Tex. for a Day, Apr. 19, 1997, Ten Best Legislators Tex. Monthly Mag., 1997, 2001, Disting. Alumnus U. Tex., 2003; inductee Nat. Hispanic Hal of Fame, 1987. Democrat. Roman Catholic. Home: PO Box 627 Laredo TX 78042-0627 Office: 1407 Washington St Laredo TX 78040-4411 Office Phone: 956-724-8379. E-mail: judith.zaffirini@senate.state.tx.us.

ZAGANO, PHYLLIS, religious studies educator; BA in English, Marymount Coll., 1969; MS in Pub. Rels., Boston U., 1970; MA in English, L.I.U., 1972; PhD in English, SUNY, Stony Brook, 1979; MA in Theology, St. John's U., Jamaica, N.Y., 1990. Program officer Nat. Humanities Ctr., N.Y.C., 1979-80; asst. prof. comms. Fordham U., Bronx, N.Y., 1980-84; rschr. Archdiocese of N.Y., 1984-86; ind. rschr. N.Y.C., 1986-88; assoc. prof. comm. Boston U., 1988—98, adj. assoc. prof. theology, 1988—98, dir. inst. for democratic comm., 1998; spl. assoc. prof. religious studies Hofstra U., Hempstead, NY, 2003—. Author: Religion and Public Affairs, 1987, Social Impact of the Mass Media, 1991, Woman to Woman, 1993, On Prayer, 1994, Ita Ford: Missionary Martyr, 1996, Twentieth Century Apostles, 1999, Things Now and Old, 1999, Holy Saturday: An Argument for the Restoration of the Formale Diaconaizs in the Catholic Church, 2000 (Book award Catholic Press Assn. 2001, Coll. Theology Soc. 2002), DorothyDay: In My Own Words, 2003, Called to Serve: A Spirituality for Deacons, 2004; monthly radio host Boston U. World of Ideas, 1992-97. Lector, lay minister Ch. St. Vincent Ferrer, NYC, 1980-92, Our Lady of the Miraculous Medal Ch., 1996—, Newman Ctr., Boston U., 1992-96. Comdr. USNR, 1976—. Faculty Rsch. grantee Fordham U., 1983, Rsch. grantee Nat. Inst. Peace, 1989, Rsch. grantee Wabash Ctr., 2003; Coolidge fellow Episcopal Divinity Sch., 1987; recipient citation for heroism Nassau County (N.Y.) Fire Commn., 1995. Mem. Am. Acad. Religion (co-chair Roman Cath. Studies, 1991-2001), Am. Cath. Philos. Assn., Assn. Profs. Religious Studies, Naval Res. Assn., Soc. for Study of Christian Spirituality. Roman Catholic. Office: 115 Hofstra Univ Hempstead NY 11549

ZAGAT, NINA, publishing executive; m. Tim Zagat, 1965; children: Ted, John. AB, Vassar Coll., 1963; LLB, Yale U.; attended, Le Cordon Bleu Ecole de Cuisine. Atty. Sherman and Sterling, N.Y.C., 1966—90; co-founder, co-pub. Zagat Survey, N.Y.C., 1979—; co-chair, co-founder Zagat.com, 1999—. Served on White House Conference on Travel and Tourism; mem. Who's Who of Food and Beverage in Am.; mem. of the corp. Culinary Institute of Am., 1994—, established lecture series, 2001. Office: Zagat Survey 4 Columbus Circle New York NY 10019*

ZAGON, LAURIE, artist; b. NYC, Feb. 4, 1950; d. Jerome and Janet (Rabinowitz) Z.; m. Joseph Sorrentino, Dec. 21, 1991. BFA, Md. Inst. Coll. Art, 1971; MFA, Syracuse U., 1973. Asst. prof. Art CUNY, NYC, 1973-87; color cons. Fieldcrest/Cannon, 1987-88. Spkr. Am. Soc. Interior Designers, Washington, 1993-97—; color, art therapit, Flagstaff, Ariz., 1996, Big Brothers/Big Sisters No. Ariz., 1996. Illustrator (book) It's Never Too Late To Have a Happy Childhood, 1989; one-woman shows include The Nat. Arts Club, NYC, 1989; group exhibits include John Szoke Gallery, NYC, Helio Galleries, NYC, CUNY Abstract Show of Shanghai, China, 1986, LA Mcpl. Gallery, 1993, The Brewery Artist Colony, 1996-2000; co-author: Power of Color, 1995. Color, art therapist for AIDS Children, LA Children's Hosp., 1994; Martin Luther Hosp., Anaheim, 1990; active painting workshops for the terminally ill, 1995—, City of Hope Nat. Cancer Ctr.; founder, pres. Art and Creativity for Healing, Inc., Laguna Niguel, Calif. Office: 26079 Getty Dr Laguna Niguel CA 92677-1233 Office Phone: 949-367-1902. E-mail: lzagon@aol.com.

ZAHM, MARY A. psychologist, educator; m. Kenneth A. Zahm, Feb. 25, 1989; children: Steven E. Kanarian, Susan B. Goulet. PhD, U. R.I., 1983; MA in Personality and Social Psychology, R.I. Coll., 1979; BA in Psychology, Roger Williams U., 1977. Cert. Human Factors Profl. Bd. of Profl. Ergonomics, 1993. Psychology prof. Bristol C.C., Fall River, Mass., 1994—; human factors engr. Raytheon Co., Portsmouth, RI, 1992—94. Author: (text book) Create Your Ideal Life;, co-author (book) Beyond SATs: 110 Strategies for Success in College. Mem.: APA, Assn. Women in Psychology (regional coord. 1989—2002), New Eng. Psychol. Assn. (pres.-elect 2003—04). Office: Bristol Community College 777 Elsbree Street Fall River MA 02720 E-mail: mzahm@bristol.mass.edu.

ZAHN, PAULA, newscaster; b. Omaha, Feb. 24, 1956; m. Richard Cohen; children: Haley Brynne, Jared Brandon, Austin Bryce. BA in journalism, Stephens Coll., Columbia, Mo., 1978. With Sta. WFAA-TV, Dallas, 1978, Sta. KFMB-TV, San Diego, 1979—81, Sta. KPRC-TV, Houston, 1981—83, Sta. WHDH-TV, Boston, 1983—85; anchor, reporter Sta. KCBS-TV, L.A., 1985—87; anchor The Health Show ABC News, N.Y.C., 1987—88, co-anchor World News This Morning, 1988—90; co-anchor CBS This Morning CBS News, N.Y.C., 1990—96, anchor CBS Evening News Sat. edit., 1996—99; anchor The Fox Report with Paula Zahn Fox News Network, N.Y.C., 1999, anchor The Edge with Paula Zahn, 1999—2001; co-anchor American Morning CNN, 2001—03, co-anchor People in the News, 2002—, anchor Paula Zahn Now, 2003—. Primetime co-host Olympic Winter Games, Albertville, France, 1992; co-anchor Olympic Winter Games, Lillehammer, Norway, 94. Musician (Cellist): Carnegie Hall Debut, 1992. Named Newscaster of Yr., Am. Women in Radio and TV, 1983; recipient Broadcasting Award, Nat. Commn. Working Women, 1982, Spirit Achievement Award, Albert Einstein Coll. Medicine, 1993, Cancer Awareness Award, Congl. Families Action for Cancer Awareness, 1994, Emmy award for outstanding coverage of a continuing news story, 1994, Spirit of Life Award, City of Hope Cancer Ctr., 2003. Office: CNN 820 1st St NE Washington DC 20002-4243

ZAHNER, DOROTHY SIMKIN, elementary school educator; b. Chengdu, Szechuan, China, May 01; d. Robert Louis and Margaret Isadore (Timberlake) Simkin; divorced; children: Mary De Avilan, Robert Louis. BA in Sociology, Whittier Coll.; MLS, U. So. Calif., L.A. Cert. tchr. Calif., Ariz. Tchr. LA and Pasadena Sch., Calif., 1969-93; dir., owner Betty Ingram Sch., North Hollywood, Calif., 1976-79; dir. Foothill Nursery Sch., La Crescenta, Calif., 1970s; tchr. L.A. Unified Sch. Dist.; guest tchr. Washington Unified Sch. Dist., Phoenix, 1994-97. Guest tchr. Osborn Sch. Dist., 1998-2000, Madison Sch. Dist., Phoenix, 1999-2001. Author: poems pub. in U.S. and Europe. Bd. dirs. Ariz. Tenants Assn., Phoenix, 1994, 95; vol. Am. Friends Svc. Com., Phila., Calif., 1985—, Common Cause, LA, 1990, Internat. Rescue Com., Dem. Candidates, LA and Phoenix. Mem.: Ariz. State Poetry Soc. (pres. 2002—03, chmn. 2004), Alameda Writers Group, Phoenix Poetry Soc. (pres. 1998, anthology editl. co. 2001, com. mem., Poet of Yr. 2000, poetry awards 1995, 2000), Phoenix Writers Club (sec. 1998). Avocations: theatre, films, music, swimming, reading.

ZAHRLY, JANICE HONEA, management educator; b. Ft. Payne, Ala., Sept. 27, 1943; d. John Wiley and Lillian (McKown) Honea. BA, U. Fla., 1964; MBA, U. Ctrl. Fla., 1980; PhD, U. Fla., 1984. Tchr. Hope Mills (N.C.) H.S., 1964-65, Satellite Beach (Fla.) H.S., 1965-69; realtor-assoc. WD Webb Realty, Melbourne, Fla., 1969-70; realtor Aero Realty, Melbourne, 1970-72, Albert J. Tuttle, Realtor, Melbourne, 1972-74; mktg. mgr. Cypress Woods Devel., Orlando, Fla., 1974-76; regional campaign mgr. Pres. Ford Com., 1976; ednl. researcher Peace Corps, Korea, 1976-78; rsch. analyst, tech. writer Rsch. Sys. Inc., Orlando, 1979-80; rsch. asst., lectr. U. Fla., Gainesville, 1980-84; asst. prof. Wayne State U., Detroit, 1984-89; assoc. prof. Old Dominion U., Norfolk, Va., 1989-94, U. N.D., Grand Forks, 1994—. Mem. Melbourne Bd. Realtors, 1969-76, orientation chair, 1972, pub. rels. chair, 1973, civic affairs chair, 1973, grievance com., 1975; cons. Wayne County Retarded Persons Assn., Detroit, 1985, Gov.'s Conf. on Women Entrepreneurs, Mich., 1986, Oakland County AAUW Conf. on Women, Mich., 1987, 88, Coll. Bus. and Pub. Adminstrn. Inst. of Mgmt., Old Dominion U., Norfolk, 1990, U.S. Army Corps Engrs., Norfolk, 1990; presenter in field. Editl. rev. bd., Case Rsch. Jour., 2000—; contbr. chpts. to books, articles to profl. jours. and procs. Vol. Tidewater AIDS Crisis Task Force, Norfolk, 1990-93, bd. dirs., 1990-92, v.p., 1991, rec. sec., 1992; mem. occupational adv. com. Brevard County Mental Health Ctr., Fla., 1973-74; mem. Brevard County Libr. Bd., 1973-74; bd. dirs. Fla. Dist. 12 Mental Health Bd., 1973-74, sec. 1973-74; bd. dirs. Alachua County Crisis Ctr., Gainesville, 1982-84, chair, 1983-84; vol. Open Door, Detroit, 1986-89; bd. dirs. United Way Grand Forks Area, 1996-97, Grand Forks Homes, 2003-; pres. bd. dirs. Cherry Arms Condominium Assn., 1996-97.

Recipient Best Paper award Midwest Soc. for Human Resources/Indsl. Rels., 1989, F.W. Lawrence award U. N.D., 1996; rsch. fellow Fed. Mogul Corp., 1987-88; rsch. grantee Wayne State U., 1985-89, Old Dominion U., 1990, U. N.D., 1995, 96, 98; recipient [illegible] award (best case) N. Am. Case Rsch. Assn. 2002. Mem. AAUW (bd. dirs. 1974-75), Acad. Mgmt., Assn. for Rsch. on Nonprofit Orgns./Vols., N.Am. Case Rsch. Assn. (nonprofit track chair 1999-2000, procs. editor 2001-2002), So. Mgmt. Assn., Hampton Rds. Gator Club (co-founder, treas. 1989-91), Alpha Omicron Pi (bd. dirs. alumnae chpt. 1969-73, v.p. 1969-73). Avocations: travel, writing fiction, photography, music. Home: 3424 Cherry St Apt A1 Grand Forks ND 58201-7692

ZAIDI, EMILY LOUISE, retired elementary school educator; b. Hoquiam, Wash., Apr. 20, 1924; d. Burdick Newton and Emily Caroline (Williams) Johnston; m. M. Baqar Abbas Zaidi, June 12, 1949 (dec. Dec. 1983). BA in Edn. and Social Studies, Ea. Wash. State U., 1948; MEd, U. Wash., 1964, EdD, 1974. Tchr. 4th grade Hoquiam Schs., 1948-49; tchr. grades 5-6 Lake Washington Sch. Dist., Kirkland, Wash., 1949-51; tchr. grades 2-3 Port Angeles (Wash.) Schs., 1951-54; tchr. grade 2 Seattle Schs., 1954-55; tchr., reading specialist Northshore sch. Dist., Bothell, Wash., 1955-69, Sacramento City Schs., 1969-87; ret. Mem. Calif. State Instructional Materials Panel, Sacramento, 1975. Mem. Sacramento Opera Assn., 1986—, Sacramento Ballet Assn., 1987-2000. Fulbright Commn. Exchange Tchr., 1961-62. Mem. Reading Club. Democrat. Avocations: writing, children's literature, reading, travel. Home: 4230 N River Way Sacramento CA 95864-6055

ZAK-DANCE, CAROL CAMILLE, human communication educator; b. Milw., Nov. 26, 1950; d. Joseph T. and Alice M. (Tatera) Zak; m. Frank E.X. Dance, July 4, 1974; children: Zachary, Gabriel, Caleb, Catherine. BA, U. Wis., Milw., 1972; MA, U. Denver, 1976, PhD, 1979. Instr. Arapahoe Cmty. Coll., Littleton, Colo., 1976-82, Regis U., Denver, 1983-85; asst. prof. U. Denver-The Women's Coll., 1984—. Adj. faculty U. Denver-Univ. Coll., 1984—; v.p. Human Comm. Cons., Denver, 1976—; guest spkr. numerous schs. and orgns. Editl. asst. Comm. Edn., Washington, 1980, editl. bd., 1985-86; author: Public Speaking, 1986, Speaking Your Mind, 1994, 2d edit., 1996; contbr. articles to profl. jours. Adv. bd. Gove Cmty. Sch., Denver, 1983-89; vol. St. Vincent de Paul Sch., Denver, 1984—, Regis Jesuit H.S., Aurora, 1994—; vol. recreation soccer coach South Ctrl. Denver Soccer, 1986—. Mem. AAUW, Speech Comm. Assn. (divsn. sec. 1983-84). Avocations: cello, tap dancing, mountain biking. Office: Womens Coll U Denver Denver CO 80237

ZAKEN, GRACE AMBROSE, project coordinator, educator; b. Pitts., Nov. 3, 1964; d. Stephen E. and Moira (Buckley) Ambrose; BA, U. New Orleans, 1986; MEd, U. Tex., 1993; EdD, Vanderbilt U., 1997. Tchr. students with visual disabilities St. Bernard Parish Sch. Bd., Arabi, La., 1987-90; play tutor for blind children Austin Tex., 1990-92; pre-sch. tchr. students with visual disabilities Austin Ind. Sch. Dist., 1992-93; orientation and mobility specialist Tex. Commn. for the Blind, Austin, 1992-93; on-line Internet instr. spl. edn. Vanderbilt U., Nashville, 1996-97; project coord., lectr. Hunter Coll., CUNY, N.Y.C., 1997—. Orientation and mobility specialist, Nashville, 1993-97, N.Y. State Commn. for the Blind and Visually Handicapped, N.Y.C., 1997—. Contbr. articles to profl. jours. and conf. procs. Vol. surrogate parent Dept. Spl. Edn.-Cavert Br. Office Met., Nashville, 1997; vol. vision screener Prevent Blindness, Nashville, 1997; state coord. Nat. Agenda for Children and Youths with Visual Impairments Including Those with Multiple Disabilities, Nashville, 1997. Recipient Reading Program for At Risk Readers award Internat. Reading St. Bernard Parish La., 1990. Mem. CEC, Assn. for Edn. of the Blind and Visually Impaired (cert. orientation and mobility specialist, chmn. O&M divsn. 2000-06), Assn. for Edn. and Rehab. of Blind and Visually Impaired. Avocations: mountain biking, cribbage, training chocolate labradors. Address: Hunter Coll of CUNY 909W Park Ave New York NY 10021-0308 Fax: (212) 650-3542. E-mail: gambrose@hunter.cuny.edu.

ZAKHEIM, BARBARA JANE, development professional; b. London, Jan. 31, 1953; d. David Sloma and Sarah Frances (Leifer) Portnoi; m. Dov Solomon Zakheim, Aug. 20, 1972 (div. 1990); children: Keith Samuel, Roger Israel, Scott Elisha; m. Ronald Kleinfeldt, Dec. 13, 1992. BA, Oxford U., Eng., 1974, MA, 1978. Economist Maxima Corp., Silver Spring, Md., 1979, U.S. Dept. Energy, Washington, 1979-80; sr. project analyst Applied Mgmt. Scis., Silver Spring, 1980-83, staff assoc., 1983-85; prin. analyst NUS Corp., Gaithersburg, Md., 1985-87, cons. analyst, 1987-89; pres. Keith R. Scott Assocs., Inc., 1989-96, African Treasures, Inc., 1990-93; dir. policy and econ. studies Sanford Cohen & Assocs., Inc., 1993-96, v.p. info. & comm. svcs. divsn., 1996-2000, COO, 2000—02; dir. devel. Save A Child's Heart Found., U.S., Inc., 2002—. U.S. rep. Coll. Petroleum Studies, Oxford, 1984-93; N.Am. rep. Twirltrade Internat. Ltd., London, 1985—; mem. adv. com. on women in bus. Theodore Roosevelt Nat. Bank, Washington, 1991-92; profl. team mem. Venture Ptnrs. Internat., Inc., N.Y.C., 1990-94. Contbr. articles to profl. jours. Bd. dirs. SE Hebrew Congregation, Silver Spring, 1977-78; sec. Stonington Woods Homeowners' Assn., 1997-98, pres., 1998-99; founder, pres. Greater Washington Jewish Coalition Against Domestic Abuse, 1999—; bd. dirs. Jewish Cmty. Coun. Greater Washington, 2002—. Mem. NAFE, Hadassah, Jewish Women Internat. Republican. Avocations: reading, travel, theater, music, ballroom dancing. Home and Office: 11247 Watermill Ln Silver Spring MD 20902-3439 E-mail: bzakheim@aol.com.

ZALESKI, CAROLINE ROB, preservationist; b. London, Eng., Jan. 15, 1948; arrived in U.S., 1960; d. Charles Granville Rob, Mary Dorothy Beazley; m. Michel Henry Zaleski, Dec. 18, 1979; children: Katharine Sabine, Olivia Mary. BA, Scripps Coll., 1969; BSN, Cornell U., 1977; MS, Columbia U., 2000. Freelance journalist, N.Y.C., 1980—97; staff writer Good Housekeeping, N.Y.C., 1997—; dir. adv. Docomomo N.Y. Tri-State, N.Y.C., 2000—. Staff historian Soc. Preservation L.I. Antiquities, Cold Spring Harbor, NY, 2000—. Author: The Glamour Guide to Pregnancy, 1982, The Caregivers Guide, 1991. Bd. dirs. Landmark West, N.Y.C., Friends of Upper East Side, N.Y.C.; leader, adv. Campaign to Save the Aaltorooms, N.Y.C., 1999—; leader adv. campaign Save the Conger Goodyear House, L.I., NY; bd. dirs. Preservation League of N.Y. State, N.Y.C., 2001—, The Preservation League of N.Y. State, 2002—. Fellow Everet fellow, Mcpl. Art Soc., 1999. Avocations: gardening, tennis, travel. Office: Docomomo NY Tri-State 300 Central Park W 29D New York NY 10024

ZALESKI, JEAN, artist; b. Birkirkara, Malta; d. John M. and Carolina (Micallef) Busuttil; children: Jeffrey, Philip, Susan. Student, Art Students League, N.Y.C., 1955—58, New Sch., 1967—69, Moore Coll. Art, Phila., 1970—71, Parsons Sch. Design, N.Y.C., 1974—75, Pratt Inst., 1976—77. Dir. art Studio 733, Great Neck, NY, 1963-67; sr. art instr. Hussian Coll. Art, Phila., 1970-71; dir. Naples (Italy) Art Studio, 1972-74; corp. sec. Women in The Arts, N.Y.C., 1974-75, exec. coord., 1976-78. Adj. lectr. Bklyn. Coll., 1974-75, Hofstra U., 1977-82, Cooper Union, 1986—. One-woman shows include Neikrug Gallery, N.Y.C., 1970, Wallnuts Gallery, Phila., 1971, Il Gabbiano Gallery, Naples, Italy, 1973, Adelphi U., 1975, Women in Arts Gallery, N.Y.C., 1975, Alonzo Gallery, 1979—80, Va. Ctr. for Creative Arts, Sweet Briar, 1981, Hodgell Galleries, Sarasota, Fla., 1982—83, Elaine Starkman Gallery, N.Y.C., 1986, Romano Gallery, Barnegat Light, N.J., 1987—88, Citicorp Ctr., N.Y.C., 1988—89, Z Gallery, 1991, Sweet Briar Coll., Va., 1993, Trinity Coll., Hartford, Conn., 1996, Myungsook Lee Gallery, N.Y.C., 1997—98, Slater Mus., Norwich, Conn., 1999, Four Decades of Painting, Retrospective Westbeth Gallery, N.Y.C., 2000, St. James Cavalier Contemporary Art Ctr., Valletta, Malta, 2002, exhibited in group shows at Art U.S.A., N.Y.C., 1969, Internat. Art Exhbn., Cannes, France, 1969, Frick Mus., Pitts., 1970, NAD, N.Y.C., 1970—71, Phila. Mus. Art, 1971, Am. Women Artists, Palazzo Vecchio, Florence, Italy, 1972, Internat. Women's Arts Festival, Milan, 1973 (Gold medal), Bklyn. Mus., 1975, Sweet Briar Coll., Va., 1977, [illegible], Mus. Hudson Highlands, 1982, Pace U. Gallery, N.Y.C., 1982, Bayly Mus., Charlottesville, Va., 1986, Allbright Knox Mus., Buffalo, 1986, E. Starkman Gallery, N.Y.C., 1987, Nabisco, 1989, Queens Coll., N.Y., 1991—92, Mus. City of N.Y., 1993, Nat. Mus. Fine Arts, Malta, 2000, Mediterranean Conf. Ctr., 2001, Westbeth Gallery, NYC, 2002—04; author: Winged Spirits, 1995; co-author: COW/LINES, 1983; Represented in permanent collections N.Y. Pub. Libr., Met. Mus. Art, Va. Ctr. for Creative Arts, Nat. Mus. Women in Arts, Mus. City of N.Y., Nat. Mus. Malta . Recipient Susan B. Anthony award NOW, 1986; MacDowell fellow, 1971—, Ragdale fellow, 1986—, Va. Ctr. for Creative Arts fellow, 1976—, Tyrone Guthrie Ctr. fellow, 1991; grantee NEA/Brown U., 1982, Artists Space, 1988; invited to White House by Pres. Carter, 1977. Mem. Artists Equity, Women in the Arts. Democrat. Roman Catholic. Avocations: music, opera, writing. E-mail: valletta@aol.com.

ZALESKI, LINDA C. retail executive; Pres. Data Projections, Houston, 1987—. Recipient Entrepreneur Yr. award, 1996, Blue Chip Enterprise Initative award, Nations Bus. Mag. and U.S. Chamber Commerce, 1995. Office: Data Projections 3036 Rogerdale Rd Houston TX 77042-4121 Fax: 713-781-3338. E-mail: getinfo@dpict.com.

ZALILA-MILI, RYM, computer scientist, educator; b. Tunis, Tunisia, Aug. 9, 1965; came to the U.S., 1995; d. Chedli and Melika (Amara) Zalila; m. Ali Mili, June 29, 1991 (div. Oct. 1998); 1 child, Noor. Pre-Engring. in Physics & Chemistry, U. Tunis, 1985, Engring. Degree in Computer Sci., 1989, Doctorat de Spécialité, 1991; PhD in Computer Sci., U. Ottawa, Ont., Can., 1997. Lectr. U. Ottawa, 1992-94, Inst. Informatics, Ottawa, 1994-95; asst. prof. U. Tex. Dallas, Richardson, 1995—. Cons. Philips, Surrey, Eng., 1998. Grantee Sandia Nat. Labs., N.Mex., 1998-99. Mem. IEEE Computer Soc., Assn. Computing Machinery. Achievements include An Effective Data Entry Method, A Cigarette Substitute. Office: Univ Tex Dallas PO Box 830688 Richardson TX 75083-0688

ZALOZNIK, ARLENE JOYCE, oncologist, retired military officer; b. Pitts., Jan. 30, 1948; d. Ernest and Frances Elizabeth (Augustin) Z. BS, Carlow Coll., 1969; MS, Duquesne U., 1972; MD, Med. Coll. Pa., 1976. Diplomate Am. Bd. Internal Medicine, Am. Bd. Oncology. Commd. U.S. Army, 1976, advanced through grades to col.; intern then resident in internal medicine Madigan Army Med. Ctr., Tacoma, 1976-77; fellow in hematology and oncology Fitzsimons Army Med. Ctr., Aurora, Colo., 1979-81, staff oncology, 1981-82, asst. chief med. oncology, 1982-84, chief hematology and oncology, 1984-86, Brooke Army Med. Ctr., Ft. Sam Houston, Tex., 1986-90; assoc. prof., chief divsn. hematology/oncology divsn. Tex. Tech. U. Health Scis., El Paso, 1997—. Clin. instr. dept. medicine U. Colo. Health Sci. Ctr., 1982-86. Contbr. articles to books and profl. jours. Active profl. edn. com. Aurora-Adams Unit Am. Cancer Soc., 1983-86, pres., 1983-86, active Colo. divsn., 1984-86. Fellow ACP; mem. AMA, Am. Soc. Clin. Oncology. Home: 324 Sharondale Dr El Paso TX 79912-4250 Office: Tex Tech U Health Scis Hematol/Oncol Divsn 4800 Alberta Ave El Paso TX 79905-2709 Office Phone: 915-545-6619. E-mail: arlene.zaloznik@ttuhsc.edu.

ZAMBANINI, SANDRA LEE, construction executive; b. Wilmington, Del., Sept. 25, 1949; d. Joseph Henry and Nellie Victoria (Elliott) Z.; 1 child, Ashley Renée. Mgr. office Coffee Pause Co., Newport, Del., 1989-91; bookkeeper Wm J. Ferschke Inc., Wilmington, 1991-93; payroll agt. Artesian Water Co., Newark, Del., 1993-97; owner, pres. Reeds Constrn. and Svc. Co. Inc., New Castle, Del., 1996—. Office: Reed's Constrn & Svc Co Inc 415 Park Ave New Castle DE 19720-4793

ZAMBRANO-DUMAUAL, CARMEN MICHELLE, molecular biologist; b. Topeka, Kans., Mar. 8, 1975; d. Mario Esteban Zambrano and Norma Ellen Smith-King; m. Alfred Christopher Dumaual, Aug. 10, 2002. BS summa cum laude, Ball State U., 1995—98; MS, Purdue U., 1998—2003. Lab. technician Pathologists Associated Med. Laboratories, Muncie, Ind., 1995—98; tchg. and rsch. asst. Ind. U.-Purdue U. at Indpls. (IUPUI), 1998—2000; rsch. assoc. Eli Lilly and Co./Kelly Sci. Services, 1997—2000; assoc. biologist Eli Lilly and Co., Rsch. Technologies and Proteins divsn., 2000—02; lab. for exptl. medicine assoc. biochemist Eli Lilly and Co., Diagnostic and Exptl. Medicine, Indpls., 2002—. Course coord. Eli Lilly and Co. Immunology course, 2001—; v.p. Sigma Zeta Hon. Sci. Soc., Muncie, Ind., 1997—98, historian, 1996—98. Mem. ACLU and ICLU (Ind. Chpt.), 2000—03. Westfield Teacher's Assn. scholarship, Westfield Wash. Teacher's Assn., 1993, Undergraduate fellowship, Ball State U., 1997. Mem.: Free the West Memphis Three Support Group, Women in Sci. and Engring., Phi Beta Kappa Hon. Soc., Golden Key Nat. Honor Soc. Avocations: marathon running, community service, animal rescue, travel, skiing. Home: 5422 Barlby Dr Indianapolis IN 46237

ZAMORA, MARJORIE DIXON, retired political science educator; b. Farm Randolph, N.Y., Nov. 8, 1933; d. Wendell Hadley and Jessie (Mercer) Dixon; m. Cornelio Raul Zamora, Dec. 20, 1969; 1 child, Daniel Cornelio. BA, Earlham Coll., 1956; MA, U. Ill., 1968; postgrad., U. Ill., Chgo., 1989—. Tchr. Ridge, Sch., Godsman Sch., Stenson Sch., various cities, 1956-62; with U.S. Peace Corps, tchr. Palmares High Sch., Costa Rica, 1963-64; reporter Lerner Newspaper, Chgo., 1965; dormitory counselor U. Ill., Urbana, 1966-68, 86; instr. Chgo. City Coll., 1968-69; prof. polit. sci. Moraine Valley C.C., Palos Hills, Ill., 1969-94, prof. emeritus, 1994—. Rschr. U. Ill., Chgo., 1985-88. Author short stories; contbr. articles on Costa Rican polit. bus. cycle and economy, land reform to publs. in U.S., Cen. Am.; contbr. short stories to mags. Dir. Coalition for a U.S. Dept. of Peace, 2001—; rep. Beijing Plus Five Regional Steering Com., 1999; appointed to planning com. for a dept. of peace bill Rep. D. Kucinich. Mem. AAUW (elected-pres. Western Spring area chpt. 1999, Ill. congressional liaison 2000—), Western Springs Band and Orch. Assn. (pres. 1990-91), Am. Assn. Ret. Persons, State Cmty. Coll. Retirees Assn. Mem. Soc. Of Friends. Avocations: skiing, swimming, writing fiction, nonfiction and filmscripts, symphonic music, scuba. Home: 3820 Lawn Ave Western Springs IL 60558-1141

ZANDER, JANET ADELE, psychiatrist; b. Miles City, Mont., Feb. 19, 1950; d. Adelbert William and Valborg Constance (Buckneberg) Z.; m. Mark Richard Ellenberger, Sept. 16, 1979; 1 child, Evan David Zander Ellenberger. BA, St. Olaf Coll., 1972; MD, U. Minn., 1976. Diplomate Am. Bd. Psychiatry and Neurology. Resident in psychiatry U. Minn., Mpls., 1976-79, fellow in psychiatry, 1979-80, asst. prof. psychiatry, 1981—; staff psychiatrist St. Paul (Minn.) Regions Hosp., 1980—, dir. edn. in psychiatry, 1980-94, dir. inpatient psychiatry, 1986—, vice chair Dept. Psychiatry, 1991-96, divsn. head behavioral health, 2002. Bd. dirs. Perry Assurance. Contbr. research articles to sci. jours. Sec. Concentus Musicus Bd. Dirs., St. Paul, 1981-89; mem. property com. St. Clement's Episcopal Ch., St. Paul, 1985. Mem. Am. Psychiat. Assn., Am. Med. Women's Assn., Minn. Psychiat. Soc. (ethics com. 1985-87, women's com. 1985-87, coun. 1994-96), Minn. Med. Assn., Ramsey County Med. Soc. (bd. dirs. 1994-96). Democrat. Avocations: singing, skiing. Home: 230 Crestway Ln West Saint Paul MN 55118-4424 Office: Regions Hosp 640 Jackson St Saint Paul MN 55101-2502 E-mail: janet.a.zander@healthpartners.com.

ZANETTI, TERESA A. state representative; b. Columbus, Ga., Jan. 20, 1958; m. Gregory Zanetti; children: Daniel, Michael. BA, Harvard U., 1979; MA, St. John's Coll., 1987. Test adminstr. Army Edn. Ctrs., Augsburg, Germany, 1982—85; bur. chief N.Mex. State Dept. Regulation and Licensing, 1989—90; faculty Albuquerque Acad., 1990—97; columnist Albuquerque Tribune, 2000—02; state rep. dist. 15 N.Mex. Ho. of Reps., Santa Fe, 2002—. Mem. N.Mex. State Bd. Edn., 2001—02, [illegible] of the Yr., Greater Albuquerque C. of C., 2002. Republican. Office: State Capitol Room 202B Santa Fe NM 87503

ZANNIERI, NINA, museum director; b. Summit, N.J., Feb. 1, 1955; d. Angelo Joseph and Louise Mary (Brumm) Z.; m. Douglas M. Vogel, Oct. 29, 1994. BA, Boston Coll., 1977; postgrad., Coll. of William & Mary, 1977-78; MA, Brown U., 1980. Curatorial asst. R.I. Hist. Soc., Providence, 1980-81, asst. curator, 1981-83, curator, 1983-86; dir. Paul Revere Meml. Assn., Boston, 1986—. Gen. editor: (exhbn. catalog) Paul Revere: The Man Behind the Myth, 1988; collaborator: (house guide) A Most Magnificent Mansion; project dir.: (exhbn. catalog) Let Virtue Be A Guide To Thee, 1983 Mem. Am. Assn. Mus.'s (bd. dirs. 1999-02, vice-chair 2002-03), New Eng. Mus. Assn. (pres. 1998-02), Am. Assn. State and Local History, Phi Beta Kappa. Office: Paul Revere Meml Assn The Paul Revere House 19 North Sq Boston MA 02113-2405*

ZANUCK, LILI FINI, film director, producer; b. Leominster, Mass., Apr. 2, 1954; m. Richard Zanuck, Sept. 23, 1978. Rsch. asst. World Bank, Washington, 1970-78; office mgr. Carnation Co., L.A., 1977-78; rsch. and devel. Zanuck-Brown Co., 1978-89; co-founder, co-owner Zanuck Co., 1989—. Prodr. films Cocoon, 1985, Cocoon: The Return, 1988, Driving Miss Daisy, 1989 (Acad. award 1989), Rich in Love, 1993, Clean Slate, 1994, Wild Bill, 1995, Dvojnik, 1995, Mulholland Falls, 1996, True Crime, 1999, Reign of Fire, 2002; dir. film Rush, 1991, TV miniseries From the Earth to the Moon (Part 3), 1998. Mem.: Calif. Film Commn. Office: The Zanuck Company 9465 Wilshire Blvd Beverly Hills CA 90212-2612*

ZAPFFE, NINA BYROM, retired elementary education educator; b. Independence, Mo., Aug. 17, 1925; d. Richmond Douglas and Nina Belle (Howell) Byrom; m. Robert Glenn Fessler, June 25, 1946 (dec. June 1947); 1 child, Robert Glenn Fessler Zapffe; m. Fred Zapffe, July 1, 1952 (dec. Dec. 1999); children: Paul Douglas, Carl Raymond. BA, So. Meth. U., 1946. Fin. sec. Tyler St. Meth. Ch., Dallas, 1948-49; tchr. Dallas Ind. Sch. Dist., 1949-52, Norman (Okla.) Pub. Schs., 1966-74; cert. chief reader for GED Writing Skills Test Part II GED Testing Svc., Am. Coun. on Edn., Washington, 1990-98. Adv. com. (Acad. Resource Ctr.) Moore-Norman Tech. Ctr., 1988—. Adv. bd. Norman Salvation Army, 1978-90, chmn., 1986; organizer, historian Norman Salvation Army Womens Aux., 1983-2000, pres., 1985; organizer, past pres. Norman Literacy Coun., 1976—; organizing com., past pres. Norman Interfaith Coun., 1974-93; organizing com., past treas. Friends of the Norman Libr., 1979—; mem. McFarlin Meml. United Meth. Ch., historian 2-in-1 Sunday Sch. class, 1990-2002, lay leader, 1980-81, adminstrv. bd., 2001-2004. Named Woman of Yr., Norman Bus. and Profl. Women, 1999; named to Literacy Hall of Fame, Pioneer Libr. Sys., Norman, 1995; recipient medal of appreciation, SAR, 2002. Mem. DAR (regent Black Beaver chpt. 1998-2000, state literacy chmn. 2000-2002, sec. 2002-2004), Nat. Soc. Daus. 1812 (state treas. 1996-2000, sec. 2002-2004), Old Regime Study Club (pres. 1998-99), Coterie Club (pres. 1996, 2002), Delta Delta Delta Alumnae. Republican. Avocation: genealogy. Home: 2717 Walnut Rd Norman OK 73072-6940

ZARCONE, DARLENE, accountant; b. Smithtown, N.Y., Sept. 28, 1973; BS, St. John's U., 1995. CPA N.Y. Mgr. Audit McGladrey & Pullen, N.Y.C., 1995—. Office: McGladrey & Pullen LLP 750 3d Ave 9th Fl New York NY 10017*

ZARGHAMI, CYMA, broadcast executive; m. George Zarghami; 1 child, Liam. Exec. v.p. Nickelodeon, gen. mgr., 1996—. Directs co. initiatives Big Help and Kids Pick the Pres. Campaign; launched Nick Jr., SNICK, Nicktoons. Office: Nickelodeon 1515 Broadway New York NY 10036

ZARK, JENNA, playwright, freelance writer; b. Bklyn., Aug. 17, 1954; d. Max and Faye (Greenberg) Z.; m. Mitchell David Kowitz, Sept. 2, 1979 (div. June 1993); 1 child, Joshua Gabriel; m. Peter Bullard Budd, Oct. 8, 1995. BS cum laude, Emerson Coll., 1976. Staff and freelance writer Scholastic mag., N.Y.C., 1987-91; playwright Circle Repertory Theatre, N.Y.C., 1994, Illusion Theatre, Mpls., co-author new commn., 1995-96. Author: (plays) Burnt House, 1990 (James Chambers award 1990), A Body of Water, 1994 (produced by Circle Repertory Co.), Fort Snelling: Wilderness Edge; co-author: Bridges of Stone, Fresh Ink series, Illusion Theater, The Magic Dreidels, Minn. Jewish Theatre, The World to Come (excerpt), Jewish Women's Theatre Project, In Coya's House, Great Am. History Theatre. Artists fellow Ind. Arts Commn., 1980, Minn. Arts Bd., 1994; advancement grantee McKnight Found., Minn., 1994. Mem. AFTRA, Dramatists Guild, Women in Comm., Chgo. Dramatists Workshop (playwright), Playwrights Ctr. (core.). Jewish. Avocations: walking, biking, family time. E-mail: thezark@bitstream.net.

ZARKY, KAREN JANE, newspaper publisher; b. St. Louis, Jan. 20, 1948; d. Herbert Lee Lawrence and Alice Ruth (Harrison) Lawrence Robison; m. Robert Gerald McCoy, Feb. 15, 1964 (div. Feb. 1982); 1 child, Karen; m. A.A. Zarky, Aug. 29, 1986. BA, Maryville Coll., St. Louis, 1988. Asst. to dir. fin. Clayton Mark Corp., Chgo., 1966-68; office mgr. A.R. Musical Enterprises, Columbus, Ind., 1969-75; owner, pres. Antique Galleries Inc., Louisville, 1975-81; sales mgr. Rainbow Graphics and Displays, St. Louis, 1981-87; pub., pres. Senior Circuit, Inc., St. Louis, 1987—; editor Francis Bus. Rev., St. Louis, 1997-98; co-pub. Todays Seniors.com, 1999—. Tchr. St. Louis C.C., 1987-89; pub. St. Louis Women on the Move, Future Plans Mo. Bd. dirs. Greeley Community Ctr., St. Louis, 1988-92; mem. reorgn. com. United Way, St. Louis, 1988-90; sec. Housing Options Provided for the Elderly, 1991-97; v.p. mktg. and comm. Women's Consortium, 1993. Mem. Nat. Assn. Women Bus. Owners, Women in Comm., Internat. Assn. Bus. Communicators, Mo. Press Women (pres. Gateway chpt. 1993-95, state treas. 1995—), Mid-Am. Mature Pubs. Assn. (sec.-treas., pres.-elect, pres.). Avocations: painting, sewing, reading.

ZARRO, JANICE ANNE, lawyer; b. Newark, June 30, 1947; BA, Rutgers U., 1969; JD, IIT-Chgo.-Kent Coll. Law, 1973. Bar: Pa. 1974. Counsel jud. com. U.S. Ho. Reps., Washington, 1973-77; profl. staff mem. counsel labor and human resources com. U.S. Senate, Washington, 1977-80; dir. Avon Products, Inc., N.Y.C., 1980-81, Washington, 1982-86, v.p., 1986-90; pres. The Novus Group, Inc., 1990-92; dir. fed. affairs Mallinckrodt Med., 1992—, v.p., 1993-94; v.p. govt. affairs Worldwide Mallinckrodt Inc., 1994-2000. Gen. counsel Nat. Italian-Am. Found., 1989-96, chair bd. trustees, 1996-99; mem. Bus. Govt. Rels. Coun., Washington, 1987—; past chair Women's Fgn. Policy Group. Past chmn. Nat. Capital chpt. Multiple Sclerosis Soc. Recipient Leadership Recognition award Nat. Women's Econ. Alliance, 1984. Home: 402 Rio Terra Venice FL 34285-2953 E-mail: j6a3n@yahoo.com.

ZEALEY, SHARON JANINE, lawyer; b. St. Paul, Aug. 30, 1959; d. Marion Edward and Freddie Zealey. BS, Xavier U. of La., 1981; JD, U. Cin., 1984. Bar: Ohio 1984; U.S. Dist. Ct. (so. dist.) Ohio 1985; U.S. Ct. Appeals (6th cir.) 1990; U.S. Supreme Ct. 1990. Law clk. U.S. Atty. for S. Dist. of Ohio, Cin., 1982; trust adminstr. Firstar Bank, Cin., 1984-86; atty. UAW Legal Svcs., Cin., 1986-88; assoc. Manley, Burke, Lipton & Fischer, Cin., 1988-91; mng. atty. and dep. atty. gen. Ohio Atty. Gen. Office, Cin., 1991-95; asst. U.S. atty. criminal div. for So. Dist. Ohio U.S. Attys. Office, Cin., 1995-97; United States atty. So. Dist. Ohio, Cin., 1997—2001; ptnr. Blank Rome LLP, 2001—. Adj. instr. lawU. Cin., 1997—; mem. U.S. Atty. Gen.'s Adv. Com., 1999—2001, chair civil rights subcom., 2001; mem. merit selection com. Sixth Cir. Ct. of Appeals Bankruptcy Ct., 1992—96, 2003. Mem. commn. Cin. Cmty. Action Now, 2001—; commr. Tall Stacks Commn., City of Cin., 1990—94, Mayor's Commn. on Children, City of

Cin., 1992—94; mem. equal employment adv. rev. panel City of Cin., 1989—91; trustee, bd. visitors U. Cin. Coll. Law, 1992—; trustee Legal Aid Soc. Cin., 1987—92. Named Career Woman of Achievement, Cin. YWCA, 1988; recipient Disting. Alumni award, Friends of Women's Studies, U. Cin., 2001, Theodore M. Berry award for outstanding achievement in politics and in svc. to cmty., Cin. chpt. NACCP, 1998, Nicholas Longworth III Alumni Achievement award for disting. pub. svc., U. Cin. Coll. Law, 1997. Mem. Black Lawyers Assn. of Cin. (pres. 1989-91, round table 1988-), Legal Aid Soc. (sec. 1991-92), ABA, Fed. Bar Assn., Ohio Bar Assn., Nat. Bar Assn. (bd. govs. 1988-1990, Mem. of Yr. region VI 1990), Cin. Bar Assn. (trustee 1989-94), Cin. CAN Commn. Democrat. Episcopalian. Office: 1700 PNC Ctr 201 E 5th St Cincinnati OH 45202 E-mail: zealey@blankRome.com.

ZEBI, SANDRA, artist; b. Sao Paulo, Brazil, Mar. 23, 1960; d. Fernando and Yvonne Landi (Visconti) Zeminian; children: Zebi Zeminian Birnbaum, Gabi Zeminian Birnbaum. BA, U. Mackenzie, Brazil, 1982; student in Architecture, Westminister Coll., London, Eng., 1983—84; student in Graphic Design, Santa Monica Coll. Artist Zebi Designs, L.A., 1990—. Prin. works include sculpture, Inglewood City Hall, Calif.

ZEBROWITZ, LESLIE ANN, psychology educator; b. Detroit, Nov. 8, 1944; d. Aaron Harry and Esther (Milgrom) Z.; m. A. Verne McArthur (div. July 1988); children: Caleb Jonathan McArthur, Loren Zachary McArthur. BA, U. Wis., 1966; MS, Yale U., 1968, PhD, 1970. Asst. prof. psychology Brandeis U., Waltham, Mass., 1970-76, assoc. prof., 1976-82, prof., 1982—, chmn. dept., 1986-91, Manuel Yellen prof. social rels., 1989—. Vis. scholar Henry Murray Rsch. Ctr. Radcliffe Coll., Cambridge, Mass., 1991-92, vis Erskine fellow, U. Canterbury, 1996; program dir. social psychology, NSF, Arlington, Va., 1994-95. Author: Social Perception, 1991, Reading Faces, 1997; editor: (with Gillian Rhodes) Facial Attractiveness, 2003; contbr. numerous articles to sci. jours. Ford. Found. faculty fellow, 1973-74; rsch. grantee NIMH, 1975-81, 87-97, NSF, 1997-2002. Fellow Am. Psychol. Assn., Am. Psychol. Soc. (charter), Soc. for Exptl. Social Pychology, Ea. Psychol. Assn., Phi Beta Kappa. Office: Brandeis U Dept Of Psychology Waltham MA 02454

ZEDLER, JOY BUSWELL, ecological sciences educator; b. Sioux Falls, S.D., Oct. 15, 1943; d. Francis H. and Charlotte (Johnson) Buswell; m. Paul H. Zedler, June 26, 1965; children: Emily and Sarah (twins). BS, Augustana Coll., 1964; MS, U. Wis., 1966, PhD, 1968. Instr. U. Mo., Columbia, 1968-69; prof. San Diego State U., 1969-97; Aldo Leopold prof. restoration ecology, arboretum, botany U. Wis., Madison, 1998—. Mem. Nat. Wetland Tech. Com., Water Sci. Tech. Bd. Nat. Rsch. Coun., 1991-94; dir. Pacific Estuarine Rsch. Lab., 1985—, Coastal and Marine Inst., 1991-93; gov. bd. The Nature Conservancy, 1995—; trustee Environ. Def. Fund, 1998—. Author: Ecology of Southern California Coastal Wetlands, 1982, Salt Marsh Restoration, 1984; co-author: A Manual for Assessing Natural and Restored Wetlands, 1990, Ecology of Tijuana Estuary, 1992, Tidal Wetland Restoration, 1996; editor: Handbook for Restoring Tidal Wetlands, 2000. Fellow San Diego Natural History Mus., mem. Ecol. Soc. Am. (mem. pub. affairs com. 1988-90), Soc. Wetlands Scientists, Soc. Ecol. Restoration. Achievements include pioneering studies of impacts of freshwater inflows to coastal wetlands in southern [illegible] contributions to understanding of coastal wetland functioning; development of methods for improving restoration projects in wetlands; identification of shortcomings of wetland restoration projects; role of diversity in the function restored ecosystems, improving the science of restoration ecology. Office: U Wis Botany Dept Madison WI 53706

ZEE, PHYLLIS C. physician, educator, researcher; b. Hong Kong, June 27, 1954; came to U.S., 1973; d. William and King Di (Wong) Cheung; m. Benjamin Zee; children: David, Caroline, Alex. BA, Mills Coll., 1976; PhD, Chgo. Med. Sch., 1980, MD, 1983. Diplomate Am. Bd. Psychiatry and Neurology, Am. Bd. Med. Examiners, Am. Bd. Sleep Medicine. NIH postdoctoral fellow Northwestern U., Evanston, Ill., 1987-89, asst. prof. neurobiology and neurology Chgo., 1989-95, assoc. prof., 1996—2000, prof., 2001—; dir. Sleep Ctr. Northwestern Meml. Hosp., Chgo., 1991—. Mem. adv. bd. Enlightened Tech., Md., 1994—; mem. bd. advisors Jour. Biol. Rhythms, 1994—; bd. dirs. Nat. Sleep Found., 2003—; mem. NIH study sect. Contbr. articles to profl. jours. Fellow Buelher Ctr. on Aging, 1995—, Brookdale Found., 1994; grantee NIH, 1994—. Fellow: Am. Sleep Disorders Assn.; mem.: Am. Neurol. Assn., Soc. Biol. Rhythms, Soc. for Neuroscience, Am. Acad. Neurology. Office: Northwestern U 710 N Lake Shore Dr Chicago IL 60611-3006

ZEFF, OPHELIA HOPE, lawyer; b. Oak Park, Ill., Aug. 19, 1934; d. Bernard Allen and Esther (Levinsohn) Gurvis; m. David Zeff, Dec. 29, 1957 (div. 1983); children: Sally Lyn Zeff Propper, Betsy Zeff Russell, Ellen, Adam; m. John Canterbury Davis, Sept. 18, 1987. BA, Calif. State U., 1956; JD, U. Pacific, 1975. Bar: Calif. 1975. Reporter Placerville (Calif.) Mountain Dem., 1956-57, Salinas Californian, 1957-59; corr. Modesto (Calif.) Bee, 1962-64; atty. ALRB, Sacramento, 1975-76, Yolo County Counsel, Woodland, Calif., 1976-78, Law Office of O.H. Zeff, Woodland, 1978-85; employee rels. officer Yolo County, 1985-87; ptnr. Littler, Mendelson, Fastiff, Tichy & Mathiason, Sacramento, 1987-98, Atkinson, Andelson, Loya, Ruud & Romo, Sacramento, 1998—. Mem. Vallejo (Calif.) Sch. Bd., 1971-74, pres., 1974; mem. Woodland Libr. Bd., 1982; v.p. LWV, Vallejo, 1972; mem. LWV, Sacramento, 1987—. Recipient Am. Jurisprudence Lawyer Coop. Pub., 1974. Mem. Sacramento County Bar, Sacramento Women Lawyers, Indsl. Rels. Assn. No. Calif., Traynor Soc. (life). Democrat. Jewish. Avocations: hiking, skiing, biking, reading, traveling. Office: Atkinson Andelson Loya Ruud & Romo 555 Capitol Mall Ste 645 Sacramento CA 95814-4502

ZEIGLER, REY, dean; b. Longmeadow, Mass., May 14, 1955; d. Shawn Patrick and Helen Mary Michaels; m. Shawn Robert Zeigler, Feb. 14, 1990; children: Jason Henry, Megan Katherine. BA, Trinity Coll., 1976; MA, Duke U., 1981, PhD, 1985. Asst. prof. St. Mary's Coll., Notre Dame, Ind., 1986—88; assoc. prof. U. Notre Dame, Notre Dame, Ind., 1990—93; prof. Meriks U., Roseburg, Oreg., 1993—2000, dean, 2000—. Mem.: Oreg. Tchg. Assn. Roman Catholic. Avocations: ping pong/table tennis, yoga, basket weaving. Office: Meriks U 442 West Riverside Dr Roseburg OR 97470-3068

ZEILIG, NANCY MEEKS, writer, editor; b. Nashville, Apr. 28, 1943; d. Edward Harvey and Nancy Evelyn (Self) Meeks; m. Lanny Kenneth Fielder, Aug. 20, 1964 (div. Dec. 1970); m. Charles Elliot Zeilig, Jan. 6, 1974 (div. Dec. 1989); 1 child, Sasha Rebecca. BA, Birmingham-So. Coll., 1964; postgrad., Vanderbilt U., 1971-73. Editorial asst. Reuben H. Donnelley, N.Y.C., 1969-70; asst. editor Vanderbilt U., Nashville, 1970-74; editor U. Minn., St. Paul, 1975; asst. editor McGraw-Hill Inc., Mpls., 1975 76; mng. editor Denver mag., 1976-80; editor Jour. Am. Water Works Assn., Denver, 1981—99; owner Nancy Zeilig Writing & Editing, Denver, 2000—. Editor, co-pub.: WomanSource, 1982, rev. edit., 1984; contbr. articles to trade and consumer mags. Co-chair arts adv. com. Denver Sch. Arts, 1994-96. Avocations: travel, reading British and Am. fiction, cooking. Subject of NBC News documentary Women Like Us, 1980. Office Phone: 303-758-7750. E-mail: nzeilig@earthlink.net.

ZEILINGER, ELNA RAE, elementary educator, gifted-talented education educator; b. Tempe, Ariz., Mar. 24, 1937; d. Clayborn Eddie and Ruby Elna (Laird) Simpson; m. Philip Thomas Zeilinger, June 13, 1970; children: Shari, Chris. BA in Edn., Ariz. State U., 1958, MA in Edn., 1966, EdS, 1980. Bookkeeper First Nat. Bank of Tempe, 1955-56; with registrar's office Ariz. State U., 1956-58; piano tchr., recreation dir. City of Tempe; tchr. Thew Sch., Tempe, 1958-61; elem. tchr. Mitchell Sch., Tempe, 1962-74, intern prin., 1976, personnel intern, 1977; specialist gifted edn. Tempe Elem. Schs., Tempe, 1977-86; elem. tchr. Holdeman Sch., Tempe, 1986-89; tchr. grades 1-12 and adult reading, lang. arts, English Zeilinger Tutoring Svc., 1991—. Grad. asst. ednl. adminstrn., Iota Workshop coordinator Ariz. State U., 1978; presenter Ariz. Gifted Conf., 1978-81; condr. survey of gifted programs, 1980; reporter pub. rels. Tempe Sch. Dist., 1978-80, Access com. for gifted programs, 1981-83. Author: Leadership Role of the Principal in Gifted Programs: A Handbook, 1980; Classified Personnel Handbook, 1977, also reports, monographs and paintings. Active Tempe Hist. Assn., liaison, 1975, Tempe Art League; freedom train com. Ariz. Bicentennial Commn., 1975-76; bd. dirs. Maple Property Owners Assn., 1994-2002; storyteller Tempe Hist. Mus., 1997—; dir. pagentry Daus. of the Nile, 2002-03. Named Outstanding Leader in Elem. and Secondary Schs., 1976' Ariz. Cattle Growers scholar, 1954-55; Elks scholar, 1954-55; recipient Judges award Tempe Art League, 1970, Best of Show, Scottsdale Art League, 1976. Mem.: Daus. of the Nile (dir. pageantry 2002—03). Democrat. Congregationalist.

ZEISER, SUSIE FEHRENBACHER, psychologist, researcher; b. Effingham, Ill., Dec. 16, 1939; d. Ralph Joseph and Faye (McKinney) Fehrenbacher; m. Leslie Howard Gargan, June 23, 1962 (div. Aug. 1966); 1 child: Carey Elizabeth Gargan-Zeiser-Dix; m. Curtis Paul Zeiser, Sept. 9, 1967; 1 child, Benton. BA in English Lang. and Lit., Calif. State U., 1962; MA in Spl. Edn., Northeastern Ill. U., 1978; cert. advanced study, Nat. Coll. Edn., 1981. Cert. sch. psychologist, Ill., N.Y. English tchr. Grove Jr. H.S., Elk Grove Village, Ill., 1962-63; mem. English dept. faculty Evanston (Ill.) Twp. H.S., 1965-71, 80-81, psychologist, 1987; staff Northwestern U. Sch. Edn., Evanston, 1971-72, faculty lectr., 1972-76; adj. faculty Nat. Coll. Edn., Evanston, 1977-79; fellow Wis. Ctr. for Edn. Rsch., Madison, 1979—97; rsch. specialist Wis. Ctr. for Edn. Rsch., U. Wis., Madison, 1997—. Tchg. asst. ednl. psychology U. Ill., fall, 1992-94; cons., presenter in field. Author: Handbook of Gifted Education in Illinois, 1976; co-author: Handbook of Gifted Education, 1997, Current Research on Occupations and Professions, 1997; contbr. articles to profl. jours. State pres. gifted divsn. Coun. Exceptional Children, 1976-78; commn. mem. Higher Edn. Dirs. Gifted Edn., 1975-76; task force State of Ill. Bd. Edn. Spl. Edn., 1978-80; pres. Ill. Coun. for the Gifted, 1974-76; bd. dirs. The Chgo. Ensemble, 1988-92, LWV, 1969-73; adv. bd. Ptnrs. in Edn., Chgo., State of Ill. grantee, 1974, 76; named one of Outstanding Young Women of Am., 1978. Mem. AAUW, Nat. Assn. Sch. Psychologists, Am. Edn. Rsch. Assn., Am. Psychol. Assn., Am. Sociological Asssn., Nature Conservancy. Avocations: cooking, gardening.

ZEITELHACK, GLORIA JEANNE, artist; b. San Diego, June 24, 1952; d. Leon Mathew and Claire Irene (Morel) Morissette; m. Don Roger Zeitelhack, Sept. 3, 1977. Artist, Tomahawk, Wis., Alto, N.Mex.; owner Many Moons Jewelry Gallery, Ruidoso, N.Mex. Inventor mother of pearl shell landscapes for jewelery, 1977— (technique copyrighted 2001). Avocations: art, music, dance. Home and Office: PO Box 419 Alto NM 88312-0419 : Many Moons Jewelry Gallery Time Sq 2501 Sudderth Ruidoso NM 88345

ZEITLIN, LAURIE, printing company executive, BA in Econs., Duke U.; MBA in Fin., U. Pa. With Touche Ross & Co., Deloitte & Touche LLP; dir. info. tech., sr. mgr. application devel. Home Depot, Inc., Atllanta, v.p. info. tech.; sr. v.p., chief info. officer Kinko's Inc., Dallas, 2003—. Office: Kinkos 13155 Noel Rd Ste 1600 Dallas TX 75240

ZEITLIN, MARIANNE LANGNER, writer; b. Toronto, Can., Mar. 3, 1928; arrived in US, 1947; d. Mordecai and Anne Langner; m. Zvi Zeitlin, May 5, 1951; children: Hillel, Leora. Author: (novels) Mira's Passage, 1986, Next of Kin, 1991, Motherless Child, (plays) A Letter to Doris Lessing.

ZEITLIN, MARILYN AUDREY, museum director; b. Newark, July 14, 1941; d. Sidney M. and Theresa Feigenblatt) Litchfield; widowed; children: Charles C. Sweedler, Milo Sweedler. Student, Vanderbilt U., 1963-65; AB in Humanities, Harvard U., 1966, MA in Teaching of English, 1967; postgrad., Cornell U., 1971-74. Dir. Ctr. Gallery, Bucknell U., Lewisburg, Pa., 1975-78; Freedman Gallery, Albright Coll., Reading, Pa., 1978-81; Anderson Gallery, Va. Commonwealth U., Richmond, 1981-87; curator, acting co-dir. Contemporary Arts Mus., Houston, 1987-90; exec. dir. Washington Projects for the Arts, 1990-92; dir. Univ. Art Mus., Ariz. State U., Tempe, 1992—. Juror Dallas Mus. of Arts, McKnight Awards, Mpls.; grant evaluator IMS; grant evaluator, panelist NEH; lectr., cons. in field. Editor, contbr. essays to art publs. Bd. dirs. Cultural Alliance Washington; curator, commr. for U.S. for 1995 Venice Biennale. Samuel H. Kress fellow, 1972-73. Mem. Assn. Coll. and Univ. Mus. and Galleries (v.p. 1986-88), Am. Assn. Mus., Coll. Art Assn. (U.S. commr. Venice Biennale 1995). Office: Ariz State U Art Mus PO Box 872911 Tempe AZ 85287-2911

ZEKMAN, PAMELA LOIS (MRS. FREDRIC SOLL), reporter; b. Chgo., Oct. 22, 1944; d. Theodore Nathan and Lois Jane (Bernstein) Z.; m. Fredric Soll, Nov. 29, 1975. BA, U. Calif. at Berkeley, 1965. Social worker Dept. Public Aid Cook County, Chgo., 1965-66; reporter City News Bur., Chgo., 1966-70, Chgo. Tribune, 1970-75, Chgo. Sun-Times, 1975-81; investigative reporter Sta. WBBM-TV, Chgo., 1981—. Recipient Pulitzer Prize awarded to Chicago Tribune for gen. local reporting on vote fraud series, 1973; Community Service award for vote fraud series UPI, 1972; Feature Series award for nursing home abuses series AP, 1971; Pub. Service award for slumlord series UPI, 1973; Newswriting award AP, 1973; In Depth Reporting award for police brutality series AP, 1974; Investigative Reporting awards Inland Daily Press Assn., 1974, 78; Investigative Reporting award for series on city waste AP, 1975; Pulitzer Prize for pub. service for series on hosp. abuses, 1976; Investigative Reporting award for series on baby selling, 1976; Pub. Service award for series on currency exchange abuses UPI, 1976; Investigative Reporting award for series on abuses in home for retarded children AP, 1977; Soc. Midland Authors Golden Rake award; UPI Public Service award; Ill. AP award; Nat. Headliners Club award; Sweepstakes award for Mirage Tavern investigative project, 1978; Nat. Disting. Service award for series on med. abuses in abortion clinics Sigma Delta Chi, 1979; named Journalist of Yr. No. Ill. U., 1979; recipient George Foster Peabody Broadcasting award, 1982, 85, RTNDA Investigative Reporting award, 1983, DuPont Columbia award 1982, 87. Office: WBBM-TV 630 N McClurg Ct Chicago IL 60611-4495

ZEKMAN, TERRI MARGARET, graphic designer; b. Chgo., Sept. 13, 1950; d. Theodore Nathan and Lois (Bernstein) Z.; m. Alan Daniels, Apr. 12, 1980; children: Jesse Logan, Dakota Caitlin. BFA, Washington U., St. Louis, 1971; postgrad, Art Inst. Chgo., 1974-75. Graphic designer (on retainer) greeting cards and related products Recycled Paper Products Co., Chgo., 1970—, Jillson Roberts, Inc., Calif.; apprenticed graphic designer Helmuth, Obata & Kassabaum, St. Louis, 1970-71; graphic designer Container Corp., Chgo., 1971; graphic designer, art dir., photographer Cuerden Advt. Design, Denver, 1971-74; art dir. D'Arcy, McManus & Masius Advt., Chgo., 1975-76; freelance graphic designer Chgo., 1976-77; art dir. Garfield Linn Advt., Chgo., 1977-78; graphic designer Keiser Design Group, Van Noy & Co., Los Angeles, 1978-79; owner and operator graphic design studio Los Angeles, 1979—. Art and photography tchr. Ctr. for Early Edn., L.A., 1996—, Buckley Sch., Sherman Oaks, 1996—; 3d grade tchr. asst., 1999—. Recipient cert. of merit St. Louis Outdoor Poster Contest, 1970, Denver Art Dirs. Club, 1973

ZELBY, RACHEL, realtor; b. Sosnowiec, Poland, May 6, 1930; came to U.S., 1955; d. Herschel Kupfermintz and Sarah Rosenblatt; m. Leon W. Zelby, Dec. 28, 1954; children: Laurie Susan, Andrew Stephen. Student, U. Pa., 1955, Realtors' Inst., Norman, Okla., 1974; grad., Realtors Inst., Oklahoma City, 1978. Lic. realtor, broker, Okla.; cert. residential specialist, Okla. Realtor, broker, ptnr. Realty World Norman Heritage, 1973-81; realtor, broker Century 21 Elite Realty, Norman, 1981—, residential specialist, 1986—. Mem. Jr. Svc. League, Norman, 1980—; charter mem. Assistance League Norman, 1970—; bd. dirs. Juvenile Svcs., Inc., Norman, 1975-76; bd. viss. Coll. Fine Arts U. Okla., 1992—. Mem. Nat. Assn. Realtors, Norman Bd. Realtors, Women's Coun. Realtors (treas. 1985), U. Okla. Women's Assn. (past pres.), Norman C. of C., LWV. Avocations: aerobics, contract bridge, theatre, music, travel. Home: 1009 Whispering Pines Dr Norman OK 73072-6912 Office: Century 21 Elite Realty 223 N Interstate Dr Norman OK 73069 Personal E-mail: rachelz@telepath.com.

ZELDES, EDITH R. freelance journalist; b. N.Y.C., Feb. 29, 1928; d. William Shakespeare and Harriet Edith (Pelikan) Herrmann; m. Benjamin Zeldes, July 4, 1948; children: Mildred R. Solomon, Hazel A., Beth E. Margulies, Ross E. BA in Fine Arts, U. Conn., 1948; MEd, Ctrl. Conn. State U., New Britain, 1970. Cert. advanced pilot New Britain Power Squadron chpt. U.S. Power Squadron. Freelance journalist. Writer features for Jour. Inquirer, Middletown Press, Imprint Publs., Life Publs. The (New Britain) Herald, The Hartford Courant. Sunday sch. tchr. Temple Sinai, Newington, Conn., Temple B'Nai Israel, New Britain, Conn.; producer, dir., publicist, booking agt., tchr. Newington Children's Theatre; dir., producer, actress, past pres. Theatre Newington On Stage; dir. Tri-Town Players, Vernon, Rockville, Conn.; dir. Aetna Players, Hartford, Conn. Mem. Theatre Newington On Stage (hon. life). Avocations: travel, boating, reading, theater. Home: 107 Lake Shore Blvd Stafford Springs CT 06076-3439 Office: 1268 Main St Newington CT 06111-3038

ZELICKSON, SUE, newspaper and cookbook editor, television reporter and host, food consultant; b. Mpls., Sept. 13, 1934; d. Harry M. and Bernice (Gross) Zipperman; m. Alvin S. Zelickson, Aug. 21, 1956; children— Barry M., Brian D. B.S. in Edn., U. Minn., 1956. Cert. elem. tchr., S.C., Minn. Tchr. various schs. Mpls., S.C., Golden Valley, Minn., 1956-79; writer, editor, columnist Mpls.-St. Paul Mag., 1980—, Buylines, Mpls., 1984— ; TV-radio reporter Sta. WCCO-KSTP, Mpls, 1980—, Lifestyles with Sue Zelickson Sta. WCCO cable; restaurant developer, cons. Mpls., 1978— ; v.p. Passage Tours, Mpls., 1984-88. Coordinator, editor: Much Ado About Food, 1978; Minnesota Heritage Cookbook, 1979; Lee Ann Chin's Chinese Cuisine, 1981; Collins Back Room Cooking Secrets, 1981; The Governor's Table Cookbook, 1981; Chocolate Days & Chocolate Nights, 1982; Food for Show, Food on the Go, 1983; Wild Rice Star of The North, 1985; Look What's Cooking Now, 1985. Contbr. articles to Sun Newspaper, Post Publs., Mpls., Tribune. Public relations, promoter, fundraiser Mpls. Boys & Girls Club, Mpls. Inst. Arts, Hennepin County Med. Soc. Aux., Ronald McDonald House, Bonaventure Mall, Women's Assn. Minn. Symphony Orchestra, Council Jewish Women, Mt. Sinai Hosp., Brandeis U. Women, Minn. Opera Assn., Guthrie Theatre, Sholom Home, Am. Cancer Soc., M.S. Soc., March of Dimes, Am. Heart Assn.; bd. dirs. U. Minn. Alumni Bd., Golden Valley State Bank. Recipient Outstanding Achievement award There's Living Proof Am. Cancer Soc., Duluth, Minn., 1984; Outstanding Achievement award Boys & Girls Club Minn., 1984. Mem. Nat. Council Jewish Women, Women's Assn. Minn. Orch., numerous others. Avocations: reading, travel; writing; painting. Home and Office: 101 [illegible] Dr Minneapolis MN 55422-5209

ZELIN, MADELEINE, think-tank executive; Prof. History and East Asian Langs. and Cultures Columbia U., dir. East Asian Inst., dir. Columbia East Asian Nat. Resource Ctr. Mem. adv. bd. Jour. Chinese Law, Chinese History Assn., bd. dirs. Chinese Bus. History Soc., curriculum com., sub. com. East Asian Langs. Presenter in field. Office: East Asian Inst Columbia U Mail Code 3333 420 W 118th St New York NY 10027-7213

ZELL, JOSEPHINE MAY, retired language educator; b. Harwood, Lancashire, England, Apr. 26, 1934; d. Joseph Henry Howe and Emily Emma Herod; m. Robert Zell, Apr. 17, 1968; children: Rosemary Thrun, Philip. BA with honors in Eng. Lang. and Lit., U. Manchester, England, 1955; MA in Latin, U. Wis., 1989. Chair Eng. dept. Milham Ford Sch., Oxford, England, 1964—68; lectr. Eng. U. Wis., Milw., 1968—71; tchr. Eng. Madison (Wis) Met. Sch. Dist., 1977—97; tchr. Latin dept. West H.S., Madison Sch. Dist., 1992—97. Author: (poetry) The Curtain Rises, 1993. Mem.: Am. Assn. Univ. Women. Methodist. Home: 3833 D Daystar Rd Madison WI 53704

ZELLER, MARILYNN KAY, retired librarian; b. Scottsbluff, Nebr., Mar. 1, 1940; d. William Harold and Dorothy Elizabeth (Wilkins) Richards; m. Robert Jerome Zeller, May 21, 1966; children: Kevin Jerome and Renae Kay. BS, Calvary Bible Coll., 1985; MLS, U. Mo., Columbia, 1989. Cert. libr. File clk. Waddell & Reed, Kansas City, Mo., 1962-65; payroll clk. Century Fin. Co., Kansas City, Mo., 1965-67, Percy Kent Bag Co., Independence, Mo., 1968-70; accounts receivable Swansons on the Pla, Kansas City, 1971-73; clk. casualty ins. Mill Mutuals, Kansas City, 1977-80; registrar's asst. Calvary Bible Coll., Kansas City, 1980-85, libr. asst., 1985-88, asst. libr., 1988-89, head libr., 1989—96. Chairperson libr. com. Calvary Bible Coll., Kansas City, 1989-96; libr. rep. Friends of the Hilda Kroeker Libr., Kansas City, 1989-96. Author: History of the Christian Librarian's Association, 1989. Mem. Christian Librs. Assn. Avocations: walking, reading, crocheting, sewing, swimming. Home: 401 13th Ave N Greenwood MO 64034-9750

ZELLER, SHIRLEY EVELYN, manufacturing executive; b. Linton, N.D., Sept. 21, 1937; d. Gordon Towne and Evelyn (Green) Ward; m. William V. Zeller, Aug. 10, 1957; children: Greg Alan, William Lee, Timothy Neil. AA in Gen. Bus., Gen. Studies, Jackson (Mich.) C.C., 1983; BA in Mgmt. of Human Resources, Spring Arbor (Mich.) U., 1984. Sec. Consumers Power Co., Jackson, 1959-66; sec., bus. mgr. Gisler, Howell & Simms, Kansas City, Mo., 1966-67; exec. sec. Commonwealth Assocs., Jackson, 1967-71, Hayes Albion Industries, Jackson, 1971-75; supr. external auditing Gilbert/Commonwealth, Jackson, 1975-89; mgr. quality assurance Constrn. Technologies, Jackson, 1989-90; sr. quality assurance engr. Mactec, San Diego, 1990-91; mgr. compliance mgmt. Westinghouse Idaho Nuclear Co., Idaho Falls, Idaho, 1991-94; mgr. quality Lockheed Idaho Techs. Co., Idaho Falls, 1994-98; mgr. quality assurance Babcock & Wilcox Tech. Co., Richland, Wash., 1998—2000; mgr. quality BWX Tech., Miamisburg, Ohio, 2000—. Commr. Mich. Transp. Commn., Lansing, 1985-91; candidate for state senate, 1986. Recipient Athena award Oldsmobile and C. of C., Jackson, Profl. Achievement award Spring Arbor Coll. Alumni, 1991, Susan B. Anthony award Jackson Y Ctr.; named Alumnae of the Yr. Jackson C.C. Mem. LWV (nat. nominating com. 1996-98), Bus. and Profl. Women (Mich. pres. 1983-84, nat. legis. com. 1989-92, Idaho pres. 1996), Jackson C. of C. (chair legis. com. 1988-91). Avocations: golf, bowling. Home: 1104 Woodknolls Dr West Carrollton OH 45449-2485

ZELLICK, SANDRA ZELDA, psychotherapist; b. Everett, Mass., Oct. 26, 1936; d. Louis Herman and Lillian Ethel (Brown) Z.; m. Norman W. Beberman, Aug. 25, 1957 (div. Feb. 1985); children: Ellen, Julie, David, Laura. BA, Brandeis U., 1957; MEd, Harvard U., 1958; MBA, Western New Eng. Coll., 1980; MS, Nova U., 1988, PhD, 1993. Lic. mental health counselor; cert. family mediator Fla. Supreme Ct., cert. hypnotherapist. Tchr. Newton (Mass.) Pub. Sch., 1957-58; rschr. Harvard U., Cambridge, Mass., 1958-59; sys. engr. IBM Corp., Balt., 1959-60; psychotherapist Family Counseling Ctr., Sarasota, 1987-89; family therapist Family Therapist Assocs., Nova U., Ft. Lauderdale, Fla., 1990-92, The Inst. for Family Therapy, Miami, Fla., 1992-95; psychotherapist in pvt. practice, Venice,

Fla., 1995—. Democrat. Jewish. Avocations: racquetball, nature, photography. Home: 1091 Covert Rd South Venice FL 34293-6733 E-mail: sandie34293@comcast.net.

ZELLIOT, ELEANOR MAE, history educator; b. Des Moines, Oct. 7, 1926; d. Ernest A. and Minnie (Hadley) Z. BA, William Penn Coll., 1948; MA, Bryn Mawr (Pa.) Coll., 1949; PhD, U. Pa., 1969. Assoc. editor The Am. Friend, Richmond, Iowa, 1950-58; tchr. Scattergood Sch., West Branch, Iowa, 1958-60; editor Pendle Hill Pubs., Wallingford, Pa., 1960-62; acting instr., asst. prof. U. Minn., Mpls., 1966-69; researcher South Asia Hist. Atlas, Mpls., 1966-69; from asst. prof. to assoc. prof. Carleton Coll., Northfield, Minn., 1969-79, prof., 1979-97, dept. chair, 1989-92, Laird Bell prof., 1993-97, prof. emerita, 1997—. Pres. Midwest Conf. on Asian Affairs, 1996-97. Author: From Untouchable to Dalit, 1992, 96, 2000; editor: Experience of Hinduism, 1988, (jour. issue) Marathi Sampler, 1982; contbr. articles to profl. jours. Mem. Dem. Farmer Labor Party, Minn., LWV. Fellowship NEH, 1987, Fulbright, 1992. Mem. Minn. Consortium for South Asia, Am. Inst. of Indian Studies (v.p. 1994-97, bd. trustees, fellowship 1985, 89), Assn. of Asian Studies (Disting. Svc. award 1999). Mem. Soc. Of Friends. Avocations: walking, cooking. Address: Carleton Coll Dept History Northfield MN 55057 E-mail: ezelliot@carleton.edu.

ZELLWEGER, RENEE, actress; b. Katy, Tex., Apr. 25, 1969; BA in English, U. Tex. Actress feature films including Reality Bites, 1994, Love and a .45, 1994, 8 Seconds, 1994, The Low Life, 1995, Empire Records, 1995, The Whole Wide World, 1996, Jerry Maguire, 1996, Texas Chainsaw Massacre: The Next Generation, 1997, Deceiver, 1997, One True Thing, 1998, A Price Above Rubies, 1998, The Bachelor, 1999, Nurse Betty, 2000 (Golden Globe award for best actress in a comedy or musical 2000), Me, Myself & Irene, 2000, Bridget Jones's Diary, 2001 (nominee Best Actress SAG award, Broadcast Film Critics Assn. award, Brit. Acad. Award and Acad. award 2001; Golden Globe award nominee best actress in a comedy or musical, 2001), White Oleander, 2002, Chicago, 2002 (Golden Globe award for best supporting actress in a comedy or musical, 2002, SAG award for Best Actress, 2003, Academy award nominee Best Actress, 2003), Down With Love, 2003, Cold Mountain, 2003 (Golden Globe for best supporting actress, 2004, Screen Actors Guild Award for best supporting actress, 2004, Acad. Award for best supporting actress, 2004). TV including Shake, Rattle and Rock Movie, 1993, Murder in the Heartland mini-series, 1994. Office: Byant Joel CAA 9830 Wilshire Blvd Beverly Hills CA 90212*

ZELMAN, SUSAN TAVE, school system administrator; DEd, U. Mich.; D in Pub. Edn. (hon.), U. Rio Grande, Ohio; D in Humanities (hon.), Youngstown U. Assoc. prof. edn. Emmanuel Coll., Boston, chair dept. edn.; assoc commr. ednl. dept. personnel Mo. Dept. Edn., Jefferson City, 1988—94; dep. commr. Mo. Dept. Elem. and Secondary Edn., Jefferson City, 1994—99; supt. pub. instrn. Ohio Dept Edn., Columbus, 1999—. Rschr. Edn. Tech. Ctr. Harvard Grad. Sch. Edn. Recipient Nat. Sci. Rsch. Opportunity award, Columbus Tchrs. Coll. Office: Ohio Dept Edn 25 S Front St Columbus OH 43215-4183

ZELON, LAURIE DEE, lawyer; b. Durham, N.C., Nov. 15, 1952; d. Irving and Doris Miriam (Baker) Z.; m. David L. George, Dec. 30, 1979; children: Jeremy, Daniel. BA in English with distinction, Cornell U., 1974; JD, Harvard U., 1977. Bar: Calif. 1977, U.S. Ct. Appeals (9th cir.) 1978, U.S. Supreme Ct. 1989. Assoc. Beardsley, Hufstedler & Kemble, L.A., 1977-81, Hufstedler, Miller, Carlson & Beardsley, L.A., 1981-82, ptnr., 1983-88, Hufstedler, Miller, Kaus & Beardsley, L.A., 1988-90, Hufstedler, Kaus & Ettinger, L.A., 1990-91, Morrison & Foerster, L.A., 1991-2000; judge L.A. Superior Ct., 2000—03; assoc. justice Calif. Ct. Appeal, L.A., 2003—. Contbg. author: West's California Litigation Forms: Civil Procedure Before Trial, 1996; editor-in-chief Harvard Civil Rights and Civil Liberties Law Rev., 1976-77 Bd. dirs. N.Y. Civil Liberties Union, 1973-74. Mem. ABA (chmn. young lawyers divsn. pro bono project 1981-83, delivery and pro bono projects com. 1983-85, subgrant competition-subgrant monitoring project 1985-86, chair standing com. on lawyers pub. svc. responsibility 1987-90, chair law firm pro bono project 1989-91, standing com. legal aid and indigent defendants 1991-97, chmn. 1993-97, mem. ho. dels. 1993—, state del. 1998—, commn. on ethics 2000 1997-2002), Calif. Bar Assn. (bd. dirs. appellate project 1995-2000, chair commn. on access to justice 1997-99), L.A. County Bar Assn. (trustee 1989-91, v.p. 1992-93, sr. v.p. 1993-94, pres.-elect 1994-95, pres. 1995-96, fed. cts. and practices com. 1984-93, vice chmn. 1987-88, chmn. 1988-89, chmn. judiciary com. 1991-92, chmn. real estate litigation subsect. 1991-92), Women Lawyers Assn. L.A., Calif. Women Lawyers Assn. Democrat. Office: Calif Ct of Appeal 2d Appellate Dist 300 S Spring St Los Angeles CA 90013

ZEMLIN, SUSAN CAROL, music educator; b. St. Paul, Apr. 23, 1965; d. Bruce Thomas and Margaret Ann (Hanson) Zemlin. BA in Music Edn., Augustan Coll., Sioux Falls, S.D., 1987; MusM in Choral Conducting, U. Minn., 2003. Choir dir. grades 6-12 Pipestone (Minn.) Cen. Sch., 1987—92; choir dir. grades 9-12 Blaine (Minn.) H.S., 1992—. Voice tchr. Son-Sheim Music Sch., Spring Lake Park, Minn., 1994—; asst. condr. Kantorei, Mpls., 1996—. Mem.: Am. Choral Dirs. Assn. Minn. (treas. 1997—99), Minn. Music Educators Assn. (choir v.p. 2001—03), Edn. Minn., Voice Care Network (substitute faculty mem. 2002), Nat. Assn. Tchrs. Singing. Lutheran.

ZEMM, SANDRA PHYLLIS, lawyer; b. Chgo., Aug. 18, 1947; d. Walter Stanley and Bernice Phyllis (Churas) Z. BS, U. Ill., 1969; JD, Fla. State U., 1974. Bar: Fla. 74, Ill. 75. With fin. dept. Sinclair Oil, Chgo., 1969-70; indsl. rels. advisor Conco Inc., Mendota, Ill., 1970-72; assoc. Seyfarth, Shaw, Fairweather & Geraldson, Chgo., 1975-82, ptnr., 1982—. Mem. Art Inst. Alliance, Chgo., 1993—; bd. dirs. Chgo. Residential Inc., 1993—97, pres., 1995—97. Mem. Ill. State Bar Assn., Fla. State Bar Assn., Univ. Club Chgo. (bd. dirs. 1991-94); Nat. Coll. of Labor and Employment Lawyers. Office: Seyfarth Shaw 55 E Monroe St Ste 4200 Chicago IL 60603-5863

ZENKER, WENDY, financial executive; BA, Radcliffe Coll., 1974. Exec. asst. to comptr. Dept. of Edn., Washington, 1981-87, chief grants ofcl., 1987-89; chief mgmt. integrity br. Office of Fed. Fin. Mgmt., Office of Mgmt. and Budget, Washington, 1989-98; COO Corp. for Nat. Svc., Washington, 1998—. Office: Corp for Nat Svc 1201 New York Ave NW Washington DC 20525-0001

ZENO, JO ANN, sales executive; b. Akron, Ohio, Sept. 25, 1952; d. Ross and Mary Francis (Gerbec) Z. BA in French and Edn., BS in Spanish, U. Akron, 1975. Tchr. French, Spanish S.E. Local, Ravenna, Ohio, 1975-77, Akron Pub. Schs., 1977-80; sales rep. Xerox Corp., Akron, Cleve., 1980-83; cert. stapling technician U.S. Surg. Corp., Norwalk, Conn., 1983-88; rep. cardiovascular surg. products Medtronic Inc., 1988-95; sales rep. Karl Storz Endoscopy-Am. Inc., Culver City, Calif., 1995-97, Vista Med. Techs., Inc., Westborough, Mass., 1997-98; Vista sales clin. specialist Medtronic, Inc., Mpls., 1998-99; area v.p. Computer Motion, Inc., Santa Barbara, Calif., 1999—2000; sr. sales specialist Zeno Med. Ltd., Stow, Okla., 2000—02; ter. mgr. Cardiac Sci. Inc., Irvine, Calif., 2002—. Home and Office: 581 N Portage Path Akron OH 44303-1264

ZEPEDA, OFELIA, linguist, educator; b. Stanfield, Ariz., Mar. 24, 1954; BA, U. Ariz., 1980, MA, 1981, PhD, 1984. Tchr. O'odham and linguistics U. Ariz., 1979-92, assoc. prof. linguistics, 1992-98, full prof., 1998—. Tchr. O'odham and Pima, Am. Indian Lang. Devel. Inst., 1980—, co-dir., 1989—. Author: A Papago Grammar, 1983, Ocean Power: Poems From the Desert, 1995, Earth Movement, 1997; editor: Mat Hekid o Ju: When It Rains: Papago and Pima Poetry, 1982; co-editor: South Corner of Time, 1980; contbr.: Returning the Gift, 1994, Home Places, 1995; series editor Sun Tracks Fellow MacArthur, 1999—; grantee, NSF, 1986, NEH, 1992. Office: U Ariz Douglass Bldg Rm 222 Tucson AZ 85721-0001 E-mail: ofelia@u.arizona.edu.

ZEPHIER, CAROL ANN, piano educator, retired organist; b. Huron, S.D., Sept. 21, 1937; d. William Arthur and Ida Isabelle Robbins; m. Richard Gene Zephier, Aug. 18, 1958; children: Kira Leigh Zephier LeCompte, Richard Donovan, Erin Dianne. BA, Yankton (S.D.) Coll., 1960. Nat. cert. tchr. piano. Elem. tchr. Aten (Nebr.) Sch. Dist., 1959-60; sec. nursing edn. Yankton State Hosp. (Human Svcs. Ctr.), 1960-62; tchr. music, K-12 Smee Sch. Dist., Wakpala, SD, 1963; piano tchr. pvt. studio McIntosh, SD, 1963-67; organist 1st Presbyn. Ch., McIntosh, 1963-67; tchr. 1st grade Northwestern Sch. Dist., Mellette, SD, 1967-71; pvt. piano tchr. Windsong Piano Studio, Mellette, SD, 1967—90, pvt. Aberdeen, SD, 1990—; organist St. Mark's Episcopal Ch., Aberdeen, 1990—2003. Author, editor: Windsong Piano Studio Notebook, 1979-99. Mem. Nat. Guild Piano Tchrs. (local chairperson 1993—), Music Tchrs. Nat. Assn., S.D. Music Tchrs. Assn. (cert. piano tchr.), Aberdeen Monday Musicale, Aberdeen Area Piano Tchrs. (treas. 2000—02), Aberdeen Music Tchrs. Assn. (pres. 2000—02, treas., 2002—). Episcopalian. Avocations: reading, genealogy, grandchildren, travel, photography. Home: 401 19th Ave NE Aberdeen SD 57401-1350 Office: Windsong Piano Studio 401 19th Ave NE Aberdeen SD 57401-1350 E-mail: windsong@nvc.net.

ZERBE, KATHRYN JANE, psychiatrist; b. Harrisburg, Pa., Oct. 17, 1951; d. Grover Franklin and Ethel (Schreckengaust) Z. BS with BA equivalent cum laude, Duke U., 1973; MD, Temple U., 1978. Diplomate Am. Bd. Psychiatry, 1984. Resident Karl Menninger Sch. Psychiatry, Topeka, 1982; staff psychiatrist Menninger Found., Topeka, 1982-2001; dean, dir. edn. and rsch. Karl Menninger Sch. Psychiatry, 1992-97; v.p. edn. and rsch. The Menninger Clinic, Topeka, 1993-97, prof., 1997-2001, Jack Aron chair in psychiat. edn., 1997-2001, apptd. tng. and supr. analyst, 1995—; prof. psychiatry, prof. ob-gyn. Oreg. Health Scis. Univ., Portland, 2001—, dir. behavioral medicine dept. women's health, 2001—; prof. psychiatry, prof. ob/gyn, dir. behavioral medicine, women's health Oreg. Health and Scis. U., Portland, chmn. psychotherapy, dir. outpatient clinic, 2003—, vice chair for psychotherapy, 2003; tng. and supr. analyst Oreg. Psychoanalytic Ctr., 2002—. Instr. numerous seminars and courses. Author: The Body Betrayed: Women, Eating Disorders and Treatment, 1993, Women's Mental Health in Primary Care, 1999, numerous articles profl. rsch. papers; editor: Womens Mental Health: Primary Care Clinics, 2001, Bull. of Menninger Clinic, 1998—2001; assoc. editor:, 1996—98, mem. editl. bd.: Eating Disorders Rev., Eating Disorders: The Jour. of Treatment and Prevention Postgrad. Medicine; editor (sect.): Current Women's Health; contbr. book revs. and articles to profl. jours. Probation officer Juvenile divsn. Dauphin County, Pa., 1973. Recipient Ann. Laughlin Merit award The Nat. Psychiat. Endowment Fund, 1982, Outstanding Paper of Profl. Programs award The Menninger Fund. Alumni Assn., 1982, Writing award Topeka Inst. for Psychoanalysis, 1985, 90, Mentorship award, 1997, Women Helping Women award, 1995, Tchr. of Yr. award, 1988, 96, 99; named one of Outstanding Young Women in Am., 1986, 88; Seeley fellow, 1979-82; Hilde Bruch lectureship, 1996. Fellow Am. Psychiat. Assn.; mem. AMA, Am. Coll. Psychiatrists, Am. Med. Women's Assn., Oreg. Med. Assn., Oreg. Psychiat. Assn., Sigma Xi, Alpha Omega Alpha. Avocations: writing, reading, art history, travel. Office: Oreg Health and Scis U Adult Psychiatry 3181 SW Sam Jackson Park Rd Portland OR 97239-3098 Office Phone: 503-494-1009.

ZERVOUDAKES, ANNETTE DIAN, reinsurance specialist; b. N.Y.C., Sept. 10, 1940; d. Abraham and Margaret (Roth) Dutchen; m. John W. Zervoudakes, June 17, 1966; children: Jason J., Alex R. Student, SUNY, Albany; grad., Career Blazers Inst., 2000. Underwriting asst. Aetna Life and Casualty, Garden City, N.Y., 1962-66; editor Rich Enterprises, Bellmore, N.Y., 1974-84; sr. reins. specialist William Penn Life, Garden City, 1984-99; hub assoc. Sears Roebuck & Co., Hicksville, NY, 1999—2001, Las Vegas, 2001—. Actor: (TV Comml.), 1981—83. Past pres. W.C. Mepham H.S. PTA, Saw Mill Rd. Sch. PTA, Bellmore-Merrick Ctr. H.S. Dist. Coun. PTAs, North Bellmore Coord. Coun. PTAs; assoc. dir. Nassau Co. Dist. PTA; hon. life mem. N.Y. State PTA; committeewoman Nassau County Dem. Party; election poll inspector Nassau County; elections clk. Clark County Elections, Nev.; sec. Mid Nassau Dem. Club. Recipient Disting. Svc. award, N.Y. State PTA, Bellmore-Merrick United Secondary Tchrs. Svc. award, 1991. Mem. W.C. Mepham Alumni Assn. (pres. 1995-99, adv., bd. dirs., class '58 rep. Meritorious Svc. award), N.Y. State PTA (hon., life). Democrat. Presbyterian. Avocations: poetry, music. Office: Sears Roebuck & Co 3450 S Maryland Pkwy Las Vegas NV 89109 E-mail: annetteZ910@msn.com.

ZETA-JONES, CATHERINE, actress; b. Swansea, Wales, Sept. 25, 1969; m. Michael Douglas, 2000. Motion picture and T.V. actress. Film appearances include Les 1001 nuits (Italy), 1990, Out of the Blue, 1991, Christopher Columbus: The Discovery, 1992, Splitting Heirs, 1993, Blue Juice, 1995, The Phantom, 1996, The Mask of Zorro, 1998, Entrapment, 1999, The Haunting, 1999, High Fidelity, 2000, Traffic, 2000, America's Sweethearts, 2001, Chicago, 2002 (Best Sup. Actress Academy award, 2003, Best Actress in Sup. Role, British Acad. Film Award (BAFTA) 2003), Sinbad: Legend of the Seven Seas (voice), 2003, Intolerable Cruelty, 2003;(T.V. films) The Return of the Native, 1994, Catherine the Great, 1995, also mini-series and T.V. guest appearances. Office: c/o ICM 8942 Wilshire Blvd Beverly Hills CA 90211*

ZETTER, LOIS C. personal manager; b. Boston, Jan. 6, 1939; d. Oscar and Pauline (Krasnov) Zetter; m. Walter S. Unterseher, Sept. 25, 1988. BA in Theatre Arts cum laude, Brandeis U., 1960. Prin. LeMond/Zetter Mgmt. Inc., Carlsbad, Calif., 1971—. Actor: (plays) Fiddler on the Roof, How to Succeed in Business Without Really Trying, Ben Bagley's Cole Porter Revue; assoc. prodr. : (films) Moment by Moment; co-prodr.: (TV series) Cover Up, Dads; prodn. cons. : (films) Grease; Blow Out; Urban Cowboy; mgr. John Travolta, Patrick Swayze, Katherine Helmond, Mickey Rourke, Mark Harmon, others. Donor Aid for AIDS, Brandeis U., Freindly Hand Found., Gaucher Disease Found. Recipient Spirit award, Brandeis U., 1995. Mem.: Women in Film, Conf. Personal Mgrs., Acad. TV Arts and Scis. Office: LeMond/Zetter Mgmt Inc 3261 Celinda Dr Carlsbad CA 92008-2070

ZEVIAR-GEESE, GABRIOLE, stock market investor, lawyer; b. LA, Apr. 10, 1948; d. Harry Lindstedt and Josephine (Conrad) Blom; m. Stephan Otto Geese, Nov. 22, 1992. Diploma in Computer Programming and Analysis, Seneca Coll. Applied Arts and Tech., 1981; BA, York U., 1991; JD, Calif. Pacific Sch. Law, 1999. Data base cons., edn. specialist Bull Internat., Toronto, Canada, 1982—91; programmer Sparta, Laguna, Niguel, Calif., 1992; stock market investor, 1994—; small claims advisor County Counsel, 1998—2000; law clk. Kern County Superior Ct., 2000; pvt. practice Bakersfield, Calif., 2001—. Tech. educator, course developer, text book writer, data base adminstr. U.S. and Can. Contbr. articles to profl. jours. Mem.: Kern County Women Lawyers Assn., Kern County Bar Assn., Calif. Bar Assn. Avocations: piano, painting, Tae Kwon Do, Lightarian Reiki master, ballroom dancing. E-mail: geeselawoffice@aol.com.

ZEVNIK-SAWATZKY, DONNA DEE, retired litigation coordinator; b. Tulsa, Dec. 15, 1946; d. Robert Joseph Z. and Dorothy Dee (Robertson) Zink; m. Kenneth Sawatzky, May 30, 1965; children: K. Brian, Kaira D. Student, U. Ctrl. Okla., 1977, Okla. State U., 1984. Cert. AIDS educator, State of Okla., 1995-97. Sec. Farmers Ins. Co., Oklahoma City, 1974-80; office mgr. S.A.F.E., Inc., Oklahoma City, 1980-83; jr. acct. Southeast Exploration Corp., Oklahoma City, 1983-84; acct. Young Bros., Inc., Oklahoma City, 1984-88, The Denman Co., Inc., Oklahoma City, 1988-89; litigation coord. ACLU Okla., Oklahoma City, 1994—2003; ret., 2003; founder, owner Otherwhere Arts, 1999—2001. Bd. dirs. ACLU Okla., 1995—; founder, CEO Otherwhere Arts. Author and illustrator: That Place--Otherwhere, 1994, Something for Otherwhere, 1995; author: At Our House, 1979-83; columnist Putnam City-N.W. News, Warr Acres, Okla., 1979-83; designer stage sets Miss Warr Acres Pageant, 1971-88. Bd. dirs. Miss Warr Acres (Okla.) Pageant, 1984-88, Warr Acres C. of C., 1981-85; treas. ACLU of Okla., 1995—, bd. dirs., 1994—; child welfare advocate Okla. State Dept. Human Svcs., Oklahoma City, 1987-89; coord. AIDS clinic Triangle Assn., Oklahoma City, 1994-97; founder Circle of Friends with Arachnoiditis World Wide Web Chronic Pain Support Group, 1997. Named Honorary Mayor of Warr Acres, 1971, Super Citizen, 1973, Outstanding Vol. Okla. State Dept. Human Svcs., 1988; recipient Svc. award Warr Acres C. of C., 1979, Legis. Commendation State of Okla., 1988, numerous Okla. Newspaper Column of Month awards Okla. Press Assn., Oklahoma City, 1981-82. Mem. NAFE, ACLU (Exec. Dir. Vol. Svc. award 1996), Nat. Notary Assn., Am. Inst. Profl. Bookkeepers, Amnesty Internat., The Interfaith Alliance, Pflag, Human Rights Campaign, Okla. Coalition to Abolish the Death Penalty. Democrat. Methodist. Avocations: painting, writing, photography, family. Office: 3000 Paseo Dr Oklahoma City OK 73103

ZEVON, SUSAN JANE, editor; b. N.Y.C., July 23, 1944; d. Louis and Rhea (Alter) Z. BA, Smith Coll., 1966. Asst. editor trends and environments House & Garden, N.Y.C., 1970-80; account supr. Jessica Dee Comm., N.Y.C., 1981-84; sr. editor architecture House Beautiful, N.Y.C., 1985—. Author: Inside Architecture, 1997, Outside Architecture, 1999; (with others) Decorating On The Cheap, 1984. Bd. dirs. The Cornerstone Learning Ctr., 1999—. Mem. Archtl. League N.Y., Smith Coll. N.Y. Club (v.p. 1987-88, pres. 1988-89), The Mcpl. Art Soc., Internat. Furnishings and Design Assn. Avocations: films, lit., gymnastics, art. Office: House Beautiful 1700 Broadway New York NY 10019-5905

ZEXTER, ELEANOR M. secondary school educator; b. Providence, R.I., Sept. 7, 1936; d. Morris and Anna Rae (Cantor) Marks; m. D. Ronald Zexter, Dec. 24, 1958; children: Francine Deborah, Judith Blair. BA, Brown U., 1958, MAT, 1962. Cert. tchr. R.I., Calif. Tchr. French and English Hope H.S., Providence, 1959—69, Nathan Bishop Mid. Sch., Providence, 1970—93; tchr. English and social studies Harkham Hillel Hebrew Acad., Beverly Hills, Calif., 1993—99. Mktg. dir. DRZ Sales; grant writer Nathan Bishop Mid. Sch., Providence, 1980-93, choral dir., 1985-93, founder Famous Authors, 1987-93; cons. substance abuse program, Brown U., 1987-93; ednl. cons. Vol. tutor Harkham Hillel Hebrew Acad., 1993-99, French club coord., Harkham Hillel Acad., 1993-99. Recipient Citizen Citation for outstanding efforts with Providence children, Mayor, 1990, McClorin award, 1991. Mem. Am. Assn. French Tchrs., Alliance Francaise, R.I. Assn. Foreign Language, Beverly Hills Country Club (tennis team capt.). Avocations: tennis, antique collecting, reading clubs, bridge, travel. Home: 8544 Burton Way Apt 401 Los Angeles CA 90048-3390

ZHA, JIANYING, writer, educator; b. Beijing; M of Philosophy in Comparative Lit., Columbia U. Writer. Vis. scholar Rice U. Author: (book) China Pop: How Soap Operas, Tabloids and Best Sellers Are Transforming a Culture, 1995 (Guggenheim fellowship, 2003). Office: The New Press 4th Fl 38 Greene St New York NY 10013

ZHANG, NIAN, research scientist, educator; d. Yiyu Xue and YouLing Zhang; m. Qiang Yao. BS, Wuhan U. Tech., China, 1996; MS, Huazhong U. Sci. and Tech., China, 1999; PhD, U. Mo., Rolla, 2004. From rsch. asst. to tchg. asst. U. Mo., Rolla, 2000—04; asst. prof. elec. and computer engring. dept. S.D. Sch. Mines and Tech., Rapid City, 2004. Cons. Wuhan U. Tech., China, 1996—99. Contbr. articles to profl. jours. Mem.: IEEE, Soc. Profl. Indsl. Engrs., IEEE Women in Engring., IEEE Neural Networks Soc. Achievements include invention of subcircuit extraction using neural networks. Office: SD Sch Mines and Tech Elect and Computer Engring Dept 501 E St Joseph St Rapid City SD 57701

ZHAO, JIA, lawyer; b. Shanghai, Sept. 23, 1940; came to U.S., 1980; BA, Beijing Fgn. Studies U., 1963; JD, Harvard U., 1983. Bar: Ill. 1985, D.C. 1986. U.S. desk officer dept. Am. and Oceanic Affairs, Fgn. Ministry People's Republic of China, 1972; atty. Arnold & Porter, Washington, Covington & Burling, Washington, Pillsbury, Madison & Sutro, San Francisco; 1st sec. dept. treaty and law, Am. and oceanic affairs Chinese Fgn. Ministry, 1986—88; with Baker & McKenzie, Chgo., 1988—, ptnr., 1994—. Mem. ABA, D.C. Bar, Chgo. Bar Assn., Beijing Fgn. Econ. Law Assn. Office: Baker and McKenzie One Prudential Plz 130 E Randolph Dr Chicago IL 60601*

ZHENG, MAGGIE (XIAOCI ZHENG), materials scientist, turbine coating specialist; b. Shanghai, Apr. 21, 1949; came to U.S., 1986; d. George and Helen (Chou) Cheng; 1 child, Dee. BS in Physics, Qufu Normal U., Shangdong, China, 1981; MSEE, U. Sci. and Tech. China, Beijing, 1984; MS in Materials Sci., U. Wis., 1988, PhD in Materials Sci., 1991. Asst. prof. Tsinghua U., Beijing, 1984-86; assoc. scientist United Techs., East Hartford, Conn., 1991-92; staff scientist Pratt & Whitney, TALEN, Rocky Hill, Conn., 1992-93; materials and coating process engr. Chromalloy Turbine Techs., Middletown, N.Y., 1993-94; sr. engr. GE Power Generation, Schenectady, N.Y., 1995-98; pres. Turbine Coatings Inc., Schenectady, N.Y., 1999—. Rsch. asst. U. Wis., Madison, 1986-91. Contbr. articles in profl. publs.; patentee in field. Mem. NAFE, Am. Metal Soc., Minerals, Metals and Materials Soc. Office: PO Box 600 Schenectady NY 12301-0600

ZHONG, DAWN HE, materials engineer; b. Shanghai, Aug. 17, 1951; came to the U.S., 1988; d. Qi Wei He and Yu Qin Shi; m. Kai Zhong, Jan. 20, 1987. BS, East China U. Chem. Tech., Shanghai, 1982; MS, Fla. Atlantic U., 1992. Rsch. engr. Shanghai Fiber Reinforced Plastics Rsch. Inst., 1982-88; sr. analytical chemist Motorola, Inc., Boynton Beach, Fla., 1993-2001; sr. engr. Tyco Sensormatic, Boca Raton, Fla., 2001—. Contbr. articles to profl. jours. Mem. Am. Chem. Soc., Chinese Assn. Sci., Econs. and Culture South Fla. Achievements include patent in field. Office: Tyco Sensormatic 6600 Congress Ave Boca Raton FL 33431

ZHOU, PING, physical engineer; b. Beijing; came to U.S., 1985; 1 child, Jie Yang. BA, Beijing U. Chem. Tech., 1964; postgrad., U. Sci. & Tech., China, 1978, Beijing U., 1982. Asst. prof. SUNY, Albany, 1985-87; engr. Chinese Acad. Scis., Beijing, 1970-90; rsch. assoc. Stanford (Calif.) U., 1990—. Vis. porf. Stanford U., 1987-88. Mem. Am. Soc. Materials Internat., Materials Rsch. Soc., Am. Vacuum Soc., Am. Phys. Soc. Achievements include development of multilayer Ti-Cu thin films for gravity probe-B gyroscope housings, BSCCO thin films with Tc above 100K; development, manufacturing, and testing of the thin film coatings and the superconducting bearings for the accelerometer for the Satellite Test of Equivalence Principle (STEP) Project. Office: Stanford Univ Hansen Lab Stanford CA 94305 E-mail: ping@relgyro.Stanford.edu.

ZHOU, SOPHIA HUAI, biomedical engineering scientist; b. Huaiyin, Jiangsu, China, Dec. 6, 1953; MS, Dalhousie U., Halifax, Can., 1987, PhD, 1991. Profl. engr., Nova Scotia. Rsch. assoc. U. Alta., Edmonton, Canada, 1991-93, asst. prof., 1993-94, St. Louis U., 1994-95; engring. scientist Hewlett-Packard Co., Andover, Mass., 1995-99; prin. scientist Agilent Techs. Inc., Andover, Mass., 1999—2001; rsch. mgr. Advanced Algorithm Rsch. Ctr.; prin. scientist Philips Med Sys., Oxnard, Calif., 2001—. Contbr. articles to profl. jours. Fellow Am. Coll. Cardiology; mem. NY Acad. Sci., Soc. Women Engrs., Internat. Soc. Electrocardiology, Internat. Soc. Computerized Electrocardiology, Am. Heart Assn. Achievements include design and development of automated ECG interpretations. Office: Philips Med Sys 1201 N Rice Ave Oxnard CA 93030 E-mail: sophia.zhou@philips.com.

ZHOU, YAN, chemist; b. Luobei, China, Jan. 23, 1963; came to U.S., 1989; d. Qingshun Zhou and Xi Chen; m. Tao Yuan, Nov. 11, 1987; 1 child, Karen. BS, Heilongjiang U., Harbin, China, 1983; MS, Ji Lin U., Changchun, China, 1986, Auburn U., 1993. Rsch. chemist Harbin Normal Univ., Harbin, China, 1986-89; grad. rsch. asst. Auburn (Ala.) U., 1990-93; prin. rsch. chemist Unilever Rsch. U.S., Edgewater, N.J., 1993—. Contbr. articles to profl. jours., patentee in field. Mem. Am. Chemical Soc. Home: 6 Crest Ter Montville NJ 07045-9608 Office: 45 River Rd Edgewater NJ 07020-1017

ZHU, AI-LAN, opera singer; b. Nanjing, Jiang Su, Peoples Republic of China, Nov. 29, 1956; arrived in U.S., 1984; d. De-Chang Zhu and Shu-hua Tsao. MusB, Cen. Conservatory Music, Beijing, 1977; Artist Diploma in Opera, Hartt Sch of Music, U. Hartford, 1986. Appeared in leading opera houses of N.Am.; leading soprano in Tex. Opera Theater, Houston, 1987, 88, Va. Opera Assn., Norfolk, 1987, Met. Opera, 1988, Opera Theater St. Louis, 1989, PepsiCo Summerfare and European tour, N.Y., 1989, Lyric Opera of Boston, 1990, Glyndebourne Opera Festival, 1990, 91, Lyric Opera of Kansas City, 1990, Caramoor Festival, N.Y., 1990, Chautauqua Opera and Orch., 1990, Opera Pacific, L.A., 1991, 92, Dayton, Ohio, 1991, Minn. Opera, 1992, Opera Co. Phila., 1992, Mich. Opera Theater, 1993, Austin Lyric Opera, 1993, 94-99, Scottish Opera, 1994, Conn. Opera, 1995, Atlanta Opera, 1995, Conn. Opera, 1995, 96, 98, Shanghai Symphony, 1996, San Antonio Symphony, 1997, San Diego Opera, 1997, Conn. Opera, 1998, 99, William Hall Master Chorals, L.A., 1998, Opera Caroline, 1999, Opera de Quebec, Chattanooga, 2000, Orlando, Fla., 2000, Opera Regina, Can., 2000, Vancouver Opera, 2000, Opera Toledo, Ohio, 2000, Austin, Tex., 2000, 01, Orlando, Fla., 2001, Conn. Opera, 2001, Vancouver Opera, 2001, 03, Poughkeepsie, NY, 2002, Ariz. Opera, 2002, Montreal (Can.) Opera, 2002 Royal Albert Hall, London, 2003; European tour Pellèas et Mèlisande, 1992-93; concert singer Chautauqua (N.Y.) Instn., 1987, Liederkranz Found., N.Y.C., 1989; recital The Theatre Musical de Paris, Chatelet, 1991; concert tour with Sherrill Milnes, Beijing, China, 1993. Finalist Luciano Pavarotti internat. vocal competition, Opera Cos. Phila., 1985; recipient 1st prize Sigma Alpha Iota vocal competition, Chautauqua, N.Y., 1986, 5th prize Liederkranz Found. vocal competition, N.Y.C., 1989. Mem. Am. Guild Mus. Artists. Office: John J Miller 889 9th Ave Ste 1 New York NY 10019 1781 Home: 27 Deer Run Dr West Hartford CT 06107-3109 E-mail: silenzal@aol.com.

ZICHEK, SHANNON ELAINE, retired secondary school educator; b. Lincoln, Nebr., May 29, 1944; d. Melvin Eddie and Dorothy Virginia (Patrick) Zichek. AA, York (Nebr.) Coll., 1965; BA, U. Nebr., Kearney, 1968; postgrad., U. Okla., Edmond, 1970—75, U. Nebr., Kearney, 1980—82, U. Nebr., 1989, postgrad., 1992. Tchr. history and English, N.W. H.S., Grand Island, Nebr., 1948-1999, ret., 1999. Republican. Home: 2730 N North Rd Grand Island NE 68803-1143

ZICKUS, ANNE, state legislator; b. Apr. 6, 1939; m. Charles Zickus, 1958; children: Kathy, Chuck. Alderman City of Palos Hills, Ill., 1973-75; state rep. Dist. 47, Ill., 1989-90, Dist. 48, Ill., 1993—; dir. Ill. State Crime Commn., 1997. Dir. Helping Hand Rehab. Ctr., 1995—. Mem. Suburban Assn. Realtors, Nat. Assn. Realtors, Republican. Home: 7909 W 112th St Palos Hills IL 60465-2731 Office: 10600 S Roberts Rd Palos Hills IL 60465-1936

ZIEGELMEIER, PATRICIA KAY, music educator, executive secretary; b. Colby, Kans., July 14, 1944; d. Lon Elmer and Mary Marie (Saddler) Sowers; m. Carl Ernest Ziegelmeier, June 9, 1963; children: Matt, Steve, Lisa, Amy, Lori. BA in Music Edn., U. Wyo., 1967; MS in Ednl. Adminstrn., Ft. Hays State U., 1991. Tchr. music, sub. tchr. Golden Plains Schs., Rexford, Kans., 1969-72; pvt. piano instr. Gem, Kans., 1972-87; ch. organist Gem and Colby, Kans., 1968—; instr. music Colby C.C., 1988—. Cmty. leader 4-H, Gem, 1980-88, 99—; bd. dirs. Thomas County Ext. Coun., Colby, 1982-86, 94-95. Mem. NEA, Music Tchrs. Nat. Assn., Kans. Music Tchrs. Assn. (bd. dirs. 1981—, exec. sec. 1987—, Outstanding Tchr. award 1994), Western Plains Arts Assn. (exec. dir. 1989—), Northwest Kans. Piano Assn. (clinic chair 1973—). Methodist. Avocations: reading, music listening, playing piano, walking. Office: Kans Music Tchrs Assn 2154 County Road 27 Gem KS 67734-9008 E-mail: patz@colby.ixks.com.

ZIEGLER, ANN E. retail executive; b. 1958; BA, Coll. William and Mary; JD, U. Chgo. With Skadden, Arps, Slate, Meagher & Flom; asst. counsel Sara Lee Corp., 1993—94, exec. dir. corp. devel., 1994—2000, v.p., 1997—2000, sr. v.p. corp. devel., 2000—01, sr. v.p. mergers and acquisitions, 2001—, CFO bakery group, 2003—, sr. v.p. adminstrn. bakery group. Bd. dirs. Unitrin, Inc. Office: Sara Lee Corp 3 First Nat Plaza Chicago IL 60602-4260*

ZIEGLER, GWENDOLYN WOODS, minister, consultant; d. William Darnell and Christine Anna Woods; children: Geraldine, Tonia Elaine, Faith Evangeline, Charity Elise. BTh, United Bible Coll., Orlando, Fla., 1988, EdM, 1990. Pastoral lic. Deliverance Evangelistic Ctrs., Inc./N.J., 1970, Evangelistic lic. Deliverance Evangelistic Ctrs., Inc./N.J., 1967. Pres./cons. G. Chafto Industries, Washington, 1990—; v.p. In The Midst, Inc., Severn, Md., 1999—2002. Spl. asst. to the pres. We Can Do Ministries, Inc., Newark, 1990—92; tchr./radio broadcaster Positive Proof Ministries, Orange, NJ, 1995—97; cons./radio broadcaster Global Ministries, South Orange, NJ, 1997—98. Author: (non-fiction book) Judgment Work - A Conclusion To The Matter. Mem.: N.Am. Bookdealers Exch. Independent. Office: G Chafto Industries PO Box 64204 Washington DC 20029-4204 Personal E-mail: gwenziegler@gchafto.com. E-mail: gwenziegler@gchafto.com.

ZIELINSKI, MELISSA L. museum director; BS, Coll. William an Mary, 1978; MS, N.C. State U., 1983. Park svc. ranger, interpreter Cape Hatteras Nat. Seashore, Buxton, N.C., 1980, 81; exhibits intern N.C. Mus. Natural Scis., Raleigh, 1980-81, 81-82, asst. curator pub. programs, 1984-92; vol. svcs. coord. N.C. State U., 1981-82, 82-83, lab. instr. vertebrate zoology lab., 1983; naturalist Durant Nature Park Raleigh (N.C.) Parks and Recreation Dept., 1983-84; mus. educator Humboldt State U. Natural History Mus., Arcata, Calif., 1992-93, dir., 1993—. Co-author, editor, illustrator vertebrate zoology lab. text, 1983-84. Sch. edn. program dir. Friends of the Dunes The Nature Conservancy, Arcata, Calif., 1993-94, mem. Mem. Am. Mus. Natural History, Nat. Assn. Interpretation, Nat. Marine Educators Assn., Guild of Natural Sci. Illustrators, Nat. Audubon Soc. Home: 1363 Mill Creek Rd Mckinleyville CA 95519-4448 Office: Humboldt State U Natural History Mus 1315 G St Arcata CA 95521-5820

ZIEMBA, KAREN, actress; Appeared in Broadway plays A Chorus Line, 42nd Street, Crazy for You, Chicago, Never Gonna Dance (Tony nom. best featured actress in a play, 2004), Contact (Tony award); (off-Broadway) And the World Goes 'Round (Drama Desk award) I Do! I Do!; (musical) Steel Pier (Tony award nominee); (tour) Crazy for You (Joseph Jefferson award), Chicago (1998-99); (regional play) Much Ado About Nothing, House and Garden, The Foreigner, Fifth of July; (opera) The Most Happy Fella, 110 in the Shade; singer Allegro, Grand Night for Singing; (TV show) Sondheim: A Celebration at Carnegie Hall, Evening at Pops, My Favorite Broadway: The Leading Ladies, Law and Order; album recs. include And the World Goes 'Round, Fifty Million Frenchmen, Lost in Boston II, Shakespeare on Broadway, 110 In The Shade, The Most Happy FElla, Ziegfeld Follies of 1936.

ZIENTARA, SUZANNAH DOCKSTADER, insurance agent; b. Wichita, Kans., Oct. 1, 1945; d. Ralph Walter and Patricia Ann (Harvey) Dockstader; m. Larry Henry Zientara, Oct. 18, 1975; 1 child, Jillian Sue Zientara Cox. Student, U. Kans., 1963-64; BS in Bus. Edn., Ft. Hays State U., 1968; MEd in Secondary Guidance and Counseling, U. Mo., St. Louis, 1973. CLU. Sec. to supt. Wichita Pub. Schs., 1968-69; tchr. bus. edn. Wichita Heights High Sch., 1969-71, Lindbergh High Sch., St. Louis, 1971-72, Holman Jr. High Sch., St. Louis, 1972-75; guidance counselor Pattonville Heights Jr. High Sch., St. Louis, 1975-79; tchr. data processing Lawrence (Kans.) High Sch., 1979-85; ins. agt. State Farm Ins. Cos., Lawrence, 1985-90, agy. mgr. Tulsa, 1990-95, agy. field exec. Topeka, 1995-98, agent, 1999—. Mem. Regional Mgr. Coun., Tulsa, 1992-93; participant Purdue Profl. Mgmt. Inst., West Lafayette, Ind., 1993. Author: Introduction to Data Processing, 1983. Mem. Williams Edn. Fund, U. Kans. Named Outstanding Young Woman of Am., 1974. Mem.: PEO, Soc. Fin. Svc. Profls., U. Kans. Alumni Assn., Mortar Bd., Shawnee Country Club, Pi Omega Pi. Republican. Episcopalian. Avocations: grandchildren, golf, snow skiing, music. Home: 3318 SE 23d Terrace Topeka KS 66605 Office Phone: 785-267-5090. Personal E-mail: agentz@cox.net. E-mail: agentz@cox.net.

ZIERATH, MARILYN JEAN, medical/surgical nurse, pediatrics nurse; b. Centralia, Wash., Jan. 24, 1942; d. Lloyd and Lolita Jeneva (Francis) Reese; m. David William Zierath, Dec. 1963; children: Carolyn, Robert, Michael. Diploma in nursing, Tacoma Gen. Hosp., 1964; BSN, U. Puget Sound, 1965; MS in Nursing, Calif. State U., Fresno, 1975. RN, Wash.; cert. in enterostomal therapy; advanced nurse practitioner. Instr. nursing Calif. State U., Fresno, 1973-75; nursing supr. med.-surg. Good Samaritan Hosp., Puyallup, Wash., 1977; clin. instr. Pacific Luth. U., Tacoma, 1977-79; med.-surg. clin. specialist, enterostomal therapy nurse Tacoma Gen. Hosp., 1979-92, nurse oper. rm., 1992-95; enterostomal therapy nurse Quad-C, Tacoma Terrace, Wash., 1995, Wash. State Nurses Assn., Seattle, 1995-96; charge nurse, enterostomal therapy nurse specialist Frank Tobey Jones Retirement Estates, Tacoma, 1996-98, Home Health Plus, Bellevue, Wash., 1997-99; program coord., instr. practical nurse program Clover Park Tech. Coll., Lakewood, Wash., 1998-99; cert. wound, ostomy, continence nurse Olsten Health Svcs., Tacoma, 1998—. Contbr. articles to nursing jours. Mem. ANA (cert. med.-surg. clni. nurse specialist), Wound, Ostomy and Continence Nurses, Assn. Enterostomal Therapy Nurses, Wash. State Nurses Assn., Puget Sound Enterostomal Nurses, Clin. Nurse Specialists Puget Sound, Phi Kappa Phi, Alpha Phi. E-mail: em42zee@aol.com.

ZIETLOW, RUTH ANN, reference librarian; b. Richland Center, Wis., Apr. 5, 1960; d. James Eldon and Dixie Ann (Doudna) Z.; m. David Robert Voigt, Aug. 22, 1992; children: Eleanor Ruth, Isabel Anna, Carl James. BA in English, U. Nebr., 1987; MA in Libr. Studies, U. Wis., 1990; cert. in info. sys., U. St. Thomas, St. Paul, 1995. English instr. Guangzhou (China) English Lang. Ctr. Zhongshan U., 1987-88; adminstrv. asst. Holm Group Lincoln, Nebr., 1988-89; circulatio supr. Sch. Edn. U. Wis., Madison, 1990-91; libr. specialist St. Paul Pub. Libr., 1991-92; reference librarian coordinator extention library svcs. U. St. Thomas, 1991—. Author manual: Electronic Communication and Information Resources Manual, 1995. Mem. Minn. Libr. Assn. (chair Distance Learning Roundtable 1999-2000). Avocations: gardening, reading. Office: U St Thomas O'Shaughnessey-Frey Libr 2115 Summit Ave Saint Paul MN 55105-1048 E-mail: razietlow@stthomas.edu.

ZIEVE, CHARLOTTE R. research scientist; b. Chgo., Sept. 17, 1926; d. Charles and Bessie Cantor; m. Edward Robert Zieve, June 15, 1947; children: Andrew, Gary, Peter, Wendy, Kathie. BS, U. Ill., 1947; MS, U. Wis., Milw., 1975; PhD, U. Wis., 1986. Chemist Farmers Chem. Co., Kalamazoo, 1947-48, Marquette Med. Sch., Milw., 1948-49; lectr. U. Wis., Milw., 1982-87, Madison, 1986-94, hon. scientist, 1990—. Rep. UN conf. Inst. for Environ. Studies, Cairo, 1994, Population Inst., 2002, UN Conf. Sustainable Devel., 2002. Contbr. articles and papers to profl. jours. and procs. Bd. dirs. Planned Parenthood, Milw., 1978-84, Future Milw., 1980, Elkhart Lake Pub. Libr., U. Wis. Sheboygan Found. 2000—; gov. commn. State of Wis., Madison, 1980; mem. Recycle Coun., Wis. 2003—, Sheboygan Co. Interfaith Coun., 1998—. Mem. Nat. Audubon Soc. (com. 1978-2003, rep. UN conf. Beijing 1995—), Wis. Audubon Soc. (pres. 1978-82, Citizens Activist award 1978), Sigma Xi. Democrat. Jewish. Avocations: travel, biking, gardening. Home: PO Box 267 Elkhart Lake WI 53020-0267 E-mail: crzieve@excel.no.

ZIGAS, RITA B. music director, musician; b. N.Y., N.Y., Feb. 22, 1960; d. Arthur L. and Irma M. Zigas. BA, San Francisco State U., 1984, tchg. credentials, 1987. Freelance musician, Calif., 1978—2001; cons. music San Francisco Unified Sch. Dist., Calif., 1986—87; dir. music San Jose (Calif.) Mid. Sch., 1987—, Corte Madera Cmty. Band, Calif., 1998—2001. Address: 1000 Sunset Pkwy Novato CA 94949-4952

ZILIANI, REGINA PETTIT, music educator; b. Spartanburg, S.C., Nov. 26, 1972; d. Joseph Ronald and Joyce Billings Pettit; m. Jeff Ziliani, May 17, 2003. BA, Converse Coll., 1995. Cert. Kindermusik Internat., 1996. Piano tchr. Self-Employed, Spartanburg, SC, 1991—2002, Pvt. Studio, San Jose, Calif., 2002—, Charlotte, NC, 2004—. Founder, moderator, piano tchr. Website/Email Group of @300 Teachers, 2000—; cons. Nat. Fedn. Music Clubs, Spartanburg, SC, 1996—2002; dir. So. Spartanburg Ch. Choir, 1997—99. Dir., organizer Piano Marath0n (Red Cross Benefit), Spartanburg, 2001—02; vol. Spl. Olympics, Raleigh, NC, 1997—2000, Silent Angels, Greenville, SC, 1997—99; dir. Make-A-Wish Found., Greensboro, NC, 1998. Recipient Daniel Music scholarship, Converse Coll., 1991—95, Spartanburg Jr. Philharm. scholarship, 1990, Hilton Meml. Music scholarship, 1989, Composition and Performance award, Nat. Piano Guild, 2001—04. Mem.: Music Teachers Nat. Assn., Nat. Guild of Piano Tchrs., Delta Omicron. Avocations: reading, music, piano, volunteering. Home: 4811 Trey View Ct Charlotte NC 28227

ZILL, ANNE BRODERICK, foundation executive; b. Phila., Nov. 25, 1941; d. John Daniel and Mary Lynna (Flynn) Broderick; children: Katherine Zill, Persephone Zill, Oriana Valentina Zill, Lydia Daniel Dennett. BA in Govt., Barnard Coll., 1963; MA in Journalism, Am. Univ., 1970. Nat news prodr. Nat. Edn. Radio, Washington, 1969-71; congrl. fellow Am. Polit. Sci. Assn., Washington, 1972-73; project staff mem. Ralph Nader Congress Project Study, Washington, 1972; rep. Stewart R. Mott Charitable Trust, 1973—; founder Women's Campaign Fund, Washington, 1974; co-founder, pres. Fund Constitutional Govt., Washington, 1974—; co-founder Ctr. Consentual Democracy, Maine, 1991; founding cons., bd. dirs. Maine Women's Fund, 1989—. Washington rep. Women's Environ. and Devel. Orgn., 1994-96; project cons. China Strategic Inst., Washington, 1995—, Inter-Am. Devel. Bank Creator Women's Leadership Fund for LAC. Contbr. articles to profl. jours. Founder, dir. Ctr. for Ethics in Action, 1997—. Congrl. fellow Am. Polit. Sci. Assn., 1972-73. Office: Ctr for Ethics in Action 716 Stevens Ave Portland ME 04103-2670 also: 122 Maryland Ave NE Washington DC 20002-5610 E-mail: annebzill@aol.com.

ZIMARINO, KAY KELLER, art educator; b. Kinston, N.C., Dec. 8, 1963; d. Roy Hamilton and Margaret Bissette Keller; m. Steven Kenneth Zimarino; children: Steven Nicklas, Logan Keller. BFA, East Carolina U., Greenville, N.C., 1988, post grad. in Sch. Adminstrn., 2003—. Cert. tchr. N.C., 1992, Nat. Bd. for Profl. Tchg. Standards, 2000. Visual arts tchr. Carteret County Schs., Beaufort, NC, 1998—; art tchr. Lenoir County Schs., Kinston, 1989—98. Mem.: Nat. Art Edn. Assn. Home: 318 Divot Ct Swansboro NC 28584 Office: Carteret County Schs 107 Safrit Drive Beaufort NC 28516 Office Phone: 252-393-7022.

ZIMMAN STETSON, NANCY See **STUART, NANCY**

ZIMMEL, TAMMY LYNN, psychologist; b. Mankato, Minn., June 9, 1963; d. James Harrold Zimmel and Sheryl Rae Otten. BS, Bemidji (Minn.) State U., 1985; MSW, Loyola U. Chgo., 1990; D in Psychology, Ill. Sch. Profl. Psychology, Chgo., 1998. Lic. psychologist Wis., Ill. Therapist Family Svcs., McHenry, Ill., 1997—2001; psychologist Wis. Dept. Corrections, Racine, Wis., 1998—; pvt. practice Racine, 2000—. Mem.: Nat. Assn. Social Workers, Am. Psychol. Assn. Avocations: sports, reading, camping, dogs. Office: 3701 Durand Ave Ste 325 Racine WI 53405

ZIMMER, MARGARET FORD, special education services professional; b. Chgo., Ill., Sept. 15, 1952; d. Kathryn Webb and Frederic Sabbaton Ford; m. Robert Michael Zimmer, June 14, 1975; children: Meghan Patricia, Andrew Michael. M, U.Houston, 1981. Licensed Specialist in School Psychology Psychology Bd. of Examiners Tex., 1998, lic. specialist in sch. psychology 1998. Spl. edn. coord. Alief Ind. Sch. Dist., Houston, 1977—. Home: 2515 Fairway Dr Sugar Land TX 77478 Office: Alief Ind Sch Dist PO Box 68 Alief TX 77411 E-mail: zimmer@alief.isd.tenet.edu.

ZIMMER, SUSAN SNEAD, music educator; b. Roswell, N.Mex., Feb. 22, 1956; d. Edward Paul Snead, Jr. and Dorothy Williams Snead; m. John LeRoy Allen, Jr., June 20, 1998; 1 child, Daniel Kirk. MusB, Tex. Tech U., 1977; MusM, Yale U., 1979. Cert. ch. musician. Dir. music First Congl. Ch., Chappaqua, NY, 1979—89, Wicomico Presbyn. Ch., Salisbury, Md., 1989—; instr. dept. music Salisbury U., 1993—. Server soup kitchen Joseph Ho., Salisbury, Md. Mem.: Presbyn. Assn. Musicians, Choristers Guild, Am. Guild English Handbell Ringers, Am. Guild Organists (past dean, sec. 1996), Phi Kappa Phi Arts and Scis., Iota Kappa Lambda, Mu Phi Epsilon Music Frat. D-Liberal. Mem. Presbyterian Ch. Avocations: reading, gardening, needlepoint, cross country skiing. Home: 26775 Nanticoke Rd Salisbury MD 21801 Office: Wicomico Presbyn Ch 129 Broad St Salisbury MD 21801

ZIMMERER, KATHY LOUISE, university art gallery director; b. Whittier, Calif., Dec. 9, 1951; BA cum laude, U. Calif., Berkeley, 1974; MA, Williams Coll., 1976. From tour guide to curatorial asst. Sterling and Francine Clark Inst., Williamstown, Mass., 1975-76; spl. asst. dept. modern art L.A. County Mus. Art, 1976-77; mus. edn. fellow Fine Arts Mus. San Francisco, 1977-78; dir. coll. art gallery SUNY, New Paltz, 1978-80; cons. in field, 1980-81; dir. univ. art gallery Calif. State U., Dominguez Hills, 1982—. Project dir. Painted Light: California Impressionist Paintings from the Gardena H.S./L.A. Unified Sch. Dist., 1996—. Mem. Internat. Assn. Art Critics, Art Table. Office: Univ Art Gallery Calif State U 1000 E Victoria St Carson CA 90747-0001 E-mail: kzimmerer@csudh.edu.

ZIMMERER, NANCY JEAN, elementary school educator, rancher; b. Torrington, Wyo., Jan. 10, 1951; d. George Frederick and Isabelle Brown Hill; m. David Lee Zimmerer, Aug. 9, 1975. AA, Ea. Wyo. Coll., Torrington, 1972; BS in Edn., Chadron (Nebr.) State Coll., 1974. Elem. tchr. Sch. Dist. # 44, Alliance, Nebr., 1974—75, Henry (Nebr.) Elem., 1975—79; tchr. grade 5 Platte County Sch. Dist. # 2, Guernsey, Wyo., tchr. grade 2, 1985—. Co-author: Let Your Light Shine, Vol. IV, 2002. Elder Lingle (Wyo.) Cmty. Presbyn. Ch., 1999—2002, tchr. Sunday sch., 2002—03, mem. choir. Recipient 3rd place Outstanding Tchr. Am. History, DAR, 1984, Nat. 3rd Place award for outstanding observance of Constitution Week, Washington DC, 1991. Mem.: DAR (state historian 1992—93, regent Elizabeth Ramsey chpt. 2001—03), Order Ea. Star (Torrington chpt. # 22), Delta Kappa Gamma (pres. Epsilon chpt. women tchrs. group 2002—04). Republican. Presbyterian. Avocations: genealogy, golf, photography, reading, crafts. Home: RR 1 Box 20 Lingle WY 82223 8537 Office: Platte County Sch Dist #2 447 S Wyoming Ave Guernsey WY 82214-0189 Office Phone: 307-836-2733.

ZIMMERMAN, AMY J. television producer, television director; b. N.Y.C., Nov. 4, 1961; d. Arthur S. and Louise (Weild) Zimmerman. BA in Journalism and History, U. So. Calif., 1983. Writer, photographer Thoroughbred Calif. Mag., Arcadia, 1981-85; prodr. Hammond Prodns., Lexington, Ky., 1985; assoc. prodr. NBC Sports, N.Y.C., 1986—; dir. broadcasting Santa Anita Pk., Arcadia, 1986—, acting dir. ops., 1999; prodr., dir. Fox Sports Net, L.A., 1996—; cons. Fox Sports, L.A., 1998—; exec. prodr. Horse Racing TV Network, 2002—. Assoc. prodr. : (TV series) Breeders' Cup, 1992 (Emmy award Best Live Sports Spl., 1992); exec. prodr.: Santa Anita Tonight: One on One, 1993 (Eclipse award hon. mention local TV), Santa Anita Today, 1996 (Eclipse award hon. mention local TV), Inside Santa Anita, 1998; exec. prodr., dir. : Best of Santa Anita, 1999 (Eclipse award local TV); assoc. prodr., editor : A Cup of Courage, 1988 (Eclipse award hon. mention local TV). Bd. dirs. U. So. Calif. Panhellenic, 1982—83, Sterling Assn. Aviva Ctr., Hollywood, Calif., 1998—. Mem.: Nat. Thoroughbred Racing Assn. (racing and TV task force, Internat. Simulcast award 2000, 2001), Turf Publicists Assn., Alpha Gamma Delta. Office: Santa Anita Park 285 W Huntington Dr Arcadia CA 91007-3439 E-mail: azimmerman@santaanita.com.

ZIMMERMAN, CAROLE LEE, public relations professional; b. Roxboro, N.C., Aug. 28, 1948; d. Ray Richard and Annie Theresa (O'Briant) Zimmerman; m. Richard A. Hoehn, Oct. 26, 1991; 1 child, Kristin Nicole Sizemore. BS in Edn., Fla. State U., 1970; publs. specialist cert., George Washington U., 1980; MA in Pub. Comm., Am. U., 1993. Accredited in pub. rels. Tchr. Gadsden County Pub. Schs., Quincy, Fla., 1971-72, Am. schs., Kaiserslautern and Darmstadt, Germany, 1974-76; editor, writer USLICO Corp., Arlington, Va., 1980-84; dir. communications Bread for the World, Washington, 1984-95; dir. comms. Nat. Coun. for Sci. and Enrivonment, Washington, 1995-97; dir. comms. and mktg. Am. Pub. Health Assn., Washington, 1997—2002; dep. exec. dir. comms. and member svcs. Am. Pub. Human Svcs. Assn., Washington, 2002—. Bd. dirs. N Street Village, 2000—. Scholar, Pub. Health Leadership Inst., 2001—02. Mem.: Assn. Women in Comms. (bd. dirs. 1996—98), Pub. Rels. Soc. Am., Am. Soc. Assn. Execs. Democrat. Office: Am Pub Human Svcs Assn 810 First St NE Washington DC 20002

ZIMMERMAN, CONNIE ANN, public administrator; AA, HACC, 1978; BS in Pub. Policy, Pa. State U., 2002. Exec. sec. DER, 1993—95, adminstrv. asst., 1995—99; pers. officer PennDOT Bureau of Design, Harrisburg, 1999—. V.p. Women's Legis. Exchange, 2001—; bd. dirs. Ctrl. Pa. Women Execs., Harrisburg, Pa., 1997—, YWCA of Greater Harrisburg, 2002—. Mem.: Am. Soc. Pub. Adminstrn., Sierra Club, Mitgleider Deutscher Verein, St. Lawrence Fraternal Union, Pi Gamma Mu. Roman Catholic. Avocations: golf, dance, music. Home: 933 Highland St Steelton PA 17113-1537

ZIMMERMAN, GAIL MARIE, medical foundation executive; b. Fort Wayne, Ind., June 23, 1945; d. Albert Douglas and Aina Dorothy (Johnson) Z. BA, U. Puget Sound, 1967. Intelligence analyst CIA, Washington, 1970-72; research asst. Arthur Young & Co., Portland, Oreg., 1972-74; emergency med. service planner Marion-Polk-Yamhill Counties, Salem, Oreg., 1975-76; health cons. Freedman Assocs., Portland, Oreg., 1976-77; legis. asst. U.S. Senator Bob Packwood, Portland, 1977-78; pres., CEO Nat. Psoriasis Found., Portland, 1979—. Mem. dermatology panel U.S. Parmacopoeial Conv., 1985-94; lay rep. Nat. Inst. Arthritis, Musculoskeletal and Skin Disease, NIH, 1990-94. Founding bd. dirs. Nat. Abortion Rights Action League, Portland, 1977; pres. bd. dirs. Oreg. Common Cause, Portland, 1977-78 Mem.: Internat. Fedn. Psoriasis Assn. (chair 1995—2001, vice chair 2001—). Avocations: tennis, flute. Office: Nat Psoriasis Found 6600 SW 92nd Ave Ste 300 Portland OR 97223-7195 Office Phone: 503-546-8366. E-mail: gzimmerman@psoriasis.org.

ZIMMERMAN, HELENE LORETTA, retired business educator; b. Rochester, N.Y., Feb. 26, 1933; d. Henry Charles and Loretta Catherine (Hobert) Z. BS, SUNY, Albany, 1953, MS, 1959; PhD, U. N.D., 1969. Cert. records mgr. [illegible] bus. dept. Williamson (N.Y.) Cen. Sch., 1953-69; asst. prof. U. Ky., Lexington, 1969-70; assoc. prof. bus. Cen. Mich. U., Mt. Pleasant, 1970-74, prof., 1974-98. Author General Business, 1977; contbg. author to records mgmt. text book, 1987. Sec. Isabella County Christmas Outreach, Mt. Pleasant, 1983—. Mem.: AAUW (pres. 1984—86), Mich. Bus. Edn. Assn. (bd. dirs. 1985—90, pres. 1988—89, bd. dirs. 1995—97), Nat. Bus. Edn. Assn., Internat. Soc. Bus. Edn. (internat. v.p. English speaking nations 1986—88, editor Internat. Rev. 1997—), Inst. Cert. Records Mgrs. (sec. 1985—89, exam. devel. com. 1993—2002), Assn. Records Mgmt. and Adminstrn., Gen. Fedn. Women's Clubs (1st v.p. Mt. Pleasant chpt. 2002—03, pres. 2004—, 2004—, Mt. Pleasant area Internat. rels. com. 2003—), Delta Kappa Gamma (state pres. 1987—89, internat. fin. com. 1990—94, internat. ad hoc com. on tech. 1996—2000). Avocations: travel, crafts. E-mail: zimmerhl@cmich.edu.

ZIMMERMAN, JEAN, lawyer; b. Berkeley, Calif., Dec. 3, 1947; d. Donald Scheel Zimmerman and Phebe Jean (Reed) Doan; m. Gilson Berryman Gray III, Nov. 25, 1982; children: Charles Donald Buffum and Catherine Elisabeth Phebe (twins); stepchildren: Alison Travis, Laura Rebecca, Gilson Berryman. BSBA, U. Md., 1970; JD, Emory U., 1975. Bar: Ga. 1975, D.C. 1976, N.Y. 1980. Asst. mgr. investments FNMA, Washington, 1970-73; assoc. counsel Fuqua Industries Inc., Atlanta, 1976-79; assoc. Sage Gray Todd & Sims, N.Y.C., 1979-84; from assoc. counsel to sr. v.p., gen. counsel, sec. IBJ Whitehall Bank & Trust Co., N.Y.C., 1984—99; sr. v.p., gen. counsel, sec., bd. dirs. IBJ Schroder Bus. Credit Corp., N.Y.C., 1996-98, Innovest Capital Mgmt., Inc., N.Y.C., 1997-99; sr. v.p., gen. counsel, sec. Innovest Corp., N.Y.C., 1997-99; from gen. counsel, sec. to exec. v.p. ops. and legal ArrowSight, Inc. (formerly ParentWatch.com), N.Y.C., 2001—. From asst. sec. to sr. v.p., gen. counsel, sec., bd. dirs. IBJ Whitehall Bus. Credit Corp., IBJ Whitehall Capital Corp., IBJ Whitehall Securities, Inc., Delphi Asset Mgmt., Inc., Innovest Asset Mgmt., Inc., N.Y.C., 1997-99; from asst. sec. to v.p., gen. counsel, sec. IBJ Schroder Internat. Bank, Miami, Fla., 1989-98; sr. v.p., gen. counsel, sec. Execution Svcs., N.Y.C., 1991-93. Founder, officer ERA Ga., Atlanta, 1977-79; bd. dirs. Ct. Apptd. Spl. Advs., 1988-94. Named one of Outstanding Atlantans, 1978-79; recipient Disting. Alumni award Emory U. Sch. Law, 1999. Mem.: ABA, LWV, Am. Soc. Corp. Secs., Inc., Ga. Assn. Women Lawyers (bd. dirs. 1977—79), Assn. Bar City N.Y., Assn. Emory Alumni (N.Y. pres. 1999—2003, bd. govs. 2001—), DAR. E-mail: jzimmer642@aol.com.

ZIMMERMAN, JO ANN, health services and educational consultant, former lieutenant governor; b. Van Buren County, Iowa, Dec. 24, 1936; d. Russell and Hazel (Ward) McIntosh; m. A. Tom Zimmerman, Aug. 26, 1956; children: Andrew, Lisa, Don and Ron (twins), Beth. Diploma, Broadlawns Sch. of Nursing, Des Moines, 1958; BA with honors, Drake U., 1973; postgrad., Iowa State U., 1973—75. RN, Iowa. Asst. head nurse maternity dept. Broadlawns Med. Ctr., Des Moines, 1958—59, weekend supr. nursing svcs., 1960—61, supr. maternity dept., 1966—68; instr. maternity nursing Broadlawns Sch. Nursing, 1968—71; health planner, community rels. assoc. Iowa Health Systems Agy., Des Moines, 1978—82; mem. Iowa Ho. Reps., 1982—86; lt. gov., pres. of Senate, State of Iowa, 1987—91; cons. health svcs., grant writing and continuing edn. Zimmerman & Assocs., Des Moines, 1991—2000; dir. patient care svcs. Nursing Svcs. Iowa, 1996—98; nurse case mgr. Olsten Health Svcs. (now Gentiva Health Svcs.), 1998—2004; founder JAZ Tours, 2002—. Ops. dir. Medlink Svcs., Inc., Des Moines, 1992-96. Contbr. articles to profl. jours. Mem. advanced registered nurse practioner task force on cert. nurse mid-wives Iowa Bd. Nursing, 1980-81, Waukee, Polk County, Iowa Health Edn. Coord. Coun., Iowa Women's Polit. Caucus, Dallas County Women's Polit. Caucus; chmn. Des Moines Area Maternity Nursing Conf. Group. 1969-70, task force on sch. health svcs. Iowa Dept. Health, 1982, task force health edn. Iowa Dept. Pub. Instruction, 1979, adv. com. health edn. assessment tool, 1980-81, Nat. Lt. Govs., chair com. on Agrl. and Rural Devel., 1989; Dallas County Dem. Ctrl. Com., 1972-84, 98—; bd. dirs. Waukee Cmty. Sch. Bd., 1976-79, pres. 1978-79; bd. dirs. Iowa PTA, 1979-83, chairperson Health Com., 1980-84; mem. steering com. ERA, Iowa, 1991-92; founder Dem. Activist Women's Network (DAWN), 1992. Mem. ANA, LWV (health chmn. met. Des Moines chpt.), Iowa Nurses Assn., Iowa League for Nursing (bd. dirs. 1979-83), Family Centered Childbirth Edn. Assn. (childbirth instr., advisor), Iowa Cattleman's Assn., Am. Lung Assn. (bd. dirs. Iowa 1988-92), Dem. Activist Women's Network (founder 1992). Mem. Christian Ch. Avocations: gardening, sewing, reading, bridge, breeding british white cattle. Office: Gentiva Health Svcs 3737 Westown Pkwy Ste 2C West Des Moines IA 50266-1028 E-mail: atzzzzz@aol.com.

ZIMMERMAN, KATHLEEN MARIE, artist; b. Floral Park, NY, Apr. 24, 1923; d. Harold G. and Evelyn M. (Andrade) Z.; m. Ralph S. Iwamoto, Nov. 23, 1963. Student, Art Students League, N.Y.C., 1942—44, Nat. Acad. Sch. Fine Arts, 1944—47, Nat. Acad. Sch. Fine Arts, 1950—54. Tchr. drawing and painting Midtown Sch. Art, N.Y.C., 1947-52. Illustrator (with Ralph S. Iwamoto) Diet for a Small Planet, 1971; one-woman shows include Westbeth Gallery, N.Y.C., 1973, 1974, St. Mary's Coll., St. Mary's City, Md., 1990, Broome St. Gallery, N.Y.C., 2002, exhibited in group shows at Woodstock Art Gallery, N.Y., 1945, Nat. Arts Club, N.Y.C., 1948—56, 1984, Emily Lowe Award Show, 1951, Contemporary Arts Gallery, N.Y.C., 1952, 1960, Village Art Ctr., 1956—61, Allied Artists Ann., N.Y.C., 1956, 1978, 1980—91, 1993—2003, Studio Gallery, 1957—60, Nat. Assn. Women Artists, N.Y.C., 1957—85, 1987—98, 2000, 2003, Art USA, 1958, ACA Gallery, 1958—59, City Ctr. Gallery, 1960, Janet Nessler Gallery, N.Y.C., 1961, Silvermine Guild, Conn., 1962, Pioneer Gallery, Cooperstown, N.Y., 1962—63, Audubon Artists, N.Y.C., 1963—2003, NAD, 1969—2001, 2003, Women Artists Award Winners, N.Y.C., 1974, Am. Watercolor Soc., 1975—78, 1980, Cheyenne (Wyo.) Western Galleries, 1975—77, Edward-Dean Mus., Cherry Valley, Calif., 1975—77, Frye Mus., Seattle, 1975—76, 1997, Boise Gallery Art, 1975, Central Wyo. Mus. Art, 1975—76, Willamette U., 1975, Yellowstone Art Ctr., Billings, Mont., 1975, Utah State U., 1975, Applewood Art Gallery, Colo., 1976, Charleston Art Gallery, W.Va., 1976, Kent State U., 1976, Cin. Art Club, 1976, Martello Mus., Key West, Fla., 1976, Buecker Gallery, N.Y.C., 1976, Anchorage Fine Arts Mus., 1976, Davis and Long Gallery, N.Y.C., 1977, Butler Inst. Am. Art, 1978, 2000, Washington Square East Gallery, NYU, 1979, Internat. Festival Women Artists, Copenhagen, 1980, Westbeth Gallery, N.Y.C., 1980, 1983, 1999—2003, City Gallery, 1981, Bergen Cmty. Mus., Paramus, N.J., 1983, Kenkeleba Gallery, N.Y.C., 1985, Adelphi U., Garden City, N.Y., 1987, Lotos Club, N.Y.C., 1987, Temperance Hall Gallery, Bellport, N.Y., 1987, Monmouth Mus., Lincroft, N.J., 1987, Marbella Gallery, N.Y.C., 1989, Knickerbocker Artists, 1990, Brownstone Gallery, N.Y.C., 1993, Viridian Gallery, 1995, Sundance Gallery, Bridgehampton, N.Y., 1996, Mcpl. Art Ctr., Athens, Greece, 1996, ISE Art Found., N.Y.C., 1996, Nat. Soc. Painters in Casein & Acrylic, 1997—2001, Zimmerli Mus., Rutgers U., New Brunswick, N.J., 1998, Gallery OneTwentyEight, N.Y.C., 2001—03, Broome St. Gallery, 2002—03, Nat. Acad. Mus., 2003, Lecei Gallery, West Concord, Mass., 2003, Represented in permanent collections Butler Inst. Am. Art, Youngstown, Ohio, Sheldon Swope Art Gallery, Terre Haute, Ind., Lauren Rogers Mus. Art, Laurel, Miss., U. Wyo. Art Mus., Laramie, U. Miami Lowe Art Mus., Coral Gables, Fla., N.C. Mus. Art, Raleigh, Swarthmore Coll., Pa., Erie Art Mus., Nat. Acad. Design, N.Y.C., Zimmerli Mus., Rutgers U., New Brunswick, Nat. Mus. Women in the Arts, Washington; bibliography James Mellow, N.Y. Times Art Rev., 1973, Hilton Kramer, N.Y. Times Rev., 1977, Helen A. Harrison, N.Y. Times Rev., 1987, William Zimmer, N.Y. Times Rev., 1999, Terry Teachout, Washington Post Review, 2003, Ken Johnson, N.Y. Times Rev., 2003, contbr. (bibliography) The Art of Collage, 1978, Mastering Color & Design in Watercolor, 1981, The Collage Handbook, 1985, Painting Without a Brush, 1992, Collage Techniques, 1994. John F. and Anna Lee Stacey scholar, 1954; recipient Nat. Soc. Painters in Casein and Acrylic award 1997, Liquitex Art award, 1999, Winsor & Newton award 2001. Mem.: NAD (Henry Ward Ranger Fund purchase prize 1976, cert. of merit 1980, Henry Ward Ranger Fund purchase prize 1982, L.G. Sawyer prize 1988, Ogden Pleissner Meml. award 1991, William A. Paton prize 1993, 1997, Zellah W. Pike prize 2001), N.Y. Artists Equity Assn. (Dr. Maury Leibovitz award 1985), Allied Artists Am. (Silver medal 1981, Jane Peterson award 1985, Creative Watercolor prize 1989, Silver medal 1991, Creative Watercolor prize 1997, Mary Lou Fitzgerald Meml. award 1998, John Young-Hunter Meml. award 2002, Pauline Law Meml. award 2003), Nat. Assn. Women Artists (14 prizes 1957—), Am. Watercolor Soc. (Barse Miller Meml. award 1976), Audubon Artists (John Wenger Meml. award 1978, Ralph Fabri medal 1981, J&E Liskin Meml. award 1987, Dick Blick award 1994, Gold Medal of Honor 2001, Art Students League award 2002). Home: 463 West St Apt 1110A New York NY 10014-2040

ZIMMERMAN, MARY ALICE, performing arts educator; BA, MA, PhD, Northwestern U. Asst. prof. performance studies Northwestern U., Evanston, Ill.; artistic assoc. Goodman and Seattle Repertory Theater; mem. Lookingglass Theater Company, Chicago. Dir.: (plays) The Notebooks of Leonardo da Vinci, The Odyssey, Arabian Nights, Journey to the West, Metamorphoses (Tony award for best director, 2002), Secret in the Wings, Eleven Rooms of Proust, Measure for Measure, Henry VIII, A Midsummer Night's Dream, All's Well That Ends Well. Active Lookingglass Theatre Co. Recipient MacArthur Fellowship, 1998, 20 Joseph Jefferson Awards for best direction. Office: Dept Performance Studies Northwestern U 1920 Campus D Evanston IL 60208*

ZIMMERMAN, MELVA JEAN, writer, retired media specialist, educator; b. El Dorado, Ks., Mar. 3, 1941; d. Virgil Leroy Zimmerman and Aldena Berneice Tidball;m. Joe Hudson Yeaman, July 6, 1968 (divorced June 1980). BA, Kansas State U., 1963; MA, U. Colo., 1970, EdS, 1973. Tchr. Jefferson County Schs., Golden, Colo., 1963-71, libr. media splst., 1971-95. Co-chaired 1976 state Conv. Colo. Assn. Sch. Librs., 1976; mem. Colo. Assn. Sch. Librs., 1971-95 (v.p. 1979-80), Jefferson County Ed. Assn. (sec. 1980-82) Lakewood. Colo., 1968-95. Contbr. chpt. to book; columnist Insight, 1983-95. Docent Wichita (Kans.) Art Mus., 1996—, events chair, 2003—; campaign treas. sch. bd. candidate, 1997, Kans. state legis. candidate, 1998, 2000; mem. Sedgwick County Dem. Party; treas. Ambassadors' Polit. Action Com., 2000—. Recipient Lifetime Achievement award, Jefferson County Edn. Assn., Jeffey award for outstanding svc., Statewide Lion award, Colo. Edn. Assn. Mem. AAUW (treas. Wichita chpt. 2000—), Sedgwick County Fedn. Dem. Women's Clubs (sec. 1998-2001, auditor 2001—). Home: 6704 Pepperwood Ct Wichita KS 67226-1609 E-mail: melzimm@southwind.net.

ZIMMERMAN, MONICA A. accountant, educator; b. Ephrata, Pa., Mar. 17, 1964; d. Leroy M. and Bonita J. Z.; m. Rudolph J. Treichel, March 8, 2003. BS, Messiah Coll., 1986; MBA, Pa. State U., 1988; PhD, Temple U., 1998. CPA. Acct. Miller & Miller CPAs, Lititz, Pa., 1988-90; pvt. practice, East Earl, Pa., 1990-93; from rsch. asst. to asst. prof. Temple U., Phila., 1993—. Project dir. micro loan fund for Temple U. Pa. Dept. Cmty. and Econ. Devel., 2001—02. Rev.: Jour. Small Bus. Strategy; contbr. articles to profl. jours. Bd. dirs. Beth Shalom, Lancaster, Pa., 1988-93; mem., reporting sec. Young Reps., Montgomery County, Pa., 1995—; chmn. Leroy Zimmerman legis. dist. re-election campaign, 2002; vol. Interfaith Hospitality Network of Mainline; mem. coll. retention com., Phila., Pa., 2000; judge Pa. 50 Best Women in Bus., Pa. Dept. Cmty. and Devel., 2001-03. Sam Walton fellow Students in Free Enterprise, 1998—2000, Irwin L. Gross Bus. Inst. Rsch. fellow, 2000—, Tchg. fellow 2000—, fellow Temple U., 2002. Mem. Acad. Mgmt., AICPA, Pa. Inst. CPA, Temple U. League for Entrepreneurial Women (co-chmn.), U.S. Assn. Small Bus. and Entrepreneurship (project dir. Coleman Found. grant program, 2001-02), Ea. Acad. Mgmt., Women's Investment Network, Nat. Assn. Women Bus. Owners, Jr. League Phila., Friends of the Am. Red Cross. Presbyterian. Avocations: walking, swimming, golf. Office: Fox Sch Temple U 201c Speakman Hall 006 00 Philadelphia PA 19122 E-mail: monica.treichel@temple.edu.

ZIMMERMAN, NANCY PICCIANO, library science educator; b. Jeannette, Pa., July 29, 1951; d. Daniel Joseph and Helen Elizabeth (Lipinski) Picciano; m. Lee W. Zimmerman, Aug. 10, 1974; children: Matthew, Renée. BA in English, Carlow Coll., Pitts., 1973; MLS in Libr. Sci., U. Pitts., 1974; MS in Computer Edn. and Cognitive Sys., U. North Tex., 1992; PhD in Libr. and Info. Studies, Tex. Woman's U., 1992. Lic. libr. media specialist, K-12, lang. arts/English 7-12. Libr. media specialist Fairfield (Calif.)-Suisun Sch. Dist., 1976-78; reference libr. Pikes Peak Libr. Dist., Colorado Springs, Colo., 1983; libr. media specialist North Pole (Alaska) H.S., 1984-85, Prince William County Schs., Woodbridge, Va., 1985-89; dir. info. retrieval lab. Tex. Woman's U., Denton, 1989-91; adj. prof., rsch. assoc. U. North Tex., Denton, 1991-92; from asst. to assoc. prof. Sch. Info. and Libr. Studies SUNY, Buffalo, 1993-99; assoc. prof. Sch. Libr. and Info. Scis. U. S.C., Columbia, 1999—. ALISE/OCLC rsch. grantee, 1994, 2004. Mem. ALA (coun. 2000—, chair Libr. Rsch. Round Table 1995-96), Am. Assn. Sch. Librs. (treas. 1996-99, pres. 2002-2003, exec. bd. 1996-99, 2001-04), Internat. Assn. Sch. Librs., N.Y. Libr. Assn. (pres. 1999), Nat. Bd. for Profl. Tchg. Stds. (sch. libr. media com. 1997-2000), Phi Delta Kappa, Beta Phi Mu (nat. exec. coun. 1994-99). Office: U SC Sch Libr and Info Scis 217 Davis Coll Columbia SC 29208-0001

ZIMMERMAN, PAMELA DIANA, elementary school educator; b. Plant City, Fla., May 21, 1952; d. Thomas Leo and Patricia Cannon Sanchez; m. Ernest L Zimmerman, Apr. 16, 1977; children: Chandler, Laura. BA Fla. State U., 1974; MEd, Stetson U., 1982; post grad, U. of Ctr. Fla., 1999—2002. Profoundly mentally handicapped, trainable mentally handicapped, educble mentally handicapped tchr. Boston Ave., 1977—85; alternative edn. tchr. Riverview, Daytona Beach, Fla., 1985—89; ESE tchr. Hurst Elem., Holly Hill, Fla., 1989—90, Seabreeze H.S., Daytona Beach, Fla., 1990—96; tchr., ESE resource Tomoka Elem. Sch., Ormond Beach, Fla., 1996—. Flare facilitator Fla. Lit. and Reading Excellence, Oveide; with Fla. Reading Assn.; tchr. adv. coun. Volusia County Sch. Bd., 2001—. Vol. Dear Neighbor Campaign- Am. Heart Assn., 2001—; mem. PTA Volusia County, 1977—. Mem.: Order of the Eastern Star. Democrat. Bapt. Avocations: walking, hiking, reading, writing, piano. Home: 26 Sand Dollar Dr Ormond Beach FL 32176

ZIMMERMAN, PAULA, writer; b. N.Y.C., Feb. 26, 1949; 1 child, Alicia Zimmerman Hofstetter. Student, Ind. U., 1967-69, NYU, 1973-75. Head pub. rels. Shiki's Restaurant, N.Y.C., 1993; writer Rsch. Assistance, Jersey City, 1995—. Author: What Should I Do About Bruce?, 1993, (screenplay) Vinnie's Omega, 1994, (poem in cassette) Sunday Night Local, 1994 (Editor's Choice award Nat. Libr. Poetry); co-author: (play) Historical Recreation of Union Square - Day of N.Y., 1994, Dreamers, Schemers, and Disbelievers, 1996; contbr. poetry to literary mag.; appeared in films Howard Stern's Private Parts, Keeping the Faith, Above the Rim. Chmn. N.Y.C. Bd. Elections, 1991-96; tenant rep. Holland House, N.Y.C., 1996; mem. Met. Coun. on Housing, 1986—, Fund for Feminist Majority, 1989—. Recipient Essence of Best award Street News, N.Y.C., 1990, mayor's letter of commendation City of N.Y.C., 1992, letter of commendation McNeil-Lehrer journalist Roger Rosenblatt, 1994. Mem. Internat. Coll. Astrology (scholar 1994), Soka Gakkai Internat. (study cert., grup chief 1994—). Buddhist. Avocations: dance, astrology, film. Address: care Jo Sea Prodns PO Box 455 New York NY 10025-0008

ZIMMERN-REED, ANNETTE WACKS, psychologist; b. Exeter, Va., Feb. 7, 1933; d. Samuel Cleve and Zella Edith (Nelson) Wacks; m. James Robert Reed; children: Kenneth Zimmern, Ronald Zimmern stepchildren: Susan, Kathleen. RN, Sinai Hosp. Sch. Nursing, 1954; BA, U. Md., 1969, MA, 1971, PhD, 1975. RN Md.; lic. [illegible] dir. substance abuse, dir. mental health divsn. USPHS, Rockville, Md., 1976—96. Asst. prof. dept. psychiatry divsn. psychology U. Tex., Dallas, 1985. Author: Violence in America, 1986. Fellow: Am. Assn. Marriage and Family Therapists; mem.: Am. Counselors Assn. Avocations: swimming, reading, writing. Home: 9213 Belle Pines Sherrills Ford NC 28673*

ZIMMERS, VIVIAN ELEANOR, development and administrative consultant; b. St. Louis, Oct. 19, 1946; d. John Dominic and Aurea Genevieve (Schottel) Baron; m. John Paul Hargis, Aug. 21, 1964 (div. Mar. 1968); m. Filomeno Mariano Ramos, June 30, 1973 (dec.); children: William S. Ramos, Kiersten E. Ramos, Leilani A. Ramos; m. Ronald Franklin Zimmers, Sept. 27, 1997 (dec.). Student, St. Louis U., 1968-69, U. Hawaii, 1986-87; BA in Mgmt., Nat. Louis U., 1991. Co-founder, owner, pres. Batts Ramos and Assocs., Inc., St. Louis, 1991—. Cons. Hawaii Govtl. Affairs Com., Honolulu, 1975—76; mem. govtl. affairs com. St. Louis Assn. Realtors, 1996—97. Bd. dirs. Mo. Orthopedically Disabled, 1993—, pres., 1997—; active Assoc. Pres.'s Youth Opportunity Program, St. Louis, 1968; vol. literacy coun., rschr. Vols. in Probation and Parole. Mem.: Mililani Mchts. Assn. (pres. 1985), St. Louis Real Estate Bd., Nat. Assn. Realtors (mem. com. pub. rels. 1987), Rotary. Democrat. Roman Catholic. Home: 70 Willow Dr Eureka MO 63025-2198

ZIMPHER, NANCY LUSK, academic administrator; b. Gallipolis, Ohio, Oct. 29, 1946; d. Aven Denzle and Elsie Gordon (Hammond) L.; 1 child from a previous marriage, William Fletcher Zimpher; m. Kenneth R. Howey, May 8, 1987. BS, Ohio State U., 1968, MA, 1971, PhD, 1976. Cert. K-12 Tchr., Ohio. English tchr. Montgomery County Schs., Md., 1968, Reynoldsburg (Ohio) Schs., 1970; substitute tchr. Rolla (Mo.) City Schs., 1970-71; tchr. Phelps County Schs., Mo., 1971-72; grad. teaching assoc. Coll. Edn. Ohio State U., Columbus, 1972-73; dir. Coll. of Edn. Ohio State U., Columbus, 1973-74, grad. adminstrn. asst. to dean, 1974-76, dir. field experiences alumni rels., 1976-80, coord. undergraduate programs, 1980-84; asst. prof. Ednl. Policy and Leadership Ohio State U., 1984-86, assoc. prof., 1986-91, full prof., 1991-98, assoc. dean, 1992, dean, 1993, exec. dean, 1994; chancellor, prof. curriculum and instrn. U. Wis., Milw., 1998—2003; pres. U. Cincinnati, 2003—. Prin. investigator U.S. Office Edn. Field Devel. Grant, 1981-83, 85-88; co-principal investigator Metro. Life Found. Grant. 1989—, 1992—; cons. The Holmes Group, Lansing, Mich., 1991—. Book rev., editor: Journal of Teacher Education, 1986-89; co-author: Book Profiles of Preservice Teacher Education, 1989, RATE Profiles, 1987-92. Chair Faculty Compensation and Benefits Commn., 1989-90, Fiscal Com., 1991-92, Spousal Equivalency Com., 1990-91, Search Com., v.p. for Fin., 1992, Ohio State U; pres., chair bd. dirs. Holmes Partnership, 1997; chair edn. vision coun. United Way Franklin County, 1997; chair bd. dirs. United Way Franklin County, 1998. Fellow Com. for Instnl. Coop., Acad. Leadership Program. 1989-90; recipient Disting. Rsch. award, Disting. Teacher Educator award Assn. Tchr. Educators, 1990, Adams Professorshi Coll. Edn. Ind. State U., 1990—, Alumni Disting. Teaching award, The Ohio State U., 1992; named YWCA Woman of Achievement, 1997. Mem. AAUP, Am. Edn. Rsch. Assn., Am. Assn. Coll. Teacher Edn. Rsch. Comm., Assn. Tchr. Educators, ASCD, Phi Delta Kappa. Episcopalian. Avocations: watercolorist, golf, sewing. Office: Univ Cin 625 Univ Pavilion PO Box 210063 Cincinnati OH 45221-0063

ZINAMAN, HELAINE MADELEINE, gifted and talented education educator; b. N.Y.C., Sept. 11, 1951; d. Harold Joseph and Charlotte (Orenstein) Z. BA, Am. U., 1973; MEd, U. Md., 1979. Spl. edn. resource tchr. John Eager Howard Elem. Sch., Capitol Heights, Md., 1973-85; coord. talented and gifted program Glenarden Woods TAG Magnet, Lanham, Md., 1985-96; coord. Owens Rd. Math., Sci. and Tech. Sch., Oxon Hill, Md., 1992-93, Walker Mill Mid. Sch., Capitol Heights, Md., 1993-94. Pvt. tutor, Washington, 1982-85, 92—; talented and gifted specialist Talented and Gifted Office, Capitol Heights, 1996-2000, talented and gifted program supr., 2000—; tchr. overview course GED, Bladensburg, Md., 1983; instr. creative thinking Prince George's Community Coll., Largo, Md., 1983, 85; instr. Thinktank, U. Md., College Park, 1989—; mem. Math., Sci. and Tech. Network, 1989; writer curriculum for gifted children, 94, 95. Asst. editor Sci. Bowl, 1990-92. Judge Md. State Odyssey of the Mind Competition; talent on "Count on Us" Cable TV Math. Show. Washington Post grantee, 1989, 95; recipient Bowie Excellence in Edn. award, 1991. Mem. Nat. Assn. for Gifted Children, Assn. for Supervision and Curriculum Devel., Md. State Tchrs. Assn., Nat. Educators Assn. Democrat. Jewish. Avocations: travel, tennis, calligraphy. Home: 4222 38th St NW Washington DC 20016-2258 Office: Talented and Gifted Office 9201 E Hampton Dr Capitol Heights MD 20743-3812

ZINBERG, DOROTHY SHORE, science policy educator; b. Boston; m. Norman E Zinberg (dec.); children: Sarah Zinberg Mandel, Anne. BA, MA, Boston U.; PhD, Harvard U., 1966. Research chemist Lever Bros., Cambridge; sr. research assoc. Daniel Yankelovich, Inc., N.Y.C., and; Cambridge Center for Research in Behavioral Scis., 1966-68; NSF research sociologist dept. chemistry U. Coll. London, 1968-69; lectr. Harvard U., 1960—. Mem. adv. com. Office Sci. Pers. NRC, Washington, 1971—74, bd. on engrng. edn., 1991; spl. adviser Aspen Inst.; cons. MacArthur Found., 1989—93; vis. scholar NAS, China, 1987, Nat. Inst. Sci. and Tech., Tokyo, 1991; vis. lectr. Inst. for Human Scis., Vienna, 1995; mem. adv. bd. Erik Erikson Inst. for Edn. and Rsch., 1996—; vis. prof. Imperial Coll., London, 2001—. Columnist: London Times Higher Educ Supplement, 1993—2001, NY Times Syndication, 1994—96. Mem. internat. sci. exchs. NAS, 1994—96, mem comt int relations, 1977—80, mem comt int human resources; chmn adv coun int div NSF, 1978—81; mem coun Int Exchange Scholars, 1978—81; mem comt int exchange engrs NAE, 1987—88; mem adv panel Office Technology Assessment Educ and Employment Scientists and Engrs, 1986—88; trustee Simon's Rock Col, 1971—75; mem panel sci and tech policy NATO, 1995—99; bd. dirs. Fine Arts Workshop, Provincetown, Mass., 1970—86, Bill T. Jones Found for Dance Promotion, 1997—99; bd dirs Gen Scanning, Inc, 1998—99; bd dirs eng educ NRC, 1990—95. Fellow: AAAS (mem comt sci freedom and responsibility 1972—74, comt opportunities in sci 1973—76, comt sci, eng, and pub policy 1982—88, comt exchange scientists with Fed Republic Germany 1987—91, 1991); mem.: NAS (mem comt to evaluate Int Sci and Technology Ctr Moscow 1995—97), Int Sci Policy Found (mem adv bd 1988—), Coun Foreign Relations, Fedn Am Scientists (mem coun 1980—85). Home: 3 Acacia St Cambridge MA 02138-4818 Office: Harvard U 79 JF Kennedy St Cambridge MA 02138 E-mail: dorothy_zinberg@harvard.edu.

ZINK, JOAN WILSON, writer, poet, composer; b. Tulsa, Dec. 17, 1928; d. Paul Almus and Gladys Emily Wilson; m. David Daniel Zink, Feb. 5, 1948; children: Laurie Zink Menard, David Paul; m. Lawrence Eugene Dalen, June 24, 1990. BA, U. Colo., 1958. Contbg. author The Ancient Stone's Speak, 1979, The Stones of Atlantis, 1978; author: (book of poetry) The Road Less Travelled, 1980; co-author (with David Zink): (book) You Are the Mystery, 1976, You Are the Mystery, new edit., 2001; contbr. articles to profl. jours., poetry to profl. pubs. Mem.: Nat. League Am. Pen Women, SPUR. Home: 4011 Saxon Dr New Smyrna Beach FL 32169

ZINKE, LAURA A. language educator; d. Casimiro and Viola Alonso; m. Franklin Zinke, May 27, 1989 (dec. Aug. 22, 2000). BA, No. Ariz. U., 1984; MA, Middlebury U., 1990. Tchr. Spanish McClintock H.S., Tempe, Ariz., 1984—; dir. Payne Acad., Tempe, 2001—02. Cons. Coll. Bd., Tempe, 1993—. Fulbright fellow, Fulbright Commn., 2003. Mem.: ACTFL, AATSP. Office: McClintock High School 1830 E Del Rio Drive Tempe AZ 85282 E-mail: lzinke.mhs@tuhsd.k12.az.us.

ZINKE, SHEILA J. music educator; b. Linton, N.D., June 6, 1958; d. Harry James Lindeman and Margaret Mary Goetz Lindeman Braun; m. Davy M. Zinke, June 14, 1980; children: Douglas D., Thomas Harry. BS in Music Edn., Valley City State U., 1980. Vocal and elem. music dir. Mt. Pleasant Sch. Dist. #4, Rolla, ND, 1988—. Mem. collaborative bargaining com. Rolla Edn. Assn. of N.D. Edn. Assn., 1995—2002; dir., founder Rolla Children's Choir, 1994—. Choir dir. St. Joachims Ch., Rolla, 1988—, cantor, 1988—. Fellow: Am. Choral Dirs. Assn. (mem. jr. high all state choir com. N.D. 2002—03); mem.: NEA, Music Educator's Nat. Conf. Roman Catholic. Avocations: gardening, sports, fishing, boating. Home: 609 Harris Ct Rolla ND 58367 Office: Mt Pleasant Sch Dist #4 201 5th St NE Rolla ND 58367 Office Phone: 701-477-3151.

ZINNER, ELLEN SCHEINER, university administrator, clinical psychologist; b. Balt., May 15, 1946; d. Louis Jack and Mary Ruth Scheiner; m. Michael J. Zinner, June 23, 1968 (div. Mar. 1977); children: Darren Edward, Daniel Elliott; m. Edward P. Dudley, May 24, 1992. BA, Goucher Coll., 1967; MA, Duke U., 1968; D in Psychology, Va. Consortium Psychology, 1989. Lic. psychologist, Md.; cert. grief therapist, death educator. Asst. prof. Frostburg (Md.) State U., 1990-92; dir. Ctr. for Loss and Grief Therapy, Kensington, Md., 1992-96; asst. prof. U. Balt., 1995-97, asst. provost, 1997-99, assoc. provost, 1999; acting assoc. vice chancellor for acad. affairs Univ. Sys. State of Md., Adelphi, 1999—2000; asst. to pres. Salisbury U., Salisbury, Md., 2000—. Mem. adv. bd. Loyola Coll. PsyD program, Balt; cons. numerous agies and univs.; founder, developer Bereavement Netline, 1996-98. Co-editor: When a Community Grieves, 1999; contbr. numerous articles to profl. jours. Fellow Md. Psychol. Assn. (pres. 1998-99); mem. AAUW, APA, Assn. for Death Edn. and Counseling (pres. 1991-92), Phi Kappa Phi. Home: 3965 Green Hill Church Rd Quantico MD 21856-2020 Office: Salisbury U 1101 Camden Ave Salisbury MD 21801 Office Phone: 410-548-3316.

ZINNERMON, SUSAN, writer; b. Coy, Ala., July 29, 1962; d. Gilbert Sr. and Ora D. Zinnermon. Grad., Talledega Coll., 1987. Substitute chr. Wilcox County, Ala., 1980-87; caregiver for elderly, 1987—. Author numerous poems. Sunday sch. tc.r. Recipient Shakespeare Trophy of Excellence, Famous Poet Soc., 2002, Poet of Yr. Gold Medallion, 2002, Poet of Yr. award, 2003. Avocations: travel, writing, reading, sewing, church. Home: Rte 1 Box 132 Coy AL 36435

ZINNES, HARRIET FICH, poet, retired English educator, literary and art critic, writer; b. Boston; d. Assir and Sarah (Goldberg) Fich; m. Irving I. Zinnes, Sept. 24, 1943 (dec. 1979); children: Clifford, Alice. BA cum laude, CUNY, 1939, MA, 1944; PhD, NYU, 1953. Editor publs. divsn. Raritan (N.J.) Arsenal, 1942-43; assoc. editor Harper's Bazaar, N.Y.C., 1944-46; tutor Hunter Coll. CUNY, N.Y.C., 1946-49; asst. prof. Queens Coll. CUNY, Flushing, 1949-53, assoc. prof., 1962-78, full prof., 1978-89, prof. emerita, 1989—; lectr. in English Rutgers U., New Brunswick, N.J., 1961-62. Vis. prof. Am. lit. U. Geneva, 1968. Author: Waiting and Other Poems, 1964, An Eye for an I, 1966, I Wanted to See Something Flying, 1976, Entropisms, 1978, Book of Ten, 1981, Lover: Short Stories, 1989, Book of Twenty, 1992, My, Haven't the Flowers Been?, 1995, (poems) Plunge, 2001, Drawing on the Wall: Poems, 2002, (stories) The Radiant Absurdity of Desire, 1998; editor: Ezra Pound and the Visual Arts, 1980; translator Blood and Feathers: Selected Poems of Jacques Prevert, 1988, rev. edit., 1993; contr. editor, Hollin's Critic, Denver Quarterly; contr. writer, N.Y. Arts Mag.; author numerous poems; contbr. articles to popular mags. MacDowell Art Colony fellow, 1972-74, 77, 2004, YADDO fellow, 1978, 81, Va. Ctr. for Creative Arts fellow, 1975-76, 81-82, 84, 86, 88-93, resident fellow, Djerassi Found., 1990, La Napouli, 2002; Am. Coun. Learned Soc. grantee, 1978, CUNY summer grantee, 1979, 81, 86. Fellow Poets Editors & Novelists, Nat. Book Critics Circle, Acad. Am. Poets, Internat. Assn. Art Critics, Poetry Soc. Am.; mem. Phi Beta Kappa. Home: 25 W 54th St New York NY 10019-5404 Office: Dept English Queens Coll Flushing NY 11367

ZINS, MARTHA LEE, elementary education educator, media specialist; b. Mankato, Minn., Dec. 14, 1945; d. Hubert Joseph and Rose Marie (Johannes) Z. BS in History, Mankato State U., 1966, BA in English, 1967; MLS, Western Mich. U., 1971; postgrad., U. Minn. Tchr. history Worthington H.S., Minn., 1966-67; sch. media generalist Hopkins West Jr. H.S., Minn., 1967-83, Curren Elem. Sch., Hopkins, Minn., 1986—2003; dir. media svcs. Hopkins Sch. Dist., Minn., 2003—. Mem. Hopkins Dist. Tech. Com., 1986—; co-chair Hopkins Elem. Sci. Com., 1991—94. Contbr. articles to profl. jours.; presenter and speaker at confs. Pres. Saddlewood Patio Homes Assn. Inc., Minnetonka, 1991-95, bd. dirs., 1987-95; mem. various Minn. Gov.'s Task Forces; del. Ngo Forum 95, Beijing; mem. WILPF's Internat. Peace Train (Helsinki to Beijing), 1995; co-chair Minn. Metro WilPF, 1998-99; mem. Metronet Adv. Com., 1994-96. Mem. NEA (bd. dirs. 1976-77, 91-97, Woman Educator of Yr. 1975), ALA, ACLU, Minn. Edn. Assn. (bd. dirs. 1975-86, 91-97, v.p. 1977-83, pres. 1983-86, Human Rels. award 1979), Minn. Civil Liberties Union (bd. dirs. 1982-95), State of Minn. Tchrs. Retirment Assn. (bd. dirs. 1989—), Minn. Ednl. Media Orgn. (co-founder, v.p 1990), Delta Kappa Gamma (Beta Beta chpt., co-founder, chpt. treas.), Beta Phi Mu, Phi Alpha Theta. Mem. Dem. Farm Labor Party. Roman Catholic. Avocations: travel, reading, photography, volunteer work, environmental/hunger concerns. Home: 17509 Saddlewood Ln Minnetonka MN 55345-2663 Office: Curren Sch Dept Media 1600 Mainstreet Hopkins MN 55343-7409 E-mail: marti_zins@hopkins.k12.mn.us.

ZINSER, ELISABETH ANN, academic administrator; b. Meadville, Pa., Feb. 20, 1940; d. Merle and Fae Zinser. BS, Stanford U., 1964; MS, U. Calif., San Francisco, 1966, MIT, 1982; PhD, U. Calif., Berkeley, 1972. Nurse VA Hosp., Palo Alto, Calif., 1964-65, San Francisco, 1969-70; instr. Sch. Nursing U. Calif., San Francisco, 1966-69; pre-doctoral fellow Nat. Inst. Health, Edn. and Welfare, 1971-72; adminstr. Sch. Medicine U. Wash., Seattle, 1972-75, Coun. Higher Edn., State of Ky., 1975-77; prof., dean. Coll. Nursing U. N.D., Grand Forks, 1977-83; vice chancellor acad. affairs U. N.C., Greensboro, 1983-89; pres. Gallaudet U., Washington, 1988, U. Idaho, Moscow, 1989-95; chancellor U. Ky., Lexington, 1995—. Bd. dirs. Am. Coun. Edn., Washington, 1995-98; chmn. commn. on outreach and tech. transfer; bd. dirs. Nat. Assn. State Univs. and Land Grant Colls., Am. Assn. Colls. and Univs., 1999—, Ctr. Acad. Integrity, 1998—; co-chair Bd. Oceans and Atmosphere, 1998—; cons. in field. Primary author: (with others) Contemporary Issues in Higher Education, 1985, Higher Education Research, 1988; spkr. in field. Bd. dirs. Humana Hosp., Greensboro, 1986-88; v.p., bd. dirs. Ea. Music Festival, Greensboro, 1987-89; trustee N.C. Coun. Econ. Edn., 1985-89, Greensboro Day Sch., 1987-89; ann. mem. Truman Found. Panel; bd. dirs. YMCA, Lexington, 1999—. Leadership fellow Bush Found., 1981-82. Office: U Ky 111 Adminstrn Bldg Lexington KY 40506-0001

ZION, ELLEN C. small business owner; b. Phoenix, Aug. 20, 1975; d. Ruth E. Helein. BA in History magna cum laude, U. Mass., 2002. Social worker Alaska Children's Svcs., Anchorage, May Inst., Hadley, Mass., 2000—01; owner No. Lights Cappuccino, Hadley, 2001—. Bd. dri. GLBT Cmty. Ctr. Project, Northampton, Mass., 2003—. Mem.: ACLU, Human Rights Campaign. Avocations: fair trade activism, gay and lesbian rights advocacy. Home: 229 Russell St Hadley MA 01035 Office: No Lights Cappuccino 229 Russell St Hadley MA 01035 Personal E-mail: ezion@intergate.com.

ZIRBES, MARY KENNETH, retired minister; b. Melrose, Minn., Sept. 4, 1926; d. Joseph Louis and Clara Bernadine (Petermeier) Z. BA in History and Edn., Coll. St. Catherine, 1960; MA in Applied Theology, Sch. Applied Theology, Berkeley, Calif., 1976. Joined Order of St. Francis, Roman Cath. Ch., 1945. Tchr. Pub. Grade Sch., St. Nicholas, Minn., 1947-52; prin. Holy Spirit Grade Sch., St. Cloud, Minn., 1953-59, St. Mary's Jr. H.S., Morris, Minn., 1960-62; coord. Franciscan Mission Team, Peru, South America, 1962-67, Franciscan Missions, Little Falls, Minn., 1967-70; dir. St. Richard's Social Justice Ministry, Richfield, Minn., 1971-80, Parish Community Devel., St. Paul, Mpls., Minn., 1980-85; councillor gen. Franciscan Sisters of Little Falls, 1960-62, 67-70; asst. dir. Renew-Archdiocese of St. Paul-Mpls., 1986-89; coord. Parish Social Justice Ministry-Archdiocese of St. Paul-Mpls., 1990-93; min. Franciscan Assocs., 1993—2003; leader of team on evangelical life Franciscan Sisters of Little Falls, 1994-96; ret., 2003. Co-developer Assn. of Pastoral Ministers, Mpls., St. Paul, 1979-81, Compañeros/Sister Parishes-Minn. and Nicaragua, 1984-89, Minn. Interfaith Ecology Coalition, 1989-92. Author: Parish Social Ministry, 1985, (manual) Acting for Justice, 1992. Organizer Twin Cities Orgn., Mpls., 1979-80; bd. dirs. Franciscan Sisters Health Care, Inc., Little Falls, 1990-93, Rice-Marion Residents Assn., St. Paul, 1991-92. Named Outstanding chair Assn. Pastoral Ministers, 1981; recipient Five Yrs. of Outstanding Svc. award Companeros, 1989. Mem. Assn. Pastoral Ministers (chair 1979), Amnesty Internat., Voices for Justice-Legis. Lobby, Audubon Soc., Network, Minn. Interfaith Ecology Coalition, Ctrl. Minn. Ecumenical Team on Racism. Avocations: water color painting, birding, golf, reading history and biography.

ZIRINSKY, SUSAN, television producer; Grad., Am. U. Sr. prodr. CBS Evening News, 1986-91, sr. broadcast prodr., 1991-93; sr. prodr. Eye to Eye, 1993-94, exec. prodr., 1994-95, CBS News, 48 Hours, N.Y.C., 1996—. Sr. prodr. CBS News coverage of 1992 Olympic Winter Games, Campaign '96. Office: CBS News 48 Hours 524 W 57th St Fl 5 New York NY 10019-2924

ZISHOLTZ-HERZOG, ELLEN NAOMI, arts administrator, consultant, cultural planner; b. N.Y.C., Dec. 27, 1942; d. David and Rose L. (Weisinger) Z.; children: Geoffrey Scott Herzog, Alessandra Lynn Herzog, Dylan Adrian Herzog, Jason Ari Herzog. BA, CCNY, 1964; postgrad., Art Students League, N.Y.C., 1970-73; MA, NYU, 1979. Tchr. N.Y.C. Pub. Schs., 1971-72; spl. asst. to mayor, press. sec. City of Passaic, N.J., 1973-74, dir. cultural affairs, 1974-76; dir. devel. George St. Playhouse, New Brunswick, N.J., 1977-79; dir. devel. and audience devel. American Place Theater, N.Y.C., 1979-80; asst. prof. Rutgers U., New Brunswick, 1979-83; producing dir. Rutgers U./Rutgers Theater Co., New Brunswick, 1980-81; prodr. Theater for Actors and Playwrights, N.Y.C., 1981-82; pub. rels. dir. Crossroads Theater Co., New Brunswick, 1982-84; exec. dir. Rod Rodgers Dance Co., N.Y.C., 1983-87; exec. dir./artistic dir. Count Basie Theater, Red Bank, N.J., 1987-92; exec. dir. Monmouth County (N.J.) Arts Coun., 1987-92, Bill T. Jones/Arnie Zane Dance Co./Found. Dance Promotion, N.Y.C., 1993; dept. cultural affairs dir. City of Savannah, Ga., 1994-96; pres. Ctr. for Creative Partnerships, N.Y.C., N.J., Nashville, 1992—; exec. dir. Sister Cities of Nashville, 1999-2000; Tenn. state coord. Sister Cities Internat., 1999-2000; dir. culture City of Trenton, 2000—. Mng. dir. Tenn. Arts Commn. grant panel, 1999-2000, INTAR-Internat. Arts Relo., N.Y.C., 1997-98; adj. faculty NYU Arts Adminstrn. Sch. Edn., 1993-94, faculty advisor interdisciplinary arts Gallatin Sch., NYU, 1997—; mem. arts in edn. team Savannah/Chatham Bd. Edn., 1996; workshop leader League Historic Am. Theaters, Tampa, 1992; mem. jazz adv. commn. MidAtlantic Arts Found., Balt., 1991-92; cons. Actors Bridge, Nashville, 1999-2000, Found. Preservation of Am. Profl. Theater, N.Y.C., 1988, Island Ctr. Performing Arts, St. Croix, V.I., 1987; cons. Miss. Assn. Preservation Robertson Sch., Jackson, [illegible] N.Y. State Coun. on the Arts for Williamsburg Music Ctr., N.Y.C., 1997, Chinese Info. and Culture Ctr., N.Y.C., 1996; tech. asst. N.Y. Found. for Arts for Annabella Gonzalez Dance Co., N.Y.C., 1997. Prodr. (world premiere concert/theater prodn.) Max Roach's To the Max, 1992; author master plan Alamo Theater: Centerpiece for Farish St. Cultural Dist., 1994, Paramount Theater and Cultural Ctr., 1992; co-author NEA internet site From Marketing to Individuals to Multi-Cultural Constituency Building, 1999; reviewer (newspaper) New Directions, 1977, From Marketing to Individuals to Multicultural Constituency Building, 1999; paintings exhibited Arts Student League Catalogue, 1973, Avante Gallery-N.Y. State Exhbn., 1977., Summit Art Ctr., 1975 (best painting prize), Rockaway Art Show, 1976 (painting prize). Founding chairperson Arts Found. N.J., New Brunswick, 1980-83; cons. Ralph Gilbert Civil Rights Mus., Savannah, 1996; mem. Passaic (N.J.) History Commn., 1974-76; pres. Morris County (N.J.) chpt. Women's Polit. Caucus, 1973; chairperson for state conf., bd. mem. Social Concerns Action Network, N.J., 1972. Cultural exch. grantee to Northern Ireland, Brit. Coun., 1996; cultural exch. grantee to Taiwan, Taiwan Coun. Cultural Affairs, 1996. Phi Alpha Theta. Jewish. Avocation: painting. Office: Divsn Culture Dept Recreation Natural Resources and Culture 319 E State St Trenton NJ 08608-1866 also: 1219 Barnwell Blf Beaufort SC 29902-4136

ZISKIN, LAURA, television producer, film producer; Co-founder Frogwood Films; pres. Fox 2000, Beverly Hills, Calif. Films include: (assoc. prodr.) Eyes of Laura Mars, 1978; (prodr.) Murphy's Romance, 1985, No Way Out, 1987, D.O.A., 1988, Everybody's An American, 1988, The Rescue, 1988, What About Bob?, 1991, The Doctor, 1991, Hero, 1992, To Die For, 1995, Spiderman, 2002; (exec. prodr.) Pretty Woman, 1990, As Good As it Gets, 1997; (TV) Fail Safe, 2000, Dinner with Friends, 2001, 74th Ann. Acad. awards, 2002, Tarzan, 2003, The Spaces, 2003., prodr.(TV) How I Learned to Drive, 2001. Office: Culver Studios 9336 Washington Blvd Culver City CA 90232-2600

ZISKIND, DEBORAH ZISKIND, public relations and legal marketing executive; b. Pitts., Mar. 4, 1961; d. Gerald N. and Norma Jean (Morris) Ziskind. BA in Internat. Rels., Tufts U., 1983. Litigation specialist, sr. case mgr., pub. affairs and client devel. assoc. Weil, Gotshal & Manges, N.Y.C., 1989-94; mgr. mktg. Reed Smith Shaw & McClay, Pitts., Phila., N.Y.C., Washington and Princeton, N.J., 1994-96; pres., CEO, Ziskind Pub. Rels. Assocs., Pitts., 1996—; founder, chmn. The Global Conf. Inst., 1996—. Pub. rels. cons. Pitts. Chamber Music Soc., U. Pitts. dept. music, 1983-85; antitrust case mgr. cons. Dickie, McCamey & Chilcote, 1985-87; exec. May Corp., Pitts., 1987-89. Contbg. columnist The Chronicle, Pitts., 1977—; columnist Resident Publs., N.Y.C., 1991-94, Actor's Resource, N.Y.C., 1992-94; bd. editors Strategies: The Journal of Legal Marketing; mem. Legal Mktg. Assn., 1992—; exec. editor for Yr. 2000, Strategies, The Jour. Legal Mktg. Mem. exec. com. New Leadership bd. Pitts. Symphony Orch., 1994—. MacJannet scholar in internat. law and economics Tufts U. and Ctr. for European Studies, Talloires, France, 1981. Mem. Tufts Media and Comm. Group, Pitts. Filmmakers (bd. dirs. 1996—), Tufts Media and Comms. Group. Avocations: international politics, music, writing, piano performance, legal ethics. Office: 4415 5th Ave Pittsburgh PA 15213-2654 Home: 50 E Bellevue Pl Apt 1901 Chicago IL 60611-1169

ZITO, JUDI, information technology executive; married; 4 children. BBA U. So. Fla.; M in Comm. and Leadership, Seton Hall U. Cert. in telecom. U. Miami. Sys. analyst Miami-Dade County, Fla., 1981, programming sys. supr., div. dir., IT Dept.; mgr. Miami-Dade County Comm. Dept., 2001—03; chief info. officer Miami Dade County, Fla., 2003—. Named one of Computer World's 100 Premier IT Leaders, 2004; recipient Quiet Storm award, Women's Power Caucus, 2003. Office: 111 NW 1st St Miami FL 33128*

ZLOWE, FLORENCE MARKOWITZ, artist; b. Allentown, Pa. d. Morris and Anna (Mandel) Markowitz; m. Irwin Zlowe, May 1, 1936. Student, Pa. Mus. Coll. Art, Phila., 1929-33; fine arts courses, NYU, 1950-53. One woman show, Charles Z. Mann Gallery, N.Y.C., 1968, Community Gallery, N.Y.C., 1978; exhibited in group shows, Nat. Acad., Riverside Mus., N.Y., Nat. Arts Club, Pen and Brush Club, Lever House, Jersey City Mus., Norfolk (Va.) Mus., Fort Lauderdale (Fla.) Mus., Joe and Emily Lowe Mus., Fla.; represented in permanent collections, Norfolk Mus., Fort Lauderdale Mus., Joe and Emily Lowe Mus., Wilson Pub. Co., N.Y.C., Phila. Mus. Art, Butler Inst. Am. Art, Minn. Mus. Art, St. Paul, Cooper-Hewitt Mus. Design, Smithsonian Instn., N.Y.C., Tweed Mus., Duluth, Minn., Evansville (Ind.) Mus., Lakeview (Ill.) Center Arts and Scis., Ga. Mus. Art, Athens, Slater Meml. Mus., Norwich, Conn. Mem. Am. Soc. Contemporary Artists (dir., treas.), N.J. Soc. Painters and Sculptors, Nat. Assn. Women Artists (1st prize ann. 1958, 12 additional awards for oils 1958-84), League Present Day Artists, Artists Equity Assn. N.Y. Studio: 41 Union Sq W New York NY 10003-3208 Home: 2 Franklin Town Blvd Apt 1606 Philadelphia PA 19103-1230

ZOBEL, JAN A. tax consultant; b. San Francisco, 1947; d. Jerome Fremont and Louise Maxine Zobel. BA, Whittier Coll., 1968; MA, U. Chgo., 1970. Tchr. Chgo. Pub. Schs., 1969-70, San Francisco Pub. Schs., 1971-78; editor, pub. People's Yellow Pages, San Francisco, 1971-81; pvt. practice tax cons. San Francisco, Oakland, 1978—. Tchr. community coll. dist., San Francisco, 1986—; tax lectr. U. Hawaii, 1989—, U. Calif., San Francisco State U., Marin C.C. Author: Minding Her Own Business: The Self-Employed Woman's Guide to Taxes and Recordkeeping, 1997, 3d edit., 2000; editor People's Yellow Pages, 1971-81 (cert. of honor San Francisco Bd. Suprs. 1974), Where the Child Things Are, 1977-80. Named Acct. Adv. of Yr., SBA, 1987; presented Key to City of Buffalo, 1970. Mem. Nat. Assn. Enrolled Agts., Calif. Assn. Enrolled Agts., Nat. Assn. Tax Preparers, Bay Area Career Women. Office: 1197 Valencia St San Francisco CA 94110-3026

ZOBEL, LOUISE PURWIN, author, educator, lecturer, writing consultant; b. Laredo, Tex., Jan. 10, 1922; d. Leo Max and Ethel Catherine (Levy) Purwin; m. Jerome Fremont Zobel, Nov. 14, 1943; children: Lenore Zobel Harris, Janice A., Robert E., Audrey Zobel Dollinger. BA cum laude, Stanford U., 1943, MA, 1976. Cert. adult edn. and community coll. tchr., Calif. Freelance mag. writer and author, Palo Alto, Calif., 1942—; writer, editor, broadcastor UP Bur., San Francisco, 1943; lectr. on writing, history, travel No. Calif., 1964—; lectr., educator U. Calif. campuses, other colls. and univs., 1969—; writing cons. to pvt. clients, 1969—; editorial asst. Assn. Coll. Unions Internat., Palo Alto, 1972-73; acting asst. prof. journalism San Jose State U., 1976. Keynote speaker, seminar leader, prin. speaker at nat. confs.; cruise/shipboard enrichment lectr. and presenter of travel slide programs; coord. TV shows; TV personality publicity and public rels. campaigns; tchr. corr. classes Writer's Digest Sch.; tchr. online writing classes for Writingschool.com, 1999—. Author: The Travel Writer's Handbook, 1980, (hard cover), 1982, (paperback) 83, 84, 85, rev. edits., 1992, 94, 97, 2002; author, narrator (90 minute cassette) Let's Have Fun in Japan, 1982; contbr. articles to anthologies, nat. mags. and newspapers; writer advertorials. Bd. dirs., publicity chair Friends of Palo Alto Libr., 1985—; officer Santa Clara County Med. Aux., Esther Clark Aux., others; past pres. PTA. Recipient award for excellence in journalism Sigma Delta Chi, 1943, awards Writers Digest, 1967-95, Armed Forces Writers League, 1972, Nat. Writers Club, 1976, All Nippon Airways and Japanese Nat. Tourist Orgn., 1997. Mem. Am. Soc. Journalists and Authors, Travel Journalists Guild, Internat. Food, Wine and Travel Writers Assn., Pacific Asia Travel Assn., Calif. Writers Club (v.p. 1988-89), AAUW (v.p. 1955-57, Nat. writing award 1969), Stanford Alumni Assn., Phi Beta Kappa. Avocations: travel, reading, writing, photography. Home and Office: 23350 Sereno Ct Unit 30 Cupertino CA 95014-6543 E-mail: lzobelwriter@cs.com.

ZOBEL, RYA WEICKERT, federal judge; b. Germany, Dec. 10, 1931; AB, Radcliffe Coll., 1953; LLB, Harvard U., 1956. Bar: Mass. 1956, U.S. Dist. Ct. Mass., 1956, U.S. Ct. Appeals (1st cir.) 1967. Assoc. Hill & Barlow, Boston, 1967-73, Goodwin, Procter & Hoar, Boston, 1973-76, ptnr., 1976-79; judge U.S. Dist. Ct. Mass., Boston, 1979—; dir. Fed. Jud. Ctr., Washington, 1995-99. Mem. Boston Bar Assn., Am. Bar Found., Mass. Bar Assn., Am. Law Inst. Office: US District Ct 1 Courthouse Way Boston MA 02210-3002

ZOCCO, PATRICIA ELIZABETH, human services manager, cardiac ultrasound technologist; b. Arlington, Va., Apr. 4, 1962; d. Natale Carmen and Barbara Elizabeth Zocco; children: Richard Natale Holloway, Matthew Tyler Holloway, Brianna Taylor Buckley. BSN, Thomas Edison State Coll., 1986, BSc, 1989; RN diploma, St. Luke's Sch. Nursing, 1983. Registered diagnostic cardiac sonographer Nat. ARDMS Allentown Hosp. Sch. Nursing. EKG tech. Lehigh Valley Hosp., Allentown, Pa., 1981—89, technologist cardiac ultrasound, 1989—96, clin. care coord./mgr. diagnostic care ctr., 1996—. Cardiac ultrasound instr. Lehigh Valley Hosp., Allentown, 1992—. Author: (tng. manual) Pediatric Training Manual for Cardiac Sonographers, 2000. Mem.: ReNew 2000-St. Catharine of Sienna Cathedral (facilitator 2000—). Roman Catholic. Achievements include development of the echo performance improvement program which is responsible for maintaining the highest level of Quality Assurance in the EchoLab at LVH; This is through biweekly continuing educational meetings that are teleconferenced nationally; These meetings have been also been approved for AMA cateogory I Type CMES for Echo technologists and physicians that attend. Avocations: jazz dancing, gardening, interior decorating, piano, cooking . Home: 925 Barn View Ln Breinigsville PA 18031 Office: Lehigh Valley Hosp 1200 S Cedar Blvd Allentown PA 18105 E-mail: PatriciaZocco@aol.com .

ZODA, SUZANNE MARIE, environmental public relations consultant; b. Washington, Apr. 12, 1947; d. Frederick A. and Alice G. (Sherer) Zoda; m. Michael A. Cohen, Jan. 28, 1967 (div. Mar. 1980); children: Adam P. Cohen, Matthew J. Cohen; m. Edmund D. Whitlock, Oct. 28, 1995. Student, Bucknell U., 1965-67; BS in Edn., U. Va., 1970; MPA, U. Colo., 1981. Tchr. secondary math. Albemarle Pub. Schs., Albemarle County, Va., 1970-71; tchr. jr./sr. h.s. Jefferson County (Colo.) Schs., 1975-79; assoc. planner, economist Briscoe, Maphis, Murray & Lamont, Boulder, Colo., 1980-83; spl. cons. U.S. EPA Office of Water, Washington, 1983-84; environ. planner, project mgr. Ch2M Hill, Denver, 1984-89; corp. mktg. mgr. RMT, Inc., Madison, Wis., 1989-91; sr. project mgr. ENSR Corp., Acton, Mass., 1991-94; owner, prin. EnviroComm Solutions, Inc., Villa Rica, Ga., 1994—. Author and presenter in field. Mem. Internat. Assn. Bus. Communicators, Air and Waste Mgmt. Assn. Democrat. Avocations: physical fitness, cooking, photography. Office: EnviroComm Solutions Inc 3002 Catamaran Cv Villa Rica GA 30180-8403

ZOLL, MARY, writer, educator; b. Newton, Mass., Aug. 21, 1947; d. Paul Maurice and Janet Jones Zoll. Diploma, The Newport (R.I.) Sch. for Girls, 1967; AB with honors, Vassar Coll., 1971; PhD, Boston U., 1980. Med. writer Harvard Med. Sch., Boston, 1971—74; tchg. fellow chemistry dept. Boston U., 1973—76; vis. asst. prof. chemistry Vassar Coll., Poughkeepsie, NY, 1980—81; tech. project mgr. Beth Israel Hosp., Boston, 1982—84; chief tech. editor Continuous Learning Corp., Cambridge, Mass., 1984—85; freelance sci. and med. writer and editor Carlisle, Mass., 1985—; instr. The Women's Tech. Inst., Boston, 1987—87; part-time lectr. Northeastern U., Boston, 1991—97, MIT, Cambridge, 1997—. Author: (poetry collection) Being, Between, Beyond; editor: Ricky. Founder and society-level mgr., spl. interest group in sci. comm. Soc. for Tech. Comm., Arlington, Va.; mem. of the planning com., stem mgr. for edn. and tng. stem, founder and mgr. for sci. and med. writing stem InterChange Conf. in Tech. Writing, Lowell, Mass., 1989—96; dir. planning com., mem. planning com. AMITA-SWE Conf., sponsored by Assn. of MIT Alumnae and Soc. of Women Engineers, Cambridge, 1985—89. Mem.: DAR, Am. Med. Writers Assn. (advanced certification in pharmaceuticals), Soc. for Tech. Comm. (founder spl. interest group in sci. comm.), Rowe Camp and Conf. Ctr., Am. Mensa (too numerous to mention). Republican. Athiest. Avocations: poetry, walking, cooking, collecting unicorns, antiques. Home: 225 School St Carlisle MA 01741-1711 Office: Mass Inst Tech 77 Massachusetts Ave 14E-303 Cambridge MA 02139

ZOLLAR, CAROLYN CATHERINE, lawyer; b. Evanston, Ill., July 5, 1947; d. Maurice Adam and Alice S. (Kelm) Z. BA, Smith Coll., Northampton, Mass., 1969; MA, Columbia U., 1970; JD, Am. U., Washington, 1976. Bar: D.C., Va. Legis. asst. Congressman William Anderson U.S. Ho. of Reps., Washington, 1970-72; planning cons. Nat. Inst. Edn., Washington, 1972, legal asst., 1973, asst. for govt. and external rels., 1973-75; assoc. Joe W. Fleming II, P.C., Washington, 1975-82; gen. counsel Nat. Assn. Rehab. Facilities, Washington, 1982-86, gen. counsel, dir. med. rehab., 1986-94; gen. counsel, v.p. policy Am. Rehab. Assn., Washington, 1994-97; v.p. govt. rels. and policy devel. Am Med. Rehab. Providers Assn., 1998—; v.p. Futures Rehab. Mgmt., 1998—. Sec. Am. Rehab. Svcs., Inc., Washington1988, 1988—94; mem. bd. advisors Ind. Living Mag., N.Y.C., 1988—97; mem. Joint Commn. Accreditation Health Care Orgns. Task Force on Rehab. Svcs., 1988; mem. various expert panels on postacute care and rehab. DHHS, 1999—. Sec. bd. dirs. Rock Creek Found., Silver Spring, Md., 1983-90; bd. dirs. Affiliated Santee Group, 1993-2002; chair Nat. Rehab. Caucus, 1991—. Mem. Am. Soc. Assn. Execs., Am. Health Lawyers Assn., Va. Bar Assn., D.C. Bar, Women in Govt. Rels. Episcopalian. Avocations: skiing, golf, singing. Office: Am Med Rehab Providers Assn 1710 N St NW Washington DC 20036

ZOLLAR, JAWOLE WILLA JO, artist, choreographer; b. Kansas City, Kans., Dec. 21, 1950; d. Alfred Jr. and Dorothy Delores Zollar; 1 child, Elizabeth Herron. BA in Dance, U. Mo., Kansas City, 1975; MFA in Dance, Fla. State U., 1979. Faculty Fla. State U., Tallahassee, 1977-80; artistic dir. Urban Bush Women, N.Y.C., 1984—; prof. dance Fla. State U., 1997—. Named Outstanding Alumni, U. Mo., 1993, Regent's lectr. dept. dance and worlds culture, UCLA, 1995—96, Alumna of Yr., Fla. State U., Tallahassee, 1997; recipient N.Y. Dance Performance award, 1992, Capezio award outstanding achievement in dance, 1994, Doris Duke awad, Am. Dance Festival, 1997; Choreography fellow, NEA, 1992, 1993, 1994, Worlds of Thought resident scholar, Mankato State U., 1994. Mem.: Internat. Assn. Blacks in Dance, Assn. Am. Cultures. Office: Urban Bush Women # 4B 138 S Oxford St Brooklyn NY 11217 also: care IMG Artists 420 W 45th St Fl 6 New York NY 10036-3503

ZOLOTOW, CHARLOTTE SHAPIRO, author, editor; b. Norfolk, Va., June 26, 1915; d. Louis J. and Ella F. (Bernstein) Shapiro; m. Maurice Zolotow, Apr. 14, 1938 (div. 1969); children: Stephen, Ellen. Student, U. Wis., 1933-36. Editor children's book dept. Harper & Row, N.Y.C., 1938-44, sr. editor, 1962-70; v.p., assoc. pub. Harper Jr. Books, 1976-81; editorial cons., editorial dir. Charlotte Zolotow Books, 1982-90; pub. emerita, advisor Harper Collins Children's Books, 1991—. Tchr. U. Colo. Writers Conf. on Children's Books, U. Ind. Writers Conf.; also lectr. children's books. Author: The Park Book, 1944, Big Brother, 1960, The Sky Was Blue, 1963, The Magic Words, 1952, Indian Indian, 1952, The Bunny Who Found Easter, 1998, new edit., 1999, In My Garden, 1960, But Not Billy, 1947, 2d edit, 1983, Not a Little Monkey, 1957, 2d edit., 1989, The Man With The Purple Eyes, 1961, Mr. Rabbit and the Lovely Present, 1962, The White Marble, 1963, A Rose, A Bridge and A Wild Black Horse, 1964, 2d edit., 1987, Someday, 1965, When I Have a Little Girl, 1965, If It Weren't for You, 1966, 2d edit., 1987, Big Sister, Little Sister, 1966, All That Sunlight, 1967, When I Have A Son, 1967, My Friend John, 1968, new edit., 1999, Summer Is, 1968, Some Things Go Together, 1969, The Hating Book, 1969, The New Friend, 1969, River Winding, 1970, 79, Lateef and His World, 1970, Yani and His World, 1970, You and Me, 1971, Wake Up and Goodnight, 1971, William's Doll, 1972, Hold My Hand, 1972, 2d edit., 1987, The Beautiful Christmas Tree, 1972, new edit., 1999, Janie, 1973, My Grandson Lew, 1974, The Summer Night, 1974, 3d edit. 1991, The Unfriendly Book, 1975, It's Not Fair, 1976, 2d edit., 1987, Someone New, 1978, Say It, 1980, If You Listen, 1980, 2d edit. 1987, The New Friend, 1981, One Step, Two ..., 1981, The Song, 1982, I Know a Lady, 1984, Timothy Too!, 1986, Everything Glistens, Everything Sings, 1987, I Like to be Little, 1987, The Poodle Who Barked at the Wind, 1987, The Quiet Mother and the Noisy Little Boy, 1988, Something's Going to Happen, 1988, This Quiet Lady, 1992, The Seashore Book, 1992, Snippets, 1992, The Moon was the Best, 1993, Peter and the Pigeons, 1993, The Old Dog, 1995, When the Wind Stops, 1995, Who is Ben, 1997, Wake Up and Goodnight, Some Things Go Together, new edits., 1998, Do You Know What I'll Do?, new edit., 2000, When I Have a Little Girl When I Have a Little Boy, 2000; Overpraised Season, Early Sorrow. Recipient Harper Gold award for editorial excellence, 1974, Kerlan award U. Minn., 1986, Corp. award for children's books Lit. Market Pl., 1990, Silver medallion U. So. Miss., 1990, Tribute for Far Reaching Contbn. to Children's Lit., ALA, 1991, Otter award, 1997; Charlotte Zolotow award for text of disting. picture book U. Wis. named in her honor, 1998. Mem. PEN, Authors League. Home: 29 Elm Pl Hastings On Hudson NY 10706-1703 Office: 10 E 53d St New York NY 10022-5244

ZOMPARELLI, WENDY, newspaper publisher; b. Chgo., 1950; d. Rocco and Eileen Zomparelli; m. André Spies; 1 child, Samuel Z. Spies. BA, Cornell U., 1971. Staff writer Raleigh (N.C.) Times, 1978-80; writer, copy editor Raleigh (N.C.) News and Observer, 1982-84; staff writer Roanoke (Va.) Times, 1984-85, asst. features editor, 1985, features editor, 1985-92, asst. to pres. and pub., 1992-95, editor, 1995-98, v.p., gen. mgr., 1998-2000, pres., pub., 2000—. Mem. Pulitzer Prize journalism awards jury, 1998-99. Mem.: Soc. Profl. Journalists, Am. Soc. Newspaper Editors, Phi Beta Kappa. Office: The Roanoke Times PO Box 2491 201 Campbell Ave SW Roanoke VA 24011-1100 E-mail: wendy.zomparelli@roanoke.com.

ZOOK, MARTHA FRANCES HARRIS, retired nursing administrator; b. Topeka, Nov. 15, 1921; d. Dwight Thacher and Helen Muriel (Houston) Harris; m. Paul Warren Zook, July 2, 1948 (dec. 1995); children: Mark Warren (dec.), Mary Elizabeth Zook Hughey. Student nurses tng., 1944—47; RN, Meriden (Conn.) Hosp. and Yale U., 1947; student, U. Kans., 1948-49, Kans. State U., 1960-61, Barton County C.C., 1970-73; BA, Stephens Coll., 1977; postgrad., Ft. Hays State U., 1978-79. Staff nurse Stormont Hosp., Topeka, 1947-48, Watkins Meml. Hosp., Lawrence, Kans., 1948-49; nursing supr. Larned State Hosp., 1949-53, sect. supr., 1956-57, dir. nursing, 1958-61, 83-86; sect. nurse Sedgewick Sect., 1961-76, clin. instr. nursing edn., 1976-77, dir. nursing edn., 1977-83; sect. supr. Dillon Bldg., Larned, 1957-58; ret., 1986. Mem. DAR, Sacred Heart Altar Soc. Democrat. Roman Catholic. Home: 2526 Illinois Ave Joplin MO 64804-2221

ZOOK, MAURINE JOYCE, artist; b. Ardmore, Okla., July 17, 1929; d. Maurice Ellsworth Linthicum and Lucia Bosinio; m. Harold Harry Zook, Aug. 5, 1950; children: Marcia, Joyce. Student, Calif. State U., Long Beach, El Camino Coll., Torrance, Calif., U. Tex., Arlington, U. Kans., Pittsburg. Cert. tchr. Art tchr. children at risk Austin Sch., 1991—94; profl. painter large oil landscapes. Mem.: Am. Watercolor Soc., Nat. Watercolor Soc. Avocations: gardening, ceramics, swimming.

ZOOK, THERESA FUETTERER, gemologist, consultant; b. Barberton, Ohio, Mar. 12, 1919; d. Charles Theodore and Ethel May (Knisely) Fuetterer; m. Donovan Quay Zook, June 21, 1941; children: Theodore Alan, Jacqueline Deborah Zook Cochran. AB, Ohio U., 1941; MA in Pub. Adminstrn., Am. U., 1946. Adminstrv. intern Nat. Inst. Pub. Affairs, Washington, 1941-42; mgmt. intern USDA, Washington, 1941-42; adminstrv. analyst Office Emergency Mgmt., Washington, 1942-43, Office Price Adminstrn., Washington, 1943-45; founder Zook and Zook Mgmt. Cons., Arlington, Va., 1945-47; tchr. ancient history and U.S. govt. Fairfax County Pub. Sch., Va., 1963-64; founder, pres. Associated Gem Cons. Lab., Alexandria, 1974—, Alpha Gate Crafts Ltd., Alexandria, 1977—. Color cons. Internat. Com. on Color in Gems, Bangkok, 1983. Author: Directory of Selected Color Resources Annotated Guide, 1982, Reunion of Descendants of David and Magdalena (Blough) Zook, 1983, Basic Machine Knitting, 1979; contbr. articles to profl. jours. Bd. dirs. Am. Embassy Com. on Edn., Montevideo, Uruguay, 1962; co-founder Workshop of Arts, Santiago, Chile, 1958; mem. Nat. Trust for Hist. Preservation, Nat. Mus. Women in Arts, Nat. Mus. [illegible] Indian, [illegible] Horticulture Soc., Textile Mus. Fellow Gemmological Assn. of Gt. Britain (diplomate); mem. AAUW, DAR, Nat. Geneal. Soc., Inter-Soc. Color Coun. (chmn. com. color in gemstones 1982-84, Appreciation cert. 1984), Accredited Gemological Assn. (co-founder, v.p.), Phi Beta Kappa, Tau Kappa Alpha, Kappa Delta Pi. Avocations: garden design, knitting, fabric creation, genealogy, music. Home: Sunrise Ste 215 8033 Holland Rd Alexandria VA 22306-3130

ZOON, KATHRYN CHRISTINE, biochemist; b. Yonkers, N.Y., Nov. 6, 1948; d. August R. and Violet T. (Pollock) Egloff; m. Robert A. Zoon, Aug. 22, 1970; children: Christine K., Jennifer R. BS, Rensselaer Poly. Inst., 1970; PhD, Johns Hopkins U., 1975. Rsch. chemist divsn. biochem. biophys. Bur. Biologics FDA, Bethesda, Md., 1980-84, rsch. chemist divsn. virology, 1984-88, rsch. chemist divsn. cytokine biology Ctr. Biologics, 1988—, divsn. dir., 1989-92; dir. Ctr. Biologics Evaluation and Rsch., 1992—2003; dep. dir. Ctr. for Cancer Rsch. Nat. Cancer Inst., NIH, 2003—. Lectr. NIH, 1994, Reigelman Lectureship, 1994; chmn. expert com. on biol. standardization WHO, 1997-98, 99, 2000, 01; mem. adv. com. of CMR, 2000-03. Contbr. articles to rsch. in biol. chemistry to sci. jours.; sect. editor Jour. Interferon and Cytokine Rsch., 1980—. Bd. dirs. Found. Advanced Edn. Scis., 1996—, 1st v.p., 1999-2003; mem. adv. bd. Def. Advance Rsch. Projects Agy., 1998-2000, Inst. Medicine Nat. Acad. Sci., 2002—. Recipient Person of the Yr. award Biopharm, 1992, Pub. Svc. and Genetic Engrng. News award, 1995, Presdl. Meritorious Exec. Rank award, 1994, Grateful Patient award Nat. Assn. Cancer Patients, 1997, Rensselaer Alumni Assn. award, 1997, Sec.'s award for disting. svc. Dept. Health and Human Svcs., 2001, 03, Disting. Alumnus award Johns Hopkins U., 2003; N.Y. State Regents fellow, 1970, Interferon rsch. fellow NIH, Bethesda, 1975-77, staff fellow, 1979-80. Mem. Am. Soc. Biochem. and Molecular Biology, Intenat. Soc. Interferon and Cytokine Rsch. (pres. elect 1998-99, pres. 2000-01), Internat. Assn. Biol. Standardization (mem. adv. coun. 2000—), Inst. of Medicine. Roman Catholic. Office: Ctr for Cancer Rsch NCI/NIH Bldg 31A Rm 3A11 31 Center Dr Bethesda MD 20892 Personal E-mail: kzoon@comcast.net. Business E-Mail: zoonk@mail.nih.gov.

ZOPF, EVELYN LANOEL MONTGOMERY, guidance counselor; b. Laurel, Miss., July 10, 1932; d. Arthur LaNoel and Ruby Lee (Lewis) Montgomery; m. Paul Edward Zopf Jr., Aug. 5, 1956; 1 child, Eric Paul. MusB in Edn., U. So. Miss., 1953, MA, 1954. Guidance counselor U. So. Miss., 1953-54, U. Fla., 1954-56; tchr. New Orleans City Schs., 1956-57; pub. sch. music tchr., band dir., choral dir. Putnam County Schs., Fla., 1957-59; pvt. music tchr. voice, piano, clarinet and trumpet, 1953-61; substitute tchr. Guilford County Schs., 1959-93; mem. arts series com. Guilford Coll., 1973-77; interim choir dir. New Garden Friends Meeting, 1961, chmn. music com., 1974-76; adviser to fgn. students, 1954-56, 59-62; mem. First Internat. Congress on Quaker Edn. Com., 1987-88, Guilford Coll.'s Sesquicentennial Com., 1985-87; speaker various religious and art groups. Vol. ARC, Boy Scouts Am.; mem. U. Fla. Union Bd., 1955-56; precinct del. County Dem. Conv., 1977, 79, precinct worker, 1980, campaign worker, 1980; bd. dirs. Greensboro Friends of Music, 1970-71, Greensboro chpt. N.C. Symphony Bd., 1979-93, mem. feeder bd. The Guilford Coll. Friends of the Lib. Bd., 1993-94, mem. exec. bd., 1994-95. Mem. United Soc. of Friends Women (pres. 1979-81), Internat. Fellowship Quaker Women, Guilford Coll. Community Chorus, Phi Mu. Clubs: Women's Soc. (dir. 1978-82), Guilford Coll. Arts Appreciation (v.p. 1980-81, pres. 1981-82), Guilford Gourmet. Home: 815 George White Rd Greensboro NC 27410-3317

ZOPP, ANDREA LYNNE, lawyer; b. Rochester, N.Y., Jan. 25, 1957; d. Reuben K. and P. Greta (Hurst) Davis; m. William E. Zopp, Jr., Oct. 7, 1989; children: Alyssa, Kelsey. BA cum laude, Harvard Coll., 1978; JD, Harvard U., 1981. Bar: Ill. 1981, U.S. Dist. Ct. (no. dist.) Ill. 1981, U.S. Ct. Appeals (7th cir.) 1982. Law clk. Hon. George N. Leighton, U.S. Dist. Ct., Chgo., 1981-83; asst. U.S. atty. U.S. Atty.'s Office, Chgo., 1983-86, dept. chief OCDETF, 1986-88, dep. chief criminal lit., 1988-90; ptnr. McDermott, Will & Emery, Chgo., 1990-91; chief narcotics prosecutions bur. Cook County State's Attys. Office, Chgo., 1991-92, first asst. state's atty., 1992—. Bd. dirs. Aux. Bd., Art Inst. Chgo., 1987—; bd. dirs. Chgo. Regional Bd. of Jr. Achievement, 1991—, Leadership Greater Chgo., 1990—, Chgo. Area Project, 1992—. Fellow Leadership Greater Chgo., 1989-90; Kizzy Scholarship Fund award, 1991-92. Mem. ABA, Chgo. Bar Assn., Chgo. Inn of Ct. Avocations: running, music, theater. Office: Cook County State's Atty 2650 S California Ave Chicago IL 60608-5146 also: Cook County State's Atty Rj Daley Ctr Rm 555 Chicago IL 60602

ZORICK, NANCY LEE, artist, actress; b. Chgo., July 24, 1946; d. William Russel and Wilma Beatrice (Fithian) Noble; m. Peter Michael Zorick, Aug. 8, 1980. Student Art Inst. Chgo., 1965-67, Second City Workshop, Chgo., 1967-68, Am. Acad. Art, 1971. Comml. artist Embosograph Display Co., Chgo., 1964-66, Stevens-Biondi-DiCiccio, Chgo., 1966-68. Illustrator: (book) Making Weight, 1991, (children's book) The Little Acorn, 1996; exhibns. include Fontana (Calif.) Arts Assn., 1988, Riverside County Art Exhibnn., 1990; appeared in plays My Sweet Charlie, Chgo., 1968, Harold, Chgo., 1969, films include Medium Cool, 1968, Jackson County Jail, 1976, Outside Chance, 1978; appeared in commercial Tastee Freeze, 1969. Mem Des Arts, 1981, historian, 1983—85, parliamentarian, 1986—93, 1996—, pres., 1993—95. Named to Taft Alumni Hall of Fame, Chgo., 2000; recipient 1st Place in Fine Arts, Nat. Date Festival, 1983, 2d place, Riverside Nat. Date Festival, 1993, 2001, 1996, Best of Show in Fine Arts, Des-Arts Show, 1988, 1st place, Des Arts, 1986, 1990, 1992, 1993, 1996, 1997, 1998, 2000, 2001, 2003, 2004, Best of Show in Fine Arts, Fontana (Calif.) Arts Assn., 1988. Avocations: teaching sunday school, ballet and art, volunteering. Home: 51-555 Monroe St #31 Indio CA 92201

ZORKIN, MELISSA WAGGENER, public relations executive; b. 1954; BA Eng., Lewis & Clark Coll. With Tektronix Inc., Beaverton, Oreg., 1975-80, Regis McKenna, Portland, 1980-83; founder Waggener Edstrom, Inc., 1983—, now pres. and CEO. Named Person of Yr., Media, Inc.; named one of 100 Most Influential People of the 20th Century in Pub. Rels., 50 Most Powerful Women in the Field, PR Week, 1999; recipient Alumni award, Lewis and Clark Coll. Office: Waggener Edstrom Inc 3 Centerpointe Dr Ste 300 Lake Oswego OR 97035-8663*

ZOSIKE, JOANIE FRITZ, theater director, actor; b. Bklyn., July 6, 1949; d. Nathan and Gloria S. (Greenberg) Hieger; m. Godson Zosike. BA in Theatre, NYU, 1980. Actor Living Theatre, N.Y.C., 1990—. Co-dir. DADAnewyork; co-founder Action Racket Theatre, N.Y.C.; artist-in-residence Living Theatre Workshops (USA), Tchrs. and Writers Collaborative. Author: (stage prodns.) You Told Me That the Carousel Was Crystal, Frames, Inside, 12 Steps to Murder; author: (with Hanon Reznikov) And Then The Heavens Closed; actress (stage prodns.) Chisciotte, Not in My Name, Mysteries and Smaller Pieces, Utopia, Anarchia, Humanity, Body of God, I and I, Midsummer Night's Dream, Mother Courage, Resistance, (solo performances) All Right So I AM the Earth, Harpies Complex, Ereshkigal's Peg, Fritzgabriel Cabaret, Alen Mak Festival (Bulgaria), Festival des Politisches Liedes (Germany), (films) Mass and Masses, Human Flesh; vocalist (radio show) Women on the Edge of Time; contbr. Between Ourselves: Letters Between Mothers and Daughters (edited by Karen Payne), Women in American Theatre (edited by Helen Krich Chinoy and Linda Walsh Jenkins); contbr. poetry and articles to artistic jours. Bd. dirs. N.Y.C. Peoples Life Fund; participating artist Theatres Against War. Mem. War Resisters League, New Yorkers Against the Death Penalty. Office: The Living Theatre 2565 Broadway #515 New York NY 10025

ZOTOS, KAREN ANN, healthcare administrator; b. Poughkeepsie, N.Y., July 28, 1967; d. Edward Charles Jr. and Janet Elizabeth Ehrlich; m. Pete Alexander Zotos, Oct. 23, 1993; children: [illegible], Alexa Ann. BA, Columbia Univ., 1989. Provider rels. rep. The Prudential, Dallas, 1991-93; network developer Anthem Health Sys., Dallas, 1993-94; contract mgr. UT Southwestern, Dallas, 1994; profl. svcs. trainer Heritage S.W. Med. Group, Irving, Tex., 1994-95; sr. provider rels. rep. Metra Health Care Plan, Dallas, 1995—96. Cons. North Tex. Podiatry Network, Dallas, 1994, 96; contr. Multiplan, Dallas, 1997-99. Mem. Jr. League Dallas, Med. Group Mgmt. Assn., PTA (life), Slipper Club of Dallas, Kappa Alpha Theta Alumnae. Episcopalian. Home: 6706 Bob O Link Dr Dallas TX 75214-3139

ZOUBAREFF, KATHY OLGA, administrative assistant; b. Hassalt, Belgium; d. Vladimir F. and Kataryna (Sarcov) Z. Grad. in TV acting, J.R. Powers Sch.-Model Agy.; BA in Polit. Sci., Wayne State U.; postgrad., Ann Parsley Sch. Dance, Clinton Twp., Mich., 1990-95, Mary Skiba Sch. Dance, 1995—; A in Gen. Studies, Drama, Macomb Community Coll.; fitness and nutrition cert., Internat. Corr. Schs. Ctr., Scranton, Pa.; voice studies, Ctr. for Creative Studies, Detroit, 1994—; drama studies, Wayne State U., 1994—; broadcasting studies, Macomb C.C., Warren, Mich., 2001. Acct./adminstrv. asst. Univ. Orthopaedic Assocs. Detroit, P.C., 1990-96, office mgr., 1996-98; with The Zoubareff Co., 1998—. Actress, dancer, fashion, TV comml. and photog. model/film screen extra, Hawaiian Tropic Pageants; fragrance model; swimsuit model Ujena; nat. spokesperson Dryell, Physique, Pantene, Oil of O'Lay, Vidal Sassoon, others. Mem. Renaissance Ctr. Fashion Panel, Detroit, 1989-91; rsch. bd. advisors Am. Biog. Inst.; mem. Internat. Biog. Centre Adv. Coun., 1992, St. Clair Shores Players. Avocations: art, drawing, exercising, reading, singing. Home: 38579 Delta Dr Clinton Township MI 48036-1711 Office: Univ Orthopaedics 28800 Ryan Rd Warren MI 48092

ZOULLAS, DEBORAH DECOTIS, private investor, entrepreneur; b. Salem, Mass., Nov. 13, 1952; d. John and Marie (Mahoney) DeC.; m. Nicholas B. Zoullas, Aug. 15, 1987. BA, Smith Coll., 1974; MBA, Stanford U., 1978. Analyst Morgan Stanley & Co. Inc., N.Y.C., 1974-76, assoc., 1978-81, v.p. London, 1982-84, prin. N.Y.C., 1985-87, mng. dir., 1988-95, adv. dir., 1996—; exec. v.p. Sotheby's Holdings, N.Y.C., 1998—2000; dir. Sotheby's Holding Corp., N.Y.C., 2000, Armor Holdings Inc., 2002—. Mem. exec. com. spl. projects com. Meml. Sloan Kettering Cancer Ctr. Mem. adv. coun. Stanford Grad. Sch. Bus., 2003—; trustee Helena Rubinstein Found. Miller scholar Stanford U., 1978. Home: 160 E 72d St New York NY 10021

ZOWADER, SHERRY LEE, volunteer; b. Washington, Feb. 28, 1946; d. Bertram and Doris (Goldberg) Hersh; m. Donald Alan Zowader, Sept. 7, 1968; 1 child, Seth. AA, N.Y. Phoenix Sch. Design, 1967. Chair N.J. state pub. affairs com., sect. rep. state pub. affairs com., chair Ida Schwartz Meml. Libr., chair Nat. Day Working Parent, nat. bd. dirs. Nat. Coun. Jewish Women; bd. dirs., women's issues dir. Raritan Valley LWV; out door art show coord. Somerset County Art Assn.; bd. dirs., chair Prescriptions for Recovery com. Coun. Human Svcs.; active Women's Agenda N.J., N.J. Commn. Sex Discrimination, Family Planning N.J., Karen Carroll for Congress, Food Bank Ctrl. N.J.; founder N.J. Women & AIDS Network, Homesharing, Choice N.J., N.J. Women's Health Collaborative; vol. art tchr., Oreg., 1981-84. Recipient Hannah G. Solomon Cmty. Svc. award Nat. Coun. Jewish Women, 1994, Somerset County (N.J.) commn. on Women, Woman of Achievement, 1994. Avocation: sculpture.

ZSCHAU, MARILYN, singer; b. Chgo., Feb. 9, 1944; d. Edwin Arthur Eugene and Helen Elizabeth (Kelly) Z. BA in Radio, TV and Motion Pictures, U. N.C.; ed., Juilliard Sch. Music; opera theatre with Christopher West, voice with Florence Page Kimball, also studied with John Lester. Toured with Met. Nat. Co., 1965-66; debut, Vienna Volksoper, in Die Tote Stadt, 1967, Vienna Staatsoper, in Ariadne auf Naxos, 1971; with N.Y.C. Opera in La Fanciulla del West, 1978; debut Royal Opera, covent Garden in La Boheme, 1982, Met. Opera, in La Boheme, 1985, La Scala, in Die Frau ohne Schatten, 1986; has toured and sung in many countries including S.Am., Japan, and Australia. Office: 4245 Wilshire Blvd Oakland CA 94602-3549

ZUBER, NORMA KEEN, career counselor, educator; b. Iuka, Miss., Sept. 27, 1934; d. William Harrington and Mary (Hebert) Keen; m. William Frederick Zuber, Sept. 14, 1958; children: William Frederick Jr., Michael, Kimberly, Karen. BS in Nursing, U. Southwestern La., 1956; MS in Counselling, Calif. Luth. U., 1984. Nat. cert. counselor, nat. cert. career counselor; registered profl. career counselor, Calif.; master career counselor. Intensive care nurse Ochsner Found. Hosp., New Orleans, 1956-59; career devel. counselor BFC Counseling Ctr., Ventura, Calif., 1984-87; founder, prin., counselor Career & Life Planning-Norma Zuber & Assocs., Ventura, 1987—. Instr. adult continuing edn. Ventura C.C., 1987—; instr. Calif. State U., Northridge, 1988-89; instr. U. Calif. Santa Barbara, Antioch U.; mem. adv. coun. on tchr. edn. Calif. Luth. U., Thousand Oaks, 1984-87; mem. adv. bd. for development of profl. career counseling cert. program U. Calif., San Diego, 1991—; co-chair legis. com. Calif. Coalition Counselor Licensure. Co-author: The Nuts and Bolts of Career Counseling: How to Set Up and Succeed in Private Practice, 1992. Chmn. bd. dirs. women's ministries Missionary Ch., Ventura, 1987-90. Recipient profl. contbn. award H.B. McDaniel Found.-Stanford U. Sch. Edn., 1988, Govt. Rels. Com. Cert. of Appreciation, Am. Assn. for Counseling and Devel., Career Devel. Practitioner of the Year award Internat. Career Conf., 1998, Spirit of Networking award Ventura Profl. Women's Network, 2001; featured in Nat. Assn. of Women bus. Owners Bravo award, Ventura, Calif. Mem. NAFE, ACA, Nat. Career Devel. Assn. (western region trustee 1994-97, master career counselor 2002—), Calif. Assn. Couseling and Devel. (chmn. legis. task force 1987-89, Jim Saum govt. rels. award 1989), Internat. Platform Assn., Nat. Career Devel. Assn. (western regional trustee 1995-98), Internat. Career Conf. (Career Devel. Practitioner of Yr. 1998), Calif. Career Devel. Assn. (bd. dirs. 1985-98, membership dir. 1991-92, pres. 1992-93, Leadership and Professionaliam award 1988, 89), Calif. Career Conf. (program chair 1993), Ventura County Profl. Women's Network (dir. membership 1990-91, pres. 1998-99), Calif. Registry Profl. Counselors and Paraprofls. (bd. dirs. 1990-94, chair 1995-97), Chi Sigma Iota. Republican. Home: 927 Sentinel Cir Ventura CA 93003-1202 Office: Career and Life Planning Norma Zuber and Assocs 3585 Maple St Ste 237 Ventura CA 93003-9117 Office Phone: 805-656-6220.

ZUBERNIS, LYNN SMITH, psychologist, counselor; d. Kevlin Walter and Carol Luckins Smith; m. James J. Zubernis, June 25, 1983 (div. Mar. 1994); children: Emily Kevlin, Jeffrey James. BA in Psychology, Rosemont Coll., 1994; MA in Sch. Psychology, Bryn Mawr Coll., 1997, PhD in Clin., Devel. and Sch. Psychology, 2002. Cert. sch. psychologist Pa., 1997. Intern psychologist Marple Newtown Sch. Dist., Newtown Square, Pa., 1996—97, Child Study Inst., Bryn Mawr, Pa., 1996—98, St. Gabriel's Hall, Audubon, Pa., 1997—98; sch. psychologist Tower Hill Sch., Wilmington, Del., 1999—; intern psychologist Friends Hosp., Phila., 2000—01; therapist Penn Friends Behl Health, Phila., 2001—02; counselor St. Josephs U., Phila., 2002—. Instr. West Chester (Pa.) State U., 1999; adj. Haverford (Pa.) Coll., 2000. Contbr. articles to profl. jours. Mem.: APA, Pa. Psychol. Assn., Delta Epsilon Sigma, Alpha Sigma Lambda. Avocations: writing, films. Office: St Josephs Univ Counseling Ctr 5600 City Ave Philadelphia PA 19131

ZUCCO, RONDA KAY, planning and marketing professional; b. Peoria, Ill, Apr. 3, 1960; d. Richard Leon Zucco. BA, So. Ill. U., 1981. Cert. addictions profl.; cert. relapse prevention specialist. Addictions counselor Parkside at BroMenn, Bloomington, Ill., 1986-89; dir. continuing care/sr.

counselor Fla. Hosp. (formerly Parkside), Orlando, Fla., 1989-95; addictions program mgr. Charter Behavioral Health Sys., Kissimmee, Fla., 1995-97; coord. outpatient svcs. Heart of Fla. Behavioral Ctr., Lakeland, Fla., 1997-99; bus. and industry rep., planning and mktg. dept. Lakeland Regional Med. Ctr., 1999—. Vol. ARC, Carbondale, Ill., 1978—81; crisis hotline vol. Jackson County Cmty. Mental Health Ctr., Carbondale, 1981; mem. AIDS spkrs. bur. BroMenn Healthcare, Bloomington, 1986—89; vol. Alliance for Mentally Ill of Greater Orlando, Fla., 1995—97, Coalition for Homeless, Orlando, 1995—97; mem. exec. bd. Drug Prevention Resource Ctr., Lakeland, Fla., pres., 1997—; vol. Spl. Olympics, 1999—; mem. Jr. League of Greater Lakeland, 2000—; Salt Lake 2002 Olympic Torchbearer; exec. bd. dirs., 2d v.p. Imperial Symphony Orch., Lakeland, 2001—. Named Outstanding Profl. of Yr., Fla. Sch. Addiction Studies, 1999; recipient State of Ill. scholar, Gen. Assembly, 1977—81, Leadership Lakeland XX, 2002—03. Mem. Am. Mktg. Assn., Am. Assn. for Counseling and Devel., Am. Mental Health Counselors Assn., Fla. Alcohol and Drug Abuse Assn., Fla. Prevention Assn., Nat. Businesswomen's Leadership Assn., Am. Bus. Women's Assn., C. of C. Greater Lakeland, Fla. Coun. on Crime and Delinquency, Kappa Delta Pi, Chi Sigma Iota. Avocations: reading, running, swimming and diving, travel, the arts. Home: 1100 Oakbridge Pkwy Apt 296 Lakeland FL 33803-5964

ZUCKER, BLANCHE MYRA, civic worker; b. Schenectady, N.Y., July 27, 1925; d. Cassius Alexander and Winifred Estelle (Davis) Millington; m. Nelson Marsh, July 7, 1947 (div. July 1967); children: Kay Patricia, Gary Nelson; m. Reuben Zucker, July 22, 1967 (dec. June 1987); m. Henry Bozarth, Feb. 13, 1994. Grad., Meth. Hosp. Sch. Nursing, Bklyn., 1946; BS in Nursing Edn., Columbia U., 1962; MEd, U. Nev., Las Vegas, 1975. RN, N.Y. Night shift head nurse Meth. Hosp., Bklyn., 1947; floor nurse Carle Meml. Hosp.Clinic, Urbana, Ill., 1947; med. librarian So. Nev. Meml. Hosp. (now Univ. Med. Ctr.), Las Vegas, 1963-66; librarian St. Viator Sch., Las Vegas, 1968-74. Del. Nev. Gov.'s Conf. on Library and Info. Services, 1978, publicity dir., 1978-79; alt. Nev. del. White House Conf. on Library and Info. Services, 1979. Mem. Univ. Med. Ctr. So. Nev. Aux, 1980—; trustee Univ. Libr. Soc., Las Vegas, 1985—2003; pres. We Can, 1985, 1986; mem. Nev. Com. for Protection of Children, 1985—2000, vice chmn., 1987—90, chmn., 1990—95; mem. Citizens Com. Victim Rights, 1986—90. Recipient Svc. award St. Viator Sch., 1975, Adminstrn. for Children, Youth and Families award U.S. Dept. Health and Human Svcs., 1985, Book of Golden Deeds award Las Vegas Exch. Club, 1986, Humanitarian award Las Vegas Women, 1986, Appreciation award We Can, Inc., 1987, Lifetime Achievement in Prevention award/20 Yr. Svc. to Children of Nev., 1994, Blanche Zucker Vol. award, 1990, named Vol. of Yr. Citizens Com. Victim Rights, 1989, Amb. of Courtesy, Las Vegas C. of C. and Las Vegas Conv. and Visitors Authority, 1998. Mem. ALA, Nev. Libr. Assn. (publicity dir. 1979, appreciation award 1979), Friends So. Nev. Libra., Clark County Med. Soc. Aux. (pres. 1971-72), Gen. Fedn. Women's Clubs (chmn. Nev. chpt. child abuse project, 1984-90, mem. Past Pres.'s Club, pres. Mesquite Club 1980-81, mem. Nat. Child Care Action Campaign, 1st place Today's Women--the Vol. award 1986, 1st Place Nat. award photography, 1986, 94). Democrat. Avocations: swimming, photography, classical music, opera, creative arts. Home: 2520 Faiss Dr Las Vegas NV 89134-7241

ZUCKER, MAUREEN T. artist; b. Bisbee, Ariz., Dec. 1, 1961; d. Howard Boardman and Cathleen Diane Taylor; m. Barry Benjamin Zucker, Apr. 21, 1956. BFA, Cooper Union U., 1984. Graphic designer George Gerard Assocs., Roslyn, N.Y.; art dir. Ross & Jacobs, Woodbury, N.Y., CMP Media, Manhasset, N.Y., Virgo Publ., Scottsdale, Ariz.; creative svcs. art dir. CWP Publ., Phoenix. Avocations: hiking, walking, drawing, painting, teaching art.

ZUCKER-FRANKLIN, DOROTHEA, internist, educator; b. Berlin, Aug. 9, 1930; came to U.S., 1949; d. Julian J. and Gertrude Zucker; m. Edward C. Franklin (dec.); 1 child, Deborah Julie. BA, CUNY, 1952, PhD in Sci. (hon.), 1996; MD, N.Y. Med. Coll., 1956. Diplomate Am. Bd. Medicine. Intern Phila. Gen. Hosp., 1956-57; resident in internal medicine Montefiore Hosp., N.Y.C., 1957-59, postdoctoral fellow in hematology, 1959-61; postdoctoral fellow in electron microscopy NYU Sch. Medicine, N.Y.C., 1961-63, asst. prof. medicine, 1963-67, assoc. prof., 1968-74, prof. medicine, 1974—; assoc. attending physician Bellevue Hosp., 1968-74, attending physician, 1974—. Assoc. attending physician Univ. Hosp., Tisch Hosp., 1968—74, attending physician, 1974—; cons. physician Manhattan VA Hosp., 1970—; meml. editl. bd. numerous publs., including Blood, 1963—76, 1980—86, Am. Jour. Pathology, 1979—, Ultrastructure Pathology, 1979—, Blood Cells, 1980, Am. Jour. Medicine, 1981—87, Hematology Oncology, 1982—, Jour. AIDS Rsch., 1987—, Hematopathology and Molecular Hematology, 1987—, others; meml. bd. reviewing editors Jour. Lab. and Clin. Medicine, 1990—; mem. hematology panel Health Rsch. Coun. City of N.Y., 1971—74; mem. pathology tng. com. Nat. Inst. Med. Scis., 1971—74; mem. allergy and immunology rsch. com. Nat. Inst. Allergy and Infectious Diseases, 1974—81; mem. U.S.-Israel Binat. Sci. Found., 1980—; mem. ad hoc promotion com. Harvard Med. Sch., 1981, 83; mem. blood products adv. com. FDA, 1981—86; mem. sci. adv. bd. and sci. rev. panel Israel Cancer Rsch. Found., 1982—90; mem. grant rev. panel VA AIDS Ctr., 1988—89; vis. fellow Assn. Claude Bernard, 1974—75. Co-author: The Physiology and Pathology of Leukocytes, 1962, Amyloidosis, 1986, Atlas of Blood Cells: Function and Pathology, 2 vols., 1981, 3d edit., 2003, Thrombopoiesis and Thrombopoietins: Molecular, Cellular, Preclinical and Clinical Biology, 1996; contbr. over 300 articles to profl. jours. Bd. dirs. Henry M. and Lillian Stratton Found., Inc., 1987-95. Named to Hall of Fame, Hunter Coll., 1977, Internat. Profl. and Bus. Women, 1994. Fellow: AAAS, N.Y. Acad. Scis.; mem.: NTLV and Related Viruses, Internat. Retrovirology Assn., N.Y. Soc. Study of Blood (chair program com. 1976—80, pres. 1981—82), N.Y. Soc. Electron Microscopists (program chair 1984, pres. 1984—85), Am. Soc. Cell Biology (program com. internat. congress 1976), Am. Soc. Exptl. Pathology, Am. Assn. Immunologists, Am. Acad. Arts and Scis., Reticuloendothelial Soc. (life; program com. 1974—76, nominating com. 1976—78, pres. 1984—85), Am. Soc. Physiology, Federated Socs. Exptl. Biology and Medicine, Am. Soc. Hematology (program com. 1973, edn. com. 1974—78, chair subcom. on leukocyte physiology 1977, chair subcom. on immunohematology 1984, com. on advanced learning resources 1986—, exec. coun. 1987—91, pres.-elect 1992, v.p. 1993, pres. 1994—95, chair adv. bd. 1996, com. on govt. affairs 2001), Am. Soc. Clin. Investigation, Am. Fedn. Clin. Rsch., Am. Assn. Physicians, Inst. Medicine NAS, Alpha Omega Alpha, Phi Beta Kappa. Office: NYU Med Ctr 550 1st Ave New York NY 10016-6402 Office Phone: 212-263-5634. E-mail: dorothea.zucker-franklin@med.nyu.edu.

ZUCKERMAN, DOROTHY ANN, elementary school educator; b. Bronx, N.Y., Aug. 26, 1932; d. Samuel and Rose (Rothbart) Sugarman; m. Jack Irwin Zuckerman, Aug. 14, 1955; children: Richard Karl, Geri Lynn. BA cum laude, Queens Coll., 1953; MLS, Stony Brook U., 1975. Cert. tchr. K-6, social studies 7-12; cert. advanced study in labor rels. Tchr. Bay Shore (N.Y.) Schs., 1953-58; 59tchr. Brentwood (N.Y.) Schs., 1958, 1969—91; retiree svcs. con. N.Y. State United Tchrs., 2000—. Pre-retirement coord. N.Y. State United Tchrs., Albany, 1980—; retirement cons. N.Y. State United Tchrs., Albany, 1990-2000; del. N.Y. State Retirement System, 1973-91; chmn. L.I. (N.Y.) Alliance Ret. Americans. Charter mem. Islip (N.Y.) Town League of Women Voters, 1961; v.p. Coalition of Labor Union Women, Massapequa, N.Y., 1982; officer, zone leader Dem. Com., Islip, 1984-88; trustee, sch. prin. Bnai Israel Reform Temple, Oakdale, N.Y., 1969-75; mediator Suffolk County Mediation Ctr., Coram, N.Y., 1985; pres. Bay Shore Tchrs., 1956-57. Mem. Am. Fedn. Tchrs. (del. 1981-2000), L.I. Fedn. of Labor (del. 1975-80), Brentwood Tchrs. Assn. (officer, negotiator 1972-80), Phi Beta Kappa. Avocations: gardening, needlework, painting, orchids, travel. Office: 150 Vanderbilt Motor Pkwy Hauppauge NY 11788

ZUCKERMAN, HARRIET, sociologist, educator; b. N.Y.C., July 19, 1937; d. Harry and Anne D. (Wiener) Z; m. Robert K. Merton, 1993. AB, Vassar Coll., 1958; PhD, Columbia U., 1965. Asst. prof. sociology Columbia U., 1965-72, assoc. prof., 1972-78, prof., 1978-92; prof. emerita, 1993—; sr. rsch. scholar, 1993—; chmn. dept. Columbia U., 1978-81; v.p. Andrew W. Mellon Found., 1991-98, sr. v.p., 1998—. Vis. scholar Russell Sage Found., 1971-72, 85-87; mem. adv. bd. Social Sci. Citation Index, Inst. Sci. Information, 1972-98; dir. Annual Revs., Inc., 1974— ; trustee Am. Savs. Bank, 1978-83 Author: Scientific Elite: Nobel Laureates in the United States, 1977, rev. edit., 1996; co-editor: Toward A Metric of Science: The Advent of Science Indictors, 1978, The Outer Circle: Women in the Scientific Community, 1991; mem. editorial bd. Scientometrics, 1977—, Am. Jour. Sociology, 1972-74, 77-79, Am. Sociol. Rev, 1972-74, 87-91, Sci., 1985-86; contbr. articles to profl. jours. Bd. dirs. Social Sci. Rsch. Coun., 1974-76, AAAS, 1980-84, Women's Forum, 1989-91; trustee Ctr. for Advanced Study in Behavioral Scis., 1976-88, 89-2001, 03—; mem. ednl. adv. bd. John Simon Guggenheim Meml. Found., 1986-93, mem. com. on selection, 1989-91. Woodrow Wilson fellow, 1958-59; Center for Advanced Study in Behavioral Scis. fellow, 1973-74; Guggenheim fellow, 1980-81; Phi Beta Kappa vis. scholar, 1982-83; recipient Dean's award for Disting. Achievement Columbia U. Grad. Sch., 1998. Mem. Am. Philos. Soc. (councillor 1997-03, chmn. Class III membership com. 2002—), Am. Acad. Arts and Scis. (chmn. class III membership com. 1991-94), Soc. Social Studies Sci. (pres. 1989-91), The Century Assn., Coun. on Fgn. Rels.

ZUCKERMAN, NANCY CAROL, learning disabilities specialist, consultant; b. Jersey City, Aug. 14, 1951; d. Bernard Milton and Shirley (Stepner) Solomon; m. Marshall Howard Zuckerman, Aug. 20, 1978; 1 child, Seth Michael. BA, Rider U., 1973; MEd, William Paterson Coll., 1977. Cert. elem. tchr., spl. edn. and learning disabilities tchr., prin., N.J. Tchr. elem. edn. North Bergen (N.J.) Bd. Edn., 1973-76; tchr. state compensatory edn. Bayonne (N.J.) Bd. Edn., 1977, tchr. cons. learning disabilities, 1977—. Chairperson Child Study Team, Bayonne, 1988-99. Mem. adv. bd., sec., asst. pack leader Cub Scouts Pack 35, Bayonne, 1996-2000, com. chair Troop 35, 2002—; bd. dirs. Temple Beth Am, Bayonne, 1975-79, 97—, edn. chmn., 1975-79. Mem. CEC, Assn. Learning Consultants, Pi Lambda Theta. Jewish. Home: 21 E 35th St Bayonne NJ 07002-3924 Office: Bayonne Bd Edn Bayonne NJ 07002 E-mail: N@LDTC@aol.com.

ZUG, ELIZABETH E. concert pianist, educator; b. Phila., Oct. 8, 1907; d. Nathan Walter and Amelia Elizabeth (Nelson) Zug. BA in Music, Irving Coll., 1928. Mem. faculty Nat. Guild Piano Tchrs., 1949. Judge piano auditions Yr. in Music, Nat. Guild Piano Tchrs., 1949. Debut N.Y. Town Hall, 1938; concert pianist, S.Am. tour, 1941. Named Outstanding N.Y. Debut as Pianist, 1938, Judge of the Yr. Nat. Guild Piano Tchrs., 1949. Mem. Music Tchrs. Nat. Assn., Pa. Music Tchrs. Assn. United Ch. Christ. Avocations: writing, designing, landscaping. Studio: 12 N 4th St Reading PA 19601-3910

ZUG, ELIZABETH KENDALL, volunteer; b. Boston, Oct. 24, 1954; d. Robert Edward Kendall and Diana (Dana) Kendall Fahrney; m. Graham F. Zug, Sept. 8, 1979; children: Keri, Amy, Kelly, Kiersten. BSBA, U. So. Calif., 1976; MBA, U. Pa., 1978, cert. fund raising mgmt., 1997. Fin. analyst FMC Corp., Chgo., [illegible] analyst, 1979-80, purchasing agt. corp. purchasing, 1980-82; cons. Individual Purchasing Cons., 1984-85; purchasing cons. Beatrice Foods, Chgo., 1984. Mem. long range planning com. bd. trustees Agnes Irwin Sch., Rosemont, Pa., 1994-96, trustee, 1996—; mem. long range planning com. subcom. of vestry Ch. of the Redeemer, Bryn Mawr, Pa., 1995—; adv. com. Bache Lewis Penrose Soc., Children's Hosp. of Phila., 1997—, mem. women's com., 1995—; mem. Gladwyne (Pa.) Libr. League, 1993—, Haverford (Pa.) Civic Assn., 1995—. Wharton scholar, 1976, 77. Mem. Nat. Soc. Fund Raising Execs., Wharton Alumni Club Phila., Alpha Lambda Delta. Avocations: travel, children's health delivery systems, financial investing, swimming, tennis. Home: 127 Rose Ln Haverford PA 19041-1724

ZUK, CARMEN VEIGA, psychiatrist; b. Buenos Aires, Mar. 5, 1939; came to U.S., 1971; d. Carlos and Carmen Villella Veiga; m. Gerald Harvey, May 7, 1974; children: Cary Elizabeth and Gabrielle Ann (twins). MD, U. Buenos Aires, 1964, cert. psychiatry, 1969. Diplomate Am. Bd. Psychiatry and Neurology. Intern Med. Coll. of Pa., Phila., 1974-75; resident in psychiatry Norristown (Pa.) State Hosp., 1977-79; child psychiatry fellowship Med. Coll. Pa. and Ea. Pa. Psychiat. Inst., Phila., 1979-81; dir. child and adolescent unit Hosp. of Med. Coll. Ga., Augusta, 1981-83; dir. treatment team New Orleans Adolescent Hosp., 1983-85; assoc. Psychiatry Med. Group, Calif., 1985-86; mental health psychiatrist L.A. County Dept. Mental Health San Fernando Mental Health Svcs., 1986-88; psychiatrist-ptnr. So. Calif. Permanente Med. Group, Van Nuys, Calif., 1988-98, ptnr., 1988-98; staff psychiatrist Santa Clarita Child and Family Ctr., 1999—2002. Asst. prof. dept. psychiatry Med. Coll. Ga., 1981-83; clin. asst. prof. dept. psychiatry and neurology Tulane U., 1983-85. Contbr. articles to profl. publs. Mem. AMA, Internat. Soc. for Adolescent Psychiatry. Avocations: reading, cooking, gardening, swimming, music. Home: 7620 Hollister Ave #219 Goleta CA 93117 Office: Santa Clarita Child and Family Ctr 21545 Redview Dr Santa Clarita CA 91350-2617 E-mail: CarmenZuk@msn.com.

ZUK, JUDITH, botanic garden administrator; b. Canandaigua, N.Y., Sept. 11, 1951; BA, Rutgers U., 1973; MS, U. Del., 1976. CEO, pres. Bklyn. Botanic Garden, 1990—. Bd. dirs. Botanic Gardens Conservation Internat., Greenwood Cemetery; mem. regional adv. bd. JP Morgan Chase. Mem. Phi Beta Kappa. Office: Bklyn Botanic Garden 1000 Washington Ave Brooklyn NY 11225-1008 E-mail: judithzuk@bbg.org.

ZULAUF, MADELINE RUTH, civilian military employee, photographer; b. Neptune, N.J., Oct. 9, 1948; d. Everett Minor and Mary Elizabeth Slocum; m. Bateston Franklin Stoddard, Jr., Apr. 2, 1967 (div. July 1972); children: Michael, Mary Beth; m. Sander William Zulauf, May 26, 1979. AA, County Coll. of Morris, 1976; BA, Montclair State U., 1978. Photographer U.S. Army Rsch., Devel. & Engring. Ctr., Picatinny Arsenal, N.J., 1979-84, TV prodr., dir., 1984-87, visual info. specialist, 1987—96, multimedia specialist, 1996—2000, visual info. mgr., 2000—. Cons. phototech. program County Coll. of Morris, Randolph, N.J., 1983-88, mem. student co-op adv. bd., 1989-94; pres. federally employed women U.S. Army Rsch., Devel. & Engring. Ctr., Picatinny Arsenal, 1984-85, chairperson fed. women's program, 1987-89. Photographer: (mag.) Horns of Plenty, 1989, (book) Above the River, 1990; photo exhbns. include Sussex City Arts Coun., 1996-97, James Wright Poetry Festival, Martins Ferry, Ohio, 1999, Mckewons Gallery, Branchville, N.J., 1997. Photographer Jersey Battered Women's Shelter, Morristown, N.J., 1985-88; dep. diocesan convs. Episcopal Diocese Newark, N.J. Recipient Humanitarian award Equal Opportunity Office, 1984. Mem. Acad. Am. Poets, Internat. Ctr. Photography. Episcopalian. Avocations: sailing, travel, hiking. Office: US Army Rsch Devel & Engring Ctr B-1 Picatinny Arsenal NJ 07806 Office Phone: 973-724-3839. E-mail: mzulawf@pica.army.mil.

ZULCH, JOAN CAROLYN, retired medical publishing company executive; b. Great Neck, N.Y., Apr. 10, 1931; d. Walter Howard and Edna Ruth (Howard) Z. BS in Biology, Allegheny Coll., 1952; postgrad., Hunter Coll., 1954. Med. sec. E.R. Squibb & Sons, N.Y.C., 1952; with Macmillan Pub. Co., N.Y.C., 1952-88, editorial asst. med. dept., 1952-56, asst. editor med. dept., 1956-58, editor med. dept., 1958-61, med. editor coll. and profl. div., 1961-75, sr. editor medicine, coll. and profl. div., 1975-78, exec. editor med. books, profl. books div., 1978-79, editor-in-chief, 1979-80, asst. v.p., editor-in-chief profl. books div., 1980-82, v.p., pub. med., nursing, health sci. dept., 1982-85, v.p., pub. med. books, sci., tech., med. dept., 1985-88. Recipient Best Illustrated Med. Book award Assn. Med. Illustrators, 1977, Outstanding Book in Health Sci. award Assn. Am. Pubs., 1982. Mem. AAAS, Post Libr. Assn., L.I.U. (rec. sec. 1990-93, exec. coun. 1990—), Friends of Locust Valley Libr. (pres. 1991-93, 94-96, 98-2000, treas. 1993-94, 96-98, 2000-02, 1st v.p. 2002—), Locust Valley C. of C. (bd. dirs. 1997—), Alpha Gamma Delta, Delta Sigma Rho. Republican. Home: 36 Wood Ln Lattingtown PO Box 547 Locust Valley NY 11560-0547

ZUMO, BILLIE THOMAS, biologist; b. Cheyenne, Wyo., Sept. 25, 1936; d. Thomas Elias and Katherine A. (Pappas); m. Charles Vincent, Aug. 21, 1959; 1 child, Thomas J. BA, U. Wyo., Laramie, 1958; MA, U. No.Colo., Greeley, 1963. Cert. tchr. Tchr. Carey Jr. H.S., Cheyenne, 1958-61, 61-63; English language tchr. McCormick Jr. H.S., Cheyenne, 1961; biology tchr. Laramie County C.C., Cheyenne; tchr. Central H.S., Cheyenne, 1963; ret., 1999. Exec. bd. Sch. Dist. curriculum adv., 1982-85; chmn. sci. dept., 1990—; mem. faculty adv. com. Central High Sch., 1988—, mem. prin. screening com., 1990-91. Football statistician Cen. Football Team, Cheyenne, 1976—; lay mem. rsch. com. of the Pharmacy Theraputics Com., 1985; judge sch. dist. sci. fair, Cheyenne, 1987-88; ch. choir dir., Cheyenne; judge Nat. Oratorical Contest, Greek Orthodox Archdiocese Am. Recipient Disting. Svc. award Sts. Constandine and Helen Orthodox Ch., 1979, Disting. Svc. award as choir dir. Archbishop Iakovas, N.Y., 1988. Mem. Nat. Assn. Biology Tchrs. (state rep. 1992-99), NEA, Cheyenne Tchrs. Edn. Assn., Wyo. Edn. Assn., Nat. Forum of Greek Orthodox Musicians, Ladies Philoptochos Soc. of Denver Diocese (treas. 1989-93, 1st v.p. 1993-95, pres. 1995-99, diocese adv. 1999-2003, diocese philoptochos bd., 2003—, editor newsletter, 1997—, appointed to nat. philoptochos bd. 1997-99, 2000—, ch. heritage com.), AAUW, Phi Delta Kappa. Democrat. Eastern Greek Orthodox. Avocations: reading, walking, music, golf. Home: 900 Ranger Dr Cheyenne WY 82009-2535

ZUMPE, DORIS, ethologist, researcher, educator; b. Berlin, May 18, 1940; came to U.S., 1972; d. Herman Frank and Eva (Wagner) Z. BSc, U. London, 1961, PhD, 1970. Asst. to K.Z. Lorenz, Max-Planck-Inst. für Verhaltensphysiologie, Seewiesen, Fed. Republic Germany, 1961-64; rsch. asst. and assoc., lectr. Inst. Psychiatry, U. London, 1965-72; rsch. assoc. Emory U. Sch. Medicine, Atlanta, 1972-74, asst. prof. psychiatry (ethology), 1974-77, assoc. prof., 1977-87, prof., 1987—. Reviewer NSF, 7 sci. jours. Contbr. over 150 articles to profl. jours. NIMH grantee, 1971-2000. Mem. AAAS, Internat. Soc. Psychoneuroendocrinology, Internat. Primatological Soc., Internat. Soc. for Human Ethology, Soc. Behavioral Neuroendocrinology, Am. Soc. Primatologists, N.Y. Acad. Scis., Earl Music Am., Viola da Gamba Soc. Am. Avocation: music. Office: Emory U Sch Medicine Dept Psychiatry Atlanta GA 30322-0001

ZUMWALT, KAREN KEPLER, education educator; b. Washington, Nov. 15, 1943; d. Povl and Helen Jean Bang-Jensen; m. Robert Eugene Zumwalt, Aug. 1, 1980; children: Christina Ann, Scott Paul; m. Michael John Kepler, June 1968 (dec. Nov. 1970). BA, Mt. Holyoke Coll., South Hadley, Mass., 1961—65; MA edn., Harvard Grad. Sch. of Edn., Cambridge, Mass., 1966—67; PhD, The U. of Chgo., Chgo., Ill., 1969—78. Cert. Permanent Secondary Social Studies Teacher NY State, 1967, Provisional Secondary Social Studies Tchr. Ohio, 1967, Spl. Social Studies, K-12 Tchg. and Supervison Ill., 1968. Social sci. analyst US [illegible] Civil Rights, Washington, 1965—66; tchr. Patrick Henry Jr. HS, Cleve., 1967—68, Ctrl. Sch., Glencoe, Ill., 1968—69; lectr. Smith Coll., Northampton, Mass., 1973—76; instr., asst. prof., assoc. prof., evenden prof. of edn. Teachers Coll., Columbia Univ., New York, NY, 1976—; dir., presvc. elem. edn. program Teachers Coll., Columbia U., New York, NY, 1976—82, dept. chair, dept. of curriculum and tchg., 1986—89, divsn. dir., divsn. of institutions and programs, 1992—94, dean and v.p. for academic affairs, 1995—2000. Author: (book chapter) Nat. Soc. for the Study of Edn. Yearbook (Am. Edn. Rsch. Assn. Interpretive Scholarship Award, 1983), Nat. Soc. for the Study of Edn., Nat. Soc. for the Study of Edn. Yearbook, Hidden Consequences of a Nat. Curriculum, (journal article) Ednl. Rschr., Teachers Coll. Record; editor (and author): (book) Improving Tchg.; author: (book chapter) Knowledge Base for Beginning Teachers, (journal article) Jour. of Tchr. Edn., (book chapter) Handbook of Rsch. on Curriculum, (journal article) Edn. and Urban Soc. Mem. Non-partisan Sch. Bd. Nominating Com., Chappaqua, NY, 1994—95; sch. bd. observer New Castle LWV, Chappaqua, NY, 2000—01; bd. mem. Roosevelt Is. Neighborhood Youth Program, New York, NY, 1977—80; co-chair Parent Adv. Com. on Elem. Sch. Growth, Dobbs Ferry, NY, 1988—88; apptd. mem. Springhurst Elem. Sch. Parent Adv. Com. to Prin., Dobbs Ferry, NY, 1990—91; mem. Dist. Parent Edn. Com., Chappaqua, NY, 1991—93; elected parent rep. and newsletter editor Roaring Brook Bldg. Level Team, Chappaqua, NY, 1993—95; chair Parent Evaluation Com., New Castle Baseball Assn., Chappaqua, NY, 1994—94. Recipient Writing prize, Nat. Ctr. for Edn. in Politics, 1964, Demonstration Tchr., Cleve. Pub. Schools, 1967-68, Mentor Award, Spencer Found., 1994-96; fellow Title IV Fellowship, Nat. Def. Edn. Act, 1969-1972; grantee Rsch. grant to study tchr. edn. in N.J., US Office of Edn., 1985-90, 1992-93., Rsch. Tng. Grant, Spencer Found., 1995-2000, 2000-2005. Mem.: Teachers Coll. Press (editl. bd. 1995—2000), Nat. Soc. for the Study of Edn. (bd. dirs. 1988—97), Am. Ednl. Rsch. Assn. (com. mem. 1975—2003, Interpretive Scholarship Award 1983). Home: 47 Spring Lane Chappaqua NY 10514 Office: Columbia University Teachers College Box 31 New York NY 10027 Business E-Mail: kkz2@columbia.edu.

ZUNGOLO, EILEEN H. dean; BS, MEd, EdD, Columbia U. Prof., dean Sch. Nursing Northeastern U., Boston, assoc. dean Bouve Coll. Health Scis. Office: Northeastern Univ Sch Nursing 360 Huntington Ave Boston MA 02115-5000 E-mail: ezungolo@lynx.dac.neu.edu.

ZUNICH, JANICE, pediatrician, geneticist, educator, health facility administrator; b. New Kensington, Pa., Sept. 2, 1953; d. Nick and Mary (Zivkovich) Z.; m. Milan Katic, June 20, 1981; children: Nikola Ilija, Milana. BS, Ohio State U., 1974, MD, 1978. Diplomate Am. Bd. Pediat., Nat. Bd. Med. Examiners, Am. Bd. Med. Genetics (clin. genetics, clin. cytogenetics). Lab. technician Cmty. Hosp., Lorain, Ohio, summer 1974, Ohio State U. Hosp., Columbus, Ohio, 1974-75; intern, then resident in pediat. Columbus Children's Hosp., Ohio, 1978-81; genetics fellow Luth. Gen. Hosp., Park Ridge, Ill., 1981-83; asst. prof. pediat. W.Va. U. Med. Ctr., Morgantown, 1983-85, assoc. dir. cytogenetics, 1984-85; clin. assoc. prof. med. genetics, dir. Genetics Ctr. N.W. Ctr. Med. Edn., Ind. U. Sch. Medicine, Gary, 1985—. Genetics cons. Cmty. Hosp., Munster, Ind., Porter Meml. Hosp., Valparaiso, Ind., St. Anthony Med. Ctr., Crown Point, Ind., Meth. Hosp., Gary and Merrillville, Ind., St. Margaret Hosp., Hammond, Ind., St. Mary Med. Ctr., Hobart, Ind., LaPort (Ind.) Hosp., Meml. Hosp., South Bend, Ind. Contbr. articles to profl. jours. Mem. med. com. Planned Parenthood, N.W.-N.E. Ind., Merrillville, 1987-99; mem. med. adv. com. Svcs. for Children with Spl. Health Care Needs, Indpls., 1989-92; chmn. Lake County Task Force on Teen Pregnancy, 1998-2000; mem. Lake County Child Fatality Rev. Com., 2003-; mem. Lake County Child Protection Team, 2000-; treas. Mental Health Assn. Lake County, 1995-99, bd. dirs., 1991-. Named Person of Yr. Down Syndrome Assn. N.W. Ind., Highland, 1988; Charles F. Whitten fellow Sickle Cell Found. N.W. Ind., 1990. Fellow: AMA, Am. Coll. Med. Genetics (founding fellow), Am. Acad. Pediat.; mem.: Lake County Med. Soc., Ind. State Med. Assn., Am. Soc. Human Genetics, Great Lakes Regional Genetics Group (financing genetics svcs. sub-com. 1988—99), Alpha Epsilon Delta, Phi Beta Kappa. Eastern Orthodox. Avocations: piano, folk dancing, choral singing, travel. Office: NW Ctr for Med Edn 3400 Broadway Gary IN 46408-1101 Office Phone: 219-980-6560. E-mail: jzunich@iun.edu.

ZUNIGA, FANNY, aerospace engineer; Postgrad., Stanford U., 2001—; BS in Aero. Engring., Syracuse U.; MS in Aero. Engring., U. So. Calif. Aerospace engr. sys. analysis br. NASA Ames Rsch. Ctr., 1990—. Office: NASA Ames Rsch Ctr Mail Stop 247-4 Bldg 258 Rm 120 Moffett Field CA 94035

ZUPAN, MARY ANNE, music educator, consultant; b. Quincy, Ill., Oct. 29, 1955; d. Robert Leo and Phyllis Arlene Orf; m. Bruce Zupan, June 11, 1977; children: Gwen Katherine, Aaron Bruce. B of Music Edn., N.E. Mo. State U., 1977; M of Music Edn., Silver Lake Coll., 1991, Kodaly cert. Music educator Kettle Moraine Sch. Dist., Wales, Wis., 1977—. Music program cons. for rsch. project VH1-Save the Music Milw. Pub. Schs. Recipient Kohl Educator fellowship, Gov. Herb Kohl, 1999, Christa McAuliffe fellowship, Dept. Edn., 2001. Mem.: Wis. Arts Alliance, Wis. Music Educators Assn. (coun. mem.), Music Educators Nat. Conf. Home: 515 W 32260 Moraine View Dr Delafield WI 53018

ZUPKUS, ELLEN CICCONE, clinical psychologist, consultant; b. Passaic, N.J., Oct. 28, 1954; d. Joseph Condoluro and Emma (Gash) Ciccone; m. Edward Walter Zupkus Jr., July 29, 1984; children: Maureen, Erin, Emily, Lauren. BA, Kean Coll. N.J., 1976; MA, Seton Hall U., 1978, PhD, 1985. Cert. sch. psychologist N.J.; Nat. cert sch. psychologist, group psychotherapist; lic. psychologist, N.J., N.Y. Adj. instr. Seton Hall U., South Orange, N.J., 1979-84; chairperson child study team Bergen County Spl. Svcs. Sch. Dist., Paramus, N.J., 1983-85; pvt. practice Holmdel, N.J., 1985—; adj. instr. Rider Coll., Lawrenceville, N.J., 1986; prin. clin. psychologist Marlboro (N.J.) Psychiat. Hosp., 1986-88; cons. psychologist Arthur Brisbane Child Treatment Ctr., Farmingdale, N.J., 1988-89; adj. instr. Monmouth Coll., West Long Branch, N.J., 1989; cons. psychologist Cedar Grove (N.J.) Residential Ctr., 1989—. Cons. psychologist Adult Diagnostic and Treatment Ctr., Avenel, N.J., 1980-82; clin. psychologist Woodbridge Child Diagnostic Ctr., Avenel, 1980-83; presenter workshop on Million Adolescent Personality Inventories, 1989, Internat. Play Therapy Conf., The Netherlands, 1996. Author: (with others) Conference on the Millon Inventories, 1987; contbr. articles to profl. jours. Mem. Monmouth County Sexual Abuse Coalition, Monmouth County Child Sexual Abuse Com., Nat. Audubon Soc., Nat. Wildlife Fedn., Vienna, Va. Mem. APA (assoc.), N.J. Psychol. Assn., N.J. Assn. Sch. Psychologists, Monmouth Ocean County Psychol. Assn., Seton Hall U. Sch. Psychology Assn. (pres. 1981), N.J. Network for Treatment Sex Offenders, Am. Coll. Forensic Examiners. Avocations: running, bird watching, hiking. Office: 51 Main St Holmdel NJ 07733-2310

ZUPON, DIANE ELIZABETH, medical technician; b. Spangler, Pa., Mar. 19, 1970; d. Patrick Evan and Theresa Louise Zupon. AS in Cardiovascular Tech., Mt. Aloysius Coll., 1993; BS in Exercise and Sport Sci., Pa. State U., 1994. Registered diagnostic cardiac sonographer, vascular specialist. Cardiac sonographer Johnstown (Pa.) Cardiovascular Assoc., 1994—99, Mayo Clinic, Rochester, Minn., 1999—2000, Geisinger Med. Ctr., State College, Pa., 2000—01, U. Pa. Med. Ctr. Lee Regional, Johnstown, 2001—02, U. Pa. Med. Ctr. Bedford Meml., 2002—. Mem.: Soc. Diagnostic Med. Sonographers, Am. Soc. Echocardiography. Roman Catholic. Avocations: reading, sports.

ZURAITIS, MARITA, insurance company executive; V.p. ceded-reins. USF&G Comml. Ins. Group, br. v.p., regional v.p., sr. v.p.; sr. v.p. U.S. ins. ops. The St. Paul Co., Inc., St. Paul, 1998—2001, exec. v.p. Comml. Lines Group, 2001—02, CEO Comml. Lines Group, 2003—. Office: The Saint Paul Cos Inc 385 Washington St Saint Paul MN 55102*

ZURAW, KATHLEEN ANN, special education and physical education educator; b. Bay City, Mich., Sept. 29, 1960; d. John Luke and Clara Josephine (Kilian) Z. AA with high honors, Delta Community Coll., 1980; BS with high honors, Mich. State U., 1984, MA, 1987. Cert. spl. edn., mentally impaired phys. edn. grade K-12, adaptive phys. edn. tchr., Mich. Summer water safety instr. Camp Midicha, Columbia, Mich., 1982, Bay Cliff Health Camp, Big Bay, Mich., 1983; summer spl. edn. tchr. Jefferson Orthopedic Sch., Honolulu, 1984, 85, 86, Ingham Intermediate Sch. Dist., Mason, Mich., 1987; spl. edn. tchr. Bay Arenac Intermediate Sch. Dist., Bay City, 1985-87, Berrien County Intermediate Sch. Dist., Berrien Springs, Mich., 1987—. Mem. citizen amb program fitness delegation People's Republic China, 1991. Area 17 coach Mich. Spl. Olympics, Berrien Springs, 1987—; mem. YMCA, St. Joseph, Mich., 1987—, Y-Ptnrs., 1989, Coun. Exceptional Children; participant Citizen Ambassador Delegation to People's Republic of China, 1991. Mem. Am. Alliance Health, Phys. Edn., Recreation and Dance, Phi Theta Kappa, Phi Kappa Phi, Phi Delta Kappa. Roman Catholic. Avocations: sports, crafts. Home: 7306 W S Saginaw Rd Bay City MI 48706

ZURAWSKI, JEANETTE, rehabilitation services professional; b. June 30, 1951; Student, U. Wis., 1969-70, Portland C.C., 1974-78; BS in Chemistry, Portland State U., 1981; MD, Oreg. Health Scis. U., 1985; postgrad. in acupuncture, UCLA, 2000. Diplomate Am. Bd. Phys. Medicine and Rehab. Resident U. Kans. Med. Ctr., Kansas City, 1985-89; med. dir. rehab. svcs. North Miss Med. Ctr., Tupelo, 1989-97; pvt. practice Tupelo, Miss. Past mem. adv. com. Medicare Carrier; presenter in field; bd. dirs. Gilbert's Home Health Care Agy. Past chair pers. com., exec. bd. mem., co-chair fund raising com. Big Brothers/Big Sisters, Lee County, Miss. Mem. AMA, Am. Acad. Phys. Medicine and Rehab. (chairperson edn. com., mem. exec. coun. resident physician sect.), Am. Med. Women's Assn., Am. Bus. Women's Assn. (chair membership com., treas., recipient Woman of the Year), Miss. State Med. Assn., Assn. Acad. Physiatrists, Am. Med. Acupuncture Assn. (bd. eligible), Iota Sigma Pi. Office: 1010 N Eason Blvd Tupelo MS 38804-7532

ZURIER, REBECCA, art history educator; AB, Harvard U., 1978; PhD, Yale U., 1988. Assoc. prof. U. Mich., Ann Arbor; Schragis fellow in modern arts Syracuse U., 1990—92. Guest curator Metropolitan Lives: The Ashcan Artists and Their New York Nat. Mus. Am. Art, Smithsonian Instn., 1995; guest curator Yale U. Art Gallery, 1986; vis. appts. U. So. Calif., Emory U., U. Pa., George Washington U., 1988—90. Author: The American Firehouse: An Architectural and Social History, 1982, Art for the Masses (1911-1917): A Radical Magazine and Its Graphics, 1988 (Alfred H. Barr award Coll. Art Assn., 1996); co-author (with Robert W. Snyder and Virginia Mecklenburg): Metropolitan Lives, 1995. Charles Warren Ctr. for Studies in Am. History, Harvard U. fellow, 1999, Getty Postdoctoral grantee, 1993. Office: Univ Mich Art History Dept 519 S State St Ann Arbor MI 48109-1357

ZUSSY, NANCY LOUISE, librarian; b. Tampa, Fla., Mar. 4, 1947; d. John David and Patsy Ruth (Stone) Roche; m. R. Mark Allen, Dec. 20, 1986. BA in Edn., U. Fla., 1969; MLS, U. So. Fla., 1977, MS in Pub. Mgmt., 1980. Cert. librarian, Wash. Ednl. evaluator State of Ga., Atlanta, 1969-70; media specialist DeKalb County Schs., Decatur, Ga., 1970-71; researcher Ga. State Libr., Atlanta, 1971; asst. to dir. reference Clearwater (Fla.) Pub. Libr., 1972-78, dir. librs., 1978-81; dep. state libr. Wash. State Libr., Olympia, 1981-86, state libr., 1986—2002. Chmn. Consortium Automated Librs., Olympia, 1982-97; cons. various pub. librs., Wash. and other U.S. states, Uzbekistan, Russia, 1981—; exec. officer Wash. Libr. Network, 1986-90; v.p. WLN (non-profit orgn.), 1990-93. Contbr. articles to profl. jours. Treas. Thurston-Mason Community Mental Health Bd., Olympia, 1983-85, bd. dirs., 1982-85; mem. race com. Seafair Hydroplane Race, Seattle, 1986—, mem. milk carton derby team, 1994—, announcer, prodr. air show; co-chair Pub. Info. Access Policy Task Force, 1995-96; mem. Gov.'s Work Group on Comml. Access to Govt. Electronic Records, 1996-97; mem. K-20 Telecomms. Oversight and Policy Com., 1996-2002. Mem. ALA, Assn. Specialized and Coop. Libr. Agys. (legis. com. 1983-86, chmn.. 1985-87, vice chmn. state libr. agys. sect. 1985-86, chmn. 1986-87, chmn. govt. affairs com. Libr. Adminstrn. and Mgmt. Assn., 1986-87), Freedom To Read Found. (bd. dirs. 1987-91), Chief Officers of State Libr. Agys. (bd. dirs.-at-large 1987-90, v.p., pres.-elect 1990-92, pres. 1992-94), Wash. Libr. Assn. (co-founder legis. planning com. 1982-2002, fed. rels. coord. 1984-2002), Fla. Libr. Assn. (legis. and planning com. 1978-81), Pacific N.W. Libr. Assn., Rotary (bd. dirs. 1995-96), Phi Kappa Phi, Phi Beta Mu. Avocations: hiking, barbershop chorus/quartet, hydroplane boat racing, cross country skiing. Office: Wash State Libr PO Box 42460 Olympia WA 98504-2460

ZUSY, CATHERINE, curator; b. Washington, May 4, 1958; d. Frederick John and Mary Jane Zusy; m. Samuel Conant Kendall, Sept. 6, 1992. BA, Bucknell U., 1981; MA in History Mus. Studies, SUNY, Oneonta, 1984. Curator of edn. Deland (Fla.) Mus., 1981-82; asst. curator State Capital Pub. Mus., Guthrie, Okla., 1982-83; rsch. asst. dept. Am. decorative arts Mus. Fine Arts, Boston, 1985-87; curator decorative arts The Bennington (Vt.) Mus., 1988-91; chief curator N.H. Hist. Soc., Concord, N.H., 1991-95; exhbn. and interpretation cons., 1996—; project dir., curator Adventures in Light and Color, 2000—02. Project dir. for exploratory excavations of the U.S. Pottery Co., Bennington, Vt., 1997, 98; project dir. exhbn. The Bicycle Takes Off, 1998-2000, Faithful Boston, 2000; lectr. L.A. County Mus. Arts, M. H. de Young Mus., San Francisco, Mus. Fine Arts, Boston. Prin. author: Highlights from the Bennington Museum, 1989; author: Norton Stoneware and American Redware: The Bennington Museum Collection, 1992; contbr. author to catalogues; contbr. articles to profl. jours. Sec. N.H. Visual Arts Coalition, 1992-94; mem. steering com. N.H. Save Outdoor Sculpture, 1992-94; mem. selection com. N.H. % for Art Program, 1994-95; co-organizer Cambridgeport Neighborhood Group. Hist. Deerfield Summer fellow, 1981, Nat. Mus. Act and Norse Found. fellow, 1983-84, Louise du Pont Crowninshield Rsch. fellow Winterthur Mus., 1990; grantee Am. Ceramic Cir., 1993-95, 98; recipient Charles F. Montgomery award Decorative Arts Soc., 1993.

ZVARA, CHRISTINE C. middle school education educator; BS in Physical Edn. and Adaptive Physical Edn., U. Wis. Mid. and secondary physical edn. specialist grades 6-12 Gibraltar Schs., Fish Creek, Wis. Coord. Dance for Heart Event; mem. swim team bd. Door County YMCA, 1991-95; vol. Sister Bay Fall Classic Run, 1988-91; mem. Sturgeon Bay Sch. Booster Club, 1992—, Sturgeon Bay Band Parents Club, 1991—, Friends of Gibraltar PTO, 1982—. Named Coord. of Yr. Wis. Northeast Dist. Jump Rope for Heart, 1993. Home: 205 S 10th Ave Sturgeon Bay WI 54235-1803 Office: Gibraltar Sch RR 1 Box 205-g Fish Creek WI 54212-9801

ZWART-LUDEMAN, THERESA, graphics designer, artist; b. Tokyo, Sept. 26, 1953; arrived in U.S., 1955; m. Curtis D. Zwart, May 31, 1970 (div. 1983); 1 child, Justin C.; m. Clifford G. Ludeman, June 30, 1996. Student, Sch. Visual Arts, N.Y.C, 1978-81, Silvermine Sch. Arts, Conn., 1982-86. Asst. art dir. Arlington Pub., Westport, Conn., 1979-81; sr. art dir. Save The Children, Westport, 1981-86; art dir. MCA/Target Market Comm., Westport, 1986-87; creative/design cons. The Common Fund, Westport, 1987-93; prin. Zwart Design, Chester, Conn., 1988—; design cons. HEH Mktg., Wilton, 1990—, Pitney Bowes, Stamford, 1993—; owner Zwart-Ludeman Studio, Chester. Bd. dirs. Rowayton Art Ctr., Conn.; affiliate 18 Marshall St. Art Cooperative, Westport Art Ctr. One woman shows include: Solo Show at Studio 18, South Norwalk, Conn., 1998, Blood Root, 1999; 4 person shows include: Studio 3/On Location, 1992; group shows include: Studio 3, 1989, Nexus Gallery, N.Y.C., 1998; exhbns., juried shows include: Northeast Ann. Show at Silvermine, 1997, 98, New Britain (Conn.) Mus. Am. Art Fair, 1998, Nat. Acad. Mus. Design N.Y.C., 1998, Bridgeport U., Conn. Landscapes, 1999, New Art Ann. '99 Stamford Mus. Nature Ctr.; commd. Feb. window display Max's Art Supplies, Westport, conn., 1998; pub. in appr. issue of Art Calendar (centerfold winner), 1999. Recipient Communicator award, Disting. award N.Y.C., 1997, award of Distinction, Zanders/Lindenmeyer, 1992, Silver award Advt. Club Fairfield County, 1983, DMA awards, 1983, 2d. prize Watercolors, Rowayton Art Ctr., 1999. Mem.: Lyme Art Assn., Essex Art Assn. Conservative Democrat. Unitarian. Home: 37 Castle View Dr Chester CT 06412-1230 Studio: Zwart/Ludeman Studio 72 Main St Chester CT 06412 E-mail: zdes@aol.com.

ZWEIG, JANET, artist; BA, Cornell U., 1971; MFA, SUNY, Rochester, 1981. Faculty RISD, 1982—; asst. prof. Boston U., 1983-84. Resident Nexus Press, Atlanta, 1981, Jacob's Pillow Dance Festival, 1986, Macdowell Colony, Peterborough, NH, 1989, Peterborough, 90, Peterborough, 93, Peterborough, 94; resident Nat. Studio program PS1 Mus., Long Island, NY, 1990—91; resident Blue Mountain Ctr., 1997, Djerassi Resident Artists Program, 1998; guest lectr. numerous instns. MIT, Sch. Mus. Fine Arts, Boston U., Wesleyan U., Worcester Art Mus., Hartford Atheneum, NYU, Harvard U., U. Mass., Folger Shakespeare Libr., Brown U., Sarah Lawrence Coll., SUNY, Purchase, Temple U. Rome, Bard Coll., Photog. Resource Ctr., Boston, Moore Coll. Art, Phila., 1980—; adj. faculty Cooper Union, Anderson Ranch Art Ctr., Emerson Coll., Mass. Coll. Art, Sch. Mus. Fine Arts, Boston, Visual Studies Workshop Summer Inst., 1982—; juror Cultural Edn. Collaborative, Boston, 1986, Ill. State Coun. on the Arts Visual Arts Fellowships, 1987; juror The Bunting Inst. Radcliffe Coll., 1992; juror Am. Acad. Rome, 1995; vis. critic Yale U., 1991. Prin. works include sculptures at List Visual Art Ctr. MIT, Cambridge, Mass., The Art Gallery U. Md., 1989, 1990, PS 1 Mus., Inst. Contemporary Art, Long Island, 1990, 1991, Wallace Gallery SUNY, Old Westbury, 1991, The Artists Mus., Lodz, Poland, 1992, The Ulrich Mus. Wichita State U., 1992, Diverse Works, Houston, 1992, Sala 1, Rome, 1993, Huntington Gallery Mass. Coll. Art, 1993, RISD Mus., Providence, 1994, DeCordova Mus., Lincoln, Mass., Computer Mus., Boston, 1994, Big Orbit Gallery, Buffalo, N.Y., 1995, Anderson Gallery, Buffalo, 1995, Motel Fine Arts, N.Y.C., 1997, 1997, Snug Harbor Cultural Ctr., S.I., N.Y., 1995, Eighth Floor Gallery, N.Y.C., 1997, Cooper Union and the Coll. Art Assn., 1997, The Rotunda Gallery, Bklyn., 1998, Neuberger Mus. Art, Purchase, 1998, Represented in permanent collections Mus. Modern Art, Whitney Mus., Boston Mus. Fine Arts, Internat. Ctr. Photography, Calif. Inst. Arts, The Houghton Libr. Harvard, Cleve. Art Inst., Wellesley Coll. Libr., Visual Studies Workshop, Mus. Contemporary Art, Chgo., Art Inst. Chgo., Walker Art Ctr., Pompidou Ctr., RISD. Recipient Englehard award, Englehard Found. Inst. Contemporary Art, Boston, 1991; fellow in new genres category, Mass. Artists Found., 1985, visual arts fellow, NEA, 1985, 1994, The Rome Prize fellow, Am. Acad. Rome, 1991—92, grantee, Art Matters, Inc., 1986—90, Faculty Devel. Fund grantee, RISD, 1987, 1990, Individual Artists grantee, Artists Space, N.Y., 1990, grantee, Arts Internat., N.Y., 1992. Home: 54 Willow St Apt 4A Brooklyn NY 11201-6955 E-mail: jzweig@quicklink.com.

ZWICK, REBECCA, education educator; BA in Psychology and Edn., Antioch Coll., 1974; MA in Quantitative Methods, U. Calif., Berkeley, 1981; PhD in Quantitative Methods, 1983; MS in Stats., Rutgers U., 1989. NIMH postdoctoral fellow L.L. Thurstone Psychometric Lab. U. N.C., Chapel Hill, 1983—84; rsch. scientist Psychometrics Rsch. Group Ednl. Testing Svc., Princeton, NJ, 1984—89, dir. data analysis and scale devel. Nat. Assessment Ednl. Progress, 1990—91, sr. rsch. scientist Rsch. Stats. Group, 1991—95, prin. rsch. scientist Rsch. Stats. Group, 1995—96; prof. dept. edn. U. Calif., Santa Barbara, 1996—. Cons., workshop presenter on psychometrics and stats. Clin. Svcs. Rsch. Tng. Program U. Calif., San Francisco, 1986—; sr. fellow Consortium of Univs. U.S. Def. Dept., 1998—; tech. design team Nat. Assessment of Adult Literacy, 1999—; reviewer for reports or proposals Nat. Ctr. for Edn. Stats., 1998, 2001, Nat. Acad. Scis., 1999, NSF, 2000, Nat. Inst. Statis. Scis., 2002, Springer Pubs., 2002. Editor: (spl. issue) Jour. Ednl. Stats., 1992, Jour. Ednl. Measurement, 1995—98; cons. editor: Jour. Consulting and Clin. Psychology, 1985—89, Psychol. Assessment, 1988—91, reviewer: Jour. Am. Statis. Assn., Psychometrika, Psychol. Methods, Applied Psychol. Measurement, Applied Measurement in Edn., Multivariate Behavioral Rsch., Jour. Ednl. Measurement, Jour. Ednl. and Behavioral Stats., Ednl. Measurement: Issues and Practice, Can. Jour. Behavioral Scis., Jour. Math. Psychology. Fellow: APA; mem.: Psychometric Soc., Nat. Coun. on Measurement in Edn. (chair publs. com. 2001—03, faculty advisor grad. student issues com. 1999—2001), Am. Stats. Assn., Am. Ednl. Rsch. Assn. (sec.-treas. 1988—90, program chair conv. 1995, pres. ednl. statisticians spl. interest group 1995—96), Soc. for Multivariate Experimental Psychology. Office: Univ Calif Santa Barbara 2216 Phelps Hall Santa Barbara CA 93106-9490

ZWICKE, DIANNE LYNN, internist, cardiologist, educator; b. Marshfield, Wis., Oct. 27, 1952; d. Edward Raymond and Donna Mae (Erickson) Z. Diploma in nursing, St. Joseph's Hosp., Marshfield, l973; BS in Nursing, Marquette U., 1975; MD, U. N.C., 1982. Diplomate Am. Bd. Internal Medicine, subspecialty cert. in cardiovascular diseases. Resident in internal medicine U. Wis.-Marshfield Clinic-St. Joseph's Hosp., l982-84, chief resident, l984-85; fellow in cardiology U. Wis. Clin. Campus-Sinai Samaritan Med. Ctr., Milw., 1985-87, assoc. prof. medicine, l987—; mem. active staff in cardiology U. Wis. Clin. Campus-St. Luke's Med. Ctr., Milw., 1987—. Attending staff Aurora Sinai Med. Ctr., St. Francis Hosp., St. Michael's Hosp., West Allis Meml. Hosp., Milw.; med. dir. hypertension clinic St. Luke's Med. Ctr.; presenter in field. Contbr. articles and abstracts to med. jours. Fellow: ACP, Am. Coll. Chest Physicians, Am. Coll. Cardiology; mem.: Milw. County Med. Soc., Wis. Med. Soc. (chmn. on continuing med. edn. 1987—97), Soc. Critical Care Medicine, Sigma Theta Tau. Avocations: classical music, oboist, handicrafts, biking, travel. Office: Ste 777 2801 W Kinnickinic River Pky Milwaukee WI 53215

ZWICKEY, SHEILA KAYE, lawyer; b. Chgo., July 9, 1951; d. Ewald Arthur Zwickey and Kathryn Allene (Hurst) Zaiden. BS, U. Wis., 1973; MSW, U. Ind., 1975, JD, 1981. Social worker Dept. of Corrections/State of Ind., Indpls., 1975-81; dep. pub. defender State of Ind., Indpls., 1981-85; pub. defender Rush County, Rushville, Ind., 1985-90, Wayne County, Richmond, Ind., 1986-90; prosecuting atty. Rush County/State of Ill., Rushville, 1991—; pvt. practice Batesville, Ind., 1991—. Bd. dirs. Ind. Pub. Defender's Coun., Indpls. Bd. dirs. Rush City Humane Soc., 1988-89; officer Rush County/Ind. Dem. Women's Club, 1991—. Mem. Kiwanis, Rush City Bar Assn. (pres. 1988-89). Democrat. Roman Catholic. Office: Prosecutors Office Rush County Ct House Rushville IN 46173

ZWICKY, BARBARINA EXITA, humanities educator, researcher; d. Fritz and Anna Margaritha Zwicky; 1 child, Christian Alexander Fritz. Diploma in fashion design, Modeschule Brunn, Zurich, 1984; AS, Pasadena City Coll., 1999, AA, 2000; BA, Pacific Oaks Coll., 2002. Cert. nursing asst. Calif., 1990. Mgr. Continental Enterprises, Pasadena, 1980—91; tchr. human devel. Pacific Oaks Coll., Pasadena, 2003—. Owner Barby's Baby Boutique, Monrovia, Calif., 1985—90. Bd. dirs. Arcadia Am. Little League, Calif., Fritz Zwicky Found., Switzerland; vol. Huntington Meml. Hosp., 1995, ARC, Pasadena, 2000; activist Rep. Party, Pasadena. Mem.: AAUW (chair pub. policy 2002—, mem. Evelyn Brandt Scholarship com. 2000—), Matterhorn Young Swiss Club, Swiss Ladies Soc., United Swiss Soc. So. Calif., Omicron Mu Delta, Alpha Gamma Sigma (hon. bd. 1999). Republican. Methodist. Avocations: skiing, art, literature, swimming. Home: 2065 Oakdale Ave Pasadena CA 91107 E-mail: barbarinaz@aol.com.

ZWILICH, ELLEN TAAFFE, composer; b. Miami, Fla., Apr. 30, 1939; d. Edward Porter and Ruth (Howard) Taaffe; m. Joseph Zwilich, June 22, 1969 (dec. June 1979). MusB, Fla. State U., 1960, MusM, 1962; D Mus. Arts, Juilliard Sch., 1975; studies with Roger Sessions and Elliott Carter; MusD (hon.), Oberlin Coll., 1987, Converse Coll., 1994; LHD (hon.), Manhattanville Coll., 1991, Marymount Manhattan Coll., 1994, N.Y. New Sch., Mannes, 1995. Francis Eppes disting. prof. Fla. State U., 1999—. Composer in residence Santa Fe Chamber Music Festival, 1990, Am. Acad. Rome, 1990; first Composer's Chair, Carnegie Hall, 1995-99. Premiere, Symposium for Orch., Pierre Boulez, N.Y.C., 1975, Chamber Symphony and Passages, Boston Musica Viva, Richard Pittman, 1979, 82. Symphony 1, Gunther Schuller, Am. Composers Orch., 1982; violinist Am. Symphony, N.Y.C., 1965-73; composer: Sonata in Three Movements, 1973-74; String Quartet, 1974; Clarino Quartet, 1977; Chamber Symphony, 1979; Passages (for Soprano and Chamber Ensemble), 1981; String Trio, 1982; Symphony 1:3 Movements for Orch., 1982 (Grammy nomination New World Records, 1987); Divertimento, 1983; Einsame Nacht, 1971; Emlekezet, 1978; Im Nebel, 1972; Passages for Soprano and Orch., 1982; Trompeten, 1974; Fantasy for Harpsichord, 1983; Intrada, 1983; Prologue and Variations, 1983; Double Quartet for Strings, Chamber Music Soc. of Lincoln Ctr., 1984; Celebration for Orch., Indpls. Symphony, John Nelson, 1984; Symphony #2 (Cello Symphony) San Francisco Symphony, Edo De Waart, 1985, Symphony #2 Louisville Orch. recording, L.L. Smith (Grammy nomination 1991); Concerto Grosso 1985, Handel Festival Orch., Steven Simon, 1986; Concerto for Piano and Orch., Detroit Symphony, Gunther Herbig, Marc-André Hamelin, 1986; Images for 2 Pianos and Orch., Nat. Symphony Orch., F. Machetti, 1987; Tanzspiel, Peter Martins N.Y.C. Ballet, 1987; Praeludium Boston chpt. AGO, 1987; Trio for piano, violin and cello; Kalichstein, Laredo, Robinson trio, 1987; Symbolon, Zubin Mehta and the N.Y. Philharm., Leningrad and Moscow (USSR), N.Y.C. (Koussevitsky Internat. Rec. award nominee 1990), 1988; concerto for trombone and orch. J. Friedman, Sir Georg Solti, Chgo. Symphony, 1989, concerto for trombone and orch. Christian Lindberg, James De Priest, Malmö Symphony, concerto for flute and orch. D.A. Dwyer, Seija Ozawa, Boston Symphony, 1990, quintet for clarinet and string quartet David Schiffrin, Chamber Music N.W., Lincoln Ctr. Chamber Mus. Soc., 1990; concerto for oboe and orch. John Mack, Christoph von Dohnanyi, Cleve. Orch., 1991; concerto for bass trombone strings, timpani and cymbals Chgo. Symphony Orch. Ch. Vernon, Daniel Barenboim, 1991; concerto for violin, violoncello and orch. Jaime Laredo, Sharon Robinson, Louisville Orch., L. Smith, 1991; Immigrant Voices Peter Leonard, St. Lukes Orch., N.Y. Internat. Festival ot the Arts Chorus, Ellis Island, 1991, concerto for flute and orch, D.A. Dwyer, J. Sedares, London Symphony Orch., 1992, Symphony # 3 (Grammy nominee 1993), J. Ling, N.Y. Philharmonic, 1993, concerto for bassoon and orch., Nancy Goeres, Lorin Maazel, Pitts. Symphony, 1993, concerto for horn and string Orch., David Jolley, Rochester Philharm., L.L. Smith., 1993, Fantasy for Orch., JoAnn Falletta, Long Beach Symphony Orch., 1994, American Concerto Doc Severinsen, J. Falletta San Diego Symphony, 1994, A Simple Magnificat, 1994, Triple Concerto Kalichstein, Laredo, Robinson Trio Zdenek Macal, Minn. Orch., 1995, for piano and orch., Peanuts Gallery, 1996, violin concerto, Pamela Frank, H. Wolff, 1997; String Quartet # 2, 1998, Emerson Quartet; Upbeat! 1998, Nat. Symphony Orch., conducted by Anthony Aibel, Symphony # 4 (orch., chorus, children's chorus) Mich. State U., L. Gregorian 2000, Lament for solo piano Carnegie Hall, 2000, Millenium Fantasy for Piano & Orch., J. Biegel, J. Cobos-Lopez, Cin. Symphony, 2000, Lament for Cello & Piano, Met. Mus., N.Y.C., 2000, Partita for Violin & String Orch., Carnegie Hall, 2001, One Nation, 2002, Openings for Orch., 2002 JoAnn Falletta Va. Symphony, Clarinet Concerto, D. Shifrin, Chamber Music Soc. of Lincoln Ctr., Buffalo Philharm, 2002; New World Records: Music By Ellen Taaffe Zwilich; N.Y. Philharm. conducted by Zubin Mehta. Bd. dirs. Copland Fund. Named Martha Baird Rockefeller Fund rec. grantee, 1977, 1979, 1982, Guggenheim fellow, 1981; named to, Fla. Artists Hall of Fame, 1994; recipient Elizabeth Sprague Coolidge Chamber Music prize, 1974, Gold medal, G.B. Viotti, Vercelli, Italy, 1975, citation, Ernst von Dohnanyi, 1981, Pulitzer prize, 1983, Composers award, Lancaster Symphony Orch., Arturo Toscanini Music Critics award, 1987, Alfred I. DuPont award, 1991, Performing Arts award, Miami Ctr. Performing Arts, 2000, named, Musical Am. Composer of Yr., 1999. Mem.: AAAL (Acad. award 1984), Guggenheim Found. (bd. dirs.), MacDowell Colony (bd. dirs.), BMI Found., Am. Music Ctr. (bd. dirs., v.p. 1982—84), Am. Fedn. Musicians (hon.; life). Home: 600 W 246th St Bronx NY 10471-3611 Office: care Music Assocs Am 224 King St Englewood NJ 07631-3026

ZWIREN, JANET, holistic professional, educator; b. Orange, N.J., Aug. 3, 1952; d. John Paul and Martha Ann (Gallik) Bachmann; m. Steven Scott Zwiren, Sept. 25, 1971 (div. Feb. 1986); children: Paula Marie, Lisa Michelle. AA in Home Econs., Centenary Coll., Hackettstown, N.J., 1975; BA in Psychology, Coll. St. Elizabeth, Convent Station, N.J., 1987; Reiki master, Unltd. Potential, West Orange. N.J., 1994; grad., Realtors Inst., Edison, N.J., 1994. Cert. residential specialist. Title searcher Chelsea Title, New Brusnwick, N.J., 1972, Stewart Title, Morristown, N.J., 1973-75; title searcher, officer Heritage Abstract, Morristown, 1976-84; mortgage banker Fin. Investement Resources, Morristown, 1987-88, Greater Metro, Wayne, N.J., 1988; realtor residential sales Weichert Realtors, Succasunna, N.J., 1988-91, Re/Max Renown Realty, Randolph, N.J., 1991-99; Reiki Master, Shamanic practitioner Universal Life Energy Healing Ctr., Succasunna, 1994—97; dir., Shaman, Reiki master Oasis for the Soul, 1997—. Pvt. cons Bus. Mktg. and Mgmt., Succasunna, 1995—. Leader Girl Scouts U.S.A., Succasunna, 1993, 1985, 88, Denville, N.J., 1981, 84; town coun. reporter League Women Voters, Randolph, 1975. Mem. Nat. Assn. Realtors, N.J. Assn. Realtors (Million Dollar Club bronze and silver awards 1988-98, Remax Internat. Hall of Fame, 1997), Morris County Bd. Realtors, Residential Spl. Coun., Grad. Realtors Inst., Remax Internat. 100 Club.

Democrat. Avocations: sailing, reading, hiking, writing, travel. Home: 16 Meadowview Ave Succasunna NJ 07876-1737 Office: Oasis for the Soul PO Box 85 Succasunna NJ 07876-0085

ZYGOCKI, RHONDA I. oil industry executive; b. St. John's, Nfld., July 1957; B.Civil Engring., Meml. U. of Nfld., 1980. Petroleum engr. Chevron Can. Resources, Calgary, Canada, gen. mgr. strategic bus. svcs., 1993—94; profit ctr. mgr. Chevron U.S.A. Prodn. Co., Houston, 1994—97; CFO Chevron Can. Resources, Calgary, 1997—99; mgr. strategic planning Chevron Corp., San Ramon, Calif., 1999—2000, advisor to chmn. bd., 2000—01; mng. dir. ChevronTexaco Australia Pty. Ltd., Perth, Australia, 2001—03; v.p. health, environment and safety Chevron Texaco Corp., San Ramon, 2003—. Mem.: Engrs. Without Borders (bd. dirs.), Internat. Petroleum Industry Environ. Conservation Assn. (bd. dirs.), Internat. Assn. Oil and Gas Prodrs. (bd. dirs.). Office: Chevron Texaco Corp 6001 Bollinger Canyon Rd San Ramon CA 94583-2324*

ZYROFF, ELLEN SLOTOROFF, information scientist, classicist, educator; b. Atlantic City, N.J., Aug. 1, 1946; d. Joseph George and Sylvia Beverly (Roth) Slotoroff; m. Jack Zyroff, June 21, 1970; children: Dena Rachel, David Aaron. AB, Barnard Coll., 1968; MA, The Johns Hopkins U., 1969, PhD, 1971; MS, Columbia U., 1973. Instr. The Johns Hopkins U., Balt., 1970-71, Yeshiva U., N.Y.C., 1971-72, Bklyn Coll., 1971-72; libr., instr. U. Calif., 1979, 81, 91, San Diego State U., 1981-85, 94; prof. San

Diego Mesa Coll., 1981-95; dir. The Reference Desk Rsch. Svcs., La Jolla, Calif., 1983—; prin. libr. San Diego County Libr., 1985—. V.p. Archaeol. Soc. Am., Balt., 1970-71. Author: The Author's Apostrophe in Epic from Homer Through Lucan, 1971, Cooperative Library Instruction for Maximum Benefit, 1989; contbr. articles to profl. jours. Pres. Women's Am. ORT, San Diego, 1979-81, Zionist Orgn. of Am., San Diego dist., 1997-2000; mem. adv. bd. With Israel Now. Mem.: ALA (chair divsn. and roundtable coms. 1982—, coun. 2003—), Libr. Congress Cataloging in Publs. Adv. Group, Assn. Jewish Librs., Am. Classical League, Calif. Libr. Assn. (assembly 1993—99, editor Calif. Libs. 1997—99, pres. mgmt. sect. 2000—01), Am. Philol. Assn., Toastmasters, Beta Phi Mu. Office: PO Box 12122 La Jolla CA 92039-2122 E-mail: eszyroff@hotmail.com.

ZYWICKI, CINDY MARY, nurse; b. Chgo., Sept. 22, 1963; d. Robert A. and Barbara J. (Hagerty) Z. BSN and BS in Psychology, Millikin U., 1986. RN Ill.; cert. profl. in utilization Interqual, Inc. Staff nurse, alt. charge nurse Highland Park (Ill.) Hosp., 1986-95, interim mgr., 1996, utilization rev. outpatient nurse, 1997—2003, case mgr., 2000—03, R.N. Condell Med. Ctr. E.R. Annex, Libertyville, Ill., 2003—. Vol. Fairy Godmother Found. Mem. Bicycle Club Lake County, Single Advantage and Conscious Connections, Alpha Phi Omega, Alpha Tau Delta. Avocations: gymnastics, travel, reading, music, nature. Office: Highland Park Hosp 718 Glenview Ave Highland Park IL 60035-2497 E-mail: CZyW687521@aol.com.

Geographic Index

UNITED STATES

ALABAMA

Abbeville
Anderson, Ruth T. *retired air traffic controller*

Adamsville
Boyd, Lisa Baker *school media specialist*

Alabaster
Sullivan, Darlene Kay *music educator*

Albertville
Hall, Ramona Shields *art educator*
Sheets, Dorothy Jane *school librarian, retired elementary school educator*

Alexander City
Graham, Betty Carol *community college administrator*

Andalusia
Cross, Charlotte Lord *retired social worker, artist*

Anniston
Harry, Robbin Nicol *music educator*
Howell, Laura Clark *biologist, educator, small business owner*
Turner, Elnora Crankfield *special education educator and administrator*
Willis, Ohandra Denise *music educator*

Atmore
Smith, Debra L. *humanities educator*

Auburn
Galbraith, Ruth Legg *retired university dean, home economist*
Guertal, Elizabeth Anderson *agronomist, educator*
Havens, Carolyn Clarice *librarian*

Bay Minette
Cabaniss, Charlotte Jones *library services director*

Bessemer
Thompson, Lula Averhart *retired educator*

Birmingham
Adams, Kaye Mabry *periodical editor*
Allen, Maryon Pittman *former senator, journalist, lecturer, interior and clothing designer*
Binion, Linda Diane *computer systems research specialist*
Blackburn, Sharon Lovelace *federal judge*
Blair, Ludie Mae Riley *retired furniture company executive*
Booth, Rachel Zonelle *nursing educator*
Carmichael, Mary Alice *artist, genealogist*
Carter, Frances Tunnell (Fran Carter) *fraternal organization administrator*
Cohen-DeMarco, Gale Maureen *pharmaceutical executive*
Crittenden, Martha A. *disability specialist*
Davis, Gwendolyn Louise *air force officer, English educator*
Diasio, Ilse Wolfartsberger *volunteer*
Drentea, Patricia *science educator, researcher*
Dubovsky, Eva Vitkova *nuclear medicine physician, educator*
Elewski, Boni Elizabeth *dermatologist, educator*
Elgavish, Ada *molecular and cellular biologist*
Finley, Sara Crews *medical geneticist, educator*
Flowers, Vonetta *Olympic athlete*
Galloway, Catherine Black *publishing executive*
Garrison, Carol Z. *academic administrator*
Gilbert, Antonia Amelia *elementary school educator, consultant*
Gilmore, Catherine Rye *arts administrator*
Goggin, Margaret Enid (Knox) *librarian, educator*
Goldstein, Jackie Lutes *psychologist, educator*
Griffin, Eleanor *magazine editor*
Gross, Iris Lee *not-for-profit association executive*
Hahn, Beatrice A. *education educator*
Hamilton, Virginia Van der Veer *historian, educator*
Holmes, Suzanne McRae *nursing supervisor*
Hopkins, Martha Ann *sculptor*
Hullett, Sandral *hospital administrator, health facility administrator*
Keller, Armor *artist, arts advocate*
Kirkley, D. Christine *non-profit organization administrator*
Kluge, Janice *art educator*
Lewis, Yvonne Antionette Fluker *secondary school educator*
Loftin, Sister Mary Frances *religious organization administrator*
Lowery, Deborah Garrison *freelance writer and editor*
Michalek, Suzanne M. *biology educator*
Moran, Mary Shanks *hydrogeologist*
Morton, Marilyn Miller *retired genealogy and history educator, lecturer, researcher, travel executive, director*
Moten, Mary Anne *gifted and talented educator, small business owner*
Mueller, Robin Sue *biology educator*
Murrell, Susan DeBrecht *librarian*
Neel, Nancee R. *counselor*
Newbern Williams, Mary Ruth *minister*
Nichols, Sandra B. *public health service officer*
Nunnelley, Carol Fishburne *editor newspaper*
Odom, Mary E. (Libby Odom) *musician, educator*
Oparil, Suzanne *cardiologist, educator, cardiologist, researcher*
Perry, Helen *medical/surgical nurse, secondary school educator*
Pittman, Constance Shen *endocrinologist, educator*
Privett, Caryl Penney *judge*
Reynolds, W(ynetka) Ann *academic administrator, educator*
Ritchie, Beth Bradley *elementary school educator*
Roberts, Susan Dianne Green *library media specialist*
Smaha, Donna Alvey *adult nurse practitioner, consultant, acute care nurse practitioner*
Todd, Judith F. *lawyer*
Wheeler, Cathy Jo *federal agency administrator*
Williams, Phyllis S. *education educator, religious organization administrator*

Blountsville
Edwards, Sheila M. *banker, educator*

Boaz
Pierce, V. Renee *music educator*

Carrollton
Winters, Janice Joyner *accountant*

Chelsea
Alicea, Yvette *special education educator*

Coy
Zinnermon, Susan *writer*

Crossville
Blessing, Maxine Lindsey *secondary school educator*

Cullman
Schgier, Linda Priest *musician, educator*
Thornton, Nancy Freebairn *psychotherapist, consultant, military officer*

Daphne
Henson, Pamela Taylor *secondary education educator*
Neese, Kristal Ann *comptroller*

Decatur
Costello, Sheri Ann *primary school educator*
Michelini, Sylvia Hamilton *auditor*
Smith, Trina *academic administrator*
Steele, Bette Hulse *medical/surgical nurse*

Demopolis
Reynolds, Louise Webb *retired volunteer, director*

Dothan
Benson, Marie Chapman *insurance agent*
Fletcher, Sarah Lee *retired elementary school educator*
Jones, Sandra Lee *dean*
Kogelschatz, Joan Lee *psychologist, psychotherapist*
Marks, Marilyn *trailer company executive*

Evergreen
Dailey, Marilyn *elementary school educator*
Lodge-Peters, Dianne Speed *writer, literature educator, researcher*
Ross, Nora Fay *poet*

Fairfield
McCaslin, LaTanya *art educator*

Fayette
Bragg, Beverly Smith *volunteer*

Florence
Knight, Karen Anne McGee *artist, educator*
Rhodes, Lisa Frances *elementary school educator*
Wright, Mildred Anne (Milly Wright) *conservator, researcher*

Fort Payne
Beasley, Mary Catherine *home economics educator, administrator, researcher*
Wilbanks, Janice Peggy *special education educator*

Gadsden
Coakley, Deirdre *writer*
Freeman, Peggy Renea *accountant*
Massaro, Traci Lynn *special education educator*

Gardendale
Hughes, Mary Virginia *secondary school educator*

Greenville
Longmire, Venus DeLoyse *minister*

Grove Hill
Clarke, Cheryl Crider *music educator*

Gurley
Patrick, Laura Daphene Layman *retired physicist*

Hamilton
Vinson, Leila Terry Walker *retired gerontological social worker*

Hartselle
Thompson, Wanda Dawson *music educator*

Hayden
Standridge, Jean *real estate executive, real estate broker*

Headland
Woodham, Patricia H. *accounting and business consultant*

Homewood
Kolb, Jennifer Akridge *special education educator*
Tucker, Rhonda Reneé *music educator*

Hoover
Kennon, Gloria Oliver *guidance counselor*

Huntsville
Archuleta, Nancy E. *engineering executive*
Blackwell, Patricia Massey *middle school educator*
Bounds, Sarah Etheline *historian*
Brown, Lashonda DeJuan *elementary school educator*
Buddington, Patricia Arrington *engineer*
Eskridge, Carole Fay *artist*
Furlow, Brenda J. *religious studies educator, consultant*
Gawronski, Elizabeth Ann *retired army officer*
Hughes, Kaylene *historian, educator*
Krueger, Kathleen Susan *special education administrator*
McIntyre-Ivy, Joan Carol *data processing executive*
Moore, Ann Roy *school system administrator*
[illegible], Susan *elementary school educator*
Plunkett, Sara L. *communications company executive*
Pruitt, Alice Fay *mathematician, engineer*
Simpson, Debra Brashear *artist*
Stewart, Verlindsey Laquetta *accounting educator*
Tucker, Eunice Jones *secondary school educator, educator*
Wu, Susan Ying Chu Lin (Ying-chu Lin) *engineering company executive, engineer*
Yarbrough, Isabel Miles *dentist, educator*

Irondale
Karr, Beverly Ann *counselor*

Jacksonville
Dunaway, Carolyn Bennett *retired sociology educator*
Lewis, Deborah Alice *tax company executive, writer*
Merrill, Martha *library media educator*

Leeds
Denton, Joy Grigg *music educator*
Westberg, Polly Pembrooke *art educator*
Wilson, Maggie Isabelle Lovell *art educator, English educator*

Lineville
Craig, Linda (Teri) Carol *science educator*

Loachapoka
Schafer, Elizabeth Diane *historian, writer*

Madison
Johnson, Kathy Virginia Lockhart *art educator*

Mc Calla
Kes, Vicki *museum director*

Millbrook
Whetstone, Charlotte Andrews *principal*

Mobile
Atkinson, Alanna Beth *music educator*
Byrd, Gwendolyn Pauline *school system superintendent*
Byrd, Mary Jane *education educator*
Clausell, Deborah Deloris *artist*
Ellis, Margaret Boland *editor, publisher*
French, Elizabeth Irene *biology educator, violinist*
Granade, Callie Virginia Smith S. *lawyer, federal district judge*
Hamner, Eugenie Lambert *English educator*
Howze, Kristi Crenshaw *music educator*
Mahoney, Margaret A. *federal judge*
Thompson, Nancy *art director*
Wisner, Pamela L. *social worker*

Monroeville
Loyd, Martha Rose *forester*

Montevallo
Neely, Evelyn Hope (Evelyn Hope Gillespie) *humanities educator, archaeologist*

Montgomery
Allen, Linda Lee *administrative assistant*
Baxley, Lucy *lieutenant governor*
Belt, Jean Rainer *art gallery owner*
Brock, Katrina Rae *music educator*
Brown, Jean Williams *state supreme court justice*
Bullard, Mary Ellen *retired religious organization administrator*
Campbell, Maria Bouchelle *lawyer, consultant*
Canary, Leura *prosecutor*
Cassels, Martha Beasley *realtor, developer*
Cauthen, Florence M. *protective services official*
Chamberlain, Kathryn Burns Browning *retired career officer*
Copeland, Jacqueline Turner *music educator*
Dillon, Jean Katherine *executive secretary, small business owner*
Escott-Russell, Sundra *state legislator*
Farshee, Marlena W. *title company executive*
Figures, Vivian Davis *state legislator*
Hertenstein, Myrna Lynn *publishing executive*
Hilliard, Lil *sales executive*
Howard, Gail Verita *special education educator*
Huffman, Mary Frances *retired secondary school educator*
Ivey, Kay Ellen *state official*
Jacobs, Jane L. *artist, state agency administrator*
Kennedy, Yvonne *state legislator*
Mandry, Christine M. *public adminstator*
Martin, Jeanne Davis *forensic specialist, consultant, writer, editor*
McCall-Thompson, Kathleen Samone *actor, educator*
McPherson, Vanzetta Penn *magistrate judge*
Napier, Cameron Mayson Freeman *historic preservationist*
Parker, Susan D. *state official, auditor*
Smith, Harri Anne *state legislator*
Sottile, Kathy Watson *publisher, writer*
Spear, Sarah G. *county administrator*
Stuart, Lyn (Jacquelyn L. Stuart) *judge*
Tullos, Barbara Waddell *art educator*
Walker, Annette *retired counseling administrator*
Worley, Nancy L. *secretary of state*

Montrose
Haynie, Betty Jo Gillmore *personal property appraiser, [illegible]*

Morris
Taylor, Brandy Miller *music educator*

Normal
Hall, Doris Spooner *music educator*
Lane, Rosalie Middleton *extension specialist*

Oxford
Johnson, Mary Murphy *social worker, writer*

Parrish
Wallace McRae, Shirley Ann *retired secondary school educator*

Phenix City
Witsell, Ethel Holden Howard *artist*

Pine Level
Boswell, Vivian Nicholson *protective services official*

Pleasant Grove
Robinson, Ella Garrett *editor, writer*

Point Clear
Englund, Gage Bush *dancer, educator*

Prattville
Lambert, Meg Stringer *construction executive, architect, interior designer*
Riddle, Sue Dorsey *primary school educator*

Prichard
Williams, Wendy *civil engineer*

Saraland
South, Sheri Cobb *writer, publishing executive*

Selma
Martin, Iona B. *guidance counselor*

Spanish Fort
Benjamin, Regina Marcia *physician, administrator*

Stevenson
Watson, Mary Elizabeth Grider *employment security officer, retailer*

Sulligent
Burleson, Emily Jane *nursing administrator*

Talladega
Jeffers, Trellie Lee James *language educator, dean*

Trussville
Ballard, Laura Clay *small business owner*

Tuscaloosa
Cook, Camille Wright *retired law educator*
Dalton, Margaret Stieg *library and information sciences educator*
Edgeworth, Emily *retired insurance agency executive, retired small business owner*
Fields, Ruth Kinniebrew *secondary and elementary educator, consultant*
Fish, Mary Martha *economics educator*
Mancini, Marilyn Elizabeth *education educator*
Orcutt, Ben Avis *retired social work educator*

Ray, Nelda Howton *financial consultant*
Reinhart, Kellee Connely *journalist*
Smalley, Donna Wesson *lawyer, educator*
von Redlich, Emily Paulette *music educator*

Tuskegee
Thomas, Elaine Freeman *artist, educator*

Tuskegee Institute
Cooley, Fannie Richardson *counselor, educator*

Warrior
Johnson, Barbara L. *retired municipal official*

ALASKA

Anchorage
Anthony, Susan *secondary school educator*
Bowie, Phyllis *secondary school educator*
Britton, Emily Maddox *sales executive*
Brown, Dean Naomi *state official, geologist*
Burke, Marianne King *state agency administrator, financial executive, consultant*
Comeau, Carol Smith *school system administrator*
Davis, Bettye Jean *academic administrator, state official*
DeLap, Miriam Anne *music educator*
Demarco, Patricia M. *state agency administrator*
Din, Herminia *art educator, museum staff member, researcher*
Fabe, Dana Anderson *state supreme court justice*
Fleming, Carolyn Elizabeth *religious organization administrator, interior designer*
Foster, Rosemary Alice *lawyer, artist*
Gazaway, Barbara Ann *music educator, art educator*
Gier, Karan Hancock *psychologist*
Gillette, Muriel Delphine *nurse*
Greenstein, Marla Nan *lawyer*
Holmes, Sandra *insurance underwriter*
Hughes, Mary Katherine *lawyer*
Jones, Jewel *social services administrator*
Keffer, Maria Jean *environmental auditor*
Kelly, Maxine Ann *retired property developer*
Matsui, Dorothy Nobuko *elementary school educator*
Myers, Leah Lynnette *military officer*
Narang, Deborah Lynn *education educator*
Obermeyer, Theresa Nangle *sociology educator*
O'Regan, Deborah *association executive, lawyer*
Sandvik, Helvi *state agency administrator*
Sedwick, Deborah *state agency administrator*
Skladal, Elizabeth Lee *retired elementary school educator*
Sturgulewski, Arliss *state legislator, director*
Thomas, Peggy Ruth *public contract and procurement consultant*
Thompson, G. Nanette *state agency administrator*
Wedel-Cowgill, Millie Redmond *secondary school educator, performing arts educator, communications educator*
Wibker, Susan Gayle *lawyer*
Willard-Jones, Donna C. *lawyer*
Williams, Eleanor Joyce *retired government air traffic control specialist*

Chugiak
Stiehr, Lizette Estelle *special education educator, director*

Cordova
Bugbee-Jackson, Joan *sculptor, educator*

Eagle River
Hayes, MaryLee *editor, writer, nurse*

Fairbanks
Alexander, Vera *dean, marine science educator*
Bodwell, Lori *lawyer*
Bryant-Wilburn, Rosita Dolores *special education educator*
Butler-Hopkins, Kathleen Margaret *musician, educator*
Corti, Lillian Zell *humanities educator, writer*
Crawford, Sarah Carter (Sally Carter Crawford) *broadcast executive*
Heckman, Jyotsna (Jo) L. *bank executive*
Jonaitis, Aldona Claire *museum administrator, art historian*
Jones-Butler, Jacqueline *painter, poet*
Lewis, Carol E. *academic administrator, management consultant*
Murakami, Gael Baxley *artist*
Schandelmeier, Linda Ann *elementary school educator*

Homer
Phillips, Gail *state legislator*

Juneau
Cissna, Sharon *state representative*
Collins, Patricia A. *lawyer, judge*
Dahlstrom, Nancy *state representative*
Green, Lyda N. *state legislator*
Guess, Gretchen *state senator*
Heinze, Cheryll Boren *state representative*
Kapsner, Mary *state representative*
Lincoln, Georgianna *state legislator*
Masek, Beverly *state representative*
McGuire, Lesil L. *state representative*
Perdue, Karen *state agency administrator*
Wilson, Peggy *state representative, registered nurse*

Kodiak
Steffey, A Kay *accountant*

Nondalton
Gay, Sarah Elizabeth *lawyer*

North Pole
James, Jeannette Adeline *state legislator, accountant*

Salcha
Alsip, Cheryl Ann *small business owner*

Valdez
Shell, Maria Christine *writing educator*
Todd, Kathleen Gail *physician*

Wasilla
Brunke, Dawn Baumann *writer, editor*

Willow
White, Gwendolyn A. *recreational facility executive*

ARIZONA

Apache Junction
Ransom, Evelyn Naill *language educator, linguist*

Bisbee
Arrowsmith, Nancy *journalist*
Gustavson, Carrie *museum director*

Carefree
Beery, Barbara Faye *secondary school educator*

Casa Grande
Landers, Patricia Glover *reading specialist*
McGillicuddy, Joan Marie *psychotherapist, consultant*
Urban, Carrie *computer specialist*

Chandler
Brunello-McCay, Rosanne *sales executive*
Casteel, Camille *school system administrator*
Elliott, Lee Ann *company executive, former government official*
Lauber, Kelli Katherine Margaret *criminal justice instructor*
Lawrence, Star *marketing executive, film company executive*
Matus, Nancy Louise *artist*
Shousha, Annette Gentry *retired critical care nurse*
Simon, Diane Rose *music educator, writer, poet*

Chinle
Quell, Margaret Anne *special education educator*

Chino Valley
Bott, Bobbie Lee *real estate broker*
Casey, Bonnie Mae *artist, educator*

Cibecue
Murphey, Margaret Janice *marriage and family therapist*

Congress
Scheall, Norma *writer, editor*

Cornville
Masters, Arlene Elizabeth *singer*
White, Judith Louise *social worker, counselor*

Cortaro
Fossland, Joeann Jones *professional speaker, personal coach*

Davis Monthan A F B
Woods, Sharhonda Michele *military officer*

Douglas
Britton, Ruth Ann Wright *elementary school educator*
Murphy, Cathy Emily *photographer, educator, journalist*

Elgin
Sebert, Michelle Ann *school system network administrator*

Flagstaff
Barlow, Nadine Gail *planetary geoscientist*
Edgerton, Debra *artist, educator*
Grandy, Jerilee *research and evaluation consultant*
Marcus, Karen Melissa *foreign language educator*
Poen, Kathryn Louise *music educator, performing arts association administrator*
Schmidt, Gretchen Erika *special education educator*
Shoemaker, Carolyn Spellman *planetary astronomer*

Fort Huachuca
Szymeczek, Peggy Lee *contract specialist*

Fountain Hills
Sarwar, Barbara Duce *education consultant*

Gilbert
Dudley, Amber Marie *music educator*
Strohmyer, Deb L. *music educator, school librarian*

Glendale
Altersitz, Janet Kinahan *principal*
Avila, Lidia D. *principal*
Chavez, Mary Lynn *pharmacy educator*
Fisher, Debra A. *communications executive, educator*
Galletti, Marie Ann *English language and linguistics educator*
Gonzales, Franceen Michelle *amusement facility executive*
Gourley, Diane *music educator*
Heathcotte, Toby Fesler *writer, retired educator*
Mahoney, Jill Elizabeth *music educator*
Scruggs, Elaine M. *mayor*
Sweat, Lynda Sue *cooking instructor, catering company owner, deaconess*

Green Valley
Greenwood, Helen Maxine *retired office manager, executive assistant*
Macafee, Susan Diane *reporter*
Shafer, Susan Wright *retired elementary school educator*

Higley
Nowatzki, Melodee *psychologist*

Kingman
Jones, Barbara Christine *linguist, creative arts designer, educator*

Marana
Green, Laura Lorraine *foundation administrator*

Mesa
Ahearn, Geraldine *medical/surgical nurse, writer, poet*
Boyd, Leona Potter *retired social worker*
Colledge, Deborah Gail *gifted and talented elementary educator*
Duvall, Debra *school system administrator*
Hess-Benish, Jenifer *protective services official, real estate agent*
Hicks, Bethany Gribben *judge, commissioner, lawyer*
Kaida, Tamarra *art and photography educator*
Winn, Kathleen Ann *bank officer, real estate broker*
Woods, Sarah Lynn *advertising executive*
Yandell, Ruth B. *music educator*
Yates, Cheryl Ann *home economist, educator*

Nogales
Lugo, Lorena Pearl *elementary school educator, band director*
Valdez, Wanda Daniel *county official*

Oracle
Garmany, Catharine Doremus *astronomer*

Oro Valley
Martinez, Margaret Anne *education organization executive, psychologist*

Page
Hart, Marian Griffith *retired reading educator*

Paradise Valley
Harnett, Lila *retired publishing executive*
McCall, Louise Harrup *artist*
Targovnik, Selma E. Kaplan *physician*

Payson
Lasys, Joan *medical nurse, writer, educator, publisher*
Salomon, Marilyn *artist*

Peoria
Bailey, Claudia Jean *retired professor, librarian, artist*
Cook, Mary Margaret *steamfitter, educator*
Hodges, Elizabeth Swanson *educational consultant, tutor*
McMahon, Maribeth Lovette *physicist*
Willard, Garcia Lou *artist*

Phoenix
Aguirre, Linda *state senator*
Allen, Janice Faye Clement *nursing administrator*
Anderson, Vicki *retired librarian*
Arzberger, Marsha *state senator*
Bateman, Jean Budington *writer, poet, home furnishings consultant*
Bechtel, Katie Ellen *art educator, artist, writer*
Berch, Rebecca White *state supreme court justice, lawyer*
Bonnell, Gayla *art educator*
Brewer, Janice Kay *state official*
Burns, Brenda *state senator*
Carpenter, Carol Settle *communications executive*
Chambliss, Linda R. *obstetrician, gynecologist, consultant*
Chavez, Nelba R. *state agency administrator, former federal agency administrator*
Cheifetz, Lorna Gale *psychologist*
Clark-Johnson, Susan *publishing executive*
Daniels, Barbara Ann *non-profit organization executive*
Daniels, Lori S. *state legislator, insurance agent*
Day, Ann *state legislator*
Dignac, Geny (Eugenia M. Bermudez) *sculptor*
Dorland, Byrl Brown *retired volunteer*
DuMoulin, Diana Cristaudo *small business owner, writer*
Duyck, Kathleen Marie *poet, musician, retired social worker*
Erwin, Barbara F. *school system administrator*
Fernandez, Helen Agnes *municipal official*
Fitzgerald, Joan *principal*
Foutz, Claudia *state agency administrator*
Gerard, Susan *state senator*
Gillom, Jennifer *professional basketball player*
Gingold, Hilary Weinberg *lawyer*
Grace, Sue *state legislator*
Grinell, Sheila *museum director*
Hagan, Judith Ann *social worker*
Hartley, Mary *state legislator*
Hellon, Toni *state senator*
Hulet, Nicole *computer consultant, poet, artist*
Hutchinson, Ann *management consultant*
Hutchinson, Edna M. *home care nurse*
Jackson, Barbara Ann *systems engineer*
Jungbluth, Connie Carlson *wealth strategist*
Karabatsos, Elizabeth Ann *career counseling services executive*
Lack, Patricia Ann *drilling and pumping company executive, consultant*
LaValle, Jennifer Suzette *marketing communications specialist, consultant*
Lawlis, Patricia Kite *air force officer, computer consultant*
Leathers, Susan Lynn *music educator*
Lee, Barbara S. *elementary school educator*
Maimon, Elaine Plaskow *English educator, university provost, campus chief executive officer*
Mariucci, Anne L. *real estate development company executive*
Martensen, Barbara *electronics executive*
Mathis, Virginia *federal judge*
McCormick, Kathryn Ellen *prosecutor*
McGregor, Ruth Van Roekel *state supreme court justice*
McKay, Kay *academic administrator*
Merritt, Nancy-Jo *lawyer*
Miel, Vicky Ann *city official*
Miller, Janice *electronics executive*
Moriarty, Karen *state agency administrator*
Mure, Barbara A. *real estate property manager*
Napolitano, Janet Ann *governor*
Nijinsky, Tamara *actress, puppeteer, author, librarian, educator*
Noone, Palmer *academic administrator*
Palacios, Christina *academic administrator*
Perry, Barbara Mitchell *retired librarian*
Ralston, Barbara Jo *bank executive*
Refo, Patricia Lee *lawyer*
Reyes, Anna Maria *broadcast executive*
Richardson, Judy McEwen *education administrator, consultant, cartoonist*
Ridenour, Joey *medical association administrator, operations research specialist*
Rollings, Judith Harvey *theater producer, actress, theater director, performing arts educator*
Roof, Sally Jean-Marie *library and information scientist, educator*
Schroeder, Mary Murphy *federal judge*
Schwartz, Nadine Susan *media specialist*
Sertich, Kelli Ann *land use planner*
Sharp, Linda *professional basketball coach*
Silver, Roslyn O. *federal judge*
Solomon, Ruth *state legislator, teacher*
Steckler, Phyllis Betty *publishing company executive*
Stewart, Nancy Sue Spurlock *education educator*
Stewart, Patricia Ann *banker*
Stone, Hazel Anne Decker *artist*
Van Sittert, Barbara C. *retired classics educator, writer*
Wade, Tyra V. *manufacturing executive*
Wells, GladysAnn *library director*
Wheaton, Marilyn *music educator, pianist, organist*
White, Annette Irene *marketing professional*
Whyte, Rachel L. *child abuse prevention specialist, social worker*
Wirtz, Dorothy Marie *retired language educator*
Wold, Kimberly G. *legislative staff member*
Wolf, Irna Lynn *psychologist*

Prescott
Churchill, Karen Lynn *curator, educator*
Halvorson, Mary Ellen *education educator, writer*
Krieger, Lois B. *retired state agency administrator*
Waterer, Bonnie Clausing *retired secondary school educator*

Prescott Valley
Beck, Doris Olson *retired library media director*
Cole, Susie Cleora *retired government employee relations official*
Conner, Eunice Eileen *city official*

San Luis
Soto, Veronica Maria *school librarian*

Scottsdale
Ailloni-Charas, Miriam Clara *interior designer, consultant*
Broe, Carolyn Waters *conductor, violist, music educator*
Brown, Shirley Margaret Kern (Peggy Brown) *interior designer*
Bullerdick, Kim H. *petroleum executive*
Burley, Barbara A. *music educator*
Carpenter, Betty O. *writer*
Coffinger, Maralin Katharyne *retired career officer, consultant*
Dalton, Phyllis Irene *library consultant*
Farney, Charlotte Eugenia *musician, music educator*
Fisher, Robyn Angela *music educator*
Fosgate Heggli, Julie Denise *producer*
Gwinn, Mary Dolores *business developer, philosopher, writer*
Harris, Marci W. *psychologist*
Hoff, Ann Marie *sales professional*
Hreniuc, Carmen Lacramioara *food service executive*
Keenan, Mary Josephine *communications executive*
Kizziar, Janet Wright *psychologist, writer, lecturer*
Kübler-Ross, Elisabeth *physician*
Lang, Margo Terzian *artist*
Lavenson, Susan Barker *hotel corporate executive, consultant*
Lillestol, Jane Brush *development consultant*
Lingle, Kathleen McCall *human resources specialist, consultant, marketing executive, entrepreneur*
MacKinnon, Sally Anne *retired fast food company executive*
Manross, Mary *mayor*
Martin-DeWitt, M. Lori *minister*
McCabe, Mary Williamson *computer systems analyst*
Milanovich, Norma JoAnne *training and development company executive*
Mohraz, Judy Jolley *foundation administrator*
Morris, Samantha A. *marketing professional, researcher*
Nelson, Mary Kathryn *bilingual counselor, artist, singer, comedienne*
O'Meara, Sara *nonprofit organization executive*
Parsons, Cynthia *writer, consultant*

Timmons, Evelyn Deering *pharmacist*
Vanier, Jerre Lynn *art director*
Wolfgang, Bonnie Arlene *musician, bassoonist*

Sedona
Catterton, Marianne Rose *occupational therapist*
Chicorel, Marietta Eva *publishing company executive, consultant*
Copeland, Suzanne Johnson *real estate executive*
Darrow, Jane *artist*
Felsted, Carla Martindell *librarian, writer, editor*
Frankel, Jennie Louise *writer, composer, playwright*
Frankel, Terrie Maxine *writer, composer, playwright, publisher, producer*
Rhines, Marie Louise *composer, violinist*
Vayanian, Solara Zakeli *artist, educator*

Sierra Vista
Boughan, Zanetta Louise *music educator*
Gignac, Judith Ann *utilities executive*
Moreno, Patricia Frazier *lawyer*

Sonoita
Browning, Sinclair *writer*
Posey, Faith E. *artist*

Springerville
Geisler, Sherry Lynn *magistrate*

Sun City
Davis, Virginia *trade show producer*
Duke, Ora Elizabeth *civic volunteer*
Kessler-Gillespie, Kathleen E. *psychotherapist*
Larkin, Mary Sue *financial planner*
Lopez, Jean Engebretsen *neuroscience nurse, researcher*
Randall, Claire *church executive*

Sun City West
Brown, Ruth Geisler *engineering supervisor*
Holloway, Diane Elaine *psychological consultant, psychotherapist, writer*
Schrag, Adele Frisbie *business education educator*

Sun Lakes
Hall, Barbara Louise *interior designer, artist*
Johnson, Marian Ilene *education educator*
Middleton, Mary *secondary school educator*
Smith, Eleanor Jane *university chancellor, retired, consultant*

Sunsites
Datcu, Ioana *visual artist*

Surprise
Bradford, Mariah *elementary school educator, consultant*
Eastman, Donna Kelly *composer*
Fennelly, Jane Corey *lawyer*
Lucchetti, Lynn L. *career officer*
Wargo, Andrea Ann *retired public health official, commissioned officer*

Taylor
Kerr, Barbara Prosser *research scientist, educator*

Tempe
Adler, Carol Ellen *publishing executive, writer*
Anchie, Toby Levine *health facility administrator*
Conrad, Cheryl Diane *behavioral neuroscientist*
Durand, Barbara *dean*
Dustman, Patricia (Jo) Allen *public school educator, educational consultant, researcher*
Ellin, Nan *architecture educator, writer*
Girón, Angela *artist, educator*
Green, Monica H. *history educator*
Guzzetti, Barbara Jean *education educator*
Herald, Cherry Lou *research educator, research director*
Honegger, Gitta *language educator*
Jefferson, Myra LaVerne Tull *sales executive*
Jennings, Marianne Moody *lawyer, educator*
Kloefkorn, Sheila *marketing professional, sales executive*
Lemmon, Nicolette *small business owner, marketing professional*
Lightfoot, Marjorie Jean *English educator*
Metros, Mary Teresa *librarian*
Papandreou-Suppappola, Antonia *electrical engineering educator*
Rowley, Beverley Davies *medical sociologist*
Ruiz, Vicki Lynn *history educator*
Smith, Carol Estes *retired councilman*
Whipkey-Louden, Harriet Beulah *fine arts and theatre productions executive*
White, Patricia Denise *dean*
Zeitlin, Marilyn Audrey *museum director*
Zinke, Laura A. *language educator*

Thatcher
Jordahl, Patricia Ann *music educator, theater director*

Tonopah
Fishgrab, Barbara Jeanne *school psychologist, mental health services professional*

Tucson
Arzoumanian, Linda Lee *early childhood educator*
Bagwell, Marsha Lynn *actor, educator*
Barber, Bonnie Lee *psychologist, educator*
Beaman, Colleen K. *education educator, choreographer*
Bedford, Felice L. *psychologist, educator*
Bermúdez, Carmen *trust company executive*
Betteridge, Frances Carpenter *retired lawyer, mediator*
Bonvicini, Joan M. *university women's basketball coach*
Boswell, Susan G. *lawyer*
Brasswel, Kerry *tax accountant*
Bryant, Marian Alanna *electric company consultant*
Cisler, Theresa Ann *osteopath*
Cooper, Corinne *communications consultant, lawyer*
Davis, Cathy *publishing executive*
Diáz, Elena R. *community health nurse*
Eberhardt, Marty Lampert *botanical garden administrator*
Emerson, Kirk *government agency administrator*
Esparza, Kacie Lynne *military officer*
Fajardo, Sarah Elizabeth Johnson *financial consultant*
Finley, Dorothy Hunt *beverage distribution company executive*
Francesconi, Louise L. *electronics executive*
Freiman, Lela Kay *retired secondary school educator*
Froman, Sandra Sue *lawyer*
Gaines, Kendra Holly *English language educator, editorial and writing consultant*
Gill, Rebecca LaLosh *aerospace engineer*
Glueck, Mary Audrey *retired psychiatric and mental health nurse*
Goldberg, Charlotte Wyman *retired educator, retired travel company executive*
Golston, Maggie *small business owner, writer*
Graham, Anna Regina *pathologist, educator*
Grant, Linda Kay *journalist*
Griffen, Agnes Marthe *library administrator*
Himmelheber, Eve *theater educator, theater director, actor*
Hoyt, Charlee Van Cleve *management executive*
Ingram, Helen Moyer *political science educator*
James, Ruby May *retired librarian*
Johnson, Elissa Sarah *speech pathology/audiology services professional, writer*
Kany, Judy C(asperson) *health policy analyst, former state senator*
Karson, Catherine June *database administrator*
Kelley, Lydia *animal trainer*
Kingsolver, Barbara Ellen *writer*
Kissinger, Karen G. *energy executive*
Lai, LiWen *molecular geneticist, educator*
Lanham, Sandra *conservationist*
Larwood, Laurie *psychologist*
Lascelles, Susan *artist*
LaCorgne, Lisette Mary *family practice nurse practitioner*
Ledin, Patricia Ann *nurse, nurse legal consultant*
Lee, Joyce Ann *computer educator*
Lovejoy, Jean Hastings *social services counselor*
Lowe, Lynn Rae *sculptor, educator, small business owner*
Martin, Julie Johnson Caldwell *journalist*
Martin, Marci *writer, former advertising specialist*
Masque, Maria L. *urban planner*
Massaro, Toni Marie *dean, law educator*
McCormick, Alma Heflin *writer, retired educator, psychologist*
McFarlin, Barbara L. *secondary school educator, small business owner*
Mendelson, Joan Rintel *lawyer*
Miles, Suzanne Laura *dean*
Miller, Elizabeth Rodriguez *city official*
Neal, Alaine (Diann Neal) *nursing administrator*
Neugebauer, Marcia *physicist, administrator*
Ohmann, Elizabeth J. *advocate*
Parra, Elena Batriz-Guadalupe *psychologist, educator*
Peterson, V. Spike *political science educator*
Pintozzi, Chestalene *librarian*
Rabuck, Donna Fontanarose *English writing educator*
Reiling, Lois Mae *librarian*
Reinius, Michele Reed *executive recruiter*
Richardson, Elaine *state legislator*
Roemer, Elizabeth *astronomer, educator*
Samet, Dee-Dee *lawyer*
Schulz, Renate Adele *German studies and second language acquisition educator*
Scott, Shirley *city council*
Simmons, Sarah R. *lawyer*
Slaper, Rachael Maree *landscape company executive, poet*
Smith, Kay Frances *social worker*
Sohnen-Moe, Cherie Marilyn *business consultant*
Sprague, Ann Louise *space scientist*
Stein, Mary Katherine *writer, editor, photographer, communications executive*
Stoffle, Carla Joy *university library dean*
Tang, Esther Don *development consultant, retired social worker*
Thompson, Kathleen Shambaugh *marriage and family counselor*
Todd, Pamela Sue *music educator*
Treadwell-Rubin, Pamela A. *lawyer*
Underwood, Jane Hainline Hammons *anthropologist, educator*
Waldt, Risa *therapist, artist, educator*
Willert, Sister St. Joan *health care corporation executive*
Witte, Marlys Hearst *internist, educator*
Wittenberg, Rachel Anne *special education educator*
Wolff, Sidney Carne *astronomer, observatory administrator*
Zepeda, Ofelia *linguist, educator*

Yuma
Anderson, Stacey Ann *school psychologist*
Hilgert, Arnie *management and marketing educator*
Houggard, Santa Carol Hall *family nurse practitioner*
Lineberry, Laurie Lawhorn *urban planner*

ARKANSAS

Arkadelphia
Sandford, Juanita Dadisman *sociologist, educator, writer*

Batesville
Bennett, Linda Lou *school librarian, educator*
Wallace, Marcia Gayle *art educator, theater educator, photographer*

Beebe
Fletcher, Maris *literature educator*

Bella Vista
Anton, Cheryl L. *sales executive*
Christensen, Margaret Anna *nurse, health management educator*

Benton
Krueger, Marlo Bush *retired lawyer*

Bentonville
Dillman, Linda *retail executive*
Swanson, Celia *retail executive*

Berryville
Brown, Frances Louise (Grandma Fran) *artist, art gallery owner*

Blytheville
Baker, Carlene Poff *real estate agent, reporter*
Estes, Pamela Jean *pastor*
Fulling, Sharon S. *college nursing program director*

Camden
Bradshaw, Otabel *retired primary school educator*
Hale, Sharon Gilbert *secondary school educator*

Cedarville
Whitaker, Ruth Reed *state legislator, retired newspaper editor*

Conway
Vanderslice, Stephanie M. *humanities educator*
Vetter, Allison Lee *sociologist, educator*
Wilson, Cheryl Lee *special education educator*

Dumas
Schexnayder, Charlotte Tillar *state legislator*

El Dorado
Botti Villegas, Maria Marta *artist, art educator*
Daymon, Joy Jones *school psychology specialist*

Elkins
Anderson, Ada *retired cattle rancher, retired court reporter*

England
Wright, Mary E. (Mary E. Guen) *clinical* [illegible]

Everton
Jones, Melba Kathryn *elementary school educator, librarian*

Fayetteville
Caldwell, Sarah *opera producer, conductor, stage director and administrator*
Cantrell, Andrea E. *library administrator*
Madison, Sue Wood *state legislator*
Mullen, Maureen Ann *social worker*
Newgent, Rebecca Ann *counselor, educator*
Prichard, Anne W.B. *librarian*
Shafer, Carol Larsen *retired book reviewer*
Stephens, Wanda Brewer *social services administrator, investor*
Webb, Lynne McGovern *communication scholar, consultant*

Flippin
Modeland, Phyllis Jo *author*

Foreman
Horn, Barbara B. *state legislator*

Fort Smith
Ashley, Ella Jane (Ella Jane Rader) *medical technologist*
Autry, Davida Marie *minister*
Decker, Josephine I. *health clinic official*
Montgomery, M. Darlene *secondary education educator, English language educator*
Shankle, Kelli Ann *social worker*
Smith-Leins, Terri L. *mathematics educator*
Walz, Patricia Jean *psychologist*

Greenbrier
Brown, Lois Heffington *health facility administrator*

Harrison
Hearn, Cynthia Ann *education educator*
McKelvy, Nikki Kay *nurse*

Heber Springs
Stroud, Peggy Ann *secondary school educator*

Helena
Stroope, Kay *mathematician, educator*

Hot Springs National Park
McDaniel, Ola Jo Peterson *retired social worker, educator*
Stuber, Irene Zelinsky *writer, researcher*

Hot Springs Village
Lihs, Marilyn Louise *retired accountant*

Humphrey
Wilson, Victoria Jane Simpson *farmer, nurse*

Huntsville
Musick, Pat *artist*

Jacksonville
Lawrence-Cox, Nancy Nell *artist, retired executive secretary*

Jonesboro
Cash, Mary Frances *minister, retired civilian military employee*
Chrisman, Nancy Carol *city manager, director, small business owner*
Sullivan, Virginia L. *public affairs educator, consultant*

Lamar
Bollman, Peggy *art educator*

Little Rock
Adams, Rose Ann *nonprofit administrator*
Bass, Evelyn Elizabeth *elementary school educator*
Bourgeois, Sharon E. *mechanical engineer*
Buehling, Cynthia Gwynne *music educator*
Casey, Paula Jean *former prosecutor*
Cherry, Sandra Wilson *lawyer*
Cline, Ann *artist, designer*
Conger, Cynthia Lynne *financial planner*
Dickey, Betty C. *judge*
Fisher, Jimmie Lou *state official*
Fowler, Jennefer Rae *sculptor*
Franks, Candace Ann *bank executive*
Gardner, Kathleen D. *gas company executive, lawyer*
Good, Mary Lowe (Mrs. Billy Jewel Good) *investment company executive, educator*
Harmon, Kay Madelon *occupational therapist*
Holland, Allison Denman *writing and film educator, film preservationist*
Imber, Annabelle Clinton *state supreme court justice*
Johananoff, Pamela *jewelry designer, manufacturer, gemologist*
Kibbe-Reed, Trudie *academic administrator*
Light, Jo Knight *stockbroker*
Mancino, Anne Rochelle *surgeon*
McCaleb, Annette Watts *executive secretary*
Mitchell, Jo Kathryn *retired hospital technical supervisor*
Moore, Helen Lucille *adult education educator, consultant*
Nunn, Patarica Dian *poet, telephone directory operator*
O'Neal, Nell Self *retired principal*
Pollan, Carolyn Joan *state legislator, job research administrator*
Priest, Sharon Devlin *association executive, former state secretary of state*
Roaf, Andree Layton *judge*
Schwartz, Deborah G. *airport manager*
Simmons, Caroline Jennermann *biomedical researcher, writer*
Smith, Mary Scott *elementary school educator, education educator*
Stockburger, Jean Dawson *lawyer*
Truex, Dorothy Adine *retired university administrator*
Walden, Catherine Jane *not-for profit director, social worker, consultant*
Waters, Zenobia Pettus *retired finance educator*
Winston, Šandra *health sciences administrator*
Witherspoon, Carolyn Brack *lawyer*
Worley, Karen Boyd *psychologist*
Wright, Susan Webber *judge*

Magnolia
Davis, Elizabeth Hawk *English language educator*

Marianna
Pruitt, Mary H. *social worker*

Mc Gehee
Wilson, Nancy LaFarra *elementary school educator, art educator, artist*

Melbourne
Sanders, Dawn Marie *special education educator*

Monticello
Webster, Linda Jean *communications educator, media consultant*

Morrilton
Crawford-Larson, Kris *minister*

Mountain View
Meyer, Eleanor Catherine *artist, educator*

Murfreesboro
Janssen, Marybeth *airframe and power plant mechanic*

Newport
Falwell, Carol *school librarian, real estate broker*

Norman
Hokanson, Carol *speech therapist, special education educator*

North Little Rock
Harrison, Angela Eve *manufacturing executive*
Wilson, LaVerne *nursing administrator*

Pangburn
Laws, Angela Kay *gifted and talented educator*

Paris
Hawkins, Naomi Ruth *nurse*

Pine Bluff
Engle, Carole Ruth *aquaculture economics educator*
Gullett, Brenda B. *state legislator*
McHan, Martha Elaine *purchasing agent*
Williams, Bettye Jean *English educator*

Pine Ridge
Hays, Annette Arlene *secondary school educator*

Quitman
Martindale, Carla Joy *retired librarian*

Russellville
Kondrick, Linda Carol *science educator*
Morris, Lois Lawson *education educator*

Trusty, Sharon *state legislator*

Scott
Rolingson, Martha *research archeologist*

Scranton
Uzman, Betty Ben Geren *pathologist, retired educator*

Searcy
Bucher, Susan A. *elementary school educator, music educator*
Whiteside, Dorothy Jean *education educator*

Sherwood
Eddy, Nancy C. *counselor*
Keaton, Frances Marlene *insurance sales representative*

Springdale
Beach, Jean Mrha *food products executive*
Cordell, Beulah Faye *special education educator*
Dunn, Jeri R. *food products executive*
Morris, Scarlett Kay *elementary school educator, music educator*
Pirozzoli, Heather Jo *food company professional*
Smith, Roblyn Carol *speech pathology/audiology services professional*

State University
McClain, Veda *education educator, department chairman*

Stuttgart
Ashley-Iverson, Mary E. *retired librarian*

White Hall
Bell, Josephine Crawford *music educator*
Dumas, Sandra Kay *music educator*

CALIFORNIA

Agoura Hills
Cannon, Nancy Gladstein *insurance agent*
Piscitelli, Nancy L. *retired special education educator*

Alameda
Carter, Roberta Eccleston *therapist, counselor*
Heiss, Claire DeYoung *manufacturing executive*
Herrick, Sylvia Anne *health service administrator*
Johnson, Beverly J. *lawyer, congressman*
Potash, Jeremy Warner *public relations executive*

Albany
Boris, Ruthanna *dancer, choreographer, dance therapist, educator*
Peterson, Nancy L. *federal agency administrator, volunteer*
Thomsen, Peggy Jean *mayor, educator, councilman*
Van Tuyl, Loraine Yvette *psychologist*

Alhambra
Austin, Elizabeth Ruth *retired elementary school educator*

Aliso Viejo
Cohen, Sasha (Alexandra Pauline Cohen) *ice skater*
Harder, Wendy Wetzel *communications executive*
Otero-Smart, Ingrid Amarillys *advertising executive*

Altadena
Johnson, Kristen Marie *art director*
Mkryan, Sonya *geophysicist, educator, research scientist*
Rabe, Elizabeth Rozina *hair stylist, horse breeder*
Seward, Grace Evangeline *retired librarian*
Willans, Jean Stone *bishop, religious organization executive*

Anaheim
Barkemeijer de Wit, Jeanne Sandra *graphic artist, illustrator, writer, multimedia consultant*
Barry, Sandra *school system administrator*
Bennett, Genevieve *artist*
Ford, Maryestelle Beverly *piano educator, music researcher*
Fyda-Mar, Mary Catherine *systems engineer, director*
Goodspeed, Kathryn Ann *pre-school educator*
Guajardo, Elisa *counselor, educator*
Jung, Charlene *city treasurer*
Lee, Donna Jean *retired hospice and respite nurse*
Orlando, Valeria *music educator, musician, artist*
Pincombe, Jodi Doris *health facility administrator*
Sandler, Michelle Gail *librarian*
Sorenson, Sandra Louise *merchandising manager*
Van Auken, Sue S. *property manager, real estate broker*
Vidergar, Teresa *music educator, musician*

Anderson
Wittmann, Jane Gordon *volunteer*

Angels Camp
Taylor, Lyda Revoire Wing *artist, gallery owner*

Antioch
Adams, Liliana Osses *music performer, harpist*
Thomson, Sondra K. *secondary school educator*

Apple Valley
Freymueller, Cynthia Louise *educational consultant*
Neal, Yolanda Kimberly Tabb *small business owner*

Aptos
Hirsch, Bette G(ross) *college administrator, foreign language educator*

Arcadia
Anderson, Holly Geis *women's health facility administrator, commentator, educator*
Baltz, Patricia Ann (Pann Baltz) *elementary school educator*
Endrusick, Rose Marie *secondary school educator*
Imbus, Sharon Haughey *neuroscience nurse*
Sloane, Beverly LeBov *writer, consultant*
Zimmerman, Amy J. *television producer, television director*

Arcata
Dojka, Jennifer Mimi *art educator, artist*
Janssen-Pellatz, Eunice Charlene *healthcare facility administrator*
Land-Weber, Ellen *photography educator*
Swanson, Carolyn Rae *news reporter, counselor*
Zielinski, Melissa L. *museum director*

Arroyo Grande
Bekey, Shirley White *psychotherapist*
Oseguera, Palma Marie *retired career officer*

Atascadero
Locke, Virginia Otis *writer*
Meyer, Lois Kathryn *graphic artist*
Rios, Evelyn Deerwester *columnist, musician, artist, writer*

Atherton
Weston, Jane Sara *plastic surgeon, educator*

Atwater
Duddy, E. Eileen *accountant*

Auburn
Burness, Maureen O'Leary *school system administrator, consultant*
Moore, Billie Jo *minister*
Patterson, Shirley Drury *genealogist, editor-in-chief*
Rothwell, Elaine B. *artist*
Sanborn, Dorothy Chappell *retired librarian*

Azusa
Aguilar, Gladys Maria *counselor, educator*
Liegler, Rosemary Menke *dean*
White, Rebecca E. *advocate*

Bakersfield
Duquette, Diane Rhea *library director*
Enriquez, Carola Rupert *museum director*
Fuller, Jean *school system administrator*
Gong, Gloria Margaret *lawyer, pharmacist*
Gunderson, Sarah Chloe (Sarah Chloe Burns) *historian, educator*
Johnson, Deborah Valerie Germaine *parish administrator*
Kegley, Jacquelyn Ann *philosophy educator*
Kelly, Diana Kay *counselor, educator*
Litherland, Donna Joyce *counselor*
Martin, Maureen Frances *medical educator*
Osterkamp, Dalene May *psychology educator, artist*
Panelli, Jewel D. *elementary school educator*
Robinson, Chalita Brossett *art educator, artist*
Ross, Katherine *librarian*
Rump, Marjorie *library director*
Saucier, Bonnie L. *dean, pediatrics nurse*
Thornton, Pauline Cecilia Eve Marie Suzanne *special education educator*

Baldwin Park
Barry, Diane Dolores (Diane Branks) *podiatrist*
Snyder, Esther *food service executive*

Banning
Finley, Margaret Mavis *retired elementary school educator*
Saubel, Katherine Siva *Indian culture consultant, educator*

Bellflower
Martin, Melissa Carol *radiological physicist*

Belmont
Hollis, Mary Frances *aerospace educator*
MacLennan, Amy Marie *poet*

Belvedere
Hugenberg, Patricia Ellen Petrie *product designer*

Berkeley
Adelman, Irma Glicman *economics educator*
Azarpay, Guitty *education educator*
Bajcsy, Ruzena *computer engineer*
Barton, Babette B. *lawyer, educator*
Bastrenta, Brigitte Elisabeth *school administrator*
Baumrind, Diana *research psychologist*
Bendix, Jane *artist, author, anthropological illustrator*
Benson, Sally M. *atmospheric scientist*
Bertozzi, Carolyn R. *chemistry educator*
Buell, Evangeline Canonizado *consumer cooperative official*
Buffler, Patricia Ann *epidemiologist, educator, retired dean*
Burch, Claire Rita *writer*
Burnside, Mary Beth *biology educator, researcher*
Campbell, Martha Madison *educational administrator*
Canfield, Judy S. *psychologist*
Chandra, Devaki *researcher in economics, analyst*
Colson, Elizabeth Florence *anthropologist*
Davis, Maggie L. *elementary teacher*
Day, Lucille Lang *museum administrator, educator, writer*
Diamond, Marian Cleeves *anatomy educator*
Diamond, Sara Rose *lawyer, writer*
Dong, Mabel H *music educator*
Edwards, Susan M. *hotel executive*
Gaillard, Mary Katharine *physics educator*
Gallagher, M. Catherine *English literature educator*
Genn, Nancy *artist*
Glenn, Evelyn Nakano *social sciences educator*
Goldstein-Erickson, Ellie *school librarian*
Grimes, Ruth Elaine *city planner*
Guest, Barbara *author, poet*
Gurgin, Vonnie Ann *social scientist, research*
Harris, Eva *molecular biology educator*
Hill, Lorie Elizabeth *psychotherapist*
Hillinger, Edith *artist*
Hoffman, Darleane Christian *chemistry educator*
Houston, Penelope *singer, songwriter, recording artist*
Hull, Glynda *language educator*
Ione, Amy *artist, researcher*
Johnson, Mary Katherine (Katie Johnson) *elementary school educator*
Jones, Patricia Bengtson *sculptor*
Josephian, Jenny Adele *acupuncturist, artist*
Joyce, Rosemary Alexandria *anthropology educator*
Katzen, Mollie *writer*
Kay, Herma Hill *education educator*
Klinman, Judith Pollock *biochemist, educator*
Kohwi-Shigematsu, Terumi *research scientist*
Kushner, Eve *writer*
Lambert, Nadine Murphy *psychologist, educator*
Lashof, Joyce Cohen *public health educator*
Lesser, Wendy *editor, writer, consultant*
Linn, Marcia Cyrog *education educator*
Little, Angela Capobianco *nutritional science educator*
Luker, Kristin *sociology educator*
Ma, Chung-Pei Michelle *astronomer, educator*
Matsumura, Vera Yoshi *pianist*
Matthews, Mildred Shapley *scientific editor, freelance writer*
McLaughlin, Sylvia Cranmer *volunteer, environmentalist*
McPhail-Geist, Karin Ruth *secondary school educator, real estate agent, musician*
Minudri, Regina Ursula *librarian, consultant*
Moran, Rachel *lawyer, educator*
Nader, Laura *anthropology educator*
Peterson, Andrea Lenore *law educator*
Polos, Iris Stephanie *artist*
Poulos, Paige M. *public relations executive*
Rapoport, Sonya *artist*
Ratcliff, Mary Curtis *artist, educator*
Ratner, Marina *mathematician, educator, researcher*
Reid, Frances Evelyn Kroll *cinematographer, director, film company executive*
Romer, Christina Duckworth *economist, educator*
Samuelson, Pamela Ann *law educator*
Savage, Elayne R. *communications educator, counselor, psychotherapist*
Schevill, Margot Blum *anthropologist*
Schild, Sylvia G. *retired elementary school educator, realtor*
Scotchmer, Suzanne Andersen *economics educator*
Siskin, Sharon Valerie *art educator*
Smith, Tanya Gay *editor*
Sorensen, Linda *lawyer*
Sussman, Wendy Rodriguez *artist, educator*
Thomas, Lisa *food service executive*
Tommelein, Iris Denise *construction engineering and management educator, consultant*
Tyson, Laura D'Andrea *dean, economist, educator*
Wake, Marvalee Hendricks *biology educator*
Waters, Alice *executive chef, restaurant owner, writer*
Weber, Molly Anne *actor*
Wehner, Kay Y. *poet*
Yellen, Janet Louise *government official, economics educator*
Yu, Bin *statistician, educator*
Yund, Mary Alice *biotechnology consultant*

Beverly Hills
Allen, Debbie *actress, choreographer, dancer, television director*
Allen, Joan *actress*
Amado, Honey Kessler *lawyer*
Amador, Miranda Barbara *artist*
Ambrose, Lauren *actress*
Anders, Allison *film director, screenwriter*
Anderson, Gillian *actress*
Anderson, Pamela *actress*
Aniston, Jennifer *actress*
Ann-Margret, (Ann-Margret Olsson) *actress, performer*
Arutt, Cheryl *clinical and forensic psychologist, educator*
Baker, Kathy Whitton *actress*
Bancroft, Anne (Mrs. Mel Brooks) *actress, scriptwriter, television director*
Bassett, Angela *actress*
Bates, Kathy *actress*
Bello, Maria Elana *actress*
Bening, Annette *actress*
Bergman, Nancy Palm *real estate investment company executive*
Berry, Halle *actress*
Bigelow, Kathryn *film director*
Blackwell, Michelle S. *media company executive*
Blakeley, Linda *psychologist, speaker*
Bland, Janeese Myra *editor*
Borgnine, Tova *cosmetics executive*
Bosworth, Kate *actress*
Boyle, Lara Flynn *actress*
Bracco, Lorraine *actress*
Branch, Michelle *musician*
Brenneman, Amy *actress*
Brockie, Pamela *motion picture executive*
Burnett, Carol *actress, comedienne, singer*
Burstyn, Ellen (Edna Rae Gillooly) *actress*
Bymel, Suzan Yvette *talent manager, film producer*
Bynes, Amanda *actress*
Campbell, Neve *actress*
Capshaw, Kate (Kathy Sue Nail) *actress*
Carroll, Diahann *actress, singer*
Carter, Dixie *actress*
Carter, Lynda *actress, entertainer*
Casey, Sue (Suzanne Marguerite Philips) *actress, real estate broker*
Castle-Hughes, Keisha *actress*
Cattrall, Kim *actress*
Channing, Carol *actress*
Cher, (Cherilyn Sarkisian) *singer, actress*
Close, Glenn *actress*
Cole, Natalie Maria *singer*
Connelly, Jennifer *actress*
Cox Arquette, Courteney *actress*
Crawford, Cindy (Cynthia Ann Crawford) *model, actress*
Cruz, Penelope *actress*
Curtis, Jamie Lee *actress*
Cusack, Joan *actress*
Daly, Tyne *actress*
Dean, Bonnie Blander *epidemiologist*
Delaney, Kim *actress*
Dennis, Karen Marie *plastic surgeon*
Diaz, Cameron *actress*
Dillard, Suzanne *interior designer*
Dragan, Alexandra *mechanical engineer, consultant, environmental engineer, researcher, engineering educator*
Drescher, Fran *actress*
Dunaway, Faye (Dorothy Dunaway) *actress*
Dussault, Nancy *actress, singer*
Duvall, Shelley *actress*
Eden, Barbara Jean *actress*
Falco, Edie *actress*
Feldshuh, Tovah S. *actress*
Fernandez, Giselle *newscaster, journalist*
Foch, Nina *actress, creative consultant, film director, educator*
Fonda, Jane *actress*
Fox, Vivica *actress*
Garofalo, Janeane *actress, comedienne*
Gellar, Sarah Michelle *actress*
Gilpin, Peri *actress*
Graham, Heather *actress*
Graham, Lauren *actress*
Griffiths, Rachel *actress*
Gyllenhaal, Maggie *actress*
Hamilton, Laurell K. *writer*
Hamilton, Lisa Gay *actress*
Hannah, Daryl *actress*
Harden, Marcia Gay *actress*
Harmon, Angie (Angie Sehorn) *actress*
Hawn, Goldie *actress*
Heaton, Patricia *actress*
Hershey, Barbara (Barbara Herzstein) *actress*
Hewitt, Jennifer Love *actress, singer*
Hines, Cheryl *actress*
Holmes, Katherine Noelle (Katie Holmes) *actor*
Hunt, Bonnie *actress*
Hunt, Helen *actress*
Hurd, Gale Anne *film producer*
Hurley, Elizabeth *actress, model, film producer*
Huston, Anjelica *actress*
Jackson, Janet Damita Jo *vocalist, dancer*
Jenkins, Patty *film director, scriptwriter*
Johansson, Scarlett *actress*
Jolie, Angelina *actress*
Jones, Cherry *actress*
Josephson, Nancy *talent agent*
Judd, Ashley *actress*
Keaton, Diane *actress*
Kelly, Moira *actress*
Kerns, Joanna de Varona *actress, writer, director*
Kidman, Nicole *actress*
Kingsley, Patricia *public relations executive*
Kingston, Alex(andra) *actress*
Klein, Renny *writer, columnist*
Lahti, Christine *actress*
Lange, Jessica *actress*
Lansbury, Angela Brigid *actress*
Leder, Mimi *television director, film director, film producer*
Leigh, Jennifer Jason (Jennifer Leigh Morrow) *actress*
Leong, Margaret *construction executive*
Lewis, Juliette *actress*
Linney, Laura *actress*
Liu, Lucy *actress*
Lopez, Jennifer *actress, dancer, singer*
Mac Dowell, Andie (Rose Anderson Mac Dowell) *actress*
MacLaine, Shirley *actress*
Manheim, Camryn *television and film actress*
Margulies, Julianna *actress*
Marshall, Penny (C. Marshall) *director, actress*
Martin, Kellie (Noelle) *actress*
Masterson, Mary Stuart *actress*
Mathis, Samantha *actress*
Matlin, Marlee *actress*
McCarthy, Jenny *actress*
McDormand, Frances *actress*
McGowan, Rose *actress*
Messing, Debra *actress*
Meyers, Nancy Jane *screenwriter, producer, director*
Midler, Bette *singer, entertainer, actress*
Moore, Demi (Demi Guynes) *actress*
Moore, Julianne (Julie Anne Smith) *actress*
Moore, Mary Tyler *actress*
Morissette, Alanis *musician*
Morton, Samantha *actress*
Mullally, Megan *actress*
Münter, Leilani Maajo *race car driver*
Najimy, Kathy *actress*
Neuwirth, Bebe (Beatrice Neuwirth) *dancer, actress, actress*
Nixon, Cynthia *actress*
Novak, Kim (Marilyn Novak) *actress*
O'Donnell, Rosie *television personality, actress, comedienne*
Paltrow, Gwyneth *actress*
Parker, Mary-Louise *actress*
Parker, Sarah Jessica *actress*
Peet, Amanda *actress*
Pfeiffer, Michelle *actress*
Portman, Natalie *actress*

Ramser, Wanda Tene *library and information scientist, educator*
Reese, Della (Deloreese Patricia Early) *singer, actress*
Ricci, Christina *actress*
Richardson, Patricia *actress*
Ringwald, Molly *actress*
Rivers, Joan *entertainer*
Roberts, Julia Fiona *actress*
Rodkin, Loree *jewelry artist*
Romijn-Stamos, Rebecca *actress, model*
Russell, Keri *actress*
Ryan, Meg *actress, film producer*
Sanford, Isabel Gwendolyn *actress*
Seeger, Melinda Wayne *realtor*
Seidel, Joan Broude *securities trader, investment advisor*
Seymour, Jane *actress*
Shepard, Kathryn Irene *public relations executive*
Shue, Elisabeth *actress*
Shuler Donner, Lauren *film producer*
Smith, Jaclyn *actress*
Smith, Marilyn Noeltner *retired science educator*
Snyder, Liza *actress*
Sorvino, Mira *actress*
Southerland, Deborah Lee *psychologist*
Spacek, Sissy (Mary Elizabeth Spacek) *actress*
Spivak, Jacque R. *bank executive*
Stiles, Julia *actress*
Stowe, Madeleine *actress*
Streep, Meryl (Mary Louise Streep) *actress*
Suvari, Mena *actress*
Swank, Hilary Ann *actress*
Tamblyn, Amber Rose *actress*
Theron, Charlize *actress*
Thompson, Caroline Warner *film director, screenwriter*
Thurman, Uma Karuna *actress*
Tierney, Maura *actress*
Turlington, Christy *model*
Turner, Kathleen *actress*
Tyler, Liv *actress*
Van Ark, Joan *actress*
Vardalos, Nia *actress, screenwriter*
Ward, Sela *actress*
Weaver, Sigourney (Susan Alexandra Weaver) *actress*
Webb, Veronica *fashion model, journalist*
Weisz, Rachel *actress*
White, Betty *actress, comedienne*
Williams, Carole Ann *retired cytotechnologist*
Winningham, Mare *actress*
Winokur, Marissa Jaret *actress*
Winters, Shelley (Shirley Schrift) *actress*
[illegible] *actress*
Yard, Sherry *chef*
Yaryan, Ruby Bell *psychologist*
Yost, Bernice *detective agency owner*
Zanuck, Lili Fini *film director, producer*
Zellweger, Renee *actress*
Zeta-Jones, Catherine *actress*

Big Sur
Spring, Barbara Ethel *sculptor*

Bodega Bay
Freeman, Donna Cook *small business owner*

Bonita
Deane, Debbe *psychologist, journalist, editor, consultant*

Boulevard
Charles, Blanche *retired elementary education educator*

Bradbury
Ackerman, Page *retired librarian, educator*

Brea
Daucher, Lynn M. *state official*
Ellis, Cynthia Bueker *musician, educator*
Missakian, Ilona Virginia *secondary school educator, bookkeeper*
Pierpoint, Karen Ann *marriage, family and child therapist*

Brentwood
Fridley, Saundra Lynn *private investigator*
Groseclose, Wanda Westman *retired elementary school educator*
Paul, Yvonne C. *retired elementary school educator*

Brisbane
Daniels, Caroline *publishing company executive*

Burbank
Boruck, Holly *artist*
Brogliatti, Barbara Spencer *television and motion picture executive*
Cohen, Valerie A. *entertainment company executive*
Cole, Paula *pop singer, songwriter*
Daniels, Susanne *broadcast executive*
DeMent, Iris *vocalist, songwriter*
Doud, Jacqueline Powers *academic administrator*
Frank, Amélie Lorraine *marketing professional*
Gomez-Falcon, Mariah Rosa *psychologist*
Hartshorn, Terry O. *health facility administrator*
Hashe, Janis Helene *editor*
Jacobson, Nina *film company executive*
Janney, Allison *actress*
Joseff, Joan Castle *manufacturing executive*
Kauffman, Marta *producer*
Kinney, Kathy *actress*
Lang, K. D. (Katherine Dawn Lang) *country music singer, composer*
Lang, Laurie *entertainment company executive*
Letterie, Kathleen *broadcast executive*
Mack, Kelly *newscaster*
Madison, Paula *broadcast executive*
Marinelli, Janice *broadcast executive*
Mc Vie, Christine Perfect *musician*
Mitchell, Joni (Roberta Joan Anderson) *singer, songwriter*
Nagra, Parminder *actress*
Neill, Ve *make-up artist*
Nurik, Cindy Bunin *educational consultant, marriage and family therapist*
Remini, Leah *actress*
Rimes, LeAnn *country music singer*
Ruiz, Michele *newscaster*
Shapiro, Angela *broadcast executive*
Sherbert, Sharon Debra *financial services executive*
Sweeney, Anne M. *cable television company executive*
Sweeny, Anne *broadcast executive*
Taubin, Dawn *film company executive*
Thomas-Graham, Pamela *communications executive*
Thompson, Lea *actress*
Ungerleider, Dorothy Fink *educational therapist*
Valdez, Denise *newscaster*
Van Arsdel, Mary Margaret *actress, voice educator*
Williams, Colleen *newscaster*
Wise, Helena Sunny *lawyer*
Younger, Laurie *broadcast executive*

Burlingame
Chalermvongsenee, Maytheenee *air freight administrator, consultant*
Garnett, Katrina A. *information technology executive*

Calabasas
Bernhard, Sandra *actress, comedienne, singer*
Hofflich, Francine K. *network architect*
Laney, Marti Olsen *psychoanalyst, researcher, social sciences educator, writer*
Wyszynski, Tori Lin *psychologist, consultant*

Camarillo
Buhr-Dupreez, Margaret Ilse *adult education educator*
Cobb, Shirley Ann Dodson *public relations consultant, journalist*

Cameron Park
Drushell, Barbara Jean *retired education educator*

Canoga Park
Alexander, Sue *writer*
Kamatoy, Lourdes Aguas *artist*
Lederer, Marion Irvine *cultural administrator*
Rosenfeld, Sarena Margaret *artist*

Canyon Country
Requa, Virginia Lee *literature educator, writer*

Capitola
Hawes, Grace Maxcy *retired archivist, researcher*
Wolff, Jean Walton *writer*

Carlsbad
Buckley, Greta Paula *auditor*
Crooke, Rosanne M. *pharmacologist*
Cuthbert, Emilie Ann (Emilie Winthrop) *interior designer*
Hartigan, Jacqueline Reneé *investigator*
Missett, Judi Sheppard *dancer, jazzercise company executive*
Oakes, Sharon Lorraine *elementary school educator, researcher*
Schmidt, Mary Louise Donnel *bank officer*
Zetter, Lois C. *personal manager*

Carmel
Boyd, Lynne Kaplan *management consultant*
Epstein-Shepherd, Bee *mental skills golf coach, hypnotist, professional speaker*
Evans, Charlotte Mortimer *communications consultant, writer*
García, Beth Baxter *sculptor, writer*
Hamilton, Beverly Lannquist *investment management professional*
Pasten, Laura Jean *veterinarian*

Carmel Valley
Sands, Sharon Louise *graphic design executive, art publisher, artist*

Carmichael
Goodin, Evelyn Marie *writer*

Carpinteria
Lopker, Pamela *technology industry executive*
Rau, Margaret E. *writer*
Shinder, Lorraine Susan *contract administrator, educator*

Carson
Davis, Carylon Lee *mortgage company executive, real estate broker*
Hirsch, Gilah Yelin *artist, writer*
Oropeza, Jenny *state official*
Palmer, Beverly Blazey *psychologist, educator*
Zimmerer, Kathy Louise *university art gallery director*

Castro Valley
Thorburn, Lisa A. *acoustical consulting company executive*

Cathedral City
Berry, Ester Lorée *vocational nurse*
Garcia, Bonnie *state official*
Hoffman, Jetha L. *piano and vocal teacher, musician*

Cayucos
Shahan, Sherry Jean *writer, educator*

Cedar Ridge
Adams, Margaret Bernice *retired museum official*

Cerritos
Solum, Pamela Byard *psychotherapist, educator*

Chatsworth
Dunwich, Gerina *writer, magazine editor, astrologer*
Henderson, Cheryl Lynne *retail executive*
Stephenson, Irene Hamlen *biorhythm analyst, consultant, editor, educator*

Chico
Bernhardt, Victoria L. *director, researcher*
King, Claudia Louan *film producer, lecturer*
Monges, Miriam M. *social studies educator*
Smith, Valene *anthropologist, educator*
Taylor, Carolyn Kay *music educator*

China Lake
Bennett, Jean Louise McPherson *physicist, research scientist*

Chino Hills
Nash, Sylvia Dotseth *consultant*
Pearson, April Virginia *lawyer*
Sanders, Nancy Ida *writer*

Chula Vista
Cohen, Elaine Helena *pediatrician, cardiologist, educator*
Hollowell, Daria Mae *social sciences educator*
Moreno-Ducheny, Denise *state senator*
Smith, Peggy O'Doniel *physicist, researcher*
Upson, Helen Rena *retired history educator*
Watley, Natasha *softball player*
Weiss-Cornwell, Amy *interior designer*

Claremont
Albaum, Jean Stirling *psychologist, educator*
Bekavac, Nancy Yavor *academic administrator, lawyer*
Christian, Suzanne Hall *financial planner*
Douglass, Enid Hart *educational program director*
Dunye, Cheryl *artist, film maker*
Gann, Pamela Brooks *academic administrator*
Halpern, Diane F. *psychology educator, professional association executive*
Lachowicz, Rachel *artist, art educator*
Moss, Myra Ellen (Myra Moss Rolle) *philosophy educator*
Rankaitis, Susan *artist*
Wents, Doris Roberta *psychologist*
Wheeler, Geraldine Hartshorn *historian, writer*

Clayton
Bower, Fay Louise *academic administrator, nursing [illegible]*

Clovis
Franklin, Heidi Ann *music educator*
Moorefield, Claudia Candyce *confectionary marketing professional*
Morgan, Alexia Baca *psychologist*

Coalinga
Russell, Beverly Ann *librarian, writer*

Colusa
Carter, Jane Foster *agriculture industry executive*

Compton
Janeway, Barbara *public relations executive*

Concord
Broadbent, Amalia Sayo Castillo *graphic arts designer*
Grosso, Lisa Therese *periodontist*
Misner, Charlotte Blanche Ruckman *retired community organization administrator*
Thompson, Tracy Lee *bank executive, voice educator*
Wood, Rosemary Ruston *environmental health scientist, consultant*

Copperopolis
McClymonds, Jean Ellen *marketing professional*

Corcoran
Martines, Eugenia Belle *elementary school educator*
Oliver, Patricia *medical assistant*

Corning
Brown, Betty J. *elementary school educator*

Corona
Everett Nollkamper, Pamela Irene *legal management company executive, educator*
Hagmann, Lillian Sue *violin instructor*
Steiner, Barbara Anne *secondary school educator*

Corona Del Mar
Dougherty, Jocelyn *retired neurologist*
Morisseau, Nan Kruger *television personality*

Coronado
Neblett, Carol *soprano*

Corte Madera
Andreini, Elizabeth B. *stockbroker, elementary education educator*
Dalpino, Ida Jane *retired secondary school educator*

Costa Mesa
Caldwell, Courtney Lynn *lawyer, real estate consultant*
Candelaria, Angie Mary *special education educator*
Dougherty, Betsey Olenick *architect*
Epstein, Susan Baerg *librarian, consultant*
Kiang, Assumpta (Amy Kiang) *brokerage house executive*
Lerner, Sandy *cosmetics executive*
Marin, Rosario *former federal agency administrator*
Marshall, Ellen Ruth *lawyer*
Martin, Felicia Dottore *mental health services professional, marriage and family therapist*
McCarthy, Mary Ann *counselor, educator*
Pettus, Candice *social sciences educator*
Sykes, Jolene *former publishing executive*
Tillman, Barbara Ann *education educator, consultant*
Willard, Shirley Fay *management executive*

Cotati
Hill, Debora Elizabeth *writer, journalist, screenwriter*

Cottonwood
Pritchett, Lori L. *real estate broker, secondary school educator*

Covina
Cottrell, Janet Ann *controller*
Durham, Betty Louise *poet*

Coyote
Keeshen, Kathleen Kearney *public relations consultant*

Crescent City
Ruffer, Joyce Sellars *poet, artist*

Culver City
Abarbanell, Gayola Havens *financial planner*
Boonshaft, Hope Judith *public affairs executive*
Evans, Linda *actress*
Fisher, Lucy *film producer*
Gordon, Florence Irene *graphic artist, illustrator*
Grant, Joan Julien *artist*
Hall, Barbara *television producer*
Maxwell-Brogdon, Florence Morency *school administrator, educational consultant*
Michaels, Helene *broadcast executive*
Pascal, Amy *film company executive*
Souza, Blase Camacho *librarian, educator*
Ziskin, Laura *television producer, film producer*

Cupertino
Dalrymple, Cheryl *retired computer company executive*
Geddes, Barbara Sheryl *communications executive, consultant*
Heinen, Nancy R. *computer company executive*
Lyon, Mary Lou *retired secondary school educator*
Zobel, Louise Purwin *author, educator, lecturer, writing consultant*

Cypress
[illegible]
Garrett, Sharon *health services company executive*

Daly City
Hargrave, Sarah Quesenberry *consulting company executive*
Kennedy, Gwendolyn Debra *artist, scriptwriter, playwright*

Dana Point
Burrows, Barbara Ann *veterinarian*

Davis
Bruch, Carol Sophie *lawyer, educator*
Burri, Betty Jane *research chemist*
DePaoli, Geri M. (Joan DePaoli) *artist, art historian*
Dickens, Janis *media services administrator*
Eastin, Delaine Andree *foundation administrator*
Franco, Elaine Adele *librarian*
Gottlieb, Leslie *geneticist, educator*
Horwitz, Barbara Ann *physiologist, educator, consultant*
Jensen, Hanne Margrete *pathology educator*
Keizer, Susan Jane *artist*
Kraft, Rosemarie *dean, educator*
Krubitzer, Leah *psychology educator, neuroscientist*
Kuhl, Tonya L. *science educator*
Liu, Gang-Yu *chemist, educator*
Meyer, Margaret Eleanor *microbiologist, educator*
Mukherjee, Amiya K. *metallurgy and materials science educator*
Ovejero, Graciela *artist*
Powers, Gay Havens-Monteagle *artist, educator*
Robert, Ellen *university administrator*
Schneeman, Barbara Olds *nutritionist, educator*
Sharrow, Marilyn Jane *library administrator*
Stern, Judith Schneider *nutritionist, researcher, educator*
Turnlund, Judith Rae *nutritionist*

Del Mar
Faludi, Susan C. *journalist, scholarly writer*
Farquhar, Marilyn Gist *cell biologist, pathologist, educator*
Rodger, Marion McGee *medical and surgical nurse, nursing administrator*

Denair
George, Cathy L. *music educator*

Diamond Bar
Cha, Grace Seungyun *financial company executive*
Usher, Charlene Lynette *lawyer*

Downey
Brooks, Lillian Drilling Ashton (Lillian Hazel Church) *adult education educator*
Diaz, Consuelo *health facility administrator*
Perry, Jacquelin *orthopedic surgeon*
Robles, Darline P. *school system administrator*
Ruecker, Martha Engels *retired special education educator*

Dublin
Ferrari, Tamara W. *benefits compensation analyst*

Earlimart
White, Kathleen *director*

East Palo Alto
Jacobs Gibson, Rose *city councilwoman, non-profit company executive*

Edwards
Larson, Jo Ann *government agency administrator*
McCarthy, Marianne *government agency administrator*

Edwards AFB
Baer-Riedhart, Jenny *aeronautical engineer*

El Cajon
Dana-Davidson, Laoma Cook *English language educator*
Kibble-Cacioppo, Maxine Lorraine *recording company executive*
Krueger, Nancy Asta *physical therapist*

El Cerrito
Conti, Isabella *psychologist, consultant*
Hargis, Barbara Louise *artist*
Kao, Yasuko Watanabe *retired library administrator*
Mendoza, Lydia *vocalist*
Schilling, Janet Naomi *nutrition consultant*
Stenmark, Jean Kerr *mathematics educator*
Tannenbaum, Judith Nettie *writer, educator*

El Granada
Heere, Karen R. *astrophysicist*

El Monte
Last, Marian Helen *social services administrator*

El Segundo
Byears, Latasha *professional basketball player*
Insprucker, Nancy Rhoades *career officer*
Leslie, Lisa DeShaun *professional basketball player*
McCarty, Shirley Carolyn *aerospace executive*
Milton-Jones, DeLisha *professional basketball player*
Olson, Jeanne Innis *technology and technical management executive*
Toler, Penny *former professional basketball player, sports team executive*
Weatherspoon, Teresa Gaye *professional basketball player*
Willis, Judy Ann *lawyer*

El Sobrante
Withrow, Sherrie Anne *financial specialist*

Elk Grove
Moe, Janet Anne *elementary school educator, church organist*
Romano, Sheila June *telecommunications industry executive, artist, writer*

Emeryville
Arguedas, Cristina C. *lawyer*
Hurst, Deborah *pediatric hematologist*
Mather, Ann *film company executive*
Spadora, Hope Georgeanne *real estate company executive*

Encinitas
Kenyon, Kendra Sue *organizational consultant*
Litvin, Inessa Elizabeth *piano educator*

Encino
Bach, Cynthia *educational program director, writer*
Badham, Julia Aileen *artist*
Francisco, Jodie E. *realtor, marketing professional, consultant*
Franklin, Bonnie Gail *actress*
Lombardini, Carol Ann *lawyer*
O'Riley, Karen E. *principal*
Ruderman, Ellen G. *psychotherapist, consultant, psychoanalyst*
Smith, Selma Moidel *lawyer, composer*
Taylor, Renee *actress, writer*
Vogel, Susan Carol *nursing administrator*

Escondido
Carey, Catherine Anita *artist, art educator*
Frawley, Sister Claire *religious studies educator*
Godone-Maresca, Lillian *lawyer*
Granet, Eileen *secondary school educator*
Hannam-Oosterbaan, Maria Gertrude *secondary school educator*
Leso, Cynthia J. *social services administrator*
Linzey, Verna May *minister, writer*
McHenry, Anita Petei *historian, archaeologist*
Mogul, Leslie Anne *business development and marketing consultant*
Rockwell, Elizabeth Goode *dance company director, consultant, educator*
Young, Gladys *business owner*

Eureka
Berg, Patty *state legislator*

Exeter
Pescosolido, Pamela Jane *arts and craft supply store owner, graphic designer*

Fair Oaks
Carrier, Lynne Thomson *journalist*

Fairfax
Ross, Sue *entrepreneur, author, fundraising executive*

Felton
Wughalter, Emily Hope *physical education educator*

Folsom
Campbell, Ann Marie *artist*
Peck, Ellie Enriquez *retired state administrator*

Sarraf, Shirley A. *secondary school educator*
Terranova, Elizabeth (Elisa) Jo *artist*

Fontana
Kirtland, Marianne Maiocco *psychologist*
Resch, Charlotte Susanna *plastic surgeon*

Forest Knolls
Floden, Roberta B. *librarian, columnist*

Fort Bragg
Dias, Michele C. *primary educator*

Foster City
Goldenstein, Lissa A. *biotechnology company executive*

Fountain Valley
Purdy, Leslie *community college president*
Smith, Marie Edmonds *real estate agent, property manager*

Frazier Park
Edwards, Sarah Anne *radio, cable TV personality, clinical social worker*

Fremont
Buswell, Debra Sue *small business owner, programmer, analyst*
Hsu, Gloria *piano teacher*
Liang, Christine *import company executive*
Macaluso, Mary Margaret *nurse, educator*
Maloney, Cheryl Ann *foundation, consultant, business executive*
Maynard, Catherine *medical researcher*
Sahatjian, Manik *nurse, psychologist*
Weinstein, Marta *packaging services company executive*
Wood, Linda May *librarian*

Fresno
Bundy-DeSoto, Teresa Mari *language educator, vocalist*
Dale, Sharon Kay *real estate broker*
Diestelkamp, Dawn Lea *government agency administrator*
DiVincenzo, Sister Mary Anne *chaplain, therapist*
Ezaki-Yamaguchi, Joyce Yayoi *dietician*
Ganulin, Judy *public relations professional*
Garrison-Finderup, Ivadelle Dalton *writer, educator*
Girvin, Shirley Eppinette *retired elementary education educator, journalist*
Lemons Odell, Lauren Sharnelle *secondary school educator*
Lumbye, Betsy *editor*
Monaghan, Kathleen M. *art museum director*
Patterson, Carolyn F. *retired English educator*
Redmond-Stewart, Audrey A. *small business owner*
Schroeder, Rita Molthen *retired chiropractor*
Stewart, Deborah Claire *dean*
Stuart, Dorothy Mae *artist*
Weymouth, Toni *social worker, writer, educator*

Fullerton
Curry, Denise *university women's basketball coach*
Dickson, Kathryn *science educator*
Donoghue, Mildred Ransdorf *education educator*
Sa, Julie *councilwoman*
Sowder, Kathleen Adams *marketing executive*
Spencer, Beverly Ann *medical administrator, health services consultant*
Tehrani, Fleur Taher *electrical engineer, educator, researcher*
Wan, Julia Chang *retired science educator*
Woyski, Margaret Skillman *retired geology educator*

Garden Grove
Schwalm, Laura *school system administrator*

Gardena
Hardison, Dee *former mayor*
Winn, Stephenie *special education program specialist*

Glendale
Dandor, Denise *newscaster*
Davidson, Suzanne Mouron *lawyer*
Dudash, Linda Christine *insurance company executive*
Edwards, Kathryn Inez *educational technology consultant*
Furtado, Nelly Kim *vocalist*
Leyva, Ellen *newscaster*
Llewellyn, Linda Garrison *foundation executive*
Michelson, Lillian *librarian, researcher*
Shelburne, Merry Clare *public information officer, educator*
Simpson, Allyson Bilich *lawyer*
Stienon, Elaine Burr *writer, music educator*
Tuzee, Michelle *newscaster*
Vara, Kathy *newscaster*
Whalen, Lucille *retired academic administrator*

Glendora
Acevedo, Elizabeth Morrison *special education educator*
Starobin, Nancy Ruth *photographer*

Goleta
Koart, Nellie Hart *real estate investor and executive*
Robinson, Nancy A. *writer*

Granada Hills
O'Connor, Betty Lou *hotel executive, food service executive*

Granite Bay
Haynes, April Michelle *band director*
Holtz, Sara *management consultant*
Kemper, Dorla Dean Eaton (Dorla Dean Eaton) *real estate broker*

Reisman, Judith Ann Gelernter *media communications executive, educator*

Grass Valley
Hayes, Cherry Ann *secondary school educator*

Gualala
Ring, Alice Ruth Bishop *retired preventive medicine physician*

Guerneville
Kozlow, Beverly Kay *physical therapist, psychologist, realtor*

Half Moon Bay
Fennell, Diane Marie *marketing professional, process engineer*

Hanford
Harris, Mildred Staeger *retired broadcast executive*

Happy Camp
Black, Barbara Ann *publisher*

Hayward
Cooper, Roberta *mayor*
De Angelis, Deborah Ann Ayars *university athletics official*
Duncan, Doris Gottschalk *information systems educator*
Garcia, Melva Ybarra *counseling administrator, educator*
Getz, Melissa B. *secondary school educator*
Harris, Penelope Claire *pre-school administrator, daycare administrator, consultant*
Laycock, Mary Chappell *gifted and talented education educator, consultant*
Meyer, Ann Jane *human development educator*
Rees, Norma S. *academic administrator*
Reevy-Manning, Gretchen Maria *psychology educator*
Spranza, Maureen *music educator, elementary school educator*
Wilson, Renee Layne *protective services official, personal trainer*

Hemet
Fitzsimmons, Terri Kathleen *career consultant, educator*
Lawrence, Paula Denise *physical therapist*
Levine, Elaine Prado *school psychologist, musician, artist*

Hermosa Beach
Chi, Lois Wang *retired biology educator, research scientist*
LaBouff, Jackie Pearson *personal care industry executive, educator*
Wickwire, Patricia Joanne Nellor *psychologist, educator*

Highland
MacQueen, Cher *interior designer, retired newscaster, sportscaster*

Hillsborough
Atwood, Mary Sanford *writer*

Hollister
Grace, Bette Frances *certified public accountant*
Miller, Alisa Dorothy Norton *artist*

Hollywood
Lore, Linda *retail executive*
Miles, Joanna *actress, playwright, director*
Minnelli, Liza *singer, actress*
Warren, Diane *song writer*

Huntington Beach
Boardman, Connie *former mayor, biologist, educator*
Boccignone, Lisa Maria *phlebotomist*
Carey, Shirley Anne *nursing consultant*
Cook, Debbie *lawyer, councilman*
De Massa, Jessie G. *media specialist*
Flakes, Susan *playwright, screenwriter, director*
Garrels, Sherry Ann *lawyer*
Isabelle, Beatrice Margaret *artist*
Jackle, Karen Dee *real estate company executive*
Sandrock, Donna *gallery director*
Schaffner-Irvin, Kristen *oil executive*
Sward, Andrea Jeanne *musician, librarian*

Idyllwild
Schneider, Margaret Perrin *writer*

Indio
Zorick, Nancy Lee *artist, actress*

Inglewood
Buss, Jeanie *professional sports team executive*
Cato, Gloria Maxine *retired secondary education educator, school program administrator*
Dixon, Tamecka *professional basketball player*
Epstein, Marsha Ann *public health administrator, physician*
Lockhart, Claudia Jo *adult education educator, department chairman*
Logan, Lynda Dianne *elementary school educator*
Marks, Laura B. *psychologist*
Patmore, Kimberly S. *financial services executive*
Wakefield, Marie Cynthia *performing arts educator, playwright, poet*

Inverness
Ciani, Judith Elaine *retired lawyer*

Inyokern
Norris, Lois Ann *elementary school educator*

Irvine
Allen, Karen Alfstad *information technology executive*
Boyd, Carolyn Patricia *history educator*

Clark, Karen Heath *lawyer*
Cox, Kathryn Cullen *laboratory executive*
Craig, Karen Lynn *accountant, controller*
Fouste, Donna H. *association executive*
Gelfand, Julia Maureen *librarian*
Greenberger, Ellen *psychologist, educator*
Kluger, Ruth *German language educator, editor*
Lee, Eva *medical educator*
Lesonsky, Rieva *editor*
Lin, Amy Yuh-Mei *industrial engineer, real estate investor*
Love, April Gaye McLean *librarian*
McClintock, Sandra Janise *writer, editor*
McPhillen, Lauri *financial analyst, product manager, educator*
Myles, Margaret Jean *real estate appraiser*
Ruttenberg, Susann I. *health sciences administrator*
Ruyter, Nancy Lee Chalfa *dance educator*
Shea, Christina *former mayor*
Smedley, Keyue Ma *engineering educator, researcher*

Kelseyville
Sandmeyer, E. E. *toxicologist, consultant*

Kentfield
Blum, Joan Kurley *fundraising executive*
Halprin, Anna Schuman (Mrs. Lawrence Halprin) *dancer*

Kingsburg
Quaday-Gray, Ailene Diann *retired speech pathology/audiology services professional*

La Canada
Clement, Cathleen McMullin *fundraiser*
Paniccia, Patricia Lynn *journalist, writer, lawyer, educator*

La Crescenta
Purcell, Lee *actress, film producer*

La Habra Heights
Agajanian, Gilda *pianist*

La Jolla
Alvariño De Leira, Angeles (Angeles Alvariño) *biologist, oceanographer*
Armstrong, Elizabeth Neilson *curator*
Baldridge, Kim *science educator*
Bardwick, Judith Marcia *management consultant*
Barlow, Carrolee *physician, scientist, educator*
Barrett-Connor, Elizabeth Louise *epidemiologist, educator*
Bastien, Jane Smisor *music educator*
Beebe, Mary Livingstone *curator*
Buchholz, Debby *lawyer*
Burbidge, E. Margaret *astronomer, educator*
Chandler, Marsha *academic administrator, educator*
Coburn, Marjorie Foster *psychologist, educator*
Cohen, Barbara Ann *artist*
Cole, Barbara Todd *bookseller*
Covell, Ruth Marie *medical educator, medical school administrator*
Covington, Stephanie Stewart *psychotherapist, writer, educator*
Dorsey, Dolores Florence *retired corporate treasurer, business executive*
Engvall, Eva *biochemist*
Falk, Julia S. *linguist, educator, dean*
Grobstein, Ruth H. *health facility administrator*
Hall, TennieBee M. *editor*
Han, Wenge *research scientist*
Henig, Suzanne *retired educator, writer, editor*
Iddings, Kathleen *poet, editor, publisher, consultant*
Janda, Kim D. *chemist, educator*
Jenik, Adriene *artist, educator*
Jorgensen, Judith Ann *psychiatrist, educator*
Kenyon, Karen Beth Smith *literature educator, writer*
Knowlton, Nancy *biologist*
Lane, Sylvia *economist, educator*
Lowe, Lisa *education educator, department chairman*
Mandler, Jean Matter *psychologist, educator*
Marshak, Celia L. *biochemist, educator*
McDonald, Marianne *classicist*
Merrim, Louise Meyerowitz *artist, actress*
Mirsky, Phyllis Simon *librarian*
North, Kathryn E. Keesey (Mrs. Eugene C. North) *retired secondary school educator*
Oreskes, Naomi *science historian*
Rearden, Carole Ann *clinical pathologist, educator*
Ride, Sally Kristen *physics educator, scientist, former astronaut*
Savoia, Maria Christina *vice dean*
Shawver, Laura K. *biotechnology company executive*
Terras, Audrey Anne *mathematics educator*
Thompson, Charlotte Ellis *pediatrician, educator, writer*
Weiner, Ferne *psychologist*
Whitaker, Eileen Monaghan (Eileen Monaghan) *artist*
White, Michelle Jo *economics educator*
Wilson, Bonnie Jean *lawyer, educator, investor*
Wong-Staal, Flossie *geneticist, medical educator*
Yuki, Goda *science educator*
Zyroff, Ellen Slotoroff *information scientist, classicist, educator*

La Mesa
Black, Eileen Mary *retired elementary school educator*
Charleton, Margaret Ann *child care administrator, consultant*
Harmening, Gail Joan *craft pattern designer*

La Mirada
Krotinger, Sheila M. *secondary school educator*

La Quinta
Adolph, Diane Joyce *retired underwriter*

Lozano-Centanino, Monica Cecilia *publishing executive*
Lucoff, Kathy Ann *art advisor*
Lunden, Joan *television personality*
Lynch, Beverly Pfeifer *education and information studies educator*
Macavinta-Tenazas, Gemorsita *family physician*
Malcolm, Dawn Grace *family physician*
Malone, Nancy *actress*
Maloney, Kristen *gymnast*
Manella, Nora M. *federal judge*
March, Kathleen Patricia *judge*
Marrow, Deborah *foundation administrator*
Marshall, Consuelo Bland *federal judge*
Marshall, Mary Jones *civic worker*
Marshall-Daniels, Meryl *communications executive, mediator*
Martin, Ann *newscaster*
Martin, Nanice S. *software company executive*
Martinez, Jean *newscaster*
Mason, Cheryl White *lawyer*
Mathias, Alice Irene *business management consultant*
McCarthy, Nobu *actress, performing company executive, educator*
McGee, Lynda Plant *guidance counselor*
Mellor, Anne Kostelanetz *English literature educator*
Mersel, Marjorie Kathryn Pedersen *lawyer*
Milligan, Sister Mary *theology educator, religious consultant*
Mohajer, Dineh *cosmetics company executive*
Money, Ruth Rowntree *infant development and care specialist, consultant*
Montoya, Velma *economist, policy consultant*
Moroto, Nadine B. *secondary school educator*
Morris, Sharon Hutson *city manager*
Moss, Susan Hecht *artist, writer*
Muldaur, Diana Charlton *actress*
Naqvi, Tasneem Zehra *cardiologist, researcher, consultant*
Nazario, Sonia *reporter*
Neely, Sally Schultz *lawyer*
Nelligan, Kate (Patricia Colleen Nelligan) *actress*
Nelson, Barbara J. *dean*
Neufeld, Elizabeth Fondal *biochemist, educator*
Nobumoto, Karen S. *prosecutor*
Norwood, Phyllis Katherene *director, educator*
O'Brien, Rosanne P. *corporate financial executive*
Ochs, Elinor *linguistics educator*
O'Connell, Taaffe Cannon *actress, publishing executive*
O'Day, Anita Belle Colton *entertainer, musician, vocalist*
O'Leary, Prentice Lee *lawyer*
Olivier, Kathy *college basketball coach*
Olsen, Ashley Fuller *actress*
Olsen, Frances Elisabeth *law educator, theorist*
Olsen, Mary-Kate *actress*
Ordin, Andrea Sheridan *lawyer*
Palmer, Pamela S. *lawyer*
Parisi, Paula Elizabeth *writer, photographer, editor*
Parkinson, Dian *actress*
Pastor, Jennifer *sculptor*
Peña, Elizabeth *actress*
Perez, Edith R. *lawyer*
Perez, Rosie *actress*
Perlmutter, Donna *music critic, dance critic*
Peters, Aulana Louise *lawyer, former government agency commissioner*
Peterson, Linda S. *lawyer*
Pfaelzer, Mariana R. *federal judge*
Philbin, Ann M. *art facility director*
Phillips, Geneva Ficker *academic editor*
Phillips, Patricia Dominis *lawyer*
Phinney, Jean Swift *psychology educator*
Plummer, Amanda *actress*
Porper, Mary *comptroller*
Porter, Verna Louise *lawyer*
Presley, Priscilla *actress*
Press, Beth *publishing executive*
Prewitt, Jean *not-for-profit organization executive*
Pruetz, Adrian Mary *lawyer*
Quinn, Patricia K. *literary agent*
Raeder, Myrna Sharon *lawyer, educator*
Rashad, Phylicia *actress, singer, dancer*
Reagan, Nancy Davis (Anne Francis Robbins) *former First Lady of the United States, volunteer*
Reeves, Barbara Ann *lawyer*
Rense, Paige *editor, publishing company executive*
Renteln, Alison Dundes *political science educator*
Resnick, Lynda *business executive*
Reyes, Susana Marie *utility executive, environmentalist*
Rice, Regina Kelly *marketing executive*
Rich, Andrea Louise *museum administrator*
Richmond, Rocsan *television and video producer, director, publicist, actress, dancer, inventor, teacher*
Rico, Suzanne *newscaster*
Ring, Trudy M. *writer, editor*
Rochelle, Dorothy *educational consultant*
Rochette, Laura Christine *literature educator*
Rohrer, Susan Earley *film producer, writer, director*
Rosenberger, Carol *concert pianist*
Rotell, Cynthia A. *lawyer*
Ruhl, Mary B. *lawyer*
Russett, Margaret E. *language educator*
Russo, Lisa Ann *registrar*
Salmon, Beth Ann *magazine editor in chief*
Saunders, Myra Kathleen *dean, law librarian, educator*
Saxe, Deborah Crandall *lawyer*
Scarlett, P. Lynn *foundation administrator, writer*
Scholefiled, Robin Marie *psychologist*
Sedaris, Amy *writer, actress*
See, Carolyn *English language educator, novelist, book critic*

Segil, Larraine Diane *materials company executive*
Shanks, Patricia L. *lawyer*
Shea, Fran *broadcast executive*
Sheindlin, Judith *television personality, judge*
Shiffman, Leslie Brown *management executive*
Shin, I. Mia *real estate broker, interior designer*
Silverstone, Alicia *actress*
Silverton, Nancy *food service executive*
Simmons, Betty Jo *civil engineer, draftsman*
Sivertsen, Linda Joyce *writer, publishing consultant, editor*
Smith, Ann Delorise *municipal official*
Smith, Jean Webb (Mrs. William French Smith) *civic worker*
Smith-Meyer, Linda Helene (Linda Smith) *artist*
Sohaili, Monira *special education educator, writer*
Spangler, Mary *college president*
Spencer, Carole A. *medical association administrator, medical educator*
Spirtos, Maria *magazine publisher*
Splichal, Christine *restaurant owner*
Squire, Molly Ann *organizational psychologist*
Stansfield, Claire *apparel designer*
Starrett, Lucinda *lawyer*
Stein, Mary Margaret *actor*
Stenge, Lynda Ann *music marketing executive*
Streisand, Barbra Joan *singer, actress, director*
Stuart, Gloria *actress*
Summer, Jena A. *writer, artist, poet*
Swartz, Roslyn Holt *real estate executive*
Swildens, Karin Johanna *sculptor*
Swit, Loretta *actress*
Szego, Clara Marian *cell biologist, educator*
Tatum, Jackie *former parks and recreation manager, municipal official*
Taylor, Minna *lawyer*
Taylor, Shelley E. *psychology researcher and educator*
Teele, Cynthia Lombard *lawyer*
Tellem, Nancy Reiss *broadcast executive*
Terrell, Ann *artist, educator*
Territo, Mary C. *health facility administrator, oncologist, educator*
Thelander, Beverly *oil company executive*
Thomas, Shirley *author, educator, business executive*
Thompson, Anne Kathleen *entertainment journalist*
Thompson, Judith Kastrup *nursing researcher*
Thompson, Sada Carolyn *actress*
Title, Gail Migdal *lawyer*
Tobias, Anita *publishing executive*
Toman, Mary Ann *federal official*
Torres, Cynthia Ann *banker*
Troy, Nancy J. *art history educator*
Tyson, Cicely *actress*
Ullman, Tracey *actress, singer*
Utz, Sarah Winifred *nursing educator*
Valerio Barrad, Catherine M. *lawyer*
Van Buren, Abigail (Jeanne Phillips) *columnist, lecturer*
Van Tilburg, JoAnne *archaeologist, educator, foundation administrator*
Vargas, Diana Lisa *television station executive*
Ver Steeg, Donna Lorraine Frank *nurse, sociologist, educator*
Von Eschen, Lisa A. *lawyer*
Vredevoe, Donna Lou *research immunologist, microbiologist, educator*
Wachtell, Wendy *foundation administrator*
Walden, Dana *broadcast executive*
Walters, Rita *councilwoman*
Ward, Leslie Allyson *journalist, editor*
Warfel, Susan Leigh *editor*
Watkins, Diane Lucille *biology educator*
Watson, Emily *actress*
Watson, Sharon Gitin *psychologist, executive*
Welch, Raquel *actress*
Wells, Annie *photographer*
Werner, Gloria S. *librarian*
White, Meg (Megan Martha White) *musician, vocalist*
White-Whitfield, Lisa Denise *social worker, grant writer*
Wiggins, Marianne *writer*
Wilkerson, LuAnn *dean, medical educator*
Williams, Julie Ford *mutual fund officer*
Williams, Roberta Gay *pediatric cardiologist, educator*
Wilson, Gayle Ann *civic worker*
Wilson, Mable Jean *paralegal*
Wilson, Miriam Geisendorfer *retired physician, educator*
Winters, Barbara Jo *musician*
Wood, Nancy Elizabeth *psychologist, educator*
Woodruff, Fay *paleoceanographer, geological researcher*
Wright, Sandra *science administrator*
Yamaguchi, Colleen S. *lawyer*
Yang, Debra W. *lawyer*
Yoshiki-Kovinick, Marian Tsugie *author*
Zacchino, Narda *newspaper editor*
Zelon, Laurie Dee *lawyer*
Zexter, Eleanor M. *secondary school educator*

Los Banos

Ellington, Karen Renae *secondary education resource specialist*

Los Gatos

Chapson, Lois Jester *interior designer*
Conaway, Margaret Grimes (Peggy Conaway) *library administrator*
Dunham, Anne *educational institute director*
Ferrari, L. Katherine *speaker, consultant, entrepreneur*
Meyers, Ann Elizabeth *sports broadcaster*

Los Osos

Polk, Emily DeSpain *conservationist, writer, designer*
Van Ekeren, Ybi *artist*

Madera

Curry, Cynthia J. R. *geneticist*

Malibu

Field, Barbara Stephenson *small business owner*
Hunt, Valerie Virginia *electrophysiologist, educator*
Marvin, Barbara Joyce *writer*
Miller-Perrin, Cindy Lou *psychology educator*
Palacio, June Rose Payne *nutritional science educator*
Raine, Melinda L. *library manager*
Smith, Yvonne Smart *advertising executive*
Tellem, Susan Mary *public relations executive*
Wilson, Rita *actress*

Manhattan Beach

King, Sharon Marie *consulting company executive*
Lee, Gloria Deane *artist, educator*

Marina

Cornell, Annie Aiko *nurse, administrator, retired military officer*
Hill, Karen Caecilia *education educator*
Mettee-McCutchon, Ila *municipal official, retired career army officer*

Marina Del Rey

Carter, Janice Joene *telecommunications executive*
Erten, Duygu *civil engineer, project manager, educator*
Gold, Carol Sapin *international management consultant, speaker*

Martinez

Baird, Laurel Cohen *clinical nurse*
DeWolfe, Martha *singer, songwriter, publisher, producer*
Kimbrell, Deborah Ann *geneticist, educator*
Tetrault, Jeanne L. *building inspector*

Marysville

Day, Colien *retired secondary school educator*
Gawel, Maureen Saltzer *newspaper executive*
Gray, Katherine *marriage, family and child therapist, writer, educator*

Mckinleyville

Morris, Marjorie Hale *artist, writer*

Mendocino

Alexander, Joyce Mary *illustrator*
Masterson, Julie Cosgrove *photographer*

Menlo Park

Baez, Joan Chandos *folk singer*
Healy, Cynthia *pharmacologist, life scientist, researcher*
Jackson, Jeanne Pellegren *apparel executive*
Jeffries, Robin *computer engineer*
Kurtzig, Sandra L. *software company executive*
Lucke, Betty Jean *dressmaker*
Middleton, Teresa Muir *Internet company executive, researcher*
Pallotti, Marianne Marguerite *foundation administrator*
Reamy, Michaelin *marriage and family therapist, educator, consultant*
Vane, Sylvia Brakke *anthropologist, writer, publishing executive, researcher*

Merced

LeCocq, Karen Elizabeth *artist*
Tomlinson-Keasey, Carol Ann *university administrator*

Midway City

Allen, Frances Michael *publisher*

Mill Valley

Burke, Kathleen J. *foundation administrator*
Mautner, Gabriella *writer, educator*
Newman, Nancy Marilyn *ophthalmologist, educator*
Rasmussen, Tina Marie *organizational development consultant, writer*
Taylor, Rose Perrin *social worker*

Milpitas

Evans, Susan A. *chemist*
Levinson, Marina *information technology executive*
Wang, Susan S. *manufacturing executive*

Mission Viejo

Austin, Berit Synnove *small business owner, central services specialist*
Burke, Kathleen J. *music director, writer*
Frederick, Roseann *retired medical/surgical nurse*
Hafner-Eaton, Chris *health services researcher, medical educator, policy analyst*
Harris, Ruby Lee *real estate agent*
Hodge, Kathleen O'Connell *academic administrator*
McAfee, Margaret Anne *retired art educator*

Modesto

Naeve, Catherine Ann *secondary school educator*
Smith, Heather Lynn *psychotherapist, recreational therapist*
Whiteside, Carol Gordon *foundation executive*

Moffett Field

Bakes, Emma *astrophysicist*
Bingham, Nancy F. *government agency administrator*
Dolci, Wendy Whiting *government agency administrator*
Friedmann, Roseli Ocampo *microbiologist, educator*
Grymes, Rose *government agency administrator*
Harper, Lynn D. *biologist*
Kwong, Jennifer *writer*
Pendleton, Yvonne *astrophysicist*
Shaw, Tianna *biomedical engineer*
Yamauchi, Gloria *aerospace engineer*

Zuniga, Fanny *aerospace engineer*

Monrovia

Brown, Gwendolyn (Williams) *music educator*
Miller, Karen *clinical psychologist, neuropsychologist*
Salaman, Maureen Kennedy *writer, nutritionist*

Montague

Faulkner, Deborah Kay *school system administrator, principal*

Montclair

Negrete McLeod, Gloria *state official*

Montebello

Bucey, Constance Virginia Russell *retired elementary school educator, education educator*
Dible, Rose Harpe McFee *special education educator*
Jacobs, Lillian Laura *secondary school educator*

Montecito

Brenken, Hanne Marie *artist*

Monterey

Aguilar, Miriam Rebecca *technology project manager*
Blair, Cynthia *meteorologist, oceanographer, researcher*
Boger, Gail Lorraine Zivna *reading specialist*
Bui-Burton, Kim Ly *library director, poet*
Gamiere, Constance Anne *education educator, counselor*
Kadushin, Karen Donna *law school dean*
Packard, Julie *aquarium administrator*
Reneker, Maxine Hohman *librarian*
Robinson, Marla Holbrook *community care nurse*

Monterey Park

Smith, Betty Denny *county official, administrator, fashion executive*
Stapleton, Jean *journalism educator*
Wilson, Linda *librarian*

Moorpark

Halperin, Kristine Briggs *insurance sales and marketing professional*
Schwabauer, Mary Ann *secondary school educator, rancher*
Young, Victoria E. *occupational health nurse, lawyer*

Moraga

Lashof, Carol Suzanne *literature educator*
O'Brien, Bea Jae *artist*
Sestanovich, Molly Brown *writer*
Silcox, Frances Eleanor *museum and exhibits planning consultant*

Moreno Valley

Hadfield, Tomi Senger *hospital administrator*
Young, Ruby Waller *medical/surgical nurse, writer, poet*

Morgan Hill

Aranda, Sandra Louise *speech pathology/audiology services professional*

Morro Bay

O'Neill, Margaret E. *psychological counselor*
Scholer, Margaret D. *adult education educator*

Mount Shasta

Mann, Karen *consultant, educator*
Stienstra, Stephani Ann *editor, writer*

Mountain View

Abel, Elizabeth A. *dermatologist*
Allen, Vicky *sales and marketing professional*
Craig, Joan Carmen *secondary school educator, performing arts educator*
Di Muccio, Mary-Jo *retired librarian*
Emmons, Victoria Ann *hospital administrator, marketing consultant*
Falcao, Veronica Grace *midwife*
Juvvadi, Anita Reddy *pediatrician*
Livermore, Ann M. *computer company executive*
Lucas, Catherine *biotechnology company executive*
Mansfield, Elaine Schultz *molecular geneticist, automation specialist*
Otus, Simone *public relations executive*
Polese, Kim *software company executive*
Quartuccio, Maryann *insurance agent, home economist*
Serebrennikova, Emiliya *musician, educator*
Serra, Patricia Janet *social services administrator*
Vanni, Deborah Ann *marriage and family therapist, educator*
Wulff, Virginia McMillan *association executive*

Murrieta

Miller, Helen F. *music educator, musician*

Napa

Coates, Verona Agnes *secondary school educator*
Gillespie, Marcia Lou *tax specialist, accountant, musician*
Lee, Margaret Anne *psychotherapist, social worker*
Loar, Peggy Ann *foundation administrator, museum administrator*
Renfrow, Patricia Anne *secondary school educator*
Woodruff, Diane Carey *college president*

National City

Quigley, Deborah Hewitt *adult education educator*

Nevada City

Hudson, Lee (Arlene Hudson) *environmental activist*

Newark
Mueller, Nancy *food products executive*

Newbury Park
Lindsey, Joanne M. *flight attendant, poet*
McCune, Sara Miller *foundation executive, publisher*
Stadler, Katherine Loy *advertising sales executive*

Newhall
Sylvers, Arlene Marder *clinical psychologist*

Newman
Carlsen, Janet Haws *retired insurance company executive*

Newport Beach
de Garcia, Lucia *marketing professional*
Duvall, Florence Marie *software engineer*
Gellman, Gloria Gae Seeburger Schick *marketing professional*
Harlan, Nancy Margaret *lawyer*
McManigal, Penny *artist*
Schiff, Laurie *lawyer*
Simon, Karen Michele *clinical psychologist, educator*
Spitz, Barbara Salomon *artist*
Vine, Naomi *museum administrator*

Nipomo
Dronen, Linda-Kay *social worker*

North Hills
Villani, Luisa *writer, educator*

North Hollywood
Charis, Barbara *nutritionist, consultant, health researcher*
Downey, Roma *actress*
Fanning, Dakota *actress*
Gallardo, Sandra Silvana *producer*
Martin, Milinda *public relations executive*
Miller, La Brenda *investment analyst, writer*
Nutt, Sandra Maria *actress, writer*
Reynolds, Debbie (Mary Frances Reynolds) *actress*
Runquist, Lisa A. *lawyer*
Schlosser, Anne Griffin *librarian*
Stone, Sharon *actress*
Taravella, Rosie *actress*
Toplitt, Gloria H. *voice educator, singer, actress*
Toussieng, Yolanda *make-up artist*

North Shore
Kopp-Kelly, Jennifer Lee *technical illustrator*

Northridge
Baker, Katherine Ramos *music educator, conductor*
Cartwright, Nancy *actress, television producer*
Curzon, Susan Carol *university administrator*
Hall, Leilani Rae *humanities educator*
Harwick, Betty Corinne Burns *sociology educator*
Heinen, Julia Margaret *music educator*
Koester, Jolene *academic administrator*
Lewis, Louise Miller *gallery director, art history educator*
Sparling, Mary Lee *biology educator*
Syms, Helen Maksym *educational administrator*
Weatherup, Wendy Gaines *graphic designer, writer*

Novato
Conolly, Katharine Farnam *editor*
Fraser, Margot *consumer products company executive*
Guadarrama, Belinda *computer company executive*
Jaeger, Patsy Elaine *retired secondary education educator, artist*
Popovic, Bozena (Bo Popovic) *artist*
Turner, Mabel Croughan *retired microbiologist*
Zigas, Rita B. *music director, musician*

Nuevo
Rogers, Marilyn Rose *special education educator*

Oak Park
Kavesh, Eden *fraud investigator, financial consultant*

Oakdale
Saletta, Mary Elizabeth (Betty Saletta) *sculptor, rancher*

Oakhurst
Gyer, Jane E. *artist, educator*

Oakland
Alba, Benny *artist*
Alford, Joan Franz *entrepreneur*
Armstrong, Saundra Brown *federal judge*
Austin, Caroline Germaine *small business owner*
Benton-Hardy, Lisa Renee *psychiatrist, educator*
Bouska Lee, Carla Ann *nursing and health care educator*
Breed, Sarah Dunford *elementary school educator, writer*
Brown, Karen *performing company executive*
Buzaljko, Grace Wilson *retired editor*
Carter, Mandy *professional organization administrator*
Carwell, Hattie Virginia *health physicist*
Cary, Alice Shepard *retired physician*
Chan, Wilma *county official*
Chodorow, Nancy Julia *psychoanalyst, psychotherapist, educator*
Coleman-Perkins, Carolyn *medical/surgical nurse*
Crocker, Joy Laksmi *concert pianist and organist, composer*
DeFazio, Lynette Stevens *dancer, educator, choreographer, violinist, actress*
DeMoro, Rose Ann *nursing administrator*
Diaz, Sharon *education administrator*
Earle, Sylvia Alice *research biologist, oceanographer*
Eis, Ruth Susanne *museum curator, artist*
Griffin, Betty Jo *elementary school educator*
Hafter, Ruth Anne *library director, educator*
Holmgren, Janet L *college president*
Isaac Nash, Eva Mae *secondary school educator*
Jeffries, Pamela Depperman *advertising executive, entrepreneur*
Kennedy, Judith Price *elementary school educator*
Killebrew, Ellen Jane (Mrs. Edward S. Graves) *cardiologist, educator*
King, Janet Carlson *nutrition educator, researcher*
Krause, Marcella Elizabeth Mason (Mrs. Eugene Fitch Krause) *retired secondary school educator*
Lake, Suzanne *singer, music educator*
Lee, Ella Louise *librarian, educator*
Light, Sally G. *cultural organization administrator*
Luterman, Alison Gina *poet*
McCarroll, Martha Hadley *music educator, conductor*
Miller, Connie Joy *assistant real estate officer, broker*
Neeley, Beverly Evon *sociologist, consultant*
Nelson, Shirley W. *bank executive*
Ocheltree, Carolyn Donine *minister, religious studies educator*
O'Hara, Delia Iglauer *family nurse practitioner*
Randisi, Elaine Marie *accountant, educator, writer*
Reynolds, Kathleen Diane Foy (KDF Reynolds) *transportation executive*
Rice, Frances Mae *physician*
Sandler, Marion Osher *savings and loan association executive*
Slack, Vickie *human services administrator*
Tchaikovsky, Leslie J. *federal judge*
Tran, Nguyet T. *accountant*
Vaccariello, Carol Polizzi
West, Natalie Elsa *lawyer*
Wilken, Claudia *judge*
Williams, Carol H. *advertising executive*
Wood, Larry (Mary Laird) *journalist, writer, public relations executive, educator, environmental consultant*
Woodbury, Marda Liggett *librarian, writer*
Zschau, Marilyn *singer*

Occidental
Granahan, Andrea Eleanor *editor, writer,* [illegible]

Oceanside
Asato, Susan Pearce *business executive, educator*
Book, Marilyn Mohr *columnist*
Druhe Brandt, Iris Claire *retired elementary school educator*
Hertweck, Alma Louise *sociology and child development educator*
Johnson, Karen Elaine *secondary school educator, tax preparer*
McIntyre, Louise S. *income tax consultant*
Munson, Lucille Marguerite (Mrs. Arthur E. Munson) *real estate broker*
Paxton, Mary Jean Wallace *science educator*
Pena, Maria Geges *academic services administrator*
Sarkisian, Pamela Outlaw *artist*
Villasenor, Barbara *book publisher*
Witbeck, Glenda M. *poet*

Ojai
Horne, Rikki *school system administrator*

Ontario
Dastrup-Hamill, Faye Myers *city official*
Maynard, Pamela Rae *architectural design firm executive*
McGehee, Sharon *school system administrator*
Peters, Jacqueline Mary *secondary school educator*
Presto, Catherine Ann (Kay Presto) *small business owner, media specialist, consultant*
Soto, Nell *state senator*

Orange
Banning, Donna Rose *retired art educator*
Bogart, Wanda Lee *interior designer*
Gibbons, Pamela R. *professional athletic trainer*
Morgan, Beverly Carver *pediatrician, educator*
Scherman, Carol E. *human resources professional*
Stevens, Cherita Wyman *social sciences educator, writer*
Strate, Jan Nicole (Niki Strate) *contractor*
Stuewe, Isabel *elementary school educator*

Orinda
Dorn, Virginia Alice *artist, art gallery director*
Epperson, Stella Marie *artist*
Lorensen, Hilda S. *librarian*
Strong, Susan Clancey *writer, communication consultant, editor*

Oroville
Strisower, Suzanne *clinical hypnotherapist, counselor*

Oxnard
Neilson, Jane Scott *mathematics educator*
Rosales, Sandra Johnson *school system administrator*
Tolmach, Jane Louise *community activist, municipal official*
Zhou, Sophia Huai *biomedical engineering scientist*

Pacific Grove
Beidleman, Linda Havighurst *biologist*
Penney, Beth *English educator, editor, writer*
Schapiro, Karen Lee *language educator*

Pacific Palisades
Helfgott, Gloria Vida *artist*
Jennings, Marcella Grady *rancher, investor*
Kaufer, Shirley Helen *artist, painter*
Kirkgaard, Valerie Anne *media group executive, syndicated talk radio host, writer, producer, consultant*
Love, Susan Margaret *surgeon, educator, writer*

Pacifica
Hall, Judith Young *nurse*

Palm Desert
Baxter, Betty Carpenter *educational administrator*
Bratrud, Linda Kay *secondary school educator*
Carangelo, Lori *writer, social activist, not-for-profit executive*
Friesz, Mary Lee *freelance/self-employed poet*
Hoffmann, Joan Carol *retired academic dean*
Kaufman, Charlotte King *artist*
Ponder, Catherine *clergywoman, author*
Reordan, Beverly Jean *artist*
Romano, Darlene *music educator, composer*
Sausman, Karen *zoological park administrator*
Vander Naald Egenes, Joan Elizabeth *small business owner, educator*

Palm Springs
Coffey, Nancy Ann *real estate broker*
Hilb, Jeane Dyer *community volunteer*
Holtz-Borders, Karen Lynn *police officer*
Tennyson, Louise H. *artist*

Palmdale
Farley, Margaret Wilhelmina *librarian*
Garcia, Beatrice Maude *social worker*
Rosete, Amy Renee *accountant, writer, editor*
Scott-Flanton, Vernita Lynn *consultant*
Vahle, Laura Miles *marriage and family therapist, educator*
Valenti, Betty Janet *resource specialist, educator*

Palo Alto
Baskins, Ann O. *lawyer, computer company executive*
Berg, Olena *investment company executive, former federal official*
Berger-Granet, Nancy Sue *nursing researcher*
Blessing-Moore, Joann Catherine *allergist*
Bowick, Susan D. *computer company executive*
Capparell, Lorraine Susan *artist, sculptor, painter*
Collins, Margery Louise *elementary school educator*
Denzel, Nora *information technology executive*
Diamond, Diana Louise *editor, graphic artist*
Dunn, Debra L. *computer company executive*
Estrin, Judith *computer company executive*
Fiorina, Carleton S. (Carly Fiorina) *computer company executive*
Goldstein, Mary Kane *physician*
Greene, Diane *information technology executive*
Gunther, Barbara *artist, educator*
Hays, Marguerite Thompson *nuclear medicine physician, educator*
Herr, Pamela Staley *writer, historian*
Hubert, Helen Betty *epidemiologist*
Jackson, Cynthia L. *lawyer*
Johnson, Allison *corporate communications specialist*
Kincaid, Judith Wells *electronics company executive*
Kirk, Carmen Zetler *data processing executive*
Litt, Iris Figarsky *pediatrics educator*
Long, Anne T. *financial analyst, investment adviser*
Love, Brenda Zejdl *writer*
Lundy, Jackelyn Ruth *consulting firm owner, economist, researcher*
McCall, Jennifer Jordan *lawyer*
McHugh, Maura *professional basketball coach*
Michie, Sara H. *pathologist, educator*
Mommsen, Katharina *retired German language and literature educator*
Moore, Cassandra Chrones *real estate broker and policy analyst*
Quinn, Helen Rhoda *physicist*
Saegesser, Marguerite M. *artist*
Scitovsky, Anne Aickelin *economist, researcher*
Spangenberg, Ruth Beahrs *psychologist, educator*
Sproule, Betty Ann *computer industry strategic consultant*
Stephens, Bess *computer company executive*
Swain, Judith Lea *cardiovascular physician, educator*
Ticknor, Carolyn M. *computer company executive*
Tirschwell-Newby, Kathy Ann *events production company executive*
Walker, Carolyn Peyton *English language educator*
Willem, Karen J. *business software company financial executive*
Winkleby, Marilyn A. *medical researcher*
Wojcicki, Esther Denise *journalist, educator*

Palos Verdes Estates
Brigden, Ann Schwartz *mediator, educator*
Kingsley, Kathryn Alexis Krah *retired elementary school educator*
McNeill, Susan *real estate marketing and sales professional*
Yarbrough, Allyson Debra *electrical engineer*

Palos Verdes Peninsula
Deveny, Charlotte Perry *musician, educator*
King, Nancy *communications educator*
Miller, Francie Loraditch *counseling administrator*
Narasimhan, Padma Mandyam *physician*
Vanderlip, Elin Brekke *philanthropic executive*

Panorama City
Janis, Elinor Raiden *artist, educator*
Jasso, Nancy *dermatologist*

Paradise
Bernstein, Elizabeth Ann *retired executive secretary*

Paramount
Williams, Vivian Lewie *retired counseling administrator*

Pasadena
Almore-Randle, Allie Louise *special education educator*
Avrech, Gloria May *psychotherapist*
Brogden-Stirbl, Shona Marie *writer, researcher*
Bunting, Anne Evelyn (Eve Bunting) *author*
Buratti, Bonnie J. *aerospace scientist*
Cepielik, Elizabeth Lindberg *elementary school educator*
Freedman, Wendy Laurel *astronomer, educator*
Hall, Cynthia Holcomb *federal judge*
Harris, Jennifer A. *aerospace engineer*
Helin, Eleanor Francis *astronomer, geologist*
Hunt, Hazel Analue Stanfield *retired accountant*
Iturbide, Graciela *photographer*
Johnson, Barbara Jean *retired judge, lawyer*
Kornfield, Julia Ann *chemical engineering educator*
Lopes, Rosaly Mutel Crocce *astronomer, planetary geologist*
Morgan, Ann Marie *psychologist*
Mosher, Sally Ekenberg *lawyer, musician*
Nelson, Dorothy Wright (Mrs. James F. Nelson) *federal judge*
Newman, Marjorie Yospin *psychiatrist*
Nicholson, Frances Mary Baum *secondary school educator, writer*
Olson, Diana Craft *image and etiquette consultant*
Pashgian, Margaret Helen *artist*
Racklin, Barbara Cohen *fundraising consultant*
Roth, Irma Doris Brubaker *editor*
Rymer, Pamela Ann *federal judge*
Sanchez, Pauline Stella *artist*
Short, Elizabeth M. *internist, educator, retired federal agency administrator*
Shuster, Marguerite *minister, educator*
Spilker, Linda Joyce *aerospace scientist*
Tan-Wang, Grace *aeronautical engineer*
Wilson, Mary Ellen *retired project administrator*
Worby, Rachel *conductor*
Yeager, Caroline Hale *radiologist, consultant*
Zwicky, Barbarina Exita *humanities educator, researcher*

Paso Robles
Buck-Moyer, Sandra Kay *marriage and family therapist*

Pebble Beach
Hoffman, Sharon Lynn *adult education educator*
Moriarty, Maureen C. *marketing professional*
Sanford-Hagus, Barbara *geneticist, consultant*

Penn Valley
Longan, Suzanne M. *retired elementary school educator*
Nix, Barbara Lois *real estate broker*

Petaluma
de Lappe, Pele Phyllis *retired journalist, artist*
Fuller-McChesney, Mary Ellen *sculptor, writer, publisher*
Hirshfield, Jane B. *poet*
Levinthal, Jeana Davison *pediatrician*
Paul, Amy *lawyer*
Sebold, Alice *writer*
Thomas, Nancy Hinckley *special education educator*

Pico Rivera
Merrill Warner, Veronique *psychologist*

Piedmont
Mayeri, Beverly *artist, ceramic sculptor, educator*

Pinedale
Falcone, Patricia Jeanne Lalim *investor, foundation administrator*

Pinole
Wold, Vera O'Bryan *retired medical/surgical nurse*

Pittsburg
Hurley, Allison Ruth *mentor coach specialist*
Williams, Elizabeth A. *financial planner, business consultant*
Williscroft-Barcus, Beverly Ruth *lawyer*

Placerville
Miller, Edna Rae Atkins *secondary school educator*
Wall, Sonja Eloise *nursing administrator*
Wickline, Marian Elizabeth *former corporate librarian*
Wilkinson, Rosemary Regina Challoner *poet, writer*

Playa Del Rey
Lutz, Charlene Joyce *special education educator, consultant*

Pleasant Hill
George, Julianne Mary *music educator, conductor*

Pleasanton
Caldwell, Nanci *software company executive*
Fine, Marjorie Lynn *lawyer*
Hilton, Shirley Shin Sil *controller*
Novak, Randi Ruth *engineer, computer scientist*
Plaisance, Melissa *retail executive*
Renda, Laree M. *retail executive*

Point Richmond
Tellier, Jen Emily *psychologist, educator*

Pollock Pines
Rickard, Margaret Lynn *retired library director*

Pomona
Adomaitis, Alyssa Dana *design educator, consultant*
Amaya-Thetford, Patricia *elementary school educator*
Callaway, Linda Marie *special education educator*
Demery, Dorothy Jean *secondary school educator*
Dishman, Rose Marie Rice *academic administrator, researcher*
Elliott, Susan Donise *secondary school educator*
Englert, Phyllis Ann *psychology educator*
Patterson, Frieda Morgan *retired medical secretary, computer professional*
Singer-Chang, Gail Leslie *social sciences educator, assistant dean for student affairs*
Tarver, Paula Diann *marketing professional*

Porterville
Vasilescu, Vasilica *psychologist, consultant*

Portola Valley
Cameron, Eleanor Cranston Fowle *writer*
Nycum, Susan Hubbell *lawyer*

Prather
Marvin, Freda Mary *art educator, nurse*

Presidio of Monterey
Dulo, Donna Ann *computer scientist, consultant*

Ramona
McAndrews, Shannon Marie *elementary school educator*
Newman, Malane L. *digital designer, cartoonist, illustrator, computer graphics designer, educator, small business owner*
Van Zant, Susan Lucille *principal*

Rancho Cordova
Hendrickson, Elizabeth Ann *retired secondary school educator*
Wilderotter, Mary Agnes *cable television executive*

Rancho Cucamonga
Horsley, Paula Rosalie *accountant*

Rancho Dominguez
Campbell, Jennifer Bradley *company official, social worker*

Rancho Mirage
Ford, Betty Ann (Elizabeth Ann Ford) *former First Lady of the United States, health facility executive*
Sheldon, Deena Lynn *television camera operator*
Wyatt, Lenore *civic worker*

Rancho Palos Verdes
Hughs, Mary Geraldine *accountant, social service specialist*
Kolosvary-Stupler, Eva *sculptor*

Rancho Santa Fe
Kranz, Kathleen Nee *pianist, music educator*
Land, Judy M. *real estate broker*
McNally, Connie Benson *magazine editor, publisher, antiques dealer*

Rancho Santa Margarita
Aguilera, Donna Conant *psychologist, researcher*
Newton, Michelle Marie *sales executive*

Redding
Caskie, Judith Maureen *physical therapist*
D'Amico, Petrina *sculptor*
Drake, Patricia Evelyn *psychologist*
Peterson, Robyn Gayle *museum curator*
Rocafort, Julia Esther *social worker*

Redlands
Auerbacher, Mary Jane *church organist*
Bumann, Daniela *movement therapist, massage therapist*
Coleman, Arlene Florence *retired pediatrics nurse*
Huenergardt, Myrna Louise *retired academic administrator, retired adult nurse practitioner*
Simone, Sharon Elizabeth *education educator, filmmaker, writer*

Redondo Beach
Battles, Roxy Edith *novelist, consultant, educator*
Engstrom, Stephanie Cloes *wildlife artist, small business owner*
McCall-Rodriguez, Leonor *entrepreneur, consultant*
McWilliams, Margaret Ann *home economics educator, author*
Oh, Angela E. *lawyer*
Richards, Denise *actress*
Shellhorn, Ruth Patricia *landscape architect*
Woike, Lynne Ann *computer scientist*

Redwood City
Davidson, Mary Ann *information technology executive*
Jones, Brenda Gail *school district administrator*
Katz, Safra *computer company executive*
Majure, Allison Scott *product marketing professional*
Sharpnack, Rayona *management consultant*
Smith, Nancy L. *information technology executive*
Spangler, Nita Reifschneider *volunteer*
Stirm, Doris Elizabeth *artist*
Woods, Jacqueline F. *telecommunications industry executive*

Reedley
Carey, Ernestine Gilbreth (Mrs. Charles E. Carey) *writer, lecturer*

Rescue
Ackerly, Wendy Saunders *construction company executive*

Rialto
Jackson, Betty Eileen *music and elementary school educator*
Johnson, Ruth Floyd *educational consultant*
King, Muriel Eileen *secondary school educator*

Richmond
Corbin, Rosemary MacGowan *former mayor*
McLeod, Jacquelyn H. *special education educator*
Quenneville, Kathleen *lawyer*

Riverside
Andersen, Frances Elizabeth Gold *religious leadership educator*
Anderson, Jolene Slover *small business owner, publishing executive, consultant*
Auth, Judith *library director*
Chang, Janice May *lawyer, naturopathic doctor, psychologist*
Chang, Sylvia Tan *health facility administrator, educator*
Dutton, Jo Sargent *education educator, researcher, consultant*
Fagundo, Ana Maria *creative writing and Spanish literature educator*
Fontana, Sandra Ellen Frankel *special education educator*
Hackwood, Susan *electrical and computer engineering educator*
James, Etta *recording artist*
Lobb, Cynthia Jean Hocking *lawyer*
Macek, Pamela Kay *tax specialist, business executive*
Meadows, Joyce Katherine *nurse*
Naugle, Charlotte June *principal, educator*
Oakes, Judy Dianne *real estate broker*
Phillips, Virginia A. *judge*
Raikhel, Natasha V. *plant cell biology educator*
Rainey, Susan J. *school system administrator*
Smith, Dorothy Ottinger *jewelry designer, civic worker*
Warren, Katherine Virginia *art gallery director*
Witman, Laura Kathleen *writer, security professional*
Wood, Brenda Jean *pastor, evangelist*
Yount, Gwendolyn Audrey *humanities educator*

Rocklin
Hyde, Geraldine Veola *retired secondary school educator*

Rohnert Park
Leeder, Elaine *sociologist, educator, writer*
Newcomb, Joan Leslie *elementary school educator*

Rolling Hills Estates
Ingerson, Nancy Nina Moore *special education educator*

Rosemead
Black, Melodee *marketing professional*
Featherstone, Diane L. *utilities executive*
Goddard, Jo Ann *investment advisor*
Parsky, Barbara *utilities executive*
Ryder, Beverly *utilities executive*
Yazdi, Mahvash *utilities executive*

Roseville
French, Leura Parker *secondary educator*
Grant, Barbara *venture capitalist*
Madden, Wanda Lois *nurse*
Potterton, Barbara Alice *artist, educator, illustrator*
Smith, Kaye Train *artist*

Ross
Godwin, Sara *writer*
Matan, Lillian Kathleen *secondary school educator, consultant, interior designer*

Sacramento
Adolphson, Vanessa *counseling administrator, educator, chemist*
Alpert, Deirdre Whittleton (Dede Alpert) *state legislator*
Amezcua, Esther Hernandez *elementary school educator*
Anderson, Rachel Lyn *behavior researcher*
Armacost, Mary Jane *healthcare company executive*
Artz, Ethel Angela Cleavenger *elementary education educator, consultant*
Barnard, Linda S. *marriage and family therapist*
Baum, Sandra Beattie *executive secretary*
Boekhoudt-Cannon, Gloria Lydia *business education educator*
Bossuat, Judy Weigert *music educator*
Bowen, Debra Lynn *lawyer, state legislator*
Bromund, Alice A. *retired elementary school educator*
Burgess, Deborah Lee *small business owner*
Chu, Judy May *psychology educator, city official*
Cohn, Rebecca *state representative*
Connell, Kathleen *state official*
Contreras, Dee (Dorothea Contreras) *municipal official, educator*
Corbett, Ellen M. *mayor*
Doyel, Cindy M. *information systems specialist*
Escutia, Martha *state senator*
Fargo, Heather *mayor*
Figueroa, Liz *state senator*
Friedman, Kenni *healthcare company official, councilwoman*
Garth-Lewis, Kimberley *state official, public policy educator*
Gibson, Patrice Vandegrift *anthropologist, educator*
Gillan, Kayla J. *lawyer*
Goldberg, Jackie *councilwoman*
Gray, Robin *stage manager*
Hancock, Loni *state legislator, former mayor*
Hardmon, Lady *professional athlete*
Hartman, Patricia Jeanne *lawyer, educator*
Heaphy, Janis Besler *newspaper executive*
Hill, Elizabeth Goodwin *legislative analyst*
Hope, Gerri Danette *telecommunications management executive*
Horton, Shirley A. *state legislator, former mayor*
Hughes, Teresa P. *state legislator*
Hunter, Patricia Rae (Tricia Hunter) *state official*
Kobe, Lisa Marie *quality assurance professional, consultant*
Kuehl, Sheila James *state legislator*
Kulp, Sherrill Irene *business educator, consultant*
Laethem, Fern Melody *lawyer*
LaVally, Rebecca Jean *research editor, journalist*
Lieber, Sally J. *state representative*
Liu, Carol *state representative*
Lucas, Donna *communications executive*
Lundstrom, Marjie *newspaper editor and columnist*
Maitoza, Colleen *professional sports team executive*
Menebroker, Ann *special education educator, writer*
Montanez, Cindy *state representative*
Morgan-Prager, Karole *lawyer, publishing executive*
Nickless, Barbara A. *primary school educator*
Nisson, Mary *elementary school educator*
Opperman, Rosanna Resendez *adult education educator*
Ortiz, Deborah V. *state legislator*
Parra, Nicole M. *state representative*
Pavley, Fran J. *state representative*
Penicheiro, Ticha Nunes *professional basketball player*
Perez, Elena N. *professional society administrator, writer*
Piskoti, Carol Lee *art educator*
Potter, Teresa Pearl *adult education educator*
Reyes, Sarah *state representative*
Romero, Gloria *state senator, government agency administrator*
Ross, Jean M. *think-tank executive*
Rounds, Barbara Lynn *psychiatrist*
Runfola, Sheila Kay *nurse*
Runner, Sharon *state representative*
Sanborn, Kathy *career planning administrator, consultant*
Santiago, Mayumi-Mae Lacaya *marriage therapist*
Scholey, Diann Patricia *accountant*
Shaw, Eleanor Jane *newspaper editor*
Smith, Marie B. *college president*
Speier, Jackie *state senator*
Stuart, Toni Freeman *priest*
Terhaar, Joyce *editor*
Tom, Gail *business educator*
Totton, Gayle *professional sports team executive*
von Friederichs-Fitzwater, Marlene Marie *health communication scholar and researcher*
Welsh, Melinda Ann *editor*
Willis, Dawn Louise *legal assistant, small business owner*
Woo, Sharon Y. *healthcare organization executive*
Work, Janice René *pediatric dentist*
Wright, Cathie *state legislator*
Wunder, Haroldene Fowler *taxation educator*
Zaidi, Emily Louise *retired elementary school educator*
Zeff, Ophelia Hope *lawyer*

Saint Helena
Allegra, Antonia *editor, writer*

Salinas
Chester, Lynne *foundation administrator, artist*
Esquivel, Mary *agricultural products company executive*
Quick, Valerie Anne *sonographer*
Sprude, Margaret *credit services company executive*

San Andreas
Buringrud, Lisa Marie *music educator*

San Anselmo
Ellenberger, Diane Marie *nurse, consultant*

San Bernardino
Brown, Marta Macías *legislative staff member, executive assistant*
Burgess, Mary Alice (Mary Alice Wickizer) *publisher*
Caballero, Sharon *academic administrator*
Clark, Phyllis Yvette *marketing professional, consultant*
Ereksen, Christa Ann *social worker, marriage and family therapist*
Evans, R. Marlene *social welfare administrator, educator*
Griffiths, Barbara Lorraine *psychologist, marriage-family therapist, writer*
Hansen, Anne Katherine *poet*
Kirkland, Bertha Theresa *project engineer*
Plotkin, Judy Ann *special education educator*
Roberts, Katharine Adair *retired bookkeeper*
Valles, Judith *mayor, former academic administrator*

San Bruno
Edwards, Kassandra Bennett *psychotherapist, consultant*
Hariton, Lorraine Jill *information technology executive*
Kell-Smith, Carla Sue *federal agency administrator*
Mangahas, Crystal Tecca *market researcher*
Olson, Julie Ann *systems consultant, educator*
White, Frances LaVonne *academic administrator*

San Carlos
Oliver, Nancy Lebkicher *artist, retired elementary education educator*
Sullivan, Shirley Ross (Shirley Ross Davis) *art collector*

San Clemente
Geyser, Lynne M. *lawyer, writer*
Meredith, Mary J. *secondary school educator*
Renk, Pamela Jean *counselor, psychotherapist*

San Diego
Aaron, Cynthia G. *judge*
Adams, Loretta *marketing executive*
Adler, Louise DeCarl *judge*
Alcosser, Sandra Beth *English language educator, writer*
Amos, Theresa Ann *marketing professional*
Amstadt, Nancy Hollis *retired language educator*
Arova, Sonia *artistic director, ballet educator*
Barone, Angela Maria *artist, researcher*
Bates-Romeo, Delores Alvenia *music educator, consultant*
Bauer, Judy Marie *minister*
Blade, Melinda Kim *archaeologist, educator, research scientist*
Blessing, Carol Ann *literature educator*
Borden, Diane Lynn *communications educator*
Bowens, Thella *senior aviation director*
Brierton, Cheryl Lynn *lawyer*
Brokaw, Meredith A. *women's health care company director*
Brown, Barbara Sproul *retired librarian, consultant, writer*
Buska, Sheila Mary *controller, writer, columnist*
Carson, Cynthia Lee *physician's assistant*
Casey, Nancy J. *women's healthcare company executive*
Chory, Joanne *plant biologist*
Clark, Ann D. *marriage and family therapist*
Clarke, Evelyn Woodman *volunteer*
Cline, Stephanie E. *food service executive*
Comrie, Sandra Melton *human resource executive*
Crawford, Debra P. *women's healthcare company executive*
Crawford, Randi *women's healthcare company executive*
Crocker, Valerie Marian *mechanical engineer*
Darby, Joanne Tyndale (Jaye Darby) *arts and humanities educator*
DiBona, Leslie Faye *librarian*
Drzewiecki, Darla Ruth *accountant*
Dubé, Susan E. *women's healthcare company executive*
Dumanis, Bonnie M. *prosecutor*
Dunlop, Marianne *retired English as second language educator*
Essex, Lauren S. *women's health care company executive*
Farmer, Janene Elizabeth *artist, educator*
Flettner, Marianne *opera administrator*
Freeman, Myrna Faye *county schools official*
Gengor, Virginia Anderson *financial planning executive, educator*
Golding, Susan G. *former mayor*
Gonzalez, Irma Elsa *federal judge*
Gray-Bussard, Dolly H. *energy company executive*
Green, Charlene *principal, speech pathology/audiology services professional*
Grossbard-Shechtman, Shoshana Amyra *economist, educator*
Haverly, Pamela Sue *nursing administrator*
Hays, Diana Joyce Watkins *consumer products company executive*
Hemmingsen, Barbara Bruff *microbiologist, educator*
Herman, Rebecca Lynn *human resources specialist*
Hogan, Sheila Maureen *biology educator, nurse*
Hollingsworth, Margaret Camille *financial services administrator, consultant*
Hoston, Germaine Annette *political science educator*
Howard, Mildred *sculptor*
Huff, Marilyn L. *federal judge*
Idos, Rosalina Vejerano *secondary school educator*
Jacob, Dianne *county official*
Jennings, Jackie *construction executive, contractor*
Johnson, Wendy S. *women's healthcare company executive*
Kaweski, Susan *plastic surgeon, naval officer*
Keep, Judith N. *federal judge*
Kehoe, Christine T. *state official*
King, Verna St. Clair *retired school counselor*
Klamerus, Karen Jean *pharmacist, researcher*
Kraus, Pansy Daegling *gemology consultant, editor, writer*
Krull, Kathleen *writer*
Krupchak, Tamara *artist*
Lacey-Parks, Rena Elizabeth *secondary school educator*
Lam, Carol C. *lawyer*
Lane, Gloria Julian *foundation administrator*
Lang, Linda A. *food service executive*
Langer, Eva Marie *video specialist*
Lindh, Patricia Sullivan *banker, former government official*
Longenecker, Martha W. *museum director*
Lucas, Eloisa B. *tax consultant, management consultant*
Lundy-Slade, Bettie B. *retired electronics professional*
Lyons, Mary E. *academic administrator*
Mahon, Maxine *performing company executive*
Martin, Julie *women's healthcare company executive*
McBrayer, Sandra L. *educational director, homeless outreach educator*
McCarty, Judy *councilman*
McKeown, Mary Margaret *federal judge*
McNeely, Delores *banker*
Morris, Sandra Joan *lawyer*
Niedermeier, Mary B. *retired nutritionist*
O'Laughlin, Joanie *broadcast executive*
Oldham, Maxine Jernigan *real estate broker*
Olson, Linda Ann Salmonson *minister*
Parthemore, Jacqueline Gail *internist, educator, hospital administrator*

San Ramon
Dennis, Patricia Diaz *lawyer*
Jue, Susan Lynne *interior designer*
[illegible] *retired controller, artist*
Peebles, Lucretia Neal Drane *policy and administration educator*
Shapiro, Fania *computer company executive*
Woertz, Patricia A. *petroleum industry executive*
Yarrington, Patricia *oil industry executive*
Zygocki, Rhonda I. *oil industry executive*

San Ysidro
Schneider, Christine Lynn *customs inspector*

Santa Ana
Arriola-Nickell, Gail Emily *development executive*
Chenhalls, Anne Marie *nurse, educator*
Cohen-Strong, Elayne Barbara *social services administrator, educator*
Danoff-Kraus, Pamela Sue *real estate developer*
Dumdum, Josefina Martinez *chemist, researcher*
Gudea, Darlene *publishing company executive*
Kato, Terri Emi *elementary school and gifted and talented educator*
Katz, Tonnie *newspaper editor*
Lyons, Linda *health science association administrator*
Myers, Marilyn Gladys *pediatric hematologist and oncologist*
Prizio, Betty J. *volunteer, retired property manager*
Storer, Maryruth *law librarian*
Stotler, Alicemarie Huber *federal judge*
Torrez, Caroline Herminia *recreation director*
Weiermiller, Kathy *publishing executive*
Wilson, Beth A. *college official*

Santa Barbara
Albanese, Catherine *religious studies educator*
Atwater, Tanya Maria *marine geophysicist, educator*
Beck, Isabel Holderman *psychologist, consultant*
Ben-Dor, Gisselle *conductor, musician*
Binion, Gayle *political science educator*
Bischel, Margaret DeMeritt *physician, managed care consultant*
Brown, J'Amy Maroney *journalist, media relations consultant, investor*
Casey, Mary A. *telecommunications company executive*
Child, Julia McWilliams (Mrs. Paul Child) *cooking expert, television personality, author*
Cunningham, Julia Woolfolk *author*
Enos, Kelly D. *telecommunications company financial executive*
Ford, Anabel *research anthropologist, archaeologist*
Gold, Calla Giselle *jewelry designer*
Higgins, Isabelle Jeanette *librarian*
Hu, Evelyn Lynn *electrical and computer engineering educator*
Hurwitz, Saundra Harriet (Sandi Hurwitz) *analyst, educator*
Ingram, Katharine Goodridge *language educator, writer*
Jackson, Hannah Beth *state legislator*
Johnson, Mary Kathryn *legal assistant*
Keator, Carol Lynne *library director*
Kelm, Bonnie G. *art museum director, educator*
Kirkpatrick, Diane Yvonne *retired speech pathology/audiology services professional*
Larsgaard, Mary Lynette *librarian, writer*
Mack, Judith Cole Schrim *political scientist, educator*
Mahlendorf, Ursula Renate *literature educator*
Mathews, Barbara Edith *gynecologist*
McCoy, Lois Clark *emergency services professional, retired county official, magazine editor*
Menkin, Eva L. *marriage and family therapist*
Mitchell, Shawne Maureen *author*
Nyborg, Vanessa Marie *psychologist, researcher, educator*
Payne, Joanne Lesley *broadcast executive*
Pritchard, Sarah Margaret *library director*
Sebastian, Suzie *producer*
Segal, Helene Rose *periodical editor*
Shea, Joan-Emma *biophysicist, educator*
Snow, Kimberley *editor, writer*
Sulzbach, Christi Rocovich *lawyer*
Tapper, Joan Judith *magazine editor*
Tucker, Shirley Lois Cotter *botany educator, researcher*
Zwick, Rebecca *education educator*

Santa Clara
Chastain, Brandi Denise *professional soccer player*
Culbertson, Leslie S. *computer company executive*
DeBartolo-York, Denise *sports team executive*
Dorchak, Glenda *electronics company executive*
Ellis, Carlene *computer company executive*
Floyd, Shelly L. *computer company executive*
Glancy, Dorothy Jean *lawyer, educator*
Hopkinson, Shirley Lois *library and information science educator*
Kamm, Barbara B. *bank executive*
Lane, Holly Diana *artist*
Lawrence, Deborah Jean *quality assurance professional*
Lehman, Cassandra *psychologist*
Ludgus, Nancy Lucke *lawyer*
Morris, Sandra K. *computer company executive*
Murray, Patricia *electronics company executive*
Pollace, Pamela L. *public relations executive*
Roberts, Janice *marketing professional*
Schapp, Rebecca Maria *museum director*
Siegal, Susan E. *biotechnology company executive*
Simmons, Janet Bryant *writer, publisher*
Weigle, Peggy *information technology executive*

Santa Clarita
Sturges, Sherry Lynn *recording industry executive*
Zuk, Carmen Veiga *psychiatrist*

Santa Cruz
Faber, Sandra Moore *astronomer, educator*
Greenwood, M. R. C. *college dean, biologist, nutrition educator*
Langenheim, Jean Harmon *biologist, educator*
Leites, Barbara L. (Ara Leites) *artist, educator*
Lenox, Catherine Corneau *volunteer*
Martinez, Alma R. *actress, theater director, educator*
Mirk, Judy Ann *retired elementary school educator*
Pletsch, Marie Eleanor *plastic surgeon*
Poulos, Clara Jean *nutritionist*
Roby, Pamela Ann *sociology educator*
Shorenstein, Rosalind Greenberg *internist*
Silver, Mary Wilcox *oceanography educator*
Suckiel, Ellen Kappy *philosophy educator*
Young, Carol Ann (Casey Young) *information systems consultant*

Santa Fe Springs
Hanzel, Mimi S. *psychotherapist*

Santa Maria
Bowker, Margaret Sheard *artist*
Hoyt, Mary G(enevieve) *artist, educator*
Meehan, Lil Euphrasia Therese *poet*
Phillips, Dorothy Lowe *nursing educator*
Sparks, Jeanne *columnist, photographer, educator*
Walton, Maurine Isabel *social worker*

Santa Monica
Amerian, Mary Lee *physician*
Berres, Frances Brandes *clinical psychologist*
Brauner, Marygail K. *engineer, systems analyst*
Carr, Ruth Margaret *plastic surgeon*
Dostal, Tamara *insurance company executive*
Eizenberg, Julie *architect*
Eve, (Eve Jihan Jeffers) *rap artist, actress*
Feniger, Susan *chef, television personality, writer*
Fisher, Frances *actress*
Foley, Jane Deborah *foundation executive*
Frot-Coutaz, Cecile *television producer*
Haroon, Nasreen *artist*
Heimbuch, Babette E. *bank executive*
Henderson, Florence (Florence Henderson Bernstein) *actress, singer*
Hersh, Kristin *vocalist, musician*
Honour, Lynda Charmaine *research scientist, educator, psychotherapist*
Hutton, Fiona S. *communications executive*
Intriligator, Devrie Shapiro *physicist*
Jones, Janet Dulin *writer, film producer*
Josepher, Susan Ann *art educator, consultant*
Kanim, Linda Elie Aliea *medical researcher*
Kaplowitz, Karen (Jill) *lawyer, business consultant*
LaBelle, Patti (Patricia Louise Holt) *singer, entertainer*
Landon, Helen Zielinski *psychologist*
Lara-Cinisomo, Sandra Luz *psychologist*
Lockhart, Sharon *artist*
Louis-Dreyfus, Julia *actress*
Magnabosco-Bower, Jennifer Lynn *mental health professional*
Milliken, Mary Sue *chef, television personality, writer*
Osbourne, Sharon Arden *music manager, actress, talk show host*
Perlman, Judith Faith *think-tank associate, researcher*
Roney, Alice Lorraine Mann *poet*
Ryan, Jane Frances *corporate communications executive*
Shamban, Ava T. *dermatologist*
Simpson, India.Arie *musician*
Smith, Anna Deavere *actress, educator, playwright*
Snedaker, Catherine Raupagh (Kit Snedaker) *editor*
Summer, Donna (La Donna Adrian Gaines) *singer, songwriter, actress*
Timmer, Barbara *state agency administrator*
Veit, Clairice Gene Tipton *measurement psychologist*
Wilfert, Catherine M. *medical association administrator, medical educator*
Wilson-Fellows, Suzanne *motion picture producer*
Wong, Diana Shui Iu *artist*
Wosk, Miriam *artist*

Santa Paula
Broughton, Margaret Martha *psychiatric nurse practitioner*
Kay, Hazel T. *local commissioner*

Santa Rosa
Christiansen, Peggy *principal*
Conway, Lois Lorraine *piano teacher*
Foster, Lucille Caster *school system administrator, retired*
Fruiht, Dolores Giustina *artist, educator, poet*
Jones, Doris (Anna Doris Vogel) *apparel buyer*
King, Gwendolyn Bair *former government staff member, public speaker*
Monk, Diana Charla *artist, stable owner*
Weare, Sally Spiegel *art educator, artist*
Wiggins, Patricia Ann *computer systems analyst, state legislator*

Santa Ynez
Rymer, Ilona Suto *artist, retired art educator*

Santee
Schenk, Susan Kirkpatrick *nursing educator, consultant, small business owner*

Saratoga
Chisholm, Margaret Elizabeth *retired library education administrator*
deBarling, Ana Maria *language educator*

Sausalito
Casals, Rosemary *retired professional tennis player*
Groah, Linda Kay *nursing administrator, educator*
Ramsey, Eleanore Edwards *design bookbinder*

Seal Beach
Wiley, Dianne *aeronautical engineer*

Seaside
Gibson-Brehon, Dawn D. *performing company executive, consultant*
Melicia, Kitty *human resources administrator, foundation administrator*

Sebastopol
Snyder, Allegra Fuller *dance educator*

Shasta Lake
Parsons, Debra Lea *elementary school educator*

Sherman Oaks
Alcott-Jardine, Susan *artist, writer*
Atwood, Colleen *costume designer*
Clark, Susan (Nora Goulding) *actress*
Dent, Ellen Margaret *writer*
Ferguson, Lisa Beryl *accountant*
Gross, Sharon Ruth *forensic psychologist, researcher*
Klimas, Elizabeth Jolanta *accountant, lawyer, economist*
Leighton, Carolyn *foundation administrator*
Little, Carole *women's apparel company executive*
Norwood, Brandy *singer, actress*
Powell, Sandy *costume designer*
Schlessinger, Laura *radio talk show host*
Sharon, Debra Melinda *psychologist*
Weiss, Julie *costume designer*
Wood, Evan Rachel *actress*

Sierra Madre
Converse, Elizabeth *artist, writer*

Simi Valley
Erzinger, Kathy McClam *nursing educator*
McBride, Joyce Browning *accountant*

Skyforest
Wagner, Cheri J. *business owner*

Solana Beach
Bays, Kathryn Michelle *interior designer, educator*
Beard, Ann Southard *diplomat, oil company executive*
Tall, Cheryl A. *artist, art educator*
Withee, Diana Keeran *art historian, art dealer, educator*

Solvang
Anderson, Barbara Ann *property manager*

Somis
Premack, Ann J. *writer*

Sonoma
Fellows, Alice Combs *artist*
Herron, Ellen Patricia *retired judge*
Hobart, Billie *education educator, consultant*
Kizer, Carolyn Ashley *poet, educator*
Minelli, Helene Marie *artist*
Pollack, Phyllis Addison *ballerina*
Racke, Anne Moller *winery executive*

Sonora
Clarke, Paula Katherine *anthropology educator, sociology educator*
Coffill, Marjorie Louise *civic leader*
Gee, Gail Marie *retired medical society executive*
Jones, Georgia Ann *publisher*
Mathias, Betty Jane *communications and community affairs consultant, writer, editor, lecturer*
Sharboneau, Lorna Rosina *artist, educator, author, poet, illustrator*

South Lake Tahoe
Barr, Lois I. *personnel administrator*
Nason, Rochelle *conservation organization administrator*

South Pasadena
Bernal, Harriet Jean Daniels *real estate agent*
Bishop, Carole C. *elementary education educator, family therapist*
Harnsberger, Therese Coscarelli *librarian*
Lynch, Annette Peters *literature educator*
Mantell, Suzanne Ruth *editor*
Yett, Sally Pugh *elementary school educator, gifted and talented educator*

South San Francisco
Desmond-Hellmann, Susan *medical products manufacturing executive*
Estrin, Judy Ann *human resources consultant*
Gerritsen, Mary Ellen *vascular and cell biologist*
Mertens, Lynne G. *retail executive*
Morris, Arlene Myers *marketing professional*
Potter, Myrtle S. *research and development company executive*
Rollence, Michele Lynette *molecular biologist*
Wong, Carrie *public relations executive*

Spring Valley
Heinecke, Margaret Theresa *librarian*
Roberts, Carolyn June *real estate broker*
Soltero, Michelle Dolores *director*

Stanford
Arvin, Ann Margaret *microbiology and immunology educator, researcher*
Babcock, Barbara Allen *law educator, lawyer*
Baker, Patricia Ann *publishing executive*
Ball, Arnetha *education educator*
Barron, Brigid *education educator*
Blau, Helen Margaret *pharmacology educator*
[illegible]
Byerwalter, Mariann *academic administrator*
Carstensen, Laura Lee *gerontology educator*
Cohen, Elizabeth G. *education and sociology educator, researcher*
Cork, Linda Katherine *veterinary pathologist, educator*
Darling-Hammond, Linda *education educator*
Derksen, Charlotte Ruth Meynink *librarian*
Donaldson, Sarah Susan *radiologist*
Ehrlich, Anne Howland *research biologist*
Emery, Jane Dailey *English literature and language educator*
Francke, Uta *medical geneticist, genetics researcher, educator*
Gold, Anne Marie *library director*
Jacobs, Charlotte De Croes *medical educator, oncologist*
Kallosh, Renata *physics educator*
Kraemer, Helena Antoinette Chmura *psychiatry educator*
Loeb, Susanna *education educator*
Long, Sharon Rugel *molecular biologist, plant biology educator*
Lotan, Rachel *education educator*
Maccoby, Eleanor Emmons *psychology educator*
Marsh, Martha *hospital administrator*
Martin, Joanne *social sciences educator*
Matson, Pamela Anne *environmental scientist, science educator*
Newman-Gordon, Pauline *French language and literature educator*
Offen, Karen Marie *historian, educator*
Paté-Cornell, Marie-Elisabeth Lucienne *management and engineering educator*
Payne, Anita Hart *reproductive endocrinologist, researcher*
Perloff, Marjorie Gabrielle *English and comparative literature educator*
Polan, Mary Lake *obstetrics and gynecology educator*
Powers, Rebecca Ann *psychiatrist, health facility administrator*
Rhode, Deborah Lynn *law educator*
Ricardo-Campbell, Rita *economist, educator*
Shapiro, Lucille *molecular biology educator*
Stipek, Deborah *education educator, dean*
Sullivan, Kathleen Marie *dean, law educator*
Suppes, Christine Johnson *publishing executive*
Traugott, Elizabeth Closs *linguist, educator, researcher*
Van Derveer, Tara *university athletic coach*
Wapnir, Irene Leonor *medical educator*
Whittemore, Alice *biostatistician*
Wotipka, Christine Min *education educator*
Zhou, Ping *physical engineer*

Stockton
Bickford, Melissa A. *internet administrator*
Cooper, Iva Jean *special education educator*
Foster, Colleen *library director*
Fung, Rosaline Lee *language educator*
Haines, Joybelle *retired elementary school educator*
Hepper, Iona Lydia *retired gallery owner*
Hitchcock, Susan Y. *school administrator, city council member*
Jackson, Jewel *retired state agency administrator*
Jacobs, Marian *advertising agency owner*
Kizer, Nancy Anne *music educator, musician*
Magness, Rhonda Ann *microbiologist*
Mann, Tori *secondary school educator*
Matthews, Barbara *state legislator*
Matuszak, Alice Jean Boyer *pharmacy educator*
Meissner, Katherine Gong *city official*
Norton, Linda Lee *pharmacist, educator*
Wilcox, Helena Marguerita (Rita) *music educator*
Wright, Evelyn Louise *artist*

Studio City
Alvarado, Sandra Jacqueline *television director*
Basinger, Kim *actress*
Boyett, Joan Reynolds *arts administrator*
Carsey, Marcia Lee Peterson *television producer*
Chambers, Clytia Montllor *public relations consultant*
Herrman, Marcia Kutz *child development specialist*
Johnston, Kristen *television personality*
King, Carole (Carole Klein) *songwriter, singer*
Lasarow, Marilyn Doris *artist, educator*
Manders, Susan Kay *artist*
Mc Donald, Meg *public relations executive*
Moseley, Chris Rosser *marketing executive*
Rotblatt, Joy J. *artist*
Weiner, Sandra Samuel *critical care nurse, nursing consultant*

Sugarloaf
Black, Victoria Lynn *writer, artist*

Suisun City
Schunke, Hildegard Heidel *accountant*

Sunnyvale
Daltchev, Ana Ranguel *sculptor*
Decker, Susan *Internet company executive*
Garner, Shirley Imogene *retired music educator*
Gupta, Vinita *communications executive*
Herscher, Penny *company executive*
Merrill, Wendy Jane *insurance company executive*
Michals, Lee Marie *travel agency administrator*
Ng, Betty *electronics executive*
Patstone, Cheryl *public relations executive*
Perdikou, Kim *information technology executive*
Seeger, Virginia Vincent *portrait painter*
Wesely, Elaine Gale *purchasing manager*

Sunol
Rebello, Marlene Munson *speech pathologist*

Sutter Creek
Sanders, Elizabeth Anne Weaver (Betsy Sanders) *management consultant*

Sylmar
Corry, Dalila Boudjellal *internist, educator*
Faye, Thalia Garin *retired microbiologist, educator*
Froelich, Beverly Lorraine *foundation director*
Hayes, Cynthia Ann (C.A. Hayes) *writer*
Tully, Susan Balsley *pediatrician, medical educator*
Yu, Katherine Kit *internist*

Tarzana
Blackburn, Greta Jeanette *writer*
Neece, Olivia Helene Ernst *investment company executive, consultant*
Rinsch, Maryann Elizabeth *occupational therapist*

Tehachapi
Smith-Thompson, Patricia Ann *public relations consultant, educator*
Sprinkle, Martha Clare *elementary school educator*

Temecula
Bathaee, Soussan *engineering technician*
Keenan, Retha Ellen Vornholt *retired nursing educator*
Sjursen, Hope Bianchi *marketing professional*

Templeton
Foster-Wells, Karen Margaret *artist*

The Sea Ranch
Baas, Jacquelynn *museum consultant, art historian*

Thermal
Montoya, Leiala *assistant principal*

Thousand Oaks
Falberg, Kathryn E. *pharmaceutical executive*
Helton, Patricia Beth *realtor*
Herman, Joan Elizabeth *healthcare company executive*
Heyer, Carol Ann *illustrator*
Mulkey, Sharon Renee *gerontology nurse*
Pakula, Anita Susan *dermatologist*
Relkin, Michele Weston *artist*
Rosenblatt, Alice F. *health products executive*
Shirley, Courtney Dymally *nurse*
Washburn, Nan *conductor*
Wolfson, Marsha *internist, nephrologist*

Toluca Lake
Gipson, Juliet Annette *real estate broker*
Powers, Mala *actress*

Topanga
McGray, Deanna Gail *retired elementary school educator*
Norwood, Virginia Tower *retired engineer*

Torrance
Adelsman, Jean (Harriette Adelsman) *newspaper editor*
Barnard, Cynthia Marie *art educator, artist*
Brasel, Jo Anne *pediatrician, educator*
Bryan, Sharon Ann *lawyer*
Carey, Kathryn Ann *foundation administrator, editor, consultant*
Ebeling, Vicki *marriage and family therapist, psychotherapist, writer*
Howroyd, Janice Bryant *personnel placement executive*
McNamara, Brenda Norma *secondary school educator*
Sorstokke, Susan Eileen *systems engineer*
Sperling, Irene R. *publishing executive*
Sun, Nora Chi-Jun *pathologist*
Van Emburgh, Joanne *lawyer*

Tracy
Harris, Kathleen Renee *marketing professional*

Truckee
Todd, Linda Marie *nutrition researcher, circulation manager, financial consultant, pilot*

Tujunga
Buri, Carolyn *management consultant*
Daly, Saralyn R. *retired humanities educator, writer*
Pozzo, Mary Lou *retired librarian, writer*

Tulare
Pinto, Marie Malania *academic administrator, consultant*
Vickrey, Herta M. *microbiologist*

Turlock
Antoniuk, Verda JoAnne *secondary school educator*
Hughes, Marvalene *academic administrator*

Tustin
Greene, Wendy Segal *special education educator*

Ukiah
Lohrli, Anne *retired English language educator, writer*
Newell, Barbara Ann *coatings company executive*

Union City
Cross, Elizabeth *apparel manufacturing company executive*
Lockhart, Patsy Marie *secondary school educator, consultant*
Velarde, Heide Marie *publisher, writer, lyricist*

Universal City
Crow, Sheryl *singer, songwriter, musician*
Fleishman, Susan Nahley *film company executive*
Gill, Libby *television executive*
Hammer, Bonnie *broadcast executive*
Menendez, Belinda *broadcast executive*
Merkerson, S. Epatha *actress*
Parent, Mary *film company executive*
Randall, Karen *film company executive*
Rocco, Nikki *film company executive*
Schulz, Diana *film company executive*
Snider, Stacey *film company executive*

Upland
Bast, Karolyn (Kay) Anne *dance educator, choreographer*
Lewis, Goldy Sarah *real estate developer, corporation executive*

Vacaville
Biscevic, Nancy Lunsford *photographer*
Leonard, Suzanne Louise *artist, photographer*

Valencia
Anguiano, Lupe *advocate*
Dolegowski, Dina C. *executive secretary*
Fogel, Jennifer Lynn *technical associate, researcher*
Parks, Suzan Lori *playwright*
Webb, Margot *writer*
Wilson, Millie L. *artist, educator*

Vallejo
Landauer, Elvie Ann Whitney *humanities educator, writer*
Murillo, Carol Ann *secondary school educator*

Valley Center
Whitten, Laura A. *secondary school educator*

Valley Village
Barkin, Elaine Radoff *composer*
Bishop, Kathryn Elizabeth *film company executive, writer*
Diller, Phyllis *actress, writer*

Van Nuys
Boone, Deborah Ann (Debby Boone) *singer*
Cook, Jenik Esterm (Jenik Esterm Cook Simonian) *artist, educator*
Lemberger, Phyllis *language educator, elementary school educator*
Vasylyeva, Anna *artist, writer*

Venice
Alf, Martha Joanne *artist*
Edelstein, Jean *artist, performance artist*
Groppe, Laura *interactive software company executive*

Ventura
Bircher, Andrea Ursula *mental health services professional*
Chandler, Juliette Anne *writer, communications executive*
Granata, Donna Assunta *photographer, educator*
Kreissman, Starrett *librarian*
Lipinski, Barbara Janina *psychologist, psychotherapist, educator, writer*
Moffatt, Mindy Ann *elementary school educator, educational training specialist*
Renger, Marilyn Hanson *elementary school educator*
Zuber, Norma Keen *career counselor, educator*

Victorville
Polley-Shellcroft, Theresa Diane *university educator*
Yochem, Barbara June (Runyan) *sales executive, lecturer*

Visalia
Lynch, Janet Nichols *English language educator, writer*
Ryan-Halley, Charlotte Muriel *oncology clinical specialist, family nurse practitioner*

Vista
Cannon, Kathleen *lawyer, educator*
Ferguson, Margaret Ann *tax consultant*
Lane, Marsha K. *medical/surgical nurse*
Linhart, Letty Lemon *editor*
Rigby, Amanda Young *paralegal firm executive*
Savage, Linda Eileen *psychologist*
Tadeo, Elvia *artist*

Walnut
McKee, Catherine Lynch *law educator, lawyer*
Weisbart, Jennifer Rachel *mathematician, educator*

Walnut Creek
Ausenbaum, Helen Evelyn *social worker, psychologist*
Cannon, Grace Bert *retired immunologist*
Carver, Dorothy Lee Eskew (Mrs. John James Carver) *retired secondary school educator*
Foster, Bonnie Gayle *operating room nurse, real estate agent*
Goldman, Anne L. *ceramic artist*
Lilly, Luella Jean *academic administrator*
Mackay, Patricia McIntosh *psychotherapist*
Pfeiffer, Phyllis Kramer *publishing executive*
Reimann, Arline Lynn *artist*
Sheen, Portia Yunn-ling *retired physician*
Van Noy, Christine Ann *restaurateur*
Wilkins, Sheila Scanlon *management consultant*

Watsonville
Hernandez, Jo Farb *music director, consultant*
Hugg, Alicia Esther *healthcare administrator*

Weed
Richard, Eleanor *minister*

West Covina
Wagner, Frances Rita *secondary school educator*

West Hills
Hawes, Bess Lomax *retired anthropologist*
Maeda, J. A. *data processing executive, consultant*

West Hollywood
Baker, Anita *singer*
Eger, Denise Leese *rabbi*
Gates, Lisa *private chef, caterer*
Goin, Suzanne *food company executive, chef*
Innes, Laura *actress*
Madonna, (Madonna Louise Veronica Ciccone) *singer, actress, producer*
Stern, Ruth Szold *business executive, artist*
Wilson, Nancy Linda *religious organization administrator*

West Sacramento
Lloyd, Sharon *marketing professional*
Teel, Joyce Raley *retail executive*

Westchester
Capetillo, Charlene Vernelle *music educator, special education educator*

Westlake Village
Steadman, Lydia Duff *symphony violinist, retired elementary school educator*
Troxell, Lucy Davis *management consultant*
Weiss, Barbara G. *artist*

Westminster
Nguyen, Lan Thi Hoang *physician, educator*
Phan, Kim Than Nguyen *psychologist, educator*

Whittier
Benavides, Greta Louise *elementary school educator, entrepreneur*
Cavanaugh, Janis Lynn *protective services official, educator*
Conly, Diane Carroll *dentist*
Gosfield, Margaret *secondary school educator, school system administrator, consultant, editor*
Harvey, Patricia Jean *special education administrator, retired*
Jacobson, Sandra Ann *music educator*
Korf, Jean Prinz *retired theater educator*
McKenna, Jeanette Ann *archaeologist*
Will, Katherine Haley *academic administrator*

Willits
Handley, Margie Lee *manufacturing executive*

Wilmington
Bornino-Glusac, Anna Maria *mathematics educator*
McAlpine, Mary Helen *nutritional science educator*

Windsor
Matkin, Judith Conway *jewelry designer and manufacturer*

Woodlake
Pace, Sally Mae *student services dean*

Woodland
Turner, Patricia Butler *mental health nurse, educator, consultant*

Woodland Hills
Berry, Carol Ann *insurance company executive*
DeWitt, Barbara Jane *journalist*
Ebin, Cynthia Rebecca *artist, sculptor*
Fung, Flora Lik-Yuen *statistician, consultant*
Harris, Barbara S. *publishing executive*
Johnson-Champ, Debra Sue *lawyer, educator, writer, artist*
Lax, Kathleen Thompson *judge*
Mund, Geraldine *judge*
Murphy, Irene Helen *publishing executive*
Rabaca, Josefina Ragsag *writer*
Rafter, Tracy *publishing executive*
Russell, Anne M. *editor-in-chief*
Stahlecker, Barbara Jean *marketing professional, consultant*
Tellez, Cora *healthcare company executive*
Wiesner, Carol A. *financial services company executive*

Woodside
Melmon, Elyce Edelman *literature educator, writer*

Yorba Linda
Naulty, Susan Louise *archivist*
Stavropoulos, Rose Mary Grant *community activist, volunteer*

Yreka
Fiock, Shari Lee *not-for-profit developer*

Yuba City
Doss-Reed, Helen Grigsby *writer*

Yucaipa
deBaun, Linda Louise *performing arts educator*

Yucca Valley
Lewis, Mary Etta *special education educator*
Styles, Beverly (Juanita Robins Carpenter) *entertainer, composer, musician*

COLORADO

Alamosa
Davis, Glenna Sue *human resources director*

Arvada
Eaves, Sally Ann *military career officer*
Halley, Diane Esther *artist*
Hammond-Blessing, DiAnn A. *elementary school educator*
Meiklejohn, Mindy June (Lorraine Meiklejohn) *political organizer, realtor*
Moorhead, Jennifer Theresa *art educator*
Williams, Marsha Kay *data processing executive*

Aspen
Hayes, Mary Eshbaugh *editor, writer*
Hough, Jennine *artist*
MacPhail, Wendy Rowena *art educator, artist*
Mitchell, Karen Frances *artist, jewelry designer*

Aurora
Adams, Nancy R. *nurse, retired military officer*
Brown, Anne Sherwin *speech pathologist, educator*
Hoffmaster, Nancy Jo Clement *social services professional, retired*
Hood, Ollie Ruth *health facilities executive*
Kellogg Fain, Karen *retired history and geography educator*
King Calkins, Carol Coleman *health sciences administrator*
Lassen, Betty Jane *gifted and talented educator*
Martinez-Nemnich, Maricela *realtor*
McKenney, Muriel Anita *art educator, engineer*
Miller, Dorothea Helen *librarian, educator*
Miller, Sarah Pearl *librarian*
Nora, Audrey Hart *physician*
Sheffield, Nancy *city agency administrator*
Sorenson, Katherine Ann *elementary school educator*
Teflian, Pamela Jane *lyricist, photographer*
Wessler, Mary Hraha *real estate company executive*

Black Hawk
Jones, Linda May *tour guide, writer*

Boulder
Arnold, Janet Nina *health care consultant*
Avery, Susan Kathryn *electrical engineering educator, research administrator*
Bintliff, Barbara Ann *law educator, library director*
Borko, Hilda *education educator*
Borysenko, Joan *psychologist, biologist*
Cadora, Karen Michele *application developer*
Civish, Gayle Ann *psychologist*
deKieffer, Kitty *volunteer*
Dilley, Barbara Jean *college administrator, choreographer, educator*
Dubofsky, Jean Eberhart *lawyer, retired state supreme court justice*
El Mallakh, Dorothea Hendry *editor, publishing executive*
Engel, Barbara Alpern *history educator*
Foland, Sara *geologist, association executive*
Forstrom, June Rochelle *professional society administrator*
Friedman, Pamela Ruth Lessing *financial consultant, writer*
Healy, Alice Fenvessy *psychology educator, researcher*
Heath, Josephine Ward *foundation administrator*
Hinkley, Caroline Lawson *dean*
Hoffman, Elizabeth *academic administrator*
Holdsworth, Janet Nott *women's health nurse*
Jin, Deborah *physicist, educator*
Joyce, Janet S. *psychologist*
Kahn, Herta Hess (Mrs. Howard Kahn) *retired securities trader*
Kintzing, Julie Alexandra *social worker*
LeMone, Margaret Anne *atmospheric scientist*
Limerick, Patricia Nelson *history educator*
Madden, Alice Donnelly *lawyer*
Malville, Nancy Jean *anthropologist*
Marie, Heather *director, consultant*
Menken, Jane Ava *demographer, educator*
Meyer, Andrea Peroutka *small business owner*
Mitchell, Joan LaVerne *research scientist*
Rienner, Lynne Carol *publishing executive*
Roberts, Pamela Ranger *secondary school educator*
Rothenberg, Elizabeth Jill *editor*
Sable, Barbara Kinsey *retired music educator*
Shumick, Diana Lynn *computer executive*
Tolbert, Margaret A. *geochemistry educator*
Verdill, Elaine Denise *artisan*
Waldman, Anne Lesley *poet, performer, editor, publisher, educational administrator*
Wallace, Stephanie Ann *music educator, conductor*
Wertheimer, Marilyn Lou *school librarian, educator*
Yan, Haiping *theatre and comparative literature educator*

Brighton
Tyrrell-Meier, Cassandra B. *banker*

Broomfield
Lybarger, Marjorie Kathryn *nurse*
Shannon, Denise Leslie *nurse*

Buena Vista
Goddard, Hazel Bryan *religious organization administrator*

Canon City
Cochran, Susan Mills *librarian*
Romano, Rebecca Kay *counselor*

Carbondale
Cowgill, Ursula Moser *biologist, educator, environmental consultant*
Keeney, Karen Elaine *photographer, educator, anthropologist*
Linden, Susan Pyles *marketing executive*

Cascade
Seger, Linda Sue *script consultant, lecturer, writer*

Castle Rock
Broer, Eileen Dennery *management consultant*
Richardson, Suzanne Mays *communication consultant*
Rogers, Pattiann *poet, educator, poet, writer*

Cherry Hills Village
Stapleton, Katharine Hall (Katie Stapleton) *food broadcaster, writer*

Colorado Springs
Abbott, Gina *municipal government executive*

Ansorge, Iona Marie *retired real estate agent, musician, educator*
Arsenault, Samantha *Olympic athlete*
Artl, Karen Ann *business owner, author*
Badger, Sandra Rae *health and physical education educator*
Bedford, Barbara J. *Olympic athlete*
Benko, Lindsay *Olympic athlete*
Bennett, Brooke *Olympic athlete*
Bobek, Nicole *professional figure skater*
Borgen, Irma R. *music educator*
Bowen, Clotilde Marion Dent *retired career officer, psychiatrist*
Bowers, Zella Zane *real estate broker*
Brierre, Micheline *artist*
Buckner-Davis, Annett *professional volleyball player*
Clugston, Angela M. *medical technician*
Corwin, Amber *figure skater*
Cutone, Kathaleen Kelly *figure skater, former skating judge, athletic representative*
Darpino, Victoria Gnojek *music educator*
Deiotte, Margaret Williams Tuckey *nonprofit consultant, grants writer*
D'Entremont, Amy *professional figure skater*
Dufer, Miriam Donyelle *military officer, writer*
Engfer, Susan Marvel *zoological park executive*
Evans, Janet *former Olympic swimmer*
Fleming, Terri *newspaper editor*
Freeman, J. P. Ladyhawk *vicar, underwater exploration, security and transportation executive, educator, fashion model, legislative advocate*
Gifford, Marilyn Joyce *emergency physician, consultant*
Granato, Catherine (Cammi Granato) *Olympic athlete*
Guy, Mildred Dorothy *retired secondary school educator*
Halber, Diane *professional figure skater*
Hawley, Nanci Elizabeth *association administrator*
Herron, Sherry Shelton *biology educator*
Hughes, Sarah *figure skater*
Hyman, Misty Dawn *Olympic athlete*
Johnson, Stephanie L. B. *small business owner, office manager*
Kwan, Karen *professional figure skater*
Kwan, Michelle *professional figure skater*
Lang, Naomi *ice skater*
Leffingwell, Denise C. *social worker*
LeMieux, Linda Dailey *museum director*
Lirette, Dorothy Lou *artist, educator*
Loo, Katherine Haughey *nonprofit organization consultant*
Mackety, Carolyn Jean *laser medicine and nursing consultant*
Makepeace, Mary Lou *former mayor*
McDivitt, Karen Louise *psychologist, writer*
McDonough, Ann Patrice *ice skater*
Meese, Frances Mildred *library administrator*
Mery, Naomi Mery *music educator*
Michels, Patricia A. *insurance agent*
Miller, Zoya Dickins (Mrs. Hilliard Eve Miller Jr.) *civic worker*
Milligan, Annette Marie *secondary school educator*
Munz, Diana *Olympic athlete*
Nikodinov, Angela *professional figure skater, Olympic athlete*
Orner, Linda Price *family therapist, counselor*
Quann, Megan *Olympic athlete*
Rhodes, Daisy Chun *writer, researcher, oral historian*
Rouss, Ruth *lawyer*
Rowan, Cynthia L. Reeves *accountant*
Rueda, Deborah Jean *music educator*
Scott, Tiffany *ice skater*
Shade, Linda Bunnell *university chancellor*
Shealy, Courtney *Olympic athlete*
Shockley-Zalabak, Pamela Sue *academic administrator*
Skadden, Vanda Sue *retired music educator*
Stienmier, Saundra Kay Young *aviation educator*
Tögel, Cornelia (Conni) D. *artist*
Torres, Dara *Olympic athlete*
Tueting, Sarah *professional hockey player*
Williams, Ruth Lee *clinical social worker*
Winfield, Karen Ann *art educator, artist, small business owner*

Commerce City
Baker, Maria Luise *retired secondary school educator*

Conifer
West, Molly Marie *music educator*

Craig
Gray, Ann Maynard *broadcasting company executive*

Creede
Hague, Angela L. *artist, gallery manager, art consultant*

Delta
Carson, Marlene Ann *artist*
Reever, Wilma Marie *educational consultant*

Denver
Adkins, Jeanne M. *state agency administrator*
Alsop, Marin *conductor*
Alvarado, Linda G. *construction executive*
Anderson, Norma V. *state legislator*
Augustine, Rosemary *vocational counselor, writer*
Bacon, Betty J. Nichols *preschool educator and administrator*
Bayes, Ginny *public relations and advertising executive*
Beldock, Joan Ellen *real estate broker*
Berry, Gayle *state representative*
Blair, Hilary *actor, performing company executive, educator*
Borodkin, Alice *state representative*
Boyd, Betty Ann *state representative*
Brownlee, Judith Marilyn *priestess, psychotherapist, psychic*
Buckstein, Caryl Sue *writer*
Burford, Anne McGill *lawyer*
Burrows, Bertha Jean *retired academic administrator*
Butcher, Dorothy *state representative*
Carroll, Kim Marie *nurse*
Carson, Janine Marie *marketing professional*
Chavez, Jeanette *editor*
Childears, Linda *banker*
Churchill, Mair Elisa Annabelle *medical educator*
Clapp, Lauri *state representative*
Coan, Patricia A. *magistrate judge*
Coe, Judith Anne *music educator, composer, performer*
Cohen-Vader, Cheryl Denise *municipal official*
Coleman, Fran Natividad *state representative*
Daley, Ann Scarlett *curator*
Dallas, Sandra *writer*
Dancik, Jo Marie *accountant, accounting company executive*
Davidson, Donetta *state official*
Decatur, Raylene *former museum director*
Dennis, Ginette E. (Gigi) *state legislator*
DePew, Marie Kathryn *retired secondary school educator*
Devine, Sharon Jean *lawyer*
Drake, Sylvie (Jurras Drake) *theater critic*
Dudden, Rosalind F. *librarian*
Dunham, Joan Roberts *administrative assistant*
Ehret, Josephine Mary *microbiologist, researcher*
Engels, Patricia A. *communications executive*
Enright, Cynthia Lee *illustrator*
Epps, Mary Ellen *state legislator*
Faatz, Jeanne Ryan *councilperson*
Fasel, Ida *English language educator, writer*
Fitz-Gerald, Joan *state senator*
Fogg, Janet *architectural firm executive*
Fujioka, Jo Ann Ota *educational administrator, consultant*
Gabow, Patricia Anne *internist*
Galloway, Judy A. *deputy commissioner*
Gampel, Elaine Susan *investment company executive, consultant*
Garcia, June Marie *librarian*
Geraci, Maria Catherine *mental health nurse practitioner, educator*
Gibson, Elisabeth Jane *retired principal*
Goeken, Deborah *editor*
Goldblatt, Barbara Janet *sex therapist, educator*
Graham, Pamela Smith *artist, distributing company executive*
Gries, Robbie Rice *geologist, gas and petroleum company executive*
Groff, JoAnn *organization administrator*
Harmsen, Dorothy *food products executive*
Harris, Ellen Gandy (Mrs. J. Ramsay Harris) *civic worker*
Hefley, Lynn A. *state representative*
Heppler, Robin Lee *project manager*
Hightower, Nancy Elizabeth *literature educator*
Hirschfeld, Arlene F. *civic worker, homemaker*
Hodge, Mary *state representative*
Hoehn, Margaret Maier *neurologist*
Hoppe, Phyllis Diane *state representative*
Horwitz, Kathryn Bloch *molecular biologist, educator, breast cancer researcher*
Hotchkiss, Heather A. *social worker, consultant*
Howse, Cathy L. *writer, researcher, entrepreneur*
Huang, Linda Chen *plastic surgeon*
Hunsaker, Jill Ann *public health administrator*
Jahn, Cheri E. *state representative*
Jarles, Ruth Sewell *education educator*
Jennett, Shirley Shimmick *health facility administrator*
Johnson, Candice Elaine Brown *pediatrics educator*
Johnson, Geraldine Esch *language specialist*
Johnston, Gwinavere Adams *public relations consultant*
Jones, Jean Correy *organization administrator*
Joyce, Mary Holt *retired social worker*
Kaczanowska, Laurie Hyson Smith *lawyer*
Kaplan, Sandra Lee *artist*
Kaplan, Sheila *academic administrator*
Keller, Maryanne *state senator*
Korslund, Annette *administrative assistant, translator, interpreter, writer*
Kourlis, Rebecca Love *state supreme court justice*
Krendl, Cathy Stricklin *lawyer*
Krieger, Marcia Smith *federal judge*
Kruger, Paula *telecommunications industry executive*
Kurtz, Maxine *personnel consultant, lawyer*
Lacy, Elsie *state legislator*
Lahey, Bonita Louise *marketing and operations consultant*
Landon, Susan Melinda *petroleum geologist*
Lefly, Dianne Louise *research psychologist*
Leydon, Debra Jean *food products executive*
Lingé, Virginia Ann *elementary school educator*
Lundy, Barbara Jean *training executive*
Mackinnon, Peggy Louise *public relations executive*
Major, Alice Jean *lawyer*
Marshall, Rosemary *state representative*
Mathews, Laurie A. *state agency administrator*
Maul, Carol Elaine *small business owner*
McAtee, Patricia Anne Rooney *medical educator*
McDonnell, Barbara *lawyer*
McDowell, Karen Ann *lawyer*
McFadyen, Liane *state representative*
McKelrath, Heidi Lee *real estate closing agent*
Merritt, Jeralyn E. *lawyer*
Merscham, Carrie *psychologist*
Moulton, Jennifer T. *city official, architect*
Muja, Kathleen Ann *state official, consultant*
Mullarkey, Mary J. *state supreme court chief justice*
Murdock, Pamela Ervilla *travel and advertising company executive*
Nelson, LeAnn Lindbeck *small business owner*
Nelson, Nevin Mary *interior designer*
Nelson, Sarah Milledge *archaeology educator*
Nemiro, Beverly Mirium Anderson *author, educator*
Nichol, Alice J. *state legislator*
Norton, Jane E. *lieutenant governor*
Orullian, B. LaRae *bank executive*
Osborn, Susan Chaney *writer, educator*
Page, Polly E. *state agency administrator*
Phillips, Dorothy Reid *retired medical library technician*
Plummer, Ora Beatrice *nursing educator, trainer*
Ragsdale, Ann F. *state representative*
Read, Patricia Ellen *administrator non-profit organization, editor*
Reece, Monique Elizabeth *marketing, advertising and sales consultant*
Reeves, Peggy *state legislator*
Rhodes, Pamela *state representative*
Rice, Nancy E. *judge*
Robinson, Cleo Parker *artistic director*
Rowe, Tina L. *government official*
Rubin, Cathy Ann *retired educator*
Rupert, Dorothy *state legislator*
Sanders, Mary Margaret *personnel director, dancer*
Sandoval, Paula E. *state senator*
Savan, Jakki L. *lawyer, writer*
Shaeffer, Thelma Jean *primary school educator*
Shaw, Priscilla *music educator, coach*
Shinabery, Kimbery Ann *minister*
Shirkey, Linda Sue *interior designer, film company executive, set designer*
Shwayder, Elizabeth Yanish *sculptor*
Simpson, Diane Jeannette *school social worker, counselor, adoption home study worker*
Smith, Sallye Wrye *librarian*
Spence, Nancy Joan *state representative*
Spradley, Lola *state representative*
Stafford, Debbie *state senator*
Stamm, Carol Ann *obstetrician, gynecologist*
Steigerwald-Clausen, Beverly *sculptor, educator*
Stott, Annette *art historian, educator*
Studevant, Laura *medical association administrator*
Sujansky, Eva Borska *pediatrician, geneticist, educator*
Takis, Stephanie *state senator*
Tanner, Gloria Travis *state legislator*
Taylor, Teresa *communications executive*
Thomas, Enolia *nutritionist, educator*
Tochtrop, Lois *state legislator, nurse consultant*
Turner, Karen *psychotherapist, educator*
Veiga, Jennifer *state representative*
Vosevich, Kathi Ann *writer, editor, scholar*
Wade, Karen *federal agency administrator*
Wagner, Judith Buck *investment firm executive*
Walcher, Jennifer Lynne *city official*
Waldstein, Gail P. *pediatric pathologist, writer*
Walker, Joan H. *marketing and communications executive*
Weinshienk, Zita Leeson *federal judge*
Welch, Carol Mae *lawyer*
Welch, J(oan) Kathleen *entrepreneur*
Wetzel, Jodi (Joy Lynn Wetzel) *history and women's studies educator*
White, Joyce Louise *librarian*
Williams, Marcia Putnam *human resources specialist*
Williams, Suzanne *state representative*
Williams, Tambor *state representative*
Windels, Sue *state senator*
Witt, Catherine Lewis *neonatal nurse practitioner, writer*
Wunnicke, Brooke *lawyer*
Zak-Dance, Carol Camille *human communication educator*

Dillon
Barron, Theodora S. *retired music educator*

Dolores
Winterer, Barbara Jean *designer, author*

Durango
Allison, Pamela Sue *special education administrator*
Balas-Whitfield, Susan *artist*
Ballantine, Morley Cowles (Mrs. Arthur Atwood Ballantine) *editor*
Korns, Leota Elsie *writer, mountain land developer, insurance broker*
MacCallum, Lorene (Edythe MacCallum) *pharmacist*
Reid-Bills, Mae *magazine editor, historian*
Tischhauser, Katherine Jetter *music educator, cellist*
Webb, Elizabeth Louise *real estate broker, artist*

Eagle
Sheaffer, Karen *county official, treasurer*

Edwards
Burdick, Margaret Seale (Marge) *interior designer*
Chambers, Joan Louise *retired librarian, retired dean*

Elizabeth
Gale, Rebecca J. *artist*

Englewood
Asarch, Elaine *interior designer, anthropologist*
Brennan, Joann *photographer, educator*
Cooper, Sharon Marsha *marketing, advertising executive*
Dunker, Amy Melissa *sales manager*
Graves, Nada Proctor *retired elementary school educator*
Keesling, Ruth Morris *foundation administrator*
Kristin, Karen *artist*
Lamb, Darlis Carol *sculptor*
Lambert, Shirley Anne *marketing professional, publisher*
Miles, Amy E. *recreational facility executive*
Oshman, Marilyn *retail executive*
Peters, Janice C. *cable company executive*
Shields, Marlene Sue *elementary school educator*
Sideman, Jill *engineering executive*
Spencer, Margaret Gilliam *lawyer*
Wham, Dorothy Stonecipher *retired state legislator*

Evergreen
Saxton, Mary Jane *management educator*

Fleming
Nichols, Lee Ann *library media specialist*

Fort Collins
Andreas, Carol *sociologist, educator*
Clark, Claudia Ann *business development manager*
Fairbank, Jane Davenport *editor, civic worker*
Gonzalez, Rosita Christine *photographer*
Grandin, Temple *industrial designer*
Honaker, Stevie Lee *career counselor, consultant*
Jensen, Margaret *real estate broker*
Ketcham, Sally Ann *historic site staff member, consultant*
Ladanyi, Branka Maria *chemist, educator*
Myrtis-Garcia, Carmen Ruth *social sciences educator*
Panik, Sharon McClain *primary education educator, writer*
Sedei Rodden, Pamela Jean *therapist*
Sprague, Amaris Jeanne *real estate broker*
Thomas, Jeanette Mae *public accountant*
Tyler, Gail Madeleine *nurse*
Wilber, Clare Marie *musician, educator*

Fort Garland
Taylor-Dunn, Corliss Leslie *marriage and family therapist*

Fountain
Wilson, Roberta (Bobbi) Gail *performing arts educator*

Fowler
Giadone, Susan *livestock office manager*

Georgetown
Hildebrandt-Willard, Claudia Joan *banker*

Gilcrest
Halley, Gail Renee *secondary school educator*

Glenwood Springs
Candlin, Frances Ann *psychotherapist, social worker, educator*

Golden
Alberts, Celia Anne *lawyer*
Arvisais, Kari Lynn *marriage and family therapist*
Brainerd, Mary *small business owner*
Fahey, Barbara Stewart Doe *public agency administrator*
Gosink, Joan P. *engineering educator*
Hopper, Sally Hunter *former state legislator*
Lott, Brenda Louise *insurance company executive*
Mathews, E. Anne Jones *library educator and administrator, consultant*
Olson, Marian Katherine *management executive, consultant, publisher*
Van Dusen, Donna Bayne *communications consultant, educator, researcher*

Grand Junction
Barger, Cathy Lynn *music educator*
Brewington, Elaine Sue *social worker*
Everhart, Dorothy L. *music educator*
Flick, Carol J. *middle school educator*
Hall, Kathryn H. *public relations executive*
Hoagland, Christina Gail *occupational therapist, industrial drafter*
Michels, Ruth Yvonne *retired cytotechnologist, consultant*
Pantenburg, Michel *hospital administrator, health educator, holistic health coordinator*
Sewell, Beverly Jean *financial executive*
Taylor, Mary Lee *retired college administrator*
Wilson, Deborah Grim *music educator*

Greeley
Afoaku, Oyibo Helisita *academic administrator*
Linde, Lucille Mae (Lucille Jacobson) *motor-perceptual specialist*
Miller, Diane Wilmarth *retired human resources director*
Richardson, Laura *psychologist, educator*
Seris, Eileen Janice *library information specialist*
Willis, Connie (Constance E. Willis) *author*
Wilson, Sharon Rose *literature educator, researcher*

Greenwood Village
Dickerson, Cynthia Rowe *marketing executive, consultant*

Guffey
McCaslin, Kathleen Denise *child abuse educator*

Highlands Ranch
Brierley, Corale L. *geological engineer*
Erickson, Linda Rae *elementary school educator*

Hotchkiss
Garber, Dorothy Helen *rancher, artist*

Idledale
Brown, Gerri Ann *physical therapist*

Jefferson
Maatsch, Deborah Joan *manufacturing executive*

Lakewood
Bailey, Zelda Chapman *hydrologist*
Burnett, Elizabeth (Betsy Burnett) *counselor*
Finnie, Doris Gould *investment company executive*
Hanna, Deanna *state senator*
Johnson, Ramey Kayes *community health nurse*

Joy, Carla Marie *history educator*
McEwen, Ruth *foundation administrator*
Meyer, Lynn Nix *lawyer*
Nichols, Vicki Anne *financial consultant, librarian*
Wallisch, Carolyn E. *principal*
Weskamp, Kelley S. *loan account manager, real estate company executive*
Woodruff, Kathryn Elaine *English language educator*
Zachman, Kathleen E. *gifted and talented educator, music educator*

Limon
Huffman, Janet Faye *secondary school educator*

Littleton
Connell-Allen, Elizabeth Ann *elementary school educator*
Greenberg, Elinor Miller *university official, consultant*
Harney, Patricia Rae *enviromental technical supervisor*
Johansson, Alicia Barbara *musician*
Keogh, Heidi Helen Dake *advocate*
King, Linda *musician, music educator*
Lesh-Laurie, Georgia Elizabeth *university administrator, biology educator, researcher*
Lohman, Loretta Cecelia *social scientist, consultant*
Miller, Betty Sue *counselor*
Pardue, Karen Reiko *elementary school educator*
Poduska, T. F. *artist*
Price, Gayl Baader *residential construction company administrator*
Ryan, Evonne Ianacone *capital management company executive*
Schomp, Lisa Juliana *automotive industry executive*
Shepherd, Donna Lou *interior designer*
Stamile, Jennifer *materials engineer*
Treybig, Edwina Hall *sales executive*
VanderLinden, Camilla Denice Dunn *telecommunications industry executive*

Longmont
Blackwood, Lois Anne *elementary school educator*
Campbell, Sally Jo *music educator, primary school educator*
Flanders, Eleanor Carlson *community volunteer*
Harrison, Sarah K. *music educator*
Jones, Beverly Ann Miller *nursing administrator, retired patient services administrator*
Lavin, L. [illegible] *executive*
McEachern, Susan Mary *information technology specialist*
Vemick, Kristie Lund *mathematics educator*
Weaver, Barbara Horning *social worker*

Louisville
Kenney, Belinda Jill Forseman *technology company executive*
Price, Julia Larkin *art educator*
Raymond, Dorothy Gill *lawyer*
Tyson, Charlotte Rose *software development manager*

Loveland
Bierbaum, Janith Marie *artist*
Carter, Laura Lee *academic librarian, psychotherapist*
Hach-Darrow, Kathryn *water testing company executive*
Johnson, Stephanie Kay *school counselor*
King, Joan Caluda *medical educator, neuroscientist*
Lee, Evelyn Marie *elementary school educator, secondary school educator*
Nossaman, Marian Alecia *manufacturing engineering executive*
Rodman, Sue A. *wholesale company executive, artist, writer*
Schockner, Jan Rosetta (Rosetta) *sculptor*
Weresh, Thelma Faye *sculptor, artist*

Mancos
Brown, Joy Alice *social services administrator*

Monte Vista
Haslar, Peggy Jo *elementary school counselor*

Montrose
Gillette, Ethel Morrow *columnist*

Morrison
Neumann, Stephanie Tower *retired librarian*

Nederland
Morrison, K. Jaydene *education counseling firm executive*

New Castle
Spuhler, Jacilyn Erickson *librarian*

Northglenn
Hemlock, Roberta Leigh *veterinary technician*
Knepel, Nancy *school librarian*
Stoian, Cristina *sales professional, real estate agent, real estate broker*

Norwood
Hollinbeck, Ethel Lindell *sculptor*

Ohio City
Dolezal, Ruth Ellen *resort owner*

Pagosa Springs
Howard, Carole Margaret Munroe *retired public relations executive*

Paonia
Marston, Betsy Pilat *newspaper editor*

Parker
Brainard, Carol Lee *realtor*
Lark, M. Ann *management consultant, strategic planner, naturalist*
Rogers, Rowena Emery *retired land manager*

Placerville
Monferrato, Angela Maria *investor, writer, designer*

Pritchett
Hall, Carol Ann *music educator*

Pueblo
Alt, Betty L. *sociology educator*
Cress, Cecile Colleen *retired librarian*
Heizer, Ida Ann *retired real estate broker*
Nimmo, Charlene *minister*
Presley, Eva Luise Von Schritlz *counselor, writer*
Ritter, Jennifer Leigh *music minister, educator*

Silverton
Voorlas, Stephanie Katherine *freelance/self-employed writer, photographer*

Steamboat Springs
Kiser-Miller, Kathy Joy *humanities educator*

Sterling
Gumina, Pamela Ray *municipal government administrator*

Superior
Forshee, Gladys Marie *writer, insurance agent*
Reagan, Melodie A. *communications executive*

Telluride
Claridge, Rhonda L. *writer, educator*

Thornton
Johnson, Carole Jean *investment company executive*

Torrance
Field, Phylis Sharon *consulting director*

Vail
Knight, Constance Bracken *writer, realtor, corporate executive*

Westminster
Hartman, Susan P(atrice) *adult education administrator*
Wolfram, Suzanne G. *minister, educator, dean*

Wheat Ridge
Hashimoto, Christine L. *physician*
Leino, Deanna Rose *business educator*
Wells, Karen Kay *medical librarian*

Wiggins
Kammerzell, Susan Jane *elementary school educator, music educator*

Windsor
Hein, Connie L. *real estate company officer, writer*

CONNECTICUT

Avon
Drapeau, Suzanne Eva *art educator*
Kling, Phradie (Phradie Kling Gold) *small business owner, educator*

Barkhamsted
Stokes, Susan *political science educator*

Berlin
Bennerup, Brooke Clara *poet, writer*
Carroll, Adorna Occhialini *real estate executive*
Grise, Cheryl *electric power industry executive*

Bethel
Shepard, Jean Heck *publishing company consultant, author, agent*

Bloomfield
Ivey, Elizabeth S. *retired physicist, educator*
Shimelman, Susan Fromm *state policy administrator*

Branford
Wright, Nancy Howell *interior designer*
Wulke, Joy *artist*

Bridgeport
Garcia, Edna I. *state legislator, secondary education educator*
Macdonald, Karen Crane *occupational therapist, geriatric counselor*
Mahmud, Shireen Dianne *photographer*
McAuliffe, Catherine A. *counselor, psychology educator, psychotherapist*
Orloski, Sharon *secondary school educator*
Simoneau, Cynthia Lambert *newspaper editor, journalism educator*

Bristol
Driessen, Christine F. *broadcast executive*
LaGanga, Donna Brandeis *sales and marketing executive, management/educational administrator*
Morales, Mary E. *social worker*
Petosa, Janet Frances *recruiting executive, publishing executive*
Roberts, Robin *sportscaster*
Vetter, Noelle I. *information technology manager*

Brookfield
Reynolds, Jean Edwards *publishing executive*

Chaplin
Bruckerhoff, Theresa *business owner, educational researcher*

Cheshire
Driscoll, Colleen Mary *writer, researcher, consultant*
Greenhalgh, Patricia Ellen Donoghue *marketing research consultant*
Holm-Cipollini, Lori Katherine *gifted and talented educator*
Markowski, Sally Hamilton *medical/surgical nurse*
McKee, Margaret Jean *federal agency administrator*

Chester
Feldmann, Shirley Clark *psychology educator*
Frost-Knappman, Elizabeth (Linda Elizabeth Frost-Knappman) *publishing executive, editor, writer*
Harwood, Eleanor Cash *librarian*
Zwart-Ludeman, Theresa *graphics designer, artist*

Clinton
Adler, Peggy Ann *writer, illustrator, consultant*
Gilman, Frances M. *genealogist, librarian*
McAllister, Nancy Elizabeth *music educator*

Columbia
Klein, Cathy M. *funeral director*

Cos Cob
Kane, Margaret Brassler *sculptor*
Leamy, Nancy M. *professional athletics coach*
Neal, Irene Collins *artist, educator*

Coventry
Halvorson, Judith Anne (Judith Anne Devaud) *elementary school educator*

Danbury
Fuller, Cassandra Miller *applications specialist*
Hawkes, Carol Ann *academic administrator*
Hellmann, Rene Braun *English as a Second Language educator, elementary school educator*
Izzo, Lucille Anne *sales representative*
Jensen-Ruopp, Helga Spitko *school program administrator, consultant*
Kendall, Marcia S. *literature educator, consultant*
Meyers, Abbey S. *foundation administrator*
Wright, Marie Anne *management information systems educator*

Darien
[illegible] *manager*
Springer, Ruth Wiren *music educator*
West, Maria McDonald *social worker*

Dayville
Nicholson, Pamela D. *school librarian*

Derby
McEvoy, Sharlene Ann *law educator*
Rinaldo, Sharon Ann *special education educator*

Durham
Ostby, Karen Jean *speech pathology/audiology services professional*

East Haddam
Clarke, Cordelia Kay Knight Mazuy *management consultant, artist*

East Hampton
Klein, Gail Beth Marantz *freelance/self-employed writer, animal breeder*
Tucceri, Clive Knowles *science writer and educator, consultant*

East Hartford
Barredo, Rita M. *auditor*
Gold, Carla Christine *commodities trader, director*
Rivers, Loretta J. *film producer, film director, consultant*
Wile, Dawn M. *protective services official*

Easton
Constantinople, Alexandra *communications executive*
Meyer, Alice Virginia *state official*

Enfield
Reuter, Joan Copson *retired program director*

Essex
Hieatt, Constance Bartlett *English language educator*

Fairfield
Barone, Rose Marie Pace *writer, retired educator, entertainer*
Browne, Elizabeth Peddle *financial assistant*
Bryan, Barbara Day *retired librarian*
Comstock, Elizabeth J. *marketing executive*
Daley, Pamela *lawyer*
Eigel, Marcia Duffy *editor*
Evans, Margaret A. *volunteer*
Fash, Victoria R. *healthcare company executive*
Ford, Maureen Morrissey *civic worker*
Hamilton, Heather Amlin *conductor, director*
Hergenhan, Joyce *public relations executive*
Howell, Karen Jane *private school educator*
Ladd, Louise *writer*
Morehouse, Sarah McCally *retired political science educator*
Newton, Lisa Haenlein *philosopher, educator*
Shaffer, Dorothy Browne *retired mathematician, educator*
Shelton, Carolyn Johnson *professional society administrator*
Turetsky, Judith *librarian, researcher*
Webster, Barbara Sheppard *art association administrator*

Falls Village
Gaschel-Clark, Rebecca Mona *special education educator*
Purcell, Mary Louise Gerlinger *retired adult education educator*
Toomey, Jeanne Elizabeth *animal activist*

Farmington
Baker, Patricia *health foundation administrator*
Grunnet, Margaret Louise *pathologist, educator*
Osborn, Mary Jane Merten *biochemist, educator*
Rothfield, Naomi Fox *physician*
Sacerdote, Frances Arlene *executive recruiter*

Gaylordsville
Dunn, Virginia *artist, community volunteer*

Georgetown
Roberts, Priscilla Warren *artist*

Glastonbury
Cassotto, Mary Lou Grace *language educator*
Googins, Sonya Forbes *state legislator, retired banker*
Hatch, D. Patricia P. *principal*
Raffles, Linda N. *secondary school educator*

Granby
Fair, Nancy Hazen *media specialist, educator*

Greenwich
Bentley, Lissa Frances *elementary school educator*
Bjornson, Edith Cameron *foundation administrator, communications consultant*
Boutelle, Jane Cronin *fitness consultant*
DeNigris, Carole Dell Cato *artist*
Griggs, Nina M. *realtor*
Hauptman, Betty *hospital official, fundraiser*
Hershaft, Elinor *space planner, interior designer*
Hess, Marilyn Ann *state legislator*
Hoberman, Mary Ann *author*
Kopenhaver, Patricia Ellsworth *podiatrist*
Kovner, Kathleen Jane *civic worker, portrait artist*
Lewis, Audrey Gersh *financial marketing, public relations, strategic communications consultant*
Marram, Ellen R. *investment company executive*
Nockler, Linda A. *corporate financial executive*
Perless, Ellen *advertising executive*
Pope, Ingrid Bloomquist *sculptor, poet*
Rudy, Kathleen Vermeulen *small business owner*
Stauffer, Valerie Vilas *civic volunteer*
Tigett-Parks, Elizabeth *arts administrator*
Wallach, Magdalena Falkenberg (Carla Wallach) *writer*

Groton
Baumann, Rebecca Ellen *minister*
DeMarinis, Nancy Ann *state legislator*
Kennedy, Evelyn Siefert *foundation executive, textile specialist*
Payson, Herta Ruth *psychotherapist, theater educator*
Stoddard, Elizabeth (Lolly) *artist, writer*

Guilford
Colish, Marcia Lillian *history educator*
McGrath, Chrystyne Mary *retail clothing store owner*
Mick, Margaret Anne *communications executive*
Stevens, Lydia Hastings *community volunteer*
Woody, Carol Clayman *data processing executive*

Hamden
Adair, Eleanor Reed *environmental biologist*
Balogh, Anne Marceline *personnel consultant*
Blumberg, Betty Lou *education educator*
Cole-Schiraldi, Marilyn Bush *occupational therapy educator*
Davis, Lorraine Jensen *writer, editor*
Lakin, Joan Field *retired water treatment plant manager*
McDonough, Kaye (Kathryn Susan McDonough) *poet, playwright*
Sola, Janet Elaine *secondary school educator*

Hartford
Bysiewicz, Susan *secretary of state*
Carey, Ellen *artist*
Carter, Annette Wheeler *state legislator*
Cocco, Jacqueline M. *state legislator*
Cook, Catherine Welles *state legislator*
Currey, Melody Alena *state legislator*
Daily, Eileen M. *state legislator*
Dandrow, Ann P. *state legislator*
deRaismes, Ann M. *insurance company executive, human resources specialist*
Dillon, Patricia Anne *state legislator*
Eberle, Mary U. *state legislator*
Elliott, Eric S *insurance company executive*
Fahrbach, Ruth C. *state legislator*
Furniss, Wendy Hagstrom *public health services administrator*
Garvey, Jeanne Wolter *state legislator, realtor*
Gerratana, Theresa B. *state legislator*
Gibbons, Mary Peyser *civic volunteer*
Glover, Ann B. *finance company executive*
Handley, Mary Ann *state legislator*
Harkin, Ruth R. *lawyer*
Harmon, Clara Chokenea *public relations/marketing executive*
Harp, Toni N. *state legislator*
Hedrick, Joan Doran *writer, university educator*
Hinsch, Cathleen Loffredo *press secretary*
Jung, Betty Chin *epidemiologist, research analyst, educator, medical/surgical nurse*
Katz, Joette *state supreme court justice*
Kedderis, Pamela Jean *academic administrator*
Kirkley-Bey, Marie Lopez *state legislator*
Knott-Twine, Laura Mae *director*
Lautzenheiser, Barbara Jean *insurance company executive*
Lyman, Peggy *artistic director, dancer, choreographer, educator*
Lyons, Moira K. *state legislator*

Martinez, Donna F. *federal judge*
McCarthy, Patrice Ann *lawyer*
McDonald, Anne B. *state legislator*
McGrattan, Mary K. *state legislator*
Murphy, Joanne M. *computer company executive*
Mushinsky, Mary M. *state legislator*
Nappier, Denise L. *state official*
Newton, Nell Jessup *dean, law educator*
Peters, Ellen Ash *judge, retired Supreme Court chief justice*
Peters, Melodie M. *state legislator*
Petty, M. S. Marty *publisher*
Prague, Edith G. *state legislator*
Rell, M. Jodi *lieutenant governor*
Roessner, Barbara *journalist*
Sawyer, Pamela Z. *state legislator*
Scalettar, Ellen *state legislator*
Sellers, Kate M. *art museum director*
Sisco, Carol *broadcast executive, educator*
Souza, Diane D *corporate financial executive*
Stillman, Andrea L. *state legislator*
Stratton, Jessie Gray *state legislator*
Stravalle-Schmidt, Ann Roberta *lawyer*
Stuart, Ann *academic administrator, writer, educator*
Truglia, Christel *state legislator*
Vertefeuille, Christine Siegrist *judge*
Winter, Miriam Therese (Gloria Frances Winter) *nun, religious education educator*
Wood, Margaret *performing company executive*
Wright, Elease *insurance company executive*
Young, Dona Davis Gagliano *lawyer, insurance executive*

Hebron
Garrett, Florence Rome *poet*

Higganum
de Brigard, Emilie *anthropologist, consultant*
Gillmor, Rogene Godding *retired medical technologist*
Miles, Deborah H. *language educator*

Ivoryton
Osborne, Judith Barbour *artist*

Kensington
Manning, Brenda Argosy *painter*

Kent
Friedman, Frances *public relations executive*

Lakeville
Restout, Denise *musician*

Litchfield
Keifer, Julia A. *retired dental hygienist*

Madison
Gianotti-Falcigno, Constance Elizabeth *special education educator*
Hedwall, Patricia Greger *municipal assessor*

Manchester
Campbell, Katherine Marie Langrehr *elementary and secondary education educator*
Hilton, Cheryl Celeste *music educator*
Sears, Sandra Lee *computer consultant*

Mansfield Center
Ciaramella, Suzanne *psychologist*
Merrill, Denise *state legislator*

Meriden
Brandt, Irene Hildegard *retired secondary school educator*
Losada-Zarate, Gloria *psychologist*
Shemchuk, Mary Elizabeth *occupational therapist*

Middlebury
Scarpetti, Angelina (Lee Scarpetti) *state legislator*

Middletown
Brown, Judith *academic administrator*
Craig, Barbara Kinkson *academic administrator*
Crenshaw, Martha *political science educator*
Heimann-Hast, Sybil Dorothea *language arts and literature educator*
Meyer, Priscilla Ann *Russian language and literature educator*
Winston, Krishna *foreign language professional*

Milford
Curt, Denise Morris *artist, limner, photographer*
Demarais, Karin *financial analyst*
Sullivan, Christine Anne *secondary school educator*

Monroe
Cote-Beaupre, Camille Yvette *artist, educator*

Mystic
Bobruff, Carole Marks *radio producer, radio personality*
Gilbert, Ellen Effman *music educator*
Rooney, Maria Dewing *photographer*
Spakoski, Marcia *insurance agent*

Naugatuck
Chrzanowski, Rose-Ann Cannizzo *art educator*
Mannweiler, Mary-Elizabeth *painter*

New Britain
Boyea, Ruthe W. *retired educator*
Brancifort, Janet Marie *hospital administrator, respiratory therapist*
Czajkowski, Eva Anna *aerospace engineer, educator*
Detmar-Pines, Gina Louise *business strategy and policy educator*
Hermes, Katherine Ann *historian, history educator*
Margiotta, Mary-Lou Ann *application developer*
Marshall, Cora Maria *art educator, artist, researcher*

Pearl, Helen Zalkan *lawyer*
Sohn, Jeanne *librarian*
Tedford, Deborah J. *lawyer*

New Canaan
Bartlett, Dede Thompson *non-profit executive*
Christensen, Donna Radovich *needlecraft designer, consultant, educator*
Grace, Julianne Alice *retired investor relations firm executive*
Jakacki, Diane Katherine *multimedia entertainment company executive*
Lione, Susan Garrett *consultant*
Penny, Susan Caroline Voelker *investment manager*
Smithers, Ruth Anne Hall *special education educator, consultant*
Thomas, Marianne Gregory *school psychologist*

New Haven
Arterton, Janet Bond *federal judge*
Barnett, Megan A. *lawyer*
Bartoshuk, Linda J. *otolaryngologist, educator*
Borroff, Marie *English language educator*
Burns, Ellen Bree *federal judge*
Caldwell-Andrews, Alison Amelia *psychologist, researcher*
Diers, Donna Kaye *nursing educator*
Doudna, Jennifer A. *molecular biologist, educator*
Dreyer, Lois Helene Goodman *reading and language arts educator, researcher*
Dudley, Kathryn Marie *anthropology and American studies educator*
Ember, Carol R. *anthropology educator, author*
Feinstein, Rochelle *artist, educator*
Ferholt, J. Deborah Lott *pediatrician*
Frank, Roberta *English language educator*
Garvey, Sheila Hickey *theater educator*
Gaudiani, Claire Lynn *retired academic administrator*
Gilliss, Catherine Lynch *nursing educator*
Glier, Ingeborg Johanna *German language and literature educator*
Greene, Liliane *French language and literature educator, editor*
Hayden, Dolores *author, architect, educator*
Hines, Roberta Leigh *medical educator*
Hostetter, Margaret K. *pediatrician, medical educator*
Huwiler, Joan P. *public relations executive, consultant*
Hyman, Paula E(llen) *history educator*
Jacob, Deirdre Ann Bradbury *manufacturing executive, business educator, consultant*
Krauss, Judith Belliveau *nursing educator*
Kwiatkowski, Jonna M. *research scientist*
Lindroth, Linda (Linda Hammer) *artist, curator, writer*
Lorimer, Linda Koch *university educator*
McCorkle, Ruth *oncological nurse, educator*
McNamara, Julia Mary *academic administrator, foreign language educator*
Meyers, Amy *museum director*
Nolan, Victoria *theater director*
Okerson, Ann Shumelda Lillian *librarian*
Oliver-Warren, Mary Elizabeth *retired library science educator*
Patterson, Peyton R. *bank executive*
Peterson, Linda H. *English language and literature educator*
Reyes, Marcia Stygles *medical technologist*
Robinson, Dorothy K. *lawyer*
Rose-Ackerman, Susan *law and political economy educator*
Ruddle, Nancy Hartman *microbiology educator, microbiologist, researcher*
Scarf, Margaret (Maggie Scarf) *author*
Seashore, Margretta Reed *physician, educator*
Shaywitz, Sally E. *pediatrics educator*
Skinner, Helen Catherine Wild *biomineralogist*
Slayman, Carolyn Walch *geneticist, educator*
Spataro, Sandra Elizabeth *business educator, consultant*
Steitz, Joan Argetsinger *biochemistry educator*
Tanaka, Kay *genetics educator*
van Altena, Alicia Mora *language educator*
Wenig, Mary Moers *law educator*
Yeazell, Ruth Bernard *English language educator*

New London
Allen, Carol Marie *radiologic technologist*
Johnson, Diana Atwood *business owner, innkeeper*
Seelbach, Anne Elizabeth *artist*
Tassinari, Melissa Sherman *toxicologist*
Wakeman, Martha Jane *artist, educator*

New Milford
Smith, Virginia *real estate broker*

New Preston Marble Dale
Biddle, Flora Miller *writer*

Newington
Foley, Patricia Jean *accountant*
Hadley, Nancy Lynne *management consultant, community foundation executive*
Zeldes, Edith R. *freelance journalist*

Newtown
Pilchard, Melissa Meyer *realtor, appraiser*

Niantic
Andersen, Susan Hackes *early childhood educator*

Norfolk
O'Malley, Margaret Parlin *marketing administrator*

North Branford
Thacher, Barbara Auchincloss *history educator*

North Haven
Fuggi, Gretchen Miller *education educator*

Weaver, Kitra K. *sales and marketing executive*

Norwalk
Babcock, Catherine Evans *artist, educator*
Bennett Minnerly, Denise Patricia *artist, art educator*
Czajkowski-Barrett, Karen Angela *human resources specialist*
Doran, Maureen *sales executive*
Freitag, Anna Carol *endocrinologist, internist*
Greene, Karen Sandra *actress, educator, singer*
Major, Flora Hoelting *music educator*
Mintz, Lenore Chaice (Lea Mintz) *consultant*
Nelson, Paula Morrison Bronson *gifted and talented educator, consultant*
Roman, Mary *city official*
Schaefer-Wicke, Elizabeth *reading consultant, educator*
Timlin-Scalera, Rebecca Mary *neuropsychologist*
Weiner, Sandra Joan *computer catalog reseller company executive*

Norwich
Buddington, Olive Joyce *shop owner, retired education educator*
Thompson, Carrie Lorraine *volunteer*

Oakdale
Dailey, Judy (Judy St. Marie) *mathematician, director, mathematician, consultant*

Old Greenwich
Kelley, Wendy Thue *fine art advisor, independent curator*
Nelson, Norma Randy deKadt *psychotherapist, consultant*
Parris, Sally Nye *real estate agent*
Whitlock, Veronica P. *interior designer, educator*

Old Lyme
St. George, Judith Alexander *author*

Old Saybrook
Geer, Lois Margaret *music educator*
Steffen, Elizabeth Ducas *political organization worker*

Orange
Dileone, Carmel Montano *dental hygienist*
Phillips, Jeannette Veronica *management consultant, gerontologist*

Plainville
Boukus, Elizabeth *state legislator*

Redding
Bailey, Mary Katherine *sculptor, writer*
Benyei, Candace Reed *psychotherapist*
Bernier, Tina *artist*

Ridgefield
Clary, Alexia Barbara *purchasing agent*
Gruen, Marsha Irene *marketing executive*
Hancock, Ellen Marie *communications executive*
Leonard, Sister Anne C. *superintendent, education director*
Lindsay, Dianna Marie *educational administrator*
Tamsett, Susan O. *architect, artist*

Riverside
Powers, Claudia McKenna *state legislator*

Salisbury
Kilner, Ursula Blanche *genealogist, educator, writer*

Sandy Hook
Dakofsky, LaDonna Jung *radiation oncologist, educator*

Shelton
Mariotti, Margaret *executive secretary*

Sherman
Cohn, Jane Shapiro *public relations executive*
Goodspeed, Barbara *artist*
Sandor, Jocelyn R. *artist*

Simsbury
Brenner, Anna (Bonnie) Hurnyak *music educator*
DiCosimo, Patricia Shields *secondary school educator*
Roberts, Celia Ann *librarian*
Wolfe, Jennifer Nan *special education educator, consultant*

South Windsor
Pasakarnis, Kathleen Fallon *health services consultant*

Southbury
Bergen, Polly *actress*
Foxworth, Johnnie Hunter *retired state agency administrator*
Vega, Marylois Purdy *journalist*

Southington
Burkhardt, Dolores Ann *library consultant*
Carrington, Virginia Gail (Vee Carrington) *marketing professional, consultant*

Stamford
Allocca, Antoinette *computer company executive*
Anderson, Susan Stuebing *business equipment company executive*
Arms, Karen G. *social sciences educator*
Aveni, Beverly A. *executive aide*
Berets, Eileen Tolkowsky *artist*
Block, Ruth *retired insurance company executive*
Burgess, Lynne A *lawyer*
Burns, Ursula *printing company executive*
Candland, Catherine C. *human resources executive*
Dennies, Sandra Lee *city official*
Di Maria, Valerie Theresa *public relations executive*

Filter, E. Margie *business equipment manufacturing executive*
Goldsmith, Donna *sports association executive*
Goodkin, Deborah Gay *corporate financial executive*
Herbert, Tiffany Amber *marketing professional*
Jason, J. Julie *portfolio manager, writer, lawyer*
Klenk, Rosemary Ellen *pediatrician*
Lamberti, Deborah Louise *psychotherapist*
Lane, Hana Umlauf *editor*
Maarbjerg, Mary Penzold *office equipment company executive*
Mayes, Michele Coleman *lawyer*
McDonald, Cassandra Burns *lawyer*
McGarry, Diane E. *marketing professional*
McMahon, Linda E. *sports association executive*
Moggio, Barbara Jean *health education specialist*
Moore, Sharon Helen Scott *gerontological nurse*
Mulcahy, Anne Marie *printing company executive*
Ortner, Toni *English language educator*
Paolillo, Regina M. *information technology consulting executive*
Preiss-Harris, Patricia *music educator, composer, pianist*
Roberts, Victoria Lynn P. *antique expert*
Ryan, Theresa Ann Julia *accountant*
Schiff, Jayne Nemerow *underwriter*
Stern, Arlene Helen *human resources specialist*
Stevenson, Alexandra *professional tennis player*
Stillings, Irene Ella Grace Cordiner *foundation executive*
Teeters, Nancy Hays *economist, director*

Stonington
Elliott, Inger McCabe *designer, textile company executive, design consultant*
Stoddard, Alexandra *designer, writer, lecturer*
Trott-Backus, Elaine Erika Aldrich *gerontologist, educator*

Storrs Mansfield
Censky, Ellen Joan *curator, biologist*
Charters, Ann *biographer, editor, educator*
Chinn, Peggy Lois *nursing educator, editor*
Croteau, Maureen Elizabeth *journalism educator*
Ford, Karrin Elizabeth *music educator, musician*
Gilbert, Margaret P. *university educator, researcher*
Price, Glenda Delores *university dean*
Taurasi, Diana *college basketball player*

Stratford
DiCicco, Margaret C. *lawyer*
DiDomenico, Maureen Ellen *art educator, muralist*
Sahagian, Lucille Bedrosian *gasoline company executive*

Suffield
Bianchi, Maria *critical care specialist, adult and acute care nurse practitioner, nursing administrator*
Hanzalek, Astrid Teicher *public information officer, consultant*

Thomaston
Donohue, Diane Frances *fine arts publisher, artist*

Tolland
O'Shaughnessy, Ellen Hodgson *elementary school educator*
Wyman, Nancy S. *state legislator*

Torrington
Di Russo, Terry *communications educator, writer*
Sexton, Diana Elizabeth *communications company executive*

Trumbull
Hayman, Helen Feeley *retired nursing director*
Herman, Elizabeth Mullee *elementary school educator*
Hochberg, Jennifer Anne *counselor*
Hofbauer, Michele Pace *illustrator, writer*
Madigan, Rita Duffy *career education coordinator*
Nevins, Lyn (Carolyn A. Nevins) *educational supervisor, trainer, consultant*
Norcel, Jacqueline Joyce Casale *educational administrator*
Smith, Gail Marie *special education educator, educational consultant*

Uncasville
Lobo, Rebecca *professional basketball player*

Vernon Rockville
Davis, Nancy Costello *retired educator*
Gallien, Sandra Jean *social worker*
Marmer, Ellen Lucille *pediatric cardiologist, mayor*

Wallingford
Bush, Linda A. *land use planner*
Fritz, Mary G. *state legislator*
Lauttenbach, Carol *artist*
Regueiro-Ren, Alicia *biomedical researcher*

Washington
Chamberlain, Frances W. *writer*
Grimes, Margaret Whitehurst *artist, educator*
Porter, Priscilla Manning *artist*

Waterbury
Bachman, Carol Christine *trust company executive*
Brown, Lillian Hill *retired academic administrator*
Meyer, Judith Chandler Pugh *history educator*
Wolfe, Harriet Munrett *lawyer*

Waterford
Commire, Anne *playwright, writer, editor*
Hinkle, Janet *project leader*

Carr, Marie Pinak *book distribution company executive*
Carroll, M(argaret) Lizbeth Carr *art educator, graphics designer, photographer*
Carson, Julia M. *congresswoman*
Carter, Yvonne Johnson *writer, editor, English educator*
Cashion, Ann *food service executive*
Casteel, Steven W. *federal agency administrator*
Catoe, Bette Lorrina *pediatrician, educator*
Chalk, Rosemary Anne *federal agency administrator*
Chalkley, Jacqueline Ann *retail company executive*
Chanin, Leah Farb *law library administrator, lawyer, consultant, law educator*
Chao, Elaine L. *secretary of labor*
Chavez, Linda *civil rights organization executive*
Chavez-Thompson, Linda *labor union administrator*
Cheney, Lynne V. *humanities educator, writer*
Chesser, Judy Lee *municipal official*
Chiechi, Carolyn Phyllis *federal judge*
Chin, Cecilia Hui-Hsin *librarian*
Chittum, Loretta Petty *federal agency administrator*
Chotin, Elizabeth Ettlinger *research organization administrator*
Christian, Betty Jo *lawyer*
Christian, Mary Jo Dinan *educational administrator, educator*
Christian-Christensen, Donna Marie *congresswoman*
Chu, Margaret S. Y. *federal agency administrator*
Chun, Shinae *federal agency administrator*
Chute, Mary L. *federal agency administrator, library director*
Cino, Maria *political organization administrator, former federal agency administrator*
Clark, Cynthia Zang Facer *federal agency administrator*
Clark, Kathryn *government agency administrator*
Clarke, Kathleen Burton *federal agency administrator*
Claussen, Eileen Barbara *federal agency administrator*
Cleary, Manon Catherine *artist, educator*
Cleave, Mary L. *environmental engineer, former astronaut*
Clift, Eleanor *magazine correspondent*
Clinton, Hillary Rodham *senator, lawyer, former First Lady of United States*
Clontz, Karen Lynn *social worker*
Coffield, Shirley Ann *lawyer, educator*
Cohen, Mary Ann *judge*
Cohen, Sarah *reporter*
Coin, Sheila Regan *organization and management development consultant*
Collins, Susan M. *senator*
Colton Skolnick, Judith A. *artist*
Combs, Ann L. *federal agency administrator*
Combs, Linda Morrison *federal agency administrator*
Comstock, Amy L. *social services administrator*
Conlin, Linda Mysliwy *federal agency administrator*
Connell, Mary Ellen *diplomat*
Conroy, Sarah Booth *columnist, writer, educator*
Cook, Beverly *federal agency administrator*
Cook, Frances D. *international business consultant*
Coons, Barbara Lynn *public relations executive, librarian*
Cooper, Jacqueline Gerson *lawyer*
Cooper, Kathleen Bell *federal agency administrator*
Cooper, Nannie Coles *education educator, consultant*
Cope, Jeannette Naylor *executive search consultant*
Corrigan, Janet M. *health services association executive*
Coulter, Ann *lawyer, author*
Covington, Eileen Queen *secondary school educator*
Cowal, Sally Grooms *diplomat, association administrator*
Cox, Carol Thayer *art therapist, educator*
Cox, Kathleen *broadcast executive, lawyer*
Craig, Susan Lyons *library director*
Crawford, Mary Louise Perri *career officer*
Crawford, Natalie Wilson *applied mathematician*
Crawford, Susan Jean *federal judge*
Crawford-Mason, Clare Wootten *television producer, journalist*
Cropp, Linda W. *city official*
Cubin, Barbara Lynn *congresswoman*
Cunningham, Sarah Bainter *dean, educator*
Curry, Sadye Beatryce *gastroenterologist, educator*
Daffron, MaryEllen *librarian*
Daly, Kay R. *public relations professional*
Daniels, Deborah Jean *federal agency administrator*
Daniels, Diana M. *lawyer*
Darr, Ann Russell *poet, educator*
Darragh, Martina *school librarian*
Dasch, Pat (Anne) *professional society administrator*
Daschle, Linda Hall *transportation industry lobbyist*
Davidson, Sarah J. *health services administrator*
Davidson, Susan Bettina *editor, writer*
Davis, Deidre *advocate*
Davis, Evelyn Y. *editor, writer*
Davis, Jo Ann S. *congresswoman*
Davis, Michele *federal agency administrator*
Davis, Ruth A. *federal agency administrator*
Davis, Susan A. *congresswoman*
Dawson, Mimi Weyforth, Sr., *public policy consultant*
Day, Doris (Doris von Kappelhoff) *singer, actress*
Day, Elizabeth Agall *press secretary*
Day, Mary *artistic director, ballet company executive*
Dean, Lisa *foundation executive*
Deaton, Valerie L. *financial researcher, consultant*
DeBusk, F. Amanda *export administration executive*
DeCosta-Willis, Miriam *education educator, writer*
Deeb, Mary-Jane *editor, educator*
DeGiovanni-Donnelly, Rosalie Frances *biology researcher, educator*
de Kanter, Adriana Alison *federal agency administrator*
DeKuyper, Mary Hundley *non-profit consultant*
DeLauro, Rosa L. *congresswoman*
Delbanco, Suzanne F. *human services administrator*
de Leon, Sylvia A. *lawyer*
Delgado, Jane *health facility administrator, writer*
DeMesme, Ruby Butler *civilian military executive*
Dempsey, Joan *federal agency administrator*
Denison, Mary Boney *lawyer*
Denny, Judith Ann *retired lawyer*
DeRocco, Emily Stover *federal agency administrator*
Dessaso, Deborah Ann *freelance/self-employed writer, corporate communications specialist*
Determan, Sara-Ann *lawyer*
DeVaul, Diane D. *policy director*
Dewar, Helen *reporter*
Didion, Catherine Jay *science association administrator*
Dillon-Ridgley, Dianne Granville *mediator, consultant, association executive*
Dobriansky, Paula Jon *federal agency administrator*
Dodge, Judith C. *musician*
Dolan, Kay Frances *human resources administrator*
Dole, Elizabeth Hanford *senator, former charitable organization administrator, former federal official*
Dominguez, Cari M. *government agency administrator*
Dominiquez, Cari M. *federal agency administrator*
Donley, Rosemary *university official*
Donlon, Claudette *performing company executive*
Donohoe, Cathryn Murray *journalist*
Dooley, Betty Parsons *educational association administrator*
Dorfman, Cynthia Hearn *government agency administrator*
Dorn, Jennifer L. *federal agency administrator*
Dorn, Jennifer Lynn *charitable organization administrator*
Dowd, Maureen *columnist*
Downey-Sargent, Kathryn T. *psychologist, researcher*
Drew, Elizabeth *television commentator, journalist, author*
Drizin, Julie Merle *public radio producer*
DuCran, Claudette Deloris *retired financial analyst*
Duke, Sara Willett *curator*
Dunn, Jennifer Blackburn *congresswoman*
Dunn, Loretta Lynn *lawyer*
Dutton, Christina Parker *interior designer, event planner*
Duval-Pierrelouis, Jeanne-Marie *educational association executive*
Dwyer, Maureen E. *lawyer*
Dwyer Southern, Kathy *museum administrator*
Dye, Rebecca Feemster *legislative counsel*
Echaveste, Maria *government official, lawyer*
Eckles, Susan *former management executive*
Edelman, Marian Wright *not-for-profit organization administrator, lawyer*
Efros, Ellen Ann *lawyer*
Elcano, Mary S. *lawyer*
Elliott, Kimberly Ann *economist*
Ely-Raphel, Nancy *diplomat*
Emely, Mary Ann *association executive*
Emerson, Jo Ann *congresswoman*
Emery, Nancy Beth *lawyer*
Emperado, Mercedes Lopez *librarian*
Engleman, Ellen G. *federal agency administrator*
Engler, Renata Johanna Martha *allergist, immunologist, internist, educator*
Epps, Roselyn Elizabeth Payne *pediatrician, educator*
Erting, Carol Jean *special education educator, researcher, anthropologist*
Escallon, Ana Maria *museum director, writer, curator*
Esfandiary, Mary S. *physical scientist, operations consultant*
Eshoo, Anna Georges *congresswoman*
Evans, Joy *foundation administrator*
Evans, Marsha Johnson *non-profit association administrator, former career officer*
Fain, Cheryl Ann *translator, editor*
Falk, Diane M. *research director, librarian, editor, writer*
Fall, Dorothy *artist, art director, administrator*
Fallon, Sally *writer*
Farr, Judith Banzer *writer, literature educator*
Feder, Judith *dean*
Feinstein, Dianne *senator*
Feld, Karen Irma *columnist, journalist, broadcaster, public speaker*
Feldman, Clarice Rochelle *lawyer*
Feldman, Sandra *labor union executive*
Fennel, Melody H. *federal agency administrator*
Ferrier, Maria Hernandez *federal official, educator*
Fidler, Shelley N. *legislative director*
Fields, Suzanne Bregman *syndicated columnist*
Fields, Wendy Lynn *lawyer*
Fifer Canby, Susan Melinda *library administrator*
Fingerhut, Marilyn Ann *federal agency administrator*
Finley, Julie Hamm *political party official*
Fischer, Elizabeth (Betsy) *television producer*
Fitzgerald, Helen Teresa *grief therapist, writer*
Flaherty, Sister Mary Jean *dean*
Flannery, Ellen Joanne *lawyer*
Flattau, Pamela Ebert *research psychologist, consultant*
Fleischer, Rebecca *federal agency administrator*
Flippo, Karen Francine *social welfare administrator*
Flowe, Carol Connor *lawyer*
Foley, Mary E. *medical association administrator, nursing administrator*
Fong, Phyllis Kamoi *federal agency administrator, lawyer*
Ford, Cecilia S. *federal agency administrator*
Ford, Elizabeth Ann *administrator, children's advocate*
Fore, Henrietta Holsman *federal agency administrator*
Foreman, Carol Lee Tucker *consumer advocate*
Forkan, Patricia Ann *foundation executive*
Forman, Lori Ann *federal agency administrator*
Forrester, Patricia Tobacco *artist*
Foscarinis, Maria *lawyer*
Fowler, Tillie Kidd *lawyer*
Fox, Sarah *lawyer*
Francis, Shari *federal agency administrator*
Francke, Gloria Niemeyer *pharmacist, editor, publisher*
Francke, Rend Rahim *ambassador*
Franklin, Barbara Hackman *business executive, former government official*
Frawley Bagley, Elizabeth *government advisor, ambassador*
Freeman, Sharee M. *federal agency administrator*
French, Hilary F. *foundation administrator*
Fresh, Linda Lou *government official*
Freund, Deborah Miriam *transportation engineer*
Friedan, Betty *writer, feminist leader*
Friend, Patricia A. *trade association administrator*
Fries, Helen Sergeant Haynes *civic leader*
Froman, Veronica Zasadni *career officer*
Fuller, Kathryn Scott *environmental association executive, lawyer*
Fusillo, Alice Elbert *retired sociologist, sculptor*
Gall, Mary Sheila *federal agency administrator*
Gallagher, Patricia E. *government agency administrator*
Galloway, Eilene Marie *space and astronautics consultant*
Gandy, Kim Allison *feminist organization executive, lawyer*
Garcia, Frances *accountant*
Garnette, Cheryl Petty *government agency administrator*
Garrels, Anne *news correspondent*
Garrison, LaTrease E. *association executive*
Garvey, Jane *public relations executive*
Gaston, Marilyn Hughes *health facility administrator*
Gati, Toby T. *international advisor*
Gatons, Anna-Marie Kilmade *government official*
Geiselman, LucyAnn *college president*
Genia, Vicky *psychologist*
Gest, Kathryn Waters *public affairs professional*
Geyer, Georgie Anne *syndicated columnist, educator, author, biographer, TV commentator*
Gibbons Tankard, Mellisa W. *education educator*
Gibson, Florence Anderson *talking book company executive, narrator*
Gilbert, Pamela *strategic services company executive*
Gilfoyle, Nathalie Floyd Preston *lawyer*
Gilliom, Judith Carr *government official*
Ginsburg, Ruth Bader *United States Supreme Court justice*
Glaser, Vera Romans *journalist*
Glassman, Cynthia A. *commissioner*
Glynn, Marilyn *lawyer*
Goldberg, Kirsten Boyd *science journalist*
Golden, Olivia A. *human service agency administrator*
Goldway, Ruth Y. *federal agency administrator*
Gonzalez-Hermosillo, Brenda *economist, researcher*
Gordon, Dorothy K. *silversmith, goldsmith*
Gore, Patricia W. *federal agency administrator*
Gorelick, Jamie Shona *lawyer*
Gorman, Joyce J(ohanna) *lawyer*
Gorman, Patricia Jane *editor*
Graham, Margaret M. *minister*
Grapin, Jacqueline G. *economist*
Grasselli, Margaret Morgan *curator*
Gray, Mary Wheat *statistician, lawyer*
Gray, Sheila Hafter *psychiatrist, psychoanalyst*
Grealy, Mary R. *medical association administrator*
Greaux, Cheryl Prejean *federal agency director*
Green, Joyce Hens *federal judge*
Greenhouse, Linda Joyce *journalist*
Gregory, Bettina Louise *journalist*
Griffin, Janice *political organization professional*
Griffin, Kelly Ann *public relations executive, consultant*
Griffith, Elizabeth Anna *communications executive, educator*
Gross, Roberta Lee *inspector general*
Grossman, Joanne Barbara *lawyer*
Guard, Patricia J. *federal agency administrator*
Gupta, Tanya *financial analyst*
Guzy, Carol *photojournalist*
Hager, Susan Kulka *public relations executive*
Hahn, Lorna *political organization executive, author*
Hale, Janet *federal agency administrator*
Hall, Betty Jean *public interest group executive, lawyer*
Hall, Kathryn Walt *ambassador*
Hallett, Carol Boyd *air transportation executive*
Halpern, Cheryl F. *federal agency administrator*
Hamburg, Margaret Ann (Peggy Hamburg) *public health administrator*
Handman, Bobbie (Barbara Handman) *foundation executive*
Harbour, Pamela Jones *lawyer*
Harlem, Susan Lynn *librarian*
Harman, Jane *congresswoman*
Harrington, Kathleen M. *federal agency administrator*
Harris, Katherine *congresswoman*
Harrison, Monika Edwards *business development executive*
Harrison, Patricia de Stacy *federal agency administrator*
Hart, Melissa Anne *congresswoman*
Hart, Sarah V. *federal agency administrator*
Hartmann, Heidi Irmgard Victoria *economist, research organization executive*
Harty, Maura *federal agency administrator, former ambassador*
Harvey, Edith M. *federal agency administrator*
Harvey, Eleanor Jones *museum curator*
Harvey, Jane Hull *church administrator*
Hasselmo, Ann Hayes Die *executive search consultant, former college president, psychologist, educator*
Hatfield, C. Maile *lobbyist*
Hattan, Susan K. *legislative staff member*
Hawkins, Lisa Lynne *lawyer, municipal official*
Hayes, Allene Valerie Farmer *government executive*
Hayes, Paula Freda *governmental official*
Hazard, Roberta Louise *career officer*
Headden, Susan M. *editor*
Hecht, Marjorie Mazel *editor*
Hedges, Kamla King *library director*
Heichel, Paula *investment company executive, financial consultant*
Height, Dorothy I. *association executive*
Heinz Kerry, Teresa F. *foundation administrator*
Heise, Dorothy Hilbert *librarian, government official*
Heivilin, Donna Mae *government executive*
Helfer, Ricki Tigert *banking consultant*
Hellwig, Monika Konrad *organization executive, theology educator*
Henderson, Karen LeCraft *federal judge*
Hennessy, Ellen Anne *lawyer, benefits compensation analyst, educator*
Henningsen, Jacqueline Vincent *civilian military official*
Hentges, Harriet *not-for-profit developer*
Herman, Andrea Maxine *newspaper editor*
Hernreich, Nancy *federal official*
Heumann, Judith *bank executive*
Hewitt, Emily Clark *judge, minister*
Higgins, Kathryn O'Leary *consulting firm executive*
Higgins, Robin L. *federal agency administrator*
Higuchi, Shirley A. *lawyer*
Hill, Eleanor Jean *lawyer*
Hill, Patrice Susan *journalist, economist*
Hillman, Jennifer Anne *commissioner, ambassador, trade negotiator*
Hills, Carla Anderson *lawyer, former federal official*
Hoffmann, Melane Kinney *marketing and public relations executive, writer*
Holdsclaw, Chamique Shaunta *professional basketball player*
Holladay, Wilhelmina Cole *interior design and museum executive*
Holland, Christie Anna *biochemist, virologist*
Holland, Joy *health care facility executive*
Hollis, Sheila Slocum *lawyer*
Hooley, Darlene *congresswoman*
Horinko, Marianne Lamant *former federal agency administrator*
Horn, Marian Blank *federal judge*
Horn, Sharon K. *government agency administrator*
Horner, Constance Joan *federal agency administrator*
Horwitz, Sari *reporter*
Howard, Barbara Viventi *research foundation executive*
Howell, Deborah *editor*
Howell, Deborah S. *career officer*
Howell, Mary L. *diversified company executive*
Howland, Nina Davis *historian*
Hu, Grace M. *economist*
Hudson, Melinda B. *foundation administrator*
Hughes, Ellen Roney *historian, museum exhibition curator*
Hughes, Marija Matich *law librarian*
Hughes, Sharon Mary *trade association executive*
Hull, Marion Hayes *communications educator, researcher*
Hunt, Lynne *federal agency administrator*
Ignagni, Karen *healthcare association executive*
Ingold, Catherine White *academic administrator*
Innis, Pauline *writer, publishing company executive*
Ireland, Patricia *not-for-profit developer*
Irving, Susan Jean *government executive*
Isaacs, Amy Fay *political organization executive*
Iverson, Kristine Ann *federal agency administrator*
Jackson, Jacquelyn C. *federal agency administrator*
Jackson, Sandra Willett *marketing professional*
Jackson Lee, Sheila *congresswoman*
Jacobs, Susan S. *ambassador*
James, Kay Coles *federal agency administrator*
Jani, Sushma Niranjan *pediatric psychiatrist*
Jarvis, Charlene Drew *university administrator, former scientist*
Jenkins, Renee R. *medical educator, pediatrician*
Jenks, Rosemary Elizabeth *lawyer*
Jeweler, Robin *lawyer*
Johns, Marie C. *telecommunications industry executive*
Johnson, Cheryl L. *nursing administrator*
Johnson, Eddie Bernice *congresswoman*
Johnson, Gloria *labor union administrator*
Johnson, Judith A. *educational administrator*
Johnson, Karen *professional society administrator*
Johnson, Karen *legislation and congressional affairs secretary*
Johnson, Nancy Lee *congresswoman*
Johnson, Sandra K. *journalist*
Jones, A. Elizabeth *federal agency administrator*

Rheintgen, Laura Dale *research center official*
Rhoades, Margaret *health care association executive*
Rice, Condoleezza *national security advisor*
Rice, Lois Dickson *former computer company executive*
Rich, Dorothy Kovitz *writer, educational administrator*
Rich, Laurie M. *federal official, educator*
Richards, Suzanne V. *lawyer*
Richardson, Ann Bishop *foundation executive, lawyer*
Richman, Phyllis Chasanow *newspaper critic*
Richmond, Marilyn Susan *lawyer*
Richwine, Heather *technology support manager*
Ridgway, Delissa Anne *lawyer*
Riedel, Bunnie *not-for-profit organization executive*
Ritchie, Elisavietta *poet, writer, educator, editor, translator*
Rivlin, Alice Mitchell *federal agency administrator, economist*
Robb, Lynda Johnson *writer*
Roberson, Jessie Hill *federal agency administrator*
Roberts, Jeanne Addison *retired literature educator*
Robinowitz, Carolyn Bauer *psychiatrist, educator*
Robinson, Sharon Porter *professional society administrator*
Roby, Cheryl J. *deputy assistant secretary*
Rocca, Christina B. *federal agency administrator*
Rodney, Bonnie M. *music educator*
Rodriguez, Rita Maria *economist*
Roessel, Faith *Indian arts and crafts administrator*
Rogers, Judith W. *federal judge*
Rogers, Julie *foundation administrator*
Rogers, Thomasina Venese *federal commissioner*
Roscher, Nina Matheny *chemistry educator*
Rosenberg, Ruth Helen Borsuk *lawyer*
Rosenstock, Linda *federal agency administrator, medical educator*
Ros-Lehtinen, Ileana *congresswoman*
Ross, Wendy Clucas *newspaper editor, journalist*
Rossotti, Barbara Jill Margulies *lawyer*
Rothstein, Barbara Jacobs *federal judge*
Rovelstad, Mathilde V(erner) *library science educator*
Rowland, Diane *health facility administrator, researcher*
Roybal-Allard, Lucille *congresswoman*
Ruiz, Vanessa *federal judge*
Russell, Judy C. *government agency administrator*
Ryan, Mary A. *diplomat*
Sabelhaus, Melanie R. *government agency administrator*
Sabol, Carolyn A. *lawyer, government official*
St. Amand, Janet G. *government relations lawyer*
St. John, Julie *mortgage company executive*
Salamon, Linda Bradley *English literature educator*
Samsami, Soona *advocate*
Samuels, Cynthia Kalish *communications executive*
Samuels, Diane *public information officer, real estate appraiser*
Sanchez, Linda T. *congresswoman*
Sanchez, Loretta *congresswoman*
Sanchez-Way, Ruth Dolores *health services administrator*
Sanderson, Janet A. *ambassador*
Sandler, Bernice Resnick *women's rights specialist*
Sankaran, Shubha Silver *musician, music educator, consultant*
Sawhill, Isabel Van Devanter *economist*
Scarlett, Patricia Lynn *federal agency administrator*
Schagh, Catherine *federal agency administrator*
Schakowsky, Janice *congresswoman*
Schapiro, Mary *federal agency administrator, lawyer*
Schechter, Geraldine Poppa *hematologist*
Schecter, Kate Sara *healthcare development executive*
Schierow, Linda-Jo *environmental policy analyst*
Schiff, Margaret Scott *newspaper publishing executive*
Schiffer, Lois Jane *lawyer*
Schlitt, Lyn M. *lawyer*
Schneider, Carol Geary *educational association administrator*
Schneider, Cynthia Perrin *art historian, educator*
Schoettle, Enid C.B. *government agency administrator*
Scholz, Jane *newspaper publisher*
Schorr, Lisbeth Bamberger *child and family policy analyst, author, educator*
Schroeder, Patricia Scott *trade association administrator, retired congresswoman*
Schulman, Heidi *broadcast executive*
Sclafani, Susan K. *federal agency administrator*
Scott, Portia Adele *paralegal*
Scott-Finan, Nancy Isabella *government administrator*
Scruggs-Leftwich, Yvonne *association executive*
Seale, N. Allison *communications specialist*
Searing, Marjory Ellen *government official, economist*
Sears, Mary Helen *lawyer*
Sebejais, Melanie *federal agency administrator*
Seelman, Katherine Dolores *institute administrator*
Segall, JoAnn Butters *retired school librarian*
Seitz, Virginia A. *lawyer*
Selin, Nina Evvie *philanthropist*
Sewall, Sarah Lee *foundation administrator*
Shaffron, J. Janet *legislative administrator*
Shamim, Mah Talat *chemist*
Shanahan, Sheila Ann *pediatrician, educator*
Shanks, Judith Weil *editor*
Sharma, Martha Bridges *geography educator*
Sharpe, Dorothy Jones *secondary education educator, researcher*
Sharples, Ruth Lissak *communications executive*
Sharpless, Mattie R. *ambassador*
Shaw, Theresa (Terri) S. *federal official*
Shay-Byrne, Olivia *lawyer*
Shear, Natalie Pickus *conference and event management executive*
Sheekey, Kathleen D. *advocate, director*
Sheeler, Harva Lee *law librarian*
Shelly, Christine Deborah *foreign service officer*
Sherman, Nancy *philosophy educator*
Shields, Carole *foundation administrator*
Shiner, Josette Sheeran *ambassador*
Shinolt, Eileen Thelma *artist*
Shrier, Diane Kesler *psychiatrist, educator*
Shute, Roberta E. *sculptor*
Silberman, Deborah F. *general counsel*
Silverman, Leslie E. *federal agency administrator*
Silverman, Marcia *public relations executive*
Simmons, Anne L. *federal official*
Simmons, Caroline Thompson *civic worker*
Simmons, Emmy B *federal agency administrator*
Simmons, Enid Brown *retired state agency administrator*
Simon, Rosalyn McCord *public relations executive*
Simon-Gillo, Jehanne E. *physicist, science administrator*
Simons, Carol Lenore *magazine editor*
Singer, Maxine Frank *retired biochemist, scientific institute executive*
Singer, Suzanne Fried *editor*
Skolfield, Melissa T. *public relations executive, government official*
Slater, Eve *federal agency administrator*
Slater, Valerie A. *lawyer*
Slaughter, Louise McIntosh *congresswoman*
Smith, Abbie Oliver *college administrator, educator*
Smith, Elaine Diana *foreign service officer*
Smith, Elise Fiber *international non-profit development agency administrator*
Smith, Jessie P. Dowling *retired social services administrator*
Smith, Linda Gene *legislative staff member*
Smith, Marie F. *small business owner, writer*
Smith, Marie Ford *small business owner*
Smith, Mignon C. *publishing executive*
Smith, Molly D. *theater director*
Smith, Nancy Lee *communications official*
Smith, Pamela Hyde *ambassador*
Smith, Patricia Grace *government official*
Smulkstys, Inga *operations and management executive*
Snider, Virginia L. *antitrust consultant*
Snow, Rebecca *lawyer*
Snowe, Olympia J. *senator*
Snyder, Andrea *performing arts association administrator*
Solberg, Mary Ann *federal agency administrator*
Solis, Hilda Lucia *congresswoman, educational administrator*
Solomon, Elinor Harris *economics educator*
Soloway, Rose Ann Gould *clinical toxicologist*
Somer-Greif, Penny Lynn *lawyer*
Sopher, Vicki Elaine *museum curator*
Sorrels, Carrie L. *federal agency administrator*
Sparacino, Joann *lawyer, consultant*
Spellings, Margaret LaMontagne *assistant to US President on domestic policy*
Spelman, Lucy H. *zoological park administrator*
Sprague, Mary Gabrielle *lawyer*
Springer, Linda *portfolio manager, controller*
Sproul, Robin *television news bureau chief*
Stabenow, Deborah Ann *senator, former congresswoman*
Stahmer, Ann Miklofsky *choral music director, producer*
Stamberg, Susan Levitt *radio broadcaster*
Stanley, Marianne *professional athletics coach*
Statom, Laurena Edith *retired special education educator*
Steele, Ana Mercedes *former government official*
Stein, Cheryl Denise *lawyer*
Steinem, Gloria *writer, editor, lecturer, activist*
Stephen, Elizabeth Hervey *sociologist, educator*
Stepp, Laura Sessions *journalist*
Sterling, Charlotte B. *hotel executive*
Stern, Paula *international trade advisor*
Stevenson, Frances Kellogg *museum program director*
Stevenson, Katherine Holler *federal agency administrator*
Stevenson, Nancy Nelson *museum executive*
Stewart, Debra Wehrle *academic administrator*
Stierle, Linda J. *military officer*
Stitch, Roberta Lynn *not-for-profit fundraiser, social worker*
Stock, Ann *federal official*
Stoiber, Susanne A. *health science organization administrator*
Stone, Florence Smith *film festival executive, consultant*
Strand, Joan H. *law educator*
Stratton, Kathleen R. *medical association administrator*
Stromberg, Jean Wilbur Gleason *lawyer*
Stroup, Sally *federal agency administrator*
Stuart, Pamela Bruce *lawyer*
Stucky, Jean Seibert *lawyer*
Styles, Angela B. *federal agency administrator*
Sullivan, Mary Anne *lawyer, government official*
Sussman, Monica Hilton *lawyer*
Sutherland, Lisa Jo *legislative staff member*
Sutter, Eleanor Bly *retired diplomat*
Swain, Susan Marie *communications executive*
Swarthworth, Sharon T. *military officer*
Sweet, Lynn D. *journalist*
Swenson, Sue *foundation administrator, former health and education administrator*
Swinton, Sonya DeVonne *government agency administrator*
Sypolt, Diane Gilbert *federal judge*
Tacha, Athena *sculptor, educator*
Tannen, Deborah Frances *writer*
Tappert, Tara Leigh *art historian, archivist, researcher*
Tate, Sheila Burke *public relations executive*
Taylor, Estelle Wormley *English educator, dean*
Taylor, Sandra E. *public relations executive*
Terry-Leonard, Brenda L. *psychologist, consultant*
Tetelman, Alice Fran *small business owner*
Theiss, Patricia Kelley *public health researcher, educator*
Thomas, Helen A. (Mrs. Douglas B. Cornell) *newspaper bureau executive*
Thomas, Mary Augusta *library administrator*
Thompson, Bernida Lamerle *principal, consultant, educator*
Thompson, Diane E. *lawyer*
Thompson, Sally Engstrom *state official*
Tidball, M. Elizabeth Peters *physiologist, educator, science administrator, researcher*
Tinsley, Nikki Lee *federal agency administrator*
Titus-Dillon, Pauline Yvonne *associate dean academic affairs, medical educator*
Tolmachoff, Willadene *accountant, auditor*
Tomb, Diane Lenegan *federal agency administrator*
Topelius, Kathleen Ellis *lawyer*
Torkelson, Jodie Rae *charitable organization executive*
Tornblom, Claudia L. *civilian military employee*
Torrey, Barbara Boyle *research council administrator*
Tosi, Laura Lowe *orthopaedic surgeon*
Totenberg, Nina *journalist*
Townsend, Ann Van Devanter *foundation administrator, art historian*
Townsend, Frances Fragos *federal agency administrator*
Townsend, Marjorie Rhodes *aerospace engineer, business executive*
Tracey, Patricia A. *career officer*
Trafford, Abigail *columnist, editor, writer*
Truitt, Anne Dean *artist*
Tse, Man-Chun Marina *educational association administrator*
Turner, Jean-Louise *public relations executive*
Tutwiler, Margaret DeBardeleben *federal agency administrator*
Tyler, Cecilia Kay *career officer US Army*
Tyler, Peggy Lynne Bailey *lawyer*
Tyner, Lee Reichelderfer *lawyer*
Unger, Laura Simone *lawyer, commissioner*
Valdez-Snelgrove, Deborah *communications executive*
Valentine, Debra A. *lawyer*
Van Allen, Barbara Martz *marketing professional*
Van de Water, Read *former federal agency administrator*
Van Metre, Lauren *foundation administrator*
Van Ummersen, Claire A(nn) *academic administrator, biologist, educator*
Vaslef, Irene *historian, librarian*
Vasques, Victoria L. *federal agency administrator*
Vazirani-Fales, Heea *legislative staff member, lawyer*
Velazquez, Nydia M. *congresswoman*
Veneman, Ann M. *secretary of agriculture*
Verstandig, Toni Grant *federal agency administrator*
Verville, Elizabeth Giavani *federal official*
Vickery, Ann Morgan *lawyer*
Victory, Nancy *federal agency administrator*
Villarreal, June Patricia *sales consultant*
Violante, Patricia *consultant, language expert, writer, translator/interpreter*
Vose, Kathryn Kahler *marketing and communication executive*
Wager, Deborah Miller *researcher, consultant*
Wagner, Annice McBryde *judge*
Wahba, Marcelle M. *ambassador*
Wald, Patricia McGowan *retired federal judge*
Walker, Mary L. *federal agency administrator, lawyer*
Walker, Savannah T. *retired executive assistant, legislative assistant*
Wallace Douglas, Jean *conservationist*
Walter, Sheryl Lynn *lawyer*
Wand, Patricia Ann *librarian*
Ward, Erica Anne *lawyer, educator*
Wasserman, Krystyna *librarian, art historian*
Waters, Jennifer Nash *lawyer*
Waters, Mary Brice Kirtley *federal agency administrator*
Waters, Maxine *congresswoman*
Watkins, Shirley Robinson *agriculture department administrator*
Watson, Diane Edith *congresswoman*
Watson, Rebecca Wunder *federal agency administrator, lawyer*
Watters, Mary Teresa *communications executive*
Watters, Susan J. *communications executive*
Weaver, Donna L. *engraver*
Wedgwood, Ruth *law educator, international affairs expert*
Weidenfeld, Sheila Rabb *television producer, author*
Weifenbach, Terri Lynn *photographer, printer*
Weinberg, Myrl *medical association administrator*
Weinhold, Linda Lillian *psychologist, researcher*
Weintraub, Ellen L. *commissioner*
Weiss, Gail Ellen *legislative staff director*
Werner, Mary Ann *lawyer*
Werronen, Betsy Warren *political organization administrator*
Wertheim, Mitzi Mallina *technology company executive*
Wesley, LaTonya Rashawn *legislative assistant*
West, Gail Berry *lawyer*
West, Mary Beth *federal agency administrator*
Wexler, Anne *government relations and public affairs consultant*
Weymouth, Elizabeth Morris Graham (Lally Weymouth) *editor, columnist*
White, Evelyn *human resources administrator*
White, Margit Triska *financial advisor*
Whittlesey, Judith Holloway *public relations executive*
Wilensky, Gail Roggin *economist, researcher*
Wilkie, Edith B. *foundation administrator*
Wilkinson, Sharon P. *department of state official, former ambassador*
Willeford, Pamela P. *ambassador*
Williams, Jody *political organization administrator*
Williams, Julie Lloyd *lawyer*
Williams, Karen Hastie *lawyer*
Williams, Mary Ellen Coster *judge*
Willner, Ann Ruth *political scientist, educator*
Willner, Dorothy *anthropologist, educator*
Wilson, Heather Ann *congresswoman*
Wilson, Joanne *federal agency administrator*
Winnie, Glenna Barbara *pediatric pulmonologist*
Winston, Judith Ann *lawyer*
Wiss, Marcia A. *lawyer*
Withrow, Mary Ellen *federal agency administrator*
Wolanin, Barbara Ann Boese *art curator, art historian*
Wolfskill, Mary Margaret *archivist*
Woodruff, Judy Carline *broadcast journalist*
Woods, Stephanie *television producer, reporter*
Woofter, Vivien Perrine *interior designer, consultant*
Woolsey, Lynn *congresswoman*
Worthy, Patricia Morris *law educator, lawyer*
Woteki, Catherine Ellen *nutritionist*
Wright, Sylvia *government agency administrator*
Yaklin, Lori Stillwagon *government agency administrator*
Yates, Allison A. *scientific organization administrator*
Yates, Mary Carlin *ambassador*
Yoder, Mary Jane Warwick *psychotherapist*
Yonts-Shepard, Susan *forest service administrator*
Yoo, Grace *legal association administrator*
Young, Jennifer B. *federal agency administrator*
Young, Marlene Annette *lawyer*
Zahn, Paula *newscaster*
Zenker, Wendy *financial executive*
Ziegler, Gwendolyn Woods *minister, consultant*
Zimmerman, Carole Lee *public relations professional*
Zollar, Carolyn Catherine *lawyer*

FLORIDA

Apopka
Bentley, Edith Louise *secondary school educator*

Archer
Lockwood, Rhonda J. *mental health services professional*

Aventura
Freshwater, Shawna Marie *neuropsychologist, clinical psychologist, cognitive neuroscientist*
Krop, Lois Pulver *psychologist*
Ross, Selma Belle *retired not-for-profit fundraiser*

Bal Harbour
Ash, Dorothy Matthews *civic worker*
Bernay, Betti *artist*

Bartow
Bentley, Joyce Elaine *customer service officer*

Bay Pines
Nolan, Marilyn Ann *health facility administrator*

Belleair
Dexter, Helen Louise *dermatologist, consultant*

Boca Raton
Adriazola, Ana *Spanish and Latin American culture educator*
Boykin, Anne J. *dean*
Dower Gold, Catherine Anne *music history educator*
Eisenberg, Robin Ledgin *religious education administrator*
Fineman, Geraldine Gottesman *artist*
Fuller, Bonnie *editor*
Grant, Diantha Hawkes *not-for-profit administrator, educator*
Hayashi, Maris Lani *librarian*
Innes-Brown, Georgette Meyer *real estate broker, insurance broker*
Jacobson, Susan Bogen *psychotherapist*
Jessup, Jan Amis *arts volunteer, writer*
Kaye, Carole *museum director and curator*
Kewley, Sharon Lynn *systems analyst, consultant*
Klasfield, Ilene *psychologist*
Konrad, Agnes Crossman *retired real estate agent, retired educator*
Kramer, Cecile E. *retired medical librarian*
Kramer, Marsha Louise Endahl *psychotherapist*
Laine, Iris Ruth *minister, public relations/advertising executive*
Land, Judith Broten *stockbroker*
Langbort, Polly *retired advertising executive*
Morris, Jill Carole *psychotherapist*
Naples, Mary Cecilia *mental health services professional, health facility administrator*
Pajunen, Grazyna Anna *electrical engineer, educator*
Pelish, Susan Marion *sculptor, painter*
Pradere, Sonia *accounting administrator*
Reeves, Mary Jane W. *interior designer*
Robben, Tricia Elizabeth *protective services official*
Rosen, Harriet R. *elementary school educator*
Rothberg-Blackman, June Simmonds *retired nursing educator, psychotherapist, psychoanalyst*
Rothschild, Barbara *artist, educator*
Shepard, Colleen *elementary school educator, art educator*
Turner, Lisa Phillips *human resources executive*
Warshaw, Carole Klein *education educator, consultant*
Yoder, Patricia Doherty *public relations executive*

Zhong, Dawn He *materials engineer*

Bonita Springs
Elliott, Donna Louise *artist*
Hauserman, Jacquita Knight *management consultant*
McManigal, Shirley Ann *university educator, dean emerita*
McNamara-Ringewald, Mary Ann Thérèse *artist, educator*

Boynton Beach
Albert, Elizabeth Ann Salisbury *elementary school educator*
Harwood, Bernice Baumel *artist, community volunteer*
Haveson, Barbara Marcia *retired elementary education educator*
Jacobs, Wendy *editor, writer, translator*
Machtiger, Harriet Gordon *retired psychoanalyst*
Morris, Nancy Lois *elementary education educator*
Parsons, Mindy (Mindy Enos) *newsletter editor, publisher, non-profit organization executive*
Polinsky, Janet Naboicheck *retired state official, former state legislator*
Rabinof, Sylvia *pianist, composer, author, educator*
Ricks, Dallis Derrick Biehl *pianist*
Srinath, Latha *physician*
Wilner, Lois Annette *retired speech and language pathologist*

Bradenton
Becker, Nancy S. *retired real estate broker, retired shop owner*
Bjorklund, Nancy Margarette Watts *music educator*
Driscoll, Constance Fitzgerald *education educator, writer, consultant*
Kournikova, Anna *professional tennis player*
LaForest, Lana Jean *lawyer*
Rahn, Saundra L. *councilwoman*
Woodson-Howard, Marlene Erdley *former state legislator*

Brandon
England, Lynne Lipton *lawyer, speech pathologist, audiologist*

Cantonment
Crook, Penny Loraine *investment broker*

Cape Canaveral
Hess, Terry Lee *writer, educator, logistician*

Cape Coral
Andert, Darlene (Darlene Andert-Schmidt) *management consultant*
Mac Master, Harriett Schuyler *retired elementary school educator*
Wendel, Joan Audrey *music educator*

Casselberry
Homayssi, Ruby Lee *small business owner*

Celebration
Crabtree, Valleri Jayne *real estate executive, lawyer*
Renard, Meredith Anne *marketing and advertising professional*

Clearwater
Bairstow, Frances Kanevsky *arbitrator, mediator, educator*
Baker-Bowens, Helen L. *administrative assistant, genealogy researcher*
Barbeau, Sandra Alene *daycare administrator*
Barry, Joyce Alice *dietician, consultant*
Bazzone, Theresa (Terry) A. *sales executive*
Dougall-Sides, Leslie K. *lawyer*
Duncan, Holly H. *foundation executive*
Edmonds, Maria Nieves *college administrator*
Eriksen, Beverly Morgan *retired primary school educator*
Fenderson, Caroline Houston *psychotherapist*
Hallam, Arlita Warrick *quality of life administrator*
Henderson, Janet Lynn *small business owner*
Jacobs, Marilyn Arlene Potoker *gifted education educator, consultant, author*
Kelsey, Linda Jean *technologist, educator*
Kessler-Hodgson, Lee Gwendolyn *actress, corporate executive*
Knoop, Maggie Pearson *language educator*
Lansky, Zena *surgeon*
Werner, Elizabeth Helen *librarian, language educator*

Clermont
Cox, Margaret Stewart *photographer*

Cocoa
Baggarly, Claire Johnson *music educator, department chairman*
McLendon, Dorothy *school psychologist*
Ollie, Pearl Lynn *artist, singer, songwriter*
Rudzik, Marcia Ann *music educator*

Cocoa Beach
Taylor, Nancy Alice *mechandiser, buyer*
Wirtschafter, Irene Nerove *tax specialist, consultant*

Coconut Grove
Adams, Belinda Jeanette Spain *nursing administrator*
Soto, Patricia McFarlane *elementary school educator*

Cooper City
Garrard, Patricia Renick *elementary school educator*

Coral Gables
Aitken, Anne E. *computer company executive*
Bacon, Lydia Leach *human resources professional*
Buchsbaum, Karen Fuson *public relations executive, consultant*
Burini, Sonia Montes de Oca *apparel manufacturing and public relations executive*
Castellanos, Maria Luisa A. *architect, general contractor*
Gustafson, Anne-Lise Dirks *lawyer, foreign consul*
Horner, Diane L. *dean*
MacLiammoir, Sandra Jean *journalist, columnist, educator*
Morales-Martin, Gisela *interior designer*
Perez, Josephine *psychiatrist, educator*
Sackstein, Rosalina Guerrero *music educator, consultant*
Schwartz, Ana Stella *art dealer, gallery owner*
Schwartztol, Holly Wechsler *psychologist*
Shalala, Donna E. *university administrator, former federal official, political scientist, educator*
Van Vliet, Carolyne Marina *physicist, researcher*
Weiner, Ruth Eileen Blower Kassewitz *retired public relations executive*

Coral Springs
Bolene, Rosalie Steele (Margaret Bolene) *bacteriologist, volunteer*
Colesanti, Roseann *medical/surgical nurse, consultant*
Faul, Maureen Patricia *healthcare and research consultant*
Halberg, Jeanne *music educator*
Kohl, Joan *non-profit administrator, social worker*
Ritter, Stacy Joy *state legislator, lawyer*

Dade City
Brown, Jessica Bree *secondary school educator, consultant*

Dania
Fernander, Karen Geneine *secondary school educator*
Satin, Claire Jeanine *sculptor, book artist*

Davie
Ross, Kathryn Amie *psychologist*

Daytona Beach
Andrews, Donna L. *professional golfer*
Barrett, Tina *professional golfer*
Chabrian, Peggy *air transportation executive*
Chesnut, Nondis Lorine *screenwriter, consultant, reading and language arts educator, instructor, counselor*
Cool, Mary L. *education specialist*
Davies, Laura *professional golfer*
DeLuca, Annette *professional golfer*
Figg-Currier, Cindy *professional golfer*
Furstman, Shirley Elise Daddow *advertising executive*
Green, Betty Nielsen *education educator, consultant*
Hill, Dora Ann (Douffas) *language educator, writer*
Inkster, Juli *professional golfer*
Jones, Rose *professional golfer*
Kane, Lorie *professional golfer*
King, Betsy *professional golfer*
Klein, Emilee *professional golfer*
Kuehne, Kelli *professional golfer*
Mallon, Meg *professional golfer*
Moodie, Janice *professional golfer*
Neumann, Liselotte *professional golfer*
Pak, Se Ri *professional golfer*
Pepper, Dottie *professional golfer*
Robbins, Kelly *professional golfer*
Schauer, Catharine Guberman *public affairs specialist*
Sheehan, Patty *professional golfer*
Sorenstam, Annika *professional golfer*
Steinhauer, Sherri *professional golfer*
Tschetter, Kris *professional golfer*
Webb, Karrie *professional golfer*
Whitworth, Kathrynne Ann *professional golfer*
Wie, Michelle Sung *amateur golfer*

De Leon Springs
Price, Artis J. *retired secondary school educator*

Deerfield Beach
Caso, Dawn Marie *lawyer, consultant, law educator*
Moran, Patricia Genevieve *corporate executive*
Wade, Brenda Lynn *chef*

Deland
Caccamise, Genevra Louise Ball (Mrs. Alfred E. Caccamise) *retired librarian*
Navarro, Lydia *language educator*
Ryan, Susan Magness *librarian, educator*
Sorensen, Jacki Faye *choreographer, aerobic dance company executive*

Delray Beach
Campbell, Cynthia *retail executive*
Carter-Miller, Jocelyn *retail executive*
Ehrlich, Geraldine Elizabeth *management consultant*
Force, Elizabeth Elma *retired pharmaceutical executive*
George, Mildred M. *retired sentencing advocate*
Gilfilen, Teri *artist*
Greenspan, Gladys *textile designer*
Leeds, Susanne *special education educator, writer*
Luechtefeld, Monica *retail executive*
Mayer, Marilyn Gooder *steel company executive*
Morrison, Patricia B. *retail executive*
Randall, Priscilla Richmond *retired travel company executive*
Rejune-Adams, Gloria Jean *museum director*
Robinson, Brenda Kay *editor, public relations professional*
Schenkel, Suzanne Chance *retired natural resource specialist*
Schwarz, Rose Oberman *artist*
Stewart, Patricia Carry *foundation administrator*
Stone, Elizabeth Walker *English educator*
Weiner, Anne Lee *social worker*
Wells, Mary Elizabeth Thompson *minister*

Deltona
Bondinell, Stephanie *counselor, academic administrator*
Schadenfroh, JoAnn *secondary school educator*

Destin
Deel, Frances Quinn *retired librarian*

Dowling Park
Lebo, Lenore B. *counselor*

Dunedin
Barlis, Bettye Montgomery *medical center administrator, elementary educator*
Cappiello, Mimi *elementary school educator*
Foley, Briana *music educator, consultant*
Gamblin, Cynthia MacDonald *mathematics educator, lobbyist*
Simmons, Patricia Ann *pharmacist, consultant*
Whiting, Susan D. *marketing professional*

Edgewater
Schubert, Jeanne *artist*

Englewood
Catterlin, Cindy Lou *English educator*
Clark, Carolyn Chambers *nurse, educator, publishing executive*
Dickson, Katharine Hayland *dance educator*
McClellan, Joan C. Osmundson *retired art educator, artist*

Estero
Mayo, Kathleen Owens *librarian*

Eustis
Alfrey, Lydia Jean *musician educator*

Fernandina Beach
Barlow, Anne Louise *pediatrician, medical research administrator*
Grant, Catherine *music educator*

Floral City
Rondot, Susan E. Sladen *nures, case manager, health facility administrator*

Fort Lauderdale
[illegible]
Bartelstone, Rona Sue *gerontologist*
Berkey-Abbott, Kristin Lee *language educator*
Carter, Marjorie Jackson *special education educator, consultant*
Carton, Cristina Silva-Bento *elementary school educator*
Castillo, Carmen *staffing company executive*
Castro, Stephanie L. *business management educator*
Cavendish, Kim L. Maher *museum administrator*
Cox, Linda Susan *allergist, immunologist*
Dawson, Muriel Amanda (Mandy Dawson) *state legislator*
Donaldson, Lisa Miller *city administration*
Dunham, Laura *elementary school educator*
Durst, Kay Horres *physician*
Friedman, Marla Ilene *director, educator*
Fruth, Beryl Rose *physician*
Gonzalez, Nancy Berger *healthcare professional, educator*
Gude, Nancy Carlson *lawyer*
Guest, Suzanne Mary *adult education educator, artist*
Gunzburger, Suzanne Nathan *municipal official, social worker*
Hallman, Cinda A. *management consultant*
Hartz, Deborah Sophia *editor, writer*
Hershenson, Miriam Hannah Ratner *librarian*
Hester, Julia A. *lawyer*
Jackson-Callandret, Shirley Lorraine *music educator*
Johnson, Mary Margaret Dickens *researcher, consultant*
Koch, Katherine Rose *communications executive*
Kornblau, Barbara L. *physical therapist*
Kropp, Stacy Anne *small business owner*
Lazarus, Arleen *lawyer*
LeRoy, Miss Joy *model, apparel designer*
Lilley, Mili Della *insurance company executive, entertainment management consultant*
Littman, Marlyn Kemper *information scientist, educator*
Loos, Roberta Alexis *advocate, artist, educator*
McCormick, Queen Esther Williams *clergyman*
Moorhead, Rolande Annette Reverdy *artist, educator*
Parrish, Lori Nance *commissioner*
Platt, Ellen L. *financial planner*
Printz, Jillian Krueger *college program administrator*
Reisinger, Sandra Sue *columnist*
Rentoumis, Ann Mastroianni *psychotherapist*
Richmond, Gail Levin *law educator*
Sands, Roberta Alyse *real estate investor*
Sargent, Jan *art appraiser*
Schear, Betty Z. *engineering executive, consultant*
Schlueter, Sherry *protective services official*
Siegel, Wilma Bulkin *oncologist, educator, artist*
Silva, Joanne Rizzo *family nurse practitioner*
Stern, Edith Lois *counselor, hypno-therapist*
Van Alstyne, Judith Sturges *retired language educator*
Wood, Linda Dee *psychologist*

Fort Myers
Aron, Eve Glicka Serenson *personal care industry executive*
Canham, Pruella Cromartie Niver *retired educator*
Colgate, Doris Eleanor *sailing school owner and administrator*
Consilio, Barbara Ann *legal administrator, management consultant*
Dean, Jean Beverly *artist*
Elliot, Kathleen Ann *school system administrator*
Frank, Mary Lou *retired elementary school educator*
Gorelik, Alla *piano educator*
Goyak, Elizabeth Fairbairn *retired public relations executive*
Gray-Vickrey, Peg *nursing educator*
Housel, Natalie Rae Norman *physical therapist*
Hugill, Chloe *artist, office administrator*
Jaye, Karen A. *human resources specialist*
Johnson, Sally A. *nurse, educator*
MacDougall, Frances Kay *marketing consultant*
Madden, Vicky J. *brokerage house executive*
Pouliot, Assunta Gallucci *retired business school owner and director, consultant*
Ranney, Mary Elizabeth *business executive*
Taylor, Donna Bloyd *vocational rehabilitation consultant*
Toney, Avia Vernet *medical products manufacturer*
Van Vleck, Pamela Kay *real estate company officer*
Weiss, Susette Maré *technical and photographic consultant, mass communications and media relations specialist, investor*
Woodbridge, Norma Jean *registered nurse, writer*

Fort Pierce
Belcher, Dorothy S. *state correctional department administrator*
Clunn, Patricia Ann *nursing educator, writer*
Fischer, Ellen E. *art gallery director*
Garde, Susan Reutershan *accountant*
Jefferson, Zanobia Bracy *art educator, artist*
Minor, Beverly June *retired social worker*
Padrick, Kerry Bridges *elementary school educator*
Peterson, Barbara Owecke *retired real estate agent, artist, nurse*
Rice, Mary Esther *biologist*
Whitaker, Diana Marie *medical/surgical nurse*

Fort Walton Beach
Bolt, Lynda Elaine *alcohol/drug abuse services professional*
Fallin, Barbara Moore *human resources director*
Hill, Carol Koelling *library director*
McDonald, Pamela Jane *educational media specialist*
Register, Annette Rowan *reading educator*
Vanderburg, Kathleen *surgical nurse*

Gainesville
Albarracín, Dolores *psychologist, educator*
Ardelt, Monika *sociologist, educator*
Behnke, Marylou *pediatrician, educator*
Brown, Myra Suzanne *university librarian*
Chestnut, Cynthia Moore *state legislator*
Coleman, Mary Stallings *retired chief justice*
Dolan, Teresa A. *dean, educator, researcher*
Drummond, Willa Hendricks *physiology and medical educator*
Green, Eleanor Myers *veterinarian, educator*
Grobman, Hulda Gross (Mrs. Arnold B. Grobman) *retired health sciences educator*
Hartigan, Karelisa Dorothy *classics educator*
Hoy, Marjorie Ann *entomology educator*
Hyatt, Mary Louise *music educator, pianist*
Johnson, Annie Cooper *music educator*
Kelly, Kathleen S(ue) *communications educator*
Kersey, Talana S. *mental health counselor*
Kirkland, Nancy Childs *secondary education educator, consultant*
Korner, Barbara Oliver *academic administrator*
Limacher, Marian Cecile *cardiologist*
Linton, Kristy Ann *primary school educator*
Lipowski, Earlene E *pharmacist, education educator*
Long, Kathleen Ann *nursing educator, dean, consultant*
Malasanos, Lois Julanne Fosse *nursing educator*
Maple, Marilyn Jean *educational media coordinator*
Marohn, Ann Elizabeth *health information management professional*
Martin, Sarah Carrier *science educator*
Morsey, Sara *actor, educator*
Paul, Ouida Fay *music educator*
Puckett, Ruby Parker *nutritionist, hospital food service administrator, consultant, author*
Robinson, Jacqueline J. *health services administrator, accountant*
Rosenberger, Margaret Adaline *retired elementary school educator, writer*
Schmidt-Nielsen, Bodil Mimi (Mrs. Roger G. Chagnon) *physiologist, educator*
Scott, Lynn Thomson *Spanish language and literature educator*
Skelton, Winifred Karger (Freddie Skelton) *advertising agency executive, painter*
Small, Natalie Settimelli *pediatric mental health counselor*
Smith, Jo Anne *writer, retired educator*
Steffee, Nina Dean *publisher*
Stipek, Kathleen *reference librarian*
Taylor, Grace Elizabeth Woodall (Betty Taylor) *law educator, law library administrator*
Wass, Hannelore Lina *educational psychology educator*
White, Susie Mae *school psychologist*
Wing, Elizabeth Schwarz *museum curator, educator*
York, Vermelle Cardwell *real estate broker and developer*

Goulds
Taylor, Millicent Ruth *elementary school educator*

Green Cove Springs
Davidson, Joy Elaine *mezzo-soprano*

Wrigley, Claudia Stephens *gifted and talented educator*

Groveland
Sides, I. Ruth S. *music educator*

Gulf Breeze
Smithey, Susan Willett *music educator*
Williams, Betty *peace activist*

Gulf Stream
FitzSimons, Marjorie Kitchen *art consultant*

Gulfport
Athanson, Mary Catheryne *school system administrator*
Davis, Ann Caldwell *history educator*

Hallandale
Engel, Tala *lawyer*
Geller, Bunny Zelda *poet, author, publisher, sculptor, artist, photographer*
Lippe, Harriet Rothfeder *retired elementary school educator*
Rentz, Bessie Elizabeth *adult education educator*
Schatken, Nancy Leah *medical editor*

Hernando
Saxe, Thelma Richards *secondary school educator, consultant*

Hialeah
Engler, Eva Kay *dental and veterinary products company executive*
Hernandez, Madeline *mental health services professional*
Jenkins, Dawn *special education educator, dancer*
Pelaez, Ofelia *addiction and HIV/AIDS counselor*
Warfel, Jill Kristin *political organization worker*

Hillsboro Beach
Gibbons, Celia Victoria Townsend (Mrs. John Sheldon) *editor, publisher*
Marshall, Jo Taylor *social worker*
McGarry, Carmen Racine *historian, artist*

Hobe Sound
Houser, Constance W. *writer, artist*

Holiday
Barney, Linda Susan *manufacturing specialist*

Hollywood
Border, Gladys Louise *piano educator*
Carmen Maria, Lopez *sales executive*
Fuentes, Denise Iris *customer service administrator, sales representative*
Giulianti, Mara Selena *mayor, civic worker*
Kelly, Cleo Parker *retired bank executive*
King, Alma Jean *retired physical education educator, healthcare educator*
Korthals, Candace Durbin *lawyer*
Krane, Jessica (Aida Jessica Kohnop-Krane) *writer, educator*
Mendez, Deborah *parochial school educator*
Pittarelli, Diana *entrepreneur*
Sadowski, Carol Johnson *artist*
Tannen, Ricki Lewis *lawyer, psychologist, educator*
Tucker, Nina Angella *hospital administrator*
Williams, Roslyn Patrice *marketing executive*

Holmes Beach
Dunne, Nancy Anne *retired social services administrator*
Ehde, Ava Louise *librarian, educator*

Homestead
Ferraro, Marie *dental hygienist*

Homosassa
Carmichael, Roberta Kay *writer*
Frank, Elizabeth Ahls (Betsy Frank) *art educator*

Hutchinson Island
Wanzer, Mary Kathryn *computer company executive, consultant*

Indialantic
Claflin, Tracie Nadine *private school educator*
Pavlakos, Ellen Tsatiri *sculptor*

Indian Harbor Beach
Tasker, Molly Jean *lawyer*
Traylor, Angelika *stained glass artist*

Indian Rocks Beach
Muneio, Patricia Anne *public health nurse*

Indian Shores
Browne, A. Pauline *accountant, writer*

Inglis
Norris, Mildred Eleanor *consultant*

Inverness
Grasso, Julia Alice *nursing educator*
Hawk, Pauletta Browning *student elementary school educator*
Kramer, Marlene Dixie *dietician*

Islamorada
Sieber, Dawn *food service executive*

Jacksonville
Aftoora, Patricia Joan *transportation executive*
Aleschus, Justine Lawrence *retired real estate broker*
Alexander, Edna M. DeVeaux *elementary school educator*
Bedell, Elizabeth Snyder (Betty Bedell) *editor-in-chief, marketing professional*
Black, Susan Harrell *judge*
Bodkin, Ruby Pate *corporate executive, real estate broker, educator*
Booth, Terri Lynne *music educator*
Cannon, Lillian *retired editor*
Constantini, JoAnn M. *small business owner, consultant*
Costin, Rea-Silvia *civil engineer*
Duncan, Shirley A. *portfolio manager*
Dundon, Margo Elaine *museum director*
Eden, F. Brown *artist*
Helganz, Beverly Buzhardt *counselor*
Holliday, Patricia Ruth McKenzie *evangelist*
Holmes, Rachel Ellen Flynn *sculptor*
Hott, Peggy A. *mortgage banker*
Huber, Mary Susan *music educator*
Kelso, Linda Yayoi *lawyer*
Kilbourne, Krystal Hewett *retired rail transportation executive*
King, Janey Hampton *music educator, vocalist, educator*
Kinne, Frances Bartlett *academic administrator*
Koeppel, Mary Sue *communications educator, writer*
Kress, Mary Elizabeth *retired newspaper editor*
Langford, Cecilia Motes *nursing educator*
Loomis, Jacqueline Chalmers *photographer*
Magill, Sherry *foundation administrator*
Main, Edna Dewey (June Main) *education educator*
Olin, Marilyn *secondary school educator*
Pavlick, Pamela Kay *nurse, consultant*
Perry, Beth Bentley *writer, artist*
Rodney, Roxanne Audrey *cardiologist, consultant*
Salem, Karen E. *information technology executive*
Sanders, Marion Yvonne *retired geriatrics nurse*
Schultz, Nancy Reilly *artist*
Scott, Kamela Koon *psychologist, educator*
Segal, Linda Gale *retired insurance company executive*
Simms, Jacqueline Kamp *secondary school educator*
Small, Patricia Ann *minister*
Smalley, Terri Barnes *social worker*
Soud, Ginger *city councilwoman*
Stanley, Helen Camille *composer, musician*
Stewart, Sandra Kay *music educator*
Stiehl, Ruth Rasco *nursing educator*
Van Deusen, Cheryl A. *business educator, consultant*
Weaver, Dianne Jay *lawyer*
Weber, Nancy Walker *charitable trust administrator*

Jacksonville Beach
Richetti, Cindy L. *mental health services professional*
Saltzman, Irene Cameron *consumer products company executive*
Urban, A. Greg M. *health facility administrator*

Jay
Cloud, Linda Beal *retired secondary school educator*

Jupiter
Colucci, Jacqueline Strupp *insurance agent, small business administration specialist, sculptor, special project coordinator*
Malm, Rita H. *securities executive*
Moseley, Karen Frances Flanigan *educational consultant, retired school system administrator, educator*
Tanis, Janet Eleanor *museum administrator, retired elementary school educator*

Kennedy Space Center
Malone, Lisa A. *federal agency administrator*

Key Biscayne
Blank, Joan Gill *journalist, illustrator*
Ross, Marilyn J. *English and communications educator*

Key Colony Beach
Crenshaw, Patricia Shryack *sales executive, consultant*

Key Largo
Kennedy, Mary Sussock *artist*

Key West
Armendariz, Alma Delia *small business owner, researcher*
Bradford, Judith Lynnell *journalist, artist*
Menendez, Teresa *communications executive*
Murphy, S(usan) (Jane Murphy) *small business owner*

Kissimmee
Buma, Judith Bergeson *music educator*
King, Susan Marie *special education educator*
O'Shaughnessy, Rosemarie Isabelle Rao *clinical nutritionist*
Severance, Jeri-Lynne White *elementary school educator*
Toothe, Karen Lee *elementary and secondary school educator*
Wallace, Evelina Velvia Joetha *elementary school educator*

LaBelle
Etgeton, Cassandra Zehntner *mathematician, educator*

Lady Lake
Head-Hammond, Anna Lucille *retired secondary school educator*

Lake City
Montgomery, June C. *musician, composer*
Norman, Alline L. *health facility administrator*

Lake Helen
Dillashaw, Eula Catherine *artist, graphic artist*

Lake Mary
Branciforte, Theresa Alice *retired business educator*
Reagan, Bettye Jean *artist*
Southward, Patricia C. *volunteer*

Lake Park
Heaton, Janet Nichols *artist, art gallery director*

Lake Worth
Asher, Kathleen May *communications educator*
Chittick, Elizabeth Lancaster *women's rights activist*
Dilgen, Regina Marie *English educator*
Gorman, Marcie Sothern *personal care industry executive*
Gough, Carolyn Harley *library director*

Lakeland
Bricker, Lisa G. *marketing professional, not-for-profit fundraiser*
Flekke, Mary Muriel *instructional services librarian*
Garrott, Frances Carolyn *architectural technician*
Markley, Kate *social worker, consultant*
Pospichal, Marcie W. *neuroscientist, psychologist, educator*
Spencer, Mary Miller *civic worker*
Wilson, Micheline *small business owner*
Zucco, Ronda Kay *planning and marketing professional*

Land O Lakes
O'Connell, Carmela Digristina *appraisal executive, consultant*
Webb, Mary Greenwald *cardiovascular clinical specialist, educator*

Lantana
Wetherby, Ivor Lois *librarian*

Largo
Carter, Jennifer Leigh *special education educator*
Hinson, Karen Renee *mental health services professional*
Szalkowski, Deborah *music educator*
Woodruff, Debra A. *occupational health nurse*

Lauderdale By The Sea
Kennedy, Beverly (Kleban) Burris *financial advisor, television and radio personality*

Lecanto
Wheatley, Deborah A. *music educator*

Leesburg
Thompson, Mary B. *writer, illustrator*
Twiss, Wanda May *interior designer*
Whalen, Norma Jean *special education educator*

Lehigh Acres
Wahlberg, Gretchen Marie *music educator*

Longboat Key
Hazan, Marcella Maddalena *writer, educator, consultant*
Molles, Emily DeMartino *artist, real estate broker*
Moulton, Katherine Klauber *hotel executive*

Longwood
Bomar, Bunnye M. *secondary school educator*
Gasperoni, Ellen Jean Lias *interior designer*
Meitin, Deborah Dorsky *cantor*
Tomasulo, Virginia Merrills *retired lawyer*

Loxahatchee
Newman, Nellie Yvonnie *nurse*

Lutz
Miller, Bonnie Sewell *marketing professional, writer*

Lynn Haven
Bonazzi, Elaine Claire *mezzo-soprano*

Maitland
Mansson, Joan *librarian, consultant*
Stephens, Patricia Ann *marketing professional*
Vallee, Judith Delaney *environmentalist, writer, fundraiser*

Manalapan
Phipard, Nancy Midwood *retired special education educator, poet*

Marathon
Vail, Elizabeth Forbus *volunteer*
Wolpe, Marcy Shear *artist, art educator*

Marco Island
Henry, Sally *assistant principal*
Hollenbeck, Karen Fern *foundation consultant*

Margate
Dexter, Jane Meiser *physical education educator*

Marianna
Connor, Catherine Brooks *educational media specialist*

Melbourne
Chaloult, Nancy Marie *nursing administrator*
Dillen, Nancy Baur *art educator, artist*
Failla, Sophia Lynn *artist, educator*
Hughes, A. N. *psychotherapist*
Jones, Elaine Hancock *humanities educator*
King, Virginia Shattuck *painter, retired school nurse practitioner, educator*
Scheuerer, Diane Thomspon *home economics educator*
Stone, Elaine Murray *author, composer, television producer*

Melrose
Harley, Ruth *artist, educator*

Merritt Island
Babcock, Hope Smith *counselor, educator, program designer*
Givens, Christine Juliano *music educator, elementary school educator*
Gross, Elizabeth Anne *elementary school educator*
Young, Nancy Mayer *retired secondary school educator, artist*

Mexico Beach
Turney, Virginia *writer*

Miami
Abril, Marcia (Ela I. Cardinas) *writer*
Algazi, Nancy *health facility administrator*
Alvarez, Ofelia Amparo *medical educator*
Amos, Betty Giles *restaurant company executive, accountant*
Austin-Hill, Suzanne S. *mathematician, educator*
Balmaseda, Liz *columnist*
Banas, Suzanne *middle school educator*
Barkett, Rosemary *circuit judge*
Baumbach, Lisa Lorraine *research scientist*
Bell, Sandra Kathleen *special education educator*
Bennett, Olga Salowich *civic worker, graphic arts researcher, consultant*
Bessette, Diane J. *homebuilding company executive*
Brondello, Sandy *professional basketball player*
Brooten, Dorothy *nursing educator, former dean*
Bullard, Larcenia J. *state legislator*
Carey-Shuler, Barbara *county commissioner*
Carnesoltas, Ana-Maria *lawyer*
Chambers, Elenora Strasel *artist*
Cheyney, Wendy *special education educator, researcher*
Collier, Courtney Carole *mathematics educator*
Colona, Jane B. *transplant nurse coordinator*
Conover, Pamela C. *cruise line executive*
Corbi, Lana *communications executive*
Cortes, Carol Solis *school system administrator*
Coulter, Beverly Norton *singer, pianist, opera director*
Cubberley, Gayle Susan *band director*
de Leon, Lidia Maria *magazine editor*
Dimitriou, Dolores Ennis *computer consultant*
Dorfman, Lisa Ann *nutritionist, consultant, educator*
DuFresne, Elizabeth Jamison *lawyer*
Durkin, Diane L. *nurse*
Engle, Mary Allen English *physician*
Feinberg, Wendie *producer*
Fichtner, Margaria *journalist*
Fine, Rana Arnold *chemical and physical oceanographer*
Gittens, Angela *airport executive*
Goin-Harding, Cecilia Margaret *poet*
Gonzalez, Ivette *biomedical engineer*
Goodman-Milone, Constance Beth *writer*
Gray, Frances Boone *minister*
Haar, Ana Maria Fernández *advertising and public relations executive*
Harmon, Monica Renee *music educator*
Hicks, Dorothy Jane *obstetrician and gynecologist, educator*
Himburg, Susan Phillips *dietician, educator*
Humphries, Joan Ropes *psychologist, educator*
Huysman, Arlene Weiss *psychologist, educator, writer*
Jackson-Holmes, Flora Marie *lawyer, educator*
Javier-Dejneka, Amelia Luisa *accountant*
Jones, Janice Cox *elementary school educator, writer*
Jones-Koch, Francena *school counselor, educator*
Jones-Wills, Eunice Stephanie *mental health nurse, researcher*
Kaplan, Betsy Hess *school board member*
Kislak, Jean Hart *art director*
Kooima, Linda Kay *neonatal and pediatrics nurse*
Korchin, Judith Miriam *lawyer*
Kowalska, Maria Teresa *research scientist, educator*
Krissel, Susan Hinkle *transportation company executive*
Laje, Zilia L. *writer, publisher, translator*
Liebes, Raquel *retired import/export company executive*
Long, Maxine Master *lawyer*
Lovio-Rodriguez, Jessica Bertha *accountant*
Lynch, Catherine Gores *social work administrator*
Margolis, Gwen *county commissioner*
Marinez, Rita Maria *writer*
Marks, Shirley Isaacson *artist*
Mauch, Diane Farrell *music educator*
McKinney, Erica Kimberly *city official*
McLaughlin, Margaret Brown *adult education educator, writer*
McNamany, Eve Weeks *clinical psychologist, marriage therapist*
McPhee, Penelope L. Ortner *foundation executive, television producer, writer*
Meadors, Marynell *former professional basketball coach, sports team executive*
Mehta, Eileen Rose *lawyer*
Mendieta, Raquelín Maria de la Concepción *artist*
Miller, Constance Johnson *elementary school educator*
Miller Udell, Bronwyn *lawyer*
Mitchell, Virginia Ann *investment company executive*
Moran, Kate *sculptor, photographer*
Morgan, Marabel *writer*
Muir, Helen *journalist, author*
Munn, Janet Teresa *lawyer*
Nestor Castellano, Brenda Diana *real estate company executive*
Neuman, Susan Catherine *public relations and marketing consultant*
O'Brien, Amy V. *apparel designer*
O'Bryon, Linda Elizabeth *television station executive*
O'Connor, Kathleen Mary *lawyer*

O'Meara, Vicki A. *lawyer*
Osman, Edith Gabriella *lawyer*
O'Sullivan, Mary J. *physician, maternal fetal medicine educator*
Pampe, Pamela Mary *textiles executive, consultant*
Parchment, Yvonne *nursing educator*
Paschal, Verona *real estate agent, small business owner*
Patrie, Cheryl Christine *elementary school educator*
Perez, Mary Christine *guidance counselor, small business owner*
Plater-Zyberk, Elizabeth Maria *architectural educator*
Poston, Rebekah Jane *lawyer*
Potocky-Tripodi, Miriam *social worker, educator*
Reno, Janet *former attorney general*
Reyes, Lory G. *entrepreneur*
Richards-Vital, Claudia *small business owner, recreational facility executive*
Rickard, Lisa Ann *lawyer*
Rodriguez-Walling, Matilde Barcelo *special education educator*
Rundle, Katherine Fernandez *state's attorney*
Saland, Deborah *psychotherapist, educator*
Seitz, Patricia Ann *federal judge*
Shipp, Theta Wanza *social service organization administrator, educator, consultant, minister*
Sorenson, Katy *county commissioner*
Sorrentino, Charlene H. *federal judge*
Spear, Laurinda Hope *architect*
Stanley, Sherry A. *lawyer*
Stiehm, Judith Hicks *university official, political science educator*
Theodoli, Katrin *manufacturing executive*
Thomas, Lise-Marie *actress*
Touby, Kathleen Anita *lawyer*
Tumpson, Joan Berna *artist*
Tuzel, Tulin *food service executive*
Ungaro-Benages, Ursula Mancusi *federal judge*
Uribe, Claudia Patricia *psychologist, educator*
Vento, M. Thérèse *lawyer*
Vogel, Malvina Graff *video and infosystems specialist*
Walkley, Mary L *voice educator, music educator*
Welsh, Judith Schenck *communications educator*
Wolff, Grace Susan *pediatrician, pediatric cardiologist*
Young, Freddie Gilliam *principal, educator*
Zito, Judi *information technology executive*

Miami Beach
Gardiner, Pamela Nan *performing arts company executive*
Gojman, Bea Answinger *retired elementary school educator*
Kalsner-Silver, Lydia *psychologist*
Kersten, Sharon *public relations executive, consultant*
Lawson, Eve Kennedy *dancer*
Membiela, Roymi Victoria *marketing professional, consultant*
Rut, Wanda E. *artist, educator, writer*

Miami Shores
Diener, Betty Jane *finance educator*
Martino Maze, Claire Denise *nursing educator*

Micco
Christoph, Frances *painter*

Middleburg
Combs, Diane Louise *elementary school educator, music educator*

Milton
Arnold, Margaret Morelock *music specialist, educator, performer*
Coston, Brenda Maria Bone *language arts educator*

Miramar
González Tricoche, Cynthia Marie *human resources specialist*
Stephens, Sallie L. *retired assistant principal, commissioner*

Mount Dora
Kirton, Jennifer Myers *artist*
Scharfenberg, Margaret Ellan *retired elementary school educator*

Mulberry
Bowman, Hazel Lois *retired English language educator*

Naples
Blumenthal, Ronnie *lawyer*
Capelle-Frank, Jacqueline Aimee *writer*
Ehlers, Kathryn Hawes (Mrs. James D. Gabler) *physician*
Evans, Judith P. *music educator*
Finger, Iris Dale Abrams *elementary school educator*
Gifford, Nancy (Mumtaz) *artist, poet*
Guerra, Mayra *insurance company executive*
Hainsworth, Melody May *information professional, researcher*
Karkut, Bonnie Lee *retired dental office manager*
Kinder, Suzanne Fonay Wemple *historian, educator*
Kvetko, Colleen M. *bank executive*
Mainwaring, Susan Adams *recreational facility executive*
Marcy, Jeannine Koonce *retired educational administrator*
McCaffrey, Judith Elizabeth *lawyer*
McDonald, Jinx *interior designer*
Mills, Dorothy Jane (Dorothy Z. Seymour) *editor, consultant*
Norton, Elizabeth Wychgel *lawyer*
Post, Barbara Joan *elementary school educator*
Rawson, Marjorie Jean *lawyer*
Strauss, RoseMarie *medical/surgical nurse*
Ward, Kelsey S. *purchasing agent*
Wroble, Lisa Ann *writer, educator*

Navarre
McLaughlin, Carolyn Lucile *elementary school educator*
Starratt, Patricia Elizabeth *writer, actress, composer, pianist*

Neptune Beach
Chambers, Ruth Coe *writer*

New Port Richey
Baker, Michele Dawn Litz *management consultant*
Cessna, Janice Lynn *systems administrator, information technology manager*
Charters, Karen Ann Elliott *critical care nurse, health facility administrator*
Robbins, Jennifer Katherine *music educator*
Sebring, Marjorie Marie Allison *former home furnishings company executive*

New Smyrna Beach
Zink, Joan Wilson *writer, poet, composer*

Niceville
Melich, Gayle Peters *writer*
Morris Schweitzer, Nancy N. *retired science educator, writer*
Valdés, Karen W. *art gallery director, educator*

Nokomis
Novak, Joyce Keen *artist, secondary school educator*
Robinson, Mary Catherine *artist*

North Miami
Birbragher-Rozencwaig, Francine *art historian, critic, editor*
Kordalewski, Lydia Maria *news correspondent, municipal employee*

North Miami Beach
MacIvor, Catherine J. *lawyer*
Sorosky, Jeri Ruth *academic administrator*

North Port
Koor, Margaret P. *medical/surgical nurse, deacon, obstetrical nurse*
Seiler, Charlotte Woody *retired educator*

Ocala
Adams, Marylyn Dewey *music educator*
Belmontez, Deborah Lynn Groves *poet, editor*
Blalock, Carol Douglass *psychologist, educator*
Booth, Jane Schuele *real estate company executive, real estate broker*
Delozier, Doris M. *retired secondary school educator*
Gatison, Karen Ann *private school educator*
Ovrebo, Judith *retired physical education educator*
Simon, Margaret B(allif) *elementary school educator, writer*
Staples, Elizabeth Ann *counselor*
Stickeler, Carl Ann Louise *professional parliamentarian*
Westbrook, Rebecca Vollmer *secondary school educator*

Ocklawaha
Silagi, Barbara Weibler *corporate administrator*

Ocoee
Blackman, Sharon Forbes *music educator*
Davis, Elena Denise *accountant*

Okeechobee
Brown, Radie Lynn *secondary school educator*
Mercer, Frances deCourcy *artist, educator*
Raulerson, Phoebe Hodges *school superintendent*

Opa Locka
Robinson, Shirley S *coach, educator*

Orange City
Schaeffer, Barbara Hamilton *retired rental leasing company executive, writer*

Orlando
Allison, Anne Marie *retired librarian*
Baggott, Brenda Jane Lamb *elementary school educator*
Bauer, Maria Casanova *computer engineer*
Bichler, Elizabeth Anne *secondary school educator, musician*
Boyd, Be (Belinda) Carolyn *theater educator*
Conway, Anne Callaghan *federal judge*
DeLorme, Denise Elizabeth *communications educator*
Dimopoulos, Linda J. *food service executive*
Fawsett, Patricia Combs *federal judge*
Flanagan, Marianne *music educator*
Good, Virginia Johnson *real estate executive*
Gouvellis, Mary C. *utilities executive*
Grice, Lorraine E. *finance educator*
Hall, Charlotte Hauch *newspaper editor*
Harris, Lani M. *theater educator*
Healy, Jane Elizabeth *newspaper editor*
Hodel, Mary Anne *library director*
Hom, Trudy A. *music educator*
Houser, Ruth G. *financial executive*
Jennemann, Karen Sue *judge*
Johnson, Rebecca J. *literature educator*
Kramer, Elaine *editor*
Leonard, Penny Sue Evans *nurse*
Leuner, Jean D'Meza *nursing administrator*
Levy, Barbara Ellen *music educator*
Lloyd, Priscilla Ann *finance educator*
Magsino, Marissa Estiva *internist, pediatrician*
Mahoney, Mary *hotel executive*
Maupin, Elizabeth Thatcher *theater critic*
Michaud, Norma Alice Palmer *paralegal, real estate investor*
Morrisey, Marena Grant *art museum administrator*
Murphrey, Elizabeth Hobgood *history educator, librarian*

Murrah, Ann Ralls Freeman *historical association executive*
Peck, Carolyn *professional basketball coach*
Powell, Elaine Marie *consultant, educator, writer*
Radloff, Marie Ulrey *music educator*
Raffa, Jean Benedict *author, educator*
Renk, Kimberly Dawn *social sciences educator*
Scarcella, Karyn Allee *coach, special education services professional*
Schultz, Victoria L. *music educator, entertainer*
Sharp, Christina Krieger *nursing educator, researcher*
Shives, Paula J *lawyer*
Thorpe, Janet Claire *judge*
Vander Weide, Cheri DeVos *sports team executive, marketing professional*
Waltz, Kathleen M. *publishing executive*
Waltz, Kathy *publishing executive*
Wirth, Melissa Kay *medical/surgical nurse, rehabilitation nurse*

Ormond Beach
Connors, Michele Perrott *wholesale beverage company executive*
Franchini, Roxanne *bank executive*
Graf, Dorothy Ann *human resources specialist*
Granville, Paulina *independent music scholar and educator*
Logan, Sharon Brooks *lawyer*
Lynn, Evelyn Joan *state senator, consultant*
Ray, Janie Machelle (J. R. Shepard) *software development executive*
Zimmerman, Pamela Diana *elementary school educator*

Osprey
Halladay, Laurie Ann *public relations consultant, former franchise executive*
Harrington, Nancy O'Connor *volunteer*
Holec, Anita Kathryn Van Tassel *civic worker*

Pace
Davis, Gail Shell *gifted and talented educator*

Palm Bay
Downes, Patricia Ann *minister*
Galitello-Wolfe, Jane Maryann *artist, writer*
Hanna, Emma Harmon *architectural designer, business owner, official*
Sampере, Roberta Lynn *English language educator, consultant*

Palm Beach
Baum, Selma *customer relations consultant*
Birmingham, Pat *pageant director*
Canary, Nancy Halliday *lawyer*
Elson, Suzanne Goodman *community activist*
Harper, Mary Sadler *financial advisor*
Hope, Margaret Lauten *civic worker*
Krois, Audrey *artist*
Robb, Babette *retired elementary school educator*
Roberts, Margot Markels *business executive*
Shulgasser-Parker, Barbara *writer*
Whiteside, Patricia Lee *fine art antique and personal property appraiser*

Palm Beach Gardens
Curwick, Deborah *realtor*
Más, Beverley Berlin *career planning advisor, counseling advisor*
Samuels, Fern Jacqueline *artist, educator*
Schurtz, Ora Sears *hypnotist, educator*
Van Allen, Veronica Elaine *marketing and public relations professional*
Wilkes, N. Tiffany *social studies educator*

Palm City
Whichello, Carol *political scientist, educator, writer*

Palm Coast
Barnes, Judith Ann *real estate executive*
Boyer, Kaye Kittle *association management executive*
Franco, Annemarie Woletz *editor*
Wiggins-Rothwell, Jeanine Ellen *artist*

Palm Harbor
Jones, Winona Nigels *retired library media specialist*
Katzen-Guthrie, Joy *performance artist, engineering services executive*
Richardson, Pamela Austin *music educator*
Rivelli, Susan Veronica *nurse*

Panama City
Reedy-Dewey, Madeline Anne *retired occupational therapist*
Robbins, Dorothy Ann *librarian*
Whitsitt, Marjorie Rae *artist, educator*

Panama City Beach
Birdwell, Michelle Marie *music educator*
Shugart, Anita Carol *research and development cosmetologist*

Parkland
Garcia, Laura Catherine *emergency and disaster preparedness consultant*
Landman, Deborah Tracy *real estate company executive, small business owner, fitness trainer*

Parrish
Corey, Kay Janis *business owner, designer, nurse*

Pembroke Pines
Corbiere, Mary Louise Sambataro *music educator, musician*
DeBiagi, Anna Lillian *retired educator*
Embergher, Mary Louise *elementary school educator*
Ferris, Rita Bernadette *social worker*

Pensacola
Appleyard, Diane Paige *human service administrator*

Burke-Fanning, Madeleine *artist*
Canady, Alexa Irene *pediatric neurosurgeon*
Costello, Arlene M. *elementary school educator*
Demars, Bonnie Macon *librarian*
Dorman, Jo-Anne *elementary school educator*
Galloway, Sharon Lynne *special education educator*
Garrett, Vikki Rae *transportation planner*
Garrison, Wanda Brown *environmental consultant*
George, Katie *lawyer*
Ivey, Denise H. *publishing executive*
Law, Carol Judith *medical psychotherapist*
Loesch, Mabel Lorraine *social worker*
Maki, Hope Marie *artist, sculptor, illustrator, poet, educator*
McCann, Mary Cheri *medical technologist, horse breeder and trainer*
McQueen, Rebecca Hodges *health care executive, consultant*
Shimmin, Margaret Ann *women's health nurse*
Sims, Pam *writer, minister*

Pinellas Park
Benedict, Gail Cleveland *music educator*
Brennan, Mary M. *state legislator*
Strader, Marlene Knocks *nursing educator*

Plant City
Durham, Susan F. *music educator*

Plantation
Ballantyne, Maree Anne Canine *artist*
Bosted, Dorothy Stack *public relations executive*
Burnett, Barbara Diane *social worker*
Clerici, Susan Marie *psychotherapist*
Newburge, Idelle Block *psychotherapist*
Nickelson, Kim René *internist*
Spigler, Karen Jensen *lawyer, accountant*

Poinciana
VanderHeyden, Carol *retired elementary school educator*

Pompano Beach
Amisano, Bernadette Parker *artist*
Bethel, Marilyn Joyce *librarian*
Corsello, Lily Joann *minister, counselor, educator*
Goldberg, Lois D. *health facility administrator, disability analyst*
Hellwege, Nancy Carol *special education educator*
Johnson, Dorothy Curfman *elementary school educator*
Kaskinen, Barbara Kay *author, composer, active musician, music educator*
Kory, Marianne Greene *lawyer*
Levine, Ruth Hannah *retired sculptor*
Potash, Vella Rosenthal *lawyer, educator*

Ponte Vedra Beach
Berry, Clare Gebert *real estate broker*
Church, Barbara Ryan *organizational psychologist*
Friedmann, Elizabeth Carroll *writer, editor*
Roland, Melissa Montgomery *accountant*
Simon, Lois Prem *interior designer, artist*
Toker, Karen Harkavy *physician*

Port Charlotte
Gehring, Karin *real estate broker*
Hollinshead, Ariel Cahill *research oncologist, educator*
Reynolds, Helen Elizabeth *management services consultant*
Wolff, Diane Patricia *writer, film producer*

Port Richey
Applefield, Sandra *small business owner*
Mueller, Lois M. *psychologist*

Port Saint Lucie
Dunbar, Shirley Eugenia-Doris *small business owner, writer*
Hammer, Elizabeth Carter Bowers *art educator*
Hogan, Roxanne Arnold *nursing consultant, risk management consultant, educator*
Holloman, Marilyn Leona Davis *nursing non profit administrator, new product developer*
Kinder, Joann Stephanie Love *music educator*

Punta Gorda
Clinton, Mariann Hancock *educational association administrator*
Faerber, Abigail Hobbs *physician*
Nash, Ruth S. *foundation administrator*
Smith-Mooney, Marilyn Patricia *city government official, management consultant and facilitator*
Spaulding, Mar *retired special education educator, therapist*

Reddick
Corwin, Joyce Elizabeth Stedman *construction company executive*

Riverview
Till, Beatriz Maria *international business consultant, translator*

Rockledge
Davis, Beth *elementary school educator*
Harris, Marcelite Jordan *retired career officer*
Sutton, Betty Sheriff *elementary school educator*

Rotonda West
Broyles, Christine Anne *art educator*
Morrison, Beth Ann *music educator, musician*

Royal Palm Beach
Curphey, Geraldine Casterline *church musician, retired*

Ruskin
Briscoe, Anne M. *retired scientist, educator*
LaComb-Williams, Linda Lou *community health nurse*

Saint Augustine
Bishop, Claire DeArment *small business owner, former librarian*
Causey, Rhonda Marie *elementary school educator*
Couture, Diane Rhea *sister, artist, educator*
Henderson, Hazel *economist, writer, lecturer*
Oliver, Elizabeth Kimball *writer*
Sappington, Sharon Anne *retired school librarian*
Sullivan, Mary Jean *elementary school educator*

Saint Cloud
Stamp, Melva Elaine *special education educator*

Saint Petersburg
Baker, Victoria Jean *anthropology educator*
Barthle, Audrey Jean *medical technician, educator*
Bass, Kimberleigh Anne *real estate company executive, risk management consultant*
Betzer, Susan Elizabeth Beers *physician, geriatrician*
Butler, Susan Belinda *environmental specialist*
Clarke, Kit Hansen *radiologist*
Coeyman, Emily Nollie Rogers *civic worker*
Craybas, Jill *professional tennis player*
Despanza-Sprenger, Lynette Charlie *small business owner*
Dunlap, Karen F. Brown *academic administrator*
Eadens, Danielle Maya *gifted and talented educator*
Freeman, Corinne *financial services, former mayor*
Gordon-Harris, Cassandra I. *curator, educator*
Granville, Laura *professional tennis player*
Gregg, Kathy Kay *school system administrator*
Hallock-Muller, Pamela *oceanography educator, biogeologist, researcher*
Harkleroad, Ashley *professional tennis player*
Henin-Hardenne, Justine *professional tennis player*
Johnson, Edna Ruth *editor*
Johnson, Pam *former newspaper editor, communications educator*
Keistler, Betty Lou *accountant, tax consultant*
Keller, Natasha Matrina Leonidow *nursing administrator*
Korn, Naomi S. *social worker, consultant*
Martin, Susan Taylor *newspaper editor*
McArdle, Barbara Virginia *elementary school educator*
McKeown, H. Mary *lawyer, law educator*
Metzger, Kathleen Ann *computer systems specialist*
Michael, Marilyn Corliss *music educator, mezzo soprano*
Molina-Gavilán, Yolanda *language educator*
Petty, Marty *publishing executive*
Reeves, Samantha *professional tennis player*
Riley, Nancy J. *real estate broker*
Schell, Joan Bruning *information specialist, business science librarian*
Shaughnessy, Meghann *professional tennis player*
Simpson, Lisa Ann *physician, educator*
Snyder-Haug, Diane Leslie *writer*
Thompson, Dayle Ann *small business owner, consultant*
Walker, Brigitte Maria *translator, linguistic consultant*
Wasserman, Susan Valesky *accountant, artist, yoga instructor*
Weaver, F. Louise Beazley *curator, director*
Weaver, Janet S. *newspaper editor*
White, June Miller *mathematics educator, educational consultant*
Williams, Minnie Caldwell *retired special education educator*
Wright, Mattie Pearl *civic worker*

Sanford
Perry, Janis Dolores *elementary school educator*
Range, Shirley Qualls *academic administrator*
Scott, Mellouise Jacqueline *retired media specialist*
Tossi, Alice Louise *special education educator*

Sanibel
Allen, Patricia J. *library director*
Keogh, Mary Cudahy *artist*

Santa Rosa Beach
Gilmore, Beverly J *retired journalist, gallery owner*

Sarasota
Brassard, Virginia *elementary school educator*
Byron, E. Lee *real estate broker*
Cauffield, Christine Anne *psychologist*
Clopine, Marjorie Showers *librarian*
Conetta, Tami Foley *lawyer*
DiPirro, Joni Marie *artist*
Elmendorf-Landgraf, Mary Lindsay *retired anthropologist*
Feldhusen, Hazel Jeanette *elementary school educator*
Forrest, Iris *publisher*
Hanscom, Marina *band director, musician*
Hanson, Virginia A. *activities director*
Hapner, Joanna Sue *humanities educator*
Harris, Judith Ann White *health occupations vocational educator, nurse*
Hentz, Susan Marie *special education educator, consultant, trainer*
Holcomb, Constance L. *sales and marketing management executive*
Honner Sutherland, B. Joan *advertising executive*
Hummel, Dana D. Mallett *librarian*
Jacobson, Jeanne McKee *humanities educator, writer*
Jelks, Mary Larson *retired pediatrician*
Jones, Sally Daviess Pickrell *writer*
Lee, Ann McKeighan *curriculum specialist*
Lee, Nancy Ranck *management consultant*
Mason, Ann Darlene *real estate broker*
McFarlin, Diane Hooten *publisher*
North, Marjorie Mary *columnist*
Pike, Nancy M. *librarian*
Plunket, Dolores *art and archaeology educator*
Retzer, Mary Elizabeth Helm *retired librarian*
Savenor, Betty Carmell *painter, printmaker*
Schoenhals, Katherine Viola *social worker*
Stedman, Myrtle Lillian *artist*
Stevens, Elisabeth Goss (Mrs. Robert Schleussner Jr.) *writer, journalist, graphic artist*
Tennant, Diane P. *editor*
Thompson, Annie Figueroa *retired academic director, educator*
Towner, Margaret Ellen *retired minister*
Williams, Tanya Dawn *art appraiser, consultant*
Winterhalter, Dolores August (Dee Winterhalter) *art educator*

Satellite Beach
Osmundsen, Barbara Ann *sculptor*

Sebastian
Mauke, Leah Rachel *retired counselor*
Parulis, Cheryl *English, drama and speech educator*
Pieper, Patricia Rita *artist*

Seffner
Straub, Susan Monica *special education educator*

Seminole
Riedling, Ann Marlow *education educator*

Sneads
Scott, Brenda D. *writer*

South Daytona
Hollandsworth, Phyllis W. *marriage and family therapist*

South Miami
Price, Anna Maria *university administrator*

South Venice
Zellick, Sandra Zelda *psychotherapist*

Spring Hill
Chase, Patricia M. *management consultant*
Del Toro-Politowicz, Lillian *medical association administrator, geriatric counselor*
Moore, Faye Annette *retired social services professional*

Stuart
Hutchinson, Janet Lois *historical society administrator, writer, consultant*
Mark, Marsha Yvonne Ismailoff *artistic director*
Spears, Doris Ann Hachmuth *entrepreneur, writer, publisher, real estate and management consultant*
Stimmell, Anne Krueger *special education educator*
Woodward, Isabel Avila *educational writer, foreign language educator*

Sugarloaf
Greenberg, Linda I. *education educator, volunteer, educator*

Sun City Center
Stanton, Vivian Brennan (Mrs. Ernest Stanton) *retired guidance counselor*

Sunrise
Kolker, Sondra G. *fund raising, special events executive*
Pasker, Debbie Ann *protective services official*
Stalker, Jacqueline D'Aoust *academic administrator, educator*

Tallahassee
Argenziano, Nancy *state legislator*
Barnett, Martha Walters *lawyer*
Baylor, Amy L. *educational technology educator*
Betancourt, Annie *state legislator*
Bish, Deborah F. *music educator*
Blair, Maudine *psychotherapist, communications executive, management consultant*
Blanton, Faye Wester *legislative staff member*
Bloom, Elaine *state legislator*
Boyd, Janegale *state legislator*
Brady, Terrie *political organization executive*
Bucuvalas, Tina *folklorist*
Burnette, Ada M. Puryear *educational administrator*
Carlton, Lisa *state legislator*
Cowin, Anna P. *state legislator, educator*
Crook, Wendy P. *management consultant, educator*
Dean, Delores A. *director*
Dinnen, Maureen *educational association administrator, educator*
Dockery, Paula *state legislator*
Edwards, Lori *state legislator*
Ford, Ann Suter *family nurse practitioner, health planner*
Frankel, Lois J. *state legislator*
Gievers, Karen A. *lawyer*
Hammer, Marion Price *association executive*
Harsanyi, Janice *soprano, educator*
Heyman, Sally Anne *state legislator, crime/loss prevention specialist*
Hood, Glenda E. *state agency administrator*
Humphrey, Louise Ireland *civic worker, equestrienne*
Hunt, Mary Alice *library science educator*
Jaber, Lila A. *state official*
Jacobs, Suzanne *state legislator*
James, Frances Crews *retired zoology educator*
Jennings, Toni *lieutenant governor*
Kessler, Mitzi Lyons *artist*
Kosmas, Suzanne *state legislator, real estate company executive*
Kurth, Patsy Ann *state legislator*
Laird, Doris Anne Marley *humanities educator, musician*
Lisenby, Dorrece Edenfield *realtor*
Maguire, Charlotte Edwards *retired pediatrician*
Marshall, Elizabeth Annette *auditor*
Mason, Marilyn Gell *library administrator, writer, consultant*
Merchant, Sharon J. *state legislator*
Morgan, Lucy Ware *journalist*
Mortham, Sandra Barringer *former state official*
Moulton, Grace Charbonnet *physics educator*
Murman, Sandra L. *state legislator, community activist*
Palladino-Craig, Allys *museum director*
Pariente, Barbara J. *state supreme court justice*
Perry-Camp, Jane *music educator, pianist*
Prewitt, Debra A. *state legislator*
Proctor, Briley Elizabeth *psychologist, educator*
Quince, Peggy A. *state supreme court justice*
Reid, Sue Titus *law educator*
Robbins, Jane Borsch *library science educator, information science educator*
Roberts-Burke, Beryl D. *state legislator, lawyer*
Rodriguez, Raquel *lawyer*
Rollins, Jennie Albin Brown *music educator*
Sapp, Lauren B. *librarian, educator*
Sawh, Ruth *English educator, writer*
Shepard, Deborah True *secondary school educator, consultant*
Smith, Erlinda Fay *occupational therapist*
Stebleton, Michelle Marie *music educator, musician*
Thompson, Jean Tanner *retired librarian*
Tourtet, Christiane Andrée *writer, human rights activist, photojournalist, reporter*
Turnbull, Marjorie Reitz *foundation executive, former state legislator*
Wasserman-Schultz, Debbie *state legislator*
Zachert, Martha Jane *retired librarian*

Tamarac
Baron-Malkin, Phyllis *artist, art educator*
Hughes, Jennifer *utilities executive, photographer*
Marged, Judith Michele *information technology educator*
Palmieri, Patricia J. *elementary school educator*

Tampa
Abell, Jan Meisterheim *architect*
Angard, Nancy Tellis *medical/surgical nurse*
Arfsten, Betty-Jane *nurse*
Bear, Marca Marie *business educator, management consultant*
Boutros, Linda Nelene Wiley *medical/surgical nurse*
Brady, Kathleen Deming *psychologist, occupational therapist, educator*
Bucella, Donna Ann *federal official*
Bucklew, Susan Cawthon *federal judge*
Caltagirone, Norma Tomasello *psychologist, educator*
Cámara, Madeline María *humanities educator*
Cancio, Margarita R. *infectious disease physician*
Castellano, Josephine Massaro *medical records specialist*
Clark, Anna M. *minister, lobbyist*
Collins, Gwendolyn Beth *health administrator*
Costello, Debra Smith *interior designer*
Culpepper, Mary Kay *publishing executive*
Cunningham, Kathleen Ann *human resources specialist, purchasing agent*
Davis, Helen Gordon *former state senator*
DeVane, Mindy Klein *financial planner*
Eddy, Colette Ann *aerial photography studio owner, photographer*
Faulkner, Melanie E. *music educator*
Fernandez, Yolanda *newscaster*
Freedman, Sandra Warshaw *former mayor*
Genshaft, Judy Lynn *psychologist, educator*
Gilbert-Barness, Enid F. *pathologist, pathology and pediatrics educator*
Guyardo, Gayle *newscaster*
Hanford, Grail Stevenson *writer*
Harkness, Mary Lou *librarian*
Harlow, Carol Jean *prospect researcher*
Haselwood, Alicia Jane *photographer*
Henard, Elizabeth Ann *controller*
Hine, Betty Dixon *design consultant*
Hoover, Betty-Bruce Howard *private school educator*
Huneycutt, Alice Ruth *lawyer*
Iorio, Pam *county official*
Jenkins, Elizabeth Ann *federal judge*
Johnson, Joy K. *biofeedback consultant, educator*
Kanter, Jennifer Lynne *curator*
Kass, Emily *art museum administrator*
Kimmel, Ellen Bishop *psychologist, educator*
Kovachevich, Elizabeth Anne *judge*
Kuzmin-Nichols, Nicole A *biotechnology research and development company executive*
LaTourrette, Kathryn *family therapist, counselor, artist*
Luddington, Betty Walles *library media specialist*
MacManus, Susan Ann *political science educator, researcher*
Maher, Irene *newscaster*
Mathis, Marsha Debra *customer relations manager*
McCook, Kathleen de la Peña *university educator*
McDevitt, Sheila Marie *lawyer, energy company executive*
McGinnis, Mary Louise *mental health services professional*
McKinney, Patricia J. *automobile company executive*
Miller, Gwendolyn M. *councilman*
Mitchell, Mozella Gordon *English language educator, minister*
Molloy, Jean Marie *psychologist, human services administrator*
Moore, Janet L.S. *music educator, dean*
Nadrotoska, Barbara Anna *art educator*
Olson, Candy *school system administrator*
Pauly, Jennifer L. *director, graphics designer*
Platt, Jan Kaminis *county official*
Plawecki, Judith Ann *nursing educator*
Powers, Pauline Smith *psychiatrist, educator, researcher*
Prest, Nerissa *newscaster*
Reed, Donna Marie *editor, newspaper*
Riley, Dorothy Joan *clinical social worker, writer*
Rojas, Mazie *pastor*
Ronson, Bonnie Whaley *literature educator*
Rugers, Tatiana Yurievna *computer programmer, consultant*
Russell, Diane Elizabeth Henrikson *career counselor*
Schaible, Stacie *newscaster*
Scialdo, Mary Ann *music educator, musician*
Sierens, Gayle *newscaster*
Simmons, Patricia T. *marketing analyst, researcher*
Steiner, Sally Ann *psychiatric nurse practitioner*
Stiles, Mary Ann *lawyer, author, lobbyist*
Strauss, Dorothy Brandfon *marriage and family therapist*
Sullivan, Anne McCrary *language educator*
Vogt, Martha Diane *lawyer*
Watkins, Joan Marie *osteopath, occupational medicine physician*
Weizmann, Maria Pia *ESL educator*
Westcott, Joan Clark *poet*
Young, Gwynne A. *lawyer*

Tarpon Springs
Crismond, Linda Fry *public relations executive*

Tavares
Osborne, Glenna Jean *health services administrator, social services administrator*

Temple Terrace
Kashdin, Gladys Shafran *painter, educator*

Tierra Verde
Schmitz, Dolores Jean *primary education educator*

Titusville
Horn, Flora Leola *retired administrative assistant*
King, Sheila Sue *music educator, elementary school educator*

Treasure Island
Williams, Bonnie Lee *city official*

Umatilla
Balandran, Stella Varona *interpreter, lyricist, composer, writer*

University Park
Davis, Tufts *artist*

Valrico
Carlucci, Marie Ann *nursing administrator, consultant*
Tirelli, Maria Del Carmen S. *retired realtor*

Venice
Balch, Nelda Caroline Kurtz *humanities educator*
Barritt, Evelyn Ruth Berryman *nurse, educator, dean*
Bluhm, Barbara Jean *communications agency executive*
Cool, Kim Patmore *retail executive, needlework consultant*
Kleinlein, Kathy Lynn *training and development executive*
Myers, Virginia Lou *education educator*
Trammell, Jean Ehrhart *real estate agent, secondary school educator*
Zarro, Janice Anne *lawyer*

Vero Beach
Binney, Jan Jarrell *publishing executive*
Bowman, Margaret Coon *retired public official, environmental educator*
Haight, Carol Barbara *lawyer*
Lange, Billie Carola *video specialist*

Wauchula
Saddler, Peggy Chandler *counselor*

Wellington
Fitch, Mary Killeen *human resources specialist*
Morales-Hendry Holguin, Maria B. *realtor, poet*

West Melbourne
Fetner, Suzanne *small business owner*

West Palm Beach
Baker, Dina Gustin *artist*
Barndt, Faith Ann *elementary school educator*
Belford, Roz *real estate broker*
Beriro, Deborah Raquel *real estate broker, investor*
Cooper, Margaret Leslie *lawyer*
Goetz, Cecelia Helen *lawyer, retired judge*
Hale, Marie Stoner *artistic director*
Jecko, Laura Ann (Laura Engel, Laura Wallace) *music educator*
Jordan, Linda Diane *music educator*
Lutey, Joyce Louise *real estate broker*
McKeen, Elisabeth Anne *oncologist*
Orr-Cahall, Christina *art museum director, art historian*
Peller, Marci Terry *realtor*
Polo, Kristine Carol *accountant, educator*
Posner, Sylvie Perez *lawyer*
Rander, JoAnn Corpaci *musician, music educator*
Robertson, Sara Stewart *private investor, entrepreneur*
Rosenberg, Leslie Karen *media buyer*
Sander, Dorothy E. *manufacturing executive*
Terwillegar, Jane Cusack *librarian, educator*
Waters, Lisa Lyle *airport administrator, consultant*

Gustin, Ann Winifred *psychologist*
Mustakova-Possardt, Elena M. *social sciences educator, counselor*
Sheesley, Mary Frank *art educator*

Cartersville
Cockrill, Annette S. *elementary school educator, music educator*
Wheeler, Susie Weems *retired educator*

Chamblee
Lass, Teresa Lee *secondary school educator, special education educator*

Clarkesville
Davis, Marilyn Ruth *artist*

Claxton
Odum, Felicia Sellers *art educator*

Clayton
Funkhouser, Catherine G. *music educator*
Monroe, Brenda *priest*

College Park
Bradley, Lynn Hecht *school librarian*
Fahy, Nancy Lee *food products marketing executive*
Ferguson, Wendell *private school educator*
Sims, Deborah Lyde *counselor*

Columbus
Averill, Ellen Corbett *secondary education science educator, administrator*
Duncan, Frances Murphy *retired special education educator*
Finch, Catherine Ann *firework display artist, aromatherapist*
Harris, Mary Cole *counselor*
Hedges, Julie Elaine *photographer*
James, Elizabeth R. *bank executive*
Owens, Deborah *artist, writer*
Riggsby, Dutchie Sellers *education educator*
Ripple, Rochelle Poyourow *educational administrator, educator*
Spencer, Kathelen V. *insurance company executive*
Tidd, Joyce Carter *etiquette educator*

Conley
Grant, Lucille *hospital administrator, social worker*

Conyers
Myers, Sheila John *artist*
Spearman, Maxie Ann *financial analyst, administrator*

Cordele
Venable, Lisa Anita *computer programmer*

Covington
Gray, Phenessa Antoinette *not-for-profit developer*

Cumming
Beaty-Gunter, Sharon E. *music teacher*
Benson, Betty Jones *retired school system administrator*
Palmer, Theresa Joan Griffin *restaurant owner executive*
Pruitt-Streetman, Shirley Irene *small business owner*

Dallas
Corley, Ginger Elaine *secondary school educator*
Harris, Celeste Acquanita *vocational rehabilitation counselor*

Dalton
Pye, Janna Lynn *music educator*

Darien
Davis, Ann Richardson *artist, sculptor, book dealer, writer*

Decatur
Bockwitz, Cynthia Lee *psychologist, psychology and women's studies educator*
Breckenridge, Betty Gayle *management development consultant*
Bullock, Mary Brown *academic administrator*
Cartman, Shirley Eleise *retired music educator*
Childrey Barksdale, Joyce *writer, social worker*
Cravey, Pamela J. *librarian*
Freemont, Andria Shamona *laboratory administrator*
Gary, Julia Thomas *retired minister*
Hale, Cynthia Lynette *religious organization administrator*
Holtzman, Mary *engineering company executive*
Pharr, Paige Elizabeth *interior designer, real estate broker*
Pryce, Monica Elizabeth *music educator*
Solomon, Hilda Pearl *wholesale executive*
Strickland, Brenda B. *music educator*
Wong, Faye Ling *public health service officer*

Douglas
Baars, Ella Jane *art educator*
Pugh, Joye Jeffries *educational administrator*
Tucker, Maureen Ann *musician*

Douglasville
Hall, Mary Hugh *retired secondary school educator*
Haynes, Reba Carol *media specialist, educator*

Dublin
Claxton, Harriett Maroy Jones *retired language educator*
Lee, Michele Cherry *counseling administrator*

Duluth
Capogna-Moras, Barbara Jean *secondary school educator*
Caruana, Laura E. *special education educator*

Gullickson, Nancy Ann *art association administrator*

Dunwoody
Duvall, Marjorie L. *English and foreign language educator*

East Point
Malcolm, Gloria J. *small business owner*
Warren, Barbara Denise *special education educator*

Eastman
Hall, Lula *retired special education educator*

Ellenwood
Pack, Bobigene *minister, writer*

Evans
Stout, Elva Carolyn Fraser *elementary school educator*
Wiggins, Margaret Reynolds *elementary school educator*
Zachert, Virginia *psychologist, educator*

Fayetteville
Cokuslu, Lynda Elizabeth McCord *medical assistant*

Fitzgerald
Rogers, Rebecca Harris *music educator*

Flowery Branch
Monroe, Melrose *retired bank executive*
Tharp, Mary Therese *elementary school educator*

Folkston
Crumbley, Esther Helen Kendrick *retired real estate agent, retired secondary school educator, councilman*
Knowles, Julie Nall *secondary school educator*
Wangsness, Genna Stead *hotel executive, innkeeper*

Forest Park
Grace-Crum, Phyllis Venetia *military officer*

Fort Benning
Livingston, Joyce Torbic *civilian military employee*

Gainesville
Davis, Connie Waters *public relations executive, marketing professional*

Grayson
Nease, Judith Allgood *marriage and family therapist*

Griffin
Shockley, Carol Frances *psychologist, psychotherapist*

Hahira
Connell, Sandra Bennett *school librarian*

Hartwell
Royston, Pamela Jean *special education educator*

Homer
Rylee, Gloria Genelle *music educator*

Hoschton
Osburn, Ella Katherine *elementary school educator*

Jackson
Bomar, Laura Beth *music educator*

Jasper
Sutter, Jean *sculptor*

Jesup
Hirvela-Aberle, Helen DeRee *lawyer*

Jonesboro
Finley, Sarah Maude Merritt *social worker*
Givens, Freda D. *school system administrator, musician*
Stephens, Sara Cecile *music educator*
Williams, Sheila A.T. *elementary education educator, consultant*

Kathleen
Uzzell-Baggett, Karon Lynette *career officer*
Wills, Lois Elaine *art gallery owner, religious education educator*

Kennesaw
Diaz, Anne Marie Theresa *music educator, musician*
Frank, Mary Lou Bryant *psychologist, educator*
Hetrick, Joan Willette *critical care nurse, administrator*
Siegel, Betty Lentz *university president*
Still, Candace Tyson *music educator*

La Fayette
Rogers, Susan Mitchell *psychotherapist*

Lagrange
Donehew, Pamela K. *reading specialist*
Greene, Annie Lucille *artist, retired art educator*
Hawkins, Frances Pam *business educator*
Olney, Nancy Helen *secondary school educator*

Lake Park
Blanton, Vallye J. *elementary school educator*

Lawrenceville
Crain, Mary Ann *elementary school educator*
Harris, Melba Iris *elementary education educator, secondary school educator, state agency administrator*
Hendrix, Jacquelyn McIntyre *elementary music educator*

Lane, Carolyn Brooks *school counselor*
Moran, Sharyn Lee *financial consulting company executive*
Reuter, Helen Hyde *psychologist*

Leesburg
Unger, Suzanne Everett *music educator, musician*

Lilburn
Parker, Venus Cristela *music educator, musician*

Ludowici
Stokes, Melanie Miller *art educator*

Mableton
Harris, Paulette Collier *pre-school administrator, educator*
Peters, Crystal Harrington *music educator, consultant*

Macon
Baima, Julie Martin *special education educator*
Brown, Nancy Childs *marriage and family therapist*
Camp, Shirley A. *nursing consultant, lawyer*
Dorsey, Donna Bagley *insurance agent*
Good, Estelle M. *minister*
Hartman Tillett, Colleen *law educator*
Huffman, Joan Brewer *history educator*
Jobe, Ann Connor *dean, educator*
Johnson, Bonnie Sue *piano educator*
Johnson, Patricia Diane *nurse anesthetist*
Kinzie, Carole G. *artist*
Konersman, Elaine Reich *nursing administrator*
Landry, Sara Griffin *social worker*
Lewis, Sandra Combs *research psychologist, writer*
Long, Shirley June Stafford *artist, educator*
Oliver, Katherine C. *museum director*
Preuit, Theresa *librarian*
Rigsby, Sheila Goree *accounting firm executive*
Terry, Doris D. *music educator*
Weaver, Jacquelyn Kunkel Ivey *artist, educator*

Madison
Short, Betsy Ann *elementary school educator*

Manchester
Ellison, Betty D. *retired elementary school educator*

Marietta
Biehle, Karen Jean *pharmacist*
Corley, Florence Fleming *retired history educator*
Crossley, Ann Cook *writer*
Devigne, Karen Cooke *retired amateur athletics executive*
Eggersman, Denise *computer engineer, educator*
Gerace, Deborah Cobb *music educator*
Hudson, Linda *health care executive*
Hutson, Jacquelyn Collins *pianist, educator*
Laframboise, Joan Carol *middle school educator*
Lahtinen, Silja Liisa *artist*
Lowe, Pamela Mary *art educator*
Neff, Marilyn Lee *nursing consultant*
Niemann, Linda Grant *railroad conductor*
Peck, Natalie Deanne *music educator*
Pou, Linda G. *interior designer, architectural designer*
Rivers, Alma Faye *secondary school educator*
Roaché, Sylvia *social worker*
Rogers, Gail Elizabeth *library director*
Rossbacher, Lisa Ann *university president, geology educator, writer*
Rutherfoord, Rebecca Hudson *computer science educator*
Shapiro, Abra Blair *real estate company executive*
Short-Mayfield, Patricia Ahlene *business owner*
Smith, Irene Helen-Nordine *music educator*
Wimberly, Linda Roberts *music educator, artist*
Wrege, Julia Bouchelle *tennis professional, physics educator*

Maxeys
Cabaniss, Barbara Lee Ferguson *counseling administrator*

Mcdonough
Brown, Joy Withers *music educator*

Milledgeville
Engerrand, Doris Dieskow *business educator*
Sargent, Diane Robertson *mathematician, educator*
Stewart, Felecia Marcia *purchasing agent*
Thrasher, Jennifer Nichols *music educator*

Monticello
Bell, Jacqueline Delores *management consultant*

Morrow
Richter, Janell Johnston *principal, minister*

Moultrie
Wright, Kathy Diane *secondary school educator*

Mountain City
Kennedy, Robinette *anthropologist, researcher*

Newnan
Golden, Lily Oliver *humanities educator*
Royal, Nancy B. *primary school educator*

Newton
Blood, Elizabeth R. *research scientist*

Norcross
Bennett, Catherine June *information technology executive, educator, consultant*
Hicks, Nanci Ann *minister, marketing professional*
Koscik, Ella M. *management and technology company executive*
Moreno, Veronica *food products executive*

Nardelli-Olkowska, Krystyna Maria *ophthalmologist, educator*

Oakwood
Jondahl, Terri Elise *importing and distribution company executive*

Peachtree City
Barnes, Marylou Riddleberger *retired academic administrator, educator*
Marsh, Carole *author, photographer, publisher*
Vires, Judy Doan *early childhood educator*
Wilde, Mary *secondary school educator*
Yother, Michele *publisher*

Reidsville
Goodman, Joy Duvall *elementary school educator*

Ringgold
Austin, Gayla Rolston *music educator, musician*
Hayes Gladson, Laura Joanna *psychologist*

Riverdale
Buchanan, Mariah Spann *artist*
Minter, Jimmie Ruth *accountant*

Robins AFB
Manley, Nancy Jane *environmental engineer*

Rome
Potts, Glenda Rue *music educator*
Watson, Mary Ann *marriage and family therapist*

Roopville
Huckeba, Emily Causey *retired elementary school educator*

Rossville
Anderson, Kristie *construction company executive*

Roswell
Atkins, Vicki Alvinda *realtor*
Devine, Libby *art educator, consultant*
Haase, Patricia Ann Thompson *retired nursing educator*
Hoskinson, Carol Rowe *middle school educator*
Krapf, Veronica Lynne Benefield *elementary school educator*
Lietch, Margie *insurance company administrator*
Mayer, Kay Magnor *writer*
Peebles, Mary Lynn *nursing home administrator*
Polatty, Rose Jackson *civic worker*
Rhau-Bernhard, Anna Frieda *women's health nurse practitioner*
Strong-Tidman, Virginia Adele *marketing professional*

Saint Marys
Hall, Lois Bremer *retired educator, volunteer*

Saint Simons Island
Austin, Jeannette Holland *genealogist, writer*
Low, Anne Douglas *nurse*
Sullivan, Barbara Boyle *management consultant*
Weinberg, Elisabeth H. *physical therapist, health facility administrator*

Savannag
Braithwaite, Margaret Evon *music educator*

Savannah
Aja-Herrera, Marie *fashion designer, educator*
Aquadro, Jeana Lauren *graphic designer, educator*
Baker, Brinda Elizabeth Garrison *infectious disease nurse*
Bertolozzi, Victoria Margaret *program analyst, community planning and development*
Burke, Suzanne Maureen *art historian, dean*
Cobb, Clara Jo *pre-school special education educator*
Cunniff, Sister Georgette *religious organization administrator*
Dandy, Beryl C. *middle school educator*
DiClaudio, Janet Alberta *health information administrator*
Dunlap, Ellen Roe *music educator*
Edeawo, Gale Sky *publishing company executive, writer*
Gabeler, Jo *artist*
Greene, Gail Purchase *medical/surgical nurse*
Gusby, Kim *newscaster*
Hatfield, Stacie H. *professional pianist*
Hill, Dorothy Bennett *community activist*
John, Selena Latricia *systems analyst*
LaSalle, Diana Margaret *company executive, writer, consultant*
Manzi, Sharon Ulrich *education educator, social worker*
Murray, Mary A. *transportation executive*
Parker, Sheila *newscaster*
Polite, Evelyn C. *retired middle school educator, counselor, evangelist*
Ramsay, Linda *architect*
Ray, Susan Davis *accountant*
Rigelwood, Diane Colleen *insurance adjuster, administrator*
Rozantine, Gayle Stubbs *clinical psychologist*
Strauss, Gwen B. *writer, editor*
Taggart, Helen M. *adult education educator, nurse*
Thomas, Regina D. *state legislator*
Thomson, Audrey Shire *volunteer*
Thorne, Kristan *newscaster*
Tyus-Shaw, Tina *newscaster*
Vonschlegel, Patricia *artist*
Wallace, Paula S. *academic administrator*
Wilder, Ginger *newscaster*

Scottdale
Borochoff, Ida Sloan *artist*

Senoia
Griffin, Tammy Lynn *industrial engineer*

Sharpsburg
Skinner, Lynn Strickland *secondary school mathematics educator*

Smyrna
Michels, Frances G. *management company executive*
Rife, Elizabeth *musician, music educator*

Snellville
Dodd, Polly *nursing educator, recreational therapist*
Magill, Dodie Burns *early childhood education educator*

Social Circle
Archibald, Claudia Jane *parapsychologist, counselor, consultant*
Dupree, Nathalie *chef, television personality, writer*
O'Connor, Patricia Eryl *telecommunications consultant*

Springfield
Demarest, Cynthia *music educator*

Statesboro
Bartels, Jean Ellen *nursing educator*
Duke-Whitaker, Lois *government and public relations educator, consultant, educator, researcher*

Statham
Anderson, Sondra C. *music educator*

Stockbridge
Cordobes, Dorothy Eskew *art educator*
Spencer-Jacobs, Jamelle Elizabeth *minister, performing company executive*
Sprayberry, Roslyn Raye *retired secondary school educator*

Stone Mountain
Gotlieb, Jaquelin Smith *pediatrician*
Pryor, Vanita Moon *music educator*

Suwanee
Tatum, Carla Maria *elementary school educator*

Swainsboro
Weatherford, Sharon Davis *music educator*

Sylvania
Brown, Barbara Hayes *elementary school educator*

Thomaston
Brown, June Dyson *elementary education educator, administrator*

Thomasville
Turner, Marta Jones *public affairs professional*

Tifton
Hobby, Zoe Elaine *musician, educator, composer*

Tiger
Ring, Yvonne Ann *special education educator*

Toccoa Falls
Brock, Dorothy Dixon *psychologist, educator*
Frederick, Leah Ruth *education educator*

Tucker
Brown, Betsy S. *hotel executive*
Franklin, Carol D. *electronics company executive*

Tybee Island
Smith, Elizabeth Mackey *financial consultant*
Smith, Tricia E. *artist*

Union City
Riley, Francena *nurse, retired non-commissioned officer*

Valdosta
Harmon, Sharon Granholm *special education educator*
Montgomery, Denise Lynne *librarian, researcher*
Shaw, Patricia Jill *retired music educator*

Villa Rica
Thompson, Jacqueline *air force officer, retired*
Zoda, Suzanne Marie *environmental public relations consultant*

Waleska
Naylor, Susan Embry *music educator*
Taylor, Sue Ann *film producer, television producer*

Warner Robins
Beck, Rhonda Joann *paramedic, educator, writer*
Harris, Naomi Litora *mental health services professional*
Lee, Glenda Dianne *accountant*

Washington
Cole, Joan Carol *music educator*

Waycross
Hoover, Mary Lou Ballentine *music educator*

West Point
Hart, Brenda Rebecca *retired gifted and talented educator*

Winder
Stoffel, Candace Jo *secondary school educator*

Woodstock
Hunt Brogden, Christine Michelle *music educator*
Streeter, Linda V. *music educator*

HAWAII

Ewa Beach
Lewis, Mary Jane *film producer, director, scriptwriter*

Fort Shafter
Emery, Carolyn Vera *non-commissioned officer*

Hanalei
Snyder, Francine *psychotherapist, registered nurse, writer*

Hilo
Ahmadia, Phyllis *lawyer*
Gersting, Judith Lee *computer scientist, educator, computer scientist, researcher*
Golian-Lui, Linda Marie *librarian*
Kinney, Jeanne Kawelolani *English studies educator, writer*
McKee, Eleanor Swetnam *retired principal*
Merk, Elizabeth Thole *investment company executive*
Tseng, Rose *academic administrator*

Holualoa
Scarr, Sandra Wood *psychology educator, researcher*
Stoddard, Sandol *freelance/self-employed writer*

Honolulu
Adcock, Betty-Lee *real estate company officer*
Aduja, Melodie Williams *state senator*
Akiba, Lorraine Hiroko *lawyer*
Antal, Ann Slaughter *adult education educator*
Baker, Helen Doyle Peil *realtor, contractor*
Baker, Rosalyn Hester *state senator*
Barbosa, Rhona *music educator*
Betts, Barbara Stoke *artist, educator*
Billings, Kathy *national monument administrator*
Black, Cobey *journalist*
Bronster, Margery S *state attorney general*
Buen, Jan Yagi *state legislator*
Chee, Gloria Y.M. *secondary school educator*
Chock, Raelene *school system administrator*
Chun, Jacqueline Clibbett *artist, educator*
Chun Oakland, Suzanne Nyuk Jun *state legislator*
Doi, Dorothy Mitsue Yano *travel company executive*
Flannelly, Laura T. *mental health nurse, nursing educator, researcher*
Fok, Agnes Kwan *retired cell biologist, educator*
Fukunaga, Carol A. *state legislator, lawyer*
Fukushima, Barbara Naomi *financial advisor*
Gillmor, Helen *federal judge*
[illegible] *school educator*
Goto Sabas, Jennifer *state official*
Hale, Helene H. *state representative*
Hamamoto, Patricia *school system administrator, educator*
Hanabusa, Colleen *state legislator, lawyer*
Hatfield, Elaine Catherine *psychology educator*
Inouye, Lorraine R. *state legislator*
Ishikawa-Fullmer, Janet Satomi *psychologist, educator*
Jensen, Barbara Wood *interior design business owner*
Jones, Pamela S. *real estate development executive*
Kaiser-Botsai, Sharon Kay *retired early childhood educator*
Kawakami, Bertha C. *state representative*
Kawamura, Georgina K. *finance company executive*
Kay, Elizabeth Alison *zoology educator*
Kennedy, Faye *retired social worker, author*
Kennedy, Reneau Charlene Ufford *forensic psychologist, consultant*
Keyes, Saundra Elise *newspaper editor*
Kim, Donna Mercado *state senator*
Kohr, Melinda Ann *psychologist, educator*
Kudo, Emiko Iwashita *former state official*
Lane, Teresa Marie *language educator*
Lee, Marilyn B. *state representative*
Lee, Pali Jae (Polly Jae Stead Lee) *retired librarian, writer*
Lee, Patricia Y. *lawyer*
Lee, Yeu-Tsu Margaret *surgeon, educator*
Leong, Antoinette Marie *musician, director*
Leong, Bertha F.K. *state representative*
Lin, Yvonne Y. *foreign language teacher*
Lingle, Linda *governor*
Loke, Joan Tso Fong *respiratory therapist*
Lowell, Virginia Lee *librarian*
Lum, Jean Loui Jin *nursing educator*
Mau-Shimizu, Patricia Ann *lawyer*
McShane, Rosemary *lawyer*
Middleton, Linda Charlene *humanities educator*
Migimoto, Fumiyo Kodani *retired secondary school educator*
Miyamoto, Robin Emi Sugihara *psychologist, researcher, supervisor*
Miyasaki, Nola *state agency administrator*
Nakayama, Paula Aiko *state supreme court justice*
Nance, Susan I. *sociologist, educator*
Nordyke, Eleanor Cole *population researcher, public health nurse*
Ogburn, Nancy Wrenn *civic volunteer*
Pagotto, Louise *English language educator*
Palumbo, Lorraine Reiko Minatoishi *architectural historian*
Peterson, Barbara Ann Bennett *history educator, television personality*
Pickens, Frances Jenkins *artist, educator*
Preble, Sarah Hamilton *art librarian, author, writer*
Reed, Nancy Ellen *computer science educator*
Saiki, Patricia (Mrs. Stanley Mitsuo Saiki) *former federal agency administrator, former congresswoman*
Schoenke, Marilyn Leilani *foundation administrator*
Schweitzer, Marsha L. *musician, consultant*
Sharma, Santosh Devraj *obstetrician/gynecologist, educator*
Spencer, Caroline *retired library director*
Stamper, Ewa Szumotalska *psychologist*
Tanoue, Donna A. *bank executive, former federal agency administrator*
Thielen, Cynthia Henry *lawyer, state legislator*
Thompson, Karen Marie *art educator*
Thurston, Kathleen *academic administrator*
Tito, Maureen Louise *educational administrator*
Uchida, Janice Yukiko *plant pathologist/mycologist, researcher*
Varner, Helen *communications educator*
Wakatsuki, Lynn Y. *commissioner*
Walker, Margaret Smith *real estate company executive*
Watanabe, Corinne Kaoru Amemiya *judge, state official, lawyer*
Wee, Christine Dijos *elementary school educator*
Weingand, Darlene Erna *librarian educator, consultant*
Wesselkamper, Sue *academic administrator*
Yeh, Hsiao Yen C. *artist*
Yokouchi, Kathy *nursing administrator*

Kahului
Domingo, Cora Maria Corazon Encarnacion *minister*
Shaw, Virginia Ruth *clinical psychologist*
Tolliver, Dorothy *librarian*

Kailua
Fine, Virginia O. *psychologist*
Grimmer, Beverley Sue *consumer products company executive*
Ivey, Andi *special education educator*
Young, Jacqueline Eurn Hai *former state legislator, consultant*

Kailua Kona
Spitze, Glenys Smith *retired educator*

Kaneohe
Coberly, Margaret *psychologist, educator*
Jackson, Jane W. *interior designer*
Lagoria, Georgianna Marie *curator, writer, editor, visual art consultant*
Nagtalon-Miller, Helen Rosete *humanities educator*
Young-Pohlman, Colette Lisa *music educator*

Kapaa
duPont, Nicole *artist*

Kapaau
Ralston, Joanne Smoot *public relations executive*

Keaau
[illegible]
actress

Kihei
Corell, Marcella Anne *community worker, retired educator*
Galesi, Deborah Lee *fine artist*

Koloa
Cobb, Rowena Noelani Blake *real estate broker*

Kula
Mueller-Fitch, Heather May *priest*

Lanai City
Keenan-Abilay, Georgia Ann *service representative*

Lihue
Kusaka, Maryanne Winona *mayor*
Lovell, Carol *museum director*

Makawao
Ayers, Katherine Stone *artist, chiropractor*
Moore, Rosemary Kuulei *art gallery administrator*

Mililani
Gardner, Sheryl Paige *gynecologist*

Pahoa
Salat, Cristina *writer*

Pearl City
Lee, Rebecca *literature educator, writer*

Volcano
Nicholson, Marilyn Lee *arts administrator*

Waialua
Pugliese Locke, Ranada Marie *nurse*
Singlehurst, Dona Geisenheyner *horse farm owner*

IDAHO

Arco
Williams, Ardith Jean *gifted and talented educator*

Boise
Ahrens, Pamela *state government administrator*
Barrett, Lenore Hardy *state legislator, mining and investment consultant*
Beaumont, Pamela Jo *marketing professional*
Boe, Donna H. *state representative*
Boyce, Carolyn *political organization administrator*
Brownson, Mary Louise *counselor, educator, artist*
Bubb, Karen Denise *art association administrator, educator*
Craig, Kara Lynn *children's home administrator*
Crow, Dolores J. *state representative*
Danielson, Judith A. *state legislator*
Douglas, Bonnie *state representative*
Dunklin, Betsy D. *state legislator*
Elg, Annette *food products executive*
Ellsworth, Julie *state representative*
Field, Debbie *state representative*
Field, Frances *state representative*
Griffin, Sylvia Gail *reading specialist*
Hendren, Merlyn Churchill *investment company executive*
Herbert, Kathy *retail executive*
Holt, Isabel Rae *radio program producer*
Howard, Marilyn *school system administrator*
Jaquet, Wendy S. *state representative*
Jones, Donna Marilyn *state agency administrator, former legislator*
Kellogg, Hilde *state representative*
Keough, Shawn *state legislator*
Lodge, Patti Anne *state senator*
McKague, Shirley *state representative*
McLaughlin, Marguerite P. *state legislator, logging company executive*
Minnich, Diane Kay *legal association administrator*
Peterson, Eileen M. *state agency administrator*
Pimble, Toni *artistic director, choreographer, educator*
Ringo, Shirley G. *state representative*
Seeliger, Lisa Kay *social worker, writer*
Shepherd, Mary Lou *state representative*
Silak, Cathy R. *lawyer, former state supreme court justice*
Skurzynski, Gloria Joan *writer*
Smith, Marsha H. *state agency administrator, lawyer*
Smith, Saliesh Anne *comptroller, payroll administrator*
Terteling-Payne, Carolyn Ann *city official*
Theis, Kristine Lynn *family practice nurse practitioner*
Thornton, Felicia *food service executive, corporate financial executive*
Uranga, Jean R. *lawyer*
Wainwright Henbest, Margaret A. *state representative*
Wood, JoAn E. *state representative*
Woods, Jean Frahm *science educator*
Wyers, Giselle Eleanor *music educator, conductor*

Coeur D Alene
Dahlgren, Dorothy *museum director*
Jaeger, Ellen Louise *small business owner*
Shriner, Darlene Kay *professional athletics coach*

Eagle
Richardson, Betty H. *lawyer, former prosecutor*
Wickman, Patricia Ann *retired social worker*

Fruitland
Sherman, Trina Arden *elementary school educator*

Glenns Ferry
King-Barrutia, Robbie L. *state senator*

Grangeville
Turner, Kathy Ann *mental health services professional*

Hailey
Liebich, Marcia Trathen *community volunteer*
Youngblood, Deborah Sue *lawyer, speech pathology/audiology services professional*

Hayden
Morris, Mary Ann *bookkeeper*

Hope
Meyers, Marlene O. *retired health facility administrator*

Idaho Falls
Barbe, Betty Catherine *marketing professional, retired financial analyst*
Kirkland, Judy Joylene *computer specialist*
Matthews, Janice C. *financial consultant*
Nicholas, Claudia Jo *music educator*
Riddoch, Hilda Johnson *accountant*
Rydalch, Ann *federal agency administrator*
Thorsen, Nancy Dain *real estate broker*
Winston, Jane Kay *secondary education educator, artist*

Jerome
Bell, Maxine Toolson *state legislator, librarian*
Ricketts, Virginia Lee *historian, researcher*

Kamiah
Mills, Carol Margaret *business consultant, public relations consultant*

Ketchum
Leonardo, Ann Adamson *marketing and sales consultant*

Lewiston
Marshall, Josie *secondary school educator*
Thomas, Dene *academic administrator, educator*

Meridian
Shaffer, Mary Louise *art educator*

Moscow
Greever, Janet Groff *history educator*
Moffitt, Christine M. *biologist, educator*
Sebald, Jama Lynn *academic administrator*
Shreeve, Jean'ne Marie *chemist, educator*

Nampa
Ivie, Christine Marie *principal*

Osburn
Calabretta, Marti Ann *senator*

Pocatello
Bott-Graham, Michelle Lynn *behavior therapist*
Heberlein, Alice LaTourrette *healthcare educator, physical education educator, coach*
Smith, Elaine E. *school system administrator*
Smith, Evelyn Elaine *language educator*
Walter, Kay J. *literature educator*

Post Falls
Hasalone Eve, Annette Leona *research and development company executive*

Rupert
Oppelt, Maren Joyce *secondary school educator*

Sagle
Price, Anita W. *music educator, consultant*

Sandpoint
Bowne, Martha Hoke *publishing consultant*
Nelson, Marcella May *volunteer*

Sun Valley
Erickson, Ann Florin *recreational facility executive, realtor*

Twin Falls
Fanselow, Julie Ruth *writer*
Yost, Kelly Lou *pianist*

ILLINOIS

Abbott Park
Amundson, Joy A. *pharmaceutical and health products executive*
Flynn, Gary L. *pharmaceutical executive*

Addison
Christopher, Doris K. *consumer products company executive*
Rose, Gail Elaine *wholesale trade company manager*

Algonquin
Lange-Connelly, Phyllis *musician, music educator*

Alton
Bazile, Anita Michele *psychologist, educator*
Davis, Anne Louise *music educator*

Arcola
Eskridge, Judith Ann *secondary school educator*

Argonne
Jonkouski, Jill Ellen *materials scientist, ceramic engineer, educator*

Arlington Heights
Falkenberg, Mary Ann Theresa *realtor*
Fields, Sara A. *travel company executive*
Griffin, Jean Latz *political strategist, writer*
Lewin, Pearl Goldman *psychologist*
Mulder, Arlene JoAnn *mayor*
Pasieka, Anne W. *elementary school educator*
Smith, Wendy L. *foundation executive*
Telleen, Judy *counselor*

Aurora
Belcher, La Jeune *automotive executive*
Cisar, Margaret *special education educator*
Cooper, Annette Lyn *music educator*
Daugherty, Patricia Ann *elementary school educator*
Dillitzer, Dianne René *sales executive*
Halfvarson, Lucille Robertson *music educator*
McCarthy, Mary Elizabeth (Beth) Constance *conductor, educator, music educator*
Sotir, Judith Sophia *educational technology consultant, researcher*

Bannockburn
Daube, Lorrie O. *sales executive*

Barrington
Fowler, Susan Michele *real estate broker, entrepreneur*
Kellogg, Joan Barrett *grief therapist, counseling astrologer, educator, author*
Lee, Catherine M. *business owner, educator*
Roland, Regina E. *elementary school educator*
Sturm, Sherri Charisse *marketing and developmental researcher, actuary*
Taylor, Jacqueline Ann *systems administrator*
Wood, Andrée Robitaille *archaeologist, researcher*

Bartlett
Markle, Sandra *publishing company executive*

Bartonville
Dina, Gwendolyn Judith *special education educator*

Batavia
Abuhl, Jeanne Marie *sales professional*
Flannigan, Sandra F. *secondary school educator*
Waranius Vass, Rosalie Jean *artist*

Beardstown
Vermillion, Julia Kathleen *music educator*

Belleville
Lane-Trent, Patricia Jean *information specialist*
Megahy, Diane Alaire *physician*
Setterlund, Tina A.M. *music educator*
Thien-Stasko, Vicki Lynn *civil engineer technician*

Bellwood
Miller, Denyce Karlina *tax specialist*
Szilagyi-Hawkins, Elizabeth Maria *social services administrator*

Bensenville
Mueller, Paula Deutsch *music educator*

Berwyn
Karasek, Mary Hapac *city treasurer, community volunteer*

Bethalto
Sabaj, Nancy J. *secondary school educator*

Talbott, Janet K. *information technology executive*

Bloomington
Axley, Dixie L. *insurance company executive*
Beeler, Charlotte Jean *oil and supply company executive, interior design business executive*
Daily, Jean A. *marketing executive*
Friedman, Joan M. *accounting educator*
Key, Otta Bischof *retired educator*
Olson, Rue Eileen *retired librarian*
Stump, Lisa Dian *marketing professional, music educator*
Sullivan, Laura Patricia *lawyer, insurance company executive*

Blue Island
Skinner, Tillian Esther *daycare administrator*

Bolingbrook
Day, Mary Ann *medical/surgical nurse*
Madori, Jan *art gallery director*
Price, Theodora Hadzisteliou *individual, child and family therapist*

Bourbonnais
Wilkey, Elmira Smith *illustrator, artist, publisher, writer, educator*

Bradley
Brown, Lana Weiss *public relations executive*

Broadview
Gockley, Barbara Jean *manufacturing executive*
Lazar, Jill Sue *home healthcare company executive*

Brookfield
Dearhammer, Nancy Ellen *educational consultant*

Buffalo Grove
Freemond-Woods, Reneé *secondary school educator*
McConville, Rita Jean *finance executive*
Serbus, Pearl Sarah Dieck *freelance writer, former editor*

Burbank
Juodvalkis, Egle (Eglé Juodvalké) *writer*

Burr Ridge
Jones, Shirley Joyce *small business owner, fashion designer*
Zaccone, Suzanne Maria *sales executive*

Caledonia
Hubbard, Marguerite *elementary school educator*

Calumet City
Fantin, Arline Marie *state legislator*
Scullion, Annette Murphy *lawyer, educator*

Canton
Hines, Daisy Marie *freelance/self-employed writer*

Carbondale
Abakoui, Roki Ann *psychologist, consultant*
Bauner, Ruth Elizabeth *library administrator, reference librarian*
Covington, Patricia Ann *university administrator*
Kawewe, Saliwe Moyo *social work educator, researcher*
Koch, Loretta Peterson *librarian, educator*
Matthews, Elizabeth Woodfin *law librarian*
Quisenberry, Nancy Lou *university administrator, educator*
Renzaglia, Karen A. *biologist, educator*
Snyder, Carolyn Ann *education educator, librarian*

Carlinville
Bellm, Joan *civic worker*
Pride, Miriam R. *college president*

Carol Stream
Franzen, Janice Marguerite Gosnell *magazine editor*
O'Dell, Lynn Marie Luegge (Mrs. Norman D. O'Dell) *librarian*

Carterville
Crews, Denise M. *educational association administrator*

Caseyville
Dayton, Jean *elementary school principal*
Stanford, Diana L. *librarian*

Catlin
Asaad, Kolleen Joyce *special education educator*

Centralia
Davidson, Karen Sue *computer software designer*
Whitten, Mary Lou *nursing educator*

Champaign
Anthony, Kathryn Harriet *architecture educator*
Bednar, Susan Gail *social worker, consultant*
Blanchard, Rosemary Ann *university program administrator, consultant, educator*
Cantor, Nancy *academic administrator*
Dulany, Elizabeth Gjelsness *university press administrator*
Gomez, Terrine *school director*
Harris, Zelema M. *academic administrator*
Hurd, Heidi M. *law educator, humanities educator, dean*
Killeen, Albertina Ellen *retail executive, consultant, personnel advisor*
Koenker, Diane P. *history educator*
Kummer, Karen Lang *historian, consultant, architecture educator*
Loeb, Jane Rupley *academic administrator, educator*

McCulloh, Judith Marie *editor*
Osborne, Margery Diane *education educator*
Rosenblatt, Karin Ann *cancer epidemiologist*
Thomas, Jo *journalist*
Turquette, Frances Bond *editor*

Charleston
Ball-Saret, Jayne Adams *small business owner*
Cooper, Carolyn Sue *translator, educator*
Surles, Carol D. *academic administrator*

Chicago
Acker, Ann *lawyer*
Adelman, Susan Hershberg *surgeon*
Ahern, Mary Ann *reporter*
Akers, Michelle Anne *professional soccer player*
Akins, Cindy S. *human resources professional*
Allen, Belle *management consulting firm executive, communications executive*
Allen, Danielle *political scientist, educator*
Allen, Julie O'Donnell *lawyer*
Altman, Edith G. *sculptor*
Amato, Isabella Antonia *real estate executive*
Andreoli, Kathleen Gainor *nurse, educator, dean*
Anthony-Perez, Bobbie Cotton Murphy *psychology educator, researcher*
Apelbaum, Phyllis L. *delivery messenger service executive*
Appel, Nina Schick *law educator, dean, academic administrator*
Apple, Kathy *medical association administrator*
Aronson, Virginia L. L. *lawyer*
Aubin, Barbara Jean *artist*
Baca, Stacey *newscaster*
Badel, Julie *lawyer*
Bae, Sue Hyun *psychologist, educator*
Baker, Pamela *lawyer*
Barbour, Claude Marie *minister, educator*
Barker, Barbara *real estate professional*
Barnes, Brenda C. *food and apparel executive*
Barney, Carol Ross *architect*
Barr, Emily L. *television station executive*
Bart, Susan T. *lawyer*
Baumgardt, Justi Michelle *professional soccer player*
Bean, Rosie M. *volunteer*
Beane, Marjorie Noterman *academic administrator*
Beaudet-Francès, Patricia Suzanne *photography editor*
Becker, Geraldine Ann *psychology educator*
Bellantoni, Maureen Blanchfield *manufacturing and retail executive*
Benedict, Kennette Mari *foundation executive, researcher*
Benson, Sara Elizabeth *real estate broker, real estate appraiser*
Bergstrom, Betty Howard *consulting executive, foundation administrator*
Berkson, Sadie *volunteer*
Berman, Cheryl R. *advertising company executive*
Bernstein, Gerda Meyer *artist*
Berryman, Diana (Kapnas) *radio personality*
Bertagnolli, Leslie A. *lawyer*
Beugen, Joan Beth *communications company executive*
Bienias, Julia Louise *medical researcher, statistician*
Birchett, Colleen Lucille *editor*
Bodi, Sonia Ellen *library director, educator*
Boggs, Catherine J. *lawyer*
Boggs, Jessica Lynn *creative director, web designer*
Bomchill, Fern Cheryl *lawyer*
Boncher, Mary *talent agent*
Bourdon, Cathleen Jane *professional society administrator*
Bowman, Barbara Taylor *early childhood educator*
Bowman, Leah *fashion designer, consultant, photographer, educator*
Boyda, Debora *advertising executive*
Bradley, Vanessa Lynn *management consultant*
Bratcher, Juanita *journalist*
Bregoli-Russo, Mauda Rita *language educator, educator*
Bristo, Marca *human services administrator*
Bro, Ruth Hill *lawyer*
Brock, Kathy *newscaster*
Brogan, Lisa S. *lawyer*
Brooks, Marion *newscaster*
Brotman, Barbara Louise *columnist, writer*
Brown, Rosellen *writer*
Bryant, Esther *investment manager, retired correspondent*
Bucklo, Elaine Edwards *United States district court judge*
Burke, Michelle C. *lawyer*
Burke, Nancy *psychologist, educator*
Burns, Diann *newscaster*
Burton, Cheryl *newscaster*
Busey, Roxane C. *lawyer*
Cafferty, Pastora San Juan *public policy educator*
Callaway, Karen A(lice) *journalist*
Campos-Pons, Maria Magdalena *artist*
Carney, Jean Kathryn *psychologist*
Carr, Anne Elizabeth *theology educator*
Case, Donni Marie *investment company executive*
Casillas, Ofelia Marie *journalist*
Castorino, Sue *communications executive*
Chandler, Estelle T. *artist*
Childers, Mary Ann *newscaster*
Choldin, Marianna Tax *librarian, educator*
Christoffel, Katherine Kaufer *pediatrician, epidemiologist, educator*
Clevenger, Penelope *international business consultant*
Coffey, Susanna Jean *art educator*
Cohen, Melanie Rovner *lawyer*
Colley, Karen J. *medical educator, medical researcher*
Colom, Vilma *alderman*
Conlon, Suzanne B. *federal judge*
Connors, Dorsey *television and radio commentator, newspaper columnist*

Cooper, Ilene Linda *magazine editor, author*
Cooper, Jo Marie *elementary school principal*
Cox, Julia Diamond *lawyer*
Cox-Hayley, Deon Melayne *geriatrics services professional*
Crane, Barbara Bachmann *photographer, educator*
Crane, Charlotte *law educator*
Crawford, Jean Andre *clinical therapist*
Cremin, Susan Elizabeth *lawyer*
Crenshaw, Carol *charitable organization administrator*
Cromwell, Amanda Caryl *former soccer player, coach*
Cross, Dolores Evelyn *former university administrator, educator*
Culp, Kristine Ann *dean, theology educator*
Culverwell, Rosemary Jean *principal, elementary education educator*
Cummings, Andrea J. *lawyer*
Cummings, Maxine Gibson *elementary school educator*
Curran, Barbara Adell *retired law foundation administrator, lawyer, writer*
Daley, Susan Jean *lawyer*
Daniel, Elnora D. *academic administrator*
Danis, Julie Marie *writer, advertising executive*
Davis, Mary Ellen K. *library director*
De, Devasmita *research aquarist*
deChaud, Christina Rita *marketing specialist, consultant*
de Hoyos, Debora M. *lawyer*
Deli, Anne Tynion *marketing executive*
Dempsey, Mary A. *library commissioner, lawyer*
Desombre, Nancy Cox *academic administrator, consultant*
DeVault, Kathy *psychiatric consultant, liaison nurse*
Diamond, Shari Seidman *law educator, psychology educator*
Dickstein, Beth J. *lawyer, accountant*
Diederichs, Janet Wood *public relations executive*
Doering, Deborah Adams *artist, educator*
Doetsch, Virginia Lamb *former advertising executive, writer*
Doherty, Sister Barbara *religious institution administrator*
Doniger, Wendy *history of religions educator*
Donovan, Dianne Francys *journalist*
Dooley, Sharon L. *obstetrician, gynecologist*
Douglas, Cynthia *executive administrative assistant*
Dowling, Doris Anderson *business owner, educator, consultant*
Drake, Robyn Renée (Robyn Fielder) *writer, painter, equestrian*
Drantz, Veronica Ellen *science educator and consultant*
Drewry, June E. *information technology executive*
Dry, Judith Kallen *dental hygienist, cable producer, writer*
Ducar, Tracy *former soccer player*
Dunlop, Karen Owen *lawyer*
Dutta, Mitra *physicist, educator*
Easley, Cheryl Eileen *nursing educator, department chairman*
Eastabrook, Dianne *news correspondent*
Easton, Lory Barsdate Barsdate *lawyer*
Eaton, Maja Campbell *lawyer*
Edelstein, Teri J. *art history educator, art administrator, small business owner*
Einoder, Camille Elizabeth *retired secondary school educator*
Elshtain, Jean Bethke *social and political ethics educator*
Eubanks-Pope, Sharon G. *real estate company executive, entrepreneur*
Evans, Mariwyn *periodical editor*
Evans, Thelma Jean Mathis *internist*
Fahnestock, Jean Howe *retired civil engineer*
Farbman, Ruth Ellen *lawyer*
Fawcett, Joy Lynn *professional soccer player*
Feigenholtz, Sara *state legislator*
Felton, Cynthia *educational administrator*
Ferguson, Diana S. *food products executive*
Ferguson, Margaret Geneva *writer, publisher, real estate broker*
Ferguson, Renee *news correspondent, reporter*
Field, Karen Ann (Karen Ann Schaffner) *real estate broker*
Flaherty, Emalee Gottbrath *pediatrician*
Flanagan, Sylvia *editor*
Foster, Teree E. *law educator, department chairman, dean*
Fotopoulos, Danielle *former soccer player*
Foudy, Julia Maurine *professional soccer player*
Fox, Elaine Saphier *lawyer*
Fox, Leslie B. *real estate company executive*
Franklin, Veronica Rena *psychotherapist*
Frederiksen, Marilynn C. *physician*
Freeman, Susan Tax *anthropologist, educator, culinary historian*
Freidheim, Ladonna *dance company director*
Friedlander, Patricia Ann *marketing professional, writer*
Friedli, Helen Russell *lawyer*
Friedman, Roselyn L. *lawyer, mediator*
Fritsch-Stewart, Antoinette M. *education educator*
Froetscher, Janet *social services administrator*
Fuchs, Elaine V. *molecular biologist, educator*
Funk, Carla Jean *library association executive*
Furth, Yvonne *advertising executive*
Gabarra, Carin Leslie *professional soccer player, professional soccer coach*
Gaines, Barbara *theater director*
Gaines, Brenda *financial services company executive*
Gaines-Masak, Anne Farley *artist, art educator*
Gajic, Ranka Pejovic *secondary school educator*
Gall, Betty Bluebaum *office services company executive*
Gand, Gayle *chef*
Gannon, Sister Ann Ida *retired philosophy educator, former college administrator*

Wagner, Alyson Kay (Aly Wagner) *professional soccer player*
Waintroob, Andrea Ruth *lawyer*
Walker, Juliet *alcohol/drug abuse services professional, educator*
Watson, Easter Jean *psychotherapist, financial program consultant*
Watson, MaryFrances Elizabeth *management consultant, librarian*
Waxler, Beverly Jean *anesthesiologist, physician*
Weaver, Donna Rae *wine company executive*
Weber, Susan A. *lawyer*
Weinberg, Lila Shaffer *writer, editor*
Weisberg, Lois *arts administrator, city official*
Weissman, Sharon Theresa *speech language pathologist*
Whalen, Sarah Eve *professional soccer player*
Wiecek, Barbara Harriet *advertising executive*
Wier, Patricia Ann *publishing executive, consultant*
Wildeisen, Rebecca Alyssa *psychologist, educator*
Wille, Lois Jean *retired newspaper editor*
Williams, Ann Claire *federal judge*
Williams, Elynor A. *public affairs specialist*
Williams, Martha *consumer products company executive, entrepreneur*
Williamson, Donna C. E. *investment company executive*
Willis, Anna L. *commissioner*
Wilson, Anne Gawthrop *artist, educator*
Wilson, Cleo Francine *entertainment company executive*
Wine-Banks, Jill Susan *lawyer*
Winfrey, Oprah *television talk show host, actress, producer*
Winker, Margaret A. *editor*
Winnecke, Joycelyn *editor*
Winter, Jane *medical educator*
Wolf, Linda S. *advertising executive*
Wolfe, Sheila A. *journalist*
Woods, Nikki *radio personality*
Wooldridge, Patrice Marie *marketing professional, martial arts and meditation educator*
Wright, Helen Kennedy *retired professional association administrator, publisher, editor, librarian*
Wright, Judith Margaret
Wright, Sharon *reporter*
Wyndewicke, Kionne Annette (Annette Johnson Moorer) *reading educator*
Young, Lauren Sue Jones *education educator*
Yu, Linda *newswoman, television anchorwoman*
Zee, Phyllis C. *physician, educator, researcher*
Zekman, Pamela Lois (Mrs. Fredric Soll) *reporter*
Zemm, Sandra Phyllis *lawyer*
Zhao, Jia *lawyer*
Ziegler, Ann E. *retail executive*
Zopp, Andrea Lynne *lawyer*

Chicago Heights
Pryga, Suzanne Marie *gender equity consultant, sociology educator, academic administrator*

Clinton
Ellerman, Linda Ann *music educator*

Coal City
Major, Mary Jo *dance school artistic director*
O'Brien, Mary Kathleen *state representative, lawyer*

Country Club Hills
McClelland, Helen *music educator*

Crestwood
Bonnes, Karen L. *clinical social worker*

Crystal Lake
Fleming, Marjorie Foster *freelance writer, artist*
Linklater, Isabelle Stanislawa Yarosh-Galazka (Lee Linklater) *foundation administrator*
Reed, Helen G. *poet*
Salvesen, B. Forbes *artist*
Thoms, Jeannine Aumond *lawyer*

Danville
Garman, Rita B. *judge*

Decatur
Brown, Lenore Francine *music educator*
Ewers, Marla Rouse *voice educator*
Litchfield, Jean Anne *nurse*
Loebl, Maragaret Margo *corporate financial executive*
Madding, Claudia *agricultural products executive*

Deerfield
Cabay, Gina Grace Angela *lawyer*
Dawson, Suzanne Stockus *lawyer*
Halpin, Mary Elizabeth *psychologist*
Huff, Gayle Compton *advertising and marketing executive*

Dekalb
Crosser, Carmen Lynn *marriage and family therapist, social worker, consultant*
Folgate, Cynthia A. *social services administrator*
Frank-Stromborg, Marilyn Laura *nursing educator*
Gómez-Vega, Ibis *humanities educator*
McSpadden, Lettie *political science educator*
Rollman, Charlotte *artist, educator*
Schmidt, Jennifer Anne *education educator*
Sons, Linda Ruth *mathematician, educator*
Stewart, Mary R *education educator, artist*
Vary, Patricia Susan *biologist, educator, retired geneticist*
Weisenthal, Rebecca G. *clinical psychologist*

Des Plaines
Clapper, Marie Anne *magazine publisher*
Drake, Ann M. *consumer products company executive*

Dvorak, Kathleen S. *business products company executive*
Giles, Phyllis Lenore Williams *retired elementary school educator*
Henrikson, Lois Elizabeth *photojournalist*
Lee, Margaret Burke *college president, English educator*
Le Menager, Lois M. *incentive merchandise and travel company executive*
Levitin, Valeria Oskar *family physician*
Meyer, Susan M. *lawyer*
O'Dwyer, Mary Ann *automotive executive*

Dixon
Hansen, Linda Marie *small business owner*
Huber, Marianne Jeanne *art dealer, appraiser*
Polascik, Mary Ann *ophthalmologist*

Downers Grove
Nichols, Karen *academic administrator*
Ozog, Diane L. *allergist*
Saricks, Joyce Goering *librarian*
Schnell, Patricia Lenore *military officer*
Stevenson, Judy G. *instrument manufacturing executive*

Dundee
Weck, Kristin Willa *bank executive*

East Alton
Abert, Amber Christine *home remodeling contractor*

East Dundee
Simons, Gail S. *artist, educator, librarian*

East Saint Louis
Dunham, Katherine *choreographer, anthropologist, dancer*
Roy, Darlene *human services administrator*
Wright, Katie Harper *educational administrator, journalist*

Edwardsville
Anderson, Mary Jane *music educator*
Dietrich, Suzanne Claire *instructional designer, communications consultant*

El Paso
Musick, Marilyn Irene *secondary school educator*
Prairie-Steber, Cheryl Lee *art educator, graphics designer*

Elgin
Aydt, Mary I. *secondary school educator*
Barnett, Sue *nurse*
Bowen, Jean Ann *school system administrator*
Colpitts, Gail Elizabeth *artist, educator*
Dodohara, Jean Noton *music educator*
Kalsow-Bernhard, Kathryn Marie *choir director*
O'Connor, Peggy Lee *communications manager*
Reimer, Judy Mills *pastor, religious executive*
Thompson, Phyllis Darlene *retired elementary school educator*

Elk Grove Village
Finney, Ann Jung *bank executive*
Herrerias, Carla Trevette *epidemiologist, health policy analyst*
Jan, Chwu-Ching Hwang *environmental chemistry consultant*

Elmhurst
Blain, Charlotte Marie *internist, educator*
Choyke, Phyllis May Ford (Mrs. Arthur Davis Choyke Jr.) *management executive, editor, poet*
Duarte, Gloria *chef*
Malo, Michele Lee *marketing professional*
Nega, Nancy Kawecki *middle school science educator*
Pruter, Margaret Franson *editor*
Seabright, Frances *volunteer*

Elmwood Park
Hofmann, Kay Joyce *sculptor, artist*

Erie
Latham, LaVonne Marlys *physical education educator*

Eureka
West, Nancy Lee *music educator, performance artist, entertainer*

Evanston
Agrawal, Amita *management consultant*
Beck, Eva-Carol *musician*
Bellow, Alexandra *mathematician, educator*
Bjorncrantz, Leslie Benton *librarian*
Blair, Virginia Ann *public relations executive*
Buchbinder, Barbara Joyce *art and architectural historian*
Cates, Jo Ann *library administrator, writer*
Crawford, Susan *library director, educator, writer*
Downing, Joan Forman *editor, writer*
Eberley, Helen-Kay *opera singer, classical record company executive, poet*
Enroth-Cugell, Christina Alma Elisabeth *neurophysiologist, educator*
Galvin, Kathleen Malone *communications educator*
Gordon, Julie Peyton *foundation administrator*
Komp, Barbara Ann *writer*
Langsley, Pauline Royal *psychiatrist*
Marian, Viorica *psychologist, educator*
McCoy, Marilyn *university official*
McCurry, Stephanie *historian, educator*
McDonough, Bridget Ann *music theatre company director*
Mineka, Susan *psychology educator*
Nueske-Perez, Barbara Allen *art educator*
Peltier, Janis Janosek *real estate agent, astrologer*
Persons, Fern *actor*

Pinsky, Joanna K. *artist, artistic director*
Power, Peggy Ann *elementary school educator*
Powers, Marian *accounting educator*
Quinn, Elizabeth Marie *performing arts educator*
Rago-McNamara, Juliet Maggio *artist*
Reiss, Lenore Ann *language educator, retired secondary school educator*
Rosenzweig, Amy *biochemist, educator*
Schwartz, Neena Betty *endocrinologist, educator*
Shanas, Ethel *sociology educator*
Taraki, Shirlee *librarian*
Thrash, Patricia Ann *educational association administrator*
Tolf, Gale Maureen *artist, educator*
Weertman, Julia Randall *materials science and engineering educator*
Willoughby, Judith Anne *conductor, music educator*
Zimmerman, Mary Alice *performing arts educator*

Evergreen Park
Michalak, Melanie S. *music educator*

Fairfield
Thomason, Nola Faye *critical care-emergency supervisor*

Forreston
Hall, Carol Beth *elementary school educator*

Frankfort
Chapel, Tennille Maria *speech pathology/audiology services professional*
Flanagan, Aileen Mary *special education educator*
Lambert, Alysia Connell *music educator*

Galatia
Foster, Jan S. *special education educator*

Galena
Alexander, Barbara Leah Shapiro *clinical social worker*

Galesburg
Pierson, Karen Arlene *poet*
Simpson, Carol *elementary school educator*
Sunderland, Jacklyn Giles *former alumni affairs director*

Geneseo
Brown, Mabel Welton *lawyer*
Crisp, Sandra Sue *procurement analyst*

Geneva
Houska-Green, Kathleen Ann *marketing professional, public relations executive*
Stephens, Gay *human services executive*

Glen Carbon
Adkerson, Donya Lynn *clinical counselor*
Anderson, Nancy Keech *music educator*

Glen Ellyn
Conti, Lee Ann *lawyer*
Hoornbeek, Lynda Ruth Couch *librarian, educator*

Glencoe
Cole, Kathleen Ann *advertising agency executive, retired social worker*
Rosen, Deborah Nodler *poet, writer*
Siske, Regina *artist*
Warren, Elizabeth Curran *retired political science educator*

Glendale Heights
Cook, Doris Marie *retired accountant, educator*
Spearing, Karen Marie *physical education educator, coach*

Glenview
Casas, Laurie Ann *plastic surgeon*
Corley, Jenny Lynd Wertheim *elementary school educator*
Coulson, Elizabeth Anne *physical therapy educator, state representative*
Franklin, Lynne *business communications consultant, writer*
Gómez, Fabiola *marketing communications professional*
King, Billie Jean Moffitt *former professional tennis player*

Godfrey
Gallagher, Kathryn Kasich *elementary school educator*

Granite City
Garber, Katherine *special education educator*

Grayslake
Choice, Priscilla Kathryn Means (Penny Choice) *educational director, international consultant*
Craven, Deborah *performing arts educator*
Krakora-Looby, Janice Marie *pediatrician*

Green Valley
Gerrietts, Vivian Jane *music educator*

Greenfield
Weller, Robin Lea *elementary school educator, secondary school educator*

Gurnee
Halsne-Baarda, Alana Michelle *secondary school educator*
Ullrich, Linda J. *medical technologist*

Hanover Park
Carter, Eleanor Elizabeth *business manager*
Renner, Jacqueline Marie *research and development company executive*

Herscher
Cessna, Katrina J. *music educator, composer*

Hickory Hills
Schultz, Barbara Marie *investment advisor representative*

Highland Park
Axelrod, Leah Joy *tour company executive*
Burman, Diane Berger *career management and organization development consultant*
Gash, Lauren Beth *lawyer, state legislator*
Greenblatt, Miriam *writer, editor, educator*
Leavitt, Sandra B. *editor*
Marder, Nancy Grace *foundation executive*
Papich, Mary Jo *secondary school educator, department chairman*
Schindel, Alice *social worker*
Slavick, Ann Lillian *retired art educator*
Stein, Paula Jean Anne Barton *hotel real estate executive, broker*
Zywicki, Cindy Mary *nurse*

Hillside
Abraham, Noël Jeanette *social worker*

Hines
Cummings, Joan E. *health facility administrator, educator*

Hinsdale
Amsler, Jana *chef*
Bazik, Edna Frances *mathematician, educator*
Szeremeta-Browar, Taisa Lydia *endodontist*

Hoffman Estates
Baier, Lucinda *corporate financial executive*
Hardin, Bianka Nicole *psychologist, educator*
Meads, Mindy *merchandising and design executive*
Purves, Karen E. *freelance/self-employed small business owner*

Homewood
Jarvis, Debra Jean *fire chief, consultant*

Hoopeston
Hicks, Carol Ann *small business owner, educator*

Hudson
Mills, Lois Jean *design company executive, retired education educator, aide*

Huntley
Plunkett, Melba Kathleen *manufacturing executive*

Itasca
Constant, Anita Aurelia *publisher*

Jacksonville
Johns, Beverley Anne Holden *special education administrator*
Moe-Fishback, Barbara Ann *counseling administrator*
Welch, Rhea Jo *special education educator*

Joliet
Bartow, Barbara Jené *university program administrator*
Crosby, Janet Marie *gifted and talented educator, writer*
Ethridge, Veree Kepley *economist, educator*
Hill, Kathleen Joy *administrative assistant*
Hooper, Denise Lynn *technologist*
Lynch, Priscilla A. *nursing educator, therapist*
Norris, Jean Marie *director*
Stahl, Arleen Marie *nursing educator*
Starner, Barbara Kazmark *marketing, advertising and export sales executive*

Kankakee
Thomas, Tammy Louise *medical/surgical nurse, writer*

Kenilworth
Clary, Rosalie Brandon Stanton *timber farm executive, civic worker*
Florian, Marianna Bolognesi *civic leader*

Kewanee
Grant, Linda Kay (Linda Kay Scott) *small business owner, sales executive*

La Grange
Kensek, Magdalene Agnes *private school educator*
Mahoney, Donna Marie *psychotherapist*
Vernerder, Gloria Jean *retired librarian*

La Grange Park
Alonzo, Loretta J. *real estate broker*
Brown, Helen Sauer *fund raising executive*
Butler, Margaret Kampschaefer *retired computer scientist*
Webster, Lois Shand *association executive*

La Moille
Carius, Christina Marie *music educator, horse trainer*

LaGrange
Lubenkov, Terry Anne *broker, realtor*

Lake Bluff
Scott, Karen Bondurant *consumer catalog company executive*

Lake Forest
Bradley, Kim Alexandra *sales and marketing specialist*
Chieger, Kathryn Jean *recreation company executive*
Frederick, Virginia Fiester *state legislator*
Goldstein, Marsha Feder *tour company executive*
Palmer, Ann Therese Darin *lawyer*
Rand, Kathy Sue *public relations executive*
Reich, Victoria J. *consumer products company executive*
Stirling, Ellen Adair *retail executive*

Swanton, Virginia Lee *writer, publishing executive*
Szaksztylo, Kathee *design technologist*
Taylor, Barbara Ann Olin *writer, educational consultant*
Van Ella, Kathleen E. *fine art consultant*
Weston, Dawn Thompson *artist, researcher*

Lake Villa
Johnson, Samira El-Chehabi *marketing professional*

Lake Zurich
Schwarz, Cheryl Marita *special education educator*

Lanark
Ling, Kathryn Wrolstad *health association administrator, minister*

Lansing
Kaplan, Huette Myra *business educator, training consultant*

Lebanon
Norris, Sandra Love *occupational therapist*

Libertyville
Conklin, Mara Loraine *public relations executive*
Devine, Barbara Armstrong *risk manager*
Gertz, Suzanne C. *artist*
Pollina, Kristen Mittl *child and adolescent psychologist*

Lincolnwood
Grossinger, Caroline *sales executive*

Lisle
Cordoba Tait, Alicia Rose *music educator*
Huffman, Louise Tolle *middle school educator*

Lombard
Kasprow, Barbara Anne *biomedical scientist, writer*

Loves Park
Schlub, Teresa Rae *minister*
Sylvester, Nancy Katherine *management consultant*

Machesney Park
Vaughn, Linda M *municipal official*

Macomb
Bailey, Martha Jane *science educator, research scientist*
Leonard, Virginia Waugh *history educator, writer, researcher*
Pawelko, Katharine Ann *recreation educator*

Madison
Purdes, Alice Marie *retired adult education educator*

Mahomet
Kennedy, Cheryl Lynn *museum director*
Thompson, Margaret M. *physical education educator*

Marion
Aikman, Elflora Anna *senior citizens center administrator*
Howell, Catherine Jeanine *retired secondary school educator*

Markham
Peacock, Marilyn Claire *primary education educator*

Maryville
Stark, Patricia Ann *psychologist*

Matteson
van der Hoek, Sherry A. *counselor*

Maywood
Albain, Kathy S. *oncologist*
Dado, Diane Valentina *plastic and reconstructive surgeon, pediatric plastic surgeon*
Ellington, Mildred L. *librarian*
Gaynor, Ellen Rose *hematologist*
Hindle, Paula Alice *nursing administrator*
Nand, Sucha *medical educator*

Mc Gaw Park
Risen-White, Angela Lorri *systems analyst*

Mchenry
Koehl, Camille Joan *accountant*

Melrose Park
Bernick, Carol Lavin *corporate executive*
Chaudhry, Marie-Laurence *elementary education educator, administrator*
Kipper, Barbara Levy *corporate executive*
Lavin, Bernice E. *cosmetics executive*
Wechter, Clari Ann *paint manufacturing company executive*

Milford
Beall, Pamela Honn *psychologist, consultant*
Coogan, Melinda Ann Strank *chemistry and biology educator*

Mokena
Pammer, Lesa Gail *marketing professional*

Moline
Curry, Kathleen Bridget *retired librarian*
Johnson, Mary Lou *lay worker, educator*
Kundert, Candice Jean *psychotherapist, social worker, educator*
Lash, Sharon C. *psychologist*
Mitchell, Lucille Anne *retired elementary school educator*
Morrison, Deborah Jean *lawyer*

Schauenberg, Susan Kay *retired counseling administrator*
Williamsen, Dannye Sue *personal development educator, health facility administrator*
Wright, Susie Flora *medical/surgical nurse*

Momence
Holland, Leslie Ann *special education educator*

Monmouth
Bruce, Mary Hanford *academic administrator, educator, writer*

Montgomery
Healy, Laura Marie *editor*

Morris
Janz, Gail Diane *media director*

Morton
Paxton, Kathleen Marie *special education educator*

Morton Grove
Friedman, Marla Lee *marketing professional*
Hoffman, Joy Yu *harpist, pianist*
Johnson, Laura Stark *secondary school educator, administrator*
Kouba, Shari L. *retired federal official*
Smolyansky, Julie *consumer products company executive*

Mount Prospect
Bailey-Mershon, Glenda Mariah *historian, educator, retired writer*
Forman, Ann Lee *music educator*
Harmon Brown, Valarie Jean *hospital laboratory director, information systems executive*

Mount Vernon
Hall, Sharon Gay *retired language educator, artist*
Kendrick-Hopgood, Debra Jo *small business owner*

Mundelein
Greene, Stephanie Harrison *marketing executive*

Murphysboro
Barrette, Linda Jones *dean*
Berry, Alice Allen *retired music educator*
Young, Linda Diane *speech pathology/audiology services professional*

Naperville
Burken, Ruth Marie *utilities executive*
Cowlishaw, Mary Lou *government educator*
Harvard, Rita Grace *real estate agent, volunteer*
Martin, Molly Erdman *music educator*
Nicotra, Mary *healthcare consultant*
Pope, Kathleen Marie *library director*
Raccah, Dominique Marcelle *publisher*
Ruyle-Hullinger, Elizabeth Smith (Beth Ruyle) *consultant, municipal financial advisor*
Sherren, Anne Terry *chemistry educator*
Stephen, Doris Moyer *music educator*
Tan, Li-Su Lin *accountant, insurance executive, investment consultant*

New Berlin
Buffington, Rosemary *secondary school educator*

New Lenox
Fries, Rebecca Kay *director, special education educator*
Ryan, Pamela Jeanne *guidance director*

Normal
Davis, Janet R. Beach *science educator*
Deany, Donna Jean *radiology technologist*
Miller, Wilma Hildruth *education educator*
Mtegha, Dorothy Mercy *education educator*
O'Dell, Lisa A. *special education educator*
Wortham, Anne Estelle *education educator*

North Chicago
Loga, Sanda *physicist, researcher*
Sladek, Celia Davis *neuroscientist, educator*

Northbrook
Cakora-Netzky, Leslie Lynn *photographer*
Crockett, Joan M. *human resources executive*
Ehrenberg, Maureen *management consultant*
Fox, Betty *financial services executive*
Goldsmith, Kimberlee Beth *special education educator*
Kahn, Sandra S. *psychotherapist*
Mandel, Karyl Lynn *accountant*
McGinn, Mary J. *lawyer, insurance company executive*
Mulhall, Kimberly A. *marketing professional*
Noeth, Carolyn Frances *speech and language pathologist*
Rosenberg, Auria Eleanor *elementary school educator*
Sudbrink, Jane Marie *sales and marketing executive*
Vasiljevic, Elizabeth Agnes *music educator, secondary school educator*
Wilson, Rita P. *insurance company executive*

Northfield
Heise, Marilyn Beardsley *public relations company executive*
Holden, Betsy D. *food products company executive*
Parker, Kathleen Kappel *state legislator*
Schneider-Criezis, Susan Marie *architect*
Sneed, Paula Ann *food products executive*

O Fallon
Belt, Beth Marie *music educator*
Guciardo, Joan *family and consumer sciences educator*
Tiemann, Jeannine E. *music educator*

Oak Brook
Babrowski, Claire Harbeck *fast food chain executive*
Barnes, Karen Kay *lawyer*
Bennett, Margaret Airola *lawyer*
Bossmann, Laurie *controller, hardware company executive*
Bower, Barbara Jean *nurse, consultant*
Congalton, Susan Tichenor *lawyer*
Crump-Caine, Lynn *food service executive*
Fields, Janice L. *food service executive*
Harless, Katherine J. *telecommunications company executive*
Hassert, Elizabeth Anne *transportation sales executive*
Iles, Eileen Marie *bank executive*
Marcus, Carol A. *information technology manager*
Santona, Gloria *lawyer*
Schultz, Karen Rose *clinical social worker, author, publisher, speaker*
Sweeney, Patrice Ellen *health administration executive*

Oak Forest
Monaghan, M. Patricia *education educator, writer*

Oak Lawn
Laird, Jean Elouise Rydeski (Mrs. Jack E. Laird) *author, adult education educator*
Noonan, Melinda Dunham *nursing administrator*

Oak Park
Bedrossian, Ursula Kay Kennedy *editor*
Desai, Pankaja Mohan *epidemiologist*
Evert, Margaret Jane *principal*
Flynn Schneider, Dana *psychologist*
McMahon, Margot Ann *sculptor, art educator*
Pearson, Gayle Marlene *writer*
Rinnan, Barbara Guy *retired non-profit organization executive*
Saxton, Carolyn Virginia *fund raising executive*
Senese, Suzanne Marie *art educator, music educator, performance artist*
Venerable, Shirley Marie *gifted education educator*

Oakbrook Terrace
Caun, Marilynn Jean *technological institute official, lawyer*
Hegenderfer, Jonita Susan *public relations executive*
Hiitola, Bethany *writer, consultant*
Moreno, Judith Wilson *psychotherapist, consultant*

Orion
Magee, Elizabeth Sherrard *civic organization volunteer*

Orland Park
Burfeind, Betty Ruth *science educator*

Oswego
Orland, Rachel Jane *elementary school educator, musician*

Ottawa
Hiltabrand, Linda Mae *state official*

Palatine
Bender, Virginia Best *computer scientist, educator*
Bontempo, Elaine *language educator*
Czerwinski, Rene D. *counselor*
Hull, Elizabeth Anne *retired English language educator*
Keres, Karen Lynne *English language educator*
von Keudell, Renate *language educator*

Palos Heights
Powell, Patricia Lynn *education educator, educator, special education educator, educator*

Palos Hills
McInerney, Noreen Linda *lawyer*
Porter, Joyce Klowden *theatre educator and director*
Schonauer, Kathleen G. *jewelry designer, small business owner*
Stratton, Pauline A. *former elementary education educator, alderman*
Zickus, Anne *state legislator*

Pana
Waddington, Irma Joann *music educator*

Paris
Essinger, Susan Jane *special education educator*

Park Forest
Billig, Etel Jewel *theater director, actor*
Bricker, Joyce Lynn *art educator*
Cribbs, Maureen Ann *artist, educator*

Park Ridge
Albert, Elizabeth Franz (Mrs. Henry B. Albert) *investor, artist, conservationist*
Bateman, Andrea R. *insurance agent*
Campbell, Dorothy May *management consultant*
Naker, Mary Leslie *legal firm executive*

Paw Paw
Heim, Alberta Jane *publishing executive, writer*

Payson
Tenhouse, Gayle Denise *secondary school educator*

Pekin
Herbstreith, Yvonne Mae *primary education educator*

Peoria
Behrll, Cathy G. *special education educator*
Jibben, Laura Ann *state agency administrator*

McCollum, Jean Hubble *medical assistant*
Murphy, Sharon Margaret *social studies educator*
Price Boday, Mary Kathryn *choreographer, small business owner, educator*
Salazar, Shirley Ann *music educator*

Peoria Heights
Taylor, Kathy Deanne *marketing executive, consultant*

Plainfield
Alander, Virginia Nickerson *retired student assistance coordinator*
Bennett-Hammerberg, Janie Marie *small business owner, writer, consultant, administrative assistant*
Stewart Nelson, Pamela *home health administrator, consultant*

Pleasant Plains
Thomas, Evelyn B. *agricultural products supplier*

Port Byron
Dennis-McDonnell, Lynn Marie *environmetal health practitioner, biologist*

Prospect Heights
Hanagan, Audrey Jeanette *training services executive*

Quincy
Adams, Beejay (Meredith Elisabeth Jane Adams) *retired sales executive*
Bohn, Donna May *music educator*
Cornell, Helen W. *manufacturing company executive*
Flinspach, Ursula R. *pharmacy technician, mathematics educator*
Wemhoener, Dolores Lucille *cultural organization administrator, entertainer*

Rantoul
Holmes, Lois Rehder *composer, piano and voice educator*

Richmond
Lopat, Romalda Regina *publisher, editor*

Richton Park
Burt, Gwen Behrens *elementary school administrator*
Pierce, Mary E. *retired educator, public relations consultant*

Ringwood
Tomlinson, Ferol Martin *reading and learning center media specialist*

River Forest
Carroll, Donna M. *academic administrator*
Harvey, Lynne Cooper *broadcasting executive, civic worker*
Prendergast, Carole Lisak *musician, educator*
Sipe, Doris Elaine *college dean*

River Grove
Gardner, Sandi B. *biology educator*
Hillert, Gloria Bonnin *anatomist, educator*
Stanton, Kathryn *retail bookstores/educ products and services executive*

Riverside
Van Cura, Joyce Bennett *librarian*

Riverwoods
Del Tiempo, Sandra Kay *sales executive*

Robinson
Newlin, Yvonne Ann *adult education educator*

Rochester
Petterchak, Janice A. *researcher, writer*

Rock Falls
Crebo, Mary Elizabeth *state agency official, assessor*
Julifs, Sandra Jean *community action agency executive*

Rock Island
Welling, Mary Ann *secondary school educator*

Rockford
Anderson, Karen Mildred *music educator*
Felder, Sheila Kay *music educator*
Gregory, Dola Bell *bishop, customer service administrator*
Heath, Alice Fairchild *retired mental health services professional*
Hendershott Love, Arles June *television community relations director*
Heuer, Beth Lee *music educator, composer, arranger*
Kampfe, Doris Elaine *storyteller, folk artist, poet*
McClelland, Patricia G. *minister*
Morrissey, Mary F. (Fran) *human resource consulting company executive*
Walhout, Justine Simon *chemistry educator*

Rockton
Cunningham, Judy Evalyn *elementary school administrator, educator*

Rolling Meadows
Strongin, Bonnie Lynn *English language educator*

Romeoville
Lifka, Mary Lauranne *history educator*

Roscoe
DeHaven-Binger, Jeanine Kay *special education educator*
Sears, Donna Mae *designer, illustrator*

Rushville
Burton, Sheila Belle *music educator*

Saint Anne
Glenn, Ruth Esther Murphy *counseling psychologist*

Saint Charles
Abts, Gwyneth Hartmann *retired dietician*
Bull, Martha *artist, educator*
LaHood, Julie Ann *small business owner*
Malinowski, Maryellen *photographer, artist*
Osowiec, Darlene Ann *clinical psychologist, educator, consultant*
Sjogren, Jaime Lynn *dancer, choreographer*

Saint Francisville
Harezi, Ilonka Jo *medical technology research executive*

Schaumburg
Adrianopoli, Barbara Catherine *librarian*
Epstein, Barbara Myrna Robbin *language educator*
Kleppe, Joan Marie *entertainment executive*
Metty, Theresa M. *communications executive*
Morse, Gloria Jeanne *executive secretary*
Tompson, Marian Leonard *professional society administrator*
Warrior, Padmasree *communications executive*
Wernette, Karen Marie *veterinarian*
Wojcik, Kathleen Louise *state representative*

Scott Air Force Base
Noland, Linda M *music educator*

Serena
Thorsen, Christine Mae *music educator*

Shorewood
Copeland, Charlene Carole *lawyer*

Skokie
Breckel, Alvina Hefeli *librarian*
Guillermo, Linda Sue *clinical social worker*
Langguth, Margaret Witty *health facility administrator*
Siegal, Rita Goran *engineering company executive*
Sloan, Judi C. *former physical education educator*
Weiss, Marcia Ann *special education educator*
Whalen, Patricia Therese *marketing and public relations educator, consultant*
Wills, Patricia Mary *controller*
Yogev, Sara *psychologist*

Sleepy Hollow
Mallers, Linda Rae *music educator*

Smithfield
Corsaw, Ardith *geriatrics nurse, administrator*

Smithton
Hostetler, Elsie J. *musician, music educator*

South Beloit
Julian, Linda S. *music educator, director*

South Holland
Worden, Michele Marie *speech pathology/audiology services professional*

Spring Grove
York, Karen Kay *accountant, farmer*

Springfield
Bartolo, Donna Marie *nursing administrator*
Blackman, Jeanne A. *community program manager*
Bowles, Evelyn Margaret *state legislator*
Chapman, Delinda (Ann) *retired state official*
Collins, Annazette R. *state representative*
Collins, Jacqueline Y *state senator*
Crotty, M. Maggie *state senator*
Currie, Barbara Flynn *state legislator*
Davis, Monique D. (Deon Davis) *state legislator*
Deal, Karen Lynne *conductor*
Doyle, Rebecca Carlisle *state agency administrator*
Erwin, Judy *state legislator*
Flowers, Mary E. *state legislator*
Fuchs, Nora Kay *business manager*
Fullerton, Faye Ellen *academic administrator*
Garrett, Susan *state senator*
Geo-Karis, Adeline Jay *state legislator*
Giamanco, Scherrie V *bank executive*
Hamos, Julie E. *state representative*
Harmon, Carolyn *adult education educator*
Hasara, Karen A. *mayor*
Howard, Constance A. *state representative*
Hundley, Elaine E. *retired nursing education administrator*
Jakobsson, Naomi D. *state representative*
Jones, Lovana S. *state legislator*
Jones, Shirley M. *state legislator*
Kaige, Alice Tubb *retired librarian*
Karpiel, Doris Catherine *state legislator*
Kelly, Robin L. *state representative*
Klingler, Gwendolyn Walbolt *state representative*
Kosel, Renée *state representative*
Krause, Carolyn H. *state legislator, lawyer*
Kuhn, Kathleen Jo *accountant*
Kurtz, Rosemary *state representative*
Lawrence, Katherine Michele *government affairs consultant*
Lightford, Kimberly A. *state legislator*
Lindley, Maralee Irwin *county official, consultant, speaker*
Martinez, Iris *state senator*
Mogerman, Susan *state agency administrator*
Moore, Andrea S. *state legislator*
Morford, Lynn Ellen *state official*
Mulligan, Rosemary Elizabeth *legislator*
Nekritz, Elaine *state representative*
Pihos, Sandra M *state representative*
Powell, Laura Elizabeth *music educator*
Radogno, Christine *state legislator*
Ramirez-Campbell, Christine M. *art council administrator*
Ronen, Carol *state legislator*
Schroeder, Joyce Katherine *state agency administrator, research analyst*
Slone, Ricca C *state representative*
Smith, Margaret *state legislator*
Steiner, Janet *educational association administrator*
Stevens, Barbara Helen *economist*
Woodson, Gayle Ellen *otolaryngologist*
Wynn, Nan L. *historic site administrator*
Yarbrough, Karen A. *state representative*

Sterling
Donahue, Shirley Ohnstad *elementary school educator*
Moran, Joan Jensen *physical education and health educator*

Swansea
Tessereau, Linda Ann *music educator*

Sycamore
Crain, Terri L. *music educator, director*
Vance Siebrasse, Kathy Ann *legislative staff member*

Table Grove
Thomson, Helen Louise *artist*

Tinley Park
Baker, Betty Louise *retired secondary school educator*
Good, Linda L. *music educator*
Nagle, Carol Ann *elementary school educator*

Tuscola
Henderson, E. Suzanne *elementary school educator*

Urbana
Baym, Nina *English educator*
Berenbaum, May Roberta *entomology educator*
Conlin, Kathleen F. *dean, theater director*
Dovring, Karin Elsa Ingeborg *writer, poet, playwright, media specialist*
Due, Jean Margaret *agricultural economist, educator*
Glick, Karen Lynne *college administrator*
Greene, Laura Helen *physicist*
Kieffer, Susan Werner *geologist, educator, media consultant*
Liebman, Judith Rae Stenzel *operations research educator*
Makri, Nancy *chemistry educator*
O'Brien, Nancy Patricia *librarian, educator*
Prussing, Laurel Lunt *public interest lobbyist, economist, auditor*
Spence, Mary Lee *historian, educator*
Tripp, April *special education services professional*
Warren, Pamela Allyson *psychologist*
Watson, Paula D. *library administrator*
Watts, Emily Stipes *English language educator*
Williams, Martha Ethelyn *information science educator*
Woodard, Beth Stuckey *librarian, educator*

Vandalia
Low, Louise O. *volunteer*

Varna
Knackstedt, Judy M. *secondary school educator*

Venice
Cunningham, Betty Jean De Bow *adult education educator*

Vernon Hills
Beckles, Ingrid *mortgage banker*
Klein, Barbara A. *information technology executive*
Leahy, Christine A. *information technology executive*
Ryg, Kathleen Schultz *municipal government official*

Villa Park
Hougen, Carlene Lenore *secondary school educator, department chairman*

Warrenville
Elder, Amy Hope *psychotherapist, counselor*

Wauconda
Gotthardt, Mary Jane *religious studies educator*

Waukegan
Drapalik, Betty R. *volunteer, artist, educator*

West Peoria
McBride, Sharon Louise *counselor, technical communication educator*

Westchester
Abbinante, Vita *sales executive, administrator*
Bauer, Beth E. *advocate, consultant*
Castellano, Christine Marie *lawyer*
Imran, Ayesha *internist*
Pavelka, Elaine Blanche *mathematics educator*
Webb, Emily *retired plant morphologist*

Western Springs
Hanson, Heidi Elizabeth *lawyer*
Tiefenthal, Marguerite Aurand *school social worker*
Zamora, Marjorie Dixon *retired political science educator*

Westmont
Babiak, Heather *nurse, food service executive*
Bellock, Patricia Rigney *state legislator*
Goring, Ruth Ann *editor, writer*
Harten, Ann M. *relocation services executive*
Hodgson, Barbara Caroline *music educator*
Nyien, Patricia *music educator*
Ryan, Joan *food company executive*
Tricase, Elizabeth *gymnast*

Wheaton
Harris, E(leanor) Lynn(e) *religious studies educator, literature educator, minister, writer*
Pape, Patricia Ann *social worker, consultant*
Tucker, Beverly Sowers *information specialist*

Wheeling
Long, Sarah Ann *librarian*

Willowbrook
Mathisen-Reid, Rhoda Sharon *international communications consultant*

Wilmette
Brindel, June Rachuy *writer*
Hass, Victoria Yusim *psychogeriatrics services professional, consultant*
McClure, Julie Anne *literature educator*
Merrier, Helen *actress, writer*
Shannon, Julie (Julie Geller) *musician, music educator, composer, lyricist*

Wilmington
Chappell, Elizabeth Irene *special education educator*

Winnetka
Huggins, Charlotte Susan Harrison *secondary school educator, author, travel specialist*
Krueger, Deborah A. Blake *school psychologist, consultant*
Peck, Annette Biemond *retired social worker, writer*

Wood Dale
Grady, Kimberly Ann *medical technician*

Woodstock
Levandowski, Barbara Sue *educational administrator*

Yorkville
McEachern, Joan *medical association administrator*

INDIANA

Anderson
Kratzner, Judith Evelyn *program manager*
Olson, Carol Lea *lithographer, educator*
Ritchey, Yvonne Kay *assistant principal*

Atwood
Creamer, Kathy Jayne *writer*

Auburn
Bash, Danielle Renee *quality control engineer*

Austin
Lacy, Dona Paulette *librarian, writer*

Beverly Shores
Collins, Moira Ann *graphics and communications company executive, calligrapher*

Bloomington
Adams, Karen Hoeve *university administrator*
Anderson, Judith Helena *English language educator*
Austin, Joan Kessner *mental health nurse*
Bair, Susanne Paulette *university foundation administrator*
Bartleson, Amy Aileen *psychotherapist*
Bornholdt, Laura Anna *university administrator*
Brehm, Sharon Stephens *psychology educator, university administrator*
Calinescu, Adriana Gabriela *museum curator, art historian*
Chafel, Judith Ann *education educator*
Collins, Dorothy Craig *retired educational administrator*
Collyer, Esther Ritz *volunteer, educator*
Ferguson, Sarah Ann *music educator*
Gealt, Adelheid Maria *museum director*
Gough, Pauline Bjerke *magazine editor*
Hutton, Deborah Spence *academic administrator*
Kane, Stephanie C. *social anthropologist, educator*
Ketterson, Ellen D. *biologist, educator*
Knudsen, Laura Georgia *linguist*
Mac Watters, Virginia Elizabeth *singer, music educator, actress*
Montgomery, Kathleen Rae *counselor*
Robel, Lauren *law educator*
Spiro, Rosann Lee *marketing professional, educator*
Srinivasan, Jayasree M. *research scientist*
Stines, Betty Irene *artist*
Svetlova, Marina *ballerina, choreographer, educator*
Wells, Kimberly K. *not-for-profit organization executive*
Williams, Camilla *soprano, voice educator*
York, Cynthia A. *retail executive*
York, Karen Sue *artist, art historian*

Blufton
Mayle, Amanda Lynn *psychologist*

Boonville
Sureck, Karen Eileen *special education educator*

Brazil
Jones, Carole Moody-Anderson *retired outreach representative*

Brownsburg
Voorhis, Lori Beth *respiratory therapist*

Burlington
Roussakis, Dorothy Ferguson *artist*

Cambridge City
Slonaker, Mary Joanna King *columnist*

Carmel
Ashcraft, Nancy Olson *mining engineer*
Brooks, Patricia Scott *principal*
Cuneo, Ngaire E. *corporate development executive*
Dean, Ann Marie Butz *secondary school educator*
Eden, Barbara Janiece *commercial and residential interior designer*
Husman, Catherine Bigot *retired insurance company executive, actuary*
Kellison, Donna Louise George *accountant, educator*
Mahoney, Margaret Ellis *accountant*
Stevens, Jocelyn Alexis *music educator*

Cedar Lake
Loudermilk, Mary Ruth *local government volunteer*

Centerville
Wendeln, Darlene Doris *English language educator*

Churubusco
Lough, Susan M. *music educator*

Clinton
Byers, Teresa Ann *music educator*

Cloverdale
Schwartz, Susan Lynn Hill *principal*

Columbus
Carter, Pamela Lynn *former state attorney general*
Engelking, Ellen Melinda *textiles executive, manufacturing executive, real estate broker*
Jorgensen, Virginia Dyer *antique dealer, museum consultant*
Shannon, Carolyn Jean *interior designer*

Corydon
Speth, Camille *engineer*

Crawfordsville
Barnes, Patience Plummer *writer, editor*
Everett, Cheryl Ann *music educator, pianist*
Karg, Thelma Aileen *writer, retired educator*

Crown Point
Akin, Donna Rae *retired elementary school educator*
Eisenhauer, Linda Ann *volunteer*

Danville
Baldwin, Patricia Ann *lawyer*

East Chicago
Fortenberry, Delores B. *dean*
Platis, Mary Lou *media specialist*
Psaltis, Helen *medical and surgical nurse*
Suhre, Edith Lavonne *adult education educator*

Elkhart
Burns, B(illye) Jane *museum director*
Eddy, Darlene Mathis *poet, educator*
Free, Helen Murray *chemist, consultant*
Mathias, Margaret Grossman *manufacturing company executive, leasing company executive*

Evansville
Baker, Ann Long *language educator*
Baker, Gloria Marie *visual artist, art educator*
Blesch, K(athy) Suzann *small business owner*
Clark, Shirley Suzanne *music educator*
Collins, Cindy Elaine *property manager*
Grabill, Virginia Lowell *retired English educator*
Hunt, Lucille(Luci) Edith *real estate agent, real estate broker*
Kinkade, Jill Annette *writer*
Overton, Sharon Faye *elementary school educator*
Roth, Carolyn Louise *art educator*
Tannenbaum, Karen Jean *library services supervisor*

Fort Wayne
Atzeff, Efrodita *fraternal organization administrator*
Brandt, Nancy G. *education educator*
Cast, Anita Hursh *small business owner*
Cummins, Kathleen K. *retired elementary school educator*
Cutshall-Hayes, Diane Marion *elementary school educator*
Gutreuter, Jill Stallings *financial consultant, financial planner*
Harwood, Virginia Ann *retired nursing educator*
Hernandez, Ann Margaret *education educator*
Jones, Louise Conley *drama and literature educator, academic administrator*
Kennedy, Elizabeth *health facility administrator*
Langhinrichs, Ruth Imler *playwright, writer*
Lord, Pamela *chemist, educator*
Neuman, Paula Anne Young *cultural organization administrator*
Oxley, Ann *television executive*
Ridderheim, Mary Margaret *psychotherapist*
Robinson, Wendy Y. *school system administrator*
Russell, Christine R. *music educator*
Sasko, Nancy Ann *insurance agent*
Scheetz, Sister Mary JoEllen *English language educator*
Stebbins, Vrina Grimes *retired elementary school educator, counselor*
Taritas, Karen Joyce *customer service administrator*
Ushenko, Audrey Andreyevna *painter, art historian, educator*
Walley, Pamela Kaye *elementary school educator*
Watkinson, Patricia Grieve *museum director*

Fortville
Demegret, A. Jean Hughes *secondary education educator, artist*

Frankfort
Borland, Kathryn Kilby *author*

Freetown
Frederick, Shelley Cannon *artist*

Gary
Hensley, Mary Kay *dietician*
Steele, Beverly J. *elementary school educator*
Steinberg, Marilyn Marie *psychotherapist*
Walker, Juanita Moffett *retired elementary school educator*
Zunich, Janice *pediatrician, geneticist, educator, health facility administrator*

Goshen
Deuschle, Constance Joan *counselor, educational consultant*
Loomis, Norma Irene *marriage and family therapist*
Nyce, Dorothy Yoder *writer, retired religious studies educator*
Showalter, Shirley H. *academic administrator*

Granger
Harmelink, Ruth Irene *marriage and family therapist, writer*
Thomas, Debi (Debra J. Thomas) *ice skater*
Yared, Linda S. *mechanical engineer*

Greenfield
Geesa, Susan Louise *special education educator*

Greenwood
Grube, Elizabeth *investment company executive*
Tomlin, Jeanne Brannon *real estate broker, small business owner*
Watson, Susan Dale *psychologist*

Griffith
Luetschwager, Mary Susan *transportation company professional*
Spires, Roberta Lynn *small business owner*

Hammond
Chandler, Melanie Lynn *surgical technologist, paralegal*
Curiel, Carolyn *ambassador*
Fehring, Mary Ann *secondary school educator*
Hogan, Mary Irene Bernadette *poet*
Smokvina, Gloria Jacqueline *nursing educator*

Hanover
Nickels, Ruth Elizabeth *band director*

Hebron
Casbon, Monica Lynn *accountant*

Highland
DeVaney, Cynthia Ann *elementary school educator, secondary school educator, real estate broker*
Mach, Michele R. *special education educator*

Hobart
Hanley, Roberta Lynn *alternative education coordinator, educator*

Howe
Bowerman, Ann Louise *writer, genealogist, educator*

Huntingburg
Heim, Tonya Sue *nurse, small business owner*

Huntington
Lindsey, Jacquelyn Maria *editor*

Indianapolis
Adamak, M. Jeanelle *broadcast executive*
Ahlrichs, Nancy Surratt *marketing professional*
Allen, Joyce Smith *librarian*
Antich-Carr, Rose Ann *state legislator*
Austin, Terri Jo *state representative*
Barcus, Mary Evelyn *primary school educator*
Barker, Sarah Evans *judge*
Batten, Kimberly Jane *Olympic athlete*
Becker, Karla Lynn *systems analyst*
Becker, Vaneta G. *state representative*
Boehm, Peggy *state agency administrator*
Bowser, Anita Olga *state legislator, education educator*
Braham, Delphine Doris *accountant, government official*
Brash, Susan Kay *principal*
Brooks, Susan W. *prosecutor*
Budak, Mary Kay *state legislator*
Budniakiewicz, Therese *writer*
Buford-Bailey, Tonja Yevette *Olympic athlete*
Burnette, Ruth Leona *retired finance company administrative assistant*
Caine, Virginia A. *city health department administrator*
Calvano, Linda Sue Ley *insurance company executive*
Catchings, Tamika *professional basketball player*
Caudell, Joan Edwards *critical care nurse, consultant*
Chase, Alyssa Ann *editor*
Cilella, Mary Winifred *director*
Cliff, Johnnie Marie *mathematics and chemistry educator*
Cohen, Marlene Lois *pharmacologist*
Colander-Richardson, LaTasha *Olympic athlete*
Cole, Elsa Kircher *lawyer*
Cole, Karen Jean *music educator*
Comiskey, Nancy *newspaper editor*
Cramer, Betty F. *life insurance company executive*
D'Amico, Carol *educational administrator*
Davis, Katherine Lyon *lieutenant governor*
Dawes, Dominique *Olympic athlete*
Dembrowski, Nancy J. *state senator*
Dickenson-Hazard, Nancy Ann *pediatric nurse practitioner, consultant*
Dickinson, Mae *state legislator*
Dishong, Linda S. *estate planner*
Donovan, Anne *professional basketball coach, coach*
Dwyer, Ruth E. *music educator*
Favor-Hamilton, Suzanne Marie *track and field athlete, Olympian*
Fine, Pamela B. *newspaper editor*
Finley, Katherine Mandusic *professional society administrator*
Fleming, Marcella *journalist*
Folco, Angelika *secondary school educator*
Fortner, Nell *professional athletics coach*
Fruehwald, Kristin G. *lawyer*
Gantz, Nancy Rollins *hospital administrator, nursing administrator, consultant*
Gard, Beverly J. *state legislator*
Garmel, Marion Bess Simon *retired arts journalist*
Gregory, Valiska *writer*
Hammontree, Marie Gertrude *writer*
Harden, Anita Joyce *nurse*
Hegel, Carolyn Marie *farm bureau executive*
Helveston, Eugene McGillis *pediatric ophthalmologist, educator*
Hennagan, Monique *Olympic athlete*
Henry, Barbara A. *publishing executive*
Hill, Beverly Ellen *health sciences educator*
Horn, Brenda Sue *lawyer*
Huffman, Rosemary Adams *lawyer, corporate executive*
Humphreys, Katie *health agency administrator*
Ilgen, Dorothy L. *arts foundation executive*
Israelov, Rhoda *financial planner, writer, entrepreneur*
Jackson, Valerie Pascuzzi *radiologist, educator*
Johnston, Joanne Spitznagel *lawyer, writing consultant*
Jones, Marion *track and field athlete*
Kendall, Rebecca O. *lawyer, pharmaceutical company executive*
King, Kay Sue *investment company executive*
Kirk, Carol *lawyer*
Kleiman, Mary Margaret *lawyer*
Klika, Cristine M. *state official*
Klinker, Sheila Ann J. *state legislator, middle school educator*
Knoebel, Suzanne Buckner *cardiologist, educator*
Koch, Edna Mae *lawyer, nurse*
Koch, Linda Brown *utility administrator*
Kovacik, Karen Marie *English literature educator*
Krueger, Betty Jane *telecommunications company executive*
Landske, Dorothy Suzanne (Sue Landske) *state legislator*
Lau, Pauline Young *chemist*
Lawson, Connie *state legislator*
Lawson, Linda *state senator*
Lee, Kristi *broadcast executive, reporter*
Leuck, Claire M. *state legislator*
Lorell, Beverly H. *medical products executive*
Lubbers, Teresa S. *state legislator, public relations executive*
Marendt, Candace L. *state legislator*
Marshall, Carolyn Ann M. *church official*
Maurer, Illene K. *retired speech pathology/audiology services professional, volunteer*
Mays, Carolene *state representative*
McIntyre, Lola Mazza *music educator*
McLaughlin, Sherry *association administrator*
Metzner, Barbara Stone *university counselor*
Miles-Clark, Jearl *olympic athlete, track and field*
Moelhman, Amy Jo *social worker*
Morrell, Ruth Ann *speech pathology/audiology services professional*
Moser, Barbara Jo *elementary school educator*
Nass, Connie Kay *state auditor*
Niederberger, Jane *information technology executive*
Nnaemeka, Obioma Grace *French language and women's studies educator, consultant, researcher*
Noe, Cindy J. *state representative*
Norwalk, Kelli Curran *retail executive, entrepreneur*
Nurok, Zita *elementary school educator*
Oldham, Phyllis Virginia Kidd *retired librarian*
Otero, Lettice Margarita *lawyer*
Perry, Jane A. *service assistant*
Phelps, Jaycie *gymnast, Olympic athlete*
Quarles, Beth *civil rights administrator*
Reed, Suellen Kinder *school system administrator*
Richardson, Kathy Kreag *state legislator*
Richter, Judith Anne *pharmacology educator*
Rogers, Earline S. *state legislator*
Rose, Mary Etta *retired educator*
Rutledge, Joanne *artist, consultant*
Schafer, Yvonne A. *human resources specialist*
Schilling, Emily Born *editor, association executive*
Scholer, Sue Wyant *state legislator*
Settles, Holly Arlene (Holly Woloszyk) *microbiologist*
Shideler, Shirley Ann Williams *lawyer*
Shields, V. Sue *federal magistrate judge*
Simmons, Roberta Johnson *public relations firm executive*
Simpson, Vi *state senator*
Sipes, Connie W. *state legislator, educator*
Skillman, Becky Sue *state legislator*
Slaughter Andrew, Anne *lawyer*
Small, Joyce Graham *psychiatrist, educator*
Sterling, Jennifer Elizabeth *application developer, educator*
Stotka, Jennifer Lynn *pharmaceutical executive, physician*
Summers, Vanessa *state legislator*
Tabler, Susan Beidler *lawyer*
Tandy, Kisha Renee *curator*
Torrence, Gwen *Olympic athlete*
Turner, Barbara A. *former dance company executive*
Uebelhor, Tara Leigh *financial analyst*
Usher, Phyllis Land *state official*
Vann, Lora Jane *reading educator, retired*
Wallace, Edna Marie *paralegal*
Watkins, Sherry Lynne *elementary school educator*
Welch, Peggy *state representative*
Wilkinson, Laura *Olympic athlete*
Williams, Judith Ellen *educational administrator*
Wolf, Katie Louise *state legislator*
Wolsiffer, Patricia Rae *retired insurance company executive*
Wyss-Treadwell, Mary Josephine *music educator, consultant*
Zambrano-Dumaual, Carmen Michelle *molecular biologist*

Jeffersonville
McMichael, Jeane Casey *real estate company executive, educator*

Kentland
Ekstrom, Lisa Marie *special education educator*

Knightstown
Richardson, Shirley Maxine *editor*

Kokomo
Beebe, Gayle L. *music educator*
Coppock, Janet Elaine *mental health nurse*
Finster, Mary Ruth *deacon, retired elementary school educator, cosmetics executive*
MacKay, Gail *librarian*

Kouts
Miller, Sarabeth *secondary school educator*

La Porte
McShane-Halik, Christine Denise *secondary school educator*
Stoler, Dorothy Anne *engineer*

Lafayette
Buckles, Judith Ann *dental educator, program administrator*
Geddes, LaNelle Evelyn *nurse, physiologist*
Gordon, Irene Marlow *radiology educator*
McBride, Angela Barron *nursing educator*
McKowen, Dorothy Keeton *librarian, educator, consultant*
Mobley, Emily Ruth *library dean, educator*
Novak, Julie Cowan *nursing educator, researcher, clinician*
Phillips, Linda *county official*
[illegible]
Scaletta, Helen Marguerite *volunteer*

Lagrange
Glick, Cynthia Susan *lawyer*

Lanesville
Cleveland, Peggy Rose Richey *cytotechnologist*

Lawrenceburg
Edwards, Marie D. *social services administrator*

Lebanon
Geisler, Kay *transportation executive*
Willing, Katherine *former state legislator*

Loogootee
Hotz, Martha Pauline *artist*

Lowell
Elkins, Jeni L. McIntosh *webmaster*

Madison
Grahn, Ann Wagoner *retired scientific policy officer*

Marion
Reaves, Lori Jo *social worker, educator*

Martinsville
Cupka, Nancy Irvine *artist, educator*
Smith, Peg L. *foundation administrator*

Merrillville
Peterson, Lauren Kay *social worker*
Protho, Jessie *vocational school educator*

Michigan City
Moldenhauer, Nancy A. *social worker, educator*

Mishawaka
Brogan-Werntz, Bonnie Bailey *retired police officer, photographer*
Lamb, Beatriz Dominguez *home health agency administrator*
Rubenstein, Pamela Silver *manufacturing executive*
Stone, Cathy Jean *elementary school educator*
Wilson, Rebecca Jo *dean, education educator*

Monroeville
Ray, Annette D. *executive secretary*
Sorgen, Elizabeth Ann *retired educator*

Monticello
Burkhardt, Mary Sue D. *secondary school educator*

Muncie
Christman, Jill Corey *literature educator, writer*
Harris, Vicki Lee *educational consultant*
Hoffman, Mary Catherine *retired nurse, anesthetist*
Irvine, Phyllis Eleanor *nursing educator, administrator*
Joles, Candace Rae *special education educator*
Kroehler, Beth Ann *librarian*
Schaefer, Patricia *librarian*
Shoemaker, Helen E. Martin Achor *civic worker*
Stewart, Rita Joan *academic administrator*
Swetnam, Ruth E. Danglade *curriculum director*

Munster
Colander, Patricia Marie *newspaper editor*
LeMonnier, Shari Smith *artist*
Moore, Carolyn Lannin *video specialist*
Neff, Bonita Dostal *communication development facilitator*

Nashville
Kriner, Sally Gladys Pearl *artist*
Wills, Katherine V. Tsiopos *English language educator*

New Albany
Crump, Claudia *geography educator*
Riehl, Jane Ellen *education educator*

New Harmony
Feiner, Arlene Marie *librarian, researcher, consultant*

New Palestine
Court Gipson, Yvette Kristina *marketing professional*

Newburgh
McKown, Martha *minister, writer*
Verley, Barbara Ann *music educator*

Notre Dame
Blum, Susan Debra *anthropologist, educator*
Doody, Margaret Anne *English language educator*
Feigl, Dorothy Marie *chemistry educator, university official*
Hallinan, Maureen Theresa *sociologist, educator*
Johnstone, Joyce Visintine *education educator*
O'Hara, Patricia A. *dean, law educator*
Sent, Esther-Mirjam *economics educator*
Stevenson, Marsha Joan *librarian*
Wiedower, Sister M. Veronique *religious organization administrator*

Oldenburg
Beiersdorfer, Elizabeth Anne *music educator*

Pendleton
Phenis-Bourke, Nancy Sue *educational administrator*

Plainfield
Lucas, Georgetta Marie Snell *retired educator, artist*

Plymouth
Jurkiewicz, Margaret Joy Gommel *secondary school educator*

Portage
Williams, Susan Marie *music educator*

Rensselaer
Orchard, Olga Sokolich *music educator*

Richmond
Kennedy, Barbara Ellen Perry *art therapist*
Tolliver, Lorraine *language educator, writer*

Rochester
Martens, Betty Joan *music educator, elementary school educator*

Rockville
Sodora, Rosalyn Harpold *elementary education educator, school librarian*

Rushville
Zwickey, Sheila Kaye *lawyer*

Saint Mary Of The Woods
Lescinski, Joan *higher education administrator, English educator*

Sandborn
Hartsburg, Judith Catherine *small business owner*

Schererville
Jarrett, Alexis *insurance agent, lawyer*

Scottsburg
Dockery-Schillig, Linda *writer*

Seymour
Lake, Nancy Jean *nursing educator, medical/surgical nurse*
Rust, Lois *food company executive*

Shelbyville
Clark, Rose Sharon *elementary school educator*

Shoals
Saenz, Ruth E. *missionary*

South Bend
Charles, Isabel *university administrator*
Colborn, Nancy Wootton *school librarian*
Emery, Margaret Ross *elementary school educator*
Hunt, Mary Reilly *organization executive*
Ivory, Goldie Lee *retired social worker, educator*
Kline, Syril Levin *writer, educational consultant*
Kuehner, Denise Ann *music educator, musician*
McDonnell, G. Darlene *retired business educator*
Rodgers, Grace Anne *university official*
Streich, Cynthia Sue *special education educator*
Torstrick, Rebecca Lee *anthropologist, educator*

South Whitley
Hinthorn, Dawn Rosa *elementary and secondary school educator*

Spencer
Coley, Brenda Ann *elementary school educator*

Sullivan
Chavez, Mary Ann *osteopathic family physician*

Tell City
Arterberry, Patricia *elementary school educator*
Guillaum, Marsha Kaye *information technology manager*

Terre Haute
De Marr, Mary Jean *English language educator*
Flick, Connie Ruth *real estate agent, real estate broker*
Hunt, Effie Neva *former college dean, former English language educator*
Lindley, Joyce E. *health facility administrator, real estate appraiser*
Stoelting, Freda Ann *special education educator*

Tipton
Hurst, Laurenda Lee *library director, music educator*

Valparaiso
Brown, Elizabeth A. *librarian, multi-media specialist*
Lawley, Deena C. Butterfield *music educator, legal assistant*
Persyn, Mary Geraldine *law librarian, law educator*
Peters, Judith Griessel *foreign language educator*
Scales, Freda S. *dean, nursing educator*
Taylor, Heather Marie *director*

Wabash
Ward, Judith A. *elementary school educator, music educator*

West Lafayette
Alsup, Janet Marie *language educator*
Anderson, Kristine Jo *librarian*
Andrews, Theodora Anne *retired librarian, educator*
Fliotsos, Anne *theater educator*
Gappa, Judith M. *university administrator*
Heise, Kathryn Ann *music educator*
Jagacinski, Carolyn Mary *psychology educator*
Johns, Janet Susan *physician*
Kirksey, Avanelle *nutrition educator*
Lefever, Maxine Lane *music educator*
Lord, Victoria Lynn *artist*
Markee, Katherine Madigan *librarian, educator*
Moyars-Johnson, Mary Annis *university official*
Nixon, Judith May *librarian*
Raskin, Rose Esther *veterinary educator*
Roberts, Anne Margaret *secondary school educator*
Sims-Curry, Kristy *women's college basketball coach*
Stetter, Aimee Rae *finance company executive*
Taber, Margaret Ruth *retired electrical engineering technology educator, electrical engineer*

Westfield
Scott, Jennifer Marie *special education educator*

Wheatfield
Woolever, Gail Waluk *elementary school educator, artist, secondary school educator*

Williamsport
Swanson, Donna Kay *elementary school educator, writer*

Winslow
McKinney, Shannon J. *retired secondary school educator*

IOWA

Ames
Alumbaugh, JoAnn McCalla *magazine editor*
Bonomi, Ferne Gater *public relations executive*
Bruene, Barbara Jane *artist, educator*
Buck, Sarah Beth *educational association administrator, director*
Crabtree, Beverly June *retired dean*
Dial, Eleanore Maxwell *foreign language educator*
Hill, Fay Gish *retired librarian*
Johnson-Richt, Cheryl Lynn *performing artist*
Mattila, Mary Jo Kalsem *elementary and art educator*
Melby, Janet Nieuwsma *research scientist*
Mitchell, Jacqueline Keaton *English language educator*
Roskey, Carol Boyd *social studies educator, dean, director*
Sanders, Calli Theisen *athletics administrator*
Wendell, Barbara Taylor *retired real estate agent*
Withers, Heather Nowell *minister*

Anita
Lloyd-Cameron, Rosemary Ann *music educator*

Ankeny
Tomb, Carol E. *retail executive*

Atlantic
Johnson, Joan (Jan) Hope Voss *communications executive, photojournalist, public relations executive*

Bettendorf
Hirsch, Lynn Christy *elementary school educator, art educator*
Webb, Carol E *school system administrator*

Bloomfield
Combs, Judy Diane *elementary school educator, civic association administrator*

Brighton
Guy, Donna S. *artist*

Burlington
Noll, Laurie Jane *secondary school educator*
Smith, Mona Riley *psychotherapist*

Cedar Falls
Maier, Donna Jane-Ellen *history educator*

Cedar Rapids
Arnold-Olson, Helen B. *nonprofit consultant*
Baermann, Donna Lee Roth *real estate property executive, retired insurance analyst*
Brooks, Debra L. *healthcare executive, neuromuscular therapist*
Hall, Kathy L. *orchestra executive*
Huber, Rita Norma *civic worker*
Magill, Nancy Gene *microbiologist, educator*
Merritt, Sandra Lee *educational consultant*
Mulvaney, Molly Marie *women's health nurse practitioner*
Novetzke, Sally Johnson *former ambassador*
O'Keefe, Ellen Margaret *special education educator*
Pike, Shirley *school psychologist*
Reppert, Nancy Lue *retired municipal official, legal consultant*
Wax, Nadine Virginia *retired bank executive*

Charles City
McCartney, Rhoda Huxsol *farm manager*

Charter Oak
Kutschinski, Dorothy Irene *elementary school educator*

Clarksville
Kattenhorn, Lisa Ann *music educator*

Clinton
Warner, Jean Lollich *poet*

Clive
O'Brien, Nancy A. *youth counselor*

Collins
Razor, Mary C. *writer*

Council Bluffs
Lawson, Patricia Lynn *technologist*

Davenport
Bannick, Janice Carol *automotive dealerships executive*
Beguhn, Sandra E. *poet, writer*
Corcoran, Janet Patricia *elementary school educator*
Goudy, Josephine Gray *social worker*
Heisner, Ellen Ann *occupational health nurse*
Irving, Nancy Irene *volunteer*
Jecklin, Lois Underwood *art corporation executive, consultant*
Keller, Nancy Anne *special education educator*
McDonald, Julie Jensen *writer, educator*
Pedersen, Karen Sue *electrical engineer*
Sheehey, Patricia Ann *secondary school educator*
Sievert, Mary Elizabeth *small business owner, retired secondary school educator*
Tinsman, Margaret Neir *state legislator*
Townsend, Julie Rae *artist, educator*
Van Dyke, Wendy Johanna *artist*
Wilson, Frances Edna *protective services official*

Decorah
Maurland, Anne Elisabeth *potter*
Meade, Birgitta Rosemary *elementary school educator*

Des Moines
Amendt, Marilyn Joan *personnel director*
Bennett, Virginia Cook *music educator, consultant*
Berry, Deborah *state representative*
Boal, Carmine *state official*
Boettger, Nancy J. *state legislator*
Bremer, Celeste F. *judge*
Buhr, Florence D. *county official*
Bukta, Polly *state representative*
Byal, Nancy Louise *food editor*
Conlin, Roxanne Barton *lawyer*
Corning, Joy Cole *retired state official*
Dandekar, Swati *state representative*
DeBoef, Betty *state representative*
DeWulf Nickell, Karol *editor*
Dukes, Vanessa Johnson *dietician*
Ellis, Mary Louise Helgeson *retired insurance company executive, business consultant*
Erickson, Elaine Mae *composer, poet*
Finley, Kerry A. *lawyer*
Freeman, Mary Louise *state legislator*
Garman, Teresa Agnes *state legislator*
Gaskill, Mary *state official*
Goodin, Julia C. *forensic pathologist, state official, educator*
Graham, Diane E. *newspaper editor*
Granzow, Polly *state representative, language educator*
Greimann, Jane *state representative, elementary school educator*
Grundberg, Betty *state legislator, property manager*
Heddens, Lisa *state official*
Henry, Phylliss Jeanette *marshal*
Hosch, Julie *state senator*
Huser, Geri D. *state official*
Isenstein, Laura *library director*
Jacobs, Libby Swanson *state official*
Jochum, Pam *state representative*
Kramer, Mary Elizabeth *state legislator, health services executive*
Lensing, Vicki *state representative, funeral home business owner*
Lund, Doris Hibbs *retired dietitian*
Mertz, Dolores Mary *farmer, state legislator*
Miller, Helen *state representative, lawyer*
Myers, Mary Kathleen *publishing executive*
Nelson, Charlotte Bowers *public administrator*
Oldson, Jo *state representative, lawyer*
Paterik, Frances Sue *secondary school educator, actress*
Pederson, Sally *lieutenant governor*
Petersen, Janet *state representative*
Ragan, Amanda *state senator*

Ramsden, Mary Catherine *substance abuse specialist*
Ratcliff, Dolores Jean *special education educator*
Rehberg, Kitty *state legislator*
Runge, Kay Kretschmar *library director*
Shaff, Karen E. *lawyer, insurance company executive*
Sheehan, Carol Sama *magazine editor*
Soukup, Betty A. *state legislator*
Stier, Mary P. *publishing executive*
Szymoniak, Elaine Eisfelder *retired state senator*
Ternus, Marsha K. *state supreme court justice*
Tymeson, Jodi *state official*
Upmeyer, Linda *state official*
Van Zante, Shirley M(ae) *magazine editor*
Wattleworth, Roberta Ann *physician, medical educator*
Wilson, Sal *systems analyst*
Winckler, Cindy *state representative*

Dubuque
Collins, Barbara Louise *retired elementary school educator*
Dunn, M. Catherine *college administrator, educator*

Fairfield
Drees, Dorothy E. *small business owner, real estate manager*

Fort Dodge
Hickey, Sharon Marie *councilman, elementary school educator, Mayoral aide*

Garner
Duregger, Karen Marie *health facility administrator*

George
Symens, Maxine Brinkert Tanner *marketing professional*

Grinnell
Carl, Janet A. *writing instructor, consultant*
Ferguson, Pamela Anderson *mathematics educator, educational administrator*
Michaels, Jennifer Tonks *foreign language educator*

Harlan
Wilson, Annette Sigrid *elementary school educator*

Humeston
Goben, Mirella Segalotto *real estate agent*

Indianola
Mace, Jerilee Marie *opera company executive*

Iowa City
Andreasen, Nancy Coover *psychiatrist, educator, neuroscientist*
Babb, Florence Evelyn *anthropologist, educator*
Buckwalter, Kathleen C. *academic administrator, educator*
Clark, Dianne Elizabeth *religious studies and reading educator*
Davis, Julia McBroom *college dean, speech pathology and audiology educator*
Dettmer, Helena R. *classics educator*
DiPardo, Anne *English language and education educator*
Dreher, Melanie Creagan *dean, nursing educator*
Gittler, Josephine *law educator*
Hettmansperger, Sue *artist*
Hovland, Jody *theater director*
Kerber, Linda Kaufman *historian, educator*
Lamping, Kathryn G. *medical educator, medical researcher*
Lee, Angie *basketball coach*
Maxson, Linda Ellen *biologist, educator*
Muir, Ruth Brooks *counselor, substance abuse service coordinator*
Niebyl, Jennifer Robinson *obstetrician, gynecologist, educator*
Packer, ZZ (Zuwena) *writer, literature educator*
Porter, Nancy Lefgren *reading recovery educator*
Scullion, Rosemarie *literature educator*
Smothers, Ann Elizabeth *museum director*
Solbrig, Ingeborg Hildegard *literature educator, writer*
Stay, Barbara *zoologist, educator*
Tsalikian, Eva *physician, educator*
Wing, Adrien Katherine *law educator*
Young, Laura Elizabeth *artist*

Iowa Falls
Sessler, Donna Jean Hotz *secondary school educator*

Janesville
Jarosh, Colleen Marie *nursing educator, consultant*

Johnston
Anderson, Sara *special education educator*

Kalona
Skaden, Anne Marie *library director*

Keokuk
Hardy, Julia Irene *elementary school educator*

Keota
Greiner, Sandra *state legislator*

Knoxville
Baker, Cynthia Joan *elementary education educator, historic site interpreter*

Lamoni
Kirkpatrick, Sharon Minton *nursing educator, college administrator*

Leon
Miller, Eleanora Genevieve *freelance/self-employed poet*

Manchester
Baumgartner, Cindy Sue *secondary school educator*

Marshalltown
Foote, Sherrill Lynne *retired manufacturing company technician*

Mason City
Iverson, Carol Jean *retired library media specialist*
Rodamaker, Marti Tomson *bank executive*
Sappenfield, Maedeane L. *piano and organ educator*

Morning Sun
Byers, Elizabeth *education educator*

Newell
Doyen, Barbara J. *literary agent*

Newton
Johnson, Jane Ann Bockwoldt *music educator, small business owner*

Oelwein
McFarlane, Beth Lucetta Troester *former mayor*

Osage
Christensen, Pamela Karen *pediatric nurse*

Oskaloosa
Burrow, Nancy Kay *special education educator*
Gleason, Carol Ann *mental health nurse, educator*

Ottumwa
Krafka, Mary Baird *lawyer*
Sager Neil, Theresa Louise *poet, author of children's books*

Prairie City
Buckingham, Betty Jo *library media consultant*

Reinbeck
Koester, Lisa *educational administrator, consultant*

Richland
Walter, Sandra S. *social worker*

Roland
Kuykendall, Tempest Anne *elementary school educator*

Sioux City
Burns, Susan Reneé *psychologist, educator*
Dillman, Kristin Wicker *elementary and middle school educator, musician*
Rants, Carolyn Jean *college official*
Wick, Sister Margaret *former college administrator*

Sioux Rapids
Thies, Heidi Marie *music educator*

Sloan
Ullrich, Roxie Ann *special education educator*

Storm Lake
McKenney, Irene June *business manager, former educator*

Walcott
Greer, Mimi (Martha) Emilie *language educator*

Waterloo
Kober, Arletta Refshauge (Mrs. Kay L. Kober) *supervisor*

Waverly
Blair, Rebecca Sue *English educator*
Juhl Zelle, Dorothy Helen *retired social worker*
Koob, Kathryn Loraine *religious studies educator*

West Branch
Mather, Mildred Eunice *retired archivist*

West Des Moines
Hubbard, Cheryl A. *director*
Zimmerman, Jo Ann *health services and educational consultant, former lieutenant governor*

West Union
Hansen, Ruth Lucille Hofer *business owner, consultant*

Woodward
Jenkins, Alice Marie *secondary school educator*

KANSAS

Arkansas City
Bruton, Rebecca Ann *mayor, commissioner*
Meeks, Cindy Lou *special education educator*

Atwood
Goodwin, Stephanie Ruth *art educator, finance educator*

Baldwin City
Baker, Margaret Moore-Fritz *retired school librarian, retired humanities educator*
English, Evonne Kludas *artist*

Basehor
Brown, Debra Rae *music educator*

Caldwell
Robinson, Alice Jean McDonnell *retired drama and speech educator*

Ashland
Cavins, Jacqueline Lou *education educator, adult nurse practitioner*

Barbourville
Floyd, Linda Smith *principal*

Benton
Brown, Sharon Webb *art educator*
Kellie, Diane *special education educator*
Shurley, Elaine P. *music educator*

Berea
Flynn, Candy Ruth *music educator*
Lamb, Irene Hendricks *medical researcher*
Stephenson, Jane Ellen *educational association administrator*

Boston
Rosenbaum, Mary Heléne Pottker *writer, editor*

Bowling Green
Garrison, Geneva *retired administrative assistant*
Keller, Patricia Huggins *music educator*
Schaeffer, Beth Bolin *pre-school educator, consultant*
Smith, Janet L. Bass *musician, educator*
Tyrie, Tina Napier *music educator*

Burlington
Hines, Tina Loree *video producer, writer, publicist, photographer*

Butler
Lustenberg, Michelle Williamson *gifted and talented educator*

Calvert City
Dowdy, Vicki J. *music educator*
Madison, Vicki DiAnne *retired music educator*

Campbellsburg
Mitchell, Mary Ann Carrico *poet*

Campbellsville
Irwin, Donna Rice *music educator*
McArthur, Lisa R. *music educator, musician*
Moore, Nevalyn *music educator*

Carrollton
Duncan, Carol Lynn *English language and literature educator*
Heilman, Mary Joanne *gifted education educator*

Catlettsburg
Selbee, Maxine Butcher *county clerk*

Corbin
Barton-Collings, Nelda Ann *political activist, newspaper, bank and nursing home executive*
Watkins, Jennie Shore *elementary school educator*

Covington
Berg, Lorine McComis *retired guidance counselor*
Fleischer-Rieveschl, Ellen Lee *real estate agent*
Littleton, Nan Elizabeth Feldkamp *psychologist, educator*
McQueen, Regenia *writer*

Custer
Egbert, Donna *elementary school educator*

Cynthiana
Ellis, E. Susan *library director, lay mminister*

Danville
Brogle, Jennifer Lynn *music educator, consultant*
Kennan, Elizabeth Topham *academic administrator, retired historian*

Eddyville
Norman, Pamela Kay *special education educator, director*

Edgewood
Ballinger, Carolyn Ann *nursing educator*

Ekron
Hamilton, Amelia Wentz (Amy Wentz) *elementary school educator*

Flatwoods
Blankenship, Dawn Olivia *pediatric nurse*
Sharp, Verna Ellen *special education educator*

Flemingsburg
Bolar, Amy Leigh *music educator*

Florence
Gorman, Gayla Marlene Osborne *consumer affairs executive*

Fort Wright
Sullivan, Connie Castleberry *artist*

Frankfort
Belcher, Carolyn R. *state representative*
Casebier, Lindy *state legislator*
Fleming, Juanita Wilson *nursing educator, academic administrator*
Fletcher, Winona Lee *theater educator emeritus*
Jenkins, Joni Lynn *state legislator*
Johns, Susan D. *state senator*
McCarthy, Lynn Cowan *genealogist, researcher*
Nowland-Curry, Betsy *state official*
Palmore, Carol M. *state official*
Palumbo, Ruth Ann *state legislator*
Patton, Nicki *former political organization executive*
Pullin, Tanya *state representative*
Robinson, Ella D. *state agency administrator*
Stein, Kathy W. *state representative*
Stine, Katie Kratz *state legislator*
Tribble, Pamela Gail *special education educator*
Williams, Ellen C. *political party official*

Georgetown
Bevins, Ann Bolton *retired journalist, retired historian*
White, Mary Ann *bank executive*

Glasgow
Duvo, Mechelle Louise *oil company executive, consultant*
Swystun-Rives, Bohdana Alexandra *dentist*

Goshen
Dahl, Marilyn Gail *psychotherapist*

Grayson
Jones, April Lynn *music educator*

Greenville
Painter, Elizabeth Marie *insurance agent, financial consultant*

Harlan
DeLong-Smith, Stephanie K. *secondary school educator*
Lee, Jeanne Ann *music educator, consultant*

Harrodsburg
Bradshaw, Phyllis Bowman *historian, historic site staff member*
Hammond, Debbie Johnson *computer analyst*
VanDiver, Betty Jean *protective services professional*

Hazard
Bryant, Renee Tabor *director, educator*

Hebron
Morrow, Debra Deola *accountant*

Henderson
Schadler, Cynthia K. *accountant*

Highland Heights
Donnelly, Sharlotte K. B. Neely *anthropology educator, author*
Forman, Sandra H. *theater educator*

Hopkinsville
Lester, Joan Stadelman *music educator*
Major, Carolyn Ledford *counselor*
Martin, Theresa Kay *minister*

La Grange
Morgan, Mary Dan *librarian*
Shaver, Lindy Carol *nursing administrator*

Lexington
Blackwell, Jeannine *foreign language educator*
Boyer, Lillian Buckley *artist, educator*
Campbell, Zenita A. D. *environmental engineer, educator, safety engineer*
Coffman, Jennifer Burcham *judge*
Daniel, Marilyn S. *lawyer*
Davis, Mary Byrd *conservationist, researcher*
Elliott, Teresa J. *music educator*
Farrar, Donna Beatrice *hospital official*
Goldman, Elisabeth Paris *lawyer*
Gornik, Kathy *electronics executive*
Gray, Lois Howard *construction company executive*
Henderson, Jerrie *realtor*
Holley, Kay Moffitt *nutrition instructor, dietitian*
Hundley, Cristi Moran *psychologist*
Hurley, Janet Lee *university health service administrator*
Isaac, Teresa Ann *mayor, lawyer*
Isenhour, Kathleen Chaney *special education educator, consultant*
Johnson, Jane Penelope *freelance/self-employed writer*
Johnson, Lizabeth Lettie *small business owner, insurance agent*
Jones, Bonnie Quantrell *automobile dealer*
Kang, Bann C. *immunologist*
Kerr, Alice Forgy *state legislator*
Miller, Pamela Gundersen *mayor*
Noonan, Jacqueline Anne *pediatrics educator*
Rowe, Melinda Grace *public health service officer*
Salisbury, Holly Buckner *university arts director*
Snowden, Ruth O'Dell Gillespie *artist*
Varellas, Sandra Motte *judge*
Williams, Carolyn Antonides *university dean*
Worell, Judith P. *psychologist, educator*
Zinser, Elisabeth Ann *academic administrator*

Louisville
Albin, Melanie Arlisse *marriage and family therapist*
Alford, Alana Floyd *art educator*
Anderson, Linda Jean *critical care nurse, psychiatric nurse practitioner*
Antoine, Janet Anne *social worker*
Becker, Gail Roselyn *museum director*
Benfield, Ann Kolb *lawyer*
Berger, Barbara Paull *social worker, marriage and family therapist*
Blake, Jane Salley *publishing, public relations, and management consultant*
Bledsoe, Linda Kay *psychologist, researcher*
Bohn, Donna Schuhmann *accountant*
Boykin, Gladys *retired religious organization administrator*
Bratton, Ida Frank *retired secondary school educator*
Carranza, Jovita *delivery service executive*
Cayce, Kay C. *accountant*
Cecil, Bonnie Susan *elementary school educator*
Colburn, Jennifer Christine *business analyst*
Columbus, Shanna S. *advertising executive*
Dale, Judy Ries *religious organization administrator, consultant*
DeMunbrun-Harmon, Donne O'Donnell *retired family physician*
Faller, Rhoda *lawyer*
Fassett, Frances Nicholas (Kitty Fassett) *pianist, record producer*
Force, Jill L. *health facility executive*

Freibert, Lucy Marie *humanities educator*
Galandiuk, Susan *colon and rectal surgeon, educator*
Garrett, Debra Anne *music educator*
Glass, Elizabeth L. *social worker, literature educator*
Goellner, Susan Kitchin *nurse midwife*
Greaver, Joanne Hutchins *mathematics educator, author*
Haddaway, Janice Lillian *psychotherapist, consultant*
Hathcock, Bonita Catherine (Bonnie Hathcock) *managed health care company executive*
Hines-Martin, Vicki Patricia *nursing educator, researcher*
Hixson, Allie Corbin *retired adult education educator, advocate*
Hoffer, Debra Humes *educational association administrator*
Ivey, Susan *tobacco company executive*
James, Virginia Lynn *contracts executive*
Johnson, Adria Elaine *financial analyst, accountant*
Keith, Penny Sue *mayor, educator*
Lake, Carol Lee *anesthesiologist, physician executive, educator*
Leonard, Mona Freeman *adult education educator*
Lloyd, Kimcherie *performing company executive*
Lyndrup, Peggy B. *lawyer*
Margulis, Heidi *managed health care company executive*
Mather, Elizabeth Vivian *healthcare executive*
McKim, Ruth Ann *financial planner*
Miller, Marilee Hebert *arts administrator, producer, director, consultant*
Murrell, Deborah Anne *music educator, speaker, writer*
Niles, Judith F. *librarian*
Peden, Katherine Graham *industrial consultant*
Rahm, Mary Ellen *statistical clerk*
Sandler, Deborah *performing company executive*
Scheu, Lynn McLaughlin *scientific publication editor, secondary school educator*
Schneider, Jayne Bangs *school librarian*
Scott, Lolita Jean *social worker*
Shelburne, Renee D. *communications executive*
Sherman, Mildred Mozelle *music educator, vocalist, actress, opera director*
Soriano, Cristina *dietician*
Stone, Marsha L. *music educator*
Theiss, Gena Lee *genealogist, researcher*
Thompson, Kathy C. *bank executive*
Turner, Sandra Chucalo *music educator*
Watts, Beverly L. *civil rights executive*
Weisenbeck, Sharon M. *healthcare regulatory administrator*
White-Walker, Roxana *elementary school educator*
Willenbrink, Rose Ann *lawyer*
Wood, Phoebe A. *food products executive*

Mackville
Scott, Donna C. *human resources specialist*

Madisonville
Grothem, Helen Marie *occupational therapist, educator*
Kemp, Ann *retired librarian*

Mc Kee
Tincher-Threlkeld, Marsha Lea *music educator*

Middlesboro
Potter-Hughes, Karen Ann *secondary school educator*
Welch, Patricia *retired nursing educator, association executive*

Morehead
Creasap, Susan Diane *music educator, conductor*

Mount Olivet
Dorton, Truda Lou *medical, surgical and geriatrics nurse*

Murray
Boston, Betty Lee *investment company executive, financial consultant, financial planner*
Ratliff, Judy Lynn *chemist, educator*
Russell, Mary Ann *secondary school educator*

Newport
Kirk, Charlotte Leidecker *director*

Nicholasville
Bender, Betty Barbee *food service professional*
Sewell, Viola L. *daycare administrator*

Olive Hill
Knipp, Jenny L. *science educator*

Owensboro
Blandford, Virginia Rose *music educator*
Freese, Laura Ann *social worker, consultant*
Mullikin, Sandra Marie *music educator*

Paducah
Farr, Carla Lake *therapist*

Pikeville
Sisco, Mary Ann *director*

Pineville
Hoskins, Barbara R(uth) Williams *elementary educator, elementary principal*

Prestonsburg
Stumbo, Janet Lynn *state supreme court justice*

Prospect
Garner, Joyce Craig *artist*

Radcliff
Labtis-Jardim, Odessa *import/export company executive*

Richmond
Adams, Constance Ewing *school psychologist, art therapist*
Hall, Kathy *nursing official*
Jackson, Cheryl Ann *music educator, director*
King, Amy Cathryne Patterson *retired mathematics educator, researcher*
Smith, Carla Anne *music educator*

Russellville
Harper, Shirley Fay *nutritionist, educator, consultant, lecturer*

Saint Catharine
Collins, Martha Layne *college president, former governor*

Shelbyville
Coffman, Lucinda Harrison *writer*
Miller, Mary Helen *retired public administrator*
Scheidt, Rebecca Lynnell *psychologist, educator*

Shepherdsville
Matson, Frances Shober *retired social worker*

Summer Shade
Smith, Ruby Lucille *retired librarian*

Union
Franklin, Dorothy Ann *guidance counselor*

Upton
Lawson, Linda Jean *elementary school educator*

Utica
Henry, Loretta Marrie *writer*
Mountjoy, Helen W. *educational association administrator*

Williamsburg
Conn, Rebecca Darlene *psychologist*

Winchester
Cantrell, Georgia Ann *realtor*
Jude, Cassandra Joy *music educator*
Skinner, Jill Suzanne *special education educator*

LOUISIANA

Alexandria
Anderson, Rose Marie *insurance agent*
Bradford, Louise Mathilde *social services administrator*
Foster, Sally *interior designer*
Ginsburgh, Judy Caplan *music specialist, vocalist, consultant*
Thevenot, Maude Travis *retired home economist*
Vandersypen, Rita DeBona *guidance counselor, academic administrator*
Welch, Kelli Carruth *secondary school counselor*

Baton Rouge
Adams, Sharon Butler *minister, philosopher, researcher*
Barnette, Kim Bailey *counseling administrator*
Blanco, Kathleen Babineaux *governor*
Boulton, Bonnie Smith *assistant principal, special education educator*
Brister, Pat *political party executive*
Buchmann, Molly O'Banion *choreographer, ballet educator*
Davis, Carol *educational association administrator, educator*
Doty, Gresdna Ann *theatre historian, educator*
Gikas, Carol Sommerfeldt *museum director*
Harrison, Betty Carolyn Cook *education educator, administrator*
Hayward, Olga Loretta Hines (Mrs. Samuel Ellsworth Hayward) *retired librarian*
Hewitt, Maureen Gilgore *scholarly book publishing executive*
Kimball, Dorothy Jean *foundation executive*
Lane, Margaret Beynon Taylor *librarian*
Lee, Betty Redding *architect*
Litton, Nancy Joan *education educator*
Lovejoy, Jennifer Carole *medical educator*
Lusk, Glenna Rae Knight (Mrs. Edwin Bruce Lusk) *librarian*
Lusted, Dona Sanders *music educator, consultant, organist*
Mathews, Sharon Walker *artistic director, secondary school educator*
Mayho, Lois Mary *social worker*
Mueller, Lisel *writer, poet*
Noland, Christine A. *magistrate judge*
Owen, Sue Ann *poet*
Rami, Janet Simmons *university dean, nursing educator*
Rutledge, Katherine Burck *artist*
Sasek, Gloria Burns *English language and literature educator*
Schechter, Lynn Renee *psychologist*
Shaw, Beverly C. *state official*
Shield, Carolyn Douglas *music educator*
Speier, Karen Rinardo *psychologist*
Stockwell, Mary Diamond *information technology manager*
Thomason, Norma Jean *librarian*
Willett, Anna Hart *composer, painter*
Yarbrough, Martha Cornelia *music educator*
Younathan, Margaret Tims *nutritionist, educator*

Bogalusa
Wood, Helen Chamblee *accountant*

Bossier City
DeFatta-Barattini, Kathryn *communications educator*
Johnson, Ruby LaVerne *retail executive*
Rankin, Mary Anne *director*

Carencro
Gorski, Hedwig Irene *poet, writer*

Cecilia
Girouard, Tina *artist, curator*

Damariscotta
Swanson, Karin *hospital administrator, consultant*

Edgecomb
Carlson, Suzanne Olive *architect*

Ellsworth
Heath, Audrey Mary *artist, jewelry designer*

Falmouth
Gulliver, Jean K. *educational association administrator*
Hathaway, Lynn McDonald *education advocate, administrator*
McCoy, Carol P. *psychologist, training executive*
Winton, Linda *corporate financial executive*

Farmington
Kalikow, Theodora June *university president*

Fort Fairfield
Shapiro, Joan Isabelle *lab administrator, medical/surgical nurse*

Freeport
Broder, Shari Bryant *arbitrator, mediator*
Cushman, Margaret Jane *home care executive, nurse*
Parkhurst, Denice Delray *music educator*

Gardiner
Nowell, Glenna Greely *librarian, consultant, city manager*
Treat, Sharon Anglin *state legislator*

Gorham
Bearce, Jeana Dale *artist, educator*
Kaschub, Michele Ellen *music educator, researcher*
Katsekas, Bette Susan *counseling education educator*

Hampden
Paonessa, M. Suzanne *budget analyst*

Kennebunk
Ward, Nina Gillson *jewelry store executive*

Kennebunkport
Ray, Virginia H. S. *columnist, writer*

Kingfield
Clapp, Millicent Evans *real estate broker*

Kittery Point
Howells, Muriel Gurdon Seabury (Mrs. William White Howells) *volunteer*

Lewiston
Hansen, Elaine Tuttle *academic administrator*
Randall, Carla Elizabeth *nursing educator*
Reich, Jill *dean*

Lincoln
Nevells, Kimberly A *medical/surgical nurse, educator*

Lisbon
Iverson, Carlene V. *principal*

Monhegan
Boehmer, Raquel Davenport *newsletter editor*
Van Houten, Elizabeth Ann *corporate communications executive, painter*

Mount Desert
Redfield, Rita Tams *art gallery owner*
Weinberger, Jane Dalton *retired nurse, volunteer*

New Harbor
Brookes, Ruth Harding *guidance counselor*

Nobleboro
Fisher, Ellen Roop *retired librarian, educator*

North Haven
Pingree, Rochelle M. *state legislator*

North Yarmouth
Kuhrt, Sharon Lee *nursing administrator*
York, Gladys Doughty *minister*

Old Town
Alex, Joanne DeFilipp *elementary school educator*
Nelligan, Annette Frances *clinical coordinator*
Scribner, Princess Rose-Marie *not-for-profit developer*

Orono
Hutchison, Sandra Lynn *writer, educator*

Pemaquid
Howell, Jeanette Helen *retired cultural organization administrator*

Port Clyde
Duarte, Patricia M. *real estate and insurance broker*

Portland
Chandler, Patricia Ann *retired special education educator*
Chapkis, Wendy Lynn *women's studies educator*
Chow, Amy *gymnast, Olympic athlete*
Courtney, Ann M. *lawyer*
Glassman, Caroline Duby *state supreme court justice*
Jamison, Elizabeth Alease *drafting and design business owner*
Khoury, Colleen A. *dean*
Miller, Buffy *dancer*
Morgan, Robin Evonne *poet, author, journalist, activist, editor*
Saufley, Leigh Ingalls *judge*
Silsby, Paula *prosecutor*

Weir, Anne *writer*
Wilkinson, Barbara J. *physician, medical educator*
Zill, Anne Broderick *foundation executive*

Presque Isle
Davidshofer, Claire H. *college instructor*
Gentile, Caroline D. *adult education educator*
Hensel, Nancy H. *academic administrator*

Rockland
Brown, Clare Winslow *accountant, writer*

Rockport
Goodwin, Doris Helen Kearns *historian*

Saco
Collins, Cynthia Jane *marriage and family therapist, priestess*
Mason, Nancy Tolman *retired state agency director*

Saint Agatha
Cyr, Elaine Marie *special education educator*

Scarborough
Russo, Joan Mildred *special education educator*
Warg, Pauline *artist, educator*

South Bristol
Hammond, Karen T. *writer, editor*
Lasher, Esther Lu *minister*

South Portland
Harris, Penny Smith *fundraising consultant*
Huntoon, Abby Elizabeth *artist, teacher*
Kandoian, Janet Adrienne *elementary school educator*

Stockton Springs
Gold, Donna Lauren *writer*

Surry
Pickett, Betty Horenstein *psychologist*

Topsham
Outhwaite, Lucille Conrad *ballerina, educator*
Palesky, Carol East *tax accountant*

Washburn
Humphrey, Mary Frances *historian, writer, retired health care recruiter*

Waterville
Cook, Susan Farwell *associate director planned giving*
Desrosiers, Muriel C. *music educator, retired nursing consultant*
Gilkes, Cheryl Louise Townsend *sociologist, educator, minister*
Muehlner, Suanne Wilson *library director*
Ring, Miranda *psychologist, photographer*
Roisman, Hanna Maslovski *classics educator*

West Baldwin
Simmonds, Rae Nichols *musician, composer, educator*

Westbrook
Oatley, Nina Karen *music educator*

Westport Island
Stedman, Susan Goodwillie *writer, consultant*

Windham
Mulvey, Mary Crowley *retired adult education director, gerontologist, senior citizen association administrator*

Wiscasset
Golden, Ellen Frances *economic development practitioner*

Woolwich
Clark, Joyce T. *piano teacher, church organist*

York
Haley, Priscilla Jane *artist, printmaker*
Hallam, Beverly (Beverly Linney) *artist*
Smart, Mary-Leigh Call (Mrs. J. Scott Smart) *civic worker*

MARYLAND

Aberdeen
Hopkins, Susan Shiplett *music educator, director*
Klien, Karen Ann *speech pathology/audiology services professional*

Aberdeen Proving Ground
Tobin, Aileen Webb *educational administrator*

Abingdon
Uzdilla, Laura Angeline *radiation oncology technician, researcher*

Adamstown
Church, Martha Eleanor *retired academic administrator, scholar*

Annapolis
Alderdice, Cynthia Lou *artist*
Battaglia, Lynne Ann *judge*
Benson, Joanne C. *state legislator*
Bowen, Linnell R. *director*
Brann, Eva Toni Helene *archaeology educator*
Cadden, Joan *state legislator*
Clagett, Virginia Parker *county official*
Connolly, Janet Elizabeth *retired sociologist and criminal justice educator*
Conroy, Mary A. *state legislator*
Conway, Joan Carter *state legislator*
Dembrow, Dana Lee *lawyer*
Dewar, Mildred Jo Eller (Mrs. Donald Norman Dewar) *librarian*
Ebinger, Mary Ritzman *pastoral counselor*

Flanagan, Susan Marie *special education educator*
Florestano, Patricia Sherer *state official*
Forehand, Jennie Meador *state legislator*
Fowler, Terri (Marie Therese Fowler) *artist*
Harrison, Hattie N. *state senator*
Healey, Anne *state legislator*
Hixson, Sheila Ellis *state legislator*
Hollinger, Paula Colodny *state legislator*
Howard, Carolyn J. B. *state legislator*
Kelley, Delores Goodwin *state legislator*
Kirk, Ruth M. *state legislator*
Klima, Martha Scanlan *state legislator*
Kopp, Nancy Kornblith *state official*
Krysiak, Carolyn *state legislator*
Libby, Jane Elliott *retired dietitian*
McIntosh, Maggie *state legislator*
McQuarrie, Beatrice Sue *financial analyst*
Menes, Pauline H. *state legislator*
Miller, Patricia A. *training services executive*
Parham, Carol Sheffey *school system administrator*
Ruben, Ida Gass *state senator*
Ryan, Michele King *marketing professional*
Schleicher, Nora Elizabeth *banker, treasurer, accountant*
Smith Tarchalski, Helen Marie *piano educator*
Snyder, Kathleen Theresa *state agency administrator*
Stern, Margaret Bassett *retired special education educator, author*
Thoms, Josephine Bowers *artist*
Trescott, Sara Lou *water resources engineer*
Wyman, L. Pilar *indexer*

Annapolis Junction
Brown, Wendy Elaine *communications consultant*
Nejib, Perri Umid-Rashid *electrical engineer*

Arnold
Smith, Martha A. *academic administrator*

Ashton
Tabler, Shirley May *retired librarian, artist*

Avenue
Price, Kathleen Vermillion *priest*

Baltimore
Abrams, Rosalie Silber *retired state agency official*
Adams, Clara I. *academic administrator*
Allan, Janet D. *dean*
Allen, Norma Ann *librarian, educator*
Alpern, Linda Lee Wevodau *health agency administrator*
Amos, Helen *hospital administrator*
Anderson, Jean R. *women's health physician*
Armstrong, Marie Cynthia *music educator*
Augustson, Edith *mental health clinician*
Baker, Susan P. *public health educator*
Ball, Marion Jokl *academic administrator*
Barnes, Adrienne *public information officer*
Barnes, Janet Lynn *artist*
Barnhart, Jo Anne B. *federal agency administrator*
Bishop, Jennifer Ann *photographer*
Blake, Catherine C. *judge*
Blakemore, Karin Jane *obstetrician, geneticist*
Bolger, Doreen *museum director*
Boughman, Joann Ashley *dean*
Bradley, Wanda Louise *librarian*
Brewer, Nevada Nancy *elementary school educator*
Bright, Margaret *sociologist*
Brock, Roslyn McCallister *association executive*
Brotman, Phyllis Block *advertising and public relations executive*
Brown, Patricia Mary Clare *health facility administrator*
Busch-Vishniac, Ilene Joy *mechanical engineering educator, researcher*
Buser, Carolyn Elizabeth *correctional education administrator*
Cain, Marcena Jean Beesley *retail executive*
Campbell, Jacquelyn C. *community health nurse*
Carper, Gertrude Esther *artist, marina owner*
Cascio, Toni Angela *social worker, educator*
Chagnoni, Kathleen *energy executive*
Chang, Debbie I-Ju *health services director*
Chapelle, Suzanne Ellery Greene *history educator*
Chaplin, Peggy Louie *lawyer*
Child-Olmsted, Gisèle Alexandra *language educator*
Chin, Katherine Moy *nutritionist, consultant*
Choudhury, Dipa *mathematician, educator*
Clements, Janice *science educator*
Clements, Mary Lou *epidemiologist, educator*
Coleman, Carolyn Quilloin *association executive*
Colomer, Veronica *medical educator, researcher*
Croushler, Sarah Isabella *dance and movement therapist*
Curl, Leigh Ann *orthopedist, surgeon*
Daniels, Susan M. *commissioner*
Davis, Katherine Sarah *physical therapy educator*
Davis, Linda L. *social welfare executive director*
Dawson, Valina L. *science educator*
DeAngelis, Catherine D. *pediatrics educator*
DeLateur, Barbara Jane *medical educator*
Del Rosso, Jeana Marie *literature educator*
D'Erasmo, Martha Jean *health company executive*
De Shields-Minnis, Tarra Ramit *lawyer*
Devan, Deborah Hunt *lawyer*
Dickinson, Jane W. *social services administrator*
Donaldson, Sue Karen *nursing educator, researcher*
Donnell, Jean Downey *education educator*
Donovan, Sharon Ann *secondary school educator*
Doory, Ann Marie *lawyer, legislator*
Dorsey, Donna Morgan *state agency administrator*
Eden-Fetzer, Dianne Toni *nurse, project coordinator*

Eldefrawi, Amira Toppozada *medical educator, toxicologist, pharmacologist, neuroscientist*
Emerson, Mia Diane *English educator*
Entwisle, Doris Roberts *sociology educator*
Evans, Judy Anne *health center administrator*
Eveleth, Janet Stidman *law association administrator*
Faden, Ruth R. *medical educator, ethicist, researcher*
Ferencz, Charlotte *pediatrician, epidemiology and preventive medicine educator*
Ferro, Elizabeth Krams *lawyer*
Fried, Linda P. *medical educator*
Friedman, Maria Andre *public relations executive*
Gauvey, Susan Kathryn *judge*
Godenne, Ghislaine Dudley *physician, psychoanalyst, educator*
Goldman, Lynn Rose *medical educator*
Grasmick, Nancy S. *school system administrator*
Greider, Carol Widney *molecular biology educator*
Grieb, Elizabeth *lawyer*
Griffin, Diane Edmund *research physician, virologist, educator*
Habermann, Helen Margaret *plant physiologist, educator*
Hahn Waranch, Helene *educational association administrator*
Hall, Marian M. *retired music educator*
Hansen, Barbara Caleen *physiologist, science educator*
Harryman, Kathleen A. *board administrator*
Helberg, Kristin Vaughan *artist*
Heller, Barbara R. *former dean, nursing educator*
Hernandez, Iris N. *clinical specialist*
Higginbotham, Eve Juliet *ophthalmologist, educator*
High, Maria Louise *artist*
Hillman, Sandra Schwartz *public relations executive, marketing professional*
Holt-Stone, C. Yvonne *judge*
Howard, Bettie Jean *surgical nurse*
Huggins, Amy Branum *music educator*
Hughes, Brenda Bethea *state legislator*
Hughes, Catherine L. (Cathy Hughes) *radio personality, broadcast executive*
Jacobson, Katherine Louise *musician, music educator*
Jamison, Kay *psychologist*
Jenkins, Louise Sherman *nursing researcher, educator*
Jenniches, F. Suzanne *engineering executive*
Jones, Hendree Evelyn *research scientist, psychologist*
Katz, Martha Lessman *lawyer*
Kemp, Suzanne Leppart *elementary school educator*
Kesselring, Linda J. *medical editor, writer*
Kim, Lillian G. Lee *retired administrative assistant*
Kramer, Norma Domenica Andrea *artist*
Kumin, Libby Barbara *speech language pathologist, educator*
Kyger, Brenda Sue *intravenous therapy nurse*
Lanier, Jacqueline Ruth *curator, artist*
Leonard, Angela Michele *librarian, educator*
Levine, Audrey Pearlstein *foundation administrator*
Li, Joanne *finance educator*
Lidtke, Doris Keefe *retired computer science educator*
Lion, Jill Altschul *sculptor*
Litrenta, Frances Marie *psychiatrist*
Lucas, Barbara B. *electrical equipment manufacturing executive*
Lungaro Cid, Lisa *educational association administrator*
Macht, Amy *real estate executive, foundation manager*
Magnuson, Nancy *librarian*
Massey-Burzio, Virginia *librarian, writer*
Massie-Burrell, Terri L. *educational association administrator*
Matheson, Nina W. *medical researcher*
Matjasko, M. Jane *anesthesiologist, educator*
Maultsby, Marilyn D. *health science association administrator*
Maumenee, Irene H. *ophthalmology educator*
McMillan, Julia A. *pediatrician*
Mensh, Suzanne Cooper *state official*
Metzger, Delores Virginia *social services professional*
Migeon, Barbara Ruben *pediatrician, geneticist*
Montgomery, Paula Kay *publisher*
Motz, Diana Gribbon *judge*
Murphy, Frances Louise, II, *retired newspaper publisher*
Norris, Karen W. *grants specialist*
Oden, Gloria *English educator, poet*
Palmer, Denise *publishing executive*
Park, Mary Woodfill *information consultant*
Peirce, Carol Marshall *English educator*
Phillips, Paula L. *foundation administrator, visual artist*
Pinkard, Anne Merrick *foundation administrator*
Pollak, Joanne E. *lawyer*
Pollak, Lisa *columnist*
Pollard, Shirley *employment training director, community services administrator, consultant*
Pratt, Joan M. *comptroller*
Prugh, Patricia Alice *psychotherapist*
Puglisi, Mary Joanna *psychologist*
Ramos, Odette Teresa *political organization worker, director*
Robinson, Carrie *pastor*
Robinson, Florine Samantha *marketing executive*
Robinson, Sally Shoemaker *lay associate church social ministries*
Rosen, Wendy Workman *arts management and publishing executive*
Rothenberg, Karen H. *dean, law educator*
Roup, Brenda Jacobs *nurse, retired military officer*
Rousuck, J. Wynn *theater critic*
Saltzberg, Joanne Maria *company executive*

Sands, Cori Eileen *artist*
Schoenrich, Edyth Hull *internal and preventive medicine physician*
Seurkamp, Mary Pat *college president*
Seydoux, Geraldine *molecular biologist*
Silbergeld, Ellen Kovner *environmental epidemiologist, researcher, toxicologist*
Smith, Carol E. *judge*
Smith, Janet Marie *sports and entertainment executive*
Starfield, Barbara Helen *pediatrician, educator*
Steinbach, Alice *journalist*
Stewart, Doris Mae *biology educator*
Stidman, Edith (Janet) Scales *parliamentarian*
Sugg, Diana K. *reporter*
Tamminga, Carol Ann *neuroscientist*
Tenser, Beth Hillary *graphics designer, art director*
Terborg-Penn, Rosalyn Marian *historian, educator*
Thomas, Jacqueline Marie *journalist, editor*
Thomas, Margaret Ann *not-for-profit developer*
Thomas, Susan Wiskemann *music educator*
Tyler, Anne (Mrs. Taghi M. Modarressi) *writer*
Ushry, Roselyn *minister*
Washington, Earline *healthcare executive*
White, Libby Kramer *librarian*
White, Pamela Janice *lawyer*
Williams, Anna M. *social worker*
Wilmot, Louise C. *charitable organization executive, retired career officer*
Yellin, Judith *small business owner*
Young, Barbara *psychiatrist, psychoanalyst, psychiatry educator, photographer*

Bel Air
Cash, LaVerne (Cynthia Cash) *physicist*
Jacobs, Nancy *state legislator*
Miller, Dorothy Eloise *education educator*
Phillips, Bernice Cecile Golden *retired vocational education educator*
Powers, Doris Hurt *retired engineering company executive*
Webster, Colleen Michael *English language educator*

Bel Alton
Quesada-Embid, Mary Regina Chamberlain *library media specialist*

Beltsville
Adams, Jean Ruth *retired entomologist, biomedical researcher*
Collins, Anita Marguerite *research geneticist*
Johnson, Phyllis Elaine *chemist, researcher*
Palm, Mary Egdahl *mycologist*
Reed, Marseeda *photographer*

Berlin
Auxer, Cathy Joan *elementary school educator*
Passwater, Barbara Gayhart *real estate broker*
Smith, Gloria Young *retired graphic artist, art educator*

Bethesda
Alving, Barbara *federal agency administrator*
Atwell, Constance Woodruff *health services executive, researcher*
Benson, Elizabeth Polk *art specialist*
Burns, Drusilla Lorene *microbiologist*
Christian, Michaele Chamblee *internist, oncologist*
Coe, Judith Lynn *retired automobile manufacturing company administrator*
Comiskey, Angela Picariello *accountant*
Cutting, Mary Dorothea *audio and audio-visual communications company executive*
Day, Marylouise Muldoon (Mrs. Richard Dayton Day) *appraiser*
Dayhoff, Nancy Belmont *artist*
de Vries, Margaret Garritsen *economist*
Dorr, Ann Pierce *science educator*
Drazin, Lisa *real estate and corporate investment banker, financial consultant*
Dulin, Maurine Stuart *volunteer*
Duncan, Constance Catharine *psychologist, educator, researcher*
Dunn, Bonnie Brill *chemist*
Dyer, Doris Anne *nursing consultant*
Ehrenfeld, Ellie (Elvera Ehrenfeld) *health science association administrator*
English, Michela *entertainment company executive*
Farci, Patrizia *medical educator, researcher*
Fleming, Patricia Stubbs *artist*
Francomano, Clair Ann *geneticist*
Free, Ann Cottrell *writer*
Gimmel, Molly Kay *business executive*
Grady, Patricia A. *health institute director, researcher*
Greenberg, Judith Horovitz *genetics and developmental biology administrator*
Guttman, Helene Nathan *biomedical research consultant, transpersonal counselor, regression therapist*
Hagberg, Viola Wilgus *lawyer*
Hartnett, Elizabeth A. *trade association administrator*
Haseltine, Florence Pat *obstetrician, gynecologist, research administrator*
Haugan, Gertrude M. *clinical psychologist*
Helke, Cinda Jane *pharmacology and neuroscience educator, researcher, academic administrator*
Herman, Edith Carol *journalist*
Herman, Mary Margaret *neuropathologist*
Humphreys, Betsy L. *librarian*
Johnson, Joyce Marie *psychiatrist, epidemiologist, public health officer*
Jordan, Elke *molecular biologist, government medical research institute executive*
Joyce, Bernita Anne *former federal government agency administrator*
Kaplan, Marjorie *broadcast executive*
Kawazoe, Robin Inada *federal official*
Kirschstein, Ruth Lillian *physician*
Klee, Claude Blenc *medical researcher*
Koenig, Elizabeth Barbara *sculptor*
Krumsiek, Barbara J. *investment company executive*
Landis, Story C. C. *neurobiologist*
Larrabee, Barbara Princelau *retired intelligence officer*
Lystad, Mary Hanemann (Mrs. Robert Lystad) *sociologist, author*
Marini, Ann Marie *medical researcher, educator*
Martin, Kathleen L. *military officer, hospital administrator*
McCray, Alexa T. *health science association administrator, director*
McHale, Judith A. (Judith Ottalloran) *broadcast executive, lawyer*
Nabel, Elizabeth G. *medical researcher, cardiologist*
Naylor, Phyllis Reynolds *writer*
Nelson, Ethelyn Barnett *civic worker*
Nimeroff, Phyllis Ruth *electronic engineer, visual artist*
Olson, Lynn *editor*
Orthmann, Rosemary Ann *editor*
Parron, Delores L. *federal agency administrator*
Penn, Audrey S. *retired federal agency administrator*
Peters, Brenda Irene *computer specialist, government official*
Pinn, Vivian W. *pathologist, federal agency administrator*
Pollard, Bette Marlene *computer scientist*
Polsby, Gail K. *psychotherapist*
Puck, Jennifer M. *physician, scientist*
Raffini, Renee Kathleen *foreign language professional, educator*
Rapoport, Judith *psychiatrist*
Reed, Miriam Bell *legislative staff member*
Roberts, Doris Emma *epidemiologist, consultant, public health nurse*
Robinson, Sharon Beth *health science association administrator*
Ruttenberg, Ruth A. *economist*
Salisbury, Tamara Paula *foundation executive*
Sarnoff, Lili-Charlotte (Lolo Sarnoff) *artist*
Singer, Dinah *federal agency administrator, immunologist, researcher*
Skirboll, Lana R. *federal health policy director*
Smith, Renae Colleen *music educator*
Spector, Eleanor Ruth *corporation executive*
Spencer, Heidi Hornold *psychotherapist, writer, educator*
Sternberg, Esther May *neuroendocrinologist, immunologist, rheumatologist*
Stover, Ellen L. *health scientist, psychologist*
Underwood, Brenda S. *information specialist, microbiologist, grants administrator*
Ungerleider, Leslie G. *neuroscientist*
Vaitukaitis, Judith Louise *medical research administrator*
Vaughan, Martha *biochemist, educator*
Volkow, Nora Dolores *medical research center director*
Wagner, Cynthia Gail *editor, writer*
White, Jeannette Lee *information technology executive*
Willoughby, Anne *health facility administrator, researcher, educator*
Wolpert-DeFilippes, Mary K. *science administrator*
Zoon, Kathryn Christine *biochemist*

Bowie
Brown, Angela Rose *social services speaker, educator*
Hillsman, Joan Rucker *music educator*
Lesh, Kathryn Ann *nursing researcher*
Tesar, Patricia Marie *academic coordinator*

Brookeville
Rico, Stephanie Allcock *art educator*

Burkittsville
Aughenbaugh, Deborah Ann *mayor, retired elementary school educator*

Burtonsville
Kammeyer, Sonia Margaretha *real estate agent*

Cabin John
Bergfors, Constance Marie *artist, educator*

California
Avram, Henriette Davidson *librarian, government official*

Cambridge
Brohawn, Virginia Bridgeman *music educator*
Eckardt, Adelaide Campbell *state legislator, psychiatric nurse*
Spahr, Elizabeth *environmental services administrator*

Capitol Heights
Zinaman, Helaine Madeleine *gifted and talented education educator*

Catonsville
Hammond, Deborah Lynn *lay worker*
Lanciotti, Judi D. *art educator*
Smith, F. Louise *elementary school educator*

Centreville
Shoemaker, Anne Cunningham *retired mathematics educator*

Chester
Shively, Bonnie Lee *pastor*

Chestertown
Docksteader, Karen Kemp *marketing professional*
Rather, Lucia Porcher Johnson *library administrator*

Chevy Chase
Allison, Adrienne Amelia *not-for-profit developer*
Brenner, Marcella Siegel *retired education educator*
Cline, Ruth Eleanor Harwood *translator*
Coble, Wilma Loretta *real estate investor, property management*
Duvall, Bernice Bettum *artist, exhibit coordinator, jewelry designer*
Eccles, Mary *writer*
Greenspoon, Irma Naiman *business executive*
Kranking, Margaret Graham *artist, educator*
Kullen, Shirley Robinowitz *psychiatric epidemiologist, consultant*
Langelan, Martha Jane (Marty) *sexual harassment expert*
Norwood, Janet Lippe *economist*
Sagawa, Shirley Sachi *lawyer*
Towsner, Cynthia Merle *vocational school educator*
Wolf, Jean D. *educational consultant, writer*
Wolf, Michele Sue *poet, writer, editor*
Wright, Helen Patton *professional society administrator*

Chillum
Malbon, Louise *nursing educator, hypnotherapist*

Churchton
Miller, Sandra Ritchie *artist, art therapist*

Clinton
Brooks, Pauline C. *computer and networking services company executive*
Cruz, Wilhelmina Mangahas *critical care physician, educator*

Cockeysville
Hager, Louise Alger *retired chaplain*

Cockeysville Hunt Valley
Elkin, Lois Shanman *business systems company executive*
Roeder Vaughan, Mimi *small business owner*

College Park
Beasley, Maurine Hoffman *journalism educator, historian*
Brazile, Donna *advocate*
Buggs, Elaine S. *financial analyst*
Collins, Merle *English and comparative literature educator*
Dill, Bonnie Thornton *sociology educator*
Doherty, Lillian Eileen *classicist, educator*
Fenselau, Catherine Clarke *chemistry educator*
Finkelstein, Barbara *education educator*
Gantt, Elisabeth *plant biology educator, researcher*
[illegible] *studies educator*
Hill, Clara Edith *psychology educator*
Hudson, Deborah M. *public relations practitioner*
Latham, Corinna Elisabeth *aerospace engineer*
Lubkin, Gloria Becker *physicist*
Morman, Shirley H. *director*
Murdoch, Amelia Clara *educational association administrator*
Oster, Rose Marie Gunhild *foreign language professional, educator*
Prentice, Ann Ethelynd *university dean*
Presser, Harriet Betty *sociology educator*
Schwab, Susan Carroll *dean*
Sorenson, Georgia Lynn Jones *political scientist, educator*
Struna, Nancy L. *social historian and American studies educator*
Szymanski, Edna Mora *dean*
White, Marilyn Domas *information science educator*
Yotsukura, Lindsay Amthor *language educator*

Columbia
Davis, Janet Marie Gorden *secondary school educator*
Gold, Susan *conference educator*
Gregoric, Corazon Arzalem *operations supervisor*
Gruhl, Andrea Morris *librarian*
Hale, Mignon S. Palmer-Flack *elementary school educator, educator*
Harrison, Elza Stanley *medical association executive*
Hartman, Lee Ann Walraff *secondary school educator, consultant*
Hyde, Rebecca Medwin *financial consultant*
Jones-Wilson, Faustine Clarisse *retired education educator*
Klein, Sami Weiner *librarian*
Lok, Joan Mei-Lok *community affairs specialist, artist*
Narvaez, Bernice Williams *financial consultant*
Queen, Sandy (Sandra Jane Queen) *psychologist, trainer*
Scates, Alice Yeomans *former government official, consultant*
Spicknall, Joan *music educator*
Weems, Helen Rachel *piano teacher, accompanist*
Williams, Mamie Alethia *minister*

Crisfield
LaRue, Lea Maylene *music educator*

Cumberland
Bennett, Sue Ellen *director*

Davidsonville
Blaxall, Martha Ossoff *economist*
Bowles, Liza K. *construction executive*

Derwood
Mizes, Maria Gabriela *cultural organization administrator, art historian*
Stadtman, Thressa Campbell *biochemist*

Easton
Colton, Elizabeth Wishart *government agency administrator*
Daniels, Marybeth Elizabeth *nurse*
Fredrick, Susan Walker *tax company manager*
Potter, Blair Burns *editor*
Reed, Carol L. *secondary school educator, writer*
Whitten, Nancy Bimmerman *clinical social worker, marriage therapist*
Wilson, Laura Ann *newspaper editor*

Edgewater
Holm, Jeanne Marjorie *writer, consultant, government official, former career officer*

Elkridge
Byrd, Alicia D. *minister, sociologist*
Calton, Sandra Jeane *accountant*
Matthews, Lois Marr *musician, music educator*

Elkton
Battee, Sharon Taylor *not-for-profit developer*
Jasinski-Caldwell, Mary L. *company executive*
Loveless, Laurel Plumstead *minister*

Ellicott City
Adkins, Sandra Kay *music educator, church musician*
Galinsky, Deborah Jean *county official*
Powell, Lillian Marie *retired music educator*

Forest Hill
Klein, Shirley Snyderman *retail executive*

Fort George G Meade
Kera, Tiiu *career officer*

Fort Washington
Cameron, Rita Giovannetti *writer, publisher*
Diercks, Elizabeth Gorman *elementary school educator*
Fielding, Elizabeth M(ay) *public relations executive, writer*

Frederick
Byron, Beverly Butcher *retired congresswoman*
Cannon, Faye E. *bank executive*
Gordon, Rita Simon *civic leader, former nurse, educator*
Hamilton, Rhoda Lillian Rosén *guidance counselor, language educator, consultant*
Henderson, Madeline Mary (Berry Henderson) *chemist, researcher, consultant*
Hogan, Ilona Modly *lawyer*
Jenkins, Nancy A. *research scientist*
Klein, Elaine Charlotte *school system administrator*
Randall, Frances *technical writer*
Schricker, Ethel Killingsworth *retired business management consultant*
Smith, Sharron Williams *chemistry educator*

Frostburg
Gira, Catherine Russell *university president*
Mills, Susan W. *music educator*

Gaithersburg
Dowd, Carolyn Lay *social worker*
Gebbie, Katharine Blodgett *physicist*
Green, Shia Toby Riner *therapist*
Hegyeli, Ruth Ingeborg Elisabeth Johnsson *pathologist, government official*
Jacox, Marilyn Esther *chemist*
Kemmerer, Sharon Jean *computer systems analyst*
Kress, Jill Clancy *human resources professional, consultant*
McDowell, Donna Schultz *lawyer, educator*
Powell, Lura J. *science association administrator*
Rosenblatt, Joan Raup *mathematical statistician*
Sengers, Johanna M. H. Levelt *thermophysicist*
Stroud, Nancy Iredell *retired secondary school educator, freelance writer, editor*
Vanasdalan, Joan Louise *music educator, musician*

Galena
Hunsperger, Elizabeth Jane *art and design consultant, educator*

Gambrills
Streeter, Carol *technology marketing executive*

Garrett Park
Stites, M(ary) Elizabeth *architecture educator*

Germantown
Collins, Karen Jeanne *music educator*
Foulke, Judith Diane *health physicist*
Isaacson, Elaine Marie *sales and training agent*
Searle, Michelle A. *music educator, webmaster*
Weiner, Claire Muriel *freelance writer*

Glen Burnie
Barteet, Barbara Boyter *retired social worker*
Endres, Eleanor Estelle *speech pathology/audiology services professional*
Hepburn, Jeanette C. *home health nurse*
Ruth, Shiela Grant *music educator*

Great Mills
Gehring, Patti J. *principal*

Greenbelt
Amato, Deborah Douglass *aerospace engineer*
Chasanow, Deborah K. *federal judge*
Hogensen, Margaret Hiner *librarian, consultant*
Kalnay, Eugenia *university administrator, meteorologist*
Kessel, Mona *space physicist*
Li, Mary J. *scientist, educator*
Obamogie, Mercy A. *physician*
Simpson, Joanne Malkus *meteorologist*
Wagner, Sally Sterrett *music educator*

Hagerstown
Butts, Mary Ellen F. *secondary school educator*
Corbett, Helen A. *chemist, chemical engineer*
Harrison, Lois Smith *hospital executive, educator*
Kelsh, Janice Eileen *club executive*

McCoy, Mildred Brookman *retired elementary education educator*
Thomas, Yvonne Shirey *family and consumer science educator*
Yost, Jean Marie *administrative assistant*

Hampstead
Rogers, Karen Cooledge *music educator*

Hanover
Schmidt, Sandra Jean *secondary school educator*

Harwood
Smith, Maria Lynn *school system administrator*

Havre de Grace
Wetter, Virginia Forwood Pate *broadcast executive*

Highland
Varga, Deborah Trigg *music educator, entertainment company owner*

Hollywood
Dietz, Laurel Patricia *music educator*

Hyattsville
Golden, Marita *English language educator, foundation executive*
Jones, Gretchen Kuykendall *computer specialist, statistician*
Raines, Charlotte Austine Butler *artist*
Rodgers, Mary Columbro *literature educator, writer, academic administrator*
Williams, Gladys Tucker *elementary school principal*

Jefferson
Dybell, Elizabeth Anne Sledden *clinical psychologist*

Jessup
Fox, Dawne Marie *safety scientist*

Joppa
Kott, Beverly Parat *financial counselor, community activist*

Kensington
Mintz, Suzanne *association executive*
Ricketts, Marijane Gnegy *poet*

La Plata
Core, Mary Carolyn W. Parsons *health facility administrator*
Fisher, Gail Feimster *epidemiologist, researcher, government agency administrator*
Raymond, Elizabeth Sollars *vault and monument company executive*

Landover
Frederick, Amy L. *science administrator*

Lanham
Godwin, Mary Jo *editor, librarian consultant*
Henderson Hall, Brenda Ford *computer company executive*

Lanham Seabrook
Barnes, Margaret Anderson *business consultant*
Corrothers, Helen Gladys *criminal justice official*
Moore, Erica *band director*
Ojinnaka, Becky *publishing executive*
Pleasant-Jackson, Tonya *therapist, consultant*
Southall, Virginia Lawrence *retired artist*

Laurel
Hunter, Edwina Earle *elementary school educator*
Landis, Donna Marie *nursing administrator, women's health nurse*

Leonardtown
Rudigier, Roberta Lynn *librarian*

Lonaconing
Lynch, Diane *volunteer*

Lutherville
Chait, Andrea Melinda *school psychologist*
Goodman, Valerie Dawson *psychiatric social worker*

Lutherville Timonium
Booth, Penelope Partridge *secondary school educator, writer, principal*
Gray, Dahli *accounting educator and administrator*

Manokin
Miles, Elizabeth Jane *social worker*

Mardela Springs
Harcum, Louise Mary Davis *retired elementary education educator*

McDaniel
Roth, Lisa Mae *writer*

Mitchellville
Chilman, Catherine Earles Street *social welfare educator, author*
Marsh, Caryl Amsterdam *museum exhibitions curator, psychologist, advisor*

Montgomery Village
Wykes, Mary Maushak *real estate agent*

Mount Airy
Johnston, Josephine Rose *chemist*
Wagner, Doris Walkling *volunteer, director*
Yocum, Carol Cosens *minister*

Mount Rainier
London, Wanda Elaine *minister*

Newburg
Mason, Christine Chapman *psychotherapist*

North Bethesda
Sherman, Deane Murray *culture organization administrator*

North East
Goldbach, Jennifer D. *bank executive*

Ocean City
Phillips, Shirley Flowers *food service executive*

Ocean Pines
Fullerton, Jean Leah *retired language educator, researcher, census researcher*

Odenton
Murray, Catherine Mary Murphy *accountant*

Olney
Hendricks, Susan McCurdy *art educator, artist*
Sodetz, Carol Jean *aquatic fitness educator*

Owings Mills
Berg, Barbara Kirsner *health education specialist*
Holdridge, Barbara *book publisher*
Ryan, Judith W. *geriatrics consultant, adult nurse practitioner, educator, researcher*
Smith, Katrina Diane *writer*
Tapp, Mamie Pearl *educational association administration*

Oxon Hill
Robinson, Cheryl Jeffreys *special education educator, consultant*
Scott, Frances Fisher Markoe *retired secondary school educator*

Pasadena
Bell, Patricia Wright *music educator*
Fastige, Nellie Marshall *elementary school educator*
Kuhn, Jolyn *artist*

Perryville
Dunne, Judith Doyle *information scientist, educator*

Pikesville
Portnoy, Leslie Snyder *art educator, artist*

Port Tobacco
Smith, Sheila Robertson *laboratory technician*

Potomac
Benton, Kay Myers *sales executive*
Carper, Fern Gayle *small business owner, writer*
Dickerman, Serafina Poerio *real estate broker, consultant*
Durek, Dorothy Mary *retired English language educator*
Eaves, Maria Perry *realtor*
Johnson, Anne Hale *educational association administrator, director*
Karch, Karen Brooke *principal*
Kernan, Barbara Desind *senior government executive*
Kuykendall, Crystal Arlene *educational consultant, lawyer*
Marincola, Elizabeth Mark *scientific society executive*
Medin, Julia Adele *mathematics educator, researcher*
Murow, Christine *music educator*
Paper, Susanne Abby Babin *science educator, writer*
Pastan, Linda Olenik *poet*
Peters, Carol Beattie Taylor (Mrs. Frank Albert Peters) *mathematician*
Roesser, Jean Wolberg *state official*
Rosenberg, Sarah Zacher *institute arts administration executive, humanities administration consultant*
Rotberg, Iris Comens *social scientist*
Sceery, Beverly Davis *genealogist, writer, educator*
Schonholtz, Joan Sondra Hirsch *banker, civic worker*
Schuessler, Isabelle Sweeny *school administrator*
Sundick, Sherry Small *author, journalist, poet*
Vadus, Gloria A. *scientific document examiner*

Princess Anne
Nnadi, Eucharia E. *academic administrator*

Randallstown
Hatch, Sally Ruth *foundation administrator, writer, consultant*
McDowell, Elizabeth Mary *retired pathology educator*

Reisterstown
Bart, Polly Turner *real estate developer*
Goethe, Elizabeth Hogue *music educator*
Tirone, Barbara Jean *health insurance administrator*

Riva
Lynch Schuster, Janice Marie *freelance/self-employed writer*

Riverdale
Bernard, Cathy S. *management corporation executive*
Kline, Nancy Meadors *non-profit company executive, consulting executive, writer*

Rockville
Alexis, Shirley Davidson *secondary school educator*
Barron, Myra Hymovich *lawyer*
Bayne, Kathryn Ann Louise *veterinarian*
Boetticher, Helene *lawyer*
Broder, Gail Steinmetz *lawyer*
Cain, Karen Mirinda *musician, educator*
Cheston, Sheila Carol *lawyer*

Clancy, Carolyn *science foundation director, researcher, educator*
Corley, Rose Ann McAfee *government official*
Culliton, Barbara J. *medical association administrator*
Cyr, Karen D. *lawyer*
Davis, Beverly Watts *government agency administrator*
Dawson, Dianne *education educator, writer*
Duke, Elizabeth M. *health facility administrator*
Fraser, Claire M. *research scientist, science administrator*
Gillick, Betsy Brinkley *pharmaceutical executive*
Gleich, Carol S. *health professions education executive*
Gordon, Joan Irma *lawyer*
Gougé, Susan Cornelia Jones *microbiologist*
Henderson, Harriet *librarian*
Hodgson, Helen *writer*
Kagan, Cheryl C. *state legislator*
Kelsey, Frances Oldham *government official*
Kiger, F. Louise *nursing administrator*
Kohlhorst, Gail Lewis *librarian*
Kurkul, Wenyi Wang *musician, educator, administrator*
MacArthur, Diana Taylor *advanced technology executive*
Marcuccio, Phyllis Rose *retired association executive, editor*
Messersmith, Stephanie Hunt *nursing administrator*
Middleton, Wanda Karen Lee *songwriter, poet, minister*
Miller, Claire Ellen *children's writer, editor, educator*
Moore, Melinda *public health physician*
Moses, Cynthia Glass *realtor*
Niewiaroski, Trudi Osmers (Gertrude Niewiaroski) *social studies educator*
Nitkin, Rebecca A. *lawyer*
Parham-Hopson, Deborah Hopson *health administrator*
Petzold, Carol Stoker *state legislator*
Power, A. Kathryn *social services administrator*
Raker, Irma *judge*
Rimer, Barbara K. *health facility administrator, educator*
Salzman, Joanna Michele *special education educator*
Smith, Shelagh Alison *public health educator*
Standing, Kimberly Anna *educational researcher*
Stratton, Margaret Adele *psychologist*
Uffen, Ellen Serlen *editor, writer*
Waidler, Beverly Mae *music teacher*
Weiss, Rita Sandra *transportation executive, educator*
Woodcock, Janet *federal official*

Royal Oak
Israel, Lesley Lowe *retired political scientist, consultant*

Ruxton
Sheldon, Louise Roberts *writer*

Saint Marys City
Clifton, Lucille Thelma *author*
Von Kellenbach, Katharina *religious studies and women's studies educator*

Saint Michaels
Wildasin, Elizabeth Sewell *band director*

Salisbury
Adkins, Patricia Ann *school system administrator, educator*
Booker, Betty Mae *poet*
Wiljanen, Lynn M. *social sciences educator*
Wilmer, Ann *public relations executive*
Zimmer, Susan Snead *music educator*
Zinner, Ellen Scheiner *university administrator, clinical psychologist*

Severna Park
Grace, Barbara Lee *retail executive*
Hall, Marcia Joy *non-profit organization administrator*
Humphreys Troy, Patricia *communications executive*
Pumphrey, Janet Kay *editor, publisher*
Sunday, Melva Dora *elementary school educator*
Sundeen, Sandra Joan *mental health nurse*
Windsor, Patricia (Katonah Summertree, Perrin Winters) *author, educator, lecturer*

Silver Spring
Adams, Diane Loretta *physician*
Ahmad, Mirza Muzaffar *economic advisor*
Altschul, B J *public relations counselor*
Beard, Lillian B. McLean *pediatrician, consultant*
Bennett, Carol(ine) Elise *retired reporter, actress*
Best-Goring, Cynthia Lovale *elementary school principal*
Bonner, Bester Davis *school system administrator*
Borkovec, Vera Z. *Russian studies educator*
Burgos-Sasscer, Ruth *chancellor emeritus*
Burke, Margaret Ann *computer and communications company specialist*
Canahuati, Judy *lactation consultant*
Cathey, Mary Ellen Jackson *religious studies educator*
Coles, Anna Louise Bailey *retired dean, nurse*
Compton, Mary Beatrice Brown (Mrs. Ralph Theodore Compton) *public relations executive, writer*
Dunkins, Betty *wedding coordinator, publisher*
Fields, Daisy Bresley *human resources specialist, writer*
Flug, Janice *librarian*
Foley, Virginia Sue Lashley *counselor, international training consultant*
Fromberg, Jean Stern *school system administrator*
Goertzel, Gwendolyn Michele *painter, priest*
Hall, Davida Karen *art educator, elementary school educator*

Hilberg, Rosemary Helen *retired human resource specialist*
Hunt, Mary Elizabeth *religious studies educator*
Jaffe, Elaine June *creative fiberwork designer*
Johnson, Karisa Ann *political activist*
Kant, Gloria Jean *retired neuroscientist, researcher*
Keating, Susan C. *credit foundation executive*
Laughlin, Naomi Myers *realtor*
Lett, Cynthia Ellen Wein *speaker, trainer, coach*
Mashin, Jacqueline Ann Cook *medical sciences administrator, nursing administrator*
Mills, Ianther Marie *minister*
Mohr, Christina *retired economist*
Moreno, Donna Marie *communications executive*
Nevans, Laurel S. *rehabilitation counselor*
Null, Elisabeth Higgins *librarian, writer*
O'Connell, Mary Ita *psychotherapist*
Ott, Mary Diederich *artist*
Papas, Irene Kalandros *English language educator, poet, writer*
Power, Barbara Louise *artist, educator*
Rayburn, Carole Ann (Mary Aida Rayburn) *psychologist, researcher, writer, consultant*
Rivera-Sinclair, Elsa *psychologist, consultant, researcher*
Roth, Harriet Steinhorn *advocate, educator, public speaker*
Sammet, Jean E. *computer scientist*
Shih-Carducci, Joan Chia-mo *cooking educator, biochemist, medical technologist, author, writer*
Stanford, Jennifer Laura *nurse, educator*
Vanzant, Iyanla *writer*
Wallace, C. Elizabeth McFarland *retired association director*
Wolfe, Pamela Kline *history educator*
Woolard, Connie Ward *artist, retired art gallery manager*
Zakheim, Barbara Jane *development professional*

Simpsonville
Altschuler, Ruth Phyllis *realtor, secondary school educator*

Snow Hill
Apson, Jane R. *public health educator*
Pusey, Ellen Pratt *home economist*

Sparks
Suarez-Murias, Marguerite C. *retired language educator, retired literature educator*

Stevenson
Hyman, Mary Bloom *science education programs coordinator*

Suitland
Vandiver, Pamela Bowren *science educator*

Sykesville
Crist, Gertrude H. *civic worker*
Perry, Nancy Trotter *former telecommunications company executive*

Takoma Park
Silverman, Charlotte *epidemiologist, educator*
von Hake, Margaret Joan *librarian*

Temple Hills
Curry, Emma Beatrice *elementary school educator*
Day, Mary Jane Thomas *cartographer*
Lawlah, Gloria Gary *state legislator, educator*

Timonium
Yorkman, Marquetta Marcye Bodine *financial professional*

Towson
Baker, Jean Harvey *history educator*
Baltzley, Patricia Creel *secondary mathematics educator*
Mueller, Alicia Kay *music educator*
Myers, Debra Taylor *elementary school educator, writer*
Nicolosi, Gianna Ruth *marketing professional*
Putzel, Constance Kellner *lawyer*
Sadak, Diane Marie *performing arts educator*
Shriver, Pamela H. *retired professional tennis player, sports analyst*

Union Bridge
Hannah, Judy Challenger *private education tutor*

Upper Marlboro
Cutright, Loretta Ann *special education educator*
Hewlett, Elizabeth M. *county official*
Rough, Marianne Christina *librarian, educator*
Street, Patricia Lynn *retired secondary school educator*
Swift-Howard, Alice Lorraine *school system administrator*

Vienna
Farnell, Mary Ann *minister*

Waldorf
Bouchard, Lynne Katherine *music educator*
Robey, Sherie Gay Southall Gordon *secondary education educator, consultant*

Walkersville
Newton, Loretta Jean *insurance agent*

Washington Grove
Anisimova, Tanya *cellist, educator*

West Bethesda
Vogelgesang, Sandra Louise *business executive, writer, consultant*

West River
Bower, Catherine Downes *communications, management consultant*
Howl, Joanne Healey *veterinarian, writer*

Adams, Jody *chef, restaurant owner*
Adams, Ruth-Anne *chef*
Amon, Angelika *medical researcher*
Arkhipova, Irina R. *biologist*
Bailyn, Lotte *psychology and management educator*
Bane, Mary Jo *political science educator*
Bartholet, Elizabeth *law educator*
Baumgartner, Mary Anne Sgarlat *academic administrator, entrepreneur*
Berlowitz, Leslie *cultural organization administrator*
Blair, Ann *historian*
Bloom, Kathryn Ruth *public relations executive*
Bonina, Mary *poet*
Burns, Virginia *social worker*
Cazden, Courtney B(orden) *education educator*
Ceyer, Sylvia T. *chemistry educator*
Chandler, Fay Martin *artist*
Chiles, Carol S. *architectural firm executive*
Chisholm, Sallie Watson *biological oceanography educator, researcher*
Clifton, Anne Rutenber *psychotherapist, educator*
Cohn, Marjorie Benedict *curator, art historian, educator*
Cole, Heather Ellen *librarian*
Cooper, Mary Campbell *information services executive*
Cordero, Mercedes Paula *director, consultant*
Crawford, Linda Sibery *lawyer, educator*
de Monteiro, Nadsa *chef*
DiCamillo, Kate *writer*
Dobson, Parrish *photographer, educator*
Drake, Elisabeth Mertz *chemical engineer, consultant*
Dresselhaus, Mildred Spiewak *physics and engineering educator*
Eisenberg, Carola *psychiatry educator*
Eurich, Nell P. *education educator*
Faust, Drew Gilpin *historian, educator*
Flannery, Susan Marie *library administrator*
Frazer, Jendayi *political science educator*
Friend, Cynthia M. *chemist, educator*
Frisch, Rose Epstein *population sciences researcher*
Funkhouser, Erica *writer, writing educator*
Gilligan, Carol *psychologist, writer*
Glendon, Mary Ann *law educator*
Goldin, Claudia Dale *economics educator*
Goldring, Elizabeth *environmental media artist, poet*
Goodman, Ellen Holtz *journalist*
Graham, Jorie *writer, educator*
Graham, Patricia Albjerg *education educator*
Gray, Elizabeth Dodson *theologian, writer, speaker*
Graybiel, Ann M. *medical educator*
Grosz, Barbara Jean *computer science educator*
Hamner, Suzanne Leath *retired history educator*
Hau, Lene *physicist, optics scientist*
Herzlinger, Regina *economist, educator*
Hewitt, Jacqueline N. *astronomy educator*
Hopkins, Nancy H. *biology educator*
Hubbard, Ruth *biology educator*
Hunt, Swanee G. *public policy educator, former ambassador*
Jones, Mary M. *landscape architect*
Kagan, Elena *law educator*
Kanwisher, Nancy G. *neuroscientist*
Kilpatrick, Maureen *food service executive*
Kistiakowsky, Vera *physics researcher, educator*
Klunder, Janice Marie *lawyer*
Koepp, Donna Pauline Petersen *librarian*
Kraus, Rozann B. *performing company executive*
Krauss, Alison *country musician*
Laiou, Angeliki Evangelos *history educator*
Langer, Ellen Jane *psychologist, educator, writer, artist*
Lauzier, Marijean *public relations executive*
Leveson, Nancy G. *aeronautical engineer*
Lipson, Pamela *information scientist*
Long, Bridget Terry *education educator*
Luu, Jane *astronomer*
Lydon, Amanda *chef*
Lynch, Nancy Ann *computer scientist, educator*
Maier, Pauline *history educator*
Martin, Lynn Morley *former secretary of labor*
Marvin, Ursula Bailey *retired geologist*
Mathews, Joan Helene *pediatrician*
Matsui, Connie L. *pharmaceutical executive*
McDonald, Christie Anne *Romance languages and literature educator, writer*
McKenna, Margaret Anne *university president*
Merrifield, Susan Ruth *education educator*
Moore, Sally Falk *anthropology educator*
Mori, Toshiko *architecture educator*
Nightingale, Deborah Seifert *systems engineer, consultant*
Pardue, Mary-Lou *biology educator*
Pierce, Naomi Ellen *biology educator, researcher*
Pollock, Rachel Elizabeth *costume designer*
Power, Samantha *academic administrator, writer*
Qualls, Roxanne *mayor*
Rayman, Paula M. *economics educator*
Raymo, Maureen Elizabeth *geologist, researcher*
Rhoda, Janice Tucker *writer, educator, musician*
Roberts, Nancy *computer educator*
Rosenkrantz, Barbara Gutmann *retired history educator*
Rowe, Mary P. *organizational ombudsman, management educator*
Sallee, Marguerite *association executive*
Samson, Leona D. *biological engineering educator, research center director, researcher*
Schuessler Fiorenza, Elisabeth *theology educator*
Slosburg-Ackerman, Jill Rose *artist, educator*
Smith, Susie Irene *histotechnologist, cytometrist*
Sortun, Ana *food service executive*
Stubbe, JoAnne *chemistry educator*
Thompson, Doreen *public relations executive*
Tocio, Mary Ann *association executive*
Torriani-Gorini, Annamaria *microbiologist, educator*
Ulrich, Laurel Thatcher *historian, educator*
Vendler, Helen Hennessy *literature educator, poetry critic*
Villa-Komaroff, Lydia *molecular biologist, educator, university official*
Warren, Elizabeth *law educator*
Watson, Rubie *museum director*
Widnall, Sheila Evans *aeronautical educator, former secretary of the airforce, former university official*
Wilcox, Maud *editor*
Wood, Julie M. *educational consultant*
Wurtman, Judith Joy *research scientist*
Wylie, Joan Blout *real estate rehabilitator, designer, ceramist*
Youngren, Virginia Rotan *psychologist*
Zinberg, Dorothy Shore *science policy educator*
Zoll, Mary *writer, educator*

Canton
Bentas, Lily Haseotes *retail executive*
Karpiak, Tanya *lawyer, educator*
Pitts, Virginia M. *human resources executive*

Centerville
Condon, Ann Blunt *psychotherapist*

Charlestown
Faustman, Denise L. *immunologist*
Washa, Kirsten Thomas *mental health services professional*

Chatham
Boudreau, Michelle E. *principal, consultant*
Cogan, Mary Hart *community activist, educator*
Popkin, Alice Brandeis *lawyer*

Chelmsford
Elwell, Barbara Lois Dow *community organizer*

Chelsea
Kuhne, Alice *oil industry executive*

Chestnut Hill
Addis, Deborah Jane *management consultant, editor*
Bando, Patricia Alice *director*
Burgess, Ann Wolbert *nursing educator*
Edward, G. Gail *investment company executive, theater operator*
Eutemey, Karen Denise *art educator, sculptor*
Grove, Shari Taylor *librarian, educator*
Hawkins, Joellen Margaret Beck *nursing educator*
Munro, Barbara Hazard *nursing educator, dean, researcher*
Nemerowicz, Gloria *academic administrator*
Valette, Rebecca Marianne *Romance languages educator*

Chicopee
Costanzo, Nanci Joy *art educator*
Masciotra, Janet Marie *elementary school educator*

Cohasset
Chenault Minot, Marilyn *legal executive*
Husband, Janet Grace *library director, writer*
Replogle, Jeanne Lonnquist *artist*
Yess, Denise Anne *speech pathology/audiology services professional, educator*

Concord
Domar, Carola Rosenthal *social worker*
Erdely, Beatrice *musician*
Gomberg, Sydelle *dancer educator*
Rice, Susan S. *social worker*

Cotuit
Crocker, Jean Hazelton *retired educator, environmental volunteer*
Thibideau, Regina *retail executive, social worker*

Danvers
Clark, Sharon Jackson *private school administrator*
O'Malley, Marie Kiernan *healthcare products company professional*

Dartmouth
Leclair, Susan Jean *hematologist, clinical laboratory scientist, educator*

Dedham
Janson, Barbara Jean *publisher*
Naughton, Marie Ann *corporate executive*

Dorchester
Garrison, Althea *government official*
Lee, June Warren *dentist*
Wideman, Carol M. *accountant, consultant*

Dover
Buyse, Marylou *pediatrician, geneticist, medical association administrator*
Salhany, Lucille S. *broadcast executive*

Duxbury
Erickson, Phyllis Traver *marketing executive*
Parris, Rebecca (Ruth Blair MacCloskey) *musician, educator*
Thrasher, Dianne Elizabeth *mathematics educator, computer consultant*

East Bridgewater
Farrell, Sharon Elaine *retired real estate broker*
Heywood, Anne *artist, educator, author*

Everett
Auger, Kimberly Ann *elementary school educator*

Fairhaven
Goes, Kathleen Ann *secondary education educator, choral director*
Lopes, Myra Amelia *writer*
Rose, Anita Carroll *retired educator*

Fall River
Andrade, Manuela Pestana *art educator*
Sullivan, Ruth Anne *librarian*
Zahm, Mary A. *psychologist, educator*

Falmouth
Fullerton, Davina *art historian, consultant, researcher*
Milkman, Marianne Friedenthal *retired city planner*

Fiskdale
Colwell-Snyder, Lucy Fay *music educator*

Fitchburg
Niemi, Beatrice Neal *social services professional*
Scannell, Ann Elizabeth *nurse, educator*
Sugrue, Teresa Gillis *multi-media specialist, secondary school educator*

Florence
Kan, Susan *publishing executive, editor*
Park, Beverly Goodman *lawyer*

Foxboro
Kennedy, Susan Marie *music educator*

Framingham
Agüero-Torres, Irene Beatriz *language educator*
Austin, Sandra Ikenberry *nursing educator, consultant*
Bogard, Carole Christine *lyric soprano*
Dawicki, Doloretta Diane *analytical chemist, research biochemist, educator*
Heineman, Helen L. *provost*
Hillman, Carol Barbara *communications executive, consultant*
Hoyt, Susan *retail stores executive*
Johnson, Maryfran *editor*
Lindsay, Leslie *packaging engineer*
Lipton, Leah *art historian, educator, museum curator*
Valakis, M. Lois *retired elementary school educator*
West, Doe *bioethicist, social justice activist, researcher*
Willinger, Rhonda Zwern *optometrist*
Wulf, Sharon Ann *management consultant*

Franklin
Alibrio-Curran, Frances J. *retired music educator*

Gloucester
Johnson, Anne Elisabeth *medical assistant*
Means, Rosaline *business executive, business educator*
Swift, Marilyn K. *artist, educator*
Swigart, Joan B. *artist, art consultant*

Great Barrington
Curtin, Phyllis *music educator, dean, vocalist*
Lewis, Karen Marie *writer, human services professional*

Greenfield
Curtiss, Carol Perry *healthcare consultant*

Groton
Anthony, Sylvia *social welfare organization executive*

Hadley
Zion, Ellen C. *small business owner*

Hanscom AFB
Kenne, Leslie F. *military officer*

Hatfield
Yolen, Jane *author*

Haydenville
Shallcross, Doris Jane *creative behavioral educator*

Hinsdale
Cijka, Michele Dawn *minister*

Holden
Sanfacon, Mary Elizabeth *French educator*

Holland
McGrory, Mary Kathleen *retired academic administrator, humanities educator*

Holyoke
Blanchard, Karen Marie *development professional*
Dearborn, Maureen Markt *speech and language clinician*
Morrissey, Jane F. *religious organization administrator*
Powell, Kathleen Trestka *artist, educator, editor*

Hubbardston
Marceau, Judith Marie *retired elementary school educator, small business owner*

Hyannis
Loughnane, Audrey Moran *town councilor*
Nicholson, Ellen Ellis *clinical social worker*

Hyde Park
Harris, Emily Louise *special education educator*

Ipswich
Moules, Deborah Ann *not-for-profit developer*

Jamaica Plain
Kadden, Judith *author, educator, journalist*

Lenox
Rudden, Marie Georgine *psychiatrist*

Leominster
Lyons, Beryl Barton Anfindsen *advertising executive*

Leverett
Shulman, Paula B(aka Phillips) *marriage and family therapist, educator*

Lexington
Bernitz, Francine S. *marketing professional*
Bombardieri, Merle Ann *psychotherapist*
Davis, Barbara M(ae) *librarian*
Garing, Ione Davis *civic worker, club woman*
Giteck, Evelyn B. *poet, educator*
Jordan, Judith Victoria *clinical psychologist, educator*
Piano, Phyllis J. *communications executive*
Rhoads, Rebecca R. *electronics executive*
Shapiro, Marian Kaplun *psychologist*
Topalian, Naomi Getsoyan *writer*
Washburn, Barbara Polk *cartographer, researcher, explorer*

Lincoln
Barrett, Beatrice Helene *psychologist*

Littleton
Crory, Mary *town official*
Lau, Joanna T. *information technology executive*

Longmeadow
Katz, Barbara S. *special education educator*
Leary, Carol Ann *academic administrator*
Schirmer-Smith, Sara Jane (Sally Schirmer-Smith) *dean, director student activities*
Teitz, Betty Beatrice Goldstein *retired interior designer*

Lowell
Clark, Sharon Ann *educational consultant, music educator*
Donoghue, Eileen M. *former mayor*
Galizzi, Monica *economics educator*
Mercier, Rita *mayor*

Lunenburg
Schnakenberg, Lori Ann *secondary school educator*

Lynnfield
Kerrigan, Nancy *professional figure skater, former Olympic athlete*

Malden
Dell, Diana Jean *writer*

Manchester
Moody, Marianna S. *dietician*
White, Sallie Snow Wilber *retired elementary school educator*

Marblehead
Gardner, Mary Josephine *management development consultant*
Heins, Esther *botanical artist, painter*
Onishi, Anna Tokiko *financial analyst*
Seamans, Beverly Benson *sculptor*
Tamaren, Michele Carol *educational consultant, writer, retired special education educator*

Marion
McPartland, Patricia Ann *health educator and administrator*

Marlborough
Bobel, Mary *video development company financial executive*
Lindsay, Janice Campbell *communications executive, writer*

Marshfield Hills
Johnson, Margaret Hill *retired educational administrator, consultant*

Marstons Mills
Martin, Susan Katherine *librarian*

Mashpee
Payne, Paula Marie *minister*

Mattapoisett
Bertram, Christine G. *artist, painter, graphics designer*
Perry, Blanche Belle *physical therapist*

Medfield
Nedder, Janet Marie *elementary school educator*
Phillips, Marion Grumman *writer, civic worker*
Woolston-Catlin, Marian *psychiatrist*

Medford
Abriola, Linda M. *civil engineer, environmental engineer*
Ambady, Nalini *social psychologist, educator, researcher*
Ch'en, Li-li *writer, Chinese language, literature and comparative literature educator*
Comeau, Lorene Anita Emerson *real estate developer*
Cowen, Lenore Jennifer *mathematician, educator, computer scientist*
Goldberg, Pamela Winer *entrepreneurship educator, director*
Goodwin, Neva R. *economist*
Jacobs, Mary Lee *lawyer*
Luria, Zella Hurwitz *psychology educator*
Mc Carthy, Kathryn A. *physicist*
Schlegel, Amy Ingrid *curator, art historian*

Melrose
Desforges, Jane Fay *internist, hematologist, educator*
McLennan, Bernice Claire *human resources professional*

Mill River
Jaffe, Katharine Weisman *retired librarian*

Milton
Randall, Lilian Maria Charlotte *museum curator*

Monson
De Santis, Sylvia *library director*

Nantucket
Bartlett, Cheryl Ann *public health service administrator*
Pollard, Margaret Louise *association administrator*

Natick
Geller, Esther (Bailey Geller) *artist*
Lebowitz, Charlotte Meyersohn *social worker*
Ma, Jing-Heng Sheng *language educator*
Sen, Laura J. *wholesale distribution executive*
Shapero, Esther Bailey Geller *artist*
Strauss, Harlee Sue *environmental consultant*

Needham
Carr, Iris Constantine *artist, writer*
Meisner, Mary Jo *editor*
Ryan, Una Scully *health sciences professional, medical educator*

New Bedford
Cordeiro, Elizabeth Dalein *law enforcement training educator*
Gonsalves, Jane Louise *city councilor, claims adjuster*
LaPorte, Adrienne Aroxie *nursing administrator*
Lincoln, Rosamond Hadley *modern painter, photographer*
Monteiro, Patricia M. *clinical social worker*
Nunes, Pricilla O. *special education educator, artist*
Raposo, Deborah F. *nursing administrator*
Silvia, Lori A. *speech pathology/audiology services professional*
Thomas, Sharon M. *city official*

New Braintree
Lesak, Alice Elaine *psychotherapist, minister*

New Town
Carton, Lonnie Caming *educational psychologist*

Newburyport
Yeomans, Katie Morse *writer*

Newton
Bassuk, Ellen Linda *psychiatrist*
Benner, Mary Wright *event planner*
Bronstein, Ilena *science administrator, consultant*
Corcoran, Nancy Helen *minister*
[illegible]
Goldweitz, Julie *lawyer*
Gullette, Margaret Morganroth *cultural critic, writer*
Havens, Candace Jean *planning consultant*
Hume, Ellen Hunsberger *media analyst, journalist*
Kelliher, Justine Oren *retired nurse, educator*
Khan, Kay *state legislator*
Matteson, Carol J. *academic administrator*
Metzer, Patricia Ann *lawyer*
O'Connell, Sister Virginia M. *school librarian*
Tannenwald, Leslie Keiter *rabbi, justice of peace, educational administrator, chaplain*

Newton Center
Parker, Jacqueline Yvonne *lawyer, educator*
Pill, Cynthia Joan *social worker*
Veeder, Nancy Walker *social work educator*
Williamson, Susan *mathematician, educator*

North Andover
Gannon, Patricia J. *academic administrator*
Lenihan, Barbara Desch *neonatal clinical nurse specialist*
Longsworth, Ellen Louise *art historian, consultant*

North Attleboro
Cote, Louise Roseanne *art director*

North Chelmsford
Garcia, Jennifer *music educator*

North Dartmouth
Noel, Barbara Hughes McMurtry *retired music educator*

North Falmouth
Green, Linda C. *education specialist administrator, researcher*

Northampton
Boutelle, Ann Edwards *poet, educator*
Christ, Carol Tecla *academic administrator*
Fabing, Suzannah *museum director*
Friedman, D. Dina *writer, educator*
Lehmann, Phyllis Williams *archaeologist, educator*
Lightburn, Anita Louise *dean, social work educator*
Rupp, Sheron Adeline *photographer, educator*
Skarda, Patricia Lyn *English language educator*
Stinson, Susan Elizabeth *director, writer*

Northfield
Knox, Carol B. *biologist, educator*
Matney, Louise Hoff *psychotherapist*

Norton
Marshall, Dale Rogers *academic administrator, political scientist, educator*
Woods, Susanne *academic administrator, educator*

Norwell
Brett, Jan Churchill *illustrator, author*

Norwood
Sidiropoulou, Eleftheria Alexandrou *minister, family therapist*

Orleans
Addison, Helen Katherine *marketing professional, art dealer*
Hogan, Ruth DeWitt *artist*
Rappaport, Margaret M.W.E. *psychologist, physician, writer, pilot, consultant*

Osterville
Kennedy, Michele Lyn *artist*
McLean, Susan O'Brien *artist*
Weber, Adelheid Lisa *former nurse, chemist*
Williams, Ann Meagher *retired hospital administrator*

Peabody
Brave, Rebecca S. Larsen *curator*
Dee, Pauline Marie *artist*
Kokoras, Victoria *retired elementary school educator*

Pittsfield
Fawcett, Gayle P. *bank executive*

Plainfield
Nash, June Caprice *anthropology educator*

Plymouth
Cully, Mikki *artist*
Flood, H(ulda) Gay *editor, consultant*
Freyermuth, Virginia Karen *art educator*
Goggin, Joan Marie *school system administrator*
Leonard-Zabel, Ann Marie T. *psychologist, educator*
Paul, Carol Ann *retired academic administrator, biology educator*

Princeton
Roney-O'Brien, Susan Frances *elementary school educator, writer*

Provincetown
Oliver, Mary *poet*
Wolfman, Brunetta Reid *education educator*

Quincy
Bunting, Carolyn Anne *writer*
Chung, Cynthia Norton *communications specialist*
Furtado, Beverly Ann *financial aid administrator*
Hayes, Mary Dianne Wixted *lawyer*
Lawler, Linda *disability examiner*
Pratt, Mary *retired educator*
Wilson, Blenda Jacqueline *foundation administrator*

Randolph
Porter, Christine Ann *music educator*

Raynham
Worrell, Cynthia Lee *bank executive*

Reading
Ellert, Lucinda Joan *musician, educator*
Frey, Joanne Alice Tupper *art educator*
Nordstrand, Nathalie Elizabeth Johnson *artist*

Revere
Ferrante, Olivia Ann *retired educator, consultant*
Recupero-Faiella, Anna Antonietta *poet*

Rockland
Blethen, Sandra Lee *pediatric endocrinologist*

Rockport
Calabro, Joanna Joan Sondra *artist*
Johnson, Janet Lou *real estate company executive, writer*

Roslindale
Driscoll, Kathleen J. *writer*

Roxbury
Alméstica, Johanna Lynnette *mental health counselor, administrator*
Simons, Elizabeth R(eiman) *biochemist, educator*

Salem
Gozemba, Patrica Andrea *women's studies and English language educator, writer*
Harrington, Nancy D. *college president*
Monahan, Martha J. *psychologist*

Seekonk
Parker, Janet Ruth *town official*

Sharon
Johnson, Addie Collins *secondary education educator, former dietitian*

Sheffield
Young, Susan Babson *retired library director*

Siasconset
Emerson, Alice Frey *political scientist, educator emerita*

Somerville
Gurley, Rhonda Jean *special education educator, consultant*
Landon, Susan N. *volunteer, poet*

South Attleboro
Hanson, Barbara Jean *education educator*

South Easton
Myers, Linda M. *writer*

South Hadley
Bronner, Kathleen M. *not-for-profit fundraiser*
Campbell, Mary Kathryn *chemistry educator*
Clancy, Marguerite Aline (Meg Clancy) *librarian*
Creighton, Joanne Vanish *academic administrator*
Elleman, Barbara *editor*
James, Vanessa *theater educator, department chairman*
Randall, Hermine Maria *retired power plant engineer*
Scanlon, Gail Gretchen *librarian, nurse*
Tatum, Beverly Daniel *psychology and education educator*
Townsend, Jane Kaltenbach *biologist, educator*

South Hamilton
Kroeger, Catherine C. *writer, educator, editor*

South Natick
Cantor, Pamela Corliss *psychologist*

South Orleans
Hale, Margaret Smith *insurance company executive, educator*

Southbridge
O'Brien, Christine Leduc *art educator*

Spencer
Robinson, Evelyn Edna *secondary school educator*

Springfield
Adams, Voleen *surgeon*
Bonemery, Anne M. *language educator*
Cohen, Beth Diane *law educator*
Dunn, Gail Pederzoli *English language educator*
Frey, Mary Elizabeth *artist*
Gordon, Ronni Anne *journalist*
Gross, Donalyn Ann *counselor*
Ingram, Renay Eloise *elementary school educator, school system administrator*
Merriman, Deborah Joy *marriage and family therapist*
Modie, Christine M. *insurance company executive*
Saia, Diane Plevock DiPiero *nutritionist, educator, legal administrator*
Stack, May Elizabeth *library director*
Susse, Sandra Slone *lawyer*
Vincensi, Avis A. *sales executive, medical educator*
Winn, Janice Gail *food products administrator*

Sterling
Lundgren, Ruth Williamson Wood (Ruth Lundgren Williamson Wood) *public relations executive, writer*

Stockbridge
Fitzpatrick, Jane *entrepreneur*

Sudbury
Ames, Lois Winslow Sisson *social worker,* [illegible]
Gruol, Mary Catherine Schuetz *human resources operations executive*
Hillery, Mary Jane Larato *columnist, television personality, television producer, writer, military officer*
Pitman, Ursula Wall *curator, educator*
Thompson, Mary Lou *elementary school educator*

Taunton
Doyle, Nancy Carolyn *writer*
Lopes, Maria Fernandina *commissioner*

Templeton
Evans, Jeanne Carol *retired military officer*

Tewksbury
Lefebvre, Sharon Elaine *psychiatric nurse practitioner*

Topsfield
Huntley-Wright, Joan Augusta (Joan Augusta Huntley) *musician*
Natale, Diane Theresa *communications executive*

Townsend
Smith, Denise Groleau *data processing professional*

Truro
Kelley, Maryellen R. *economist, management consultant*
Woolley, Catherine (Jane Thayer) *writer*

Turners Falls
Finley-Morin, Kimberley K. *secondary school educator*

Vineyard Haven
Jacobs, Gretchen Huntley *psychiatrist*

Waban
Etter, Faye Madalyn *interior design company executive*
Hewlett-Kierstead, Nancy Carrick *psychologist, educator*

Wakefield
Menard, Joan M. *state legislator*

Waltham
Corbato, Emily S. *photographer, researcher, musician*
Curnan, Susan P. *social policy and management educator*
Delaney, Mary Anne *retired theology studies educator*
Domar, Alice Diane *psychologist, educator*
Flynn, Patricia Marie *economics educator*
Gray-Nix, Elizabeth Whitwell *occupational therapist*
Hahn, Bessie King *library administrator, lecturer*
Hale, Jane Alison *French and comparative literature educator*
Hayes, Ailish Maire *pediatrician*
Jones, Jacqueline *historian*
Lees, Marjorie Berman *biochemist, neuroscientist*
McCulloch, Rachel *economics researcher, educator*
Mitchell, Janet Brew *health services researcher*
O'Donnell, Teresa Hohol *application developer, electrical engineer*
Preve, Roberta Jean *librarian, researcher*
Schwartz, Paula Mae *communications company executive*
Staves, Susan *English educator*
Warren, Susan Hanke Murphy *international marketing business development executive*
Zebrowitz, Leslie Ann *psychology educator*

Wareham
Gayoski, Kathleen Mary *counselor, minister*
Monty, Ruthelaine *musician, educator*

Watertown
Boland, Elizabeth *social services company financial executive*
Rivers, Wilga Marie *foreign language educator*

Wayland
Anderson, Monica Luffman *school librarian, educator, real estate broker*
Caristo-Verrill, Janet Rose *international management consultant*
Harrington, Kay Lorraine *executive secretary*
Humphrey, Diana Young *fund raiser*
Smith, Joan Trimble *artist*

Wellesley
Heartt, Charlotte Beebe *university official*
Jacobs, Ruth Harriet *poet, playwright, sociologist, gerontologist*
Jacoff, Rachel *Italian language and literature educator*
Lefkowitz, Mary Rosenthal *Greek literature educator*
McGibbon, Phyllis Isabel *art educator, artist*
Miller, Linda B. *political scientist*
Mistacco, Vicki E. *foreign language educator*
Palmerio, Elvira Castano *art gallery director, art historian*
Piper, Adrian Margaret Smith *philosopher, artist, educator*
Putnam, Ruth Anna *philosopher, educator*
Walsh, Diana Chapman *academic administrator, sociologist, educator*

Wellesley Hills
Clarkson, Cheryl Lee *healthcare executive*

Wellfleet
Piercy, Marge *poet, writer*

West Chatham
Dimm, Susan Tyner *art educator, artist*

West Dennis
Amidon, Barbara Stone *forensic specialist, psychologist*

West Hyannisport
Devine, Nancy *postmaster*

West Newbury
Dooley, Ann Elizabeth *freelance writers cooperative executive, editor*

West Newton
Logan, Georgiana Marie *psychotherapist*

West Roxbury
Cohen, Carolyn Alta *healthcare educator*
Roach, Maureen S. *primary school educator*

West Springfield
Desai, Veena Balvantrai *obstetrician, gynecologist, educator*
McKenzie-Anderson, Rita Lynn *psychologist*
Sumaryono, Karen L. *secondary school educator, consultant*

West Stockbridge
Levine, Toby Kleban *communications executive, educational media developer*

Westborough
Antalek, Eileen Elizabeth *educational consultant*
Bok, Joan Toland *utility executive*
Horwitz, Eleanor Catherine *information and education official*
Staffier, Pamela Moorman *psychologist*

Westfield
Conant, Tara Patricia *photographer*
Dunphy, Maureen Milbier *reading educator*

Westford
Endyke, Debra Joan *data communications marketing professional*
Geary, Marie Josephine *art association administrator*
Weston, Joan Spencer *editorial and production director, communications executive*

Weston
Fine, Sally Solfisburg *artist, educator*
Higgins, Sister Therese *English educator, former college president*
Lin, Alice Lee Lan *physicist, researcher, educator*
Marshall, Jean McElroy *physiologist*
Nolan-Conners, Elizabeth Ann *director, educator*
Rearick, Anne *photographer, educator*
Sanzone, Donna S. *publishing executive*
Schwartz, Ann Simmons *retired publishing executive*
Smick, Susan Schnee *manufacturing executive, tile designer, marketing professional*
Tenney, Sarah G. *music educator*

Westport
Sexton, Janice Louise *artist*

Weymouth
Parks, Kristin M. *pediatrics health nurse, educator and practitioner*

Williamstown

Blair, Phyllis E. *artist*
Conklin, Susan Joan *psychotherapist, educator, corporate staff developer, TV talk show host*
Cramer, Phebe *psychologist*
Driscoll, Genevieve Bosson (Jeanne Bosson Driscoll) *management and organization development consultant*
Glück, Louise Elisabeth *poet, educator*
Graver, Suzanne Levy *English literature educator*
Hill, Catharine B. *provost, economics educator*

Wilmington

Raven, Linda F. *mechanical engineer*

Winchester

Baumann, Priscilla *medieval art history educator, researcher*
Blackham, Ann Rosemary (Mrs. J. W. Blackham) *realtor*
Furui, Sachiko *language educator, consultant, artist*

Winthrop

Brown, Patricia Irene *retired law librarian, lawyer*
Lutze, Ruth Louise *retired textbook editor, public relations executive*

Woburn

O'Doherty, Kathleen Marie *library director*
Paul, Lois *public relations company executive*
Speerstra, Karen M. *former publishing executive*

Worcester

Bowen, Alice Frances *school system administrator*
Dunlap, Ellen S. *library administrator*
Dyer-Cole, Pauline *school psychologist, educator*
Hatfield, Renee S.J. *music educator*
Kennedy, Linda Mann *neuroscience educator, researcher*
Lish, Jennifer D. *psychologist*
Ravnikar, Veronika A. *reproductive endocrinologist, educator*
Upshur, Carole Christofk *psychologist, educator*
Vick, Susan *playwright, educator, director, actress*

Worthington

Schrade, Rolande Maxwell Young *composer, pianist, educator*

Yarmouth Port

McGill, Grace Anita *retired occupational health nurse*

MICHIGAN

Allegan

Drozd, Phyllis Ann *agricultural products supplier*

Allen Park

Bizon, Emma Djafar *management consultant*

Allendale

Fernandez-Levin, Rosa *language educator*
Miller, Jo Ellen *humanities educator*
Murray, Diane Elizabeth *librarian*
Salazar, Laura Alice Gardner *retired theater educator*

Alma

Tracy, Saundra J. *academic administrator*

Ann Arbor

Akil, Huda *neuroscientist, educator, researcher*
Aller, Margo Friedel *astronomer*
Apperson, Jean *psychologist*
Arlinghaus, Sandra Judith Lach *mathematical geographer, educator*
Bachelder, Cheryl Anne *marketing professional*
Ball, Deborah Loewenberg *education educator*
Beaubien, Anne Kathleen *librarian*
Benamou, Catherine Laure *filmmaker, educator*
Beutler, Suzanne A. *retired secondary school educator, artist*
Bloom, Jane Maginnis *emergency physician*
Britt, Margaret Mary *communications director*
Bryant, Barbara Everitt *academic researcher, market research consultant, former federal agency administrator*
Busard, Roberta Ann *artist, educator*
Cerniglia, Alice May *museum program director, consultant*
Clark, Noreen Morrison *behavioral science educator, researcher*
Conway, Lynn *computer scientist, electrical engineer, educator*
Copeland, Carolyn Abigail *retired dean*
Daub, Peggy Ellen *library administrator*
Dede, Bonnie Aileen *librarian, educator*
deJesus-Burgos, Sylvia Teresa *security and risk management officer*
Dominguez, Kathryn Mary *political scientist, educator*
Doyle, Constance Talcott Johnston *physician, educator, medical association administrator*
Dumas, Rhetaugh Etheldra Graves *university official*
Dunlap, Connie *librarian*
Eccles, Jacquelynne S. *psychology educator*
Eisenstein, Elizabeth Lewisohn *historian, educator*
Feldman, Eva Lucille *neurology educator*
Fleming, Suzanne Marie *academic administrator, freelance/self-employed writer*
Forsyth, Ilene Haering *art historian*
Freese, Katherine *physicist, researcher*
Garcia, Elisa Dolores *lawyer*
Gomberg, Edith S. *psychologist, educator*
Gregerson, Linda Karen *poet, language educator, critic*

Guardo, Carol J. *association executive*
Heath, Angela Mary *academic advisor*
Hefferlin, Earline Dawdy *retired writer*
Hertz, Dawn Leslie *lawyer*
Herzig, Phyllis Glicksberg *social worker*
Hill, Helen Morey Williams *English literature educator*
Hinshaw, Ada Sue *dean, nursing educator*
Kalisch, Beatrice Jean *nursing educator, consultant*
Kendall, Kay Lynn *interior designer, consultant*
Ketefian, Shaké *nursing educator*
Leary, Margaret *law librarian, library director*
Lindsay, June Campbell McKee *communications executive*
Lozoff, Betsy *pediatrician*
Ludwig, Martha *biochemist, educator*
MacKinnon, Catharine Alice *lawyer, law educator, legal scholar, writer*
McCloud, Patricia Carolyn Kaiser *nurse educator, consultant*
McLaughlin, Catherine G. *healthcare educator*
Mitchell, Anna-Marie Rajala *quality/outcomes analyst*
Murnane, Margaret Mary *engineering and physics educator*
Nelson, Virginia Simson *pediatrician, educator, physiatrist*
Oakley, Deborah Jane *researcher, educator*
Prins, Johanna *literature educator*
Ray, Elise *gymnast*
Reame, Nancy *nursing educator*
Ross, Theresa Mae *secondary school educator*
Scharp-Radovic, Carol Ann *choreographer, classical ballet educator, artistic director*
Scodel, Ruth *humanities educator*
Sears, JoAnn Marie *school librarian*
Sheldon, Ingrid Kristina *former mayor, bookkeeper*
Singer, Eleanor *sociologist, editor*
Sloat, Barbara Furin *cell biologist, educator*
Snyder, Lucy Karla *lawyer, finance company executive*
Strang, Ruth Hancock *pediatric educator, pediatric cardiologist, priest*
Toronto, Ellen Leslie Kaylor *psychologist*
Unterburger, Amy L. *editor*
Verrett, Shirley *soprano*
Walter, Lynn M. *geologist, educator*
Waltz, Susan *international relations educator*
Whitman, Marina Von Neumann *economist, educator*
Zurier, Rebecca *art history educator*

Auburn Hills

De Martin, Colleen Dianne *college official, interior designer, consultant*
Drexler, Mary Sanford *financial executive*
Etefia, Florence Victoria *school psychologist*
Nelson, Debra Jean *journalist, public relations executive, consultant*
Palmer, Wendy *professional basketball player*

Bath

Wildt, Janeth Kae *small business owner*

Battle Creek

Banks, Donna Jo *food products executive*
Davis, Laura Arlene *retired foundation administrator*
Kelly, Janet Langford *lawyer*
Lincoln, Margaret *library media specialist*
Matthews, Wyhomme S. *retired music educator, academic administrator*
Wendt, Linda M. *educational association administrator*

Bay City

Frahm, Karen Foley *epidemiologist*
Vader-McCormick, Nancy Jane *humanities educator*
Zuraw, Kathleen Ann *special education and physical education educator*

Belmont

Whiteman, Martha Joyce *retired elementary school educator*

Berkley

Leland, Janet K. *social work therapist*

Berrien Center

Dunbar, Mable Cleone *counselor education, family*

Berrien Springs

Summitt, April *history educator*

Beulah

Tanner, Helen Hornbeck *historian, researcher*

Beverly Hills

Tolias, Linda Puroff *music educator*

Big Rapids

Weis-Taylor, Carrie Lynn *curator, artist*

Bingham Farms

Banas, C(hristine) Leslie *lawyer*
Krevsky, Margery Brown *talent agency executive*

Birmingham

Ashleigh, Caroline *art and antiques appraiser*
Reeves, Kathleen Walker *English and French language educator*
Robinson, Marietta S. *lawyer*

Bloomfield Hills

Ball, Patricia Ann *physician*
Bass, Janis *musician*
Bird, Linda C. *psychotherapist, educator*
Burnett, Patricia Hill *portrait artist, author, sculptor, lecturer*
Haidostian, Alice Berberian *concert pianist, volunteer, not-for-profit fundraiser*
Jurkiewicz, Mary Louise *elementary school educator*

Lapadot, Sonee Spinner *retired automobile manufacturing company official*
Levin, Carolyn Bible *volunteer*
Miller, Dorothy Anne Smith *retired cytogenetics educator*
Nuss, Shirley Ann *computer coordinator, educator*
Panush, Irene E(sther) *social worker*
Simon, Evelyn *lawyer*
Starkman, Betty Provizer *genealogist, writer, educator*
Wermuth, Mary Louella *secondary school educator*

Bloomfield Township

Brown, Lynette Ralya *journalist, publicist*

Brighton

Jensen, Baiba *principal*

Brownstown

Slingerland, Mary Jo *literature educator*

Buchanan

Stromswold, Dorothy *retired secondary school educator*

Burton

Johnson-Brown, Linda Lee *music educator*

Cadillac

Fisher, Christine Lynne *art educator, artist*

Camden

Falls, Kathleene Joyce *photographer*

Canton

Price, Linda K. *small business owner*
Schulz, Karen Alice *psychologist, medical psychotherapist, medical and vocational case manager*

Capac

Wagner, Dorothy Marie *retired senior creative designer, artist*

Charlotte

Herrick, Kathleen Magara *social worker*

Chesaning

Swartzmiller, Mildred M. *art gallery owner*

Chesterfield

Broad, Cynthia Ann Morgan *special education educator, consultant*
Wilson-Pleiness, Christine Joyce *writer, poet, columnist, real estate investor*

Clarkston

Pieknik, Rebecca Anne *technologist, educator*
Snow, Sandra Inez *mortgage company executive*

Clifford

Staples, Lynne Livingston Mills *retired psychologist, educator, consultant*

Clinton

Anderson, Denice Anna *editor*
Scott, Sharon Ann *retired librarian, archivist*

Clinton Township

Childress, Janet Lynn *logistician*
Noraas, Diane Rice *computer scientist, educator*

Clio

Hammond, Jane Pamela *adult education educator*

Coldwater

Kibiloski, Catherine Kay *real estate appraiser*
Scheidler, Elana Dawn *elementary school educator, art educator*

Dearborn

Ardisana, Beth *communications company executive*
Beauford, Sandra *registered nurse, data processing executive*
Buckingham, Lorie *automotive executive*
Byars, Leisa *marketing professional, automotive executive*
Fox, Stacy *automotive executive*
Frank, Nancy Kathleen *minister*
Hess, Margaret Johnston *religious writer, educator*
Ibbotson, Patricia Ann *occupational health nurse, writer*
Linnansalo, Vera *engineer*
McKeage, Alice Jane *computer programmer*
Meyer, Lisa Marie *elementary school educator*
Odeh, Kristin S. *information technology executive*
Orlowska-Warren, Lenore Alexandria *art educator, fiber artist*
Pacheco, Susan *automotive executive*
Petrauskas, Helen O. *automobile manufacturing company executive*
Wang, Liyan *product design engineer*

Dearborn Heights

Carter, Julia Marie *secondary school educator*
Johns, Diana *secondary school educator*

Detroit

Aaron-Taylor, Susan Wendy *sculptor, educator*
Acton, Elizabeth S *corporate financial executive*
Aguirre, Pamela Ann *manufacturing executive*
Ashley, Lois A. *retired university reference librarian*
Barclay, Kathleen S. *automotive executive*
Barrett, Nancy Smith *university administrator*
Beale, Susan M. *electric power industry executive*
Bell Wilson, Carlotta A. *state official, consultant*
Booth, Betty Jean *retired daycare administrator, poet*

Bully-Cummings, Ella M. *protective services official*
Burzynski, Susan Marie *newspaper editor*
Chauderlot, Fabienne-Sophie *foreign language educator*
Chen, Ping *physician*
Colby, Joy Hakanson *critic*
Corbitt, Eumiller Mattie *elementary and secondary education educator, special education educator*
Corrigan, Maura Denise *judge*
Darlow, Julia Donovan *lawyer*
Diebolt, Judith *newspaper editor*
Dixson, J. B. *communications executive*
Dooley, Gayle Darlene *special education educator, consultant*
Edmunds, Nancy Garlock *federal judge*
Edwards, Esther G. *museum administrator, former record, film and entertainment company executive*
Engelhardt, Regina *cosmetologist, artist, small business owner*
Fay, Sister Maureen A. *university president*
Feldhouse, Lynn *automotive company executive*
Ferguson, Tamara *clinical sociologist*
Gibbs, Mary L. *writer, writers' services provider*
Greenwood, Harriet Lois *environmental banker, researcher*
Heppner, Gloria Hill *medical science administrator, educator*
Hill, Elizabeth Marie *research scientist*
Hood, Antoinette Foote *dermatologist*
Hood, Denise Page *federal judge*
Hutton, Carole Leigh *newspaper editor*
Ilitch, Denise *food services executive*
Ilitch, Marian *professional hockey team executive, food service executive*
Jacox, Ada Kathryn *nurse, educator*
James, Phyllis A. *lawyer*
James, Sheryl Teresa *journalist*
Jenkins-Anderson, Barbara Jeanne *pathologist, educator*
Jiang, Wei *chemist*
Kantrowitz, Jean *health products executive*
Keys, Elizabeth A. *accountant, business executive*
Kline, Mable Cornelia Page *retired secondary school educator*
Laughlin, Nancy *newspaper editor*
Lowery, Elizabeth *automotive executive*
Madgett, Naomi Long *poet, editor, publisher, educator*
Mahaffey, Maryann *councilwoman*
Mahoney, Joan *law educator*
McCracken, Caron Francis *computer company executive, consultant*
McGee, Sherry *retail executive*
McIntosh, Deborah V. *elementary school educator*
Mitchell, Connie *director*
Moldenhauer, Judith A. *graphic design educator*
Morgan, Virginia Mattison *magistrate judge*
Muszynski, Stacy *editor, writer*
Newman, Andrea Fischer *air transportation executive*
Noland, Mariam Charl *foundation executive*
Parks, Rosa Louise *civil rights activist*
Parsons, Anne *performing company executive*
Redfield, Jean M. *electric power company executive*
Redman, Barbara Klug *nursing educator*
Ridley, Andrew Jean *small business owner*
Rozof, Phyllis Claire *lawyer*
Salter, Linda Lee *security officer*
Shannon, Margaret Anne *lawyer*
Smith, Valerie Christine *registered nurse, writer*
Stallworth, Alma Grace *former state legislator*
Stark, Susan R. *film critic*
Sufalko, Dynah Naomi Juliette *marketing professional*
Sutton, Lynn Sorensen *librarian*
Tallet, Margaret Anne *theatre executive*
Taylor, Anna Diggs *federal judge*
Titus, Susan Anne *association executive*
Tolia, Vasundhara K. *pediatric gastroenterologist, educator*
Toney, Creola Sarah *minister*
Tushman, J. Lawrence *wholesale distribution executive*
Valentine, Cheryl Ann Whitney *music educator*
Walker, Deborah Sue *nurse midwife, educator*
Wesley, Ruby LaVerne *nursing educator, administrator, researcher*
White, Katherine E. *law educator*

Douglas

Karamas, Joyce Efthemia *art educator, consultant, artist*

Dowagiac

Mulder, Patricia Marie *education educator*

East Lansing

Bandes, Susan Jane *museum director, educator*
Bassett, Debra Lyn *lawyer, educator*
Burnett, Jean Bullard (Mrs. James R. Burnett) *biochemist, educator*
Draper, Penny Kaye Pekrul *music educator*
Fairfax, Kathleen M *director*
Fluck, Michele M(arguerite) *biology educator*
Force, Christine *small business developer*
Gass, Gertrude Zemon *psychologist, researcher*
Krishnan, Ranjani *finance educator*
Kronegger, Maria Elisabeth *French and comparative literature educator*
Lewis, Tina *music educator, writer*
McMeekin, Dorothy *botany, plant pathology educator*
Mitstifer, Dorothy Irwin *honor society administrator*
Palac, Judith Ann *music educator*
Patterson, Maria Jevitz *microbiology-pediatric infectious disease educator*
Rothert, Marilyn L. *dean, nursing educator*
Schemmel, Rachel Anne *food science and human nutrition educator, researcher*
Simon, Lou Anna Kimsey *academic administrator*

South Haven
Llorens, Merna Gee *elementary school educator, music educator*

Southfield
Acton, Ellen Hall *minister, educator*
Barnett, Marilyn *advertising agency executive*
Baughman, Leonora Knoblock *lawyer*
Bledsoe, Laurita *small business owner, publisher*
Catallo, Heather *newscaster*
Davis-Yancey, Gwendolyn *lawyer*
Gayle, Monica *broadcast journalist*
Hartman-Abramson, Ilene *medical educator*
Hudson, Cheryl L. *communications executive*
Jones, Marceline Yvonne *secondary school educator*
Makupson, Amyre Porter *television station executive*
Margolis, Sherry *newscaster*
Martin, Marcella Edric *retired community health nurse*
McNelis, Kathleen Ann *medical/surgical nurse*
Pickett, Sherry M. *social worker*
Portnoy, Lynn Ann *fashion retailer*
Primo, Joan Erwina *retail and real estate consulting business owner*
Schmidt, Mary Teresa *retired elementary school educator*
Sedler, Rozanne Friedlander *social worker, educator*
Shilts, Nancy S. *automotive executive, lawyer*
Stinger, Fanchon *newscaster*
Wagner, Muriel Ginsberg *nutrition therapist*
Weiner, Karen Colby (Karen Lynn Colby) *psychologist, lawyer*

Southgate
Torok, Margaret Louise *insurance company executive*

Sparta
Bomhof, Robyn *artist, educator*
McDonald, Lois Alice *elementary school educator*

Sterling Heights
Empson, Heather Leigh (Parmann) *elementary school educator*
Hammond-Kominsky, Cynthia Cecelia *optometrist*
Matthews Ellis, Bonnie *management consultant*

Stockbridge
Clarke, Jane Carol *academic administrator, director, principal*

Tecumseh
Sackett, Dianne Marie *city treasurer, accountant*
Staples, Alice Marie *elementary school educator*

Three Rivers
Pierce, Sue *sales executive*

Traverse City
Bullis, Jo Louise *social services administrator, educator*
Burton, Betty June *retired pastor*
Weaver, Elizabeth A. *state supreme court justice*

Trenton
Beebe, Grace Ann *retired special education educator*

Troy
Arking, Lucille Musser *nurse, epidemiologist*
Austin, Karen *retail executive*
Elder, Irma *retail automotive executive*
Esler, Barbara Hart *accountant, consultant*
Harrison, Christine Delane *company executive*
Healy, Karen *automotive executive*
Kelly, Janet G. *retail executive*
LaDuke, Nancie *lawyer, corporate executive*
Lorencz, Mary *public relations executive*
Maierle, Bette Jean *director nursery school*
McLaren, Karen Lynn *advertising executive*
Meyers, Christine Laine *marketing and media executive, consultant*
Schafer, Sharon Marie *anesthesiologist*
Updike, Linda S. *personnel placement firm executive*
Walker, Bette *automotive executive*
Wettergren, Sandra Marie *personnel consultant*
White, Tommi A. *human resources firm executive*

Union Pier
Howland, Bette *writer*

University Center
May, Margrethe *health educator*
Riegle, Rosalie Genevieve *English educator, writer*
Schaab, Nancy A. *education educator, consultant*

Walled Lake
Remer, Deborah Jane *secondary school educator*
Schmitz, Carol Ann *speech pathology/audiology services professional*

Warren
Gilbert, Suzanne Harris *advertising executive*
Morton, Katie Marie *special education educator*
White, Gaye Lee *elementary school educator*
Zoubareff, Kathy Olga *administrative assistant*

Waterford
Anderson, Francile Mary *secondary school educator*

West Bloomfield
Mamut, Mary Catherine *retired entrepreneur*
Miller, Nancy Ellen *computer consultant*
Smith, Nancy Hohendorf *retired sales and marketing executive*
Starr, Monica *company executive*
Williamson, Marilyn Lammert *English educator, university administrator*

Westland
Coates, Dianne Kay *social worker*

White Lake
Boyle, Patricia Jean *retired state supreme court justice*

White Pigeon
Pavel, Patricia L. *elementary school educator*

Whitmore Lake
White, Susan Rochelle *psychologist, investor*

Williamston
Ellis, Sharon Alston *lawyer, political organization worker*

Woodhaven
Kim, Hyo Sook *anesthesiologist*

Wyandotte
Dunn, Gloria Jean *artist*

Wyoming
Carey, JoAnna *financial consultant, writer*

Ypsilanti
Coykendall, Abby Lynn *literature educator*
Schwartz, Ellen C. *art historian, educator*
Warner, Jo F. *mathematics educator*

Zeeland
Nickels, Elizabeth Anne *office furniture manufacturing executive*

MINNESOTA

Albert Lea
Schwab, Grace S. *state legislator*

Andover
Peterson, Jill Susan *elementary school educator*

Apple Valley
Bronner, Katherine Elizabeth *high school counselor*
Haaheim, Patricia Jane Dando *pastor, consultant*
Kettle, Sally Anne *consulting company executive, educator*
Sagen, Judy *secondary education choral director*

Bemidji
Christenson, Eileen Esther *geriatrics nurse*
Erickson, Nancy Carolyn *dean*
Martinson, Ida Marie *nursing educator, physiologist, medical/surgical nurse*

Blaine
Yecke, Cheri Pearson *education agency administrator, columnist, author*

Bloomington
Avery, Maurine Ann *health record administrator*
Brokke, Catherine Juliet *mission executive*
Jeffries, Mary *public relations executive*
Nichols, Donna Mardell *nurse anesthetist*
Powell, Christa Ruth *educational training executive*
Taylor, Susan S. *communications executive*

Blue Earth
Ellingsen, Susan P. *music educator*

Brainerd
Russell, Maxine *poet, writer*
Wannamaker, Mary Ruth *music educator*

Brandon
Bettermann, Hilda *state legislator*

Brooklyn Park
Boutiette, Mary Antonia *language educator*

Buffalo
Carter, Barbara Possis *elementary school educator*

Byron
Westerlund, Frezil Daniel-Ellis *pastor*

Chisholm
Peterson, Marjorie *former mayor*

Circle Pines
Yanta, Kristin *publishing executive*

Comfrey
Nohner, Sharon *nun, minister*

Coon Rapids
Angrist, Georgene Leiter *social studies educator*
Bordner, Patricia Anne *insurance agent, writer*
Goodstein-Shapiro, Florence (Florence Goodstein Walton) *artist, art historian*
Wilson, Sylvia Alyce *musician, educator*

Dilworth
DiAllesandro, Connie Lyn *family practice nurse practitioner*

Duluth
Gruver, Nancy *publishing executive*
Heller, Lois Jane *physiologist, educator, researcher*
Henrikson, Vickie L. *social worker*
Martin, Kathryn A. *academic administrator*
Regan, Laura Anderson *aviation maintenance technician*
Salmela, Lynn Marie *clinical nurse specialist*
Stoddard, Patricia Florence Coulter *retired psychologist*

Eagan
Kraskey, Carolyn Reneé *small business owner*

East Grand Forks
Engel, Carol Louise *music educator*

East Gull Lake
Hemkin-Kavanaugh, Sue *music educator*

Eden Prairie
Cervilla, Constance Marlene *marketing consultant*
De Bono, Luella Elizabeth *music educator*
Engel, Susan E. *retail executive*
Erickson, Kim *consumer products company executive*
Gullickson, Brandy Klingel *conductor, music educator*
Knous, Pamela K. *wholesale distribution executive*
McCombs, Charline *professional sports team executive*
Petersen, Maureen Jeanette Miller *management information consultant, former nurse*
Ruffenach, Rosemary Anne *English and writing educator*

Edina
Emmerich, Karol Denise *foundation executive, daylily hybridizer, former retail executive*
Holman, Iletta Marcella *retired art educator*
Kata, Marie L. *securities dealer, brokerage house executive*
King, Heather Ann *freelance journalist*
Kirchner, Mary Katherine *musician, educator*
Nelson, Patricia Joan Pingenot *retired educator*
Schwarzrock, Shirley Pratt *writer, educator*
Weber, Gail Mary *lawyer*

Elbow Lake
Lohse, Susan Faye *county official, educator*

Elk River
Goss, Cynthia Lee *tax accountant*

Elysian
Thayer, Edna Louise *medical facility and nursing administrator*

Excelsior
Henke, Janice Carine *educational software developer and marketer*

Falcon Heights
Kreuter, Gretchen V. *academic administrator*

Foley
Cross, Eunice D. *elementary school educator*

Forest Lake
Broecker, Sherry *state legislator*

Fridley
Larson, Marilyn J. *retired elementary music educator*

Gaylord
Strouth, Lenore Eileen *music educator*

Glencoe
Delagardelle, Linda *food executive*

Golden Valley
Leppik, Margaret White *municipal official*
Lester, Susan E. *bank executive*

Goodridge
Hanson, Norma Lee *farmer*

Grand Marais
Napadensky, Hyla Sarane *engineering consultant*

Hackensack
Marquart, Petra A. *training consultant*

Hastings
Avent, Sharon L. Hoffman *manufacturing company executive*
Jacobsen-Theel, Hazel M. *retired historian*

Hibbing
Gentile, Glenna Lee *psychologist, educator*
Lahdelma, Gladys Linda *elementary school educator*
Lilyquist, Candace Louise *labor union administrator*

Hokah
Fishel, Rachel Therese *principal, elementary school educator*

Hopkins
Hoard, Heidi Marie *lawyer*
Young, Margaret Labash *librarian, information consultant, editor*
Zins, Martha Lee *elementary education educator, media specialist*

Janesville
Frank, Sister Elaine Lou *sister*

Lake Elmo
Tomljanovich, Esther M. *retired judge*

Lakeland
Larsen, Peg *state legislator*

Lakeville
McGowan, Monica S. *performing company executive, sales executive*

Lindstrom
Messin, Marlene Ann *plastics company executive*

Long Lake
Hofkin, Ann Ginsburgh *photographer, poet*

Loretto
Veit, Gae *construction executive*

Mankato
Huot, Rachel Irene *biomedical educator, research scientist, physician*
Mink, Jo Anna Stephens *humanities educator*
Preska, Margaret Louise Robinson *education historian, administrator*
Roisum Foley, Amy Kathryn *music educator, director*

Maple Grove
Leiseth, Patricia Schutz *educational technology specialist*
Prins, LaVonne Kay *programmer analyst*
Riesgraf, Kim Marie Wogensen *director*

Mapleton
Carpenter, Rebecca Lee *secondary school educator, music educator*

Maplewood
St. Germain, Sharon Marie *writer*

Marshall
Clark, Lynnette Faye *music educator*
Wilson, Judy Robinson *language educator, writer*

Mentor
Jerdee, Sylvia Ann *minister*

Minneapolis
Adlis, Susan Annette *biostatistician*
Ahlers, Linda L. *retail executive*
Alton, Ann Leslie *judge, lawyer, educator*
Atkinson, Christine Anne *curator*
Bancroft, Ann E. *polar explorer*
Battle, Willa Lee Grant *clergywoman, educational administrator*
Bell, Constance Conklin *child care association administrator*
Bernhardson, Ivy Schutz *lawyer*
Berscheid, Ellen S. *psychology educator, writer, researcher*
Bonner, Brigid Ann *marketing professional*
Brooks, Gladys Sinclair *retired public affairs consultant*
Campbell, Karlyn Kohrs *speech and communication educator*
Carlson, Jennie Peaslack *bank executive*
Casey, Lynn M. *public relations executive*
Chavers, Blanche Marie *pediatrician, educator, researcher*
Chemberlin, Peg *clergy, religious organization administrator*
Comstock, Rebecca Ann *lawyer*
Corbine Espinosa, Juanita Grace *cultural association administrator*
Crosby, Jacqueline Garton *newspaper editor, journalist*
Durdahl, Carol Lavaun *psychiatric nurse*
Dworsky, Mary *interior designer*
Edwardson, Sandra *dean, nursing educator*
Eich, Susan *public relations executive*
Feldman, Nancy Jane *health organization executive*
Fergus, Patricia Marguerita *English language educator, writer, editor*
Feuss, Linda Anne Upsall *lawyer*
Filloon, Karen *radio personality*
Firchow, Evelyn Scherabon *German language and literature educator, writer*
Flanagan, Barbara *journalist*
Fleezanis, Jorja Kay *violinist, educator*
Forneris, Jeanne M. *lawyer*
Fraser, Arvonne Skelton *former United Nations ambassador*
French, Catherine E. Wolfgram *engineering educator, researcher*
Fruen, Lois *secondary school educator*
Gajl-Peczalska, Kazimiera J. *retired surgical pathologist, pathology educator*
Gardebring, Sandra S. *academic administrator*
Garner, Shirley Nelson *English language educator*
Gavin, Sara *public relations executive*
Gerberich, Susan Goodwin *epidemiologist, educator, medical researcher*
Gerdner, Linda Ann *nursing researcher, educator*
Gilbert, Helen DeLong *psychologist, psychoanalyst*
Goldberg, Luella Gross *corporation executive*
Griffith, Sima Lynn *investment banker, consultant*
Grodsky, Jamie Anne *law educator*
Gudmundson, Barbara Rohrke *ecologist*
Hand, Mary Jane *artist*
Hansen, Jo-Ida Charlotte *psychology educator, researcher*
Harper, Patricia Nelsen *psychiatrist*
Harp-Jirschele, Mary *communications executive*
Hawley, Sandra Sue *electrical engineer*
Hill, Tessa *president non profit environmental group*
Houlton, Lise *performing company executive*
Howland, Joan Sidney *law librarian, educator*
Jeffrey-Smith, Lilli Ann *biofeedback specialist, educator, administrator*
Jeffries, Kim *radio personality*
Johnson, Badri Nahvi *sociology educator, real estate company officer*
Johnson, Carol R. *school system administrator*
Johnson, Cheri Marie *writer, humanities educator*
Johnson, Lola Norine *retired advertising and public relations executive, educator*
Johnson, Margaret Ann (Peggy) *library administrator*
Jones, Susie *radio personality*
Joseph, Marilyn Susan *gynecologist*
Karlins, Miriam *mental health and volunteer services consultant*
Kaufman, Anne Mull *education educator*
King, Lyndel Irene Saunders *art museum director*
King, Reatha Clark *community foundation executive*
Kirtley, Jane Elizabeth *law educator*

Kohlstedt, Sally Gregory *history educator*
Kulig, Martha *stage manager*
Laing, Karel Ann *magazine publishing executive*
Lange, Katherine J. *writer*
Leuchovius, Deborah *advocate, special education services professional, consultant*
Logan, Veryle Jean *retail executive, realtor*
Lyon, Joyce *artist, art educator*
Maloney, Rita *radio personality*
Mamayek, Telly *radio personality*
Marling, Karal Ann *art history and social sciences educator, curator*
Marshall, Siri Swenson *lawyer*
Mason, Barbara Fountain *minister*
Mathews, Kathleen Ann *social worker, psychotherapist*
McConnell Serio, Suzie Theresa *former professional basketball player, professional basketball coach*
McDaniel, Jan *television station executive*
Mickelson, Stacey *state legislator*
Mondale, Joan Adams *wife of former Vice President of United States*
Montgomery, Ann D. *federal judge, educator*
Murphy, Diana E. *federal judge*
Murphy, Edrie Lee *laboratory administrator*
Musacchio, Laura R. *planning and design educator*
Nelson, Kari J. *psychologist, educator*
Nelson, Marilyn C. *hotel executive, travel company executive, food service executive, marketing professional*
Neville, Cara Lee T. *judge*
Nortwen, Patricia Harman *music educator*
Oakes, Laura *radio personality*
O'Keefe, Nancy Jean *retired real estate company executive*
Palmer, Deborah Jean *lawyer*
Paul, Nora Marie *media studies educator*
Pejsa, Jane Elizabeth *writer, retired computer scientist*
Peterson, Patty *radio personality*
Porter, Jeannette Upton *elementary school educator*
Porter, Jennifer Madeleine *producer, director*
Pour-El, Marian Boykan *mathematician, educator*
Powell, Deborah Elizabeth *pathologist, dean*
Rahman, Yueh-Erh *biologist*
Rajkumar, Roshini Anne *reporter*
Raynolds, Virginia Crane *nurse*
Reichgott Junge, Ember D. *former state senator, lawyer, writer, broadcast analyst, radio personality*
Rogers, Karen Beckstead *gifted studies educator, researcher, consultant*
Sayles Belton, Sharon *former mayor*
Schneider, Elaine Carol *lawyer, researcher, writer*
Serstock, Doris Shay *retired microbiologist, educator, civic worker*
Sloan, Debra Lynne *interior designer*
Slocum, Rosemarie *physician services consultant, recruiter*
Smith, Katie *professional basketball player*
Spake, Mary Barbara *music educator*
Stanfield, Rebecca *radio personality*
Steen-Hinderlie, Diane Evelyn *social worker, musician*
Stephenson, Nancy Louise *medical products company professional*
Stephenson, Vivian M. *former retail executive*
Struthers, Margo S. *lawyer*
Tunheim, Kathryn H. *public relations executive*
Vainschtein, Arkady *physics educator*
Veldey, Bonnie *special education educator*
Watson, Catherine Elaine *journalist*
Wilhelm, Gretchen *retired secondary school educator, volunteer*
Wille, Karin L. *lawyer*
Younger, Judith Tess *law educator*
Zelickson, Sue *newspaper and cookbook editor, television reporter and host, food consultant*

Minnetonka
DiGeso, Amy *mail order company executive*
Jacobson, Anna Sue *finance company executive*
McCarron, Merne Christine *writer, public relations consultant*
Quam, Lois *healthcare company executive*
Rivet, Jeannine M. *health plan administrator*
Vanstrom, Marilyn June Christensen *retired elementary school educator*
Wigfield, Rita L. *elementary school educator*

Monticello
Sonbuchner, Gail Murphy *secondary special education educator*

Moorhead
Kent, Jill *midwife*
Morrison, Barbara Sheffield *Japanese translator and interpreter, consultant, educator*

Morris
Ordway, Ellen *biologist, educator, entomologist, researcher*

Mounds View
Thomason, Lynne *councilwoman, medical laser technician*

New Brighton
Carlson, Kaye Lilien *retired music educator*
Heston, Renate *nursing administrator*
Kieffer, Kathleen Cecil *elementary school educator*

New Prague
Gallagher, Sandra Ann *music educator*

Northfield
McKinsey, Elizabeth *humanities educator, consultant*
Yandell, Cathy Marleen *language educator*
Zelliot, Eleanor Mae *history educator*

Oakdale
Cederburg, Barbara M. *printing company executive*

Ortonville
Schrom, Elizabeth Ann *retired writer*

Owatonna
Aune, Debra Bjurquist *lawyer*
Larson, Diane LaVerne Kusler *principal*
Schroeder, Mary Ellen *adult education educator*

Palisade
Kilde, Sandra Jean *nurse, anesthetist, educator, consultant*

Paynesville
Bungum, Cheryl Nancy *music educator, director*

Plymouth
Hurlburt, Anne Wedewer *municipal official*

Preston
Schommer, Trudy Marie *pastoral minister, religion education*

Richfield
Devlin, Barbara Jo *school district administrator*
Fischer, Colleen Theresa *music educator*
Reilly, Jill Marlene *school system administrator*
Schuett, Carol Ann *travel industry business analyst*

Rochester
Frusti, Doreen Kaye *nursing administrator*
Gervais, Sister Generose *hospital consultant*
Goodman, Julie *nurse midwife*
Grosset, Jessica Ariane *computer analyst*
Hiniker, LuAnn *management consultant, educator, researcher, grants consultant*
Hodgson, Harriet W. *non-fiction writer*
Hodgson, Jane Elizabeth *obstetrician, gynecologist, consultant*
Kinney, Carolyn *executive secretary*
Kummeth, Patricia Joan *nursing educator*
Nienow, Beth Marie *librarian*
Schmieding, Rebecca Sue *information technology manager*
Shepard, Laura Ann *microbiologist, researcher*
Shulman, Carole Karen *professional society administrator*
Stelck, Mickie Joann *technologist*
Swenson, Constance N. *artist*

Roseville
[illegible] Jean Marie *media specialist, educator*
McMillan, Mary Bigelow *retired minister, volunteer*

Saginaw
Stauber, Marilyn Jean *retired secondary school educator, retired elementary school educator*

Saint Cloud
Boltuck, Mary A. *retired psychologist, educator*
McIntyre, Vicky Joyce *business owner*
McKay, Joane Williams *dean*
Olson, Barbara Ford *physician*
Reha, Rose Krivisky *retired finance educator*

Saint James
Jones, Patricia Louise *elementary counselor*

Saint Louis Park
Husen, Aino Maria *retired elementary school educator*

Saint Paul
Anderson, Ellen Ruth *state legislator*
Archabal, Nina M(archetti) *historical society director*
Bachmann, Michele *state legislator*
Barry, Anne M. *public health officer*
Beers, Anne *protective services official*
Berglin, Linda *state legislator*
Blatz, Kathleen Anne *judge, state agency administrator, state legislator*
Bly, Carol McLean *writer, educator*
Boudreau, Lynda L. *state legislator*
Clark, Karen *state legislator*
Close, Elizabeth Scheu *retired architect*
Critzer, Susan L. *health products company executive*
Davis, Joy Lee *English language educator*
Davis, Margaret Bryan *paleoecology researcher, educator*
DeMaris, Heather *occupational therapist*
Doescher, Jill Train *lawyer*
Doyle, Florence Elizabeth *retired secondary school educator*
Dutcher, Judi *state auditor*
Dybvig, Mary McIlvaine *educational consultant, psychologist*
Ehlke, Nancy Jo *agronomist*
Esposito, Bonnie Lou *marketing professional*
Fischbach, Michelle L. *state legislator*
Flynn, Carol *state legislator*
Franey, Billie Nolan *political activist*
Fruehling, Rosemary Therese *publishing executive, author*
Gagnon, Laura Christine *financial analyst*
Glancy, Helen Diane *literature educator*
Greiling, Mindy *state legislator*
Hall, Beverly Joy *police officer*
Hansen, Robyn L. *lawyer*
Hanson, Paula E. *state legislator*
Harder, Elaine Rene *state legislator*
Harris, Duchess *social sciences educator*
Harvey, Patricia A. *school system administrator*
Higgins, Linda I. *state legislator*
Huber, Sister Alberta *college president*
Hultman, Carol Linda *elementary school educator*
Johnson, Alice M. *state legislator*
Kahn, Phyllis *state legislator*
Kerr, Sylvia Joann *science educator*
Kiffmeyer, Mary *state official*
Kilbourne, Barbara Jean *health and housing executive*
Kimberly, Susan Elizabeth *state legislative director, city program administrator*
Kiscaden, Sheila M. *state legislator*
Krentz, Jane *state legislator, elementary school educator*
Lebedoff, Randy Miller *lawyer*
Lee, Andrea Jane *academic administrator, nun*
Lesewski, Arlene *state legislator, insurance agent*
Lofquist, Vicki L. *journalist*
Matteson, Clarice Chris *artist, educator*
May, Georgiana *biologist, educator*
McGuire, Mary Jo *state legislator*
Meyer, Helen M. *judge*
Molnau, Carol *lieutenant governor*
Monson, Dianne Lynn *literacy educator*
Murphy, Mary C. *state legislator*
Nylander, Patricia Marie *pilot*
O'Brien, Odessa Louise *protective services official*
O'Connor, Genevieve *pharmaceutical executive*
Olson, Bettye Johnson *artist, retired educator*
Olson, Gen *state legislator*
Oswald, Eva Sue Aden *retired insurance company executive*
Padelford, Nicole *accountant*
Pampusch, Anita Marie *foundation administrator*
Pappas, Sandra Lee *state senator*
Pariseau, Patricia *state legislator*
Paulos, Christine Ann *academic administrator*
Portoghese, Caroline Louise Parke *occupational therapist*
Ranum, Jane Barnhardt *state senator, lawyer*
Reinhardt, Victoria Ann *county official, environmentalist*
Rest, Ann H. *state legislator*
Ring, Twyla L. *state legislator, newspaper editor*
Robertson, Martha Rappaport *state legislator, consultant*
Robling, Claire A. *state legislator*
Runbeck, Linda C. *state legislator*
Rydell, Catherine M. *former state legislator*
Schaefer, Elzbieta A. *music educator*
Scheid, Linda J. *state legislator*
Schumacher, Leslie *state legislator, artist*
Seagren, Alice *state legislator*
Shepard, Sue Annette *director fund raising*
Smith, Lucy *intercultural communication specialist*
Smith, Mary Hill *volunteer*
Smith, Rosemary *artist, educator*
Starling, Elizabeth Anne *strategic planner*
Straight, Cathy *editor*
Stroud, Rhoda M. *elementary school educator*
Tyrrell, [illegible] *community health educator*
Victor, Lorraine Carol *critical care nurse*
Wagner, Mary Margaret *library and information science educator*
Wejcman, Linda *state legislator*
Wheelock, Pam *financial executive*
Zander, Janet Adele *psychiatrist*
Zietlow, Ruth Ann *reference librarian*
Zuraitis, Marita *insurance company executive*

Shakopee
Kelso, Becky *former state legislator*

Stewartville
Tlougan, Jessica Elise *music educator*
Wilson, Diane E. *music educator*

Stillwater
Asch, Susan McClellan *pediatrician*
Buck, Anita Emily *newswriter*

Taylors Falls
Yeager, Debra Lyn *science educator*

Thief River Falls
Jauquet-Kalinoski, Barbara *library director*

Two Harbors
Gredzens, Sandra May Pillsbury *art educator*

Wabasha
Brelsford, Mary J. *music educator*

Waconia
Scanlon Hobbs, Laurie Ann *public relations professional*

Winona
Heukeshoven, Janet Kay *music educator*
Holm, Joy Alice *psychology educator, goldsmith, artist, art educator*
Merchlewitz, Ann Elizabeth *lawyer*
Sullivan, Kathryn Ann *librarian, educator*

Worthington
Meyer, Helen Bernadine *financial services company executive*

Zumbrota
Fredrickson, Marilyn H. *secondary school educator, art educator, artist*
Post, Diana Constance *retired librarian*

MISSISSIPPI

Amory
Brannon, Pat *poet*

Ashland
Massengill, Belinda B. *voice educator*

Batesville
Rivers, Nettie Taylor *hearing impaired educator*

Bay Saint Louis
Foster, Willetta Jean *music educator*

Biloxi
Brown, Sheba Ann *elementary school educator*
Manners, Pamela Jeanne *middle school educator*
McCaughan, Della Marie *retired science educator*

Blue Mountain
Mounce, Carolyn P. *school librarian*

Bolton
Byrd, Lisa Marie *family nurse practitioner, lecturer*

Booneville
Hardon, Imogene M. *elementary school educator*

Brandon
Bishop, Faira Lee *library educator*
Schoolar, Laurel Ann *artist, educator*

Brookhaven
Hyde-Smith, Cindy *state legislator*

Brooklyn
Gerald, Carolyn Aileen T. *emergency physician*

Byhalia
Tackett, Maresa D. *medical technician*

Calhoun City
Macon, Myra Faye *retired library director*

Canton
Hammack, Julia Kathryn *music educator*

Clarksdale
Presley, Vivian Mathews *junior college administrator*
Walton, SuzAnne W. *elementary school educator*

Cleveland
Taylor, Donna Buescher *marriage and family therapist*

Clinton
Bigelow, Martha Mitchell *retired historian*
Causey, Carley Claire *art educator, consultant, art therapist, researcher*
Whitlock, Betty *retired secondary school educator*

Columbus
Labensky, Sarah Ross *culinary educator*
Nawrocki, Susan Jean *librarian*
Reynolds, Gail Smith *accountant, bank officer*

Corinth
Howell, Teresa Christine Wallin *elementary school educator*
Stafford Humbers, Linda Logan *family practice nurse practitioner*

Crystal Springs
Bates, Lura Wheeler *retired trade association executive*

Ellisville
Ross, Lisa Sims *special education educator*
Smith, Nina J. *music educator*

Goodman
King, Kathy Cooper *music educator*

Greenville
Potter, Suzanne Peyton *elementary school educator*

Greenwood
Wacht, Leny Nowag *art educator*

Grenada
Thomas, Ouida Power *music educator*

Gulfport
Price, Helen Hoggatt *counseling administrator*

Hattiesburg
Bedenbaugh, Angela Lea Owen *chemistry educator, researcher*
Curry, Martha Ann *music educator*
D'Arpa, Josephine *music educator*
Davis, Doris Johnson *retired music educator*
McRaney, Joan Katherine *artist*
Reinshagen, Yolanda P. *elementary school educator*
Slade, Barbie Evette Delk *special education educator*
Taylor, Elizabeth Ann (Beth Taylor) *advertising and marketing executive, video producer*

Hazlehurst
Blakeney, Margaret Elizabeth Fleming *counselor, educator*

Itta Bena
Henderson, Robbye Robinson *library director*

Iuka
Barnes, Betty Jean *educational administrator*

Jackson
Anderson, Roslyn *newscaster*
Baltz, Mary Melissa *lawyer*
Blackmon, Barbara Martin *state legislator, lawyer*
Brumfield, Dana Kristine *music educator, medical transcriptionist*
Carlton, Neely C. *state legislator, lawyer*
Chambers-Mangum, Fransenna Ethel *special education educator*
Clarke, Alyce Griffin *state legislator*
Cobb, Kay Beevers *state supreme court justice, former state senator*
Coleman, Linda *state legislator*
Coleman, Mary H. *state legislator*
Collins, Deloris Williams *secondary school educator*
Creel, Sue Cloer *secondary school educator*
Dickson, Reecy L. *state legislator*

Fillingane, Joey *lawyer, state representative*
Frazel-Lasseter, Cheryl *newscaster*
Fredericks, Frances M. *state legislator, nurse*
Harden, Alice V. *state legislator*
Harrison, Esther M. *elementary school educator, state representative*
Hiatt, Jane Crater *arts agency administrator*
Hoban-Moore, Patricia A. *federal agency administrator*
Holly, Ellistine Perkins *music educator*
Houston, Gerry Ann *oncologist*
Jackson, Valerie Lynnette *social worker*
Jennings, Wanda T. *state legislator*
Leonard, Pamela Dian *architect, artist*
Martinson, Rita R. *state legislator*
McLemore-Wheeler, Linda M. *literature educator*
Miller, Patricia K. *former state legislator*
Patterson, Chan *food service executive*
Peranich, Diane C. *state legislator*
Phillips, Karen Suzanne *psychologist*
Robertson, Valeria Brower *state legislator, land developer*
Rubisoff, Deborah L. *state agency administrator*
Scott, Eloise Hale *state legislator*
Scott, Omeria McDonald *state legislator*
Segal, Jane *newscaster*
Shaifer, Audrey Virginia *director*
Smith, Sharman Bridges *former state librarian*
Somekawa, Mina C. *pianist, educator*
Srinivasan, Seetha *publishing company executive*
Stevens, Mary Ann *state legislator*
Thomas, Sara R. *state legislator*
Thompson, Marsha *newscaster*
Tuck, Amy *lieutenant governor*
Wade, Maggie *newscaster*
Wolfe, Mildred Nungester *artist*

Keesler AFB
Harrell, Elizabeth Ann *career officer*

Lauderdale
Van Doren, Henrietta Lambert *nurse, anesthetist*

Laurel
Asmar, Kathleen *educational association administrator*
Harper, Peggy Sue *music educator*

Leland
Stott, Barbara Paxton *volunteer*

Madison
Fordice, Patricia Owens *civic leader, former state first lady*

Marks
Kaufman, Raylene Dyane *secondary school educator*

Mccomb
Jackson, Alfreda Murraye *adult education educator*

Meridian
Smith, Lois Adkins *science educator*
Wilson-Jones, Linda *guidance counselor*

Minter City
Mitchell, Patsy Malier *religious school founder and administrator*

Mississippi State
Crudden, Adele Louise *social work research educator*
Delgado, Marica LaDonne *librarian, educator*
Henington, Carlen *psychologist, educator*
Rent, Clyda Stokes *academic administrator*
Wall, Diane Eve *political science educator*
Wiltrout, Ann Elizabeth *foreign language educator*

Moss Point
Bolton, Betty J. *medical/surgical nurse, poet*
Stephens, Cecile Higdon *artist*

Natchez
Anderson, Rose L. Dyess *elementary school educator, poet*
Branyan, Cheryl Munyer *museum administrator, consultant*
Marion, Ann *school psychologist, educator*

Nettleton
Hairald, Mary Payne *vocational education educator, coordinator*

Ocean Springs
Parker, Rebecca Mary *special education facility administrator, educator*
Vinsonhaler, Chris *storyteller, musician, consultant*

Olive Branch
Kern, Angeline Frazier *educational administrator, guidance counselor*

Oxford
Wickham, Kathleen Woodruff *education educator*
Winter, Karen Knight Alice *special education educator*

Pass Christian
Dawkins, Deborah Jeanne *state legislator*
Henrion, Rosemary P. *mental health professional*

Pearl
Grison, Deborah D. *publishing executive*

Philadelphia
Watson, Sheila Nelson *secondary school educator*
Williamson, Gloria *state legislator*

Picayune
Carter, Enita Joy *conductor*

Poplarville
Peterson, Katherine Dianne *ministry assistant*

Port Gibson
Alford, Constance Keith *recreational facility executive, artist*

Purvis
Evans, V. Faye *postmaster*

Raymond
Bee, Anna Cowden *dance educator*

Richton
Edwards, Claudette LeCoq *speech pathology/audiology services professional*

Ridgeland
Crittenden, Antoinette *marketing professional*
Jones, Sarah Ashley *realtor, consultant*

Southaven
Johnson, Joyce Thedford *state agency administrator*

Starkville
Dampier, Caryn *self-defense instructor*
Dumas, Joyce Pendleton *social worker*
Durst, Jo *artist, educator*
Hoffman, Helene *lawyer*
Looby, Eugenie Joan *dean, educator*

Sunflower
Powell, Anice Carpenter *retired librarian*

Tupelo
Doxey-Tate, Sarah Rolston *retired elementary school educator*
Holland, Gloria Temple *psychotherapist*
Radojcsics, Anne Parsons *librarian*
Weaver, Laura Fisher *financial planner*
Zurawski, Jeanette *rehabilitation services professional*

Union
Johnson, Denise Horton *speech pathology/audiology services professional*

Vicksburg
Joyner, Elizabeth *curator*
Keulegan, Emma Pauline *special education educator*

Walls
Tharnish, Rose Maries Lehman *veterinarian*

Whitfield
Swann, Melissa Lynne *psychologist*

MISSOURI

Archie
Whiteside, Jennie Susan *elementary school educator, secondary school educator*

Ballard
Talbot, Phyllis Mary *reading educator*

Ballwin
Beckmann, Nancy Bourke *retired elementary school educator*
Corno, Donna A. *retired public relations executive, consultant*
Guinther, Christine Louise *special education educator*
Pallozola, Christine *non-profit administrator*
Rothermich, Gayla *music educator, director*

Belton
Brown, Doris Jane *medical technician*

Bourbon
Heitsch, Leona Mason *artist, writer*

Branson
Ford, Jean Elizabeth *former English language educator*
Herron, Gayle Ann *forensic psychologist, mental health consultant, psychotherapist, health facility administrator, columnist*

Bridgeton
Hylla, Linda Kay *sister, social worker*

Butler
Baxter, Myrtle Mae (Bobbi Baxter) *artist*
Cochran, Beth *gifted and talented educator*

Camdenton
Harris, Deanna Lynn *special education educator, writer*

Canton
Howe, Sandra Jo *library director*

Charleston
Wallhausen, Mildred Carolyn *publisher*

Chesterfield
Baker, Sandra Kay *music educator*
Finley, Marlynn Holt *elementary educator consultant*
Fowler, Marti *fine arts consultant*
Kruse, Margaret M. *art educator*
Landram, Christina Louella *librarian*
Mitchell, Carolyn Joyce *music educator*
Phariss, Susan Willis *dietitian*
Ridenhour, Marilyn Housel *accountant, consultant*
Robinson, Patricia Elaine *women's health nurse practitioner*
Schwind, Wanda Ruth *retail executive*
Stevens, Anne Bickett Parker *architectural designer*

Clarkton
Dooley, Wendy Brooke *vocalist, music educator*

Clayton
Mach, Ruth *principal*

Columbia
Adams, Algalee Pool *college dean, art educator*
Alexander, Martha Sue *retired librarian*
Bank, Barbara J. *sociology educator*
Beedle, Dawn Danene *recruiting and training administrator*
Burgoyne, Suzanne *theater educator, writer*
Cunningham, Milamari Antoinella *anesthesiologist*
DeJarnette, Shirley Shea *treasurer*
Findley-Liles, Shannon Marie *sales executive*
Flournoy, Nancy *statistician, educator*
Flynn, Margaret Alberi *nutritionist, dietitian*
Grundler, Mary Jane Lang *business education educator*
Hensley, Elizabeth Catherine *nutritionist, educator*
Horner, Winifred Bryan *humanities educator, researcher, consultant, writer*
James, Elizabeth Joan Plogsted *pediatrician, educator*
Kyllonen, Frances Thompson *retired educator*
Libby, Wendy B. *academic administrator*
Looser, Devoney Kay *English literature educator*
Miller, Karen Marie *county commissioner*
Morrow, Constance Prescott *music educator*
Mustard, Cindy Singleton *social worker, administrator*
Northway, Wanda I. *real estate company executive*
Plummer, Patricia Lynne Moore *chemistry and physics educator*
Pringle, Norma Jean Poarch *translator, educator*
Randall, Linda Lea *biochemist, educator*
Robins, Betty Dashew *antiques and arts dealer*
Snively, Carol A. *social worker, educator*
Swan, Shanna Helen *epidemiologist, researcher*
Tarnove, Lorraine *medical association executive*
Wallach, Barbara Price *classicist, educator*

Creve Coeur
Kemper, Christina *small business owner, respiratory therapist, elementary school educator*
Manne, Deborah Sue *dental hygienist, educator*
Myers, Debra Annella *speech pathology/audiology services professional*

Defiance
Brail, Katrina Irene *epidemiologist*
LeMaster, Sherry Renee *fundraising administrator, foundation administrator, consultant*

Dexter
Owens, Debra Ann *chiropractor*

Earth City
Frontiere, Georgia *professional football team executive*
Kiry-Ryan, Rita Irene *computer scientist, educator*

El Dorado Springs
Hochstedler, Lisa Inez *educational association administrator*

Eureka
Lindsey, Susan Lyndaker *zoologist*
Zimmers, Vivian Eleanor *development and administrative consultant*

Fair Grove
Piech, Mary Lou Rohling *medical psychotherapist, consultant*

Farmington
Huck, Linda A. *music educator*
Welch Dickerman, Tanya L. *speech pathology/audiology services professional, consultant, small business owner*

Fayette
Inman, Marianne Elizabeth *college administrator*

Fenton
Hughes, Barbara Bradford *manufacturing executive, real estate manager, community health nurse*
Marcus, Michelle *computer scientist*

Ferguson
Lawrence, Trudy Kay *art educator*

Florissant
Ashhurst, Anna Wayne *foreign language educator*
Ferguson, Audrey Diane *elementary school educator*
James, Dorothy Louise King *special education educator*
Schutzius, Mary Jane *volunteer activist*
Stokan, Lana J. Ladd *state legislator*

Forsyth
Klinefelter, Sarah Stephens *retired division dean, radio station manager*

Franklin
Becker, Barbara Ann Stulac (Bobbie Becker) *small business owner*

Fredericktown
Sudmeyer, Alice Jean *artist, poet*

Fulton
Bierdeman-Fike, Jane Elizabeth *social worker, educator*
Reifsteck, Dorothy L. *retired health facility executive*

Golden City
Howard, Joanne Frances *marketing executive, researcher, funeral director*

Greenwood
Zeller, Marilynn Kay *retired librarian*

Hamilton
Hawley, Lucretia Marlene *retired accounting educator*

Hannibal
Richmond, Deborah Vance *civil engineer*

Hazelwood
Agre, Joy Elaine *music educator*
Kostecki, Mary Ann *financial tax consultant, small business consultant*

Hermann
Mahoney, Catherine Ann *artist, educator*

High Ridge
Karll, Jo Ann *retired judge, lawyer*

Hillsboro
Phillips, Amy Renea *assistant principal*

Holden
Martin, Laurabelle *real estate and farm land owner and manager*

Hollister
Canfield, Cindy Sue *art educator*
Hopper, Ruby Lou *clergy member*

Houston
Morgan, Brenda Gaye *art educator*

Independence
Booz, Gretchen Arlene *marketing executive*
Dorshow-Gordon, Ellen *epidemiologist*
Evans, Margaret Ann *human resources administrator, business owner*
Henley, Patricia Joan *principal*
Johnson, Sharon Elaine *elementary school educator*
Kilpatrick, Laura Shelby *music educator*
Lundy, Sadie Allen *small business owner*
Marlow, Lydia Lou *elementary school educator*
Mortimer, Anita Louise *minister*
Nordsieck, Karen Ann *custom apparel company executive*
Peake, Candice K. Loper *data processing professional*
Potts, Barbara Joyce *retired historical society executive*
Starks, Carol Elizabeth *retired principal*
Stoner, Connie Kay *special education educator*
Willett, Teri Kay *art educator*

Ironton
Sebastian, Phylis Sue (Ingram) *real estate broker, antique appraiser*

Jefferson City
Backer, Gracia Yancey *state legislator*
Bland, Mary Groves *state legislator*
Bray, Joan *state legislator*
Bussabarger, Mary Louise *mental health services professional*
Carter, Paula J. *state legislator*
Days, Rita Denise *state legislator*
Farmer, Nancy *state official*
Fues, Marianne Cole *multi-media specialist*
Hagan-Harrell, Mary M. *state legislator*
Hanaway, Catherine *state representative, lawyer*
Hoskins, Rhonda Sue *real estate appraiser*
Kasten, Mary Alice C. *state legislator*
Kauffman, Sandra Daley *state legislator*
Kelly, Glenda Marie *state legislator*
Long, Elizabeth L. *state legislator, small business owner*
Lumpe, Sheila *state commissioner, former state legislator*
Mays, Carol Jean *state legislator*
McCaskill, Claire *auditor*
McClelland, Emma L. *state legislator*
McDaniel, Sue Powell *writer, speaker*
Murray, Connie Wible *state official, former state legislator*
Ostmann, Cindy *state legislator*
Parker, Sara Ann *librarian, consultant*
Ridgeway, Luann *state legislator*
Robirds, Estel *state legislator*
Sallee, Mary Lou *state legislator*
Scheve, May E. *state legislator, political organization worker*
Sims, Betty *state legislator*
Stith, Laura Denvir *state supreme court justice*
Wagner, Ann *political organization executive*
Williams, Deleta *state legislator*
Williams, Marilyn *state legislator*

Joplin
Arguello, Barbara Ann *nursing assistant*
Zook, Martha Frances Harris *retired nursing administrator*

Kahoka
Jones, Mary D. *court clerk*

Kansas City
Adams, Beverly Josephine *data processing specialist*
Aylward, Marcia Eileen *artist, educator*
Bacon, Jennifer Gille *lawyer*
Barnes, Kay *mayor*
Bartlett, Sherie *printing company executive*
Belzer, Ellen J. *negotiations and communications trainer, consultant*
Bennett, Teresa Ann (Terri) *social worker, counselor*
Blake, Darcie Kay *radio news director, anchor*
Boysen, Melicent Pearl *finance company executive*
Brent, Elizabeth Maria *education educator*

Busby, Marjean (Marjorie Jean Busby) *retired journalist*
Byers-Pevitts, Beverley *college administrator, educator*
Cahill, Patricia Deal *radio station executive*
Caulfield, Joan *director, educator*
Clegg, Karen Kohler *lawyer*
Coon, Saundra Kay *home health nurse, small business owner*
Courson, Marna B.P. *public relations executive*
Danner, Kathleen Frances Steele *federal official*
Davis, Florea Jean *social worker*
Davis, Mary Bronaugh *music educator*
DeParle, Nancy-Ann Min *former federal agency administrator, lawyer*
Donovan, Ann Burcham *medical office administrator*
Drees, Betty *dean, educator*
Dumovich, Loretta *real estate and transportation company executive*
Ethern, Aberdeen *music educator*
Fairchild, Sharon Elaine *corrections administrator*
Garrison, F. Elaine *copy editor*
Guilliland, Martha W. *academic administrator*
Guisewite, Cathy Lee *cartoonist*
Hamerle, Jill Christine *secondary school educator*
Hebenstreit, Jean Estill Stark *religion educator, practitioner*
Hirsch, Irma Lou Kolterman *retired nurse*
Hutson, Betty Switzer *art educator, artist*
Kloth, Carolyn *meteorologist*
Krause, Heather Dawn *data processing executive*
Krieg, Nancy Kay *social worker, poet, musician*
Kuenn, Marjorie Asp *music educator*
Latza, Beverly Ann *accountant*
Laughrey, Nanette Kay *judge, federal*
Lawrence, Susan *art dealer*
Lee, Margaret Norma *artist*
Leigh, Cheri J. *engineering consulting executive*
Leighton, Carol *retired educator*
Levings, Theresa Lawrence *lawyer*
Lindenbaum, Sharon *publishing executive*
Lindsay, Twyla Lynn *music educator*
Lombard, Regina A. *elementary school educator*
Manson, Anne *music director*
Martin Bowen, Lindsey *freelance writer*
Mast, Kande White *artist*
McElwreath, Sally Chin *corporate communications executive*
Mustard, Mary Carolyn *financial executive*
Nagle, Jean Susan Karabacz *sociologist, psychologist*
Nichols, Virginia Violet *independent insurance* [illegible]
Norris, Ruth Ann *social worker*
O'Dell, Jane *automotive company executive*
Parisi, Cheryl Lynn *music educator*
Parker, Marietta *prosecutor*
Phalp-Rathbun, Stephanie Dawn *music educator*
Plax, Karen Ann *lawyer*
Rice, Levina Ruth (Sally) *city council person, former government official*
Rocha, Catherine Tomasa *municipal official*
Rose, Teresa Beth *psychologist, educator*
Roush, Sue *newspaper editor*
Rove, Frances Ann *lawyer*
Sanchez, Beatrice Rivas *art institute executive, artist*
Satterlee, Terry Jean *lawyer*
Sauer, Elisabeth Ruth *lawyer*
Scott, Deborah Emont *curator*
Setser, Patricia A. *music educator*
Smith, Audrey Lee *psychologist, consultant*
Solberg, Elizabeth Transou *public relations executive*
Spalding, Helen H. *library director*
Stevens, Jane *advertising executive*
Stroup, Kala Mays *educational alliance administrator, former state higher education commissioner*
Stuckel, Ruth F. *philosopher, educator, nun*
Svadlenak, Jean Hayden *museum consultant*
Taylor, Marilyn Levere *management consultant, educator*
Thomas, Marcia Markowitz *library director, educator*
Van Dyne, Michele Miley *information engineer*
Welles, Ferne Bingham Malcolm *retired archivist*
Whittaker, Judith Ann Cameron *lawyer*
Willsie, Sandra K. *dean, internist, educator*
Yarmo, Fanny F. *not-for-profit fundraiser*
Youmans, Joyce M. *curator, researcher*

Kearney
Wood, Debra Lynn *music educator*

Kennett
Smith, Donna Dale *music educator*

Kirksville
Davis, Andrea Barbara *language educator*
Dixon, Barbara Bruinekool *academic administrator*
McLane-Iles, Betty Louise *academic administrator, educator, writer*
Presley, Paula Lumpkin *retired editor*

Kirkwood
Collins, Nancy Lee *mathematician, educator*
Hoglen, Jewel Pamela *retired secondary school educator*

Knob Noster
Engle, Cynthia Louise *art educator*

Lake Ozark
DeShazo, Marjorie White *occupational therapist*

Lebanon
Drennan, Heidi Marie *music educator*

Lees Summit
Barfield, Cynthia K. *social worker, psychotherapist*
Duke, Ellen Kay *planned giving administrator*
Headley, Carol Ann *elementary and secondary school educator*
Linder, Beverly L. *elementary school educator*
Lord, Heaven *theology studies educator, consultant, minister, translator*
Smith, Geraldine May *nutritionist*

Lewistown
Terpening, Virginia Ann *artist*

Lexington
Vinson, Lynette D. *speech pathology/audiology services professional*

Liberty
Gronlund, Sally Ann *special education educator*
Seward, Nancy H. *retired band director, composer*

Lockwood
Wehrman, Natalie Ann *retired music educator*

Macon
Maddox, Wilma *health facility administrator*

Marshall
Lines, Cheryl Elaine *music educator*
Ransom, Judy Lynn *music educator*

Maryville
Gorman, Karen Machmer *optometric physician*
Schultz, Patricia Bowers *vocal music educator, performer*
Strating, Sharon L. *elementary school educator, professional staff developer, educational consultant*

Mexico
Teague, Deborah Gant *elementary school educator*

Moberly
Werner, Karen Elaine *music educator*

Monett
Cooke, Bette Louise *retired library director*

Mount Vernon
Stemmons, Randee Smith *lawyer*

Neosho
Allman, Margaret Ann Lowrance *counseling administrator*

Nevada
Wassenberg, Evelyn M. *medical and surgical nurse, nursing educator*

New Bloomfield
Melton, June Marie *nursing educator*

New Cambria
Guilford, Kimberly Sue *music educator*

New Haven
Roth, Nancy Louise *former nurse, veterinarian*

O Fallon
Wood, Leslie Ann *retail administrator*

Osage Beach
Childers, Brenda Sue *medical/surgical nurse*

Overland
Clark, Maxine *retail executive*

Owensville
Leick, Carol Lynn *special education educator*

Pacific
Wilson, Jill Marie *early childhood educator*

Park Hills
Moore, Carol Jean *music educator, musician*

Parkville
Schultis, Gail Ann *library director*

Platte City
Kalin, D(orothy) Jean *artist, educator*
Knight, Betty Ann *county commissioner*
Nash, Donna Cecile *county official*

Pleasant Hill
Goosey, Karmen Eileen *nurse*

Pleasant Valley
Nelson, Freda Nell Hein *librarian*

Poplar Bluff
Allen, Brenda Kay *elementary school educator*

Raytown
Coppenbarger, Cecelia Marie *special education educator*
Siegel, Kim Annette *speech pathology/audiology services professional*

Richmond
Richardson, Opal Mae *music educator, director*
Stoenner, Jessamine *music educator*

Rogersville
Davis, Evelyn Marguerite Bailey *artist, musician*

Rolla
Brewster, Louise Boone *artist, educator*
Sauerwein, Amanda Marie *small business owner*
Sotiriou-Leventis, Chariklia *chemist, educator, researcher*
Steelman, Sarah *state legislator*

Saint Charles
Bax, Debra *real estate agent*
Brown, C. Alison *counselor*
Castro, Jan Garden *writer, arts consultant, educator*
Dorsey, Mary Elizabeth *lawyer*
Panagos, Rebecca Jean Huffman *university educator, researcher, consultant*
Reed, Warlene Patricia *retired librarian*
Tabaka, Sandra Lee *medical/surgical nurse*

Saint James
Stevens, Helen Jean *music educator*

Saint Joseph
Correu, Sandra Kay *special education educator*
Murphy, Janet Gorman *college president*
Rachow, Sharon Dianne *realtor*
Schneider, Julia *library director*
Thomas, Eleanor Shepherd *health facility administrator*

Saint Louis
Albee, Lenore K. *management consultant*
Atwood, Hollye Stolz *lawyer*
Baker, Nannette A. *lawyer, city official*
Baker, Shirley Kistler *university administrator*
Bateman, Sharon Louise *public relations executive*
Baum, M(ary) Carolyn *occupational therapist*
Beck, Lois Grant *anthropologist, educator, author*
Bellville, Margaret (Maggie Bellville) *communications executive*
Bennett, Patricia Ann *radio executive*
Bextermiller Metzger, Theresa Marie *architect, computer engineer*
Bockenkamp, Karen Ann *bank administrator*
Boggs, Beth Clemens *lawyer*
Bolanos, Maria Cecilia Maruqez *medical association administrator*
Bonacorsi, Mary Catherine *lawyer*
Bourne, Carol Elizabeth Mulligan *biology educator, phycologist*
Bradley, Marilynne Gail *advertising executive, advertising educator*
Brauer, Camilla Thompson (Kimmy Thompson Brauer) *civic leader*
Breckenridge, Joanne *political organization administrator*
Briccetti, Joan Therese *theater manager, arts management consultant*
Brickey, Kathleen Fitzgerald *law educator*
Briggs, Cynthia Anne *educational administrator, clinical psychologist*
Brown, JoBeth Goode *food products executive, lawyer*
Bryant, Ruth Alyne *banker*
Campbell, Anita Joyce *computer company executive*
Carpenter, Sharon Quigley *municipal official*
Case-Schmidt, Mary E. *pathologist, educator*
Chervitz, Randi S *art gallery director, artist*
Cima, Cheryl Ann *medical/surgical nurse*
Corbett, Suzanne Elaine *food writer, marketing executive, food historian*
Covington, Ann K. *lawyer, former state supreme court justice*
Crews, Janet M. *elementary school educator*
Dawson, M. Susan *nursing educator, psychiatric clinical specialist*
Devers, Gail *track and field athlete*
De Voe, Pamela Ann *anthropologist, educator*
Diekemper, Rita Garbs *landscape company executive*
Dugan, Jean Brodshaug *public relations consultant*
Duhig, Susan Caroline *writer*
Duhme, Carol McCarthy *civic worker*
Edwards, Judith Elizabeth *advertising executive*
Ehrlich, Ava *television executive*
Elliott, Susan Spoehrer *information technology executive*
Entessar, Tahmineh *political scientist, educator*
Ezenwa, Josephine Nwabuoku *social worker*
Faherty, Annalee *social worker, nun*
Farhatt, Kendra *travel company executive*
Fischer, Emily Christina *primary school educator*
Fitch, Rachel Farr *health policy analyst*
Fitzpatrick, Susan *biochemist, neurologist, foundation executive*
Foster, Scarlett Lee *investor relations executive*
Gfeller, Donna Kvinge *clinical psychologist*
Gilligan, Sandra Kaye *private school director*
Goldberg, Anne Carol *physician, educator*
Gooch, Audrey Smith *retired education educator*
Grant, Michele Byrd *secondary school educator*
Green, Darlene *controller, municipal official*
Greenley, Beverly Jane *lawyer, educator*
Griffin, Monica Victoria *military officer, writer*
Haley, Johnetta Randolph *musician, educator, university official*
Hall, Mary Taussig *professional volunteer*
Hamilton, Jean Constance *judge*
Handelman, Alice Samuels *public relations professional, writer*
Harris, Teresa Maria *visual artist*
Hawkins, Peggy Anne *veterinarian*
Hays, Ruth *lawyer*
Haywood, Kathleen Marie *university educator, dean*
Hemish, Carol Marie *liturgist/spiritual director, musician*
Hicks, Shirley E. *director*
Hilyard, Veronica Marie *education administrator*
Hinkle, Christina Nicole *primary school educator*
Hinshaw, Juanita *electric distributor executive*
Hoeffken, Rebecca Lynn *private school educator*
Holmes, Nancy Elizabeth *pediatrician*
Holt, Leslie Edmonds *librarian*
Hood, Phyllis Ilene *special education educator*
Horn, Joan Kelly *political research and consulting firm executive*
Horvath, Frances Louise *retired dean*
Hrubetz, Joan *dean, nursing educator*
Jackson, Carol E. *federal judge*
Jackson, Rebecca R. *lawyer*
Johnson, Susan L. B. *human resource administrator*
Johnston, Marilyn Frances-Meyers *physician, medical educator*
Joyner Kersee, Jacqueline *former track and field athlete*
Kennelly, Sister Karen Margaret *retired academic administrator, church administrator, nun*
Kincaid, Marilyn Coburn *medical educator*
Kohnen, Carol Ann *librarian*
Korando, Donna Kay *journalist*
Lackey, Kayle Diann *elementary school educator*
Lauenstein, Ann Gail *librarian*
Leek, Diane Webb *nurse*
Leonard, Judith Price *educational advisor*
Lindsey, Linda Lee *sociology educator*
Lipan, Petruta E. *semiotician, curator, artist*
Loepker, Patricia M. *marketing manager*
Mann, Judith Walker *curator*
McDonald, Brenda Denise *librarian*
McTyer-Clarke, Wanda Kathleen *interior designer*
Medler, Mary Ann L. *federal judge*
Megivern, Deborah Mary *social worker, educator*
Mitchell, Louise Tyndall *special education educator*
Monteleone, Patricia *dean*
Moore, Patricia Kay *investor, public relations director*
Mosley, Karen D. *retired elementary school educator*
Newman, Joan Meskiel *lawyer*
North, Carol Sue *psychiatrist, educator*
Olsen, Tava Maryanne Lennon *industrial and operations engineering educator*
O'Neill, Sheila *principal*
Ott, Sabina *art educator*
Ozawa, Martha Naoko *social work educator*
Payne, Meredith Jorstad *physician*
Pearson, Barbara Joy *small business owner*
Perotti, Rose Norma *lawyer*
Perry, Catherine D. *judge*
Posgay, Betty Marie *medical equipment company executive, artist*
Purkerson, Mabel Louise *physician, physiologist, educator*
Reidy, Frances Ryan *English language educator, editor, writer*
Reilly, Catherine Herbert *librarian, educator*
Rice, Patricia Jane *journalist*
Richardson, Pollie *principal*
Rifkind, Irene Glassman *legal secretary*
Robins, Lee Nelken *medical educator*
Robins, Marjorie McCarthy (Mrs. George Kenneth Robins) *civic worker*
Rodriguez, Mercedes M. *psychiatrist*
Rosen, Adrienne *artist, educator*
Rosenblum, Sharon *interior designer*
Rudd, Susan *retail executive*
Ruwitch, Ann Rubenstein *urban planner*
Ryall, Jo-Ellyn M. *psychiatrist*
Ryan, Sister Mary Jean *health facility executive*
Sago, Janis Lynn *photography educator*
Schaal, Barbara Anna *evolutionary biologist, educator*
Scheffing, Dianne Elizabeth *special education educator*
Schindler, Laura Ann *piano teacher, accompanist*
Schlafly, Phyllis Stewart *writer*
Schoene, Kathleen Snyder *lawyer*
Searls, Eileen Haughey *retired lawyer, librarian, educator*
Shea, Kathleen E. *cultural resources specialist*
Sherby, Kathleen Reilly *lawyer*
Shodean, Lisa Diane *military officer*
Shrauner, Barbara Wayne Abraham *electrical engineer, educator*
Shucart, Evelyn Ann *artist, educator*
Soeteber, Ellen *journalist, editor*
Steiner, Hope Elizabeth *school counselor*
Storandt, Martha *psychologist*
Sutherland, Mary (Marcus) *composer, musician, music company executive*
Sutter, Jane Elizabeth *science educator, writer, conservationist*
Ternberg, Jessie Lamoin *pediatric surgeon*
Thetford, Frances Alicia *social services group administrator*
Thompson, Vetta Lynn Sanders *psychologist, educator*
Todorova-Moreno, Ilina *psychologist, educator*
Vandiver, Donna *public relations executive*
Waddington, Bette Hope (Elizabeth Crowder) *violinist, educator*
Walentik, Corinne Anne *pediatrician*
Ward-Brown, Denise *sculptor, educator*
Warner, Susan *federal agency administrator*
Watson, Patty Jo *anthropology educator*
Weese, Cynthia Rogers *architect, educator*
Weldon, Virginia V. *retired corporate executive, pediatrician*
Williams, Nellie James Batt *secondary school educator, educator*
Wilson, Margaret Bush *lawyer*
Winter, Mildred M. *educational administrator*
Woodward, Mary Lou *retired elementary education educator*
Wright, Diane *procurement manager*
Yeckel, Anita T. *state legislator*
Young, Virginia McLain *information technology consulting executive*

Saint Peters
Poettker, Mary Therese *music educator*
Purcell, Cheryl Linn *music educator*

Sedalia
McClain, Cindy Dunstan *music educator*
Miller, Toni M. Andrews *critical care nurse*
Waldo, Susan Lauderdale *psychologist*

Seneca
Kolb, Jimmie Lois *marriage and family therapist*

Seymour
Rudolph, Wanda *art educator*

Sibley
Morrow, Elizabeth Hostetter *sculptress, museum administrator, farmer, educator*

Sikeston
Tesseneer-Street, Susan *photographer, artist, writer*

Springfield
Bohnenkamper, Katherine Elizabeth *library science educator*
Brennan, Deborah Ann *artist*
Busch, Annie *library director*
Champion, Norma Jean *communications educator, state legislator*
Easley, June Ellen Price *genealogist*
Gonzalez, Judith R. *psychologist, marriage and family therapist*
Groves, Sharon Sue *elementary school educator*
Holloway, Wanda Kaye *psychotherapist, consultant*
Hutson, Sheila *psychologist*
Jayne, Arlene Mae *artist*
Kaiser, Dorothy Carolyn *social worker*
Levesque, Chantal *psychologist, researcher*
Martin, Nancy Jane *music educator*
Mathis, Alicia *biologist*
Montgomery, Linda Stroupe *county official*
Morris, Ann Haseltine Jones *social welfare administrator*
Moss, Elizabeth Lucille (Betty Moss) *retired transportation executive*
Peebles, Sheila Kay *music educator*
Quiroga, Ninoska *university official*
Stewart, Lois *humanities educator, curriculum coordinator*
Williams, Juanita (Tudie Williams) *home health care nurse, administrator*
Wommack, Janice Marie *insurance company executive*

Stella
Yeagley, Joan Howerton *writer*

Stockton
Jackson, Betty L. Deason *real estate developer*

Stover
Reynolds, Sallie Blackburn *artist, civic volunteer*

Sturgeon
Dawkins, Amy *artist*

Sweet Springs
Long, Helen Halter *writer, educator*

Town And Country
Lachenicht-Berkeley, Angela Marie *marketing professional*

Trenton
Hannaford, Karla *college official*

Troy
Burkemper, Sarah B. *state agency administrator*
McClellan, Betty *county official*

Unity Village
Boehm, Toni Georgene *seminary dean, nurse, minister*

University City
Bogenschneider, Gayle Mueller *small business owner, interior designer*
Gatlin, Novella Anna Maria *collection specialist, business consultant*

Urbana
Frey, Lucille Pauline *social studies educator, consultant*

Van Buren
Dee, Diane Marie *rancher, farmer*

Vandalia
Brookshier, Elaine Marie *counseling administrator, psychology examiner, social worker*

Viburnum
West, Roberta Bertha *writer*

Warrensburg
Desmond, Kathleen Kadon *critic, educator, artist*
Engle, Mary Elizabeth *dietician, educator*
Heming, Carol Piper *historian, educator*
Limback, E(dna) Rebecca *vocational education educator*
Resch, Rita Marie *music educator*
Young, Mary Ann *lawyer*

Weatherby Lake
Hawkins, Geri Sue *interior designer, jewelry designer, realtor*

Webb City
James, Kathryn A. *secondary school educator*

Webster Groves
Carr, Margaret *elementary school educator*
Gergeceff-Cooper, Lorraine *artist, consultant*
Schenkenberg, Mary Martin *principal*
Whittemore, Joan M. *music educator*

West Plains
Buxton, Gina LeeAnn *music educator*

Wildwood
Colletti, Teresa Ann *polymer chemist*

Willow Springs
East, LeEtta Joyce *elementary school educator, music educator*

Windyville
Condron, Barbara O'Guinn *metaphysics educator, school administrator, publisher*

MONTANA

Anaconda
McCarthy, Bea *state legislator*

Antelope
Olson, Betty-Jean *retired elementary education educator*

Belgrade
Aveson, Martha Caralyn *pharmaceutical company executive*

Bigfork
Wetzel, Betty Preat *writer*

Billings
Deschner, Jane Waggoner *photo artist, public relations consultant*
Gallinger, Lorraine D. *prosecutor*
Kolstad, Candice (Candy) Carol *pre-school educator, special needs coordinator*
Lorenz, Marianne *curator*
Park, Janie C. *provost*

Bonner
Smith, Annick *writer*

Bozeman
Acord, Lea *dean*
Billau, Robin Louise *engineering and consulting executive*
Exley, Maureen Catherine *music educator*
Gibson, Luanne Eileen *visual artist, educator*
Piazza, Rosanna Joy *paralegal*

Butte
Clark, Gloria A. *music educator*
Garvey, Arlene P. *library media specialist*
Kohler, Nora Helen *music educator*
Ouellette, Debra Lee *administrative assistant, consultant*
Shea, Debbie Bowman *state legislator*
Shea, Stephanie *music educator*

Clancy
Ekanger, Laurie *retired state official, retired contractor*

Crow Agency
Deernose, Kitty *curator*
Pease-Pretty On Top, Janine B. *community college administrator*

Cut Bank
Schilling, Brenda Gail *music educator*

Eureka
Cheek, Cheryl A. *language educator*

Fairfield
Ratliff, Kari Lynne *music educator*

Forsyth
Lincoln, Sharon Ann *retired county official*

Glendive
Shields, Lisa A. *music educator*

Great Falls
Franklin, Eve *state legislator*
Lauzon, Marcia Louise *performing company executive*
Ledesma-Nicholson, Charmaine *psychotherapist*
Schmidt, Rita *retired library media specialist*
Swaby, Barbara Emilie *music educator*

Hamilton
Soden, Ruth M. *geriatrics nurse, educator*
Tonkens, Rebecca Annette *maternal/women's health nurse, rehabilitation nurse*

Harlowton
Huning, Devon Gray *actress, audiologist, dancer, photographer*

Havre
Coffman, Barbara LeAnn *environmentalist*
Mayer Lossing, Emily Ann *city official*
Van Cleave, Vicki L. *psychologist, educator*

Helena
Bartlett, Sue *retired state legislator*
Cocchiarella, Vicki Marshall *state legislator*
Cotter, Patricia O'Brien *state supreme court justice*
Craig, Mary Lauri *accountant*
Eck, Dorothy Fritz *state legislator*
Fitzpatrick, Lois Ann *library administrator*
Franz, Holly Jo *lawyer, partner*
Gray, Karla Marie *judge*
Hanson, Marian W. *state legislator*
Hill, Betti Christie *government executive*
Keenan, Nancy A. *state agency administrator*
Manuel, Vivian *public relations executive*
McCulloch, Linda *state official*
Meadows, Judith Adams *law librarian, educator*
Schlesinger, Deborah Lee *librarian*
Seiler, Karen Peake *organizational psychologist*
Stonington, Emily S. *state legislator*
Strege, Karen *library director*
Toole, Joan Trimble *financial consultant*
Waterman, Mignon Redfield *public relations executive, state legislator*
Wickham, Dianne *nursing administrator*

Hobson
Otis, Gertrude Maxine *home economist*

Kalispell
Gallagher-Dalton, Tonya Marie *family support specialist*
Klang, Mary Margaret *secondary school educator*

Lame Deer
Williams, Deeanna Maxine *secondary school educator*

Lewistown
Edwards, Linda L. *former elementary education educator*

Livingston
Hillegass, Christine Ann *psychologist*

Malta
Watts, Alice L. *nurse*

Martinsdale
Rostad, Lee B. *rancher, writer*

Medicine Lake
Nelson, Linda J. *state legislator*

Miles City
Thomason, Suzanne Irene *health services professional, researcher*
Walden, Alice *artist, educator*

Missoula
Barnett, Mary Louise *elementary school educator*
Millin, Laura Jeanne *museum director*
Wigfied-Phillip, Ruth Genivea *genealogist, author, researcher*
Wollersheim, Janet Puccinelli *psychology educator*
Yungmeyer Olson, Jane Elizabeth *conservationist*

Roundup
Harant, Patricia A. *minister*
Stanfel, Jane Ellen *artist, adult education educator*

Troy
Sherman, Signe Lidfeldt *portfolio manager, former research chemist*

Victor
Stewart, JoAnne *director*

Whitefish
Morgan, Susan McGrath *Jungian analyst*

NEBRASKA

Bancroft
Neihardt, Hilda *lawyer, foundation administrator, writer, educator, lawyer*

Bayard
Tillman, Tamra (Tammy) K. *secondary school educator*

Bellevue
Braun, Sally A. *elementary school educator, music educator*

Benkelman
Owens, Judith L(ynn) *lawyer*
Whiteley, Rose Marie *city clerk, treasurer*

Boys Town
Wright Sapone, Tanya D *director*

Brewster
Teahon, Jean Ann *county official*

Central City
Wischmeier, Elaine Alice *music educator*

Chadron
Buschkopf, Debora J. *court reporter*
Lecher, Belvadine (Belvadine Reeves) *museum curator*
Limbach, Barbara June *management educator*

Columbus
Micek, Isabelle *music educator*

Curtis
Wiiest, Joan Eloise *secondary school educator*

Elkhorn
Bluford, Michelle A. *music educator*

Elm Creek
Whitney, Marilyn Beth *music educator*

Fremont
Winans, Anna Jane *dietician*

Gering
Meier, Nancy Jo *nursing consultant*

Grand Island
Abernethy, Irene Margaret *civic worker, retired county official*
Weseman, Vicki Lynne *elementary school educator*
Zichek, Shannon Elaine *retired secondary school educator*

Gretna
Druliner, Marcia Marie *education educator*

Harrison
Coffee, Virginia Claire *civic worker, former mayor*
Knudson, Ruthann *environmental consultant*

Hastings
Bohlke, Ardyce *state legislator*
Kort, Betty *secondary school educator*

Holdrege
De Wald, Vicky Coleen *theater director, performing company executive, theater educator*

Kearney
Hoffman, M. Kathy *graphic designer, packaging designer*
Johnston, Gladys Styles *university official*
Young, Ann Elizabeth O'Quinn *historian, educator*

Kilgore
Rothleutner, Phyllis Harriet *rancher*

Lincoln
Bargen, Nancy Lee *music educator*
Boyle, Anne C. *state commissioner*
Brown, Pam *state legislator*
Byrd, Lorelee *state treasurer*
Connor, Carol J. *library director*
Crosby, LaVon Kehoe Stuart *state legislator, civic leader*
Davis, LuAnn Raelene *fund raising executive*
Epp, Dianne Naomi *secondary educator*
Fleharty, Mary Sue *state government staff member*
Frobom, LeAnn Larson *lawyer*
Gray, Joni Nadine *state agency administrator*
Grew, Priscilla Croswell *university official, geology educator*
Hac, Lucile Rose *biochemistry educator*
Hasselbalch, Marilyn Jean *state official*
Henderson, Robyn Lee *project manager*
Holmes, Mary Anne *geologist, research scientist*
Hottovy, Susan Elizabeth *music educator*
LeValley, Joan Catherine *accountant*
Levin, Carole *history educator*
Miller-Lerman, Lindsey *state supreme court justice*
Moul, Maxine Burnett *state official*
Mulvaney, Mary Jean *physical education educator, department chairman*
Neal, Mo (P. Maureen Neal) *sculptor*
Nicoll, Gayle *chemistry educator*
Ogle, Robbin Sue *criminal justice educator*
Oman, Deborah Sue *health science facility administrator*
Price, Marian L. *state legislator*
Raz, Hilda *editor-in-chief periodical, English educator*
Redfield, Pamela A. *state legislator*
Robak, Jennie *state legislator*
Robak, Kim M. *academic administrator, lawyer*
Rohren, Brenda Marie Anderson *therapist, educator*
Schimek, DiAnna Ruth Rebman *state legislator*
Schizas, Jennifer Anne *law association administrator*
Seng, Coleen Joy *mayor*
Stuhr, Elaine Ruth *state legislator*
Sullivan, Mary Ann *retired school psychologist*
Suttle, Deborah S. *state legislator*
Thompson, Nancy P. *state legislator*
Tonack, DeLoris *elementary school educator*
Vidaver, Anne Marie *plant pathology educator*
Wallis, Deborah *curator*
Wiegand, Sylvia Margaret *mathematician, educator*
Witek, Kate *state senator, trucking company executive*
Young, Jeannette Rose *music educator*

Mc Cook
Watts, Susan Helene *theater educator*

Newman Grove
Anderson, Joyce Lorraine *nurse*

Norfolk
Mortensen-Say, Marlys *school system administrator*

Odell
Lindblad, Cynthia Merrill *music educator*

Ogallala
Brown, Jo Etta *elementary school educator, librarian*

Omaha
Batchelder, Anne Stuart *retired publishing executive, political organization worker*
Belck, Nancy Garrison *dean, educator*
Bouma, Lyn Ann Nichols *music educator*
Brailey, Susan Louise *quality analyst, educator*
Brimmerman, Barbara Jane *language educator*
Bruckner, Martha *academic administrator*
Buffett, Susan Thompson *investment company executive*
Burris, Janice Elaine *educational administrator*
Cherney, Isabelle Denise *education educator, researcher*
Cleary, Pamela Ann *symphony executive*
Dufner, Donna Kane *management information systems, project management educator*
Fyfe, Doris Mae *elementary school educator*
Gallagher, Paula Marie *real estate appraiser*
Graves, Maureen Ann *self esteem and spirituality consultant*
Gray-Ventry, Tina L. *minister*
Heim, Megan Alyssa *biomedical engineer*
Jones-Thurman, Rosanna M. *psychologist*
Kessinger, Margaret Anne *medical educator*
Lechowicz, Lisa Marie *retired insurance company executive*
Leininger, Madeleine Monica *nursing educator, consultant, anthropologist, therorist, editor, writer*
Lindsay, Cosimano *marketing professional*
Lindsey, Ada Marie *dean, nursing educator*
Longo, Amy L. *lawyer*
Mactier, Ann Dickinson *state agency administrator*
Patrick, Erline M. *federal agency administrator*
Phares, Lynn Levisay *public relations communications executive*
Pirsch, Carol McBride *county official, former state senator, community relations manager*
Ranks, Anne Elizabeth *retired elementary and secondary education educator*

Dunham, Vivian L. *state legislator*
McKinney, Betsy *state legislator*
Parten, Priscilla M. *medical and psychiatric social worker, educator*
Verani, Patricia Lewis *sculptor*

Loudon
Moore, Beatrice *religious organization administrator*

Lyme
Wise, Joanne Herbert *art director*

Manchester
Arnold, Barbara Eileen *state legislator*
Belanger, Traci L. *psychotherapist, writer*
Bolduc, Diane Eileen Mary Buchholz *psychotherapist*
Cusson-Cail, Kathleen *consulting company executive*
Holden, Carol H. *county official*
Krueger, Patricia *state representative*
Lyons, Elisabeth Helene *peer counselor*
Marchesseault, Anita *music educator*
Merideth, Susan Carol *business administration educator*
Prew, Diane Schmidt *information systems executive*
Stimpson, Patricia *software company executive*
Sullivan, Kathleen N. *political organization administrator, lawyer*
Sysyn, Mary A. *alderman*
Totten, Mary Anne *internist*

Marlow
McCracken, Linda *librarian, commercial artist*

Mason
Jones, Elizabeth Orton *artist, author*

Merrimack
Cunningham, Patricia Ann Cahoy *band director, musician*
Gallup, Patricia *computer company executive*

Milford
Dokmo, Cynthia J. *state legislator*

Munsonville
Kirk, Jane Seaver *municipal government administrator*

Nashua
Descoteaux, Carol J. *health facility administrator*
Franks, Suzan L. R. *state legislator*
Lerch, Carol M. *mathematics educator*
Nolan-Piteri, Dawn C. *state legislator*
Pignatelli, Debora Becker *state legislator*
Provencher, Jeanne Stansfield *secondary school educator*

New Durham
Sullivan, Mary Ann *author, marketing professional*

New London
Sheerr, Deirdre McCrystal *architectural firm executive*
Vernon, Alison F. *nursing administrator, artist*

Newmarket
Getchell, Sylvia Fitts *librarian*

Newport
Gayvoronsky, Ludmila *artist, educator*
Stamatakis, Carol Marie *lawyer, former state legislator*

North Hampton
Pazdon, Denise Joan *speech pathology/audiology services professional*

North Woodstock
Ham, Bonnie Davis *state legislator*

Nottingham
Case, Margaret A. *state legislator*

Ossipee
Bartlett, Diane Sue *counselor*

Peterborough
Thomas, Elizabeth Marshall *writer*

Pittsfield
Brown, Mary Ellen *former state legislator, accountant*

Plainfield
Brown, Judith Olans *lawyer, educator*

Plaistow
Senter, Merilyn P(atricia) *former state legislator and freelance reporter*

Plymouth
DeCotis, Ruth Janice *career planning administrator, educator*
Morth-Fraser, Grace M. *social sciences educator*
Petersen, Meg Joanna *education educator, language educator*
Santore, Marcia Lucinda Green *editor, artist*

Portsmouth
Day, Frances Ann *writer, educator*
Hopkins, Jeannette Ethel *book publisher, editor*
Nylander, Jane Louise *museum director, lecturer, writer*
Pantelakos, Laura C. *state legislator*
Ward, Bonnie J. *insurance company executive*

Randolph
Bradley, Paula E. *former state legislator*

Raymond
Fosher, Mary Jane *humanities educator*

Rindge
Emerson, Susan *oil company executive*

Rochester
Brown, Julie M. *state legislator*
Grassie, Anne C. *state legislator*
McCarley, Caroline *state legislator*
Rogers, Rose Marie *state legislator*

Rye Beach
Langley, Jane S. *state legislator*

Spofford
Trumbull, Virginia Hardesty *retired special education educator*

Stratham
Terry, Elizabeth Hays *needlepoint designer*

Temple
Weston, Priscilla Atwood *library director*

Tilton
Lombardo, Janet Vogt *priest*
Wolf, Sharon Ann *psychotherapist*

Walpole
Hunter, Barbara Way *public relations consultant*

Weare
White, Karen Ruth Jones *information systems executive*

West Lebanon
Malik, Shazia Mumtaz *education educator, researcher*

Wilton
Mellon, Nancy Scott *arts therapist*

Windham
Arndt, Janet S. *state legislator*
Khanbegian, Jean M. *artist*

Wolfeboro
Bonin, Suzanne Jean *artist*
Hutchins, Carleen Maley *acoustical engineer, consultant*

NEW JERSEY

Absecon
Paparone, Pamela Ann *nurse practitioner*

Allendale
DiBlasi, Dianne Clark *editor*
Long, Jo-Nelle Desmond *editor, consultant, historian*

Andover
Pavone, Marianne *medical/surgical nurse*

Annandale
Baugh, Lisa Saunders (Lisa Saunders Boffa) *research chemist*

Asbury Park
McTague-Dougherty, Amy Elizabeth *speech pathology/audiology services professional*
Rosenbloom, Norma Frisch *lawyer*

Atlantic City
Oswell, Audrey S. *casino executive*

Avalon
Johnson, Adele Cunningham *marina executive*

Avon By The Sea
Potter, Emma Josephine Hill *language educator*

Basking Ridge
Besch, Lorraine W. *special education educator*
Frediani, Diane Marie *graphics designer, interior designer, executive secretary*
Marrero, Teresa *lawyer*
Samuelson, Cynthia *information technology executive*

Bayonne
Graham, Theresa Anne *art educator*
Zuckerman, Nancy Carol *learning disabilities specialist, consultant*

Bayville
Albano, Paige Lynne *small business owner*

Beach Haven
Schreiber, Eileen Sher *artist*

Bedminster
Dabney, Michelle Sheila *administrative assistant*
Delehanty, Martha *human services administrator*
Weaver, Constance *communications executive*
Yannuzzi, Elaine Victoria *food and home products executive*

Belle Mead
Aloisi, Carol Ann *marketing executive*
Brown, Elizabeth Schmeck *fashion historian*
Moevs, Maria Teresa Marabini *archaeologist*

Bellmawr
Wilke, Constance Regina *elementary school educator*

Bergenfield
Janow, Lydia Frances *meeting planner*

Berkeley Heights
Schwarzwald, Julie Nanette *elementary school educator*

Bernardsville
Boquist, Diana D. *mayor, real estate agent*
Burbank, Claudia *poet*

Blackwood
Huls, Glenna L. *sociology educator, photographer*

Blairstown
Horn-Alsberge, Michele Maryann *school psychologist*
Wenner, Judith Wills *secondary school educator*

Bloomfield
Barros, Lydia *elementary school educator*
Lordi, Katherine Mary *lawyer*
Shogen, Kuslima *pharmaceutical executive*

Bloomingdale
Farrell, Donna Marie *photographer, graphic artist*

Bogota
Koshimitsu, Keiko *artist*
Livingston, Kathryn E. *writer*

Boonton
Bridges, Beryl Clarke *marketing executive*

Bound Brook
Blumberg, Adele Rosenberg *volunteer*
Chandler, Marguerite Nella *real estate corporation executive*

Bradley Beach
Shrem, Eileen Merry *insurance planner*

Bridgeton
Chanatry-Howell, Lorraine Marie *artist, designer, educator*

Bridgewater
Bernson, Marcella S. *psychiatrist*
Glesmann, Sylvia-Maria *artist*

Brielle
McIntyre, Elizabeth Jones *multi-media specialist, educator*

Brigantine
Kickish, Margaret Elizabeth *elementary school educator*

Budd Lake
Bauer, Jean Marie *accountant*
Davis-Kalupin, Dorinne Sue *audiologist*
Hilbert, Rita L. *librarian*
Shepherd, Deborah Gulick *elementary school educator*

Burlington
Hancock, Beverly J. *counseling consultant, secondary school educator*
Mustokoff, Henrietta M. *music educator*

Caldwell
Palombo, Lisa *artist*
Randall, Lynn Ellen *librarian*
Werner, Patrice (Patricia Ann Werner) *dean*

Califon
Clipsham, Jacqueline Ann *artist*
Rosen, Carol Mendes *artist*

Camden
Baltimore, Pamela A. Grayson *social worker, consultant*
Bell, Kathy Dawn *medical/surgical nurse*
Coney, Stephné Reniá *communications and telecommunications educator*
Daniels, Albertina Diana *secondary school educator*
Kaden, Ellen Oran *lawyer, consumer products company executive*
Markey, Charlotte Nicole *psychologist, educator*
Marshall, Sara
Watkins, LaSandra *science educator*

Cape May Court House
Cohen, Susan Lois *writer*

Carteret
John, Dolores *architect, consultant*
Scott, Eileen Rose *retail executive*

Cedar Grove
Carlozzi, Catherine L. *corporate communications consultant, writer*
Helwig, Annette L. *retired elementary school educator*

Cedarville
Marsella, Julia *music educator*

Chatham
Earle, Jean Buist *financial officer*
Glover, Janet Briggs *artist*

Cherry Hill
Collier-Evans, Demetra Frances *veterans benefits counselor*
Gutin, Myra Gail *communications educator*
Johnson, Catherine Graham *religious organization administrator*
Kole, Janet Stephanie *lawyer, writer, photographer*
Robinson, Mary Jo *pathologist*

Chester
Maddalena, Lucille Ann *management consultant*

Cliffside Park
Fox, Margery Q. *anthropology educator*
Lombardi, Tracey Anne *financial administrator, medical assistant*
Perhacs, Marylouise Helen *musician, educator*

Clifton
Bronkesh, Annette Cylia *public relations executive*
Hochman, Naomi Lipson *special education educator, consultant*
Kalata, Mary Ann Catherine *architect*
Ressetar, Nancy *foreign language educator*
Silber, Judy G. *dermatologist*

Clinton
Lish, Donna Lee *art educator*
Moore, Alma Donst *writer, lyricist*

Closter
Garbe-Morillo, Patricia Ann *preservationist*

Collingswood
Creamer-Franke, Shannon *graphic design company executive*

Colonia
Cohen, Diane A. *rabbi*
Wiesenfeld, Bess G. *interior designer*

Columbia
Timcenko, Lydia Teodora *biochemist, chemist*

Convent Station
Scheierman, Mindy *music educator, consultant*

Cranford
Crow, Lynne Campbell Smith *insurance company representative*

Dayton
Adickes, Sandra Elaine *English language educator, writer*

Delanco
Lane, Carrie Belle (Hairston) *retired music educator*

Denville
Fisher, Sharon Mary *musician*
Veech, Lynda Anne *musician, educator*

Deptford
Kelly, Barbara Sue *psychologist*

Dover
Hammond-Rector, Susan Glynn *illustrator, photographer, sculptor*
Kassell, Paula Sally *editor, publisher*

Dunellen
Minson, Mary Beth *music educator, elementary school educator, musician*

East Brunswick
Brandenburg, Lois Sue *special education educator*
Burns, Barbara *lawyer*
Dombrowski, Anne Wesseling *retired microbiologist, researcher*
Meningall, Evelyn L. *educational media specialist*
Savio, Frances Margaret Cammarotta *music educator*
Weiss, Judith Ann *music educator*

East Hanover
Davidson, Anne Stowell *lawyer*
Jenkins, Twylah La'Triece *pharmacuetical sales representative*
Nemecek, Georgina Marie *molecular pharmacologist*
O'Byrne, Elizabeth Milikin *pharmacologist, researcher*

East Orange
Anderson, Zina-Diane *real estate company executive*
Corbitt, Ann Marie *municipal official*
Fielo, Muriel Bryant *interior designer*
Hudson-Zonn, Eliza *nurse, psychologist*
Omoregie, Irene O. *accountant*

East Rutherford
Alberta, Frances Rita *principal*
Blate, Alissa *advertising executive*

Eatontown
Priesand, Sally Jane *rabbi*

Edgewater
Paci, Ruth A. *freelance/self-employed writer*
Zhou, Yan *chemist*

Edison
Buono, Barbara *state legislator*
Currence, Anna *publishing executive*
Haberman, Louise Shelly *consulting company executive*
Kushinsky, Jeanne Alice *humanities educator*

Egg Harbor City
Farris, Vera King *former college president*

Elizabeth
Bell-Bowe, Jacqueline *mental health nurse, consultant, nursing educator*
Blowe, Arnethia *religious studies educator*
Fulmore, MaryAnn *state agency administrator*
Miller-Duffy, Merritt *insurance agent, assistant camp director*
Pineros, Elizabeth *social services administrator, psychotherapist*

Emerson
Hannon, Patricia Ann *library director*

Englewood
Chiorazzi, Mary Lorraine *psychiatrist*
de Gramont, Carol Carmel *writer*
Fay, Toni Georgette *communications executive*
Zwilich, Ellen Taaffe *composer*

Monroe Township
Cushman, Helen Merle Baker *retired management consultant*
Naumik, Maria Charlene *academic administrator, educator*
Wolfe, Deborah Cannon Partridge *government education consultant, educator, minister*

Montclair
Anselmi, Elvira *psychologist, researcher*
Blooston, Roselee *cultural organization administrator, writer*
Brown, Geraldine Reed *lawyer, management consultant*
Castiglione, Anita *pianist, music educator*
Cole, Susan A. *university president, English language educator*
Gill, Nia H. *state legislator*
Kawecki, Jean Mary *sculptor*
Mason, Lucile Gertrude *fundraiser, consultant*
McConnell, Lorelei Catherine *retired library director*
Murphy, Betty Jagoda *small business owner*
Phillips, Ann Y. *art advisor*
Pransky, Joan E. *lawyer, community organizer*
Schoch, Clarissa Anthony *singer, educator, executive assistant*

Montvale
Cervantez, Michelle *marketing professional*
Falk, Ellen Stein *media specialist, educator*
Margolin, Deborah Susan *performance artist, educator, writer*
Politi, Beth Kukkonen *publishing services company executive*

Moorestown
Weiss, Eva *retired bridge commissioner*

Morganville
Lechtanski, Cheryl Lee *chiropractor*
Marder, Carol *advertising specialist and premium firm executive*

Morris Plains
Gulfo, Adele Madelyn *pharmaceutical marketing executive*
Inez, Donna Lee *hospital administrator*
Wyskowski, Barbara Jean *lawyer*

Morristown
Armstrong, Diana Rose *financial consultant*
Bernstein, Jan Lenore *lawyer*
Cucco, Judith Elene *international marketing professional*
Finkel, Marion Judith *internist, pharmaceutical administrator*
Flynn, Marie Cosgrove *portfolio manager, corporate financial executive*
Gorrell, Nancy S. *English language educator*
Handler, Lauren E. *lawyer*
LaVecchia, Jaynee *state supreme court justice*
MacKinnis, Ann Phelps *municipal government and land use management executive*
Mooney, Patricia Anne *secondary school educator*
Prince, Leah Fanchon *art educator and research institute administrator*
Selman, Carol *retired secondary school educator*
Sherman, Sandra Brown *lawyer*
Walters, Teresa *musician, music educator, concert pianist*

Mount Holly
Mancini, Lois Jean *elementary school educator*

Mount Laurel
Bark, Martha W. *state legislator*
Li, Pearl Nei-Chien Chu *technology company executive*

Mountain Lakes
Doane, Eileen Maloney *learning disabilities teacher consultant*
Loomis, Rebecca C. *psychology educator*
Starger, Victoria Gondek *artist*

Mountainside
James, Barbara Frances *school nurse, special education educator*
Lipton, Bronna Jane *marketing communications executive*
Nielsen, Gwyn English *writer, illustrator, publishing executive*

Murray Hill
Bruch, Ruth E. *information technology executive*
Christy, Cindy *telecommunications industry executive*
Davidson, Janet G. *telecommunications industry executive*

Neptune
Haag, Jane *education educator*

Neshanic Station
Castellon, Christine New *information systems specialist, real estate agent*

New Brunswick
Bachmann, Gloria Ann *obstetrician, gynecologist, educator*
Bancila, Edita *pathologist, educator*
Bunch, Charlotte *advocate*
Buto, Kathleen A. *health products executive*
Casey, Heather Anne Kenyon *education educator*
Chasek, Arlene Shatsky *academic director*
Corbett, Siobhan Aiden *surgeon*
Day-Salvatore, Debra Lynn *medical geneticist*
Formica, Palma Elizabeth *physician*
Goffen, Rona *art educator, educator*
Gottlieb, Alice B. *dermatologist*
Hartman, Mary S. *historian, educator*
Heisen, JoAnn Heffernan *health care company executive*
Henry, Paula Louise (Paula Louise Henry Coover) *academic administrator*
Jenkins, Alyce Mitchem *writer*
Kuhn, Melanie R. *literature educator, consultant*
Laraya-Cuasay, Lourdes Redublo *pediatric pulmonologist, educator*
Leventhal, Elaine A. *internist*
Liao, Mei-June *biopharmaceutical company executive*
Louis, Barbara *psychologist, educator*
Machado, Kety Gonzalez *mathematician, educator*
Mandel, Ruth Blumenstock *politics educator, educational association administrator, researcher*
Mills, Dorothy Allen *investor*
Mora, Gabriela *language educator, researcher*
Morrow, Lesley Mandel *literacy and elementary education educator*
Ostriker, Alicia Suskin *poet*
Poon, Christine A. *pharmaceutical executive*
Ralston, Sarah Lucille *veterinarian, educator*
Rodgers, Denise V. *medical educator*
Rosenthal, Susan R. *pediatrician, educator*
Russell, Louise Bennett *economist, educator*
Saidi, Parvin *hematologist, medical educator*
Scanlon, Jane Cronin *mathematics educator*
Snyder, Barbara K. *pediatrician, educator*
Strickland, Dorothy *education educator*
Tigeleiro, Susana *corporate financial executive*
Todd, Mary Beth *medical oncologist, researcher*
Turock, Betty Jane *library and information science educator*
Weiss, Lynne S. *pediatrician, educator*
Willett, Laura R. *internist*
Yorke, Marianne *lawyer, real estate executive*

New Milford
Spiegel, Edna Z. *lawyer*

New Providence
Bernstein, Nadia J. *lawyer*
Celler, Adeline (Lynn) Marie *art educator*
Cooper, Carol Diane *publishing company executive*
Murray, Cherry Ann *physicist, researcher*
Rivo, Shirley Winthrope *artist*
Russo, Patricia F. *communications executive*
Sivco, Deborah Lee *research materials scientist*
White, Alice Elizabeth *physicist, researcher*
Wright, Margaret Hagen *computer scientist, administrator*

Newark
Baer, Susan M. *airport executive*
Banta, Vivian L. *insurance company executive*
Barry, Maryanne Trump *federal judge*
Bizub, Johanna Catherine *law librarian*
Bolden, Marion A. *school system administrator*
Brazil, Aine M. *engineering company executive*
Cheng, Mei-Fang *psychobiology educator, neuroethology researcher, biologist, educator*
Clowney, Mary L. *educational media specialist, librarian*
Corbin Walker, Karol *lawyer*
Creenan, Katherine Heras *lawyer*
Dauth, Frances Kutcher *journalist, newspaper editor*
Davis, Yvonne D. *county official*
Defeis, Elizabeth Frances *law educator, lawyer*
Dennery, Linda *newspaper publishing executive*
Ferris-Waks, Arlene Susan *compliance officer*
Fox, Jeanne Marie *lawyer*
Gilbert, Margaret Barbour *literature educator, poet*
Griffith, Hurdis M. *dean*
Guron, Gunwant K. *oncologist*
Hadas, Rachel *poet, educator*
Hamarman, Stephanie *psychiatrist, educator*
Harrison, Roslyn Siman *lawyer*
Healy-Sova, Phyllis M. Cordasco *school social worker*
Hiltz, Starr Roxanne *sociologist, educator, computer scientist, writer, lecturer, consultant*
Hochberg, Faith S. *US district court judge*
Johnson, Evelyn *minister, educator*
Koster, Barbara *insurance company executive*
Labaj, Pamela Joan *lawyer*
Liman, Joan Pamela *university dean*
Monty, Gloria *former television producer, film executive*
Moore, Mattie H. *clergy, folk artist, retired educator*
Myers, Priscilla A. *insurance company executive*
Nash, Alicia *computer programmer, physicist*
Norwood, Carolyn Virginia *business educator*
Price, Mary Sue Sweeney *museum director*
Raveché, Elizabeth Scott *immunologist, educator*
Reynolds, Valrae *museum curator*
Shain, Jo-Ann *editor*
Storch, Susan Borowski *lawyer*
Weis, Judith Shulman *biology educator*
Wright-White, Kimberly Zenora *vice principal*

Newfoundland
Divinsky, Miriam *psychotherapist*

Newton
Case, Tammy *bank executive*
MacMurren, Margaret Patricia *secondary education educator, consultant*
McHose, Alison Littell *assemblywoman*

North Arlington
Borowski, Jennifer Lucile *corporate administrator*

North Bergen
Karp, Roberta S. *wholesale apparel and accessories executive*

North Branch
Jones, Cori *education educator, writer*

North Brunswick
Walker, Carolyn Mae *secondary school educator*

Northvale
Heslin, Cathleen Jane *artist, designer, entrepreneur*

Nutley
Seyffarth, Linda Jean Wilcox *corporate executive*
Tropiano, JoAnn Alma *librarian, library director*

Oakland
Schwager, Linda Helen *lawyer*

Oaklyn
Miranda, Minda *chemist, pharmacy technician*

Ocean City
Guokas, Joan Ellen (Mrs. Matthew Guokas Sr.) *retired elementary school educator*

Old Tappan
Gaffin, Joan Valerie *secondary school educator*

Oldwick
Svoboda, Joanne Dzitko *artist, educator*

Oradell
Struck, Norma Johansen *artist*

Paramus
Blue, Catherine Anne *lawyer*
Carunchio, Florence Regina *financial planner*
Fader, Shirley Sloan *writer*
Forman, Beth Rosalyne *specialty food trade executive*
Teichman, Evelyn *antiques appraiser, educator, estate liquidator*

Park Ridge
An, Samantha Hae Jung *executive recruiter, social worker*

Parsippany
Azzarone, Carol Ann *marketing executive*
Pedescleaux-Muckle, Gail *business analyst, writer*
Sangiuliano, Barbara Ann *tax consultant*
Timmins, Maryanne *real estate accountant, educator*

Passaic
Johnson, Myrtle Alice Harris *elementary and secondary school educator*
Johnson, Sakinah *paralegal*

Paterson
Daniels, Cheryl Lynn *pediatrics nurse, case manager*
Pou, Nellie *assemblywoman*

Pennington
Gundeck, Caroline Nyklewicz *investment company executive*
Mitchell, Janet Aldrich *fund raising executive, reference materials publisher*

Pennsauken
Ramos, Mildred *administrative assistant*
Southard, Ruth Audrey *medical/surgical nurse*
Sygnecki, Christina *sales executive*

Pennsville
Whittinghill, Elizabeth Jane *speech pathology/audiology services professional*

Perth Amboy
Lavin-Pennyfeather, Rose *artist*
Reyes, Irma V. *adult education educator*
Richardson-Melech, Joyce Suzanne *music educator, singer*
Santiago, Theresa Marie *special education educator*

Petersburg
Orlando-Spinelli, Josephine *gifted and talented educator, educational consultant*

Picatinny Arsenal
Zulauf, Madeline Ruth *civilian military employee, photographer*

Piscataway
Champe, Pamela Chambers *biochemistry educator, writer*
Coppola, Sarah Jane *special education educator*
Essien, Francine B. *geneticist, educator*
Kenney, Mary R. *software engineer*
Klein, Lisa Carol *materials scientist, educator*
Lee, Barbara Anne *law educator, dean*
Liu, Alice Y. C. *biology educator*
McCrady, Barbara Sachs *psychologist, educator*
Rosalsky, Barbara Ellen *artist, home health aide*
Trontell, Marie Celestine *dean*
Urban, Cathleen Andrea *graphic designer*
Wagner-Westbrook, Bonnie Joan *management professional*
Wasserman, Marlie P(arker) *publisher*
White, Helene R. *sociologist, educator*

Pittstown
Bennett, Joan Hierholzer *artist*

Plainfield
Bober, Joanne L. *lawyer*

Plainsboro
Spiegel, Phyllis *public relations consultant, journalist*

Pleasantville
London, Charlotte Isabella *secondary education educator, reading specialist*

Pomona
Bukowski, Elaine Louise *physical therapist, educator*
Comfort, Priscilla Maria *retired college official, human resources professional*
Dagavarian-Bonar, Debra Aghavni *college administrator, consultant*
Vito, Marilyn Elaine *business educator*

Port Monmouth
Walling, Debra Ann *recreational therapist, director*

Princeton
Altmann, Jeanne *zoologist, educator*
Bassler, Bonnie *molecular biologist*
Beidler, Marsha Wolf *lawyer*
Bermann, Sandra Lekas *English language educator*
Berridge, Mary Lloyd *photographer*
Blackman, Sue Anne Batey *economics researcher*
Boretz, Naomi Messinger *artist, educator*
Broad, Barbara Prentice *retired real estate agent*
Campbell, Mildred Corum *business owner, nurse*
Chang, Sun-Yung Alice *mathematics educator*
Cheadle, Louise *concert pianist, educator*
Chedid, Lisa Leasure *food scientist*
Crossley, Helen Martha *public opinion analyst, research consultant*
De Lung, Jane Solberger *independent sector executive*
Diller, Elizabeth E. *architect, educator, artist*
Drakeman, Lisa N. *biotechnology company executive*
Dubrovsky, Gertrude Wishnick *journalist, researcher*
Duncan, Dianne Walker *elementary school educator*
Elliott-Moskwa, Elaine Sally *psychologist, researcher*
Finn, Frances Mary *biochemistry researcher*
Flanagan, Theresa *quality assurance professional*
Fox, Mary Ann Williams *librarian*
Fried, Eleanor Reingold *psychologist, educator*
Galloway, Patricia Denese *civil engineer*
Girgus, Joan Stern *psychologist, university administrator*
Goldfarb, Irene Dale *retired financial planner*
Gould, Elizabeth *neuroscientist, educator*
Greenman, Jane Friedlieb *lawyer, human resources executive*
Gutmann, Amy *political science and philosophy educator, academic administrator*
Hearn, Ruby Puryear *foundation executive*
Helm, Jocelyn B. *retired gerontologist*
Jenson, Pauline Alvino *retired speech and hearing educator*
Johnson, Barbara Piasecka *philanthropist, art historian and collector, business investor*
Kahn, Eiko Taniguchi *artist*
Kaple, Deborah A. *writer*
Keller, Suzanne *sociologist, psychotherapist*
Krulewicz, Rita Gloria *special education educator*
Lavizzo-Mourey, Risa Juanita *academic administrator, medical association administrator*
Lincoln, Anna *publishing executive*
Logue, Judith Felton *psychoanalyst, educator, professional coach*
Malkiel, Nancy Weiss *dean, historian, educator*
Marshall, Carol Joyce *clinical project director*
Morrison, Toni (Chloe Anthony Morrison) *novelist*
Nichols, Karen *architect*
Orphanides, Nora Charlotte *ballet educator*
Painter, Nell Irvin *historian, educator, writer*
Sandoval, Amada *education program director*
Shear, Ione Mylonas *archaeologist*
Showalter, Elaine *humanities educator, educator*
Stern, Gail Frieda *historical association director*
Tienda, Marta *demographer, educator*
Tilghman, Shirley Marie *academic administrator, biology educator*
Vizzini, Carol Redfield *symphony musician, music educator*
Weiss, Renée Karol *editor, musician*
Witkin, Evelyn Maisel *retired geneticist*

Princeton Junction
Mauro, Jean Cranstoun *music educator*
Rose, Peggy Jane *artist, art educator, gifted education advocate*

Prospect Park
Blair, Sherry Ann *psychotherapist, educator*

Rahway
Chen, Liya *chemist*
Garcia, Maria Luisa *biochemist, researcher*
Strack, Alison Merwin *neurobiologist*

Ramsey
O'Dell, Elizabeth Ann *controller*

Randolph
Greenberger, Marsha Moses *sales executive*
Oliveira, Theresa Razzano *secondary school educator*
Oppenheimer, Sonya *advertising executive, graphics designer*
Rathore, Uma Pandey *utilities executive*
Stoskus, Joanna Jorzysta *computer information systems educator*
Tomaino, Leah Karratoglou *artist*
Whildin, Leonora Porreca *retired nursing educator*

Red Bank
Brown, Valerie Anne *psychiatric social worker, educator*
Groves, Lizabeth A. *accountant, local area network administrator*
Gutentag, Patricia Richmond *social worker, family counselor, occupational therapist*
McWhinney, Madeline H. (Mrs. John Denny Dale) *economist, director*

Ridgefield
Riggs, Rory B. *pharmaceutical executive*

Ridgefield Park
Meidhof, Sister Patricia E. *school system administrator*

Ridgewood
Beresford, Madeleine Rosamond Sylvia *theater director, puppeteer*
Clements, Lynne Fleming *marriage and family therapist, application developer*
Friedrich, Margret Cohen *guidance and student assistance counselor*
Harris, Micalyn Shafer *lawyer, educator, arbitrator, consultant, mediator*

Ringoes
Santin, Jean *cosmetic company executive, consultant*
Tema-Lyn, Laurie *management consultant*

Ringwood
Day, Ann Elizabeth *artist, educator*
Murphy, Gloria Walter *novelist, screenwriter*
Paliga-Tanzola, Rhonda *special education educator*

Riverton
Gorman, Nancy Jane *executive secretary*

Rochelle Park
Olzerowicz, Sharon *information technology executive*

Rockaway
Allen, Dorothea *secondary school educator*
Carboy, Beverly J. *humanities educator*
Kelsey, Ann Lee *library administrator*
Kurtz, Ellen R. *journalist*
Laine, Cleo (Clementina Dinah Dankworth) *singer*

Rocky Hill
Lott, Joyce Greenberg *English language educator*

Roseland
Bolger, Mary Phyllis Judge *special education educator*
Foster, M. Joan *lawyer*
Graham, Patricia *information technology executive*
Steidl, Mary Catherine *food service executive*

Roselle
Di Marco, Barbaranne Yanus *principal*
Meister, Karen Olivia *secondary school educator*
Riley, Barbara Polk *retired librarian*
Tanner-Oliphant, Karen M. *family and consumer science educator*

Roselle Park
Brown, Reni (Arlene Patricia Theresa Brown) *artist*
Loredo, Linda S. *marketing executive*

Rumson
Topham, Sally Jane *ballet educator*

Rutherford
Driscoll, Lorraine Eva *obstetrician-gynecologist*

Saddle Brook
Ballone, Eileen Marie *music educator, musician, organist*
Clifton, Nelida *social worker*

Saddle River
Lasser, Gail Maria *psychologist, educator*
Lehmann, Doris Elizabeth *elementary school educator*
O'Connor, Denise Lynn *marketing communications executive*
Peters, Eleanor White *retired mental health nurse*
Weissmann, Heidi Seitelblum *radiologist, educator*

Salem
Carpenter, Margaret S. (Molly Carpenter) *artist*

Scotch Plains
Johnsen, Karen Kennedy *marketing professional*

Sea Isle City
Bruno, Carol Jeanette *library media specialist, gifted and talented education educator, innkeeper*
Tull, Theresa Anne *retired diplomat*

Seaside Park
Golembeski, Beverly Long *artist, art educator*

Secaucus
Blackman, Brenda *newscaster*
Cho, Alina *anchor*
O'Rourke, Ann Marie Cecilia *social worker*
Pinsker, Penny Collias (Pangeota Pinsker) *television producer*
Syms, Marcy *retail executive*

Sewell
Crocker, Jane Lopes *library director*
Meyer, Norma Weintraub *conductor*

Short Hills
Friedman, Frances Wolf *political fund raiser*
Henn, Cynthia *artist, educator*
Ogden, Maureen Black *retired state legislator*
Robbins-Wilf, Marcia *educational consultant*
Spector, Shelly *company executive*
Winter, Ruth Grosman (Mrs. Arthur Winter) *journalist*

Shrewsbury
Westerman, Liane Marie *research scientist executive*

Skillman
Brill, Yvonne Claeys *engineer, consultant*
Cummings, Peggy Ann *counseling administrator*

Somers Point
Hagerthey, Gwendolyn Irene *retired music educator*
McCullough, Eileen (Eileen McCullough LePage, Elli McCullough) *financial consultant, writer, editor, educator*

Somerset
Becker, Phyllis *systems analyst*
Lee, Thai Theresa *information technology executive*
Robinson-Hilton, Lorraine Ann *music educator*

Somerville
D'Alessio, Jacqueline Ann *English educator*
Dobrinsky, Susan Elizabeth *human resources director*
Gross, Carol Ann *lawyer*
Weisblatt, Barbara Ann *secondary school educator*

South Bound Brook
Weir, Sonja Ann *artist*

South Hackensack
Wille, Rosanne Louise *higher education administrator*

South Orange
Budin, Wendy C. *nursing educator, researcher*
Delo, Ellen Sanderson *lawyer*
Greene, Rebecca Rachel *lawyer*
Hecht, Marion B. *mental health counselor, mental health therapist*
Steiner, Gloria Litwin *psychologist*
Williams, Veronica Ann *marketing professional, consultant, information technology executive*
Wright, Barbara Wincklhofer *nursing educator*

Sparta
Guida, Pat *information broker, literature chemist*

Springfield
Baker, Alden *artist*
DeVone, Denise *artist, educator*

Stewartsville
Busch, Beverly Gail *English language educator, literature educator, instructional resource center administrator*

Stockton
Taylor, Rosemary *artist*

Succasunna
Romance, Mary C. *library director*
[illegible], Janet *holistic professional educator*

Summit
Call, Denise Hodgins *curator, artist, freelance/self-employed writer*
Clynes, Carolann Elizabeth *realtor*
Good, Joan Duffey *artist*
Hall, Pamela Elizabeth *psychologist*
Rousseau, Irene Victoria *artist*
Starks, Florence Elizabeth *retired special education educator*
Tator, Adriennne Maria *director*
Vandenberg, Joka Maria *physicist, researcher*

Teaneck
Baldwin, Dorothy Leila *secondary school educator*
Brudner, Helen Gross *social sciences educator*
Czin, Felicia Tedeschi *Italian language and literature educator, small business owner*
Dowd, Janice Lee *foreign language educator*
Enteen, Vicki L. *public relations executive*
Graham, Janet Lorraine *music educator*
Halper, June *medical center director*
Indick, Janet *sculptor*
Jackson, Millie *vocalist, songwriter, playwright, producer*
Lehmann, Esther Strauss *investment company executive*
Lightman, Marjorie *historian*
Nagy, Christa Fiedler *biochemist*
Smith, Susan Elizabeth *guidance director*
Stucker, Eleanor Marie *social worker, psychotherapist*
Walensky, Dorothy Charlotte *language educator*
Walker, Lucy Doris *secondary school educator, writer*
Weinberg, Loretta *state legislator*

Tenafly
Blank, Marion Sue *psychologist, educator*
Brown, Shirley Ann *speech-language pathologist*
Schoenberg, Coco *sculptor*

Tinton Falls
Butler, Nancy Taylor *gender equity specialist, program director*

Toms River
Bosley, Karen Lee *English and journalism educator*
Donaldson, Marcia Jean *lay worker*
Engelhardt, Catherine *elementary school educator*
Kudryasheva, Aleksandra A. *scientist, researcher, educator*
Leone, Judith Gibson *educational media specialist, video production company executive*
Matteo, Christine E. *librarian*
Schockaert, Barbara Ann *marketing professional*
Schwartz, Anna R. *music educator, musician*
Willetts, Elizabeth M. *humanities lecturer, actress*

Towaco
Gasperini, Elizabeth Carmela (Lisa Gasperini) *marketing consultant, graphic designer*

Trenton
Allen, Diane Betzendahl *state legislator*
Bakke, Holly *bank commission official*
Binder, Elaine Kotell *associations consultant*
Blake, Allison *social worker, educator*
Bowker, Linda Barbara *lobbyist*
Brearley, Candice *fashion designer*
Cardinali, Noreen Sadler *state agency administrator*
Castro, Ida L. *state official, former federal official*
Chavooshian, Marge *artist, educator*
Christopherson, Elizabeth Good *broadcast executive*
Coleman, Bonnie Watson *assemblywoman*
Cooper, Mary Little *federal judge, former banking commissioner*
Dahme, Maud *educational association administrator*
Dimasi, Linda Grace *epidemiologist*
Dixon, Kathryn A. *social worker*
Himm, Emilie Gina *administrative analyst, records and information manager, consultant*
Joseph, Edith Hoffman *retired editor*
Kelman, Marybeth *health care consultant, health policy analyst*
Levin, Susan Bass *lawyer*
Long, Virginia *state supreme court justice*
Manno, Rita *state agency administrator*
McCann, Colleen Mary *public affairs specialist, lobbyist*
McGowan, Joan Yuhas *development researcher*
Miller, Velvet G. *healthcare administrator*
Obed, Leonora Rita Villegas *writer*
Poritz, Deborah T. *state supreme court chief justice, former attorney general*
Russell, Joyce Anne Rogers *librarian*
Stein, Sandra Lou *educational psychologist, educator*
Suter, Karen L. *former state banking department administrator*
Thomas, Regena L. *secretary of state*
Thompson, Anne Elise *federal judge*
Vandervalk, Charlotte *state legislator*
Watson-Coleman, Bonnie *state legislator*
Zisholtz-Herzog, Ellen Naomi *arts administrator, consultant, cultural planner*

Turnersville
Richie, Michelle Tracey *special education educator*

Union
Chen-Hafteck, Lily *music educator*
Darden, Barbara S. *library director*
Fabyanski, Mary Irene *nursing administrator*
Gronewold, Sue Ellen *history educator*
Kuzan, Kathleen *speech pathology services professional, educator*
Lederman, Susan Sturc *public administration educator*
Whitelaw, Dolores Fahey *artist*
Williams, Carol Jorgensen *social work educator*

Union City
Bull, Inez Stewart *special education, gifted music educator, coloratura soprano, pianist, editor, author, curator*

Upper Montclair
Cass, Mary Louise *librarian*
Mandel, Charlotte *poet, literature educator, editor*

Upper Saddle River
Farmer, Martha Louise *retired college administrator*
Marron, Darlene Lorraine *real estate company executive*
Smith, Miranda Constance *writer, educator*

Ventnor City
Robbins, Hulda Dornblatt *artist, printmaker*

Verona
Poor, Suzanne Donaldson *advertising and public relations executive*

Vineland
Blevins, Amy L. *financial advisor, investment advisor*
Hesser, Lorraine M *special education educator*
Popp, Charlotte Louise *health facility administrator*
Santucci, L. Michelle *adult nurse practitioner, nutrition consultant*

Voorhees
Carter, Catherine Louise *elementary school educator*

Waldwick
Lynch, Carol *director special services, psychologist*
Samuelson, Billie Margaret *artist*

Warren
Baxter, Nancy *medical writer*
Hennings, Dorothy Grant (Mrs. George Hennings) *education educator*
Kozberg, Donna Walters *rehabilitation administration executive*

Washington
Myers, Connie *assemblywoman*

Watchung
Abrams, Donna Marie *art educator*
Grey, Ruthann E. *communications specialist, management consultant*

Wayne
Brockett, Francesca L. *retail executive*
Bronstein, Jagoda Ewa *pediatrician*
Derby, Deborah *retail executive*
Einreinhofer, Nancy Anne *art gallery director*
Garcia, Ofelia *dean*
Makarec, Katherine *psychologist, educator*
Salny, Abbie Feinstein *psychologist*

Weehawken
Metallo, Frances Rosebell *mathematics educator*

West New York
Kelly, Lucie Stirm Young *nursing educator*
Murphy, Melinda *TV host, reporter*

West Orange
Bogstahl, Deborah Marcelle *global strategic planner*
Bojsza, Joan E. *elementary school educator*
Hutcheon, Barbara Silver *lawyer*

Westfield
Brown, Shirley Mark *retired science administrator*
Burton, Barbara *marketing executive*
Roll, Marilyn Rita Brownlie *social worker*

Whippany
Meola, Janice Grace *lawyer*
Papera, Rosemarie Marucci *speech pathologist*
Petitto, Barbara Buschell *artist*

Whitehouse Station
Avedon, Marcia J. *pharmaceutical executive*
Lewent, Judy Carol *pharmaceutical executive*
McGlynn, Margaret G. *pharmaceutical executive*
Yarno, Wendy *pharmaceutical executive*

Wildwood
Callinan, Patricia Ann *legal secretary*

Willingboro
Coppock, Kristen Anne K. *newswriter, editor*
Denslow, Deborah Pierson *primary education educator*
Green, Riva Lee *social worker, minister*
Suber, Sharon L. *technology coordinator*

Woodbridge
Bupathi, Kavita K. *pediatrician*
DeMatteo, Gloria Jean *financial counselor*
Estok, Rosemarie DeNorscio *educational administrator*
Friscia, Arline M. *assemblywoman*
Paugh, Nancy Adele *secondary school educator, school system administrator*

Woodbury
Murphy, Ann Marie *special education educator*
O'Bryant, Cathy *retired social worker, evangelist*

Woodcliff Lake
Nachtigal, Patricia *lawyer*

Woodstown
Tatnall, Ann Weslager *reading educator*

Wyckoff
Cropper, Susan Peggy *veterinarian*
Marcus, Linda Susan *dermatologist*
Stahl, Alice Slater *retired psychiatrist*

NEW MEXICO

Abiquiu
Howlett, Phyllis Lou *retired athletics conference administrator*

Alamogordo
Carnes, Colleen Kennedy *writer, retired military officer*
Denney, Shawna LeAnn *music educator*
McFadin, Helen Lozetta *retired elementary education educator*
Wilson, Jennifer *psychologist*

Albuquerque
Abraham, Karen A. *university administrator*
Abrams, Fay Pfaelzer *art gallery owner, educator*
Archulata, Margie Baca *city clerk*
Bernard, Marilyn Thomas *director, vocalist*
Best, Marcia A. *graphics designer, artist*
Betts, Dorothy Anne *elementary school educator*
Blake, Renée *broadcast executive*
Chang, Barbara Karen *medical educator*
Clark, Teresa Watkins *psychotherapist, clinical counselor*
Cole, Terri Lynn *organization administrator*
Coleman, Barbara McReynolds *artist*
Collins, Julie *healthcare organization executive*
Condie, Carol Joy *anthropologist, research facility administrator*
Cook, Marcella Kay *retired theater educator*
Culpepper, Mabel Claire *artist*
Dal Santo, Diane *writer, retired judge*
Davis, Betty Bourbonia *real estate investment executive*
Desantis, Sherolyn Smith *foundation executive*
DeWitt, Mary Therese *forensic anthropologist, archaeologist*
Ellen, Jane *composer, music educator, researcher*
Evans, Pauline D. *physicist, researcher*
Everitt, Elizabeth M. *school system administrator*
Feldman, Dede *state legislator*
Freeman, Patricia Elizabeth *library and education specialist*
Fuchs, Beth Ann *research engineer*
Fuller, Anne Elizabeth Havens *English language and literature educator, consultant*
Gahala, Estella Marie *writer, consultant*
Gorham, Ramsay L. *state legislator, political organization administrator*
Graff, Pat Stuever *secondary school educator*
Green, Mae Maera *artist*
Grossetete, Ginger Lee *retired gerontology administrator, consultant*
Gutierrez, Joni Marie *landscape architect, political organization worker*
Hadas, Elizabeth Chamberlayne *editor*
Hahn, Betty *artist, photographer, educator*

Harlow, Judith Leigh *educational institute executive, consultant*
Henderson, Rogene Faulkner *toxicologist, researcher*
Jaramillo, Mari-Luci *retired federal agency administrator*
Kaehele, Bettie Louise *accountant*
King-Pimentel, Cara Shannon *music educator*
Kotchian, Sarah Bruff *municipal official*
Kroken, Patricia Ann *health science association administrator*
Kushlis, Patricia Hogin *foreign affairs writer, analyst*
Landis, Ellen Jamie *art curator*
Leesman, Beverly Jean *artist, art critic, art educator*
Lopez, Linda M. *state legislator*
Loss, Lynne Franklin *artist, volunteer*
Lowrance, Muriel Edwards *program specialist*
Marks, Martha Alford *writer*
McBride, Teresa *information systems specialist*
McGuire, Susan Grayson *legislative staff member*
Miera, Lucille Catherine Miera *artist, retired art educator*
Montoya, Patricia T. *federal agency administrator*
Moody, Patricia Ann *psychiatric nurse, artist, small business owner*
Moses, Karen *editor*
Mulcahy, Lucille Burnett *freelance writer*
Multhaup, Merrel Keyes *artist*
Myers, Carol McClary *retired sales administrator, editor*
Navarro, Janyte Janine *real estate executive*
Nelson, Mary Carroll *artist, writer*
Neufeld, Frances Foss *sculptor*
Nevin, Jean Shaw *artist*
Olson, Jean A. *psychotherapist*
Ortiz, Kathleen Lucille *travel consultant*
Owens, Georgia Katherine *human resources specialist, consultant*
Palmer, Sharon-Joy *agricultural research company executive*
Paster, Janice Dubinsky *lawyer, former state legislator*
Pohl, Elizabeth *contracting company executive*
Ramo, Roberta Cooper *lawyer*
Rice, Linda Angel *music educator*
Richter, Harvena *retired english literature and creative writing teacher, writer*
Riordan, Jennifer L. *media relations manager*
Saland, Linda Carol *anatomy educator, neuroscience researcher*
Seiser, Virginia *librarian*
Smith, Jean *interior design firm executive*
Snell, Patricia Poldervaart *librarian, consultant*
Steider, Doris *artist*
Stewart, Mimi (Miriam) (Kay) (Mimi Stewart) *state legislator, educator*
Stuart, Cynthia Morgan *university administrator*
Tangman, Ruth S. *educational administrator*
Torres, Barbara Wood *technical services professional*
Trojahn, Lynn *academic administrator*
Twigg, Nancy L. *nursing association administrator*
Valdez, Dianna Marie *language educator, consultant*
White, Jennifer Phelps *counselor*
Wilkinson, Frances Catherine *librarian, educator*
Wilson, Sue *state legislator*

Alto
Zeitelhack, Gloria Jeanne *artist*

Arroyo Hondo
Greenwood Levy, Phaedra Jean *photojournalist, writer*

Bayard
Lopez, Linda Carol *social sciences educator*

Belen
Chicago, Judy *artist*
Smith, Helen Elizabeth *retired career officer*
Turner, Aileen Archunde *artist*

Bernalillo
Pritchard, Betty Jean *retired art educator*

Bloomfield
Sledzinski, Jessica K. *elementary school educator*

Caballo
Massengill, Barbara Daves *artist*

Carlsbad
Mills, Dolores Elizabeth *speech pathology/audiology services professional*
Paviet-Hartmann, Patricia *chemist, researcher*
Queen, Dorothy *distribution company executive*
Regan Gossage, Muriel *librarian*

Cloudcroft
Starling, Virginia R. *music educator, consultant*

Clovis
Barnard, Janet Kinzy *music educator, elementary school educator*
Rehorn, Lois M(arie) (Lois Marie Smith) *nursing administrator*
Shade, Marsha J. *elementary school educator, music educator*

Corrales
Eaton, Pauline *artist, educator*
Eisenstadt, Pauline Doreen Bauman *investment company executive, state legislator*
Foryst, Carole *computer electronics executive*
Williams, Juanita Rosalie *artist*

Crownpoint
Alexander, Judith Elaine *psychologist*

Dona Ana
Garcia, Mary Jane Madrid *state legislator*

Edgewood
Villagomez, Deborah Lynn *medical/surgical nurse, horse breeder*

El Prado
Tsoodle-Marcus, Charlene *education educator, school system administrator*

Farmington
Anderson, Evelyn Louise *elementary teacher*
Doig, Beverly Irene *retired systems specialist*
Evans, Helen Ruth *music educator, pianist*
Luttrell, Mary Lou *elementary school educator*
Mathers, Margaret *reference librarian, archivist*
Riddle, Claudine *real estate company executive*
Wilmer, Pamela Sue *music educator*

Galisteo
Lippard, Lucy Rowland *writer, lecturer*

Gallup
Cattaneo, Jacquelyn Annette Kammerer *artist, educator*
Fellin, Octavia Antoinette *retired librarian, historical researcher*
Garcia, Mother Magda Leticia *sister, consultant*
Lundstrom, Patricia *state government administrator*
Mouttet, Jane Elizabeth *librarian*

Hobbs
Ebler, Marilyn Ann *graphic designer, educator*
Garey, Patricia Martin *artist*
Weldy, Lana Gail *secondary school educator*

Kirtland
Nelson, Theresa Veronica *medical technologist, small business owner*

Kirtland Afb
Anderson, Christine Marlene *software engineer*

La Mesa
Cantu, Delia *training services executive*

Las Cruces
Anderson, Joyce Ann *lawyer*
Bell, M. Joy Miller *financial planner, real estate broker*
Bird, Mary Francis *secondary school educator*
Branch, Dori Alice *music educator*
Crnkovic, Anise Elaine *marriage and family therapist*
Mata, Josefina *health education coordinator, educator*
Merrick, Beverly Georgianne *journalism, communications educator*
Nelson, Antonya *writer*
Reese, Janet Kay *purchasing agent*
Rosile, GraceAnn *business management educator*
Selden, Annie *mathematics educator*

Las Vegas
Casey, Barbara A. Perea *state legislator, school superintendent*
Simpson, Dorothy Audrey *retired speech educator*

Los Alamos
Bauer, Eve *research scientist*
Benjamin, Susan Selton *elementary school educator*
Flaherty, Anne H. *advocate*
Gonzales, Stephanie *state official*
Livesay, Valorie Ann *security program analyst*
Lu, Ningping *environmental chemist*
Mendius, Patricia Dodd Winter *editor, educator, writer*
Orndoff, Elizabeth Carlson *retired junior college librarian, educator*
Smith, Fredrica Emrich *rheumatologist, internist*
Thompson, Lois Jean Heidke Ore *psychologist*
Wallace, Jeannette Owens *state legislator*

Los Lunas
Behrend, Betty Ann *municipal official*
Denzler, Mary Joanne *special education educator*

Lovington
Stuart, Lillian Mary *writer*
Trujillo, Anna *food company administrator, city official*

Nogal
Moeller, Susan Elaine *artist*

Placitas
McElhinney, Susan Kay (Kate Echeverria) (Kate McElhinney) *executive assistant*

Playas
Clifton, Judy Raelene *association administrator*

Portales
Edwards, Carolyn Mullenax *public relations executive*

Prewitt
Droll, Ruth Lucille *missionary pastor*

Ranchos De Taos
Marx, Nicki Diane *sculptor, painter*

Rio Rancho
Duitman, Lois Robinson *artist*
Meyerson, Barbara Tobias *elementary school educator*
Peters, Evelyn Joan *artist*
Weber, Alois Hughes *principal*

Rociada
Reed, Carol Louise *designer*

Roswell
Anderson, Sally Midgette *social services administrator, linguist*
Hedin, Edna Jenks *musician, educator*
Munroe, Shirley Ann *retired hospital association executive, health care consultant*
Padilla, Sandra Lynn *counselor, consultant*
Watson, Marilyn Fern *writer*
Weikel, Sandra G. *music educator*

Ruidoso
Ayers, Kathy Venita Moore *librarian*
Reeder, Karen Emerald *artist, educator*
Stover, Carolyn Nadine *middle school educator*

Ruidoso Downs
Templeton, Ann *artist, educator*

Sandia Park
Weitz, Jeanne Stewart *artist, educator*

Santa Ana Pueblo
Burns, Corrina Jessica *marketing professional, public relations executive*

Santa Fe
Andreeva, Tatiana *art gallery owner*
Arnold-Jones, Janice E. *state representative*
Beam, Gail C. *state representative*
Bergé, Carol *writer*
Caplan, Jessica Marie *small business owner, artist*
Cerny, Charlene Ann *director*
Chacon, Mari B. *counseling administrator*
Cohen, Marcia Friedlander *writer, editor-in-chief, journalist*
Dehn, Virginia *visual artist*
Denish, Diane D. *lieutenant governor*
Erdman, Barbara *visual artist*
Gagan, Jamie Lisa *emergency physician, artist*
Gallagher, Paula *minister, musician*
Garcia, Mary Helen *state representative*
Hanson, Linda N. *academic administrator, educator*
Harding, Marie *ecological executive, artist*
Helin, Jacquelyn Mae *classical musician, music educator*
Howell, Vicky Sue *health researcher*
Howes, Gloria *state legislator*
Kelly, Ruth *state agency administrator*
Kinderwater, Diane *state official*
Kingman, Elizabeth Yelm *anthropologist*
Kirk, Flora Kay Stude *artist, accountant*
Lichtenberg, Margaret Klee *publishing company executive*
Lippincott, Janet *artist, art educator*
Loftin, Thelma Tee *writer*
Lovejoy, Lynda M. *state agency administrator*
Madrid, Patricia A. *state attorney general*
Maes, Petra Jimenez *state supreme court justice*
Melnick, Alice Jean (AJ Melnick) *counselor*
Miller-Engel, Marjorie *foundation administrator, commissioner, small business owner*
Minzner, Pamela Burgy *state supreme court justice*
Moll, Deborah Adelaide *lawyer*
Myers, Charlotte Will *biology educator*
Nava, Cynthia L. *state legislator*
Otten, Robin Dozier *state agency administrator*
Papen, Mary Kay *state senator*
Perroni, Carol *artist, painter*
Perry, Nancy Estelle *psychologist*
Powdrell-Culbert, Jane E. *state representative*
Pulitzer, Roslyn Kitty *social worker, psychotherapist*
Ribble, Judith Glenn *medical educator*
Rodello, Debbie A. *state representative*
Rodriguez, Nancy *state legislator*
Sanchez, Bernadette M. *state senator*
Shubart, Dorothy Louise Tepfer *artist, educator*
Sickler, Joan Louise *retail store owner*
Sloan, Jeanette Pasin *artist*
Snyder, Helen Diane *state senator*
Stapleton, Sheryl Williams *state representative*
Stieber, Tamar *journalist*
Taylor, Beverly Lacy *musician, educator, stringed instrument restorer*
Tokheim, Sara Ann *writer, information technology professional*
Townsend, Sandra L. *state representative*
Vaughn, Gloria C. *state representative*
Vazquez, Martha Alicia *judge*
Vigil-Giron, Rebecca *state official*
Weckesser, Susan Oneacre *lawyer*
Wiese, Neva *critical care nurse*
Wilson, Avon W. *state representative*
Wilson, Laura Eleanor *landscape architect*
Yalman, Ann *judge, lawyer*
York, Star Liana *sculptor*
Zanetti, Teresa A. *state representative*

Santa Rosa
Campos, Christina Rivas *finance officer, restaurant owner*

Shiprock
Atcitty, Fannie L. *elementary school educator, education educator*

Silver City
Bettison, Cynthia Ann *museum director, archaeologist*
Hall, Jean Quintero *communications and history educator*

Taos
Aspenwind, Linda Eileen *social worker*
Bolls, Imogene Lamb *English language educator, poet*
Garcia, Christine *academic administrator, educator, researcher*
Lipscomb, Anna Rose Feeny *entrepreneur, arts organizer, fundraiser*
Martin, Agnes *artist*
Winslow, Bette Killingsworth *dance studio owner*

Tesuque
MacGraw, Ali *actress*

Tijeras
Hoffman, Robyn Brown *lawyer*

Tularosa
Duran, Dianna J. *state legislator*

Vadito
Patten, Christine Taylor *artist*

NEW YORK

Addison
Haines, Caryl *retired medical/surgical nurse*

Albany
Alvarez, Christina *counselor*
Amodeo-Smargon, Christine Joanne *adult education educator, real estate rehabilitator*
Arroyo, Carmen Elsie *state legislator*
Barnard, Sylvia Evans *classicist, educator*
Berman, Carol *commissioner*
Bowen, Mary Lu *ecumenical administrator*
Branigan, Helen Marie *educational consultant, administrator*
Brewer, Aida M. *treasurer*
Carman, Joanne G. *consultant*
Castro, Bernadette *state official*
Catalano, Jane Donna *lawyer*
Chretien, Margaret Cecilia *public administrator*
Christensen, Joan K. *state legislator*
Clifford, Lisa Mary *marketing professional*
Cloud, Gary Lynn *food and nutrition services administrator*
DeBuono, Barbara Ann *physician, state official*
Destito, RoAnn M. *state legislator*
Dominian, Julie *human resources specialist*
Donohue, Mary *lieutenant governor*
Ferrara, Donna *state legislator*
Fitzgerald, Norma Anne *emergency nurse*
Galus, Clara P. *philosopher, educator*
Glick, Deborah J. *state legislator*
Graffeo, Victoria A. *state appeals court judge*
Greene, Aurelia *state legislator*
Hassell-Thompson, Ruth *state legislator*
Hitchcock, Karen Ruth *biology educator, university dean, academic administrator*
Hooper, Earlene *state legislator*
Howard, Lyn Jennifer *medical educator*
Hunziker, Sudha *social worker*
Jacobs, Rhoda S. *state legislator*
Johnson, Jacqueline *psychologist, researcher*
Kaye, Judith Smith *state appeals court chief judge*
Kelley, Sister Helen *health facility executive*
Krueger, Liz *state legislator*
Langer, Judith Ann *literacy educator*
Lawton, Nancy *artist*
Leone, Gilda C. *adult education educator*
Lustenader, Barbara Diane *human resources specialist*
Mancinelli-Cahill, Maggie *theater director*
Mayersohn, Nettie *state legislator*
Mendez, Olga A. *state legislator*
Miles, Christine Marie *museum director*
Morris, Margretta Elizabeth *conservationist*
Nolan, Catherine T. *state legislator*
Novello, Antonia Coello *state health commissioner, former surgeon general, pediatric nephrologist, educator, retired federal agency administrator*
Olmsted, Ruth Martin *humanities educator*
Pheffer, Audrey Iris *state legislator*
Poleto, Mary Margaret *orthopedic nurse*
Read, Susan Phillips *state appeals court judge*
Smith, Ada L. *state legislator*
Smith, Bethany Rae *accountant*
Stavisky, Toby Ann *state legislator*
Stewart, Margaret McBride *biology educator, researcher*
Sullivan, Frances Taylor *state legislator*
Van Nortwick, Barbara Louise *library director*
Weinstein, Helene E. *state legislator*
Wick-Pelletier, Joan *academic administrator, mathematician*
Williman, Pauline *shorthand reporter, farm foundation administrator*

Albion
Allamon, Karen Henn *minister*

Alfred
Goodman, Robyn S. *communications educator*

Amagansett
Fleetwood, M. Freile *psychiatrist, educator*

Amenia
Gagne, Nancy Lynn *music educator, musician*

Amherst
Kester, Gunilla Theander *poet, literature educator, music educator*
Messinger, Penny *historian, educator*
Monpere, Lisa Renee *budget and personnel administrator, entrepreneur*
Pachan, Mary Jude Kathryn Dorothy *guidance counselor*
Wiesenberg, Jacqueline Leonardi *social sciences educator*

Amity Harbor
O'Hanlon, Carol Ann *minister*

Amityville
Angeles, Carmen M. *pathologist*
Citrano-Cummiskey, Debra Moira *chemist, network technician*

Amsterdam
Ossenfort, Stephanie Helen *music educator, secondary school educator, special education educator*

Malkiewicz, Elizabeth Mary *art director*
Merini, Rafika *foreign language, cultures and literatures educator*
Nowak, Carol Ann *city official*
O'Donnell, Denise Ellen *lawyer*
O'Loughlin, Sandra S. *lawyer*
Overton, Nicole Yolanda *program analyst*
Payne, Frances Anne *literature educator, researcher*
Peoples, Crystal D. *state legislator*
Piech, Margaret Ann *mathematics educator*
Rubin, Lois S. *lawyer*
Samuels, Hanna *artist*
Sarmiento, Shirley Jean *counselor, court advocate*
Seitz, Mary Lee *mathematics educator*
Smith, Sara D. *minister, lawyer*
Sullivan, Margaret M. *editor*
Tedlock, Barbara Helen *anthropologist, educator, academic administrator*
Temperato, Susan *mental health counselor, clinical supervisor*
Wagner, Barbara Lee *musician*
Williams, Lillian Serece *educator*
Wright, Dana Jace *retired emergency nurse practitioner*

Buskirk
Johanson, Patricia Maureen *artist, architect, park designer*

Cairo
Ludwig, Laura Lonshein *poet*

Calverton
Troge, Darlene I. *director*

Camillus
Alvaro, Maureen Teresa *music educator*

Canandaigua
Chappelle, Lou Jo *physical therapist assistant*
Malinowski, Patricia A. *community college educator*
Ristuccia, Lavern K. Cole *psychologist, consultant*
Story, Amy Taylor *music educator*

Canton
Auster, Nancy Eileen Ross *economics educator*
Bucher, Mary *school librarian*
Daniels, Cindy Lou *writer, educator*
Goldberg, Rita Maria *foreign language educator*

Cape Vincent
Stiefel, Linda Shields *lawyer*

Carle Place
Russo, Joni K. *director*

Carmel
Calegari, Maria *ballerina*

Castleton On Hudson
Wagner, Mary Susan *academic administrator*

Catskill
Wolfe, Geraldine *administrator*

Cedarhurst
Lipsky, Linda Ethel *health facility administrator*
Solymosy, Hattie May *writer, publisher, storyteller, educator*
Van Raalte, Polly Ann *reading and writing specialist, photojournalist*

Centereach
Stern, Marci Ann *English educator*

Central Islip
Cyganowski, Melanie L. *bankruptcy judge*
Eisenberg, Dorothy *federal judge*
Seybert, Joanna *federal judge*
Wiggins, Gloria *nonprofit organization administrator, television producer*

Central Nyack
Margolis, Patt *minister*

Central Square
BuMann, Sharon Ann *sculptor*

Chappaqua
George, Jean Craighead *author, illustrator*
Hurford, Carol *retired lawyer*

Chatham
Squier, Rita Ann Holmberg *graphic designer*

Chautauqua
Campbell, Joan Brown *religious organization executive*
Yurth, Helene Louise *librarian*

Chazy
Ratner, Gayle *special education educator*

Cheektowaga
Berkun, Rose *anesthesiologist*
Rogers, Cheryl Ann *speech pathology services professional*

Cherry Valley
Dallemagne-Cookson, Elise Camille *writer*

Chester
Karen, Linda Tricarico *interior designer*

Chichester
Kaye/Kantrowitz, Melanie *writer, educator*

Cicero
Pink, (Alecia Moore) *singer*
Schiess, Betty Bone *priest*

Clarence
Stringer, Gretchen Engstrom *consulting volunteer administrator*

Claverack
Martin, Mary Elaine *psychologist*

Clayton
Musser, Gloria J. *retired composer*

Clifton Park
Glasgow, Constance Lenore *pediatrician*

Clifton Springs
DeRuyter, Marilyn *real estate broker*

Clinton
Havens, Pamela Ann *college official*

Clinton Corners
McDermott, Patricia Ann *nursing administrator*

Cobleskill
Colony, Pamela Cameron *medical researcher, educator*

Cohocton
Kowulich, Barbara Ann *physician assistant*

Cohoes
Vallee, Catherine E. *music educator*

Cold Spring
Battersby, Katherine Sue *elementary school educator*
Milner, Debbi Elissa *computer company executive*

Commack
Cohen, Judith W. *retired academic administrator*
Nilson, Patricia *clinical psychologist*
Price, Amelia Ruth *not-for-profit foundation president, artist, small business owner*
Richardson, Ellen Morris *music educator*

Congers
Voce, Patricia Maria *medical/surgical nurse*

Cooperstown
Cossa, Joanne *performing company executive*

Copake
Wahlers, Linda Ann Ford *writer*

Coram
Celella, Karen Ann *music teacher, author*

Corning
Cicerchi, Eleanor Ann Tomb *fundraising executive*
Hauselt, Denise Ann *lawyer*
Peaslee, Jayne Marie *computer scientist, educator*
Spillman, Jane Shadel *curator, researcher, writer*

Cornwall On Hudson
Abrams-Collens, Vivien *artist*
Burke, Ann Therese *social worker, educator*
D'Alvia, Marlene *medical social worker, clinical social worker*

Corona
Maruca, Rita *real estate company executive, real estate broker*

Cortland
Bulger, Marcia S. *physical education educator*

Cortlandt Manor
Genis, Alice Singer *psychologist*
Keating, Laura Lee M. *historian, records management professional*
Rosenberg, Marilyn Rosenthal *artist, visual poet*

Cross River
Thorn, Susan Howe *interior designer*

Croton On Hudson
Cotton, Cornelia *photographer, art dealer*
Wandel, Sharon Lee *sculptor*

Crugers
Norman, Jessye *soprano*

De Ruyter
Jeschke, Carol T. *arts/theater consultant, real estate investor*

Deer Park
Gerbino, Robinann Louise *real estate agent, pharmaceutical executive*
Martone, Jeanette Rachele *artist*
Pariag, Haimwattie Ramkistodas *information management administrator*

Delhi
Duncan, Mary Ellen *academic administrator*
Townsend, Sue Joyce *retired air traffic controller*

Delmar
Button, Rena Pritsker *public affairs executive*
Campas, Anna Penelope *civil engineer, architect*
Hoffman, Rita Mary *counselor, cosmetics executive, consultant*
Redlich, Allison Dyan *research psychologist*
Rice, Ruth Elaine *music educator*
Schwarz, Louise A. *band director*

Deposit
Myrick, Katherine Julia *minister*

Derby
Kieffer, Marcia S. *psychotherapist*

Dewitt
Berg, Francine Judith *music educator*

Dix Hills
Blumstein, Reneé J. *educational research consultant, grant writer, program developer*
Fouladvand, Hengameh *artist*
Gordon, Jacqueline Alicia *guidance counselor, protective services official*
Somerville, Daphine Holmes *retired elementary education educator*
Virostko, Joan *elementary school educator*

Dobbs Ferry
Hotchkiss, Janet McCann *secondary school educator*
Kraetzer, Mary C. *sociologist, educator, consultant*
Lesack, Beatriz Díaz *secondary school educator*
Maiocchi, Christine *lawyer*
Sailors, Emma Lou *pediatrician*

Downsville
Hornick, Susan Florence Stegmuller *secondary education educator, fine arts educator, curriculum specialist, artist*

Dunkirk
Lewis, Amy Beth *newswriter, reporter, writer, photographer*

East Amherst
Allen, Maureen Janet *music educator*
Kirdani, Esther May *school counselor*
Weiss, Elinor *elementary school educator*

East Aurora
Woodard, Carol Jane *educational consultant*

East Greenbush
Jacobson, Dorothy Troup *English and education educator*

East Hampton
Goldstein, Judith Shelley *reading and learning specialist*
Jaudon, Valerie *artist*
Lichtenstein, Therese Ellen *art educator*
Schetlin, Eleanor M. *retired university official*
Scott, Rosa Mae *art educator, artist*
Vered, Ruth *art gallery director, owner*

East Islip
Cullen, Valerie Adelia *secondary school educator*
Donohue, Claire P. *school librarian*
Harrington, Carolyn Marie *accountant, artist, jewelry designer*
Weaver, Joyce R. *hypnotherapist*

East Meadow
Kalin, Karin Bea *retired secondary school educator, consultant*
Price, Marilyn *lawyer*

East Moriches
Guthrie, Teresa Irene *pediatric nurse practitioner*

East Northport
Mateer, Anne Frances *multi-media specialist, elementary school educator*

East Otto
Anderson, Ursula M. *pediatrician*

East Quogue
Setlow, Neva Delihas *artist, research biologist*

East Setauket
Kefalas, Jessie Ae *visual merchandiser, artist*

East Syracuse
Duffy, Nancy Keogh *television broadcast professional*

Eastchester
Burgess, Carol Ann *educational association administrator, literature educator*
Weinberg, Dale Glaser *technical writer, consultant, trainer*

Elizabethtown
Sayward, Teresa R. *state representative*

Elma
Tichy, Susan Hastings *music educator*

Elmhurst
Markey, Margaret M. *state legislator*
Matsa, Loula Zacharoula *social services administrator, educator*
Przystawski, Karen Ann *registered nurse*

Elmira
Bruzee, Kristen K. *nursing administrator*
Kerr-Nowlan, Donna Courtney *pre-school administrator*
Mitchell, Sharon *artist, designer*
Runer, Evelyn Rosario *endocrinologist*
Van den Blink, Nelson Mooers *light industrial manufacturing executive*

Elmont
Butera, Ann Michele *consulting company executive*

Endicott
Englehart, Joan Anne *consultant*

Fairport
Graham, Susette Ryan *retired English educator*
Holtzclaw, Diane Smith *elementary school educator*
Radell, Carol K. *elementary school educator*

Far Rockaway
Mitchell, Lillian Adassa *principal*
Sussman, Laureen Glicklin *junior high school educator*
Titus, Michele R. *state legislator*

Farmingdale
Lindsley, Michelle A. *theater educator*
Lobel, Sharon *retail executive*
O'Brien, Joan Susan *lawyer, educator*
Segale, Althea Frances *music educator*

Fayetteville
Hadyk-Wepf, Sonia Margaret *artist, real estate manager*

Feura Bush
Lawson, Nancy Louise *computer scientist, educator*

Flushing
Baik-Han, Won H. *pediatrician, educator, consultant*
Bezrod, Norma R. *artist*
Brooks, Helene Margaret *editorial consultant*
Carlson, Cynthia Joanne *artist, educator*
Electra, Carmen *actress*
Flechner, Roberta Fay *graphic designer*
Givens, Janet Eaton *writer*
Gomez, Pastora *medical/surgical nurse*
Li, Qin *television anchor, reporter, director, producer*
Malow-Iroff, Micheline Susan *psychologist, educator*
Raines, Judi Belle *language educator, historian*
Ranald, Margaret Loftus *English literature educator, author*
Roberts, Kathleen Joy Doty *secondary school educator*
Rosen-Supnick, Elaine Renee *physical therapist*
Sanborn, Anna Lucille *pension and insurance consultant*
Schnall, Edith Lea *microbiologist, educator*
Schwartz, Estar Alma *lawyer*
Smith-Campbell, Charmaine *secondary school educator*
Unsal-Tunay, Nuran *geological engineer, researcher*
Vigorito, Rosaria Susanna *law librarian, adult education educator, lawyer, artist*
Yeo, Kim Eng *artist*
Zinnes, Harriet Fich *poet, retired English educator, literary and art critic, writer*

Forest Hills
Alsapiedi, Consuelo Veronica *psychoanalytic psychotherapist, consultant*
Dessylas, Ann Atsaves *human resources and office management executive*
Flowers, Cynthia *investment company executive*
Kra, Pauline Skornicki *French language educator*
Mac Innes, Virginia Lewis *real estate broker*
Prager, Alice Heinecke *music company executive*
Torrence-Thompson, Juanita Lee *public relations executive*

Fort Covington
Dumas, Charlene Anne *music educator*

Frankfort
Conigilaro, Phyllis Ann *retired elementary education educator*

Franklin Square
Bergen, Jeannine Evelyn *psychologist*

Fredonia
Royal, Susan *classical musician, music educator*
Smith, Claire Laremont *language educator*
Strada, Christina Bryson *retired humanities educator, librarian*

Freeport
Faraci, Diana *social worker, department chairman*
Martorana, Barbara Joan *secondary school educator*

Fresh Meadows
Jackson, Rhonda *telecommunications professional, poet*
Soto Baltrusitis, Arleane *financial analyst/benefits compensation analyst*
Yang, Susan Xia *business consultant, massage therapist*

Garden City
Berka, Marianne Guthrie *health and physical education educator*
Caputo, Kathryn Mary *paralegal*
Doucette, Mary-Alyce *computer company executive*
Healy, Margaret Mary *retail marketing executive*
Jason, Kathrine *language educator, writer*
Korshak, Yvonne *art historian*
O'Dwyer, Joan *judge*
Podwall, Kathryn Stanley *biology educator*
Slater, Nancy Lynne *special education educator, marketing professional, consultant*
Steil, Janice M. *social psychology educator*
Weess, Pamela R. *financial services representative*

Geneseo
Myers, Helen Marie *education educator, choreographer*

Geneva
Harkness, Mabel Gleason *retired librarian*
Lucas, Karen *music educator*

Glen Head
Heath-Psyd, Pamela B. Wasserman *psychologist*

Glens Falls
Little, Elizabeth O'Connor *state legislator*
Tucker, Bernadine *patient registrar*

Gouverneur
Scozzafava, Dede *state representative*
Stacy, Trudy L. *elementary school educator*

Grahamsville
McInerney, Ellen Eustis *management consultant*

Grand Island
DiVita, Angela Marie *music educator*
Lokken, Carolyn Grace *music educator*

Great Neck
Aronson, Margaret Rupp *school psychologist*
Blumberg, Barbara Salmanson (Mrs. Arnold G. Blumberg) *retired state housing official, housing consultant*
Fiel, Maxine Lucille *journalist, behavior analyst, educator*
Gross, Lillian *psychiatrist, educator*
Helstein, Ivy Rae *communications executive, psychotherapist, writer*
Hurwitz, Johanna (Johanna Frank) *writer*
Mayer, Susan Lee *nurse, educator*
Roth, Gladys Thompson *retired early childhood and special education educator*
Schussheim, Joan Lana *mathematics educator*
Sears, Victoria Conason *psychiatrist*
Seidler, Doris *artist*
Seo, Christine C. *real estate broker*
Soleymani, Nancy *psychologist, researcher*
Sterling, Lorraine *volunteer*
Strickon, Linda Meltzer *music educator*

Greenlawn
Starost, Diane Joan *music educator*

Greenport
Richland, Lisa *library director*

Greenvale
Westermann-Cicio, Mary Louise *academic administrator, library studies educator*

Greenwich
Johnson-Siebold, Judith Eloise *minister*

Guilderland
Escobar, Deborah Ann *gifted and talented education educator*

Halesite
Grey-Bethiel, Shari *artist, sculptress, jewelry designer*

Hamburg
Ortolano, Mary Kay *music educator*

Hamilton
Chopp, Rebecca S. *university president*
Pinchin, Jane *literature educator*
Staley, Lynn *English education*

Hartsdale
Fishman, Helene Beth *social worker*
Greenawalt, Peggy Freed Tomarkin *advertising executive*
McMann, Edith Brozak *performance artist, visual artist*

Hastings On Hudson
Barolini, Helen *writer, translator, educator*
Benedis, Sheila Meyer *sculptor*
Cooper, Doris Jean *market research executive*
Del Duca, Rita *language educator*
Stillman, Jeanne Betsock *public health administrator, consultant*

Hauppauge
Kruger, Frances Petronelle *lawyer*
Zuckerman, Dorothy Ann *elementary school educator*

Hempstead
Ancrum, Cheryl Denise *dentist*
Barlow, Linda *social services administrator, trainer*
Freese, Melanie Louise *librarian, educator, assistant dean*
Graffeo, Mary Thérèse *music educator, performer*
McPhee, Martha *literature educator*
Raney, Carolyn E. *educational consultant*
Roble, Carole Marcia *accountant*
Weiss, Sara C. *religious organization administrator*
Zagano, Phyllis *religious studies educator*

Herkimer
Martin, Lorraine B. *humanities educator*

Heuvelton
Ponko, Vera *artist, museum intrepreter*

Hewlett
Wolff, Eleanor Blunk *actress*

Hicksville
Ballweg, Sallyanne K. *finance company executive*
Kronowitz, Pamela Renee *music educator*
Reedy, Catherine Irene *elementary school educator*
Waxberg, Emily Steinhardt *educator*

Highland
Ratick, Randie H. *music educator, elementary school educator*

Highland Mills
Da Silva, Ann Marie Katherine *psychotherapist, consultant*

Hillsdale
Kersten, Mary Lou *real estate broker*

Holbrook
Watkins, Linda Theresa *educational researcher*

Holley
Ruck, Rosemarie Ulissa *retired social worker, freelance/self-employed writer*

Hollis
Stephens, B. Consuela *minister, consultant*

Honeoye
Kates, Cheryl L. *legal nursing consultant*

Hopewell Junction
Conti, AnnaLee Cousart *minister, writer*
Cznarty, Donna Mae *secondary school educator*

Hornell
Swift, Katharine I. *cytotechnologist*

Horseheads
Andrake, Nancy Carolyn *secondary school educator*

Houghton
Machamer, Cynthia G. *editor, writer*

Howard Beach
Chwalek, Constance *real estate broker, mortgage broker*
Powell, Jeanne Marie *accountant*

Hudson
Miner, Jacqueline *political consultant*
Vile, Sandra Jane *leadership training educator*

Huntington
German, June Resnick *lawyer*
Maglione, Lili *artist, consultant*
Munson, Nancy K. *lawyer*
Roberts, Elizabeth Anne Stephens *educational consultant*
Shih, Patricia Alice *musician, writer, artist*
Vale, Margo Rose *physician*

Huntington Station
Cannistraci, Diane Frances *sales account executive*
Devlin, Jean Theresa *education educator, storyteller*
Smith, Sharon Elaine *music educator*
Williams, Una Joyce *psychiatric social worker*
Yacobian, Sonia Simone *metals company executive*

Hurley
Darrow, Marianne Rosina *speech pathology/audiology services professional, editor, writer*
Davila, Elisa *language educator, literature educator*
Mazzilli, Roslyn *sculptor*
Petruski, Jennifer Andrea *speech and language pathologist*

Hurleyville
Hilfstein, Erna *science historian, educator*

Hyde Park
Beckmann, Kathleen Ann *music educator*
Blackman, Drusilla Denise *dean*
Rider, Kathleen Mary *dietician*

Ilion
Edwards, Christine Utley *social services administrator, consultant*
Nemyier, Margaret Gertrude *sales executive*

Inwood
Neumann, Tammy Leigh *speech pathology/audiology services professional*
Soffer, Grace Florey *retired elementary school educator, artist*

Irvington
Rainer, Renata Urbach *artist, photographer, educator*

Island Park
Pal, Cheryl Lynn *music teacher*

Islip Terrace
Miller, Alyson Rebecca *school psychologist*

Ithaca
Arquit, Nora Harris *retired music educator, writer*
Assie-Lumumba, N'Dri T. *Africana studies educator*
Beneria, Lourdes *economist, educator*
Benson, A. LeGrace Gupton *humanities educator, researcher*
Brazell, Karen Woodard *Japanese literature educator*
Colby-Hall, Alice Mary *Romance studies educator*
Cope, Caroline Bancroft *special education educator*
Cornish, Elizabeth Turverey *stockbroker*
DeLaurentis, Louise Budde *writer*
Firebaugh, Francille Maloch *university official*
Garrison, Elizabeth Jane *artist*
Germain, Claire Madeleine *law librarian, educator, lawyer*
Grainger, Mary Maxon *civic volunteer*
Hammond, Jane Laura *retired law librarian, lawyer*
Henderson, Cynthia Anne *theater educator, actress*
Howley, Teresa Moorehouse *artist*
Kane, Marilyn A. *occupational therapist, educator*
Lifton, Barbara *state legislator, secondary school educator*
Lurie, Alison *writer*
Martin, Carolyn A. (Biddy Martin) *provost*
McKinney, Cynthia Ann *former congresswoman*
Mueller, Betty Jeanne *social work educator*
Nasrallah, June *plant pathologist, department chairman*
Norton, Mary Beth *history educator, writer*

Park, Dorothy Goodwin Dent (Mrs. Roy Hampton Park) *broadcast executive, publishing executive*
Pelto, Gretel H. *nutritional anthropologist, educator*
Perry, Margaret *librarian, writer*
Radzinowicz, Mary Ann *language educator*
Rasmussen, Kathleen Maher *nutritional sciences educator*
Seibert, Mary Lee *college official*
Seraji-Bozorgzad, Nasrine *architecture educator*
Stycos, Maria Nowakowska *adult education educator*
Varona-Lacey, Gladys María *language educator*
Wavle, Elizabeth Margaret *college official*
Whitaker, Susanne Kanis *veterinary medical librarian*
Williams, Peggy Ryan *academic administrator*

Jackson Heights
Chang, Lydia Liang-Hwa *social worker, educator*
Fischbarg, Zulema F. *pediatrician, educator*
Gall, Lenore Rosalie *educational administrator*
Stevenson, Amanda (Sandy Stevens) *librettist, composer, document examiner*

Jamaica
Becker, Nancy Jane *information science educator*
Brockway, Laurie Sue *editor, journalist, author, minister*
Cocchiarelli, Maria *artist, educator*
Davis-Jerome, Eileen George *principal*
Ekbatani, Glayol *language educator, director, writer*
Faust, Naomi Flowe *education educator*
Feldman, Arlene Butler *aviation industry executive*
Geffner, Donna Sue *speech pathology/audiology services professional, audiologist, educator*
Isaac-Emmons, Merlyn Maria *religious studies educator, academic administrator*
Jawin, Ann Juliano *human resource specialist*
Jones, Cynthia Teresa Clarke *artist*
Kahn, Faith-Hope *nurse, administrator, author*
Malewitz, Joan *elementary school educator, library and information scientist*
Mithaug, Deirdre Kristen *special education educator, researcher*
Moskowitz, Randi Zucker *nurse*
Vellucci, Sherry Lynn *library and information science educator*

Jamestown
Keefer, Judith E. *elementary school educator*
Pitt, Ruth Anne *school system administrator, music education*
Reale, Sara Jane *museum education director*
Thompson, Birgit Dolores *civic worker, writer*

Jamesville
DeCrow, Karen *lawyer, writer, educator*

Jeffersonville
Harms, Elizabeth Louise *artist*
Hoering, Helen G. *elementary school educator*

Jericho
Auster, Ellen *finance company executive*
Beal, Carol Ann *lawyer*
Dore, Kathleen A. *broadcast executive*

Johnstown
Rumrill Zullo, Patricia Robbin *music educator*

Katonah
Brownlee, Delphine *actress, musician*

Kew Gardens
Aldea, Patricia *architect*
Wesley, Irma R. *art historian, educator*

Kingston
Ione, Carole *psychotherapist, writer, playwright, director*
Johnson, Marie-Louise Tully *dermatologist, educator*

Lagrangeville
Davis, Mary Lou *secondary school educator*

Lake George
Nellis, Nora LaJoy *special education educator, writer*

Lake Placid
Bakken, Jill *Olympic athlete*
Gale, Tristan *Olympic athlete*
Rickard, Anne Colton *art educator, artist*

Lakewood
McConnon, Virginia Fix *dietician*

Lancaster
Kappan, Sandra Jean *elementary school educator*
Meides, Holly Sue *music educator*

Larchmont
Greenwald, Carol Schiro *professional services marketing research executive*
Hinerfeld, Ruth G. *civic organization executive*
Swire, Edith Wypler *music educator, musician, violist, violinist*

Latham
Caruso, Aileen Smith *managed care consultant*
LeRoy, Beth Seperack *jazz musician, piano teacher*

Lattingtown
Burke-Spence, Bonnie *psychologist, social worker, alcohol/drug abuse services professional*

Lawrence
Cohen, Elana Ungar *psychotherapist, researcher, consultant*

Okos, Mildred *city manager*

Lewiston
Askins, Nancy Ellen Paulsen *training and organizational development professional*
Laurie, Margaret Sanders *retired English educator*
LoTempio, Julia Matild *retired accountant*
Moraca-Sawicki, Anne Marie *oncology nurse*

Lindenhurst
Boltz, Mary Ann *aerospace materials company executive, travel agency executive*
Sanna, Catherine Lee *special education educator*

Lisbon
Walsh, Lisa J. *elementary school educator*

Little Neck
Overton, Rosilyn Gay Hoffman *financial services executive*

Liverpool
Egan, Marsha Christine *school psychologist*

Lockport
Ragusa, Karen Ann *music educator*

Locust Valley
Bentel, Carol Rusche *architect*
Zulch, Joan Carolyn *retired medical publishing company executive*

Long Beach
Thompson, Dorothy Barnard *elementary school educator*

Long Island City
DiGiovanni, Eleanor Elma *scaffold installation company executive*
Donneson, Seena Sand *artist*
Goldstein, Katherine H. *technology educator, computer consultant*
Heiss, Alanna *museum director*
Hoffman, Merle Holly *political activist, social psychologist, writer*
Lieberman, Janet Elaine *academic administrator*
Lutz, Karen *finance company executive*
Markus, Maura *bank executive*
Munro, Roxie Jean *artist, educator, illustrator, writer*
Popian, Lucia *artist*
Rychlak, Bonnie Lee *artist, museum curator*

Loudonville
Jonquières, Lynne *travel agent*

Lowville
Colton, Bonnie Myers *writer, folklorist*

Lynbrook
Cline, Starr *elementary school educator, educator*

Macedon
Moore, Shanna La'Von *chemical company executive*

Mahopac
Castronovo, Bernadine Marro *music educator*
Havens, Cheryl Ciano *music educator*
Talbot, Deborah Ann *assistant principal*
Vigliotti, Patricia Noreen *welder, sculptor*

Malverne
Alesse, Judith *special education educator*
Ryan, Suzanne Irene *nursing educator*

Mamaroneck
Carty, Mary Ellen *psychologist*
Kaneko-Adams, Naoko *business executive*
Merskey-Zeger, Marie Gertrude Fine *retired librarian*

Manhasset
Croce, Anne Lally *nurse, commissioner*
Foley, Cornelia MacIntyre *retired artist*
Fountain, Karen Schueler *physician*
Galante, Ann Muriel *municipal official*
Montane, Fran *poet, film producer*
Seftel, Donna Selene *architect*
Spetsieris, Phoebe George *physicist, application developer, researcher*

Manlius
Brophy, Mary O'Reilly *environmental scientist*
Gibson, Judith W. *clinical therapist*
Gray, Judith A. *retired school librarian, educator*
Harriff, Suzanna Elizabeth (Bahner) *advertising consultant*
Koch, Catherine Ann *music educator, musician*

Marcellus
Corrigan-Syrocki, Patricia Ann *art educator*

Maryknoll
Guerrieri, Sister Antonia Maria, Arcangiolina Veronica *sister*

Massapequa
Batt, Alyse Schwartz *technical officer*
Goldberg, Beth Sheba *artist, educator, art therapist*
Kappenberg, Marilyn Kascius *library director*
Pearl, Alison B. *music educator*
Turk, Elizabeth Ann *music educator*

Mattituck
Berman, Patricia Karatsis *arts specialist*

Medford
Klement, Diane *educational assistant*

Melville
Basile, Sheila *secondary education educator, consultant*
Carter, Sylvia *journalist*

Christiansen, Lauri A. *marketing professional*
Garrett, Laurie *science correspondent*
Krenek, Debby *newspaper editor*
Noguere, Suzanne *publishing manager, poet*
Ponzi Kay, Marylou *human resources specialist*
Richards, Carol Ann Rubright *editor, columnist*
Saul, Stephanie *journalist*
Sobol, Elise Schwarcz *music educator*
Webber, Pamela D. *information technology executive*

Merrick
Beckman, Judith Kalb *financial counselor and planner, educator, writer*
Fleischman, Francine D. *elementary school educator*
Harrison, Marjorie Freeman *secondary education educator, librarian*

Mexico
Walters, Natalie A. *music educator*

Middle Island
Andrews, Gaylen *measurable response public relations expert*
Crowder, Lillie Mae Brown *retired architectural engineer*

Middle Village
Heyd, Eva *photographer*

Middleburgh
Lennon, Amy Jo *elementary school educator, principal*

Middletown
Bedell, Barbara Lee *journalist*
D'Agostino, Gloria M. *secondary school educator*
McCord, Jean Ellen *secondary art educator, coach*
Moore, Virginia Lee Smith *elementary school educator*

Millbrook
Flexner, Josephine Moncure *musician, educator*
Hall, Penelope Coker *writer, magazine editor*

Miller Place
Callahan, Jean M. *personnel administrator*

Millerton
Paretsky, Sara N. *writer*

Millwood
Durst, Carol Goldsmith *food studies educator*

Mineola
Hammer, Deborah Marie *librarian, paralegal*
Lelyveld, Gail Annick *actress*
Shaheen Alesi, Barbara *lawyer*
Tankoos, Sandra Maxine *court reporting services executive*

Monroe
Centeno-Dainty, Sonia Margarita *artist*
Gocek, Matilda Arkenbout (Mrs. John A. Gocek) *librarian*

Montauk
Hartsough, Cheryl Marie *nutritionist, director*

Moravia
Welch, Joan Minde *elementary school educator*

Morrisville
Cleland, Gladys Lee *university administrator, adult education educator*
Weiler, Angela M. *librarian, writer*

Mount Kisco
Bithoney, Carmen C. D'Amborsio *artistic director*
Hodara, Susan Mina *writer*
Keesee, Patricia Hartford *volunteer*

Mount Vernon
Griffith, Katherine Scott *librarian*

Narrowsburg
Krause, Gloria Rose *music educator*

Nesconset
Mac Millan, Janet Susan *elementary school educator, education educator*

New City
Samimi, Sandra *lawyer*

New Hampton
Sinnard, Elaine Janice *painter, sculptor*

New Hartford
Chapin, Mary Q. *television personality, arbitrator, mediator, writer, performing artist*
Dyman, Kathleen Eleanor *medical association administrator*
Paciello, Linda Katherine *psychologist*

New Hyde Park
Armstrong, Denise Grace *medical association administrator*
Seltzer, Vicki Lynn *obstetrician, gynecologist*

New Paltz
Davidson, Thyra *artist, sculptor*
Emanuel-Smith, Robin Lesley *special education educator*
Goodell, Kathy Susan *artist, educator*
Harris, Kristine *historian, educator*
Irvine, Rose Loretta Abernethy *retired communications educator, consultant*
Kahl, Mary L(ouise) *communication educator*
Pine, Patricia Palmer *aging services administrator*
Upton, Barbara *hypnotherapist, small business owner*

New Rochelle
Adato, Linda Joy *artist, educator*
Berlage, Gai Ingham *sociologist, educator*
Black, Page Morton *civic worker*
Cutney, Barbara Ann *philosophy educator*
Fitch, Nancy Elizabeth *historian, educator*
Golub, Sharon Bramson *psychologist, educator*
Goodman, Joan Frances *avionics manufacturing executive*
Grimes, Tresmaine Judith Rubain *psychology educator*
Miller, Rita *personnel consultant, diecasting company executive*
Reddington, Mary Jane *retired secondary school educator*
St. John, Patricia Anne *art educator*
Schreibman, Thelma Rabinowitz *psychotherapist, educator*
Tassone, Gelsomina (Gessie Tassone) *metal processing executive*

New Windsor
Calhoun, Nancy *state legislator*
Saunders, Joanne Hines *elementary school educator*

New York
Abate, Catherine M. *former state senator*
Abella, Mercedes *occupational therapist*
Abish, Cecile *artist*
Abrams, Roz *newscaster*
Abramson, Jill *newspaper publishing executive*
Abramson, Sara Jane *radiologist, educator*
Ackerman, Valerie B. *sports association executive*
Adams, Cindy *journalist*
Adler, Margot Susanna *journalist, radio producer*
Adri, (Adri Steckling Coen) *fashion designer*
Agard, Emma Estornel *psychotherapist*
Aguilera, Christina *vocalist*
Ahrendts, Angela *apparel executive*
Ahrens, Lynn *lyricist*
Aigen, Betsy Paula *psychotherapist*
Albee, Gloria *playwright*
Alenikoff, Frances *choreographer, performer, writer, dancer, artist*
Alex, Paula Ann *foundation administrator*
Alexander, Jane *actress, former federal agency administrator, producer, author, theater educator*
Allen, Alice *communications and marketing executive*
Allen, Betty (Mrs. Ritten Edward Lee III) *mezzo-soprano*
Alter, Eleanor Breitel *lawyer*
Altfest, Karen Caplan *diversified financial services company executive, director*
Altschul, Serena *newscaster*
Altschuler, Marjorie *advertising executive*
Alvarez, Julia *writer*
Amenta, Joyce Ann *United Nations executive*
Amster, Linda Evelyn *newspaper executive, consultant*
Ananiashvili, Nina *ballerina*
Andersen, Susan Marie *political scientist, educator, researcher, clinician, policy advisor*
Andora, Suzanne E. *communications company executive*
Angelo, Larian *economist*
Anthony, Michele *entertainment executive*
Antman, Karen *oncologist*
Antonacci, Lori (Loretta Marie Antonacci) *marketing executive, consultant*
Appel, Gloria *advertising executive*
Appel, Marsha Ceil *association executive*
Appelbaum, Ann Harriet *lawyer*
Apter, Emily *language educator*
Arlen, Jennifer Hall *law educator*
Armitage, Karole *dancer*
Arms, Anneli (Anna Elizabeth Arms) *artist, educator*
Arndt, Carmen Gloria *secondary school educator*
Arnot-Heaney, Susan Eileen *not-for-profit fundraiser*
Arnow, Pat *freelance writer, editor, photographer*
Aronson, Esther Leah *retired foundation administrator, psychotherapist*
Arvio, Sarah *poet*
Arystanbekova, Akmaral Khaidarovna *diplomat*
Asakawa, Takako *dancer, dance teacher, director, choreographer*
Ash, Jennifer Gertrude *writer, editor*
Ashdown, Marie Matranga (Mrs. Cecil Spanton Ashdown Jr.) *writer, educator, lecturer, cultural organization administrator*
Ashley, Elizabeth *actress*
Ashton, Dore *writer, educator*
Atkinson, Holly Gail *physician, journalist, business executive, author, lecturer, human rights activist*
Atwood, Margaret Eleanor *writer*
Augustine, Cynthia H. *lawyer*
Axthelm, Nancy *advertising executive*
Azrielant, Aya *jewelry manufacturing executive*
Bacall, Lauren *actress*
Bacher, Judith St. George *executive search consultant*
Bachner, Barbara LaVerdiere *artist*
Bachrach, Nancy *advertising executive*
Backstedt, Roseanne Joan *artist*
Bacon, Chantal *retail executive*
Baderinwa, Sade *newscaster*
Badu, Erykah *singer*
Bahr, Lauren S. *publishing company executive*
Bailey, Darlyne *social worker, educator*
Bailey, Janet Dee *publishing company executive*
Bains, Leslie Elizabeth *banker*
Baird, Penny Drue *interior designer*
Baird, Zoë *foundation president, lawyer*
Baker, Elizabeth Calhoun *magazine editor*
Balaban, Vivian *librarian, elementary school educator*
Balaz, Beverly Ann *publishing executive*
Balogh, Mary *writer*
Balter, Bernice *religious organization administrator*
Bancel, Marilyn *fund raising management consultant*
Bancroft, Margaret Armstrong *lawyer*
Banfield, Ashleigh Dennistoun *news correspondent*
Banks, Tyra *model, actress*
Baquero, Lynda *newscaster, reporter*
Baranauckas, Carla May *journalist*
Baranski, Joan Sullivan *publisher*
Barbosa, Shameka Brown *copywriter*
Barbour, Celia *editor*
Bardach, Joan Lucile *clinical psychologist*
Bardin, Mary Beth *telecommunications company executive*
Barker, Barbara Ann *ophthalmologist*
Barker, Sylvia Margaret *nurse*
Barlow, Barbara Ann *surgeon*
Barnao, Laura *management assistant*
Barnes, Jhane Elizabeth *fashion design company executive, designer*
Barnett, Amy DuBois *editor-in-chief*
Barnett, Vivian Endicott *curator*
Barnum, Barbara Stevens *writer, retired nursing educator*
Barolini, Teodolinda *literary critic*
Baron, Sheri *advertising agency executive*
Barrett, Elizabeth Ann Manhart *nursing educator, psychotherapist, consultant*
Barrio, Soledad *dancer*
Barrish, Carol Lampert *psychologist*
Barry, Nancy Marie *bank executive*
Bartoli, Cecilia *soprano*
Barton, Alice *physician, educator*
Bartow, Diane Grace *marketing and sales executive*
Barzilay, Judith Morgenstern *federal judge*
Basquin, Mary Smyth (Kit Basquin) *museum administrator*
Bastianich, Lidia Matticchio *chef, food service executive*
Battiste, Janice Louise *editor, writer*
Battle, Pat *reporter*
Batts, Deborah A. *judge*
Bauer, Marion Dane *writer*
Bauer, Tricia *publishing executive, writer*
Bauman, Susan *communications executive*
Bawden, Nina (Mary Bawden) *author*
Beattie, Ann *writer*
Beausoleil, Doris Mae *federal agency housing specialist*
Becker, Barbara Lynn *lawyer*
Becker, Helane Renée *securities analyst, financial executive*
Beerbower, Cynthia Gibson *lawyer*
Begley, Sharon Lynn *journalist*
Behar, Joy *television personality*
Beinecke, Candace Krugman *lawyer*
Belag, Andrea Susan *artist*
Bel Geddes, Joan *writer*
Bellamy, Carol *international organization executive*
Belloni, Alessandra *artistic director*
Bemis, Mary Ferguson *magazine editor*
Bender, Judith *journalist, editor*
Benedek, Melinda *television executive*
Benshoof, Janet Lee *lawyer, association executive*
Berger, Pearl *library director*
Bergstrom, Elaine *novelist*
Berkery, Rosemary T. *lawyer, investment company executive*
Berkowitz, Susan J. *investment banking executive*
Berman, Ariane R. *artist*
Berman, Carol Wendy *psychiatrist*
Berman, Phyllis Ocean *adult education educator*
Berman, Rachel *dancer*
Berner, Mary *publisher*
Bernstein, Bonnie *sportscaster*
Bernstein, Phyllis J. *financial consultant*
Berresford, Susan Vail *philanthropic foundation executive*
Berry, Gail W. *psychiatrist, educator*
Bertini, Catherine Ann *international organization official*
Beshar, Christine *lawyer*
Betanzos, Amalia V. *social services administrator*
Beverley, Cordia Luvonne *gastroenterologist*
Beyer, Lisa *journalist*
Beyoncé, (Beyoncé Giselle Knowles) *vocalist*
Bibliowicz, Jessica M. *financial analyst*
Biedel, Alexis *actress*
Bird, Mary Lynne Miller *professional society administrator*
Bird, Sharlene *clinical psychologist*
Birnbaum, Sheila L. *lawyer, educator*
Birstein, Ann *writer, educator*
Bisbee, Joyce Evelyn *utility company manager, retired*
Bischoff, Theresa A. *not-for-profit association administrator, former medical center executive*
Bishop, Susan Katharine *executive search company executive*
Bishopric, Susan Ehrlich *public relations executive*
Black, Barbara Aronstein *legal history educator*
Black, Carole *broadcast executive*
Black, Cathleen Prunty *publishing executive*
Black, Shawn Morgado *dancer*
Blackman, Cindy *musician, composer*
Blake, Grace *cultural organization administrator*
Blalock, Sherrill *investment advisor*
Blanchard, Kimberly Staggers *lawyer, educator*
Blazejowski, Carol A. *professional sports team executive, retired professional basketball player*
Blige, Mary Jane *recording artist*
Block, Francesca Lia *writer*
Bloomgarden, Kathy Finn *public relations executive*
Blum, Barbara B. *foundation administrator*
Blume, Judy *author*
Blumkin, Linda Ruth *lawyer*
Blythe, Christina Josephine *business analyst, consultant*
Bonfante, Larissa *classics educator*
Bonino, Fernanda *art dealer*
Booth, Barbara Ribman *civic worker*
Booth, Margaret A(nn) *communications company executive*
Booth, Tami *editor*
Borhi, Carol *data processing executive, finance company executive*
Borree, Yvonne *dancer*
Boskey, Adele Ludin *biochemistry educator, researcher*
Boston, Gretha *actress, vocalist*
Boufford, Jo Ivey *health and human services administrator*
Bourgeois, Louise *sculptor*
Bowden, Sally Ann *choreographer, educator, dancer*
Bowers, Patricia Eleanor Fritz *economist*
Bowie, Angie *accounting company official*
Boylan, Elizabeth Shippee *academic administrator, biologist, educator*
Braden, Martha Brooke *concert pianist, educator*
Bradford, Barbara Taylor *writer, journalist*
Bradshaw, Dove *artist*
Brady, Adelaide Burks *public relations agency executive, giftware catalog executive*
Brant, Sandra J. *magazine publisher*
Bratten, Millie Martini *editor-in-chief*
Braudy, Susan Orr *writer*
Bravo, Dominique *lawyer*
Braxton, Toni *popular musician*
Breakstone, Kay Louise *public relations executive*
Brenner, Beth Fuchs *publishing executive*
Breslow, Esther May Greenberg *biochemistry educator, researcher*
Bressman, Susan Berliner *health facility administrator*
Brett, Nancy Heléne *artist*
Brewer, Karen *librarian*
Bricard, Yolanda Borras *music educator, music program administrator*
Brightman, Sarah *singer, actress*
Brinkley, Christie *model, spokesperson, designer*
Brinson, Monica E. *pharmaceutical sales representative*
Brisman, Jennifer *event planning executive*
Bristor, Katherine M. *lawyer*
Bristow, Louise Alice *mental health nurse*
Britton, Monica Ena Louise *community health nurse, public health nurse*
Britz Lotti, Diane Edward *investment company executive*
Brodie-Baldwin, Helen Sylvia *retired college and human services administrator*
Brody, Jane Ellen *journalist, researcher*
Brooks, Anita Helen *public relations executive*
Brooks, Laurie *playwright, educator*
Brothers, Joyce Diane *television personality, psychologist*
Browar, Lisa Muriel *librarian*
Brown, Bobbi *cosmetics executive*
Brown, Campbell *commentator*
Brown, Carolyn Rice *dancer, choreographer, writer, filmmaker*
Brown, Helen Gurley *editor, writer*
Brown, Joyce F. *academic administrator*
Brown, Lyn *newscaster*
Brown, Renee *sports association executive*
Brown, Rita Mae *writer*
Brown, Tina *journalist, television personality*
Brown, Trisha *dancer*
Brown, Tyese Andrea *music educator*
Browne, Joy *psychologist, radio personality*
Brownell, Patricia Jane *social worker, educator*
Browning, Candace *corporate financial executive*
Brownmiller, Susan *author, feminist activist*
Bruneau, Lise *actor*
Buchanan, Edna *journalist*
Buchwald, Naomi Reice *judge*
Buckley, Priscilla Langford *magazine editor*
Buckley, Susan *lawyer*
Buckley, Virginia Laura *editor*
Bucolo, Gail Ann *biotechnologist*
Bugge, Carole Elizabeth *writer, actress*
Bujold, Lois McMaster *writer*
Bull, Helen May *artist*
Bumbry, Grace *soprano*
Burbank, Jane Richardson *language educator*
Burgman, Dierdre Ann *lawyer*
Burkhardt, Ann *occupational therapist, clinical educator*
Burns, Red *academic administrator*
Burrell, Pamela *actress*
Bush, Lauren *model*
Bushnell, Candance *columnist, writer*
Busquet, Anne M. *Internet company executive*
Bussert, Meg *actress, educator*
Butler, Kerry *actress*
Butte, Amy S. *securities trader*
Buttner, Jean Bernhard *diversified financial services company executive*
Byer, Diana *performing arts company executive*
Cafiero, Jennifer Annette *academic administrator, educator*
Cahan, Cora *not-for-profit developer*
Cahill, Catherine M. *orchestra executive*
Cairns, Anne Marie *public relations executive*
Calabrese, Rosalie Sue *management consultant, writer*
Calame, Kathryn Lee *microbiologist, educator*
Caldwell, Zoe *actress, film director*
Calisher, Hortense (Mrs. Curtis Harnack) *writer*
Calvi, Mary *reporter*
Campagnolo, Ann-Casey *retail executive*
Campbell, Judith E. *retired insurance company executive*
Campbell, Mary Schmidt *dean*
Campbell, Naomi *model*
Cantor, Linda C. *retired history educator*
Cantrell, Lana *actress, lawyer, singer*
Caploe, Roberta *magazine editor*
Capriati, Jennifer Maria *professional tennis player*
Capucilli, Terese *performing company executive*
Caputo, Lisa M. *finance company executive*
Carlson, P(atricia) M(cElroy) *writer*
Caroff, Phyllis M. *social work educator*

Graves, Hillary *marketing professional*
Gray, Deborah Dolia *business writing consultant*
Gray, Lois Spier *labor relations educator, consultant*
Green, Barbara Strawn *psychotherapist*
Green, Jean Hess *psychotherapist*
Greene, Adele S. *management consultant*
Greene Oster, Selmaree *medical anthropologist, researcher*
Greenfield, Rachel *magazine executive*
Greenman, Paula S. *lawyer*
Greenwald, Sheila Ellen *writer, illustrator*
Griffith, Nicola *writer*
Griffiths, Sylvia Preston *physician, educator*
Grimes, Suzanne *publishing executive*
Grocholski, Basia (Barbara) G. *art director*
Groh, Jennifer Calfa *law librarian*
Gross, Amy *publishing executive*
Gross, Karen Charal *lawyer*
Grossman, Melanie *dermatologist*
Grossman, Nancy *artist*
Grubin, Sharon E. *lawyer*
Grunwald, Ilana Shlomit *psychologist*
Guerra, Juanita Patricia *psychologist, educator*
Guerrero, Lisa (Lisa Guerrero-Coles) *sports reporter*
Guillermoprieto, Alma *journalist, non-fiction writer*
Gumpert, Lynn *gallery director*
Gund, Agnes *former art museum administrator*
Gusoff, Carolyn *reporter*
Gustafson, Judith *federal association administrator*
Habachy, Suzan Salwa Saba *development economist, non profit administrator*
Haddad, Colleen *institutional marketing executive*
Hadden, Margaret (Peggy Hadden) *writer*
Hadley, Leila Eliott-Burton (Mrs. Henry Luce III) *writer*
Haegele, Patricia *publishing executive*
Hafner, Genevieve *photographer*
Haggerty, Rosanne *entrepreneur*
Halberstam, Malvina *law educator, lawyer*
Hall, Lisa G. *broadcast executive, lawyer*
Hall, Nancy Christensen *publishing company executive, author, editor*
Hallingby, Jo Davis *lawyer, arbitrator*
Halsband, Frances *architect*
Hamilton, Jane *writer*
Hamilton, Linda Helen *clinical psychologist*
Hammond, Lou Rena Charlotte *public relations executive*
Hamoy, Carol *artist*
Hampton, Kym *professional basketball player*
Hamura, Kaori *artist*
Hanauer, Linda *venture capitalist*
Hand, Joni Marie *art educator*
Hann, Lucy Ellen *radiologist*
Hannigan, Pamela S. *economist, educator*
Hanson, Jane *newscaster*
Hanson, Jean Elizabeth *lawyer*
Hanson, Paula *sports association executive*
Harbutt, Sarah *photographer, director*
Hardwick, Elizabeth *writer*
Hargitay, Mariska *actress*
Hariri, Gisue *architect, educator*
Harley, Naomi Hallden *radiation specialist, environmental medicine educator*
Harlow, Ruth *lawyer*
Harmon, Jane *producer*
Harrington, E.B. *art dealer*
Harris, Anne M. *interior designer, educator*
Harris, Carla Ann *investment company executive*
Harris, Harriet *actress*
Harris, Julie (Julie Ann Harris) *actress*
Harris, Katherine Safford *speech and hearing educator*
Harris, Patricia E. *deputy mayor*
Harrison, Judith Anne *human resources executive*
Hart, Karen Ann *advertising executive*
Hart, Kitty Carlisle *arts administrator*
Hartman, Joan Edna *English educator*
Harvey, Julie L. *artist*
Haskell, Barbara *curator*
Hastings, Deborah *bass guitarist*
Hatfield, Juliana *vocalist*
Haubegger, Christy *media consultant, publishing executive*
Hauck, Marguerite Hall *broadcast executive*
Haukeness, Helen *journalist, writer*
Hauser, Joyce Roberta *marketing professional*
Hauser, Rita Eleanore Abrams *lawyer*
Hawkins, Katherine Ann *hematologist, lawyer*
Hayes, Constance J. *pediatric cardiologist*
Hayes, Joyce Merriweather *secondary school educator*
Hayes, Nancy Eveylin *anthropologist, geographer, researcher*
Hayman, Linda C. *lawyer*
Hays, Kathleen *news correspondent*
Hays, Sorrel (Doris) *composer*
Hazzard, Shirley *author*
Head, Elizabeth *lawyer*
Heck, Melissa Eileen *speech pathology/audiology services professional*
Heckel, Sally *independent filmmaker*
Helmsley, Leona Mindy *hotel executive*
Henderson, Maxine Olive Book (Mrs. William Henderson III) *foundation executive*
Henriques, Diana Blackmon *journalist*
Henry, Sally McDonald *lawyer*
Henschel, Shirley Myra *licensing agent*
Henschke, Claudia Ingrid *physician, radiologist*
Herman, Mindy *broadcast executive*
Hermann, Mildred L. *artist*
Hernstadt, Judith Filenbaum *city planner, real estate executive, broadcasting executive*
Herrera, Carolina *fashion designer*
Herrera, Paloma *dancer*
Herron, Cindy *actress, vocalist*
Herzeca, Lois Friedman *lawyer*
Herzig, Rita Wynne *critical care nurse, soprano*
Hesse, Karen (Karen Sue Hesse) *writer, educator*
Hesselbein, Frances Richards *foundation executive, consultant, editor*
Hewitt, Vivian Ann Davidson (Mrs. John Hamilton Hewitt Jr.) *retired librarian*
Heyde, Martha Bennett (Mrs. Ernest R. Heyde) *psychologist*
Heyzer, Noeleen *international organization official*
Hickey, Catherine Josephine *school system administrator*
Hill, Lauryn *vocalist, actress*
Hill, May Brawley *art historian*
Hillenbrand, Laura *writer*
Himmel, Leslie Wohlman *real estate manager*
Hinojosa, Maria L. *news correspondent*
Hirsch, Roseann Conte *publisher*
Hirschhorn, Rochelle *genetics educator*
Ho, Betty Juenyü Yulin *physiological educator, researcher*
Ho, Weifan Lee *merchandise executive*
Hoag, Tami *writer*
Hochlerin, Diane *pediatrician, educator*
Hoffman, Alice *writer*
Hoffman, Linda M. *chemist, educator*
Hoffman, Linda R. *social services administrator*
Hoffman, Nancy *art gallery director*
Hoffmann, Anne Marie *health facility administrator*
Hoffmann, Elinor R. *lawyer*
Hoffner, Marilyn *university administrator*
Hohauser, Marilyn *artist*
Hollis, Loucille *risk control administrator, educator*
Holmes, Anna-Marie *ballerina, ballet mistress*
Holmes, Miriam H. *publisher*
Holt, Thelma *theatrical producer*
Holtzman, Elizabeth *lawyer*
Holtzman, Ellen A. *foundation executive*
Hommo, Harumi *accountant*
Honig, Ethelyn *artist*
Hopkins, Deborah C. *diversified financial services company executive*
Hopkins, Jan *journalist, newscaster*
Horn, Shirley *vocalist, pianist*
Horne, Marilyn *mezzo-soprano*
Horowitz, Frances Degen *academic administrator, psychology educator*
Horvath, Annette *home care administrator*
Horvath, Polly *writer*
Hotchner, Holly *curator, museum director, conservator*
House, Jane E. *director, writer, actress*
House, Karen Elliott *company executive, former editor, reporter*
Howe, Florence *English educator, writer*
Howe, Tina *playwright*
Howson, Tamar D. *pharmaceutical executive*
Hricik, Lorraine E. *bank executive*
Hsu, Cindy Kwang-Mei *news correspondent, anchor*
Hudes, Nana Brenda *marketing professional*
Huff, Janice *newscaster, meteorologist*
Hughes, Brigid *editor*
Hughes, Norah Ann O'Brien *bank securities executive*
Hull, Cathy *artist, illustrator*
Humphreys, Josephine *novelist*
Hunter-Stiebel, Penelope *art historian*
Hurd, Ruth *publishing executive*
Hurley, Cheryl Joyce *book publishing executive*
Hussung, Alleen Mosette *literary agent*
Huttner, Constance S. *lawyer*
Huxtable, Ada Louise *architecture critic*
Hyatt, Carole S. *author, speaker, coach*
Hynde, Chrissie *musician*
Hynes, Patricia Mary *lawyer*
Ilchman, Alice Stone *foundation administrator, former college president, former government official*
Ilse-Neuman, Ursula *curator*
Imperato-McGinley, Julianne Leonore *endocrinologist, educator*
Ina, Kyoko *professional figure skater*
Innesa, Levkova-Lamm *art critic, writer, curator*
Intilli, Sharon Marie *television director, small business owner*
Iqbal, Syma U. *corporate financial executive*
Isaacs, Barbara Shivitz *painter*
Isay, Jane Franzblau *publisher*
Isbin, Sharon *classical guitarist, guitar educator*
Istomin, Marta Casals *performing arts administrator, former educator*
Ivanick, Carol W. Trencher *lawyer*
Ives, Colta Feller *museum curator, educator*
Jacker, Corinne Litvin *playwright, writer*
Jackson, Anne (Anne Jackson Wallach) *actress*
Jackson, Wynelle Redding *children's services educational administrator, tax preparer*
Jackson, Yvonne *pharmaceutical executive*
Jackson McCabe, Jewell *not-for-profit developer*
Jacobsen, Sally *communications executive*
Jacquette, Yvonne Helene *artist*
Jaffe, Susan *ballerina*
James, Cheryl *vocalist*
Jamison, Jayne *publishing executive*
Jamison, Judith *dancer*
Jamison, Sheila Ann English *stockbroker, retirement planning specialist*
Jasso, Guillermina *sociologist, educator*
Javens, Kathleen Elizabeth *artist*
Jean-Baptiste, Tricia *public relations executive*
Jefferson, Denise *dance school director*
Jefferson, Margo L. *journalist*
Jelinek, Vera *university director*
Jenkins, Zeretha Lenore *publishing executive*
Jett, Joan (Joan Larkin) *musician*
Jewel, (Jewel Kilcher) *folk singer, songwriter*
Jeynes, Mary Kay *college dean*
Jhabvala, Ruth Prawer *writer*
Joachim, Brigitta Golden *writer, advertising agency executive, media consultant*
Johnson, Betsey Lee *fashion designer*
Johnson, Brooke Bailey *consultant, former television executive*
Johnson, Verdia E. *marketing professional*
Johnson, Vickie *professional basketball player*
Johnston, Diane Miller *librarian*
Johnston, Lynn Beverley *animator*
Jonas, Ruth Haber *psychologist*
Jones, Diana Wynne *writer*
Jones, Laurie Lynn *magazine editor*
Jones, Maxine *vocalist*
Jones, Star (Starlet Marie Jones) *television host*
Jong, Erica Mann *writer*
Jordan, Theresa Joan *psychologist, educator*
Josell, Jessica (Jessica Wechsler) *public relations executive*
Joseph, Ellen R. *lawyer*
Joseph, Wendy Evans *architect*
Josephson, Diana Hayward *not-for-profit company executive*
Juliber, Lois D. *manufacturing executive*
Jung, Andrea *cosmetics executive*
Jung, Doris *dramatic soprano*
Juran, Sylvia Louise *editor*
Jurka, Edith Mila *psychiatrist, researcher*
Just, Gemma Rivoli *retired advertising executive*
Kafka, Barbara Poses *writer*
Kaggen, Lois Sheila *non-profit organization executive*
Kahan, Marlene *professional association executive*
Kahn, Nancy Valerie *publishing and entertainment executive, consultant*
Kaish, Luise Clayborn *sculptor, former educator*
Kakutani, Michiko *critic*
Kalajian-Lagani, Donna *publishing executive*
Kalayjian, Anie *psychotherapist, nurse, educator, consultant*
Kallir, Jane Katherine *art gallery director, author*
Kamali, Norma *fashion designer*
Kambour, Annaliese Spofford *lawyer*
Kamerman, Sheila Brody *social worker, educator*
Kamm, Linda Heller *lawyer*
Kan, Diana Artemis Mann Shu *painter, art educator, writer*
Kane, Alice Theresa *lawyer*
Kane, Marilyn *real estate company executive*
Kanick, Virginia *retired radiologist*
Kanner, Bernice *columnist*
Kanter, Stacy J. *lawyer*
Kapelman, Barbara Ann *internist, gastroenterologist, educator*
Kaplan, Daile *photographer*
Kaplan, Deborah Renee *artist*
Kaplan, Madeline *legal administrator*
Kaplan, Rosalind Perlow *ophthalmologist*
Kapner, Lori *marketing professional*
Karan, Donna (Donna Faske) *fashion designer*
Kardon, Janet *museum director, curator, educator*
Karlin, Susan *design company executive*
Karpen, Marian Joan *financial executive*
Karr, Kathleen *writer*
Karsen, Sonja Petra *retired American-Hispanic literature educator*
Kasakove, Susan *interior designer*
Kassel, Catherine M. *community, maternal, and women's health nurse, consultant*
Kassel, Virginia Weltmer *television producer, writer*
Katen, Karen L. *pharmaceutical executive*
Katz, Jane *swimming educator*
Katz, Lois Anne *internist, nephrologist*
Katz, Marcia *public relations company executive*
Katzowitz Shenfield, Lauren *philanthropic consultant, foundation executive*
Kaufman, Bel *author, educator*
Kavaler-Adler, Susan *clinical psychologist, psychoanalyst*
Kavovit, Barbara *entrepreneur*
Kayse, Kathleen *publishing executive*
Kearse, Amalya Lyle *federal judge*
Keating, Isabel *actress*
Keefe, Diane Marie *portfolio manager*
Keenan, Terry *anchor, correspondent*
Kehret, Peg *writer*
Kellar, Charlotte Avrutis *writer*
Kelly, Christina *editor*
Kemether, Eileen *psychiatrist*
Kenan, Brunette Johnella *graphics designer*
Kennedy, Adrienne Lita *playwright*
Kenny, Jane Marie *government agency administrator*
Kent, Julie *ballet dancer, actress, model*
Kent, Linda Gail *dancer*
Kerz, Louise *historian*
Keys, Alicia *vocalist, musician, songwriter*
Khedoori, Toba *artist*
Khidekel, Regina P. *art historian, curator, lecturer*
Kim, Tong Rim *art foundation administrator*
Kinberg, Judy *television producer, director*
Kind, Phyllis *art gallery owner*
King, Marcia Gygli *artist*
Kinney, Catherine R. *stock exchange executive*
Kinsman, Sarah Markham *investment company executive*
Kirnos, Dina *technology support professional*
Kirschenbaum, Lisa L. *portfolio manager, financial advisor*
Kirschner, Joyce *art dealer*
Kiser, Molly *musician*
Kitagawa, Audrey Emiko *retired lawyer*
Kitahata-Sporn, Amy *movement educator*
Kitt, Eartha Mae *actress, singer*
Kjellberg, Ann C. *editor*
Klagsbrun, Francine *writer, editor*
Klein, Laura *publishing executive*
Klein, Nancy Lynn *fine jewelry company owner, consultant*
Klotz, Florence *costume designer*
Kmiotek-Welsh, Jacqueline *lawyer*
Knapp, Ellen M. *financial company executive*
Knight, Shirley *actress*
Kober, Jane *lawyer*
Konner, Joan Weiner *academic administrator, educator, television producer, writer*
Kopp, Wendy *teaching program administrator*
Koppelman, Dorothy Myers *artist, consultant*
Korff, Phyllis G. *lawyer*
Korot, Beryl *artist*
Koslow, Sally *editor-in-chief*
Koster, Elaine Landis *publishing executive*
Koteff, Ellen *periodical editor*
Kothera, Lynne Maxine *clinical psychologist*
Kotuk, Andrea Mikotajuk *public relations executive, writer*
Kourides, Ione Anne *endocrinologist, researcher, educator*
Kove, Miriam *psychotherapist*
Kowroski, Maria *dancer*
Kozak, Harley Jane *actress, writer*
Kozik, Susan S. *information technology executive*
Kozlowski, Cheryl M. *principal*
Kraemer, Lillian Elizabeth *lawyer*
Kram, Shirley Wohl *federal judge*
Kramer, Jane *writer*
Kramer, Michelle *reporter*
Krantz, Judith Tarcher *novelist*
Kraus, Norma Jean *industrial relations executive*
Krauss, Judith Scheer *art dealer*
Krawcheck, Sallie L. *investment company executive*
Kreek, Mary Jeanne *physician*
Krementz, Jill *photographer, author*
Kress, Nancy *writer*
Krinsky, Carol Herselle *art history educator*
Krizer, Jodi *performing arts executive*
Kroeger, Brooke W. *journalist, writer*
Krominga, Lynn *cosmetic and health care company executive, lawyer*
Kropf, Susan J. *cosmetics company executive*
Kruger, Louise Virginia *sculptor*
Kuck, Lea Haber *lawyer*
Kugelman, Stephanie *advertising executive*
Kunes, Ellen *editor-in-chief*
Kuo, Charlene *finance professional*
Kurian, Marian *surgeon*
Kurman, Juta *music educator*
Kurtzman, Susan Joan *school system administrator, speech pathology/audiology services professional*
Kurzweil, Edith *sociology educator, editor*
Kutosh, Sue *artist*
Kyriakou, Linda Grace *communications executive*
Labovitz, Deborah Rose Rubin *occupational therapist, educator*
Lagomasino, Maria Elena *bank executive*
Laing, Jennifer *advertising executive*
Lakatos, Susan Carol *investment banker, artist*
Lake, Ricki *talk show host, actress*
Lambert, Judith A. Ungar *lawyer*
Lamont, Lee *music management executive*
Lamont, Rosette Clementine *Romance languages educator, theatre journalist, translator*
Land, Irene Stokvis *marketing executive*
Landy, Joanne Veit *foreign policy and health policy reform analyst*
Lane, Nancy *editor, human rights activist*
Lang, Enid Asher *psychiatrist*
Lang, Pearl *dancer, choreographer*
Lange, Liz Steinberg *apparel designer and executive*
LaNicca Albanese, Ellen *public relations executive*
Lanquetot, E. Roxanne *retired special education educator*
Lappin, Joan E. *financial executive*
LaRose, Melba Lee *performing company executive, actress, playwright, theater director*
Lassiter, Sheri L. *insurance company executive*
Lauber, Patricia Grace *writer*
Lauder, Aerin *cosmetics executive*
Lauder, Evelyn H. *cosmetics executive*
Lauper, Cyndi *musician*
Lavori, Nora *real estate executive, lawyer*
Lawhon, Charla *editor*
Lawrence, Lauren *author, dreams expert, psychoanalytical theorist, psychoanalyst*
Laybourne, Geraldine B. *broadcast executive*
Lazarus, Rochelle Braff (Shelly Lazarus) *advertising executive*
Leach, Mary Jane *composer*
Leahey, Lynn *editor-in-chief*
Lebenthal, Alexandra *investment firm executive*
LeCompte, Elizabeth *theater director*
Le Count, Virginia G. *communications company executive*
Lederman, Sally Ann *nutrition researcher*
Lee, Amy *singer*
Lee, Catherine *sculptor, painter*
Lee, Frances Helen *editor*
Lee, Sally A. *editor-in-chief*
Leet, Mildred Robbins *corporate executive, consultant*
Leff, Ilene J(afnel) *management consultant, corporate and government executive*
Leff, Sandra H. *gallery director, consultant*
Lehmkuhl, Lynn *publishing executive*
Lehrman, Marceline Barbara *psychotherapist*
Leibovitz, Annie *photographer*
Leiman, Joan Maisel *hospital and university administrator, hospital administrator*
Leive, Cindi *editor-in-chief*
L'Engle, Madeleine (Mrs. Hugh Franklin) *writer*
Leonard, Zoe *artist*
Lesk, Ann Berger *lawyer*
Lester, Pamela Robin *lawyer*
Leven, Ann Ruth *museum financial officer*
Levine, Ellen R. *editor*
Levine, Naomi Bronheim *academic administrator*
Lewis, Loida Nicolas *food products holding company executive*
Lewis, Marcia *actress*
Lewyn, Ann Salfeld *retired English as a second language educator*
Lieberman, Nancy Ann *lawyer*
Limmroth, Karin Leigh *international producer, television correspondent*
Lin, Maria C. H. *lawyer*
Lipin, Joan Carol *healthcare executive, consultant*
Lippman, Donna Robin *psychotherapist*
Lipton, Joan Elaine *advertising executive*
Lisovicz, Susan *anchor, correspondent*
Little, Judith *cultural organization administrator*
Livingston, Julie *publicist*
Lockwood, Helshi *advertising executive*

Rivera, Chita (Conchita del Rivero) *actress, singer, dancer*
Rivera, Sophie *photographer*
Rizer, Maggie *model*
Roach, Margaret *editor-in-chief*
Robbins, Carrie F(ishbein) *costume designer, educator*
Roberts, Denise (Denise Roberts Hurlin) *dancer*
Roberts, Dorothy Hyman *accessory company executive*
Roberts, Madelyn Alpert *publishing executive*
Roberts, Nancy Cohen *art dealer, marketing professional*
Roberts, Nora *writer*
Robertson, Anne Ferratt *language educator, researcher*
Robinson, Barbara Paul *lawyer*
Robinson, Janet L. *publishing executive*
Robinson, Nan Senior *not-for-profit organization consultant*
Robinson Derossi, Flavia *photographer, foundation executive*
Robles-Roman, Carol A. *municipal official*
Rockas, Anastasia T. *lawyer*
Rockefeller, Allison Hall W. *conservationist*
Rocklen, Kathy Hellenbrand *lawyer*
Rodin, Rita A. *lawyer*
Rodriguez, Darlene *newscaster*
Rohrbach, Heidi A. *lawyer*
Rollin, Betty *writer, television journalist, lecturer*
Ronstadt, Linda Marie *singer*
Roome, Kristine Ann *college administrator*
Root, Nina J. *librarian, writer*
Rosa, Margarita *agency chief executive, lawyer*
Rosado, Rossana *publishing executive, editor-in-chief*
Rose, Joanna Semel *cultural activist*
Rose, Joanne W. *rating service executive*
Rose, Leatrice *artist, educator*
Rose, Merrill *public relations counselor*
Rosen, Ruth Chier *retired editor-in-chief*
Rosenbaum, Joan Hannah *museum director*
Rosenberg, Ellen Y. *religious association administrator*
Rosenberg, Tina *international relations educator, writer*
Rosensaft, Jean Bloch *university administrator*
Rosenthal, Donna Myra *social worker*
Rosenthal, Jane *film company executive*
Rosenthal, Nan *curator, educator, author*
Rosenthal, Shirley Lord *cosmetics magazine executive, novelist*
Rosenwasser, Donna *management consulting company executive*
Ross, Audrey *theatrical publicist*
Ross, Diana Ernestine Earle *singer, actress, entertainer, fashion designer*
Ross, Karen *information technology executive*
Ross, Rhoda *artist*
Rossbach, Janet B. *art association administrator, not-for-profit fundraiser*
Rossi, Marianne *financial analyst*
Rossi, Norma M. *management consultant*
Roth, Daryl *theater producer*
Roth, Judith Shulman *lawyer*
Rothman, Carol *theater director*
Rothman, Sheila Miller *public health educator*
Rotolo, Susan *artist*
Rowen, Ruth Halle *musicologist, educator*
Rowland, Esther E(delman) *retired dean*
Roy, Arundhati *writer*
Rubenstein, Atoosa Behnegar *editor-in-chief*
Rubinstein, Rosalinda *allergist, medical association administrator*
Ruckert, Ann Johns *musician, singer*
Rudolph, Lisa Beth *news correspondent*
Rudolph, Maya *actress, comedienne*
Ruiz-Valera, Phoebe Lucile *law librarian*
Russell, Charlotte Sananes *biochemistry educator, researcher*
Russell, Maryanne *photographer*
Russo, Melissa *reporter*
Russo, Rosalie J. *social worker, vocational rehabilitation counselor, educator*
Rylant, Cynthia *author*
Rzeszotarski, Pamela Sue (Pamela Sue Dougherty) *banker*
Rzewnicki, Janet C. *state official*
Sabino, Catherine Ann *magazine editor*
Sacksteder, Elizabeth M. *lawyer*
Sadik, Nafis *United Nations administrator*
Safro, Millicent *small business owner, decorative arts scholar, writer*
St. Germain, Jean Mary *medical physicist*
St. John, Suzan *astrologer, illustrator, writer, vocalist*
St. Lifer Kennedy, Jane *art appraiser, curator*
Saint-Ouen Leung, Brigitte *art dealer, consultant*
Salembier, Valerie Birnbaum *publishing executive*
Salerno-Sonnenberg, Nadja *violinist*
Salonga, Lea *actress, singer*
Salter, Mary Jo *poet*
Saltzstein, Susan L. *lawyer*
Samelson, Judy *editor*
Samuels, Dorothy J. *journalist, writer*
Sanchez, Hazel *reporter*
Sanders, Summer *Olympic athlete, news correspondent, newscaster*
Sand Lee, Inger *artist*
Sandler, Lucy Freeman *art history educator*
Santaella, Irma Vidal *retired state supreme court justice*
Sarachik, Myriam Paula Morgenstein *physics educator*
Sarandon, Susan Abigail *actress*
Sard, Susannah Ellen *non-profit executive*
Sargent, Pamela *writer*
Sasman, Irene Deak Handberg *educational publishing executive*
Savage, Veronica Rivera *social worker, educator*
Savitt, Susan Schenkel *lawyer*
Sawyer, Diane (L. Diane Sawyer) *newscaster, journalist*
Sawyer, Linda *advertising executive*
Saxton, Catherine Patricia *public relations executive*
Scaffidi, Judith Ann *academic administrator*
Scanlon, Rosemary *economist*
Scherber, Amy *food service executive*
Schindler, Teri *sports association executive*
Schine, Cathleen *writer*
Schlain, Barbara Ellen *lawyer*
Schlein, Miriam *author*
Schless, Phyllis Ross *investment banker*
Schmertz, Mildred Floyd *editor, writer*
Schneider, Jane Harris *sculptor*
Schneider, JoAnne *artist*
Schneider, Willys Hope *lawyer*
Schneirov, Allison R. *lawyer*
Schoen, Regina Neiman *psychotherapist*
Schoonmaker Powell, Thelma *film editor*
Schoonover, Jean Way *public relations consultant*
Schorer, Suki *ballet teacher*
Schuch, Beverly *anchor*
Schuhart, Anne Dashley (Susan Schuhart Zito) *actress*
Schulhoff, Karen L. *information specialist*
Schulman, Amy Weinfeld *lawyer*
Schulz, Susan *magazine editor*
Schuman, Patricia Glass *publishing company executive, educator*
Schuster, Carlotta Lief *psychiatrist*
Schwartz, Anna Jacobson *economic historian*
Schwartz, Carol Vivian *lawyer*
Schwartz, Renee Gerstler *lawyer*
Scott, Adrienne *social worker, psychotherapist*
Scott, Margaret Simon *retired mortgage broker*
Scott, Mimi Koblenz *psychotherapist, actress, publicist, journalist, playwright*
Scott, Susan Craig *plastic surgeon*
Scotti, Rita Angelica *novelist*
Scotto, Rosanna *newscaster*
Seborovski, Carole *artist*
See, Saw-Teen *structural engineer*
Seelig, Jill *publishing executive*
Segal, Lore *writer*
Seidenberg, Rita Nagler *education educator*
Selby, Cecily Cannan *dean, educator, scientist*
Seldes, Marian *actress*
Seligman, Nicole K. *broadcast executive, lawyer*
Semaya, Francine Levitt *lawyer*
Serota, Susan Perlstadt *lawyer, educator*
Sevely, Maria *architect*
Sevilla-Sacasa, Frances Aldrich *bank executive*
Seymour, Lesley Jane *magazine editor-in-chief*
Seymour, Stephanie *model*
Shafer, Yvonne *theater educator, writer*
Shaffler, Rhonda *news correspondent*
Shainwald, Sybil *lawyer*
Shames, Germaine W. *journalist, writer*
Shane, Rita *opera singer, educator*
Shapiro, Judith R. *academic administrator, anthropology educator*
Sharbel, Jean M. *editor*
Sharp, Anne Catherine *artist, educator*
Shatter, Susan Louise *artist*
Sheehan, Susan *writer*
Sheehy, Gail Henion *author*
Sheldon, Eleanor Harriet Bernert *sociologist, writer*
Shelley, Carole *actress*
Shepard, Sarah *public relations company executive*
Shepherd, Kathleen Shearer Maynard *television executive*
Sheridan LaBarge, Joan Ruth *publishing executive*
Sherman, Cindy *artist*
Shern, Stephanie Marie *investment company executive, accountant*
Shientag, Florence Perlow *lawyer*
Shier, Shelley M. *production company executive*
Shocked, Michelle *vocalist, songwriter*
Shohen, Saundra Anne *health care communications and public relations executive*
Shoss, Cynthia Renée *lawyer*
Shull, Mikki *media consultant*
Sidamon-Eristoff, Anne Phipps *community trust executive*
Sidran, Miriam *retired physics educator, researcher*
Siebert, Muriel (Mickie) *brokerage house executive, former state banking official*
Siegal, Peggy *public relations executive*
Siegel, Lucy Boswell *public relations executive*
Sifton, Elisabeth *book publisher*
Sigal-Ibsen, Rose *artist*
Sigmond, Carol Ann *lawyer*
Sikander, Shahzia *artist*
Sills, Beverly (Mrs. Peter B. Greenough) *performing arts organization executive, coloratura soprano*
Silver, Joan Micklin *film director, screenwriter*
Silverman, Marylin A. *advertising agency executive*
Silvers, Sally *choreographer, performing company executive*
Silvestri, Heather L. *psychologist*
Simmons, Sue *newscaster*
Simon, Jacqueline Albert *political scientist, journalist*
Simpson, Elizabeth *archaeologist, educator*
Simpson, Jessica Ann *vocalist*
Simpson, Mary Michael *priest, psychotherapist*
Sinclair, Daisy *casting executive*
Singer, Barbara Helen *photographer*
Singer, Davida *poet, journalist, educator*
Singer, Niki *media consultant*
Sischy, Ingrid Barbara *editor, art critic*
Sitarz, Anneliese Lotte *pediatrics educator, physician*
Sitomer, Sheila Marie *television producer, director*
Skerl, Diana M. *stockbroker*
Skigen, Patricia Sue *lawyer*
Slavin, Arlene *artist*
Slavin, Rosanne Singer *textile converter*
Slawsky, Donna Susan *librarian, singer*
Sleigh, Sylvia *artist, educator*
Slitkin, Barbara Ann *artist*
Slone, Sandi *artist*
Sloss, Merle *shoe company executive*
Slutsky, Lorie A.(Ann) *foundation executive*
Smiley, Jane Graves *author, educator*
Smith, Angela Lantz *psychiatrist, researcher*
Smith, Anna Nicole (Vickie Lynn Hogan) *television personality, model*
Smith, Barbara *food service executive, model*
Smith, Betty *writer, nonprofit foundation executive*
Smith, Karen Lynn *principal*
Smith, Kathryn Ann *art educator*
Smith, Kiki *artist*
Smith, Liz (Mary Elizabeth Smith) *newspaper columnist, broadcast journalist*
Smith, Patricia Lynne *visual artist*
Smith, Shirley *artist*
Smith-Loeb, Margaret *marketing educator*
Smits, Helen Lida *physician, medical administrator, educator*
Snyderman, Selma Eleanore *pediatrician, educator*
Soave, Rosemary *internist*
Sohl, Joyce Darlene *religious organization administrator*
Sokoloff, Audrey L. *lawyer*
Solnit, Rebecca *writer, art critic*
Solomon, Gail Ellen *physician*
Somogyi, Jennie *dancer*
Sonneman, Eve *artist*
Sontag, Susan *writer*
Sorensen, Gillian Martin *United Nations official*
Soriano, Nancy Mernit *editor-in-chief*
Soros, Susan Weber *educational administrator*
Sotomayor, Sonia *federal judge*
Southworth, Linda Jean *artist, critic, educator, poet*
Soyster, Margaret Blair *lawyer*
Spade, Kate (Katherine Noel Spade) *apparel designer*
Spears, Britney *vocalist, actress*
Spector, Johanna Lichtenberg *ethnomusicologist, former educator*
Spence, Sique (Mary Stewart Spence) *art dealer*
Speransky, Helen I. *psychotherapist, consultant*
Spero, Joan Edelman *foundation president*
Squire, Gilda N. *brand manager, publicist, writer*
Stack, Teresa Marie *publishing executive*
Stacom, Darcy A. *real estate company executive*
Stahl, Lesley R. *news correspondent*
Stanger, Ila *writer, editor*
Stark, Robin Caryl *psychotherapist, consultant*
Stecher, Esta E. *lawyer, investment company executive*
Steck, Jodi *photojournalist*
Steedman, Doria Lynne Silberberg *organization executive*
Steel, Danielle Fernande *author*
Steichen, Joanna T(aub) *psychotherapist, writer*
Stein, Ellen Gail *executive manager*
Stein, Emily Jo *psychologist*
Stein, Zena A. *health facility administrator, psychiatry educator*
Steinberg, Nancy *healthcare public relations executive*
Stern, Lynn Solinger *photographer*
Stern, Madeleine Bettina *rare books dealer, author*
Stern, Roslyne Paige *magazine publisher*
Stern-Larosa, Caryl M. *advocate, educational association administrator*
Stevens, Risë *performing arts company administrator*
Steves, Gale C. *marketing professional, writer, editor-in-chief, publishing executive*
Stewart, Leora Klaymer *textile artist, educator*
Stewart, Ruth Ann *public policy educator*
Stiassny, Melanie L.J. *curator*
Stimpson, Catharine Roslyn *English language educator, writer*
Stine, Catherine Morris *artist*
Stokes, Lori *newscaster*
Stone, Amy *reporter*
Stone, Caroline Fleming *artist*
Storey, Susan Lynne *investment banker*
Storm, Hannah *newscaster*
Storm, Jackie *nutritionist, health education specialist*
Storrs, Immi Casagrande *sculptor*
Stratas, Teresa (Anastasia Strataki) *opera singer, soprano*
Stroer, Rosemary Ann *real estate broker*
Stroman, Susan *choreographer, theater director*
Strossen, Nadine *legal association administrator, law educator*
Stuart, Alice Melissa *lawyer*
Stuart, Lori Ames *public relations executive*
Studin, Jan *publishing executive*
Sullivan, Irene A. *lawyer*
Sullivan, Mary Brosnahan *advocate, social services administrator*
Susman, Sally *cosmetics executive*
Susskind, Emily H. *broadcast executive*
Sutherland, Dame Joan *retired soprano*
Sutherland, Susan J. *lawyer*
Sutton, Karen E. *administrator*
Swartz, Linda Z. *lawyer*
Sweed, Phyllis *publishing executive*
Swenson, Tree (Holly) *poet*
Swergold, Marcelle Miriam *sculptor*
Swift, Mary Lou *art dealer, financial consultant*
Syler, Rene *newscaster*
Symonette, Lys *foundation executive, musician, writer*
Szeto, Yvonne *architectural firm executive*
Szymkowiak, Mary L. *non-profit organization administrator*
Tafoya, Michele *sports reporter*
Takamura, Jeanette Chiyoko *dean*
Talese, Nan Ahearn *publishing company executive*
Tallmer, Margot Sallop *psychologist, psychoanalyst, gerontologist*
Tamony, Katie *editor-in-chief*
Tan, Amy Ruth *writer*
Tanaka, Patrice Aiko *public relations executive*
Tannenbaum, Bernice Salpeter *national religious organization executive*
Tanner, Lois *magazine editor*
Tarnofsky-Ostroff, Dawn *broadcast executive*
Taylor, Barbara Alden *public relations executive*
Taylor, Felicia *newscaster*
Taylor, Jean Ellen *mathematics researcher and educator*
Taylor, Marilyn Jordan *architectural firm executive*
Taylor, Mildred D. *author*
Taylor, Nicole Renée *model*
Taylor, Terry R. *editor, educator*
Taymor, Julie *theater, film and opera director and designer*
Teichner, Martha Alice *network television news correspondent*
Temin, Davia B. *marketing executive*
Templeton, Fiona *performance artist, writer, director*
Terris, Lillian Dick *psychologist, association executive*
Tesori, Jeanine *composer*
Thaler, Linda Kaplan *communications executive*
Theut-Toplyn, Elizabeth Ann *psychologist*
Thierry, Lauren *anchor*
Thomas, Violeta de los Angeles *real estate broker*
Thomasos, Denyse *artist*
Thornton, Yvonne Shirley *physician, author, musician*
Thoyer, Judith Reinhardt *lawyer*
Thurston, Sally A. *lawyer*
Tighe, Mary Ann *real estate company executive*
Tillman, Vickie A. *diversified financial services company executive*
Tischler, Judith Blanche *retired music publishing executive, educator*
Tobach, Ethel *retired curator*
Toben, Doreen A. *corporate financial executive*
Tober, Barbara D. (Mrs. Donald Gibbs Tober) *editor*
Todd, Kim A. *actress*
Toepfer, Susan Jill *editor*
Toff, Nancy Ellen *book editor*
Tolchin, Joan Gubin *psychiatrist, educator*
Toldalagi, Marianne *foundation administrator*
Tolkoff, Esther Phyllis *writer, magazine editor*
Toll, Barbara Elizabeth *art gallery director*
Tong, Kaity *anchor*
Toote, Gloria E. A. *real estate developer, lawyer, columnist*
Torchin, Mimi *periodical editor*
Tortora, Leslie C. *finance company executive*
Touby, Linda *artist*
Toulantis, Marie *retail executive*
Townsend, Alair Ane *publisher, municipal official*
Townsend, Kathleen Kennedy *former lieutenant governor*
Townsend-Butterworth, Diana Barnard *educational consultant, author*
Tozer, Elizabeth Farran *interior and floral designer*
Tracy, Janet Ruth *legal educator, librarian*
Trauthwein, Christina *editor-in-chief*
Trevens, Francine Linda *writer, publishing executive*
Trombetta, Annamarie *artist*
Trump, Martha Lindley Blaine Beard *philanthropist*
Tudryn, Joyce Marie *professional society administrator*
Turner, Alice Kennedy *editor*
Turo, Joann K. *psychoanalyst, psychotherapist, consultant*
Turturro, Aida *actress*
Tuttle, Ashley *dancer*
Tyler, Dana *anchor*
Uggams, Leslie *entertainer*
Umansky, Diane *publishing executive*
Umeh, Marie Arlene *English language educator*
Ungaro, Susan Kelliher *magazine editor*
Updike, Helen Hill *investment manager, financial advisor*
Upright, Diane Warner *art dealer*
Urban, Amanda (Binky Urban) *literary agent*
Urdang, Alexandra *book publishing executive*
Valenstein, Suzanne Gebhart *art historian*
Valla, Teressa Marie *artist, textile designer*
Valletta, Amber *model*
Van de Bovenkamp, Sue Erpf *charitable organization executive*
Vanden Heuvel, Katrina *magazine editor*
Vander Heyden, Marsha Ann *business owner*
Van Goethem, Nancy Ann *painter, educator*
Vargas, Martha *government liaison*
Vass, Joan *apparel designer*
Vaughan, Linda *publishing executive*
Velez-Mitchell, Anita *entertainer, writer*
Vendela, *model*
Vennum, Joan Fay *artist*
Vermeer, Maureen Dorothy *sales executive*
Vickers, Marcia *journalist*
Vieira, Meredith *television personality*
Vladeck, Judith Pomarlen *lawyer*
Volk, Kristin *advertising agency executive*
von Baillou, Astrid *executive search consultant*
von Fraunhofer-Kosinski, Katherina *bank executive*
Von Stade, Frederica *mezzo-soprano*
Vrancik, Barbara A. *lawyer*
Wainwright, Cynthia Crawford *banker*
Wajsfeld, Annie R. *volunteer*
Wald, Sylvia *artist*
Walden, Janet C. *lawyer*
Walker, Alice *writer*
Walker, Kara *artist*
Walker, Sally Barbara *retired glass company executive*
Wallace, Barbara Faith *linguistics educator*
Wallace, Carol *editor at large*
Wallace, Joyce Irene Malakoff *internist*
Wallace, Michele *media company executive*
Wallace, Nora Ann *lawyer*
Walters, Barbara Ann *television journalist*

Walzer, Judith Borodovko *academic administrator, educator*
Wang, Vera *fashion designer*
Ward, Sarah M. *lawyer*
Waricha, Joan *publishing executive*
Warrick, Ruth *actress*
Warshauer, Irene C. *lawyer*
Warwick, Dionne *singer*
Washburn, Joan Thomas *business owner, art gallery director*
Wasserstein, Wendy *playwright*
Watanabe, Nana *photographer*
Waters, Crystal *vocalist, songwriter*
Waters, Sylvia *dance company artistic director*
Watson, Marlan *reporter*
Wattleton, Faye (Alyce Faye Wattleton) *educational association administrator*
Waxman, Anita *producer*
Weber, Lisa M. *insurance company executive*
Webster, Lesley Daniels *bank executive*
Wedgeworth, Ann *actress*
Weeks, Brigitte *publishing executive*
Weems, Carrie Mae *photographer*
Weese, Miranda *dancer*
Weiksner, Sandra S. *lawyer*
Weil-Garris Brandt, Kathleen (Kathleen Brandt) *art historian*
Weinberg, H. Barbara *art historian, educator, curator paintings and sculpture*
Weingarten, Rhonda *lawyer*
Weinshenker, Naomi Joyce *clinical psychiatrist, educator, researcher*
Weinstein, Ellen *performing company executive*
Weinstein, Ruth Joseph *lawyer*
Weinstein, Sharon Schlein *corporate communications executive, educator*
Weiss, Myrna Grace *financial planner*
Weissler, Fran *theatrical producer*
Welch, Martha Grace *physician, researcher*
Wells, Linda Ann *editor-in-chief*
Wells, Patricia Trent *retail marketing executive*
Wender, Phyllis Bellows *literary agent*
West, Betsy *broadcast executive*
Westheimer, Ruth Siegel (Karola Westheimer) *psychologist, television personality*
Weston, Michele J. *apparel executive, consultant*
Wexler, Nancy Sabin *clinical neuropsychology educator*
Whelan, Elizabeth Ann Murphy *epidemiologist*
Whelchel, Betty Anne *lawyer*
White, Kate *editor-in-chief*
White, Lillias *actress*
White, Mary Jo *former prosecutor, lawyer*
Whitney, Phyllis Ayame *author*
Wiggers, Charlotte Suzanne Ward *magazine* [illegible]
Wijnberg, Sandra S. *professional services company executive*
Wilkins, Amy P. *publishing executive*
Willett, Roslyn Leonore *public relations executive, food service consultant, writer*
Willett Bird, Susan *public and motivational speaker*
Williams, Diane *writer, editor*
Williams, Harriet Clarke *retired academic administrator*
Williams, Lena *sportswriter*
Williams, Lucinda *country musician*
Williams, Reba White *financial executive, writer*
Williams, Sue *artist*
Williams, Terrie Michelle *publicity agency executive*
Williams, Vanessa *recording artist, actress*
Williamson, Philemona *artist*
Willis, Beverly Ann *architect*
Willis, Gerri *news correspondent*
Wils, Madelyn *film company executive*
Wilson, Cassandra *singer*
Wilson, Marie C. *foundation administrator*
Wilson, Pamela K. *corporate financial executive*
Winchell, Kristina Anne *psychologist, school system administrator*
Winston, Mary A. *publishing executive*
Wintour, Anna *editor*
Wiseman, Cynthia Sue *language educator*
Witherell, Mary *editor*
Wittner-Kaufman, Michele Susan *psychologist*
Wizen, Sarabeth Margolis *financial consultant*
Wolff, Margaret Louise *lawyer*
Wolff, Virginia Euwer *writer*
Wood, Kimba M. *judge*
Woodward, Joanne Gignilliat *actress*
Worthing, Marcia Lynn *outplacement services executive*
Wright, Faith-dorian *artist*
Wright, Gwendolyn *art center director, writer, educator*
Wrubel, Barbara *lawyer, educator, former editor*
WuDunn, Sheryl *journalist, correspondent*
Wunderman, Jan Darcourt *artist*
Wylde, Kathryn S. *not-for-profit developer*
Wyschogrod, Edith *philosophy educator*
Wyse, Lois *advertising executive*
Yablonski, Janice Beth *museum administrator, publishing executive*
Yetman, Leith Eleanor *academic administrator*
Yglesias, Helen Bassine *author, educator*
Yin, Beatrice Wei-Tze *medical researcher*
York, Alexandra *writer, lecturer*
York, Janet Brewster *nurse, family and sex therapist, artist*
Yoshiuchi, Ellen Haven *health educator, clinical counselor*
Young, Alice *lawyer*
Young, Estelle Irene *dermatologist, educator*
Young, Genevieve Leman *publishing executive, editor*
Young, Jayne *recording industry executive*
Young, Paula Eva *city official, journalist, writer*
Yousef, Mona Lee *psychotherapist*
Yu, Pauline Ruth *former dean, educational association administrator*
Yurchenco, Henrietta Weiss *ethnomusicologist, writer*
Yuspeh-Hidalgo, Denise Anne *juvenile writer, editor*
Zagat, Nina *publishing executive*
Zaken, Grace Ambrose *project coordinator, educator*
Zaleski, Caroline Rob *preservationist*
Zarcone, Darlene *accountant*
Zarghami, Cyma *broadcast executive*
Zelin, Madeleine *think-tank executive*
Zevon, Susan Jane *editor*
Zha, Jianying *writer, educator*
Zhu, Ai-Lan *opera singer*
Zimmerman, Kathleen Marie *artist*
Zimmerman, Paula *writer*
Zirinsky, Susan *television producer*
Zlowe, Florence Markowitz *artist*
Zolotow, Charlotte Shapiro *author, editor*
Zosike, Joanie Fritz *theater director, actor*
Zoullas, Deborah Decotis *private investor, entrepreneur*
Zucker-Franklin, Dorothea *internist, educator*
Zumwalt, Karen Kepler *education educator*

Newark
Hemmings, Madeleine Blanchet *management consultant, media consultant, not-for-profit fundraiser*
Henderson, Elizabeth Ann *farmer*

Newark Valley
Griffith, Jewel Ann *music educator*

Newburgh
Adams, Barbara *English language educator, poet, writer*
Fallon, Rae Mary *psychology educator, early childhood consultant*
Joyce, Mary Ann *principal*
Mucci, Louise Catherine *family practice nurse practitioner, health care negotiator*
Sabini, Barbara Dorothy *artist, educator*
Sakac, Sister Ann

Niagara Falls
Clark, Patsy Vedder *retired educator and staff developer*
DelMonte, Francine *state legislator*
Douglas, Frances Sonia *minister*
Jones, Suzanne P. *public relations executive*

Niagara University
Green, Sharon Anne *reading specialist, educator*

Niskayuna
Brinkman, Paula H. *music educator*
Fitzroy, Nancy deLoye *engineering executive, mechanical engineer*
Standfast, Susan J(ane) *retired state official, educator, researcher*
Steeley, Dolores Ann *music educator*

North Bellmore
Connell, S. Clare *minister*
Trigoboff, Sybelle *artist, art educator, lecturer*

North Massapequa
Capone, Maryann *financial planner*

North Syracuse
Bakeman, JoAnne *alcohol/drug abuse services professional, educator*
McDonald, Elizabeth Lynne *speech pathology/audiology services professional*
Williamson, Donna Maria *pastoral counselor*

North Tonawanda
Strong, Audrey Farone *music educator*

North Woodmere
Aviles, Alice Alers *psychologist*

Northport
Hohenberger, Patricia Julie *fine arts and antique appraiser, consultant*

Northville
Popp, Ann L. *elementary school educator, music educator*

Norwood
Musante, Patricia W. *library director*

Nyack
Carey, Lois J. *psychotherapist*
Lieberman, Rita Leah *psychologist*
Pease, Eleanor Jeanne *humanities educator*
Price, Helen (Lois) Burdon *artist, retired nurse educator*
Scott-Battle, Gladys Natalie *retired social worker*

Oakland Gardens
Bernabo, Lois *social worker, educator*

Oceanside
Vaccaro, Joann *psychologist*

Odessa
Stillman-Myers, Joyce L. *artist, educator, writer, illustrator, consultant*

Ogdensburg
Smith, Carol Ann *academic administrator*

Olean
McGee, Patricia K. *state legislator*
Young, Catharine M. *state legislator*

Oneida
Bennett, Colleen T. *music educator*
Closson, Helga C. *councilwoman*

Oneonta
Carney, Margaret E. *administrative assistant, small business owner*
Dean, Carol *secondary school educator*
Desjarlais, Georgia Kathrine *retired military officer*
Helterline, Marilyn *sociology educator*
Kaufman, Janice Horner *foreign language educator, women's and gender studies educator*
Sharpe, Yolanda Ruby *art educator, vocalist*

Ontario
Blackman, Lani Modica *copy editor*

Orangeburg
Penney, Dixianne McCall *mental health services researcher, administrator*
Pratt, Christina Carver *social work and women's studies educator*
Siegel, Carole Ethel *mathematician*

Orchard Park
Greenwood, Audrey Gates *retired librarian*

Ossining
Galef, Sandra Risk *state legislator, teacher*
Gilbert, Joan Stulman *retired public relations executive*

Oswego
Huff, JoAn *retired physicial education/dance educator*
Loveridge-Sanbonmatsu, Joan Meredith *communication studies and women's studies educator, poet*
Smiley, Marilynn Jean *musicologist*

Owego
Coppens, Laura Kathryn *special education educator*

Oyster Bay
Russell, Mary Wendell Vander Poel *non-profit organization executive*
Smith, Pamela Rosevear *air transportation executive*

Ozone Park
Catalfo, Betty Marie *health service executive, nutritionist*

Painted Post
Ogden, Anita Bushey *nursing educator*

Palisades
Davis, Dorothy Salisbury *writer*
Hyams, Harriet *artist*
Knowlton, Grace Farrar *sculptor, photographer, painter*
Porta, Siena Gillann *sculptor, educator*

Panama
Dolce, Anne Frances *elementary school educator*

Patchogue
Maldonado, Judith Ann Batorski *art association administrator*
McPherson, Sherry Lynn *social worker*
Yee, Janice *dentist*

Pawling
Light, Sybil Elizabeth *executive secretary*
Peale, Ruth Stafford (Mrs. Norman Vincent Peale) *religious leader*

Pearl River
Bryant, Karen Worstell *financial advisor, investment company executive*

Peekskill
Bennett, Lisa *artist*
Finnigan, Claire Marie *media specialist, librarian*
Jackson, Linda B. *social worker*
Wiggins, Ida Silver *elementary school educator*

Penfield
Ahlstedt, Linda Foxx *music educator*
Hamilton, Candis Lee *religious organization administrator*
Klose, Charlotte Ann *insurance agency owner*
Marbach, Donna Maureen *writer*
Monti, Rena Marie *music educator*

Piermont
Brechtel, Unda Jurka *library director*
Madawick, Paula Christian *artist, educator*

Pittsford
Estin-Klein, Libbyada *advertising executive, medical writer*
Templeton, Karen Schroer *music educator*
Utterback, Betty Harris *editor*

Plainview
Fein, Leona Moss *artist*

Plattsburgh
Rech, Susan Anita *obstetrician, gynecologist*
Worthington, Janet Evans *retired academic dean, English language educator*

Pleasant Valley
Hankamp, Margaret *lawyer*
Marshall, Natalie Junemann *economics educator*

Pleasantville
Cesarini, Danielle Kristin *psychologist*
Havens, Jeanette Lynn *public relations executive*
Keller, Mary Beth *consumer research consultant*
Leo, Jacqueline M. *editor-in-chief*
McEwen, Laura *publishing executive*
Nelson, K. Bonita *literary agent*
Rockwood, Marcia *magazine editor*

Pomona
Landau, Lauri Beth *accountant, tax consultant*

Port Chester
Brescia, Alicia *science educator, vice principal*
Dessereau, April *art educator*
Duveen, Anneta *artist*
Oppenheimer, Suzi *state legislator*

Port Jefferson
Lipitz, Elaine Kappel *secondary education fine arts educator*

Port Washington
Cox, Jane *writer*
Schneider, Greta *economist, speaker, author, security consultant*
van Schenkhof, Carol Dougherty (Carol Dovan) *soprano, music educator*
Weiner, Mina Rieur *museum consultant, civic worker*

Porter Corners
Blom, Carol Barnes *music educator*

Potsdam
Bouchard, Kimberley A. *performing arts educator*
Garg, Rajni *chemist, researcher*
Regan, Marie Carbone *retired language educator*
Scott, Jean A. *university president*
Sennett, Patricia M. *artist, educator*
Skandera-Trombley, Laura Elise *language professional, English*
Usher, Bethany McKay *biological anthropology educator*

Poughkeepsie
Berlin, Doris Ada *psychiatrist*
Berry, Maryann Paradiso *minister*
Brakas, Nora Jachym *education educator*
Carino, Aurora Lao *psychiatrist, hospital administrator*
Daniels, Elizabeth Adams *English language educator*
Deiters, Sister Joan Adele *psychoanalyst, nun, chemistry educator*
Dolamore, Jeanne Porcino *music educator*
Fergusson, Frances Daly *college president, educator*
Hansen, Karen Thornley *accountant*
Hill, Carla Larsen *physical education educator, gymnastics judge*
Hytier, Adrienne Doris *French language educator*
Jacobi, Kerry Lee *information systems specialist*
LaGreca, Carla Irene *activist*
Millett, Kate (Katherine Murray Millett) *political activist, sculptor, artist, writer*
Mitchell, Katherine Sarah *not-for-profit developer*
Moysey, Carol Anne *investigator*
Pisterzi, Candy *special education educator*
Teal, Arabella W. *lawyer, former state attorney general*
VanBuren, Denise Doring *corporate* [illegible]
Willard, Nancy Margaret *writer, educator*

Pound Ridge
Schwebel, Renata Manasse *sculptor*

Purchase
Bannon, Nancy *performing arts educator*
Ehrman, Lee *geneticist, educator*
Finnerty, Louise Hoppe *beverage and food company executive*
Frost, Elizabeth Ann McArthur *physician*
Gedeon, Lucinda Heyel *museum director*
Moore, Margaret D. *human resources specialist*
Newton, Esther Mary *anthropologist, educator*
Nooyi, Indra K. *food products company executive*
Parrs, Marianne M. *paper and lumber company executive*
Sullivan, Margaret M. *university program administrator*

Queens Village
Clark, Barbara Marlene *state legislator*
Heckman, Lucy T. *librarian*
Megherian, Yefkin *sculptor*

Queensbury
Cackener, Helen Lewis *retired English educator, writer*
Depan, Mary Elizabeth *civic volunteer, nurse*

Rego Park
Guerra, C. Ines *real estate broker*
Tsui, Soo Hing *educational research consultant*

Rensselaer
Nack, Claire Durani *artist, author*

Rhinebeck
Campbell, Elizabeth Rose *astrologer, writer, videographer*
Rabinovich, Raquel *painter, sculptor*

Richfield Springs
Walters, Marjorie Anne *interior designer, consultant*

Ridgewood
Monroe, Leonora *surgeon*

Riverdale
Katz, Sheri Lynn *learning disabilities specialist, tutor*

Riverhead
Acampora, Patricia L. *state legislator*

Rochester
Adams, Carol H. *dean*
Aydelotte, Myrtle Kitchell *retired nursing administrator*
Bidlack, Jean Marie *pharmacologist, educator, medical researcher*
Blondell, Debra Brown *chemist, researcher*
Buckingham, Barbara Rae *social studies educator*
Cahn, Ruth Patricia *director, musician*
Chiverton, Patricia Ann *nursing educator, dean*
Ciaio, Laura Ashmore *accountant*

Conwell, Esther Marly *physicist, researcher*
Coon, Penny K. *human services administrator*
Dolin, Lonny H. *lawyer*
Eichenlaub, Rosemary Waring *music educator*
Fitzmorris, Pamela S. *music educator*
Fox, Donna Brink *music educator*
Frear, Lorrie *graphic designer, educator*
Freeman, Leslie Jean *neuropsychologist, researcher*
Friauf, Katherine Elizabeth *metal company executive*
Furness, Janet Elisabeth *social work educator*
Glatzer, Jenna *writer*
Glazer, Jane *company executive*
Goldberg-Schaible, Jocelyn Hope Schnier *market research professional*
Gootnick, Margery Fischbein *lawyer*
Goyer, Virginia L. *accountant*
Grant, Marilynn Patterson *secondary educator*
Guarnere, Joanne *protective services official*
Harris, Diane Carol *merger and acquisition consulting firm executive*
Haywood, Anne Mowbray *pediatrician, educator*
Herminghouse, Patricia Anne *foreign language educator*
Herrera, Charlotte Mae *medical office administrator*
Hollis, Susan Tower *history educator*
Huddleston, Vicki Jean *diplomat*
Hughes, Deborah L. *minister, director*
Hurt, Davina Theresa *secondary school educator*
Hyland, Sharon Ann *adult nurse practitioner*
John, Susan V. *state representative*
Johnson, B. Jean *music educator, musician*
Kehoe, Jennifer Spungin *English language educator, writer*
Kelly, Angela Mary *photographer, educator*
Klinke, Louise Hoyt *volunteer*
Lacey, Dorothy Ellen *theology studies educator, religious organization administrator*
Lank, Edith Handleman *columnist, educator*
Lawrence, Ruth Anderson *pediatrician, clinical toxicologist*
Lipsky, S. Kate *retired social worker*
Loquasto, Eileen Grace *sociologist*
Magnuson, Karen M. *editor*
Manley, Cathey Neracker *interior design executive*
Marini, Jane Marie *music educator*
Marriott, Marcia Ann *business and economics educator, health facility administrator*
McAnarney, Elizabeth R. *pediatrician, educator*
McWilliams, Dawn Suzanne *marketing professional, consultant*
Morrison, Patrice B. *lawyer*
Niznik, Carol Ann *electrical engineer, educator, consultant*
Ornt, Jeanine Arden *lawyer*
Palvino, Nancy Mangin *retired librarian*
Parrinello, Kathleen Ann Mulholland *nursing administrator, educator*
Pavone, Jill Russell *special education educator*
Penneys, Rebecca Ann *musician*
Portanova, Carolyn Amick *religious organization administrator*
Pratt, Alice S. *music educator*
Rissone, Donna *language educator*
Robbins, Nancy Slinker *volunteer*
Robfogel, Susan Salitan *lawyer*
Rodgers, Suzanne Hooker *ergonomics consultant, physiologist*
Santos, Wilma *missionary*
Schneider, Sue R. *music educator*
Seymour, Dawn Yvonne *manufacturing executive*
Smith, Julia Ladd *medical oncologist, hospice physician*
Spurrier, Mary Eileen *investment advisor, financial planner*
Steward, Jennifer A. *academic administrator*
Stewart, Sue S. *lawyer*
Strand, Marion Delores *social service administrator*
Sutter, Jane E. *editor*
Swanton, Susan Irene *retired library director*
Tobin, Barbara Kay *minister*
Toribara, Masako Ono *voice educator*
Truesdale, Carol A. *music educator*
Young, Mary Elizabeth *history educator*

Rockaway Park
Goldsmith, Cathy Ellen *retired special education educator*

Rockville Centre
Beyer, Suzanne *advertising agency executive*
Fitzgerald, Janet Anne *philosophy educator, academic administrator*

Rocky Point
Irizarry, Debra Edith *artist*

Rome
Sanders, Robin Renee *diplomat*

Roslyn Heights
Newmark, Marilyn *sculptor*
Rubrum, Erica Courtney *family therapist, school counselor*

Ruby
Cole, Max *artist*

Rush
Smith, Katherine Teresa *history educator*

Rushville
Carpenter, Florence Erika *retired human services administrator*

Rye
Casson Madden, Chris *entrepreneur, interior designer*
McDonnell, Mary Theresa *travel service executive*
Olver, Ruth Carol *social worker, retired*
Vauclair, Marguerite Renée *communications and sales promotion executive*
Vernon, Lillian *mail order company executive*

Rye Brook
Lo Russo, Diane *radiologist*

Sabael
Morrill-Cummins, Carolyn *social worker, consultant*

Sag Harbor
Brathwaite, Harriet Louisa *nursing educator, educator*
Brody, Jacqueline *editor*
Diamond, Mary E(lizabeth) B(aldwin) *artist*

Sagaponack
Cedering, Siv *poet, writer*

Saint Albans
Miller, Gwendolyn Doris *special education educator, retired*

Saint James
Van Dover, Karen *middle and elementary school educator, curriculum consultant, language arts specialist, lecturer*

Saint Johnsville
Schoff, Marcia Anne *elementary school educator*

Salisbury Mills
Satkowski, Sharon Kathleen Kennedy *elementary school educator*

Salt Point
Botway, Jaclyn Cooper *antiques dealer, consultant*
Lackey, Mary Michele *physician assistant*

Sanborn
Robinson, Deborah J. *counselor, educator, educational consultant*

Sands Point
Cohen, Ida Bogin (Mrs. Savin Cohen) *import and export executive*
Cullinan, Bernice E(llinger) *education educator*
Olian, JoAnne Constance *curator, art historian*
Tane, Susan Jaffe *retired manufacturing company executive*

Sandy Creek
Miller, Cheryl Marie *special education educator, business owner*

Saranac Lake
Cooper, Susan Lee Gensel *institutional advancement administrator*

Saratoga Springs
Carey, Margot Beckmann *fundraiser*
Martínez, Nicola Marie *choreographer, educator*
Muller, Susan Marie *physician*
O'Baire, Marika *community health nurse, writer*
Ratzer, Mary Boyd *secondary education educator, librarian*
Richardson, Elaina *foundation administrator, former magazine editor*

Saugerties
Starobin, Christina F. *artist, educator*

Sayville
Leuzzi, Linda *writer*
Lippman, Sharon Rochelle *art historian, art therapist, filmmaker*
Wurtz, Margaret Johnston *artist, calligrapher*

Scarborough
Stigall, Phyllis Graham *retired librarian*

Scarsdale
Bayar, Julia Beryl *interior designer*
Breslow, Marilyn Ganon *portfolio manager*
Bruck Lieb Port, Lilly *retired consumer advisor, broadcaster, columnist*
Callaghan, Georgann Mary *lawyer*
Clehane, Diane Catherine *journalist, writer, communications executive*
Liston, Mary Frances *retired nursing educator*
Newman, Stacey Clarfield *artist, curator*
Paulin, Amy Ruth *civic activist, consultant*
Schweitzer, Caren S. *social worker*
Shaw, Grace Goodfriend (Mrs. Herbert Franklin Shaw) *publisher, editor*
Topping, Audrey Ronning *photojournalist*
Wolfzahn, Annabelle Forsmith *psychologist*

Schenectady
Atchinson, Judy Fitzner *composer*
DuBrey, Patricia A. *medical technician*
Fabens, Sally Fisher *communications executive, consultant*
Smallin, Michelle DeAnne *marketing professional*
Sorum, Christina Elliott *academic administrator*
Zheng, Maggie (Xiaoci Zheng) *materials scientist, turbine coating specialist*

Sea Cliff
Bolin, Mary Jane *director*
Popova, Nina *dancer, choreographer, director*

Seaford
Spencer, Jean *food products executive*

Selden
Chin, Jing-Yi Syz *chemist, educator*
Sather, Voleen Rotunda *coroner*

Seneca Falls
Norman, Mary Marshall *alcohol/drug abuse services professional*

Setauket
Davenport, Deborah Morgan *obstetrician, gynecologist*

Shelter Island Heights
Culbertson, Janet Lynn *artist*

Sherburne
Rinaldo, Ginger Lee *music educator*

Shrub Oak
Vaccaro, Annette Andréa *music educator*

Sidney
Marsi, Janice Michaels *religious organization administrator*

Skaneateles
Filkins, Susan Esther *small business owner*

Sleepy Hollow
Flynn-Connors, Elizabeth Kathryn *editor*
Maun, Mary Ellen *computer consultant*
St. Vincent, Katharine Neyman *secondary school educator*

Slingerlands
Childs, Rhonda Louise *motivational speaker*
Jacobs, Karen Louise *medical technologist*

Smithtown
Kalabza-Balsamo, Debra Alyce *music educator*

Somers
Hall, Kathleen Yanarella *financial executive*
Lemke, Judith A. *lawyer*
Ryan, Cathleen Reneer *management consultant*
Sanford, Linda S. *information technology executive*

Sound Beach
Preuss, Linda Palmbaum *music educator*

South Bethlehem
Shirikian-Hesselton, Joan Lee *safety engineer*

South Ozone Park
Cook, Vivian *state legislator*

Southampton
Freeman, Elaine Lavalle *sculptor*
McLauchlen, Jennifer *art dealer*
Shapiro, Anna *microbiologist, researcher*

Southold
Alexander, Dolores Anne *retired journalist, advocate*
Giardi, Diane M. *ceramics educator, sculptor*
Small, Bertrice W. *writer*

Sparkill
Dahl, Arlene *actress, writer, apparel designer, cosmetics executive*
Myers, Adele Anna *artist, educator, nun*
Nelson, Marguerite Hansen *special education educator*

Sparrow Bush
Miiller, Susan Diane *artist*

Spring Valley
Ligonde-Minor, Gina *social worker, consultant*

Springfield Gardens
Moore, Deborah Chantay *protective services official, psychotherapist*
Williams, Vida Veronica *guidance counselor*

Staten Island
Berman, Barbara *educational consultant*
Dobis, Joan Pauline *education administrator*
Fung, Amy Shu-Fong *accountant*
Garcia, Minerva A.F. *bacteriologist, research and clinical laboratory scientist*
Lockhart, Patricia Ann *elementary school educator*
McGinn, Loretta *food service administrator*
Popp, Lilian Mustaki *writer, educator*
Robison, Paula Judith *flutist*
Springer, Marlene *university administrator, educator*
Vinitskaya, Marina *language educator, education educator*
Woodford, Ann Marguerite *social services administrator, social worker*

Stone Ridge
Ebersole, Patricia Sue *advertising executive, design educator*

Stony Brook
Brandwein, Ruth Ann *social welfare educator, administrator, author*
Harvey, Christine Lynn *publishing executive*
Kenny, Shirley Strum *academic administrator*
Lane, Dorothy Spiegel *preventive medicine physician*
Leske, M. Cristina *medical educator, medical researcher*
McClean, Lenora James *nursing educator, dean*
Mueller, Jean Margaret *nursing consultant*
Pindell, Howardena Doreen *artist*
Stone, Elizabeth Cecilia *anthropology educator*
Tanur, Judith Mark *sociologist, educator*

Stuyvesant
Tripp, Susan Gerwe *museum director*

Suffern
Badau, Karen Snyder *psychologist, researcher*
Bay, Libby *college administrator, English language educator*
Hawver, Carolyn Dunn *pharmaceutical production executive*

Syosset
Denton, Michele Anne *music educator*
Grenzig, Gail A. *assistant principal, consultant*
Kniffin, Paula Sichel *insurance sales executive*

Syracuse
Boghosian, Paula der *computer business consultant*
Chickadonz, Grace Harlow *dean*
Darrow, Gretchen *costume designer*
DeSiato, Donna Jean *school system administrator*
Duerr, Dianne Marie *sports medicine consultant, educator*
Fiske, Sandra Rappaport *psychologist, educator*
Giacchi, Judith Adair *elementary school educator*
Gilman, Karen Frenzel *legal assistant*
Hoffmann, Nancy Larraine *state legislator*
Horst, Pamela Sue *medical educator, family physician*
Jeannotte, Mary Elizabeth *psychologist, educator*
Johnson, Denise Eva *director, researcher*
Kerr, Darlene Dixon *electric power company executive*
King, Marcia Jones *potter, physicist, photographer*
Manley, Michelle S. *social worker, educator*
Numann, Patricia Joy *surgeon, educator*
Rogers, Sherry Anne *physician*
Skoler, Celia Rebecca *retired art gallery director*
Streeten, Barbara Wiard *ophthalmologist, medical educator*
Trop, Sandra *museum administrator*
Von Braunsberg, Mary Jane *clinical psychologist*
Waddy, Patricia A. *architectural history educator*
Wadley, Susan Snow *anthropologist*
Walker, Amy Melissa *English as second language educator*
Wilkinson, Louise Cherry *psychology educator, dean*
Wolff, Catherine Elizabeth *opera company executive*

Tannersville
Kline, Linda *employment consultant*

Tappan
Fox, Muriel *retired public relations executive*
Golbert, Sandra *artist*

Tarrytown
Kirsch, Abigail *culinary productions executive*
O'Brien, Anne Therese *chemist*

Thompsonville
Dalli, Inalbys R. *accountant*

Tillson
Debrosky, Christine Anne *painter, educator*
Kelly, Patricia Ellen *information technology manager*

Tivoli
Cranna, Christina M. *social services specialist*

Tonawanda
Glickman, Marlene *non-profit organization administrator*
Peterson, Dorothy Lulu *artist*

Troy
Burch, Mary Seelye Quinn *law librarian, consultant*
Friedman, Sue Tyler *technical publications executive*
Jackson, Shirley Ann *academic administrator, physicist*
Krause, Sonja *chemistry educator*
Medicus, Hildegard Julie *retired dentist, orthodontist, educator*
Neff, Jeanne Henry *academic administrator*
Snyder, Patricia Di Benedetto *theater director and administrator*
Tanguay, Janet *expressive arts therapist, writer, filmmaker*

Trumansburg
Frederick, Susan Ann (Pentz) *music educator*
Kredell, Carol Ruth *artist*
Van Buren, Mary Lou *retired religious organization administrator*

Truxton
Schultz, Helen Welkley *marriage and family therapist, minister*

Tuxedo Park
Buckley, Maureen A. *speech pathology/audiology services professional*
Regan, Ellen Frances (Mrs. Walston Shepard Brown) *ophthalmologist, educator*

Uniondale
Adams, Velma M. *assistant principal, consultant*
Meng, M. Kathryn *lawyer*

Upton
Fowler, Joanna S. *chemist*
Setlow, Jane Kellock *biophysicist*

Utica
Donovan, Donna Mae *newspaper publisher*
Droz, Elizabeth Jane *foundation administrator*
Stormer, Nancy Rose *lawyer*

Valhalla
Campbell, Debra Lynn *marketing and new venture consultant*
Keesler, Deborah Elizabeth *civil engineer*
Kline, Susan Anderson *medical school official and dean, internist*
McGoldrick, Kathryn Elizabeth *anesthesiologist, educator, writer*

Valley Cottage
Mahan, Jacqueline Francis *artist, educator*

Valley Stream
Ellis, Bernice *financial planning company executive, investment advisor*
Lehner, Remy D. *publishing executive*

Bradford, Anne Harden *director*
Breland-Noble, Alfiee Matiese *psychologist, researcher*
Buckley, Rebecca Hatcher *allergist, immunologist, pediatrician, educator*
Burgess, Paula Lashenske *health facility administrator*
Champagne, Mary T. *dean*
Clark, Mary Cannon *art educator*
Coard, Stephanie Irby *psychologist, researcher*
Demott, Deborah Ann *lawyer, educator*
Denlinger, Ann T. *school system administrator*
Goestenkors, Gail *basketball coach*
Gosselin, Tracy Karen *nursing administrator*
Hoffman, Jennifer Anne *vascular technician, director*
Hogan, Brigid L. *molecular biologist*
Holder, Angela Roddey *lawyer, educator*
Johnson, Kristina M. *technology director*
Kaplan, Alice *humanities educator, writer*
Kaprielian, Victoria Susan *medical educator*
Keohane, Nannerl Overholser *university president, political scientist*
Kerckhoff, Sylvia Stansbury *mayor*
Kurtzberg, Joanne *pediatrics educator*
Ladd, Marcia Lee *medical equipment and supplies company executive*
Lischer, Tracy Kenyon *lawyer*
Markert, Mary Louise *pediatrics educator*
Martinez, Maria Dolores *pediatrician*
McClain, Paula Denice *political scientist, educator*
Mickiewicz, Ellen Propper *political and social science educator*
Murphy, Barbara Anne *emergency physician, surgery educator*
Nelson, Denise Grau *special education educator, consultant*
Page, Bernadette Ryan *emergency physician*
Pericak-Vance, Margaret A. *health facility administrator*
Richardson, Lily Pendarvis *retired occupational health nurse*
Rouse, Doris Jane *physiologist, research administrator*
Schiffman, Susan Stolte *medical psychologist, educator*
Scott, Anne Byrd Firor *history educator*
Semans, Mary Duke Biddle Trent *foundation administrator*
Thibodeau, Patricia Leona *medical librarian*
Watkins, Melynda *research scientist, chemist*

Eden
Sanders, Barbara Fayne *artist, educator*

Elizabeth City
Pierce, Dianne S. *city clerk*
Williams, Rita Carroll *language educator, poet*

Fayetteville
Jordan, Karla Salge *early childhood education educator*
Kem, Katherine Frances *urban planner*
Lydon, Kerry Raines *elementary school educator*
McMillan, Bettie Barney *English language educator*
Mohn, Amy Elizabeth Brennan *special education educator, retail consultant*
Rivers, Stephanie Denise Wall *elementary school educator*
Ross, Bernadette Marie-Teresa *librarian*
Swoope, Janice Robins *music educator*
Townsend, Susan Stockstill *elementary school educator, music educator*
Turner, Gwendolyn Marie *band director, musician*

Fort Bragg
Carnahan, Doris Jean *budget analyst*
Nichols, Carol-Lee *real estate broker, property manager*

Franklin
Earhart, Eileen Magie *retired child and family life educator*

Garner
Barbour, Charlene *management firm executive*
Henderson, Shirley Elizabeth *minister*

Gastonia
Randall, Sheila R. *real estate company executive*

Goldsboro
Aldridge, Helen Belinda Oliver *primary school educator*
Harper, Linda Ruth *disabilities educator, consultant*
Turlington, Patricia Renfrew *artist, educator*

Graham
Stanberry, D(osi) Elaine *English literature educator, writer*

Granite Quarry
Trivette, Susan Brown *music educator*

Greensboro
Archibald, Brigitte Edith *language educator*
Barnett, Dorothy Prince *retired dean*
Black, Sylvia Sloan *business educator*
Bland, Annie Ruth (Ann Bland) *nursing educator*
Bynum, Magnolia Virginia Wright *retired secondary school educator*
Champlin, Deborah Louise *medical/surgical nurse, consultant*
Cole, Johnnetta Betsch *academic administrator, educator*
Cummings, Candace S. *apparel company executive*
Dillon, Terri L. *consulting firm executive*
Dyer, Karen Marie *education educator*
Gill, Diane Louise *psychology educator, university official*
Gill, Evalyn Pierpoint *editor, writer, publisher*
Green, Jill I. *dance educator, researcher*
Harris-Offutt, Rosalyn Marie *counselor, consultant, mental health nurse, writer*
Hazelip, Edwina Kay *critical care nurse*
Helms VanStone, Mary Wallace *anthropology educator*
Henley, Jody Dale Hartig *music educator, consultant*
Hudgens, Jeanne Ellis *advocate*
Jeffus, Margaret M. (Maggie Jeffus) *state representative, retired elementary school educator*
Kovacs, Beatrice *library studies educator*
Lenard, Mary Jane *accounting and information systems educator*
Lloyd, Lila G. *business educator*
Nesbitt, Eleanor Troutman *elementary school educator, music educator*
Nieman, Valerie Gail *editor*
Oliver, Donna H. *secondary school educator*
Pearcey, Lynne G. *university dean, nursing educator*
Penninger, Frieda Elaine *retired English language educator*
Richardson, Erika *special education educator*
Roerden, Chris (Claire Roerden) *editor, business owner, publishing consultant*
Russell, Anne Wrenn *property manager*
Russell, Peggy Taylor *soprano, educator*
Scott, Gloria Randle *college president*
Shaw, Linda Dare Owens *county commissioner*
Smith, Rebecca McCulloch *human relations educator*
Stone, Theresa M. *communications executive*
Styles, Teresa Jo *producer, educator*
Sullivan, Patricia A. *academic administrator*
Villaverde, Leila E. *education educator*
Wagoner, Anna Mills *prosecutor*
Wallace, Becky Whitley *protective services official*
Ward, Angie *radio personality*
Watson, Betty *artist*
White, Gladys Hope Franklin *reading specialist*
Zopf, Evelyn LaNoel Montgomery *guidance counselor*

Greenville
Faircloth, Mary Williams *minister, educator*
Johnson, Cynda Ann *physician, educator*
Page, Mary Stancill *insurance agency executive*
Reichelt, Susan Ann *career and techical educator*
Tripp, Linda A. Lynn *court reporter*
Turnage, Karen L. *medical technologist*

Grimesland
Phillips, Paula Brady *speech pathology/audiology services professional*

Halifax
Phillips, Margaret Rackley *retired elementary school educator*

Havelock
Stroud, Carrie Hoggard *elementary school educator*

Hayesville
Gibson, Jennifer Williams *music educator*

Henderson
Williams, Ruth Russell *artist*

Hendersonville
Butcher, Diane *chaplain, bereavement facilitator*
Heil, Mary Ruth *former counselor*
Keefauver, Nancy Ann *pre-school educator*
Kingsbury, Carolyn Ann *aerospace engineer, craftsman, writer*
Van Boer, Helen Shirley *counselor, educator*

Hertford
Sutton, Louise Nixon *retired mathematics educator*

Hickory
Mason, Anne R. Hardin *municipal official*

High Point
Bennett-Wilkes, Theresa Williams *writer, educator*
Draelos, Zoe Diana *dermatologist, consultant*
Flack, Teresa Hopper *music educator*
Howard, Lou Dean Graham *elementary school educator*

Hillsborough
Richmond, Donna *speech-language pathologist*
Stephens, Brenda Wilson *librarian*

Holden Beach
Blecha, Diane Louise *business consultant*

Hope Mills
Williams, LaVerne Carmen *performance artist, poet, musician*

Hubert
Howell, Nelda Kay *commissioner*
Lloyd, Margaret Harris *entrepreneur, educator*

Huntersville
McCall, Debra Knight *art educator*
Petersen, Ruth Anne *performing arts educator*

Jacksonville
Fischer, Violeta Pèrez Cubillas *Spanish literature and linguistics educator*

Jamestown
Moorefield, Susan Morgan *music educator*

Jefferson
Maney, Lois Jean *postmaster*

Kernersville
Cappel, Linda Greenwood *education educator*
Craven, Betty *educational association administrator*
Hosier, Linda Grube *gifted and talented educator*

King
Shanahan, Elizabeth Anne *art educator*

Kings Mountain
Aderholdt, Traci Eaves *music educator*

Kinston
Richardson, Vanessa *education educator*

Kitty Hawk
Berger, Tina *hotel executive*
Elliott, Candice K. *interior designer*

Knightdale
Braswell, Jackie Terry *medical, surgical nurse*

Lake Waccamaw
Spaulding, Lila Bernice *marriage and family counselor*

Laurel Springs
Gilbert-Strawbridge, Anne Wieland *journalist*

Laurinburg
Hamby, Sherry Lynne *psychologist, researcher*
Tate, Alicia Salemme *special education educator*

Leasburg
Treacy, Sandra Joanne Pratt *artist, educator*

Leland
Jones, Jacqueline Lee *health facility administrator*
Karch, Jacqueline *artist*

Lexington
Wood, April Carthena *judge*

Lumberton
Canonizado, Gloria M. *choreographer, educator*

Manteo
Evans, Michelle T. *county official*
Hollins, April Rife *music educator*

Matthews
Kocsis, Joan Bosco *elementary education educator, administrative assistant, assistant principal*

Monroe
Helms, Katie Mae *artist*
Little, Wanda Vickery *school system administrator*
Radke, Anne Marie *assistant principal, writer*
Rorie, Nancy Catherine *retired elementary and secondary school educator*
Wallace, Patricia Ellen *minister*

Mooresboro
Goode, Elizabeth Ann *music educator*

Mooresville
Dow, Leslie Wright *communications company executive, photographer, writer*
Earnhardt, Teresa *race team owner*
La Monica, Patricia C. *real estate broker*

Morehead City
Jones, Hilda Hobbs *minister*

Morganton
McDaniel, Janet B. *principal*
Singleton, Stella Wood *nurse*

Morrisville
Cannon, Alice Grace *counselor*
Rauch, Kathleen *computer executive*

Mount Gilead
McNeill, Maxine Currie *county official*

Mount Holly
Whobrey, Virginia Jean *retired director*

Murphy
Ashley, Mary J. *media specialist*
Dickey, Jeannetta Burkett *social worker*

New Bern
Crecca, Pamela Michelle *small business owner*
Hemphill, Jean Hargett *college dean*
Phipps, Patsy Duncan *retired auditor*
White, Rhea Amelia *information scientist, consciousness researcher*

Newland
Lustig, Susan Gardner *occupational therapist*

Newport
Mundine, Rachel Quinn *music educator*

Newton
Daniels, Glennie Overman *family and consumer educator*
Reinhardt, Susan Elaine Gantt *family resource center administrator, counselor*

North Wilkesboro
Parsons, Irene Adelaide *management consultant*

Otto
Harwell, Joanne Brindley *music educator*

Oxford
Dorton, Louise *library director*
Harvey, Gloria-Stroud *physician assistant*

Pembroke
Sexton, Jean Elizabeth *librarian*
Thompson, Debra Anne *speech pathology/audiology services professional, educator*
Tyner, Bessie Hubbard *mechanical engineer, mathematician*

Pilot Mountain
Collins, Sherri Smith *music educator*

Pinnacle
Ayers, Carole Annette *social studies educator*

Pittsboro
Betts, Doris June Waugh *writer, English language educator*
Handler, Enid Irene *health care administrator, consultant*
Schwinn-Jordan, Barbara (Barbara Schwinn) *painter*

Raeford
Abreu, Sue Hudson *physician, army officer, organizational and healthcare consultant*

Raleigh
Allen, Barbara Kirkman *politcal organization administrator*
Anderson, Jala *newscaster*
Barker, Gloria S. *government and community affairs professional*
Berry, Cherie Killian *commissioner*
Berry, Joni Ingram *hospice pharmacist, educator*
Bhandari, Rajika *psychologist*
Bowie, Joanne Walker (Joni Bowie) *state legislator*
Bradley, Elizabeth Clay *financial planner, educator*
Burkholder, Joann M. *botany educator*
Byrd, Emily *newscaster*
Carter, Jean Gordon *lawyer*
Cauthen, Carmen Wimberley *legislative staff member, jewelry designer*
Chaney, Ethel Scotland *English language educator*
Conley, Christine *music educator*
Deja, Heidi *newscaster*
Delaney, Sharon *newscaster*
Duncan, Allyson K. *federal judge*
Faulkner, Janice H. *state official*
Florin, Julie A. *music educator*
Fox, Marye Anne *university chancellor, chemistry educator*
Foxx, Virginia Ann *state legislator, small business owner*
Fredenburgh, Lisa Marie *music educator*
Garriss, Phyllis Weyer *music educator, performer*
Garrou, Linda *state legislator*
Geller, Janice Grace *nurse*
Genardo, Kim *newscaster*
Gulledge, Karen Stone *educational administrator*
Hagan, Kay R. *state legislator, lawyer*
Harnish, Margaret Ann *music educator*
Hartford, Maureen A. *academic administrator*
Henry, Janice K. *construction materials company executive*
Hiday, Virginia Aldigé *sociologist educator*
Howard, Julia C. *state legislator*
Hughes, Francis P. *medical organization executive*
Hynus, Anita Eileen *music educator*
Johnson, Mary Pauline (Polly Johnson) *nursing executive*
Johnston, Linda Tidwell *municipal official*
Jones, Janice *newscaster*
Jordan, Brenda Moore *artist*
Joyner, Lorinzo Little *commissioner*
Kauffman, Terry *broadcast and creative arts communication educator, artist*
Kimbrough, Lorelei *elementary school educator*
Kinnaird, Eleanor Gates *state legislator, lawyer*
Kurz, Mary Elizabeth *lawyer*
Lasher, Harriet Pinsker *director, educator*
Lucas, Jeanne Hopkins *state senator, retired educational administrator*
Maidon, Carolyn Howser *director*
Malling, Martha Hale Shackford *social worker, educator*
Marsh, Melissa *newscaster*
Marshall, Elaine Folk *state official*
McGee, Linda Mace *judge, lawyer*
McKinney, Carolyn *educational association administrator, educator*
Nelson, Cynthia Kaye *infrastructure security engineer*
Occhetti, Dianne *psychologist, writer*
Olevsky, Kathy Kilmartin *owner, instructor karate school*
Osteryoung, Janet Gretchen *chemistry educator*
Page, Anne Ruth *gifted education educator, education specialist*
Parker, Sarah Elizabeth *state supreme court justice*
Parramore, Barbara Mitchell *education educator*
Peele, Katherine N. *architect*
Perdue, Beverly E. *lieutenant governor, geriatric consultant*
Ridgeway, Johanna Bohacek *language educator*
Ross, Deborah Koff *lawyer, state legislator*
Russell, Carolyn B. *state legislator*
Sanford, Jo Anne *state agency administrator*
Santucci, Angela Maria *performing arts educator, actress, singer*
Shaw, Sandra *newscaster*
Sill, Melanie *editor*
Steed, Michelle Elnora *special education educator, counselor*
Stukes, Reesie *communications executive*
Suber, Dianne Boardley *educational administrator*
Tally, Lura Self *state legislator*
Thorton, Angelica *newscaster*
Triantaphyllou, H. H. *plant pathologist*
Whitworth, Camille *newscaster*

Research Triangle Park
Haynes, Victoria F. *science administrator*
League, Charle Allport (Charlene League) *federal official, minister*

Rockingham
Evans, Patricia McCormick *clinical therapist*

Rocky Mount
Dickens, Alice McKnight *minister*

Rougemont
Nilsson, Mary Ann *music educator*

Roxboro
Broyles, Bonita Eileen *nursing educator*

Salisbury
Brautigan, June Marie *artist, poet*
Fisher, Ada Markita *physician, health services administrator, writer, poet*
Hall, Telka Mowery Elium *retired educational administrator*
Julian, Rose Rich *music educator, director*
Snipes, Mignonne Elvira *academic administrator*
Troxler, Willie Thomasene *retired elementary school educator*
Ward, Brenda Robinson *social worker*

Sanford
Wesner, Jennifer Isla *music educator*

Shallotte
Weaver, Lyn Ann Simmons *psychologist*

Shelby
Bess, Angela Paige *music educator*
Edgar, Ruth R. *retired elementary school educator*

Sherrills Ford
Stynes, Barbara Bilello *integrative health professional, educator*
Zimmern-Reed, Annette Wacks *psychologist*

Southern Pines
Cardwell, Nina Fern *special education educator*
Kaufmann, Rachel Norsworthy *social sciences educator*
Martin, Lorna Campbell *English language educator*

Stoneville
Halpin, Margaret Renee *music educator*

Sylva
Karcher, Susan Marie *speech pathology/audiology services professional*

Tryon
McDermott, Renée R(assler) *lawyer*

Valdese
Hildebran, Frances Elaine *municipal clerk*

Wake Forest
Jerose, Terese M.J. *librarian*

Walstonburg
Beaman, Joyce Proctor *retired secondary and elementary school educator, writer*

Warrenton
Kearney, Irene Spruill *elementary school educator*
Weddington, Elizabeth Gardner (Liz Gardner) *actress*

Waxhaw
Edwards, Irene Elizabeth (Libby Edwards) *dermatologist, educator, medical researcher*

Waynesville
Ingle, Marti Annette *protective services official, educator*

Weaverville
Chamberlain, Elizabeth Simmons *retired English language educator*

West End
Hodge, Katherine Rhodes *retired school guidance counselor*

Whispering Pines
Catullo, Doris Jane *sculptor*

Wilkesboro
Anderson, Theresa A. *retail executive*
Dale, Brenda Stephens *gifted and talented educator*
Klark, Denise J. *special education educator, consultant*

Williamston
Hoggard, Minnie Coltrain *gifted education educator, consultant*

Wilmington
Baldridge, Jane L. *graphic artist, fine artist*
Bomhan, Ruth Walker *social studies educator*
Cameron, Kay *conductor, music director, arranger*
Charles, Catherine Elaine *music educator*
Clinton, Lottie Dry Edwards *retired state agency administrator*
Coté, Debra Nan *surgical nurse*
DePaolo, Rosemary *dean, academic administrator*
Foglia, Michelle Lynn *psychologist*
Israel, Margie Olanoff *psychotherapist*
Kelley, Patricia Hagelin *geology educator*
Kelley, Virginia Wiard (Judy Kelley) *dance educator*
Lavin, Linda *actress*
Lawson, Pamela Ann *musician, educator*
Maness, Eleanor Palmer *research analyst*
Midgett, Carol Wickham *mathematics educator, consultant*
Nubel, Marianne Kunz *cultural administrator, writer, composer*
Robinson, Robin Wicks *lawyer*
Seapker, Janet Kay *museum and architectural history consultant*

Wilson
McCain, Betty Landon Ray (Mrs. John Lewis McCain) *political party official, state official*
Morris, Sharon Louise Stewart *emergency medical technician, paramedic*

Wingate
Bostic, Polly Thomas *music educator*

Winston Salem
Carruthers, Catharine *federal judge*
Cieszewski, Sandra Josephine *artist, retired manufacturing company manager*
Crowder, Lena Belle *retired special education educator*
Dykers, Carol Reese *communications educator*
Evans, Lisbeth *business networking executive, political party official*
Ferree, Carolyn Ruth *radiation oncologist, educator*
Gala, Candelas S. *literature educator, language educator*
Graham, Gloria Flippin *dermatologist*
Graybeal, Barbara *editor, writer*
Jarrell, Iris Bonds *elementary school educator, business executive*
Jenkins, Barbara Alexander *pastor and overseer*
Karnes, Lucia Rooney *psychologist*
Kaufman, Charlotte S. *communications executive*
Kelly, Katherine Theresa *psychologist, consultant*
Ludolf, Marilyn Marie Keaton *lay worker*
Mueller, Margaret S. *musician, educator*
Pera, McCall *newscaster*
Roth, Marjory Joan Jarboe *special education educator*
Smunt, Marsha Lynn Haeflinger *financial executive*
Stewart, Gwendolyn Johns *music educator*
Thrift, Julianne Still *academic administrator*
Volz, Annabelle Wekar *learning disabilities educator, consultant*
Wallace, Roanne *hosiery company executive*
Walters, Doris Lavonne *retired pastoral counselor, counseling services facility administrator*
Wood, Mary Elizabeth *retired physician assistant*
Yeatts, Dorothy Elizabeth Freeman *nurse, educator, retired county official*

Winton
Williams, Sue Darden *library director*

Wrightsville Beach
[illegible], Kathryn Watkins *personal and professional success coach*
McDonald, Wylene Booth *former nurse, pharmaceutical sales professional*

Zebulon
Platt, Katrina Vontelle *music educator*
Ruffing, Anne Elizabeth *artist*

NORTH DAKOTA

Bisbee
Keller, Michelle R. *science educator, secondary education educator*

Bismarck
Dixon, Dotti S. *school counselor*
Evanson, Barbara Jean *middle school education educator*
Gilmore, Kathi *state treasurer*
Gray, Arlene *music educator, musician*
Gulleson, Pam *state legislator*
Joersz, Fran Woodmansee *secondary school educator*
Kapsner, Carol Ronning *state supreme court justice*
Kelsch, RaeAnn *state legislator*
Ketterling, Debra M. *secondary school educator*
Lundberg, Susan Ona *musical organization administrator*
Maring, Mary Muehlen *state supreme court justice*
Neas, Sherry Lee *purchasing agent, procurement manager*
Nelson, Carolyn *state legislator*
Ott, Doris Ann *librarian*
Price, Clara Sue *state legislator*
Sandvig, Sally *state legislator*
Schwartz, Judy Ellen *cardiothoracic surgeon*
Stoller, Rose *think-tank executive*
Wefald, Susan *state commissioner*

Calvin
Magnus, Elsie L. *music educator*

Devils Lake
Moyer Klemetsrud, Kandace Marie *artist*

Dickinson
Medlar, Deborah Starkey *secondary school educator*
Nelson, Debra L. *consultant for non-profit organizations*
Schubert, Yvette Marie *music educator*

Edinburg
Myrdal, Rosemarie Caryle *state official, former state legislator*

Fargo
Fossum, Ruth N. *musician*
Holman, Maureen *lawyer*
Klein, Karen K. *federal judge*
Lardy, Sister Susan Marie *academic administrator*
Mathern, Deb *state legislator*
Nickel, Janet Marlene Milton *geriatrics nurse*
Sanford, Glenda Levonne *educational administrator*
Slobin, Kathleen Overin *sociology educator, researcher, consultant*
Wegenast, Judy H. *elementary school educator, consultant*

Fort Yates
Chief Eagle, Joan *secondary school educator*

Golden Valley
Nordgren, Mary Kathleen *secondary school educator*

Grand Forks
Ashe, Kathy Rae *special education educator*
Burns, Elizabeth Ann *physician, educator*
Caldwell, Mary Ellen *English language educator*
Christenson, Linda *state legislator*
Delmore, Lois M. *state legislator*
DeMers, Judy Lee *former state legislator, university dean*
Harken, Shelby Elaine *librarian*
Mondry, Diane *secondary school educator*
Page, Sally Jacquelyn *university official, management educator*
Rakow, Lana F. *communications educator, humanities educator*
Sobus, Kerstin MaryLouise *physician, physical therapist*
Warnke, Amy Nicholle *state legislator*
Zahrly, Janice Honea *management educator*

Hazen
Eustice, Esther *elementary school educator*

Hettinger
Burrer, Ardath Rose *elementary school educator, music educator*

Killdeer
Bergstedt, Sonja K. *elementary school educator*

Maddock
Aadland, Kathleen A. *counselor, army intelligence officer*

Mandan
Heitkamp, Heidi *former state attorney general*
Hollingsworth, Rebecca A. *speech pathology/audiology services professional*

Mayville
Karaim, Betty June *retired librarian*

Minot
Anderson, Denise W. *publishing executive, musician*
Krebsbach, Karen K. *state legislator*
[illegible]
Watne, Darlene Claire *state legislator*

Rhame
Kulish, Carma C. *music educator*

Rolla
Zinke, Sheila J. *music educator*

Saint John
Haas, Judith *elementary school educator*

Stanley
Eliason, Bonnie Mae *county treasurer*

Steele
Dewitz, Lynn Marlene *art educator, consultant*

Taylor
Miller, Jean Patricia Salmon *art educator*

Towner
Gunter, G. Jane *state legislator*

Valley City
Fischer, Mary Elizabeth *library director*

Washburn
Hall, Gwen Marie *music educator*

West Fargo
Jordahl, Susan Marie *music educator*

OHIO

Ada
Herr, Sharon Marie *librarian*
Sycks, Linda B. *music educator*

Akron
Bowman-Dalton, Burdene Kathryn *education testing coordinator, computer consultant*
Buzzelli, Charlotte Grace *special education educator*
Capers, Cynthia Flynn *dean, nursing educator*
Cocain Hastler, Cynthia Lucille *artist, graphic designer*
Deason, Lucinda Marie *accountant, educator*
Dietz, Margaret Jane *retired public information director*
Donehey, Marilyn Moss *foundation administrator*
Graham, DeBorah Denise *minister, educator*
Korow, Elinore Maria *artist, educator*
Kuster, Doreen K. *accountant*
Lesner, Sharon A. *audiologist, educator*
Livingston, Kriemhilde Irmgard Reinfriede *retired language educator, translator, interpreter*
Milsted, Amy *biomedical educator*
Myers, Mary Elizabeth *police officer*
Piirma, Irja *chemist, educator*
Rothkin, Marilyn Mae *psychotherapist*
Scheel, Karen Rae *psychologist*
Shea-Stonum, Marilyn *federal judge*
Simmons, Debra Adams *editor*
Smith, Priscilla R. *social sciences educator*
Usher, Ann L. *music educator*
Vespoli, Leila L. *lawyer, energy executive*
Wang, Ya-Hui *conductor*
Zeno, Jo Ann *sales executive*

Alliance
Clem, Harriet Frances *library director*
Fugelberg, Nancy Jean *retired music educator*
Woods, Rose Mary *former presidential assistant, consultant*

Amherst
Gall, Simone Ellen *music educator*
Gerstenberger, Valerie *media coordinator*

Ashland
Drushal, Mary Ellen *education educator, former academic administrator*
Ford, Lucille Garber *economist, educator*
Reidenbach, Faith E. *medical editor, writer*

Athens
Dugan, JoAnn Rubino *education educator*
Heindl, Christine *artist, educator*
Helsel, Elsie Dressler *retired special education educator*
Jellison, Katherine Kay *historian, educator*
Krendl, Kathy *dean*
Miller, Peggy McLaren *retired management educator*
Parrotti, Laura Davidian *theater educator*
Sarnoff, Susan Kiss *social worker, educator*
Whealey, Lois Deimel *humanities scholar*

Aurora
Nelson, Hedwig Potok *marketing executive*

Avon
Grmek, Dorothy Antonia *accountant*

Avon Lake
Kent, Deborah *automotive executive*

Batavia
Muskopf, Beth A. *curriculum consultant*

Bath
Hoffer, Alma Jeanne *nursing educator*

Beachwood
Curran, Audrey Harwell *psychologist, educator*
Eagleeve-Lord, Amy S. *editor*
Farley, Carolyn Juanita *music educator*
Fufuka, Natika Njeri Yaa *retail executive*
Liebow, Joanne Elisabeth *poet and freelance publicist*
Strauss, Marilyn Sheperd *public relations executive*

Beavercreek
Busch, Sharon Lynne *elementary and secondary education educator*
Focht, Sandra Jean *elementary school educator*
Rinta, Christine Evelyn *nurse, air force officer*

Bedford
Shauf, Jennifer Elaine *music educator*

Berea
Jones, Erin Marguerite *music educator*

Bergholz
Goddard, Sandra Kay *elementary school educator*

Bexley
Osnes, Pamela Grace *behavior analyst*
Unverferth, Barbara Patten *small business owner*

Blacklick
Robinson, Bernice Joyce *secondary school educator*

Bowling Green
Berger, Bonnie G. *sport psychologist, educator*
Clark, Eloise Elizabeth *biologist, educator*
Dobb, Linda Sue *university official, librarian*
Filippova, Daria Vladimirovna *private school educator*
Heckman, Carol A. *biology educator*
Leetch, Nancy Wikoff *artist*
Singer, Carol Ann *librarian, researcher*
Williams, Theresa Ann Aleshire *poet, writer, educator*
Wolcott, Nancy Bookout *music director*

Bratenahl
DesRosiers, Anne Booke *performing arts administrator, consultant*

Brecksville
Pappas, Effie Vamis *language educator, finance educator, writer, poet, artist*

Broadview Heights
Jergens, Maribeth Joie *school counselor*

Brookpark
Cotton, Barbara Jean *systems analyst*

Brunswick
Fabich, Penelope Jane *humanities educator*

Bryan
Nowak, Carol Lee *art educator*

Bucyrus
Cooper, April Helen *family nurse practitioner*

Cadiz
Thompson, Sandra Lee *library administrator*

Cambridge
Barzda, Susan Marie *special education educator, art educator*
Ryan, Mary Esther *music educator*

Canton
Bernstein, Penny L. *biologist, educator*

Gleckler, Lois Eileene *occupational therapist*
Kilcullen, Maureen *librarian, educator*
Klotz, Leora Nylee *retired music educator, vocalist*
Moorhouse, Linda Virginia *symphony orchestra administrator*
Morgart, Michele *psychologist, consultant*
Moses, Marcia Swartz *artist*
Patrick, Beth Pelletier *art educator*
Rubin, Patricia *internist*
Snyder, Judith Lynn *fund development consultant*
Thomas, Suzanne Ward *public relations executive, communications educator, radio personality*
Traveria, Beth M. *mental health counselor*

Centerville

Coyle, Diane R. *artist, educator*
Geier, Sharon Lee *special education educator*
Kauffold, Ruth Elizabeth *clinical psychologist*
Rahe, Peggy Ann *realtor*
Wasson-Shaw, Carol R. *music teacher*

Chagrin Falls

Brown, Jeanette Grasselli *retired university official*
Cordes, Loverne Christian *interior designer*
Cortese, Julia F. *retired elementary school educator*
Cox, Cynthia A. *art education specialist*
Kuby, Barbara Eleanor *personnel director, management consultant*
Ostendorf, Joan Donahue *fund raiser, volunteer*
Robertson, Linda F. *educational adminstrator*
Ross, Sally Price *artist, painter*
Vail, Iris Jennings *civic worker*

Chandlersville

Herron, Janet Irene *industrial manufacturing engineer*

Chardon

Reinhard, Sister Mary Marthe *educational organization administrator*

Chesterland

Aster, Ruth Marie Rhydderch *business owner*

Chillicothe

Atwood, Joyce Charlene *curriculum and instruction administrator, consultant*
Copley, Cynthia Sue Love *insurance adjuster*
Greene, Judy *elementary school educator*
Reed, Faith Patricia *health services administrator*

Cincinnati

Anderson, Joan Balyeat *religion educator, minister*
Anderson, Judith Ann *artist, writer*
Arnold, Susan E. *consumer products company executive*
Ashley, Lynn *social sciences educator, consultant*
Attee, Joyce Valerie Jungclas *artist*
Aumiller, Wendy L. *utilities executive*
Aylesworth, Julie Ann *writer, personal care professional*
Beckwith, Barbara Jean *journalist*
Beckwith, Sandra Shank *judge*
Beggs, Patricia Kirk *performing company executive*
Bench, Barbara Anne *chemist*
Bestehorn, Ute Wiltrud *retired librarian*
Bollen, Sharon Kesterson *artist, educator*
Boyd, Deborah Ann *pediatrician*
Braunstein, Mary *energy consulting company executive*
Brestel, Mary Beth *librarian*
Briskin, Madeleine *paleo-oceanographer, paleoclimatologist, micropaleontologist*
Brown, Dale Patrick *retired advertising executive*
Brown, Jacqueline I. *medical assistant*
Brown, Lillie Harrison *music educator*
Bruns, Patricia Ann *art educator, consultant*
Bruvold, Kathleen Parker *lawyer*
Buchanan, Margaret *publishing executive*
Carvey, Julie Amber *behavior specialist, educational consultant*
Church, Sonia Jane Shutter *librarian*
Cook, Deborah L. *judge, former state supreme court justice*
Croskery, Beverly Ann *education consultant*
Curran, Mary Ann *chemical engineer*
De Courten-Myers, Gabrielle Marguerite *neuropathologist*
DeLong, Deborah *lawyer*
Di Benedetto, Ann Louise *accounting administrator*
Dlott, Susan Judy *judge, lawyer*
Dunevant, Carol Dary *music educator, conductor*
Einbinder, Susan Leslie *literature educator, rabbi*
Emmich, Linda L. *private school educator*
Everett, Karen Joan *retired librarian, genealogist, educator*
Everson, Jean Watkins Dolores *librarian, media consultant, educator*
Faller, Susan Grogan *lawyer*
Fenoglio-Preiser, Cecilia Mettler *pathologist, educator*
Flanagan, Martha Lang *publishing executive*
Foley, Cheryl M. *electric power industry executive*
Friedman, Penny *lawyer*
Galloway, Lillian Carroll *modeling agency executive, consultant*
Garfinkel, Jane E. *lawyer*
Gehlert, Sally Oyler *dental hygienist, consultant*
Goodman, Phyllis L. *public relations executive*
Govern, Maureen *information technology executive*
Greenwald, Theresa McGowan *medical administrator, nurse*
Grove, Janet E. *retail executive*
Hall, Madelon Carol Syverson *elementary school educator*
Heekin, Mary Ann *oncology social worker*
Henney, Jane Ellen *health facility administrator, educator, oncologist*
Henretta, Deb *consumer products company executive*
Hess, Evelyn Victorine *medical educator*
Hess, Marcia Wanda *retired secondary school educator*
Hodgson, Irene Belle *language educator, translator*
Hoguet, Karen M. *retail department store executive*
Holdren, Jamie Lynn *music educator*
Horrell, Karen Holley *insurance company executive, lawyer*
Irwin, Miriam Dianne Owen *book publisher, writer*
Isburgh, Anne Marie *engineering manager*
James, Jefferson Ann *performing company executive, choreographer*
Janson, Julia S. *utilities executive*
Jenkins, Kathleen Maria *web site design company executive*
Johnson, Betty Lou *secondary school educator*
Kalven, Janet *education educator, writer, consultant*
Karle-Swails, Jeanine *neuroscience clinical nurse specialist*
Kelly, Holly Andrea *real estate developer*
Kendle, Candace *pharmaceutical executive*
Kennedy, Cornelia Groefsema *federal judge*
King, Margaret Ann *communications educator*
Koebel, Sister Celestia *health care system executive*
Kollstedt, Paula Lubke *communications executive, writer*
Kronick, Susan D. *retail executive*
Laney, Sandra Eileen *service company executive*
Levin, Debbe Ann *lawyer*
Lindell, Andrea Regina *dean, nurse*
Loggie, Jennifer Mary Hildreth *medical educator, physician*
Lucky, Anne Weissman *dermatologist*
Manning, Alleen Blesi *art educator, artist*
McDaniels, Audrey Evelyn *microbiologist*
McMullin, Ruth Roney *publishing executive, trustee, management fellow*
Meal, Larie *chemistry educator, researcher, consultant*
Metcalf, Elyse N. *small business owner*
Meyers, Pamela Sue *lawyer*
Miller, Sari Elizabeth (Sally Derby) *writer*
Monroe, Erin *psychiatric nurse practitioner*
Morgan, Victoria *performing company executive, choreographer*
Morris, Margaret Elizabeth *marketing professional*
Murphy, Molly Ann *investment company executive*
Noonan, Sheila M. *energy consulting company executive*
Otto, Charlotte R. *consumer products company executive*
Parker, Linda Bates *professional development organization administrator*
Patterson, Claire Ann *career techincal educator*
Petty, Priscilla Hayes *writer, columnist, producer*
Phillips, Lynn Alice *pre-school educator*
Pirtle, Laurie Lee *women's university basketball coach*
Rexroth, Nancy Louise *photographer*
Rosen, Roberta *philosophy educator*
Runyan, Anne Sisson *political science educator*
St. John, Maria Ann *nurse anesthetist*
Schmidt, Leeanne *artist*
Schutzius, Lucy Jean *retired librarian*
Sedgwick, Sally Belle *publishing company executive*
Sierra-Amor, Rosa Isabel *health facility administrator*
Skavlem, Melissa Kline *publisher*
Solomon, Susanne Nina *podiatrist, surgeon*
Spencer, Marian Alexander *volunteer*
Stanton, Jeanne Frances *retired lawyer*
Steinberg, Janet Eckstein *journalist*
Stinson, Mary Florence *retired nursing educator*
Sullivan, Sandra Long *retired human resources specialist*
Ten Eyck, Dorothea Fariss *real estate agent*
Thomas, Hannah H. *retired educator*
Thompson, Adrienne *secondary school educator*
Timpano, Anne *museum director, art historian*
Tuttle, Martha Benedict *artist*
Wellington, Jean Susorney *librarian*
Winchell, Margaret J. *realtor*
Zealey, Sharon Janine *lawyer*
Zimpher, Nancy Lusk *academic administrator*

Cleveland

Ainsworth, Joan Horsburgh *university development director*
Aldrich, Ann *federal judge*
Baranova, Elena *professional basketball player*
Beall, Cynthia *anthropologist, educator*
Berger, Molly *historian, educator*
Bixenstine, Kim Fenton *lawyer*
Borchert, Catherine Glennan *minister*
Bowen, Chieh-Chen *psychology educator, consultant*
Brennan, Maureen *lawyer*
Burke, Kathleen B. B. *lawyer*
Byrd-Bennett, Barbara *school system administrator*
Campbell, Jane Louise *mayor*
Carrick, Kathleen Michele *law librarian*
Crandall, Karen *government agency administrator*
Cudak, Gail Linda *lawyer*
Curnow, Kathy *art historian, educator*
Dadley, Arlene Jeanne *sleep technologist*
Davis, Pamela Bowes *pediatric pulmonologist*
Dirksen, Marlene Kay *music educator*
Dougherty, Ursel Thielbeule *communications and marketing executive*
Douglas, Janice Green *physician, educator*
Drake, Grace L. *retired state senator, cultural organization administrator*
Dunbar, Mary Asmundson *communications executive, investor and public relations consultant*
Dylag, Helen Marie *healthcare administrator*
Eagan, Susan Lajoie *finance educator, consultant*
Edwards, Michelle Denise *professional basketball player*
Fallon, Pat *artist, educator*
Fijalkowski, Isabelle *professional basketball player*
Fischer, Michelle K. *lawyer*
Fitzpatrick, Joyce J. *nursing educator, former dean*
Foster, Faith Wilhelmina *school counselor, educational consultant*
Gaughan, Patricia Anne *judge*
Goins, Frances Floriano *lawyer*
Gould, Bonnie M(arincic) *realtor*
Griffith, Mary H. *corporate communications executive*
Guffey, Edith Ann *religious organization administrator*
Hafner, Laurinda Marie *minister*
Hamilton, Nancy Beth *data processing executive*
Harf, Patricia Jean Kole *syndicated columnist, educational consultant, lecturer, clinical and behavioral psychologist, family therapist*
Hemann, Patricia A. *federal judge*
Jaffe, Marcia Weissman *elementary school educator*
Jensen, Kathryn Patricia (Kit) *public radio and television station executive*
Jindra, Christine *editor*
Johnson, Mattiedna *medical/surgical nurse*
Jorgenson, Mary Ann *lawyer*
Joseph, Eleanor Ann *health science association administrator, consultant*
Key, Helen Elaine *accountant, educator, consulting company executive*
Kilbane, Catherine M. *lawyer*
Kilbane, Sally Conway *economics educator*
Knieriem, Beulah White *retired elementary school educator, minister*
Kohn, Mary Louise Beatrice *nurse*
Kovacs, Rosemary *newspaper editor*
Kovel, Terry Horvitz (Mrs. Ralph Kovel) *writer, antiques authority*
Kronenberg, Janet Lois *lawyer*
Lawrence, Estelene Yvonne *musician, transportation executive*
Lazar, Kathy Pittak *lawyer*
Lennox, Heather *lawyer*
Leukart, Barbara J. J. *lawyer*
Lopez, Nancy *former professional golfer*
Maloney, Mary D. *lawyer*
Mantzell, Betty Lou *school health administrator*
Martin Burghard, Stephanie Marie *pilot, educator*
Mast, Bernadette Mihalic *lawyer*
Mayne, Lucille Stringer *finance educator*
McCormick, Maureen Olivea *computer systems programmer*
Mc Farlane, Karen Elizabeth *concert artists manager*
Michney-Heipp, Karen Marie *secondary education educator*
Miller, Genevieve *retired medical historian*
Moceanu, Dominique *retired Olympic athlete*
Monihan, Mary Elizabeth *lawyer*
Moore, Karen Nelson *judge*
Moravec, Christine D. Schomis *medical educator*
Nelson, Sue Grodsky *humanities educator, consultant*
Nemcova, Eva *professional basketball player*
Nemeth, Dian Jean *secondary school educator*
Norrington, Eileen O'Hickey *military officer, chaplain*
Oakar, Mary Rose *congresswoman*
Olness, Karen Norma *pediatrics and international health educator*
Olson, Sandra *aerospace engineer*
O'Malley, Kathleen M. *federal judge*
Petras, Cheryl Ann *nursing administrator*
Pierson, Marilyn Ehle *financial planner*
Pollack, Florence K.Z. *management consultant*
Potter, Susan K. *bank executive*
Pringle, Barbara Carroll *state legislator*
Pucko, Diane Bowles *public relations executive*
Queen, Joyce Ellen *elementary school educator*
Quigney, Theresa Ann *special education educator*
Rawson, Rachel L. *lawyer*
Rehm, Susan *physician*
Reid, Katharine Lee *museum director*
Reveiz, Maria Cristina *osteopath*
Richardson, Allison *financial services company official*
Rickert, Jeanne Martin M. *lawyer*
Roberts-Mamone, Lisa A. *lawyer*
Robinson, Alice Helene *English language educator, administrative assistant*
Schlotfeldt, Rozella May *nursing educator, educator*
Seifert, Shelley Jane *bank executive, human resources specialist*
Seles, Monica *professional tennis player*
Shellito, Sonia (Sunny) Terese *financial analyst, accountant*
Slone, Charlotte M. *telecommunications executive*
Smith, Barbara Jean *lawyer*
Smith, Beverly Harriett *elementary school educator*
Smith, Kestra Jan *prosecutor*
Striefsky, Linda A(nn) *lawyer*
Sweeney, Emily Margaret *prosecutor*
Swetkis, Doreen L. *advocate, educator, writer*
Taft, Frances Prindle *art history educator*
Taylor, Margaret Wischmeyer *retired language educator*
Thimmig, Diana M. *lawyer*
Thornton, Glenda Ann *librarian*
Thornton, Jerry Sue *community college president*
Torgerson, Katherine P. *diversified business media company executive*
Trapp, Mary Jane *lawyer*
Velasco, Esda Nury *speech and language professional*
Weir, Dame Gillian Constance *concert organist, harpsichordist*
Wells, Lesley *federal judge*
Wertheim, Sally Harris *academic administrator, dean, education educator, consultant*
Will, Sandra Gail *controller*
Wright, Clifflora L. *social worker, educator, alcohol/drug abuse services professional, consultant*
Wykle, May L. *dean, educator, researcher*

Cleveland Heights

Jablow, Bernice R. *architectural designer and space consultant*
Sandburg, Helga *author*
Soltis, Katherine *editor*

Columbia Station

Goll, Paulette Susan *education educator*

Columbus

Allen, Dixie J. *state representative*
Allen, Lois Arlene Height (Mrs. James Pierpont Allen) *musician*
Anderson, Carole Ann *nursing educator, academic administrator*
Bachman, Sister Janice *healthcare executive, religious order administrator*
Barrett, Catherine L. *state representative*
Beatty, Joyce *state representative*
Benjamin, Ann Womer *former state legislator, lawyer*
Benton-Borghi, Beatrice Hope *secondary school educator, consultant, writer, director*
Berndt, Ellen German *lawyer*
Bloomfield, Clara Derber *oncologist, medical institute administrator*
Boyd, Hazel *minister*
Bradley, Jennette *lieutenant governor*
Brown, Edna *state representative*
Caracciolo, Sandra Nicol *voice educator*
Carter, Melinda *municipal official*
Cirelli, Mary M. *state representative*
Clancy, Patricia *state representative*
Codogni, Iwona M. *scientific information analyst, chemist*
Crowder, Marjorie Briggs *lawyer*
Cuddihy, June Tuck *pediatrics nurse*
Curtis, Loretta O'Ellen *retired construction executive*
Davidson, Jo Ann *former state legislator*
Dervin, Brenda Louise *communications educator*
Donovan, Maureen Hildegarde *librarian, educator*
Dresser, Karen Kerns *state agency administrator*
Fedor, Teresa *state senator*
Ferderber, June H. *state legislator*
Fessler, Diana M. *state representative*
Foucht, Joan Lucille *retired elementary school educator, retired counseling administrator*
Franano, Susan Margaret Ketteman *arts consultant and adminstrator, musician*
Fraser, Pamela *artist*
Freece, Debbie Ann *trade association executive*
Furney, Linda Jeanne *state legislator*
Gillmor, Karen Lako *state agency administrator*
Goorey, Nancy Jane *dentist*
Grant, Jean Terry *educational consultant*
Grendell, Diane V. *state legislator, nurse*
Gruliow, Agnes Forrest *artist, educator*
Guy, Jennifer Louise *nursing administrator*
Hailey, V. Ann *retail executive*
Haque, Malika Hakim *pediatrician*
Harwood, Sandra Stabile *lawyer, state representative*
Hatler, Patricia Ruth *lawyer*
Hentz-Polk, Nicey *secondary school educator*
Hill, Kathleen Blickenstaff *lawyer, mental health nurse, nursing educator*
Hill, Terri *diversified financial services company executive*
Hollis-Allbritton, Cheryl Dawn *retail paper supply store executive*
Hollister, Nancy *state legislator*
Holman-Rao, Marie *retail executive*
Holonitch, Roxanne Michelle *art educator*
Holtz, Diane *retail executive*
Huber, Joan Althaus *sociology educator*
Huheey, Marilyn Jane *ophthalmologist, educator*
Jackson, Janet Elizabeth *city attorney, association executive*
Jacobs, Alexis A. *automobile company executive*
James, Donna A. *diversified financial services company executive*
Johnson, Julia F. *bank executive*
Julia, Maria *social worker, educator, consultant*
Katz, Janyce C(harlene) *lawyer*
Kearns, Merle Grace *state representative*
Keister, Lisa A. *social studies educator*
Key, Annie L. *state representative*
Kiecolt-Glaser, Janice Kay *psychologist*
King, Norah McCann *federal judge*
Kinser, Diane *communications educator, writer*
Koeppel, Holly *electric power industry executive*
Krakoff, Diane Elizabeth Butts *medical/surgical nurse*
Kreager, Eileen Davis *administrative consultant*
Kyte, Susan Janet *lawyer, consultant*
Laderer, Patricia M. *career planning administrator*
Lander, Ruth A. *medical group and association administrator*
Landrum-Bittles, Jenita *artist, educator*
Larzelere, Kathy Lynn Heckler *paralegal*
Laufman, Leslie Rodgers *hematologist, oncologist*
Lawrence, Joan Wipf *former state legislator*
Lefavre, Hadia *human resources executive*
Leitzel, Joan Ruth *university president emerita*
Lewis, Nina *social worker*
Long, Sarah Elizabeth Brackney *physician*
Long, Teresa C. *city health department administrator*
Mead, Priscilla *state legislator*
Mencer, Jetta *lawyer*

Meredith, Meri Hill *reference librarian, educator*
Montgomery, Betty Dee *state auditor, former state attorney general, former state legislator*
Moroi, Kazue Elizabeth *sculptor*
Morrison, Jacqueline Ann *social worker, psychologist*
Moser, Debra Kay *medical educator*
Newman, Diana S. *development consultant*
Nucklos, Shirley *health facility administrator, consultant*
O'Connor, Maureen *judge*
Oxley, Margaret Carolyn Stewart *elementary school educator*
Pastore, Donna Lee *physical education educator*
Perrini, Nancy Brown *writer, consultant*
Perry, Jeanine *state representative*
Pfahl, Floradelle Atwater *civic worker*
Prentiss, C. J. *state legislator*
Reardon, Nancy Anne *human resource executive*
Reece, Beth Elaine *music educator*
Reed, Constance Louise *materials management and purchasing consultant*
Reidelbach, Linda *state representative*
Resnick, Alice Robie *judge*
Richardson, Laurel Walum *sociology educator*
Ricord, Kathy *diversified financial services company executive*
Roeder, Rebecca Emily *software engineer*
Rogers, Nancy Hardin *dean, law educator*
Rosenstock, Susan Lynn *orchestra administrator*
Saunders, Mary L. *career officer*
Sawyers, Elizabeth Joan *librarian, administrator*
Schmidt, Jean *state representative*
Schneider, Cindy E. Gower (Lones) *financial advisor*
Schneider, Michelle G. *state representative*
Scott, Misty Anne *marketing professional*
Seiling, Sharon Lee *family economics educator*
Selby, Diane Ray Miller *fraternal organization administrator*
Sellers, Barbara Jackson *federal judge*
Setzer, Arlene J. *state representative, retired secondary school educator*
Sevel, Francine *advocate, researcher*
Simson, Bevlyn *artist*
Smith, Marcia J. *pastor*
Smith, Shirley A. *state legislator, state representative*
Snyder, Susan Leach *science educator, writer*
Sommer, Annemarie *pediatrician*
Stratton, Evelyn Lundberg *judge*
Sullivan, Kathryn D. *geologist, former astronaut*
Sutton, Betty *state legislator*
Sykes, Barbara *state legislator, state representative*
Taylor, Celianna Isley *information systems specialist*
Taylor, Mary *state representative*
Turney, Sharon Jester *retail executive*
Vesper, Rose *state legislator*
Walcher, Kathleen *state official*
Walker-Griffin, Donna Fay *information technology manager*
Weinhold, Virginia Beamer *interior designer*
Westman, Judith Ann *clinical geneticist*
Whitacre, Caroline Clement *immunologist, researcher*
Winkler, Cheryl J. *state legislator*
Woltz, Mary Lynn Monaco *management consultant*
Woodard, Claudette J. *state representative, retired educational association administrator*
Zelman, Susan Tave *school system administrator*

Copley
Broda, C. Denise *education educator*
Smith, Joan H. *retired women's health nurse, educator*

Cortland
Bryner, E. Jeanne *medical/surgical nurse*
Lane, Sarah Marie Clark *elementary school educator*

Cuyahoga Falls
Deemer, (Norma) Jean *artist*
Shane, Sandra Kuli *postal service administrator*
Smith, Margaret A. (Maggie Carroll Smith) *community volunteer*
Stewart, Christine Marie *church music director*
Walker, Suzannah Wolf *language educator*

Dayton
Anderson, Ruth Yarnnelle *real estate professional, educator*
Barr, Ann Helen *director*
Boice, Martha Hibbert *writer, publisher*
Cameron, Joyce *human factors and ergonomics specialist, music educator*
Carrier, Rachel Esther *music educator, director*
Carson, Dora A. *secondary school educator*
Cunningham, Kima Hicks *minister, client services manager*
Dunn, Margaret M. *general surgeon, educator, university official*
Eby, Marlene Jean *retired secondary school educator*
Farkas, Nancy A. *realtor*
Gambrel, Kimberly *lawyer*
Goldenberg, Kim *academic administrator, internist*
Grant, Colleen *information systems specialist*
Hanna, Marsha L. *artistic director*
Harden, Oleta Elizabeth *English educator, university administrator*
Harris, Bonnie *psychological education specialist*
Hitch, Melanie Audrey *orthopaedics nurse*
Jelus, Susan Crum *writer, editor*
King-Cooper, Jennifer Laine *social sciences educator*
Klinck, Cynthia Anne *library director*
Lansaw, Judy W. *public utility executive*
MacGregor, Shawna Anne *lawyer, educator*
Martin, Patricia *dean, nursing educator*
Matheny, Ruth Ann *editor*
McLin, Rhine Lana *mayor, former state legislator*
Monk, Susan Marie *pediatrician, educator*
Nanagas, Maria Teresita Cruz *pediatrician, educator*
O'Malley, Patricia *critical care nurse*
Pflum, Barbara Ann *pediatrician, allergist*
Reid, Marilyn Joanne *state legislator, lawyer*
Shaffer, Joanne Tyler *music educator*
Stefanics, Charlotte Louise *retired mental health nurse*
Taylor, Elisabeth Coler *retired secondary school educator*
Thomas, Marianna *volunteer community activist, writer, speaker*
Versic, Linda Joan *nurse educator, research company executive*
Wasson, Barbara Hickam *music educator*
Wightman, Ann *lawyer*
Young, Yvonne Delease *elementary school educator*

Defiance
Strata, Jane *music educator*

Delaware
Fry, Anne Evans *zoology educator*
Gardner, Bonnie Milne *theater educator*
Schlichting, Catherine Fletcher Nicholson *librarian, educator*

Delta
Miller, Beverly White *former college president, educational consultant, consultant*

Dublin
Anderson, Kerrii B. *food service executive*
Baker, Mary Evelyn *retired librarian*
Bordelon, Carolyn Thew *elementary school educator*
Davids, Jody *pharmaceutical and medical supply executive*
Meyer, Betty Jane *former librarian*
Pollner, Julia A. *financial executive*
Rhoades, Nancy Lybarger *retired librarian*
Spies, Phyllis Bova *information services company executive*
Tenuta, Luigia *lawyer*
Watkins, Carole S. *human resources specialist, health facility administrator*
White, Kathy Brittain *medical association executive*

East Cleveland
Davis, Dianne *music educator*
Soule, Lucile Snyder *pianist, music educator*

East Liberty
Head, Teresa Rena *electrical engineer*

East Liverpool
Gailey, Joan Dale *retired finance educator*

Eaton
Kendall, Susan Haines *library director*

Elyria
Bonnell-Mihalis, Pamela Gay *library director*
Manner, Jennifer Fouse *social worker*

Enon
DeVore, Barbara Jane Egan *corporate finance executive*

Euclid
Harasym, Jean Louise *music educator*

Fairborn
Moore, Margaret Anne *retired civilian military employee*

Fairfield
Bender, Jacqueline *music educator*
Sheehan, Samantha *gymnast*

Fairlawn
Brubaker, Karen Sue *small business owner*
France, Dorothy Daniel *minister*

Fairport Harbor
Priddy, Jean Marie *music educator, voice educator*

Fairview Park
Flynn, Patricia M. *director, special education educator, gifted and talented educator*

Findlay
Drake, Jeanette Wenig *communications educator, public relations consultant, writer*
Stephani, Nancy Jean *social worker, journalist*

Fort Jennings
Warnecke, Rose Mary *music educator*

Fostoria
Howard, Kathleen *computer company executive*
Underwood, Carole Ann *English and Spanish language educator*

Fremont
Sattler, Nancy Joan *educational administrator*

Gahanna
Sherman, Ruth Todd *government advisor, counselor, consultant*

Galion
Harter, Lonna *city manager*

Gambier
Buchsbaum, Julianne *writer, educator*
Nugent, S. Georgia *academic administrator*
Ponder, Anne *dean*

Geneva
Arkkelin, Cora Rink *realtor*
Carrel, Marianne Eileen *music educator*

Genoa
Loy, Stephanie Lynn *music educator*

Georgetown
Conway, Dorothy Jean Williams *economist*

Grand River
Abel, Mary Ellen Kathryn *quality control executive, chemist*

Grove City
Kimethu, Susan Wanja *computer specialist, database manager*

Hamilton
Fein, Linda Ann *nurse anesthetist, consultant*
Hornsby, Judith Elizabeth *special education educator*
New, Rosetta Holbrock *home economics educator, nutrition consultant*
Quay, Jacquelyn Sue *art educator, consultant*
Ridner, Melanie Marie *writer, composer*

Hannibal
Guyette, Diana *minister*

Harrison
Kocher, Juanita Fay *retired auditor*

Hebron
Slater, Wanda Marie Worth *property manager*

Highland Hills
Sender, Maryann *director*

Hilliard
Cooper, Almeta E. *lawyer, medical association administrator*

Holland
D'Anniballe-Holdren, Priscilla Lucille *contracting company executive*

Hubbard
Trucksis, Theresa A. *retired library director*

Hudson
Carducci, Judith Weeks Barker *artist, former social worker*
Elliott, Frances Carano *lawyer, educator*
Goheen, Janet Moore *counseling administrator, sales executive*
Hallenbeck, Linda S. *elementary school educator*
Snyder, Virginia Anne *gifted and talented educator*
Sorgi, Mercedes Prieto *psychologist*

Huron
Leser, Anne Elizabeth *education educator*

Independence
Boyle, Kammer *estate planner, financial analyst*

Kent
Apseloff, Marilyn Fain *English educator*
Cartwright, Carol Ann *university president*
Cielinski-Kessler, Audrey Ann *writer, publishing executive, small business owner*
Gosnell, Davina J. *dean, nursing educator*
Khol, Charel L. *psychologist*
Kristof, Cindy *librarian, educator*
Scillia, Diane Graybowski *art historian, researcher*
Sonnhalter, Carolyn Therese *physical therapist, consultant*
Tuan, Debbie Fu-Tai *chemist, educator*

Kettering
Denlinger, Vicki Lee *secondary school educator, physical education educator*
Hoffman, Sue Ellen *retired elementary school educator*
Martin, Margaret Gately *elementary school educator*

Kingsville
Poluga, Judith *education educator*

Lakewood
Barrett, Linda *insurance company executive*
Cain, Madeline Ann *mayor*
Ellis, Deborah Marie *art educator*
Heston, Sara Smith *art educator, artist*
Olson, Carol Joan *foundation administrator, consultant*

Lebanon
McDonel, Jennifer Sutton *music educator*
Ruder, Diane G. *fund raising executive*

Liberty Center
Grieser, Ilsa Adele *elementary school educator, music educator*
Jones, Marlene Ann *retired education supervisor*

Liberty Township
Conditt, Margaret Karen *research scientist, policy analyst*

Lima
Lovett, Katherine Van Every *special education educator*
Meek, Violet Imhof *retired dean*
Riggs, Jane L. *performing arts association administrator, consultant*

Lisbon
Dailey, Coleen Hall *magistrate, lawyer*

Lodi
Langlotz, Jennifer Cook *music educator*

Lorain
Comer, Brenda Warmee *elementary school educator, real estate company officer*

Loudonville
Gault, Jeannie Suzanne *elementary school educator*

Lucasville
Crotty, Ladonna Deane *librarian*

Lyndhurst
Dellas, Marie C. *retired psychology educator and consultant*
Packer, Diana *retired reference librarian*
Silver, Thelma *social worker*

Lynx
Watters, Cora Tula *musician, educator*

Macedonia
Levy, Beth Ann *music educator*

Maineville
Cook, Janice Eleanor Nolan *retired elementary school educator*

Mansfield
Converse, Sandra *city finance director, financial planner*
Crittenden, Sophie Marie *communications executive*
Gregory, Deirdre Dianne *secondary educator*
Hunt, Pamela Sue *elementary school educator, music educator*

Maple Heights
Sargent, Liz Elaine (Elizabeth Sargent) *safety consulting executive*

Marietta
Francis, Lynne Ann *elementary school educator, music educator*

Marion
Bower, Anne Lieberman *English educator*
Burris, Lynette Sue *music educator*
Fassler, Crystal G. *marketing consultant*
Rowe, Lisa Dawn *computer programmer/analyst, computer consultant*

Marysville
Baik-Kromalic, Sue S. *metallurgical engineer*
Jones-Morton, Pamela *human resources specialist*

Mason
Snyder, Barbara Royalty *pharmaceutical executive*

Massillon
Green, Angela LaVonne *band director*
Penczarski, Jennifer Marie *music educator*
Vaughn, Lisa Dawn *physician, educator*

Maumee
McBride, Beverly Jean *lawyer*

Mechanicsburg
Maynard, Joan *education educator*

Medina
Batchelder, Alice M. *federal judge*
DeMars, Judith M. *elementary school educator*
Jeffers, Lynette A. *anesthetist*
Moll, Sara H. *psychologist, volunteer*

Mentor
Miller, Frances Suzanne *historic site curator*

Miamisburg
Lucius, Mary Albus *dietician*
Thompson, Holley Marker *lawyer, marketing professional*

Middleburg Heights
Maciuszko, Kathleen Lynn *librarian, educator*

Middlefield
Jaite, Gail Ann *music educator*

Middleport
Cantrell, Carol Howe *municipal administrator*

Middletown
Gilmore, June Ellen *psychologist*
Marine, Susan Sonchik *analytical chemist, educator*
Tucker, Catherine L. *financial advisor*

Milford
Conover, Nellie Coburn *retired retail furniture company executive*

Millersburg
Yoder, Anna A. *elementary school educator*

Mineral City
Girard, Susan Marie *manufacturing executive*

Mount Orab
Raines, Tami Jo *principal*

Mount Pleasant
Aspenwall, Kathryn DeBlasis *music educator*

Mount Vernon
Wells-Maxwell, Violet *writer, artist*

Munroe Falls
Clawson, Judith Louise *middle school educator*

Napoleon
Meekison, MaryFran *writer*

Nelsonville
Mingus, Judy Ellen *special education educator, secondary school educator*

New Albany
Page, Linda Kay *bank executive*

Riley, Susan Jean *retail executive*

New Carlisle
Leffler, Carole Elizabeth *mental health nurse, women's health nurse*
Peters, Elizabeth Ann Hampton *retired nursing educator*

New Concord
Schumann, Laura Elaine *conductor*
Wagner, Vivian Audrey *communications educator, writer*

New Lebanon
Dillman, Karin Christine *elementary school educator*

New Matamoras
Brown, Blanche Y. *secondary education educator, genealogy researcher*

New Philadelphia
Barlock, Ida Belle *county board of elections clerk*
Doughten, Mary Katherine (Molly Doughten) *retired secondary school educator*
Hendrix, Christine Janet *retired government agency administrator, retired small business owner, volunteer*

New Richmond
Fisher, Virginia Carolyn *music educator, director*

Newark
Paul, Rochelle Carole *special education educator*
Simpson, Linda Sue *elementary school educator*
Wallace, Sarah Reese *banker*
Williams, Gale Cady *secondary school educator*

Newbury
Proctor, Cheryl Ann *music educator*

Niles
Linden, Carol Marie *special education educator*
Rizer, Janet Marlene *city tax administrator*

North Canton
Edwards, Sharon Marie *minister, educator*

North Ridgeville
Stewart, Arden Ruth *automotive aftermarket manufacturing executive*

North Royalton
Pamin, Diana Dolhancyk (Diana Dolhancyk) *poet*

Northfield
Sleeman, Mary (Mrs. John Paul Sleeman) *retired librarian*

Norwalk
Fresch, Marie Beth *court reporting company executive*
Lang, Wilma Jean *special education educator*

Norwood
Beresford, Mary Jo Theresa *theatre educator*

Oak Harbor
Witt, Beth M. *music educator*

Oberlin
Collins, Martha *English language educator, writer*
Dye, Nancy Schrom *academic administrator, historian, educator*
Greenberg, Eva Mueller *librarian*
Kruks, Sonia R. *social sciences educator, researcher*
MacKay, Gladys Godfrey *adult education educator*
Rutstein, Sedmara Zakarian *piano educator, concert pianist*

Olmsted Falls
Semple, Jane Frances *health facility administrator*

Oregon
Poad, Flora Virginia *retired librarian and educator, retired elementary school educator*

Orrville
Mackus, Eloise L. *food products company executive*

Orwell
Strong, Marcella Lee *music specialist, educator*

Oxford
Brewer, Nancy Ellen *communications executive, writer*
Ewing, Susan R. *art educator, artist*
Gallehue, Dawn E. *voice educator*
Messman-Moore, Terri Lyn *psychologist, educator*
Presnell, Jenny Lynn *librarian*
Rypstra, Ann *zoology educator*
Saas, Deborah Anne *investment advisor, securities broker*
Sessions, Judith Ann *librarian, university library dean*
Thompson, Bertha Boya *retired education educator, antique dealer and appraiser*
Yost, Nancy Runyon *artist, small business owner*

Painesville
Blyth, Ann Marie *secondary school educator*
Davis, Barbara Snell *education educator*
Luhta, Caroline Naumann *airport manager, flight educator*

Parma
Plasterer, Tamara J. *music educator, theater educator*
Reichheld, Deborah Ann *secondary school music educator*
Romanovich, Patricia M. *parochial school educator*
Salzgeber, Karen A. *secondary school educator*
Scheffel, Donna Jean *elementary school educator*
Tener, Carol Joan *retired elementary school educator*

Pataskala
Honnold, Kathryn S. *real estate agent*

Paulding
Moore, Pamela Rae *elementary school educator*

Pemberville
King, Laura Jane *librarian, genealogist*

Peninsula
Cooke, Honore Guilbeau *artist, educator*

Pepper Pike
Stano, Sister Diana *academic administrator*

Perrysburg
Autry, Carolyn *artist, art history educator*
Billnitzer, Bonnie Jeanne *nurse, gerontologist*
Schwier, Priscilla Lamb Guyton *television broadcasting company executive*
Williams, Pamela Sue *music educator*

Pickerington
Callander, Kay Eileen Paisley *business owner, retired education educator, writer*
Collins, Arlene *secondary school educator*
Lang, Lisa Ann *music educator*
Palmer, Noreen E. *psychotherapist*

Plain City
Karrer, Carol Converse *nursing educator, consultant*

Plymouth
Hartman, Ruth Campbell *director, educator*

Port Clinton
Ewersen, Mary Virginia *retired school system administrator, poet*
Taylor, Jane Ellen *elementary school educator*

Powell
Spangler, Edra Mildred *clinical psychologist*

Ravenna
O'Brien, Jane *special education educator*

Reynoldsburg
Blair, Jennifer Marie *music educator, consultant*
Garling, Tina Louise *data processing coordinator*
Maratta Snyder, Grace Elvira *volunteer*
Nichols, Grace A. *retail executive*

Richfield
Lewis, Sylvia Davidson *foundation executive*

Rocky River
Briscar-Martel, Nancy Marie *agent, musician, educator*
Hudson, Judith Ann *elementary school educator*

Rootstown
Nora, Lois Margaret *neurologist, educator, academic administrator, dean*
Woodall, Susan Elaine *minister*

Saint Marys
Ball, Judy Kay *minister*

Saint Paris
Phillips, Raelene E. *writer, educator*

Salem
Moss, Susan *nurse, retail store owner*

Sandusky
Shaylor, Karen Ann *artist, educator*

Sardinia
Evans, C(aroline) Sue *social sciences educator*

Seaman
Cartaino, Carol Ann *editor*

Shaker Heights
Aulicino, Christine Wilkinson *education educator*
Donnem, Sarah Lund *financial analyst, non-profit and political organization consultant*
Hill, Felicity Jane *editor*
Katz, Linda M. *social worker*
Trefts, Joan Landenberger *retired educator, administrator*

Shelby
Phelan, Martha Armstrong *realtor*

Somerset
Green, Tammie *professional golfer*

South Euclid
Miller Schear, Annice Mara *music educator*

Sparta
Ruffing, Eileen Mary *elementary school educator, music educator*

Springfield
Beatty, Betty Joy *library educator*
Dobson, Janet Louise *writer*
Fry, Maureen Shea *director, educator*
Gardunia, Sharon Strawsburg *secondary school educator*
Gesalman, Carol *minister*
Patterson, Martha Ellen *artist, art educator*
Pitzer, Betty Braun *social services administrator*
Rowland-Raybold, Roberta *insurance agent, music educator*
Stelzer, Patricia Jacobs *retired secondary school educator*
Woodhouse, Elizabeth C. *retired government agency administrator*

Stow
Mikes, Judith Pauline *music educator*

Strongsville
Taghizadeh, Georgeanne Marie *medical/surgical nurse, diagnostic cardiac sonographer*

Swanton
Barko, Helen Marie *music educator*

Sylvania
Buckenmeyer, Janet *director, education educator, director*
Sampson, Earldine Robison *education educator*
Verhesen, Anna Maria Hubertina *social worker*

Thornville
Taylor, Leslie Carole *minister*

Tiffin
Hillmer, Margaret Patricia *library director*
Spellerberg, Elinor M. *riding instructor*

Tipp City
Ahmed, Gail R. *music educator*
Tighe-Moore, Barbara Jeanne *electronics executive*

Toledo
Dahl Reeves, Gretchen *occupational therapy educator*
Danko-McGhee, Katherina Elaine *art educator, consultant*
Goldstein, Margaret Franks *special education educator*
Jauregui, Connie Lee *internist*
Johnson, Cheryl L. *labor association administrator, activist*
Knuth, Marya Danielle *special education educator*
Lessick, Mira Lee *nursing educator*
Machin, Barbara E. *lawyer*
Mills, Anna M. *realtor*
Nordin, Phyllis Eck *sculptor, painter, consultant*
Overmyer, Janet Elaine *counselor*
Rabideau, Margaret Catherine *retired media center director*
Rejent, Marian Magdalen *retired pediatrician*
Smale, Ann-Laura *public relations company executive, writer, researcher*
Spruce, Simone Renee *art educator*
Wolter, Virginia Lynn *librarian*
Worley, Debere *educational consultant*

Trotwood
Staggs, Barbara J. *vice mayor*

Troy
DeHart, Karen Trautmann *artist, educator*
Miller, Rebecca S. *financial analyst*

University Heights
Goral, Judith Ann *language educator*
Mahon, Marinna Fairbank *secondary education educator, writer, consultant*
Starcher-Dell'Aquila, Judy Lynn *special education educator*

Urbana
Meyers, Marsha Lynn *retired social worker*
Stolz, Claudia Grace *humanities educator, consultant*

Valley View
Miller, Susan Ann *school system administrator*

Van Wert
Huffman, Laura Christine *computer programmer, educator*

Wadsworth
Ross, Jane Arlene *music educator*
Thomas, Jennifer Butler *special education educator, coach*

Walbridge
Cox, Brenda Lynn *information technology manager*
Wiseman, Gretchen Renee *personal care industry executive*

Walton Hills
Cieszewski, Joyce Catherine *writer, educator*

Wapakoneta
Lusk, Mary Margaret *music educator*

Warren
Cremeans, Sharon Lu *medical/surgical nurse*
Seachrist, Denise *music educator*
Smith, Paula Marie *medical technologist*
VanAuker, Lana *recreational therapist, educator*

Washington Court House
Febo, Diana Lucile *counseling administrator*
Fichthorn, Fonda Gay *gifted and talented educator, retired principal*
Johnson, Penny Sue *auditor*

Wauseon
Stutzman, Donna J. *minister*

West Carrollton
Zeller, Shirley Evelyn *manufacturing executive*

West Chester
Reed, Valerie V. *school librarian*
Ulrich, Jody L. *accountant*
Verbesselt, Martine Carole *primary school educator*

West Farmington
Smith, Agnes Monroe *history educator*

West Jefferson
Puckett, Helen Louise *retired tax consulting company executive*

West Manchester
Long, Valerie Jean *pastor*

Westerville
Diersing, Carolyn Virginia *educational administrator*
Krueger-Horn, Cheryl *apparel executive*
Lott, Vera Naomi *artist, educator*
Van Sant, Joanne Frances *academic administrator*

Westfield Center
Bock, Carolyn A. *writer, small business owner*

Westlake
Coeling, Harriet Van Ess *nursing educator, editor*
Lahiff, Marilyn J. *nursing administrator*
Loehr, Marla *spiritual care coordinator*
Schroth, Joyce Able *social worker*

Whitehall
Van Camp, Diana J. *music educator*

Wickliffe
Fisher, Nancy DeButts *library director*
Graves, Pamela Kay *music educator*
Haffey, Susan M. *treasurer*
Krause, Marjorie N. *biochemist*
Wainio, Melody F. *dean*

Wilberforce
Walker-Taylor, Yvonne *retired academic administrator*

Willoughby
Corrigan, Faith *journalist, educator, historian*
Grossman, Mary Margaret *elementary school educator*
Linsenmeier, Carol Vincent *music educator*

Wilmington
Evans, Elizabeth Ann West *retired real estate agent*

Wooster
Patterson, Gina Lynn *psychologist*
Saif, Linda J. *animal scientist*

Worthington
Bernhagen, Lillian Flickinger *retired school health consultant*
Winston, Janet Margaret *real estate agent, civic volunteer*

Wright Patterson Afb
Chelette, Tamara Lynne *biomedical engineer*
Newsome, Kathy Noel *accountant*

Xenia
Nutter, Zoe Dell Lantis *retired public relations executive*

Yellow Springs
Graham, Jewel Freeman *social worker, lawyer, educator*
Straumanis, Joan *academic administrator*

Youngstown
Bartlett, Shirley Anne *accountant*
Bond, Christina M. *magistrate, lawyer*
Bowers, Bege K. *English educator, academic administrator*
Byrd, Swettie Lee *minister*
Camardese, Amy Hoffman *education educator*
Catoline-Ackerman, Pauline Dessie *small business owner*
Checcone, Iole Carlesimo *foreign language educator*
Gransee, Marsha L. *federal agency executive*
Kenner, Marilyn Sferra *civil engineer*
Lambert, Jean Marjorie *health care executive*
Marks, Esther L. *metals company executive*
Popio, Donna Marie *music educator*
Tyson, Edith Slosson *retired librarian, writer*

Zanesville
Brown, Karen Rima *orchestra manager, Spanish language educator*
Fulkerson, Sue Ellen *poet*
O'Sullivan, Christine *retired executive director social service agency, consultant*
Porto, Marisa Josetta *editor*
Show, Renee Deane *music educator*
Stainbrook, Margaret Collins *retired school system administrator*

Zoar
Fernandez, Kathleen M. *cultural organization administrator*

OKLAHOMA

Ada
Baker, Judith Ann *retired computer technician*
Davenport, Ann Adele Mayfield *retired home care agency administrator*
Dempsey, B. *artist*
Frye, Linda Beth (Linda Beth Hisle) *elementary, secondary education educator*
Parham, Betty Ely *credit bureau executive*
Scott, Rita Fay *art educator*

Adair
Notley, Thelma A. *retired librarian, educator*

Altus
Runyan, Mary Lynn *music educator*

Anadarko
Kidd, Lovetta Monza *music educator*

Bartlesville
Chambers, Imogene Klutts *school system administrator, financial consultant*
Risner, Anita Jane *vocational school educator*
Yao, Jianhua *chemist, researcher*

Bixby
Wetzel, Marlene Reed *freelance/self-employed writer*

Broken Arrow
Lobser, Heather A. *music educator*
Muller, Patricia Ann *nursing administrator, educator*

Cache
Ayers, Betty Lou *missionary, pastor*

Chelsea
Geyer, Kathy Van Ness *retailer*
Taylor, Connie *minister*

Chickasha
Cook, Catharine *library director*
Davis, Margaret Schlitt *social services administrator*

Choctaw
Glavan, Denise Lynn *minister*

Cleveland
Anderson, Patricia Sue *writer*
Henry, Kathleen Marie *marketing executive*

Clinton
Askew, Penny Sue *choreographer, artistic director, ballet instructor*

Coalgate
Willis, Tricia Lee *special education educator*

Del City
Wallace, Fannie Margaret *minister, religious organization administrator*

Dewey
White, Joy Kathryn *retired claims consultant, artist*

Drumright
Geyer, Karen Lea *writer*
Pruitt, Linda Kay *special education educator*

Duncan
Austin, Diana Sue *elementary school educator*

Durant
Hooser, Helen *artist*
Wilkins, Carolyn Ann *music educator*

Earlsboro
Smart, Ella Jo *special education educator*

Edmond
Charoenwongse, Chindarat *pianist, music educator*
Dedmon, Angela Marie Maxine *psychologist*
Harryman, Rhonda L. *education educator*
Haywood, B(etty) J(ean) *anesthesiologist*
Loman, Mary LaVerne *retired mathematics educator*
Loving, Susan Brimer *lawyer, former state official*
Maye, S. Elizabeth Beth *artist, small business owner*
Miller, Shannon *Olympic athlete*
Necco, E(dna) Joanne *school psychologist*
Osgood, Virginia M. *vocational educator*
Pydynkowsky, Joan Anne *journalist*
Stewart, Ann Tefertiller *interior designer, secondary school educator*
Thompson, Stephanie Denise *newspaper columnist, radio host*
Wylie, Quineta G. Beagle *state political party executive*
Zabel, Vivian Ellouise *secondary school educator*

El Reno
Buendia, Imelda Bernardo *health facility administrator, physician*

Elgin
Leonard, Nedra V. *music educator*

Elk City
Beaty, Deborah Joyce *music educator*

Enid
Hanousek, Victoria A. *real estate broker*
Hildebrand, Kaye *music educator*
Russell, Rhonda Cheryl *piano educator, recording artist*
Seem, Evelyn Ashcraft *music educator*
Varnell, Maxine Ann *minister*

Eufaula
Dawson, Cindy Marie *lawyer*

Forgan
Husted, Charlene E. *library media specialist, educator*

Fort Cobb
Rexroat, Vicki Lynn *occupational child development educator*

Grove
Penquite, Mary C. *realtor*

Healdton
Lewis, Reba Jolene *secondary school educator, consultant*

Jenks
Dominguez, Monica Raye *special education educator*

Lamont
Covalt, Edna Irene *retired medical/surgical nurse*

Lawton
Cashion, Patricia Sue *minister*
Ellenbrook, Carolyn Kay *religious organization administrator*
McKeown, Rebecca J. *principal*
Nalley, Elizabeth Ann *chemistry educator*
Wonsewitz, Pom Cha *artist, horticulturist*

Lexington
Looman, Mary Dale *psychologist, forensic specialist, consultant*

Mannford
Dehn-Wittke, Barbara Ann *music educator*

Marlow
Hines, Deborah Sue *special education educator*

Miami
Taylor, Vesta Fisk *real estate broker, educator*
Vanpool, Cynthia Paula *special education educator, special services consultant*

Midwest City
Cheek, Norma Jean *retired educator*
Robinson, Emily Sue *music educator*
Saulmon, Sharon Ann *college librarian*

Mounds
Fellows, Esther Elizabeth *musician, music educator*

Muskogee
Carvajal, Victoria Lavone *customer service administrator*
Hilbern, Sandra J. *library director*
Shelton, Nancy Sue *music educator*

Mustang
Hutter, Teresa Ann *art educator*
Laurent, J(erry) Suzanna *technical communications specialist*
McDonald, Terre Reese *elementary school educator*

Newkirk
Eisenhauer, Gayle Ann *elementary school educator, secondary school educator*
Newport, L. Joan *clinical social worker, retired psychotherapist*

Noble
Watrous, Naoma Dicksion *retired clinical psychologist*

Norman
Affleck, Marilyn *sociology educator*
Bethel, Joann D. *computer programmer, analyst*
Carroll, Frances Laverne *librarian, educator*
Cochran, Gloria Grimes *retired pediatrician*
Dalton, Deborah Whitmore *dean*
Day, Adrienne Carol *artist*
Garner, Lani Aloha *music educator*
Gass, Cynthia Ann *music educator*
Kemp, Betty Ruth *retired librarian*
Lester, June *library information studies educator*
Loeffelholz, Diane *art educator*
MacFarland, Miriam Katherine (Mimi MacFarland) *writer*
Madden, Glenda Gail *sales professional*
Nelson, Donna Jean *chemistry educator, researcher*
Petersen, Catherine Holland *lawyer*
Phillips, Joan Elizabeth *recreational therapist, educator*
Price, Linda Rice *community development administrator*
Provine, Lorraine *retired mathematics educator*
Rupp-Serrano, Karen *school librarian*
Sharp, Susan F. *sociologist, educator*
Sherman, Mary Angus *public library administrator*
Smith, Beulah Mae *music educator*
Tackwell, Elizabeth Miller *social worker*
Wagner, Brenda Marcyea *music educator, musician*
Wood, Betty Jean *conceptual artist, art educator*
Zapffe, Nina Byrom *retired elementary education educator*
Zelby, Rachel *realtor*

Okemah
DeShields, Elizabeth Peggy Bowen *artist, educator, poet*

Oklahoma City
Allbright, Karan Elizabeth *psychologist, consultant*
Askins, Jari *lawyer, department chairman, state representative*
Atlee, Debbie Gayle *sales consultant, medical educator*
Bahr, Carman Bloedow *internist*
Bentley, Karen Gail *elementary school educator*
Blackburn, Debbie *elementary school educator, state representative*
Blochowiak, Mary Ann *cultural organization administrator, writer*
Bode, Denise Anne *petroleum association executive*
Boston, Billie *costume designer, costume history educator*
Boyd, Betty *government official*
Brooks, Norma Newton *legal assistant*
Cadamy, Shelley R. *economic development professional*
Campbell, Brenda Dianne *protective services official*
Campbell, Virginia Hopper *piano concert artist, composer, educator*
Cauthron, Robin J. *federal judge*
Chiles, Mary Jane *secondary school educator*
Coleman, Carolyn *state legislator*
Cox, Kevin *state representative*
Crowder, Carolyn *educational association administrator, educator*
Douty, Sheila *softball player*
Easley, Mary *retired elementary school educator, state representative*
Fallin, Mary Copeland *lieutenant governor*
Felts, Rebecca Nancy *elementary school educator*
Fernandez, Lisa *softball player*
Forni, Patricia Rose *dean*
Forrest, Linda Sue *music educator*
Frates, Mex (Mrs. Clifford Leroy Frates) *civic worker*
Garrett, Sandy Langley *school system administrator*
Gatewood, Tela Lynne *lawyer*
Geopfert, Kelli Renee *rehabilitation services professional*
Graves, Brenda Vanessa *small business owner*
Greenwood, Joan *state representative*
Hale, Sue A. *editor*
Hall, Nancy K. *college dean*
Halpin, Anna Marie *architect, writer*
Hamilton, Rebecca *state representative*
Hampton, Carol McDonald *priest, educator, historian*
Harrison-Bridgeman, Ann Marie *claims adjuster*
Henderson, Molly *academic administrator, educator*
Holt, Karen Anita Young *English educator*
Horner, Maxine Edwyna Cissel *state legislator*
Jones, Renee Kauerauf *health care administrator*
Kerr, Lou C. *foundation administrator*
Lambird, Mona Salyer *lawyer*
LaMotte, Janet Allison *retired management specialist*
Lashley, Karen Huggins *psychologist, educator*
Lawler, Daisy *state senator, elementary school educator, farmer, rancher*
Martin, Caroline June *state senator*
Mather, Ruth Elsie *writer*
Mather, Stephanie June *lawyer*
McClellan, Mary Ann *pediatric nurse practitioner*
McEwen, Irene Ruble *physical therapy educator*
McIntyre, Judy *social worker, state representative*
Miles-La Grange, Vicki *judge*
Monson, Angela Zoe *state legislator*
Moore, Joanne Iweita *pharmacologist, educator*
Morris, Phyllis *legislative staff member*
Morris, Theresa Linthicum *retired medical social worker*
[illegible]
school educator
Osborn, Lynda Pauwels *social worker*
Pain, Betsy M. *lawyer*
Price, Donna J. *nurse*
Prichard, Barbara Ann *English educator*
Regier, Elaine Roxanne *elementary school educator, school librarian*
Richardson, Dot (Dorothy Gay) *softball player, physician*
Ridley, Betty Ann *religous educator, lay worker*
Riley, Nancy C. *state legislator*
Savage, Susan M. *state official, former mayor*
Shackleton, Jean L. *music educator*
Shaffer, Kimberly Saundra *medical technician*
Sharpe, Bobbie Mahon *author*
Staggs, Barbara *state representative*
Tibbs, Sue *state representative*
Twyman, Nita (Venita Twyman) *music educator*
Weedn, Trish *state legislator*
Whitener, Carolyn Raye *artist*
Wilcoxson, Kathleen Louise *state legislator, educator*
Williams, Mary Ann *musical instrument executive, music educator*
Williamson, Marvel *dean, nursing administrator, sexologist, educator, writer*
Winchester, Susan *human resources specialist, state representative*
Wood, Paula Davidson *lawyer*
Wynn, Brenda Reneau *trade association executive*
Zevnik-Sawatzky, Donna Dee *retired litigation coordinator*

Owasso
Sandford, Brenda Lynne *executive secretary*

Park Hill
Mankiller, Wilma Pearl *tribal leader, retired*

Pauls Valley
Pesterfield, Linda Carol *retired school administrator, educator*

Pawnee
Brown, Paula Ann *pre-school administrator*

Perkins
Lewis, Mary May Smith *retired family practice nurse practitioner*

Ponca City
Barraclough, Mary Jane *music educator*
Rice, Sue Ann *dean, industrial and organizational psychologist*
Warren, Maxine Wood *artist, art educator*

Pryor
Rice, Susan K. *school librarian, educator*

Sapulpa
Weinstock Rad, Katheryn Louise *music educator*

Seminole
Branscum, Carla Jeanne *special education educator*
Gillespie, Norma *educational advisor*

Snow
Minshall, Dorothy Kathleen *music educator*

Stillwater
Burr, Meghan LeRa *researcher*
DeLacerda, Melissa Griner *lawyer*

Tahlequah
Brown, Sara Nordholm *social work educator*
Grant, Kay Lallier *early childhood education educator*

Tinker Afb
Penn, Vernita Lynn *government agency administrator*
Scott, Carol Lee *child care educator*
Velasco, Jodi Marie *military lawyer*

Tulsa
Arnold-Chapman, Ingrid M *writer*
Arrington, Rebecca Carol *occupational health nurse*
Barnes, Cynthia Lou *retired gifted and talented educator*
Blackstock, Virginia Lee Lowman (Mrs. LeRoy Blackstock) *civic worker*
Buthod, Mary Clare *school administrator*
Candreia, Peggy Jo *financial analyst*
Cardwell, Sandra Gayle Bavido *university admissions professional*
Carpenter, Nancy J. *health science association administrator*
Clark, Marian Wilson *writer*
Collins, Laura Jane *music educator, singer, accompanist*
Dexter, Deirdre O'Neil Elizabeth *lawyer*
Ellerbach, Susan *editor*
Frazier, Mary Ann *artist*
Freesemann, LeAnne Clair (Luikart) *music educator*
Gottschalk, Sister Mary Therese *nun, hospital administrator*
Howerton, Helen F. *artist*
Hyland, Cheryl C. *health services administrator*
Imhoff, Pamela M. *marketing educator*
Knox, Teresa Louise *entrepreneur, small business owner*
Kukura, Rita Anne *pre-school educator*
Larkin, Moscelyne *retired artistic director, dancer*
Lewis, Corinne Hemeter *psychotherapist, educator*
Manhart, Marcia Y(ockey) *art museum director*
Marshall, Linda Lantow *pediatrics nurse*
Mojtabai, Ann Grace *author, educator*
Osborn, La Donna Carol *clergywoman*
Owens, Jana Jae *entertainer*
Price, Alice Lindsay *writer*
Redfearn, Charlotte Marie *nursing administrator*
Seymour, Stephanie Kulp *federal judge*
[illegible]
Thompson, Lori Raquel *marriage and family therapist, consultant*
Williams, Penny *state legislator*
Wood, Emily Churchill *special education educator, social studies educator, consultant*
Wyckoff, Lydia Lloyd *art curator*

Vinita
Wright, Jo Anne *Episcopal priest*

Wagoner
Durham, Nancy Ruth *elementary school educator, music educator*

Warr Acres
Swain, Joye Raechel *writer*

Welling
Varner, Joyce Ehrhardt *retired librarian*

Woodward
Fisher, Deena Kaye *social studies education administrator*

Yukon
Myers, Kandy Kay *music educator*

OREGON

Albany
Chowning, Orr-Lyda Brown *dietician*
Haralson, Linda Jane *communications executive*
Smart, Ann Catherine *dean*

Aloha
Gorea, Lucia-Iosefina *English educator, writer, poet*
Pronovost, Vicki S. *special education educator*

Ashland
Appel, Libby *theater director*
Fujitsubo, Lani Charlene *psychology educator*
Hegler, Ellen Marie *business executive, retired educator*
Mannix, Alicia Gutman *artist, marketing consultant*
Meese, Celia Edwards *pharmaceutical company executive*

Baker City
Trohkimoinen, Judith Lorraine *elementary school educator*

Beaverton
de Sá e Silva, Elizabeth Anne *secondary school educator*
McElligott, Ann Theresa *accountant*
Mitchell, Bettie Phaenon *religious organization administrator*
Pepper, Floy Childers *educational consultant*
Pond, Patricia Brown *library science educator, university administrator*

Bend
Clarno, Beverly Ann *state legislator, farmer*
Collins, Sally Duke *forest service manager*

Evers-Williams, Myrlie *cultural organization administrator*
Forbes Johnson, Mary Gladys *retired secondary school educator*
Goodman, Susan Kathleen *charitable organization administrator, educator*
Loewenthal, Nessa Parker *intercultural communications consultant*
Moss, Patricia L. *bank executive*
Thompson, Mari Hildenbrand *medico-legal and administrative consultant*

Boring
Robinson, Jeanne Louise *writer, educator*

Canby
Flinn, Roberta Jeanne *management, computer applications consultant*
Jarvey, Paulette Sue *publishing executive*
Sundquist, Leah Renata *physical education specialist*

Cannon Beach
Hellyer, Constance Anne (Connie Anne Conway) *writer, musician*
Wismer, Patricia Ann *retired secondary school educator*

Central Point
Ingraham, Laura *lawyer, political commentator*

Christmas Valley
Johnson, Mary Alice *magazine editor*

Corvallis
Achterman, Gail Louise *lawyer*
Chau, May Ying *librarian, educator*
Engle, Molly *program evaluator, preventive medicine researcher, medical educator*
Huyer, Adriana *oceanographer, educator*
Lambert, Deborah Sue *data processing professional*
Landers, Teresa Price *librarian*
Leibowitz, Flora Lynn *philosophy educator*
Lubchenco, Jane *marine biologist, educator*
Lumpkin, Margaret Catherine *retired education educator*
McKee-Ryan, Frances M *education educator*
Shoemaker, Clara Brink *retired chemistry researcher*
Verts, Lita Jeanne *university administrator*
Wechsler, Susan Linda *research and development software manager*
Wilkins, Caroline Hanke *consumer agency administrator, political worker*

Culver
Siebert, Diane Dolores *author, poet*

Dayton
Angaran, Sally Jean *school system administrator*

Eagle Point
Blanchard, Shirley Lynn *primary school educator, consultant*

Eugene
Aldave, Barbara Bader *law educator, lawyer*
Bailey, Exine Margaret Anderson *soprano, educator*
Baker, Bridget Downey *publishing executive*
Bascom, Ruth F. *retired mayor*
Bassett, Carol Ann *journalism educator, writer*
Benson, Joan *musician, music educator*
Camp, Delpha Jeanne *counselor*
Chambers, Carolyn Silva *communications company executive*
Collas-Dean, Angela G. *former state commissioner, small business owner*
Dorn, Kathie Lee *medical/surgical nurse*
Freyd, Jennifer Joy *psychology educator*
Gillespie, Penny Hannig *business owner*
Gourley, Paula Marie *art educator, artist, designer bookbinder, writer, publisher*
Hess, Suzanne Harriet *newspaper publisher, photographer*
Kilgore, Nancy *educational association administrator*
Langlois, Alicia Jean *business development planner, small business owner*
Lansdowne, Karen Myrtle *retired English language and literature educator*
Leeds, Elizabeth Louise *miniature collectibles executive*
McMillan, Adell *retired educational administrator*
Peterson, Donna Rae *gerontologist*
Sisley, Becky Lynn *physical education educator*
Warpinski, Terri L. *academic administrator, artist*
Wilhelm, Kate (Katy Gertrude) *author*
Woolley, Donna Pearl *lumber company executive*

Falls City
Thex, Alberta Hughes *secondary education educator*

Forest Grove
Coleman, Deborah Ann *electronics company executive*
Gibby-Smith, Barbara *psychologist, nurse*
Ginn, Sharon Patrick *mechanical engineer*

Gladstone
Frank, Dee *artist, educator*
Landers, Patricia Burneice *writer*

Grants Pass
Agricola, Dianne G. *secondary education educator, tutor*
Comeaux, Katharine Jeanne *realtor*
McDonald, Saranne *human services professional*
Murdock, Doris Dean *special education educator*
Nankervis, Medora B. *artist*
Remington, Mary *artist, author*
Roberts, Susan Sturgeon *art educator, writer*

Gresham
Light, Betty Jensen Pritchett *former college dean*
Webb, Donna Louise *academic director, educator*

Hillsboro
Dyess, Kirby A. *computer company executive*
Furse, Elizabeth *former congresswoman, small business owner*
Imbrie, Barbara Marie *musician, music educator*

Keizer
Beranek, Kim Marie *music educator*

Klamath Falls
Dow, Martha Anne *biology educator*
Hoggarth, Karen *lumber company executive*
Klepper, Carol Herdman *mental health therapist*
Koch, Margaret Rau *writer, artist, historian*
Stevens, Kendra Ann *speech-language pathologist*

La Grande
Ewing, Marilyn *English educator*

Lake Oswego
Chula, Margaret Jean *poet, writer*
Edstrom, Pam *public relations executive*
Finley, Patricia Ann *psychologist, artist*
Largent, Margie *retired architect*
Lenderman, Joanie *elementary school educator*
Marietta, Elizabeth Ann *industrial engineer*
Meltebeke, Renette *career counselor*
Miller, Barbara Stallcup *development consultant*
Wirtz, Doris W. *secondary school educator*
Zorkin, Melissa Waggener *public relations executive*

Mcminnville
Bull, Vivian Ann *college president*
Burchard, Rachael C. *literary critic, poet, playwright*
Fread, Phyllis Jean *counselor, educator*
Nelson, Donna Gayle *state representative, aviation executive, business owner, educator, writer, journalist*

Medford
Gregory, Rosamund Ann *actor*
Harris, Linda Ruth *obstetrician and gynecologist*
Hennion, Carolyn Laird (Lyn Hennion) *investment executive*
Lantis, Donna Lea *retired banker, art educator, artist*
Linn, Carole Anne *dietician*

Merrill
Porter, Roberta Ann *counselor, educator, school system administrator*

Milwaukie
Davis, Terri Lee *graphics designer, writer, artist*
Eichinger, Marilynne Hildegarde *museum administrator*

Monmouth
Dunn, Doris Marjory *retired educator, volunteer*

Myrtle Creek
Kuk, Mary Halvorson *secondary school educator*

Newberg
Austin, Joan D. *personal care industry executive*
Keith, Pauline Mary *artist, illustrator, writer*
O'Donnell, Susan Lynee *psychologist, educator*

North Bend
Mahon, Barbara Joanne *art educator*

Oceanside
Wadlow, Joan Krueger *retired academic administrator, construction executive*

Pacific City
Perez, Rose (Rose A. Perez) *painter*

Pendleton
Bedford, Amy Aldrich *public relations executive*
Klepper, Elizabeth Lee *physiologist*

Philomath
Leckle, Cheryl Ann *special education educator*

Phoenix
Dodd, Darlene Mae *nurse, retired military officer*

Portland
Adams, Julie Karen *clinical psychologist*
Anthony, Wilma Tylinda *customer representative*
Baker, Diane R.H. *dermatologist*
Balkowiec, Agnieszka Zofia *science educator, researcher*
Blumberg, Naomi *symphony musician, educator*
Bottomly, Therese *editor*
Bowyer, Joan Elizabeth *medical technologist, realtor*
Boyle, Gertrude *sportswear company executive*
Bunza, Linda Hathaway *editor, writer, composer, institution director*
Cassetta, Rhondda King *statistician*
Clausing, Kimberly Anne *economics educator*
Collins, Maribeth Wilson *foundation president*
Cooper, Ginnie *library director*
Corbett, Alice Catherine *investor*
Dailey, Dianne K. *lawyer*
Davis, Gloria Zeal *counseling administrator, educator*
Denhart, Gun *direct mail order company executive*
Detweiler-Bedell, Jerusha Beth *social sciences educator*
Dow, Mary Alexis *auditor*
Ebert, Leslie *artist*
Fritz, Barbara Jean *occupational health nurse*
Frolick, Patricia Mary *retired elementary school educator*
Frye, Helen Jackson *federal judge*
Giffin, Sandra Lee *nursing administrator*
Glass, Laurel Ellen *gerontologist, developmental biologist, physician, retired educator*
Gordly, Avel Louise *state legislator, community activist*
Halupowski, Rachel Elizabeth *fundraising campaign administrator*
Hanchett, Suzanne Lorraine *anthropologist, consultant*
Hargrove, Linda *professional basketball coach*
Helmer, M(artha) Christie *lawyer*
Hickcox, Leslie Kay *health educator, consultant, counselor*
Higdon, Polly Susanne *federal judge*
Hill, Mary Lou *accountant, business consultant*
Hooker, Elaine Norton *news executive*
Jensen, Marion Pauline *singer*
Johansen, Judith A. *lawyer*
Kaluza, Sheryle Siegfried *music educator, vocalist, composer*
Karant-Nunn, Susan Catherine *history educator*
Katz, Vera *mayor, former college administrator, state legislator*
Kleim, E. Denise *city official*
Korb, Christine Ann *music therapist, researcher, educator*
Larson, Wanda Z. *writer, poet*
Leupp, Edythe Peterson *retired education educator*
Lilly, Elizabeth Giles *small business owner*
Lorenz, Nancy *artist*
MacArthur, Carol Jeanne *pediatric otolaryngology educator*
Martin, Lucy Z. *public relations executive*
Massee, Judith Tyle *editor, educator*
Mendelson, Lottie M. *retired pediatric nurse practitioner, writer*
Merrill, Norma *video producer, copy writer*
Meyer, Paulette Ann *history educator*
Milton, Catherine Higgs *social service entrepreneur*
Mittelstaedt, Janet Rugen *music educator, composer*
Morten, Ann Keane *nurse midwife*
Mullane, Jeanette Leslie *artist, educator*
Olson, Kristine *prosecutor*
Patterson, Beverly Ann Gross *not-for-profit fundraiser, consultant, social services administrator*
Porter, Elsa Allgood *writer, lecturer*
Potempa, Kathleen *dean*
Robbins, Jeanette Lee *sales and manufacturing executive*
Robinson, Helene M. *retired music educator*
Robinson, Ruth Carleson *retired secondary school educator*
Rooks, Charles S. *foundation administrator*
Rooks, Judith Pence *midwife, public health consultant*
Rosenbaum, Lois Omenn *lawyer*
Rosenblum, Ellen F. *judge*
Rowe, Sandra Mims *editor*
Sedgwick, Levonne *retired school program administrator*
Sokol, Jan D. *lawyer*
Steinman, Lisa Malinowski *English literature educator, writer*
Stephens, Alice Elizabeth (Alice Wanke Stephens) *artist*
Stewart, Janice Mae *federal judge*
Taylor, J(ocelyn) Mary *museum administrator, zoologist, educator*
Teller, Susan Elaine *lawyer*
Thomas, Carol F. *educational association administrator*
Thompson, Jill Lynette Long *federal agency administrator, former congresswoman*
Thompson, Terrie Lee *graphic designer*
Vanderslice, Ellen *architect*
VanSickle, Sharon Dee *public relations executive*
Wageman, Virginia Farley *editor, writer*
Watts, Sara Kathryn *musician, educator*
Whitsell, Helen Jo *lumber executive*
Witherspoon, Sophia *professional basketball player*
Zerbe, Kathryn Jane *psychiatrist*
Zimmerman, Gail Marie *medical foundation executive*

Prineville
Schulz, Suzon Louise *fine artist*

Redmond
Dey, Charlotte Jane *retired community health nurse*

Rhododendron
Williamson, Diana Jean *nurse*

Roseburg
Eddy, Wanda Criger *music educator*
Ferguson, Cynthia Claire *music educator, consultant*
Oleskowicz, Jeanette *physician*
Zeigler, Rey *dean*

Salem
Anderson, Laurie Monnes *state representative*
Bentley, Sara *newspaper publishing executive*
Berger, Vicki *state representative*
Beyer, Elizabeth Terry *state representative*
Brown, Kate *state legislator*
Burdick, Ginny *state legislator*
Castillo, Susan *school system administrator*
Close, Betsy L. *state representative*
Dingfelder, Jackie *state representative*
Dukes, Joan *state legislator*
Flores, Linda *state representative*
Gallegos, Mary *state representative*
Hopson, Elaine M. *state representative*
Kafoury, Deborah *state representative*
Kirk, Jill *educational association administrator*
Marshall, Cak (Catherine Elaine Marshall) *music educator, composer*
Milbrath, Mary Merrill Lemke *quality assurance professional*
Minnis, Karen *state representative*
Morgan, Susan H. *state representative*
Nolan, Mary *state representative*
Page, Cheryl Miller *elementary school educator*
Qutub, Eileen *state legislator, real estate appraiser*
Robertson, Marian Ella (Marian Ella Hall) *small business owner, handwriting analyst*
Rosenbaum, Diane M. *state representative*
Shannon, Marylin Linfoot *state legislator, educator*
Smith, Patti *state representative*
Smith, Tootie *state representative*
Taylor, Janet R. *mayor*
Tomei, Carolyn *state representative*
Verger, Joanne *state representative*
Walker, Vicki L. *state senator*
Warnath, Maxine Ammer *organizational psychologist, mediator*
Winters, Jackie F. *small business owner, foundation administrator*
Wirth, Kelley K. *state representative*
Yih, Mae Dunn *state legislator*

Seaside
Bishop, Virginia Wakeman *retired librarian and humanities educator, small business owner*

Silverton
Brown, Bethany Joy *advocate*
Stone, Jane Buffington *artist, writer*

Springfield
Smith, Vangy Edith *accountant, consultant, writer, artist*

Sutherlin
Johnson, Barbara E. *adult education educator*
Rose, Sarah Elizabeth *genealogist, counselor*

West Linn
Harris, Debra Coral *physical education educator*
Stoddard-Hayes, Marlana Kay *artist, educator*

White City
Whelan, Mary Jane *accountant, writer, photographer*

Wilsonville
McKay, Laura L. *banker, consultant*
Talus, Donna J. *secondary school educator*

Yachats
Robeck, Mildred Coen *education educator, writer*

Zigzag
Chappell, Annie-Dear *retired information technology company official*

PENNSYLVANIA

Abington
Bard, Ellen Marie *state legislator, former small business owner, small business owner*
Lauck, Donna L. *mental health nurse*
Schuster, Ingeborg Ida *chemistry educator*

Acme
Babcock, Marguerite Lockwood *addictions treatment therapist, educator, writer*

Akron
Livingston, Margery Elsie *missionary, clinical psychologist*

Allentown
Bedics, Lynn Fay *nurse*
Beltzner, Gail Ann *music educator*
Blaney, Dorothy Gulbenkian *academic administrator*
Buenaflor, Judith Luray *secondary school educator*
Cole, Joan (Ellen) Blyler *financial executive*
Flores, Robin Ann *social worker, social services administrator*
Glaessmann, Doris Ann *former county official, consultant*
Hunt, L. Susan *publishing executive*
Langman, Madeleine Charna *psychologist*
Martyska, Barbara *composer, performer, teacher*
Moeller, MaryAnn *music educator*
Nippert, Carolyn Cochrane *college official, information scientist*
Pribanich, Cheryl Marie *music educator*
Saab, Deanne Keltum *real estate appraiser, real estate broker*
Sacks, Patricia Ann *librarian, consultant*
Taylor, Sherri Kearise *obstetrician, gynecologist, writer*
Zocco, Patricia Elizabeth *human services manager, cardiac ultrasound technologist*

Allison Park
Guffey, Barbara Braden *elementary school educator*
Reagan, Patricia L. *secondary school counselor*

Altoona
Arpino, Denise Marie *minister*
Kinney, Janis Marie *librarian, consultant*

Ambler
Pazicky, Diana Loercher *literature educator*
Swansen, Donna Maloney *landscape designer, consultant*

Annville
Condran, Cynthia Marie *gospel musician*
Riegle Kinch, Marie Eileen *art educator*
Verhoek, Susan Elizabeth *botany educator*

Ardmore
Dagna, Jeanne Marie *special education educator*
Lockett-Egan, Marian Workman *advertising executive*
Rodriguez, Kathleen Moore *art educator*

Aston
Mirenda, Rosalie M. *nursing educator, administrator*

Athens
Lane, Elizabeth Ann *music educator*
Luther-Lemmon, Carol Len *elementary school educator*
Miller, Vina Elizabeth *music educator*
Murphy, Sylvia J. Harris *secondary school educator*

Baden
Pellegrino, Sister Mary R. *nun*

Bala Cynwyd
Armani, Aida Mary *small business executive*
Cohen, Rachel Rutstein *financial planner*
Dorwart, Bonnie Brice *historian, retired rheumatologist*
Kane-Vanni, Patricia Ruth *lawyer, paleontology educator*
Peret, Karen Krzyminski *health services administrator, consultant*
Ringpfeil, Fraziska *dermatologist*

Bangor
Pensack, Susan *elementary school educator*

Beaver Falls
Hemphill, Diane Eilene *music educator*
Mahosky, Nancy Lynne *secondary school educator*
Miller, Kathleen S. *management and accounting professional*
Smith, Nancy Irene *director*

Belle Vernon
Stimmell, Tamara *special education educator*

Bensalem
Bern, Dorrit J. *apparel company executive*
Gentile, Mary O'Connor *principal*
Jurowicz, Kimberly Deborah *special education educator, elementary school educator*

Benton
Hopkins, Mary Bazemore *landscape designer, consultant*

Berwyn
Ahlquist, Janet Sue *musician, music educator*
Gingles, Marjorie Stanke *music educator, educator*
Langford, Linda Kosmin *library consultant*

Bethel Park
Douds, Virginia Lee *elementary school educator*

Bethlehem
Allen, Beatrice *music educator, pianist*
Dienel, Nancy Alduma Roberts *health insurance underwriter*
Dorward, Judith A. *business ordering customer service representative*
Herbst, Patricia Carlisle *lay worker*
Korsak, Barbara A. *geriatrics nurse*
Moeller, Rachel Nelson *career development specialist*
Schattschneider, Doris Jean *retired mathematics educator*
Simons, Audrey Kay *music educator*
Teicher, Stacy Ellen *publishing executive*
Yatsonsky, Joan Marie *nursing educator*

Biglerville
Marks, Nora Maralea *retired secondary school educator*

Birdsboro
Sipotz, Naomi C. *music educator*

Bloomsburg
Kozloff, Jessica S. *university president*
Perner, Darlene E. *special education educator, consultant, editor*

Blue Bell
Furman, Sue *owner public relations agency*
Halas, Cynthia Ann *business information specialist*
Haugen, Janet B. *corporate financial executive*
Roden, Carol Looney *retired language educator*
Sundheim, Nancy Straus *lawyer*

Boalsburg
Isler, Erika Lisbeth *journalist*

Boiling Springs
Oxenreider, Laura Elizabeth *elementary guidance counselor*

Boothwyn
Giordano, Patricia A. *music educator*

Boyertown
Craner, Wanda Dietz *clergywoman, therapist*
Woods Coggins, Alma *artist*

Bradfordwoods
Allardice, Susan M. *manufacturing executive*

Breinigsville
de Limantour, Clarice Barr *food scientist*

Bridgeville
Fox, Debra L. *educational association administrator, business owner*

Brodheadsville
Snyder, Nadine Eldora *music educator*

Broomall
Saunders, Sally Love *poet, educator*

Bryn Mawr
Cooney, Patricia Ruth *civic worker*
Crawford, Maria Luisa Buse *geology educator*
Fellinger-Buzby, Linda *interior and industrial designer*
Fletcher, Marjorie Amos *librarian*
Gaisser, Julia Haig *classics educator*
King, Willard Fahrenkamp (Mrs. Edmund Ludwig King) *Spanish language educator*
Lane, Barbara Miller (Barbara Miller-Lane) *humanities educator*
Lang, Mabel Louise *classics educator*
Porter, Judith Deborah Revitch *sociologist, educator*
Smith, Nona Coates *academic administrator*
Vickers, Nancy J. *academic administrator*

Burlington
Papa, Kathleen Nicole *music educator*

Butler
Day, Margaret Ann *research librarian, information specialist*
Hawk, Kathleen Patricia *broadcast consultant*

California
Langham, Norma E. *playwright, educator, poet, composer, inventor*

Cambridge Springs
Ferringer-Burdick, Susan *elementary school educator*
Ralph, NancyJo *music educator*

Camp Hill
Besch, Nancy Adams *county official*
Crist, Christine Myers *consulting executive*
Parry-Solá, Cheryl Lee *critical care nurse*
Romberger, Jean Louise *retired educator*
Rugen, Karen *manufacturing executive, corporate communications specialist*
Sammons, Mary F. *retail executive*

Carlisle
Cook, Ann Harris Shackleton *gifted and talented educator, psychotherapist*
Kot, Heather A. (Heather A. Oliver) *soprano, educator*
Streidl, Isabelle Roberts Smiley *economist*
Strong, Sara Dougherty *psychologist, family therapist, custody mediator*
Talley, Carol Lee *newspaper editor*

Center Valley
Bartolacci, Paulette Marie *middle school educator, aerobics instructor*

Centre Hall
Fry, Theresa Eileen *therapeutic foster care aide*

Chadds Ford
Swensson, Evelyn Dickenson *conductor, composer, librettist*
Werner DeNadai, Mary *architectural firm executive*

Chalfont
Ashley, Kathleen Labonis *music educator*
Wilson, Jean L. *retired state legislator*

Chambersburg
Broadwater, Shirley Marie *psychologist*
Gilbreath, Sarah Burkhart Gelbach *health facility administrator*

Cheltenham
Kuziemski, Naomi Elizabeth *educational consultant, counselor*
Selekman, Meridith *psychologist*

Chester
Ciociola, Cecilia Mary *development specialist*
Lieberman, Ilene D. *art history and humanities educator*

Cheyney
Bagley, Edythe Scott *theater educator*
Ellis-Scruggs, Jan *theater arts educator*

Clarion
Dingle, Patricia A. *education educator, artist*
Grejda, Gail Fulton *dean*
Miller, Andrea Lynn *library science educator*
Reinhard, Diane L. *university president*

Clarks Summit
Weiss, Tammy Lee *information technology manager*

Clearfield
Boykiw, Norma Severne *retired nutritionist, educator*
Krebs, Margaret Eloise *publishing executive*

Coatesville
Rodkey, Frances Theresa *elementary school educator*
Simmons, Barbara Ann *music educator*
Smith, Patricia Anne *special education educator*

Collegeville
Barnes, Jo Anne *investment advisor*
Maco, Teri Regan *accountant, engineer*

Columbia
Steiner-Houck, Sandra Lynn *interior designer*
Trout, Gwenn Louise *minister*

Coraopolis
Stage, Ginger Rooks *psychologist*
Stevens, Paulette *daycare administrator*
Vandertie, Suzan Mary *music educator*
Wilkins, Arlene *social worker*

Custer City
Cavallero, Ann Freaney *literature educator*

Darby
Wardell, Lindy Constance *nonprofit organization administrator*

Delaware Water Gap
Chamberlin, Marjorie Ruth *elementary school educator*

Dickson City
Kearns, Colleen *physical therapist*

Donora
Todd, Norma Ross *retired government official*

Downingtown
Crescenz, Valerie J. *music educator*

Doylestown
Dimond, Roberta Ralston *psychology and sociology educator*
McCafferty, Barbara Jean (BJ McCafferty) *sales executive*
Meyer, Diane Christine *social worker*
Thomas, Ellen Louise *school system administrator*
Waite, Frances W. *librarian, professional genealogist*
Wolfinger, Audrey Jane *retired librarian*

Dresher
Michael, Dorothy Ann *nursing administrator, naval officer*

Drexel Hill
Bay, Joann Reeder *financial planner*
Boyer, Anna Marie *music educator*
Turnbull, Mary Regina *secondary school educator*

Du Bois
Mortimer, Pamela S. *printing company executive*
Williams, Kathryn Blake *retired librarian*

Duncannon
Butt, Elizabeth Kathryn Moffatt *journalist, photographer, newspaper editor*

Dunmore
Pencek, Carolyn Carlson *treasurer, educator*

East Petersburg
Kunkle, Mary Lou *counselor*

East Stroudsburg
Baril, Nancy Ann *gerontological nurse practitioner, consultant*
Braithwaite, Barbara J. *secondary school educator*
Hauner-Morris, Phyllis Marie *systems analyst*
Miller, Edith Fisher *special education educator*

Easton
Kistler, Loretta M. *social worker, consultant*
Lutte, Carole Anne *music educator*
Miller, Marie Gelsinger *music educator*
Reibman, Jeanette Fichman *retired state senator*
Schlueter, June Mayer *English educator, author*
Stitt, Dorothy Jewett *journalist*

Ebensburg
Pereira, Melany *elementary school educator*

Edinboro
Kowalski, Kathe A. *art educator, photographer*
Marszalek, Marilyn *elementary school educator*
Paul, Charlotte Patricia Peggram *nursing educator*
Snyder, Heather *social sciences educator*

Eighty Four
Magerko, Maggie Hardy *lumber company executive*

Elizabethtown
Bartoli, Jill Sunday *reading and language arts researcher and educator*
Chesbro, Karen E. Henise *registered nurse*

Elkins Park
Erlebacher, Martha Mayer *artist, educator*

Emmaus
Favorule, Denise *publishing executive*
Rodale, Ardath Harter *publishing executive*

Ephrata
Sweigart, Anne B. *communications company executive*

Erdenheim
Murphy, Mary Marguerite *artist*

Erie
Andrian-Ceciu, Roxanne R. *engineer, program manager*
Azicri, Nicolette Maly *art educator, artist*
Begley, Charlene *electronics executive*
Brunner-Martinez, Kirstin Ellen *pediatrician, psychiatrist*
Bruno, Mia Noelle Claudia *archaeological organization administrator*
Earll, Jane *state legislator, lawyer*
Foltz, Katrina Marie *music educator*
Jenkins, Janet S. *minister*
Mattis, Constance Marie *controller*
McKinney, Betty Louise *musician*
Waldron, Allene *insurance group executive*

Erwinna
Auerbach, Kathryn Ann *architecture and preservation educator, consultant*

Etters
Steps, Barbara Jill *lawyer*

Evans City
Mustovic, Faithann Marian (Faithann Grigalunas) *pharmacist*

Everett
Snow, Linda Sue *family educator, consumer sciences educator, secondary school educator*

Exton
Chu, Deh-Ying *chemist, researcher*
Ellis, Staci Elaine *psychotherapist, actress*
Webber, Helen *artist, designer*

Factoryville
Simmons, Ruth Doris *retired women's health nurse, educator*

Fairfield
Mikesell, Pamela Prestwood *guidance counselor*

Fairless Hills
Hess, Frances Elizabeth *retired secondary school educator, retired director*

Fairview
Sanford, Carolyn Ann *music educator*

Farrell
Pawluk, Annette Marie *secondary school educator*

Feasterville Trevose
Thee, Cynthia Urban *psychotherapist*

Flinton
Burket, Darla Eileen *music educator*

Fogelsville
Crooker, Barbara Ann *writer, educator*

Fort Washington
Fulton, Cheryl L. *customer service administrator*
Minniti, Martha Jean *home healthcare company executive*

Franklin
Sauer, Mary Julia *special education educator*

Franklin Center
Resnick, Lynda Rae *consumer products company executive*

Gap
Beller, Anne F. *food company executive*
Tindall, Janice Clough *family physician*

Gettysburg
Gritsch, Ruth Christine Lisa *editor*
Nelson-Small, Kathy Ann *foundation administrator*
Schein, Virginia Ellen *psychologist, editor*

Gibsonia
Haas, Eileen Marie *homecare advocate*
Krause, Helen Fox *otolaryngologist*

Gladwyne
Allen, Theresa Ohotnicky *neurobiologist, consultant*
Morrison, Gail *internist, nephrologist, educator*
Stick, Alyce Cushing *systems administrator, consultant*

Glen Mills
Dunion, Celeste Mogab *consultant, business manager, township official*
Shields, Martha Buckley *elementary school educator*
Turner, Janet Sullivan *painter, sculptor*

Glenmoore
Humphreys-Heckler, Maureen Kelly *nursing home administrator*

Glenshaw
Stevens, Christine Treml *music educator*

Glenside
Crivelli-Kovach, Andrea *public health and nutrition consultant, educator*
Doman, Janet Joy *professional society administrator*
Fine, Elsa Honig *editor, publishing executive*
Landman, Bette Emeline *academic administrator*
Medel, Rebecca Rosalie *artist*

Grantville
Sudor, Cynthia Ann *sales and marketing professional*

Greencastle
Fremgen, Darlene *manufacturing specialist*

Greensburg
Blazina, Carole Marie *nun*
Duck, Patricia Mary *librarian*
Fajt, Karen Elaine *art educator*
Shafer-Kenney, Jolie E. *writer, columnist*

Gwynedd Valley
Owens, Kathleen C. *academic administrator*

Halifax
Stauffer, Joanne Rogan *steel company official*

Hamburg
Schappell, Abigail Susan *speech, language, hearing and massage therapist*

Hanover
Barnhart, Nikki Lynn Clark *elementary school educator*
Clark, Sandra Marie *school administrator*
Davis, Ruth Carol *pharmacy educator*

Harrisburg

Antoun, Annette Agnes *newspaper editor, publisher*
Baehre, Edna Victoria *college president*
Baker Knoll, Catherine *lieutenant governor*
Barron, Cate *editor*
Bebko-Jones, Linda *state legislator*
Bishop, Louise Williams *state legislator*
Boscola, Lisa M. *state legislator*
Burns, Rebecca Ann *elementary school educator, librarian*
Butler, Jessie D. *community activist, retired educator and counselor*
Chambers, Clarice Lorraine *clergy, educational consultant*
Cohen, Lita Indzel *state legislator*
Comoss, Patricia B. *cardiac rehabilitation nurse, consultant*
Cooper, Jane Todd (J. C. Todd) *poet, writer, educator*
Crahalla, Jacqueline R. *state representative*
Ellenbogen, Elisabeth Alice *retired accountant*
Filardo, Janet Becherer *lobbyist*
Forcier, Teresa Elaine *state legislator*
Franco, Barbara Alice *museum director*
Gingrich, Mauree A. *state representative*
Hafer, Barbara *state official*
Hample, Judy G. *academic administrator*
Houstoun, Feather O'Connor *state official*
Kane, Yvette *lawyer, judge*
Knackstedt, Mary V. *interior designer*
Koken, M. Diane *commissioner, state*
Laughlin, Susan *state legislator*
Lederer, Marie A. *state legislator*
Mackereth, Beverly D. *state representative*
Mann, Jennifer L. *state representative*
Martine, Andrea Schultz *secondary school educator*
Maunus, Eileen Susan *lawyer*
Miller, Leslie Anne *lawyer*
Miller, Sheila *state legislator*
Phillips, Vicki L. *school system administrator*
Pickett, Tina L. *state representative*
Pizzingrilli, Kim *state official*
Pletz, Darcy L. *sales executive*
Pringle, Rebecca *elementary school educator*
Prioleau, Sara Nelliene *dentist*
Rambo, Sylvia H. *federal judge*
Ross, Ellyn N. *educational association administrator, consultant*
Schmedlen, Jeanne Hearn *writer, legislative staff member, consultant*
Schwartz, Allyson Y. *state legislator*
Tartaglione, Christine M. *state legislator*
Taylor, Elinor Zimmerman *state legislator*
True, Katie *state legislator*
Tyson, Gail L. *health federation administrator*
Vance, Patricia H. *state legislator*
Watson, Katharine M. *state representative*
Weber, Melissa Murphy *state representative*
West, Eileen M. *caseworker*
White, Mary Jo *state legislator, lawyer*
Williams, Constance *state senator*
Wissler-Thomas, Carrie *professional society administrator, artist*
Yenchko, Suzanne *research and development company executive*

Harrison City

Rubright, Beverly Jean *music educator*

Harveys Lake

Wolensky, Joan *occupational therapist, interfaith minister*

Hatboro

Carroll, Lucy Ellen *choral director, music coordinator, educator*

Hatfield

Madden, Theresa Marie *elementary school educator*

Haverford

de Laguna, Frederica *anthropology educator emeritus, writer, publisher*
Jorden, Eleanor Harz *linguist, educator*
Mellink, Machteld Johanna *archaeologist, educator*
Stiller, Jennifer Anne *lawyer*
Zug, Elizabeth Kendall *volunteer*

Havertown

Garletts, Twila Umbel *advocate*
Hoffman, Elizabeth Parkinson *librarian*
Wright, Cecilia Powers *gifted and talented educator*

Hellertown

Kunkel-Christman, Debra Ann *educator*

Hershey

Butterfield, Andrea Christine *elementary school educator, adult education educator, psychology educator*
Hopper, Anita Klein *molecular genetics educator*
Kruger, Nancy R. *university program director, nurse*
Testa, Donna Marie *physician*

Holland

Ryalls, Barbara Taylor *freelance/self-employed editor, critic*

Hollidaysburg

McPhee, Norma Howatt *publishing executive, author*

Honesdale

Clark, Christine May *editor, author*
Roos, Paula Sparrow *manufacturer's representative*

Houtzdale

McGowan, Diane Joyce *psychologist*

Hulmeville

Jackson, Mary L. *health services executive*

Huntingdon Valley

Stephenson, Helene Ruth *painter, consultant*

Immaculata

Fadden, Sister R. Patricia *academic administrator, nun*
Kriebel, Dawn Kastanek *psychologist, educator, researcher*

Indiana

Craig, Chauna Janene *language educator*
LaRoche, Lynda *artist, educator*
Reynolds, Virginia Edith *sociologist, anthropologist, educator, artist*
Ruddock, Ellen Sylves *business consultant*
Steelman, Sara Gerling *art association administrator*
Tobin, Lois Moore *home economist, educator, retired*

Jenkintown

Dickstein, Joan Borteck *arbitrator, conflict management consultant*
Goldman, Janice Goldin *psychologist, educator*
Greenspan-Margolis, June E. *psychiatrist*
Leiter, Barbara F. *music educator*
Lowry, Karen M. *biomedical research scientist, pharmacist*
O'Neill, Judith Jones *insurance agent*
Roediger, Janice Anne *artist, educator*

Jessup

Karluk, Lori Jean *craft designer, copy editor*

Johnstown

Fattman, Anne Carilyn *elementary school educator*
George, Christine *mental health services professional, supervisor, writer*
Puto, Anne-Marie *reading specialist*

Kempton

Lenhart, Cynthia Rae *conservation organization executive*

Kennett Square

Harrington, Anne Wilson *medical librarian*
Lippincott, Sarah Lee *astronomer, graphologist*
Pensyl, Christina A. *special education educator*

King Of Prussia

Helmetag, Diana *music educator*
McCairns, Regina Carfagno *pharmaceutical executive*
Phipps, Judith A. *social worker*
Schneider, Pam Horvitz *lawyer*
Schumann, Paula M. L. *writer*
Swank, Annette Marie *software designer*

Kingsley

McNabb, Corrine Radtke *librarian*

Kingston

Weisberger, Barbara *artistic director, educator, choreographer*

Knox

Rupert, Elizabeth Anastasia *retired dean*

Kutztown

Meyer, Susan Moon *speech language pathologist, educator*
Speirs, Peg *art educator, artist, researcher*

Lafayette Hill

Delacato, Janice Elaine *learning consultant, educator*
Duncalfe Holt, Lucinda Bromwyn *marketing executive*

Lake Ariel

Casper, Marie Lenore *middle school educator*

Lake Winola

Driscole, Melissa Rees *conductor, educator*

Lancaster

Bernard, Ruth Faye *artist, educator*
Brunner, Lillian Sholtis *nurse, writer*
Daugherty, Ruth Alice *religious association consultant*
Drum, Alice *academic administrator, educator*
Geiger, Carol Lynn *educational therapist*
Horein, Kathleen Marie *music educator*
Hubbard, Jayne Elizabeth *minister, marriage and family therapist*
Jordan, Lois Wenger *foundation official*
Nast, Dianne Martha *lawyer*
Poser, Joan Rapps *artists agent*
Shenk, Lois Elaine Landis *writer*
Stewart, Arlene Jean Golden *designer, stylist*
Taylor, Ann *human resources specialist, educator*
Trupe, Mary-Ann *secondary school educator*
Veri, Frances Gail *musician, educator*
Whare, Wanda Snyder *lawyer*
Young, Brenda Ann *nurse*

Landisville

Steiner, Donna Forbes *minister, executive consultant*

Langhorne

Haimbach, Marjorie Anne *music educator*
Paetzold, Mary E. *agricultural products supplier*
Wychock, Karen Marie *principal, set designer, craftsman*

Lansdale

Holloway, M(ary) Katharine *research scientist, chemist*
Richards, Jane C. *music educator*
Robinson, Joan Lenore *retired dietitian*
Sokolowski, Elizabeth Catherine *music educator*

Lenhartsville

Ryan, Christine Brett *music educator*

Levittown

Camer, Mary Martha *retired secretary*
Walker, Patricia Ann Dixon *retired elementary school educator, real estate rehabilitator*

Lewisburg

Brill, Marilyn *community-based collaboration consultant*
Lenhart, Lorraine Margaret *county official*
Neuman, Nancy Adams Mosshammer *civic leader*
Roberts, Ruth W. *retired elementary school educator*
Rote, Nelle Fairchild Hefty *management consultant*
Smith, Marguerite Irene *gifted and talented educator*

Lititz

Hudelson, Judith Giantomass *elementary school educator*
Whitson, Sandra Joyce *antiques dealer*

Littlestown

Gall, Pamela Jane *art educator*

Lock Haven

Almes, June *retired education educator, librarian*
Bowers, Gloria Mills *secondary education art educator*
Chang, Shirley Lin (Hsiu-Chu Chang) *librarian, educator*
Hoff, Joan Whitman *philosophy educator, women's studies coordinator, director*

Loretto

Clark, Rose Ann *chemist, educator*
Sackin, Claire *retired social work educator*

Loysburg

Stuckey, Ellen Mae *music educator*

Macungie

Nenstiel, Susan Kisthart *fundraising professional*

Mahaffey

Lieb, Susan M. *elementary school educator*

Malvern

Brighton, Ruth Louise *lay worker, educator*
Colosimo, Lisa Marie *software engineer*
Dolores, Fidishun *librarian, educator*
Fisher, Sallie Ann *chemist*

Mansfield

Donahue, Martha *librarian, educator, retired*
Sidell, Nancy L. *adult education educator*

Maple Glen

Jacobson, Bonnie Brown *writer, energy executive, statistician, researcher*
Weaver-Stroh, Joanne Mateer *education educator, consultant*

Mar Lin

Studlack, Cindy June *speech pathology/audiology services professional*

Marietta

Mendenhall, Hollie Christine *music educator*

Mc Donald

Maurer, Karen Ann *special education educator*
Starkey, Aleta Rae *music educator*

Mc Keesport

Lodor, Marci Ann *dietician*

Mc Murray

Cmar, Janice Butko *home economics educator*

Meadville

Dixon, Armendia Pierce *school program administrator*
Karns, Cynthia Denise *art educator*
Stewart, Anne Williams *historian, writer, researcher*

Mechanicsburg

Bitner, Jerri Lynne *information technology professional, consultant*
Harper, Diane Marie *retired communications retailer*
Snider, Karen *human services administrator*

Media

Gordon, Lisa Diane *psychologist*
Stevenson, Karen Lee (Rizzo) *psychologist, consultant*
Turner, Letitia Rhodes *artist*

Mercersburg

Mufson, Laurie Ethel *theater educator, director, actress*

Merion Station

Camp, Kimberly N. *museum administrator, artist*
Mitchell, Joann M. *music educator*

Midland

Dunlap, Barbara J. *music educator*

Midway

Pierrard-Mutton, Mary V. *artist, educator*

Milford

Le Guin, Ursula Kroeber *writer*

Milford Square

Sewell, Gloriana *piano teacher*

Millersville

Bensur, Barbara Jean *art educator, researcher*
Hess, Patricia Ann *dietician*
Saunders, Kendra J. *psychologist, educator*

Millerton

Kipferl, Christiana A. *special education educator*

Monaca

Soltes, Joann Margaret *retired music educator, realtor*

Monongahela

Yovanof, Silvana *physician*

Monroeville

Baker, Faith Mero *retired elementary education educator*
Kennedy, Kathy Kay *library director*
Skolnick, Marilyn *civic worker*

Montoursville

Woolever, Naomi Louise *retired editor-in-chief*

Moon Township

Martin, Diana Williams *music educator*

Moon Township,

Pociernicki, Janice Louise *artist*

Morgantown

Quinn, Elysia D. *finance company executive*

Morrisville

Kuronya, Carol Gasco *tour guide*

Moscow

Lisandrelli, Elaine Slivinski *secondary school educator*

Mount Gretna

Warshaw, Roberta Sue *lawyer*

Mount Joy

Sater, Denise M. *journalist, editor*

Nanticoke

Donohue, Patricia Carol *academic administrator*

Narberth

Pauxtis, Mary Jo *academic administrator*
Pollack, Sonya A. *artist*

Nazareth

Simpson, Veronica Ann *photographer, lab technician*

New Alexandria

Sehring, Hope Hutchinson *library science educator*

New Brighton

Ficca, Rhonda Lee *music educator*

New Castle

Halm, Nancye Studd *retired academic administrator*
Roux, Mildred Anna *retired secondary school educator*
Sands, Christine Louise *English educator*

New Cumberland

Rose, Bonnie Lou *state official*
Wilson, Wanda Mae French *animal association administrator*

New Florence

Melville, Cathy Louise *administrative assistant*

New Freedom

Sedlak, Valerie Frances *retired English language educator, retired academic administrator*

New Holland

Fanus, Pauline Rife *librarian*

New Hope

Brandes, Doris *artist, art administrator, journalist*
Van Pelt, Janet Ruth *retired insurance company executive*

New Oxford

Martin, Sandra Ann *special education educator, writer*

New Stanton

Black, Cora Jean *evangelist, wedding consultant*

New Tripoli

Hess, Darla Bakersmith *cardiologist, educator*

New Wilmington

Bolger, Dorita Yvonne Ferguson *librarian*
Magyary, Cynthia Marie *elementary school educator, music educator*

Newport

Switzer, Karen Belle Ringers *music educator*

Newtown

Jorczak, Nancy *history educator*
Latzel, Greta *marketing professional, director*
Letizi, Sunny Selma *social worker*
McLaughlin, Judith Ann *secondary school educator*
Somers, Anne Ramsay *retired medical educator*

Newtown Square

de Rivas, Carmela Foderaro *psychiatrist, health facility administrator*
Pacini, Renee Annette *software company executive*
Vela, Laurie Story *illustrator, writer, publisher, producer*

Norristown

DeCaro, Monica Ward *finance administrator*
Del Collo, Mary Anne Demetris *school administrator*
D'Ulisse-Caldwell, Maryellen Cecilia *music educator*

Rial, Martha *photographer*
Ross, Eunice Latshaw *judge*
Ross, Madelyn Ann *newspaper editor*
Rudy, Ellen Beam *nursing educator*
Schaub, Marilyn McNamara *religion educator*
Scheuble, Kathryn Jean *social worker, family therapist*
Schock, Barbara Jean *educational consultant*
Schorr-Ribera, Hilda Keren *psychologist*
Schultheiss, Emily Ekonen *management consultant, writer*
Sensenich, Ila Jeanne *federal judge*
Shaw, Mary M. *computer science educator*
Somova, Marla Jo *counseling administrator, psychologist*
Southworth, Jamie MacIntyre *retired education educator*
Steytler, C. Anne Webster *clinical social worker*
Strick, Sadie Elaine *psychologist*
Stunja, Valerie Ann *aircraft dispatcher*
Vergun, Olga Victorovna *physiologist, researcher*
Verlich, Jean Elaine *writer, public relations consultant*
Warner, Judith (Anne) Huss *elementary school educator*
Wenger, Sharon Louise *pediatrics educator, researcher, cytogeneticist*
Werner, Jane *museum administrator*
Wilde, Patricia *retired artistic director*
Wohleber, Lynne Farr *archivist, librarian*
Wooten, Carol Campbell *academic administrator*
Worley, Virginia King *microbiologist*
Yourison, Karola Maria *librarian services professional*
Ziskind, Deborah Ziskind *public relations and legal marketing executive*

Plymouth
Campbell, Leanne Hays *pastor*
Castner, Deborah A. *librarian*

Plymouth Meeting
Blessing, Carole Anne *human resources manager*
Sauer, Elizabeth Mason *school social worker*

Pocono Lake
Caramelli, Iraina R. *artist, educator*

Port Allegany
McJunkin, Evon Marie Lloyd *minister*

Port Matilda
Ritti, Alyce Rae *artist*

Pottstown
Hollingsworth, Debra Lynn *elementary school educator*

Pottsville
Whalen, Denise Lasco *family therapist*

Presto
Moeller, Audrey Carolyn *retired energy company executive, corporate secretary*

Punxsutawney
Dinsmore, Roberta Joan Maier *library director*

Quakertown
Emig, Carol A. *music educator, musician*
Laincz, Betsy Ann *nurse*

Radnor
Flagg, Helen Clawson *writer*
Harris, Mary Howard *finance educator*
Iadarola, Antoinette *college president*
Thompson, Pamela Padwick *public relations executive*

Reading
Bell, Frances Louise *medical technologist*
Dietrich, Renée Long *fund raising executive*
Hackenberg, Barbara Jean Collar *retired advertising and public relations executive*
Hurwitz, Ellen Stiskin *college president, historian*
McVey, Diane Elaine *accountant*
Sauer, Elissa Swisher *nursing educator*
Shultz, Lois Frances Casho *nursing supervisor*
Ulshafer, Sharon A. *accountant, educator*
Zug, Elizabeth E. *concert pianist, educator*

Rices Landing
Cottle, Kimberly Lynn *municipal official*

Richboro
Burtt, Larice Annadel Roseman *artist*

Ridley Park
Brown, Ruth Ann *pharmacist*

Riegelsville
Banko, Ruth Caroline *retired library director*

Rural Valley
Forringer, Deborah Lee *music educator*

Russellton
Cicco, Cecilia Victoria *music educator*
Curtis, Paula Annette *elementary and secondary education educator*

Sayre
Bentley, Dianne H. Glover *minister, consultant*
Brittain, Nancy Hammond *accountant*
Smith, Robin L. *municipal official*

Scranton
Balint, Annette *church administrator*
Garrett, Jill Hope *broadcast journalist*
Lemoncelli, Lorine Barbara *counselor, elementary school educator*
Nee, Sister Mary Coleman *college president emeritus*
Reap, Sister Mary Margaret *college administrator*
Turock, Jane Parsick *nutritionist*
Williams, Holly Thomas *retired business executive*

Selinsgrove
Connolly, Elma Troutman *artist, contractor, designer*
Pineno, Mariam Davis *retired music educator, poet*

Sellersville
Dodson, Lois Alderdice *psychotherapist, consultant*

Sewickley
Jackson, Velma Louise *lawyer*
Silva, Pat A. *artist*

Shamokin
Styer, Sharon Louise *music educator*

Sharon
Matejka, Barbara A. *draftsman*

Shavertown
Fioti, Jean K. *pharmacist*
Motyka, Susanne Victoria *music educator*

Shippensburg
Stone, Susan Ridgaway *marketing educator*

Solebury
Gilleo, Sandra V. *elementary school educator*

Somerset
Thomas, Darlene Jean *state employee*

South Park
Lotze, Barbara *retired physicist*

Southampton
Schmidt, Catherine Ann *psychologist*

Spring Grove
Alcon, Sonja L. *retired medical social worker*
Helberg, Shirley Adelaide Holden *artist, educator*

Springfield
Sellers, Lois Eileen Wagner *art director*

State College
Chiswick, Nancy Rose *psychologist*
Darnell, Doris Hastings *performance artist*
Erem, Suzan *writer*
Link, Phoebe Forrest *secondary school educator, writer*
Lintner, Karen Louise *art educator*
MacBride, Elizabeth Cummings *editor, writer, media consultant*
McKeel, Lillian Phillips *retired education educator*
Phillips, Janet Colleen *retired educational association executive, editor*
Roy, Della Martin *materials science educator, researcher*

Steelton
Zimmerman, Connie Ann *public administrator*

Stroudsburg
Pope, Arlette Farrar *insurance company professional*
Wormack, Karen Elise *small business owner, poet*

Summerdale
Pickel, Diane Dunn *education educator*

Sunbury
Maue, Leta Jo *special education administrator*

Swarthmore
Baskin, Maureen Louise *special education educator*
Berger, Dianne Gwynne *family life educator, consultant*
Hungerford, Constance Cain *art educator*
Kaufman, Antoinette D. *business services company executive*
Keith, Jennie *anthropology educator and administrator, writer*
Marecek, Jeanne *psychologist, educator*
Morgan, Kathryn Lawson *retired historian, educator*
North, Helen Florence *classicist, educator*
Sawyers, Claire Elyce *arboretum administrator*
Valen, Nanine Elisabeth *psychotherapist, poet*

Titusville
Altomare, Erica Von Scheven *psychologist*
Campasino, Ellen Marie *elementary school educator*

Towanda
Rockefeller, Shirley E. *court clerk*

Trevose
Barbetta, Maria Ann *health information management consultant*
Quinn, Holli Jo Bardo *social worker, educator*

Unionville
Martin, Helen Elizabeth *educational consultant*

University Park
Askov, Eunice May *adult education educator*
Bazirjian, Rosann V. *dean, librarian*
Coupland, Jennifer Chang *finance educator*
Eaton, Nancy Ruth Linton *librarian, dean*
Fedoroff, Nina Vsevolod *research scientist, consultant, educator*
Fuhrman, Susan H *education educator*
Fullerton, Stephanie Malia *research scientist*
Garrison, Barbara Jane *chemistry educator*
Grosholz, Emily Rolfe *philosophy educator, poet*
Guthrie, Helen A. *nutrition educator, registered dietitian*
Halsey, Martha Taliaferro *Spanish language educator*
Hamburger, Susan *librarian*
Holt, Frieda M. *nursing educator, former academic director*
Irwin, Mary Jane *engineering educator*
Kasdorf, Julia Mae *language educator, poet*
Kellerman, Lydia Suzanne (Sue) *librarian*
MacEwan, Bonnie *librarian*
Muhlert, Jan Keene *art museum director*
Newsome, Lee Ann *anthropologist, educator*
Ross, A. Catharine *biochemist, educator*
Shannon, Barbara *dean, nutrition educator*
Todd Copley, Judith A. *materials and metallurgical engineering educator*
Zabel, Diane Marion *school librarian*

Upper Black Eddy
McIntyre, Linnea Andren *landscaping company executive*

Upper Darby
Kahler, Nancy J. *music educator, director*
Toney, Angela M. *medical administrator and educator*

Upper Saint Clair
Anderson, Catherine M. *consulting company executive*
Dunkis, Patricia B. *school system administrator*
Smith, Gloria S. *local commissioner, educator*

Valley Forge
Harvey, Carole (Kate Harvey) *minister, church official*
Miller, Betty Brown *freelance writer*

Vandergrift
Stitt, Theresa Mary *special education educator*

Villanova
Alter, Maria Pospischil *language educator*
Beck, Christine Safford *photographer, publisher, volunteer*
Fitzpatrick, M. Louise *dean, nursing educator*
Gould, Lilian *writer*
Lesch, Ann Mosely *political scientist, educator*
McDiarmid, Lucy *English educator, author*
Olsen, Judith Johnson *reference librarian*
Sewell, Lisa *literature educator*
Vander Veer, Suzanne *aupair business executive*

Wallingford
Parker, Jennifer Ware *chemical engineer, researcher*
Purcell, Mary Hamilton *speech educator*

Warrendale
Gaetano, Joy M. *human resources executive*
Meury, Veronica Kmec *foundation administrator*
Snyder, Linda Ann *editor*

Warrington
Heckler, Maureen Kelly *nursing home administrator*

Washington
Gregg, Cynthia Louise *music educator*
Knight, Sherry Ann *art educator*

Washington Crossing
Knupp, Judi Bulkowski *nutritionist*
Roche, Gail Connor *editor*

Waverly
Quesada, Francine Barbara *social services administrator, therapist, educator*

Wayne
Burton, B.J. (Betty Jane) *playwright*
Rabii, Patricia Berg *church administrator*
Rolleri, Denise Marie *radiation therapist, business owner*
Rubley, Carole A. *state legislator*
Santo, Melissa Marie *chemist*
Thompson, Gloria Matthews *marketing and statistics educator*

Waynesburg
Maguire, Mildred May *chemistry educator, magnetic resonance researcher*

Wellsboro
Driskell, Lucile G. *artist*

West Chester
Abbott, Ann Augustine *social worker, educator*
Adler, Madeleine Wing *academic administrator*
Albert, Kristen Ann *music educator*
Beaumont, Mary *artist, art educator*
Bove, Patrice Magee *elementary school educator*
Cinelli, Bethann *school health educator*
Flood, Dorothy Garnett *neuroscientist*
Garrahan-Masters, Mary Patricia *retired social worker, writer*
Hanson, Diane Charske *management consultant*
Keiser, Mary Ann Myers *special education educator*
Knuth Fischer, Cynthia Strout *environmental consultant*
McCullough, Mary W. *social work educator, therapist*
Rizzo, Joyce A. *environmental services executive*
Silverthorne, Holly Appel *sculptor, educator*
Simons, Nancy *naturopathic physician, hypnotherapist*

West Conshohocken
Newman, Sandra Schultz *state supreme court justice*

West Grove
Allman, Margo Hutz *sculptor, painter*
Loveland, Christine Frances *psychologist*

West Lawn
Borelli, Cynthia Ann *vocal educator, chorus director*

West Middlesex
Hoffman, Ada Jean *music educator*

West Mifflin
Archey, Mary Frances Elaine (Onofaro) *academic administrator, educator*

West Point
Gehris, Tamar K. *biologist*

West Sunbury
Ferrere, Rita L. *band director, music educator*

Whitehall
Collina, Kathleen Alice *corrugated box company executive*
Tufton, Janie Lee (Jane Tufton) *dental hygienist, animal rights lobbyist, activist*

Wilkes Barre
Kaufer, Karen Evans *academic administrator*

Williamsport
Clarke, Louise Rigdon *gifted student program administrator, principal*
Parks, Michelle M. *academic administrator*
Rosebrough, Carol Belville *cable television company executive*

Willow Grove
Burtt, Anne Dampman *special education educator*

Winfield
Wert, Barbara J. Yingling *special education consultant*

Wyalusing
Goodman, Carol Hockenbury *retired elementary school educator, consultant*

Wyncote
Boyer, Sister Mary Veronica *nun, art educator*
Schaffner, Roberta Irene *retired medical, surgical nurse*
Weiss, Mili Dunn *artist, educator*

Wynnewood
Frankl, Razelle *management educator*
Koprowska, Irena *cytopathologist, cancer researcher*
Lodish, Susan Fischer *theater director*
Meyers, Mary Ann *foundation administrator, writer, consultant*

Wyomissing
Williams-Wennell, Kathi *human resources specialist*

Yardley
Huret, Marilynn Joyce *editor*
Newsom, Carolyn Cardall *management consultant*
Soultoukis, Donna Zoccola *library director*

York
Ardison, Linda G. *author, writing educator*
Jackson, Renée Bernadette *English language educator*
Livingston, Pamela A. *corporate image and marketing management consultant*
Lloyd, June Burk *librarian, archivist*
Snyder, Jan Louise *administrative aide*
Wright, Tiffany Erin *secondary school educator*

Youngsville
Montgomery, Christina Lynn *music educator*
Pearson, Denise Anne *music educator*
Scheid, Cynthia Loiuse *music educator*

Youngwood
Duvall, Hollie Jean *music educator*

RHODE ISLAND

Adamsville
Cumming, Patricia A. *writer*
Quick, Joan B. *state legislator*

Block Island
Connolly, Violette M. *small business owner*

Bristol
Grota, Barbara Lynn *academic administrator, educator*
Parella, Mary A. *state legislator*

Central Falls
Bolandrina, Grethel Ramos *nurse*

Charlestown
Walsh, Donna M. *state legislator*

Chepachet
Jubinska, Patricia Ann *ballet instructor, choreographer, artist, anthropologist, archaeologist*

Cranston
Ferguson, Christine C. *lawyer, state agency administrator*
Goldberg, Barbara M. *consultant*
Hetherington, Nancy *state legislator*
Lanzi, Beatrice A. *state legislator*
Moffitt, Kathleen *marketing professional, writer, educator*

East Providence
Freda, Lisa M. *psychologist*
Furtado-Lavoie, Julia *management consultant, accountant*

Greenville
Hopkins, Catherine Lee *music educator*

Jamestown
Logan, Nancy Allen *library media specialist*
Worden, Katharine Cole *sculptor*

Johnston
Thomas, Carol Lee *massage therapist*

Kingston
Caldwell, Naomi Rachel *library and information scientist, educator*
Gilton, Donna Louise *library and information scientist, educator*
Hufnagel, Linda Ann *biology educator, researcher*
Markin, Karen Mary *research scientist, journalist*
Newman, Barbara Miller *psychologist, educator*
Smith, Sareba G. *special education educator*

Lincoln
Marsden, Herci Ivana *classical ballet artistic director*

Middletown
Ottaviano, Doris Baginski *librarian*
Reed, Julia Constance *financial services executive*

Newport
Brown, Jane G. *sports association executive*
Coxe, Trudy *museum administrator, former state official*
Higgins, Harriet Pratt *investment advisor*
Liotus, Sandra Mary *lighting designer, small business owner, consultant*
Ramey, Linda Dee *literature educator, poet*
Scoll, Eulalie Elizabeth *writer, researcher*
Tinney, Harle Hope Hanson *museum administrator, owner*

North Kingstown
Benson, Melvoid J. *state legislator*
Kilguss, Elsie Schaich *artist, gallery owner*

North Providence
Bain, Marissa *social worker*
Maciel, Patricia Ann *development professional*

Pawtucket
Boghossian, Joan Thompson *artist*
Ferland, Darlene Frances *management consultant*
Lepore, Lisa *principal*
Orson, Barbara Tuschner *actress*

Portsmouth
Byassee, Margaret Foley *art educator, poet, vocalist*

Providence
Ackerman, Felicia *philosophy educator, writer*
Ajello, Edith H. *state legislator*
Anderson, Mabel M. *state legislator*
Biron, Christine Anne *medical science educator, researcher*
Blasing, Mutlu Konuk *English language educator*
Blumstein, Sheila Ellen *former academic administrator, linguistics educator*
Bogan, Mary Flair *stockbroker*
Bright, Deborah *artist, educator*
Brisson, Harriet Eldredge *art educator*
Callahan, Christine H. *state legislator*
Cambio, Bambilyn Breece *state legislator*
Coderre, Elaine Ann *state representative*
Coffman, Teresa Susan *music educator*
Cox, Dawn Everlina *paralegal*
Farmer, Susan Lawson *broadcasting executive, former secretary of state*
Farrell, Margaret Dawson *lawyer*
Gallo, Hanna M. *state legislator*
Gerbi, Susan Alexandra *biology educator*
Gibbs, June Nesbitt *state legislator*
Goldberg, Maureen McKenna *state supreme court justice*
Goldscheider, Frances K. *sociologist, educator*
Goodwin, Maryellen *state legislator*
Graziano, Catherine Elizabeth *state legislator, retired nursing educator*
Green, Angel Yvonne *literature educator*
Harleman, Ann *English language educator, writer*
Harman, Carole Moses *retired art educator, artist*
Harwood, Patricia L. *judge*
Hay, Susan Stahr Heller *museum curator*
Hedlund, Ellen Louise *state agency administrator, educator*
Henseler, Suzanne Marie *state legislator, social studies educator, majority whip*
Howes, Lorraine de Wet *fashion designer, educator*
Iannitelli, Susan B. *state legislator*
Jenness, Rebecca Estella *artist, educator*
Johnson, Melody *school system administrator*
Kacir, Barbara Brattin *lawyer*
Kagan, Marilyn D. *retired architect*
Kane, Agnes Brezak *pathologist, educator*
Killeen, Johanne *small business owner*
Leviten, Riva Shamray *artist*
Lima, Charlene *state legislator*
Lisi, Mary M. *federal judge*
Long, Beverly Glenn *retired lawyer*
Lopes, Maria J. *state legislator*
Lopez-Morillas, Frances M. *translator*
Marek, Kiersten L. *social worker*
McCann, Gail Elizabeth *lawyer*
Monteiro, Lois Ann *medical science educator*
Murphy, Christine *medical facility administrator*
Nolan, Patricia Ann *public health officer*
O'Keefe, Beverly Disbrow *state official, federal official*
Olmsted, Audrey June *communications educator, department chairman*
Paiva-Weed, M. Teresa *state legislator*
Pivin, Jeanette Eva *psychotherapist*
Price, Alicia Hemmalin *psychotherapist, researcher*
Reed, Cynthia S. *manufacturing executive*
Richards, Priscilla Ann *medical/surgical nurse*
Richardson, Julie G. *investment company executive*
Roberts, Elizabeth H. *state legislator*
Sasso, Eleanor Catherine *state senator*
Schmitt, Johanna Marie *plant population biologist, educator*
Simmons, Ruth J. *academic administrator*
Sosnowski, V. Susan *state legislator*
Triedman, Karen *design educator, consultant*
Vogel, Paula Anne *playwright*
Waite-Franzen, Ellen Jane *academic administrator*
Waldrop, Rosmarie *writer*
Widgoff, Mildred *physicist, researcher*
Williams, Anastasia P. *state legislator*
Young, Carol J. *editor*

Riverside
Lekas, Mary Despina *retired otolaryngologist*
Schwegler, Nancy Ann *librarian, writer*

Rumford
Nichols, Alice Marshall *manufacturing executive*

Saunderstown
Tener, Lisa C. *writer*

Slatersville
Pannullo, Deborah Paolino *lawyer, training and consulting company executive*

Smithfield
Kosowski, Mary *artist, educator*
Morahan-Martin, Janet May *psychologist, educator*
Weiss, Susan F. *accountant*

Wakefield
Doody, Agnes G. *communications educator, management and communication consultant*

Warwick
Charette, Sharon Juliette *library administrator*
Jennings, Julianne *cultural organization administrator*
Markward, Cheri D. *music educator*

Westerly
Hindle, Marguerita Cecelia *textile chemist, consultant*
Lin, Foong-Yi *physician*

Woonsocket
Morris, Mary Elizabeth *pastor*

SOUTH CAROLINA

Aiken
Cope, Esther Owens *genealogical researcher*
Hickey, Delina Rose *retired education educator*
Johnston, Carolyn Judith *construction engineer*
Rudnick, Irene Krugman *lawyer, former state legislator, educator*
Santos, Karey Michale *elementary school educator*
Wood, Susan *applied technology center executive*

Anderson
Beattie, Stephanie Shannon *social worker*
Jarrett, Jinger Elaine *freelance/self-employed writer*
Mandrell, Marion D. *psychology educator*
Rhoe, Wilhelmina Robinson *retired science educator*

Batesburg
Long, Drucilla *special education educator*
Moon, Linda Walker *music educator*

Beaufort
Eggen, Belinda Lay *education educator*
Moussatos, Martha Ann Tyree *librarian*
Raines, Karen Cornell *secondary school educator*
Tombe, Sheila Joan *language educator, editor*

Beech Island
Bartley, Jacqueline Prior *public relations executive, journalist*

Bishopville
Roycroft, Cheryl *secondary school educator*

Bluffton
Cann, Sharon Lee *retired health science librarian*
Cork, Holly A. *former state legislator*
Hawn, Judith Rady *medical/surgical nurse*
Scovel, Mary Alice *retired music therapy educator*
Windham, Melba B. *real estate broker*

Camden
Blackwell, Dorothy Patton *artist*
Craig, Joanna Burbank *historic site director*
Koestner, Carol Ann *information technology manager, consultant*

Cayce
Cox, Donna (Bozard) *music educator*

Central
Bell, Gloria Jean *academic administrator, literature educator, dean*

Chapin
Bowers, Linda *educational administrator*
Freitag, Carol Wilma *state official, political scientist*

Charleston
Adelson, Gloria Ann *financial executive*
Ballard, Mary Melinda *financial communications and marketing/advertising executive, consumer advocate*
Bradham, Tamala Selke *audiologist*
Brown, Ann Catherine *investment company executive*
Buvinger, Jan *library director*
Cordova, Maria Asuncion *dentist*
Ferguson, Esther B. *philanthropist*
Fraser, Mary Edna *artist, educator*
Grauer, Sandra Lee *environmentalist, educator*
Hoffman, Brenda Joyce *gastroenterology educator*
Huang, Peng *statistician*
Karesh, Janice Lehrer *special education consultant*
Key, Janice Dixon *physician, medical educator*
Langley, Lynne Spencer *newspaper editor, columnist*
Lovinger, Sophie Lehner *child psychologist*
Luton, Mary Katherine *language educator*
Mikell, Nancy Theresa *pharmacist*
Nations, Janice McKinney *music educator*
Nordquist, Sonya Lynn *information technology executive*
Perry, Evelyn Reis *communications company executive*
Powell, Marilyn Lindeberg *minister*
Pridgen, Heather Dawn *financial analyst*
Rhea, Marcia Chandler *accountant*
Sharpe, Kathryn Moye *psychologist*
Siddons, Anne Rivers (Sybil Anne Rivers Siddons) *writer*
Simms, Lois Averetta *retired secondary school educator*
Williams, Barbara Stambaugh *editor*

Clemson
Hare, Eleanor O'Meara *computer science educator*
Krause, Lois Ruth Breur *chemistry educator*
Nielsen, Barbara Stock *state educational administrator*
Petzel, Florence Eloise *textiles educator*
Wilson, Paulette Adassa *language educator, writer*

Columbia
Aelion, C. Marjorie *adult education educator*
Allison, Merita Ann *state legislator*
Arias-Haskins, Gloria *state representative*
Badders, Rebecca Susanne *military officer, educator, writer*
Barnum, Mary Ann Mook *information management manager*
Black, Rita Dutton *media specialist*
Boyce, Corrie Mosby *music educator*
[illegible] *administrator*
Ceips, Catherine C. *state representative*
Chappell, Barbara Kelly *child welfare consultant*
Clyburn, Mignon L. *commissioner*
Cobb-Hunter, Gilda *state representative, social worker*
Currie, Cameron McGowan *federal judge*
Currin, Lynne Irene *art educator*
Duggan, Carol Cook *research director*
Dunnam, Marie McClure *social worker*
Ettel, Zita Moak *nursing administrator, food services executive*
Fields, Harriet Gardin *counselor, educator, consultant*
Fowler, Linda McKeever *health facility administrator, educator*
Freeman, Mary Beth *state representative*
Fry, Catherine Howard *publishing executive*
Gasque, Diane Phillips *mortgage manager*
Gilham, JoAnne *state representative*
Glover, Maggie Wallace *state legislator*
Gray, Elizabeth Van Doren *lawyer*
Greene, Claudia *education associate*
Griffin, Mary Frances *retired library media consultant*
Grimball, Caroline Gordon *retail sales professional*
Herrin, Loretta Rasberry *physical education educator*
Hinson, Shirley Rogers *state representative*
Hoffman, Mary Ann Hartman *principal*
Holmes, Cecile Searson *religion editor*
James, Nancy Ellen *art educator*
Kay, Carol McGinnis *literature educator*
Lee, Brenda *state representative*
Martin, Becky Rogers *state representative, realtor*
McCulloch, Anne Merline Jacobs *college dean*
McGill, Jennifer Houser *non-profit association administrator*
McNeely, Patricia Gantt *journalism educator*
Miller, Vida O. *state representative, art gallery owner*
Moody-Lawrence, Bessie *state representative, education educator*
Newton, Rhonwen Leonard *writer, microcomputer consultant, data processing executive, consultant*
Parks, J. Anne *state representative, funeral director*
Paschal, Rhoda Jones *voice educator*
Paulson-Crawford, Carol *conservator, educator*
Phillips, Vicky Lynn *elementary school educator*
Rabb, Gael Caution *mental health consultant*
Rawlinson, Helen Ann *librarian*
Richardson, Becky D. *state representative*
Roberts, Pamela J. *lawyer*
Ruff, Cheryl Anderson *health facility administrator*
Scott, Bernice G. *county official*
Seigler, Ruth Queen *college nursing administrator, educator, consultant, nurse*
Shifflett, Audrey Horton *academic administrator, researcher*
Short, Linda Huffstetler *state legislator*
Sinclair, Linda Drumwright *educational consultant*
Stamps, Laura Anne *writer, poet*
Sutherland-Abel, Anne Elizabeth *pediatrician*
Synnott, Marcia Graham *history educator*
Tenenbaum, Inez Moore *superintendent of education*
Toal, Jean Hoefer *state supreme court chief justice*
Tunstall, Dorothy Fiebrich *early childhood educator*
Waites, Candy Yaghjian *former state official*
Walters, Rebecca Russell Yarborough *medical technologist*
Washington, Nancy Jane Hayes *librarian*
Weber, Lynn *sociology educator*
Young, Annette D. *state representative*
Zimmerman, Nancy Picciano *library science educator*

Conway
Johnson-Leeson, Charleen Ann *former elementary school educator, insurance agent, insurance consultant, regional executive assistant*
Palm, Linda J. *psychology educator*

Denmark
Boyd-Scotland, Joann *college president*

Dillon
Chandler, Marcia Shaw Barnard *farmer*

Duncan
Clarke, Jean Alderman *orchestra director*
Rollins, Wendy Milwood *media specialist*

Easley
Densmore, Jacqueline Jean *financial accountant*
Snider, Patricia Stapleton *assistant principal*
Stone, Lisa Murphy *elementary school educator, music educator*

Edisto Island
Van Metre, Margaret Cheryl *artistic director, dance educator*

Effingham
Taylor, Sherry Michelle Mills *elementary school educator*

Florence
Rutherford, Vicky Lynn *special education educator*
Sease, Susan G. *social worker*

Fort Mill
Bowles, Crandall Close *textiles executive*

Fountain Inn
Mozoski, Diane Marie *information technology executive*

Gaffney
Griffin, Penni Oncken *dean, social worker*
Suttle, Helen Jayson *retired education educator*

Galivants Ferry
Christy, Connie Annette *music educator, webmaster*

Georgetown
Ragland, Mary Ruth *music educator*
Williams, Rynn Mobley *community health nurse*

Goose Creek
Todoro, Mary Elizabeth *process engineer*
Vogt, Kathleen Cunningham *musician, music educator*

Greenville
Campbell, Heidi Denice *communications educator*
Cureton, Claudette Hazel Chapman *biology educator*
Davis, Joan Carroll *retired museum director*
Earle, Patricia Nelson *artist*
Glenn, Idella Goodson *director*
Hancock, Donna *secondary school educator*
Hendrix, Susan Clelia Derrick *civic worker*
Hill, Grace Lucile Garrison *education educator, consultant*
Hogg, Judith E. *neurologist, educator*
Jordan, Katie L. *minister*
Lloyd, Wanda Smalls *newspaper editor*
Manly, Sarah Letitia *retired state legislator, ophthalmic photographer, angiographer*
McCune, Linda Williams *artist, educator*
Seibert, Lesa Marie *university educator*
Steed, Connie Mantle *nurse*
Stoller, Patricia Sypher *structural engineer, engineering executive*
Wang, Ming De *engineer*
Westrope, Martha Randolph *psychologist, consultant*
Williams, Martha Garrison *lawyer*

Greenwood
Cushing, Sara Elizabeth *English language educator, writer*
Marino, Sheila Burris *education educator*

Greer
Cooper, Rose Marie *composer*

Hardeeville
Kadar, Karin Patricia *librarian*

Hartsville
Grove, Pecolia J. *social worker*

Hilton Head Island
Brock, Karena Diane *dancer, educator*
Kearney-Nunnery, Rose *nursing administrator, educator, consultant*
Reed, Frances Boogher *writer, actress*

Hopkins
Garrett, Robin Scott *public information officer*

Inman
Eleazer, Nila Kay Lankford *speech pathology/audiology services professional*

Isle Of Palms
McKinley, Debra Lynn McKinley *small business owner, dog show judge, real estate agent*
Wohltmann, Hulda Justine *pediatric endocrinologist, diabetologist*

Iva
Gentry, Margaret Burton *retired elementary school teacher*
Standridge, Diane H. *secondary school educator*

Johns Island
Carter, Mary Andrews *paralegal*

Kershaw
Wall, Kathy Elliott *secondary school educator*

Kingstree
Burgess, Pamela Shawnta *music educator, director*
Fulton, Addie Ruth *minister, social worker*
Holliday, Jennifer Nexsen *elementary school educator, music educator*

Ladys Island
Yates, Linda Snow *financial services marketing executive, real estate*

Lake City
Hawkins, Linda Parrott *school system administrator*
Stone, Betty Frances *music educator*

Lancaster
Garris, Annette D. Faile *medical, surgical, and rehabilitation nurse*

Laurens
Henderson, Rita Beatrice *county official*

Lexington
Floyd, Ann R. *elementary school educator*
Holland, Gene Grigsby (Scottie Holland) *artist*

Manning
Samuels, Yvonne James *retired special education educator*

Mauldin
Norris, Joan Clafette Hagood *retired assistant principal*
Wood, Myra Linden Frank *consultant*

Mc Cormick
Clayton, Verna Lewis *retired state legislator*

Moncks Corner
Collins, Jenny Lynn *music educator*

Moore
King, Tamara Powers *music educator, musician*

Mount Pleasant
Falkowski, Brenda Lisle *business executive, consultant*
Gregory, Yvonne E. *interior designer*
Hill, Larkin Payne *real estate company operations administrator*
Winter-Switz, Cheryl Donna *travel company executive*

Murrells Inlet
Howard, Joan Alice *artist*

Myrtle Beach
Marsh, Carol K. *adult community administrator*
Todd, Cheryl *art educator*

Newberry
Johnson, Melissa Carol *poet, educator*
Pollard, Wendy Higgins *counselor*

Orangeburg
Gamble, Jacquelyn Valdena *secondary school educator*
Hare, Ester Rose *physician*
Nwafor, Bernadette Ego *educational psychologist, educator*
Quick, Julia May *music educator, musician*
Ramsey, Kim N. *information technology manager*
Robinson, Ruth Hubbard *retired elementary school educator*
Sibley, Rebecca Leigh Cardwell *dietician*
Thompson, Marguerite Myrtle Graming (Mrs. Ralph B. Thompson) *librarian*

Pawleys Island
Cromley, Jane Meadors *music educator*
Ford, Anna Maria *language educator*

Pickens
Hicks, Virginia Buchholz *secondary school educator*

Piedmont
Blume, Deborah Davenport *music educator*
Winter-Neighbors, Gwen Carole *special education educator, art educator, consultant*

Prosperity
Hause, Edith Collins *college administrator*

Ridgeville
Hill, Jacquelyn Louise Harrison *secondary school educator*

Rock Hill
Barbaree, Dorothy A. *secondary school educator, antique dealer*
Russell, Cynthia M. *college president*
Wishert, Jo Ann Chappell *music educator, elementary and secondary education educator*

Yeager, Bernice Whittaker *elementary and secondary school educator*

Roebuck
Baier, Susan Lovejoy *music educator*

Seneca
Byars, Betsy (Cromer) *writer*

Simpsonville
Hill, Holly Traynham *choral director, music minister*
Selvy, Barbara *dance instructor*
Somervill, Barbara Ann *small business owner, writer*
Stevenson, Susan Marie *music educator*

Spartanburg
Agnew, Janet Burnett *secondary school educator*
Barrick, Donna Matz *music educator*
Foy, Patricia Solesbee *music educator*
Gray, Gwen Cash *real estate broker*
Gray, Nancy Ann Oliver *college administrator*
Kuhn, Hans Heinrich *retired chemist*
Kuntz, Janet Ruth *musician, music educator*
Lucktenberg, Jerrie Cadek *music educator*
McCraw, Kathy *elementary school educator, special education educator*
Sellars, Christi von Lehe *music educator*
Walker, Melissa A. *historian, educator*

Sullivans Island
Norton, Fran *parks and recreation director*

Summerville
Reisman, Rosemary Moody Canfield *writer, humanities educator*
Sepulveda, Sonja Marian Atkinson *choral director, accompanist*

Sumter
Blassengale, Michelle Yvette *music educator*
Moore, Verna *county official*
Rogers, Penny M. *music educator*
van Bulck, Margaret West *accountant, financial planner, educator*

Surfside Beach
Calo, Tina Carol *school counselor*
Favaro, Mary Kaye Asperheim *pediatrician, writer*

Waterloo
Grigsby, Amanda Moore *special education educator*

West Columbia
Byars, Merlene Hutto *accountant, visual artist, writer*
Byrne, Eleanor *artist*
Carter, Saralee Lessman *immunologist, microbiologist*
Moore, Shirley Throckmorton (Mrs. Elmer Lee Moore) *accountant*
Perkins, Esther Tye *pastor*
Walter, Jolene Kendra *music educator*

Williamston
Hawkins-Sneed, Janet Lynn *school psychologist, human resources administrator, small business owner*
Parrish, Cathy Waldron *elementary school educator*

SOUTH DAKOTA

Aberdeen
Fouberg, Glenna M. *career planning administrator*
Omland, Jacqueline Leigh-Knute *secondary school educator, small business owner*
Pesicka, Harlene Neave *mental health services professional*
Zephier, Carol Ann *piano educator, retired organist*

Black Hawk
Maicki, G. Carol *former state senator, consultant*

Brookings
Hall, Teresa Joanne Keys *manufacturing engineer, educator*
McClure-Bibby, Mary Anne *former state legislator*
Miller, Peggy Gordon Elliott *university president*
Torson, Dianna May *small business owner*
Williams, Elizabeth Evenson *writer*

Canton
Forelle, Helen (Grace Janet Leih) *publishing executive, writer, poet*

Dakota Dunes
Hagan, Sheila B. *corporate lawyer*

Freeman
Graber, Muriel *music educator, lay worker*
Koller, Berneda Joleen *library administrator*

Gettysburg
Schreiber, Lola F. *former state legislator*

Hot Springs
Collins, Mary Alise *music educator, non-commissioned officer*

Humboldt
Johnson, June Marilyn *music educator*

Huron
Clatworthy, Catherine Lynn *educational trainer, graphics designer*

Keystone
Wagner, Mary Kathryn *sociology educator, former state legislator*

Miller
Morford, JoAnn (JoAnn Morford-Burg) *state senator, investment company executive*

Mitchell
Clemens, Deb Fischer *state legislator, nursing administrator*
Russell, Annika Renee *secondary school educator, financial consultant*

Mobridge
Hall, Jo(sephine) Marian *editor*

Mud Butte
Ingalls, Marie Cecelie *former state legislator, retail executive*

Pierre
Adam, Patricia Ann *legislative aide*
Everist, Barbara *state legislator*
Fiegen, Kristie K. *state legislator*
Hackenjos-Butler, Genie Marie *minister*
Ham, Arlene H. *state legislator*
Johnson, Julie Marie *lawyer, lobbyist, judge*
Olson, Judith Mary Reedy *retired public information officer, former state senator*
Schoenfelder, Laska *commissioner, farmer*
Weyer, Dianne Sue *health facility administrator*

Platte
Pennington, Beverly Melcher *financial services company executive*

Rapid City
Callahan, Susan Jane Whitney *accountant*
Chamberlain Hayman, Susan Denise *psychotherapist, pain management therapist*
Lee, Jamie Lee *video specialist*
Moore, Mary Kathryn *psychologist*
Rogers, Deborah S. *human biology educator, writer*
Schreier, Karen Elizabeth *judge*
Tesch, Marie Louise *music educator, artist*
Zhang, Nian *research scientist, educator*

Redfield
Schoen, Jill F. *psychologist, educator*

Saint Lawrence
Lockner, Vera Joanne *farmer, rancher, legislator*

Sioux Falls
Ashworth, Julie *elementary school educator*
Callison, JoJean Faye *educational association administrator*
Carlson Aronson, Marilyn A. *English language and education educator*
Dunn, Rebecca Jo *state legislator*
Eckhoff, Kristine Kay *mental health therapist*
Egan, Lora Rae *music educator*
Haig, Susan *conductor*
Kuntz, Carol B. *psychologist, educator*
Meierhenry, Judith Knittel *judge, lawyer*
Niemann, Patricia *nurse*
Richards, LaClaire Lissetta Jones (Mrs. George A. Richards) *social worker*
Thompson, Ronelle Kay Hildebrandt *library director*
Trujillo, Angelina *endocrinologist*
VanDemark, Michelle Volin *critical care, neuroscience nurse*
Volin, Suzanne *former laboratory administrator*

Spearfish
Hubbard, Constance E. *language educator, piano teacher*
Wishard, Della Mae *former newspaper editor*

Viborg
Ehrke, Mindy Jo *minister*

Watertown
Natale, Fernanda Maria Maddalena *conservator, artist*
Welch, Sharon I. *customer service representative, artist*

Wessington Springs
Christopherson, Karen Marie *education educator*

Winner
Maule, Theresa Moore *lawyer*

Yankton
Piper, Kathleen *former political organization administrator*

TENNESSEE

Alamo
Finch, Evelyn Vorise *financial planner*

Antioch
Bluing-Osborne, Karen Louise *executive assistant*
Sandlin, Debbie Crowe *critical care nurse*

Arlington
Lake, Martha M. *engineer*

Athens
Brown, Sandra Lee *arts management consultant, watercolorist*
Fisher, Nancy M. *educator, poet*
Higdon, Linda Hampton *congressional staff*

Bartlett
Crudup, Pamela Tracy Parham *science educator, writer*

Big Sandy
Hancock, Sandra Olivia *secondary school educator, elementary school educator*

Brentwood
Berry, Kathryn-Grace *geriatrics nurse*
Bolton, Martha O. *writer*
Gotterer, Shelley McCullough *elementary school educator*
Tucker, Tanya Denise *singer*

Bristol
Holler, Ann K. *music educator*

Brownsville
Scott-Wilson, Susan Rice *vice principal*

Charlotte
Frazier, Linda Joyce *county official*

Chattanooga
Altekruse, Joan Morrissey *retired preventive medicine educator*
Bechtel, Sherrell Jean *psychotherapist*
Fouquet, Anne (Judy Fuqua) *musician, music educator*
Gould, Mary Christa *small business owner*
McFarland, Jane Elizabeth *librarian*
McNeill-Murray, Joan Reagin *volunteer consultant*
Rath, Linda Joann *professional organization executive*
Riggs, Claudesta Lavern *professional storyteller*
Steele, Shirley Sue *retired special resource educator*
Turner, Brenda Kaye *state legislator*
Vital, Patricia Best *lawyer*
Washburn, Sandra Paynter *art educator*
Young, Sonia Winer *public relations executive, educator*

Clarksville
Johnson, Barbara Ella Jackson *city official*
Myers, Linda Shafer *secondary educator*
Riggins, Carolyn Frances *music educator*
Sharpe, Patricia La Vonne *artist*
Wilson, Deborah Lynn *secondary school educator, music educator*
Wilson, Patti L. *psychologist, educator*

Cleveland
Garrett, Susan *music educator*
Hamid, Suzanne L *academic administrator*
Lockhart, Madge Clements *educational organization executive*
Posner, Linda Irene *retired government official, marketing consultant*

Clinton
Hutchens, Gail R. *chemist*

Collegedale
Bennett, Peggy Elizabeth *librarian, library director, educator*

Collierville
Hays, Louise Stovall *retail fashion executive*

Columbia
Cantrell, Sharron Caulk *principal*

Cookeville
Asanbe, Comfort Bola *psychologist, educator*
Musacchio, Marilyn Jean *nurse midwife, educator*
Pierce, Sarah Faith *counseling administrator, secondary school educator, elementary school educator*
Underwood, Lucinda Jean *poet, playwright, small business owner, researcher*

Cordova
Cheatham, Wanda M. *music educator*
Diggs, Beatrice M. *research assistant*
Kalbach, Audrey A. *family practice nurse practitioner, psychiatric nurse practitioner*
Pugh, Dorothy Gunther *artistic director*

Crossville
Kinslow, Norma Jean *musician, educator*
Ralstin, Betty Lou *religious organization administrator*
Spivey, (Dolores) Joanne *retired music educator*

Dandridge
Weatherly-McWaters, Barbara Cannon *artist*

Dickson
Thomas, Janey Sue *elementary school principal*
Tucker, Julie Robyn *illustrator, art educator*

Dover
Page, Patricia (Patty) Newton *real estate broker, real estate company executive*

Dunlap
Carr, Marsha Hamblen *elementary school principal*

Enville
Campbell, Nell *mayor*

Fairview
Hutchison, Barbara Bailey *singer, songwriter*

Franklin
Cliff, Karissa *consumer researcher, recruiter*
Daniel, Cathy Brooks *tutor, educational consultant*
Douglass, Dorris Callicott *librarian, historian, genealogist*
Hughey, Brenda Joyce *supervisor*
McClellan, Dixie *secondary school educator*
Smolenski, Lisabeth Ann *family practice physician*

Gatlinburg
Flanagan, Judy *special events professional, entertainment and marketing specialist, professional public speaker*

GEOGRAPHICAL INDEX 1617 TENNESSEE

Germantown
Bensman, Harriet Landsman *speech pathology/audiology services professional*

Goodlettsville
DePriest, Tiffany Boals *music educator, music director*

Greeneville
Breckenridge, Judith Watts *writer, educator*
Dannecker, Tanja Michaela *electrical engineer*
Ford, Sally J. *physical education educator*
Justice, Sarah C. *social worker, volunteer*
Parsons, Marcia Phillips *judge*

Harriman
Hoppe, Sherry Lee *academic administrator*
Laxton, Patricia M. *technologist*

Henderson
Cypress, Karen Lenett *special education educator*

Hendersonville
Towe, Linda Miller *music educator*

Hermitage
Castner, Catherine S. *information technology administrator*
Jared, Margaret Ellen *music educator*
Reid, Donna Joyce *small business owner*
White, Mary Beth *guidance counselor, adult education educator*

Hickory Valley
Weaver, Peggy (Marguerite McKinnie Weaver) *plantation owner*

Hilham
Ashburn, Sue Lawson Fisher *geriatrics nurse*

Hixson
Prichard, Lona Ann *retired elementary education educator*

Huntsville
Lewallen Reynolds, Cynthia Maire *city administrator, small business owner*

Jackson
Agee, Nelle Hulme *retired art history educator*
Dennison, Norma Mae *art educator*
Eddleman, Dian P. *music educator*
Hearn, Beverly Jean *secondary education educator, librarian*

Jefferson City
Hodges, Mary Bozeman *literature educator*

Johnson City
Drinkard-Hawkshawe, Dorothy Lee *historian, educator, writer*
Edwards, Joellen Beckett *dean, community health nurse educator*
Fredericks, Dolores Elizabeth *music educator*
McIntosh, Cecilia Ann *biochemist, educator*
Pumariega, JoAnne Buttacavoli *mathematics educator*
Rasch, Ellen Myrberg *cell biology educator*
Schneider, Valerie Lois *speech educator*

Jonesborough
Rose, Anita *journalist, minister*

Kenton
Jenkins-Brady, Terri Lynn *publishing executive, journalist*

Kingsport
Abbott, Verna Ruth *social studies educator*
Eason, Eleanor Wilson *realtor*
Egan, Martha Avaleen *history educator, archivist, consultant*
Runyan, Carol Reid *audiologist*
Sass, Candace Elaine *research associate*
Wilhoit, Trisha C. *elementary school educator*
Wolfe, Margaret Ripley *historian, educator, consultant*
Woods, Bernice Irene *graphics specialist, small business owner*

Knoxville
Aguilar, Julia Shell *publishing executive*
Anderson, Ilse Janell *clinical geneticist*
Andrews, Rosalind *probation officer*
Blanton, Priscilla White *social sciences educator, psychologist, researcher*
Cottrell, Jeannette Elizabeth *retired librarian*
Creasia, Joan Catherine *dean, nursing educator*
Dinkins, M. Jean *goverment official*
Drennen, Jean Cobble *retired public relations executive, linguist*
Drinnon, Janis Bolton *artist, poet, volunteer*
Drumheller, Janet Louise *librarian*
Earl, Martha Frances *librarian, researcher*
Eaves, Dorothy Ann Greene *music educator*
Edge, Lara *editor*
Felder-Hoehne, Felicia Harris *librarian*
Garrison, Arlene Allen *engineering executive, engineering educator*
Griffin, Mary Jane Ragsdale *educational consultant, writer, small business owner*
Harris, Diana Koffman *sociologist, educator*
Harris, Skila *government agency administrator*
Hatton, Barbara R. *academic administrator*
Holman, Rosalind Denise *music educator*
Krauter, Lana Cain *retail executive*
Lobins, Christine Marie *accounts sales administrator*
Maginnis, Sherry Ann *musician, educator, composer*
Marshall-Hardin, Floy Jeanne *art school educator*
Matteson, Karla J. *health science association administrator*
McGuire, Sandra Lynn *nursing educator*
Moore, Louise Hill *surgical technologist*
Penn, Dawn Tamara *entrepreneur*
Pirkle, Mãnya Higdon *artist, craftsman*
Reeves, Pamela *lawyer*
Rice, Charlene Russell *human resources professional, consultant*
Roberts, Esther Lois *patent attorney, piano educator, composer, writer*
Siler, Susan Reeder *communications educator*
Smith, Vicky Lynn *geriatrics nurse*
Tenopir, Carol *information science educator*
Walsh, Joanne Elizabeth *retired elementary school educator, librarian*
Watson, Patricia L. *library director*
Wilhite, Nancy Jane *evangelist*
Worthington, Carole Yard Lynch *lawyer*

La Follette
Williams, Jane Crouch *mental health counselor, social worker*

Lafayette
Carter, Anna Dean *volunteer*
Crowder, Bonnie Walton *small business owner, composer*
Oliver, Barbara Ann *retired apparel executive*

Lexington
Swatzell, Marilyn Louise *nurse*

Loudon
Brakebill, Elizabeth M. *music educator*
Hallstrand, Sarah Laymon *denomination executive*
Hicks, Betty Harris *real estate agent, real estate company executive*

Madison
Cage, Allie M. *communications executive*
Haber, Melissa Ann *psychologist*

Martin
Wade, Reba *music teacher, pianist*
Welden, Alicia Galaz-Vivar *foreign language educator*

Maryville
Ratledge, Elizabeth Ann Gentry *social worker*

Mc Minnville
Brock, Angela Eulene Douglass *education educator*

Memphis
Anthony, Nakia Lacquers *healthcare educator*
Bargagliotti, Lillian Antoinette *nursing dean*
Brooks, Kathleen *journalist*
Caffrey, Margaret Mary *humanities educator, researcher*
Coleman, Veronica Freeman *prosecutor*
Cook, Mary Phelps *chemistry educator*
Crane, Laura Jane *research chemist*
Crawford, Sheila Jane *elementary education librarian, reading consultant*
De Mere-Dwyer, Leona *medical illustrator*
Demir, Semahat Siddika *engineering educator*
Donahue, Joan Elizabeth *elementary school educator*
Donald, Bernice B. *judge*
Drescher, Judith Altman *library director*
Edwards, Doris Porter *computer specialist*
Elfervig, Lucie Theresa Savoie *ophthalmic consultant*
Geter, Jennifer L. *psychologist*
Getske, Kathrine *psychiatric social worker*
Gibbons, Julia Smith *federal judge*
Harris, Cora Lee *science educator, small business owner*
Hirsch, Callie Clark *instructional facilitator*
Hofmann, Polly A. *physiologist, science educator*
Holder, Janice Marie *state supreme court justice*
Hord, Pauline Jones *primary school educator, educator*
Howe, Martha Morgan *microbiologist, educator*
Indingaro, Margaret Ann *supervisor*
Jalenak, Peggy Eichenbaum *volunteer*
Jallepalli, Raji *food service executive*
Jordan, Cynthia *counselor, educator*
Joyner, Marguerite Austin *secondary school educator*
Kaplan, Claudette S. (Claudia Kaplan) *volunteer*
Karp, Harvey Lawrence *metal products manufacturing executive*
Kaste, Sue Creviston *pediatric radiologist, researcher*
Kelley, Linda Rose *human resources specialist*
Lee, Theresa K. *chemicals executive*
Madlock, Yvonne *city health department administrator*
Mardis, Elma Hubbard *county administrator, consultant*
McRee, Celia *composer, singer, actress, writer, producer*
Morreim, E. Haavi *medical ethics educator*
O'Neill Tate, Frances *construction executive*
Piazza, Marguerite *opera singer, actress, entertainer*
Pourmotabbed, Tayebeh *biochemist*
Presley, Lisa Marie *musician*
Raines, Shirley Carol *academic administrator*
Riely, Caroline Armistead *physician, medical educator*
Riser, Kathleen Walsh *secondary school educator*
Sams Schreiber, Carol Marie Houser *artist, graphic designer*
Scales, Patricia Kathleen *psychological therapist*
Shafer, Anne Whalen *volunteer civic worker*
Tibbs, Martha Jane Pullen *civic worker*
Turner, Bernice Hilburn *recording industry executive*
Vescovo, Diane Kirkland *federal judge*
Walters, Jane *state agency administrator*
Watson, Ella H. *principal*
Whitehead, Jenifer Barron *corporate communications specialist, consultant*
Winters, Darcy LaFountain *medical management company executive*
Wright Carrier, J. T. *business owner*

Morristown
Johnson, Evelyn Bryan *airport terminal executive*

Mount Juliet
Williams, Vicky Ann *music educator, musician*

Murfreesboro
Doyle, Delores Marie *retired principal*
Garrison, Kathryn Ann *retired nutritionist*
Gilbert, Linda Arms *education educator, educational administrator*
Reed, Angelica Denise *sculptor, writer, illustrator*
Rupprecht, Nancy Ellen *historian, educator*
Wehofer, Donna Lynn *music educator*

Nashville
Albright, Julia Szur *artist*
Anderson, Lynn (Rene Anderson) *singer*
Bailey, Stephanie B.C. *city health department administrator*
Benbow, Camilla Persson *psychology educator, researcher*
Bigham, Wanda Durrett *religious organization administrator*
Bird, Caroline *author*
Bramlett, Shirley Marie Wilhelm *interior decorator, artist*
Brown, Tommie Florence *social work educator*
Brown, Wendy Weinstock *nephrologist, educator*
Burks, Charlotte *state legislator*
Butler, Carol Green *music educator*
Clark, Terri *singer*
Cleveland, Ashley *musician*
Clinton, Barbara Marie *university health services director, social worker*
Collins, Joe Lena *retired secondary school educator*
Conway-Welch, Colleen *dean, nurse midwife*
Cook, Ann Jennalie *English language educator*
Cooper, Mary Berry *retired legal assistant, association executive*
Cornwell, Ilene Jones *writer, editor*
Crosswhite, Jeanette Elvira *art educator*
Daughtrey, Martha Craig *federal judge*
Dauser, Kimberly Ann *physician assistant*
DeBerry, Lois Marie *state legislator*
Dimengo, Josephine *medical/surgical nurse*
Eckles, Mary Ann *state legislator*
Etherington, Carol A. *medical association administrator*
[illegible], Katherine Fenton *elementary school educator*
Giallombardo, Leslie *publishing executive*
Goggin, Wendy *prosecutor*
Gore, Tipper (Mary Elizabeth Gore) *wife of the former vice president of the United States*
Grant, Amy *singer, songwriter*
Graves, Jo Ann *state legislator*
Green, Lisa Cannon *online editor*
Greene, Lydia Abbi Jwuan *elementary school educator*
Griffith, Nanci *singer, songwriter*
Gusky, Diane Elizabeth *state agency administrator, planner*
Guy, Sharon Kaye *state agency executive*
Halteman Harwell, Beth *state legislator*
Hammond, Charlene Foster *writer, choreographer, musician, artist, educator*
Harper, Thelma *state legislator*
Harris, Emmylou *singer*
Harwell, Beth H. *political organization worker*
Higgs, Mary Phil Egerton *editor*
Hill, Faith *musician*
Ingram, Martha Rivers *publishing executive*
James, Kay Louise *management consultant, healthcare executive*
Jones, Evelyn Gloria *medical technologist, educator*
Judd, Naomi *country music entertainer, singer, songwriter, writer*
Keith, Suzanne Gregory *legal association administrator*
Kessler, Ingrid Anderson *musician, music educator*
Kurita, Rosalind *state legislator*
Kyle, Sara *state agency administrator*
Loper, Linda Sue *special collections librarian*
Lyle, Virginia Reavis *retired archivist, genealogist*
Lynn, Loretta Webb (Mrs. Oliver Lynn Jr.) *singer*
Maguire, Martha Elenor Erwin (Martie Maguire) *musician*
Maines, Natalie Louise *musician*
Mandrell, Barbara Ann *singer, entertainer, actress, producer, writer*
Mauksch, Ingeborg Grosser *nursing educator*
Mayden, Barbara Mendel *lawyer*
McBride, Martina *vocalist*
McKeel, Sheryl Wilson *pharmacist*
McMurry, Idanelle Sam *educational consultant*
Oates, Sherry Charlene *portraitist, artist, photographer*
Orgebin-Crist, Marie-Claire *biology educator*
Parton, Stella Mae *entertainer*
Pearson, Sela *poet, speaker*
Penterman, Carol A. *opera company executive*
Pierce, Patricia Ann *university administrator*
Ragan, Lisa Carol *editor*
Richey, Kimberly Kay *singer, actress, composer*
Risko, Victoria J. *language educator*
Rizor, Nancy Lucile *retired bookkeeper, retired librarian, genealogist*
Roberts, Sandra *editor*
Robison, Emily Burns *musician*
Rodgers, Roberta Walker *music educator*
Seivers, Lana C. *commissioner of education*
Shaw, Carole *editor, publisher*
Shaw-Cohen, Lori Eve *magazine editor*
Sheffield, Stephanie S. *portfolio and marketing management consultant*
Short, Sallie Lee *physical plant service worker*
Smith Heinz, Amy *publishing executive*
Stahlman, Mildred Thornton *pediatrics and pathology educator, researcher*
Swing, Marilyn S. *metropolitan clerk*
Thomas, Hazel Beatrice *state official*
Torrey, Claudia Olivia *lawyer*
Trauger, Aleta Arthur *judge*
Twain, Shania (Eilleen Regina Edwards) *country musician*
Wadley, Fredia Stovall *state commissioner*
Watkins, Sara *musician*
Whitten-Frickey, Wendy Elise *entertainer*
Willis, Eleanor Lawson *not-for-profit developer*
Wilson, Carolyn Taylor *librarian*
Winstead, Elisabeth Weaver *poet, writer, English language educator*
Young, Rebecca Payne *secondary school educator*
Young, Tommie Morton *social psychology educator, writer*

New Market
Humphreys, Rebecca *music educator, elementary school educator*

Newport
Gregg, Ella Mae *writer*
Kridler, Jamie Branam *children's advocate, social psychologist*

Nolensville
Heeney, Susan Welch *interior designer, educator*
Lessard, Lisa Kathleen Hamlin *spiritual counselor*

Oak Ridge
Cragle, Donna Lynne *university administrator, researcher*
Ergen, Viola S. *accountant*
Evans, Carole Clinton *special education educator*
Foust, Donna Elaine Marshall *women's health nurse*
Fox, Janie *environmental engineer*
Holloway, Jacqueline *county commissioner*
Johnson, Ruth Crumley *economics educator*
Jones, Virginia McClurkin *retired social worker*
Regan-Stanton, Christa Maria *artist*
Slusher, Kimberly Goode *researcher*
Swierbut, Wendi Marie *electrochemist*
Thompson, Dorothea Kathleen *microbiologist*
Watson, Evelyn Egner *radiation scientist*
Wurth, Patsy Ann *geographic information systems specialist*

Old Hickory
[illegible] *English language educator*

Oliver Springs
Davis, Sara Lea *pharmacist*
Heacker, Thelma Weaks *retired elementary school educator*

Paris
Hawkins, Angela *music educator*
McFarlin, Shannon Dianne *writer, researcher*
Wiedemann, Ramona Diane *occupational therapist*

Pigeon Forge
Parton, Dolly Rebecca *singer, composer, actress*

Portland
Miller, Sandra Perry *middle school educator*
Wiggins, Kelley J.K. *music educator*

Primm Springs
Carlson, Karen *actress*

Pulaski
Calvert, Lois Prince *health facility administrator, geriatrics nurse*

Readyville
Merrill, Mary Margaret *secondary school educator*

Savannah
Folkerts, Linda Jo *publishing executive*

Selmer
Prather, Sophie S. *educational administrator*

Sevierville
Etherton, Jane *retired sales executive, marketing professional*
Heldman, Betty Lou Faulkner *retired health facility administrator*
Koff, Shirley Irene *writer*

Sewanee
Watson, Gail H. *retired librarian*

Seymour
Burkhart, Elvira (Jean) *language educator, music educator*

Shelbyville
Nelson, Clara Singleton *human resources consultant*

Smithville
Hinton, Susan Frazier *secondary school educator*
Vaughn, Eulalia Cobb *retired science educator, mathematician*

Smyrna
Faules, Barbara Ruth *retired elementary education educator*
Guitard, Margaret Mary *elementary school educator*

Soddy Daisy
Frazier, Douglas Almeda McRee *volunteer, former energy facility analyst*

Randall, Kay Temple *accountant, retired real estate agent*

Sparta
Keisling, Mary West *volunteer*
Young, Olivia Knowles *retired librarian*

Spring Hill
Lafevor, Kimberly Ann *human resources specialist, educator*
Trudell, Cynthia *automotive executive*

Strawberry Plains
Blanchard, Pamela Snyder *special education educator*
Snodderly, Louise Davis *librarian*

Sweetwater
Forkner, Geraldine G. *art educator, artist*

Trenton
McCullough, Kathryn T. Baker *social worker*

Tullahoma
Hill, Susan Sloan *safety engineer*
Majors, Betty-Joyce Moore *genealogist, writer*

Whiteville
Allen, Yvonne *principal*

TEXAS

Abilene
Boone, Celia Trimble *lawyer*
Freeman, Carol Lyn *business administrator*
Kiel, Martha Guillet *art educator*
McGrew, Pamela Kay *health facility administrator*
Owen, Dian Grave *investment corporation executive*
Specht, Alice Wilson *university libraries dean*

Addison
Baskett, Christina St. Clair *fund raising executive*
Cotter, Ka *real estate company executive*
Ragusa, Elysia *real estate company executive*
Smith, Cece *venture capitalist*

Aledo
Rowe, Sheryl Ann *librarian*

Alice
Dyer, Stephanie Jo *anesthesiologist*
Thomas, Katherine Carol *special education educator*

Alief
Zimmer, Margaret Ford *special education services professional*

Allen
Anderson, Robin Marie *secondary school educator*
Clifton, Melanie Fairlight *bank executive*
Fryman, Alison Leigh *bank executive*

Alpine
Fairlie, Carol Hunter *artist, art educator*

Alvord
King, Barbara Jean *nurse*

Amarillo
Arnold, Winnie Jo *retired mental health nurse, nursing administrator*
Hicks, Ann Neuwirth *clinical social worker*
Huff, Earleen *education educator*
Knutson, Bonnie Rae *secondary education educator, commercial artist*
McCall, Colleen Whiting *social worker*
Parker, Lynda Michele *psychiatrist*
Robertson, Pauline Durrett *publishing executive*
Robinson, Mary Lou *federal judge*
Robinson, Ola Mae *accountant*
Stapleton, Claudia Ann *school director*
Stovich, Joy *chemistry educator*

Angleton
Allen, Nancy Janette *school librarian*

Aransas Pass
Stehn, Lorraine Strelnick *physician*

Arlington
Buckley Green, Deborah Fern *nursing educator*
Burke, Toni Scotto *primary school educator*
Burson, Betsy Lee *librarian*
English, Marlene Cabral *management consultant*
Hall, Anna Christene *retired government official*
Liu, Hanli *biomedical engineer, educator*
McKeen, Sally Werst *volunteer*
Pickard, Myrna Rae *dean*
Poster, Elizabeth C. *dean*
Savage, Ruth Hudson *poet, writer, speaker*
Sawyer, Dolores *motel chain executive*
Shabazz, Cheryl Antoinette *legal assistant*
Swanson, Peggy Eubanks *finance educator*
Thomas, Lois C. *organist, music educator*
Willoughby, Sarah-Margaret C. *chemist, educator, chemical engineer, consultant*

Aubrey
Pizzamiglio, Nancy Alice *performing company executive*

Austin
Ables-Flatt, Jean Ann *commissioner*
Aboussie, Marilyn *retired state justice*
Alford, Frances Holliday *artist, retired elementary school educator*
Baker, Mary Ann *program manager*
Banks, Virginia Anne (Ginger Banks) *association administrator*
Bennett, Catherine Margaret *music educator*
Bingham, Ouita Hyams *librarian*
Branch, Brenda Sue *library director*
Brannon-Peppas, Lisa *chemical engineer, researcher*
Brown, Shirley Jean *health care facility manager, nurse*
Brown, Vivian Anderson *retired government agency administrator*
Caldwell, Shirley W. *commissioner*
Calfee, Laura Pickett *university administrator, photographer*
Cantú, Norma V. *law educator, former federal official*
Christian, Cheryl Lynn *editor, writer*
Clay, Lareatha H. *commissioner*
Combs, Susan *commissioner of agriculture*
Conradt, Jody *basketball coach*
Corredor, Mary B. *language educator, consultant, translator*
Covington, Veronica Pro *librarian, educator*
Cullum, Bonnie Brooks *theater producer, theater director, educator*
Curle, Robin Lea *computer software industry executive*
Dabbs Riley, Jeanne Kernodle *retired public relations executive*
Danburg, Debra *state legislator*
Dealey, Amanda Mayhew *former foundation administrator*
Denny, Mary Craver *state legislator, business owner*
DeWitt-Morette, Cécile *physicist*
Drummond Borg, Lesley Margaret *clinical geneticist*
Easley, Christa Birgit *nurse, researcher*
Ehrlich, Stacy Wheeler *school fundraiser, administrator*
Eldredge, Linda Gaile *psychologist*
Fisk, Doris Rosalie Scanlan *volunteer*
Fletcher, Robin Mary *health care administrator*
Friedman, Alice Diane *internist, gastroenterologist, educator*
Fryxell, Greta Albrecht *marine botany educator, oceanographer*
Furman, Laura *writer, educator*
Galbreath, Margaret Anne *market research analyst*
Garcia, Sara Kruger *lawyer*
Golden, Kimberly Kay *critical care nurse*
Green, Shirley Moore *retired public affairs and communications executive*
Greer, Carolyn A. *guidance counselor*
Gregory, Marilyn *primary school educator*
Hagerty, Polly Martiel *financial analyst, construction executive*
Hall, Beverly Adele *nursing educator*
Hamilton, Dagmar Strandberg *lawyer, educator*
Hammer, Katherine Gonet *software company executive*
Hamouda, Amy Bice *artist*
Hayes, Patricia Ann *health facility administrator*
Hayman, Carol Anne *anthropology educator, photographer*
Henson, Glenda Maria *newspaper writer*
Herrington-Borre, Frances June *sign language school director*
Hinojosa, Tish (Leticia Hinojosa) *vocalist*
Hitchcock, Joanna *publisher*
Holtzman, Joan King *musician, composer*
Hornbeck, Nita Lou McClennan *university and secondary school educator*
Hughes, Judy Lynne *political organization executive*
Hutchins, Karen Leslie *psychotherapist*
Johnson, Eileen *curator, educator, commissioner*
Johnson, Lady Bird (Mrs. Claudia Alta Taylor) *former First Lady of the United States*
Keller, Sharon Faye *judge*
Kirk, Lynda Pounds *biofeedback therapist, neurotherapist, counselor*
Klein, Rebecca *commissioner*
Lafferty, Joyce G. Zvonar *retired elementary school educator*
Larkam, Beverley McCosham *clinical social worker, family therapist*
Lehmann-Carssow, Nancy Beth *secondary school educator, coach*
Lenoir, Gloria Cisneros *consultant, educator*
Little, Emily Browning *architect*
Maar, Rosina *medical organization executive*
Mauzy, (Martha) Anne *retired deaf educator, audiologist*
McDaniel, Myra Atwell *lawyer, former state official*
McElroy, Mary M. (Mickie McElroy) *educational writer*
McElroy, Maurine Davenport *financier, educator*
McEvoy, Grace Elizabeth *photographer*
McKean, Maureen Catherine *city official, systems analyst*
McKeown-Moak, Mary Park *educational consultant*
McKnight, Mamie *commissioner*
Minault, Gail *history educator*
Monteverde, Frances Elaine *social sciences educator*
Moore, Colleen *piano and voice instructor*
Morrow, Sandra Kay *librarian*
Mueller, Peggy Jean *dance educator, choreographer, rancher*
Mullenix, Linda Susan *lawyer, educator*
O'Neill, Harriet *state supreme court justice*
Owen, Priscilla Richman *state supreme court justice*
Owens, Margaret Alma *educational administrator*
Pate, Jacqueline Hail *retired data processing company executive*
Pettigrew, Jo Arnold *educational association administrator*
Pingree, Dianne *sociologist, educator, psychotherapist*
Popma, Rena M. *psychologist*
Qunell, Kerri Wynn *marketing professional*
Richards, Ann Willis *former governor*
Richards-Kortum, Rebecca Rae *biomedical engineering educator*
Robbins, Mary *concert pianist*
Rogers, Lorene Lane *university president emeritus*
Rostow, Elspeth Davies *political science educator*
Ruiz, Cookie *performing company executive*
Ryan, Randa Catherine *university administrator, business owner*
Sands, Dolores S. *dean*
Sawyer, Margo Lucy *artist, educator*
Schaeffer, Nancy Ellen *liberal arts educator*
Schloss, Hadassah *open records program administrator*
Shapiro, Florence *state legislator, advertising, public relations executive*
Shea, Gwyn *secretary of state*
Simon, Erica Cecelia *research scientist, consultant*
Simon, Sandra Ruth Waldman *state agency administrator*
Simpson, Beryl Brintnall *botany educator*
Slavin, Alexandra Nadal *artistic director, educator*
Smith, Bert Kruger *retired mental health services professional*
Sober, Debra Evonne *environmental services administrator*
Spector, Rose *state supreme court justice*
Spicer, Beverly White *writer, photojournalist, artist*
Spielman, Barbara Helen New *editor, consultant*
Stout, Patricia A. *communications educator*
Strayhorn, Carole Keeton *comptroller*
Sullivan, Teresa Ann *law and sociology educator, academic administrator*
Sutton, Beverly Jewell *psychiatrist*
Swanson, Elizabeth Ann *special education educator, researcher*
Trabulsi, Judy *advertising and marketing executive*
Uhlenbeck, Karen Keskulla *mathematician, educator*
Vandel, Diana Geis *management consultant*
Wakeman, Olivia Van Horn *marketing professional*
Walter, Virginia Lee *psychologist, educator*
Watson, Brenda Bennett *insurance company executive*
Watson, Elizabeth Marion *protective services official*
Watson, Irene *seminar and retreat facilitator, author, artist*
Weddington, Susan *political party official*
Weinberg, Louise *law educator, author*
Williams, Diane Elizabeth *architectural historian, photographer*
Williams, Mary Pearl *judge*
Witt, Doreen Marie *business executive*
Worthing, Carol Marie *minister*
Wurzbach, Linda *educational consultant*
York, Candace A. *marketing professional, writer*
Young, Joan Crawford *advertising executive*

Beaumont
Alter, Shirley Jacobs *jewelry store owner*
Gagne, Mary *academic administrator*
Hawkins, Emma B. *humanities educator*
Hunt, Madelyn Dora *biologist, educator, director*
Lewin, Nancy S. *actress*
Lord, Evelyn Marlin *mayor*
Mueller, Lisa Maria *chemical engineer*
Phan, Tâm Thanh *medical educator, psychotherapist, consultant, researcher*
Wohler, Marjorie Lynn Coulter *medical and surgical nurse, health facility administrator*

Bedford
Newell, Karin Barnes *bank executive*
Turnbull, Dana *psychologist*

Bellaire
Ballanfant, Kathleen Gamber *newspaper executive, public relations company executive*
Rumfolo, Marilu *financial analyst, non-profit corporation executive*
Smeal, Janis Lea *osteopath*

Bellville
Krueger, Betty Adel *county official*
Mann, Laura Susan *editor*
Wentworth, Bette Wilson *artist, educator*

Belton
Fontaine-White, Barbara Frances *art educator*
Traver, Janice Weygandt *horse breeder*

Benbrook
Margolis, Susan Ellen *psychiatric clinical nurse specialist, artist*

Bertram
Albert, Susan Wittig *writer, English educator*

Boerne
Daugherty, Linda Hagaman *real estate company executive*

Brenham
Brown, Marguerite Johnson *music educator*
Lubbock, Mildred Marcelle (Midge Lubbock) *former small business owner*

Brookshire
Utley, Jane Beson *poet*

Brownsville
Garcia, Juliet Villarreal *university administrator*
Gorman, Margaret Norine *probation officer, chemical dependency counselor*
Halaby, Margarita Gonzalez *marketing professional, communications executive*
Mendoza, Melissa Ann *lab administrator, technologist*
Rodriguez, Nora Hilda *social worker*
Soldan, Angelika *philosopher, political scientist, educator*
Tarrant, Susan Kathryn *art educator*

Brownwood
Owens, Diane Dobray *music educator*
Roby, Annie Beth Brian *librarian*

Bryan
Guitry, Loraine Dunn *community health nurse*
Van Ouwerkerk, Anita Harrison *reading educator*

Buchanan Dam
Miloy, Leatha Faye *university program director*

Burleson
Buford, Evelyn Claudene Shilling *retired consumer products company executive*
Lisi, Lori A. (Lori Fredeking) *freelance/self-employed editor, writer*

Burnet
Gurno, Mary Ann *school system administrator*

Calvert
Alemán, Marthanne Payne *environmental planner, consultant*

Canyon
Brasher, Treasure Ann Kees *physics educator*
Haraden, Mary Clyde *language educator, musician*
Rice, Lois *mayor*

Canyon Lake
Reinhardt, Linda Kay *minister*

Carrollton
Daily, Ellen Wilmoth Matthews *technical publications specialist*
Estilette, Kathleen C. *music educator*
Hart, Elizabeth Ann *foundation administrator*
Heath, Jinger L. *cosmetics executive*
Last, Susan Walker *training developer*
Lieberman-Cline, Nancy *sports commentator, former professional basketball coach, former player*
Moellering, Charlotte Lareson *music educator*
Mohle, Brenda Simonson *art appraiser*
Odem, Joyce Marie *human resources specialist*
Ratliff, Mary Jean Dougherty *fine arts educator*
Withrow, Lucille Monnot *nursing home administrator*

Carthage
Cooke, Walta Pippen *automobile dealership owner*

Castroville
Eyre, Pamela Catherine *retired career officer*

Cat Spring
Ramsey, Mary Catherine *mechanical engineer, consultant*

Cedar Hill
Findley, Milla Jean *nutritionist*
Hickman, Traphene Parramore *retired library director, storyteller, library and library building consultant*
Moore, Jacquelyn *art educator*

Cedar Park
Duke, Carol Michiels *personal care industry executive*
Lam, Pauline Poha *library director*
Porterfield, Sherri Lou *music educator*

Channelview
Wallace, Betty Jean *elementary school educator, lay minister*

Channing
Brian, Mary H. *librarian*

Chireno
Mayhar, Ardath Frances (Frank Cannon) *author*

Cleburne
Arnold, Sandra Ruth Kouns *photographer*
Gorman, Charlotte A. *family and consumer sciences agent*

Cleveland
Campbell, Selaura Joy *lawyer*

College Station
Beaver, Bonnie Veryle *veterinarian, educator*
Cantrell, Carol Whitaker *educational administrator*
Darensbourg, Marcetta York *chemistry educator*
Edwards, Janine C. *educational administrator*
Ezell, Margaret J. *language educator*
Jones, Kristen Gae *chemistry educator*
Lu, Mi *computer engineer, educator*
Martin, Carol Jacquelyn *artist, educator*
McCann, Janet *language educator, poet*
Ory, Marcia Gail *social science researcher*
Perry, Helen Thomas *artist*
Seifert, Kathryn Ann Hawkins *language educator*
Unterberger, Betty Miller *history educator, writer*
Vandiver, Renee Lillian Aubry *interior designer, architectural preservator*

Colleyville
Bush, Holly Newsom *management consultant*
Donnelly, Barbara Schettler *retired medical technologist*
Tigue, Virginia Beth (Ginny Tigue) *volunteer*

Comanche
Droke, Edna Faye *retired elementary school educator*

Commerce
Scott, Joyce Alaine *university official*
Thompson, Jane Ann *elementary school educator, researcher*

Yaites, LilliAnn *minister*

Fredericksburg
Gibson, Frances Ernst *music educator*
Wahrmund, Peggy Stieler *artist, rancher*

Fresno
Shaw, Teshetesa S. *pre-school educator*

Frisco
de Veritch, Nina *cellist, music educator*
Doone, Michele Marie *chiropractor*
Meadows, Patricia Blachly *art curator, civic worker*
Meyer, Amy Allen *counselor*
Taylor, Teresa Marie *realtor*

Galveston
Goodwin, Jean McClung *psychiatrist*
Goodwin, Sharon Ann *academic administrator*
Gugliuzza, Kristene Koontz *transplant and general surgery educator*
Holcomb, Mary Anne *councilwoman, municipal official*
LaGrone, Lavenia Whiddon *chemist, real estate broker*
Phillips, Linda Goluch *plastic surgeon, educator, researcher*

Garland
Brumit, Jo Ann *sheet metal manufacturing executive*
Hodges, Kathleen McGill *art educator*
Lord, Jacqueline Ward *accountant, photographer, artist*
Michaels, Cindy Whitfill (Cynthia G. Michaels) *educational consultant*
Rogers, Sharon *art educator*
Syphers, Mary Frances *music educator*

Georgetown
Earney, Mary K. *writer, educator*
James, Karen Dawn *performing arts educator*
Ramsey, Margie *librarian*
Smitheram, Margaret Etheridge *health facility administrator, director*

Giddings
Dismukes, Carol Jaehne *county official*

Gladewater
Cox-Beaird, Dian Sanders *middle school educator*

Glen Rose
Blankenship, Jenny Mary *museum administrator*

Gonzales
Ince, Laurel T. *music educator*

Grand Prairie
Horak, Trish *city government worker*
Mathis, Prudence Marchman *real estate company executive*
McMillan, Helen Berneice *sales executive*
Ritterhouse, Kathy Lee *librarian*

Grapevine
Blair, Sylvia H. *computer project engineer, small business owner*
Bloyd, Ruthanne *gifted and talented mathematics educator*
Hirsh, Cristy J. *principal*

Hale Center
Courtney, Carolyn Ann *school librarian*

Hallsville
Hutcherson, Donna Dean *retired music educator*

Harker Heights
Gunter, Wanda Brock *special education educator*

Harlingen
Knight, Normah Louise *artist*
Roberts-Parast, Ann Talbot *English and foreign language educator*

Hempstead
Propst, Catherine Lamb *biotechnology company executive*

Henderson
Knapp, Virginia Estella *retired secondary school educator*
Rhoades, Eva Yvonne *retired elementary school educator*

Honey Grove
Thurman, Mary Anne *foundation administrator*

Houston
Adams, Joyce M. *academic administrator*
Adams-Allen, June Evelyn *real estate broker*
Aday, Luann *social science educator*
Addison, Linda Leuchter *lawyer, writer*
Adkins, Susan *health services administrator*
Aguilar-Bryan, Lydia *medical educator, medical researcher*
Amador, Anne *architect, composer*
Anderson, Claire W. *gifted and talented educator*
Anderson, Doris Ehlinger *lawyer*
Andrews, Sally S. *lawyer*
Arceneaux, Janice Harmon *director*
Atlas, Nancy Friedman *judge*
Atwood, Carol Ann *healthcare executive*
Auchter, Norma Holmes *musician, music educator*
Baker, Ellen Shulman *astronaut, physician*
Baldwin, Bonnie *physician*
Ballantyne, Christie Mitchell *medical educator*
Ballard, Linda Christine *financial aid director*
Baranovich, Diana Lea *music educator*
Bartling, Phyllis McGinness *oil company executive*
Bazelides, Diane *public relations executive*
Beckingham, Kathleen Mary *education educator, researcher*
Belk, Joan Pardue *English educator*
Berg, Michele *health services administrator*
Berniard, Susan K. *business writer/editor*
Bevers, Therese Bartholomew *physician, medical educator*
Bischoff, Susan Ann *newspaper editor*
Black, Margaret Louise *accountant, educator*
Black, Marilyn Hammer *non-profit organization executive*
Blackburn, Sadie Gwin Allen *business executive*
Boutwell, Sharon Marie *school system administrator, educator*
Bridges, Margaret Elizabeth *physician*
Brosh, Rita *performing company executive*
Brown, Glenda Ann Walters *ballet director*
Brown, Karen Kennedy *judge*
Bryan, Mary Ann *interior designer*
Burnett, Susan Walk *personnel service company owner*
Bush, Jill A. *medical educator*
Bush, Sharon L *director*
Butel, Janet Susan *research scientist, virology educator*
Butts, Cherie LaVaughn *biomedical researcher*
Cagle, Yvonne Darlene *astronaut*
Caldwell, Tracy Ellen *surface chemist, researcher*
Callender, Norma Anne *psychology educator, counselor*
Campbell, Eileen M. *oil industry executive*
Carriere, Margaret E. *energy executive*
Carrillo, Laurie Yvette *aerospace engineer*
Caskey, Caroline *lab administrator*
Catchings, Kelly Suzanne *photographer*
Chance, Jane *English literature educator*
Chiou-Tan, Faye *physician, educator*
Clark, Letitia Z. *federal judge*
Cline, Vivian Melinda *lawyer*
Coker, Sally Jo (Bozeman) *sociology educator*
Coleman, Catherine G. *astronaut*
Condit, Linda Faulkner *economist*
Cooper, Cynthia *professional baseball player*
Cooper, Valerie Gail *minister*
Crawford, Mary Ellen *secondary school educator*
Currie, Nancy Jane *astronaut*
Curtis, Barbara *consumer products company professional*
Daniels, Davetta Mills *principal*
Darst, Mary Lou *secondary school educator*
Davis, N. Jan *astronaut, mechanical engineer*
Davis-Lewis, Bettye *nursing educator*
DeArmond, Patti Jo *hotel administrator*
DeBakey, Lois *science communications educator, editor, writer*
DeBakey, Selma *science communications educator, writer, editor, lecturer*
de Kanter, Ellen Ann *English and foreign language educator*
Dent, Leanna Gail *secondary art educator*
desVignes-Kendrick, Mary *municipal official*
de Vries, Robbie Ray Parsons *writer, illustrator, international consultant*
Dinkins, Carol Eggert *lawyer*
Dorman, Margaret K. *oil equipment manufacturer*
Drew, Katherine Fischer *history educator*
Duganier, Barbara J. *corporate financial executive*
Dunbar, Bonnie J. *engineer, astronaut*
Durham, Susan K. *research scientist*
Dworsky, Clara Weiner *lawyer, former merchandise brokerage executive*
Ehlig-Economides, Christine A. *petroleum engineer*
Eisner, Diana *pediatrician*
Ellis, Juliet S. *bank executive*
Esmaeli, BitA *ophthalmologist*
Ewen, Pamela Binnings *lawyer*
Faison, Holly *state official*
Farenthold, Frances Tarlton *lawyer*
Feeback, Cynthia Ann *corporate financial executive, accountant*
Feigon, Judith Tova *ophthalmologist, surgeon, educator*
Fenn, Sandra Ann *programmer, analyst*
Finch, Diane Shields *retail sales executive*
Fisher, Anna Lee *physician, astronaut*
Fisher, Janet Warner *secondary school educator*
Florian-Lacy, Dorothy *therapist, educator*
Foote, Jill *film producer, educator, investment banker*
Friday, Leah Rebecca *portfolio manager*
Garrett, Mary Jane *director*
Gaucher, Jane Heyck *retail executive*
Gerhart, Glenna Lee *pharmacist*
Ghiglieri, Catherine A. *auto loan company executive*
Gibson, Kathleen Rita *anatomy and anthropology educator*
Gigli, Irma *dermatologist, educator, academic administrator*
Gilmore, Vanessa D. *federal judge*
Girouard, Peggy Jo Fulcher *ballet educator*
Graebner, Carol F. *lawyer*
Greco, Janice Teresa *psychology educator*
Green, Sharon Jordan *interior decorator*
Griffith, Martha *controller*
Grossett, Deborah Lou *psychologist, consultant*
Gunn, Joan Marie *health facility administrator*
Halstead, Trazanna *newscaster*
Hambly, Ann Alle *appliance company executive*
Hamilton, Jacqueline *art consultant*
Harmon, Melinda Furche *federal judge*
Harris, Deborah Ann *science educator*
Harris, Venita Van Caspel *retired financial planner*
Hartland, Carol D. *real estate broker*
Heeg, Peggy A. *lawyer, former gas industry executive*
Heinsen, Lindsay *newspaper editor*
Helms, Susan Jane *astronaut*
Hempfling, Linda Lee *nurse*
Henderson, (Ruejenuia) Secret *social worker*
Heslop, Helen E. *physician, educator, health facility administrator*
Higginbotham, Joan E. *astronaut*
Hinton, Paula Weems *lawyer*
Holmes, Ann Hitchcock *journalist*
Hoppe, Laura *air traffic controller*
Horan, Shelly *marketing professional*
Hornak, Anna Frances *library administrator*
Hughes, Mary Katherine *nurse*
Ivins, Marcia S. *astronaut*
Jackson, Donna Ann *musician, piano instructor*
Jackson, Felicia Denise *elementary school educator*
Jackson, Susanne Leora *retired creative placement firm executive*
Jaramillo, Sandra Julier *nutritionist, researcher*
Jeevarajan, Judith A. *chemist*
Jemison, Mae Carol *physician, engineer, entrepreneur, philanthropist, educator, former astronaut*
Jenkins, Peggy Ann *counselor*
Jernigan, Tamara E. *astronaut*
Jhingran, Anuja *oncologist, educator*
Johnson, Sandra Ann *counselor, educator*
Johnson, Sandra G. *engineering company executive*
Johnston, Marguerite *journalist, author*
Jones, Edith Hollan *federal judge*
Jones, Edith Irby *physician*
Jones, Florence M. *music educator*
Jones, Sonia Josephine *advertising agency executive*
Kasi, Leela Peshkar *pharmaceutical chemist*
Kavandi, Janet Lynn *aerospace power engineer, chemist*
Kelley, Michaelann *art educator*
Kelly, Dorothy Helen *pediatrician, educator*
Kelly, Kay *social worker, administrator*
Kiang, Ching-Hwa *chemical engineering educator*
Kilrain, Susan *astronaut*
King, Carolyn Dineen *federal judge*
King, Kay Wander *academic administrator, design educator, fashion designer, consultant*
Kirkland, Rebecca Trent *pediatric endocrinologist*
Knickel, Carin S. *oil industry executive*
Konefal, Margaret Moore *health facility administrator, critical care nurse, nursing consultant, educator*
Kornbleet, Lynda Mae *insulation, fireproofing and acoustical contractor*
Kupiec, Suzanne L. *utilities executive*
Lake, Kathleen Cooper *lawyer*
Landers, Susan Mae *psychotherapist, professional counselor*
Lawrence, Wendy B. *astronaut*
Lee, Janie C. *curator*
Lehne, Kathy Prasnicki *gas industry executive*
Leichtman, Maria Luisa *mental health services professional*
Leins, Cynthia Marie *school nurse practitioner*
Lenox, Angela Cousineau *healthcare consultant*
Leslie, Mae Sue *writer*
Lewis, Lisa *psychologist, administrator*
Lu, May *psychologist, counselor, writer, watercolorist*
Lubbat, Nancy Parmar *secondary school educator*
Lucid, Shannon W. *biochemist, astronaut*
Lumgair, Mary Elizabeth *energy executive*
Malik, T. Sophia *political scientist, educator*
Mallia-Hughes, Marianne *medical writer*
Mampre, Virginia Elizabeth *communications executive*
Marek, Joycelyn *publishing executive*
Marion, Suzanne Margaret *music educator*
Mark, Rebecca P. *environmental services administrator*
Marshall, Jane Pretzer *newspaper editor*
Martin, Randi Christine *psychology educator*
Matthews, Kathleen Shive *biochemistry educator*
Mayes, Maureen Davidica *physician, educator*
Mayo, Carolyn *marketing professional, public relations executive*
McDonald, Marilyn A. *academic assistant*
McDonald, Rebecca Ann *natural gas company executive*
McEvoy-Jamil, Patricia Ann *English language educator*
McPhail, JoAnn Winstead *writer, publisher, art dealer*
McPherson, Alice Ruth *ophthalmologist, educator*
Melroy, Pamela Ann *astronaut*
Mercer, Nancy Owens Dunn *art industry purchasing agent, artist, educator*
Mermelstein, Isabel Mae Rosenberg *financial consultant*
Merrill, Connie Lange *chemical company executive*
Milburn, Diane Suzane *healthcare industry executive, writer*
Miller, Janel Howell *psychologist*
Mitcham, Carla J. *utilities executive*
Moneypenny, Naomi Felina *research and development company executive*
Montgomery, Denise Karen *nurse*
Moroney, Linda L.S. (Muffie) *lawyer, educator*
Munson, Sylvia Frances Farris *energy company manager*
Nacol, Mae *lawyer*
Neuhaus, Joan T. *finance company executive, private investigator*
Newton, Gloria Jones *accountant, feminist activist*
Nicklas, Theresa Ann *nutritionist, educator, researcher*
Ochoa, Ellen *astronaut*
O'Malley, Kimberly Joy *psychometrician, researcher*
Orr, Carole *artist*
Parle, Bertha Ibarra *writer*
Pasternak, Joanna Murray *humanities educator*
Peabody, Arlene L. Howland Bayar *retired, nurse*
Perkyns, Jane Elizabeth *music educator, composer*
Pfeiffer, Angela McGlaun *psychologist*
Pinson, Artie Frances *retired elementary school educator*
Pospisil, JoAnn *historian, archivist*
Potenza, Daisy McKaskle *newspaper executive*
Prestridge, Pamela Adair *lawyer*
Pruden, Nancy Paris *artist*
Rance, Sharon Lee *speech pathology/audiology services professional*
Randall, Beverly Marilyn *theater director*
Randolph, Lynn Moore *artist*
Rapoport, Nancy B. *dean, law educator*
Reed, Kathlyn Louise *occupational therapist, educator*
Reid, Katherine Louise *artist, educator, author*
Reiff, Patricia Hofer *space physicist, educator*
Reiter, Eunice Harris *accountant*
Ribble, Anne Hoerner *communications executive*
Robbins, Susan Paula *social work educator*
Rodgers, Amber Gayle *speech pathology/audiology services professional*
Roos, Sybil Friedenthal *retired elementary school educator*
Rosenthal, Lee H. *federal judge*
Ross, Patti Jayne *obstetrics and gynecology educator*
Saizan, Paula Theresa *oil company executive*
Sanderson, Mary Louise *medical association administrator*
Santi, Kristi L. *special education educator, researcher*
Sazama, Kathleen *pathologist, lawyer*
Scarbrough, Sara Eunice *librarian, archivist, consultant*
Schachtel, Barbara Harriet Levin *epidemiologist, educator*
Scharold, Mary Louise *psychoanalyst, educator*
Schell, Mary Elizabeth *secondary school educator*
Scholin, Margo S. *lawyer*
Schulz, Amanda Jean *real estate consultant, lawyer*
Schumacher, Diane Kosmach *manufacturing executive, lawyer*
Seaton, Alberta Jones *biologist, educator, consultant*
Sewell, Beth Perry *gas industry executive*
Sheehan, Linda Suzanne *education administrator*
Shore, Lisa *flight controller, trainer*
Shuart, Carey Chenoweth *farmer, volunteer*
Skidmore, Margaret Cooke *fundraiser*
Slade, Priscilla Dean *academic administrator*
Smith, Alison Leigh *lawyer*
Smith, Andrea Dawn *financial planner*
Smith, Claire *chef*
Snowden, Bernice Rives *former construction company executive*
Solomon, Marsha Harris *draftsman, artist*
Sondock, Ruby Kless *retired judge*
Stacy, Frances H. *federal judge*
Stewart, Pamela L. *lawyer*
Stripling, Kaye *school system administrator*
Strommer, Anne Elizabeth Rivard *retired librarian*
Sweet, Portia Ann *retired human resources specialist*
Swoopes, Sheryl Denise *professional basketball player*
Thomas, Katherine Jane *magazine and newspaper columnist*
Thomas, M. Ann *bank executive*
Thompson, Ewa M. *foreign language educator*
Thompson, Tina *professional basketball player*
Thompson-Draper, Cheryl L. *electronics executive, real estate executive*
Tice, Pamela Paradis *scientific editor, writer*
Tilney, Elizabeth A. *marketing executive*
Tripp, Karen Bryant *lawyer*
Tucker, Anne Wilkes *curator, photography historian and critic, lecturer*
Urbina, Febe Gloria *elementary school principal*
Vallbona, Rima-Gretel Rothe *foreign language educator, writer*
Vassilopoulou-Sellin, Rena *clinician investigator*
Vilas, Faith *aerospace scientist*
Vollmer, Helen *public relations executive*
Voss, Janice E. *astronaut*
Wagner, Charlene Brook *publishing consultant, elementary school educator*
Walls, Martha Ann Williams (Mrs. B. Carmage Walls) *publishing executive*
Wardle, Victoria Sarah *business analyst*
Watkins, Lisa M. *financial analyst*
Webb, Marty Fox *principal*
Weber, Mary Ellen *astronaut*
Wejman, Janet P. *information technology executive, air transportation executive*
Williams, Dorothy S. *consultant nurse*
Williams, Sunita L. *astronaut*
Wilson, Carolyn Campbell *art historian*
Wood, Susan *poet, literature educator*
Wray, Nelda P. *medical association administrator*
Wright, B. Ann *academic administrator*
Yi, Jenny Kisuk *public health educator*
Yiu, Fang *structural engineer, researcher*
Young, Jeanette Cochran *corporate planner, reporter, analyst*
Zaleski, Linda C. *retail executive*

Hubbard
Schronk, Patricia Lynn *secondary school educator*

Humble
Schellinger, Ann Goodwin *medical manager*

Hunt
Shaifer, Margaret S. *artist*

Huntsville
Gratz, Cindy Carpenter *dance educator, choreographer*
Gullette, Valencia Deshae *counselor*

Bowden, Virginia Massey *librarian*
Brewster, Olive Nesbitt *retired librarian*
Brown, Mary Rose *energy executive*
Bunten, Brenda Arlene *geriatrics nurse*
Carr, Cassandra Colvin *communications company executive*
Condos, Barbara Seale *real estate broker, developer, investor*
Corrigan, Helen González *retired cytologist*
Cruz, Rosalina Sedillo *marriage and family therapist*
Dacbert-Friese, Sharyn Varhely *social worker, evangelist*
Deal, Sarah R. *psychotherapist, educator*
DeNice, Marcella L. *counseling administrator*
deTiege-Campos, Alicea Lynnette *special education educator*
Diehl, Kimberly A. *researcher*
Dixon, Ernestine Othree *secondary school educator*
Donelson, Rosemarie Quiroz Carvajal *human services professional, state official*
Endresen, Lisa Castro *curatorial assistant*
Estep, Myrna Lynne *systems analyst, philosophy educator*
Flaherty, Sergina Maria *ophthalmic medical technologist*
Galvan, Alicia Zavala *pharmacist*
Garner, Jo Ann Starkey *retired elementary and special education educator*
Glueck, Sylvia Blumenfeld *writer*
Godin, Christine C. *library director*
Guerrero, Monica Elaine *judge*
Harvey, Candi *professional basketball coach*
Hawken, Patty Lynn *retired nursing educator, dean of faculty*
Heloise, *columnist, writer*
Henderson, Connie Chorlton *city planner, artist and writer*
Hogan, Donna Helen *school librarian, educator*
Hood, Sandra Dale *librarian*
Jacobson, Helen Gugenheim (Mrs. David Jacobson) *civic worker*
Johnson, Anne Stuckly *retired lawyer*
Johnson, Sammye LaRue *communications educator*
Johnson, Shannon *professional basketball player*
Kamada-Cole, Mika M. *allergist, immunologist, medical educator*
Kaye, Celia Ilene *pediatrics educator*
Kickbusch, Consuelo Castillo *educational association administrator, consultant, former military officer*
Kretzschmar, Angelina Genzer *small business owner, paralegal*
Labenz-Hough, Marlene *dispute resolution professional*
Lehrmann, Ruby Jean *protective services official*
Lenke, Joanne Marie *publishing executive*
Macon, Jane Haun *lawyer*
Madrid, Olga Hilda Gonzalez *retired elementary education educator, association executive*
Maloney, Marynell *lawyer*
Marshall, Karolyn Margaret *private school educator*
Masters, Bettie Sue Siler *biochemist, educator*
Mathews, Jennifer Pauline *anthropologist, educator, archaeologist*
McClinton, Dorothy Hardaway *former business educator*
McSorley, Rita Elizabeth *adult education educator*
Mills, Linda S. *public relations executive*
Montecel, Maria Robledo (Cuca Robledo Montecel) *educational association administrator*
Morris, Lissa Camille *music educator*
Mott, Peggy Laverne *sociologist, educator*
Nance, Betty Love *librarian*
Nava, Carmen P. *communications executive*
Newton, Virginia *archivist, historian, librarian*
Nowak, Nancy Stein *judge*
Oppenheim, Martha Kunkel *pianist, educator*
Passty, Jeanette Nyda *English language educator, writer*
Penrod, Hazel L. *music educator*
Pfanstiel Parr, Dorothea Ann *interior designer*
Pliego-Stout, Patricia *travel company executive*
Potts, Martha Lou *elementary school educator*
Reed, Susan D. *prosecutor*
Rhodes, Linda Jane *psychiatrist*
Rodriguez, Helen G. *retired social worker*
Rogers, Frances Evelyn *author, retired educator and librarian*
Sabo, Corinne Mae *volunteer*
Sanchez, Susie Riojas *elementary school educator*
Schuk, Linda Lee *legal assistant, business educator*
Sinkin, Fay Marie *environmentalist*
Spears, Sally *lawyer*
Summers, Barbara June *artist*
Tarazon, Maureen Reeves *landscape artist, conservator*
Titzman, Donna M. *energy executive*
Van de Putte, Leticia *pharmacist, state legislator*
von Raffler-Engel, Walburga (Walburga Engel) *linguist, cross-cultural communications specialist, lecturer, writer*
Wang, Yufeng *science educator*
Weiner, Marcia Myra *judge*
Weyel, Peggy Ann *secondary school educator*
Wilson, F. Jill *real estate executive, Internet consultant*
Wilson, Janie Menchaca *nursing educator, researcher*
Winik, Joanne *broadcast executive*
Winstead, Antoinette Fay *performing arts educator*
Wisniewski, Mary Josephine *art educator, religious organization administrator*
Yerkes, Susan Gamble *newspaper columnist*

San Benito
Cavazos, Ana A. *librarian*

San Marcos
Barragán, Celia Silguero *elementary school educator*
Carman, Mary Ann *retired special education educator*
Martin, Jerri Whan *public relations executive*
Monroe, Debra F. *writer, educator*
Moore, Betty Jean *retired education educator*
Moore, Patsy Sites *food service consultant*
Stovall, Frances Middagh *writer, preservationist*
Taylor, Ruth Arleen Lesher *marketing educator*
Treanor, Betty McKee *interior design educator*

Santa Fe
Jernigan, Vicki Louise MacKechney *clinical nurse specialist*
Lambert, Willie Lee Bell *mobile equipment company owner, educator*
McLean, Dianne Kay *music educator*

Seabrook
Sterling, Shirley Frampton *artist, educator*

Sealy
Stevens, Rhea Christina *lawyer*

Shelbyville
Lifshutz, Melanie Janet Bell *patient education, medical, and surgical nurse*

Sheppard AFB
Cook, Sharla J. *career officer*

Sherman
Carnes, La Zetta *elementary school educator*
Ellington, Jane Elizabeth *experimental psychologist*
Williams, Ruby Jo *retired principal*

Silsbee
Wilson, Mary Elizabeth *priest*

Smithville
Clark, LaVerne Harrell *writer*

Snyder
Barnes, Maggie Lue Shifflett (Mrs. Lawrence Barnes) *nurse*

Somerset
Holder, Linda Kay *librarian*

Southlake
Grosklos, Hollie Jo *music educator*
Herrmann, Debra McGuire *chemist, educator*
Kelly, Carol A. *travel company executive*
Somerstein-Campbell, Jasmine Aurora Abrera *preschool administrator, educator*
Sorge, Karen Lee *commercial printing company executive, consultant*
Wuetig, Joyce Linda *realtor*

Spring
Jackson, Guida Myrl *writer, magazine editor, book editor, publisher*
Mackay, Cynthia Jean *music educator*
Maxfield, Mary Constance *management consultant*
Treasure-Terrell, Suzanne Marie *marketing and sales professional, writer, poet, lyricist*
Westover, Diana Kay *interior designer, recruitment company executive*

Stafford
Forbes, Sharon Elizabeth *software engineer*
Krenek, Mary Louise *political scientist, researcher*
Le, Duy-Loan *electrical engineer*
Polinger, Iris Sandra *dermatologist*

Stephenville
Huffman-Moser, Barbara S. *criminal investigator*
Huggins, Mary Louise White *English educator, small business owner*
Levisay, Leesa Dawn *music educator, composer*
McElroy, Linda Sue *retired elementary school educator*
Stricker, Mary Fran *music educator*

Sugar Land
Keefe, Carolyn Joan *tax accountant*
Matney, Judy McCaleb *secondary school educator*
Vangellow, Deborah Sophia *sports educator, administrator*

Sulphur Springs
Clayton, Pamela Sanders *special education educator*
Gibson, Jannette Poe *educational consultant*

Sunnyvale
Bassett, Henrietta Elizabeth *music educator*

Taylor
Cernosek, Kitty *interior decorator*

Temple
Chamlee, Ann Combest *music educator*
Staten, Donna Kay *elementary school educator*

Terrell
Wilson, Melanie D *rancher*

Texarkana
Floyd, Stacy Y. *retail executive*
Hubbard, Sonia Y. *retail executive*
Malcolm, Molly Beth *political party official, counselor*

The Woodlands
Hall, Nancy Kay *music educator*
Jack, Nancy Rayford *supplemental resource company executive, consultant*
Jones, Susan Chafin *management consultant*
Mock, Cherry L. *marriage and family therapist, child therapist*
Page, Linda Ann *special education educator, language educator*
Sharman, Diane Lee *secondary school educator*
Welch, Kathy Jane *information technology executive*

Three Rivers
Barnes, Patricia Ann *art educator*

Tomball
Bates, Cheryl A *university educator*
Burgoyne, Mojie Adler *clinical social worker*
Moore, Marcia G. *human resources specialist*

Trophy Club
Caffee, Virginia Maureen *executive assistant*

Tye
Hill, Emma Lee *education educator*

Tyler
Brock, Dee Sala *television executive, educator, writer, consultant*
Cleveland, Mary Louise *librarian, media specialist*
Coker, Melinda Louise *counselor*
Guthrie, Judith K. *federal judge*
Walker, Alice R. *mechanical engineer*
Waller, Wilma Ruth *retired secondary school educator and librarian*
West, Syntha Jane Traughber *mental health services professional*
Wright, Mary Ellen *theater educator*
Yeager, Ruth *lawyer*

Universal City
Glover, Katherine Denise *musician*
Lamoureux, Gloria Kathleen *nurse, consultant, retired military officer*
Trevor, Leslie Jean *special education educator*

Van Alstyne
Hazelton, Juanita Louise *librarian*

Vernon
Hodsden, Sara Marie *minister*
Mikkelsen, Barbara Berry *retired retail executive, rancher*

Victoria
Lorenzen, Janice Ruth *physician*

Waco
Dwyer, Theresa *utilities executive*
Girouard, Tandy Denise *special education educator, psychology educator*
Hillman, Kathy Robinson *librarian*
Hollingsworth, Martha Lynette *secondary school educator*
Lewis, Martha Nell *Christian educator, minister, expressive arts therapist*
McCullagh, Janice Mary *adult education educator*
Owens-Dwyer, Dina *utilities executive*
Roberts, Betty Jo *retired librarian, speech therapist*

Weatherford
Bergman, Anne Newberry *civic leader*
Buckner-Reitman, Joyce *psychologist, educator*
Miller, Dixie Davis *elementary school educator*
Pyle, Carol Lynn Horsley *small business owner*

White Settlement
Cook, Margaret Moyer *special education educator*

Whitehouse
Brewer, Edith Gay *librarian, educator*
Killian, Christine Lynn Coe *art educator*

Wichita Falls
Evans, Melinda Dianne *elementary school educator*
Farris, Charlye Ola *lawyer*
Haynes, Linda Rose *medical/surgical nurse*
Rousey, Anne *social worker*

Wiergate
Hunter, Georgia L. *clergywoman*

Wimberley
Taylor, Mary Ross *art administrator*
Troester, Waltraud *artist, graphic designer, consultant*

UTAH

Bountiful
Bertelsen, Karyn *school system administrator, principal*
Peterson, Rose Ann *artist*

Brigham City
Tolle, Melinda Edith *engineer, scientist*

Dammeron Valley
McAnally, Ann *puzzle constructor*

Highland
Jolley, Cathy Jenna *music educator*
Mayberry, Marilyn Marie *community outreach advocate-mediator*

Layton
Rigby, Maria Dean *interpreter, advocate*

Logan
Dobson, Dorothy Lynn Watts *elementary school educator*
Newell, Ellen Elizabeth *landscape manager*
Shultz, Leila McReynolds *botanist, educator*
Van Dusen, Lani Marie *psychologist*
Wheeler, Dolores *food products executive*

Midvale
Greene, Enid *retired congresswoman*
Vigil, Debbie Saxon *surgical technician*

Murray
Webster, Linda Jane *clinical social worker, consultant*

Ogden
Davis, Lori *foundation executive*
Harrington, Mary Evelina Paulson (Polly Harrington) *religious journalist, writer, educator*
Runolfson, Marilyn Dolores *special education educator*

Park City
Carter, La Rae Dunn *music educator*
Clark, Kelly *Olympic athlete*
Corradini, Deedee *real estate company executive, former mayor*
Dunn, Shannon *Olympic athlete*
Finney, Lynne Dratler *writer, educator, retired psychotherapist, lawyer*
Solomon, Dorothy Jeanne Allred *writer, communications executive*
Stone, Nikki *motivational speaker, retired Olympic athlete*
Street, Picabo *Olympic athlete*
Witty, Christine (Chris Witty) *speed skater*

Provo
Ballif-Spanvill, Bonnie *psychologist, educator*
Densley, Colleen T. *principal*
Konecny-Costa, Jennifer *computer company executive*

Riverside
Reveal, Arlene Hadfield *retired librarian, consultant*

Riverton
Willmore, LeAnna *music educator*

Saint George
Chilow, Barbara Gail *social worker*
Wiltsey, Susan A. *secondary school educator, priest*

Salt Lake City
Arrington, Harriet Ann Horne *historian, biographer, researcher, writer*
Bartmess, Michele *public relations specialist*
Benjamin, Lorna Smith *psychologist*
Bowen, Melanie *legislative staff administrator*
Brandon, Kathryn Elizabeth Beck *pediatrician*
Campbell, Tena *judge*
Cannell, Cyndy Michelle *elementary school principal*
Carroll, Karen Colleen *physician, infectious disease educator, medical microbiologist*
Christensen, Patricia Anne Watkins *lawyer*
Clark, Deanna Dee *civic leader and volunteer*
Cole, Sally J. (Sarah Jewell Cole) *archaeologist, researcher*
Conway, Nancy Ann *newspaper editor*
Dahmen-Ray, Patricia *professional society administrator*
Durham, Christine Meaders *state supreme court chief justice*
Dydek, Margo *professional basketball player*
Emerson, Sharon B. *biology researcher and educator*
Evans, Beverly Ann *state legislator, school system administrator*
Ewers, Anne *opera company director*
Fields, Debbi *cookie franchise executive*
Foxley, Cecelia Harrison *commissioner*
George, Sarah B. *museum director*
Hale, Karen *state legislator*
Hatch, Wilda Gene *broadcast company executive*
Hlede, Korie *professional basketball player*
Holbrook, Meghan Zanolli *fundraiser, public relations specialist, political organization chairman*
Horn, Susan Dadakis *statistics educator*
Huefner, Dixie Snow *special education educator*
Jensen, Susan *instructional designer, multimedia producer*
Julander, Paula Foil *health care and political consultant, state senator*
Keefe, Maureen Ruth *dean*
Kristensen, Kathleen Howard *music educator*
Kumpfer, Karol Linda *research psychologist*
Lewis, Amy C. *finance educator, researcher*
Lustica, Katherine Grace *marketing executive, artist, consultant*
McAllister, Lynette J. *financial consultant*
McIntosh, Terrie Tuckett *lawyer*
Miller, Lorraine *business owner*
Minson, Dixie L. *legislative staff member*
Moore, Annette B. *legislative staff member*
Moore, Debra *lawyer*
Morris, Elizabeth Treat *physical therapist*
Oakes, Claudia *museum administrator*
Osherow, Jacqueline Sue *poet, English language educator*
Owen, Amy *library director*
Parrish, Jill N. *judge*
Paulsen, Vivian *magazine editor*
Perkins, Nancy Ann *nurse*
Peterson, Millie M. *state senator*
Romney-Manookin, Elaine Clive *music educator, composer*
St. John, Katherine Iva *artistic director, dance educator*
Schutz, Roberta Maria (Bobbi Schutz) *social worker*
Shaw, Karen Jane *special education educator*
Shepherd, Karen *retired congresswoman*
Smith, Janet Hugie *lawyer*
Sparks, Mildred Thomas *state agency administrator, educator*
Stock, Peggy A(nn) *college president, educator*
Struhs, Rhoda Jeanette *civic and political worker*
Ungricht, Yvette Scharffs *musician, music educator*

Van Ert, Heidi *gifted education educator, artist, art therapist*
Varela, Vicki *state official*
Walker, Carlene Martin *state senator*
Walker, Olene S. *governor*
Wanji, Sue *nurse*
White, Constance Burnham *state official*
Williams, Natalie *professional basketball player, restaurant executive*

Sandy
Snell, Marilyn Nelson *psychologist, researcher, director*

Springville
Mayne, Marianne *special education educator*

Stansbury Park
Moyer, Linda Lee *artist, educator, author*

West Jordan
Bland, Dorothy Ann *construction executive, real estate agent*

West Valley City
Bandeka, Faun Ann *elementary school educator*

VERMONT

Barnard
Duckworth, Ruth *sculptor*

Belvidere Center
Lipke, Kathryn *artist, educator*

Bennington
Bernard, April *poet, literature educator*
Coleman, Elizabeth *college president*
Morrissey, Mary *state representative*

Benson
Hair, Jennie (M. Virginia Reppert) *counseling administrator, poet*

Bethel
Wells, Wendy *art educator*

Brattleboro
Bussino, Melinda Holden *human services administrator*
Hammond, Deborah D.J. *school librarian, researcher*
Lappe, Frances Moore *author, lecturer*
Milkey, Virginia A. *state legislator*
Nichols, Joann Edith Heselton *retired legal secretary*
Smiley, Carol Anne *home health administrator, sculptor*
Steffens, Annie Laurie *sign language educator, interpreter*

Burlington
Bouchey, Heather Ann *psychologist*
Carlisle, Lilian Matarose Baker (Mrs. E. Grafton Carlisle Jr.) *writer, lecturer*
Della Santa, Laura *principal*
Donovan, Johannah L. *state representative, educator*
Hearon, Shelby *writer, lecturer, educator*
Heffernan, Patricia Conner *management consultant*
Hendley, Edith Di Pasquale *physiology and neuroscience educator*
Kunin, Madeleine May *former ambassador to Switzerland, former governor*
Lafayette, Karen Moran *state legislator*
Longmaid, Kate Jessamyn *psychologist*
Miller, Hinda *state senator, management consultant*
Paul, Karen S. *diversified financial services company executive*
Stone, Judith Elise *artist, English educator*
Sullivan, Mary Margaret *state legislator*
Tamarkin, Kate *conductor*
Tracy, John Patrick *state legislator*
Van Raalte, Barbara G. *retired realtor*

Castleton
Meloy, Judith Marie *humanities educator*

Charlotte
Robinson, Sally Winston *artist*
Russell, Eleanor M. *retired technologist*

Chelsea
Kennedy, Sylvia C. *state representative*

Chester
Carey, Erron J. *merchant banker, state representative*

Colchester
Dakin, Maureen P. *state representative*
Edmundson, Lorna Duphiney *academic administrator*
Sweeney, Joyce C. *state representative*

Craftsbury
Shambaugh, Joan Dibble *literature educator, writer*

East Calais
Alfano, Elaine *state representative*
Elliott, Susan Auguste *psychologist, psychotherapist, consultant*

East Thetford
Cummings Rockwell, Patricia Guilbault *psychiatric nurse*

Enosburg Falls
Gervais, Avis L. *state representative, consumer products company executive*

Essex Junction
Kirker, Linda *state representative, health facility administrator*
Myers, Linda K. *retired editor, state representative*
Sweetser, Susan W. *lawyer, advocate, former state legislator*
Tedd, Monique Micheline *artist*

Fairfield
Kittell, Sara Branon *state legislator*

Georgia
Branagan, Carolyn W. *state representative*

Hinesburg
Snelling, Diane *state senator, artist*

Hyde Park
Bartlett, Susan J. *state legislator*
Bourdeau, Stephanie *state representative*

Jacksonville
Hein, Karen Kramer *pediatrician, epidemiologist*

Jericho
Symington, Gaye R. *state representative*

Johnson
Rice, Rebecca Kynoch *writer, consultant, educator*
Whitehill, Angela Elizabeth *artistic director*

Lower Waterford
Burnham, Patricia White *consultant, advocate, writer, business executive*

Ludlow
Buswell, Jane H. *lay pastor*
Mueller, Diane *hotel executive*
Nitka, Alice W. *social services administrator, state representative*

Lyndonville
Elmes, Martha L. *art educator*
Moore, Carol A. *academic administrator*

Middlebury
Berens, Betty Kathryn McAdam *community program administrator*
Ginevan, Anne V. *state representative*
Lamberti, Marjorie *retired social studies educator*
Mock, Susan E. *pre-school educator, consultant*
Nuovo, Betty A. *state representative*

Milton
Rivero, Marilyn Elaine Keith *state legislator*

Montpelier
Backus, Jan *state legislator*
Blanchard, Margaret Moore *author, educator*
Cummings, Ann E. *state legislator*
Emmons, Alice M. *state legislator*
Errecart, Joyce Hier *lawyer*
Erskine, Kali (Wendy Colman) *psychoanalyst*
Fox, Sally G. *state legislator, lawyer*
Johnson, Denise Reinka *state supreme court justice*
Klein, Tony *public relations executive, state representative*
Markowitz, Deborah Lynn *state government official*
Metcalf, Cindy W. *political organization administrator*
Munt, Janet S. *state legislator*
Peaslee, Janice L. *state legislator, agricultural products executive*
Peterson, Julie *public information officer*
Ready, Elizabeth M. *state legislator*
Riehle, Helen S. *state senator*
Rivers, Cheryl P. *state legislator*
Saxman, Anna Esther *lawyer*
Seibert, Ann *state legislator, physical therapist*
Sheltra, Nancy J. *state legislator, legal assistant, auditor*
Skoglund, Marilyn *state supreme court justice*
Towne, Ruth H. *state legislator*

Moretown
Grad, Maxine J. *state representative, law educator*
Hartshorn, Brenda Bean *elementary school educator*

Morrisville
Furey, Annemarie Patricia *apparel designer*
Lechevalier, Mary Pfeil *retired microbiologist, educator*

Newark
Van Vliet, Claire *artist*

North Bennington
Feidner, Mary P. *retired speech and language pathologist*

North Ferrisburg
Tulin, Marna *psychotherapist*

North Pomfret
Shepherd, Gaal *artist*

Norwich
Carlson, Elizabeth Borden *historian, educator*
Flanders, Janet Huessy *travel company executive*
Lamperti, Claudia Jane McKay *editor*

Peacham
Scott, Jutta R. *retired librarian*

Pittsfield
Wacker, Susan Regina *creative design director*

Pittsford
Flory, Margaret K. *state representative, lawyer*

Plymouth
Bittinger, Cynthia Douglas *foundation executive*

Putney
Loring, Honey *small business owner*
Rodgers, Joyce Ellen *humanities educator*
White, Jeanette K. *state senator, health facility administrator*

Randolph
French, Patsy J. *property manager, state representative*

Richmond
Doyle, Patricia R. *state representative*

Rutland
Duffy, Virginia *state representative, artist*
Ferraro, Betty Ann *former state senator*
Mazzariello, Mary C. *state representative*
Merrihew, Mary Albee *counselor*
Thompson, Marie Angela *computer engineer, consultant*

Saint Albans
Keenan, Kathleen *state legislator*

Shelburne
Robert, Elisabeth B. *toy company executive*

South Burlington
Head, Helen *state representative, management consultant*
Pugh, Anne D. *state legislator*

South Duxbury
Villemaire, Diane Davis *adult education educator*

South Hero
Johnson, Mitzi *state representative*

South Royalton
McLaughlin, Rosemary *horse trainer, state representative*

Stowe
Beach, Lisa (Elizabeth) Forster *artist, educator*

Swanton
LaVoie, Kathy L. *state representative*

Thetford
Paley, Grace *author, educator*

Tinmouth
Fallar, Gail M. *state representative, town clerk*

Underhill
Hummel, Margaret P. *state representative*

Vergennes
Houston, Constance T. *state legislator*
Sandy, Catherine Ellen *librarian*

Vernon
O'Donnell, Pat A. *state representative*

Warren
Connell, Kinny *state representative*

Waterbury
Hilton, Linda D. *academic administrator*
Steele, Karen Kiarsis *retired state legislator*
Vincent, Val D. *state legislator*

West Rutland
Crowley, Judy B. *state representative*

Westford
Heath, Martha *state legislator*

Weybridge
Ayer, Claire D. *state representative, women's health nurse*

White River Junction
Bohi, Lynn *state legislator*
Davis, Emily S. *lawyer*
Rutter, Frances Tompson *publisher*

Williston
Ankeney, Jean B. *state legislator*
Carter, Ruth B. (Mrs. Joseph C. Carter) *foundation administrator*
Lyons, Virginia *state legislator*
Peterson, Mary N. *state representative, lawyer*
Podhajski, Blanche Rita *language foundation administrator*

Windham
Partridge, Carolyn *farmer, state representative*

Windsor
Sweaney, Donna *state representative*

Woodstock
Crocker, Patricia Conway *former state legislator*

VIRGINIA

Abingdon
Ball, Amy Catherine *education program manager*
Humphreys, Lois H. *realtor*
Ramos-Cano, Hazel Balatero *caterer, chef, innkeeper, restaurateur, entrepreneur*
Williams, Barbara Kitty *nursing educator*

Afton
McCoy, Sue *retired surgeon, biochemist*

Aldie
Weaver, Kitty Dunlap *author*

Alexandria
Alderson, Margaret Northrop *arts administrator, educator, artist*
Alexander, Marian G. *elementary school educator*
Bellon, Venetia Rochelle *financial consultant, educator*
Berger, Patricia Wilson *retired librarian*
Bond, Frances Torino *academic administrator, consultant*
Brinkema, Leonie Milhomme *federal judge*
Brown, Lillie Deloris *elementary school educator, adult education educator*
Brown, Quincalee *professional society administrator*
Bryant, Anne Lincoln *educational association executive*
Bynum, Gayela A. *public affairs specialist*
Carvalho, Julie Ann *psychologist*
Collins, Cardiss *retired congresswoman*
Collins, Mary *writer, educator*
Cooper, Edythe E.D. *political organization administrator*
Cross, Dorothy Abigail *retired librarian*
Davis, Ruth Margaret (Mrs. Benjamin Franklin Lohr) *information technology executive*
De Barbieri, Mary Ann *nonprofit management consultant*
Diachenko, Marge *political organization administrator*
Edgell, Karin Jane *reading specialist, special education educator*
Ellison, Pamela Ion *secondary school educator, consultant*
Erion, Carol Elizabeth *music educator*
Fisher, Colleen M. *trade association administrator*
Fosdick, Cora Prifold (Cora Prifold Beebe) *management consultant*
Foutch, Karan *marketing professional*
Franklin, Jeanne F. *lawyer*
Freeman-Wilson, Karen *former attorney general, prosecutor, educational association administrator*
Galles, Kristen *lawyer*
Gaynor, Margaret Cryor *program director*
Gil, Libia Socorro *school system administrator*
Goodman, Sherri Wasserman *lawyer*
Greenstein, Ruth Louise *research institute executive, lawyer*
Hallman, Lynda *medical association administrator*
Haygood, Alma Jean *elementary school educator*
Henry, Catherine Ann *health science association administrator*
Herrera, Clarita *medical association administrator*
Higgins, Mary Celeste *lawyer, researcher*
Hughes, Grace-Flores *business exeucitve*
Jackson, Nancy Morrison *architect*
Johnson, JoAnn Mardelle *federal agency administrator*
Johnson, Marlys Marlene *elementary school educator*
Jones-Lukács, Elizabeth Lucille *physician*
Jordan, Carole Jean *political organization administrator*
Kaufman, Beverly *political organization administrator*
Kaye, Ruth Lincoln *historical researcher*
Kim, Sook Cha *artist*
Krebs, Martha *physicist, federal science agency administrator*
Lauderdale, Katherine Sue *lawyer*
Lendsey, Jacquelyn L. *foundation administrator*
Leonhart, Michele Marie *government agency administrator*
Lightner, Candace Lynne *nonprofit management consultant, advocate*
Lipnick, Anne Ruth *advocate*
Matz, Deborah *federal agency administrator*
McMiller, Anita Williams *leasing company executive*
Miller, Marian *professional society administrator*
Nodeen, Janey Price *company executive*
Paulson, Gwen O. Gampel *government relations consultant*
Rainwater, Joan Lucille Morse *investment company executive*
Rassai, Rassa *electrical engineering educator*
Reiley, Mame Carrigan *political consultant*
Richman, Arleen *professional society administrator*
Riel, Pauline *association executive*
Schofield, Regina Brown *lobbyist, political consultant*
Shoaee, Rokhsareh Sarah *marriage and family therapist, counselor*
Simonds, Marie Celeste *architect*
Smith, Ann Wheeler *exercise specialist*
Smith, Canda Banks *educational consultant*
Smith, Heidi *political organization administrator*
Stone, Ann E.W. *direct marketing company executive*
Sturtevant, Brereton *retired lawyer, former government official*
Tandy, Karen P. *government agency administrator*
Thayer, Marilyn *political organization executive, civic worker*
Thomas, Ramonia *political organization executive, civic worker*
Ticer, Patricia *state senator*
Van Cleve, Ruth Gill *retired lawyer, government official*
Wallace, Barbara Brooks *writer*
Wasko-Flood, Sandra Jean *artist, educator*
Watts, Sonja Marie *assistant principal, educational consultant*
Welburn, Brenda Lilienthal *professional society administrator*
Wells, Fay Gillis *writer, lecturer, broadcaster, aviation historian*
Whitson, Elizabeth Temple *graphics designer*
Winzer, P.J. *lawyer*
Woolley, Mary Elizabeth *research administrator*
Zook, Theresa Fuetterer *gemologist, consultant*

Amelia Court House
Hughes, Corry Hankinson *special education educator*

Annandale
Abdellah, Faye Glenn *retired public health service executive*
Baditoi, Barbara Ellen *information scientist, educator*
Bohen, Dolores Boylston *retired school system administrator*
Burchett, Brenda Jean Harnage *secondary school educator, writer*
Del Conte, L. Catherine *special education educator*
Freeman, Baba Foster *editor*
Grosso, Camille M. *nurse*
Heyer, Laura Miriam *special education educator*
Wilhelmi, Mary Charlotte *education educator, college official*

Arlington
Adreon, Beatrice Marie Rice *pharmacist*
Alexander, Myrna B. *psychologist, counselor*
Alford, Paula N. *federal agency administrator*
Askey, Thelma J. *federal agency administrator*
Austin, Rebecca Lynne *anthropologist, consultant*
Barak, Eve Ida *science administrator*
Basterrechea, Ivette *research analyst*
Bengalee Miller, Amatul-Mannan Q. Katherine *activist*
Berger, Gisela Porsch *psychotherapist*
Berry Bodoh, Emily *dancer, choreographer, educator*
Beyer, Barbara Lynn *aviation consultant*
Binkowski, Sylvia Julia *water transportation executive, consultant*
Brennan, Christine *journalist, columnist*
Buchanan, Louise *political organization worker, consultant*
Bune, Karen Louise *criminal justice official*
Carson, Mary Smith *marketing and communications consultant*
Cavanaugh, Margaret Anne *chemist*
Chipman, Susan Elizabeth *psychologist, researcher*
Choksi, Mary *investment company executive*
Cinca, Silvia (Roberta King) *writer, producer*
Clutter, Mary Elizabeth *federal official*
Cragin, Maureen Patricia *aerospace transportation executive, former federal agency administrator*
Dalglish, Lucy Ann *lawyer, organization executive*
Davis, Lynn Etheridge *political scientist, educator*
Dentzer, Susan *journalist*
Draeger, Susanne Yarbrough *interior designer*
Ericsson, Sally Claire *not-for-profit organization administrator*
Estes, Valerie *independent consultant*
Finta, Frances Mickna *secondary school educator*
Flynn, Laurie M. *social worker*
Foxwell, Elizabeth Marie *editor*
Gallagher, Anne Porter *communications executive*
Gramm, Wendy Lee *economics educator, former government official*
Haggett, Rosemary Romanowski *academic administrator*
Hamed, Martha Ellen *government administrator*
Hassett, Valerie Jane *interior designer, architect, educator*
Hastings, Melanie (Melanie Jean Wotring) *television news anchor*
Headley, Jennifer Lynn *art educator*
Heatwole, Mary Phyllis *lawyer*
Hickman, Elizabeth Podesta *retired counselor, educator*
Irizarry, Estelle Diane *foreign language educator, writer, editor*
Johnson, Rosemary Wrucke *personnel management specialist*
Koury, Agnes Lillian *real estate property manager*
Krusa-Dossin, Mary Ann *military officer*
Langley, Patricia Ann *lobbyist*
Lean, Judith *physicist, researcher*
Leinen, Margaret Sandra *oceanographic researcher*
Lieber, Carole Marguerite Renee *human resources specialist, consultant*
Long, Madeleine J. *mathematics and science educator*
Lurie, Nicole *former health science association administrator*
McCarthy, Jane McGinnis *retired consultant*
Mc Donald, Gail Faber *musician, educator*
Milkman, Beverly L. *federal agency administrator*
Myers, Elissa Matulis *publisher, association executive*
Ochoa-Brillembourg, Hilda Margarita *investment banker*
Park, Susan Young *radar systems engineer*
Pfister, Karstin Ann *human services administrator*
Queen, Sally Ann Crannell *entrepreneur*
Rabbit, Linda *construction executive*
Ramaley, Judith Aitken *former university president, endocrinologist*
Redd, Vivian Cortezza *government agency administrator*
Reiss, Susan Marie *editor, writer*
Reynolds, Rochelle Annetta *flight attendant*
Roane, Lelia Denise *music educator*
Rockefeller, Sharon Percy *broadcast executive*
Rogers, Sharon J. *education consultant*
Shannon, Jacqueline *association executive*
Siddayao, Corazón Morales *economist, educator, consultant*
Silberstang, Joyce Esther *psychologist, consultant*
Smeal, Eleanor Cutri *civil rights executive*
Stokes, Jeanett Barrett *editor*
Stout, Mary Webb *education program specialist*
Strelau, Renate *historical researcher, artist*
Swenson, Diane Kay *lawyer*
Tarr-Whelan, Linda *policy center executive*
Vaught, Wilma L. *foundation executive, retired air force officer*
Weidemann, Celia Jean *social scientist, management consultant, financial consultant*
Weiss, Susan *newspaper editor*
Wheeler, Barbara Monica *lawyer*
Whyte, Nancy Gooch *microbiologist, chemist*
Widener, Peri Ann *business development executive*
Wilcox, Shirley Jean Langdon *genealogist*
Wood, Heidi *commissioner*

Ashburn
Mitchell, Barbara Ann *marketing professional*

Assawoman
Holley, Pamela Spencer *retired librarian*

Barboursville
Slater, Valerie Periolat *volunteer*

Bedford
Wills, Sherian Atkins *editor, writer*

Berryville
Martin, Alison Cady *interior designer*

Big Island
Durham, Betty Bethea *therapist*

Blacksburg
Bliznakov, Milka Tcherneva *architect, educator*
Bosniak, Kanta *artist*
Campbell, Joan Virginia Loweke *secondary school educator, language educator*
Connerley, Mary L. *psychologist, educator*
Edwards, Patricia Klobus *former dean, architecture/urban studies educator*
Gablik, Suzi *art educator, writer*
Henrickson, Bonnie *college basketball coach*
Katz, Marya Ruth *music educator*
Lynch, Sherry Kay *counselor*
McKee, Charlotte Hickerson *music educator*
Meszaros, Peggy S. *academic administrator*
Soniat, Katherine Thompson *English educator, poet*
Sweeney, Lucy Graham *psychologist*
Trent, Tiffany Leone *English educator, writer, editor*
Weaver, Pamela Ann *hospitality research professional*
Young, Deborah Elspeth *industrial hygienist, educator*

Bluemont
Johnson, Evelyn Porterfield *journalist, educator*

Bridgewater
Bittel, Muriel Albers *managing editor*

Bristol
Brittle, Linda Vaughan *reading and behavioral science educator*
Hagy, Teresa Jane *elementary school educator*

Bristow
Insalaco-De Nigris, Anna Maria Theresa *middle school educator*
Mac Donald, Margaret Clark *retired real estate agent*
Roketenetz, Annemarie *professional society administrator*

Buena Vista
Harvey, Susan Ann *music educator, conductor, educator*

Burke
Austin, Sandra J. *small business owner*
Emery, Vicki Morris *school library media administrator*

Capeville
Spady, Joanne Smith *secondary school educator*

Catawba
Bartizal, Denise *psychologist*

Centreville
Hand, Antoinette Marie *accountant*

Chantilly
Chrzanowski, Leye Jeannette *publisher*
Gunnerson, Debra Ann *piano teacher*
Lardin, Jessica Elizabeth *vocalist*
Rogin, Ronne Ann *retired government contract specialist*
Sullivan, Penelope Dietz *computer software development company executive*

Charlottesville
Andrews, Minerva Wilson *retired lawyer*
Bishop, Ruth Ann *coloratura soprano, voice educator*
Bly-Monnen, April M. *quality assurance professional*
Chase, Karen Susan *English literature educator*
Cohen, Helen Herz *camp owner, director*
Currie, Jo Anne *art educator*
Dalton, Claudette Ellis Harloe *anesthesiologist, educator, university official*
Dove, Rita Frances *poet, English language educator*
Essig, Nancy Claire *publishing executive*
Fernbach, Louise Oftedal *physician, educator*
Foard, Susan Lee *editor*
Friedman, Susan Lynn Bell *economic development professional*
Frye, LaToya Aisha Hortense *banking administrator*
Gaskin, Felicia *biochemist, educator*
Greville, Florence Nusim *secondary school educator, mathematician*
Grohskopf, Bernice *writer*
Hanft, Ruth S. Samuels *healthcare consultant, educator, economist*
Hartz, Jill *museum director*
Hetherington, Eileen Mavis *psychologist, educator*
Horton, Madeline Mary *financial planner, consultant*
Hostler, Sharon Lee *pediatrics educator, rehabilitation center executive*
Jagger, Janine *epidemiologist*
Johnson, Cornelia *city sheriff, gift shop owner*
Kaiserlian, Penelope Jane *publishing company executive*
Kuhlmann-Wilsdorf, Doris *materials scientist, educator*
Lane, Ann Judith *history and women's studies educator*
Linden, Peppy G. *museum director*
Loo, Beverly Jane *publishing company executive*
Lupton, Mary Hosmer *retired small business owner*
MacIlwaine, Mary Jarratt *public relations executive*
McDuffie, Marcia Jensen *pediatrics educator, researcher*
Miller, Margaret Alison *education educator*
Minehart, Jean Besse *tax accountant*
Moreno, Zerka Toeman *psychodrama educator*
Norment, Rachel Gobbel *artist, educator, writer*
Ohira, Akemi *art educator*
Parshall, Karen Virginia Hunger *mathematics and science historian*
Priest, Hartwell Wyse *artist*
Schutte, Anne Jacobson *historian, educator*
Sibert, Polly Lou *conductor, music educator*
Smith, Sarah Bagwell *sculptor, artist, printmaker*
Spacks, Patricia Meyer *English educator*
Thornton, Kathryn C. *physicist, astronaut*
Verstegen, Deborah A. *finance educator*
Weinberger, Adrienne *artist, appraiser*
Worrell, Anne Everette Rowell *newspaper publisher*
Worsham, Christine Behrens *healthcare administrator*

Chesapeake
Allen, Elizabeth Maresca *marketing and telecommunications executive*
Byrum, Edith Ward *music educator*
Green, Barbara Marie *publisher, journalist, poet, writer*
Hoster-Burandt, Norma J. *musician, fundraiser*
Kringel, Deanna Lynn *music educator*
Lewter, Helen Clark *elementary education educator, retired*
Owens, Susan Elizabeth *realtor*
Pearce, Patsy Beasley *elementary education educator*
Potter, Cynthia M. *art educator, artist*
Skrip, Linda Jean *nurse*
Stillman, Margaret D. *library director*

Chester
Jilcott, Rebecca Ann *music educator*
Paden, Mary Grace Nuckols *humanities educator*

Chesterfield
Davis, Bonnie Christell *judge*
Hill, Ida Johnson *education consultant, technologist, administrator*

Christiansburg
Burkhart, Katherine West *music educator, adult education educator*

Clarksville
Worth, Lynn Harris *writer*

Clifton
Cavileer, Sharon E. *writer, public relations executive, consultant*
Hoffman, Karla Leigh *mathematician, educator*

Clifton Forge
Stump, Pamela Ferris *music educator*

Colonial Heights
Crowder, Dorothy Sholes *nursing educator*
Grizzard-Barham, Barbara Lee *artist*
Martin, Cynthia Marek *art educator*

Covesville
Williams, Patricia Anne *philosopher, writer*

Covington
Cauthron, Kathleen Downie *protective services official*
Spurlock, Evelyn Harvey *retired elementary school educator, minister*

Danville
Clark, Rebecca Leigh *sociology educator*
Fountain, Clara Garrett *archivist, librarian*

Dinwiddie
Ballard, Caroline Susan *music educator*
McCray, Doris Raines *minister*

Draper
Whitehurst, Mary Tarr *artist, poet, writer*

Dublin
Clark, Shelia Roxanne *sports association executive, legislative analyst*
Lineberry, Rebecca J. *municipal official, treasurer*

Dumfries
Gaudet, Jean Ann *retired librarian, educator*
Thrall, Eileen Fowler *real estate broker, government staff official*

Eastville
Williams, Ida Jones *consumer and home economics educator, writer*

Emporia
Butler, Tammy J. Wiley *medical, surgical, and pediatric nurse*

Ettrick
Davis, Minnie Louise *writer*

Fairfax
Bailey, Helen McShane *historian*
Bohan, Gloria *travel retail executive*
Cahill, Anne Pickford *economist, demographer*
Carr, Patricia Warren *adult education educator*
Carty, Rita Mary *dean, nurse*
Fisher, Linda Alice *physician*
Harper, Doreen C. *nursing educator*
Haskett, Dianne Louise *former mayor, lawyer, consultant*
Hicks, Jocelyn Muriel *laboratory medicine specialist*
Kitsantas, Anastasia *educational psychologist*
Knee, Ruth Irelan (Mrs. Junior K. Knee) *social worker, health care consultant*
Lavine, Thelma Zeno *philosophy educator*
Lowery, Sabra Annette *special education educator*
Miller, Emilie F. *former state senator, consultant*
Monahan, Danielle Joan *renal nutritionist*
Mulvaney, Mary Frederica *systems analyst*
Pan, Elizabeth Lim *information systems company executive*
Parrish-St. John, Florence Tucker *writer, educator, retired government official*
Powell, Karan Hinman *academic administrator*
Ryder, Michele Cain *counselor, speech therapist*
Slade-Martin, Phyllis E. *director*
Tolchin, Susan Jane *public administration educator, writer*
Tucker, Calanthia Rallings *school administrator*
Vehrs, Nancy Joyce *county official*
Welles, Judith *public affairs executive*
Woods, Jane Haycock *state legislator*

Fairfax Station
Barringer, Joan Marie *counselor, educator, artist, writer*
Crissey, Rebecca Lynn *special education educator*
St. John, Jennifer Kathleen *gifted and talented educator*

Falls Church
Bankson, Marjory Zoet *former religious association administrator*
Berg, Lillian Douglas *chemistry educator*
Byrne, Leslie Larkin *state legislator*
Calkins, Susannah Eby *retired economist*
Cianciolo-Carney, Rossana *investigative analyst*
Cole, Patricia A. *federal agency administrator*
Cooper, Jean Saralee *judge*
Dunne, Mary Maguire *federal agency administrator, lawyer*
East, Mary Ann Hildegarde *vocalist*
Elderkin, Helaine Grace *lawyer*
Elliott, Virginia F. Harrison *retired anatomist, publisher, educator, investment advisor*
Fink, Cathy DeVito *small business owner*
Finney, Kathryn Rebecca *music educator*
Honigberg, Carol Crossman *lawyer*
Inzana, Barbara Ann *professional musician, educator*
Jones, Linda R. Wolf *company executive*
Kay, Peg (Marjorie A. Kay) *information technology executive*
Kotler, Wendy Illene *art educator, social studies educator, grants coordinator*
Lambert, Vickie Ann *dean emerita, international nursing consultant*
Leighton, Frances Spatz *writer, journalist*
Mathon, Lauren R. *judge*
Miller, Mary Jeannette *office management specialist*
Padgett, Gail Blanchard *lawyer*
Stanford, Elaine P. *secondary school educator*
Swerdlow, Roberta Dyas *educational consultant*
Thomas, Lydia Waters *research and development executive*
Todd, Shirley Ann *school system administrator*
Travis, Tracy Leigh *emergency physician*
Waylonis, Jean Lynnette *elementary school educator*
Work, Jane Magruder *retired professional society administrator*

Farmville
Cormier, Patricia Picard *academic executive*
Craft, Carolyn M. *English literature educator, priest, religion educator*
Shield, Julie Marie Karst *retired art educator, artist*

Fisherville
Moore, Marianne *special education services professional, educator*

Flint Hill
Forbush, Sandra M. *artist, educator*

Floyd
Lineberry, Betty O. *hotel executive*

Fort Belvoir
Clark, Trudy H. *career officer*
Lane, Karen Gale *operations research analyst*
Smith, Margherita *writer, editor*

Franktown
Holcomb, Caramine Kellam *volunteer*
Johnson, Claudia Anderson *psychologist, Jungian analyst, educator*

Fredericksburg
Dahnk, Jean Patricia *lawyer*
Hickman, Margaret Capellini *advertising executive*
Jenks-Davies, Kathryn Ryburn *retired daycare provider and owner, civic worker*
Merrill, Judith Robin *artist*

Jones, Jeanne Pitts *pre-school administrator*
Jones-Atkins, DeBorah Kaye *state official*
Joynes, Barbara Cole *marketing executive*
Kinnier, Emily P. *artist*
Kinser, Cynthia D. *state supreme court justice*
Kirschbaum, Pamela Gale *editor, writer*
Lacy, Elizabeth Bermingham *state supreme court justice*
Langston, Nancy Sue Friedrich *dean*
Lanier, Nancy McDaniel *researcher*
Levit, Héloïse B. (Ginger Levit) *art historian, art dealer, art consultant, journalist*
Linkonis, Suzanne Newbold *probation officer, counselor*
Mallory-Parker, Suzanne *performing arts educator*
Maneker, Deanna Marie *advertising executive*
Massenburg, Johnnye Smith *speech pathology/audiology services professional, minister*
McClenahan, Mary Tyler Freeman *civic and community volunteer*
McDermid, Margaret E. *information technology executive, engineer*
McQuigg, Michele Berger *state legislator*
Melcher, Elizabeth (Elizabeth Melcher Winger) *musician*
Miller, Sherrie Lynn *artist*
Minor, Marian Thomas *elementary and secondary school educational consultant*
Morgan, Elizabeth Seydel *writer, educator, retired writer*
Parke, Carol Reeves *retired librarian*
Petera, Anne Pappas *state official*
Puller, Linda Todd *state legislator*
Ragland, Ines Colom *principal*
Rapp, Melanie L. *state legislator, primary school educator*
Reynolds, Sheri *writer*
Rhodes, Anne Gregory (Panny Rhodes) *state legislator*
Rigsby, Linda Flory *lawyer*
Rimler, Anita A. *secretary of state*
Roberts, Betty Winkler *retired health agency administrator*
Rubinstein, Phyllis M. *lawyer*
Schaar, Susan Clarke *state legislative staff member*
Schlatter, Elizabeth *museum administrator*
Schmidt, Karen Lee *marketing professional, sales executive*
Seals, Louise Crumrine *editor*
Seals, Margaret Louise *newspaper editor*
Suit, Terrie L. *state representative*
Thoma, Colleen Ann *educator*
Treadway, Sandra Gioia *library director*
Turner, Elaine S. *allergist, immunologist*
Tyler, Payne Bouknight *museum executive*
Wagner, Jody M. *treasurer*
Wheelan, Belle S. *state agency administrator*
Whipple, Mary Margaret *state legislator*
Whitfield, Patricia Ann Rainwater *education educator*
Wilder, Eunice *city official*
Williams, Karen Johnson *federal judge*
Winslett, Stoner *artistic director*
Wood, Jeanne Clarke *charitable organization executive*
Worden, Marny *artist, musician*
Young, Sharon Wisdom *retired music educator*

Roanoke

Barnes, Sharon D. *academic advisor, music educator*
Burcham, Darlene *state agency administrator*
Effel, Laura *lawyer*
Fitzgerald, Mary Eileen *museum program director*
Gaylor, Susan Roland *social worker*
Hankla, Cathy *English language educator, writer*
Johnson, Sharon Brabson *music educator*
Klein-Davis, Stephanie Ann *photojournalist*
Logan Lawson, Anna *social services administrator*
Miller, Gretchen M. *music educator*
Street, Terri Evans *counselor, consultant*
Taubman, Jenny *museum program director*
Taylor, Janet Droke *legal secretary*
Waldron, Karen *development, construction, and management company executive*
Wall-Lievsay, Bonnie Lee *human resources specialist, educator*
Zomparelli, Wendy *newspaper publisher*

Rocky Mount

Nichols, Freda Carol *elementary school educator, artist*

Ruckersville

Clark, Mizzell Phillips (Mitzi Clark) *school librarian*

Rural Retreat

Dronsick, Margery Sutton *social worker*

Rustburg

Hughes, Deborah Enoch *circuit court clerk*

Salem

Crowder, Rebecca Byrum *music educator, elementary school educator*

Sandston

Herrera, Linda R. *pharmacist*

Sedley

Briggs, Martha Wren *publishing executive, writer*

South Boston

Ferrell, Denise Moore *music educator*

South Hill

Brooks, Arlene Sheffield *secondary school educator*
Clay, Carol Ann *family nurse practitioner*

Spotsylvania

Hardy, Dorcas Ruth *business and government relations executive*
Pritchard, Tiffany Maxwell *writer, educator*

Springfield

Dake, Marcia Allene *retired nursing educator, university dean*
Dodson, Alicejean Leigh *nursing administrator*
Edwards-LeBoeuf, Renee Camille *public relations professional, logistics engineer*
Kratovil, Jane Lindley *think tank associate, developer/fundraiser*
Leavitt, Mary Janice Deimel *special education educator, civic worker*
McDonald, Joanne *business executive*
Rankin, Jacqueline Annette *communications expert, educator*
Siddons, Joy Garbee *music educator*
Watts, Helena Roselle *military analyst*
Williams, Cecilia Lee Pursel *optometrist*

Stafford

Snyder, Deborah Shusman *literature educator, columnist, poet*

Stanardsville

Anns, Arlene Eiserman *publishing company executive*

Staunton

Arnold, Ruth Southgate *librarian*
Bryant, Brenda Louise *director, educator*
Firehock, Barbara A. *interior designer*
Grewe, Marjorie Jane *retired protective services official*

Sterling

Bartow, Nicole A. *secondary school educator*
Cowen, Jean *employee benefits consultant*
Davidson-Meyer, Noreen Hanna *financial services company executive*
Jefferson, Sandra Traylor *choreographer*
Naquin, Deborah Ann *humanities educator*
Newton, Cheryl Kay *music educator*

Suffolk

Logan-Sutton, Floretta R. *elementary school educator*
McAdoo, Clarissa Eileen *city agency administrator*

Surry

Sprouse, Earlene Pentecost *special education educator*

Sweet Briar

Muhlenfeld, Elisabeth S. *college president, educator, author*

Tappahannock

McGuire, Lillian (Elizabeth) Hill *historian, researcher, retired education educator, writer*

Tazewell

Garner, June Brown *journalist*

Upperville

Powell Gebhard, Joy Lee (Bok Sin Lee) *small business owner*
Smart, Edith Merrill *civic worker*

Vienna

Artz, Cherie B. *lawyer*
Colón, Eugenia Valinda *development executive*
Damon, Shirley Stockton *art gallery owner*
Gardenier, Turkan Kumbaraci *statistical company executive, researcher*
Higginbotham, Wendy Jacobson *political adviser, writer*
Kinsolving, Sylvia Crockett *musician, educator*
Lorfano, Pauline Davis *artist*
Miller, Christine Marie *marketing executive, public relations executive*
Milton, Carol Lynne *artist*
Peltz, Paulette Beatrice *corporate lawyer*
Price, Ilene Rosenberg *lawyer*
Slowik, Sharon A. *real estate agent*
Tordiff, Hazel Midgley *education director*
Townsend, Irene Fogleman *accountant, tax specialist*
Vachher, Sheila Ann *information systems consultant*
Yamaguchi, Yuriko Fujita *artist*

Virginia Beach

Baker, Claudia Muller *reading specialist*
Cehelska, Olga M. *music educator, flight instructor*
Clark, Suzanne Underwood *writer*
DiCarlo, Susanne Helen *financial analyst*
Duke, Elizabeth (Betsy) A. *bank executive*
Gibbs, Jordan Smith *music educator, artist*
Guckert, Nora Jane Gaskill *medical and surgical nurse, hospice nurse, holistic consultant*
Hughes, Lesley Lynne *assistant principal*
Jacobson, Frances M. *history educator*
Jones, Felicia M. *director*
Kawczynski, Diane Marie *elementary and middle school educator, composer*
Keenan, Barbara Milano *judge*
Kiernan, Margaret M. *adult education educator*
Lawson, Beth Ann Reid *strategic planner*
Oberndorf, Meyera E. *mayor*
Powell, Michele Hall *music educator*
Reece-Porter, Sharon Ann *international human rights educator*
Simmons, Marsha Thrift *science and reading educator, musician*
Sims, Martha J. *library director*
Stanton, Pamela Freeman *interior designer, writer*
Suggs Wallace, Vanessa *marketing professional, writer*
Tuskey, Laura Jeanne *music educator, pharmacologist*
Von Mosch, Wanda Gail *middle school educator*

Watkins, Brenda L. *music educator*
Weck, Mary Katherine *special education educator*

Warrenton

Greene, Cynthia Bain *elementary school educator*
Gullace, Marlene Frances *information engineer, systems analyst, consultant*

Washington

Lamma, Candace McDaniel *guidance counselor, primary school educator, elementary school educator*

Waynesboro

Ross, Ellen Hardman *graphic designer*
Spilman, Patricia *artist, educator*

White Stone

Duer, Ellen Ann Dagon *anesthesiologist, general practitioner*

Williamsburg

Bell, Christine Marie *secondary educator*
Cappetta, Pamela Guyler *counselor*
Chandler, Kimberley Lynn *educational administrator*
Christison, Muriel Branham *retired art museum director, fine arts educator*
Coffman, Orene Burton *hotel executive*
Drum, Joan Marie McFarland *federal agency administrator, educator*
Durrant, Rita Delores *poet, educator*
Kellogg, Ann Marie *retired publishing executive, consultant*
McLennan, Barbara Nancy *international tax specialist*
Myatt, Sue Henshaw *nursing home administrator*
Nettels, Elsa *English language educator*
Pierce, Catherine Maynard *history educator*
Spaeth, Barbette Stanley *classics educator*
Stanley, Shirley Davis *artist*
Van Tassel-Baska, Joyce Lenore *education educator*
Voorhess, Mary Louise *pediatric endocrinologist*
Windsor, Joan Ruth *author, professional counselor*

Winchester

Branescu-Hurt, Ana *music educator*
Russell, Melinda Farrar *music educator*
Tisinger, Catherine Anne *history and economics educator*

Woodbridge

Denison, Cynthia Lee *accountant, tax specialist*
Englert, Helen Wiggs *writer*
Flori, Anna Marie DiBlasi *health facility administrator, nurse anesthetist, educational administrator*
Lee, Barbara Mahoney *career officer, educator*
McMahon, Janet Mankiewich *critical care nurse*
Peck, Dianne Kawecki *architect*
Phillips-LeSane, Fay M. *mental health professional*
Thornton-Artson, Linda Elizabeth *psychiatric nurse*
Williams, Cynthia Ann *small business owner, pediatrics nurse*

Woodstock

Maggiolo, Paulette Blanche *writer*

Yorktown

Douthat, Rebecca Arlene *secondary school educator*

WASHINGTON

Aberdeen

Hill, Christine Marie *voice educator, music educator*
Wilhelms, Patricia Sue *choral director*

Arlington

Bullington, Gayle Rogers *writer, researcher*

Auburn

Blum, Sarah Leah *nurse psychotherapist*

Bainbridge Island

Berg, Darla Gaye *service representative*
Burns, Shirley M. *artist, educator*
Stewart, Kay Boone *writer, retired educator and administrator*

Bellevue

Chi, Hannah T. *poet, writer*
Dodge, Kirstin Sue *lawyer*
Douglas, Diane Miriam *museum director*
Dykstra, Gail Sullivan *information scientist, consultant*
Hackett, Carol Ann Hedden *physician*
Nowik, Dorothy Adam *medical equipment company executive*
O'Keefe, Kathleen Mary *state government official*
Phillips, Zaiga Alksnis *pediatrician*
Skillman, Judith Anne *humanities educator*
Sygeel, Crystal Renee *minister, consultant*
Tee, Virginia *lawyer*
Wallace, Mary Colette *architectural researcher, designer*

Bellingham

Clark-Langager, Sarah Ann *curator, director, university official*
Graves, Vicki Lloyd *retired mechanical engineer*
Haensly, Patricia Anastacia *psychology educator*
Jack, Dana Crowley *psychologist, educator*
James, Helen Ann *plastic surgeon*
Meals, Pamela F. *publishing executive*
Morse, Karen Williams *academic administrator*
Murdock, Mary-Elizabeth *history educator*
Ross, June Rosa Pitt *biologist, educator*

Whyte, Nancy Marie *performing arts educator*

Benton City

Kromminga, An-Marie *special education educator*

Black Diamond

Walker, Minerva E. Gilara *retail executive, poet*

Bothell

Hawthorne, Nan Louise *Internet resources consultant, web site designer, writer*
Jacobus, Elizabeth Loomis *volunteer*

Bremerton

Hower, Jeanne Louise *landscape designer*

Burien

McKamey, Frances Helene *music educator*

Camano Island

Hartley, Celia Love *nursing consultant, writer, retired nursing educator, nursing administrator*

Camas

Liem, Annie *pediatrician*

Carnation

Beshur, Jacqueline E. *special education educator*

Chehalis

Dennis, Linda Susan *nonprofit organization executive*
McQueen, Deva Revell *minister*
Neal-Parker, Shirley Anita *obstetrician, gynecologist*

Chelan

Korn, Theresa Marie *former electrical engineer, consulting firm co-owner, technical writer*

Cheney

Feeney, Kendall Greer *art director, music educator*
Kondas, Patricia Ann *film studies educator*

Clarkston

Smith, Phyllis Mae *healthcare consultant, educator*

Coulee City

George, Kristi Kay *music educator*

Coupeville

Canfield, Stella Stojanka *artist, art gallery owner, educator*

East Wenatchee

Kissler, Cynthia Eloise *geologist, consultant*
Marion, Sarah Kathleen *music educator*

Edmonds

Bell, Nancy Lee Hoyt *real estate investor, middle school educator, volunteer*
Deering, Anne-Lise *artist, retired real estate salesperson*
Johnson, d'Elaine Ann Herard *artist, consultant*
Polikowsky, Mary Elizabeth *retired English educator*
Terry, Melinda Lee *elementary school educator*

Ellensburg

McIntyre, Jerilyn Sue *university administrator*
Rosell, Sharon Lynn *physics and chemistry educator, researcher*
Thomas, Spring Ursula *not-for-profit developer, educator, photographer*

Elma

Houle, LouAnn *minister*

Everett

Boschok, Jackie *labor union administrator*
Brynildsen-Smith, Kristine Ann *principal*
Nelson, Carol Kobuke *bank executive*
Olsen-Estie, Jeanne Lindell *golf course owner*
Ostergaard, Joni Hammersla *lawyer*
Rimbach, Evangeline Lois *retired music educator*
Van Ry, Ginger Lee *school psychologist*
Vaughn, Kathy *municipal official*

Federal Way

Muzyka-McGuire, Amy *marketing professional, nutrition consultant*
Rossi, Ruth Harris *special education educator*

Gig Harbor

Wissmann, Carol Reneé *sales executive*

Hansville

Blalock, Ann Bonar *evaluation researcher*

Hoodsport

Gray, Jennifer Francine *photographer, illustrator*

Hoquiam

Lamb, Isabelle Smith *manufacturing executive*

Issaquah

Cain, Coleen W. *writer, educator*
Duncan, Elizabeth Charlotte *retired marriage and family therapist, educational therapist, educator*
Frederick, Paula F. *health facility administrator*

Kenmore

Montague, Deborah Marie *elementary school educator, music educator, consultant*

Kennewick

Fann, Margaret Ann *counselor*
Sullivan-Schwebke, Karen Jane *lawyer*

Kent

Dumitrescu, Cristina M. *intensive care nurse*

GEOGRAPHICAL INDEX 1627 WASHINGTON

McGuire, Robin Christine *special education educator*
Mong, Michelle Denise *marriage and family therapist*
Personette, Louise Metzger (Sister Mary Roger Metzger) *mathematics educator*

Kettle Falls
Pancoast, Brandy Elizabeth *music educator*

Kirkland
Barto, Deborah Ann *physician*
Szablya, Helen Mary *writer, language professional, lecturer*
Witte, Peggy *metal products executive*

Lacey
Evans, Mari *art educator*
Miller, Linda Jean *music educator, writer*

Langley
Cammermeyer, Margarethe *retired medical/surgical nurse*

Lilliwaup
McGrady, Corinne Young *design company executive*

Longbranch
Ehrhardt, Margaret Wright *retired librarian*

Lynnwood
Floten, Barbara Jean *educational dean*

Marysville
Bartholomew, Shirley Kathleen *municipal official*
Wolfkill-Hoff, Ramona Lea *music educator*

Medina
Ward, Marilyn Beeman *commissioner*

Mercer Island
Carey, Susan M. *psychologist*
Kessler, Gale Suzanne *psychologist, educator*
Langhout-Nix, Nelleke *artist*

Monroe
Kirwan, Katharyn Grace (Mrs. Gerald Bourke Kirwan Jr.) *retail executive*

Moses Lake
Aur, Marina V. *choir conductor, music educator*
Sanderson, Holladay Worth *priest*

Mountlake Terrace
Cannon, Christine Anne *veterinarian*
Johnson, LuAn *disaster management consultant*
Townsend, Wendy *marketing executive*

Mukilteo
Black, Jackie John *artist*

Naches
Assink, Nellie Grace *agricultural executive*

Newcastle
Rosa-Bray, Marilyn *physician*

Nordland
Denniston, Martha Kent *small business owner, writer*
Kepner, Rita Marie *sculptor, writer, editor, educator*

Oak Harbor
Lightbourne, Alesa M. *writer*

Ocean Park
Lee, Martha *artist, writer*

Olympia
Anderson, Vicki Susan *legislative staff member, travel consultant*
Bergeson, Teresa *school system administrator*
Bridge, Bobbe J. *state supreme court justice*
Brown, Lisa J. *state legislator, educator*
Costa, Jeralita *state legislator*
Eide, Tracey J. *state legislator*
Fairhurst, Mary E. *judge*
Fairley, Darlene *state legislator*
Fisher, Nancy Louise *pediatrician, medical geneticist, former nurse*
Fleskes, Carol Lynn *environmental engineer*
Franklin, Rosa G. *state legislator, retired nurse*
Fraser, Karen *state legislator*
Gardner, Georgia Anne *state legislator*
Gregoire, Christine O. *state attorney general*
Hale, Patricia S. *state legislator*
Haugen, Mary Margaret *state legislator*
Howell, Helen *state agency administrator*
Hutchins, Diane Elizabeth Rider *librarian*
Ireland, Faith *state supreme court justice*
Kells, Kari Joy *indexer, librarian*
Kessler, Lynn Elizabeth *state legislator*
Long, Jeanine Hundley *retired state legislator*
Long, Marsha Tadano *state official*
Macduff, Ilone Margaret *music educator*
Madsen, Barbara A *state supreme court justice*
McAuliffe, Rosemary *state legislator*
Myers, Sharon Diane *auditor*
Mylroie, Willa Wilcox *transportation engineer, regional planner*
Owens, Susan *state supreme court justice*
Parlette, Linda Evans *state senator*
Patterson, Julia *state legislator*
Prentice, Margarita *state legislator, nurse*
Randlett, Mary Willis *photographer*
Rasmussen, Marilyn *state legislator*
Regala, Debbie *state senator*
Roach, Pam *state legislator*
Russman, Irene Karen *artist*
Senn, Deborah *insurance commissioner*
Sheldon, Betti L. *state legislator*
Showalter, Marilyn Grace *state agency administrator*
Spanel, Harriet *state legislator*
Sparrow, Ruth S. *lawyer*
Stevens, Val *state legislator*
Thibaudeau, Patricia *state legislator*
Thomas-John, Yvonne Maree *artist, interior designer*
Tremblay, Gail Elizabeth *art educator*
Walker, Yvonne Denise *research analyst*
Winsley, Shirley J. *state legislator, insurance agent*
Zussy, Nancy Louise *librarian*

Outlook
Mears, Catherine Louise *principal*

Port Angeles
Kinney, Beverly Jean *English language educator*
McCormick, Karen Louise *savings and loan association executive*
Muller, Carolyn Bue *physical therapist, volunteer*

Port Orchard
Huber, Virginia Rollo *photojournalist, educator, artist*

Port Townsend
Buhler, Jill Lorie *editor, writer*
Harrington, LaMar *retired curator*
Wallin, Madge Marie *retired librarian, musician*

Poulsbo
Pack, Nancy J. *special education educator, speech therapist*

Pullman
Kelley, Margaret Mary *music educator, musician*
McSweeney, Frances Kaye *psychology educator*
Mills, Paulette Everett *human development educator, consultant*
Petura, Barbara Bradley *academic administrator*
Sprunger, Leslie Karen *physiologist, educator*
Stammerjohan, Elizabeth Claire Allison *finance educator*
Thomashow, Linda Suzanne *microbiologist*

Puyallup
Phillips, Gail Susan *elementary school educator*

Rainier
Curtis, Suzanne M. *school system administrator, educator*

Redmond
Ambrose, Adele D. *communications executive*
Andrew, Jane Hayes *non-profit organization executive*
Black, Deborah [illegible]
Brummel, Lisa *information technology executive*
Butler, Jannette Sue *human resources professional*
Doman, Margaret Horn *government policy and process consultant, civic official*
Elliot, Gerri *information technology executive*
Hebert, Kathleen *information technology executive*
Martinez, Maria *computer software company executive*
Marvin, D. Jane *consumer products company executive*
Mathews, Mich *computer company executive*
Moore, Lori *information technology executive*
Oaks, Lucy Moberley *retired social worker*
Stonesifer, Patricia Q. *information systems executive*

Renton
Stanley, Carol Lynn *psychologist*

Republic
Sale, Dorothy O. *psychotherapist*

Richland
Ristow, Gail Ross *art educator, paralegal, children's rights advocate*
Sinerius-Rupp-Bloor, Sharon Kay *sculptor*

Seatac
Green, Suzanne Lundy *music educator*

Seattle
Anang, Amma Cecilia *dance company administrator*
Armstrong, Mary M. *insurance company executive*
Barnard, Kathryn Elaine *nursing educator, researcher*
Barnes, Susan Lewis *lawyer*
Beaumonte, Phyllis Ilene *retired secondary school educator*
Berkowitz, Bobbie *medical educator*
Berman, Gizel *sculptor*
Bird, Sue *professional basketball player*
Blase, Nancy Gross *librarian*
Blomdahl, Sonja *artist*
Boersma, P. Dee *marine biologist, educator*
Boggs, Paula Elaine *lawyer*
Boxx, Karen Elizabeth *lawyer, educator*
Brown, Janiece Alfreida *pilot*
Brownstein, Barbara Lavin *geneticist, educator, university official*
Burrows, Elizabeth MacDonald *religious organization executive, educator*
Butler, Octavia Estelle *free-lance writer*
Card, Deborah Frances *orchestra administrator*
Cardenas, Diana Delia *physician, educator*
Chapman, Fay L. *lawyer*
Char, Patricia Helen *lawyer*
Condrea, Lydia *linguist, educator, researcher*
Cottingham, Mary Patricia *vocational rehabilitation counselor*
Cottle, Gail Ann *retail executive*
Covey, Joy D. *finance and administration executive*
Covington, Germaine Ward *municipal agency administrator*
Dally, Lynn *choreographer, performing company executive, educator*
Dannenhold, Kathleen E. *writer, director*
Davison, Audrey M. *lawyer, consultant*
Dawson, Patricia Lucille *surgeon*
de Chesnay, Mary *nursing educator*
Deming, Jody Wheeler *oceanography educator*
de Tornyay, Rheba *nursing educator, retired dean*
Dillard, Marilyn Dianne *property manager*
Dimmick, Carolyn Reaber *federal judge*
Disteche, Christine M. *geneticist*
Dresher, Olivia Whitaker *publishing executive, writer*
Duckworth, Tara Ann *insurance company executive*
Dunn, Lin *professional basketball coach*
Ellis, Janice Rider *nursing educator, consultant*
El-Moslimany, Ann Paxton *paleoecologist, educator, writer*
Farr, Sheila G. *critic, poet*
Fetterly, Mary E. *counseling administrator*
Fidel, Raya *library science educator*
Fletcher, Betty Binns *federal judge*
Fluke, Lyla Schram (Mrs. John M. Fluke Sr.) *publisher*
Garvens, Ellen Jo *art educator, educator, artist*
Gayle, Helene D. *public health physician*
Georgulas, Susan Beth *sales and marketing executive*
Gerstenberger, Donna Lorine *humanities educator*
Gibbs, Nancy Patricia *lawyer*
Giblett, Eloise Rosalie *hematologist, educator*
Ginorio, Angela Beatriz *university research administrator, educator*
Glover, Karen E. *lawyer*
Godden, Jean W. *columnist*
Gonzalez, Carmen Gracia *law educator*
Gowdey, Dorothy E. *artist*
Greggs, Elizabeth May Bushnell (Mrs. Raymond John Greggs) *retired librarian*
Gustafson, Alice Fairleigh *lawyer*
Gwinn, Mary Ann *newspaper reporter*
Hannaford, Janet Kirtley *software administrative manager*
Hazelton, Penny Ann *law librarian, educator*
Hegyvary, Sue Thomas *nursing school dean, editor, nursing educator*
Henderson, Maureen McGrath *medical educator*
Hendrickson, Anita Elizabeth *biology educator*
Herring, Susan Weller *dental educator, oral anatomist*
Hills, Regina J. *journalist*
Humphries, Edna Bevan *music educator, choir director*
Isaki, Lucy Power Slyngstad *lawyer*
Jackson, Lauren *professional basketball player*
[illegible] *librarian*
Jessen, Joel Anne *not-for-profit executive, art educator*
Johnson, Mildred Grace Mash *investment company executive*
Kalonji, Gretchen *engineering educator*
Kaplan, Sydney Janet *English educator*
Karl, Helen Weist *pediatric anesthesia and pain management educator, researcher*
Kelley, Lucille Marie Kindely *dean, psychosocial nurse*
Kelly, Carolyn Sue *newspaper executive*
Kelsey, Norma L. *labor union administrator*
Kennedy, Mary Virginia *diplomat*
King, Mary-Claire *geneticist, educator*
Knox, Venerria L. *city official*
Kolbeson, Marilyn Hopf *holistic practitioner, educator, artist, poet, advertising executive, poet*
Kraft, Elaine Joy *community relations and communications official*
Kraus, Naomi *retired biochemistry educator*
Kunkel, Georgie Bright *freelance writer, retired school counselor*
Law, Marcia Elizabeth *aide*
Lawless, Janine A. *lawyer*
Levi, Margaret *humanities educator*
Lightner, Janet (Jan) Anderson *information technology manager, consultant, writer*
Lindsey, Gina Marie *airport executive*
Mahdaviani, Miriam *choreographer, educator*
Mastroianni, Anna Catherine *law educator*
Matesky, Nancy Lee *music educator*
McConney, Mary E. *information technology executive*
McDunn, Adrienne *human behavior consultant*
McFarland, Lynne Vernice *pharmaceutical executive*
McHugh, Heather *poet*
Melendez, Rosa Maria *protective services official*
Mini, Anne Alexandra Apostolides *writer, educator*
Monsen, Elaine Ranker *nutritionist, educator, editor*
Moudon, Anne Vernez *urban design educator*
Murdock, Tullisse Antoinette (Toni Murdock) *academic administrator*
Nash, Cynthia Jeanne *journalist*
Nellermoe, Leslie Carol *lawyer*
Nelson, Arleen Bruce *social worker*
Niemi, Janice *retired lawyer, retired state legislator*
Nuxoll, Carla *federal official*
Oakley, Carolyn Le *state legislator, small business owner*
Olmstead, Marjorie Ann *physics educator*
Oppenheimer, Deanna Watson *bank executive*
Ostrom, Katherine Elma *retired educator*
Ott, Sharon *artistic director*
Overstreet, Karen A. *federal bankruptcy judge*
Ozaki, Nancy Junko *performance artist, performing arts educator*
Pagon, Roberta Anderson *pediatrics educator*
Parker, H. Stewart *biotechnology company executive*
Parks, Patricia Jean *lawyer*
Pascal, Naomi Brenner *editor-at-large, publishing executive*
Pearl, Nancy Linn *librarian*
Perthou, Alison Chandler *interior designer*
Peterson, Jane White *nursing educator, anthropologist*
Pflaumer, Katrina C. *lawyer*
Pizzorno, Lara Elise *medical writer, editor*
Rainbow, Dee Dee *retired art educator, sculptor*
Reis, Jean Stevenson *administrative secretary*
Riddiford, Lynn Moorhead *zoologist, educator*
Russell, Francia *ballet director, educator*
Sandahl, Bonnie Beardsley *health services executive and provider, educator*
Sandstrom, Alice Wilhelmina *accountant*
Schwartz, Pepper Judith *sociologist, educator*
Sellick, Kathleen A. *hospital administrator*
Sherland, Barbara C. *lawyer*
Shirley, Donna *former aerospace engineer, management consultant, speaker*
Snow-Smith, Joanne Inloes *art history educator*
So, Connie Ching *ethnic studies educator*
Somerman, Martha J. *academic administrator*
Stanford, Janet Lee *physician, epidemiologist*
Steele, Cynthia *literary critic, translator, educator*
Sterkovsky, Julia Ellen *activist, organizer*
Strombom, Cathy Jean *transportation planner, consultant*
Stroup, Elizabeth Faye *librarian*
Su, Judy Ya Hwa Lin *pharmacologist*
Szkody, Paula *astronomy educator, researcher*
Thomas, Karen P. *composer, conductor*
Thomassen, Pauline Frances *medical and surgical nurse*
Tift, Mary Louise *artist*
Trenkler, Tina Louise *nuclear engineer*
Van Schoiack Edstrom, Leihua Cathleen *psychologist, researcher*
Vestal, Josephine Burnet *lawyer*
Voegtlin-Anderson, Mary Margaret *secondary school educator, music educator*
von Bargen, Sally *stock image photography company executive*
Wagner, Patricia Hamm *lawyer*
Wechsler, Mary Heyrman *lawyer*
Whitson, Barbara Lee *psychologist, consultant*
Wick, Laurie Clare *director, consultant*
Wight, Julia Helen *secondary school educator*
Williams, Jeanette K. *association executive*
Williams, Joan Elaine *podiatric surgeon, educator*
Wilson, Pamela *microbiologist, educator*
Woo, Cathy M. *artist*
Woods, Nancy Fugate *dean, women's health nurse, educator*
Wright, Rachel *curator*
Young, Elizabeth *minister*
Young, Nora Jane *actuary, consultant*
Yue, Agnes Kau-Wah *otolaryngologist*

Sedro-Woolley
Weaver, Diane [illegible]

Selah
Ring, Lucile Wiley *lawyer*

Sequim
Guilmet, Glenda Jean *artist*
McGee, Jane Marie *retired elementary school educator*
Robinson, June P. *columnist, retired special education educator*

Shoreline
Geer, Jerri Diane *retired career officer, photographer*

Silverdale
Balcomb, Mary Nelson *design studio owner*
Shaw, Annita Louise *art educator*

Snohomish
Guzak, Karen Jean Wahlstrom *artist*
Hill, Valerie Charlotte *nurse*
Sahlstrom, Jill Louise *elementary school educator*

Spanaway
Parker, Lynda Christine Rylander *secondary school educator*
Roberts-Dempsey, Patricia E. *secondary school educator*

Spokane
Babcock, M. Sandra *administrative assistant, writer*
Bender, Betty Wion *librarian*
Chadwick, Laurie L. *secondary school educator*
Chamberlain, Barbara Kaye *small business owner, communications executive*
Clarke, Judy *lawyer*
Coker, Charlotte Noel *political activist*
Colford, Ann M. *freelance/self-employed writer*
Cooke, Becky Jill Berg *principal*
Cope, Kathleen Adelaide *critical care nurse, parish nurse, educator*
Danke, Virginia *educational administrator, travel consultant*
Gilpatrick, Janet *public affairs and public relations consultant*
Gilpin-Gordon, Mary Ann *retired educational association administrator*
Girvin, Lila Shaw *artist*
Greenwood, Collette P. *municipal official, finance officer*
Halvorson, Marjory *opera director*
Hendershot, Carol Miller *physical therapist*
Hirsch, Anne *dean*
Horton, Susan Pittman *bank executive*
Imbrogno, Cynthia *magistrate judge*
Koch, Lisa Michelle *psychologist*
Lee, Sun Myung *physician*
Metcalf, Ginger (Virginia) Arvan *psychotherapist, consultant*
Mobley, Karen Ruth *art gallery director*
Nemetz Mills, Patricia Louise *engineer, educator*
Powers, Theresa Mack *medical/surgical nurse, psychotherapist*
Steele, Karen Dorn *journalist*
Thompson, Patricia A. *lawyer*
Williams, Patricia C. *federal judge*

Sultan
Duffy, Anne M. *artist*

Sumner
Wickizer, Cindy Louise *retired elementary school educator*

Tacoma
Bartlett, Norma Thyra *retired administrative assistant*
Bertoia, Rénate *special education educator*
Brenner, Elizabeth (Betsy Brenner) *publishing executive*
Burns, Robin C(arol) *mathematics theoretician, accountant*
Callan, Josi Irene *museum director*
Crisman, Mary Frances Borden *librarian*
Crotto, Denice *elementary school educator*
Dahl, Barbara Jean *psychologist*
Don, Audrey *clinical psychologist, neuropsychologist*
Harris, Marian S. *social work educator*
Hinkley, Nancy Emily Engstrom *foundation administrator, educator*
Pribble, Elizabeth J. *retired airline administrator*
Reigstad, Ruth Elaine *lay worker, retired physical therapy consultant*
Wanwig, Annette Clare *nursing administrator*
West, Carolyn Marie *psychologist, educator, writer*

Toledo
Welch, Kathryn Anne *music educator*

Toppenish
Ross, Kathleen Anne *academic administrator*

University Place
Pliskow, Vita Sari *anesthesiologist*

Vancouver
Grant, Nancy Marie *marketing professional, journalist*
Griffith, Linda Marie (Lynne) *county government official*
Ingalls, Sudi-Suzanne L. *artist*
Lollar, Katherine Louise *tour director, social worker, therapist*
Lusky, JoAnn *psychotherapist, coach*
Ogden, Valeria Munson *management consultant, state representative*
Smith, Linda A. *retired congresswoman*
Tuttle, Marcia *retired elementary school educator, music educator*

Vashon
Henderson, Sally Kathleen *advertising, communications and marketing executive*

Veradale
Cadwallader, Gwen Natalie *elementary school educator, music educator*

Wenatchee
Davies, Lois A. *educational association administrator, adult education educator*
Rappé, Teri Wahl *piano educator*

Woodway
Kent, Aimee Bernice Petersen *small business owner, interior designer, landscape architect, artist*

Yakima
Newland, Ruth Laura *small business owner*
Savage, Carla Lee *insurance agent*
Spracher, Nancy A. *psychotherapist*
Ullas, Yvonne Lee *primary school educator*
Walker, Lorene *retired elementary school educator*

WEST VIRGINIA

Beaver
White, Barbara Ann *physical science technician*

Beckley
Lee, Carol *artist, songwriter*
Wills, Connie Sue *special education educator*

Belington
McCartney, Rose Marie *minister*

Bluefield
Brown, Sheri Lynn *artist, poet, educator*
Davenport, Dorothy Dean *retired medical/surgical nurse*
Loundmon-Clay, Juanita L. *academic administrator, educator, dean*

Bridgeport
Bennett, C. Lynn *educational consultant*
Jones, Mary Lou *real estate broker, real estate company executive*

Charles Town
Bauer, Irene Susan *elementary school educator*

Charleston
Arrington, Carolyn Ruth *education consultant*
Betts, Rebecca A. *lawyer*
Bias, Sharon G. *state commissioner*
Boley, Donna Jean *state legislator*
Chilton, Elizabeth Easley Early *newspaper executive*
Davis, Robin Jean *state supreme court justice*
Hallanan, Elizabeth Virginia *federal judge*
King, Rebecca Jane *nursing educator*
Lane, Charlotte *lawyer*
Leasor, Jane *religion and philosophy educator, musician*
Mellert, Lucie Anne *writer, photographer*
Meschke, Debra JoAnn *polymer chemist*
Minear, Sarah M. *state legislator*
Offutt, Rebecca Sue *business and sales executive*
Palumbo, Louise Corey *fashion and special events administrator*
Redd, Marie E. *state legislator, criminal justice educator*
Richardson, Sally Keadle *health care administrator*
Smith, Stuart Lewis *volunteer*
Stanley, Mary Elizabeth *judge*
Walker, Martha Yeager *state senator, businesswoman*

Clarksburg
Forinash, Carolyn Cosner *medical/surgical nurse*
Keeley, Irene Patricia Murphy *federal judge*

Dunbar
Eliason, Pamela Parker *minister, social worker*
Given, Melissa Ann *elementary school educator, educational consultant*

Elkins
Marshall, Elizabeth *performing company executive*
Mullens, Susan Lynn *psychologist, educator*
Murphy, Patricia Ann *physician, otolaryngologist*
Payne, Gloria Marquette *business educator*
Seaman, Judith D. *retired adult education educator*
Super, Deborah H. *secondary school educator*

Fairmont
DeVito, Teresa Marie *artist*
Dudley-Eshbach, Janet *university president*
Ford, Alma Regina *union official, educator*
Skidmore, Dorothy L. *music educator*
Swiger, Elizabeth Davis *chemist, educator*
York, Linda Kay *real estate appraiser, real estate company executive*

Falling Waters
Braithwaite, Marilyn Jean *realtor*

Fayetteville
Seay-Bell, Margaretta *pastoral counselor*

Forest Hill
Martin-Weikle, Mary Jane *medical/surgical nurse*

Frankford
Mazzio-Moore, Joan L. *retired radiology educator, physician*

Gallipolis Ferry
Brown, Nancy Jane *human resources specialist*

Glenville
Grogg, Ann Marie *director*

Great Cacapon
Coe, Diana Ward (Dina Coe) *language educator, writer*

Harpers Ferry
Cooley, Hilary Elizabeth *county official*

Huntington
Campbell, Nausha Coury *speech pathology/audiology services professional, educator*
Dean-Toler, Bethany Francine *psychologist*
Engle, Jeannette Cranfill *medical technologist*
Fannin, Josephine Jewell *social services administrator*
Howerton, Cheryl Alley *secondary school educator*
Pratt, Mary Louise *librarian, writer*
Smith, Sherri Lee *law educator*
Welch, Lynne Brodie *nursing school dean*
Whitley, Angela Jane *social worker*
Wiebe, Kimberly P. *music educator*

Inwood
Cloyd, Helen Mary *accountant, educator*

Kearneysville
Lotze, Evie Daniel *psychodramatist*

Keyser
Falkowski, Theresa Gae *chemistry educator*

Kingwood
Moyers, Sylvia Dean *retired medical librarian*

Lewisburg
Kennedy, Leila *accounting educator*

Lost Creek
Smith, Babs G. *music educator*

Mannington
Reese, Katherine Rose *music educator*

Martinsburg
Brooks, Hillary Afton *social worker*
Cogle, Monica R. *social worker*
Hoak, Carolyn Clarke *physician assistant*

Morgantown
Allamong, Betty D. *academic administrator*
Barba, Roberta Ashburn *retired social worker, writer*
Beattie, Diana Scott *biochemistry educator*
Beresford, Annette Diana *researcher*
Blaydes, Sophia Boyatzies *English language educator*
Drvar, Margaret Adams *vocational education educator*
Jackson, Ruth Moore *academic administrator*
Kinsey, Donna Lee *music educator*
Peterson, Sophia *international studies educator*
Saeler, Penelope *music educator*
Sikora, Rosanna Dawn *emergency physician, educator*
Wilson, Mary Alice *violinist, music teacher*

New Cumberland
Ford, Irene Elaine *pastor*
Schwab, Denise Margaret *speech pathology/audiology services professional*

New Martinsville
Francis, Elizabeth Romine *secondary school educator, theater director*

Ona
Smalley, Rhonda E. *music educator*

Parkersburg
Brum, Brenda *state legislator, librarian*
Bush, Roberta B. *psychotherapist, accountant*
Gunter, Norma *artistic director*
Thorp, Carol Lyn *elementary school music educator*

Princeton
Moody, Frances Marie *former performing arts educator, musician*

Ranson
Rudacille, Sharon Victoria *medical technologist*

Ravenswood
Woods, Abbi Johnson *music educator*

Ronceverte
Hooper, Anne Dodge *pathologist, educator*

Saint Albans
Alderson, Gloria Frances Dale *rehabilitation specialist*
Ennis, Jill Ann *medical/surgical nurse, educator*

Saint Marys
Moffett, Patricia Lou *music educator*

Salem
Raad, Virginia *pianist, lecturer*

Shepherdstown
Elliott, Jean Ann *librarian emeritus*
Shurbutt, Sylvia Bailey *English language educator*
Wilson, Rebecca Ann *retired English and special education educator*

Shinnston
Spears, Jae *state legislator*

South Charleston
Boyles, Elizabeth Kelley *psychologist, educator*
Herzog, Valerie Wirth *computer company executive*
Stedman, Molly Renee *special education educator, researcher*

Wayne
Davis, Paula May *music educator*

Webster Springs
Moore, Alma Merle *association executive*

Wellsburg
Viderman, Linda Jean *paralegal, corporate executive*

West Columbia
Fowler, Sandra Lynn *poet*

Weston
Hamric, Carolyn Marie *legal assistant, small business owner*
Riddle, Anna Lee *retired elementary school educator, retired music educator*

Wheeling
Heceta, Estherbelle Aguilar *anesthesiologist*
Hogan, Susan Cox *association executive*
Phillis, Marilyn Hughey *artist*
Thurston, Bonnie Bowman *religious educator, minister, poet*

Williamsburg
Scott, Pamela Moyers *physician assistant*

WISCONSIN

Antigo
Beck-Hafner, Janene M. *assistant principal*

Appleton
Amm, Sophia Jadwiga *artist, educator*
Drescher, Kathleen Ebben *lawyer*
Hasselbacher, Darlene M. *human resources executive*
Hinkens, Kay L. *social services association executive*
Meyer, Cheryl Lorraine *music educator*
Rice, Ferill Jeane *writer, civic worker*
Richards, Susan Lynne *library director*

Balsam Lake
Mattson, Carol Linnette *social services administrator*

Baraboo
Baymiller, Lynda Doern *social worker*
Umhoefer, Aural M. *retired dean, educational consultant*

Barron
Anderson, Ruth Ilene Monier *music educator*
Johnson, Eleanor Mae *education educator*

Bassett
Filipiak, Debra Ann *speech pathology/audiology services professional*

Belgium
Pohl, Catherine M. *principal, educator*

Beloit
Lowry, Cheryl Ann *music educator, church musician*
Story, Kendra *wholesale distribution executive*

Black River Falls
Reichenbach, Laura Jean *art educator*

Brookfield
Cifaldi, Rosalie *private investigator*
Pottebaum, Sharon Mitchell *health educator*
Rooney, Carol Bruns *dietician*

Burlington
Oestmann, Mary Jane *retired senior radiation specialist*

Cascade
Baumann, Carol Edler *retired political science educator*

Casco
Bartel, Teresa J. *art educator*

Chaseburg
Jackson, Gloria Leigh *genealogist, retired archivist*

Chippewa Falls
Schmider, Mary Ellen Heian *American studies educator, academic administrator*

Colfax
Ralph, LeAnn Rae *writer, editor*

Crivitz
Gerhart, Lorraine Pfeiffer *reading specialist, educator*

De Pere
Hoell, Victoria Ann *special education educator*
Molnar, Kathleen Kay *management information systems educator*

Delafield
Zupan, Mary Anne *music educator, consultant*

Delavan
Lepke, Charma Davies *musician, educator*

Drummond
Lintula, Margaret M. *elementary and secondary school educator*

Eau Claire
Biegel, Eileen Mae *retired hospital executive*
Clark, Judy *newscaster*
Cohen, Maryjo R. *manufacturing executive*
Dusk, Brooke *meteorologist*
Hugo, Miriam Jeanne *counseling psychologist, educator*
Kreibich, Robin G. *state legislator*
Lippold, Judith Rosenthal *retired occupational therapist*
Rupnor, Jennifer *journalist*
Tiefel, Virginia May *librarian*
Tubbs, Virginia Carol *music director*
Tuckner, Michelle *newscaster*

Edgerton
Douglas, Susan *data processing specialist, consultant*

Elkhart Lake
Zieve, Charlotte R. *research scientist*

Elkhorn
Reinke, Doris Marie *retired elementary school educator*

Fennimore
Croft, Candace Ann *psychology educator, academic administrator*

Fish Creek
Zvara, Christine C. *middle school education educator*

Fond Du Lac
Eby, Patricia Lynn *music educator*
Towne, Kristine Marie *title company executive*
Upadhyay, Wendy Schutt *psychotherapist*

Fort Atkinson
Lorman, Barbara K. *former state senator*

Franklin
Roark, Barbara Ann *librarian*

Gillett
Brown, Kathryn Ann *music educator*
Nichols, Diane Colleen *municipal official*

Gordon
La Liberte, Ann Gillis *graphic artist, consultant, designer, educator*

Grafton
Duback, Sally Wood *artist, educator*
Schneider, Carol Ann *staffing services company executive*

Green Bay
Capelle, Elaine M. *financial planner*
Erickson, Ruth Alice *poet, artist*
Handrich, Heidi Leah *speech pathology/audiology services professional*
Hardy, Deborah Lewis *dean, educator, dental hygienist*
Kelso, Carol *state legislator*
McIntosh, Elaine Virginia *nutrition educator*

Greendale
Kaiser, Ann Christine *magazine editor*
Kuhn, Roseann *sports association administrator*
Pohl, Kathleen Sharon *editor*

Greenfield
Jirovec, Mary Ann *music educator*
McKillip, Patricia Claire *operatic soloist*

Hales Corners
Case, Karen Ann *lawyer*

Hancock
Vroman, Barbara Fitz *writer, educator*

Hartland
Schabow, Nancy A. Dexter *music educator*
Stamsta, Jean F. *artist*

Holcombe
Randall, Rhonda Michaele *music educator*

Ixonia
Peebles, Allene Kay *manufactured housing company executive*
Reul, Betty A. *construction executive*

Janesville
Detert-Moriarty, Judith Anne *graphic designer, educator, volunteer*
Roth, Sarah Eve *occupational safety professional*
Thomas, Margaret Ann *educational administrator, art educator*

Johnson Creek
Quest, Kristina Kay *art educator, small business owner*

Kaukauna
Brewster, Margaret Emelia *artist*

Kenosha
Amborn, Pauline Gall *music educator*
Armstrong, Leona May Bottrell *retired counselor, educator*
Helman, Iris Barca *elementary school educator, consultant*
Kolb, Vera M. *chemist, educator*
Rothstein, Marian *humanities educator*
Teegarden, Nicolee *art educator*

Kiel
Bauer, Cheryl Kristine *music educator*

Kimberly
Kading, Laura J *special education educator*

Kohler
[illegible]
Kohler, Laura E. *human resources executive*

La Crosse
Anderson, Gwyn C. *computer company executive, computer consultant*
Hatfield, Mary Lou *flight nurse, paramedic*
Hitch, Elizabeth *academic administrator*
Oswalt, Sally Hundt *small business owner*
Thomas-Williams, Pamela Rae *publishing executive, writer*

Lake Mills
Lazaris, Pamela Adriane *community planning and development consultant*

Laona
Sturzl, Alice A. *school library administrator*

Madison
Ashley, Renee *writer, creative writing educator, consultant*
Baldwin, Janice Murphy *lawyer*
Banfield, Jillian *mineralogist, geomicrobiologist, educator*
Barnick, Helen *retired judicial clerk*
Bartell, Angela Gina Baldi *judge*
Bauman, Susan Joan Mayer *mayor, lawyer*
Berceau, Terese L. *state representative*
Beyer-Mears, Annette *physiologist*
Bishop, Carolyn Benkert *public relations counselor*
Blankenburg, Julie J. *librarian*
Bochert, Linda H. *lawyer*
Braden, Betty Jane *legal association administrator*
Bradley, Ann Walsh *state supreme court justice*
Brandt, Deborah *English educator*
Brennan, Patricia Flatley *nursing educator, systems engineer, educator*
Burmaster, Elizabeth *school system administrator*
Burns, Elizabeth Murphy *media executive*
Charo, Robin Alta *law educator*
Ciplijauskaite, Birute *humanities educator*
Coppersmith, Susan Nan *physicist*
Crabb, Barbara Brandriff *federal judge*
Cronin, Patti Adrienne Wright *state agency administrator*
Darling, Alberta Statkus *state legislator, marketing executive, former art museum executive*
Deer, Ada E. *former federal agency official, social worker, educator*
Dott, Nancy Robertson *geologist*
Dubrow, Heather *English educator*
Dunwoody, Sharon Lee *journalism and communications educator*
Engelman, Marjorie Jeckel *retired higher education administrator*
Fasse, Jane Ellen *art educator*
Faulkner, Julia Ellen *opera singer*
Foley Mullaney, Ellen Madaline *journalist*
Fowler, Barbara Hughes *classics educator*
Gavin, Mary Jane *medical and surgical nurse*
Gronemus, Barbara *state legislator*
Hanson, Doris J. *state legislator*
Heim, Marcy Lynn Schultz *foundation executive*
Honold, Linda Kaye *political organization executive, human resources development executive*
Huelsman, Joanne B. *state legislator*
Hundertmark, Jean L. *state representative*
Hutchison, Jane Campbell *art history educator, researcher*
Jeskewitz, Suzanne E. *state representative*
Johnson, Jean Elaine *nursing educator*
Johnson, Maryl Rae *cardiologist*
Kerkman, Samantha *state representative*
Kiessling, Laura Lee *chemist, researcher*
Kim, Kyung-Sun *library and information scientist, educator*
Kimble, Judith E. *molecular biologist, cell biologist*
Korenic, Lynette Marie *librarian*
Krawczyk, Judy *state representative*
Krug, Shirley *state legislator*
Krusick, Margaret Ann *state legislator*
Lassa, Julie M. *state representative*
Lautenschlager, Peggy A. *state attorney general*
Lawton, Barbara *lieutenant governor*
Leavitt, Judith Walzer *history of medicine educator*
Leckie, Carol Mavis *retired state government administrator*
Littlefield, Vivian Moore *nursing educator, administrator*
Lyall, Katharine C(ulbert) *academic administrator, economist, educator*
Marlett, Judith Ann *nutritional sciences educator, researcher*
Marrett, Cora B. *science educator*
McCallum, Laurie Riach *lawyer, state government*
McCormick, Terri *state legislator*
Melli, Marygold Shire *law educator*
Murray, Julia Killin *art history educator*
Nischke, Ann M. *state legislator*
Owens, Carol *state legislator*
Panzer, Mary E. *state legislator*
Parrino, Cheryl Lynn *federal agency administrator*
Piper, Odessa *chef*
Plache, Kimberly Marie *state legislator*
Pope-Roberts, Sondy *state legislator*
Rhoades, Kitty *state legislator*
Rice, Joy Katharine *psychologist, educational policy studies and women's studies educator*
Riley, Jocelyn Carol *writer, television producer*
Roberson, Linda *lawyer*
Robson, Judith Biros *state legislator*
Roessler, Carol Ann *state legislator*
Rosenzweig, Peggy A. *state legislator*
Rosser, Annetta Hamilton *composer*
Rowe, Marieli Dorothy *media literacy education consultant, organization executive*
Schmidt, Martha Bubeck *social sciences educator*
Seratti, Lorraine M. *state legislator*
Shilling, Jennifer *state official*
Sims, Terre Lynn *insurance company executive*
Sinicki, Christine *state official*
Skochelak, Susan E. *college dean*
Sobkowicz, Hanna Maria *neurology researcher*
Spring, Terri *political organization executive*
Sproule, Deborah W. *art educator, artist*
Steele, Ramona Grace Jesse *physical therapist*
Steingass, Susan R. *lawyer*
Stepp, Cathy *state senator*
Stites, Susan Kay *writer, human resources consultant*
Strier, Karen Barbara *anthropologist, educator*
Sykes, Diane S. *state supreme court justice*
Thompson, Barbara Storck *state official*
Toth, Susan Irene *surgeon, educator*
Towns, Debi *state legislator*
Tullis, Tricia M. *marketing professional*
Vruwink, Amy Sue *state legislator*
Vukmir, Leah *state legislator*
Weber, Becky *state legislator*
Whitney, Lori Ann *legislative staff member*
Williams, Annette Polly *state legislator*
Williams, Mary *state legislator*
Wilson, Pamela Aird *physician*
Wolfe, Barbara L. *economics educator, researcher*
Young, Rebecca Mary Conrad *retired state legislator*
Zedler, Joy Buswell *ecological sciences educator*
Zell, Josephine May *retired language educator*

Manitowoc
Gaus, Lynn Shebesta *school administrator*
Hickok, Sister Alice Marie *special education educator*

Marathon
Natzke, Paulette Ann *manufacturing executive*

Marinette
Malmstadt, Mary Jane *music educator*

Marshfield
Schafer, Lorraine *psychologist, researcher*

Menasha
Streeter, Stephanie Anne *printing company executive*

Menomonee Falls
Blanc, Caryn *retail executive*
Dynek, Sigrid *corporate lawyer, retail executive*
Janzen, Norine Madelyn Quinlan *medical technologist*
Meier, Arlene *retail executive*

Menomonie
Clausing, Alice *state legislator*
Cutnaw, Mary-Frances *retired communications educator, writer, editor, publisher*
Furst-Bowe, Julie *academic administrator*
Lueder, Dianne Carol *library director*

Mequon
Beaudry, Diane Fay Puta *medical quality management executive*
Denton, Peggy *occupational therapy educator, researcher*
Dohmen, Mary Holgate *retired primary school educator*
Mandel, Trudy Ann *medical/surgical nurse, theology studies educator*
Tucholke, Christel-Anthony *artist, educator*

Merrill
Bierman, Jane *wood products company executive*
McCauley, Diane Lynn *secondary school educator, music educator*

Middleton
Conaway, Jane Ellen *elementary school educator*
Jacobs, Eleanor R. *retired volunteer*
Rowland, Pleasant *publisher, toy company executive*
Semmes, Sally Peterson *choreographer, educator, performer*
Taylor, Fannie Turnbull *social education and arts administration educator*

Milton
Parker, Letitia *secondary school educator*

Milwaukee
Alexander, Jennifer Lynn *marketing professional*
Babcock, Janice Beatrice *healthcare coordinator*
Baez, JoAnne Marie *school psychologist*
Ballman, Patricia Kling *lawyer*
Blumberg, Sherry Helene *Jewish education educator*
Carter, Charlene Ann *psychologist*
Carter, Valerie *food products executive*
Curtain, Helena Hambuch *foreign language specialist*
Dale, Kathleen A. *literature educator*
Daniels-Carter, Valerie *food franchise executive*
Davis, Susan F. *human resources specialist*
Dawson, Kim *reporter*
Delgado, Mary Louise *elementary school educator, secondary school educator, consultant, Internet company executive*
Dobbs, Yvette Marie *director*
Eaton Adams, Elizabeth Susan *retired middle school educator, jazz musician*
Eirich, Michelle A. *editor, writer*
Elliot, Tammy *newscaster*
Esterly, Nancy Burton *physician*
Felbab, Amanda Jane *marketing professional, consultant*
Ferguson, Nancy L. *psychotherapist, social worker*
Gallop, Jane (Jane Anne Gallop) *women's studies educator, writer*
Garcia, Astrid J. *newspaper executive*
Geske, Janine Patricia *law educator, former state supreme court justice*
Gondek, Mary Jane (Mary Jane Suchorski) *property manager*
Grider, Barbara Jean *real estate broker, consultant*
Hammer, (Beth) Mary Elizabeth *adult nurse practitioner*
Harris, Christine *dance company executive*
Hatton, Janie R. Hill *principal*
Hegerty, Nannette H. *police chief*
Heim, Kathryn Marie *psychiatric nurse, author*
Hidson, Patricia Diane *artist, educator*
Hipp, Kristine Kiefer *adult education educator*
Hudson, Katherine Mary *manufacturing executive*
Huf, Carol Elinor *tax service company executive*
Huff, Marsha Elkins *lawyer*
Hunt, Courtney Lanel *foundation administrator*
Huston, Kathleen Marie *library administrator*
Jallings, Jessica *reporter, newscaster*
Johannes, Kay L. *insurance company executive*
Kessler, Joan F. *lawyer*
Kleefisch, Rebecca *reporter*
Kraut, Joanne Lenora *computer programmer, analyst*
Kupst, Mary Jo *psychologist, researcher*
Kwak, Eun-Joo *concert pianist, music educator*
Lange, Marilyn *social worker*
Lea, Filomena *English language educator, writer*
Lenz, Debra Lynn *financial analyst*
Loehr, Stephanie Schmahl *social worker*
Maker, Azmaira Hamid *psychologist, educator*
McGarity, Margaret Dee *federal judge*
McMahon, Christine Caroline *sales professional, trainer, consultant*
Meyer, Jenne L. *marketing professional*
Murphy, Judith Chisholm *trust company executive*
Mykleby, Kathy *newscaster, reporter*
Nielson, Kristy Ann *psychology educator, researcher*
Niskala Apps, Jennifer A. *pediatric neuropsychologist, researcher, educator*
Paul, Mary *automotive executive*
Peltz, Cissie Jean *art gallery director, cartoonist*
Pitts, Gertrude Louise *minister*
Potter, Rosemary *state legislator*
Preston, Patricia Ann *language educator, researcher*
Read, Sister Joel *academic administrator*
Rheams, Annie Elizabeth *education educator*
Rhoten, Juliana Theresa *retired principal*
Rivera-Velazquez, Maria Jesus *marketing professional*
Romer, Denise Patrice *lawyer*
Schaub, Theresa Marie *early childhood educator*
Schneider, Mary Lea *college administrator*
Schumann, Gail L. *plant pathologist, educator*
Selig-Prieb, Wendy *sports team executive*
Severson, Sally *meteorologist*
Shapiro, Robyn Sue *lawyer, educator*
Smith, Lois Ann *real estate executive*
Stafford, Lori *reporter*
Stokes, Kathleen Sarah *dermatologist, educator*
Taylor, Katherine *social service administrator*
Wake, Madeline Musante *academic administrator, nursing educator*
Waldbaum, Jane Cohn *art history educator*
Walsh, Kathleen *lawyer*
Weiner, Wendy L. *elementary school educator, writer*
White-Winters, Jill Mary *nursing educator*
Zwicke, Dianne Lynn *internist, cardiologist, educator*

Mondovi
Alexander, Michelle Lynn *music educator*

Monroe
Bean, Virginia Ann (Ginny Bean) *marketing executive*
Bennett, Judy A. *music educator*

Neenah
Brehm-Gruber, Therese Frances *minister, consulting psychologist*
Rieder, Mary Catherine (Ahern) *language educator*

Nekoosa
Ramirez, Mary Catherine *retired secondary school educator*

New Berlin
Belich, Kay S. *music educator*
Czarnezki, Mary Elaine *media specialist*
Marsh, Clare Teitgen *retired school psychologist*
Winkler, Dolores Eugenia *retired health facility administrator*

New London
Fitzgerald, Laurine Elisabeth *university dean, educator*

Oconomowoc
Conrader, Constance Ruth *artist, writer, librarian*
Driscoll, Virgilyn Mae (Schaetzel) *retired art educator, artist, consultant*
Handrich, Wendy Elizabeth *education educator, consultant*
Muehlmeier, Ruth Ewart *painter, sculptor, art historian*

Oconto
Dorner, Darlene A. *music educator*
Watson-Boone, Rebecca A. *library and information studies researcher, educator*

Oregon
Glodowski, Shelley Jean *administrator, writer, musician*

Oshkosh
Alderson, Jo Bartels *writer, poet*
Buser, Rose M. *elementary school educator*
Cooper, Janelle Lunette *neurologist, educator*
Klusman, Judith Anderson *state legislator*
Ristow, Thelma Frances *elementary school educator*
Smith, Merilyn Roberta *art educator*

Patch Grove
Wadding, Tonia J. *multi-media specialist*

Pelican Lake
Martin, Mary Wolf *newspaper editor*

Pewaukee
Farrow, Margaret Ann *former state official*

Pittsville
Normington, Norma Shotwell *secretary*

Port Washington
Provis, Dorothy L(ouise) *retired artist, sculptor*

Racine
Baker, Joyce Mildred *medical/surgical nurse, volunteer*
Constantine, Margaret L(ouise) (Peggy Constantine) *newspaper reporter, freelance writer*
Gannaway, Carolyn Marie *elementary school educator*
Hoelzel, Sally Ann *lawyer*
Jensen, Sande Kelsey *technologist, church administrator*
Johnson-Leipold, Helen P. *outdoor recreation company executive*
Ladwig, Bonnie L. *state legislator*
McPheron, JoAnn Marie *music educator, poet*
Miller, Yolanda *publisher, writer*
Rubico-Jamir, Sonia Mendoza *sensory/food scientist, consumer researcher*
Rupinski, Janette Marie *banker*
Schoening, Ruth Irene *retired music educator, musician*
Wright, Betty Ren *children's book writer*
Zimmel, Tammy Lynn *psychologist*

Redgranite
Borchardt, Betsy Olk *artist*

Reedsburg
Olson, Jeanne M. *real estate broker*

Reedsville
Glaza, Mary Margaret *primary school educator*

Rhinelander
Bennett, Demara B. *psychologist*
Hansen, Paula J. *academic administrator*
Pekol, Marilyn Patricia *music educator, musician*

Rice Lake
Hubler, Mary *state legislator*

Ripon
Prissel, Barbara Ann *paralegal, law educator*

River Falls
Harsdorf, Sheila Eloise *state legislator, farmer*

Saint Croix Falls
Lane, Kathleen Margaret *refrigeration company official*

Sauk City
Lins, Debra *bank executive*

Saukville
Gulan, Bonnie Marion *writer, researcher*

Schofield
Plein, Kathryn Anne *retired secondary school educator*

Sheboygan
Linse, Marion Marilyn *art educator*
Meisenbech, Annette Marie *elementary school educator*
Mueller, Jeanne Karen *music educator*

Shorewood
Bowers, Jane Meredith *music educator*

Sobieski
Richards, Rhonda Sue *accountant*

Sparta
Hagen, Joanne R. *elementary school educator*

Stevens Point
Doherty, Patricia Anne *psychologist*
Holter, Patra Jo *artist, art education consultant*
Isaacson, Marjorie Jean *retired elementary school educator*

Sturgeon Bay
Ebbeson, Karen Ann *retired social worker*
Korb, Joan *lawyer*
Maher, Virginia Jones *art historian, educator*
Skadden, Nancy Lee Mackey *information technology manager*

Sturtevant
Brandes, Jo Anne *lawyer*

Sun Prairie
Deaner, Nancy Marcy *religious studies educator, religious organization administrator*

Superior
Robek, Mary Frances *business education educator*
Vance, Mary *academic administrator*

Tomah
Johnson, Linda Arlene *transportation executive*

Two Rivers
Beth, Joyce Elizabeth *elementary school educator*

Verona
White, Carolyn Louise *music educator*

Warrens
Potter, June Anita *small business owner*

Washburn
Krutsch, Phyllis *academic administrator*

Waterford
Rindo, Linda Sue *music educator*

Watertown
Burns, Noëlle Ann *art educator*
Ruesink, Linda Joan *music educator*

Waukesha
Backhaus, Patricia Dawn *musician, educator*
Bellovary, Cathy *aging services administrator, volunteer*
Floeter, Valerie Ann *music educator*
Gustafson, Mardel Emma *secondary school educator, writer*
Leatherberry, Anne Knox Clark *architect*
Leekley, Marie Valpoon *secondary school educator*
Tegge, Patricia Ann *administrative assistant*
Wehmeier, Sarah E. *secondary school educator, director, music educator*

Waunakee
King, Judith Marie *librarian, educator*

Wausau
Builer, Dorothy Marion *business owner*
Gruling, Kay Ann *family physician*
Prey, Yvonne Mary *real estate broker*

West Allis
Bautz, Jennifer Jean *music educator*
Koch, Suzanne M. *interior designer*
Ramazzini, Judith Williams *curator*

West Bend
Dries, Kathleen Marie *social worker*
Melinski, Margaret *realtor*
VanBrunt-Kramer, Karen *business administration educator*
Wysocky, Karen Ann *music educator*

Weyauwega
Hanneman, Elaine Esther *salesperson*

Whitefish Bay
Stillman, Sharon J. *real estate broker*

Whitehall
Nordhagen, Hallie Huerth *nursing home administrator*

Whitewater
Gauger, Michele Roberta *photographer, studio administrator, corporate executive*

WYOMING

Buffalo
Fehir, Kim Michele *oncologist, hematologist*
Madden, Cheryl Beth *state legislator*
Smelser, Ruth Malone *volunteer*

Casper
Boyer, Patricia Ann *social worker, educator*
Constantino, Becky *political organization administrator*
Elliott, Marian Kay *real estate manager*
Stoval, Linda *political party official*
True, Jean Durland *entrepreneur, oil industry executive, gas industry executive*

Cheyenne
Berger, Rosie M. *state representative*
Boughton, Lesley D. *library director*
Carlson, Kathleen Bussart *law librarian*
Catchpole, Judy *state official*
Dale, Marcia Lyn *nursing educator*
Devin, Irene K. *state legislator, nurse*
Friess, Lynn *state agency administrator*
Fritz, Mary Ann *elementary school educator*
Gentile, Liz *state representative*
Green, Laurie *state agency administrator*
Harvey, Elaine *state representative*
Johnson, Lorna *state representative*
Kite, Marilyn S. *state supreme court justice, lawyer*
Kunz, April Brimmer *state legislator, lawyer*
Law, Carlene *state agency administrator*
Lummis, Cynthia Marie *state official, lawyer*
McDowell, Sherrie Lorraine *secondary school educator*
Miller, Monica Jeanne *educational association administrator*
Mockler, Esther Jayne *state senator*
Moore, Mary French (Muffy Moore) *potter, advocate*
Moser, Diane *state agency administrator*
Parrish, Denise Kay *regulatory accountant*
Robertson, Susan Joyce Coe *special education educator*
Robinson, Ann *state representative*
Rodekohr, Diane E. *state official*
Sessions, Kathryn L. *state legislator, educator*
Simons, Lynn Osborn *educational consultant*
Thomson, Thyra Godfrey *former state official*
Warren, Jane *state representative*
Woodhouse, Gay Vanderpoel *former state attorney general, lawyer*
Zumo, Billie Thomas *biologist*

Cody
Coe, Margaret Louise Shaw *community service volunteer*
Grimes, Daphne Buchanan *priest, artist*
Kraft, Janice Kay *accounting educator*
Shreve, Peg *retired state legislator, retired elementary school educator*

Dubois
Glasser, Pamela Jean *musician, music educator*

Edgerton
Malson, Verna Lee *special education educator*

Ethete
Tepper, Marcy Elizabeth *drug education director*

Evanston
Connelly, Diane *elementary educator*

Gillette
Reardon, Cindy Lu *gifted and talented educator*
Wise, Kitty *writer, composer*

Green River
Albers, Dolores M. *secondary school educator*
Evans, Eileen *music teacher*

Guernsey
Zimmerer, Nancy Jean *elementary school educator, rancher*

Jackson
Decker, Carol Arne *magazine publishing consultant*
Ferguson, Jean Kennan *psychotherapist*
Law, Clarene Alta *small business owner, state legislator*

Lander
Bakke, Luanne Kaye *music educator*
Nunley, Cynthia Ann *special education educator*

Laramie
Darnall, Roberta Morrow *association executive*
Franks, Beverly Matthews *psychotherapist, consultant*
Fulton, Jo Ann *lawyer*
Hansen, Matilda Joyner *former state legislator*
Hardy, Deborah Welles *history educator*
Kinney, Lisa Frances *lawyer*
McBride, Judith *elementary school educator*
Renaud, Paula Marie *researcher*
Schmitt, Diana Mae *elementary school educator*
Sorini, Susan Santina *chemist*
Spiegelberg, Emma Jo *business education educator, academic administrator*

Lovell
Dickson, Linnea E. *music educator*

Newcastle
Engle, Kathleen Faye *elementary education educator*

Powell
Bruscino, Leah *state agency administrator*
Dean, Patricea Louise *lawyer, law educator, small business owner*

Riverton
Girard, Nettabell *lawyer*

Rock Springs
Arambel, Phyllis Ann *elementary school educator*
Jackman Dabb, Holly Pieper *publisher*
Job, Rae Lynn *state legislator*
Thompson, Josie *nurse*

Sheridan
Aguirre-Batty, Mercedes *Spanish and English language and literature educator*
Moore, Pamela Sue *music educator*
Pilch, Margaret L. *grant consultant*
Robertson, Lisa Rae *music educator*
Tonak, Loretta Jean *music educator, librarian*

Thermopolis
Gear, Kathleen O'Neal *archaeologist, writer*

Torrington
Olenyik, Debra Ann *minister*

Worland
Staab, Margaret E. *social services administrator*
Bartol, Katherine Aurelia *music educator, mezzo soprano*
Clifford, Cheryl Kuchta *Christian education administrator*
Edwards, Sarah R. *state representative*
Ethridge, Sally Annette *music educator*
Rice, Ashley Lynn *writer, illustrator*
Wajda, Shirley Teresa *historian*

TERRITORIES OF THE UNITED STATES

AMERICAN SAMOA

Pago Pago
Fung-Chen-Pen, Emma Talauna Solaita *librarian, program director*

GUAM

Barrigada
Cruz, Teofila Perez *nursing administrator*

Hagatna
Maraman, Katherine Ann *judge*
Tydingco-Gatewood, Frances Marie *judge*

Mangilao
Duenas, Laurent Flores *health and nursing consultant*

Tamuning
Cahinhinan, Nelia Agbada *retired public health nurse, administrator*

NORTHERN MARIANA ISLANDS

Saipan
Inos, Rita Hocog *school system administrator*
Kaufer, Connie Tenorio *retired reading specialist*

PUERTO RICO

Aguadilla
Cuebas Irizarry, Ana E. *director*
Jaramillo, Juana Segarra *chancellor*

Bayamon
Rosa, Helen *dean*

Carolina
Reyes-Hernández, Migdalia *counselor*

Guaynabo
de Cacho, Graciela Eleta *marketing executive*
Lambert, Christina *telecommunications executive*

Hato Rey
Cerezo, Carmen Consuelo *federal judge*

Mayaguez
Rodriguez, Grisell *librarian, educator*

San German
Mojica, Agnes *academic administrator*

San Juan
Andujar, Norma Burgos *former state official*
Burgos, Norma *former secretary of state*
Calderón, Sila M. *governor*
Casiano, Kimberly *publishing executive*
Delgado-Colon, Aida M. *federal judge*
de Taboas, Hilda Rivera *occupational health nurse*
Guzman, Maritza *director*
Lambert, Cristina *telecommunications executive*
Lugo, Sonia I. *pharmacist, educator*
Luna Padilla, Nitza Enid *photography educator*
Merly, Miriam Naveira *state supreme court justice*
Rivera-Urrutia, Beatriz Dalila *psychology and rehabilitation counseling educator*
Rodriguez, Annabelle *state attorney general*
Rosso de Irizarry, Carmen (Tutty Rosso de Irizarry) *finance executive*
San Miguel, Lolita *artistic director*
Velez Silva, Xenia *Puerto Rican government official*

VIRGIN ISLANDS

Charlotte Amalie
Garfield, Winifred L. *nursing administrator*
Stapleton, Marylyn Alecia *diplomat*

Christiansted
Welcome, Patricia *lawyer*

Cruz Bay
Blitz, Peggy Sanderfur *corporate travel management company official*

Kingshill
Male, Cynthia Lee *elementary school educator, artist*

St Thomas
Berry, Lorraine L. *state senator*
Creque, Linda Ann *non-profit educational and research executive, former education commissioner*
Michael, Noreen *commissioner, educator*
Ragster, LaVerne E. *academic administrator*

MILITARY ADDRESSES OF THE UNITED STATES

AA

Apo
Watt, Linda E. *ambassador*

AE

APO
Morella, Constance Albanese *ambassador, former congresswoman*
Ohman, Diana J. *government agency administrator, former state official*
Schoonover, Brenda B. *ambassador*
Simpson, Sandra Kay *logistics management specialist*

Apo
Corwin, Elizabeth A. *foreign service officer*

AP
Corrigan, Paula Ann *career officer, internist*

CANADA

ALBERTA

Calgary
Hlavay, Sarah Inez *fundraising executive*
Southern, Nancy C. *utilities executive*

Calmar
Tomaszeski, Josephine Gallas *retired nursing educator*

Edmonton
Fraser, Catherine Anne *Canadian chief justice*
Hughes, Linda J. *newspaper publisher*

BRITISH COLUMBIA

Burnaby
Kimura, Doreen *psychology educator, researcher*
Switlo, Janice Georgina Alice E. *barrister, solicitor, mediator, legal and business consultant, strategist*

Powell River
Carsten, Arlene Desmet *financial executive*

Prince George
Kerr, Nancy Karolyn *pastor, mental health services professional*

Richmond
Smith, Deborah K. *human resources executive*

Salt Spring Island
Raginsky, Nina *artist*

Sidney
Bigelow, Margaret Elizabeth Barr (M.E. Barr) *mycology educator*
Saddlemyer, Ann (Eleanor Saddlemyer) *humanities educator, critic, theater historian*

Vancouver
Baird, Patricia Ann *physician, educator*
Bonifacho, Bratsa *artist*
Chiavario, Nancy Anne *business and community relations executive*
Jones, Norah *vocalist, musician*
Krall, Diana *musician*
Lavigne, Avril *musician*
Levy, Julia *immunology educator, researcher*
Marchak, Maureen Patricia *anthropology and sociology educator*
McGeer, Edith Graef *neurological science educator*
Murray, Anne *singer*
Piternick, Anne Brearley *librarian, educator*
Salcudean, Martha Eva *mechanical engineer, educator*
Yaffe, Barbara Marlene *journalist*

West Vancouver
Rae, Barbara Joyce *former employee placement company executive*

NEW BRUNSWICK

Saint John
Mowatt, E. Ann *women's voluntary leader, lawyer*

NEWFOUNDLAND

Torbay
Dabinett, Diana Frances *visual artist*

NEW ZEALAND

Wellington
Paquin, Anna *actress*

NICARAGUA

Managua
Moore, Barbara C. *ambassador*

PAKISTAN

Islamabad
Powell, Nancy J. *ambassador*

REPUBLIC OF KOREA

Seoul
Park, Kathleen Jeongsoo *portfolio manager, risk management consultant*

RUSSIA

Moscow
Collins, Mary *health science association administrator, retired legislator*

RWANDA

Kigali
McMillion, Margaret Kim *foreign service officer*

SPAIN

Barcelona
Haley, Kathleen M. *communications executive*

Canary Islands
Wells, Melissa Foelsch *foreign service officer*

SWEDEN

Stockholm
Johnson, Antonia Axson *corporate executive*

SWITZERLAND

Bern
Carlson, Dale Bick *writer*

Geneva
Deily, Linnet Frazier *ambassador*
Maglacas, A. Mangay *nursing researcher, educator*

Küsnacht
Jones Dame, Gwyneth *soprano*

SYRIA

Damascus
Scobey, Margaret *ambassador*

THAILAND

Bangkok
Kruck, Donna Jean *special education educator, consultant*

TURKMENISTAN

Ashgabat
Jacobson, Tracey Ann *ambassador*

Niamey
Mathieu, Gail Dennise *ambassador*

WEST INDIES

Grand Cayman Island
Ronald, Pauline Carol *retired art educator*

ADDRESS UNPUBLISHED

Abbe, Elfriede Martha *sculptor, graphic artist*
Abbey, Linda Rowe *artist, educator*
Abbott, Linda Joy *stained glass artisan, educator, photographer*
Abbott, Rebecca Phillips *museum director, art consultant, photographer*
Abbott, Regina A. *neurodiagnostic technologist, consultant, business owner*
Abeles, Kim Victoria *artist*
Abell, Anna Ellen *primary school educator*
Abell, Sara Nightingale *music educator, musician*
Abernathy, Vicki Marie *retired nurse*
Abernethy, Sharron Gray *language educator*
Abey, Kathy Michele *district representative, congressional caseworker*
Abood, Denise Maroon *finance company executive*
Abrahamson, Shirley Schlanger *state supreme court chief justice*
Abrams, Stephanie Bass *performing company executive*
Absher, Donna Atkins *textile designer*
Acevedo-Rhodes, Eileen *psychologist, educator*
Adamitis, Tina Theresa *art educator, artist*
Adams, Carolyn Lee *poet, artist*
Adams, Christine Beate Lieber *psychiatrist, educator*
Adams, Frances Grant, II, *lawyer*
Adams, Susan Lois *music educator*
Adamson, Jane Nan *retired elementary school educator*
Adamson, Lynda G. *literature educator, writer*
Adams-Passey, Suellen S. *retired elementary school educator*
Adato, Perry Miller *documentary producer, director, writer*
Adcroft, Patrice Gabriella *former editor*
Addicott, Beverly Jeanne *retired elementary school educator*
Adekson, Mary Olufunmilayo *therapist, counselor, educator*
Adiletta, Debra Jean Olson *business analyst consultant*
Adkins, Kathy Forester *music educator*
Adkins Campbell, Angela Dawn *speech-language pathologist*
Adler, Posy (Roslyn Adler) *artist, educator*
Adolph, Kathryn Ann *passenger service employee*
Adsit, Robin Viva *artist, educator*
Aehlert, Barbara June *health services executive*
Aftel, Mandy *perfumer*
Agard, Nancey Patricia *nursing administrator, consultant*
Aghdashloo, Shohreh *actress*
Agonito, Rosemary *publishing company executive*
Agrait, Nilsa Ivette *speech language pathologist*
Ahearn, Holly Ande *music educator*
Ai, Amy Lee *medical educator*
Aiello, Kimberly Jean *surgical technologist*
Aiken, Ann L. *federal judge*
Aikens, Martha Brunette *national park service administrator*
Aitchison, Anne Catherine *retired environmental activist*
Aitchison, Bridget Mary *theater educator, theater director*
Akin, Ann Foster *special education educator*
Alaimo, Terry M. *financial consultant*
Alarcon, Sylvia M. *music educator*
Albagli, Louise Martha *psychologist*
Albers, Sheryl Kay *state legislator*
Albreski, Melody Louise *emergency nurse practitioner*
Albright, Madeleine Korbel *former secretary of state*
Alday, Marta Perdomo *library technology consultant, media consultant, art dealer*
Alderman, Shirley M. *insurance agent*
Aldredge, Theoni Vachliotis *costume designer*
Aldrich, Patricia Anne Richardson *retired magazine editor*
Alexakos, Frances Marie *counselor, business owner, psychology educator, researcher, producer, editor*
Alexander, Barbara Toll *financial consultant*
Alexander, Icie M. *communications executive*
Alexander, Marjorie Anne *artist, art consultant*
Alexander, Nancy A. *information technology manager, consultant*
Alexander, S. Allan *magistrate judge*
Alford, Renee Marie *speech pathology/audiology services professional, educator*
Aliga, Olivia R. *music teacher, choral director*
Alinder, Mary Street *writer, lecturer*
Allen, Charity E. *music educator*
Allen, Charlotte *secondary school educator*
Allen, Cynthia Lea *nurse*
Allen, Leatrice Delorice *psychologist*
Allen, Linda S. *editor, writer*
Allen, Louise *writer, educator*
Allen, Marilyn Myers Pool *theater director, video producer*
Allen, Roberta *fiction and nonfiction writer, conceptual artist, photographer*
Allen, Victoria Taylor *archivist*
Alley, Kirstie *actress*
Allison, Carrie Frances *English language educator*
Allston, Charita Capers *music educator*
Aloff, Mindy *writer*
Alpers, Denise Kay Anderson *music educator*
Alpers, Svetlana Leontief *art educator*
Alpert, Ann Sharon *retired insurance claims examiner*
Altman, Adele Rosenhain *radiologist*
Alvarez, Aida *former federal agency administrator*
Amadio, Bari Ann *metal fabrication executive, former nurse*
Amaki, Amalia *curator*
Amancio, Ruth Carson *safety engineer*
Amend, Kate *film editor, educator*
Amgott, Madeline *television producer, media consultant*
Amos, Linda K. *academic administrator*
Amos-Mandela, Tiye Uhura *systems analyst, researcher*
Anastole, Dorothy Jean *retired electronics company executive*
Ancker-Johnson, Betsy *physicist, engineer, retired automotive company executive*
Anderegg, Karen Klok *business executive*
Anders, Kathryn *artist, educator*
Anderson, Allamay Eudoris *health educator, home economist*
Anderson, Amy Lee *realtor*
Anderson, Cherine E. *television and film production manager, special events planner, marketing executive*
Anderson, Dorothy Fisher *social worker, psychotherapist*
Anderson, Elizabeth Ann *special education educator*
Anderson, Georgia Griffin *educational designer*
Anderson, Geraldine Louise *medical researcher*
Anderson, Glenda *special education educator, sales executive, financial planner*
Anderson, Jane Ellsworth *retired secondary school educator*
Anderson, Mary Jane *public library consultant*
Anderson, Peggy Rees *accountant*
Anderson, Rachael Keller *retired library administrator*
Anderson, Ruth Lucille *interior designer, educator, artist, librarian, archivist*
Anderson-Spivy, Alexandra *writer, editor*
Andersson, Helen Demitrous *artist*
Andleton, Suzanne Spurlock *art educator*
Andrade, Carolyn L. *foreign language educator*
Andrade, Edna *artist, art educator*
Andrau, Maya Hedda *physical therapist*
Andreae, Christine Ewing *writer*
Andreason, (Sharon) Lee *sculptor*
Andreatta, Susan L. *anthropologist*
Andrew, Dolores Molcan *art educator, artist*
Andrews, Janice D. *elementary school educator*
Andrews, Jean *artist*
Andrews, Dame Julie (Julia Elizabeth Wells) *actress, singer*
Anton, Barbara *writer*
Apel-Brueggeman, Myrna L. *entrepreneur*
Aponte, Elsie *conservationist*
Appell, Louise Sophia *consulting company executive*
Applegate, Christina *actress*
Aptaker, Janet Marcia *social worker*
Arden, Sherry W. *publishing company executive*
Areen, Judith Carol *law educator, dean*
Arenal, Julie (Mrs. Barry Primus) *choreographer*
Aretz, Barbara Jane *reading specialist, educator*
Argers, Helen *novelist, playwright*
Ariens, Karla Rae *library director*
Arifi, Fatana Baktash *artist, educator*
Ariosa, Corazon Encila *accountant*
Armacost, Mary-Linda Sorber Merriam *former academic administrator, consultant*
Armatrading, Joan *singer, songwriter*
Armentrout, Keri Janelle *minister, educator*
Armistead, Katherine Kelly (Mrs. Thomas B. Armistead III) *interior designer, travel consultant, civic worker*
Armstrong, Anne Legendre (Mrs. Tobin Armstrong) *retired ambassador*
Armstrong, Karen Lee *special education educator*
Armstrong Squall, Paula Estelle *executive secretary*
Arndt, Dianne Joy *artist, photographer*
Arnold, Jean Ann *health science facility administrator*
Arnold-Rogers, Judy *education educator, language educator, coach*
Arnone, Mary Grace *radiologic technologist*
Arntz, Barbara C. *elementary school educator*
Aronson, Luann Marie *actress*
Arp, Arlene *pre-school educator*
Arp Lotter, Donna *venture capitalist, investor*
Arrieu-King, Cynthia M. *echocardiographer, poet, educator*
Arrott, Patricia Graham *artist, art instructor*
Arthur, Beatrice *actress*
Arting, Patricia Dee *special education educator*
Arutyunyan, Emma *radio broadcaster*
Aschheim, Eve Michele *artist, educator*
Ascone, Teresa Palmer *artist, educator*
Ashkin, Roberta Ellen *lawyer*
Ashton, Betsy Finley *broadcast journalist, author, lecturer*
Assael, Alyce *artist*
Astor, Brooke *foundation administrator, philanthropist, writer*
Atamian, Susan *nurse*
Atcheson, Sue Hart *business educator*
Athias, Lori R. *real estate broker*
Atkins, Jeannine Catherine *writer*
Atwater, Phyllis Y. *municipal administrator*
Aukofer, Clare Elizabeth *newspaper editor*
Aukon-Shoaff, Larisa *art educator, artist*
Aunio, Irene M. *artist*
Aurelio, Kristen Joan *school psychologist*
Aurori, Michele Dawn *music educator*
Aust, Elizabeth Ann (Betty) *artist*
Autolitano, Astrid *consumer products executive*
Autry, Lola Mae *music educator*
Auyong, Jan *biologist*
Avery, Carolyn Elizabeth *artist*
Avrett, Roz (Rosalind Case) *writer, advertising creative director*
Ayres, Mary Jo *professional speaker, writer, composer*
Azarian, Mary *illustrator*
Azelton, Rebecca Joy *music educator*
Baba, Marietta Lynn *business anthropologist, university administrator*
Baber, Yongsook Kim *musician*
Babitzke, Theresa Angeline *health facility administrator*
Backlar, Patricia *education educator*
Backowski-Dawson, Therese Marie *editor*
Bacon, Caroline Sharfman *investor relations consultant*
Bacon, Jeri Ann *music educator*
Baerwald, Susan Grad *television broadcasting company executive producer*
Bahr, Christine Marie *special education educator*
Bahr, Jane Marie *writer, retired English educator*
Bahret, Mary Ellen *lobbyist*
Bailar, Barbara Ann *statistician, researcher*
Bailey, Carla Lynn *nursing administrator*
Bailey, Joy Y. *art educator*
Bailey, Rita Maria *investment advisor, psychologist*
Bailey-Stein, Deena Tamara *health care administrator*
Baillos, Marianne Tkach *secondary school educator*
Baiman, Gail *real estate broker*
Bainbridge, Dona Bardelli *marketing professional*
Bainbridge, Susan W. *elementary school educator*
Baker, Diane Louise *financial professional*
Baker, Gwendolyn Calvert *United Nations official*
Baker, Jane E. *secondary school educator*
Baker, Lesliegh *bank officer, lawyer*
Baker, Lucinda *writer*
Baker, Nancy Kassebaum (Nancy Kassebaum) *former senator, foundation official*
Baker, Susan Marie Victoria *writer, artist, musician*
Balaban-Perry, Eleanor *retired advertising executive*
Baldrige, Letitia *writer, management training consultant*
Baldwin, Marie Hunsucker *retired secondary school educator*
Balis, Jennifer Lynn *retired academic administrator, computer technology educator*
Ball, Marcia *vocalist*
Ballard, Marion Scattergood *software development professional*
Ballard, Tina Rowann *music educator*
Ballou, Claudia Arceneaux *artist*
Balog, Rita Jean *retired librarian*
Balsam, Marion Joyce *pediatrician, retired naval officer*
Balter, Frances Sunstein *civic worker*
Baltimore, Linda Owlett *psychologist, educator*
Ban, Margo A. *elementary school educator*
Banaszynski, Carol Jean *secondary school educator*
Baney, Lori A. *education educator*
Banfill, Sally Anne *painter*
Banks, Deirdre Margaret *retired church organization administrator*
Barad, Jill Elikann *family products company executive*
Baranski, Christine *actress*
Barber, Joan Marie *artist*
Barber, Marsha *business company executive*
Barbey, Adélaïde *publisher*
Barbo, Dorothy Marie *obstetrician, gynecologist, educator*
Barca, Kathleen *marketing executive*
Barcus, Nancy B. *fine arts educator, writer*
Bard, Marjorie *social welfare administrator*
Bardeen-Henschel, Ann *anesthesiology educator*
Barker, Hilda Jean *retired library director*
Barker, Virginia Lee *nursing educator*
Barlow, Jean *art educator, painter*
Barmore, Heather A *music educator, vocalist*
Barnes-Kempton, Isabel Janet *microbiology educator, college dean*
Barnett, Peggy G. *music educator*
Barnhill, Wendy Renee *music educator*
Baron, Jennifer Lynne *museum education director*
Barone, Kerri Lynn *music educator*
Barr, Marlene Joy *volunteer*
Barranger, Milly Slater *theater educator, writer*
Barrett, Barbara McConnell *ranch owner, community leader, lawyer*
Barrett, Janet Tidd *academic administrator*
Barrett, Jessica (Donna Ann Nipert) *psychotherapist*
Barrett, Krista E. *psychotherapist, educator*
Barrett, Lida Kittrell *mathematics educator*
Barrett, Linda L. *real estate consultant*
Barrett, Lora McNeece *art educator, artist*
Barrett, Paulette Singer *public relations executive*
Barron, Peggy Pennisi *management consultant*
Barry, Carolyn McNamara *psychologist, educator*
Barry, Janet Cecilia *retired elementary school educator*
Barry, Miranda Robbins *internet and television producer, writer, educator*
Barrymore, Drew *actress*
Bartelli, Alice Hill *librarian, secondary education educator*
Bartels, Betty Jane *nurse*
Bartenstein, Jeuli *federal agency administrator*
Barth, Frances *artist*
Bartoletti, Gina P. *assistant principal, art educator*
Bartolotti, Virginia L. *retired principal*
Barton, Ann Elizabeth *retired corporate financial executive*
Basch, Reva *information services company executive*
Bashore, Irene Saras *art association administrator*
Basinger, Karen Lynn *renal dietitian*
Bass, Betsy Daves *ophthalmic assistant, artist*
Bass, Lynda D. *retired medical/surgical nurse, nursing educator*
Bass, Ruth Mary Haskins *journalist*
Bassett, Elizabeth Ewing (Libby Bassett) *writer, editor*
Bassey, Idara E. *lawyer, educator*
Bates, Beverly Joyce *retired educator and computer professional*
Bates, Margaret P. *historian*
Bates, Shirley Graves *music educator*
Bateson, Mary Catherine *anthropology educator emerita*
Bates Stoklosa, Evelynne (Eve Bates Stoklosa) *educational consultant, educator*
Batory, Joan Anne *solid waste and environmental administrator*
Battin, Patricia Meyer *librarian*
Battiste, Michele C. *poet, literature educator*
Bauer, Barbara Ann *marketing consultant*
Bauer, Louise May *minister, educator*
Baum, Eleanor *electrical engineering educator, academic administrator*
Baum, Susan Jean *vocalist, voice educator*
Baumol, Hilda *management consultant*
Baur, Susan W. *psychologist, writer*
Baxter, Barbara Morgan *Internet service provider executive, educator*
Baxter, Kathleen Byrne *academic administrator*

Butler, Kathleen Marie *editor*
Butler Yank, Leslie Ann *artist, writer, editor*
Butterbrodt, Patricia Ann *music educator*
Butterfield, Deborah Kay *sculptor*
Buttram, Christine Ruth *music educator*
Butts, Carol Henderson *human resources specialist, consultant*
Buyanovsky, Sophia *linguist, educator*
Byrne, Judy Susanne *writer, educator*
Byrne, Loretta Daum *artist, writer*
Cabanas, Elizabeth Ann *nutritionist, educator*
Cahill, Verna Eleanore *writer*
Cai, Ming Zhi *film producer*
Calamar, Gloria *artist*
Calder, Diane *artist, art educator, writer*
Caldicott, Helen *physician*
Caldwell, Judy Carol *advertising executive, public relations executive, consultant, writer, designer*
Caldwell-Smith, Gaetana Lee *writer*
Calhoun, Ramona *human services administrator, academic administrator, consultant*
Callard, Carole Crawford *librarian, educator*
Callaway, Julienne Morriss *financial consultant*
Callen, Paulette Marie *writer, advocate*
Calmenson, Stephanie Lyn *writer*
Calooy, Sonya Renee *advertising executive, consultant*
Calvert, Jeanne Anne *historian, educator*
Cameron, Donna *artist, art educator*
Cameron, Lucille Wilson *retired dean*
Cameron, Susan Kay *government and public relations executive*
Cammack, Ann *librarian, secondary school educator*
Camp, Alethea Taylor *executive and organizational design consultant*
Campbell, Andrea S. *writer*
Campbell, Claire Patricia *nurse practitioner, educator*
Campbell, Heather Sue *credit manager, religious studies educator*
Campbell, Jane Turner *retired realtor, retired secondary school educator, retired adult education educator*
Campbell, Josephine Anne Conrad *news service executive*
Candido, Viola Jeane Heimberger *writer*
Canfield, Constance Dale *retired accountant, retired medical/surgical nurse, retired military officer*
Cannistraro, Carolyn Marie *financial recruiter*
Cannon, Patricia Althen *librarian, writer*
Cano, Leah Marie *music educator, writer, musician*
Cano, Marta Mendendez *securities company executive, financial consultant*
Canulla, Theresa *microbiologist*
Capell, Cydney Lynn *editor*
Capello, Linda *artist*
Caplan, Paula Joan *actress, playwright*
Cappello, Eve *speaker, trainer, author*
Caputo, Carrie Dawn *music educator, musician*
Cardone, Bonnie Jean *freelance photojournalist*
Cardwell, Nancy Lee *editor, writer*
Carideo, Marguerite *painter*
Carl, Susan Marie *photographer, photojournalist*
Carlin, Betty *education educator*
Carlisle-Frank, Pamela L. *writer, researcher, consultant, management consultant*
Carlsen, Mary Baird *clinical psychologist*
Carlson, Alisa M. *secondary school educator*
Carlson, Janet Frances *psychologist, educator*
Carmack, Mildred Jean *retired lawyer*
Carman, Susan Hufert *nurse coordinator*
Carmichael, Judy Lea *record industry executive, concert jazz pianist*
Carnahan, Jean *former senator*
Carney, Patricia *Canadian government official*
Carpenter, Candice *writer, former media executive*
Carpenter, Dorothy Fulton *retired state legislator*
Carpenter, Janella Ann *retired librarian*
Carpenter, Liz (Elizabeth Sutherland Carpenter) *journalist, writer, equal rights leader, lecturer*
Carpenter, Susan Karen *defender*
Carpenter-Mason, Beverly Nadine *quality assurance professional, medical/surgical nurse*
Carr, Bessie *retired elementary school educator*
Carraher, Mary Lou Carter *art educator*
Carrillo, Juanita *gerontological services consultant*
Carroll, Barbara *musician, composer, singer*
Carroll, E Jean *columnist, writer*
Carroll, Mary Patricia *writer*
Carson, Regina E. *healthcare administrator, geriatric specialist, pharmacist, educator*
Carstairs, Sharon *legislator*
Carswell, Jane Triplett *retired family physician*
Carter, Barbara Dale *pianist, piano teacher, clinical counselor*
Carter, Betsy L. *magazine editor*
Carter, Harriet Rodes *language educator*
Carter, Jaine M(arie) *human resources specialist, director*
Carter, Nanette Carolyn *artist*
Carter, Rosalynn Smith *former First Lady of the United States*
Carver, Juanita Ash *plastic company executive*
Casadesus, Penelope Ann *advertising executive, film producer*
Casei, Nedda *mezzo-soprano*
Caseiras, Jo Ann Striga *artist, educator*
Casey, Darla Diann *elementary school educator*
Cash, Deanna Gail *retired nursing educator*
Cassian, Nina *poet, composer*
Cassidy, Esther Christmas *retired government official*
Castiglia, Patricia Anne Thorson *dean, nursing educator*
Castle, Janine *psychologist*
Castle, Nancy Margaret Timma *accountant, banker*
Castor, Betty *academic administrator*
Castro, Judith Ana *social worker*
Castro, Maria Graciela *medical educator, geneticist, researcher*
Castro, Sandra Ivette *special education educator*
Caswell, Dorothy Ann Cottrell *visual artist, arts administrator*
Caswell, Frances Pratt *retired English language educator*
Cathou, Renata Egone *chemist, consultant*
Cattell, Heather Birkett *psychologist*
Caulfield, Kathleen Marie *medical association administrator, medical/surgical nurse*
Cawley, Juanita Sandgren *director*
Cawley, Patricia Blonts *secondary school educator*
Cazalas, Mary Rebecca Williams *lawyer, nurse*
Cell, Gillian Townsend *historian, educator*
Centafont, Lucy Ann Alexander *occupational therapy consultant*
Cerven, Laura Kay *language educator, translator, music educator*
Chaffin, Virginia Louise *licensed practical nurse*
Chafkin, Rita M. *dermatologist*
Chait, Fay Klein *health administrator*
Chalcraft, Elena Marie *actress, singer*
Chalfant-Allen, Linda Kay *retired Spanish language educator*
Chamberlain, Cara Lee *literature educator, writer*
Chamberlain, Patricia Ann *writer, farmer, retired environmental manager, land use planner*
Chambers, Marjorie Bell *historian*
Champey, Elaine *science and technology research coordinator*
Chance, M. Sue *psychiatrist, author, publisher*
Chandler, Alice *higher education consultant, university president*
Chandler, Kathleen *retired executive secretary*
Chang, Helen Chung-Hung Hsiang *music educator*
Chapman, Alison Beaton *music educator*
Chapman, Linda Lee *computer company executive, consultant*
Chapman, Robyn Lemon *music educator*
Chappell, Annette M. *higher education consultant, minister*
Chardavoyne, Lara J. *social worker*
Charette, Cecile M. *music educator*
Charlton, Shirley Marie *educational consultant*
Charnin, Jade Hobson *magazine executive*
Chase, Doris Totten *sculptor, educator, filmmaker*
Chatterji, Angana P. *anthropologist*
Chaudoir, Jean Hamilton (Jean Hamilton) *secondary school educator*
Chave, Carolyn Margaret *arbitrator, retired lawyer*
Cheatham, Belzora *writer*
Chee, Ann-Ping *music educator*
Cheek, Barbara Lee *college reading program director, educator*
Cherepanov, Elena *psychologist, educator*
Chermayeff, Alexandra Sasha *artist*
Chesney, Susan Talmadge *writer, developer*
Chess, Sonia Mary *retired language educator*
Child, Abigail *filmmaker, educator*
Childers, Carol Louise *elementary school educator, music educator, musician*
Childers, Pamela Barnard *secondary school educator*
Childers, Susan Lynn Bohn *special education educator, administrator, human resources and transition specialist, consultant*
Childs, Lucinda *choreographer*
Childs, Wenetta Grybas *artist*
Chill, Myrtle N. *advertising copywriter, promoter*
Chin, Janet Sau-Ying *data processing executive, consultant*
Chisholm, Shirley Anita St. Hill *former congresswoman, educator, lecturer*
Chiu, Bella Chao *astrophysicist, writer*
Chludzinski, Carol A. *medical products executive*
Choi, Theresa Sun *performing arts association administrator*
Choukas-Bradley, Melanie *writer, photographer*
Chow, Rita Kathleen *nursing consultant*
Chretien, Carol Ann *chemical engineer*
Chretien, Jane Henkel *internist*
Christensen, Karen Kay *lawyer*
Christian, Brenda Jean *physician assistant, educator*
Christian, Pearl C *musician*
Christopher, Sharon A. Brown *bishop*
Chughtai, Raana Lynn *psychiatric nurse practitioner*
Chung, Caroline *foreign service officer*
Chung, Connie (Constance Yu-hwa Chung) *broadcast journalist*
Ciancio, Marilyn *television producer*
Cimino, Ann Mary *education educator*
Citron, Beatrice Sally *law librarian, lawyer, educator*
Claes, Gayla Christine *writer, editorial consultant*
Claiborne, Liz (Elisabeth Claiborne Ortenberg) *fashion designer*
Clark, Alicia Garcia *political party official*
Clark, Barbara June *elementary school educator*
Clark, Beverly Ann *lawyer*
Clark, Candy *actress*
Clark, Eve Vivienne *linguistics educator*
Clark, Margaret Ann-Cynthia *television producer, writer*
Clark, Mary Etta *science writing consultant*
Clark, Mary Higgins *writer, communications executive*
Clark, Nancy Lucinda Brown *retired music teacher*
Clark, Paula Irene *elementary school educator, consultant*
Clark, Peggy Rillann *principal*
Clarke, Maryanna *theater director*
Clarke, Victoria *federal agency administrator*
Clawson, Roxann Eloise *college administrator, computer company executive*
Clayton, Eva M. *retired congresswoman, former commissioner*
Cleaver, Lydia Ruth *musician, educator*
Cleland, Nora Temple *writer, editor*
Clement, Hope Elizabeth Anna *retired librarian*
Clemetson, Cheryl Price *minister, consultant*
Clemons, Julie Payne *telephone company manager*
Cline, Janet E. Safford *school district administrator, desktop publisher*
Cline, Pauline M. *educational administrator*
Cobb, Ruth *artist*
Cobb, Sue McCourt *lawyer, educator*
Cochran, Carolyn *library director*
Cochran, Jacqueline Louise *management executive*
Codo, Christina *securities executive*
Cody, Arlene J. Clark Brattain *interior designer*
Cody, Judith *composer, writer*
Coen, Mary Ellen *adult education educator, secondary school educator, chemist*
Coffey, Joanne Christine *dietician*
Coffin, Bertha Louise *telephone company executive*
Coggins, Ruthanne L. Gable *music educator*
Coggins, Suzanne Bridges *music educator*
Cohen, Roberta Jane *government executive*
Cohen, Sharleen Cooper *interior designer, writer*
Cohen, Shirley Mason *retired secondary school educator, volunteer*
Cohn, Marianne Winter Miller *civic activist*
Colage, Beatrice Elvira *education educator*
Colburn, Nancy Douglas *social worker, educator*
Cole, Jean Anne *artist*
Cole, Nancy Stooksberry *educational research executive*
Cole, Rachel P. *science educator*
Coleman, Claire Kohn *public relations executive*
Coleman, Jean Black *nurse, physician assistant*
Coleman, Mary Sue *academic administrator*
Collette, Frances Madelyn *retired tax specialist, lawyer, consultant, advocate*
Colline, Marguerite Richnavsky *maternal, women's health and pediatrics nurse*
Collins, Eileen Marie *astronaut*
Collins, Irma Helen *music educator, consultant*
Collins, Jean Katherine *English educator*
Collins, Joan Henrietta *actress*
Collins, Kathleen Anne *artistic director*
Collins-Brown, E. Dorlee (E. Dorlee Woodyard) *systems support specialist*
Collinson, Vivienne Ruth *education educator, researcher, consultant*
Collins-Pravel, Paula Marie *marketing professional*
Colwell, Rita Rossi *microbiologist, former federal agency administrator, medical educator*
Comar, Mary Alice *art educator, farmer*
Comfrey, Kathleen Marie *lawyer*
Comola, Jacqueline Petermann *management consultant*
Compton, Norma Haynes *retired university dean, artist*
Cone, Frances McFadden *data processing consultant*
Conley, Ruth Irene *poet*
Conley, Sarah Ann *health facility administrator*
Connell, Shirley Hudgins *public relations professional*
Connelly, Amy Reece *career planning administrator, consultant*
Connelly, Barbara Catherine *organization administrator*
Connelly, Elizabeth Ann *retired state legislator*
Connelly, Sharon Rudolph *lawyer*
Conover, Mona Lee *retired adult education educator*
Conover, Nancy Anderson *retired secondary school counselor*
Conover-Carson, Anne *writer*
Conrad-England, Roberta Lee *pathologist*
Conte, Andrea *retail executive, healthcare consultant, advocate*
Cook, Beth Marie *volunteer, poet*
Cook, Kathy H. *elementary school educator, conductor, composer*
Cook, Sister M(ary) Mercedes *secondary school educator, principal*
Cook, Rebecca McDowell *former state official*
Cooke, Chantelle Anne *writer*
Cooks, Pamala Aniece *insurance agent*
Cooper, Elva June *artist*
Cooper, Jamie Lee *writer*
Cooper, Josephine Smith *trade association and public affairs executive*
Cooper, Judith Kase *retired theater educator, playwright*
Cooper, Rebecca *art dealer*
Cooper, Signe Skott *retired nursing educator*
Cooper-González, Angela *counseling administrator*
Coover, Doris Dimock *artist*
Cope, Melba Darlene *volunteer, photographer*
Copenhaver, Kirsten Jeannette *health facility administrator, consultant*
Corbett, Lenora Meade *mathematician, community college educator*
Corcoran, Denise Marie (Lacey) *music educator*
Cordell, Joann Meredith *music educator*
Corkran, Virginia B. *retired real estate agent*
Cornell, Carole Anne Walcutt *nurse*
Cornwell, Nancy Dunn *secondary school educator*
Corson, Mary Louise *special education educator*
Cortez, Marti *marketing professional*
Corto, Diana Maria *lyric-coloratura, producer, educator*
Cosman, Francene Jen *former government official*
Costantini, Mary Ann C. *writer, editor, retired elementary educator*
Coté, Kathryn Marie *psychotherapist, stress management educator*
Cothran, Anne Jennette *educational administrator*
Cotten, Annie Laura *psychologist, educator*
Cotter, Emily Rexann *social worker, marriage and family therapist*
Cottingham, Martha Maxfield *journalist, volunteer*
Cottrell, Mary-Patricia Tross *bank executive*
Coughran, Jane Nora *writer, editor, researcher*
Coulter, Cynthia Jean *artist, educator*
Couto, Nancy Vieira *poet, literary consultant*
Coutret, Kay Elizabeth *financial analyst*
Cowles, Elizabeth Hall *program consultant*
Cowles, Lois Anne Fort *social worker, educator*
Cox, Joy Dean *small business owner*
Coyle, Marie Bridget *retired microbiologist, retired lab administrator*
Cozzens, Mimi *actress, director*
Crabb, Virginia Geany Ruth *librarian*
Crabtree, Davida Foy *minister*
Craig, Carol Mills *marriage, family and child counselor*
Craig, Jenny *weight management executive*
Craig, Judith *bishop*
Craig, Terri L. *social worker*
Crandall, Nancy Lee *mayor*
Cranston, Pamela Lee *priest, writer*
Craven, Elizabeth *pediatrician*
Crawford, Carol Tallman *law educator*
Crawford, Helene Hope *elementary school principal*
Crawford, Lela Burch *school nurse*
Crawford, Muriel Laura *lawyer, author, educator*
Crawford-Dickerson, Carrie Cae *art gallery director*
Crenshaw, Tena Lula *librarian*
Creswell, Dorothy Anne *computer consultant*
Crews, Judith Young *career planning administrator*
Crino, Marjanne Helen *anesthesiologist*
Crispell, Marilyn B. *jazz musician*
Criswell, Kimberly Ann *executive coach, communications consultant, performing artist*
Critelli, Nancy Barbara *music educator, cellist*
Crittendon, Donna Elizabeth *customer service administrator*
Crocker, Barbara Jean *clinical nurse specialist*
Crocker, Saone Baron *lawyer*
Croft, Kathryn Delaine *business executive, consultant*
Cromwell, Florence Stevens *occupational therapist*
Cronacher, Karen Jan *playwright, educator*
Croog, Roslyn Zeporah *chief systems engineer*
Crooker, Diane Kay *accountant*
Crosby, Kathryn Grandstaff (Grant Crosby) *actress*
Crosby, Marena Lienhard *retired college administrator*
Cross, Goldie K. *telecommunications engineer*
Cross, Kathryn Patricia *education educator*
Crouse, Lindsay *actress*
Crow, Elizabeth Smith *editor*
Crowder, Jane Nelson *middle school educator*
Crowder, Mary Ellen *art educator, real estate agent*
Crowley, Liska Anne *historian*
Crown, Nancy Elizabeth *lawyer*
Crozier, Prudence Slitor *economist*
Cruikshank, Margaret Louise *humanities educator, writer*
Crumpton, Evelyn *psychologist, educator*
Cruver, Suzanne Lee *communications executive, writer*
Cruz-Romo, Gilda *soprano*
Cuba, Nan Brindley *small business owner, writer*
Cuccinello, Darlene Ann *retirement home administrator, physical education educator*
Culleeney, Maureen Ann *information technology executive, educator*
Cullen-Rivera, Amy Janene *management consultant*
Cullingford, Hatice Sadan *chemical engineer*
Cullum, Lee Brooks *journalist*
Culp, Faye Berry *state legislator*
Culp, Mildred Louise *corporate executive*
Cummings, Erika Helga *business consultant*
Cummings, Mary Voigt *counselor*
Cummins, Nancyellen Heckeroth *electronics engineer*
Cunha, Jane *artist, consultant*
Cunningham, Andrea Lee *public relations executive*
Cunningham, Nancy Schieffelin *business educator*
Curley, Nancy Palmer *marriage and family therapist*
Curnutte, Mary E. *artist, restorer of painting, educator*
Curran-Smith, Anita Stiles *retired public health medicine educator, dean*
Currier, Ruth *dancer, choreographer and educator*
Curtis, Candace A. *former state legislator*
Curtis, Dolores Rogers *writer*
Curtis, Mary E. (Mary Curtis Horowitz) *publishing company executive*
Custureri, Mary Catherine Foca *literature educator*
Cutler, Cathy Gordon *women's health nurse practitioner*
Cuttler, Dona Lou *music educator, writer*
Dacey, Kathleen Ryan *lawyer, former federal judge*
Daggett, Roxann *state legislator*
Dahl, Bren Bennington *photography studio co-owner*
Dahlstrom, Patricia Margaret *real estate appraiser*
Dailey, Irene *actress, educator*
Dailey, Janet *writer*
D'Alessio, Valaida Corrine *artist, consultant*
Daley, Linda *lawyer*
Dallmann, Carolyn E. *auditor*
Daly, Linda *artist, educator*
Damp, Katie *actor, educator, community relations administrator*
Danaher, Mallory Millett (Mallory Jones) *actress, photographer, film producer, theater producer*
Danes, Claire *actress*
D'Angelo, Lihong Lilly *chemist*
D'Angelo, Renée Young *special education educator*
Daniel, Beth *professional golfer*

Daniel, Winifred Yvonne *elementary school educator*
Daniels, Arlene Kaplan *sociology educator*
Danner, Patsy Ann (Mrs. C. M. Meyer) *former congresswoman*
Danziger, Gertrude Seelig *metal fabricating executive*
Dapper, Karen Lynn *psychologist, educator*
D'Arcangelo, Marcia Diane *educational media producer*
Darkovich, Sharon Marie *nurse administrator*
Darlington, Hilda Walker *real estate company officer*
Darnell, Susan Laura Browne *retired air force officer*
Dart, Deborah Gordon *artist*
Daubenas, Jean Dorothy Tenbrinck *librarian, educator*
Davidson, Bonnie Jean *gymnastics educator, sports management consultant*
Davidson, Jeannie *costume designer*
Davies, Terri Lynn *pharmaceutical sales representative*
Davies-McNair, Jane *retired educational consultant*
Davila, Rebecca Tober *physical education educator*
Davion, Ethel Johnson *school system administrator, curriculum specialist*
Davis, Ada Romaine *nursing educator*
Davis, Anna Jane Ripley *elementary school educator*
Davis, Barbara Jean Siemens *service company executive*
Davis, Charlotte MacLean *secondary school educator*
Davis, Debra Greer *music educator, pianist*
Davis, Diann Holmes *elementary school educator*
Davis, Donna Lee *small business owner, writer*
Davis, Elba Lucila *veterans affairs nurse*
Davis, Erlynne P. *social work educator*
Davis, Geena (Virginia Davis) *actress*
Davis, Joanne Fatse *lawyer*
Davis, Jonni K. *secondary school educator, writer*
Davis, June Fiksdal *medical facility owner, floral designer*
Davis, Karen Ann (Karen Ann Falconer) *special education educator*
Davis, Keigh Leigh *aerospace engineer*
Davis, Lisa Anne *secondary school educator*
Davis, Maggie (Marie Hill) *writer*
Davis, Margaret Thacker *retired critical care, medical and surgical nurse*
Davis, Mary Helen *psychiatrist, psychoanalyst, educator*
Davis, Nicole D. *executive secretary, entrepreneur*
Davis, Norma Stites *conductor, music educator*
Davis, Sharon Cade *secondary school educator*
Davis, Sheila Kay *administrative assistant*
Davis, Sue Ellen H. *elementary and secondary music educator*
Davis, Suzanne Spiegel *retired information specialist*
Davis, Wanda Rose *lawyer*
Davis-Goga, Muriel E. *elementary school educator*
Davis-Townsend, Helen Irene *retired art educator*
Dawkins, Marva Phyllis *psychologist, educator*
Dawson, Donna L. *secondary school educator*
Dawson, Martha Bromley *administrative assistant, software developer*
Dawson, Virginia Sue *retired editor*
Day, Anne White *retired nurse*
Day, Victoria Lynn *principal*
De Amorim, Valdivia Vânia Siqueira *translator*
Dean, Carole Lee *film company executive*
Dean, Diane (H.) Sweet *artist, retired credit manager*
Deane, Sally Jan *health services management, consultant*
DeAngelo, Judith *artist*
De Both, Tanya *statistician*
Debs, Barbara Knowles *former college president, consultant*
Debus, Eleanor Viola *retired business management company executive*
DeClercq, Marissa Helena *actress*
Deeds, Virginia Williams *volunteer*
Deere, Kelli Beth *music educator*
DeFrancis, Suellen Maria *interior architect*
Degann, Sona Irene *obstetrician, gynecologist, educator*
DeGeneres, Ellen *actress, comedienne*
De Gette, Diana Louise *congresswoman, lawyer*
Degrenia, Lisa Ann Moss *minister*
DeHority, Miriam A. (Miriam Newman) *artist*
Deitz, Susan Rose *columnist*
DeJack, Jacqueline Elvadeana *artist, educator*
de Lacerda, Maria Assunçaõ Escobar *social worker, consultant*
Delaney, Marion Patricia *retail executive*
DeLapp, Tina Davis *retired nursing educator*
Del Papa, Frankie Sue *former state attorney general*
Demetrakeas, Regina Cassar *social worker*
DeMita, Geraldine *librarian*
DeMitchell, Terri Ann *law educator*
Denenberg, Katharine W. Hornberger (Tinka Denenberg) *artist, educator*
Denious, Sharon Marie *retired publishing executive*
Dennany, Kelly *mechanical engineer, test engineer*
Dennick, Lori Ann (L. Anne Carrington) *editor*
deNobriga, Kathie Elizabeth *consultant*
Densen-Gerber, Judianne *psychiatrist, lawyer, educator*
Dent, Julie *director*
Denton, Judy Ann *art educator*
Deoul, Kathleen Boardsen *publishing executive*
de Planque, E. Gail *physicist*
de Planque, J. Kathryn *psychologist*
Dern, Laura *actress*
Derrickson, Denise Ann *secondary school educator, educator*
Derrico, Georgia Santangelo *banker*
DeShields, Sheila Beth *writer*
Desjardins, Judith Anne *psychotherapist*
DeStaffany, Sandra Russell *childbirth educator, author*
Detert, Miriam Anne *chemical analyst*
Detwiler, Christina LeFevre *elementary school educator*
Deutschman, Louise Tolliver *curator*
Deutz, Natalie Rubinstein *actress, consultant*
DeVaris, Jeannette Mary *psychologist*
de Varona, Donna *sports reporter, former Olympic swimmer*
Devaughan, Jewell L. *music educator*
DeVera, Gertrude Quenano *education educator*
Devine, Katherine *environmental consultant, educator*
De Voe, Tamara Lynne *art director, painter*
DeVore, Kimberly K. *business executive*
DeVos, Elisabeth (Betsy) *political association executive*
Dewane-Pope, Peggy *elementary school educator, public relations executive, consultant*
Dewey, Ariane *artist, illustrator*
Dewey, Helen Scamell *retired humanities educator*
DeWitt, Sallie Lee *realtor*
D'Haiti, Felicia Kathleen (Felicia Kathleen Messina) *fine arts educator*
Dhillon, Sukhbans K. *retired computer services executive*
Diamant, Anita *writer*
Diamond, Estelle *education educator, state legislator*
Diamond, Nancy Kay *environmentalist, consultant*
Diamond, Susan Zee *management consultant*
Dias, Mari Nardolillo *education educator, consultant*
DiBattiste, Carol A. *lawyer*
DiCarlo, Laurette Mary *nurse*
Dicciani, Nance Katherine *chemical company executive, chemical engineer*
Dickens, Alycia Thompson *nurse practitioner*
Dickens, Joyce Rebecca *addictions therapist, educator*
Dickerson, Betty *secondary education educator, consultant, tester*
Dickerson, Claire Moore *lawyer, educator*
Dickey, Linda Ann *learning center director*
Dickinson, Carol Rittgers *arts administrator, writer, executive director*
[illegible] *educator*
Dickson, Eva Mae *credit manager*
Diede, Norma Dale *retired private school educator*
Diehl, Deborah Hilda *lawyer*
Diehl, Jennifer L. *counselor*
Diemer, Emma Lou *composer, educator*
Dietderich, Shirley (Jane Rohlfing) *interior decorator*
Dietz, Janis Camille *business educator*
Di Giacomo, Fran *artist*
DiGiamarino, Marian Eleanor *retired realty administrator*
Dike, Margaret Hopcraft *retired education administrator*
DiLiberti, Lara Marie *music educator*
Dillon, Joan Kent *civic worker, volunteer consultant*
Dillon, Toni Ann *emotional support educator*
DiMartino, Sandra Louise *theater educator*
DiMento, Carol A.G. *lawyer*
Dincecco, Jennie Elizabeth Williams Swanson *healthcare administrator, mentor, healthcare educator, volunteer*
Ding, Ai-Yue *conductor, music educator*
Dinkins, Jennifer Lynn *special education educator*
Diorio, Eileen Patricia *retired medical technologist, philosophy educator*
Di Paolo, Maria Grazia *language educator, writer*
Diston, Lorraine Diana *clinical psychologist, educator*
Dixon, Pauline K. *retired secondary school educator*
Doan, Mary Frances *advertising executive*
Dockstader, Deborah Ruth *minister*
Dodds, Linda Carol *special education educator*
Doderer, Minnette Frerichs *retired state legislator*
Doebler, Bettie Anne *language educator, researcher, writer*
Doherty, Evelyn Marie *data processing consultant*
Doherty, Shannon *actress*
Doland, Judy Ann *administrative assistant, retired financial rating company associate*
Doll, Patricia Marie *marketing professional, public relations executive, consultant*
Dominic, Magie *writer*
Dominick, Lisa Marie *elementary school educator*
Domzella, Janet *retired library director*
Donahue, Donna Charlene *computer company executive, marketing professional*
Donahue, Laura Kent *former state senator*
Donahue, Mary Beth *human services administrator*
Donald, Aida DiPace *retired publishing executive*
Donaldson, Myrtle Norma *music educator, musician*
Donaldson, Wilma Crankshaw *elementary school educator*
Donath, Therese *artist, author*
Donlou-Richmond, Doris Julia *scriptwriter*
Donnelly, Christina Wos *poet*
Donohue, Anne Emlen *software engineer*
Donovan, Kathleen A. *water transportation executive, county official*
Dooley, Jo Ann Catherine *retired publishing executive*
Dooreck, Lisa *special education educator, writer*
Doorley, Mathilda Doerseln *chemist, educator*
Doornink, Barbara *military officer*
Dorighi, Nancy S. *computer engineer*
Dorman, Angelia Hardy *writer*
Dorman, Hattie Lawrence *management consultant, trainer, former government agency official*
Dorsey, Rhoda Mary *retired academic administrator*
Dosti, Rose *newspaper columnist, author*
Dotson, Nancy Jean Davis *secondary school educator*
Dougherty, Barbara Lee *artist, writer*
Dougherty, Karla R. *writer*
Douglas, Mary Younge Riley *retired secondary school educator*
Douglas, Roxanne Grace *secondary school educator*
Douglass, Jane Dempsey *theology educator*
Doviak, Ingrid Ellinger *elementary school educator*
Dowben, Carla Lurie *lawyer, educator*
Dowdell, Sharonlyn Scott *accountant*
Downey, Deborah Ann *systems specialist*
Downing, Cynthia Hurst *therapist, addiction and abuse specialist*
Downs, Kathleen Anne *health facility administrator*
Doyle, Gillian *actress*
Doyle, Irene Elizabeth *electronic sales executive, nurse*
Doyle, Jacqueline Griffith Larcombe *psychologist*
Doyle, Judith Marie *principal*
Doyle, Judith Stovall *retired real estate executive*
Doyle, Nancy Hazlett *artist*
Dozier, Eleanor Cameron *computer company executive, writer*
Dozier, Therese Knecht *educational association administrator, educator*
Drake, Carolyn A. *administrative assistant*
Drake, Evelyn Downie *secondary school educator*
Drayson, Pamela K. *library director*
Drechsel, Joanne J. *writer, educator*
Dresbach, Mary Louise *state educational administrator*
Drew, Elizabeth Heineman *publishing executive*
Driver-Barstow, Susannah *editor*
Droke, Marilyn Lois *music educator*
Drost, Marianne *lawyer*
Drucker, Ana Bueno *healthcare marketing and public relations executive, writer*
Du Boise, Kim Rees *artist, photographer, art educator*
Duhs, Gloria L. *artist, realtor*
[illegible]
Duckwitz, Erika *music educator*
Dudics-Dean, Susan Elaine *interior designer*
Dudley, Elizabeth Hymer *retired security executive, community volunteer*
Duffey, Rosalie Ruth *elementary school educator*
Duguid, Dorothy Ann Ramseyer *artist*
Dumitru, Mirela *accountant*
Dumler, Patricia Ann *critical care nurse*
Duncan, Cleo *state legislator*
Duncan, Jennifer R. *secondary school educator*
Duniphan, J. P. *state legislator, small business owner*
Dunlop, Dorothy D. *statistician*
Dunmeyer, Sarah Louise Fisher *retired health care consultant*
Dunn, Carola *writer*
Dunn, Grace Veronica *retired executive secretary*
Dunn, Melanie Lea *information technology manager*
Dunne, Donnalee *artist, educator, writer*
Dunning, Lisa Anne *marriage and family therapist*
Dunn Kelly, Ruth Emma *management consultant*
Durgin, Diane *arbitrator, lawyer, mediator*
Durham, Thena Monts *microbiologist, researcher, management executive*
DuRocher, Frances A. *retired physician, educator*
Dustman, Elizabeth *art educator, designer*
Dwinell, Ann Jones *retired special education educator*
Dworin, Micki (Maxine Dworin) *automobile dealership executive*
Dwyer, Judith A. *marriage and family therapist*
Dyar, Kathryn Wilkin *pediatrician*
Dye, Linda Kaye *elementary school educator*
Dyer, Arlene Thelma *retail company owner*
Dyrstad, Joanell M. *former lieutenant governor, consultant*
Dyson, Anne Haas *English language educator*
Dzamba, Anne O. *history and women's studies educator*
Dziewanowska, Zofia Elizabeth *neuropsychiatrist, pharmaceutical executive, researcher, educator*
Eacho, Esther MacLively *special education educator*
Eason, Linda Lee *music educator*
Eason-Watkins, Barbara June *principal*
East, Janette Diane *marketing consultant*
Easton, Kelly Anne *writer, educator*
Easton, Michelle *foundation executive*
Eastwood, Kathleen J. *medical/surgical nurse*
Eaton, Emma Parker *special education educator*
Eaton, Shirley M. *medical/surgical nurse*
Ebersole, Andree D. *finance company executive, consultant*
Ebert, Dorothy Elizabeth *retired county clerk*
Ebinger, Linda Ann *nurse*
Ebisuzaki, Yukiko *retired chemistry educator*
Ebrahim, Ada *special education educator*
Echols, Mary Evelyn *travel consultant*
Ecton, Donna R. *management consultant, retired food products executive*
Edelsberg, Sally Comins *physical therapy educator and administrator*
Edelson, Zelda Sarah Toll *retired editor, artist*
Edelstein, Rosemarie (Rosemarie Hublou) *medical/surgical nurse, educator, medical and legal consultant*
Edens, Betty Joyce *reading recovery educator*
Edge, Charlene L. *writer*
Edmo, Jean Umiokalani *artist, poet*
Edmonds, Anne Carey *librarian*
Edmonds, Eileen Celeste *music educator, musician, composer*
Edmunds, Jane Clara *communications consultant*
Edwards, Ardis Lavonne Quam *retired elementary education educator*
Edwards, Christine Annette *retired lawyer, securities firm executive*
Edwards, Helen Thom *physicist*
Edwards, Kathleen *real estate broker, former educator*
Edwards, Lydia Justice *state official*
Edwards, Lynn A. *retired school system administrator*
Edwards, Patricia Burr *small business owner, counselor, consultant*
Egan, Moira *poet, educator*
Eid, Cynthia Ann *metalsmith, jeweler, designer, educator*
Eimers, Jeri Anne *retired therapist*
Eisenberg, Patricia Lee *medical/surgical nurse*
Eisenberg, Phyllis Rose *author*
Ekelchik, Jodi *management consultant*
Elcik, Elizabeth Mabie *fashion illustrator*
Elder, Mary Louise *librarian*
Elias, Rosalind *mezzo-soprano*
Ellie, Beth Joy *writer*
Elliot, Janet Lee *occupational medicine physician*
Elliott, Cindy Sue *academic administrator*
Elliott-Zahorik, Bonnie *nurse, administrator*
Ellis, Anne Elizabeth *fundraiser*
Ellis, Betty Graham *radiographer, sonographer*
Ellis, Carolyn Terry *lawyer*
Ellis, J. Renee Eley *special events administrator*
Ellis, Patricia Weathers *small business owner, retired electronic technician*
Ellner, Carolyn Lipton *not-profit organization executive, retired dean, consultant, dean, consultant*
Else, Carolyn Joan *retired library director*
Elwood-Akers, Virginia Edythe *retired librarian, archivist*
Emek, Sharon Helene *risk management consultant*
Emerling, Carol G(reenbaum) *consultant*
Emerson, Donna Lucille *social worker, educator*
Emrich, Jeanne Ann *poet, artist*
Endicott, Jennifer Jane Reynolds *education educator*
Engelbreit, Mary *art licensing entrepreneur*
Engels, Beatrice Ann *retired real estate company executive, poet, artist*
English, Lauren Jackson *media specialist,* [illegible]
English-Anderson, San Dei *minister*
Ensey, Suzanne Clinton Gorman *volunteer*
Ephron, Nora *writer*
Erlebacher, Arlene Cernik *retired lawyer*
Erlichson, Miriam *fundraiser*
Ernest, Pamela Kay *business consultant*
Erni, Corinne *writer, cultural projects manager*
Erwin, Judith Ann (Judith Ann Peacock) *writer, photographer, lawyer*
Espenlaub, Margo Linn *women's studies educator, writer, artist*
Essa, Lisa Beth *elementary school educator*
Essig, Kathleen Susan *university official, management consultant*
Essman, Saundra Carol *music educator*
Estes, Elaine Rose Graham *retired librarian*
Esther, Queen *playwright, scriptwriter, songwriter, solo performer, actor, musician*
Estrin, Thelma Austern *retired electrical engineer*
Etheridge, Diana Carol *internet business executive*
Ethridge, Brenda Kay *advertising employee*
Ettenger, Deborah Jean *music educator*
Etzel, Deborah Anne *computer technician, consultant*
Etzel, Ruth Ann *pediatrician, epidemiologist, educator*
Eu, March Fong *ambassador*
Euster, Joanne Reed *retired librarian*
Eustis, Jennifer Marie *language educator*
Evangelista, Anita Loretta *freelance writer, psychologist, nurse, publishing executive*
Evans, Bonita Dianne *adult education educator*
Evans, Gene M. *publishing executive*
Evans, Geraldine Ann *academic administrator*
Evans, Pamela R. *sales and marketing executive*
Evans, Patricia Marie *sales executive*
Evans, Sue Hollis *journalist, public relations executive*
Evans-Freed, Nancy Jane *secondary school educator*
Evdokimova, Eva *prima ballerina assoluta, choreographer, director, producer, actress*
Everett, Donna Raney *finance educator*
Evert, Chris (Christine Marie Evert) *retired professional tennis player*
Ewell, Miranda Juan *journalist*
Ewing, Elisabeth Anne Rooney *priest*
Ewing, Robyn *writer, educator*
Eyring, Maxine Louise *small business owner, esthetician*
Fadiman, Anne *writer, editor*
Fadley, Ann Miller *retired literature educator, literature educator*
Fahringer, Catherine Hewson *retired savings and loan association executive*
Fair, Marcia Jeanne Hixson *retired educational administrator*
Faison, Lugenia Marion *special education educator*
Faiz, Alexandria *nonfiction writer, researcher*
Falconer, Marguerite Elizabeth *artist*
Faletto, Kimberly Elizabeth *art educator*
Falguiere, Sharon Ellen *costume designer*
Falk, Melanie Kay *art director*
Fanos, Kathleen Hilaire *osteopathic physician, podiatrist*
Farina, Laura *lawyer*
Farmer, Ann Dahlstrom *English language educator*

Holiday, Edith Elizabeth *former presidential adviser, cabinet secretary*
Holifield, Pearl Kam (Kam Holifield, Momi Kam Holifield) *poet*
Holland, Beth *actress*
Holland, Ellen C. *music educator*
Holland, Rosemary Sheridan *program evaluation consultant*
Holland, Ruby Mae *social welfare administrator*
Hollander, Anne *writer*
Holleb, Doris B. *urban planner, economist*
Holleman, Sandy Lee *religious organization administrator*
Holliday, Polly Dean *actress*
Hollis, Jacquelyn Wilson *music educator*
Hollis, Janice Denise *publishing executive, minister*
Hollister, Patricia Hackett *psychotherapist, educator, marriage and family therapist*
Holm, Celeste *actress*
Holmes, Erline Morrison *retired educational administrator, consultant*
Holmes, Genta Hawkins *former diplomat*
Holmes, Joan *retired social welfare administrator*
Holmes, Susan G. *music educator*
Holmes, Wilhelmina Kent *community health nurse*
Holsinger, Adena Seguine *music educator, community volunteer*
Holt, Marjorie Jensen *artist*
Holt, Marjorie Sewell *lawyer, retired congresswoman*
Holte, Debra Leah *investment executive, financial analyst*
Holthaus, Joan Marie *elementary school educator*
Holt-Hunter, Tracy Lynn *language educator, artist*
Holtkamp, Susan Charlotte *elementary school educator*
Holton, Grace Holland *accountant*
Holtzscher, Denise Erin *music educator*
Holzer, Jenny *artist*
Holzman, Elizabeth Esther *artist, director*
Hombordy, Hanna Lore *artist*
Honanie, Jeannette *special education educator*
Honea, Joyce Clayton *critical care nurse*
Honeycutt, Janice Louise *nurse*
Hood, Luann Sandra *special education educator*
Hoover, Katherine Lacy *composer*
Hopper, Tammy Jane *art educator*
Horlick, Ruth *photographer*
Hornbaker, Alice Joy *writer*
Hornby-Anderson, Sara Ann *metallurgical engineer, marketing professional*
Horner, Matina Souretis *retired academic administrator, corporate financial executive*
Horowitz, Diana J. *artist*
Horsman, Lenore Lynde (Eleanora Lynde) *soprano, educator, actress*
Horstman, Suzanne Rucker *financial planner*
Horton, Joann *academic administrator*
Horton, Patricia Mathews *artist, violist and violinist*
Horton-Wright, Alma Irene *retired elementary school educator*
Hosman, Sharon Lee *music educator*
Houghtaling, Pamela Ann *technology marketing professional, writer*
Houghton, Katharine *actress*
Hourani, Laurel Lockwood *epidemiologist*
Houseman, Ann Elizabeth Lord *educational administrator, state official*
Houston, Whitney *vocalist, recording artist*
Houx, Shirley Ann *personal and business services company executive, consultant, researcher*
Howard, Barbara Byers *public policy consultant*
Howard, Cynthia Stotts *adult education educator*
Howard, Janet C. *former state legislator*
Howard, Susan J. *small business owner*
Howard-Peebles, Patricia N. *clinical cytogeneticist*
Howe, Virginia Hoffman *nurse administrator*
Howell, Janet D. *state legislator*
Howes, Sophia DuBose *writer*
Hricak, Hedvig *radiologist*
Hubbard, Elizabeth *actress*
Huckabee, Phyllis *human resources specialist*
Hudalla, Karen *court reporting educator, academic administrator*
Hudkins, Carol L. *state legislator*
Hudson, Carolyn Brauer *application developer, educator*
Hudson, Kate *actress*
Huegel, Donna *historian, writer, artist, archivist*
Huerta, Dolores Fernandez *labor union administrator*
Huffington, Anita *sculptor*
Huffman, Cady *actress*
Huffman, Carol Cicolani *music educator, consultant*
Hughes, Ann Hightower *retired economist, international trade consultant*
Hughes, Debra *writer, educator*
Hughes, Jacqueline Emma *information systems specialist*
Hughes, Karen Parfitt *former federal official*
Hughes, Michaela Kelly *actress*
Hugley, Carolyn Fleming *state legislator*
Huie, Carol P. *information systems educator*
Hulin, Frances C. *retired prosecutor*
Hull, Jane Dee *former governor, former state legislator*
Hull, Louise Knox *retired elementary educator, administrator*
Humbach, Miriam Jane *publishing executive*
Hume, Susan Rachel *finance and economics educator*
Hummel, Marian *retired art educator, photographer*
Hummel, Marilyn Mae *elementary school educator*
Humphries Barker, Dedria *humanities educator*
Hundley, Jill L. *special education educator*
Hunsberger, Christine Lee *accountant*
Hunt, Martha *sales executive, researcher*
Hunt, Mary Melinda *artist*
Hunte, Beryl Eleanor *mathematics educator, consultant*
Hunter, Frances Ellen Croft *music educator*
Hunter, Helen Frances *social worker*
Hunter, Holly *actress*
Hurd, Veronica Terez *career officer*
Hurlbut, Geraldine *retired elementary education educator*
Hurst, Susan Henthorn *music educator*
Hurwood, Rebecca Mayre *art association administrator*
Huston, Joan Bonfiglio *psychotherapist*
Huston, Margo *journalist*
Huszai, Kristy Renee *insurance agent*
Hutcheon, Linda Ann *English language educator*
Hutcherson, Rene Ridens *medical social services administrator*
Hutchin, Nancy Lee *corporate financial executive*
Hutchison, Edna Ruth *artist*
Hutchison, Kay Bailey *senator*
Hutt, Evelyn Ann *geriatrician, researcher*
Hutton, Lauren (Mary Laurence Hutton) *model, actress*
Huyser, Cynthia Gaye *computer programmer, poet*
Hyler, Sheryl Root *application developer*
Hyman, Trina Schart *illustrator*
Iasiello, Dorothy Barbara *clinical social worker, former brokerage company executive*
Ignatius, Nancy Weiser *fundraising and administrative executive*
Iltis, Carolee Ellen *psychologist*
Iman, (Iman Abdulmajid) *model*
Imlah, MaryPat *sales, advertising and marketing executive*
Impellizzeri, Anne Elmendorf *insurance company executive, non-profit executive*
Infante-Ogbac, Daisy Inocentes *sales executive, marketing executive, real estate broker*
Ingle, Beverly Dawn *elementary school educator*
Ingram, Barbara Averett *minister*
Ingram, Diana Joyce *construction executive*
Inscho, Jean Anderson *retired social worker, landscape artist*
Intrater, Cheryl Watson Waylor *career management consultant*
Irey, Charlotte York *dance educator*
Irwin, Denise Anne *human resources specialist*
Irwin, Linda Belmore *public relations/marketing consultant*
Isaac, Bina Susan *data processing executive*
Isaacs, Susan *novelist, screenwriter*
Isbell, Rita Anette *special education educator*
Isenor, Linda Darlene *grocery retailer, marketing professional*
Iskander, Sylvia Wiese *English literature educator*
Ittelson, Mary Elizabeth *museum director*
Iwuanyanwu, Eucharia Chiege *physician assistant*
Jablonski, Valerie *librarian*
Jack, Morgann Tayllor *writer, artist*
Jack-Moore, Phyllis *strategist, educational consultant*
Jackson, Clora Ellis *counselor, psychologist, educator*
Jackson, Donna E. *legal secretary, administrative assistant*
Jackson, Felicity Anne *performing arts organization administrator*
Jackson, Heather *secondary school educator*
Jackson, Lola Hirdler *art educator*
Jackson, Nicole Renée *mechanical engineer, educator*
Jackson, Robbi Jo *agricultural products executive, lawyer*
Jackson, Victoria Lynn *actress, comedienne*
Jackson-Tkac, Stephanie Ann *nurse*
Jacob, Christina Marie *social worker*
Jacob, Rosamond Tryon *librarian*
Jacobowitz, Ellen Sue *museum curator, museum and temple administrator*
Jacobs, Annette M. *music educator*
Jacobs, Eleanor *art consultant, retired art administrator*
Jacobs, Grace Gaines *retired gerontologist, adult education educator*
Jacobs, Judith *county legislator*
Jacobs, Lois Elizabeth *art educator*
Jacobs, Nancy Carolyn Baker *writer*
Jacobs, Patricia H. *social welfare organization executive*
Jacobsen, Diane DeMell *business executive and foreign policy specialist*
Jacobsen, Magdalena Gretchen *former mediator, former federal agency executive*
Jacobson, Joan Leiman *writer*
Jacoby, Beverly Schreiber *art consultant*
Jacoby, Teresa Michelle *animal behaviorist, business owner, entrepreneur*
James, Estelle *economist, educator*
Jameson, Patricia Marian *government agency administrator*
Jameson, Paula Ann *lawyer*
Jamison, Suzanne *management consultant*
Janko, May *graphic artist*
Jansen, Angela Bing *artist, educator*
Janssen, Anne L. *music educator*
Jaques, Kathryn Misbach *tax consultant*
Jaranilla, Sarah J. *critical care nurse, consultant*
Jarcho, Judith Lynn *artist*
Jarrow, Gail *literature educator, writer*
Jarvik, Gail Pairitz *medical geneticist*
Jay, Norma Joyce *artist*
Jayne, Cynthia Elizabeth *psychologist*
Jean, Claudette R. *retired elementary school educator*
Jefferson, Kathleen Henderson *retired secondary school educator*
Jeffress, Lynn *writer, education educator*
Jelsma, Elizabeth Barbara *music educator*
Jenkins, Billie Beasley *film company executive*
Jenkins, Brenda Gwenetta *early childhood and special education specialist*
Jenkins, Sebetha *college president*
Jennings, Carol *marketing executive*
Jennings, Gabrielle *artist*
Jensen, Eva Marie *medical/surgical nurse*
Jervis, Jane Lise *college official, science historian*
Jessup, Constance M. *music educator*
Jewell, Deborah Lynn *minister, educator*
Jewett, Mary (Betsy) Elizabeth *artist, conservationist*
Jiles, Kendra D'Antoinette *special education educator*
Jobe, Muriel Ida *medical technologist, educator*
Joffe, Barbara Lynne *computer management professional, computer artist*
Johansen, Karen Lee *retired sales executive*
Johnsen, Barbara Parrish *writer, educator*
Johnson, Amanda A. *computer scientist*
Johnson, Brenda Ann *special education educator*
Johnson, Carol Ann *editor*
Johnson, Carolyn M. *librarian, writer*
Johnson, Charlene Elizabeth *adult education educator, language arts consultant, educator*
Johnson, Crystal Duane *psychologist*
Johnson, Dolores Estelle *retired small business owner*
Johnson, Erma Jean *human services administrator*
Johnson, Freda S. *public finance consultant*
Johnson, Jana E. *pathologist*
Johnson, J(anet) Susan *psychologist*
Johnson, Jennie *chaplain, social worker*
Johnson, Joann K. *management consultant*
Johnson, Joyce *retired military officer*
Johnson, Karla Ann *county official*
Johnson, Katherine Holthaus *health care marketing professional*
Johnson, Kay Durbahn *real estate manager, consultant*
Johnson, Kysa Nicole *artist*
Johnson, Linda Sue *academic administrator, state agency administrator, retired state legislator*
Johnson, Margaret Kathleen *business educator*
Johnson, Marlene M. *nonprofit executive*
Johnson, Mary P. *freelance writer*
Johnson, Patricia B *medical, surgical nurse, mental health nurse*
Johnson, Rosalind B. *psychologist, researcher*
Johnson, Susan Ann *writer*
Johnson, Sylvia Sue *university administrator, educator*
Johnson, Ursula Anne *artist*
Johnson Hirt, Jacqueline Marie *elementary school educator*
Johnson-MIller, Charleen V. *teacher coordinator*
Johnson-Watson, Reva Mae *non-commissioned officer, consultant*
Johnston, Kristen Elizabeth *psychologist, researcher*
Jolivette, Carola Kate *assistant principal*
Jonas, Trudy Ann *principal*
Jones, Anita Katherine *computer scientist, educator*
Jones, Carolyn Evans *writer, speaker*
Jones, Christine Massey *retired furniture company executive*
Jones, Elaine R. *civil rights advocate*
Jones, Gwenyth Ellen *publishing information systems/technology executive*
Jones, Hettie Cohen *writer, educator*
Jones, Jan Laverty *mayor*
Jones, Joan Megan *anthropologist*
Jones, Pauline Reid *speech pathology/audiology services professional*
Jones, Phyllis Gene *judge*
Jones, Shirley *actress, singer*
Jones, Shirley Carol *music educator*
Jordan, Michelle Denise *lawyer*
Jordan, Tamecia Michelle *computer engineer*
Joseph, Geri Mack (Geraldine Joseph) *former ambassador, educator, journalist*
Joseph, Shirley Troyan *retired executive*
Joshi, Pratibha C. *immunologist, researcher*
Joyce, Diana *psychologist, education educator*
Judd, Barbara Ann Eastwood *financial management professional, union activist*
Judge, Jean Frances *management consultant*
Judge, Nancy Elizabeth *obstetrician, gynecologist*
Judge, Rajinder *psychiatrist*
Juenemann, Sister Jean *hospital executive*
Juffer, Kristin Ann *research analyst*
Julian, Frances Bloch *volunteer*
Junger, Patricia Carol *nurse*
Jurgensen, Karen *former newspaper editor*
Jurgutis, Danguole *artist*
Kaabar, JoAnne Florence *special education educator, poet*
Kabrich, Jeanine Renee *broadcaster, educator*
Kachur, Betty Rae *elementary school educator*
Kahana, Eva Frost *sociology educator*
Kahn, Lesly Jane *performing arts educator*
Kahn, Susan *artist*
Kahn, Victoria Elaine Hopkins *special education educator*
Kaimann, Diane S. *writer, educator*
Kaiser, Carlene Pearl *counseling administrator, media specialist*
Kaiser, Karen Sue *elementary school educator*
Kaiser, Nina Irene *health care consultant*
Kaliski, Mary *psychologist*
Kallman, Kathleen Barbara *marketing and business development professional*
Kalvin-Stiefel, Judy *public relations executive*
Kaminski, Patricia Joyce *lab administrator*
Kaminsky, Alice Richkin *English language educator*
Kane, Karen Marie *public affairs consultant*
Kane, Patricia Lanegran *language professional, educator*
Kane Hittner, Marcia Susan *bank executive*
Kanin, Fay *screenwriter*
Kannenstine, Margaret Lampe *artist*
Kantrowitz, Susan Lee *lawyer*
Kanuk, Leslie Lazar *management consultant, educator*
Kanyo, Deborah Sue *elementary school educator, music educator*
Kaplan, Erica Lynn *typing and word processing service company executive, pianist, educator*
Kaplan, Gabriela Diana *radiologist*
Kaplan, Grisel Arias *bank executive*
Kaplan, Helene Lois *lawyer*
Kaplan, Phyllis *artist, composer*
Kaplan, Sharon Barbara Bernstein *music educator*
Kaplun Braun, Jeannette *announcer, communications consultant*
Kappner, Augusta Souza *academic administrator*
Karakey, Sherry JoAnne *real estate company executive, interior designer*
Karalekas, Anne *business executive*
Karnofsky, Mollyne *artist, educator, poet*
Karp, Rosanne *oncology and women's health nurse*
Kaslow, Florence Whiteman *psychologist, educator, family business consultant*
Kaster, Laura A. *lawyer*
Kathan, Joyce C. *social worker, administrator*
Katz, Susan Arons *language arts specialist, author, poet*
Kauffman, B. Suzanne *investment company professional*
Kauffman, Kaethe Coventon *artist, writer, art educator*
Kauger, Yvonne *state supreme court justice*
Kavanagh, Cornelia Kubler *sculptor*
Kavanaugh, Bonnie B. *corporate communications executive*
Kavner, Julie *actress*
Kay, Bonnie Kathryn *management consultant*
Kaye, Janet Miriam *psychologist, educator*
Kazmarek, Linda Adams *secondary school educator*
Kearns, Amy Elizabeth Bankert *chemist*
Keating, Regina G. *computer analyst consultant*
Keebler, Lois Marie *elementary school educator*
Keech, Elowyn Ann *interior designer*
Keefer, Susan *voice educator*
Keene-Burgess, Ruth Frances *military official*
Keets, Elizabeth *artist, educator*
Keim, Betty Lou *actress, literary consulant*
Keiper, Marilyn Morrison *elementary school educator*
Keiser, Nanette Marie *research associate, project administrator*
Kelehear, Carole Marchbanks Spann *legal administrator*
Kellaigh, Kathleen *conservatory artistic director*
Kelley, Mary Elizabeth (Mary LaGrone) *information technology executive*
Kelley, Sheila Seymour *public relations consultant*
Kelly, Anastasia Donovan *lawyer*
Kelly, Sister Dorothy Ann *Ursuline Provincial college chancellor*
Kelly, Kathleen Dennis *international government affairs consultant*
Kelly, Sister Mary Elizabeth *principal*
Kelly, Nancy Folden *arts administrator*
Kelman, Lori Macellaro *biology educator, molecular biology researcher*
Kennedy, Claudia J. *retired military officer*
Kennedy, Colleen Michelle *academic administrator, educator*
Kennedy, Debra Joyce *marketing professional*
Kennedy, Jerrie Ann Preston *public relations executive*
Kennedy, Joanie Tiska *artist, painter, sculptor*
Kennedy, Kathleen *film producer*
Kennedy, Marla Catherine *psychologist*
Kenny, Deborah *marketing professional, educator*
Kenyon, Daphne Anne *economics educator*
Kercher, Kelli S. *special education educator*
Kerney, Yolonda V. *music historian*
Kernochan, Sarah M. *film director, scriptwriter, composer*
Kerr, Janet Spence *physiologist, pharmacologist, researcher*
Kerr, Linda *executive secretary*
Kerrigan, Kelly Ann *special education educator*
Kerzhnerman, Irina *psychologist*
Ketchum, Irene Frances *library director*
Key, Fleda *administrative assistant*
Keyes, Joan Ross Rafter *education educator, writer*
Keyes, Margaret Naumann *home economics educator*
Kezer, Pauline Ryder *state government executive, management consultant*
Kezlarian, Nancy Kay *marriage and family therapist*
Khan, Arfa *radiologist, educator*
Kibbe, Thana M. *pastor*
Kidd, Debra Jean *communications executive*
Kiel, Shelley *state senator*
Kienitz, LaDonna Trapp *lawyer, librarian, municipal official*
Killen, Kathleen Elizabeth *systems engineer, retired military officer*
Killoran, Cynthia Lockhart *retired educator*
Kim, Christina K.(yung) *investment company executive*
Kimbriel-Eguia, Susan *engineering planner, small business owner*
Kinard, Agnes Dodds *retired real estate company executive, historian, writer, lawyer*
Kincaid, Jamaica *writer*
King, Bonnie La Verne *education educator*
King, Imogene M. *retired nursing educator*
King, Jane Cudlip Coblentz *volunteer educator*
King, Joy Rainey *poet, executive secretary*
King, Joy Riemer *art educator*
King, Lynda *counselor*
King, Rosalyn Mercita *social sciences educator, researcher*
King, Susan Bennett *retired glass company executive*
King, Tamara Lynn *counselor*
Kingery, Brenda L. *artist, volunteer*
Kingston, Maxine Hong *writer, educator*
Kinley, Christine T. *certified physician assistant*

Mabee, Sandra Ivonne timpanist, percussionist, educator, clergyman
Macaskill, Bridget finance company executive
MacCarthy, Talbot Leland civic volunteer
MacCormack, Jean F. academic administrator
Macdonald, Sheila de Marillac company executive
Macklin, Ericka Monique career planning administrator
MacLean, Judith E. writer, editor
MacLennan, Beryce Winifred psychologist
MacPherson, Shirley clinical therapist
Madariaga, Lourdes Mercedes accountant
Maday, Christine Verga artist, illustrator
Maddox, Marjorie Lee (Marjorie Lee Maddox-Hafer) English educator
Madsen, Susan Arrington writer
Mady, Beatrice M. artist
Magarian, Karen S. chiropractor, consultant
Maglio, Gesomina V. clinical social worker
Magoon, Nancy Amelia art association administrator
Maguire-Zinni, Deirdre federal community development management analyst
Maher, Fran advertising agency executive
Maher, Lisa Krug editor
Mahfouz, Ilham Badreddine artist
Mahoney, Heather M. social worker
Mainwaring-Healey, Pepper equestrian, writer
Makkreel, Karen Emiko lawyer
Malek, Marlene Anne healthcare advocate, foundation administrator
Mallin, Jennifer internet company executive, writer
Mallo-Garrido, Josephine Ann advertising agency owner
Malme, Jane Hamlett lawyer, educator, advisor
Malone, Claudine Berkeley management consultant
Maloney, Therese Adele insurance company executive
Malott, Adele Renee editor
Malouf, Pamela Bonnie film editor, video editor
Maltby, Florence Helen library science educator
Manasc, Vivian architect, consultant
Mancini Brown, Sheree L education educator, writer
Mandel, Adrienne Abramson state legislator
Mandravelis, Patricia Jean retired healthcare administrator
Maner, Diana financial consultant
Mangan, Patricia Ann Pritchett statistician
Manglona, Ramona V. state attorney general, judge
Mangold, Sylvia Plimack artist
Manhart, Shawna Hope music educator
Manion, Kelley Michelle surgical technician
Manis, Laura Glance retired psychology educator
Manley, Joan A(dele) Daniels retired publishing executive
Manley, Judith L. director
Mann, Emily Betsy writer, artistic director, theater director
Mann, Joan Ellona artist, editor
Mannes, Elena Sabin film and television producer, director
Manning, Elaine S. retired art educator
Manning, Joan Elizabeth health association administrator
Manning, Nancy Christine elementary school educator
Manuelian, Lucy Der art educator, architecture educator
Manus, Nancy Manning writer, former social services administrator
Maple, Opal Lucille school psychologist
Maplesden, Carol Harper marital and family therapist, music educator
Marcdante, Karen Jean medical educator
Marceau, Yvonne ballroom dancer, educator
March, Jacqueline Front retired chemist
Marcinek, Margaret Ann nursing educator
Marcinko, Jacqueline Michele social worker
Marcinko, Kristy Eileen special education educator
Marco, Patricia Louise music educator
Marcoux, Julia A. midwife
Marcus, Kelly Stein psychologist, health science association administrator
Marcus, Sandra L. special education educator, consultant
Marez, Trinnie Marie marketing professional
Margolis, Peppy Sylvia (Pearl Margolis) elementary education educator, consultant
Margrave, Kathy Christine nurse anesthetist
Marino, Mary Q. research scientist
Marinoff, Isabella Blumenstock English educator
Marion, Marjorie Anne English language educator, education consultant
Mark, Judi actress, choreographer
Markle, Cheri Virginia Cummins nurse
Marko, Marlene psychiatrist
Markovich, Patricia Helen economist
Markowitz, Phyllis Frances retired mental health services professional, retired psychologist
Marlar, Janet Cummings retired public relations officer
Marlow, Marcia Marie secondary school educator, publishing executive
Marlowe, Willie artist, fine arts educator
Maroney, Jane P. former state legislator, consultant
Maroni, Donna Farolino biologist, researcher
Marot, Lola retired accountant
Marple, Jill M. music educator
Marquardt, Sandra Mary activist, lobbyist, researcher
Marquez, Michelle F. elementary school educator
Marquis, Harriet Hill social worker
Marr, Carmel Carrington retired lawyer, retired state official
Marron, Amy M. band director
Marsee, Susanne Irene mezzo-soprano
Marsh, Joan Knight educational film, video and computer software company executive, publisher children's books
Marsh, Lisa A. musician
Marsh, Merrilyn Delano sculptor, painter
Marshall, Kathryn Sue lawyer
Marshall, Navarre retired secondary school educator
Marth, Mary Ellen (Kim Martin) entertainer
Martin, Alice Howze prosecutor
Martin, Andrea Louise actress, comedienne, writer
Martin, Dale health facility administrator
Martin, Dianne Leslie artist, educator
Martin, Ione Edwards social worker
Martin, Leanna Wright minister
Martin, Marilyn Mann retired library media specialist
Martin, Mary secondary school educator
Martinelli, Janet Sue artist, educator
Martino, Donna Frances newspaper sales administrator
Martyl, (Mrs. Alexander Langsdorf Jr.) artist
Martz, Judy Helen governor
Maruoka, Jo Ann Elizabeth retired information systems manager
Marx, Anne (Mrs. Frederick E. Marx) poet
Mascheroni, Eleanor Earle marketing communications executive
Masi, Mary Elizabeth editor, writer
Mason, Lois E. (J. Day Mason) painter, poet, actress, educator
Mason, Margaret Crather elementary school educator
Mason, Marsha actress, theater director, writer
Massaro, Linda P. science foundation executive
Masten, Jacqueline Gwendolyn small business owner
Masters, Ann Browning education educator, poet
Mastracchio-Hardt, Dina Raphaella elementary school educator
Mata, Linda Sue Proctor writer, consultant
Matasovic, Marilyn Estelle manufacturing executive
Matelic, Candace Tangorra museum studies educator, consultant, museum director
Mater, Maud lawyer
Matera, Frances Lorine elementary school educator
Materia, Kathleen Patricia Ayling nurse
Mathieu, Michele Suzanne computer scientist, consultant
Mathis, Karen McHugh artist
Mathis, Sharon Bell author, retired elementary educator and librarian
Mattern, Joanne writer, educator
Matterson, Joan McDevitt physical therapist
Matteucci, Sherry Scheel former prosecutor
Matthew, Lyn sales executive, consultant, marketing professional, consultant
Matthews, Glenna Christine historian
Matthews, Mary Kostielney political organization worker, consultant
Maxfield, Louisa Fonda Gribble executive secretary
Maxwell, Dorothea Bost Andrews volunteer
Maxwell, Mary Ellen school system administrator
May, Phyllis Jean financial executive
Mayer, Kristine I. small business owner, writer
Mayer, Mona R. music educator
Mayer, Susan Martin art educator
Maynard, Natalie Ryshna pianist, educator
Mazzoni, Kerry former state agency administrator
McArdle, Kathleen Ann elementary school educator
McAteer, Deborah Grace travel executive
McBride, Sandra Teague psychiatric nurse
McCafferty, Lorna Marie (Lorna Supernor) computer electronics engineer
McCandless, Carolyn Keller retired human resources executive
McCann, Diana Rae secondary school educator
McCann, Elizabeth Ireland theater, television and motion picture producer, lawyer
McCann, Joyce Jeannine retired elementary education educator
McCargar, Eleanor Barker artist
McCarthy, Mary Armao professional society administrator
McCarthy, Mary Frances medical foundation administrator, not-for-profit fundraiser, consultant
McCarthy, Rose Marie medical/surgical nurse
McCaughey Ross, Elizabeth P. (Betsy McCaughey) former lieutenant governor
McCauley, Floyce Reid psychiatrist
McCauley, Jane Reynolds journalist
McClain, Lena Alexandria protective services official
Mc Clellan, Catharine anthropologist, educator
McClure, Ann Crawford judge, lawyer
McClure, Evelyn Susan historian, photographer
McCombs, Kelly Fritz dietician
McCormack, Marjorie Guth psychology educator, career counselor, communications educator, public relations consultant
McCormick, Donna Lynn social worker
McCourt, Lisa writer
McCoy, Donna Lee elementary school educator
McCoy, Mary Nell music educator
McCuistion, Peg Orem retired hospice administrator
McCulley, Lana Janeen museum administrator, consultant
McCully, Emily Arnold illustrator, writer
McCurdy, Gisela Ann physician
McDaniel, Anna S. language educator
McDaniel, Sara Sherwood (Sally McDaniel) trainer, consultant
McDarrah, Gloria Schoffel editor, author
McDermott, Agnes Charlene Senape philosophy educator
McDermott, Lucinda Mary ecumenical minister, teacher, philosopher, poet, author, psychologist
McDonald, Roxanne Marie English language educator, writer
McDonald, Sally J. lawyer
McDonald-UmBayemake, Linda librarian, rehabilitation counselor
Mc Donnell, Loretta Wade lawyer
McDougal, Amy Nicole poet
McDowell, Elaine retired federal government executive, educator
McDyer, Susan Spear academic administrator
McElwee, Doris Ryan psychotherapist
McEntire, Reba N. country singer
McEwen, Joan Grace (Joanie Lawrence) actress, recording industry executive
McFadden, Nancy Elizabeth lawyer
McFadden, Robbyn Kilbane interior designer, public policy specialist, artist, advocate
McFall, Catherine Gardner poet, critic, educator
McFate, Patricia Ann foundation executive, science educator
McGann, Lisa B. Napoli language educator
McGarry, Marcia retired community service coordinator
McGee, Carrie L. artist
McGervey, Teresa Ann technical information specialist
McGhee, Carla Renee professional basketball player
McGinn, Mary Lyn real estate company executive
McGinn Miller, Janet Scrivner elementary school educator, writer
McGlynn, Marilyn Hutchison medical/surgical nurse, educator
McGrath, Anna Fields retired librarian
McGrath, Eileen Marie pediatric nurse
McGraw, A. Michelle music educator
McGraw, Janet Goller executive secretary, office coordinator
McGreevy, Mary Sharron former psychology educator
McGunigle, Dorothy Greene interior designer, artist
McHugh, Annette S. artist, educator, playwright
McIntosh, Amy Bennett publishing/internet company executive
McIntosh, Carolyn Meade retired educational administrator
Mc Intyre, Vonda Neel writer
McKay, Renee artist
McKelly, Beverly artist, educator
McKenney, Gladys Holdeman educational consultant, artist, storyteller
McKeown, Lorraine Laredo travel company executive, writer
McKinney, Cara Lynn music educator
McKinnie, Nancy Elliott bank executive
McKune, Elizabeth Walter education educator, psychologist
McLain, Thelma Louise retired librarian
McLaughlin, Dara Dawn freelance/self-employed writer, freelance/self-employed artist
McLaughlin, Goldie Carter music educator
McLaughlin, Jean Wallace art director, artist
McLaughlin, Joan B. literature and writing educator, writer
McLean, Julianne Drew concert pianist, educator
McLemore, Carol Lee accountant
McMahon Mastroddi, Marcia A. secondary school educator, artist, writer
McMaster, Belle Miller religious organization administrator
McMaster, Juliet Sylvia English language educator
McMillan, Terry L. writer, educator
McMillen, Sarah Anne marriage and family therapist, adult education educator
McMinn, Virginia Ann human resources consulting company executive
McMorrow, Margaret Mary (Peg McMorrow) retired secondary school educator
McMullen, Jennifer Anne secondary school educator
McMullin, Joyce Anne general contractor
McNeely, Bonnie L. (K.W. Rowe Jr.) retired internist and educator
McNees, Pat (Patricia Ann McNees) writer, editor
McNeil Staudenmaier, Heidi Loretta lawyer
McNulty, Kathleen Anne clinical social worker, psychotherapist, business consultant,
McPeters, Sharon Jenise artist, writer
McPhearson, Geraldine June medical/surgical nurse
McVeigh-Pettigrew, Sharon Christine communications consultant
McVey, Alice Lloyd social worker
McWethy, Patricia Joan educational association administrator
McWhirter, Jamila LeAnn choral conductor
Meagher, Sandra Krebs artist
Meaker, Marijane Agnes author
Meara, Anne actress, playwright, writer
Mebane, Felicia Eugenia health policy, news media educator, researcher
Medaglia, Elizabeth Ellen small business owner
Medina, Janie not-for-profit fundraiser
Medina, Kathryn Bach book editor
Medina, Sandra social worker, educator
Medlin, Veronica B. benefits compensation analyst
Meek, Carrie P. former congresswoman
Mehring, Nancy medical and surgical nurse, administrator
Meier, Debi Dawn secondary school educator
Meier, Heather M. music educator
Meil, Kate sculptor
Meilan, Celia food products executive
Meitner, Erika poet, education educator
Melanson, Susan C. small business owner
Melesio, Kathryn Mary oncological nurse, educator
Melka, Janet Patricia medical/surgical nurse
Melman, Cynthia Sue special education educator
Melnick, Jodi dancer
Melton, Roberta Lynn-Kong financial consultant
Meltzer, E. Alyne elementary school educator, social worker, volunteer
Menaker, Shirley Ann Lasch psychology educator, academic administrator
Mendelsohn, Carol S. television producer
Mendez, C. Beatriz obstetrician, gynecologist, educator, gynecologist, consultant
Mendoza, Ruth art educator
Menna, Sári artist, educator
Menzel, Marybelle Proctor volunteer
Mercuri, Joan B. museum administrator
Merlis, Annette Forbes artist
Mermelstein, Betty Jane elementary school educator
Merrifield, Theresa L. assistant principal, consultant
Merrill, Jean Fairbanks writer
Mesa, Yolanda Del Carmen artist
Mesch, Helene W. retired social worker
Mesrobian, Arpena Sachaklian publisher, editor, consultant
Metcalf, Karen retired foundation executive
Metcalf, Pauline Cabot architectural historian
Metzler, Ruth Horton genealogical educator
Meyer, Frances Margaret Anthony elementary and secondary school educator, health education specialist
Meyer, Pucci newspaper editor
Meyer, Ruth Krueger museum administrator, educator, art historian
Meyers, Jan retired congresswoman
Mezacapa, Edna S. music educator, elementary school educator
Michaels, Marion Cecelia newswriter, editor, news syndicate executive
Michel, Aimee Katherine theater director, educator
Michel, Elizabeth Cheney social reform consultant
Michelle, Stefl music educator, choral director, soprano
Michels, Dia Loren publishing executive, writer
Mickelson, Rhoda Ann speech pathology/audiology services professional
Middel, Marjorie social worker, consultant
Miedema, Barbara Jane music educator
Miele, Denise Marie special education educator
Miguel, Jennifer Marie adult education educator
Mikan, Kathleen Joyce Kehrer medical/surgical nurse, educator
Mikiewicz, Anna Daniella marketing and international business exporter
Mikles, Alicia Genevieve artist, publishing executive
Mikulski, Barbara Ann senator
Milano, Alyssa actress
Miles, Joan Fowle journalist, writer
Miles, Laveda Ann advertising executive
Milewski, Barbara Anne pediatrics nurse, neonatal/perinatal nurse practitioner, critical care nurse
Milholland, Sandra Jane marriage and family therapist
Militello, Roberta Jan artist, illustrator, designer
Millane, Lynn retired town official
Miller, Alice state representative
Miller, Alice Ann state utilities regulation executive
Miller, Catherine Lynn mental health services professional, writer
Miller, Cheryl DeAnn former professional basketball coach, broadcaster
Miller, Diane Doris executive search consultant
Miller, Elaine Wilson computer consultant
Miller, Elizabeth Jean geologist
Miller, Ellen S. marketing communications executive
Miller, Emily Elizabeth elementary school educator, editor
Miller, Eunice A. marriage and family therapist, sex therapist, foundation administrator
Miller, Gay Davis lawyer
Miller, Harriet Sanders former art center director
Miller, Jacqueline Winslow library director
Miller, Lenore Wolf Daniels speech-language pathologist
Miller, Linda Karen retired secondary school educator, social studies educator, law educator
Miller, Loretta Marie dispatcher, writer
Miller, Marilyn Lea library science educator
Miller, Mary Hotchkiss lay worker
Miller, Nancy Ann music educator
Miller, Patricia Louise state legislator, nurse
Miller, Roberta Doris elementary school educator
Miller(Gordon), Michelle Renee music educator
Millman, Amy J. government official
Millman, Marilyn Estelle elementary school educator
Mills, Celeste Louise dog breeder, hypnotherapist, professional magician
Mills, Dale Douglas journalist
Mills, Elizabeth Shown genealogist, editor, writer
Mills, Gloria Adams energy service consultant
Milnor, Hazel nurse
Mims, Clarice Roberta financial advisor
Minatee, Stefanie Reneé vocal educator
Mindas, Mary L. music educator, composer
Mindnich, Ellen sales executive
Minieri, Joan community organization director
Minkoff, Hilda Bressler secondary and adult education educator
Minor, Addine E. civic leader
Minor, Clara Mae election judge
Minot, Eliza writer
Mintz, Gwendolyn Joyce writer, educator
Miquelon, Miriam F. former prosecutor, lawyer
Miracle, Doris Jean retired medical/surgical nurse
Miscella, Maria Diana humanities educator
Miskill, Dee Shelton design graphics executive
Misner, Lorraine laboratory technologist
Misrack, Tana Marie counselor, minister, writer
Mitchell, Carlena Michelle school system administrator

Mitchell, Carolyn Cochran *foundation administrator's executive assistant*
Mitchell, Edith (Bertsche) *secondary school educator*
Mitchell, Gina Lynn *health facility administrator*
Mitchell, Marcia Jeanne *freelance/self-employed writer, events producer*
Mitchell, Margaret Yvonne *forester*
Mitchell, Mary Lu *information researcher, civic volunteer, retired*
Mitchell, Pamela Ann *airline pilot*
Mitchell, Patricia Edenfield *television executive*
Mitchem, Cheryl E. *accounting educator*
Mitchem, Mary Teresa *publishing executive*
Mitchum, Beth *freelance/self-employed editor, writer*
Mitelman, Bonnie Cossman *editor, writer*
Mitgang, Iris Feldman *retired lawyer*
Mitrany, Devora *writer, editor*
Mitts, Marybeth Frazier *real estate company executive, consultant*
Moberly, Bonnie Lou *travel services executive*
Mockler, Anna *writer, ecologist*
Moen, Margaret *print company editor*
Moffat, MaryBeth *consulting company executive*
Moffatt, Katy (Katherine Louella Moffatt) *musician, vocalist, songwriter*
Mohr, Barbara Jeanne *secondary school educator*
Moistner, Mona Sue *adult education educator*
Molden, A(nna) Jane *counselor*
Molina, Richelle Julietta *music educator*
Molinaro, Valerie Ann *lawyer*
Molloy, Sylvia *Latin American literature educator, writer*
Molnar, Violet *mental health nurse*
Monck, Maureen F. *psychoanalyst*
Monczewski, Maureen R. *secondary art educator, visual artist*
Monkman, Betty Claire *curator*
Monroe, Barbara Jean *writer, educator*
Montbertrand, Lois Shiner *lawyer*
Montgomery, Helen Janet *social worker*
Montgomery, Marilyn Ruth *elementary school educator, consultant*
Monzingo, Agnes Yvonne *veterinary technician*
Mooney, Sara *media specialist*
Moore, Betty Jo *legal assistant*
Moore, Emily Allyn *pharmacologist*
Moore, Fay Linda *systems engineer*
Moore, Jean E. *social worker, academic administrator, educator, radio personality*
Moore, Margaret Ann *musician, composer*
Moore, Marsha Lynn *elementary school educator, counseling administrator*
Moore, Susanna *writer*
Moosbrugger, Sabine Andrea *education educator, writer*
Morales, Marcia Paulette Merry *language educator, archaeologist*
Moran, Sheila Kathleen *journalist*
Morang, Diane Judy *writer, television producer, business entrepreneur*
Morelan, Paula Kay *choreographer*
Moreland, Cheryl *psychologist*
Morgan, Ann M. *artist, educator*
Morgan, Anne Marie G. *broadcast journalist, educator*
Morgan, Donna Jean *psychotherapist*
Morgan, Evelyn Buck *retired nursing educator*
Morgan, Jane Hale *retired library director*
Morgan, Linda Gail *producer*
Morgan, Linda Joan *former federal agency administrator*
Morgan, Lynn *sports association executive*
Morgan, M. Jane *computer systems consultant*
Morgan, Marianne *corporate professional*
Morgan, Mary Lou *retired education educator, volunteer*
Morgan, Paulette Elise *state official, researcher*
Morgan, Ruth Prouse *academic administrator, educator*
Moritz, Jean Loris *elementary school educator*
Morrell, Tanya M. *psychologist*
Morrill, Penny Chittim *art historian*
Morris, Dorothy Kay *writer*
Morris, Harriet R. *elementary school educator*
Morris, Martha Marnel *music educator*
Morris, Maureen Sauter *bank officer*
Morris-Blacker, Marilyn Eileen *librarian*
Morrison, Ann Hess *information technology specialist*
Morrison, Francine Darlene *psychiatrist, massage therapist, herbal simplist*
Morrison, Margaret L. *artist, educator, consultant*
Morrison, Nancy Jane *art educator*
Morrison, Sarah Lyddon *author*
Morrison, Shelley *actress*
Morrow, Martha F. *elementary school educator*
Morrow, Nena Renee *medical/surgical nurse*
Morrow, Susan Dagmar *psychic, medium educator, writer, consultant*
Morse, Anne Bernadette *educational consultant*
Morse, Jean Avnet *higher education administrator, lawyer*
Morse, Terri Fraser *engineering administrator*
Morse-McNeely, Patricia *poet, writer, retired middle school educator*
Moseley, Carol June *security supervisor, small business owner*
Moseley, Julia W. *music teacher, historic preservationist*
Moseley-Braun, Carol *former senator, former ambassador*
Mosely, Elaine W. *school librarian*
Moskovitz, Elisa McMillan *music educator, musician*
Moskovitz, Nancy Siegel *artist, elementary school educator*
Moskowitz, Rebecca C. *systems analyst*
Moslak, Judith *retired music educator*
Mossel, Patricia L. *retired opera executive*
Mott, Mary Elizabeth *retired educational administrator*
Motzer, Robin Lynne *interior designer, writer, artist, poet, singer*

Mould, Joan Powell *social worker*
Mowrer-Reynolds, Elizabeth Louise *educational psychology educator*
Moy, Audrey *retired retail buyer*
Moyers, Kelli R. *psychotherapist*
Muehl, Lois Baker *writer, retired language educator*
Mueller, Barbara Stewart (Bobbie Mueller) *youth drug use prevention specialist, volunteer*
Muhammad, Claudette Marie *religious organization administrator*
Muhammad, LaTonja Walker *control engineer*
Muhn, Judy Ann *psychologist, genealogist*
Mulcahy, Joanne B. *literature educator*
Mull, Beth A. *counseling educator*
Mullen, Terri Ann *retired special education educator*
Mullette, Julienne Patricia *health facility administrator*
Mullins, Barbara J. *financial executive*
Mulryan, Lenore Hoag *art curator, author*
Mundorff Shrestha, Sheila Ann *cariologist*
Munn, Carol Louise *private school educator*
Muñoz Dones De Carrascal, Eloisa *hospital administrator, pediatrician, consultant, educator*
Muñoz-Solá, Haydeé Socorro *library administrator*
Munsell, Elsie Louise *lawyer*
Munson, Lynne Ann *cultural critic*
Munson, Susan Marie *special education educator*
Munsterman, Ingrid Anita *assistant principal*
Murphey, Sheila Ann *infectious diseases physician, educator, researcher*
Murphy, Ann Pleshette *magazine editor-in-chief*
Murphy, Elisabeth Maria *physical design engineer, consultant*
Murphy, Evelyn Frances *economist*
Murphy, Jean B. *principal*
Murphy, Kathleen Mary *former law firm executive, alternative healing professional*
Murphy, Margaret A. *nursing educator, adult nurse practitioner*
Murphy, Michelle Zick *special education educator*
Murphy, Sandra Robison *lawyer*
Murphy, Thelma Arabella *elementary school educator, photographer*
Murtha, Pamela Berry *secondary school educator*
Musilli Messano, Ester Anna *music educator*
Muskopf, Margaret Rose *elementary school educator*
[illegible] *mechanical engineering researcher, consultant*
Myers, Libby Ann *retired medical/surgical nurse*
Myers, Margaret Jane (Dee Dee Myers) *television personality, editor*
Myers, Sue Bartley *artist*
Myers-Morrison, Cynthia Jean *marriage and family therapist, educator*
Nagys, Elizabeth Ann *environmental issues educator*
Nahumck, Nadia Chilkovsky *performer, dance educator, choreographer, author*
Naidu, Jenny *principal*
Natividad, Lisalinda Salas *family advocacy outreach manager*
Natsuyama, Harriet Hatsune Kagiwada *mathematician, educator*
Navratilova, Martina *professional tennis player*
Neal, Cynthia Ann *elementary school educator, composer*
Neal, Teresa Schreibeis *secondary school educator*
Neale, Diane Yunck *artist*
Neary, Patricia Elinor *ballet director*
Nederveld, Ruth Elizabeth *retired real estate executive*
Nedza, Sandra Louise *manufacturing executive*
Needham, Tracy Lee *marketing professional, consultant*
Neel, Judy Murphy *association executive*
Neeley, Abigail English *music educator*
Neff, Diane Irene *university administrator*
Neff, Jennifer Ellen *painter, artist*
Nelson, Alice Carlstedt *retired nursing educator*
Nelson, Charlene Dess *elementary school educator*
Nelson, Doreen Kae *mental health counselor, educator, reserve military officer*
Nelson, Hope Linda *pilot*
Nelson, JoAnn *secondary school educator, educational consultant*
Nelson, Kay Ellen *speech and language pathologist*
Nelson, Marcia Z. *writer, educator*
Nelson, Martha Jane *magazine editor*
Nemec-Kessel, Charlene *artist, educator*
Nemeroff, Robin Kim *psychologist, educator, researcher*
Nemiroff, Maxine Celia *art educator, gallery owner, consultant*
Neu, Jennifer Elizabeth *music educator*
Neuerburg-Denzer, Ursula *theater director, educator, actress*
Neuman, Linda Kinney *retired state supreme court justice, lawyer*
Neumann, Irma Wanda *musician, educator*
Neville, Phoebe *choreographer, dancer, educator*
Neville, Regina Frances Lickteig *performing arts company executive, educator*
Nevins, Sheila *television programmer and producer*
New, Anne Latrobe *public relations, fund raising executive*
Newell, Jane Ann *retired elementary school educator*
Newhall, Edith Allerton *writer*
Newman, Rachel *editor*
Newman, Rebecca K. *principal*
Newman, Robin Gorman *communications executive, writer*
Newman, Suzanne Dinkes *web site development executive*

Newmar, Julie Chalane *actress, dancer, real estate businesswoman*
Newton, Elizabeth Purcell *counselor, consultant, writer*
Newton, Juanita *social worker, educator*
Nguyen, Mai (Mai Tuyet Nguyen) *writer*
Nicholas, Lynn Holman *historian, researcher, writer*
Nichols, Allene Rasmussen *writer, educator*
Nichols, Cherie L. *publishing executive, composer*
Nichols, Elizabeth Grace *nursing educator, dean*
Nichols, Iris Jean *illustrator*
Nichols, Natalie Rega *development consultant*
Nichols, Sandra Jean *secondary school educator, coach*
Nicholson, Jennifer Denise *workers' compensation claims administrator*
Nicholson, June C. Daniels *retired speech pathologist*
Nicks, Stevie (Stephanie Lynn Nicks) *singer, songwriter*
Nicolodi, Theresa Anne *speech pathologist*
Nicols, Angela C. *software engineer, computer consultant*
Nielsen, Jacqueline Anne *music specialist*
Nielsen, Linda Miller *city councilwoman*
Nielson, Alyce Mae *poet*
Niguidula, Kathleen Ann *music educator, musician*
Nixon, Carol Holladay *retired park and recreation director*
Nixon, Marni *singer*
Nixon, Shirnette *pharmaceutical company administrator*
Noah, Julia Jeanine *retired librarian*
Nobert, Frances *music educator*
Nochman, Lois Wood Kivi (Mrs. Marvin Nochman) *retired educator*
Noddings, Nel *education educator, writer*
Noddings, Sarah Ellen *lawyer*
Nodelman, Nancy Ziegler *sculptor, designer*
Noe, Elnora (Ellie Noe) *retired chemicals executive*
Noel, Cheryl Elaine *artist, poet*
Nolan, Joan T. *elementary school educator*
Noll, Jeanne C. *retired music educator*
Noolan, Julie Anne Carroll *management consultant*
Noonan, Shauna Gay *petroleum engineer*
Norbeck, Jane S. *retired nursing educator*
Norkin, Cynthia Clair *retired physical therapist*
Norman, E. Gladys *retired business computer educator, consultant*
Normore, Lorraine Frances *information systems researcher*
North, Anita *secondary school educator*
Northern, Ernestine *gifted and talented educator*
Norton, Karen Ann *accountant*
Nott, Tara Lee *Olympic athlete*
Novack, Barbara *writer, educator*
Novak, Barbara *art history educator*
Novotny, Deborah A. *management consultant*
Noyes, Judith Mitchell *sales executive*
Noziglia, Carla Miller *forensic scientist, consultant*
Nugent, Jane Kay *retired utilities executive*
Nuss, Joanne Ruth *sculptor, artist*
Nuttelman, Doris Graves *nursing administrator*
Oakes, Ellen Ruth *psychotherapist, health institute administrator*
O'Brien, K. Patricia *product development engineer*
O'Brien, Kathy Mosdal *director, educator*
O'Brien, Orin Ynez *musician, educator*
O'Brien, Sheila Marie *judge*
Occhipinti, Lisa *artist*
O'Connor, Catherine Marie *music educator*
O'Connor, Doris Julia *non-profit fundraiser, consultant*
O'Connor Taylor, Sheryl Ann *medical services administrator*
Odegaard, Cynthia *sales executive*
O'Dell, Joan Elizabeth *lawyer, mediator, business executive, educator*
Odom, Judy *software company executive*
O'Donell, Rosa Elia *assistant principal, educator*
O'Donnell, Kathleen C. *artist*
O'Donnell Rich, Dorothy Juanita *small business owner*
Ofstad, Evelyn Larsen Boyl *retired primary school educator, radio personality, film producer*
Ogden, Ann *writer*
Oglesby, Jerri Burdette *elementary school educator*
O'Hara, Catherine *actress, comedienne*
Okolski, Cynthia Antonia *psychotherapist, social worker*
Okoshi-Mukai, Sumiye *artist*
Olds, Jacqueline *psychiatrist, educator*
O'Leary, Kathleen Ann *writer*
Olesen, Carolyn McDonald *dance educator, choreographer*
O'Loughlin, Katie Eileen Bridget *poet*
Olsen, Virginia *human services manager*
Olson, Joanne J. *artist, art educator*
Olson, Lynn Ann *psychologist, educator*
Olson, Margaret Smith *program director, hospitality professional*
O'Neal, Patricia Jane *human resources specialist*
O'Neill, Mary Jane *not-for-profit administrator, consultant*
O'Neill Wotanowski, Eileen Mary *special education educator*
Ongas, Sharon *elementary school educator*
Oppenheim-Schreiner, Elissa *composer*
Ord, Linda Banks *artist*
Oritsky, Mimi *artist, educator*
Ormai-Buza, Ildiko *soprano, composer, organist, music educator*
Orner, Patricia Ann *desktop publishing administrator, writer*
O'Rourke, Joan B. Doty Werthman *retired school system administrator*
Orozco, Edith Dell *counselor*

Orr, Amy J. *sociologist, educator*
Orr, Marjorie *poet, dancer, publishing executive*
Ortega, Lorraine G. *state land office executive*
Ortiz - Robledo, Cinda Aurelia *music educator*
Osborn, Susan Titus *editor*
Osborne, Carrie Lynn *special education educator*
O'Shea, Catherine Large *marketing and public relations consultant*
Oskin, JoEllen Ross *special education educator, school librarian*
Osmond, Marie *singer*
Ostermann, Grace Gentile *librarian, media specialist*
Otis, Lee Liberman *lawyer, educator*
Otto, Jean Hammond *journalist*
Otwell, Donna Sharon *history educator*
Ovadiah, Janice *non-profit organization consultant, cultural institute executive*
Owen, Carol Thompson *artist, educator, writer*
Owen, Suzanne *retired savings and loan association executive*
Owens, Luvie Moore *association consultant*
Oxell, Loie Gwendolyn *fashion and beauty educator, consultant, columnist*
Ozick, Cynthia *writer*
Pack, Susan Joan *art consultant*
Padberg, Harriet Ann *mathematics educator*
Paddock, Sandra Constance *music educator*
Padgett, Cynthia S. *artist*
Paegle, Julie Sophia *writer, editor, educator*
Pagano, Michelina Olimpia *art director, writer*
Pagel, Inga Ann *accountant*
Painter, Vanessa L. *music educator*
Pakenham, Rosalie Muller Wright *magazine and newspaper editor*
Palchik, Anna *book designer, writer*
Pallart, Cheryl *literature educator, writer*
Pall-Pallant, Teri *paleontologist, inventor, behavioral scientist, design engineer, advertising agency executive*
Palmer, Faye Diane *music educator*
Palmer, Irene Sabelberg *university dean and educator emeritus, nurse, researcher, historian, genealogist*
Palmer, Jocelyn Beth *volunteer*
Palmer, Mary Ann *videoconference product manager, sales engineer*
Palmer, Rose Ann *television producer, writer, educator*
Palumbo, Lucille A. *microbiologist*
Panzer, Mary Caroline *historian, museum curator*
Paolucci, Anne Attura *playwright, poet, English and comparative literature educator, educational consultant*
[illegible] *communications technbology executive, communications engineer*
Pappal, Jennifer M. *musician, educator*
Parashak, Debra Sue *civil engineer*
Parham, Ellen Speiden *nutrition educator*
Parke, Janet Diane *interior designer*
Parke, Marilyn Neils *writer*
Parker, Susan Brooks *healthcare executive*
Parks, Grace Susan *bank official*
Parks, Jean Anne *retired acute care nurse practitioner*
Parode, Ann *lawyer*
Parrette, Anne Marie *music educator, conductor, musician*
Parris, Nina Gumpert *curator, writer, researcher, photographer*
Parrish-Porter, Vallerie *controller*
Parrott, Lois Anne *humanities educator*
Parry-Roland, Ann *writing educator*
Parsons, Christina Anne *writer, photographer*
Parsons, Lisa Kay *artist, writer*
Pascale, Jane Fay *pathologist*
Pascoe, Clara P. *public relations executive, property manager*
Pascoe, Patricia Hill *former state legislator*
Paskawicz, Jeanne Frances *pain specialist*
Pastula, Leah Lynn *mental health services professional*
Patchin, Rebecca J. *anesthesiologist, educator, administrator*
Patrick, Mary Kathleen *freelance/self-employed writer, food service executive*
Patrick, Michele Mary *government official*
Patterson, Denise Quitina *principal*
Patterson, Elizabeth Johnston *retired congresswoman*
Patterson, Mildred Lucas *retired teaching specialist*
Paul, Eve W. *retired lawyer*
Paul, Julia *ancient history researcher*
Pauley, Jane *television journalist*
Paulik, Mary Theresa *retired municipal official, researcher*
Paulus, Norma Jean Petersen *lawyer*
Payne, Mary Libby *retired judge*
Payne, Susan Frantz *fundraiser, artist*
Peacock, Mary Willa *magazine editor*
Peacock, Virginia C. *artist*
Pearce, Serena Ray *performing arts educator, music director*
Pearson, Carolyn Sue *primary school educator*
Peaslee, Margaret Mae Hermanek *zoology educator*
Peattie, Lisa Redfield *urban anthropology educator*
Peckham, Ellen *artist, poet*
Pedrick, Jean *poet*
Peek, Stephanie *artist*
Peele-Burkholder, Tammy Sue *nurse*
Peifer, Millie R. *computer company executive*
Peiris, Suhithi Mahesica *research chemist*
Pellicciotto, Nicole Alyssa *special education services professional, consultant*
Pence, Jean Virginia (Jean Pence) *retired real estate broker*
Pendleton, Gail Ruth *newspaper editor, writer, educator*
Pendleton, Joan Marie *microprocessor designer*
Penniman, Linda Simmons *real estate agent*
Pepelea, Kimberli Rae *case manager*

Perdigó, Luisa Marina *foreign language and literature educator*
Perdue, Kathy *operations research specialist*
Peretsman, Nancy B. *investment banker*
Peretti, Marilyn Gay Woerner *human services professional*
Perez, Dianne M. *medical researcher*
Perez, Luz Lillian *psychologist*
Pergal, Theresa Maria *artist*
Perham, Leigh Wellington *art educator, art historian*
Peri, Linda Carol *librarian*
Perkins, Nancy Jane *industrial designer*
Perlov, Dadie *management consultant, consultant*
Perraud, Pamela Brooks *human resources professional*
Perriguey, Georgia Désirée *poet, educator*
Perry, Dawn Anna *music educator*
Pervall, Stephanie Joy *management consultant*
Peters, Carol Ann Dudycha *counselor*
Peters, Mary Catherine *journalist, researcher, broadcaster*
Petersen, Stephanie Burton *bond analyst*
Peterson, Ann Sullivan *physician, health care consultant*
Peterson, Clara Margaret *elementary school educator*
Peterson, Veronica Marie (Ronnie Peterson) *clinical nurse manager*
Petree, Betty Chapman *anesthetist*
Petrelis, Stella Marsha *writer*
Petrie, Amy Elizabeth *speech pathology/audiology services professional*
Pettigrew, L. Eudora *retired academic administrator*
Pettinato, Maureen J. *special education educator*
Pettine, Linda Faye *physical therapist*
Pettis-Roberson, Shirley McCumber *retired congresswoman*
Pevear, Roberta Charlotte *retired state legislator*
Pfaff, Judy *artist*
Pfeiffer-Kennedy, Natalie Patricia Anita *public relations executive, social sciences educator, consultant*
Pham, Lara Bach-Vien *small business owner*
Phelan, Ellen *artist*
Phelan, Mary Michenfelder *public relations executive, writer*
Phelps, Gerry Charlotte *economist, minister*
Phillips, Dorothy Kay *lawyer*
Phillips, Glynda Ann *editor*
Phillips, Jill Meta *novelist, critic, astrologer*
Phillips, M. Catherine *elementary school educator*
Phillips, Michelle Gilliam *actress, writer*
Phillips, Winifred Patricia *radio producer, composer*
Picket, Lynn Snowden *magazine editor, writer*
Pickus, Gloria B. *retired secondary school educator*
Piculin, Laurette M. *mediator*
Pielou, Evelyn C. *biologist*
Pierce, Diane Jean *artist*
Pierce, Hilda (Hilda Herta Harmel) *painter*
Pierce, Lisa Margaret *telecommunications executive, product and market development manager, lecturer*
Pierce, Marian Marie *writer, educator*
Pierce, Ponchitta Ann *TV host, producer, journalist, writer, consultant*
Pierce, Shaheeda Laura *midwife, consultant*
Pierce, Susan Resneck *academic administrator, literature educator*
Pierik, Marilyn Anne *retired librarian, piano teacher*
Pilette, Patricia Chehy *healthcare organizational management consultant*
Pilgrim, Dianne Hauserman *retired museum director*
Pillote, Barbara Wiegand *volunteer*
Pilon, A. Barbara *language and literature educator*
Pimental, Nancy M. *scriptwriter, actress*
Pincus, Nancy *architect, web site designer*
Pinkett-Smith, Jada *actress*
Pinkham, Robin Remick *corporate financial executive*
Pinto, Rosalind *retired educator, civic volunteer*
Pinton, Cristina Costantina *artist, educator*
Pipchick, Margaret Hopkins *advance practice nurse, marriage and family therapist*
Piper, Margarita Sherertz *retired school system administrator*
Pipkin, Mary Margaret *artist*
Pisciotta, Vivian Virginia *psychotherapist*
Pitcher, Susan Ingrid *art dealer*
Pitilli, Loretta Ann *special education educator*
Place, Janey *banking consultant, former bank executive*
Plaisted, Carole Anne *elementary school educator*
Plank, Judith Anne *television production coordinator*
Platti, Rita Jane *secondary school educator, draftsman, writer, inventor*
Player, Audrey Nell *research scientist*
Pledger, Myrna Joan *counselor*
Pleshette, Suzanne *actress*
Plette, Sandra Lee *retired insurance company executive*
Plimpton, Peggy Lucas *trustee*
Plottel, Gloria Susanne Stone *marketing professional*
Plouffe, Diane Marie *music educator*
Podell, Jean Elizabeth Mesberg *artist*
Podsiadlo, Maria J. *human resources analyst*
Poe, Cheryl Toni *music educator*
Poe, Laura *nursing educator, administrator*
Pohlmann, Evelyn Gawley *music educator, consultant*
Pokras, Sheila Frances *retired judge*
Poleshuk, Alicia L. *alcohol/drug abuse services professional*
Polite, Carlene Hatcher *writer, educator*
Polk, Dora Beale *literature educator*
Pollock, Karen Anne *computer analyst*
Poncelet, Paulette *school system administrator*
Pond, Phyllis Joan Ruble *state legislator, educator*
Ponzo, Karen Diane *music educator*
Poor, Janet Meakin, III, *landscape designer*
Poppler, Doris Swords *lawyer*
Porter, Jennie Lee *health facility administrator, entrepreneur*
Porter, Leah LeEarle *biological researcher, industry executive*
Porter, Marie Ann *neonatal nurse*
Portnoy, Sara S. *lawyer*
Potsic, Amie Sharon *photographer, educator, artist*
Potts, Alison Jean *neuroscience medical liaison*
Poulton, Roberta Doris *nurse, consultant*
Povich, Lynn *journalist, magazine editor, internet executive*
Powell, Alma Johnson *writer, advocate, foundation administrator*
Powell, Patricia Hruby *writer, dancer*
Powell, Ruth Aregood *music educator*
Power, Mary Susan *political scientist, educator*
Powers, Elizabeth Whitmel *lawyer*
Poynter, Deena Roush *elementary school educator, music educator*
Prather, Lenore Loving *former state supreme court chief justice*
Prazak, Bessmarie Lillian *science educator*
Preeshl, Artemis Susan *choreographer, actor, director*
Preis, Mary Louise *commissioner, former state legislator*
Prescott, Barbara Lodwich *educational administrator*
Prespare, Deborah Sun *financial analyst*
Press, Aida Kabatznick *former editor, writer, poet*
Pressley-Ulmer, Dara Ayanna *web site designer*
Preston, Colleen Ann *lawyer*
Preston, Kelly *actress*
Preszler, Sharon Marie *psychiatric home health nurse*
Price, Barbara Gillette *college administrator, artist*
Price, Betty Jeanne *choirchime soloist, writer*
Price, Ruthe Geier *actress, writer, educator*
Primerano, Lavina S. *volunteer*
Prince, Ginger Lee *actress, choreographer, educator*
Prinz, Kristie Dawn *lawyer*
Privette, Nancy Annette *school system administrator*
Proctor, Barbara Gardner *advertising agency executive, writer*
Proctor, Betty Jane *English language and literature educator*
Proenza, Theresa Butler *adult education educator, writer*
Prokop, Susan *disability rights advocate*
Prout, Kathleen Soliozy *realtor*
Provensen, Alice Rose Twitchell *artist, author*
Pruden, Treva Ann *music educator*
Pruett-Lawson, Jo Ann *marketing professional, special events coordinator*
Pruitt, Anne Loring *academic administrator, education educator*
Przybylski, Mercedes *retired medical and surgical nurse, health facility administrator*
Pucci Giles, Michelle *legislative staff member, writer*
Pudick, Donna Eastman *writer, educator*
Puetz, Pamela Ann *human resources executive*
Pugliese, Karen Olsen *freelance public relations counsel*
Pulitizer, Lilly (Lillian McKim Rousseau) *apparel designer, writer*
Pullen, Penny Lynne *non-profit organization administrator, former state legislator*
Punch, Shawna Lynnette *special education educator*
Putterman, Florence Grace *artist, printmaker*
Pyle, Wilma J. *retired education educator*
Quade, Vicki *editor, writer, playwright, producer*
Quaife, Marjorie Clift *retired nursing educator*
Quast, Pearl Elizabeth Kolb *retired elementary school educator*
Quattrone-Carroll, Diane Rose *clinical social worker*
Quay, Joyce Crosby *writer*
Quayle, Marilyn Tucker *lawyer, wife of former vice president of United States*
Quinlan, Kathleen *actress*
Quinn, Barbara Ann *writer*
Quinn, Brenda Whalen *writer, poet*
Quintana, Ana M. *media specialist*
Quist, Jeanette Fitzgerald *television production educator, choreographer*
Raash, Kathleen Forecki *artist*
Rabkin, Peggy Ann *retired lawyer*
Radice, Anne-Imelda *museum director*
Radkowsky, Karen *advertising research specialist*
Radzikowski, Antonina Angelina *retired elementary education educator*
Ragans, Rosalind Dorothy *textbook author, retired art educator*
Rahbar, Zita Ina *insurance company executive*
Rahms, Beatrix Anna *accountant, artist*
Rail, Kathy Lynn Parish *accountant*
Rainer, Luise *actor*
Rako, Susan *psychiatrist, author*
Raleigh, Jean W *museum staff member*
Rambo, Domingo H. *elementary school educator*
Ramirez, Maria C(oncepción) *retired educational administrator*
Ramo, Virginia M. Smith *civic worker*
Ramsay, Karin Kinsey *publisher, educator*
Ramsden, Sally Ann *pianist*
Ramsden, Willa Oldham *retired organization executive, columnist, historian, consultant*
Ramsey, Lucie Avra *small business owner, consultant*
Ramsey, Lynn Allison *trade association, public relations professional*
Ranada, Rose Marie *retired elementary school educator*
Rand, Joella Mae *retired nursing educator, counselor*
Randinelli, Tracey Anne *magazine editor*
Randolph, Beverley *production stage manager*
Ranney, Helen Margaret *internist, hematologist, educator*
Ransom, Nancy Alderman *sociology and women's studies educator, university administrator*
Rasberry, Dawn Yvette *counselor*
Rasnick, Melissa Hope *music educator, musician*
Rasor, Dina Lynn *investigator, journalist*
Ratcliffe, Walterene Harris *social worker, educator*
Rathfon, Jeanne Lorraine *artist*
Ravin, Linda *actress*
Rawls Oltmanns, Sandra Kay *interior designer, educator*
Ray, Debra Ann *music educator*
Ray, Diane Marie Ayers *music educator*
Raya, Madhavi *controller*
Razoharinoro, *archivist, historian, researcher*
Rea, Ann Hadley Kuehn *retired social organization marketing administrator*
Reast, Deborah Stanek *small business owner*
Reber, Cheryl Ann *consultant, social worker, trainer*
Reciniello, Karen Mary *language educator*
Redmon, Cynthia Boudreaux *art educator*
Reece, Geraldine Maxine *elementary school educator*
Reed, Diane Marie *psychologist*
Reed, Mary Carolyn Camblin *retired music educator, retired county official*
Reed-Ford, Lillie Mae *geriatrics services professional*
Reedy, Susan *painter*
Reeves, Barbara *writer, educator*
Reeves, Diana Crimhilda Aslan *chemist, researcher*
Reeves, Lucy Mary *retired secondary school educator*
Regan, Helen Brooks *education educator, educational consultant*
Regn Fraher, Bonnie *special education educator*
Rehnke, Mary Ann *academic administrator*
Rehnquist, Janet *federal agency administrator*
Reich, Denise Elizabeth *writer, researcher*
Reichmanis, Elsa *chemist*
Reid, Joan Evangeline *lawyer, stockbroker*
Reifler, Nelly *writer*
Reil, Beverly Jean *director, educator*
Reinke, Linda Jeanette *retired social worker*
Reljac, Mary Catherine *principal*
Remer, Jane Toba *author, arts education consultant*
Renaud, Bernadette Marie Elise *author*
Rendl-Marcus, Mildred *artist, economist*
Renfro, Linda Grossetta *elementary school educator, librarian*
Renshaw, Jean Rehkop *management educator, consultant*
Repko, Lisa *medical/surgical nurse*
Resing, Maryloretto Rachel *guidance counseling administrator, elementary school educator, pastoral counselor*
Revere, Virginia Lehr *clinical psychologist*
Revoal, Deborah Anne Leyde *primary school educator*
Reynolds, Billie Iles *insurance agent*
Reynolds, Louise Maxine Kruse *retired school nurse*
Rezac, Roselyn Ann *graphic designer, business owner*
Rezendes, Tara Melissa *music educator*
Rhoades, Marcia Diane *career counselor*
Rhode, Kim *Olympic athlete*
Rhodes, Karren *public information officer*
Rhody, Susan M. *director*
Rhone, Diane Caruso *music educator*
Rhone, Sylvia Marie Miller *recording industry executive*
Rice, Donna S. *educational administrator*
Rice, Patricia Oppenheim Levin *special education educator, consultant*
Rice, Susan F. *fundraising consultant*
Rice-Gould, Norma Jane *home school administrator*
Richard, Candace L. *music educator*
Richard, Susan Mathis *communications executive, screenwriter*
Richards, Ann *actress, educator, poet*
Richards, Carmeleete A. *computer training executive, network administrator, consultant*
Richards, Lynn *company training executive, consultant*
Richards, Susan R. *management consultant*
Richardson, Brownie F. *accountant*
Richardson, Margaret Milner *former accounting firm executive, lawyer*
Richardson, Natasha Jane *actress*
Richardson, Patricia Jean *librarian*
Richardson, Susan *health facility administrator, writer*
Riche, Wendy *television producer*
Richstone, Beverly June *psychologist, writer*
Rickard, Ruth David *retired history and political science educator*
Rickel, Annette Urso *psychology and psychiatry researcher, educator*
Ricketts, Sondra Lou *librarian*
Ricks, Joycia Camilla *retired lawyer*
Riddle, Elsie Kathleen *elementary school educator, school librarian*
Rideout, Patricia Irene *operatic, oratorio and concert singer*
Rider, Fae B. *freelance writer*
Ridgway, Rozanne LeJeanne *retired diplomat*
Ridley, JoAnn D. *writer, public relations executive*
Riehecky, Janet Ellen *writer*
Riffle, Rhonda Lorene *construction executive*
Rifman, Eileen *music educator*
Riikonen, Charlene Boothe *international health administrator*
Riley, Johnna Waller *principal*
Riley-Davis, Shirley Merle *advertising agency executive, marketing consultant, writer*
Rimel, Rebecca Webster *foundation administrator*
Ring, Nancy Gail *writer*
Ring, Renee Etheline *lawyer*
Ringler, Lenore *educational psychologist, educator*
Ripstein, Jacqueline *artist*
Riskin, Victoria *former trade association administrator*
Ristich, Katharine Alexandra *journalist*
Rittel, Kathleen Ann *former assistant principal and school system administrator, middle school educator*
Ritter, Elise Dawn *therapist, clinical social worker, writer, artist*
Ritter, Madeliene *practical nurse, surgical technologist*
Rivero, Andria *education educator*
Rivers, Beverly D. *former secretary of the district*
Rivers, Joan Nadia *graphics designer*
Rivers, Lynn N. *former congresswoman*
Rizzi, Alicia *protective services official*
Roark, Candice Renau *lawyer*
Roarty, Louise R. *writer, realtor*
Robbins, Alexandra *journalist, writer*
Roberts, Corinne Boggs (Cokie Roberts) *correspondent, news analyst*
Roberts, Debra S. *secondary school educator*
Roberts, Doris *actress*
Roberts, Janet Moats *retired secondary school educator*
Roberts, Judith Marie *librarian, educator*
Roberts, Kathleen Mary *school system administrator, retired*
Roberts, Kathy Desmond *executive director educational facility*
Roberts, Linda *truck transportation services company executive*
Roberts, Margaret Harold *editor, publisher*
Roberts, Marie Dyer *retired computer systems specialist*
Roberts, Reba Gill *literature educator*
Roberts, Suzanne Catherine *artist*
Robertson, Heather Anderson *music educator, musician*
Robertson, Wyndham Gay *university official, journalist*
Robiner, Linda Goodman *writer, educator*
Robinson, Angela Tomei *clinical laboratory technologist, laboratory manager*
Robinson, Annettmarie *entrepreneur*
Robinson, Carol Susan *special education educator*
Robinson, Crystal *professional basketball player*
Robinson, Gail Patricia *retired mental health counselor*
Robinson, Glenda Carole *pharmacist*
Robinson, Judith Ruttenberg *educator*
Robinson, Laurie Overby *former assistant attorney general*
Robinson, Linda Gosden *communications executive*
Robinson, Linda Schultz *art educator, artist*
Robinson, Lynda Hickox *artist*
Robinson, Marguerite Stern *anthropologist, educator, consultant*
Robinson, Mary Elizabeth Goff *retired historian, researcher*
Robinson, Myrna L(orraine) *business analyst/program control specialist*
Robinson, Nancy Ellen *artist*
Robinson, Nancy Nowakowski *academic administrator*
Robinson, Verna Cotten *retired librarian, property management owner*
Rocco, Vanessa M. *art historian, curator, educator*
Roche, Barbara Anne *retired minister, editor*
Roche, Pauline Jennifer *artist*
Rochelle, Lugenia *academic administrator*
Rock, Caro *publisher*
Rock, Mary Ann *fine artist, educator, consultant*
Rockburne, Dorothea Grace *artist*
Rockman, Ilene Frances *librarian, educator, editor*
Rodenberg, Joy D. *sports association executive*
Rodriguez, Donna Jeanne Anglin *dietician, writer*
Rodriguez, Ellen Kay *special education educator*
Roe, Wanda Jeraldean *artist, retired educator, lecturer*
Roffé, Sarina *public relations executive*
Rogers, Elizabeth Parker *chemistry educator*
Rogers, Eva Marie VanLeuven *artist, poet*
Rogers, Kate Ellen *interior design educator*
Rogers, Olivia Johnson *elementary school counselor*
Rogers, Rosemary *author*
Rogers, Stacey A. *mechanical engineer*
Rohner, Bonnie-Jean *small business owner, computer consultant*
Rohse, Elaine Dahl *newswriter*
Roitman, Judith *mathematician, educator*
Roland, Lenore Susan *writer*
Rolland, Clara *pianist, educator*
Rollin, Miriam Ann *child advocate*
Roman, Nancy Grace *astronomer, consultant*
Roman, Twyla I. *state legislator*
Romana, Kathleen *writer*
Romano, Mena N. *artist, educator*
Romero, Sylvia *social worker*
Romero-Rainey, Rebeca *bank executive*
Rondeau, Ann E. *career officer*
Rondeau, Doris Jean *entrepreneur, consultant*
Roney, Judith Rose *marriage and family therapist*
Rook, Judith Rawie *television producer, writer*
Rooks, Linda *writer*
Roop, Karen Danstedt *elementary and secondary school educator*
Root, Janet Greenberg *private school educator*
Root, Phyllis Idalene *writer*
Rosado, Sharon L. *marketing professional*

Smith, Barbara Jeanne *retired librarian*
Smith, Betty Mallett *philosopher, educator*
Smith, Betty Pauline *television producer*
Smith, Carole Dianne *retired lawyer, editor, writer, product developer*
Smith, Charlotte Reed *retired music educator*
Smith, Cheryl Diane *music educator*
Smith, D(aisy) Mullett *publisher*
Smith, Debbie Ilee Randall *elementary school educator*
Smith, Deborah L. *music educator, secondary school educator*
Smith, Doris Irene *music educator*
Smith, Esther Marian Greenwell *education educator*
Smith, Fern M. *judge*
Smith, Gayle Sue Swartz *theater director, choreographer*
Smith, Gloria Richardson *nursing educator*
Smith, Gwendolyn *elementary school educator*
Smith, Jamesetta Delorise *author*
Smith, Jean Kennedy *former ambassador*
Smith, Julie Shelton *artist*
Smith, Karen Ann *visual artist*
Smith, Leila Hentzen *artist*
Smith, Leonore Rae *artist*
Smith, Linda Ann Glidewell *accountant*
Smith, Lois Arlene *actress, writer*
Smith, Margaret (Peggy) Jane *psychologist*
Smith, Margaret Taylor *volunteer*
Smith, Marie Burnley *music educator*
Smith, Marilyn Paulette *guidance counselor*
Smith, Marji L. *artist*
Smith, Marjorie Aileen Matthews *museum director*
Smith, Martha Virginia Barnes *retired elementary school educator*
Smith, Marthe Elisabeth *retired pathologist*
Smith, Mary Louise *real estate broker*
Smith, Marya Jean *writer*
Smith, Maura Abeln *lawyer*
Smith, Michele Kathleen *marriage and family therapist*
Smith, Michele Lindsay *music educator*
Smith, Nancy Angelynn *federal agency administrator*
Smith, Patricia *state representative*
Smith, Sarah Jane (Sally Smith) *state agency administrator*
Smith, Susan J *music educator, flutist*
Smith, Vme Edom (Verna Mae Edom Smith) *sociology educator, freelance writer, photographer*
Smith, Wendy Carol *music educator*
Smith, Wendy Haimes *federal agency administrator*
Smith Brinton, Marcia *psychologist, consultant*
Smith-Buckingham, Minnie M. *surgery technologist*
Smith-Epstein, Mary Kathleen *dancer*
Smolek, Rochelle Thérèse *interior designer*
Snelling, Barbara W. *retired state legislator*
Sniffen, Frances P. *artist*
Snodgrass, Lynn *small business owner, former state legislator*
Snow, Marina Sexton *writer*
Snow, Sue *principal*
Snowden, Ruth *artist, educator, executive secretary*
Snyder, Carolyn L. Smith *medical writing director*
Snyder, Colleen M. *music educator*
Snyder, Katharine A. *social sciences educator, researcher*
Snyder, Patricia *volunteer*
Sobel, Faye Walton *elementary school educator*
Softic, Tanja *artist*
Soles, Ada Leigh *former state legislator, government advisor*
Solomon, Susan *chemist, scientist*
Solotar, Anne Paula *real estate agent*
Solow, Jamie Elise *psychologist, vocalist*
Somers, Suzanne Marie *actress, writer, singer*
Somerville, Diana Elizabeth *author*
Sommerfeld, Marianna *retired social worker, writer*
Sonderegger, Theo Brown *psychology educator*
Sonnier, Patricia Bennett *business management educator*
Sonsteby, Kristi Lee *healthcare consultant*
Sopkin, Carole A. *realtor*
SoRelle, Ruth Doyle *medical writer, journalist*
Sorensen, Elizabeth Julia *retired cultural administrator*
Sorensen, Sheila *state legislator*
Sorstokke, Ellen Kathleen *marketing executive, educator*
Souders, Jean Swedell *artist, educator*
Souther, Lisa *music educator*
Spake, Kluane *minister, writer*
Spanninger, Beth Anne *lawyer*
Sparrow, Alison Kidder *painter, sculptor*
Spears, Rebecca Ann *writer, educator*
Speed, Christa A. Witt *music educator*
Spelman, Nancy Latting *developmental psychologist*
Spier, Paula *retired dean*
Spillman, Marjorie Rose *producer, dancer*
Spirn, Michele Sobel *communications professional, writer*
Spivak, Carol *investment manager, philanthropist*
Spivak, Joan Carol *healthcare communications specialist*
Sprince, Leila Joy *librarian*
Sproat, Kezia Vanmeter *communications executive, writer*
Squire, Beverly *business owner, entrepreneur*
Squires, Connie Jo *special education educator*
Srere, Linda Jean *former advertising executive*
Stadler, Selise McNeil *laboratory and x-ray technician*
Staffel, Megan *writer, educator*
Stafford, Rebecca *retired academic administrator, sociologist, education consultant*
Stagen, Mary-Patricia Healy *marketing executive*
Staheli, Linda Anne *social science executive*
Stalker, Linda J. *retired secondary school educator*
Stallings, Viola Patricia Elizabeth *systems engineer, educational systems specialist, retired information technology manager*
Stallworth-Barron, Doris A. Carter *librarian, educator*
Stancil, Irene Mack *family counselor*
Standiford, Natalie Anne *writer*
Stanford, Kathleen Theresa *secondary school educator*
Stanley, Frances Lucille *human resources manager, fire commissioner*
Stanley, Karen Gweneith *vocational nurse*
Stanley, Margaret King *performing arts administrator*
Stanley, Marlyse Reed *horse breeder*
Stanley, Martha Barbee *music educator*
Stanley, Myrtle Brooks *minister, educational and religious consultant*
Stansil, Sheryl *medical/surgical nurse*
Star, Gloria Gay *astrologer, writer, educator, consultant*
Stark, Andrea Marie *theater educator*
Stark, Diana *public relations executive*
Stark, Joan Scism *education educator*
Stark, Nellie May *forester, ecologist, educator*
Starnes, Susan Smith *elementary school educator*
Stash, Susan Michele *critical care nurse*
Stearns, Marilyn Tarpy *music educator*
Steck, Linda Marie *elementary school educator*
Steelman, Deborah Macon *pharmaceutical consultant*
Steen, Nancy G. *volunteer, retired rare books librarian*
Stefani, Gwen Renee *musician*
Steffen, Penny Dawn *interior designer, consultant, writer*
Steffy, Marion Nancy *state agency administrator*
Steinberg, Joan Emily *retired secondary school educator*
Steinberg-Epstein, Robin Beth *pediatrician, educator*
Steiner, Carol Seaton *social worker, educator*
Steiner, Shari Yvonne *publisher, editor, journalist*
Steinhauser, Janice Maureen *arts administrator, educator, artist*
Stendahl, Brita Kristina *humanities educator, social studies educator*
Stephens, Martha *retired psychiatrist*
Steptoe, Mary Lou *lawyer*
Sterling, Sarah L. *archaeologist, educator*
Stern, Marilyn *photographer, writer, picture editor*
Sternhagen, Frances *actress*
Stevens, Connie *actress, singer*
Stevens, May *artist*
Stewart, Barbara Lynn *church secretary, bookkeeper*
Stewart, Barbara Lynne *geriatrics nursing educator*
Stewart, Dorothy K. *librarian*
Stewart, Idalee Adel *educational administrator, consultant*
Stewart, Janet *artist*
Stewart, Joan Hinde *academic administrator*
Stewart, Karen Elizabeth Victoria *research scientist, artist*
Stewart, Lucille Marie *retired special education educator*
Stewart-Pérez, Renice Ann *technology writer, internal systems professional*
Stewart Tyler, Vivian DeLois *primary school educator*
Stickles, Bonnie Jean *nurse*
Stickney, Jessica *former state legislator*
Stillman, Elinor Hadley *retired lawyer*
Stinsmuehlen-Amend, Susan *artist*
Stirling, Christine Anne *music educator*
Stockar, Helena Marie Magdalena *artist*
Stocklin, Alma Katherine *retired public relations executive*
Stoddard, Erin *actress, artist*
Stoffel, Peggi Smith *music educator*
Stohlman, Connie Suzanne *obstetrical gynecological nurse*
Stoica, Susana *computer/electrical engineer, scientist, author, healer*
Stokstad, Marilyn Jane *art history educator, curator*
Stomfay-Stitz, Aline Maria *education educator*
Stone, Cynthia S. *director*
Stone, Dee Wallace *actress*
Stone, Marilyn *foreign language educator, consultant*
Stoppel, Sheree' Sue *music educator*
Storey, Joyce R. *writer, actress*
Stout, Elizabeth West *foundation administrator*
Stover, Laura Elkins *artist*
Strang, Heidi Cordova *art educator*
Stratton, Mariann *retired naval nursing administrator*
Straus, A. Susan *volunteer*
Strider, Marjorie Virginia *artist, educator*
Striegel, Nicole Susette *director*
Strike, Kimberly Therese *principal*
Stringer, C. Vivian *college basketball coach*
Stringer, Mary Evelyn *art historian, educator*
Stringfield, Sherry *actress*
Stringham, Renée *physician*
Stripling, Betty Keith *artist, medical/surgical nurse*
Strom, Doris Marie *music educator*
Stronach, Belinda *former retail executive*
Strong, Christina Cordaire *author, artist*
Strong, Virginia Wilkerson *freelance writer, former educator*
Stroud, Betsy Dillard *artist*
Strouse, Jean *writer*
Struble, Susan C. *artist, volunteer art therapist*
Stuart, Nancy Rubin (Nancy Zimman Stetson) *journalist, author, writer, producer*
Stuart, Sandra Joyce *computer information scientist*
Stubbs, Katrina Childs *business consultant*
Stucky, Nancy L. *special education educator*
Studer, Kathy Lynn *music educator*
Sturns, Debera C. *marketing professional*
Stutzman, Sandra Louise *advanced nurse practitioner*
Stutzman, Sarah E. *music educator*
Suber, Robin Hall *former medical and surgical nurse*
Subkowsky, Elizabeth *insurance company executive*
Substad Lokensgard, Kathryn Ann *small business owner, career consultant*
Sudanowicz, Elaine Marie *government executive*
Sugar, Sandra Lee *art consultant*
Sullivan, Cela Marie *social sciences educator*
Sullivan, Kathryn Meara *telecommunications company executive*
Sullivan, Mary Rose *English language educator*
Sullivan, Nell Inklebarger *retired administrative official, counselor*
Sullivan, Sarah Louise *management and technology consultant*
Summers, Cathleen Ann *film producer*
Summers, Lorraine Dey Schaeffer *retired librarian*
Summitt, Patricia Head *basketball coach*
Sunderland, Holly Brown *church musician*
Sundstrom, Barbara Ann *scriptwriter, film producer, educator*
Suppa-Friedman, Janice DeStefano *secondary school educator, consultant*
Surley, Leslie K. *marketing professional*
Sussman, Janet I. *social sciences educator*
Sutcliffe, Mary Ogden *clinical social worker*
Sutlin, Vivian *advertising executive*
Sutton, Dolores *actress, writer*
Sutton, Julia *musicologist, dance historian*
Sutton, Julia Zeigler *retired special education educator*
Sutton, Nancy Thurmond *music educator*
Sutton, Sharon Marie *emergency services nurse*
Swallum, Maryann *musician, music educator*
Swan, Beth Ann *nursing administrator*
Swaner-Smoot, Paula Margetts *clinical psychologist*
Sweetland, Loraine Fern *librarian, educator*
Sweig, Cherry Elizabeth *artist, painter*
Swensen, Mary Jean Hamilton *graphic artist*
Swift, Jane Maria *former governor*
Swig, Roselyne Chroman *community consultant*
Swing, Marce *producer, publisher*
Swinney, Jeanne Lyn *music educator*
Switzer, Toccoa *artist*
Swoboda, Melanie Ruth *elementary school educator, music educator*
Sword, Teresa Le *music educator*
Sykora, Barbara Zwach *state legislator*
Synnestvedt, Kirstin *musician, educator*
Sze, Sarah *sculptor*
Szymanski, Therese *marketing professional, writer*
Szyszka, Roswita Evelyn *artist*
Tableman, Claudette *principal*
Tabor, Linda J. *performing arts educator*
Tacha, Deanell Reece *federal judge*
Tadlock, Anita Conner *volunteer*
Tagiuri, Consuelo Keller *child psychiatrist, educator*
Tagliente, Josephine Marlene *artist*
Tainatonga, Rosie R. *former director of education*
Tait, Heather Jean *artist*
Takanishi, Ruby N. *foundation administrator, researcher*
Talbot-Elliott, Susan *artist*
Tallerico, Delma Dolores *elementary school educator*
Tallett, Elizabeth Edith *biopharmaceutical company executive*
Tamen, Harriet *lawyer*
Tamor-Amodo, Florence Marie *medical technologist*
Tanenbaum, Leora *writer, editor*
Tanner, Laurel Nan *education educator*
Tanner, Lynn *actress*
Tarbuck, Barbara Joan *actor*
Tardos, Anne *artist, writer, composer*
Tarrody, Janet Faulstich *retired congressional executive*
Tasman, Alice Lea Mast *not-for-profit fundraiser*
Tassos, Alice Crowley *writer*
Tate, Sheila Diane *music educator*
Tatlock, Anne M. *trust company executive*
Tatrow, Kristin *research scientist*
Tauscher, Ellen O. *congresswoman*
Tavares, Charleta B. *former state legislator*
Tayler, Irene *English literature educator*
Taylor, Connie J. *real estate company executive*
Taylor, Edna Jane *retired employment program counselor*
Taylor, Elizabeth Rosemond *actress*
Taylor, Gwendolyn Nadine *elementary school educator*
Taylor, Karen Annette *mental health nurse*
Taylor, Kathleen (Christine Taylor) *physical chemist, researcher*
Taylor, Kathleen N. *state legislator*
Taylor, L. Ann *financial analyst*
Taylor, Lesli Ann *pediatric surgery educator*
Taylor, Linda Rathbun *investment manager*
Taylor, Margaret Turner *apparel designer, economist, writer, architectural designer*
Taylor, Michelle Y. *human resources consultant*
Taylor, Nathalee Britton *retired nutritionist*
Taylor, Ruth Anne *lawyer*
Taylor-Kidder, Pamela Sue *special education educator*
Taylor-Pickell, LaVonne Troy *editor*
Taylor Song, Stephanie Ingram *nutritionist*
Teater, Dorothy Seath *retired county official*
Teater, Tricia L. *human resources specialist*
Tebedo, MaryAnne *state legislator*
Teeple, Fiona Diane *librarian, lawyer*
Tejedor, Marcela Alejandra *sales executive, consultant*
Telnaes, Ann *cartoonist*
Temelkoff, Vonda Lee *counselor, therapist*
Tepper, Arielle *theater producer*
Terada, Alice Masae *retired elementary school educator*
Terani, Cindy *music educator*
Ternovitz, Ruth *mathematics and computer educator*
Terris, Susan *physician, cardiologist*
Terry, Barbara L. *human services administrator*
Terry, Kay Adell *marketing executive*
Terry, Sandra Eleanor *visual artist*
Teten, Melody-Leigh *library media specialist*
Tharp, Twyla *dancer*
Thern, Peggy Huang *literature educator, small business owner*
Thiele, Gloria Day *retired librarian, small business owner*
Thomas, Angela M. *marketing professional*
Thomas, Betty *director, actress*
Thomas, Beverly Irene *special education educator, educational diagnostician, substance abuse counselor*
Thomas, Christine A. *writer, editor, educator*
Thomas, Patricia Anne *retired law librarian*
Thomas, Patricia Goodnow *journalist*
Thomas, Rhonda Robbins *marketing educator, consultant*
Thomas, Sylvia Elizabeth *artist*
Thomas, Teresa Ann *microbiologist, educator*
Thomerson, Anne Spach *counselor*
Thompson, Ana Calzada *secondary education educator, mathematician*
Thompson, Andrea *TV host former newscaster and actress*
Thompson, Claire Louisa *nurse, educator*
Thompson, Eve Katherine *literature educator, department chairman*
Thompson, Jennifer B. *Olympic swimmer*
Thompson, Joyce Lurine *retired information systems specialist*
Thompson, Julia Ann *physicist, educator*
Thompson, Laura Jill *curator, educator*
Thompson, Margie Ann *artist*
Thompson, Mary Eileen *chemistry educator*
Thompson-Lorenzo, Angela Christine *music educator*
Thon, Melanie Rae *writer*
Thornburg, Linda A. *writer*
Thorsen, Marie Kristin *radiologist, educator*
Thrasher, Rose Marie *critical care nurse, community health nurse*
Threadcraft, Kelli King *speech pathology/audiology services professional*
Thurman, Karen L. *former congresswoman, lobbyist*
Thurner, Agnes H. *retired administrative secretary*
Thurston, Tina L. *archaeologist, educator*
Tiedge-Lafranier, Jeanne Marie *editor*
Tiemann, Barbara Jean *special education educator*
Tillman, Mercia V. *musician*
Tillman, Shirley *retired military officer*
Timmons, Debra *surgical technologist*
Tinner, Franziska Paula *social worker, artist, apparel designer, educator, entrepreneur*
Tipton, Melanie Carol *music educator*
Tirello, Maria Eugenia Duke *artist*
Tishner, Keri Lynn *visual art education consultant*
Toay, Thelma M. *columnist, poet*
Tobias, Judy *university development executive*
Tobias, Sheila *writer, educator*
Tobiassen, Virginia Hege *editor, author*
Todd, Ruth *artist*
Toensing, Victoria *lawyer*
Tolstedt, Buffy D. *music educator, musician*
Tom, Lauren *actress, singer*
Tomasky, Susan *corporate officer*
Tomkow, Gwen Adelle *artist*
Tomlin, Lily *actress*
Tompkins, Julie Lynberg *market research consultant*
Toms, Justine Willis *educational organization executive*
Tong, Rosemarie *medical humanities and philosophy educator, consultant and researcher*
Tooman, Stephanie *performing arts educator*
Topolewski-Green, Mary Jo Therese *small business owner*
Topolski, Catherine *science educator*
Torrence, Margaret Ann Johnson *company executive, consultant, paralegal, therapist, human resources manager, training instructor*
Torres-Mabasa, Virginia Maria *physician assistant*
Torresyap, Pearl Marie *surgical nurse*
Toshach, Clarice Oversby *real estate developer, former computer executive*
Toter, Kimberly Mrowiec *nurse*
Touhill, Blanche Marie *retired university chancellor, history-education educator*
Towe, A. Ruth *retired museum director*
Trampusch, Christine Ann *music educator*
Transou, Lynda Lou *advertising art administrator*
Trautman, Alta Louise *nurse, funeral director, writer*
Traxler, Eva Maria *marketing professional*
Traylor, Gayla S. *music educator, composer*
Trego, Nancy ReMine *not-for-profit fundraiser*
Treichel, Dixie Ann *composer, sound designer, consultant*
Tremaglio, Michelle T. *merchant banker*
Trenhaile, Jennifer Ann *music educator*
Treppler, Irene Esther *retired state senator*
Trettin, Rosemary Elizabeth *fraternal organization administrator*
Triana, Gladys *artist*
Triece, Anne Gallagher *magazine publisher*
Triipan, Maive *library director*
Trinchero, Agnes Theresa *social services consultant, administrator, educator*
Triplett, Arlene Ann *management consultant*
Tripp, Aili Mari *political science educator*
Troll, Kitty *actress, writer*
Trombley, Deborah Pelkey *crossword puzzle constructor*

Wood, Jane Semple *editor, writer*
Wood, Marian Starr *publishing company executive*
Wood, Roberta Susan *retired foreign service officer*
Wood, Valerie J. *public information officer, writer*
Wood, Vivian Poates *mezzo soprano, educator, writer*
Woodard, Alfre *actress*
Woodruff, Mary Brennan *elementary school educator, educator*
Woodruff, Virginia *broadcast journalist, writer*
Woodrum, Patricia Ann *librarian*
Woods, Eleanor C. *music educator*
Woods, Harriett Ruth *retired political organization president*
Woods, Phyllis Michalik *librarian*
Woods, Sandra Kay *real estate executive*
Woodson, Jacqueline *writer*
Woodsworth, Anne *university administrator, librarian*
Woodward, Debbie Carol *special education educator*
Wooley, Geraldine Hamilton *poet, writer*
Woolworth, Susan Valk *primary school educator*
Wooten, Carol G. *conductor, music educator*
Wooten, Joan Hedrich *minister*
Workman, Kayleen Marie *special education and adult education educator*
Workman, Margaret Lee *lawyer*
Woronov, Mary Peter *actress*
Worrell, Mary Thora *loan officer*
Worthington, Carol Pearce *writer, editor*
Wos, Carol Elaine *small business owner*
Wostrel, Rebekah A. *artist, educator*

Wright, Cheryl Diane *marketing professional*
Wright, Dixie Lee *special needs persons consultant*
Wright, Gladys Stone *music educator, composer, writer*
Wright, Judith Rae *retired accountant*
Wright, Linda Jean *manufacturing executive*
Wright, Peggy Sue Espy *elementary school educator*
Wright, Romona Xylena *music educator*
Wriston, Kathryn Dineen *lawyer, financial consultant*
Wroblowa, Halina Stefania *electrochemist*
Wulff, Julie Bader *purchasing agent*
Wunsch, Kathryn Sutherland *retired lawyer*
Wuthrick, Eileen B. *special education educator*
Wyatt, Judith Lois *psychotherapist, consultant*
Wyatt, Marcia Jean *fine arts educator, administrative assistant*
Wylan, Barbara *artist*
Wyman, Viola Bousquet *elementary school educator*
Wynn, Karla Wray *artist, agricultural products company executive*
Wyse, Karen Ann *artist*
Yacoub, Allison *music educator*
Yaeger, Therese Francis *management professional*
Yaes, Joyce *musician, artist, educator*
Yamaguchi, Kristi Tsuya *ice skater*
Yancey, Elizabeth Stilphen *political scientist*
Yancey, Victoria Francine *education educator*
Yanda, Cathy L. *counselor, illustrator*
Yarbrough, Kathryn Davis *public health nurse*
Yard, Molly *social activist*
Yates, Kimberly Nicole *school psychologist*

Yates, Mildred Campbell *retired literature educator*
Yde, Jacqulyn Rae *interior designer, architectural colorist*
Yearwood, Trisha *country music singer, songwriter*
Yee, Nancy W. *travel consultant*
Yerkovich, Gloria *social service administrator*
Yerxa, Jane Anne *artist*
Yeterian, Isabelle M.C. *lawyer*
Yih, Ann *writer, journalist*
Ying, Jackie *chemical engineer, educator*
Yitts, Rose Marie *nursery school executive*
Ynda, Mary Lou *artist, educator*
Yntema, Mary Katherine *retired mathematics educator*
Yoder, Elizabeth Jane *neuroscience researcher*
Yokum, Jane *music educator*
Young, Candace C. *educational consultant, researcher*
Young, Christine E *writer, journalist, private investigator*
Young, Deborah (Deborah Ayling Yanowitz) *social worker, librarian*
Young, Elizabeth Bell *consultant*
Young, Emily Elizabeth *religious studies educator*
Young, Grace May-En *pediatrician, educator*
Young, Judith Anne *animal conservationist*
Young, Teresa Gail Hilger *retired adult education educator*
Young, Theresa Elizabeth Jennifer *music educator*
Youngblood, Daisy *ceramist*
Young-Stevens, Katherine Tratebas *occupational health nurse*

Yowell, Nancy T. *photographer, retired elementary educator*
Yu, Jessica *director, producer, writer, editor*
Zablocki, Elaine *writer*
Zach, Grace Rebecca *retired secondary school educator*
Zahner, Dorothy Simkin *elementary school educator*
Zaleski, Jean *artist*
Zark, Jenna *playwright, freelance writer*
Zarky, Karen Jane *newspaper publisher*
Zebi, Sandra *artist*
Zeilig, Nancy Meeks *writer, editor*
Zeilinger, Elna Rae *elementary educator, gifted-talented education educator*
Zeiser, Susie Fehrenbacher *psychologist, researcher*
Zeitlin, Marianne Langner *writer*
Zekman, Terri Margaret *graphic designer*
Zemlin, Susan Carol *music educator*
Zeviar-Geese, Gabriole *stock market investor, lawyer*
Ziemba, Karen *actress*
Zierath, Marilyn Jean *medical/surgical nurse, pediatrics nurse*
Zimmerman, Helene Loretta *retired business educator*
Zimmerman, Jean *lawyer*
Zirbes, Mary Kenneth *retired minister*
Zook, Maurine Joyce *artist*
Zowader, Sherry Lee *volunteer*
Zucker, Maureen T. *artist*
Zuckerman, Harriet *sociologist, educator*
Zupon, Diane Elizabeth *medical technician*
Zusy, Catherine *curator*

Professional Index

Columbus
Shannon, Carolyn Jean *interior designer*

LOUISIANA

Alexandria
Foster, Sally *interior designer*

Baton Rouge
Lee, Betty Redding *architect*

New Orleans
Hence, Jane Knight *designer*

MAINE

Brunswick
deLyra, Elizabeth M. *product designer*

Edgecomb
Carlson, Suzanne Olive *architect*

MARYLAND

Garrett Park
Stites, M(ary) Elizabeth *architecture educator*

MASSACHUSETTS

Boston
Goody, Joan Edelman *architect*
Wedge, Carole C. *architectural firm executive*

Cambridge
Chiles, Carol S. *architectural firm executive*
Jones, Mary M. *landscape architect*
Mori, Toshiko *architecture educator*

Longmeadow
Teitz, Betty Beatrice Goldstein *retired interior designer*

Waban
Etter, Faye Madalyn *interior design company executive*

MICHIGAN

Ann Arbor
Kendall, Kay Lynn *interior designer, consultant*

Frankenmuth
Rau, Louise Billie *interior designer*

MINNESOTA

Minneapolis
Dworsky, Mary *interior designer*
Musacchio, Laura R. *planning and design educator*
Sloan, Debra Lynne *interior designer*

Saint Paul
Close, Elizabeth Scheu *retired architect*

MISSISSIPPI

Jackson
Leonard, Pamela Dian *architect, artist*

MISSOURI

Chesterfield
Stevens, Anne Bickett Parker *architectural designer*

Saint Louis
Bextermiller Metzger, Theresa Marie *architect, computer engineer*
McTyer-Clarke, Wanda Kathleen *interior designer*
Rosenblum, Sharon *interior designer*
Weese, Cynthia Rogers *architect, educator*

Weatherby Lake
Hawkins, Geri Sue *interior designer, jewelry designer, realtor*

NEW HAMPSHIRE

New London
Sheerr, Deirdre McCrystal *architectural firm executive*

NEW JERSEY

Bernardsville
Lazor, Patricia Ann *interior designer*

Carteret
John, Dolores *architect, consultant*

Clifton
Kalata, Mary Ann Catherine *architect*

Colonia
Wiesenfeld, Bess G. *interior designer*

East Orange
Fielo, Muriel Bryant *interior designer*

Haddon Heights
Westfield, Margaret Ann Hoyert *architect*

Princeton
Diller, Elizabeth E. *architect, educator, artist*
Nichols, Karen *architect*

NEW MEXICO

Albuquerque
Gutierrez, Joni Marie *landscape architect, political organization worker*
Smith, Jean *interior design firm executive*

Santa Fe
Wilson, Laura Eleanor *landscape architect*

NEW YORK

Brooklyn
Lev, Darleen Katherine *interior designer, writer*
Woolley, Margaret Anne (Margot Woolley) *architect*

Brookville
Otte, Debra Bergsma *designer, educator, art administrator*

Buffalo
Belfer, Nancy B. *design educator*

Chester
Karen, Linda Tricarico *interior designer*

Cross River
Thorn, Susan Howe *interior designer*

Ithaca
Seraji-Bozorgzad, Nasrine *architecture educator*

Kew Gardens
Aldea, Patricia *architect*

Locust Valley
Bentel, Carol Rusche *architect*

Manhasset
Seftel, Donna Selene *architect*

New York
Baird, Penny Drue *interior designer*
Daniels, J. Yolande *architectural firm executive, educator*
Edelman, Judith H. *architect*
Gath, Jean Marie *architectural firm executive*
Georgopoulos, Maria *architect, artist, inventor*
Halsband, Frances *architect*
Hariri, Gisue *architect, educator*
Harris, Anne M. *interior designer, educator*
Huxtable, Ada Louise *architecture critic*
Joseph, Wendy Evans *architect*
Karlin, Susan *design company executive*
Kasakove, Susan *interior designer*
Sevely, Maria *architect*
Szeto, Yvonne *architectural firm executive*
Taylor, Marilyn Jordan *architectural firm executive*
Tozer, Elizabeth Farran *interior and floral designer*
Willis, Beverly Ann *architect*

Richfield Springs
Walters, Marjorie Anne *interior designer, consultant*

Rochester
Manley, Cathey Neracker *interior design executive*

Scarsdale
Bayar, Julia Beryl *interior designer*

Westhampton Beach
Flood, Angela *interior designer, artist*

NORTH CAROLINA

Kitty Hawk
Elliott, Candice K. *interior designer*

Raleigh
Peele, Katherine N. *architect*

OHIO

Chagrin Falls
Cordes, Loverne Christian *interior designer*

Cleveland Heights
Jablow, Bernice R. *architectural designer and space consultant*

Columbus
Weinhold, Virginia Beamer *interior designer*

OKLAHOMA

Edmond
Stewart, Ann Tefertiller *interior designer, secondary school educator*

Oklahoma City
Halpin, Anna Marie *architect, writer*

OREGON

Lake Oswego
Largent, Margie *retired architect*

Portland
Vanderslice, Ellen *architect*

PENNSYLVANIA

Ambler
Swansen, Donna Maloney *landscape designer, consultant*

Benton
Hopkins, Mary Bazemore *landscape designer, consultant*

Bryn Mawr
Fellinger-Buzby, Linda *interior and industrial designer*

Chadds Ford
Werner DeNadai, Mary *architectural firm executive*

Columbia
Steiner-Houck, Sandra Lynn *interior designer*

Erwinna
Auerbach, Kathryn Ann *architecture and preservation educator, consultant*

Harrisburg
Knackstedt, Mary V. *interior designer*

Philadelphia
Brown, Denise Scott *architect, urban planner*
Keefe, Mary *architectural firm executive*
Maxman, Susan Abel *architect*
Santos, Adele Naude *architect, educator*
Tyng, Anne Griswold *architect*
Winkler, Gail Caskey *design historian, writer, educator*

Pittsburgh
Kingsbury, Lisa R. *instructional design consultant*
Loftness, Vivian Ellen *architecture educator, department chairman*

Sharon
Matejka, Barbara A. *draftsman*

Upper Black Eddy
McIntyre, Linnea Andren *landscaping company executive*

RHODE ISLAND

Providence
Kagan, Marilyn D. *retired architect*

SOUTH CAROLINA

Mount Pleasant
Gregory, Yvonne E. *interior designer*

TENNESSEE

Nashville
Bramlett, Shirley Marie Wilhelm *interior decorator, artist*

Nolensville
Heeney, Susan Welch *interior designer, educator*

TEXAS

Austin
Little, Emily Browning *architect*

College Station
Vandiver, Renee Lillian Aubry *interior designer, architectural preservator*

Corpus Christi
Angell, Ellen *interior designer*

Dallas
Charriere, Suzanne *architectural firm executive*
Spencer, Mary Helen *interior designer*
Wilson, Trisha *interior architectural designer*

El Paso
Benning, Mary Etzold *interior designer*
Korth, Charlotte Williams *furniture and interior design firm executive*

Houston
Amador, Anne *architect, composer*
Bryan, Mary Ann *interior designer*
Green, Sharon Jordan *interior decorator*
Solomon, Marsha Harris *draftsman, artist*

San Antonio
Pfanstiel Parr, Dorothea Ann *interior designer*
Tarazon, Maureen Reeves *landscape artist, conservator*

San Marcos
Treanor, Betty McKee *interior design educator*

Spring
Westover, Diana Kay *interior designer, recruitment company executive*

Taylor
Cernosek, Kitty *interior decorator*

VIRGINIA

Alexandria
Jackson, Nancy Morrison *architect*
Simonds, Marie Celeste *architect*

Arlington
Draeger, Susanne Yarbrough *interior designer*

Hassett, Valerie Jane *interior designer, architect, educator*

Berryville
Martin, Alison Cady *interior designer*

Blacksburg
Bliznakov, Milka Tcherneva *architect, educator*

Reston
Holthausen, Martha Anne *interior designer*

Richmond
Frazer, Susan Hume *independent scholar and consultant*
Jamgochian, Victoria *interior designer*

Staunton
Firehock, Barbara A. *interior designer*

Virginia Beach
Stanton, Pamela Freeman *interior designer, writer*

Woodbridge
Peck, Dianne Kawecki *architect*

WASHINGTON

Bellevue
Wallace, Mary Colette *architectural researcher, designer*

Bremerton
Hower, Jeanne Louise *landscape designer*

Seattle
Moudon, Anne Vernez *urban design educator*
Perthou, Alison Chandler *interior designer*

WISCONSIN

Waukesha
Leatherberry, Anne Knox Clark *architect*

West Allis
Koch, Suzanne M. *interior designer*

CANADA

ONTARIO

Toronto
van Ginkel, Blanche Lemco *architect, educator*

ENGLAND

London
Gavin, Lesley Catherine *architecture educator, consultant*

ADDRESS UNPUBLISHED

Anderson, Ruth Lucille *interior designer, educator, artist, librarian, archivist*
Armistead, Katherine Kelly (Mrs. Thomas B. Armistead III) *interior designer, travel consultant, civic worker*
Berry, Sharon Elaine *interior designer*
Cody, Arlene J. Clark Brattain *interior designer*
Cohen, Sharleen Cooper *interior designer, writer*
DeFrancis, Suellen Maria *interior architect*
Dietderich, Shirley (Jane Rohlfing) *interior decorator*
Dudics-Dean, Susan Elaine *interior designer*
Friedman, Mildred *architectural and design educator, curator, consultant*
Gallup, Patricia Sue *architect*
Hastings, L(ois) Jane *architect, architecture educator*
Keech, Elowyn Ann *interior designer*
Knoll, Florence Schust *architect, designer*
Kobza, Julia Colleen *drafter, building designer*
Konon, Neena Nicholai *design strategist*
Labiner, Caroline *architect*
Lapin, Sharon Joyce Vaughn *interior designer*
Lin, Maya *architect, sculptor*
Love, Dian *interior architect, educator*
Lyn, Jean *interior designer*
Manasc, Vivian *architect, consultant*
McFadden, Robbyn Kilbane *interior designer, public policy specialist, artist, advocate*
McGunigle, Dorothy Greene *interior designer, artist*
Motzer, Robin Lynne *interior designer, writer, artist, poet, singer*
Parke, Janet Diane *interior designer*
Perkins, Nancy Jane *industrial designer*
Pincus, Nancy *architect, web site designer*
Poor, Janet Meakin, III, *landscape designer*
Rawls Oltmanns, Sandra Kay *interior designer, educator*
Rogers, Kate Ellen *interior design educator*
Ross, Molly Owings *jewelry designer, sculptor, small business owner*
Schuth, Mary McDougle *interior designer, educator*
Selig, Phyllis Sims *retired architect*
Silver, Lynne Miller *garden designer*
Sirola, Linda F. *interior designer*
Smolek, Rochelle Thérèse *interior designer*
Steffen, Penny Dawn *interior designer, consultant, writer*
Webber, Linda Judith Ritz *interior designer*
White, Othell *interior designer*
White, Pauline M. *interior decorator*
Wiebenson, Dora Louise *architectural historian, editor, author*

Yde, Jacqulyn Rae *interior designer, architectural colorist*

ARTS: LITERARY *See also* COMMUNICATIONS MEDIA

UNITED STATES

ALABAMA

Coy
Zinnermon, Susan *writer*

Evergreen
Lodge-Peters, Dianne Speed *writer, literature educator, researcher*
Ross, Nora Fay *poet*

Saraland
South, Sheri Cobb *writer, publishing executive*

ALASKA

Wasilla
Brunke, Dawn Baumann *writer, editor*

ARIZONA

Congress
Scheall, Norma *writer, editor*

Glendale
Heathcotte, Toby Fesler *writer, retired educator*

Phoenix
Bateman, Jean Budington *writer, poet, home furnishings consultant*
Dnyck, Kathleen Marie *poet, musician, retired social worker*

Scottsdale
Carpenter, Betty O. *writer*
Parsons, Cynthia *writer, consultant*

Sedona
Frankel, Jennie Louise *writer, composer, playwright*
Frankel, Terrie Maxine *writer, composer, playwright, publisher, producer*

Sonoita
Browning, Sinclair *writer*

Tucson
Kingsolver, Barbara Ellen *writer*
Martin, Marci *writer, former advertising specialist*
McCormick, Alma Heflin *writer, retired educator, psychologist*

ARKANSAS

Fayetteville
Shafer, Carol Larsen *retired book reviewer*

Flippin
Modeland, Phyllis Jo *author*

Hot Springs National Park
Stuber, Irene Zelinsky *writer, researcher*

Little Rock
Holland, Allison Denman *writing and film educator, film preservationist*
Nunn, Patarica Dian *poet, telephone directory operator*

CALIFORNIA

Arcadia
Sloane, Beverly LeBov *writer, consultant*

Atascadero
Locke, Virginia Otis *writer*

Belmont
MacLennan, Amy Marie *poet*

Berkeley
Burch, Claire Rita *writer*
Guest, Barbara *author, poet*
Katzen, Mollie *writer*
Kushner, Eve *writer*
Wehner, Kay Y. *poet*

Beverly Hills
Hamilton, Laurell K. *writer*
Klein, Renny *writer, columnist*
Meyers, Nancy Jane *screenwriter, producer, director*

Canoga Park
Alexander, Sue *writer*

Capitola
Wolff, Jean Walton *writer*

Carmichael
Goodin, Evelyn Marie *writer*

Carpinteria
Rau, Margaret E. *writer*

Cayucos
Shahan, Sherry Jean *writer, educator*

Chatsworth
Dunwich, Gerina *writer, magazine editor, astrologer*

Chino Hills
Sanders, Nancy Ida *writer*

Cotati
Hill, Debora Elizabeth *writer, journalist, screenwriter*

Covina
Durham, Betty Louise *poet*

Crescent City
Ruffer, Joyce Sellars *poet, artist*

Cupertino
Zobel, Louise Purwin *author, educator, lecturer, writing consultant*

El Cerrito
Tannenbaum, Judith Nettie *writer, educator*

Fresno
Garrison-Finderup, Ivadelle Dalton *writer, educator*

Glendale
Stienon, Elaine Burr *writer, music educator*

Goleta
Robinson, Nancy A. *writer*

Hillsborough
Atwood, Mary Sanford *writer*

Huntington Beach
Flakes, Susan *playwright, screenwriter, director*

Idyllwild
Schneider, Margaret Perrin *writer*

Irvine
McClintock, Sandra Janise *writer, editor*

La Jolla
Iddings, Kathleen *poet, editor, publisher, consultant*

Lafayette
James, Muriel Marshall *writer, lecturer, psychotherapist*

Lakeside
Koski, Donna Faith *poet*

Landers
Landers, Vernette Trosper *writer, educator, association executive*

Los Angeles
Dew, Joan King *freelance/self-employed writer*
Elias, Merle *writer, consultant*
Good, Edith Elissa (Pearl Williams) *writer*
Johnson, Carole A. *writer, artist*
Kaplan, Nadia *writer*
Quinn, Patricia K. *literary agent*
Ring, Trudy M. *writer, editor*
Sedaris, Amy *writer, actress*
Sivertsen, Linda Joyce *writer, publishing consultant, editor*
Summer, Jena A. *writer, artist, poet*
Thomas, Shirley *author, educator, business executive*
Wiggins, Marianne *writer*
Yoshiki-Kovinick, Marian Tsugie *author*

Malibu
Marvin, Barbara Joyce *writer*

Mill Valley
Mautner, Gabriella *writer, educator*

Moffett Field
Kwong, Jennifer *writer*

Monrovia
Salaman, Maureen Kennedy *writer, nutritionist*

Moraga
Sestanovich, Molly Brown *writer*

North Hills
Villani, Luisa *writer, educator*

Oakland
Luterman, Alison Gina *poet*

Oceanside
Witbeck, Glenda M. *poet*

Orinda
Strong, Susan Clancey *writer, communication consultant, editor*

Palm Desert
Carangelo, Lori *writer, social activist, not-for-profit executive*
Friesz, Mary Lee *freelance/self-employed poet*

Palo Alto
Herr, Pamela Staley *writer, historian*
Love, Brenda Zejdl *writer*

Pasadena
Brogden-Stirbl, Shona Marie *writer, researcher*
Bunting, Anne Evelyn (Eve Bunting) *author*

Petaluma
Hirshfield, Jane B. *poet*
Sebold, Alice *writer*

Placerville
Wilkinson, Rosemary Regina Challoner *poet, writer*

Portola Valley
Cameron, Eleanor Cranston Fowle *writer*

Redondo Beach
Battles, Roxy Edith *novelist, consultant, educator*

Reedley
Carey, Ernestine Gilbreth (Mrs. Charles E. Carey) *writer, lecturer*

Riverside
Witman, Laura Kathleen *writer, security professional*

Ross
Godwin, Sara *writer*

San Bernardino
Hansen, Anne Katherine *poet*

San Diego
Krull, Kathleen *writer*
Stein, Eleanor Benson (Ellie Stein) *playwright, writer*

San Francisco
Cohn, Kathleen Mandry *writer*
Field, Carol Hart *writer, journalist, foreign correspondent*
Sachs, Marilyn Stickle *author, lecturer, editor*
Wayburn, Peggy (Cornelia Elliott Wayburn) *writer, editor*

San Luis Rey
Williams, Elizabeth Yahn *writer, lecturer, lawyer*

San Marcos
Winebrenner, Susan Kay *writer, consultant*

San Marino
Hull, Suzanne White *writer, retired administrator*

San Rafael
Marcus, Adrianne Stuhl *writer*

Santa Barbara
Cunningham, Julia Woolfolk *author*
Mitchell, Shawne Maureen *author*

Santa Clara
Simmons, Janet Bryant *writer, publisher*

Santa Maria
Meehan, Lil Euphrasia Therese *poet*

Santa Monica
Jones, Janet Dulin *writer, film producer*
Roney, Alice Lorraine Mann *poet*

Sherman Oaks
Dent, Ellen Margaret *writer*

Somis
Premack, Ann J. *writer*

Sonoma
Kizer, Carolyn Ashley *poet, educator*

Sugarloaf
Black, Victoria Lynn *writer, artist*

Sylmar
Hayes, Cynthia Ann (C.A. Hayes) *writer*

Tarzana
Blackburn, Greta Jeanette *writer*

Valencia
Parks, Suzan Lori *playwright*
Webb, Margot *writer*

Ventura
Chandler, Juliette Anne *writer, communications executive*

Woodland Hills
Rabaca, Josefina Ragsag *writer*

Yuba City
Doss-Reed, Helen Grigsby *writer*

COLORADO

Boulder
Waldman, Anne Lesley *poet, performer, editor, publisher, educational administrator*

Cascade
Seger, Linda Sue *script consultant, lecturer, writer*

Castle Rock
Rogers, Pattiann *poet, educator, poet, writer*

Colorado Springs
Rhodes, Daisy Chun *writer, researcher, oral historian*

Denver
Buckstein, Caryl Sue *writer*
Dallas, Sandra *writer*
Howse, Cathy L. *writer, researcher, entrepreneur*
Nemiro, Beverly Mirium Anderson *author, educator*
Osborn, Susan Chaney *writer, educator*
Vosevich, Kathi Ann *writer, editor, scholar*

Durango
Korns, Leota Elsie *writer, mountain land developer, insurance broker*

Greeley
Willis, Connie (Constance E. Willis) *author*

Silverton
Voorlas, Stephanie Katherine *freelance/self-employed writer, photographer*

Telluride
Claridge, Rhonda L. *writer, educator*

Vail
Knight, Constance Bracken *writer, realtor, corporate executive*

CONNECTICUT

Berlin
Bennerup, Brooke Clara *poet, writer*

Cheshire
Driscoll, Colleen Mary *writer, researcher, consultant*

Clinton
Adler, Peggy Ann *writer, illustrator, consultant*

East Hampton
Klein, Gail Beth Marantz *freelance/self-employed writer, animal breeder*
Tucceri, Clive Knowles *science writer and educator, consultant*

Fairfield
Barone, Rose Marie Pace *writer, retired educator, entertainer*
Ladd, Louise *writer*

Greenwich
Hoberman, Mary Ann *author*
Wallach, Magdalena Falkenberg (Carla Wallach) *writer*

Hamden
Davis, Lorraine Jensen *writer, editor*
McDonough, Kaye (Kathryn Susan McDonough) *poet, playwright*

Hartford
Hedrick, Joan Doran *writer, university educator*

Hebron
Garrett, Florence Rome *poet*

New Haven
Hayden, Dolores *author, architect, educator*
Scarf, Margaret (Maggie Scarf) *author*

New Preston Marble Dale
Biddle, Flora Miller *writer*

Old Lyme
St. George, Judith Alexander *author*

Washington
Chamberlain, Frances W. *writer*

Waterford
Commire, Anne *playwright, writer, editor*

West Hartford
Schweitzer, N. Tina *fiction writer, photojournalist, television producer, director, international consultant public relations, media relations, government relations*

Westbrook
Fuller, Martha M. *poet*
Hall, Jane Anna *writer, model, artist*

Westport
Manners, Ruth Ann *writer*

Winsted
Wilson, Mary Flynn *writer, educator*

DELAWARE

Hockessin
Mertz, Anne Morris *writer, researcher, journalist, educator*

DISTRICT OF COLUMBIA

Washington
Angell, Lois Louise *writer, comedienne, poet*
Atlas, Liane Wiener *writer*
Barras, Jonetta Rose *writer*
Carter, Yvonne Johnson *writer, editor, English educator*
Darr, Ann Russell *poet, educator*
Dessaso, Deborah Ann *freelance/self-employed writer, corporate communications specialist*
Fallon, Sally *writer*
Friedan, Betty *writer, feminist leader*
Goldberg, Kirsten Boyd *science journalist*
Innis, Pauline *writer, publishing company executive*
Levy, Ellen J. *writer, educator*
Mann-Bondat, Lydia Rachel *writer, researcher*
Miller, Hope Ridings *author*
Murphy, Joanne Becker *writer*
Ritchie, Elisavietta *poet, writer, educator, editor, translator*
Robb, Lynda Johnson *writer*
Steinem, Gloria *writer, editor, lecturer, activist*
Tannen, Deborah Frances *writer*
Violante, Patricia *consultant, language expert, writer, translator/interpreter*

FLORIDA

Cape Canaveral
Hess, Terry Lee *writer, educator, logistician*

Daytona Beach
Chesnut, Nondis Lorine *screenwriter, consultant, reading and language arts educator, instructor, counselor*

Gainesville
Smith, Jo Anne *writer, retired educator*

Hallandale
Geller, Bunny Zelda *poet, author, publisher, sculptor, artist, photographer*

Hobe Sound
Houser, Constance W. *writer, artist*

Hollywood
Krane, Jessica (Aida Jessica Kohnop-Krane) *writer, educator*

Homosassa
Carmichael, Roberta Kay *writer*

Jacksonville
Perry, Beth Bentley *writer, artist*

Leesburg
Thompson, Mary B. *writer, illustrator*

Longboat Key
Hazan, Marcella Maddalena *writer, educator, consultant*

Melbourne
Stone, Elaine Murray *author, composer, television producer*

Mexico Beach
Turney, Virginia *writer*

Miami
Abril, Marcia (Ela I. Cardinas) *writer*
Goin-Harding, Cecilia Margaret *poet*
Goodman-Milone, Constance Beth *writer*
Laje, Zilia L. *writer, publisher, translator*
Marinez, Rita Maria *writer*
Morgan, Marabel *writer*

Naples
Capelle-Frank, Jacqueline Aimee *writer*
Wroble, Lisa Ann *writer, educator*

Navarre
Starratt, Patricia Elizabeth *writer, actress, composer, pianist*

Neptune Beach
Chambers, Ruth Coe *writer*

New Smyrna Beach
Zink, Joan Wilson *writer, poet, composer*

Niceville
Melich, Gayle Peters *writer*

Ocala
Belmontez, Deborah Lynn Groves *poet, editor*

Orlando
Powell, Elaine Marie *consultant, educator, writer*
Raffa, Jean Benedict *author, educator*

Pensacola
Sims, Pam *writer, minister*

Pompano Beach
Kaskinen, Barbara Kay *author, composer, songwriter, musician, music educator*

Ponte Vedra Beach
Friedmann, Elizabeth Carroll *writer, editor*

Port Charlotte
Wolff, Diane Patricia *writer, film producer*

Saint Augustine
Oliver, Elizabeth Kimball *writer*

Saint Petersburg
Snyder-Haug, Diane Leslie *writer*

Sarasota
Jones, Sally Daviess Pickrell *writer*

Sneads
Scott, Brenda D. *writer*

Stuart
Woodward, Isabel Avila *educational writer, foreign language educator*

Tallahassee
Tourtet, Christiane Andrée *writer, human rights activist, photojournalist, reporter*

Tampa
Hanford, Grail Stevenson *writer*
Westcott, Joan Clark *poet*

GEORGIA

Atlanta
Austin, Judy Essary *scriptwriter*
Corriher, Shirley *food writer*
Edson, Margaret *playwright*
Tavaras, Tasha Neanda *writer*
Trethewey, Natasha *poet, literature educator*

Barnesville
Brown, Angelia *poet*

Decatur
Childrey Barksdale, Joyce *writer, social worker*

Marietta
Crossley, Ann Cook *writer*

Peachtree City
Marsh, Carole *author, photographer, publisher*

Roswell
Mayer, Kay Magnor *writer*

Savannah
Strauss, Gwen B. *writer, editor*

HAWAII

Holualoa
Stoddard, Sandol *freelance/self-employed writer*

Pahoa
Salat, Cristina *writer*

IDAHO

Boise
Skurzynski, Gloria Joan *writer*

Twin Falls
Fanselow, Julie Ruth *writer*

ILLINOIS

Buffalo Grove
Serbus, Pearl Sarah Dieck *freelance writer, former editor*

Burbank
Juodvalkis, Egle (Eglé Juodvalké) *writer*

Canton
Hines, Daisy Marie *freelance/self-employed writer*

Charleston
Cooper, Carolyn Sue *translator, educator*

Chicago
Brown, Rosellen *writer*
Danis, Julie Marie *writer, advertising executive*
Drake, Robyn Renée (Robyn Fielder) *writer, painter, equestrian*
Ferguson, Margaret Geneva *writer, publisher, real estate broker*
Hilliard, Celia *writer, educator*
Lach, Alma Elizabeth *food and cooking writer, consultant*
Powell, Enid Levinger *writer, educator*

Crystal Lake
Fleming, Marjorie Foster *freelance writer, artist*
Reed, Helen G. *poet*

Evanston
Komp, Barbara Ann *writer*

Galesburg
Pierson, Karen Arlene *poet*

Glencoe
Rosen, Deborah Nodler *poet, writer*

Highland Park
Greenblatt, Miriam *writer, editor, educator*

Lake Forest
Swanton, Virginia Lee *writer, publishing executive*
Taylor, Barbara Ann Olin *writer, educational consultant*

Oak Lawn
Laird, Jean Elouise Rydeski (Mrs. Jack E. Laird) *author, adult education educator*

Oak Park
Pearson, Gayle Marlene *writer*

Oakbrook Terrace
Hiitola, Bethany *writer, consultant*

Rockford
Kampfe, Doris Elaine *storyteller, folk artist, poet*

Roscoe
Sears, Donna Mae *designer, illustrator*

Urbana
Dovring, Karin Elsa Ingeborg *writer, poet, playwright, media specialist*

Wilmette
Brindel, June Rachuy *writer*

INDIANA

Atwood
Creamer, Kathy Jayne *writer*

Crawfordsville
Barnes, Patience Plummer *writer, editor*

Elkhart
Eddy, Darlene Mathis *poet, educator*

Evansville
Kinkade, Jill Annette *writer*

Fort Wayne
Langhinrichs, Ruth Imler *playwright, writer*

Frankfort
Borland, Kathryn Kilby *author*

Goshen
Nyce, Dorothy Yoder *writer, retired religious studies educator*

Hammond
Hogan, Mary Irene Bernadette *poet*

Howe
Bowerman, Ann Louise *writer, genealogist, educator*

Indianapolis
Budniakiewicz, Therese *writer*
Gregory, Valiska *writer*
Hammontree, Marie Gertrude *writer*

Scottsburg
Dockery-Schillig, Linda *writer*

South Bend
Kline, Syril Levin *writer, educational consultant*

IOWA

Clinton
Warner, Jean Lollich *poet*

Collins
Razor, Mary C. *writer*

Davenport
Beguhn, Sandra E. *poet, writer*
McDonald, Julie Jensen *writer, educator*

Grinnell
Carl, Janet A. *writing instructor, consultant*

Iowa City
Packer, ZZ (Zuwena) *writer, literature educator*

Leon
Miller, Eleanora Genevieve *freelance/self-employed poet*

Newell
Doyen, Barbara J. *literary agent*

KANSAS

Leawood
Garwood, Julie *writer*

KENTUCKY

Boston
Rosenbaum, Mary Heléne Pottker *writer, editor*

Campbellsburg
Mitchell, Mary Ann Carrico *poet*

Covington
McQueen, Regenia *writer*

Lexington
Johnson, Jane Penelope *freelance/self-employed writer*

Shelbyville
Coffman, Lucinda Harrison *writer*

Utica
Henry, Loretta Marrie *writer*

LOUISIANA

Baton Rouge
Mueller, Lisel *writer, poet*
Owen, Sue Ann *poet*

Eunice
Attole, Mary Bertha *writer*

Gretna
Kennedy, Maydra Jane Penisson (J.P. Kennedy) *poet*

Metairie
Grau, Shirley Ann (Mrs. James Kern Feibleman) *writer*
Reinike, Irma *writer, fine artist, poet, lyricist*
Scruggs, Sandra Nell *writer, former school teacher*

New Orleans
Friedmann, Patricia Ann *writer*

MAINE

Allagash
Hafford, Faye O'Leary *writer*

Bangor
King, Tabitha *author*

Brunswick
Heiser, Nancy E. *freelance/self-employed writer, coach*

Orono
Hutchison, Sandra Lynn *writer, educator*

Portland
Morgan, Robin Evonne *poet, author, journalist, activist, editor*
Weir, Anne *writer*

South Bristol
Hammond, Karen T. *writer, editor*

Stockton Springs
Gold, Donna Lauren *writer*

Westport Island
Stedman, Susan Goodwillie *writer, consultant*

MARYLAND

Baltimore
Tyler, Anne (Mrs. Taghi M. Modarressi) *writer*

Bethesda
Free, Ann Cottrell *writer*
Naylor, Phyllis Reynolds *writer*

Chevy Chase
Eccles, Mary *writer*
Wolf, Michele Sue *poet, writer, editor*

Edgewater
Holm, Jeanne Marjorie *writer, consultant, government official, former career officer*

Fort Washington
Cameron, Rita Giovannetti *writer, publisher*

Frederick
Randall, Frances *technical writer*

Germantown
Weiner, Claire Muriel *freelance writer*

Kensington
Ricketts, Marijane Gnegy *poet*

McDaniel
Roth, Lisa Mae *writer*

Owings Mills
Smith, Katrina Diane *writer*

Potomac
Pastan, Linda Olenik *poet*
Sundick, Sherry Small *author, journalist, poet*

Riva
Lynch Schuster, Janice Marie *freelance/self-employed writer*

Rockville
Hodgson, Helen *writer*

Ruxton
Sheldon, Louise Roberts *writer*

Saint Marys City
Clifton, Lucille Thelma *author*

Salisbury
Booker, Betty Mae *poet*

Severna Park
Windsor, Patricia (Katonah Summertree, Perrin Winters) *author, educator, lecturer*

Silver Spring
Vanzant, Iyanla *writer*

MASSACHUSETTS

Amherst
Holland, Noy *writer, educator*
Sandweiss, Martha A. *author, American studies and history educator*

Andover
Murray, Sabina *writer*

Belmont
McEvoy, Frances Jane Coman *writer, editor*

Boston
Angelou, Maya (Marguerite Johnson) *writer, playwright, actress, activist*
Lahiri, Jhumpa *writer*
Lowry, Lois (Lois Hammersberg) *writer*
Martin, Jacqueline Briggs *author juvenile prose*
Ocko, Stephanie *writer, journalist*
Sklar, Holly L. *nonfiction writer*
Treadway, Jessica *writer, educator*
Warren, Rosanna *poet*

Brewster
Hughes, Libby *writer*

Cambridge
Bonina, Mary *poet*
DiCamillo, Kate *writer*
Funkhouser, Erica *writer, writing educator*
Graham, Jorie *writer, educator*
Rhoda, Janice Tucker *writer, educator, musician*
Zoll, Mary *writer, educator*

Fairhaven
Lopes, Myra Amelia *writer*

Great Barrington
Lewis, Karen Marie *writer, human services professional*

Hatfield
Yolen, Jane *author*

Lexington
Giteck, Evelyn B. *poet, educator*
Topalian, Naomi Getsoyan *writer*

Malden
Dell, Diana Jean *writer*

Medfield
Phillips, Marion Grumman *writer, civic worker*

Newburyport
Yeomans, Katie Morse *writer*

Northampton
Boutelle, Ann Edwards *poet, educator*
Friedman, D. Dina *writer, educator*
Stinson, Susan Elizabeth *director, writer*

Provincetown
Oliver, Mary *poet*

Quincy
Bunting, Carolyn Anne *writer*

Revere
Recupero-Faiella, Anna Antonietta *poet*

South Easton
Myers, Linda M. *writer*

South Hamilton
Kroeger, Catherine C. *writer, educator, editor*

Taunton
Doyle, Nancy Carolyn *writer*

Truro
Woolley, Catherine (Jane Thayer) *writer*

Wellesley
Jacobs, Ruth Harriet *poet, playwright, sociologist, gerontologist*

Wellfleet
Piercy, Marge *poet, writer*

West Newbury
Dooley, Ann Elizabeth *freelance writers cooperative executive, editor*

Williamstown
Glück, Louise Elisabeth *poet, educator*

Worcester
Vick, Susan *playwright, educator, director, actress*

MICHIGAN

Ann Arbor
Gregerson, Linda Karen *poet, language educator, critic*
Hefferlin, Earline Dawdy *retired writer*

Chesterfield
Wilson-Pleiness, Christine Joyce *writer, poet, columnist, real estate investor*

Detroit
Gibbs, Mary L. *writer, writers' services provider*
Madgett, Naomi Long *poet, editor, publisher, educator*

East Lansing
Wakoski, Diane *poet, educator*

Flint
Bobb, Carolyn Ruth *science writer*
Campbell, M. Edith *writer, public relations consultant*

Grand Rapids
Henry, Karen Lee *writer, lecturer*

Lansing
Behrens, Ellen Elizabeth Cox *writer, counselor, educator*

New Era
Minty, Judith Makinen *poet, literature and creative writing educator*

Oshtemo
Arnold, Nancy Kay *writer*

Pontiac
Tamez, Myriam *poet*

Powers
Kleikamp, Beverly *poet, writer, publisher*

Union Pier
Howland, Bette *writer*

MINNESOTA

Brainerd
Russell, Maxine *poet, writer*

Edina
Schwarzrock, Shirley Pratt *writer, educator*

Maplewood
St. Germain, Sharon Marie *writer*

Minneapolis
Johnson, Cheri Marie *writer, humanities educator*
Lange, Katherine J. *writer*
Pejsa, Jane Elizabeth *writer, retired computer scientist*

Minnetonka
McCarron, Merne Christine *writer, public relations consultant*

Ortonville
Schrom, Elizabeth Ann *retired writer*

Rochester
Hodgson, Harriet W. *non-fiction writer*

Saint Paul
Bly, Carol McLean *writer, educator*

MISSISSIPPI

Amory
Brannon, Pat *poet*

MISSOURI

Jefferson City
McDaniel, Sue Powell *writer, speaker*

Kansas City
Martin-Bowen, Lindsey *freelance writer*

Saint Charles
Castro, Jan Garden *writer, arts consultant, educator*

Saint Louis
Corbett, Suzanne Elaine *food writer, marketing executive, food historian*
Duhig, Susan Caroline *writer*
Schlafly, Phyllis Stewart *writer*

Stella
Yeagley, Joan Howerton *writer*

Sweet Springs
Long, Helen Halter *writer, educator*

Viburnum
West, Roberta Bertha *writer*

MONTANA

Bigfork
Wetzel, Betty Preat *writer*

Bonner
Smith, Annick *writer*

NEVADA

Las Vegas
Palmer, Lynne *writer, astrologer*

NEW HAMPSHIRE

Cornish Flat
Erdrich, Louise (Karen Erdrich) *fiction writer, poet*

New Durham
Sullivan, Mary Ann *author, marketing professional*

Peterborough
Thomas, Elizabeth Marshall *writer*

Portsmouth
Day, Frances Ann *writer, educator*

NEW JERSEY

Bernardsville
Burbank, Claudia *poet*

Bogota
Livingston, Kathryn E. *writer*

Cape May Court House
Cohen, Susan Lois *writer*

Edgewater
Paci, Ruth A. *freelance/self-employed writer*

Englewood
de Gramont, Carol Carmel *writer*

Fair Haven
Derchin, Dary Bret Ingham *writer*

Lebanon
Barto, Susan Carol *writer*

Long Branch
Stewart, Georgiana Liccione *writer*

Mountainside
Nielsen, Gwyn English *writer, illustrator, publishing executive*

New Brunswick
Jenkins, Alyce Mitchem *writer*
Ostriker, Alicia Suskin *poet*

Newark
Hadas, Rachel *poet, educator*

Paramus
Fader, Shirley Sloan *writer*

Princeton
Kaple, Deborah A. *writer*
Morrison, Toni (Chloe Anthony Morrison) *novelist*

Ringwood
Murphy, Gloria Walter *novelist, screenwriter*

Trenton
Obed, Leonora Rita Villegas *writer*

Upper Montclair
Mandel, Charlotte *poet, literature educator, editor*

Upper Saddle River
Smith, Miranda Constance *writer, educator*

Warren
Baxter, Nancy *medical writer*

NEW MEXICO

Alamogordo
Carnes, Colleen Kennedy *writer, retired military officer*

Albuquerque
Gahala, Estella Marie *writer, consultant*
Kushlis, Patricia Hogin *foreign affairs writer, analyst*
Marks, Martha Alford *writer*
Mulcahy, Lucille Burnett *freelance writer*
Richter, Harvena *retired english literature and creative writing teacher, writer*

Galisteo
Lippard, Lucy Rowland *writer, lecturer*

Las Cruces
Nelson, Antonya *writer*

Lovington
Stuart, Lillian Mary *writer*

Roswell
Watson, Marilyn Fern *writer*

Santa Fe
Bergé, Carol *writer*
Cohen, Marcia Friedlander *writer, editor-in-chief, journalist*
Loftin, Thelma Tee *writer*

NEW YORK

Amherst
Kester, Gunilla Theander *poet, literature educator, music educator*

Bronx
Bingham, June *writer, playwright*
Leighton, Anne Renita *writer, educator*

Bronxville
Silber, Joan Karen *writer, educator*
Swann, Lois Lorraine *writer, editor, educator*

Brooklyn
Blue, Rose *writer, educator*
Cummings, Josephine Anna *writer, consultant, advertising executive*
Gioseffi, Daniela (Dorothy Daniela Gioseffi) *poet, writer, playwright*
Montanarelli, Lisa *writer, researcher*
Pearlman, Ellen Lois *writer, photographer, computer consultant*
Reynolds, Nancy Remick *writer, researcher, editor*

Cairo
Ludwig, Laura Lonshein *poet*

Canton
Daniels, Cindy Lou *writer, educator*

Cedarhurst
Solymosy, Hattie May *writer, publisher, storyteller, educator*

Chappaqua
George, Jean Craighead *author, illustrator*

Cherry Valley
Dallemagne-Cookson, Elise Camille *writer*

Chichester
Kaye/Kantrowitz, Melanie *writer, educator*

Eastchester
Weinberg, Dale Glaser *technical writer, consultant, trainer*

Flushing
Givens, Janet Eaton *writer*
Zinnes, Harriet Fich *poet, retired English educator, literary and art critic, writer*

Great Neck
Hurwitz, Johanna (Johanna Frank) *writer*

Hastings On Hudson
Barolini, Helen *writer, translator, educator*

Ithaca
DeLaurentis, Louise Budde *writer*
Lurie, Alison *writer*

Lowville
Colton, Bonnie Myers *writer, folklorist*

Manhasset
Montane, Fran *poet, film producer*

Millerton
Paretsky, Sara N. *writer*

Mount Kisco
Hodara, Susan Mina *writer*

New York
Albee, Gloria *playwright*
Alvarez, Julia *writer*
Arnow, Pat *freelance writer, editor, photographer*
Arvio, Sarah *poet*
Ash, Jennifer Gertrude *writer, editor*
Ashdown, Marie Matranga (Mrs. Cecil Spanton Ashdown Jr.) *writer, educator, lecturer, cultural organization administrator*
Ashton, Dore *writer, educator*
Atwood, Margaret Eleanor *writer*
Balogh, Mary *writer*
Bauer, Marion Dane *writer*
Bawden, Nina (Mary Bawden) *author*
Beattie, Ann *writer*
Bel Geddes, Joan *writer*

Bergstrom, Elaine *novelist*
Birstein, Ann *writer, educator*
Block, Francesca Lia *writer*
Blume, Judy *author*
Bradford, Barbara Taylor *writer, journalist*
Braudy, Susan Orr *writer*
Brooks, Laurie *playwright, educator*
Brown, Rita Mae *writer*
Brownmiller, Susan *author, feminist activist*
Bugge, Carole Elizabeth *writer, actress*
Bujold, Lois McMaster *writer*
Calisher, Hortense (Mrs. Curtis Harnack) *writer*
Carlson, P(atricia) M(cElroy) *writer*
Carol, Joy Haupt *writer, educator, cultural organization administrator*
Charbonnet, Gabrielle *writer*
Christina, Sonja (Alisa Morris) *writer, poet*
Cisneros, Sandra *poet, short story writer, essayist*
Cleary, Beverly Atlee (Mrs. Clarence T. Cleary) *writer*
Cole, Diane Joyce *writer*
Cole, Harriett *writer, media consultant*
Collins, Jackie *writer*
Cornwell, Patricia Daniels *writer*
Creech, Sharon *children's author*
Cryer, Gretchen *playwright, lyricist, actress*
Curry, Jane Louise *writer*
Cushman, Karen Lipski *writer*
Davis, Patti *writer*
deCoppet, Laura *writer, editor*
Decter, Midge *writer*
Deveraux, Jude (Jude Gilliam White) *writer*
De Voe, Milda M. *writer*
Diamonstein-Spielvogel, Barbaralee *writer, television interviewer/ producer*
Didion, Joan *writer*
Diggs, Elizabeth F(rancis) *playwright, educator*
Dillard, Annie *writer*
Eckstut, Arielle *literary agent, writer*
Fennell Robbins, Sally *writer*
Finch, Sheila *writer*
Fitch, Janet *writer*
Fleesler, Faith B. *writer*
Fleming, Alice Carew Mulcahey *writer*
Fogarassy, Helen Catherine *writer*
Fox, Paula (Mrs. Martin Greenberg) *writer*
Fritz, Jean Guttery *writer*
Gabaldon, Diana *writer*
Gaydos, Mary *writer, researcher, actress*
Gibbons, Kaye *writer*
Goldsmith, Barbara *writer, historian, journalist*
Goldstein, Lisa Joy *writer*
Gordon, Mary Catherine *writer*
Goreau, Angeline Wilson *writer*
Grafton, Sue *novelist*
Grant, Cynthia D. *writer*
Gray, Deborah Dolja *business writing consultant*
Greenwald, Sheila Ellen *writer, illustrator*
Griffith, Nicola *writer*
Hadden, Margaret (Peggy Hadden) *writer*
Hadley, Leila Eliott-Burton (Mrs. Henry Luce III) *writer*
Hamilton, Jane *writer*
Hardwick, Elizabeth *writer*
Hazzard, Shirley *author*
Hesse, Karen (Karen Sue Hesse) *writer, educator*
Hillenbrand, Laura *writer*
Hoag, Tami *writer*
Hoffman, Alice *writer*
Horvath, Polly *writer*
Howe, Tina *playwright*
Humphreys, Josephine *novelist*
Hussung, Alleen Mosette *literary agent*
Hyatt, Carole S. *author, speaker, coach*
Jacker, Corinne Litvin *playwright, writer*
Jhabvala, Ruth Prawer *writer*
Joachim, Brigitta Golden *writer, advertising agency executive, media consultant*
Jones, Diana Wynne *writer*
Jong, Erica Mann *writer*
Kafka, Barbara Poses *writer*
Karr, Kathleen *writer*
Kaufman, Bel *author, educator*
Kehret, Peg *writer*
Kellar, Charlotte Avrutis *writer*
Kennedy, Adrienne Lita *playwright*
Klagsbrun, Francine *writer, editor*
Kramer, Jane *writer*
Krantz, Judith Tarcher *novelist*
Kress, Nancy *writer*
Lauber, Patricia Grace *writer*
L'Engle, Madeleine (Mrs. Hugh Franklin) *writer*
Lorch, Maristella De Panizza *writer, educator*
Lord, M. G. *writer*
Lunardini, Christine Anne *writer, historian, school administrator*
Macer-Story, Eugenia Ann *writer*
Macklin, Elizabeth (Jean) *poet, editor*
MacLachlan, Patricia *author*
Manning, Martha Mary *writer, psychologist*
Mason, Bobbie Ann *novelist, short story writer*
McCorduck, Pamela Ann *writer, educator*
McDermott, Alice *writer*
McWhorter, Diane *writer*
Menza, Claudia Marcella *literary agent*
Mills, Stephanie Ellen *writer*
Minarik, Else Holmelund (Bigart Minarik) *author*
Mitchard, Jacquelyn *writer*
Monk Kidd, Sue *writer*
Munro, Alice *author*
Munro, Eleanor *writer, lecturer*
Murphy, Patrice Ann (Pat Murphy) *writer*
Navarra, Tova *writer*
Nesbit, Lynn *literary agent*
Newberg, Esther *literary agent*
Nixon, Agnes Eckhardt *television writer, producer*
Noonan, Peggy *writer*
Oates, Joyce Carol *author*
Olsen, Tillie *author*
Osborne, Mary Pope *writer*
Paley, Maggie *writer, editor*
Pall, Ellen Jane *writer*
Papell, Helen Gertrude *poet, retired librarian*
Park, Linda Sue *writer*
Parkhurst, Carolyn *writer*

Patchett, Ann *writer*
Paterson, Katherine Womeldorf *writer*
Pogrebin, Letty Cottin *writer, lecturer*
Pool, Mary Jane *writer, lecturer*
Proula, (Edna) Annie *writer*
Quilter, Deborah *writer, consultant, educator*
Rabinowitz, Anna *poet*
Rathmann, Peggy *writer, illustrator*
Reig, June Wilson *scriptwriter, television director, television producer*
Replansky, Naomi *poet*
Resuché, Barbara T. *writer*
Rice, Anne *writer*
Rice, Luanne *writer*
Rich, Adrienne *writer*
Roberts, Nora *writer*
Rollin, Betty *writer, television journalist, lecturer*
Roy, Arundhati *writer*
Rylant, Cynthia *author*
Salter, Mary Jo *poet*
Sargent, Pamela *writer*
Schine, Cathleen *writer*
Schlein, Miriam *writer*
Scotti, Rita Angelica *novelist*
Segal, Lore *writer*
Sheehan, Susan *writer*
Sheehy, Gail Henion *author*
Singer, Davida *poet, journalist, educator*
Smiley, Jane Graves *author, educator*
Smith, Betty *writer, nonprofit foundation executive*
Solnit, Rebecca *writer, art critic*
Sontag, Susan *writer*
Squire, Gilda N. *brand manager, publicist, writer*
Steel, Danielle Fernande *author*
Swenson, Tree (Holly) *poet*
Tan, Amy Ruth *writer*
Taylor, Mildred D. *author*
Trevens, Francine Linda *writer, publishing executive*
Urban, Amanda (Binky Urban) *literary agent*
Walker, Alice *writer*
Wasserstein, Wendy *playwright*
Wender, Phyllis Bellows *literary agent*
Whitney, Phyllis Ayame *author*
Williams, Diane *writer, editor*
Wolff, Virginia Euwer *writer*
Yglesias, Helen Bassine *author, educator*
York, Alexandra *writer, lecturer*
Yuspeh-Hidalgo, Denise Anne *juvenile writer, editor*
Zha, Jianying *writer, educator*
Zimmerman, Paula *writer*
Zolotow, Charlotte Shapiro *author, editor*

Palisades
Davis, Dorothy Salisbury *writer*

Penfield
Marbach, Donna Maureen *writer*

Pleasantville
Nelson, K. Bonita *literary agent*

Port Washington
Cox, Jane *writer*

Poughkeepsie
Willard, Nancy Margaret *writer, educator*

Rochester
Glatzer, Jenna *writer*

Sagaponack
Cedering, Siv *poet, writer*

Sayville
Leuzzi, Linda *writer*

Southold
Small, Bertrice W. *writer*

Staten Island
Popp, Lilian Mustaki *writer, educator*

Troy
Tanguay, Janet *expressive arts therapist, writer, filmmaker*

Warwick
Linnéa, Sharon *writer, playwright*

Whitesboro
O'Hara, Cynthia O'Connor *writer, columnist, food consultant*

Woodstock
Godwin, Gail Kathleen *writer*

NORTH CAROLINA

Asheville
Hunter, Brenda Ann *writer, psychologist*

Chapel Hill
Spencer, Elizabeth *author*

Charlotte
Coffey, Marilyn June *writer, educator*
Finley, Glenna *writer*

Columbus
Sauvé, Carolyn Opal *writer, journalist, poet*

Cullowhee
Stripling Byer, Kathryn *poet*

High Point
Bennett-Wilkes, Theresa Williams *writer, educator*

Pittsboro
Betts, Doris June Waugh *writer, English language educator*

OHIO

Beachwood
Liebow, Joanne Elisabeth *poet and freelance publicist*

Bowling Green
Williams, Theresa Ann Aleshire *poet, writer, educator*

Cincinnati
Aylesworth, Julie Ann *writer, personal care professional*
Miller, Sari Elizabeth (Sally Derby) *writer*

Cleveland
Kovel, Terry Horvitz (Mrs. Ralph Kovel) *writer, antiques authority*

Cleveland Heights
Sandburg, Helga *author*

Columbus
Perrini, Nancy Brown *writer, consultant*

Dayton
Boice, Martha Hibbert *writer, publisher*
Jelus, Susan Crum *writer, editor*

Gambier
Buchsbaum, Julianne *writer, educator*

Hamilton
Ridner, Melanie Marie *writer, composer*

Kent
Cielinski-Kessler, Audrey Ann *writer, publishing executive, small business owner*

Mount Vernon
Wells-Maxwell, Violet *writer, artist*

Napoleon
Meekison, MaryFran *writer*

North Royalton
Pamin, Diana Dolhancyk (Diana Dolhancyk) *poet*

Saint Paris
Phillips, Raelene E. *writer, educator*

Springfield
Dobson, Janet Louise *writer*

Walton Hills
Cieszewski, Joyce Catherine *writer, educator*

Westfield Center
Bock, Carolyn A. *writer, small business owner*

Zanesville
Fulkerson, Sue Ellen *poet*

OKLAHOMA

Bixby
Wetzel, Marlene Reed *freelance/self-employed writer*

Cleveland
Anderson, Patricia Sue *writer*

Drumright
Geyer, Karen Lea *writer*

Norman
MacFarland, Miriam Katherine (Mimi MacFarland) *writer*

Oklahoma City
Mather, Ruth Elsie *writer*
Sharpe, Bobbie Mahon *author*

Tulsa
Arnold-Chapman, Ingrid M *writer*
Clark, Marian Wilson *writer*
Mojtabai, Ann Grace *author, educator*
Price, Alice Lindsay *writer*

Warr Acres
Swain, Joye Raechel *writer*

OREGON

Boring
Robinson, Jeanne Louise *writer, educator*

Cannon Beach
Hellyer, Constance Anne (Connie Anne Conway) *writer, musician*

Culver
Siebert, Diane Dolores *author, poet*

Eugene
Wilhelm, Kate (Katy Gertrude) *author*

Gladstone
Landers, Patricia Burneice *writer*

Klamath Falls
Koch, Margaret Rau *writer, artist, historian*

Lake Oswego
Chula, Margaret Jean *poet, writer*

Mcminnville
Burchard, Rachael C. *literary critic, poet, playwright*

Portland
Larson, Wanda Z. *writer, poet*
Porter, Elsa Allgood *writer, lecturer*

PENNSYLVANIA

Broomall
Spunberg, Sally Lees *poet, educator*

California
Langham, Norma E. *playwright, educator, poet, composer, inventor*

Fogelsville
Crooker, Barbara Ann *writer, educator*

Greensburg
Shafer-Kenney, Jolie E. *writer, columnist*

Harrisburg
Cooper, Jane Todd (J. C. Todd) *poet, writer, educator*
Schmedlen, Jeanne Hearn *writer, legislative staff member, consultant*

King Of Prussia
Schumann, Paula M. L. *writer*

Lancaster
Shenk, Lois Elaine Landis *writer*

Maple Glen
Jacobson, Bonnie Brown *writer, energy executive, statistician, researcher*

Milford
Le Guin, Ursula Kroeber *writer*

Philadelphia
Axelrod, Jean Kolb *writer*
Fine, Andrea Joiner *writer*
Goldstein, Melissa Anne *writer*
Granato, Carol Anne *writer*
Greenspun, Adele Aron *writer, educator, photographer*
Owens, Rochelle *poet, playwright*
Paglia, Camille *writer, humanities educator*
Scanlon, Elizabeth C. *poet, editor*
Stewart, Susan *writer*

Pittsburgh
Bleier, Carol Stein *writer, researcher*
Chewning, Lisa Lee *writer, educator*
Edelman, Barbara Jane *writer, educator*
Hodges, Margaret Moore *author, educator*
Verlich, Jean Elaine *writer, public relations consultant*

Radnor
Flagg, Helen Clawson *writer*

State College
Erem, Suzan *writer*

Valley Forge
Miller, Betty Brown *freelance writer*

Villanova
Gould, Lilian *writer*

Wayne
Burton, B.J. (Betty Jane) *playwright*

Wynnewood
Meyers, Mary Ann *foundation administrator, writer, consultant*

York
Ardison, Linda G. *author, writing educator*

RHODE ISLAND

Adamsville
Cumming, Patricia A. *writer*

Newport
Scoll, Eulalie Elizabeth *writer, researcher*

Providence
Lopez-Morillas, Frances M. *translator*
Vogel, Paula Anne *playwright*
Waldrop, Rosmarie *writer*

Saunderstown
Tener, Lisa C. *writer*

SOUTH CAROLINA

Anderson
Jarrett, Jinger Elaine *freelance/self-employed writer*

Charleston
Siddons, Anne Rivers (Sybil Anne Rivers Siddons) *writer*

Columbia
Newton, Rhonwen Leonard *writer, microcomputer consultant, data processing executive, consultant*
Stamps, Laura Anne *writer, poet*

Hilton Head Island
Reed, Frances Boogher *writer, actress*

Newberry
Johnson, Melissa Carol *poet, educator*

Seneca
Byars, Betsy (Cromer) *writer*

Summerville
Reisman, Rosemary Moody Canfield *writer, humanities educator*

SOUTH DAKOTA

Brookings
Williams, Elizabeth Evenson *writer*

TENNESSEE

Brentwood
Bolton, Martha O. *writer*

Chattanooga
Riggs, Claudesta Lavern *professional storyteller*

Cookeville
Underwood, Lucinda Jean *poet, playwright, small business owner, researcher*

Greeneville
Breckenridge, Judith Watts *writer, educator*

Nashville
Bird, Caroline *author*
Cornwell, Ilene Jones *writer, editor*
Hammond, Charlene Foster *writer, choreographer, musician, artist, educator*
Pearson, Sela *poet, speaker*
Winstead, Elisabeth Weaver *poet, writer, English language educator*

Newport
Gregg, Ella Mae *writer*

Old Hickory
Vivelo, Jacqueline Jean *author, English language educator*

Paris
McFarlin, Shannon Dianne *writer, researcher*

Sevierville
Koff, Shirley Irene *writer*

TEXAS

Arlington
Savage, Ruth Hudson *poet, writer, speaker*

Austin
Furman, Laura *writer, educator*
McElroy, Mary M. (Mickie McElroy) *educational writer*
Spicer, Beverly White *writer, photojournalist, artist*

Bertram
Albert, Susan Wittig *writer, English educator*

Brookshire
Utley, Jane Beson *poet*

Chireno
Mayhar, Ardath Frances (Frank Cannon) *author*

Dallas
Harte, Sherri Jean *technical writer*
Jones, Peggy W. *poet*
Phillips, Betty Lou (Elizabeth Louise Phillips) *writer, interior designer*

Denton
Wood, Jane Roberts *writer*

Dripping Springs
Fierstien, Nancy Louise *writer*

Flower Mound
Hawkins, Kathleen L. *writer, training services executive*

Fort Worth
de Toledo, Catherine Holt *medical writer*
Laughlin, Christel Renate *translator, consultant*

Georgetown
Earney, Mary K. *writer, educator*

Houston
Berniard, Susan K. *business writer/editor*
de Vries, Robbie Ray Parsons *writer, illustrator, international consultant*
Leslie, Mae Sue *writer*
McPhail, JoAnn Winstead *writer, publisher, art dealer*
Parle, Bertha Ibarra *writer*
Wood, Susan *poet, literature educator*

Kyle
Brown, Valerie *writer*

Lubbock
Bronwell, Nancy Brooker *writer*

Marfa
McBride, Elizabeth Anne Wilmore *writer*

Plano
Gallardo, Henrietta Castellanos *writer*

Pottsboro
Jackson, Nona Armour *writer, illustrator*

Round Top
Kilgore, Carolyn Harrell (Carolyn Lawton Harrell) *writer*

Salado
Black, Mary Lee *writer, educator*

San Antonio
Glueck, Sylvia Blumenfeld *writer*
Rogers, Frances Evelyn *author, retired educator and librarian*

San Marcos
Monroe, Debra F. *writer, educator*

Smithville
Clark, LaVerne Harrell *writer*

UTAH

Dammeron Valley
McAnally, Ann *puzzle constructor*

Park City
Finney, Lynne Dratler *writer, educator, retired psychotherapist, lawyer*
Solomon, Dorothy Jeanne Allred *writer, communications executive*

Salt Lake City
Osherow, Jacqueline Sue *poet, English language educator*

VERMONT

Bennington
Bernard, April *poet, literature educator*

Brattleboro
Lappe, Frances Moore *author, lecturer*

Burlington
Carlisle, Lilian Matarose Baker (Mrs. E. Grafton Carlisle Jr.) *writer, lecturer*
Hearon, Shelby *writer, lecturer, educator*

Johnson
Rice, Rebecca Kynoch *writer, consultant, educator*

Thetford
Paley, Grace *author, educator*

VIRGINIA

Aldie
Weaver, Kitty Dunlap *author*

Alexandria
Collins, Mary *writer, educator*
Kaye, Ruth Lincoln *historical researcher*
[illegible]
Wells, Fay Gillis *writer, lecturer, broadcaster, aviation historian*

Arlington
Cinca, Silvia (Roberta King) *writer, producer*

Charlottesville
Dove, Rita Frances *poet, English language educator*
Grohskopf, Bernice *writer*

Clarksville
Worth, Lynn Harris *writer*

Clifton
Caviloer, Sharon E. *writer, public relations executive, consultant*

Ettrick
Davis, Minnie Louise *writer*

Fairfax
Parrish-St. John, Florence Tucker *writer, educator, retired government official*

Falls Church
Leighton, Frances Spatz *writer, journalist*

Fort Belvoir
Smith, Margherita *writer, editor*

Fredericksburg
Westebbe, Barbara Liebst *writer, sculptor*

Free Union
LeBoutillier, Megan *writer*

Leesburg
Johnson, Julia A. *writer*

Lexington
Solod, Lisa *writer*

Newport News
Smith, Barbara Ruthjena Drucker *writer, educator*

Richmond
Morgan, Elizabeth Seydel *writer, educator, retired writer*
Reynolds, Sheri *writer*

Spotsylvania
Pritchard, Tiffany Maxwell *writer, educator*

Virginia Beach
Clark, Suzanne Underwood *writer*

Williamsburg
Durrant, Rita Delores *poet, educator*
Windsor, Joan Ruth *author, professional counselor*

Woodbridge
Englert, Helen Wiggs *writer*

Woodstock
Maggiolo, Paulette Blanche *writer*

WASHINGTON

Arlington
Bullington, Gayle Rogers *writer, researcher*

Bainbridge Island
Stewart, Kay Boone *writer, retired educator and administrator*

Bellevue
Chi, Hannah T. *poet, writer*

Issaquah
Cain, Coleen W. *writer, educator*

Kirkland
Szablya, Helen Mary *writer, language professional, lecturer*

Oak Harbor
Lightbourne, Alesa M. *writer*

Seattle
Butler, Octavia Estelle *free-lance writer*
Dannenhold, Kathleen E. *writer, director*
Kunkel, Georgie Bright *freelance writer, retired school counselor*
McHugh, Heather *poet*
Mini, Anne Alexandra Apostolides *writer, educator*
Pizzorno, Lara Elise *medical writer, editor*

Spokane
Colford, Ann M. *freelance/self-employed writer*

WEST VIRGINIA

Charleston
Mellert, Lucie Anne *writer, photographer*

West Columbia
Fowler, Sandra Lynn *poet*

WISCONSIN

Appleton
Rice, Ferill Jeane *writer, civic worker*

Colfax
Ralph, LeAnn Rae *writer, editor*

Green Bay
Erickson, Ruth Alice *poet, artist*

Hancock
Vroman, Barbara Fitz *writer, educator*

Madison
Ashley, Renee *writer, creative writing educator, consultant*
Riley, Jocelyn Carol *writer, television producer*

Oshkosh
Alderson, Jo Bartels *writer, poet*

Racine
Wright, Betty Ren *children's book writer*

Saukville
Gulan, Bonnie Marion *writer, researcher*

WYOMING

Gillette
Wise, Kitty *writer, composer*
Rice, Ashley Lynn *writer, illustrator*

CANADA

ONTARIO

London
Barfoot, Joan *writer*

Toronto
Peacock, Molly *poet, educator*

MEXICO

Puerto Vallarta
Pordon, Judith *writer, poet, artist*

ENGLAND

London
Desai, Anita *writer*
Fine, Anne *author*
Galloway, Janice *writer, editor*
Hunter Blair, Pauline Clarke *writer*
James, P(hyllis) D(orothy) (Baroness James of Holland Park of Southwold in County of Suffolk) *author*
Paton Walsh, Jill *writer*
Rowling, J.K. (Joanne Kathleen Rowling) *writer*

SWITZERLAND

Bern
Carlson, Dale Bick *writer*

ADDRESS UNPUBLISHED

Adams, Carolyn Lee *poet, artist*
Alinder, Mary Street *writer, lecturer*
Allen, Louise *writer, educator*
Allen, Roberta *fiction and nonfiction writer, conceptual artist, photographer*
Aloff, Mindy *writer*
Anderson-Spivy, Alexandra *writer, editor*
Andreae, Christine Ewing *writer*
Anton, Barbara *writer*
Argers, Helen *novelist, playwright*
Atkins, Jeannine Catherine *writer*
Avrett, Roz (Rosalind Case) *writer, advertising creative director*
Bahr, Jane Marie *writer, retired English educator*
Baker, Lucinda *writer*
Baker, Susan Marie Victoria *writer, artist, musician*
Baldrige, Letitia *writer, management training consultant*
Barcus, Nancy B. *fine arts educator, writer*
Bassett, Elizabeth Ewing (Libby Bassett) *writer, editor*
Battiste, Michele C. *poet, literature educator*
Beard, Bernice Talbott *writer, publisher*
Beatts, Anne Patricia *writer, producer*
Beisch, June *freelance/self-employed writer, literature educator, poet*
Berman, Eleanor *writer*
Bertram, Anne *playwright, application developer*
Bertram, Jean DeSales *writer*
Blos, Joan W. *author, critic, lecturer*
Blunt, Kathryn London *screenwriter, author*
Blythe, Carolita Antoinette *writer*
Bonanni, Victoria *writer*
Bracken, Peg *writer*
Brandler, Marcielle Y. *poet, educator*
Braz-Valentine, Claire *writer, playwright*
Brewer, Rogenna Wynne *writer*
Brookner, Anita *writer, educator*
Brown, Crystal Jeanine *writer*
Brown, Denise *poet*
Brown, Marcia Joan *author, artist, photographer*
Brown, Rebecca *writer, educator*
Brown, Sandra *writer*
Brubach, Holly Beth *writer*
Brussel, Marika H. *writer, educator*
Buckingham, Deidre Lyn *writer, musician*
Bush, Yvonne *writer, counselor*
Byrne, Judy Susanne *writer, educator*
Cahill, Verna Eleanore *writer*
Caldwell-Smith, Gaetana Lee *writer*
Callen, Paulette Marie *writer, advocate*
Calmenson, Stephanie Lyn *writer*
Campbell, Andrea S. *writer*
Candido, Viola Jeane Heimberger *writer*
Carlisle-Frank, Pamela L. *writer, researcher, consultant, management consultant*
[illegible]
Cassian, Nina *poet, composer*
Chamberlain, Patricia Ann *writer, farmer, retired environmental manager, land use planner*
Cheatham, Delzora *writer*
Chesney, Susan Talmadge *writer, developer*
Choukas-Bradley, Melanie *writer, photographer*
Claes, Gayla Christine *writer, editorial consultant*
Clark, Mary Higgins *writer, communications executive*
Cleland, Nora Temple *writer, editor*
Conley, Ruth Irene *poet*
Conover-Carson, Anne *writer*
Cooke, Chantelle Anne *writer*
Cooper, Jamie Lee *writer*
Costantini, Mary Ann C. *writer, editor, retired elementary educator*
Coughran, Jane Nora *writer, editor, researcher*
Couto, Nancy Vieira *poet, literary consultant*
Cronacher, Karen Jan *playwright, educator*
Curtis, Dolores Rogers *writer*
Dailey, Janet *writer*
Davis, Maggie (Marie Hill) *writer*
De Amorim, Valdivia Vânia Siqueira *translator*
DeShields, Sheila Beth *writer*
Diamant, Anita *writer*
Dominic, Magic *writer*
Donlou-Richmond, Doris Julia *scriptwriter*
Donnelly, Christina Wos *poet*
Dorman, Angelia Hardy *writer*
Dougherty, Karla R. *writer*
Drechsel, Joanne J. *writer, educator*
Dunn, Carola *writer*
Easton, Kelly Anne *writer, educator*
Edge, Charlene L. *writer*
Egan, Moira *poet, educator*
Eisenberg, Phyllis Rose *author*
Ellie, Beth Joy *writer*
Emrich, Jeanne Ann *poet, artist*
Ephron, Nora *writer*
Erni, Corinne *writer, cultural projects manager*
Erwin, Judith Ann (Judith Ann Peacock) *writer, photographer, lawyer*
Esther, Queen *playwright, scriptwriter, songwriter, solo performer, actor, musician*
Evangelista, Anita Loretta *freelance writer, psychologist, nurse, publishing executive*
Ewing, Robyn *writer, educator*
Faiz, Alexandria *nonfiction writer, researcher*
Fearrington, Ann Peyton *writer, illustrator, newspaper reporter, portraitist*
Fiedler, Johanna *writer*
Filleman, Teresa Ellen *technical writer*
Finn, Ange Dickson *freelance/self-employed writer*
Fisher, Nancy *writer, producer, director*
Forrest, Katherine Virginia *writer*
Fouquet, Kristin K. *writer, photographer*
Fraser, Kathleen Joy *poet, creative writing educator*
Freid, Stephanie Lynne *writer, educator*
French, Marilyn *writer, critic*
Friday, Nancy *author*
Furst, Greta Lenetska *entertainer, writer, travel agent*
Gallimore, Margaret Martin *poet*
Garceau, Jo Mills *writer*
Garfield-Woodbridge, Nancy *writer*
Garfinkle, Elaine Myra *writer*
Gavriloff, Katrina *writer*
George, Linda Shumaker *freelance/self-employed writer*
Gersoni-Edelman, Diane Claire *author, editor*
Giffin, Marjie G. *writer*
Gifford, Heidi *writer, editor*
Gilchrist, Ellen Louise *writer*
Gilmer, Ellen Louise *writer, artist*
Glenn, Rosemary *writer*
Glick, Ruth Burtnick *author, lecturer*
Goldfarb, Ruth *poet, educator*
Goldsmith, Jill *scriptwriter, television producer*
Gordimer, Nadine *author*
Grambs, Jennifer *writer*
Gray, Francine du Plessix *author*
Greenberg, Carol *poet*
Greensides, Catherine May *poet*
Greer, Germaine *author*
Grossman, Edith Marian *translator, critic, editor*
Guirado, Tamara A. *writer, educator*
Gunn, S. Jeanne *writer, natural healer*
Guy, Eleanor Bryenton *writer*
Hageman, Anna Robbins *writer*
Hahn, Mary Downing *writer*
Harrison, Sue Ann McHaney *writer*
Haskell, Molly *writer*
Hazard, Barbara Ward *writer, artist*
Herbert, Mary Katherine Atwell *writer*
Herrnkind, Hilda Marie *writer, military volunteer*
Higdon, Pamela Leis *writer*
Hill, Donna Marie *writer, retired librarian*
Hillman, Marguerite Agnes *literary agent, consultant*
Himes, Barbara Alison (Sydney Kendall) *writer*
Holifield, Pearl Kam (Kam Holifield, Momi Kam Holifield) *poet*
Hollander, Anne *writer*
Hornbaker, Alice Joy *writer*
Howes, Sophia DuBose *writer*
Hughes, Debra *writer, educator*
Isaacs, Susan *novelist, screenwriter*
Jack, Morgann Tayllor *writer, artist*
Jacobs, Nancy Carolyn Baker *writer*
Jacobson, Joan Leiman *writer*
Jeffress, Lynn *writer, education educator*
Johnsen, Barbara Parrish *writer, educator*
Johnson, Mary P. *freelance writer*
Johnson, Susan Ann *writer*
Jones, Carolyn Evans *writer, speaker*
Jones, Hettie Cohen *writer, educator*
Kaimann, Diane S. *writer, educator*
Kanin, Fay *screenwriter*
Kincaid, Jamaica *writer*
King, Joy Rainey *poet, executive secretary*
Kingston, Maxine Hong *writer, educator*
Kirchner, Bharti N. *writer*
Kleine, Andrea *playwright, actor, choreographer*
Konecky, Edith *writer*
Konigsburg, Elaine Lobl *writer*
Krupat, Kitty Weiss *writer, educator*
Kumin, Maxine Winokur *poet, writer*
Kutlich, Anna *writer*
Langham, Gail B. *writer*
Lansing, Jewel Beck (Jewel Anne Beck) *writer, auditor*
Lapidus, Jacqueline *poet, editor, educator*
Lapore, Janyce Catherine *writer*
Larkin, Joan *poet, English educator*
LaRoche, Linda *writer*
Larsdotter, Anna-Lisa *retired translator, artist*
Lawrence, Ruth *writer, illustrator*
Lawton, Violet *writer*
Lazo, Caroline Evensen *writer*
LeBlanc, Adrian Nicole *writer*
LeBlanc, Jean Eva *writer, poet, educator*
Ledford, Brenda Kay *writer*
Leiter, Elaine Carol *technical writer*
Leventhal, Ann Z. *writer, educator*
Lingle, Marilyn Felkel *freelance writer, columnist, author*
Long, Elaine *writer, editor*
Lubell, Ellen *writer*
MacLean, Judith E. *writer, editor*
Madsen, Susan Arrington *writer*
Mann, Emily Betsy *writer, artistic director, theater director*
Manus, Nancy Manning *writer, former social services administrator*
Marx, Anne (Mrs. Frederick E. Marx) *poet*
Mata, Linda Sue Proctor *writer, consultant*
Mathis, Sharon Bell *author, retired elementary educator and librarian*
Mattern, Joanne *writer, educator*
McCourt, Lisa *writer*
McDougal, Amy Nicole *poet*
McFall, Catherine Gardner *poet, critic, educator*
Mc Intyre, Vonda Neel *writer*
McLaughlin, Dara Dawn *freelance/self-employed writer, freelance/self-employed artist*
McMillan, Terry L. *writer, educator*
McNees, Pat (Patricia Ann McNees) *writer, editor*
Meaker, Marijane Agnes *author*
Meitner, Erika *poet, education educator*
Merrill, Jean Fairbanks *writer*
Minot, Eliza *writer*
Mintz, Gwendolyn Joyce *writer, educator*
Mitchell, Marcia Jeanne *freelance/self-employed writer, events producer*
Mitrany, Devora *writer, editor*
Mockler, Anna *writer, ecologist*
Monroe, Barbara Jean *writer, educator*
Moore, Susanna *writer*
Morang, Diane Judy *writer, television producer, business entrepreneur*
Morris, Dorothy Kay *writer*
Morrison, Sarah Lyddon *author*
Morse-McNeely, Patricia *poet, writer, retired middle school educator*
Muehl, Lois Baker *writer, retired language educator*
Newhall, Edith Allerton *writer*
Nguyen, Mai (Mai Tuyet Nguyen) *writer*
Nichols, Allene Rasmussen *writer, educator*
Nielson, Alyce Mae *poet*
Novack, Barbara *writer, educator*
Ogden, Ann *writer*
O'Leary, Kathleen Ann *writer*

O'Loughlin, Katie Eileen Bridget *poet*
Orr, Marjorie *poet, dancer, publishing executive*
Ozick, Cynthia *writer*
Paegle, Julie Sophia *writer, editor, educator*
Paolucci, Anne Attura *playwright, poet, English and comparative literature educator, educational consultant*
Parke, Marilyn Neils *writer*
Parsons, Christina Anne *writer, photographer*
Patrick, Mary Kathleen *freelance/self-employed writer, food service executive*
Pedrick, Jean *poet*
Perriguey, Georgia Désirée *poet, educator*
Petrelis, Stella Marsha *writer*
Phillips, Jill Meta *novelist, critic, astrologer*
Pierce, Marian Marie *writer, educator*
Pimental, Nancy M. *scriptwriter, actress*
Polite, Carlene Hatcher *writer, educator*
Powell, Alma Johnson *writer, advocate, foundation administrator*
Powell, Patricia Hruby *writer, dancer*
Pudick, Donna Eastman *writer, educator*
Quay, Joyce Crosby *writer*
Quinn, Barbara Ann *writer*
Quinn, Brenda Whalen *writer, poet*
Ragans, Rosalind Dorothy *textbook author, retired art educator*
Reeves, Barbara *writer, educator*
Reich, Denise Elizabeth *writer, researcher*
Reifler, Nelly *writer*
Renaud, Bernadette Marie Elise *author*
Rider, Fae B. *freelance writer*
Ridley, JoAnn D. *writer, public relations executive*
Riehecky, Janet Ellen *writer*
Ring, Nancy Gail *writer*
Roarty, Louise R. *writer, realtor*
Robiner, Linda Goodman *writer, educator*
Rogers, Rosemary *author*
Roland, Lenore Susan *writer*
Romana, Kathleen *writer*
Rooks, Linda *writer*
Root, Phyllis Idalene *writer*
Rose, Joy H. *playwright, poet*
Rosen, Diana *writer*
Rosmus, Anna Elisabeth *writer*
Rowse, Cynthia (Cindy) Lynn *writer*
Rubenstein, Sharon Lynn *poet*
Russ, Joanna *author*
Russell, Pamela Redford *writer, film documentarian*
Russell, Sofia *writer*
Ryan, Joyce Ethel *artist, author*
Sanders-Self, Melissa Lynn *author*
Santini, Rosemarie *writer*
Schaefer, Christina Kassabian *writer, genealogist*
Schanstra, Carla Ross *technical writer*
Schecter, Ellen L. *scriptwriter, television producer, educational consultant*
Schiff, Stacy *writer*
Schindler, Holly Suzanne *freelance/self-employed writer*
Schlossberg, Caroline Bouvier Kennedy (Caroline Kennedy) *writer, lawyer*
Schneider, Phyllis Leah *writer, editor*
Schremp, Faith Maryanne *writer*
Schumm-Burgess, Nancy Lynn *freelance/self-employed writer*
Schwartz, Joan Ruth *writer*
Scott, Joyce *writer*
Senerchia, Dorothy Sylvia *author, urban planner*
Sengstacke, Astrid Pryor *poet, journalist*
Sheldon, Edith Louise Thach *writer*
Sherman, Carol *poet, educator*
Shortz, Wilma Wildes *writer, utilities executive*
Shreve, Susan Richards *writer, educator*
Siefker, Judith Marie *writer*
Siegel, Mary Ann Garvin *writer*
Singer, Donna Lea *writer, editor, educator*
Singer, Ella Norris *writer, artist*
Smith, Jamesetta Delorise *author*
Smith, Marya Jean *writer*
Snow, Marina Sexton *writer*
Somerville, Diana Elizabeth *author*
SoRelle, Ruth Doyle *medical writer, journalist*
Spears, Rebecca Ann *writer, educator*
Staffel, Megan *writer, educator*
Standiford, Natalie Anne *writer*
Storey, Joyce R. *writer, actress*
Strong, Christina Cordaire *author, artist*
Strong, Virginia Wilkerson *freelance writer, former educator*
Strouse, Jean *writer*
Sundstrom, Barbara Ann *scriptwriter, film producer, educator*
Tanenbaum, Leora *writer, editor*
Tassos, Alice Crowley *writer*
Thomas, Christine A. *writer, editor, educator*
Thon, Melanie Rae *writer*
Thornburg, Linda A. *writer*
Tobias, Sheila *writer, educator*
Tobiassen, Virginia Hege *editor, author*
Trombley, Deborah Pelkey *crossword puzzle constructor*
Trudeau, Susan (Smoky Trudeau) *writer*
Truman, Margaret *author*
Ucko, Barbara Clark *writer*
Unger, Barbara *poet, retired educator*
Utz, Heidi M. *writer*
Van Duyn, Mona Jane *poet, educator*
Vargo, Beth Copeland *writer*
Vesey, Mary Frances *writer, educator*
Vestal, Marilyn Anita *writer, researcher, educator*
Viorst, Judith Stahl *writer*
Voigt, Cynthia *writer*
Volk, Patricia Gay *fiction writer, essayist*
Von Gizycki, Alkistis Romanoff *research scientist, educator, scholar, writer*
Wagner, Marilyn Schoefer *writer*
Waldron, Ann W. *writer*
Wallace, Michele *writer, educator*
Wallace-Brodeur, Ruth Myrna *writer*
Weis, Margaret Edith *writer, editor*
Whelchel, Sandra Jane *writer*
Whiley, Julia Helen *writer, actor*
Whouley, Kate *book industry consultant, writer*
Wilder, Eleanor Marie (Nora Roberts Wilder) *writer*
Willenz, June Adele *writer, public affairs executive, playwright, screenwriter*
Williams, Darcel Patrice *writer, editor*
Williams, Jennifer Lynne *writer*
Wolfe, Linda *writer*
Woodson, Jacqueline *writer*
Wooley, Geraldine Hamilton *poet, writer*
Worthington, Carol Pearce *writer, editor*
Yih, Ann *writer, journalist*
Young, Christine E *writer, journalist, private investigator*
Zablocki, Elaine *writer*
Zark, Jenna *playwright, freelance writer*
Zeitlin, Marianne Langner *writer*

ARTS: PERFORMING

UNITED STATES

ALABAMA

Alabaster
Sullivan, Darlene Kay *music educator*

Anniston
Harry, Robbin Nicol *music educator*
Willis, Shandra Denise *music educator*

Birmingham
Gilmore, Catherine Rye *arts administrator*
Odom, Mary E. (Libby Odom) *musician, educator*

Boaz
Pierce, V. Renee *music educator*

Cullman
Schgier, Linda Priest *musician, educator*

Grove Hill
Clarke, Cheryl Crider *music educator*

Hartselle
Thompson, Wanda Dawson *music educator*

Homewood
Tucker, Rhonda Reneé *music educator*

Leeds
Denton, Joy Grigg *music educator*

Mobile
Atkinson, Alanna Beth *music educator*
Howze, Kristi Crenshaw *music educator*

Montgomery
Brock, Katrina Rae *music educator*
Copeland, Jacqueline Turner *music educator*
McCall-Thompson, Kathleen Samone *actor, educator*

Morris
Taylor, Brandy Miller *music educator*

Normal
Hall, Doris Spooner *music educator*

Point Clear
Englund, Gage Bush *dancer, educator*

Tuscaloosa
von Redlich, Emily Paulette *music educator*

ALASKA

Anchorage
DeLap, Miriam Anne *music educator*
Gazaway, Barbara Ann *music educator, art educator*

Fairbanks
Butler-Hopkins, Kathleen Margaret *musician, educator*

ARIZONA

Chandler
Simon, Diane Rose *music educator, writer, poet*

Cornville
Masters, Arlene Elizabeth *singer*

Flagstaff
Poen, Kathryn Louise *music educator, performing arts association administrator*

Gilbert
Dudley, Amber Marie *music educator*
Strohmyer, Deb L. *music educator, school librarian*

Glendale
Gourley, Diane *music educator*
Mahoney, Jill Elizabeth *music educator*

Mesa
Yandell, Ruth B. *music educator*

Phoenix
Leathers, Susan Lynn *music educator*
Nijinsky, Tamara *actress, puppeteer, author, librarian, educator*
Rollings, Judith Harvey *theater producer, actress, theater director, performing arts educator*
Wheaton, Marilyn *music educator, pianist, organist*

Scottsdale
Broe, Carolyn Waters *conductor, violist, music educator*
Burley, Barbara A. *music educator*
Farney, Charlotte Eugenia *musician, music educator*
Fisher, Robyn Angela *music educator*
Fosgate Heggli, Julie Denise *producer*
Wolfgang, Bonnie Arlene *musician, bassoonist*

Sedona
Rhines, Marie Louise *composer, violinist*

Sierra Vista
Boughan, Zanetta Louise *music educator*

Surprise
Eastman, Donna Kelly *composer*

Tempe
Whipkey-Louden, Harriet Beulah *fine arts and theatre productions executive*

Thatcher
Jordahl, Patricia Ann *music educator, theater director*

Tucson
Bagwell, Marsha Lynn *actor, educator*
Himmelheber, Eve *theater educator, theater director, actor*
Todd, Pamela Sue *music educator*

ARKANSAS

Fayetteville
Caldwell, Sarah *opera producer, conductor, stage director and administrator*

Little Rock
Buehling, Cynthia Gwynne *music educator*

White Hall
Bell, Josephine Crawford *music educator*
Dumas, Sandra Kay *music educator*

CALIFORNIA

Albany
Boris, Ruthanna *dancer, choreographer, dance therapist, educator*

Altadena
Rabe, Elizabeth Rozina *hair stylist, horse breeder*

Anaheim
Ford, Maryestelle Beverly *piano educator, music researcher*
Orlando, Valeria *music educator, musician, artist*
Vidergar, Teresa *music educator, musician*

Antioch
Adams, Liliana Osses *music performer, harpist*

Arcadia
Zimmerman, Amy J. *television producer, television director*

Berkeley
Dong, Mabel H *music educator*
Houston, Penelope *singer, songwriter, recording artist*
Matsumura, Vera Yoshi *pianist*
Reid, Frances Evelyn Kroll *cinematographer, director, film company executive*
Weber, Molly Anne *actor*

Beverly Hills
Allen, Debbie *actress, choreographer, dancer, television director*
Allen, Joan *actress*
Ambrose, Lauren *actress*
Anders, Allison *film director, screenwriter*
Anderson, Gillian *actress*
Anderson, Pamela *actress*
Aniston, Jennifer *actress*
Ann-Margret, (Ann-Margret Olsson) *actress, performer*
Baker, Kathy Whitton *actress*
Bancroft, Anne (Mrs. Mel Brooks) *actress, scriptwriter, television director*
Bassett, Angela *actress*
Bates, Kathy *actress*
Bello, Maria Elana *actress*
Bening, Annette *actress*
Berry, Halle *actress*
Bigelow, Kathryn *film director*
Bosworth, Kate *actress*
Boyle, Lara Flynn *actress*
Bracco, Lorraine *actress*
Branch, Michelle *musician*
Brenneman, Amy *actress*
Brockie, Pamela *motion picture executive*
Burnett, Carol *actress, comedienne, singer*
Burstyn, Ellen (Edna Rae Gillooly) *actress*
Bymel, Suzan Yvette *talent manager, film producer*
Bynes, Amanda *actress*
Campbell, Neve *actress*
Capshaw, Kate (Kathy Sue Nail) *actress*
Carroll, Diahann *actress, singer*
Carter, Dixie *actress*
Carter, Lynda *actress, entertainer*
Casey, Sue (Suzanne Marguerite Philips) *actress, real estate broker*
Castle-Hughes, Keisha *actress*
Cattrall, Kim *actress*
Channing, Carol *actress*
Cher, (Cherilyn Sarkisian) *singer, actress*
Close, Glenn *actress*
Cole, Natalie Maria *singer*
Connelly, Jennifer *actress*
Cox Arquette, Courteney *actress*
Crawford, Cindy (Cynthia Ann Crawford) *model, actress*
Cruz, Penelope *actress*
Curtis, Jamie Lee *actress*
Cusack, Joan *actress*
Daly, Tyne *actress*
Delaney, Kim *actress*
Diaz, Cameron *actress*
Drescher, Fran *actress*
Dunaway, Faye (Dorothy Dunaway) *actress*
Dussault, Nancy *actress, singer*
Duvall, Shelley *actress*
Eden, Barbara Jean *actress*
Falco, Edie *actress*
Feldshuh, Tovah S. *actress*
Foch, Nina *actress, creative consultant, film director, educator*
Fonda, Jane *actress*
Fox, Vivica *actress*
Garofalo, Janeane *actress, comedienne*
Gellar, Sarah Michelle *actress*
Gilpin, Peri *actress*
Graham, Heather *actress*
Graham, Lauren *actress*
Griffiths, Rachel *actress*
Gyllenhaal, Maggie *actress*
Hamilton, Lisa Gay *actress*
Hannah, Daryl *actress*
Harden, Marcia Gay *actress*
Harmon, Angie (Angie Sehorn) *actress*
Hawn, Goldie *actress*
Heaton, Patricia *actress*
Hershey, Barbara (Barbara Herzstein) *actress*
Hewitt, Jennifer Love *actress, singer*
Hines, Cheryl *actress*
Holmes, Katherine Noelle (Katie Holmes) *actor*
Hunt, Bonnie *actress*
Hunt, Helen *actress*
Hurd, Gale Anne *film producer*
Hurley, Elizabeth *actress, model, film producer*
Huston, Anjelica *actress*
Jackson, Janet Damita Jo *vocalist, dancer*
Jenkins, Patty *film director, scriptwriter*
Johansson, Scarlett *actress*
Jolie, Angelina *actress*
Jones, Cherry *actress*
Josephson, Nancy *talent agent*
Judd, Ashley *actress*
Keaton, Diane *actress*
Kelly, Moira *actress*
Kerns, Joanna de Varona *actress, writer, director*
Kidman, Nicole *actress*
Kingston, Alex(andra) *actress*
Lahti, Christine *actress*
Lange, Jessica *actress*
Lansbury, Angela Brigid *actress*
Leder, Mimi *television director, film director, film producer*
Leigh, Jennifer Jason (Jennifer Leigh Morrow) *actress*
Lewis, Juliette *actress*
Linney, Laura *actress*
Liu, Lucy *actress*
Lopez, Jennifer *actress, dancer, singer*
Mac Dowell, Andie (Rose Anderson Mac Dowell) *actress*
MacLaine, Shirley *actress*
Manheim, Camryn *television and film actress*
Margulies, Julianna *actress*
Marshall, Penny (C. Marshall) *director, actress*
Martin, Kellie (Noelle) *actress*
Masterson, Mary Stuart *actress*
Mathis, Samantha *actress*
Matlin, Marlee *actress*
McCarthy, Jenny *actress*
McDormand, Frances *actress*
McGowan, Rose *actress*
Messing, Debra *actress*
Midler, Bette *singer, entertainer, actress*
Moore, Demi (Demi Guynes) *actress*
Moore, Julianne (Julie Anne Smith) *actress*
Moore, Mary Tyler *actress*
Morissette, Alanis *musician*
Morton, Samantha *actress*
Mullally, Megan *actress*
Najimy, Kathy *actress*
Neuwirth, Bebe (Beatrice Neuwirth) *dancer, actress, actress*
Nixon, Cynthia *actress*
Novak, Kim (Marilyn Novak) *actress*
O'Donnell, Rosie *television personality, actress, comedienne*
Paltrow, Gwyneth *actress*
Parker, Mary-Louise *actress*
Parker, Sarah Jessica *actress*
Peet, Amanda *actress*
Pfeiffer, Michelle *actress*
Portman, Natalie *actress*
Reese, Della (Deloreese Patricia Early) *singer, actress*
Ricci, Christina *actress*
Richardson, Patricia *actress*
Ringwald, Molly *actress*
Rivers, Joan *entertainer*
Roberts, Julia Fiona *actress*
Romijn-Stamos, Rebecca *actress, model*
Russell, Keri *actress*
Ryan, Meg *actress, film producer*
Sanford, Isabel Gwendolyn *actress*
Seymour, Jane *actress*
Shue, Elisabeth *actress*
Shuler Donner, Lauren *film producer*
Smith, Jaclyn *actress*
Snyder, Liza *actress*
Sorvino, Mira *actress*
Spacek, Sissy (Mary Elizabeth Spacek) *actress*
Stiles, Julia *actress*
Stowe, Madeleine *actress*
Streep, Meryl (Mary Louise Streep) *actress*
Suvari, Mena *actress*
Swank, Hilary Ann *actress*
Tamblyn, Amber Rose *actress*
Theron, Charlize *actress*

Thompson, Caroline Warner *film director, screenwriter*
Thurman, Uma Karuna *actress*
Tierney, Maura *actress*
Turlington, Christy *model*
Turner, Kathleen *actress*
Tyler, Liv *actress*
Van Ark, Joan *actress*
Vardalos, Nia *actress, screenwriter*
Ward, Sela *actress*
Weaver, Sigourney (Susan Alexandra Weaver) *actress*
Webb, Veronica *fashion model, journalist*
Weisz, Rachel *actress*
White, Betty *actress, comedienne*
Winningham, Mare *actress*
Winokur, Marissa Jaret *actress*
Winters, Shelley (Shirley Schrift) *actress*
Witherspoon, Reese (Laura Jean Witherspoon) *actress*
Zanuck, Lili Fini *film director, producer*
Zellweger, Renee *actress*
Zeta-Jones, Catherine *actress*

Brea
Ellis, Cynthia Bueker *musician, educator*

Burbank
Cole, Paula *pop singer, songwriter*
DeMent, Iris *vocalist, songwriter*
Janney, Allison *actress*
Kauffman, Marta *producer*
Kinney, Kathy *actress*
Lang, K. D. (Katherine Dawn Lang) *country music singer, composer*
Mc Vie, Christine Perfect *musician*
Mitchell, Joni (Roberta Joan Anderson) *singer, songwriter*
Nagra, Parminder *actress*
Neill, Ve *make-up artist*
Remini, Leah *actress*
Rimes, LeAnn *country music singer*
Thompson, Lea *actress*
Van Arsdel, Mary Margaret *actress, voice educator*

Calabasas
Bernhard, Sandra *actress, comedienne, singer*

Carlsbad
Missett, Judi Sheppard *dancer, jazzercise company executive*
Zetter, Lois C. *personal manager*

Cathedral City
Hoffman, John L. *piano and vocal teacher, musician*

Chico
King, Claudia Louan *film producer, lecturer*
Taylor, Carolyn Kay *music educator*

Clovis
Franklin, Heidi Ann *music educator*

Corona
Hagmann, Lillian Sue *violin instructor*

Corona Del Mar
Morisseau, Nan Kruger *television personality*

Coronado
Neblett, Carol *soprano*

Culver City
Evans, Linda *actress*
Fisher, Lucy *film producer*
Hall, Barbara *television producer*
Ziskin, Laura *television producer, film producer*

Denair
George, Cathy L. *music educator*

El Cajon
Kibble-Cacioppo, Maxine Lorraine *recording company executive*

El Cerrito
Mendoza, Lydia *vocalist*

Encinitas
Litvin, Inessa Elizabeth *piano educator*

Encino
Franklin, Bonnie Gail *actress*
Taylor, Renee *actress, writer*

Escondido
Rockwell, Elizabeth Goode *dance company director, consultant, educator*

Frazier Park
Edwards, Sarah Anne *radio, cable TV personality, clinical social worker*

Fremont
Hsu, Gloria *piano teacher*

Glendale
Furtado, Nelly Kim *vocalist*

Granite Bay
Haynes, April Michelle *band director*

Hayward
Spranza, Maureen *music educator, elementary school teacher*

Hollywood
Miles, Joanna *actress, playwright, director*
Minnelli, Liza *singer, actress*
Warren, Diane *song writer*

Huntington Beach
Sward, Andrea Jeanne *musician, librarian*

Inglewood
Wakefield, Marie Cynthia *performing arts educator, playwright, poet*

Irvine
Ruyter, Nancy Lee Chalfa *dance educator*

Kentfield
Halprin, Anna Schuman (Mrs. Lawrence Halprin) *dancer*

La Crescenta
Purcell, Lee *actress, film producer*

La Habra Heights
Agajanian, Gilda *pianist*

La Jolla
Bastien, Jane Smisor *music educator*

La Quinta
Knoblauch, Mary Reilly (Mary Louise Reilly) *retired music educator, writer*

Lake Elsinore
Bouslog, Robbin Raye *performing arts educator, art educator*

Lake View Terrace
Coolidge, Martha *film director*

Littleriver
Van Dyck, Wendy *dancer*

Long Beach
deAlbuquerque, Joan Marie *band director*
Helferich, Christine Mary *musician, music educator*

Los Altos
Ward, Lillian Hazel *music educator*

Los Angeles
Abdul, Paula (Julie) *singer, dancer, choreographer*
Balaski, Belinda L. *actress, educator*
Bell, Lee Phillip *television personality, television producer*
Benatar, Pat (Pat Andrzejewski) *rock singer*
Bergman, Marilyn Keith *lyricist, writer*
Biel, Jessica *actress, model*
Black, Lisa Hartman *actress, singer*
Bloom, Claire *actress*
Borda, Deborah *symphony orchestra executive*
Bridgewater, Dee Dee *jazz singer, diplomat*
Brown, Carol *make-up artist*
Butler, Kim C. *communications, media*
Chapman, Carolyn *broadcasting director*
Cho, Margaret *comedienne, actress*
Combs, Holly Marie *actress*
Conley, Darlene Ann *actress*
Coston, Suzanne *television producer*
Davis, Kristin *actress*
Dee, Ruby (Ruby Dee Davis) *actress, writer, director*
Diehl, Dolores *communication arts director*
Donahue, Ann M. *television producer*
Dunst, Kirsten *actress*
Elrod, Lu *music educator, actress, author*
Everhart, Angie *model*
Ferrell, Conchata Galen *actress, performing arts educator*
Finneran, Katie *actress*
Flanagan, Fionnula Manon *actress, writer, theater director*
Flockhart, Calista *actress*
Foster, Jodie (Alicia Christian Foster) *actress, film director, film producer*
Franz, Elizabeth *actress*
Gibbons, Leeza *television talk show host, entertainment reporter*
Hart, Mary *television talk show host*
Howard, Sandy *motion picture producer*
Hu, Kelly *actress*
Ireland, Kathy *actor, apparel designer*
Jackson, Kate *actress*
Kaczmarek, Jane *actress*
Kellerman, Sally Claire *actress*
Kurtz, Swoosie *actress*
Landers, Audrey *actress, singer*
Lansing, Sherry Lee (Heimann) *motion picture executive*
Leeves, Jane *actress*
Lunden, Joan *television personality*
Malone, Nancy *actress*
McCarthy, Nobu *actress, performing company executive, educator*
Muldaur, Diana Charlton *actress*
Nelligan, Kate (Patricia Colleen Nelligan) *actress*
O'Connell, Taaffe Cannon *actress, publishing executive*
O'Day, Anita Belle Colton *entertainer, musician, vocalist*
Olsen, Ashley Fuller *actress*
Olsen, Mary-Kate *actress*
Parkinson, Dian *actress*
Peña, Elizabeth *actress*
Perez, Rosie *actress*
Plummer, Amanda *actress*
Presley, Priscilla *actress*
Rashad, Phylicia *actress, singer, dancer*
Richmond, Rocsan *television and video producer, director, publicist, actress, dancer, inventor, teacher*
Rohrer, Susan Earley *film producer, writer, director*
Rosenberger, Carol *concert pianist*
Sheindlin, Judith *television personality, judge*
Silverstone, Alicia *actress*
Stein, Mary Margaret *actor*
Stenge, Lynda Ann *music marketing executive*
Streisand, Barbra Joan *singer, actress, director*
Stuart, Gloria *actress*
Swit, Loretta *actress*
Thompson, Sada Carolyn *actress*
Tyson, Cicely *actress*

Ullman, Tracey *actress, singer*
Watson, Emily *actress*
Welch, Raquel *actress*
White, Meg (Megan Martha White) *musician, vocalist*
Winters, Barbara Jo *musician*

Malibu
Wilson, Rita *actress*

Martinez
DeWolfe, Martha *singer, songwriter, publisher, producer*

Menlo Park
Baez, Joan Chandos *folk singer*

Mission Viejo
Burke, Kathleen J. *music director, writer*

Monrovia
Brown, Gwendolyn (Williams) *music educator*

Mountain View
Serebrennikova, Emiliya *musician, educator*

Murrieta
Miller, Helen F. *music educator, musician*

North Hollywood
Downey, Roma *actress*
Fanning, Dakota *actress*
Gallardo, Sandra Silvana *producer*
Nutt, Sandra Maria *actress, writer*
Reynolds, Debbie (Mary Frances Reynolds) *actress*
Stone, Sharon *actress*
Taravella, Rosie *actress*
Toplitt, Gloria H. *voice educator, singer, actress*
Toussieng, Yolanda *make-up artist*

Northridge
Baker, Katherine Ramos *music educator, conductor*
Cartwright, Nancy *actress, television producer*
Heinen, Julia Margaret *music educator*

Novato
Zigas, Rita B. *music director, musician*

Oakland
Brown, Karen *performing company executive*
Crocker, Joy Laksmi *concert pianist and organist, composer*
DeFazio, Lynette Stevens *dancer, educator, choreographer, violinist, actress*
Laley, Lyndelle *singer, music administrator*
McCarroll, Martha Hadley *music educator, conductor*
Zschau, Marilyn *singer*

Pacific Palisades
Kirkgaard, Valerie Anne *media group executive, syndicated talk radio host, writer, producer, consultant*

Palm Desert
Romano, Darlene *music educator, composer*

Palo Alto
Tirschwell-Newby, Kathy Ann *events production company executive*

Palos Verdes Peninsula
Deveny, Charlotte Perry *musician, educator*

Pasadena
Worby, Rachel *conductor*

Pleasant Hill
George, Julianne Mary *music educator, conductor*

Rancho Santa Fe
Kranz, Kathleen Nee *pianist, music educator*

Redlands
Auerbacher, Mary Jane *church organist*

Redondo Beach
Richards, Denise *actress*

Riverside
James, Etta *recording artist*

Sacramento
Bossuat, Judy Weigert *music educator*
Gray, Robin *stage manager*

San Andreas
Buringrud, Lisa Marie *music educator*

San Diego
Arova, Sonia *artistic director, ballet educator*
Bates-Romeo, Delores Alvenia *music educator, consultant*
Flettner, Marianne *opera administrator*
Langer, Eva Marie *video specialist*
Mahon, Maxine *performing company executive*

San Francisco
Cisneros, Evelyn *dancer*
Etheridge, Melissa Lou *singer, songwriter*
Greenawald, Sheri *performing company executive*
Hutchinson, Brenda Irene *sound artist, sound designer, audio engineer*
Jenkins, Margaret Ludmilla *choreographer, dancer*
LeBlanc, Tina *dancer*
Lee, Iara *filmmaker*
Maffre, Muriel *ballet dancer*
Perloff, Carey *performing company executive, theater director, playwright*
Rosenberg, Pamela *performing company executive, conductor*

San Jose
Dalis, Irene *mezzo-soprano, opera company administrator, music educator*
Kordestani, Kayvon Kim *music educator, choreographer*
Near, Timothy *theater director*
Shuster, Diana *former artistic director*
Stevens, Dorothy Frost *retired television producer*

San Marino
Santoso, Michelle Jo *music educator, pianist*

Santa Barbara
Ben-Dor, Gisselle *conductor, musician*
Child, Julia McWilliams (Mrs. Paul Child) *cooking expert, television personality, author*
Sebastian, Suzie *producer*

Santa Cruz
Martinez, Alma R. *actress, theater director, educator*

Santa Monica
Eve, (Eve Jihan Jeffers) *rap artist, actress*
Fisher, Frances *actress*
Frot-Coutaz, Cecile *television producer*
Henderson, Florence (Florence Henderson Bernstein) *actress, singer*
Hersh, Kristin *vocalist, musician*
LaBelle, Patti (Patricia Louise Holt) *singer, entertainer*
Louis-Dreyfus, Julia *actress*
Simpson, India.Arie *musician*
Smith, Anna Deavere *actress, educator, playwright*
Summer, Donna (La Donna Adrian Gaines) *singer, songwriter, actress*
Wilson-Fellows, Suzanne *motion picture producer*

Santa Rosa
Conway, Lois Lorraine *piano teacher*

Seaside
Gibson-Brehon, Dawn D. *performing company executive, consultant*

Sebastopol
Snyder, Allegra Fuller *dance educator*

Sherman Oaks
Clark, Susan (Nora Goulding) *actress*
Norwood, Brandy *singer, actress*
Schlessinger, Laura *radio talk show host*
Wood, Evan Rachel *actress*

Sonoma
Pollack, Phyllis Addison *ballerina*

Stockton
Kizer, Nancy Anne *music educator, musician*
Wilcox, Helena Marguerita (Rita) *music educator*

Studio City
Alvarado, Sandra Jacqueline *television director*
Basinger, Kim *actress*
Carsey, Marcia Lee Peterson *television producer*
Johnston, Kristen *television personality*
King, Carole (Carole Klein) *songwriter, singer*

Sunnyvale
Garner, Shirley Imogene *retired music educator*

Thousand Oaks
Washburn, Nan *conductor*

Toluca Lake
Powers, Mala *actress*

Universal City
Crow, Sheryl *singer, songwriter, musician*
Merkerson, S. Epatha *actress*

Upland
Bast, Karolyn (Kay) Anne *dance educator, choreographer*

Valley Village
Barkin, Elaine Radoff *composer*
Diller, Phyllis *actress, writer*

Van Nuys
Boone, Deborah Ann (Debby Boone) *singer*

West Hollywood
Baker, Anita *singer*
Innes, Laura *actress*
Madonna, (Madonna Louise Veronica Ciccone) *singer, actress, producer*

Westchester
Capetillo, Charlene Vernelle *music educator, special education educator*

Whittier
Jacobson, Sandra Ann *music educator*
Korf, Jean Prinz *retired theater educator*

Yucaipa
deBaun, Linda Louise *performing arts educator*

Yucca Valley
Styles, Beverly (Juanita Robins Carpenter) *entertainer, composer, musician*

COLORADO

Aurora
Teflian, Pamela Jane *lyricist, photographer*

Boulder
Sable, Barbara Kinsey *retired music educator*

Wallace, Stephanie Ann *music educator, conductor*
Yan, Haiping *theatre and comparative literature educator*

Colorado Springs
Borgen, Irma R. *music educator*
Darpino, Victoria Gnojek *music educator*
Mery, Naomi Mery *music educator*
Rueda, Deborah Jean *music educator*
Skadden, Vanda Sue *retired music educator*

Conifer
West, Molly Marie *music educator*

Denver
Alsop, Marin *conductor*
Blair, Hilary *actor, performing company executive, educator*
Coe, Judith Anne *music educator, composer, performer*
Robinson, Cleo Parker *artistic director*
Shaw, Priscilla *music educator, coach*

Dillon
Barron, Theodora S. *retired music educator*

Durango
Tischhauser, Katherine Jetter *music educator, cellist*

Fort Collins
Wilber, Clare Marie *musician, educator*

Fountain
Wilson, Roberta (Bobbi) Gail *performing arts educator*

Grand Junction
Barger, Cathy Lynn *music educator*
Everhart, Dorothy L. *music educator*
Wilson, Deborah Grim *music educator*

Littleton
Johansson, Alicia Barbara *musician*
King, Linda *musician, music educator*

Longmont
Campbell, Sally Jo *music educator, primary school educator*
Harrison, Sarah K. *music educator*

Paonia
Marston, Betsy Pilat *newspaper editor*

Pritchett
Hall, Carol Ann *music educator*

CONNECTICUT

Clinton
McAllister, Nancy Elizabeth *music educator*

Darien
Springer, Ruth Wiren *music educator*

East Hartford
Rivers, Loretta J. *film producer, film director, consultant*

Fairfield
Hamilton, Heather Amlin *conductor, director*

Hartford
Lyman, Peggy *artistic director, dancer, choreographer, educator*
Wood, Margaret *performing company executive*

Lakeville
Restout, Denise *musician*

Manchester
Hilton, Cheryl Celeste *music educator*

Mystic
Bobruff, Carole Marks *radio producer, radio personality*
Gilbert, Ellen Effman *music educator*

New Haven
Garvey, Sheila Hickey *theater educator*
Nolan, Victoria *theater director*

Norwalk
Greene, Karen Sandra *actress, educator, singer*
Major, Flora Hoelting *music educator*

Old Saybrook
Geer, Lois Margaret *music educator*

Simsbury
Brenner, Anna (Bonnie) Hurnyak *music educator*

Southbury
Bergen, Polly *actress*

Stamford
Preiss-Harris, Patricia *music educator, composer, pianist*

Storrs Mansfield
Ford, Karrin Elizabeth *music educator, musician*

West Hartford
Howard, Karen *music educator, conductor*

Weston
Fredrik, Burry *theatrical producer, director*

Woodbridge
Just, Jennifer Ramsay *television and video producer, writer*

DELAWARE

Lewes
Buchert, Stephanie Nicole *music educator*

Wilmington
Syer, Fontaine *theater director*

DISTRICT OF COLUMBIA

Washington
Anderson, Mary Ann Grasso *theater association executive*
Berman, Karen Judith *theater director, educator*
Bradley, Barbra Bailey *musician, educator, accompanist*
Crawford-Mason, Clare Wootten *television producer, journalist*
Day, Doris (Doris von Kappelhoff) *singer, actress*
Day, Mary *artistic director, ballet company executive*
Dodge, Judith C. *musician*
Donlon, Claudette *performing company executive*
Drizin, Julie Merle *public radio producer*
Fischer, Elizabeth (Betsy) *television producer*
Leissner, Janet *television news bureau chief*
Moore, Elvi *performing company executive*
Ratner, Ellen Faith *radio talk show host, writer*
Rodney, Bonnie M. *music educator*
Sankaran, Shubha Silver *musician, music educator, consultant*
Smith, Molly D. *theater director*
Snyder, Andrea *performing arts association administrator*
Sproul, Robin *television news bureau chief*
Stahmer, Ann Miklofsky *choral music director, producer*
Weidenfeld, Sheila Rabb *television producer, author*
Woods, Stephanie *television producer, reporter*

FLORIDA

Boca Raton
Dower Gold, Catherine Anne *music history educator*

Boynton Beach
Rabinof, Sylvia *pianist, composer, author, educator*
Ricks, Dallis Derrick Biehl *pianist*

Bradenton
Bjorklund, Nancy Margarette Watts *music educator*

Cape Coral
Wendel, Joan Audrey *music educator*

Clearwater
Kessler-Hodgson, Lee Gwendolyn *actress, corporate executive*

Cocoa
Baggarly, Claire Johnson *music educator, department chairman*
Rudzik, Marcia Ann *music educator*

Coral Gables
Sackstein, Rosalina Guerrero *music educator, consultant*

Coral Springs
Halberg, Jeanne *music educator*

Deland
Sorensen, Jacki Faye *choreographer, aerobic dance company executive*

Dunedin
Foley, Briana *music educator, consultant*

Englewood
Dickson, Katharine Hayland *dance educator*

Eustis
Alfrey, Lydia Jean *musician educator*

Fernandina Beach
Grant, Catherine *music educator*

Fort Lauderdale
Jackson-Callandret, Shirley Lorraine *music educator*
LeRoy, Miss Joy *model, apparel designer*

Fort Myers
Gorelik, Alla *piano educator*

Gainesville
Hyatt, Mary Louise *music educator, pianist*
Johnson, Annie Cooper *music educator*
Morsey, Sara *actor, educator*
Paul, Ouida Fay *music educator*

Green Cove Springs
Davidson, Joy Elaine *mezzo-soprano*

Groveland
Sides, I. Ruth S. *music educator*

Gulf Breeze
Smithey, Susan Willett *music educator*

Hollywood
Border, Gladys Louise *piano educator*

Jacksonville
Booth, Terri Lynne *music educator*
Huber, Mary Susan *music educator*
King, Janey Hampton *music educator, vocalist, educator*
Stanley, Helen Camille *composer, musician*

Stewart, Sandra Kay *music educator*

Kissimmee
Buma, Judith Bergeron *music educator*

Lake City
Montgomery, June C. *musician, composer*

Largo
Szalkowski, Deborah *music educator*

Lecanto
Wheatley, Deborah A. *music educator*

Lehigh Acres
Wahlberg, Gretchen Marie *music educator*

Lynn Haven
Bonazzi, Elaine Claire *mezzo-soprano*

Merritt Island
Givens, Christine Juliano *music educator, elementary school educator*

Miami
Coulter, Beverly Norton *singer, pianist, opera director*
Cubberley, Gayle Susan *band director*
Feinberg, Wendie *producer*
Harmon, Monica Renee *music educator*
Mauch, Diane Farrell *music educator*
Thomas, Lise-Marie *actress*
Vogel, Malvina Graff *video and infosystems specialist*
Walkley, Mary L *voice educator, music educator*

Miami Beach
Gardiner, Pamela Nan *performing arts company executive*
Lawson, Eve Kennedy *dancer*

Milton
Arnold, Margaret Morelock *music specialist, educator, performer*

Naples
Evans, Judith P. *music educator*

New Port Richey
Robbins, Jennifer Katherine *music educator*

Ocala
Adams, Marylyn Dewey *music educator*

Ocoee
Blackman, Sharon Forbes *music educator*

Orlando
Boyd, Be (Belinda) Carolyn *theater educator*
Flanagan, Marianne *music educator*
Harris, Lani M. *theater educator*
Hom, Trudy A. *music educator*
Levy, Barbara Ellen *music educator*
Radloff, Marie Ulrey *music educator*
Schultz, Victoria L. *music educator, entertainer*

Ormond Beach
Granville, Paulina *independent music scholar and educator*

Palm Harbor
Katzen-Guthrie, Joy *performance artist, engineering services executive*
Richardson, Pamela Austin *music educator*

Panama City Beach
Birdwell, Michelle Marie *music educator*

Pembroke Pines
Corbiere, Mary Louise Sambataro *music educator, musician*

Pinellas Park
Benedict, Gail Cleveland *music educator*

Plant City
Durham, Susan F. *music educator*

Port Saint Lucie
Kinder, Joann Stephanie Love *music educator*

Rotonda West
Morrison, Beth Ann *music educator, musician*

Royal Palm Beach
Curphey, Geraldine Casterline *church musician, retired*

Saint Petersburg
Michael, Marilyn Corliss *music educator, mezzo soprano*

Sarasota
Hanscom, Marina *band director, musician*

Stuart
Mark, Marsha Yvonne Ismailoff *artistic director*

Tallahassee
Bish, Deborah F. *music educator*
Harsanyi, Janice *soprano, educator*
Perry-Camp, Jane *music educator, pianist*
Rollins, Jennie Albin Brown *music educator*
Stebleton, Michelle Marie *music educator, musician*

Tampa
Faulkner, Melanie E. *music educator*
Moore, Janet L.S. *music educator, dean*
Scialdo, Mary Ann *music educator, musician*

Titusville
King, Sheila Sue *music educator, elementary school educator*

Vero Beach
Lange, Billie Carola *video specialist*

West Palm Beach
Hale, Marie Stoner *artistic director*
Jecko, Laura Ann (Laura Engel, Laura Wallace) *music educator*
Jordan, Linda Diane *music educator*
Rander, JoAnn Corpaci *musician, music educator*
Rosenberg, Leslie Karen *media buyer*

Winter Haven
Arens, Christine M. *pianist, educator, composer*

GEORGIA

Adel
Grimsley, Joy Elizabeth *music educator*

Albany
Bell, Theresa Marie *music educator*

Alpharetta
Ali Ahmad, Susan Vaughan *music educator*
Stalling, Janet Kitts *music educator*

Armuchee
Burgess, Ann Dalton *music educator*

Athens
David, Martha Lena Huffaker *retired music educator, retired sales executive*
Granum, Doris R. *music educator, director*

Atlanta
Booth, Susan Virginia *theater director*
Chen, Joie *cable news anchor*
Domingo, Esther *music educator*
Furcron, Charne Delise *dancer*
Goodman, Lula Carolyn *music educator*
Hutton, Jenny *music educator*
Parnell, Janine E. *conductor, violinist*
Poorman, Christine K. *television producer*
Rice, Elizabeth Osburn *music educator, conductor*
Tillotson, Mary *cable television host*
Vulgamore, Allison *performing arts administrator*
Wylly, Barbara Bentley *performing arts association administrator*

Augusta
Colton, Zanne Beaufort *performing company executive*
Floyd, Rosalyn Wright *pianist, accompanist, educator*

Bainbridge
Lucas, Tammi Michelle *music educator*

Canton
Frady, Rita R. *music educator, information technology manager*
Lokey, Linda H. *music educator*

Clayton
Funkhouser, Catherine G. *music educator*

Cumming
Beaty-Gunter, Sharon E. *music teacher*

Dalton
Pye, Janna Lynn *music educator*

Decatur
Cartman, Shirley Eleise *retired music educator*
Pryce, Monica Elizabeth *music educator*
Strickland, Brenda B. *music educator*

Douglas
Tucker, Maureen Ann *musician*

Fitzgerald
Rogers, Rebecca Harris *music educator*

Homer
Rylee, Gloria Genelle *music educator*

Jackson
Bomar, Laura Beth *music educator*

Jonesboro
Stephens, Sara Cecile *music educator*

Kennesaw
Diaz, Anne Marie Theresa *music educator, musician*
Still, Candace Tyson *music educator*

Lawrenceville
Hendrix, Jacquelyn McIntyre *elementary music educator*

Leesburg
Unger, Suzanne Everett *music educator, musician*

Lilburn
Parker, Venus Cristela *music educator, musician*

Mableton
Peters, Crystal Harrington *music educator, consultant*

Macon
Johnson, Bonnie Sue *piano educator*
Terry, Doris D. *music educator*

Marietta
Gerace, Deborah Cobb *music educator*
Hutson, Jacquelyn Collins *pianist, educator*
Peck, Natalie Deanne *music educator*
Smith, Irene Helen-Nordine *music educator*
Wimberly, Linda Roberts *music educator, artist*

Mcdonough
Brown, Joy Withers *music educator*

Milledgeville
Thrasher, Jennifer Nichols *music educator*

Ringgold
Austin, Gayla Rolston *music educator, musician*

Rome
Potts, Glenda Rue *music educator*

Savannag
Braithwaite, Margaret Evon *music educator*

Savannah
Dunlap, Ellen Roe *music educator*
Hatfield, Stacie H. *professional pianist*

Smyrna
Rife, Elizabeth *musician, music educator*

Springfield
Demarest, Cynthia *music educator*

Statham
Anderson, Sondra C. *music educator*

Stone Mountain
Pryor, Vanita Moon *music educator*

Swainsboro
Weatherford, Sharon Davis *music educator*

Tifton
Hobby, Zoe Elaine *musician, educator, composer*

Valdosta
Shaw, Patricia Jill *retired music educator*

Waleska
Naylor, Susan Embry *music educator*
Taylor, Sue Ann *film producer, television producer*

Washington
Cole, Joan Carol *music educator*

Waycross
Hoover, Mary Lou Ballentine *music educator*

Woodstock
Hunt Brogden, Christine Michelle *music educator*
Streeter, Linda V. *music educator*

HAWAII

Ewa Beach
Lewis, Mary Jane *film producer, director, scriptwriter*

Honolulu
Barbosa, Rhona *music educator*
Leong, Antoinette Marie *musician, director*
Schweitzer, Marsha L. *musician, consultant*

Kaneohe
Young-Pohlman, Colette Lisa *music educator*

Keaau
Bremer, Nina Shipman *performing arts educator, actress*

IDAHO

Boise
Holt, Isabel Rae *radio program producer*
Pimble, Toni *artistic director, choreographer, educator*
Wyers, Giselle Eleanor *music educator, conductor*

Idaho Falls
Nicholas, Claudia Jo *music educator*

Sagle
Price, Anita W. *music educator, consultant*

Twin Falls
Yost, Kelly Lou *pianist*

ILLINOIS

Algonquin
Lange-Connelly, Phyllis *musician, music educator*

Alton
Davis, Anne Louise *music educator*

Aurora
Cooper, Annette Lyn *music educator*
Halfvarson, Lucille Robertson *music educator*
McCarthy, Mary Elizabeth (Beth) Constance *conductor, educator, music educator*

Beardstown
Vermillion, Julia Kathleen *music educator*

Belleville
Setterlund, Tina A.M. *music educator*

Bensenville
Mueller, Paula Deutsch *music educator*

Chicago
Berryman, Diana (Kapnas) *radio personality*
Boncher, Mary *talent agent*
Freidheim, Ladonna *dance company director*
Gaines, Barbara *theater director*
Heider, Anne Harrington *music educator*
Higgins, Ruth Ellen *theatre producer*
Kalver, Gail Ellen *dance company executive, musician*
Kenas-Heller, Jane Hamilton *musician*

Lavey, Martha *theater director*
Lazar, Ludmila *concert pianist, music educator, pedagogue*
Lustrea, Anita *radio personality*
May, Aviva Rabinowitz *music educator, linguist, musician*
Moffatt, Joyce Anne *performing company executive*
Myers-Rami, Masequa *theatrical company executive, theater producer*
Naudzius, Aldona Kanauka *pianist, music educator*
Ran, Shulamit *composer*
Savage, Terry *television personality, journalist, stockbroker*
Stratman, Deborah *filmmaker, film and video educator*
Tallchief, Maria *ballerina*
Taylor, Koko *singer*
Winfrey, Oprah *television talk show host, actress, producer*
Woods, Nikki *radio personality*
Yu, Linda *newswoman, television anchorwoman*

Clinton
Ellerman, Linda Ann *music educator*

Coal City
Major, Mary Jo *dance school artistic director*

Country Club Hills
McClelland, Helen *music educator*

Decatur
Brown, Lenore Francine *music educator*
Ewers, Marla Rouse *voice educator*

East Saint Louis
Dunham, Katherine *choreographer, anthropologist, dancer*

Edwardsville
Anderson, Mary Jane *music educator*

Elgin
Dodohara, Jean Noton *music educator*
Kalsow-Bernhard, Kathryn Marie *choir director*

Eureka
West, Nancy Lee *music educator, performance artist, entertainer*

Evanston
Beck, Eva-Carol *musician*
Eberley, Helen-Kay *opera singer, classical record company executive, poet*
McDonough, Bridget Ann *music theatre company director*
Persons, Fern *actor*
Quinn, Elizabeth Marie *performing arts educator*
Willoughby, Judith Anne *conductor, music educator*
Zimmerman, Mary Alice *performing arts educator*

Evergreen Park
Michalak, Melanie S. *music educator*

Frankfort
Lambert, Alysia Connell *music educator*

Glen Carbon
Anderson, Nancy Keech *music educator*

Grayslake
Craven, Deborah *performing arts educator*

Green Valley
Gerrietts, Vivian Jane *music educator*

Herscher
Cessna, Katrina J. *music educator, composer*

La Moille
Carius, Christina Marie *music educator, horse trainer*

Lisle
Cordoba Tait, Alicia Rose *music educator*

Morton Grove
Hoffman, Joy Yu *harpist, pianist*

Mount Prospect
Forman, Ann Lee *music educator*

Murphysboro
Berry, Alice Allen *retired music educator*

Naperville
Martin, Molly Erdman *music educator*
Stephen, Doris Moyer *music educator*

Northbrook
Vasiljevic, Elizabeth Agnes *music educator, secondary school educator*

O Fallon
Belt, Beth Marie *music educator*
Tiemann, Jeannine E. *music educator*

Palos Hills
Porter, Joyce Klowden *theatre educator and director*

Pana
Waddington, Irma Joann *music educator*

Park Forest
Billig, Etel Jewel *theater director, actor*

Peoria
Price Boday, Mary Kathryn *choreographer, small business owner, educator*
Salazar, Shirley Ann *music educator*

Quincy
Bohn, Donna May *music educator*

Rantoul
Holmes, Lois Rehder *composer, piano and voice educator*

River Forest
Prendergast, Carole Lisak *musician, educator*

Rockford
Anderson, Karen Mildred *music educator*
Felder, Sheila Kay *music educator*
Hendershott Love, Arles June *television community relations director*
Heuer, Beth Lee *music educator, composer, arranger*

Rushville
Burton, Sheila Belle *music educator*

Saint Charles
Sjogren, Jaime Lynn *dancer, choreographer*

Schaumburg
Kleppe, Joan Marie *entertainment executive*

Scott Air Force Base
Noland, Linda M *music educator*

Serena
Thorsen, Christine Mae *music educator*

Sleepy Hollow
Mallers, Linda Rae *music educator*

Smithton
Hostetler, Elsie J. *musician, music educator*

South Beloit
Julian, Linda S. *music educator, director*

Springfield
Deal, Karen Lynne *conductor*
Powell, Laura Elizabeth *music educator*

Swansea
Tessereau, Linda Ann *music educator*

Sycamore
Crain, Terri L. *music educator, director*

Tinley Park
Good, Linda L. *music educator*

Westmont
Hodgson, Barbara Caroline *music educator*
Nyien, Patricia *music educator*

Wilmette
Merrier, Helen *actress, writer*
Shannon, Julie (Julie Geller) *musician, music educator, composer, lyricist*

INDIANA

Bloomington
Ferguson, Sarah Ann *music educator*
Mac Watters, Virginia Elizabeth *singer, music educator, actress*
Svetlova, Marina *ballerina, choreographer, educator*
Williams, Camilla *soprano, voice educator*

Carmel
Stevens, Jocelyn Alexis *music educator*

Churubusco
Lough, Susan M. *music educator*

Clinton
Byers, Teresa Ann *music educator*

Crawfordsville
Everett, Cheryl Ann *music educator, pianist*

Evansville
Clark, Shirley Suzanne *music educator*

Fort Wayne
Jones, Louise Conley *drama and literature educator, academic administrator*
Russell, Christine R. *music educator*

Hanover
Nickels, Ruth Elizabeth *band director*

Indianapolis
Cole, Karen Jean *music educator*
Dwyer, Ruth E. *music educator*
Ilgen, Dorothy L. *arts foundation executive*
McIntyre, Lola Mazza *music educator*
Turner, Barbara A. *former dance company executive*
Wyss-Treadwell, Mary Josephine *music educator, consultant*

Kokomo
Beebe, Gayle L. *music educator*

Munster
Moore, Carolyn Lannin *video specialist*

Newburgh
Verley, Barbara Ann *music educator*

Oldenburg
Beiersdorfer, Elizabeth Anne *music educator*

Portage
Williams, Susan Marie *music educator*

Rensselaer
Orchard, Olga Sokolich *music educator*

Rochester
Martens, Betty Joan *music educator, elementary school educator*

South Bend
Kuehner, Denise Ann *music educator, musician*

Valparaiso
Lawley, Deena C. Butterfield *music educator, legal assistant*

West Lafayette
Fliotsos, Anne *theater educator*
Heise, Kathryn Ann *music educator*
Lefever, Maxine Lane *music educator*

IOWA

Ames
Johnson-Richt, Cheryl Lynn *performing artist*

Anita
Lloyd-Cameron, Rosemary Ann *music educator*

Cedar Rapids
Hall, Kathy L. *orchestra executive*

Clarksville
Kattenhorn, Lisa Ann *music educator*

Des Moines
Bennett, Virginia Cook *music educator, consultant*
Erickson, Elaine Mae *composer, poet*

Indianola
Mace, Jerilee Marie *opera company executive*

Iowa City
Hovland, Jody *theater director*

Mason City
Sappenfield, Maedeane L. *piano and organ educator*

Newton
Johnson, Jane Ann Bockwoldt *music educator, small business owner*

Sioux Rapids
Thies, Heidi Marie *music educator*

KANSAS

Basehor
Brown, Debra Rae *music educator*

Caldwell
Robinson, Alice Jean McDonnell *retired drama and speech educator*

Colby
Koel, Jennifer Jo Weber *music educator*

Dodge City
Ross, Connie L. *music educator*
Smoot, Donna Jean *music educator*

El Dorado
Mack, Valerie Lippoldt *music educator, performing arts educator, freelance/self-employed choreographer*

Ellsworth
Keith, Susan Jayne *music educator*

Emporia
DeBauge, Janice B. *musician*

Gem
Ziegelmeier, Patricia Kay *music educator, executive secretary*

Hutchinson
Wendelburg, Norma Ruth *composer, pianist, educator*

Independence
Delacour, JoNell *music educator*

Iola
Marsh, Alma Fern *retired music educator, director, organist*

Junction City
Baker, Kristi Ann *music educator, composer*
Day, Christine Susan *music educator*

Leoti
Koehn, Tori JoAnn *music educator*

Maize
Morrell, Karen Kay *music educator*

Olathe
Colson, Judy C. *music educator*
McCabe, Melissa Christine *music educator, researcher*
Meis, Rebecca G. *orchestra director*
Smith, Katheryn Jeanette *music educator*

Ottawa
Hoge, Medora Davidson *dance educator*

Overland Park
Barkley, Brenna C. *music educator*

Parsons
Myers, Margaret Alice *music educator*

Rose Hill
Davidson, Karen Lea *music educator*

Shawnee Mission
Herbert, Cheryl Sue Chapman *music educator*
Julien, Gail Leslie *model, public relations professional*
McGhee-Hensel, Karen Sue *music educator*

Topeka
Smith, Linda S. *music educator, musician*

Wetmore
Armstrong, Carol Sue *music educator*

Wichita
Chambers, Sara Lynn *music educator*

KENTUCKY

Benton
Shurley, Elaine P. *music educator*

Berea
Flynn, Candy Ruth *music educator*

Bowling Green
Keller, Patricia Huggins *music educator*
Smith, Janet L. Bass *musician, educator*
Tyrie, Tina Napier *music educator*

Burlington
Hines, Tina Loree *video producer, writer, publicist, photographer*

Calvert City
Dowdy, Vicki J. *music educator*
Madison, Vicki DiAnne *retired music educator*

Campbellsville
Irwin, Donna Rice *music educator*
McArthur, Lisa R. *music educator, musician*
Moore, Nevalyn *music educator*

Danville
Brogle, Jennifer Lynn *music educator, consultant*

Flemingsburg
Bolar, Amy Leigh *music educator*

Frankfort
Fletcher, Winona Lee *theater educator emeritus*

Grayson
Jones, April Lynn *music educator*

Harlan
Lee, Jeanne Ann *music educator, consultant*

Highland Heights
Forman, Sandra H. *theater educator*

Hopkinsville
Lester, Joan Stadelman *music educator*

Lexington
Elliott, Teresa J. *music educator*

Louisville
Fassett, Frances Nicholas (Kitty Fassett) *pianist, record producer*
Garrett, Debra Anne *music educator*
Lloyd, Kimcherie *performing company executive*
Miller, Marilee Hebert *arts administrator, producer, director, consultant*
Murrell, Deborah Anne *music educator, speaker, writer*
Sandler, Deborah *performing company executive*
Sherman, Mildred Mozelle *music educator, vocalist, actress, opera director*
Stone, Marsha L. *music educator*
Turner, Sandra Chucalo *music educator*

Mc Kee
Tincher-Threlkeld, Marsha Lea *music educator*

Morehead
Creasap, Susan Diane *music educator, conductor*

Owensboro
Blandford, Virginia Rose *music educator*
Mullikin, Sandra Marie *music educator*

Richmond
Jackson, Cheryl Ann *music educator, director*
Smith, Carla Anne *music educator*

Winchester
Jude, Cassandra Joy *music educator*

LOUISIANA

Alexandria
Ginsburgh, Judy Caplan *music specialist, vocalist, consultant*

Baton Rouge
Buchmann, Molly O'Banion *choreographer, ballet educator*
Lusted, Dona Sanders *music educator, consultant, organist*
Mathews, Sharon Walker *artistic director, secondary school educator*
Shield, Carolyn Douglas *music educator*
Willett, Anna Hart *composer, painter*
Yarbrough, Martha Cornelia *music educator*

Chalmette
Cotogno, Denise Leto *music educator, assistant principal*

Gray
Jones, Angela Diane *music educator*

Houma
Roper, Denise Michelle *music educator*

Lafayette
Stravinska, Sarah *dance educator*

Metairie
deMoruelle, Charmaine *music educator*
Downs, Betty Ratcliff *music educator*

New Orleans
Blackwell, Karen Elaine *music educator*
Downing, Johnette *musician, educator*
Litwin, Sharon *orchestra executive*

New Roads
Hambrick, Myra Jean *musician, poet*

Pineville
Carpenter, Terri Rudd *music educator*

Shreveport
Rettelle, Kathryne W. *music educator*

Slidell
Herron, Florine Pernell *retired music educator*
Larson, Sandra Pauline *music educator*

Sulphur
Fuller, Betty Stamps *music educator*

Zachary
Rogillio, Kathy June *musician, piano rebuilder, educator*

MAINE

Biddeford
Delorge, Amy Beth *music educator*

Freeport
Parkhurst, Denice Delray *music educator*

Gorham
Kaschub, Michele Ellen *music educator, researcher*

Portland
Miller, Buffy *dancer*

Topsham
Outhwaite, Lucille Conrad *ballerina, educator*

Waterville
Desrosiers, Muriel C. *music educator, retired nursing consultant*

West Baldwin
Simmonds, Rae Nichols *musician, composer, educator*

Westbrook
Oatley, Nina Karen *music educator*

Woolwich
Clark, Joyce T. *piano teacher, church organist*

MARYLAND

Aberdeen
Hopkins, Susan Shiplett *music educator, director*

Annapolis
Smith Tarchalski, Helen Marie *piano educator*

Baltimore
Armstrong, Marie Cynthia *music educator*
Hall, Marian M. *retired music educator*
Huggins, Amy Branum *music educator*
Hughes, Catherine L. (Cathy Hughes) *radio personality, broadcast executive*
Jacobson, Katherine Louise *musician, music educator*
Thomas, Susan Wiskemann *music educator*

Bethesda
Smith, Renae Colleen *music educator*

Bowie
Hillsman, Joan Rucker *music educator*

Cambridge
Brohawn, Virginia Bridgeman *music educator*

Columbia
Spicknall, Joan *music educator*
Weems, Helen Rachel *piano teacher, accompanist*

Crisfield
LaRue, Lea Maylene *music educator*

Elkridge
Matthews, Lois Marr *musician, music educator*

Ellicott City
Adkins, Sandra Kay *music educator, church musician*

Frostburg
Mills, Susan W. *music educator*

Gaithersburg
Vanasdalan, Joan Louise *music educator, musician*

Germantown
Collins, Karen Jeanne *music educator*
Searle, Michelle A. *music educator, webmaster*

Glen Burnie
Ruth, Shiela Grant *music educator*

Greenbelt
Wagner, Sally Sterrett *music educator*

Hampstead
Rogers, Karen Cooledge *music educator*

Highland
Varga, Deborah Trigg *music educator, entertainment company owner*

Hollywood
Dietz, Laurel Patricia *music educator*

Lanham Seabrook
Moore, Erica *band director*

Pasadena
Bell, Patricia Wright *music educator*

Potomac
Murow, Christine *music educator*

Reisterstown
Goethe, Elizabeth Hogue *music educator*

Rockville
Cain, Karen Mirinda *musician, educator*
Kurkul, Wenyi Wang *musician, educator, administrator*
Middleton, Wanda Karen Lee *songwriter, poet, minister*
Waidler, Beverly Mae *music teacher*

Saint Michaels
Wildasin, Elizabeth Sewell *band director*

Salisbury
Zimmer, Susan Snead *music educator*

Towson
Mueller, Alicia Kay *music educator*
Sadak, Diane Marie *performing arts educator*

Waldorf
Bouchard, Lynne Katherine *music educator*

Washington Grove
Anisimova, Tanya *cellist, educator*

MASSACHUSETTS

Amherst
Donohue, Therese Brady *artistic director, choreographer, designer*

Beverly
Pilanen, Carolyn L. *music educator*

Boston
Anderson, Jewelle Lucille *musician, educator*
Bacon, A. Smoki *television host*
Del Sesto, Janice Mancini *opera company executive*
FitzGibbon, Katherine Lenore *music educator, director*
Jochum, Veronica *pianist*
Klein, Wendy Lee *music educator*
LaForgia, Jeanne Ellen *performing arts educator*
Young, Laura *dance educator, choreographer*

Braintree
Shetler, Rachel Kirsten *music educator, director*

Brookline
Rizzi, Marguerite Claire *music educator*

Cambridge
Kraus, Rozann B. *performing company executive*
Krauss, Alison *country musician*

Concord
Erdely, Beatrice *musician*
Gomberg, Sydelle *dancer educator*

Duxbury
Parris, Rebecca (Ruth Blair MacCloskey) *musician, educator*

Fiskdale
Colwell-Snyder, Lucy Fay *music educator*

Foxboro
Kennedy, Susan Marie *music educator*

Framingham
Bogard, Carole Christine *lyric soprano*

Franklin
Alibrio-Curran, Frances J. *retired music educator*

Great Barrington
Curtin, Phyllis *music educator, dean, vocalist*

Marlborough
Bobel, Mary *video development company financial executive*

North Chelmsford
Garcia, Jennifer *music educator*

North Dartmouth
Noel, Barbara Hughes McMurtry *retired music educator*

Randolph
Porter, Christine Ann *music educator*

Reading
Ellert, Lucinda Joan *musician, educator*

South Hadley
James, Vanessa *theater educator, department chairman*

Topsfield
Huntley-Wright, Joan Augusta (Joan Augusta Huntley) *musician*

Wareham
Monty, Ruthelaine *musician, educator*

Weston
Tenney, Sarah G. *music educator*

Worcester
Hatfield, Renee S.J. *music educator*

Worthington
Schrade, Rolande Maxwell Young *composer, pianist, educator*

MICHIGAN

Allendale
Salazar, Laura Alice Gardner *retired theater educator*

Ann Arbor
Benamou, Catherine Laure *filmmaker, educator*
Scharp-Radovic, Carol Ann *choreographer, classical ballet educator, artistic director*
Verrett, Shirley *soprano*

Battle Creek
Matthews, Wyhomme S. *retired music educator, academic administrator*

Beverly Hills
Tolias, Linda Puroff *music educator*

Bloomfield Hills
Bass, Janis *musician*
Haidostian, Alice Berberian *concert pianist, volunteer, not-for-profit fundraiser*

Burton
Johnson-Brown, Linda Lee *music educator*

Detroit
Parsons, Anne *performing company executive*
Valentine, Cheryl Ann Whitney *music educator*

East Lansing
Draper, Penny Kaye Pekrul *music educator*
Lewis, Tina *music educator, writer*
Palac, Judith Ann *music educator*
Verdehr, Elsa Ludewig (Elsa Ludewig Verderber) *music educator*
Whiting Dobson, Lisa Lorraine *video production educator, producer, director*

Erie
Herman, Jayne E. *music educator*

Flushing
Arndt, Rebecca Dewey *music educator*

Midland
Buechner, Margaret *composer, music educator*
Diehl, Ann *radio personality*

New Baltimore
Sheldrick, Barbara England *music educator, consultant*

Oden
Thibideau, Carolyn C. *musician, educator*

Okemos
Mancini, Gilda Mariann *musician, music educator*

Rochester Hills
Eisenhower, Laurie *performing company executive*

Saginaw
Coughlin, Jeannine M. *music educator*

MINNESOTA

Blue Earth
Ellingsen, Susan P. *music educator*

Brainerd
Wannamaker, Mary Ruth *music educator*

Coon Rapids
Wilson, Sylvia Alyce *musician, educator*

East Grand Forks
Engel, Carol Louise *music educator*

East Gull Lake
Hemkin-Kavanaugh, Sue *music educator*

Eden Prairie
De Bono, Luella Elizabeth *music educator*
Gullickson, Brandy Klingel *conductor, music educator*

Edina
Kirchner, Mary Katherine *musician, educator*

Gaylord
Strouth, Lenore Eileen *music educator*

Lakeville
McGowan, Monica S. *performing company executive, sales executive*

Mankato
Roisum Foley, Amy Kathryn *music educator, director*

Marshall
Clark, Lynnette Faye *music educator*

Minneapolis
Filloon, Karen *radio personality*
Fleezanis, Jorja Kay *violinist, educator*
Houlton, Lise *performing company executive*

Jeffries, Kim *radio personality*
Jones, Susie *radio personality*
Kulig, Martha *stage manager*
Maloney, Rita *radio personality*
Mamayek, Telly *radio personality*
Nortwen, Patricia Harman *music educator*
Oakes, Laura *radio personality*
Peterson, Patty *radio personality*
Porter, Jennifer Madeleine *producer, director*
Spake, Mary Barbara *radio personality*
Stanfield, Rebecca *radio personality*

New Brighton
Carlson, Kaye Lilien *retired music educator*

New Prague
Gallagher, Sandra Ann *music educator*

Paynesville
Bungum, Cheryl Nancy *music educator, director*

Richfield
Fischer, Colleen Theresa *music educator*

Saint Paul
Schaefer, Elzbieta A. *music educator*

Stewartville
Tlougan, Jessica Elise *music educator*
Wilson, Diane E. *music educator*

Wabasha
Brelsford, Mary J. *music educator*

Winona
Heukeshoven, Janet Kay *music educator*

MISSISSIPPI

Ashland
Massengill, Belinda B. *voice educator*

Bay Saint Louis
Foster, Willetta Jean *music educator*

Canton
Hammack, Julia Kathryn *music educator*

Ellisville
Smith, Nina J. *music educator*

Goodman
King, Kathy Cooper *music educator*

Grenada
Thomas, Ouida Power *music educator*

Hattiesburg
Curry, Martha Ann *music educator*
D'Arpa, Josephine *music educator*
Davis, Doris Johnson *retired music educator*

Jackson
Brumfield, Dana Kristine *music educator, medical transcriptionist*
Holly, Ellistine Perkins *music educator*
Somekawa, Mina C. *pianist, educator*

Laurel
Harper, Peggy Sue *music educator*

Ocean Springs
Vinsonhaler, Chris *storyteller, musician, consultant*

Picayune
Carter, Enita Joy *conductor*

Raymond
Bee, Anna Cowden *dance educator*

MISSOURI

Ballwin
Rothermich, Gayla *music educator, director*

Chesterfield
Baker, Sandra Kay *music educator*
Mitchell, Carolyn Joyce *music educator*

Clarkton
Dooley, Wendy Brooke *vocalist, music educator*

Columbia
Burgoyne, Suzanne *theater educator, writer*
Morrow, Constance Prescott *music educator*

Farmington
Huck, Linda A. *music educator*

Hazelwood
Agre, Joy Elaine *music educator*

Independence
Kilpatrick, Laura Shelby *music educator*

Kansas City
Blake, Darcie Kay *radio news director, anchor*
Davis, Mary Bronaugh *music educator*
Ethern, Aberdeen *music educator*
Kuenn, Marjorie Asp *music educator*
Lindsay, Twyla Lynn *music educator*
Manson, Anne *music director*
Parisi, Cheryl Lynn *music educator*
Phalp-Rathbun, Stephanie Dawn *music educator*
Setser, Patricia A. *music educator*

Kearney
Wood, Debra Lynn *music educator*

Kennett
Smith, Donna Dale *music educator*

Lebanon
Drennan, Heidi Marie *music educator*

Liberty
Seward, Nancy H. *retired band director, composer*

Lockwood
Wehrman, Natalie Ann *retired music educator*

Marshall
Lines, Cheryl Elaine *music educator*
Ransom, Judy Lynn *music educator*

Maryville
Schultz, Patricia Bowers *vocal music educator, performer*

Moberly
Werner, Karen Elaine *music educator*

New Cambria
Guilford, Kimberly Sue *music educator*

Park Hills
Moore, Carol Jean *music educator, musician*

Richmond
Richardson, Opal Mae *music educator, director*
Stoenner, Jessamine *music educator*

Saint James
Stevens, Helen Jean *music educator*

Saint Louis
Briccetti, Joan Therese *theater manager, arts management consultant*
Haley, Johnetta Randolph *musician, educator, university official*
Schindler, Laura Ann *piano teacher, accompanist*
Sutherland, Mary (Marcus) *composer, musician, music company executive*
Waddington, Bette Hope (Elizabeth Crowder) *violinist, educator*

Saint Peters
Poettker, Mary Therese *music educator*
Purcell, Cheryl Linn *music educator*

Sedalia
McClain, Cindy Dunstan *music educator*

Springfield
Martin, Nancy Jane *music educator*
Peebles, Sheila Kay *music educator*

Warrensburg
Resch, Rita Marie *music educator*

Webster Groves
Whittemore, Joan M. *music educator*

West Plains
Buxton, Gina LeeAnn *music educator*

MONTANA

Bozeman
Exley, Maureen Catherine *music educator*

Butte
Clark, Gloria A. *music educator*
Kohler, Nora Helen *music educator*
Shea, Stephanie *music educator*

Cut Bank
Schilling, Brenda Gail *music educator*

Fairfield
Ratliff, Kari Lynne *music educator*

Glendive
Shields, Lisa A. *music educator*

Great Falls
Lauzon, Marcia Louise *performing company executive*
Swaby, Barbara Emilie *music educator*

Harlowton
Huning, Devon Gray *actress, audiologist, dancer, photographer*

NEBRASKA

Central City
Wischmeier, Elaine Alice *music educator*

Columbus
Micek, Isabelle *music educator*

Elkhorn
Bluford, Michelle A. *music educator*

Elm Creek
Whitney, Marilyn Beth *music educator*

Holdrege
De Wald, Vicky Coleen *theater director, performing company executive, theater educator*

Lincoln
Bargen, Nancy Lee *music educator*
Hottovy, Susan Elizabeth *music educator*
Young, Jeannette Rose *music educator*

Mc Cook
Watts, Susan Helene *theater educator*

Odell
Lindblad, Cynthia Merrill *music educator*

Omaha
Bouma, Lyn Ann Nichols *music educator*
Cleary, Pamela Ann *symphony executive*
Smith, Sharon Marie *music educator*
Young, Mary Kathryn *vocalist, educator*

Platte Center
Goering, Pamela Jo *music educator, bank officer*

Schuyler
Johnson, Dolores DeBower *consultant*

Wilber
Vrbka, Judith Mary *music educator*

NEVADA

Carson City
Mielke, Nancy E. *music educator*

Henderson
DeVol, Luana *vocalist, consultant*

Las Vegas
Bernstein, Maureen Ann *theater educator, director*
Bond-Brown, Barbara Ann *musician, educator*
Davies, Alma (Alma Rosita) *producer, playwright, lyricist, composer, designer, sculptor*
Deal, Amy Suzanne *choral director*
Healy, Mary (Mrs. Peter Lind Hayes) *singer, actress*
Knight, Gladys (Gladys Maria Knight) *singer*
Stephen, Anne DiIorio *music educator*
Tyler, Janet Irene *music educator*

Reno
Hudson, Karen Ann Sampson *music educator*

Sparks
Walsh, Barbara Jean *music educator*

NEW HAMPSHIRE

Bath
Page, Patti (Clara Ann Fowler) *vocalist*

Concord
Church, Gail Graham *television producer, consultant*

Gorham
[illegible]

Manchester
Marchesseault, Anita *music educator*

Merrimack
Cunningham, Patricia Ann Cahoy *band director, musician*

NEW JERSEY

Burlington
Mustokoff, Henrietta M. *music educator*

Cedarville
Marsella, Julia *music educator*

Cliffside Park
Perhacs, Marylouise Helen *musician, educator*

Convent Station
Scheierman, Mindy *music educator, consultant*

Delanco
Lane, Carrie Belle (Hairston) *retired music educator*

Denville
Fisher, Sharon Mary *musician*
Veech, Lynda Anne *musician, educator*

Dunellen
Minson, Mary Beth *music educator, elementary school educator, musician*

East Brunswick
Savio, Frances Margaret Cammarotta *music educator*
Weiss, Judith Ann *music educator*

Englewood
Zwilich, Ellen Taaffe *composer*

Fort Lee
Amara, Lucine *opera and concert singer*
Herera, Sue *television host*

Freehold
Cheng, Grace Zheng-Ying *music educator*

Hamilton
Plumstead, Kristine Laura *music educator*
Pucciatti, Sandra Milstein *opera company director*

Hightstown
Petri, Christine Ann *music educator*

Jersey City
Queen Latifah, (Dana Owens) *recording artist, actress*

Lawrenceville
Onyshkevych, Larissa M. L. Zaleska *theater educator, editor*

Leonia
Deutsch, Nina *pianist, vocalist*

Lincroft
Benham, Helen *music educator*

Livingston
Clark, Carolyn *performing company executive*

Lodi
Arella, Ann Marietta *music educator, vocalist*

Long Valley
Falk, Barbara Higinbotham *music educator*
Gorman, Tara Ann *music educator*

Madison
Monte, Bonnie J. *performing arts company executive, director, educator*

Margate City
Rose, Jodi *opera company founder and artistic director*

Medford
Saltus, Phyllis Borzelliere *music educator*

Millburn
Conrad, Karen M. *music educator, musician*

Montclair
Castiglione, Anita *pianist, music educator*
Schoch, Clarissa Anthony *singer, educator, executive assistant*

Montvale
Margolin, Deborah Susan *performance artist, educator, writer*

Morristown
Walters, Teresa *musician, music educator, concert pianist*

Newark
Monty, Gloria *former television producer, film executive*

Perth Amboy
Richardson-Melech, Joyce Suzanne *music educator, singer*

Princeton
Cheadle, Louise *concert pianist, educator*
Orphanides, Nora Charlotte *ballet educator*
Vizzini, Carol Redfield *symphony musician, music educator*

Princeton Junction
Mauro, Jean Cranstoun *music educator*

Ridgewood
Beresford, Madeleine Rosamond Sylvia *theater director, puppeteer*

Rockaway
Laine, Cleo (Clementina Dinah Dankworth) *singer*

Rumson
Topham, Sally Jane *ballet educator*

Saddle Brook
Ballone, Eileen Marie *music educator, musician, organist*

Secaucus
Pinsker, Penny Collias (Pangeota Pinsker) *television producer*

Sewell
Meyer, Norma Weintraub *conductor*

Somers Point
Hagerthey, Gwendolyn Irene *retired music educator*

Somerset
Robinson-Hilton, Lorraine Ann *music educator*

Teaneck
Graham, Janet Lorraine *music educator*
Jackson, Millie *vocalist, songwriter, playwright, producer*

Toms River
Schwartz, Anna R. *music educator, musician*

Union
Chen-Hafteck, Lily *music educator*

West New York
Murphy, Melinda *TV host, reporter*

NEW MEXICO

Alamogordo
Denney, Shawna LeAnn *music educator*

Albuquerque
Cook, Marcella Kay *retired theater educator*
Ellen, Jane *composer, music educator, researcher*
King-Pimentel, Cara Shannon *music educator*
Rice, Linda Angel *music educator*

Cloudcroft
Starling, Virginia R. *music educator, consultant*

Clovis
Barnard, Janet Kinzy *music educator, elementary school educator*

Farmington
Evans, Helen Ruth *music educator, pianist*
Wilmer, Pamela Sue *music educator*

Las Cruces
Branch, Dori Alice *music educator*

Roswell
Hedin, Edna Jenks *musician, educator*
Weikel, Sandra G. *music educator*

Santa Fe
Helin, Jacquelyn Mae *classical musician, music educator*
Taylor, Beverly Lacy *musician, educator, stringed instrument restorer*

Tesuque
MacGraw, Ali *actress*

NEW YORK

Albany
Mancinelli-Cahill, Maggie *theater director*

Amenia
Gagne, Nancy Lynn *music educator, musician*

Amsterdam
Ossenfort, Stephanie Helen *music educator, secondary school educator, special education educator*

Armonk
Scotto, Renata *soprano*

Astoria
Sirignano, Monica Ann *performing company executive, playwright*

Bellmore
Baer, Karen Faust *music educator, musician*

Bellport
Esnes, Valerie June *music educator*

Binghamton
Valencia, Melanie Laine *music educator, performer*

Brewerton
Walczyk, Eugenia C. *music educator*

Briarcliff Manor
Ostrofsky, Anna *music educator, violinist*

Bronx
Isaacman, Carrie Edel *actor, educator*
Mittler, Diana (Diana Mittler-Battipaglia) *music educator, administrator, pianist*
Nelson, Esther *dance educator*

Brooklyn
Delahunt, Suzanne Mary *music educator, musician*
Garber, Nara Thea *filmmaker*
Giordano, Marie-Christine *choreographer, dancer, educator, performing company executive, director*
Ham, Karen *musician, music educator*
Harpham, Heather Elise *performing arts educator*
Hopkins, Karen Brooks *performing arts executive*
Rucker, Bronwyn *actress, writer, social worker*
Vidal, Maureen Eris *theater educator, actress*
Villegas, Alma *theater director, actor, writer*
Zabriskie, Sherry LaFollette *filmmaker, author, actress*

Buffalo
DiFranco, Ani *music executive, musician*
Kiefer, Ann Marie *music educator*
Kordinak, Irma L. *piano teacher, musician*
Wagner, Barbara Lee *musician*

Camillus
Alvaro, Maureen Teresa *music educator*

Canandaigua
Story, Amy Taylor *music educator*

Carmel
Calegari, Maria *ballerina*

Cicero
Pink, (Alecia Moore) *singer*

Clayton
Musser, Gloria J. *retired composer*

Cohoes
Vallee, Catherine E. *music educator*

Commack
Richardson, Ellen Morris *music educator*

Cooperstown
Cossa, Joanne *performing company executive*

Coram
Celella, Karen Ann *music teacher, author*

Crugers
Norman, Jessye *soprano*

De Ruyter
Jeschke, Carol T. *arts/theater consultant, real estate investor*

Delmar
Rice, Ruth Elaine *music educator*

Dewitt
Berg, Francine Judith *music educator*

East Amherst
Allen, Maureen Janet *music educator*

Elma
Tichy, Susan Hastings *music educator*

Farmingdale
Lindsley, Michelle A. *theater educator*
Segale, Althea Frances *music educator*

Flushing
Electra, Carmen *actress*
Li, Qin *television anchor, reporter, director, producer*

Fort Covington
Dumas, Charlene Anne *music educator*

Fredonia
Royal, Susan *classical musician, music educator*

Geneva
Lucas, Karen *music educator*

Grand Island
DiVita, Angela Marie *music educator*
Lokken, Carolyn Grace *music educator*

Great Neck
Strickon, Linda Meltzer *music educator*

Greenlawn
Starost, Diane Joan *music educator*

Hamburg
Ortolano, Mary Kay *music educator*

Hartsdale
McMann, Edith Brozak *performance artist, visual artist*

Hempstead
Graffeo, Mary Thérèse *music educator, performer*

Hewlett
Wolff, Eleanor Blunk *actress*

Hicksville
Kronowitz, Pamela Renee *music educator*

Highland
Ratick, Randie H. *music educator, elementary school educator*

Huntington
Shih, Patricia Alice *musician, writer, artist*

Huntington Station
Smith, Sharon Elaine *music educator*

Hurley
O'Boyle, Maureen *television show host*

Hyde Park
Beckmann, Kathleen Ann *music educator*

Ithaca
Arquit, Nora Harris *retired music educator, writer*
Henderson, Cynthia Anne *theater educator, actress*

Jackson Heights
Stevenson, Amanda (Sandy Stevens) *librettist, composer, document examiner*

Johnstown
Rumrill Zullo, Patricia Robbin *music educator*

Katonah
Brownlee, Delphine *actress, musician*

Lancaster
Meides, Holly Sue *music educator*

Larchmont
Swire, Edith Wypler *music educator, musician, violist, violinist*

Latham
LeRoy, Beth Seperack *jazz musician, piano teacher*

Lockport
Ragusa, Karen Ann *music educator*

Mahopac
Castronovo, Bernadine Marro *music educator*
Havens, Cheryl Ciano *music educator*

Manlius
Koch, Catherine Ann *music educator, musician*

Massapequa
Pearl, Alison B. *music educator*
Turk, Elizabeth Ann *music educator*

Melville
Sobol, Elise Schwarcz *music educator*

Mexico
Walters, Natalie A. *music educator*

Millbrook
Flexner, Josephine Moncure *musician, educator*

Mineola
Lelyveld, Gail Annick *actress*

Narrowsburg
Krause, Gloria Rose *music educator*

New York
Aguilera, Christina *vocalist*
Ahrens, Lynn *lyricist*
Alenikoff, Frances *choreographer, performer, writer, dancer, artist*
Alexander, Jane *actress, former federal agency administrator, producer, author, theater educator*
Allen, Betty (Mrs. Ritten Edward Lee III) *mezzo-soprano*

Ananiashvili, Nina *ballerina*
Armitage, Karole *dancer*
Asakawa, Takako *dancer, dance teacher, director, choreographer*
Ashley, Elizabeth *actress*
Bacall, Lauren *actress*
Badu, Erykah *singer*
Banks, Tyra *model, actress*
Barrio, Soledad *dancer*
Bartoli, Cecilia *soprano*
Behar, Joy *television personality*
Belloni, Alessandra *artistic director*
Berman, Rachel *dancer*
Beyoncé, (Beyoncé Giselle Knowles) *vocalist*
Biedel, Alexis *actress*
Black, Shawn Morgado *dancer*
Blackman, Cindy *musician, composer*
Blige, Mary Jane *recording artist*
Borree, Yvonne *dancer*
Boston, Gretha *actress, vocalist*
Bowden, Sally Ann *choreographer, educator, dancer*
Braden, Martha Brooke *concert pianist, educator*
Braxton, Toni *popular musician*
Bricard, Yolanda Borras *music educator, music program administrator*
Brightman, Sarah *singer, actress*
Brinkley, Christie *model, spokesperson, designer*
Brothers, Joyce Diane *television personality, psychologist*
Brown, Carolyn Rice *dancer, choreographer, writer, filmmaker*
Brown, Trisha *dancer*
Brown, Tyese Andrea *music educator*
Bruneau, Lise *actor*
Bumbry, Grace *soprano*
Burrell, Pamela *actress*
Bush, Lauren *model*
Bussert, Meg *actress, educator*
Butler, Kerry *actress*
Byer, Diana *performing arts company executive*
Cahill, Catherine M. *orchestra executive*
Caldwell, Zoe *actress, film director*
Campbell, Naomi *model*
Cantrell, Lana *actress, lawyer, singer*
Capucilli, Terese *performing company executive*
Carpenter, Mary Chapin *singer, songwriter*
Cash, Rosanne *country singer, songwriter*
Castro-Pozo, Talía *dancer, educator*
Cazeaux, Isabelle Anne Marie *retired musicology educator*
Chang, Marian S. *filmmaker, composer*
Channing, Stockard (Susan Stockard) *actress*
Chao, Yu Chen *musician, cellist, educator*
Chenoweth, Kristin *actress*
Chesler, Gail *arts organization development executive*
Clarkson, Patricia *actress*
Collins, Judy Marjorie *singer, songwriter*
Colvin, Shawn *recording artist, songwriter*
Conroy, Frances *actress*
Coppola, Sofia Carmina *film director, scriptwriter, actress*
Curran, Leigh *actress, playwright*
Curtin, Jane Therese *actress, writer*
D'Abruzzo, Stephanie *actress*
D'Addario, Edith *performing company executive*
Dakin, Christine Whitney *dancer, educator*
Danitz, Marilynn Patricia *choreographer, videographer*
Deen, Paula H. *television personality, chef, restaurant owner*
De Luca, Eva *vocalist, writer, composer*
de Matteo, Drea *actress*
Devorah, Ruth *vocalist, actress, composer, artist, costume designer*
Dion, Celine *musician*
DiScala, Jamie Lynn *actress*
Dlugoszewski, Lucia *artistic director*
Douglas, Ashanti S. (Ashanti) *vocalist*
Duff, Hillary Ann *actress, singer*
Dukakis, Olympia *actress*
Dunham, Christine *dancer*
Earle, Eugenia *music educator*
Elliott, Missy *musician*
Ellis, Terry *vocalist*
Emme, *model, apparel designer*
Emmerich, Constance *musician*
Eterovich Maguire, Karen Ann *actress, writer*
Evangelista, Linda *model*
Evans, Faith *singer*
Falletta, Jo Ann *conductor*
Farley, Carole *soprano*
Federman, Simone *theater educator, theater director*
Felious, Odetta *vocalist*
Fey, Tina *actress*
Filarski Hasselbeck, Elizabeth *television host/personality*
Flack, Roberta *singer*
Fleming, Renée L. *opera singer*
Ford, Eileen Otte (Mrs. Gerard W. Ford) *modeling agency executive*
Foster, Sutton *actress*
Fowler, Beth *actress*
Franklin, Aretha *singer*
Fuchs, Lillian *classical musician, educator, composer*
Glasberg, Lisa *radio personality*
Goodacre, Jill *model*
Goto, Midori *classical violinist*
Graff, Randy *actress*
Hargitay, Mariska *actress*
Harmon, Jane *producer*
Harris, Harriet *actress*
Harris, Julie (Julie Ann Harris) *actress*
Hastings, Deborah *bass guitarist*
Hatfield, Juliana *vocalist*
Hays, Sorrel (Doris) *composer*
Herrera, Paloma *dancer*
Herron, Cindy *actress, vocalist*
Hill, Lauryn *vocalist, actress*
Holmes, Anna-Marie *ballerina, ballet mistress*
Holt, Thelma *theatrical producer*
Horn, Shirley *vocalist, pianist*
Horne, Marilyn *mezzo-soprano*
Hynde, Chrissie *musician*

Intilli, Sharon Marie *television director, small business owner*
Isbin, Sharon *classical guitarist, guitar educator*
Istomin, Marta Casals *performing arts administrator, former educator*
Jackson, Anne (Anne Jackson Wallach) *actress*
Jaffe, Susan *ballerina*
James, Cheryl *vocalist*
Jamison, Judith *dancer*
Jefferson, Denise *dance school director*
Jett, Joan (Joan Larkin) *musician*
Jewel, (Jewel Kilcher) *folk singer, songwriter*
Jones, Maxine *vocalist*
Jung, Doris *dramatic soprano*
Kassel, Virginia Weltmer *television producer, writer*
Keating, Isabel *actress*
Kent, Julie *ballet dancer, actress, model*
Kent, Linda Gail *dancer*
Keys, Alicia *vocalist, musician, songwriter*
Kinberg, Judy *television producer, director*
Kiser, Molly *musician*
Kitahata-Sporn, Amy *movement educator*
Kitt, Eartha Mae *actress, singer*
Knight, Shirley *actress*
Kowroski, Maria *dancer*
Kozak, Harley Jane *actress, writer*
Krizer, Jodi *performing arts executive*
Kurman, Juta *music educator*
Lake, Ricki *talk show host, actress*
Lang, Pearl *dancer, choreographer*
LaRose, Melba Lee *performing company executive, actress, playwright, theater director*
Lauper, Cyndi *musician*
Leach, Mary Jane *composer*
LeCompte, Elizabeth *theater director*
Lee, Amy *singer*
Lewis, Marcia *actress*
Limmroth, Karin Leigh *international producer, television correspondent*
Love, Laura *singer, songwriter*
Loveless, Patty (Patty Ramey) *country music singer*
Lucci, Susan *actress*
Ludwig, Karen *actor*
Lynn, Judith *opera singer, artist, voice teacher*
Macpherson, Elle *model*
Malm, Mia *actress*
Mamlok, Ursula *composer, educator*
Manahan, Anna *actress*
Mandabach, Caryn *television producer*
Marshall, Kathleen *choreographer, theater director, theater producer*
Maxwell, Carla Lena *dancer, choreographer, educator*
May, Elaine *actress, theatre and film director*
Mazzo, Kay *ballet dancer, educator*
McDonald, Audra Ann *actress*
McGrady, Phyllis *television producer*
McKerrow, Amanda *ballet dancer*
McLachlan, Sarah *composer, musician*
Meadow, Lynne (Carolyn Meadow) *theater producer*
Menzel, Idina *actress, lyricist*
Merchant, Natalie Anne *musician, singer*
Meunier, Monique *dancer*
Miller, Bebe *choreographer*
Miller, Beth McCarthy *television director*
Miller, Erika *on-air business news reporter*
Monk, Meredith Jane *artistic director, composer, choreographer, filmmaker, director*
Moore, Mandy (Amanda Leigh Moore) *singer, actress*
Moore, Rachel Suzanne *performing company executive, dancer*
Moyers, Judith Davidson *television producer*
Muller, Jennifer *choreographer, dancer*
Murphy, Carolyn *model*
Murphy, Donna *actress*
Murphy, Rosemary *actress*
Nugent, Nelle *theater, film and television producer*
Olim, Dorothy *theater administrator*
Osborne, Joan (Elizabeth) *singer, songwriter*
Parker, Alice *composer*
Parsons, Estelle *actress, film director, film producer*
Payton-Wright, Pamela *actress*
Peters, Bernadette (Bernadette Lazzara) *actress*
Peters, Roberta *soprano*
Phair, Liz *recording artist, pop vocalist*
Pinkins, Tonya *actress*
Posin, Kathryn Olive *choreographer*
Pratt, Suzanne *producer, reporter*
Price, Leontyne *concert and opera singer, soprano*
Queler, Eve *conductor*
Quivers, Robin *radio personality*
Ramirez, Tina *artistic director*
Raphael, Sally Jessy *talk-show host*
Reinking, Ann H. *dancer, actress*
Rennie, Milbrey Tower *television news producer*
Reuben, Gloria *actress*
Rice, Barbara Lynn *stage manager*
Richard, Ellen *theater executive*
Rigg, Dame Diana *actress*
Ringer, Jennifer *dancer*
Ripa, Kelly Maria *television personality*
Rivera, Chita (Conchita del Rivero) *actress, singer, dancer*
Rizer, Maggie *model*
Roberts, Denise (Denise Roberts Hurlin) *dancer*
Ronstadt, Linda Marie *singer*
Ross, Audrey *theatrical publicist*
Ross, Diana Ernestine Earle *singer, actress, entertainer, fashion designer*
Roth, Daryl *theater producer*
Rothman, Carol *theater director*
Ruckert, Ann Johns *musician, singer*
Rudolph, Maya *actress, comedienne*
Salerno-Sonnenberg, Nadja *violinist*
Salonga, Lea *actress, singer*
Sarandon, Susan Abigail *actress*
Schoonmaker Powell, Thelma *film editor*
Schorer, Suki *ballet teacher*
Schuhart, Anne Dashley (Susan Schuhart Zito) *actress*

Seldes, Marian *actress*
Seymour, Stephanie *model*
Shafer, Yvonne *theater educator, writer*
Shane, Rita *opera singer, educator*
Shelley, Carole *actress*
Shocked, Michelle *vocalist, songwriter*
Silver, Joan Micklin *film director, screenwriter*
Silvers, Sally *choreographer, performing company executive*
Simpson, Jessica Ann *vocalist*
Sinclair, Daisy *casting executive*
Sitomer, Sheila Marie *television producer, director*
Smith, Anna Nicole (Vickie Lynn Hogan) *television personality, model*
Somogyi, Jennie *dancer*
Spears, Britney *vocalist, actress*
Stevens, Risë *performing arts company administrator*
Stratas, Teresa (Anastasia Strataki) *opera singer, soprano*
Stroman, Susan *choreographer, theater director*
Sutherland, Dame Joan *retired soprano*
Taylor, Nicole Renée *model*
Taymor, Julie *theater, film and opera director and designer*
Tesori, Jeanine *composer*
Tischler, Judith Blanche *retired music publishing executive, educator*
Todd, Kim A. *actress*
Turturro, Aida *actress*
Tuttle, Ashley *dancer*
Uggams, Leslie *entertainer*
Valletta, Amber *model*
Velez-Mitchell, Anita *entertainer, writer*
Vendela, *model*
Vieira, Meredith *television personality*
Von Stade, Frederica *mezzo-soprano*
Wallace, Michele *media company executive*
Warrick, Ruth *actress*
Warwick, Dionne *singer*
Waters, Crystal *vocalist, songwriter*
Waters, Sylvia *dance company artistic director*
Waxman, Anita *producer*
Wedgeworth, Ann *actress*
Weese, Miranda *dancer*
Weinstein, Ellen *performing company executive*
Weissler, Fran *theatrical producer*
White, Lillias *actress*
Williams, Lucinda *country musician*
Williams, Terrie Michelle *publicity agency executive*
Williams, Vanessa *recording artist, actress*
Wilson, Cassandra *singer*
Woodward, Joanne Gignilliat *actress*
Zhu, Ai-Lan *opera singer*
Zimmerman, Pegeen *television producer*
Zosike, Joanie Fritz *theater director, actor*

Newark Valley
Griffith, Jewel Ann *music educator*

Niskayuna
Brinkman, Paula H. *music educator*
Steeley, Dolores Ann *music educator*

North Tonawanda
Strong, Audrey Farone *music educator*

Oneida
Bennett, Colleen T. *music educator*

Oswego
Huff, JoAn *retired physicial education/dance educator*

Penfield
Ahlstedt, Linda Foxx *music educator*
Monti, Rena Marie *music educator*

Pittsford
Templeton, Karen Schroer *music educator*

Port Washington
van Schenkhof, Carol Dougherty (Carol Dovan) *soprano, music educator*

Porter Corners
Blom, Carol Barnes *music educator*

Potsdam
Bouchard, Kimberley A. *performing arts educator*

Poughkeepsie
Dolamore, Jeanne Porcino *music educator*

Purchase
Bannon, Nancy *performing arts educator*

Rochester
Eichenlaub, Rosemary Waring *music educator*
Fitzmorris, Pamela S. *music educator*
Fox, Donna Brink *music educator*
Johnson, B. Jean *music educator, musician*
Marini, Jane Marie *music educator*
Penneys, Rebecca Ann *musician*
Pratt, Alice S. *music educator*
Schneider, Sue R. *music educator*
Toribara, Masako Ono *voice educator*
Truesdale, Carol A. *music educator*

Saratoga Springs
Martínez, Nicola Marie *choreographer, educator*

Schenectady
Atchinson, Judy Fitzner *composer*

Sea Cliff
Popova, Nina *dancer, choreographer, director*

Sherburne
Rinaldo, Ginger Lee *music educator*

Shrub Oak
Vaccaro, Annette Andréa *music educator*

Smithtown
Kalabza-Balsamo, Debra Alyce *music educator*

Sound Beach
Preuss, Linda Palmbaum *music educator*

Sparkill
Dahl, Arlene *actress, writer, apparel designer, cosmetics executive*

Staten Island
Robison, Paula Judith *flutist*

Syosset
Denton, Michele Anne *music educator*

Syracuse
Wolff, Catherine Elizabeth *opera company executive*

Troy
Snyder, Patricia Di Benedetto *theater director and administrator*

Trumansburg
Frederick, Susan Ann (Pentz) *music educator*

Victor
Bechler, Susan Keifer *music educator*

Walden
Murphy, Pamela Ann *music educator*

Warrensburg
Gallup Ricci, Janice Elizabeth *music educator*

Webster
Nitsch, Brenda Sue *music educator*

West Islip
Hayes, Judith M. *music educator, elementary school educator, secondary school educator*

Willow
Bley, Carla Borg *composer*

NORTH CAROLINA

Aberdeen
Sinclair, Ruth Spears Smith *piano teacher*

Asheville
Seeger, Peggy *musician, singer, songwriter*

Bayboro
Wilson, Anne Forlaw *music educator*

Bear Creek
Enloe, Loraine Alexander Davis *music educator*

Boone
Cole, Susan Stockbridge *theatre educator*

Burnsville
Boulter, Elizabeth Catherine *music educator*

Cary
Bruce, Brenda *pianist*

Chapel Hill
Froeber, Sarah Marjorie *actress, playwright, educator*
Peacock, Florence F. *professional musician, soprano, voice teacher*

Charlotte
Engen, Rebecca Lynn *music educator*
Higgins, Diane W. *music teacher*
Hock, Joanne Means *film director, cinematographer*
Iley, Martha Strawn *music educator*
Penninger, Beverly Lynn *television producer, writer*
Ziliani, Regina Pettit *music educator*

Clayton
Banks, Susan Rebecca *music educator*

Fayetteville
Swoope, Janice Robins *music educator*
Turner, Gwendolyn Marie *band director, musician*

Granite Quarry
Trivette, Susan Brown *music educator*

Greensboro
Green, Jill I. *dance educator, researcher*
Henley, Jody Dale Hartig *music educator, consultant*
Russell, Peggy Taylor *soprano, educator*
Styles, Teresa Jo *producer, educator*
Ward, Angie *radio personality*

Hayesville
Gibson, Jennifer Williams *music educator*

High Point
Flack, Teresa Hopper *music educator*

Hope Mills
Williams, LaVerne Carmen *performance artist, poet, musician*

Huntersville
Petersen, Ruth Anne *performing arts educator*

Jamestown
Moorefield, Susan Morgan *music educator*

Kings Mountain
Aderholdt, Traci Eaves *music educator*

Lumberton
Canonizado, Gloria M. *choreographer, educator*

Manteo
Hollins, April Rife *music educator*

Mooresboro
Goode, Elizabeth Ann *music educator*

Newport
Mundine, Rachel Quinn *music educator*

Otto
Harwell, Joanne Brindley *music educator*

Pilot Mountain
Collins, Sherri Smith *music educator*

Raleigh
Conley, Christine *music educator*
Florin, Julie A. *music educator*
Fredenburgh, Lisa Marie *music educator*
Garriss, Phyllis Weyer *music educator, performer*
Harnish, Margaret Ann *music educator*
Hynus, Anita Eileen *music educator*
Santucci, Angela Maria *performing arts educator, actress, singer*

Rougemont
Nilsson, Mary Ann *music educator*

Salisbury
Julian, Rose Rich *music educator, director*

Sanford
Wesner, Jennifer Isla *music educator*

Shelby
Bess, Angela Paige *music educator*

Stoneville
Halpin, Margaret Renee *music educator*

Warrenton
Weddington, Elizabeth Gardner (Liz Gardner) *actress*

Wilmington
Cameron, Kay *conductor, music director, arranger*
Charles, Catherine Elaine *music educator*
Kelley, Virginia Wiard (Judy Kelley) *dance educator*
Lavin, Linda *actress*
Lawson, Pamela Ann *musician, educator*

Wingate
Bostic, Polly Thomas *music educator*

Winston Salem
Mueller, Margaret S. *musician, educator*
Stewart, Gwendolyn Johns *music educator*

Zebulon
Platt, Katrina Vontelle *music educator*

NORTH DAKOTA

Bismarck
Gray, Arlene *music educator, musician*
Lundberg, Susan Ona *musical organization administrator*

Calvin
Magnus, Elsie L. *music educator*

Dickinson
Schubert, Yvette Marie *music educator*

Fargo
Fossum, Ruth N. *musician*

Minot
Starr, Sandra Schjeldahl *music educator*

Rhame
Kulish, Carma C. *music educator*

Rolla
Zinke, Sheila J. *music educator*

Washburn
Hall, Gwen Marie *music educator*

West Fargo
Jordahl, Susan Marie *music educator*

OHIO

Ada
Sycks, Linda B. *music educator*

Akron
Usher, Ann L. *music educator*
Wang, Ya-Hui *conductor*

Alliance
Fugelberg, Nancy Jean *retired music educator*

Amherst
Gall, Simone Ellen *music educator*

Athens
Parrotti, Laura Davidian *theater educator*

Beachwood
Farley, Carolyn Juanita *music educator*

Bedford
Shauf, Jennifer Elaine *music educator*

Berea
Jones, Erin Marguerite *music educator*

Bowling Green
Wolcott, Nancy Bookout *music director*

Bratenahl
DesRosiers, Anne Booke *performing arts administrator, consultant*

Cambridge
Ryan, Mary Esther *music educator*

Canton
Klotz, Leora Nylee *retired music educator, vocalist*
Moorhouse, Linda Virginia *symphony orchestra administrator*

Centerville
Wasson-Shaw, Carol R. *music teacher*

Cincinnati
Beggs, Patricia Kirk *performing company executive*
Brown, Lillie Harrison *music educator*
Dunevant, Carol Dary *music educator, conductor*
Galloway, Lillian Carroll *modeling agency executive, consultant*
Holdren, Jamie Lynn *music educator*
James, Jefferson Ann *performing company executive, choreographer*
Morgan, Victoria *performing company executive, choreographer*

Cleveland
Dirksen, Marlene Kay *music educator*
Lawrence, Estelene Yvonne *musician, transportation executive*
Mc Farlane, Karen Elizabeth *concert artists manager*
Weir, Dame Gillian Constance *concert organist, harpsichordist*

Columbus
Allen, Lois Arlene Height (Mrs. James Pierpont Allen) *musician*
Caracciolo, Sandra Nicol *voice educator*
Reece, Beth Elaine *music educator*
Rosenstock, Susan Lynn *orchestra administrator*

Cuyahoga Falls
Stewart, Christine Marie *church music director*

Dayton
Carrier, Rachel Esther *music educator, director*
Hanna, Marsha L. *artistic director*
Shaffer, Joanne Tyler *music educator*
Wasson, Barbara Hickam *music educator*

Defiance
Strata, Jane *music educator*

Delaware
Gardner, Bonnie Milne *theater educator*

East Cleveland
Davis, Dianne *music educator*
Soule, Lucile Snyder *pianist, music educator*

Euclid
Harasym, Jean Louise *music educator*

Fairfield
Bender, Jacqueline *music educator*

Fairport Harbor
Priddy, Jean Marie *music educator, voice educator*

Fort Jennings
Warnecke, Rose Mary *music educator*

Geneva
Carrel, Marianne Eileen *music educator*

Genoa
Loy, Stephanie Lynn *music educator*

Lebanon
McDonel, Jennifer Sutton *music educator*

Lima
Riggs, Jane L. *performing arts association administrator, consultant*

Lodi
Langlotz, Jennifer Cook *music educator*

Lynx
Watters, Cora Tula *musician, educator*

Macedonia
Levy, Beth Ann *music educator*

Marion
Burris, Lynette Sue *music educator*

Massillon
Green, Angela LaVonne *band director*
Penczarski, Jennifer Marie *music educator*

Middlefield
Jaite, Gail Ann *music educator*

Mount Pleasant
Aspenwall, Kathryn DeBlasis *music educator*

New Concord
Schumann, Laura Elaine *conductor*

New Richmond
Fisher, Virginia Carolyn *music educator, director*

Newbury
Proctor, Cheryl Ann *music educator*

Norwood
Beresford, Mary Jo Theresa *theatre educator*

Oak Harbor
Witt, Beth M. *music educator*

Oberlin
Rutstein, Sedmara Zakarian *piano educator, concert pianist*

Oxford
Gallehue, Dawn E. *voice educator*

Parma
Plasterer, Tamara J. *music educator, theater educator*

Perrysburg
Williams, Pamela Sue *music educator*

Pickerington
Lang, Lisa Ann *music educator*

Reynoldsburg
Blair, Jennifer Marie *music educator, consultant*

Rocky River
Briscar-Martel, Nancy Marie *agent, musician, educator*

South Euclid
Miller Schear, Annice Mara *music educator*

Stow
Mikes, Judith Pauline *music educator*

Swanton
Barko, Helen Marie *music educator*

Tipp City
Ahmed, Gail R. *music educator*

Wadsworth
Ross, Jane Arlene *music educator*

Wapakoneta
Lusk, Mary Margaret *music educator*

Warren
Seachrist, Denise *music educator*

Whitehall
Van Camp, Diana J. *music educator*

Wickliffe
Graves, Pamela Kay *music educator*

Willoughby
Linsenmeier, Carol Vincent *music educator*

Youngstown
Popio, Donna Marie *music educator*

Zanesville
Brown, Karen Rima *orchestra manager, Spanish language educator*
Show, Renee Deane *music educator*

OKLAHOMA

Altus
Runyan, Mary Lynn *music educator*

Anadarko
Kidd, Lovetta Monza *music educator*

Broken Arrow
Lobser, Heather A. *music educator*

Clinton
Askew, Penny Sue *choreographer, artistic director, ballet instructor*

Durant
Wilkins, Carolyn Ann *music educator*

Edmond
Charoenwongse, Chindarat *pianist, music educator*

Elgin
Leonard, Nedra V. *music educator*

Elk City
Beaty, Deborah Joyce *music educator*

Enid
Hildebrand, Kaye *music educator*
Russell, Rhonda Cheryl *piano educator, recording artist*
Seem, Evelyn Ashcraft *music educator*

Mannford
Dehn-Wittke, Barbara Ann *music educator*

Midwest City
Robinson, Emily Sue *music educator*

Mounds
Fellows, Esther Elizabeth *musician, music educator*

Muskogee
Shelton, Nancy Sue *music educator*

Norman
Garner, Lani Aloha *music educator*
Gass, Cynthia Ann *music educator*
Smith, Beulah Mae *music educator*
Wagner, Brenda Marcyea *music educator, musician*

Oklahoma City
Campbell, Virginia Hopper *piano concert artist, composer, educator*
Forrest, Linda Sue *music educator*
Shackleton, Jean L. *music educator*
Twyman, Nita (Venita Twyman) *music educator*

Ponca City
Barraclough, Mary Jane *music educator*

Sapulpa
Weinstock Rad, Katheryn Louise *music educator*

Snow
Milslian, Dorothy Kathleen *music educator*

Tulsa
Collins, Laura Jane *music educator, singer, accompanist*
Freesemann, LeAnne Clair (Luikart) *music educator*
Larkin, Moscelyne *retired artistic director, dancer*
Owens, Jana Jae *entertainer*

Yukon
Myers, Kandy Kay *music educator*

OREGON

Ashland
Appel, Libby *theater director*

Eugene
Bailey, Exine Margaret Anderson *soprano, educator*
Benson, Joan *musician, music educator*

Hillsboro
Imbrie, Barbara Marie *musician, music educator*

Keizer
Beranek, Kim Marie *music educator*

Medford
Gregory, Rosamund Ann *actor*

Portland
Blumberg, Naomi *symphony musician, educator*
Jensen, Marion Pauline *singer*
Kaluza, Sheryle Siegfried *music educator, vocalist, composer*
Merrill, Norma *video producer, copy writer*
Mittelstaedt, Janet Rugen *music educator, composer*
Robinson, Helene M. *retired music educator*
Watts, Sara Kathryn *musician, educator*

Roseburg
Eddy, Wanda Criger *music educator*
Ferguson, Cynthia Claire *music educator, consultant*

Salem
Marshall, Cak (Catherine Elaine Marshall) *music educator, composer*

PENNSYLVANIA

Allentown
Beltzner, Gail Ann *music educator*
Martyska, Barbara *composer, performer, teacher*
Moeller, MaryAnn *music educator*
Pribanich, Cheryl Marie *music educator*

Annville
Condran, Cynthia Marie *gospel musician*

Athens
Lane, Elizabeth Ann *music educator*
Miller, Vina Elizabeth *music educator*

Beaver Falls
Hemphill, Diane Eilene *music educator*

Berwyn
Ahlquist, Janet Sue *musician, music educator*
Gingles, Marjorie Stanke *music educator, educator*

Bethlehem
Allen, Beatrice *music educator, pianist*
Simons, Audrey Kay *music educator*

Birdsboro
Sipotz, Naomi C. *music educator*

Boothwyn
Giordano, Patricia A. *music educator*

Brodheadsville
Snyder, Nadine Eldora *music educator*

Burlington
Papa, Kathleen Nicole *music educator*

Cambridge Springs
Ralph, NancyJo *music educator*

Carlisle
Kot, Heather A. (Heather A. Oliver) *soprano, educator*

Chadds Ford
Swensson, Evelyn Dickenson *conductor, composer, librettist*

Chalfont
Ashley, Kathleen Labonis *music educator*

Cheyney
Bagley, Edythe Scott *theater educator*
Ellis-Scruggs, Jan *theater arts educator*

Coatesville
Simmons, Barbara Ann *music educator*

Coraopolis
Vandertie, Suzan Mary *music educator*

Downingtown
Crescenz, Valerie J. *music educator*

Drexel Hill
Boyer, Anna Marie *music educator*

Easton
Lutte, Carole Anne *music educator*
Miller, Marie Gelsinger *music educator*

Erie
Foltz, Katrina Marie *music educator*
McKinney, Betty Louise *musician*

Fairview
Sanford, Carolyn Ann *music educator*

Flinton
Burket, Darla Eileen *music educator*

Glenshaw
Stevens, Christine Treml *music educator*

Harrison City
Rubright, Beverly Jean *music educator*

Hatboro
Carroll, Lucy Ellen *choral director, music coordinator, educator*

Jenkintown
Leiter, Barbara F. *music educator*

King Of Prussia
Helmetag, Diana *music educator*

Kingston
Weisberger, Barbara *artistic director, educator, choreographer*

Lake Winola
Driscole, Melissa Rees *conductor, educator*

Lancaster
Horein, Kathleen Marie *music educator*
Veri, Frances Gail *musician, educator*

Langhorne
Haimbach, Marjorie Anne *music educator*

Lansdale
Richards, Jane C. *music educator*
Sokolowski, Elizabeth Catherine *music educator*

Lenhartsville
Ryan, Christine Brett *music educator*

Loysburg
Stuckey, Ellen Mae *music educator*

Marietta
Mendenhall, Hollie Christine *music educator*

Mc Donald
Starkey, Aleta Rae *music educator*

Mercersburg
Mufson, Laurie Ethel *theater educator, director, actress*

Merion Station
Mitchell, Joann M. *music educator*

Midland
Dunlap, Barbara J. *music educator*

Milford Square
Sewell, Gloriana *piano teacher*

Monaca
Soltes, Joann Margaret *retired music educator, realtor*

Moon Township
Martin, Diana Williams *music educator*

New Brighton
Ficca, Rhonda Lee *music educator*

Newport
Switzer, Karen Belle Ringers *music educator*

Norristown
D'Ulisse-Caldwell, Maryellen Cecilia *music educator*

North Versailles
Crawford, Melinda Heather *music educator, musician*

Patton
Galczynski, Valerie Ertter *music educator, soprano*

Philadelphia
Burton, Katherine Gale *music educator, recording industry executive, musician*
Davis, Paige *television host/personality*
Fauntleroy, Angela Colleen *music educator*
Garonzik, Sara Ellen *stage producer*
Ingolfsson-Fassbind, Ursula G. *music educator*
Myers Brown, Joan *dance company executive*
Volansky, Michele *dramaturg, educator*

Pittsburgh
Bardyguine, Patricia Wilde *ballerina, ballet theatre executive*
Desiree, Laura *dancer*
Dreyer, Melanie Ann *theater educator*
Li, Ying *dancer*
Posvar, Mildred Miller *opera singer*
Wilde, Patricia *retired artistic director*

Quakertown
Emig, Carol A. *music educator, musician*

Reading
Zug, Elizabeth E. *concert pianist, educator*

Rural Valley
Forringer, Deborah Lee *music educator*

Russellton
Cicco, Cecilia Victoria *music educator*

Selinsgrove
Pineno, Mariam Davis *retired music educator, poet*

Shamokin
Styer, Sharon Louise *music educator*

Shavertown
Motyka, Susanne Victoria *music educator*

State College
Darnell, Doris Hastings *performance artist*

Upper Darby
Kahler, Nancy J. *music educator, director*

Washington
Gregg, Cynthia Louise *music educator*

West Chester
Albert, Kristen Ann *music educator*

West Lawn
Borelli, Cynthia Ann *vocal educator, chorus director*

West Middlesex
Hoffman, Ada Jean *music educator*

West Sunbury
Ferrere, Rita L. *band director, music educator*

Wynnewood
Lodish, Susan Fischer *theater director*

Youngsville
Montgomery, Christina Lynn *music educator*
Pearson, Denise Anne *music educator*
Scheid, Cynthia Loiuse *music educator*

Youngwood
Duvall, Hollie Jean *music educator*

RHODE ISLAND

Chepachet
Jubinska, Patricia Ann *ballet instructor, choreographer, artist, anthropologist, archaeologist*

Greenville
Hopkins, Catherine Lee *music educator*

Lincoln
Marsden, Herci Ivana *classical ballet artistic director*

Pawtucket
Orson, Barbara Tuschner *actress*

Providence
Coffman, Teresa Susan *music educator*

Warwick
Markward, Cheri D. *music educator*

SOUTH CAROLINA

Batesburg
Moon, Linda Walker *music educator*

Cayce
Cox, Donna (Bozard) *music educator*

Charleston
Nations, Janice McKinney *music educator*

Columbia
Boyce, Corrie Mosby *music educator*
Paschal, Rhoda Jones *voice educator*

Duncan
Clarke, Jean Alderman *orchestra director*

Edisto Island
Van Metre, Margaret Cheryl *artistic director, dance educator*

Galivants Ferry
Christy, Connie Annette *music educator, webmaster*

Georgetown
Ragland, Mary Ruth *music educator*

Goose Creek
Vogt, Kathleen Cunningham *musician, music educator*

Greer
Cooper, Rose Marie *composer*

Hilton Head Island
Brock, Karena Diane *dancer, educator*

Kingstree
Burgess, Pamela Shawnta *music educator, director*

Lake City
Stone, Betty Frances *music educator*

Moncks Corner
Collins, Jenny Lynn *music educator*

Moore
King, Tamara Powers *music educator, musician*

Manassas
Livingston, Jo Ellen Brooks *music educator*

Midlothian
Jennings, Elizabeth Forrest *music educator*

Mount Crawford
German, Lynne Cummings *music educator*

New Kent
Whitman, Sharon May *music educator*

Newport News
Hines, Mary Susan *musician, educator*
Morant, Jocelyn Juanita Johnson *music educator*
Trachuk, Lillian Elizabeth *music educator*

Norfolk
Hurwitz, Linda *music educator, musician*
Ibarra, Avelina C. *music educator*
Musgrave, Thea *composer, conductor*

Oakton
Drummond, Carol Cramer *voice educator, singer, artist, writer*

Portsmouth
Clary, Inez Harris *music educator*
Weber, Marie Florence Morano *music educator*

Pound
Mccoy, Edna Rose *music educator*

Radford
James, Clarity (Carolyne Faye James) *mezzo-soprano*

Reston
Cravey, Clara *dancer, performing arts association administrator*
Hepworth-Woolston, Connie Jo *choreographer*
Wawrejko Cochran, Diane *performing arts association administrator*

Richmond
Bray, Patricia Shannon *music educator, musician, small business owner*
Hammel, Alice Maxine *music educator*
Mallory-Parker, Suzanne *performing arts educator*
Melcher, Elizabeth (Elizabeth Melcher Winger) *musician*
Winslett, Stoner *artistic director*
Young, Sharon Wisdom *retired music educator*

Roanoke
Johnson, Sharon Brabson *music educator*
Miller, Gretchen M. *music educator*

Salem
Crowder, Rebecca Byrum *music educator, elementary school educator*

South Boston
Ferrell, Denise Moore *music educator*

Springfield
Siddons, Joy Garbee *music educator*

Sterling
Jefferson, Sandra Traylor *choreographer*
Newton, Cheryl Kay *music educator*

Vienna
Kinsolving, Sylvia Crockett *musician, educator*

Virginia Beach
Cehelska, Olga M. *music educator, flight instructor*
Gibbs, Jordan Smith *music educator, artist*
Powell, Michele Hall *music educator*
Tuskey, Laura Jeanne *music educator, pharmacologist*
Watkins, Brenda L. *music educator*

Winchester
Branescu-Hurt, Ana *music educator*
Russell, Melinda Farrar *music educator*

WASHINGTON

Aberdeen
Hill, Christine Marie *voice educator, music educator*
Wilhelms, Patricia Sue *choral director*

Bellingham
Whyte, Nancy Marie *performing arts educator*

Burien
McKamey, Frances Helene *music educator*

Coulee City
George, Kristi Kay *music educator*

East Wenatchee
Marion, Sarah Kathleen *music educator*

Everett
Rimbach, Evangeline Lois *retired music educator*

Kettle Falls
Pancoast, Brandy Elizabeth *music educator*

Lacey
Miller, Linda Jean *music educator, writer*

Marysville
Wolfkill-Hoff, Ramona Lea *music educator*

Moses Lake
Aur, Marina V. *choir conductor, music educator*

Olympia
Macduff, Ilone Margaret *music educator*

Pullman
Kelley, Margaret Mary *music educator, musician*

Seatac
Green, Suzanne Lundy *music educator*

Seattle
Anang, Amma Cecilia *dance company administrator*
Card, Deborah Frances *orchestra administrator*
Dally, Lynn *choreographer, performing company executive, educator*
Humphries, Edna Bevan *music educator, choir director*
Mahdaviani, Miriam *choreographer, educator*
Matesky, Nancy Lee *music educator*
Ott, Sharon *artistic director*
Ozaki, Nancy Junko *performance artist, performing arts educator*
Russell, Francia *ballet director, educator*
Thomas, Karen P. *composer, conductor*

Sedro-Woolley
Weaver, Diane Celeste *music educator*

Spokane
Halvorson, Marjory *opera director*

Toledo
Welch, Kathryn Anne *music educator*

Wenatchee
Rappé, Teri Wahl *piano educator*

WEST VIRGINIA

Elkins
Marshall, Elizabeth *performing company executive*

Fairmont
Skidmore, Dorothy L. *music educator*

Huntington
Wiebe, Kimberly P. *music educator*

Lost Creek
Smith, Babs G. *music educator*

Mannington
Reese, Katherine Rose *music educator*

Morgantown
Kinsey, Donna Lee *music educator*
Saeler, Penelope *music educator*
Wilson, Mary Alice *violinist, music teacher*

Ona
Smalley, Rhonda E. *music educator*

Parkersburg
Gunter, Norma *artistic director*
Thorp, Carol Lyn *elementary school music educator*

Princeton
Moody, Frances Marie *former performing arts educator, musician*

Ravenswood
Woods, Abbi Johnson *music educator*

Saint Marys
Moffett, Patricia Lou *music educator*

Salem
Raad, Virginia *pianist, lecturer*

Wayne
Davis, Paula May *music educator*

WISCONSIN

Appleton
Meyer, Cheryl Lorraine *music educator*

Barron
Anderson, Ruth Ilene Monier *music educator*

Beloit
Licary, Cheryl Ann *music educator, church musician*

Delafield
Zupan, Mary Anne *music educator, consultant*

Delavan
Lepke, Charma Davies *musician, educator*

Eau Claire
Tubbs, Virginia Carol *music director*

Fond Du Lac
Eby, Patricia Lynn *music educator*

Gillett
Brown, Kathryn Ann *music educator*

Greenfield
Jirovec, Mary Ann *music educator*
McKillip, Patricia Claire *operatic soloist*

Hartland
Schabow, Nancy A. Dexter *music educator*

Holcombe
Randall, Rhonda Michaele *music educator*

Kenosha
Amborn, Pauline Gall *music educator*

Kiel
Bauer, Cheryl Kristine *music educator*

Madison
Faulkner, Julia Ellen *opera singer*
Rosser, Annetta Hamilton *composer*

Marinette
Malmstadt, Mary Jane *music educator*

Middleton
Semmes, Sally Peterson *choreographer, educator, performer*

Milwaukee
Harris, Christine *dance company executive*
Kwak, Eun-Joo *concert pianist, music educator*

Mondovi
Alexander, Michelle Lynn *music educator*

Monroe
Bennett, Judy A. *music educator*

New Berlin
Belich, Kay S. *music educator*

Oconto
Dorner, Darlene A. *music educator*

Racine
McPheron, JoAnn Marie *music educator, poet*
Schoening, Ruth Irene *retired music educator, musician*

Rhinelander
Pekol, Marilyn Patricia *music educator, musician*

Sheboygan
Mueller, Jeanne Karen *music educator*

Shorewood
Bowers, Jane Meredith *music educator*

Verona
White, Carolyn Louise *music educator*

Waterford
Rindo, Linda Sue *music educator*

Watertown
Ruesink, Linda Joan *music educator*

Waukesha
Backhaus, Patricia Dawn *musician, educator*
Floeter, Valerie Ann *music educator*

West Allis
Bautz, Jennifer Jean *music educator*

West Bend
Wysocky, Karen Ann *music educator*

WYOMING

Dubois
Glasser, Pamela Jean *musician, music educator*

Green River
Evans, Eileen *music teacher*

Lander
Bakke, Luanne Kaye *music educator*

Lovell
Dickson, Linnea E. *music educator*

Sheridan
Moore, Pamela Sue *music educator*
Robertson, Lisa Rae *music educator*
Tonak, Loretta Jean *music educator, librarian*
Bartol, Katherine Aurelia *music educator, mezzo soprano*
Ethridge, Sally Annette *music educator*

TERRITORIES OF THE UNITED STATES

PUERTO RICO

San Juan
San Miguel, Lolita *artistic director*

CANADA

BRITISH COLUMBIA

Vancouver
Jones, Norah *vocalist, musician*
Krall, Diana *musician*
Lavigne, Avril *musician*
Murray, Anne *singer*

ONTARIO

Toronto
Goh, Chan Hon *ballerina*
Hodgkinson, Greta *dancer*

QUEBEC

Montreal
Von Gencsy, Eva *dancer, choreographer, educator*

Kingston
Dokken, Aurora Dawne *music educator*

Montreal
Moss, David *conductor*

AUSTRALIA

Darlinghurst
Davis, Judy *actress*

Redfern
Campion, Jane *director, screenwriter*

DENMARK

Copenhagen
Martin, Vivian *soprano*

ENGLAND

Leeds
Ichino, Yoko *ballet dancer*

London
Arman Gelenbe, Deniz *concert pianist*
Duncan, Lindsay Vere *actress*
Glover, Jane Alison *conductor*
Minton, Yvonne Fay *mezzo-soprano*
Osbourne, Kelly Lee *television personality, singer*
Uchida, Mitsuko *pianist*

Richmond
Te Kanawa, Kiri *opera and concert singer*

FRANCE

Paris
de Havilland, Olivia Mary *actress*

IRELAND

Galway
Mullen, Marie *actress*

ITALY

Milano
Brown, Deborah Elizabeth *television producer, consultant*

Palermo
Smith-Lombardini, Maryelizabeth Anne *opera singer, artistic director*

NEW ZEALAND

Wellington
Paquin, Anna *actress*

SWITZERLAND

Küsnacht
Jones Dame, Gwyneth *soprano*

ADDRESS UNPUBLISHED

Abell, Sara Nightingale *music educator, musician*
Abrams, Stephanie Bass *performing company executive*
Adams, Susan Lois *music educator*
Adato, Perry Miller *documentary producer, director, writer*
Adkins, Kathy Forester *music educator*
Aghdashloo, Shohreh *actress*
Ahearn, Holly Ande *music educator*
Aitchison, Bridget Mary *theater educator, theater director*
Alarcon, Sylvia M. *music educator*
Aliga, Olivia R. *music teacher, choral director*
Allen, Charity E. *music educator*
Allen, Marilyn Myers Pool *theater director, video producer*
Alley, Kirstie *actress*
Allston, Charita Capers *music educator*
Alpers, Denise Kay Anderson *music educator*
Amend, Kate *film editor, educator*
Amgott, Madeline *television producer, media consultant*
Anderson, Cherine E. *television and film production manager, special events planner, marketing executive*
Andrews, Dame Julie (Julia Elizabeth Wells) *actress, singer*
Applegate, Christina *actress*
Arenal, Julie (Mrs. Barry Primus) *choreographer*
Armatrading, Joan *singer, songwriter*
Aronson, Luann Marie *actress*
Arthur, Beatrice *actress*
Aurori, Michele Dawn *music educator*
Autry, Lola Mae *music educator*
Azelton, Rebecca Joy *music educator*
Baber, Yongsook Kim *musician*
Bacon, Jeri Ann *music educator*
Baerwald, Susan Grad *television broadcasting company executive producer*
Ball, Marcia *vocalist*
Ballard, Tina Rowann *music educator*

Rolland, Clara *pianist, educator*
Rook, Judith Rawie *television producer, writer*
Rose, Debbie J *music educator*
Roseanne, (Roseanne Barr) *actress, comedienne, television producer, writer*
Rowlands, Gena *actress*
Rowley, Kara Dawn *music educator*
Rudner, Sara *dancer*
Russell, Elise Beckett *piano teacher*
Russo, Kristen Danielle *music educator*
Rutter, Marie E. *music educator*
Ruviella-Knorr, Jeanne L. *music educator, consultant, clinician*
Ryder, Winona (Winona Laura Horowitz) *actress*
Saint, Eva Marie *actress*
Salz, Sue *music educator*
Sapp, Gina Leann *music educator*
Sarry, Christine *ballerina*
Savage, Jill A. *music educator*
Scarwid, Diana Elizabeth *actress*
Schiffer, Claudia *model*
Schmidt, Angela Marie *music educator, musician*
Schmidt, Sheri Lynn *band director*
Schmitt, Elizabeth Marie *music educator*
Schoeniger, Jane *music educator*
Schubert, Barbara Schuele *retired performing company executive*
Schuur, Diane Joan *vocalist*
Sciorra, Annabella *actress*
Scott, Sue A. *music educator*
Seaman, Mary *theater educator*
Seibel, Sharon *music educator*
Seifert-King, Lori Ann *performing company executive*
Seiter, Kati Elizabeth *music educator*
Shaftman, Rachel Ellen *music educator, musician*
Shanks, Ann Zane *filmmaker, producer/director, photographer, writer*
Shannon, Charlotte P. *music educator*
Shatin, Judith *music composing educator*
Shaver, Michelle M. *music educator*
Shelby, Peggy Lee *music educator*
Shepherd, Cybill Lynne *actress, singer*
Shields, Brooke Christa Camille *actress, model*
Shire, Talia Rose *actress*
Shoemaker, Jennifer Lynn *music educator*
Shull, Claire *documentary film producer, casting director*
Sikes, Cynthia Lee *actress, children's advocate, singer*
Silverstein, Barbara Ann *conductor, artistic director*
Simmons, Deidre Warner *retired performing company executive, arts consultant*
Simmons, Jonathan Kimble (J.K. Simmons) *actor*
Simon, Jami Lea *actress*
Sisemore, Claudia *educational films and videos producer, director*
Skilling, Marie L. *music educator*
Skylar, Alayne *television producer, writer, talent scout, talent agent, educator*
Slipko, Natalie M. *actress, choreographer, dancer, writer*
Sluga, Yvonne Marie *radio producer, announcer*
Smith, Betty Pauline *television producer*
Smith, Charlotte Reed *retired music educator*
Smith, Cheryl Diane *music educator*
Smith, Deborah L. *music educator, secondary school educator*
Smith, Doris Irene *music educator*
Smith, Gayle Sue Swartz *theater director, choreographer*
Smith, Lois Arlene *actress, writer*
Smith, Marie Burnley *music educator*
Smith, Michele Lindsay *music educator*
Smith, Susan J *music educator, flutist*
Smith, Wendy Carol *music educator*
Smith-Epstein, Mary Kathleen *dancer*
Snyder, Colleen M. *music educator*
Somers, Suzanne Marie *actress, writer, singer*
Souther, Lisa *music educator*
Speed, Christa A. Witt *music educator*
Spillman, Marjorie Rose *producer, dancer*
Stanley, Margaret King *performing arts administrator*
Stanley, Martha Barbee *music educator*
Stark, Andrea Marie *theater educator*
Stearns, Marilyn Tarpy *music educator*
Stefani, Gwen Renee *musician*
Sternhagen, Frances *actress*
Stevens, Connie *actress, singer*
Stirling, Christine Anne *music educator*
Stoddard, Erin *actress, artist*
Stoffel, Peggi Smith *music educator*
Stone, Dee Wallace *actress*
Stoppel, Sheree' Sue *music educator*
Stringfield, Sherry *actress*
Strom, Doris Marie *music educator*
Studer, Kathy Lynn *music educator*
Stutzman, Sarah E. *music educator*
Summers, Cathleen Ann *film producer*
Sunderland, Holly Brown *church musician*
Sutton, Dolores *actress, writer*
Sutton, Nancy Thurmond *music educator*
Swallum, Maryann *musician, music educator*
Swing, Marce *producer, publisher*
Swinney, Jeanne Lyn *music educator*
Sword, Teresa Le *music educator*
Synnestvedt, Kirstin *musician, educator*
Tabor, Linda J. *performing arts educator*
Tanner, Lynn *actress*
Tarbuck, Barbara Joan *actor*
Tate, Sheila Diane *music educator*
Taylor, Elizabeth Rosemond *actress*
Tepper, Arielle *theater producer*
Teresi, Cindy *music educator*
Tharp, Twyla *dancer*
Thomas, Betty *director, actress*
Thompson-Lorenzo, Angela Christine *music educator*
Tillman, Mercia V. *musician*
Tipton, Melanie Carol *music educator*
Tolstedt, Buffy D. *music educator, musician*
Tom, Lauren *actress, singer*
Tomlin, Lily *actress*

Tooman, Stephanie *performing arts educator*
Trampusch, Christine Ann *music educator*
Traylor, Gayla S. *music educator, composer*
Treichel, Dixie Ann *composer, sound designer, consultant*
Trenhaile, Jennifer Ann *music educator*
Troll, Kitty *actress, writer*
Tubb, Betty Lou *music educator*
Tugend, Jennie Lew *film producer*
Turner, Tina (Anna Mae Bullock) *singer*
Tyrrell, Rosemary *performing company executive, educator*
Uken, Marcile Rena *music educator*
Upbin, Shari *theatrical producer, director, agent, educator*
Upham, Esther J. *music educator*
Urista, Diane Jean *music educator, researcher*
Vaccaro, Brenda *actress*
Vani, Anita H. *music educator, voice educator*
Varis, Jina Aleksandra *voice educator*
Vedder, Nena Helene *music educator*
Von Brandenstein, Patrizia *production designer*
von Furstenberg, Betsy *actress, writer*
Vozheiko Wheaton, Lena *music educator, pianist*
Wagner, Melinda *musician, composer*
Wallace, Sarah Fitzgerald *music educator*
Wallis, Diana Lynn *artistic director*
Wallner, Amanda Ober *retired music educator*
Walsh, Diane *pianist*
Walston, Barbara H. *music educator*
Warberg, Willetta *concert pianist, writer, piano educator*
Ward, Anne Starr Minton *music educator, musician*
Warren-MacNaught, Felicia *music educator, musician*
Warrick, Lola June *agent*
Watson, Vera K. *music educator, pianist, conductor*
Webb, Lucy Jane *actress, film producer, consultant*
Webb, Martha Jeanne *author, speaker, film producer*
Weeks, Skyla Gay *music educator*
Weimer, Jessica R. *music educator*
Weiner-Heuschkel, Sydell *theater educator*
Wells, Kitty (Muriel Deason Wright) *country western singer*
Wen, Gwen GuoYao *music educator*
West, Karen Marie *music educator, musician*
West, Nettie J.R. *music educator*
Westbrook, Deborah Kay *music educator*
White, Loray Betty *TV talk show host, writer, television producer, vocalist, actress, television director*
White, Roslyn R. *music educator*
White, Shelby Kathryn *music educator*
Wiener, Cheryl Renee *music educator, musician*
Wiese, Denise Kay *music educator*
Wiest, Dianne *actress*
Williams, Jeanne Elizabeth *music educator*
Wilmoth, Jennnifer Lynn *music educator*
Winter, Kathryn *music educator, writer*
Wise, Patricia *opera singer and educator*
Wolf, Muriel Hebert *soprano, performing company executive, music educator*
Wood, Vivian Poates *mezzo soprano, educator, writer*
Woodard, Alfre *actress*
Woods, Eleanor C. *music educator*
Wooten, Carol G. *conductor, music educator*
Woronov, Mary Peter *actress*
Wright, Gladys Stone *music educator, composer, writer*
Wright, Romona Xylena *music educator*
Yacoub, Allison *music educator*
Yaes, Joyce *musician, artist, educator*
Yearwood, Trisha *country music singer, songwriter*
Yokum, Jane *music educator*
Young, Theresa Elizabeth Jennifer *music educator*
Yu, Jessica *director, producer, writer, editor*
Zemlin, Susan Carol *music educator*
Ziemba, Karen *actress*

ARTS: VISUAL

UNITED STATES

ALABAMA

Albertville
Hall, Ramona Shields *art educator*

Birmingham
Carmichael, Mary Alice *artist, genealogist*
Hopkins, Martha Ann *sculptor*
Keller, Armor *artist, arts advocate*
Kluge, Janice *art educator*

Fairfield
McCaslin, LaTanya *art educator*

Florence
Knight, Karen Anne McGee *artist, educator*

Huntsville
Eskridge, Carole Fay *artist*
Simpson, Debra Brashear *artist*

Leeds
Westberg, Polly Pembrooke *art educator*
Wilson, Maggie Isabelle Lovell *art educator, English educator*

Madison
Johnson, Kathy Virginia Lockhart *art educator*

Mobile
Clausell, Deborah Deloris *artist*

Thompson, Nancy *art director*

Montgomery
Jacobs, Jane L. *artist, state agency administrator*
Tullos, Barbara Waddell *art educator*

Phenix City
Witsell, Ethel Holden Howard *artist*

Tuskegee
Thomas, Elaine Freeman *artist, educator*

ALASKA

Anchorage
Din, Herminia *art educator, museum staff member, researcher*

Cordova
Bugbee-Jackson, Joan *sculptor, educator*

Fairbanks
Jones-Butler, Jacqueline *painter, poet*
Murakami, Gael Baxley *artist*

ARIZONA

Chandler
Matus, Nancy Louise *artist*

Chino Valley
Casey, Bonnie Mae *artist, educator*

Douglas
Murphy, Cathy Emily *photographer, educator, journalist*

Flagstaff
Edgerton, Debra *artist, educator*

Mesa
Kaida, Tamarra *art and photography educator*

Paradise Valley
McCall, Louise Harrup *artist*

Payson
Salomon, Marilyn *artist*

Peoria
Willard, Garcia Lou *artist*

Phoenix
Bechtel, Katie Ellen *art educator, artist, writer*
Bonnell, Gayla *art educator*
Dignac, Geny (Eugenia M. Bermudez) *sculptor*
Stone, Hazel Anne Decker *artist*

Scottsdale
Lang, Margo Terzian *artist*
Vanier, Jerre Lynn *art director*

Sedona
Darrow, Jane *artist*
Vayanian, Solara Zakeli *artist, educator*

Sonoita
Posey, Faith E. *artist*

Sun Lakes
Hall, Barbara Louise *interior designer, artist*

Sunsites
Datcu, Ioana *visual artist*

Tempe
Girón, Angela *artist, educator*

Tucson
Lascelles, Susan *artist*
Lowe, Lynn Rae *sculptor, educator, small business owner*

ARKANSAS

Batesville
Wallace, Marcia Gayle *art educator, theater educator, photographer*

Berryville
Brown, Frances Louise (Grandma Fran) *artist, art gallery owner*

El Dorado
Botti Villegas, Maria Marta *artist, art educator*

Huntsville
Musick, Pat *artist*

Jacksonville
Lawrence-Cox, Nancy Nell *artist, retired executive secretary*

Lamar
Bollman, Peggy *art educator*

Little Rock
Cline, Ann *artist, designer*
Fowler, Jennefer Rae *sculptor*
Johananoff, Pamela *jewelry designer, manufacturer, gemologist*

Mountain View
Meyer, Eleanor Catherine *artist, educator*

CALIFORNIA

Altadena
Johnson, Kristen Marie *art director*

Anaheim
Barkemeijer de Wit, Jeanne Sandra *graphic artist, illustrator, writer, multimedia consultant*
Bennett, Genevieve *artist*

Angels Camp
Taylor, Lyda Revoire Wing *artist, gallery owner*

Arcata
Dojka, Jennifer Mimi *art educator, artist*
Land-Weber, Ellen *photography educator*

Atascadero
Meyer, Lois Kathryn *graphic artist*

Auburn
Rothwell, Elaine B. *artist*

Bakersfield
Robinson, Chalita Brossett *art educator, artist*

Berkeley
Bendix, Jane *artist, author, anthropological illustrator*
Genn, Nancy *artist*
Hillinger, Edith *artist*
Ione, Amy *artist, researcher*
Jones, Patricia Bengtson *sculptor*
Polos, Iris Stephanie *artist*
Rapoport, Sonya *artist*
Ratcliff, Mary Curtis *artist, educator*
Siskin, Sharon Valerie *art educator*
Sussman, Wendy Rodriguez *artist, educator*

Beverly Hills
Amador, Miranda Barbara *artist*
Rodkin, Loree *jewelry artist*

Big Sur
Spring, Barbara Ethel *sculptor*

Burbank
Boruck, Holly *artist*

Canoga Park
Kamatoy, Lourdes Aguas *artist*
Rosenfeld, Sarena Margaret *artist*

Carmel
García, Beth Baxter *sculptor, writer*

Carmel Valley
Sands, Sharon Louise *graphic design executive, art publisher, artist*

Carson
Hirsch, Gilah Yelin *artist, writer*

Claremont
Dunye, Cheryl *artist, film maker*
Lachowicz, Rachel *artist, art educator*
Rankaitis, Susan *artist*

Concord
Broadbent, Amalia Sayo Castillo *graphic arts designer*

Culver City
Gordon, Florence Irene *graphic artist, illustrator*
Grant, Joan Julien *artist*

Daly City
Kennedy, Gwendolyn Debra *artist, scriptwriter, playwright*

Davis
DePaoli, Geri M. (Joan DePaoli) *artist, art historian*
Keizer, Susan Jane *artist*
Ovejero, Graciela *artist*
Powers, Gay Havens-Monteagle *artist, educator*

El Cerrito
Hargis, Barbara Louise *artist*

Encino
Badham, Julia Aileen *artist*

Escondido
Carey, Catherine Anita *artist, art educator*

Folsom
Campbell, Ann Marie *artist*
Terranova, Elizabeth (Elisa) Jo *artist*

Fresno
Stuart, Dorothy Mae *artist*

Glendora
Starobin, Nancy Ruth *photographer*

Hollister
Miller, Alisa Dorothy Norton *artist*

Huntington Beach
Isabelle, Beatrice Margaret *artist*

Indio
Zorick, Nancy Lee *artist, actress*

La Jolla
Cohen, Barbara Ann *artist*
Jenik, Adriene *artist, educator*
Merrim, Louise Meyerowitz *artist, actress*
Whitaker, Eileen Monaghan (Eileen Monaghan) *artist*

La Mesa
Harmening, Gail Joan *craft pattern designer*

Lafayette
Monheit, Molly Jane *artist*
Shurtleff, Akiko Aoyagi *artist, consultant*

Laguna Beach
Powers, Runa Skötte *artist*

Laguna Hills
Block, Amanda Roth *artist*
Schachter, Bernice *sculptor, educator, writer*

Laguna Niguel
Zagon, Laurie *artist*

Lake Isabella
Ozanich, Ruth Shultz *artist, poet, retired elementary educator*

Larkspur
Napoles, Veronica *graphic designer, consultant*

Loleta
Schoenfeld, Diana Lindsay *photographer, educator*

Long Beach
Bowen, Fern Chambers *artist, educator*
Pizzo, Pia *artist, educator*
Sanders, Joan Skogsberg *artist*

Los Alamitos
Rippo, Olga Alicia *art director*

Los Altos
Sherwood, Patricia Waring *artist, educator*

Los Angeles
Apple, Jacki (Jacqueline B. Apple) *artist, writer, educator*
Baca, Judith F. *art educator*
Benedict, Cheyann *apparel designer*
Burbank, Lynda A. *painter*
Caroompas, Carole Jean *artist, educator*
Crawford, M. Holly *artist, writer, educator*
De Larios, Dora *artist*
Dismukes, Valena Grace Broussard *photographer, former physical education educator*
Hamilton, Patricia Rose *art dealer*
Hoffman, Margaret Ann Hovland *artist, activist*
Johnston, Ynez *artist, educator*
Kupper, Ketti *artist*
LeMay, Nancy *graphic designer, painter*
Lucoff, Kathy Ann *art advisor*
Moss, Susan Hecht *artist, writer*
Pastor, Jennifer *sculptor*
Smith-Meyer, Linda Helene (Linda Smith) *artist*
Stansfield, Claire *apparel designer*
Swildens, Karin Johanna *sculptor*
Terrell, Ann *artist, educator*
Wells, Annie *photographer*

Los Osos
Van Ekeren, Ybi *artist*

Manhattan Beach
Lee, Gloria Deane *artist, educator*

Mckinleyville
Morris, Marjorie Hale *artist, writer*

Mendocino
Alexander, Joyce Mary *illustrator*
Masterson, Julie Cosgrove *photographer*

Merced
LeCocq, Karen Elizabeth *artist*

Mission Viejo
McAfee, Margaret Anne *retired art educator*

Montecito
Brenken, Hanne Marie *artist*

Moraga
O'Brien, Bea Jae *artist*

Newport Beach
McManigal, Penny *artist*
Spitz, Barbara Salomon *artist*

North Shore
Kopp-Kelly, Jennifer Lee *technical illustrator*

Northridge
Weatherup, Wendy Gaines *graphic designer, writer*

Novato
Popovic, Bozena (Bo Popovic) *artist*

Oakdale
Saletta, Mary Elizabeth (Betty Saletta) *sculptor, rancher*

Oakhurst
Gyer, Jane E. *artist, educator*

Oakland
Alba, Benny *artist*

Oceanside
Sarkisian, Pamela Outlaw *artist*

Orange
Banning, Donna Rose *retired art educator*

Orinda
Dorn, Virginia Alice *artist, art gallery director*
Epperson, Stella Marie *artist*

Pacific Palisades
Helfgott, Gloria Vida *artist*
Kaufer, Shirley Helen *artist, painter*

Palm Desert
Kaufman, Charlotte King *artist*
Reordan, Beverly Jean *artist*

Palm Springs
Tennyson, Louise H. *artist*

Palo Alto
Capparell, Lorraine Susan *artist, sculptor, painter*
Gunther, Barbara *artist, educator*
Saegesser, Marguerite M. *artist*

Panorama City
Janis, Elinor Raiden *artist, educator*

Pasadena
Iturbide, Graciela *photographer*
Pashgian, Margaret Helen *artist*
Sanchez, Pauline Stella *artist*

Petaluma
Fuller-McChesney, Mary Ellen *sculptor, writer, publisher*

Piedmont
Mayeri, Beverly *artist, ceramic sculptor, educator*

Prather
Marvin, Freda Mary *art educator, nurse*

Ramona
Newman, Malane L. *digital designer, cartoonist, illustrator, computer graphics designer, educator, small business owner*

Rancho Palos Verdes
Kolosvary-Stupler, Eva *sculptor*

Redding
D'Amico, Petrina *sculptor*

Redondo Beach
Engstrom, Stephanie Cloes *wildlife artist, small business owner*

Redwood City
Stirm, Doris Elizabeth *artist*

Riverside
Smith, Dorothy Ottinger *jewelry designer, civic worker*

Roseville
Potterton, Barbara Alice *artist, educator, illustrator*
Smith, Kaye Train *artist*

Sacramento
Piskoti, Carol Lee *art educator*

San Carlos
Oliver, Nancy Lebkicher *artist, retired elementary education educator*
Sullivan, Shirley Ross (Shirley Ross Davis) *art collector*

San Diego
Barone, Angela Maria *artist, researcher*
Farmer, Janene Elizabeth *artist, educator*
Howard, Mildred *sculptor*
Krupchak, Tamara *artist*
Sorrentino, Renate Maria *illustrator*

San Francisco
Calvin, Carolina *apparel executive, designer*
Chin, Sue Soone Marian (Suchin Chin) *conceptual artist, portraitist, photographer, community affairs activist*
Davis, Joan Elan *artist*
Dickinson, Eleanor Creekmore *artist, educator*
Dignan, Eleanor A. *artist*
Frey, Viola *sculptor, educator*
Hardin, Heidi *artist, educator*
Hershman, Lynn Lester *artist*
Lamanet LaLonde, Shari *artist*
McClintock, Jessica *fashion designer*
Pearlman, Amalia Cecile *artist, educator*
Raciti, Cherie *artist*
Van Hoesen, Beth Marie *artist, printmaker*

San Gabriel
Smith, June Sylvia Kolbe *artist, educator*

San Jose
Abbott, Barbara Louise *artist, educator*
Ballarian, Anna Nevarte *retired art educator*
Burkhart, Sandra Marie *art dealer*
Caywood, Barbara May *artist, educator*
Landauer, Susan E. *art historian*
Purpura, Grace *artist, retired art educator*

San Juan Capistrano
Burns, Toni Anthony *artist*

San Pedro
Parkhurst, Violet Kinney *artist*

Santa Barbara
Gold, Calla Giselle *jewelry designer*

Santa Clara
Lane, Holly Diana *artist*

Santa Cruz
Leites, Barbara L. (Ara Leites) *artist, educator*

Santa Maria
Bowker, Margaret Sheard *artist*
Hoyt, Mary G(enevieve) *artist, educator*

Santa Monica
Haroon, Nasreen *artist*
Josepher, Susan Ann *art educator, consultant*
Lockhart, Sharon *artist*
Wong, Diana Shui Iu *artist*
Wosk, Miriam *artist*

Santa Rosa
Fruiht, Dolores Giustina *artist, educator, poet*
Monk, Diana Charla *artist, stable owner*
Weare, Sally Spiegel *art educator, artist*

Santa Ynez
Rymer, Ilona Suto *artist, retired art educator*

Sausalito
Ramsey, Eleanore Edwards *design bookbinder*

Sherman Oaks
Alcott-Jardine, Susan *artist, writer*
Atwood, Colleen *costume designer*
Powell, Sandy *costume designer*
Weiss, Julie *costume designer*

Sierra Madre
Converse, Elizabeth *artist, writer*

Solana Beach
Tall, Cheryl A. *artist, art educator*

Sonoma
Fellows, Alice Combs *artist*
Minelli, Helene Marie *artist*

Sonora
Sharboneau, Lorna Rosina *artist, educator, author, poet, illustrator*

Stockton
Wright, Evelyn Louise *artist*

Studio City
Boyett, Joan Reynolds *arts administrator*
Lasarow, Marilyn Doris *artist, educator*
Manders, Susan Kay *artist*
Rotblatt, Joy J. *artist*

Sunnyvale
Daltchev, Ana Ranguel *sculptor*
Seeger, Virginia Vincent *portrait painter*

Templeton
Foster-Wells, Karen Margaret *artist*

Thousand Oaks
Heyer, Carol Ann *illustrator*
Relkin, Michele Weston *artist*

Torrance
Barnard, Cynthia Marie *art educator, artist*

Vacaville
Biscevic, Nancy Lunsford *photographer*
Leonard, Suzanne Louise *artist, photographer*

Valencia
Wilson, Millie L. *artist, educator*

Van Nuys
Cook, Jenik Esterm (Jenik Esterm Cook Simonian) *artist, educator*
Vasylyeva, Anna *artist, writer*

Venice
Alf, Martha Joanne *artist*
Edelstein, Jean *artist, performance artist*

Ventura
Granata, Donna Assunta *photographer, educator*

Vista
Tadeo, Elvia *artist*

Walnut Creek
Goldman, Anne L. *ceramic artist*
Reimann, Arline Lynn *artist*

Westlake Village
Weiss, Barbara G. *artist*

Windsor
Matkin, Judith Conway *jewelry designer and manufacturer*

Woodland Hills
Ebin, Cynthia Rebecca *artist, sculptor*

COLORADO

Arvada
Halley, Diane Esther *artist*
Moorhead, Jennifer Theresa *art educator*

Aspen
Hough, Jennine *artist*
MacPhail, Wendy Rowena *art educator, artist*
Mitchell, Karen Frances *artist, jewelry designer*

Aurora
McKenney, Muriel Anita *art educator, engineer*

Boulder
Verdill, Elaine Denise *artisan*

Carbondale
Keeney, Karen Elaine *photographer, educator, anthropologist*

Colorado Springs
Brierre, Micheline *artist*
Lirette, Dorothy Lou *artist, educator*
Tögel, Cornelia (Conni) D. *artist*
Winfield, Karen Ann *art educator, artist, small business owner*

Creede
Hague, Angela L. *artist, gallery manager, art consultant*

Delta
Carson, Marlene Ann *artist*

Denver
Enright, Cynthia Lee *illustrator*
Graham, Pamela Smith *artist, distributing company executive*
Kaplan, Sandra Lee *artist*

Shwayder, Elizabeth Yanish *sculptor*
Steigerwald-Clausen, Beverly *sculptor, educator*

Dolores
Winterer, Barbara Jean *designer, author*

Durango
Balas-Whitfield, Susan *artist*

Elizabeth
Gale, Rebecca J. *artist*

Englewood
Brennan, Joann *photographer, educator*
Kristin, Karen *artist*
Lamb, Darlis Carol *sculptor*

Fort Collins
Gonzalez, Rosita Christine *photographer*

Littleton
Poduska, T. F. *artist*

Louisville
Price, Julia Larkin *art educator*

Loveland
Bierbaum, Janith Marie *artist*
Schockner, Jan Rosetta (Rosetta) *sculptor*
Weresh, Thelma Faye *sculptor, artist*

Norwood
Hollinbeck, Ethel Lindell *sculptor*

CONNECTICUT

Avon
Drapeau, Suzanne Eva *art educator*

Branford
Wulke, Joy *artist*

Bridgeport
Mahmud, Shireen Dianne *photographer*

Chester
Zwart-Ludeman, Theresa *graphics designer, artist*

Cos Cob
Kane, Margaret Brassler *sculptor*
Neal, Irene Collins *artist, educator*

Gaylordsville
Dunn, Virginia *artist, community volunteer*

Georgetown
Roberts, Priscilla Warren *artist*

Greenwich
DeNigris, Carole Dell Cato *artist*
Pope, Ingrid Bloomquist *sculptor, poet*

Groton
Stoddard, Elizabeth (Lolly) *artist, writer*

Hartford
Carey, Ellen *artist*

Ivoryton
Osborne, Judith Barbour *artist*

Kensington
Manning, Brenda Argosy *painter*

Milford
Curt, Denise Morris *artist, limner, photographer*

Monroe
Cote-Beaupre, Camille Yvette *artist, educator*

Mystic
Rooney, Maria Dewing *photographer*

Naugatuck
Chrzanowski, Rose-Ann Cannizzo *art educator*
Mannweiler, Mary-Elizabeth *painter*

New Britain
Marshall, Cora Maria *art educator, artist, researcher*

New Canaan
Christensen, Donna Radovich *needlecraft designer, consultant, educator*

New Haven
Feinstein, Rochelle *artist, educator*
Lindroth, Linda (Linda Hammer) *artist, curator, writer*

New London
Seelbach, Anne Elizabeth *artist*
Wakeman, Martha Jane *artist, educator*

Norwalk
Babcock, Catherine Evans *artist, educator*
Bennett Minnerly, Denise Patricia *artist, art educator*

Old Greenwich
Kelley, Wendy Thue *fine art advisor, independent curator*

Redding
Bailey, Mary Katherine *sculptor, writer*
Bernier, Tina *artist*

Sherman
Goodspeed, Barbara *artist*
Sandor, Jocelyn R. *artist*

Stamford
Berets, Eileen Tolkowsky *artist*
Roberts, Victoria Lynn P. *antique expert*

Stonington
Elliott, Inger McCabe *designer, textile company executive, design consultant*

Trumbull
Hofbauer, Michele Pace *illustrator, writer*

Wallingford
Lauttenbach, Carol *artist*

Washington
Grimes, Margaret Whitehurst *artist, educator*
Porter, Priscilla Manning *artist*

West Hartford
Uccello, Vincenza Agatha *artist, director, educator emerita*

Weston
Reinker, Nancy Cooke *artist*

Westport
Chernow, Ann Levy *artist, art educator*
Kraus, Hilda *designer, artist*
McTague-Stock, Nancy A. *painter, printmaker*
Reilly, Nancy (Anne Caulfield Reilly) *painter*
Siff, Marlene Ida *artist, designer*

DELAWARE

Dagsboro
Davis, Marica Nanci Ella Riggin *retired artist*
Hanna, Anne Marie *artist*

Greenville
Cooch, Nancy duPont (Mrs. Edward W. Cooch Jr.) *sculptor*

Lewes
Costigan, Constance Frances *artist, educator*

New Castle
Keane, Marie Jeanette (Maria Keane) *art educator, artist*

Wilmington
Bounds-Seemans, Pamella J. *artist*

DISTRICT OF COLUMBIA

Washington
Biddle, Catharina Baart *artist*
Bowman, Dorothy Louise *artist*
Brown, Pamela Wedd *artist*
Carroll, M(argaret) Lizbeth Carr *art educator, graphics designer, photographer*
Cleary, Manon Catherine *artist, educator*
Colton Skolnick, Judith A. *artist*
Fall, Dorothy *artist, art director, administrator*
Forrester, Patricia Tobacco *artist*
Gordon, Dorothy K. *silversmith, goldsmith*
Kapikian, Catherine Andrews *artist*
Kelso, Gwendolyn Lee *silver appraiser, consultant*
Lorens, Emalie Sigrid *artist, educator, museum staff member*
Polan, Annette Lewis *artist, educator*
Ravenal, Carol Bird Myers *artist*
Shinolt, Eileen Thelma *artist*
Shute, Roberta E. *sculptor*
Tacha, Athena *sculptor, educator*
Truitt, Anne Dean *artist*
Weaver, Donna L. *engraver*
Weifenbach, Terri Lynn *photographer, printer*

FLORIDA

Bal Harbour
Bernay, Betti *artist*

Boca Raton
Fineman, Geraldine Gottesman *artist*
Pelish, Susan Marion *sculptor, painter*
Rothschild, Barbara *artist, educator*

Bonita Springs
Elliott, Donna Louise *artist*
McNamara-Ringewald, Mary Ann Thérèse *artist, educator*

Boynton Beach
Harwood, Bernice Baumel *artist, community volunteer*

Clermont
Cox, Margaret Stewart *photographer*

Cocoa
Ollie, Pearl Lynn *artist, singer, songwriter*

Coral Gables
Schwartz, Ana Stella *art dealer, gallery owner*

Dania
Satin, Claire Jeanine *sculptor, book artist*

Delray Beach
Gilfilen, Teri *artist*
Greenspan, Gladys *textile designer*
Schwarz, Rose Oberman *artist*

Edgewater
Schubert, Jeanne *artist*

Englewood
McClellan, Joan C. Osmundson *retired art educator, artist*

Fort Lauderdale
Ambrose, Judith Ann *designer*
Moorhead, Rolande Annette Reverdy *artist, educator*
Sargent, Jan *art appraiser*

Fort Myers
Dean, Jean Beverly *artist*
Hugill, Chloe *artist, office administrator*
Weiss, Susette Maré *technical and photographic consultant, mass communications and media relations specialist, investor*

Fort Pierce
Jefferson, Zanobia Bracy *art educator, artist*

Gulf Stream
FitzSimons, Marjorie Kitchen *art consultant*

Hollywood
Sadowski, Carol Johnson *artist*

Homosassa
Frank, Elizabeth Ahls (Betsy Frank) *art educator*

Indialantic
Pavlakos, Ellen Tsatiri *sculptor*

Indian Harbor Beach
Traylor, Angelika *stained glass artist*

Jacksonville
Eden, F. Brown *artist*
Holmes, Rachel Ellen Flynn *sculptor*
Loomis, Jacqueline Chalmers *photographer*
Schultz, Nancy Reilly *artist*

Key Largo
Kennedy, Mary Sussock *artist*

Lake Helen
Dillashaw, Eula Catherine *artist, graphic artist*

Lake Mary
Reagan, Bettye Jean *artist*

Lake Park
Heaton, Janet Nichols *artist, art gallery director*

Longboat Key
Molles, Emily DeMartino *artist, real estate broker*

Marathon
Wolpe, Marcy Shear *artist, art educator*

Melbourne
Dillen, Nancy Baur *art educator, artist*
Failla, Sophia Lynn *artist, educator*
King, Virginia Shattuck *painter, retired school nurse practitioner, educator*

Melrose
Harley, Ruth *artist, educator*

Miami
Chambers, Elenora Strasel *artist*
Kislak, Jean Hart *art director*
Marks, Shirley Isaacson *artist*
Mendieta, Raquelín Maria de la Concepción *artist*
Moran, Kate *sculptor, photographer*
O'Brien, Amy V. *apparel designer*
Tumpson, Joan Berna *artist*

Miami Beach
Rut, Wanda E. *artist, educator, writer*

Micco
Christoph, Frances *painter*

Mount Dora
Kirton, Jennifer Myers *artist*

Naples
Gifford, Nancy (Mumtaz) *artist, poet*

Nokomis
Novak, Joyce Keen *artist, secondary school educator*
Robinson, Mary Catherine *artist*

Okeechobee
Mercer, Frances deCourcy *artist, educator*

Palm Bay
Galitello-Wolfe, Jane Maryann *artist, writer*

Palm Beach
Krois, Audrey *artist*

Palm Beach Gardens
Samuels, Fern Jacqueline *artist, educator*

Palm Coast
Wiggins-Rothwell, Jeanine Ellen *artist*

Panama City
Whitsitt, Marjorie Rae *artist, educator*

Pensacola
Burke-Fanning, Madeleine *artist*
Maki, Hope Marie *artist, sculptor, illustrator, poet, educator*

Plantation
Ballantyne, Maree Anne Canine *artist*

Pompano Beach
Amisano, Bernadette Parker *artist*
Levine, Ruth Hannah *retired sculptor*

Port Saint Lucie
Hammer, Elizabeth Carter Bowers *art educator*

Rotonda West
Broyles, Christine Anne *art educator*

Sanibel
Keogh, Mary Cudahy *artist*

Sarasota
DiPirro, Joni Marie *artist*

Plunket, Dolores *art and archaeology educator*
Savenor, Betty Carmell *painter, printmaker*
Stedman, Myrtle Lillian *artist*
Williams, Tanya Dawn *art appraiser, consultant*
Winterhalter, Dolores August (Dee Winterhalter) *art educator*

Satellite Beach
Osmundsen, Barbara Ann *sculptor*

Sebastian
Pieper, Patricia Rita *artist*

Tallahassee
Kessler, Mitzi Lyons *artist*

Tamarac
Baron-Malkin, Phyllis *artist, art educator*

Tampa
Haselwood, Alicia Jane *photographer*
Hine, Betty Dixon *design consultant*
Nadrotoska, Barbara Anna *art educator*

Temple Terrace
Kashdin, Gladys Shafran *painter, educator*

University Park
Davis, Tufts *artist*

West Palm Beach
Baker, Dina Gustin *artist*

Weston
Deleuze, Margarita *artist*
Napp, Gudrun F. *artist*
Piken, Michele Reneé (Penn) *artist, photographer*

GEORGIA

Alpharetta
Sirlin, Deanna Louise *artist*

Atlanta
Alexander, Constance Joy (Connie Alexander) *stone sculptor*
Blalock, Clara Dodd *artist*
Cone-Skelton, Annette *artist, museum director*
Fisher, Carlyn Feldman *artist, writer*
James, Rose Victoria *sculptor, poet*
Rhodes, Ann Frances Bloodworth *artist, art history lecturer*
Richards, Jacqueline *artist, curator*
Rodríguez, Rocío *artist*
Venzer, Dolores *artist*
Wilmer, Mary Charles *artist*
Winslow, Anne Branan *artist*

Augusta
Schultz, Nancy Jansson *artist*

Avondale Estates
Carroll, Jane Hammond *artist, writer, poet*

Carrollton
Sheesley, Mary Frank *art educator*

Clarkesville
Davis, Marilyn Ruth *artist*

Claxton
Odum, Felicia Sellers *art educator*

Columbus
Hedges, Julie Elaine *photographer*
Owens, Deborah *artist, writer*

Conyers
Myers, Sheila John *artist*

Darien
Davis, Ann Richardson *artist, sculptor, book dealer, writer*

Douglas
Baars, Ella Jane *art educator*

Jasper
Sutter, Jean *sculptor*

Lagrange
Greene, Annie Lucille *artist, retired art educator*

Ludowici
Stokes, Melanie Miller *art educator*

Macon
Kinzie, Carole G. *artist*
Long, Shirley June Stafford *artist, educator*
Weaver, Jacquelyn Kunkel Ivey *artist, educator*

Marietta
Lahtinen, Silja Liisa *artist*
Lowe, Pamela Mary *art educator*

Riverdale
Buchanan, Mariah Spann *artist*

Roswell
Devine, Libby *art educator, consultant*

Savannah
Aja-Herrera, Marie *fashion designer, educator*
Aquadro, Jeana Lauren *graphic designer, educator*
Gabeler, Jo *artist*
Vonschlegel, Patricia *artist*

Scottdale
Borochoff, Ida Sloan *artist*

Stockbridge
Cordobes, Dorothy Eskew *art educator*

Tybee Island
Smith, Tricia E. *artist*

HAWAII

Honolulu
Betts, Barbara Stoke *artist, educator*
Chun, Jacqueline Clibbett *artist, educator*
Pickens, Frances Jenkins *artist, educator*
Thompson, Karen Marie *art educator*
Yeh, Hsiao Yen C. *artist*

Kapaa
duPont, Nicole *artist*

Kihei
Galesi, Deborah Lee *fine artist*

Makawao
Ayers, Katherine Stone *artist, chiropractor*

IDAHO

Meridian
Shaffer, Mary Louise *art educator*

ILLINOIS

Batavia
Waranius Vass, Rosalie Jean *artist*

Bourbonnais
Wilkey, Elmira Smith *illustrator, artist, publisher, writer, educator*

Chicago
Altman, Edith G. *sculptor*
Aubin, Barbara Jean *artist*
Bernstein, Gerda Meyer *artist*
Boggs, Jessica Lynn *creative director, web designer*
Bowman, Leah *fashion designer, consultant, photographer, educator*
Campos-Pons, Maria Magdalena *artist*
Chandler, Estelle T. *artist*
Coffey, Susanna Jean *art educator*
Crane, Barbara Bachmann *photographer, educator*
Doering, Deborah Adams *artist, educator*
Gaines-Masak, Anne Farley *artist, art educator*
Kenney, Estelle Koval *artist, educator*
La Civita, Jennifer *artist, columnist, cultural organization administrator*
Look, Dona Jean *artist*
Lycardi, Joan C. *artist*
MacNamara, Ann Margaret *artist, educator*
McGrail, Jeane Kathryn *artist, educator, poet, curator*
Migdal, Ruth Aizuss *sculptor, educator*
Pallasch, Magdalena Helena (Mrs. Bernhard Michael Pallasch) *artist*
Sigler, Hollis *artist, educator, author*
Smith-Romer, Helene Bonnie *artist, educator*
Smoller, Irene Mildred *artist, educator*
Wilson, Anne Gawthrop *artist, educator*

Crystal Lake
Salvesen, B. Forbes *artist*

Dekalb
Rollman, Charlotte *artist, educator*

Dixon
Huber, Marianne Jeanne *art dealer, appraiser*

East Dundee
Simons, Gail S. *artist, educator, librarian*

El Paso
Prairie-Steber, Cheryl Lee *art educator, graphics designer*

Elgin
Colpitts, Gail Elizabeth *artist, educator*

Elmwood Park
Hofmann, Kay Joyce *sculptor, artist*

Evanston
Nueske-Perez, Barbara Allen *art educator*
Pinsky, Joanna K. *artist, artistic director*
Rago-McNamara, Juliet Maggio *artist*
Tolf, Gale Maureen *artist, educator*

Glencoe
Siske, Regina *artist*

Highland Park
Slavick, Ann Lillian *retired art educator*

Lake Forest
Van Ella, Kathleen E. *fine art consultant*
Weston, Dawn Thompson *artist, researcher*

Libertyville
Gertz, Suzanne C. *artist*

Northbrook
Cakora-Netzky, Leslie Lynn *photographer*

Oak Park
McMahon, Margot Ann *sculptor, art educator*
Senese, Suzanne Marie *art educator, music educator, performance artist*

Palos Hills
Schonauer, Kathleen G. *jewelry designer, small business owner*

Park Forest
Bricker, Joyce Lynn *art educator*
Cribbs, Maureen Ann *artist, educator*

Saint Charles
Bull, Martha *artist, educator*
Malinowski, Maryellen *photographer, artist*

Table Grove
Thomson, Helen Louise *artist*

INDIANA

Anderson
Olson, Carol Lea *lithographer, educator*

Beverly Shores
Collins, Moira Ann *graphics and communications company executive, calligrapher*

Bloomington
Stines, Betty Irene *artist*
York, Karen Sue *artist, art historian*

Burlington
Roussakis, Dorothy Ferguson *artist*

Evansville
Baker, Gloria Marie *visual artist, art educator*
Roth, Carolyn Louise *art educator*

Fort Wayne
Ushenko, Audrey Andreyevna *painter, art historian, educator*

Freetown
Frederick, Shelley Cannon *artist*

Indianapolis
Rutledge, Joanne *artist, consultant*

Loogootee
Hotz, Martha Pauline *artist*

Martinsville
Cupka, Nancy Irvine *artist, educator*

Munster
LeMonnier, Shari Smith *artist*

Nashville
Kriner, Sally Gladys Pearl *artist*

Richmond
Kennedy, Barbara Ellen Perry *art therapist*

West Lafayette
Lord, Victoria Lynn *artist*

IOWA

Ames
Bruene, Barbara Jane *artist, educator*

Brighton
Guy, Donna S. *artist*

Davenport
Jecklin, Lois Underwood *art corporation executive, consultant*
Townsend, Julie Rae *artist, educator*
Van Dyke, Wendy Johanna *artist*

Decorah
Maurland, Anne Elisabeth *potter*

Iowa City
Hettmansperger, Sue *artist*
Young, Laura Elizabeth *artist*

KANSAS

Atwood
Goodwin, Stephanie Ruth *art educator, finance educator*

Baldwin City
English, Evonne Kludas *artist*

Chase
Stull, Evalyn Marie *artist*

Emporia
Henry, Elaine Olafson *artist, educator*

Kansas City
Amundson, Beverly Carden *artist*

LaCygne
Tillery-Kriske, Charlene *art educator*

Lawrence
Ramberg, Laura Louise *sculptor*

Overland Park
Riordan, Rosemary Ann *art educator, consultant*

Prairie Village
Schmitz, Jennifer Dawn *art educator*

Topeka
Lee, Karen *art appraiser*
Peters, Barb Waterman *artist, educator*

Wa Keeney
Kerth, Roberta Jean *artist*

KENTUCKY

Benton
Brown, Sharon Webb *art educator*

Fort Wright
Sullivan, Connie Castleberry *artist*

Lexington
Boyer, Lillian Buckley *artist, educator*
Snowden, Ruth O'Dell Gillespie *artist*

Louisville
Alford, Alana Floyd *art educator*

Prospect
Garner, Joyce Craig *artist*

LOUISIANA

Baton Rouge
Rutledge, Katherine Burck *artist*

Cecilia
Girouard, Tina *artist, curator*

Covington
Rohrbough, Elsa Claire Hartman *artist*

Lafayette
Barry, Mildred Castille *artist*

Metairie
Ales, Beverly Gloria Rushing *artist*
Bonvillian, Pauline *artist*
Crosby, Deborah Berry *artist*
Foucha, Laura Theresa *computer graphics designer, film maker, writer*

New Orleans
Best, Susan Marie *artist, educator*
Emery, Lin *sculptor*
Jordan, Louise Herron *art educator*

Shreveport
Hughes, Mary Sorrows *artist*
Morelock, Jasmine Crawford *artist*
Wray, Geraldine Smitherman (Jerry Wray) *artist*

Slidell
Risher, Mary Lou Bishop *artist*

Zachary
Mills, Elizabeth Jennings *art educator*

MAINE

Anson
Harwood, Lynne *artist, book designer*

Biddeford
Riley, Pamela Jennings *artist*

Cape Neddick
Morphew, Dorothy Richards-Bassett *artist, real estate broker*

Ellsworth
Heath, Audrey Mary *artist, jewelry designer*

Gorham
Bearce, Jeana Dale *artist, educator*

Scarborough
Warg, Pauline *artist, educator*

South Portland
Huntoon, Abby Elizabeth *artist, teacher*

York
Haley, Priscilla Jane *artist, printmaker*
Hallam, Beverly (Beverly Linney) *artist*

MARYLAND

Annapolis
Alderdice, Cynthia Lou *artist*
Fowler, Terri (Marie Therese Fowler) *artist*
Thoms, Josephine Bowers *artist*

Baltimore
Barnes, Janet Lynn *artist*
Bishop, Jennifer Ann *photographer*
Carper, Gertrude Esther *artist, marina owner*
Helberg, Kristin Vaughan *artist*
High, Maria Louise *artist*
Kramer, Norma Domenica Andrea *artist*
Lion, Jill Altschul *sculptor*
Sands, Cori Eileen *artist*
Tenser, Beth Hillary *graphics designer, art director*

Beltsville
Reed, Marseeda *photographer*

Berlin
Smith, Gloria Young *retired graphic artist, art educator*

Bethesda
Day, Marylouise Muldoon (Mrs. Richard Dayton Day) *appraiser*
Dayhoff, Nancy Belmont *artist*
Fleming, Patricia Stubbs *artist*
Koenig, Elizabeth Barbara *sculptor*
Sarnoff, Lili-Charlotte (Lolo Sarnoff) *artist*

Brookeville
Rico, Stephanie Allcock *art educator*

Cabin John
Bergfors, Constance Marie *artist, educator*

Catonsville
Lanciotti, Judi D. *art educator*

Chevy Chase
Duvall, Bernice Bettum *artist, exhibit coordinator, jewelry designer*
Kranking, Margaret Graham *artist, educator*

Churchton
Miller, Sandra Ritchie *artist, art therapist*

Galena
Hunsperger, Elizabeth Jane *art and design consultant, educator*

Hyattsville
Raines, Charlotte Austine Butler *artist*

Lanham Seabrook
Southall, Virginia Lawrence *retired artist*

Olney
Hendricks, Susan McCurdy *art educator, artist*

Pasadena
Kuhn, Jolyn *artist*

Pikesville
Portnoy, Leslie Snyder *art educator, artist*

Silver Spring
Goertzel, Gwendolyn Michele *painter, priest*
Hall, Davida Karen *art educator, elementary school educator*
Jaffe, Elaine June *creative fiberwork designer*
Ott, Mary Diederich *artist*
Power, Barbara Louise *artist, educator*
Woolard, Connie Ward *artist, retired art gallery manager*

Woodbine
Nuss, Barbara Gough *artist*

MASSACHUSETTS

Amherst
Elman, Naomi Geist *artist, producer*
Lasch, Pat *artist, educator*

Andover
Hastings, Cynthia Lampros *graphic artist, photographer*

Auburn
Berg, G. Vivian *artist*

Barnstable
Lummus, Carol Travers *artist, printmaker*

Boston
Ablow, Roz Karol (Roselyn Karol Ablow) *painter, curator*
Baker, Sam Ann Kontoff *environmental artist, art educator*
Gallagher, Ellen *artist*
Nierman, Meredith Alisa *multimedia producer*
Parker, Olivia *photographer*

Brookline
Barron, Ros *artist*

Burlington
DeCrosta, Susan Elyse *graphic designer*

Cambridge
Chandler, Fay Martin *artist*
Dobson, Parrish *photographer, educator*
Goldring, Elizabeth *environmental media artist, poet*
Pollock, Rachel Elizabeth *costume designer*
Slosburg-Ackerman, Jill Rose *artist, educator*

Chestnut Hill
Eutemey, Karen Denise *art educator, sculptor*

Chicopee
Costanzo, Nanci Joy *art educator*

Cohasset
Replogle, Jeanne Lonnquist *artist*

East Bridgewater
Heywood, Anne *artist, educator, author*

Fall River
Andrade, Manuela Pestana *art educator*

Gloucester
Swift, Marilyn K. *artist, educator*
Swigart, Joan B. *artist, art consultant*

Holyoke
Powell, Kathleen Trestka *artist, educator, editor*

Marblehead
Heins, Esther *botanical artist, painter*
Seamans, Beverly Benson *sculptor*

Mattapoisett
Bertram, Christine G. *artist, painter, graphics designer*

Natick
Geller, Esther (Bailey Geller) *artist*
Shapero, Esther Bailey Geller *artist*

Needham
Carr, Iris Constantine *artist, writer*

New Bedford
Lincoln, Rosamond Hadley *modern painter, photographer*

North Attleboro
Cote, Louise Roseanne *art director*

Northampton
Rupp, Sheron Adeline *photographer, educator*

Norwell
Brett, Jan Churchill *illustrator, author*

Orleans
Hogan, Ruth DeWitt *artist*

Osterville
Kennedy, Michele Lyn *artist*
McLean, Susan O'Brien *artist*

Peabody
Dee, Pauline Marie *artist*

Plymouth
Cully, Mikki *artist*
Freyermuth, Virginia Karen *art educator*

Reading
Frey, Joanne Alice Tupper *art educator*
Nordstrand, Nathalie Elizabeth Johnson *artist*

Rockport
Calabro, Joanna Joan Sondra *artist*

Southbridge
O'Brien, Christine Leduc *art educator*

Springfield
Frey, Mary Elizabeth *artist*

Waltham
Corbato, Emily S. *photographer, researcher, musician*

Wayland
Smith, Joan Trimble *artist*

Wellesley
McGibbon, Phyllis Isabel *art educator, artist*

West Chatham
Dimm, Susan Tyner *art educator, artist*

Westfield
Conant, Tara Patricia *photographer*

Weston
Fine, Sally Solfisburg *artist, educator*
Rearick, Anne *photographer, educator*

Westport
Sexton, Janice Louise *artist*

Williamstown
Blair, Phyllis E. *artist*

MICHIGAN

Ann Arbor
Busard, Roberta Ann *artist, educator*

Birmingham
Ashleigh, Caroline *art and antiques appraiser*

Bloomfield Hills
Burnett, Patricia Hill *portrait artist, author, sculptor, lecturer*

Cadillac
Fisher, Christine Lynne *art educator, artist*

Camden
Falls, Kathleene Joyce *photographer*

Capac
Wagner, Dorothy Marie *retired senior creative designer, artist*

Dearborn
Orlowska-Warren, Lenore Alexandria *art educator, fiber artist*

Detroit
Aaron-Taylor, Susan Wendy *sculptor, educator*
Moldenhauer, Judith A. *graphic design educator*

Douglas
Karamas, Joyce Efthemia *art educator, consultant, artist*

Farmington Hills
Eisner, Gail Ann *artist, educator*

Grand Rapids
Bolt, Eunice Mildred DeVries *artist*
Frye, Della Mae *portrait artist*
Jackoboice, Sandra Kay *artist*
Stewart, Debbie Elaine *artist, librarian, artist*

Grosse Ile
Stump, M. Pamela *sculptor*

Grosse Pointe
Disanto, Carol L. (Carol La Chiusa) *artist*

Grosse Pointe Farms
Thibodeau, Virginia Durbin *artist*

Holland
Van Noord, Diane C. *artist, educator*

Houghton
Beckwith, Mary Ann *art educator*

Kalamazoo
Brodbeck, Mary Lou *artist, furniture designer*
Ruttinger, Jacquelyn *director of exhibitions*

Lansing
Brendahl, Marcia *artist, illustrator, designer*

Mount Pleasant
Hiar, Danielle Marie *graphics designer, educator*
Traines, Rose Wunderbaum *sculptor, educator*
Wood, Sigrid Lynn *art educator*

Okemos
Wager, Paula Jean *artist*

Petoskey
Switzer, Carolyn Joan *artist, educator*
Thomson, Valerie Anne *artist, art gallery owner*

Plainwell
Flower, Jean Frances *art educator*

Port Sanilac
Emerich, Suzan Marie *art educator, artist*

Royal Oak
Chambers-McCarty, Lorraine *painter, educator*

Saint Clair Shores
Kachman, Frances Guiducci *artist*
Valetti, Leota May *artist*

Sparta
Bomhof, Robyn *artist, educator*

Wyandotte
Dunn, Gloria Jean *artist*

MINNESOTA

Coon Rapids
Goodstein-Shapiro, Florence (Florence Goodstein Walton) *artist, art historian*

Edina
Holman, Iletta Marcella *retired art educator*

Long Lake
Hofkin, Ann Ginsburgh *photographer, poet*

Minneapolis
Hand, Mary Jane *artist*
Lyon, Joyce *artist, art educator*

Rochester
Swenson, Constance N. *artist*

Saint Paul
Matteson, Clarice Chris *artist, educator*
Olson, Bettye Johnson *artist, retired educator*
Smith, Rosemary *artist, educator*

Two Harbors
Gredzens, Sandra May Pillsbury *art educator*

MISSISSIPPI

Brandon
Schoolar, Laurel Ann *artist, educator*

Clinton
Causey, Carley Claire *art educator, consultant, art therapist, researcher*

Greenwood
Wacht, Leny Nowag *art educator*

Hattiesburg
McRaney, Joan Katherine *artist*

Jackson
Wolfe, Mildred Nungester *artist*

Moss Point
Stephens, Cecile Higdon *artist*

Starkville
Durst, Jo *artist, educator*

MISSOURI

Bourbon
Heitsch, Leona Mason *artist, writer*

Butler
Baxter, Myrtle Mae (Bobbi Baxter) *artist*

Chesterfield
Fowler, Marti *fine arts consultant*
Kruse, Margaret M. *art educator*

Columbia
Robins, Betty Dashew *antiques and arts dealer*

Ferguson
Lawrence, Trudy Kay *art educator*

Fredericktown
Sudmeyer, Alice Jean *artist, poet*

Hermann
Mahoney, Catherine Ann *artist, educator*

Hollister
Canfield, Cindy Sue *art educator*

Houston
Morgan, Brenda Gaye *art educator*

Independence
Willett, Teri Kay *art educator*

Kansas City
Aylward, Marcia Eileen *artist, educator*
Hutson, Betty Switzer *art educator, artist*
Lawrence, Susan *art dealer*
Lee, Margaret Norma *artist*
Mast, Kande White *artist*
Sanchez, Beatrice Rivas *art institute executive, artist*

Knob Noster
Engle, Cynthia Louise *art educator*

Lewistown
Terpening, Virginia Ann *artist*

Platte City
Kalin, D(orothy) Jean *artist, educator*

Rogersville
Durio, Evelyn Marguerite Dailey *artist, musician*

Rolla
Brewster, Louise Boone *artist, educator*

Saint Louis
Bradley, Marilynne Gail *advertising executive, advertising educator*
Harris, Teresa Maria *visual artist*
Lipan, Petruta E. *semiotician, curator, artist*
Ott, Sabina *art educator*
Rosen, Adrienne *artist, educator*
Sago, Janis Lynn *photography educator*
Shucart, Evelyn Ann *artist, educator*
Ward-Brown, Denise *sculptor, educator*

Seymour
Rudolph, Wanda *art educator*

Sibley
Morrow, Elizabeth Hostetter *sculptress, museum administrator, farmer, educator*

Sikeston
Tesseneer-Street, Susan *photographer, artist, writer*

Springfield
Brennan, Deborah Ann *artist*
Jayne, Arlene Mae *artist*

Stover
Reynolds, Sallie Blackburn *artist, civic volunteer*

Sturgeon
Dawkins, Amy *artist*

Webster Groves
Gergeceff-Cooper, Lorraine *artist, consultant*

MONTANA

Billings
Deschner, Jane Waggoner *photo artist, public relations consultant*

Bozeman
Gibson, Luanne Eileen *visual artist, educator*

Miles City
Walden, Alice *artist, educator*

Roundup
Stanfel, Jane Ellen *artist, adult education educator*

NEBRASKA

Kearney
Hoffman, M. Kathy *graphic designer, packaging designer*

Lincoln
Neal, Mo (P. Maureen Neal) *sculptor*

Whitney
Tejeda-Brown, Mary Louise *artist*

NEVADA

Fallon
Venturacci, Toni Marie *artist, substitute educator*

Henderson
Hara-Isa, Nancy Jeanne *graphic designer, county official*

Incline Village
Ealy, Cynthia Pike *artist, realtor*

Las Vegas
Oettinger, Kathleen Linda *artist*
Slade, Barbara Ann *art educator*

Mesquite
Alcorn, Karen Zefting Hogan *artist, art educator, journalist*

North Las Vegas
Sullivan, Barbara Jean *artist*

Reno
Newberg, Dorothy Beck (Mrs. William C. Newberg) *portrait artist*

NEW HAMPSHIRE

Alstead
Beetle, Kate *designer, illustrator, calligrapher*

Canaan
Taussig, Margaret C. *artist*

Hampstead
Bolton, Elizabeth (Margaret Bolton) *artist, poet*

Hanover
Silliman, Nancy Priscilla *artist, writer*

Londonderry
Verani, Patricia Lewis *sculptor*

Lyme
Wise, Joanne Herbert *art director*

Mason
Jones, Elizabeth Orton *artist, author*

Newport
Gayvoronsky, Ludmila *artist, educator*

Stratham
Terry, Elizabeth Hays *needlepoint designer*

Windham
Khanbegian, Jean M. *artist*

Wolfeboro
Bonin, Suzanne Jean *artist*

NEW JERSEY

Basking Ridge
Frediani, Diane Marie *graphics designer, interior designer, executive secretary*

Bayonne
Graham, Theresa Anne *art educator*

Beach Haven
Schreiber, Eileen Sher *artist*

Bernardsville
Spofford, Sally (Sally Hyslop) *artist*

Bloomingdale
Farrell, Donna Marie *photographer, graphic artist*

Bogota
Koshimitsu, Keiko *artist*

Bridgeton
Chanatry-Howell, Lorraine Marie *artist, designer, educator*

Bridgewater
Glesmann, Sylvia-Maria *artist*

Caldwell
Palombo, Lisa *artist*

Califon
Clipsham, Jacqueline Ann *artist*
Rosen, Carol Mendes *artist*

Chatham
Glover, Janet Briggs *artist*

Clinton
Lish, Donna Lee *art educator*

Collingswood
Creamer-Franke, Shannon *graphic design company executive*

Dover
Hammond-Rector, Susan Glynn *illustrator, photographer, sculptor*

Englewood Cliffs
Lerner, Renée *artist*

Fairfield
de Smet, Lorraine May *artist*

Franklin Lakes
Baker, Cornelia Draves *artist*

Hoboken
Rose, Roslyn *artist*

Jamesburg
Sinclaire, Estelle Foster *appraiser, writer, former educator*

Jersey City
Barney, Christine J. *artist*

Lake Hiawatha
Andreucci-Budney, Deborah Ann *artist*

Leonia
Thiesfeldt, Sheila M. *artist, educator, small business owner*
Wilson, Marcia Sandmeyer *artist*

Linwood
Chernoff, Deborah Shelley *art educator*

Maplewood
Woods, Krystyna Janina *artist, pharmacist*

Margate City
Pronesti, Rosa C. *artist*

Marlboro
Moskowitz, Danielle Mara *art educator, artist*

Marlton
Cullen, Mary Lynne *artist*

Matawan
Luis, Belinda *graphic designer*

Medford
Mayer, Joyce Harris *artist*

Mendham
Smith, Elizabeth *artist*

Metuchen
Ackerson, Patricia Kathleen Freis *art educator, artist*
Arbeiter, Joan *artist, educator*
Fasciale, Yvonne M. *art educator, musician*

Montclair
Kawecki, Jean Mary *sculptor*
Phillips, Ann Y. *art advisor*

Morristown
Prince, Leah Fanchon *art educator and research institute administrator*

Mountain Lakes
Starger, Victoria Gondek *artist*

New Brunswick
Goffen, Rona *art educator, educator*

New Providence
Celler, Adeline (Lynn) Marie *art educator*
Rivo, Shirley Winthrope *artist*

Northvale
Heslin, Cathleen Jane *artist, designer, entrepreneur*

Oldwick
Svoboda, Joanne Dzitko *artist, educator*

Oradell
Struck, Norma Johansen *artist*

Paramus
Teichman, Evelyn *antiques appraiser, educator, estate liquidator*

Perth Amboy
Lavin-Pennyfeather, Rose *artist*

Piscataway
Rosalsky, Barbara Ellen *artist, home health aide*

Pittstown
Bennett, Joan Hierholzer *artist*

Princeton
Berridge, Mary Lloyd *photographer*
Boretz, Naomi Messinger *artist, educator*
Kahn, Eiko Taniguchi *artist*

Princeton Junction
Rose, Peggy Jane *artist, art educator, gifted education advocate*

Randolph
Tomaino, Leah Karratoglou *artist*

Ringwood
Day, Ann Elizabeth *artist, educator*

Roselle Park
Brown, Reni (Arlene Patricia Theresa Brown) *artist*

Salem
Carpenter, Margaret S. (Molly Carpenter) *artist*

Seaside Park
Golembeski, Beverly Long *artist, art educator*

Short Hills
Henn, Cynthia *artist, educator*

South Bound Brook
Weir, Sonja Ann *artist*

Springfield
Baker, Alden *artist*
DeVone, Denise *artist, educator*

Stockton
Taylor, Rosemary *artist*

Summit
Good, Joan Duffey *artist*
Rousseau, Irene Victoria *artist*

Teaneck
Indick, Janet *sculptor*

Tenafly
Schoenberg, Coco *sculptor*

Trenton
Brearley, Candice *fashion designer*
Chavooshian, Marge *artist, educator*

Union
Whitelaw, Dolores Fahey *artist*

Ventnor City
Robbins, Hulda Dornblatt *artist, printmaker*

Waldwick
Samuelson, Billie Margaret *artist*

Watchung
Abrams, Donna Marie *art educator*

Whippany
Petitto, Barbara Buschell *artist*

NEW MEXICO

Albuquerque
Best, Marcia A. *graphics designer, artist*
Coleman, Barbara McReynolds *artist*
Culpepper, Mabel Claire *artist*
Green, Mae Maera *artist*
Hahn, Betty *artist, photographer, educator*
Leesman, Beverly Jean *artist, art critic, art educator*
Loss, Lynne Franklin *artist, volunteer*
Miera, Lucille Catherine Miera *artist, retired art educator*
Multhaup, Merrel Keyes *artist*
Nelson, Mary Carroll *artist, writer*
Neufeld, Frances Foss *sculptor*
Nevin, Jean Shaw *artist*
Steider, Doris *artist*

Alto
Zeitelhack, Gloria Jeanne *artist*

Belen
Chicago, Judy *artist*
Turner, Aileen Archunde *artist*

Bernalillo
Pritchard, Betty Jean *retired art educator*

Caballo
Massengill, Barbara Daves *artist*

Corrales
Eaton, Pauline *artist, educator*
Williams, Juanita Rosalie *artist*

Gallup
Cattaneo, Jacquelyn Annette Kammerer *artist, educator*

Hobbs
Ebler, Marilyn Ann *graphic designer, educator*
Garey, Patricia Martin *artist*

Nogal
Moeller, Susan Elaine *artist*

Ranchos De Taos
Marx, Nicki Diane *sculptor, painter*

Rio Rancho
Duitman, Lois Robinson *artist*
Peters, Evelyn Joan *artist*

Rociada
Reed, Carol Louise *designer*

Ruidoso
Reeder, Karen Emerald *artist, educator*

Ruidoso Downs
Templeton, Ann *artist, educator*

Sandia Park
Weitz, Jeanne Stewart *artist, educator*

Santa Fe
Dehn, Virginia *visual artist*
Erdman, Barbara *visual artist*
Kirk, Flora Kay Stude *artist, accountant*
Lippincott, Janet *artist, art educator*
Perroni, Carol *artist, painter*
Shubart, Dorothy Louise Tepfer *artist, educator*
Sloan, Jeanette Pasin *artist*
York, Star Liana *sculptor*

Taos
Martin, Agnes *artist*

Vadito
Patten, Christine Taylor *artist*

NEW YORK

Albany
Lawton, Nancy *artist*

Ancramdale
Weinstein, Joyce *artist*

Ardsley
Sokolow, Isobel Folb *sculptor*

Astoria
Cannon, Carol Ann *painter*

Bay Shore
Baradzi, Amelia *stained glass artist, restorationist*

Bearsville
Ruellan, Andree *artist*

Binghamton
Adour, Colleen McNulty *art educator*
Niles, Kathryn M. *artist, art educator*
Weissman, Ann Paley *art educator, artist, consultant*

Brainard
Johnsen, May Ann *artist, sculptor*

Bronx
Adams, Alice *sculptor*
Bacarella, Flavia *artist, educator*
Greenberg, Arline Francine *artist*
Kassoy, Hortense (Honey Kassoy) *artist, sculptor, painter, printmaker*
Kitt, Olga *artist*

Bronxville
Neblett, Marcia Amelia *artist, educator*

Brookhaven
Grucci Butler, Donna *fireworks company executive*

Brooklyn
Bangs, Mary Constance (C Bangs) *artist, curator*
Biondi, Florence *freelance/self-employed artist*
Brody-Lederman, Stephanie *artist*
Carlile, Janet Louise *artist, educator*
Dantzic, Cynthia Maris *artist, educator*
Diamond, Jessica *artist*
Gianlorenzi, Nona Elena *painter, art dealer, educator*
Giusti, Karin F. *artist, educator*
Henning, Roni Anita *printmaker, artist*
Jones, Susan Emily *fashion educator, administrator, educator emeritus*
Kjok, Sol *artist, art historian, linguist, translator*
Lanzillotto, Ann Rachele *performance artist, writer*
Moore, Anne Frances *arts administrator, consultant, educator, art appraiser*
Natsume, Kaori Takami *artist, small business owner*
Plaut, Jane Margaret *art educator*
Purcell, Ann Kathryn *artist, educator, painter*
Rauschenbusch, Stephanie *artist, educator, poet*
Schaefer, Marilyn Louise *artist, writer, educator*
Shechter, Laura Judith *artist*
von Rydingsvard, Ursula Karoliszyn *sculptor*
Wilkinson, Jeanne Carol *artist, educator*
Zollar, Jawole Willa Jo *artist, choreographer*
Zweig, Janet *artist*

Buffalo
Brown, Renee *painter, art educator, minister*
Janiga, Mary Ann *art educator*
Malkiewicz, Elizabeth Mary *art director*
Samuels, Hanna *artist*

Buskirk
Johanson, Patricia Maureen *artist, architect, park designer*

Central Square
BuMann, Sharon Ann *sculptor*

Chatham
Squier, Rita Ann Holmberg *graphic designer*

Copake
Wahlers, Linda Ann Ford *writer*

Cornwall On Hudson
Abrams-Collens, Vivien *artist*

Cortlandt Manor
Rosenberg, Marilyn Rosenthal *artist, visual poet*

Croton On Hudson
Cotton, Cornelia *photographer, art dealer*
Wandel, Sharon Lee *sculptor*

Deer Park
Martone, Jeanette Rachele *artist*

Dix Hills
Fouladvand, Hengameh *artist*

East Hampton
Jaudon, Valerie *artist*
Lichtenstein, Therese Ellen *art educator*
Scott, Rosa Mae *art educator, artist*

East Quogue
Setlow, Neva Delihas *artist, research biologist*

Elmira
Mitchell, Sharon *artist, designer*

Fayetteville
Hadyk-Wepf, Sonia Margaret *artist, real estate manager*

Flushing
Bezrod, Norma R. *artist*
Carlson, Cynthia Joanne *artist, educator*
Flechner, Roberta Fay *graphic designer*
Yeo, Kim Eng *artist*

Great Neck
Seidler, Doris *artist*

Halesite
Grey-Bethiel, Shari *artist, sculptress, jewelry designer*

Hastings On Hudson
Benedis, Sheila Meyer *sculptor*

Heuvelton
Ponko, Vera *artist, museum intrepreter*

Huntington
Maglione, Lili *artist, consultant*

Hurley
Mazzilli, Roslyn *sculptor*

Irvington
Rainer, Renata Urbach *artist, photographer, educator*

Ithaca
Garrison, Elizabeth Jane *artist*
Howley, Teresa Moorehouse *artist*

Jamaica
Cocchiarelli, Maria *artist, educator*
Jones, Cynthia Teresa Clarke *artist*

Jeffersonville
Harms, Elizabeth Louise *artist*

Lake Placid
Rickard, Anne Colton *art educator, artist*

Long Island City
Donneson, Seena Sand *artist*
Munro, Roxie Jean *artist, educator, illustrator, writer*
Popian, Lucia *artist*
Rychlak, Bonnie Lee *artist, museum curator*

Manhasset
Foley, Cornelia MacIntyre *retired artist*

Marcellus
Corrigan-Syrocki, Patricia Ann *art educator*

Massapequa
Goldberg, Beth Sheba *artist, educator, art therapist*

Mattituck
Berman, Patricia Karatsis *arts specialist*

Middle Village
Heyd, Eva *photographer*

Monroe
Centeno-Dainty, Sonia Margarita *artist*

New Hampton
Sinnard, Elaine Janice *painter, sculptor*

New Paltz
Davidson, Thyra *artist, sculptor*
Goodell, Kathy Susan *artist, educator*

New Rochelle
Adato, Linda Joy *artist, educator*
St. John, Patricia Anne *art educator*

New York
Abish, Cecile *artist*
Adri, (Adri Steckling Coen) *fashion designer*
Arms, Anneli (Anna Elizabeth Arms) *artist, educator*
Bachner, Barbara LaVerdiere *artist*
Backstedt, Roseanne Joan *artist*
Belag, Andrea Susan *artist*
Berman, Ariane R. *artist*
Bonino, Fernanda *art dealer*
Bourgeois, Louise *sculptor*
Bradshaw, Dove *artist*
Brett, Nancy Heléne *artist*
Bull, Helen May *artist*
Casella, Margaret Mary *artist*
Castoro, Rosemarie *sculptor*
Celmins, Vija *artist*
Chu, Lili *jewelry designer, consultant*
Chwatsky, Ann *photographer, educator*
Cohen, Cora *artist*
Cooper, Paula *art dealer*
Cutler, Ronnie *artist*
Davidson, Nancy Brachman *artist, educator*
Davis, Doris Rosenbaum (Dee Davis) *artist, writer*
Davis, Lisa Corinne *artist*
DeLuccia, Paula *artist*
DeMonte, Claudia Ann *artist, educator*
Denes, Agnes C. *environmental artist*
Dennis, Donna Frances *sculptor, art educator*
Dodd, Lois *artist, art educator*
Donegan, Cheryl *artist*
Drexler, Joanne Lee *art appraiser*
Drum, Sydney Maria *artist*
Dunkelman, Loretta *artist*
Edelson, Mary Beth *artist, educator*
Eisenberg, Sonja Miriam *artist*
Eisner, Carole Swid *artist*
Enders, Elizabeth McGuire *artist*
Feuerman, Carole A. *sculptor, artist*
Field, Patricia *apparel designer*
Firestone, Susan Paul *artist*
Florendo, Andrea Oliva *art director, artist, educator*
Foster, Kim *art dealer, gallery owner*
Frankenthaler, Helen *artist*
Gage, Beau *artist*
Gering, Sandra Eileen *art dealer, curator*
Gitler, Wendy *artist, art historian, writer*
Gold, Lois Meyer *artist*
Gold, Sharon Cecile *artist, educator*
Goldsmith, Caroline L. *arts executive*
Gordon, Tina *sculptor, art therapist*
Grocholski, Basia (Barbara) G. *art director*
Grossman, Nancy *artist*
Hafner, Genevieve *photographer*
Hamoy, Carol *artist*
Hamura, Kaori *artist*
Hand, Joni Marie *art educator*
Harbutt, Sarah *photographer, director*
Harrington, E.B. *art dealer*
Harvey, Julie L. *artist*
Hermann, Mildred L. *artist*
Herrera, Carolina *fashion designer*
Hohauser, Marilyn *artist*
Honig, Ethelyn *artist*
Hull, Cathy *artist, illustrator*
Isaacs, Barbara Shivitz *painter*
Jacquette, Yvonne Helene *artist*
Javens, Kathleen Elizabeth *artist*
Johnson, Betsey Lee *fashion designer*
Johnston, Lynn Beverley *animator*
Kaish, Luise Clayborn *sculptor, former educator*
Kamali, Norma *fashion designer*
Kan, Diana Artemis Mann Shu *painter, art educator, writer*
Kaplan, Daile *photographer*
Kaplan, Deborah Renee *artist*
Karan, Donna (Donna Faske) *fashion designer*
Kenan, Brunette Johnella *graphics designer*
Khedoori, Toba *artist*
King, Marcia Gygli *artist*
Kirschner, Joyce *art dealer*
Klotz, Florence *costume designer*
Koppelman, Dorothy Myers *artist, consultant*
Korot, Beryl *artist*
Krauss, Judith Scheer *art dealer*
Krementz, Jill *photographer, author*
Kruger, Louise Virginia *sculptor*
Kutosh, Sue *artist*
Lange, Liz Steinberg *apparel designer and executive*
Lee, Catherine *sculptor, painter*
Leibovitz, Annie *photographer*
Leonard, Zoe *artist*
Lou, Liza *artist*
Margolin, Jean Spielberg *artist*
Maryschuk, Olga Yaroslava *artist, executive assistant*
Mayer, Rosemary *artist*
McHugh, Caril Eisenstein Dreyfuss *art dealer, art gallery director, consultant*
McKenzie, Mary Beth *artist*
McKinley-Haas, Mary *artist*
McNeely, Juanita *artist*
Meiselas, Susan Clay *photographer*
Miller, Nancy Suzanne *technology consultant, artist*
Miller, Nicole Jacqueline *fashion designer*
Mori, Mariko *artist*
Nengudi, Senga *artist, educator*
Niccolini, Dianora *photographer*
Ono, Yoko *conceptual artist, singer, recording artist*
Opie, Catherine *photographer*
Parker, Nancy Winslow *artist, writer*
Plavinskaya, Anna Dmitrievna *artist*
Porter, Liliana Alicia *artist, photographer, painter, print and filmaker*
Prieto, Monique N. *artist*
Recanati, Dina *artist*
Reininghaus, Ruth *retired artist*
Remington, Deborah Williams *artist*
Ringgold, Faith *artist*
Rivera, Sophie *photographer*
Robbins, Carrie F(ishbein) *costume designer, educator*
Roberts, Nancy Cohen *art dealer, marketing professional*
Robinson Derossi, Flavia *photographer, foundation executive*
Rose, Leatrice *artist, educator*
Ross, Rhoda *artist*
Rotolo, Susan *artist*
Russell, Maryanne *photographer*
St. Lifer Kennedy, Jane *art appraiser, curator*
Saint-Ouen Leung, Brigitte *art dealer, consultant*
Sand Lee, Inger *artist*
Schneider, Jane Harris *sculptor*
Schneider, JoAnne *artist*
Seborovski, Carole *artist*
Sharp, Anne Catherine *artist, educator*
Shatter, Susan Louise *artist*
Sherman, Cindy *artist*
Sigal-Ibsen, Rose *artist*
Sikander, Shahzia *artist*
Singer, Barbara Helen *photographer*
Slavin, Arlene *artist*
Sleigh, Sylvia *artist, educator*
Slitkin, Barbara Ann *artist*
Slone, Sandi *artist*
Smith, Kathryn Ann *art educator*
Smith, Kiki *artist*
Smith, Patricia Lynne *visual artist*
Smith, Shirley *artist*
Sonneman, Eve *artist*
Southworth, Linda Jean *artist, critic, educator, poet*
Spade, Kate (Katherine Noel Spade) *apparel designer*
Spence, Sique (Mary Stewart Spence) *art dealer*
Stern, Lynn Solinger *photographer*
Stewart, Leora Klaymer *textile artist, educator*
Stine, Catherine Morris *artist*
Stone, Caroline Fleming *artist*
Storrs, Immi Casagrande *sculptor*
Swergold, Marcelle Miriam *sculptor*
Swift, Mary Lou *art dealer, financial consultant*
Templeton, Fiona *performance artist, writer, director*
Thomasos, Denyse *artist*
Touhy, Linda *artist*
Trombetta, Annamarie *artist*
Upright, Diane Warner *art dealer*
Valla, Teressa Marie *artist, textile designer*
Van Goethem, Nancy Ann *painter, educator*
Vass, Joan *apparel designer*
Vennum, Joan Fay *artist*
Wald, Sylvia *artist*
Walker, Kara *artist*
Wang, Vera *fashion designer*
Watanabe, Nana *photographer*
Weems, Carrie Mae *photographer*
Williams, Sue *artist*
Williamson, Philemona *artist*
Wright, Faith-dorian *artist*
Wunderman, Jan Darcourt *artist*
Zimmerman, Kathleen Marie *artist*
Zlowe, Florence Markowitz *artist*

Newburgh
Sabini, Barbara Dorothy *artist, educator*

North Bellmore
Trigoboff, Sybelle *artist, art educator, lecturer*

Northport
Hohenberger, Patricia Julie *fine arts and antique appraiser, consultant*

Nyack
Price, Helen (Lois) Burdon *artist, retired nurse educator*

Odessa
Stillman-Myers, Joyce L. *artist, educator, writer, illustrator, consultant*

Oneonta
Sharpe, Yolanda Ruby *art educator, vocalist*

Palisades
Hyams, Harriet *artist*
Knowlton, Grace Farrar *sculptor, photographer, painter*
Porta, Siena Gillann *sculptor, educator*

Peekskill
Bennett, Lisa *artist*

Piermont
Madawick, Paula Christian *artist, educator*

Plainview
Fein, Leona Moss *artist*

Port Chester
Dessereau, April *art educator*
Duveen, Anneta *artist*

Potsdam
Sennett, Patricia M. *artist, educator*

Pound Ridge
Schwebel, Renata Manasse *sculptor*

Queens Village
Megherian, Yefkin *sculptor*

Rensselaer
Nack, Claire Durani *artist, author*

Rhinebeck
Rabinovich, Raquel *painter, sculptor*

Rochester
Frear, Lorrie *graphic designer, educator*
Kelly, Angela Mary *photographer, educator*

Rocky Point
Irizarry, Debra Edith *artist*

Roslyn Heights
Newmark, Marilyn *sculptor*

Ruby
Cole, Max *artist*

Sag Harbor
Diamond, Mary E(lizabeth) B(aldwin) *artist*

Saugerties
Starobin, Christina F. *artist, educator*

Sayville
Wurtz, Margaret Johnston *artist, calligrapher*

Scarsdale
Newman, Stacey Clarfield *artist, curator*

Shelter Island Heights
Culbertson, Janet Lynn *artist*

Southampton
Freeman, Elaine Lavalle *sculptor*
McLauchlen, Jennifer *art dealer*

Southold
Giardi, Diane M. *ceramics educator, sculptor*

Sparkill
Myers, Adele Anna *artist, educator, nun*

Sparrow Bush
Miiller, Susan Diane *artist*

Stony Brook
Pindell, Howardena Doreen *artist*

Syracuse
Darrow, Gretchen *costume designer*
King, Marcia Jones *potter, physicist, photographer*

Tappan
Golbert, Sandra *artist*

Tillson
Debrosky, Christine Anne *painter, educator*

Tonawanda
Peterson, Dorothy Lulu *artist*

Trumansburg
Kredell, Carol Ruth *artist*

Valley Cottage
Mahan, Jacqueline Francis *artist, educator*

Valley Stream
Wasserman, Muriel *artist*

Victor
McCann, Jean Friedrichs *artist, educator*

Wading River
Marlow, Audrey Swanson *artist, designer*

Wainscott
Uehling, Judith Olson *artist, painter, printmaker, sculptor*

Westbury
Sherbell, Rhoda *artist, sculptor*

Westernville
Hart, Pamela Walker *artist, educator, writer*

White Plains
Erla, Karen *artist, painter, collagist, printmaker*

Woodmere
Winick, Bernyce Alpert *artist, photographer*

Woodstock
Banks, Rela *sculptor*
Segal, Sabra Lee *artist, graphics designer, illustrator, actress*

Yorktown Heights
Jones, Lauretta Marie *artist, designer, computer science researcher*

NORTH CAROLINA

Ahoskie
Adams, Martha Jean Morris *art educator, artist*

Beaufort
Zimarino, Kay Keller *art educator*

Brevard
Dillon, Doris (Doris Dillon Kenofer) *artist, art historian, educator*

Carthage
Chambers, Margaret-Anne *art educator, muralist*

Cary
Daniels, Astar *artist*

Castalia
Wilder, Dorothy May *artist, educator, librarian*

Chapel Hill
Stevens, Phyllis A. *conceptual artist*

Charlotte
Campbell, Suzane Eva *computer graphics designer, freelance/self-employed interior designer*
Maney, Cheryl Little *art educator, arts facilitator*
Triplette, Laurance Daltroff *art advisor and appraiser*

Concord
Brown, Deborah Parke *art educator*

Davidson
Grosch, Laura Dudley *artist, teacher*

Durham
Clark, Mary Cannon *art educator*

Eden
Sanders, Barbara Fayne *artist, educator*

Goldsboro
Turlington, Patricia Renfrew *artist, educator*

Greensboro
Watson, Betty *artist*

Henderson
Williams, Ruth Russell *artist*

Huntersville
McCall, Debra Knight *art educator*

King
Shanahan, Elizabeth Anne *art educator*

Leasburg
Treacy, Sandra Joanne Pratt *artist, educator*

Leland
Karch, Jacqueline *artist*

Monroe
Helms, Katie Mae *artist*

Pittsboro
Schwinn-Jordan, Barbara (Barbara Schwinn) *painter*

Raleigh
Jordan, Brenda Moore *artist*

Salisbury
Brautigan, June Marie *artist, poet*

Whispering Pines
Catullo, Doris Jane *sculptor*

Wilmington
Baldridge, Jane L. *graphic artist, fine artist*

Winston Salem
Cieszewski, Sandra Josephine *artist, retired manufacturing company manager*

Zebulon
Ruffing, Anne Elizabeth *artist*

NORTH DAKOTA

Devils Lake
Moyer Klemetsrud, Kandace Marie *artist*

Steele
Dewitz, Lynn Marlene *art educator, consultant*

Taylor
Miller, Jean Patricia Salmon *art educator*

OHIO

Akron
Cocain Hastler, Cynthia Lucille *artist, graphic designer*
Korow, Elinore Maria *artist, educator*

Athens
Heindl, Christine *artist, educator*

Bowling Green
Leetch, Nancy Wikoff *artist*

Bryan
Nowak, Carol Lee *art educator*

Canton
Moses, Marcia Swartz *artist*
Patrick, Beth Pelletier *art educator*

Centerville
Coyle, Diane R. *artist, educator*

Chagrin Falls
Cox, Cynthia A. *art education specialist*
Ross, Sally Price *artist, painter*

Cincinnati
Anderson, Judith Ann *artist, writer*
Attee, Joyce Valerie Jungclas *artist*
Bollen, Sharon Kesterson *artist, educator*
Bruns, Patricia Ann *art educator, consultant*
Manning, Alleen Blesi *art educator, artist*
Rexroth, Nancy Louise *photographer*
Schmidt, Leeanne *artist*
Tuttle, Martha Benedict *artist*

Cleveland
Fallon, Pat *artist, educator*

Columbus
Fraser, Pamela *artist*
Gruliow, Agnes Forrest *artist, educator*
Holonitch, Roxanne Michelle *art educator*
Landrum-Bittles, Jenita *artist, educator*

Moroi, Kazue Elizabeth *sculptor*
Simson, Bevlyn *artist*

Cuyahoga Falls
Deemer, (Norma) Jean *artist*

Hamilton
Quay, Jacquelyn Sue *art educator, consultant*

Hudson
Carducci, Judith Weeks Barker *artist, former social worker*

Lakewood
Ellis, Deborah Marie *art educator*
Heston, Sara Smith *art educator, artist*

Oxford
Ewing, Susan R. *art educator, artist*
Yost, Nancy Runyon *artist, small business owner*

Peninsula
Cooke, Honore Guilbeau *artist, educator*

Perrysburg
Autry, Carolyn *artist, art history educator*

Sandusky
Shaylor, Karen Ann *artist, educator*

Springfield
Patterson, Martha Ellen *artist, art educator*

Toledo
Danko-McGhee, Katherina Elaine *art educator, consultant*
Nordin, Phyllis Eck *sculptor, painter, consultant*
Spruce, Simone Renee *art educator*

Troy
DeHart, Karen Trautmann *artist, educator*

Westerville
Lott, Vera Naomi *artist, educator*

OKLAHOMA

Ada
Dempsey, B. *artist*
Scott, Rita Fay *art educator*

Durant
Hooser, Helen *artist*

Edmond
Maye, S. Elizabeth Beth *artist, small business owner*

Lawton
Wonsewitz, Pom Cha *artist, horticulturist*

Mustang
Hutter, Teresa Ann *art educator*

Norman
Day, Adrienne Carol *artist*
Loeffelholz, Diane *art educator*
Wood, Betty Jean *conceptual artist, art educator*

Okemah
DeShields, Elizabeth Peggy Bowen *artist, educator, poet*

Oklahoma City
Boston, Billie *costume designer, costume history educator*
Whitener, Carolyn Raye *artist*

Ponca City
Warren, Maxine Wood *artist, art educator*

Tulsa
Frazier, Mary Ann *artist*
Howerton, Helen F. *artist*

OREGON

Ashland
Mannix, Alicia Gutman *artist, marketing consultant*

Eugene
Gourley, Paula Marie *art educator, artist, designer bookbinder, writer, publisher*

Gladstone
Frank, Dee *artist, educator*

Grants Pass
Nankervis, Medora B. *artist*
Remington, Mary *artist, author*
Roberts, Susan Sturgeon *art educator, writer*

Milwaukie
Davis, Terri Lee *graphics designer, writer, artist*

Newberg
Keith, Pauline Mary *artist, illustrator, writer*

North Bend
Mahon, Barbara Joanne *art educator*

Pacific City
Perez, Rose (Rose A. Perez) *painter*

Portland
Ebert, Leslie *artist*
Lorenz, Nancy *artist*
Mullane, Jeanette Leslie *artist, educator*
Stephens, Alice Elizabeth (Alice Wanke Stephens) *artist*
Thompson, Terrie Lee *graphic designer*

Prineville
Schulz, Suzon Louise *fine artist*

Silverton
Stone, Jane Buffington *artist, writer*

West Linn
Stoddard-Hayes, Marlana Kay *artist, educator*

PENNSYLVANIA

Annville
Riegle Kinch, Marie Eileen *art educator*

Ardmore
Rodriguez, Kathleen Moore *art educator*

Boyertown
Woods Coggins, Alma *artist*

Edinboro
Kowalski, Kathe A. *art educator, photographer*

Elkins Park
Erlebacher, Martha Mayer *artist, educator*

Erdenheim
Murphy, Mary Marguerite *artist*

Erie
Azicri, Nicolette Maly *art educator, artist*

Exton
Webber, Helen *artist, designer*

Glen Mills
Turner, Janet Sullivan *painter, sculptor*

Glenside
Medel, Rebecca Rosalie *artist*

Greensburg
Fajt, Karen Elaine *art educator*

Huntingdon Valley
Stephenson, Helene Ruth *painter, consultant*

Indiana
LaRoche, Lynda *artist, educator*

Jenkintown
Roediger, Janice Anne *artist, educator*

Jessup
Karluk, Lori Jean *craft designer, copy editor*

Kutztown
Speirs, Peg *art educator, artist, researcher*

Lancaster
Bernard, Ruth Faye *artist, educator*
Poser, Joan Rapps *artists agent*
Stewart, Arlene Jean Golden *designer, stylist*

Littlestown
Gall, Pamela Jane *art educator*

Meadville
Karns, Cynthia Denise *art educator*

Media
Turner, Letitia Rhodes *artist*

Midway
Pierrard-Mutton, Mary V. *artist, educator*

Millersville
Bensur, Barbara Jean *art educator, researcher*

Moon Township,
Pociernicki, Janice Louise *artist*

Narberth
Pollack, Sonya A. *artist*

Nazareth
Simpson, Veronica Ann *photographer, lab technician*

New Hope
Brandes, Doris *artist, art administrator, journalist*

Newtown Square
Vela, Laurie Story *illustrator, writer, publisher, producer*

Philadelphia
Fine, Miriam Brown *artist, educator, poet, writer*
Levy, Rochelle Feldman *artist*
Miyamori, Keiko *artist, educator*
Pildes, Sara *artist*
Saul, April *photographer*
Schaff, Barbara Walley *artist*
Spandorfer, Merle Sue *artist, educator, author*
Wolovitz, Vivian Toby *fine arts educator, artist*

Pittsburgh
Bickel, Minnette Duffy *artist*
McLean, Katherine *photographer, artist*

Pocono Lake
Caramelli, Iraina R. *artist, educator*

Port Matilda
Ritti, Alyce Rae *artist*

Richboro
Burtt, Larice Annadel Roseman *artist*

Selinsgrove
Connolly, Elma Troutman *artist, contractor, designer*

Sewickley
Silva, Pat A. *artist*

Spring Grove
Helberg, Shirley Adelaide Holden *artist, educator*

Springfield
Sellers, Lois Eileen Wagner *art director*

State College
Lintner, Karen Louise *art educator*

Swarthmore
Hungerford, Constance Cain *art educator*

Villanova
Beck, Christine Safford *photographer, publisher, volunteer*

Washington
Knight, Sherry Ann *art educator*

Wellsboro
Driskell, Lucile G. *artist*

West Chester
Beaumont, Mary *artist, art educator*
Silverthorne, Holly Appel *sculptor, educator*

West Grove
Allman, Margo Hutz *sculptor, painter*

Wyncote
Weiss, Mili Dunn *artist, educator*

RHODE ISLAND

Jamestown
Worden, Katharine Cole *sculptor*

Newport
Liotus, Sandra Mary *lighting designer, small business owner, consultant*

North Kingstown
Kilguss, Elsie Schaich *artist, gallery owner*

Pawtucket
Boghossian, Joan Thompson *artist*

Portsmouth
Byassee, Margaret Foley *art educator, poet, vocalist*

Providence
Bright, Deborah *artist, educator*
Brisson, Harriet Eldredge *art educator*
Harman, Carole Moses *retired art educator, artist*
Howes, Lorraine de Wet *fashion designer, educator*
Jenness, Rebecca Estella *artist, educator*
Leviten, Riva Shamray *artist*
Triedman, Karen *design educator, consultant*

Smithfield
Kosowski, Mary *artist, educator*

SOUTH CAROLINA

Camden
Blackwell, Dorothy Patton *artist*

Charleston
Fraser, Mary Edna *artist, educator*

Columbia
Currin, Lynne Irene *art educator*
James, Nancy Ellen *art educator*

Greenville
Earle, Patricia Nelson *artist*
McCune, Linda Williams *artist, educator*

Lexington
Holland, Gene Grigsby (Scottie Holland) *artist*

Murrells Inlet
Howard, Joan Alice *artist*

Myrtle Beach
Todd, Cheryl *art educator*

West Columbia
Byrne, Eleanor *artist*

SOUTH DAKOTA

Huron
Clatworthy, Catherine Lynn *educational trainer, graphics designer*

TENNESSEE

Chattanooga
Washburn, Sandra Paynter *art educator*

Clarksville
Sharpe, Patricia La Vonne *artist*

Dandridge
Weatherly-McWaters, Barbara Cannon *artist*

Dickson
Tucker, Julie Robyn *illustrator, art educator*

Jackson
Dennison, Norma Mae *art educator*

Kingsport
Woods, Bernice Irene *graphics specialist, small business owner*

Knoxville
Drinnon, Janis Bolton *artist, poet, volunteer*
Pirkle, Mänya Higdon *artist, craftsman*

Memphis
Crawford, Sheila Jane *elementary education librarian, reading consultant*
De Mere-Dwyer, Leona *medical illustrator*
Sams Schreiber, Carol Marie Houser *artist, graphic designer*

Murfreesboro
Reed, Angelica Denise *sculptor, writer, illustrator*

Nashville
Albright, Julia Szur *artist*
Crosswhite, Jeanette Elvira *art educator*
Oates, Sherry Charlene *portraitist, artist, photographer*

Oak Ridge
Regan-Stanton, Christa Maria *artist*

Sweetwater
Forkner, Geraldine G. *art educator, artist*

TEXAS

Abilene
Kiel, Martha Guillet *art educator*

Alpine
Fairlie, Carol Hunter *artist, art educator*

Austin
Alford, Frances Holliday *artist, retired elementary school educator*
Hamouda, Amy Bice *artist*
McEvoy, Grace Elizabeth *photographer*
Sawyer, Margo Lucy *artist, educator*

Bellville
Wentworth, Bette Wilson *artist, educator*

Belton
Fontaine-White, Barbara Frances *art educator*

Brownsville
Tarrant, Susan Kathryn *art educator*

Carrollton
Mohle, Brenda Simonson *art appraiser*
Ratliff, Mary Jean Dougherty *fine arts educator*

Cedar Hill
Moore, Jacquelyn *art educator*

Cleburne
Arnold, Sandra Ruth Kouns *photographer*

College Station
Martin, Carol Jacquelyn *artist, educator*
Perry, Helen Thomas *artist*

Corpus Christi
Bluntzer, Chispa Hernández *artist, educator*

Corsicana
Senkarik, Mikki *oil painter*

Cumby
Lytle, Debora Schubert *art educator*

Dallas
Lawrence, Annette *artist*
McKnight, Pamela Ann *art educator*
Schulz, Sandra E. *art educator*
Stephenson, Jane Connell *artist, educator*
Thompson, Tara D. *writer, career advisor, educator, illustrator*
Walsh, Dawna Hamm *art educator*

Denton
McMath, Elizabeth Moore *graphic artist*

Diboll
Tannery, Ginger *art educator*

El Paso
Martin, Conny *artist, educator*

Elgin
Hallenbeck, Pomona Juanita *artist*

Flower Mound
West, Frances Lee *retired doll artist, freelance writer*

Fort Worth
Durham, Jo Ann Fanning *artist*
Kellerman, Shirley Rose *artist*
Kimerer, Alice Louise *artist, educator*
Ray, Jessica B. *artist, poet, educator*

Fredericksburg
Wahrmund, Peggy Stieler *artist, rancher*

Garland
Hodges, Kathleen McGill *art educator*
Rogers, Sharon *art educator*

Harlingen
Knight, Normah Louise *artist*

Houston
Catchings, Kelly Suzanne *photographer*
Hamilton, Jacqueline *art consultant*
Jackson, Susanne Leora *retired creative placement firm executive*
Kelley, Michaelann *art educator*

King, Kay Wander *academic administrator, design educator, fashion designer, consultant*
Orr, Carole *artist*
Pruden, Nancy Paris *artist*
Randolph, Lynn Moore *artist*
Reid, Katherine Louise *artist, educator, author*

Hunt
Shaifer, Margaret S. *artist*

Hurst
Ivy, Marilyn Atkinson *artist, educator, art director*

Irving
Doneham, Shawna Elyse *set designer*

Kilgore
Hearne, Carolyn Fox *artist, historian, museum director*

Lakehills
Spears, Diane Shields *artist, retired art academy administrator*

Laredo
Gómez, Angela González *art educator*
Krueger, Janet Eager *artist, educator*
Watson, Helen Richter *artist, educator*

Lometa
Thompson, Mary Koleta *sculptor, non-profit organization management consultant*

Mabank
Smith, Thelma Tina Harriette *gallery owner, artist*

Marfa
Meyer, Ellen Adams *arts and small business development specialist*

Mcallen
Roberts Veliz, Senorina *artist, educator*

Midland
King, Mary Lou *artist, medical technologist*

New Braunfels
Alexander, Anna Margaret *artist, writer, educator*

North Zulch
Hill, Ellen Annette *artist*

Plano
Kuddes, Kathryn M. *fine arts director*
Lizvia, Ruth Ann Forbus *artist*

Richardson
Lelewicz, Deborah Gatlin (Debbi Lelewicz) *artist*

Rusk
Cook, Doris Adele *artist*

San Antonio
Summers, Barbara June *artist*
Wisniewski, Mary Josephine *art educator, religious organization administrator*

Seabrook
Sterling, Shirley Frampton *artist, educator*

Three Rivers
Barnes, Patricia Ann *art educator*

Whitehouse
Killian, Christine Lynn Coe *art educator*

Wimberley
Troester, Waltraud *artist, graphic designer, consultant*

UTAH

Bountiful
Peterson, Rose Ann *artist*

Salt Lake City
Jensen, Susan *instructional designer, multimedia producer*

Stansbury Park
Moyer, Linda Lee *artist, educator, author*

VERMONT

Barnard
Duckworth, Ruth *sculptor*

Belvidere Center
Lipke, Kathryn *artist, educator*

Bethel
Wells, Wendy *art educator*

Burlington
Stone, Judith Elise *artist, English educator*

Charlotte
Robinson, Sally Winston *artist*

Essex Junction
Tedd, Monique Micheline *artist*

Lyndonville
Elmes, Martha L. *art educator*

Morrisville
Furey, Annemarie Patricia *apparel designer*

Newark
Van Vliet, Claire *artist*

North Pomfret
Shepherd, Gaal *artist*

Stowe
Beach, Lisa (Elizabeth) Forster *artist, educator*

VIRGINIA

Alexandria
Alderson, Margaret Northrop *arts administrator, educator, artist*
Kim, Sook Cha *artist*
Wasko-Flood, Sandra Jean *artist, educator*
Whitson, Elizabeth Temple *graphics designer*

Arlington
Headley, Jennifer Lynn *art educator*

Blacksburg
Bosniak, Kanta *artist*
Gablik, Suzi *art educator, writer*

Charlottesville
Currie, Jo Anne *art educator*
Norment, Rachel Gobbel *artist, educator, writer*
Ohira, Akemi *art educator*
Priest, Hartwell Wyse *artist*
Smith, Sarah Bagwell *sculptor, artist, printmaker*
Weinberger, Adrienne *artist, appraiser*

Colonial Heights
Grizzard-Barham, Barbara Lee *artist*
Martin, Cynthia Marek *art educator*

Draper
Whitehurst, Mary Tarr *artist, poet, writer*

Falls Church
Kotler, Wendy Illene *art educator, social studies educator, grants coordinator*

Farmville
Shield, Julie Marie Karst *retired art educator, artist*

Flint Hill
Forbush, Sandra M. *artist, educator*

Fredericksburg
Merrill, Judith Robin *artist*

Front Royal
Harrison, (Hilde) *artist*

Glade Hill
Leitenberger, Maureen Doris *art educator*

Great Falls
Ganley, Betty *artist*

Harrisonburg
Banks, Diane P. *art educator, artist*
Theodore, Crystal *artist, retired educator*

Lynchburg
Massie, Anne Adams Robertson *artist*

Mc Lean
Edmondson, Mary Ellen *artist*
Francis, Karen *painter, television producer*
Freyer, Victoria C. *fashion and interior design executive*
Harrison, Carol Love *fine art photographer*
Scott, Concetta Ciotti *artist, art educator*
Young, Cynthia Myers *artist*

Merrifield
Judelsohn, Jennifer *artist, psychotherapist*

Midlothian
Morse, Kimberly Deane *artist*

Millboro
Sams, Ann Grasty *artist, educator*

Newport
Hutson, Patricia Fain *artist, writer*

Newport News
Camp, Hazel Lee Burt *artist*
Keech, Ann Marie *training design and multimedia consultant*

Norfolk
Frieden, Jane Heller *art educator*

Radford
Kessler, Kendall Seay Feriozi *artist*

Richmond
Kinnier, Emily P. *artist*
Miller, Sherrie Lynn *artist*
Worden, Marny *artist, musician*

Vienna
Lorfano, Pauline Davis *artist*
Milton, Carol Lynne *artist*
Yamaguchi, Yuriko Fujita *artist*

Waynesboro
Ross, Ellen Hardman *graphic designer*
Spilman, Patricia *artist, educator*

Williamsburg
Stanley, Shirley Davis *artist*

WASHINGTON

Bainbridge Island
Burns, Shirley M. *artist, educator*

Cheney
Feeney, Kendall Greer *art director, music educator*

Kondas, Patricia Ann *film studies educator*

Coupeville
Canfield, Stella Stojanka *artist, art gallery owner, educator*

Edmonds
Deering, Anne-Lise *artist, retired real estate salesperson*
Johnson, d'Elaine Ann Herard *artist, consultant*

Hoodsport
Gray, Jennifer Francine *photographer, illustrator*

Lacey
Evans, Mari *art educator*

Lilliwaup
McGrady, Corinne Young *design company executive*

Mercer Island
Langhout-Nix, Nelleke *artist*

Mukilteo
Black, Jackie John *artist*

Nordland
Kepner, Rita Marie *sculptor, writer, editor, educator*

Ocean Park
Lee, Martha *artist, writer*

Olympia
Randlett, Mary Willis *photographer*
Russman, Irene Karen *artist*
Thomas-John, Yvonne Maree *artist, interior designer*
Tremblay, Gail Elizabeth *art educator*

Richland
Ristow, Gail Ross *art educator, paralegal, children's rights advocate*
Sinerius-Rupp-Bloor, Sharon Kay *sculptor*

Seattle
Berman, Gizel *sculptor*
Blomdahl, Sonja *artist*
Garvens, Ellen Jo *art educator, educator, artist*
Gowdey, Dorothy E. *artist*
Rainbow, Dee Dee *retired art educator, sculptor*
Tift, Mary Louise *artist*
Woo, Cathy M. *artist*

Sequim
Guilmet, Glenda Jean *artist*

Silverdale
Balcomb, Mary Nelson *design studio owner*
Shaw, Annita Louise *art educator*

Snohomish
Guzak, Karen Jean Wahlstrom *artist*

Spokane
Girvin, Lila Shaw *artist*

Sultan
Duffy, Anne M. *artist*

Vancouver
Ingalls, Sudi-Suzanne L. *artist*

WEST VIRGINIA

Beckley
Lee, Carol *artist, songwriter*

Bluefield
Brown, Sheri Lynn *artist, poet, educator*

Charleston
Palumbo, Louise Corey *fashion and special events administrator*

Fairmont
DeVito, Teresa Marie *artist*

Wheeling
Phillis, Marilyn Hughey *artist*

WISCONSIN

Appleton
Amm, Sophia Jadwiga *artist, educator*

Black River Falls
Reichenbach, Laura Jean *art educator*

Casco
Bartel, Teresa J. *art educator*

Gordon
La Liberte, Ann Gillis *graphic artist, consultant, designer, educator*

Grafton
Duback, Sally Wood *artist, educator*

Hartland
Stamsta, Jean F. *artist*

Janesville
Detert-Moriarty, Judith Anne *graphic designer, educator, volunteer*

Johnson Creek
Quest, Kristina Kay *art educator, small business owner*

Kaukauna
Brewster, Margaret Emelia *artist*

Kenosha
Teegarden, Nicolee *art educator*

Madison
Fasse, Jane Ellen *art educator*
Sproule, Deborah W. *art educator, artist*

Mequon
Tucholke, Christel-Anthony *artist, educator*

Milwaukee
Hidson, Patricia Diane *artist, educator*

Oconomowoc
Conrader, Constance Ruth *artist, writer, librarian*
Driscoll, Virgilyn Mae (Schaetzel) *retired art educator, artist, consultant*
Muehlmeier, Ruth Ewart *painter, sculptor, art historian*

Oshkosh
Smith, Merilyn Roberta *art educator*

Port Washington
Provis, Dorothy L(ouise) *retired artist, sculptor*

Redgranite
Borchardt, Betsy Olk *artist*

Sheboygan
Linse, Marion Marilyn *art educator*

Stevens Point
Holter, Patra Jo *artist, art education consultant*

Watertown
Burns, Noëlle Ann *art educator*

Whitewater
Gauger, Michele Roberta *photographer, studio administrator, corporate executive*

WYOMING

Cheyenne
Moore, Mary French (Muffy Moore) *potter, advocate*

TERRITORIES OF THE UNITED STATES

PUERTO RICO

San Juan
Luna Padilla, Nitza Enid *photography educator*

CANADA

BRITISH COLUMBIA

Salt Spring Island
Raginsky, Nina *artist*

Vancouver
Bonifacho, Bratsa *artist*

NEWFOUNDLAND

Torbay
Dabinett, Diana Frances *visual artist*

NOVA SCOTIA

Halifax
Kulyk, Karen Gay *visual artist*

ONTARIO

Toronto
Astman, Barbara Ann *artist, educator*
Bolley, Andrea *artist*
Braswell, Paula Ann *artist*
Jaworska, Tamara *painter, tapestry maker*
Kooluris Dobbs, Linda Kia *artist*

QUEBEC

Saint-Adele
Rousseau-Vermette, Mariette *artist*

MEXICO

Mexico City
De La Riva, Myriam Ann *artist*

Naucalpan
Salis, Jeanne Elaine *artist*

BRAZIL

Uberlândia
Hinkle, Erika Galvão *art educator, digital artist*

ENGLAND

London
Edwards, Sylvia Ann *artist*

Richmond Surrey
Armfield, Diana Maxwell *artist, educator*

FRANCE

Benerville-Sur-Mer
Feiler, Jo Alison *artist*

Malaucene Vaucluse
Langenkamp, Mary Alice (M.A. Langenkamp) *artist, educator*

WEST INDIES

Grand Cayman Island
Ronald, Pauline Carol *retired art educator*

ADDRESS UNPUBLISHED

Abbe, Elfriede Martha *sculptor, graphic artist*
Abbey, Linda Rowe *artist, educator*
Abbott, Linda Joy *stained glass artisan, educator, photographer*
Abeles, Kim Victoria *artist*
Absher, Donna Atkins *textile designer*
Adamitis, Tina Theresa *art educator, artist*
Adler, Posy (Roslyn Adler) *artist, educator*
Adsit, Robin Viva *artist, educator*
Aldredge, Theoni Vachliotis *costume designer*
Alexander, Marjorie Anne *artist, art consultant*
Alpers, Svetlana Leontief *art educator*
Anders, Kathryn *artist, educator*
Andersson, Helen Demitrous *artist*
Andleton, Suzanne Spurlock *art educator*
Andrade, Edna *artist, art educator*
Andreason, (Sharon) Lee *sculptor*
Andrew, Dolores Molcan *art educator, artist*
Andrews, Jean *artist*
Arifi, Fatana Baktash *artist, educator*
Arndt, Dianne Joy *artist, photographer*
Arrott, Patricia Graham *artist, art instructor*
Aschheim, Eve Michele *artist, educator*
Ascone, Teresa Palmer *artist, educator*
Assael, Alyce *artist*
Aukon-Shoaff, Larisa *art educator, artist*
Aunio, Irene M. *artist*
Aust, Elizabeth Ann (Betty) *artist*
Avery, Carolyn Elizabeth *artist*
Azarian, Mary *illustrator*
Bailey, Joy Y. *art educator*
Ballou, Claudia Arceneaux *artist*
Banfill, Sally Anne *painter*
Barber, Joan Marie *artist*
Barlow, Jean *art educator, painter*
Barrett, Lora McNeece *art educator, artist*
Barth, Frances *artist*
Beerman, Miriam *artist, educator*
Begley, June Alice *art educator*
Behr, Marion Ray *artist, writer, business executive*
Bellamy, Jennifer Wiggins *artist*
Bellospirito, Robyn Suzanne *artist, writer*
Berard, Maria Dolores *clothing designer*
Berman, Eleanore *artist*
Berry, Martha Katheryn *artist*
Bethlen, Ilona R. *designer, educator*
Bierman, Sandra *artist*
Birchard, Catherine Suzanne Sieh *artist*
Birdsong, Cynthia Price *artist, art educator*
Bishop, Delores Ann *artist, educator*
Bittel, Linda Lee *art educator*
Bodie, Phyllis Jean *art educator, watercolorist*
Bogdanowicz, Loretta Mae *artist, educator*
Bohannon, Janice Gail Treadway *art educator, artist*
Boldovitch, Gerri *art educator*
Bonassi, Jodi *artist, marketing consultant*
Bowen, Ginger Ann *artist*
Bowman, Laura *artist*
Bradshaw, Melissa Wahlquist *art educator*
Braisted, Madeline Charlotte *artist, visual artist, retired financial planner, army officer*
Brennan, Frances Anstett *artist*
Brenton, Hatice *painter, graphics designer*
Brigeois, Evelyne Brigitte *artist, publisher*
Bronkar, Eunice Dunalee *artist, educator*
Brown, Alice Elste *artist*
Brown, Carol Rose *artist*
Browne, Diana Gayle *artist, social worker*
Bryant, Daryl Leslie *painter, educator*
Butler Yank, Leslie Ann *artist, writer, editor*
Butterfield, Deborah Kay *sculptor*
Byrne, Loretta Daum *artist, writer*
Calamar, Gloria *artist*
Calder, Diane *artist, art educator, writer*
Cameron, Donna *artist, art educator*
Capello, Linda *artist*
Carideo, Marguerite *painter*
Carl, Susan Marie *photographer, photojournalist*
Carraher, Mary Lou Carter *art educator*
Carter, Nanette Carolyn *artist*
Caseiras, Jo Ann Striga *artist, educator*
Chase, Doris Totten *sculptor, educator, filmmaker*
Chermayeff, Alexandra Sasha *artist*
Childs, Wenetta Grybas *artist*
Claiborne, Liz (Elisabeth Claiborne Ortenberg) *fashion designer*
Cobb, Ruth *artist*
Cole, Jean Anne *artist*
Comar, Mary Alice *art educator, farmer*
Cooper, Elva June *artist*
Cooper, Rebecca *art dealer*
Coover, Doris Dimock *artist*
Coulter, Cynthia Jean *artist, educator*
Crowder, Mary Ellen *art educator, real estate agent*
Cunha, Jane *artist, consultant*
Curnutte, Mary E. *artist, restorer of painting, educator*
D'Alessio, Valaida Corrine *artist, consultant*
Daly, Linda *artist, educator*
Dart, Deborah Gordon *artist*
Davidson, Jeannie *costume designer*
Davis-Townsend, Helen Irene *retired art educator*
Dean, Diane (H.) Sweet *artist, retired credit manager*
DeAngelo, Judith *artist*
DeHority, Miriam A. (Miriam Newman) *artist*
DeJack, Jacqueline Elvadeana *artist, educator*
Denenberg, Katharine W. Hornberger (Tinka Denenberg) *artist, educator*
Denton, Judy Ann *art educator*
De Voe, Tamara Lynne *art director, painter*
Dewey, Ariane *artist, illustrator*
Di Giacomo, Fran *artist*
Donath, Therese *artist, author*
Dougherty, Barbara Lee *artist, writer*
Doyle, Nancy Hazlett *artist*
Du Boise, Kim Rees *artist, photographer, art educator*
Dubs, Gloria L. *artist, realtor*
Duguid, Dorothy Ann Ramseyer *artist*
Dunne, Donnalee *artist, educator, writer*
Dustman, Elizabeth *art educator, designer*
Edmo, Jean Umiokalani *artist, poet*
Elcik, Elizabeth Mabie *fashion illustrator*
Falconer, Marguerite Elizabeth *artist*
Faletto, Kimberly Elizabeth *art educator*
Falguiere, Sharon Ellen *costume designer*
Falk, Melanie Kay *art director*
Farrar, Elaine Willardson *artist*
Feeback, Loreta Dotaline Kreeger *artist*
Feuerstein, Penny *artist*
Fish, Janet Isobel *artist*
Flavin, Sonja *artist*
Flinn, Mary Agnes *artist, educator*
Ford, Jennifer *art educator*
Ford, Jo Anne *artist, educator*
Frank, JoAnn *photographer*
Fratkin, Leslie *photographer*
Frauenhoffer, Rose Marie *visual artist, cosmetologist*
Frederick, Elizabeth Eleanor Tatum *watercolor artist, retired educator*
Freeman, Anne Frances *artist, freelance/self-employed illustrator*
Freidel, Judy Ann *artist*
Freilicher, Jane *artist*
Friday, Katherine Orwoll *artist*
Frink, Jeanne Rae Rundell *artist*
Fulkerson, Julie Maria *illustrator*
Furth, Karen J. *artist*
Galen, Elaine *painter*
Gallagher, Cynthia *artist, educator*
Galvis y Assmus, Patricia *computer animator, educator, filmmaker*
Gamble, Desirata *artist, poet*
Gardner, Elizabeth Ann Hunt *artist, poet, genealogist*
Gass, Rosario *artist*
Gerhardt, Carol Ashby *visual artist*
Gilliland, Lucille Mary *artist, writer*
Gitman, Leda Victoria *artist*
Glen, Niki *artist*
Gold, Sarae R. *art educator*
Goldberger, Blanche Rubin *sculptor, jeweler*
Golden, Judith Greene *artist, educator*
Gonzalez-Crespo, Teresita *art educator*
Goulet, Lorrie *sculptor*
Graham, K(athleen) M. (K. M. Graham) *artist*
Grames-Lyra, Judith Ellen *artist*
Gray, Barbara May *artist*
Gray, Linda Alyn *artist, educator*
Greene, Liza M *creative services director, writer*
Greene, Lynne Jeannette *fashion designer*
Griffin, Sallie T. *artist, photographer, sculptor, former radiologic technologist*
Grim, Ellen Townsend *artist, retired art educator*
Gurwitz-Hall, Barbara Ann *artist*
Hall, Susan Laurel *artist, educator, writer*
Hamilton, Ann Katherine *artist*
Handa, Eugenie Quan *graphic designer*
Hannaman, Alberta Anna *artist*
Hannon, Sherrill Ann *artist*
Hanson, Janice Crawford *artist*
Hanson, Jo *artist, lecturer, writer*
Hardwicke, Catherine Helen *motion picture production designer*
Harris, Jeannette Frances *artist*
Hawkins, Cynthia *artist, educator*
Head, Melva Ann *artist*
Heft, Carol Beth *artist*
Heller, Mary Wheeler *photographer*
Helpern, Joan (Joan Marshall) *designer, business executive*
Henderson Rollyson, Tonya Rene *artist*
Henson Scales, Meg D(iane) *artist, writer, publisher*
Hernandez, Robin Renee *artist, graphics designer*
Herranen, Kathy *artist*
Hess, Wendy K. *art curator, researcher, writer*
Hessinger, Jill A. *art educator*
Heyer, Marilee *illustrator*
Hickman, Patricia *artist, craftswoman*
Higgins, Larkin Maureen *artist, poet, educator*
Hillard, Wonda Yvette *art educator, artist*
Hilton, Nicky (Nicholai Olivia Hilton) *apparel designer*
Hintzke, Teresa Anna *illustrator*
Hixon, Emily Earl *artist, educator*
Holbrow, Gwendolyn Jane *artist, writer*
Holden, Rebecca Lynn *artist*
Holt, Marjorie Jensen *artist*
Holzer, Jenny *artist*
Holzman, Elizabeth Esther *artist, director*
Hombordy, Hanna Lore *artist*
Hopper, Tammy Jane *art educator*
Horlick, Ruth *photographer*
Horowitz, Diana J. *artist*
Huffington, Anita *sculptor*
Hummel, Marian *retired art educator, photographer*
Hunt, Mary Melinda *artist*
Hutchison, Edna Ruth *artist*
Hyman, Trina Schart *illustrator*

Jackson, Lola Hirdler *art educator*
Jacobs, Lois Elizabeth *art educator*
Jacoby, Beverly Schreiber *art consultant*
Janko, May *graphic artist*
Jansen, Angela Bing *artist, educator*
Jarcho, Judith Lynn *artist*
Jay, Norma Joyce *artist*
Jennings, Gabrielle *artist*
Jewett, Mary (Betsy) Elizabeth *artist, conservationist*
Johnson, Kysa Nicole *artist*
Johnson, Ursula Anne *artist*
Jurgutis, Danguole *artist*
Kahn, Susan *artist*
Kannenstine, Margaret Lampe *artist*
Kaplan, Phyllis *artist, composer*
Karnofsky, Mollyne *artist, educator, poet*
Kauffman, Kaethe Coventon *artist, writer, art educator*
Kavanagh, Cornelia Kubler *sculptor*
Kennedy, Joanie Tiska *artist, painter, sculptor*
King, Joy Riemer *art educator*
Kingery, Brenda L. *artist, volunteer*
Kirsch, Roslyn Ruth *art educator, painter, printmaker*
Klein, Charlotte Feuerstein *art consultant*
Klein, Lynn Ellen *artist*
Klein, Sheri Rose *art educator*
Klement, Vera *artist*
Knapp, Candace Louise *sculptor*
Kocher, Jeannine M. *art educator*
Kohn, Karen Josephine *graphic and exhibition designer*
Korr, Marla *artist*
Kouzel, Mildred *artist*
Kraft, Yvette *art educator*
Krebs, Mary *art educator*
Krulik, Barbara S. *director, writer, curator*
Kunin, Jacqueline Barlow *art educator*
Kuppers, Petra *art educator, artist*
Kvalheim, Ethel M. (Margete) *artist*
Kwong, Eva *artist, art educator*
Kyle, Gene Magerl *merchandise presentation artist*
LaCroix, Sophia Marie *artist*
Lake, Marilyn Hope (Waide) Warn *artist*
LaPierre, Eileen Marie *technical service manager*
La Rocca, Isabella *artist, educator*
Lawrence, Mary Josephine (Josie Lawrence) *artist, retired library official, retired library director*
LÊ, An-My *photographer, educator*
Leak, Nancy Maric *artist*
Leeds, Nancy Brecker *sculptor, lyricist*
Leiber, Judith Maria *designer, manufacturer*
[illegible] Wertheimer *art consultant*
Leone, Jeanne *artist*
Lewie, Reva Goodwin *artist, educator*
Lewy, Helen Crosby *artist, writer, translator, painter*
Lindenfeld, Naomi *ceramic artist*
Linhares, Judith Yvonne *artist, educator*
Livingston-MacIrelan, Joan Persilla *artist*
Lodeski, Lisa *artist, consultant*
Lonstein, Shoshanna *fashion designer*
Lundeen, Marga Laird *art educator*
Lundgren, Cissi *artist, poet*
Lynn, Sharon *artist*
Maday, Christine Verga *artist, illustrator*
Mady, Beatrice M. *artist*
Mahfouz, Ilham Badreddine *artist*
Mangold, Sylvia Plimack *artist*
Mann, Joan Ellona *artist, editor*
Manning, Elaine S. *retired art educator*
Manuelian, Lucy Der *art educator, architecture educator*
Marlowe, Willie *artist, fine arts educator*
Marsh, Merrilyn Delano *sculptor, painter*
Martin, Dianne Leslie *artist, educator*
Martinelli, Janet Sue *artist, educator*
Martyl, (Mrs. Alexander Langsdorf Jr.) *artist*
Mason, Lois E. (J. Day Mason) *painter, poet, actress, educator*
Mathis, Karen McHugh *artist*
Mayer, Susan Martin *art educator*
McCargar, Eleanor Barker *artist*
McCully, Emily Arnold *illustrator, writer*
McGee, Carrie L. *artist*
McHugh, Annette S. *artist, educator, playwright*
McKay, Renee *artist*
McKelly, Beverly *artist, educator*
McLaughlin, Jean Wallace *art director, artist*
McPeters, Sharon Jenise *artist, writer*
Meagher, Sandra Krebs *artist*
Meil, Kate *sculptor*
Mendoza, Ruth *art educator*
Menna, Sári *artist, educator*
Merlis, Annette Forbes *artist*
Mesa, Yolanda Del Carmen *artist*
Mikles, Alicia Genevieve *artist, publishing executive*
Militello, Roberta Jan *artist, illustrator, designer*
Monczewski, Maureen R. *secondary art educator, visual artist*
Morgan, Ann M. *artist, educator*
Morrison, Margaret L. *artist, educator, consultant*
Morrison, Nancy Jane *art educator*
Moskovitz, Nancy Siegel *artist, elementary school educator*
Myers, Sue Bartley *artist*
Neale, Diane Yunck *artist*
Neff, Jennifer Ellen *painter, artist*
Nemec-Kessel, Charlene *artist, educator*
Nemiroff, Maxine Celia *art educator, gallery owner, consultant*
Nichols, Iris Jean *illustrator*
Nodelman, Nancy Ziegler *sculptor, designer*
Noel, Cheryl Elaine *artist, poet*
Nuss, Joanne Ruth *sculptor, artist*
Occhipinti, Lisa *artist*
O'Donnell, Kathleen C. *artist*
Okoshi-Mukai, Sumiye *artist*
Olson, Joanne J. *artist, art educator*
Ord, Linda Banks *artist*
Oritsky, Mimi *artist, educator*
Orner, Patricia Ann *desktop publishing administrator, writer*
Owen, Carol Thompson *artist, educator, writer*
Oxell, Loie Gwendolyn *fashion and beauty educator, consultant, columnist*
Pack, Susan Joan *art consultant*
Padgett, Cynthia S. *artist*
Pagano, Michelina Olimpia *art director, writer*
Palchik, Anna *book designer, writer*
Parsons, Lisa Kay *artist, writer*
Peacock, Virginia C. *artist*
Peckham, Ellen *artist, poet*
Peek, Stephanie *artist*
Pergal, Theresa Maria *artist*
Perham, Leigh Wellington *art educator, art historian*
Pfaff, Judy *artist*
Phelan, Ellen *artist*
Pierce, Diane Jean *artist*
Pierce, Hilda (Hilda Herta Harmel) *painter*
Pinton, Cristina Costantina *artist, educator*
Pipkin, Mary Margaret *artist*
Pitcher, Susan Ingrid *art dealer*
Podell, Jean Elizabeth Mesberg *artist*
Potsic, Amie Sharon *photographer, educator, artist*
Provensen, Alice Rose Twitchell *artist, author*
Pulitizer, Lilly (Lillian McKim Rousseau) *apparel designer, writer*
Putterman, Florence Grace *artist, printmaker*
Raash, Kathleen Forecki *artist*
Rathfon, Jeanne Lorraine *artist*
Redmon, Cynthia Boudreaux *art educator*
Reedy, Susan *painter*
Rendl-Marcus, Mildred *artist, economist*
Rezac, Roselyn Ann *graphic designer, business owner*
Ripstein, Jacqueline *artist*
Rivers, Joan Nadia *graphics designer*
Roberts, Suzanne Catherine *artist*
Robinson, Linda Schultz *art educator, artist*
Robinson, Lynda Hickox *artist*
Robinson, Nancy Ellen *artist*
Roche, Pauline Jennifer *artist*
Rock, Mary Ann *fine artist, educator, consultant*
Rockburne, Dorothea Grace *artist*
Roe, Wanda Jeraldean *artist, retired educator, lecturer*
Rogers, Eva Marie VanLeuven *artist, poet*
Romano, Mena N. *artist, educator*
Rosenbaum, Belle Sara *appraiser, interior designer, museum director, educator*
Rosenberg, Carole *art dealer, real estate broker, foundation executive*
Ross, Joan Stuart *artist, art educator*
Ross, Sharon D. *artist, art gallery owner*
Rossman, Ruth Scharff *artist, educator*
Rothschild, Jennifer Ann *artist, educator*
Rubin, Sandra Mendelsohn *artist*
Rubinstein, Eva (Anna) *photographer*
Rudy, Sandra Roberson *photographer*
Rule, Mary Shand (Mary Shand) *artist, educator*
Rush, Julia Ann Halloran (Mrs. Richard Henry Rush) *artist, writer*
Rutherford, Doreen *artist, excavating company executive*
Rutschke, Annamarie *artist*
Sakai, Kiyoko *artist*
Saks, Judith-Ann *artist*
Salerno, Cherie Ann (C. S. Mau) *artist*
Santini, Debrah Ann *art educator, artist*
Sauerbrun, Susan Jo *artist*
Savedra, Jeannine Evangeline *artist, educator, art educator*
Schabner, Dawn Freeble *art educator, artist*
Schmitz, Barbara *art preservationist*
Schultz, Eileen Hedy *graphic designer*
Schwalb, Klaudia *painter, critic*
Schwartz, Lillian Feldman *artist, filmmaker, art analyst, writer, nurse*
Schwegman, Monica Joan *artist*
Schwind, Audrey Frances *artist, educator*
Scotland, Susan Jane *artist, art educator*
Scott, Deborah L. *costume designer*
Scott, Jane Wooster *artist*
Searles, Edna Lowe *artist, illustrator, composer*
Segal, Rena Beth *artist*
Segil, Laura Chipman *art dealer, consultant*
Seligson, Judith *artist*
Shaderowfsky, Eva Maria *photographer, writer, computer communications specialist*
Shamy, Jennifer Ann *art educator*
Shaughnessy, Marie Kaneko *artist*
Shaw, Gloria Doris *art educator*
Sheridan, Sonia Landy *artist, retired art educator*
Sherwood, Gloria N. *graphic and literary artist, genealogy researcher*
Shiershke, Nancy Fay *artist, educator, property manager*
Shikashio, Hiroko *artist, interpreter, educator*
Shulman, Mildred *artist*
Shuss, Jane Margaret *artist*
Simeone, Cheryl *artist*
Sklarin, Ann H. *artist*
Smith, Julie Shelton *artist*
Smith, Karen Ann *visual artist*
Smith, Leila Hentzen *artist*
Smith, Leonore Rae *artist*
Smith, Marji L. *artist*
Sniffen, Frances P. *artist*
Snowden, Ruth *artist, educator, executive secretary*
Softic, Tanja *artist*
Souders, Jean Swedell *artist, educator*
Sparrow, Alison Kidder *painter, sculptor*
Stern, Marilyn *photographer, writer, picture editor*
Stevens, May *artist*
Stewart, Janet *artist*
Stinsmuehlen-Amend, Susan *artist*
Stockar, Helena Marie Magdalena *artist*
Stover, Laura Elkins *artist*
Strang, Heidi Cordova *art educator*
Strider, Marjorie Virginia *artist, educator*
Stripling, Betty Keith *artist, medical/surgical nurse*
Stroud, Betsy Dillard *artist*
Struble, Susan C. *artist, volunteer art therapist*
Sugar, Sandra Lee *art consultant*
Sweig, Cherry Elizabeth *artist, painter*
Swensen, Mary Jean Hamilton *graphic artist*
Switzer, Toccoa *artist*
Sze, Sarah *sculptor*
Szyszka, Roswita Evelyn *artist*
Tagliente, Josephine Marlene *artist*
Tait, Heather Jean *artist*
Talbot-Elliott, Susan *artist*
Tardos, Anne *artist, writer, composer*
Taylor, Margaret Turner *apparel designer, economist, writer, architectural designer*
Terry, Sandra Eleanor *visual artist*
Thomas, Sylvia Elizabeth *artist*
Thompson, Margie Ann *artist*
Tirello, Maria Eugenia Duke *artist*
Tishner, Keri Lynn *visual art education consultant*
Todd, Ruth *artist*
Tomkow, Gwen Adelle *artist*
Triana, Gladys *artist*
Turner, Bonese Collins *artist, educator*
Turner, Bracha *Naive Landscape painter*
Turner, Florence Frances *ceramist*
Turner, Peggy Ann *graphics designer, artist, educator*
Tyrrell, Lilian *craftsperson, artist*
Unithan, Dolly *visual artist*
Vahradian, Melinda *fine artist*
Vanderbilt, Gloria Morgan *artist, actress, fashion designer*
Van Hooser, Patricia Lou Scott *art educator*
Vergano, Lynn (Marilynn Bette Vergano) *artist*
Vernazza, Trish Brown (Trish Eileen Brown) *visual artist, art therapist, sculptor*
Versch, Esther Marie *artist*
Villachica, Andrea Luisa *art educator*
Villoch, Kelly Carney *art director*
Von Furstenberg, Diane Simone Michelle *fashion designer, writer, entrepreneur*
VonSchulze-Delitzsch, Marilyn Wandling (Lady VonSchulze-Delitzsch) *artist, writer*
Walker, Bernice Baker *artist*
Wallach-Levy, Wendee Esther *astrophotographer*
Walsh, Nan *artist, painter, sculptor, consultant*
Warner, Ruth E. *art educator*
Warren, Alice Louise *artist*
Wasserman, Helene Waltman *art dealer, artist*
Watts, Ginny (Virginia C. Watts) *artist*
Weiss, Nancy P. *artist*
Weld, Alison Gordon *artist*
West, Alexandra (Annie West) *artist, creative director*
Westbie, Barbara Jane *retired graphics designer*
Weston, Peggy Hutson *artist, art educator*
Williams, Eleanor Claflin (Claffy Williams) *artist*
Williams, Monica Bernardette Ellen *jewelry designer*
Wilson, Jane *artist*
Winokur, Paula Colton *artist, educator*
Witt, Nancy Camden *artist*
Wolpert Richard, Chava *artist*
Wood, Christie Ann *artist*
Wostrel, Rebekah A. *artist, educator*
Wylan, Barbara *artist*
Wynn, Karla Wray *artist, agricultural products company executive*
Wyse, Karen Ann *artist*
Yerxa, Jane Anne *artist*
Ynda, Mary Lou *artist, educator*
Youngblood, Daisy *ceramist*
Yowell, Nancy T. *photographer, retired elementary educator*
Zaleski, Jean *artist*
Zebi, Sandra *artist*
Zekman, Terri Margaret *graphic designer*
Zook, Maurine Joyce *artist*
Zucker, Maureen T. *artist*

ASSOCIATIONS AND ORGANIZATIONS *See also* specific fields

UNITED STATES

ALABAMA

Birmingham
Carter, Frances Tunnell (Fran Carter) *fraternal organization administrator*
Diasio, Ilse Wolfartsberger *volunteer*
Gross, Iris Lee *not-for-profit association executive*
Kirkley, D. Christine *non-profit organization administrator*

Demopolis
Reynolds, Louise Webb *retired volunteer, director*

Fayette
Bragg, Beverly Smith *volunteer*

ALASKA

Anchorage
Jones, Jewel *social services administrator*
O'Regan, Deborah *association executive, lawyer*

ARIZONA

Marana
Green, Laura Lorraine *foundation administrator*

Phoenix
Daniels, Barbara Ann *non-profit organization executive*
Dorland, Byrl Brown *retired volunteer*
Whyte, Rachel L. *child abuse prevention specialist, social worker*

Scottsdale
Milanovich, Norma JoAnne *training and development company executive*
Mohraz, Judy Jolley *foundation administrator*
O'Meara, Sara *nonprofit organization executive*

Sun City
Duke, Ora Elizabeth *civic volunteer*

Tucson
Lovejoy, Jean Hastings *social services counselor*
Ohmann, Elizabeth J. *advocate*

ARKANSAS

Fayetteville
Stephens, Wanda Brewer *social services administrator, investor*

Little Rock
Adams, Rose Ann *nonprofit administrator*
Walden, Catherine Jane *not-for profit director, social worker, consultant*

CALIFORNIA

Anderson
Wittmann, Jane Gordon *volunteer*

Azusa
White, Rebecca E. *advocate*

Berkeley
Buell, Evangeline Canonizado *consumer cooperative official*
Campbell, Martha Madison *educational administrator*
McLaughlin, Sylvia Cranmer *volunteer, environmentalist*

Canoga Park
Lederer, Marion Irvine *cultural administrator*

Concord
Misner, Charlotte Blanche Ruckman *retired community organization administrator*

[illegible]
Friess, Donna Lewis *children's rights advocate*

Davis
Eastin, Delaine Andree *foundation administrator*

El Monte
Last, Marian Helen *social services administrator*

Escondido
Leso, Cynthia J. *social services administrator*

Fremont
Maloney, Cheryl Ann *foundation, consultant, business executive*

Glendale
Llewellyn, Linda Garrison *foundation executive*

Irvine
Fouste, Donna H. *association executive*

Kentfield
Blum, Joan Kurley *fundraising executive*

La Canada
Clement, Cathleen McMullin *fundraiser*

Lodi
Nusz, Phyllis Jane *not-for-profit fundraiser, consultant, educational consultant*

Loma Linda
Pendergraft, Janice Gayle *volunteer*

Long Beach
Heggeness, Julie Fay *foundation administrator, lawyer*

Los Altos
Orr, Susan Packard *business owner*

Los Angeles
Dunn, Anne Yvonne *advocacy organization executive*
Jaggers, Velma Mary Lee *foundation administrator, educator*
Kipke, Michele Diane *education and social services administrator, former hospital director*
Marrow, Deborah *foundation administrator*
Marshall, Mary Jones *civic worker*
Prewitt, Jean *not-for-profit organization executive*
Scarlett, P. Lynn *foundation administrator, writer*
Smith, Jean Webb (Mrs. William French Smith) *civic worker*
Wachtell, Wendy *foundation administrator*
Wilson, Gayle Ann *civic worker*

Menlo Park
Pallotti, Marianne Marguerite *foundation administrator*

Mill Valley
Burke, Kathleen J. *foundation administrator*

Modesto
Whiteside, Carol Gordon *foundation executive*

Mount Shasta
Mann, Karen *consultant, educator*

Mountain View
Serra, Patricia Janet *social services administrator*
Wulff, Virginia McMillan *association executive*

Napa
Loar, Peggy Ann *foundation administrator, museum administrator*

Nevada City
Hudson, Lee (Arlene Hudson) *environmental activist*

Newbury Park
McCune, Sara Miller *foundation executive, publisher*

Oakland
Carter, Mandy *professional organization administrator*
Light, Sally G. *cultural organization administrator*

Oxnard
Tolmach, Jane Louise *community activist, municipal official*

Palm Springs
Hilb, Jeane Dyer *community volunteer*

Palos Verdes Peninsula
Vanderlip, Elin Brekke *philanthropic executive*

Pasadena
Racklin, Barbara Cohen *fundraising consultant*

Rancho Mirage
Wyatt, Lenore *civic worker*

Redwood City
Spangler, Nita Reifschneider *volunteer*

Sacramento
Perez, Elena N. *professional society administrator, writer*
Ross, Jean M. *think-tank executive*

Salinas
Chester, Lynne *foundation administrator, artist*

San Bernardino
Evans, R. Marlene *social welfare administrator, educator*

San Diego
Clarke, Evelyn Woodman *volunteer*
Lane, Gloria Julian *foundation administrator*
Rossi, Norma J. *not-for-profit executive, advocate*
Spira, Patricia Goodsitt *association executive*
Swanson, Mary Catherine *educational reform program founder*

San Francisco
Bitterman, Mary Gayle Foley *foundation executive*
Brown, Bernice Leona Baynes *foundation consultant, educator, consultant*
Chang, Patti *foundation administrator*
Clarey, Patricia *association executive*
Harvey, Glen H. *educational association administrator*
Lord, Mia W. *advocate*
Metz, Mary Seawell *foundation administrator, retired academic administrator*
Pipes, Sally C. *think-tank executive*
Reading, Phyllis Ann *social welfare administrator*
Simon, Lateefah *foundation administrator, director*
Soler, Esta *foundation administrator*
Steele, Shari *think-tank executive*
Toussaint, T. Nicolette *writer, nonprofit organization official*

San Jose
Orton, Eva Dorothy *civic worker*

Santa Ana
Cohen-Strong, Elayne Barbara *social services administrator, educator*
Prizio, Betty J. *volunteer, retired property manager*

Santa Barbara
McCoy, Lois Clark *emergency services professional, retired county official, magazine editor*

Santa Cruz
Lenox, Catherine Corneau *volunteer*

Santa Monica
Foley, Jane Deborah *foundation executive*
Perlman, Judith Faith *think-tank associate, researcher*

Sherman Oaks
Leighton, Carolyn *foundation administrator*

Sonora
Coffill, Marjorie Louise *civic leader*

Sylmar
Froelich, Beverly Lorraine *foundation director*

Torrance
Carey, Kathryn Ann *foundation administrator, editor, consultant*

Valencia
Anguiano, Lupe *advocate*

Whittier
Harvey, Patricia Jean *special education administrator, retired*

Yorba Linda
Stavropoulos, Rose Mary Grant *community activist, volunteer*

Yreka
Fiock, Shari Lee *not-for-profit developer*

COLORADO

Arvada
Meiklejohn, Mindy June (Lorraine Meiklejohn) *political organizer, realtor*

Boulder
deKieffer, Kitty *volunteer*
Forstrom, June Rochelle *professional society administrator*
Heath, Josephine Ward *foundation administrator*

Colorado Springs
Deiotte, Margaret Williams Tuckey *nonprofit consultant, grants writer*
Hawley, Nanci Elizabeth *association administrator*
Loo, Katherine Haughey *nonprofit organization consultant*
Miller, Zoya Dickins (Mrs. Hilliard Eve Miller Jr.) *civic worker*

Denver
Fujioka, Jo Ann Ota *educational administrator, consultant*
Groff, JoAnn *organization administrator*
Harris, Ellen Gandy (Mrs. J. Ramsay Harris) *civic worker*
Hirschfeld, Arlene F. *civic worker, homemaker*
Jones, Jean Correy *organization administrator*
Read, Patricia Ellen *administrator non-profit organization, editor*
Simpson, Diane Jeannette *school social worker, counselor, adoption home study worker*

Englewood
Keesling, Ruth Morris *foundation administrator*

Fort Collins
Fairbank, Jane Davenport *editor, civic worker*

Lakewood
McEwen, Ruth *foundation administrator*

Littleton
Keogh, Heidi Helen Dake *advocate*

Longmont
Flanders, Eleanor Carlson *community volunteer*
Lovins, L. Hunter *public policy institute executive*

Mancos
Brown, Joy Alice *social services administrator*

CONNECTICUT

Danbury
Meyers, Abbey S. *foundation administrator*

Fairfield
Evans, Margaret A. *volunteer*
Ford, Maureen Morrissey *civic worker*
Shelton, Carolyn Johnson *professional society administrator*
Webster, Barbara Sheppard *art association administrator*

Falls Village
Toomey, Jeanne Elizabeth *animal activist*

Farmington
Baker, Patricia *health foundation administrator*

Greenwich
Bjornson, Edith Cameron *foundation administrator, communications consultant*
Kovner, Kathleen Jane *civic worker, portrait artist*
Stauffer, Valerie Vilas *civic volunteer*
Tigett-Parks, Elizabeth *arts administrator*

Groton
Kennedy, Evelyn Siefert *foundation executive, textile specialist*

Guilford
Stevens, Lydia Hastings *community volunteer*

Hartford
Gibbons, Mary Peyser *civic volunteer*

New Canaan
Bartlett, Dede Thompson *non-profit executive*

Norwich
Thompson, Carrie Lorraine *volunteer*

Old Saybrook
Steffen, Elizabeth Ducas *political organization worker*

Stamford
Stillings, Irene Ella Grace Cordiner *foundation executive*

DELAWARE

Dover
Friedland, Billie Louise *former human services administrator*

Lewes
Spence, Sandra *retired professional society administrator*

Newark
Townsend, Brenda S. *educational association administrator*

Wilmington
Baxter, Beverley Velons *economic association administrator, educator*
Fleming, Blanche Miles *educational administrator*
Spence, Janet Blake Conley (Mrs. Alexander Pyott Spence) *civic worker*

DISTRICT OF COLUMBIA

Washington
Aall, Pamela R. *foundation administrator*
Anderson, Jane Louise *association executive*
Andrews, Laureen E. *foundation administrator*
Avery, Byllye Yvonne *health association administrator*
Babby, Ellen Reisman *education administrator*
Bednash, Geraldine Polly *educational association administrator*
Bode, Barbara *Internet entrepreneur, foundation executive, freelance/self-employed writer*
Bonosaro, Carol Alessandra *professional association executive, former government official*
Brosnan, Carol Raphael Sarah *retired arts administrator, musician*
Brown, Ann W. *not-for-profit developer*
Bulger, Peggy Anne *cultural organization administrator*
Bushkin, Kathryn A. *foundation administrator*
Callahan, Debra Jean *professional society administrator*
Canja, Esther *foundation administrator*
Chavez, Linda *civil rights organization executive*
Chavez-Thompson, Linda *labor union administrator*
Cino, Maria *political organization administrator, former federal agency administrator*
Comstock, Amy L. *social services administrator*
Dasch, Pat (Anne) *professional society administrator*
Daschle, Linda Hall *transportation industry lobbyist*
Davis, Deidre *advocate*
Dean, Lisa *foundation executive*
DeKuyper, Mary Hundley *non-profit consultant*
Dooley, Betty Parsons *educational association administrator*
Dorn, Jennifer Lynn *charitable organization administrator*
Duval-Pierrelouis, Jeanne-Marie *educational association executive*
Edelman, Marian Wright *not-for-profit organization administrator, lawyer*
Emely, Mary Ann *association executive*
Evans, Joy *foundation administrator*
Evans, Marsha Johnson *non-profit association administrator, former career officer*
Feldman, Sandra *labor union executive*
Finley, Julie Hamm *political party official*
Flippo, Karen Francine *social welfare administrator*
Ford, Elizabeth Ann *administrator, children's advocate*
Foreman, Carol Lee Tucker *consumer advocate*
Forkan, Patricia Ann *foundation executive*
French, Hilary F. *foundation administrator*
Friend, Patricia A. *trade association administrator*
Fries, Helen Sergeant Haynes *civic leader*
Fuller, Kathryn Scott *environmental association executive, lawyer*
Gandy, Kim Allison *feminist organization executive, lawyer*
Garrison, LaTrease E. *association executive*
Griffin, Janice *political organization professional*
Hahn, Lorna *political organization executive, author*
Hall, Betty Jean *public interest group executive, lawyer*
Handman, Bobbie (Barbara Handman) *foundation executive*
Harrison, Monika Edwards *business development executive*
Hatfield, C. Maile *lobbyist*
Heinz Kerry, Teresa F. *foundation administrator*
Hentges, Harriet *not-for-profit developer*
Howard, Barbara Viventi *research foundation executive*
Hudson, Melinda B. *foundation administrator*
Hughes, Sharon Mary *trade association executive*
Ireland, Patricia *not-for-profit developer*
Isaacs, Amy Fay *political organization executive*
Johnson, Gloria *labor union administrator*
Johnson, Karen *professional society administrator*
Kauffman, Amy *political organization worker*
Kelley, Colleen M. *labor union administrator*
Knippers, Diane LeMasters *association executive*
Lachance, Janice Rachel *educational association administrator, former federal agency administrator, lawyer*
Lampl, Peggy Ann *public policy administrator*
Lenn, Marjorie Peace *education association administrator, consultant*
Levine, Felice *educational association administrator*
Lichtman, Judith L. *lawyer, organization administrator*
Lief, Beth *educational association administrator*
Limon, Lavinia *social services administrator*
Marks, Susan Collin *foundation administrator*
Matheis, Cheryl *nonprofit association administrator*
McGinnis, Patricia Gwaltney *nonprofit organization executive*
Mc Kay, Emily Gantz *civil rights professional*
Michelman, Kate *advocate*
Moore, Jacquelyn Cornelia *labor union official, editor*
Moore, Minvon *political organization worker*
Muir, Patricia Allen *professional association administrator*
Nickens, Paula *political organization administrator*
Obrecht, Margaret M. H. *cultural organization administrator*
O'Kane, Margaret E. *non-profit organization executive*
Oliphant, Martha Carmichael *civic worker*
O'Neill, Catherine *cultural organization administrator*
Otremba, Geraldine Marie *congressional and international relations executive*
Pensky, Carol *political organization administrator*
Petito, Margaret L. *foundation administrator*
Raizen, Senta Amon *educational administrator, researcher*
Rich, Dorothy Kovitz *writer, educational administrator*
Richardson, Ann Bishop *foundation executive, lawyer*
Riedel, Bunnie *not-for-profit organization executive*
Robinson, Sharon Porter *professional society administrator*
Roessel, Faith *Indian arts and crafts administrator*
Rogers, Julie *foundation administrator*
Samsami, Soona *advocate*
Sandler, Bernice Resnick *women's rights specialist*
Schneider, Carol Geary *educational association administrator*
Schroeder, Patricia Scott *trade association administrator, retired congresswoman*
Scruggs-Leftwich, Yvonne *association executive*
Sewall, Sarah Lee *foundation administrator*
Sheekey, Kathleen D. *advocate, director*
Shields, Carole *foundation administrator*
Simmons, Caroline Thompson *civic worker*
Smith, Elise Fiber *international non-profit development agency administrator*
Smith, Jessie P. Dowling *retired social services administrator*
Stern, Paula *international trade advisor*
Stitch, Roberta Lynn *not-for-profit fundraiser, social worker*
Swenson, Sue *foundation administrator, former health and education administrator*
Torkelson, Jodie Rae *charitable organization executive*
Townsend, Ann Van Devanter *foundation administrator, art historian*
Tse, Man-Chun Marina *educational association administrator*
Van Metre, Lauren *foundation administrator*
Werronen, Betsy Warren *political organization administrator*
Wesley, LaTonya Rashawn *legislative assistant*
Wilkie, Edith B. *foundation administrator*
Williams, Jody *political organization administrator*

FLORIDA

Aventura
Ross, Selma Belle *retired not-for-profit fundraiser*

Bal Harbour
Ash, Dorothy Matthews *civic worker*

Boca Raton
Grant, Diantha Hawkes *not-for-profit administrator, educator*
Jessup, Jan Amis *arts volunteer, writer*

Clearwater
Duncan, Holly H. *foundation executive*

Coral Springs
Kohl, Joan *non-profit administrator, social worker*

Delray Beach
George, Mildred M. *retired sentencing advocate*
Stewart, Patricia Carry *foundation administrator*

Fort Lauderdale
Loos, Roberta Alexis *advocate, artist, educator*

Gulf Breeze
Williams, Betty *peace activist*

Hialeah
Warfel, Jill Kristin *political organization worker*

Holmes Beach
Dunne, Nancy Anne *retired social services administrator*

Jacksonville
Magill, Sherry *foundation administrator*
Weber, Nancy Walker *charitable trust administrator*

Lake Mary
Southward, Patricia C. *volunteer*

Lake Worth
Chittick, Elizabeth Lancaster *women's rights activist*

Lakeland
Spencer, Mary Miller *civic worker*

Marathon
Vail, Elizabeth Forbus *volunteer*

Marco Island
Hollenbeck, Karen Fern *foundation consultant*

North Bethesda
Sherman, Deane Murray *culture organization administrator*

Owings Mills
Tapp, Mamie Pearl *educational association administration*

Potomac
Johnson, Anne Hale *educational association administrator, director*
Marincola, Elizabeth Mark *scientific society executive*
Rosenberg, Sarah Zacher *institute arts administration executive, humanities administration consultant*

Randallstown
Hatch, Sally Ruth *foundation administrator, writer, consultant*

Rockville
Marcuccio, Phyllis Rose *retired association executive, editor*
Power, A. Kathryn *social services administrator*
Standing, Kimberly Anna *educational researcher*

Severna Park
Hall, Marcia Joy *non-profit organization administrator*

Silver Spring
Johnson, Karisa Ann *political activist*
Roth, Harriet Steinhorn *advocate, educator, public speaker*
Wallace, C. Elizabeth McFarland *retired association director*
Zakheim, Barbara Jane *development professional*

Sykesville
Crist, Gertrude H. *civic worker*

MASSACHUSETTS

Arlington
Deal, Patricia Marie *political activist*

Boston
Deissler, Mary Alice *foundation executive*
Garcia, Frieda *community foundation executive*
Hughes, Judith Elaine *not-for-profit developer, director*
Inman, Jean A. *political party official*
Leff, Deborah *government executive*

Cambridge
Berlowitz, Leslie *cultural organization administrator*
Sallee, Marguerite *association executive*
Tocio, Mary Ann *association executive*

Chatham
Cogan, Mary Hart *community activist, educator*

Chelmsford
Elwell, Barbara Lois Dow *community organizer*

Fitchburg
Niemi, Beatrice Neal *social services professional*

Groton
Anthony, Sylvia *social welfare organization executive*

Holyoke
Blanchard, Karen Marie *development professional*

Ipswich
Moules, Deborah Ann *not-for-profit developer*

Lexington
Garing, Ione Davis *civic worker, club woman*

Nantucket
Pollard, Margaret Louise *association administrator*

Quincy
Wilson, Blenda Jacqueline *foundation administrator*

Somerville
Landon, Susan N. *volunteer, poet*

South Hadley
Bronner, Kathleen M. *not-for-profit fundraiser*

Watertown
Boland, Elizabeth *social services company financial executive*

Wayland
Humphrey, Diana Young *fund raiser*

Westford
Geary, Marie Josephine *art association administrator*

MICHIGAN

Ann Arbor
Guardo, Carol J. *association executive*

Battle Creek
Davis, Laura Arlene *retired foundation administrator*
Wendt, Linda M. *educational association administrator*

Bloomfield Hills
Levin, Carolyn Bible *volunteer*

Detroit
Noland, Mariam Charl *foundation executive*
Parks, Rosa Louise *civil rights activist*
Titus, Susan Anne *association executive*

East Lansing
Mitstifer, Dorothy Irwin *honor society administrator*

Flint
Maynard, Olivia P. *foundation administrator*

Hancock
Tuisku, Mary Joan *volunteer, advocate*

Kalamazoo
Moore, Stephanie LaFaye *advocate, director*
Petersen, Anne C.(Cheryl) *foundation administrator, educator*

Traverse City
Bullis, Jo Louise *social services administrator, educator*

MINNESOTA

Hibbing
Lilyquist, Candace Louise *labor union administrator*

Minneapolis
Bell, Constance Conklin *child care association administrator*
Corbine Espinosa, Juanita Grace *cultural association administrator*
King, Reatha Clark *community foundation executive*
Leuchovius, Deborah *advocate, special education services professional, consultant*

Rochester
Shulman, Carole Karen *professional society administrator*

Saint Paul
Archabal, Nina M(archetti) *historical society director*
Franey, Billie Nolan *political activist*
Pampusch, Anita Marie *foundation administrator*
Smith, Mary Hill *volunteer*

MISSISSIPPI

Crystal Springs
Bates, Lura Wheeler *retired trade association executive*

Jackson
Hiatt, Jane Crater *arts agency administrator*

Laurel
Asmar, Kathleen *educational association administrator*

Leland
Stott, Barbara Paxton *volunteer*

Madison
Fordice, Patricia Owens *civic leader, former state first lady*

MISSOURI

Defiance
LeMaster, Sherry Renee *fundraising administrator, foundation administrator, consultant*

El Dorado Springs
Hochstedler, Lisa Inez *educational association administrator*

Florissant
Schutzius, Mary Jane *volunteer activist*

Independence
Potts, Barbara Joyce *retired historical society executive*

Jefferson City
Wagner, Ann *political organization executive*

Kansas City
Yarmo, Fanny F. *not-for-profit fundraiser*

Saint Louis
Brauer, Camilla Thompson (Kimmy Thompson Brauer) *civic leader*
Breckenridge, Joanne *political organization administrator*
Duhme, Carol McCarthy *civic worker*
Hall, Mary Taussig *professional volunteer*
Horn, Joan Kelly *political research and consulting firm executive*
Robins, Marjorie McCarthy (Mrs. George Kenneth Robins) *civic worker*
Shea, Kathleen E. *cultural resources specialist*
Thetford, Frances Alicia *social services group administrator*
Winter, Mildred M. *educational administrator*

Springfield
Morris, Ann Haseltine Jones *social welfare administrator*

NEBRASKA

Bancroft
Neihardt, Hilda *lawyer, foundation administrator, writer, educator, lawyer*

Grand Island
Abernethy, Irene Margaret *civic worker, retired county official*

Harrison
Coffee, Virginia Claire *civic worker, former mayor*

Lincoln
Davis, LuAnn Raelene *fund raising executive*

Omaha
Burris, Janice Elaine *educational administrator*

NEVADA

Carson City
Ayres, Janice Ruth *social services administrator*

Las Vegas
Martinez, Adriana *political organization worker, photographer*
Segerblom, Sharon B. *social services administrator*
Spencer, Carol Brown *association executive*
Vilardo, Carole *research association administrator*
Zucker, Blanche Myra *civic worker*

Pahrump
Nowell, Linda Gail *organization executive*

NEW HAMPSHIRE

Littleton
Merritt, Mary Jane *community volunteer*

Manchester
Lyons, Elisabeth Helene *peer counselor*
Sullivan, Kathleen N. *political organization administrator, lawyer*

NEW JERSEY

Bound Brook
Blumberg, Adele Rosenberg *volunteer*

Camden
Coney, Stephné Reniá *communications and telecommunications educator*

Elizabeth
Pineros, Elizabeth *social services administrator, psychotherapist*

Jackson
Landau-Crawford, Dorothy Ruth *retired social services administrator*

Jersey City
Beeman, Barbara *social work supervisor*

Keyport
Gilmartin, Clara T. *volunteer*

Lebanon
O'Neill, Elizabeth Sterling *trade association administrator*

Lyndhurst
Gallagher, Elizabeth Worrell *fund raising consultant*

Montclair
Blooston, Roselee *cultural organization administrator, writer*
Mason, Lucile Gertrude *fundraiser, consultant*

New Brunswick
Bunch, Charlotte *advocate*

Pennington
Mitchell, Janet Aldrich *fund raising executive, reference materials publisher*

Princeton
De Lung, Jane Solberger *independent sector executive*
Hearn, Ruby Puryear *foundation executive*
Johnson, Barbara Piasecka *philanthropist, art historian and collector, business investor*
Stern, Gail Frieda *historical association director*

Short Hills
Friedman, Frances Wolf *political fund raiser*

Trenton
Binder, Elaine Kotell *associations consultant*
Bowker, Linda Barbara *lobbyist*
Dahme, Maud *educational association administrator*
Zisholtz-Herzog, Ellen Naomi *arts administrator, consultant, cultural planner*

NEW MEXICO

Albuquerque
Cole, Terri Lynn *organization administrator*
Desantis, Sherolyn Smith *foundation executive*

Los Alamos
Flaherty, Anne H. *advocate*

Playas
Clifton, Judy Raelene *association administrator*

Roswell
Anderson, Sally Midgette *social services administrator, linguist*

Santa Fe
Miller-Engel, Marjorie *foundation administrator, commissioner, small business owner*

NEW YORK

Albany
Carman, Joanne G. *consultant*
Williman, Pauline *shorthand reporter, farm foundation administrator*

Bedford Hills
Waller, Wilhelmine Kirby (Mrs. Thomas Mercer Waller) *civic worker, organization official*

Binghamton
Crocker, Margaret Suydam Smith *art association executive director, art historian*

Brooklyn
Horowitz, Sara *labor organizer*
Morgan, Mary Louise Fitzsimmons *fund raising executive, lobbyist*

Buffalo
Clarkson, Elisabeth Ann Hudnut *volunteer*
Hunt, Jane Helfrich *volunteer*

Central Islip
Wiggins, Gloria *nonprofit organization administrator, television producer*

Clarence
Stringer, Gretchen Engstrom *consulting volunteer administrator*

Commack
Price, Amelia Ruth *not-for-profit foundation president, artist, small business owner*

Corning
Cicerchi, Eleanor Ann Tomb *fundraising executive*

Eastchester
Burgess, Carol Ann *educational association administrator, literature educator*

Elmhurst
Matsa, Loula Zacharoula *social services administrator, educator*

Endicott
Englehart, Joan Anne *consultant*

Great Neck
Sterling, Lorraine *volunteer*

Hempstead
Barlow, Linda *social services administrator, trainer*

Hudson
Miner, Jacqueline *political consultant*

Ilion
Edwards, Christine Utley *social services administrator, consultant*

Ithaca
Grainger, Mary Maxon *civic volunteer*

Jamestown
Thompson, Birgit Dolores *civic worker, writer*

Larchmont
Hinerfeld, Ruth G. *civic organization executive*

Long Island City
Hoffman, Merle Holly *political activist, social psychologist, author*

Mount Kisco
Keesee, Patricia Hartford *volunteer*

New Rochelle
Black, Page Morton *civic worker*

New York
Alex, Paula Ann *foundation administrator*
Appel, Marsha Ceil *association executive*
Arnot-Heaney, Susan Eileen *not-for-profit fundraiser*
Aronson, Esther Leah *retired foundation administrator, psychotherapist*
Baird, Zoë *foundation president, lawyer*
Bellamy, Carol *international organization executive*
Berresford, Susan Vail *philanthropic foundation executive*
Bertini, Catherine Ann *international organization official*
Betanzos, Amalia V. *social services administrator*
Bird, Mary Lynne Miller *professional society administrator*
Bischoff, Theresa A. *not-for-profit association administrator, former medical center executive*
Blake, Grace *cultural organization administrator*
Blum, Barbara B. *foundation administrator*
Booth, Barbara Ribman *civic worker*
Cahan, Cora *not-for-profit developer*
Catley-Carlson, Margaret *not-for-profit executive*
Chatfield-Taylor, Adele *historic preservationist*
Christensen, Kathleen Elizabeth *foundation administrator*
Coffin, Anne Gagnebin *art association administrator, editor*
Cole, Elma Phillipson (Mrs. John Strickler Cole) *social welfare executive*
Coly, Lisette *foundation executive*
Dajani, Virginia *arts association administrator*
Davis, Karen *fund executive*
Davis, Kathryn Wasserman *foundation executive, writer, lecturer*

Greenville
Hendrix, Susan Clelia Derrick *civic worker*

SOUTH DAKOTA

Sioux Falls
Callison, JoJean Faye *educational association administrator*

Yankton
Piper, Kathleen *former political organization administrator*

TENNESSEE

Athens
Brown, Sandra Lee *arts management consultant, watercolorist*

Chattanooga
McNeill-Murray, Joan Reagin *volunteer consultant*
Rath, Linda Joann *professional organization executive*

Cleveland
Lockhart, Madge Clements *educational organization executive*

Lafayette
Carter, Anna Dean *volunteer*

Memphis
Jalenak, Peggy Eichenbaum *volunteer*
Kaplan, Claudette S. (Claudia Kaplan) *volunteer*
Shafer, Anne Whalen *volunteer civic worker*
Tibbs, Martha Jane Pullen *civic worker*

Nashville
Harwell, Beth H. *political organization worker*
Willis, Eleanor Lawson *not-for-profit developer*

Newport
Kridler, Jamie Branam *children's advocate, social psychologist*

Soddy Daisy
Frazier, Douglas Almeda McRee *volunteer, former energy facility analyst*

Sparta
Keisling, Mary West *volunteer*

TEXAS

Addison
Baskett, Christina St. Clair *fund raising executive*

Arlington
McKeen, Sally Werst *volunteer*

Austin
Banks, Virginia Anne (Ginger Banks) *association administrator*
Dealey, Amanda Mayhew *former foundation administrator*
Fisk, Doris Rosalie Scanlan *volunteer*
Green, Shirley Moore *retired public affairs and communications executive*
Hughes, Judy Lynne *political organization executive*
Pettigrew, Jo Arnold *educational association administrator*
Weddington, Susan *political party official*

Carrollton
Hart, Elizabeth Ann *foundation administrator*

Colleyville
Tigue, Virginia Beth (Ginny Tigue) *volunteer*

Corpus Christi
French, Dorris Towers Bryan *volunteer*

Dallas
Bonner, Cathy *foundation administrator*
Braun, Susan J. *foundation administrator*
Ellis, Kay Crosby *fundraiser*
Evans, Linda Perryman *foundation administrator*
Hamilton, Wendy J. *foundation administrator*
Smith, Suzanne Naomi *lobbyist*

Dickinson
Sawyer, Cheryl Lynne *foundation administrator, consultant*

El Paso
Goodman, Gertrude Amelia *civic worker*

Fort Worth
Eudaly, Olivia Coggin *not-for-profit executive, educator*
Taylor, Susan Vogel *cultural organization administrator*

Honey Grove
Thurman, Mary Anne *foundation administrator*

Houston
Black, Marilyn Hammer *non-profit organization executive*
Skidmore, Margaret Cooke *fundraiser*

Jacksonville
Lewis, Mary Sals *social services administrator, educator*

Laredo
Lozano, Araceli E. *foundation administrator, consultant*

Lubbock
Livermore, Jane *foundation executive*

Orange
Bengkanstain, Eunice R. *foundation administrator*

Plano
Carver, Rita *fundraising consultant*

San Antonio
Atherton, Flora Cameron *volunteer*
Jacobson, Helen Gugenheim (Mrs. David Jacobson) *civic worker*
Kickbusch, Consuelo Castillo *educational association administrator, consultant, former military officer*
Montecel, Maria Robledo (Cuca Robledo Montecel) *educational association administrator*
Sabo, Corinne Mae *volunteer*

Texarkana
Malcolm, Molly Beth *political party official, counselor*

Weatherford
Bergman, Anne Newberry *civic leader*

UTAH

Highland
Mayberry, Marilyn Marie *community outreach advocate-mediator*

Ogden
Davis, Lori *foundation executive*

Salt Lake City
Clark, Deanna Dee *civic leader and volunteer*
Dahmen-Ray, Patricia *professional society administrator*
Holbrook, Meghan Zanolli *fundraiser, public relations specialist, political organization chairman*
Julander, Paula Foil *health care and political consultant, organizer, state senator*
Struhs, Rhoda Jeanette *civic and political worker*

VERMONT

Ludlow
Nitka, Alice W. *social services administrator, state representative*

Middlebury
Berens, Betty Kathryn McAdam *community program administrator*

Montpelier
Metcalf, Cindy W. *political organization administrator*

Plymouth
Bittinger, Cynthia Douglas *foundation executive*

Williston
Carter, Ruth B. (Mrs. Joseph C. Carter) *foundation administrator*
Podhajski, Blanche Rita *language foundation administrator*

VIRGINIA

Alexandria
Brown, Quincalee *professional society administrator*
Bryant, Anne Lincoln *educational association executive*
Cooper, Edythe E.D. *political organization administrator*
De Barbieri, Mary Ann *nonprofit management consultant*
Diachenko, Marge *political organization administrator*
Fisher, Colleen M. *trade association administrator*
Greenstein, Ruth Louise *research institute executive, lawyer*
Jordan, Carole Jean *political organization administrator*
Kaufman, Beverly *political organization administrator*
Lendsey, Jacquelyn L. *foundation administrator*
Lipnick, Anne Ruth *advocate*
Miller, Marian *professional society administrator*
Richman, Arleen *professional society administrator*
Riel, Pauline *association executive*
Schofield, Regina Brown *lobbyist, political consultant*
Smith, Heidi *political organization administrator*
Thayer, Marilyn *political organization executive, civic worker*
Thomas, Ramonia *political organization executive, civic worker*
Welburn, Brenda Lilienthal *professional society administrator*

Arlington
Bengalee Miller, Amatul-Mannan Q. Katherine *activist*
Buchanan, Louise *political organization worker, consultant*
Ericsson, Sally Claire *not-for-profit organization administrator*
Hickman, Elizabeth Podesta *retired counselor, educator*
Langley, Patricia Ann *lobbyist*
Shannon, Jacqueline *association executive*
Smeal, Eleanor Cutri *civil rights executive*
Tarr-Whelan, Linda *policy center executive*

Vaught, Wilma L. *foundation executive, retired air force officer*

Barboursville
Slaten, Valerie Perlolat *volunteer*

Bristow
Roketenetz, Annemarie *professional society administrator*

Charlottesville
Friedman, Susan Lynn Bell *economic development professional*

Falls Church
Jones, Linda R. Wolf *company executive*
Work, Jane Magruder *retired professional society administrator*

Franktown
Holcomb, Caramine Kellam *volunteer*

Great Falls
Dinger, Ann Monroe *association executive, interior designer*

Keswick
Nosanow, Barbara Shissler *art association administrator*

Lynchburg
Craddock, Mary Spencer Jack *volunteer*

Mc Lean
Bragg, Lynn Munroe *trade association administrator, former federal commissioner*
Trout, Margie Marie Mueller *civic worker*

Newport News
Mazur, Rhoda Himmel *community volunteer*

Norfolk
Lochen, Lynne Carol *tourism organization administrator*

Reston
Brennan, Norma Jean *professional society publications director*
Madry-Taylor, Jacquelyn Yvonne *educational administrator*

Richmond
Bankos, Jean *educational association administrator, educator*
Brackenridge, N. Lynn *not-for-profit developer*
Dell, Willie Jones *social services executive, educator*
McClenahan, Mary Tyler Freeman *civic and community volunteer*
Wood, Jeanne Clarke *charitable organization executive*

Roanoke
Logan Lawson, Anna *social services administrator*

Spotsylvania
Hardy, Dorcas Ruth *business and government relations executive*

Springfield
Kratovil, Jane Lindley *think tank associate, developer/fundraiser*

Upperville
Smart, Edith Merrill *civic worker*

Vienna
Colón, Eugenia Valinda *development executive*

Virginia Beach
Reece-Porter, Sharon Ann *international human rights educator*

WASHINGTON

Bothell
Jacobus, Elizabeth Loomis *volunteer*

Chehalis
Dennis, Linda Susan *nonprofit organization executive*

Ellensburg
Thomas, Spring Ursula *not-for-profit developer, educator, photographer*

Everett
Boschok, Jackie *labor union administrator*

Redmond
Andrew, Jane Hayes *non-profit organization executive*

Seattle
Jessen, Joel Anne *not-for-profit executive, art educator*
Kelsey, Norma L. *labor union administrator*
Sterkovsky, Julia Ellen *activist, organizer*
Williams, Jeanette K. *association executive*

Spokane
Coker, Charlotte Noel *political activist*
Gilpin-Gordon, Mary Ann *retired educational association administrator*

Tacoma
Hinkley, Nancy Emily Engstrom *foundation administrator, educator*

Wenatchee
Davies, Lois A. *educational association administrator, adult education educator*

WEST VIRGINIA

Charleston
Smith, Stuart Lewis *volunteer*

Fairmont
Ford, Alma Regina *union official, educator*

Huntington
Fannin, Josephine Jewell *social services administrator*

Webster Springs
Moore, Alma Merle *association executive*

Wheeling
Hogan, Susan Cox *association executive*

WISCONSIN

Appleton
Hinkens, Kay L. *social services association executive*

Balsam Lake
Mattson, Carol Linnette *social services administrator*

Madison
Heim, Marcy Lynn Schultz *foundation executive*
Honold, Linda Kaye *political organization executive, human resources development executive*
Spring, Terri *political organization executive*

Middleton
Jacobs, Eleanor R. *retired volunteer*

Milwaukee
Hunt, Courtney Lanel *foundation administrator*
Taylor, Katherine *social service administrator*

Waukesha
Bellovary, Cathy *aging services administrator, volunteer*

WYOMING

Buffalo
Smelser, Ruth Malone *volunteer*

Casper
Constantino, Becky *political organization administrator*
Stoval, Linda *political party official*

Cheyenne
Miller, Monica Jeanne *educational association administrator*

Cody
Coe, Margaret Louise Shaw *community service volunteer*

Laramie
Darnall, Roberta Morrow *association executive*

Worland
Staab, Margaret E. *social services administrator*

TERRITORIES OF THE UNITED STATES

VIRGIN ISLANDS

St Thomas
Creque, Linda Ann *non-profit educational and research executive, former education commissioner*

CANADA

ALBERTA

Calgary
Hlavay, Sarah Inez *fundraising executive*

NEW BRUNSWICK

Saint John
Mowatt, E. Ann *women's voluntary leader, lawyer*

ONTARIO

Ottawa
Maxwell, Judith *think-tank executive, economist*
Rodger, Ginette *professional association executive, nurse*

QUEBEC

Rosemere
Hopper, Carol *meeting and incentive trip administrator*

AUSTRALIA

Altona
Daniel-Dreyfus, Susan B. Russe *civic worker*

ATHLETICS

Opa Locka
Robinson, Shirley S. *coach, educator*

Orlando
Peck, Carolyn *professional basketball coach*
Scarcella, Karyn Allee *coach, special education services professional*
Vander Weide, Cheri DeVos *sports team executive, marketing professional*

Saint Petersburg
Craybas, Jill *professional tennis player*
Granville, Laura *professional tennis player*
Harkleroad, Ashley *professional tennis player*
Henin-Hardenne, Justine *professional tennis player*
Reeves, Samantha *professional tennis player*
Shaughnessy, Meghann *professional tennis player*

GEORGIA

Marietta
Devigne, Karen Cooke *retired amateur athletics executive*
Wrege, Julia Bouchelle *tennis professional, physics educator*

IDAHO

Coeur D Alene
Shriner, Darlene Kay *professional athletics coach*

ILLINOIS

Chicago
Akers, Michelle Anne *professional soccer player*
Baumgardt, Justi Michelle *professional soccer player*
Cromwell, Amanda Caryl *former soccer player, coach*
Ducar, Tracy *former soccer player*
Fawcett, Joy Lynn *professional soccer player*
Fotopoulos, Danielle *former soccer player*
Foudy, Julia Maurine *professional soccer player*
Gabarra, Carin Leslie *professional soccer player, professional soccer coach*
Gregg, Lauren *women's soccer coach*
Hamm, Mia (Mariel Margaret Hamm) *professional soccer player*
Heinrichs, April *coach*
Hucles, Angela Khalia *professional soccer player*
Keller, Deborah Kim *former soccer player*
Lenti Ponsetto, Jean *athletic director*
Lilly, Kristine Marie *professional soccer player*
MacMillan, Shannon Ann *professional soccer player*
Milbrett, Tiffeny Carleen *professional soccer player*
Overbeck, Carla Werden *soccer player, coach*
Parlow, Cynthia Maria *professional soccer player*
Pearce, Christie Patricia *professional soccer player*
Reddick, Catherine Anne (Cat Reddick) *professional soccer player*
Roberts, Tiffany Marie *former soccer player*
Schwoy, Laurie Annette *professional soccer player*
Scurry, Briana Collette *professional soccer player*
Slaton, Danielle Victoria *professional soccer player*
Sobrero, Kate (Kathryn Michele Sobrero) *professional soccer player*
Staples, Thori Yvette *former soccer player*
Streiffer, Jenny *former soccer player*
Venturini, Tisha Lea *professional soccer player*
Wagner, Alyson Kay (Aly Wagner) *professional soccer player*
Whalen, Sarah Eve *professional soccer player*

Erie
Latham, LaVonne Marlys *physical education educator*

Glendale Heights
Spearing, Karen Marie *physical education educator, coach*

Glenview
King, Billie Jean Moffitt *former professional tennis player*

Mahomet
Thompson, Margaret M. *physical education educator*

Sterling
Moran, Joan Jensen *physical education and health educator*

Westmont
Tricase, Elizabeth *gymnast*

INDIANA

Granger
Thomas, Debi (Debra J. Thomas) *ice skater*

Indianapolis
Batten, Kimberly Jane *Olympic athlete*
Buford-Bailey, Tonja Yevette *Olympic athlete*
Catchings, Tamika *professional basketball player*
Colander-Richardson, LaTasha *Olympic athlete*
Dawes, Dominique *Olympic athlete*
Donovan, Anne *professional basketball coach, coach*

Favor-Hamilton, Suzanne Marie *track and field athlete, Olympian*
Fortner, Nell *professional athletics coach*
Hennagan, Monique *Olympic athlete*
Jones, Marion *track and field athlete*
Miles-Clark, Jearl *olympic athlete, track and field*
Phelps, Jaycie *gymnast, Olympic athlete*
Torrence, Gwen *Olympic athlete*
Wilkinson, Laura *Olympic athlete*

West Lafayette
Sims-Curry, Kristy *women's college basketball coach*

IOWA

Ames
Sanders, Calli Theisen *athletics administrator*

Iowa City
Lee, Angie *basketball coach*

KANSAS

Lawrence
Washington, Marian *women's basketball coach*

Manhattan
Patterson, Deb *university women's head basketball coach*

Overland Park
Voska, Kathryn Caples *consultant, facilitator*

MAINE

Bangor
Kelley, Barbara Bannin *physical education educator*

Portland
Chow, Amy *gymnast, Olympic athlete*

MARYLAND

Baltimore
Smith, Janet Marie *sports and entertainment executive*

Olney
Sodetz, Carol Jean *aquatic fitness educator*

Towson
Shriver, Pamela H. *retired professional tennis player, sports analyst*

MASSACHUSETTS

Arlington
Samuelson, Joan Benoit *professional runner*

Lynnfield
Kerrigan, Nancy *professional figure skater, former Olympic athlete*

MICHIGAN

Ann Arbor
Ray, Elise *gymnast*

Auburn Hills
Palmer, Wendy *professional basketball player*

Detroit
Ilitch, Marian *professional hockey team executive, food service executive*

MINNESOTA

Eden Prairie
McCombs, Charline *professional sports team executive*

Minneapolis
McConnell Serio, Suzie Theresa *former professional basketball player, professional basketball coach*
Smith, Katie *professional basketball player*

MISSOURI

Earth City
Frontiere, Georgia *professional football team executive*

Saint Louis
Devers, Gail *track and field athlete*
Joyner Kersee, Jacqueline *former track and field athlete*

NEBRASKA

Lincoln
Mulvaney, Mary Jean *physical education educator, department chairman*

NEW HAMPSHIRE

Goshen
Wright, Lilyan Boyd *physical education educator*

NEW JERSEY

Flemington
Castelgrant, Elizabeth Ann Saylor *physical education educator, consultant*

Gladstone
O'Connor, Karen Lende *Olympic athlete*

NEW MEXICO

Abiquiu
Howlett, Phyllis Lou *retired athletics conference administrator*

NEW YORK

Bellmore
MacCoy, Marilyn *physical education educator, volleyball coach*

Bronx
Afterman, Jean *professional sports team executive*

Cortland
Bulger, Marcia S. *physical education educator*

Garden City
Berka, Marianne Guthrie *health and physical education educator*

Lake Placid
Bakken, Jill *Olympic athlete*
Gale, Tristan *Olympic athlete*

New York
Ackerman, Valerie B. *sports association executive*
Blazejowski, Carol A. *professional sports team executive, retired professional basketball player*
Brown, Renee *sports association executive*
Capriati, Jennifer Maria *professional tennis player*
Chen, Lu *figure skater*
Cook, Traci *sports association executive*
Hampton, Kym *professional basketball player*
Hanson, Paula *sports association executive*
Ina, Kyoko *professional figure skater*
Johnson, Vickie *professional basketball player*
Katz, Jane *swimming educator*
Phillips, Tari *professional basketball player*
Sanders, Summer *Olympic athlete, news correspondent, newscaster*
Schindler, Teri *sports association executive*

Poughkeepsie
Hill, Carla Larsen *physical education educator, gymnastics judge*

Syracuse
Duerr, Dianne Marie *sports medicine consultant, educator*

White Plains
Davenport, Lindsay *professional tennis player*
Frazier, Amy *professional tennis player*
Garrison-Jackson, Zina *retired professional tennis player*
Grossman, Ann *professional tennis player*
McNeil, Lori Michelle *professional tennis player*
Morariu, Corina *professional tennis player*
Raymond, Lisa *professional tennis player*
Rubin, Chanda *professional tennis player*
Williams, Serena *professional tennis player*
Williams, Venus *professional tennis player*

NORTH CAROLINA

Charlotte
Lacey, Trudi *professional athletics coach*
Mapp, Rhonda *professional basketball player*
Reid, Tracy *professional basketball player*
Robinson, Shawna *race car driver*
Staley, Dawn *professional basketball player*
Stinson, Andrea Maria *professional basketball player*

Durham
Goestenkors, Gail *basketball coach*

Mooresville
Earnhardt, Teresa *race team owner*

Raleigh
Olevsky, Kathy Kilmartin *owner, instructor karate school*

Wrightsville Beach
Marcolina, Kathryn Watkins *personal and professional success coach*

OHIO

Cincinnati
Pirtle, Laurie Lee *women's university basketball coach*

Cleveland
Baranova, Elena *professional basketball player*
Edwards, Michelle Denise *professional basketball player*
Fijalkowski, Isabelle *professional basketball player*
Lopez, Nancy *former professional golfer*
Moceanu, Dominique *retired Olympic athlete*
Nemcova, Eva *professional basketball player*
Seles, Monica *professional tennis player*

Columbus
Pastore, Donna Lee *physical education educator*

Fairfield
Sheehan, Samantha *gymnast*

Somerset
Green, Tammie *professional golfer*

Tiffin
Spellerberg, Elinor M. *riding instructor*

OKLAHOMA

Edmond
Miller, Shannon *Olympic athlete*

Oklahoma City
Douty, Sheila *softball player*
Fernandez, Lisa *softball player*
Richardson, Dot (Dorothy Gay) *softball player, physician*

Tulsa
Smith, Betty Gene *physical education educator*

OREGON

Canby
Sundquist, Leah Renata *physical education specialist*

Eugene
Sisley, Becky Lynn *physical education educator*

Portland
Hargrove, Linda *professional basketball coach*
Witherspoon, Sophia *professional basketball player*

West Linn
Harris, Debra Coral *physical education educator*

PENNSYLVANIA

Philadelphia
Boyer, Lisa *basketball coach*

Pittsburgh
Berenato, Agnus McGlade *women's basketball coach*

RHODE ISLAND

Newport
Brown, Jane G. *sports association executive*

SOUTH CAROLINA

Columbia
Herrin, Loretta Rasberry *physical education educator*

TENNESSEE

Greeneville
Ford, Sally J. *physical education educator*

TEXAS

Austin
Conradt, Jody *basketball coach*

Carrollton
Lieberman-Cline, Nancy *sports commentator, former professional basketball coach, former player*

Dallas
Hudel, Chestella Alvis *athletics educator*

Houston
Cooper, Cynthia *professional baseball player*
Swoopes, Sheryl Denise *professional basketball player*
Thompson, Tina *professional basketball player*

Lubbock
Sharp, Marsha *basketball coach*

San Antonio
Azzi, Jennifer L. *professional basketball player*
Harvey, Candi *professional basketball coach*
Johnson, Shannon *professional basketball player*

Sugar Land
Vangellow, Deborah Sophia *sports educator, administrator*

UTAH

Park City
Clark, Kelly *Olympic athlete*
Dunn, Shannon *Olympic athlete*
Stone, Nikki *motivational speaker, retired Olympic athlete*
Street, Picabo *Olympic athlete*
Witty, Christine (Chris Witty) *speed skater*

Salt Lake City
Dydek, Margo *professional basketball player*
Hlede, Korie *professional basketball player*
Williams, Natalie *professional basketball player, restaurant executive*

Universal City
Fleishman, Susan Nahley *film company executive*
Gill, Libby *television executive*
Hammer, Bonnie *broadcast executive*
Menendez, Belinda *broadcast executive*
Parent, Mary *film company executive*
Randall, Karen *film company executive*
Rocco, Nikki *film company executive*
Schulz, Diana *film company executive*
Snider, Stacey *film company executive*

Valley Village
Bishop, Kathryn Elizabeth *film company executive, writer*

Vista
Linhart, Letty Lemon *editor*

Walnut Creek
Pfeiffer, Phyllis Kramer *publishing executive*

Woodland Hills
DeWitt, Barbara Jane *journalist*
Harris, Barbara S. *publishing executive*
Murphy, Irene Helen *publishing executive*
Rafter, Tracy *publishing executive*
Russell, Anne M. *editor-in-chief*

COLORADO

Aspen
Hayes, Mary Eshbaugh *editor, writer*

Boulder
El Mallakh, Dorothea Hendry *editor, publishing executive*
Rienner, Lynne Carol *publishing executive*
Rothenberg, Elizabeth Jill *editor*

Castle Rock
Richardson, Suzanne Mays *communication consultant*

Cherry Hills Village
Stapleton, Katharine Hall (Katie Stapleton) *food broadcaster, writer*

Colorado Springs
Fleming, Terri *newspaper editor*

Craig
Gray, Ann Maynard *broadcasting company executive*

Denver
Chavez, Jeanette *editor*
Drake, Sylvie (Jurras Drake) *theater critic*
Goeken, Deborah *editor*

Durango
Ballantine, Morley Cowles (Mrs. Arthur Atwood Ballantine) *editor*
Reid-Bills, Mae *magazine editor, historian*

Englewood
Peters, Janice C. *cable company executive*

Montrose
Gillette, Ethel Morrow *columnist*

CONNECTICUT

Bethel
Shepard, Jean Heck *publishing company consultant, author, agent*

Bridgeport
Simoneau, Cynthia Lambert *newspaper editor, journalism educator*

Bristol
Driessen, Christine F. *broadcast executive*
Roberts, Robin *sportscaster*

Brookfield
Reynolds, Jean Edwards *publishing executive*

Chester
Frost-Knappman, Elizabeth (Linda Elizabeth Frost-Knappman) *publishing executive, editor, writer*

Fairfield
Eigel, Marcia Duffy *editor*

Granby
Fair, Nancy Hazen *media specialist, educator*

Hartford
Roessner, Barbara *journalist*
Sisco, Carol *broadcast executive, educator*

Newington
Zeldes, Edith R. *freelance journalist*

Southbury
Vega, Marylois Purdy *journalist*

Stamford
Lane, Hana Umlauf *editor*

Storrs Mansfield
Croteau, Maureen Elizabeth *journalism educator*

Thomaston
Donohue, Diane Frances *fine arts publisher, artist*

Torrington
Di Russo, Terry *communications educator, writer*

DELAWARE

New Castle
Henley, Deborah S. *newspaper editor*

DISTRICT OF COLUMBIA

Washington
Adams, Lorraine *reporter*
Angier, Natalie Marie *science journalist*
Applebaum, Anne *journalist, writer*
Arena, Kelli *news correspondent*
Attkisson, Sharyl T. *newscaster, correspondent, writer*
Boo, Katherine *newswriter*
Borger, Gloria *journalist, editor*
Bourke, Dale Hanson *publishing company owner*
Butterworth, Ritajean Hartung *broadcast executive*
Clift, Eleanor *magazine correspondent*
Cohen, Sarah *reporter*
Conroy, Sarah Booth *columnist, writer, educator*
Cox, Kathleen *broadcast executive, lawyer*
Davidson, Susan Bettina *editor, writer*
Davis, Evelyn Y. *editor, writer*
Deeb, Mary-Jane *editor, educator*
Dewar, Helen *reporter*
Donohoe, Cathryn Murray *journalist*
Dowd, Maureen *columnist*
Drew, Elizabeth *television commentator, journalist, author*
Feld, Karen Irma *columnist, journalist, broadcaster, public speaker*
Fields, Suzanne Bregman *syndicated columnist*
Garrels, Anne *news correspondent*
Geyer, Georgie Anne *syndicated columnist, educator, author, biographer, TV commentator*
Gibson, Florence Anderson *talking book company executive, narrator*
Glaser, Vera Romans *journalist*
Gorman, Patricia Jane *editor*
Greenhouse, Linda Joyce *journalist*
Gregory, Bettina Louise *journalist*
Guzy, Carol *photojournalist*
Headden, Susan M. *editor*
Hecht, Marjorie Mazel *editor*
Herman, Andrea Maxine *newspaper editor*
Hill, Patrice Susan *journalist, economist*
Horwitz, Sari *reporter*
Howell, Deborah *editor*
Hull, Marion Hayes *communications educator, researcher*
Johnson, Sandra K. *journalist*
Jones, Leonade Diane *media publishing company executive*
Jordan, Mary *editor-in-chief, reporter*
Joyce, Anne Raine *editor, director of publications*
Judd, Jacqueline Dee (Jackie Judd) *journalist, reporter*
Kempley, Rita A. *film critic, editor*
Kilian, Pamela Reeves *journalist, writer*
King, Nina Davis *journalist*
Knight, Athelia Wilhelmenia *journalist*
Lajoux, Alexandra Reed *editor, educator*
Lawson, Jennifer *broadcast executive*
Lee, Debra L. *broadcast executive*
Lehrman, Margaret McBride *television news executive, producer*
Loker, Elizabeth St. John *newspaper executive*
Lumpkin, Beverley Carson *reporter, producer*
Mamer, Louisan Elizabeth *home economist, journalist*
Maxwell, Maureen Kay *media specialist, educator*
McBee, Susanna Barnes *retired journalist*
McFeatters, Ann Carey *journalist*
Milner Anderson, Katherine *broadcast executive*
Mitchell, Andrea *journalist*
Murphy, Caryle Marie *foreign correspondent*
O'Brien, Soledad *newscaster, news anchor*
Ong, Laureen E. *broadcast executive*
Palmer, Stacy Ella *periodical editor*
Paull, Elsie Behrend *editorial stylist, interpreter*
Porter, Barbara *anchorwoman, writer, educator*
Potter, Deborah Ann *news correspondent, educator*
Pratt, Carin *television executive*
Richman, Phyllis Chasanow *newspaper critic*
Ross, Wendy Clucas *newspaper editor, journalist*
Schiff, Margaret Scott *newspaper publishing executive*
Scholz, Jane *newspaper publisher*
Schulman, Heidi *broadcast executive*
Shanks, Judith Weil *editor*
Simons, Carol Lenore *magazine editor*
Singer, Suzanne Fried *editor*
Smith, Mignon C. *publishing executive*
Stamberg, Susan Levitt *radio broadcaster*
Stepp, Laura Sessions *journalist*
Sweet, Lynn D. *journalist*
Thomas, Helen A. (Mrs. Douglas B. Cornell) *newspaper bureau executive*
Totenberg, Nina *journalist*
Trafford, Abigail *columnist, editor, writer*
Valdez-Snelgrove, Deborah *communications executive*
Weymouth, Elizabeth Morris Graham (Lally Weymouth) *editor, columnist*
Woodruff, Judy Carline *broadcast journalist*
Zahn, Paula *newscaster*

FLORIDA

Boca Raton
Fuller, Bonnie *editor*

Boynton Beach
Jacobs, Wendy *editor, writer, translator*
Parsons, Mindy (Mindy Enos) *newsletter editor, publisher, non-profit organization executive*

Coral Gables
MacLiammoir, Sandra Jean *journalist, columnist, educator*

Delray Beach
Robinson, Brenda Kay *editor, public relations professional*

Fort Lauderdale
Hartz, Deborah Sophia *editor, writer*
Reisinger, Sandra Sue *columnist*

Fort Walton Beach
McDonald, Pamela Jane *educational media specialist*

Gainesville
Kelly, Kathleen S(ue) *communications educator*
Maple, Marilyn Jean *educational media coordinator*

Hallandale
Schatken, Nancy Leah *medical editor*

Hillsboro Beach
Gibbons, Celia Victoria Townsend (Mrs. John Sheldon) *editor, publisher*

Jacksonville
Bedell, Elizabeth Snyder (Betty Bedell) *editor-in-chief, marketing professional*
Cannon, Lillian *retired editor*
Koeppel, Mary Sue *communications educator, writer*
Kress, Mary Elizabeth *retired newspaper editor*

Key Biscayne
Blank, Joan Gill *journalist, illustrator*

Key West
Bradford, Judith Lynnell *journalist, artist*

Lake Worth
Asher, Kathleen May *communications educator*

Miami
Balmaseda, Liz *columnist*
de Leon, Lidia Maria *magazine editor*
Fichtner, Margaria *journalist*
Muir, Helen *journalist, author*
O'Bryon, Linda Elizabeth *television station executive*
Welsh, Judith Schenck *communications educator*

Naples
Mills, Dorothy Jane (Dorothy Z. Seymour) *editor, consultant*

North Miami
Kordalewski, Lydia Maria *news correspondent, municipal employee*

Orlando
DeLorme, Denise Elizabeth *communications educator*
Hall, Charlotte Hauch *newspaper editor*
Healy, Jane Elizabeth *newspaper editor*
Kramer, Elaine *editor*
Maupin, Elizabeth Thatcher *theater critic*
Waltz, Kathleen M. *publishing executive*
Waltz, Kathy *publishing executive*

Palm Beach
Shulgasser-Parker, Barbara *writer*

Palm Coast
Franco, Annemarie Woletz *editor*

Pensacola
Ivey, Denise H. *publishing executive*

Saint Petersburg
Johnson, Edna Ruth *editor*
Johnson, Pam *former newspaper editor, communications educator*
Martin, Susan Taylor *newspaper editor*
Petty, Marty *publishing executive*
Weaver, Janet S. *newspaper editor*

Sanford
Scott, Mellouise Jacqueline *retired media specialist*

Santa Rosa Beach
Gilmore, Beverly J *retired journalist, gallery owner*

Sarasota
North, Marjorie Mary *columnist*
Stevens, Elisabeth Goss (Mrs. Robert Schleussner Jr.) *writer, journalist, graphic artist*
Tennant, Diane P. *editor*

Tallahassee
Morgan, Lucy Ware *journalist*

Tampa
Culpepper, Mary Kay *publishing executive*
Fernandez, Yolanda *newscaster*
Guyardo, Gayle *newscaster*
Maher, Irene *newscaster*
Prest, Nerissa *newscaster*
Reed, Donna Marie *editor, newspaper*
Schaible, Stacie *newscaster*
Sierens, Gayle *newscaster*

GEORGIA

Alpharetta
Lynn, Kristina *journalist, actress, writer, producer*

Atlanta
Allen, Natalie *cable news anchor*
Bennett, Lorraine Martin *editor*
Chambers, Anne Cox *newspaper executive, former diplomat*
Charles, Cory Anne *television guest booking director*
Clayton, Xernona *media executive*
Dobson, Bridget McColl Hursley *television executive, writer*
Evans, Gail Hirschorn *television news executive*
Fortin, Judy *cable news anchor*
Grogan, Paula Cataldi *newspaper editor*
Kaufman, Monica *newscaster*
McGill, Sylviette Delphine *editor*
Robelot, Jane *anchor*
Roth, Teresa Ann *broadcast executive*
Scott, Marian Alexis *journalist*
Sloan, Mary Jean *retired media specialist*
Tucker, Cynthia Anne *journalist*
Wallace, Julia Diane *newspaper editor*
Ward, Janet Lynn *magazine editor, sports wire reporter*
Whitworth, Wendy Walker *cable network executive*
Wilson, Debora J. *broadcast executive*

Douglasville
Haynes, Reba Carol *media specialist, educator*

Savannah
Edeawo, Gale Sky *publishing company executive, writer*
Gusby, Kim *newscaster*
Parker, Sheila *newscaster*
Thorne, Kristan *newscaster*
Tyus-Shaw, Tina *newscaster*
Wilder, Ginger *newscaster*

HAWAII

Honolulu
Black, Cobey *journalist*
Keyes, Saundra Elise *newspaper editor*
Varner, Helen *communications educator*

IDAHO

Sandpoint
Bowne, Martha Hoke *publishing consultant*

ILLINOIS

Bartlett
Markle, Sandra *publishing company executive*

Carol Stream
Franzen, Janice Marguerite Gosnell *magazine editor*

Champaign
McCulloh, Judith Marie *editor*
Thomas, Jo *journalist*
Turquette, Frances Bond *editor*

Chicago
Ahern, Mary Ann *reporter*
Baca, Stacey *newscaster*
Barr, Emily L. *television station executive*
Beaudet-Francès, Patricia Suzanne *photography editor*
Birchett, Colleen Lucille *editor*
Bratcher, Juanita *journalist*
Brock, Kathy *newscaster*
Brooks, Marion *newscaster*
Brotman, Barbara Louise *columnist, writer*
Burns, Diann *newscaster*
Burton, Cheryl *newscaster*
Callaway, Karen A(lice) *journalist*
Casillas, Ofelia Marie *journalist*
Childers, Mary Ann *newscaster*
Connors, Dorsey *television and radio commentator, newspaper columnist*
Cooper, Ilene Linda *magazine editor, author*
Donovan, Dianne Francys *journalist*
Eastabrook, Dianne *news correspondent*
Evans, Mariwyn *periodical editor*
Ferguson, Renee *news correspondent, reporter*
Flanagan, Sylvia *editor*
Garza, Melita Marie *journalist*
Gomez, Sylvia *newscaster*
Grumman, Cornelia *newswriter*
Guillen, Alita (Alita Haytayan) *newscaster*
Guy, Sandra *journalist, telecommunications writer*
Hast, Adele *editor, historian*
Hefner, Christie Ann *multi-media entertainment executive*
Hill, Darlene *newscaster*
Hsu, Judy *newscaster*
Idol, Anna Catherine *magazine editor*
Jones, Linda *communications educator*
Jordan, Karen *newscaster*
Kelly, Maura Anne *reporter*
King, Jennifer Elizabeth *editor*
Klaviter, Helen Lothrop *magazine editor*
Kramer, Weezie Crawford *former broadcast executive*
Krueger, Bonnie Lee *editor, writer*
Kwan, Nesita *newscaster*
Lipinski, Ann Marie *newspaper editor*
Loesch, Katharine Taylor (Mrs. John George Loesch) *communication and theatre educator*
Lythcott, Marcia A. *newspaper editor*
Martinez, Natalie *newscaster*
Migala, Lucyna J. *journalist, arts administrator, radio station executive*
Needleman, Barbara *newspaper executive*
Pender, Nancy *newscaster*
Peres, Judith May *journalist*
Perez, Sylvia *newscaster, reporter*
Rice, Linda Johnson *publishing executive*
Robinson, Robin *newscaster*
Rosati, Allison *newscaster*
Sneed, Michael (Michele Sneed) *columnist*
Weinberg, Lila Shaffer *writer, editor*
Wier, Patricia Ann *publishing executive, consultant*

Wille, Lois Jean *retired newspaper editor*
Winker, Margaret A. *editor*
Winnecke, Joycelyn *editor*
Wolfe, Sheila A. *journalist*
Wright, Sharon *reporter*
Zekman, Pamela Lois (Mrs. Fredric Soll)
  reporter

Des Plaines
Clapper, Marie Anne *magazine publisher*
Henrikson, Lois Elizabeth *photojournalist*

Elmhurst
Pruter, Margaret Franson *editor*

Evanston
Downing, Joan Forman *editor, writer*
Galvin, Kathleen Malone *communications
  educator*

Highland Park
Leavitt, Sandra B. *editor*

Montgomery
Healy, Laura Marie *editor*

Oak Park
Bedrossian, Ursula Kay Kennedy *editor*

Paw Paw
Heim, Alberta Jane *publishing executive, writer*

Richmond
Lopat, Romalda Regina *publisher, editor*

River Forest
Harvey, Lynne Cooper *broadcasting executive,
  civic worker*

Westmont
Goring, Ruth Ann *editor, writer*

INDIANA

Bloomington
Gough, Pauline Bjerke *magazine editor*

Cambridge City
Slonaker, Mary Joanna King *columnist*

Crawfordsville
Karg, Thelma Aileen *writer, retired educator*

East Chicago
Platis, Mary Lou *media specialist*

Fort Wayne
Oxley, Ann *television executive*

Huntington
Lindsey, Jacquelyn Maria *editor*

Indianapolis
Adamak, M. Jeanelle *broadcast executive*
Chase, Alyssa Ann *editor*
Comiskey, Nancy *newspaper editor*
Fine, Pamela B. *newspaper editor*
Fleming, Marcella *journalist*
Garmel, Marion Bess Simon *retired arts
  journalist*
Henry, Barbara A. *publishing executive*
Lee, Kristi *broadcast executive, reporter*
Schilling, Emily Born *editor, association
  executive*

Knightstown
Richardson, Shirley Maxine *editor*

Lafayette
Renzetti, Phyllis Jean *retired technical editor*

Munster
Colander, Patricia Marie *newspaper editor*
Neff, Bonita Dostal *communication development
  facilitator*

IOWA

Ames
Alumbaugh, JoAnn McCalla *magazine editor*

Des Moines
Byal, Nancy Louise *food editor*
DeWulf Nickell, Karol *editor*
Graham, Diane E. *newspaper editor*
Myers, Mary Kathleen *publishing executive*
Sheehan, Carol Sama *magazine editor*
Stier, Mary P. *publishing executive*
Van Zante, Shirley M(ae) *magazine editor*

KANSAS

Hutchinson
Baumer, Beverly Belle *journalist*

Logan
Manion, Kay Daureen *newspaper executive*

North Newton
Snider, Marie Anna *syndicated columnist*

Russell
Soetaert, Pamela Joyce *journalist, editor*

Shawnee Mission
Martin, Donna Lee *publishing company
  executive, retired*

Wichita
Zimmerman, Melva Jean *writer, retired media
  specialist, educator*

KENTUCKY

Georgetown
Bevins, Ann Bolton *retired journalist, retired
  historian*

Louisville
Scheu, Lynn McLaughlin *scientific publication
  editor, secondary school educator*

LOUISIANA

Bossier City
DeFatta-Barattini, Kathryn *communications
  educator*

Carencro
Gorski, Hedwig Irene *poet, writer*

Hammond
Sullivan, Jane St. Amant *editor, educator*

La Place
Fiffie Proctor, JoAnn *media and technology
  specialist*

New Orleans
Ball, Millie (Mildred Porteous Ball) *editor,
  journalist*
Boswell, Stephanie *newscaster*
Curry, Dale Blair *retired journalist*
Fairbairn, Kriss *newscaster*
Moreno, Helena *newscaster*
Orr, Margaret *newscaster*
Sanders, Melanie *newscaster*

Slidell
Johnson, Patricia Lucille *editor, writer*
Lovell, Emily Kalled *retired journalist*

MAINE

Belfast
Griffith, Patricia King *journalist*

Kennebunkport
Ray, Virginia H. S. *columnist, writer*

Monhegan
Boehmer, Raquel Davenport *newsletter editor*

MARYLAND

Annapolis
Wyman, L. Pilar *indexer*

Baltimore
Kesselring, Linda J. *medical editor, writer*
Murphy, Frances Louise, II, *retired newspaper
  publisher*
Palmer, Denise *publishing executive*
Pollak, Lisa *columnist*
Rousuck, J. Wynn *theater critic*
Steinbach, Alice *journalist*
Sugg, Diana K. *reporter*
Thomas, Jacqueline Marie *journalist, editor*

Bethesda
English, Michela *entertainment company
  executive*
Herman, Edith Carol *journalist*
Kaplan, Marjorie *broadcast executive*
McHale, Judith A. (Judith Ottalloran) *broadcast
  executive, lawyer*
Olson, Lynn *editor*
Orthmann, Rosemary Ann *editor*
Wagner, Cynthia Gail *editor, writer*

College Park
Beasley, Maurine Hoffman *journalism educator,
  historian*

Easton
Potter, Blair Burns *editor*
Wilson, Laura Ann *newspaper editor*

Havre de Grace
Wetter, Virginia Forwood Pate *broadcast
  executive*

Lanham
Godwin, Mary Jo *editor, librarian consultant*

Lanham Seabrook
Ojinnaka, Becky *publishing executive*

Owings Mills
Holdridge, Barbara *book publisher*

Rockville
Miller, Claire Ellen *children's writer, editor,
  educator*
Uffen, Ellen Serlen *editor, writer*

Severna Park
Pumphrey, Janet Kay *editor, publisher*

Silver Spring
Bennett, Carol(ine) Elise *retired reporter, actress*

MASSACHUSETTS

Beverly
Daya, Jackie *publishing company executive*

Boston
Adams, Phoebe-Lou *journalist*
Baldassano, Corinne Leslie *radio executive*
Buckingham, Virginia *editor*
Caldwell, Gail *book critic*
Cohen, Rachelle Sharon *journalist*

Collins, Monica Ann *journalist*
Donovan, Helen W. *newspaper editor*
Flaherty, Lois Talbot *editor, psychiatrist,
  educator*
Foreman, Judy *journalist*
Grimes, Heilan Yvette *publishing executive*
Lawrence, Merloyd Ludington *editor*
McNamee, Linda Rose *broadcast executive*
Mills, Kathryn *publishing executive, director*
Stevens, Marilyn Ruth *editor*
Strothman, Wendy Jo *book publisher*

Cambridge
Goodman, Ellen Holtz *journalist*
Wilcox, Maud *editor*

Dover
Salhany, Lucille S. *broadcast executive*

Florence
Kan, Susan *publishing executive, editor*

Framingham
Johnson, Maryfran *editor*

Needham
Meisner, Mary Jo *editor*

Newton
Gullette, Margaret Morganroth *cultural critic,
  writer*
Hume, Ellen Hunsberger *media analyst,
  journalist*

Plymouth
Flood, H(ulda) Gay *editor, consultant*

Quincy
Chung, Cynthia Norton *communications
  specialist*

Roslindale
Driscoll, Kathleen J. *writer*

South Hadley
Elleman, Barbara *editor*

Springfield
Gordon, Ronni Anne *journalist*

Sudbury
Hillery, Mary Jane Larato *columnist, television
  personality, television producer, writer,
  military officer*

Weston
Schwartz, Donna S. *publishing executive*
Schwartz, Ann Simmons *retired publishing
  executive*

Winthrop
Lutze, Ruth Louise *retired textbook editor, public
  relations executive*

Woburn
Speerstra, Karen M. *former publishing executive*

MICHIGAN

Ann Arbor
Unterburger, Amy L. *editor*

Bloomfield Township
Brown, Lynette Ralya *journalist, publicist*

Clinton
Anderson, Denice Anna *editor*

Detroit
Burzynski, Susan Marie *newspaper editor*
Colby, Joy Hakanson *critic*
Diebolt, Judith *newspaper editor*
Hutton, Carole Leigh *newspaper editor*
James, Sheryl Teresa *journalist*
Laughlin, Nancy *newspaper editor*
Muszynski, Stacy *editor, writer*
Stark, Susan R. *film critic*

Farmington Hills
Bryfonski, Dedria Anne *publishing company
  executive*

Grand Rapids
Wheeler, Kathryn S. *editor*

Grosse Pointe
Whittaker, Jeanne Evans *former newspaper
  columnist*

Grosse Pointe Farms
Holsapple, Linda Harris *retired editor*

Grosse Pointe Woods
McWhirter, Glenna Suzanne (Nickie McWhirter)
  retired newspaper columnist

Kalamazoo
DeRitter, Margaret Catherine *journalist*

Lansing
Brown, Nancy Field *editor*

Midland
Messing, Carol Sue *communications educator*

Petoskey
Vernon, Doris Schaller *retired writer*

Saginaw
Heitkamp, Lynn Elizabeth *journalist*
Killingbeck, Janice Lynelle (Mrs. Victor Lee
  Killingbeck) *journalist*

Shelby Township
Argirokastritis, Diane Marie *media specialist*

Southfield
Catallo, Heather *newscaster*
Gayle, Monica *broadcast journalist*
Makupson, Amyre Porter *television station
  executive*
Margolis, Sherry *newscaster*
Stinger, Fanchon *newscaster*

West Bloomfield
Starr, Monica *company executive*

MINNESOTA

Circle Pines
Yanta, Kristin *publishing executive*

Duluth
Gruver, Nancy *publishing executive*

Edina
King, Heather Ann *freelance journalist*

Minneapolis
Crosby, Jacqueline Garton *newspaper editor,
  journalist*
Flanagan, Barbara *journalist*
Laing, Karel Ann *magazine publishing executive*
McDaniel, Jan *television station executive*
Paul, Nora Marie *media studies educator*
Rajkumar, Roshini Anne *reporter*
Watson, Catherine Elaine *journalist*
Zelickson, Sue *newspaper and cookbook editor,
  television reporter and host, food consultant*

Roseville
Arndt, Joan Marie *media specialist, educator*

Saint Paul
Fruehling, Rosemary Therese *publishing
  executive, author*
Lofquist, Vicki L. *journalist*
Straight, Cathy *editor*

Stillwater
Buck, Anita Emily *newswriter*

MISSISSIPPI

Jackson
Anderson, Roslyn *newscaster*
Frazel-Lasseter, Cheryl *newscaster*
Segal, Jane *newscaster*
Srinivasan, Seetha *publishing company executive*
Thompson, Marsha *newscaster*
Wade, Maggie *newscaster*

Pearl
Grison, Deborah D. *publishing executive*

MISSOURI

Kansas City
Busby, Marjean (Marjorie Jean Busby) *retired
  journalist*
Cahill, Patricia Deal *radio station executive*
Garrison, F. Elaine *copy editor*
Guisewite, Cathy Lee *cartoonist*
Lindenbaum, Sharon *publishing executive*
Roush, Sue *newspaper editor*

Kirksville
Presley, Paula Lumpkin *retired editor*

Saint Louis
Bennett, Patricia Ann *radio executive*
Ehrlich, Ava *television executive*
Korando, Donna Kay *journalist*
Rice, Patricia Jane *journalist*
Soeteber, Ellen *journalist, editor*

Springfield
Champion, Norma Jean *communications
  educator, state legislator*

Warrensburg
Desmond, Kathleen Kadon *critic, educator, artist*

NEBRASKA

Chadron
Buschkopf, Debora J. *court reporter*

Lincoln
Raz, Hilda *editor-in-chief periodical, English
  educator*

Omaha
Batchelder, Anne Stuart *retired publishing
  executive, political organization worker*
Sands, Deanna *editor*

NEVADA

Las Vegas
Miller, Valerie Carol *journalist*
Norman, Jean Reid *journalist*

Reno
Crowe, Jennifer *newspaper reporter*
Cunning, Tonia *newspaper managing editor*
Weniger-Phelps, Nancy Ann *media specialist,
  photographer*

NEW HAMPSHIRE

Keene
Salcetti, Marianne *newswriter, educator*

Plymouth
Santore, Marcia Lucinda Green *editor, artist*

Portsmouth
Hopkins, Jeannette Ethel *book publisher, editor*

NEW JERSEY

Allendale
DiBlasi, Dianne Clark *editor*
Long, Jo-Nelle Desmond *editor, consultant, historian*

Cherry Hill
Gutin, Myra Gail *communications educator*

Dover
Kassell, Paula Sally *editor, publisher*

Edison
Currence, Anna *publishing executive*

Englewood Cliffs
Dobrzynski, Judith Helen *journalist, commentator*
Saible, Stephanie Irene *magazine editor*
Vane, Dena *magazine editor-in-chief*

Fort Lee
Bohner, Kate *correspondent*
Epperson, Sharon *television correspondent*
MacCallum, Martha *correspondent*
Stuart, Carole *publishing executive*

Garwood
Smith, Joan Lowell *syndicated columnist, feature writer*

Gillette
Nathanson, Linda Sue *publisher, author, technical writer*

Hackensack
Waixel, Vivian *journalist*

Haworth
Biesel, Diane Jane *editor, publishing executive*

Hillsborough
Yuster-Freeman, Leigh Carol *broadcast executive*

Long Branch
Lagowski, Barbara Jean *writer, book editor*

Martinsville
Squire, Laurie Rubin *media consultant*

Montvale
Falk, Ellen Stein *media specialist, educator*
Politi, Beth Kukkonen *publishing services company executive*

New Providence
Cooper, Carol Diane *publishing company executive*

Newark
Clowney, Mary L. *educational media specialist, librarian*
Dauth, Frances Kutcher *journalist, newspaper editor*
Dennery, Linda *newspaper publishing executive*
Shain, Jo-Ann *editor*

Piscataway
Urban, Cathleen Andrea *graphic designer*

Princeton
Dubrovsky, Gertrude Wishnick *journalist, researcher*
Lincoln, Anna *publishing executive*
Weiss, Renée Karol *editor, musician*

Rockaway
Kurtz, Ellen R. *journalist*

Sea Isle City
Bruno, Carol Jeanette *library media specialist, gifted and talented education educator, innkeeper*

Secaucus
Blackman, Brenda *newscaster*
Cho, Alina *anchor*

Short Hills
Winter, Ruth Grosman (Mrs. Arthur Winter) *journalist*

Toms River
Leone, Judith Gibson *educational media specialist, video production company executive*

Trenton
Christopherson, Elizabeth Good *broadcast executive*
Joseph, Edith Hoffman *retired editor*

Willingboro
Coppock, Kristen Anne K. *newswriter, editor*

NEW MEXICO

Albuquerque
Blake, Renée *broadcast executive*
Hadas, Elizabeth Chamberlayne *editor*
Moses, Karen *editor*
Riordan, Jennifer L. *media relations manager*

Arroyo Hondo
Greenwood Levy, Phaedra Jean *photojournalist, writer*

Las Cruces
Merrick, Beverly Georgianne *journalism, communications educator*

Los Alamos
Mendius, Patricia Dodd Winter *editor, educator, writer*

Santa Fe
Lichtenberg, Margaret Klee *publishing company executive*
Stieber, Tamar *journalist*

Silver City
Hall, Jean Quintero *communications and history educator*

NEW YORK

Alfred
Goodman, Robyn S. *communications educator*

Armonk
Slosek, Theresa J. *media specialist, school librarian*

Bainbridge
Goerlich, Shirley Alice Boyce *publishing executive, educator, media consultant*

Bellport
Townsend, Terry *publishing executive*

Bethpage
Albergo, Margaret *broadcast executive*
Mahony, Sheila Anne *broadcast executive*

Bronx
Ahmose, Nefertari A. *journalism educator*
Silverman, Francine Terry *writer*

Bronxville
Civiello, Mary *correspondent*
Rosenthal, Lucy Gabrielle *writer, educator, editor*

Brooklyn
Daly, Joe Ann Godown *publishing company executive*
De Lisi, Joanne *media consultant, educator*
Giuliani, Cristina Lynn *broadcast technician, scriptwriter*

Buffalo
Sullivan, Margaret M. *editor*

Dunkirk
Lewis, Amy Beth *newswriter, reporter, writer, photographer*

East Syracuse
Duffy, Nancy Keogh *television broadcast professional*

Flushing
Brooks, Helene Margaret *editorial consultant*

Forest Hills
Prager, Alice Heinecke *music company executive*

Great Neck
Fiel, Maxine Lucille *journalist, behavior analyst, educator*

Houghton
Machamer, Cynthia G. *editor, writer*

Ithaca
Park, Dorothy Goodwin Dent (Mrs. Roy Hampton Park) *broadcast executive, publishing executive*

Jamaica
Brockway, Laurie Sue *editor, journalist, author, minister*

Jericho
Dore, Kathleen A. *broadcast executive*

Locust Valley
Zulch, Joan Carolyn *retired medical publishing company executive*

Melville
Carter, Sylvia *journalist*
Garrett, Laurie *science correspondent*
Krenek, Debby *newspaper editor*
Noguere, Suzanne *publishing manager, poet*
Richards, Carol Ann Rubright *editor, columnist*
Saul, Stephanie *journalist*

Middletown
Bedell, Barbara Lee *journalist*

Millbrook
Hall, Penelope Coker *writer, magazine editor*

New Paltz
Irvine, Rose Loretta Abernethy *retired communications educator, consultant*

New York
Abrams, Roz *newscaster*
Abramson, Jill *newspaper publishing executive*
Adams, Cindy *journalist*
Adler, Margot Susanna *journalist, radio producer*
Altschul, Serena *newscaster*
Amster, Linda Evelyn *newspaper executive, consultant*
Anthony, Michele *entertainment executive*
Atkinson, Holly Gail *physician, journalist, business executive, author, lecturer, human rights activist*
Baderinwa, Sade *newscaster*

Bahr, Lauren S. *publishing company executive*
Bailey, Janet Dee *publishing company executive*
Baker, Elizabeth Calhoun *magazine editor*
Balaz, Beverly Ann *publishing executive*
Banfield, Ashleigh Dennistoun *news correspondent*
Baquero, Lynda *newscaster, reporter*
Baranauckas, Carla May *journalist*
Barbosa, Shameka Brown *copywriter*
Barbour, Celia *editor*
Barnett, Amy DuBois *editor-in-chief*
Barolini, Teodolinda *literary critic*
Battiste, Janice Louise *editor, writer*
Battle, Pat *reporter*
Bauer, Tricia *publishing executive, writer*
Begley, Sharon Lynn *journalist*
Bemis, Mary Ferguson *magazine editor*
Bender, Judith *journalist, editor*
Benedek, Melinda *television executive*
Bernstein, Bonnie *sportscaster*
Beyer, Lisa *journalist*
Black, Carole *broadcast executive*
Black, Cathleen Prunty *publishing executive*
Booth, Tami *editor*
Brant, Sandra J. *magazine publisher*
Bratten, Millie Martini *editor-in-chief*
Brenner, Beth Fuchs *publishing executive*
Brody, Jane Ellen *journalist, researcher*
Brown, Campbell *commentator*
Brown, Helen Gurley *editor, writer*
Brown, Lyn *newscaster*
Brown, Tina *journalist, television personality*
Buchanan, Edna *journalist*
Buckley, Priscilla Langford *magazine editor*
Buckley, Virginia Laura *editor*
Bushnell, Candance *columnist, writer*
Calvi, Mary *reporter*
Caploe, Roberta *magazine editor*
Carr, Gladys Justin *publishing company executive, consultant, editor, writer*
Caruso, Ann S. *fashion editor, stylist*
Cassidy, Catherine *editor-in-chief*
Centrello, Gina *publishing executive*
Chan, Janet *publishing executive*
Chang, Jeannette *publishing executive*
Chast, Roz *cartoonist*
Chen, Julie *newscaster*
Chen, Lena *broadcast executive*
Chesnutt, Jane *publishing executive*
Chira, Susan *editor*
Christoforous, Alexis *reporter*
Chwat, Anne *recording industry executive*
Cohane, Heather Christina *magazine publisher, editor*
Cohen, Claudia *journalist, television personality*
Cole, Kirsten *reporter*
Colletti, Roseanne *reporter*
Collins, Gail *editor*
Constantino, Yamila *journalist, media executive*
Cooley, Lisa *television news anchor*
Cooney, Joan Ganz *broadcast executive, director*
Cooper, Gloria *editor, press critic*
Cortina, Betty *magazine editor*
Couric, Katie (Katherine Anne Couric) *broadcast journalist*
Coyne, Judith *editor*
Crandell, Susan *magazine editor*
Crist, Judith *film and drama critic*
Croce, Arlene Louise *critic*
Crone, Penny *reporter*
Cross, Mary S. *photojournalist*
Curry, Ann *correspondent, anchor*
Daly, Cheryl *broadcast executive*
Danziger, Lucy *editor*
De Angelis, Judy *anchorwoman*
Deitz, Paula *magazine editor*
Delbourgo, Joëlle Lily *publishing executive*
Demillo, Ernabel *reporter*
Disney, Anthea *publishing executive*
Dolan, Daria *news correspondent*
Dozier, Kimberly *reporter*
Dyson, Esther *publisher, editor*
Eaker, Sherry Ellen *entertainment newspaper editor*
Eckman, Fern Marja *journalist*
Egen, Maureen Mahon *publishing executive*
Epstein, Barbara *editor*
Evans, Linda Kay *publishing company executive*
Farber, Jackie *editor*
Farrell, Margaret *magazine publisher*
Fine, Deborah *publishing executive*
Fiori, Pamela *publishing executive, magazine editor, writer*
Foley, Ann *broadcast executive*
Forden, Diane Claire *magazine editor*
Franks, Lucinda Laura *journalist*
Friedman, Jane *publishing executive*
Fuentez, Tania Michele *journalist*
Gables, Shon *newscaster*
Gaffney, Elizabeth Mallory *editor, writer, literature educator, translator*
Gardner, Janet Paxton *journalist, film/video producer*
Gatto, Carolyn Michele *editor-in-chief*
Gayle, King *editor*
Geary, Hilary R. *society editor*
Geiser, Elizabeth Able *publishing company executive*
Gewirtz-Friedman, Gerry *editor*
Gharib, Susie *television newscaster*
Goldenberg, Elizabeth Leigh *editor*
Golon, Maryanne *photojournalist*
Gora, Susannah Porter Martin *journalist, poet*
Grader, Patricia Alison Lande *editor*
Greenfield, Rachel *magazine executive*
Grimes, Suzanne *publishing executive*
Gross, Amy *publishing executive*
Guerrero, Lisa (Lisa Guerrero-Coles) *sports reporter*
Guillermoprieto, Alma *journalist, non-fiction writer*
Gusoff, Carolyn *reporter*
Haegele, Patricia *publishing executive*
Hall, Lisa G. *broadcast executive, lawyer*
Hall, Nancy Christensen *publishing company executive, author, editor*
Hanson, Jane *newscaster*

Haubegger, Christy *media consultant, publishing executive*
Hauck, Marguerite Hall *broadcast executive*
Haukeness, Helen *journalist, writer*
Hays, Kathleen *news correspondent*
Heckel, Sally *independent filmmaker*
Henriques, Diana Blackmon *journalist*
Herman, Mindy *broadcast executive*
Hinojosa, Maria L. *news correspondent*
Hopkins, Jan *journalist, newscaster*
Hsu, Cindy Kwang-Mei *news correspondent, anchor*
Huff, Janice *newscaster, meteorologist*
Hughes, Brigid *editor*
Hurd, Ruth *publishing executive*
Hurley, Cheryl Joyce *book publishing executive*
Innesa, Levkova-Lamm *art critic, writer, curator*
Jamison, Jayne *publishing executive*
Jefferson, Margo L. *journalist*
Jenkins, Zeretha Lenore *publishing executive*
Johnson, Brooke Bailey *consultant, former television executive*
Jones, Laurie Lynn *magazine editor*
Jones, Star (Starlet Marie Jones) *television host*
Juran, Sylvia Louise *editor*
Kahn, Nancy Valerie *publishing and entertainment executive, consultant*
Kakutani, Michiko *critic*
Kalajian-Lagani, Donna *publishing executive*
Kanner, Bernice *columnist*
Kayse, Kathleen *publishing executive*
Keenan, Terry *anchor, correspondent*
Kelly, Christina *editor*
Kjellberg, Ann C. *editor*
Klein, Laura *publishing executive*
Koslow, Sally *editor-in-chief*
Koster, Elaine Landis *publishing executive*
Koteff, Ellen *periodical editor*
Kramer, Michelle *reporter*
Kroeger, Brooke W. *journalist, writer*
Kunes, Ellen *editor-in-chief*
Lane, Nancy *editor, human rights activist*
Lawhon, Charla *editor*
Laybourne, Geraldine B. *broadcast executive*
Leahey, Lynn *editor-in-chief*
Lee, Frances Helen *editor*
Lee, Sally A. *editor-in-chief*
Lehmkuhl, Lynn *publishing executive*
Leive, Cindi *editor-in-chief*
Levine, Ellen R. *editor*
Lisovicz, Susan *anchor, correspondent*
Long, Lisa Valk *communications company executive*
Longley, Marjorie Watters *newspaper executive*
Loomis, Carol J. *journalist*
Lovenheim, Barbara Irene *editor*
Mabrey, Vicki *news correspondent, anchor*
MacGowan, Sandra Firelli *publishing executive, publishing educator*
Mann, Maria *photojournalist, director*
Marsh, Michele *former newscaster*
Martin, Denise Belisle *magazine editor*
Martin, Judith Sylvia *journalist, author*
McAniff, Nora P. *publishing executive*
McCarthy, Pamela Maffei *magazine editor*
McCarty, V.K. *publisher, chaplain, librarian*
McGrath, Eleanor Burns *editor, writer*
McGrath, Judith *broadcast executive*
Miller, Caroline *editor-in-chief*
Mohler, Mary Gail *magazine editor*
Moldow, Susan *publishing executive*
Moore, Ann S. *magazine executive*
Morgan, Mary E. *publishing executive*
Morgenson, Gretchen C. *reporter*
Morris, Valerie *news correspondent*
Murphy, Helen *recording industry executive*
Nadelman, Cynthia J. *writer, editor*
Newhouse, Nancy Riley *newspaper editor*
Newman, Nancy *publishing executive*
Nielsen, Nancy *publishing executive*
Norman, Christina *broadcast executive*
Norville, Deborah Anne *news correspondent*
Novogrod, Nancy Gerstein *editor*
O'Kelley, Winnie *editor*
Pak, SuChin *newscaster*
Palmer, Marcella *reporter*
Palsho, Dorothea Coccoli *information services executive*
Pesin, Ella Michele *journalist, public relations professional*
Pfeiffer, Jane Cahill *former broadcasting company executive, consultant*
Phillips, Reneé *editor-in-chief, writer, educator*
Plagemann, Susan *publishing executive*
Podd, Ann *newspaper editor*
Poster, Meryl *film company executive*
Pulos, Virginia Kate *communications consultant*
Quindlen, Anna *journalist, author*
Quinn, Jane Bryant *journalist, writer*
Rabinowitz, Dorothy *television critic*
Raven, Abbe *broadcast executive*
Rawson, Eleanor S. *publishing company executive*
Regan, Judith Terrance *publishing executive*
Reichl, Ruth Molly *editor*
Resnick, Rosalind *multimedia executive*
Rhoads, Geraldine Emeline *editor, consultant*
Ridell, Carol Anne *reporter*
Roach, Margaret *editor-in-chief*
Roberts, Madelyn Alpert *publishing executive*
Robinson, Janet L. *publishing executive*
Rodriguez, Darlene *newscaster*
Rosado, Rossana *publishing executive, editor-in-chief*
Rosen, Ruth Chier *retired editor-in-chief*
Rosenthal, Jane *film company executive*
Rosenthal, Shirley Lord *cosmetics magazine executive, novelist*
Rubenstein, Atoosa Behnegar *editor-in-chief*
Rudolph, Lisa Beth *news correspondent*
Russo, Melissa *reporter*
Sabino, Catherine Ann *magazine editor*
Salembier, Valerie Birnbaum *publishing executive*
Samelson, Judy *editor*
Samuels, Dorothy J. *journalist, writer*
Sanchez, Hazel *reporter*

Nashville
Giallombardo, Leslie *publishing executive*
Green, Lisa Cannon *online editor*
Higgs, Mary Phil Egerton *editor*
Ingram, Martha Rivers *publishing executive*
Ragan, Lisa Carol *editor*
Roberts, Sandra *editor*
Shaw, Carole *editor, publisher*
Shaw-Cohen, Lori Eve *magazine editor*
Smith Heinz, Amy *publishing executive*

Savannah
Folkerts, Linda Jo *publishing executive*

TEXAS

Amarillo
Robertson, Pauline Durrett *publishing executive*

Austin
Christian, Cheryl Lynn *editor, writer*
Henson, Glenda Maria *newspaper writer*
Spielman, Barbara Helen New *editor, consultant*
Stout, Patricia A. *communications educator*

Bellaire
Ballanfant, Kathleen Gamber *newspaper executive, public relations company executive*

Bellville
Mann, Laura Susan *editor*

Burleson
Lisi, Lori A. (Lori Fredeking) *freelance/self-employed editor, writer*

Carrollton
Daily, Ellen Wilmoth Matthews *technical publications specialist*

Dallas
Blessen, Karen Alyce *freelance/self-employed journalist, artist*
Blumenthal, Karen *newspaper executive*
Brown, Colleen *broadcast executive*
Creany, Cathleen Annette *television station executive*
Diaz Meyer, Cheryl *photojournalist*
Griffith, Dotty (Dorothy Griffith Stephenson) *journalist, writer*
Harasta, Cathy Ann *journalist*
Kutner, Janet *art critic, book reviewer*
Pederson, Rena *newspaper editor*
Smith, Nancy Woolverton *journalist, real estate agent*
Smith, Sue Frances *newspaper editor*
Vick, Frances Brannen *publishing executive*

Devine
Whitaker, Ruth M. *newswriter, photographer, horse breeder*

Houston
Bischoff, Susan Ann *newspaper editor*
Halstead, Trazanna *newscaster*
Heinsen, Lindsay *newspaper editor*
Holmes, Ann Hitchcock *journalist*
Johnston, Marguerite *journalist, author*
Marek, Joycelyn *publishing executive*
Marshall, Jane Pretzer *newspaper editor*
Potenza, Daisy McKaskle *newspaper executive*
Thomas, Katherine Jane *magazine and newspaper columnist*
Tice, Pamela Paradis *scientific editor, writer*
Wagner, Charlene Brook *publishing consultant, elementary school educator*
Walls, Martha Ann Williams (Mrs. B. Carmage Walls) *publishing executive*

Kyle
Saunders, Patricia Gene Knight *freelance writer, editor*

Plano
Gray, Bonnie Ann Lawry *publishing executive*

San Antonio
Heloise, *columnist, writer*
Johnson, Sammye LaRue *communications educator*
Lenke, Joanne Marie *publishing executive*
Winik, Joanne *broadcast executive*
Yerkes, Susan Gamble *newspaper columnist*

San Marcos
Stovall, Frances Middagh *writer, preservationist*

Spring
Jackson, Guida Myrl *writer, magazine editor, book editor, publisher*

Tyler
Brock, Dee Sala *television executive, educator, writer, consultant*

UTAH

Salt Lake City
Conway, Nancy Ann *newspaper editor*
Hatch, Wilda Gene *broadcast company executive*
Paulsen, Vivian *magazine editor*

VERMONT

Essex Junction
Myers, Linda K. *retired editor, state representative*

Norwich
Lamperti, Claudia Jane McKay *editor*

VIRGINIA

Alexandria
Reiley, Mame Carrigan *political consultant*

Annandale
Freeman, Baba Foster *editor*

Arlington
Brennan, Christine *journalist, columnist*
Dentzer, Susan *journalist*
Foxwell, Elizabeth Marie *editor*
Hastings, Melanie (Melanie Jean Wotring) *television news anchor*
Myers, Elissa Matulis *publisher, association executive*
Reiss, Susan Marie *editor, writer*
Rockefeller, Sharon Percy *broadcast executive*
Stokes, Jeanett Barrett *editor*
Weiss, Susan *newspaper editor*

Bedford
Wills, Sherian Atkins *editor, writer*

Bluemont
Johnson, Evelyn Porterfield *journalist, educator*

Bridgewater
Bittel, Muriel Albers *managing editor*

Charlottesville
Essig, Nancy Claire *publishing executive*
Foard, Susan Lee *editor*
Kaiserlian, Penelope Jane *publishing company executive*
Loo, Beverly Jane *publishing company executive*
Worrell, Anne Everette Rowell *newspaper publisher*

Chesapeake
Green, Barbara Marie *publisher, journalist, poet, writer*

Grafton
Cubberly, Margaret Therese *columnist, freelance writer*

Lexington
Luecke, Pamela *professor, former editor*

Lynchburg
Turyn, Noreen Audrey *television news anchor, reporter*
Vaughn, Susan Marie *journalist, educator*

Manassas
Bahner, Sue (Florence Suzanna Bahner) *radio broadcasting executive*

Marion
Elledge, Glenna Ellen Tuell *journalist*

Mc Lean
Bullard, Marcia *publishing executive*
Feller, Millicent (Mimi) A. *newspaper publishing executive*
Leinwand, Donna Claire *journalist*
Mathews, Linda McVeigh *newspaper editor*

Newport News
Matthews, Rondra J. *publishing executive*

Norfolk
Addis, Kay Tucker *newspaper editor*
Carpenter, Dee *publishing executive*
Dryer, Barbara Ferrell *media specialist, educator*
Jackson, Kathy Merlock *communications educator*

Reston
Powell, Anne Elizabeth *editor*

Richmond
Curran, Colleen A. *editor, writer*
Kirschbaum, Pamela Gale *editor, writer*
Seals, Louise Crumrine *editor*
Seals, Margaret Louise *newspaper editor*

Roanoke
Klein-Davis, Stephanie Ann *photojournalist*
Zomparelli, Wendy *newspaper publisher*

Sedley
Briggs, Martha Wren *publishing executive, writer*

Springfield
Rankin, Jacqueline Annette *communications expert, educator*

Stanardsville
Anns, Arlene Eiserman *publishing company executive*

Tazewell
Garner, June Brown *journalist*

Williamsburg
Kellogg, Ann Marie *retired publishing executive, consultant*

WASHINGTON

Bellingham
Meals, Pamela F. *publishing executive*

Port Orchard
Huber, Virginia Rollo *photojournalist, educator, artist*

Port Townsend
Buhler, Jill Lorie *editor, writer*

Seattle
Dresher, Olivia Whitaker *publishing executive, writer*
Farr, Sheila G. *critic, poet*
Godden, Jean W. *columnist*
Gwinn, Mary Ann *newspaper reporter*
Hills, Regina J. *journalist*
Kelly, Carolyn Sue *newspaper executive*
Nash, Cynthia Jeanne *journalist*
Pascal, Naomi Brenner *editor-at-large, publishing executive*
Steele, Cynthia *literary critic, translator, educator*

Sequim
Robinson, June P. *columnist, retired special education educator*

Spokane
Steele, Karen Dorn *journalist*

Tacoma
Brenner, Elizabeth (Betsy Brenner) *publishing executive*

WEST VIRGINIA

Charleston
Chilton, Elizabeth Easley Early *newspaper executive*

WISCONSIN

Eau Claire
Clark, Judy *newscaster*
Rupnor, Jennifer *journalist*
Tuckner, Michelle *newscaster*

Greendale
Kaiser, Ann Christine *magazine editor*
Pohl, Kathleen Sharon *editor*

La Crosse
Thomas-Williams, Pamela Rae *publishing executive, writer*

Madison
Burns, Elizabeth Murphy *media executive*
Dunwoody, Sharon Lee *journalism and communications educator*
Foley Mullaney, Ellen Madaline *journalist*
Rowe, Marieli Dorothy *media literacy education consultant, organization executive*

Menomonie
Cutnaw, Mary-Frances *retired communications educator, writer, editor, publisher*

Middleton
Rowland, Pleasant *publisher, toy company executive*

Milwaukee
Dawson, Kim *reporter*
Eirich, Michelle A. *editor, writer*
Elliot, Tammy *newscaster*
Garcia, Astrid J. *newspaper executive*
Jallings, Jessica *reporter, newscaster*
Kleefisch, Rebecca *reporter*
Mykleby, Kathy *newscaster, reporter*
Stafford, Lori *reporter*

New Berlin
Czarnezki, Mary Elaine *media specialist*

Pelican Lake
Martin, Mary Wolf *newspaper editor*

Racine
Constantine, Margaret L(ouise) (Peggy Constantine) *newspaper reporter, freelance writer*
Miller, Yolanda *publisher, writer*

WYOMING

Jackson
Decker, Carol Arne *magazine publishing consultant*

TERRITORIES OF THE UNITED STATES

PUERTO RICO

San Juan
Casiano, Kimberly *publishing executive*

CANADA

ALBERTA

Edmonton
Hughes, Linda J. *newspaper publisher*

BRITISH COLUMBIA

Vancouver
Yaffe, Barbara Marlene *journalist*

NOVA SCOTIA

Glasgow
Williams, Edna Aleta Theadora Johnston *journalist*

ONTARIO

North York
Gasparrini-Etheridge, Claudia *publishing company executive, scientist, writer*

ENGLAND

London
Scardino, Marjorie Morris *publishing company executive*

ADDRESS UNPUBLISHED

Adcroft, Patrice Gabriella *former editor*
Agonito, Rosemary *publishing company executive*
Aldrich, Patricia Anne Richardson *retired magazine editor*
Allen, Linda S. *editor, writer*
Arden, Sherry W. *publishing company executive*
Arutyunyan, Emma *radio broadcaster*
Ashton, Betsy Finley *broadcast journalist, author, lecturer*
Aukofer, Clare Elizabeth *newspaper editor*
Ayres, Mary Jo *professional speaker, writer, composer*
Backowski-Dawson, Therese Marie *editor*
Bass, Ruth Mary Haskins *journalist*
Behrmann, Joan Gail *newspaper editor*
Berlin, Meredith Rise *editor*
Bernstein, Henrietta Ruth *publishing executive, writer*
Betts, Katherine *editor-in-chief, publisher*
Bieber-Roberts, Peggy Eilene *communications educator, editor, journalist, researcher*
Bingham, Jinsie Scott *broadcast company executive*
Blount, Delores Overman *publishing executive*
Blyth, Myrna Greenstein *publishing executive, editor, author*
Borysewicz, Mary Louise *editor*
Brady-Borland, Karen *retired reporter, columnist*
Bratzler, Mary Kathryn *desktop publisher*
Brekke, Gail Louise *broadcasting administrator*
Brown, Fay *editor, writer*
Bucciarelli, Patrice Denice *journalist*
Budny, Lorraine *freelance writer, newspaper reporter*
Buhagiar, Marion *editor, author*
Butler, Kathleen Marie *editor*
Campbell, Josephine Anne Conrad *news service executive*
Capell, Cydney Lynn *editor*
Cardone, Bonnie Jean *freelance photojournalist*
Cardwell, Nancy Lee *editor, writer*
Carpenter, Liz (Elizabeth Sutherland Carpenter) *journalist, writer, equal rights leader, lecturer*
Carroll, E Jean *columnist, writer*
Carter, Betsy L. *magazine editor*
Charnin, Jade Hobson *magazine executive*
Chung, Connie (Constance Yu-hwa Chung) *broadcast journalist*
Cottingham, Martha Maxfield *journalist, volunteer*
Crow, Elizabeth Smith *editor*
Cullum, Lee Brooks *journalist*
Culp, Mildred Louise *corporate executive*
Curtis, Mary E. (Mary Curtis Horowitz) *publishing company executive*
Dawson, Virginia Sue *retired editor*
Dean, Carole Lee *film company executive*
Deitz, Susan Rose *columnist*
Denious, Sharon Marie *retired publishing executive*
Dennick, Lori Ann (L. Anne Carrington) *editor*
Deoul, Kathleen Boardsen *publishing executive*
de Varona, Donna *sports reporter, former Olympic swimmer*
Dickinson, Gail Krepps *communications educator*
Donald, Aida DiPace *retired publishing executive*
Dooley, Jo Ann Catherine *retired publishing executive*
Dosti, Rose *newspaper columnist, author*
Drew, Elizabeth Heineman *publishing executive*
Driver-Barstow, Susannah *editor*
Edelson, Zelda Sarah Toll *retired editor, artist*
Edmunds, Jane Clara *communications consultant*
English, Lauren Jackson *media specialist, secondary school educator*
Evans, Gene M. *publishing executive*
Evans, Sue Hollis *journalist, public relations executive*
Ewell, Miranda Juan *journalist*
Fadiman, Anne *writer, editor*
Farnsworth, Elizabeth *broadcast journalist*
Fitzpatrick, Nancy Hecht *editor*
Fortenberry, Vanessa Lea *media specialist, voice educator*
Francke, Linda Bird *journalist*
Franse, Karen Balch *editor, small business owner*
Frazier, Cynthia Ellen *journalist, writer*
Fuchs, Anne Sutherland *magazine publisher*
Gates, Susan Inez *magazine publisher*
Gay, Susan Matthews *publishing professional*
Godoff, Ann *book editor*
Godwin, Naomi Nadine *editor*
Gowler, Vicki Sue *newspaper editor, journalist*
Grahn, Barbara Ascher *retired publishing executive*
Grann, Phyllis *former publisher, editor*
Grant, Frances Bethea *editor*
Green, Nancy Loughridge *publishing executive*
Greene, Bernadette *media specialist*
Griffin, Terri Duggan *media specialist*
Grossman, Janice *former magazine publishing company executive*
Hahn, Helene B. *motion picture company executive*
Hall, Marnye E. *journalist, newswriter*
Hamilton, Valerie Michelle *editor, administrative assistant*

EDUCATION *See also* specific fields for postsecondary education

UNITED STATES

Kibbe-Reed, Trudie *academic administrator*
Moore, Helen Lucille *adult education educator, consultant*
O'Neal, Nell Self *retired principal*
Smith, Mary Scott *elementary school educator, education educator*
Truex, Dorothy Adine *retired university administrator*

Mc Gehee
Wilson, Nancy LaFarra *elementary school educator, art educator, artist*

Melbourne
Sanders, Dawn Marie *special education educator*

Newport
Falwell, Carol *school librarian, real estate broker*

Pangburn
Laws, Angela Kay *gifted and talented educator*

Pine Ridge
Hays, Annette Arlene *secondary school educator*

Russellville
Morris, Lois Lawson *education educator*

Searcy
Bucher, Susan A. *elementary school educator, music educator*
Whiteside, Dorothy Jean *education educator*

Springdale
Cordell, Beulah Faye *special education educator*
Morris, Scarlett Kay *elementary school educator, music educator*

State University
McClain, Veda *education educator, department chairman*

CALIFORNIA

Agoura Hills
Piscitelli, Nancy L. *retired special education educator*

Alameda
Carter, Roberta Eccleston *therapist, counselor*

Alhambra
Austin, Elizabeth Ruth *retired elementary school educator*

Anaheim
Barry, Sandra *school system administrator*
Goodspeed, Kathryn Ann *pre-school educator*
Guajardo, Elisa *counselor, educator*

Antioch
Thomson, Sondra K. *secondary school educator*

Apple Valley
Freymueller, Cynthia Louise *educational consultant*

Aptos
Hirsch, Bette G(ross) *college administrator, foreign language educator*

Arcadia
Baltz, Patricia Ann (Pann Baltz) *elementary school educator*
Endrusick, Rose Marie *secondary school educator*

Auburn
Burness, Maureen O'Leary *school system administrator, consultant*

Azusa
Aguilar, Gladys Maria *counselor, educator*
Liegler, Rosemary Menke *dean*

Bakersfield
Fuller, Jean *school system administrator*
Panelli, Jewel D. *elementary school educator*
Saucier, Bonnie L. *dean, pediatrics nurse*
Thornton, Pauline Cecilia Eve Marie Suzanne *special education educator*

Banning
Finley, Margaret Mavis *retired elementary school educator*

Berkeley
Azarpay, Guitty *education educator*
Bastrenta, Brigitte Elisabeth *school administrator*
Davis, Maggie L. *elementary teacher*
Goldstein-Erickson, Ellie *school librarian*
Johnson, Mary Katherine (Katie Johnson) *elementary school educator*
Kay, Herma Hill *education educator*
Linn, Marcia Cyrog *education educator*
McPhail-Geist, Karin Ruth *secondary school educator, real estate agent, musician*
Schild, Sylvia G. *retired elementary school educator, realtor*
Tyson, Laura D'Andrea *dean, economist, educator*

Boulevard
Charles, Blanche *retired elementary education educator*

Brea
Missakian, Ilona Virginia *secondary school educator, bookkeeper*

Brentwood
Groseclose, Wanda Westman *retired elementary school educator*
Paul, Yvonne C. *retired elementary school educator*

Burbank
Doud, Jacqueline Powers *academic administrator*
Nurik, Cindy Bunin *educational consultant, marriage and family therapist*

Camarillo
Buhr-Dupreez, Margaret Ilse *adult education educator*

Cameron Park
Drushell, Barbara Jean *retired education educator*

Carlsbad
Oakes, Sharon Lorraine *elementary school educator, researcher*

Chico
Bernhardt, Victoria L. *director, researcher*

Claremont
Bekavac, Nancy Yavor *academic administrator, lawyer*
Douglass, Enid Hart *educational program director*
Gann, Pamela Brooks *academic administrator*

Clayton
Bower, Fay Louise *academic administrator, nursing educator*

Corcoran
Martines, Eugenia Belle *elementary school educator*

Corning
Brown, Betty J. *elementary school educator*

Corona
Steiner, Barbara Anne *secondary school educator*

Corte Madera
Dalpino, Ida Jane *retired secondary school educator*

Costa Mesa
Candelaria, Angie Mary *special education educator*
Tillman, Barbara Ann *education educator, consultant*

Culver City
Maxwell-Brogdon, Florence Morency *school administrator, educational consultant*

Cupertino
Lyon, Mary Lou *retired secondary school educator*

Davis
Kraft, Rosemarie *dean, educator*
Robert, Ellen *university administrator*

Downey
Brooks, Lillian Drilling Ashton (Lillian Hazel Church) *adult education educator*
Robles, Darline P. *school system administrator*
Ruecker, Martha Engels *retired special education educator*

Earlimart
White, Kathleen *director*

Elk Grove
Moe, Janet Anne *elementary school educator, church organist*

Encino
Bach, Cynthia *educational program director, writer*
O'Riley, Karen E. *principal*

Escondido
Granet, Eileen *secondary school educator*
Hannam-Oosterbaan, Maria Gertrude *secondary school educator*

Folsom
Sarraf, Shirley A. *secondary school educator*

Fort Bragg
Dias, Michele C. *primary educator*

Fountain Valley
Purdy, Leslie *community college president*

Fresno
Girvin, Shirley Eppinette *retired elementary education educator, journalist*
Lemons Odell, Lauren Sharnelle *secondary school educator*
Stewart, Deborah Claire *dean*

Fullerton
Donoghue, Mildred Ransdorf *education educator*

Garden Grove
Schwalm, Laura *school system administrator*

Gardena
Winn, Stephenie *special education program specialist*

Glendale
Edwards, Kathryn Inez *educational technology consultant*
Whalen, Lucille *retired academic administrator*

Glendora
Acevedo, Elizabeth Morrison *special education educator*

Grass Valley
Hayes, Cherry Ann *secondary school educator*

Hayward
Garcia, Melva Ybarra *counseling administrator, educator*
Getz, Melissa B. *secondary school educator*
Harris, Penelope Claire *pre-school administrator, daycare administrator, consultant*
Laycock, Mary Chappell *gifted and talented education educator, consultant*
Rees, Norma S. *academic administrator*

Hemet
Fitzsimmons, Terri Kathleen *career consultant, educator*

Inglewood
Cato, Gloria Maxine *retired secondary education educator, school program administrator*
Lockhart, Claudia Jo *adult education educator, department chairman*
Logan, Lynda Dianne *elementary school educator*

Inyokern
Norris, Lois Ann *elementary school educator*

La Jolla
Chandler, Marsha *academic administrator, educator*
Henig, Suzanne *retired educator, writer, editor*
Lowe, Lisa *education educator, department chairman*
North, Kathryn E. Keesey (Mrs. Eugene C. North) *retired secondary school educator*
Savoia, Maria Christina *vice dean*

La Mesa
Black, Eileen Mary *retired elementary school educator*
Charleton, Margaret Ann *child care administrator, consultant*

La Mirada
Krotinger, Sheila M. *secondary school educator*

La Quinta
Tebbs, Carol Ann *secondary school educator, academic administrator*

La Verne
Ebersole, Helen Brownsberger *elementary school educator*
Rahmani, Loretta Hardie *university administrator*

Laguna Beach
Martinez, Vera *academic administrator*

Laguna Niguel
André, Joy LaRae *elementary school educator, adult education educator, language educator*
Gunning, Monica Olwen Minott *elementary school educator*

Lake Elsinore
Wilson, Sonja Mary *retired secondary school educator, poet*

Lakeside
Walker, Wanda Medora *retired elementary school educator, consultant*

Lancaster
Walsh, Patricia Maack *special education educator*

Lathrop
Swanson, Jeannie Marie *special education educator*

Livermore
Davis, Lisa Rene *special education educator, consultant*
Roshong, Dee Ann Daniels *dean, educator*

Lodi
Bishop-Graham, Barbara *secondary school educator, journalist*
Reinold, Christy Diane *school counselor, consultant*
Vaughan, Berniece Miller *retired school system administrator, writer*

Loma Linda
King, Helen Emori *dean*

Long Beach
Duke, Phyllis Louise Kellogg Henry *school administrator, consultant*
Fleming, Jane Williams *retired educator, writer*
Lofland, Patricia Lois *secondary school educator, travel company executive*
Mandarino, Candida Ann *education educator, consultant*
Writer, Sharon Lisle *secondary school educator*

Los Altos
Fong, Bernadine Chuck *academic administrator*
Rainville, Anna Mary *elementary school educator*

Los Angeles
Aldahl, Deborah Campbell *elementary school educator*
Bernstein, Leslie *academic administrator, biostatistician*
Brandon, Kathleen Alma *director*
Burman, Sheila Flexer Zola *special education educator*
Coker, Sybil Jane Thomas *counseling administrator*
Fitz-Carter, Aleane *elementary school educator, composer*
Fountila, Sallie Marie *educational specialist*
Geller, Debra F. *academic administrator, educator*
Grose, Elinor Ruth *retired elementary education educator*

Haley, Roslyn Trezevant *educational program director*
Heath, Berthann Jones *education administrator*
Lee, Jennifer Morita *secondary school educator*
Leonard, Kandi *English language educator*
Lynch, Beverly Pfeifer *education and information studies educator*
McGee, Lynda Plant *guidance counselor*
Money, Ruth Rowntree *infant development and care specialist, consultant*
Moroto, Nadine B. *secondary school educator*
Nelson, Barbara J. *dean*
Norwood, Phyllis Katherene *director, educator*
Rochelle, Dorothy *educational consultant*
Russo, Lisa Ann *registrar*
Saunders, Myra Kathleen *dean, law librarian, educator*
Sohaili, Monira *special education educator, writer*
Spangler, Mary *college president*
Wilkerson, LuAnn *dean, medical educator*
Zexter, Eleanor M. *secondary school educator*

Los Banos
Ellington, Karen Renae *secondary education resource specialist*

Los Gatos
Dunham, Anne *educational institute director*
Ferrari, L. Katherine *speaker, consultant, entrepreneur*

Malibu
Raine, Melinda L. *library manager*

Marina
Hill, Karen Caecilia *education educator*

Marysville
Day, Colien *retired secondary school educator*

Merced
Tomlinson-Keasey, Carol Ann *university administrator*

Mill Valley
Rasmussen, Tina Marie *organizational development consultant, writer*

Mission Viejo
Hodge, Kathleen O'Connell *academic administrator*

Modesto
Naeve, Catherine Ann *secondary school educator*

Montague
Faulkner, Deborah Kay *school system administrator, principal*

Montebello
Bucey, Constance Virginia Russell *retired elementary school educator, education educator*
Dible, Rose Harpe McFee *special education educator*
Jacobs, Lillian Laura *secondary school educator*

Monterey
Boger, Gail Lorraine Zivna *reading specialist*
Gamiere, Constance Anne *education educator, counselor*
Kadushin, Karen Donna *law school dean*

Moorpark
Schwabauer, Mary Ann *secondary school educator, rancher*

Morro Bay
Scholer, Margaret D. *adult education educator*

Mountain View
Craig, Joan Carmen *secondary school educator, performing arts educator*

Napa
Coates, Verona Agnes *secondary school educator*
Renfrow, Patricia Anne *secondary school educator*
Woodruff, Diane Carey *college president*

National City
Quigley, Deborah Hewitt *adult education educator*

Northridge
Curzon, Susan Carol *university administrator*
Koester, Jolene *academic administrator*
Syms, Helen Maksym *educational administrator*

Novato
Jaeger, Patsy Elaine *retired secondary education educator, artist*

Nuevo
Rogers, Marilyn Rose *special education educator*

Oakland
Breed, Sarah Dunford *elementary school educator, writer*
Diaz, Sharon *education administrator*
Griffin, Betty Jo *elementary school educator*
Holmgren, Janet L *college president*
Isaac Nash, Eva Mae *secondary school educator*
Kennedy, Judith Price *elementary school educator*
Krause, Marcella Elizabeth Mason (Mrs. Eugene Fitch Krause) *retired secondary school educator*

Oceanside
Druhe Brandt, Iris Claire *retired elementary school educator*
Johnson, Karen Elaine *secondary school educator, tax preparer*

Pena, Maria Geges *academic services administrator*

Ojai
Horne, Rikki *school system administrator*

Ontario
McGehee, Sharon *school system administrator*
Peters, Jacqueline Mary *secondary school educator*

Orange
Stuewe, Isabel *elementary school educator*

Oxnard
Rosales, Sandra Johnson *school system administrator*

Palm Desert
Baxter, Betty Carpenter *educational administrator*
Bratrud, Linda Kay *secondary school educator*
Hoffmann, Joan Carol *retired academic dean*

Palmdale
Valenti, Betty Janet *resource specialist, educator*

Palo Alto
Collins, Margery Louise *elementary school educator*

Palos Verdes Estates
Kingsley, Kathryn Alexis Krah *retired elementary school educator*

Palos Verdes Peninsula
Miller, Francie Loraditch *counseling administrator*

Paramount
Williams, Vivian Lewie *retired counseling administrator*

Pasadena
Almore-Randle, Allie Louise *special education educator*
Cepielik, Elizabeth Lindberg *elementary school educator*
Nicholson, Frances Mary Baum *secondary school educator, writer*

Pebble Beach
Hoffman, Sharon Lynn *adult education educator*

Penn Valley
Longan, Suzanne M. *retired elementary school educator*

Petaluma
Thomas, Nancy Hinckley *special education educator*

Pittsburg
Hurley, Allison Ruth *mentor coach specialist*

Placerville
Miller, Edna Rae Atkins *secondary school educator*

Playa Del Rey
Lutz, Charlene Joyce *special education educator, consultant*

Pomona
Amaya-Thetford, Patricia *elementary school educator*
Callaway, Linda Marie *special education educator*
Demery, Dorothy Jean *secondary school educator*
Dishman, Rose Marie Rice *academic administrator, researcher*
Elliott, Susan Donise *secondary school educator*

Ramona
McAndrews, Shannon Marie *elementary school educator*
Van Zant, Susan Lucille *principal*

Rancho Cordova
Hendrickson, Elizabeth Ann *retired secondary school educator*

Redlands
Huenergardt, Myrna Louise *retired academic administrator, retired adult nurse practitioner*
Simone, Sharon Elizabeth *education educator, filmmaker, writer*

Redwood City
Jones, Brenda Gail *school district administrator*

Rialto
Jackson, Betty Eileen *music and elementary school educator*
Johnson, Ruth Floyd *educational consultant*
King, Muriel Eileen *secondary school educator*

Richmond
McLeod, Jacquelyn H. *special education educator*

Riverside
Dutton, Jo Sargent *education educator, researcher, consultant*
Fontana, Sandra Ellen Frankel *special education educator*
Naugle, Charlotte June *principal, educator*
Rainey, Susan J. *school system administrator*

Rocklin
Hyde, Geraldine Veola *retired secondary school educator*

Rohnert Park
Newcomb, Joan Leslie *elementary school educator*

Rolling Hills Estates
Ingerson, Nancy Nina Moore *special education educator*

Roseville
French, Leura Parker *secondary educator*

Ross
Matan, Lillian Kathleen *secondary school educator, consultant, interior designer*

Sacramento
Adolphson, Vanessa *counseling administrator, educator, chemist*
Amezcua, Esther Hernandez *elementary school educator*
Artz, Ethel Angela Cleavenger *elementary education educator, consultant*
Bromund, Alice A. *retired elementary school educator*
Menebroker, Ann *special education educator, writer*
Nickless, Barbara A. *primary school educator*
Nisson, Mary *elementary school educator*
Opperman, Rosanna Resendez *adult education educator*
Potter, Teresa Pearl *adult education educator*
Sanborn, Kathy *career planning administrator, consultant*
Smith, Marie B. *college president*
Zaidi, Emily Louise *retired elementary school educator*

San Bernardino
Caballero, Sharon *academic administrator*
Plotkin, Judy Ann *special education educator*

San Bruno
White, Frances LaVonne *academic administrator*

San Clemente
Meredith, Mary J. *secondary school educator*

San Diego
Green, Charlene *principal, speech pathology/audiology services professional*
Idos, Rosalina Vejerano *secondary school educator*
King, Verna St. Clair *retired school counselor*
Lacey-Parks, Rena Elizabeth *secondary school educator*
Lyons, Mary E. *academic administrator*
McBrayer, Sandra L. *educational director, homeless outreach educator*
Ulen, Gene Eldridge *elementary school educator*
Uribe, Jennie Ann *elementary school educator*
Williams, Carolyn *secondary school educator*
Young, Sarah Moskowitz *educational and computer consultant, journalist*

San Dimas
Cameron, Judith Lynne *secondary education educator, hypnotherapist*

San Francisco
Ackerman, Arlene *school system administrator*
Ada, Alma Flor *education educator, writer*
Albino, Judith Elaine Newsom *university president*
Bibbs, Cheryl Susheel *education educator, researcher*
Boyden, Jaclyne Witte *university vice dean*
Clifford, Geraldine Joncich (Mrs. William F. Clifford) *education educator*
Hudson, Suncerray Ann *analyst, research grants manager*
Kane, Mary Kay *dean*
Pierce, Deborah Mary *educational administrator*
Stephens, Elisa *college president*
Wara, Diane *dean*
Won, Cynthia Jane *secondary school educator*

San Jose
Bain, Linda L. *academic administrator*
Best, Amy L. *education educator*
Covey, Susan Cowles *director*
Holyer, Erna Maria *adult education educator, writer, artist*
Jordan, Bernice Bell *retired elementary school educator*
Lobig, Janie Howell *special education educator*
Okerlund, Arlene Naylor *university official*
Rose, Virginia Shottenhamer *secondary school educator*

San Leandro
Chohlis, Dana Marie *elementary school educator, theater director*

San Luis Obispo
Kulp, Bette Joneve *retired educator, wallpaper installation business owner*

San Marcos
Haynes, Karen Sue *academic administrator, educator*

San Mateo
Mark, Lillian Gee *educational administrator*

San Pedro
Bailey, Dorothy Jean *secondary school educator, consultant*

San Rafael
Adcock, Muriel W. *special education educator*

San Ramon
Peebles, Lucretia Neal Drane *policy and administration educator*

Santa Ana
Kato, Terri Emi *elementary school and gifted and talented educator*
Wilson, Beth A. *college official*

Santa Barbara
Hurwitz, Saundra Harriet (Sandi Hurwitz) *analyst, educator*
Zwick, Rebecca *education educator*

Santa Cruz
Greenwood, M. R. C. *college dean, biologist, nutrition educator*
Mirk, Judy Ann *retired elementary school educator*

Santa Rosa
Christiansen, Peggy *principal*
Foster, Lucille Caster *school system administrator, retired*

Shasta Lake
Parsons, Debra Lea *elementary school educator*

Sonoma
Hobart, Billie *education educator, consultant*

South Pasadena
Bishop, Carole C. *elementary education educator, family therapist*
Yett, Sally Pugh *elementary school educator, gifted and talented educator*

Spring Valley
Soltero, Michelle Dolores *director*

Stanford
Ball, Arnetha *education educator*
Barron, Brigid *education educator*
Boaler, Jo *education educator*
Byerwalter, Mariann *academic administrator*
Cohen, Elizabeth G. *education and sociology educator, researcher*
Darling-Hammond, Linda *education educator*
Loeb, Susanna *education educator*
Lotan, Rachel *education educator*
Stipek, Deborah *education educator, dean*
Sullivan, Kathleen Marie *dean, law educator*
Wotipka, Christine Min *education educator*

Stockton
Cooper, Iva Jean *special education educator*
Haines, Joybelle *retired elementary school educator*
Hitchcock, Susan Y. *school administrator, city council member*
Mann, Tori *secondary school educator*

Tehachapi
Sprinkle, Martha Clare *elementary school educator*

Thermal
Montoya, Leiala *assistant principal*

Topanga
McGray, Deanna Gail *retired elementary school educator*

Torrance
McNamara, Brenda Norma *secondary school educator*

Tulare
Pinto, Marie Malania *academic administrator, consultant*

Turlock
Antoniuk, Verda JoAnne *secondary school educator*
Hughes, Marvalene *academic administrator*

Tustin
Greene, Wendy Segal *special education educator*

Union City
Lockhart, Patsy Marie *secondary school educator, consultant*

Vallejo
Murillo, Carol Ann *secondary school educator*

Valley Center
Whitten, Laura A. *secondary school educator*

Ventura
Moffatt, Mindy Ann *elementary school educator, educational training specialist*
Renger, Marilyn Hanson *elementary school educator*
Zuber, Norma Keen *career counselor, educator*

Victorville
Polley-Shellcroft, Theresa Diane *university educator*

Walnut Creek
Carver, Dorothy Lee Eskew (Mrs. John James Carver) *retired secondary school educator*
Lilly, Luella Jean *academic administrator*

West Covina
Wagner, Frances Rita *secondary school educator*

Westlake Village
Steadman, Lydia Duff *symphony violinist, retired elementary school educator*

Whittier
Benavides, Greta Louise *elementary school educator, entrepreneur*
Gosfield, Margaret *secondary school educator, school system administrator, consultant, editor*
Will, Katherine Haley *academic administrator*

Woodlake
Pace, Sally Mae *student services dean*

Yucca Valley
Lewis, Mary Etta *special education educator*

COLORADO

Arvada
Hammond-Blessing, DiAnn A. *elementary school educator*

Aurora
Kellogg Fain, Karen *retired history and geography educator*
Lassen, Betty Jane *gifted and talented educator*
Sorenson, Katherine Ann *elementary school educator*

Boulder
Borko, Hilda *education educator*
Dilley, Barbara Jean *college administrator, choreographer, educator*
Hinkley, Caroline Lawson *dean*
Hoffman, Elizabeth *academic administrator*
Marie, Heather *director, consultant*
Roberts, Pamela Ranger *secondary school educator*
Wertheimer, Marilyn Lou *school librarian, educator*

Colorado Springs
Guy, Mildred Dorothy *retired secondary school educator*
Meese, Frances Mildred *library administrator*
Milligan, Annette Marie *secondary school educator*
Shade, Linda Bunnell *university chancellor*
Shockley-Zalabak, Pamela Sue *academic administrator*

Commerce City
Baker, Maria Luise *retired secondary school educator*

Delta
Reever, Wilma Marie *educational consultant*

Denver
Augustine, Rosemary *vocational counselor, writer*
Bacon, Betty J. Nichols *preschool educator and administrator*
Burrows, Bertha Jean *retired academic administrator*
DePew, Marie Kathryn *retired secondary school educator*
Gibson, Elisabeth Jane *retired principal*
Jarles, Ruth Sewell *education educator*
Kaplan, Sheila *academic administrator*
Lingé, Virginia Ann *elementary school educator*
Rubin, Cathy Ann *retired educator*
[illegible], Thelma Jean *primary school educator*

Durango
Allison, Pamela Sue *special education administrator*

Englewood
Graves, Nada Proctor *retired elementary school educator*
Shields, Marlene Sue *elementary school educator*

Fort Collins
Panik, Sharon McClain *primary education educator, writer*

Gilcrest
Halley, Gail Renee *secondary school educator*

Grand Junction
Flick, Carol J. *middle school educator*
Taylor, Mary Lee *retired college administrator*

Greeley
Afoaku, Oyibo Helisita *academic administrator*

Highlands Ranch
Erickson, Linda Rae *elementary school educator*

Lakewood
Wallisch, Carolyn E. *principal*
Zachman, Kathleen E. *gifted and talented educator, music educator*

Limon
Huffman, Janet Faye *secondary school educator*

Littleton
Connell-Allen, Elizabeth Ann *elementary school educator*
Greenberg, Elinor Miller *university official, consultant*
Lesh-Laurie, Georgia Elizabeth *university administrator, biology educator, researcher*
Pardue, Karen Reiko *elementary school educator*

Longmont
Blackwood, Lois Anne *elementary school educator*

Loveland
Johnson, Stephanie Kay *school counselor*
Lee, Evelyn Marie *elementary school educator, secondary school educator*

Monte Vista
Haslar, Peggy Jo *elementary school counselor*

Nederland
Morrison, K. Jaydene *education counseling firm executive*

Northglenn
Knepel, Nancy *school librarian*

Westminster
Hartman, Susan P(atrice) *adult education administrator*

Wiggins
Kammerzell, Susan Jane *elementary school educator, music educator*

CONNECTICUT

Bridgeport
Orloski, Sharon *secondary school educator*

Chaplin
Bruckerhoff, Theresa *business owner, educational researcher*

Cheshire
Holm-Cipollini, Lori Katherine *gifted and talented educator*

Coventry
Halvorson, Judith Anne (Judith Anne Devaud) *elementary school educator*

Danbury
Hawkes, Carol Ann *academic administrator*
Jensen-Ruopp, Helga Spitko *school program administrator, consultant*

Dayville
Nicholson, Pamela D. *school librarian*

Derby
Rinaldo, Sharon Ann *special education educator*

Enfield
Reuter, Joan Copson *retired program director*

Fairfield
Howell, Karen Jane *private school educator*

Falls Village
Gaschel-Clark, Rebecca Mona *special education educator*
Purcell, Mary Louise Gerlinger *retired adult education educator*

Glastonbury
Hatch, D. Patricia P. *principal*
Raffles, Linda N. *secondary school educator*

Greenwich
Bentley, Lissa Frances *elementary school educator*

Hamden
Blumberg, Betty Lou *education educator*
Sola, Janet Elaine *secondary school educator*

Hartford
Kedderis, Pamela Jean *academic administrator*
Knott-Twine, Laura Mae *director*
Newton, Nell Jessup *dean, law educator*
Stuart, Ann *academic administrator, writer, educator*

Madison
Gianotti-Falcigno, Constance Elizabeth *special education educator*

Manchester
Campbell, Katherine Marie Langrehr *elementary and secondary education educator*

Meriden
Brandt, Irene Hildegard *retired secondary school educator*

Middletown
Brown, Judith *academic administrator*
Craig, Barbara Kinkson *academic administrator*

Milford
Sullivan, Christine Anne *secondary school educator*

New Britain
Boyea, Ruthe W. *retired educator*

New Canaan
Smithers, Ruth Anne Hall *special education educator, consultant*

New Haven
Gaudiani, Claire Lynn *retired academic administrator*
Lorimer, Linda Koch *university educator*
McNamara, Julia Mary *academic administrator, foreign language educator*

Niantic
Andersen, Susan Hackes *early childhood educator*

North Haven
Fuggi, Gretchen Miller *education educator*

Norwalk
Nelson, Paula Morrison Bronson *gifted and talented educator, consultant*
Schaefer-Wicke, Elizabeth *reading consultant, educator*

Ridgefield
Leonard, Sister Anne C. *superintendent, education director*
Lindsay, Dianna Marie *educational administrator*

Simsbury
DiCosimo, Patricia Shields *secondary school educator*
Wolfe, Jennifer Nan *special education educator, consultant*

Storrs Mansfield
Gilbert, Margaret P. *university educator, researcher*
Price, Glenda Delores *university dean*

Stratford
DiDomenico, Maureen Ellen *art educator, muralist*

Tolland
O'Shaughnessy, Ellen Hodgson *elementary school educator*

Trumbull
Herman, Elizabeth Mullee *elementary school educator*
Madigan, Rita Duffy *career education coordinator*
Nevins, Lyn (Carolyn A. Nevins) *educational supervisor, trainer, consultant*
Norcel, Jacqueline Joyce Casale *educational administrator*
Smith, Gail Marie *special education educator, educational consultant*

Waterbury
Brown, Lillian Hill *retired academic administrator*

West Hartford
Coleman, Winifred Ellen *academic administrator*
Echols, Ivor Tatum *retired educator, assistant dean*
Gaumond, Lynn E. *elementary school educator*

West Haven
Farquharson, Patrice Ellen *primary school educator*

Westport
Gordon, Thelma Stone *retired audio-visual specialist, librarian*
Hunter, Gloria Eleanore *secondary school educator*

Willimantic
Wilson, Margaret Sullivan *retired executive dean, consultant*

Winsted
Baccus, R. Eileen Turner *academic administrator*

DELAWARE

Dover
Sorenson, Liane Beth McDowell *women's affairs director, state legislator*
Wagner, Nancy Hughes *secondary school educator, state legislator*

Georgetown
Cooper, Lorraine W. *special education educator*

Hockessin
Alexander, Michele Yermack *private school educator*

Magnolia
Berry, Teresa E.S. *adult education educator*

New Castle
Doberstein, Audrey K. *college president*
George, Margaret Y. *retired educator*
Martin, Jean Ann *retired school system administrator, educator*
Williamson, Sandra Kaye *education educator*

Newark
Carter, Mae Riedy *retired academic official, consultant*
Keppler, Mary Louise *elementary school educator*

Wilmington
Chagnon, Lucille Tessier *workforce development and literacy specialist*
DeHart, Deborah Lee *private school educator, composer*
Evans, Margaret Utz *secondary school educator*
Garvin, Geraldine McKinley *retired psychology educator*
Higgins, Roxanne Snelling *educational consultant*
Witcher, Phyllis Herrmann *secondary school educator*

DISTRICT OF COLUMBIA

Washington
Acker, Rose L. *elementary school educator*
Alexander, Marianne Ellis *academic administrator*
Anderson, Beverly Jacques *academic administrator*
Anroman, Gilda Marie *college program director, lecturer, educator*
Arnez, Nancy Levi *educational leadership educator*
Bader, Rochelle Linda (Shelley Bader) *educational administrator*
Boudreaux, Angela Lois *elementary school educator*
Brown, Dorothy M. *academic administrator*
Bullock, Alice Gresham *university dean*
Caputo, Anne Spencer *knowledge and learning programs director*
Christian, Mary Jo Dinan *educational administrator, educator*
Cooper, Nannie Coles *education educator, consultant*
Covington, Eileen Queen *secondary school educator*
Cunningham, Sarah Bainter *dean, educator*
Darragh, Martina *school librarian*
DeCosta-Willis, Miriam *education educator, writer*
Donley, Rosemary *university official*

Erting, Carol Jean *special education educator, researcher, anthropologist*
Feder, Judith *dean*
Flaherty, Sister Mary Jean *dean*
Geiselman, LucyAnn *college president*
Gibbons Tankard, Mellisa W. *education educator*
Ingold, Catherine White *academic administrator*
Jarvis, Charlene Drew *university administrator, former scientist*
Johnson, Judith A. *educational administrator*
Jones, Judith Miller *director*
Kirkien-Rzeszotarski, Alicja Maria *academic administrator, researcher, educator*
Kopper, Mary Carll *director*
Kyhos, M. Gaither Galleher *private school educator*
Lederer, Laura J. *educational program administrator*
Lovett, Clara Maria *university administrator, historian*
Manley, Audrey Forbes *retired academic administrator, pediatrician, military officer*
Mantyla, Karen *distance learning consultant*
Miller, Annie Christmas *secondary school educator*
Miller, Mary Rita *former college educator*
Mills, Kim I. *director*
Mohrman, Kathryn J *academic administrator*
Pasmanick, Frances Virginia Cohen *admissions director*
Petty, Rachel *academic administrator*
Segall, JoAnn Butters *retired school librarian*
Sharpe, Dorothy Jones *secondary education educator, researcher*
Smith, Abbie Oliver *college administrator, educator*
Statom, Laurena Edith *retired special education educator*
Stewart, Debra Wehrle *academic administrator*
Thompson, Bernida Lamerle *principal, consultant, educator*
Titus-Dillon, Pauline Yvonne *associate dean academic affairs, medical educator*
Van Ummersen, Claire A(nn) *academic administrator, biologist, educator*

FLORIDA

Apopka
Bentley, Edith Louise *secondary school educator*

Boca Raton
Boykin, Anne J. *dean*
Rosen, Harriet R. *elementary school educator*
Shepard, Colleen *elementary school educator, art educator*
Warshaw, Carole Klein *education educator, consultant*

Bonita Springs
McManigal, Shirley Ann *university educator, dean emerita*

Boynton Beach
Albert, Elizabeth Ann Salisbury *elementary school educator*
Haveson, Barbara Marcia *retired elementary education educator*
Morris, Nancy Lois *elementary education educator*

Bradenton
Driscoll, Constance Fitzgerald *education educator, writer, consultant*

Cape Coral
Mac Master, Harriett Schuyler *retired elementary school educator*

Clearwater
Barbeau, Sandra Alene *daycare administrator*
Edmonds, Maria Nieves *college administrator*
Eriksen, Beverly Morgan *retired primary school educator*
Jacobs, Marilyn Arlene Potoker *gifted education educator, consultant, author*

Coconut Grove
Soto, Patricia McFarlane *elementary school educator*

Cooper City
Garrard, Patricia Renick *elementary school educator*

Coral Gables
Horner, Diane L. *dean*
Shalala, Donna E. *university administrator, former federal official, political scientist, educator*

Dade City
Brown, Jessica Bree *secondary school educator, consultant*

Dania
Fernandez, Karen Geneine *secondary school educator*

Daytona Beach
Cool, Mary L. *education specialist*
Green, Betty Nielsen *education educator, consultant*

De Leon Springs
Price, Artis J. *retired secondary school educator*

Delray Beach
Leeds, Susanne *special education educator, writer*

Deltona
Schadenfroh, JoAnn *secondary school educator*

Dunedin
Cappiello, Mimi *elementary school educator*

Gamblin, Cynthia MacDonald *mathematics educator, lobbyist*

Fort Lauderdale
Carter, Marjorie Jackson *special education educator, consultant*
Carton, Cristina Silva-Bento *elementary school educator*
Dunham, Laura *elementary school educator*
Friedman, Marla Ilene *director, educator*
Guest, Suzanne Mary *adult education educator, artist*
Printz, Jillian Krueger *college program administrator*

Fort Myers
Canham, Pruella Cromartie Niver *retired educator*
Elliot, Kathleen Ann *school system administrator*
Frank, Mary Lou *retired elementary school educator*
Pouliot, Assunta Gallucci *retired business school owner and director, consultant*

Fort Pierce
Padrick, Kerry Bridges *elementary school educator*

Fort Walton Beach
Register, Annette Rowan *reading educator*

Gainesville
Dolan, Teresa A. *dean, educator, researcher*
Kirkland, Nancy Childs *secondary education educator, consultant*
Korner, Barbara Oliver *academic administrator*
Linton, Kristy Ann *primary school educator*
Rosenberger, Margaret Adaline *retired elementary school educator, writer*

Goulds
Taylor, Millicent Ruth *elementary school educator*

Green Cove Springs
Wrigley, Claudia Stephens *gifted and talented educator*

Gulfport
Athanson, Mary Catheryne *school system administrator*

Hallandale
Lippe, Harriet Rothfeder *retired elementary school educator*
Rentz, Bessie Elizabeth *adult education educator*

Hernando
Saxe, Thelma Richards *secondary school educator, consultant*

Hialeah
Jenkins, Dawn *special education educator, dancer*

Hollywood
Mendez, Deborah *parochial school educator*

Indialantic
Claflin, Tracie Nadine *private school educator*

Inverness
Hawk, Pauletta Browning *student elementary school educator*

Jacksonville
Alexander, Edna M. DeVeaux *elementary school educator*
Kinne, Frances Bartlett *academic administrator*
Main, Edna Dewey (June Main) *education educator*
Olin, Marilyn *secondary school educator*
Simms, Jacqueline Kamp *secondary school educator*

Jay
Cloud, Linda Beal *retired secondary school educator*

Jupiter
Moseley, Karen Frances Flanigan *educational consultant, retired school system administrator, educator*

Kissimmee
King, Susan Marie *special education educator*
Severance, Jeri-Lynne White *elementary school educator*
Toothe, Karen Lee *elementary and secondary school educator*
Wallace, Evelina Velvia Joetha *elementary school educator*

Lady Lake
Head-Hammond, Anna Lucille *retired secondary school educator*

Lake Mary
Branciforte, Theresa Alice *retired business educator*

Largo
Carter, Jennifer Leigh *special education educator*

Leesburg
Whalen, Norma Jean *special education educator*

Longwood
Bomar, Bunnye M. *secondary school educator*

Manalapan
Phipard, Nancy Midwood *retired special education educator, poet*

Marco Island
Henry, Sally *assistant principal*

Marianna
Connor, Catherine Brooks *educational media specialist*

Melbourne
Scheuerer, Diane Thomspon *home economics educator*

Merritt Island
Gross, Elizabeth Anne *elementary school educator*
Young, Nancy Mayer *retired secondary school educator, artist*

Miami
Banas, Suzanne *middle school educator*
Bell, Sandra Kathleen *special education educator*
Brooten, Dorothy *nursing educator, former dean*
Cheyney, Wendy *special education educator, researcher*
Cortes, Carol Solis *school system administrator*
Jones, Janice Cox *elementary school educator, writer*
Jones-Koch, Francena *school counselor, educator*
Kaplan, Betsy Hess *school board member*
McLaughlin, Margaret Brown *adult education educator, writer*
Miller, Constance Johnson *elementary school educator*
Patrie, Cheryl Christine *elementary school educator*
Perez, Mary Christine *guidance counselor, small business owner*
Rodriguez-Walling, Matilde Barcelo *special education educator*
Stiehm, Judith Hicks *university official, political science educator*
Young, Freddie Gilliam *principal, educator*

Miami Beach
Gopman, Beth Alswanger *retired elementary school educator*

Middleburg
Combs, Diane Louise *elementary school educator, music educator*

Miramar
Stephens, Sallie L. *retired assistant principal, commissioner*

Mount Dora
Sobottenyty, Margaret Ellan *retired elementary school educator*

Naples
Finger, Iris Dale Abrams *elementary school educator*
Marcy, Jeannine Koonce *retired educational administrator*
Post, Barbara Joan *elementary school educator*

Navarre
McLaughlin, Carolyn Lucile *elementary school educator*

North Miami Beach
Sorosky, Jeri Ruth *academic administrator*

Ocala
Delozier, Doris M. *retired secondary school educator*
Gatison, Karen Ann *private school educator*
Ovrebo, Judith *retired physical education educator*
Simon, Margaret B(allif) *elementary school educator, writer*
Westbrook, Rebecca Vollmer *secondary school educator*

Okeechobee
Brown, Radie Lynn *secondary school educator*
Raulerson, Phoebe Hodges *school superintendent*

Orlando
Baggott, Brenda Jane Lamb *elementary school educator*
Bichler, Elizabeth Anne *secondary school educator, musician*

Ormond Beach
Zimmerman, Pamela Diana *elementary school educator*

Pace
Davis, Gail Shell *gifted and talented educator*

Palm Beach
Robb, Babette *retired elementary school educator*

Palm Beach Gardens
Más, Beverley Berlin *career planning advisor, counseling advisor*

Pembroke Pines
DeBiagi, Anna Lillian *retired educator*
Embergher, Mary Louise *elementary school educator*

Pensacola
Costello, Arlene M. *elementary school educator*
Dorman, Jo-Anne *elementary school educator*
Galloway, Sharon Lynne *special education educator*

Poinciana
VanderHeyden, Carol *retired elementary school educator*

Pompano Beach
Hellwege, Nancy Carol *special education educator*
Johnson, Dorothy Curfman *elementary school educator*

Punta Gorda
Spaulding, Mar *retired special education educator, therapist*

Rockledge
Davis, Beth *elementary school educator*
Sutton, Betty Sheriff *elementary school educator*

Saint Augustine
Causey, Rhonda Marie *elementary school educator*
Sappington, Sharon Anne *retired school librarian*
Sullivan, Mary Jean *elementary school educator*

Saint Cloud
Stamp, Melva Elaine *special education educator*

Saint Petersburg
Dunlap, Karen F. Brown *academic administrator*
Eadens, Danielle Maya *gifted and talented educator*
Gregg, Kathy Kay *school system administrator*
McArdle, Barbara Virginia *elementary school educator*
Williams, Minnie Caldwell *retired special education educator*

Sanford
Perry, Janis Dolores *elementary school educator*
Range, Shirley Qualls *academic administrator*
Tossi, Alice Louise *special education educator*

Sarasota
Brassard, Virginia *elementary school educator*
Feldhusen, Hazel Jeanette *elementary school educator*
Hentz, Susan Marie *special education educator, consultant, trainer*
Lee, Ann McKeighan *curriculum specialist*
Thompson, Annie Figueroa *retired academic director, educator*

Seffner
Straub, Susan Monica *special education educator*

Seminole
Riedling, Ann Marlow *education educator*

South Miami
Price, Anna Maria *university administrator*

Stuart
Shipworth, Anne Krueger *special education educator*

Sugarloaf
Greenberg, Linda I. *education educator, volunteer, educator*

Sun City Center
Stanton, Vivian Brennan (Mrs. Ernest Stanton) *retired guidance counselor*

Sunrise
Stalker, Jacqueline D'Aoust *academic administrator, educator*

Tallahassee
Baylor, Amy L. *educational technology educator*
Burnette, Ada M. Puryear *educational administrator*
Dean, Delores A. *director*
Shepard, Deborah True *secondary school educator, consultant*

Tamarac
Palmieri, Patricia J. *elementary school educator*

Tampa
Harlow, Carol Jean *prospect researcher*
Hoover, Betty-Bruce Howard *private school educator*
Johnson, Joy K. *biofeedback consultant, educator*
Luddington, Betty Walles *library media specialist*
McCook, Kathleen de la Peña *university educator*
Olson, Candy *school system administrator*
Pauly, Jennifer L. *director, graphics designer*

Tierra Verde
Schmitz, Dolores Jean *primary education educator*

Venice
Myers, Virginia Lou *education educator*

West Palm Beach
Barndt, Faith Ann *elementary school educator*

Winter Garden
Gillet, Pamela Kipping *special education educator*

Winter Haven
Peck, Maryly VanLeer *retired academic administrator, chemical engineer*

Winter Park
Allen, Nancy Jean *adult education educator*
Bornstein, Rita *academic administrator*
Carver, Robin Campbell *business software educator*
McDowell, Annie R. *retired counselor*

Winter Springs
Briggs, Debra A. *secondary school educator*

GEORGIA

Acworth
Tate, Dianne Evans *program coordinator*

Adel
Darby, Marianne Talley *elementary school educator*

Albany
Keith, Carolyn Austin *secondary school counselor*
Shields, Portia Holmes *academic administrator*

Athens
Amstutz, Margaret *academic administrator*
Coley, Linda Marie *retired secondary school educator*
Herrman, Margaret Susan *university official, sociologist*

Atlanta
Affonso, Dyanne D. *dean*
Chatlen, Martha Cahill *middle school counselor*
Gordon, Jasmine Rosetta *elementary school educator*
Hall, Beverly L. *school system administrator*
Lovewell, Marjorie Klingensmith *secondary school educator*
Lucas-Tauchar, M. Frances *university administrator*
Maddox-Adams, Sherry *secondary school educator*
Meyer, Ellen L. *academic administrator*
Rosser, Sue V. *dean, educator*
Towslee, Janet L. *special education educator*

Augusta
Jackson, Rosa M. *retired elementary school educator*
Lewis, Shirley Ann Redd *college president*
Williams, Carolyn *school counselor*

Avondale Estates
Fowler, Andrea *teachers academy administrator*

Bremen
Ayers, Janet *technical college president*

Brunswick
Essick, Carol Easterling *elementary school educator*
Pittman, Catherine Sylvia *secondary school educator*

Cartersville
Cockrill, Annette S. *elementary school educator, music educator*
Wheeler, Susie Weems *retired educator*

Champton
Lane, Lenora Lee *secondary school educator, special education educator*

College Park
Bradley, Lynn Hecht *school librarian*
Ferguson, Wendell *private school educator*

Columbus
Averill, Ellen Corbett *secondary education science educator, administrator*
Duncan, Frances Murphy *retired special education educator*
Riggsby, Dutchie Sellers *education educator*
Ripple, Rochelle Poyourow *educational administrator, educator*
Tidd, Joyce Carter *etiquette educator*

Cumming
Benson, Betty Jones *retired school system administrator*

Dallas
Corley, Ginger Elaine *secondary school educator*
Harris, Celeste Acquanita *vocational rehabilitation counselor*

Decatur
Bullock, Mary Brown *academic administrator*

Douglas
Pugh, Joye Jeffries *educational administrator*

Douglasville
Hall, Mary Hugh *retired secondary school educator*

Dublin
Lee, Michele Cherry *counseling administrator*

Duluth
Capogna-Moras, Barbara Jean *secondary school educator*
Caruana, Laura E. *special education educator*

East Point
Warren, Barbara Denise *special education educator*

Eastman
Hall, Lula *retired special education educator*

Evans
Stout, Elva Carolyn Fraser *elementary school educator*
Wiggins, Margaret Reynolds *elementary school educator*

Flowery Branch
Tharp, Mary Therese *elementary school educator*

Folkston
Knowles, Julie Nall *secondary school educator*

Hahira
Connell, Sandra Bennett *school librarian*

Hartwell
Royston, Pamela Jean *special education educator*

Hoschton
Osburn, Ella Katherine *elementary school educator*

Jonesboro
Givens, Freda D. *school system administrator, musician*
Williams, Sheila A.T. *elementary education educator, consultant*

Kennesaw
Siegel, Betty Lentz *university president*

Lagrange
Donehew, Pamela K. *reading specialist*
Olney, Nancy Helen *secondary school educator*

Lake Park
Blanton, Vallye J. *elementary school educator*

Lawrenceville
Crain, Mary Ann *elementary school educator*
Harris, Melba Iris *elementary education educator, secondary school educator, state agency administrator*
Lane, Carolyn Brooks *school counselor*

Mableton
Harris, Paulette Collier *pre-school administrator, educator*

Macon
Baima, Julie Martin *special education educator*
Jobe, Ann Connor *dean, educator*

Madison
Short, Betsy Ann *elementary school educator*

Manchester
Ellison, Betty D. *retired elementary school educator*

Marietta
Laframboise, Joan Carol *middle school educator*
Rivers, Alma Faye *secondary school educator*
Rossbacher, Lisa Ann *university president, geology educator, writer*

Maxeys
Cabaniss, Barbara Lee Ferguson *counseling administrator*

Morrow
Richter, Janell Johnston *principal, minister*

Moultrie
Wright, Kathy Diane *secondary school educator*

Newnan
Royal, Nancy B. *primary school educator*

Peachtree City
Barnes, Marylou Riddleberger *retired academic administrator, educator*
Vires, Judy Doan *early childhood educator*
Wilde, Mary *secondary school educator*

Reidsville
Goodman, Joy Duvall *elementary school educator*

Roopville
Huckeba, Emily Causey *retired elementary school educator*

Roswell
Hoskinson, Carol Rowe *middle school educator*
Krapf, Veronica Lynne Benefield *elementary school educator*

Saint Marys
Hall, Lois Bremer *retired educator, volunteer*

Savannah
Cobb, Clara Jo *pre-school special education educator*
Dandy, Beryl C. *middle school educator*
Manzi, Sharon Ulrich *education educator, social worker*
Polite, Evelyn C. *retired middle school educator, counselor, evangelist*
Taggart, Helen M. *adult education educator, nurse*
Wallace, Paula S. *academic administrator*

Sharpsburg
Skinner, Lynn Strickland *secondary school mathematics educator*

Snellville
Magill, Dodie Burns *early childhood education educator*

Stockbridge
Sprayberry, Roslyn Raye *retired secondary school educator*

Suwanee
Tatum, Carla Maria *elementary school educator*

Sylvania
Brown, Barbara Hayes *elementary school educator*

Thomaston
Brown, June Dyson *elementary education educator, administrator*

Tiger
Ring, Yvonne Ann *special education educator*

Toccoa Falls
Frederick, Leah Ruth *education educator*

Valdosta
Harmon, Sharon Granholm *special education educator*

West Point
Hart, Brenda Rebecca *retired gifted and talented educator*

Winder
Stoffel, Candace Jo *secondary school educator*

HAWAII

Hilo
McKee, Eleanor Swetnam *retired principal*
Tseng, Rose *academic administrator*

Honolulu
Antal, Ann Slaughter *adult education educator*
Chee, Gloria Y.M. *secondary school educator*
Chock, Raelene *school system administrator*
Gonsalves, Margaret Leboy *elementary school educator*
Hamamoto, Patricia *school system administrator, educator*
Kaiser-Botsai, Sharon Kay *retired early childhood educator*
Lin, Yvonne Y. *foreign language teacher*
Migimoto, Fumiyo Kodani *retired secondary school educator*
Thurston, Kathleen *academic administrator*
Tito, Maureen Louise *educational administrator*
Wee, Christine Dijos *elementary school educator*
Wesselkamper, Sue *academic administrator*

Kailua
Ivey, Andi *special education educator*

Kailua Kona
Spitze, Glenys Smith *retired educator*

IDAHO

Arco
Williams, Ardith Jean *gifted and talented educator*

Boise
Griffin, Sylvia Gail *reading specialist*
Howard, Marilyn *school system administrator*

Fruitland
Sherman, Trina Arden *elementary school educator*

Idaho Falls
Winston, Jane Kay *secondary education educator, artist*

Lewiston
Marshall, Josie *secondary school educator*
Thomas, Dene *academic administrator, educator*

Moscow
Sebald, Jama Lynn *academic administrator*

Nampa
Ivie, Christine Marie *principal*

Pocatello
Smith, Elaine E. *school system administrator*

Rupert
Oppelt, Maren Joyce *secondary school educator*

ILLINOIS

Arcola
Eskridge, Judith Ann *secondary school educator*

Arlington Heights
Pasieka, Anne W. *elementary school educator*

Aurora
Cisar, Margaret *special education educator*
Daugherty, Patricia Ann *elementary school educator*
Sotir, Judith Sophia *educational technology consultant, researcher*

Barrington
Roland, Regina E. *elementary school educator*

Bartonville
Dina, Gwendolyn Judith *special education educator*

Batavia
Flannigan, Sandra F. *secondary school educator*

Bethalto
Sabaj, Nancy J. *secondary school educator*

Bloomington
Key, Otta Bischof *retired educator*

Blue Island
Skinner, Tillian Esther *daycare administrator*

Brookfield
Dearhammer, Nancy Ellen *educational consultant*

Buffalo Grove
Freemond-Woods, Reneé *secondary school educator*

Caledonia
Hubbard, Marguerite *elementary school educator*

Carbondale
Covington, Patricia Ann *university administrator*
Quisenberry, Nancy Lou *university administrator, educator*
Snyder, Carolyn Ann *education educator, librarian*

Carlinville
Pride, Miriam R. *college president*

Caseyville
Dayton, Jean *elementary school principal*

Catlin
Asaad, Kolleen Joyce *special education educator*

Champaign
Blanchard, Rosemary Ann *university program administrator, consultant, educator*
Cantor, Nancy *academic administrator*
Dulany, Elizabeth Gjelsness *university press administrator*
Gomez, Terrine *school director*
Harris, Zelema M. *academic administrator*
Loeb, Jane Rupley *academic administrator, educator*
Osborne, Margery Diane *education educator*

Charleston
Surles, Carol D. *academic administrator*

Chicago
Beane, Marjorie Noterman *academic administrator*
Bowman, Barbara Taylor *early childhood educator*
Cafferty, Pastora San Juan *public policy educator*
Cooper, Jo Marie *elementary school principal*
Cross, Dolores Evelyn *former university administrator, educator*
Culp, Kristine Ann *dean, theology educator*
Culverwell, Rosemary Jean *principal, elementary education educator*
Cummings, Maxine Gibson *elementary school educator*
Daniel, Elnora D. *academic administrator*
Desombre, Nancy Cox *academic administrator, consultant*
Einoder, Camille Elizabeth *retired secondary school educator*
Felton, Cynthia *educational administrator*
Fritsch-Stewart, Antoinette M. *education educator*
Gajic, Ranka Pejovic *secondary school educator*
Gantz, Suzi Grahn *special education educator*
Gold, Carol R. *dean, nursing educator*
Harris, Shirley *elementary, secondary and adult education educator*
Hart, Katherine Miller *college dean*
Hawkins, Loretta Ann *retired secondary school educator, playwright*
Hayes, Alice Bourke *academic administrator, biologist, researcher*
Howard, Janet *elementary school educator*
Howell, Lynnette *elementary school principal*
Johnson, Mary Ann *vocational school owner*
Kim, Mi Ja *dean, academic administrator*
Kubistal, Patricia Bernice *educational consultant*
Matasar, Ann B. *former dean, business and political science educator*
Mindes, Gayle Dean *education educator*
Mirza, Leona Lousin *elementary school educator, director*
Morris-Rogers, Cheryl-Ann *daycare provider, director, educator*
Normand, Beverly Ann *counseling administrator*
Parker, Pamela Jean *vice principal*
Petitan, Debra Ann Burke *elementary school educator*
Roberts, Jo Ann Wooden *school system administrator*
Sampey, Debra A. *middle school principal*
Schwarzkopf, Gloria A. *education educator, psychotherapist*
Scrimshaw, Susan Crosby *dean*
Seals, Teresa McCray *elementary school educator*
Shaver, Joan Louise Fowler *adult education educator*
Steinberg, Salme Elizabeth Harju *academic administrator, historian*
Stephens, Helen Janssens *principal*
Traudt, Mary B. *elementary school educator*
Wyndewicke, Kionne Annette (Annette Johnson Moorer) *reading educator*
Young, Lauren Sue Jones *education educator*

Dekalb
Schmidt, Jennifer Anne *education educator*
Stewart, Mary R *education educator, artist*

Des Plaines
Giles, Phyllis Lenore Williams *retired elementary school educator*
Lee, Margaret Burke *college president, English educator*

Downers Grove
Nichols, Karen *academic administrator*

East Saint Louis
Wright, Katie Harper *educational administrator, journalist*

El Paso
Musick, Marilyn Irene *secondary school educator*

Elgin
Aydt, Mary I. *secondary school educator*
Bowen, Jean Ann *school system administrator*
Thompson, Phyllis Darlene *retired elementary school educator*

Elmhurst
Nega, Nancy Kawecki *middle school science educator*

Evanston
McCoy, Marilyn *university official*
Power, Peggy Ann *elementary school educator*

Forreston
Hall, Carol Beth *elementary school educator*

Frankfort
Flanagan, Aileen Mary *special education educator*

Galatia
Foster, Jan S. *special education educator*

Galesburg
Simpson, Carol *elementary school educator*
Sunderland, Jacklyn Giles *former alumni affairs director*

Glenview
Corley, Jenny Lynd Wertheim *elementary school educator*

Godfrey
Gallagher, Kathryn Kasich *elementary school educator*

Granite City
Garber, Katherine *special education educator*

Grayslake
Choice, Priscilla Kathryn Means (Penny Choice) *educational director, international consultant*

Greenfield
Weller, Robin Lea *elementary school educator, secondary school educator*

Gurnee
Halsne-Baarda, Alana Michelle *secondary school educator*

Highland Park
Papich, Mary Jo *secondary school educator, department chairman*

Jacksonville
Johns, Beverley Anne Holden *special education administrator*
Moe-Fishback, Barbara Ann *counseling administrator*
Welch, Rhea Jo *special education educator*

Joliet
Bartow, Barbara Jené *university program administrator*
Crosby, Janet Marie *gifted and talented educator, writer*
Norris, Jean Marie *director*

La Grange
Kensek, Magdalene Agnes *private school educator*

Lake Forest
Szaksztylo, Kathee *design technologist*

Lake Zurich
Schwarz, Cheryl Marita *special education educator*

Lisle
Huffman, Louise Tolle *middle school educator*

Madison
Purdes, Alice Marie *retired adult education educator*

Marion
Howell, Catherine Jeanine *retired secondary school educator*

Markham
Peacock, Marilyn Claire *primary education educator*

Melrose Park
Chaudhry, Marie-Laurence *elementary education educator, administrator*

Moline
Mitchell, Lucille Anne *retired elementary school educator*
Schauenberg, Susan Kay *retired counseling administrator*

Momence
Holland, Leslie Ann *special education educator*

Monmouth
Bruce, Mary Hanford *academic administrator, educator, writer*

Morris
Janz, Gail Diane *media director*

Morton
Paxton, Kathleen Marie *special education educator*

Morton Grove
Johnson, Laura Stark *secondary school educator, administrator*

Murphysboro
Barrette, Linda Jones *dean*

New Berlin
Buffington, Rosemary *secondary school educator*

New Lenox
Fries, Rebecca Kay *director, special education educator*
Ryan, Pamela Jeanne *guidance director*

Normal
Miller, Wilma Hildruth *education educator*
Mtegha, Dorothy Mercy *education educator*
O'Dell, Lisa A. *special education educator*
Wortham, Anne Estelle *education educator*

Northbrook
Goldsmith, Kimberlee Beth *special education educator*

Rosenberg, Auria Eleanor *elementary school educator*

O Fallon
Guciardo, Joan *family and consumer sciences educator*

Oak Forest
Monaghan, M. Patricia *education educator, writer*

Oak Park
Evert, Margaret Jane *principal*
Venerable, Shirley Marie *gifted education educator*

Oakbrook Terrace
Cason, Marilynn Jean *technological institute official, lawyer*

Oswego
Orland, Rachel Jane *elementary school educator, musician*

Palos Heights
Powell, Patricia Lynn *education educator, educator, special education educator, educator*

Palos Hills
Stratton, Pauline A. *former elementary education educator, alderman*

Paris
Essinger, Susan Jane *special education educator*

Payson
Tenhouse, Gayle Denise *secondary school educator*

Pekin
Herbstreith, Yvonne Mae *primary education educator*

Peoria
Behrll, Cathy G. *special education educator*

Plainfield
Alander, Virginia Nickerson *retired student assistance coordinator*

Richton Park
Burt, Gwen Behrens *elementary school administrator*
Pierce, Mary E. *retired educator, public relations consultant*

Ringwood
Tomlinson, Ferol Martin *reading and learning center media specialist*

River Forest
Carroll, Donna M. *academic administrator*
Sipe, Doris Elaine *college dean*

Robinson
Newlin, Yvonne Ann *adult education educator*

Rock Island
Welling, Mary Ann *secondary school educator*

Rockton
Cunningham, Judy Evalyn *elementary school administrator, educator*

Roscoe
DeHaven-Binger, Jeanine Kay *special education educator*

Skokie
Sloan, Judi C. *former physical education educator*
Weiss, Marcia Ann *special education educator*

Springfield
Fullerton, Faye Ellen *academic administrator*
Harmon, Carolyn *adult education educator*

Sterling
Donahue, Shirley Ohnstad *elementary school educator*

Tinley Park
Baker, Betty Louise *retired secondary school educator*
Nagle, Carol Ann *elementary school educator*

Tuscola
Henderson, E. Suzanne *elementary school educator*

Urbana
Conlin, Kathleen F. *dean, theater director*
Glick, Karen Lynne *college administrator*

Varna
Knackstedt, Judy M. *secondary school educator*

Venice
Cunningham, Betty Jean De Bow *adult education educator*

Villa Park
Hougen, Carlene Lenore *secondary school educator, department chairman*

West Peoria
McBride, Sharon Louise *counselor, technical communication educator*

Wilmington
Chappell, Elizabeth Irene *special education educator*

Winnetka
Huggins, Charlotte Susan Harrison *secondary school educator, author, travel specialist*

Woodstock
Levandowski, Barbara Sue *educational administrator*

INDIANA

Anderson
Ritchey, Yvonne Kay *assistant principal*

Bloomington
Adams, Karen Hoeve *university administrator*
Bair, Susanne Paulette *university foundation administrator*
Bornholdt, Laura Anna *university administrator*
Chafel, Judith Ann *education educator*
Collins, Dorothy Craig *retired educational administrator*
Hutton, Deborah Spence *academic administrator*

Boonville
Sureck, Karen Eileen *special education educator*

Carmel
Brooks, Patricia Scott *principal*
Dean, Ann Marie Butz *secondary school educator*

Cloverdale
Schwartz, Susan Lynn Hill *principal*

Crown Point
Akin, Donna Rae *retired elementary school educator*

East Chicago
Fortenberry, Delores B. *dean*
Suhre, Edith Lavonne *adult education educator*

Evansville
Overton, Sharon Faye *elementary school educator*

Fort Wayne
Brandt, Nancy G. *education educator*
Cummins, Kathleen K. *retired elementary school educator*
Cutshall-Hayes, Diane Marion *elementary school educator*
Hernandez, Ann Margaret *education educator*
Robinson, Wendy Y. *school system administrator*
Stebbins, Vrina Grimes *retired elementary school educator, counselor*
Walley, Pamela Kaye *elementary school educator*

Fortville
Demegret, A. Jean Hughes *secondary education educator, artist*

Gary
Steele, Beverly J. *elementary school educator*
Walker, Juanita Moffett *retired elementary school educator*

Goshen
Showalter, Shirley H. *academic administrator*

Greenfield
Geesa, Susan Louise *special education educator*

Hammond
Fehring, Mary Ann *secondary school educator*

Highland
DeVaney, Cynthia Ann *elementary school educator, secondary school educator, real estate broker*
Mach, Michele R. *special education educator*

Hobart
Hanley, Roberta Lynn *alternative education coordinator, educator*

Indianapolis
Barcus, Mary Evelyn *primary school educator*
Brash, Susan Kay *principal*
Cilella, Mary Winifred *director*
D'Amico, Carol *educational administrator*
Folco, Angelika *secondary school educator*
Kovacik, Karen Marie *English literature educator*
Metzner, Barbara Stone *university counselor*
Moser, Barbara Jo *elementary school educator*
Nurok, Zita *elementary school educator*
Reed, Suellen Kinder *school system administrator*
Rose, Mary Etta *retired educator*
Vann, Lora Jane *reading educator, retired*
Watkins, Sherry Lynne *elementary school educator*
Williams, Judith Ellen *educational administrator*

Kentland
Ekstrom, Lisa Marie *special education educator*

Kouts
Miller, Sarabeth *secondary school educator*

La Porte
McShane-Halik, Christine Denise *secondary school educator*

Merrillville
Protho, Jessie *vocational school educator*

Mishawaka
Stone, Cathy Jean *elementary school educator*
Wilson, Rebecca Jo *dean, education educator*

Monroeville
Sorgen, Elizabeth Ann *retired educator*

Monticello
Burkhardt, Mary Sue D. *secondary school educator*

Muncie
Harris, Vicki Lee *educational consultant*
Joles, Candace Rae *special education educator*
Stewart, Rita Joan *academic administrator*
Swetnam, Ruth E. Danglade *curriculum director*

New Albany
Riehl, Jane Ellen *education educator*

Notre Dame
Johnstone, Joyce Visintine *education educator*
O'Hara, Patricia A. *dean, law educator*

Pendleton
Phenis-Bourke, Nancy Sue *educational administrator*

Plainfield
Lucas, Georgetta Marie Snell *retired educator, artist*

Plymouth
Jurkiewicz, Margaret Joy Gommel *secondary school educator*

Rockville
Sodora, Rosalyn Harpold *elementary education educator, school librarian*

Saint Mary Of The Woods
Lescinski, Joan *higher education administrator, English educator*

Shelbyville
Clark, Rose Sharon *elementary school educator*

South Bend
Charles, Isabel *university administrator*
Colborn, Nancy Wootton *school librarian*
Emery, Margaret Ross *elementary school educator*
Rodgers, Grace Anne *university official*
Streich, Cynthia Sue *special education educator*

South Whitley
Hinthorn, Dawn Rosa *elementary and secondary school educator*

Spencer
Coley, Brenda Ann *elementary school educator*

Tell City
Arterberry, Patricia *school educator*

Terre Haute
Aton, Eric Newton *former x x x x former English language educator*
Stoelting, Freda Ann *special education educator*

Valparaiso
Scales, Freda S. *dean, nursing educator*
Taylor, Heather Marie *director*

Wabash
Ward, Judith A. *elementary school educator, music educator*

West Lafayette
Gappa, Judith M. *university administrator*
Moyars-Johnson, Mary Annis *university official*
Roberts, Anne Margaret *secondary school educator*

Westfield
Scott, Jennifer Marie *special education educator*

Wheatfield
Woolever, Gail Waluk *elementary school educator, artist, secondary school educator*

Williamsport
Swanson, Donna Kay *elementary school educator, writer*

Winslow
McKinney, Shannon J. *retired secondary school educator*

IOWA

Ames
Crabtree, Beverly June *retired dean*
Mattila, Mary Jo Kalsem *elementary and art educator*

Bettendorf
Hirsch, Lynn Christy *elementary school educator, art educator*
Webb, Carol E *school system administrator*

Bloomfield
Combs, Judy Diane *elementary school educator, civic association administrator*

Burlington
Noll, Laurie Jane *secondary school educator*

Cedar Rapids
Merritt, Sandra Lee *educational consultant*
O'Keefe, Ellen Margaret *special education educator*

Charter Oak
Kutschinski, Dorothy Irene *elementary school educator*

Clive
O'Brien, Nancy A. *youth counselor*

Davenport
Corcoran, Janet Patricia *elementary school educator*
Keller, Nancy Anne *special education educator*
Sheehey, Patricia Ann *secondary school educator*

Decorah
Meade, Birgitta Rosemary *elementary school educator*

Des Moines
Paterik, Frances Sue *secondary school educator, actress*
Ratcliff, Dolores Jean *special education educator*

Dubuque
Collins, Barbara Louise *retired elementary school educator*
Dunn, M. Catherine *college administrator, educator*

Harlan
Wilson, Annette Sigrid *elementary school educator*

Iowa City
Buckwalter, Kathleen C. *academic administrator, educator*
Davis, Julia McBroom *college dean, speech pathology and audiology educator*
Dreher, Melanie Creagan *dean, nursing educator*
Porter, Nancy Lefgren *reading recovery educator*

Iowa Falls
Sessler, Donna Jean Hotz *secondary school educator*

Johnston
Anderson, Sara *special education educator*

Keokuk
Hardy, Julia Irene *elementary school educator*

Knoxville
Baker, Cynthia Joan *elementary education educator, historic site interpreter*

Manchester
Baumgartner, Cindy Sue *secondary school educator*

Morning Sun
Byers, Elizabeth *education educator*

Oskaloosa
Burrow, Nancy Kay *special education educator*

Reinbeck
Koester, Lisa *educational administrator, consultant*

Roland
Weisendahl, Tempest Anne *elementary school educator*

Sioux City
Dillman, Kristin Wicker *elementary and middle school educator, musician*
Rants, Carolyn Jean *college official*
Wick, Sister Margaret *former college administrator*

Sloan
Ullrich, Roxie Ann *special education educator*

Waterloo
Kober, Arletta Refshauge (Mrs. Kay L. Kober) *supervisor*

West Des Moines
Hubbard, Cheryl A. *director*

Woodward
Jenkins, Alice Marie *secondary school educator*

KANSAS

Arkansas City
Meeks, Cindy Lou *special education educator*

Baldwin City
Baker, Margaret Moore-Fritz *retired school librarian, retired humanities educator*

Caney
McVey, Teresa Lynn *special education educator*

Carbondale
McCollum, Susan *elementary school educator*

De Soto
Davis, Pamela Jo *special education educator*

Dodge City
Sapp, Nancy L. *educational administrator*

Emporia
Schallenkamp, Kay *academic administrator*

Fort Riley
Truitt, Karen Reneé *special education educator*

Great Bend
Rittenhouse, Nancy Carol *elementary school educator*

Hays
Karlin, Lisa Marie *academic administrator*

Holton
McDonald, Sharon Holliday *special education educator*

Horton
Radford, Virginia Rodriguez *retired secondary education educator, librarian*

Kansas City
Atkinson, Barbara F. *dean, medical educator, academic administrator*
Bach, Michele *education educator*

Miller
Miller, Karen L. *dean, nursing educator*
Wendel, Shirley Anne *college dean*

Lawrence
Brasseur, Irma Faye *special education educator*
Lyerla, Karen Dale *special education educator*
Peterson, Nancy *special education educator*
Turnbull, Ann Patterson *special educator, consultant, research director*

Leavenworth
James, Verla Alice *academic administrator, educator*

Liberal
Rodenberg, Anita Jo *academic administrator*
Wilkerson, Rita Lynn *special education educator, consultant*

Lindsborg
Humphrey, Karen Ann *college director*

Mcpherson
Stevens, Leota Mae *retired elementary education educator*

Meade
Brannan, Cleo Estella *retired elementary education educator*
Coles, Lori Jane *secondary school educator*

Oakley
Oelke, Anita Jean *special education educator*

Olathe
Allen, Dawn *secondary school educator, writer*
Dennis, Patricia Lyon *adult education educator*
Goodwin, Becky K. *educational technology resource educator*
Hackler, Ruth Ann *retired educator*
Stevens, Diana Lynn *elementary school educator*
Williams, Carol Marie *retired secondary school educator*

Overland Park
Brun, Pamela Ann *special education educator*

Parker
Gowing, Patricia M. *retired elementary education educator*

Pittsburg
Stuckey, Donna Sue Pintar *information services executive*

Pleasanton
Starr, Darlene R. *special education educator, education educator*

Pomona
Gentry, Alberta Elizabeth *elementary school educator*

Roeland Park
Viveros, Mary L. *principal*

Russell
Craven, Charmarose Lanelle *technology coordinator*

Shawnee
Scanlon, Vicki E. *secondary school educator*

Shawnee Mission
Barton, Betty Louise *school system administrator*
Crooks, Lisa Zahn *elementary school educator*
Kaplan, Marjorie Ann Pashkow *school district administrator*

Sublette
Swinney, Carol Joyce *secondary school educator*

Topeka
Greene, Jane *health educator*
Renauer, Marita *educational consultant*

Wichita
Erickson, Sheryl Laraine *education educator*
Gibson, Kay Lynn *education educator*
Ines, Amy *elementary school educator*
Van Arendonk, Susan Carole *elementary school educator*

KENTUCKY

Ashland
Cavins, Jacqueline Lou *education educator, adult nurse practitioner*

Barbourville
Floyd, Linda Smith *principal*

Benton
Kellie, Diane *special education educator*

Bowling Green
Schaeffer, Beth Bolin *pre-school educator, consultant*

Butler
Lustenberg, Michelle Williamson *gifted and talented educator*

Carrollton
Heilman, Mary Joanne *gifted education educator*

Corbin
Watkins, Jennie Shore *elementary school educator*

Covington
Berg, Lorine McComis *retired guidance counselor*

Custer
Egbert, Donna *elementary school educator*

Danville
Kennan, Elizabeth Topham *academic administrator, retired historian*

Eddyville
Norman, Pamela Kay *special education educator, director*

Ekron
Hamilton, Amelia Wentz (Amy Wentz) *elementary school educator*

Flatwoods
Sharp, Verna Ellen *special education educator*

Frankfort
Tribble, Pamela Gail *special education educator*

Harlan
DeLong-Smith, Stephanie K. *secondary school educator*

Hazard
Bryant, Renee Tabor *director, educator*

Lexington
Hurley, Janet Lee *university health service administrator*
Isenhour, Kathleen Chaney *special education educator, consultant*
Salisbury, Holly Buckner *university arts director*
Williams, Carolyn Antonides *university dean*
Zinser, Elisabeth Ann *academic administrator*

Louisville
Bratton, Ida Frank *retired secondary school educator*
Cecil, Bonnie Susan *elementary school educator*
Hixson, Allie Corbin *retired adult education educator, advocate*
Leonard, Mona Freeman *adult education educator*
Schneider, Jayne Bangs *school librarian*
White-Walker, Roxana *elementary school educator*

Middlesboro
Potter-Hughes, Karen Ann *secondary school educator*

Murray
Russell, Mary Ann *secondary school educator*

Newport
Kirk, Charlotte Leidecker *director*

Nicholasville
Sewell, Viola L. *daycare administrator*

Pikeville
Sisco, Mary Ann *director*

Pineville
Hoskins, Barbara R(uth) Williams *elementary educator, elementary principal*

Saint Catharine
Collins, Martha Layne *college president, former governor*

Union
Franklin, Dorothy Ann *guidance counselor*

Upton
Lawson, Linda Jean *elementary school educator*

Winchester
Skinner, Jill Suzanne *special education educator*

LOUISIANA

Alexandria
Vandersypen, Rita DeBona *guidance counselor, academic administrator*
Welch, Kelli Carruth *secondary school counselor*

Baton Rouge
Barnette, Kim Bailey *counseling administrator*
Boulton, Bonnie Smith *assistant principal, special education educator*
Harrison, Betty Carolyn Cook *education educator, administrator*
Litton, Nancy Joan *education educator*
Rami, Janet Simmons *university dean, nursing educator*

Chalmette
Crouchet, Kathleen Hunt *elementary educator, reading educator*
Williamson, Ramona Diane *special education educator*

Covington
Bourgeois, Priscilla Elzey *educational administrator*
Stahr, Beth A. *school librarian*

Crowley
Tall, Carol Dailey *special education educator, speech pathology/audiology services professional*

Grambling
Warner, Neari Francois *university president*

Gretna
Tross-Tanner, Marsha Lynn *elementary school educator*

Houma
Bordelon, Dena Cox Yarbrough *retired special education educator, director*

Jennings
Romine, Donna Mae *gifted and talented program educator*

Lafayette
Colbert-Cormier, Patricia A. *secondary school educator*
Marceaux, Linda d'Augereau *elementary school educator*
Redding, Evelyn A. *dean*
Ventress, Mary Ellen *school system administrator*

Lake Arthur
Dronet, Judy Lynn *elementary school educator, librarian*

Lake Charles
Fields-Gold, Anita *retired dean*

Metairie
Johnson, Beth Michael *school administrator*

Monroe
Hall, Donna Marie *director*

New Iberia
Hockless, Mary Fontenot *educational consultant*

New Orleans
Hassenboehler, Donalyn *principal*
Longstreet, Wilma S. *curriculum and instruction educator*

New Roads
Gauthier, Amy *campus administrator*

Newllano
Boren, Lynda Sue *gifted education educator*

Pineville
Smith, Mabel Hargis *retired secondary school educator, musician*

Port Vincent
Foster, Crystal Ann *elementary school educator*

Ruston
Freasier, Aileen W. *special education educator*

Shreveport
Morehead, Deborah Elizabeth Betts *gifted and talented educator, music minister*
Pierson, Juanita (Nita Pierson) *secondary school educator*

Slidell
Faust, Marilyn B. *middle school principal*

Springhill
Thomas, Faye Evelyn J. *elementary and secondary school educator*

Westlake
Grantham, Camille Renee Theriot *high school librarian, media specialist*

Winnfield
Ward, Charlotte Lowrey *guidance counselor*

MAINE

Auburn
Appleby, Penny E. *secondary school educator*
Bailey, Linda Karen *special education educator*

Augusta
vonHerrlich, Phyllis Herrick *academic administrator*
Wilder, Elaine Kathryn *university official*

Bangor
Sullivan, Mary E. *retired secondary educator, past state legislator*

Bar Harbor
Swazey, Judith Pound *academic administrator, sociomedical science educator*

Biddeford
Featherman, Sandra *academic administrator, political science educator*

Boothbay
Watson, Caroline *elementary school educator*

Bremen
Wilson, Linda Smith *academic administrator*

Bridgton
Hill, Marilynn Irene Reynolds *secondary school educator*

Cumberland Center
Thompson, Deborah Carpenter *private school educator*

Farmington
Kalikow, Theodora June *university president*

Lewiston
Hansen, Elaine Tuttle *academic administrator*
Reich, Jill *dean*

Lisbon
Iverson, Carlene V. *principal*

New Harbor
Brookes, Ruth Harding *guidance counselor*

Old Town
Alex, Joanne DeFilipp *elementary school educator*

Portland
Chandler, Patricia Ann *retired special education educator*
Tenbury, Colleen A. *dean*

Presque Isle
Davidshofer, Claire H. *college instructor*
Gentile, Caroline D. *adult education educator*
Hensel, Nancy H. *academic administrator*

Saint Agatha
Cyr, Elaine Marie *special education educator*

Scarborough
Russo, Joan Mildred *special education educator*

South Portland
Kandoian, Janet Adrienne *elementary school educator*

Waterville
Cook, Susan Farwell *associate director planned giving*

MARYLAND

Adamstown
Church, Martha Eleanor *retired academic administrator, scholar*

Annapolis
Bowen, Linnell R. *director*
Flanagan, Susan Marie *special education educator*
Parham, Carol Sheffey *school system administrator*
Stern, Margaret Bassett *retired special education educator, author*

Arnold
Smith, Martha A. *academic administrator*

Baltimore
Adams, Clara I. *academic administrator*
Allan, Janet D. *dean*
Ball, Marion Jokl *academic administrator*
Boughman, Joann Ashley *dean*
Brewer, Nevada Nancy *elementary school educator*
Buser, Carolyn Elizabeth *correctional education administrator*
Donnell, Jean Downey *education educator*
Donovan, Sharon Ann *secondary school educator*
Grasmick, Nancy S. *school system administrator*
Heller, Barbara R. *former dean, nursing educator*
Kemp, Suzanne Leppart *elementary school educator*
Norris, Karen W. *grants specialist*
Rothenberg, Karen H. *dean, law educator*
Seurkamp, Mary Pat *college president*

Bel Air
Miller, Dorothy Eloise *education educator*
Phillips, Bernice Cecile Golden *retired vocational education educator*

Berlin
Auxer, Cathy Joan *elementary school educator*

Bowie
Tesar, Patricia Marie *academic coordinator*

Capitol Heights
Zinaman, Helaine Madeleine *gifted and talented education educator*

Catonsville
Smith, F. Louise *elementary school educator*

Centreville
Shoemaker, Anne Cunningham *retired mathematics educator*

Chevy Chase
Brenner, Marcella Siegel *retired education educator*
Towsner, Cynthia Merle *vocational school educator*
Wolf, Jean D. *educational consultant, writer*

College Park
Finkelstein, Barbara *education educator*
Morman, Shirley H. *director*
Prentice, Ann Ethelynd *university dean*
Schwab, Susan Carroll *dean*
Szymanski, Edna Mora *dean*

Columbia
Davis, Janet Marie Gorden *secondary school educator*
Gold, Susan *conference educator*
Hale, Mignon S. Palmer-Flack *elementary school educator, educator*
Hartman, Lee Ann Walraff *secondary school educator, consultant*
Jones-Wilson, Faustine Clarisse *retired education educator*

Cumberland
Bennett, Sue Ellen *director*

Easton
Reed, Carol L. *secondary school educator, writer*

Ellicott City
Powell, Lillian Marie *retired music educator*

Fort Washington
Diercks, Elizabeth Gorman *elementary school educator*

Frederick
Hamilton, Rhoda Lillian Rosen *guidance counselor, language educator, consultant*
Klein, Elaine Charlotte *school system administrator*

Frostburg
Gira, Catherine Russell *university president*

Gaithersburg
Stroud, Nancy Iredell *retired secondary school educator, freelance writer, editor*

Great Mills
Gehring, Patti J. *principal*

Greenbelt
Kalnay, Eugenia *university administrator, meteorologist*

Hagerstown
Butts, Mary Ellen F. *secondary school educator*
McCoy, Mildred Brookman *retired elementary education educator*

Hanover
Schmidt, Sandra Jean *secondary school educator*

Harwood
Smith, Maria Lynn *school system administrator*

Hyattsville
Williams, Gladys Tucker *elementary school principal*

Laurel
Hunter, Edwina Earle *elementary school educator*

Lutherville Timonium
Booth, Penelope Partridge *secondary school educator, writer, principal*

Mardela Springs
Harcum, Louise Mary Davis *retired elementary education educator*

Owings Mills
Berg, Barbara Kirsner *health education specialist*

Oxon Hill
Robinson, Cheryl Jeffreys *special education educator, consultant*
Scott, Frances Fisher Markoe *retired secondary school educator*

Pasadena
Fastige, Nellie Marshall *elementary school educator*

Potomac
Karch, Karen Brooke *principal*
Kuykendall, Crystal Arlene *educational consultant, lawyer*
Schuessler, Isabelle Sweeny *school administrator*

Princess Anne
Nnadi, Eucharia E. *academic administrator*

Rockville
Alexis, Shirley Davidson *secondary school educator*
Dawson, Dianne *education educator, writer*
Salzman, Joanna Michele *special education educator*

Salisbury
Adkins, Patricia Ann *school system administrator, educator*
Zinner, Ellen Scheiner *university administrator, clinical psychologist*

Severna Park
Sunday, Melva Dora *elementary school educator*

Silver Spring
Best-Goring, Cynthia Lovale *elementary school principal*
Bonner, Bester Davis *school system administrator*
Burgos-Sasscer, Ruth *chancellor emeritus*
Coles, Anna Louise Bailey *retired dean, nurse*
Fromberg, Jean Stern *school system administrator*

Stevenson
Hyman, Mary Bloom *science education programs coordinator*

Temple Hills
Curry, Emma Beatrice *elementary school educator*

Towson
Baltzley, Patricia Creel *secondary mathematics educator*
Myers, Debra Taylor *elementary school educator, writer*

Union Bridge
Hannah, Judy Challenger *private education tutor*

Upper Marlboro
Cutright, Loretta Ann *special education educator*
Street, Patricia Lynn *retired secondary school educator*
Swift-Howard, Alice Lorraine *school system administrator*

Waldorf
Robey, Sherie Gay Southall Gordon *secondary education educator, consultant*

Westminster
Coley, Joan Develin *education educator, academic administrator*

Kroeger Smith, Marilyn Beth *adult education educator, researcher*
Pappalardo, Faye *academic administrator*

Wheaton
Davis, Marie Elaine *elementary school educator*
Davis, Patricia Anne *secondary school educator, art educator*

Wye Mills
Schisler, Amy MacWilliams *school librarian, graphics designer*

MASSACHUSETTS

Amherst
MacKnight, Carol Bernier *educational administrator*

Bedford
Wasson, Lila Elizabeth *educational consultant*

Boston
Berkman, Lisa F. *public health educator*
Caldwell, Ann Wickins *academic administrator*
Celestino-Arguinzoni, Wilma *academic administrator*
Coleman, K(atherine) Ann *behavioral psychology educator*
Dluhy, Deborah Haigh *college dean*
Dujon, Diane Marie *director, activist*
Eisner, Sister Janet Margaret *college president*
Gora, JoAnn M. *university chancellor*
Liebergott, Jacqueline W. *academic administrator*
Love, Carol *dean*
Meier, Deborah *principal*
Paine, Lynn *academic administrator*
Penney, Sherry Hood *university president, educator*
Piscatelli, Nancy Marie *secondary school educator*
Prothrow-Stith, Deborah *academic administrator, public health educator*
Shore, Eleanor Gossard *medical school dean*
Simmons, Sylvia Jeanne Quarles (Mrs. Herbert G. Simmons Jr.) *university administrator, educator, executive*
Tornow, Barbara *academic administrator*
Yarborough, Nellie Constance *principal, minister*
Zungolo, Eileen H. *dean*

Bridgewater
Tinsley, Adrian *college president*

Brockton
Demers, Catherine Mary *parochial school educator*

Cambridge
Baumgartner, Mary Anne Sgarlat *academic administrator, entrepreneur*
Cazden, Courtney B(orden) *education educator*
Cordero, Mercedes Paula *director, consultant*
Eurich, Nell P. *education educator*
Graham, Patricia Albjerg *education educator*
Long, Bridget Terry *education educator*
McKenna, Margaret Anne *university president*
Merrifield, Susan Ruth *education educator*
Power, Samantha *academic administrator, writer*
Rowe, Mary P. *organizational ombudsman, management educator*
Wood, Julie M. *educational consultant*

Chatham
Boudreau, Michelle E. *principal, consultant*

Chestnut Hill
Bando, Patricia Alice *director*
Nemerowicz, Gloria *academic administrator*

Chicopee
Masciotra, Janet Marie *elementary school educator*

Cotuit
Crocker, Jean Hazelton *retired educator, environmental volunteer*

Danvers
Clark, Sharon Jackson *private school administrator*

Everett
Auger, Kimberly Ann *elementary school educator*

Fairhaven
Goes, Kathleen Ann *secondary education educator, choral director*
Rose, Anita Carroll *retired educator*

Framingham
Heineman, Helen L. *provost*
Valakis, M. Lois *retired elementary school educator*

Holland
McGrory, Mary Kathleen *retired academic administrator, humanities educator*

Hubbardston
Marceau, Judith Marie *retired elementary school educator, small business owner*

Hyde Park
Harris, Emily Louise *special education educator*

Longmeadow
Katz, Barbara S. *special education educator*
Leary, Carol Ann *academic administrator*
Schirmer-Smith, Sara Jane (Sally Schirmer-Smith) *dean, director student activities*

Lowell
Clark, Sharon Ann *educational consultant, music educator*

Lunenburg
Schnakenberg, Lori Ann *secondary school educator*

Manchester
White, Sallie Snow Wilber *retired elementary school educator*

Marblehead
Tamaren, Michele Carol *educational consultant, writer, retired special education educator*

Marshfield Hills
Johnson, Margaret Hill *retired educational administrator, consultant*

Medfield
Nedder, Janet Marie *elementary school educator*

New Bedford
Nunes, Pricilla O. *special education educator, artist*

Newton
Matteson, Carol J. *academic administrator*
O'Connell, Sister Virginia M. *school librarian*

North Andover
Gannon, Patricia J. *academic administrator*

North Falmouth
Green, Linda C. *education specialist administrator, researcher*

Northampton
Christ, Carol Tecla *academic administrator*
Lightburn, Anita Louise *dean, social work educator*

Norton
Marshall, Dale Rogers *academic administrator, political scientist, educator*
Woods, Susanne *academic administrator, educator*

Peabody
Kokoras, Victoria *retired elementary school educator*

Plymouth
Goggin, Joan Marie *school system administrator*
Paul, Carol Ann *retired academic administrator, biology educator*

Princeton
Roney-O'Brien, Susan Frances *elementary school educator, writer*

Provincetown
Wolfman, Brunetta Reid *education educator*

Quincy
Furtado, Beverly Ann *financial aid administrator*
Pratt, Mary *retired educator*

Revere
Ferrante, Olivia Ann *retired educator, consultant*

Salem
Harrington, Nancy D. *college president*

Sharon
Johnson, Addie Collins *secondary education educator, former dietitian*

Somerville
Gurley, Rhonda Jean *special education educator, consultant*

South Attleboro
Hanson, Barbara Jean *education educator*

South Hadley
Creighton, Joanne Vanish *academic administrator*

Spencer
Robinson, Evelyn Edna *secondary school educator*

Springfield
Ingram, Renay Eloise *elementary school educator, school system administrator*

Sudbury
Thompson, Mary Lou *elementary school educator*

Turners Falls
Finley-Morin, Kimberley K. *secondary school educator*

Wayland
Anderson, Monica Luffman *school librarian, educator, real estate broker*

Wellesley
Heartt, Charlotte Beebe *university official*
Walsh, Diana Chapman *academic administrator, sociologist, educator*

West Roxbury
Roach, Maureen S. *primary school educator*

West Springfield
Sumaryono, Karen L. *secondary school educator, consultant*

Westborough
Antalek, Eileen Elizabeth *educational consultant*

Westfield
Dunphy, Maureen Milbier *reading educator*

Weston
Nolan-Conners, Elizabeth Ann *director, educator*

Williamstown
Hill, Catharine B. *provost, economics educator*

Worcester
Bowen, Alice Frances *school system administrator*

MICHIGAN

Alma
Tracy, Saundra J. *academic administrator*

Ann Arbor
Ball, Deborah Loewenberg *education educator*
Beutler, Suzanne A. *retired secondary school educator, artist*
Copeland, Carolyn Abigail *retired dean*
Dumas, Rhetaugh Etheldra Graves *university official*
Fleming, Suzanne Marie *academic administrator, freelance/self-employed writer*
Heath, Angela Mary *academic advisor*
Hinshaw, Ada Sue *dean, nursing educator*
Ross, Theresa Mae *secondary school educator*
Sears, JoAnn Marie *school librarian*

Auburn Hills
De Martin, Colleen Dianne *college official, interior designer, consultant*

Bay City
Zuraw, Kathleen Ann *special education and physical education educator*

Belmont
Whiteman, Martha Joyce *retired elementary school educator*

Bloomfield Hills
Jurkiewicz, Mary Louise *elementary school educator*
Wermuth, Mary Louella *secondary school educator*

Brighton
Jensen, Baiba *principal*

Buchanan
Stromswold, Dorothy *retired secondary school educator*

Chesterfield
Broad, Cynthia Ann Morgan *special education educator, consultant*

Clio
Hammond, Jane Pamela *adult education educator*

Coldwater
Scheidler, Elana Dawn *elementary school educator, art educator*

Dearborn
Meyer, Lisa Marie *elementary school educator*

Dearborn Heights
Carter, Julia Marie *secondary school educator*
Johns, Diana *secondary school educator*

Detroit
Barrett, Nancy Smith *university administrator*
Booth, Betty Jean *retired daycare administrator, poet*
Corbitt, Eumiller Mattie *elementary and secondary education educator, special education educator*
Dooley, Gayle Darlene *special education educator, consultant*
Fay, Sister Maureen A. *university president*
Kline, Mable Cornelia Page *retired secondary school educator*
McIntosh, Deborah V. *elementary school educator*
Mitchell, Connie *director*

Dowagiac
Mulder, Patricia Marie *education educator*

East Lansing
Fairfax, Kathleen M *director*
Rothert, Marilyn L. *dean, nursing educator*
Simon, Lou Anna Kimsey *academic administrator*
Velicer, Janet Schafbuch *retired elementary school educator*

Escanaba
Bennett, Kathleen Marourneen *elementary school educator*

Farmington Hills
Sparrow, Laura *secondary educator*

Franklin
Reinhart, Anne Christine *special education educator, consultant*

Gaylord
Magsig, Judith Anne *retired early childhood education educator*

Grand Rapids
May, Dawn Arlene *counseling administrator*

Grosse Pointe Woods
Robie, Joan *elementary school principal*

Harbor Springs
Cappel, Constance *educational consultant, writer*

Henderson
Miller, Kathleen Mae *intermediate school administrator*

Holt
Thompson, Teresa Ackerman *special education educator*

Hopkins
Manchip, Nancy *special education educator*

Jackson
Straayer, Carole Kathleen *retired elementary education educator*

Kalamazoo
Bailey, Judith Irene *university official, consultant*
Gordon, Alice Jeannette Irwin *secondary and elementary education educator*
Howard-Wyne, Josie *elementary school educator*
Lennon, Elizabeth Marie *retired educator*
Morton, Natalie Elaine *director*

Kewadin
Klinefelter, Donna Jean *secondary school educator*

Lake Orion
Leonard, Jacquelyn Ann *retired elementary school educator*

Lanse
Berggren-Moilanen, Bonnie Lee *education educator*

Lansing
Marazita, Eleanor Marie Harmon *retired secondary school educator*
Straus, Kathleen Nagler *education administrator, consultant*

Livonia
Kujawa, Sister Rose Marie *academic administrator*
Van de Vyver, Sister Mary Francilene *academic administrator*

Marquette
Koskiniemi, Donna Louise Rogers *elementary school educator, music educator*

Michigan Center
Savick, Cecily Bianca Simon *secondary school educator*

Midland
Grzesiak, Katherine Ann *primary educator*

Monroe
Siciliano, Elizabeth Marie *secondary school educator*

Owosso
Reynolds, Pauline Phyllis *retired early education educator, accountant*

Pleasant Ridge
Sneed, Marie Eleanor Wilkey *retired secondary school educator*

Pontiac
Anderson, Anita A. *secondary school educator*

Riverview
Thompson, LaVerne Elizabeth Thomas *college official*

Rochester
Packard, Sandra Podolin *education educator, consultant*

Rochester Hills
Anderson, Susan Elaine Mosshamer *educational consultant, organization consultant, musician, mezzo soprano*
Mills, Helene Audrey *education educator*

Saint Clair
Ratliff, Linda Susan *special education educator, consultant*

Saint Clair Shores
Kavadas-Pappas, Iphigenia Katherine *preschool administrator, educator, consultant*
Skoney, Sophie Essa *educational administrator*

Sault Sainte Marie
Youngblood, Betty J. *academic administrator*

Sidney
Rice, Sharon Jean *secondary school educator*

South Haven
Llorens, Merna Gee *elementary school educator, music educator*

Southfield
Jones, Marceline Yvonne *secondary school educator*
Schmidt, Mary Teresa *retired elementary school educator*

Sparta
McDonald, Lois Alice *elementary school educator*

Sterling Heights
Empson, Heather Leigh (Parmann) *elementary school educator*

Stockbridge
Clarke, Jane Carol *academic administrator, director, principal*

Tecumseh
Staples, Alice Marie *elementary school educator*

Trenton
Beebe, Grace Ann *retired special education educator*

Troy
Mallerie, Bette Jean *director nursery school*

University Center
Schaab, Nancy A. *education educator, consultant*

Walled Lake
Remer, Deborah Jane *secondary school educator*

Warren
Morton, Katie Marie *special education educator*
White, Gaye Lee *elementary school educator*

Waterford
Anderson, Francile Mary *secondary school educator*

White Pigeon
Pavel, Patricia L. *elementary school educator*

MINNESOTA

Andover
Peterson, Jill Susan *elementary school educator*

Apple Valley
Bronner, Katherine Elizabeth *high school counselor*
Sagen, Judy *secondary education choral director*

Bemidji
Erickson, Nancy Carolyn *dean*

Blaine
Yecke, Cheri Pearson *education agency administrator, columnist, author*

Bloomington
Powell, Christa Ruth *educational training executive*

Buffalo
Carter, Barbara Possis *elementary school educator*

Duluth
Martin, Kathryn A. *academic administrator*

Edina
Nelson, Patricia Joan Pingenot *retired educator*

Falcon Heights
Kreuter, Gretchen V. *academic administrator*

Foley
Cross, Eunice D. *elementary school educator*

Fridley
Larson, Marilyn J. *retired elementary music educator*

Hibbing
Lahdelma, Gladys Linda *elementary school educator*

Hokah
Fishel, Rachel Therese *principal, elementary school educator*

Hopkins
Zins, Martha Lee *elementary education educator, media specialist*

Mankato
Preska, Margaret Louise Robinson *education historian, administrator*

Maple Grove
Leiseth, Patricia Schutz *educational technology specialist*
Riesgraf, Kim Marie Wogensen *director*

Mapleton
Carpenter, Rebecca Lee *secondary school educator, music educator*

Minneapolis
Edwardson, Sandra *dean, nursing educator*
Fruen, Lois *secondary school educator*
Gardebring, Sandra S. *academic administrator*
Johnson, Carol R. *school system administrator*
Kaufman, Anne Mull *education educator*
Porter, Jeannette Upton *elementary school educator*
Rogers, Karen Beckstead *gifted studies educator, researcher, consultant*
Veldey, Bonnie *special education educator*
Wilhelm, Gretchen *retired secondary school educator, volunteer*

Minnetonka
Vanstrom, Marilyn June Christensen *retired elementary school educator*
Wigfield, Rita L. *elementary school educator*

Monticello
Sonbuchner, Gail Murphy *secondary special education educator*

New Brighton
Kieffer, Kathleen Cecil *elementary school educator*

Owatonna
Larson, Diane LaVerne Kusler *principal*
Schroeder, Mary Ellen *adult education educator*

Richfield
Devlin, Barbara Jo *school district administrator*
Reilly, Jill Marlene *school system administrator*

Saginaw
Stauber, Marilyn Jean *retired secondary school educator, retired elementary school educator*

Saint Cloud
McKay, Joane Williams *dean*

Saint James
Jones, Patricia Louise *elementary counselor*

Saint Louis Park
Husen, Aino Maria *retired elementary school educator*

Saint Paul
Doyle, Florence Elizabeth *retired secondary school educator*
Dybvig, Mary McIlvaine *educational consultant, psychologist*
Harvey, Patricia A. *school system administrator*
Huber, Sister Alberta *college president*
Hultman, Carol Linda *elementary school educator*
Lee, Andrea Jane *academic administrator, nun*
Paulos, Christine Ann *academic administrator*
Shepard, Sue Annette *director fund raising*
Stroud, Rhoda M. *elementary school educator*

Zumbrota
Fredrickson, Marilyn H. *secondary school educator, art educator, artist*

MISSISSIPPI

Batesville
Rivers, Nettie Taylor *hearing impaired educator*

Biloxi
Brown, Sheba Ann *elementary school educator*
Manners, Pamela Jeanne *middle school educator*

Blue Mountain
Mounce, Carolyn P. *school librarian*

Booneville
Hardon, Imogene M. *elementary school educator*

Clarksdale
Presley, Vivian Mathews *junior college administrator*
Walton, SuzAnne W. *elementary school educator*

Clinton
Whitlock, Betty *retired secondary school educator*

Corinth
Howell, Teresa Christine Wallin *elementary school educator*

Ellisville
Ross, Lisa Sims *special education educator*

Greenville
Potter, Suzanne Peyton *elementary school educator*

Gulfport
Price, Helen Hoggatt *counseling administrator*

Hattiesburg
Reinshagen, Yolanda P. *elementary school educator*
Slade, Barbie Evette Delk *special education educator*

Hazlehurst
Blakeney, Margaret Elizabeth Fleming *counselor, educator*

Iuka
Barnes, Betty Jean *educational administrator*

Jackson
Chambers-Mangum, Fransenna Ethel *special education educator*
Collins, Deloris Williams *secondary school educator*
Creel, Sue Cloer *secondary school educator*
Harrison, Esther M. *elementary school educator, state representative*
Shaifer, Audrey Virginia *director*

Marks
Kaufman, Raylene Dyane *secondary school educator*

Mccomb
Jackson, Alfreda Murraye *adult education educator*

Meridian
Wilson-Jones, Linda *guidance counselor*

Mississippi State
Rent, Clyda Stokes *academic administrator*

Natchez
Anderson, Rose L. Dyess *elementary school educator, poet*
Marion, Ann *school psychologist, educator*

Nettleton
Hairald, Mary Payne *vocational education educator, coordinator*

Olive Branch
Kern, Angeline Frazier *educational administrator, guidance counselor*

Oxford
Wickham, Kathleen Woodruff *education educator*
Winter, Karen Knight Alice *special education educator*

Philadelphia
Watson, Sheila Nelson *secondary school educator*

Starkville
Dampier, Caryn *self-defense instructor*
Looby, Eugenie Joan *dean, educator*

Tupelo
Doxey-Tate, Sarah Rolston *retired elementary school educator*

Vicksburg
Keulegan, Emma Pauline *special education educator*

MISSOURI

Archie
Whiteside, Jennie Susan *elementary school educator, secondary school educator*

Ballwin
Beckmann, Nancy Bourke *retired elementary school educator*
Guinther, Christine Louise *special education educator*

Butler
Cochran, Beth *gifted and talented educator*

Camdenton
Harris, Deanna Lynn *special education educator, writer*

Chesterfield
Finley, Marlynn Holt *elementary educator consultant*

Clayton
Mach, Ruth *principal*

Columbia
Adams, Algalee Pool *college dean, art educator*
Kyllonen, Frances Thompson *retired educator*
Libby, Wendy B. *academic administrator*

Fayette
Inman, Marianne Elizabeth *college administrator*

Florissant
Ferguson, Audrey Diane *elementary school educator*
James, Dorothy Louise King *special education educator*

Forsyth
Klinefelter, Sarah Stephens *retired division dean, radio station manager*

Hillsboro
Phillips, Amy Renea *assistant principal*

Independence
Henley, Patricia Joan *principal*
Johnson, Sharon Elaine *elementary school educator*
Marlow, Lydia Lou *elementary school educator*
Starks, Carol Elizabeth *retired principal*
Stoner, Connie Kay *special education educator*

Kansas City
Brent, Elizabeth Maria *education educator*
Byers-Pevitts, Beverley *college administrator, educator*
Caulfield, Joan *director, educator*
Drees, Betty *dean, educator*
Guilliland, Martha W. *academic administrator*
Hamerle, Jill Christine *secondary school educator*
Leighton, Carol *retired educator*
Lombard, Regina A. *elementary school educator*
Willsie, Sandra K. *dean, internist, educator*

Kirksville
Dixon, Barbara Bruinekool *academic administrator*
McLane-Iles, Betty Louise *academic administrator, educator, writer*

Kirkwood
Hoglen, Jewel Pamela *retired secondary school educator*

Lees Summit
Headley, Carol Ann *elementary and secondary school educator*
Linder, Beverly L. *elementary school educator*

Liberty
Gronlund, Sally Ann *special education educator*

Maryville
Strating, Sharon L. *elementary school educator, professional staff developer, educational consultant*

Mexico
Teague, Deborah Gant *elementary school educator*

Neosho
Allman, Margaret Ann Lowrance *counseling administrator*

Owensville
Leick, Carol Lynn *special education educator*

Pacific
Wilson, Jill Marie *early childhood educator*

Poplar Bluff
Allen, Brenda Kay *elementary school educator*

Raytown
Coppenbarger, Cecelia Marie *special education educator*

Saint Joseph
Correu, Sandra Kay *special education educator*
Murphy, Janet Gorman *college president*

Saint Louis
Baker, Shirley Kistler *university administrator*
Briggs, Cynthia Anne *educational administrator, clinical psychologist*
Crews, Janet M. *elementary school educator*
Fischer, Emily Christina *primary school educator*
Gilligan, Sandra Kaye *private school director*
Gooch, Audrey Smith *retired education educator*
Grant, Michele Byrd *secondary school educator*
Haywood, Kathleen Marie *university educator, dean*
Hicks, Shirley E. *director*
Hilyard, Veronica Marie *education administrator*
Hinkle, Christina Nicole *primary school educator*
Hoeffken, Rebecca Lynn *private school educator*
Hood, Phyllis Ilene *special education educator*
Horvath, Frances Louise *retired dean*
Hrubetz, Joan *dean, nursing educator*
Kennelly, Sister Karen Margaret *retired academic administrator, church administrator, nun*
Lackey, Kayle Diann *elementary school educator*
Leonard, Judith Price *educational advisor*
Mitchell, Louise Tyndall *special education educator*
Monteleone, Patricia *dean*
Mosley, Karen D. *retired elementary school educator*
O'Neill, Sheila *principal*
Richardson, Pollie *principal*
Scheffing, Dianne Elizabeth *special education educator*
Steiner, Hope Elizabeth *school counselor*
Williams, Nellie James Batt *secondary school educator, educator*
Woodward, Mary Lou *retired elementary education educator*

Springfield
Groves, Sharon Sue *elementary school educator*
Quiroga, Ninoska *university official*

Trenton
Hannaford, Karla *college official*

Unity Village
Boehm, Toni Georgene *seminary dean, nurse, minister*

Vandalia
Brookshier, Elaine Marie *counseling administrator, psychology examiner, social worker*

Warrensburg
Limback, E(dna) Rebecca *vocational education educator*

Webb City
James, Kathryn A. *secondary school educator*

Webster Groves
Carr, Margaret *elementary school educator*
Schenkenberg, Mary Martin *principal*

Willow Springs
East, LeEtta Joyce *elementary school educator, music educator*

MONTANA

Antelope
Olson, Betty-Jean *retired elementary education educator*

Billings
Kolstad, Candice (Candy) Carol *pre-school educator, special needs coordinator*
Park, Janie C. *provost*

Bozeman
Acord, Lea *dean*

Crow Agency
Pease-Pretty On Top, Janine B. *community college administrator*

Kalispell
Klang, Mary Margaret *secondary school educator*

Lame Deer
Williams, Deeanna Maxine *secondary school educator*

Lewistown
Edwards, Linda L. *former elementary education educator*

Missoula
Barnett, Mary Louise *elementary school educator*

Victor
Stewart, JoAnne *director*

NEBRASKA

Bayard
Tillman, Tamra (Tammy) K. *secondary school educator*

Bellevue
Braun, Sally A. *elementary school educator, music educator*

Boys Town
Wright Sapone, Tanya D *director*

Curtis
Wiiest, Joan Eloise *secondary school educator*

Grand Island
Weseman, Vicki Lynne *elementary school educator*
Zichek, Shannon Elaine *retired secondary school educator*

Gretna
Druliner, Marcia Marie *education educator*

Hastings
Kort, Betty *secondary school educator*

Kearney
Johnston, Gladys Styles *university official*

Lincoln
Epp, Dianne Naomi *secondary educator*
Grew, Priscilla Croswell *university official, geology educator*
Nicoll, Gayle *chemistry educator*
Robak, Kim M. *academic administrator, lawyer*
Tonack, DeLoris *elementary school educator*

Norfolk
Mortensen-Say, Marlys *school system administrator*

Ogallala
Brown, Jo Etta *elementary school educator, librarian*

Omaha
Belck, Nancy Garrison *dean, educator*
Bruckner, Martha *academic administrator*
Cherney, Isabelle Denise *education educator, researcher*
Fyfe, Doris Mae *elementary school educator*
Lindsey, Ada Marie *dean, nursing educator*
Ranks, Anne Elizabeth *retired elementary and secondary education educator*
Roland, Sally *secondary resource teacher*
Ryan, Sheila A. *nursing educator, former dean*

Oneill
Thoendel, Julie R. *retired secondary school educator, education educator*

Sutherland
Robert, Teresa Lynn *elementary and secondary school music educator*

NEVADA

Boulder City
Calvo, Rhonda Lynne *special education educator*

Henderson
Chairsell, Christine *academic administrator*
Ekanger, Karin L. *educational consultant*

Las Vegas
Butz, Janet Avery *school system administrator*
Gaspar, Anna Louise *retired elementary school educator, consultant*
Harter, Carol Clancey *university president, English language educator*
Holmes, BarbaraAnn Krajkoski *secondary school educator*
Johnson, Mary Elizabeth *retired elementary education educator*
Joyce, Phyllis Norma *educational administrator*
McComb, Karla Joann *educational curriculum and instruction administrator, consultant*
Mercier, Linda Ann *secondary school educator*
Pierce, Thresia Korte (Tish Pierce) *primary school educator*
Shriner, Joan Ward *secondary school educator*
Skoll, Pearl A. *retired mathematics and special education educator*

Minden
Tyndall, Gaye Lynn *secondary school educator*

North Las Vegas
Savello, Cheryl Adamson *secondary school educator*
Smith, Stephanie S. *middle school educator, councilwoman*

Reno
Mulert, Lynne Carol *school counselor*
Perry, Jean Louise *dean*
Swanson, Dolores *special education educator, musician*

Silver Springs
O'Malia, Mary Frances *special education educator*

NEW HAMPSHIRE

Concord
Twomey, Elizabeth Ann Molloy *education educator*

Dover
Pelletier, Marsha Lynn *secondary school educator, poet*

Durham
Hart, Ann Weaver *educational administration educator*

Hanover
Dow, Christine Detscher *library assistant, educational consultant*

Manchester
Merideth, Susan Carol *business administration educator*

Nashua
Provencher, Jeanne Stansfield *secondary school educator*

Plymouth
DeCotis, Ruth Janice *career planning administrator, educator*
Petersen, Meg Joanna *education educator, language educator*

Spofford
Trumbull, Virginia Hardesty *retired special education educator*

West Lebanon
Malik, Shazia Mumtaz *education educator, researcher*

NEW JERSEY

Basking Ridge
Besch, Lorraine W. *special education educator*

Bayonne
Zuckerman, Nancy Carol *learning disabilities specialist, consultant*

Bellmawr
Wilke, Constance Regina *elementary school educator*

Berkeley Heights
Schwarzwald, Julie Nanette *elementary school educator*

Blairstown
Wenner, Judith Wills *secondary school educator*

Bloomfield
Barros, Lydia *elementary school educator*

Brigantine
Kickish, Margaret Elizabeth *elementary school educator*

Budd Lake
Shepherd, Deborah Gulick *elementary school educator*

Burlington
Hancock, Beverly J. *counseling consultant, secondary school educator*

Caldwell
Werner, Patrice (Patricia Ann Werner) *dean*

Camden
Daniels, Albertina Diana *secondary school educator*

Cedar Grove
Helwig, Annette L. *retired elementary school educator*

Clifton
Hochman, Naomi Lipson *special education educator, consultant*

East Brunswick
Brandenburg, Lois Sue *special education educator*
Mendingall, Evelyn L. *educational media specialist*

East Rutherford
Alberta, Frances Rita *principal*

Egg Harbor City
Farris, Vera King *former college president*

Englishtown
Jones, Sarah Lucille *supervisor, consultant*

Ewing
Gitenstein, Donna M. *academic administrator*
Hamm, Claire Rose *development information services administrator*

Fair Lawn
Aitchison, Suann *elementary school educator*

Flemington
Wolfson, Barbara Libensperger *guidance counselor*

Forked River
Ruffalo, Maria Therese *secondary school educator*

Freehold
Paul, Connie Sue *educational media specialist, school librarian*

Galloway
Hamaty, Julie Armbruster *secondary school educator*

Green Brook
Balsamello, Melissa (Marley) *elementary school educator*

Hackensack
Williamson, (Eulah) Elaine *elementary school educator*

Haddon Heights
Weinberg, Ruthmarie Louise *special education educator, researcher*

Hamilton
Kilbourne, Claire Anne *retired gifted and talented education educator*

Highlands
Lofstrom, Arlene Katherine *primary school educator*

Hillside
Aragonés-Enda, Lillian Estella *elementary school educator*

Ho Ho Kus
O'Loughlin, Judith Beryl *elementary and special education educator*

Howell
Pearson, Clara *elementary school educator, music educator*

Jackson
Carney, Rita J. *educational administrator*

Jersey City
Wilson, Tina Marie *special education educator*

Lakewood
Balbach, Ruth T. *elementary school educator*
Prachar, Michele C. *elementary school educator*
Williams, Barbara Anne *retired academic administrator*

Layton
Seely, Maribeth Walsh *elementary school educator*

Lincoln Park
Aleman, Sheila B. *special education educator*

Linden
Bedrick, Bernice *retired science educator, consultant*

Long Valley
Duane, Jeannine Morrissey *retired elementary school educator*

Mahwah
Geiling, Louise Elizabeth *elementary school educator, secondary school educator*

Manahawkin
Barton, Noreen E. *high school educator*

Marlboro
Francisco, Deborah Antosh *educational administrative professional*
Geier, Denise B. *director*
Kayafas, Stephanie Ann *special education educator, consultant, supervisor, actress*

Matawan
Liggett, Twila Marie Christensen *academic administrator, public television executive*

Mendham
Posunko, Linda Mary *retired elementary education educator*

Midland Park
Dunn, Patricia Ann *school system administrator, English language educator*

Monroe Township
Naumik, Maria Charlene *academic administrator, educator*
Wolfe, Deborah Cannon Partridge *government education consultant, educator, minister*

Montclair
Cole, Susan A. *university president, English language educator*

Morristown
Mooney, Patricia Anne *secondary school educator*
Selman, Carol *retired secondary school educator*

Mount Holly
Mancini, Lois Jean *elementary school educator*

Mountain Lakes
Doane, Eileen Maloney *learning disabilities teacher consultant*

Neptune
Haag, Jane *education educator*

New Brunswick
Casey, Heather Anne Kenyon *education educator*
Chasek, Arlene Shatsky *academic director*
Henry, Paula Louise (Paula Louise Henry Coover) *academic administrator*
Morrow, Lesley Mandel *literacy and elementary education educator*
Strickland, Dorothy *education educator*

Newark
Bolden, Marion A. *school system administrator*
Griffith, Hurdis M. *dean*
Liman, Joan Pamela *university dean*
Wright-White, Kimberly Zenora *vice principal*

Newton
MacMurren, Margaret Patricia *secondary education educator, consultant*

North Branch
Jones, Cori *education educator, writer*

North Brunswick
Walker, Carolyn Mae *secondary school educator*

Ocean City
Guokas, Joan Ellen (Mrs. Matthew Guokas Sr.) *retired elementary school educator*

Old Tappan
Gaffin, Joan Valerie *secondary school educator*

Passaic
Johnson, Myrtle Alice Harris *elementary and secondary school educator*

Perth Amboy
Reyes, Irma V. *adult education educator*
Santiago, Theresa Marie *special education administrator, educator*

Petersburg
Orlando-Spinelli, Josephine *gifted and talented educator, educational consultant*

Piscataway
Coppola, Sarah Jane *special education educator*
Trontell, Marie Celestine *dean*

Pleasantville
London, Charlotte Isabella *secondary education educator, reading specialist*

Pomona
Comfort, Priscilla Maria *retired college official, human resources professional*
Dagavarian-Bonar, Debra Aghavni *college administrator, consultant*

Princeton
Duncan, Dianne Walker *elementary school educator*
Krulewicz, Rita Gloria *special education educator*
Lavizzo-Mourey, Risa Juanita *academic administrator, medical association administrator*
Malkiel, Nancy Weiss *dean, historian, educator*
Sandoval, Amada *education program director*
Tilghman, Shirley Marie *academic administrator, biology educator*

Randolph
Oliveira, Theresa Razzano *secondary school educator*

Ridgefield Park
Meidhof, Sister Patricia E. *school system administrator*

Ridgewood
Friedrich, Margret Cohen *guidance and student assistance counselor*

Ringwood
Paliga-Tanzola, Rhonda *special education educator*

Rockaway
Allen, Dorothea *secondary school educator*

Roseland
Bolger, Mary Phyllis Judge *special education educator*

Roselle
Di Marco, Barbaranne Yanus *principal*
Meister, Karen Olivia *secondary school educator*
Tanner-Oliphant, Karen M. *family and consumer science educator*

Saddle River
Lehmann, Doris Elizabeth *elementary school educator*

Short Hills
Robbins-Wilf, Marcia *educational consultant*

Skillman
Cummings, Peggy Ann *counseling administrator*

Somerville
Weisblatt, Barbara Ann *secondary school educator*

South Hackensack
Wille, Rosanne Louise *higher education administrator*

Summit
Starks, Florence Elizabeth *retired special education educator*
Tator, Adriennne Maria *director*

Teaneck
Baldwin, Dorothy Leila *secondary school educator*
Smith, Susan Elizabeth *guidance director*
Walker, Lucy Doris *secondary school educator, writer*

Toms River
Engelhardt, Catherine *elementary school educator*

Trenton
Stein, Sandra Lou *educational psychologist, educator*

Turnersville
Richie, Michelle Tracey *special education educator*

Union
Lederman, Susan Sturc *public administration educator*

Union City
Bull, Inez Stewart *special education, gifted music educator, coloratura soprano, pianist, editor, author, curator*

Upper Saddle River
Farmer, Martha Louise *retired college administrator*

Vineland
Hesser, Lorraine M *special education educator*

Voorhees
Carter, Catherine Louise *elementary school educator*

Waldwick
Lynch, Carol *director special services, psychologist*

Warren
Hennings, Dorothy Grant (Mrs. George Hennings) *education educator*

Wayne
Garcia, Ofelia *dean*

West Orange
Bojsza, Joan E. *elementary school educator*

Willingboro
Denslow, Deborah Pierson *primary education educator*

Woodbridge
Paugh, Nancy Adele *secondary school educator, school system administrator*

Woodbury
Murphy, Ann Marie *special education educator*

Woodstown
Tatnall, Ann Weslager *reading educator*

NEW MEXICO

Alamogordo
McFadin, Helen Lozetta *retired elementary education educator*

Albuquerque
Abraham, Karen A. *university administrator*
Bernard, Marilyn Thomas *director, vocalist*
Betts, Dorothy Anne *elementary school educator*
Everitt, Elizabeth M. *school system administrator*
Graff, Pat Stuever *secondary school educator*
Harlow, Judith Leigh *educational institute executive, consultant*
Stuart, Cynthia Morgan *university administrator*
Tangman, Ruth S. *educational administrator*
Trojahn, Lynn *academic administrator*

Bloomfield
Sledzinski, Jessica K. *elementary school educator*

Clovis
Shade, Marsha J. *elementary school educator, music educator*

El Prado
Tsoodle-Marcus, Charlene *education educator, school system administrator*

Farmington
Anderson, Evelyn Louise *elementary teacher*
Luttrell, Mary Lou *elementary school educator*

Hobbs
Weldy, Lana Gail *secondary school educator*

Las Cruces
Bird, Mary Francis *secondary school educator*

Los Alamos
Benjamin, Susan Selton *elementary school educator*

Los Lunas
Denzler, Mary Joanne *special education educator*

Rio Rancho
Meyerson, Barbara Tobias *elementary school educator*
Weber, Alois Hughes *principal*

Ruidoso
Stover, Carolyn Nadine *middle school educator*

Santa Fe
Cerny, Charlene Ann *director*
Chacon, Mari B. *counseling administrator*
Hanson, Linda N. *academic administrator, educator*

Shiprock
Atcitty, Fannie L. *elementary school educator, education educator*

Taos
Garcia, Christine *academic administrator, educator, researcher*

NEW YORK

Albany
Amodeo-Smargon, Christine Joanne *adult education educator, real estate rehabilitator*
Branigan, Helen Marie *educational consultant, administrator*
Langer, Judith Ann *literacy educator*
Leone, Gilda C. *adult education educator*
Wick-Pelletier, Joan *academic administrator, mathematician*

Amherst
Pachan, Mary Jude Kathryn Dorothy *guidance counselor*

Astoria
Arholekas, Irene *secondary school educator*

Aurora
Ryerson, Lisa M. *academic administrator*

Babylon
Schwarz, Barbara Ruth Ballou *elementary school educator*

Batavia
Hawkins, Susan Ann *special education educator*

Bellmore
Feldman, Harriet Ruth *dean*
Moore, Tara *secondary school educator*

Binghamton
Coffey, Margaret Tobin *education educator, county official*
DeFleur, Lois B. *university president, sociology educator*
Suriner, Noreen P. *rector, priest*
Swain, Mary Ann Price *university official*

Bluff Point
Fitch, Linda Bauman *elementary school educator*

Brockport
Campbell, Jill Frost *university official*

Bronx
Damico, Debra Lynn *college official, English and French educator*
Murphy, Sheila Ann *elementary school educator*
Shanklin, Elizabeth E. *secondary school educator*
Ukponmwan, Lucy *elementary school educator*
Wertheim, Mary Danielle *elementary education coordinator*

Bronxville
Myers, Michele Tolela *academic administrator*

Brooklyn
Avraham, Regina *retired secondary school educator*
Bakakos, Diana *middle school educator*
Browne, Nicole N. *elementary school educator*
Carielli, Carol Leggio *guidance counselor*
Cohen, Gloria Ernestine *elementary education educator*
Gover, Kathleen Ann *dean, director*
Hill, Elizabeth Anne *academic administrator, lawyer*
Kovat, Robin M. *secondary school educator*
Meade, Dorothy Winifred *retired educational administrator*
O'Connor, Sister George Aquin (Margaret M. O'Connor) *academic administrator, sociology educator*
O'Keefe, Katherine Patricia *elementary school educator*
Riccardelli, Rosanne Sharon *primary school educator*
Schweikert, Mary Lou *elementary school educator*
Washington, Tyona *adult education educator*
Wexler, Joan G. *dean*
Wolfe, Ethyle Renee (Mrs. Coleman Hamilton Benedict) *college administrator*

Buffalo
Amato, Rosalie *secondary school educator*
Cañedo, Marion *school system administrator*
Cathey, Patrice Antoinette *secondary school educator, director*
Fuda, Siri Narayan K.K. (Elaine T. Barber) *director*
Gielow, Kathleen Louise *career planning administrator, consultant, special education educator*
Howard, Muriel A. *academic administrator*
Williams, Lillian Serece *educator*

Calverton
Troge, Darlene I. *director*

Canandaigua
Malinowski, Patricia A. *community college educator*

Canton
Bucher, Mary *school librarian*

Carle Place
Russo, Joni K. *director*

Castleton On Hudson
Wagner, Mary Susan *academic administrator*

Catskill
Wolfe, Geraldine *administrator*

Cedarhurst
Van Raalte, Polly Ann *reading and writing specialist, photojournalist*

Chazy
Ratner, Gayle *special education educator*

Clinton
Havens, Pamela Ann *college official*

Cold Spring
Battersby, Katherine Sue *elementary school educator*

Commack
Cohen, Judith W. *retired academic administrator*

Delhi
Duncan, Mary Ellen *academic administrator*

Dix Hills
Gordon, Jacqueline Alicia *guidance counselor, protective services official*
Somerville, Daphine Holmes *retired elementary education educator*
Virostko, Joan *elementary school educator*

Dobbs Ferry
Hotchkiss, Janet McCann *secondary school educator*
Lesack, Beatriz Díaz *secondary school educator*

Downsville
Hornick, Susan Florence Stegmuller *secondary education educator, fine arts educator, curriculum specialist, artist*

East Amherst
Kirdani, Esther May *school counselor*
Weiss, Elinor *elementary school educator*

East Aurora
Woodard, Carol Jane *educational consultant*

East Hampton
Goldstein, Judith Shelley *reading and learning specialist*
Schetlin, Eleanor M. *retired university official*

East Islip
Cullen, Valerie Adelia *secondary school educator*
Donohue, Claire P. *school librarian*

East Meadow
Kalin, Karin Bea *retired secondary school educator, consultant*

Elmira
Kerr-Nowlan, Donna Courtney *pre-school administrator*

Fairport
Holtzclaw, Diane Smith *elementary school educator*
Radell, Carol K. *elementary school educator*

Far Rockaway
Mitchell, Lillian Adassa *principal*
Sussman, Laureen Glicklin *junior high school educator*

Flushing
Roberts, Kathleen Joy Doty *secondary school educator*
Smith-Campbell, Charmaine *secondary school educator*

Frankfort
Conigilaro, Phyllis Ann *retired elementary education educator*

Freeport
Martorana, Barbara Joan *secondary school educator*

Garden City
Slater, Nancy Lynne *special education educator, marketing professional, consultant*

Geneseo
Myers, Helen Marie *education educator, choreographer*

Gouverneur
Stacy, Trudy L. *elementary school educator*

Great Neck
Roth, Gladys Thompson *retired early childhood and special education educator*

Greenvale
Westermann-Cicio, Mary Louise *academic administrator, library studies educator*

Guilderland
Escobar, Deborah Ann *gifted and talented education educator*

Hamilton
Chopp, Rebecca S. *university president*

Hauppauge
Zuckerman, Dorothy Ann *elementary school educator*

Hempstead
Raney, Carolyn E. *educational consultant*

Hicksville
Reedy, Catherine Irene *elementary school educator*
Waxberg, Emily Steinhardt *educator*

Holbrook
Watkins, Linda Theresa *educational researcher*

Hopewell Junction
Cznarty, Donna Mae *secondary school educator*

Horseheads
Andrake, Nancy Carolyn *secondary school educator*

Hudson
Vile, Sandra Jane *leadership training educator*

Huntington
Roberts, Elizabeth Anne Stephens *educational consultant*

Huntington Station
Devlin, Jean Theresa *education educator, storyteller*

Hyde Park
Blackman, Drusilla Denise *dean*

Inwood
Soffer, Grace Florey *retired elementary school educator, artist*

Island Park
Pal, Cheryl Lynn *music teacher*

Ithaca
Cope, Caroline Bancroft *special education educator*
Firebaugh, Francille Maloch *university official*
Martin, Carolyn A. (Biddy Martin) *provost*
Seibert, Mary Lee *college official*
Stycos, Maria Nowakowska *adult education educator*
Wavle, Elizabeth Margaret *college official*
Williams, Peggy Ryan *academic administrator*

Jackson Heights
Gall, Lenore Rosalie *educational administrator*

Jamaica
Davis-Jerome, Eileen George *principal*
Faust, Naomi Flowe *education educator*
Malewitz, Joan *elementary school educator, library and information scientist*
Mithaug, Deirdre Kristen *special education educator, researcher*

Jamestown
Keefer, Judith E. *elementary school educator*
Pitt, Ruth Anne *school system administrator, music educator*

Jeffersonville
Hoering, Helen G. *elementary school educator*

Lagrangeville
Davis, Mary Lou *secondary school educator*

Lake George
Nellis, Nora LaJoy *special education educator, writer*

Lancaster
Kappan, Sandra Jean *elementary school educator*

Lindenhurst
Sanna, Catherine Lee *special education educator*

Lisbon
Walsh, Lisa J. *elementary school educator*

Long Beach
Thompson, Dorothy Barnard *elementary school educator*

Long Island City
Lieberman, Janet Elaine *academic administrator*

Lynbrook
Cline, Starr *elementary school educator*

Mahopac
Talbot, Deborah Ann *assistant principal*

Malverne
Alesse, Judith *special education educator*

Medford
Klement, Diane *educational assistant*

Melville
Basile, Sheila *secondary education educator, consultant*

Merrick
Fleischman, Francine D. *elementary school educator*
Harrison, Marjorie Freeman *secondary education educator, librarian*

Middleburgh
Lennon, Amy Jo *elementary school educator, principal*

Middletown
D'Agostino, Gloria M. *secondary school educator*
McCord, Jean Ellen *secondary art educator, coach*
Moore, Virginia Lee Smith *elementary school educator*

Millwood
Durst, Carol Goldsmith *food studies educator*

Moravia
Welch, Joan Minde *elementary school educator*

Morrisville
Cleland, Gladys Lee *university administrator, adult education educator*

Nesconset
Mac Millan, Janet Susan *elementary school educator, education educator*

New Paltz
Emanuel-Smith, Robin Lesley *special education educator*

New Rochelle
Reddington, Mary Jane *retired secondary school educator*

New Windsor
Saunders, Joanne Hines *elementary school educator*

New York
Arndt, Carmen Gloria *secondary school educator*
Berman, Phyllis Ocean *adult education educator*
Boylan, Elizabeth Shippee *academic administrator, biologist, educator*
Brown, Joyce F. *academic administrator*

PROFESSIONAL INDEX 1701 EDUCATION

Burns, Red *academic administrator*
Cafiero, Jennifer Annette *academic administrator, educator*
Campbell, Mary Schmidt *dean*
Claster, Jill Nadell *university administrator, history educator*
Consagra, Sophie Chandler *academic administrator*
Dendy, Terri Anita *secondary school educator*
Dimino, Sylvia Theresa *elementary and secondary educator*
Duldner, Marianne *director, educator*
Durkin, Dorothy Angela *university official*
Ellenbogen, Marjorie *elementary school educator*
Essandoh, Hilda Brathwaite *kindergarten educator*
Finegold, Amy Beth *elementary school educator, consultant*
Gray, Lois Spier *labor relations educator, consultant*
Hayes, Joyce Merriweather *secondary school educator*
Hickey, Catherine Josephine *school system administrator*
Hoffner, Marilyn *university administrator*
Horowitz, Frances Degen *academic administrator, psychology educator*
House, Jane E. *director, writer, actress*
Jelinek, Vera *university director*
Jeynes, Mary Kay *college dean*
Konner, Joan Weiner *academic administrator, educator, television producer, writer*
Kopp, Wendy *teaching program administrator*
Kozlowski, Cheryl M. *principal*
Kurtzman, Susan Joan *school system administrator, speech pathology/audiology services professional*
Lanquetot, E. Roxanne *retired special education educator*
Leiman, Joan Maisel *hospital and university administrator, hospital administrator*
Levine, Naomi Bronheim *academic administrator*
Mandelbaum, Jean *director, educator*
Marks, Lillian Shapiro *secretarial studies educator, author*
Morgan, Allyson Suzanne *elementary school educator*
Morgan, Arlene Notoro *university administrator*
Pigott, Irina Vsevolodovna *educational administrator*
Prutzman, Penelope Elizabeth *elementary school educator*
Pulanco, Tonya Beth *special education educator*
Rabb, Harriet Schaffer *academic administrator, educator, lawyer, government official*
Reid, Deborah E. *director*
Roome, Kristine Ann *college administrator*
Rosensaft, Jean Bloch *university administrator*
Rowland, Esther E(delman) *retired dean*
Scaffidi, Judith Ann *academic administrator*
Seidenberg, Rita Nagler *education educator*
Selby, Cecily Cannan *dean, educator, scientist*
Shapiro, Judith R. *academic administrator, anthropology educator*
Smith, Karen Lynn *principal*
Soros, Susan Weber *educational administrator*
Takamura, Jeanette Chiyoko *dean*
Townsend-Butterworth, Diana Barnard *educational consultant, author*
Walzer, Judith Borodovko *academic administrator, educator*
Williams, Harriet Clarke *retired academic administrator*
Yetman, Leith Eleanor *academic administrator*
Yu, Pauline Ruth *former dean, educational association administrator*
Zaken, Grace Ambrose *project coordinator, educator*
Zumwalt, Karen Kepler *education educator*

Newburgh
Joyce, Mary Ann *principal*

Niagara Falls
Clark, Patsy Vedder *retired educator and staff developer*

Niagara University
Green, Sharon Anne *reading specialist, educator*

Northville
Popp, Ann L. *elementary school educator, music educator*

Ogdensburg
Smith, Carol Ann *academic administrator*

Oneonta
Dean, Carol *secondary school educator*

Owego
Coppens, Laura Kathryn *special education educator*

Panama
Dolce, Anne Frances *elementary school educator*

Peekskill
Finnigan, Claire Marie *media specialist, librarian*
Wiggins, Ida Silver *elementary school educator*

Plattsburgh
Worthington, Janet Evans *retired academic dean, English language educator*

Port Jefferson
Lipitz, Elaine Kappel *secondary education fine arts educator*

Potsdam
Scott, Jean A. *university president*

Poughkeepsie
Brakas, Nora Jachym *education educator*
Fergusson, Frances Daly *college president, educator*
Pisterzi, Candy *special education educator*

Purchase
Sullivan, Margaret M. *university program administrator*

Rego Park
Tsui, Soo Hing *educational research consultant*

Riverdale
Katz, Sheri Lynn *learning disabilities specialist, tutor*

Rochester
Adams, Carol H. *dean*
Cahn, Ruth Patricia *director, musician*
Grant, Marilynn Patterson *secondary educator*
Hurt, Davina Theresa *secondary school educator*
Pavone, Jill Russell *special education educator*
Steward, Jennifer A. *academic administrator*

Rockaway Park
Goldsmith, Cathy Ellen *retired special education educator*

Saint Albans
Miller, Gwendolyn Doris *special education educator, retired*

Saint James
Van Dover, Karen *middle and elementary school educator, curriculum consultant, language arts specialist, lecturer*

Saint Johnsville
Schoff, Marcia Anne *elementary school educator*

Salisbury Mills
Satkowski, Sharon Kathleen Kennedy *elementary school educator*

Sands Point
Cullinan, Bernice E(llinger) *education educator*

Sandy Creek
Miller, Cheryl Marie *special education educator, business owner*

Saratoga Springs
Ratzer, Mary Boyd *secondary education educator, librarian*

Schenectady
Sorum, Christina Elliott *academic administrator*

Sea Cliff
Bolin, Mary Jane *director*

Sleepy Hollow
St. Vincent, Katharine Neyman *secondary school educator*

Sparkill
Nelson, Marguerite Hansen *special education educator*

Springfield Gardens
Williams, Vida Veronica *guidance counselor*

Staten Island
Berman, Barbara *educational consultant*
Dobis, Joan Pauline *education administrator*
Lockhart, Patricia Ann *elementary school educator*
Springer, Marlene *university administrator, educator*

Stony Brook
Kenny, Shirley Strum *academic administrator*
McClean, Lenora James *nursing educator, dean*

Suffern
Bay, Libby *college administrator, English language educator*

Syosset
Grenzig, Gail A. *assistant principal, consultant*

Syracuse
Chickadonz, Grace Harlow *dean*
DeSiato, Donna Jean *school system administrator*
Giacchi, Judith Adair *elementary school educator*
Johnson, Denise Eva *director, researcher*

Troy
Jackson, Shirley Ann *academic administrator, physicist*
Neff, Jeanne Henry *academic administrator*

Uniondale
Adams, Velma M. *assistant principal, consultant*

West Hempstead
Conway-Gervais, Kathleen Marie *reading specialist, educational consultant*

West Nyack
Coffey, Kimberly E. *secondary school educator*
Kanyuk, Joyce Stern *secondary art educator*

Westbury
Neziri, Maria G. De Lucia *elementary school educator*
Ross-Lee, Barbara *dean, educator*

Whitesboro
Voce, Joan A. Cifonelli *retired elementary school educator*

Whitney Point
Belanger, Randi Colleen *special education educator*

Wolcott
Wiggins, Dorothy L. *retired primary school educator*

Woodbury
Rosenthal, Marilyn *school librarian, educator*

Yonkers
Liggio, Jean Vincenza *adult education educator, artist*
Weston, Francine Evans *secondary school educator*

Yorkshire
Friedhaber-Hard, Susan Margaret *school media specialist, educator*

NORTH CAROLINA

Aberdeen
Ross, Deshan Jackson *elementary school educator*

Ahoskie
Phelps, Mary Ann Bazemore *elementary school educator*

Asheboro
Williams, Gwendolyn Sue *principal, educator*

Asheville
Ensley, Renné Whitaker *secondary school educator, artist*
Reed, Patsy Bostick *former academic administrator*
Sgro, Beverly Huston *day school administrator, educator, state official*

Belmont
Abernathy, Dixie Friend *elementary school educator, principal*

Boone
Wyatt, Jennifer Lynne *director*

Brasstown
Deslauriers, Suzanne Dawsey *secondary school educator, artist*

Chapel Hill
Broad, Margaret Corbett (Molly Broad) *academic administrator*
Brown, Betsy Etheridge *academic administrator*
Cronenwett, Linda Houk *dean*
Freund, Cynthia M. *dean*
Stewart, Sarah *elementary school educator*

Charlotte
Clark, Ann Blakeney *educational administrator*
Hardin, Elizabeth Ann *academic administrator*
Mercer, Evelyn Lois *retired guidance counselor*
Tobias, Dorothy Burton *retired elementary school music educator, consultant*
Tyson, Cynthia Haldenby *academic administrator*
Wall, Audrey G. *secondary school educator*
Yancy, Dorothy Cowser *college president*

Clayton
Harris, Patricia Ann Brady *principal, educational consultant*

Dallas
Moore, Judith Marie *assistant principal*

Davidson
Winkler, Mary Bernice *special education educator*

Denver
Eppley, Frances Fielden *retired secondary education educator, writer*

Durham
Bradford, Anne Harden *director*
Champagne, Mary T. *dean*
Denlinger, Ann T. *school system administrator*
Keohane, Nannerl Overholser *university president, political scientist*
Nelson, Denise Grau *special education educator, consultant*

Fayetteville
Jordan, Karla Salge *early childhood education educator*
Lydon, Kerry Raines *elementary school educator*
Mohn, Amy Elizabeth Brennan *special education educator, retail consultant*
Rivers, Stephanie Denise Wall *elementary school educator*
Townsend, Susan Stockstill *elementary school educator, music educator*

Goldsboro
Aldridge, Helen Belinda Oliver *primary school educator*

Greensboro
Barnett, Dorothy Prince *retired dean*
Bynum, Magnolia Virginia Wright *retired secondary school educator*
Cole, Johnnetta Betsch *academic administrator, educator*
Dyer, Karen Marie *education educator*
Nesbitt, Eleanor Troutman *elementary school educator, music educator*
Oliver, Donna H. *secondary school educator*
Pearcey, Lynne G. *university dean, nursing educator*
Richardson, Erika *special education educator*
Scott, Gloria Randle *college president*
Sullivan, Patricia A. *academic administrator*
Villaverde, Leila E. *education educator*
White, Gladys Hope Franklin *reading specialist*
Zopf, Evelyn LaNoel Montgomery *guidance counselor*

Greenville
Reichelt, Susan Ann *career and techical educator*

Halifax
Phillips, Margaret Rackley *retired elementary school educator*

Havelock
Stroud, Carrie Hoggard *elementary school educator*

Hendersonville
Keefauver, Nancy Ann *pre-school educator*

High Point
Howard, Lou Dean Graham *elementary school educator*

Kernersville
Cappel, Linda Greenwood *education educator*
Hosier, Linda Grube *gifted and talented educator*

Kinston
Richardson, Vanessa *education educator*

Laurinburg
Tate, Alicia Salemme *special education educator*

Matthews
Kocsis, Joan Bosco *elementary education educator, administrative assistant, assistant principal*

Monroe
Little, Wanda Vickery *school system administrator*
Radke, Anne Marie *assistant principal, writer*
Rorie, Nancy Catherine *retired elementary and secondary school educator*

Morganton
McDaniel, Janet B. *principal*

Mount Holly
Whobrey, Virginia Jean *retired director*

New Bern
Hemphill, Jean Hargett *college dean*

Newton
Daniels, Glennie Overman *family and consumer educator*

Raleigh
Fox, Marye Anne *university chancellor, chemistry educator*
Gulledge, Karen Stone *educational administrator*
Hartford, Maureen A. *academic administrator*
Kimbrough, Lorelei *elementary school educator*
Lasher, Harriet Pinsker *director, educator*
Maidon, Carolyn Howser *director*
Page, Anne Ruth *gifted education educator, education specialist*
Parramore, Barbara Mitchell *education educator*
Steed, Michelle Elnora *special education educator, counselor*
Suber, Dianne Boardley *educational administrator*

Salisbury
Hall, Telka Mowery Elium *retired educational administrator*
Snipes, Mignonne Elvira *academic administrator*
Troxler, Willie Thomasene *retired elementary school educator*

Shelby
Edgar, Ruth R. *retired elementary school educator*

Southern Pines
Cardwell, Nina Fern *special education educator*

Walstonburg
Beaman, Joyce Proctor *retired secondary and elementary school educator, writer*

Warrenton
Kearney, Irene Spruill *elementary school educator*

West End
Hodge, Katherine Rhodes *retired school guidance counselor*

Wilkesboro
Dale, Brenda Stephens *gifted and talented educator*
Klark, Denise J. *special education educator, consultant*

Williamston
Hoggard, Minnie Coltrain *gifted education educator, consultant*

Wilmington
DePaolo, Rosemary *dean, academic administrator*

Winston Salem
Crowder, Lena Belle *retired special education educator*
Jarrell, Iris Bonds *elementary school educator, business executive*
Roth, Marjory Joan Jarboe *special education educator*
Thrift, Julianne Still *academic administrator*
Volz, Annabelle Wekar *learning disabilities educator, consultant*

NORTH DAKOTA

Bismarck
Dixon, Dotti S. *school counselor*
Evanson, Barbara Jean *middle school education educator*
Joersz, Fran Woodmansee *secondary school educator*
Ketterling, Debra M. *secondary school educator*

Dickinson
Medlar, Deborah Starkey *secondary school educator*

Fargo
Lardy, Sister Susan Marie *academic administrator*
Sanford, Glenda Levonne *educational administrator*
Wegenast, Judy H. *elementary school educator, consultant*

Fort Yates
Chief Eagle, Joan *secondary school educator*

Golden Valley
Nordgren, Mary Kathleen *secondary school educator*

Grand Forks
Ashe, Kathy Rae *special education educator*
Mondry, Diane *secondary school educator*
Page, Sally Jacquelyn *university official, management educator*

Hazen
Eustice, Esther *elementary school educator*

Hettinger
Burrer, Ardath Rose *elementary school educator, music educator*

Killdeer
Bergstedt, Sonja K. *elementary school educator*

Saint John
Haas, Judith *elementary school educator*

OHIO

Akron
Bowman-Dalton, Burdene Kathryn *education testing coordinator, computer consultant*
Buzzelli, Charlotte Grace *special education educator*
Capers, Cynthia Flynn *dean, nursing educator*
Dietz, Margaret Jane *retired public information director*

Amherst
Gerstenberger, Valerie *media coordinator*

Ashland
Drushal, Mary Ellen *education educator, former academic administrator*

Athens
Dugan, JoAnn Rubino *education educator*
Helsel, Elsie Dressler *retired special education educator*
Krendl, Kathy *dean*

Batavia
Muskopf, Beth A. *curriculum consultant*

Beavercreek
Busch, Sharon Lynne *elementary and secondary education educator*
Focht, Sandra Jean *elementary school educator*

Bergholz
Goddard, Sandra Kay *elementary school educator*

Bexley
Osnes, Pamela Grace *behavior analyst*

Blacklick
Robinson, Bernice Joyce *secondary school educator*

Bowling Green
Dobb, Linda Sue *university official, librarian*
Filippova, Daria Vladimirovna *private school educator*

Broadview Heights
Jergens, Maribeth Joie *school counselor*

Cambridge
Barzda, Susan Marie *special education educator, art educator*

Centerville
Geier, Sharon Lee *special education educator*

Chagrin Falls
Brown, Jeanette Grasselli *retired university official*
Cortese, Julia F. *retired elementary school educator*
Robertson, Linda F. *educational adminstrator*

Chillicothe
Atwood, Joyce Charlene *curriculum and instruction administrator, consultant*
Greene, Judy *elementary school educator*

Cincinnati
Croskery, Beverly Ann *education consultant*
Emmich, Linda L. *private school educator*
Hall, Madelon Carol Syverson *elementary school educator*
Hess, Marcia Wanda *retired secondary school educator*

Johnson, Betty Lou *secondary school educator*
Kalven, Janet *education educator, writer, consultant*
Lindell, Andrea Regina *dean, nurse*
Patterson, Claire Ann *career techincal educator*
Phillips, Lynn Alice *pre-school educator*
Thomas, Hannah H. *retired educator*
Thompson, Adrienne *secondary school educator*
Zimpher, Nancy Lusk *academic administrator*

Cleveland
Ainsworth, Joan Horsburgh *university development director*
Byrd-Bennett, Barbara *school system administrator*
Foster, Faith Wilhelmina *school counselor, educational consultant*
Jaffe, Marcia Weissman *elementary school educator*
Knieriem, Beulah White *retired elementary school educator, minister*
Michney-Heipp, Karen Marie *secondary education educator*
Nemeth, Dian Jean *secondary school educator*
Queen, Joyce Ellen *elementary school educator*
Quigney, Theresa Ann *special education educator*
Smith, Beverly Harriett *elementary school educator*
Thornton, Jerry Sue *community college president*
Wertheim, Sally Harris *academic administrator, dean, education educator, consultant*
Wykle, May L. *dean, educator, researcher*

Columbia Station
Goll, Paulette Susan *education educator*

Columbus
Benton-Borghi, Beatrice Hope *secondary school educator, consultant, writer, director*
Foucht, Joan Lucille *retired elementary school educator, retired counseling administrator*
Grant, Jean Terry *educational consultant*
Hentz-Polk, Nicey *secondary school educator*
Laderer, Patricia M. *career planning administrator*
Leitzel, Joan Ruth *university president emerita*
Oxley, Margaret Carolyn Stewart *elementary school educator*
Rogers, Nancy Hardin *dean, law educator*
Zelman, Susan Tave *school system administrator*

Copley
Broda, C. Denise *education educator*

Cortland
Lane, Sarah Marie Clark *elementary school educator*

Dayton
Barr, Ann Helen *director*
Carson, Dora A. *secondary school educator*
Eby, Marlene Jean *retired secondary school educator*
Goldenberg, Kim *academic administrator, internist*
Harris, Bonnie *psychological education specialist*
Martin, Patricia *dean, nursing educator*
Taylor, Elisabeth Coler *retired secondary school educator*
Young, Yvonne Delease *elementary school educator*

Delta
Miller, Beverly White *former college president, educational consultant, consultant*

Dublin
Bordelon, Carolyn Thew *elementary school educator*

Fairview Park
Flynn, Patricia M. *director, special education educator, gifted and talented educator*

Fremont
Sattler, Nancy Joan *educational administrator*

Gambier
Nugent, S. Georgia *academic administrator*
Ponder, Anne *dean*

Hamilton
Hornsby, Judith Elizabeth *special education educator*

Highland Hills
Sender, Maryann *director*

Hudson
Goheen, Janet Moore *counseling administrator, sales executive*
Hallenbeck, Linda S. *elementary school educator*
Snyder, Virginia Anne *gifted and talented educator*

Huron
Leser, Anne Elizabeth *education educator*

Kent
Cartwright, Carol Ann *university president*
Gosnell, Davina J. *dean, nursing educator*

Kettering
Denlinger, Vicki Lee *secondary school educator, physical education educator*
Hoffman, Sue Ellen *retired elementary school educator*
Martin, Margaret Gately *elementary school educator*

Kingsville
Poluga, Judith *education educator*

Liberty Center
Grieser, Ilsa Adele *elementary school educator, music educator*

Jones, Marlene Ann *retired education supervisor*

Lima
Lovett, Katherine Van Every *special education educator*
Meek, Violet Imhof *retired dean*

Lorain
Comer, Brenda Warmee *elementary school educator, real estate company officer*

Loudonville
Gault, Jeannie Suzanne *elementary school educator*

Maineville
Cook, Janice Eleanor Nolan *retired elementary school educator*

Mansfield
Gregory, Deirdre Dianne *secondary educator*
Hunt, Pamela Sue *elementary school educator, music educator*

Marietta
Francis, Lynne Ann *elementary school educator, music educator*

Mechanicsburg
Maynard, Joan *education educator*

Medina
DeMars, Judith M. *elementary school educator*

Millersburg
Yoder, Anna A. *elementary school educator*

Mount Orab
Raines, Tami Jo *principal*

Munroe Falls
Clawson, Judith Louise *middle school educator*

Nelsonville
Mingus, Judy Ellen *special education educator, secondary school educator*

New Lebanon
Dillman, Karin Christine *elementary school educator*

New Matamoras
Brown, Blanche Y. *secondary education educator, genealogy researcher*

New Philadelphia
Doughten, Mary Katherine (Molly Doughten) *retired secondary school educator*

Newark
Paul, Rochelle Carole *special education educator*
Simpson, Linda Sue *elementary school educator*
Williams, Gale Cady *secondary school educator*

Niles
Linden, Carol Marie *special education educator*

Norwalk
Lang, Wilma Jean *special education educator*

Oberlin
Dye, Nancy Schrom *academic administrator, historian, educator*
MacKay, Gladys Godfrey *adult education educator*

Orwell
Strong, Marcella Lee *music specialist, educator*

Oxford
Thompson, Bertha Boya *retired education educator, antique dealer and appraiser*

Painesville
Blyth, Ann Marie *secondary school educator*
Davis, Barbara Snell *education educator*

Parma
Reichheld, Deborah Ann *secondary school educator*
Romanovich, Patricia M. *parochial school educator*
Salzgeber, Karen A. *secondary school educator*
Scheffel, Donna Jean *elementary school educator*
Tener, Carol Joan *retired elementary school educator*

Paulding
Moore, Pamela Rae *elementary school educator*

Pepper Pike
Stano, Sister Diana *academic administrator*

Pickerington
Collins, Arlene *secondary school educator*

Plymouth
Hartman, Ruth Campbell *director, educator*

Port Clinton
Ewersen, Mary Virginia *retired school system administrator, poet*
Taylor, Jane Ellen *elementary school educator*

Ravenna
O'Brien, Jane *special education educator*

Rocky River
Hudson, Judith Ann *elementary school educator*

Shaker Heights
Aulicino, Christine Wilkinson *education educator*
Trefts, Joan Landenberger *retired educator, administrator*

Sparta
Ruffing, Eileen Mary *elementary school educator, music educator*

Springfield
Fry, Maureen Shea *director, educator*
Gardunia, Sharon Strawsburg *secondary school educator*
Stelzer, Patricia Jacobs *retired secondary school educator*

Sylvania
Buckenmeyer, Janet *director, education educator, director*
Sampson, Earldine Robison *education educator*

Toledo
Goldstein, Margaret Franks *special education educator*
Knuth, Marya Danielle *special education educator*
Rabideau, Margaret Catherine *retired media center director*
Worley, Debere *educational consultant*

University Heights
Mahon, Marinna Fairbank *secondary education educator, writer, consultant*
Starcher-Dell'Aquila, Judy Lynn *special education educator*

Valley View
Miller, Susan Ann *school system administrator*

Wadsworth
Thomas, Jennifer Butler *special education educator, coach*

Washington Court House
Febo, Diana Lucile *counseling administrator*
Fichthorn, Fonda Gay *gifted and talented educator, retired principal*

West Chester
Reed, Valerie V. *school librarian*
Verbesselt, Martine Carole *primary school educator*

Westerville
Diersing, Carolyn Virginia *educational administrator*
Van Sant, Joanne Frances *academic administrator*

Westlake
Loehr, Marla *spiritual care coordinator*

Wickliffe
Wainio, Melody F. *dean*

Wilberforce
Walker-Taylor, Yvonne *retired academic administrator*

Willoughby
Grossman, Mary Margaret *elementary school educator*

Yellow Springs
Straumanis, Joan *academic administrator*

Youngstown
Camardese, Amy Hoffman *education educator*

Zanesville
Stainbrook, Margaret Collins *retired school system administrator*

OKLAHOMA

Ada
Frye, Linda Beth (Linda Beth Hisle) *elementary, secondary education educator*

Bartlesville
Chambers, Imogene Klutts *school system administrator, financial consultant*
Risner, Anita Jane *vocational school educator*

Coalgate
Willis, Tricia Lee *special education educator*

Drumright
Pruitt, Linda Kay *special education educator*

Duncan
Austin, Diana Sue *elementary school educator*

Earlsboro
Smart, Ella Jo *special education educator*

Edmond
Harryman, Rhonda L. *education educator*
Osgood, Virginia M. *vocational educator*
Zabel, Vivian Ellouise *secondary school educator*

Fort Cobb
Rexroat, Vicki Lynn *occupational child development educator*

Healdton
Lewis, Reba Jolene *secondary school educator, consultant*

Jenks
Dominguez, Monica Raye *special education educator*

Lawton
McKeown, Rebecca J. *principal*

Marlow
Hines, Deborah Sue *special education educator*

Miami
Vanpool, Cynthia Paula *special education educator, special services consultant*

Midwest City
Cheek, Norma Jean *retired educator*
Saulmon, Sharon Ann *college librarian*

Mustang
McDonald, Terre Reese *elementary school educator*

Newkirk
Eisenhauer, Gayle Ann *elementary school educator, secondary school educator*

Norman
Dalton, Deborah Whitmore *dean*
Rupp-Serrano, Karen *school librarian*
Zapffe, Nina Byrom *retired elementary education educator*

Oklahoma City
Bentley, Karen Gail *elementary school educator*
Blackburn, Debbie *elementary school educator, state representative*
Chiles, Mary Jane *secondary school educator*
Easley, Mary *retired elementary school educator, state representative*
Felts, Rebecca Nancy *elementary school educator*
Forni, Patricia Rose *dean*
Garrett, Sandy Langley *school system administrator*
Hall, Nancy K. *college dean*
Henderson, Molly *academic administrator, educator*
Noakes, Betty LaVonne *retired elementary school educator*
Regier, Elaine Roxanne *elementary school educator, school librarian*
Williamson, Marvel *dean, nursing administrator, sexologist, educator, writer*

Pauls Valley
Pesterfield, Linda Carol *retired school administrator, educator*

Pawnee
Brown, Paula Ann *pre-school administrator*

Ponca City
Rice, Sue Ann *dean, industrial and organizational psychologist*

Pryor
Rice, Susan K. *school librarian, educator*

Seminole
Branscum, Carla Jeanne *special education educator*
Gillespie, Norma *educational advisor*

Tahlequah
Grant, Kay Lallier *early childhood education educator*

Tinker Afb
Scott, Carol Lee *child care educator*

Tulsa
Barnes, Cynthia Lou *retired gifted and talented educator*
Buthod, Mary Clare *school administrator*
Cardwell, Sandra Gayle Bavido *university admissions professional*
Kukura, Rita Anne *pre-school educator*
Wood, Emily Churchill *special education educator, social studies educator, consultant*

Wagoner
Durham, Nancy Ruth *elementary school educator, music educator*

Woodward
Fisher, Deena Kaye *social studies education administrator*

OREGON

Albany
Smart, Ann Catherine *dean*

Aloha
Pronovost, Vicki S. *special education educator*

Baker City
Trohkimoinen, Judith Lorraine *elementary school educator*

Beaverton
de Sá e Silva, Elizabeth Anne *secondary school educator*
Pepper, Floy Childers *educational consultant*

Bend
Forbes Johnson, Mary Gladys *retired secondary school educator*

Cannon Beach
Wismer, Patricia Ann *retired secondary school educator*

Corvallis
Lumpkin, Margaret Catherine *retired education educator*
McKee-Ryan, Frances M *education educator*
Verts, Lita Jeanne *university administrator*

Dayton
Angaran, Sally Jean *school system administrator*

Eagle Point
Blanchard, Shirley Lynn *primary school educator, consultant*

Eugene
McMillan, Adell *retired educational administrator*
Warpinski, Terri L. *academic administrator, artist*

Grants Pass
Agricola, Dianne G. *secondary education educator, tutor*
Murdock, Doris Dean *special education educator*

Gresham
Light, Betty Jensen Pritchett *former college dean*
Webb, Donna Louise *academic director, educator*

Lake Oswego
Lenderman, Joanie *elementary school educator*
Meltebeke, Renette *career counselor*
Wirtz, Doris W. *secondary school educator*

Mcminnville
Bull, Vivian Ann *college president*

Merrill
Porter, Roberta Ann *counselor, educator, school system administrator*

Monmouth
Dunn, Doris Marjory *retired educator, volunteer*

Myrtle Creek
Kuk, Mary Halvorson *secondary school educator*

Oceanside
Wadlow, Joan Krueger *retired academic administrator, construction executive*

Philomath
Leckle, Cheryl Ann *special education educator*

Portland
Davis, Gloria Zeal *counseling administrator, educator*
Frolick, Patricia Mary *retired elementary school educator*
Leupp, Edythe Peterson *retired education educator*
Potempa, Kathleen *dean*
Robinson, Ruth Carleson *retired secondary school educator*
Sedgwick, Levonne *retired school program administrator*

Roseburg
Zeigler, Key *dean*

Salem
Castillo, Susan *school system administrator*
Page, Cheryl Miller *elementary school educator*

Sutherlin
Johnson, Barbara E. *adult education educator*

Wilsonville
Talus, Donna J. *secondary school educator*

Yachats
Robeck, Mildred Coen *education educator, writer*

PENNSYLVANIA

Allentown
Blaney, Dorothy Gulbenkian *academic administrator*
Buenaflor, Judith Luray *secondary school educator*
Nippert, Carolyn Cochrane *college official, information scientist*

Allison Park
Guffey, Barbara Braden *elementary school educator*
Reagan, Patricia L. *secondary school counselor*

Ardmore
Dagna, Jeanne Marie *special education educator*

Athens
Luther-Lemmon, Carol Len *elementary school educator*
Murphy, Sylvia J. Harris *secondary school educator*

Bangor
Pensack, Susan *elementary school educator*

Beaver Falls
Mahosky, Nancy Lynne *secondary school educator*
Smith, Nancy Irene *director*

Belle Vernon
Stimmell, Tamara *special education educator*

Bensalem
Gentile, Mary O'Connor *principal*
Jurowicz, Kimberly Deborah *special education educator, elementary school educator*

Bethel Park
Douds, Virginia Lee *elementary school educator*

Bethlehem
Moeller, Rachel Nelson *career development specialist*

Biglerville
Marks, Nora Maralea *retired secondary school educator*

Bloomsburg
Kozloff, Jessica S. *university president*

Perner, Darlene E. *special education educator, consultant, editor*

Boiling Springs
Oxenreider, Laura Elizabeth *elementary guidance counselor*

Bryn Mawr
Smith, Nona Coates *academic administrator*
Vickers, Nancy J. *academic administrator*

Cambridge Springs
Ferringer-Burdick, Susan *elementary school educator*

Camp Hill
Romberger, Jean Louise *retired educator*

Carlisle
Cook, Ann Harris Shackleton *gifted and talented educator, psychotherapist*

Center Valley
Bartolacci, Paulette Marie *middle school educator, aerobics instructor*

Cheltenham
Kuziemski, Naomi Elizabeth *educational consultant, counselor*

Clarion
Dingle, Patricia A. *education educator, artist*
Reinhard, Diane L. *university president*

Coatesville
Rodkey, Frances Theresa *elementary school educator*
Smith, Patricia Anne *special education educator*

Coraopolis
Stevens, Paulette *daycare administrator*

Delaware Water Gap
Chamberlin, Marjorie Ruth *elementary school educator*

Doylestown
Thomas, Ellen Louise *school system administrator*

Drexel Hill
Turnbull, Mary Regina *secondary school educator*

East Stroudsburg
Braithwaite, Barbara J. *secondary school educator*
Miller, Edith Fisher *special education educator*

Ebensburg
Pereira, Melany *elementary school educator*

Edinboro
Marszalek, Marilyn *elementary school educator*

Everett
Snow, Linda Sue *family educator, consumer sciences educator, secondary school educator*

Fairfield
Mikesell, Pamela Prestwood *guidance counselor*

Fairless Hills
Hess, Frances Elizabeth *retired secondary school educator, retired director*

Farrell
Pawluk, Annette Marie *secondary school educator*

Franklin
Sauer, Mary Julia *special education educator*

Glen Mills
Shields, Martha Buckley *elementary school educator*

Glenside
Landman, Bette Emeline *academic administrator*

Gwynedd Valley
Owens, Kathleen C. *academic administrator*

Hanover
Barnhart, Nikki Lynn Clark *elementary school educator*
Clark, Sandra Marie *school administrator*

Harrisburg
Baehre, Edna Victoria *college president*
Burns, Rebecca Ann *elementary school educator, librarian*
Hample, Judy G. *academic administrator*
Martine, Andrea Schultz *secondary school educator*
Phillips, Vicki L. *school system administrator*
Pringle, Rebecca *elementary school educator*

Hatfield
Madden, Theresa Marie *elementary school educator*

Havertown
Wright, Cecilia Powers *gifted and talented educator*

Hellertown
Kunkel-Christman, Debra Ann *educator*

Hershey
Butterfield, Andrea Christine *elementary school educator, adult education educator, psychology educator*

Immaculata
Fadden, Sister R. Patricia *academic administrator, nun*

Johnstown
Fattman, Anne Carilyn *elementary school educator*
Puto, Anne-Marie *reading specialist*

Kennett Square
Pensyl, Christina A. *special education educator*

Knox
Rupert, Elizabeth Anastasia *retired dean*

Lafayette Hill
Delacato, Janice Elaine *learning consultant, educator*

Lake Ariel
Casper, Marie Lenore *middle school educator*

Lancaster
Drum, Alice *academic administrator, educator*
Geiger, Carol Lynn *educational therapist*
Trupe, Mary-Ann *secondary school educator*

Langhorne
Wychock, Karen Marie *principal, set designer, craftsman*

Levittown
Walker, Patricia Ann Dixon *retired elementary school educator, real estate rehabilitator*

Lewisburg
Roberts, Ruth W. *retired elementary school educator*
Smith, Marguerite Irene *gifted and talented educator*

Lititz
Hudelson, Judith Giantomass *elementary school educator*

Lock Haven
Almes, June *retired education educator, librarian*
Bowers, Gloria Mills *secondary education art educator*

Mahaffey
Lieb, Susan M. *elementary school educator*

Mansfield
Sidell, Nancy L. *adult education educator*

Maple Glen
Weaver-Stroh, Joanne Mateer *education educator, consultant*

Mc Donald
Maurer, Karen Ann *special education educator*

Mc Murray
Omar, Janice Butko *home economics educator*

Meadville
Dixon, Armendia Pierce *school program administrator*

Millerton
Kipferl, Christiana A. *special education educator*

Monroeville
Baker, Faith Mero *retired elementary education educator*

Moscow
Lisandrelli, Elaine Slivinski *secondary school educator*

Nanticoke
Donohue, Patricia Carol *academic administrator*

Narberth
Pauxtis, Mary Jo *academic administrator*

New Alexandria
Sehring, Hope Hutchinson *library science educator*

New Castle
Halm, Nancye Studd *retired academic administrator*
Roux, Mildred Anna *retired secondary school educator*

New Oxford
Martin, Sandra Ann *special education educator, writer*

New Wilmington
Magyary, Cynthia Marie *elementary school educator, music educator*

Newtown
McLaughlin, Judith Ann *secondary school educator*

Norristown
Del Collo, Mary Anne Demetris *school administrator*

Patton
Pompa, Louise Elaine *secondary school educator*

Perkasie
Ferry, Joan Evans *school counselor*

Philadelphia
Austin, Patricia Davis *academic administrator*
Aversa, Dolores Sejda *educational administrator*
Christman, Jolley Bruce *educational research executive, educator*
Cooke, Sara Mullin Graff *daycare provider, kindergarten educator, medical assistant*
Delaney, Anna T. *director*
Donnelly, Gloria Ferraro *university dean*
Dunn, Mary Maples *former university dean*

Fernandez, Happy Craven (Gladys Fernandez) *academic administrator*
Gur, Raquel E. *academic administrator*
Guyer, Hedy-Ann Klein *special education educator*
Jamieson, Kathleen Hall *dean, communications educator*
Lobel, Grace *education educator*
Meghan, Murray Patrice *director*
Onley, Sister Francesca *academic administrator*
Presseisen, Barbara Zemboch *retired educational director, researcher*
Reid, Mary Wallace *retired secondary school educator*
Rice, Carrie Sottile *public relation director, retired principal*
Rodin, Judith Seitz *academic administrator*
Sibolski, Elizabeth Hawley *higher education administrator*
Sklar, Gail Janice *secondary special education educator*
Slaughter-Defoe, Diana Tresa *education educator*

Philipsburg
Genesi, Susan Petrovich *school system administrator*

Phoenixville
Harkin, Ann Winifred *elementary school educator, psychotherapist*

Pittsburgh
Barazzone, Esther Lynn *academic administrator, educator*
Boyce, Doreen Elizabeth *lecturer, civic development foundation executive*
Bradick, Angella Velvet *special education educator*
Fox, Mariann Palombo *supervisor, music educator*
Geibel, Sister Grace Ann *college president*
Haas, Marlene Ringold *special education educator*
Linke, Erika C. *school librarian*
McBride, Mildred Maylea *retired elementary school educator*
McHoes, Ann McIver *academic administrator, computer systems consultant*
Packard, Rochelle Sybil *elementary school educator*
Rago, Ann D'Amico *university official, public relations professional*
Schock, Barbara Jean *educational consultant*
Somova, Marla Jo *counseling administrator, psychologist*
Southworth, Jamie MacIntyre *retired education educator*
Warner, Judith (Anne) Huss *elementary school educator*
Wooten, Carol Campbell *academic administrator*

Pottstown
Hollingsworth, Debra Lynn *elementary school educator*

Radnor
Iadarola, Antoinette *college president*

Reading
Hurwitz, Ellen Stiskin *college president, historian*

Russellton
Curtis, Paula Annette *elementary and secondary education educator*

Scranton
Nee, Sister Mary Coleman *college president emeritus*
Reap, Sister Mary Margaret *college administrator*

Solebury
Gilleo, Sandra V. *elementary school educator*

State College
Link, Phoebe Forrest *secondary school educator, writer*
McKeel, Lillian Phillips *retired education educator*

Summerdale
Pickel, Diane Dunn *education educator*

Sunbury
Maue, Leta Jo *special education administrator*

Swarthmore
Baskin, Maureen Louise *special education educator*
Berger, Dianne Gwynne *family life educator, consultant*

Titusville
Campasino, Ellen Marie *elementary school educator*

Unionville
Martin, Helen Elizabeth *educational consultant*

University Park
Askov, Eunice May *adult education educator*
Bazirjian, Rosann V. *dean, librarian*
Fuhrman, Susan H *education educator*
Shannon, Barbara *dean, nutrition educator*
Zabel, Diane Marion *school librarian*

Upper Saint Clair
Dunkis, Patricia B. *school system administrator*

Vandergrift
Stitt, Theresa Mary *special education educator*

Villanova
Fitzpatrick, M. Louise *dean, nursing educator*

West Chester
Adler, Madeleine Wing *academic administrator*
Bove, Patrice Magee *elementary school educator*
Keiser, Mary Ann Myers *special education educator*

West Mifflin
Archey, Mary Frances Elaine (Onofaro) *academic administrator, educator*

Wilkes Barre
Kaufer, Karen Evans *academic administrator*

Williamsport
Clarke, Louise Rigdon *gifted student program administrator, principal*
Parks, Michelle M. *academic administrator*

Willow Grove
Burtt, Anne Dampman *special education educator*

Winfield
Wert, Barbara J. Yingling *special education consultant*

Wyalusing
Goodman, Carol Hockenbury *retired elementary school educator, consultant*

York
Wright, Tiffany Erin *secondary school educator*

RHODE ISLAND

Bristol
Grota, Barbara Lynn *academic administrator, educator*

Kingston
Smith, Sareba G. *special education educator*

Pawtucket
Lepore, Lisa *principal*

Providence
Blumstein, Sheila Ellen *former academic administrator, linguistics educator*
Johnson, Melody *school system administrator*
Simmons, Ruth J. *academic administrator*
Waite-Franzen, Ellen Jane *academic administrator*

SOUTH CAROLINA

Aiken
Hickey, Delina Rose *retired education educator*
Santos, Karey Michale *elementary school educator*

Batesburg
Long, Drucilla *special education educator*

Beaufort
Eggen, Belinda Lay *education educator*
Raines, Karen Cornell *secondary school educator*

Bishopville
Roycroft, Cheryl *secondary school educator*

Central
Bell, Gloria Jean *academic administrator, literature educator, dean*

Chapin
Bowers, Linda *educational administrator*

Charleston
Karesh, Janice Lehrer *special education consultant*
Simms, Lois Averetta *retired secondary school educator*

Columbia
Aelion, C. Marjorie *adult education educator*
Fields, Harriet Gardin *counselor, educator, consultant*
Greene, Claudia *education associate*
Hoffman, Mary Ann Hartman *principal*
McCulloch, Anne Merline Jacobs *college dean*
Phillips, Vicky Lynn *elementary school educator*
Shifflett, Audrey Horton *academic administrator, researcher*
Sinclair, Linda Drumwright *educational consultant*
Tunstall, Dorothy Fiebrich *early childhood educator*

Conway
Johnson-Leeson, Charleen Ann *former elementary school educator, insurance agent, insurance consultant, regional executive assistant*

Denmark
Boyd-Scotland, Joann *college president*

Easley
Snider, Patricia Stapleton *assistant principal*
Stone, Lisa Murphy *elementary school educator, music educator*

Effingham
Taylor, Sherry Michelle Mills *elementary school educator*

Florence
Rutherford, Vicky Lynn *special education educator*

Gaffney
Griffin, Penni Oncken *dean, social worker*
Suttle, Helen Jayson *retired education educator*

Greenville
Glenn, Idella Goodson *director*
Hancock, Donna *secondary school educator*
Hill, Grace Lucile Garrison *education educator, consultant*
Seibert, Lesa Marie *university educator*

Greenwood
Marino, Sheila Burris *education educator*

Iva
Gentry, Margaret Burton *retired elementary school teacher*
Standridge, Diane H. *secondary school educator*

Kershaw
Wall, Kathy Elliott *secondary school educator*

Kingstree
Holliday, Jennifer Nexsen *elementary school educator, music educator*

Lake City
Hawkins, Linda Parrott *school system administrator*

Lexington
Floyd, Ann R. *elementary school educator*

Manning
Samuels, Yvonne James *retired special education educator*

Mauldin
Norris, Joan Clafette Hagood *retired assistant principal*

Orangeburg
Gamble, Jacquelyn Valdena *secondary school educator*
Robinson, Ruth Hubbard *retired elementary school educator*

Pickens
Hicks, Virginia Buchholz *secondary school educator*

Piedmont
Winter-Neighbors, Gwen Carole *special education educator, art educator, consultant*

Prosperity
Hause, Edith Collins *college administrator*

Ridgeville
Hill, Jacquelyn Louise Harrison *secondary school educator*

Rock Hill
Barbaree, Dorothy A. *secondary school educator, antique dealer*
Russell, Cynthia M. *college president*
Yeager, Bernice Whittaker *elementary and secondary school educator*

Spartanburg
Agnew, Janet Burnett *secondary school educator*
Gray, Nancy Ann Oliver *college administrator*
McCraw, Kathy *elementary school educator, special education educator*

Surfside Beach
Calo, Tina Carol *school counselor*

Waterloo
Grigsby, Amanda Moore *special education educator*
Parrish, Cathy Waldron *elementary school educator*

SOUTH DAKOTA

Aberdeen
Fouberg, Glenna M. *career planning administrator*
Omland, Jacqueline Leigh-Knute *secondary school educator, small business owner*

Brookings
Miller, Peggy Gordon Elliott *university president*

Mitchell
Russell, Annika Renee *secondary school educator, financial consultant*

Sioux Falls
Ashworth, Julie *elementary school educator*

Wessington Springs
Christopherson, Karen Marie *education educator*

TENNESSEE

Athens
Fisher, Nancy M. *educator, poet*

Big Sandy
Hancock, Sandra Olivia *secondary school educator, elementary school educator*

Brentwood
Gotterer, Shelley McCullough *elementary school educator*

Brownsville
Scott-Wilson, Susan Rice *vice principal*

Chattanooga
Steele, Shirley Sue *retired special resource educator*

Clarksville
Myers, Linda Shafer *secondary educator*

Cleveland
Hamid, Suzanne L *academic administrator*

Columbia
Cantrell, Sharron Caulk *principal*

Cookeville
Pierce, Sarah Faith *counseling administrator, secondary school educator, elementary school educator*

Dickson
Thomas, Janey Sue *elementary school principal*

Dunlap
Carr, Marsha Hamblen *elementary school principal*

Franklin
Daniel, Cathy Brooks *tutor, educational consultant*
Hughey, Brenda Joyce *supervisor*
McClellan, Dixie *secondary school educator*

Harriman
Hoppe, Sherry Lee *academic administrator*

Henderson
Cypress, Karen Lenett *special education educator*

Hermitage
White, Mary Beth *guidance counselor, adult education educator*

Hixson
Prichard, Lona Ann *retired elementary education educator*

Jackson
Hearn, Beverly Jean *secondary education educator, librarian*

Johnson City
Edwards, Joellen Beckett *dean, community health nurse educator*

Kingsport
Wilhoit, Trisha C. *elementary school educator*

Knoxville
Creasia, Joan Catherine *dean, nursing educator*
Griffin, Mary Jane Ragsdale *educational consultant, writer, small business owner*
Hatton, Barbara R. *academic administrator*
Marshall-Hardin, Floy Jeanne *art school educator*
Walsh, Joanne Elizabeth *retired elementary school educator, librarian*

Mc Minnville
Brock, Angela Eulene Douglass *education educator*

Memphis
Donahue, Joan Elizabeth *elementary school educator*
Hirsch, Callie Clark *instructional facilitator*
Hord, Pauline Jones *primary school educator, educator*
Indingaro, Margaret Ann *supervisor*
Joyner, Marguerite Austin *secondary school educator*
Raines, Shirley Carol *academic administrator*
Riser, Kathleen Walsh *secondary school educator*
Watson, Ella H. *principal*

Murfreesboro
Doyle, Delores Marie *retired principal*
Gilbert, Linda Arms *education educator, educational administrator*

Nashville
Clinton, Barbara Marie *university health services director, social worker*
Collins, Joe Lena *retired secondary school educator*
Conway-Welch, Colleen *dean, nurse midwife*
Fitzwater, Katherine Sauter *elementary school educator*
Greene, Lydia Abbi Jwuan *elementary school educator*
Loper, Linda Sue *special collections librarian*
McMurry, Idanelle Sam *educational consultant*
Pierce, Patricia Ann *university administrator*
Young, Rebecca Payne *secondary school educator*

Oak Ridge
Cragle, Donna Lynne *university administrator, researcher*
Evans, Carole Clinton *special education educator*

Oliver Springs
Heacker, Thelma Weaks *retired elementary school educator*

Portland
Miller, Sandra Perry *middle school educator*

Readyville
Merrill, Mary Margaret *secondary school educator*

Selmer
Prather, Sophie S. *educational administrator*

Smithville
Hinton, Susan Frazier *secondary school educator*

Wichita Falls
Evans, Melinda Dianne *elementary school educator*

UTAH

Bountiful
Bertelsen, Karyn *school system administrator, principal*

Logan
Dobson, Dorothy Lynn Watts *elementary school educator*

Ogden
Runolfson, Marilyn Dolores *special education educator*

Provo
Densley, Colleen T. *principal*

Saint George
Wiltsey, Susan A. *secondary school educator, priest*

Salt Lake City
Cannell, Cyndy Michelle *elementary school principal*
Huefner, Dixie Snow *special education educator*
Keefe, Maureen Ruth *dean*
Shaw, Karen Jane *special education educator*
Stock, Peggy A(nn) *college president, educator*
Van Ert, Heidi *gifted education educator, artist, art therapist*

Springville
Mayne, Marianne *special education educator*

West Valley City
Bandeka, Faun Ann *elementary school educator*

VERMONT

Bennington
Coleman, Elizabeth *college president*

Benson
Hair, Jennie (M. Virginia Reppert) *counseling administrator, poet*

Brattleboro
Hammond, Deborah D.J. *school librarian, researcher*
Steffens, Annie Laurie *sign language educator, interpreter*

Burlington
Della Santa, Laura *principal*

Colchester
Edmundson, Lorna Duphiney *academic administrator*

Lyndonville
Moore, Carol A. *academic administrator*

Middlebury
Mock, Susan E. *pre-school educator, consultant*

Montpelier
Blanchard, Margaret Moore *author, educator*

Moretown
Hartshorn, Brenda Bean *elementary school educator*

South Duxbury
Villemaire, Diane Davis *adult education educator*

Waterbury
Hilton, Linda D. *academic administrator*

VIRGINIA

Abingdon
Ball, Amy Catherine *education program manager*

Alexandria
Alexander, Marian G. *elementary school educator*
Bond, Frances Torino *academic administrator, consultant*
Brown, Lillie Deloris *elementary school educator, adult education educator*
Edgell, Karin Jane *reading specialist, special education educator*
Ellison, Pamela Ion *secondary school educator, consultant*
Gil, Libia Socorro *school system administrator*
Haygood, Alma Jean *elementary school educator*
Johnson, Marlys Marlene *elementary school educator*
Smith, Canda Banks *educational consultant*
Watts, Sonja Marie *assistant principal, educational consultant*

Amelia Court House
Hughes, Corry Hankinson *special education educator*

Annandale
Bohen, Dolores Boylston *retired school system administrator*
Burchett, Brenda Jean Harnage *secondary school educator, writer*
Del Conte, L. Catherine *special education educator*
Heyer, Laura Miriam *special education educator*
Wilhelmi, Mary Charlotte *education educator, college official*

Arlington
Finta, Frances Mickna *secondary school educator*
Haggett, Rosemary Romanowski *academic administrator*
Ramaley, Judith Aitken *former university president, endocrinologist*
Rogers, Sharon J. *education consultant*
Stout, Mary Webb *education program specialist*

Blacksburg
Campbell, Joan Virginia Loweke *secondary school educator, language educator*
Edwards, Patricia Klobus *former dean, architecture/urban studies educator*
Meszaros, Peggy S. *academic administrator*

Bristol
Hagy, Teresa Jane *elementary school educator*

Bristow
Insalaco-De Nigris, Anna Maria Theresa *middle school educator*

Burke
Emery, Vicki Morris *school library media administrator*

Capeville
Spady, Joanne Smith *secondary school educator*

Charlottesville
Greville, Florence Nusim *secondary school educator, mathematician*
Miller, Margaret Alison *education educator*

Chesapeake
Lewter, Helen Clark *elementary education educator, retired*
Pearce, Patsy Beasley *elementary education educator*
Potter, Cynthia M. *art educator, artist*

Chesterfield
Hill, Ida Johnson *education consultant, technologist, administrator*

Covington
Spurlock, Evelyn Harvey *retired elementary school educator, minister*

Fairfax
Carr, Patricia Warren *adult education educator*
Carty, Rita Mary *dean, nurse*
Lowery, Sabra Annette *special education educator*
Powell, Karan Hinman *academic administrator*
Slade-Martin, Phyllis E. *director*
Tucker, Calanthia Rallings *school administrator*

Fairfax Station
Crissey, Rebecca Lynn *special education educator*
St. John, Jennifer Kathleen *gifted and talented educator*

Falls Church
Lambert, Vickie Ann *dean emerita, international nursing consultant*
Stanford, Elaine P. *secondary school educator*
Swerdlow, Roberta Dyas *educational consultant*
Todd, Shirley Ann *school system administrator*
Waylonis, Jean Lynnette *elementary school educator*

Farmville
Cormier, Patricia Picard *academic executive*

Fredericksburg
Jenks-Davies, Kathryn Ryburn *retired daycare provider and owner, civic worker*
Potter, Sylvia *education educator*

Gainesville
Burke, Marjorie Tisdale *retired special education educator*

Glen Allen
Bosdell, Melony *special education educator*

Great Falls
Andrews, Betty Bauserman *retired secondary school educator, property manager*

Hampton
Betts, Christina Pinkston *education educator*
Carrington, Marian Denise *university administrator, counselor, motivational speaker*
Silva, Monica *gifted education educator*
Vernon, Lisa Jo *reading and special education educator*

Harrisonburg
Gonzalez, Teresa Ann *academic administrator, psychologist, educator*

Heathsville
Sisson, Jean Cralle *retired primary school educator*

Herndon
Botsis, Beth Ann *director*

Leesburg
Hronik, Rebecca Jane Leake *educator*

Lexington
Elrod, Mimi Cobb Milner *academic administrator*
McCloud, Anece Faison *academic administrator*

Locust Grove
Ingalls, Jane *university program director*

Lovettsville
Ryan-Griffith, Mary Kate *special education educator*

Lynchburg
Bowman, Kathleen Gill *academic administrator*
Herndon, Merle Puckette *principal*
Schewel, Rosel Hoffberger *education educator*
Webb, Evelyn Dunbar *elementary school educator*

Marion
Groseclose, Joanne Stowers *special education educator*

Mc Dowell
Harkleroad, Jo-Ann Decker *special education educator*

Mc Lean
Brown, Betty J. *director*

Mechanicsville
Watkins, Carol A. *special education educator*

Middleburg
Kaplan, Jean Gaither (Norma Kaplan) *reading specialist, retired educator*
New, Margaret Ann *educational consultant*

Midlothian
Böer, Susanne Ella *secondary school educator, translator*
Romig, Deborah Lynn *secondary school educator*

New Kent
Hammond, Susan Meeks *elementary school educator*

Newport News
Eanes, Janet Teresa *elementary school educator, music educator*
Smith, Kelly McCoig *secondary school educator*

Norfolk
Golembiewski, Gae S. *gifted education educator*
Hill, Deborah Nixon *elementary school educator, minister*
Little, Grace Ruiz *computer services administrator*
McDemmond, Marie Valentine *academic administrator, consultant*
Notti, Donna Betts *special education educator*
Runte, Roseann *academic administrator*
Sebren, Lucille Griggs *retired private school educator, public school educator*
Wingate, Tanya Williams *school disciplinarian*

Poquoson
Tuck, Carolyn Weaver *middle school educator*

Portsmouth
Hill, Dorothy Monroe *retired educator*
Taylor, Gwendolyn Barnett *school system administrator*
Williams, Lena Harding *educational administrator*

Radford
Nelson, Beth Carlson *educational consultant*

Reston
Pavek, Bryn Carpenter *director arts administration*

Richmond
Christenbury, Leila *education educator*
Harris, Grace E. *academic administrator*
Jewell-Sherman, Deborah *school system administrator*
Jones, Jeanne Pitts *pre-school administrator*
Langston, Nancy Sue Friedrich *dean*
Minor, Marian Thomas *elementary and secondary school educational consultant*
Ragland, Ines Colom *principal*
Thoma, Colleen Ann *educator*
Whitfield, Patricia Ann Rainwater *education educator*

Roanoke
Barnes, Sharon D. *academic advisor, music educator*
Street, Terri Evans *counselor, consultant*

Rocky Mount
Nichols, Freda Carol *elementary school educator, artist*

Ruckersville
Clark, Mizell Phillips (Mitzi Clark) *school librarian*

South Hill
Brooks, Arlene Sheffield *secondary school educator*

Springfield
Leavitt, Mary Janice Deimel *special education educator, civic worker*

Staunton
Bryant, Brenda Louise *director, educator*

Sterling
Bartow, Nicole A. *secondary school educator*

Suffolk
Logan-Sutton, Floretta R. *elementary school educator*

Surry
Sprouse, Earlene Pentecost *special education educator*

Sweet Briar
Muhlenfeld, Elisabeth S. *college president, educator, author*

Vienna
Tordiff, Hazel Midgley *education director*

Virginia Beach
Baker, Claudia Muller *reading specialist*
Hughes, Lesley Lynne *assistant principal*
Jones, Felicia M. *director*
Kawczynski, Diane Marie *elementary and middle school educator, composer*
Kiernan, Margaret M. *adult education educator*
Von Mosch, Wanda Gail *middle school educator*
Weck, Mary Katherine *special education educator*

Warrenton
Greene, Cynthia Bain *elementary school educator*

Washington
Lamma, Candace McDaniel *guidance counselor, primary school educator, elementary school educator*

Williamsburg
Bell, Christine Marie *secondary educator*
Chandler, Kimberley Lynn *educational administrator*
Van Tassel-Baska, Joyce Lenore *education educator*

Yorktown
Douthat, Rebecca Arlene *secondary school educator*

WASHINGTON

Bellingham
Morse, Karen Williams *academic administrator*

Benton City
Kromminga, An-Marie *special education educator*

Carnation
Beshur, Jacqueline E. *special education educator*

Edmonds
Terry, Melinda Lee *elementary school educator*

Ellensburg
McIntyre, Jerilyn Sue *university administrator*

Everett
Brynildsen-Smith, Kristine Ann *principal*

Federal Way
Rossi, Ruth Harris *special education educator*

Kenmore
Montague, Deborah Marie *elementary school educator, music educator, consultant*

Kent
McGuire, Robin Christine *special education educator*

Lynnwood
Floten, Barbara Jean *educational dean*

Olympia
Bergeson, Teresa *school system administrator*

Outlook
Mears, Catherine Louise *principal*

Poulsbo
Pack, Nancy J. *special education educator, speech therapist*

Pullman
Mills, Paulette Everett *human development educator, consultant*
Petura, Barbara Bradley *academic administrator*

Puyallup
Phillips, Gail Susan *elementary school educator*

Rainier
Curtis, Suzanne M. *school system administrator, educator*

Seattle
Beaumonte, Phyllis Ilene *retired secondary school educator*
Cottingham, Mary Patricia *vocational rehabilitation counselor*
Fetterly, Mary E. *counseling administrator*
Ginorio, Angela Beatriz *university research administrator, educator*
Hegyvary, Sue Thomas *nursing school dean, editor, nursing educator*
Kelley, Lucille Marie Kindely *dean, psychosocial nurse*
Murdock, Tullisse Antoinette (Toni Murdock) *academic administrator*
Ostrom, Katherine Elma *retired educator*
Somerman, Martha J. *academic administrator*
Voegtlin-Anderson, Mary Margaret *secondary school educator, music educator*
Wick, Laurie Clare *director, consultant*
Wight, Julia Helen *secondary school educator*
Woods, Nancy Fugate *dean, women's health nurse, educator*

Sequim
McGee, Jane Marie *retired elementary school educator*

Snohomish
Sahlstrom, Jill Louise *elementary school educator*

Spanaway
Parker, Lynda Christine Rylander *secondary school educator*
Roberts-Dempsey, Patricia E. *secondary school educator*

Buckler, Marilyn Lebow *school psychologist, educational consultant*
Bullock, Molly *retired elementary school educator*
Bursley-Hamilton, Susan *secondary school educator*
Bush, Sandi Tokoa *elementary school educator*
Cameron, Lucille Wilson *retired dean*
Carlin, Betty *education educator*
Carlson, Alisa M. *secondary school educator*
Carr, Bessie *retired elementary school educator*
Casey, Darla Diann *elementary school educator*
Castiglia, Patricia Anne Thorson *dean, nursing educator*
Castor, Betty *academic administrator*
Castro, Sandra Ivette *special education educator*
Cawley, Juanita Sandgren *director*
Cawley, Patricia Blonts *secondary school educator*
Chandler, Alice *higher education consultant, university president*
Chappell, Annette M. *higher education consultant, minister*
Charlton, Shirley Marie *educational consultant*
Chaudoir, Jean Hamilton (Jean Hamilton) *secondary school educator*
Cheek, Barbara Lee *college reading program director, educator*
Childers, Carol Louise *elementary school educator, music educator, musician*
Childers, Pamela Barnard *secondary school educator*
Childers, Susan Lynn Bohn *special education educator, administrator, human resources and transition specialist, consultant*
Cimino, Ann Mary *education educator*
Clark, Barbara June *elementary school educator*
Clark, Paula Irene *elementary school educator, consultant*
Clark, Peggy Rillann *principal*
Clawson, Roxann Eloise *college administrator, computer company executive*
Cline, Janet E. Safford *school district administrator, desktop publisher*
Cline, Pauline M. *educational administrator*
Coen, Mary Ellen *adult education educator, secondary school educator, chemist*
Cohen, Shirley Mason *retired secondary school educator, volunteer*
Colage, Beatrice Elvira *education educator*
Cole, Nancy Stooksberry *educational research executive*
Coleman, Mary Sue *academic administrator*
Collinson, Vivienne Ruth *education educator, researcher, consultant*
Compton, Norma Haynes *retired university dean, artist*
Connelly, Amy Reece *career planning administrator, consultant*
Conover, Mona Lee *retired adult education educator*
Conover, Nancy Anderson *retired secondary school counselor*
Cook, Kathy H. *elementary school educator, conductor, composer*
Cook, Sister M(ary) Mercedes *secondary school educator, principal*
Cooper-González, Angela *counseling administrator*
Cornwell, Nancy Dunn *secondary school educator*
Corson, Mary Louise *special education educator*
Crawford, Helene Hope *elementary school principal*
Crews, Judith Young *career planning administrator*
Crosby, Marena Lienhard *retired college administrator*
Cross, Kathryn Patricia *education educator*
Crowder, Jane Nelson *middle school educator*
D'Angelo, Renée Young *special education educator*
Daniel, Winifred Yvonne *elementary school educator*
Davies-McNair, Jane *retired educational consultant*
Davion, Ethel Johnson *school system administrator, curriculum specialist*
Davis, Anna Jane Ripley *elementary school educator*
Davis, Charlotte MacLean *secondary school educator*
Davis, Diann Holmes *elementary school educator*
Davis, Jonni K. *secondary school educator, writer*
Davis, Karen Ann (Karen Ann Falconer) *special education educator*
Davis, Lisa Anne *secondary school educator*
Davis, Sharon Cade *secondary school educator*
Davis, Sue Ellen H. *elementary and secondary music educator*
Davis-Goga, Muriel E. *elementary school educator*
Dawson, Donna L. *secondary school educator*
Day, Victoria Lynn *principal*
Debs, Barbara Knowles *former college president, consultant*
Dent, Julie *director*
Derrickson, Denise Ann *secondary school educator, educator*
Detwiler, Christina LeFevre *elementary school educator*
DeVera, Gertrude Quenano *education educator*
Dewane-Pope, Peggy *elementary school educator, public relations executive, consultant*
D'Haiti, Felicia Kathleen (Felicia Kathleen Messina) *fine arts educator*
Diamond, Estelle *education educator, state legislator*
Dias, Mari Nardolillo *education educator, consultant*
Dickerson, Betty *secondary education educator, consultant, tester*
Dickey, Linda Ann *learning center director*
Diede, Norma Dale *retired private school educator*
Dike, Margaret Hopcraft *retired education administrator*
Dillon, Toni Ann *emotional support educator*
Dinkins, Jennifer Lynn *special education educator*
Dixon, Pauline K. *retired secondary school educator*
Dodds, Linda Carol *special education educator*
Dominick, Lisa Marie *elementary school educator*
Donaldson, Wilma Crankshaw *elementary school educator*
Dooreck, Lisa *special education educator, writer*
Dorsey, Rhoda Mary *retired academic administrator*
Dotson, Nancy Jean Davis *secondary school educator*
Douglas, Mary Younge Riley *retired secondary school educator*
Douglas, Roxanne Grace *secondary school educator*
Doviak, Ingrid Ellinger *elementary school educator*
Doyle, Judith Marie *principal*
Drake, Evelyn Downie *secondary school educator*
Dresbach, Mary Louise *state educational administrator*
Duffey, Rosalie Ruth *elementary school educator*
Duncan, Jennifer R. *secondary school educator*
Dwinell, Ann Jones *retired special education educator*
Dye, Linda Kaye *elementary school educator*
Eacho, Esther MacLively *special education educator*
Eason-Watkins, Barbara June *principal*
Eaton, Emma Parker *special education educator*
Ebrahim, Ada *special education educator*
Edens, Betty Joyce *reading recovery educator*
Edwards, Ardis Lavonne Quam *retired elementary education educator*
Edwards, Lynn A. *retired school system administrator*
Elliott, Cindy Sue *academic administrator*
Endicott, Jennifer Jane Reynolds *education educator*
Essa, Lisa Beth *elementary school educator*
Essig, Kathleen Susan *university official, management consultant*
Evans, Bonita Dianne *adult education educator*
Evans, Geraldine Ann *academic administrator*
Evans-Freed, Nancy Jane *secondary school educator*
Fair, Marcia Jeanne Hixson *retired educational administrator*
Faison, Lugenia Marion *special education educator*
Faucette, Merilon Cooper *retired secondary school educator*
Feldman, Lillian Maltz *early childhood education consultant*
Felty, Sharon J. *elementary school educator*
Filchock, Ethel *education educator*
Filomeno, Linda Jean Harvey *elementary school educator*
Fink, Alma *retired elementary education educator*
Fishburn, Janet Forsythe *university dean*
Fodrea, Carolyn Wrobel *educational researcher, publisher, consultant*
Foote-Kragbe, Marilyn *elementary school educator*
Ford, Loretta C. *retired dean, educator, consultant, nurse*
Ford, Natalie Ruth *education educator*
Forney, Virginia Sue *educational counselor*
Fowlkes, Janet Studard *secondary school educator*
Franey, Catherine T. *elementary school educator*
Frank, Jean Marie *educational administrator, researcher*
Franke-Barringer, Michele Annette *elementary school educator*
French, Candace Lee *elementary school educator, music educator*
Frey, Margo Walther *career counselor, columnist*
Fullerton, Gail Jackson *retired academic administrator*
Fusco, Aurilla Marie *director*
Gabel, Katherine *retired academic administrator*
Gammill, Kathryn Denise *elementary school educator*
Garber, Beth Carol *early childhood educator, music educator*
Garcia, Julia Theresa *secondary school educator*
Gedo, Julie *secondary school educator*
Gentilcore, Eileen Marie Belsito *elementary school principal*
Gershansky, Libby Meg *secondary school educator*
Gibson, Glenda Gale *special education educator, secondary school educator*
Gibson, Lisette L. *elementary school educator, music educator*
Giegel, Kathleen A. *elementary school educator*
Gilmore, Connie Sue *director*
Gittman, Elizabeth *education educator*
Glasgow, Karen *principal*
Glass, M. Susan *principal*
Glave, Dianne D. *education educator*
Glaze, Lynn Ferguson *development consultant*
Gleue, Lorine Anna *elementary school educator*
Glismann, Clementine *elementary school educator, researcher*
Goode, Janet Weiss *elementary school educator*
Goodman, Lillian Rachel *dean, nursing educator*
Gorelova, Linda M. *elementary school educator*
Gorman, Jane Marilyn *retired elementary school educator*
Goron, Mara J. *social studies educator, assistant principal*
Gosser-Drummond, Tara O. *counseling administrator, music educator*
Gouthro, Barbara Ann *elementary school educator*
Grady, Irene Hart *reading specialist*
Graham, Sylvia Swords *secondary school educator, retired*
Graves, Ruth Parker *educational executive, educator*
Gray, Hazel Irene *retired special education educator, counselor, consultant*
Greco, Margaret Elizabeth *secondary school educator*
Green, Patricia Pataky *school system administrator, consultant*
Greer, Cheryl L. *middle school educator*
Griffin, Gloria Jean *retired elementary school educator*
Griffin, Laura Mae *retired elementary and secondary school educator*
Grotto, Beth Anne *educational consultant*
Grove, Myrna Jean *elementary school educator*
Groves, B C *educational consultant, writer*
Groves, Bernice Ann *retired elementary and secondary school coordinator, educator*
Gudnitz, Ora M. Cofey *secondary school educator*
Guerrero, Olive Ciridon *retired educator, civic worker*
Gunning, Carolyn Sue *dean, provost, nursing educator*
Gustafson, Sandra Lynne *retired secondary school educator*
Haab, Lucille Helen *primary school educator*
Haas, Carolyn Buhai *elementary education educator, publisher, writer, consultant*
Hagerman, Lana Lee *reading educator*
Halamicek, Tina Marie *special education educator*
Hamilton, Sara Darlene *special education educator*
Hammer, Rebecca Elaine *secondary school educator*
Hand, Sharon S. *assistant principal*
Haneke, Dianne Myers *retired education educator*
Hanna, Noreen Anelda *retired adult education administrator, consultant*
Hanson, Jennifer Renee *elementary school educator, music educator*
Hardage, Page Taylor *elementary school educator*
Hare, Norma Q. *retired school system administrator*
Harper, Janet Sutherlin Lane *retired educational administrator, writer*
Harrington, Jean Patrice *college president*
Harris, Dolores M. *retired academic administrator*
Harris, Merle Wiener *college administrator, educator*
Harvey, Judith Gootkin *elementary school educator, real estate agent*
Hathcox, Cathy Brizendine *special education educator*
Haugland, Susan Warrell *education educator, consultant*
Haupt, Patricia A. *principal*
Hawkins, Jacquelyn *elementary and secondary education educator*
Hayden, Colleen *advanced placement secondary school educator*
Hazel, Mary Belle *university administrator*
Heap, Sylvia Stuber *adult education educator*
Heathcote, Diana Kay *special education educator*
Hedgecock, Jane Clarkson *secondary school educator*
Heinonen, Elana Rae *elementary school educator*
Heinrichs, Mary Ann *former dean*
Helm, Monica M. *elementary school educator, mental health therapist*
Henderson, Catherine Lynn *retired secondary education educator, writer*
Henricks, Mary Sigrid *retired elementary school educator*
Hensley, Patricia Drake *principal*
Herold, Rochelle Snyder *early childhood educator*
Hertel, Suzanne Marie *training and development specialist*
Hibbs, Dawn Wilcox *elementary school educator*
Hickman, Shirley Anna *secondary school educator*
Higginbotham, Elizabeth Rebecca Osborne *special education educator*
Higgins, Dorothy Marie *dean, educator*
Hill, Emita Brady *academic administrator, consultant*
Hillery, Susie Moore *retired elementary school educator*
Hines, Voncile *special education educator*
Hing, Barbara Lim *elementary school educator, assistant principal, data processing executive*
Hinman, Eve Caison *retired academic administrator*
Hinson, Claudia Burns *elementary school educator*
Hinton, Karolyn Kay *retired elementary school educator*
Hoberecht, Reynotta Jahnke *school system administrator, educator*
Hoff, Mary Ellen *educational consultant*
Hoffman, Judy Greenblatt *preschool director*
Holmes, Erline Morrison *retired educational administrator, consultant*
Holthaus, Joan Marie *elementary school educator*
Holtkamp, Susan Charlotte *elementary school educator*
Honanie, Jeannette *special education educator*
Hood, Luann Sandra *special education educator*
Horner, Matina Souretis *retired academic administrator, corporate financial executive*
Horton, Joann *academic administrator*
Horton-Wright, Alma Irene *retired elementary school educator*
Houseman, Ann Elizabeth Lord *educational administrator, state official*
Howard, Cynthia Stotts *adult education educator*
Hudalla, Karen *court reporting educator, academic administrator*
Huie, Carol P. *information systems educator*
Hull, Louise Knox *retired elementary educator, administrator*
Hummel, Marilyn Mae *elementary school educator*
Hundley, Jill L. *special education educator*
Hurlbut, Geraldine *retired elementary education educator*
Ingle, Beverly Dawn *elementary school educator*
Isbell, Rita Anette *special education educator*
Jackson, Clora Ellis *counselor, psychologist, educator*
Jackson, Heather *secondary school educator*
Jean, Claudette R. *retired elementary school educator*
Jefferson, Kathleen Henderson *retired secondary school educator*
Jenkins, Brenda Gwenetta *early childhood and special education specialist*
Jenkins, Sebetha *college president*
Jervis, Jane Lise *college official, science historian*
Jiles, Kendra D'Antoinette *special education educator*
Johnson, Brenda Ann *special education educator*
Johnson, Charlene Elizabeth *adult education educator, language arts consultant, educator*
Johnson, Linda Sue *academic administrator, state agency administrator, retired state legislator*
Johnson, Sylvia Sue *university administrator, educator*
Johnson Hirt, Jacqueline Marie *elementary school educator*
Johnson-MIller, Charleen V. *teacher coordinator*
Jolivette, Carola Kate *assistant principal*
Jonas, Trudy Ann *principal*
Kaabar, JoAnne Florence *special education educator, poet*
Kachur, Betty Rae *elementary school educator*
Kahn, Victoria Elaine Hopkins *special education educator*
Kaiser, Carlene Pearl *counseling administrator, media specialist*
Kaiser, Karen Sue *elementary school educator*
Kanyo, Deborah Sue *elementary school educator, music educator*
Kappner, Augusta Souza *academic administrator*
Kazmarek, Linda Adams *secondary school educator*
Keebler, Lois Marie *elementary school educator*
Keiper, Marilyn Morrison *elementary school educator*
Kelly, Sister Dorothy Ann *Ursuline Provincial college chancellor*
Kelly, Sister Mary Elizabeth *principal*
Kennedy, Colleen Michelle *academic administrator, educator*
Kercher, Kelli S. *special education educator*
Kerrigan, Kelly Ann *special education educator*
Keyes, Joan Ross Rafter *education educator, writer*
Killoran, Cynthia Lockhart *retired educator*
King, Bonnie La Verne *education educator*
Kirk, Rea Helene (Rea Helene Glazer) *special education educator*
Klein, Mary Ann *special education educator*
Kliebhan, Sister M(ary) Camille *academic administrator*
Kolakoski, Dawn Laymond *education educator, consultant, music educator*
Kolb, Dorothy Gong *elementary school educator*
Kosa, Jaymie Reeber *middle school educator*
Kramer, Carole Ree *retired special education educator*
Kranowitz, Carol Stock *pre-school educator, writer*
Krueger, Beth Ann *academic administrator*
Lacey, Vera Lavonne *secondary school educator, researcher, retired minister*
Lai, Feng-Qi *instructional designer, educator*
Lancaster, Jeanette (Barbara Lancaster) *dean, nursing educator*
Langley, Dawn Elaine *dean, writer*
Lanning, Yvonne Bradshaw *elementary school educator*
Lantz, Joanne Baldwin *retired academic administrator*
Lauer, Jeanette Carol *college dean, history educator, writer*
Lawrence, Sally Clark *retired academic administrator*
Leather, Victoria Potts *college librarian*
LeBlanc, Eugenia Talbert *counselor, educator*
LeBlanc, Victoria Anne *elementary school educator*
Ledet, Phyllis L. *educational administrator*
Lee, Barbara Catherine *career counselor*
Leidig, Margot Helene *retired elementary and secondary education educator*
Leslie, Maureen Heelan *university director*
Lester, Virginia Laudano *education administrator*
Light, Marion Jessel *retired elementary education educator*
Little, Claire Long *education educator, humanities educator*
Little, Teresa Clinton *special education educator*
Lockette, Daphney D. *elementary school educator*
Love, Sara Elizabeth *retired elementary school educator*
Lowenberg, Georgina Grace *retired elementary school educator*
Lowrie, Kathryn Yanacek *special education educator*
Lucente, Rosemary Dolores *retired academic administrator*
Luft, Cecile E. *music educator*
Lundin, Shirley Matcouff *pre-school administrator, adult education educator, consultant*
Lynam, Gloria *elementary school educator*
Lyne, Dorothy-Arden *secondary school educator*
Lynn, Naomi B. *academic administrator*
MacCormack, Jean F. *academic administrator*
Macklin, Ericka Monique *career planning administrator*

Zeilinger, Elna Rae *elementary educator, gifted-talented education educator*

ENGINEERING

UNITED STATES

ALABAMA

Huntsville
Archuleta, Nancy E. *engineering executive*
Buddington, Patricia Arrington *engineer*
Wu, Susan Ying Chu Lin (Ying-chu Lin) *engineering company executive, engineer*

Prichard
Williams, Wendy *civil engineer*

ARIZONA

Phoenix
Jackson, Barbara Ann *systems engineer*

Sun City West
Brown, Ruth Geisler *engineering supervisor*

Tempe
Papandreou-Suppappola, Antonia *electrical engineering educator*

Tucson
Gill, Rebecca LaLosh *aerospace engineer*

ARKANSAS

Little Rock
Bourgeois, Sharon E. *mechanical engineer*

CALIFORNIA

Anaheim
Fyda-Mar, Mary Catherine *systems engineer, director*

Belmont
Hollis, Mary Frances *aerospace educator*

Berkeley
Bajcsy, Ruzena *computer engineer*
Tommelein, Iris Denise *construction engineering and management educator, consultant*

Beverly Hills
Dragan, Alexandra *mechanical engineer, consultant, environmental engineer, researcher, engineering educator*

Edwards AFB
Baer-Riedhart, Jenny *aeronautical engineer*

Fullerton
Tehrani, Fleur Taher *electrical engineer, educator, researcher*

Irvine
Lin, Amy Yuh-Mei *industrial engineer, real estate investor*
Smedley, Keyue Ma *engineering educator, researcher*

Los Angeles
Simmons, Betty Jo *civil engineer, draftsman*

Marina Del Rey
Erten, Duygu *civil engineer, project manager, educator*

Menlo Park
Jeffries, Robin *computer engineer*

Moffett Field
Shaw, Tianna *biomedical engineer*
Yamauchi, Gloria *aerospace engineer*
Zuniga, Fanny *aerospace engineer*

Oxnard
Zhou, Sophia Huai *biomedical engineering scientist*

Palos Verdes Estates
Yarbrough, Allyson Debra *electrical engineer*

Pasadena
Harris, Jennifer A. *aerospace engineer*
Kornfield, Julia Ann *chemical engineering educator*
Tan-Wang, Grace *aeronautical engineer*

Pleasanton
Novak, Randi Ruth *engineer, computer scientist*

Riverside
Hackwood, Susan *electrical and computer engineering educator*

San Bernardino
Kirkland, Bertha Theresa *project engineer*

San Diego
Crocker, Valerie Marian *mechanical engineer*

San Francisco
Burkey, Marcia B. *engineering executive*
Kammerer, Ann Marie *geotechnical engineer*

San Gabriel
Tomich-Bolognesi, Vera *engineering executive*

San Jose
Ma, Xing *optical engineer*
Phan, Christina *electronic analog design executive*

Santa Barbara
Hu, Evelyn Lynn *electrical and computer engineering educator*

Santa Monica
Brauner, Marygail K. *engineer, systems analyst*

Seal Beach
Wiley, Dianne *aeronautical engineer*

Stanford
Zhou, Ping *physical engineer*

Temecula
Bathaee, Soussan *engineering technician*

Topanga
Norwood, Virginia Tower *retired engineer*

Torrance
Sorstokke, Susan Eileen *systems engineer*

COLORADO

Boulder
Avery, Susan Kathryn *electrical engineering educator, research administrator*

Englewood
Sideman, Jill *engineering executive*

Golden
Gosink, Joan P. *engineering educator*

Highlands Ranch
Brierley, Corale L. *geological engineer*

Littleton
Stamile, Jennifer *materials engineer*

Loveland
Nossaman, Marian Alecia *manufacturing engineering executive*

CONNECTICUT

New Britain
Czajkowski, Eva Anna *aerospace engineer, educator*

Waterford
Hinkle, Muriel Ruth Nelson *naval warfare analysis company executive*

DISTRICT OF COLUMBIA

Washington
Campbell, Patricia Lindsey *mechanical engineer, lawyer*
Cleave, Mary L. *environmental engineer, former astronaut*
Freund, Deborah Miriam *transportation engineer*
Marechaux, Toni Grobstein *engineer, consultant*
Townsend, Marjorie Rhodes *aerospace engineer, business executive*

FLORIDA

Boca Raton
Pajunen, Grazyna Anna *electrical engineer, educator*
Zhong, Dawn He *materials engineer*

Fort Lauderdale
Schear, Betty Z. *engineering executive, consultant*

Jacksonville
Costin, Rea-Silvia *civil engineer*

Miami
Gonzalez, Ivette *biomedical engineer*

Orlando
Bauer, Maria Casanova *computer engineer*

Pensacola
Garrett, Vikki Rae *transportation planner*

GEORGIA

Alpharetta
Salay, Cindy Rolston *systems engineer*

Atlanta
Ehrlich, Margaret Isabella Gorley *systems engineer, mathematics educator, consultant*
Perry, Kathryn Abbott *telecommunications engineer*

Decatur
Holtzman, Mary *engineering company executive*

Marietta
Eggersman, Denise *computer engineer, educator*

Robins AFB
Manley, Nancy Jane *environmental engineer*

Senoia
Griffin, Tammy Lynn *industrial engineer*

ILLINOIS

Belleville
Thien-Stasko, Vicki Lynn *civil engineer technician*

Chicago
Fahnestock, Jean Howe *retired civil engineer*

Quincy
Cornell, Helen W. *manufacturing company executive*

Skokie
Siegal, Rita Goran *engineering company executive*

INDIANA

Auburn
Bash, Danielle Renee *quality control engineer*

Carmel
Ashcraft, Nancy Olson *mining engineer*

Corydon
Speth, Camille *engineer*

Granger
Yared, Linda S. *mechanical engineer*

La Porte
Stoler, Dorothy Anne *engineer*

West Lafayette
Taber, Margaret Ruth *retired electrical engineering technology educator, electrical engineer*

IOWA

Davenport
Pedersen, Karen Sue *electrical engineer*

KANSAS

Overland Park
Daniel, Karen *engineering and design company executive*

KENTUCKY

Lexington
Campbell, Zenita A. D. *environmental engineer, educator, safety engineer*

LOUISIANA

New Orleans
Keller, Deborah Ducote *civil engineer*
O'Connor, Kim Claire *chemical engineering and biotechnology educator, researcher, inventor*

MARYLAND

Annapolis
Trescott, Sara Lou *water resources engineer*

Annapolis Junction
Nejib, Perri Umid-Rashid *electrical engineer*

Baltimore
Busch-Vishniac, Ilene Joy *mechanical engineering educator, researcher*
Jenniches, F. Suzanne *engineering executive*

Bel Air
Powers, Doris Hurt *retired engineering company executive*

Bethesda
Nimeroff, Phyllis Ruth *electronic engineer, visual artist*

College Park
Lathan, Corinna Elisabeth *aerospace engineer*

Greenbelt
Amato, Deborah Douglass *aerospace engineer*

MASSACHUSETTS

Cambridge
Drake, Elisabeth Mertz *chemical engineer, consultant*
Leveson, Nancy G. *aeronautical engineer*
Nightingale, Deborah Seifert *systems engineer, consultant*
Samson, Leona D. *biological engineering educator, research center director, researcher*

Framingham
Lindsay, Leslie *packaging engineer*

Medford
Abriola, Linda M. *civil engineer, environmental engineer*

South Hadley
Randall, Hermine Maria *retired power plant engineer*

Wilmington
Raven, Linda F. *mechanical engineer*

MICHIGAN

Dearborn
Linnansalo, Vera *engineer*
Wang, Liyan *product design engineer*

Farmington Hills
Hurd, Mary K. *civil engineer, writer*

MINNESOTA

Grand Marais
Napadensky, Hyla Sarane *engineering consultant*

Minneapolis
French, Catherine E. Wolfgram *engineering educator, researcher*
Hawley, Sandra Sue *electrical engineer*

MISSOURI

Hannibal
Richmond, Deborah Vance *civil engineer*

Kansas City
Leigh, Cheri J. *engineering consulting executive*

Saint Louis
Olsen, Tava Maryanne Lennon *industrial and operations engineering educator*
Shrauner, Barbara Wayne Abraham *electrical engineer, educator*

MONTANA

Bozeman
Billau, Robin Louise *engineering and consulting executive*

NEBRASKA

Omaha
Heim, Megan Alyssa *biomedical engineer*

NEVADA

Dayton
Clements, Linda L. *materials engineer, educator, journalist*

Las Vegas
Thomas, Helen Hazer *electrical engineer*

NEW HAMPSHIRE

Hanover
Garmire, Elsa Meints *electrical engineering educator, consultant*

Wolfeboro
Hutchins, Carleen Maley *acoustical engineer, consultant*

NEW JERSEY

Newark
Brazil, Aine M. *engineering company executive*

Princeton
Galloway, Patricia Denese *civil engineer*

Skillman
Brill, Yvonne Claeys *engineer, consultant*

NEW MEXICO

Albuquerque
Fuchs, Beth Ann *research engineer*

NEW YORK

Brooklyn
Nakanishi, Yuko Julie *engineering educator, consultant*

Delmar
Campas, Anna Penelope *civil engineer, architect*

Flushing
Unsal-Tunay, Nuran *geological engineer, researcher*

Middle Island
Crowder, Lillie Mae Brown *retired architectural engineer*

New York
Perez, Julie Anna *audio engineer*
See, Saw-Teen *structural engineer*

Niskayuna
Fitzroy, Nancy deLoye *engineering executive, mechanical engineer*

Rochester
Niznik, Carol Ann *electrical engineer, educator, consultant*

South Bethlehem
Shirikian-Hesselton, Joan Lee *safety engineer*

Valhalla
Keesler, Deborah Elizabeth *civil engineer*

NORTH CAROLINA

Chapel Hill
Lucas, Carol Lee *biomedical engineer*

Hendersonville
Kingsbury, Carolyn Ann *aerospace engineer, craftsman, writer*

Pembroke
Tyner, Bessie Hubbard *mechanical engineer, mathematician*

Raleigh
Nelson, Cynthia Kaye *infrastructure security engineer*

OHIO

Chandlersville
Herron, Janet Irene *industrial manufacturing engineer*

Cincinnati
Curran, Mary Ann *chemical engineer*
Isburgh, Anne Marie *engineering manager*

Cleveland
Olson, Sandra *aerospace engineer*

East Liberty
Head, Teresa Rena *electrical engineer*

Marysville
Baik-Kromalic, Sue S. *metallurgical engineer*

Wright Patterson Afb
Chelette, Tamara Lynne *biomedical engineer*

Youngstown
Kenner, Marilyn Sferra *civil engineer*

OREGON

Forest Grove
Ginn, Sharon Patrick *mechanical engineer*

Lake Oswego
Marietta, Elizabeth Ann *industrial engineer*

PENNSYLVANIA

Erie
Andrian-Ceciu, Roxanne R. *engineer, program manager*

Philadelphia
Winston, Flaura K. *engineering researcher*

University Park
Irwin, Mary Jane *engineering educator*
Todd Copley, Judith A. *materials and metallurgical engineering educator*

Wallingford
Parker, Jennifer Ware *chemical engineer, researcher*

SOUTH CAROLINA

Aiken
Johnston, Carolyn Judith *construction engineer*

Goose Creek
Todoro, Mary Elizabeth *process engineer*

Greenville
Stoller, Patricia Sypher *structural engineer, engineering executive*
Wang, Ming De *engineer*

SOUTH DAKOTA

Brookings
Hall, Teresa Joanne Keys *manufacturing engineer, educator*

TENNESSEE

Arlington
Lake, Martha M. *engineer*

Greeneville
Dannecker, Tanja Michaela *electrical engineer*

Knoxville
Garrison, Arlene Allen *engineering executive, engineering educator*

Memphis
Demir, Semahat Siddika *engineering educator*

Oak Ridge
Fox, Janie *environmental engineer*

Tullahoma
Hill, Susan Sloan *safety engineer*

TEXAS

Arlington
Liu, Hanli *biomedical engineer, educator*

Austin
Brannon-Peppas, Lisa *chemical engineer, researcher*

Richards-Kortum, Rebecca Rae *biomedical engineering educator*

Beaumont
Mueller, Lisa Maria *chemical engineer*

Cat Spring
Ramsey, Mary Catherine *mechanical engineer, consultant*

College Station
Lu, Mi *computer engineer, educator*

Dallas
Gass, Wanda *engineering executive*
Wang, Cong *electrical engineer*

Fort Worth
Roberson, Janet L. *aircraft manufacturing company official*

Grapevine
Blair, Sylvia H. *computer project engineer, small business owner*

Houston
Carrillo, Laurie Yvette *aerospace engineer*
Dunbar, Bonnie J. *engineer, astronaut*
Ehlig-Economides, Christine A. *petroleum engineer*
Johnson, Sandra G. *engineering company executive*
Kavandi, Janet Lynn *aerospace power engineer, chemist*
Kiang, Ching-Hwa *chemical engineering educator*
Yiu, Fang *structural engineer, researcher*

Irving
McCormack, Grace Lynette *civil engineering technician*

Plano
Stone, Juanita Jane *telecommunications engineer*

Stafford
Le, Duy-Loan *electrical engineer*

Tyler
Walker, Alice R. *mechanical engineer*

UTAH

Brigham City
Tolle, Melinda Edith *engineer, scientist*

VERMONT

Rutland
Thompson, Marie Angela *computer engineer, consultant*

VIRGINIA

Alexandria
Rassai, Rassa *electrical engineering educator*

Arlington
Park, Susan Young *radar systems engineer*

Falls Church
Thomas, Lydia Waters *research and development executive*

Hampton
Amer, Tahani R. *aerospace engineer*
Bangert, Linda S. *aeronautical engineer*
Fay, Catharine C. *aerospace engineer*

Hayes
Martinez Fallon, Alma Urania *mechanical engineer*

Lynchburg
Groshner, Maria Star *nuclear engineer*

Newport News
Noblitt, Nancy Anne *aerospace engineer*

Reston
Young, Janet Cheryl *electrical engineer*

WASHINGTON

Bellingham
Graves, Vicki Lloyd *retired mechanical engineer*

Chelan
Korn, Theresa Marie *former electrical engineer, consulting firm co-owner, technical writer*

Olympia
Fleskes, Carol Lynn *environmental engineer*
Mylroie, Willa Wilcox *transportation engineer, regional planner*

Seattle
Kalonji, Gretchen *engineering educator*
Shirley, Donna *former aerospace engineer, management consultant, speaker*
Trenkler, Tina Louise *nuclear engineer*

Spokane
Nemetz Mills, Patricia Louise *engineer, educator*

CANADA

BRITISH COLUMBIA

Vancouver
Salcudean, Martha Eva *mechanical engineer, educator*

ADDRESS UNPUBLISHED

Amancio, Ruth Carson *safety engineer*
Baum, Eleanor *electrical engineering educator, academic administrator*
Becerra-Fernandez, Irma *electrical engineer, researcher, educator*
Brozowski, Laura Adrienne *mechanical engineer*
Chretien, Carol Ann *chemical engineer*
Cross, Goldie K. *telecommunications engineer*
Cullingford, Hatice Sadan *chemical engineer*
Cummins, Nancyellen Heckeroth *electronics engineer*
Davis, Keigh Leigh *aerospace engineer*
Dennany, Kelly *mechanical engineer, test engineer*
Dorighi, Nancy S. *computer engineer*
Estrin, Thelma Austern *retired electrical engineer*
Francis, Juanita Rose *environmental engineer, chemist*
Gant, Lesyle K. *systems engineer*
Gimpelson, Laura J. *environmental engineer, safety engineer*
Hanson, Wendy Karen *retired chemical engineer*
Herrin, Stephanie Ann *retired aerospace engineer, astrobiotical engineer*
Hornby-Anderson, Sara Ann *metallurgical engineer, marketing professional*
Jackson, Nicole Renée *mechanical engineer, educator*
Jordan, Tamecia Michelle *computer engineer*
Killen, Kathleen Elizabeth *systems engineer, retired military officer*
Kimbriel-Eguia, Susan *engineering planner, small business owner*
Longobardo, Anna Kazanjian *engineering executive*
Lyon, Martha Sue *research engineer, retired military officer*
McCafferty, Lorna Marie (Lorna Supernor) *computer electronics engineer*
Moore, Fay Linda *systems engineer*
Morse, Terri Fraser *engineering administrator*
Muhammad, LaTonja Walker *control engineer*
Murphy, Elisabeth Maria *physical design engineer*
Muszynska, Agnieszka (Agnes Muszynska) *mechanical engineering researcher, consultant*
Noonan, Shauna Gay *petroleum engineer*
O'Brien, K. Patricia *product development engineer*
Parashak, Debra Sue *civil engineer*
Rogers, Stacey A. *mechanical engineer*
Seldner, Betty Jane *environmental engineer, consultant, aerospace transportation executive*
Stallings, Viola Patricia Elizabeth *systems engineer, educational systems specialist, retired information technology manager*
Stoica, Susana *computer/electrical engineer, scientist, author, healer*
Wang, Qin *computer engineer, researcher*
Ying, Jackie *chemical engineer, educator*

FINANCE: BANKING SERVICES
See also FINANCE: INVESTMENT SERVICES

UNITED STATES

ALABAMA

Blountsville
Edwards, Sheila M. *banker, educator*

ALASKA

Fairbanks
Heckman, Jyotsna (Jo) L. *bank executive*

ARIZONA

Mesa
Winn, Kathleen Ann *bank officer, real estate broker*

Phoenix
Ralston, Barbara Jo *bank executive*
Stewart, Patricia Ann *banker*

Tucson
Bernmúdez, Carmen *trust company executive*

ARKANSAS

Little Rock
Franks, Candace Ann *bank executive*

CALIFORNIA

Beverly Hills
Spivak, Jacque R. *bank executive*

Carlsbad
Schmidt, Mary Louise Donnel *bank officer*

Carson
Davis, Carylon Lee *mortgage company executive, real estate broker*

Concord
Thompson, Tracy Lee *bank executive, voice educator*

Lakewood
Kozakiewicz, Sandi *bank executive*

Los Angeles
Brown, Kathleen *bank executive, lawyer*
Torres, Cynthia Ann *banker*

Oakland
Nelson, Shirley W. *bank executive*
Sandler, Marion Osher *savings and loan association executive*

San Diego
Lindh, Patricia Sullivan *banker, former government official*
McNeely, Delores *banker*

San Francisco
August-deWilde, Katherine *banker*
Braasch, Barbara Lynn *banker, consultant*
Callahan, Patricia R. *bank executive*
Gillette, Frankie Jacobs *retired savings and loan executive, social worker, government administrator*
Ho, Doreen Woo *bank executive*
Lee, Pamela Anne *bank executive, accountant, business analyst*
Tolstedt, Carrie L. *bank executive*
Yao, Hilda Maria Hsiang *banker, strategic planner*

Santa Clara
Kamm, Barbara B. *bank executive*

Santa Monica
Heimbuch, Babette E. *bank executive*

COLORADO

Brighton
Tyrrell-Meier, Cassandra B. *banker*

Denver
Childears, Linda *banker*
Orullian, B. LaRae *bank executive*

Georgetown
Hildebrandt-Willard, Claudia Joan *banker*

Lakewood
Weskamp, Kelley S. *loan account manager, real estate company executive*

CONNECTICUT

New Haven
Patterson, Peyton R. *bank executive*

Waterbury
Bachman, Carol Christine *trust company executive*

DISTRICT OF COLUMBIA

Washington
Helfer, Ricki Tigert *banking consultant*
Heumann, Judith *bank executive*
St. John, Julie *mortgage company executive*

FLORIDA

Hollywood
Kelly, Cleo Parker *retired bank executive*

Jacksonville
Hott, Peggy A. *mortgage banker*

Naples
Kvetko, Colleen M. *bank executive*

Ormond Beach
Franchini, Roxanne *bank executive*

Palm Beach
Harper, Mary Sadler *financial advisor*

GEORGIA

Atlanta
Biggins, J. Veronica *bank executive*
Chau, Pin Pin *bank executive*
Halwig, Nancy Diane *banker*
Hayworth, Laura *bank officer, real estate analyst*

Columbus
James, Elizabeth R. *bank executive*

Flowery Branch
Monroe, Melrose *retired bank executive*

HAWAII

Honolulu
Tanoue, Donna A. *bank executive, former federal agency administrator*

ILLINOIS

Chicago
Hart, Pamela Heim *banker*
Lorenz, Katherine Mary *bank executive*
Moody, Susan R. *bank executive*
Thomas, Cynthia C. *mortgage company executive*

Dundee
Weck, Kristin Willa *bank executive*

Elk Grove Village
Finney, Ann Jung *bank executive*

Oak Brook
Iles, Eileen Marie *bank executive*

Springfield
Giamanco, Scherrie V *bank executive*

Vernon Hills
Beckles, Ingrid *mortgage banker*

IOWA

Cedar Rapids
Wax, Nadine Virginia *retired bank executive*

Mason City
Rodamaker, Marti Tomson *bank executive*

KANSAS

Coldwater
Adams, Elizabeth Herrington *banker*

Overland Park
Whitaker, Freda N. *trust company executive*

Scott City
Berning, Louise Justine *bank executive*

Tonganoxie
Torneden, Connie Jean *bank officer*

Topeka
Wagnon, Joan *banker, former mayor*

KENTUCKY

Georgetown
White, Mary Ann *bank executive*

Louisville
Thompson, Kathy C. *bank executive*

MARYLAND

Annapolis
Schleicher, Nora Elizabeth *banker, treasurer, accountant*

Frederick
Cannon, Faye E. *bank executive*

North East
Goldbach, Jennifer D. *bank executive*

Potomac
Schonholtz, Joan Sondra Hirsch *banker, civic worker*

MASSACHUSETTS

Boston
Mullin, Patricia Jones *banker*
Szostak, M. Anne *bank executive*

Pittsfield
Fawcett, Gayle P. *bank executive*

Raynham
Worrell, Cynthia Lee *bank executive*

MICHIGAN

Clarkston
Snow, Sandra Inez *mortgage company executive*

Detroit
Greenwood, Harriet Lois *environmental banker, researcher*

Grosse Pointe Park
Harmon, Phyllis Darnell *mortgage banker*

MINNESOTA

Golden Valley
Lester, Susan E. *bank executive*

Minneapolis
Carlson, Jennie Peaslack *bank executive*
Griffith, Sima Lynn *investment banker, consultant*

MISSOURI

Saint Louis
Bockenkamp, Karen Ann *bank administrator*
Bryant, Ruth Alyne *banker*

NEBRASKA

Waterloo
O'Brien, Nancy Lynn *bank executive*

NEVADA

Las Vegas
Hansen, Janet M. *bank executive*

NEW JERSEY

Jackson
Gasparro, Madeline *banker*

Newton
Case, Tammy *bank executive*

Trenton
Bakke, Holly *bank commission official*

NEW YORK

Long Island City
Markus, Maura *bank executive*

New York
Bains, Leslie Elizabeth *banker*
Barry, Nancy Marie *bank executive*
Casey, Karen Anne *banker*
Considine, Jill *banker*
Dogancay, Angela *banker*
Drew, Ina R. *bank executive*
Dublon, Dina *bank executive*
Eshleman, Diane Varrin *bank executive*
Flaherty, Pamela Potter *bank executive*
Flynn, Elizabeth E. *bank executive*
Godridge, Leslie V. *bank executive*
Hricik, Lorraine E. *bank executive*
Hughes, Norah Ann O'Brien *bank securities executive*
Lagomasino, Maria Elena *bank executive*
Magner, Marjorie *bank executive*
Myerberg, Marcia *investment banker*
Prager-Kamel, Nancy Ann *investment banker, artist, business development firm executive*
Putney, Mary Lynn *bank administrator, educator*
Rzeszotarski, Pamela Sue (Pamela Sue Dougherty) *banker*
Schless, Phyllis Ross *investment banker*
Scott, Margaret Simon *retired mortgage broker*
Sevilla-Sacasa, Frances Aldrich *bank executive*
Storey, Susan Lynne *investment banker*
von Fraunhofer-Kosinski, Katherina *bank executive*
Wainwright, Cynthia Crawford *banker*
Webster, Lesley Daniels *bank executive*

Yonkers
Singer, Cecile Doris *bank executive, former state legislator*

NORTH CAROLINA

Charlotte
Bessant, Catherine Pombier *bank executive, marketing professional*
Brinkley, Amy Woods *bank executive*
Clark, Ranjana B. *bank executive*
Davis, Jean E. *bank executive*
Desoer, Barbara J. *bank executive*
Erwin, Betty *bank executive*
Lehman, Alice *bank executive*
Nichols, Debra *bank executive*
Sutton, Cecilia (Cece Sutton) *bank executive*
Wilson, Constance Kramer *bank officer*

OHIO

Cleveland
Potter, Susan K. *bank executive*
Seifert, Shelley Jane *bank executive, human resources specialist*

Columbus
Johnson, Julia F. *bank executive*

New Albany
Page, Linda Kay *bank executive*

Newark
Wallace, Sarah Reese *banker*

OREGON

Bend
Moss, Patricia L. *bank executive*

Medford
Lantis, Donna Lea *retired banker, art educator, artist*

Wilsonville
McKay, Laura L. *banker, consultant*

PENNSYLVANIA

Philadelphia
Bogaczyk, Kathryn *conversion specialist, executive, consultant*
Cohen, Betsy Z. *bank executive*

Pittsburgh
Gulley, Joan Long *banker*

SOUTH CAROLINA

Columbia
Gasque, Diane Phillips *mortgage manager*

TEXAS

Allen
Clifton, Melanie Fairlight *bank executive*
Fryman, Alison Leigh *bank executive*

Bedford
Newell, Karin Barnes *bank executive*

Houston
Ellis, Juliet S. *bank executive*
Ghiglieri, Catherine A. *auto loan company executive*
Thomas, M. Ann *bank executive*

VERMONT

Chester
Carey, Erron J. *merchant banker, state representative*

VIRGINIA

Arlington
Ochoa-Brillembourg, Hilda Margarita *investment banker*

Charlottesville
Frye, LaToya Aisha Hortense *banking administrator*

Newport News
Ward, Judy Kitchen *bank executive*

Virginia Beach
Duke, Elizabeth (Betsy) A. *bank executive*

WASHINGTON

Everett
Nelson, Carol Kobuke *bank executive*

Port Angeles
McCormick, Karen Louise *savings and loan association executive*

Seattle
Oppenheimer, Deanna Watson *bank executive*

Spokane
Horton, Susan Pittman *bank executive*

WISCONSIN

Milwaukee
Murphy, Judith Chisholm *trust company executive*

Racine
Rupinski, Janette Marie *banker*

Sauk City
Lins, Debra *bank executive*

CANADA

ONTARIO

Toronto
Denham, Jill H. *bank executive*
Lawson, Jane Elizabeth *bank executive*
Story, Susan *merchant banker*

INDIA

Fort Mumbai
Woodard, Nina Elizabeth *banker*

ADDRESS UNPUBLISHED

Baker, Lesliegh *bank officer, lawyer*
Cottrell, Mary-Patricia Tross *bank executive*
Derrico, Georgia Santangelo *banker*
Fahringer, Catherine Hewson *retired savings and loan association executive*
Figlar, Anita Wise *retired bank executive*
Flugger, Penelope Ann *banker*
Friars, Eileen M. *bank executive*
Gillard, Beryl L. *mortgage company executive*
Hayes, Mary Phyllis *retired savings and loan association executive*
Kane Hittner, Marcia Susan *bank executive*
Kaplan, Grisel Arias *bank executive*
Lawer, Betsy *banker*
McKinnie, Nancy Elliott *bank executive*
Morris, Maureen Sauter *bank officer*
Owen, Suzanne *retired savings and loan association executive*
Parks, Grace Susan *bank official*
Peretsman, Nancy B. *investment banker*
Place, Janey *banking consultant, former bank executive*
Romero-Rainey, Rebeca *bank executive*
Salamone-Kochowicz, Jean Gloria *retired bank executive*
Seeds, Sharon Lynn *bank processor*
Tatlock, Anne M. *trust company executive*
Tremaglio, Michelle T. *merchant banker*

Walton, Alice L. *bank executive*
Wilson, S. Liane *bank executive*
Worrell, Mary Thora *loan officer*

FINANCE: FINANCIAL SERVICES

UNITED STATES

ALABAMA

Carrollton
Winters, Janice Joyner *accountant*

Daphne
Neese, Kristal Ann *comptroller*

Decatur
Michelini, Sylvia Hamilton *auditor*

Gadsden
Freeman, Peggy Renea *accountant*

Headland
Woodham, Patricia H. *accounting and business consultant*

Huntsville
Stewart, Verlindsey Laquetta *accounting educator*

Jacksonville
Lewis, Deborah Alice *tax company executive, writer*

Tuscaloosa
Ray, Nelda Howton *financial consultant*

ALASKA

Kodiak
Steffey, A Kay *accountant*

ARIZONA

Phoenix
Jungbluth, Connie Carlson *wealth strategist*
Richardson, Judy McEwen *education administrator, consultant, cartoonist*

Sun City
Larkin, Mary Sue *financial planner*

Sun City West
Schrag, Adele Frisbie *business education educator*

Tucson
Brasswel, Kerry *tax accountant*
Fajardo, Sarah Elizabeth Johnson *financial consultant*

ARKANSAS

Hot Springs Village
Lihs, Marilyn Louise *retired accountant*

Little Rock
Conger, Cynthia Lynne *financial planner*
Waters, Zenobia Pettus *retired finance educator*

CALIFORNIA

Atwater
Duddy, E. Eileen *accountant*

Brentwood
Fridley, Saundra Lynn *private investigator*

Burbank
Sherbert, Sharon Debra *financial services executive*

Carlsbad
Buckley, Greta Paula *auditor*

Claremont
Christian, Suzanne Hall *financial planner*

Covina
Cottrell, Janet Ann *controller*

Culver City
Abarbanell, Gayola Havens *financial planner*

Diamond Bar
Cha, Grace Seungyun *financial company executive*

Dublin
Ferrari, Tamara W. *benefits compensation analyst*

El Sobrante
Withrow, Sherrie Anne *financial specialist*

Hollister
Grace, Bette Frances *certified public accountant*

Inglewood
Patmore, Kimberly S. *financial services executive*

Irvine
Craig, Karen Lynn *accountant, controller*

McPhillen, Lauri *financial analyst, product manager, educator*

La Jolla
Dorsey, Dolores Florence *retired corporate treasurer, business executive*

Laguna Beach
Pories, Muriel H. *business executive, loan consultant*

Laguna Niguel
Bauer, Barbara A. *financial consultant*

Lakewood
Bogdan, Carolyn Louetta *financial specialist*

Lincoln
Dorn, Mary Ann *retired auditor*

Los Altos
Sanchez, Marla Rena *retired controller*

Los Angeles
Allen, Suzanne *financial planning executive, insurance agent, writer*
O'Brien, Rosanne P. *corporate financial executive*
Porper, Mary *comptroller*
Williams, Julie Ford *mutual fund officer*

Napa
Gillespie, Marcia Lou *tax specialist, accountant, musician*

Oak Park
Kavesh, Eden *fraud investigator, financial consultant*

Oakland
Randisi, Elaine Marie *accountant, educator, writer*
Tran, Nguyet T. *accountant*

Oceanside
McIntyre, Louise S. *income tax consultant*

Palmdale
Rosete, Amy Renee *accountant, writer, editor*

Pasadena
Hunt, Hazel Analue Stanfield *retired accountant*

Pittsburg
Williams, Elizabeth A. *financial planner, business consultant*

Pleasanton
Hilton, Shirley Shin Sil *controller*

Rancho Cucamonga
Horsley, Paula Rosalie *accountant*

Rancho Palos Verdes
Hughs, Mary Geraldine *accountant, social service specialist*

Riverside
Macek, Pamela Kay *tax specialist, business executive*

Sacramento
Kulp, Sherrill Irene *business educator, consultant*
Scholey, Diann Patricia *accountant*
Tom, Gail *business educator*
Wunder, Haroldene Fowler *taxation educator*

Salinas
Sprude, Margaret *credit services company executive*

San Diego
Buska, Sheila Mary *controller, writer, columnist*
Drzewiecki, Darla Ruth *accountant*
Gengor, Virginia Anderson *financial planning executive, educator*
Hollingsworth, Margaret Camille *financial services administrator, consultant*
Lucas, Eloisa B. *tax consultant, management consultant*

San Francisco
Duncan, Deborah L. *finance company executive*
Kahn, Linda McClure *actuary, consultant*
Lynn, Evadna Saywell *investment analyst*
Richey, Ellen *credit card company executive*
Silverman, Victoria Lillian *consultant, fundraiser, cultural organization administrator*
Tornese, Judith M. *financial institution executive*
Zobel, Jan A. *tax consultant*

San Marino
Gouw, Julia Suryapranata *accountant*

San Ramon
King Hauser, Ann Marie B. *retired controller, artist*

Sherman Oaks
Ferguson, Lisa Beryl *accountant*
Klimas, Elizabeth Jolanta *accountant, lawyer, economist*

Simi Valley
McBride, Joyce Browning *accountant*

Suisun City
Schunke, Hildegard Heidel *accountant*

Vista
Ferguson, Margaret Ann *tax consultant*

Woodland Hills
Wiesner, Carol A. *financial services company executive*

COLORADO

Boulder
Friedman, Pamela Ruth Lessing *financial consultant, writer*

Colorado Springs
Rowan, Cynthia L. Reeves *accountant*

Denver
Dancik, Jo Marie *accountant, accounting company executive*
Lahey, Bonita Louise *marketing and operations consultant*

Evergreen
Saxton, Mary Jane *management educator*

Fort Collins
Thomas, Jeanette Mae *public accountant*

Grand Junction
Sewell, Beverly Jean *financial executive*

Lakewood
Nichols, Vicki Anne *financial consultant, librarian*

Littleton
Ryan, Evonne Ianacone *capital management company executive*

Wheat Ridge
Leino, Deanna Rose *business educator*

CONNECTICUT

East Hartford
Barredo, Rita M. *auditor*

Greenwich
Nockler, Linda A. *corporate financial executive*

Hartford
Glover, Ann B. *finance company executive*
Souza, Diane D *corporate financial executive*

Milford
Demarais, Karin *financial analyst*

New Britain
Detmar-Pines, Gina Louise *business strategy and policy educator*

New Haven
Snataro, Sandra Elizabeth *business educator, consultant*

Newington
Foley, Patricia Jean *accountant*

Stamford
Goodkin, Deborah Gay *corporate financial executive*
Jason, J. Julie *portfolio manager, writer, lawyer*
Ryan, Theresa Ann Julia *accountant*

Westport
McElroy, Abby Lucille Wolman *financial advisor*
Simone, Albertina *accountant*

Woodbridge
Vasileff, Lili Alexandra *financial planner*

DELAWARE

Wilmington
Rogoski, Patricia Diana *financial executive*

DISTRICT OF COLUMBIA

Washington
Armstrong, Alexandra *financial advisor*
Bondurant, Amy Laura *retired corporate financial executive*
Brown-Daniels, Patricia *budget analyst, wedding consultant*
Campbell, Ruth Ann *retired budget analyst*
Deaton, Valerie L. *financial researcher, consultant*
DuCran, Claudette Deloris *retired financial analyst*
Garcia, Frances *accountant*
Gupta, Tanya *financial analyst*
Knight, Linda K. *financial company executive*
Logan, Ann D. *financial company executive*
Morgan, Joan *financial planner*
Springer, Linda *portfolio manager, controller*
Tolmachoff, Willadene *accountant, auditor*
White, Margit Triska *financial advisor*
Zenker, Wendy *financial executive*

FLORIDA

Boca Raton
Pradere, Sonia *accounting administrator*

Cocoa Beach
Wirtschafter, Irene Nerove *tax specialist, consultant*

Deerfield Beach
Moran, Patricia Genevieve *corporate executive*

Fort Lauderdale
Castro, Stephanie L. *business management educator*
Platt, Ellen L. *financial planner*

Fort Pierce
Garde, Susan Reutershan *accountant*

Indian Shores
Browne, A. Pauline *accountant, writer*

Jacksonville
Duncan, Shirley A. *portfolio manager*
Van Deusen, Cheryl A. *business educator, consultant*

Lauderdale By The Sea
Kennedy, Beverly (Kleban) Burris *financial advisor, television and radio personality*

Miami
Javier-Dejneka, Amelia Luisa *accountant*
Lovio-Rodriguez, Jessica Bertha *accountant*

Miami Shores
Diener, Betty Jane *finance educator*

Ocklawaha
Silagi, Barbara Weibler *corporate administrator*

Ocoee
Davis, Elena Denise *accountant*

Orlando
Grice, Lorraine E. *finance educator*
Lloyd, Priscilla Ann *finance educator*

Ponte Vedra Beach
Roland, Melissa Montgomery *accountant*

Saint Petersburg
Keistler, Betty Lou *accountant, tax consultant*
Wasserman, Susan Valesky *accountant, artist, yoga instructor*

Tallahassee
Marshall, Elizabeth Annette *auditor*

Tampa
Bear, Marca Marie *business educator, management consultant*
DeVane, Mindy Klein *financial planner*
Henard, Elizabeth Ann *controller*
Simmons, Patricia T. *marketing analyst, researcher*

West Palm Beach
Polo, Kristine Carol *accountant, educator*

Winter Haven
Goodman, Karen Lacerte *financial services executive*

Winter Springs
Bevc, Carol-Lynn Anne *accountant*

GEORGIA

Alpharetta
Sabaan, Otdria *finance company executive*

Atlanta
Ackerman, Arlene Alice *accountant, business consultant, artist, writer*
Charles, Sally Allen *financial analyst*
Curtis, Lisa A. *accountant, administrator*
Dial, Carmen Miranda *financial counselor, evangelist*
Grove, Denise Whitlock *accounting and financial professional*
Gundersen, Mary Lisa Kranitzky *finance company executive*
Lincoln, Patricia J. *auditor*
Peterson, Darlene Denise *budget officer*
Robertson, Sandra Dee (Graen) *tax director*
Simpson, Agnes Monika *financial advisor*
Tome, Carol *corporate financial executive*

Calhoun
Broyles, Judith Ann *accountant*

Conyers
Spearman, Maxie Ann *financial analyst, administrator*

Lagrange
Hawkins, Frances Pam *business educator*

Lawrenceville
Moran, Sharyn Lee *financial consulting company executive*

Macon
Rigsby, Sheila Goree *accounting firm executive*

Milledgeville
Engerrand, Doris Dieskow *business educator*

Riverdale
Minter, Jimmie Ruth *accountant*

Savannah
Ray, Susan Davis *accountant*

Tybee Island
Smith, Elizabeth Mackey *financial consultant*

Warner Robins
Lee, Glenda Dianne *accountant*

HAWAII

Honolulu
Fukushima, Barbara Naomi *financial advisor*
Kawamura, Georgina K. *finance company executive*

IDAHO

Boise
Smith, Saliesh Anne *comptroller, payroll administrator*

Hayden
Morris, Mary Ann *bookkeeper*

Idaho Falls
Matthews, Janice C. *financial consultant*
Riddoch, Hilda Johnson *accountant*

ILLINOIS

Bellwood
Miller, Denyce Karlina *tax specialist*

Bloomington
Friedman, Joan M. *accounting educator*

Buffalo Grove
McConville, Rita Jean *finance executive*

Chicago
Gaines, Brenda *financial services company executive*
Goldfein, Iris *financial company executive*
Mallow, Kathleen Kelly *accountant*
Miller, Heidi G. *diversified financial company executive*
Morisato, Susan Cay *actuary*
Rodgers, Cynthia *anchor, correspondent*

Decatur
Loebl, Maragaret Margo *corporate financial executive*

Evanston
Powers, Marian *accounting educator*

Glendale Heights
Cook, Doris Marie *retired accountant, educator*

Hickory Hills
Schultz, Barbara Marie *investment advisor representative*

Hoffman Estates
Baier, Lucinda *corporate financial executive*

Mchenry
Koehl, Camille Joan *accountant*

Naperville
Ruyle-Hullinger, Elizabeth Smith (Beth Ruyle) *consultant, municipal financial advisor*
Tan, Li-Su Lin *accountant, insurance executive, investment consultant*

Northbrook
Fom, Betty *financial...*
Mandel, Karyl Lynn *accountant*

Oak Brook
Bossmann, Laurie *controller, hardware company executive*

Skokie
Wills, Patricia Mary *controller*

Spring Grove
York, Karen Kay *accountant, farmer*

Springfield
Kuhn, Kathleen Jo *accountant*

INDIANA

Carmel
Kellison, Donna Louise George *accountant, educator*
Mahoney, Margaret Ellis *accountant*

Fort Wayne
Gutreuter, Jill Stallings *financial consultant, financial planner*

Hebron
Casbon, Monica Lynn *accountant*

Indianapolis
Braham, Delphine Doris *accountant, government official*
Burnette, Ruth Leona *retired finance company administrative assistant*
Israelov, Rhoda *financial planner, writer, entrepreneur*
Uebelhor, Tara Leigh *financial analyst*

South Bend
McDonnell, G. Darlene *retired business educator*

West Lafayette
Stetter, Aimee Rae *finance company executive*

KANSAS

Leawood
White, Shanon Kathleen *accountant, consultant*

Manhattan
Swanson, Diane L. *business management and economics educator, researcher*

Shawnee Mission
Robinson, Mary Lu *retired accountant, artist*

Topeka
Mc Candless, Barbara J. *financial consultant*
Wilson, Carol Ann *retired business manager*

Wichita
Green, Shawna Marie *accountant*

KENTUCKY

Hebron
Morrow, Debra Deola *accountant*

Henderson
Schadler, Cynthia K. *accountant*

Louisville
Bohn, Donna Schuhmann *accountant*
Cayce, Kay C. *accountant*
Colburn, Jennifer Christine *business analyst*
Johnson, Adria Elaine *financial analyst, accountant*
McKim, Ruth Ann *financial planner*

LOUISIANA

Bogalusa
Wood, Helen Chamblee *accountant*

Hammond
LaFargue, Melba Faye Fulmer *credit manager, realtor*

Harvey
Ditta, Phyllis Ann *treasurer*

Mandeville
Aaron, Shirley Mae *tax consultant*

Pineville
Conway, Evelyn Atkinson *accountant, financial analyst*

MAINE

Augusta
Sheive, Doreen Laurel *fiscal administrator*

Camden
Dyer, Barbara F. *retired accountant, writer*

Falmouth
Winton, Linda *corporate financial executive*

Hampden
Paonessa, M. Suzanne *budget analyst*

Rockland
Brown, Clare Winslow *accountant, writer*

Topsham
Palesky, Carol East *tax accountant*

MARYLAND

Annapolis
McQuarrie, Beatrice Sue *financial analyst*

Baltimore
Li, Joanne *finance educator*
Pratt, Joan M. *comptroller*

Bethesda
Comiskey, Angela Picariello *accountant*

College Park
Buggs, Elaine S. *financial analyst*

Columbia
Hyde, Rebecca Medwin *financial consultant*
Lok, Joan Mei-Lok *community affairs specialist, artist*
Narvaez, Bernice Williams *financial consultant*

Easton
Fredrick, Susan Walker *tax company manager*

Elkridge
Calton, Sandra Jeane *accountant*

Joppa
Kott, Beverly Parat *financial counselor, community activist*

Lutherville Timonium
Gray, Dahli *accounting educator and administrator*

Odenton
Murray, Catherine Mary Murphy *accountant*

Silver Spring
Keating, Susan C. *credit foundation executive*

Timonium
Yorkman, Marquetta Marcye Bodine *financial professional*

MASSACHUSETTS

Belmont
Gray, Margaret Ann *management educator, consultant*

Boston
Fletcher, Cathy Ann *auditor*
Kanter, Rosabeth Moss *management educator, consultant, writer*
MacArthur, Sandra Lea *financial services executive*
Schneider, Mary Etta *finance company executive*
Schnitzer, Iris Taymore *diversified financial services company executive, lawyer, arbitrator, mediator*

Dorchester
Wideman, Carol M. *accountant, consultant*

Marblehead
Onishi, Anna Tokiko *financial analyst*

Medford
Goldberg, Pamela Winer *entrepreneurship educator, director*

Waltham
Curnan, Susan P. *social policy and management educator*

MICHIGAN

Auburn Hills
Drexler, Mary Sanford *financial executive*

Detroit
Acton, Elizabeth S *corporate financial executive*
Keys, Elizabeth A. *accountant, business executive*

East Lansing
Krishnan, Ranjani *finance educator*

Monroe
Mlocek, Sister Frances Angeline *financial executive*

Novi
Holforty, Pearl Martha *accountant*

Troy
Esler, Barbara Hart *accountant, consultant*

Wyoming
Carey, JoAnna *financial consultant, writer*

MINNESOTA

Elk River
Goss, Cynthia Lee *tax accountant*

Minneapolis
Goldberg, Luella Gross *corporation executive*

Minnetonka
Jacobson, Anna Sue *finance company executive*

Saint Cloud
Reha, Rose Krivisky *retired finance educator*

Saint Paul
Dutcher, Judi *state auditor*
Gagnon, Laura Christine *financial analyst*
Padelford, Nicole *accountant*
Starling, Elizabeth Anne *strategic planner*
Wheelock, Pam *financial executive*

Worthington
Meyer, Helen Bernadine *financial services company executive*

MISSISSIPPI

Columbus
Reynolds, Gail Smith *accountant, bank officer*

Tupelo
Weaver, Laura Fisher *financial planner*

MISSOURI

Chesterfield
Ridenhour, Marilyn Housel *accountant, consultant*

Columbia
DeJarnette, Shirley Shea *treasurer*
Grundler, Mary Jane Lang *business education educator*

Hamilton
Hawley, Lucretia Marlene *retired accounting educator*

Hazelwood
Kostecki, Mary Ann *financial tax consultant, small business consultant*

Jefferson City
McCaskill, Claire *auditor*

Kansas City
Boysen, Melicent Pearl *finance company executive*
Latza, Beverly Ann *accountant*
Mustard, Mary Carolyn *financial executive*

Saint Louis
Green, Darlene *controller, municipal official*
Weldon, Virginia V. *retired corporate executive, pediatrician*

MONTANA

Helena
Craig, Mary Lauri *accountant*
Toole, Joan Trimble *financial consultant*

Troy
Sherman, Signe Lidfeldt *portfolio manager, former research chemist*

NEBRASKA

Lincoln
Byrd, Lorelee *state treasurer*
LeValley, Joan Catherine *accountant*

NEVADA

Elko
Ballew, Kathy I. *controller*

Las Vegas
Kobberoe, Birthe *corporate financial executive, accountant*
Nold, Aurora Ramirez *business and economics educator*

Reno
Garcia, Katherine Lee *controller, accountant*
Holder, Anna Maria *holding company executive*

NEW HAMPSHIRE

Goffstown
Martel, Eva Leona *accountant*

NEW JERSEY

Budd Lake
Bauer, Jean Marie *accountant*

Chatham
Earle, Jean Buist *financial officer*

Cliffside Park
Lombardi, Tracey Anne *financial administrator, medical assistant*

East Orange
Omoregie, Irene O. *accountant*

Flemington
Simonds, Theresa M. Troegner *accountant*

Hackensack
Donahoe, Maureen Alice *accounting consultant*

Hasbrouck Heights
Savva, Andrea *financial consultant*

Hazlet
Aumack, Shirley Jean *financial planner, tax preparer*

Mendham
Hesselink, Ann Patrice *financial executive, lawyer*

Morristown
Armstrong, Diana Rose *financial consultant*
Flynn, Marie Cosgrove *portfolio manager, corporate financial executive*

New Brunswick
Tigeleiro, Susana *corporate financial executive*

Newark
Norwood, Carolyn Virginia *business educator*

Paramus
Carunchio, Florence Regina *financial planner*

Parsippany
Pedescleaux-Muckle, Gail *business analyst, writer*
Sangiuliano, Barbara Ann *tax consultant*

Pomona
Vito, Marilyn Elaine *business educator*

Princeton
Goldfarb, Irene Dale *retired financial planner*

Ramsey
O'Dell, Elizabeth Ann *controller*

Red Bank
Groves, Lizabeth A. *accountant, local area network administrator*

Somers Point
McCullough, Eileen (Eileen McCullough LePage, Elli McCullough) *financial consultant, writer, editor, educator*

Vineland
Blevins, Amy L. *financial advisor, investment advisor*

Woodbridge
DeMatteo, Gloria Jean *financial counselor*

NEW MEXICO

Albuquerque
Kaehele, Bettie Louise *accountant*

Las Cruces
Bell, M. Joy Miller *financial planner, real estate broker*
Rosile, GraceAnn *business management educator*

NEW YORK

Albany
Brewer, Aida M. *treasurer*
Smith, Bethany Rae *accountant*

Bath
Simonson, Donna Jeanne *accountant*

Briarcliff Manor
Atwood, Donna Elaine *retired financial manager*

Brooklyn
Abrams, Roni *business education educator, communications consultant, trainer*
Fischman, Myrna Leah *accountant, educator*
Satterfield-Harris, Rita *workers compensation representative*

East Islip
Harrington, Carolyn Marie *accountant, artist, jewelry designer*

Flushing
Sanborn, Anna Lucille *pension and insurance consultant*

Fresh Meadows
Soto Baltrusitis, Arleane *financial analyst/benefits compensation analyst*

Garden City
Weess, Pamela R. *financial services representative*

Hempstead
Roble, Carole Marcia *accountant*

Hicksville
Ballweg, Sallyanne K. *finance company executive*

Howard Beach
Powell, Jeanne Marie *accountant*

Jericho
Auster, Ellen *finance company executive*

Lewiston
LoTempio, Julia Matild *retired accountant*

Little Neck
Overton, Rosilyn Gay Hoffman *financial services executive*

Long Island City
Lutz, Karen *finance company executive*

Merrick
Beckman, Judith Kalb *financial counselor and planner, educator, writer*

New York
Altfest, Karen Caplan *diversified financial services company executive, director*
Becker, Helane Renée *securities analyst, financial consultant*
Bernstein, Phyllis J. *financial consultant*
Bibliowicz, Jessica M. *financial analyst*
Blythe, Christina Josephine *business analyst, consultant*
Bowie, Angie *accounting company official*
Browning, Candace *corporate financial executive*
Buttner, Jean Bernhard *diversified financial services company executive*
Caputo, Lisa M. *finance company executive*
Coles, Dianna Robyn *benefits compensation analyst*
Corbet, Kathleen A. *diversified financial services company executive*
Cronson, Caroline Mary *financial executive*
De Lisi, Nancy *corporate financial executive*
Etienne, Michele *financial consultant*
Farley, Peggy Ann *finance company executive*
Glaeser, Betsy *financial services company executive*
Hommo, Harumi *accountant*
Hopkins, Deborah C. *diversified financial services company executive*
Iqbal, Syma U. *corporate financial executive*
Jamison, Sheila Ann English *stockbroker, retirement planning specialist*
Karpen, Marian Joan *financial executive*
Keefe, Diane Marie *portfolio manager*
Kirschenbaum, Lisa L. *portfolio manager, financial advisor*
Knapp, Ellen M. *financial company executive*
Kuo, Charlene *finance professional*
Lappin, Joan E. *financial executive*
Masterson, Ellen Hornberger *accountant*
Meehan, Sandra Gotham *corporate financial executive, consultant*
Militello, Michelle Leigh *securitization specialist*
Monrad, Elizabeth A. *corporate financial executive*
Openshaw, Jennifer *finance company executive*
Reiss, Dale Anne *accounting executive, investment company executive*
Ritch, Kathleen *diversified company executive*
Rossi, Marianne *financial analyst*
Smith-Loeb, Margaret *marketing educator*
Tillman, Vickie A. *diversified financial services company executive*
Toben, Doreen A. *corporate financial executive*
Tortora, Leslie C. *finance company executive*
Weiss, Myrna Grace *financial planner*
Williams, Reba White *financial executive, writer*
Wilson, Pamela K. *corporate financial executive*
Wizen, Sarabeth Margolis *financial consultant*
Zarcone, Darlene *accountant*

North Massapequa
Capone, Maryann *financial planner*

Pearl River
Bryant, Karen Worstell *financial advisor, investment company executive*

Pomona
Landau, Lauri Beth *accountant, tax consultant*

Poughkeepsie
Hansen, Karen Thornley *accountant*

Rochester
Ciaio, Laura Ashmore *accountant*
Goyer, Virginia L. *accountant*
Marriott, Marcia Ann *business and economics educator, health facility administrator*

Scarsdale
Breslow, Marilyn Ganon *portfolio manager*

Somers
Hall, Kathleen Yanarella *financial executive*

Staten Island
Fung, Amy Shu-Fong *accountant*

Thompsonville
Dalli, Inalbys R. *accountant*

Valley Stream
Ellis, Bernice *financial planning company executive, investment advisor*

Webster
Iulianello, Carmela *tax specialist*

Windsor
Warner, Roberta Arlene *retired accountant, financial services executive*

NORTH CAROLINA

Asheville
Letzig, Betty Jean *financial consultant*
Mack, Carole *financial consultant*
Scully, Bonnie Diane *financial planner*

Cary
Coderre, Nancy Adele *financial analyst*

Charlotte
Garner, Cindy Anne *account executive*
Knox, Havolyn Crocker *financial consultant*

Fort Bragg
Carnahan, Doris Jean *budget analyst*

Greensboro
Black, Sylvia Sloan *business educator*
Lenard, Mary Jane *accounting and information systems educator*
Lloyd, Lila G. *business educator*

New Bern
Phipps, Patsy Duncan *retired auditor*

Raleigh
Bradley, Elizabeth Clay *financial planner, educator*

NORTH DAKOTA

Grand Forks
Zahrly, Janice Honea *management educator*

Stanley
Eliason, Bonnie Mae *county treasurer*

OHIO

Akron
Deason, Lucinda Marie *accountant, educator*
Kuster, Doreen K. *accountant*

Athens
Miller, Peggy McLaren *retired management educator*

Avon
Grmek, Dorothy Antonia *accountant*

Cincinnati
Di Benedetto, Ann Louise *accounting administrator*

Cleveland
Eagan, Susan Lajoie *finance educator, consultant*
Key, Helen Elaine *accountant, educator, consulting company executive*
Mayne, Lucille Stringer *finance educator*
Pierson, Marilyn Ehle *financial planner*
Richardson, Allison *financial services company official*
Shellito, Sonia (Sunny) Terese *financial analyst, accountant*
Will, Sandra Gail *controller*

Columbus
Hill, Terri *diversified financial services company executive*
James, Donna A. *diversified financial services company executive*
Kreager, Eileen Davis *administrative consultant*
Ricord, Kathy *diversified financial services company executive*
Schneider, Cindy E. Gower (Lones) *financial advisor*

Dublin
Pollner, Julia A. *financial executive*

East Liverpool
Gailey, Joan Dale *retired finance educator*

Enon
DeVore, Barbara Jane Egan *corporate finance executive*

Harrison
Kocher, Juanita Fay *retired auditor*

Independence
Boyle, Kammer *estate planner, financial analyst*

Middletown
Tucker, Catherine L. *financial advisor*

Oxford
Saas, Deborah Anne *investment advisor, securities broker*

Shaker Heights
Donnem, Sarah Lund *financial analyst, non-profit and political organization consultant*

Troy
Miller, Rebecca S. *financial analyst*

Washington Court House
Johnson, Penny Sue *auditor*

West Chester
Ulrich, Jody L. *accountant*

Wickliffe
Haffey, Susan M. *treasurer*

Wright Patterson Afb
Newsome, Kathy Noel *accountant*

Youngstown
Bartlett, Shirley Anne *accountant*

OKLAHOMA

Ada
Parham, Betty Ely *credit bureau executive*

Tulsa
Candreia, Peggy Jo *financial analyst*
Imhoff, Pamela M. *marketing educator*

OREGON

Beaverton
McElligott, Ann Theresa *accountant*

Portland
Dow, Mary Alexis *auditor*
Hill, Mary Lou *accountant, business consultant*

Springfield
Smith, Vangy Edith *accountant, consultant, writer, artist*

White City
Whelan, Mary Jane *accountant, writer, photographer*

PENNSYLVANIA

Allentown
Cole, Joan (Ellen) Blyler *financial executive*

Bala Cynwyd
Cohen, Rachel Rutstein *financial planner*

Blue Bell
Haugen, Janet B. *corporate financial executive*

Collegeville
Maco, Teri Regan *accountant, engineer*

Drexel Hill
Bay, Joann Reeder *financial planner*

Dunmore
Pencek, Carolyn Carlson *treasurer, educator*

Erie
Mattis, Constance Marie *controller*

Harrisburg
Ellenbogen, Elisabeth Alice *retired accountant*

Morgantown
Quinn, Elysia D. *finance company executive*

Norristown
DeCaro, Monica Ward *finance administrator*

Paoli
Gotshall, Jan Doyle *financial planner*

Philadelphia
Goldsmith, Nancy Carrol *business and health services management educator*
Scogno, Stacie Joy *financial services company executive*
Zimmerman, Monica A. *accountant, educator*

Pittsburgh
Haggerty, Gretchen R. *accounting and finance executive*
Ludin, Pamela S. *accountant*

Radnor
Harris, Mary Howard *finance educator*

Reading
McVey, Diane Elaine *accountant*
Ulshafer, Sharon A. *accountant, educator*

Sayre
Brittain, Nancy Hammond *accountant*

University Park
Coupland, Jennifer Chang *finance educator*

Wayne
Thompson, Gloria Matthews *marketing and statistics educator*

Wynnewood
Frankl, Razelle *management educator*

RHODE ISLAND

Middletown
Reed, Julia Constance *financial services executive*

Smithfield
Weiss, Susan F. *accountant*

SOUTH CAROLINA

Charleston
Adelson, Gloria Ann *financial executive*
Pridgen, Heather Dawn *financial analyst*
Rhea, Marcia Chandler *accountant*

Easley
Densmore, Jacqueline Jean *financial accountant*

Sumter
van Bulck, Margaret West *accountant, financial planner, educator*

West Columbia
Byars, Merlene Hutto *accountant, visual artist, writer*
Moore, Shirley Throckmorton (Mrs. Elmer Lee Moore) *accountant*

SOUTH DAKOTA

Platte
Pennington, Beverly Melcher *financial services company executive*

Rapid City
Callahan, Susan Jane Whitney *accountant*

TENNESSEE

Alamo
Finch, Evelyn Vorise *financial planner*

Nashville
Rizor, Nancy Lucile *retired bookkeeper, retired librarian, genealogist*

Oak Ridge
Ergen, Viola S. *accountant*

Soddy Daisy
Randall, Kay Temple *accountant, retired real estate agent*

TEXAS

Amarillo
Bul... , Ola Mae *accountant*

Arlington
Swanson, Peggy Eubanks *finance educator*

Austin
Hagerty, Polly Marticl *financial analyst, construction executive*
McElroy, Maurine Davenport *financier, educator*
Schloss, Hadassah *open records program administrator*
Strayhorn, Carole Keeton *comptroller*

Bellaire
Rumfolo, Marilu *financial analyst, non profit corporation executive*

Cypress
Hlozek, Carole Diane Quast *finance company executive*

Dallas
Hoyt, Rosemary Ellen *trust advisor*
Jimenez, Mercy *corporate financial executive*
McElyea, Jacquelyn Suzanne *accountant, real estate consultant*
Wilbur, Janis A. *financial consultant, sales professional*

Denton
Henley, Marie Suzanne *accountant, consultant*

Dripping Springs
Guess, Aundrea Kay *accounting educator*

El Paso
Preston, Letricia Elayne *financial planner*

Fort Worth
Dominiak, Geraldine Florence *accounting educator, retired*

Garland
Lord, Jacqueline Ward *accountant, photographer, artist*

Houston
Black, Margaret Louise *accountant, educator*
Duganier, Barbara J. *corporate financial executive*
Feeback, Cynthia Ann *corporate financial executive, accountant*
Friday, Leah Rebecca *portfolio manager*
Griffith, Martha *controller*
Harris, Venita Van Caspel *retired financial planner*
Mermelstein, Isabel Mae Rosenberg *financial consultant*
Neuhaus, Joan T. *finance company executive, private investigator*
Newton, Gloria Jones *accountant, feminist activist*
Reiter, Eunice Harris *accountant*
Smith, Andrea Dawn *financial planner*
Wardle, Victoria Sarah *business analyst*
Watkins, Lisa M. *financial analyst*
Young, Jeanette Cochran *corporate planner, reporter, analyst*

Irving
Geisinger, Janice Allain *accountant*

Laredo
Mayfield, Jacqueline Rowley *business educator, department chairman*

Leander
Craddock, Catherine Todd *accountant*

Plano
Wayne, Jeanette Marie *auditor*

Prairie View
De Luna-Gonzalez, Elma *accountant*

San Antonio
Baeza Flores, Virginia *audit specialist*

San Marcos
Taylor, Ruth Arleen Lesher *marketing educator*

Sugar Land
Keefe, Carolyn Joan *tax accountant*

UTAH

Salt Lake City
Lewis, Amy C. *finance educator, researcher*
McAllister, Lynette J. *financial consultant*

VERMONT

Burlington
Paul, Karen S. *diversified financial services company executive*

VIRGINIA

Alexandria
Bellon, Venetia Rochelle *financial consultant, educator*

Centreville
Hand, Antoinette Marie *accountant*

Charlottesville
Horton, Madeline Mary *financial planner, consultant*
Minehart, Jean Besse *tax accountant*
Verstegen, Deborah A. *finance educator*

Mc Lean
Drew, K. *financial advisor, management consultant*
Edgar, Janelle Diane Ward *financial services executive*
Young, Loretta Ann *auditor*

Norfolk
Shumadine, Anne Ballard *financial advisor, lawyer*

Quantico
Evans, Gaye Lois *comptroller*

Radford
Bienstock, Carol Cook *finance educator*
Kitts, Deborah L. *accountant*

Reston
Polemitou, Olga Andrea *accountant*

Richmond
Hull, Rita Prizler *retired accounting educator*
Wagner, Jody M. *treasurer*

Sterling
Davidson-Meyer, Noreen Hanna *financial services company executive*

Vienna
Townsend, Irene Fogleman *accountant, tax specialist*

Virginia Beach
DiCarlo, Susanne Helen *financial analyst*
Lawson, Beth Ann Reid *strategic planner*

Williamsburg
McLennan, Barbara Nancy *international tax specialist*

Woodbridge
Denison, Cynthia Lee *accountant, tax specialist*

WASHINGTON

Olympia
Myers, Sharon Diane *auditor*
Walker, Yvonne Denise *research analyst*

Pullman
Stammerjohan, Elizabeth Claire Allison *finance educator*

Seattle
Covey, Joy D. *finance and administration executive*
Sandstrom, Alice Wilhelmina *accountant*
Young, Nora Jane *actuary, consultant*

WEST VIRGINIA

Elkins
Payne, Gloria Marquette *business educator*

Inwood
Cloyd, Helen Mary *accountant, educator*

Lewisburg
Kennedy, Leila *accounting educator*

WISCONSIN

Green Bay
Capelle, Elaine M. *financial planner*

Milwaukee
Huf, Carol Elinor *tax service company executive*
Lenz, Debra Lynn *financial analyst*

Sobieski
Richards, Rhonda Sue *accountant*

Superior
Robek, Mary Frances *business education educator*

West Bend
VanBrunt-Kramer, Karen *business administration educator*

WYOMING

Cheyenne
Parrish, Denise Kay *regulatory accountant*

Cody
Kraft, Janice Kay *accounting educator*

Laramie
Spiegelberg, Emma Jo *business education educator, academic administrator*

Sheridan
Pilch, Margaret L. *grant consultant*

TERRITORIES OF THE UNITED STATES

PUERTO RICO

San Juan
Rosso de Irizarry, Carmen (Tutty Rosso de Irizarry) *finance executive*

CANADA

BRITISH COLUMBIA

Powell River
Carsten, Arlene Desmet *financial executive*

ONTARIO

Toronto
Mercier, Eileen Ann *corporate financial executive*

REPUBLIC OF KOREA

Seoul
Park, Kathleen Jeongsoo *portfolio manager, risk management consultant*

ADDRESS UNPUBLISHED

Abood, Denise Maroon *finance company executive*
Alaimo, Terry M. *financial consultant*
Alexander, Barbara Toll *financial consultant*
Anderson, Peggy Rees *accountant*
Ariosa, Corazon Encila *accountant*
Atcheson, Sue Hart *business educator*
Baker, Diane Louise *financial professional*
Barton, Ann Elizabeth *retired corporate financial executive*
Beard, Deborah Faye *accounting and finance educator*
Beller, Luanne Evelyn *accountant*
Bolt, Dawn Maria *financial coach, stock trader*
Bowne, Shirlee Pearson *finance and housing consultant*
Boyer, Heidi Hild *public policy consultant*
Brainard, Melissa *accountant*
Brdlik, Carola Emilie *retired accountant*
Bretz, Kelly Jean Rydel *actuary, consultant*
Callaway, Julienne Morriss *financial consultant*
Campbell, Heather Sue *credit manager, religious studies educator*
Canfield, Constance Dale *retired accountant, retired medical/surgical nurse, retired military officer*
Cannistraro, Carolyn Marie *financial recruiter*
Castle, Nancy Margaret Timma *accountant, banker*
Collette, Frances Madelyn *retired tax specialist, lawyer, consultant, advocate*
Coutret, Kay Elizabeth *financial analyst*
Crooker, Diane Kay *accountant*
Cummings, Erika Helga *business consultant*
Cunningham, Nancy Schieffelin *business educator*
Dallmann, Carolyn E. *auditor*
Dickson, Eva Mae *credit manager*
Dowdell, Sharonlyn Scott *accountant*
Dumitru, Mirela *accountant*
Ebersole, Andree D. *finance company executive, consultant*
Everett, Donna Raney *finance educator*
Faucette, Gloria Marie *accountant, educator*

FitzSimons, Sharon Russell *international financial and treasury executive*
Flantroy, Tammy L. *financial analyst*
Fletcher, Denise Koen *strategic and financial consultant*
Foisy, Renée Thérèse *financial consultant*
Forman, Danna *financial analyst*
Fox, Kelly Diane *financial advisor*
Gallagher, Lindy Allyn *banker, financial consultant*
Gehrke, Karen Marie *retired accountant*
Genét, Barbara Ann *accountant, travel counselor*
Givens, Courtney Michelle *finance company executive*
Goehring, Maude Cope *retired business educator*
Gronau, Crystal Lynn *accountant*
Hanson, Tamara Shields *accountant*
Hargrove, Sandra Leigh *financial planner*
Harris, Susan Louise *financial services company executive*
Hayek, Carolyn Jean *financial consultant, retired judge*
Holton, Grace Holland *accountant*
Horstman, Suzanne Rucker *financial planner*
Hunsberger, Christine Lee *accountant*
Hutchin, Nancy Lee *corporate financial executive*
Jaques, Kathryn Misbach *tax consultant*
Johnson, Freda S. *public finance consultant*
Johnson, Margaret Kathleen *business educator*
Judd, Barbara Ann Eastwood *financial management professional, union activist*
Lamb, Sloane Trelles *finance company executive*
Lang-Piasecki, Vera Jean *financial consultant*
Lauff, Jennifer *corporate financial executive*
Lester, Alicia Louise *financial analyst*
Loken, Barbara *marketing educator, social psychologist*
Lombard, Marjorie Ann *financial officer*
Longden, Claire Suzanne *retired financial planner, investment advisor*
Lucas, Karen Williams *controller*
Macaskill, Bridget *finance company executive*
Macdonald, Sheila de Marillac *company executive*
Madariaga, Lourdes Mercedes *accountant*
Maner, Diana *financial consultant*
Marot, Lola *retired accountant*
May, Phyllis Jean *financial executive*
McLemore, Carol Lee *accountant*
Medlin, Veronica B. *benefits compensation analyst*
Melton, Roberta Lynn-Kong *financial consultant*
Mims, Clarice Roberta *financial advisor*
Mitchem, Cheryl E. *accounting educator*
Mullins, Barbara J. *financial executive*
Norton, Karen Ann *accountant*
Pagel, Inga Ann *accountant*
Parrish-Porter, Vallerie *controller*
Petersen, Stephanie Burton *bond analyst*
Pinkham, Robin Remick *corporate financial executive*
Plimpton, Peggy Lucas *trustee*
Prespare, Deborah Sun *financial analyst*
Rahms, Beatrix Anna *accountant, artist*
Rail, Kathy Lynn Parish *accountant*
Raya, Madhavi *controller*
Richardson, Brownie F. *accountant*
Richardson, Margaret Milner *former accounting firm executive, lawyer*
Robinson, Myrna L(orraine) *business analyst/program control specialist*
Saidens, Susan M. *accountant, consultant*
Saunders, Donna M. *accountant*
Savage, Sondra L. *finance educator*
Schulz, Marianne *accountant*
Sexton, Carol Burke *consultant*
Smith, Linda Ann Glidewell *accountant*
Sonnier, Patricia Bennett *business management educator*
Taylor, L. Ann *financial analyst*
Taylor, Linda Rathbun *investment manager*
Tyler, Rachel *finance specialist*
Wagner, Barbara Ann *accountant, writer*
Washington-Velazquez, Sarah Elizabeth *tax auditor*
Wells, Toni Lynn *accountant*
Whyte, Bettina Marshall *financial crisis manager*
Williams, Helen Margaret *retired accountant*
Williams-Lockett, Lolita Monique *accountant*
Wilson, Linda Lee *finance company executive*
Wright, Judith Rae *retired accountant*
Zimmerman, Helene Loretta *retired business educator*

FINANCE: INSURANCE

UNITED STATES

ALABAMA

Dothan
Benson, Marie Chapman *insurance agent*

Tuscaloosa
Edgeworth, Emily *retired insurance agency executive, retired small business owner*

ALASKA

Anchorage
Holmes, Sandra *insurance underwriter*

ARKANSAS

Sherwood
Keaton, Frances Marlene *insurance sales representative*

CALIFORNIA

Agoura Hills
Cannon, Nancy Gladstein *insurance agent*

Glendale
Dudash, Linda Christine *insurance company executive*

La Quinta
Adolph, Diane Joyce *retired underwriter*

Moorpark
Halperin, Kristine Briggs *insurance sales and marketing professional*

Mountain View
Quartuccio, Maryann *insurance agent, home economist*

Newman
Carlsen, Janet Haws *retired insurance company executive*

San Francisco
Allen, Lola *insurance agent*

San Rafael
Keegan, Jane Ann *insurance executive, consultant*

Santa Monica
Dostal, Tamara *insurance company executive*

Sunnyvale
Merrill, Wendy Jane *insurance company executive*

Woodland Hills
Berry, Carol Ann *insurance company executive*

COLORADO

Colorado Springs
Michels, Patricia A. *insurance agent*

Golden
Lott, Brenda Louise *insurance company executive*

Superior
Forshee, Gladys Marie *writer, insurance agent*

CONNECTICUT

Hartford
deRaismes, Ann M. *insurance company executive, human resources specialist*
Elliott, Eric S *insurance company executive*
Lautzenheiser, Barbara Jean *insurance company executive*
Wright, Elease *insurance company executive*

Mystic
Spakoski, Marcia *insurance agent*

Stamford
Block, Ruth *retired insurance company executive*
Schiff, Jayne Nemerow *underwriter*

DISTRICT OF COLUMBIA

Washington
Martin, Julie A. *retired insurance company executive*
Oakley, Diane *insurance executive, benefit consultant*
Snider, Virginia L. *antitrust consultant*

FLORIDA

Fort Lauderdale
Lilley, Mili Della *insurance company executive, entertainment management consultant*

Jacksonville
Segal, Linda Gale *retired insurance company executive*

Naples
Guerra, Mayra *insurance company executive*

GEORGIA

Alpharetta
Fowler, Vivian Delores *insurance company executive*
Horton, Rosalyn *underwriter*

Columbus
Spencer, Kathelen V. *insurance company executive*

Macon
Dorsey, Donna Bagley *insurance agent*

Roswell
Lietch, Margie *insurance company administrator*

Savannah
Rigelwood, Diane Colleen *insurance adjuster, administrator*

ILLINOIS

Bloomington
Axley, Dixie L. *insurance company executive*

Chicago
Grant, Beatrice *underwriter, consultant*
Hinkelman, Ruth Amidon *insurance company executive*
Janecek, Lenore Elaine *insurance specialist, consultant*
Johnson, Caroline Janice *insurance company executive*

Northbrook
Wilson, Rita P. *insurance company executive*

Park Ridge
Bateman, Andrea R. *insurance agent*

INDIANA

Carmel
Husman, Catherine Bigot *retired insurance company executive, actuary*

Fort Wayne
Sasko, Nancy Ann *insurance agent*

Indianapolis
Calvano, Linda Sue Ley *insurance company executive*
Cramer, Betty F. *life insurance company executive*
Wolsiffer, Patricia Rae *retired insurance company executive*

Schererville
Jarrett, Alexis *insurance agent, lawyer*

IOWA

Des Moines
Ellis, Mary Louise Helgeson *retired insurance company executive, business consultant*

KANSAS

Newton
Morford, Marie Arlene *insurance company executive*

Overland Park
Sikyta, Jayne A. *insurance agent*

Topeka
Zientara, Suzannah Dockstader *insurance agent*

Wichita
Johnstone, Marva Jean (Jeanie Johnstone) *insurance agency executive*

KENTUCKY

Greenville
Painter, Elizabeth Marie *insurance agent, financial consultant*

LOUISIANA

Alexandria
Anderson, Rose Marie *insurance agent*

MARYLAND

Reisterstown
Tirone, Barbara Jean *health insurance administrator*

Walkersville
Newton, Loretta Jean *insurance agent*

MASSACHUSETTS

Boston
Bunker, Beryl H. *retired insurance company executive, volunteer*
Ford, Maureen R. *insurance company executive*
McAneny, Deborah H. *insurance company executive*

South Orleans
Hale, Margaret Smith *insurance company executive, educator*

Springfield
Modie, Christine M. *insurance company executive*

MICHIGAN

Saginaw
Othersen-Khalifa, Cheryl Lee *insurance agent, realtor*

Southgate
Torok, Margaret Louise *insurance company executive*

MINNESOTA

Coon Rapids
Bordner, Patricia Anne *insurance agent, writer*

Minnetonka
Rivet, Jeannine M. *health plan administrator*

Saint Paul
Oswald, Eva Sue Aden *retired insurance company executive*

Zuraitis, Marita *insurance company executive*

MISSOURI

Kansas City
Nichols, Virginia Violet *independent insurance agent, accountant*

Springfield
Wommack, Janice Marie *insurance company executive*

NEBRASKA

Omaha
Lechowicz, Lisa Marie *retired insurance company executive*

NEVADA

Henderson
Johnson, Joan Bray *insurance company consultant*

Las Vegas
Zervoudakes, Annette Dian *reinsurance specialist*

NEW HAMPSHIRE

Dover
Bergerson, Nancy Dahl *life and health underwriter, paralegal*

Portsmouth
Ward, Bonnie J. *insurance company executive*

NEW JERSEY

Bradley Beach
Shrem, Eileen Merry *insurance planner*

Cranford
Crow, Lynne Campbell Smith *insurance company representative*

Elizabeth
Miller-Duffy, Merritt *insurance agent, assistant camp director*

Madison
Leak, Margaret Elizabeth *insurance company executive*

Newark
Banta, Vivian L. *insurance company executive*
Koster, Barbara *insurance company executive*
Myers, Priscilla A. *insurance company executive*

NEW YORK

Brooklyn
Chavis, Katherine (Kitty Chavis) *disability consultant, artist*

New York
Campbell, Judith E. *retired insurance company executive*
Hollis, Loucille *risk control administrator, educator*
Lassiter, Sheri L. *insurance company executive*
Martino, Cheryl Derby *insurance company secretary*
Rein, Catherine Amelia *retired insurance company executive, lawyer*
Weber, Lisa M. *insurance company executive*

Penfield
Klose, Charlotte Ann *insurance agency owner*

Syosset
Kniffin, Paula Sichel *insurance sales executive*

Westbury
Borut, Josephine *retired insurance company executive*

NORTH CAROLINA

Charlotte
Dunn, Sandra E. *insurance agent*
Howard, Grazell *risk management executive*

Greenville
Page, Mary Stancill *insurance agency executive*

OHIO

Chillicothe
Copley, Cynthia Sue Love *insurance adjuster*

Cincinnati
Horrell, Karen Holley *insurance company executive, lawyer*

Lakewood
Barrett, Linda *insurance company executive*

Springfield
Rowland-Raybold, Roberta *insurance agent, music educator*

OKLAHOMA

Dewey
White, Joy Kathryn *retired claims consultant, artist*

Oklahoma City
Harrison-Bridgeman, Ann Marie *claims adjuster*

PENNSYLVANIA

Bethlehem
Dienel, Nancy Alduma Roberts *health insurance underwriter*

Erie
Waldron, Allene *insurance group executive*

Jenkintown
O'Neill, Judith Jones *insurance agent*

New Hope
Van Pelt, Janet Ruth *retired insurance company executive*

Olyphant
Paoloni, Virginia Ann *insurance company executive*

Philadelphia
Anania, Andrea *insurance company executive*
Soltz, Judith E. *insurance company executive, lawyer*

Pittsburgh
Chipman, Debra Decker *title insurance executive*

Stroudsburg
Pope, Arlette Farrar *insurance company professional*

TEXAS

Austin
Watson, Brenda Bennett *insurance company executive*

Cypress
Jordan, Raylene O. *insurance agent*

Dallas
Madden, Teresa Darleen *insurance agency owner*

Palestine
Douthitt, Shirley Ann *insurance agent*

Richardson
White, Irene *insurance professional*

San Antonio
Balbaugh, Ethel L. *insurance agent*

VIRGINIA

Glen Allen
Jones, Carolyn *insurance company executive*

Mc Lean
Connelly, Mary Creedon *insurance company executive*

WASHINGTON

Olympia
Senn, Deborah *insurance commissioner*

Seattle
Armstrong, Mary M. *insurance company executive*
Duckworth, Tara Ann *insurance company executive*

Yakima
Savage, Carla Lee *insurance agent*

WISCONSIN

Madison
Sims, Terre Lynn *insurance company executive*

Milwaukee
Johannes, Kay L. *insurance company executive*

ADDRESS UNPUBLISHED

Alderman, Shirley M. *insurance agent*
Alpert, Ann Sharon *retired insurance claims examiner*
Becker, JoAnn Elizabeth *insurance company executive*
Cooks, Pamala Aniece *insurance agent*
Emek, Sharon Helene *risk management consultant*
Hawk, Carole Lynn *retired insurance company executive, research analyst*
Haynes, Marcia Margaret *insurance agent*
Hellenbrand, Sherri *insurance company executive*
Huszai, Kristy Renee *insurance agent*
Impellizzeri, Anne Elmendorf *insurance company executive, non-profit executive*
Knizeski, Justine Estelle *insurance company executive*
Lamel, Linda Helen *professional society executive, former insurance company executive, former college president, lawyer*
Lardakis, Moira Gambrill *insurance executive, lawyer*

Maloney, Therese Adele *insurance company executive*
Plette, Sandra Lee *retired insurance company executive*
Rahbar, Zita Ina *insurance company executive*
Reynolds, Billie Iles *insurance agent*
Saber, Lisa Marie *insurance agent*
Subkowsky, Elizabeth *insurance company executive*
Weir, Linda Woodruff *insurance broker, theater director*

FINANCE: INVESTMENT SERVICES

UNITED STATES

ARKANSAS

Little Rock
Good, Mary Lowe (Mrs. Billy Jewel Good) *investment company executive, educator*
Light, Jo Knight *stockbroker*

CALIFORNIA

Beverly Hills
Seidel, Joan Broude *securities trader, investment advisor*

Carmel
Hamilton, Beverly Lannquist *investment management professional*

Corte Madera
Andreini, Elizabeth B. *stockbroker, elementary education educator*

Costa Mesa
Kiang, Assumpta (Amy Kiang) *brokerage house executive*

Fairfax
Ross, Sue *entrepreneur, author, fundraising executive*

Los Angeles
Ashwell, Rachel *entrepreneur, interior designer*
Geraldez, Maria-Teresa De Jesus *investment advisor, small business owner*
Jarrell, Leeann *investment company executive*

North Hollywood
Miller, La Brenda *investment analyst, writer*

Oakland
Alford, Joan Franz *entrepreneur*

Palo Alto
Berg, Olena *investment company executive, former federal official*
Long, Anne T. *financial analyst, investment adviser*

Pinedale
Falcone, Patricia Jeanne Lalim *investor, foundation administrator*

Redondo Beach
McCall-Rodriguez, Leonor *entrepreneur, consultant*

Rosemead
Goddard, Jo Ann *investment advisor*

Roseville
Grant, Barbara *venture capitalist*

San Francisco
Dunn, Patricia C. *investment company executive*
Marduel, Alix *venture capitalist*
Morgan, Christina *venture capital firm executive*
Winblad, Ann *investment company executive*

Tarzana
Neece, Olivia Helene Ernst *investment company executive, consultant*

COLORADO

Boulder
Kahn, Herta Hess (Mrs. Howard Kahn) *retired securities trader*

Denver
Gampel, Elaine Susan *investment company executive, consultant*
Wagner, Judith Buck *investment firm executive*
Welch, J(oan) Kathleen *entrepreneur*

Lakewood
Finnie, Doris Gould *investment company executive*

Placerville
Monferrato, Angela Maria *investor, writer, designer*

Thornton
Johnson, Carole Jean *investment company executive*

CONNECTICUT

East Hartford
Gold, Carla Christine *commodities trader, director*

Greenwich
Marram, Ellen R. *investment company executive*

New Canaan
Grace, Julianne Alice *retired investor relations firm executive*
Lione, Susan Garrett *consultant*
Penny, Susan Caroline Voelker *investment manager*

Westport
Stewart, Martha Kostyra *entrepreneur, lecturer, author*

DISTRICT OF COLUMBIA

Washington
Abramson, Patty *investment company executive*
Heichel, Paula *investment company executive, financial consultant*
McCaul, Elizabeth *investment advisor, former state agency administrator*

FLORIDA

Boca Raton
Land, Judith Broten *stockbroker*

Cantonment
Crook, Penny Loraine *investment broker*

Fort Lauderdale
Sands, Roberta Alyse *real estate investor*

Fort Myers
Madden, Vicky J. *brokerage house executive*

Hollywood
Pittarelli, Diana *entrepreneur*

Jupiter
Malm, Rita H. *securities executive*

Miami
Mitchell, Virginia Ann *investment company executive*
Reyes, Lory G. *entrepreneur*

Stuart
Spears, Doris Ann Hachmuth *entrepreneur, writer, publisher, real estate and management consultant*

West Palm Beach
Robertson, Sara Stewart *private investor, entrepreneur*

GEORGIA

Atlanta
Jackson, Geraldine *entrepreneur*
Moore, Darla D. *investment company executive*
Sanger, Hazel A D *investment company executive*

Austell
Orr, Zellie *entrepreneur, educator, writer, researcher*

HAWAII

Hilo
Merk, Elizabeth Thole *investment company executive*

IDAHO

Boise
Hendren, Merlyn Churchill *investment company executive*

ILLINOIS

Chicago
Bryant, Esther *investment manager, retired correspondent*
Case, Donni Marie *investment company executive*
Gilbert, Debbie Rose *entrepreneur*
Hobson, Mellody *investment company executive*
Reece, Beth Pauley *commodities broker*
Rosenberg, Sheli Z. *investment company executive*
Williamson, Donna C. E. *investment company executive*

Park Ridge
Albert, Elizabeth Franz (Mrs. Henry B. Albert) *investor, artist, conservationist*

INDIANA

Carmel
Cuneo, Ngaire E. *corporate development executive*

Greenwood
Grube, Elizabeth *investment company executive*

Indianapolis
King, Kay Sue *investment company executive*

KENTUCKY

Murray
Boston, Betty Lee *investment company executive, financial consultant, financial planner*

LOUISIANA

Mandeville
Colomb, Marjorie Monroe *investor, volunteer*

Ruston
Marbury, Virginia Lomax *insurance and investment executive*

MARYLAND

Bethesda
Drazin, Lisa *real estate and corporate investment banker, financial consultant*
Krumsiek, Barbara J. *investment company executive*

MASSACHUSETTS

Boston
Johnson, Abigail *investment company executive*
Ling, Chiew Sing *investment company executive*
Marshall, Sheryl *venture capitalist*
Morby, Jacqueline *venture capitalist*
Tempel, Jean Curtin *venture capitalist*

Chestnut Hill
Edward, G. Gail *investment company executive, theater operator*

Stockbridge
Fitzpatrick, Jane *entrepreneur*

MICHIGAN

Farmington Hills
Ellmann, Sheila Frenkel *investment company executive*

Muskegon
Cirona, Jane Callahan *investment company executive*

West Bloomfield
Mamut, Mary Catherine *retired entrepreneur*

MINNESOTA

Edina
Kata, Marie L. *securities dealer, brokerage house executive*

MISSOURI

Saint Louis
Foster, Scarlett Lee *investor relations executive*
Moore, Patricia Kay *investor, public relations director*

NEBRASKA

Omaha
Buffett, Susan Thompson *investment company executive*

NEVADA

Las Vegas
Roberts, Lia *investor, political organization worker*

NEW JERSEY

Haddonfield
Carter, Joan Pauline *investment company executive*

New Brunswick
Mills, Dorothy Allen *investor*

Newark
Ferris-Waks, Arlene Susan *compliance officer*

Pennington
Gundeck, Caroline Nyklewicz *investment company executive*

Teaneck
Lehmann, Esther Strauss *investment company executive*

NEW MEXICO

Corrales
Eisenstadt, Pauline Doreen Bauman *investment company executive, state legislator*

Taos
Lipscomb, Anna Rose Feeny *entrepreneur, arts organizer, fundraiser*

NEW YORK

Bay Shore
Williams, Tonda *entrepreneur, consultant*

Forest Hills
Flowers, Cynthia *investment company executive*

Ithaca
Cornish, Elizabeth Turverey *stockbroker*

New York
Berkowitz, Susan J. *investment banking executive*
Blalock, Sherrill *investment advisor*
Britz Lotti, Diane Edward *investment company executive*
Butte, Amy S. *securities trader*
Clemente, Lilia Calderon *capital company executive*
Cohen, Abby Joseph *investment strategist*
Cohen, Claire Gorham *investors service company executive*
Cole, Carolyn Jo *brokerage company executive*
Cruz, Zoe *investment company executive*
Ezrati, Susan Graham *investment company executive, economist*
Gavin, Paula Lance *investment company executive*
Haggerty, Rosanne *entrepreneur*
Hanauer, Linda *venture capitalist*
Harris, Carla Ann *investment company executive*
House, Karen Elliott *company executive, former editor, reporter*
Kavovit, Barbara *entrepreneur*
Kinney, Catherine R. *stock exchange executive*
Kinsman, Sarah Markham *investment company executive*
Krawcheck, Sallie L. *investment company executive*
Lakatos, Susan Carol *investment banker, artist*
Lebenthal, Alexandra *investment firm executive*
Main, Patricia Englander *investor*
Mc Crann, Deborah Theresa *securities trader*
Meeker, Mary *stock brokerage executive*
Morrissey, Dolores Josephine *investment executive*
Nascimento, Ana Paula *entrepreneur, food service executive*
Neustein, Robin *investment company executive*
Nichols, Carol D. *real estate professional*
O'Grady, Beverly Troxler *investment executive, counselor*
Shern, Stephanie Marie *investment company executive, accountant*
Siebert, Muriel (Mickie) *brokerage house executive, former state banking official*
Skerl, Diana M. *stockbroker*
Updike, Helen Hill *investment manager, financial advisor*
Zoullas, Deborah Decotis *private investor, entrepreneur*

Rochester
Spurrier, Mary Eileen *investment advisor, financial planner*

Rye
Casson Madden, Chris *entrepreneur, interior designer*

NORTH CAROLINA

Hubert
Lloyd, Margaret Harris *entrepreneur, educator*

Winston Salem
Smunt, Marsha Lynn Haeflinger *financial executive*

OHIO

Cincinnati
Murphy, Molly Ann *investment company executive*

OKLAHOMA

Tulsa
Knox, Teresa Louise *entrepreneur, small business owner*

OREGON

Medford
Hennion, Carolyn Laird (Lyn Hennion) *investment executive*

Portland
Corbett, Alice Catherine *investor*

PENNSYLVANIA

Collegeville
Barnes, Jo Anne *investment advisor*

Philadelphia
Simpson, Carol Louise *investment company executive*

RHODE ISLAND

Newport
Higgins, Harriet Pratt *investment advisor*

Providence
Bogan, Mary Flair *stockbroker*
Richardson, Julie G. *investment company executive*

SOUTH CAROLINA

Charleston
Brown, Ann Catherine *investment company executive*

TENNESSEE

Knoxville
Penn, Dawn Tamara *entrepreneur*

TEXAS

Abilene
Owen, Dian Grave *investment corporation executive*

Addison
Smith, Cece *venture capitalist*

Dallas
Byrne, Susan M. *investment company executive*
Crockett, Dodee Frost *brokerage firm executive*

Desoto
Harrington, Betty Byrd *entrepreneur*

VIRGINIA

Alexandria
Rainwater, Joan Lucille Morse *investment company executive*

Arlington
Choksi, Mary *investment company executive*
Queen, Sally Ann Crannell *entrepreneur*

WASHINGTON

Seattle
Johnson, Mildred Grace Mash *investment company executive*

WYOMING

Casper
True, Jean Durland *entrepreneur, oil industry executive, gas industry executive*

MEXICO

Mexico City
de Brun, Shauna Doyle *industrialist, investment banker*

MONGOLIA

Ulaanbaatar
Mandel, Leslie Ann *investment advisor, business owner, author*

ADDRESS UNPUBLISHED

Apel-Brueggeman, Myrna L. *entrepreneur*
Arp Lotter, Donna *venture capitalist, investor*
Bacon, Caroline Sharfman *investor relations consultant*
Bailey, Rita Maria *investment advisor, psychologist*
Blum, Barbara Davis *investor*
Bowles, Barbara Landers *investment company executive*
Brooks, Velma *entrepreneur, small business owner*
Burns, Barbara Belton *investment company executive*
Cano, Marta Mendendez *securities company executive, financial consultant*
Codo, Christina *securities executive*
Engelbreit, Mary *art licensing entrepreneur*
Fitts, Catherine Austin *investment advisor*
Godwin, Pamela June *financial services executive*
Gouletas, Evangeline *investment executive*
Hapner, Mary Lou *securities trader and dealer, writer*
Hartness, Sandra Jean *venture capitalist*
Holte, Debra Leah *investment executive, financial analyst*
Kauffman, B. Suzanne *investment company professional*
Kim, Christina K.(yung) *investment company executive*
Lambert, Rebecca Fotouhi *investment company executive*
Levinson, Kathy *former investment company executive, philanthropist*
Lieberman, Gail Forman *investment company executive*
Robinson, Annettmarie *entrepreneur*
Rondeau, Doris Jean *entrepreneur, consultant*
Scher, Laura Susan *financial company executive*
Schwartz, Carol Ann *investment company executive*
Spivak, Carol *investment manager, philanthropist*
Squire, Beverly *business owner, entrepreneur*
Urato, Barbra Casale *entrepreneur*
Wadsworth, Jacqueline Dorèt *private investor*
Wilkey, Mary Huff *investor, writer, publisher*
Zeviar-Geese, Gabriole *stock market investor, lawyer*

GOVERNMENT: AGENCY ADMINISTRATION

UNITED STATES

ALABAMA

Birmingham
Wheeler, Cathy Jo *federal agency administrator*

Montgomery
Cauthen, Florence M. *protective services official*
Mandry, Christine M. *public adminstator*
Martin, Jeanne Davis *forensic specialist, consultant, writer, editor*
Parker, Susan D. *state official, auditor*

Pine Level
Boswell, Vivian Nicholson *protective services official*

ALASKA

Anchorage
Burke, Marianne King *state agency administrator, financial executive, consultant*
Demarco, Patricia M. *state agency administrator*
Sandvik, Helvi *state agency administrator*
Sedwick, Deborah *state agency administrator*
Thompson, G. Nanette *state agency administrator*

Juneau
Perdue, Karen *state agency administrator*

ARIZONA

Chandler
Lauber, Kelli Katherine Margaret *criminal justice instructor*

Mesa
Hess-Benish, Jenifer *protective services official, real estate agent*

Phoenix
Chavez, Nelba R. *state agency administrator, former federal agency administrator*
Foutz, Claudia *state agency administrator*
Moriarty, Karen *state agency administrator*

Prescott
Krieger, Lois B. *retired state agency administrator*

Tucson
Emerson, Kirk *government agency administrator*

CALIFORNIA

Albany
Peterson, Nancy L. *federal agency administrator, volunteer*

Costa Mesa
Marin, Rosario *former federal agency administrator*

Edwards
Larson, Jo Ann *government agency administrator*
McCarthy, Marianne *government agency administrator*

Fresno
Diestelkamp, Dawn Lea *government agency administrator*

Glendale
Shelburne, Merry Clare *public information officer, educator*

Hayward
Wilson, Renee Layne *protective services official, personal trainer*

Lancaster
Davison, Dawn Sherry *correctional administrator, educator*

Moffett Field
Bingham, Nancy F. *government agency administrator*
Dolci, Wendy Whiting *government agency administrator*
Grymes, Rose *government agency administrator*

Palm Springs
Holtz-Borders, Karen Lynn *police officer*

San Bruno
Kell-Smith, Carla Sue *federal agency administrator*

San Francisco
Coye, Molly Joel *state agency administrator*
Fong, Heather J. *protective services official*
Fujii, Sharon M. *federal agency administrator*
Lynch, Loretta *state agency administrator*

LOUISIANA

New Orleans
Adams, Ingrid G. *federal government intelligence specialist*

Shreveport
Foggin, Brenda Frazier *retired state agency administrator, volunteer*

MAINE

Saco
Mason, Nancy Tolman *retired state agency director*

MARYLAND

Annapolis
Snyder, Kathleen Theresa *state agency administrator*

Baltimore
Abrams, Rosalie Silber *retired state agency official*
Barnes, Adrienne *public information officer*
Barnhart, Jo Anne B. *federal agency administrator*
Dorsey, Donna Morgan *state agency administrator*
Harryman, Kathleen A. *board administrator*

Bethesda
Alving, Barbara *federal agency administrator*
Joyce, Bernita Anne *former federal government agency administrator*
Larrabee, Barbara Princelau *retired intelligence officer*
Parron, Delores L. *federal agency administrator*
Penn, Audrey S. *retired federal agency administrator*
Singer, Dinah *federal agency administrator, immunologist, researcher*
Skirboll, Lana R. *federal health policy director*

Easton
Colton, Elizabeth Wishart *government agency administrator*

Rockville
Davis, Beverly Watts *government agency administrator*
Kelsey, Frances Oldham *government official*

MASSACHUSETTS

Boston
Hill, Vicki Kaufman *civil rights investigator*
O'Toole, Kathleen M. *police commissioner*

New Bedford
Cordeiro, Elizabeth Dalein *law enforcement training educator*

West Dennis
Amidon, Barbara Stone *forensic specialist, psychologist*

Westborough
Horwitz, Eleanor Catherine *information and education official*

MICHIGAN

Detroit
Bully-Cummings, Ella M. *protective services official*

Flint
Anderson, Mary Elizabeth *protection services official*

Lanse
Butler, Patricia *protective services official*

Lansing
Wilbur, Kathleen *state agency administrator*

Muskegon
Ohst, Wendy Joan *government agency administrator, educator*

Novi
Crane, Patricia Sue *probation services administrator, social worker*

Royal Oak
Thomson, Kathleen Kepner *state agency administrator, researcher*

MINNESOTA

Saint Paul
Beers, Anne *protective services official*
Hall, Beverly Joy *police officer*
O'Brien, Odessa Louise *protective services official*

MISSISSIPPI

Jackson
Hoban-Moore, Patricia A. *federal agency administrator*
Rubisoff, Deborah L. *state agency administrator*

Southaven
Johnson, Joyce Thedford *state agency administrator*

MISSOURI

Kansas City
Fairchild, Sharon Elaine *corrections administrator*

Saint Louis
Warner, Susan *federal agency administrator*

Troy
Burkemper, Sarah B. *state agency administrator*

MONTANA

Helena
Keenan, Nancy A. *state agency administrator*

NEBRASKA

Lincoln
Fleharty, Mary Sue *state government staff member*
Gray, Joni Nadine *state agency administrator*

Omaha
Mactier, Ann Dickinson *state agency administrator*
Patrick, Erline M. *federal agency administrator*

NEVADA

Carson City
Chanos, Adriana Escobar *state agency administrator*
Peterson, Mary L. *state agency official*

Las Vegas
Chevers, Wilda Anita Yarde *former state official and educator*
Klein, Freda *retired state agency administrator*
Lally, Norma Ross *retired federal agency administrator*

NEW HAMPSHIRE

Concord
Millerick, Jayne Marcucci *Republican party chairman*

NEW JERSEY

Elizabeth
Fulmore, MaryAnn *state agency administrator*

Little Falls
Reid, Desirée Andréa *forensic scientist*

Maplewood
Rabadeau, Mary Frances *protective services official*

Mays Landing
Connor, Wilda *government health agency administrator*

Trenton
Cardinali, Noreen Sadler *state agency administrator*
Manno, Rita *state agency administrator*
Suter, Karen L. *former state banking department administrator*

NEW MEXICO

Albuquerque
Jaramillo, Mari-Luci *retired federal agency administrator*
Montoya, Patricia T. *federal agency administrator*

Santa Fe
Kelly, Ruth *state agency administrator*
Lovejoy, Lynda M. *state agency administrator*
Otten, Robin Dozier *state agency administrator*

NEW YORK

Albany
Novello, Antonia Coello *state health commissioner, former surgeon general, pediatric nephrologist, educator, retired federal agency administrator*

Bronxville
Conway, Elaine Wingate *state agency administrator*

Great Neck
Blumberg, Barbara Salmanson (Mrs. Arnold G. Blumberg) *retired state housing official, housing consultant*

New York
Beausoleil, Doris Mae *federal agency housing specialist*
Gustafson, Judith *federal association administrator*
Kenny, Jane Marie *government agency administrator*
Rosa, Margarita *agency chief executive, lawyer*
Sorensen, Gillian Martin *United Nations official*

Niskayuna
Standfast, Susan J(ane) *retired state official, educator, researcher*

Rochester
Guarnere, Joanne *protective services official*

Selden
Sather, Voleen Rotunda *retired*

Springfield Gardens
Moore, Deborah Chantay *protective services official, psychotherapist*

NORTH CAROLINA

Greensboro
Wallace, Becky Whitley *protective services official*

Jefferson
Maney, Lois Jean *postmaster*

Raleigh
Sanford, Jo Anne *state agency administrator*

Waynesville
Ingle, Marti Annette *protective services official, educator*

Wilmington
Clinton, Lottie Dry Edwards *retired state agency administrator*

OHIO

Akron
Myers, Mary Elizabeth *police officer*

Cleveland
Crandall, Karen *government agency administrator*

Columbus
Dresser, Karen Kerns *state agency administrator*
Gillmor, Karen Lako *state agency administrator*
Long, Teresa C. *city health department administrator*

Cuyahoga Falls
Shane, Sandra Kuli *postal service administrator*

New Philadelphia
Hendrix, Christine Janet *retired government agency administrator, retired small business owner, volunteer*

Springfield
Woodhouse, Elizabeth C. *retired government agency administrator*

Zanesville
O'Sullivan, Christine *retired executive director social service agency, consultant*

OKLAHOMA

Oklahoma City
Campbell, Brenda Dianne *protective services official*

Tinker Afb
Penn, Vernita Lynn *government agency administrator*

OREGON

Portland
Thompson, Jill Lynette Long *federal agency administrator, former congresswoman*

PENNSYLVANIA

Norristown
Raquet, Maureen Graham *protective services official, educator*

Philadelphia
Brown, Betty Marie *government agency administrator*

RHODE ISLAND

Providence
Hedlund, Ellen Louise *state agency administrator, educator*

SOUTH CAROLINA

Chapin
Freitag, Carol Wilma *state official, political scientist*

Clemson
Nielsen, Barbara Stock *state educational administrator*

Hopkins
Garrett, Robin Scott *public information officer*

SOUTH DAKOTA

Pierre
Olson, Judith Mary Reedy *retired public information officer, former state senator*

TENNESSEE

Knoxville
Andrews, Rosalind *probation officer*

Rochester

Dinkins, M. Jean *government official*
Harris, Skila *government agency administrator*

Memphis
Maddock, Yvonne *city health department administrator*
Walters, Jane *state agency administrator*

Nashville
Bailey, Stephanie B.C. *city health department administrator*
Gusky, Diane Elizabeth *state agency administrator, planner*
Guy, Sharon Kaye *state agency executive*
Kyle, Sara *state agency administrator*

TEXAS

Austin
Brown, Vivian Anderson *retired government agency administrator*
Simon, Sandra Ruth Waldman *state agency administrator*
Watson, Elizabeth Marion *protective services official*

Brownsville
Gorman, Margaret Norine *probation officer, chemical dependency counselor*

Dallas
Cain, Sally H. *federal agency administrator*
Lancaster, Karine R. *city health department administrator*

El Paso
Hardesty, Barbara Lynne *revenue agent, auditor*

San Antonio
Lehrmann, Ruby Jean *protective services official*

Stephenville
Huffman-Moser, Barbara S. *criminal investigator*

UTAH

Salt Lake City
Sparks, Mildred Thomas *state agency administrator, educator*

VERMONT

Montpelier
Peterson, Julie *public information officer*

VIRGINIA

Alexandria
Bynum, Gayela A. *public affairs specialist*
Hughes, Grace-Flores *business exeucitve*
Johnson, JoAnn Mardelle *federal agency administrator*
Leonhart, Michele Marie *government agency administrator*
Matz, Deborah *federal agency administrator*
Tandy, Karen P. *government agency administrator*

Arlington
Alford, Paula N. *federal agency administrator*
Askey, Thelma J. *federal agency administrator*
McCarthy, Jane McGinnis *retired consultant*
Milkman, Beverly L. *federal agency administrator*
Redd, Vivian Cortezza *government agency administrator*

Charlottesville
Johnson, Cornelia *city sheriff, gift shop owner*

Covington
Cauthron, Kathleen Downie *protective services official*

Falls Church
Cianciolo-Carney, Rossana *investigative analyst*
Cole, Patricia A. *federal agency administrator*
Dunne, Mary Maguire *federal agency administrator, lawyer*

Mc Lean
Lion, Linda N. *retired federal agency administrator*

Portsmouth
DaMoude, Denise Ann *postal worker*

Richmond
Wheelan, Belle S. *state agency administrator*

Roanoke
Burcham, Darlene *state agency administrator*

Staunton
Grewe, Marjorie Jane *retired protective services official*

Williamsburg
Drum, Joan Marie McFarland *federal agency administrator, educator*

WASHINGTON

Bellevue
O'Keefe, Kathleen Mary *state government official*

Olympia
Howell, Helen *state agency administrator*

Showalter, Marilyn Grace *state agency administrator*

Seattle
Melendez, Rosa Maria *protective services official*

WISCONSIN

Madison
Cronin, Patti Adrienne Wright *state agency administrator*
Deer, Ada E. *former federal agency official, social worker, educator*
Leckie, Carol Mavis *retired state government administrator*
Parrino, Cheryl Lynn *federal agency administrator*

Milwaukee
Hegerty, Nannette H. *police chief*

WYOMING

Cheyenne
Friess, Lynn *state agency administrator*
Green, Laurie *state agency administrator*
Law, Carlene *state agency administrator*
Moser, Diane *state agency administrator*

Powell
Bruscino, Leah *state agency administrator*

MILITARY ADDRESSES OF THE UNITED STATES

EUROPE

APO
Ohman, Diana J. *government agency administrator, former state official*

CANADA

ONTARIO

Ottawa
Fraser, Sheila *government agency administrator*

ADDRESS UNPUBLISHED

Alvarez, Aida *former federal agency administrator*
Bartenstein, Jeuli *federal agency administrator*
Benton, Marjorie Craig *federal agency administrator*
Billings, Judith A. *state education official*
Bishop, C. Diane *state agency administrator, educator*
Burgess, Marjorie Laura *retired protective services official*
Cassidy, Esther Christmas *retired government official*
Clarke, Victoria *federal agency administrator*
Fisher, Linda J. *federal agency administrator*
Franklin, Bonnie Selinsky *retired federal agency administrator*
Golding, Carolyn May *former government senior executive, consultant*
Grandguist, Betty L. *former director elder affairs*
Gruber Spinks, Melody Mitchell *protective services official*
Hay, Sandra Kay Gilletti *state agency administrator*
Jameson, Patricia Marian *government agency administrator*
Kezer, Pauline Ryder *state government executive, management consultant*
Korologos, Ann McLaughlin *public policy, communications executive*
Kyer, Maureen Mary *protective services official*
Lissakers, Karin Margareta *former federal agency administrator*
Lovelace, Rose Marie Sniegon *federal space agency administrator*
Lynch, Caryn A. *government agency administrator*
Mazzoni, Kerry *former state agency administrator*
McClain, Lena Alexandria *protective services official*
McDowell, Elaine *retired federal government executive, educator*
McGarry, Marcia *retired community service coordinator*
Miller, Loretta Marie *dispatcher, writer*
Millman, Amy J. *government official*
Morgan, Linda Joan *former federal agency administrator*
Noziglia, Carla Miller *forensic scientist, consultant*
Rehnquist, Janet *federal agency administrator*
Rhodes, Karren *public information officer*
Rizzi, Alicia *protective services official*
Schrenko, Linda C. *former state agency administrator*
Schultz, Janet W. *intelligence research analyst*
Smith, Nancy Angelynn *federal agency administrator*
Smith, Sarah Jane (Sally Smith) *state agency administrator*
Smith, Wendy Haimes *federal agency administrator*
Steffy, Marion Nancy *state agency administrator*
Whisler, Elizabeth Anne *government agency administrator*
Wood, Valerie J. *public information officer, writer*

GOVERNMENT: EXECUTIVE ADMINISTRATION

UNITED STATES

ALABAMA

Montgomery
Baxley, Lucy *lieutenant governor*
Ivey, Kay Ellen *state official*
Spear, Sarah G. *county administrator*
Worley, Nancy L. *secretary of state*

Warrior
Johnson, Barbara L. *retired municipal official*

ALASKA

Anchorage
Brown, Dean Naomi *state official, geologist*

ARIZONA

Glendale
Scruggs, Elaine M. *mayor*

Nogales
Valdez, Wanda Daniel *county official*

Phoenix
Brewer, Janice Kay *state official*
Fernandez, Helen Agnes *municipal official*
Miel, Vicky Ann *city official*
Napolitano, Janet Ann *governor*

Prescott Valley
Connor, Eunice Eileen *city official*

Scottsdale
Manross, Mary *mayor*

Tucson
Miller, Elizabeth Rodriguez *city official*
Scott, Shirley *city council*

ARKANSAS

Jonesboro
Chrisman, Nancy Carol *city manager, director, small business owner*

Little Rock
Fisher, Jimmie Lou *state official*
Priest, Sharon Devlin *association executive, former state secretary of state*

CALIFORNIA

Albany
Thomsen, Peggy Jean *mayor, educator, councilman*

Anaheim
Jung, Charlene *city treasurer*

Berkeley
Yellen, Janet Louise *government official, economics educator*

Brea
Daucher, Lynn M. *state official*

Carson
Oropeza, Jenny *state official*

Cathedral City
Garcia, Bonnie *state official*

Folsom
Peck, Ellie Enriquez *retired state administrator*

Fullerton
Sa, Julie *councilwoman*

Gardena
Hardison, Dee *former mayor*

Hayward
Cooper, Roberta *mayor*

Huntington Beach
Boardman, Connie *former mayor, biologist, educator*

Irvine
Shea, Christina *former mayor*

Laguna Niguel
Bates, Patricia C. *state official*

Livermore
Brown, Cathie *city official*

Long Beach
O'Neill, Beverly Lewis *mayor, former college president*
Sato, Eunice Noda *former mayor, consultant*

Los Angeles
Galanter, Ruth *city official*
Morris, Sharon Hutson *city manager*
Reagan, Nancy Davis (Anne Francis Robbins) *former First Lady of the United States, volunteer*
Smith, Ann Delorise *municipal official*
Toman, Mary Ann *federal official*

Marina
Mettee-McCutchon, Ila *municipal official, retired career army officer*

Montclair
Negrete McLeod, Gloria *state official*

Monterey Park
Smith, Betty Denny *county official, administrator, fashion executive*

Oakland
Chan, Wilma *county official*

Ontario
Dastrup-Hamill, Faye Myers *city official*

Rancho Mirage
Ford, Betty Ann (Elizabeth Ann Ford) *former First Lady of the United States, health facility executive*

Richmond
Corbin, Rosemary MacGowan *former mayor*

Sacramento
Connell, Kathleen *state official*
Contreras, Dee (Dorothea Contreras) *municipal official, educator*
Corbett, Ellen M. *mayor*
Fargo, Heather *mayor*
Garth-Lewis, Kimberley *state official, public policy educator*
Hunter, Patricia Rae (Tricia Hunter) *state official*

San Bernardino
Valles, Judith *mayor, former academic administrator*

San Diego
Freeman, Myrna Faye *county schools official*
Golding, Susan G. *former mayor*
Jacob, Dianne *county official*
Kehoe, Christine T. *state official*

San Francisco
Achtenberg, Roberta *former federal official*
Islambouly, Hagar Abdel-Hamid *consul general*
Ward, Doris M. *county official*

San Jose
Edwards, Frances Lavinia *city official*

Santa Paula
Kay, Hazel T. *local commissioner*

Solana Beach
Beard, Ann Southard *diplomat, oil company executive*

Stockton
Meissner, Katherine Gong *city official*

COLORADO

Aurora
Sheffield, Nancy *city agency administrator*

Colorado Springs
Abbott, Gina *municipal government executive*
Makepeace, Mary Lou *former mayor*

Denver
Cohen-Vader, Cheryl Denise *municipal official*
Davidson, Donetta *state official*
Galloway, Judy A. *deputy commissioner*
Moulton, Jennifer T. *city official, architect*
Muja, Kathleen Ann *state official, consultant*
Norton, Jane E. *lieutenant governor*
Rowe, Tina L. *government official*
Walcher, Jennifer Lynne *city official*

Eagle
Sheaffer, Karen *county official, treasurer*

Golden
Fahey, Barbara Stewart Doe *public agency administrator*

Sterling
Gumina, Pamela Ray *municipal government administrator*

CONNECTICUT

Easton
Meyer, Alice Virginia *state official*

Hartford
Bysiewicz, Susan *secretary of state*
Hinsch, Cathleen Loffredo *press secretary*
Nappier, Denise L. *state official*
Rell, M. Jodi *lieutenant governor*

Madison
Hedwall, Patricia Greger *municipal assessor*

Norwalk
Roman, Mary *city official*

Stamford
Dennies, Sandra Lee *city official*

DELAWARE

Dover
Minner, Ruth Ann *governor*
Windsor, Harriet Smith *state official*
Woodruff, Valerie *secretary of education*

Wilmington
Brady, M. Jane *state attorney general*

DISTRICT OF COLUMBIA

Washington
Anthony, Sheila Foster *government official*
Apodaca, Clara R. *federal official*
Argrett, Loretta Collins *assistant attorney general, educator*
Ayres, Mary Ellen *government official*
Baasan, Ragchaa *diplomat*
Brazeal, Aurelia Erskine *ambassador*
Breathitt, Linda K. *federal commissioner*
Bridgewater, Pamela E. *ambassador*
Brown, Elizabeth Ann *foreign service officer*
Bush, Laura Welch *First Lady of United States*
Bushnell, Prudence *diplomat, former management consultant, trainer*
Chesser, Judy Lee *municipal official*
Connell, Mary Ellen *diplomat*
Cowal, Sally Grooms *diplomat, association administrator*
Cropp, Linda W. *city official*
Echaveste, Maria *government official, lawyer*
Ely-Raphel, Nancy *diplomat*
Ferrier, Maria Hernandez *federal official, educator*
Francke, Rend Rahim *ambassador*
Franklin, Barbara Hackman *business executive, former government official*
Frawley Bagley, Elizabeth *government advisor, ambassador*
Gatons, Anna-Marie Kilmade *government official*
Gilliom, Judith Carr *government official*
Glassman, Cynthia A. *commissioner*
Hall, Kathryn Walt *ambassador*
Hayes, Allene Valerie Farmer *government executive*
Heivilin, Donna Mae *government executive*
Hernreich, Nancy *federal official*
Hillman, Jennifer Anne *commissioner, ambassador, trade negotiator*
Irving, Susan Jean *government executive*
Jacobs, Susan S. *ambassador*
Jordan, Mary Lucille *commissioner*
Karaer, Arma Jane *ambassador*
Kraemer, Sylvia Katharine *government official, historian*
Levy, Leah Garrigan *federal official*
Lewis, Ann Frank *former government official*
Lieberman, Evelyn S. *diplomat*
Lino, Marisa Rose *diplomat*
Lowe, Mary Frances *federal government official*
Lowrey, Barbara R. *federal official*
Marcoulis, Erato [illegible]
Martinez, Carmen M. *ambassador*
Mathews, Jessica Tuchman *executive, foreign policy expert*
McElveen-Hunter, Bonnie *ambassador*
Miller, Judith A. *federal official*
Miller, Marcia E. *federal government official*
Morrissey, Patricia A. *commissioner*
Nesbitt, Wanda L. *ambassador*
Ness, Susan *federal official*
Norton, Gale Ann *secretary of interior*
Oakley, Phyllis Elliott *retired diplomat*
O'Day, Kathleen M. *federal official*
Orr, Bobette Kay *diplomat*
Pearce, Drue *government official, former state legislator*
Phillips, Jeanne L. *ambassador*
Plaisted, Joan M. *diplomat*
Quinn, Maureen E. *ambassador*
Raphel, Robin *ambassador*
Reef, Grace *government official*
Rees, Nina Shokraii *federal official, writer*
Remez, Shereen G. *government executive*
Render, Arlene *ambassador*
Rice, Condoleezza *national security advisor*
Rich, Laurie M. *federal official, educator*
Roby, Cheryl J. *deputy assistant secretary*
Rogers, Thomasina Venese *federal commissioner*
Ryan, Mary A. *diplomat*
Sanderson, Janet A. *ambassador*
Scott-Finan, Nancy Isabella *government administrator*
Searing, Marjory Ellen *government official, economist*
Sharpless, Mattie R. *ambassador*
Shaw, Theresa (Terri) S. *federal official*
Shelly, Christine Deborah *foreign service officer*
Shiner, Josette Sheeran *ambassador*
Simmons, Anne L. *federal official*
Smith, Elaine Diana *foreign service officer*
Smith, Pamela Hyde *ambassador*
Smith, Patricia Grace *government official*
Spellings, Margaret LaMontagne *assistant to US President on domestic policy*
Stock, Ann *federal official*
Sutter, Eleanor Bly *retired diplomat*
Thompson, Sally Engstrom *state official*
Veneman, Ann M. *secretary of agriculture*
Verville, Elizabeth Giavani *federal official*
Wahba, Marcelle M. *ambassador*
Weintraub, Ellen L. *commissioner*
Wexler, Anne *government relations and public affairs consultant*
Wilkinson, Sharon P. *department of state official, former ambassador*
Willeford, Pamela P. *ambassador*
Yates, Mary Carlin *ambassador*

FLORIDA

Boynton Beach
Polinsky, Janet Naboicheck *retired state official, former state legislator*

Fort Lauderdale
Gunzburger, Suzanne Nathan *municipal official, social worker*

Parrish, Lori Nance *commissioner*

Hollywood
Giulianti, Mara Selena *mayor, civic worker*

Miami
Carey-Shuler, Barbara *county commissioner*
Margolis, Gwen *county commissioner*
McKinney, Erica Kimberly *city official*
Reno, Janet *former attorney general*
Sorenson, Katy *county commissioner*

Punta Gorda
Smith-Mooney, Marilyn Patricia *city government official, management consultant and facilitator*

Tallahassee
Jaber, Lila A. *state official*
Jennings, Toni *lieutenant governor*
Mortham, Sandra Barringer *former state official*

Tampa
Bucella, Donna Ann *federal official*
Freedman, Sandra Warshaw *former mayor*
Iorio, Pam *county official*
Platt, Jan Kaminis *county official*

Treasure Island
Williams, Bonnie Lee *city official*

Vero Beach
Bowman, Margaret Coon *retired public official, environmental educator*

GEORGIA

Alpharetta
Johnson, Sandra Bartlett *city official*

Atlanta
Burke, Karen Keith *county official*
Cox, Cathy *state official*
Franklin, Shirley Clarke *mayor*

HAWAII

Honolulu
Bronster, Margery S *state attorney general*
Goto Sabas, Jennifer *state official*
Lingle, Linda *governor*
Wakatsuki, Lynn Y. *commissioner*

Lihue
Kusaka, Maryanne Winona *mayor*

IDAHO

Boise
Terteling-Payne, Carolyn Ann *city official*

ILLINOIS

Arlington Heights
Mulder, Arlene JoAnn *mayor*

Berwyn
Karasek, Mary Hapac *city treasurer, community volunteer*

Chicago
Madigan, Lisa *state attorney general*
Robbins, Audrey *county official*
Topinka, Judy Baar *state official, political organization worker*
Willis, Anna L. *commissioner*

Machesney Park
Vaughn, Linda M. *municipal official*

Morton Grove
Kouba, Shari L. *retired federal official*

Ottawa
Hiltabrand, Linda Mae *state official*

Springfield
Chapman, Delinda (Ann) *retired state official*
Hasara, Karen A. *mayor*
Lindley, Maralee Irwin *county official, consultant, speaker*
Morford, Lynn Ellen *state official*

Urbana
Prussing, Laurel Lunt *public interest lobbyist, economist, auditor*

Vernon Hills
Ryg, Kathleen Schultz *municipal government official*

INDIANA

Columbus
Carter, Pamela Lynn *former state attorney general*

Hammond
Curiel, Carolyn *ambassador*

Indianapolis
Davis, Katherine Lyon *lieutenant governor*
Klika, Cristine M. *state official*
Nass, Connie Kay *state auditor*
Usher, Phyllis Land *state official*

Lafayette
Phillips, Linda *county official*

IOWA

Cedar Rapids
Novetzke, Sally Johnson *former ambassador*
Reppert, Nancy Lue *retired municipal official, legal consultant*

Des Moines
Boal, Carmine *state official*
Buhr, Florence D. *county official*
Corning, Joy Cole *retired state official*
Gaskill, Mary *state official*
Heddens, Lisa *state official*
Huser, Geri D. *state official*
Jacobs, Libby Swanson *state official*
Pederson, Sally *lieutenant governor*
Tymeson, Jodi *state official*
Upmeyer, Linda *state official*

Oelwein
McFarlane, Beth Lucetta Troester *former mayor*

KANSAS

Arkansas City
Bruton, Rebecca Ann *mayor, commissioner*

Garden Plain
Stovall, Carla Jo *former state attorney general*

Marion
Bateman, Jeannine Ann *county official*

Topeka
Glasscock, Joyce H. *state official*
Jenkins, Lynn M. *state official, former state legislator*
Sebelius, Kathleen Gilligan *governor*

KENTUCKY

Catlettsburg
Selbee, Maxine Butcher *county clerk*

Frankfort
Nowland-Curry, Betsy *state official*
Palmore, Carol M. *state official*

Lexington
Isaac, Teresa Ann *mayor, lawyer*
Miller, Pamela Gundersen *mayor*

Louisville
Keith, Penny Sue *mayor, educator*

Shelbyville
Miller, Mary Helen *retired public administrator*

LOUISIANA

Baton Rouge
Blanco, Kathleen Babineaux *governor*
Shaw, Beverly C. *state official*

New Orleans
Gates, Audrey Castine *city government administrator*

MAINE

Augusta
Gendron, Susan Ann *commissioner, educator*
McCormick, Dale *state treasurer*

MARYLAND

Annapolis
Clagett, Virginia Parker *county official*
Florestano, Patricia Sherer *state official*
Kopp, Nancy Kornblith *state official*

Baltimore
Daniels, Susan M. *commissioner*
Mensh, Suzanne Cooper *state official*

Bethesda
Kawazoe, Robin Inada *federal official*

Burkittsville
Aughenbaugh, Deborah Ann *mayor, retired elementary school educator*

Columbia
Scates, Alice Yeomans *former government official, consultant*

Ellicott City
Galinsky, Deborah Jean *county official*

Potomac
Kernan, Barbara Desind *senior government executive*
Roesser, Jean Wolberg *state official*

Rockville
Corley, Rose Ann McAfee *government official*
Woodcock, Janet *federal official*

Upper Marlboro
Hewlett, Elizabeth M. *county official*

MASSACHUSETTS

Boston
Healey, Kerry Murphy *lieutenant governor*
O'Brien, Shannon Patricia *state treasurer*

Cambridge
Hunt, Swanee G. *public policy educator, former ambassador*
Martin, Lynn Morley *former secretary of labor*
Qualls, Roxanne *mayor*

Dorchester
Garrison, Althea *government official*

Littleton
Crory, Mary *town official*

Lowell
Donoghue, Eileen M. *former mayor*
Mercier, Rita *mayor*

New Bedford
Thomas, Sharon M. *city official*

Seekonk
Parker, Janet Ruth *town official*

Taunton
Lopes, Maria Fernandina *commissioner*

West Hyannisport
Devine, Nancy *postmaster*

MICHIGAN

Ann Arbor
Sheldon, Ingrid Kristina *former mayor, bookkeeper*

Detroit
Bell Wilson, Carlotta A. *state official, consultant*

Flint
Conyers, Jean Louise *chamber of commerce executive*

Lansing
Christian, Sandra Svec *retired state official*
Granholm, Jennifer Mulhern *governor*
Land, Terri Lynn *state official*

Mount Clemens
Kolakowski, Diana Jean *county commissioner*

Tecumseh
Sackett, Dianne Marie *city treasurer, accountant*

MINNESOTA

Chisholm
Peterson, Marjorie *former mayor*

Elbow Lake
Lohse, Susan Faye *county official, educator*

Golden Valley
Leppik, Margaret White *municipal official*

Minneapolis
Fraser, Arvonne Skelton *former United Nations ambassador*
Mondale, Joan Adams *wife of former Vice President of United States*
Sayles Belton, Sharon *former mayor*

Plymouth
Hurlburt, Anne Wedewer *municipal official*

Saint Paul
Kiffmeyer, Mary *state official*
Molnau, Carol *lieutenant governor*
Reinhardt, Victoria Ann *county official, environmentalist*

MISSISSIPPI

Jackson
Tuck, Amy *lieutenant governor*

MISSOURI

Columbia
Miller, Karen Marie *county commissioner*

Jefferson City
Farmer, Nancy *state official*
Lumpe, Sheila *state commissioner, former state legislator*

Kansas City
Barnes, Kay *mayor*
Danner, Kathleen Frances Steele *federal official*
Rocha, Catherine Tomasa *municipal official*
Stroup, Kala Mays *educational alliance administrator, former state higher education commissioner*

Platte City
Knight, Betty Ann *county commissioner*
Nash, Donna Cecile *county official*

Saint Louis
Carpenter, Sharon Quigley *municipal official*

Springfield
Montgomery, Linda Stroupe *county official*

Troy
McClellan, Betty *county official*

MONTANA

Clancy
Ekanger, Laurie *retired state official, retired contractor*

Forsyth
Lincoln, Sharon Ann *retired county official*

Havre
Mayer Lossing, Emily Ann *city official*

Helena
Hill, Betti Christie *government executive*
McCulloch, Linda *state official*

NEBRASKA

Benkelman
Whiteley, Rose Marie *city clerk, treasurer*

Brewster
Teahon, Jean Ann *county official*

Lincoln
Boyle, Anne C. *state commissioner*
Hasselbalch, Marilyn Jean *state official*
Moul, Maxine Burnett *state official*
Seng, Coleen Joy *mayor*

Omaha
Pirsch, Carol McBride *county official, former state senator, community relations manager*

NEVADA

Carson City
Hunt, Lorraine T. *lieutenant governor*

Dayton
Hudgens, Sandra Lawler *retired state official*

Henderson
McKinney, Sally Vitkus *state official*

Las Vegas
Augustine, Kathy Marie *state controller, state legislator, secondary education educator*
Vandever, Judith Ann *county official*

NEW HAMPSHIRE

Concord
Thomas, Georgie A. *state official*

Hanover
Haselton, Mary Michelson *retired foreign service officer, artist*

Manchester
Holden, Carol H. *county official*

Munsonville
Kirk, Jane Seaver *municipal government administrator*

NEW JERSEY

Bernardsville
Boquist, Diana D. *mayor, real estate agent*

East Orange
Corbitt, Ann Marie *municipal official*

Jersey City
Bowen-Thompson, Frances Octavia *county official, nonprofit organization consultant*
Mizzi, Charlotte H. *city director*

Little Ferry
Navarro-Steinel, Catherine A. *municipal official*

Moorestown
Weiss, Eva *retired bridge commissioner*

Morristown
MacKinnis, Ann Phelps *municipal government and land use management executive*

Newark
Davis, Yvonne D. *county official*

Sea Isle City
Tull, Theresa Anne *retired diplomat*

Trenton
Castro, Ida L. *state official, former federal official*
Thomas, Regena L. *secretary of state*

NEW MEXICO

Albuquerque
Archulata, Margie Baca *city clerk*
Kotchian, Sarah Bruff *municipal official*

Gallup
Lundstrom, Patricia *state government administrator*

Los Alamos
Gonzales, Stephanie *state official*

Los Lunas
Behrend, Betty Ann *municipal official*

Santa Fe
Denish, Diane D. *lieutenant governor*
Kinderwater, Diane *state official*
Madrid, Patricia A. *state attorney general*
Vigil-Giron, Rebecca *state official*

NEW YORK

Albany
Berman, Carol *commissioner*
Castro, Bernadette *state official*
Chretien, Margaret Cecilia *public administrator*
Donohue, Mary *lieutenant governor*

Brewster
Bates, Barbara J. Neuner *retired municipal official*

Buffalo
Nowak, Carol Ann *city official*

Lawrence
Okos, Mildred *city manager*

Manhasset
Galante, Ann Muriel *municipal official*

New York
Amenta, Joyce Ann *United Nations executive*
Arystanbekova, Akmaral Khaidarovna *diplomat*
Dawson, Stephanie Elaine *city manager*
Dayson, Diane Harris *superintendent, park ranger*
Durrant, M. Patricia *diplomat*
Ferguson, Sarah *The Duchess of York*
Finauri, Graciela Maria *foreign service professional*
Harris, Patricia E. *deputy mayor*
Løj, Ellen Margrethe *ambassador*
Robles-Roman, Carol A. *municipal official*
Rzewnicki, Janet C. *state official*
Sadik, Nafis *United Nations administrator*
Townsend, Kathleen Kennedy *former lieutenant governor*
Young, Paula Eva *city official, journalist, writer*

Rochester
Huddleston, Vicki Jean *diplomat*

Rome
Sanders, Robin Renee *diplomat*

NORTH CAROLINA

Concord
Sossamon, Nancy H. *city official*

Durham
Kerckhoff, Sylvia Stansbury *mayor*

Elizabeth City
Pierce, Dianne S. *city clerk*

Greensboro
Shaw, Linda Dare Owens *county commissioner*

Hickory
Mason, Anne R. Hardin *municipal official*

Hubert
Howell, Nelda Kay *commissioner*

Manteo
Evans, Michelle T. *county official*

Mount Gilead
McNeill, Maxine Currie *county official*

Raleigh
Berry, Cherie Killian *commissioner*
Faulkner, Janice H. *state official*
Johnston, Linda Tidwell *municipal official*
Joyner, Lorinzo Little *commissioner*
Marshall, Elaine Folk *state official*
Perdue, Beverly E. *lieutenant governor, geriatric consultant*

Research Triangle Park
League, Charle Allport (Charlene League) *federal official, minister*

Valdese
Hildebran, Frances Elaine *municipal clerk*

NORTH DAKOTA

Bismarck
Gilmore, Kathi *state treasurer*
Wefald, Susan *state commissioner*

Edinburg
Myrdal, Rosemarie Caryle *state official, former state legislator*

Mandan
Heitkamp, Heidi *former state attorney general*

OHIO

Alliance
Woods, Rose Mary *former presidential assistant, consultant*

Cleveland
Campbell, Jane Louise *mayor*

Columbus
Bradley, Jennette *lieutenant governor*
Carter, Melinda *municipal official*
Montgomery, Betty Dee *state auditor, former state attorney general, former state legislator*
Walcher, Kathleen *state official*

Dayton
McLin, Rhine Lana *mayor, former state legislator*

Gahanna
Sherman, Ruth Todd *government advisor, counselor, consultant*

Galion
Harter, Lonna *city manager*

Lakewood
Cain, Madeline Ann *mayor*

Mansfield
Converse, Sandra *city finance director, financial planner*

Middleport
Cantrell, Carol Howe *municipal administrator*

New Philadelphia
Barlock, Ida Belle *county board of elections clerk*

Niles
Rizer, Janet Marlene *city tax administrator*

Trotwood
Staggs, Barbara J. *vice mayor*

Youngstown
Gransee, Marsha L. *federal agency executive*

OKLAHOMA

Norman
Price, Linda Rice *community development administrator*

Oklahoma City
Boyd, Betty *government official*
Fallin, Mary Copeland *lieutenant governor*
Savage, Susan M. *state official, former mayor*

Park Hill
Mankiller, Wilma Pearl *tribal leader, retired*

OREGON

Eugene
Bascom, Ruth F. *retired mayor*
Collas-Dean, Angela G. *former state commissioner, small business owner*

Portland
Katz, Vera *mayor, former college administrator, state legislator*
Kleim, F. Denise *city official*

Salem
Taylor, Janet R. *mayor*

PENNSYLVANIA

Allentown
Glaessmann, Doris Ann *former county official, consultant*

Camp Hill
Besch, Nancy Adams *county official*

Donora
Todd, Norma Ross *retired government official*

Glen Mills
Dunion, Celeste Mogab *consultant, business manager, township official*

Harrisburg
Baker Knoll, Catherine *lieutenant governor*
Hafer, Barbara *state official*
Houstoun, Feather O'Connor *state official*
Koken, M. Diane *commissioner, state*
Pizzingrilli, Kim *state official*

Lewisburg
Lenhart, Lorraine Margaret *county official*

New Cumberland
Rose, Bonnie Lou *state official*

Philadelphia
DiBona, Margaret Rose *retired state official*
Kaplan, Barbara Jane *retired city planner*
Latsios, Barbara Lynn *government official*
Miller, Donna Reed *city official*
Murray, Kathleen *municipal official*

Pittsburgh
Crawford, Robin Yvette *county caseworker*

Rices Landing
Cottle, Kimberly Lynn *municipal official*

Sayre
Smith, Robin L. *municipal official*

Somerset
Thomas, Darlene Jean *state employee*

Upper Saint Clair
Smith, Gloria S. *local commissioner, educator*

RHODE ISLAND

Providence
O'Keefe, Beverly Disbrow *state official, federal official*

SOUTH CAROLINA

Columbia
Clyburn, Mignon L. *commissioner*

Scott, Bernice G. *county official*
Tenenbaum, Inez Moore *superintendent of education*
Waites, Candy Yaghjian *former state official*

Laurens
Henderson, Rita Beatrice *county official*

Sumter
Moore, Verna *county official*

SOUTH DAKOTA

Pierre
Schoenfelder, Laska *commissioner, farmer*

TENNESSEE

Charlotte
Frazier, Linda Joyce *county official*

Clarksville
Johnson, Barbara Ella Jackson *city official*

Cleveland
Posner, Linda Irene *retired government official, marketing consultant*

Enville
Campbell, Nell *mayor*

Huntsville
Lewallen Reynolds, Cynthia Maire *city administrator, small business owner*

Memphis
Mardis, Elma Hubbard *county administrator, consultant*

Nashville
Gore, Tipper (Mary Elizabeth Gore) *wife of the former vice president of the United States*
Seivers, Lana C. *commissioner of education*
Swing, Marilyn S. *metropolitan clerk*
Thomas, Hazel Beatrice *state official*
Wadley, Fredia Stovall *state commissioner*

Oak Ridge
Holloway, Jacqueline *county commissioner*

TEXAS

Arlington
Hall, Anna Christene *retired government official*

Austin
Ables-Flatt, Jean Ann *commissioner*
Caldwell, Shirley W. *commissioner*
Clay, Lareatha H. *commissioner*
Combs, Susan *commissioner of agriculture*
Johnson, Lady Bird (Mrs. Claudia Alta Taylor) *former First Lady of the United States*
Klein, Rebecca *commissioner*
McKean, Maureen Catherine *city official, systems analyst*
McKnight, Mamie *commissioner*
Richards, Ann Willis *former governor*

Beaumont
Lord, Evelyn Marlin *mayor*

Bellville
Krueger, Betty Adel *county official*

Canyon
Rice, Lois *mayor*

Dallas
Cottingham, Jennifer Jane *city official*
Miller, Laura *mayor, journalist*

Edinburg
García, Norma Garza *county treasurer*

Giddings
Dismukes, Carol Jaehne *county official*

Grand Prairie
Horak, Trish *city government worker*

Houston
desVignes-Kendrick, Mary *municipal official*
Faison, Holly *state official*

Lubbock
Sitton, Windy *mayor*

Pecos
Florez, Diane O. *county clerk*

Plano
Evans, Pat *mayor*

San Antonio
Henderson, Connie Chorlton *city planner, artist and writer*

UTAH

Salt Lake City
Foxley, Cecelia Harrison *commissioner*
Varela, Vicki *state official*
Walker, Olene S. *governor*
White, Constance Burnham *state official*

VERMONT

Burlington
Kunin, Madeleine May *former ambassador to Switzerland, former governor*

Montpelier
Markowitz, Deborah Lynn *state government official*

VIRGINIA

Alexandria
Freeman-Wilson, Karen *former attorney general, prosecutor, educational association administrator*

Arlington
Bune, Karen Louise *criminal justice official*
Clutter, Mary Elizabeth *federal official*
Hamed, Martha Ellen *government administrator*
Wood, Heidi *commissioner*

Chantilly
Rogin, Ronne Ann *retired government contract specialist*

Dublin
Lineberry, Rebecca J. *municipal official, treasurer*

Fairfax
Haskett, Dianne Louise *former mayor, lawyer, consultant*
Vehrs, Nancy Joyce *county official*

Gate City
Edwards, Barbara Ann *county official*

Manassas
Lawson, Nancy P. *retired county official*

Mc Lean
Gregus, Linda Anna *government official*
Healy, Theresa Ann *former ambassador*

Morattico
Dawson, Carol Gene *former commissioner, writer, consultant*

Richmond
DeMary, Jo Lynne *state official, elementary school educator*
Jones-Atkins, DeBorah Kaye *state official*
Linkonis, Suzanne Newbold *probation officer, counselor*
Petera, Anne Pappas *state official*
Wilder, Eunice *city official*

Suffolk
McAdoo, Clarissa Eileen *city agency administrator*

Virginia Beach
Oberndorf, Meyera E. *mayor*

WASHINGTON

Everett
Vaughn, Kathy *municipal official*

Marysville
Bartholomew, Shirley Kathleen *municipal official*

Medina
Ward, Marilyn Beeman *commissioner*

Olympia
Gregoire, Christine O. *state attorney general*
Long, Marsha Tadano *state official*

Seattle
Covington, Germaine Ward *municipal agency administrator*
Kennedy, Mary Virginia *diplomat*
Knox, Venerria L. *city official*
Nuxoll, Carla *federal official*

Spokane
Greenwood, Collette P. *municipal official, finance officer*

Vancouver
Griffith, Linda Marie (Lynne) *county government official*

WEST VIRGINIA

Charleston
Bias, Sharon G. *state commissioner*

Harpers Ferry
Cooley, Hilary Elizabeth *county official*

WISCONSIN

Gillett
Nichols, Diane Colleen *municipal official*

Madison
Bauman, Susan Joan Mayer *mayor, lawyer*
Lautenschlager, Peggy A. *state attorney general*
Lawton, Barbara *lieutenant governor*
Shilling, Jennifer *state official*
Sinicki, Christine *state official*
Thompson, Barbara Storck *state official*

Pewaukee
Farrow, Margaret Ann *former state official*

WYOMING

Cheyenne
Catchpole, Judy *state official*
Lummis, Cynthia Marie *state official, lawyer*
Rodekohr, Diane E. *state official*

Thomson, Thyra Godfrey *former state official*
Woodhouse, Gay Vanderpoel *former state attorney general, lawyer*

TERRITORIES OF THE UNITED STATES

PUERTO RICO

San Juan
Andujar, Norma Burgos *former state official*
Burgos, Norma *former secretary of state*
Calderón, Sila M. *governor*
Rodriguez, Annabelle *state attorney general*
Velez Silva, Xenia *Puerto Rican government official*

VIRGIN ISLANDS

Charlotte Amalie
Stapleton, Marylyn Alecia *diplomat*

St Thomas
Michael, Noreen *commissioner, educator*

MILITARY ADDRESSES OF THE UNITED STATES

ATLANTIC

Apo
Watt, Linda E. *ambassador*

EUROPE

APO
Morella, Constance Albanese *ambassador, former congresswoman*
Schoonover, Brenda B. *ambassador*

Apo
Corwin, Elizabeth A. *foreign service officer*

CANADA

ONTARIO

Ottawa
Augustine, Jean Magdalene *Canadian government official, member of parliament*
Caplan, Elinor *former Canadian government official*
Clarkson, Adrienne *Governor General of Canada*
Copps, Sheila *former Canadian government official*
Fairbairn, Joyce *Canadian government official*
Grey, Deborah Cleland *Canadian government official*
Guarnieri, Albina *Canadian government official, Canadian legislator*
Lalonde, Francine *member of parliament*
Marleau, Diane *Canadian government official*
Martin, Sheila Ann *wife of Canadian Prime Minister*
McLellan, A. Anne *Canadian government official*
Minna, Maria *member of Canadian Parliament*
Poulin, Marie *Canadian government official*
Robillard, Lucienne *Canadian government official*
Roland, Anne *registrar Supreme Court of Canada*

QUEBEC

Hull
Blondin-Andrew, Ethel D. *Canadian government official*
Bradshaw, Claudette *Canadian government official*

Pointe-Claire
Lapointe, Lucie *Canadian government official*

SASKATCHEWAN

Regina
Haverstock, Lynda M. *lieutenant governor*

MEXICO

Delegacion Miguel Hidalgo CP
de Fox, Marta Sahagun *First Lady of Mexico*

AUSTRALIA

Canberra
Vanstone, Amanda *Australian government official*

Double Bay
Peacock, Penne Korth *ambassador*

BANGLADESH

Baridhara Dhaka
Peters, Mary Ann *ambassador*

BRAZIL

Quadra
Hrinak, Donna Jean *ambassador*

COSTA RICA

San Jose
McClanahan, Kay Marie *government official, lawyer*

ECUADOR

Quito
Kenney, Kristie Anne *ambassador*

EGYPT

Cairo
Pendleton, Mary Catherine *foreign service officer*

ENGLAND

London
Elizabeth, Her Majesty, II, (Elizabeth Alexandra Mary) *Queen of United Kingdom of Great Britain, Northern Ireland and Canada, and her other Realms and Territories, head of the Commonwealth, Defender of the Faith*
Hewitt, Patricia Hope *English government official, political scientist, researcher, broadcaster*

ISRAEL

Jerusalem
Edighoffer-Murray, Anna Barbel *procurement officer, political scientist, pharmacist*

MALAYSIA

Kuala Lumpur
Huhtala, Marie Therese *diplomat*

MONGOLIA

Ulaanbaatar
Slutz, Pamela Jo Howell *ambassador*

MOZAMBIQUE

Maputo
La Lime, Helen R. Meagher *ambassador*

NICARAGUA

Managua
Moore, Barbara C. *ambassador*

PAKISTAN

Islamabad
Powell, Nancy J. *ambassador*

RWANDA

Kigali
McMillion, Margaret Kim *foreign service officer*

SPAIN

Canary Islands
Wells, Melissa Foelsch *foreign service officer*

SWITZERLAND

Geneva
Deily, Linnet Frazier *ambassador*

SYRIA

Damascus
Scobey, Margaret *ambassador*

TURKMENISTAN

Ashgabat
Jacobson, Tracey Ann *ambassador*

Niamey
Mathieu, Gail Dennise *ambassador*

ADDRESS UNPUBLISHED

Albright, Madeleine Korbel *former secretary of state*

Armstrong, Anne Legendre (Mrs. Tobin Armstrong) *retired ambassador*
Atwater, Phyllis Y. *municipal administrator*
Baker, Gwendolyn Calvert *United Nations official*
Bayless, Betsey *state official*
Benson, Joanne E. *former lieutenant governor*
Berlincourt, Marjorie Alkins *government official, retired*
Binsfeld, Connie Berube *former state official*
Black, Shirley Temple (Mrs. Charles A. Black) *former ambassador, former actress*
Broadrick-Allen, Sandra Carol *retired city manager, consultant, civic worker*
Brown, June Gibbs *retired government official*
Brown, Kay (Mary Kathryn Brown) *retired state official, consultant*
Bumpas, Diane DeWare *commissioner*
Bush, Barbara Pierce *former First Lady of the United States, volunteer*
Carney, Patricia *Canadian government official*
Carter, Rosalynn Smith *former First Lady of the United States*
Chung, Caroline *foreign service officer*
Cohen, Roberta Jane *government executive*
Cook, Rebecca McDowell *former state official*
Cosman, Francene Jen *former government official*
Crandall, Nancy Lee *mayor*
Del Papa, Frankie Sue *former state attorney general*
Dyrstad, Joanell M. *former lieutenant governor, consultant*
Ebert, Dorothy Elizabeth *retired county clerk*
Edwards, Lydia Justice *state official*
Ellis, J. Renee Eley *special events administrator*
Eu, March Fong *ambassador*
Goldsmith, Jocelyn Stone *retired state employment professional*
Graham, Janet C. *former state attorney general*
Growe, Joan Anderson *former state official*
Han, Soo J. *governmental administrator*
Hazeltine, Joyce *former state official*
Henry, Sherrye P. *former political advisor*
Herman, Alexis M. *former secretary of labor*
Hester, Nancy Elizabeth *county government official*
Hillard, Carole *former lieutenant governor*
Hinds, Sallie Ann *retired township official*
Hirono, Mazie Keiko *former lieutenant governor*
Holiday, Edith Elizabeth *former presidential adviser, cabinet secretary*
Holmes, Genta Hawkins *former diplomat*
Howard, Barbara Byers *public policy consultant*
Hughes, Karen Parfitt *former federal official*
Hull, Jane Dee *former governor, former state legislator*
Jacobs, Judith *county legislator*
Johnson, Karla Ann *county official*
Jones, Jan Laverty *mayor*
Joseph, Geri Mack (Geraldine Joseph) *former ambassador, educator, journalist*
Joseph, Shirley Troyan *retired executive*
Likins, Rose Marie *foreign service officer*
Maguire-Zinni, Deirdre *federal community development management analyst*
Manglona, Ramona V. *state attorney general, judge*
Martz, Judy Helen *governor*
McCaughey Ross, Elizabeth P. (Betsy McCaughey) *former lieutenat governor*
Millane, Lynn *retired town official*
Morgan, Paulette Elise *state official, researcher*
Ortega, Lorraine G. *state land office executive*
Paulik, Mary Theresa *retired municipal official, researcher*
Preis, Mary Louise *commissioner, former state legislator*
Ridgway, Rozanne LeJeanne *retired diplomat*
Rivers, Beverly D. *former secretary of the district*
Robinson, Laurie Overby *former assistant attorney general*
Rosenthal, Helen Nagelberg *county official, advocate*
Rudin, Anne *retired mayor, nursing educator*
Rundio, Joan Peters (Jo Rundio) *public administrator*
Salsitz, Elena L. *city official*
Sampas, Dorothy Myers *retired government official*
Sauerbrey, Ellen Elaine Richmond *diplomat*
Savocchio, Joyce A. *former mayor*
Schoettler, Gail Sinton *former ambassador*
Schunk, Mae Gasparac *former state official*
Schwartz, Carol Levitt *government official*
Sentenne, Justine *corporate ombudsman consultant*
Shaheen, C. Jeanne *former governor*
Smith, Jean Kennedy *former ambassador*
Sudanowicz, Elaine Marie *government executive*
Swift, Jane Maria *former governor*
Tarrody, Janet Faulstich *retired congressional executive*
Teater, Dorothy Seath *retired county official*
Tomasky, Susan *corporate officer*
Ulmer, Frances Ann *former lieutenant governor*
Ushijima, Jean M. *retired city official*
Wallach, Patricia *councilwoman, retired mayor*
Whitman, Christine Todd *former governor*
Whitney, Jane *foreign service officer*
Wilson, Eleanor McElroy *county official*
Wood, Corinne *former lieutenant governor*

Wood, Roberta Susan *retired foreign service officer*

GOVERNMENT: LEGISLATIVE ADMINISTRATION

UNITED STATES

ALABAMA

Birmingham
Allen, Maryon Pittman *former senator, journalist, lecturer, interior and clothing designer*

Montgomery
Escott-Russell, Sundra *state legislator*
Figures, Vivian Davis *state legislator*
Kennedy, Yvonne *state legislator*
Smith, Harri Anne *state legislator*

ALASKA

Anchorage
Sturgulewski, Arliss *state legislator, director*

Homer
Phillips, Gail *state legislator*

Juneau
Cissna, Sharon *state representative*
Dahlstrom, Nancy *state representative*
Green, Lyda N. *state legislator*
Guess, Gretchen *state senator*
Heinze, Cheryll Boren *state representative*
Kapsner, Mary *state representative*
Lincoln, Georgianna *state legislator*
Masek, Beverly *state representative*
McGuire, Lesil L. *state representative*
Wilson, Peggy *state representative, registered nurse*

North Pole
James, Jeannette Adeline *state legislator, accountant*

ARIZONA

Phoenix
Aguirre, Linda *state senator*
Arzberger, Marsha *state senator*
Burns, Brenda *state senator*
Daniels, Lori S. *state legislator, insurance agent*
Day, Ann *state legislator*
Gerard, Susan *state senator*
Grace, Sue *state legislator*
Hartley, Mary *state legislator*
Hellon, Toni *state senator*
Solomon, Ruth *state legislator, teacher*
Wold, Kimberly G. *legislative staff member*

Tempe
Smith, Carol Estes *retired councilman*

Tucson
Richardson, Elaine *state legislator*

ARKANSAS

Dumas
Schexnayder, Charlotte Tillar *state legislator*

Fayetteville
Madison, Sue Wood *state legislator*

Foreman
Horn, Barbara B. *state legislator*

Little Rock
Pollan, Carolyn Joan *state legislator, job research administrator*

Pine Bluff
Gullett, Brenda B. *state legislator*

Russellville
Trusty, Sharon *state legislator*

CALIFORNIA

Chula Vista
Moreno-Ducheny, Denise *state senator*

East Palo Alto
Jacobs Gibson, Rose *city councilwoman, non-profit company executive*

Eureka
Berg, Patty *state legislator*

Long Beach
Karentte, Betty *state legislator*
Karnette, Betty *state senator*

Los Angeles
Chick, Laura *councilwoman*
Walters, Rita *councilwoman*

Ontario
Soto, Nell *state senator*

Sacramento
Alpert, Deirdre Whittleton (Dede Alpert) *state legislator*
Cohn, Rebecca *state representative*
Escutia, Martha *state senator*
Figueroa, Liz *state senator*
Goldberg, Jackie *councilwoman*
Hancock, Loni *state legislator, former mayor*
Hill, Elizabeth Goodwin *legislative analyst*
Horton, Shirley A. *state legislator, former mayor*
Hughes, Teresa P. *state legislator*
Kuehl, Sheila James *state legislator*
Lieber, Sally J. *state representative*
Liu, Carol *state representative*
Montanez, Cindy *state representative*
Ortiz, Deborah V. *state legislator*
Parra, Nicole M. *state representative*
Pavley, Fran J. *state representative*
Reyes, Sarah *state representative*
Romero, Gloria *state senator, government agency administrator*
Runner, Sharon *state representative*
Speier, Jackie *state senator*
Wright, Cathie *state legislator*

San Bernardino
Brown, Marta Macías *legislative staff member, executive assistant*

San Diego
McCarty, Judy *councilman*
Stallings, Valerie Aileen *retired councilwoman, consultant*

Santa Barbara
Jackson, Hannah Beth *state legislator*

Santa Rosa
King, Gwendolyn Bair *former government staff member, public speaker*

Stockton
Matthews, Barbara *state legislator*

COLORADO

Denver
Anderson, Norma V. *state legislator*
Berry, Gayle *state representative*
Borodkin, Alice *state representative*
Boyd, Betty Ann *state representative*
Butcher, Dorothy *state representative*
Clapp, Lauri *state representative*
Coleman, Fran Natividad *state representative*
Duggin, Ginette E. (Gigi) *state legislator*
Epps, Mary Ellen *state legislator*
Faatz, Jeanne Ryan *councilperson*
Fitz-Gerald, Joan *state senator*
Hefley, Lynn A. *state representative*
Hodge, Mary *state representative*
Hoppe, Phyllis Diane *state representative*
Jahn, Cheri E. *state representative*
Keller, Maryanne *state senator*
Lacy, Elsie *state legislator*
Marshall, Rosemary *state representative*
McFadyen, Liane *state representative*
Nichol, Alice J. *state legislator*
Ragsdale, Ann F. *state representative*
Reeves, Peggy *state legislator*
Rhodes, Pamela *state representative*
Rupert, Dorothy *state legislator*
Sandoval, Paula E. *state senator*
Spence, Nancy Joan *state representative*
Spradley, Lola *state representative*
Stafford, Debbie *state senator*
Takis, Stephanie *state senator*
Tanner, Gloria Travis *state legislator*
Tochtrop, Lois *state legislator, nurse consultant*
Veiga, Jennifer *state representative*
Williams, Suzanne *state representative*
Williams, Tambor *state representative*
Windels, Sue *state senator*

Englewood
Wham, Dorothy Stonecipher *retired state legislator*

Golden
Hopper, Sally Hunter *former state legislator*

Lakewood
Hanna, Deanna *state senator*

CONNECTICUT

Bridgeport
Garcia, Edna I. *state legislator, secondary education educator*

Glastonbury
Googins, Sonya Forbes *state legislator, retired banker*

Greenwich
Hess, Marilyn Ann *state legislator*

Groton
DeMarinis, Nancy Ann *state legislator*

Hartford
Carter, Annette Wheeler *state legislator*
Cocco, Jacqueline M. *state legislator*
Cook, Catherine Welles *state legislator*
Currey, Melody Alena *state legislator*
Daily, Eileen M. *state legislator*
Dandrow, Ann P. *state legislator*
Dillon, Patricia Anne *state legislator*
Eberle, Mary U. *state legislator*
Fahrbach, Ruth C. *state legislator*
Garvey, Jeanne Wolter *state legislator, realtor*
Gerratana, Theresa B. *state legislator*
Handley, Mary Ann *state legislator*
Harp, Toni N. *state legislator*
Kirkley-Bey, Marie Lopez *state legislator*
Lyons, Moira K. *state legislator*
McDonald, Anne B. *state legislator*
McGrattan, Mary K. *state legislator*
Mushinsky, Mary M. *state legislator*
Peters, Melodie M. *state legislator*
Prague, Edith G. *state legislator*
Sawyer, Pamela Z. *state legislator*
Scalettar, Ellen *state legislator*
Stillman, Andrea L. *state legislator*
Stratton, Jessie Gray *state legislator*
Truglia, Christel *state legislator*

Mansfield Center
Merrill, Denise *state legislator*

Middlebury
Scarpetti, Angelina (Lee Scarpetti) *state legislator*

Plainville
Boukus, Elizabeth *state legislator*

Riverside
Powers, Claudia McKenna *state legislator*

Stamford
Aveni, Beverly A. *executive aide*

Tolland
Wyman, Nancy S. *state legislator*

Wallingford
Fritz, Mary G. *state legislator*

Westport
Freedman, Judith Greenberg *state legislator, importer*

DELAWARE

Dover
Cloutier, Catherine A. *state legislator*
Connor, Dorinda A. *state legislator*
Cook, Nancy W. *state legislator*
Fallon, Tina K. *state legislator*

Wilmington
Blevins, Patricia M. *state legislator*

DISTRICT OF COLUMBIA

Washington
Baldwin, Tammy *congresswoman*
Berkley, Shelley *congresswoman*
Biggert, Judith Borg *congresswoman, lawyer*
Blackburn, Marsha *congresswoman*
Bono, Mary Whitaker *congresswoman*
Bordallo, Madeleine Mary (Mrs. Ricardo Jerome Bordallo) *congresswoman*
Boxer, Barbara *senator*
Brown, Corrine *congresswoman*
Cantwell, Maria E. *senator*
Capito, Shelley Moore *congresswoman*
Capps, Lois Ragnhild Grimsrud *congresswoman, former school nurse*
Carson, Julia M. *congresswoman*
Christian-Christensen, Donna Marie *congresswoman*
Clinton, Hillary Rodham *senator, lawyer, former First Lady of United States*
Collins, Susan M. *senator*
Cubin, Barbara Lynn *congresswoman*
Davis, Jo Ann S. *congresswoman*
Davis, Susan A. *congresswoman*
DeLauro, Rosa L. *congresswoman*
Dole, Elizabeth Hanford *senator, former charitable organization administrator, former federal official*
Dunn, Jennifer Blackburn *congresswoman*
Emerson, Jo Ann *congresswoman*
Eshoo, Anna Georges *congresswoman*
Feinstein, Dianne *senator*
Fidler, Shelley N. *legislative director*
Harman, Jane *congresswoman*
Harris, Katherine *congresswoman*
Hart, Melissa Anne *congresswoman*
Hattan, Susan K. *legislative staff member*
Hooley, Darlene *congresswoman*
Jackson Lee, Sheila *congresswoman*
Johnson, Eddie Bernice *congresswoman*
Johnson, Karen *legislation and congressional affairs secretary*
Johnson, Nancy Lee *congresswoman*
Jones, Stephanie Tubbs *congresswoman, lawyer*
Kaptur, Marcia Carolyn *congresswoman*
Kelly, Sue W. *congresswoman*
Kennan, Stephanie Ann *policy advisor*
Kennelly, Barbara B. *former congresswoman, federal agency administrator*
Kilpatrick, Carolyn Cheeks *congresswoman*
Landrieu, Mary L. *senator*
Lee, Barbara *congresswoman*
Lincoln, Blanche Lambert *senator*
Lofgren, Zoe *congresswoman*
Lowey, Nita M. *congresswoman*
Majette, Denise *congresswoman*
Maloney, Carolyn Bosher *congresswoman*
McCarthy, Carolyn *congresswoman*
McCarthy, Karen P. *congresswoman, former state legislator*
McCollum, Betty *congresswoman*
McDonald, Patricia Ann *legislative administrator*
McGuire, Carole Baker *legislative staff member*
Millender-McDonald, Juanita *congresswoman, school system administration*
Miller, Candice S. *congresswoman*
Molinari, Susan *congresswoman*
Murkowski, Lisa *senator*
Murray, Patty *senator*
Musgrave, Marilyn N. *congresswoman*
Napolitano, Grace F. *congresswoman*
Nardi Riddle, Clarine *legislative staff member*
Northup, Anne Meagher *congresswoman*
Norton, Eleanor Holmes *congresswoman, lawyer, educator*
Pelosi, Nancy *congresswoman*
Pryce, Deborah D. *congresswoman*
Ros-Lehtinen, Ileana *congresswoman*
Roybal-Allard, Lucille *congresswoman*
Sanchez, Linda T. *congresswoman*
Sanchez, Loretta *congresswoman*
Schakowsky, Janice *congresswoman*
Shaffron, J. Janet *legislative administrator*
Slaughter, Louise McIntosh *congresswoman*
Smith, Linda Gene *legislative staff member*
Snowe, Olympia J. *senator*
Solis, Hilda Lucia *congresswoman, educational administrator*
Stabenow, Deborah Ann *senator, former congresswoman*
Sutherland, Lisa Jo *legislative staff member*
Vazirani-Fales, Heea *legislative staff member, lawyer*
Velazquez, Nydia M. *congresswoman*
Waters, Maxine *congresswoman*
Watson, Diane Edith *congresswoman*
Weiss, Gail Ellen *legislative staff director*
Wilson, Heather Ann *congresswoman*
Woolsey, Lynn *congresswoman*
Yonts-Shepard, Susan *forest service administrator*

FLORIDA

Bradenton
Rahn, Saundra L. *councilwoman*
Woodson-Howard, Marlene Erdley *former state legislator*

Coral Springs
Ritter, Stacy Joy *state legislator, lawyer*

Fort Lauderdale
Dawson, Muriel Amanda (Mandy Dawson) *state legislator*

Gainesville
Chestnut, Cynthia Moore *state legislator*

Jacksonville
Soud, Ginger *city councilwoman*

Miami
Bullard, Larcenia J. *state legislator*

Ormond Beach
Lynn, Evelyn Joan *state senator, consultant*

Pinellas Park
Brennan, Mary M. *state legislator*

Tallahassee
Argenziano, Nancy *state legislator*
Betancourt, Annie *state legislator*
Blanton, Faye Wester *legislative staff member*
Bloom, Elaine *state legislator*
Boyd, Janegale *state legislator*
Carlton, Lisa *state legislator*
Cowin, Anna P. *state legislator, educator*
Dockery, Paula *state legislator*
Edwards, Lori *state legislator*
Frankel, Lois J. *state legislator*
Heyman, Sally Anne *state legislator, crime/loss prevention specialist*
Jacobs, Suzanne *state legislator*
Kosmas, Suzanne *state legislator, real estate company executive*
Kurth, Patsy Ann *state legislator*
Merchant, Sharon J. *state legislator*
Murman, Sandra L. *state legislator, community activist*
Prewitt, Debra A. *state legislator*
Roberts-Burke, Beryl D. *state legislator, lawyer*
Wasserman-Schultz, Debbie *state legislator*

Tampa
Davis, Helen Gordon *former state senator*
Miller, Gwendolyn M. *councilman*

GEORGIA

Atlanta
Blitch, Peg *state legislator*
Buckner, Gail *state legislator*
Bunn, Barbara Jean *state legislator*
Butler, Gloria Singleton *state legislator*
Cable, Susan W. *state legislator*
Davis, Grace W. *state legislator*
Felton, Dorothy *state legislator*
Hegstrom, June *state legislator*
Jackson, Carol *state legislator*
James, Donzella *state legislator*
Jamieson, Mary Jeanette *state legislator*
Kemp, Rene D. *state legislator*
Manning, Judith Hubert *state legislator, real estate executive*
McBee, Mary Louise *state legislator, former academic administrator*
McClinton, JoAnn *state legislator*
Mobley, Barbara Jean *state legislator*
Mueller, Anne *legislator*
Oliver, Mary Margaret *state legislator*
Orrock, Nan *state legislator*
Purcell, Ann Rushing *state legislator, office manager*
Sinkfield, Georganna T. *state legislator*
Smith, Faye *state legislator*
Stanley, Lanett Lorraine *state legislator*
Stanley, Pamela Aurelia *state legislator*
Stokes, Connie *state legislator*
Tate, Horencena *state legislator, software company executive*
Taylor, Maretta Mitchell *state legislator*
Teague, Sharon Beasley *state legislator*
Thomas, Nadine *state senator, nurse*
Trense, Sharon *state legislator*

Savannah
Thomas, Regina D. *state legislator*

HAWAII

Honolulu
Aduja, Melodie Williams *state senator*
Baker, Rosalyn Hester *state senator*
Buen, Jan Yagi *state legislator*
Chun Oakland, Suzanne Nyuk Jun *state legislator*
Fukunaga, Carol A. *state legislator, lawyer*
Hale, Helene H. *state representative*
Hanabusa, Colleen *state legislator, lawyer*
Inouye, Lorraine R. *state legislator*
Kawakami, Bertha C. *state representative*
Kim, Donna Mercado *state senator*
Lee, Marilyn B. *state representative*
Leong, Bertha F.K. *state representative*

Kailua
Young, Jacqueline Eurn Hai *former state legislator, consultant*

IDAHO

Boise
Barrett, Lenore Hardy *state legislator, mining and investment consultant*
Boe, Donna H. *state representative*
Crow, Dolores J. *state representative*
Danielson, Judith A. *state legislator*
Douglas, Bonnie *state representative*
Dunklin, Betsy D. *state legislator*
Ellsworth, Julie *state representative*
Field, Debbie *state representative*
Field, Frances *state representative*
Jaquet, Wendy S. *state representative*
Kellogg, Hilde *state representative*
Keough, Shawn *state legislator*
Lodge, Patti Anne *state senator*
McKague, Shirley *state representative*
McLaughlin, Marguerite P. *state legislator, logging company executive*
Ringo, Shirley G. *state representative*
Shepherd, Mary Lou *state representative*
Wainwright Henbest, Margaret A. *state representative*
Wood, JoAn E. *state representative*

Glenns Ferry
King-Barrutia, Robbie L. *state senator*

Jerome
Bell, Maxine Toolson *state legislator, librarian*

Osburn
Calabretta, Marti Ann *senator*

ILLINOIS

Calumet City
Fantin, Arline Marie *state legislator*

Chicago
Colom, Vilma *alderman*
Feigenholtz, Sara *state legislator*
Stern, Grace Mary *former state legislator*

Coal City
O'Brien, Mary Kathleen *state representative, lawyer*

Lake Forest
Frederick, Virginia Fiester *state legislator*

Northfield
Parker, Kathleen Kappel *state legislator*

Palos Hills
Zickus, Anne *state legislator*

Schaumburg
Wojcik, Kathleen Louise *state representative*

Springfield
Bowles, Evelyn Margaret *state legislator*
Collins, Annazette R. *state representative*
Collins, Jacqueline Y *state senator*
Crotty, M. Maggie *state senator*
Currie, Barbara Flynn *state legislator*
Davis, Monique D. (Deon Davis) *state legislator*
Erwin, Judy *state legislator*
Flowers, Mary E. *state legislator*
Garrett, Susan *state senator*
Geo-Karis, Adeline Jay *state legislator*
Hamos, Julie E. *state representative*
Howard, Constance A. *state representative*
Jakobsson, Naomi D. *state representative*
Jones, Lovana S. *state legislator*
Jones, Shirley M. *state legislator*
Karpiel, Doris Catherine *state legislator*
Kelly, Robin L. *state representative*
Klingler, Gwendolyn Walbolt *state representative*
Kosel, Renée *state representative*
Krause, Carolyn H. *state legislator, lawyer*
Kurtz, Rosemary *state representative*
Lightford, Kimberly A. *state legislator*
Martinez, Iris *state senator*
Moore, Andrea S. *state legislator*
Mulligan, Rosemary Elizabeth *legislator*
Nekritz, Elaine *state representative*
Pihos, Sandra M *state representative*
Radogno, Christine *state legislator*
Ronen, Carol *state legislator*
Slone, Ricca C *state representative*
Smith, Margaret *state legislator*
Yarbrough, Karen A. *state representative*

Sycamore
Vance Siebrasse, Kathy Ann *legislative staff member*

Westmont
Bellock, Patricia Rigney *state legislator*

INDIANA

Indianapolis
Antich-Carr, Rose Ann *state legislator*
Austin, Terri Jo *state representative*
Becker, Vaneta G. *state representative*
Bowser, Anita Olga *state legislator, education educator*
Budak, Mary Kay *state legislator*
Dembrowski, Nancy J. *state senator*
Dickinson, Mae *state legislator*
Gard, Beverly J. *state legislator*
Klinker, Sheila Ann J. *state legislator, middle school educator*
Landske, Dorothy Suzanne (Sue Landske) *state legislator*
Lawson, Connie *state legislator*
Lawson, Linda *state senator*
Leuck, Claire M. *state legislator*
Lubbers, Teresa S. *state legislator, public relations executive*
Marendt, Candace L. *state legislator*
Mays, Carolene *state representative*
Noe, Cindy J. *state representative*
Richardson, Kathy Kreag *state legislator*
Rogers, Earline S. *state legislator*
Scholer, Sue Wyant *state legislator*
Simpson, Vi *state senator*
Sipes, Connie W. *state legislator, educator*
Skillman, Becky Sue *state legislator*
Summers, Vanessa *state legislator*
Welch, Peggy *state representative*
Wolf, Katie Louise *state legislator*

Lebanon
Willing, Katherine *former state legislator*

IOWA

Davenport
Tinsman, Margaret Neir *state legislator*

Des Moines
Berry, Deborah *state representative*
Boettger, Nancy J. *state legislator*
Bukta, Polly *state representative*
Dandekar, Swati *state representative*
DeBoef, Betty *state representative*
Freeman, Mary Louise *state legislator*
Garman, Teresa Agnes *state legislator*
Granzow, Polly *state representative, language educator*
Greimann, Jane *state representative, elementary school educator*
Grundberg, Betty *state legislator, property manager*
Hosch, Julie *state senator*
Jochum, Pam *state representative*
Kramer, Mary Elizabeth *state legislator, health services executive*
Lensing, Vicki *state representative, funeral home business owner*
Miller, Helen *state representative, lawyer*
Oldson, Jo *state representative, lawyer*
Petersen, Janet *state representative*
Ragan, Amanda *state senator*
Rehberg, Kitty *state legislator*
Soukup, Betty A. *state legislator*
Szymoniak, Elaine Eisfelder *retired state senator*
Winckler, Cindy *state representative*

Fort Dodge
Hickey, Sharon Marie *councilman, elementary school educator, Mayoral aide*

Keota
Greiner, Sandra *state legislator*

KANSAS

Concordia
Freeborn, Joann Lee *state legislator, farmer, former educator*

Haddam
Hardenburger, Janice *state legislator*

Herington
Weber, Shari *state legislator*

Inman
Downey, Christine *state legislator*

Lawrence
Ballard, Barbara W. *state legislator*

Neodesha
Chronister, Rochelle Beach *former state legislator*

Olathe
O'Connor, Kay F. *state legislator*

Prairie Village
Langworthy, Audrey Hansen *state legislator*

Shawnee Mission
Sader, Carol Hope *former state legislator*

Stafford
Teichman, Ruth *state senator*

Topeka
Allen, Barbara *state legislator*
Barbieri-Lightner, Patricia *state representative*
Bleeker, Laurie *state legislator*
Brownlee, Karin S. *state legislator*
Carlin, Sydney *state representative*
Craft, Barbara J. *state representative*
Flaharty, Geraldine *state representative*
Flower, Joann *state legislator*
Gilmore, Phyllis *state legislator*
Goodwin, Greta Hall *state legislator*
Gordon, Lana G. *state representative*
Kirk, Nancy A. *state legislator, nursing home administrator*
Kuether, Annie *state representative*
Lee, Janis K. *state legislator*
Long-Mast, Peggy *state representative*
McClure, Laura *state legislator*
Oleen, Lana *state legislator*
Pauls, Janice Long *state legislator*
Petty, Marge D. *state senator*
Praeger, Sandy *state legislator*
Ruff, L. Candy *state legislator*
Salisbury, Alicia Laing *state senator*
Saville, Pat *state senate official*
Schodorf, Jean *state legislator*
Schwartz, Sharon J. *state representative*
Showalter, Judy *state representative*
Storm, Suzanne *state representative*
Toelkes, Dixie E. *state legislator*
Welshimer, Gwen R. *state legislator, real estate broker, appraiser*
Winn, Valdenia C. *state representative*

Wichita
Ott, Belva Joleen *former state legislator*
Pottorff, Jo Ann *state legislator*
Wagle, Susan *state legislator, small business owner*

KENTUCKY

Frankfort
Belcher, Carolyn R. *state representative*
Casebier, Lindy *state legislator*
Jenkins, Joni Lynn *state legislator*
Johns, Susan D. *state senator*
Palumbo, Ruth Ann *state legislator*
Pullin, Tanya *state representative*
Stein, Kathy W. *state representative*
Stine, Katie Kratz *state legislator*

Lexington
Kerr, Alice Forgy *state legislator*

LOUISIANA

Deridder
Iles, Kay C. *state representative*

Grambling
Wilkerson, Pinkie Carolyn *state legislator, lawyer*

Harahan
Bowler, Shirley *state legislator*

Lake Charles
Mount, Willie Landry *state legislator*

Natchitoches
Morrow, Sylvia Marie *councilwoman, volunteer*

New Orleans
Bajoie, Diana E. *state legislator*
Boggs, Corinne Claiborne (Lindy Boggs) *retired congresswoman*
Irons, Paulette Riley *state legislator, lawyer*
Pratt, Renee Gill *state legislator*

Parks
Durand, Sydnie Mae M. *state legislator*

MAINE

Auburn
Douglass, Neria Gay *state legislator, lawyer*

Augusta
Amero, Jane Adams *state senator*
Bromley, Lynn *state legislator*
Cathcart, Mary R. *state legislator*
Daggett, Beverly Clark *state legislator*
Edmonds, Beth A. *state legislator*
Hatch, Pamela H. *state legislator*
Kilkelly, Marjorie Lee *state legislator, community development official*
Kontos, Carol A. *state senator, educator*
Mitchell, Betty Lou *state legislator, retired operations director*
Paradis, Judy *state legislator*
Rotundo, Margaret R. *state legislator*
Savage, Christine R. *state legislator*
Saxl, Jane Wilhelm *state legislator*
Small, Mary E. *state legislator*
Townsend, Elizabeth *state legislator*

Bar Harbor
Goldthwait, Jill Murdoch *state legislator*

Brunswick
Pfeiffer, Sophia Douglass *state legislator, lawyer*

Gardiner
Treat, Sharon Anglin *state legislator*

North Haven
Pingree, Rochelle M. *state legislator*

MARYLAND

Annapolis
Benson, Joanne C. *state legislator*
Cadden, Joan *state legislator*
Conroy, Mary A. *state legislator*
Conway, Joan Carter *state legislator*
Forehand, Jennie Meador *state legislator*
Harrison, Hattie N. *state senator*
Healey, Anne *state legislator*
Hixson, Sheila Ellis *state legislator*
Hollinger, Paula Colodny *state legislator*
Howard, Carolyn J. B. *state legislator*
Kelley, Delores Goodwin *state legislator*
Kirk, Ruth M. *state legislator*
Klima, Martha Scanlan *state legislator*
Krysiak, Carolyn *state legislator*
McIntosh, Maggie *state legislator*
Menes, Pauline H. *state legislator*
Ruben, Ida Gass *state senator*

Baltimore
Hughes, Brenda Bethea *state legislator*

Bel Air
Jacobs, Nancy *state legislator*

Bethesda
Reed, Miriam Bell *legislative staff member*

Cambridge
Eckardt, Adelaide Campbell *state legislator, psychiatric nurse*

Frederick
Byron, Beverly Butcher *retired congresswoman*

Rockville
Kagan, Cheryl C. *state legislator*
Petzold, Carol Stoker *state legislator*

Temple Hills
Lawlah, Gloria Gary *state legislator, educator*

MASSACHUSETTS

Boston
Atkins, Cory *state legislator, writer*
Balser, Ruth B. *state legislator, psychologist*
Blumer, Deborah *state legislator*
Callahan, Jennifer *state legislator, education educator*
Canavan, Christine Estelle *state legislator*
Candaras, Gale D. *state legislator, lawyer*
Chandler, Harriette Levy *state legislator, management consultant, educator*
Chesky, Evelyn G. *state legislator*
Cleven, Carol Chapman *state legislator*
Creedon, Geraldine *state legislator*
Creem, Cynthia Stone *state legislator, lawyer*
Donovan, Carol Ann *state legislator*
Fargo, Susan C. *state legislator*
Flavin, Nancy Ann *state legislator*
Fox, Gloria L. *state representative, state legislator*
Garry, Colleen M. *state legislator*
Gobi, Anne *state legislator, lawyer*
Gomes, Shirley *state legislator*
Haddad, Patricia A. *state legislator*
Hahn, Celia Ferner *state representative, broadcaster*
Harkins, Lida E. *state legislator, educator*
Hyland, Barbara Claire *state legislator*
Jacques, Cheryl Ann *state legislator*
Jehlen, Patricia D. *state legislator*
Kaprielian, Rachel *state legislator*
L'italien, Barbara A. *state legislator, social worker*
Malia, Elizabeth A. *state representative, state legislator*
Melconian, Linda Jean *state legislator, lawyer*
Murray, Therese *state legislator*
Owens-Hicks, Shirley *state legislator*
Paulsen, Anne M. *state legislator*
Peisch, Alice Hanlon *state legislator*
Poirier, Elizabeth A. *state representative, state legislator*
Pope, Susan W. *state legislator*
Provost, Ruth W. *state legislator*
Reinstein, Kathi-Anne *state representative, state legislator*
Resor, Pamela P. *state legislator*
Rivera, Cheryl A. *state representative, lawyer*
Rogeness, Mary Speer *state legislator*
St. Fleur, Marie P. *state representative, state legislator*
Simmons, Mary Jane *state legislator*
Spiliotis, Joyce A. *state legislator*
Spilka, Karen *state legislator, lawyer*
Sprague, Jo Ann *state legislator*
Stanley, Harriett Lari *state legislator*
Story, Ellen *state legislator*
Teahan, Kathleen M. *state legislator, educator*
Tucker, Susan Carol *state legislator*
Walrath, Patricia A. *state legislator*
Walsh, Marian C. *state legislator*
Wilkerson, Dianne *state legislator*
Williams Gifford, Susan *state legislator*
Wolf, Alice K. *state legislator, former mayor*

Hyannis
Loughnane, Audrey Moran *town councilor*

New Bedford
Gonsalves, Jane Louise *city councilor, claims adjuster*

Newton
Khan, Kay *state legislator*

Wakefield
Menard, Joan M. *state legislator*

MICHIGAN

Detroit
Mahaffey, Maryann *councilwoman*
Stallworth, Alma Grace *former state legislator*

Farmington Hills
Dolan, Jan Clark *former state legislator*

Lansing
Brater, Elizabeth *state legislator*
Byrum, Dianne *state legislator, small business owner*
DeHart, Eileen *state legislator*
Emmons, Joanne *state legislator*
Hammerstrom, Beverly Swoish *state legislator*
Scott, Martha G. *state legislator*
Van Regenmorter, William *state legislator*

Mount Clemens
Rocca, Sue *state legislator*

Rochester
Crissman, Penny M. *state legislator*

MINNESOTA

Albert Lea
Schwab, Grace S. *state legislator*

Brandon
Bettermann, Hilda *state legislator*

Forest Lake
Broecker, Sherry *state legislator*

Lakeland
Larsen, Peg *state legislator*

Minneapolis
Mickelson, Stacey *state legislator*
Reichgott Junge, Ember D. *former state senator, lawyer, writer, broadcast analyst, radio personality*

Mounds View
Thomason, Lynne *councilwoman, medical laser technician*

Saint Paul
Anderson, Ellen Ruth *state legislator*
Bachmann, Michele *state legislator*
Berglin, Linda *state legislator*
Boudreau, Lynda L. *state legislator*
Clark, Karen *state legislator*
Fischbach, Michelle L. *state legislator*
Flynn, Carol *state legislator*
Greiling, Mindy *state legislator*
Hanson, Paula E. *state legislator*
Harder, Elaine Rene *state legislator*
Higgins, Linda I. *state legislator*
Johnson, Alice M. *state legislator*
Kahn, Phyllis *state legislator*
Kimberly, Susan Elizabeth *state legislative director, city program administrator*
Kiscaden, Sheila M. *state legislator*
Krentz, Jane *state legislator, elementary school educator*
Lesewski, Arlene *state legislator, insurance agent*
McGuire, Mary Jo *state legislator*
Murphy, Mary C. *state legislator*
Olson, Gen *state legislator*
Pappas, Sandra Lee *state senator*
Pariseau, Patricia *state legislator*
Ranum, Jane Barnhardt *state senator, lawyer*
Rest, Ann H. *state legislator*
Ring, Twyla L. *state legislator, newspaper editor*
Robertson, Martha Rappaport *state legislator, consultant*
Robling, Claire A. *state legislator*
Runbeck, Linda C. *state legislator*
Rydell, Catherine M. *former state legislator*
Scheid, Linda J. *state legislator*
Schumacher, Leslie *state legislator, artist*
Seagren, Alice *state legislator*
Wejcman, Linda *state legislator*

Shakopee
Kelso, Becky *former state legislator*

MISSISSIPPI

Brookhaven
Hyde-Smith, Cindy *state legislator*

Jackson
Blackmon, Barbara Martin *state legislator, lawyer*
Carlton, Neely C. *state legislator, lawyer*
Clarke, Alyce Griffin *state legislator*
Coleman, Linda *state legislator*
Coleman, Mary H. *state legislator*
Dickson, Reecy L. *state legislator*
Fredericks, Frances M. *state legislator, nurse*
Harden, Alice V. *state legislator*
Jennings, Wanda T. *state legislator*
Martinson, Rita R. *state legislator*
Miller, Patricia K. *former state legislator*
Peranich, Diane C. *state legislator*
Robertson, Valeria Brower *state legislator, land developer*
Scott, Eloise Hale *state legislator*
Scott, Omeria McDonald *state legislator*
Stevens, Mary Ann *state legislator*
Thomas, Sara R. *state legislator*

Pass Christian
Dawkins, Deborah Jeanne *state legislator*

Philadelphia
Williamson, Gloria *state legislator*

MISSOURI

Florissant
Stokan, Lana J. Ladd *state legislator*

Jefferson City
Backer, Gracia Yancey *state legislator*
Bland, Mary Groves *state legislator*
Bray, Joan *state legislator*
Carter, Paula J. *state legislator*
Days, Rita Denise *state legislator*

Hagan-Harrell, Mary M. *state legislator*
Hanaway, Catherine *state representative, lawyer*
Kasten, Mary Alice C. *state legislator*
Kauffman, Sandra Daley *state legislator*
Kelly, Glenda Marie *state legislator*
Long, Elizabeth L. *state legislator, small business owner*
Mays, Carol Jean *state legislator*
McClelland, Emma L. *state legislator*
Murray, Connie Wible *state official, former state legislator*
Ostmann, Cindy *state legislator*
Ridgeway, Luann *state legislator*
Robirds, Estel *state legislator*
Sallee, Mary Lou *state legislator*
Scheve, May E. *state legislator, political organization worker*
Sims, Betty *state legislator*
Williams, Deleta *state legislator*
Williams, Marilyn *state legislator*

Kansas City
Rice, Levina Ruth (Sally) *city council person, former government official*

Rolla
Steelman, Sarah *state legislator*

Saint Louis
Yeckel, Anita T. *state legislator*

MONTANA

Anaconda
McCarthy, Bea *state legislator*

Butte
Shea, Debbie Bowman *state legislator*

Great Falls
Franklin, Eve *state legislator*

Helena
Bartlett, Sue *retired state legislator*
Cocchiarella, Vicki Marshall *state legislator*
Eck, Dorothy Fritz *state legislator*
Hanson, Marian W. *state legislator*
Stonington, Emily S. *state legislator*

Medicine Lake
Nelson, Linda J. *state legislator*

NEBRASKA

Hastings
Bohlke, Ardyce *state legislator*

Lincoln
Brown, Pam *state legislator*
Crosby, LaVon Kehoe Stuart *state legislator, civic leader*
Price, Marian L. *state legislator*
Redfield, Pamela A. *state legislator*
Robak, Jennie *state legislator*
Schimek, DiAnna Ruth Rebman *state legislator*
Stuhr, Elaine Ruth *state legislator*
Suttle, Deborah S. *state legislator*
Thompson, Nancy P. *state legislator*
Witek, Kate *state senator, trucking company executive*

NEVADA

Carson City
O'Connell, Mary Ann *state legislator, small business owner*
Titus, Alice Cestandina (Dina Titus) *state legislator*

Hawthorne
Chenoweth-Hage, Helen P. *former congresswoman*

Henderson
Tiffany, Sandra L. *state legislator*

Las Vegas
Carlton, Maggie *state legislator*

Reno
Mathews, Bernice Martin *state legislator, small business owner*

NEW HAMPSHIRE

Barrington
DeChane, Marlene M. *state legislator*

Bow
Sytek, Donna P. *former state legislator*

Center Harbor
Patten, Betsey Leland *state legislator*

Concord
Clark, Martha Fuller *state legislator, architectural historian, preservation consultant*
Clemons, Jane Andrea *state legislator*
Cote, Patricia L. *state legislator*
Crosby, Toni M. *state legislator*
Drabinowicz, A. Theresa *state legislator*
Dunlap, Patricia C. *state legislator*
Ferland, Brenda L. *state representative*
Flanagan, Natalie Smith *state representative*
Flora, Kathleen M. *state representative*
Foster, Linda Timberlake *state legislator*
Francoeur, Sheila T. *state representative*
Fraser, Marilyn Anne *state legislator*
Ginsburg, Ruth *state representative*
Griffin, Mary E. *state representative*
Hager, Elizabeth Sears *state legislator, social services organization administrator*
Hall, Betty B. *state legislator, manufacturing executive*
Hutchinson, Rebecca *state representative*
Kaen, Naida *state representative*
Kane, Cecelia Drapeau *state legislator, registered nurse*
Keans, Sandra B. *state legislator*
Larsen, Sylvia B. *state legislator*
Lozeau, Donnalee M. *state legislator*
Lynch, Margaret A. *state legislator*
Lynott, Margaret *state legislator*
Martin, Mary Ellen *state legislator, human development specialist*
McRae, Karen K. *state legislator*
Merritt, Deborah Foote *state legislator, vocational coordinator*
Messier, Irene M. *state legislator*
Moore, Carol *state legislator*
Nichols, Avis B. *state legislator*
Nordgren, Sharon L. *state legislator*
Norelli, Terie Thompson *state legislator*
O'Hearn, Jane E. *state legislator*
O'Keefe, Patricia M. *state legislator*
Packard, Bonnie Bennett *former state legislator*
Pratt, Irene Agnes *state legislator*
Reardon, Tara G. *state legislator*
Richardson, Barbara Hull *state legislator, social worker*
Roberge, M. Sheila *state legislator*
Seldin, Gloria *state legislator*
Smith, Marjorie K. *state legislator*
Snyder, Clair A. *state legislator*
Stickney, Nancy Carver *state legislator*
Wall, Janet G. *state legislator*
Wallin, Jean R. *state legislator*
Wallner, Mary Jane *state legislator, director child care organization*
Weatherspoon, Jackie K. *state legislator*
Wiggins, Celestine K. *state legislator*
Williams, Carol Ann *state legislator*

Durham
Estabrook, Iris W. *state representative*

Etna
Copenhaver, Marion Lamson *former state legislator*

Hanover
Crory, Elizabeth L. *former state legislator*

Henniker
French, Barbara C. *state representative*

Hollis
Durham, Susan B. *state legislator*

[illegible]
Horton, Lynn C. *state legislator*

Littleton
Eaton, Stephanie *state legislator*

Londonderry
Dunham, Vivian L. *state legislator*
McKinney, Betsy *state legislator*

Manchester
Arnold, Barbara Eileen *state legislator*
Krueger, Patricia *state representative*
Sysyn, Mary A. *alderman*

Milford
Dokmo, Cynthia J. *state legislator*

Nashua
Franks, Suzan L. R. *state legislator*
Nolan-Piteri, Dawn C. *state legislator*
Pignatelli, Debora Becker *state legislator*

North Woodstock
Ham, Bonnie Davis *state legislator*

Nottingham
Case, Margaret A. *state legislator*

Pittsfield
Brown, Mary Ellen *former state legislator, accountant*

Plaistow
Senter, Merilyn P(atricia) *former state legislator and freelance reporter*

Portsmouth
Pantelakos, Laura C. *state legislator*

Randolph
Bradley, Paula E. *former state legislator*

Rochester
Brown, Julie M. *state legislator*
Grassie, Anne C. *state legislator*
McCarley, Caroline *state legislator*
Rogers, Rose Marie *state legislator*

Rye Beach
Langley, Jane S. *state legislator*

Windham
Arndt, Janet S. *state legislator*

NEW JERSEY

Edison
Buono, Barbara *state legislator*

Ewing
Turner, Shirley Kersey *state legislator*

Freehold
Farragher, Clare M. *state legislator*
Karcher, Ellen M. *state senator*

Jersey City
Quigley, Joan Marie *state legislator*

Lodi
Heck, Rose *state legislator*

Monroe
Greenstein, Linda R. *assemblywoman*

Montclair
Gill, Nia H. *state legislator*

Mount Laurel
Bark, Martha W. *state legislator*

Newton
McHose, Alison Littell *assemblywoman*

Paterson
Pou, Nellie *assemblywoman*

Short Hills
Ogden, Maureen Black *retired state legislator*

Teaneck
Weinberg, Loretta *state legislator*

Trenton
Allen, Diane Betzendahl *state legislator*
Coleman, Bonnie Watson *assemblywoman*
McCann, Colleen Mary *public affairs specialist, lobbyist*
Vandervalk, Charlotte *state legislator*
Watson-Coleman, Bonnie *state legislator*

Washington
Myers, Connie *assemblywoman*

Woodbridge
Friscia, Arline M. *assemblywoman*

NEW MEXICO

Albuquerque
Feldman, Dede *state legislator*
Gorham, Ramsay L. *state legislator, political organization administrator*
Lopez, Linda M. *state legislator*
McGuire, Susan Grayson *legislative staff member*
Stewart, Mimi (Miriam) (Kay) (Mimi Stewart) *state legislator, educator*
Wilson, Sue *state legislator*

Dona Ana
Garcia, Mary Jane Madrid *state legislator*

Las Vegas
Casey, Barbara A. Perea *state legislator, school superintendent*

Los Alamos
Wallace, Jeannette Owens *state legislator*

Santa Fe
Arnold-Jones, Janice E. *state representative*
Beam, Gail C. *state representative*
Garcia, Mary Helen *state representative*
Howes, Gloria *state legislator*
Nava, Cynthia L. *state legislator*
Papen, Mary Kay *state senator*
Powdrell-Culbert, Jane E. *state representative*
Rodello, Debbie A. *state representative*
Rodriguez, Nancy *state legislator*
Sanchez, Bernadette M. *state senator*
Snyder, Helen Diane *state senator*
Stapleton, Sheryl Williams *state representative*
Townsend, Sandra L. *state representative*
Vaughn, Gloria C. *state representative*
Wilson, Avon W. *state representative*
Zanetti, Teresa A. *state representative*

Tularosa
Duran, Dianna J. *state legislator*

NEW YORK

Albany
Arroyo, Carmen Elsie *state legislator*
Christensen, Joan K. *state legislator*
Destito, RoAnn M. *state legislator*
Ferrara, Donna *state legislator*
Glick, Deborah J. *state legislator*
Greene, Aurelia *state legislator*
Hassell-Thompson, Ruth *state legislator*
Hooper, Earlene *state legislator*
Jacobs, Rhoda S. *state legislator*
Krueger, Liz *state legislator*
Mayersohn, Nettie *state legislator*
Mendez, Olga A. *state legislator*
Nolan, Catherine T. *state legislator*
Pheffer, Audrey Iris *state legislator*
Smith, Ada L. *state legislator*
Stavisky, Toby Ann *state legislator*
Sullivan, Frances Taylor *state legislator*
Weinstein, Helene E. *state legislator*

Bayside
Carrozza, Ann-Margaret E. *state legislator, lawyer*

Bedford
Matusow, Naomi C. *state legislator*

Brooklyn
Cohen, Adele *state legislator, lawyer, elementary school educator*
Gordon, Diane *state legislator*
Millman, Joan *state legislator*
Montgomery, Velmanette *state senator*
Robinson, Annette *councilwoman*

Buffalo
Peoples, Crystal D. *state legislator*

Elizabethtown
Sayward, Teresa R. *state representative*

Elmhurst
Markey, Margaret M. *state legislator*

Far Rockaway
Titus, Michele R. *state legislator*

Glens Falls
Little, Elizabeth O'Connor *state legislator*

Gouverneur
Scozzafava, Dede *state representative*

Ithaca
Lifton, Barbara *state legislator, secondary school educator*
McKinney, Cynthia Ann *former congresswoman*

New Windsor
Calhoun, Nancy *state legislator*

New York
Abate, Catherine M. *former state senator*

Niagara Falls
DelMonte, Francine *state legislator*

Olean
McGee, Patricia K. *state legislator*
Young, Catharine M. *state legislator*

Oneida
Closson, Helga C. *councilwoman*

Ossining
Galef, Sandra Risk *state legislator, teacher*

Port Chester
Oppenheimer, Suzi *state legislator*

Queens Village
Clark, Barbara Marlene *state legislator*

Riverhead
Acampora, Patricia L. *state legislator*

Rochester
John, Susan V. *state representative*

South Ozone Park
Cook, Vivian *state legislator*

Syracuse
Hoffmann, Nancy Larraine *state legislator*

Westbury
O'Connell, Marueen C. *state legislator, lawyer*

Williamsville
Rath, Mary Lou *state legislator*

NORTH CAROLINA

Advance
Cochrane, Betsy Lane *former state senator*

Burlington
Holt, Bertha Merrill *state legislator*

Charlotte
Myrick, Sue *congresswoman, former mayor*

Greensboro
Jeffus, Margaret M. (Maggie Jeffus) *state representative, retired elementary school educator*

Raleigh
Bowie, Joanne Walker (Joni Bowie) *state legislator*
Cauthen, Carmen Wimberley *legislative staff member, jewelry designer*
Foxx, Virginia Ann *state legislator, small business owner*
Garrou, Linda *state legislator*
Hagan, Kay R. *state legislator, lawyer*
Howard, Julia C. *state legislator*
Kinnaird, Eleanor Gates *state legislator, lawyer*
Lucas, Jeanne Hopkins *state senator, retired educational administrator*
Russell, Carolyn B. *state legislator*
Tally, Lura Self *state legislator*

NORTH DAKOTA

Bismarck
Gulleson, Pam *state legislator*
Kelsch, RaeAnn *state legislator*
Nelson, Carolyn *state legislator*
Price, Clara Sue *state legislator*
Sandvig, Sally *state legislator*

Fargo
Mathern, Deb *state legislator*

Grand Forks
Christenson, Linda *state legislator*
Delmore, Lois M. *state legislator*
DeMers, Judy Lee *former state legislator, university dean*
Warnke, Amy Nicholle *state legislator*

Minot
Krebsbach, Karen K. *state legislator*
Watne, Darlene Claire *state legislator*

Towner
Gunter, G. Jane *state legislator*

OHIO

Cleveland
Drake, Grace L. *retired state senator, cultural organization administrator*

Oakar, Mary Rose *congresswoman*
Pringle, Barbara Carroll *state legislator*

Columbus
Allen, Dixie J. *state representative*
Barrett, Catherine L. *state representative*
Beatty, Joyce *state representative*
Benjamin, Ann Womer *former state legislator, lawyer*
Brown, Edna *state representative*
Cirelli, Mary M. *state representative*
Clancy, Patricia *state representative*
Davidson, Jo Ann *former state legislator*
Fedor, Teresa *state senator*
Ferderber, June H. *state legislator*
Fessler, Diana M. *state representative*
Furney, Linda Jeanne *state legislator*
Grendell, Diane V. *state legislator, nurse*
Hollister, Nancy *state legislator*
Kearns, Merle Grace *state representative*
Key, Annie L. *state representative*
Lawrence, Joan Wipf *former state legislator*
Mead, Priscilla *state legislator*
Perry, Jeanine *state representative*
Prentiss, C. J. *state legislator*
Reidelbach, Linda *state representative*
Schmidt, Jean *state representative*
Schneider, Michelle G. *state representative*
Setzer, Arlene J. *state representative, retired secondary school educator*
Smith, Shirley A. *state legislator, state representative*
Sutton, Betty *state legislator*
Sykes, Barbara *state legislator, state representative*
Taylor, Mary *state representative*
Vesper, Rose *state legislator*
Winkler, Cheryl J. *state legislator*
Woodard, Claudette J. *state representative, retired educational association administrator*

Dayton
Reid, Marilyn Joanne *state legislator, lawyer*

OKLAHOMA

Oklahoma City
Coleman, Carolyn *state legislator*
Cox, Kevin *state representative*
Greenwood, Joan *state representative*
Hamilton, Rebecca *state representative*
Horner, Maxine Edwyna Cissel *state legislator*
Lawler, Daisy *state senator, elementary school educator, farmer, rancher*
Martin, Caroline June *state senator*
Monson, Angela Zoe *state legislator*
Morris, Phyllis *legislative staff member*
Riley, Nancy C. *state legislator*
Staggs, Barbara *state representative*
Tibbs, Sue *state representative*
Weedn, Trish *state legislator*
Wilcoxson, Kathleen Louise *state legislator, educator*

Tulsa
Williams, Penny *state legislator*

OREGON

Bend
Clarno, Beverly Ann *state legislator, farmer*

Hillsboro
Furse, Elizabeth *former congresswoman, small business owner*

Mcminnville
Nelson, Donna Gayle *state representative, aviation executive, business owner, educator, writer, journalist*

Portland
Gordly, Avel Louise *state legislator, community activist*

Salem
Anderson, Laurie Monnes *state representative*
Berger, Vicki *state representative*
Beyer, Elizabeth Terry *state representative*
Brown, Kate *state legislator*
Burdick, Ginny *state legislator*
Close, Betsy L. *state representative*
Dingfelder, Jackie *state representative*
Dukes, Joan *state legislator*
Flores, Linda *state representative*
Gallegos, Mary *state representative*
Hopson, Elaine M. *state representative*
Kafoury, Deborah *state representative*
Minnis, Karen *state representative*
Morgan, Susan H. *state representative*
Nolan, Mary *state representative*
Qutub, Eileen *state legislator, real estate appraiser*
Rosenbaum, Diane M. *state representative*
Shannon, Marylin Linfoot *state legislator, educator*
Smith, Patti *state representative*
Smith, Tootie *state representative*
Tomei, Carolyn *state representative*
Verger, Joanne *state representative*
Walker, Vicki L. *state senator*
Wirth, Kelley K. *state representative*
Yih, Mae Dunn *state legislator*

PENNSYLVANIA

Abington
Bard, Ellen Marie *state legislator, former small business owner, small business owner*

Chalfont
Wilson, Jean L. *retired state legislator*

Easton
Reibman, Jeanette Fichman *retired state senator*

Erie
Earll, Jane *state legislator, lawyer*

Harrisburg
Bebko-Jones, Linda *state legislator*
Bishop, Louise Williams *state legislator*
Boscola, Lisa M. *state legislator*
Cohen, Lita Indzel *state legislator*
Crahalla, Jacqueline R. *state representative*
Forcier, Teresa Elaine *state legislator*
Gingrich, Mauree A. *state representative*
Laughlin, Susan *state legislator*
Lederer, Marie A. *state legislator*
Mackereth, Beverly D. *state representative*
Mann, Jennifer L. *state representative*
Miller, Sheila *state legislator*
Pickett, Tina L. *state representative*
Schwartz, Allyson Y. *state legislator*
Tartaglione, Christine M. *state legislator*
Taylor, Elinor Zimmerman *state legislator*
True, Katie *state legislator*
Vance, Patricia H. *state legislator*
Watson, Katharine M. *state representative*
Weber, Melissa Murphy *state representative*
White, Mary Jo *state legislator, lawyer*
Williams, Constance *state senator*

Philadelphia
Josephs, Babette *state legislator*
Kitchen, Shirley *state legislator, social worker*

Wayne
Rubley, Carole A. *state legislator*

RHODE ISLAND

Adamsville
Quick, Joan B. *state legislator*

Bristol
Parella, Mary A. *state legislator*

Charlestown
Walsh, Donna M. *state legislator*

Cranston
Hetherington, Nancy *state legislator*
Lanzi, Beatrice A. *state legislator*

North Kingstown
Benson, Melvoid J. *state legislator*

Providence
Ajello, Edith H. *state legislator*
Anderson, Mabel M. *state legislator*
Callahan, Christine H. *state legislator*
Cambio, Bambilyn Breece *state legislator*
Coderre, Elaine Ann *state representative*
Gallo, Hanna M. *state legislator*
Gibbs, June Nesbitt *state legislator*
Goodwin, Maryellen *state legislator*
Graziano, Catherine Elizabeth *state legislator, retired nursing educator*
Henseler, Suzanne Marie *state legislator, social studies educator, majority whip*
Iannitelli, Susan B. *state legislator*
Lima, Charlene *state legislator*
Lopes, Maria J. *state legislator*
Paiva-Weed, M. Teresa *state legislator*
Roberts, Elizabeth H. *state legislator*
Sasso, Eleanor Catherine *state senator*
Sosnowski, V. Susan *state legislator*
Williams, Anastasia P. *state legislator*

SOUTH CAROLINA

Bluffton
Cork, Holly A. *former state legislator*

Columbia
Allison, Merita Ann *state legislator*
Arias-Haskins, Gloria *state representative*
Ceips, Catherine C. *state representative*
Cobb-Hunter, Gilda *state representative, social worker*
Freeman, Mary Beth *state representative*
Gilham, JoAnne *state representative*
Glover, Maggie Wallace *state legislator*
Hinson, Shirley Rogers *state representative*
Lee, Brenda *state representative*
Martin, Becky Rogers *state representative, realtor*
Miller, Vida O. *state representative, art gallery owner*
Moody-Lawrence, Bessie *state representative, education educator*
Parks, J. Anne *state representative, funeral director*
Richardson, Becky D. *state representative*
Short, Linda Huffstetler *state legislator*
Young, Annette D. *state representative*

Greenville
Manly, Sarah Letitia *retired state legislator, ophthalmic photographer, angiographer*

Mc Cormick
Clayton, Verna Lewis *retired state legislator*

SOUTH DAKOTA

Black Hawk
Maicki, G. Carol *former state senator, consultant*

Brookings
McClure-Bibby, Mary Anne *former state legislator*

Gettysburg
Schreiber, Lola F. *former state legislator*

Miller
Morford, JoAnn (JoAnn Morford-Burg) *state senator, investment company executive*

Mitchell
Clemens, Deb Fischer *state legislator, nursing administrator*

Mud Butte
Ingalls, Marie Cecelie *former state legislator, retail executive*

Pierre
Adam, Patricia Ann *legislative aide*
Everist, Barbara *state legislator*
Fiegen, Kristie K. *state legislator*
Ham, Arlene H. *state legislator*

Sioux Falls
Dunn, Rebecca Jo *state legislator*

TENNESSEE

Athens
Higdon, Linda Hampton *congressional staff*

Chattanooga
Turner, Brenda Kaye *state legislator*

Nashville
Burks, Charlotte *state legislator*
DeBerry, Lois Marie *state legislator*
Eckles, Mary Ann *state legislator*
Graves, Jo Ann *state legislator*
Halteman Harwell, Beth *state legislator*
Harper, Thelma *state legislator*
Kurita, Rosalind *state legislator*

TEXAS

Austin
Danburg, Debra *state legislator*
Denny, Mary Craver *state legislator, business owner*
Shapiro, Florence *state legislator, advertising, public relations executive*
Shea, Gwyn *secretary of state*

Flower Mound
Nelson, Jane Gray *state legislator, small business owner, educator*

Fort Worth
Mowery, Anna Renshaw *state legislator*
Palmer, Sue *former state legislator, oil industry executive*

Galveston
Holcomb, Mary Anne *councilwoman, municipal official*

Laredo
Zaffirini, Judith *state legislator, small business owner*

Nacogdoches
Kirchhoff, Mary Virginia *city council member*

UTAH

Midvale
Greene, Enid *retired congresswoman*

Salt Lake City
Bowen, Melanie *legislative staff administrator*
Evans, Beverly Ann *state legislator, school system administrator*
Hale, Karen *state legislator*
Minson, Dixie L. *legislative staff member*
Moore, Annette B. *legislative staff member*
Peterson, Millie M. *state senator*
Shepherd, Karen *retired congresswoman*
Walker, Carlene Martin *state senator*

VERMONT

Bennington
Morrissey, Mary *state representative*

Brattleboro
Milkey, Virginia A. *state legislator*

Burlington
Donovan, Johannah L. *state representative, educator*
Lafayette, Karen Moran *state legislator*
Miller, Hinda *state senator, management consultant*
Sullivan, Mary Margaret *state legislator*
Tracy, John Patrick *state legislator*

Chelsea
Kennedy, Sylvia C. *state representative*

Colchester
Dakin, Maureen P. *state representative*
Sweeney, Joyce C. *state representative*

East Calais
Alfano, Elaine *state representative*

Enosburg Falls
Gervais, Avis L. *state representative, consumer products company executive*

Essex Junction
Kirker, Linda *state representative, health facility administrator*

Fairfield
Kittell, Sara Branon *state legislator*

Georgia
Branagan, Carolyn W. *state representative*

Hinesburg
Snelling, Diane *state senator, artist*

Hyde Park
Bartlett, Susan J. *state legislator*
Bourdeau, Stephanie *state representative*

Jericho
Symington, Gaye R. *state representative*

Middlebury
Ginevan, Anne V. *state representative*
Nuovo, Betty A. *state representative*

Milton
Rivero, Marilyn Elaine Keith *state legislator*

Montpelier
Backus, Jan *state legislator*
Cummings, Ann E. *state legislator*
Emmons, Alice M. *state legislator*
Fox, Sally G. *state legislator, lawyer*
Munt, Janet S. *state legislator*
Peaslee, Janice L. *state legislator, agricultural products executive*
Ready, Elizabeth M. *state legislator*
Riehle, Helen S. *state senator*
Rivers, Cheryl P. *state legislator*
Seibert, Ann *state legislator, physical therapist*
Sheltra, Nancy J. *state legislator, legal assistant, auditor*
Towne, Ruth H. *state legislator*

Moretown
Grad, Maxine J. *state representative, law educator*

Pittsford
Flory, Margaret K. *state representative, lawyer*

Putney
White, Jeanette K. *state senator, health facility administrator*

Richmond
Doyle, Patricia R. *state representative*

Rutland
Duffy, Virginia *state representative, artist*
Ferraro, Betty Ann *former state senator*
Mazzariello, Mary C. *state representative*

Saint Albans
Keenan, Kathleen *state legislator*

South Burlington
Head, Helen *state representative, management consultant*
Pugh, Anne D. *state legislator*

South Hero
Johnson, Mitzi *state representative*

Swanton
LaVoie, Kathy L. *state representative*

Tinmouth
Fallar, Gail M. *state representative, town clerk*

Underhill
Hummel, Margaret P. *state representative*

Vergennes
Houston, Constance T. *state legislator*

Vernon
O'Donnell, Pat A. *state representative*

Warren
Connell, Kinny *state representative*

Waterbury
Steele, Karen Kiarsis *retired state legislator*
Vincent, Val D. *state legislator*

West Rutland
Crowley, Judy B. *state representative*

Westford
Heath, Martha *state legislator*

Weybridge
Ayer, Claire D. *state representative, women's health nurse*

White River Junction
Bohi, Lynn *state legislator*

Williston
Ankeney, Jean B. *state legislator*
Lyons, Virginia *state legislator*
Peterson, Mary N. *state representative, lawyer*

Windsor
Sweaney, Donna *state representative*

Woodstock
Crocker, Patricia Conway *former state legislator*

VIRGINIA

Alexandria
Collins, Cardiss *retired congresswoman*
Ticer, Patricia *state senator*

Fairfax
Miller, Emilie F. *former state senator, consultant*
Woods, Jane Haycock *state legislator*

Falls Church
Byrne, Leslie Larkin *state legislator*

Mc Lean
Burke, Sheila P. *federal administrator*

Newport News
Keator, Margaret Whitley *legislative aide*

Norfolk
Miller, Yvonne Bond *state legislator, educator*
Sears, Winsome Earle *state representative*

Richmond
Crittenden, Flora Davis *state legislator*
Darner, Leslie Karen *state legislator*
Devolites, Jeanne Marie Aragona *state legislator*
Drake, Thelma Day *state legislator*
McQuigg, Michele Berger *state legislator*
Puller, Linda Todd *state legislator*
Rapp, Melanie L. *state legislator, primary school educator*
Rhodes, Anne Gregory (Panny Rhodes) *state legislator*
Rimler, Anita A. *secretary of state*
Schaar, Susan Clarke *state legislative staff member*
Suit, Terrie L. *state representative*
Whipple, Mary Margaret *state legislator*

Vienna
Higginbotham, Wendy Jacobson *political adviser, writer*

WASHINGTON

Olympia
Anderson, Vicki Susan *legislative staff member, travel consultant*
Brown, Lisa J. *state legislator, educator*
Costa, Jeralita *state legislator*
Eide, Tracey J. *state legislator*
Fairley, Darlene *state legislator*
Franklin, Rosa G. *state legislator, retired nurse*
Fraser, Karen *state legislator*
Gardner, Georgia Anne *state legislator*
Hale, Patricia S. *state legislator*
Haugen, Mary Margaret *state legislator*
Kessler, Lynn Elizabeth *state legislator*
Long, Jeanine Hundley *retired state legislator*
McAuliffe, Rosemary *state legislator*
Parlette, Linda Evans *state senator*
Patterson, Julia *state legislator*
Prentice, Margarita *state legislator, nurse*
Rasmussen, Marilyn *state legislator*
Regala, Debbie *state legislator*
Roach, Pam *state legislator*
Sheldon, Betti L. *state legislator*
Spanel, Harriet *state legislator*
Stevens, Val *state legislator*
Thibaudeau, Patricia *state legislator*
Winsley, Shirley J. *state legislator, insurance agent*

Seattle
Law, Marcia Elizabeth *aide*
Oakley, Carolyn Le *state legislator, small business owner*

Vancouver
Smith, Linda A. *retired congresswoman*

WEST VIRGINIA

Charleston
Boley, Donna Jean *state legislator*
Minear, Sarah M. *state legislator*
Redd, Marie E. *state legislator, criminal justice educator*
Walker, Martha Yeager *state senator, businesswoman*

Parkersburg
Brum, Brenda *state legislator, librarian*

Shinnston
Spears, Jae *state legislator*

WISCONSIN

Eau Claire
Kreibich, Robin G. *state legislator*

Fort Atkinson
Lorman, Barbara K. *former state senator*

Green Bay
Kelso, Carol *state legislator*

Madison
Berceau, Terese L. *state representative*
Darling, Alberta Statkus *state legislator, marketing executive, former art museum executive*
Gronemus, Barbara *state legislator*
Hanson, Doris J. *state legislator*
Huelsman, Joanne B. *state legislator*
Hundertmark, Jean L. *state representative*
Jeskewitz, Suzanne E. *state representative*
Kerkman, Samantha *state representative*
Krawczyk, Judy *state representative*
Krug, Shirley *state legislator*
Krusick, Margaret Ann *state legislator*
Lassa, Julie M. *state representative*
McCormick, Terri *state legislator*
Nischke, Ann M. *state legislator*
Owens, Carol *state legislator*
Panzer, Mary E. *state legislator*
Plache, Kimberly Marie *state legislator*
Pope-Roberts, Sondy *state legislator*
Rhoades, Kitty *state legislator*
Robson, Judith Biros *state legislator*
Roessler, Carol Ann *state legislator*
Rosenzweig, Peggy A. *state legislator*
Seratti, Lorraine M. *state legislator*
Stepp, Cathy *state senator*

Towns, Debi *state legislator*
Vruwink, Amy Sue *state legislator*
Vukmir, Leah *state legislator*
Weber, Becky *state legislator*
Whitney, Lori Ann *legislative staff member*
Williams, Annette Polly *state legislator*
Williams, Mary *state legislator*
Young, Rebecca Mary Conrad *retired state legislator*

Menomonie
Clausing, Alice *state legislator*

Milwaukee
Potter, Rosemary *state legislator*

Oshkosh
Klusman, Judith Anderson *state legislator*

Racine
Ladwig, Bonnie L. *state legislator*

Rice Lake
Hubler, Mary *state legislator*

River Falls
Harsdorf, Sheila Eloise *state legislator, farmer*

WYOMING

Buffalo
Madden, Cheryl Beth *state legislator*

Cheyenne
Berger, Rosie M. *state representative*
Devin, Irene K. *state legislator, nurse*
Gentile, Liz *state representative*
Harvcy, Elaine *state representative*
Johnson, Lorna *state representative*
Kunz, April Brimmer *state legislator, lawyer*
Mockler, Esther Jayne *state senator*
Robinson, Ann *state representative*
Sessions, Kathryn L. *state legislator, educator*
Warren, Jane *state representative*

Cody
Shreve, Peg *retired state legislator, retired elementary school educator*

Laramie
Hansen, Matilda *former state legislator*

Rock Springs
Job, Rae Lynn *state legislator*
Edwards, Sarah R. *state representative*

TERRITORIES OF THE UNITED STATES

VIRGIN ISLANDS

St Thomas
Berry, Lorraine L. *state senator*

CANADA

ONTARIO

Essex
Whelan, Susan *member of parliament*

Ottawa
Andreychuk, Raynell *Canadian senator*
Bacon, Lise *Canadian senator*
Chalifoux, Thelma *Canadian senator*
Christensen, Ione *Canadian senator*
Cook, Joan *Canadian senator*
Cools, Anne C. *Canadian senator*
Cordy, Jane *Canadian senator*
Dalphond-Guiral, Madeleine *member of Canadian parliament*
Finnerty, Isobel *Canadian senator*
Hervieux-Payette, Céline *Canadian senator*
Jaffer, Mobina S.B. *Canadian senator*
Johnson, Janis G. *Canadian senator*
LeBreton, Marjory *senator*
Léger, Viola *Canadian senator*
Losier-Cool, Rose Marie *Canadian senator*
Maheu, Shirley *Canadian legislator*
Milne, Lorna *Canadian senator*
Pearson, Landon *Canadian senator*
Poy, Vivienne *Canadian senator*
Robertson, Brenda *senator*
Rossiter, Eileen *Canadian senator*
St. Hilaire, Caroline *member of parliament*
Ur, Rose-Marie *member of parliament*
Wayne, Elsie Eleanore *Canadian parliament member*
Hubley, Elizabeth *Canadian senator*

ADDRESS UNPUBLISHED

Abey, Kathy Michele *district representative, congressional caseworker*
Albers, Sheryl Kay *state legislator*
Baker, Nancy Kassebaum (Nancy Kassebaum) *former senator, foundation official*
Beals, Nancy Farwell *former state legislator*
Benoit, Nancy Louise *former state legislator, secondary school educator*
Blanchard, MaryAnn N. *state legislator*
Bodem, Beverly A. *state legislator*
Bonsack, Rose Mary Hatem *state legislator, physician*
Boyd, Barbara *state legislator*
Brown-Waite, Virginia (Ginny Brown-Waite) *congresswoman*

Burton, R. Johnnie Medinger *state official, data processing executive, finance company executive*
Carnahan, Jean *former senator*
Carpenter, Dorothy Fulton *retired state legislator*
Carstairs, Sharon *legislator*
Chisholm, Shirley Anita St. Hill *former congresswoman, educator, lecturer*
Clayton, Eva M. *retired congresswoman, former commissioner*
Connelly, Elizabeth Ann *retired state legislator*
Culp, Faye Berry *state legislator*
Curtis, Candace A. *former state legislator*
Daggett, Roxann *state legislator*
Danner, Patsy Ann (Mrs. C. M. Meyer) *former congresswoman*
De Gette, Diana Louise *congresswoman, lawyer*
Doderer, Minnette Frerichs *retired state legislator*
Donahue, Laura Kent *former state senator*
Duncan, Cleo *state legislator*
Duniphan, J. P. *state legislator, small business owner*
Finestone, Sheila *former legislator*
Gile, Mary Stuart *state legislator, educational executive*
Granger, Kay *congresswoman*
Hawkins, Mary Ellen Higgins (Mary Ellen Higgins) *former state legislator, public relations consultant*
Hearn, Joyce Camp *retired state legislator, educator, consultant*
Henry, Margaret Rose *state legislator*
Hickey, Winifred E(spy) *former state legislator, social worker*
Howard, Janet C. *former state legislator*
Howell, Janet D. *state legislator*
Hudkins, Carol L. *state legislator*
Hugley, Carolyn Fleming *state legislator*
Hutchison, Kay Bailey *senator*
Kiel, Shelley *state legislator*
Koch, Christine *legislative aide*
Lebowitz, Catharine Koch *state legislator*
Mandel, Adrienne Abramson *state legislator*
Maroney, Jane P. *former state legislator, consultant*
Meek, Carrie P. *former congresswoman*
Meyers, Jan *retired congresswoman*
Mikulski, Barbara Ann *senator*
Miller, Alice *state representative*
Miller, Patricia Louise *state legislator, nurse*
Moseley-Braun, Carol *former senator, former ambassador*
Nielsen, Linda Miller *city councilwoman*
Pascoe, Patricia Hill *former state legislator*
Patrick, Michele Mary *government official*
Patterson, Elizabeth Johnston *retired*
Pettis-Roberson, Shirley McCumber Jerrea *congresswoman*
Pevear, Roberta Charlotte *retired state legislator*
Pond, Phyllis Joan Ruble *state legislator, educator*
Pucci Giles, Michelle *legislative staff member, writer*
Rivers, Lynn N. *former congresswoman*
Roman, Twyla I. *state legislator*
Roukema, Margaret Scafati *congresswoman*
Rudy, Ruth Corman *former state legislator*
Salerno, Amy *state legislator*
Satterthwaite, Helen Foster *retired state legislator*
Simpers, Mary Palmer *state legislator*
Skinner, Patricia Morag *state legislator*
Smith, Alma Wheeler *state legislator*
Smith, Patricia *state representative*
Snelling, Barbara W. *retired state legislator*
Soles, Ada Leigh *former state legislator, government advisor*
Sorensen, Sheila *state legislator*
Stickney, Jessica *former state legislator*
Sykora, Barbara Zwach *state legislator*
Tauscher, Ellen O. *congresswoman*
Tavares, Charleta B. *former state legislator*
Taylor, Kathleen N. *state legislator*
Tebedo, MaryAnne *state legislator*
Thurman, Karen L. *former congresswoman, lobbyist*
Treppler, Irene Esther *retired state senator*
Vellenga, Kathleen Osborne *retired state legislator*
Vucanovich, Barbara Farrell *retired congressman*
Walkup, Mary Roe *state legislator*
Wojahn, R. Lorraine *retired state senator*

HEALTHCARE: DENTISTRY

UNITED STATES

ALABAMA

Huntsville
Yarbrough, Isabel Miles *dentist, educator*

CALIFORNIA

Concord
Grosso, Lisa Therese *periodontist*

Sacramento
Work, Janice René *pediatric dentist*

San Francisco
Greenspan, Deborah *dental educator*

Whittier
Conly, Diane Carroll *dentist*

CONNECTICUT

Litchfield
Keifer, Julia A. *retired dental hygienist*

Orange
Dileone, Carmel Montano *dental hygienist*

DELAWARE

Wilmington
Wachstein, Joan Martha *dental hygienist*

FLORIDA

Homestead
Ferraro, Marie *dental hygienist*

Winter Park
Bush, Christine Gay *dental hygienist*

ILLINOIS

Chicago
Dry, Judith Kallen *dental hygienist, cable producer, writer*

Hinsdale
Szeremeta-Browar, Taisa Lydia *endodontist*

INDIANA

Lafayette
Buckles, Judith Ann *dental educator, program administrator*

KANSAS

Wichita
Huntley, Diane E. *dental hygiene educator*

KENTUCKY

Glasgow
Swystun-Rives, Bohdana Alexandra *dentist*

MASSACHUSETTS

Arlington
Immanuel, Laura Amelia *dentist*

Dorchester
Lee, June Warren *dentist*

MISSOURI

Creve Coeur
Manne, Deborah Sue *dental hygienist, educator*

NEW HAMPSHIRE

Bedford
Twarjan, Colleen Ann *dental hygienist*

NEW JERSEY

Hammonton
Stephanick, Carol Ann *dentist, consultant*

NEW YORK

Hempstead
Ancrum, Cheryl Denise *dentist*

Patchogue
Yee, Janice *dentist*

Troy
Medicus, Hildegard Julie *retired dentist, orthodontist, educator*

OHIO

Cincinnati
Gehlert, Sally Oyler *dental hygienist, consultant*

Columbus
Goorey, Nancy Jane *dentist*

PENNSYLVANIA

Harrisburg
Prioleau, Sara Nelliene *dentist*

Whitehall
Tufton, Janie Lee (Jane Tufton) *dental hygienist, animal rights lobbyist, activist*

SOUTH CAROLINA

Charleston
Cordova, Maria Asuncion *dentist*

TEXAS

Dallas
Blanton, Patricia Louise *periodontal surgeon*

Eden, Becky DeSpain *dental educator*
McWhorter, Kathleen *orthodontist*

WASHINGTON

Seattle
Herring, Susan Weller *dental educator, oral anatomist*

ADDRESS UNPUBLISHED

Mundorff Shrestha, Sheila Ann *cariologist*
Sinkford, Jeanne Craig *dental association administrator, retired dentist, retired dean, educator*

HEALTHCARE: HEALTH SERVICES

UNITED STATES

ALABAMA

Andalusia
Cross, Charlotte Lord *retired social worker, artist*

Birmingham
Booth, Rachel Zonelle *nursing educator*
Crittenden, Martha A. *disability specialist*
Holmes, Suzanne McRae *nursing supervisor*
Hullett, Sandral *hospital administrator, health facility administrator*
Neel, Nancee R. *counselor*
Nichols, Sandra B. *public health service officer*
Perry, Helen *medical/surgical nurse, secondary school educator*
Smaha, Donna Alvey *adult nurse practitioner, consultant, acute care nurse practitioner*

Cullman
Thornton, Nancy Freebairn *psychotherapist, consultant, military officer*

Decatur
Steele, Bette Hulse *medical/surgical nurse*

Hamilton
Vinson, Leila Terry Walker *retired gerontological social worker*

Irondale
Karr, Beverly Ann *counselor*

Mobile
Wisner, Pamela L. *social worker*

Oxford
Johnson, Mary Murphy *social worker, writer*

Sulligent
Burleson, Emily Jane *nursing administrator*

Tuscaloosa
Orcutt, Ben Avis *retired social work educator*

Tuskegee Institute
Cooley, Fannie Richardson *counselor, educator*

ALASKA

Anchorage
Gillette, Muriel Delphine *nurse*

Eagle River
Hayes, MaryLee *editor, writer, nurse*

ARIZONA

Casa Grande
McGillicuddy, Joan Marie *psychotherapist, consultant*

Chandler
Shousha, Annette Gentry *retired critical care nurse*

Cibecue
Murphey, Margaret Janice *marriage and family therapist*

Cornville
White, Judith Louise *social worker, counselor*

Glendale
Chavez, Mary Lynn *pharmacy educator*

Mesa
Ahearn, Geraldine *medical/surgical nurse, writer, poet*
Boyd, Leona Potter *retired social worker*

Payson
Lasys, Joan *medical nurse, writer, educator, publisher*

Phoenix
Allen, Janice Faye Clement *nursing administrator*
Hagan, Judith Ann *social worker*
Hutchinson, Edna M. *home care nurse*

Scottsdale
Nelson, Mary Kathryn *bilingual counselor, artist, singer, comedienne*
Timmons, Evelyn Deering *pharmacist*

Sedona
Catterton, Marianne Rose *occupational therapist*

Sun City
Kessler-Gillespie, Kathleen E. *psychotherapist*
Lopez, Jean Engebretsen *neuroscience nurse, researcher*

Sun City West
Holloway, Diane Elaine *psychological consultant, psychotherapist, writer*

Surprise
Wargo, Andrea Ann *retired public health official, commissioned officer*

Tempe
Anchie, Toby Levine *health facility administrator*

Tucson
Diáz, Elena R. *community health nurse*
Glueck, Mary Audrey *retired psychiatric and mental health nurse*
Johnson, Elissa Sarah *speech pathology/audiology services professional, writer*
Kany, Judy C(asperson) *health policy analyst, former state senator*
LeCorgne, Lisette Mary *family practice nurse practitioner*
Ledin, Patricia Ann *nurse, nurse legal consultant*
Neal, Alaine (Diann Neal) *nursing administrator*
Smith, Kay Frances *social worker*
Thompson, Kathleen Shambaugh *marriage and family counselor*
Waldt, Risa *therapist, artist, educator*

Yuma
Houggard, Santa Carol Hall *family nurse practitioner*

ARKANSAS

Bella Vista
Christensen, Margaret Anna *nurse, health management educator*

Fayetteville
Mullen, Maureen Ann *social worker*
Newgent, Rebecca Ann *counselor, educator*

Fort Smith
Ashley, Ella Jane (Ella Jane Rader) *medical technologist*
Decker, Josephine I. *health clinic official*
Shankle, Kelli Ann *social worker*

Greenbrier
Brown, Lois Heffington *health facility administrator*

Harrison
McKelvy, Nikki Kay *nurse*

Hot Springs National Park
McDaniel, Ola Jo Peterson *retired social worker, educator*

Little Rock
Harmon, Kay Madelon *occupational therapist*
Mitchell, Jo Kathryn *retired hospital technical supervisor*
Winston, Sandra *health sciences administrator*

Marianna
Pruitt, Mary H. *social worker*

Norman
Hokanson, Carol *speech therapist, special education educator*

North Little Rock
Wilson, LaVerne *nursing administrator*

Paris
Hawkins, Naomi Ruth *nurse*

Sherwood
Eddy, Nancy C. *counselor*

Springdale
Smith, Roblyn Carol *speech pathology/audiology services professional*

CALIFORNIA

Alameda
Herrick, Sylvia Anne *health service administrator*

Anaheim
Lee, Donna Jean *retired hospice and respite nurse*
Pincombe, Jodi Doris *health facility administrator*

Arcadia
Anderson, Holly Geis *women's health facility administrator, commentator, educator*
Imbus, Sharon Haughey *neuroscience nurse*

Arcata
Janssen-Pellatz, Eunice Charlene *healthcare facility administrator*

Arroyo Grande
Bekey, Shirley White *psychotherapist*

Bakersfield
Kelly, Diana Kay *counselor, educator*
Litherland, Donna Joyce *counselor*

Berkeley
Hill, Lorie Elizabeth *psychotherapist*
Lashof, Joyce Cohen *public health educator*
Little, Angela Capobianco *nutritional science educator*

Brea
Pierpoint, Karen Ann *marriage, family and child therapist*

Burbank
Hartshorn, Terry O. *health facility administrator*
Ungerleider, Dorothy Fink *educational therapist*

Carlsbad
Hartigan, Jacqueline Reneé *investigator*

Cathedral City
Berry, Ester Lorée *vocational nurse*

Cerritos
Solum, Pamela Byard *psychotherapist, educator*

Corcoran
Oliver, Patricia *medical assistant*

Costa Mesa
Martin, Felicia Dottore *mental health services professional, marriage and family therapist*
McCarthy, Mary Ann *counselor, educator*

Davis
Schneeman, Barbara Olds *nutritionist, educator*
Stern, Judith Schneider *nutritionist, researcher, educator*
Turnlund, Judith Rae *nutritionist*

Del Mar
Rodger, Marion McGee *medical and surgical nurse, nursing administrator*

Downey
Diaz, Consuelo *health facility administrator*

El Cajon
Krueger, Nancy Asta *physical therapist*

El Cerrito
Schilling, Janet Naomi *nutrition consultant*

Encino
Ruderman, Ellen G. *psychotherapist, consultant, psychoanalyst*
Vogel, Susan Carol *nursing administrator*

Fremont
Macaluso, Mary Margaret *nurse, educator*
Sahatjian, Manik *nurse, psychologist*

Fresno
Ezaki-Yamaguchi, Joyce Yayoi *dietician*
Schroeder, Rita Molthen *retired chiropractor*
Weymouth, Toni *social worker, writer, educator*

Fullerton
Spencer, Beverly Ann *medical administrator, health services consultant*

Guerneville
Kozlow, Beverly Kay *physical therapist, psychologist, realtor*

Hemet
Lawrence, Paula Denise *physical therapist*

Huntington Beach
Boccignone, Lisa Maria *phlebotomist*
Carey, Shirley Anne *nursing consultant*

Inglewood
Epstein, Marsha Ann *public health administrator, physician*

Irvine
Cox, Kathryn Cullen *laboratory executive*
Ruttenberg, Susann I. *health sciences administrator*

Kingsburg
Quaday-Gray, Ailene Diann *retired speech pathology/audiology services professional*

La Jolla
Covington, Stephanie Stewart *psychotherapist, writer, educator*
Grobstein, Ruth H. *health facility administrator*

Laguna Beach
Gress, Donna Mary *health facility administrator*
Jensen, Gloria Veronica *adult nurse practitioner*

Laguna Hills
Anderson, Mikki Melinda *massage therapist, small business owner*
Banuelos, Betty Lou *rehabilitation nurse*

Lake Arrowhead
Keller, Sharon Pillsbury *speech pathologist*

Lake Elsinore
Young, Patricia Janean *speech pathologist*

Lake Forest
Boccia, Judy Elaine Stacy *home health agency executive, consultant*

Lake View Terrace
McCraven, Eva Stewart Mapes *health service administrator*

Lakeport
Niquette, Geraldine Norma *marriage and family therapist*

Lompoc
Boone, Donna Clausen *physical therapist, biostatistician, researcher*
Wagner, Geraldine Marie *nursing educator, consultant*

Long Beach
Mullins, Ruth Gladys *nurse*

Los Altos
Lathrop, Jennifer Fargo *audiologist*

Los Angeles
Banks, Mattie Mary *nurse*
Bingham-Newman, Ann Marie *marriage and family therapist, educator*
Carson, Margaret *human services administrator*
Cowan, Marie Jeanette *nurse, pathology and cardiology educator*
Edelman, Barbara J. *cancer registrar*
Gillies, Esther Herroon *social worker, educator*
Harrison, Gail G. *public health educator*
Katzin, Carolyn Fernanda *nutritionist, consultant*
Lindsey, Carol Annette *nursing administrator, educator*
Looney, Claudia Arlene *healthcare administrator*
Territo, Mary C. *health facility administrator, oncologist, educator*
Thompson, Judith Kastrup *nursing researcher*
Utz, Sarah Winifred *nursing educator*
Ver Steeg, Donna Lorraine Frank *nurse, sociologist, educator*
White-Whitfield, Lisa Denise *social worker, grant writer*

Malibu
Palacio, June Rose Payne *nutritional science educator*

Marina
Cornell, Annie Aiko *nurse, administrator, retired military officer*

Martinez
Baird, Laurel Cohen *clinical nurse*

Marysville
Gray, Katherine *marriage, family and child therapist, writer, educator*

Menlo Park
Reamy, Michaelin *marriage and family therapist, educator, consultant*

Mill Valley
Taylor, Rose Perrin *social worker*

Mission Viejo
Frederick, Roseann *retired medical/surgical nurse*

Modesto
Smith, Heather Lynn *psychotherapist, recreational therapist*

Monterey
Robinson, Marla Holbrook *community care nurse*

Moorpark
Young, Victoria E. *occupational health nurse, lawyer*

Moreno Valley
Hadfield, Tomi Senger *hospital administrator*
Young, Ruby Waller *medical/surgical nurse, writer, poet*

Morgan Hill
Aranda, Sandra Louise *speech pathology/audiology services professional*

Morro Bay
O'Neill, Margaret E. *psychological counselor*

Mountain View
Emmons, Victoria Ann *hospital administrator, marketing consultant*
Falcao, Veronica Grace *midwife*
Lucas, Catherine *biotechnology company executive*
Vanni, Deborah Ann *marriage and family therapist, educator*

Napa
Lee, Margaret Anne *psychotherapist, social worker*

Nipomo
Dronen, Linda-Kay *social worker*

North Hollywood
Charis, Barbara *nutritionist, consultant, health researcher*

Oakland
Bouska Lee, Carla Ann *nursing and health care educator*
Chodorow, Nancy Julia *psychoanalyst, psychotherapist, educator*
Coleman-Perkins, Carolyn *medical/surgical nurse*
DeMoro, Rose Ann *nursing administrator*
King, Janet Carlson *nutrition educator, researcher*
O'Hara, Delia Iglauer *family nurse practitioner*
Slack, Vickie *human services administrator*

Oroville
Strisower, Suzanne *clinical hypnotherapist, counselor*

Pacifica
Hall, Judith Young *nurse*

Palmdale
Garcia, Beatrice Maude *social worker*

Vahle, Laura Miles *marriage and family therapist, educator*

Palo Alto
Berger-Granet, Nancy Sue *nursing researcher*

Pasadena
Avrech, Gloria May *psychotherapist*

Paso Robles
Buck-Moyer, Sandra Kay *marriage and family therapist*

Pinole
Wold, Vera O'Bryan *retired medical/surgical nurse*

Placerville
Wall, Sonja Eloise *nursing administrator*

Redding
Caskie, Judith Maureen *physical therapist*
Rocafort, Julia Esther *social worker*

Redlands
Bumann, Daniela *movement therapist, massage therapist*
Coleman, Arlene Florence *retired pediatrics nurse*

Riverside
Chang, Sylvia Tan *health facility administrator, educator*
Meadows, Joyce Katherine *nurse*

Roseville
Madden, Wanda Lois *nurse*

Sacramento
Armacost, Mary Jane *healthcare company executive*
Barnard, Linda S. *marriage and family therapist*
Friedman, Kenni *healthcare company official, councilwoman*
Runfola, Sheila Kay *nurse*
Santiago, Mayumi-Mae Lacaya *marriage therapist*
von Friederichs-Fitzwater, Marlene Marie *health communication scholar and researcher*
Woo, Sharon Y. *healthcare organization executive*

Salinas
Quick, Valerie Anne *sonographer*

San Anselmo
Ellenberger, Diane Marie *nurse, consultant*

San Bernardino
Ereksen, Christa Ann *social worker, marriage and family therapist*

San Bruno
Edwards, Kassandra Bennett *psychotherapist, consultant*

San Clemente
Renk, Pamela Jean *counselor, psychotherapist*

San Diego
Brokaw, Meredith A. *women's health care company director*
Carson, Cynthia Lee *physician's assistant*
Clark, Ann D. *marriage and family therapist*
Crawford, Debra P. *women's healthcare company executive*
Crawford, Randi *women's healthcare company executive*
Dubé, Susan E. *women's healthcare company executive*
Essex, Lauren S. *women's health care company executive*
Haverly, Pamela Sue *nursing administrator*
Johnson, Wendy S. *women's healthcare company executive*
Klamerus, Karen Jean *pharmacist, researcher*
Martin, Julie *women's healthcare company executive*
Niedermeier, Mary D. *retired nutritionist*
Phillips, Angela L. *psychotherapist*
Robinson, Cheryl Jean *human services specialist, advocate*
Rodgers, Janet Ahalt *nursing educator, dean*
Steele, Dale F. *women's healthcare company executive*
Varga, Jeanne-Marie *women's healthcare company executive*

San Francisco
Auerback, Sandra Jean *social worker*
Chater, Shirley Sears *health educator*
Claypool, Nancy *social worker*
Dracup, Kathleen Anne *nursing educator*
Eng, Catherine *health care facility administrator, physician, medical educator*
Grossman, Melanie Durand *social worker, researcher*
Harrington, Charlene Ann *sociology and health policy educator*
Kaplan, Ruth Jean *mental health services professional, social worker*
Nix, Katherine Jean *medical case manager*
Rosales, Suzanne Marie *hospital coordinator*
Salbec, Patricia R. *emergency medical technician*
Smith, Cecilia May *hospital official*
Solday, Alidra (Linda Brown) *psychotherapist, psychoanalyst, filmmaker*
Styles, Margretta Madden *nursing educator*
Ventura, Jacqueline N. *retired nurse, researcher*
Wu-Chu, Stella Chwenyea *nutritionist, consultant*
Xu, Fran Feng *financial researcher*

San Jose
Cunnane, Patricia S. *medical facility administrator*

Lu, Nancy Chao *nutrition and food science educator*
Sawyer-Schlaepfer, Colene *marriage and family therapist, writer*
Vierra, Amanda Rose *counselor*

San Lorenzo
Arca, Patricia Genevieve *retired mental health nurse*

San Marcos
Ball, Betty Jewel *retired social worker, consultant*

San Pedro
McMullen, Sharon Joy Abel *life coach, marriage and family therapist*

Santa Ana
Chenhalls, Anne Marie *nurse, educator*
Lyons, Linda *health science association administrator*

Santa Barbara
Kirkpatrick, Diane Yvonne *retired speech pathology/audiology services professional*
Menkin, Eva L. *marriage and family therapist*

Santa Cruz
Poulos, Clara Jean *nutritionist*

Santa Fe Springs
Hanzel, Mimi S. *psychotherapist*

Santa Maria
Phillips, Dorothy Lowe *nursing educator*
Walton, Maurine Isabel *social worker*

Santa Monica
Magnabosco-Bower, Jennifer Lynn *mental health professional*

Santa Paula
Broughton, Margaret Martha *psychiatric nurse practitioner*

Santee
Schenk, Susan Kirkpatrick *nursing educator, consultant, small business owner*

Sausalito
Groah, Linda Kay *nursing administrator, educator*

Simi Valley
Erzinger, Kathy McClam *nursing educator*

Sonora
Gee, Gail Marie *retired medical society executive*

Stanford
Marsh, Martha *hospital administrator*

Stockton
Matuszak, Alice Jean Boyer *pharmacy educator*
Norton, Linda Lee *pharmacist, educator*

Studio City
Herrman, Marcia Kutz *child development specialist*
Weiner, Sandra Samuel *critical care nurse, nursing consultant*

Sunol
Rebello, Marlene Munson *speech pathologist*

Tarzana
Rinsch, Maryann Elizabeth *occupational therapist*

Temecula
Keenan, Retha Ellen Vornholt *retired nursing educator*

Thousand Oaks
Herman, Joan Elizabeth *healthcare company executive*
Mulkey, Sharon Renee *gerontology nurse*
Shirley, Courtney Dymally *nurse*

Torrance
Ebeling, Vicki *marriage and family therapist, psychotherapist, writer*

Truckee
Todd, Linda Marie *nutrition researcher, circulation manager, financial consultant, pilot*

Ventura
Bircher, Andrea Ursula *mental health services professional*

Visalia
Ryan-Halley, Charlotte Muriel *oncology clinical specialist, family nurse practitioner*

Vista
Lane, Marsha K. *medical/surgical nurse*

Walnut Creek
Ausenbaum, Helen Evelyn *social worker, psychologist*
Foster, Bonnie Gayle *operating room nurse, real estate agent*
Mackay, Patricia McIntosh *psychotherapist*

Watsonville
Hugg, Alicia Esther *healthcare administrator*

Woodland
Turner, Patricia Butler *mental health nurse, educator, consultant*

Woodland Hills
Tellez, Cora *healthcare company executive*

COLORADO

Aurora
Adams, Nancy R. *nurse, retired military officer*
Brown, Anne Sherwin *speech pathologist, educator*
Hood, Ollie Ruth *health facilities executive*
King Calkins, Carol Coleman *health sciences administrator*

Boulder
Arnold, Janet Nina *health care consultant*
Holdsworth, Janet Nott *women's health nurse*
Kintzing, Julie Alexandra *social worker*

Broomfield
Lybarger, Marjorie Kathryn *nurse*
Shannon, Denise Leslie *nurse*

Canon City
Romano, Rebecca Kay *counselor*

Colorado Springs
Clugston, Angela M. *medical technician*
Leffingwell, Denise C. *social worker*
Mackety, Carolyn Jean *laser medicine and nursing consultant*
Orner, Linda Price *family therapist, counselor*
Williams, Ruth Lee *clinical social worker*

Denver
Carroll, Kim Marie *nurse*
Geraci, Maria Catherine *mental health nurse practitioner, educator*
Goldblatt, Barbara Janet *sex therapist, educator*
Hotchkiss, Heather A. *social worker, consultant*
Hunsaker, Jill Ann *public health administrator*
Jennett, Shirley Shimmick *health facility administrator*
Joyce, Mary Holt *retired social worker*
Plummer, Ora Beatrice *nursing educator, trainer*
Thomas, Enolia *nutritionist, educator*
Turner, Karen *psychotherapist, educator*
Witt, Catherine Lewis *neonatal nurse practitioner, writer*

Durango
MacCallum, Lorene (Edythe MacCallum) *pharmacist*

Fort Collins
Sedei Rodden, Pamela Jean *therapist*
Tyler, Gail Madeleine *nurse*

Fort Garland
Taylor-Dunn, Corliss Leslie *marriage and family therapist*

Glenwood Springs
Candlin, Frances Ann *psychotherapist, social worker, educator*

Golden
Arvisais, Kari Lynn *marriage and family therapist*

Grand Junction
Brewington, Elaine Sue *social worker*
Hoagland, Christina Gail *occupational therapist, industrial drafter*
Michels, Ruth Yvonne *retired cytotechnologist, consultant*
Pantenburg, Michel *hospital administrator, health educator, holistic health coordinator*

Greeley
Linde, Lucille Mae (Lucille Jacobson) *motor-perceptual specialist*

Guffey
McCaslin, Kathleen Denise *child abuse educator*

Idledale
Brown, Gerri Ann *physical therapist*

Lakewood
Burnett, Elizabeth (Betsy Burnett) *counselor*
Johnson, Ramey Kayes *community health nurse*

Littleton
Miller, Betty Sue *counselor*

Longmont
Jones, Beverly Ann Miller *nursing administrator, retired patient services administrator*
Weaver, Barbara Horning *social worker*

Pueblo
Presley, Eva Luise Von Schriltz *counselor, writer*

CONNECTICUT

Bridgeport
Macdonald, Karen Crane *occupational therapist, geriatric counselor*
McAuliffe, Catherine A. *counselor, psychology educator, psychotherapist*

Bristol
Morales, Mary E. *social worker*

Cheshire
Markowski, Sally Hamilton *medical/surgical nurse*

Darien
West, Maria McDonald *social worker*

Durham
Ostby, Karen Jean *speech pathology/audiology services professional*

Greenwich
Hauptman, Betty *hospital official, fundraiser*

Groton
Payson, Herta Ruth *psychotherapist, theater educator*

Hamden
Cole-Schiraldi, Marilyn Bush *occupational therapy educator*

Hartford
Furniss, Wendy Hagstrom *public health services administrator*

Higganum
Gillmor, Rogene Godding *retired medical technologist*

Meriden
Shemchuk, Mary Elizabeth *occupational therapist*

New Britain
Brancifort, Janet Marie *hospital administrator, respiratory therapist*

New Haven
Diers, Donna Kaye *nursing educator*
Gilliss, Catherine Lynch *nursing educator*
Krauss, Judith Belliveau *nursing educator*
McCorkle, Ruth *oncological nurse, educator*
Reyes, Marcia Stygles *medical technologist*

New London
Allen, Carol Marie *radiologic technologist*

Old Greenwich
Nelson, Norma Randy deKadt *psychotherapist, consultant*

Redding
Benyei, Candace Reed *psychotherapist*

South Windsor
Pasakarnis, Kathleen Fallon *health services consultant*

Stamford
Lamberti, Deborah Louise *psychotherapist*
Moggio, Barbara Jean *health education specialist*
Moore, Sharon Helen Scott *gerontological nurse*

Storrs Mansfield
Chinn, Peggy Lois *nursing educator, editor*

Suffield
Bianchi, Maria *critical care specialist, adult and acute care nurse practitioner, nursing administrator*

Trumbull
Hauser, Hazel Mary *retired nursing director*
Hochberg, Jennifer Anne *counselor*

Vernon Rockville
Gallien, Sandra Jean *social worker*

West Hartford
Gebo, Susan Claire *consulting nutritionist*
Gobes, Landy *psychotherapist*
Hugg, Geraldine Bertha Novotny *retired gerontology specialist, journalist*

Westport
Boles, Lenore Utal *nurse psychotherapist, educator*

Wethersfield
Nesteruk, Julia Ann *marriage and family counselor*

DELAWARE

Hockessin
Croyle, Barbara Ann *health care management executive*

Long Neck
Landgrebe, Marilyn Ann *nutritionist, electrochemical company executive*

Newark
Talbert, Dorothy Georgie Burkett *social worker*

Smyrna
McClellan, Stephanie Ann *speech pathology/audiology services professional*

Wilmington
Johnson, Constance Green *health facility administrator*
Miranda-Evans, Valetta Lee *social worker, human services manager*
Riddle, Audrey Maxwell *healthcare administrator*

DISTRICT OF COLUMBIA

Washington
Adams-Campbell, Lucille L. *health facility administrator*
Alward, Ruth Rosendall *nursing consultant*
Baigis, Judith Ann *nursing educator, academic administrator*
Baldwin Anderson, Janet E. *researcher*
Bassiwa, LizaMarie *medical technologist*
Briggins, Vikki Marie *medical/surgical nurse*
Clontz, Karen Lynn *social worker*
Corrigan, Janet M. *health services association executive*
Cox, Carol Thayer *art therapist, educator*
Davidson, Sarah J. *health services administrator*
Delbanco, Suzanne F. *human services administrator*
Delgado, Jane *health facility administrator, writer*

Fitzgerald, Helen Teresa *grief therapist, writer*
Francke, Gloria Niemeyer *pharmacist, editor, publisher*
Gaston, Marilyn Hughes *health facility administrator*
Golden, Olivia A. *human service agency administrator*
Holland, Joy *health care facility executive*
Ignagni, Karen *healthcare association executive*
Johnson, Cheryl L. *nursing administrator*
Martin, Kathleen *medical center administrator*
Martinez, Rose Marie *health facility administrator*
Masi, Dale A. *research company executive, social work educator*
McCarter, Katherine Sauter *association executive*
Michnich, Marie E. *health policy analyst, consultant, educator*
Miller, Linda B. *administrator*
Njie, Veronica P.S. *clinical nurse, educator*
Obrams, Gunta Iris *medical officer*
Rheintgen, Laura Dale *research center official*
Rowland, Diane *health facility administrator, researcher*
Sanchez-Way, Ruth Dolores *health services administrator*
Schecter, Kate Sara *healthcare development executive*
Schorr, Lisbeth Bamberger *child and family policy analyst, author, educator*
Seelman, Katherine Dolores *institute administrator*
Stoiber, Susanne A. *health science organization administrator*
Theiss, Patricia Kelley *public health researcher, educator*
Wager, Deborah Miller *researcher, consultant*
Woteki, Catherine Ellen *nutritionist*
Yoder, Mary Jane Warwick *psychotherapist*

FLORIDA

Archer
Lockwood, Rhonda J. *mental health services professional*

Bay Pines
Nolan, Marilyn Ann *health facility administrator*

Boca Raton
Jacobson, Susan Bogen *psychotherapist*
Kramer, Marsha Louise Endahl *psychotherapist*
Morris, Jill Carole *psychotherapist*
Naples, Mary Cecilia *mental health services professional, health facility administrator*
Rothberg-Blackman, June Simmonds *retired nursing educator, psychotherapist, psychoanalyst*

Boynton Beach
Machtiger, Harriet Gordon *retired psychoanalyst*
Wilner, Lois Annette *retired speech and language pathologist*

Clearwater
Barry, Joyce Alice *dietician, consultant*
Fenderson, Caroline Houston *psychotherapist*
Kelsey, Linda Jean *technologist, educator*

Coconut Grove
Adams, Belinda Jeanette Spain *nursing administrator*

Coral Gables
Weiner, Ruth Eileen Blower Kassewitz *retired public relations executive*

Coral Springs
Colesanti, Roseann *medical/surgical nurse, consultant*

Delray Beach
Weiner, Anne Lee *social worker*

Deltona
Bondinell, Stephanie *counselor, academic administrator*

Dowling Park
Lebo, Lenore B. *counselor*

Dunedin
Simmons, Patricia Ann *pharmacist, consultant*

Englewood
Clark, Carolyn Chambers *nurse, educator, publishing executive*

Floral City
Rondot, Susan E. Sladen *nures, case manager, health facility administrator*

Fort Lauderdale
Gonzalez, Nancy Berger *healthcare professional, educator*
Kornblau, Barbara L. *physical therapist*
Rentoumis, Ann Mastroianni *psychotherapist*
Silva, Joanne Rizzo *family nurse practitioner*
Stern, Edith Lois *counselor, hypno-therapist*

Fort Myers
Gray-Vickrey, Peg *nursing educator*
Housel, Natalie Rae Norman *physical therapist*
Johnson, Sally A. *nurse, educator*
Taylor, Donna Bloyd *vocational rehabilitation consultant*
Woodbridge, Norma Jean *registered nurse, writer*

Fort Pierce
Clunn, Patricia Ann *nursing educator, writer*
Minor, Beverly June *retired social worker*
Whitaker, Diana Marie *medical/surgical nurse*

Fort Walton Beach
Bolt, Lynda Elaine *alcohol/drug abuse services professional*
Vanderburg, Kathleen *surgical nurse*

Gainesville
Kersey, Talana S. *mental health counselor*
Lipowski, Earlene E *pharmacist, education educator*
Long, Kathleen Ann *nursing educator, dean, consultant*
Malasanos, Lois Julanne Fosse *nursing educator*
Marohn, Ann Elizabeth *health information management professional*
Puckett, Ruby Parker *nutritionist, hospital food service administrator, consultant, author*
Robinson, Jacqueline J. *health services administrator, accountant*
Small, Natalie Settimelli *pediatric mental health counselor*

Hialeah
Hernandez, Madeline *mental health services professional*
Pelaez, Ofelia *addiction and HIV/AIDS counselor*

Hillsboro Beach
Marshall, Jo Taylor *social worker*

Hollywood
Tucker, Nina Angella *hospital administrator*

Indian Rocks Beach
Muneio, Patricia Anne *public health nurse*

Inverness
Grasso, Julia Alice *nursing educator*
Kramer, Marlene Dixie *dietician*

Jacksonville
Helganz, Beverly Buzhardt *counselor*
Langford, Cecilia Motes *nursing educator*
Pavlick, Pamela Kay *nurse, consultant*
Sanders, Marion Yvonne *retired geriatrics nurse*
Smalley, Terri Barnes *social worker*
Stiehl, Ruth Rasco *nursing educator*

Jacksonville Beach
Richetti, Cindy L. *mental health services professional*
Urban, A. Greg M. *health facility administrator*

Kissimmee
O'Shaughnessy, Rosemarie Isabelle Rao *clinical nutritionist*

Lake City
Norman, Alline L. *health facility administrator*

Lakeland
Markley, Kate *social worker, consultant*

Land O Lakes
Webb, Mary Greenwald *cardiovascular clinical specialist, educator*

Largo
Hinson, Karen Renee *mental health services professional*
Woodruff, Debra A. *occupational health nurse*

Loxahatchee
Newman, Nellie Yvonnie *nurse*

Melbourne
Chaloult, Nancy Marie *nursing administrator*
Hughes, A. N. *psychotherapist*

Merritt Island
Babcock, Hope Smith *counselor, educator, program designer*

Miami
Algazi, Nancy *health facility administrator*
Colona, Jane B. *transplant nurse coordinator*
Dorfman, Lisa Ann *nutritionist, consultant, educator*
Durkin, Diane L. *nurse*
Himburg, Susan Phillips *dietician, educator*
Jones-Wills, Eunice Stephanie *mental health nurse, researcher*
Kooima, Linda Kay *neonatal and pediatrics nurse*
Parchment, Yvonne *nursing educator*
Potocky-Tripodi, Miriam *social worker, educator*
Saland, Deborah *psychotherapist, educator*

Miami Shores
Martino Maze, Claire Denise *nursing educator*

Naples
Karkut, Bonnie Lee *retired dental office manager*
Strauss, RoseMarie *medical/surgical nurse*

New Port Richey
Charters, Karen Ann Elliott *critical care nurse, health facility administrator*

North Port
Koor, Margaret P. *medical/surgical nurse, deacon, obstetrical nurse*

Ocala
Staples, Elizabeth Ann *counselor*

Orlando
Leonard, Penny Sue Evans *nurse*
Leuner, Jean D'Meza *nursing administrator*
Sharp, Christina Krieger *nursing educator, researcher*
Wirth, Melissa Kay *medical/surgical nurse, rehabilitation nurse*

Palm Beach Gardens
Schurtz, Ora Sears *hypnotist, educator*

Palm Harbor
Rivelli, Susan Veronica *nurse*

Panama City
Reedy-Dewey, Madeline Anne *retired occupational therapist*

Pembroke Pines
Ferris, Rita Bernadette *social worker*

Pensacola
Appleyard, Diane Paige *human service administrator*
Law, Carol Judith *medical psychotherapist*
Loesch, Mabel Lorraine *social worker*
McCann, Mary Cheri *medical technologist, horse breeder and trainer*
Shimmin, Margaret Ann *women's health nurse*

Pinellas Park
Strader, Marlene Knocks *nursing educator*

Plantation
Burnett, Barbara Diane *social worker*
Clerici, Susan Marie *psychotherapist*
Newburge, Idelle Block *psychotherapist*

Pompano Beach
Goldberg, Lois D. *health facility administrator, disability analyst*

Ponte Vedra Beach
Church, Barbara Ryan *organizational psychologist*

Port Saint Lucie
Hogan, Roxanne Arnold *nursing consultant, risk management consultant, educator*
Holloman, Marilyn Leona Davis *nursing non profit administrator, new product developer*

Ruskin
LaComb-Williams, Linda Lou *community health nurse*

Saint Petersburg
Barthle, Audrey Jean *medical technician, educator*
Freeman, Corinne *financial services, former mayor*
Keller, Natasha Matrina Leonidow *nursing administrator*
Korn, Naomi S. *social worker, consultant*

Sarasota
Hanson, Virginia A. *activities director*
Harris, Judith Ann White *health occupations vocational educator, nurse*
Schoenhals, Katherine Viola *social worker*

Sebastian
Mauke, Leah Rachel *retired counselor*

South Daytona
Hollandsworth, Phyllis W. *marriage and family therapist*

South Venice
Zellick, Sandra Zelda *psychotherapist*

Tallahassee
Blair, Maudine *psychotherapist, communications executive, management consultant*
Ford, Ann Suter *family nurse practitioner, health planner*
Smith, Erlinda Fay *occupational therapist*

Tampa
Angard, Nancy Tellis *medical/surgical nurse*
Arfsten, Betty-Jane *nurse*
Boutros, Linda Nelene Wiley *medical/surgical nurse*
Castellano, Josephine Massaro *medical records specialist*
Collins, Gwendolyn Beth *health administrator*
Kuzmin-Nichols, Nicole A *biotechnology research and development company executive*
LaTourrette, Kathryn *family therapist, counselor, artist*
McGinnis, Mary Louise *mental health services professional*
Plawecki, Judith Ann *nursing educator*
Riley, Dorothy Joan *clinical social worker, writer*
Russell, Diane Elizabeth Henrikson *career counselor*
Steiner, Sally Ann *psychiatric nurse practitioner*
Strauss, Dorothy Brandfon *marriage and family therapist*

Tavares
Osborne, Glenna Jean *health services administrator, social services administrator*

Valrico
Carlucci, Marie Ann *nursing administrator, consultant*

Venice
Barritt, Evelyn Ruth Berryman *nurse, educator, dean*

Wauchula
Saddler, Peggy Chandler *counselor*

GEORGIA

Acworth
Ramachandran, Patricia Pates *retired social worker*

Alpharetta
Mock, Melinda Smith *orthopedic nurse specialist, consultant*

Atlanta
Bales, Virginia Shankle *health administrator*
Beaton, Rebecca Andrea *psychotherapist*
de Harven, Gerry S. *healthcare educator, consultant*
Ferdinand, Lisa G. *psychotherapist*
Holloway, Barbara R. *health science association administrator*
Huff, Sara Davis *nursing manager*
Kelly, Karen Deloris *addiction counselor, administrator*
Lattimore, Barbara *healthcare administrator, consultant*
Parrott, Janice Morton *medical and surgical nurse, nursing researcher*
Salmon, Marla E. *nursing educator, dean*
Slocum, Susanne Tunno *medical/surgical nurse*
Turner, Myrtle Inez *training facility director, research scientist*
Walton, Carole Lorraine *clinical social worker*

Augusta
Barab, Patsy Lee *nutritionist, consultant, realtor*
Feldman, Elaine Bossak *medical nutritionist, educator*
Logan, Betty Mulherin *human services specialist*

Brunswick
Bennett, Anne Marie *nursing administrator*
Herndon, Alice Patterson Latham *public health nurse*
Riner, Deborah Lillian *mental health services professional*

Canton
Sperin, Amelia Harrison *medical/surgical nurse, obstetrics/gynecological nurse*

College Park
Sims, Deborah Lyde *counselor*

Columbus
Harris, Mary Cole *counselor*

Conley
Grant, Lucille *hospital administrator, social worker*

Decatur
Wong, Faye Ling *public health service officer*

Fayetteville
Cokuslu, Lynda Elizabeth McCord *medical assistant*

Grayson
Nease, Judith Allgood *marriage and family therapist*

Jonesboro
Finley, Sarah Maude Merritt *social worker*

Kennesaw
Hetrick, Joan Willette *critical care nurse, administrator*

La Fayette
Rogers, Susan Mitchell *psychotherapist*

Macon
Brown, Nancy Childs *marriage and family therapist*
Camp, Shirley A. *nursing consultant, lawyer*
Johnson, Patricia Diane *nurse anesthetist*
Konersman, Elaine Reich *nursing administrator*
Landry, Sara Griffin *social worker*

Marietta
Biehle, Karen Jean *pharmacist*
Hudson, Linda *health care executive*
Neff, Marilyn Lee *nursing consultant*
Roaché, Sylvia *social worker*

Rome
Watson, Mary Ann *marriage and family therapist*

Roswell
Haase, Patricia Ann Thompson *retired nursing educator*
Peebles, Mary Lynn *nursing home administrator*
Rhau-Bernhard, Anna Frieda *women's health nurse practitioner*

Saint Simons Island
Low, Anne Douglas *nurse*
Weinberg, Elisabeth H. *physical therapist, health facility administrator*

Savannah
Baker, Brinda Elizabeth Garrison *infectious disease nurse*
DiClaudio, Janet Alberta *health information administrator*
Greene, Gail Purchase *medical/surgical nurse*

Snellville
Dodd, Polly *nursing educator, recreational therapist*

Statesboro
Bartels, Jean Ellen *nursing educator*

Union City
Riley, Francena *nurse, retired non-commissioned officer*

Warner Robins
Beck, Rhonda Joann *paramedic, educator, writer*
Harris, Naomi Litora *mental health services professional*

HAWAII

Hanalei
Snyder, Francine *psychotherapist, registered nurse, writer*

Honolulu
Flannelly, Laura T. *mental health nurse, nursing educator, researcher*
Kennedy, Faye *retired social worker, author*
Loke, Joan Tso Fong *respiratory therapist*
Lum, Jean Loui Jin *nursing educator*
Yokouchi, Kathy *nursing administrator*

Waialua
Pugliese Locke, Ranada Marie *nurse*

IDAHO

Boise
Brownson, Mary Louise *counselor, educator, artist*
Seeliger, Lisa Kay *social worker, writer*
Theis, Kristine Lynn *family practice nurse practitioner*

Eagle
Wickman, Patricia Ann *retired social worker*

Grangeville
Turner, Kathy Ann *mental health services professional*

Hope
Meyers, Marlene O. *retired health facility administrator*

Pocatello
Bott-Graham, Michelle Lynn *behavior therapist*
Heberlein, Alice LaTourrette *healthcare educator, physical education educator, coach*

ILLINOIS

Arlington Heights
Telleen, Judy *counselor*

Barrington
Kellogg, Joan Barrett *grief therapist, counseling astrologer, educator, author*

Bolingbrook
Day, Mary Ann *medical/surgical nurse*
Price, Theodora Hadzisteliou *individual, child and family therapist*

Carbondale
Kawewe, Saliwe Moyo *social work educator, researcher*

Centralia
Whitten, Mary Lou *nursing educator*

Champaign
Bednar, Susan Gail *social worker, consultant*

Chicago
Andreoli, Kathleen Gainor *nurse, educator, dean*
Bristo, Marca *human services administrator*
Cox-Hayley, Deon Melayne *geriatrics services professional*
Crawford, Jean Andre *clinical therapist*
DeVault, Kathy *psychiatric consultant, liaison nurse*
Easley, Cheryl Eileen *nursing educator, department chairman*
Franklin, Veronica Rena *psychotherapist*
Goldsmith, Ethel Frank *medical social worker*
Hill, Barbara Benton *healthcare executive*
Kumar, Faith *clinical professional counselor*
Logemann, Jerilyn Ann *speech pathologist, educator*
Nielsen, Nancy H. *health organization executive*
Proctor, Millicent Carlé *social worker*
Raheja, Krishna Kumari *retired medical/surgical nurse*
Reed, Vastina Kathryn (Tina Reed) *child and adolescent psychotherapist, family development specialist*
Rodts, Mary Faut *medical/surgical nurse*
Rosenheim, Margaret Keeney *social welfare policy educator*
Rudnick, Ellen Ava *healthcare executive*
Scott, Nancy L. *health facility administrator, consultant*
Sebring, Penny Bender *researcher*
Simon, Bernece Kern *retired social work educator*
Smalley, Penny Judith *healthcare technology consultant*
Vigen, Kathryn L. Voss *nursing administrator, educator*
Villalon, Dalisay Manuel *nurse, real estate broker*
Walker, Juliet *alcohol/drug abuse services professional, educator*
Watson, Easter Jean *psychotherapist, financial program consultant*
Weissman, Sharon Theresa *speech language pathologist*

Crestwood
Bonnes, Karen L. *clinical social worker*

Decatur
Litchfield, Jean Anne *nurse*

Dekalb
Crosser, Carmen Lynn *marriage and family therapist, social worker, consultant*
Frank-Stromborg, Marilyn Laura *nursing educator*

East Saint Louis
Roy, Darlene *human services administrator*

Elgin
Barnett, Sue *nurse*

Fairfield
Thomason, Nola Faye *critical care-emergency supervisor*

Frankfort
Chapel, Tennille Maria *speech pathology/audiology services professional*

Galena
Alexander, Barbara Leah Shapiro *clinical social worker*

Geneva
Stephens, Gay *human services executive*

Glen Carbon
Adkerson, Donya Lynn *clinical counselor*

Glenview
Coulson, Elizabeth Anne *physical therapy educator, state representative*

Gurnee
Ullrich, Linda J. *medical technologist*

Highland Park
Schindel, Alice *social worker*
Zywicki, Cindy Mary *nurse*

Hillside
Abraham, Noël Jeanette *social worker*

Hines
Cummings, Joan E. *health facility administrator, educator*

Joliet
Hooper, Denise Lynn *technologist*
Lynch, Priscilla A. *nursing educator, therapist*
Stahl, Arleen Marie *nursing educator*

Kankakee
Thomas, Tammy Louise *medical/surgical nurse, writer*

La Grange
Mahoney, Donna Marie *psychotherapist*

Lanark
Ling, Kathryn Wrolstad *health association administrator, minister*

Lebanon
Norris, Sandra Love *occupational therapist*

Matteson
van der Hoek, Sherry A. *counselor*

Maywood
Hindle, Paula Alice *nursing administrator*

Moline
Kundert, Candice Jean *psychotherapist, social worker, educator*
Williamsen, Dannye Sue *personal development educator, health facility administrator*
Wright, Susie Flora *medical/surgical nurse*

Mount Prospect
Harmon Brown, Valarie Jean *hospital laboratory director, information systems executive*

Murphysboro
Young, Linda Diane *speech pathology/audiology services professional*

Naperville
Nicotra, Mary *healthcare consultant*

Normal
Deany, Donna Jean *radiology technologist*

Northbrook
Kahn, Sandra S. *psychotherapist*
Noeth, Carolyn Frances *speech and language pathologist*

Oak Brook
Bower, Barbara Jean *nurse, consultant*
Schultz, Karen Rose *clinical social worker, author, publisher, speaker*
Sweeney, Patrice Ellen *health administration executive*

Oak Lawn
Noonan, Melinda Dunham *nursing administrator*

Oakbrook Terrace
Moreno, Judith Wilson *psychotherapist, consultant*

Palatine
Czerwinski, Rene D. *counselor*

Peoria
McCollum, Jean Hubble *medical assistant*

Plainfield
Stewart Nelson, Pamela *home health administrator, consultant*

Port Byron
Dennis-McDonnell, Lynn Marie *environmetal health practitioner, biologist*

Quincy
Flinspach, Ursula R. *pharmacy technician, mathematics educator*

Rockford
Heath, Alice Fairchild *retired mental health services professional*

Saint Charles
Abts, Gwyneth Hartmann *retired dietician*

Saint Francisville
Harezi, Ilonka Jo *medical technology research executive*

Skokie
Guillermo, Linda Sue *clinical social worker*
Langguth, Margaret Witty *health facility administrator*

Smithfield
Corsaw, Ardith *geriatrics nurse, administrator*

South Holland
Worden, Michele Marie *speech pathology/audiology services professional*

Springfield
Bartolo, Donna Marie *nursing administrator*
Hundley, Elaine E. *retired nursing education administrator*

Urbana
Tripp, April *special education services professional*

Warrenville
Elder, Amy Hope *psychotherapist, counselor*

Western Springs
Tiefenthal, Marguerite Aurand *school social worker*

Westmont
Babiak, Heather *nurse, food service executive*

Wheaton
Pape, Patricia Ann *social worker, consultant*

Wilmette
Hass, Victoria Yusim *psychogeriatrics services professional, consultant*

Winnetka
Peck, Annette Biemond *retired social worker, writer*

Wood Dale
Grady, Kimberly Ann *medical technician*

INDIANA

Anderson
Kratzner, Judith Evelyn *program manager*

Bloomington
Austin, Joan Kessner *mental health nurse*
Bartleson, Amy Aileen *psychotherapist*
Montgomery, Kathleen Rae *counselor*

Brownsburg
Voorhis, Lori Beth *respiratory therapist*

East Chicago
Psaltis, Helen *medical and surgical nurse*

Fort Wayne
Harwood, Virginia Ann *retired nursing educator*
Kennedy, Elizabeth *health facility administrator*
Ridderheim, Mary Margaret *psychotherapist*

Gary
Hensley, Mary Kay *dietician*
Steinberg, Marilyn Marie *psychotherapist*

Goshen
Deuschle, Constance Joan *counselor, educational consultant*
Loomis, Norma Irene *marriage and family therapist*

Granger
Harmelink, Ruth Irene *marriage and family therapist, writer*

Hammond
Chandler, Melanie Lynn *surgical technologist, paralegal*
Smokvina, Gloria Jacqueline *nursing educator*

Huntingburg
Heim, Tonya Sue *nurse, small business owner*

Indianapolis
Caudell, Joan Edwards *critical care nurse, consultant*
Dickenson-Hazard, Nancy Ann *pediatric nurse practitioner, consultant*
Gantz, Nancy Rollins *hospital administrator, nursing administrator, consultant*
Harden, Anita Joyce *nurse*
Humphreys, Katie *health agency administrator*
Maurer, Illene K. *retired speech pathology/audiology services professional, volunteer*
Moelhman, Amy Jo *social worker*
Morrell, Ruth Ann *speech pathology/audiology services professional*

Kokomo
Coppock, Janet Elaine *mental health nurse*

Lafayette
Geddes, LaNelle Evelyn *nurse, physiologist*
McBride, Angela Barron *nursing educator*
Novak, Julie Cowan *nursing educator, researcher, clinician*

Marion
Reaves, Lori Jo *social worker, educator*

Merrillville
Peterson, Lauren Kay *social worker*

Michigan City
Moldenhauer, Nancy A. *social worker, educator*

Mishawaka
Lamb, Beatriz Dominguez *home health agency administrator*

Muncie
Hoffman, Mary Catherine *retired nurse, anesthetist*
Irvine, Phyllis Eleanor *nursing educator, administrator*

Seymour
Lake, Nancy Jean *nursing educator, medical/surgical nurse*

South Bend
Ivory, Goldie Lee *retired social worker, educator*

Terre Haute
Lindley, Joyce E. *health facility administrator, real estate appraiser*

West Lafayette
Kirksey, Avanelle *nutrition educator*

IOWA

Burlington
Smith, Mona Riley *psychotherapist*

Cedar Rapids
Brooks, Debra L. *healthcare executive, neuromuscular therapist*
Mulvaney, Molly Marie *women's health nurse practitioner*

Council Bluffs
Lawson, Patricia Lynn *technologist*

Davenport
Goudy, Josephine Gray *social worker*
Heinner, Ellen Ann *occupational health nurse*

Des Moines
Dukes, Vanessa Johnson *dietician*
Lund, Doris Hibbs *retired dietitian*
Ramsden, Mary Catherine *substance abuse specialist*

Garner
Duregger, Karen Marie *health facility administrator*

Iowa City
Muir, Ruth Brooks *counselor, substance abuse service coordinator*

Janesville
Jarosh, Colleen Marie *nursing educator, consultant*

Lamoni
Kirkpatrick, Sharon Minton *nursing educator, college administrator*

Osage
Christensen, Pamela Karen *pediatric nurse*

Oskaloosa
Gleason, Carol Ann *mental health nurse, educator*

Richland
Walter, Sandra S. *social worker*

Waverly
Juhl Zelle, Dorothy Helen *retired social worker*

West Des Moines
Zimmerman, Jo Ann *health services and educational consultant, former lieutenant governor*

KANSAS

Council Grove
Flott, Carman Marie *mobile intensive care technician, instructor*

Courtland
Johnson, Dorothy Phyllis *retired counselor, art therapist*

Dighton
Schwartz, Janice Marie *dietician*

Garden City
Lisk, Martha Ann *vocational rehabilitation counselor*

Humboldt
Lee, Tracy D. *speech pathology/audiology services professional*

Kansas City
Boal, Marcia Anne Riley *clinical social worker, administrator*
Gilliland, Marcia Ann *nursing administrator*
Jerome, Norge Winifred *nutritionist, anthropologist*

Lawrence
Siemsen, Susan Anne *physician assistant*

Leavenworth
Heim, Dixie Sharp *family practice nurse practitioner*

Manhattan
Spears, Marian Caddy *dietetics and institutional management education*

Nashville
Huss, Bonnie Jean *intensive cardiac care nurse*

Ottawa
DeShazer, Ruth Shomler *health facility administrator, consultant*

Pratt
Westerhaus, Catherine K. *social worker*

Shawnee Mission
Breen, Katherine Anne *speech and language pathologist*

Topeka
Bauman-Bork, Marceil *health services administrator*
Horsley, Gail Patricia *retired mental health nurse*
Thompson, Pamela J. *nurse*
Varner, Charleen LaVerne McClanahan (Mrs. Robert B. Varner) *nutritionist, educator, administrator, dietitian*

Wellington
White, Helen Lou *school nurse practitioner*

Wichita
Dorr, Stephanie Tilden *psychotherapist*
Guthrie, Diana Fern *nursing educator*

KENTUCKY

Albany
Tallent, Brenda Colene *social worker, psychotherapist*

Edgewood
Ballinger, Carolyn Ann *nursing educator*

Flatwoods
Blankenship, Dawn Olivia *pediatric nurse*

Frankfort
Fleming, Juanita Wilson *nursing educator, academic administrator*

Goshen
Dahl, Marilyn Gail *psychotherapist*

Hopkinsville
Major, Carolyn Ledford *counselor*

La Grange
Shaver, Lindy Carol *nursing administrator*

Lexington
Farrar, Donna Beatrice *hospital official*
Holley, Kay Moffitt *nutrition instructor, dietitian*
Rowe, Melinda Grace *public health service officer*

Louisville
Albin, Melanie Arlisse *marriage and family therapist*
Anderson, Linda Jean *critical care nurse, psychiatric nurse practitioner*
Antoine, Janet Anne *social worker*
Berger, Barbara Paull *social worker, marriage and family therapist*
Force, Jill L. *health facility executive*
Glass, Elizabeth L. *social worker, literature educator*
Goellner, Susan Kitchin *nurse midwife*
Haddaway, Janice Lillian *psychotherapist, consultant*
Hathcock, Bonita Catherine (Bonnie Hathcock) *managed health care company executive*
Hines-Martin, Vicki Patricia *nursing educator, researcher*
Margulis, Heidi *managed health care company executive*
Mather, Elizabeth Vivian *healthcare executive*
Scott, Lolita Jean *social worker*
Soriano, Cristina *dietician*
Weisenbeck, Sharon M. *healthcare regulatory administrator*

Madisonville
Grothem, Helen Marie *occupational therapist, educator*

Middlesboro
Welch, Patricia *retired nursing educator, association executive*

Mount Olivet
Dorton, Truda Lou *medical, surgical and geriatrics nurse*

Owensboro
Freese, Laura Ann *social worker, consultant*

Paducah
Farr, Carla Lake *therapist*

Richmond
Hall, Kathy *nursing official*

Russellville
Harper, Shirley Fay *nutritionist, educator, consultant, lecturer*

Shepherdsville
Matson, Frances Shober *retired social worker*

LOUISIANA

Baton Rouge
Mayho, Lois Mary *social worker*
Younathan, Margaret Tims *nutritionist, educator*

Destrehan
Richmond-Frank, Sherry Dee *marriage and family therapist*

Franklinton
Wheeler, Gwen *medical, surgical, and critical care nurse*

Hammond
Theriot, Lisa Marie *social worker*

La Place
Lodwick, Judith Lynne *nursing educator*

Lafayette
LaHaye, Laura Launey *medical/surgical nurse*

Leesville
Gutman, Lucy Toni *school social worker, educator, counselor*

Mandeville
Pittman, Jacquelyn *retired mental health nurse, nursing educator*
Treuting, Edna Gannon *retired nursing administrator, retired nursing educator*

Metairie
Evans, Carol Rockwell *nursing administrator*
Floersch, Shirley Patten *dietician, consultant*
Friedman, Lynn Joseph *counselor*

Monroe
Corder, Jan Busby *nursing educator, university dean*
Murphy, Deborah Margaret *mental health services professional, social worker*

New Orleans
Brown, Mary Willoughby *health facilities administrator*
Higgins, Oleda Jackson *retired medical and surgical nurse*
Humphrey, Elizabeth Ann *women's health nurse*
Joyce, Marie Caldwell *medical, surgical, and mental health nurse*
Le Blanc, Alice Isabelle *public health program, academic program administrator*
Setlow, Valerie Petit *health science association director*

Pineville
Adams, Jane Miller *retired psychotherapist*

Ruston
Bourgeois, Patricia McLin *women's health and pediatrics nurse, educator*

Shreveport
Credeur, Catherine *social worker*
Sutton, G. Katherine Hallett *nurse*

Slidell
Jacob, Susan Marie *nurse*

MAINE

Bangor
Ballesteros, Paula Mitchell *nurse*
Marks, Joan Florence *social worker*

Brooklin
Schmidt, Lynda Wheelwright *psychotherapist*

Canton
Parsons, Lorraine Leighton *nurse, pre-school administrator*

Caribou
Swanson, Shirley June *emergency room nurse, travel nurse, adult education educator*

Damariscotta
Swanson, Karin *hospital administrator, consultant*

Fort Fairfield
Shapiro, Joan Isabelle *lab administrator, medical/surgical nurse*

Freeport
Cushman, Margaret Jane *home care executive, nurse*

Gorham
Katsekas, Bette Susan *counseling education educator*

Lewiston
Randall, Carla Elizabeth *nursing educator*

Lincoln
Nevells, Kimberly A *medical/surgical nurse, educator*

Mount Desert
Weinberger, Jane Dalton *retired nurse, volunteer*

North Yarmouth
Kuhrt, Sharon Lee *nursing administrator*

Old Town
Nelligan, Annette Frances *clinical coordinator*

Saco
Collins, Cynthia Jane *marriage and family therapist, priestess*

MARYLAND

Aberdeen
Klien, Karen Ann *speech pathology/audiology services professional*

Annapolis
Ebinger, Mary Ritzman *pastoral counselor*
Libby, Jane Elliott *retired dietitian*

Baltimore
Amos, Helen *hospital administrator*
Augustoch, Edith *mental health clinician*
Brown, Patricia Mary Clare *health facility administrator*
Campbell, Jacquelyn C. *community health nurse*
Cascio, Toni Angela *social worker, educator*
Chin, Katherine Moy *nutritionist, consultant*
Croushler, Sarah Isabella *dance and movement therapist*
Davis, Katherine Sarah *physical therapy educator*
Donaldson, Sue Karen *nursing educator, researcher*
Eden-Fetzer, Dianne Toni *nurse, project coordinator*
Evans, Judy Anne *health center administrator*
Hernandez, Iris N. *clinical specialist*
Howard, Bettie Jean *surgical nurse*
Jenkins, Louise Sherman *nursing researcher, educator*
Kumin, Libby Barbara *speech language pathologist, educator*
Kyger, Brenda Sue *intravenous therapy nurse*
Maultsby, Marilyn D. *health science association administrator*
Metzger, Delores Virginia *social services professional*
Prugh, Patricia Alice *psychotherapist*
Roup, Brenda Jacobs *nurse, retired military officer*
Washington, Earline *healthcare executive*
Williams, Anna M. *social worker*

Bethesda
Atwell, Constance Woodruff *health services executive, researcher*
Dyer, Doris Anne *nursing consultant*
Ehrenfeld, Ellie (Elvera Ehrenfeld) *health science association administrator*
McCray, Alexa T. *health science association administrator, director*
Polsby, Gail K. *psychotherapist*
Robinson, Sharon Beth *health science association administrator*
Spencer, Heidi Honnold *psychotherapist, writer, educator*
Stover, Ellen L. *health scientist, psychologist*
Willoughby, Anne *health facility administrator, researcher, educator*

Bowie
Lesh, Kathryn Ann *nursing researcher*

Chillum
Malbon, Louise *nursing educator, hypnotherapist*

Easton
Daniels, Marybeth Elizabeth *nurse*
Whitten, Nancy Bimmerman *clinical social worker, marriage therapist*

Gaithersburg
Dowd, Carolyn Lay *social worker*
Green, Shia Toby Riner *therapist*

Glen Burnie
Barteet, Barbara Boyter *retired social worker*
Endres, Eleanor Estelle *speech pathology/audiology services professional*
Hepburn, Jeanette C. *home health nurse*

Hagerstown
Harrison, Lois Smith *hospital executive, educator*

La Plata
Core, Mary Carolyn W. Parsons *health facility administrator*

Lanham Seabrook
Pleasant-Jackson, Tonya *therapist, consultant*

Laurel
Landis, Donna Marie *nursing administrator, women's health nurse*

Lutherville
Goodman, Valerie Dawson *psychiatric social worker*

Manokin
Miles, Elizabeth Jane *social worker*

Mitchellville
Chilman, Catherine Earles Street *social welfare educator, author*

Newburg
Mason, Christine Chapman *psychotherapist*

Owings Mills
Ryan, Judith W. *geriatrics consultant, adult nurse practitioner, educator, researcher*

Port Tobacco
Smith, Sheila Robertson *laboratory technician*

Rockville
Duke, Elizabeth M. *health facility administrator*
Gleich, Carol S. *health professions education executive*
Kiger, F. Louise *nursing administrator*
Messersmith, Stephanie Hunt *nursing administrator*
Moore, Melinda *public health physician*

Parham-Hopson, Deborah Hopson *health administrator*
Rimer, Barbara K. *health facility administrator, educator*
Smith, Shelagh Alison *public health educator*

Severna Park
Sundeen, Sandra Joan *mental health nurse*

Silver Spring
Canahuati, Judy *lactation consultant*
Foley, Virginia Sue Lashley *counselor, international training consultant*
Mashin, Jacqueline Ann Cook *medical sciences administrator, nursing administrator*
Nevans, Laurel S. *rehabilitation counselor*
O'Connell, Mary Ita *psychotherapist*
Stanford, Jennifer Laura *nurse, educator*

Snow Hill
Apson, Jane R. *public health educator*

White Plains
McCants, Zaditu Esther *social worker*

MASSACHUSETTS

Amherst
Breslin, Eileen Theresa *women's health nurse*

Auburndale
Kibrick, Anne *retired nursing educator and university dean*

Bedford
Herlihy, Maura Ann *psychology technician*

Billerica
Barnes, Shirley Moore *retired psychiatric social worker, genealogist*

Boston
Andrews, Sally May *healthcare administrator*
Blakeney, Barbara A. *public health service officer*
Bonanno, Theresa M. *nursing administrator*
Delahanty, Linda Michele *dietician*
Dwyer, Johanna Todd *nutrition research scientist, clinical nutritionist, educator*
Greenstein, Sharon Diane *health facility administrator, educator*
Lowenstein, Arlene Jane *nursing educator, health facility administrator*
Millar, Sally Gray *nurse*
Reinherz, Helen Zarsky *researcher, social services educator*
Ullian, Elaine S. *health facility administrator*

Brockton
Moore, Mary Johnson *nurse*

Brookline
Gewirtz, Mindy L. *organizational and human relations consultant*

Burlington
Rogers, Carol Rosenstein *social worker, educator*

Cambridge
Burns, Virginia *social worker*
Clifton, Anne Rutenber *psychotherapist, educator*

Centerville
Condon, Ann Blunt *psychotherapist*

Charlestown
Washa, Kirsten Thomas *mental health services professional*

Chestnut Hill
Burgess, Ann Wolbert *nursing educator*
Hawkins, Joellen Margaret Beck *nursing educator*
Munro, Barbara Hazard *nursing educator, dean, researcher*

Cohasset
Yess, Denise Anne *speech pathology/audiology services professional, educator*

Concord
Domar, Carola Rosenthal *social worker*
Rice, Susan S. *social worker*

Fitchburg
Scannell, Ann Elizabeth *nurse, educator*

Framingham
Austin, Sandra Ikenberry *nursing educator, consultant*
Willinger, Rhonda Zwern *optometrist*

Gloucester
Johnson, Anne Elisabeth *medical assistant*

Greenfield
Curtiss, Carol Perry *healthcare consultant*

Holyoke
Dearborn, Maureen Markt *speech and language clinician*

Hyannis
Nicholson, Ellen Ellis *clinical social worker*

Leverett
Shulman, Paula B(aka Phillips) *marriage and family therapist, educator*

Lexington
Bombardieri, Merle Ann *psychotherapist*

Manchester
Moody, Marianna S. *dietician*

Marion
McPartland, Patricia Ann *health educator and administrator*

Mattapoisett
Perry, Blanche Belle *physical therapist*

Nantucket
Bartlett, Cheryl Ann *public health service administrator*

Natick
Lebowitz, Charlotte Meyersohn *social worker*

Needham
Ryan, Una Scully *health sciences professional, medical educator*

New Bedford
LaPorte, Adrienne Aroxie *nursing administrator*
Monteiro, Patricia M. *clinical social worker*
Raposo, Deborah F. *nursing administrator*
Silvia, Lori A. *speech pathology/audiology services professional*

New Braintree
Lesak, Alice Elaine *psychotherapist, minister*

Newton
Kelliher, Justine Oren *retired nurse, educator*

Newton Center
Pill, Cynthia Joan *social worker*
Veeder, Nancy Walker *social work educator*

North Andover
Lenihan, Barbara Desch *neonatal clinical nurse specialist*

Northfield
Matney, Louise Hoff *psychotherapist*

Osterville
Weber, Adelheid Lisa *former nurse, chemist*
Williams, Ann Meagher *retired hospital administrator*

Roxbury
Alméstica, Johanna Lynnette *mental health counselor, administrator*

Springfield
Gross, Donalyn Ann *counselor*
Merriman, Deborah Joy *marriage and family therapist*
Saia, Diane Plevock DiPiero *nutritionist, educator, legal administrator*

Sudbury
Ames, Lois Winslow Sisson *social worker, educator, writer*

Tewksbury
Lefebvre, Sharon Elaine *psychiatric nurse practitioner*

Waltham
Gray-Nix, Elizabeth Whitwell *occupational therapist*
Mitchell, Janet Brew *health services researcher*

Wareham
Gayoski, Kathleen Mary *counselor, minister*

West Newton
Logan, Georgiana Marie *psychotherapist*

West Roxbury
Cohen, Carolyn Alta *healthcare educator*

Weymouth
Parks, Kristin M. *pediatrics health nurse, educator and practitioner*

Williamstown
Conklin, Susan Joan *psychotherapist, educator, corporate staff developer, TV talk show host*

Worcester
Ravnikar, Veronika A. *reproductive endocrinologist, educator*

Yarmouth Port
McGill, Grace Anita *retired occupational health nurse*

MICHIGAN

Ann Arbor
Clark, Noreen Morrison *behavioral science educator, researcher*
Herzig, Phyllis Glicksberg *social worker*
Kalisch, Beatrice Jean *nursing educator, consultant*
Ketefian, Shaké *nursing educator*
McCloud, Patricia Carolyn Kaiser *nurse educator, consultant*
McLaughlin, Catherine G. *healthcare educator*
Oakley, Deborah Jane *researcher, educator*
Reame, Nancy *nursing educator*

Berkley
Leland, Janet K. *social work therapist*

Berrien Center
Dunbar, Mable Cleone *counselor education, family*

Bloomfield Hills
Bird, Linda C. *psychotherapist, educator*
Panush, Irene E(sther) *social worker*

Charlotte
Herrick, Kathleen Magara *social worker*

Clarkston
Pieknik, Rebecca Anne *technologist, educator*

Dearborn
Beauford, Sandra *registered nurse, data processing executive*
Ibbotson, Patricia Ann *occupational health nurse, writer*

Detroit
Heppner, Gloria Hill *medical science administrator, educator*
Jacox, Ada Kathryn *nurse, educator*
Redman, Barbara Klug *nursing educator*
Smith, Valerie Christine *registered nurse, writer*
Walker, Deborah Sue *nurse midwife, educator*
Wesley, Ruby LaVerne *nursing educator, administrator, researcher*

East Lansing
Schemmel, Rachel Anne *food science and human nutrition educator, researcher*

Farmington
Burns, Sister Elizabeth Mary *hospital administrator*

Farmington Hills
Abrams, Roberta Busky *hospital administrator, nurse*
Pallares, Annette Marie *dietician*
Rinker, Marianne Marie *rehabilitation nurse*

Flint
Alarie-Anderson, Peggy Sue *physician assistant*
Williams, Veronica Myres *psychotherapist, social worker*

Franklin
Sax, Mary Randolph *speech and language pathologist*

Gladstone
Larson, Patricia Joan *clinical therapist*

Grand Rapids
Brent, Helen Teressa *school nurse*
Chase, Sandra Lee *clinical pharmacist, consultant*
Gemmell-Akalis, Donni Jean *psychotherapist*
Jackson, Wendy S. Lewis *social worker*
Kramer, Carol Gertrude *marriage and family counselor*
List, Annita *social worker, educator*
VanDerTuuk-Perkins, Jennifer Elizabeth *counselor, psychologist*

Grosse Pointe Park
Knapp, Mildred Florence *retired social worker*

Huntington Woods
Katser, Donna Durham *critical care nurse, educator*

Ionia
Ulmer, Evonne Gail *health science facility executive*

Kalamazoo
Bartz, Judith Anderson *nurse*
Fredericks, Sharon Kay *nurse's aide*
Grover, Kathron Claire *counselor, social worker*
Lander, Joyce Ann *nursing educator, medical/surgical nurse*
Ortiz-Button, Olga *social worker*
Yoder-Gagnon, Pamala S. *retired orthopedic nurse*

Laingsburg
Collins, Mary Alice *psychiatric social worker*

Lansing
Loftus, Kay Douglas Colgan *social worker*

Lincoln Park
Russell, Harriet Shaw *social worker*

Livonia
Gepford, Barbara Beebe *retired nutrition educator*

Marquette
Edgell, Isabel Julie Hoff *hospice nurse*
Sherony, Cheryl Anne *dietician*

Monroe
McCracken, Kathryn Angela *clinical social worker*

Muskegon
Cusick Reimink, Ruth Elizabeth *community health nurse*

Negaunee
Matero, Janet Louise *counselor, educator*

North Muskegon
Heyen, Beatrice J. *psychotherapist*

Novi
Pelham, Judith *health system administrator*

Oak Park
Rutherford, Guinevere Faye *surgical technician*

Ortonville
Coffel, Patricia K. *retired social worker*

Petoskey
Krancevich-Shaw, Cynthia Ann *health facility professional*

Pinckney
McNamara, Ann Dowd *medical technologist*

Rapid River
Olson, Marian Edna *nursing consultant, social psychologist*

Redford
Aubertin, Madeline Katherine *retired nursing educator, medical/surgical nurse, mental health services professional*

Southfield
Martin, Marcella Edric *retired community health nurse*
McNelis, Kathleen Ann *medical/surgical nurse*
Pickett, Sherry M. *social worker*
Sedler, Rozanne Friedlander *social worker, educator*
Wagner, Muriel Ginsberg *nutrition therapist*

Sterling Heights
Hammond-Kominsky, Cynthia Cecelia *optometrist*

Troy
Arking, Lucille Musser *nurse, epidemiologist*

University Center
May, Margrethe *health educator*

Walled Lake
Schmitz, Carol Ann *speech pathology/audiology services professional*

Westland
Coates, Dianne Kay *social worker*

MINNESOTA

Bemidji
Christenson, Eileen Esther *geriatrics nurse*
Martinson, Ida Marie *nursing educator, physiologist, medical/surgical nurse*

Bloomington
Avery, Maurine Ann *health record administrator*
Nichols, Donna Mardell *nurse anesthetist*

Dilworth
DiAllesandro, Connie Lyn *family practice nurse practitioner*

Duluth
Henrikson, Vickie L. *social worker*
Salmela, Lynn Marie *clinical nurse specialist*

Elysian
Thayer, Edna Louise *medical facility and nursing administrator*

Minneapolis
Dundahl, Carol Lamm *psychiatric nurse*
Feldman, Nancy Jane *health organization executive*
Gerdner, Linda Ann *nursing researcher, educator*
Gilbert, Helen DeLong *psychologist, psychoanalyst*
Karlins, Miriam *mental health and volunteer services consultant*
Mathews, Kathleen Ann *social worker, psychotherapist*
Murphy, Edrie Lee *laboratory administrator*
Raynolds, Virginia Crane *nurse*
Steen-Hinderlie, Diane Evelyn *social worker, musician*

Minnetonka
Quam, Lois *healthcare company executive*

Moorhead
Kent, Jill *midwife*

New Brighton
Heston, Renate *nursing administrator*

Palisade
Kilde, Sandra Jean *nurse, anesthetist, educator, consultant*

Rochester
Frusti, Doreen Kaye *nursing administrator*
Gervais, Sister Generose *hospital consultant*
Goodman, Julie *nurse midwife*
Kummeth, Patricia Joan *nursing educator*
Stelck, Mickie Joann *technologist*

Saint Paul
Barry, Anne M. *public health officer*
DeMaris, Heather *occupational therapist*
Kilbourne, Barbara Jean *health and housing executive*
Portoghese, Caroline Louise Parke *occupational therapist*
Tyrrell, Mary Margaret *community health educator*
Victor, Lorraine Carol *critical care nurse*

MISSISSIPPI

Bolton
Byrd, Lisa Marie *family nurse practitioner, lecturer*

Byhalia
Tackett, Maresa D. *medical technician*

Cleveland
Taylor, Donna Buescher *marriage and family therapist*

Corinth
Stafford Humbers, Linda Logan *family practice nurse practitioner*

Jackson
Jackson, Valerie Lynnette *social worker*

Lauderdale
Van Doren, Henrietta Lambert *nurse, anesthetist*

Mississippi State
Crudden, Adele Louise *social work research educator*

Moss Point
Bolton, Betty J. *medical/surgical nurse, poet*

Ocean Springs
Parker, Rebecca Mary *special education facility administrator, educator*

Pass Christian
Henrion, Rosemary P. *mental health professional*

Richton
Edwards, Claudette LeCoq *speech pathology/audiology services professional*

Starkville
Dumas, Joyce Pendleton *social worker*

Tupelo
Holland, Gloria Temple *psychotherapist*
Zurawski, Jeanette *rehabilitation services professional*

Union
Johnson, Denise Horton *speech pathology/audiology services professional*

MISSOURI

Belton
Brown, Doris Jane *medical technician*

Chesterfield
Phariss, Susan Willis *dietitian*
Robinson, Patricia Elaine *women's health nurse practitioner*

Columbia
Flynn, Margaret Alberi *nutritionist, dietitian*
Hensley, Elizabeth Catherine *nutritionist, educator*
Mustard, Cindy Singleton *social worker, administrator*
Snively, Carol A. *social worker, educator*

Creve Coeur
Myers, Debra Annella *speech pathology/audiology services professional*

Dexter
Owens, Debra Ann *chiropractor*

Fair Grove
Piech, Mary Lou Rohling *medical psychotherapist, consultant*

Farmington
Welch Dickerman, Tanya L. *speech pathology/audiology services professional, consultant, small business owner*

Fulton
Bierdeman-Fike, Jane Elizabeth *social worker, educator*
Reifsteck, Dorothy L. *retired health facility executive*

Jefferson City
Bussabarger, Mary Louise *mental health services professional*

Joplin
Arguello, Barbara Ann *nursing assistant*
Zook, Martha Frances Harris *retired nursing administrator*

Kansas City
Bennett, Teresa Ann (Terri) *social worker, counselor*
Coon, Saundra Kay *home health nurse, small business owner*
Davis, Florea Jean *social worker*
DeParle, Nancy-Ann Min *former federal agency administrator, lawyer*
Hirsch, Irma Lou Kolterman *retired nurse*
Krieg, Nancy Kay *social worker, poet, musician*
Norris, Ruth Ann *social worker*

Lake Ozark
DeShazo, Marjorie White *occupational therapist*

Lees Summit
Barfield, Cynthia K. *social worker, psychotherapist*
Smith, Geraldine May *nutritionist*

Lexington
Vinson, Lynette D. *speech pathology/audiology services professional*

Macon
Maddox, Wilma *health facility administrator*

Maryville
Gorman, Karen Machmer *optometric physician*

Nevada
Wassenberg, Evelyn M. *medical and surgical nurse, nursing educator*

New Bloomfield
Melton, June Marie *nursing educator*

Osage Beach
Childers, Brenda Sue *medical/surgical nurse*

Pleasant Hill
Goosey, Karmen Eileen *nurse*

Raytown
Siegel, Kim Annette *speech pathology/audiology services professional*

Saint Charles
Brown, C. Alison *counselor*
Panagos, Rebecca Jean Huffman *university educator, researcher, consultant*
Tabaka, Sandra Lee *medical/surgical nurse*

Saint Joseph
Thomas, Eleanor Shepherd *health facility administrator*

Saint Louis
Baum, M(ary) Carolyn *occupational therapist*
Cima, Cheryl Ann *medical/surgical nurse*
Dawson, M. Susan *nursing educator, psychiatric clinical specialist*
Ezenwa, Josephine Nwabuoku *social worker*
Faherty, Annalee *social worker, nun*
Fitch, Rachel Farr *health policy analyst*
Leek, Diane Webb *nurse*
Megivern, Deborah Mary *social worker, educator*
Ozawa, Martha Naoko *social work educator*
Ryan, Sister Mary Jean *health facility executive*

Sedalia
Miller, Toni M. Andrews *critical care nurse*

Seneca
Kolb, Jimmie Lois *marriage and family therapist*

Springfield
Holloway, Wanda Kaye *psychotherapist, consultant*
Kaiser, Dorothy Carolyn *social worker*
Williams, Juanita (Tudie Williams) *home health care nurse, administrator*

Warrensburg
Engle, Mary Elizabeth *dietician, educator*

MONTANA

Great Falls
Ledesma-Nicholson, Charmaine *psychotherapist*

Hamilton
Soden, Ruth M. *geriatrics nurse, educator*
Tonkens, Rebecca Annette *maternal/women's health nurse, rehabilitation nurse*

Helena
Wickham, Dianne *nursing administrator*

Malta
Watts, Alice L. *nurse*

Miles City
Thomason, Suzanne Irene *health services professional, researcher*

Whitefish
Morgan, Susan McGrath *Jungian analyst*

NEBRASKA

Fremont
Winans, Anna Jane *dietician*

Gering
Meier, Nancy Jo *nursing consultant*

Lincoln
Henderson, Robyn Lee *project manager*
Oman, Deborah Sue *health science facility administrator*

Newman Grove
Anderson, Joyce Lorraine *nurse*

Omaha
Graves, Maureen Ann *self esteem and spirituality consultant*
Leininger, Madeleine Monica *nursing educator, consultant, anthropologist, therorist, editor, writer*
Schinzel, Sue Madeline *registered nurse*

NEVADA

Carson City
Ayers, Janice R. *social service administrator*
Schwerin, Kathy Ann *marriage and family therapist*

Las Vegas
Gage, Miriam Betts *retired nutritionist*
Gilchrist, Ann Roundey *hospice nurse*
MacDonald, Erin E. *healthcare company executive*
Michel, Mary Ann Kedzuf *nursing educator*
Weber-Javers, Florence R. *nurse*

Minden
Hare, Dawn Michelle Ervin *alcohol/drug abuse services professional*

North Las Vegas
Fry, Judy Arline *hypnotherapist*

Reno
Bramwell, Marvel Lynnette *mental health nurse, social worker*

NEW HAMPSHIRE

Brentwood
Thompson, Eleanor Dumont *nurse*

Concord
McCall, Junietta Baker *psychotherapist, minister*

Conway
Phillips, Linda Fox *social worker, consultant, healthcare educator*

Hampstead
Parke, Paula Marie *nurse*

Lebanon
Boardman, Maureen Bell *community health nurse, educator*
Thompson, Pamela A. *nurse administrator*

Londonderry
Parten, Priscilla M. *medical and psychiatric social worker, educator*

Manchester
Belanger, Traci L. *psychotherapist, writer*
Bolduc, Diane Eileen Mary Buchholz *psychotherapist*

Nashua
Descoteaux, Carol J. *health facility administrator*

New London
Vernon, Alison F. *nursing administrator, artist*

North Hampton
Pazdon, Denise Joan *speech pathology/audiology services professional*

Ossipee
Bartlett, Diane Sue *counselor*

Tilton
Wolf, Sharon Ann *psychotherapist*

Wilton
Mellon, Nancy Scott *arts therapist*

NEW JERSEY

Absecon
Paparone, Pamela Ann *nurse practitioner*

Andover
Pavone, Marianne *medical/surgical nurse*

Asbury Park
McTague-Dougherty, Amy Elizabeth *speech pathology/audiology services professional*

Bedminster
Delehanty, Martha *human services administrator*

Budd Lake
Davis-Kalugin, Dorinne Sue *audiologist*

Camden
Baltimore, Pamela A. Grayson *social worker, consultant*
Bell, Kathy Dawn *medical/surgical nurse*
Marshall, Sara

Cherry Hill
Collier-Evans, Demetra Frances *veterans benefits counselor*

East Orange
Hudson-Zonn, Eliza *nurse, psychologist*

Elizabeth
Bell-Bowe, Jacqueline *mental health nurse, consultant, nursing educator*

Fair Lawn
Bowman, Delores *medical cost management administrator*

Flemington
Van Ost, Lynn *physical therapist, Olympic team official*

Fort Lee
Schirmer, Helga *retired chiropractor*

Freehold
Wilson, Nancy Jeanne *laboratory consultant, medical technologist*

Glassboro
Magnan, Ruthann *nurse, social worker*

Hackensack
Imus, Deirdre *health facility administrator*

Hamilton Square
Ridolfi, Dorothy Porter Boulden *nurse*

Harrington Park
Salmon, Margaret Belais *nutritionist, dietitian*

Haworth
Mango, Christina Rose *psychiatric art therapist*

Hazlet
Bradley, Carolyn Ann *social worker*

Highland Park
Blum, Lisa Carrie *social worker, researcher*
Grady, Joyce (Marian Joyce Grady) *psychotherapist, consultant*

Holmdel
Tambaro, Marie Grace *health specialist, nursing educator*

Jackson
Thomas, Doris Amelia *family practice nurse practitioner*

Jersey City
Gipson, Gloria Lorraine *social worker*
Mastropaolo, Joan Arena *healthcare management executive*
Milton, Barbara Ella, II, *psychotherapist*

Landing
Wolahan, Caryle Goldsack *nursing educator*

Linwood
Cohen, Diana Louise *psychology, educator, psychotherapist, consultant*

Long Branch
Vandebunte, Eileen J. *health facility administrator*

Lumberton
Losse, Catherine Ann *pediatric nurse, critical care nurse, educator, clinical nurse specialist, family nurse practitioner*

Morganville
Lechtanski, Cheryl Lee *chiropractor*

Morris Plains
Inez, Donna Lee *hospital administrator*

Mountainside
James, Barbara Frances *school nurse, special education educator*

Newark
Healy-Sova, Phyllis M. Cordasco *school social worker*

Newfoundland
Divinsky, Miriam *psychotherapist*

Paterson
Daniels, Cheryl Lynn *pediatrics nurse, case manager*

Pennsauken
Southard, Ruth Audrey *medical/surgical nurse*

Pennsville
Whittinghill, Elizabeth Jane *speech pathology/audiology services professional*

Pomona
Bukowski, Elaine Louise *physical therapist, educator*

Port Monmouth
Walling, Debra Ann *recreational therapist, director*

Princeton
Logue, Judith Felton *psychoanalyst, educator, professional coach*

Prospect Park
Blair, Sherry Ann *psychotherapist, educator*

Randolph
Whildin, Leonora Porreca *retired nursing educator*

Red Bank
Brown, Valerie Anne *psychiatric social worker, educator*
Gutentag, Patricia Richmand *social worker, family counselor, occupational therapist*

Ridgewood
Clements, Lynne Fleming *marriage and family therapist, application developer*

Saddle Brook
Clifton, Nelida *social worker*

Saddle River
Peters, Eleanor White *retired mental health nurse*

Secaucus
O'Rourke, Ann Marie Cecilia *social worker*

South Orange
Budin, Wendy C. *nursing educator, researcher*
Hecht, Marion B. *mental health counselor, mental health therapist*
Wright, Barbara Wincklhofer *nursing educator*

Succasunna
Zwiren, Janet *holistic professional, educator*

Teaneck
Stucker, Eleanor Marie *social worker, psychotherapist*

Tenafly
Brown, Shirley Ann *speech-language pathologist*

Trenton
Blake, Allison *social worker, educator*
Dixon, Kathryn A. *social worker*
Kelman, Marybeth *health care consultant, health policy analyst*
Miller, Velvet G. *healthcare administrator*

Union
Fabyanski, Mary Irene *nursing administrator*
Kuzan, Kathleen *speech pathology services professional, educator*
Williams, Carol Jorgensen *social work educator*

Vineland
Popp, Charlotte Louise *health facility administrator*
Santucci, L. Michelle *adult nurse practitioner, nutrition consultant*

Warren
Kozberg, Donna Walters *rehabilitation administration executive*

West New York
Kelly, Lucie Stirm Young *nursing educator*

Westfield
Roll, Marilyn Rita Brownlie *social worker*

Whippany
Papera, Rosemarie Marucci *speech pathologist*

Willingboro
Green, Riva Lee *social worker, minister*

Woodbridge
Estok, Rosemarie DeNorscio *educational administrator*

Woodbury
O'Bryant, Cathy *retired social worker, evangelist*

NEW MEXICO

Albuquerque
Clark, Teresa Watkins *psychotherapist, clinical counselor*
Kroken, Patricia Ann *health science association administrator*
Lowrance, Muriel Edwards *program specialist*
Moody, Patricia Ann *psychiatric nurse, artist, small business owner*
Olson, Jean A. *psychotherapist*
White, Jennifer Phelps *counselor*

Carlsbad
Mills, Dolores Elizabeth *speech pathology/audiology services professional*

Clovis
Rehorn, Lois M(arie) (Lois Marie Smith) *nursing administrator*

Edgewood
Villagomez, Deborah Lynn *medical/surgical nurse, horse breeder*

Kirtland
Nelson, Theresa Veronica *medical technologist, small business owner*

Las Cruces
Crnkovic, Anise Elaine *marriage and family therapist*
Mata, Josefina *health education coordinator, educator*

Roswell
Padilla, Sandra Lynn *counselor, consultant*

Santa Fe
Melnick, Alice Jean (AJ Melnick) *counselor*
Pulitzer, Roslyn Kitty *social worker, psychotherapist*
Wiese, Neva *critical care nurse*

Santa Rosa
Campos, Christina Rivas *finance officer, restaurant owner*

Taos
Aspenwind, Linda Eileen *social worker*

NEW YORK

Addison
Haines, Caryl *retired medical/surgical nurse*

Albany
Alvarez, Christina *counselor*
Cloud, Gary Lynn *food and nutrition services administrator*
Fitzgerald, Norma Anne *emergency nurse*
Hunziker, Sudha *social worker*
Kelley, Sister Helen *health facility executive*
Poleto, Mary Margaret *orthopedic nurse*

Astoria
Matheson, Linda *retired social worker*

Averill Park
Catullo, Laura A. *psychotherapist, artist*

Baldwin
Parker, Arlene Sandra *social worker*

Binghamton
Bansky-Donovan, Bonita A. *social worker*

Bloomfield
Thomas, Sheila Faye *pediatric nurse practitioner*

Bronx
Mills, Rosie Erica *nursing educator*
Simpson-Jeff, Wilma *social worker*

Brooklyn
Browne, Ruth *health science association administrator*
Dia, Mabel Perillo *dietician*
Eisenberg, Karen Sue Byer *nurse*
Jimenez, Kathryn Fisher *nurse, patient educator*
Jones, Blanche *nursing administrator*
Koenig, Leah *marriage and family therapist*
Logan, Janet Artisam *mental health nurse*
Mosquera, Zoila Bianca *social worker*
Murillo-Rohde, Ildaura Maria *marriage and family therapist, consultant, educator, dean*
Phillips, Gretchen *social worker*
Pine, Bessie Miriam *social worker, editor, columnist*
Segal, Beatrice Ann *social worker*
Sullivan, Ann Catherine *health facility administrator*
Watson-Byers, Eloisa *social worker*

Buffalo
Hoffman, Faith Louise *social worker*
Jervis-Herbert, Gwendolyn Theresa *mental health services professional*
Sarmiento, Shirley Jean *counselor, court advocate*
Temperato, Susan *mental health counselor, clinical supervisor*
Wright, Dana Jace *retired emergency nurse practitioner*

Canandaigua
Chappelle, Lou Jo *physical therapist assistant*

Cedarhurst
Lipsky, Linda Ethel *health facility administrator*

Cheektowaga
Rogers, Cheryl Ann *speech pathology services professional*

Clinton Corners
McDermott, Patricia Ann *nursing administrator*

Cohocton
Kowulich, Barbara Ann *physician assistant*

Congers
Voce, Patricia Maria *medical/surgical nurse*

Cornwall On Hudson
Burke, Ann Therese *social worker, educator*
D'Alvia, Marlene *medical social worker, clinical social worker*

Deer Park
Pariag, Haimwattie Ramkistodas *information management administrator*

Delmar
Hoffman, Rita Mary *counselor, cosmetics executive, consultant*

Derby
Kieffer, Marcia S. *psychotherapist*

East Islip
Weaver, Joyce R. *hypnotherapist*

East Moriches
Guthrie, Teresa Irene *pediatric nurse practitioner*

Elmhurst
Przystawski, Karen Ann *registered nurse*

Elmira
Bruzee, Kristen K. *nursing administrator*

Flushing
Gomez, Pastora *medical/surgical nurse*
Rosen-Supnick, Elaine Renee *physical therapist*

Forest Hills
Alsapiedi, Consuelo Veronica *psychoanalytic psychotherapist, consultant*

Freeport
Faraci, Diana *social worker, department chairman*

Glens Falls
Tucker, Bernadine *patient registrar*

Great Neck
Mayer, Susan Lee *nurse, educator*

Hartsdale
Fishman, Helene Beth *social worker*

Hastings On Hudson
Stillman, Jeanne Betsock *public health administrator, consultant*

Highland Mills
Da Silva, Ann Marie Katherine *psychotherapist, consultant*

Holley
Ruck, Rosemarie Ulissa *retired social worker, freelance/self-employed writer*

Honeoye
Kates, Cheryl L. *legal nursing consultant*

Hornell
Swift, Katharine I. *cytotechnologist*

Huntington Station
Williams, Una Joyce *psychiatric social worker*

Hurley
Darrow, Marianne Rosina *speech pathology/audiology services professional, editor, writer*
Petruski, Jennifer Andrea *speech and language pathologist*

Hyde Park
Rider, Kathleen Mary *dietician*

Inwood
Neumann, Tammy Leigh *speech pathology/audiology services professional*

Ithaca
Kane, Marilyn A. *occupational therapist, educator*
Mueller, Betty Jeanne *social work educator*
Rasmussen, Kathleen Maher *nutritional sciences educator*

Jackson Heights
Chang, Lydia Liang-Hwa *social worker, educator*

Jamaica
Geffner, Donna Sue *speech pathology/audiology services professional, audiologist, educator*
Kahn, Faith-Hope *nurse, administrator, author*
Moskowitz, Randi Zucker *nurse*

Kingston
Ione, Carole *psychotherapist, writer, playwright, director*

Lakewood
McConnon, Virginia Fix *dietician*

Latham
Caruso, Aileen Smith *managed care consultant*

Lawrence
Cohen, Elana Ungar *psychotherapist, researcher, consultant*

Lewiston
Moraca-Sawicki, Anne Marie *oncology nurse*

Malverne
Ryan, Suzanne Irene *nursing educator*

Manhasset
Croce, Anne Lally *nurse, commissioner*

Manlius
Gibson, Judith W. *clinical therapist*

Montauk
Hartsough, Cheryl Marie *nutritionist, director*

New Paltz
Pine, Patricia Palmer *aging services administrator*
Upton, Barbara *hypnotherapist, small business owner*

New Rochelle
Schreibman, Thelma Rabinowitz *psychotherapist, educator*

New York
Abella, Mercedes *occupational therapist*
Agard, Emma Estornel *psychotherapist*
Aigen, Betsy Paula *psychotherapist*
Bailey, Darlyne *social worker, educator*
Barker, Sylvia Margaret *nurse*
Barnum, Barbara Stevens *writer, retired nursing educator*
Barrett, Elizabeth Ann Manhart *nursing educator, psychotherapist, consultant*
Boufford, Jo Ivey *health and human services administrator*
Bressman, Susan Berliner *health facility administrator*
Bristow, Louise Alice *mental health nurse*
Britton, Monica Ena Louise *community health nurse, public health nurse*
Brodie-Baldwin, Helen Sylvia *retired college and human services administrator*
Brownell, Patricia Jane *social worker, educator*
Burkhardt, Ann *occupational therapist, clinical educator*
Caroff, Phyllis M. *social work educator*
Cathcart, Jane Wilson *recreational therapist, social worker, psychotherapist*
Dinerman, Miriam *social work educator*
Dorn, Sue Bricker *consultant, retired hospital administrator*
Duckett-Wallace, Barbara Monica *hospital administrator*
Eichel, Beverly *apparel company executive*
Ethan, Carol Baehr *psychotherapist*
Friedman, Danielle *social worker*
Garrett, Celia Erica *human services administrator, consultant*
Glassman, Carol *psychotherapist*
Grandizio, Lenore *social worker*
Green, Barbara Strawn *psychotherapist*
Green, Jean Hess *psychotherapist*
Heck, Melissa Eileen *speech pathology/audiology services professional*
Herzig, Rita Wynne *critical care nurse, soprano*
Hoffmann, Anne Marie *health facility administrator*
Horvath, Annette *home care administrator*
Kalayjian, Anie *psychotherapist, nurse, educator, consultant*
Kamerman, Sheila Brody *social worker, educator*
Kassel, Catherine M. *community, maternal, and women's health nurse, consultant*
Kove, Miriam *psychotherapist*
Labovitz, Deborah Rose Rubin *occupational therapist, educator*
Lawrence, Lauren *author, dreams expert, psychoanalytical theorist, psychoanalyst*
Lederman, Sally Ann *nutrition researcher*
Lehrman, Marceline Barbara *psychotherapist*
Lippman, Donna Robin *psychotherapist*
Lombardi, Linda Catherine *health facility administrator, educator*
Mandracchia, Violet Ann Palermo *psychotherapist, educator*
Marshak, Hilary Wallach *psychotherapist, owner, small business owner*
Matorin, Susan *social work administrator, educator*
McLoughlin, Carol A. *health facility administrator*
Moffat Salant, Marilyn *physical therapist, educator*
Morgan, Florence Murdina *nurse*
Mundinger, Mary O'Neil *nursing educator*
Murphy, Stacia *health service association executive*
Naegle, Madeline Anne *mental health nurse, educator*
Niles, Barbara Elliott *psychoanalyst*
O'Neill McGivern, Diane *nursing educator, educator*
Ossenberg, Hella Svetlana *psychoanalyst*
Pakter, Jean *maternal and child health consultant*
Patterson Dehn, Cathleen *pediatrics administrator*
Paulson, Loretta Nancy *psychoanalyst*
Rehr, Helen *social worker*
Resnick, Rhoda Brodowsky *psychotherapist*
Rosenthal, Donna Myra *social worker*
Rothman, Sheila Miller *public health educator*
Russo, Rosalie J. *social worker, vocational rehabilitation counselor, educator*
Savage, Veronica Rivera *social worker, educator*
Schoen, Regina Neiman *psychotherapist*
Scott, Adrienne *social worker, psychotherapist*
Scott, Mimi Koblenz *psychotherapist, actress, publicist, journalist, playwright*
Shohen, Saundra Anne *health care communications and public relations executive*
Speransky, Helen I. *psychotherapist, consultant*
Stark, Robin Caryl *psychotherapist, consultant*
Steichen, Joanna T(aub) *psychotherapist, writer*
Stein, Zena A. *health facility administrator, psychiatry educator*
Storm, Jackie *nutritionist, health education specialist*
Turo, Joann K. *psychoanalyst, psychotherapist, consultant*
York, Janet Brewster *nurse, family and sex therapist, artist*
Yoshiuchi, Ellen Haven *health educator, clinical counselor*
Yousef, Mona Lee *psychotherapist*

Newburgh
Mucci, Louise Catherine *family practice nurse practitioner, health care negotiator*

North Syracuse
Bakeman, JoAnne *alcohol/drug abuse services professional, educator*
McDonald, Elizabeth Lynne *speech pathology/audiology services professional*

Nyack
Carey, Lois J. *psychotherapist*
Scott-Battle, Gladys Natalie *retired social worker*

Oakland Gardens
Bernabo, Lois *social worker, educator*

Orangeburg
Penney, Dixianne McCall *mental health services researcher, administrator*
Pratt, Christina Carver *social work and women's studies educator*

Ozone Park
Catalfo, Betty Marie *health service executive, nutritionist*

Painted Post
Ogden, Anita Bushey *nursing educator*

Patchogue
McPherson, Sherry Lynn *social worker*

Peekskill
Jackson, Linda B. *social worker*

Rochester
Aydelotte, Myrtle Kitchell *retired nursing administrator*
Chiverton, Patricia Ann *nursing educator, dean*
Coon, Penny K. *human services administrator*
Furness, Janet Elisabeth *social work educator*
Herrera, Charlotte Mae *medical office administrator*
Hyland, Sharon Ann *adult nurse practitioner*
Lipsky, S. Kate *retired social worker*
Parrinello, Kathleen Ann Mulholland *nursing administrator, educator*

Roslyn Heights
Rubrum, Erica Courtney *family therapist, school counselor*

Rushville
Carpenter, Florence Erika *retired human services administrator*

Rye
Olver, Ruth Carol *social worker, retired*

Sabael
Morrill-Cummins, Carolyn *social worker, consultant*

Sag Harbor
Brathwaite, Harriet Louisa *nursing educator, educator*

Salt Point
Lackey, Mary Michele *physician assistant*

Sanborn
Robinson, Deborah J. *counselor, educator, educational consultant*

Saratoga Springs
O'Baire, Marika *community health nurse, writer*

Scarsdale
Liston, Mary Frances *retired nursing educator*
Schweitzer, Caren S. *social worker*

Schenectady
DuBrey, Patricia A. *medical technician*

Seneca Falls
Norman, Mary Marshall *alcohol/drug abuse services professional*

Slingerlands
Jacobs, Karen Louise *medical technologist*

Spring Valley
Ligonde-Minor, Gina *social worker, consultant*

Stony Brook
Mueller, Jean Margaret *nursing consultant*

Syracuse
Manley, Michelle S. *social worker, educator*

Truxton
Schultz, Helen Welkley *marriage and family therapist, minister*

Tuxedo Park
Buckley, Maureen A. *speech pathology/audiology services professional*

West Seneca
Siegel, Carolyn Augusta *social worker, lawyer*

White Plains
Fowlkes, Nancy Lanetta Pinkard *social worker*
Hariton, Jo Rosenberg *psychotherapist, educator*

Williamson
Thomason-Mussen, Janis Faye *human services administrator*

Woodside
VanArsdale, Diana Cort *social worker*

Wyandanch
Hodges-Robinson, Chettina M. *nursing administrator*

Yonkers
Roberson, Doris Jean Herold *retired social worker*

NORTH CAROLINA

Benson
Taylor, Martha McClintock *marriage and family therapist, researcher*

Buies Creek
Blalock, Mary Wright *counselor*

Calabash
Mack, Mary Elkin *counselor*

Cary
LaBelle, Ginger Sullivan *pediatric nurse practitioner*
Tittle, Vicki Marks *healthcare business manager*

Chapel Hill
Martikainen, A(une) Helen *retired health education specialist*

Charlotte
Crawford, Jenny Lynn Sluder *medical/surgical nurse, educator*
Swartz, Sharon Marie *physician assistant*

Concord
Fleck, Lisa C. *physician assistant, dietician*

Conover
Williams, Nancy Carole *nursing researcher*

Durham
Burgess, Paula Lashenske *health facility administrator*
Gosselin, Tracy Karen *nursing administrator*
Hoffman, Jennifer Anne *vascular technician, director*
Pericak-Vance, Margaret A. *health facility administrator*
Richardson, Lily Pendarvis *retired occupational health nurse*

Goldsboro
Harper, Linda Ruth *disabilities educator, consultant*

Greensboro
Bland, Annie Ruth (Ann Bland) *nursing educator*
Champlin, Deborah Louise *medical/surgical nurse, consultant*
Harris-Offutt, Rosalyn Marie *counselor, consultant, mental health nurse, writer*
Hazelip, Edwina Kay *critical care nurse*
Smith, Rebecca McCulloch *human relations educator*

Greenville
Turnage, Karen L. *medical technologist*

Grimesland
Phillips, Paula Brady *speech pathology/audiology services professional*

Hendersonville
Heil, Mary Ruth *former counselor*
Van Boer, Helen Shirley *counselor, educator*

Hillsborough
Richmond, Donna *speech-language pathologist*

Knightdale
Braswell, Jackie Terry *medical, surgical nurse*

Lake Waccamaw
Spaulding, Lila Bernice *marriage and family counselor*

Leland
Jones, Jacqueline Lee *health facility administrator*

Morganton
Singleton, Stella Wood *nurse*

Morrisville
Cannon, Alice Grace *counselor*

Murphy
Dickey, Jeannetta Burkett *social worker*

Newland
Lustig, Susan Gardner *occupational therapist*

Oxford
Harvey, Gloria-Stroud *physician assistant*

Pembroke
Thompson, Debra Anne *speech pathology/audiology services professional, educator*

Pittsboro
Handler, Enid Irene *health care administrator, consultant*

Raleigh
Berry, Joni Ingram *hospice pharmacist, educator*
Geller, Janice Grace *nurse*
Malling, Martha Hale Shackford *social worker, educator*

Rockingham
Evans, Patricia McCormick *clinical therapist*

Roxboro
Broyles, Bonita Eileen *nursing educator*

Salisbury
Ward, Brenda Robinson *social worker*

Sherrills Ford
Stynes, Barbara Bilello *integrative health professional, educator*

Sylva
Karcher, Susan Marie *speech pathology/audiology services professional*

Wilmington
Coté, Debra Nan *surgical nurse*
Israel, Margie Olanoff *psychotherapist*

Wilson
Morris, Sharon Louise Stewart *emergency medical technician, paramedic*

Winston Salem
Walters, Doris Lavonne *retired pastoral counselor, counseling services facility administrator*
Wood, Mary Elizabeth *retired physician assistant*
Yeatts, Dorothy Elizabeth Freeman *nurse, educator, retired county official*

Wrightsville Beach
McDonald, Wylene Booth *former nurse, pharmaceutical sales professional*

NORTH DAKOTA

Fargo
Nickel, Janet Marlene Milton *geriatrics nurse*

Maddock
Aadland, Kathleen A. *counselor, army intelligence officer*

Mandan
Hollingsworth, Rebecca A. *speech pathology/audiology services professional*

OHIO

Akron
Lesner, Sharon A. *audiologist, educator*
Rothkin, Marilyn Mae *psychotherapist*

Athens
Sarnoff, Susan Kiss *social worker, educator*

Bath
Hoffer, Alma Jeanne *nursing educator*

Beavercreek
Rinta, Christine Evelyn *nurse, air force officer*

Bucyrus
Cooper, April Helen *family nurse practitioner*

Canton
Gleckler, Lois Eileene *occupational therapist*
Traveria, Beth M. *mental health counselor*

Chillicothe
Reed, Faith Patricia *health services administrator*

Cincinnati
Greenwald, Theresa McGowan *medical administrator, nurse*
Heekin, Mary Ann *oncology social worker*
Henney, Jane Ellen *health facility administrator, educator, oncologist*
Karle-Swails, Jeanine *neuroscience clinical nurse specialist*
Koebel, Sister Celestia *health care system executive*
Monroe, Erin *psychiatric nurse practitioner*
St. John, Maria Ann *nurse anesthetist*
Sierra-Amor, Rosa Isabel *health facility administrator*
Stinson, Mary Florence *retired nursing educator*

Cleveland
Dadley, Arlene Jeanne *sleep technologist*
Douglas, Janice Green *physician, educator*
Dylag, Helen Marie *healthcare administrator*

Fitzpatrick, Joyce J. *nursing educator, former dean*
Johnson, Mattiedna *medical/surgical nurse*
Joseph, Eleanor Ann *health science association administrator, consultant*
Kohn, Mary Louise Beatrice *nurse*
Mantzell, Betty Lou *school health administrator*
Petras, Cheryl Ann *nursing administrator*
Schlotfeldt, Rozella May *nursing educator, educator*
Wright, Clifflora L. *social worker, educator, alcohol/drug abuse services professional, consultant*

Columbus
Anderson, Carole Ann *nursing educator, academic administrator*
Bachman, Sister Janice *healthcare executive, religious order administrator*
Cuddihy, June Tuck *pediatrics nurse*
Guy, Jennifer Louise *nursing administrator*
Julia, Maria *social worker, educator, consultant*
Krakoff, Diane Elizabeth Butts *medical/surgical nurse*
Lewis, Nina *social worker*
Morrison, Jacqueline Ann *social worker, psychologist*
Nucklos, Shirley *health facility administrator, consultant*

Copley
Smith, Joan H. *retired women's health nurse, educator*

Cortland
Bryner, E. Jeanne *medical/surgical nurse*

Dayton
Hitch, Melanie Audrey *orthopaedics nurse*
O'Malley, Patricia *critical care nurse*
Stefanics, Charlotte Louise *retired mental health nurse*
Versic, Linda Joan *nurse educator, research company executive*

Dublin
White, Kathy Brittain *medical association executive*

Elyria
Manner, Jennifer Fouse *social worker*

Findlay
Stephani, Nancy Jean *social worker, journalist*

Hamilton
Fein, Linda Ann *nurse anesthetist, consultant*

Kent
Sonnhalter, Carolyn Therese *physical therapist, consultant*

Lyndhurst
Silver, Thelma *social worker*

Miamisburg
Lucius, Mary Albus *dietician*

New Carlisle
Leffler, Carole Elizabeth *mental health nurse, women's health nurse*
Peters, Elizabeth Ann Hampton *retired nursing educator*

Olmsted Falls
Semple, Jane Frances *health facility administrator*

Perrysburg
Billnitzer, Bonnie Jeanne *nurse, gerontologist*

Pickerington
Palmer, Noreen E. *psychotherapist*

Plain City
Karrer, Carol Converse *nursing educator, consultant*

Salem
Moss, Susan *nurse, retail store owner*

Shaker Heights
Katz, Linda M. *social worker*

Strongsville
Taghizadeh, Georgeanne Marie *medical/surgical nurse, diagnostic cardiac sonographer*

Sylvania
Verhesen, Anna Maria Hubertina *social worker*

Toledo
Dahl Reeves, Gretchen *occupational therapy educator*
Lessick, Mira Lee *nursing educator*
Overmyer, Janet Elaine *counselor*

Urbana
Meyers, Marsha Lynn *retired social worker*

Warren
Cremeans, Sharon Lu *medical/surgical nurse*
Smith, Paula Marie *medical technologist*
VanAuker, Lana *recreational therapist, educator*

Westlake
Coeling, Harriet Van Ess *nursing educator, editor*
Lahiff, Marilyn J. *nursing administrator*
Schroth, Joyce Able *social worker*

Worthington
Bernhagen, Lillian Flickinger *retired school health consultant*

Youngstown
Lambert, Jean Marjorie *health care executive*

OKLAHOMA

Ada
Davenport, Ann Adele Mayfield *retired home care agency administrator*

Broken Arrow
Muller, Patricia Ann *nursing administrator, educator*

Edmond
Thompson, Stephanie Denise *newspaper columnist, radio host*

El Reno
Buendia, Imelda Bernardo *health facility administrator, physician*

Lamont
Covalt, Edna Irene *retired medical/surgical nurse*

Newkirk
Newport, L. Joan *clinical social worker, retired psychotherapist*

Norman
Phillips, Joan Elizabeth *recreational therapist, educator*
Tackwell, Elizabeth Miller *social worker*

Oklahoma City
Geopfert, Kelli Renee *rehabilitation services professional*
Jones, Renee Kauerauf *health care administrator*
McClellan, Mary Ann *pediatric nurse practitioner*
McEwen, Irene Ruble *physical therapy educator*
McIntyre, Judy *social worker, state representative*
Morris, Theresa Linthicum *retired medical social worker*
Osborn, Lynda Pauwels *social worker*
Price, Donna J. *nurse*
Shaffer, Kimberly Saundra *medical technician*

Perkins
Lewis, Mary May Smith *retired family practice nurse practitioner*

Stillwater
Burr, Meghan LeRa *researcher*

Tahlequah
Brown, Sara Nordholm *social work educator*

Tulsa
Arrington, Rebecca Carol *occupational health nurse*
Carpenter, Nancy J. *health science association administrator*
Hyland, Cheryl C. *health services administrator*
Lewis, Corinne Hemeter *psychotherapist, educator*
Marshall, Linda Lantow *pediatrics nurse*
Redfearn, Charlotte Marie *nursing administrator*
Thompson, Lori Raquel *marriage and family therapist, consultant*

OREGON

Albany
Chowning, Orr-Lyda Brown *dietician*

Bend
Thompson, Mari Hildenbrand *medico-legal and administrative consultant*

Eugene
Camp, Delpha Jeanne *counselor*
Dorn, Kathie Lee *medical/surgical nurse*

Grants Pass
McDonald, Saranne *human services professional*

Klamath Falls
Klepper, Carol Herdman *mental health therapist*
Stevens, Kendra Ann *speech-language pathologist*

Mcminnville
Fread, Phyllis Jean *counselor, educator*

Medford
Linn, Carole Anne *dietician*

Phoenix
Dodd, Darlene Mae *nurse, retired military officer*

Portland
Bowyer, Joan Elizabeth *medical technologist, realtor*
Fritz, Barbara Jean *occupational health nurse*
Giffin, Sandra Lee *nursing administrator*
Hickcox, Leslie Kay *health educator, consultant, counselor*
Korb, Christine Ann *music therapist, researcher, educator*
Mendelson, Lottie M. *retired pediatric nurse practitioner, writer*
Morten, Ann Keane *nurse midwife*
Rooks, Judith Pence *midwife, public health consultant*

Redmond
Dey, Charlotte Jane *retired community health nurse*

Rhododendron
Williamson, Diana Jean *nurse*

PENNSYLVANIA

Abington
Lauck, Donna L. *mental health nurse*

Acme
Babcock, Marguerite Lockwood *addictions treatment therapist, educator, writer*

Allentown
Bedics, Lynn Fay *nurse*
Flores, Robin Ann *social worker, social services administrator*
Zocco, Patricia Elizabeth *human services manager, cardiac ultrasound technologist*

Aston
Mirenda, Rosalie M. *nursing educator, administrator*

Bala Cynwyd
Peret, Karen Krzyminski *health services administrator, consultant*

Bethlehem
Korsak, Barbara A. *geriatrics nurse*
Yatsonsky, Joan Marie *nursing educator*

Camp Hill
Parry-Solá, Cheryl Lee *critical care nurse*

Centre Hall
Fry, Theresa Eileen *therapeutic foster care aide*

Chambersburg
Gilbreath, Sarah Burkhart Gelbach *health facility administrator*

Clearfield
Boykiw, Norma Severne *retired nutritionist, educator*

Coraopolis
Wilkins, Arlene *social worker*

Dickson City
Kearns, Colleen *physical therapist*

Doylestown
Meyer, Diane Christine *social worker*

Dresher
Michael, Dorothy Ann *nursing administrator, naval officer*

East Petersburg
Kunkle, Mary Lou *counselor*

East Stroudsburg
Baril, Nancy Ann *gerontological nurse practitioner, consultant*

Easton
Kistler, Loretta M. *social worker, consultant*

Edinboro
Paul, Charlotte Patricia Peggram *nursing educator*

Elizabethtown
Chesbro, Karen E. Henise *registered nurse*

Evans City
Mustovic, Faithann Marian (Faithann Grigalunas) *pharmacist*

Exton
Ellis, Staci Elaine *psychotherapist, actress*

Factoryville
Simmons, Ruth Doris *retired women's health nurse, educator*

Feasterville Trevose
Thee, Cynthia Urban *psychotherapist*

Fort Washington
Minniti, Martha Jean *home healthcare company executive*

Glenmoore
Humphreys-Heckler, Maureen Kelly *nursing home administrator*

Glenside
Crivelli-Kovach, Andrea *public health and nutrition consultant, educator*

Hamburg
Schappell, Abigail Susan *speech, language, hearing and massage therapist*

Hanover
Davis, Ruth Carol *pharmacy educator*

Harrisburg
Comoss, Patricia B. *cardiac rehabilitation nurse, consultant*
Tyson, Gail L. *health federation administrator*
West, Eileen M. *caseworker*

Harveys Lake
Wolensky, Joan *occupational therapist, interfaith minister*

Hershey
Kruger, Nancy R. *university program director, nurse*

Hulmeville
Jackson, Mary L. *health services executive*

Jenkintown
Lowry, Karen M. *biomedical research scientist, pharmacist*

Johnstown
George, Christine *mental health services professional, supervisor, writer*

King Of Prussia
Phipps, Judith A. *social worker*

Meyer, Amy Allen *counselor*

Georgetown
Smitheram, Margaret Etheridge *health facility administrator, director*

Houston
Adkins, Susan *health services administrator*
Berg, Michele *health services administrator*
Caskey, Caroline *lab administrator*
Davis-Lewis, Bettye *nursing educator*
Florian-Lacy, Dorothy *therapist, educator*
Gerhart, Glenna Lee *pharmacist*
Gunn, Joan Marie *health facility administrator*
Hempfling, Linda Lee *nurse*
Henderson, (Ruejenuia) Secret *social worker*
Hughes, Mary Katherine *nurse*
Jaramillo, Sandra Julier *nutritionist, researcher*
Jenkins, Peggy Ann *counselor*
Johnson, Sandra Ann *counselor, educator*
Kelly, Kay *social worker, administrator*
Konefal, Margaret Moore *health facility administrator, critical care nurse, nursing consultant, educator*
Leichtman, Maria Luisa *mental health services professional*
Leins, Cynthia Marie *school nurse practitioner*
Lenox, Angela Cousineau *healthcare consultant*
Mallia-Hughes, Marianne *medical writer*
Montgomery, Denise Karen *nurse*
Nicklas, Theresa Ann *nutritionist, educator, researcher*
O'Malley, Kimberly Joy *psychometrician, researcher*
Peabody, Arlene L. Howland Bayar *retired, nurse*
Rance, Sharon Lee *speech pathology/audiology services professional*
Reed, Kathlyn Louise *occupational therapist, educator*
Robbins, Susan Paula *social work educator*
Rodgers, Amber Gayle *speech pathology/audiology services professional*
Williams, Dorothy S. *consultant nurse*
Yi, Jenny Kisuk *public health educator*

Humble
Schellinger, Ann Goodwin *medical manager*

Huntsville
Gullette, Valencia Deshae *counselor*

Irving
Jorden, Yon Yoon *health services company executive*

Italy
Lawson, Diane Marie *counselor*

Keene
Adams, Lavonne Marilyn Beck *critical care nurse, nursing educator*

Keller
Hewlett, Sandra Marie *clinical consultant*

La Porte
Levi, Janice Lawan *counselor*

Lago Vista
Garcia y Carrillo, Martha Xochitl *pharmacist*

Lewisville
Browne, M. Lynne *optician, artist*

Lubbock
Broselow, Linda Latt *medical office technician, aviculturist*
Dersch, Charette Alyse *marriage and family therapist*
Young, Teri Ann Butler *pharmacist*

Mcallen
Guerra, Edna *pharmacist*
Ramirez, Linda Manning *counselor*

Mexia
Chambers, Linda Dianne Thompson *social worker*

Midland
Ienatsch, Gayleen Elizabeth *nursing educator*

Missouri City
Taylor, Beth L. *counselor*
Watson, Loretta *medical/surgical nurse*

Montgomery
Gooch, Carol Ann *psychotherapist consultant*

New Braunfels
English, Mildred Oswalt *retired nurse supervisor*

Plano
Becker, Doreen Doris *medical/surgical nurse*
Calabro, Sara Louise *mental health therapist, consultant*

Port Arthur
Vinecour, Oneida Agnes *nurse*
Wade, Ernestine *public health nurse*

Rockport
Acker, Virginia Margaret *nursing educator*

San Antonio
Adcox, Mary Sandra *dietician, consultant*
Bunten, Brenda Arlene *geriatrics nurse*
Cruz, Rosalina Sedillo *marriage and family therapist*
Dacbert-Friese, Sharyn Varhely *social worker, evangelist*
Deal, Sarah R. *psychotherapist, educator*
Diehl, Kimberly A. *researcher*
Donelson, Rosemarie Quiroz Carvajal *human services professional, state official*

Flaherty, Sergina Maria *ophthalmic medical technologist*
Galvan, Alicia Zavala *pharmacist*
Hawken, Patty Lynn *retired nursing educator, dean of faculty*
Rodriguez, Helen G. *retired social worker*
Van de Putte, Leticia *pharmacist, state legislator*
Wilson, Janie Menchaca *nursing educator, researcher*

Santa Fe
Jernigan, Vicki Louise MacKechney *clinical nurse specialist*

Shelbyville
Lifshutz, Melanie Janet Bell *patient education, medical, and surgical nurse*

Snyder
Barnes, Maggie Lue Shifflett (Mrs. Lawrence Barnes) *nurse*

The Woodlands
Mock, Cherry L. *marriage and family therapist, child therapist*

Tomball
Burgoyne, Mojie Adler *clinical social worker*

Tyler
Coker, Melinda Louise *counselor*
West, Syntha Jane Traughber *mental health services professional*

Universal City
Lamoureux, Gloria Kathleen *nurse, consultant, retired military officer*

Wichita Falls
Haynes, Linda Rose *medical/surgical nurse*
Rousey, Anne *social worker*

UTAH

Midvale
Vigil, Debbie Saxon *surgical technician*

Murray
Webster, Linda Jane *clinical social worker, consultant*

Saint George
Chilow, Barbara Gail *social worker*

Salt Lake City
Morris, Elizabeth Treat *physical therapist*
Perkins, Nancy Ann *nurse*
Schutz, Roberta Maria (Bobbi Schutz) *social worker*
Wanji, Sue *nurse*

VERMONT

Brattleboro
Bussino, Melinda Holden *human services administrator*
Smiley, Carol Anne *home health administrator, sculptor*

Charlotte
Russell, Eleanor M. *retired technologist*

East Thetford
Cummings Rockwell, Patricia Guilbault *psychiatric nurse*

Montpelier
Erskine, Kali (Wendy Colman) *psychoanalyst*

North Bennington
Feidner, Mary P. *retired speech and language pathologist*

North Ferrisburg
Tulin, Marna *psychotherapist*

Rutland
Merrihew, Mary Albee *counselor*

VIRGINIA

Abingdon
Williams, Barbara Kitty *nursing educator*

Alexandria
Henry, Catherine Ann *health science association administrator*
Shoaee, Rokhsareh Sarah *marriage and family therapist, counselor*

Annandale
Abdellah, Faye Glenn *retired public health service executive*
Grosso, Camille M. *nurse*

Arlington
Adreon, Beatrice Marie Rice *pharmacist*
Berger, Gisela Porsch *psychotherapist*
Flynn, Laurie M. *social worker*
Lurie, Nicole *former health science association administrator*
Pfister, Karstin Ann *human services administrator*

Big Island
Durham, Betty Bethea *therapist*

Blacksburg
Lynch, Sherry Kay *counselor*

Charlottesville
Hanft, Ruth S. Samuels *healthcare consultant, educator, economist*

Worsham, Christine Behrens *healthcare administrator*

Chesapeake
Skrip, Linda Jean *nurse*

Colonial Heights
Crowder, Dorothy Sholes *nursing educator*

Emporia
Butler, Tammy J. Wiley *medical, surgical, and pediatric nurse*

Fairfax
Harper, Doreen C. *nursing educator*
Knee, Ruth Irelan (Mrs. Junior K. Knee) *social worker, health care consultant*
Monahan, Danielle Joan *renal nutritionist*
Ryder, Michele Cain *counselor, speech therapist*

Fairfax Station
Barringer, Joan Marie *counselor, educator, artist, writer*

Fisherville
Moore, Marianne *special education services professional, educator*

Hampton
Davis, Bertha Lane *psychiatric nursing educator*

Hopewell
Vartanian, Isabel Sylvia *retired dietitian*

Keysville
Frayser, Mary Stokes *human services administrator, consultant*

Lawrenceville
Stransky, Maria Soledad *psychotherapist*

Manassas
Lytton, Linda Rountree *marriage and family therapist, consultant*
Naylor, Illana *pediatrics nurse*

Mc Lean
Walsh, Marie Leclerc *nurse*

Newport News
Moore, Mildred Thorpe *dietician*
Price, JoAnna Saegusa *psychotherapist*
Shepard, Jean Moye *nurse*

Norfolk
Anderson, Darleen Shircliffe *hospital system administrator*
Hinsdale, Stephanie M. *social worker*
Nichols, Brenda Sue *nursing educator*

Radford
Carter, Kimberly Ferren *nursing educator*
Southern, Ann Gayle *medical/surgical nurse, educator*

Reston
Di Trapani, Marcia A. *health facility administrator, community health nurse, educator*

Richmond
Brown-Glover, Patricia *special education services professional*
Durrett, Nancy Kashner *health science association administrator*
Freund, Emma Frances *medical technologist*
Hargette, Julie Lynn *social worker*
Homestead, Susan E. (Susan Freedlender) *psychotherapist*
Lanier, Nancy McDaniel *researcher*
Massenburg, Johnnye Smith *speech pathology/audiology services professional, minister*
Roberts, Betty Winkler *retired health agency administrator*

Roanoke
Gaylor, Susan Roland *social worker*

Rural Retreat
Dronsick, Margery Sutton *social worker*

Sandston
Herrera, Linda R. *pharmacist*

South Hill
Clay, Carol Ann *family nurse practitioner*

Springfield
Dake, Marcia Allene *retired nursing educator, university dean*
Dodson, Alicejean Leigh *nursing administrator*
Williams, Cecilia Lee Pursel *optometrist*

Virginia Beach
Guckert, Nora Jane Gaskill *medical and surgical nurse, hospice nurse, holistic consultant*

Williamsburg
Cappetta, Pamela Guyler *counselor*
Myatt, Sue Henshaw *nursing home administrator*

Woodbridge
Flori, Anna Marie DiBlasi *health facility administrator, nurse anesthetist, educational administrator*
McMahon, Janet Mankiewich *critical care nurse*
Phillips-LeSane, Fay M. *mental health professional*
Thornton-Artson, Linda Elizabeth *psychiatric nurse*

WASHINGTON

Auburn
Blum, Sarah Leah *nurse psychotherapist*

Camano Island
Hartley, Celia Love *nursing consultant, writer, retired nursing educator, nursing administrator*

Clarkston
Smith, Phyllis Mae *healthcare consultant, educator*

Issaquah
Duncan, Elizabeth Charlotte *retired marriage and family therapist, educational therapist, educator*
Frederick, Paula F. *health facility administrator*

Kennewick
Fann, Margaret Ann *counselor*

Kent
Dumitrescu, Cristina M. *intensive care nurse*
Mong, Michelle Denise *marriage and family therapist*

Langley
Cammermeyer, Margarethe *retired medical/surgical nurse*

Port Angeles
Muller, Carolyn Bue *physical therapist, volunteer*

Redmond
Oaks, Lucy Moberley *retired social worker*

Republic
Sale, Dorothy O. *psychotherapist*

Seattle
Barnard, Kathryn Elaine *nursing educator, researcher*
de Chesnay, Mary *nursing educator*
de Tornyay, Rheba *nursing educator, retired dean*
Ellis, Janice Rider *nursing educator, consultant*
Kolbeson, Marilyn Hopf *holistic practitioner, educator, artist, poet, advertising executive, poet*
Monsen, Elaine Ranker *nutritionist, educator, editor*
Nelson, Arleen Bruce *social worker*
Peterson, Jane White *nursing educator, anthropologist*
Sandahl, Bonnie Beardsley *health services executive and provider, educator*
Sellick, Kathleen A. *hospital administrator*
Thomassen, Pauline Frances *medical and surgical nurse*

Snohomish
Hill, Valerie Charlotte *nurse*

Spokane
Cope, Kathleen Adelaide *critical care nurse, parish nurse, educator*
Hendershot, Carol Miller *physical therapist*
Metcalf, Ginger (Virginia) Arvan *psychotherapist, consultant*
Powers, Theresa Mack *medical/surgical nurse, psychotherapist*

Tacoma
Wanwig, Annette Clare *nursing administrator*

Vancouver
Lollar, Katherine Louise *tour director, social worker, therapist*
Lusky, JoAnn *psychotherapist, coach*

Yakima
Spracher, Nancy A. *psychotherapist*

WEST VIRGINIA

Bluefield
Davenport, Dorothy Dean *retired medical/surgical nurse*

Charleston
King, Rebecca Jane *nursing educator*
Richardson, Sally Keadle *health care administrator*

Clarksburg
Forinash, Carolyn Cosner *medical/surgical nurse*

Forest Hill
Martin-Weikle, Mary Jane *medical/surgical nurse*

Huntington
Campbell, Nausha Coury *speech pathology/audiology services professional, educator*
Engle, Jeannette Cranfill *medical technologist*
Whitley, Angela Jane *social worker*

Kearneysville
Lotze, Evie Daniel *psychodramatist*

Martinsburg
Brooks, Hillary Afton *social worker*
Cogle, Monica R. *social worker*
Hoak, Carolyn Clarke *physician assistant*

Morgantown
Barba, Roberta Ashburn *retired social worker, writer*
Beresford, Annette Diana *researcher*

New Cumberland
Schwab, Denise Margaret *speech pathology/audiology services professional*

Parkersburg
Bush, Roberta B. *psychotherapist, accountant*

Ranson
Rudacille, Sharon Victoria *medical technologist*

Saint Albans
Alderson, Gloria Frances Dale *rehabilitation specialist*
Ennis, Jill Ann *medical/surgical nurse, educator*

Williamsburg
Scott, Pamela Moyers *physician assistant*

WISCONSIN

Baraboo
Baymiller, Lynda Doern *social worker*

Bassett
Filipiak, Debra Ann *speech pathology/audiology services professional*

Brookfield
Pottebaum, Sharon Mitchell *health educator*
Rooney, Carol Bruns *dietician*

Burlington
Oestmann, Mary Jane *retired senior radiation specialist*

Eau Claire
Biegel, Eileen Mae *retired hospital executive*
Lippold, Judith Rosenthal *retired occupational therapist*

Fond Du Lac
Upadhyay, Wendy Schutt *psychotherapist*

Green Bay
Handrich, Heidi Leah *speech pathology/audiology services professional*
McIntosh, Elaine Virginia *nutrition educator*

La Crosse
Hatfield, Mary Lou *flight nurse, paramedic*

Madison
Brennan, Patricia Flatley *nursing educator, systems engineer, educator*
Gavin, Mary Jane *medical and surgical nurse*
Johnson, Jean Elaine *nursing educator*
Littlefield, Vivian Moore *nursing educator, administrator*
Marlett, Judith Ann *nutritional sciences educator, researcher*
Steele, Ramona Grace Jesse *physical therapist*

Menomonee Falls
Janzen, Norine Madelyn Quinlan *medical technologist*

Mequon
Beaudry, Diane Fay Puta *medical quality management executive*
Denton, Peggy *occupational therapy educator, researcher*
Mandel, Trudy Ann *medical/surgical nurse, theology studies educator*

Milwaukee
Babcock, Janice Beatrice *healthcare coordinator*
Ferguson, Nancy L. *psychotherapist, social worker*
Hammer, (Beth) Mary Elizabeth *adult nurse practitioner*
Heim, Kathryn Marie *psychiatric nurse, author*
Lange, Marilyn *social worker*
Loehr, Stephanie Schmahl *social worker*
White-Winters, Jill Mary *nursing educator*

New Berlin
Winkler, Dolores Eugenia *retired health facility administrator*

Racine
Baker, Joyce Mildred *medical/surgical nurse, volunteer*
Jensen, Sande Kelsey *technologist, church administrator*

Sturgeon Bay
Ebbeson, Karen Ann *retired social worker*

West Bend
Dries, Kathleen Marie *social worker*

Whitehall
Nordhagen, Hallie Huerth *nursing home administrator*

WYOMING

Casper
Boyer, Patricia Ann *social worker, educator*

Cheyenne
Dale, Marcia Lyn *nursing educator*

Ethete
Tepper, Marcy Elizabeth *drug education director*

Jackson
Ferguson, Jean Kennan *psychotherapist*

Laramie
Franks, Beverly Matthews *psychotherapist, consultant*
Renaud, Paula Marie *researcher*

Rock Springs
Thompson, Josie *nurse*

TERRITORIES OF THE UNITED STATES

GUAM

Barrigada
Cruz, Teofila Perez *nursing administrator*

Mangilao
Duenas, Laurent Flores *health and nursing consultant*

Tamuning
Cahinhinan, Nelia Agbada *retired public health nurse, administrator*

PUERTO RICO

Carolina
Reyes-Hernández, Migdalia *counselor*

San Juan
de Taboas, Hilda Rivera *occupational health nurse*
Lugo, Sonia I. *pharmacist, educator*

VIRGIN ISLANDS

Charlotte Amalie
Garfield, Winifred L. *nursing administrator*

CANADA

ALBERTA

Calmar
Tomaszeski, Josephine Gallas *retired nursing educator*

ONTARIO

Owen Sound
Jones, Phyllis Edith *nursing educator*

Toronto
McRae, Marion Eleanor *critical care nurse*

QUEBEC

Montreal
Messing, Karen *occupational health researcher*

ENGLAND

London
de Savorgnani, Adriane Aldrich *health care administrator, nurse*

JAPAN

Tokyo
Murray, Julia Kaoru (Mrs. Joseph E. Murray) *occupational therapist*

RUSSIA

Moscow
Collins, Mary *health science association administrator, retired legislator*

SWITZERLAND

Geneva
Maglacas, A. Mangay *nursing researcher, educator*

ADDRESS UNPUBLISHED

Abbott, Regina A. *neurodiagnostic technologist, consultant, business owner*
Abernathy, Vicki Marie *retired nurse*
Adekson, Mary Olufunmilayo *therapist, counselor, educator*
Adkins Campbell, Angela Dawn *speech-language pathologist*
Aehlert, Barbara June *health services executive*
Agard, Nancey Patricia *nursing administrator, consultant*
Agrait, Nilsa Ivette *speech language pathologist*
Aiello, Kimberly Jean *surgical technologist*
Albreski, Melody Louise *emergency nurse practitioner*
Alford, Renee Marie *speech pathology/audiology services professional, educator*
Allen, Cynthia Lea *nurse*
Anderson, Allamay Eudoris *health educator, home economist*
Anderson, Dorothy Fisher *social worker, psychotherapist*
Andrau, Maya Hedda *physical therapist*
Aptaker, Janet Marcia *social worker*
Arnold, Jean Ann *health science facility administrator*
Arrieu-King, Cynthia M. *echocardiographer, poet, educator*
Atamian, Susan *nurse*

Babitzke, Theresa Angeline *health facility administrator*
Bailey, Carla Lynn *nursing administrator*
Bailey-Stein, Deena Tamara *health care administrator*
Barker, Virginia Lee *nursing educator*
Barrett, Jessica (Donna Ann Nipert) *psychotherapist*
Barrett, Krista E. *psychotherapist, educator*
Bartels, Betty Jane *nurse*
Basinger, Karen Lynn *renal dietitian*
Bass, Lynda D. *retired medical/surgical nurse, nursing educator*
Beaton, Meredith *enterostomal therapy clinical nurse specialist*
Becker, Kathy Gail *medical/surgical nurse*
Becker, Nancy May *nursing educator*
Bell, Rebecca *psychotherapist, journalist*
Bell, Susan Jane *nurse*
Bendheim, Leonore Caroline *psychotherapist*
Berger, Miriam Roskin *creative arts therapy director, educator, therapist*
Berger-Kraemer, Nancy *speech and language pathologist, artist*
Berkley, Gail Winnick *psychotherapist*
Berner, Judith *mental health nurse*
Bertram, Susan *rehabilitation counselor*
Billingsley, Florence Ilona *nurse, case manager*
Black, Patricia Jean *medical technologist*
Blakeney, Karen Elizabeth *social service and community health program executive, consultant*
Blauvelt, Barbara Louise *nutritionist*
Blazej, Penny Annette *clinical social worker, writer, artist*
Boer, Linda Karen *medical/surgical nurse*
Bogard, Margaret Joan *nurse*
Borden, Michelle *health facility administrator*
Borg, Ruth I. *home nursing care provider*
Bottone, JoAnn *health services executive*
Brady, Kristylynne *social worker, speech pathology/audiology services professional*
Brame, Marillyn A. *hypnotherapist*
Brandt, Leota Fay *medical/surgical nurse*
Brault, G. Lorain *healthcare executive*
Braun, Mary Lucile Dekle (Lucy Braun) *therapist, consultant, counselor, educator*
Breasure, Joyce M. *counselor, educator*
Breslin, Evalynne Louise Wood-Robertson *retired psychiatric nurse*
Brewer, Jennifer A. *respiratory care practioner*
Bronson, Carol E. *health facility administrator*
Brown, Barbara June *hospital and nursing administrator*
Brown, Billye Jean *retired nursing educator*
Brown, Geraldine *nurse, freelance writer*
Bryant, Bernice R. *speech pathology/audiology services professional*
Bryant, Bertha Estelle *retired medical/surgical nurse*
Budd, Margaret Jane *retired physical therapist*
Büsch, Annemarie *retired mental health nurse*
Cabanas, Elizabeth Ann *nutritionist, educator*
Calhoun, Ramona *human services administrator, academic administrator, consultant*
Campbell, Claire Patricia *nurse practitioner, educator*
Carman, Susan Hufert *nurse coordinator*
Carson, Regina E. *healthcare administrator, geriatric specialist, pharmacist, educator*
Cash, Deanna Gail *retired nursing educator*
Castro, Judith Ana *social worker*
Centafont, Lucy Ann Alexander *occupational therapy consultant*
Chaffin, Virginia Louise *licensed practical nurse*
Chait, Fay Klein *health administrator*
Chardavoyne, Lara J. *social worker*
Chow, Rita Kathleen *nursing consultant*
Christian, Brenda Jean *physician assistant, educator*
Chughtai, Raana Lynn *psychiatric nurse practitioner*
Coffey, Joanne Christine *dietician*
Colburn, Nancy Douglas *social worker, educator*
Coleman, Jean Black *nurse, physician assistant*
Colline, Marguerite Richnavsky *maternal, women's health and pediatrics nurse*
Conley, Sarah Ann *health facility administrator*
Cooper, Signe Skott *retired nursing educator*
Copenhaver, Kirsten Jeannette *health facility administrator, consultant*
Cornell, Carole Anne Walcutt *nurse*
Coté, Kathryn Marie *psychotherapist, stress management educator*
Cotter, Emily Rexann *social worker, marriage and family therapist*
Cowles, Lois Anne Fort *social worker, educator*
Craig, Carol Mills *marriage, family and child counselor*
Craig, Terri L. *social worker*
Crawford, Lela Burch *school nurse*
Crocker, Barbara Jean *clinical nurse specialist*
Cromwell, Florence Stevens *occupational therapist*
Cuccinello, Darlene Ann *retirement home administrator, physical education educator*
Cummings, Mary Voigt *counselor*
Curley, Nancy Palmer *marriage and family therapist*
Curran-Smith, Anita Stiles *retired public health medicine educator, dean*
Cutler, Cathy Gordon *women's health nurse practitioner*
Darkovich, Sharon Marie *nurse administrator*
Davis, Ada Romaine *nursing educator*
Davis, Elba Lucila *veterans affairs nurse*
Davis, Erlynne P. *social work educator*
Davis, June Fiksdal *medical facility owner, floral designer*
Davis, Margaret Thacker *retired critical care, medical and surgical nurse*
Day, Anne White *retired nurse*
Deane, Sally Jan *health services management, consultant*
de Lacerda, Maria Assunçaõ Escobar *social worker, consultant*
DeLapp, Tina Davis *retired nursing educator*

Demetrakeas, Regina Cassar *social worker*
Desjardins, Judith Anne *psychotherapist*
DeStaffany, Sandra Russell *childbirth educator, author*
DiCarlo, Laurette Mary *nurse*
Dickens, Alycia Thompson *nurse practitioner*
Dickens, Joyce Rebecca *addictions therapist, educator*
Diehl, Jennifer L. *counselor*
Dincecco, Jennie Elizabeth Williams Swanson *healthcare administrator, mentor, healthcare educator, volunteer*
Diorio, Eileen Patricia *retired medical technologist, philosophy educator*
Donahue, Mary Beth *human services administrator*
Downing, Cynthia Hurst *therapist, addiction and abuse specialist*
Downs, Kathleen Anne *health facility administrator*
Dumler, Patricia Ann *critical care nurse*
Dunmeyer, Sarah Louise Fisher *retired health care consultant*
Dunning, Lisa Anne *marriage and family therapist*
Dwyer, Judith A. *marriage and family therapist*
Eastwood, Kathleen J. *medical/surgical nurse*
Eaton, Shirley M. *medical/surgical nurse*
Ebinger, Linda Ann *nurse*
Edelsberg, Sally Comins *physical therapy educator and administrator*
Edelstein, Rosemarie (Rosemarie Hublou) *medical/surgical nurse, educator, medical and legal consultant*
Eimers, Jeri Anne *retired therapist*
Eisenberg, Patricia Lee *medical/surgical nurse*
Elliott-Zahorik, Bonnie *nurse, administrator*
Emerson, Donna Lucille *social worker, educator*
Farrar, Mary Caroline *speech and language pathologist*
Farrington, Bertha Louise *retired nursing administrator*
Faruque, Cathleen Jo *social worker, educator*
Feathers, Gail M. Wratny *social worker*
Fehr, Lola Mae *health organization administrator*
Ferguson, Paula Irene *nursing administrator*
Fidone, Laura Peebles *social worker*
Fields, Velma Archie *medical/surgical nurse*
Fitzgerald-Verbonitz, Dianne Elizabeth *healthcare executive*
Forest, Eva Brown *nursing administrator, songwriter*
Fountain, Linda Kathleen *health science association executive*
Foust, Jean Louise *physical therapist*
Fralix-Gold, Carolyn *nursing educator, consultant, medical/surgical nurse*
Fusillo, Nancy Marie *medical/surgical, oncological, pediatric, community health and family nurse practitioner*
Gabriel, Judith A. *bodywork therapist, educator, writer*
Gagen, Gina *psychotherapist*
Garbacz, Patricia Frances *school social worker, therapist*
Garity, Kathleen *medical/surgical nurse, director*
Garrabrant, Dorothy Olson *retired social worker, psychotherapist*
Garrett, Shirley Gene *nuclear medicine technologist*
Gendreau, Bernice Marie *retired women's health nurse*
Gerry, Debra Prue *psychotherapist, recording artist, writer*
Gerstner, Mary Jane *nurse*
Gilmore, Louisa Ruth *retired nurse*
Gimenes, Sonia Regina Rosendo *family therapist, psychologist*
Girouard, Shirley Ann *nurse, policy analyst*
Gladden, Vivianne Cervantes *healthcare consultant, writer*
Glashan, Constance Elaine *retired nurse, civic worker*
Gleason, Harriet Hall *nurse*
Goldie, Dorothy Roberta *retired suicide prevention counselor, educator*
Gordon, Audrey Kramen *healthcare educator*
Gorske, Margot Elizabeth *nurse administrator*
Grant, Janett Ulrica *medical/surgical nurse*
Gray, Michele Diane *psychotherapist, art gallery owner*
Green, Flora Hungerford *lactation consultant, nurse*
Green, Linda Gail *retired international healthcare and management consultant, nurse educator*
Greene, Monica Lynn Banks *recreational therapist, director*
Greenfield, Linda Sue *nursing educator*
Greggs, Elanora *social worker*
Grosso-Proulx, Deborah *medical/surgical nurse*
Hadley, Jane Byington *psychotherapist*
Hanni, Geraldine Marie *retired therapist*
Hanratty, Carin Gale *pediatric nurse practitioner*
Hardman, Angela Gayle Bontemps *social worker*
Harms, Nancy Ann *nursing educator*
Harren, Julie Catherine *marriage and family therapist*
Harris, Deborah A. *counselor, consultant*
Hart-Duling, Jean Macaulay *clinical social worker*
Hartman, Deanna Mears *retired family counselor, addiction counselor*
Hartman, Lenore Anne *physical therapist*
Hass, Lisa M. *freelance/self-employed counselor*
Hasselmeyer, Eileen Grace *medical research administrator*
Haviland, Kay Lynn (Kade Haviland) *mental health services professional*
Hayes, Judith *psychotherapist, educator*
Healy, Sonya Ainslie *retired health facility administrator*
Heim, Hazel *nurse*
Held, Nancy B. *perinatal nurse, lactation consultant*
Helms Guba, Lisa Marie *nursing administrator*

Henry, Sue *social worker, educator*
Heubusch, Louise Madeline *physical therapist, educator*
Hickman, Lucille *physical therapist*
Hill, Beverley Jane *physician assistant*
Hill, Martha N. *community health nurse*
Hiner, Cheryl Lynn *adult nurse practitioner*
Hiner, Elizabeth Ellen *pharmacist*
Hobson, Alesa *medical/surgical nurse*
Hobson, Diane Marie *social worker*
Hodnicak, Victoria Christine *pediatrics nurse*
Holguin, Roxanna R. *speech pathology/audiology services professional*
Holland, Rosemary Sheridan *program evaluation consultant*
Hollister, Patricia Hackett *psychotherapist, educator, marriage and family therapist*
Holmes, Wilhelmina Kent *community health nurse*
Honea, Joyce Clayton *critical care nurse*
Honeycutt, Janice Louise *nurse*
Howe, Virginia Hoffman *nurse administrator*
Hunter, Helen Frances *social worker*
Huston, Joan Bonfiglio *psychotherapist*
Hutcherson, Rene Ridens *medical social services administrator*
Iasiello, Dorothy Barbara *clinical social worker, former brokerage company executive*
Inscho, Jean Anderson *retired social worker, landscape artist*
Iwuanyanwu, Eucharia Chiege *physician assistant*
Jackson-Tkac, Stephanie Ann *nurse*
Jacob, Christina Marie *social worker*
Jaranilla, Sarah J. *critical care nurse, consultant*
Jensen, Eva Marie *medical/surgical nurse*
Jobe, Muriel Ida *medical technologist, educator*
Johnson, Erma Jean *human services administrator*
Johnson, Katherine Holthaus *health care marketing professional*
Johnson, Patricia B *medical, surgical nurse, mental health nurse*
Jones, Pauline Reid *speech pathology/audiology services professional*
Juenemann, Sister Jean *hospital executive*
Junger, Patricia Carol *nurse*
Kaiser, Nina Irene *health care consultant*
Kaminski, Patricia Joyce *lab administrator*
Karp, Rosanne *oncology and women's health nurse*
Kathan, Joyce C. *social worker, administrator*
Kezlarian, Nancy Kay *marriage and family therapist*
King, Imogene M. *retired nursing educator*
King, Lynda *counselor*
King, Tamara Lynn *counselor*
Klein, Rosalyn Finkelstein *social worker*
Kleinhenz, Nancy Alison *medical/surgical nurse*
Knopf, Tana Darlene *counselor, music educator*
Koerber, Marilynn Eleanor *gerontology nursing educator, consultant, nurse*
Kohn, Jean Gatewood *retired health facility administrator, pediatrician*
Kopf, Randi *family and oncology nurse practitioner, lawyer*
Krehtinkoff-Yarlovsky, Nina *nursing administrator, medical-legal consulting firm owner*
Krobath, Krista Ann *pharmacist*
Krug, Ellen J. *social worker, medical educator*
Kuehn, Mildred May *retired social worker*
Kuhler, Deborah Gail *grief therapist, former state legislator*
Kurtz, Gillian L. *medical/surgical nurse*
Kuzmowych, Chrystyna Prytula *optometrist*
Lane, Patricia Peyton *retired nursing consultant*
Langenkamp, Sandra Carroll *retired human services administrator*
Langrehr, Jocelyn Clare *counselor*
Larsen-Denning, Lorie *critical care nurse, risk management consultant, insurance broker, insurance agent*
Larson, Vicki Lord *communication disorders educator*
La Torre, Carissa Danitza *counselor*
Lautenschlager, Yetta Elizabeth *clinical social worker*
Leach, Cynthia Elizabeth *social worker, communications executive*
Leddy, Susan *nursing educator*
Lehmkuhler, Elaine Louise *speech pathology/audiology services professional*
Lentz, Sandra M. *family practice nurse practitioner*
Leon, Jeannette Caridad *mental health services professional, consultant*
Lindquist, Kirsten Mary *critical care nurse*
Lippman Salovesh, Dorothy *nurse practitioner*
Long-Middleton, Ellen *family nurse practitioner, educator, researcher*
Lopez Lysne, Robin *counselor, writer, artist*
Lubic, Ruth Watson *health facility administrator, nurse midwife*
Lucero, Anne *critical care nurse*
Luddy, Paula Scott *nursing educator*
Lynch-Polansky, Patricia *health services executive*
Lyons, Gloria Rogers *medical, surgical nurse, clinical nurse specialist*
Lyons, Natalie Beller *family counselor*
MacPherson, Shirley *clinical therapist*
Magarian, Karen S. *chiropractor, consultant*
Maglio, Gesomina V. *clinical social worker*
Mahoney, Heather M. *social worker*
Malek, Marlene Anne *healthcare advocate, foundation administrator*
Mandravelis, Patricia Jean *retired healthcare administrator*
Manion, Kelley Michelle *surgical technician*
Manning, Joan Elizabeth *health association administrator*
Maplesden, Carol Harper *marital and family therapist, music educator*
Marcinek, Margaret Ann *nursing educator*
Marcinko, Jacqueline Michele *social worker*
Marcoux, Julia A. *midwife*
Margrave, Kathy Christine *nurse anesthetist*
Markle, Cheri Virginia Cummins *nurse*
Markowitz, Phyllis Frances *retired mental health services professional, retired psychologist*
Marquis, Harriet Hill *social worker*
Martin, Dale *health facility administrator*
Martin, Ione Edwards *social worker*
Materia, Kathleen Patricia Ayling *nurse*
Matterson, Joan McDevitt *physical therapist*
McBride, Sandra Teague *psychiatric nurse*
McCarthy, Rose Marie *medical/surgical nurse*
McCombs, Kelly Fritz *dietician*
McCormick, Donna Lynn *social worker*
McCuistion, Peg Orem *retired hospice administrator*
McElwee, Doris Ryan *psychotherapist*
McGlynn, Marilyn Hutchison *medical/surgical nurse, educator*
McGrath, Eileen Marie *pediatric nurse*
McMillen, Sarah Anne *marriage and family therapist, adult education educator*
McNulty, Kathleen Anne *clinical social worker, psychotherapist, business consultant,*
McPhearson, Geraldine June *medical/surgical nurse*
McVey, Alice Lloyd *social worker*
Mebane, Felicia Eugenia *health policy, news media educator, researcher*
Medina, Sandra *social worker, educator*
Mehring, Nancy *medical and surgical nurse, administrator*
Melesio, Kathryn Mary *oncological nurse, educator*
Melka, Janet Patricia *medical/surgical nurse*
Mesch, Helene W. *retired social worker*
Mickelson, Rhoda Ann *speech pathology/audiology services professional*
Middel, Marjorie *social worker, consultant*
Mikan, Kathleen Joyce Kehrer *medical/surgical nurse, educator*
Milewski, Barbara Anne *pediatrics nurse, neonatal/perinatal nurse practitioner, critical care nurse*
Milholland, Sandra Jane *marriage and family therapist*
Miller, Catherine Lynn *mental health services professional, writer*
Miller, Eunice A. *marriage and family therapist, sex therapist, foundation administrator*
Miller, Lenore Wolf Daniels *speech-language pathologist*
Milnor, Hazel *nurse*
Miracle, Doris Jean *retired medical/surgical nurse*
Misner, Lorraine *laboratory technologist*
Misrack, Tana Marie *counselor, minister, writer*
Mitchell, Gina Lynn *health facility administrator*
Molden, A(nna) Jane *counselor*
Molnar, Violet *mental health nurse*
Monck, Maureen F. *psychoanalyst*
Montgomery, Helen Janet *social worker*
Moore, Jean E. *social worker, academic administrator, educator, radio personality*
Morgan, Donna Jean *psychotherapist*
Morgan, Evelyn Buck *retired nursing educator*
Morrow, Nena Renee *medical/surgical nurse*
Mould, Joan Powell *social worker*
Moyers, Kelli R. *psychotherapist*
Mueller, Barbara Stewart (Bobbie Mueller) *youth drug use prevention specialist, volunteer*
Mullette, Julienne Patricia *health facility administrator*
Muñoz Dones De Carrascal, Eloisa *hospital administrator, pediatrician, consultant, educator*
Murphy, Margaret A. *nursing educator, adult nurse practitioner*
Myers, Libby Ann *retired medical/surgical nurse*
Myers-Morrison, Cynthia Jean *marriage and family therapist, educator*
Natividad, Lisalinda Salas *family advocacy outreach manager*
Nelson, Alice Carlstedt *retired nursing educator*
Nelson, Doreen Kae *mental health counselor, educator, reserve military officer*
Nelson, Kay Ellen *speech and language pathologist*
Newton, Juanita *social worker, educator*
Nichols, Elizabeth Grace *nursing educator, dean*
Nicholson, June C. Daniels *retired speech pathologist*
Nicolodi, Theresa Anne *speech pathologist*
Norbeck, Jane S. *retired nursing educator*
Norkin, Cynthia Clair *retired physical therapist*
Nuttelman, Doris Graves *nursing administrator*
Oakes, Ellen Ruth *psychotherapist, health institute administrator*
O'Connor Taylor, Sheryl Ann *medical services administrator*
Okolski, Cynthia Antonia *psychotherapist, social worker*
Olsen, Virginia *human services manager*
Parham, Ellen Speiden *nutrition educator*
Parker, Susan Brooks *healthcare executive*
Parks, Jean Anne *retired acute care nurse practitioner*
Paskawicz, Jeanne Frances *pain specialist*
Pastula, Leah Lynn *mental health services professional*
Peele-Burkholder, Tammy Sue *nurse*
Pellicciotto, Nicole Alyssa *special education services professional, consultant*
Pepelea, Kimberli Rae *case manager*
Peters, Carol Ann Dudycha *counselor*
Peterson, Veronica Marie (Ronnie Peterson) *clinical nurse manager*
Petree, Betty Chapman *anesthetist*
Petrie, Amy Elizabeth *speech pathology/audiology services professional*
Pettine, Linda Faye *physical therapist*
Pierce, Shaheeda Laura *midwife, consultant*
Pipchick, Margaret Hopkins *advance practice nurse, marriage and family therapist*
Pisciotta, Vivian Virginia *psychotherapist*
Pledger, Myrna Joan *counselor*
Poe, Laura *nursing educator, administrator*
Poleshuk, Alicia L. *alcohol/drug abuse services professional*
Porter, Jennie Lee *health facility administrator, entrepreneur*
Porter, Marie Ann *neonatal nurse*
Poulton, Roberta Doris *nurse, consultant*
Preszler, Sharon Marie *psychiatric home health nurse*
Przybylski, Mercedes *retired medical and surgical nurse, health facility administrator*
Quaife, Marjorie Clift *retired nursing educator*
Quattrone-Carroll, Diane Rose *clinical social worker*
Rand, Joella Mae *retired nursing educator, counselor*
Rasberry, Dawn Yvette *counselor*
Ratcliffe, Walterene Harris *social worker, educator*
Reber, Cheryl Ann *consultant, social worker, trainer*
Reed-Ford, Lillie Mae *geriatrics services professional*
Reinke, Linda Jeanette *retired social worker*
Repko, Lisa *medical/surgical nurse*
Reynolds, Louise Maxine Kruse *retired school nurse*
Rhoades, Marcia Diane *career counselor*
Richardson, Susan *health facility administrator, writer*
Riikonen, Charlene Boothe *international health administrator*
Ritter, Elise Dawn *therapist, clinical social worker, writer, artist*
Ritter, Madeliene *practical nurse, surgical technologist*
Robinson, Angela Tomei *clinical laboratory technologist, laboratory manager*
Robinson, Gail Patricia *retired mental health counselor*
Robinson, Glenda Carole *pharmacist*
Rodriguez, Donna Jeanne Anglin *dietician, writer*
Romero, Sylvia *social worker*
Roney, Judith Rose *marriage and family therapist*
Rosenstein, Mary Elisabeth Mallory *retired social worker*
Rothbard, Barbara *allergy and dermatology nurse*
Rothman-Bernstein, Lisa J. *occupational health nurse*
Rubin, Phyllis Getz *health association executive*
Saari, Joy Ann *family nurse practitioner, geriatrics medical and surgical nurse*
Santina, Dalia *nutritionist, writer, skin care specialist*
Sastrowardoyo, Teresita Manejar *nurse*
Savoy, Suzanne Marie *advanced practice nurse*
Sawyer-Morse, Mary Kaye *nutritionist, educator*
Scarlett, Novlin Rose *public health nurse, educator*
Schoenberg, April Mindy *nursing administrator*
Schroeder, LaVerne *medical/surgical nurse*
Schwartz, Ilene *psychotherapist*
Scott, Justine Ford *counselor, educator*
Seaton, Joyah A. *nursing assistant*
Sewell, Laura J. Pollock *social worker*
Shaffer, Deborah Bland *adult nurse practitioner*
Shannon, Margaret T. *nursing administrator, educator*
Sheaffer, Suzanne Frances *geriatrics nurse*
Sheehan, Sophia Ann *marriage and family therapist, department chairman*
Shelton, Margaret *counselor*
Sherwood-Fabre, Liese Anne *public health service officer*
Silverman, Ellen-Marie *speech and language pathologist*
Silvers, Ann *peri-operative nurse, educator*
Simon-Boyd, Gail Deborah *psychotherapist*
Simons, Sheila R. *healthcare educator*
Sinclair, Sara Voris *health facility administrator, nurse*
Skelley, Billie Holladay *clinical nurse specialist*
Smith, Barbara Anne *health facility administrator, consultant*
Smith, Gloria Richardson *nursing educator*
Smith, Michele Kathleen *marriage and family therapist*
Smith-Buckingham, Minnie M. *surgery technologist*
Sommerfeld, Marianna *retired social worker, writer*
Sonsteby, Kristi Lee *healthcare consultant*
Stadler, Selise McNeil *laboratory and x-ray technician*
Stancil, Irene Mack *family counselor*
Stanley, Karen Gweneith *vocational nurse*
Stansil, Sheryl *medical/surgical nurse*
Stash, Susan Michele *critical care nurse*
Steelman, Deborah Macon *pharmaceutical consultant*
Steiner, Carol Seaton *social worker, educator*
Stewart, Barbara Lynne *geriatrics nursing educator*
Stickles, Bonnie Jean *nurse*
Stohlman, Connie Suzanne *obstetrical gynecological nurse*
Stratton, Mariann *retired naval nursing administrator*
Stutzman, Sandra Louise *advanced nurse practitioner*
Suber, Robin Hall *former medical and surgical nurse*
Sutcliffe, Mary Ogden *clinical social worker*
Sutton, Sharon Marie *emergency services nurse*
Swan, Beth Ann *nursing administrator*
Tamor-Amodo, Florence Marie *medical technologist*
Taylor, Edna Jane *retired employment program counselor*
Taylor, Karen Annette *mental health nurse*
Taylor, Nathalee Britton *retired nutritionist*
Taylor Song, Stephanie Ingram *nutritionist*
Temelkoff, Vonda Lee *counselor, therapist*
Terry, Barbara L. *human services administrator*
Thomerson, Anne Spach *counselor*
Thompson, Claire Louisa *nurse, educator*
Thrasher, Rose Marie *critical care nurse, community health nurse*
Threadcraft, Kelli King *speech pathology/audiology services professional*
Timmons, Debra *surgical technologist*
Tinner, Franziska Paula *social worker, artist, apparel designer, educator, entrepreneur*
Torres-Mabasa, Virginia Maria *physician assistant*
Torresyap, Pearl Marie *surgical nurse*
Toter, Kimberly Mrowiec *nurse*
Trautman, Alta Louise *nurse, funeral director, writer*
Tsai, Ruth Man-kam *nurse*
Tyson, Lucille R. *health facility administrator, geriatrics nurse*
Ulmen, Kathryn T. *neuroscience clinical nurse specialist*
Uris, Patricia Firme *health science association administrator*
Usinger, Martha Putnam *counselor, educator, dean*
Valfre, Michelle Williams *nursing educator, administrator, writer*
Vogel, H. Victoria *psychotherapist, trauma, post-traumatic stress disorder and addiction recovery counselor and educator, author*
Von Thurn, Jelena *health science specialist*
Voreacos, Sally A. *social worker*
Wallace, Scyatta A *public health researcher, program consultant*
Walling, Mary Jo Anne *women's health nurse*
Wanley, Patricia Ann *medical/surgical nurse*
Waring, Mary Louise *retired social worker*
Warres, Margie Black *social work administrator, department chairman, human services manager, department chairman*
Warwick, Margaret Ann *health science facility administrator, consultant*
Weaver, Victoria Ann *nursing researcher*
Wedge, Barbara Jane *women's health nurse*
Weightman, Esther Lynn *emergency trauma nurse*
Weinstein, Lori Jill *social worker*
Westrick, Heidi Lynn *medical/surgical nurse*
White, Sarah Jowilliard *retired counselor*
Whittier, Sandra M. *nursing services administrator*
Wiggerly, Deborah Jean *speech pathology/audiology services professional, educator*
Wilamowski, Doris *psychotherapist*
Wilson, Carrie Lynn *technologist*
Wilson, Karen Lee *researcher*
Wilt, Maureen Moffitt *social worker, educator*
Wyatt, Judith Lois *psychotherapist, consultant*
Yanda, Cathy L. *counselor, illustrator*
Yarbrough, Kathryn Davis *public health nurse*
Young, Deborah (Deborah Ayling Yanowitz) *social worker, librarian*
Young-Stevens, Katherine Tratebas *occupational health nurse*
Zierath, Marilyn Jean *medical/surgical nurse, pediatrics nurse*
Zupon, Diane Elizabeth *medical technician*

HEALTHCARE: MEDICINE

UNITED STATES

ALABAMA

Birmingham
Dubovsky, Eva Vitkova *nuclear medicine physician, educator*
Elewski, Boni Elizabeth *dermatologist, educator*
Oparil, Suzanne *cardiologist, educator, cardiologist, researcher*
Pittman, Constance Shen *endocrinologist, educator*

Spanish Fort
Benjamin, Regina Marcia *physician, administrator*

ALASKA

Valdez
Todd, Kathleen Gail *physician*

ARIZONA

Paradise Valley
Targovnik, Selma E. Kaplan *physician*

Phoenix
Chambliss, Linda R. *obstetrician, gynecologist, consultant*
Ridenour, Joey *medical association administrator, operations research specialist*

Scottsdale
Kübler-Ross, Elisabeth *physician*

Tempe
Rowley, Beverley Davies *medical sociologist*

Tucson
Cisler, Theresa Ann *osteopath*
Graham, Anna Regina *pathologist, educator*
Witte, Marlys Hearst *internist, educator*

ARKANSAS

Little Rock
Mancino, Anne Rochelle *surgeon*

PROFESSIONAL INDEX 1743 HEALTHCARE: MEDICINE

Simmons, Caroline Jennermann *biomedical researcher, writer*

Scranton
Uzman, Betty Ben Geren *pathologist, retired educator*

CALIFORNIA

Atherton
Weston, Jane Sara *plastic surgeon, educator*

Bakersfield
Martin, Maureen Frances *medical educator*

Baldwin Park
Barry, Diane Dolores (Diane Branks) *podiatrist*

Berkeley
Buffler, Patricia Ann *epidemiologist, educator, retired dean*
Diamond, Marian Cleeves *anatomy educator*
Josephian, Jenny Adele *acupuncturist, artist*

Beverly Hills
Dean, Bonnie Blander *epidemiologist*
Dennis, Karen Marie *plastic surgeon*
Williams, Carole Ann *retired cytotechnologist*

Calabasas
Laney, Marti Olsen *psychoanalyst, researcher, social sciences educator, writer*

Carlsbad
Crooke, Rosanne M. *pharmacologist*

Chatsworth
Stephenson, Irene Hamlen *biorhythm analyst, consultant, editor, educator*

Chula Vista
Cohen, Elaine Helena *pediatrician, cardiologist, educator*

Corona Del Mar
Dougherty, Jocelyn *retired neurologist*

Davis
Jensen, Hanne Margrete *pathology educator*

Downey
Perry, Jacquelin *orthopedic surgeon*

[illegible]
Hurst, Deborah *pediatric hematologist*

Fontana
Resch, Charlotte Susanna *plastic surgeon*

Fremont
Maynard, Catherine *medical researcher*

Gualala
Ring, Alice Ruth Bishop *retired preventive medicine physician*

Irvine
Lee, Eva *medical educator*

La Jolla
Barlow, Carrolee *physician, scientist, educator*
Barrett-Connor, Elizabeth Louise *epidemiologist, educator*
Covell, Ruth Marie *medical educator, medical school administrator*
Jorgensen, Judith Ann *psychiatrist, educator*
Rearden, Carole Ann *clinical pathologist, educator*
Thompson, Charlotte Ellis *pediatrician, educator, writer*

La Verne
McDonough-Treichler, Judith Dianne *medical educator, consultant*

Laguna Hills
Widyolar, Sheila Gayle *dermatologist*

Loma Linda
Behrens, Berel Lyn *physician, academic and healthcare administrator*

Long Beach
Tabrisky, Phyllis Page *physiatrist, educator*

Los Angeles
Alkon, Ellen Skillen *physician*
Anderson, Kathryn D. *surgeon*
Ashley, Sharon Anita *pediatric anesthesiologist*
Barrett, Cynthia Townsend *neonatologist*
Giesser, Barbara Susan *neurologist, educator*
Guze, Phyllis Arlene *internist, educator, academic administrator*
Henriksen, Eva H. *former anesthesiology educator*
Jalali, Behnaz *psychiatrist, educator*
Kamil, Elaine Scheiner *pediatric nephrologist, educator*
Korsch, Barbara M. *pediatrician*
Lee, Joselyn C.R. *physician, researcher*
Macavinta-Tenazas, Gemorsita *family physician*
Malcolm, Dawn Grace *family physician*
Naqvi, Tasneem Zehra *cardiologist, researcher, consultant*
Spencer, Carole A. *medical association administrator, medical educator*
Vredevoe, Donna Lou *research immunologist, microbiologist, educator*
Williams, Roberta Gay *pediatric cardiologist, educator*
Wilson, Miriam Geisendorfer *retired physician, educator*

Menlo Park
Healy, Cynthia *pharmacologist, life scientist, researcher*

Mill Valley
Newman, Nancy Marilyn *ophthalmologist, educator*

Mission Viejo
Hafner-Eaton, Chris *health services researcher, medical educator, policy analyst*

Mountain View
Abel, Elizabeth A. *dermatologist*
Juvvadi, Anita Reddy *pediatrician*

Oakland
Benton-Hardy, Lisa Renee *psychiatrist, educator*
Cary, Alice Shepard *retired physician*
Killebrew, Ellen Jane (Mrs. Edward S. Graves) *cardiologist, educator*
Rice, Frances Mae *physician*

Orange
Morgan, Beverly Carver *pediatrician, educator*

Pacific Palisades
Love, Susan Margaret *surgeon, educator, writer*

Palo Alto
Blessing-Moore, Joann Catherine *allergist*
Goldstein, Mary Kane *physician*
Hays, Marguerite Thompson *nuclear medicine physician, educator*
Hubert, Helen Betty *epidemiologist*
Litt, Iris Figarsky *pediatrics educator*
Michie, Sara H. *pathologist, educator*
Swain, Judith Lea *cardiovascular physician, educator*
Winkleby, Marilyn A. *medical researcher*

Palos Verdes Peninsula
Narasimhan, Padma Mandyam *physician*

Panorama City
Jasso, Nancy *dermatologist*

Pasadena
Newman, Marjorie Yospin *psychiatrist*
Short, Elizabeth M. *internist, educator, retired federal agency administrator*
Yeager, Caroline Hale *radiologist, consultant*

Petaluma
Levinthal, Jeana Davison *pediatrician*

Riverside
Chang, Janice May *lawyer, naturopathic doctor, immunologist*

Sacramento
Anderson, Rachel Lyn *behavior researcher*
Rounds, Barbara Lynn *psychiatrist*

San Diego
Kaweski, Susan *plastic surgeon, naval officer*
Parthemore, Jacqueline Gail *internist, educator, hospital administrator*
Wallace, Helen Margaret *pediatrician, preventive medicine physician, educator*

San Francisco
Ascher, Nancy Louise *surgeon*
Bainton, Dorothy Ford *pathology educator, researcher*
Behrens, M. Kathleen *medical researcher*
Chesney, Margaret A. *medical educator, medical researcher*
Clever, Linda Hawes *physician*
Fu, Karen King-Wah *radiation oncologist*
Gibbs, Patricia Hellman *physician*
Goode, Erica Tucker *internist*
Gooding, Gretchen Ann Wagner *physician, educator*
Kenyon, Cynthia *medical researcher*
Koda-Kimble, Mary Anne *medical educator, pharmacologist, dean*
Lucia, Marilyn Reed *physician*
McGrath, Mary Helena *plastic surgeon, educator*
McNamara, Margaret M. *pediatrician*
Ponton, Lynn E. *psychiatrist, educator*
Seebach, Lydia Marie *physician*
Snyderman, Nancy *surgeon, medical journalist*
Terr, Lenore Cagen *psychiatrist, writer*

San Pablo
Woodruff, Kay Herrin *pathologist, educator*

Santa Ana
Myers, Marilyn Gladys *pediatric hematologist and oncologist*

Santa Barbara
Bischel, Margaret DeMeritt *physician, managed care consultant*
Mathews, Barbara Edith *gynecologist*

Santa Clarita
Zuk, Carmen Veiga *psychiatrist*

Santa Cruz
Pletsch, Marie Eleanor *plastic surgeon*
Shorenstein, Rosalind Greenberg *internist*

Santa Monica
Amerian, Mary Lee *physician*
Carr, Ruth Margaret *plastic surgeon*
Kanim, Linda Elie Aliea *medical researcher*
Shamban, Ava T. *dermatologist*
Wilfert, Catherine M. *medical association administrator, medical educator*

Stanford
Blau, Helen Margaret *pharmacology educator*
Carstensen, Laura Lee *gerontology educator*
Donaldson, Sarah Susan *radiologist*
Jacobs, Charlotte De Croes *medical educator, oncologist*
Kraemer, Helena Antoinette Chmura *psychiatry educator*
Payne, Anita Hart *reproductive endocrinologist, researcher*
Polan, Mary Lake *obstetrics and gynecology educator*
Powers, Rebecca Ann *psychiatrist, health facility administrator*
Wapnir, Irene Leonor *medical educator*

Sylmar
Corry, Dalila Boudjellal *internist, educator*
Tully, Susan Balsley *pediatrician, medical educator*
Yu, Katherine Kit *internist*

Thousand Oaks
Pakula, Anita Susan *dermatologist*
Wolfson, Marsha *internist, nephrologist*

Torrance
Brasel, Jo Anne *pediatrician, educator*
Sun, Nora Chi-Jun *pathologist*

Walnut Creek
Cannon, Grace Bert *retired immunologist*
Sheen, Portia Yunn-ling *retired physician*

Westminster
Nguyen, Lan Thi Hoang *physician, educator*

COLORADO

Aurora
Nora, Audrey Hart *physician*

Colorado Springs
Gifford, Marilyn Joyce *emergency physician, consultant*

Denver
Churchill, Mair Elisa Annabelle *medical educator*
Gabow, Patricia Anne *internist*
Hoehn, Margaret Maier *neurologist*
Huang, Linda Chen *plastic surgeon*
Johnson, Candice Elaine Brown *pediatrics educator*
McAtee, Patricia Anne Rooney *medical educator*
Stamm, Carol Ann *obstetrician, gynecologist*
Studevant, Laura *medical association administrator*
Sujansky, Eva Borska *pediatrician, geneticist, educator*
Waldstein, Gail P. *pediatric pathologist, writer*

Loveland
King, Joan Caluda *medical educator, neuroscientist*

Wheat Ridge
Hashimoto, Christine L. *physician*
Wells, Karen Kay *medical librarian*

CONNECTICUT

Farmington
Grunnet, Margaret Louise *pathologist, educator*
Rothfield, Naomi Fox *physician*

Greenwich
Kopenhaver, Patricia Ellsworth *podiatrist*

Hartford
Jung, Betty Chin *epidemiologist, research analyst, educator, medical/surgical nurse*

New Haven
Bartoshuk, Linda J. *otolaryngologist, educator*
Ferholt, J. Deborah Lott *pediatrician*
Hines, Roberta Leigh *medical educator*
Hostetter, Margaret K. *pediatrician, medical educator*
Seashore, Margretta Reed *physician, educator*
Shaywitz, Sally E. *pediatrics educator*

Norwalk
Freitag, Anna Carol *endocrinologist, internist*

Sandy Hook
Dakofsky, LaDonna Jung *radiation oncologist, educator*

Stamford
Klenk, Rosemary Ellen *pediatrician*

Vernon Rockville
Marmer, Ellen Lucille *pediatric cardiologist, mayor*

Wallingford
Regueiro-Ren, Alicia *biomedical researcher*

Waterford
Pierson, Anne Bingham *physician*

West Hartford
Sousa, Marilyn Felske *medical educator, consultant*

Westport
Lopker, Anita Mae *psychiatrist, researcher*

DELAWARE

Wilmington
Inselman, Laura Sue *pediatrician, educator*

DISTRICT OF COLUMBIA

Washington
Anthony, Virginia Quinn Bausch *medical association executive*
Aschenbrener, Carol Ann *pathologist, educator*
Benoit, Marilyn B. *psychiatrist, medical association administrator*
Blumenthal, Susan Jane *psychiatrist, educator, public health official*
Catoe, Bette Lorrina *pediatrician, educator*
Curry, Sadye Beatryce *gastroenterologist, educator*
Engler, Renata Johanna Martha *allergist, immunologist, internist, educator*
Epps, Roselyn Elizabeth Payne *pediatrician, educator*
Foley, Mary E. *medical association administrator, nursing administrator*
Gray, Sheila Hafter *psychiatrist, psychoanalyst*
Grealy, Mary R. *medical association administrator*
Hamburg, Margaret Ann (Peggy Hamburg) *public health administrator*
Jani, Sushma Niranjan *pediatric psychiatrist*
Jenkins, Renee R. *medical educator, pediatrician*
Lynn, D. Joanne *physician, ethicist, health services researcher*
Nowak, Judith Ann *psychiatrist*
Oertel, Yolanda Castillo *pathologist, educator, diagnostician*
Perez, Lucille C. Norville *medical association administrator, pediatrician*
Pincus, Stephanie Hoyer *dermatologist*
Ramphele, Mamphela A. *medical educator*
Rhoades, Margaret *health care association executive*
Robinowitz, Carolyn Bauer *psychiatrist, educator*
Schechter, Geraldine Poppa *hematologist*
Shanahan, Sheila Ann *pediatrician, educator*
Shrier, Diane Kesler *psychiatrist, educator*
Stratton, Kathleen R. *medical association administrator*
Tosi, Laura Lowe *orthopaedic surgeon*
Weinberg, Myrl *medical association administrator*
Winnie, Glenna Barbara *pediatric pulmonologist*
Yates, Allison A. *scientific organization administrator*

FLORIDA

Belleair
Dexter, Helen Louise *dermatologist, consultant*

Boca Raton
Kramer, Cecile E. *retired medical librarian*

Boynton Beach
Srinath, Latha *physician*

Clearwater
Lansky, Zena *surgeon*

Coral Gables
Perez, Josephine *psychiatrist, educator*

Coral Springs
Faul, Maureen Patricia *healthcare and research consultant*

Dunedin
Barlis, Bettye Montgomery *medical center administrator, elementary educator*

Fernandina Beach
Barlow, Anne Louise *pediatrician, medical research administrator*

Fort Lauderdale
Cox, Linda Susan *allergist, immunologist*
Durst, Kay Horres *physician*
Fruth, Beryl Rose *physician*
Siegel, Wilma Bulkin *oncologist, educator, artist*

Gainesville
Behnke, Marylou *pediatrician, educator*
Limacher, Marian Cecile *cardiologist*

Jacksonville
Rodney, Roxanne Audrey *cardiologist, consultant*

Miami
Alvarez, Ofelia Amparo *medical educator*
Engle, Mary Allen English *physician*
Hicks, Dorothy Jane *obstetrician and gynecologist, educator*
O'Sullivan, Mary J. *physician, maternal fetal medicine educator*
Wolff, Grace Susan *pediatrician, pediatric cardiologist*

Naples
Ehlers, Kathryn Hawes (Mrs. James D. Gabler) *physician*

Orlando
Magsino, Marissa Estiva *internist, pediatrician*

Pensacola
Canady, Alexa Irene *pediatric neurosurgeon*

Plantation
Nickelson, Kim René *internist*

Ponte Vedra Beach
Toker, Karen Harkavy *physician*

Port Charlotte
Hollinshead, Ariel Cahill *research oncologist, educator*

Punta Gorda
Faerber, Abigail Hobbs *physician*

Saint Petersburg
Betzer, Susan Elizabeth Beers *physician, geriatrician*
Clarke, Kit Hansen *radiologist*
Simpson, Lisa Ann *physician, educator*

Sarasota
Jelks, Mary Larson *retired pediatrician*

Spring Hill
Del Toro-Politowicz, Lillian *medical association administrator, geriatric counselor*

Tallahassee
Maguire, Charlotte Edwards *retired pediatrician*

Tampa
Cancio, Margarita R. *infectious disease physician*
Gilbert-Barness, Enid F. *pathologist, pathology and pediatrics educator*
Powers, Pauline Smith *psychiatrist, educator, researcher*
Watkins, Joan Marie *osteopath, occupational medicine physician*

West Palm Beach
McKeen, Elisabeth Anne *oncologist*

GEORGIA

Atlanta
Broome, Claire Veronica *epidemiologist, researcher*
Frank, Erica *preventive medicine physician*
Heimburger, Elizabeth Morgan *psychiatrist*
Kimani, Grace Alexandra *internist*
Klein, Luella Voogd *obstetrics-gynecology educator*
Wenger, Nanette Kass *cardiology educator, cardiologist, researcher*
Yeargin-Allsopp, Marshalyn *medical epidemiologist, pediatrician*
Zumpe, Doris *ethologist, researcher, educator*

Augusta
Fincher, Ruth Marie Edla *medical educator, dean*
Guill, Margaret Frank *pediatrician, educator, medical researcher*
Pryor, Carol Graham *obstetrician, gynecologist*
Wray, Betty Beasley *allergist, immunologist, pediatrician*

Norcross
Nardelli-Olkowska, Krystyna Maria *ophthalmologist, educator*

Stone Mountain
Gotlieb, Jaquelin Smith *pediatrician*

HAWAII

Honolulu
Lee, Yeu-Tsu Margaret *surgeon, educator*
Sharma, Santosh Devraj *obstetrician/gynecologist, educator*

Mililani
Gardner, Sheryl Paige *gynecologist*

ILLINOIS

Belleville
Megahy, Diane Alaire *physician*

Champaign
Rosenblatt, Karin Ann *cancer epidemiologist*

Chicago
Adelman, Susan Hershberg *surgeon*
Apple, Kathy *medical association administrator*
Bienias, Julia Louise *medical researcher, statistician*
Christoffel, Katherine Kaufer *pediatrician, epidemiologist, educator*
Colley, Karen J. *medical educator, medical researcher*
Dooley, Sharon L. *obstetrician, gynecologist*
Evans, Thelma Jean Mathis *internist*
Flaherty, Emalee Gottbrath *pediatrician*
Frederiksen, Marilynn C. *physician*
Gapstur, Susan Mary *cancer epidemiologist, educator, researcher*
Gewurz, Anita Tartell *medical association administrator*
Grammer, Leslie Carroll *allergist*
Gregory, Stephanie Ann *hematologist, educator*
Hackett, Karen L. *medical association administrator*
Hambrick, Ernestine *retired colon and rectal surgeon*
Hibbard, Judith Usher *obstetrician*
Holst, Ruth Mary *medical librarian*
Jonasson, Olga *surgeon, educator*
Kinslow, Monica M. *forensic scientist*
Kirschner, Barbara Starrels *pediatric gastroenterologist*
Kloss, Linda L. *medical association administrator*
Koenig, Heidi Margret *medical educator*
Lunz, Ellen Deitelbaum *speech and language pathologist*
Mendelson, Ellen B. *radiologist, educator*
Morris, Naomi Carolyn Minner *clinical pediatrician, medical researcher, educator, health facility administrator*
Nakajima, Yasuko *medical educator*
Olson, Sandra Forbes *neurologist*
Ramsey-Goldman, Rosalind *physician*
Robinson, June Kerswell *dermatologist, educator*
Roizen, Nancy J. *physician, educator*
Rotman, Carlotta Hill *physician*
Rowley, Janet Davison *physician*
Scarse, Olivia Marie *cardiologist, consultant*
Seeler, Ruth Andrea *pediatrician, educator*
Shannon, Iris Reed *health consultant*
Short, Marion Priscilla *neurogenetics educator*
Southgate, Marie Therese *physician, editor*
Starr, Ann Elizabeth *obstetrician, gynecologist, educator*
Telfer, Margaret Clare *internist, hematologist, oncologist*
Thomas, Leona Marlene *health information educator*
Volgman, Annabelle Santos *cardiologist, educator*
Waxler, Beverly Jean *anesthesiologist, physician*
Winter, Jane *medical educator*
Zee, Phyllis C. *physician, educator, researcher*

Des Plaines
Levitin, Valeria Oskar *family physician*

Dixon
Polascik, Mary Ann *ophthalmologist*

Downers Grove
Ozog, Diane L. *allergist*

Elk Grove Village
Herrerias, Carla Trevette *epidemiologist, health policy analyst*

Elmhurst
Blain, Charlotte Marie *internist, educator*

Evanston
Enroth-Cugell, Christina Alma Elisabeth *neurophysiologist, educator*
Langsley, Pauline Royal *psychiatrist*
Schwartz, Neena Betty *endocrinologist, educator*

Glenview
Casas, Laurie Ann *plastic surgeon*

Grayslake
Krakora-Looby, Janice Marie *pediatrician*

Lombard
Kasprow, Barbara Anne *biomedical scientist, writer*

Maywood
Albain, Kathy S. *oncologist*
Dado, Diane Valentina *plastic and reconstructive surgeon, pediatric plastic surgeon*
Gaynor, Ellen Rose *hematologist*
Nand, Sucha *medical educator*

Oak Park
Desai, Pankaja Mohan *epidemiologist*

River Grove
Hillert, Gloria Bonnin *anatomist, educator*

Springfield
Woodson, Gayle Ellen *otolaryngologist*

Westchester
Imran, Ayesha *internist*

Yorkville
McEachern, Joan *medical association administrator*

INDIANA

Gary
Zunich, Janice *pediatrician, geneticist, educator, health facility administrator*

Indianapolis
Cohen, Marlene Lois *pharmacologist*
Helveston, Eugene McGillis *pediatric ophthalmologist, educator*
Hill, Beverly Ellen *health sciences educator*
Jackson, Valerie Pascuzzi *radiologist, educator*
Knoebel, Suzanne Buckner *cardiologist, educator*
Richter, Judith Anne *pharmacology educator*
Small, Joyce Graham *psychiatrist, educator*

Lafayette
Gordon, Irene Marlow *radiology educator*

Sullivan
Chavez, Mary Ann *osteopathic family physician*

West Lafayette
Johns, Janet Susan *physician*

IOWA

Des Moines
Goodin, Julia C. *forensic pathologist, state official, educator*
Wattleworth, Roberta Ann *physician, medical educator*

Iowa City
Andreasen, Nancy Coover *psychiatrist, educator, neuroscientist*
Lamping, Kathryn G. *medical educator, medical researcher*
Niebyl, Jennifer Robinson *obstetrician, gynecologist, educator*
Tsalikian, Eva *physician, educator*

KANSAS

Greenwich
Shaughnessy, Elizabeth Ann *surgeon, researcher*

Kansas City
Johnson, Joy Ann *diagnostic radiologist*
Lynch, Sharon Glynn *neurologist, educator*

Shawnee Mission
Bell, Deloris Wiley *physician*

Topeka
Johnson, Patsy *nursing association administrator*

Wichita
Haynes, Deborah Gene *physician*

KENTUCKY

Berea
Lamb, Irene Hendricks *medical researcher*

Lexington
Kang, Bann C. *immunologist*
Noonan, Jacqueline Anne *pediatrics educator*

Louisville
DeMunbrun-Harmon, Donne O'Donnell *retired family physician*
Galandiuk, Susan *colon and rectal surgeon, educator*
Lake, Carol Lee *anesthesiologist, physician executive, educator*

LOUISIANA

Baton Rouge
Lovejoy, Jennifer Carole *medical educator*

Houma
Eschete, Mary Louise *internist*

Mandeville
Young, Lucy Cleaver *physician*

New Orleans
Duncan, Margaret Caroline *physician*
Gatipon, Betty Becker *medical educator, consultant*
Hartz, Renee Semo *cardiothoracic surgeon*
O'Quinn, April Gale *obstetrician, gynecologist, educator*

Shreveport
Blondin, Joan *nephrologist educator*
Mancini, Mary Catherine *cardiothoracic surgeon, researcher*

Slidell
McBurney, Elizabeth Innes *dermatologist, physician, educator*

MAINE

Bangor
Austin, Linda S. *psychiatrist*

Portland
Wilkinson, Barbara J. *physician, medical educator*

MARYLAND

Abingdon
Uzdilla, Laura Angeline *radiation oncology technician, researcher*

Baltimore
Alpern, Linda Lee Wevodau *health agency administrator*
Anderson, Jean R. *women's health physician*
Baker, Susan P. *public health educator*
Blakemore, Karin Jane *obstetrician, geneticist*
Clements, Mary Lou *epidemiologist, educator*
Colomer, Veronica *medical educator, researcher*
Curl, Leigh Ann *orthopedist, surgeon*
DeAngelis, Catherine D. *pediatrics educator*
DeLateur, Barbara Jane *medical educator*
Eldefrawi, Amira Toppozada *medical educator, toxicologist, pharmacologist, neuroscientist*
Faden, Ruth R. *medical educator, ethicist, researcher*
Ferencz, Charlotte *pediatrician, epidemiology and preventive medicine educator*
Fried, Linda P. *medical educator*
Godenne, Ghislaine Dudley *physician, psychoanalyst, educator*
Goldman, Lynn Rose *medical educator*
Griffin, Diane Edmund *research physician, virologist, educator*
Higginbotham, Eve Juliet *ophthalmologist, educator*
Litrenta, Frances Marie *psychiatrist*
Matheson, Nina W. *medical researcher*
Matjasko, M. Jane *anesthesiologist, educator*
Maumenee, Irene H. *ophthalmology educator*
McMillan, Julia A. *pediatrician*
Migeon, Barbara Ruben *pediatrician, geneticist*
Schoenrich, Edyth Hull *internal and preventive medicine physician*
Silbergeld, Ellen Kovner *environmental epidemiologist, researcher, toxicologist*
Starfield, Barbara Helen *pediatrician, educator*
Young, Barbara *psychiatrist, psychoanalyst, psychiatry educator, photographer*

Bethesda
Christian, Michaele Chamblee *internist, oncologist*
Farci, Patrizia *medical educator, researcher*
Haseltine, Florence Pat *obstetrician, gynecologist, research administrator*
Helke, Cinda Jane *pharmacology and neuroscience educator, researcher, academic administrator*
Herman, Mary Margaret *neuropathologist*
Johnson, Joyce Marie *psychiatrist, epidemiologist, public health officer*
Kirschstein, Ruth Lillian *physician*
Klee, Claude Blenc *medical researcher*
Marini, Ann Marie *medical researcher, educator*
Nabel, Elizabeth G. *medical researcher, cardiologist*
Pinn, Vivian W. *pathologist, federal agency administrator*
Puck, Jennifer M. *physician, scientist*
Rapoport, Judith *psychiatrist*
Roberts, Doris Emma *epidemiologist, consultant, public health nurse*
Sternberg, Esther May *neuroendocrinologist, immunologist, rheumatologist*
Vaitukaitis, Judith Louise *medical research administrator*
Volkow, Nora Dolores *medical research center director*

Chevy Chase
Kullen, Shirley Robinowitz *psychiatric epidemiologist, consultant*

Clinton
Cruz, Wilhelmina Mangahas *critical care physician, educator*

Columbia
Harrison, Elza Stanley *medical association executive*

Gaithersburg
Hegyeli, Ruth Ingeborg Elisabeth Johnsson *pathologist, government official*

Greenbelt
Obamogie, Mercy A. *physician*

La Plata
Fisher, Gail Feimster *epidemiologist, researcher, government agency administrator*

Randallstown
McDowell, Elizabeth Mary *retired pathology educator*

Rockville
Culliton, Barbara J. *medical association administrator*

Silver Spring
Adams, Diane Loretta *physician*
Beard, Lillian B. McLean *pediatrician, consultant*

Takoma Park
Silverman, Charlotte *epidemiologist, educator*

Wheaton
White, Martha Vetter *allergy and immunology physician, researcher*

MASSACHUSETTS

Boston
Abrahm, Janet Lee *hematologist, oncologist, palliative care specialist, educator*
Ampola, Mary G. *pediatrician, geneticist*
Angell, Marcia *pathologist, editor-in-chief*
Angelo, E. Joanne *child, adolescent and adult psychiatrist*
Avery, Mary Ellen *pediatrician, educator*
Bigby, JudyAnn *medical educator*
Briggs, Susan Miller *surgeon*
Brugge, Joan S. *medical educator*
Buck, Linda B. *physician, medical educator*
David, Michele Marie Aline *physician, researcher*
Donahoe, Patricia Kilroy *surgeon*
Doyle, Jennifer *surgical educator, scholar*
Duncan, Lyn M. *pathology educator*
Eckstein, Marlene R. *vascular radiologist*
Gilchrest, Barbara Ann *dermatologist*
Goldberg, Marcia B. *medical educator*
Goldstein, Jill M. *psychiatric epidemiologist, clinical neuroscientist, psychiatry educator*
Goumnerova, Liliana Christova *physician, neurosurgeon, educator*
Hay, Elizabeth Dexter *embryology researcher, educator*
Iezzoni, Lisa I. *medical educator, healthcare educator, researcher*
Kandarian, Susan Christine *medical educator*
Manson, JoAnn Elisabeth *endocrinologist*
Maratos-Flier, Eleftheria *medical educator, physician*
McCormick, Marie Clare *pediatrician, educator*
McNeil, Barbara Joyce *radiologist, educator*
Mesholam, Raquelle Ilyse *neuropsychologist, researcher*
Messerle, Judith Rose *medical librarian, public relations director*
Nadelson, Carol Cooperman *psychiatrist, educator*
Nour, Nawal M. *obstetrician, gynecologist, health facility administrator*
Pallotta, Johanna Antonia (Johanna Stephen) *physician, educator, researcher*
Ravid, Katya *medical educator*
Reid, Lynne McArthur *pathologist*
Schaller, Jane Green *pediatrician*
Seddon, Johanna Margaret *ophthalmologist, epidemiologist*
Seidman, Christine E. *medical educator*
Solomon, Caren Grossbard *internist*
Van Marter, Linda Joanne *pediatrician, educator, neonatologist, researcher*
Young, Anne B. *neurologist, educator*
Yuan, Junying *medical educator, researcher*

Brockton
Carlson, Desiree Anice *pathologist*

Brookline
Jakab, Irene *psychiatrist*
Jordan, Ruth Ann *physician*
Sarfaty, Suzanne *internist, educator*

Cambridge
Amon, Angelika *medical researcher*
Eisenberg, Carola *psychiatry educator*
Graybiel, Ann M. *medical educator*
Mathews, Joan Helene *pediatrician*
Smith, Susie Irene *histotechnologist, cytometrist*

Weinshenker, Naomi Joyce *clinical psychiatrist, educator, researcher*
Welch, Martha Grace *physician, researcher*
Whelan, Elizabeth Ann Murphy *epidemiologist*
Yin, Beatrice Wei-Tze *medical researcher*
Young, Estelle Irene *dermatologist, educator*
Zucker-Franklin, Dorothea *internist, educator*

Plattsburgh
Rech, Susan Anita *obstetrician, gynecologist*

Poughkeepsie
Berlin, Doris Ada *psychiatrist*
Carino, Aurora Lao *psychiatrist, hospital administrator*

Purchase
Frost, Elizabeth Ann McArthur *physician*

Ridgewood
Monroe, Leonora *surgeon*

Rochester
Bidlack, Jean Marie *pharmacologist, educator, medical researcher*
Haywood, Anne Mowbray *pediatrician, educator*
Lawrence, Ruth Anderson *pediatrician, clinical toxicologist*
McAnarney, Elizabeth R. *pediatrician, educator*
Smith, Julia Ladd *medical oncologist, hospice physician*

Rye Brook
Lo Russo, Diane *radiologist*

Saratoga Springs
Muller, Susan Marie *physician*

Setauket
Davenport, Deborah Morgan *obstetrician, gynecologist*

Stony Brook
Lane, Dorothy Spiegel *preventive medicine physician*
Leske, M. Cristina *medical educator, medical researcher*

Syracuse
Horst, Pamela Sue *medical educator, family physician*
Numann, Patricia Joy *surgeon, educator*
Rogers, Sherry Anne *physician*
Streeten, Barbara Wiard *ophthalmologist, medical educator*

Tuxedo Park
Regan, Ellen Frances (Mrs. Walston Shepard Brown) *ophthalmologist, educator*

Valhalla
Kline, Susan Anderson *medical school official and dean, internist*
McGoldrick, Kathryn Elizabeth *anesthesiologist, educator, writer*

Warsaw
Dy-Ang, Anita C. *pediatrician*

West Islip
Elkowitz, Sheryl Sue *radiologist*

White Plains
Monteferrante, Judith Catherine *cardiologist*
Pfeffer, Cynthia Roberta *psychiatrist, educator*

NORTH CAROLINA

Advance
Guth, Caryl Joy *retired anesthesiologist*

Asheville
Turcot, Marguerite Hogan *medical researcher*

Chapel Hill
Fletcher, Suzanne Wright *epidemiologist, medical educator, editor*
Hulka, Barbara Sorenson *epidemiologist, educator*
Mitchell, Beverly Shriver *hematologist, oncologist, educator*
Trejo, JoAnn *medical researcher*

Charlotte
Saikevych, Irene A. *pathologist*
Visser, Valya Elizabeth *physician*

Durham
Buckley, Rebecca Hatcher *allergist, immunologist, pediatrician, educator*
Kaprielian, Victoria Susan *medical educator*
Kurtzberg, Joanne *pediatrics educator*
Markert, Mary Louise *pediatrics educator*
Martinez, Maria Dolores *pediatrician*
Murphy, Barbara Anne *emergency physician, surgery educator*
Page, Bernadette Ryan *emergency physician*
Thibodeau, Patricia Leona *medical librarian*

Greenville
Johnson, Cynda Ann *physician, educator*

High Point
Draelos, Zoe Diana *dermatologist, consultant*

Raeford
Abreu, Sue Hudson *physician, army officer, organizational and healthcare consultant*

Raleigh
Hughes, Francis P. *medical organization executive*
Johnson, Mary Pauline (Polly Johnson) *nursing executive*

Salisbury
Fisher, Ada Markita *physician, health services administrator, writer, poet*

Waxhaw
Edwards, Irene Elizabeth (Libby Edwards) *dermatologist, educator, medical researcher*

Winston Salem
Ferree, Carolyn Ruth *radiation oncologist, educator*
Graham, Gloria Flippin *dermatologist*

NORTH DAKOTA

Bismarck
Schwartz, Judy Ellen *cardiothoracic surgeon*

Grand Forks
Burns, Elizabeth Ann *physician, educator*
Sobus, Kerstin MaryLouise *physician, physical therapist*

OHIO

Akron
Milsted, Amy *biomedical educator*

Canton
Rubin, Patricia *internist*

Cincinnati
Boyd, Deborah Ann *pediatrician*
Brown, Jacqueline I. *medical assistant*
De Courten-Myers, Gabrielle Marguerite *neuropathologist*
Fenoglio-Preiser, Cecilia Mettler *pathologist, educator*
Hess, Evelyn Victorine *medical educator*
Loggie, Jennifer Mary Hildreth *medical educator, physician*
Lucky, Anne Weissman *dermatologist*
Solomon, Susanne Nina *podiatrist, surgeon*

Cleveland
Davis, Pamela Bowes *pediatric pulmonologist*
Moravec, Christine D. Schomis *medical educator*
Olness, Karen Norma *pediatrics and international health educator*
Rehm, Susan *physician*
Reveiz, Maria Cristina *osteopath*

Columbus
Bloomfield, Clara Derber *oncologist, medical institute administrator*
Haque, Malika Hakim *pediatrician*
Huheey, Marilyn Jane *ophthalmologist, educator*
Lander, Ruth A. *medical group and association administrator*
Laufman, Leslie Rodgers *hematologist, oncologist*
Long, Sarah Elizabeth Brackney *physician*
Moser, Debra Kay *medical educator*
Sommer, Annemarie *pediatrician*
Whitacre, Caroline Clement *immunologist, researcher*

Dayton
Dunn, Margaret M. *general surgeon, educator, university official*
Monk, Susan Marie *pediatrician, educator*
Nanagas, Maria Teresita Cruz *pediatrician, educator*
Pflum, Barbara Ann *pediatrician, allergist*

Massillon
Vaughn, Lisa Dawn *physician, educator*

Medina
Jeffers, Lynette A. *anesthetist*

Rootstown
Nora, Lois Margaret *neurologist, educator, academic administrator, dean*

Toledo
Jauregui, Connie Lee *internist*
Rejent, Marian Magdalen *retired pediatrician*

OKLAHOMA

Edmond
Haywood, B(etty) J(ean) *anesthesiologist*

Norman
Cochran, Gloria Grimes *retired pediatrician*

Oklahoma City
Bahr, Carman Bloedow *internist*
Moore, Joanne Iweita *pharmacologist, educator*

OREGON

Corvallis
Engle, Molly *program evaluator, preventive medicine researcher, medical educator*

Medford
Harris, Linda Ruth *obstetrician and gynecologist*

Portland
Baker, Diane R.H. *dermatologist*
Glass, Laurel Ellen *gerontologist, developmental biologist, physician, retired educator*
MacArthur, Carol Jeanne *pediatric otolaryngology educator*
Zerbe, Kathryn Jane *psychiatrist*
Zimmerman, Gail Marie *medical foundation executive*

Roseburg
Oleskowicz, Jeanette *physician*

PENNSYLVANIA

Allentown
Taylor, Sherri Kearise *obstetrician, gynecologist, writer*

Bala Cynwyd
Ringpfeil, Fraziska *dermatologist*

Erie
Brunner-Martinez, Kirstin Ellen *pediatrician, psychiatrist*

Gap
Tindall, Janice Clough *family physician*

Gibsonia
Krause, Helen Fox *otolaryngologist*

Gladwyne
Morrison, Gail *internist, nephrologist, educator*

Hershey
Testa, Donna Marie *physician*

Jenkintown
Greenspan-Margolis, June E. *psychiatrist*

Kennett Square
Harrington, Anne Wilson *medical librarian*

Monongahela
Yovanof, Silvana *physician*

New Tripoli
Hess, Darla Bakersmith *cardiologist, educator*

Newtown
Somers, Anne Ramsay *retired medical educator*

Newtown Square
de Rivas, Carmela Foderaro *psychiatrist, health facility administrator*

Pennsburg
Shuhler, Phyllis Marie *physician*

Philadelphia
Ballard, Roberta A. *pediatrics educator*
Bibbo, Marluce *physician, educator*
Bilaniuk, Larissa Tetiana *neuroradiologist, educator*
Bowman, Marjorie Ann *family practice physician, educator*
Cassel, Christine Karen *physician*
Conlay, Lydia *physician, health sciences administrator*
Danzon, Patricia M. *medical educator*
Dunn, Linda Kay *physician*
Foti, Margaret *medical association administrator, editor, consultant*
Gary, Nancy Elizabeth *nephrologist, academic administrator*
Glick, Jane Mills *biomedical researcher, educator*
Gordon, Susan Joan *physician, educator*
Gueson, Emerita Torres *obstetrician, gynecologist*
Holzbaur, Erika L. *medical educator*
Ildstad, Suzanne T. *transplant surgeon, immunologist, educator*
Joseph, Rosaline Resnick *hematologist and oncologist*
Kaji, Hideko *pharmacology educator*
Klinghoffer, June Florence *physician, educator*
Kruc, Antoinette Campion *family physician*
Lee, Virginia M. Y. *medical educator, health science association administrator*
Levit, Edithe Judith *physician*
Lipshutz, Laurel Sprung *psychiatrist*
Long, Sarah Sundborg *pediatrician, educator*
Margo, Katherine Lane *family physician, educator*
Pugliese, Maria Alessandra *psychiatrist*
Ritter, Deborah Elizabeth *anesthesiologist, educator*
Rorke, Lucy Balian *neuropathologist*
Rosen, Rhoda *obstetrician, gynecologist*
Russo, Irma Haydee Alvarez de *pathologist*
Sabili, Erlinda Asa *internist, psychiatrist, pastoral care minister*
Stuart, Marie Jean *physician, hematologist, researcher*
Weller, Elizabeth Boghossian *child and adolescent psychiatrist*
Young, Terri L. *ophthalmologist*

Phoenixville
Hanaway, Andrea Stein *emergency physician*

Pittsburgh
Brady, Mary Clemmer *medical association administrator, actress*
Cockerham, Kimberly Peele *ophthalmologist, educator*
Frank, Ellen *medical educator, psychiatrist, psychologist, researcher*
Karol, Meryl Helene *medical educator, researcher, health facility administrator, science educator*
Kent, Georgia L. *obstetrician-gynecologist, healthcare executive, educator*
Lewis, Jennifer L. *internist, educator*
Lyjak Chorazy, Anna Julia *pediatrician, medical administrator, educator*
Wenger, Sharon Louise *pediatrics educator, researcher, cytogeneticist*

Upper Darby
Toney, Angela M. *medical administrator and educator*

West Chester
Simons, Nancy *naturopathic physician, hypnotherapist*

Wynnewood
Koprowska, Irena *cytopathologist, cancer researcher*

RHODE ISLAND

Providence
Biron, Christine Anne *medical science educator, researcher*
Kane, Agnes Brezak *pathologist, educator*

Riverside
Lekas, Mary Despina *retired otolaryngologist*

Westerly
Lin, Foong-Yi *physician*

SOUTH CAROLINA

Charleston
Hoffman, Brenda Joyce *gastroenterology educator*
Key, Janice Dixon *physician, medical educator*

Columbia
Sutherland-Abel, Anne Elizabeth *pediatrician*

Greenville
Hogg, Judith E. *neurologist, educator*

Isle Of Palms
Wohltmann, Hulda Justine *pediatric endocrinologist, diabetologist*

Orangeburg
Hare, Ester Rose *physician*

Surfside Beach
Favaro, Mary Kaye Asperheim *pediatrician, writer*

West Columbia
Carter, Saralee Lessman *immunologist, microbiologist*

SOUTH DAKOTA

Sioux Falls
Trujillo, Angelina *endocrinologist*

TENNESSEE

Chattanooga
Altekruse, Joan Morrissey *retired preventive medicine educator*

Cordova
Diggs, Beatrice M. *research assistant*

Franklin
Smolenski, Lisabeth Ann *family practice physician*

Memphis
Kaste, Sue Creviston *pediatric radiologist, researcher*
Morreim, E. Haavi *medical ethics educator*
Riely, Caroline Armistead *physician, medical educator*

Nashville
Brown, Wendy Weinstock *nephrologist, educator*
Etherington, Carol A. *medical association administrator*
Stahlman, Mildred Thornton *pediatrics and pathology educator, researcher*

TEXAS

Alice
Dyer, Stephanie Jo *anesthesiologist*

Amarillo
Parker, Lynda Michele *psychiatrist*

Aransas Pass
Stehn, Lorraine Strelnick *physician*

Austin
Friedman, Alice Diane *internist, gastroenterologist, educator*
Sutton, Beverly Jewell *psychiatrist*

Beaumont
Phan, Tâm Thanh *medical educator, psychotherapist, consultant, researcher*

Bellaire
Smeal, Janis Lea *osteopath*

Corpus Christi
Sisley, Nina Mae *physician, public health service officer*

Dallas
Berry, Priscilla Marie Burch *ophthalmologist*
Helm, Phala Aniece *physiatrist*
Johnson, Jane Elaine *medical educator*
Kindberg, Shirley Jane *pediatrician*
Phillips, Margaret A. *pharmacology educator*
Roberts, Lynne Jeanine *physician*
Schneider, Nancy Reynolds *pathologist, educator*
Taliaferro, Ellen *medical educator*

Danville
Robertson, Rose Marie *cardiologist, educator*

HUMANITIES: LIBERAL STUDIES

UNITED STATES

ALABAMA

Birmingham
Hamilton, Virginia Van der Veer *historian, educator*
Morton, Marilyn Miller *retired genealogy and history educator, lecturer, researcher, travel executive, director*

Huntsville
Bounds, Sarah Etheline *historian*
Hughes, Kaylene *historian, educator*

Loachapoka
Schafer, Elizabeth Diane *historian, writer*

Mobile
Hamner, Eugenie Lambert *English educator*

Montevallo
Neely, Evelyn Hope (Evelyn Hope Gillespie) *humanities educator, archaeologist*

Montgomery
Napier, Cameron Mayson Freeman *historic preservationist*

Talladega
Jeffers, Trellie Lee James *language educator, dean*

ALASKA

Fairbanks
Corti, Lillian Zell *humanities educator, writer*

ARIZONA

Apache Junction
Ransom, Evelyn Naill *language educator, linguist*

Flagstaff
Marcus, Karen Melissa *foreign language educator*

Glendale
Galletti, Marie Ann *English language and linguistics educator*

Kingman
Jones, Barbara Christine *linguist, creative arts designer, educator*

Phoenix
Maimon, Elaine Plaskow *English educator, university provost, campus chief executive officer*
Van Sittert, Barbara C. *retired classics educator, writer*
Wirtz, Dorothy Marie *retired language educator*

Tempe
Green, Monica H. *history educator*
Honegger, Gitta *language educator*
Lightfoot, Marjorie Jean *English educator*
Ruiz, Vicki Lynn *history educator*
Zinke, Laura A. *language educator*

Tucson
Gaines, Kendra Holly *English language educator, editorial and writing consultant*
Rabuck, Donna Fontanarose *English writing educator*
Schulz, Renate Adele *German studies and second language acquisition educator*
Zepeda, Ofelia *linguist, educator*

ARKANSAS

Beebe
Fletcher, Maris *literature educator*

Conway
Vanderslice, Stephanie M. *humanities educator*

Magnolia
Davis, Elizabeth Hawk *English language educator*

Pine Bluff
Williams, Bettye Jean *English educator*

CALIFORNIA

Auburn
Patterson, Shirley Drury *genealogist, editor-in-chief*

Bakersfield
Gunderson, Sarah Chloe (Sarah Chloe Burns) *historian, educator*
Kegley, Jacquelyn Ann *philosophy educator*

Berkeley
Gallagher, M. Catherine *English literature educator*
Hull, Glynda *language educator*

Canyon Country
Requa, Virginia Lee *literature educator, writer*

Chula Vista
Upson, Helen Rena *retired history educator*

Claremont
Moss, Myra Ellen (Myra Moss Rolle) *philosophy educator*
Wheeler, Geraldine Hartshorn *historian, writer*

El Cajon
Dana-Davidson, Laoma Cook *English language educator*

Escondido
McHenry, Anita Petei *historian, archaeologist*

Fresno
Bundy-DeSoto, Teresa Mari *language educator, vocalist*
Patterson, Carolyn F. *retired English educator*

Irvine
Boyd, Carolyn Patricia *history educator*
Kluger, Ruth *German language educator, editor*

La Jolla
Falk, Julia S. *linguist, educator, dean*
Kenyon, Karen Beth Smith *literature educator, writer*
McDonald, Marianne *classicist*
Oreskes, Naomi *science historian*

Long Beach
Beebe, Sandra E. *retired English language educator, artist, writer*
Nguyen, Huong Tran *English language professional, federal agency official*

Los Angeles
Appleby, Joyce Oldham *historian, educator*
Dumitrescu, Domnita *Spanish language educator, researcher*
Dusa, Joan Elizabeth *history educator*
Hadda, Janet Ruth *Yiddish language educator, lay psychoanalyst*
Hsu, Kylie *language educator, researcher, linguist*
Lawrence, Gwynn Lewis *language educator*
Levin, Carol Arlene *language educator*
Lionnet, Francoise *French and comparative literature educator*
Mellor, Anne Kostelanetz *English literature educator*
Ochs, Elinor *linguistics educator*
Rochette, Laura Christine *literature educator*
Russett, Margaret E. *language educator*
See, Carolyn *English language educator, novelist, book critic*
Troy, Nancy J. *art history educator*

Moraga
Lashof, Carol Suzanne *literature educator*

Northridge
Hall, Leilani Rae *humanities educator*

Pacific Grove
Penney, Beth *English educator, editor, writer*
Schapiro, Karen Lee *language educator*

Palo Alto
Mommsen, Katharina *retired German language and literature educator*
Walker, Carolyn Peyton *English language educator*

Pasadena
Zwicky, Barbarina Exita *humanities educator, researcher*

Riverside
Fagundo, Ana Maria *creative writing and Spanish literature educator*
Yount, Gwendolyn Audrey *humanities educator*

San Diego
Alcosser, Sandra Beth *English language educator, writer*
Amstadt, Nancy Hollis *retired language educator*
Blessing, Carol Ann *literature educator*
Darby, Joanne Tyndale (Jaye Darby) *arts and humanities educator*
Dunlop, Marianne *retired English as second language educator*

San Francisco
Batchelor, Karen Lee *English language educator*
Hansen, Carol Louise *English language educator*
Polk, Constance Christine *language educator, education educator*

San Jose
Kerkoc, Ruth Ann *Spanish educator*

San Marcos
Rolle-Rissetto, Silvia *foreign languages educator, writer, artist*

San Marino
Stefansson, Wanda Gae *language educator, literature educator*

Santa Barbara
Ingram, Katharine Goodridge *language educator, writer*
Mahlendorf, Ursula Renate *literature educator*

Santa Cruz
Suckiel, Ellen Kappy *philosophy educator*

Saratoga
deBarling, Ana Maria *language educator*

Solana Beach
Withee, Diana Keeran *art historian, art dealer, educator*

South Pasadena
Lynch, Annette Peters *literature educator*

Stanford
Emery, Jane Dailey *English literature and language educator*
Newman-Gordon, Pauline *French language and literature educator*
Offen, Karen Marie *historian, educator*
Perloff, Marjorie Gabrielle *English and comparative literature educator*

Traugott, Elizabeth Closs *linguist, educator, researcher*

Stockton
Fung, Rosaline Lee *language educator*

Tujunga
Daly, Saralyn R. *retired humanities educator, writer*

Ukiah
Lohrli, Anne *retired English language educator, writer*

Vallejo
Landauer, Elvie Ann Whitney *humanities educator, writer*

Van Nuys
Lemberger, Phyllis *language educator, elementary school educator*

Visalia
Lynch, Janet Nichols *English language educator, writer*

Woodside
Melmon, Elyce Edelman *literature educator, writer*

COLORADO

Boulder
Engel, Barbara Alpern *history educator*
Limerick, Patricia Nelson *history educator*

Denver
Fasel, Ida *English language educator, writer*
Hightower, Nancy Elizabeth *literature educator*
Johnson, Geraldine Esch *language specialist*
Stott, Annette *art historian, educator*
Wetzel, Jodi (Joy Lynn Wetzel) *history and women's studies educator*

Greeley
Wilson, Sharon Rose *literature educator, researcher*

Lakewood
Joy, Carla Marie *history educator*
Woodruff, Kathryn Elaine *English language educator*

Steamboat Springs
Kiser-Miller, Kathy Joy *humanities educator*

CONNECTICUT

Clinton
Gilman, Frances M. *genealogist, librarian*

Danbury
Hellmann, Rene Braun *English as a Second Language educator, elementary school educator*
Kendall, Marcia S. *literature educator, consultant*

Essex
Hieatt, Constance Bartlett *English language educator*

Fairfield
Newton, Lisa Haenlein *philosopher, educator*

Glastonbury
Cassotto, Mary Lou Grace *language educator*

Guilford
Colish, Marcia Lillian *history educator*

Higganum
Miles, Deborah H. *language educator*

Middletown
Heimann-Hast, Sybil Dorothea *language arts and literature educator*
Meyer, Priscilla Ann *Russian language and literature educator*
Winston, Krishna *foreign language professional*

New Britain
Hermes, Katherine Ann *historian, history educator*

New Haven
Borroff, Marie *English language educator*
Dreyer, Lois Helene Goodman *reading and language arts educator, researcher*
Frank, Roberta *English language educator*
Glier, Ingeborg Johanna *German language and literature educator*
Greene, Liliane *French language and literature educator, editor*
Hyman, Paula E(llen) *history educator*
Peterson, Linda H. *English language and literature educator*
van Altena, Alicia Mora *language educator*
Yeazell, Ruth Bernard *English language educator*

North Branford
Thacher, Barbara Auchincloss *history educator*

Salisbury
Kilner, Ursula Blanche *genealogist, educator, writer*

Stamford
Ortner, Toni *English language educator*

Storrs Mansfield
Charters, Ann *biographer, editor, educator*

Waterbury
Meyer, Judith Chandler Pugh *history educator*

West Hartford
Collins, Alma Jones *English educator, writer*
Hodnicki, Jill Ann *historian, researcher*

Woodbridge
Ecklund, Constance Cryer *French language educator*
Kleiner, Diana Elizabeth Edelman *art history educator, administrator*

DELAWARE

Dover
Haskins, Linda L. *English educator*

Frederica
Miller, Mary-Emily *history educator*

Newark
Isaacs, Diane Scharfeld *English educator*

Wilmington
Kneavel, Ann Callanan *humanities educator, communications consultant*

DISTRICT OF COLUMBIA

Washington
Albrecht, Kathe Hicks *art historian, visual resources manager*
Bennett, Betty T. *English literature educator, university dean, writer*
Broun, Elizabeth *art historian, museum administrator*
Cheney, Lynne V. *humanities educator, writer*
Fain, Cheryl Ann *translator, editor*
Farr, Judith Banzer *writer, literature educator*
Howland, Nina Davis *historian*
Hughes, Ellen Roney *historian, museum exhibition curator*
Kreinheder, Hazel Fuller *genealogist, historian*
Marr, Phebe Ann *retired historian, educator*
McAuliffe, Jane Dammen *religious studies and Islamic studies educator*
Miller, Jeanne-Marie Anderson (Mrs. Nathan J. Miller) *English language educator, academic administrator*
Park, Alice Mary Crandall *genealogist*
Reagon, Bernice Johnson *cultural historian, educator, curator, singer, composer*
Reed, Berenice Anne *art historian, artist, government official*
Roberts, Jeanne Addison *retired literature educator*
Salamon, Linda Bradley *English literature educator*
Schneider, Cynthia Perrin *art historian, educator*
Sherman, Nancy *philosophy educator*
Stone, Florence Smith *film festival executive, consultant*
Tappert, Tara Leigh *art historian, archivist, researcher*
Taylor, Estelle Wormley *English educator, dean*
Vaslef, Irene *historian, librarian*

FLORIDA

Boca Raton
Adriazola, Ana *Spanish and Latin American culture educator*

Clearwater
Knoop, Maggie Pearson *language educator*

Daytona Beach
Hill, Dora Ann (Douffas) *language educator, writer*

Deland
Navarro, Lydia *language educator*

Delray Beach
Stone, Elizabeth Walker *English educator*

Englewood
Catterlin, Cindy Lou *English educator*

Fort Lauderdale
Berkey-Abbott, Kristin Lee *language educator*
Van Alstyne, Judith Sturges *retired language educator*

Gainesville
Hartigan, Karelisa Dorothy *classics educator*
Scott, Lynn Thomson *Spanish language and literature educator*

Gulfport
Davis, Ann Caldwell *history educator*

Hillsboro Beach
McGarry, Carmen Racine *historian, artist*

Key Biscayne
Ross, Marilyn J. *English and communications educator*

Lake Worth
Dilgen, Regina Marie *English educator*

Melbourne
Jones, Elaine Hancock *humanities educator*

Milton
Coston, Brenda Maria Bone *language arts educator*

Mulberry
Bowman, Hazel Lois *retired English language educator*

Naples
Kinder, Suzanne Fonay Wemple *historian, educator*

North Miami
Birbragher-Rozencwaig, Francine *art historian, critic, editor*

North Port
Seiler, Charlotte Woody *retired educator*

Orlando
Johnson, Rebecca J. *literature educator*
Murphrey, Elizabeth Hobgood *history educator, librarian*

Palm Bay
Sampere, Roberta Lynn *English language educator, consultant*

Saint Petersburg
Molina-Gavilán, Yolanda *language educator*
Walker, Brigitte Maria *translator, linguistic consultant*

Sarasota
Hapner, Joanna Sue *humanities educator*
Jacobson, Jeanne McKee *humanities educator, writer*

Sebastian
Parulis, Cheryl *English, drama and speech educator*

Tallahassee
Bucuvalas, Tina *folklorist*
Laird, Doris Anne Marley *humanities educator, musician*
Sawh, Ruth *English educator, writer*

Tampa
Cámara, Madeline María *humanities educator*
Mitchell, Mozella Gordon *English language educator, minister*
Ronson, Bonnie Whaley *literature educator*
Sullivan, Anne McCrary *language educator*
Weizmann, Maria Pia *ESL educator*

Umatilla
Balandran, Stella Varona *interpreter, lyricist, composer, writer*

Venice
Balch, Nelda Caroline Kurtz *humanities educator*

Winter Garden
Earls, Irene Anne *art history educator*

Winter Haven
McShay, Yvonne Mangram Al'media *English educator, consultant*

Winter Park
Mésavage, Ruth Matilde *language educator*

GEORGIA

Alpharetta
Harrison, Stephanie A. *language educator, director*

Athens
Ranson, Diana L. *language educator*
Troutt Powell, Eve *historian, educator*

Atlanta
Chafee, Ingrid Roberta Hoover Coleman *French language educator*
Fox-Genovese, Elizabeth Ann Teresa *humanities educator, educator*
Kuntz, Marion Lucile Leathers *classicist, historian*
Sheftall, Beverly Guy *women's studies educator*
Wing, Jennifer Mary *literature educator*

Brunswick
Choate, Jean Marie *historian, humanities educator*

Dublin
Claxton, Harriett Maroy Jones *retired language educator*

Dunwoody
Duvall, Marjorie L. *English and foreign language educator*

Macon
Huffman, Joan Brewer *history educator*

Marietta
Corley, Florence Fleming *retired history educator*

Newnan
Golden, Lily Oliver *humanities educator*

Saint Simons Island
Austin, Jeannette Holland *genealogist, writer*

Savannah
Burke, Suzanne Maureen *art historian, dean*

HAWAII

Hilo
Kinney, Jeanne Kawelolani *English studies educator, writer*

Honolulu
Lane, Teresa Marie *language educator*
Middleton, Linda Charlene *humanities educator*
Pagotto, Louise *English language educator*

Peterson, Barbara Ann Bennett *history educator, television personality*

Kaneohe
Nagtalon-Miller, Helen Rosete *humanities educator*

Pearl City
Lee, Rebecca *literature educator, writer*

IDAHO

Jerome
Ricketts, Virginia Lee *historian, researcher*

Moscow
Greever, Janet Groff *history educator*

Pocatello
Smith, Evelyn Elaine *language educator*
Walter, Kay J. *literature educator*

ILLINOIS

Champaign
Koenker, Diane P. *history educator*
Kummer, Karen Lang *historian, consultant, architecture educator*

Chicago
Bregoli-Russo, Mauda Rita *language educator, educator*
Edelstein, Teri J. *art history educator, art administrator, small business owner*
Elshtain, Jean Bethke *social and political ethics educator*
Gannon, Sister Ann Ida *retired philosophy educator, former college administrator*
Gray, Hanna Holborn *history educator*
Hoover, Polly Ruth *humanities educator*
Hsia, Sophie S. *language educator, researcher*
Johnson, Raymonda Theodora Greene *humanities educator*
Manning, Sylvia *English studies educator*
Nakamura, Kimiko *language educator*
Nussbaum, Martha Craven *philosophy and classics educator*
Palmer, Rose *humanities educator, writer*
Romano-Magner, Patricia R. *English studies educator, researcher*
Sedgwick, Sally Stowell *philosophy educator*
Sitton, Ann Marie *educator*
Trumpener, Katie *literature educator*

Dekalb
Gómez Vega, Ibis *humanities educator*

Evanston
Buchbinder, Barbara Joyce *art and architectural historian*
McCurry, Stephanie *historian, educator*
Reiss, Lenore Ann *language educator, retired secondary school educator*

Macomb
Leonard, Virginia Waugh *history educator, writer, researcher*

Mount Prospect
Bailey-Mershon, Glenda Mariah *historian, educator, retired writer*

Mount Vernon
Hall, Sharon Gay *retired language educator, artist*

Palatine
Bontempo, Elaine *language educator*
Hull, Elizabeth Anne *retired English language educator*
Keres, Karen Lynne *English language educator*
von Keudell, Renate *language educator*

Rolling Meadows
Strongin, Bonnie Lynn *English language educator*

Romeoville
Lifka, Mary Lauranne *history educator*

Schaumburg
Epstein, Barbara Myrna Robbin *language educator*

Urbana
Baym, Nina *English educator*
Spence, Mary Lee *historian, educator*
Watts, Emily Stipes *English language educator*

Wilmette
McClure, Julie Anne *literature educator*

INDIANA

Bloomington
Anderson, Judith Helena *English language educator*
Knudsen, Laura Georgia *linguist*

Centerville
Wendeln, Darlene Doris *English language educator*

Evansville
Baker, Ann Long *language educator*
Grabill, Virginia Lowell *retired English educator*

Fort Wayne
Scheetz, Sister Mary JoEllen *English language educator*

Indianapolis
Nnaemeka, Obioma Grace *French language and women's studies educator, consultant, researcher*

Muncie
Christman, Jill Corey *literature educator, writer*

Nashville
Wills, Katherine V. Tsiopos *English language educator*

Notre Dame
Doody, Margaret Anne *English language educator*

Richmond
Tolliver, Lorraine *language educator, writer*

Terre Haute
De Marr, Mary Jean *English language educator*

Valparaiso
Peters, Judith Griessel *foreign language educator*

West Lafayette
Alsup, Janet Marie *language educator*

IOWA

Ames
Dial, Eleanore Maxwell *foreign language educator*
Mitchell, Jacqueline Keaton *English language educator*

Cedar Falls
Maier, Donna Jane-Ellen *history educator*

Grinnell
Michaels, Jennifer Tonks *foreign language educator*

Iowa City
Dettmer, Helena R. *classics educator*
DiPardo, Anne *English language and education educator*
Kerber, Linda Kaufman *historian, educator*
Scullion, Rosemarie *literature educator*
Solbrig, Ingeborg Hildegard *literature educator, writer*

Walcott
Greer, Mimi (Martha) Emilie *language educator*

Waverly
Blair, Rebecca Sue *English educator*

KANSAS

Dighton
Stanley, Ellen May *historian, consultant*

Great Bend
Gunn, Mary Elizabeth *retired English language educator*

Lawrence
Dusenbury, Mary McClintock *arts scholar, farmer, rancher*
Kuznesof, Elizabeth Anne *history educator*
Trulove, Sarah Chappell *humanities educator*

Salina
Collins, Judith Ann *literature educator*

Shawnee Mission
Lazzo, Janelle *humanities educator, writer*

KENTUCKY

Carrollton
Duncan, Carol Lynn *English language and literature educator*

Frankfort
McCarthy, Lynn Cowan *genealogist, researcher*

Harrodsburg
Bradshaw, Phyllis Bowman *historian, historic site staff member*

Lexington
Blackwell, Jeannine *foreign language educator*

Louisville
Freibert, Lucy Marie *humanities educator*
Theiss, Gena Lee *genealogist, researcher*

LOUISIANA

Baton Rouge
Doty, Gresdna Ann *theatre historian, educator*
Sasek, Gloria Burns *English language and literature educator*

Natchitoches
Wells, Carol McConnell *genealogist, retired archivist*

New Orleans
Roberts, Louise Nisbet *philosopher, educator*

Ruston
Dodge Robbins, Dorothy Ellin *English educator*
Lewis, Karen DeWitt *English language educator*

MAINE

Portland
Chapkis, Wendy Lynn *women's studies educator*

Rockport
Goodwin, Doris Helen Kearns *historian*

Washburn
Humphrey, Mary Frances *historian, writer, retired health care recruiter*

Waterville
Roisman, Hanna Maslovski *classics educator*

MARYLAND

Baltimore
Chapelle, Suzanne Ellery Greene *history educator*
Child-Olmsted, Gisèle Alexandra *language educator*
Del Rosso, Jeana Marie *literature educator*
Emerson, Mia Diane *English educator*
Oden, Gloria *English educator, poet*
Peirce, Carol Marshall *English educator*
Stidman, Edith (Janet) Scales *parliamentarian*
Terborg-Penn, Rosalyn Marian *historian, educator*

Bel Air
Webster, Colleen Michael *English language educator*

Bethesda
Benson, Elizabeth Polk *art specialist*
Raffini, Renee Kathleen *foreign language professional, educator*

Chevy Chase
Cline, Ruth Eleanor Harwood *translator*

College Park
Collins, Merle *English and comparative literature educator*
Doherty, Lillian Eileen *classicist, educator*
Hallett, Judith Peller *classical studies educator*
Oster, Rose Marie Gunhild *foreign language professional, educator*
Struna, Nancy L. *social historian and American studies educator*
Yotsukura, Lindsay Amthor *language educator*

Hyattsville
Golden, Marita *English language educator, foundation executive*
Rodgers, Mary Columbro *literature educator, writer, academic administrator*

Ocean Pines
Fullerton, Jean Leah *retired language educator, researcher, census researcher*

Potomac
Durek, Dorothy Mary *retired English language educator*
Sceery, Beverly Davis *genealogist, writer, educator*

Silver Spring
Borkovec, Vera Z. *Russian studies educator*
Papas, Irene Kalandros *English language educator, poet, writer*
Wolfe, Pamela Kline *history educator*

Sparks
Suarez-Murias, Marguerite C. *retired language educator, retired literature educator*

Towson
Baker, Jean Harvey *history educator*

MASSACHUSETTS

Amherst
Alexander, Alison F. *communication educator*
Baker, Lynne Rudder *philosophy educator*
Partee, Barbara Hall *linguist, educator*
Taubman, Jane Andelman *Russian literature educator*
Wilson, Mary Christina *history educator*

Andover
Miller, Francine Koslow *art history educator, art critic*

Boston
Scanlon, Dorothy Therese *history educator*

Bridgewater
Farrar, Ruth Doris *reading and literacy educator*

Burlington
Nash, Mildred Jean *English educator, poet*

Cambridge
Blair, Ann *historian*
Faust, Drew Gilpin *historian, educator*
Hamner, Suzanne Leath *retired history educator*
Laiou, Angeliki Evangelos *history educator*
Maier, Pauline *history educator*
McDonald, Christie Anne *Romance languages and literature educator, writer*
Rosenkrantz, Barbara Gutmann *retired history educator*
Ulrich, Laurel Thatcher *historian, educator*
Vendler, Helen Hennessy *literature educator, poetry critic*

Chestnut Hill
Valette, Rebecca Marianne *Romance languages educator*

Falmouth
Fullerton, Davina *art historian, consultant, researcher*

Framingham
Agüero-Torres, Irene Beatriz *language educator*

Lipton, Leah *art historian, educator, museum curator*

Holden
Sanfacon, Mary Elizabeth *French educator*

Medford
Ch'en, Li-li *writer, Chinese language, literature and comparative literature educator*

Natick
Ma, Jing-Heng Sheng *language educator*

North Andover
Longsworth, Ellen Louise *art historian, consultant*

Northampton
Skarda, Patricia Lyn *English language educator*

Salem
Gozemba, Patrica Andrea *women's studies and English language educator, writer*

Springfield
Bonemery, Anne M. *language educator*
Dunn, Gail Pederzoli *English language educator*

Waltham
Hale, Jane Alison *French and comparative literature educator*
Jones, Jacqueline *historian*
Staves, Susan *English educator*

Watertown
Rivers, Wilga Marie *foreign language educator*

Wellesley
Jacoff, Rachel *Italian language and literature educator*
Lefkowitz, Mary Rosenthal *Greek literature educator*
Mistacco, Vicki E. *foreign language educator*
Piper, Adrian Margaret Smith *philosopher, artist, educator*
Putnam, Ruth Anna *philosopher, educator*

Weston
Higgins, Sister Therese *English educator, former college president*

Williamstown
Graver, Suzanne Levy *English literature educator*

Winchester
Baumann, Priscilla *medieval art history educator, researcher*
Furui, Sachiko *language educator, consultant, artist*

MICHIGAN

Allendale
Fernandez-Levin, Rosa *language educator*
Miller, Jo Ellen *humanities educator*

Ann Arbor
Eisenstein, Elizabeth Lewisohn *historian, educator*
Forsyth, Ilene Haering *art historian*
Hill, Helen Morey Williams *English literature educator*
Prins, Johanna *literature educator*
Scodel, Ruth *humanities educator*
Zurier, Rebecca *art history educator*

Bay City
Vader-McCormick, Nancy Jane *humanities educator*

Berrien Springs
Summitt, April *history educator*

Beulah
Tanner, Helen Hornbeck *historian, researcher*

Birmingham
Reeves, Kathleen Walker *English and French language educator*

Bloomfield Hills
Starkman, Betty Provizer *genealogist, writer, educator*

Brownstown
Slingerland, Mary Jo *literature educator*

Detroit
Chauderlot, Fabienne-Sophie *foreign language educator*

East Lansing
Kronegger, Maria Elisabeth *French and comparative literature educator*

Flint
Leeds, Valerie Ann *art historian, curator, writer*

Kalamazoo
Easterday, Shanda Hansma Blue *language educator, writer*
Julien, Catherine *history educator*
Raaberg, Gloria Gwen *literature educator*

Livonia
Holtzman, Roberta Lee *French and Spanish language educator*

Saginaw
Houshiar, Bobbie Kay *language arts educator*

University Center
Riegle, Rosalie Genevieve *English educator, writer*

West Bloomfield
Williamson, Marilyn Lammert *English educator, university administrator*

Ypsilanti
Coykendall, Abby Lynn *literature educator*
Schwartz, Ellen C. *art historian, educator*

MINNESOTA

Brooklyn Park
Boutiette, Mary Antonia *language educator*

Eden Prairie
Ruffenach, Rosemary Anne *English and writing educator*

Hastings
Jacobsen-Theel, Hazel M. *retired historian*

Mankato
Mink, Jo Anna Stephens *humanities educator*

Marshall
Wilson, Judy Robinson *language educator, writer*

Minneapolis
Campbell, Karlyn Kohrs *speech and communication educator*
Fergus, Patricia Marguerita *English language educator, writer, editor*
Firchow, Evelyn Scherabon *German language and literature educator, writer*
Garner, Shirley Nelson *English language educator*
Kohlstedt, Sally Gregory *history educator*
Marling, Karal Ann *art history and social sciences educator, curator*

Moorhead
Morrison, Barbara Sheffield *Japanese translator and interpreter, consultant, educator*

Northfield
McKinsey, Elizabeth *humanities educator, consultant*
Yandell, Cathy Marleen *language educator*
Zelliot, Eleanor Mae *history educator*

Saint Paul
Davis, Joy Lee *English language educator*
Glancy, Helen Diane *literature educator*
Monson, Dianne Lynn *literacy educator*

MISSISSIPPI

Clinton
Bigelow, Martha Mitchell *retired historian*

Jackson
McLemore-Wheeler, Linda M. *literature educator*

Mississippi State
Wiltrout, Ann Elizabeth *foreign language educator*

MISSOURI

Ballard
Talbot, Phyllis Mary *reading educator*

Branson
Ford, Jean Elizabeth *former English language educator*

Columbia
Horner, Winifred Bryan *humanities educator, researcher, consultant, writer*
Looser, Devoney Kay *English literature educator*
Pringle, Norma Jean Poarch *translator, educator*
Wallach, Barbara Price *classicist, educator*

Florissant
Ashhurst, Anna Wayne *foreign language educator*

Kansas City
Stuckel, Ruth F. *philosopher, educator, nun*

Kirksville
Davis, Andrea Barbara *language educator*

Saint Louis
Reidy, Frances Ryan *English language educator, editor, writer*

Springfield
Easley, June Ellen Price *genealogist*
Stewart, Lois *humanities educator, curriculum coordinator*

Warrensburg
Heming, Carol Piper *historian, educator*

MONTANA

Eureka
Cheek, Cheryl A. *language educator*

Missoula
Wigfied-Phillip, Ruth Genivea *genealogist, author, researcher*

NEBRASKA

Kearney
Young, Ann Elizabeth O'Quinn *historian, educator*

Lincoln
Levin, Carole *history educator*

Omaha
Brimmerman, Barbara Jane *language educator*

Trenton
Goodenberger, Mary Ellen *literature educator*

NEVADA

Incline Village
Saraceno, June Sylvester *literature educator, department chairman*

North Las Vegas
Miller, Eleanor *English language and literature educator*

NEW HAMPSHIRE

Center Sandwich
Folch-Pi, Willa Babcock *romance language educator*

Durham
Gold, Janet Nowakowski *Spanish language educator*
James, Marion E. *retired humanities educator*
Linden, Blanche Marie Gemrose *history educator*
Lukens, E.A. Nancy *language educator, writer*

Henniker
Donovan, Martha Andrews *humanities educator*

Raymond
Fosher, Mary Jane *humanities educator*

NEW JERSEY

Avon By The Sea
Potter, Emma Josephine Hill *language educator*

Belle Mead
Brown, Elizabeth Schmeck *fashion historian*

Clifton
Ressetar, Nancy *foreign language educator*

Dayton
Adickes, Sandra Elaine *English language educator, writer*

Edison
Kushinsky, Jeanne Alice *humanities educator*

Ewing
Hollander, Jean *literature educator, poet*

Jersey City
D'Ambra, Eve *art historian*
Jennings, Sister Vivien *English language educator*

Livingston
Rothbard, Susan Kaye *humanities educator*
Saffer, Amy Beth *foreign language educator*

Madison
Denholtz, Elaine Grudin *literature educator, writer*

Mahwah
Weinberg, Sydney Stahl *historian*

Manasquan
Hope, Jaime Lynn *foreign language educator*

Morristown
Gorrell, Nancy S. *English language educator*

New Brunswick
Hartman, Mary S. *historian, educator*
Kuhn, Melanie R. *literature educator, consultant*
Mora, Gabriela *language educator, researcher*

Newark
Gilbert, Margaret Barbour *literature educator, poet*

Princeton
Bermann, Sandra Lekas *English language educator*
Gutmann, Amy *political science and philosophy educator, academic administrator*
Jenson, Pauline Alvino *retired speech and hearing educator*
Painter, Nell Irvin *historian, educator, writer*
Showalter, Elaine *humanities educator, educator*

Rockaway
Carboy, Beverly J. *humanities educator*

Rocky Hill
Lott, Joyce Greenberg *English language educator*

Somerville
D'Alessio, Jacqueline Ann *English educator*

Stewartsville
Busch, Beverly Gail *English language educator, literature educator, instructional resource center administrator*

Teaneck
Czin, Felicia Tedeschi *Italian language and literature educator, small business owner*
Dowd, Janice Lee *foreign language educator*
Lightman, Marjorie *historian*
Walensky, Dorothy Charlotte *language educator*

Toms River
Bosley, Karen Lee *English and journalism educator*
Willetts, Elizabeth M. *humanities lecturer, actress*

Union
Gronewold, Sue Ellen *history educator*

NEW MEXICO

Albuquerque
Fuller, Anne Elizabeth Havens *English language and literature educator, consultant*
Valdez, Dianna Marie *language educator, consultant*

Las Vegas
Simpson, Dorothy Audrey *retired speech educator*

Taos
Bolls, Imogene Lamb *English language educator, poet*

NEW YORK

Albany
Barnard, Sylvia Evans *classicist, educator*
Galus, Clara P. *philosopher, educator*
Olmsted, Ruth Martin *humanities educator*

Amherst
Messinger, Penny *historian, educator*

Aurora
French, Sara Lillian *humanities educator, writer*
Greenwood, Pilar Fernández-Cañadas *language and literature educator*

Bayport
Mohanty, Christine Ann *retired language educator, actress*

Binghamton
Gaddis Rose, Marilyn *literature educator, translator*
Sklar, Kathryn Kish *historian, educator*

Bronx
Bullaro, Grace Russo *literature, film and foreign language educator, speaker, book reviewer*
Cammarata, Joan Frances *Spanish language and literature educator*
Glickman, Benita *language educator, writer, poet*
González, Diana M. *language educator*
Leifer, Erica Haft *speech therapist*

Bronxville
Peters, Sarah Whitaker *art historian, writer, lecturer*

Brooklyn
Chase, Norah Carol *English language educator*
Jaffe, Louise *English language educator, creative writer*
King, Margaret Leah *history educator*
Lobron, Barbara L. *speech educator, writer, editor, photographer*
Schlissel, Lillian *English educator, writer*

Brookville
Maillet, Lucienne *humanities educator*

Buffalo
Merini, Rafika *foreign language, cultures and literatures educator*
Payne, Frances Anne *literature educator, researcher*

Canton
Goldberg, Rita Maria *foreign language educator*

Centereach
Stern, Marci Ann *English educator*

Cortlandt Manor
Keating, Laura Lee M. *historian, records management professional*

Delmar
Schwarz, Louise A. *band director*

East Greenbush
Jacobson, Dorothy Troup *English and education educator*

Fairport
Graham, Susette Ryan *retired English educator*

Flushing
Raines, Judi Belle *language educator, historian*
Ranald, Margaret Loftus *English literature educator, author*

Forest Hills
Kra, Pauline Skornicki *French language educator*

Fredonia
Smith, Claire Laremont *language educator*
Strada, Christina Bryson *retired humanities educator, librarian*

Garden City
Jason, Kathrine *language educator, writer*
Korshak, Yvonne *art historian*

Hamilton
Pinchin, Jane *literature educator*
Staley, Lynn *English educator*

Hastings On Hudson
Del Duca, Rita *language educator*

Hempstead
McPhee, Martha *literature educator*

Herkimer
Martin, Lorraine B. *humanities educator*

Hurley
Davila, Elisa *language educator, literature educator*

Hurleyville
Hilfstein, Erna *science historian, educator*

Ithaca
Benson, A. LeGrace Gupton *humanities educator, researcher*
Brazell, Karen Woodard *Japanese literature educator*
Colby-Hall, Alice Mary *Romance studies educator*
Norton, Mary Beth *history educator, writer*
Radzinowicz, Mary Ann *language educator*
Varona-Lacey, Gladys María *language educator*

Jamaica
Ekbatani, Glayol *language educator, director, writer*

Kew Gardens
Wesley, Irma R. *art historian, educator*

Lewiston
Laurie, Margaret Sanders *retired English educator*

New Paltz
Harris, Kristine *historian, educator*

New Rochelle
Cutney, Barbara Ann *philosophy educator*
Fitch, Nancy Elizabeth *historian, educator*

New York
Apter, Emily *language educator*
Bonfante, Larissa *classics educator*
Burbank, Jane Richardson *language educator*
Cantor, Linda C. *retired history educator*
Cavallo, Jo Ann *Italian language educator*
Caws, Mary Ann *French language and comparative literature educator, critic*
Clark, Elizabeth Lamb *art historian, researcher*
Cook, Blanche Wiesen *history educator, journalist*
Driver, Martha Westcott *English language educator, writer, researcher*
Ferrante, Joan Marguerite *language educator, literature educator, writer*
Frank, Elizabeth *literature educator, writer*
Frey, Julia Bloch *French language educator, art historian educator*
Gluck, Carol *history educator*
Harris, Katherine Safford *speech and hearing educator*
Hartman, Joan Edna *English educator*
Hill, May Brawley *art historian*
Howe, Florence *English educator, writer*
Hunter-Stiebel, Penelope *art historian*
Karsen, Sonja Petra *retired American-Hispanic literature educator*
Kerz, Louise *historian*
Khidekel, Regina P. *art historian, curator, lecturer*
Krinsky, Carol Herselle *art history educator*
Lamont, Rosette Clementine *Romance languages educator, theatre journalist, translator*
Lewyn, Ann Salfeld *retired English as a second language educator*
Lord, Carla *retired art history educator*
May, Gita *language educator, literature educator*
Maysilles, Elizabeth *speech communication professional, educator*
Middlebrook, Diane Wood *English language educator, writer*
Miller, Nancy K. *literature educator*
Nims, Kelly Michelle *literature educator, researcher*
Plottel, Jeanine Parisier *foreign language educator*
Quinn, Alice Freeman *literature educator*
Quiñones Keber, Eloise *art historian, educator*
Ragusa, Olga Maria *retired Italian language educator*
Ravitch, Diane Silvers *historian, educator, author, government official*
Raymond, Dorothy Sarnoff *communications consultant, former actress and singer*
Riback, Estelle Posner *art historian*
Robertson, Anne Ferratt *language educator, researcher*
Rowen, Ruth Halle *musicologist, educator*
Sandler, Lucy Freeman *art history educator*
Spector, Johanna Lichtenberg *ethnomusicologist, former educator*
Stimpson, Catharine Roslyn *English language educator, writer*
Umeh, Marie Arlene *English language educator*
Valenstein, Suzanne Gebhart *art historian*
Wallace, Barbara Faith *linguistics educator*
Weil-Garris Brandt, Kathleen (Kathleen Brandt) *art historian*
Weinberg, H. Barbara *art historian, educator, curator paintings and sculpture*
Willett Bird, Susan *public and motivational speaker*
Wiseman, Cynthia Sue *language educator*
Wyschogrod, Edith *philosophy educator*
Yurchenco, Henrietta Weiss *ethnomusicologist, writer*

Newburgh
Adams, Barbara *English language educator, poet, writer*

Nyack
Pease, Eleanor Jeanne *humanities educator*

Oneonta
Kaufman, Janice Horner *foreign language educator, women's and gender studies educator*

Oswego
Smiley, Marilynn Jean *musicologist*

Potsdam
Regan, Marie Carbone *retired language educator*
Skandera-Trombley, Laura Elise *language professional, English*

Poughkeepsie
Daniels, Elizabeth Adams *English language educator*
Hytier, Adrienne Doris *French language educator*

Queensbury
Cackener, Helen Lewis *retired English educator, writer*

Rochester
Herminghouse, Patricia Anne *foreign language educator*
Hollis, Susan Tower *history educator*
Kehoe, Jennifer Spungin *English language educator, writer*
Rissone, Donna *language educator*
Young, Mary Elizabeth *history educator*

Rockville Centre
Fitzgerald, Janet Anne *philosophy educator, academic administrator*

Rush
Smith, Katherine Teresa *history educator*

Sayville
Lippman, Sharon Rochelle *art historian, art therapist, filmmaker*

Slingerlands
Childs, Rhonda Louise *motivational speaker*

Staten Island
Vinitskaya, Marina *language educator, education educator*

Syracuse
Waddy, Patricia A. *architectural history educator*
Walker, Amy Melissa *English as second language educator*

Yellow Stream
Lois, Dolores Carmen *literature educator*

Webster
Baden, Joan H. *retired language educator*

Yonkers
Viola, Mary Jo *art history educator*

NORTH CAROLINA

Asheville
Voigt, Ellen *literature educator*

Chapel Hill
Davis, Sarah Irwin *retired English language educator*
Levine, Madeline Geltman *Slavic literatures educator, translator*
Raphael, Bonnie Nanette *voice, speech, text and dialect coach, educator*

Charlotte
Hill, Ruth Foell *language consultant*

Durham
Kaplan, Alice *humanities educator, writer*
Scott, Anne Byrd Firor *history educator*

Elizabeth City
Williams, Rita Carroll *language educator, poet*

Fayetteville
McMillan, Bettie Barney *English language educator*

Graham
Stanberry, D(osi) Elaine *English literature educator, writer*

Greensboro
Archibald, Brigitte Edith *language educator*
Penninger, Frieda Elaine *retired English language educator*

Jacksonville
Fischer, Violeta Pèrez Cubillas *Spanish literature and linguistics educator*

Raleigh
Chaney, Ethel Scotland *English language educator*
Ridgeway, Johanna Bohacek *language educator*

Southern Pines
Martin, Lorna Campbell *English language educator*

Weaverville
Chamberlain, Elizabeth Simmons *retired English language educator*

Winston Salem
Gala, Candelas S. *literature educator, language educator*

NORTH DAKOTA

Grand Forks
Caldwell, Mary Ellen *English language educator*

OHIO

Akron
Livingston, Kriemhilde Irmgard Reinfriede *retired language educator, translator, interpreter*

Athens
Jellison, Katherine Kay *historian, educator*
Whealey, Lois Deimel *humanities scholar*

Brecksville
Pappas, Effie Vamis *language educator, finance educator, writer, poet, artist*

Brunswick
Fabich, Penelope Jane *humanities educator*

Cincinnati
Einbinder, Susan Leslie *literature educator, rabbi*
Hodgson, Irene Belle *language educator, translator*
Rosen, Roberta *philosophy educator*

Cleveland
Berger, Molly *historian, educator*
Curnow, Kathy *art historian, educator*
Miller, Genevieve *retired medical historian*
Nelson, Sue Grodsky *humanities educator, consultant*
Robinson, Alice Helene *English language educator, administrative assistant*
Taft, Frances Prindle *art history educator*
Taylor, Margaret Wischmeyer *retired language educator*
Velasco, Esda Nury *speech and language professional*

Cuyahoga Falls
Walker, Suzannah Wolf *language educator*

Dayton
Harden, Oleta Elizabeth *English language educator, university administrator*

Fostoria
Underwood, Carole Ann *English and Spanish language educator*

Kent
Apseloff, Marilyn Fain *English educator*
Scillia, Diane Graybowski *art historian, researcher*

Marion
Bower, Anne Lieberman *English educator*

Oberlin
Collins, Martha *English language educator, writer*

University Heights
Goral, Judith Ann *language educator*

Urbana
Stolz, Claudia Grace *humanities educator, consultant*

West Farmington
Smith, Agnes Monroe *history educator*

Youngstown
Bowers, Bege K. *English educator, academic administrator*
Checcone, Iole Carlesimo *foreign language educator*

OKLAHOMA

Oklahoma City
Holt, Karen Anita Young *English educator*
Prichard, Barbara Ann *English educator*

OREGON

Aloha
Gorea, Lucia-Iosefina *English educator, writer, poet*

Corvallis
Leibowitz, Flora Lynn *philosophy educator*

Eugene
Lansdowne, Karen Myrtle *retired English language and literature educator*

La Grande
Ewing, Marilyn *English educator*

Portland
Karant-Nunn, Susan Catherine *history educator*
Meyer, Paulette Ann *history educator*
Steinman, Lisa Malinowski *English literature educator, writer*

Sutherlin
Rose, Sarah Elizabeth *genealogist, counselor*

PENNSYLVANIA

Ambler
Pazicky, Diana Loercher *literature educator*

Bala Cynwyd
Dorwart, Bonnie Brice *historian, retired rheumatologist*

Blue Bell
Roden, Carol Looney *retired language educator*

Bryn Mawr
Gaisser, Julia Haig *classics educator*

King, Willard Fahrenkamp (Mrs. Edmund Ludwig King) *Spanish language educator*
Lane, Barbara Miller (Barbara Miller-Lane) *humanities educator*
Lang, Mabel Louise *classics educator*

Chester
Lieberman, Ilene D. *art history and humanities educator*

Custer City
Cavallero, Ann Freaney *literature educator*

Easton
Schlueter, June Mayer *English educator, author*

Elizabethtown
Bartoli, Jill Sunday *reading and language arts researcher and educator*

Haverford
Jorden, Eleanor Harz *linguist, educator*

Indiana
Craig, Chauna Janene *language educator*

Kutztown
Meyer, Susan Moon *speech language pathologist, educator*

Lock Haven
Hoff, Joan Whitman *philosophy educator, women's studies coordinator, director*

Meadville
Stewart, Anne Williams *historian, writer, researcher*

New Castle
Sands, Christine Louise *English educator*

New Freedom
Sedlak, Valerie Frances *retired English language educator, retired academic administrator*

Newtown
Jorczak, Nancy *history educator*

Philadelphia
Kaplan, Janet Ann *art historian, educator*
Logan, Marie-Rose van Stynvoort *literature educator, publishing executive, writer*
Matus-Mendoza, Mariadelaluz *language educator, sociologist*
Sanchez, Sonia *English literature educator*
Risser, Rosemary A. *medicine and public health historian*
Woodside, Lisa Nicole *humanities educator*

Phoenixville
Clark, Kathleen Mulhern *foreign language and literature educator*

Pittsburgh
Harris, Ann Birgitta Sutherland *art historian*
Rawski, Evelyn Sakakida *history educator*

Swarthmore
Morgan, Kathryn Lawson *retired historian, educator*
North, Helen Florence *classicist, educator*

University Park
Grosholz, Emily Rolfe *philosophy educator, poet*
Halsey, Martha Taliaferro *Spanish language educator*
Kasdorf, Julia Mae *language educator, poet*

Villanova
Alter, Maria Pospischil *language educator*
McDiarmid, Lucy *English educator, author*
Sewell, Lisa *literature educator*

Wallingford
Purcell, Mary Hamilton *speech educator*

York
Jackson, Renée Bernadette *English language educator*

RHODE ISLAND

Newport
Ramey, Linda Dee *literature educator, poet*

Providence
Ackerman, Felicia *philosophy educator, writer*
Blasing, Mutlu Konuk *English language educator*
Green, Angel Yvonne *literature educator*
Harleman, Ann *English language educator, writer*

SOUTH CAROLINA

Aiken
Cope, Esther Owens *genealogical researcher*

Beaufort
Tombe, Sheila Joan *language educator, editor*

Charleston
Luton, Mary Katherine *language educator*

Clemson
Wilson, Paulette Adassa *language educator, writer*

Columbia
Kay, Carol McGinnis *literature educator*
Synnott, Marcia Graham *history educator*

Greenwood
Cushing, Sara Elizabeth *English language educator, writer*

Pawleys Island
Ford, Anna Maria *language educator*

Spartanburg
Walker, Melissa A. *historian, educator*

SOUTH DAKOTA

Sioux Falls
Carlson Aronson, Marilyn A. *English language and education educator*

Spearfish
Hubbard, Constance E. *language educator, piano teacher*

TENNESSEE

Jackson
Agee, Nelle Hulme *retired art history educator*

Jefferson City
Hodges, Mary Bozeman *literature educator*

Johnson City
Drinkard-Hawkshawe, Dorothy Lee *historian, educator, writer*
Schneider, Valerie Lois *speech educator*

Kingsport
Egan, Martha Avaleen *history educator, archivist, consultant*
Wolfe, Margaret Ripley *historian, educator, consultant*

Martin
Welden, Alicia Galaz-Vivar *foreign language educator*

Memphis
Caffrey, Margaret Mary *humanities educator, researcher*

Murfreesboro
Rupprecht, Nancy Ellen *historian, educator*

Nashville
Cook, Ann Jennalie *English language educator*
Risko, Victoria J. *language educator*

Seymour
Burkhart, Elvira (Jean) *language educator, music educator*

Tullahoma
Majors, Betty-Joyce Moore *genealogist, writer*

TEXAS

Austin
Corredor, Mary B. *language educator, consultant, translator*
Minault, Gail *history educator*
Williams, Diane Elizabeth *architectural historian, photographer*

Beaumont
Hawkins, Emma B. *humanities educator*

Brownsville
Soldan, Angelika *philosopher, political scientist, educator*

Bryan
Van Ouwerkerk, Anita Harrison *reading educator*

Canyon
Haraden, Mary Clyde *language educator, musician*

College Station
Ezell, Margaret J. *language educator*
McCann, Janet *language educator, poet*
Seifert, Kathryn Ann Hawkins *language educator*
Unterberger, Betty Miller *history educator, writer*

Dallas
Chawner, Lucia Martha *English educator*
Comini, Alessandra *art historian, educator*
Davis, Daisy Sidney *history educator*
Dean, Sherry Lynn *language educator, speech professional*

Denison
Rushing, Dorothy M. *retired historian, writer*

Denton
DeMoss, Dorothy Dell *historian, educator*

El Paso
Clement-Fouts, Shirley George *educational services executive*
Lujan, Rosa Emma *bilingual specialist, trainer, consultant, assistant principal, assistant principal*
Moya, Elizabeth *language educator*

Fort Worth
Robin, Clara Nell (Claire Robin) *English language educator*

Harlingen
Roberts-Parast, Ann Talbot *English and foreign language educator*

Houston
Belk, Joan Pardue *English educator*
Chance, Jane *English literature educator*
de Kanter, Ellen Ann *English and foreign language educator*
Drew, Katherine Fischer *history educator*
McEvoy-Jamil, Patricia Ann *English language educator*
Pasternak, Joanna Murray *humanities educator*
Pospisil, JoAnn *historian, archivist*
Thompson, Ewa M. *foreign language educator*
Vallbona, Rima-Gretel Rothe *foreign language educator, writer*
Wilson, Carolyn Campbell *art historian*

Kingsville
Smith, Julia Amelia *retired English language educator*

Klein
Thompson, Patricia Rather *literature educator, department chairman*

Lubbock
Angstadt, Frances Virginia *language arts and theatre arts educator*
Hurst, Mary Jane *English language educator*

Mesquite
Davis, Vivian *English language educator*

Nacogdoches
McGrath, Sylvia Wallace *historian, educator*

Odessa
Forsyth, Beverly K. *language educator, writer*
Toruño, Rhina M. *Literature educator, researcher, writer*

Port Arthur
Terrell, Janice *language educator*

San Antonio
Passty, Jeanette Nyda *English language educator, writer*
von Raffler-Engel, Walburga (Walburga Engel) *linguist, cross-cultural communications specialist, lecturer, writer*

Stephenville
Huggins, Mary Louise White *English educator, small business owner*

UTAH

Layton
Rigby, Maria Dean *interpreter, advocate*

Salt Lake City
Arrington, Harriet Ann Horne *historian, biographer, researcher, writer*

VERMONT

Castleton
Meloy, Judith Marie *humanities educator*

Craftsbury
Shambaugh, Joan Dibble *literature educator, writer*

Norwich
Carlson, Elizabeth Borden *historian, educator*

Putney
Rodgers, Joyce Ellen *humanities educator*

VIRGINIA

Arlington
Irizarry, Estelle Diane *foreign language educator, writer, editor*
Strelau, Renate *historical researcher, artist*
Wilcox, Shirley Jean Langdon *genealogist*

Blacksburg
Soniat, Katherine Thompson *English educator, poet*
Trent, Tiffany Leone *English educator, writer, editor*

Charlottesville
Chase, Karen Susan *English literature educator*
Lane, Ann Judith *history and women's studies educator*
Schutte, Anne Jacobson *historian, educator*
Spacks, Patricia Meyer *English educator*

Chester
Paden, Mary Grace Nuckols *humanities educator*

Covesville
Williams, Patricia Anne *philosopher, writer*

Fairfax
Bailey, Helen McShane *historian*
Lavine, Thelma Zeno *philosophy educator*

Farmville
Craft, Carolyn M. *English literature educator, priest, religion educator*

Fredericksburg
Nobles, Susanne Lee *language educator*

Great Falls
Castro-Klaren, Sara *Latin American literature educator*
Kagan, Constance Henderson *philosopher, educator, consultant*

Lexington
Simpson, Pamela Hemenway *art historian, educator*

Lynchburg
Bell, Carolyn Wilkerson *English educator*
Lassaletta, Antonia Mir *language educator*

Martinsville
Smith, Jean Katherine Martin *English language educator*

Mc Lean
Scribner, Sherlie Ann *language educator*

Newport News
Hurst, Rebecca McNabb *language educator*

Norfolk
Thompson, Thelma Barnaby *English educator, university dean*

Poquoson
Sommer, Deborah Kelly *language educator*

Richmond
Levit, Héloïse B. (Ginger Levit) *art historian, art dealer, art consultant, journalist*

Roanoke
Hankla, Cathy *English language educator, writer*

Stafford
Snyder, Deborah Shusman *literature educator, columnist, poet*

Sterling
Naquin, Deborah Ann *humanities educator*

Tappahannock
McGuire, Lillian (Elizabeth) Hill *historian, researcher, retired education educator, writer*

Virginia Beach
Jacobson, Frances M. *history educator*

Williamsburg
Nettels, Elsa *English language educator*
Pierce, Catherine Maynard *history educator*
Spaeth, Barbette Stanley *classics educator*

Winchester
Tisinger, Catherine Anne *history and economics educator*

WASHINGTON

Bellevue
Skillman, Judith Anne *humanities educator*

Bellingham
Murdock, Mary-Elizabeth *history educator*

Edmonds
Polikowsky, Mary Elizabeth *retired English educator*

Port Angeles
Kinney, Beverly Jean *English language educator*

Seattle
Condrea, Lydia *linguist, educator, researcher*
Gerstenberger, Donna Lorine *humanities educator*
Kaplan, Sydney Janet *English educator*
Levi, Margaret *humanities educator*
Snow-Smith, Joanne Inloes *art history educator*
So, Connie Ching *ethnic studies educator*

WEST VIRGINIA

Great Cacapon
Coe, Diana Ward (Dina Coe) *language educator, writer*

Morgantown
Blaydes, Sophia Boyatzies *English language educator*

Shepherdstown
Shurbutt, Sylvia Bailey *English language educator*

WISCONSIN

Chaseburg
Jackson, Gloria Leigh *genealogist, retired archivist*

Chippewa Falls
Schmider, Mary Ellen Heian *American studies educator, academic administrator*

Kenosha
Rothstein, Marian *humanities educator*

Madison
Brandt, Deborah *English educator*
Ciplijauskaite, Birute *humanities educator*
Dubrow, Heather *English educator*
Fowler, Barbara Hughes *classics educator*
Hutchison, Jane Campbell *art history educator, researcher*
Leavitt, Judith Walzer *history of medicine educator*
Murray, Julia Killin *art history educator*
Zell, Josephine May *retired language educator*

Milwaukee
Curtain, Helena Hambuch *foreign language specialist*
Dale, Kathleen A. *literature educator*

Gallop, Jane (Jane Anne Gallop) *women's studies educator, writer*
Lea, Filomena *English language educator, writer*
Preston, Patricia Ann *language educator, researcher*
Waldbaum, Jane Cohn *art history educator*

Neenah
Rieder, Mary Catherine (Ahern) *language educator*

Sturgeon Bay
Maher, Virginia Jones *art historian, educator*

WYOMING

Laramie
Hardy, Deborah Welles *history educator*

Sheridan
Aguirre-Batty, Mercedes *Spanish and English language and literature educator*
Wajda, Shirley Teresa *historian*

CANADA

BRITISH COLUMBIA

Sidney
Saddlemyer, Ann (Eleanor Saddlemyer) *humanities educator, critic, theater historian*

ONTARIO

Downsview
Thomas, Clara McCandless *retired English language educator, biographer*

MEXICO

Baja California Sur
Dorantes De Fischer, Diana L. *language educator*

JAPAN

Kashiwara
Hori, Keiko *English literature educator*

Shimonoseki
MacLelland, Jackie Lynn *English educator*

ADDRESS UNPUBLISHED

Abernethy, Sharron Gray *language educator*
Adamson, Lynda G. *literature educator, writer*
Allison, Carrie Frances *English language educator*
Andrade, Carolyn L. *foreign language educator*
Bates, Margaret P. *historian*
Beale, Georgia Robison *historian, educator*
Becker, Susan D. *retired history educator*
Ben-Arieh, Josefa *language educator*
Benario, Janice Martin *retired classics educator*
Bok, Sissela *philosopher, writer*
Bolsterli, Margaret Jones *English educator, farmer*
Branham, Lorraine E. *literature educator, director*
Brewster, Elizabeth Winifred *English language educator, poet, novelist*
Brown, Mary Jane *history educator*
Burrill, Kathleen R. F. (Kathleen R. F. Griffin-Burrill) *language educator*
Buyanovsky, Sophia *linguist, educator*
Calvert, Jeanne Anne *historian, educator*
Carter, Harriet Rodes *language educator*
Caswell, Frances Pratt *retired English language educator*
Cell, Gillian Townsend *historian, educator*
Cerven, Laura Kay *language educator, translator, music educator*
Chalfant-Allen, Linda Kay *retired Spanish language educator*
Chamberlain, Cara Lee *literature educator, writer*
Chambers, Marjorie Bell *historian*
Chess, Sonia Mary *retired language educator*
Clark, Eve Vivienne *linguistics educator*
Collins, Jean Katherine *English educator*
Crowley, Liska Anne *historian*
Cruikshank, Margaret Louise *humanities educator, writer*
Custureri, Mary Catherine Foca *literature educator*
Dewey, Helen Scamell *retired humanities educator*
Di Paolo, Maria Grazia *language educator, writer*
Doebler, Bettie Anne *language educator, researcher, writer*
Dyson, Anne Haas *English language educator*
Dzamba, Anne O. *history and women's studies educator*
Espenlaub, Margo Linn *women's studies educator, writer, artist*
Eustis, Jennifer Marie *language educator*
Fadley, Ann Miller *retired literature educator, literature educator*
Farmer, Ann Dahlstrom *English language educator*
Ferguson, Patricia Anne *language educator*
Fisher, Anita Jeanne (Kit Fisher) *language educator*
Geiselhart, Lorene Annetta *English language educator*

Gerlach, Jeanne Elaine *English language educator*
Gerrard, Ruth Ann *retired English educator*
Gillett, Mary Caperton *military historian*
Goldenberg, Myrna Gallant *English language/literature and Holocaust educator*
Goldstein, Phyllis Ann *art historian, educator*
Grant, Linda Hess *language educator*
Greenberg, Barbara Levenson *literature educator, poet*
Greene, Elinore Aschah *speech and drama professional, writer*
Hankin, Lisa Bush *art and architectural historian, consultant*
Haring, Ellen Stone (Mrs. E. S. Haring) *philosophy educator*
Hartman, Marilyn D. *English and art educator*
Holt-Hunter, Tracy Lynn *language educator, artist*
Huegel, Donna *historian, writer, artist, archivist*
Humphries Barker, Dedria *humanities educator*
Hutcheon, Linda Ann *English language educator*
Iskander, Sylvia Wiese *English literature educator*
Jarrow, Gail *literature educator, writer*
Kaminsky, Alice Richkin *English language educator*
Kane, Patricia Lanegran *language professional, educator*
Katz, Susan Arons *language arts specialist, author, poet*
Kerney, Yolonda V. *music historian*
Kohler, Sheila M. *humanities educator, writer*
Korsgaard, Christine Marion *philosophy educator*
Kravitz, Ellen King *musicologist, educator*
Lederer, Katherine Gay *English language educator*
Lee, Corinne Adams *retired English teacher*
Lindboe, Berit Roberg *language educator, literature educator*
Lindsey, Roberta Lewise *music researcher, historian*
Lott, Erin Elizabeth *literature educator*
Lowenthal, Constance *art historian, consultant*
Lukomsky, Vera *musicologist, pianist, music educator*
Luschnig, Cecelia Eaton *humanities educator*
Maddox, Marjorie Lee (Marjorie Lee Maddox-Hafer) *English educator*
Marinoff, Isabella Blumenstock *English educator*
Marion, Marjorie Anne *English language educator, education consultant*
Matthews, Glenna Christine *historian*
McClure, Evelyn Susan *historian, photographer*
McDaniel, Anna S. *language educator*
McDermott, Agnes Charlene Senape *philosophy educator*
McDonald, Roxanne Marie *English language educator, writer*
McGann, Lisa B. Napoli *language educator*
McLaughlin, Joan B. *literature and writing educator, writer*
McMaster, Juliet Sylvia *English language educator*
Metcalf, Pauline Cabot *architectural historian*
Mills, Elizabeth Shown *genealogist, editor, writer*
Miscella, Maria Diana *humanities educator*
Molloy, Sylvia *Latin American literature educator, writer*
Morales, Marcia Paulette Merry *language educator, archaeologist*
Morrill, Penny Chittim *art historian*
Mulcahy, Joanne B. *literature educator*
Nicholas, Lynn Holman *historian, researcher, writer*
Nochman, Lois Wood Kivi (Mrs. Marvin Nochman) *retired educator*
Novak, Barbara *art history educator*
Pallart, Cheryl *literature educator, writer*
Panzer, Mary Caroline *historian, museum curator*
Parrott, Lois Anne *humanities educator*
Paul, Julia *ancient history researcher*
Perdigó, Luisa Marina *foreign language and literature educator*
Pilon, A. Barbara *language and literature educator*
Polk, Dora Beale *literature educator*
Proctor, Betty Jane *English language and literature educator*
Ransom, Nancy Alderman *sociology and women's studies educator, university administrator*
Reciniello, Karen Mary *language educator*
Rickard, Ruth David *retired history and political science educator*
Roberts, Reba Gill *literature educator*
Robinson, Mary Elizabeth Goff *retired historian, researcher*
Rocco, Vanessa M. *art historian, curator, educator*
Ryan, Marleigh Grayer *language educator*
Salgado, Susana *musicologist, researcher, consultant*
Saveri, Francesca *humanities educator, consultant*
Sawai, Dahleen Emi *language educator*
Schadow, Karen E. *public speaking trainer/educator*
Schendel, Kelly Ryan *literature educator, writer*
Schoen, Carol Bronston *retired English language educator*
Sessions, Bettye Jean *humanities educator*
Shepard, Suzanne V. *English language educator*
Shillingsburg, Miriam Jones *English educator, academic administrator*
Sicherman, Dara *art historian, researcher*
Smith, Betty Mallett *philosopher, educator*
Stendahl, Brita Kristina *humanities educator, social studies educator*
Stokstad, Marilyn Jane *art history educator, curator*
Stone, Marilyn *foreign language educator, consultant*
Stringer, Mary Evelyn *art historian, educator*

Sullivan, Mary Rose *English language educator*
Sutton, Julia *musicologist, dance historian*
Tayler, Irene *English literature educator*
Thern, Peggy Huang *literature educator, small business owner*
Thompson, Eve Katherine *literature educator, department chairman*
Tong, Rosemarie *medical humanities and philosophy educator, consultant and researcher*
Tufte, Virginia James *humanities educator, writer*
Valencia, Margarita *Spanish language educator*
Vaz, Katherine Anne *language educator*
Vesper, Ethel Rose *language educator, consultant*
Weisert, Mary Carol *language educator*
Wheatley, Lynn Marie *humanities educator*
Wiseman, Mary Bittner *philosopher, educator*
Wizenberg, Chanah Liora *language educator, poet*
Wolff, Cynthia Griffin *humanities educator, author*
Wyatt, Marcia Jean *fine arts educator, administrative assistant*
Yates, Mildred Campbell *retired literature educator*

HUMANITIES: LIBRARIES

UNITED STATES

ALABAMA

Auburn
Havens, Carolyn Clarice *librarian*

Bay Minette
Cabaniss, Charlotte Jones *library services director*

Birmingham
Goggin, Margaret Enid (Knox) *librarian, educator*
Murrell, Susan DeBrecht *librarian*

Tuscaloosa
Dalton, Margaret Stieg *library and information sciences educator*

ARIZONA

Peoria
Bailey, Claudia Jean *retired professor, librarian, artist*

Phoenix
Anderson, Vicki *retired librarian*
Perry, Barbara Mitchell *retired librarian*
Roof, Sally Jean-Marie *library and information scientist, educator*
Wells, GladysAnn *library director*

Prescott Valley
Beck, Doris Olson *retired library media director*

Scottsdale
Dalton, Phyllis Irene *library consultant*

Sedona
Felsted, Carla Martindell *librarian, writer, editor*

Tempe
Metros, Mary Teresa *librarian*

Tucson
Griffen, Agnes Marthe *library administrator*
James, Ruby May *retired librarian*
Pintozzi, Chestalene *librarian*
Reiling, Lois Mae *librarian*

ARKANSAS

Fayetteville
Cantrell, Andrea E. *library administrator*
Prichard, Anne W.B. *librarian*

Quitman
Martindale, Carla Joy *retired librarian*

Stuttgart
Ashley-Iverson, Mary E. *retired librarian*

CALIFORNIA

Altadena
Seward, Grace Evangeline *retired librarian*

Anaheim
Sandler, Michelle Gail *librarian*

Auburn
Sanborn, Dorothy Chappell *retired librarian*

Bakersfield
Duquette, Diane Rhea *library director*
Ross, Katherine *librarian*
Rump, Marjorie *library director*

Berkeley
Minudri, Regina Ursula *librarian, consultant*

Beverly Hills
Ramser, Wanda Tene *library and information scientist, educator*

Bradbury
Ackerman, Page *retired librarian, educator*

Capitola
Hawes, Grace Maxcy *retired archivist, researcher*

Coalinga
Russell, Beverly Ann *librarian, writer*

Costa Mesa
Epstein, Susan Baerg *librarian, consultant*

Culver City
Souza, Blase Camacho *librarian, educator*

Davis
Franco, Elaine Adele *librarian*
Sharrow, Marilyn Jane *library administrator*

El Cerrito
Kao, Yasuko Watanabe *retired library administrator*

Forest Knolls
Floden, Roberta B. *librarian, columnist*

Fremont
Wood, Linda May *librarian*

Glendale
Michelson, Lillian *librarian, researcher*

Irvine
Gelfand, Julia Maureen *librarian*
Love, April Gaye McLean *librarian*

La Jolla
Mirsky, Phyllis Simon *librarian*

Lafayette
Morehouse, Valerie Jeanne *librarian*

Livermore
Love, Sandra Rae *information specialist*

Long Beach
Strait, Viola Edwina Washington *librarian*

Los Angeles
Bates, Marcia Jeanne *information scientist educator*
Ciccone, Amy Navratil *art librarian*
Kent, Susan *library director, consultant*
Werner, Gloria S. *librarian*

Los Gatos
Conaway, Margaret Grimes (Peggy Conaway) *library administrator*

Monterey
Bui-Burton, Kim Ly *library director, poet*
Reneker, Maxine Hohman *librarian*

Monterey Park
Wilson, Linda *librarian*

Mountain View
Di Muccio, Mary-Jo *retired librarian*

North Hollywood
Schlosser, Anne Griffin *librarian*

Oakland
Hafter, Ruth Anne *library director, educator*
Lee, Ella Louise *librarian, educator*
Woodbury, Marda Liggett *librarian, writer*

Orinda
Lorensen, Hilda S. *librarian*

Palmdale
Farley, Margaret Wilhelmina *librarian*

Placerville
Wickline, Marian Elizabeth *former corporate librarian*

Pollock Pines
Rickard, Margaret Lynn *retired library director*

Riverside
Auth, Judith *library director*

San Diego
Brown, Barbara Sproul *retired librarian, consultant, writer*
DiBona, Leslie Faye *librarian*

San Francisco
Bocobo-Balunsat, Dalisay *librarian, journalist*
Futch, Dorothy Helen *librarian, paralegal*
McQuown, Eloise *librarian*

San Jose
Woolls, Esther Blanche *library science educator*

San Marcos
Ciurczak, Alexis *librarian*

San Marino
Robertson, Mary Louise *archivist, art historian*

Santa Barbara
Higgins, Isabelle Jeanette *librarian*
Keator, Carol Lynne *library director*
Larsgaard, Mary Lynette *librarian, writer*
Pritchard, Sarah Margaret *library director*

Santa Clara
Hopkinson, Shirley Lois *library and information science educator*

Saratoga
Chisholm, Margaret Elizabeth *retired library education administrator*

South Pasadena
Harnsberger, Therese Coscarelli *librarian*

Spring Valley
Heinecke, Margaret Theresa *librarian*

Stanford
Derksen, Charlotte Ruth Meynink *librarian*
Gold, Anne Marie *library director*

Stockton
Foster, Colleen *library director*

Tujunga
Pozzo, Mary Lou *retired librarian, writer*

Ventura
Kreissman, Starrett *librarian*

Yorba Linda
Naulty, Susan Louise *archivist*

COLORADO

Aurora
Miller, Dorothea Helen *librarian, educator*
Miller, Sarah Pearl *librarian*

Canon City
Cochran, Susan Mills *librarian*

Denver
Dudden, Rosalind F. *librarian*
Garcia, June Marie *librarian*
Phillips, Dorothy Reid *retired medical library technician*
Smith, Sallye Wrye *librarian*
White, Joyce Louise *librarian*

Edwards
Chambers, Joan Louise *retired librarian, retired dean*

Fleming
Nichols, Lee Ann *library media specialist*

Golden
Mathews, E. Anne Jones *library educator and administrator, consultant*

Greeley
Seris, Eileen Janice *library information specialist*

Loveland
Carter, Laura Lee *academic librarian, psychotherapist*

Morrison
Neumann, Stephanie Tower *retired librarian*

New Castle
Spuhler, Jacilyn Erickson *librarian*

Pueblo
Cress, Cecile Colleen *retired librarian*

CONNECTICUT

Chester
Harwood, Eleanor Cash *librarian*

Fairfield
Bryan, Barbara Day *retired librarian*
Turetsky, Judith *librarian, researcher*

New Britain
Sohn, Jeanne *librarian*

New Haven
Okerson, Ann Shumelda Lillian *librarian*
Oliver-Warren, Mary Elizabeth *retired library science educator*

Simsbury
Roberts, Celia Ann *librarian*

Southington
Burkhardt, Dolores Ann *library consultant*

Westport
Campbell, Marta Smith *librarian*

Wilton
Poundstone, Sally Hill *library director*

DISTRICT OF COLUMBIA

Washington
Basa, Enikö Molnár *librarian*
Chin, Cecilia Hui-Hsin *librarian*
Craig, Susan Lyons *library director*
Daffron, MaryEllen *librarian*
Emperado, Mercedes Lopez *librarian*
Falk, Diane M. *research director, librarian, editor, writer*
Fifer Canby, Susan Melinda *library administrator*
Harlem, Susan Lynn *librarian*
Hedges, Kamla King *library director*
Heise, Dorothy Hilbert *librarian, government official*
Knezo, Genevieve Johanna *science and technology policy researcher*
Lofaro, Nanette *information services administrator*
Lowe, Dorothy Ann *library technician*
Marcum, Deanna Bowling *library administrator*
Meyer, Margaret Vaughan *librarian, educator*
Murphy, Kathryn Marguerite *archivist*
Player, Thelma B. *librarian*
Renninger, Mary Karen *librarian*
Rovelstad, Mathilde V(erner) *library science educator*

Thomas, Mary Augusta *library administrator*
Wand, Patricia Ann *librarian*
Wasserman, Krystyna *librarian, art historian*
Wolfskill, Mary Margaret *archivist*

FLORIDA

Boca Raton
Hayashi, Maris Lani *librarian*

Clearwater
Werner, Elizabeth Helen *librarian, language educator*

Deland
Caccamise, Genevra Louise Ball (Mrs. Alfred E. Caccamise) *retired librarian*
Ryan, Susan Magness *librarian, educator*

Destin
Deel, Frances Quinn *retired librarian*

Estero
Mayo, Kathleen Owens *librarian*

Fort Lauderdale
Hershenson, Miriam Hannah Ratner *librarian*

Fort Walton Beach
Hill, Carol Koelling *library director*

Gainesville
Brown, Myra Suzanne *university librarian*
Stipek, Kathleen *reference librarian*

Holmes Beach
Ehde, Ava Louise *librarian, educator*

Lake Worth
Gough, Carolyn Harley *library director*

Lakeland
Flekke, Mary Muriel *instructional services librarian*

Lantana
Wetherby, Ivor Lois *librarian*

Maitland
Mansson, Joan *librarian, consultant*

Naples
Hainsworth, Melody May *information professional, researcher*

Orlando
Allison, Anne Marie *retired librarian*
Hodel, Mary Anne *library director*

Palm Harbor
Jones, Winona Nigels *retired library media specialist*

Panama City
Robbins, Dorothy Ann *librarian*

Pensacola
Demars, Bonnie Macon *librarian*

Pompano Beach
Bethel, Marilyn Joyce *librarian*

Saint Petersburg
Schell, Joan Bruning *information specialist, business science librarian*

Sanibel
Allen, Patricia J. *library director*

Sarasota
Clopine, Marjorie Showers *librarian*
Hummel, Dana D. Mallett *librarian*
Pike, Nancy M. *librarian*
Retzer, Mary Elizabeth Helm *retired librarian*

Tallahassee
Hunt, Mary Alice *library science educator*
Mason, Marilyn Gell *library administrator, writer, consultant*
Robbins, Jane Borsch *library science educator, information science educator*
Sapp, Lauren B. *librarian, educator*
Thompson, Jean Tanner *retired librarian*
Zachert, Martha Jane *retired librarian*

Tampa
Harkness, Mary Lou *librarian*

West Palm Beach
Terwillegar, Jane Cusack *librarian, educator*

GEORGIA

Americus
Tietjen, Mildred Campbell *librarian, college official*

Athens
Abolins, Ruta *archivist*

Atlanta
Brown, Lorene B(yron) *retired library educator, educational administrator*
Drake, Miriam Anna *librarian, educator, writer*
Flagg Davis, Vivian Annette *librarian, researcher, public policy consultant*
McDavid, Sara June *librarian*
Wallace, Gladys Baldwin *librarian*
Yates, Ella Gaines *library consultant*

Decatur
Cravey, Pamela J. *librarian*

Macon
Preuit, Theresa *librarian*

Marietta
Bogaм, Geil Elizabeth [illegible]

Valdosta
Montgomery, Denise Lynne *librarian, researcher*

HAWAII

Hilo
Golian-Lui, Linda Marie *librarian*

Honolulu
Lee, Pali Jae (Polly Jae Stead Lee) *retired librarian, writer*
Lowell, Virginia Lee *librarian*
Preble, Sarah Hamilton *art librarian, author, writer*
Spencer, Caroline *retired library director*
Weingand, Darlene Erna *librarian educator, consultant*

Kahului
Tolliver, Dorothy *librarian*

ILLINOIS

Bloomington
Olson, Rue Eileen *retired librarian*

Carbondale
Bauner, Ruth Elizabeth *library administrator, reference librarian*
Koch, Loretta Peterson *librarian, educator*

Carol Stream
O'Dell, Lynn Marie Luegge (Mrs. Norman D. O'Dell) *librarian*

Caseyville
Stanford, Diana L. *librarian*

Chicago
Bodi, Sonia Ellen *library director, educator*
Choldin, Marianna Tax *librarian, educator*
Davis, Mary Ellen K. *library director*
Dempsey, Mary A. *library commissioner, lawyer*
Funk, Carla Jean *library association executive*
Hanrath, Linda Carol *librarian, archivist*
Kim, Charlotte Chung-Sook *retired librarian, administrator*
Maloy, Frances *librarian*
Parr, Virginia Helen *retired librarian*
Sullivan, Peggy (Peggy Anne Sullivan) *librarian, consultant*
Vondruska, Eloise Marie *librarian*

Downers Grove
Saricks, Joyce Goering *librarian*

Evanston
Bjorncrantz, Leslie Benton *librarian*
Cates, Jo Ann *library administrator, writer*
Crawford, Susan *library director, educator, writer*
Taraki, Shirlee *librarian*

Glen Ellyn
Hoornbeek, Lynda Ruth Couch *librarian, educator*

La Grange
Vernerder, Gloria Jean *retired librarian*

Maywood
Ellington, Mildred L. *librarian*

Moline
Curry, Kathleen Bridget *retired librarian*

Naperville
Pope, Kathleen Marie *library director*

Riverside
Van Cura, Joyce Bennett *librarian*

Rochester
Petterchak, Janice A. *researcher, writer*

Schaumburg
Adrianopoli, Barbara Catherine *librarian*

Skokie
Breckel, Alvina Hefeli *librarian*

Springfield
Kaige, Alice Tubb *retired librarian*

Urbana
O'Brien, Nancy Patricia *librarian, educator*
Watson, Paula D. *library administrator*
Woodard, Beth Stuckey *librarian, educator*

Wheaton
Tucker, Beverly Sowers *information specialist*

Wheeling
Long, Sarah Ann *librarian*

INDIANA

Austin
Lacy, Dona Paulette *librarian, writer*

Evansville
Tannenbaum, Karen Jean *library services supervisor*

Indianapolis
Allen, Joyce Smith *librarian*
Oldham, Phyllis Virginia Kidd *retired librarian*

Kokomo
MacKay, Gail *librarian*

Lafayette
McKown, Dorothy Keeton *librarian, educator, consultant*
Mobley, Emily Ruth *library dean, educator*

Muncie
Kroehler, Beth Ann *librarian*
Schaefer, Patricia *librarian*

New Harmony
Feiner, Arlene Marie *librarian, researcher, consultant*

Notre Dame
Stevenson, Marsha Joan *librarian*

Tipton
Hurst, Laurenda Lee *library director, music educator*

Valparaiso
Brown, Elizabeth A. *librarian, multi-media specialist*

West Lafayette
Anderson, Kristine Jo *librarian*
Andrews, Theodora Anne *retired librarian, educator*
Markee, Katherine Madigan *librarian, educator*
Nixon, Judith May *librarian*

IOWA

Ames
Hill, Fay Gish *retired librarian*

Des Moines
Isenstein, Laura *library director*
Runge, Kay Kretschmar *library director*

Kalona
Skaden, Anne Marie *library director*

Mason City
Iverson, Carol Jean *retired library media specialist*

Prairie City
Buckingham, Betty Jo *library media consultant*

West Branch
Mather, Mildred Eunice *retired archivist*

KANSAS

Clay Center
Bachand, Alice Jeanne *school library media specialist*

Lawrence
Fredrickson, Karen Loraine *librarian*

Olathe
Nightingale, Susie *librarian*

Wichita
Berner Harris, Cynthia Kay *librarian*
Woolf, Amy Kaspar *librarian, storyteller*

KENTUCKY

Cynthiana
Ellis, E. Susan *library director, lay mminister*

La Grange
Morgan, Mary Dan *librarian*

Louisville
Niles, Judith F. *librarian*

Madisonville
Kemp, Ann *retired librarian*

Summer Shade
Smith, Ruby Lucille *retired librarian*

LOUISIANA

Baton Rouge
Hayward, Olga Loretta Hines (Mrs. Samuel Ellsworth Hayward) *retired librarian*
Lane, Margaret Beynon Taylor *librarian*
Lusk, Glenna Rae Knight (Mrs. Edwin Bruce Lusk) *librarian*
Thomason, Norma Jean *librarian*

Kenner
Duplessis, Sandra Walsh *librarian, educator*

Lafayette
Carstens, Jane Ellen *retired library science educator*

Lake Charles
Curol, Helen Ruth *librarian, English language educator*

New Iberia
Garcia, Susan Breaux *multi-media specialist, consultant*

New Orleans
Arceneaux, Pamela Davis *librarian*
Jumonville, Florence M. *librarian, historian*
Mangipano, Adele C. *librarian, educator*

Schriever
Shaffer, Margaret Minor *retired library director*

MAINE

Bangor
Rea, Ann W. *librarian*

Camden
Moran, Elizabeth Ames *library director*

Gardiner
Nowell, Glenna Greely *librarian, consultant, city manager*

Nobleboro
Fisher, Ellen Roop *retired librarian, educator*

Waterville
Muehlner, Suanne Wilson *library director*

MARYLAND

Annapolis
Dewar, Mildred Jo Eller (Mrs. Donald Norman Dewar) *librarian*

Ashton
Tabler, Shirley May *retired librarian, artist*

Baltimore
Allen, Norma Ann *librarian, educator*
Bradley, Wanda Louise *librarian*
Leonard, Angela Michele *librarian, educator*
Magnuson, Nancy *librarian*
Massey-Burzio, Virginia *librarian, writer*
White, Libby Kramer *librarian*

Bel Alton
Quesada-Embid, Mary Regina Chamberlain *library media specialist*

Bethesda
Humphreys, Betsy L. *librarian*

California
Avram, Henriette Davidson *librarian, government official*

Chestertown
Rather, Lucia Porcher Johnson *library administrator*

Columbia
Gruhl, Andrea Morris *librarian*
Klein, Sami Weiner *librarian*

Greenbelt
Hogensen, Margaret Hiner *librarian, consultant*

Leonardtown
Rudigier, Roberta Lynn *librarian*

Rockville
Henderson, Harriet *librarian*
Kohlhorst, Gail Lewis *librarian*

Silver Spring
Flug, Janice *librarian*
Null, Elisabeth Higgins *librarian, writer*

Takoma Park
von Hake, Margaret Joan *librarian*

Upper Marlboro
Rough, Marianne Christina *librarian, educator*

MASSACHUSETTS

Amesbury
Dowd, Frances Connelly *retired librarian*

Boston
Chen, Ching-chih *information science educator, consultant*
Christopher, Irene *librarian, consultant*
Desnoyers, Megan Floyd *archivist, educator*
Kowal, Ruth Elizabeth *library administrator*
Loscalzo, Anita Beth *librarian*
Preece, Barbara G. *librarian*
von Fettweis, Yvonne Caché *archivist, historian*

Cambridge
Cole, Heather Ellen *librarian*
Flannery, Susan Marie *library administrator*
Koepp, Donna Pauline Petersen *librarian*

Chestnut Hill
Grove, Shari Taylor *librarian, educator*

Cohasset
Husband, Janet Grace *library director, writer*

Fall River
Sullivan, Ruth Anne *librarian*

Fitchburg
Sugrue, Teresa Gillis *multi-media specialist, secondary school educator*

Lexington
Davis, Barbara M(ae) *librarian*

Marstons Mills
Martin, Susan Katherine *librarian*

Mill River
Jaffe, Katharine Weisman *retired librarian*

Monson
De Santis, Sylvia *library director*

Newton
Glick-Weil, Kathy *library director*

Sheffield
Young, Susan Babson *retired library director*

South Hadley
Clancy, Marguerite Aline (Meg Clancy) *librarian*
Scanlon, Gail Gretchen *librarian, nurse*

Springfield
Stack, May Elizabeth *library director*

Waltham
Hahn, Bessie King *library administrator, lecturer*
Preve, Roberta Jean *librarian, researcher*

Woburn
O'Doherty, Kathleen Marie *library director*

Worcester
Dunlap, Ellen S. *library administrator*

MICHIGAN

Allendale
Murray, Diane Elizabeth *librarian*

Ann Arbor
Beaubien, Anne Kathleen *librarian*
Daub, Peggy Ellen *library administrator*
Dede, Bonnie Aileen *librarian, educator*
Dunlap, Connie *librarian*

Battle Creek
Lincoln, Margaret *library media specialist*

Clinton
Scott, Sharon Ann *retired librarian, archivist*

Detroit
Ashley, Lois A. *retired university reference librarian*
Sutton, Lynn Sorensen *librarian*

Farmington Hills
Papai, Beverly Daffern *library director*

Holt
Smith, Betty W. *librarian*

Interlochen
Tacke, Eleanor *archivist*

Kalamazoo
Grotzinger, Laurel Ann *librarian, educator*
Pinkham, Eleanor Humphrey *retired university librarian*

Livonia
Emerson, Carol Marie *librarian*

Monroe
Carlen, Sister Claudia *librarian, consultant*

Mount Pleasant
Smallwood, Carol *librarian, writer*

Owosso
Bentley, Margaret Ann *librarian*

Port Huron
Miller, Theresa L. *library director*

Redford
Karpinski, Huberta Elaine *library trustee*

MINNESOTA

Hopkins
Young, Margaret Labash *librarian, information consultant, editor*

Minneapolis
Johnson, Margaret Ann (Peggy) *library administrator*

Rochester
Nienow, Beth Marie *librarian*

Saint Paul
Wagner, Mary Margaret *library and information science educator*
Zietlow, Ruth Ann *reference librarian*

Thief River Falls
Jauquet-Kalinoski, Barbara *library director*

Winona
Sullivan, Kathryn Ann *librarian, educator*

Zumbrota
Post, Diana Constance *retired librarian*

MISSISSIPPI

Brandon
Bishop, Faira Lee *library educator*

Calhoun City
Macon, Myra Faye *retired library director*

Columbus
Nawrocki, Susan Jean *librarian*

Itta Bena
Henderson, Robbye Robinson *library director*

Jackson
Smith, Sharman Bridges *former state librarian*

Mississippi State
Delgado, Marica LaDonne *librarian, educator*

Sunflower
Powell, Anice Carpenter *retired librarian*

Tupelo
Radojcsics, Anne Parsons *librarian*

MISSOURI

Canton
Howe, Sandra Jo *library director*

Chesterfield
Landram, Christina Louella *librarian*

Columbia
Alexander, Martha Sue *retired librarian*

Greenwood
Zeller, Marilyn Kay *retired librarian*

Jefferson City
Fues, Marianne Cole *multi-media specialist*
Parker, Sara Ann *librarian, consultant*

Kansas City
Spalding, Helen H. *library director*
Thomas, Marcia Markowitz *library director, educator*
Welles, Ferne Bingham Malcolm *retired archivist*

Monett
Cooke, Bette Louise *retired library director*

Parkville
Schultis, Gail Ann *library director*

Pleasant Valley
Nelson, Freda Nell Hein *librarian*

Saint Charles
Reed, Warlene Patricia *retired librarian*

Saint Joseph
Schneider, Julia *library director*

Saint Louis
Holt, Leslie Edmonds *librarian*
Kohnen, Carol Ann *librarian*
Lauenstein, Ann Gail *librarian*
McDonald, Brenda Denise *librarian*
Reilly, Catherine Herbert *librarian, educator*

Springfield
Bohnenkamper, Katherine Elizabeth *library science educator*
Busch, Annie *library director*

MONTANA

Billings
Garvey, Arlene P. *library media specialist*

Great Falls
Schmidt, Rita *retired library media specialist*

Helena
Fitzpatrick, Lois Ann *library administrator*
Schlesinger, Deborah Lee *librarian*
Strege, Karen *library director*

NEBRASKA

Lincoln
Connor, Carol J. *library director*

NEVADA

Carson City
Jones, Sara Sue Fisher *librarian*

Henderson
Derner, Carol A. *retired librarian*

Las Vegas
Honsa, Vlasta *retired librarian*

NEW HAMPSHIRE

Berlin
Doherty, Katherine Mann *librarian, writer*

Exeter
Thomas, Jacquelyn May *librarian*

Hanover
Otto, Margaret Amelia *librarian*

Londonderry
Ballard, Susan Doyon *library director*

Marlow
McCracken, Linda *librarian, commercial artist*

Newmarket
Getchell, Sylvia Fitts *librarian*

Temple
Weston, Priscilla Atwood *library director*

NEW JERSEY

Brielle
McIntyre, Elizabeth Jones *multi-media specialist, educator*

Budd Lake
Hilbert, Rita L. *librarian*

Caldwell
Randall, Lynn Ellen *librarian*

Emerson
Hannon, Patricia Ann *library director*

Fort Lee
Altomara, Rita Ecke *library director, writer*

Glassboro
Martin, Marilyn Joan *library director*

Haledon
Dougherty, June Eileen *librarian*

Highland Park
Coughlin, Caroline Mary *librarian, educator, director*

Hopewell
Baeckler, Virginia Van Wynen *librarian*

Laurel Springs
Cleveland, Susan Elizabeth *library administrator, researcher*

Leonia
Berliner, Barbara *retired librarian, consultant*

Lindenwold
Clarke, Betty Ann *librarian, minister*

Livingston
Sikora, Barbara Jean *library director*

Monmouth Junction
Lawton, Deborah Simmons *library director, educational media specialist*

Monroe
Post, JoAnn Jesson *librarian*

Montclair
McConnell, Lorelei Catherine *retired library director*

New Brunswick
Turock, Betty Jane *library and information science educator*

Nutley
Tropiano, JoAnn Alma *librarian, library director*

Princeton
Fox, Mary Ann Williams *librarian*

Rockaway
Kelsey, Ann Lee *library administrator*

Roselle
Riley, Barbara Polk *retired librarian*

Sewell
Crocker, June Lopez *library director*

Succasunna
Romance, Mary C. *library director*

Toms River
Matteo, Christine E. *librarian*

Trenton
Russell, Joyce Anne Rogers *librarian*

Union
Darden, Barbara S. *library director*

Upper Montclair
Cass, Mary Louise *librarian*

NEW MEXICO

Albuquerque
Freeman, Patricia Elizabeth *library and education specialist*
Seiser, Virginia *librarian*
Snell, Patricia Poldervaart *librarian, consultant*
Wilkinson, Frances Catherine *librarian, educator*

Carlsbad
Regan Gossage, Muriel *librarian*

Farmington
Mathers, Margaret *reference librarian, archivist*

Gallup
Fellin, Octavia Antoinette *retired librarian, historical researcher*
Mouttet, Jane Elizabeth *librarian*

Los Alamos
Orndoff, Elizabeth Carlson *retired junior college librarian, educator*

Ruidoso
Ayers, Kathy Venita Moore *librarian*

NEW YORK

Albany
Van Nortwick, Barbara Louise *library director*

Bayside
Stoyan, Hortensia Rodríguez-Sánchez *library administrator*

Beechhurst
Wingate, Constance Blandy *librarian*

Brightwaters
Kavanagh, Eileen J. *librarian*

Bronx
Ostrow, Rona Lynn *librarian, educator*
Skurdenis, Juliann Veronica *librarian, educator, writer, editor*

Brooklyn
Bostic, Mary Jones *librarian*
Hill, Leda Katherine *librarian*

Langstaff, Eleanor Marguerite *retired library science educator*
Lehner-Quam, Alison Lynn *library administrator*
Moore, Jane Ross *librarian, educator*
Stukes, Geraldine Hargro *library and information scientist, educator*

Buffalo
De La Tierra, Tatiana *librarian, writer*
Hopkins, Judith *librarian*
Kreizman-Reczek, Karen Ingrid *librarian*

Chautauqua
Yurth, Helene Louise *librarian*

East Northport
Mateer, Anne Frances *multi-media specialist, elementary school educator*

Geneva
Harkness, Mabel Gleason *retired librarian*

Greenport
Richland, Lisa *library director*

Hempstead
Freese, Melanie Louise *librarian, educator, assistant dean*

Ithaca
Perry, Margaret *librarian, writer*

Jamaica
Becker, Nancy Jane *information science educator*
Vellucci, Sherry Lynn *library and information science educator*

Mamaroneck
Merskey-Zeger, Marie Gertrude Fine *retired librarian*

Manlius
Gray, Judith A. *retired school librarian, educator*

Massapequa
Kappenberg, Marilyn Kascius *library director*

Mineola
Hammer, Deborah Marie *librarian, paralegal*

Monroe
Gocek, Matilda Arkenbout (Mrs. John A. Gocek) *librarian*

Morrisville
Weiler, Angela M. *librarian, writer*

Mount Vernon
Griffith, Katherine Scott *librarian*

New York
Balaban, Vivian *librarian, elementary school educator*
Berger, Pearl *library director*
Brewer, Karen *librarian*
Browar, Lisa Muriel *librarian*
Cohen, Selma *reference librarian, researcher*
Hewitt, Vivian Ann Davidson (Mrs. John Hamilton Hewitt Jr.) *retired librarian*
Johnston, Diane Miller *librarian*
LoSchiavo, Linda Bosco *library director*
Lubetski, Edith Esther *librarian*
Mackey, Patricia Elaine *university librarian*
Margalith, Helen Margaret *retired librarian*
Miller, Barbara Kenton *retired librarian*
Root, Nina J. *librarian, writer*
Slawsky, Donna Susan *librarian, singer*

Norwood
Musante, Patricia W. *library director*

Orchard Park
Greenwood, Audrey Gates *retired librarian*

Piermont
Brechtel, Unda Jurka *library director*

Queens Village
Heckman, Lucy T. *librarian*

Rochester
Palvino, Nancy Mangin *retired librarian*
Swanton, Susan Irene *retired library director*

Saranac Lake
Cooper, Susan Lee Gensel *institutional advancement administrator*

Scarborough
Stigall, Phyllis Graham *retired librarian*

West Point
Watson, Georgianna *librarian*

White Plains
Scott-Williams, Wendy Lee *information technology specialist*

NORTH CAROLINA

Asheville
Boyce, Emily Stewart *retired library and information science educator*
Stockdale, Kay Little *librarian*

Chapel Hill
Moran, Barbara Burns *librarian, educator*
Orr, Adriana Pannevis *retired librarian*

Charlotte
Welch, Jeanie Maxine *librarian*

Cove City
Hawkins, Elinor Dixon (Mrs. Carroll Woodard Hawkins) *retired librarian*

Fayetteville
Ross, Bernadette Marie-Teresa *librarian*

Greensboro
Kovacs, Beatrice *library studies educator*

Hillsborough
Stephens, Brenda Wilson *librarian*

New Bern
White, Rhea Amelia *information scientist, consciousness researcher*

Oxford
Dorton, Louise *library director*

Pembroke
Sexton, Jean Elizabeth *librarian*

Wake Forest
Jerose, Terese M.J. *librarian*

Winton
Williams, Sue Darden *library director*

NORTH DAKOTA

Bismarck
Ott, Doris Ann *librarian*

Grand Forks
Harken, Shelby Elaine *librarian*

Mayville
Karaim, Betty June *retired librarian*

Valley City
Fischer, Mary Elizabeth *library director*

OHIO

Ada
Herr, Sharon Marie *librarian*

Alliance
Clem, Harriet Frances *library director*

Bowling Green
Singer, Carol Ann *librarian, researcher*

Cadiz
Thompson, Sandra Lee *library administrator*

Canton
Kilcullen, Maureen *librarian, educator*

Cincinnati
Bestehorn, Ute Wiltrud *retired librarian*
Brestel, Mary Beth *librarian*
Church, Sonia Jane Shutter *librarian*
Everett, Karen Joan *retired librarian, genealogist, educator*
Everson, Jean Watkins Dolores *librarian, media consultant, educator*
Schutzius, Lucy Jean *retired librarian*
Wellington, Jean Susorney *librarian*

Cleveland
Thornton, Glenda Ann *librarian*

Columbus
Donovan, Maureen Hildegarde *librarian, educator*
Meredith, Meri Hill *reference librarian, educator*
Sawyers, Elizabeth Joan *librarian, administrator*

Dayton
Klinck, Cynthia Anne *library director*

Delaware
Schlichting, Catherine Fletcher Nicholson *librarian, educator*

Dublin
Baker, Mary Evelyn *retired librarian*
Meyer, Betty Jane *former librarian*
Rhoades, Nancy Lybarger *retired librarian*

Eaton
Kendall, Susan Haines *library director*

Elyria
Bonnell-Mihalis, Pamela Gay *library director*

Hubbard
Trucksis, Theresa A. *retired library director*

Kent
Kristof, Cindy *librarian, educator*

Lucasville
Crotty, Ladonna Deane *librarian*

Lyndhurst
Packer, Diana *retired reference librarian*

Middleburg Heights
Maciuszko, Kathleen Lynn *librarian, educator*

Northfield
Sleeman, Mary (Mrs. John Paul Sleeman) *retired librarian*

Oberlin
Greenberg, Eva Mueller *librarian*

Oregon
Poad, Flora Virginia *retired librarian and educator, retired elementary school educator*

Oxford
Presnell, Jenny Lynn *librarian*
Sessions, Judith Ann *librarian, university library dean*

Pemberville
King, Laura Jane *librarian, genealogist*

Springfield
Beatty, Betty Joy *library educator*

Tiffin
Hillmer, Margaret Patricia *library director*

Toledo
Wolter, Virginia Lynn *librarian*

Wickliffe
Fisher, Nancy DeButts *library director*

Youngstown
Tyson, Edith Slosson *retired librarian, writer*

OKLAHOMA

Adair
Notley, Thelma A. *retired librarian, educator*

Chickasha
Cook, Catharine *library director*

Muskogee
Hilbern, Sandra J. *library director*

Norman
Carroll, Frances Laverne *librarian, educator*
Kemp, Betty Ruth *retired librarian*
Lester, June *library information studies educator*
Sherman, Mary Angus *public library administrator*

Welling
Varner, Joyce Ehrhardt *retired librarian*

OREGON

Beaverton
Pond, Patricia Brown *library science educator, university administrator*

Corvallis
Chau, May Ying *librarian, educator*
Landers, Teresa Price *librarian*

Portland
Cooper, Ginnie *library director*

Seaside
Bishop, Virginia Wakeman *retired librarian and humanities educator, small business owner*

PENNSYLVANIA

Allentown
Sacks, Patricia Ann *librarian, consultant*

Altoona
Kinney, Janis Marie *librarian, consultant*

Berwyn
Langford, Linda Kosmin *library consultant*

Bryn Mawr
Fletcher, Marjorie Amos *librarian*

Butler
Day, Margaret Ann *research librarian, information specialist*

Clarion
Miller, Andrea Lynn *library science educator*

Doylestown
Waite, Frances W. *librarian, professional genealogist*
Wolfinger, Audrey Jane *retired librarian*

Du Bois
Williams, Kathryn Blake *retired librarian*

Greensburg
Duck, Patricia Mary *librarian*

Havertown
Hoffman, Elizabeth Parkinson *librarian*

Kingsley
McNabb, Corrine Radtke *librarian*

Lock Haven
Chang, Shirley Lin (Hsiu-Chu Chang) *librarian, educator*

Malvern
Dolores, Fidishun *librarian, educator*

Mansfield
Donahue, Martha *librarian, educator, retired*

Monroeville
Kennedy, Kathy Kay *library director*

New Holland
Fanus, Pauline Rife *librarian*

New Wilmington
Bolger, Dorita Yvonne Ferguson *librarian*

Philadelphia
Barnett-Stewart, Barbara Anne *library catalog technician, writer*
Cole, C. Suzanne *librarian*
Gendron, Michèle Marguerite Madeleine *librarian*
Lane, Laura Alice *librarian*

Pittsburgh
Collins, Sandra Ann *librarian*

Wohleber, Lynne Farr *archivist, librarian*
Yourison, Karola Maria *librarian services professional*

Plymouth
Castner, Deborah A. *librarian*

Punxsutawney
Dinsmore, Roberta Joan Maier *library director*

Riegelsville
Banko, Ruth Caroline *retired library director*

University Park
Eaton, Nancy Ruth Linton *librarian, dean*
Hamburger, Susan *librarian*
Kellerman, Lydia Suzanne (Sue) *librarian*
MacEwan, Bonnie *librarian*

Villanova
Olsen, Judith Johnson *reference librarian*

Yardley
Soultoukis, Donna Zoccola *library director*

York
Lloyd, June Burk *librarian, archivist*

RHODE ISLAND

Jamestown
Logan, Nancy Allen *library media specialist*

Kingston
Caldwell, Naomi Rachel *library and information scientist, educator*
Gilton, Donna Louise *library and information scientist, educator*

Middletown
Ottaviano, Doris Baginski *librarian*

Riverside
Schwegler, Nancy Ann *librarian, writer*

Warwick
Charette, Sharon Juliette *library administrator*

SOUTH CAROLINA

Beaufort
Moussatos, Martha Ann Tyree *librarian*

Bluffton
Cann, Sharon Lee *retired health science librarian*

Charleston
Buvinger, Jan *library director*

Columbia
Duggan, Carol Cook *research director*
Griffin, Mary Frances *retired library media consultant*
Paulson-Crawford, Carol *conservator, educator*
Rawlinson, Helen Ann *librarian*
Washington, Nancy Jane Hayes *librarian*
Zimmerman, Nancy Picciano *library science educator*

Hardeeville
Kadar, Karin Patricia *librarian*

Orangeburg
Thompson, Marguerite Myrtle Graming (Mrs. Ralph B. Thompson) *librarian*

SOUTH DAKOTA

Freeman
Koller, Berneda Joleen *library administrator*

Sioux Falls
Thompson, Ronelle Kay Hildebrandt *library director*

TENNESSEE

Chattanooga
McFarland, Jane Elizabeth *librarian*

Collegedale
Bennett, Peggy Elizabeth *librarian, library director, educator*

Franklin
Douglass, Dorris Callicott *librarian, historian, genealogist*

Knoxville
Cottrell, Jeannette Elizabeth *retired librarian*
Drumheller, Janet Louise *librarian*
Earl, Martha Frances *librarian, researcher*
Felder-Hoehne, Felicia Harris *librarian*
Watson, Patricia L. *library director*

Memphis
Drescher, Judith Altman *library director*

Nashville
Lyle, Virginia Reavis *retired archivist, genealogist*
Wilson, Carolyn Taylor *librarian*

Sewanee
Watson, Gail H. *retired librarian*

Sparta
Young, Olivia Knowles *retired librarian*

Strawberry Plains
Snodderly, Louise Davis *librarian*

TEXAS

Abilene
Specht, Alice Wilson *university libraries dean*

Aledo
Rowe, Sheryl Ann *librarian*

Arlington
Burson, Betsy Lee *librarian*

Austin
Bingham, Ouita Hyams *librarian*
Branch, Brenda Sue *library director*
Covington, Veronica Pro *librarian, educator*
Morrow, Sandra Kay *librarian*

Brownwood
Roby, Annie Beth Brian *librarian*

Cedar Hill
Hickman, Traphene Parramore *retired library director, storyteller, library and library building consultant*

Cedar Park
Lam, Pauline Poha *library director*

Channing
Brian, Mary H. *librarian*

Corpus Christi
Erwin, Linda McIntosh *librarian, consultant*

Dallas
Howell, Bradley Sue *librarian*

Denton
Nichols, Margaret Irby *librarian, educator, library and information scientist*
Poole, Eva Duraine *librarian*
Snapp, Elizabeth *librarian, educator*

El Paso
Gardner, Kerry Ann *librarian*

Fort Davis
Gadberry, Vicki Lynn Himes *librarian*

Fort Worth
Allmand, Linda F(aith) *retired library director*
Miller, Carol Lynn *librarian*
Scholl, Belinda K. *librarian*

Georgetown
Ramsey, Margie *librarian*

Grand Prairie
Ritterhouse, Kathy Lee *librarian*

Houston
Hornak, Anna Frances *library administrator*
Scarbrough, Sara Eunice *librarian, archivist, consultant*
Strommer, Anne Elizabeth Rivard *retired librarian*

Irving
Sherlock, Jo Anne C. *librarian*

Kingsville
Beach, Regina Lee *librarian*

Laredo
Weber, Janice Ann *library director, grant writer*

Lufkin
Harmon, Jacqueline Baas *librarian, infosystems specialist*

Marshall
Magrill, Rose Mary *library director*

Mesquite
Duncan, Donna Jean *librarian, educator*

Round Rock
Ricklefs, Dale Lynne *library director*

San Angelo
Chatfield, Mary Van Abshoven *librarian*
Richardson, Shirley R. *librarian*

San Antonio
Bowden, Virginia Massey *librarian*
Brewster, Olive Nesbitt *retired librarian*
Godin, Christine C. *library director*
Hood, Sandra Dale *librarian*
Nance, Betty Love *librarian*
Newton, Virginia *archivist, historian, librarian*

San Benito
Cavazos, Ana A. *librarian*

Somerset
Holder, Linda Kay *librarian*

Tyler
Cleveland, Mary Louise *librarian, media specialist*

Van Alstyne
Hazelton, Juanita Louise *librarian*

Waco
Hillman, Kathy Robinson *librarian*
Roberts, Betty Jo *retired librarian, speech therapist*

Whitehouse
Brewer, Edith Gay *librarian, educator*

UTAH

Riverside
Reveal, Arlene Hadfield *retired librarian, consultant*

Salt Lake City
Owen, Amy *library director*

VERMONT

Peacham
Scott, Jutta R. *retired librarian*

Vergennes
Sandy, Catherine Ellen *librarian*

VIRGINIA

Alexandria
Berger, Patricia Wilson *retired librarian*
Cross, Dorothy Abigail *retired librarian*

Assawoman
Holley, Pamela Spencer *retired librarian*

Chesapeake
Stillman, Margaret D. *library director*

Danville
Fountain, Clara Garrett *archivist, librarian*

Dumfries
Gaudet, Jean Ann *retired librarian, educator*

Harrisonburg
Swope, Frances Alderson *retired librarian*

Hudgins
Story, Martha vanBeuren *retired librarian*

Lexington
Krantz, Linda Law *librarian*

Lynchburg
Schwedt, Rachel Elaine *librarian*

Newport News
Boykin, Amy Williams *librarian*

Poquoson
Tai, Elizabeth Shi-Jue Lee *library director*

Richmond
Parke, Carol Reeves *retired librarian*
Treadway, Sandra Gioia *library director*

Staunton
Arnold, Ruth Southgate *librarian*

Virginia Beach
Sims, Martha J. *library director*

WASHINGTON

Longbranch
Ehrhardt, Margaret Wright *retired librarian*

Olympia
Hutchins, Diane Elizabeth Rider *librarian*
Kells, Kari Joy *indexer, librarian*
Zussy, Nancy Louise *librarian*

Port Townsend
Wallin, Madge Marie *retired librarian, musician*

Seattle
Blase, Nancy Gross *librarian*
Fidel, Raya *library science educator*
Greggs, Elizabeth May Bushnell (Mrs. Raymond John Greggs) *retired librarian*
Jacobs, Deborah L. *librarian*
Pearl, Nancy Linn *librarian*
Stroup, Elizabeth Faye *librarian*

Spokane
Bender, Betty Wion *librarian*

Tacoma
Crisman, Mary Frances Borden *librarian*

WEST VIRGINIA

Huntington
Pratt, Mary Louise *librarian, writer*

Shepherdstown
Elliott, Jean Ann *librarian emeritus*

WISCONSIN

Appleton
Richards, Susan Lynne *library director*

Eau Claire
Tiefel, Virginia May *librarian*

Franklin
Roark, Barbara Ann *librarian*

Madison
Blankenburg, Julie J. *librarian*
Kim, Kyung-Sun *library and information scientist, educator*
Korenic, Lynette Marie *librarian*

Menomonie
Lueder, Dianne Carol *library director*

Milwaukee
Huston, Kathleen Marie *library administrator*

Patch Grove
Wadding, Tonia J. *multi-media specialist*

Waunakee
King, Judith Marie *librarian, educator*

WYOMING

Cheyenne
Boughton, Lesley D. *library director*

TERRITORIES OF THE UNITED STATES

AMERICAN SAMOA

Pago Pago
Fung-Chen-Pen, Emma Talauna Solaita *librarian, program director*

PUERTO RICO

Mayaguez
Rodriguez, Grisell *librarian, educator*

CANADA

BRITISH COLUMBIA

Vancouver
Piternick, Anne Brearley *librarian, educator*

NOVA SCOTIA

Halifax
Dykstra Lynch, Mary Elizabeth *library and information science educator*

ONTARIO

Ottawa
Scott, Marianne M.......... *librarian, educator*

Toronto
Bryant, Josephine Harriet *library executive*
Corman, Linda Wilson *librarian*
Moore, Carole Irene *librarian*

SASKATCHEWAN

Saskatoon
Kennedy, Marjorie Ellen *librarian*

CZECH REPUBLIC

Prague
Turková, Helga *library director*

MALDIVES

Male
Habeeb, Habeeba Hussain *library director*

ADDRESS UNPUBLISHED

Alday, Marta Perdomo *library technology consultant, media consultant, art dealer*
Allen, Victoria Taylor *archivist*
Anderson, Mary Jane *public library consultant*
Anderson, Rachael Keller *retired library administrator*
Ariens, Karla Rae *library director*
Balog, Rita Jean *retired librarian*
Barker, Hilda Jean *retired library director*
Bartelli, Alice Hill *librarian, secondary education educator*
Battin, Patricia Meyer *librarian*
Blackburn, Joy Martin *librarian*
Bloxom, Marguerite Doris *bibliographer*
Bogie, Lana Cecil *librarian*
Bowen, Jean *retired librarian, consultant*
Brady, Jean Stein *retired librarian*
Brakel, Lisa Elaine *multi-media specialist*
Brooks Shoemaker, Virginia Lee *librarian*
Bullard, Sharon Welch *librarian*
Callard, Carole Crawford *librarian, educator*
Cammack, Ann *librarian, secondary school educator*
Cannon, Patricia Althen *librarian, writer*
Carpenter, Janella Ann *retired librarian*
Clement, Hope Elizabeth Anna *retired librarian*
Cochran, Carolyn *library director*
Crabb, Virginia Geany Ruth *librarian*
Crenshaw, Tena Lula *librarian*
Daubenas, Jean Dorothy Tenbrinck *librarian, educator*
DeMita, Geraldine *librarian*
Domzella, Janet *retired library director*
Drayson, Pamela K. *library director*
Edmonds, Anne Carey *librarian*
Elder, Mary Louise *librarian*
Else, Carolyn Joan *retired library director*
Elwood-Akers, Virginia Edythe *retired librarian, archivist*

Estes, Elaine Rose Graham *retired librarian*
Euster, Joanne Reed *retired librarian*
Fasick, Adele Mongan *information services consultant*
Ford, Barbara Jean *library studies educator*
Foster, Joy Via *retired library media specialist*
Funk, Vicki Jane *librarian*
Giebel, Miriam Catherine *librarian, genealogist*
Gould, Martha Bernice *retired librarian*
Gray, Gloria Meador *librarian*
Gray, Patricia B. *retired librarian, information specialist*
Greenberg, Hinda Feige *library director*
Gregor, Dorothy Deborah *retired librarian*
Gross, Dorothy-Ellen *library director, educator*
Habich, Elizabeth Chamberlain *librarian*
Hazekamp, Phyllis Wanda Alberts *retired library director*
Heanue, Anne Allen *retired librarian*
Hebert, Mary Olivia *retired librarian*
Hempleman, Barbara Florence *archivist*
Hertzel, Dorothy *librarian*
Hezel, Amy R. *librarian, educator*
Hoke, Sheila Wilder *retired librarian*
Jablonski, Valerie *librarian*
Jacob, Rosamond Tryon *librarian*
Johnson, Carolyn M. *librarian, writer*
Ketchum, Irene Frances *library director*
Kirby, Marcia Karen *librarian*
Kiser, Nagiko Sato *retired librarian*
Klein, Susan Elaine *librarian*
Krinsky, Sharon Frances *librarian, editor, writer*
Kubie, Rachel *librarian, writer*
Labriola, Angelina Marie *librarian*
Landry, Abbie Vestal *librarian*
LaPolt, Margaret *librarian*
Liu, Rhonda Louise *librarian*
Lovelace, Julianne *former library director*
Maltby, Florence Helen *library science educator*
McDonald-UmBayemake, Linda *librarian, rehabilitation counselor*
McGrath, Anna Fields *retired librarian*
McLain, Thelma Louise *retired librarian*
Miller, Jacqueline Winslow *library director*
Miller, Marilyn Lea *library science educator*
Mitchell, Mary Lu *information researcher, civic volunteer, retired*
Morgan, Jane Hale *retired library director*
Morris-Blacker, Marilyn Eileen *librarian*
Muñoz-Solá, Haydeé Socorro *library administrator*
Noah, Julia Jeanine *retired librarian*
Ostermann, Grace Gentile *librarian, media specialist*
Peri, Linda Carol *librarian*
Pienik, Marilyn Anne *retired librarian, piano teacher*
Razoharinoro, *archivist, historian, researcher*
Richardson, Patricia Jean *librarian*
Ricketts, Sondra Lou *librarian*
Roberts, Judith Marie *librarian, educator*
Robinson, Verna Cotten *retired librarian, property management owner*
Rockman, Ilene Frances *librarian, educator, editor*
Rusaw, Sally Ellen *librarian*
Ryavec, Isabel Seaton *librarian, media specialist*
Scheiberg, Susan L. *librarian*
Schneider, Sherri *library clerk*
Scott, Alice Holly *retired librarian*
Scott, Catherine Dorothy *librarian, information consultant*
Shickley, Margaret S. *librarian*
Shultz, Linda Joyce *retired library director*
Siefert-Kazanjian, Donna *corporate librarian*
Smith, Barbara Jeanne *retired librarian*
Sprince, Leila Joy *librarian*
Stallworth-Barron, Doris A. Carter *librarian, educator*
Stewart, Dorothy K. *librarian*
Summers, Lorraine Dey Schaeffer *retired librarian*
Sweetland, Loraine Fern *librarian, educator*
Teeple, Fiona Diane *librarian, lawyer*
Teten, Melody-Leigh *library media specialist*
Thiele, Gloria Day *retired librarian, small business owner*
Triipan, Maive *library director*
VanMeter, Vandelia L. *retired director*
Van Orden, Phyllis Jeanne *librarian, educator*
Weaver, Barbara Frances *librarian, consultant*
Whitmore, Menandra M. *librarian*
Wilson, Patricia Potter *library science and reading educator, educational and library consultant*
Wingate, Bettye Faye *librarian, educator*
Wolf, Cynthia Tribelhorn *librarian, library educator*
Woodrum, Patricia Ann *librarian*
Woods, Phyllis Michalik *librarian*

HUMANITIES: MUSEUMS

UNITED STATES

ALABAMA

Florence
Wright, Mildred Anne (Milly Wright) *conservator, researcher*

Mc Calla
Kes, Vicki *museum director*

Montgomery
Belt, Jean Rainer *art gallery owner*

ALASKA

Fairbanks
Jonaitis, Aldona Claire *museum administrator, art historian*

ARIZONA

Bisbee
Gustavson, Carrie *museum director*

Phoenix
Grinell, Sheila *museum director*

Prescott
Churchill, Karen Lynn *curator, educator*

Tempe
Zeitlin, Marilyn Audrey *museum director*

CALIFORNIA

Arcata
Zielinski, Melissa L. *museum director*

Bakersfield
Enriquez, Carola Rupert *museum director*

Berkeley
Day, Lucille Lang *museum administrator, educator, writer*

Carson
Zimmerer, Kathy Louise *university art gallery director*

Cedar Ridge
Adams, Margaret Bernice *retired museum official*

Fresno
Monaghan, Kathleen M. *art museum director*

Huntington Beach
Sandrock, Donna *gallery director*

La Jolla
Armstrong, Elizabeth Neilson *curator*
Beebe, Mary Livingstone *curator*

Laguna Niguel
Solon, Deborah Epstein *curator*

Long Beach
Glenn, Constance White *art museum director, art consultant*

Los Angeles
Barron, Stephanie *curator*
Fontenote-Jamerson, Belinda *museum director*
Gribbon, Deborah *museum director*
Hirano, Irene Ann Yasutake *museum director*
Holo, Selma Reuben *museum director, educator*
Philbin, Ann M. *art facility director*
Rich, Andrea Louise *museum administrator*

Moraga
Silcox, Frances Eleanor *museum and exhibits planning consultant*

Newport Beach
Vine, Naomi *museum administrator*

Northridge
Lewis, Louise Miller *gallery director, art history educator*

Oakland
Eis, Ruth Susanne *museum curator, artist*

Redding
Peterson, Robyn Gayle *museum curator*

Riverside
Warren, Katherine Virginia *art gallery director*

San Diego
Longenecker, Martha W. *museum director*

San Francisco
Sano, Emily Joy *museum director*

San Jose
Norberg, Deborah Dorsey *museum administrator*

Santa Barbara
Kelm, Bonnie G. *art museum director, educator*

Santa Clara
Schapp, Rebecca Maria *museum director*

Stockton
Hepper, Iona Lydia *retired gallery owner*

The Sea Ranch
Baas, Jacquelynn *museum consultant, art historian*

Watsonville
Hernandez, Jo Farb *music director, consultant*

COLORADO

Colorado Springs
LeMieux, Linda Dailey *museum director*

Denver
Daley, Ann Scarlett *curator*
Decatur, Raylene *former museum director*

Fort Collins
Ketcham, Sally Ann *historic site staff member, consultant*

CONNECTICUT

Hartford
Sellers, Kate M. *art museum director*

New Haven
Meyers, Amy *museum director*

Storrs Mansfield
Censky, Ellen Joan *curator, biologist*

DISTRICT OF COLUMBIA

Washington
Archambault, JoAllyn *museum administrator, anthropologist*
Bloomfield, Sara J. *museum director*
Bretzfelder, Deborah May *retired museum staff member*
Buhler, Leslie Lynn *museum director*
Carr, Carolyn Kinder *deputy director and chief curator*
Duke, Sara Willett *curator*
Dwyer Southern, Kathy *museum administrator*
Escallon, Ana Maria *museum director, writer, curator*
Grasselli, Margaret Morgan *curator*
Harvey, Eleanor Jones *museum curator*
Larson, Judy L. *museum director, curator*
Legro, Patrice *museum director*
Noe, Adrianne *museum administrator*
Patton, Sharon F. *museum director*
Rathbone, Eliza E. *curator*
Selin, Nina Evvie *philanthropist*
Sopher, Vicki Elaine *museum curator*
Stevenson, Frances Kellogg *museum program director*
Stevenson, Nancy Nelson *museum executive*
Wolanin, Barbara Ann Boese *art curator, art historian*

FLORIDA

Boca Raton
Kaye, Carole *museum director and curator*

Delray Beach
Rejune-Adams, Gloria Jean *museum director*

Fort Lauderdale
Cavendish, Kim L. Maher *museum administrator*

Fort Pierce
Fischer, Ellen E. *art gallery director*

Gainesville
Wing, Elizabeth Schwarz *museum curator, educator*

Jacksonville
Dundon, Margo Elaine *museum director*

Jupiter
Tanis, Janet Eleanor *museum administrator, retired elementary school educator*

Niceville
Valdés, Karen W. *art gallery director, educator*

Orlando
Morrisey, Marena Grant *art museum administrator*

Saint Petersburg
Gordon-Harris, Cassandra I. *curator, educator*
Weaver, F. Louise Beazley *curator, director*

Tallahassee
Palladino-Craig, Allys *museum director*

Tampa
Kanter, Jennifer Lynne *curator*
Kass, Emily *art museum administrator*

West Palm Beach
Orr-Cahall, Christina *art museum director, art historian*

GEORGIA

Atlanta
Davis, Eleanor Kay *museum administrator*
King, Linda Orr *museum director, consultant*
Raney, Jean Puckett *art gallery director, artist*

Augusta
Moore Shaffer, Patricia Ann *museum educator, art association administrator*

Kathleen
Wills, Lois Elaine *art gallery owner, religious education educator*

Macon
Oliver, Katherine C. *museum director*

HAWAII

Honolulu
Billings, Kathy *national monument administrator*

Kaneohe
Lagoria, Georgianna Marie *curator, writer, editor, visual art consultant*

Lihue
Lovell, Carol *museum director*

Makawao
Moore, Rosemary Kuulei *art gallery administrator*

IDAHO

Coeur D Alene
Dahlgren, Dorothy *museum director*

ILLINOIS

Bolingbrook
Madori, Jan *art gallery director*

Chicago
Hanner, Erika Varricchio *museum program director*
Kubida, Judith Ann *museum administrator*
Weisberg, Lois *arts administrator, city official*

Mahomet
Kennedy, Cheryl Lynn *museum director*

Springfield
Wynn, Nan L. *historic site administrator*

INDIANA

Bloomington
Calinescu, Adriana Gabriela *museum curator, art historian*
Gealt, Adelheid Maria *museum director*

Elkhart
Burns, B(illye) Jane *museum director*

Fort Wayne
Watkinson, Patricia Grieve *museum director*

Indianapolis
Tandy, Kisha Renee *curator*

IOWA

Iowa City
Smothers, Ann Elizabeth *museum director*

KANSAS

Dodge City
Clifton-Smith, Rhonda Darleen *art educator, art center administrator*

Lawrence
Norris, Andrea Spaulding *art museum director*

KENTUCKY

Louisville
Becker, Gail Roselyn *museum director*

LOUISIANA

Baton Rouge
Gikas, Carol Sommerfeldt *museum director*

Deridder
Mallory, Patricia Jody *museum curator*

New Orleans
Smith, Geraldine *historic site administrator*

MAINE

Mount Desert
Redfield, Rita Tams *art gallery owner*

MARYLAND

Baltimore
Bolger, Doreen *museum director*
Lanier, Jacqueline Ruth *curator, artist*

Mitchellville
Marsh, Caryl Amsterdam *museum exhibitions curator, psychologist, advisor*

MASSACHUSETTS

Acton
Gilpin, Deborah J. *museum administrator*

Boston
Cronin, Bonnie Kathryn Lamb *museum director*
Curran, Emily Katherine *museum director*
Emerson, Anne Devereux *museum administrator*
Freed, Rita Evelyn *curator, Egyptologist, educator*
Hawley, Anne *museum director*
Hills, Patricia Gorton Schulze *curator*
Medvedow, Jill *museum director*
Zannieri, Nina *museum director*

Cambridge
Cohn, Marjorie Benedict *curator, art historian, educator*
Watson, Rubie *museum director*

Medford
Schlegel, Amy Ingrid *curator, art historian*

Milton
Randall, Lilian Maria Charlotte *museum curator*

Northampton
Fabing, Suzannah *museum director*

Peabody
Brave, Rebecca S. Larsen *curator*

Sudbury
Pitman, Ursula Wall *curator, educator*

Wellesley
Palmerio, Elvira Castano *art gallery director, art historian*

MICHIGAN

Ann Arbor
Cerniglia, Alice May *museum program director, consultant*

Big Rapids
Weis-Taylor, Carrie Lynn *curator, artist*

Chesaning
Swartzmiller, Mildred M. *art gallery owner*

Detroit
Edwards, Esther G. *museum administrator, former record, film and entertainment company executive*

East Lansing
Bandes, Susan Jane *museum director, educator*

Lansing
Homer, Elizabeth Ann *curator*

MINNESOTA

Minneapolis
Atkinson, Christine Anne *curator*
King, Lyndel Irene Saunders *art museum director*

MISSISSIPPI

Natchez
Branyan, Cheryl Munyer *museum administrator, consultant*

Vicksburg
Joyner, Elizabeth *curator*

MISSOURI

Ballwin
Pallozola, Christine *non-profit administrator*

Kansas City
Scott, Deborah Emont *curator*
Svadlenak, Jean Hayden *museum consultant*
Youmans, Joyce M. *curator, researcher*

Saint Louis
Chervitz, Randi S *art gallery director, artist*
Mann, Judith Walker *curator*

MONTANA

Billings
Lorenz, Marianne *curator*

Crow Agency
Deernose, Kitty *curator*

Missoula
Millin, Laura Jeanne *museum director*

NEBRASKA

Chadron
Lecher, Belvadine (Belvadine Reeves) *museum curator*

Lincoln
Wallis, Deborah *curator*

NEVADA

Baker
Mills, Rebecca *national park administrator*

Elko
Seymour, Lisa *museum director*

Las Vegas
Gillespie, Marilyn *museum administrator*
Le Blanc, Suzanne *museum director*
Lewis, Oli Parepa *curator*

NEW HAMPSHIRE

Portsmouth
Nylander, Jane Louise *museum director, lecturer, writer*

NEW JERSEY

Ho Ho Kus
Ciannella, Joeen Moore *museum director*

Newark
Price, Mary Sue Sweeney *museum director*
Reynolds, Valrae *museum curator*

Summit
Call, Denise Hodgins *curator, artist, freelance/self-employed writer*

Wayne
Einreinhofer, Nancy Anne *art gallery director*

NEW MEXICO

Albuquerque
Abrams, Fay Pfaelzer *art gallery owner, educator*
Landis, Ellen Jamie *art curator*

Santa Fe
Andreeva, Tatiana *art gallery owner*

Silver City
Bettison, Cynthia Ann *museum director, archaeologist*

NEW YORK

Albany
Miles, Christine Marie *museum director*

Blue Mountain Lake
Day, Jacqueline Frances *museum director*

Brooklyn
Enseki, Carol *museum director*
Ferber, Linda S. *museum curator*
Shubert, Gabrielle S. *museum executive director*

Buffalo
Bayles, Jennifer Lucene *museum program director, educator*

Corning
Spillman, Jane Shadel *curator, researcher, writer*

East Hampton
Vered, Ruth *art gallery director, owner*

Jamestown
Reale, Sara Jane *museum education director*

Long Island City
Heiss, Alanna *museum director*

Mount Kisco
Bithoney, Carmen C. D'Amborsio *artistic director*

New York
Barnett, Vivian Endicott *curator*
Basquin, Mary Smyth (Kit Basquin) *museum administrator*
Carr, Claudia *art gallery director, owner, artist*
Cooke, Lynne Catherine *curator*
De Ferrari, Gabriella *curator, writer*
Desai, Vishakha N. *museum director, professional society administrator*
Dunne, Linda *museum administrator*
Faunce, Sarah Cushing *former museum curator*
Fox, Ingrid *curator*
Futter, Ellen Victoria *museum administrator*
Globus, Dorothy Twining *museum director*
Goodman, Susan *curator*
Gumpert, Lynn *gallery director*
Gund, Agnes *former art museum administrator*
Haskell, Barbara *curator*
Hoffman, Nancy *art gallery director*
Hotchner, Holly *curator, museum director, conservator*
Ilse-Neuman, Ursula *curator*
Ives, Colta Feller *museum curator, educator*
Kallir, Jane Katherine *art gallery director, author*
Kardon, Janet *museum curator, curator, educator*
Kind, Phyllis *art gallery owner*
Leff, Sandra H. *gallery director, consultant*
Leven, Ann Ruth *museum financial officer*
Martin, Mary Anne *art gallery owner*
McGovern, Maureen Ann *curator*
Mertens, Joan R. *museum curator, art historian*
O'Brien, Catherine Louise *museum administrator*
Pesner, Carole Manishin *art gallery owner*
Rosenbaum, Joan Hannah *museum director*
Rosenthal, Nan *curator, educator, author*
Stiassny, Melanie L.J. *curator*
Sutton, Karen E. *administrator*
Tobach, Ethel *retired curator*
Toll, Barbara Elizabeth *art gallery director*
Wright, Gwendolyn *art center director, writer, educator*
Yablonski, Janice Beth *museum administrator, publishing executive*

Purchase
Gedeon, Lucinda Heyel *museum director*

Sands Point
Olian, JoAnne Constance *curator, art historian*

Stuyvesant
Tripp, Susan Gerwe *museum director*

Syracuse
Skoler, Celia Rebecca *retired art gallery director*
Trop, Sandra *museum administrator*

NORTH CAROLINA

Charlotte
Nicholson, Freda Hyams *museum executive, medical educator*

OHIO

Cincinnati
Timpano, Anne *museum director, art historian*

Cleveland
Reid, Katharine Lee *museum director*

Mentor
Miller, Frances Suzanne *historic site curator*

PROFESSIONAL INDEX

OKLAHOMA

Tulsa
Manhart, Marcia Y(ockey) *art museum director*
Wyckoff, Lydia Lloyd *art curator*

OREGON

Milwaukie
Eichinger, Marilynne Hildegarde *museum administrator*

Portland
Taylor, J(ocelyn) Mary *museum administrator, zoologist, educator*

PENNSYLVANIA

Harrisburg
Franco, Barbara Alice *museum director*

Merion Station
Camp, Kimberly N. *museum administrator, artist*

Philadelphia
Bantel, Linda Mae *former museum curator, consultant*
d'Harnoncourt, Anne *museum director, museum administrator*
Gould, Claudia *museum director*
Kolb, Nancy Dwyer *museum director*
Rouse, Terrie S. *museum administrator*
Shoemaker, Innis Howe *art museum curator*

Pittsburgh
Culan, Kristin Lynn *museum staff member*
Dawson, Mary Ruth *curator, educator*
Jaffe, Gwen Daner *museum educator*
King, Elaine A. *curator, art historian, critic*
Werner, Jane *museum administrator*

Swarthmore
Sawyers, Claire Elyce *arboretum administrator*

University Park
Muhlert, Jan Keene *art museum director*

RHODE ISLAND

Newport
Coxe, Trudy *museum administrator, former state official*
Tilley, Marie Hope Hanson *museum administrator, owner*

Providence
Hay, Susan Stahr Heller *museum curator*

SOUTH CAROLINA

Camden
Craig, Joanna Burbank *historic site director*

Greenville
Davis, Joan Carroll *retired museum director*

SOUTH DAKOTA

Watertown
Natale, Fernanda Maria Maddalena *conservator, artist*

TEXAS

Austin
Johnson, Eileen *curator, educator, commissioner*

Frisco
Meadows, Patricia Blachly *art curator, civic worker*

Glen Rose
Blankenship, Jenny Mary *museum administrator*

Houston
Lee, Janie C. *curator*
Tucker, Anne Wilkes *curator, photography historian and critic, lecturer*

Post
Neff, Marie Taylor *museum director, artist*

San Antonio
Endresen, Lisa Castro *curatorial assistant*

UTAH

Salt Lake City
George, Sarah B. *museum director*
Oakes, Claudia *museum administrator*

VIRGINIA

Alexandria
Gaynor, Margaret Cryor *program director*

Charlottesville
Hartz, Jill *museum director*
Linden, Peppy G. *museum director*

Norfolk
Marsden-Atlass, Lynn Dean *curator, museum administrator*

Richmond
Schlatter, Elizabeth *museum administrator*

Tyler, Payne Bouknight *museum executive*

Roanoke
Fitzgerald, Mary Eileen *museum program director*
Taubman, Jenny *museum program director*

Vienna
Damon, Shirley Stockton *art gallery owner*

Williamsburg
Christison, Muriel Branham *retired art museum director, fine arts educator*

WASHINGTON

Bellevue
Douglas, Diane Miriam *museum director*

Bellingham
Clark-Langager, Sarah Ann *curator, director, university official*

Port Townsend
Harrington, LaMar *retired curator*

Seattle
Wright, Rachel *curator*

Spokane
Mobley, Karen Ruth *art gallery director*

Tacoma
Callan, Josi Irene *museum director*

WISCONSIN

Milwaukee
Peltz, Cissie Jean *art gallery director, cartoonist*

West Allis
Ramazzini, Judith Williams *curator*

CANADA

ONTARIO

London
Poole, Nancy Geddes *art gallery curator*

ADDRESS UNPUBLISHED

Abbott, Rebecca Phillips *museum director, art consultant, photographer*
Amaki, Amalia *curator*
Baron, Jennifer Lynne *museum education director*
Belkov, Meredith Ann *landmark administrator*
Black, Ruth Idella *museum curator*
Booker, Nana Laurel *art gallery owner, honorary consul*
Crawford-Dickerson, Carrie Cae *art gallery director*
Dahl, Bren Bennington *photography studio co-owner*
Deutschman, Louise Tolliver *curator*
Follmer, Helene Greene *retired museum administrator, civic worker*
Harrington, Beverly *museum director*
Ittelson, Mary Elizabeth *museum director*
Jacobowitz, Ellen Sue *museum curator, museum and temple administrator*
Jacobs, Eleanor *art consultant, retired art administrator*
Knowles, Elizabeth Pringle *museum director*
Matelic, Candace Tangorra *museum studies educator, consultant, museum director*
McCulley, Lana Janeen *museum administrator, consultant*
Mercuri, Joan B. *museum administrator*
Meyer, Ruth Krueger *museum administrator, educator, art historian*
Monkman, Betty Claire *curator*
Mulryan, Lenore Hoag *art curator, author*
Parris, Nina Gumpert *curator, writer, researcher, photographer*
Pilgrim, Dianne Hauserman *retired museum director*
Radice, Anne-Imelda *museum director*
Raleigh, Jean W *museum staff member*
Rouse, Terrie Suzitte *former museum director*
Russell, Helen Diane *retired museum curator, educator*
Schneider, Janet M. *arts administrator, curator, painter*
Smith, Marjorie Aileen Matthews *museum director*
Steinhauser, Janice Maureen *arts administrator, educator, artist*
Thompson, Laura Jill *curator, educator*
Towe, A. Ruth *retired museum director*
Walker, Roslyn Adele *museum director*
White, Katharine Stone *museum administrator*

Zusy, Catherine *curator*

INDUSTRY: MANUFACTURING
See also **FINANCE: FINANCIAL SERVICES**

UNITED STATES

ALABAMA

Birmingham
Cohen-DeMarco, Gale Maureen *pharmaceutical executive*

Dothan
Marks, Marilyn *trailer company executive*

Prattville
Lambert, Meg Stringer *construction executive, architect, interior designer*

ARIZONA

Chandler
Elliott, Lee Ann *company executive, former government official*

Peoria
Cook, Mary Margaret *steamfitter, educator*

Phoenix
Martensen, Barbara *electronics executive*
Miller, Janice *electronics executive*
Wade, Tyra V. *manufacturing executive*

Tucson
Finley, Dorothy Hunt *beverage distribution company executive*
Francesconi, Louise L. *electronics executive*

ARKANSAS

North Little Rock
Harrison, Angela Eve *manufacturing executive*

Springdale
Beach, Jean Mrha *food products executive*
Dunn, Jeri K. *food products executive*
Pirozzoli, Heather Jo *food company professional*

CALIFORNIA

Alameda
Heiss, Claire DeYoung *manufacturing executive*

Beverly Hills
Borgnine, Tova *cosmetics executive*
Leong, Margaret *construction executive*

Burbank
Joseff, Joan Castle *manufacturing executive*

Castro Valley
Thorburn, Lisa A. *acoustical consulting company executive*

Colusa
Carter, Jane Foster *agriculture industry executive*

Costa Mesa
Lerner, Sandy *cosmetics executive*

Cypress
Garrett, Sharon *health services company executive*

La Jolla
Shawver, Laura K. *biotechnology company executive*

Lodi
Puerta, Christy L. *construction executive*

Los Altos
Beer, Clara Louise Johnson *retired electronics executive*
Greetham, Elizabeth M. *health products executive*

Los Angeles
Hutchins, Joan Morthland *manufacturing executive, farmer*
Mohajer, Dineh *cosmetics company executive*
Segil, Larraine Diane *materials company executive*

Menlo Park
Jackson, Jeanne Pellegren *apparel executive*
Lucke, Betty Jean *dressmaker*

Milpitas
Wang, Susan S. *manufacturing executive*

Newark
Mueller, Nancy *food products executive*

Orange
Strate, Jan Nicole (Niki Strate) *contractor*

INDUSTRY: MANUFACTURING

Palo Alto
Kincaid, Judith Wells *electronics company executive*

Rancho Dominguez
Campbell, Jennifer Bradley *company official, social worker*

Rescue
Ackerly, Wendy Saunders *construction company executive*

Salinas
Esquivel, Mary *agricultural products company executive*

San Diego
Casey, Nancy J. *women's healthcare company executive*
Jennings, Jackie *construction executive, contractor*
Piskor, Chrystal Lea *service company owner*

San Francisco
Calvin, Jamie Duif *interactive designer*
Hill, Emma *apparel executive*
Ming, Jenny J. *retail apparel company executive*
Morris-Tyndall, Lucy *construction executive*
Proctor, Georganne C. *company executive*
Smith, Cheryl T. *pharmaceutical executive, public relations executive*
Tompkins, Susie *apparel company executive, creative director*

San Rafael
Neuburger, Karen *apparel executive*
Parker, Pam *apparel manufacturing company executive*

Santa Clara
Dorchak, Glenda *electronics company executive*
Murray, Patricia *electronics company executive*

Sherman Oaks
Little, Carole *women's apparel company executive*

South San Francisco
Desmond-Hellmann, Susan *medical products manufacturing executive*
Potter, Myrtle S. *research and development company executive*

Sunnyvale
Ng, Betty *electronics executive*

Thousand Oaks
Belluzzo, Kathryn P. *pharmaceutical executive*
Rosenblatt, Alice F. *health products executive*

Ukiah
Newell, Barbara Ann *coatings company executive*

Union City
Cross, Elizabeth *apparel manufacturing company executive*

West Hollywood
Stern, Ruth Szold *business executive, artist*

Willits
Handley, Margie Lee *manufacturing executive*

COLORADO

Denver
Alvarado, Linda G. *construction executive*
Harmsen, Dorothy *food products executive*
Leydon, Debra Jean *food products executive*

Jefferson
Maatsch, Deborah Joan *manufacturing executive*

Littleton
Price, Gayl Baader *residential construction company administrator*

Louisville
Kenney, Belinda Jill Forseman *technology company executive*

CONNECTICUT

Fairfield
Fash, Victoria R. *healthcare company executive*

New Haven
Jacob, Deirdre Ann Bradbury *manufacturing executive, business educator, consultant*

Stamford
Anderson, Susan Stuebing *business equipment company executive*
Filter, E. Margie *business equipment manufacturing executive*
Maarbjerg, Mary Penzold *office equipment company executive*

Wilton
Oberstar, Helen Elizabeth *retired cosmetics company executive*

DELAWARE

New Castle
Zambanini, Sandra Lee *construction executive*

Wilmington
Gulyas, Diane H. *manufacturing executive*
Kullman, Ellen J. *manufacturing executive*
McLeer, Laureen Dorothy *drug development and pharmaceutical professional*
Vary, Eva Maros *retired chemicals executive*

DISTRICT OF COLUMBIA

Washington
Howell, Mary L. *diversified company executive*

FLORIDA

Coral Gables
Burini, Sonia Montes de Oca *apparel manufacturing and public relations executive*

Delray Beach
Force, Elizabeth Elma *retired pharmaceutical executive*
Mayer, Marilyn Gooder *steel company executive*

Fort Myers
Toney, Avia Vernet *medical products manufacturer*

Hialeah
Engler, Eva Kay *dental and veterinary products company executive*

Holiday
Barney, Linda Susan *manufacturing specialist*

Miami
Pampe, Pamela Mary *textiles executive, consultant*
Theodoli, Katrin *manufacturing executive*

New Port Richey
Sebring, Marjorie Marie Allison *former home furnishings company executive*

Ocala
Stickeler, Carl Ann Louise *professional parliamentarian*

Ormond Beach
Connors, Michele Perrott *wholesale beverage company executive*

Pensacola
McQueen, Rebecca Hodges *health care executive, consultant*

Reddick
Corwin, Joyce Elizabeth Stedman *construction company executive*

Tampa
McKinney, Patricia J. *automobile company executive*

West Palm Beach
Sander, Dorothy E. *manufacturing executive*

GEORGIA

Atlanta
Camac, Margaret Victoria *construction company executive*
Isaac, Yvonne Renee *construction executive*
Jones, Ingrid Saunders *food products executive*
Love, Gay McLawhorn *manufacturing executive*
Minnick, Mary E. *food products executive*
Palmer, Vicki R. *food products executive*
Reiniche, Dominique *food products executive*
Tilley, Tana Marie *pharmaceutical executive*

College Park
Fahy, Nancy Lee *food products marketing executive*

Norcross
Moreno, Veronica *food products executive*

Rossville
Anderson, Kristie *construction company executive*

Savannah
LaSalle, Diana Margaret *company executive, writer, consultant*

Tucker
Franklin, Carol D. *electronics company executive*

IDAHO

Boise
Elg, Annette *food products executive*

Post Falls
Hasalone Eve, Annette Leona *research and development company executive*

ILLINOIS

Abbott Park
Amundson, Joy A. *pharmaceutical and health products executive*
Flynn, Gary L. *pharmaceutical executive*

Addison
Rose, Gail Elaine *wholesale trade company manager*

Aurora
Belcher, La Jeune *automotive executive*

Broadview
Gockley, Barbara Jean *manufacturing executive*

Chicago
Barnes, Brenda C. *food and apparel executive*
Bellantoni, Maureen Blanchfield *manufacturing and retail executive*
Ferguson, Diana S. *food products executive*
Gordon, Ellen Rubin *candy company executive*
Koeliner, Laurette *manufacturing executive, human resources specialist*
Markle, Shelley Ekermeyer *construction executive*
Miglin, Marilyn *cosmetics executive*
Sprieser, Judith A. *food products company executive*
Stotler, Edith Ann *retired grain company executive, financial planner*

Decatur
Madding, Claudia *agricultural products executive*

Des Plaines
O'Dwyer, Mary Ann *automotive executive*

Downers Grove
Stevenson, Judy G. *instrument manufacturing executive*

East Alton
Abert, Amber Christine *home remodeling contractor*

Hanover Park
Renner, Jacqueline Marie *research and development company executive*

Huntley
Plunkett, Melba Kathleen *manufacturing executive*

Melrose Park
Lavin, Bernice E. *cosmetics executive*
Wechter, Clari Ann *paint manufacturing company executive*

Northfield
Holden, Betsy D. *food products company executive*
Sneed, Paula Ann *food products executive*

Westmont
Ryan, Joan *food company executive*

INDIANA

Columbus
Engelking, Ellen Melinda *textiles executive, manufacturing executive, real estate broker*

Elkhart
Mathias, Margaret Grossman *manufacturing company executive, leasing company executive*

Indianapolis
Lorell, Beverly H. *medical products executive*
Stotka, Jennifer Lynn *pharmaceutical executive, physician*

Mishawaka
Rubenstein, Pamela Silver *manufacturing executive*

Seymour
Rust, Lois *food company executive*

IOWA

Davenport
Bannick, Janice Carol *automotive dealerships executive*

Marshalltown
Foote, Sherrill Lynne *retired manufacturing company technician*

KANSAS

Topeka
Stroud, Jacqueline Lucille *medical supply company executive*

KENTUCKY

Lexington
Gornik, Kathy *electronics executive*
Gray, Lois Howard *construction company executive*

Louisville
James, Virginia Lynn *contracts executive*
Wood, Phoebe A. *food products executive*

MAINE

Bath
Simone, Gail Elisabeth *manufacturing executive*

MARYLAND

Baltimore
D'Erasmo, Martha Jean *health company executive*
Lucas, Barbara B. *electrical equipment manufacturing executive*

Bethesda
Spector, Eleanor Ruth *corporation executive*

Davidsonville
Bowles, Liza K. *construction executive*

La Plata
Raymond, Elizabeth Sollars *vault and monument company executive*

Rockville
Gillick, Betsy Brinkley *pharmaceutical executive*

MASSACHUSETTS

Boston
Murphy, Kathleen Ann *diversified manufacturing company executive*
Tremblay, Joan Louise *district manager*

Cambridge
Matsui, Connie L. *pharmaceutical executive*

Danvers
O'Malley, Marie Kiernan *healthcare products company professional*

Dedham
Naughton, Marie Ann *corporate executive*

Lexington
Rhoads, Rebecca R. *electronics executive*

Springfield
Winn, Janice Gail *food products administrator*

Wellesley Hills
Clarkson, Cheryl Lee *healthcare executive*

Weston
Smick, Susan Schnee *manufacturing executive, tile designer, marketing professional*

MICHIGAN

Battle Creek
Banks, Donna Jo *food products executive*

Bloomfield Hills
Lapadot, Sonee Spinner *retired automobile manufacturing company official*

Dearborn
Buckingham, Lorie *automotive executive*
Fox, Stacy *automotive executive*
Pacheco, Susan *automotive executive*
Petrauskas, Helen O. *automobile manufacturing company executive*

Detroit
Aguirre, Pamela Ann *manufacturing executive*
Barclay, Kathleen S. *automotive executive*
Kantrowitz, Jean *health products executive*
Lowery, Elizabeth *automotive executive*

Ferndale
Dodd, Geralda *metal products executive*

Grosse Pointe Farms
Obolensky, Marilyn Wall (Mrs. Serge Obolensky) *metals company executive*

Midland
Bader, Kathleen M. *chemicals executive*

Novi
Ligocki, Kathleen A. *auto parts company executive*

Pontiac
Mahone, Barbara Jean *automotive company executive*

Portage
Farrand, Lois Barbara *pharmaceutical company administrator*

Saint Johns
Grubaugh, Sally Jo *automotive executive*

Southfield
Shilts, Nancy S. *automotive executive, lawyer*

Troy
Elder, Irma *retail automotive executive*
Healy, Karen *automotive executive*
Walker, Bette *automotive executive*

Zeeland
Nickels, Elizabeth Anne *office furniture manufacturing executive*

MINNESOTA

Lindstrom
Messin, Marlene Ann *plastics company executive*

Loretto
Veit, Gae *construction executive*

Minneapolis
Stephenson, Nancy Louise *medical products company professional*

Saint Paul
Critzer, Susan L. *health products company executive*
O'Connor, Genevieve *pharmaceutical executive*

MISSOURI

Fenton
Hughes, Barbara Bradford *manufacturing executive, real estate manager, community health nurse*

Independence
Nordsieck, Karen Ann *custom apparel company executive*

Kansas City
O'Dell, Jane *automotive company executive*

Saint Louis
Brown, JoBeth Goode *food products executive, lawyer*
Posgay, Betty Marie *medical equipment company executive, artist*

NEVADA

Hendersonville
Niemeyer, Erin Janice *pharmaceutical sales consultant, journalist, editor*

Las Vegas
Hawks, Shirley Lynn *manufacturing executive, writer*
Strahan, Julia Celestine *electronics company executive*

NEW JERSEY

Bedminster
Yannuzzi, Elaine Victoria *food and home products executive*

Bloomfield
Shogen, Kuslima *pharmaceutical executive*

New Brunswick
Buto, Kathleen A. *health products executive*
Heisen, JoAnn Heffernan *health care company executive*
Liao, Mei-June *biopharmaceutical company executive*
Poon, Christine A. *pharmaceutical executive*

Nutley
Seyffarth, Linda Jean Wilcox *corporate executive*

Paramus
Forman, Beth Rosalyne *specialty food trade executive*

Princeton
Drakeman, Lisa N. *biotechnology company executive*

Ridgefield
Riggs, Rory B. *pharmaceutical executive*

Ringoes
Santin, Jean *cosmetic company executive, consultant*

Whitehouse Station
Avedon, Marcia J. *pharmaceutical executive*
Lewent, Judy Carol *pharmaceutical executive*
McGlynn, Margaret G. *pharmaceutical executive*
Yarno, Wendy *pharmaceutical executive*

NEW MEXICO

Albuquerque
Collins, Julie *healthcare organization executive*
Palmer, Sharon-Joy *agricultural research company executive*
Pohl, Elizabeth *contracting company executive*

NEW YORK

Armonk
Sydney, Doris S. *sports touring company executive, interior designer*

Bay Shore
Shreve, Sue Ann Gardner *retired health products company administrator*

Elmira
Van den Blink, Nelson Mooers *light industrial manufacturing executive*

Fresh Meadows
Yang, Susan Xia *business consultant, massage therapist*

Huntington Station
Yacobian, Sonia Simone *metals company executive*

Lindenhurst
Boltz, Mary Ann *aerospace materials company executive, travel agency executive*

Long Island City
DiGiovanni, Eleanor Elma *scaffold installation company executive*

Macedon
Moore, Shanna La'Von *chemical company executive*

Mahopac
Vigliotti, Patricia Noreen *welder, sculptor*

New Rochelle
Goodman, Joan Frances *avionics manufacturing executive*
Tassone, Gelsomina (Gessie Tassone) *metal processing executive*

New York
Ahrendts, Angela *apparel executive*
Azrielant, Aya *jewelry manufacturing executive*

Barnes, Jhane Elizabeth *fashion design company executive, designer*
Brinson, Monica E. *pharmaceutical sales representative*
Brown, Bobbi *cosmetics executive*
Choi, Jay Lee *women's apparel executive*
Dwyer, Katherine *cosmetic company executive*
Edmands, Susan Banks *consulting company executive*
Howson, Tamar D. *pharmaceutical executive*
Jackson, Yvonne *pharmaceutical executive*
Juliber, Lois D. *manufacturing executive*
Jung, Andrea *cosmetics executive*
Katen, Karen L. *pharmaceutical executive*
Krominga, Lynn *cosmetic and health care company executive, lawyer*
Kropf, Susan J. *cosmetics company executive*
Lauder, Aerin *cosmetics executive*
Lauder, Evelyn H. *cosmetics executive*
Lewis, Loida Nicolas *food products holding company executive*
McFadden, Mary Josephine *fashion industry executive*
Natori, Josie Cruz *apparel executive*
Pollard, Veronica *automotive executive*
Roberts, Dorothy Hyman *accessory company executive*
Slavin, Rosanne Singer *textile converter*
Sloss, Merle *shoe company executive*
Susman, Sally *cosmetics executive*
Walker, Sally Barbara *retired glass company executive*
Weston, Michele J. *apparel executive, consultant*

Purchase
Finnerty, Louise Hoppe *beverage and food company executive*
Nooyi, Indra K. *food products company executive*
Parrs, Marianne M. *paper and lumber company executive*

Rochester
Friauf, Katherine Elizabeth *metal company executive*
Seymour, Dawn Yvonne *manufacturing executive*

Sands Point
Tane, Susan Jaffe *retired manufacturing company executive*

Seaford
Spencer, Jean *food products executive*

Suffern
Hawver, Carolyn Dunn *pharmaceutical executive*

Webster
Walter, Deana A. *electronics executive, small business owner*

Williamsville
Krzyzan, Judy Lynn *automotive executive*

NORTH CAROLINA

Greensboro
Cummings, Candace S. *apparel company executive*

Raleigh
Henry, Janice K. *construction materials company executive*

Winston Salem
Wallace, Roanne *hosiery company executive*

OHIO

Avon Lake
Kent, Deborah *automotive executive*

Cincinnati
Kendle, Candace *pharmaceutical executive*
Laney, Sandra Eileen *service company executive*

Columbus
Curtis, Loretta O'Ellen *retired construction executive*

Dublin
Davids, Jody *pharmaceutical and medical supply executive*

Holland
D'Anniballe-Holdren, Priscilla Lucille *contracting company executive*

Mason
Snyder, Barbara Royalty *pharmaceutical executive*

Mineral City
Girard, Susan Marie *manufacturing executive*

North Ridgeville
Stewart, Arden Ruth *automotive aftermarket manufacturing executive*

Orrville
Mackus, Eloise L. *food products company executive*

Tipp City
Tighe-Moore, Barbara Jeanne *electronics executive*

West Carrollton
Zeller, Shirley Evelyn *manufacturing executive*

Westerville
Krueger-Horn, Cheryl *apparel executive*

Youngstown
Marks, Esther L. *metals company executive*

OREGON

Ashland
Meese, Celia Edwards *pharmaceutical company executive*

Eugene
Woolley, Donna Pearl *lumber company executive*

Forest Grove
Coleman, Deborah Ann *electronics company executive*

Klamath Falls
Hoggarth, Karen *lumber company executive*

Portland
Boyle, Gertrude *sportswear company executive*
Whitsell, Helen Jo *lumber executive*

PENNSYLVANIA

Bensalem
Bern, Dorrit J. *apparel company executive*

Bradfordwoods
Allardice, Susan M. *manufacturing executive*

Camp Hill
Rugen, Karen *manufacturing executive, corporate communications specialist*

Eighty Four
Magerko, Maggie Hardy *lumber company executive*

Erie
Begley, Charlene *electronics executive*

Gap
Beiler, Anne F. *food company executive*

Greencastle
Fremgen, Darlene *manufacturing specialist*

Halifax
Stauffer, Joanne Rogan *steel company official*

Harrisburg
Yenchko, Suzanne *research and development company executive*

King Of Prussia
McCairns, Regina Carfagno *pharmaceutical executive*

Philadelphia
Liberati, Maria Theresa *fashion production company executive*
Sohn, Catherine Angell *pharmaceutical executive, pharmacist*

Pittsburgh
Horowitz, Carole Spiegel *landscape contractor*

Swarthmore
Kaufman, Antoinette D. *business services company executive*

RHODE ISLAND

Providence
Reed, Cynthia S. *manufacturing executive*

Rumford
Nichols, Alice Marshall *manufacturing executive*

SOUTH CAROLINA

Clemson
Petzel, Florence Eloise *textiles educator*

Fort Mill
Bowles, Crandall Close *textiles executive*

TENNESSEE

Lafayette
Oliver, Barbara Ann *retired apparel executive*

Memphis
Karp, Harvey Lawrence *metal products manufacturing executive*
Lee, Theresa K. *chemicals executive*
O'Neill Tate, Frances *construction executive*

Spring Hill
Trudell, Cynthia *automotive executive*

TEXAS

Austin
Maar, Rosina *medical organization executive*

Carrollton
Heath, Jinger L. *cosmetics executive*

Coppell
Minyard, Liz *food products executive*
Williams, Gretchen Minyard *food store executive*

Dallas
Gold, Christina A. *cosmetics company executive*
Sammons, Elaine D. *corporate executive*
Tyson, Lisa N. *food products executive*

Fort Worth
Pearce, Betty McMurray *retired manufacturing executive*

Garland
Brumit, Jo Ann *sheet metal manufacturing executive*

Houston
Hambly, Ann Alle *appliance company executive*
Kornbleet, Lynda Mae *insulation, fireproofing and acoustical contractor*
Merrill, Connie Lange *chemical company executive*
Moneypenny, Naomi Felina *research and development company executive*
Schumacher, Diane Kosmach *manufacturing executive, lawyer*
Snowden, Bernice Rives *former construction company executive*
Thompson-Draper, Cheryl L. *electronics executive, real estate executive*

Irving
Seifert, Kathi P. *manufacturing executive*

Magnolia
James, Loma Gayle *construction executive, realtor*

Montgomery
Steed, Theresa Jean *manufacturing executive*

Pasadena
Gross, Cynthia Sue *petrochemicals manufacturing executive*

Plano
Cumming, Marilee *apparel company executive*

Port Lavaca
Fisher, Jewel Tanner (Mary Fisher) *retired construction company executive*

Richardson
Goodspeed, Linda A. *manufacturing executive*

Richmond
Barratt, Cynthia Louise *pharmaceutical company executive*

Santa Fe
Lambert, Willie Lee Bell *mobile equipment company owner, educator*

UTAH

Logan
Wheeler, Dolores *food products executive*

West Jordan
Bland, Dorothy Ann *construction executive, real estate agent*

VERMONT

Pittsfield
Wacker, Susan Regina *creative design director*

Shelburne
Robert, Elisabeth B. *toy company executive*

VIRGINIA

Arlington
Rabbit, Linda *construction executive*

Harrisonburg
McCurdy, Donna T. *food products company executive*

Herndon
Griffin, Luanne Marie *automotive corporation executive*

Lynchburg
DePew, Carol Ann *pharmaceutical sales representative*

Mc Lean
Mars, Jacqueline Badger *food products executive*

Norfolk
Alexander, Christine E. *manufacturing executive*

Roanoke
Waldron, Karen *development, construction, and management company executive*

WASHINGTON

Bellevue
Nowik, Dorothy Adam *medical equipment company executive*

Hoquiam
Lamb, Isabelle Smith *manufacturing executive*

Kirkland
Witte, Peggy *metal products executive*

Naches
Assink, Nellie Grace *agricultural executive*

Seattle
McFarland, Lynne Vernice *pharmaceutical executive*
Parker, H. Stewart *biotechnology company executive*

WISCONSIN

Eau Claire
Cohen, Maryjo R. *manufacturing executive*

Ixonia
Peebles, Allene Kay *manufactured housing company executive*
Reul, Betty A. *construction executive*

Marathon
Natzke, Paulette Ann *manufacturing executive*

Merrill
Bierman, Jane *wood products company executive*

Milwaukee
Carter, Valerie *food products executive*
Daniels-Carter, Valerie *food franchise executive*
Hudson, Katherine Mary *manufacturing executive*
Paul, Mary *automotive executive*

CANADA

ONTARIO

Ottawa
Beare-Rogers, Joyce Louise *former research executive*

ADDRESS UNPUBLISHED

Amadio, Bari Ann *metal fabrication executive, former nurse*
Anastole, Dorothy Jean *retired electronics company executive*
Barber, Marsha *business company executive*
Bergman, Janet Eisenstein *food industry executive*
Blum, Betty Ann *footwear company executive*
Bowen, Linda Florence *pharmaceutical executive*
Carver, Juanita Ash *plastic company executive*
Chludzinski, Carol A. *medical products executive*
Danziger, Gertrude Seelig *metal fabricating executive*
Dicciani, Nance Katherine *chemical company executive, chemical engineer*
Doyle, Irene Elizabeth *electronic sales executive, nurse*
Gates, Martina Marie *food products company executive*
Goldberg, Lee Winicki *furniture company executive*
Goodale, Toni Krissel *development consultant*
Greaser, Constance Udean *automotive industry executive*
Grenz, M. Kay *manufacturing executive*
Haberkorn, Judith R. *former manufacturing executive*
Hauptli, Barbara Beatrice *program administrator*
Ingram, Diana Joyce *construction executive*
Jackson, Robbi Jo *agricultural products executive, lawyer*
Jones, Christine Massey *retired furniture company executive*
King, Susan Bennett *retired glass company executive*
Krise, Patricia Love *automotive industry executive*
Kulik, Rosalyn Franta *food company executive, consultant*
Lewis, Rita Hoffman *plastic products manufacturing company executive*
Litzenberger, Lesley Margaret *textiles executive*
Matasovic, Marilyn Estelle *manufacturing executive*
McMullin, Joyce Anne *general contractor*
Meilan, Celia *food products executive*
Nedza, Sandra Louise *manufacturing executive*
Noe, Elnora (Ellie Noe) *retired chemicals executive*
Olson, Margaret Smith *program director, hospitality professional*
Riffle, Rhonda Lorene *construction executive*
Rosen, Ana Beatriz *electronics executive*
Schultz, Audrey Lynn *construction executive, consultant*
Sherman, Patsy O'Connell *technical development administrator, chemist*
Simmons, Marguerite Saffold *pharmaceutical sales professional*
Snyder, Carolyn L. Smith *medical writing director*
Tallett, Elizabeth Edith *biopharmaceutical company executive*
Torrence, Margaret Ann Johnson *company executive, consultant, paralegal, therapist, human resources manager, training instructor*
Turczyn-Toles, Doreen Marie *pharmaceutical consultant*
Vanaltenburg, Betty Marie *lumber company executive*
Watts, Wendy Hazel *wine consultant*

Weinberger, Diane *motivation and image consultant*
Williams, Carolyn Elizabeth *manufacturing executive*
Williams, Dorothy Standridge *soft drink company official, civic worker*
Wright, Linda Jean *manufacturing executive*

INDUSTRY: SERVICE

UNITED STATES

ALABAMA

Huntsville
McIntyre-Ivy, Joan Carol *data processing executive*
Plunkett, Sara L. *communications company executive*

Montgomery
Allen, Linda Lee *administrative assistant*
Dillon, Jean Katherine *executive secretary, small business owner*
Hilliard, Lil *sales executive*

Stevenson
Watson, Mary Elizabeth Grider *employment security officer, retailer*

ALASKA

Anchorage
Britton, Emily Maddox *sales executive*
Thomas, Peggy Ruth *public contract and procurement consultant*

Willow
White, Gwendolyn A. *recreational facility executive*

ARIZONA

Chandler
Brunello-McCay, Rosanne *sales executive*
Lawrence, Star *marketing executive, film company executive*

Cortaro
Fossland, Joeann Jones *professional speaker, personal coach*

Fort Huachuca
Szymeczek, Peggy Lee *contract specialist*

Glendale
Fisher, Debra A. *communications executive, educator*
Gonzales, Franceen Michelle *amusement facility executive*

Green Valley
Greenwood, Helen Maxine *retired office manager, executive assistant*

Mesa
Woods, Sarah Lynn *advertising executive*

Phoenix
Carpenter, Carol Settle *communications executive*
Hutchinson, Ann *management consultant*
Lack, Patricia Ann *drilling and pumping company executive, consultant*
LaValle, Jennifer Suzette *marketing communications specialist, consultant*
White, Annette Irene *marketing professional*

Prescott Valley
Cole, Susie Cleora *retired government employee relations official*

Scottsdale
Gwinn, Mary Dolores *business developer, philosopher, writer*
Hoff, Ann Marie *sales professional*
Hreniuc, Carmen Lacramioara *food service executive*
Keenan, Mary Josephine *communications executive*
Lavenson, Susan Barker *hotel corporate executive, consultant*
Lillestol, Jane Brush *development consultant*
Lingle, Kathleen McCall *human resources specialist, consultant, marketing executive, entrepreneur*
MacKinnon, Sally Anne *retired fast food company executive*
Morris, Samantha A. *marketing professional, researcher*

Sun City
Davis, Virginia *trade show producer*

Tempe
Jefferson, Myra LaVerne Tull *sales executive*
Kloefkorn, Sheila *marketing professional, sales executive*

Tucson
Cooper, Corinne *communications consultant, lawyer*
Eberhardt, Marty Lampert *botanical garden administrator*
Hoyt, Charlee Van Cleve *management executive*
Lee, Joyce Ann *computer educator*
Reinius, Michele Reed *executive recruiter*

Slaper, Rachael Maree *landscape company executive, poet*
Sohnen-Moe, Cherie Marilyn *business consultant*
Willert, Sister St. Joan *health care corporation executive*

Yuma
Hilgert, Arnie *management and marketing educator*

ARKANSAS

Bella Vista
Anton, Cheryl L. *sales executive*

Fayetteville
Webb, Lynne McGovern *communication scholar, consultant*

Jonesboro
Sullivan, Virginia L. *public affairs educator, consultant*

Little Rock
McCaleb, Annette Watts *executive secretary*

Monticello
Webster, Linda Jean *communications educator, media consultant*

Pine Bluff
McHan, Martha Elaine *purchasing agent*

CALIFORNIA

Alameda
Potash, Jeremy Warner *public relations executive*

Aliso Viejo
Harder, Wendy Wetzel *communications executive*
Otero-Smart, Ingrid Amarillys *advertising executive*

Anaheim
Sorenson, Sandra Louise *merchandising manager*

Baldwin Park
Snyder, Esther *food service executive*

Berkeley
Edwards, Susan M. *hotel executive*
Poulos, Paige M. *public relations executive*
Thomas, Lisa *food service executive*
Waters, Alice *executive chef, restaurant owner, writer*

Beverly Hills
Kingsley, Patricia *public relations executive*
Shepard, Kathryn Irene *public relations executive*
Yard, Sherry *chef*
Yost, Bernice *detective agency owner*

Burbank
Cohen, Valerie A. *entertainment company executive*
Frank, Amélie Lorraine *marketing professional*
Thomas-Graham, Pamela *communications executive*

Burlingame
Chalermvongsenee, Maytheenee *air freight administrator, consultant*

Camarillo
Cobb, Shirley Ann Dodson *public relations consultant, journalist*

Carmel
Boyd, Lynne Kaplan *management consultant*
Evans, Charlotte Mortimer *communications consultant, writer*

Carpinteria
Lopker, Pamela *technology industry executive*
Shinder, Lorraine Susan *contract administrator, educator*

Clovis
Moorefield, Claudia Candyce *confectionary marketing professional*

Compton
Janeway, Barbara *public relations executive*

Copperopolis
McClymonds, Jean Ellen *marketing professional*

Costa Mesa
Willard, Shirley Fay *management executive*

Coyote
Keeshen, Kathleen Kearney *public relations consultant*

Culver City
Boonshaft, Hope Judith *public affairs executive*

Cupertino
Dalrymple, Cheryl *retired computer company executive*
Geddes, Barbara Sheryl *communications executive, consultant*
Heinen, Nancy R. *computer company executive*

Daly City
Hargrave, Sarah Quesenberry *consulting company executive*

El Segundo
Olson, Jeanne Innis *technology and technical management executive*

Encinitas
Kenyon, Kendra Sue *organizational consultant*

Escondido
Mogul, Leslie Anne *business development and marketing consultant*

Fremont
Weinstein, Marta *packaging services company executive*

Fresno
Ganulin, Judy *public relations professional*

Fullerton
Sowder, Kathleen Adams *marketing executive*

Granada Hills
O'Connor, Betty Lou *hotel executive, food service executive*

Granite Bay
Holtz, Sara *management consultant*
Reisman, Judith Ann Gelernter *media communications executive, educator*

Half Moon Bay
Fennell, Diane Marie *marketing professional, process engineer*

Hermosa Beach
LaBouff, Jackie Pearson *personal care industry executive, educator*

La Jolla
Bardwick, Judith Marcia *management consultant*
Cole, Barbara Todd *bookseller*

La Quinta
Connerly, Dianna Jean *business official*

Laguna Niguel
Greenberg, Lenore *public relations professional*

Lake Forest
Hopp, Terry A. *computer company executive*

Long Beach
Brown, Roxanne (Jerene Roxanne Brown) *sales executive*

Los Angeles
Amey, Rae *project management and development consultant*
Bianchi, Carisa *advertising company executive*
Bohle, Sue *public relations executive*
Coots, Laurie *advertising executive*
Davidson, Judi *public relations executive*
Doll, Lynne Marie *public relations agency executive*
Flynn, Elizabeth Anne *advertising and public relations company executive*
Frank, Lillian Gorman *human resources executive, psychologist, management consultant*
Giffin, Margaret Ethel (Peggy Giffin) *management consultant*
Hale, Kaycee *research marketing professional*
Hartsough, Gayla Anne Kraetsch *management consultant*
Hill, Bonnie Guiton *consulting company executive*
Hirsh, Cynthia *food service executive*
Hodal, Melanie *public relations executive*
Hull, LeAnne von Neumeyer *public relations and communications executive, research consultant, writer*
Irwin-Hentschel, Noël *travel company executive*
Jacobs, Alicia Melvina *account executive*
Kleiman, Evan *chef*
Klein, Elaine *advertising executive*
Knox, Gertie R. *company executive, accountant*
LeMaster, Susan M. *marketing executive, writer*
Logan, Nancy Jane *broadcast sales and marketing executive*
Marshall-Daniels, Meryl *communications executive, mediator*
Mathias, Alice Irene *business management consultant*
Resnick, Lynda *business executive*
Rice, Regina Kelly *marketing executive*
Shiffman, Leslie Brown *management executive*
Silverton, Nancy *food service executive*
Splichal, Christine *restaurant owner*
Tatum, Jackie *former parks and recreation manager, municipal official*

Malibu
Smith, Yvonne Smart *advertising executive*
Tellem, Susan Mary *public relations executive*

Marina Del Rey
Gold, Carol Sapin *international management consultant, speaker*

Martinez
Tetrault, Jeanne L. *building inspector*

Menlo Park
Kurtzig, Sandra L. *software company executive*
Middleton, Teresa Muir *Internet company executive, researcher*

Mission Viejo
Austin, Berit Synnove *small business owner, central services specialist*

Mountain View
Allen, Vicky *sales and marketing professional*
Livermore, Ann M. *computer company executive*
Otus, Simone *public relations executive*
Polese, Kim *software company executive*

Newbury Park
Stadler, Katherine Loy *advertising sales executive*

Newport Beach
de Garcia, Lucia *marketing professional*
Gellman, Gloria Gae Seeburger Schick *marketing professional*

North Hollywood
Martin, Milinda *public relations executive*

Novato
Fraser, Margot *consumer products company executive*
Guadarrama, Belinda *computer company executive*

Oakland
Jeffries, Pamela Depperman *advertising executive, entrepreneur*
Williams, Carol H. *advertising executive*

Oceanside
Asato, Susan Pearce *business executive, educator*

Orange
Scherman, Carol E. *human resources professional*

Palmdale
Scott-Flanton, Vernita Lynn *consultant*

Palo Alto
Bowick, Susan D. *computer company executive*
Dunn, Debra L. *computer company executive*
Estrin, Judith *computer company executive*
Fiorina, Carleton S. (Carly Fiorina) *computer company executive*
Johnson, Allison *corporate communications specialist*
Kirk, Carmen Zetler *data processing executive*
Stephens, Bess *computer company executive*
Ticknor, Carolyn M. *computer company executive*
Willem, Karen J. *business software company financial executive*

Palos Verdes Estates
McNeill, Susan *real estate marketing and sales professional*

Paradise
Bernstein, Elizabeth Ann *retired executive secretary*

Pasadena
Wilson, Mary Ellen *retired project administrator*

Pebble Beach
Moriarty, Maureen C. *marketing professional*

Pomona
Patterson, Frieda Morgan *retired medical secretary, computer professional*
Tarver, Paula Diann *marketing professional*

Rancho Santa Margarita
Newton, Michelle Marie *sales executive*

Redwood City
Katz, Safra *computer company executive*
Majure, Allison Scott *product marketing professional*
Sharpnack, Rayona *management consultant*

Rosemead
Black, Melodee *marketing professional*

Sacramento
Baum, Sandra Beattie *executive secretary*
Boekhoudt-Cannon, Gloria Lydia *business education educator*
Hope, Gerri Danette *telecommunications management executive*
Kobe, Lisa Marie *quality assurance professional, consultant*
Lucas, Donna *communications executive*

San Bernardino
Clark, Phyllis Yvette *marketing professional, consultant*
Roberts, Katharine Adair *retired bookkeeper*

San Bruno
Mangahas, Crystal Tecca *market researcher*

San Diego
Adams, Loretta *marketing executive*
Amos, Theresa Ann *marketing professional*
Cline, Stephanie E. *food service executive*
Comrie, Sandra Melton *human resource executive*
Hays, Diana Joyce Watkins *consumer products company executive*
Herman, Rebecca Lynn *human resources specialist*
Lang, Linda A. *food service executive*
Lundy-Slade, Bettie B. *retired electronics professional*
Reno, Rosemary *marketing professional, real estate agent*
Wozniak, Joyce Marie *sales executive*

San Francisco
Blanc, Maureen *public relations executive*
Boehlke, Christine *public relations executive*
Brinkley, Susan *executive pastry chef*
Butenhoff, Susan G. *public relations executive*
Calvin, Dorothy Ver Strate *computer company executive*
D'Errico, Didi *public relations executive*
Des Jardins, Traci *chef, restaurant owner*
Everett-Thorp, Kate *digital marketing executive*
Gordon, Judith *communications consultant, writer*
Hall, Shannon *marketing professional, public relations executive, writer, photographer*
Henderson, Nancy Grace *marketing and technical documentation executive*
Hernandez, Aileen C(larke) *urban consultant*

Horn, Sabrina *public relations executive*
Hudson, Patricia Ann Siegel *association management specialist*
Hynes, Aedhmar *public relations executive*
Johnson, Camille *media executive*
Leondakis, Niki Anna *food service executive*
Mahesh, Shripriya *Internet company executive*
Martin-O'Neill, Mary Evelyn *advertising, marketing, business writing, sales training consultant*
McEvoy, Nan Tucker *publishing company executive, olive rancher*
Murphy, Kathleen Anne Foley *communications executive*
Oakes, Nancy *chef, restaurant owner*
Owades, Ruth Markowitz *marketing company executive*
Parker, Diana Lynne *restaurant manager, special events director*
Rosenfield, Ruth *advertising executive*
Torme, Margaret Anne *public relations executive, communications consultant*
Wernick, Sandra Margot *advertising and public relations executive*
Winkler, Agnieszka M. *marketing and software executive*

San Jose
Hawley, Kimra *software company executive*
Monia, Joan *retired management consultant*

San Rafael
Bartz, Carol *software company executive*
Saunders, Kathryn A. *retired data processing administrator*

San Ramon
Shapiro, Fania *computer company executive*

Santa Ana
Arriola-Nickell, Gail Emily *development executive*
Torrez, Caroline Herminia *recreation director*

Santa Clara
Culbertson, Leslie S. *computer company executive*
Ellis, Carlene *computer company executive*
Floyd, Shelly L. *computer company executive*
Lawrence, Deborah Jean *quality assurance professional*
Morris, Sandra K. *computer company executive*
Pollace, Pamela L. *public relations executive*
Roberts, Janice *marketing professional*

Santa Monica
Feniger, Susan *chef, television personality, writer*
Hutton, Fiona S. *communications executive*
Milliken, Mary Sue *chef, television personality, writer*
Ryan, Jane Frances *corporate communications executive*

Santa Rosa
Jones, Doris (Anna Doris Vogel) *apparel buyer*

Seaside
Melicia, Kitty *human resources administrator, foundation administrator*

Sonora
Mathias, Betty Jane *communications and community affairs consultant, writer, editor, lecturer*

South Lake Tahoe
Barr, Lois I. *personnel administrator*
Nason, Rochelle *conservation organization administrator*

South San Francisco
Estrin, Judy Ann *human resources consultant*
Morris, Arlene Myers *marketing professional*
Wong, Carrie *public relations executive*

Stanford
Paté-Cornell, Marie-Elisabeth Lucienne *management and engineering educator*

Stockton
Jacobs, Marian *advertising agency owner*

Studio City
Chambers, Clytia Montllor *public relations consultant*
Mc Donald, Meg *public relations executive*
Moseley, Chris Rosser *marketing executive*

Sunnyvale
Decker, Susan *Internet company executive*
Gupta, Vinita *communications executive*
Herscher, Penny *company executive*
Michals, Lee Marie *travel agency administrator*
Patstone, Cheryl *public relations executive*
Wesely, Elaine Gale *purchasing manager*

Sutter Creek
Sanders, Elizabeth Anne Weaver (Betsy Sanders) *management consultant*

Tehachapi
Smith-Thompson, Patricia Ann *public relations consultant, educator*

Temecula
Sjursen, Hope Bianchi *marketing professional*

Torrance
Howroyd, Janice Bryant *personnel placement executive*

Tracy
Harris, Kathleen Renee *marketing professional*

Tujunga
Buri, Carolyn *management consultant*

Valencia
Dolegowski, Dina C. *executive secretary*

Victorville
Yochem, Barbara June (Runyan) *sales executive, lecturer*

Walnut Creek
Wilkins, Sheila Scanlon *management consultant*

West Hills
Maeda, J. A. *data processing executive, consultant*

West Hollywood
Gates, Lisa *private chef, caterer*
Goin, Suzanne *food company executive, chef*

West Sacramento
Lloyd, Sharon *marketing professional*

Westlake Village
Troxell, Lucy Davis *management consultant*

Woodland Hills
Stahlecker, Barbara Jean *marketing professional, consultant*

COLORADO

Alamosa
Davis, Glenna Sue *human resources director*

Arvada
Williams, Marsha Kay *data processing executive*

Aurora
Hoffmaster, Nancy Jo Clement *social services professional, retired*

Black Hawk
Jones, Linda May *tour guide, writer*

Boulder
Shumick, Diana Lynn *computer executive*

Carbondale
Linden, Susan Pyles *marketing executive*

Castle Rock
Broer, Eileen Dennery *management consultant*

Denver
Bayes, Ginny *public relations and advertising executive*
Carson, Janine Marie *marketing professional*
Dunham, Joan Roberts *administrative assistant*
Engels, Patricia A. *communications executive*
Johnston, Gwinavere Adams *public relations consultant*
Korslund, Annette *administrative assistant, translator, interpreter, writer*
Kurtz, Maxine *personnel consultant, lawyer*
Lundy, Barbara Jean *training executive*
Mackinnon, Peggy Louise *public relations executive*
Murdock, Pamela Ervilla *travel and advertising company executive*
Reece, Monique Elizabeth *marketing, advertising and sales consultant*
Sanders, Mary Margaret *personnel director, dancer*
Taylor, Teresa *communications executive*
Walker, Joan H. *marketing and communications executive*
Williams, Marcia Putnam *human resources specialist*
Zak-Dance, Carol Camille *human communication educator*

Englewood
Cooper, Sharon Marsha *marketing, advertising executive*
Dunker, Amy Melissa *sales manager*
Lambert, Shirley Anne *marketing professional, publisher*
Miles, Amy E. *recreational facility executive*

Fort Collins
Clark, Claudia Ann *business development manager*
Honaker, Stevie Lee *career counselor, consultant*

Golden
Van Dusen, Donna Bayne *communications consultant, educator, researcher*

Grand Junction
Hall, Kathryn H. *public relations executive*

Greeley
Miller, Diane Wilmarth *retired human resources director*

Greenwood Village
Dickerson, Cynthia Rowe *marketing executive, consultant*

Littleton
Schomp, Lisa Juliana *automotive industry executive*
Treybig, Edwina Hall *sales executive*

Louisville
Tyson, Charlotte Rose *software development manager*

Loveland
Hach-Darrow, Kathryn *water testing company executive*

Northglenn
Stoian, Cristina *sales professional, real estate agent, real estate broker*

Ohio City
Dolezal, Ruth Ellen *resort owner*

Pagosa Springs
Howard, Carole Margaret Munroe *retired public relations executive*

Parker
Lark, M. Ann *management consultant, strategic planner, naturalist*

Superior
Reagan, Melodie A. *communications executive*

Torrance
Field, Phylis Sharon *consulting director*

CONNECTICUT

Bristol
LaGanga, Donna Brandeis *sales and marketing executive, management/educational administrator*
Petosa, Janet Frances *recruiting executive, publishing executive*

Cheshire
Greenhalgh, Patricia Ellen Donoghue *marketing research consultant*

Columbia
Klein, Cathy M. *funeral director*

Danbury
Izzo, Lucille Anne *sales representative*

Darien
Cappiello, Angela *meeting and marketing manager*

East Haddam
Clarke, Cordelia Kay Knight Mazuy *management consultant, artist*

Easton
Constantinople, Alexandra *communications executive*

Fairfield
Browne, Elizabeth Peddle *financial assistant*
Comstock, Elizabeth J. *marketing executive*
Hergenhan, Joyce *public relations executive*

Farmington
Sacerdote, Frances Arlene *executive recruiter*

Greenwich
Lewis, Audrey Gersh *financial marketing, public relations, strategic communications consultant*
Perless, Ellen *advertising executive*

Guilford
Mick, Margaret Anne *communications executive*
Woody, Carol Clayman *data processing executive*

Hamden
Balogh, Anne Marceline *personnel consultant*

Hartford
Harmon, Clara Chokenea *public relations/marketing executive*
Murphy, Joanne M. *computer company executive*

Kent
Friedman, Frances *public relations executive*

New Canaan
Jakacki, Diane Katherine *multimedia entertainment company executive*

New Haven
Huwiler, Joan P. *public relations executive, consultant*

Newington
Hadley, Nancy Lynne *management consultant, community foundation executive*

Norfolk
O'Malley, Margaret Parlin *marketing administrator*

North Haven
Weaver, Kitra K. *sales and marketing executive*

Norwalk
Czajkowski-Barrett, Karen Angela *human resources specialist*
Doran, Maureen *sales executive*
Mintz, Lenore Chaice (Lea Mintz) *consultant*
Weiner, Sandra Joan *computer catalog reseller company executive*

Orange
Phillips, Jeannette Veronica *management consultant, gerontologist*

Ridgefield
Clary, Alexia Barbara *purchasing agent*
Gruen, Marsha Irene *marketing executive*
Hancock, Ellen Marie *communications executive*

Shelton
Mariotti, Margaret *executive secretary*

Sherman
Cohn, Jane Shapiro *public relations executive*

Southington
Carrington, Virginia Gail (Vee Carrington) *marketing professional, consultant*

Stamford
Allocca, Antoinette *computer company executive*
Burns, Ursula *printing company executive*
Candland, Catherine C. *human resources executive*
Di Maria, Valerie Theresa *public relations executive*
Herbert, Tiffany Amber *marketing professional*
McGarry, Diane E. *marketing professional*
Mulcahy, Anne Marie *printing company executive*
Paolillo, Regina M. *information technology consulting executive*
Stern, Arlene Helen *human resources specialist*

Torrington
Sexton, Diana Elizabeth *communications company executive*

Waterford
Hinkle, Janet *project leader*

West Haven
Trumbley, Betty Jo Wilson *retired purchasing executive*

Wilton
Flesher, Margaret Covington *communications consultant, writer*
Lewis, Margaret Mary *marketing professional*

Woodbury
Peck, Carole *food service executive*

DELAWARE

Newark
Gore, Genevieve Walton *company executive*

Wilmington
Davis, Mary Kathryn *marketing professional*
Douglas, Victoria Jean *marketing professional, communications executive*
Trageser, Theresa Helen *project manager*

DISTRICT OF COLUMBIA

Washington
Beecraft, Carolyn Howland *communications executive*
Berman, Ellen Sue *energy and telecommunications executive, theatre producer*
Boza, Clara Brizcida *marketing professional*
Broaddus, Andrea Lynn *environmental policy advocate*
Brown, Jeanette L. *environmental protection administrator*
Cafritz, Peggy Cooper *communications executive*
Cashion, Ann *food service executive*
Coin, Sheila Regan *organization and management development consultant*
Cook, Frances D. *international business consultant*
Coons, Barbara Lynn *public relations executive, librarian*
Cope, Jeannette Naylor *executive search consultant*
Daly, Kay R. *public relations professional*
Dawson, Mimi Weyforth, Sr., *public policy consultant*
DeVaul, Diane D. *policy director*
Dolan, Kay Frances *human resources administrator*
Eckles, Susan *former management executive*
Garvey, Jane *public relations executive*
Gest, Kathryn Waters *public affairs professional*
Griffin, Kelly Ann *public relations executive, consultant*
Griffith, Elizabeth Anna *communications executive, educator*
Hager, Susan Kulka *public relations executive*
Hasselmo, Ann Hayes Die *executive search consultant, former college president, psychologist, educator*
Higgins, Kathryn O'Leary *consulting firm executive*
Hoffmann, Melane Kinney *marketing and public relations executive, writer*
Jackson, Sandra Willett *marketing professional*
Jordan, Sandra *public relations professional*
Kraus, Margery *management consultant, communications company executive*
Krumholz, Mimi *human resources administrator*
Lambert, Deborah Ketchum *public relations executive*
Lassen-Feldman, Wendy Anne *sales executive, lawyer*
Lattimore, Patricia *administration and management administrator*
Levinson, Nanette Segal *international relations educator, administrator*
Lisboa-Farrow, Elizabeth Oliver *public and government relations consultant*
Louison, Deborah Finley *global public affairs consultant*
Marshall, Maryann Chorba *office administrator*
Mayer, Susan *telecommunications company executive*
Mederos, Carolina Luisa *public policy consultant*
Minarczik, Jennifer Ann *communications company executive*
Nesbitt, Veronica A. *management executive*
Nielsen, Louisa Augusta *broadcast association executive*
Novak, Vicki Ann *human resources specialist*
Oliver-Simon, Gloria Craig *human resources advisor, consultant, lawyer*
Othello, Maryann Cecilia *quality assurance professional*
Pouillon, Nora Emanuela *food service executive*
Pyle, Cassandra A. *service organization executive*
Rainey, Jean Osgood *public relations executive*
Rice, Lois Dickson *former computer company executive*

Richwine, Heather *technology support manager*
Samuels, Cynthia Kalish *communications executive*
Seale, N. Allison *communications specialist*
Sharples, Ruth Lissak *communications executive*
Shear, Natalie Pickus *conference and event management executive*
Silverman, Marcia *public relations executive*
Simon, Rosalyn McCord *public relations executive*
Skolfield, Melissa T. *public relations executive, government official*
Smith, Nancy Lee *communications official*
Smulkstys, Inga *operations and management executive*
Sterling, Charlotte B. *hotel executive*
Swain, Susan Marie *communications executive*
Tate, Sheila Burke *communications executive*
Taylor, Sandra E. *public relations executive*
Turner, Jean-Louise *public relations executive*
Van Allen, Barbara Martz *marketing professional*
Villarreal, June Patricia *sales consultant*
Vose, Kathryn Kahler *marketing and communication executive*
Walker, Savannah T. *retired executive assistant, legislative assistant*
Watters, Mary Teresa *communications executive*
Watters, Susan J. *communications executive*
Wertheim, Mitzi Mallina *technology company executive*
White, Evelyn *human resources administrator*
Whittlesey, Judith Holloway *public relations executive*
Zimmerman, Carole Lee *public relations professional*

FLORIDA

Bartow
Bentley, Joyce Elaine *customer service officer*

Boca Raton
Langbort, Polly *retired advertising executive*
Turner, Lisa Phillips *human resources executive*
Yoder, Patricia Doherty *public relations executive*

Bonita Springs
Hauserman, Jacquita Knight *management consultant*

Cape Coral
Andert, Darlene (Darlene Andert-Schmidt) *management consultant*

Celebration
Renard, Meredith Anne *marketing and advertising professional*

Clearwater
Baker-Bowens, Helen L. *administrative assistant, genealogy researcher*
Bazzone, Theresa (Terry) A. *sales executive*
Hallam, Arlita Warrick *quality of life administrator*

Coral Gables
Aitken, Anne E. *computer company executive*
Bacon, Lydia Leach *human resources professional*
Buchsbaum, Karen Fuson *public relations executive, consultant*

Daytona Beach
Furstman, Shirley Elise Daddow *advertising executive*
Schauer, Catharine Guberman *public affairs specialist*

Deerfield Beach
Wade, Brenda Lynn *chef*

Delray Beach
Ehrlich, Geraldine Elizabeth *management consultant*
Randall, Priscilla Richmond *retired travel company executive*

Dunedin
Whiting, Susan D. *marketing professional*

Fort Lauderdale
Castillo, Carmen *staffing company executive*
Donaldson, Lisa Miller *city administration*
Hallman, Cinda A. *management consultant*
Johnson, Mary Margaret Dickens *researcher, consultant*
Koch, Katherine Rose *communications executive*

Fort Myers
Aron, Eve Glicka Serenson *personal care industry executive*
Goyak, Elizabeth Fairbairn *retired public relations executive*
Jaye, Karen A. *human resources specialist*
MacDougall, Frances Kay *marketing consultant*

Fort Walton Beach
Fallin, Barbara Moore *human resources director*

Gainesville
Skelton, Winifred Karger (Freddie Skelton) *advertising agency executive, painter*

Hollywood
Carmen Maria, Lopez *sales executive*
Fuentes, Denise Iris *customer service administrator, sales representative*
Williams, Roslyn Patrice *marketing executive*

Hutchinson Island
Wanzer, Mary Kathryn *computer company executive, consultant*

Inglis
Norris, Mildred Eleanor *consultant*

Islamorada
Sieber, Dawn *food service executive*

Jacksonville
Bodkin, Ruby Pate *corporate executive, real estate broker, educator*

Jacksonville Beach
Saltzman, Irene Cameron *consumer products company executive*

Jupiter
Colucci, Jacqueline Strupp *insurance agent, small business administration specialist, sculptor, special project coordinator*

Key Colony Beach
Crenshaw, Patricia Shryack *sales executive, consultant*

Key West
Menendez, Teresa *communications executive*

Lake Worth
Gorman, Marcie Sothern *personal care industry executive*

Lakeland
Bricker, Lisa G. *marketing professional, not-for-profit fundraiser*
Zucco, Ronda Kay *planning and marketing professional*

Land O Lakes
O'Connell, Carmela Digristina *appraisal executive, consultant*

Longboat Key
Moulton, Katherine Klauber *hotel executive*

Lutz
Miller, Bonnie Sewell *marketing professional, writer*

Maitland
Stephens, Patricia Ann *marketing professional*

Miami
Amos, Betty Giles *restaurant company executive, accountant*
Bessette, Diane J. *homebuilding company executive*
Conover, Pamela C. *cruise line executive*
Corbi, Lana *communications executive*
Haar, Ana Maria Fernández *advertising and public relations executive*
Neuman, Susan Catherine *public relations and marketing consultant*
Tuzel, Tulin *food service executive*

Miami Beach
Kersten, Sharon *public relations executive, consultant*
Membiela, Roymi Victoria *marketing professional, consultant*

Miramar
González Tricoche, Cynthia Marie *human resources specialist*

Naples
Mainwaring, Susan Adams *recreational facility executive*
Ward, Kelsey S. *purchasing agent*

New Port Richey
Baker, Michele Dawn Litz *management consultant*

Orange City
Schaeffer, Barbara Hamilton *retired rental leasing company executive, writer*

Orlando
Dimopoulos, Linda J. *food service executive*
Mahoney, Mary *hotel executive*

Ormond Beach
Graf, Dorothy Ann *human resources specialist*
Ray, Janie Machelle (J. R. Shepard) *software development executive*

Osprey
Halladay, Laurie Ann *public relations consultant, former franchise executive*

Palm Beach
Baum, Selma *customer relations consultant*
Birmingham, Pat *pageant director*
Whiteside, Patricia Lee *fine art antique and personal property appraiser*

Palm Beach Gardens
Van Allen, Veronica Elaine *marketing and public relations professional*

Panama City Beach
Shugart, Anita Carol *research and development cosmetologist*

Plantation
Bosted, Dorothy Stack *public relations executive*

Port Charlotte
Reynolds, Helen Elizabeth *management services consultant*

Riverview
Till, Beatriz Maria *international business consultant, translator*

Sarasota
Holcomb, Constance L. *sales and marketing management executive*
Honner Sutherland, B. Joan *advertising executive*
Lee, Nancy Ranck *management consultant*

Spring Hill
Chase, Patricia M. *management consultant*

Tallahassee
Crook, Wendy P. *management consultant, educator*

Tampa
Cunningham, Kathleen Ann *human resources specialist, purchasing agent*
Mathis, Marsha Debra *customer relations manager*

Tarpon Springs
Crismond, Linda Fry *public relations executive*

Titusville
Horn, Flora Leola *retired administrative assistant*

Venice
Bluhm, Barbara Jean *communications agency executive*

Vero Beach
Binney, Jan Jarrell *publishing executive*

Wellington
Fitch, Mary Killeen *human resources specialist*

Windermere
DeRubertis, Patricia Uhl *software company executive*

Winter Park
Safian, Shelley Carole *advertising executive*

GEORGIA

Alpharetta
Brebner, Kimberly Kay *marketing professional*

Atlanta
Barnard, Patricia A. *human resources specialist*
Beres, Mary Elizabeth *management educator, organizational consultant*
Brown-Olmstead, Amanda *public relations executive*
Crackett, Delores *womens bureau administrator*
Hines, Alida N. *marketing professional, researcher*
Kelly, Carol White *company executive*
Lanier, Martha I. *human resources specialist*
McDonald Rackley, Collette Lynn *management consultant*
McKenzie, Kay Branch *public relations executive*
Quatrano, Anne *chef, restaurant owner*
Reising, Juliet M. *information systems executive*
Timm-Brock, Barbara *chief product officer*
Ward, Jackie M. *computer company executive*
Weidman, Sheila *marketing professional*
Wilding, Diane *marketing, financial and information systems executive*
Wilson, Alexandra M. *communications executive*
Winograd, Audrey Lesser *retired advertising executive*

Augusta
Nevins, Frances (Frankie) Rush *tourism professional*

Bainbridge
Burkhalter, Myra Sheram *company official*

Columbus
Finch, Catherine Ann *firework display artist, aromatherapist*

Cumming
Palmer, Theresa Joan Griffin *restaurant owner executive*

Decatur
Breckenridge, Betty Gayle *management development consultant*

Folkston
Wangsness, Genna Stead *hotel executive, innkeeper*

Gainesville
Davis, Connie Waters *public relations executive, marketing professional*

Milledgeville
Stewart, Felecia Marcia *purchasing agent*

Monticello
Bell, Jacqueline Delores *management consultant*

Norcross
Koscik, Ella M. *management and technology company executive*

Oakwood
Jondahl, Terri Elise *importing and distribution company executive*

Roswell
Strong-Tidman, Virginia Adele *marketing professional*

Saint Simons Island
Sullivan, Barbara Boyle *management consultant*

Smyrna
Michels, Frances G. *management company executive*

Social Circle
Dupree, Nathalie *chef, television personality, writer*

Thomasville
Turner, Marta Jones *public affairs professional*

Tucker
Brown, Betsy S. *hotel executive*

Villa Rica
Zoda, Suzanne Marie *environmental public relations consultant*

HAWAII

Honolulu
Doi, Dorothy Mitsue Yano *travel company executive*

Kailua
Grimmer, Beverley Sue *consumer products company executive*

Kapaau
Ralston, Joanne Smoot *public relations executive*

Lanai City
Keenan-Abilay, Georgia Ann *service representative*

IDAHO

Boise
Beaumont, Pamela Jo *marketing professional*
Thornton, Felicia *food service executive, corporate financial executive*

Idaho Falls
Barbe, Betty Catherine *marketing professional, retired financial analyst*

Kamiah
Mills, Carol Margaret *business consultant, public relations consultant*

Ketchum
Leonardo, Ann Adamson *marketing and sales consultant*

Sun Valley
Erickson, Ann Florin *recreational facility executive, realtor*

ILLINOIS

Addison
Christopher, Doris K. *consumer products company executive*

Arlington Heights
Fields, Sara A. *travel company executive*

Aurora
Dillitzer, Dianne René *sales executive*

Bannockburn
Daube, Lorrie O. *sales executive*

Barrington
Lee, Catherine M. *business owner, educator*
Sturm, Sherri Charisse *marketing and developmental researcher, actuary*

Batavia
Abuhl, Jeanne Marie *sales professional*

Bloomington
Daily, Jean A. *marketing executive*
Stump, Lisa Dian *marketing professional, music educator*

Bradley
Brown, Lana Weiss *public relations executive*

Broadview
Lazar, Jill Sue *home healthcare company executive*

Burr Ridge
Zaccone, Suzanne Maria *sales executive*

Chicago
Akins, Cindy S. *human resources professional*
Allen, Belle *management consulting firm executive, communications executive*
Bergstrom, Betty Howard *consulting executive, foundation administrator*
Berman, Cheryl R. *advertising company executive*
Beugen, Joan Beth *communications company executive*
Boyda, Debora *advertising executive*
Bradley, Vanessa Lynn *management consultant*
Castorino, Sue *communications executive*
deChaud, Christina Rita *marketing specialist, consultant*
Deli, Anne Tynion *marketing executive*
Diederichs, Janet Wood *public relations executive*
Doetsch, Virginia Lamb *former advertising executive, writer*
Douglas, Cynthia *executive administrative assistant*
Friedlander, Patricia Ann *marketing professional, writer*
Furth, Yvonne *advertising executive*
Gand, Gayle *chef*
Gidwitz, Teri Lynne *marketing professional*
Gray, Dawn Plambeck *work-family consultant*
Green, RuthAnn *marketing and management consultant*
Healy, Sondra Anita *consumer products company executive*
Hoey, Rita *public relations executive*
Kindzred, Diana *communications company executive*

Kloster, Carol Good *book and magazine distribution company*
Leigh, Sherren *communications executive, editor, publisher*
Levy, Deborah *security company executive*
Lewis, Evelyn *management consultant*
Lieberman, Pamela Forbes *consumer products company executive*
Mackiewicz, Laura *advertising agency executive*
MacWilliams, Diane *communications executive*
Maczulski, Margaret Louise *event marketing professional, meeting manager*
McCann, Renetta *advertising executive*
Miller, Ellen *advertising executive*
Mosley-McCall, Jeraldine *funeral director*
Moster, Mary Clare *public relations executive*
O'Shea, Lynne Edeen *management consultant, educator*
Paitich, Olivia *project coordinator, office manager*
Petrillo, Nancy *public relations executive*
Phillips, Carolyn Kae *marketing professional*
Plank, Betsy (Mrs. Sherman V. Rosenfield) *public relations counsel*
Pope, Lena Elizabeth *human resources specialist*
Posner, Kathy Robin *communications executive*
Prather, Susan Lynn *public relations executive*
Provus, Barbara Lee *executive search consultant*
Rich, S. Judith *public relations executive*
Schindler, Judi(th) (Judith Kay Schindler) *public relations executive, marketing professional, consultant*
Seebert, Kathleen Anne *international sales and marketing executive*
Segal, Mindy *chef*
Shimokubo, Janice Teruko *marketing professional*
Shirley, Virginia Lee *advertising executive*
Singer, Emel *staffing industry executive*
Stenger, Sarah *chef*
Strubel, Ella Doyle *advertising executive, public relations executive*
Talbot, Pamela *public relations executive*
Taylor, Collette *public relations executive*
Thompson, Jayne Carr *public relations and communications executive, lawyer*
Tripp, Marian Barlow Loofe *retired public relations executive*
Vaughn, Connie Marie *marketing professional, writer*
Vilim, Nancy Catherine *advertising agency executive*
Watson, MaryFrances Elizabeth *management consultant, librarian*
Weaver, Donna Rae *wine company executive*
Wiecek, Barbara Harriet *advertising executive*
Williams, Flynor A. *public affairs specialist*
Williams, Martha *consumer products company executive, entrepreneur*
Wolf, Linda S. *advertising executive*
Wooldridge, Patrice Marie *marketing professional, martial arts and meditation educator*

Deerfield
Huff, Gayle Compton *advertising and marketing executive*

Des Plaines
Drake, Ann M. *consumer products company executive*
Dvorak, Kathleen S. *business products company executive*
Le Menager, Lois M. *incentive merchandise and travel company executive*

Edwardsville
Dietrich, Suzanne Claire *instructional designer, communications consultant*

Elgin
O'Connor, Peggy Lee *communications manager*

Elmhurst
Choyke, Phyllis May Ford (Mrs. Arthur Davis Choyke Jr.) *management executive, editor, poet*
Duarte, Gloria *chef*
Malo, Michele Lee *marketing professional*

Evanston
Agrawal, Amita *management consultant*
Blair, Virginia Ann *public relations executive*

Geneseo
Crisp, Sandra Sue *procurement analyst*

Geneva
Houska-Green, Kathleen Ann *marketing professional, public relations executive*

Glencoe
Cole, Kathleen Ann *advertising agency executive, retired social worker*

Glenview
Franklin, Lynne *business communications consultant, writer*
Gómez, Fabiola *marketing communications professional*

Hanover Park
Carter, Eleanor Elizabeth *business manager*

Highland Park
Axelrod, Leah Joy *tour company executive*
Burman, Diane Berger *career management and organization development consultant*

Hinsdale
Amsler, Jana *chef*

Hudson
Mills, Lois Jean *design company executive, retired education educator, aide*

Joliet
Hill, Kathleen Joy *administrative assistant*
Starner, Barbara Kazmark *marketing, advertising and export sales executive*

Lake Bluff
Scott, Karen Bondurant *consumer catalog company executive*

Lake Forest
Bradley, Kim Alexandra *sales and marketing specialist*
Chieger, Kathryn Jean *recreation company executive*
Goldstein, Marsha Feder *tour company executive*
Rand, Kathy Sue *public relations executive*
Reich, Victoria J. *consumer products company executive*

Lake Villa
Johnson, Samira El-Chehabi *marketing professional*

Lansing
Kaplan, Huette Myra *business educator, training consultant*

Libertyville
Conklin, Mara Loraine *public relations executive*
Devine, Barbara Armstrong *risk manager*

Lincolnwood
Grossinger, Caroline *sales executive*

Loves Park
Sylvester, Nancy Katherine *management consultant*

Macomb
Pawelko, Katharine Ann *recreation educator*

Melrose Park
Bernick, Carol Lavin *corporate executive*
Kipper, Barbara Levy *corporate executive*

Mokena
Pammer, Lesa Gail *marketing professional*

Morton Grove
Friedman, Marla Lee *marketing professional*
Smolyansky, Julie *consumer products company executive*

Mundelein
Greene, Stephanie Harrison *marketing executive*

Northbrook
Crockett, Joan M. *human resources executive*
Ehrenberg, Maureen *management consultant*
Mulhall, Kimberly A. *marketing professional*
Sudbrink, Jane Marie *sales and marketing executive*

Northfield
Heise, Marilyn Beardsley *public relations company executive*

Oak Brook
Babrowski, Claire Harbeck *fast food chain executive*
Crump-Caine, Lynn *food service executive*
Fields, Janice L. *food service executive*
Hassert, Elizabeth Anne *transportation sales executive*

Oakbrook Terrace
Hegenderfer, Jonita Susan *public relations executive*

Park Ridge
Campbell, Dorothy May *management consultant*

Peoria Heights
Taylor, Kathy Deanne *marketing executive, consultant*

Prospect Heights
Hanagan, Audrey Jeanette *training services executive*

Quincy
Adams, Beejay (Meredith Elisabeth Jane Adams) *retired sales executive*

Riverwoods
Del Tiempo, Sandra Kay *sales executive*

Rockford
Morrissey, Mary F. (Fran) *human resource consulting company executive*

Schaumburg
Metty, Theresa M. *communications executive*
Morse, Gloria Jeanne *executive secretary*
Warrior, Padmasree *communications executive*

Skokie
Whalen, Patricia Therese *marketing and public relations educator, consultant*

Springfield
Fuchs, Nora Kay *business manager*

Westchester
Abbinante, Vita *sales executive, administrator*

Willowbrook
Mathisen-Reid, Rhoda Sharon *international communications consultant*

INDIANA

Bloomington
Spiro, Rosann Lee *marketing professional, educator*

Brazil
Jones, Carole Moody-Anderson *retired outreach representative*

Fort Wayne
Taritas, Karen Joyce *customer service administrator*

Indianapolis
Ahlrichs, Nancy Surratt *marketing professional*
Dishong, Linda S. *estate planner*
Perry, Jane A. *service assistant*
Schafer, Yvonne A. *human resources specialist*
Simmons, Roberta Johnson *public relations firm executive*

Monroeville
Ray, Annette D. *executive secretary*

New Palestine
Court Gipson, Yvette Kristina *marketing professional*

IOWA

Ames
Bonomi, Ferne Gater *public relations executive*

Atlantic
Johnson, Joan (Jan) Hope Voss *communications executive, photojournalist, public relations executive*

Des Moines
Amendt, Marilyn Joan *personnel director*

George
Symens, Maxine Brinkert Tanner *marketing professional*

Ottumwa
Sager Neil, Theresa Louise *poet, author of children's books*

Storm Lake
McKenney, Irene June *business manager, former educator*

KANSAS

Colby
Baldwin, Irene S. *corporate executive, real estate investor*

Great Bend
Siebert, Deborah Ann *public relations and marketing executive*

Leavenworth
Franklin, Shirley Marie *marketing consultant*

Leawood
Joslin, Janine Elizabeth *preservation consultant*

Mission
Alexander, Anne A. *sales consultant*

Oakley
Ratliff-Smith, Dee Ann *bookkeeper*

Overland Park
Davis, Dianne Louise *marketing professional*

Topeka
Sipes, Karen Kay *communications executive*

KENTUCKY

Albany
Smith, Eugenia Sewell *funeral home executive*

Bowling Green
Garrison, Geneva *retired administrative assistant*

Florence
Gorman, Gayla Marlene Osborne *consumer affairs executive*

Louisville
Blake, Jane Salley *publishing, public relations, and management consultant*
Columbus, Shanna S. *advertising executive*
Ivey, Susan *tobacco company executive*
Peden, Katherine Graham *industrial consultant*
Shelburne, Renee D. *communications executive*

Mackville
Scott, Donna C. *human resources specialist*

Nicholasville
Bender, Betty Barbee *food service professional*

LOUISIANA

Baton Rouge
Hewitt, Maureen Gilgore *scholarly book publishing executive*
Kimball, Dorothy Jean *foundation executive*

Bossier City
Rankin, Mary Anne *director*

Jefferson
Darce, Shirl Johnson *computer sales director*

Lafayette
Ferguson, Tamela *management consultant, educator*

Mandeville
Gavin, Mary Ellen *consultant*

Metairie
Doody, Barbara Pettett *computer specialist*
Gereighty, Andrea Saunders *polling company executive, poet*
Nix, Linda Anne Bean *public relations executive*
Schwegmann, Melinda *supermarket executive, former state official*

New Orleans
Barden, Janice Kindler *personnel company executive*
Brennan, Lally *food service executive*
Bridges, Elizabeth Ann *project administrator*
Creppel, Claire Binet *hotel owner*
Davis, Pamela Marie *administrative analyst*
de la Vergne, Marie Louise Beatrice *antiques and fine art consultant*
Fertel, Ruth U. *restaurant owner*
Kearney, Anne *chef*
Spicer, Susan *food service executive*
Tahir, Mary Elizabeth (Liz Tahir) *marketing professional, consultant, speaker, writer*

Pineville
Cummings, Karen Sue *retired corrections classification administrator*

Shreveport
Giles, Katharine Emily (J. K. Piper) *administrative assistant, writer*
Wright, Marie Beulah Battey *retired advertising executive*

MAINE

Monhegan
Van Houten, Elizabeth Ann *corporate communications executive, painter*

MARYLAND

Annapolis
Miller, Patricia A. *training services executive*
Ryan, Michele King *marketing professional*

Baltimore
Brotman, Phyllis Block *advertising and public relations executive*
Friedman, Maria Andre *public relations executive*
Hillman, Sandra Schwartz *public relations executive, marketing professional*
Kim, Lillian G. Lee *retired administrative assistant*
Pollard, Shirley *employment training director, community services administrator, consultant*
Robinson, Florine Samantha *marketing executive*
Saltzberg, Joanne Maria *company executive*

Bethesda
Coe, Judith Lynn *retired automobile manufacturing company administrator*
Cutting, Mary Dorothea *audio and audio-visual communications company executive*
Gimmel, Molly Kay *business executive*

Cambridge
Spahr, Elizabeth *environmental services administrator*

Chestertown
Docksteader, Karen Kemp *marketing professional*

Chevy Chase
Greenspoon, Irma Naiman *business executive*

Clinton
Brooks, Pauline C. *computer and networking services company executive*

College Park
Hudson, Deborah M. *public relations practitioner*

Elkton
Jasinski-Caldwell, Mary L. *company executive*

Fort Washington
Fielding, Elizabeth M(ay) *public relations executive, writer*

Frederick
Schricker, Ethel Killingsworth *retired business management consultant*

Gaithersburg
Kress, Jill Clancy *human resources professional, consultant*

Gambrills
Streeter, Carol *technology marketing executive*

Germantown
Isaacson, Elaine Marie *sales and training agent*

Hagerstown
Yost, Jean Marie *administrative assistant*

Jessup
Fox, Dawne Marie *safety scientist*

Lanham
Henderson Hall, Brenda Ford *computer company executive*

Lanham Seabrook
Barnes, Margaret Anderson *business consultant*

Ocean City
Phillips, Shirley Flowers *food service executive*

Potomac
Benton, Kay Myers *sales executive*

Riverdale
Bernard, Cathy S. *management corporation executive*
Kline, Nancy Meadors *non-profit company executive, consulting executive, writer*

Rockville
MacArthur, Diana Taylor *advanced technology executive*

Salisbury
Wilmer, Ann *public relations executive*

Severna Park
Humphreys Troy, Patricia *communications executive*

Silver Spring
Altschul, B J *public relations counselor*
Burke, Margaret Ann *computer and communications company specialist*
Compton, Mary Beatrice Brown (Mrs. Ralph Theodore Compton) *public relations executive, writer*
Fields, Daisy Bresley *human resources specialist, writer*
Hilberg, Rosemary Helen *retired human resource specialist*
Lett, Cynthia Ellen Wein *speaker, trainer, coach*
Moreno, Donna Marie *communications executive*
Shih-Carducci, Joan Chia-mo *cooking educator, biochemist, medical technologist, author, writer*

Towson
Nicolosi, Gianna Ruth *marketing professional*

West Bethesda
Vogelgesang, Sandra Louise *business executive, writer, consultant*

West River
Bower, Catherine Downes *communications, management consultant*
Pratt, Katherine Merrick *environmental consulting company executive*

MASSACHUSETTS

Belmont
Fahey, Ellen McKenney *recreation director*

Boston
Argyropoulos, Ursula *food service executive*
Berman, Lisa *advertising executive*
Biro, Kathy *advertising executive*
Coady, Nicole *food service executive*
Cone, Carol Lynn *public relations executive*
Cornwall, Deborah Joyce *consulting firm executive, management consultant*
Coville, Andrea *public relations executive*
Finucane, Anne M. *communications and marketing executive*
FitzGerald, Maura *public relations executive*
Gadiesh, Orit *management consulting executive*
Hardy, Victoria Elizabeth *management educator*
Lerner, Linda Joyce *human resources executive*
Lynch, Barbara *chef, restaurant owner*
Martel, Lisa *food service executive*
McArdle, Patricia Anne *security company executive*
Regis, Susan *food service executive*
Sander, Alison Bishop *international consultant*
Schneider, Joan *public relations company owner*
Shire, Lydia *food service executive*
Swaysland, Janet *advertising executive*
Torpey, Tara Jane *sales executive*

Burlington
McWade, Jessica Christy *marketing professional*
Reeve, Pamela *communications executive*

Cambridge
Adams, Jody *chef, restaurant owner*
Adams, Ruth-Anne *chef*
Bloom, Kathryn Ruth *public relations executive*
de Monteiro, Nadsa *chef*
Kilpatrick, Maureen *food service executive*
Lauzier, Marijean *public relations executive*
Lydon, Amanda *chef*
Sortun, Ana *food service executive*
Thompson, Doreen *public relations executive*

Canton
Pitts, Virginia M. *human resources executive*

Chestnut Hill
Addis, Deborah Jane *management consultant, editor*

Duxbury
Erickson, Phyllis Traver *marketing executive*

Framingham
Hillman, Carol Barbara *communications executive, consultant*
Wulf, Sharon Ann *management consultant*

Gloucester
Means, Rosaline *business executive, business educator*

Leominster
Lyons, Beryl Barton Anfindsen *advertising executive*

Lexington
Bernitz, Francine S. *marketing professional*
Piano, Phyllis J. *communications executive*

Marblehead
Gardner, Mary Josephine *management development consultant*

Marlborough
Lindsay, Janice Campbell *communications executive, writer*

Melrose
McLennan, Bernice Claire *human resources professional*

Newton
Benner, Mary Wright *event planner*

Orleans
Addison, Helen Katherine *marketing professional, art dealer*

Quincy
Lawler, Linda *disability examiner*

Springfield
Vincensi, Avis A. *sales executive, medical educator*

Sterling
Lundgren, Ruth Williamson Wood (Ruth Lundgren Williamson Wood) *public relations executive, writer*

Sudbury
Gruol, Mary Catherine Schuetz *human resources operations executive*

Topsfield
Natale, Diane Theresa *communications executive*

Townsend
Smith, Denise Groleau *data processing professional*

Waltham
Schwartz, Paula Mae *communications company executive*
Warren, Susan Hanke Murphy *international marketing business development executive*

Wayland
Caristo-Verrill, Janet Rose *international management consultant*
Harrington, Kay Lorraine *executive secretary*

West Stockbridge
Levine, Toby Kleban *communications executive, educational media developer*

Westford
Endyke, Debra Joan *data communications marketing professional*
Weston, Joan Spencer *editorial and production director, communications executive*

Williamstown
Driscoll, Genevieve Bosson (Jeanne Bosson Driscoll) *management and organization development consultant*

Woburn
Paul, Lois *public relations company executive*

MICHIGAN

Allen Park
Bizon, Emma Djafar *management consultant*

Ann Arbor
Bachelder, Cheryl Anne *marketing professional*
Britt, Margaret Mary *communications director*
Bryant, Barbara Everitt *academic researcher, market research consultant, former federal agency administrator*
Lindsay, June Campbell McKee *communications executive*
Mitchell, Anna-Marie Rajala *quality/outcomes analyst*

Auburn Hills
Nelson, Debra Jean *journalist, public relations executive, consultant*

Dearborn
Ardisana, Beth *communications company executive*
Byars, Leisa *marketing professional, automotive executive*

Detroit
Dixson, J. B. *communications executive*
Engelhardt, Regina *cosmetologist, artist, small business owner*
Ilitch, Denise *food services executive*
McCracken, Caron Francis *computer company executive, consultant*
Salter, Linda Lee *security officer*
Sufalko, Dynah Naomi Juliette *marketing professional*
Tallet, Margaret Anne *theatre executive*

East Lansing
Force, Christine *small business developer*

Eaton Rapids
Hall, Rebecca Ann *executive secretary*

Farmington Hills
Bassett, Tina *communications executive*
Benedict, Elise *moving company executive*
Corwell, Ann Elizabeth *public relations executive*

Grand Rapids
Bruyn, Kimberly Ann *public relations executive, consultant*
Greco, Marie Danielle *advertising executive, director*
Purchase-Owens, Francena *human resources specialist, educator*
Seyferth, Virginia M. *public relations executive*

Grosse Pointe Woods
Cusmano, J. Joyce *public relations executive*

Kalamazoo
Sowles, Beth A. *secretary*

Keego Harbor
Gee, Sharon Lynn *funeral director, educator*

Lansing
Robinson, Melissa Sue *communications executive, national association administrator*

Livonia
Yax, Ellen Marie *photography finisher*

Madison Heights
Woodruff, Jane *sales executive*

Marquette
Earle, Mary Margaret *marketing executive*

Muskegon
Gundy-Reed, Frances Darnell *marketing executive*

Pontiac
Popadak, Geraldine L. *organizational development consultant, educator*

Saginaw
Thomas, Carol Marie *business manager, lawyer*

Saline
Low, Louise Anderson *consulting company executive*

Southfield
Barnett, Marilyn *advertising agency executive*
Hudson, Cheryl L. *communications executive*

Sterling Heights
Matthews Ellis, Bonnie *management consultant*

Three Rivers
Pierce, Sue *sales executive*

Troy
Harrison, Christine Delane *company executive*
Lorencz, Mary *public relations executive*
McLaren, Karen Lynn *advertising executive*
Meyers, Christine Laine *marketing and media executive, consultant*
Updike, Linda S. *personnel placement firm executive*
Wettergren, Sandra Marie *personnel consultant*
White, Tommi A. *human resources firm executive*

Warren
Gilbert, Suzanne Harris *advertising executive*
Zoubareff, Kathy Olga *administrative assistant*

West Bloomfield
Smith, Nancy Hohendorf *retired sales and marketing executive*

MINNESOTA

Apple Valley
Kettle, Sally Anne *consulting company executive, educator*

Bloomington
Jeffries, Mary *public relations executive*
Taylor, Susan S. *communications executive*

Eden Prairie
Cervilla, Constance Marlene *marketing consultant*
Erickson, Kim *consumer products company executive*
Petersen, Maureen Jeanette Miller *management information consultant, former nurse*

Glencoe
Delagardelle, Linda *food executive*

Hackensack
Marquart, Petra A. *training consultant*

Hastings
Avent, Sharon L. Hoffman *manufacturing company executive*

Minneapolis
Bonner, Brigid Ann *marketing professional*
Brooks, Gladys Sinclair *retired public affairs consultant*
Casey, Lynn M. *public relations executive*
Eich, Susan *public relations executive*
Gavin, Sara *public relations executive*
Harp-Jirschele, Mary *communications executive*
Johnson, Lola Norine *retired advertising and public relations executive, educator*
Nelson, Marilyn C. *hotel executive, travel company executive, food service executive, marketing professional*
Tunheim, Kathryn H. *public relations executive*

Oakdale
Cederburg, Barbara M. *printing company executive*

Richfield
Schuett, Carol Ann *travel industry business analyst*

Rochester
Hiniker, LuAnn *management consultant, educator, researcher, grants consultant*
Kinney, Carolyn *executive secretary*

Saint Cloud
McIntyre, Vicky Joyce *business owner*

Saint Paul
Esposito, Bonnie Lou *marketing professional*
Smith, Lucy *intercultural communication specialist*

Waconia
Scanlon Hobbs, Laurie Ann *public relations professional*

MISSISSIPPI

Columbus
Labensky, Sarah Ross *culinary educator*

Hattiesburg
Taylor, Elizabeth Ann (Beth Taylor) *advertising and marketing executive, video producer*

Jackson
Patterson, Chan *food service executive*

Port Gibson
Alford, Constance Keith *recreational facility executive, artist*

Purvis
Evans, V. Faye *postmaster*

Ridgeland
Crittenden, Antoinette *marketing professional*

MISSOURI

Ballwin
Corno, Donna A. *retired public relations executive, consultant*

Columbia
Beedle, Dawn Danene *recruiting and training administrator*
Findley-Liles, Shannon Marie *sales executive*

Golden City
Howard, Joanne Frances *marketing executive, researcher, funeral director*

Independence
Booz, Gretchen Arlene *marketing executive*
Evans, Margaret Ann *human resources administrator, business owner*

Kansas City
Adams, Beverly Josephine *data processing specialist*
Bartlett, Sherie *printing company executive*
Belzer, Ellen J. *negotiations and communications trainer, consultant*
Courson, Marna B.P. *public relations executive*
Donovan, Ann Burcham *medical office administrator*
Krause, Heather Dawn *data processing executive*
McElwreath, Sally Chin *corporate communications executive*
Solberg, Elizabeth Transou *public relations executive*
Stevens, Jane *advertising executive*
Taylor, Marilyn Levere *management consultant, educator*

Lees Summit
Duke, Ellen Kay *planned giving administrator*

Saint Louis
Albee, Lenore K. *management consultant*
Bateman, Sharon Louise *public relations executive*
Bellville, Margaret (Maggie Bellville) *communications executive*
Campbell, Anita Joyce *computer company executive*
Diekemper, Rita Garbs *landscape company executive*
Dugan, Jean Brodshaug *public relations consultant*
Edwards, Judith Elizabeth *advertising executive*
Farhatt, Kendra *travel company executive*
Handelman, Alice Samuels *public relations professional, writer*
Johnson, Susan L. B. *human resource administrator*
Loepker, Patricia M. *marketing manager*
Vandiver, Donna *public relations executive*
Wright, Diane *procurement manager*

Town And Country
Lachenicht-Berkeley, Angela Marie *marketing professional*

University City
Gatlin, Novella Anna Maria *collection specialist, business consultant*

MONTANA

Belgrade
Aveson, Martha Caralyn *pharmaceutical company executive*

Butte
Ouellette, Debra Lee *administrative assistant, consultant*

Helena
Manuel, Vivian *public relations executive*
Waterman, Mignon Redfield *public relations executive, state legislator*

NEBRASKA

Chadron
Limbach, Barbara June *management educator*

Omaha
Brailey, Susan Louise *quality analyst, educator*
Lindsay, Cosimano *marketing professional*
Phares, Lynn Levisay *public relations communications executive*
Scholz, Denise Lienemann *office manager*

NEVADA

Henderson
Absher, Robin Dawn *security firm executive, private investigator*
Atkins, Candi *management consultant, small business owner*
Bruno, Cathy Eileen *management consultant, former state official, social sciences educator*

Las Vegas
Beagles, Dorothy Boetticher *office administrator, homeopathic consultant*
Blau, Elizabeth Anne *restaurant executive*
Goodwin, Nancy Lee *corporate executive*
Huston, Joyce A. *web site design company executive*
Mataseje, Veronica Julia *sales executive*
Safford, Florence Viray Sunga *travel agent, consultant*
Shively, Judith Carolyn (Judy Shively) *contract administrator*
Sivoli-Kramer, Dianne *management analyst, social worker*

Reno
Sklar, Louise Margaret *computer company executive*

NEW HAMPSHIRE

Bedford
Hall, Pamela S. *environmental consulting firm executive*

Gilford
Kennedy, Deborah *writer, editor, business owner*

Manchester
Cusson-Cail, Kathleen *consulting company executive*
Prew, Diane Schmidt *information systems executive*
Stimpson, Patricia *software company executive*

Merrimack
Gollup, Patricia *computer company executive*

Walpole
Hunter, Barbara Way *public relations consultant*

NEW JERSEY

Atlantic City
Oswell, Audrey S. *casino executive*

Avalon
Johnson, Adele Cunningham *marina executive*

Bedminster
Dabney, Michelle Sheila *administrative assistant*
Weaver, Constance *communications executive*

Belle Mead
Aloisi, Carol Ann *marketing executive*

Bergenfield
Janow, Lydia Frances *meeting planner*

Boonton
Bridges, Beryl Clarke *marketing executive*

Cedar Grove
Carlozzi, Catherine L. *corporate communications consultant, writer*

Chester
Maddalena, Lucille Ann *management consultant*

Clifton
Bronkesh, Annette Cylia *public relations executive*

East Hanover
Jenkins, Twylah La'Triece *pharmaceutical sales representative*

East Rutherford
Blate, Alissa *advertising executive*

Edison
Haberman, Louise Shelly *consulting company executive*

Englewood
Fay, Toni Georgette *communications executive*

Englewood Cliffs
Henderson, Mary R. (Nina) *food/consumer products executive*

Ewing
D'Antonio, Cynthia Maria *sales and marketing executive*

Far Hills
Alexandre, Kristin Kuhns *public relations executive, writer*
Bruett, Karen Diesl *sales and fundraising consultant*

Flemington
Bennett, Margaret Ann *cook*

Florham Park
Fischer, Pamela Shadel *public relations executive*

Fort Lee
Schelling, Joyce Elaine *communications executive, educator*

Franklin Lakes
Mattie, Jeanne Marie *public relations and communications consultant*

Glen Rock
Davis, Alison B. *company executive*

Glenwood
Greilich, Audrey *administrative assistant*

Guttenberg
Pozniakoff, Rita Oppenheim *education software consultant*

Hillsborough
Butcher, Deborah *public relations and communications consultant*

Holmdel
Hudson, Wendy Joy *software manager*

Jersey City
Dupey, Michele Mary *communications specialist*

Kenilworth
Johnson Velazco, Nancy Ruth *marketing professional*

Lawrenceville
Adams, Christine Hanson *advertising executive*
Cox, Teri P. *public relations executive*

Livingston
Scarano-Ilutzi, Donna Lee *community and business development executive*

Madison
O'Brien, Mary Devon *communications executive, consultant*

Mahwah
Wagner, Susan Jane *sales and marketing consulting company executive*

Manalapan
Reisman, Joan Ann *executive secretary*

Maplewood
Hamburger, Mary Ann *medical management consultant*
Safian, Gail Robyn *public relations executive*

Marlton
Farnath, Dorothy Whitmyer *recruitment company executive*
Farwell, Nancy Larraine *public relations executive*
Klein, Anne Sceia *public relations executive*

Metuchen
Rakov, Barbara Streem *marketing executive*

Middletown
Heng, Siang Gek *communications executive*

Milford
Sautner, Zenobia Zoe *office manager*

Monroe Township
Cushman, Helen Merle Baker *retired management consultant*

Montvale
Cervantez, Michelle *marketing professional*

Morganville
Marder, Carol *advertising specialist and premium firm executive*

Morris Plains
Gulfo, Adele Madelyn *pharmaceutical marketing executive*

Morristown
Cucco, Judith Elene *international marketing professional*

Mountainside
Lipton, Bronna Jane *marketing communications executive*

New Providence
Russo, Patricia F. *communications executive*

North Arlington
Borowski, Jennifer Lucile *corporate administrator*

Park Ridge
An, Samantha Hae Jung *executive recruiter, social worker*

Parsippany
Azzarone, Carol Ann *marketing executive*

Pennsauken
Ramos, Mildred *administrative assistant*
Sygnecki, Christina *sales executive*

Piscataway
Wagner-Westbrook, Bonnie Joan *management professional*

Plainsboro
Spiegel, Phyllis *public relations consultant, journalist*

Princeton
Crossley, Helen Martha *public opinion analyst, research consultant*
Flanagan, Theresa *quality assurance professional*

Randolph
Greenberger, Marsha Moses *sales executive*
Oppenheimer, Sonya *advertising executive, graphics designer*

Ringoes
Tema-Lyn, Laurie *management consultant*

Riverton
Gorman, Nancy Jane *executive secretary*

Roseland
Steidl, Mary Catherine *food service executive*

Roselle Park
Loredo, Linda S. *marketing executive*

Saddle River
O'Connor, Denise Lynn *marketing communications executive*

Scotch Plains
Johnsen, Karen Kennedy *marketing professional*

Short Hills
Spector, Shelly *company executive*

Somerville
Dobrinsky, Susan Elizabeth *human resources director*

South Orange
Williams, Veronica Ann *marketing professional, consultant, information technology executive*

Teaneck
Enteen, Vicki L. *public relations executive*

Toms River
Schockaert, Barbara Ann *marketing professional*

Towaco
Gasperini, Elizabeth Carmela (Lisa Gasperini) *marketing consultant, graphic designer*

Verona
Poor, Suzanne Donaldson *advertising and public relations executive*

Watchung
Grey, Ruthann E. *communications specialist, management consultant*

West Orange
Bogstahl, Deborah Marcelle *global strategic planner*

Westfield
Burton, Barbara *marketing executive*

NEW MEXICO

Albuquerque
Myers, Carol McClary *retired sales administrator, editor*
Ortiz, Kathleen Lucille *travel consultant*
Owens, Georgia Katherine *human resources specialist, consultant*

Corrales
Foryst, Carole *computer electronics executive*

La Mesa
Cantu, Delia *training services executive*

Las Cruces
Reese, Janet Kay *purchasing agent*

Los Alamos
Livesay, Valorie Ann *security program analyst*

Lovington
Trujillo, Anna *food company administrator, city official*

Placitas
McElhinney, Susan Kay (Kate Echeverria) (Kate McElhinney) *executive assistant*

Portales
Edwards, Carolyn Mullenax *public relations executive*

Santa Ana Pueblo
Burns, Corrina Jessica *marketing professional, public relations executive*

NEW YORK

Albany
Clifford, Lisa Mary *marketing professional*
Dominian, Julie *human resources specialist*
Lustenader, Barbara Diane *human resources specialist*

Amherst
Monpere, Lisa Renee *budget and personnel administrator, entrepreneur*

Annandale On Hudson
Darrow, Emily M. *public relations executive, writer*

Armonk
Kohnstamm, Abby E. *marketing executive*

Astoria
Sheridan, Ruth Stewart *business development consultant, playwright*

Bellport
Hendrie, Elaine *public relations executive*

Berlin
Pelz, Caroline Duncombe *retired educational administrator*

Brewster
Mahoney, Joëlle Katherine *astrological consultant, communications educator*

Briarcliff Manor
Driver, Sharon Humphreys *marketing executive*

Bronx
Capodilupo, Jeanne Hatton *public relations executive*
Iadavaia, Elizabeth Ann *marketing professional*

Brooklyn
Greenwood, Monique *innkeeper, writer, restaurant owner*
Hendra, Barbara Jane *public relations executive*
Isaacson, Arline Levine *food association administrator*
Logan, Paula M. *entertainment company executive, accountant*
Martinez, Joanne *consultant*
Nayer, Jo Ann Elizabeth *executive, multimedia producer*
Quamina, Joyce *management consultant*
Rike, Susan *public relations executive*

Buffalo
Daley, Ruth Margaret *advertising agency administrator*

Cold Spring
Milner, Debbi Elissa *computer company executive*

Delmar
Button, Rena Pritsker *public affairs executive*

Elmont
Butera, Ann Michele *consulting company executive*

Forest Hills
Dessylas, Ann Atsaves *human resources and office management executive*
Torrence-Thompson, Juanita Lee *public relations executive*

Garden City
Doucette, Mary-Alyce *computer company executive*
Healy, Margaret Mary *retail marketing executive*

Grahamsville
Montcomeryj Ellen Marie *executive*

Great Neck
Helstein, Ivy Rae *communications executive, psychotherapist, writer*

Hartsdale
Greenawalt, Peggy Freed Tomarkin *advertising executive*

Hastings On Hudson
Cooper, Doris Jean *market research executive*

Huntington Station
Cannistraci, Diane Frances *sales account executive*

Ilion
Nemyier, Margaret Gertrude *sales executive*

Jamaica
Jawin, Ann Juliano *human resource specialist*

Larchmont
Greenwald, Carol Schiro *professional services marketing research executive*

Lewiston
Askins, Nancy Ellen Paulsen *training and organizational development professional*

Loudonville
Jonquières, Lynne *travel agent*

Mamaroneck
Kaneko-Adams, Naoko *business executive*

Manlius
Harriff, Suzanna Elizabeth (Bahner) *advertising consultant*

Melville
Christiansen, Lauri A. *marketing professional*
Ponzi Kay, Marylou *human resources specialist*

Middle Island
Andrews, Gaylen *measurable response public relations expert*

Miller Place
Callahan, Jean M. *personnel administrator*

New Paltz
Kahl, Mary L(ouise) *communication educator*

New Rochelle
Miller, Rita *personnel consultant, diecasting company executive*

New York
Allen, Alice *communications and marketing executive*
Altschuler, Marjorie *advertising executive*
Andora, Suzanne E. *communications company executive*
Antonacci, Lori (Loretta Marie Antonacci) *marketing executive, consultant*
Appel, Gloria *advertising executive*
Axthelm, Nancy *advertising executive*

Bacher, Judith St. George *executive search consultant*
Bachrach, Nancy *advertising executive*
Bancel, Marilyn *fund raising management consultant*
Barnao, Laura *management assistant*
Baron, Sheri *advertising agency executive*
Bartow, Diane Grace *marketing and sales executive*
Bastianich, Lidia Matticchio *chef, food service executive*
Bauman, Susan *communications executive*
Bishop, Susan Katharine *executive search company executive*
Bishopric, Susan Ehrlich *public relations executive*
Bloomgarden, Kathy Finn *public relations executive*
Booth, Margaret A(nn) *communications company executive*
Borhi, Carol *data processing executive, finance company executive*
Brady, Adelaide Burks *public relations agency executive, giftware catalog executive*
Breakstone, Kay Louise *public relations executive*
Brisman, Jennifer *event planning executive*
Brooks, Anita Helen *public relations executive*
Busquet, Anne M. *Internet company executive*
Cairns, Anne Marie *public relations executive*
Calabrese, Rosalie Sue *management consultant, writer*
Carter, Carolyn Houchin *advertising agency executive*
Casey, Barbara Jeanne *marketing professional*
Chang, Ling Wei *consulting services executive*
Cheslak, Monica Lynn *marketing professional, director*
Coyne, Nancy Carol *advertising executive*
Cutler, Laurel *advertising agency executive*
Damer, Cara Joy *marketing professional*
Danielides, Joannie C. *public relations executive*
DeAngelis, Susan Penny *human resources professional*
DeMonte, Cynthia Maria *investor relations and management consultant*
Deuser, Jane *marketing professional*
DeVard, Jerri *marketing professional*
de Vries, Madeline *public relations executive*
Dienstag, Eleanor Foa *corporate communications consultant*
Dimant, Rose Jearolmen *personnel testing specialist, psychometrician*
Dolan, Regina A. *security firm executive*
Dugan, Lynn *communications company executive*
Duke, Robin Chandler Tippett *retired public relations executive*
Eisler, Susan Krawetz *advertising executive*
Exposito, Daisy *advertising executive*
Fairbairn, Ursula Farrell *human resources executive*
Farinelli, Jean L. *public relations executive*
Feigin, Barbara Sommer *marketing consultant*
Fili-Krushel, Patricia *media company executive*
Flaherty, Tina Santi *corporate communications executive, writer*
Fleischman, Barbara Greenberg *public relations consultant*
Foxworth, Jo *advertising agency executive*
Fudge, Ann Marie *advertising executive*
Gerard-Sharp, Monica Fleur *communications executive*
Gerberg, Judith Levine *human resource company executive*
Girard, Andrea Eaton *communications executive, consultant*
Gitelson, Susan Aurelia *business executive, civic leader*
Gold, Mari S. *public relations executive*
Graves, Hillary *marketing professional*
Greene, Adele S. *management consultant*
Haddad, Colleen *institutional marketing executive*
Hammond, Lou Rena Charlotte *public relations executive*
Harrison, Judith Anne *human resources executive*
Hart, Karen Ann *advertising executive*
Hauser, Joyce Roberta *marketing professional*
Helmsley, Leona Mindy *hotel executive*
Henschel, Shirley Myra *licensing agent*
Hudes, Nana Brenda *marketing professional*
Jacobsen, Sally *communications executive*
Jean-Baptiste, Tricia *public relations executive*
Johnson, Verdia E. *marketing professional*
Josell, Jessica (Jessica Wechsler) *public relations executive*
Just, Gemma Rivoli *retired advertising executive*
Kapner, Lori *marketing professional*
Katz, Marcia *public relations company executive*
Kotuk, Andrea Mikotajuk *public relations executive, writer*
Kraus, Norma Jean *industrial relations executive*
Kugelman, Stephanie *advertising executive*
Kyriakou, Linda Grace *communications executive*
Laing, Jennifer *advertising executive*
Lamont, Lee *music management executive*
Land, Irene Stokvis *marketing executive*
LaNicca Albanese, Ellen *public relations executive*
Lazarus, Rochelle Braff (Shelly Lazarus) *advertising executive*
Le Count, Virginia G. *communications company executive*
Leet, Mildred Robbins *corporate executive, consultant*
Leff, Ilene J(afnel) *management consultant, corporate and government executive*
Lipin, Joan Carol *healthcare executive, consultant*
Lipton, Joan Elaine *advertising executive*
Livingston, Julie *publicist*
Lockwood, Helshi *advertising executive*
Lorber, Barbara Heyman *communications executive*
Lotas, Judith Patton *advertising executive*
Maio, Elsie Regina *communications consultant*

Maneker, Roberta S(ue) *public relations executive*
Mayer, Eve Orlans *retired public relations and marketing consultant, writer*
Mays, Leslie A. *human resources specialist*
McCaslin, Teresa Eve *human resources executive*
Merritt, Jean *consulting firm executive, psychotherapist*
Meyer, Pearl *executive compensation consultant*
Moden, Joleen *communications executive*
Mortimer, Ann O. *executive secretary*
Moulton, Sara *chef, magazine editor*
Murphy, Elva Glenn *executive assistant*
Nadler-Hurvich, Hedda Carol *public relations executive*
Newman, Geraldine Anne *advertising executive, inventor*
Nichols, Edie Diane *executive recruiter*
Noonan, Susan Abert *public relations executive*
Ogden, Peggy A. *retired personnel director*
Olbrick, Valerie Lyn *management consultant, information technologist*
Olinger, Carla D(ragan) *medical advertising executive*
Paine, Katharine Delahaye *communications research company executive*
Paulus, Eleanor Bock *professional speaker, author*
Pearson, Margit Linnea *management advisor*
Perlmutter, Diane F. *marketing executive*
Phillips, Elizabeth Joan *marketing professional*
Pollock-O'Brien, Louise Mary *public relations executive*
Quinlan, Mary Lou *advertising executive*
Rackow, Sylvia *business consultant, educator*
Ray, Rachael *chef*
Reals Ellig, Janice *marketing professional, human resources specialist*
Reges, Marianna Alice *marketing executive*
Renna, Cathy *communications executive, activist*
Richardson, Grace Elizabeth *consumer products company executive*
Rose, Merrill *public relations counselor*
Rosenberg, Tina *international relations educator, writer*
Rosenwasser, Donna *management consulting company executive*
Rossi, Norma M. *management consultant*
Sawyer, Linda *advertising executive*
Saxton, Catherine Patricia *public relations executive*
Scherber, Amy *food service executive*
Schoonover, Jean Way *public relations consultant*
Shepard, Sarah *public relations company executive*
Siegal, Peggy *public relations executive*
Siegel, Lucy Boswell *public relations executive*
Silverman, Marylin A. *advertising agency executive*
Smith, Barbara *food service executive, model*
Steinberg, Nancy *healthcare public relations executive*
Stuart, Lori Ames *public relations executive*
Tanaka, Patrice Aiko *public relations executive*
Taylor, Barbara Alden *public relations executive*
Temin, Davia B. *marketing executive*
Thaler, Linda Kaplan *communications executive*
Vargas, Martha *government liaison*
Vermeer, Maureen Dorothy *sales executive*
Volk, Kristin *advertising agency executive*
von Baillou, Astrid *executive search consultant*
Weinstein, Sharon Schlein *corporate communications executive, educator*
Wells, Patricia Trent *retail marketing executive*
Wijnberg, Sandra S. *professional services company executive*
Willett, Roslyn Leonore *public relations executive, food service consultant, writer*
Worthing, Marcia Lynn *outplacement services executive*
Wyse, Lois *advertising executive*

Newark
Hemmings, Madeleine Blanchet *management consultant, media consultant, not-for-profit fundraiser*

Niagara Falls
Jones, Suzanne P. *public relations executive*

Oneonta
Carney, Margaret E. *administrative assistant, small business owner*

Ossining
Gilbert, Joan Stulman *retired public relations executive*

Pawling
Light, Sybil Elizabeth *executive secretary*

Pittsford
Estin-Klein, Libbyada *advertising executive, medical writer*

Pleasantville
Havens, Jeanette Lynn *public relations executive*
Keller, Mary Beth *consumer research consultant*

Poughkeepsie
Moysey, Carol Anne *investigator*
VanBuren, Denise Doring *corporate communications executive*

Purchase
Moore, Margaret D. *human resources specialist*

Rhinebeck
Campbell, Elizabeth Rose *astrologer, writer, videographer*

Rochester
Glazer, Jane *company executive*
Goldberg-Schaible, Jocelyn Hope Schnier *market research professional*

Harris, Diane Carol *merger and acquisition consulting firm executive*
McWilliams, Dawn Suzanne *marketing professional, consultant*

Rockville Centre
Beyer, Suzanne *advertising agency executive*

Rye
McDonnell, Mary Theresa *travel service executive*
Vauclair, Marguerite Renée *communications and sales promotion executive*
Vernon, Lillian *mail order company executive*

Scarsdale
Clehane, Diane Catherine *journalist, writer, communications executive*

Schenectady
Fabens, Sally Fisher *communications executive, consultant*
Smallin, Michelle DeAnne *marketing professional*

Somers
Ryan, Cathleen Reneer *management consultant*

Staten Island
McGinn, Loretta *food service administrator*

Stone Ridge
Ebersole, Patricia Sue *advertising executive, design educator*

Syracuse
Boghosian, Paula der *computer business consultant*

Tappan
Fox, Muriel *retired public relations executive*

Tarrytown
Kirsch, Abigail *culinary productions executive*

Valhalla
Campbell, Debra Lynn *marketing and new venture consultant*

Victor
Van Bortel, Mary Catherine *sales executive*

West Hempstead
Krohley, Patricia Anne *marketing professional*

Westhampton Beach
Maas, Jane Brown *advertising executive*

Woodbury
Berezin, Evelyn *management consultant*

Woodhaven
Bolster, Jacqueline Neben (Mrs. John A. Bolster) *communications consultant*

Yonkers
Pickover, Betty Abravanel *retired executive legal secretary, civic volunteer*
Wen, Sheree *computer company executive*

NORTH CAROLINA

Canton
Dixon, Shirley Juanita *retired restaurant owner*

Chapel Hill
Hunt, Katrina Weisner *marketing professional*

Charlotte
Brehio, Renee Marie *public relations executive, consultant*
Butler, Carol King *advertising executive*
Carino, Linda Susan *business consultant*
Doherty, Barbara Whitehurst *chemical purchasing manager*
Lyerly, Elaine Myrick *advertising executive*
Mickle, Deloris B. *credit manager, artist*
Moore, Bealer Gwen *transcription company executive*

Durham
Ladd, Marcia Lee *medical equipment and supplies company executive*

Garner
Barbour, Charlene *management firm executive*

Greensboro
Dillon, Terri L. *consulting firm executive*
Stone, Theresa M. *communications executive*

Holden Beach
Blecha, Diane Louise *business consultant*

Kitty Hawk
Berger, Tina *hotel executive*

Mooresville
Dow, Leslie Wright *communications company executive, photographer, writer*

Morrisville
Rauch, Kathleen *computer executive*

North Wilkesboro
Parsons, Irene Adelaide *management consultant*

Raleigh
Barker, Gloria S. *government and community affairs professional*
Stukes, Reesie *communications executive*

Wilmington
Maness, Eleanor Palmer *research analyst*

Winston Salem
Evans, Lisbeth *business networking executive, political party official*
Kaufman, Charlotte S. *communications executive*

NORTH DAKOTA

Bismarck
Neas, Sherry Lee *purchasing agent, procurement manager*

Dickinson
Nelson, Debra L. *consultant for non-profit organizations*

OHIO

Akron
Zeno, Jo Ann *sales executive*

Aurora
Nelson, Hedwig Potok *marketing executive*

Beachwood
Strauss, Marilyn Sheperd *public relations executive*

Canton
Thomas, Suzanne Ward *public relations executive, communications educator, radio personality*

Chagrin Falls
Kuby, Barbara Eleanor *personnel director, management consultant*

Cincinnati
Arnold, Susan E. *consumer products company executive*
Brown, Dale Patrick *retired advertising executive*
Goodman, Phyllis L. *public relations executive*
Henretta, Deb *consumer products company executive*
Jenkins, Kathleen Maria *web site design company executive*
Kollstedt, Paula Lubke *communications executive, writer*
Morris, Margaret Elizabeth *marketing professional*
Otto, Charlotte R. *consumer products company executive*
Sullivan, Sandra Long *retired human resources specialist*

Cleveland
Dougherty, Ursel Thielbeule *communications and marketing executive*
Dunbar, Mary Asmundson *communications executive, investor and public relations consultant*
Griffith, Mary H. *corporate communications executive*
Hamilton, Nancy Beth *data processing executive*
Pollack, Florence K.Z. *management consultant*
Pucko, Diane Bowles *public relations executive*

Columbus
Jacobs, Alexis A. *automobile company executive*
Lefavre, Hadia *human resources executive*
Reardon, Nancy Anne *human resource executive*
Reed, Constance Louise *materials management and purchasing consultant*
Scott, Misty Anne *marketing professional*
Woltz, Mary Lynn Monaco *management consultant*

Dayton
Cameron, Joyce *human factors and ergonomics specialist, music educator*

Dublin
Anderson, Kerrii B. *food service executive*
Watkins, Carole S. *human resources specialist, health facility administrator*

Fostoria
Howard, Kathleen *computer company executive*

Grand River
Abel, Mary Ellen Kathryn *quality control executive, chemist*

Mansfield
Crittenden, Sophie Marie *communications executive*

Maple Heights
Sargent, Liz Elaine (Elizabeth Sargent) *safety consulting executive*

Marion
Fassler, Crystal G. *marketing consultant*

Marysville
Jones-Morton, Pamela *human resources specialist*

Miamisburg
Thompson, Holley Marker *lawyer, marketing professional*

Oxford
Brewer, Nancy Ellen *communications executive, writer*

Reynoldsburg
Garling, Tina Louise *data processing coordinator*

Toledo
Smale, Ann-Laura *public relations company executive, writer, researcher*

Walbridge
Wiseman, Gretchen Renee *personal care industry executive*

Xenia
Nutter, Zoe Dell Lantis *retired public relations executive*

OKLAHOMA

Cleveland
Henry, Kathleen Marie *marketing executive*

Muskogee
Carvajal, Victoria Lavone *customer service administrator*

Norman
Madden, Glenda Gail *sales professional*

Oklahoma City
Atlee, Debbie Gayle *sales consultant, medical educator*
LaMotte, Janet Allison *retired management specialist*
Williams, Mary Ann *musical instrument executive, music educator*
Winchester, Susan *human resources specialist, state representative*

Owasso
Sandford, Brenda Lynne *executive secretary*

OREGON

Albany
Haralson, Linda Jane *communications executive*

Ashland
Hegler, Ellen Marie *business executive, retired educator*

Canby
Flinn, Roberta Jeanne *management, computer applications consultant*

Corvallis
Lambert, Deborah Sue *data processing professional*

Eugene
Chambers, Carolyn Silva *communications company executive*
Langlois, Alicia Jean *business development planner, small business owner*
Leeds, Elizabeth Louise *miniature collectibles executive*

Hillsboro
Dyess, Kirby A. *computer company executive*

Lake Oswego
Edstrom, Pam *public relations executive*
Zorkin, Melissa Waggener *public relations executive*

Newberg
Austin, Joan D. *personal care industry executive*

Pendleton
Bedford, Amy Aldrich *public relations executive*

Portland
Denhart, Gun *direct mail order company executive*
Martin, Lucy Z. *public relations executive*
Robbins, Jeanette Lee *sales and manufacturing executive*
VanSickle, Sharon Dee *public relations executive*

Salem
Milbrath, Mary Merrill Lemke *quality assurance professional*

PENNSYLVANIA

Ardmore
Lockett-Egan, Marian Workman *advertising executive*

Beaver Falls
Miller, Kathleen S. *management and accounting professional*

Bethlehem
Dorward, Judith A. *business ordering customer service representative*

Blue Bell
Furman, Sue *owner public relations agency*

Camp Hill
Crist, Christine Myers *consulting executive*

Doylestown
McCafferty, Barbara Jean (BJ McCafferty) *sales executive*

Du Bois
Mortimer, Pamela S. *printing company executive*

Fort Washington
Fulton, Cheryl L. *customer service administrator*

Franklin Center
Resnick, Lynda Rae *consumer products company executive*

Grantville
Sudor, Cynthia Ann *sales and marketing professional*

Harrisburg
Pletz, Darcy L. *sales executive*

Honesdale
Roos, Paula Sparrow *manufacturer's representative*

Indiana
Ruddock, Ellen Sylves *business consultant*

Lafayette Hill
Duncalfe Holt, Lucinda Bromwyn *marketing executive*

Lancaster
Taylor, Ann *human resources specialist, educator*

Levittown
Camer, Mary Martha *retired secretary*

Lewisburg
Brill, Marilyn *community-based collaboration consultant*
Rote, Nelle Fairchild Hefty *management consultant*

Morrisville
Kuronya, Carol Gasco *tour guide*

New Florence
Melville, Cathy Louise *administrative assistant*

Newtown
Latzel, Greta *marketing professional, director*

Newtown Square
Pacini, Renee Annette *software company executive*

Philadelphia
Adawi, Nadia Sharon *energy cooperative executive*
Banse, Amy L. *communications executive, lawyer*
Bodner, Susan Rachel *marketing and communications executive*
Brown, Delores Russell *health management company official*
Burns, Marian Law *human resources specialist*
Cabot, Diana Marie *marketing professional, travel and transportation executive*
Coulson, Zoe Elizabeth *retired consumer marketing executive*
DeMarco, Carolyn Beth *human resources specialist*
Dooner, Marlene B. *communications executive*
Dougherty Buchholz, Karen *communications executive*
Friedman, Polly *public relations executive, marketing professional*
Old, Marnie Lorraine *sommelier, consultant*
Perfetto, Lisa Ann *quality assurance professional*
Presser, Janice *business executive*
Scott-Williams, Mildred P. *food service specialist*
Waite, Helen Eleanor *funeral director*

Pittsburgh
Arbutina, Petra *advertising executive*
Bish, Melody Ann *public administration professional*
Buchanan, Gloria Jean *sales executive*
O'Hare, Virginia Lewis *human resources administrator*
Paugh, Patricia Lou *business consultant*
Peterman, Donna Cole *communications executive*
Rathke, Sheila Wells *strategic and marketing consultant*
Reichblum, Audrey Rosenthal *public relations executive, publishing executive*
Schultheiss, Emily Ekonen *management consultant, writer*
Ziskind, Deborah Ziskind *public relations and legal marketing executive*

Plymouth Meeting
Blessing, Carole Anne *human resources manager*

Radnor
Thompson, Pamela Padwick *public relations executive*

Reading
Hackenberg, Barbara Jean Collar *retired advertising and public relations executive*

Scranton
Williams, Holly Thomas *retired business executive*

Shippensburg
Stone, Susan Ridgaway *marketing educator*

Steelton
Zimmerman, Connie Ann *public administrator*

Upper Saint Clair
Anderson, Catherine M. *consulting company executive*

Warrendale
Gaetano, Joy M. *human resources executive*

West Chester
Hanson, Diane Charske *management consultant*
Rizzo, Joyce A. *environmental services executive*

Wyomissing
Williams-Wennell, Kathi *human resources specialist*

Yardley
Newsom, Carolyn Cardall *management consultant*

York
Livingston, Pamela A. *corporate image and marketing management consultant*
Snyder, Jan Louise *administrative aide*

RHODE ISLAND

Cranston
Goldberg, Barbara M. *consultant*
Moffitt, Kathleen *marketing professional, writer, educator*

East Providence
Furtado-Lavoie, Julia *management consultant, accountant*

Pawtucket
Ferland, Darlene Frances *management consultant*

Wakefield
Doody, Agnes G. *communications educator, management and communication consultant*

SOUTH CAROLINA

Beech Island
Bartley, Jacqueline Prior *public relations executive, journalist*

Charleston
Ballard, Mary Melinda *financial communications and marketing/advertising executive, consumer advocate*
Perry, Evelyn Reis *communications company executive*

Columbia
Barnum, Mary Ann Mook *information management manager*
Grimball, Caroline Gordon *retail sales professional*

Ladys Island
Yates, Linda Snow *financial services marketing executive, real estate*

Mauldin
Wood, Myra Linden Frank *consultant*

Mount Pleasant
Falkowski, Brenda Lisle *business executive, consultant*
Hill, Larkin Payne *real estate company operations administrator*
Summerville, Cheryl Fannin *travel company executive*

Sullivans Island
Norton, Fran *parks and recreation director*

SOUTH DAKOTA

Watertown
Welch, Sharon I. *customer service representative, artist*

TENNESSEE

Antioch
Bluing-Osborne, Karen Louise *executive assistant*

Chattanooga
Young, Sonia Winer *public relations executive, educator*

Franklin
Cliff, Karissa *consumer researcher, recruiter*

Gatlinburg
Flanagan, Judy *special events professional, entertainment and marketing specialist, professional public speaker*

Knoxville
Drennen, Jean Cobble *retired public relations executive, linguist*
Lobins, Christine Marie *accounts sales administrator*
Rice, Charlene Russell *human resources professional, consultant*

Madison
Cage, Allie M. *communications executive*

Memphis
Edwards, Doris Porter *computer specialist*
Jallepalli, Raji *food service executive*
Kelley, Linda Rose *human resources specialist*
Whitehead, Jenifer Barron *corporate communications specialist, consultant*

Nashville
James, Kay Louise *management consultant, healthcare executive*
Sheffield, Stephanie S. *portfolio and marketing management consultant*
Short, Sallie Lee *physical plant service worker*

Sevierville
Etherton, Jane *retired sales executive, marketing professional*

Shelbyville
Nelson, Clara Singleton *human resources consultant*

Spring Hill
Lafevor, Kimberly Ann *human resources specialist, educator*

TEXAS

Abilene
Freeman, Carol Lyn *business administrator*

Arlington
English, Marlene Cabral *management consultant*
Sawyer, Dolores *motel chain executive*

Austin
Curle, Robin Lea *computer software industry executive*
Dabbs Riley, Jeanne Kernodle *retired public relations executive*
Galbreath, Margaret Anne *market research analyst*
Hammer, Katherine Gonet *software company executive*
Lenoir, Gloria Cisneros *consultant, educator*
Pate, Jacqueline Hail *retired data processing company executive*
Qunell, Kerri Wynn *marketing professional*
Sober, Debra Evonne *environmental services administrator*
Trabulsi, Judy *advertising and marketing executive*
Vandel, Diana Geis *management consultant*
Wakeman, Olivia Van Horn *marketing professional*
Watson, Irene *seminar and retreat facilitator, author, artist*
Witt, Doreen Marie *business executive*
York, Candace A. *marketing professional, writer*
Young, Joan Crawford *advertising executive*

Brownsville
Halaby, Margarita Gonzalez *marketing professional, communications executive*

Burleson
Buford, Evelyn Claudene Shilling *retired consumer products company executive*

Carrollton
Odem, Joyce Marie *human resources specialist*

Cedar Park
Duke, Carol Michiels *personal care industry executive*

Colleyville
Bush, Holly Newsom *management consultant*

Coppell
Owen, Cynthia Carol *sales executive*

Corpus Christi
DuVall, Lorraine *recreation center owner*
Stamford, Jane Herring *management consultant and educator, author*

Dallas
Bushey, Marilyn *communications executive*
Coomer, Donna R. *communications executive*
Dao, Khanh Phuong Thi *automotive executive, sales professional*
Duplantier, Dawn Elizabeth *communications executive*
Dykeman, Alice Marie *public relations executive*
England, Julie Spicer *computer company executive*
Frank, Paula Feldman *business executive*
Fulton, Carla Rae *human resources manager*
Harris, Melissa M. *communications executive*
Hunt, Caroline Rose *hotel executive*
Loveless, Kathy Lynne *client services executive*
McPherson, Gail *advertising and real estate executive*
O'Shea, Karen *public relations executive*
Perich, Toni Annette *sales executive*
Robertson, Jane Ryding *marketing executive*
Stibbens, Beverly *marketing professional, director*
Zeitlin, Laurie *printing company executive*

El Paso
Deerman, Ruth Gillett *sales executive*

Flower Mound
Ross, Lesa Moore *quality assurance professional*

Fort Worth
Davis, Carol Lyn *administrative assistant*
Genett-Schrader, Ann G. *public relations executive*
Michalski, Jeanne Ann *human resources professional*
Williams, Emma *management executive*

Grand Prairie
McMillan, Helen Berneice *sales executive*

Houston
Atwood, Carol Ann *healthcare executive*
Bazelides, Diane *public relations executive*
Blackburn, Sadie Gwin Allen *business executive*
Burnett, Susan Walk *personnel service company owner*
Curtis, Barbara *consumer products company professional*
DeArmond, Patti Jo *hotel administrator*
Finch, Diane Shields *retail sales executive*
Horan, Shelly *marketing professional*
Jones, Sonia Josephine *advertising agency executive*
Mampre, Virginia Elizabeth *communications executive*
Mark, Rebecca P. *environmental services administrator*
Mayo, Carolyn *marketing professional, public relations executive*
Mercer, Nancy Owens Dunn *art industry purchasing agent, artist, educator*
Milburn, Diane Suzane *healthcare industry executive, writer*
Ribble, Anne Hoerner *communications executive*
Smith, Claire *chef*

Sweet, Portia Ann *retired human resources specialist*
Tilney, Elizabeth A. *marketing executive*
Vollmer, Helen *public relations executive*

Irving
Forte, Mary L. *consumer products company executive*
Munger, Sharon *market research firm executive*

Junction
Evans, Jo Burt *communications executive, rancher*

Llano
Zachary, Jean *workforce development specialist*

Mc Kinney
Hansen, Elizabeth (Beth) Stevens *human resources consultant*

Plainview
Ticer, Terri Jean *sales executive*

Plano
Flores, Marion Thomas *advertising executive*
Norwood, Cecilia Stubbs *communications executive*
Sivinski, Tina M. *human resources specialist*

Port Aransas
Peters, Jean Theresa *sales executive*

Port Lavaca
Boyd, Ann Fisher *office administrator*

Round Rock
Crawford, Kim *computer company executive*
Goodman, Kim *marketing professional, computer company executive*

San Antonio
Carr, Cassandra Colvin *communications company executive*
Labenz-Hough, Marlene *dispute resolution professional*
McClinton, Dorothy Hardaway *former business educator*
Mills, Linda S. *public relations executive*
Nava, Carmen P. *communications executive*
Pliego-Stout, Patricia *travel company executive*

San Marcos
Martin, Jerri Whan *public relations executive*
Moore, Patsy Sites *food service consultant*

Southlake
Kelly, Carol A. *travel company executive*
Sorge, Karen Lee *commercial printing company executive, consultant*

Spring
Maxfield, Mary Constance *management consultant*
Treasure-Terrell, Suzanne Marie *marketing and sales professional, writer, poet, lyricist*

The Woodlands
Jack, Nancy Rayford *supplemental resource company executive, consultant*
Jones, Susan Chafin *management consultant*

Tomball
Moore, Marcia G. *human resources specialist*

Trophy Club
Caffee, Virginia Maureen *executive assistant*

UTAH

Logan
Newell, Ellen Elizabeth *landscape manager*

Provo
Konecny-Costa, Jennifer *computer company executive*

Salt Lake City
Bartmess, Michele *public relations specialist*
Lustica, Katherine Grace *marketing executive, artist, consultant*

VERMONT

Burlington
Heffernan, Patricia Conner *management consultant*

Lower Waterford
Burnham, Patricia White *consultant, advocate, writer, business executive*

Ludlow
Mueller, Diane *hotel executive*

Montpelier
Klein, Tony *public relations executive, state representative*

Norwich
Flanders, Janet Huessy *travel company executive*

VIRGINIA

Abingdon
Ramos-Cano, Hazel Balatero *caterer, chef, innkeeper, restaurateur, entrepreneur*

Alexandria
Fosdick, Cora Prifold (Cora Prifold Beebe) *management consultant*
Foutch, Karan *marketing professional*

Lightner, Candace Lynne *nonprofit management consultant, advocate*
McMiller, Anita Williams *leasing company executive*
Nodeen, Janey Price *company executive*
Paulson, Gwen O. Gampel *government relations consultant*
Stone, Ann E.W. *direct marketing company executive*

Arlington
Carson, Mary Smith *marketing and communications consultant*
Estes, Valerie *independent consultant*
Gallagher, Anne Porter *communications executive*
Johnson, Rosemary Wrucke *personnel management specialist*
Lieber, Carole Marguerite Renee *human resources specialist, consultant*
Widener, Peri Ann *business development executive*

Ashburn
Mitchell, Barbara Ann *marketing professional*

Blacksburg
Weaver, Pamela Ann *hospitality research professional*
Young, Deborah Elspeth *industrial hygienist, educator*

Chantilly
Sullivan, Penelope Dietz *computer software development company executive*

Charlottesville
Bly-Monnen, April M. *quality assurance professional*
Cohen, Helen Herz *camp owner, director*
MacIlwaine, Mary Jarratt *public relations executive*

Chesapeake
Allen, Elizabeth Maresca *marketing and telecommunications executive*

Fairfax
Pan, Elizabeth Lim *information systems company executive*
Welles, Judith *public affairs executive*

Falls Church
Miller, Mary Jeannette *office management specialist*

Floyd
Lineberry, Betty O. *hotel executive*

Fredericksburg
Hickman, Margaret Capellini *advertising executive*

Hardy
Harriett, Rebecca *park director*

Mc Lean
Rose, Susan Porter *consultant*
Smith, Esther Thomas *communications executive*
Symonds, Stacey Gabrielle *marketing professional*

Midlothian
Doumlele, Ruth Hailey *communications company executive, broadcast accounting consultant*

Newport News
Behlmar, Cindy Lee *business manager, consultant, speaker*

Reston
Brooker, Susan Gay *employment consulting firm executive*
Clark, Katherine Karen *software company executive*
Dietrich, Dawn *software company executive*
Long, Jodi L. *office manager*
Miller, Lynne Marie *environmental company executive*
Posey, Ada Louise *human resources specialist*
Sarreals, Sonia *data processing consultant*
Wultich, Donna Marie *sales professional*

Richmond
Bohannon, Sarah Virginia *personnel professional*
Brown, Patricia A. *customer service representative*
Edwards, Gloria Taylor *public relations executive*
Hoskie, Lorraine *consumer products representative, poet*
Joynes, Barbara Cole *marketing executive*
Maneker, Deanna Marie *advertising executive*
Schmidt, Karen Lee *marketing professional, sales executive*

Roanoke
Wall-Lievsay, Bonnie Lee *human resources specialist, educator*

Springfield
Edwards-LeBoeuf, Renee Camille *public relations professional, logistics engineer*
McDonald, Joanne *business executive*

Sterling
Cowen, Jean *employee benefits consultant*

Vienna
Gardenier, Turkan Kumbaraci *statistical company executive, researcher*
Miller, Christine Marie *marketing executive, public relations executive*

Virginia Beach
Suggs Wallace, Vanessa *marketing professional, writer*

Williamsburg
Coffman, Orene Burton *hotel executive*

WASHINGTON

Bainbridge Island
Berg, Darla Gaye *service representative*

Bothell
Hawthorne, Nan Louise *Internet resources consultant, web site designer, writer*

Federal Way
Muzyka-McGuire, Amy *marketing professional, nutrition consultant*

Gig Harbor
Wissmann, Carol Reneé *sales executive*

Mountlake Terrace
Johnson, LuAn *disaster management consultant*
Townsend, Wendy *marketing executive*

Redmond
Ambrose, Adele D. *communications executive*
Butler, Jannette Sue *human resources professional*
Martinez, Maria *computer software company executive*
Marvin, D. Jane *consumer products company executive*
Mathews, Mich *computer company executive*

Seattle
Georgulas, Susan Beth *sales and marketing executive*
Hannaford, Janet Kirtley *software administrative manager*
Kraft, Elaine Joy *community relations and communications official*
Reis, Jean Stevenson *administrative secretary*
von Bargen, Sally *stock image photography company executive*

Spokane
Babcock, M. Sandra *administrative assistant, writer*
Gilpatrick, Janet *public affairs and public relations consultant*

Tacoma
Bartlett, Norma Thyra *retired administrative assistant*

Vancouver
Grant, Nancy Marie *marketing professional, journalist*
Ogden, Valeria Munson *management consultant, state representative*

Vashon
Henderson, Sally Kathleen *advertising, communications and marketing executive*

WEST VIRGINIA

Charleston
Offutt, Rebecca Sue *business and sales executive*

Gallipolis Ferry
Brown, Nancy Jane *human resources specialist*

South Charleston
Herzog, Valerie Wirth *computer company executive*

WISCONSIN

Appleton
Hasselbacher, Darlene M. *human resources executive*

Brookfield
Cifaldi, Rosalie *private investigator*

Edgerton
Douglas, Susan *data processing specialist, consultant*

Grafton
Schneider, Carol Ann *staffing services company executive*

Janesville
Roth, Sarah Eve *occupational safety professional*

Kohler
Kohler, Laura E. *human resources executive*

La Crosse
Anderson, Gwyn C. *computer company executive, computer consultant*

Madison
Bishop, Carolyn Benkert *public relations counselor*
Piper, Odessa *chef*
Stites, Susan Kay *writer, human resources consultant*
Tullis, Tricia M. *marketing professional*

Menasha
Streeter, Stephanie Anne *printing company executive*

Milwaukee
Alexander, Jennifer Lynn *marketing professional*
Davis, Susan F. *human resources specialist*

Felbab, Amanda Jane *marketing professional, consultant*
McMahon, Christine Caroline *sales professional, trainer, consultant*
Meyer, Jenne L. *marketing professional*
Rivera-Velazquez, Maria Jesus *marketing professional*

Monroe
Bean, Virginia Ann (Ginny Bean) *marketing executive*

Oregon
Glodowski, Shelley Jean *administrator, writer, musician*

Pittsville
Normington, Norma Shotwell *secretary*

Racine
Johnson-Leipold, Helen P. *outdoor recreation company executive*
Rubico-Jamir, Sonia Mendoza *sensory/food scientist, consumer researcher*

Waukesha
Tegge, Patricia Ann *administrative assistant*

Weyauwega
Hanneman, Elaine Esther *salesperson*

TERRITORIES OF THE UNITED STATES

PUERTO RICO

Guaynabo
de Cacho, Graciela Eleta *marketing executive*

VIRGIN ISLANDS

Cruz Bay
Blitz, Peggy Sanderfur *corporate travel management company official*

MILITARY ADDRESSES OF THE UNITED STATES

EUROPE

APO
Simpson, Sandra Kay *logistics management specialist*

CANADA

BRITISH COLUMBIA

Richmond
Smith, Deborah K. *human resources executive*

Vancouver
Chiavario, Nancy Anne *business and community relations executive*

West Vancouver
Rae, Barbara Joyce *former employee placement company executive*

MEXICO

El Zalate Playa
Brunswig, Jessie *executive assistant*

CZECH REPUBLIC

Prague
Cox, Marjorie Milham *marketing manager*

ENGLAND

Letchworth
Everitt-Newton, Katherine Evelyn *international management consultant*

SPAIN

Barcelona
Haley, Kathleen M. *communications executive*

SWEDEN

Stockholm
Johnson, Antonia Axson *corporate executive*

ADDRESS UNPUBLISHED

Alexander, Icie M. *communications executive*
Anderegg, Karen Klok *business executive*
Appell, Louise Sophia *consulting company executive*
Armstrong Squall, Paula Estelle *executive secretary*
Autolitano, Astrid *consumer products executive*

PROFESSIONAL INDEX 1771 INDUSTRY: SERVICE

Bainbridge, Dona Bardelli *marketing professional*
Balaban-Perry, Eleanor *retired advertising executive*
Ballard, Marion Scattergood *software development professional*
Barad, Jill Elikann *family products company executive*
Barca, Kathleen *marketing executive*
Barrett, Paulette Singer *public relations executive*
Barron, Peggy Pennisi *management consultant*
Batory, Joan Anne *solid waste and environmental administrator*
Bauer, Barbara Ann *marketing consultant*
Baumol, Hilda *management consultant*
Baxter, Barbara Morgan *Internet service provider executive, educator*
Beasley, Barbara Starin *sales executive, marketing professional*
Beider, Marlys Anna *hotel executive, writer*
Bell, Jacqueline Michelle *marketing professional, public relations executive*
Berman-Hammer, Susan *public relations executive*
Bertelsen, Delora Pearl *human resources professional, mayor*
Binder, Amy Finn *public relations company executive*
Binks, Rebecca Anne *communications executive*
Bisconti, Ann Stouffer *public opinion research company executive*
Black, Kris Susan Lynn *marketing company executive, speaker, author, poet*
Blacker, Harriet *public relations executive*
Black McCoy, Debra Marlene *sales executive*
Blatz, Linda Jeanne *management professional*
Boatwright, Charlotte Jeanne *marketing professional, public relations executive*
Bowers, Patricia Newsome *communications executive*
Brand, Donna J. *career consultant, mental health counselor*
Brannick, Ellen Marie *retired management consultant*
Brecht, Sally Ann *quality assurance executive*
Brennan, Donna Lesley *public relations company executive*
Broderson, Thelma Sylvia *marketing professional*
Broedling, Laurie Adele *human resources consultant, psychologist, educator*
Broughton, Carolyn Miles *multimedia executive, public relations executive*
Brown, Patricia Donnelly *computer company executive*
[illegible] Gail C. *marketing professional*
Buck, Linda Dee *executive recruiting company executive*
Bugbee, Joan Barthelme *retired corporate communications executive*
Bunt, Kathleen Ann *human resources specialist*
Burgess, Sandra Jean *marketing consultant*
Burnett, Iris Jacobson *corporate communications specialist*
Butts, Carol Henderson *human resources specialist, consultant*
Caldwell, Judy Carol *advertising executive, public relations executive, consultant, writer, designer*
Calooy, Sonya Renee *advertising executive, consultant*
Cameron, Susan Kay *government and public relations executive*
Camp, Alethea Taylor *executive and organizational design consultant*
Cappello, Eve *speaker, trainer, author*
Carpenter, Candice *writer, former media executive*
Carpenter-Mason, Beverly Nadine *quality assurance professional, medical/surgical nurse*
Carter, Jaine M(arie) *human resources specialist, director*
Casadesus, Penelope Ann *advertising executive, film producer*
Chandler, Kathleen *retired executive secretary*
Chapman, Linda Lee *computer company executive, consultant*
Chill, Myrtle N. *advertising copywriter, promoter*
Chin, Janet Sau-Ying *data processing executive, consultant*
Cochran, Jacqueline Louise *management executive*
Coleman, Claire Kohn *public relations executive*
Collins-Pravel, Paula Marie *marketing professional*
Comola, Jacqueline Petermann *management consultant*
Cone, Frances McFadden *data processing consultant*
Connell, Shirley Hudgins *public relations professional*
Cortez, Marti *marketing professional*
Cothran, Anne Jennette *educational administrator*
Craig, Jenny *weight management executive*
Criswell, Kimberly Ann *executive coach, communications consultant, performing artist*
Crittendon, Donna Elizabeth *customer service administrator*
Croft, Kathryn Delaine *business executive, consultant*
Cruver, Suzanne Lee *communications executive, writer*
Cullen-Rivera, Amy Janene *management consultant*
Cunningham, Andrea Lee *public relations executive*
Davies, Terri Lynn *pharmaceutical sales representative*
Davis, Barbara Jean Siemens *service company executive*
Davis, Nicole D. *executive secretary, entrepreneur*
Davis, Sheila Kay *administrative assistant*
Dawson, Martha Bromley *administrative assistant, software developer*
deNobriga, Kathie Elizabeth *consultant*
DeVore, Kimberly K. *business executive*
Dhillon, Sukhbans K. *retired computer services executive*
Diamond, Susan Zee *management consultant*
Dietz, Janis Camille *business educator*
Doan, Mary Frances *advertising executive*
Doherty, Evelyn Marie *data processing consultant*
Doland, Judy Ann *administrative assistant, retired financial rating company associate*
Doll, Patricia Marie *marketing professional, public relations executive, consultant*
Donahue, Donna Charlene *computer company executive, marketing professional*
Dorman, Hattie Lawrence *management consultant, trainer, former government agency official*
Dozier, Eleanor Cameron *computer company executive, writer*
Drake, Carolyn A. *administrative assistant*
Drucker, Ana Bueno *healthcare marketing and public relations executive, writer*
Dudley, Elizabeth Hymer *retired security executive, community volunteer*
Dunn, Grace Veronica *retired executive secretary*
Dunn Kelly, Ruth Emma *management consultant*
East, Janette Diane *marketing consultant*
Echols, Mary Evelyn *travel consultant*
Ecton, Donna R. *management consultant, retired food products executive*
Ekelchik, Jodi *management consultant*
Emerling, Carol G(reenbaum) *consultant*
Ernest, Pamela Kay *business consultant*
Ethridge, Brenda Kay *advertising employee*
Evans, Pamela R. *sales and marketing executive*
Evans, Patricia Marie *sales executive*
Faron, Fay Cheryl *private investigator, writer*
Fast, Betty Blockman *travel agency owner*
Faunce, Lori *marketing professional, graphics designer*
Feinberg, Glenda Joyce *restaurant chain executive*
Feiner, Ava Sophia *public affairs and management consultant, economist*
Feld, Carole Leslie *marketing executive*
Ferguson, Sharon C. *community relations and planning specialist*
Ford, Kay Louise *innovation consulting executive*
Forester, Jean Martha Brouillette *innkeeper, retired librarian, educator*
Fox, Gretchen Hovemeyer *freelance editor, genealogical consultant*
Fox-Clarkson, Anne C. *computer company executive*
Gaia, Jennifer T. *customer support specialist*
Galbraith, Nanette Elaine Gerks *forensic and management sciences company executive*
Gallup, Janet Louise *management consultant*
Gambrell, Luck Flanders *corporate executive*
Geltzer, Sheila Simon *public relations executive*
Giddings, Helen *personnel management executive*
Gill, Gail Stoorza *corporate professional*
Gillespie, Helen Davys *marketing/industry consultant, analyst, writer*
Gillice, Sondra Jupin (Mrs. Gardner Russell Brown) *sales and marketing executive*
Glacel, Barbara Pate *management consultant*
Godfrey, Janet K *human resources specialist*
Goldfarb, Muriel Bernice *marketing consultant, advertising consultant*
Gootee, Tara Renee *independent kitchen consultant*
Grace, Marcia Bell *advertising executive*
Grindal, Mary Ann *former sales professional*
Gross, Laura Ann *marketing and communications professional, acupuncturist, herbalist*
Gross, Leslie Pamela *sales executive, consultant*
Gross, Rosalie-Ethelyn *secretary*
Grosso, Dee *human resources executive*
Guin, Catherine *marketing professional, public relations executive, consultant*
Gustafson, Kristen *advertising executive*
Hall, Adrienne A. *international marketing executive, venture capitalist consultant*
Hall, Cindy Maureen *internet consultant, educator, actress*
Hamlin, Sonya B. *communications specialist*
Hammargren, Marjorie Dolores *printing company executive*
Han, Sue Xu *marketing professional, application developer*
Hapka, Catherine M. *Internet executive*
Harden, Mary Louise *human resources consultant, real estate broker, real estate appraiser*
Harr, Lucy Loraine *public relations executive*
Hartsock, Linda Sue *educational and management association executive*
Hausman, Harriet Seceley *administrator*
Haver-Allen, Ann *communications director*
Hayes, Janet Gray *retired business manager, former mayor*
Heagy, Lorraine Mary *office manager*
Hemann, Phyllis A (nn) *public relations executive*
Henley, Katherine I. *human resources specialist, consultant*
Henselmeier, Sandra Nadine *retired training and development consulting firm executive*
Heuer, Margaret B. *retired microcomputer laboratory coordinator*
Hickman, Terrie Taylor *administrator*
Hicks, Lois Rosa *personal care industry executive, educational assistant*
Hillmer, Lois Margurite *retired receptionist*
Hirahara, Patti *public relations executive*
Hochschild, Carroll Shepherd *computer company and medical equipment executive, educator*
Holcomb, Rita *landscaper*
Houghtaling, Pamela Ann *technology marketing professional, writer*
Houx, Shirley Ann *personal and business services company executive, consultant, researcher*
Huckabee, Phyllis *human resources specialist*
Hunt, Martha *sales executive, researcher*
Imlah, MaryPat *sales, advertising and marketing executive*
Infante-Ogbac, Daisy Inocentes *sales executive, marketing executive, real estate broker*
Intrater, Cheryl Watson Waylor *career management consultant*
Irwin, Denise Anne *human resources specialist*
Irwin, Linda Belmore *public relations/marketing consultant*
Isaac, Bina Susan *data processing executive*
Jackson, Donna E. *legal secretary, administrative assistant*
Jamison, Suzanne *management consultant*
Jennings, Carol *marketing executive*
Joffe, Barbara Lynne *computer management professional, computer artist*
Johansen, Karen Lee *retired sales executive*
Johnson, Joann K. *management consultant*
Judge, Jean Frances *management consultant*
Kallman, Kathleen Barbara *marketing and business development professional*
Kalvin-Stiefel, Judy *public relations executive*
Kane, Karen Marie *public affairs consultant*
Kanuk, Leslie Lazar *management consultant, educator*
Kaplan, Erica Lynn *typing and word processing service company executive, pianist, educator*
Karalekas, Anne *business executive*
Kavanaugh, Bonnie B. *corporate communications executive*
Kay, Bonnie Kathryn *management consultant*
Kelley, Sheila Seymour *public relations consultant*
Kennedy, Debra Joyce *marketing professional*
Kennedy, Jerrie Ann Preston *public relations executive*
Kenny, Deborah *marketing professional, educator*
Kerr, Linda *executive secretary*
Key, Fleda *administrative assistant*
Kidd, Debra Jean *communications executive*
Klein, Charlotte Conrad *public relations executive*
Klein, Irma Molligan *career development educator, consultant*
Koelmel, Lorna Lee *data processing executive*
Kramer, Lora L. *executive assistant*
Kult, Amy Elaine *marketing consultant*
Lami, Judith Irene *advertising executive*
Lampert, Eleanor Verna *retired human resources specialist*
Langford, [illegible] *executive, ratings analyst*
Lavallee, Deirdre Justine *marketing professional*
Lee, Jeanne Kit Yew *administrative officer*
Lee, Linda M. *technical recruiter*
Letcher, Naomi Jewell *quality engineer, educator, counselor*
Lewis, Josephine Victoria *retired marketing executive*
Lipton, Nina Anne *healthcare executive*
Livingstone, Susan Morrisey *management consultant, former federal agency administrator*
Lokmer, Stephanie Ann *international business development consultant*
Longaberger, Tami *home decor accessories company executive*
Luce, Priscilla Mark *public relations executive*
Luciano, Roselle Patricia *advertising executive, editor*
Luna, Patricia Adele *marketing executive*
Lynch, Charlotte Andrews *retired communications executive, consultant*
Maher, Fran *advertising agency executive*
Malone, Claudine Berkeley *management consultant*
Marez, Trinnie Marie *marketing professional*
Marlar, Janet Cummings *retired public relations officer*
Martino, Donna Frances *newspaper sales administrator*
Mascheroni, Eleanor Earle *marketing communications executive*
Matthew, Lyn *sales executive, consultant, marketing professional, consultant*
Maxfield, Louisa Fonda Gribble *executive secretary*
McAteer, Deborah Grace *travel executive*
McCandless, Carolyn Keller *retired human resources executive*
McGraw, Janet Goller *executive secretary, office coordinator*
McKeown, Lorraine Laredo *travel company executive, writer*
McMinn, Virginia Ann *human resources consulting company executive*
McVeigh-Pettigrew, Sharon Christine *communications consultant*
Mikiewicz, Anna Daniella *marketing and international business exporter*
Miles, Laveda Ann *advertising executive*
Miller, Diane Doris *executive search consultant*
Miller, Ellen S. *marketing communications executive*
Mills, Celeste Louise *dog breeder, hypnotherapist, professional magician*
Mills, Gloria Adams *energy service consultant*
Mindnich, Ellen *sales executive*
Mitelman, Bonnie Cossman *editor, writer*
Moberly, Bonnie Lou *travel services executive*
Moffat, MaryBeth *consulting company executive*
Morgan, Marianne *corporate professional*
Morrow, Susan Dagmar *psychic, medium educator, writer, consultant*
Moseley, Carol June *security supervisor, small business owner*
Needham, Tracy Lee *marketing professional, consultant*
New, Anne Latrobe *public relations, fund raising executive*
Newman, Robin Gorman *communications executive, writer*
Newman, Suzanne Dinkes *web site development executive*
Nichols, Natalie Rega *development consultant*
Nicholson, Jennifer Denise *workers' compensation claims administrator*
Nixon, Carol Holladay *retired park and recreation director*
Nixon, Shirnette *pharmaceutical company administrator*
Noolan, Julie Anne Carroll *management consultant*
Novotny, Deborah A. *management consultant*
Noyes, Judith Mitchell *sales executive*
Odegaard, Cynthia *sales executive*
Odom, Judy *software company executive*
O'Neal, Patricia Jane *human resources specialist*
O'Shea, Catherine Large *marketing and public relations consultant*
Papathomas, Georgia Nikolakopoulou *communications technbology executive, communications engineer*
Pascoe, Clara P. *public relations executive, property manager*
Peifer, Millie R. *computer company executive*
Peretti, Marilyn Gay Woerner *human services professional*
Perlov, Dadie *management consultant, consultant*
Perraud, Pamela Brooks *human resources professional*
Pervall, Stephanie Joy *management consultant*
Pfeiffer-Kennedy, Natalie Patricia Anita *public relations executive, social sciences educator, consultant*
Phelan, Mary Michenfelder *public relations executive, writer*
Pilette, Patricia Chehy *healthcare organizational management consultant*
Plottel, Gloria Susanne Stone *marketing professional*
Podsiadlo, Maria J. *human resources analyst*
Proctor, Barbara Gardner *advertising agency executive, writer*
Pruett-Lawson, Jo Ann *marketing professional, special events coordinator*
Puetz, Pamela Ann *human resources executive*
Pugliese, Karen Olsen *freelance public relations counsel*
Radkowsky, Karen *advertising research specialist*
Rasor, Dina Lynn *investigator, journalist*
Renshaw, Jean Rehkop *management educator, consultant*
Richard, Susan Mathis *communications executive, screenwriter*
Richards, Carmeleete A. *computer training executive, network administrator, consultant*
Richards, Lynn *company training executive, consultant*
Richards, Susan R. *management consultant*
Riley-Davis, Shirley Merle *advertising agency executive, marketing consultant, writer*
Robinson, Linda Gosden *communications executive*
Roffé, Sarina *public relations executive*
Rosado, Sharon L. *marketing professional*
Rosen, Beth Dee *travel agency executive*
Rountree, Neva Dixon *public relations executive*
Russell, Carol Ann *personnel service company executive*
Ruyle, Julie Marie *marketing professional*
Rypczyk, Candice Leigh *employee relations executive*
Sacks, Temi J. *public relations executive*
Sanders, Kim Theresa *marketing professional, consultant*
Saucier, Guylaine *corporate director*
Schocket, Sandra Klamkin *career management consultant, writer*
Schubert, Helen Celia *public relations executive*
Schur Kaufman, Susan *retired public affairs consultant*
Schwab, Barbara *advertising executive*
Sibilla, Suzanne Rose *training and organizational development consultant*
Silva, Albertina *computer company executive*
Simecka, Betty Jean *marketing executive*
Simmons, Sylvia (Sylvia Simmons Neumann) *advertising executive, writer*
Simone, Heather Ann *management consultant*
Simpson, Andrea Lynn *communications executive*
Slater, Lori Annette *project manager*
Sorstokke, Ellen Kathleen *marketing executive, educator*
Spirn, Michele Sobel *communications professional, writer*
Spivak, Joan Carol *healthcare communications specialist*
Sproat, Kezia Vanmeter *communications executive, writer*
Srere, Linda Jean *former advertising executive*
Stagen, Mary-Patricia Healy *marketing executive*
Stanley, Frances Lucille *human resources manager, fire commissioner*
Stark, Diana *public relations executive*
Stocklin, Alma Katherine *retired public relations executive*
Stubbs, Katrina Childs *business consultant*
Sturns, Debera C. *marketing professional*
Sullivan, Nell Inklebarger *retired administrative official, counselor*
Sullivan, Sarah Louise *management and technology consultant*
Surley, Leslie K. *marketing professional*
Sutlin, Vivian *advertising executive*
Szymanski, Therese *marketing professional, writer*
Taylor, Michelle Y. *human resources consultant*
Teater, Tricia L. *human resources specialist*
Tejedor, Marcela Alejandra *sales executive, consultant*
Terry, Kay Adell *marketing executive*
Thomas, Angela M. *marketing professional*
Thomas, Rhonda Robbins *marketing educator, consultant*

Thurner, Agnes H. *retired administrative secretary*
Tompkins, Julie Lynberg *market research consultant*
Transou, Lynda Lou *advertising art administrator*
Traxler, Eva Maria *marketing professional*
Triplett, Arlene Ann *management consultant*
Tuft, Mary Ann *executive search firm executive*
Tytler, Linda Jean *communications and public affairs executive, retired state legislator*
Vega, Raynette Norma *hotel official*
Wagner, Leana Moree *computer executive, graphic designer, fine artist*
Walker, Betsy Ellen *consulting and systems integration company executive*
Wall, Carolyn Raimondi *communications executive*
Wallington, Patricia McDevitt *computer company executive*
Wardlaw, Sonya Carol *customer service administrator, educator*
Watson, Rebecca Elaine *human resources specialist, consultant*
Watson, Renée *marketing professional, special events consultant*
Webb, Doris McIntosh *human resources specialist*
Weiner, Sharon Rose *public relations executive*
Werkman, Rosemarie Anne *former public relations professional, civic worker*
Wheeler, Barbara J. *management consultant*
Whisenhunt, Livia L. *marketing executive*
Whitaker, Shirley Ann *telecommunications company marketing executive*
White, Bonnie Yvonne *management consultant, retired educator*
Wilds, Karen R. *housing authority executive*
Williams, Freda Berry *administrative assistant*
Wilson-Stewart, Marilyn Lucille *retired human resources director*
Winter, Nancy Fitz *media and public relations executive*
Wise, Susan Tamsberg *management and communications consultant, speaker*
Woerner, Louise *hotel executive*
Wright, Cheryl Diane *marketing professional*
Wulff, Julie Bader *purchasing agent*
Yaeger, Therese Francis *management professional*
Yee, Nancy W. *travel consultant*
Young, Elizabeth Bell *consultant*

INDUSTRY: TRADE

UNITED STATES

ALABAMA

Birmingham
Blair, Ludie Mae Riley *retired furniture company executive*

Montrose
Haynie, Betty Jo Gillmore *personal property appraiser, antiques dealer*

Trussville
Ballard, Laura Clay *small business owner*

ALASKA

Salcha
Alsip, Cheryl Ann *small business owner*

ARIZONA

Phoenix
DuMoulin, Diana Cristaudo *small business owner, writer*

Tempe
Lemmon, Nicolette *small business owner, marketing professional*

Tucson
Golston, Maggie *small business owner, writer*

ARKANSAS

Bentonville
Dillman, Linda *retail executive*
Swanson, Celia *retail executive*

CALIFORNIA

Apple Valley
Neal, Yolanda Kimberly Tabb *small business owner*

Bodega Bay
Freeman, Donna Cook *small business owner*

Chatsworth
Henderson, Cheryl Lynne *retail executive*

Escondido
Young, Gladys *business owner*

Exeter
Pescosolido, Pamela Jane *arts and craft supply store owner, graphic designer*

Fremont
Buswell, Debra Sue *small business owner, programmer, analyst*

Liang, Christine *import company executive*

Fresno
Redmond-Stewart, Audrey A. *small business owner*

Hollywood
Lore, Linda *retail executive*

Laguna Beach
Sieg, Sandra Nishkian *entrepreneur, dental hygienist*

Lancaster
Noble, Sunny A. *business owner*

Lockeford
Walker, Nancy Anne *small business owner, history educator, art educator*

Long Beach
Altman, Mimi Angster *business owner*

Los Angeles
Brewton, Michele Eileen *small business owner, consultant*
Condrill, Jo Ellaresa *freelance/self-employed small business owner, writer, consultant*

Malibu
Field, Barbara Stephenson *small business owner*

Manhattan Beach
King, Sharon Marie *consulting company executive*

Oakland
Austin, Caroline Germaine *small business owner*

Ontario
Presto, Catherine Ann (Kay Presto) *small business owner, media specialist, consultant*

Palm Desert
Vander Naald Egenes, Joan Elizabeth *small business owner, educator*

Pasadena
Olson, Diana Craft *image and etiquette consultant*

Pleasanton
Plaisance, Melissa *retail executive*
Renda, Laree M. *retail executive*

Riverside
Anderson, Jolene Slover *small business owner, publishing executive, consultant*

Sacramento
Burgess, Deborah Lee *small business owner*

San Francisco
Gust, Anne Baldwin *retail apparel company executive*
McCollam, Sharon L. *retail executive*
Nicolaï, Judithe *international business executive*
Sage-Gavin, Eva Marie *retail executive*

Skyforest
Wagner, Cheri J. *business owner*

South San Francisco
Mertens, Lynne G. *retail executive*

Walnut Creek
Van Noy, Christine Ann *restaurateur*

West Sacramento
Teel, Joyce Raley *retail executive*

COLORADO

Boulder
Meyer, Andrea Peroutka *small business owner*

Colorado Springs
Artl, Karen Ann *business owner, author*
Johnson, Stephanie L. B. *small business owner, office manager*

Denver
Maul, Carol Elaine *small business owner*
Nelson, LeAnn Lindbeck *small business owner*

Englewood
Oshman, Marilyn *retail executive*

Golden
Brainerd, Mary *small business owner*

Loveland
Rodman, Sue A. *wholesale company executive, artist, writer*

CONNECTICUT

Avon
Kling, Phradie (Phradie Kling Gold) *small business owner, educator*

Greenwich
Rudy, Kathleen Vermeulen *small business owner*

Guilford
McGrath, Chrystyne Mary *retail clothing store owner*

New London
Johnson, Diana Atwood *business owner, innkeeper*

Norwich
Buddington, Olive Joyce *shop owner, retired education educator*

West Haven
Mendez, Angela M. *small business owner*

DISTRICT OF COLUMBIA

Washington
Carr, Marie Pinak *book distribution company executive*
Chalkley, Jacqueline Ann *retail company executive*
DeBusk, F. Amanda *export administration executive*
McGraw, Lavinia Morgan *retired retail executive*
Pelavin, Diane Christine *small business owner*
Smith, Marie F. *small business owner, writer*
Smith, Marie Ford *small business owner*
Tetelman, Alice Fran *small business owner*

FLORIDA

Casselberry
Homayssi, Ruby Lee *small business owner*

Clearwater
Henderson, Janet Lynn *small business owner*

Cocoa Beach
Taylor, Nancy Alice *merchandiser, buyer*

Delray Beach
Campbell, Cynthia *retail executive*
Carter-Miller, Jocelyn *retail executive*
Luechtefeld, Monica *retail executive*
Morrison, Patricia B. *retail executive*

Fort Lauderdale
Kropp, Stacy Anne *small business owner*

Fort Myers
Colgate, Doris Eleanor *sailing school owner and administrator*
Ranney, Mary Elizabeth *business executive*

Jacksonville
Constantini, JoAnn M. *small business owner, consultant*

Key West
Armendariz, Alma Delia *small business owner, researcher*
Murphy, S(usan) (Jane Murphy) *small business owner*

Lakeland
Wilson, Micheline *small business owner*

Miami
Liebes, Raquel *retired import/export company executive*
Richards-Vital, Claudia *small business owner, recreational facility executive*

Palm Beach
Roberts, Margot Markels *business executive*

Parrish
Corey, Kay Janis *business owner, designer, nurse*

Port Richey
Applefield, Sandra *small business owner*

Port Saint Lucie
Dunbar, Shirley Eugenia-Doris *small business owner, writer*

Saint Augustine
Bishop, Claire DeArment *small business owner, former librarian*

Saint Petersburg
Despanza-Sprenger, Lynette Charlie *small business owner*
Thompson, Dayle Ann *small business owner, consultant*

Tampa
Eddy, Colette Ann *aerial photography studio owner, photographer*

Venice
Cool, Kim Patmore *retail executive, needlework consultant*

West Melbourne
Fetner, Suzanne *small business owner*

GEORGIA

Atlanta
Howard, Karen S. *retail executive*
Martineau, Lynn *retail executive*
Weeks, Helen Ballard *retail executive*
Wilson, Faye *retail executive*

Cumming
Pruitt-Streetman, Shirley Irene *small business owner*

Decatur
Solomon, Hilda Pearl *wholesale executive*

East Point
Malcolm, Gloria J. *small business owner*

Marietta
Short-Mayfield, Patricia Ahlene *business owner*

IDAHO

Boise
Herbert, Kathy *retail executive*

Coeur D Alene
Jaeger, Ellen Louise *small business owner*

ILLINOIS

Burr Ridge
Jones, Shirley Joyce *small business owner, fashion designer*

Champaign
Killeen, Albertina Ellen *retail executive, consultant, personnel advisor*

Charleston
Ball-Saret, Jayne Adams *small business owner*

Chicago
Dowling, Doris Anderson *business owner, educator, consultant*
Gall, Betty Bluebaum *office services company executive*
Gin, Sue Ling *retail executive*
Hunt, Holly *small business owner*
Ziegler, Ann E. *retail executive*

Dixon
Hansen, Linda Marie *small business owner*

Hoffman Estates
Meads, Mindy *merchandising and design executive*
Purves, Karen E. *freelance/self-employed small business owner*

Hoopeston
Hicks, Carol Ann *small business owner, educator*

Kewanee
Grant, Linda Kay (Linda Kay Scott) *small business owner, sales executive*

Lake Forest
Stirling, Ellen Adair *retail executive*

Mount Vernon
Kendrick-Hopgood, Debra Jo *small business owner*

Plainfield
Bennett-Hammerberg, Janie Marie *small business owner, writer, consultant, administrative assistant*

River Grove
Stanton, Kathryn *retail bookstores/educ products and services executive*

Saint Charles
LaHood, Julie Ann *small business owner*

INDIANA

Bloomington
York, Cynthia A. *retail executive*

Columbus
Jorgensen, Virginia Dyer *antique dealer, museum consultant*

Evansville
Blesch, K(athy) Suzann *small business owner*

Fort Wayne
Cast, Anita Hursh *small business owner*

Griffith
Spires, Roberta Lynn *small business owner*

Indianapolis
Norwalk, Kelli Curran *retail executive, entrepreneur*

Sandborn
Hartsburg, Judith Catherine *small business owner*

IOWA

Ankeny
Tomb, Carol E. *retail executive*

Davenport
Sievert, Mary Elizabeth *small business owner, retired secondary school educator*

Fairfield
Drees, Dorothy E. *small business owner, real estate manager*

West Union
Hansen, Ruth Lucille Hofer *business owner, consultant*

KANSAS

Ellis
Eveleigh, Arlene *marine business owner, county commissioner*

Fairway
Minkoff, Jill S. *business owner, entrepreneur, educator*

Wichita
Moore, Peggy Sue *corporation executive*

Lubbock
Willingham, Mary Maxine *fashion retailer*

Muleshoe
Logsdon, Judith Kay Logsdon *merchandiser, small business owner*

Pearland
Williams, Lynn Stenstrom *small business owner*

Round Mountain
McReynolds, Mary Maureen *small business owner*

San Antonio
Kretzschmar, Angelina Genzer *small business owner, paralegal*

Texarkana
Floyd, Stacy Y. *retail executive*
Hubbard, Sonia Y. *retail executive*

Vernon
Mikkelsen, Barbara Berry *retired retail executive, rancher*

Weatherford
Pyle, Carol Lynn Horsley *small business owner*

UTAH

Salt Lake City
Fields, Debbi *cookie franchise executive*
Miller, Lorraine *business owner*

VERMONT

Putney
Loring, Honey *small business owner*

VIRGINIA

Burke
Austin, Sandra J. *small business owner*

Charlottesville
Lupton, Mary Hosmer *retired small business owner*

Fairfax
Bohan, Gloria *travel retail executive*

Falls Church
Fink, Cathy DeVito *small business owner*

Richmond
Austin-Stephens, Ann-Marie *retail executive*
Bloomsburg, Anne Elizabeth *small business owner, writer*
Casini, Jane Sloan *wholesale distribution executive*
Dias, Fiona P. *retail executive*

Upperville
Powell Gebhard, Joy Lee (Bok Sin Lee) *small business owner*

Woodbridge
Williams, Cynthia Ann *small business owner, pediatrics nurse*

WASHINGTON

Black Diamond
Walker, Minerva E. Gilara *retail executive, poet*

Everett
Olsen-Estie, Jeanne Lindell *golf course owner*

Monroe
Kirwan, Katharyn Grace (Mrs. Gerald Bourke Kirwan Jr.) *retail executive*

Nordland
Denniston, Martha Kent *small business owner, writer*

Seattle
Cottle, Gail Ann *retail executive*

Spokane
Chamberlain, Barbara Kaye *small business owner, communications executive*

Woodway
Kent, Aimee Bernice Petersen *small business owner, interior designer, landscape architect, artist*

Yakima
Newland, Ruth Laura *small business owner*

WISCONSIN

Beloit
Story, Kendra *wholesale distribution executive*

La Crosse
Oswalt, Sally Hundt *small business owner*

Menomonee Falls
Blanc, Caryn *retail executive*
Meier, Arlene *retail executive*

Warrens
Potter, June Anita *small business owner*

Wausau
Buller, Dorothy Marion *business owner*

WYOMING

Jackson
Law, Clarene Alta *small business owner, state legislator*

CANADA

ONTARIO

Ottawa
Wendling, Louise *wholesale distribution executive*

ADDRESS UNPUBLISHED

Alexakos, Frances Marie *counselor, business owner, psychology educator, researcher, producer, editor*
Beavers, Karen Marjorie *small business owner*
Binder, Madeline Dotti *retail executive*
Bird, Patricia Coleen *business owner*
Brabec, Rosemary Jean *retail executive*
Brabenec, Stacey Marie *retail buyer*
Bravo, Rose Marie *retail executive*
Brooks, Suzanne Rayetta *small business owner*
Busch, Joyce Ida *small business owner*
Conte, Andrea *retail executive, healthcare consultant, advocate*
Cox, Joy Dean *small business owner*
Cuba, Nan Brindley *small business owner, writer*
Davis, Donna Lee *small business owner, writer*
Delaney, Marion Patricia *retail executive*
Dworin, Micki (Maxine Dworin) *automobile dealership executive*
Dyer, Arlene Thelma *retail company owner*
Edwards, Patricia Burr *small business owner, counselor, consultant*
Ellis, Patricia Weathers *small business owner, retired electronic technician*
Eyring, Maxine Louise *small business owner, esthetician*
Farr, Ivanne Estelle *small business owner, consultant, artist, sculptor*
Ferrari, Donna Mae *retired autobody shop owner*
Franzetti, Lillian Angelina *former automobile dealership owner*
Gatch, Frances Anne *retired small business owner*
Goldberg, Nancy G. *business owner, community volunteer*
Goodman, Gail Busman *small business owner*
Gray, Deborah Mary *wine importer*
Groth, Jenice Joy *small business owner*
Guzman, Carole L. *small business owner*
Hambrecht, Patricia G. *retail executive*
Hedman, Janice Lee *business executive*
Howard, Susan J. *small business owner*
Isenor, Linda Darlene *grocery retailer, marketing professional*
Johnson, Dolores Estelle *retired small business owner*
Kramer, Susan Rose *small business owner, skier, educator*
LaBudde, Bessie Freeman *retired small business owner, retired director*
Lay, Robin Renee *small business owner*
Love, Margaret Marks *business owner*
Lowry, Marilyn Jean *horticultural retail company executive*
Masten, Jacqueline Gwendolyn *small business owner*
Mayer, Kristine I. *small business owner, writer*
Medaglia, Elizabeth Ellen *small business owner*
Melanson, Susan C. *small business owner*
Moy, Audrey *retired retail buyer*
O'Donnell Rich, Dorothy Juanita *small business owner*
Pham, Lara Bach-Vien *small business owner*
Ramsey, Lucie Avra *small business owner, consultant*
Reast, Deborah Stanek *small business owner*
Rohner, Bonnie-Jean *small business owner, computer consultant*
Scott, Sylvia Jane *small business owner*
Shackelford, Nancy Kay *retail executive*
Sims, Karen Sue *small business owner*
Singh, DeAnn Coates *small business owner, artist, educator*
Slater, Kristie *small business owner*
Snodgrass, Lynn *small business owner, former state legislator*
Stronach, Belinda *former retail executive*
Substad Lokensgard, Kathryn Ann *small business owner, career consultant*
Topolewski-Green, Mary Jo Therese *small business owner*
Turner, Natalie A. *retired small business owner, consultant*
Vandenburg, Kathy Helen *small business owner, career coach, resume writer*
Ward, Darlene Marie *retail buyer*
Wos, Carol Elaine *small business owner*

INDUSTRY: TRANSPORTATION

UNITED STATES

ALABAMA

Abbeville
Anderson, Ruth T. *retired air traffic controller*

ALASKA

Anchorage
Williams, Eleanor Joyce *retired government air transportation professional*

ARKANSAS

Little Rock
Schwartz, Deborah S. *airport manager*

Murfreesboro
Janssen, Marybeth *airframe and power plant mechanic*

CALIFORNIA

El Segundo
McCarty, Shirley Carolyn *aerospace executive*

Los Angeles
Kennard, Lydia H. *airport terminal executive*
Knowles, Marie L. *transportation executive*

Newbury Park
Lindsey, Joanne M. *flight attendant, poet*

Oakland
Reynolds, Kathleen Diane Foy (KDF Reynolds) *transportation executive*

San Diego
Bowens, Thella *senior aviation director*
Williams, Lisa Rochelle *logistics and transportation educator*

San Francisco
Royer, Kathleen Rose *pilot*

COLORADO

Colorado Springs
Stienmier, Saundra Kay Young *aviation educator*

CONNECTICUT

Hamden
Lakin, Joan Field *retired water treatment plant manager*

DISTRICT OF COLUMBIA

Washington
Hallett, Carol Boyd *air transportation executive*

FLORIDA

Daytona Beach
Chabrian, Peggy *air transportation executive*

Jacksonville
Aftoora, Patricia Joan *transportation executive*
Kilbourne, Krystal Hewett *retired rail transportation executive*

Miami
Gittens, Angela *airport executive*
Krissel, Susan Hinkle *transportation company executive*

West Palm Beach
Waters, Lisa Lyle *airport administrator, consultant*

GEORGIA

Atlanta
Escarra, Vicki B. *airline company executive*
Palko, Lorri M. *automotive company executive*

Marietta
Niemann, Linda Grant *railroad conductor*

Savannah
Murray, Mary A. *transportation executive*

ILLINOIS

Chicago
Apelbaum, Phyllis L. *delivery messenger service executive*
Koelliner, Laurette T. *aerospace transportation executive*
Loney, Mary Rose *airport administrator*
McNeil, Sue *transportation system educator*
Sookik, Bonnie W. *air transportation executive*

INDIANA

Griffith
Luetschwager, Mary Susan *transportation company professional*

Lebanon
Geisler, Kay *transportation executive*

KENTUCKY

Louisville
Carranza, Jovita *delivery service executive*

LOUISIANA

New Orleans
Chetta, Holly Ann *transportation executive*

MAINE

Bangor
Hupp, Rebecca *airport terminal executive*

MARYLAND

Rockville
Weiss, Rita Sandra *transportation executive, educator*

MASSACHUSETTS

Cambridge
Widnall, Sheila Evans *aeronautical educator, former secretary of the airforce, former university official*

MICHIGAN

Detroit
Feldhouse, Lynn *automotive company executive*
Newman, Andrea Fischer *air transportation executive*

MINNESOTA

Duluth
Regan, Laura Anderson *aviation maintenance technician*

Saint Paul
Nylander, Patricia Marie *pilot*

MISSOURI

Springfield
Moss, Elizabeth Lucille (Betty Moss) *retired transportation executive*

NEW HAMPSHIRE

Hancock
Baddour, Anne Bridge *pilot*

NEW JERSEY

Newark
Baer, Susan M. *airport executive*

NEW YORK

Delhi
Townsend, Sue Joyce *retired air traffic controller*

Jamaica
Feldman, Arlene Butler *aviation industry executive*

Oyster Bay
Smith, Pamela Rosevear *air transportation executive*

NORTH CAROLINA

Chapel Hill
Waller, Patricia Fossum *transportation executive, researcher, psychologist*

Charlotte
Stearns, Cheryl Ann *commercial airline pilot*

OHIO

Cleveland
Martin Burghard, Stephanie Marie *pilot, educator*

Painesville
Luhta, Caroline Naumann *airport manager, flight educator*

PENNSYLVANIA

Pittsburgh
Stunja, Valerie Ann *aircraft dispatcher*

TENNESSEE

Morristown
Johnson, Evelyn Bryan *airport terminal executive*

TEXAS

Dallas
Barrett, Colleen Crotty *airline executive*

Euless
Tunnell, Clida Diane *air transportation specialist*

Fort Worth
Oliver, Susan M. *air transportation executive*

Houston
Baker, Ellen Shulman *astronaut, physician*
Cagle, Yvonne Darlene *astronaut*
Coleman, Catherine G. *astronaut*
Currie, Nancy Jane *astronaut*
Davis, N. Jan *astronaut, mechanical engineer*
Helms, Susan Jane *astronaut*
Higginbotham, Joan E. *astronaut*
Hoppe, Laura *air traffic controller*
Ivins, Marcia S. *astronaut*
Jernigan, Tamara E. *astronaut*
Kilrain, Susan *astronaut*
Lawrence, Wendy B. *astronaut*
Melroy, Pamela Ann *astronaut*
Ochoa, Ellen *astronaut*
Shore, Lisa *flight controller, trainer*
Voss, Janice E. *astronaut*
Weber, Mary Ellen *astronaut*
Williams, Sunita L. *astronaut*

VIRGINIA

Arlington
Beyer, Barbara Lynn *aviation consultant*
Binkowski, Sylvia Julia *water transportation executive, consultant*
Cragin, Maureen Patricia *aerospace transportation executive, former federal agency administrator*
Reynolds, Rochelle Annetta *flight attendant*

Hampton
Daniels, Cindy Lou *space agency executive*

WASHINGTON

Seattle
Brown, Janiece Alfreida *pilot*
Lindsey, Gina Marie *airport executive*
Strombom, Cathy Jean *transportation planner, consultant*

Tacoma
Pribble, Elizabeth J. *retired airline administrator*

WISCONSIN

Tomah
Johnson, Linda Arlene *transportation executive*

ADDRESS UNPUBLISHED

Adolph, Kathryn Ann *passenger service employee*
Collins, Eileen Marie *astronaut*
Donovan, Kathleen A. *water transportation executive, county official*
Glover, Lisa Marie *transportation executive, consultant*
Gornick, Melanie Dawn *flight attendant, entrepreneur*
Hahn, Virginia Lynn *reservations agent*
Heidish, Louise Oridge-Schwallie *retired transportation specialist*
Mitchell, Pamela Ann *airline pilot*
Nelson, Hope Linda *pilot*
Roberts, Linda *truck transportation services company executive*
Savitz, Maxine Lazarus *aerospace company executive*
Warner, Emily Hanrahan Howell *retired pilot, writer*

INDUSTRY: UTILITIES, ENERGY, RESOURCES

UNITED STATES

ARIZONA

Scottsdale
Bullerdick, Kim H. *petroleum executive*

Sierra Vista
Gignac, Judith Ann *utilities executive*

Tucson
Bryant, Marian Alanna *electric company consultant*
Kissinger, Karen G. *energy executive*

ARKANSAS

Little Rock
Gardner, Kathleen D. *gas company executive, lawyer*

CALIFORNIA

Elk Grove
Romano, Sheila June *telecommunications industry executive, artist, writer*

Huntington Beach
Schaffner-Irvin, Kristen *oil executive*

Los Angeles
Greenberg, Kate *telecommunications industry executive*

Reyes, Susana Marie *utility executive, environmentalist*
Thelander, Beverly *oil company executive*

Marina Del Rey
Carter, Janice Joene *telecommunications executive*

Redwood City
Woods, Jacqueline F. *telecommunications industry executive*

Rosemead
Featherstone, Diane L. *utilities executive*
Parsky, Barbara *utilities executive*
Ryder, Beverly *utilities executive*
Yazdi, Mahvash *utilities executive*

San Diego
Gray-Bussard, Dolly H. *energy company executive*

San Francisco
Hirzel, Katherine Renee *communication strategist, geographer, photographer*

San Jose
Bodensteiner, Lisa M. *utilities executive, lawyer*
Curtis, Ann B. *utilities executive*

San Ramon
Woertz, Patricia A. *petroleum industry executive*
Yarrington, Patricia *oil industry executive*
Zygocki, Rhonda I. *oil industry executive*

Santa Barbara
Casey, Mary A. *telecommunications company executive*
Enos, Kelly D. *telecommunications company financial executive*

COLORADO

Denver
Kruger, Paula *telecommunications industry executive*

Littleton
VanderLinden, Camilla Denice Dunn *telecommunications industry executive*

CONNECTICUT

Berlin
Grise, Cheryl *electric power industry executive*

Stratford
Sahagian, Lucille Bedrosian *gasoline company executive*

DELAWARE

Wilmington
Graham, Barbara S. *electric power industry executive*

DISTRICT OF COLUMBIA

Washington
Johns, Marie C. *telecommunications industry executive*
King, Gwendolyn S. *retired utility company executive, former federal official*
Miller, Susan M. *telecommunications industry executive*

FLORIDA

Orlando
Gouvellis, Mary C. *utilities executive*
Houser, Ruth G. *financial executive*

Parkland
Garcia, Laura Catherine *emergency and disaster preparedness consultant*

Tamarac
Hughes, Jennifer *utilities executive, photographer*

GEORGIA

Atlanta
Adams, Valencia I. *telecommunications industry executive*
Burns, M. Michele *energy executive, former air transportation executive*
Dunn, Rebecca M. *telecommunications industry executive*
Fuller, S(heri) Marce *energy executive*
Funderburg, Jan *telecommunications industry executive*
Greene, Margaret H. *telecommunications industry executive*
Latham, Deborah L. *energy marketing and services company executive*
Wentworth, Lynn A. *telecommunications industry executive*

Social Circle
O'Connor, Patricia Eryl *telecommunications consultant*

ILLINOIS

Bloomington
Beeler, Charlotte Jean *oil and supply company executive, interior design business executive*

Chicago
Gillis, Ruth Ann M. *electric company executive*
Rogers, Desiree Glapion *utilities executive*
Strobel, Pamela B. *energy executive*

Naperville
Burken, Ruth Marie *utilities executive*

Oak Brook
Harless, Katherine J. *telecommunications company executive*

INDIANA

Indianapolis
Koch, Linda Brown *utility administrator*
Krueger, Betty Jane *telecommunications company executive*

KANSAS

Overland Park
Strandjord, M. Jeannine *telecommunications industry executive*
Walker, Kathryn A. *telecommunications industry executive*

KENTUCKY

Glasgow
Duvo, Mechelle Louise *oil company executive, consultant*

LOUISIANA

New Orleans
Quirk, Kathleen L. *mining executive*

MARYLAND

Baltimore
Chagnoni, Kathleen *energy executive*

Sykesville
Perry, Nancy Trotter *former telecommunications company executive*

MASSACHUSETTS

Chelsea
Kuhne, Alice *oil industry executive*

Westborough
Bok, Joan Toland *utility executive*

MICHIGAN

Detroit
Beale, Susan M. *electric power industry executive*
Redfield, Jean M. *electric power company executive*

NEVADA

Reno
Brennan, Susan Mallick *utilities executive*

Winnemucca
Hesse, Martha O. *gas industry executive*

NEW HAMPSHIRE

Littleton
Wogaman, Dierdre E. *retired pipeline operator, real estate agent*

Rindge
Emerson, Susan *oil company executive*

NEW JERSEY

Kirkwood Voorhees
Wolf, Ellen C. *water company executive*

Murray Hill
Christy, Cindy *telecommunications industry executive*
Davidson, Janet G. *telecommunications industry executive*

Randolph
Rathore, Uma Pandey *utilities executive*

NEW YORK

Fresh Meadows
Jackson, Rhonda *telecommunications professional, poet*

New York
Bardin, Mary Beth *telecommunications company executive*
Bisbee, Joyce Evelyn *utility company manager, retired*
Freilich, Joan Sherman *utilities executive*

Syracuse
Kerr, Darlene Dixon *electric power company executive*

Whitestone
Bocchino, Frances Lucia *retired oil company official*

NORTH CAROLINA

Charlotte
Shaw, Ruth G. *energy company executive*

OHIO

Cincinnati
Aumiller, Wendy L. *utilities executive*
Braunstein, Mary *energy consulting company executive*
Foley, Cheryl M. *electric power industry executive*
Janson, Julia S. *utilities executive*
Noonan, Sheila M. *energy consulting company executive*

Cleveland
Slone, Charlotte M. *telecommunications executive*

Columbus
Koeppel, Holly *electric power industry executive*

Dayton
Lansaw, Judy W. *public utility executive*

OKLAHOMA

Oklahoma City
Bode, Denise Anne *petroleum association executive*

OREGON

Portland
Anthony, Wilma Tylinda *customer representative*

PENNSYLVANIA

Ephrata
Sweigart, Anne B. *communications company executive*

Philadelphia
Fretz, Deborah McDermott *oil industry executive*
Mulé, Ann C. *oil industry executive*

Presto
Moeller, Audrey Carolyn *retired energy company executive, corporate secretary*

TEXAS

Dallas
Mackenzie, Nanci *gas company executive*
Sentell, Susan B. *telecommunications company executive*

El Paso
Shelton, Patricia A. *gas company executive*

Fort Worth
Moncrief, William Alvin, Jr., *oil and gas producer*

Houston
Bartling, Phyllis McGinness *oil company executive*
Campbell, Eileen M. *oil industry executive*
Carriere, Margaret E. *energy executive*
Dorman, Margaret K. *oil equipment manufacturer*
Knickel, Carin S. *oil industry executive*
Kupiec, Suzanne L. *utilities executive*
Lehne, Kathy Prasnicki *gas industry executive*
Lumgair, Mary Elizabeth *energy executive*
McDonald, Rebecca Ann *natural gas company executive*
Mitcham, Carla J. *utilities executive*
Munson, Sylvia Frances Farris *energy company manager*
Saizan, Paula Theresa *oil company executive*
Sewell, Beth Perry *gas industry executive*

Irving
Cavanaugh, Lucille J. *oil industry executive*
Crowley, L. C. *telecommunications company executive*

Midland
Grover, Rosalind Redfern *oil and gas company executive*

Port Isabel
Michael, Carol M. *utilities executive, consultant*

San Antonio
Brown, Mary Rose *energy executive*
Titzman, Donna M. *energy executive*

Waco
Dwyer, Theresa *utilities executive*
Owens-Dwyer, Dina *utilities executive*

VIRGINIA

Reston
Hammick, Patricia A. *utilities company executive*

Richmond
Hopkins, Sandra Parker *power company administrator*

WISCONSIN

Saint Croix Falls
Lane, Kathleen Margaret *refrigeration company official*

TERRITORIES OF THE UNITED STATES

PUERTO RICO

Guaynabo
Lambert, Christina *telecommunications executive*

San Juan
Lambert, Cristina *telecommunications executive*

CANADA

ALBERTA

Calgary
Southern, Nancy C. *utilities executive*

NETHERLANDS

The Hague
Hodge, Susan *oil industry executive*

ADDRESS UNPUBLISHED

Bernard, Betsy J. *former telecommunications industry executive*
Blackman, Ghita Waucheta *natural energy consultant*
Clemons, Julie Payne *telephone company manager*
Coffin, Bertha Louise *telephone company executive*
Helton, Sandra Lynn *telecommunications industry executive*
Miller, Alice Ann *state utilities regulation executive*
Nugent, Jane Kay *retired utilities executive*
Pierce, Lisa Margaret *telecommunications executive, product and market development manager, lecturer*
Sullivan, Kathryn Meara *telecommunications company executive*
Wessner, Deborah Marie *telecommunications executive, information systems consultant*

INFORMATION TECHNOLOGY
See also SCIENCE: MATHEMATICS AND COMPUTER SCIENCE

UNITED STATES

ARIZONA

Tucson
Karson, Catherine June *database administrator*

CALIFORNIA

Burlingame
Garnett, Katrina A. *information technology executive*

Calabasas
Hofflich, Francine K. *network architect*

Irvine
Allen, Karen Alfstad *information technology executive*

Los Angeles
Martin, Nanice S. *software company executive*

Milpitas
Levinson, Marina *information technology executive*

Monterey
Aguilar, Miriam Rebecca *technology project manager*

Palo Alto
Denzel, Nora *information technology executive*
Greene, Diane *information technology executive*

Pleasanton
Caldwell, Nanci *software company executive*

Redwood City
Davidson, Mary Ann *information technology executive*
Smith, Nancy L. *information technology executive*

Sacramento
Doyel, Cindy M. *information systems specialist*

San Bruno
Hariton, Lorraine Jill *information technology executive*

San Francisco
Malloy, Sandra Miriam *information specialist*
Pure, Pamela *information technology executive*

San Jose
Whitman, Margaret C. (Meg Whitman) *internet company executive*

San Mateo
Larkin, Nelle Jean *retired application developer, systems analyst*

Santa Clara
Weigle, Peggy *information technology executive*

Santa Cruz
Young, Carol Ann (Casey Young) *information systems consultant*

Sunnyvale
Perdikou, Kim *information technology executive*

Venice
Groppe, Laura *interactive software company executive*

COLORADO

Boulder
Cadora, Karen Michele *application developer*

Denver
Heppler, Robin Lee *project manager*

CONNECTICUT

Bristol
Vetter, Noelle I. *information technology manager*

Danbury
Fuller, Cassandra Miller *applications specialist*

New Britain
Margiotta, Mary-Lou Ann *application developer*

DISTRICT OF COLUMBIA

Washington
Jorstad, Tamara J. *information technology manager*
McCaleb, Margaret Anne Sheehan *application developer*

FLORIDA

Boca Raton
Kewley, Sharon Lynn *systems analyst, consultant*

Jacksonville
Salem, Karen E. *information technology executive*

Miami
Zito, Judi *information technology executive*

New Port Richey
Cessna, Janice Lynn *systems administrator, information technology manager*

Saint Petersburg
Metzger, Kathleen Ann *computer systems specialist*

Tamarac
Marged, Judith Michele *information technology educator*

Tampa
Rugers, Tatiana Yurievna *computer programmer, consultant*

Venice
Kleinlein, Kathy Lynn *training and development executive*

GEORGIA

Atlanta
Coley, Barbara Yvonne *computer software consultant*

Cordele
Venable, Lisa Anita *computer programmer*

Savannah
Bertolozzi, Victoria Margaret *program analyst, community planning and development*

HAWAII

Honolulu
Reed, Nancy Ellen *computer science educator*

ILLINOIS

Barrington
Taylor, Jacqueline Ann *systems administrator*

Belleville
Lane-Trent, Patricia Jean *information specialist*

Bethalto
Talbott, Janet K. *information technology executive*

Centralia
Davidson, Karen Sue *computer software designer*

Chicago
Drewry, June E. *information technology executive*

Oak Brook
Marcus, Carol A. *information technology manager*

Vernon Hills
Klein, Barbara A. *information technology executive*
Leahy, Christine A. *information technology executive*

INDIANA

Indianapolis
Niederberger, Jane *information technology executive*
Sterling, Jennifer Elizabeth *application developer, educator*

Lowell
Elkins, Jeni L. McIntosh *webmaster*

Tell City
Guillaum, Marsha Kaye *information technology manager*

KANSAS

Topeka
Freden, Sharon Elsie Christman *state education official*

LOUISIANA

Baton Rouge
Stockwell, Mary Diamond *information technology manager*

MARYLAND

Annapolis Junction
Brown, Wendy Elaine *communications consultant*

Baltimore
Park, Mary Woodfill *information consultant*

Bethesda
Peters, Brenda Irene *computer specialist, government official*
White, Jeannette Lee *information technology executive*

Cockeysville Hunt Valley
Elkin, Lois Shanman *business systems company executive*

Gaithersburg
Kemmerer, Sharon Jean *computer systems analyst*

MASSACHUSETTS

Boston
Lane, Kathy S. *information technology executive, consumer products company executive*

Cambridge
Cooper, Mary Campbell *information services executive*

Littleton
Lau, Joanna T. *information technology executive*

Waltham
O'Donnell, Teresa Hohol *application developer, electrical engineer*

MICHIGAN

Ann Arbor
deJesus-Burgos, Sylvia Teresa *security and risk management officer*

Dearborn
McKeage, Alice Jane *computer programmer*
Odeh, Kristin S. *information technology executive*

Kalamazoo
Morris, Martha Josephine *information services administrator*

MINNESOTA

Excelsior
Henke, Janice Carine *educational software developer and marketer*

Maple Grove
Prins, LaVonne Kay *programmer analyst*

Rochester
Schmieding, Rebecca Sue *information technology manager*

MISSOURI

Saint Louis
Elliott, Susan Spoehrer *information technology executive*
Young, Virginia McLain *information technology consulting executive*

NEBRASKA

Omaha
Dufner, Donna Kane *management information systems, project management educator*

NEVADA

Reno
Ragavan, Anpalaki Jeyabalasinkham *software developer, researcher*

NEW HAMPSHIRE

Weare
White, Karen Ruth Jones *information systems executive*

NEW JERSEY

Basking Ridge
Samuelson, Cynthia *information technology executive*

Fort Dix
McCormack, Sheila Ann *network technician*

Marlton
Kuster, Diane M. *computer technician*

Mount Laurel
Li, Pearl Nei-Chien Chu *technology company executive*

Murray Hill
Bruch, Ruth E. *information technology executive*

Neshanic Station
Castellon, Christine New *information systems specialist, real estate agent*

Newark
Nash, Alicia *computer programmer, physicist*

Piscataway
Kenney, Mary R. *software engineer*

Randolph
Stoskus, Joanna Jorzysta *computer information systems educator*

Rochelle Park
Olzerowicz, Sharon *information technology executive*

Roseland
Graham, Patricia *information technology executive*

Somerset
Lee, Thai Theresa *information technology executive*

Sparta
Guida, Pat *information broker, literature chemist*

Trenton
Himm, Emilie Gina *administrative analyst, records and information manager, consultant*

Willingboro
Suber, Sharon L. *technology coordinator*

NEW MEXICO

Albuquerque
McBride, Teresa *information systems specialist*

Kirtland Afb
Anderson, Christine Marlene *software engineer*

NEW YORK

Brooklyn
Gilmore, Jennifer A.W. *computer specialist, educator*

Buffalo
Overton, Nicole Yolanda *program analyst*

Melville
Webber, Pamela D. *information technology executive*

New York
Cutrone, Agatha Michele *information systems specialist*
Kozik, Susan S. *information technology executive*
Petti, Nancy A. *information technology manager*
Ross, Karen *information technology executive*

Poughkeepsie
Jacobi, Kerry Lee *information systems specialist*

Somers
Sanford, Linda S. *information technology executive*

Tillson
Kelly, Patricia Ellen *information technology manager*

Weedsport
Ellinger-Labulis, Kathleen Marie *application developer, consultant*

NORTH CAROLINA

Chapel Hill
Smith, Janet Sue *systems specialist*

Charlotte
Maclean, Rhonda *information technology executive*

OHIO

Cincinnati
Govern, Maureen *information technology executive*

Cleveland
McCormick, Maureen Olivea *computer systems programmer*

Columbus
Roeder, Rebecca Emily *software engineer*
Taylor, Celianna Isley *information systems specialist*
Walker-Griffin, Donna Fay *information technology manager*

Dayton
Grant, Colleen *information systems specialist*

Dublin
Spies, Phyllis Bova *information services company executive*

Marion
Rowe, Lisa Dawn *computer programmer/analyst, computer consultant*

Van Wert
Huffman, Laura Christine *computer programmer, educator*

Walbridge
Cox, Brenda Lynn *information technology manager*

OKLAHOMA

Ada
Baker, Judith Ann *retired computer technician*

Mustang
Laurent, J(erry) Suzanna *technical communications specialist*

OREGON

Corvallis
Wechsler, Susan Linda *research and development software manager*

Zigzag
Chappell, Annie-Dear *retired information technology company official*

PENNSYLVANIA

Clarks Summit
Weiss, Tammy Lee *information technology manager*

Gladwyne
Stick, Alyce Cushing *systems administrator, consultant*

King Of Prussia
Swank, Annette Marie *software designer*

Malvern
Colosimo, Lisa Marie *software engineer*

Mechanicsburg
Bitner, Jerri Lynne *information technology professional, consultant*

Philadelphia
Wilms, Anne M. *information technology executive*

SOUTH CAROLINA

Camden
Koestner, Carol Ann *information technology manager, consultant*

Charleston
Nordquist, Sonya Lynn *information technology executive*

Fountain Inn
Mozoski, Diane Marie *information technology executive*

Orangeburg
Ramsey, Kim N. *information technology manager*

TEXAS

Dallas
Kruse, Ann Gray *computer programmer*

Fort Hood
Anderson, Nanci Louise *computer analyst*

Fort Worth
Moore, Terri Kramer *information technology manager*

Houston
Wejman, Janet P. *information technology executive, air transportation executive*

Katy
Floyed, Cheryl W. *web site designer*

Nederland
Anderson, Tess *information technology manager, education educator*

Pecos
McCracken, Peggy Jane *webmaster, publishing executive*

Stafford
Forbes, Sharon Elizabeth *software engineer*

The Woodlands
Welch, Kathy Jane *information technology executive*

VIRGINIA

Alexandria
Davis, Ruth Margaret (Mrs. Benjamin Franklin Lohr) *information technology executive*

Falls Church
Kay, Peg (Marjorie A. Kay) *information technology executive*

Reston
Heine, Karen Marieke *software development tutor, consultant*

Richmond
McDermid, Margaret F. *information technology executive, engineer*

WASHINGTON

Redmond
Black, Deborah *information technology executive*
Brummel, Lisa *information technology executive*
Elliot, Gerri *information technology executive*
Hebert, Kathleen *information technology professional*
Moore, Lori *information technology executive*
Stonesifer, Patricia Q. *information systems executive*

Seattle
Lightner, Janet (Jan) Anderson *information technology manager, consultant, writer*
McConney, Mary E. *information technology executive*

WISCONSIN

De Pere
Molnar, Kathleen Kay *management information systems educator*

Milwaukee
Kraut, Joanne Lenora *computer programmer, analyst*

Sturgeon Bay
Skadden, Nancy Lee Mackey *information technology manager*

ADDRESS UNPUBLISHED

Adiletta, Debra Jean Olson *business analyst consultant*
Alexander, Nancy A. *information technology manager, consultant*
Behnke, Doleen *computer and environmental specialist, consultant*
Bender, Caroline Helen *senior technical trainer*
Bluitt, Karen *information technology executive*
Bramhall, Debra A. *information technology manager, consultant*
Burns, Pat Ackerman Gonia *information systems specialist, software engineer*
Collins-Brown, E. Dorlee (E. Dorlee Woodyard) *systems support specialist*
Creswell, Dorothy Anne *computer consultant*
Culleeney, Maureen Ann *information technology executive, educator*
Davis, Suzanne Spiegel *retired information specialist*
Donohue, Anne Emlen *software engineer*
Dunn, Melanie Lea *information technology manager*
Etheridge, Diana Carol *internet business executive*
Etzel, Deborah Anne *computer technician, consultant*
Gibbs, Johnie Elizabeth *information technology manager, educator, consultant*
Greene Lloyd, Nancy Ellen *retired infosystems specialist, physicist*
Heck, Debra Upchurch *information technology, procurement professional*
Hill, Judith Swigost *business analyst, information systems manager*
Hudson, Carolyn Brauer *application developer, educator*
Hughes, Jacqueline Emma *information systems specialist*
Huyser, Cynthia Gaye *computer programmer, poet*

Hyler, Sheryl Root *application developer*
Jones, Gwenyth Ellen *publishing information systems/technology executive*
Kelley, Mary Elizabeth (Mary LaGrone) *information technology executive*
Kun, Rebecca *information technology executive*
Latimer, Helen *information resource manager, writer, researcher*
Levy, Leslie Ann *application developer*
Maruoka, Jo Ann Elizabeth *retired information systems manager*
McGervey, Teresa Ann *technical information specialist*
Morgan, M. Jane *computer systems consultant*
Nicols, Angela C. *software engineer, computer consultant*
Normore, Lorraine Frances *information systems researcher*
Pressley-Ulmer, Dara Ayanna *web site designer*
Roberts, Marie Dyer *retired computer systems specialist*
Rose, Brita May *web site designer, writer, peace activist*
Schneider, Sharon M. *systems administrator, information technologist*
Scruggs, Terri LaGuardia *systems support specialist*
Shei, Juliana Chiang *information technology manager*
Thompson, Joyce Lurine *retired information systems specialist*
Visocki, Nancy Gayle *information services consultant*
Weekes, Wanda L. *information technology manager*
Wilkins, Rita Denise *product development, research and technology director*

INTERNET *See* INFORMATION TECHNOLOGY

LAW: JUDICIAL ADMINISTRATION

UNITED STATES

ALABAMA

Birmingham
Blackburn, Sharon Lovelace *federal judge*
Privett, Caryl Penney *judge*

Mobile
Mahoney, Margaret A. *federal judge*

Montgomery
Brown, Jean Williams *state supreme court justice*
McPherson, Vanzetta Penn *magistrate judge*
Stuart, Lyn (Jacquelyn L. Stuart) *judge*

ALASKA

Anchorage
Fabe, Dana Anderson *state supreme court justice*

ARIZONA

Mesa
Hicks, Bethany Gribben *judge, commissioner, lawyer*

Phoenix
Berch, Rebecca White *state supreme court justice, lawyer*
Mathis, Virginia *federal judge*
McGregor, Ruth Van Roekel *state supreme court justice*
Schroeder, Mary Murphy *federal judge*
Silver, Roslyn O. *federal judge*

Springerville
Geisler, Sherry Lynn *magistrate*

ARKANSAS

Little Rock
Dickey, Betty C. *judge*
Imber, Annabelle Clinton *state supreme court justice*
Roaf, Andree Layton *judge*
Wright, Susan Webber *judge*

CALIFORNIA

Los Angeles
Baird, Lourdes G. *federal judge*
Carroll, Ellen A. *judge, lawyer*
Chapman, Rosalyn M. *federal judge*
Collins, Audrey B. *judge*
Fischer, Dale Susan *judge*
Manella, Nora M. *federal judge*
March, Kathleen Patricia *judge*
Marshall, Consuelo Bland *federal judge*
Pfaelzer, Mariana R. *federal judge*

Oakland
Armstrong, Saundra Brown *federal judge*
Tchaikovsky, Leslie J. *federal judge*
Wilken, Claudia *judge*

Pasadena
Hall, Cynthia Holcomb *federal judge*
Johnson, Barbara Jean *retired judge, lawyer*
Nelson, Dorothy Wright (Mrs. James F. Nelson) *federal judge*
Rymer, Pamela Ann *federal judge*

Riverside
Phillips, Virginia A. *judge*

San Diego
Aaron, Cynthia G. *judge*
Adler, Louise DeCarl *judge*
Gonzalez, Irma Elsa *federal judge*
Huff, Marilyn L. *federal judge*
Keep, Judith N. *federal judge*
McKeown, Mary Margaret *federal judge*
Porter, Louisa S. *federal judge*

San Francisco
Berzon, Marsha S. *federal judge*
Breall, Susan *judge*
Brown, Janice Rogers *state supreme court justice*
Callahan, Consuelo Maria *federal judge*
Chesney, Maxine M. *judge*
Graber, Susan P. *federal judge*
Illston, Susan Y. *federal judge*
James, Maria-Elena *federal judge*
Kennard, Joyce L. *judge*
Patel, Marilyn Hall *judge*
Wardlaw, Kim A.M. *federal judge*
Werdegar, Kathryn Mickle *state supreme court justice*

San Jose
Morgan, Marilyn *federal judge*

Santa Ana
Stotler, Alicemarie Huber *federal judge*

Sonoma
Herron, Ellen Patricia *retired judge*

Woodland Hills
Lax, Kathleen Thompson *judge*
Mund, Geraldine *judge*

COLORADO

Denver
Coan, Patricia A. *magistrate judge*
Kourlis, Rebecca Love *state supreme court justice*
Krieger, Marcia Smith *federal judge*
Mullarkey, Mary J. *state supreme court chief justice*
Rice, Nancy E. *judge*
Weinshienk, Zita Leeson *federal judge*

CONNECTICUT

Hartford
Katz, Joette *state supreme court justice*
Martinez, Donna F. *federal judge*
Peters, Ellen Ash *judge, retired Supreme Court chief justice*
Vertefeuille, Christine Siegrist *judge*

New Haven
Arterton, Janet Bond *federal judge*
Burns, Ellen Bree *federal judge*

DELAWARE

Wilmington
Balick, Helen Shaffer *retired judge*
Berger, Carolyn *state supreme court justice*
Robinson, Sue L(ewis) *federal judge*
Roth, Jane Richards *federal judge*

DISTRICT OF COLUMBIA

Washington
Bacon, Sylvia *judge, law educator*
Bartnoff, Judith *judge*
Braden, Susan Gertrude *federal judge, lawyer, consultant*
Chiechi, Carolyn Phyllis *federal judge*
Cohen, Mary Ann *judge*
Crawford, Susan Jean *federal judge*
Ginsburg, Ruth Bader *United States Supreme Court justice*
Green, Joyce Hens *federal judge*
Henderson, Karen LeCraft *federal judge*
Hewitt, Emily Clark *judge, minister*
Horn, Marian Blank *judge*
Kessler, Gladys *federal judge*
Kollar-Kotelly, Colleen *federal judge*
Kroupa, Diane Lynn *federal judge*
Mack, Julia Cooper *retired judge*
Marvel, L. Paige *judge*
McGranery, Regina C. *judge*
Miller, Christine Odell Cook *judge*
Newman, Pauline *federal judge*
O'Connor, Sandra Day *United States Supreme Court Justice*
Parr, Carolyn Miller *federal judge*
Prost, Sharon *federal judge*
Queen, Evelyn E. Crawford *judge, law educator*
Rogers, Judith W. *federal judge*
Rothstein, Barbara Jacobs *federal judge*
Ruiz, Vanessa *federal judge*
Sypolt, Diane Gilbert *federal judge*
Wagner, Annice McBryde *judge*
Wald, Patricia McGowan *retired federal judge*
Williams, Mary Ellen Coster *judge*

FLORIDA

Gainesville
Coleman, Mary Stallings *retired chief justice*

Jacksonville
Black, Susan Harrell *judge*

Miami
Barkett, Rosemary *circuit judge*
Seitz, Patricia Ann *federal judge*
Sorrentino, Charlene H. *federal judge*
Ungaro-Benages, Ursula Mancusi *federal judge*

Orlando
Conway, Anne Callaghan *federal judge*
Fawsett, Patricia Combs *federal judge*
Jennemann, Karen Sue *judge*
Thorpe, Janet Claire *judge*

Tallahassee
Pariente, Barbara J. *state supreme court justice*
Quince, Peggy A. *state supreme court justice*

Tampa
Bucklew, Susan Cawthon *federal judge*
Jenkins, Elizabeth Ann *federal judge*
Kovachevich, Elizabeth Anne *judge*

GEORGIA

Atlanta
Bihary, Joyce *federal judge*
Carnes, Julie Elizabeth *judge*
Evans, Orinda D. *federal judge*
Hatchett, Glenda A. *municipal judge*
Hull, Frank Mays *federal judge*
Hunstein, Carol *state supreme court justice*
Kravitch, Phyllis A. *federal judge*
Martin, Beverly *federal judge*
Murphy, Margaret Hackett *US bankruptcy judge*
Sears, Leah J. *state supreme court justice*

HAWAII

Honolulu
Gillmor, Helen *federal judge*
Nakayama, Paula Aiko *state supreme court justice*
Watanabe, Corinne Kaoru Amemiya *judge, state official, lawyer*

ILLINOIS

Chicago
Bucklo, Elaine Edwards *United States district court judge*
Conlon, Suzanne B. *federal judge*
Gottschall, Joan B. *judge*
Jones, Dorothy F. *judge*
Manning, Blanche M. *federal judge*
McMorrow, Mary Ann G. *state supreme court chief justice*
Pallmeyer, Rebecca Ruth *judge*
Rovner, Ilana Kara Diamond *federal judge*
Sonderby, Susan Pierson *federal judge*
Williams, Ann Claire *federal judge*

Danville
Garman, Rita B. *judge*

INDIANA

Indianapolis
Barker, Sarah Evans *judge*
Shields, V. Sue *federal magistrate judge*

IOWA

Des Moines
Bremer, Celeste F. *judge*
Ternus, Marsha K. *state supreme court justice*

KANSAS

Kansas City
Vratil, Kathryn Hoefer *federal judge*

Lawrence
Briscoe, Mary Beck *federal judge*

Topeka
Luckert, Marla Jo *state supreme court justice*
McFarland, Kay Eleanor *state supreme court chief justice*
Robinson, Julie Ann *judge*

KENTUCKY

Lexington
Coffman, Jennifer Burcham *judge*
Varellas, Sandra Motte *judge*

Prestonsburg
Stumbo, Janet Lynn *state supreme court justice*

LOUISIANA

Baton Rouge
Noland, Christine A. *magistrate judge*

New Orleans
Berrigan, Helen Ginger *federal judge*
Clement, Edith Brown *federal judge*
Johnson, Bernette J. *state supreme court justice*

Kimball, Catherine D. *state supreme court justice*
Knoll, Jeannette Theriot *state supreme court justice*

MAINE

Augusta
Calkins, Susan W. *state supreme court justice*

Portland
Glassman, Caroline Duby *state supreme court justice*
Saufley, Leigh Ingalls *judge*

MARYLAND

Annapolis
Battaglia, Lynne Ann *judge*

Baltimore
Blake, Catherine C. *judge*
Gauvey, Susan Kathryn *judge*
Holt-Stone, C. Yvonne *judge*
Motz, Diana Gribbon *judge*
Smith, Carol E. *judge*

Greenbelt
Chasanow, Deborah K. *federal judge*

Rockville
Raker, Irma *judge*

MASSACHUSETTS

Boston
Bowler, Marianne Bianca *federal judge*
Cowin, Judith A. *state supreme court judge*
Dreben, Raya Spiegel *judge*
Feeney, Joan N. *judge*
Gertner, Nancy *federal judge, educator*
Kenner, Carol J. *federal bankruptcy judge*
Lynch, Sandra Lea *federal judge*
Marshall, Margaret Hilary *state supreme court chief justice*
Saris, Patti Barbara *federal judge*
Sosman, Martha B. *state supreme court justice*
Zobel, Rya Weickert *federal judge*

Cambridge
Abrams, Ruth Ida *retired state supreme court justice*

MICHIGAN

Detroit
Corrigan, Maura Denise *judge*
Edmunds, Nancy Garlock *federal judge*
Hood, Denise Page *federal judge*
Morgan, Virginia Mattison *magistrate judge*
Taylor, Anna Diggs *federal judge*

Grand Rapids
Stevenson, Jo Ann C. *federal bankruptcy judge*

Lansing
Kelly, Marilyn *state supreme court justice*

Traverse City
Weaver, Elizabeth A. *state supreme court justice*

White Lake
Boyle, Patricia Jean *retired state supreme court justice*

MINNESOTA

Lake Elmo
Tomljanovich, Esther M. *retired judge*

Minneapolis
Alton, Ann Leslie *judge, lawyer, educator*
Montgomery, Ann D. *federal judge, educator*
Murphy, Diana E. *federal judge*
Neville, Cara Lee T. *judge*

Saint Paul
Blatz, Kathleen Anne *judge, state agency administrator, state legislator*
Meyer, Helen M. *judge*

MISSISSIPPI

Jackson
Cobb, Kay Beevers *state supreme court justice, former state senator*

MISSOURI

High Ridge
Karll, Jo Ann *retired judge, lawyer*

Jefferson City
Stith, Laura Denvir *state supreme court justice*

Kansas City
Laughrey, Nanette Kay *judge, federal*

Saint Louis
Hamilton, Jean Constance *judge*
Jackson, Carol E. *federal judge*
Medler, Mary Ann L. *federal judge*
Perry, Catherine D. *judge*

MONTANA

Helena
Cotter, Patricia O'Brien *state supreme court justice*
Gray, Karla Marie *judge*

NEBRASKA

Lincoln
Miller-Lerman, Lindsey *state supreme court justice*

NEVADA

Carson City
Agosti, Deborah Ann *state supreme court justice*

Las Vegas
Becker, Nancy Anne *state supreme court justice*
Rawlinson, Johnnie Blakeney *federal judge*

NEW HAMPSHIRE

Concord
Dalianis, Linda Stewart *judge*

NEW JERSEY

Morristown
LaVecchia, Jaynee *state supreme court justice*

Newark
Barry, Maryanne Trump *federal judge*
Hochberg, Faith S. *US district court judge*

Trenton
Cooper, Mary Little *federal judge, former banking commissioner*
Long, Virginia *state supreme court justice*
Poritz, Deborah T. *state supreme court chief justice, former attorney general*
Thompson, Anne Elise *federal judge*

NEW MEXICO

Albuquerque
Dal Santo, Diane *writer, retired judge*

Santa Fe
Maes, Petra Jimenez *state supreme court justice*
Minzner, Pamela Burgy *state supreme court justice*
Vazquez, Martha Alicia *judge*
Yalman, Ann *judge, lawyer*

NEW YORK

Albany
Graffeo, Victoria A. *state appeals court judge*
Kaye, Judith Smith *state appeals court chief judge*
Read, Susan Phillips *state appeals court judge*

Bronx
Bamberger, Phylis Skloot *judge*

Brooklyn
Amon, Carol Bagley *federal judge*
Gershon, Nina *federal judge*
Raggi, Reena *circuit judge*

Buffalo
Heckman, Carol E. *lawyer*

Central Islip
Cyganowski, Melanie L. *bankruptcy judge*
Eisenberg, Dorothy *federal judge*
Seybert, Joanna *federal judge*

Garden City
O'Dwyer, Joan *judge*

New York
Barzilay, Judith Morgenstern *federal judge*
Batts, Deborah A. *judge*
Buchwald, Naomi Reice *judge*
Cedarbaum, Miriam Goldman *federal judge*
Ciparick, Carmen Beauchamp *judge*
Cote, Denise Louise *federal judge*
Freedman, Helen E. *justice*
Kearse, Amalya Lyle *federal judge*
Kram, Shirley Wohl *federal judge*
Lowe, Mary Johnson *federal judge*
Motley, Constance Baker (Mrs. Joel Wilson Motley) *federal judge, former city official*
Nelson, Barbara Anne *judge*
Pooler, Rosemary S. *federal judge*
Preska, Loretta A. *federal judge*
Restani, Jane A. *federal judge*
Santaella, Irma Vidal *retired state supreme court justice*
Sotomayor, Sonia *federal judge*
Wood, Kimba M. *judge*

NORTH CAROLINA

Lexington
Wood, April Carthena *judge*

Raleigh
Duncan, Allyson K. *federal judge*
McGee, Linda Mace *judge, lawyer*
Parker, Sarah Elizabeth *state supreme court justice*

Winston Salem
Carruthers, Catharine *federal judge*

NORTH DAKOTA

Bismarck
Kapsner, Carol Ronning *state supreme court justice*
Maring, Mary Muehlen *state supreme court justice*

Fargo
Klein, Karen K. *federal judge*

OHIO

Akron
Shea-Stonum, Marilyn *federal judge*

Cincinnati
Beckwith, Sandra Shank *judge*
Cook, Deborah L. *judge, former state supreme court justice*
Dlott, Susan Judy *judge, lawyer*
Kennedy, Cornelia Groefsema *federal judge*

Cleveland
Aldrich, Ann *federal judge*
Gaughan, Patricia Anne *judge*
Hemann, Patricia A. *federal judge*
Moore, Karen Nelson *judge*
O'Malley, Kathleen M. *federal judge*
Wells, Lesley *federal judge*

Columbus
King, Norah McCann *federal judge*
O'Connor, Maureen *judge*
Resnick, Alice Robie *judge*
Sellers, Barbara Jackson *federal judge*
Stratton, Evelyn Lundberg *judge*

Lisbon
Dailey, Coleen Hall *magistrate, lawyer*

Medina
Batchelder, Alice M. *federal judge*

Youngstown
Bond, Christina M. *magistrate, lawyer*

OKLAHOMA

Oklahoma City
Cauthron, Robin J. *federal judge*
Miles-La Grange, Vicki *judge*

Tulsa
Seymour, Stephanie Kulp *federal judge*

OREGON

Portland
Frye, Helen Jackson *federal judge*
Higdon, Polly Susanne *federal judge*
Rosenblum, Ellen F. *judge*
Stewart, Janice Mae *federal judge*

PENNSYLVANIA

Harrisburg
Rambo, Sylvia H. *federal judge*

Philadelphia
Angell, M(ary) Faith *federal magistrate judge*
Rendell, Marjorie O. *federal judge*
Shapiro, Norma Sondra Levy *federal judge*
Sigmund, Diane Weiss *judge*
Sloviter, Dolores Korman *federal judge*
Welsh, Diane M. *federal judge*

Pittsburgh
Ambrose, Donetta W. *federal judge*
Conti, Joy Flowers *judge*
Fitzgerald, Judith Klaswick *federal judge*
Ross, Eunice Latshaw *judge*
Sensenich, Ila Jeanne *federal judge*

West Conshohocken
Newman, Sandra Schultz *state supreme court justice*

RHODE ISLAND

Providence
Goldberg, Maureen McKenna *state supreme court justice*
Harwood, Patricia L. *judge*
Lisi, Mary M. *federal judge*

SOUTH CAROLINA

Columbia
Currie, Cameron McGowan *federal judge*
Toal, Jean Hoefer *state supreme court chief justice*

SOUTH DAKOTA

Rapid City
Schreier, Karen Elizabeth *judge*

Sioux Falls
Meierhenry, Judith Knittel *judge, lawyer*

TENNESSEE

Greeneville
Parsons, Marcia Phillips *judge*

Memphis
Donald, Bernice B. *judge*
Gibbons, Julia Smith *federal judge*
Holder, Janice Marie *state supreme court justice*
Vescovo, Diane Kirkland *federal judge*

Nashville
Daughtrey, Martha Craig *federal judge*
Trauger, Aleta Arthur *judge*

TEXAS

Amarillo
Robinson, Mary Lou *federal judge*

Austin
Aboussie, Marilyn *retired state justice*
Keller, Sharon Faye *judge*
O'Neill, Harriet *state supreme court justice*
Owen, Priscilla Richman *state supreme court justice*
Spector, Rose *state supreme court justice*
Williams, Mary Pearl *judge*

Corpus Christi
Jack, Janis Graham *judge*
Tagle, Hilda Gloria *former judge*

Dallas
Hankinson, Deborah G. *former state supreme court justice*
Lynn, Barbara Michele *judge*

Houston
Atlas, Nancy Friedman *judge*
Brown, Karen Kennedy *judge*
Clark, Letitia Z. *federal judge*
Gilmore, Vanessa D. *federal judge*
Harmon, Melinda Furche *federal judge*
Jones, Edith Hollan *federal judge*
King, Carolyn Dineen *federal judge*
Rosenthal, Lee H. *federal judge*
Sondock, Ruby Kless *retired judge*
Stacy, Frances H. *federal judge*

San Antonio
Guerrero, Monica Elaine *judge*
Nowak, Nancy Stein *judge*

Tyler
Guthrie, Judith K. *federal judge*

UTAH

Salt Lake City
Campbell, Tena *judge*
Durham, Christine Meaders *state supreme court chief justice*
Parrish, Jill N. *judge*

VERMONT

Montpelier
Johnson, Denise Reinka *state supreme court justice*
Skoglund, Marilyn *state supreme court justice*

VIRGINIA

Alexandria
Brinkema, Leonie Milhomme *federal judge*

Chesterfield
Davis, Bonnie Christell *judge*

Falls Church
Cooper, Jean Saralee *judge*
Mathon, Lauren R. *judge*

Lynchburg
Harris, Dale Hutter *retired judge, lecturer*

Mc Lean
Anthony, Joan Caton *administrative judge*

Norfolk
Smith, Rebecca Beach *federal judge*

Richmond
Kinser, Cynthia D. *state supreme court justice*
Lacy, Elizabeth Bermingham *state supreme court justice*
Williams, Karen Johnson *federal judge*

Virginia Beach
Keenan, Barbara Milano *judge*

WASHINGTON

Olympia
Bridge, Bobbe J. *state supreme court justice*
Fairhurst, Mary E. *judge*
Ireland, Faith *state supreme court justice*
Madsen, Barbara A *state supreme court justice*
Owens, Susan *state supreme court justice*

Seattle
Dimmick, Carolyn Reaber *federal judge*
Fletcher, Betty Binns *federal judge*
Overstreet, Karen A. *federal bankruptcy judge*

Spokane
Imbrogno, Cynthia *magistrate judge*
Williams, Patricia C. *federal judge*

WEST VIRGINIA

Charleston
Davis, Robin Jean *state supreme court justice*
Hallanan, Elizabeth Virginia *federal judge*
Stanley, Mary Elizabeth *judge*

Clarksburg
Keeley, Irene Patricia Murphy *federal judge*

WISCONSIN

Madison
Bartell, Angela Gina Baldi *judge*
Bradley, Ann Walsh *state supreme court justice*
Crabb, Barbara Brandriff *federal judge*
Sykes, Diane S. *state supreme court justice*

Milwaukee
McGarity, Margaret Dee *federal judge*

WYOMING

Cheyenne
Kite, Marilyn S. *state supreme court justice, lawyer*

TERRITORIES OF THE UNITED STATES

GUAM

Hagatna
Maraman, Katherine Ann *judge*
Tydingco-Gatewood, Frances Marie *judge*

PUERTO RICO

Hato Rey
Cerezo, Carmen Consuelo *federal judge*

San Juan
Delgado-Colon, Aida M. *federal judge*
Merly, Miriam Naveira *state supreme court justice*

CANADA

ALBERTA

Edmonton
Fraser, Catherine Anne *Canadian chief justice*

NOVA SCOTIA

Halifax
Glube, Constance Rachelle *Canadian chief justice*

ONTARIO

Ottawa
McLachlin, Beverley *Canadian supreme court chief justice*

QUEBEC

Quebec City
L'Heureux-Dubé, Claire *judge*

ADDRESS UNPUBLISHED

Abrahamson, Shirley Schlanger *state supreme court chief justice*
Aiken, Ann L. *federal judge*
Alexander, S. Allan *magistrate judge*
Beck, Ronna Lee *judge*
Boulden, Judith Ann *judge*
Breslin, Peg M. *judge*
Buchanan, Theresa Carroll *judge*
Bush, Lynn Jeanne *judge*
Firestone, Nancy B. *federal judge*
Gardner, Anne Lancaster *judge*
Garibaldi, Marie Louise *former state supreme court justice*
Goldstein, Debra Holly *judge*
Gorence, Patricia Josetta *judge*
Grant, Isabella Horton *retired judge*
Jones, Phyllis Gene *judge*
Kauger, Yvonne *state supreme court justice*
Krupansky, Ethel Blanche *retired judge*
Lancaster, Joan Ericksen *state supreme court justice*
Lee, Barbara A. *retired federal magistrate judge*
Leeson, Susan M. *former state supreme court judge*
McClure, Ann Crawford *judge, lawyer*
Neuman, Linda Kinney *retired state supreme court justice, lawyer*
O'Brien, Sheila Marie *judge*
Payne, Mary Libby *retired judge*
Pokras, Sheila Frances *retired judge*
Prather, Lenore Loving *former state supreme court chief justice*
Senechal, Alice R. *federal judge, lawyer*
Shearing, Miriam Naveira *state supreme court justice*
Smith, Fern M. *judge*
Tacha, Deanell Reece *federal judge*
Trout, Linda Copple *state supreme court chief justice*

Wood, Diane Pamela *judge*

LAW: LAW PRACTICE AND ADMINISTRATION

UNITED STATES

ALABAMA

Birmingham
Todd, Judith F. *lawyer*

Mobile
Granade, Callie Virginia Smith S. *lawyer, federal district judge*

Montgomery
Campbell, Maria Bouchelle *lawyer, consultant*
Canary, Leura *prosecutor*

Tuscaloosa
Cook, Camille Wright *retired law educator*
Smalley, Donna Wesson *lawyer, educator*

ALASKA

Anchorage
Foster, Rosemary Alice *lawyer, artist*
Greenstein, Marla Nan *lawyer*
Hughes, Mary Katherine *lawyer*
Wibker, Susan Gayle *lawyer*
Willard-Jones, Donna C. *lawyer*

Fairbanks
Bodwell, Lori *lawyer*

Juneau
Collins, Patricia A. *lawyer, judge*

Nondalton
Gay, Sarah Elizabeth *lawyer*

ARIZONA

Phoenix
Gingold, Hilary Weinberg *lawyer*
McCormick, Kathryn Ellen *prosecutor*
Merritt, Nancy Jo *lawyer*
Refo, Patricia Lee *lawyer*

Sierra Vista
Moreno, Patricia Frazier *lawyer*

Surprise
Fennelly, Jane Corey *lawyer*

Tempe
Jennings, Marianne Moody *lawyer, educator*

Tucson
Betteridge, Frances Carpenter *retired lawyer, mediator*
Boswell, Susan G. *lawyer*
Froman, Sandra Sue *lawyer*
Mendelson, Joan Rintel *lawyer*
Samet, Dee-Dee *lawyer*
Simmons, Sarah R. *lawyer*
Treadwell-Rubin, Pamela A. *lawyer*

ARKANSAS

Benton
Krueger, Marlo Bush *retired lawyer*

Little Rock
Casey, Paula Jean *former prosecutor*
Cherry, Sandra Wilson *lawyer*
Stockbarger, Jean Dawson *lawyer*
Witherspoon, Carolyn Brack *lawyer*

CALIFORNIA

Alameda
Johnson, Beverly J. *lawyer, congressman*

Bakersfield
Gong, Gloria Margaret *lawyer, pharmacist*

Berkeley
Barton, Babette B. *lawyer, educator*
Diamond, Sara Rose *lawyer, writer*
Moran, Rachel *lawyer, educator*
Peterson, Andrea Lenore *law educator*
Samuelson, Pamela Ann *law educator*
Sorensen, Linda *lawyer*

Beverly Hills
Amado, Honey Kessler *lawyer*

Burbank
Wise, Helena Sunny *lawyer*

Chino Hills
Pearson, April Virginia *lawyer*

Corona
Everett Nollkamper, Pamela Irene *legal management company executive, educator*

Costa Mesa
Caldwell, Courtney Lynn *lawyer, real estate consultant*
Marshall, Ellen Ruth *lawyer*

Davis
Bruch, Carol Sophie *lawyer, educator*

Diamond Bar
Usher, Charlene Lynette *lawyer*

El Segundo
Willis, Judy Ann *lawyer*

Emeryville
Arguedas, Cristina C. *lawyer*

Encino
Lombardini, Carol Ann *lawyer*
Smith, Selma Moidel *lawyer, composer*

Escondido
Godone-Maresca, Lillian *lawyer*

Glendale
Davidson, Suzanne Mouron *lawyer*
Simpson, Allyson Bilich *lawyer*

Huntington Beach
Cook, Debbie *lawyer, councilman*
Garrels, Sherry Ann *lawyer*

Inverness
Ciani, Judith Elaine *retired lawyer*

Irvine
Clark, Karen Heath *lawyer*

La Jolla
Buchholz, Debby *lawyer*
Wilson, Bonnie Jean *lawyer, educator, investor*

Laguna Hills
Reinglass, Michelle Annette *lawyer*

Lompoc
Keller, Janice N. *lawyer, councilwoman*

Long Beach
Helwick, Christine *lawyer*

Los Angeles
Abramson, Leslie Hope *lawyer*
Allred, Gloria Rachel *lawyer*
Azad, Susan S. *lawyer*
Barrett, Jane Hayes *lawyer*
Bendix, Helen Irene *lawyer*
Black, Donna Ruth *lawyer*
Blendell, Elizabeth A. *lawyer*
Boras, Kim *lawyer*
Bryan, Karen Smith *lawyer*
Buhai, Vernon Winona Dauberdta (Mrs. William A. Burke) *lawyer*
Byrd, Christine Waterman Swent *lawyer*
Christ, Roxanne E. *lawyer*
Cohen, Cynthia Marylyn *lawyer*
Cook, Melanie K. *lawyer*
Dryden, Mary Elizabeth *law librarian, writer, actress*
Dudziak, Mary Louise *law educator, lecturer*
Fenning, Lisa Hill *lawyer, mediator, former federal judge*
Fisher, Ruth E. *lawyer*
Grauman, Nancy *lawyer*
Griffey, Linda Boyd *lawyer*
Gross, Ariela Julie *law educator*
Hemminger, Pamela Lynn *lawyer*
Hernandez, Antonia *lawyer*
Howard, Nancy E. *lawyer*
Hoye, Maria Pilar *lawyer*
Hufstedler, Shirley Mount (Mrs. Seth M. Hufstedler) *lawyer, former federal judge*
Hyman, Ursula H. *lawyer*
Jordan, Martha B. *lawyer*
Kanoff, Mary Ellen *lawyer*
Kelly, Pamela B. *lawyer*
Kirwan, Betty Jane Jane *lawyer*
Klinger, Marilyn Sydney *lawyer*
Levenson, Laurie I. *law educator*
Mason, Cheryl White *lawyer*
Mersel, Marjorie Kathryn Pedersen *lawyer*
Neely, Sally Schultz *lawyer*
Nobumoto, Karen S. *prosecutor*
O'Leary, Prentice Lee *lawyer*
Olsen, Frances Elisabeth *law educator, theorist*
Ordin, Andrea Sheridan *lawyer*
Palmer, Pamela S. *lawyer*
Perez, Edith R. *lawyer*
Peters, Aulana Louise *lawyer, former government agency commissioner*
Peterson, Linda S. *lawyer*
Phillips, Patricia Dominis *lawyer*
Porter, Verna Louise *lawyer*
Pruetz, Adrian Mary *lawyer*
Raeder, Myrna Sharon *lawyer, educator*
Reeves, Barbara Ann *lawyer*
Rotell, Cynthia A. *lawyer*
Ruhl, Mary B. *lawyer*
Saxe, Deborah Crandall *lawyer*
Shanks, Patricia L. *lawyer*
Starrett, Lucinda *lawyer*
Taylor, Minna *lawyer*
Teele, Cynthia Lombard *lawyer*
Title, Gail Migdal *lawyer*
Valerio Barrad, Catherine M. *lawyer*
Von Eschen, Lisa A. *lawyer*
Wilson, Mable Jean *paralegal*
Yamaguchi, Colleen S. *lawyer*
Yang, Debra W. *lawyer*
Zelon, Laurie Dee *lawyer*

Newport Beach
Harlan, Nancy Margaret *lawyer*
Schiff, Laurie *lawyer*

North Hollywood
Runquist, Lisa A. *lawyer*

Oakland
West, Natalie Elsa *lawyer*

Palo Alto
Baskins, Ann O. *lawyer, computer company executive*
Jackson, Cynthia L. *lawyer*
McCall, Jennifer Jordan *lawyer*

Palos Verdes Estates
Brigden, Ann Schwartz *mediator, educator*

Pasadena
Mosher, Sally Ekenberg *lawyer, musician*

Petaluma
Paul, Amy *lawyer*

Pittsburg
Williscroft-Barcus, Beverly Ruth *lawyer*

Pleasanton
Fine, Marjorie Lynn *lawyer*

Portola Valley
Nycum, Susan Hubbell *lawyer*

Redondo Beach
Oh, Angela E. *lawyer*

Richmond
Quenneville, Kathleen *lawyer*

Riverside
Lobb, Cynthia Jean Hocking *lawyer*

Sacramento
Bowen, Debra Lynn *lawyer, state legislator*
Gillan, Kayla J. *lawyer*
Hartman, Patricia Jeanne *lawyer, educator*
Laethem, Fern Melody *lawyer*
Morgan-Prager, Karole *lawyer, publishing executive*
Willis, Dawn Louise *legal assistant, small business owner*
Zeff, Ophelia Hope *lawyer*

San Clemente
Geyser, Lynne M. *lawyer, writer*

San Diego
Brierton, Cheryl Lynn *lawyer*
Dumanis, Bonnie M. *prosecutor*
Lam, Carol C. *lawyer*
Morris, Sandra Joan *lawyer*
Shippey, Sandra Lee *lawyer*

San Francisco
Alexis, Geraldine M. *lawyer*
Buccieri, Shirley H. *lawyer*
Cabraser, Elizabeth Joan *lawyer*
Chung, Amy Teresa *lawyer, property manager*
Clopton, Karen Valentia *lawyer, president civil services commission*
Coffin, Judy Sue *lawyer*
Corcoran, Maureen Elizabeth *lawyer*
Deane, Elaine *lawyer*
Edwards, Robin Morse *lawyer*
Fisher, Kathleen V. *lawyer*
Garvey, Joanne Marie *lawyer*
Gill, Margaret Gaskins *lawyer*
Knutzen, Martha Lorraine *lawyer*
Libbin, Anne Edna *lawyer*
McKelvey, Judith Grant *lawyer, educator, university dean*
Perry, E. Lynn *lawyer*
Rembe, Toni *lawyer, director*
Soberon, Presentacion Zablan *state bar administrator*
Studley, Jamienne Shayne *lawyer, educator*
Veaco, Kristina *lawyer*
Welborn, Caryl Bartelman *lawyer*

San Jose
Cottle, Karen Olson *lawyer*
Gallo, Joan Rosenberg *lawyer*
Kuklin, Susan Beverly *law librarian, lawyer*
Stevenson, Karen *lawyer*

San Mateo
Chong, Rachelle B. *lawyer, federal communications commissioner*

San Rafael
Edwards, Priscilla Ann *paralegal, business owner*

San Ramon
Dennis, Patricia Diaz *lawyer*

Santa Ana
Storer, Maryruth *law librarian*

Santa Barbara
Johnson, Mary Kathryn *legal assistant*
Sulzbach, Christi Rocovich *lawyer*

Santa Clara
Glancy, Dorothy Jean *lawyer, educator*
Ludgus, Nancy Lucke *lawyer*

Santa Monica
Kaplowitz, Karen (Jill) *lawyer, business consultant*

Stanford
Babcock, Barbara Allen *law educator, lawyer*
Rhode, Deborah Lynn *law educator*

Torrance
Bryan, Sharon Ann *lawyer*
Van Emburgh, Joanne *lawyer*

Vista
Cannon, Kathleen *lawyer, educator*
Rigby, Amanda Young *paralegal firm executive*

Walnut
McKee, Catherine Lynch *law educator, lawyer*

Woodland Hills
Johnson-Champ, Debra Sue *lawyer, educator, writer, artist*

COLORADO

Boulder
Bintliff, Barbara Ann *law educator, library director*
Dubofsky, Jean Eberhart *lawyer, retired state supreme court justice*
Madden, Alice Donnelly *lawyer*

Colorado Springs
Rouss, Ruth *lawyer*

Denver
Burford, Anne McGill *lawyer*
Devine, Sharon Jean *lawyer*
Kaczanowska, Laurie Hyson Smith *lawyer*
Krendl, Cathy Stricklin *lawyer*
Major, Alice Jean *lawyer*
McDonnell, Barbara *lawyer*
McDowell, Karen Ann *lawyer*
Merritt, Jeralyn E. *lawyer*
Savan, Jakki L. *lawyer, writer*
Welch, Carol Mae *lawyer*
Wunnicke, Brooke *lawyer*

Englewood
Spencer, Margaret Gilliam *lawyer*

Golden
Alberts, Celia Anne *lawyer*

Lakewood
Meyer, Lynn Nix *lawyer*

Louisville
Raymond, Dorothy Gill *lawyer*

CONNECTICUT

Derby
McEvoy, Sharlene Ann *law educator*

Fairfield
Daley, Pamela *lawyer*

Hartford
Harkin, Ruth R. *lawyer*
McCarthy, Patrice Ann *lawyer*
Stravalle-Schmidt, Ann Roberta *lawyer*
Young, Dona Davis Gagliano *lawyer, insurance executive*

New Britain
Pearl, Helen Zalkan *lawyer*
Tedford, Deborah J. *lawyer*

New Haven
Barnett, Megan A. *lawyer*
Robinson, Dorothy K. *lawyer*
Rose-Ackerman, Susan *law and political economy educator*
Wenig, Mary Moers *law educator*

Stamford
Burgess, Lynne A *lawyer*
Mayes, Michele Coleman *lawyer*
McDonald, Cassandra Burns *lawyer*

Stratford
DiCicco, Margaret C. *lawyer*

Waterbury
Wolfe, Harriet Munrett *lawyer*

DELAWARE

Wilmington
Hannigan, Patricia C. *prosecutor*
Jolles, Janet K. Pilling *lawyer*
Meitner, Pamela *lawyer, educator*
Mullen, Regina Marie *lawyer*

DISTRICT OF COLUMBIA

Washington
Agranov, Sharon Duke *paralegal*
Amron, Cory M. *lawyer*
Armen, Margaret Meis *lawyer*
Bachrach, Eve Elizabeth *lawyer*
Barrie, Julie Anne *lawyer*
Barshefsky, Charlene *lawyer, former diplomat*
Becker, Grace Chung *lawyer*
Bello, Judith Hippler *lawyer, trade association administrator*
Bergner, Jane Cohen *lawyer*
Berliner, Dana *lawyer*
Billauer, Barbara Pfeffer *lawyer, educator*
Bingaman, Anne K. *lawyer*
Birnbaum, S. Elizabeth *lawyer*
Blazek-White, Doris *lawyer*
Bloch, Susan Low *law educator*
Bondareff, Joan M. *retired government official, lawyer*
Born, Brooksley Elizabeth *lawyer*
Braceras, Jennifer C. *lawyer*
Bradley, Leigh A. *government official, lawyer*
Brenner, Janet Maybin Walker *lawyer*
Brooks, Sharon Diane *lawyer*
Buc, Nancy Lillian *lawyer*
Burke, Beverly J. *lawyer, energy executive*
Bushmiller, Ann E. *lawyer*
Carey, Sarah Collins *lawyer*
Caro, Luisa *lawyer*
Carpenter, Sheila Jane *lawyer*
Chanin, Leah Farb *law library administrator, lawyer, consultant, law educator*
Christian, Betty Jo *lawyer*
Coffield, Shirley Ann *lawyer, educator*
Cooper, Jacqueline Gerson *lawyer*
Coulter, Ann *lawyer, author*
Daniels, Diana M. *lawyer*
de Leon, Sylvia A. *lawyer*
Denison, Mary Boney *lawyer*
Denny, Judith Ann *retired lawyer*
Determan, Sara-Ann *lawyer*
Dillon-Ridgley, Dianne Granville *mediator, consultant, association executive*
Dunn, Loretta Lynn *lawyer*
Dwyer, Maureen E. *lawyer*
Dye, Rebecca Feemster *legislative counsel*
Efros, Ellen Ann *lawyer*
Elcano, Mary S. *lawyer*
Emery, Nancy Beth *lawyer*
Feldman, Clarice Rochelle *lawyer*
Fields, Wendy Lynn *lawyer*
Flannery, Ellen Joanne *lawyer*
Flowe, Carol Connor *lawyer*
Foscarinis, Maria *lawyer*
Fowler, Tillie Kidd *lawyer*
Fox, Sarah *lawyer*
Gati, Toby T. *international advisor*
Gilfoyle, Nathalie Floyd Preston *lawyer*
Glynn, Marilyn *lawyer*
Gorelick, Jamie Shona *lawyer*
Gorman, Joyce J(ohanna) *lawyer*
Gross, Roberta Lee *inspector general*
Grossman, Joanne Barbara *lawyer*
Harbour, Pamela Jones *lawyer*
Hawkins, Lisa Lynne *lawyer, municipal official*
Hennessy, Ellen Anne *lawyer, benefits compensation analyst, educator*
Higuchi, Shirley A. *lawyer*
Hill, Eleanor Jean *lawyer*
Hills, Carla Anderson *lawyer, former federal official*
Hollis, Sheila Slocum *lawyer*
Hughes, Marija Matich *law librarian*
Jenks, Rosemary Elizabeth *lawyer*
Jeweler, Robin *lawyer*
Jones, Mary Gardiner *lawyer, educator, consumer interest organization executive*
Kaplan, Elaine D. *lawyer*
Kappler, Ann M. *lawyer, finance company executive*
Katz, Deborah A. *lawyer*
Katzen, Sally *lawyer, educator*
Kennard, Mary Elizabeth *lawyer*
Kiddoo, Jean Lynn *lawyer*
King, Patricia Ann *law educator*
Klee, Ann *lawyer*
Knapp, Rosalind Ann *lawyer*
Koch, Kathleen Day *lawyer*
Kuperman, Frances Pergericht *lawyer*
Lamm, Carolyn Beth *lawyer*
Lanam, Linda Lee *lawyer*
Laster, Gail W. *lawyer*
Latimer, Allie B. *retired lawyer*
Lautrup, Greer Olsen *lawyer*
Leary, Mary Lou *prosecutor*
Lewis, Eleanor Roberts *lawyer*
Lewis, Wilma Antoinette *lawyer, former prosecutor and federal agency admin*
Lichtenstein, Elissa Charlene *legal association executive*
Lurensky, Marcia Adele *lawyer*
Mahaffie, Lynn Boynton *lawyer, government official*
Martin, Kate Abbott *lawyer*
Matthews, Barbara Caridad *lawyer*
Mays, Janice Ann *lawyer*
Mazzaferri, Katherine Aquino *lawyer, bar association executive*
McCluskey, Susan D. *lawyer*
McDavid, Janet Louise *lawyer*
McGrath, Kathryn Bradley *lawyer*
McGuire, Patricia A. *lawyer, academic administrator*
McGuirl, Marlene Dana Callis *law librarian, educator*
Medaglia, Mary-Elizabeth *lawyer*
Melamed, Carol Drescher *lawyer*
Menkel-Meadow, Carrie Joan *law educator*
Mirvahabi, Farin *lawyer*
Mitchelson, Mary Sue *lawyer*
Moler, Elizabeth Anne *lawyer*
Mooney, Marilyn *lawyer*
Moore, Amy Norwood *lawyer*
Murphy, Betty Southard (Mrs. Cornelius F. Murphy) *lawyer*
Murphy, Laura *legal association administrator*
Norwood, Deborah Anne *law librarian*
O'Connor, Jennifer *lawyer*
Olson, Diane Dowd *lawyer*
Olson, Pamela Faith *lawyer*
O'Sullivan, Judith Roberta *lawyer, author, artist*
O'Sullivan, Lynda Troutman *lawyer*
Padgett, Nancy Weeks *law librarian, consultant, lawyer*
Perkins, Nancy Leeds *lawyer*
Pfeiffer, Margaret Kolodny *lawyer*
Pittman, Lisa *lawyer*
Plaine, Lloyd Leva *lawyer*
Pollock, Melany Tawanda *paralegal, legal assistant*
Quarterman, Cynthia Louise *lawyer*
Reade, Claire Elizabeth *lawyer*
Reid, Inez Smith *lawyer, educator*
Richards, Suzanne V. *lawyer*
Richmond, Marilyn Susan *lawyer*
Ridgway, Delissa Anne *lawyer*
Rosenberg, Ruth Helen Borsuk *lawyer*
Rossotti, Barbara Jill Margulies *lawyer*
Sabol, Carolyn A. *lawyer, government official*
St. Amand, Janet G. *government relations lawyer*
Schiffer, Lois Jane *lawyer*
Schlitt, Lyn M. *lawyer*
Scott, Portia Adele *paralegal*
Sears, Mary Helen *lawyer*
Seitz, Virginia A. *lawyer*
Shay-Byrne, Olivia *lawyer*
Sheeler, Harva Lee *law librarian*
Silberman, Deborah F. *general counsel*
Slater, Valerie A. *lawyer*
Snow, Rebecca *lawyer*
Somer-Greif, Penny Lynn *lawyer*
Sparacino, Joann *lawyer, consultant*
Sprague, Mary Gabrielle *lawyer*
Stein, Cheryl Denise *lawyer*
Strand, Joan H. *law educator*
Stromberg, Jean Wilbur Gleason *lawyer*
Stuart, Pamela Bruce *lawyer*
Stucky, Jean Seibert *lawyer*
Sullivan, Mary Anne *lawyer, government official*
Sussman, Monica Hilton *lawyer*
Thompson, Diane E. *lawyer*
Topelius, Kathleen Ellis *lawyer*
Tyler, Peggy Lynne Bailey *lawyer*
Tyner, Lee Reichelderfer *lawyer*
Unger, Laura Simone *lawyer, commissioner*
Valentine, Debra A. *lawyer*
Vickery, Ann Morgan *lawyer*
Walter, Sheryl Lynn *lawyer*
Ward, Erica Anne *lawyer, educator*
Waters, Jennifer Nash *lawyer*
Wedgwood, Ruth *law educator, international affairs expert*
Werner, Mary Ann *lawyer*
West, Gail Berry *lawyer*
Williams, Julie Lloyd *lawyer*
Williams, Karen Hastie *lawyer*
Winston, Judith Ann *lawyer*
Wiss, Marcia A. *lawyer*
Worthy, Patricia Morris *law educator, lawyer*
Yoo, Grace *legal association administrator*
Young, Marlene Annette *lawyer*
Zollar, Carolyn Catherine *lawyer*

FLORIDA

Bradenton
LaForest, Lana Jean *lawyer*

Brandon
England, Lynne Lipton *lawyer, speech pathologist, audiologist*

Clearwater
Bairstow, Frances Kanevsky *arbitrator, mediator, educator*
Dougall-Sides, Leslie K. *lawyer*

Coral Gables
Gustafson, Anne-Lise Dirks *lawyer, foreign consul*

Deerfield Beach
Caso, Dawn Marie *lawyer, consultant, law educator*

Fort Lauderdale
Gude, Nancy Carlson *lawyer*
Hester, Julia A. *lawyer*
Lazarus, Arleen *lawyer*
Richmond, Gail Levin *law educator*

Fort Myers
Consilio, Barbara Ann *legal administrator, management consultant*

Gainesville
Taylor, Grace Elizabeth Woodall (Betty Taylor) *law educator, law library administrator*

Hallandale
Engel, Tala *lawyer*

Hollywood
Korthals, Candace Durbin *lawyer*
Tannen, Ricki Lewis *lawyer, psychologist, educator*

Indian Harbor Beach
Tasker, Molly Jean *lawyer*

Jacksonville
Kelso, Linda Yayoi *lawyer*
Weaver, Dianne Jay *lawyer*

Longwood
Tomasulo, Virginia Merrills *retired lawyer*

Miami
Carnesoltas, Ana-Maria *lawyer*
DuFresne, Elizabeth Jamison *lawyer*
Jackson-Holmes, Flora Marie *lawyer, educator*
Korchin, Judith Miriam *lawyer*
Long, Maxine Master *lawyer*
Mehta, Eileen Rose *lawyer*
Miller Udell, Bronwyn *lawyer*
Munn, Janet Teresa *lawyer*
O'Connor, Kathleen Mary *lawyer*
O'Meara, Vicki A. *lawyer*
Osman, Edith Gabriella *lawyer*
Poston, Rebekah Jane *lawyer*
Rickard, Lisa Ann *lawyer*
Rundle, Katherine Fernandez *state's attorney*
Stanley, Sherry A. *lawyer*
Touby, Kathleen Anita *lawyer*
Vento, M. Thérèse *lawyer*

Naples
Blumenthal, Ronnie *lawyer*
McCaffrey, Judith Elizabeth *lawyer*
Norton, Elizabeth Wychgel *lawyer*
Rawson, Marjorie Jean *lawyer*

North Miami Beach
MacIvor, Catherine J. *lawyer*

Orlando
Michaud, Norma Alice Palmer *paralegal, real estate investor*
Shives, Paula J *lawyer*

Ormond Beach
Logan, Sharon Brooks *lawyer*

Palm Beach
Canary, Nancy Halliday *lawyer*

Susse, Sandra Slone *lawyer*

Winthrop
Brown, Patricia Irene *retired law librarian, lawyer*

MICHIGAN

Ann Arbor
Garcia, Elisa Dolores *lawyer*
Hertz, Dawn Leslie *lawyer*
Leary, Margaret *law librarian, library director*
MacKinnon, Catharine Alice *lawyer, law educator, legal scholar, writer*
Snyder, Lucy Karla *lawyer, finance company executive*

Battle Creek
Kelly, Janet Langford *lawyer*

Bingham Farms
Banas, C(hristine) Leslie *lawyer*

Birmingham
Robinson, Marietta S. *lawyer*

Bloomfield Hills
Simon, Evelyn *lawyer*

Detroit
Darlow, Julia Donovan *lawyer*
James, Phyllis A. *lawyer*
Mahoney, Joan *law educator*
Rozof, Phyllis Claire *lawyer*
Shannon, Margaret Anne *lawyer*
White, Katherine E. *law educator*

East Lansing
Bassett, Debra Lyn *lawyer, educator*

Farmington Hills
Fershtman, Julie Ilene *lawyer*

Grand Rapids
Chiara, Margaret Mary *United States attorney*

Grosse Pointe Park
McIntyre, Anita Grace Jordan *lawyer*

Lansing
Linder, Iris Kay *lawyer*
Tombers, Evelyn Charlotte *lawyer, law educator*

Niles
Pasula, Angela Marie *lawyer*

Rochester
Pope, Melissa Lopez *law educator*

Southfield
Baughman, Leonora Knoblock *lawyer*
Davis-Yancey, Gwendolyn *lawyer*

Troy
LaDuke, Nancie *lawyer, corporate executive*

Williamston
Ellis, Sharon Alston *lawyer, political organization worker*

MINNESOTA

Edina
Weber, Gail Mary *lawyer*

Hopkins
Hoard, Heidi Marie *lawyer*

Minneapolis
Bernhardson, Ivy Schutz *lawyer*
Comstock, Rebecca Ann *lawyer*
Feuss, Linda Anne Upsall *lawyer*
Forneris, Jeanne M. *lawyer*
Grodsky, Jamie Anne *law educator*
Howland, Joan Sidney *law librarian, educator*
Kirtley, Jane Elizabeth *law educator*
Marshall, Siri Swenson *lawyer*
Palmer, Deborah Jean *lawyer*
Schneider, Elaine Carol *lawyer, researcher, writer*
Struthers, Margo S. *lawyer*
Wille, Karin L. *lawyer*
Younger, Judith Tess *law educator*

Owatonna
Aune, Debra Bjurquist *lawyer*

Saint Paul
Doescher, Jill Train *lawyer*
Hansen, Robyn L. *lawyer*
Lebedoff, Randy Miller *lawyer*

Winona
Merchlewitz, Ann Elizabeth *lawyer*

MISSISSIPPI

Jackson
Baltz, Mary Melissa *lawyer*
Fillingane, Joey *lawyer, state representative*

Starkville
Hoffman, Helene *lawyer*

MISSOURI

Kahoka
Jones, Mary D. *court clerk*

Kansas City
Bacon, Jennifer Gille *lawyer*
Clegg, Karen Kohler *lawyer*

Levings, Theresa Lawrence *lawyer*
Parker, Marietta *prosecutor*
Plax, Karen Ann *lawyer*
Rove, Frances Ann *lawyer*
Satterlee, Terry Jean *lawyer*
Sauer, Elisabeth Ruth *lawyer*
Whittaker, Judith Ann Cameron *lawyer*

Mount Vernon
Stemmons, Randee Smith *lawyer*

Saint Charles
Dorsey, Mary Elizabeth *lawyer*

Saint Louis
Atwood, Hollye Stolz *lawyer*
Baker, Nannette A. *lawyer, city official*
Boggs, Beth Clemens *lawyer*
Bonacorsi, Mary Catherine *lawyer*
Brickey, Kathleen Fitzgerald *law educator*
Covington, Ann K. *lawyer, former state supreme court justice*
Greenley, Beverly Jane *lawyer, educator*
Hays, Ruth *lawyer*
Jackson, Rebecca R. *lawyer*
Newman, Joan Meskiel *lawyer*
Perotti, Rose Norma *lawyer*
Rifkind, Irene Glassman *legal secretary*
Schoene, Kathleen Snyder *lawyer*
Searls, Eileen Haughey *retired lawyer, librarian, educator*
Sherby, Kathleen Reilly *lawyer*
Wilson, Margaret Bush *lawyer*

Warrensburg
Young, Mary Ann *lawyer*

MONTANA

Billings
Gallinger, Lorraine D. *prosecutor*

Bozeman
Piazza, Rosanna Joy *paralegal*

Helena
Franz, Holly Jo *lawyer, partner*
Meadows, Judith Adams *law librarian, educator*

NEBRASKA

Benkelman
Owens, Judith L(ynn) *lawyer*

Lincoln
Frobom, LeAnn Larson *lawyer*
Ogle, Robbin Sue *criminal justice educator*
Schizas, Jennifer Anne *law association administrator*

Omaha
Longo, Amy L. *lawyer*

NEVADA

Las Vegas
Bersi, Ann *lawyer*
Hill, Judith Deegan *retired lawyer*
Landreth, Kathryn E. *lawyer*
Sturman, Glorida J. *lawyer*

NEW HAMPSHIRE

Hanover
Prager, Susan Westerberg *law educator, provost*

Newport
Stamatakis, Carol Marie *lawyer, former state legislator*

Plainfield
Brown, Judith Olans *lawyer, educator*

NEW JERSEY

Asbury Park
Rosenbloom, Norma Frisch *lawyer*

Basking Ridge
Marrero, Teresa *lawyer*

Bloomfield
Lordi, Katherine Mary *lawyer*

Camden
Kaden, Ellen Oran *lawyer, consumer products company executive*

Cherry Hill
Kole, Janet Stephanie *lawyer, writer, photographer*

East Brunswick
Burns, Barbara *lawyer*

East Hanover
Davidson, Anne Stowell *lawyer*

Flemington
Meagher, Deirdra M. *lawyer*

Freehold
Scarola, Susan Margaret *lawyer*

Hackettstown
Mulligan, Elinor Patterson *lawyer*

Iselin
Walker, Linda Lee *lawyer*

Livingston
Cummis Sandlaufer, Deborah Gwen *lawyer*

Montclair
Brown, Geraldine Reed *lawyer, management consultant*
Pransky, Joan E. *lawyer, community organizer*

Morris Plains
Wyskowski, Barbara Jean *lawyer*

Morristown
Bernstein, Jan Lenore *lawyer*
Handler, Lauren E. *lawyer*
Sherman, Sandra Brown *lawyer*

New Brunswick
Yorke, Marianne *lawyer, real estate executive*

New Milford
Spiegel, Edna Z. *lawyer*

New Providence
Bernstein, Nadia J. *lawyer*

Newark
Bizub, Johanna Catherine *law librarian*
Corbin Walker, Karol *lawyer*
Creenan, Katherine Heras *lawyer*
Defeis, Elizabeth Frances *law educator, lawyer*
Fox, Jeanne Marie *lawyer*
Harrison, Roslyn Siman *lawyer*
Labaj, Pamela Joan *lawyer*
Storch, Susan Borowski *lawyer*

Oakland
Schwager, Linda Helen *lawyer*

Paramus
Blue, Catherine Anne *lawyer*

Passaic
Johnson, Sakinah *paralegal*

Piscataway
Lee, Barbara Anne *law educator, dean*

Plainfield
Bober, Joanne L. *lawyer*

Princeton
Beidler, Marsha Wolf *lawyer*
Greenman, Jane Friedlieb *lawyer, human resources executive*

Ridgewood
Harris, Micalyn Shafer *lawyer, educator, arbitrator, consultant, mediator*

Roseland
Foster, M. Joan *lawyer*

Somerville
Gross, Carol Ann *lawyer*

South Orange
Delo, Ellen Sanderson *lawyer*
Greene, Rebecca Rachel *lawyer*

Trenton
Levin, Susan Bass *lawyer*

West Orange
Hutcheon, Barbara Silver *lawyer*

Whippany
Meola, Janice Grace *lawyer*

Wildwood
Callinan, Patricia Ann *legal secretary*

Woodcliff Lake
Nachtigal, Patricia *lawyer*

NEW MEXICO

Albuquerque
Paster, Janice Dubinsky *lawyer, former state legislator*
Ramo, Roberta Cooper *lawyer*

Las Cruces
Anderson, Joyce Ann *lawyer*

Santa Fe
Moll, Deborah Adelaide *lawyer*
Weckesser, Susan Oneacre *lawyer*

Tijeras
Hoffman, Robyn Brown *lawyer*

NEW YORK

Albany
Catalano, Jane Donna *lawyer*

Ballston Spa
Brown, Ifigenia Theodore *lawyer*

Brooklyn
Barabash, Claire *lawyer, special education administrator, psychologist*
Karmel, Roberta Segal *lawyer, educator*
Mauskopf, Roslynn R. *prosecutor*
Roth, Pamela Susan *lawyer*

Buffalo
Freedman, Maryann Saccomando *lawyer*
Heilman, Pamela Davis *lawyer*
O'Donnell, Denise Ellen *lawyer*
O'Loughlin, Sandra S. *lawyer*
Rubin, Lois S. *lawyer*

Cape Vincent
Stiefel, Linda Shields *lawyer*

Chappaqua
Hurford, Carol *retired lawyer*

Corning
Hauselt, Denise Ann *lawyer*

Dobbs Ferry
Maiocchi, Christine *lawyer*

East Meadow
Price, Marilyn *lawyer*

Farmingdale
O'Brien, Joan Susan *lawyer, educator*

Flushing
Schwartz, Estar Alma *lawyer*
Vigorito, Rosaria Susanna *law librarian, adult education educator, lawyer, artist*

Garden City
Caputo, Kathryn Mary *paralegal*

Hauppauge
Kruger, Frances Petronelle *lawyer*

Huntington
German, June Resnick *lawyer*
Munson, Nancy K. *lawyer*

Ithaca
Germain, Claire Madeleine *law librarian, educator, lawyer*
Hammond, Jane Laura *retired law librarian, lawyer*

Jamesville
DeCrow, Karen *lawyer, writer, educator*

Jericho
Beal, Carol Ann *lawyer*

Mineola
Shaheen Alesi, Barbara *lawyer*
Tankoos, Sandra Maxine *court reporting services executive*

New City
Samimi, Sandra *lawyer*

New Hartford
Chapin, Mary Q. *television personality, arbitrator, mediator, writer, performing artist*

New York
Alter, Eleanor Breitel *lawyer*
Appelbaum, Ann Harriet *lawyer*
Arlen, Jennifer Hall *law educator*
Augustine, Cynthia H. *lawyer*
Bancroft, Margaret Armstrong *lawyer*
Becker, Barbara Lynn *lawyer*
Beerbower, Cynthia Gibson *lawyer*
Beinecke, Candace Krugman *lawyer*
Benshoof, Janet Lee *lawyer, association executive*
Berkery, Rosemary T. *lawyer, investment company executive*
Beshar, Christine *lawyer*
Birnbaum, Sheila L. *lawyer, educator*
Black, Barbara Aronstein *legal history educator*
Blanchard, Kimberly Staggers *lawyer, educator*
Blumkin, Linda Ruth *lawyer*
Bravo, Dominique *lawyer*
Bristor, Katherine M. *lawyer*
Buckley, Susan *lawyer*
Burgman, Dierdre Ann *lawyer*
Chaitman, Helen Davis *lawyer*
Champion, Sara Stewart *lawyer*
Chapman, Shelley C. *lawyer*
Chasey, Jacqueline *lawyer*
Chell, Beverly C. *lawyer, media company executive*
Chin, Sylvia Fung *lawyer*
Chromow, Sheri P. *lawyer*
Clark, Carolyn Cochran *lawyer*
Coffinas, Eleni *lawyer*
Cohen, Marcy Sharon *lawyer*
Colamarino, Katrin Belenky *lawyer*
Constantine, Jan Friedman *lawyer*
Cornish, Kelley A. *lawyer*
Cranney, Marilyn Kanrek *lawyer*
Crough, Maureen M. *lawyer*
Curtis, Susan M. *lawyer*
Dacey, Eileen M. *lawyer*
Darrow, Jill E(llen) *lawyer*
Degener, Carol M. *lawyer*
DeNiro, Mary Lyn S. *lawyer*
Diamant, Aviva F. *lawyer*
Donahue, Anne de la Blanchetai *lawyer*
Donovan, Maureen Driscoll *lawyer*
Dreizen, Alison M. *lawyer*
Drucker, Jacquelin F. *lawyer, arbitrator, author*
Feltenstein, Martha *lawyer*
Finkelstein, Nancy R. *lawyer*
Fisher, Ann Bailen *lawyer*
Fishman, Ellen Beth *lawyer*
Flanagan, Deborah Mary *lawyer*
Fodor, Susanna Serena *lawyer*
Freyer, Dana Hartman *lawyer*
Garcia, Angela G. *lawyer*
Gatting, Carlene J. *lawyer*
Gay, Faith E. *lawyer, educator*
Gelb, Judith Anne *lawyer*
Genova, Diane Melisano *lawyer*
Gill, E. Ann *lawyer*
Gilligan, Mary Ann *law librarian*
Goldstein, Marcia Landweber *lawyer*
Goldstein, Sandra Cara *lawyer*
Greenman, Paula S. *lawyer*
Groh, Jennifer Calfa *law librarian*
Gross, Karen Charal *lawyer*
Grubin, Sharon E. *lawyer*
Halberstam, Malvina *law educator, lawyer*
Hallingby, Jo Davis *lawyer, arbitrator*

Hanson, Jean Elizabeth *lawyer*
Harlow, Ruth *lawyer*
Hauser, Rita Eleanore Abrams *lawyer*
Hayman, Linda C. *lawyer*
Head, Elizabeth *lawyer*
Henry, Sally McDonald *lawyer*
Herzeca, Lois Friedman *lawyer*
Hoffmann, Elinor R. *lawyer*
Holtzman, Elizabeth *lawyer*
Huttner, Constance S. *lawyer*
Hynes, Patricia Mary *lawyer*
Ivanick, Carol W. Trencher *lawyer*
Joseph, Ellen R. *lawyer*
Kambour, Annaliese Spofford *lawyer*
Kamm, Linda Heller *lawyer*
Kane, Alice Theresa *lawyer*
Kanter, Stacy J. *lawyer*
Kaplan, Madeline *legal administrator*
Kitagawa, Audrey Emiko *retired lawyer*
Kmiotek-Welsh, Jacqueline *lawyer*
Kober, Jane *lawyer*
Korff, Phyllis G. *lawyer*
Kraemer, Lillian Elizabeth *lawyer*
Kuck, Lea Haber *lawyer*
Lambert, Judith A. Ungar *lawyer*
Lesk, Ann Berger *lawyer*
Lester, Pamela Robin *lawyer*
Lieberman, Nancy Ann *lawyer*
Lin, Maria C. H. *lawyer*
Lopo, Diana M. *lawyer*
Loss, Margaret Ruth *lawyer*
Luria, Mary Mercer *lawyer*
Lynch, Loretta E. *lawyer, former prosecutor*
Marafioti, Kayalyn A. *lawyer*
Marshall, Sheila Hermes *lawyer*
Martone, Patricia Ann *lawyer*
Mayerson, Sandra Elaine *lawyer*
McCaffrey, Carlyn Sundberg *lawyer*
McHale, Catherine A. *lawyer*
McKay, Donna *legal association administrator*
Merris, Donna Rose *lawyer*
Mikumo, Akiko *lawyer*
Miller, Yvette *lawyer, publishing executive*
Molino, Virginia Louise *lawyer*
Moran, Patricia *lawyer*
Mueller, Shirley Anne *lawyer, real estate broker*
Nearing, Vivienne W. *lawyer*
Norden, Melissa Shari *lawyer*
Nusbacher, Gloria Weinberg *lawyer*
Oberly, Kathryn Anne *lawyer, diversified financial services company executive*
Odoner, Ellen J. *lawyer*
Olshan, Regina *lawyer*
Parent, Louise Marie *lawyer*
Polevoy, Nancy Tally *lawyer, social worker, genealogist*
Pollack, Jessica Glass *lawyer*
Posen, Susan Orzack *lawyer*
Quinn, Yvonne Susan *lawyer*
Rahm, Susan Berkman *lawyer*
Ranney-Marinelli, Alesia *lawyer*
Rappaport, Linda Ellen *lawyer*
Reilly, Catherine Regina *law administrator*
Rigolosi, Elaine La Monica *lawyer, educator, consultant*
Ritter, Ann L. *lawyer*
Robinson, Barbara Paul *lawyer*
Rockas, Anastasia T. *lawyer*
Rocklen, Kathy Hellenbrand *lawyer*
Rodin, Rita A. *lawyer*
Rohrbach, Heidi A. *lawyer*
Rose, Joanne W. *rating service executive*
Roth, Judith Shulman *lawyer*
Ruiz-Valera, Phoebe Lucile *law librarian*
Sacksteder, Elizabeth M. *lawyer*
Saltzstein, Susan L. *lawyer*
Savitt, Susan Schenkel *lawyer*
Schlain, Barbara Ellen *lawyer*
Schneider, Willys Hope *lawyer*
Schneirov, Allison R. *lawyer*
Schulman, Amy Weinfeld *lawyer*
Schwartz, Carol Vivian *lawyer*
Schwartz, Renee Gerstler *lawyer*
Semaya, Francine Levitt *lawyer*
Serota, Susan Perlstadt *lawyer, educator*
Shainwald, Sybil *lawyer*
Shientag, Florence Perlow *lawyer*
Shoss, Cynthia Renée *lawyer*
Sigmond, Carol Ann *lawyer*
Skigen, Patricia Sue *lawyer*
Sokoloff, Audrey L. *lawyer*
Soyster, Margaret Blair *lawyer*
Stecher, Esta E. *lawyer, investment company executive*
Strossen, Nadine *legal association administrator, law educator*
Stuart, Alice Melissa *lawyer*
Sullivan, Irene A. *lawyer*
Sutherland, Susan J. *lawyer*
Swartz, Linda Z. *lawyer*
Thoyer, Judith Reinhardt *lawyer*
Thurston, Sally A. *lawyer*
Tracy, Janet Ruth *legal educator, librarian*
Vladeck, Judith Pomarlen *lawyer*
Vrancik, Barbara A. *lawyer*
Walden, Janet C. *lawyer*
Wallace, Nora Ann *lawyer*
Ward, Sarah M. *lawyer*
Warshauer, Irene C. *lawyer*
Weiksner, Sandra S. *lawyer*
Weingarten, Rhonda *lawyer*
Weinstein, Ruth Joseph *lawyer*
Whelchel, Betty Anne *lawyer*
White, Mary Jo *former prosecutor, lawyer*
Wolff, Margaret Louise *lawyer*
Wrubel, Barbara *lawyer, educator, former editor*
Young, Alice *lawyer*

Pleasant Valley
Hankamp, Margaret *lawyer*

Poughkeepsie
Teal, Arabella W. *lawyer, former state attorney general*

Rochester
Dolin, Lonny H. *lawyer*

Gootnick, Margery Fischbein *lawyer*
Morrison, Patrice B. *lawyer*
Ornt, Jeanine Arden *lawyer*
Robfogel, Susan Salitan *lawyer*
Stewart, Sue S. *lawyer*

Scarsdale
Callaghan, Georgann Mary *lawyer*

Somers
Lemke, Judith A. *lawyer*

Syracuse
Gilman, Karen Frenzel *legal assistant*

Troy
Burch, Mary Seelye Quinn *law librarian, consultant*

Uniondale
Meng, M. Kathryn *lawyer*

Utica
Stormer, Nancy Rose *lawyer*

Valley Stream
Levine, Marilyn Markovich *lawyer, arbitrator*

White Plains
Jacobson, Sandra W. *lawyer*

NORTH CAROLINA

Asheville
Wilson, Susan Elizabeth *lawyer*

Chapel Hill
Wegner, Judith Welch *law educator, former dean*

Durham
Bartlett, Katharine Tiffany *law educator*
Demott, Deborah Ann *lawyer, educator*
Holder, Angela Roddey *lawyer, educator*
Lischer, Tracy Kenyon *lawyer*

Greensboro
Wagoner, Anna Mills *prosecutor*

Raleigh
Carter, Jean Gordon *lawyer*
Kurz, Mary Elizabeth *lawyer*
Ross, Deborah Koff *lawyer, state legislator*

Tryon
McDermott, Renée R(oseler) *lawyer*

Wilmington
Robinson, Robin Wicks *lawyer*

NORTH DAKOTA

Fargo
Holman, Maureen *lawyer*

OHIO

Akron
Vespoli, Leila L. *lawyer, energy executive*

Cincinnati
Bruvold, Kathleen Parker *lawyer*
DeLong, Deborah *lawyer*
Faller, Susan Grogan *lawyer*
Friedman, Penny *lawyer*
Garfinkel, Jane E. *lawyer*
Levin, Debbe Ann *lawyer*
Meyers, Pamela Sue *lawyer*
Stanton, Jeanne Frances *retired lawyer*
Zealcy, Sharon Janine *lawyer*

Cleveland
Bixenstine, Kim Fenton *lawyer*
Brennan, Maureen *lawyer*
Burke, Kathleen B. B. *lawyer*
Carrick, Kathleen Michele *law librarian*
Cudak, Gail Linda *lawyer*
Fischer, Michelle K. *lawyer*
Goins, Frances Floriano *lawyer*
Jorgenson, Mary Ann *lawyer*
Kilbane, Catherine M. *lawyer*
Kronenberg, Janet Lois *lawyer*
Lazar, Kathy Pittak *lawyer*
Lennox, Heather *lawyer*
Leukart, Barbara J. J. *lawyer*
Maloney, Mary D. *lawyer*
Mast, Bernadette Mihalic *lawyer*
Monihan, Mary Elizabeth *lawyer*
Rawson, Rachel L. *lawyer*
Rickert, Jeanne Martin M. *lawyer*
Roberts-Mamone, Lisa A. *lawyer*
Smith, Barbara Jean *lawyer*
Smith, Kestra Jan *prosecutor*
Striefsky, Linda A(nn) *lawyer*
Sweeney, Emily Margaret *prosecutor*
Thimmig, Diana M. *lawyer*
Trapp, Mary Jane *lawyer*

Columbus
Berndt, Ellen German *lawyer*
Crowder, Marjorie Briggs *lawyer*
Harwood, Sandra Stabile *lawyer, state representative*
Hatler, Patricia Ruth *lawyer*
Hill, Kathleen Blickenstaff *lawyer, mental health nurse, nursing educator*
Jackson, Janet Elizabeth *city attorney, association executive*
Katz, Jayce C(harlene) *lawyer*
Kyte, Susan Janet *lawyer, consultant*
Larzelere, Kathy Lynn Heckler *paralegal*
Mencer, Jetta *lawyer*

Dayton
Gambrel, Kimberly *lawyer*
MacGregor, Shawna Anne *lawyer, educator*
Wightman, Ann *lawyer*

Dublin
Tenuta, Luigia *lawyer*

Hilliard
Cooper, Almeta E. *lawyer, medical association administrator*

Hudson
Elliott, Frances Carano *lawyer, educator*

Maumee
McBride, Beverly Jean *lawyer*

Norwalk
Fresch, Marie Beth *court reporting company executive*

Toledo
Machin, Barbara E. *lawyer*

OKLAHOMA

Edmond
Loving, Susan Brimer *lawyer, former state official*

Eufaula
Dawson, Cindy Marie *lawyer*

Norman
Petersen, Catherine Holland *lawyer*

Oklahoma City
Askins, Jari *lawyer, department chairman, state representative*
Brooks, Norma Newton *legal assistant*
Gatewood, Tela Lynne *lawyer*
Lambird, Mona Salyer *lawyer*
Mather, Stephanie June *lawyer*
Pain, Betsy M. *lawyer*
Wood, Paula Davidson *lawyer*
Zevnik-Sawatzky, Donna Dee *retired litigation coordinator*

Stillwater
DeLacerda, Melissa Griner *lawyer*

Tulsa
Dexter, Deirdre O'Neil Elizabeth *lawyer*

OREGON

Central Point
Ingraham, Laura *lawyer, political commentator*

Corvallis
Achterman, Gail Louise *lawyer*

Eugene
Aldave, Barbara Bader *law educator, lawyer*

Portland
Dailey, Dianne K. *lawyer*
Helmer, M(artha) Christie *lawyer*
Johansen, Judith A. *lawyer*
Olson, Kristine *prosecutor*
Rosenbaum, Lois Omenn *lawyer*
Sokol, Jan D. *lawyer*
Teller, Susan Elaine *lawyer*

PENNSYLVANIA

Bala Cynwyd
Kane-Vanni, Patricia Ruth *lawyer, paleontology educator*

Blue Bell
Sundheim, Nancy Straus *lawyer*

Etters
Steps, Barbara Jill *lawyer*

Harrisburg
Kane, Yvette *lawyer, judge*
Maunus, Eileen Susan *lawyer*
Miller, Leslie Anne *lawyer*

Haverford
Stiller, Jennifer Anne *lawyer*

Jenkintown
Dickstein, Joan Borteck *arbitrator, conflict management consultant*

King Of Prussia
Schneider, Pam Horvitz *lawyer*

Lancaster
Nast, Dianne Martha *lawyer*
Whare, Wanda Snyder *lawyer*

Mount Gretna
Warshaw, Roberta Sue *lawyer*

Philadelphia
Berkley, Emily Carolan *lawyer*
Boss, Amelia Helen *law educator, lawyer*
Brier, Bonnie Susan *lawyer*
Comisky, Hope A. *lawyer*
Cutrona, Cheryl F. *mediator*
Fickler, Arlene *lawyer*
Gale, Martha Jayne *lawyer*
Harris, Judith E. *lawyer*
Isdale, Margaret Holly *lawyer*
Kaiser, Linda Susan *lawyer*
Levy, Dale Penneys *lawyer*
Lillie, Charisse Ranielle *lawyer, educator*
Moyer, Louise Eileen *lawyer*

Dayton (continued — Pittsburgh, etc.)

Packer, Rekha Desai *lawyer*
Plaza, Eva M. *lawyer*
Resnick, Stephanie *lawyer*
Rhodes, Alice Graham *lawyer*
Stern, Joan Naomi *lawyer*
Stoner, Olivia Hatchett *lawyer, financial planner*
Wrobleski, Jeanne Pauline *lawyer*
Young, Roma Skeen *lawyer*

Pittsburgh
Blum, Eva Tansky *lawyer*
Buchanan, Mary Beth *prosecutor*
Candris, Laura A. *lawyer*
Johnson, Barbara Elizabeth *lawyer*
Kelly, Linda L. *prosecutor*
Kikel, Suzanne *patent agent*
Litman, Roslyn Margolis *lawyer*
Myers, Barbara Ann *lawyer*

Sewickley
Jackson, Velma Louise *lawyer*

Towanda
Rockefeller, Shirley E. *court clerk*

RHODE ISLAND

Cranston
Ferguson, Christine C. *lawyer, state agency administrator*

Providence
Cox, Dawn Everlina *paralegal*
Farrell, Margaret Dawson *lawyer*
Kacir, Barbara Brattin *lawyer*
Long, Beverly Glenn *retired lawyer*
McCann, Gail Elizabeth *lawyer*

Slatersville
Pannullo, Deborah Paolino *lawyer, training and consulting company executive*

SOUTH CAROLINA

Aiken
Rudnick, Irene Krugman *lawyer, former state legislator, educator*

Columbia
Gray, Elizabeth Van Doren *lawyer*
Roberts, Pamela J. *lawyer*

Greenville
Williams, Martha Garrison *lawyer*

Johns Island
Carter, Mary Andrews *paralegal*

SOUTH DAKOTA

Dakota Dunes
Hagan, Sheila B. *corporate lawyer*

Pierre
Johnson, Julie Marie *lawyer, lobbyist, judge*

Winner
Maule, Theresa Moore *lawyer*

TENNESSEE

Chattanooga
Vital, Patricia Best *lawyer*

Knoxville
Reeves, Pamela *lawyer*
Roberts, Esther Lois *patent attorney, piano educator, composer, writer*
Worthington, Carole Yard Lynch *lawyer*

Memphis
Coleman, Veronica Freeman *prosecutor*

Nashville
Cooper, Mary Berry *retired legal assistant, association executive*
Goggin, Wendy *prosecutor*
Keith, Suzanne Gregory *legal association administrator*
Mayden, Barbara Mendel *lawyer*
Torrey, Claudia Olivia *lawyer*

TEXAS

Abilene
Boone, Celia Trimble *lawyer*

Arlington
Shabazz, Cheryl Antoinette *legal assistant*

Austin
Cantú, Norma V. *law educator, former federal official*
Garcia, Sara Kruger *lawyer*
Hamilton, Dagmar Strandberg *lawyer, educator*
McDaniel, Myra Atwell *lawyer, former state official*
Mullenix, Linda Susan *lawyer, educator*
Sullivan, Teresa Ann *law and sociology educator, academic administrator*
Weinberg, Louise *law educator, author*

Cleveland
Campbell, Selaura Joy *lawyer*

Dallas
Anderson, Barbara McComas *lawyer*
Boyle, Jane J. *lawyer*
Cover, Kathi A. *lawyer*
Davis, Clarice McDonald *lawyer*

Demarest, Sylvia M. *lawyer*
Dutton, Diana Cheryl *lawyer*
Fenner, Suzan Ellen *lawyer*
Flood, Joan Moore *paralegal*
Freytag, Sharon Nelson *lawyer*
Goolsby, Michelle *lawyer, food products executive*
Hansen, Eugenia S. *lawyer*
Henkel, Kathryn Gundy *lawyer*
Houser, Barbara J. *lawyer*
Jayson, Melinda Gayle *lawyer*
Jennings, Susan Jane *lawyer*
Keith, Susan S. *lawyer, business executive*
Lang-Miers, Elizabeth Ann *lawyer*
McCurley, Mary Johanna *lawyer*
McNamara, Anne H. *lawyer, corporate executive*
Miers, Harriet E. *lawyer*
Nelson, Elaine Edwards *lawyer*
Ostolaza, Yvette *lawyer*
Pennington, Karen Harder *lawyer*
Raggio, Louise Ballerstedt *lawyer*
West, Susan D. *lawyer*
Whitaker, Elizabeth *lawyer*

El Paso
Delgado, Graciela *court interpreter*

Fort Worth
Reade, Kathleen Margaret *paralegal, author, educator*

Houston
Addison, Linda Leuchter *lawyer, writer*
Anderson, Doris Ehlinger *lawyer*
Andrews, Sally S. *lawyer*
Cline, Vivian Melinda *lawyer*
Dinkins, Carol Eggert *lawyer*
Dworsky, Clara Weiner *lawyer, former merchandise brokerage executive*
Ewen, Pamela Binnings *lawyer*
Farenthold, Frances Tarlton *lawyer*
Graebner, Carol F. *lawyer*
Heeg, Peggy A. *lawyer, former gas industry executive*
Hinton, Paula Weems *lawyer*
Lake, Kathleen Cooper *lawyer*
Moroney, Linda L.S. (Muffie) *lawyer, educator*
Nacol, Mae *lawyer*
Prestridge, Pamela Adair *lawyer*
Scholin, Margo S. *lawyer*
Smith, Alison Leigh *lawyer*
Stewart, Pamela L. *lawyer*
Tripp, Karen Bryant *lawyer*

Irving
de Mars, Susan S. *lawyer, health products executive*
Duran, Lois Janine *lawyer*

Little Elm
Middleton, Linda Jean Greathouse *lawyer*

Midland
Arizaga, Lavora Spradlin *retired lawyer*

Plano
Weeks, Tresi Lea *lawyer*

Pottsboro
Thomas, Ann Van Wynen *law educator*

Richardson
Austin, Ann Sheree *lawyer*

Rockport
Benningfield, Carol Ann *lawyer*

San Antonio
Biery, Evelyn Hudson *lawyer*
Johnson, Anne Stuckly *retired lawyer*
Macon, Jane Haun *lawyer*
Maloney, Marynell *lawyer*
Reed, Susan D. *prosecutor*
Schuk, Linda Lee *legal assistant, business educator*
Spears, Sally *lawyer*
Weiner, Marcia Myra *judge*

Sealy
Stevens, Rhea Christina *lawyer*

Tyler
Yeager, Ruth *lawyer*

Wichita Falls
Farris, Charlye Ola *lawyer*

UTAH

Salt Lake City
Christensen, Patricia Anne Watkins *lawyer*
McIntosh, Terrie Tuckett *lawyer*
Moore, Debra *lawyer*
Smith, Janet Hugie *lawyer*

VERMONT

Brattleboro
Nichols, Joann Edith Heselton *retired legal secretary*

Essex Junction
Sweetser, Susan W. *lawyer, advocate, former state legislator*

Montpelier
Errecart, Joyce Hier *lawyer*
Saxman, Anna Esther *lawyer*

White River Junction
Davis, Emily S. *lawyer*

VIRGINIA

Alexandria
Franklin, Jeanne F. *lawyer*
Galles, Kristen *lawyer*
Goodman, Sherri Wasserman *lawyer*
Higgins, Mary Celeste *lawyer, researcher*
Lauderdale, Katherine Sue *lawyer*
Sturtevant, Brereton *retired lawyer, former government official*
Van Cleve, Ruth Gill *retired lawyer, government official*
Winzer, P.J. *lawyer*

Arlington
Basterrechea, Ivette *research analyst*
Dalglish, Lucy Ann *lawyer, organization executive*
Heatwole, Mary Phyllis *lawyer*
Swenson, Diane Kay *lawyer*
Wheeler, Barbara Monica *lawyer*

Charlottesville
Andrews, Minerva Wilson *retired lawyer*

Falls Church
Elderkin, Helaine Grace *lawyer*
Honigberg, Carol Crossman *lawyer*
Padgett, Gail Blanchard *lawyer*

Fredericksburg
Dahnk, Jean Patricia *lawyer*

Glen Allen
Weaver, Mollie Little *lawyer*

Lexington
Wiant, Sarah Kirsten *law library administrator, educator, director*

Lynchburg
Packert, G(ayla) Beth *retired lawyer*

Mc Lean
LeSourd, Nancy Susan Oliver *lawyer, writer*
Noonan, Jean *lawyer*
Susko, Carol Lynne *lawyer, accountant*
Wall, Barbara Wartelle *lawyer*

Norfolk
Poston, Anita Owings *lawyer*

Petersburg
Burns, Cassandra Stroud *prosecutor*
Everitt, Alice Lubin *labor arbitrator*

Reston
Butler, Katherine E. *lawyer*
Keler, Marianne Martha *lawyer*

Richmond
Brissette, Martha Blevins *lawyer*
Carpi, Janice E. *lawyer*
Fitzsimmons, Ellen Marie *lawyer*
Hackney, Virginia Howitz *lawyer*
Rigsby, Linda Flory *lawyer*
Rubinstein, Phyllis M. *lawyer*

Roanoke
Effel, Laura *lawyer*
Taylor, Janet Droke *legal secretary*

Rustburg
Hughes, Deborah Enoch *circuit court clerk*

Vienna
Artz, Cherie B. *lawyer*
Peltz, Paulette Beatrice *corporate lawyer*
Price, Ilene Rosenberg *lawyer*

WASHINGTON

Bellevue
Dodge, Kirstin Sue *lawyer*
Tee, Virginia *lawyer*

Everett
Ostergaard, Joni Hammersla *lawyer*

Kennewick
Sullivan-Schwebke, Karen Jane *lawyer*

Olympia
Sparrow, Ruth S. *lawyer*

Seattle
Barnes, Susan Lewis *lawyer*
Boggs, Paula Elaine *lawyer*
Boxx, Karen Elizabeth *lawyer, educator*
Chapman, Fay L. *lawyer*
Char, Patricia Helen *lawyer*
Davison, Audrey M. *lawyer, consultant*
Gibbs, Nancy Patricia *lawyer*
Glover, Karen E. *lawyer*
Gonzalez, Carmen Gracia *law educator*
Gustafson, Alice Fairleigh *lawyer*
Hazelton, Penny Ann *law librarian, educator*
Isaki, Lucy Power Slyngstad *lawyer*
Lawless, Janine A. *lawyer*
Mastroianni, Anna Catherine *law educator*
Nellermoe, Leslie Carol *lawyer*
Niemi, Janice *retired lawyer, retired state legislator*
Parks, Patricia Jean *lawyer*
Pflaumer, Katrina C. *lawyer*
Sherland, Barbara C. *lawyer*
Vestal, Josephine Burnet *lawyer*
Wagner, Patricia Hamm *lawyer*
Wechsler, Mary Heyrman *lawyer*

Selah
Ring, Lucile Wiley *lawyer*

Spokane
Clarke, Judy *lawyer*

Thompson, Patricia A. *lawyer*

WEST VIRGINIA

Charleston
Betts, Rebecca A. *lawyer*
Lane, Charlotte *lawyer*

Huntington
Smith, Sherri Lee *law educator*

Wellsburg
Viderman, Linda Jean *paralegal, corporate executive*

Weston
Hamric, Carolyn Marie *legal assistant, small business owner*

WISCONSIN

Appleton
Drescher, Kathleen Ebben *lawyer*

Hales Corners
Case, Karen Ann *lawyer*

Kohler
Black, Natalie A. *lawyer*

Madison
Baldwin, Janice Murphy *lawyer*
Barnick, Helen *retired judicial clerk*
Bochert, Linda H. *lawyer*
Braden, Betty Jane *legal association administrator*
Charo, Robin Alta *law educator*
McCallum, Laurie Riach *lawyer, state government*
Melli, Marygold Shire *law educator*
Roberson, Linda *lawyer*
Steingass, Susan R. *lawyer*

Menomonee Falls
Dynek, Sigrid *corporate lawyer, retail executive*

Milwaukee
Ballman, Patricia Kling *lawyer*
Geske, Janine Patricia *law educator, former state supreme court justice*
Huff, Marsha Elkins *lawyer*
Kessler, Joan F. *lawyer*
Romer, Denise Patrice *lawyer*
Shapiro, Robyn Sue *lawyer, educator*
Walsh, Kathleen *lawyer*

Racine
Hoelzel, Sally Ann *lawyer*

Ripon
Prissel, Barbara Ann *paralegal, law educator*

Sturgeon Bay
Korb, Joan *lawyer*

Sturtevant
Brandes, Jo Anne *lawyer*

WYOMING

Cheyenne
Carlson, Kathleen Bussart *law librarian*

Laramie
Fulton, Jo Ann *lawyer*
Kinney, Lisa Frances *lawyer*

Powell
Dean, Patricea Louise *lawyer, law educator, small business owner*

Riverton
Girard, Nettabell *lawyer*

TERRITORIES OF THE UNITED STATES

VIRGIN ISLANDS

Christiansted
Welcome, Patricia *lawyer*

CANADA

BRITISH COLUMBIA

Burnaby
Switlo, Janice Georgina Alice E. *barrister, solicitor, mediator, legal and business consultant, strategist*

ONTARIO

Ottawa
Dawson, Mary E. *lawyer*

FRANCE

Draguignan
Frame, Nancy Davis *lawyer*

ADDRESS UNPUBLISHED

Adams, Frances Grant, II, *lawyer*
Areen, Judith Carol *law educator, dean*
Ashkin, Roberta Ellen *lawyer*
Bassey, Idara E. *lawyer, educator*
Bea, Barbara Ann *legal secretary*
Berman, Lori Beth *lawyer*
Booher, Alice Ann *lawyer*
Bower, Jean Ramsay *lawyer, writer*
Bradford, Barbara Reed *lawyer*
Bradford, Mary Rosen *lawyer*
Bradley, Amelia Jane *lawyer*
Brown, Margaret deBeers *lawyer*
Carmack, Mildred Jean *retired lawyer*
Carpenter, Susan Karen *defender*
Cazalas, Mary Rebecca Williams *lawyer, nurse*
Chave, Carolyn Margaret *arbitrator, retired lawyer*
Christensen, Karen Kay *lawyer*
Citron, Beatrice Sally *law librarian, lawyer, educator*
Clark, Beverly Ann *lawyer*
Cobb, Sue McCourt *lawyer, educator*
Comfrey, Kathleen Marie *lawyer*
Connelly, Sharon Rudolph *lawyer*
Crawford, Carol Tallman *law educator*
Crawford, Muriel Laura *lawyer, author, educator*
Crocker, Saone Baron *lawyer*
Crown, Nancy Elizabeth *lawyer*
Dacey, Kathleen Ryan *lawyer, former federal judge*
Daley, Linda *lawyer*
Davis, Joanne Fatse *lawyer*
Davis, Wanda Rose *lawyer*
DeMitchell, Terri Ann *law educator*
DiBattiste, Carol A. *lawyer*
Dickerson, Claire Moore *lawyer, educator*
Diehl, Deborah Hilda *lawyer*
DiMento, Carol A.G. *lawyer*
Dowben, Carla Lurie *lawyer, educator*
Drost, Marianne *lawyer*
Durgin, Diane *arbitrator, lawyer, mediator*
Edwards, Christine Annette *retired lawyer, securities firm executive*
Ellis, Carolyn Terry *lawyer*
Erlebacher, Arlene Cernik *retired lawyer*
Farina, Laura *lawyer*
Farmer, Cornelia Griffin *lawyer, consultant, hearings official*
Ferraro, Geraldine Anne *lawyer, former congresswoman*
Finelsen, Libbi June *lawyer*
Fox, Eleanor Mae Cohen *lawyer, educator, writer*
Fuentes, Sonia Pressman *lawyer*
Geloso-Barone, Rosalia A. *lawyer*
George, Gay *lawyer*
George, Joyce Jackson *lawyer, judge emeritus*
Georges, Mara Stacy *lawyer*
Gerwin, Leslie Ellen *lawyer, public affairs and community relations executive*
Gibb, Roberta Louise *lawyer, artist*
Goodman, Elizabeth Ann *retired lawyer*
Green, Carol H. *lawyer, educator, journalist*
Green, Carole L. *lawyer*
Grutman, Jewel Humphrey *lawyer, writer*
Hackel-Sims, Stella Bloomberg *lawyer, former government official*
Hahn, Jessica Fortner *lawyer*
Hauver, Constance Longshore *lawyer*
Heppe, Karol Virginia *lawyer, educator*
Herringer, Maryellen Cattani *lawyer*
Holt, Marjorie Sewell *lawyer, retired congresswoman*
Hulin, Frances C. *retired prosecutor*
Jack-Moore, Phyllis *strategist, educational consultant*
Jacobsen, Magdalena Gretchen *former mediator, former federal agency executive*
Jameson, Paula Ann *lawyer*
Jordan, Michelle Denise *lawyer*
Kantrowitz, Susan Lee *lawyer*
Kaplan, Helene Lois *lawyer*
Kaster, Laura A. *lawyer*
Kelehear, Carole Marchbanks Spann *legal administrator*
Kelly, Anastasia Donovan *lawyer*
Kienitz, LaDonna Trapp *lawyer, librarian, municipal official*
Kjos, Victoria *lawyer*
Kolbert, Kathryn *lawyer, educator*
Kotcher, Shirley J. W. *lawyer*
Kravetz, Katharine *law educator*
Landy, Lisa Anne *lawyer*
Laney, Meredith Hart *paralegal*
Laudone, Anita Helene *lawyer*
Lichtenstein, Sarah Carol *lawyer*
Lidsky, Ella *retired law librarian*
Liebeler, Susan Wittenberg *lawyer*
Linde, Maxine Helen *lawyer, business executive, private investor*
Lundy, Sheila Edwards *lawyer*
Makkreel, Karen Emiko *lawyer*
Malme, Jane Hamlett *lawyer, educator, advisor*
Marr, Carmel Carrington *retired lawyer, retired state official*
Marshall, Kathryn Sue *lawyer*
Martin, Alice Howze *prosecutor*
Mater, Maud *lawyer*
Matteucci, Sherry Scheel *former prosecutor*
McDonald, Sally J. *lawyer*
Mc Donnell, Loretta Wade *lawyer*
McFadden, Nancy Elizabeth *lawyer*
McNeil Staudenmaier, Heidi Loretta *lawyer*
Miller, Gay Davis *lawyer*
Minor, Clara Mae *election judge*
Miquelon, Miriam F. *former prosecutor, lawyer*
Mitgang, Iris Feldman *retired lawyer*
Molinaro, Valerie Ann *lawyer*
Montbertrand, Lois Shiner *lawyer*
Moore, Betty Jo *legal assistant*
Munsell, Elsie Louise *lawyer*
Murphy, Kathleen Mary *former law firm executive, alternative healing professional*
Murphy, Sandra Robison *lawyer*
Noddings, Sarah Ellen *lawyer*

O'Dell, Joan Elizabeth *lawyer, mediator, business executive, educator*
Otis, Lee Liberman *lawyer, educator*
Parode, Ann *lawyer*
Paul, Eve W. *retired lawyer*
Paulus, Norma Jean Petersen *lawyer*
Phillips, Dorothy Kay *lawyer*
Piculin, Laurette M. *mediator*
Poppler, Doris Swords *lawyer*
Portnoy, Sara S. *lawyer*
Powers, Elizabeth Whitmel *lawyer*
Preston, Colleen Ann *lawyer*
Prinz, Kristie Dawn *lawyer*
Quayle, Marilyn Tucker *lawyer, wife of former vice president of United States*
Rabkin, Peggy Ann *retired lawyer*
Reid, Joan Evangeline *lawyer, stockbroker*
Ricks, Joycia Camilla *retired lawyer*
Ring, Renee Etheline *lawyer*
Roark, Candice Renau *lawyer*
Rollin, Miriam Ann *child advocate*
Rosenberg, Sheli Zysman *lawyer, financial management executive*
Ross, Catherine Jane *lawyer, social policy analyst*
Rosseel-Jones, Mary Louise *lawyer*
Rothenberger, Dolores Jane *legal association administrator, actress, singer*
Rowe, Audrey *paralegal*
Ryan, Cynthia Rhoades *lawyer*
Ryan, Kelly *lawyer*
Saunders, Lonna Jeanne *lawyer, newscaster, talk show host*
Schwab, Eileen Caulfield *lawyer, educator*
Sciacchetano, Gail Mary *lawyer*
Seeger, Leinaala Robinson *law librarian, educator*
Segel, Karen Lynn Joseph *lawyer, taxation specialist*
Seidman, Ellen Shapiro *lawyer, government official*
Shattuck, Cathie Ann *lawyer, former government official*
Shinevar, Karen Kay *lawyer*
Siemer, Deanne Clemence *lawyer*
Smith, Carole Dianne *retired lawyer, editor, writer, product developer*
Smith, Maura Abeln *lawyer*
Spanninger, Beth Anne *lawyer*
Steptoe, Mary Lou *lawyer*
Stillman, Elinor Hadley *retired lawyer*
Tamen, Harriet *lawyer*
Taylor, Ruth Anne *lawyer*
Thomas, Patricia Anne *retired law librarian*
Toensing, Victoria *lawyer*
Vallianos, Carole Wagner *lawyer*
Van Bogaert, Cynthia A. *lawyer*
Villa, Atlis Maria *lawyer, academic administration, educator*
Voight, Elizabeth Anne *lawyer*
Wallack, Rina Evelyn *lawyer*
Walters, Bette Jean *lawyer*
Wang, Nina *prosecutor*
Wesely, Marissa Celeste *lawyer*
Wetzel-Williams, Kimberly *lawyer*
White, Jill Carolyn *lawyer*
Wise, Sandra Casber *lawyer*
Workman, Margaret Lee *lawyer*
Wriston, Kathryn Dineen *lawyer, financial consultant*
Wunsch, Kathryn Sutherland *retired lawyer*
Yeterian, Isabelle M.C. *lawyer*
Zimmerman, Jean *lawyer*

MEDICINE See HEALTHCARE: MEDICINE

MILITARY

UNITED STATES

ALABAMA

Birmingham
Davis, Gwendolyn Louise *air force officer, English educator*

Huntsville
Gawronski, Elizabeth Ann *retired army officer*

ALASKA

Anchorage
Myers, Leah Lynnette *military officer*

ARIZONA

Davis Monthan A F B
Woods, Sharhonda Michele *military officer*

Phoenix
Lawlis, Patricia Kite *air force officer, computer consultant*

Scottsdale
Coffinger, Maralin Katharyne *retired career officer, consultant*

Surprise
Lucchetti, Lynn L. *career officer*

Tucson
Esparza, Kacie Lynne *military officer*

CALIFORNIA

Arroyo Grande
Oseguera, Palma Marie *retired career officer*

El Segundo
Insprucker, Nancy Rhoades *career officer*

San Francisco
Gifford, Fereuza *retired military officer*

COLORADO

Arvada
Eaves, Sally Ann *military career officer*

Colorado Springs
Bowen, Clotilde Marion Dent *retired career officer, psychiatrist*
Dufer, Miriam Donyelle *military officer, writer*

DISTRICT OF COLUMBIA

Washington
Crawford, Mary Louise Perri *career officer*
DeMesme, Ruby Butler *civilian military executive*
Froman, Veronica Zasadni *career officer*
Hazard, Roberta Louise *career officer*
Henningsen, Jacqueline Vincent *civilian military official*
Howell, Deborah S. *career officer*
Paige, Kathleen K. *naval officer*
Pamerleau, Susan L. *career officer*
Potter, Lorraine K. *career military officer*
Stierle, Linda J. *military officer*
Swarthworth, Sharon T. *military officer*
Tornblom, Claudia L. *civilian military employee*
Tracey, Patricia A. *career officer*
Tyler, Cecilia Kay *career officer US Army*

FLORIDA

Rockledge
Harris, Marcelite Jordan *retired career officer*

GEORGIA

Forest Park
Grace-Crum, Phyllis Venetia *military officer*

Fort Benning
Livingston, Joyce Torbic *civilian military employee*

Kathleen
Uzzell-Baggett, Karon Lynette *career officer*

Villa Rica
Thompson, Jacqueline *air force officer, retired*

HAWAII

Fort Shafter
Emery, Carolyn Vera *non-commissioned officer*

ILLINOIS

Downers Grove
Schnell, Patricia Lenore *military officer*

MARYLAND

Bethesda
Martin, Kathleen L. *military officer, hospital administrator*

Fort George G Meade
Kera, Tiiu *career officer*

MASSACHUSETTS

Hanscom AFB
Kenne, Leslie F. *military officer*

Templeton
Evans, Jeanne Carol *retired military officer*

MISSISSIPPI

Keesler AFB
Harrell, Elizabeth Ann *career officer*

MISSOURI

Saint Louis
Griffin, Monica Victoria *military officer, writer*
Shodean, Lisa Diane *military officer*

NEW JERSEY

Picatinny Arsenal
Zulauf, Madeline Ruth *civilian military employee, photographer*

NEW MEXICO

Belen
Smith, Helen Elizabeth *retired career officer*

NEW YORK

Oneonta
Desjarlais, Georgia Kathrine *retired military officer*

OHIO

Cleveland
Norrington, Eileen O'Hickey *military officer, chaplain*

Columbus
Saunders, Mary L. *career officer*

Fairborn
Moore, Margaret Anne *retired civilian military employee*

OKLAHOMA

Tinker Afb
Velasco, Jodi Marie *military lawyer*

SOUTH CAROLINA

Columbia
Badders, Rebecca Susanne *military officer, educator, writer*

TEXAS

Castroville
Eyre, Pamela Catherine *retired career officer*

Dallas
Richard, Diana Marie *retired military officer*

Fort Hood
Johnson, Jennifer Toby *military officer*

Fort Sam Houston
Williams, Pat L. *military officer*

Kelly A F B
Elliott, Carol C. *career officer*

Sheppard A F B
Cook, Sharla J. *career officer*

VIRGINIA

Arlington
Krusa-Dossin, Mary Ann *military officer*

Fort Belvoir
Clark, Trudy H. *career officer*

Springfield
Watts, Helena Roselle *military analyst*

Woodbridge
Lee, Barbara Mahoney *career officer, educator*

WASHINGTON

Shoreline
Geer, Jerri Diane *retired career officer, photographer*

MILITARY ADDRESSES OF THE UNITED STATES

PACIFIC

Apo
Corrigan, Paula Ann *career officer, internist*

ADDRESS UNPUBLISHED

Boardman, Elizabeth Drake *naval reserve officer*
Darnell, Susan Laura Browne *retired air force officer*
Doornink, Barbara *military officer*
Fishburne, Lillian E. *career officer*
Foote, Evelyn Patricia *retired military officer*
Hallaren, Mary *career officer, social service administrator*
Hurd, Veronica Terez *career officer*
Johnson, Joyce *retired military officer*
Johnson-Watson, Reva Mae *non-commissioned officer, consultant*
Keene-Burgess, Ruth Frances *military official*
Kennedy, Claudia J. *retired military officer*
Lynch, Jessica *military officer*
Rondeau, Ann E. *career officer*
Simmons, Bettye H. *career officer*
Tillman, Shirley *retired military officer*
Truckenbrodt, Yolanda Bernabe *retired air force officer, consultant*
Watson, Mary Ann *military officer, counselor*

Wilson, Frances C. *career military officer*

REAL ESTATE

UNITED STATES

ALABAMA

Hayden
Standridge, Jean *real estate executive, real estate broker*

Montgomery
Cassels, Martha Beasley *realtor, developer*
Farshee, Marlena W. *title company executive*

ALASKA

Anchorage
Kelly, Maxine Ann *retired property developer*

ARIZONA

Chino Valley
Bott, Bobbie Lee *real estate broker*

Phoenix
Mariucci, Anne L. *real estate development company executive*
Mure, Barbara A. *real estate property manager*
Sertich, Kelli Ann *land use planner*

Sedona
Copeland, Suzanne Johnson *real estate executive*

Tucson
Lanham, Sandra *conservationist*
Masque, Maria L. *urban planner*
Tang, Esther Don *development consultant, retired social worker*

Yuma
Lineberry, Laurie Lawhorn *urban planner*

ARKANSAS

Blytheville
Baker, Carlene Poff *real estate agent, reporter*

CALIFORNIA

Anaheim
Van Auken, Sue S. *property manager, real estate broker*

Berkeley
Grimes, Ruth Elaine *city planner*

Beverly Hills
Bergman, Nancy Palm *real estate investment company executive*
Seeger, Melinda Wayne *realtor*

Cottonwood
Pritchett, Lori L. *real estate broker, secondary school educator*

Emeryville
Spadora, Hope Georgeanne *real estate company executive*

Encino
Francisco, Jodie E. *realtor, marketing professional, consultant*

Fountain Valley
Smith, Marie Edmonds *real estate agent, property manager*

Fresno
Dale, Sharon Kay *real estate broker*

Goleta
Koart, Nellie Hart *real estate investor and executive*

Granite Bay
Kemper, Dorla Dean Eaton (Dorla Dean Eaton) *real estate broker*

Huntington Beach
Jackle, Karen Dee *real estate company executive*

Irvine
Myles, Margaret Jean *real estate appraiser*

Long Beach
Davies, Grace Lucille *real estate educator*
Rosenberg, Jill *realtor, civic leader*

Los Alamitos
Spiegel, Marilyn Harriet *real estate executive*

Los Angeles
Shin, I. Mia *real estate broker, interior designer*
Swartz, Roslyn Holt *real estate executive*

Los Osos
Polk, Emily DeSpain *conservationist, writer, designer*

Mission Viejo
Harris, Ruby Lee *real estate agent*

Oakland
Miller, Connie Joy *assistant real estate officer, broker*

Oceanside
Munson, Lucille Marguerite (Mrs. Arthur E. Munson) *real estate broker*

Palm Springs
Coffey, Nancy Ann *real estate broker*

Palo Alto
Moore, Cassandra Chrones *real estate broker and policy analyst*

Penn Valley
Nix, Barbara Lois *real estate broker*

Rancho Santa Fe
Land, Judy M. *real estate broker*

Riverside
Oakes, Judy Dianne *real estate broker*

San Diego
Oldham, Maxine Jernigan *real estate broker*

San Fernando
Aguilar, Julia Elizabeth *real estate company executive*

San Francisco
Allen, Gloria Ann *realtor*
Wang, An-Yi (Anne) Chou *real estate broker*

San Marcos
Wingert, Hannelore Christiane *real estate agent, chemical company executive*

San Marino
Scheid, Ann Frances *preservation planner, consultant*

San Mateo
Messinger, Marina Trabanino *real estate investor*

Santa Ana
Danoff-Kraus, Pamela Sue *real estate developer*

Solvang
Anderson, Barbara Ann *property manager*

South Pasadena
Bernal, Harriet Jean Daniels *real estate agent*

Spring Valley
Roberts, Carolyn June *real estate broker*

Thousand Oaks
Helton, Patricia Beth *realtor*

Toluca Lake
Gipson, Juliet Annette *real estate broker*

Upland
Lewis, Goldy Sarah *real estate developer, corporation executive*

COLORADO

Aurora
Martinez-Nemnich, Maricela *realtor*
Wessler, Mary Hraha *real estate company executive*

Colorado Springs
Ansorge, Iona Marie *retired real estate agent, musician, educator*
Bowers, Zella Zane *real estate broker*

Denver
Beldock, Joan Ellen *real estate broker*
McKelrath, Heidi Lee *real estate closing agent*

Durango
Webb, Elizabeth Louise *real estate broker, artist*

Fort Collins
Jensen, Margaret *real estate broker*
Sprague, Amaris Jeanne *real estate broker*

Parker
Brainard, Carol Lee *realtor*
Rogers, Rowena Emery *retired land manager*

Pueblo
Heizer, Ida Ann *retired real estate broker*

Windsor
Hein, Connie L. *real estate company officer, writer*

CONNECTICUT

Berlin
Carroll, Adorna Occhialini *real estate executive*

Greenwich
Griggs, Nina M. *realtor*

New Milford
Smith, Virginia *real estate broker*

Newtown
Pilchard, Melissa Meyer *realtor, appraiser*

Old Greenwich
Parris, Sally Nye *real estate agent*

Wallingford
Bush, Linda A. *land use planner*

DELAWARE

Dover
Taylor, Suzonne Berry Stewart *real estate broker*

Rehoboth Beach
Truitt, Suzanne *real estate broker*

Wilmington
Maley, Patricia Ann *preservation planner*

DISTRICT OF COLUMBIA

Washington
Jones, Susan Dorfman *real estate broker, writer*
Oge, Margo Tsirigotis *environmentalist*
Wallace Douglas, Jean *conservationist*

FLORIDA

Boca Raton
Innes-Brown, Georgette Meyer *real estate broker, insurance broker*
Konrad, Agnes Crossman *retired real estate agent, retired educator*

Bradenton
Becker, Nancy S. *retired real estate broker, retired shop owner*

Celebration
Crabtree, Valleri Jayne *real estate executive, lawyer*

Fort Myers
Van Vleck, Pamela Kay *real estate company officer*

Fort Pierce
Peterson, Barbara Owecke *retired real estate agent, artist, nurse*

Gainesville
York, Vermelle Cardwell *real estate broker and developer*

Jacksonville
Aleschus, Justine Lawrence *retired real estate broker*

Maitland
Vallee, Judith Delaney *environmentalist, writer, fundraiser*

Miami
Nestor Castellano, Brenda Diana *real estate company executive*
Paschal, Verona *real estate agent, small business owner*

Ocala
Booth, Jane Schuele *real estate company executive, real estate broker*

Orlando
Good, Virginia Johnson *real estate executive*

Palm Beach Gardens
Curwick, Deborah *realtor*

Palm Coast
Barnes, Judith Ann *real estate executive*

Parkland
Landman, Deborah Tracy *real estate company executive, small business owner, fitness trainer*

Ponte Vedra Beach
Berry, Clare Gebert *real estate broker*

Port Charlotte
Gehring, Karin *real estate broker*

Saint Petersburg
Bass, Kimberleigh Anne *real estate company executive, risk management consultant*
Riley, Nancy J. *real estate broker*

Sarasota
Byron, E. Lee *real estate broker*
Mason, Ann Darlene *real estate broker*

Tallahassee
Lisenby, Dorrece Edenfield *realtor*

Valrico
Tirelli, Maria Del Carmen S. *retired realtor*

Venice
Trammell, Jean Ehrhart *real estate agent, secondary school educator*

Wellington
Morales-Hendry Holguin, Maria B. *realtor, poet*

West Palm Beach
Belford, Roz *real estate broker*
Beriro, Deborah Raquel *real estate broker, investor*
Lutey, Joyce Louise *real estate broker*
Peller, Marci Terry *realtor*

GEORGIA

Athens
Meyer, Gail Barry *retired real estate broker*

Atlanta
Motley, Charlotte Juanita *real estate company executive, consultant*
Nichols, Elizabeth Litterer *real estate developer*
Ossewaarde, Anne Winkler *real estate company executive*

Folkston
Crumbley, Esther Helen Kendrick *retired real estate agent, retired secondary school educator, councilman*

Marietta
Shapiro, Abra Blair *real estate company executive*

Roswell
Atkins, Vicki Alvinda *realtor*

HAWAII

Honolulu
Adcock, Betty-Lee *real estate company officer*
Baker, Helen Doyle Peil *realtor, contractor*
Jones, Pamela S. *real estate development executive*
Walker, Margaret Smith *real estate company executive*

Koloa
Cobb, Rowena Noelani Blake *real estate broker*

IDAHO

Idaho Falls
Thorsen, Nancy Dain *real estate broker*

ILLINOIS

Arlington Heights
Falkenberg, Mary Ann Theresa *realtor*

Barrington
Fowler, Susan Michele *real estate broker, entrepreneur*

Chicago
Amato, Isabella Antonia *real estate executive*
Barker, Barbara *real estate professional*
Benson, Sara Elizabeth *real estate broker, real estate appraiser*
Eubanks-Pope, Sharon G. *real estate company executive, entrepreneur*
Field, Karen Ann (Karen Ann Schaffner) *real estate broker*
Fox, Leslie B. *real estate company executive*
Julmy, Camille P. *real estate company executive*
Pacher, Nancy A. *real estate company executive*

Evanston
Peltier, Janis Janosek *real estate agent, astrologer*

Highland Park
Stein, Paula Jean Anne Barton *hotel real estate executive, broker*

La Grange Park
Alonzo, Loretta J. *real estate broker*

LaGrange
Lubenkov, Terry Anne *broker, realtor*

Naperville
Harvard, Rita Grace *real estate agent, volunteer*

Westmont
Harten, Ann M. *relocation services executive*

INDIANA

Evansville
Collins, Cindy Elaine *property manager*
Hunt, Lucille(Luci) Edith *real estate agent, real estate broker*

Greenwood
Tomlin, Jeanne Brannon *real estate broker, small business owner*

Jeffersonville
McMichael, Jeane Casey *real estate company executive, educator*

Terre Haute
Flick, Connie Ruth *real estate agent, real estate broker*

IOWA

Ames
Wendell, Barbara Taylor *retired real estate agent*

Cedar Rapids
Baermann, Donna Lee Roth *real estate property executive, retired insurance analyst*

Humeston
Goben, Mirella Segalotto *real estate agent*

KANSAS

Topeka
Barnett, Mary Lorene *real estate manager*

KENTUCKY

Covington
Fleischer-Rieveschl, Ellen Lee *real estate agent*

Lexington
Davis, Mary Byrd *conservationist, researcher*
Henderson, Jerrie *realtor*

Winchester
Cantrell, Georgia Ann *realtor*

LOUISIANA

Metairie
Myers, Iona Raymer *real estate property manager*

MAINE

Kingfield
Clapp, Millicent Evans *real estate broker*

Port Clyde
Duarte, Patricia M. *real estate and insurance broker*

MARYLAND

Baltimore
Macht, Amy *real estate executive, foundation manager*

Berlin
Passwater, Barbara Gayhart *real estate broker*

Burtonsville
Kammeyer, Sonia Margaretha *real estate agent*

Chevy Chase
Coble, Wilma Loretta *real estate investor, property management*

Montgomery Village
Wykes, Mary Maushak *real estate agent*

Potomac
Dickerman, Serafina Poerio *real estate broker, consultant*
Eaves, Maria Perry *realtor*

Reisterstown
Bart, Polly Turner *real estate developer*

Rockville
Moses, Cynthia Glass *realtor*

Silver Spring
Laughlin, Naomi Myers *realtor*

Simpsonville
Altschuler, Ruth Phyllis *realtor, secondary school educator*

Westminster
Erb, Betty Jane *retired real estate agent, activist*

MASSACHUSETTS

Ayer
Holmes, Jean Louise *real estate investor, Holocaust scholar, educator*

Boston
Wiggleworth, Margaret *property manager*

Cambridge
Wylie, Joan Blout *real estate rehabilitator, designer, ceramist*

East Bridgewater
Farrell, Sharon Elaine *retired real estate broker*

Falmouth
Milkman, Marianne Friedenthal *retired city planner*

Medford
Comeau, Lorene Anita Emerson *real estate developer*

Natick
Strauss, Harlee Sue *environmental consultant*

Newton
Havens, Candace Jean *planning consultant*

Rockport
Johnson, Janet Lou *real estate company executive, writer*

Winchester
Blackham, Ann Rosemary (Mrs. J. W. Blackham) *realtor*

MICHIGAN

Coldwater
Kibiloski, Catherine Kay *real estate appraiser*

Farmington Hills
Beron, Gail Laskey *real estate analyst, appraiser, consultant*

Niles
Tenney, Jane Morris *real estate developer*

MINNESOTA

Minneapolis
O'Keefe, Nancy Jean *retired real estate company executive*

MISSISSIPPI

Ridgeland
Jones, Sarah Ashley *realtor, consultant*

Falling Waters
Braithwaite, Marilyn Jean *realtor*

WISCONSIN

Fond Du Lac
Towne, Kristine Marie *title company executive*

Lake Mills
Lazaris, Pamela Adriane *community planning and development consultant*

Milwaukee
Gondek, Mary Jane (Mary Jane Suchorski) *property manager*
Grider, Barbara Jean *real estate broker, consultant*
Smith, Lois Ann *real estate executive*

Reedsburg
Olson, Jeanne M. *real estate broker*

Wausau
Prey, Yvonne Mary *real estate broker*

West Bend
Melinski, Margaret *realtor*

Whitefish Bay
Stillman, Sharon J. *real estate broker*

WYOMING

Casper
Elliott, Marian Kay *real estate manager*

ADDRESS UNPUBLISHED

Anderson, Amy Lee *realtor*
Aponte, Elsie *conservationist*
Athias, Lori R. *real estate broker*
Baiman, Gail *real estate broker*
Barrett, Linda L. *real estate consultant*
Berliner, Ruth Shirley *real estate company executive*
Bland, Eveline Mae *real estate broker, musician, music instructor*
Brown, Ann Lenora *community and business development professional*
Bryan, Mary Jo W. *realtor, artist, art educator*
Bryant, Rhona E. *real estate company executive*
Campbell, Jane Turner *retired realtor, retired secondary school educator, retired adult education educator*
Corkran, Virginia B. *retired real estate agent*
Dahlstrom, Patricia Margaret *real estate appraiser*
Darlington, Hilda Walker *real estate company officer*
DeWitt, Sallie Lee *realtor*
Diamond, Nancy Kay *environmentalist, consultant*
DiGiamarino, Marian Eleanor *retired realty administrator*
Doyle, Judith Stovall *retired real estate executive*
Edwards, Kathleen *real estate broker, former educator*
Engels, Beatrice Ann *retired real estate company executive, poet, artist*
Gault-Stovall, Sheri Zelda-Lynn *property manager, consultant*
Gong, Carolyn Lei Chu *real estate agent*
Gunn, Lucy Davis *realtor*
Hedrich, Cleda Pollard *real estate broker, writer*
Hemstreet, Pamela S. *real estate broker*
Holleb, Doris B. *urban planner, economist*
Johnson, Kay Durbahn *real estate manager, consultant*
Karakey, Sherry JoAnne *real estate company executive, interior designer*
Kinard, Agnes Dodds *retired real estate company executive, historian, writer, lawyer*
Kremer, Honor Frances (Noreen Kremer) *real estate broker, small business owner*
Lamy, M(ary) Rebecca *consultant, land developer, government official*
Lopez-Munoz, Maria Rosa P. *real estate development company executive*
Lowenthal, Susan *realtor, artist*
McGinn, Mary Lyn *real estate company executive*
Mitts, Marybeth Frazier *real estate company executive, consultant*
Nederveld, Ruth Elizabeth *retired real estate executive*
Pence, Jean Virginia (Jean Pence) *retired real estate broker*
Penniman, Linda Simmons *real estate agent*
Prout, Kathleen Soliozy *realtor*
Ross, Beverley Long *real estate broker*
Roths, Beverly Owen *environmentalist*
Sanquist, Nancy Johnson *facitliy management consultant, real estate consultant*
Schneider, Rita Joyce *property management company executive, real estate broker, mortgage broker*
Schultz, Phyllis May *financial property manager*
Smith, Mary Louise *real estate broker*
Solotar, Anne Paula *real estate agent*
Sopkin, Carole A. *realtor*
Taylor, Connie J. *real estate company executive*
Toshach, Clarice Oversby *real estate developer, former computer executive*
Walker, Helen Smith *retired real estate broker*
White, Lani Nyla *real estate developer*
Williams, Phyllis Cutforth *retired realtor*

Woods, Sandra Kay *real estate executive*

RELIGION

UNITED STATES

ALABAMA

Birmingham
Loftin, Sister Mary Frances *religious organization administrator*
Newbern Williams, Mary Ruth *minister*

Greenville
Longmire, Venus DeLoyse *minister*

Huntsville
Furlow, Brenda J. *religious studies educator, consultant*

Montgomery
Bullard, Mary Ellen *retired religious organization administrator*

ALASKA

Anchorage
Fleming, Carolyn Elizabeth *religious organization administrator, interior designer*

ARIZONA

Scottsdale
Martin-DeWitt, M. Lori *minister*

Sun City
Randall, Claire *church executive*

ARKANSAS

Blytheville
Estes, Pamela Jean *pastor*

Fort Smith
Autry, Davida Marie *minister*

Jonesboro
Cash, Mary Frances *minister, retired civilian military employee*

Morrilton
Crawford-Larson, Kris *minister*

CALIFORNIA

Altadena
Willans, Jean Stone *bishop, religious organization executive*

Auburn
Moore, Billie Jo *minister*

Bakersfield
Johnson, Deborah Valerie Germaine *parish administrator*

Chino Hills
Nash, Sylvia Dotseth *consultant*

Escondido
Frawley, Sister Claire *religious studies educator*
Linzey, Verna May *minister, writer*

Fresno
DiVincenzo, Sister Mary Anne *chaplain, therapist*

Happy Camp
Black, Barbara Ann *publisher*

Los Angeles
Daya Mata, Sri (Faye Wright) *clergywoman*
Milligan, Sister Mary *theology educator, religious consultant*

Midway City
Allen, Frances Michael *publisher*

Oakland
Ocheltree, Carolyn Donine *minister, religious studies educator*

Palm Desert
Ponder, Catherine *clergywoman, author*

Pasadena
Shuster, Marguerite *minister, educator*

Riverside
Andersen, Frances Elizabeth Gold *religious leadership educator*
Wood, Brenda Jean *pastor, evangelist*

Sacramento
Stuart, Toni Freeman *priest*

San Bernardino
Burgess, Mary Alice (Mary Alice Wickizer) *publisher*

San Diego
Bauer, Judy Marie *minister*
Olson, Linda Ann Salmonson *minister*
Robinson, Rosie Lee *minister*

San Mateo
Kelly, Leontine T. C. *clergywoman*

Santa Barbara
Albanese, Catherine *religious studies educator*

Sonora
Jones, Georgia Ann *publisher*

Union City
Velarde, Heide Marie *publisher, writer, lyricist*

Weed
Richard, Eleanor *minister*

West Hollywood
Eger, Denise Leese *rabbi*
Wilson, Nancy Linda *religious organization administrator*

COLORADO

Buena Vista
Goddard, Hazel Bryan *religious organization administrator*

Colorado Springs
Freeman, J. P. Ladyhawk *vicar, underwater exploration, security and transportation executive, educator, fashion model, legislative advocate*

Denver
Brownlee, Judith Marilyn *priestess, psychotherapist, psychic*
Shinabery, Kimbery Ann *minister*

Pueblo
Nimmo, Charlene *minister*
Ritter, Jennifer Leigh *music minister, educator*

Westminster
Wolfram, Suzanne G. *minister, educator, dean*

CONNECTICUT

Groton
Baumann, Rebecca Ellen *minister*

Hartford
Petty, M. S. Marty *publisher*
Winter, Miriam Therese (Gloria Frances Winter) *nun, religious education educator*

West Hartford
Edwards, Sarah Alexander *minister, educator*

DELAWARE

Wilmington
Linderman, Jeanne Herron *priest*

DISTRICT OF COLUMBIA

Washington
Graham, Margaret M. *minister*
Harvey, Jane Hull *church administrator*
Height, Dorothy I. *association executive*
Hellwig, Monika Konrad *organization executive, theology educator*
Kane, Annette Pieslak *religious organization executive*
Leckey, Dolores R. *religious organization administrator, writer*
Mead, Christina Dykstra *church administrator*
Pendleton, Gloria Bell *lay worker*
Ziegler, Gwendolyn Woods *minister, consultant*

FLORIDA

Boca Raton
Eisenberg, Robin Ledgin *religious education administrator*
Laine, Iris Ruth *minister, public relations/advertising executive*

Delray Beach
Wells, Mary Elizabeth Thompson *minister*

Fort Lauderdale
McCormick, Queen Esther Williams *clergyman*

Gainesville
Steffee, Nina Dean *publisher*

Jacksonville
Holliday, Patricia Ruth McKenzie *evangelist*
Small, Patricia Ann *minister*

Longwood
Meitin, Deborah Dorsky *cantor*

Miami
Gray, Frances Boone *minister*

Palm Bay
Downes, Patricia Ann *minister*

Pompano Beach
Corsello, Lily Joann *minister, counselor, educator*

Saint Augustine
Couture, Diane Rhea *sister, artist, educator*

Sarasota
Forrest, Iris *publisher*
McFarlin, Diane Hooten *publisher*
Towner, Margaret Ellen *retired minister*

Tampa
Clark, Anna M. *minister, lobbyist*
Rojas, Mazie *pastor*

Winter Haven
Lindsey, Jane Willann *minister*

GEORGIA

Albany
Sciamanda Szpak, Sylvia Anne *religious studies educator, director*

Athens
Henderson, Alma *religious studies educator*
Spears, Louise Elizabeth *minister, secondary school educator*

Atlanta
King, Barbara Lewis *minister, lecturer*
Rhodes, Lisa Diane *minister*

Bowersville
Bowers, Martha Vassar *religious studies educator*

Clayton
Monroe, Brenda *priest*

Decatur
Gary, Julia Thomas *retired minister*
Hale, Cynthia Lynette *religious organization administrator*

Ellenwood
Pack, Bobigene *minister, writer*

Macon
Good, Estelle M. *minister*

Norcross
Hicks, Nanci Ann *minister, marketing professional*

Peachtree City
Yother, Michele *publisher*

Savannah
Cunniff, Sister Georgette *religious organization administrator*

Stockbridge
Spencer-Jacobs, Jamelle Elizabeth *minister, performing company executive*

HAWAII

Kahului
Domingo, Cora Maria Corazon Encarnacion *minister*

Kula
Mueller-Fitch, Heather May *priest*

ILLINOIS

Chicago
Barbour, Claude Marie *minister, educator*
Carr, Anne Elizabeth *theology educator*
Doherty, Sister Barbara *religious institution administrator*
Doniger, Wendy *history of religions educator*
Harris, Mildred Clopton *clergy member, educator*
Hughes, Michelle D. *minister, educator*
James, Marie Moody *clergywoman, musician, vocal music educator*
Jegen, Sister Carol Frances *religion educator*
Lathon, Sheraine *clergyman*
McDonald, Theresa Beatrice Pierce (Mrs. Ollie McDonald) *church official, minister*
Poethig, Eunice Blanchard *clergywoman*
Ramey, Eudora Malois *minister*

Elgin
Reimer, Judy Mills *pastor, religious executive*

Itasca
Constant, Anita Aurelia *publisher*

Loves Park
Schlub, Teresa Rae *minister*

Moline
Johnson, Mary Lou *lay worker, educator*

Naperville
Raccah, Dominique Marcelle *publisher*

Rockford
Gregory, Dola Bell *bishop, customer service administrator*
McClelland, Patricia G. *minister*

Wauconda
Gotthardt, Mary Jane *religious studies educator*

Wheaton
Harris, E(leanor) Lynn(e) *religious studies educator, literature educator, minister, writer*

INDIANA

Indianapolis
Marshall, Carolyn Ann M. *church official*

Kokomo
Finster, Mary Ruth *deacon, retired elementary school educator, cosmetics executive*

Newburgh
McKown, Martha *minister, writer*

Notre Dame
Wiedower, Sister M. Veronique *religious organization administrator*

Shoals
Saenz, Ruth E. *missionary*

IOWA

Ames
Withers, Heather Nowell *minister*

Iowa City
Clark, Dianne Elizabeth *religious studies and reading educator*

Waverly
Koob, Kathryn Loraine *religious studies educator*

KANSAS

Clifton
Compton, Doris Martha *lay worker*

Lawrence
Ahl, Sally Webb *religious studies educator*

Overland Park
Liston, Helen J. *minister*

Wichita
Fotovich, Sister Ursula Ann *nun, religious organization administrator*

KENTUCKY

Hopkinsville
Martin, Theresa Kay *minister*

Louisville
Boykin, Gladys *retired religious organization administrator*
Dale, Judy Ries *religious organization administrator, consultant*

LOUISIANA

Baton Rouge
Adams, Olivia Butler *minister, philosopher, researcher*

Metairie
Feurtado, Rhonda Elizabeth *minister*

New Iberia
Ambers, Ann *bishop, educator*

Shreveport
Flournoy, Linda Wesley *minister, educator*

MAINE

Bridgton
Normann, Margaret Ella *deacon, educator*

North Yarmouth
York, Gladys Doughty *minister*

South Bristol
Lasher, Esther Lu *minister*

MARYLAND

Avenue
Price, Kathleen Vermillion *priest*

Baltimore
Montgomery, Paula Kay *publisher*
Robinson, Carrie *pastor*
Robinson, Sally Shoemaker *lay associate church social ministries*
Ushry, Roselyn *minister*

Catonsville
Hammond, Deborah Lynn *lay worker*

Chester
Shively, Bonnie Lee *pastor*

Cockeysville
Hager, Louise Alger *retired chaplain*

Columbia
Williams, Mamie Alethia *minister*

Elkridge
Byrd, Alicia D. *minister, sociologist*

Elkton
Loveless, Laurel Plumstead *minister*

Mount Airy
Yocum, Carol Cosens *minister*

Mount Rainier
London, Wanda Elaine *minister*

Saint Marys City
Von Kellenbach, Katharina *religious studies and women's studies educator*

Silver Spring
Cathey, Mary Ellen Jackson *religious studies educator*
Hunt, Mary Elizabeth *religious studies educator*
Mills, Ianther Marie *minister*

Vienna
Farnell, Mary Ann *minister*

MASSACHUSETTS

Auburndale
Gulbrandsen, Natalie Webber *religious association administrator*

Boston
Harris, Barbara C(lementine) *bishop*
Harris, Virginia *religious organization administrator, publisher*
Kessler, Diane Cooksey *religious organization administrator, minister*

Brookline
Bullitt-Jonas, Margaret Morley *priest, writer*
Skeete, Helen Watkins *minister, counselor*

Cambridge
Gray, Elizabeth Dodson *theologian, writer, speaker*
Schuessler Fiorenza, Elisabeth *theology educator*

Dedham
Janson, Barbara Jean *publisher*

Hinsdale
Cijka, Michele Dawn *minister*

Holyoke
Morrissey, Jane F. *religious organization administrator*

Mashpee
Payne, Paula Marie *minister*

Newton
Corcoran, Nancy Helen *minister*
Tannenwald, Leslie Keiter *rabbi, justice of peace, educational administrator, chaplain*

Norwood
Sidiropoulou, Eleftheria Alexandrou *minister, family therapist*

Waltham
Delaney, Mary Anne *retired theology studies educator*

MICHIGAN

Dearborn
Frank, Nancy Kathleen *minister*
Hess, Margaret Johnston *religious writer, educator*

Detroit
Toney, Creola Sarah *minister*

Flint
Spencer, Mary Elizabeth *minister*

Marshall
Nelson, Ann Bryan *religious studies educator*

River Rouge
Myhand, Cheryl *minister, educator*

Southfield
Acton, Ellen Hall *minister, educator*

Traverse City
Burton, Betty June *retired pastor*

MINNESOTA

Apple Valley
Haaheim, Patricia Jane Dando *pastor, consultant*

Bloomington
Brokke, Catherine Juliet *mission executive*

Byron
Westerlund, Frezil Daniel-Ellis *pastor*

Comfrey
Nohner, Sharon *nun, minister*

Janesville
Frank, Sister Elaine Lou *sister*

Mentor
Jerdee, Sylvia Ann *minister*

Minneapolis
Battle, Willa Lee Grant *clergywoman, educational administrator*
Chemberlin, Peg *clergy, religious organization administrator*
Mason, Barbara Fountain *minister*

Preston
Schommer, Trudy Marie *pastoral minister, religion education*

Roseville
McMillan, Mary Bigelow *retired minister, volunteer*

MISSISSIPPI

Minter City
Mitchell, Patsy Malier *religious school founder and administrator*

Poplarville
Peterson, Katherine Dianne *ministry assistant*

MISSOURI

Bridgeton
Hylla, Linda Kay *sister, social worker*

Charleston
Wallhausen, Mildred Carolyn *publisher*

Hollister
Hopper, Ruby Lou *clergy member*

Independence
Mortimer, Anita Louise *minister*

Kansas City
Hebenstreit, Jean Estill Stark *religion educator, practitioner*

Lees Summit
Lord, Heaven *theology studies educator, consultant, minister, translator*

Saint Louis
Hemish, Carol Marie *liturgist/spiritual director, musician*

MONTANA

Roundup
Harant, Patricia A. *minister*

NEBRASKA

Omaha
Gray-Ventry, Tina L. *minister*

NEVADA

Carson City
Morgan, Elaine Ludlum *minister*

NEW HAMPSHIRE

Hanover
Hemphill, Margaret Ayars *priest, artist*

Jaffrey
Van Ness, Patricia Wood *religious studies educator, consultant, author*

Loudon
Moore, Dantzine *religious organization administrator*

Tilton
Lombardo, Janet Vogt *priest*

NEW JERSEY

Cherry Hill
Johnson, Catherine Graham *religious organization administrator*

Clinton
Moore, Alma Donst *writer, lyricist*

Colonia
Cohen, Diane A. *rabbi*

Eatontown
Priesand, Sally Jane *rabbi*

Elizabeth
Blowe, Arnethia *religious studies educator*

Hightstown
Hull, Gretchen Gaebelein *lay worker, writer, lecturer*

Jersey City
Katz, Colleen *publisher*

Little Falls
Glasser, Lynn Schreiber *publisher*

Newark
Johnson, Evelyn *minister, educator*
Moore, Mattie H. *clergy, folk artist, retired educator*

Piscataway
Wasserman, Marlie P(arker) *publisher*

Toms River
Donaldson, Marcia Jean *lay worker*

NEW MEXICO

Gallup
Garcia, Mother Magda Leticia *sister, consultant*

Prewitt
Droll, Ruth Lucille *missionary pastor*

Santa Fe
Gallagher, Paula *minister, musician*

NEW YORK

Albany
Bowen, Mary Lu *ecumenical administrator*

Albion
Allamon, Karen Henn *minister*

Amity Harbor
O'Hanlon, Carol Ann *minister*

Arverne
Fullard, Henrietta *minister*

Bronx
Kirmse, Sister Anne-Marie Rose *nun, educator, researcher*
Ruffing, Janet Kathryn *spirituality educator*

Brooklyn
Staggers, Mary E. *minister*

Buffalo
Brady, Sister Patricia Ann *minister, director*
Smith, Sara D. *minister, lawyer*

Central Nyack
Margolis, Patt *minister*

Chautauqua
Campbell, Joan Brown *religious organization executive*

Cicero
Schiess, Betty Bone *priest*

Deposit
Myrick, Katherine Julia *minister*

Greenwich
Johnson-Siebold, Judith Eloise *minister*

Hempstead
Weiss, Sara C. *religious organization administrator*
Zagano, Phyllis *religious studies educator*

Hollis
Stephens, B. Consuela *minister, consultant*

Hopewell Junction
Conti, AnnaLee Cousart *minister, writer*

Jamaica
Isaac-Emmons, Merlyn Hulda *religious studies educator, academic administrator*

Maryknoll
Guerrieri, Sister Antonia Maria, Arcangiolina Veronica *sister*

New York
Balter, Bernice *religious organization administrator*
Baranski, Joan Sullivan *publisher*
Berner, Mary *publisher*
Conlon, Peggy Eileen *publisher*
Gracey, Janet English *church administrator*
Hirsch, Roseann Conte *publisher*
Holmes, Miriam H. *publisher*
Isay, Jane Franzblau *publisher*
McGeady, Sister Mary Rose *retired religious organization administration*
Nusim, Roberta *publisher*
Ochs, Carol Rebecca *theologian, philosophy and religion educator*
Oshin, Diane *publisher*
Patterson, Mary Jane *religious organization administrator*
Reidy, Carolyn Kroll *publisher*
Rosenberg, Ellen Y. *religious association administrator*
Simpson, Mary Michael *priest, psychotherapist*
Sohl, Joyce Darlene *religious organization administrator*
Tannenbaum, Bernice Salpeter *national religious organization executive*

Niagara Falls
Douglas, Frances Sonia *minister*

North Bellmore
Connell, S. Clare *minister*

North Syracuse
Williamson, Donna Maria *pastoral counselor*

Pawling
Peale, Ruth Stafford (Mrs. Norman Vincent Peale) *religious leader*

Penfield
Hamilton, Candis Lee *religious organization administrator*

Poughkeepsie
Berry, Maryann Paradiso *minister*

Rochester
Hughes, Deborah L. *minister, director*
Lacey, Dorothy Ellen *theology studies educator, religious organization administrator*
Portanova, Carolyn Amick *religious organization administrator*
Santos, Wilma *missionary*
Tobin, Barbara Kay *minister*

Sidney
Marsi, Janice Michaels *religious organization administrator*

Trumansburg
Van Buren, Mary Lou *retired religious organization administrator*

Yorktown Heights
Braddock, Nonnie Clarke *religious organization administrator*

NORTH CAROLINA

Charlotte
Bender, Carol Till (Pinky Bender) *minister*
Ferm, Lois Roughan *religious organization administrator*

McKay-Wilkinson, Julie Ann *minister, marriage and family therapist*

Dunn
Davis, Dolly *religious organization administrator*

Garner
Henderson, Shirley Elizabeth *minister*

Greenville
Faircloth, Mary Williams *minister, educator*

Hendersonville
Butcher, Diane *chaplain, bereavement facilitator*

Monroe
Wallace, Patricia Ellen *minister*

Morehead City
Jones, Hilda Hobbs *minister*

Rocky Mount
Dickens, Alice McKnight *minister*

Winston Salem
Jenkins, Barbara Alexander *pastor and overseer*
Ludolf, Marilyn Marie Keaton *lay worker*

OHIO

Akron
Graham, DeBorah Denise *minister, educator*

Cincinnati
Anderson, Joan Balyeat *religion educator, minister*
Skavlem, Melissa Kline *publisher*

Cleveland
Borchert, Catherine Glennan *minister*
Guffey, Edith Ann *religious organization administrator*
Hafner, Laurinda Marie *minister*

Columbus
Boyd, Hazel *minister*
Smith, Marcia J. *pastor*

Dayton
Cunningham, Kima Hicks *minister, client services manager*

Fairlawn
France, Dorothy Daniel *minister*

Hannibal
Guyette, Diana *minister*

North Canton
Edwards, Sharon Marie *minister, educator*

Rootstown
Woodall, Susan Elaine *minister*

Saint Marys
Ball, Judy Kay *minister*

Springfield
Gesalman, Carol *minister*

Thornville
Taylor, Leslie Carole *minister*

Wauseon
Stutzman, Donna J. *minister*

West Manchester
Long, Valerie Jean *pastor*

Youngstown
Byrd, Swettie Lee *minister*

OKLAHOMA

Cache
Ayers, Betty Lou *missionary, pastor*

Chelsea
Taylor, Connie *minister*

Choctaw
Glavan, Denise Lynn *minister*

Del City
Wallace, Fannie Margaret *minister, religious organization administrator*

Enid
Varnell, Maxine Ann *minister*

Lawton
Cashion, Patricia Sue *minister*
Ellenbrook, Carolyn Kay *religious organization administrator*

Oklahoma City
Hampton, Carol McDonald *priest, educator, historian*
Ridley, Betty Ann *religious educator, lay worker*

Tulsa
Gottschalk, Sister Mary Therese *nun, hospital administrator*
Osborn, La Donna Carol *clergywoman*

Vinita
Wright, Jo Anne *Episcopal priest*

OREGON

Beaverton
Mitchell, Bettie Phaenon *religious organization administrator*

PENNSYLVANIA

Akron
Livingston, Margery Elsie *missionary, clinical psychologist*

Altoona
Arpino, Denise Marie *minister*

Baden
Pellegrino, Sister Mary R. *nun*

Bethlehem
Herbst, Patricia Carlisle *lay worker*

Boyertown
Craner, Wanda Dietz *clergywoman, therapist*

Clarion
Grejda, Gail Fulton *dean*

Columbia
Trout, Gwenn Louise *minister*

Erie
Jenkins, Janet S. *minister*

Greensburg
Blazina, Carole Marie *nun*

Harrisburg
Chambers, Clarice Lorraine *clergy, educational consultant*

Lancaster
Daugherty, Ruth Alice *religious association consultant*
Hubbard, Jayne Elizabeth *minister, marriage and family therapist*

Landisville
Steiner, Donna Forbes *minister, executive consultant*

Malvern
Brighton, Ruth Louise *lay worker, educator*

New Stanton
Black, Cora Jean *evangelist, wedding consultant*

Peckville
Miner, Virginia Ann *minister*

Philadelphia
Bracey, Cookie Frances Lee *minister*
Marple, Dorothy Jane *retired church executive*

Pittsburgh
Collins, Rose Ann *minister*
Muto, Susan Annette *religion educator, academic administrator*
Schaub, Marilyn McNamara *religion educator*

Plymouth
Campbell, Leanne Hays *pastor*

Port Allegany
McJunkin, Evon Marie Lloyd *minister*

Sayre
Bentley, Dianne H. Glover *minister, consultant*

Scranton
Balint, Annette *church administrator*

Valley Forge
Harvey, Carole (Kate Harvey) *minister, church official*

Wayne
Rabii, Patricia Berg *church administrator*

Wyncote
Boyer, Sister Mary Veronica *nun, art educator*

RHODE ISLAND

Woonsocket
Morris, Mary Elizabeth *pastor*

SOUTH CAROLINA

Charleston
Powell, Marilyn Lindeberg *minister*

Greenville
Jordan, Katie L. *minister*

Kingstree
Fulton, Addie Ruth *minister, social worker*

West Columbia
Perkins, Esther Tye *pastor*

SOUTH DAKOTA

Pierre
Hackenjos-Butler, Genie Marie *minister*

Viborg
Ehrke, Mindy Jo *minister*

TENNESSEE

Crossville
Ralstin, Betty Lou *religious organization administrator*

Knoxville
Wilhite, Nancy Jane *evangelist*

Loudon
Hallstrand, Sarah Laymon *denomination executive*

Nashville
Bigham, Wanda Durrett *religious organization administrator*

Nolensville
Lessard, Lisa Kathleen Hamlin *spiritual counselor*

TEXAS

Austin
Hitchcock, Joanna *publisher*
Worthing, Carol Marie *minister*

Canyon Lake
Reinhardt, Linda Kay *minister*

Conroe
Hinson, Cynthia Thomas *minister*

Dallas
Austin-Thorn, Cynthia Kay *religious organization administrator, poet*
Gross, Harriet P. Marcus *religious studies and writing educator*
Pauley, Shirley Stewart *religious organization executive*

Fort Worth
Lawson, Carole Jean *religious educator, author, poet*
Stratton, Margaret Anne *minister*
Yaites, LilliAnn *minister*

Houston
Cooper, Valerie Gail *minister*

Lake Dallas
Beard, Patricia Claire *minister, apparel designer*

Nacogdoches
Sims, Rita Louise *minister*

Pasadena
Hackler, Lisa Marguerite *minister*

Silsbee
Wilson, Mary Elizabeth *priest*

Vernon
Hodsden, Sara Marie *minister*

Waco
Lewis, Martha Nell *Christian educator, minister, expressive arts therapist*

Wiergate
Hunter, Georgia L. *clergywoman*

UTAH

Ogden
Harrington, Mary Evelina Paulson (Polly Harrington) *religious journalist, writer, educator*

VERMONT

Ludlow
Buswell, Jane H. *lay pastor*

White River Junction
Rutter, Frances Tompson *publisher*

VIRGINIA

Chantilly
Chrzanowski, Leye Jeannette *publisher*

Dinwiddie
McCray, Doris Raines *minister*

Falls Church
Bankson, Marjory Zoet *former religious association administrator*

Martinsville
Jones, Claudia Fentress *minister, artist*

Norfolk
Holley, Sharon Land *minister*

Oakton
Terzian, Grace Paine *publisher*

Richmond
Aigner, Emily Burke *Christian lay minister*

WASHINGTON

Bellevue
Sygeel, Crystal Renee *minister, consultant*

Chehalis
McQueen, Deva Revell *minister*

Elma
Houle, LouAnn *minister*

Moses Lake
Sanderson, Holladay Worth *priest*

Seattle
Burrows, Elizabeth MacDonald *religious organization executive, educator*

Fluke, Lyla Schram (Mrs. John M. Fluke Sr.) *publisher*
Young, Elizabeth *minister*

Tacoma
Reigstad, Ruth Elaine *lay worker, retired physical therapy consultant*

WEST VIRGINIA

Belington
McCartney, Rose Marie *minister*

Charleston
Leasor, Jane *religion and philosophy educator, musician*

Dunbar
Eliason, Pamela Parker *minister, social worker*

Fayetteville
Seay-Bell, Margaretta *pastoral counselor*

New Cumberland
Ford, Irene Elaine *pastor*

Wheeling
Thurston, Bonnie Bowman *religious educator, minister, poet*

WISCONSIN

Milwaukee
Blumberg, Sherry Helene *Jewish education educator*
Pitts, Gertrude Louise *minister*

Neenah
Brehm-Gruber, Therese Frances *minister, consulting psychologist*

Sun Prairie
Deaner, Nancy Marcy *religious studies educator, religious organization administrator*

WYOMING

Cody
Grimes, Daphne Buchanan *priest, artist*

Rock Springs
Jackman Dabb, Holly Pieper *publisher*

Torrington
Olenyik, Debra Ann *minister*

CANADA

BRITISH COLUMBIA

Prince George
Kerr, Nancy Karolyn *pastor, mental health services professional*

ONTARIO

Ottawa
Squire, Anne Marguerite *religious leader*

Toronto
McWilliam, Joanne Elizabeth *retired religion educator*

CHILE

Talca
McNamee, Sister Catherine *theology studies educator*

INDIA

Kerala
Devi, Amritanandamayi (Sri Mata Amritanandamayi Devi) *spiritual advisor*

ADDRESS UNPUBLISHED

Armentrout, Keri Janelle *minister, educator*
Banks, Deirdre Margaret *retired church organization administrator*
Barbey, Adélaïde *publisher*
Bauer, Louise May *minister, educator*
Born, Ethel Wolfe *religious writer*
Brostowski, Gayle A. *minister*
Brown, Othelia Victoria *minister*
Browne, Bonnie Esther *minister*
Burris-Schnur, Catherine *minister, pastoral psychotherapist, medical/surgical nurse, nursing educator*
Christopher, Sharon A. Brown *bishop*
Clemetson, Cheryl Price *minister, consultant*
Crabtree, Davida Foy *minister*
Craig, Judith *bishop*
Cranston, Pamela Lee *priest, writer*
Degrenia, Lisa Ann Moss *minister*
Dockstader, Deborah Ruth *minister*
Douglass, Jane Dempsey *theology educator*
English-Anderson, San Dei *minister*
Ewing, Elisabeth Anne Rooney *priest*
Fazio, Evelyn M. *publisher*
Finnegan, Sara Anne (Sara F. Lycett) *publisher*
Frankson-Kendrick, Sarah Jane *publisher*
Frost, Linda Gail *clergyman, hospital chaplain*

Fry, Hedy *member of parliament*
Gerald, Emma Jane *minister*
Giese, Judith Marie *minister*
Gregory, Myra May *religious organization administrator, educator*
Holleman, Sandy Lee *religious organization administrator*
Ingram, Barbara Averett *minister*
Jewell, Deborah Lynn *minister, educator*
Johnson, Jennie *chaplain, social worker*
Kibbe, Thana M. *pastor*
Kutz, Margaret *minister*
Latiano, Sister Olivia Maria *minister, secondary school educator*
Martin, Leanna Wright *minister*
McDermott, Lucinda Mary *ecumenical minister, teacher, philosopher, poet, author, psychologist*
McMaster, Belle Miller *religious organization administrator*
Miller, Mary Hotchkiss *lay worker*
Muhammad, Claudette Marie *religious organization administrator*
Nelson, Marcia Z. *writer, educator*
Roche, Barbara Anne *retired minister, editor*
Rock, Caro *publisher*
Rourke, Arlene Carol *publisher*
Rupp, Joyce M. *nun, writer*
Savitripriya, Swami *Hindu religious leader, author*
Sherrill, Katherine Clontz *minister*
Siegmund, Mary Kay *priest, counselor, marriage and family therapist*
Smith, D(aisy) Mullett *publisher*
Spake, Kluane *minister, writer*
Stanley, Myrtle Brooks *minister, educational and religious consultant*
Stewart, Barbara Lynn *church secretary, bookkeeper*
Ware, Sandra Marie *minister, music educator, composer*
Weber, Gloria Richie *retired minister, retired state legislator*
Weihmuller, Patricia A *retired minister, artist*
Weinkauf, Mary Louise Stanley *clergywoman*
Wharton, Margaret Mary *nun, education educator*
Whiting, Carol Louise *pastor*
Wilson, Lois M. *minister*
Wisehart, Mary Ruth *retired religious organization administrator*
Wolford, Kathryn Frances *religious organization executive*
Wooten, Joan Hedrich *minister*
Young, Emily Elizabeth *religious studies educator*
Zahar, Emily Elizabeth *religious studies minister*

SCIENCE: LIFE SCIENCE

UNITED STATES

ALABAMA

Anniston
Howell, Laura Clark *biologist, educator, small business owner*

Auburn
Guertal, Elizabeth Anderson *agronomist, educator*

Birmingham
Drentea, Patricia *science educator, researcher*
Elgavish, Ada *molecular and cellular biologist*
Finley, Sara Crews *medical geneticist, educator*
Michalek, Suzanne M. *biology educator*
Mueller, Robin Sue *biology educator*

Lineville
Craig, Linda (Teri) Carol *science educator*

Mobile
French, Elizabeth Irene *biology educator, violinist*

Monroeville
Loyd, Martha Rose *forester*

ARIZONA

Flagstaff
Grandy, Jerilee *research and evaluation consultant*

Taylor
Kerr, Barbara Prosser *research scientist, educator*

Tempe
Conrad, Cheryl Diane *behavioral neuroscientist*

Tucson
Kelley, Lydia *animal trainer*
Lai, LiWen *molecular geneticist, educator*

ARKANSAS

Russellville
Kondrick, Linda Carol *science educator*

CALIFORNIA

Berkeley
Burnside, Mary Beth *biology educator, researcher*
Harris, Eva *molecular biology educator*

Kohwi-Shigematsu, Terumi *research scientist*
Wake, Marvalee Hendricks *biology educator*
Yund, Mary Alice *biotechnology consultant*

Beverly Hills
Smith, Marilyn Noeltner *retired science educator*

Carmel
Pasten, Laura Jean *veterinarian*

Dana Point
Burrows, Barbara Ann *veterinarian*

Davis
Gottlieb, Leslie *geneticist, educator*
Horwitz, Barbara Ann *physiologist, educator, consultant*
Kuhl, Tonya L. *science educator*
Meyer, Margaret Eleanor *microbiologist, educator*

Del Mar
Farquhar, Marilyn Gist *cell biologist, pathologist, educator*

Foster City
Goldenstein, Lissa A. *biotechnology company executive*

Fullerton
Dickson, Kathryn *science educator*

Hermosa Beach
Chi, Lois Wang *retired biology educator, research scientist*

Kelseyville
Sandmeyer, E. E. *toxicologist, consultant*

La Jolla
Alvariño De Leira, Angeles (Angeles Alvariño) *biologist, oceanographer*
Baldridge, Kim *science educator*
Han, Wenge *research scientist*
Knowlton, Nancy *biologist*
Wong-Staal, Flossie *geneticist, medical educator*
Yuki, Goda *science educator*

Los Angeles
Craft, Cheryl Mae *neurobiologist, anatomist, researcher*
Szego, Clara Marian *cell biologist, educator*
Watkins, Diane Lucille *biology educator*
Wright, Sandra *science administrator*

Madera
Uan, Lyanna T. W. *pediatrician*

Malibu
Hunt, Valerie Virginia *electrophysiologist, educator*

Martinez
Kimbrell, Deborah Ann *geneticist, educator*

Moffett Field
Friedmann, Roseli Ocampo *microbiologist, educator*
Harper, Lynn D. *biologist*

Monterey
Packard, Julie *aquarium administrator*

Mountain View
Mansfield, Elaine Schultz *molecular geneticist, automation specialist*

Northridge
Sparling, Mary Lee *biology educator*

Novato
Turner, Mabel Croughan *retired microbiologist*

Oakland
Earle, Sylvia Alice *research biologist, oceanographer*

Oceanside
Paxton, Mary Jean Wallace *science educator*

Pacific Grove
Beidleman, Linda Havighurst *biologist*

Palm Desert
Sausman, Karen *zoological park administrator*

Pebble Beach
Sanford-Hugus, Barbara *geneticist, consultant*

Riverside
Raikhel, Natasha V. *plant cell biology educator*

San Diego
Chory, Joanne *plant biologist*
Hemmingsen, Barbara Bruff *microbiologist, educator*
Hogan, Sheila Maureen *biology educator, nurse*

San Francisco
Bargmann, Cornelia I. *neuroscientist, science educator*
Blackburn, Elizabeth Helen *molecular biologist*
Dallman, Mary F. *physiologist, science educator*
Guo, Su *science educator*
Schimenti, Cheryl D. *retired research scientist*
Werb, Zena *cell biologist, educator*

San Jose
Moates, Betty Carolyn *microbiologist, computer consultant*
Moore, Melanie Ruth *veterinary technician*

San Juan Capistrano
White, Beverly Jane *cytogeneticist*

San Luis Obispo
Waldo, Anna Lee *retired science educator, writer*

Santa Barbara
Tucker, Shirley Lois Cotter *botany educator, researcher*

Santa Clara
Siegal, Susan E. *biotechnology company executive*

Santa Cruz
Langenheim, Jean Harmon *biologist, educator*

Santa Monica
Honour, Lynda Charmaine *research scientist, educator, psychotherapist*

South San Francisco
Gerritsen, Mary Ellen *vascular and cell biologist*
Rollence, Michele Lynette *molecular biologist*

Stanford
Arvin, Ann Margaret *microbiology and immunology educator, researcher*
Cork, Linda Katherine *veterinary pathologist, educator*
Ehrlich, Anne Howland *research biologist*
Francke, Uta *medical geneticist, genetics researcher, educator*
Long, Sharon Rugel *molecular biologist, plant biology educator*
Shapiro, Lucille *molecular biology educator*

Stockton
Magness, Rhonda Ann *microbiologist*

Sylmar
Faye, Thalia Garin *retired microbiologist, educator*

Tulare
Vickrey, Herta M. *microbiologist*

Valencia
Fogel, Jennifer Lynn *technical associate, researcher*

Wilmington
McAlpine, Mary Helen *nutritional science educator*

COLORADO

Boulder
Mitchell, Joan LaVerne *research scientist*

Carbondale
Cowgill, Ursula Moser *biologist, educator, environmental consultant*

Colorado Springs
Engfer, Susan Marvel *zoological park executive*
Herron, Sherry Shelton *biology educator*

Denver
Ehret, Josephine Mary *microbiologist, researcher*
Horwitz, Kathryn Bloch *molecular biologist, educator, breast cancer researcher*

Northglenn
Hemlock, Roberta Leigh *veterinary technician*

CONNECTICUT

Hamden
Adair, Eleanor Reed *environmental biologist*

New Haven
Doudna, Jennifer A. *molecular biologist, educator*
Kwiatkowski, Jonna M. *research scientist*
Ruddle, Nancy Hartman *microbiology educator, microbiologist, researcher*
Slayman, Carolyn Walch *geneticist, educator*
Tanaka, Kay *genetics educator*

New London
Tassinari, Melissa Sherman *toxicologist*

DISTRICT OF COLUMBIA

Washington
Berg, Patricia Elene *molecular biologist*
Chotin, Elizabeth Ettlinger *research organization administrator*
DeGiovanni-Donnelly, Rosalie Frances *biology researcher, educator*
Didion, Catherine Jay *science association administrator*
Kleiman, Devra Gail *zoologist, zoological park research scientist*
Nightingale, Elena Ottolenghi *geneticist, pediatrician, academic administrator, educator*
Pellmar, Terry C. *neurophysiologist, researcher*
Soloway, Rose Ann Gould *clinical toxicologist*
Spelman, Lucy H. *zoological park administrator*
Tidball, M. Elizabeth Peters *physiologist, educator, science administrator, researcher*
Torrey, Barbara Boyle *research council administrator*
Watkins, Shirley Robinson *agriculture department administrator*

FLORIDA

Coral Springs
Bolene, Rosalie Steele (Margaret Bolene) *bacteriologist, volunteer*

Fort Pierce
Rice, Mary Esther *biologist*

Gainesville
Drummond, Willa Hendricks *physiology and medical educator*
Green, Eleanor Myers *veterinarian, educator*
Grobman, Hulda Gross (Mrs. Arnold B. Grobman) *retired health sciences educator*
Hoy, Marjorie Ann *entomology educator*
Martin, Sarah Carrier *science educator*
Schmidt-Nielsen, Bodil Mimi (Mrs. Roger G. Chagnon) *physiologist, educator*

Lakeland
Pospichal, Marcie W. *neuroscientist, psychologist, educator*

Miami
Baumbach, Lisa Lorraine *research scientist*

Niceville
Morris Schweitzer, Nancy N. *retired science educator, writer*

Ruskin
Briscoe, Anne M. *retired scientist, educator*

Tallahassee
James, Frances Crews *retired zoology educator*

GEORGIA

Athens
Meyer, Judy L. *science educator, director*

Atlanta
Gyamfi, Phyllis *research scientist, researcher*

Augusta
Kutlar, Ferdane *genetics educator, researcher*

Decatur
Freemont, Andria Shamona *laboratory administrator*

Newton
Blood, Elizabeth R. *research scientist*

HAWAII

Honolulu
Fok, Agnes Kwan *retired cell biologist, educator*
Kay, Elizabeth Alison *zoology educator*
Uchida, Janice Yukiko *plant pathologist/mycologist, researcher*

IDAHO

Boise
Woods, Jean Frahm *science educator*

Moscow
Moffitt, Christine M. *biologist, educator*

ILLINOIS

Carbondale
Renzaglia, Karen A. *biologist, educator*

Chicago
De, Devasmita *research aquarist*
Drantz, Veronica Ellen *science educator and consultant*
Fuchs, Elaine V. *molecular biologist, educator*
Lindquist, Susan Lee *biology and microbiology educator*
McClintock, Martha K. *biologist, educator*
Mullins, Obera *retired microbiologist*
Rothman-Denes, Lucia Beatriz *biology educator*
Straus, Lorna Puttkammer *biology educator*

Dekalb
Vary, Patricia Susan *biologist, educator, retired geneticist*

Macomb
Barclay, Martha Jane *science educator, research scientist*

Normal
Davis, Janet R. Beach *science educator*

North Chicago
Sladek, Celia Davis *neuroscientist, educator*

Orland Park
Burfeind, Betty Ruth *science educator*

River Grove
Gardner, Sandi B. *biology educator*

Schaumburg
Wernette, Karen Marie *veterinarian*

Urbana
Berenbaum, May Roberta *entomology educator*

Westchester
Webb, Emily *retired plant morphologist*

INDIANA

Bloomington
Ketterson, Ellen D. *biologist, educator*

Indianapolis
Cliff, Johnnie Marie *mathematics and chemistry educator*
Settles, Holly Arlene (Holly Woloszyk) *microbiologist*
Zambrano-Dumaual, Carmen Michelle *molecular biologist*

Lanesville
Cleveland, Peggy Rose Richey *cytotechnologist*

Madison
Grahn, Ann Wagoner *retired scientific policy officer*

West Lafayette
Raskin, Rose Esther *veterinary educator*

IOWA

Ames
Melby, Janet Nieuwsma *research scientist*

Cedar Rapids
Magill, Nancy Gene *microbiologist, educator*

Iowa City
Maxson, Linda Ellen *biologist, educator*
Stay, Barbara *zoologist, educator*

KANSAS

Hays
Talbott, Nancy Costigan *science educator*

Isabel
Brant, Dorris Ellen Stapleton *bacteriologist, music educator*

Lawrence
Lane, Meredith Anne *botany educator, museum curator*

Manhattan
Kirkham, M. B. *plant physiologist, educator*

KENTUCKY

Olive Hill
Knipp, Jenny L. *science educator*

LOUISIANA

New Orleans
Beard, Elizabeth Letitia *physiologist, educator*
Ivens, Mary Sue *microbiologist, mycologist*
Lingle, Sarah Elizabeth *research scientist*
Pedersen, Pedie *physiology educator*

MAINE

Castine
Jones, Kerri-Ann *director scientific organization*

MARYLAND

Baltimore
Clements, Janice *science educator*
Dawson, Valina L. *science educator*
Greider, Carol Widney *molecular biology educator*
Habermann, Helen Margaret *plant physiologist, educator*
Hansen, Barbara Caleen *physiologist, science educator*
Seydoux, Geraldine *molecular biologist*
Stewart, Doris Mae *biology educator*
Tamminga, Carol Ann *neuroscientist*

Beltsville
Adams, Jean Ruth *retired entomologist, biomedical researcher*
Collins, Anita Marguerite *research geneticist*
Palm, Mary Egdahl *mycologist*

Bethesda
Burns, Drusilla Lorene *microbiologist*
Dorr, Ann Pierce *science educator*
Francomano, Clair Ann *geneticist*
Greenberg, Judith Horovitz *genetics and developmental biology administrator*
Guttman, Helene Nathan *biomedical research consultant, transpersonal counselor, regression therapist*
Jordan, Elke *molecular biologist, government medical research institute executive*
Underwood, Brenda S. *information specialist, microbiologist, grants administrator*
Ungerleider, Leslie G. *neuroscientist*
Wolpert-DeFilippes, Mary K. *science administrator*

College Park
Gantt, Elisabeth *plant biology educator, researcher*

Frederick
Jenkins, Nancy A. *research scientist*

Gaithersburg
Powell, Lura J. *science association administrator*

Landover
Frederick, Amy L. *science administrator*

Potomac
Paper, Susanne Abby Babin *science educator, writer*

Rockville
Bayne, Kathryn Ann Louise *veterinarian*
Clancy, Carolyn *science foundation director, researcher, educator*
Fraser, Claire M. *research scientist, science administrator*
Gougé, Susan Cornelia Jones *microbiologist*

Silver Spring
Kant, Gloria Jean *retired neuroscientist, researcher*

Suitland
Vandiver, Pamela Bowren *science educator*

West River
Howl, Joanne Healey *veterinarian, writer*

MASSACHUSETTS

Amherst
Litsky, Bertha Yanis *microbiologist, artist*
Margulis, Lynn (Lynn Alexander) *evolutionist, educator*
Palser, Barbara F. *botany researcher, retired educator*

Boston
Hochschild, Ann *molecular biologist*
Krolewski, Bozena K. *molecular biologist, researcher, cell biologist*
Leeman, Susan Epstein *neuroscientist, educator*
Mathis, Diane *cell biologist, educator*
Morton, Cynthia C. *geneticist*
Ratner, Marcia *research scientist*
Shatz, Carla J. *biology educator*
Yee, Amy Sumei *science educator*

Cambridge
Arkhipova, Irina R. *biologist*
Hopkins, Nancy H. *biology educator*
Hubbard, Ruth *biology educator*
Kanwisher, Nancy G. *neuroscientist*
Pardue, Mary-Lou *biology educator*
Pierce, Naomi Ellen *biology educator, researcher*
Torriani-Gorini, Annamaria *microbiologist, educator*
Villa-Komaroff, Lydia *molecular biologist, educator, university official*
Wurtman, Judith Joy *research scientist*

Newton
Bronstein, Irena *science administrator, consultant*

Northfield
Knox, Carol B. *biologist, educator*

South Hadley
Townsend, Jane Kaltenbach *biologist, educator*

Weston
Marshall, Jean McElroy *physiologist*

Worcester
Kennedy, Linda Mann *neuroscience educator, researcher*

MICHIGAN

Ann Arbor
Akil, Huda *neuroscientist, educator, researcher*
Sloat, Barbara Furin *cell biologist, educator*

Bloomfield Hills
Miller, Dorothy Anne Smith *retired cytogenetics educator*

Detroit
Hill, Elizabeth Marie *research scientist*

East Lansing
Fluck, Michele M(arguerite) *biology educator*
McMeekin, Dorothy *botany, plant pathology educator*
Patterson, Maria Jevitz *microbiology-pediatric infectious disease educator*

Rockford
Irish, Diana Maria *wildlife rehabilitation agent*

MINNESOTA

Duluth
Heller, Lois Jane *physiologist, educator, researcher*

Minneapolis
Gudmundson, Barbara Rohrke *ecologist*
Hill, Tessa *president non profit environmental group*
Rahman, Yueh-Erh *biology educator*
Serstock, Doris Shay *retired microbiologist, educator, civic worker*

Morris
Ordway, Ellen *biologist, educator, entomologist, researcher*

Rochester
Shepard, Laura Ann *microbiologist, researcher*

Saint Paul
Davis, Margaret Bryan *paleoecology researcher, educator*
Ehlke, Nancy Jo *agronomist*
Kerr, Sylvia Joann *science educator*
May, Georgiana *biologist, educator*

Taylors Falls
Yeager, Debra Lyn *science educator*

MISSISSIPPI

Biloxi
McCaughan, Della Marie *retired science educator*

Meridian
Smith, Lois Adkins *science educator*

Walls
Tharnish, Rose Maries Lehman *veterinarian*

MISSOURI

Eureka
Lindsey, Susan Lyndaker *zoologist*

New Haven
Roth, Nancy Louise *former nurse, veterinarian*

Saint Louis
Bourne, Carol Elizabeth Mulligan *biology educator, phycologist*
Hawkins, Peggy Anne *veterinarian*
Schaal, Barbara Anna *evolutionary biologist, educator*
Sutter, Jane Elizabeth *science educator, writer, conservationist*

Springfield
Mathis, Alicia *biologist*

Windyville
Condron, Barbara O'Guinn *metaphysics educator, school administrator, publisher*

NEBRASKA

Lincoln
Vidaver, Anne Marie *plant pathology educator*

Omaha
Rogan, Eleanor Groeniger *cancer researcher, educator*
Wong, Yoke Cheng *food scientist, musician*

NEW HAMPSHIRE

Hanover
Burchenal, Joan Riley *science educator*
Spiegel, Evelyn Sclufer *biology educator, researcher*

NEW JERSEY

Camden
Watkins, LaSandra *science educator*

East Brunswick
Dombrowski, Anne Wesseling *retired microbiologist, researcher*

East Hanover
Nemecek, Georgina Marie *molecular pharmacologist*

Haddonfield
Collins, Angelo *science educator*

Kenilworth
Kravec, Cynthia Vallen *microbiologist*

New Brunswick
Ralston, Sarah Lucille *veterinarian, educator*

Newark
Weis, Judith Shulman *biology educator*

Piscataway
Essien, Francine B. *geneticist, educator*
Liu, Alice Y. C. *biology educator*

Princeton
Altmann, Jeanne *zoologist, educator*
Bassler, Bonnie *molecular biologist*
Chedid, Lisa Leasure *food scientist*
Gould, Elizabeth *neuroscientist, educator*
Marshall, Carol Joyce *clinical project director*
Witkin, Evelyn Maisel *retired geneticist*

Rahway
Strack, Alison Merwin *neurobiologist*

Shrewsbury
Westerman, Liane Marie *research scientist executive*

Toms River
Kudryasheva, Aleksandra A. *scientist, researcher, educator*

Westfield
Brown, Shirley Mark *retired science administrator*

Wyckoff
Cropper, Susan Peggy *veterinarian*

NEW MEXICO

Albuquerque
Henderson, Rogene Faulkner *toxicologist, researcher*

Santa Fe
Harding, Marie *ecological executive, artist*
Myers, Charlotte Will *biology educator*

NEW YORK

Albany
Hitchcock, Karen Ruth *biology educator, university dean, academic administrator*
Stewart, Margaret McBride *biology educator, researcher*

Bronx
Cannizzaro, Linda Ann *geneticist, researcher*
Waelsch, Salome Gluecksohn *geneticist, educator*

Bronxville
Hutchison, Dorris Jeannette *retired microbiologist, educator*

Brooklyn
Altura, Bella T. *physiologist, educator*
Carswell, Lois Malakoff *botanical gardens executive, consultant*
Gootman, Phyllis Myrna *physiology, neuroscience and biophysics educator*
Jacobson, Leslie Sari *biologist, educator*
Oley, Nancy H. *psychobiologist, educator*
Patan, Sybill Petra *research scientist*
Zuk, Judith *botanic garden administrator*

Flushing
Schnall, Edith Lea *microbiologist, educator*

Garden City
Podwall, Kathryn Stanley *biology educator*

Ithaca
Nasrallah, June *plant pathologist, department chairman*

New York
Bucolo, Gail Ann *biotechnologist*
Calame, Kathryn Lee *microbiologist, educator*
Clarke, Marjorie Jane *environmental educator, consultant, author, researcher*
Davis, Jessica G. *clinical geneticist, pediatrician*
Eckhardt, Laurel Ann *biologist, researcher, educator*
Grafstein, Bernice *physiology and neuroscience educator, researcher*
Hirschhorn, Rochelle *genetics educator*
Ho, Betty Juenyü Yulin *physiological educator, researcher*
Mei, Dolores Marie *research administrator*
Prives, Carol *biologist, educator*

Port Chester
Brescia, Alicia *science educator, vice principal*

Potsdam
Usher, Bethany McKay *biological anthropology educator*

Purchase
Ehrman, Lee *geneticist, educator*

Rochester
Rodgers, Suzanne Hooker *ergonomics consultant, physiologist*

Southampton
Shapiro, Anna *microbiologist, researcher*

Staten Island
Garcia, Minerva A.F. *bacteriologist, research and clinical laboratory scientist*

NORTH CAROLINA

Chapel Hill
Farber, Rosann Alexander *geneticist, educator*
Mueller, Nancy Schneider *retired biology educator*

Durham
Hogan, Brigid L. *molecular biologist*
Rouse, Doris Jane *physiologist, research administrator*
Watkins, Melynda *research scientist, chemist*

Raleigh
Burkholder, Joann M. *botany educator*
Triantaphyllou, H. H. *plant pathologist*

Research Triangle Park
Haynes, Victoria F. *science administrator*

NORTH DAKOTA

Bisbee
Keller, Michelle R. *science educator, secondary education educator*

OHIO

Bowling Green
Clark, Eloise Elizabeth *biologist, educator*
Heckman, Carol A. *biology educator*

Canton
Bernstein, Penny L. *biologist, educator*

Cincinnati
McDaniels, Audrey Evelyn *microbiologist*

Columbus
Snyder, Susan Leach *science educator, writer*
Westman, Judith Ann *clinical geneticist*

Delaware
Fry, Anne Evans *zoology educator*

Oxford
Rypstra, Ann *zoology educator*

Wooster
Saif, Linda J. *animal scientist*

OREGON

Bend
Collins, Sally Duke *forest service manager*

Corvallis
Lubchenco, Jane *marine biologist, educator*

Klamath Falls
Dow, Martha Anne *biology educator*

Pendleton
Klepper, Elizabeth Lee *physiologist*

Portland
Balkowiec, Agnieszka Zofia *science educator, researcher*

PENNSYLVANIA

Annville
Verhoek, Susan Elizabeth *botany educator*

Breinigsville
de Limantour, Clarice Barr *food scientist*

Gladwyne
Allen, Theresa Ohotnicky *neurobiologist, consultant*

Hershey
Hopper, Anita Klein *molecular genetics educator*

Lansdale
Holloway, M(ary) Katharine *research scientist, chemist*

Philadelphia
Davies, Helen C. *microbiology educator*
DiBerardino, Marie Antoinette *developmental biologist, educator*
Eisenstein, Toby K. *microbiology educator*
McKeon, Judith C. *horticulturist, writer*
Patrick, Ruth (Mrs. Ruth Hodge Van Dusen) *limnologist, diatom taxonomist, educator*
Schneider, Adele Sandra *clinical geneticist*
Skalka, Anna Marie *molecular biologist, virologist*
Van Bockstaele, Elisabeth Jeanne *neuroscientist, researcher*

Pittsburgh
Cruz, Robyn Flaum *research scientist, clinician*
Edmonds, Mary Patricia *biological sciences educator*
Gollin, Susanne Merle *cytogeneticist, cell biologist*
Jones, Elizabeth Winifred *biology educator*
Marazita, Mary Louise *genetics researcher*
Morgan, Olga Plumauri *microbiologist, researcher*
Worley, Virginia King *microbiologist*

University Park
Fedoroff, Nina Vsevolod *research scientist, consultant, educator*
Fullerton, Stephanie Malia *research scientist*

West Chester
Flood, Dorothy Garnett *neuroscientist*

West Point
Gehris, Tamar K. *biologist*

RHODE ISLAND

Kingston
Hufnagel, Linda Ann *biology educator, researcher*
Markin, Karen Mary *research scientist, journalist*

Providence
Gerbi, Susan Alexandra *biology educator*
Schmitt, Johanna Marie *plant population biologist, educator*

SOUTH CAROLINA

Aiken
Wood, Susan *applied technology center executive*

Anderson
Rhoe, Wilhelmina Robinson *retired science educator*

Greenville
Cureton, Claudette Hazel Chapman *biology educator*

SOUTH DAKOTA

Rapid City
Rogers, Deborah S. *human biology educator, writer*

TENNESSEE

Bartlett
Crudup, Pamela Tracy Parham *science educator, writer*

Johnson City
Rasch, Ellen Myrberg *cell biology educator*

Knoxville
Anderson, Ilse Janell *clinical geneticist*

Memphis
Harris, Cora Lee *science educator, small business owner*
Hofmann, Polly A. *physiologist, science educator*
Howe, Martha Morgan *microbiologist, educator*

Nashville
Orgebin-Crist, Marie-Claire *biology educator*

Oak Ridge
Thompson, Dorothea Kathleen *microbiologist*

Smithville
Vaughn, Eulalia Cobb *retired science educator, mathematician*

TEXAS

Austin
Drummond Borg, Lesley Margaret *clinical geneticist*
Fryxell, Greta Albrecht *marine botany educator, oceanographer*
Simon, Erica Cecelia *research scientist, consultant*
Simpson, Beryl Brintnall *botany educator*

Beaumont
Hunt, Madelyn Dora *biologist, educator, director*

College Station
Beaver, Bonnie Veryle *veterinarian, educator*

Dallas
Vitetta, Ellen Shapiro *microbiologist educator, immunologist*

Hempstead
Propst, Catherine Lamb *biotechnology company executive*

Houston
Butel, Janet Susan *research scientist, virology educator*
DeBakey, Lois *science communications educator, editor, writer*
DeBakey, Selma *science communications educator, writer, editor, lecturer*
Durham, Susan K. *research scientist*
Harris, Deborah Ann *science educator*
Seaton, Alberta Jones *biologist, educator, consultant*

San Antonio
Corrigan, Helen González *retired cytologist*
Wang, Yufeng *science educator*

UTAH

Logan
Shultz, Leila McReynolds *botanist, educator*

Salt Lake City
Emerson, Sharon B. *biology researcher and educator*

VERMONT

Burlington
Hendley, Edith Di Pasquale *physiology and neuroscience educator*

Morrisville
Lechevalier, Mary Pfeil *retired microbiologist, educator*

VIRGINIA

Alexandria
Woolley, Mary Elizabeth *research administrator*

Arlington
Barak, Eve Ida *science administrator*
Whyte, Nancy Gooch *microbiologist, chemist*

Bristol
Brittle, Linda Vaughan *reading and behavioral science educator*

Manassas
Isbister, Jenifer Diane Wilkinson *microbiologist, researcher, educator, consultant*

Richmond
Gregory, Jean Winfrey *ecologist, educator*

Virginia Beach
Simmons, Marsha Thrift *science and reading educator, musician*

WASHINGTON

Bellingham
Ross, June Rosa Pitt *biologist, educator*

Mountlake Terrace
Cannon, Christine Anne *veterinarian*

Pullman
Sprunger, Leslie Karen *physiologist, educator*
Thomashow, Linda Suzanne *microbiologist*

Seattle
Boersma, P. Dee *marine biologist, educator*
Brownstein, Barbara Lavin *geneticist, educator, university official*
Disteche, Christine M. *geneticist*
Hendrickson, Anita Elizabeth *biology educator*
King, Mary-Claire *geneticist, educator*
Riddiford, Lynn Moorhead *zoologist, educator*
Wilson, Pamela *microbiologist, educator*

WISCONSIN

Elkhart Lake
Zieve, Charlotte R. *research scientist*

Madison
Beyer-Mears, Annette *physiologist*
Kimble, Judith E. *molecular biologist, cell biologist*
Marrett, Cora B. *science educator*
Zedler, Joy Buswell *ecological sciences educator*

Milwaukee
Schumann, Gail L. *plant pathologist, educator*

WYOMING

Cheyenne
Zumo, Billie Thomas *biologist*

CANADA

BRITISH COLUMBIA

Sidney
Bigelow, Margaret Elizabeth Barr (M.E. Barr) *mycology educator*

ONTARIO

Ottawa
Adams, Gabrielle *biologist*

QUEBEC

Montreal
Gibbs, Sarah Preble *biologist, educator*

AUSTRALIA

Melbourne
Bishop, Ruth Frances *microbiologist, research scientist, educator*

ADDRESS UNPUBLISHED

Aikens, Martha Brunette *national park service administrator*
Auyong, Jan *biologist*
Barnes-Kempton, Isabel Janet *microbiology educator, college dean*
Bick, Katherine Livingstone *neurobiologist, international liaison, consultant*
Black, Sharon Sue Gibbons *veterinary pathologist, educator*
Block, Barbara Ann *biology educator*
Brenchley, Jean Elnora *microbiologist, researcher, science administrator*
Burdett, Barbra Elaine *biology educator*
Canulla, Theresa *microbiologist*
Champey, Elaine *science and technology research coordinator*
Clark, Mary Etta *science writing consultant*
Cole, Rachel P. *science educator*
Colwell, Rita Rossi *microbiologist, former federal agency administrator, medical educator*
Coyle, Marie Bridget *retired microbiologist, retired lab administrator*
Durham, Thena Monts *microbiologist, researcher, management executive*
Feir, Dorothy Jean *entomologist, physiologist, educator*
Glass, Glenda June *clinical microbiologist*
Grand, Cindy *foundation director*
Harlin, Marilyn Miler *marine botany educator, researcher, consultant*
Hildebrand, Verna Lee *human ecology educator*
Howard-Peebles, Patricia N. *clinical cytogeneticist*
Jacoby, Teresa Michelle *animal behaviorist, business owner, entrepreneur*
Keiser, Nanette Marie *research associate, project administrator*
Kelman, Lori Macellaro *biology educator, molecular biology researcher*
Kerr, Janet Spence *physiologist, pharmacologist, researcher*
Leventhal, Ruth *retired parasitology educator, university official*
Marino, Mary Q. *research scientist*
Maroni, Donna Farolino *biologist, researcher*
Massaro, Linda P. *science foundation executive*
Metzler, Ruth Horton *genealogical educator*
Mitchell, Margaret Yvonne *forester*
Monzingo, Agnes Yvonne *veterinary technician*
Palumbo, Lucille A. *microbiologist*
Peaslee, Margaret Mae Hermanek *zoology educator*
Pielou, Evelyn C. *biologist*
Player, Audrey Nell *research scientist*
Porter, Leah LeEarle *biological researcher, industry executive*
Potts, Alison Jean *neuroscience medical liaison*
Prazak, Bessmarie Lillian *science educator*
Russell, Liane Brauch *retired geneticist*
Samuels, Linda S. *science administrator*
Scheuerle, Angela Elizabeth *geneticist*
Setser, Carole Sue *food science educator*
Shands, Gail Maxine *environmental scientist*
Shepard, Katherine *science educator, consultant*
Stark, Nellie May *forester, ecologist, educator*
Stewart, Karen Elizabeth Victoria *research scientist, artist*
Tatrow, Kristin *research scientist*
Thomas, Teresa Ann *microbiologist, educator*
Topolski, Catherine *science educator*
Washington, Josephine Harriet *biologist, endocrinologist, educator*
Willson, Mary Frances *ecology researcher, educator*
Yoder, Elizabeth Jane *neuroscience researcher*
Young, Judith Anne *animal conservationist*

SCIENCE: MATHEMATICS AND COMPUTER SCIENCE *See also* **INFORMATION TECHNOLOGY**

UNITED STATES

ALABAMA

Birmingham
Binion, Linda Diane *computer systems research specialist*

Huntsville
Pruitt, Alice Fay *mathematician, engineer*

ARIZONA

Casa Grande
Urban, Carrie *computer specialist*

Phoenix
Hulet, Nicole *computer consultant, poet, artist*

Scottsdale
McCabe, Mary Williamson *computer systems analyst*

ARKANSAS

Fort Smith
Smith-Leins, Terri L. *mathematics educator*

Helena
Stroope, Kay *mathematician, educator*

CALIFORNIA

Berkeley
Ratner, Marina *mathematician, educator, researcher*
Yu, Bin *statistician, educator*

El Cerrito
Stemmark, Joan Kerr *mathematics educator*

Hayward
Duncan, Doris Gottschalk *information systems educator*

La Jolla
Terras, Audrey Anne *mathematics educator*
Zyroff, Ellen Slotoroff *information scientist, classicist, educator*

Laguna Hills
Green, Millie Ann *mathematician, educator*

Los Angeles
Dabrowska, Dorota Maria *statistician, educator*

Newport Beach
Duvall, Florence Marie *software engineer*

Oxnard
Neilson, Jane Scott *mathematics educator*

Palo Alto
Sproule, Betty Ann *computer industry strategic consultant*

Presidio of Monterey
Dulo, Donna Ann *computer scientist, consultant*

Redondo Beach
Woike, Lynne Ann *computer scientist*

San Bruno
Olson, Julie Ann *systems consultant, educator*

San Jose
Ho, Yinhsin *retired mathematician, artist*

San Luis Obispo
Itnyre, Jacqueline Harriet *systems analyst*
McQuaid, Patricia A. *information systems educator*

San Marino
Lashley, Virginia Stephenson Hughes *retired computer science educator*

San Rafael
Barker, Celeste Arlette *computer scientist*

Santa Rosa
Wiggins, Patricia Ann *computer systems analyst, state legislator*

Stanford
Whittemore, Alice *biostatistician*

Stockton
Bickford, Melissa A. *internet administrator*

Walnut
Weisbart, Jennifer Rachel *mathematician, educator*

Wilmington
Bornino-Glusac, Anna Maria *mathematics educator*

Woodland Hills
Fung, Flora Lik-Yuen *statistician, consultant*

COLORADO

Longmont
McEachern, Susan Mary *information technology specialist*
Venrick, Kristie Lund *mathematics educator*

CONNECTICUT

Danbury
Wright, Marie Anne *management information systems educator*

Fairfield
Shaffer, Dorothy Browne *retired mathematician, educator*

Manchester
Sears, Sandra Lee *computer consultant*

Oakdale
Dailey, Judy (Judy St. Marie) *mathematician, director, mathematician, consultant*

Vernon Rockville
Davis, Nancy Costello *retired educator*

DISTRICT OF COLUMBIA

Washington
Bailey, Judy Long *outreach and education specialist, social worker*
Baran, Christine *systems analyst*
Crawford, Natalie Wilson *applied mathematician*
Gray, Mary Wheat *statistician, lawyer*
Kahlow, Barbara Fenvessy *statistician*
Powell, Margaret Ann Simmons *computer scientist*
Raphael, Louise Arakelian *mathematician, educator*

FLORIDA

Fort Lauderdale
Littman, Marlyn Kemper *information scientist, educator*

LaBelle
Etgeton, Cassandra Zehntner *mathematician, educator*

Miami
Austin-Hill, Suzanne S. *mathematician, educator*
Collier, Courtney Carole *mathematics educator*
Dimitriou, Dolores Ennis *computer consultant*

Saint Petersburg
White, June Miller *mathematics educator, educational consultant*

GEORGIA

Alpharetta
Sedivec, Mary Lynn *systems development manager*

Augusta
Craig, Cynthia Mae *mathematics educator*

Brunswick
Mihal, Sandra Powell *systems analyst*

Marietta
Rutherfoord, Rebecca Hudson *computer science educator*

Milledgeville
Sargent, Diane Robertson *mathematician, educator*

Norcross
Bennett, Catherine June *information technology executive, educator, consultant*

Savannah
John, Selena Latricia *systems analyst*

HAWAII

Hilo
Gersting, Judith Lee *computer scientist, educator, computer scientist, researcher*

IDAHO

Idaho Falls
Kirkland, Judy Joylene *computer specialist*

ILLINOIS

Chicago
Kirkpatrick, Anne Saunders *systems analyst*
Larson, Nancy Celeste *computer systems manager*

Dekalb
Sons, Linda Ruth *mathematician, educator*

Evanston
Bellow, Alexandra *mathematician, educator*

Hinsdale
Bazik, Edna Frances *mathematician, educator*

La Grange Park
Butler, Margaret Kampschaefer *retired computer scientist*

Mc Gaw Park
Risen-White, Angela Lorri *systems analyst*

Palatine
Bender, Virginia Best *computer scientist, educator*

Urbana
Liebman, Judith Rae Stenzel *operations research educator*
Williams, Martha Ethelyn *information science educator*

Westchester
Pavelka, Elaine Blanche *mathematics educator*

INDIANA

Indianapolis
Becker, Karla Lynn *systems analyst*

IOWA

Des Moines
Wilson, Sal *systems analyst*

Grinnell
Ferguson, Pamela Anderson *mathematics educator, educational administrator*

KANSAS

Kansas City
Davis, Kathy E. *information analyst*

Wichita
Palmer, Ada Margaret *systems analyst, consultant*

KENTUCKY

Harrodsburg
Hammond, Debbie Johnson *computer analyst*

Louisville
Greaver, Joanne Hutchins *mathematics educator, author*
Rahm, Mary Ellen *statistical clerk*

Richmond
King, Amy Cathryne Patterson *retired mathematics educator, researcher*

LOUISIANA

Minden
Kimball, Charlotte Elizabeth *systems analyst, writer, retired military officer*

MARYLAND

Baltimore
Choudhury, Dipa *mathematician, educator*
Lidtke, Doris Keefe *retired computer science educator*

Bethesda
Pollard, Bette Marlene *computer scientist*

College Park
White, Marilyn Domas *information science educator*

Columbia
Gregorie, Corazon Arzalem *operations supervisor*

Gaithersburg
Rosenblatt, Joan Raup *mathematical statistician*

Hyattsville
Jones, Gretchen Kuykendall *computer specialist, statistician*

Perryville
Dunne, Judith Doyle *information scientist, educator*

Potomac
Medin, Julia Adele *mathematics educator, researcher*
Peters, Carol Beattie Taylor (Mrs. Frank Albert Peters) *mathematician*

Silver Spring
Sammet, Jean E. *computer scientist*

MASSACHUSETTS

Boston
Schribman, Shelley Iris *database engineer, consultant*

Brookline
Schnipper, Sydra *mathematics educator*

Cambridge
Grosz, Barbara Jean *computer science educator*
Lipson, Pamela *information scientist*
Lynch, Nancy Ann *computer scientist, educator*
Roberts, Nancy *computer educator*

Duxbury
Thrasher, Dianne Elizabeth *mathematics educator, computer consultant*

Medford
Cowen, Lenore Jennifer *mathematician, educator, computer scientist*

Newton Center
Williamson, Susan *mathematician, educator*

MICHIGAN

Ann Arbor
Conway, Lynn *computer scientist, electrical engineer, educator*

Bloomfield Hills
Nuss, Shirley Ann *computer coordinator, educator*

Clinton Township
Childress, Janet Lynn *logistician*
Noraas, Diane Rice *computer scientist, educator*

Northville
Hansen, Jean Marie *math and computer educator*

Pontiac
Jack, Dixie Lynn *software consultant, social worker*

West Bloomfield
Miller, Nancy Ellen *computer consultant*

Ypsilanti
Warner, Jo F. *mathematics educator*

MINNESOTA

Minneapolis
Adlis, Susan Annette *biostatistician*
Pour-El, Marian Boykan *mathematician, educator*

Rochester
Grosset, Jessica Ariane *computer analyst*

MISSOURI

Columbia
Flournoy, Nancy *statistician, educator*

Earth City
Kiry-Ryan, Rita Irene *computer scientist, educator*

Fenton
Marcus, Michelle *computer scientist*

Independence
Peake, Candice K. Loper *data processing professional*

Kansas City
Van Dyne, Michele Miley *information engineer*

Kirkwood
Collins, Nancy Lee *mathematician, educator*

NEBRASKA

Lincoln
Wiegand, Sylvia Margaret *mathematician, educator*

Omaha
Wilhelmi, Cynthia Joy *information technology professional, consultant*

NEVADA

Las Vegas
Blattner, Meera McCuaig *computer science educator*

NEW HAMPSHIRE

Nashua
Lerch, Carol M. *mathematics educator*

NEW JERSEY

Jersey City
Poiani, Eileen Louise *mathematics educator, college administrator, higher education planner*

New Brunswick
Machado, Kety Gonzalez *mathematician, educator*
Scanlon, Jane Cronin *mathematics educator*

New Providence
Wright, Margaret Hagen *computer scientist, administrator*

Princeton
Chang, Sun-Yung Alice *mathematics educator*

Somerset
Becker, Phyllis *systems analyst*

Weehawken
Metallo, Frances Rosebell *mathematics educator*

NEW MEXICO

Farmington
Doig, Beverly Irene *retired systems specialist*

Las Cruces
Selden, Annie *mathematics educator*

Santa Fe
Tokheim, Sara Ann *writer, information technology professional*

NEW YORK

Brewster
Dominicus, Adele M. *mathematician, educator*

Buffalo
Goodberry, Diane Jean (Diane Oberkircher) *mathematics educator, tax accountant*
Piech, Margaret Ann *mathematics educator*
Seitz, Mary Lee *mathematics educator*

Corning
Peaslee, Jayne Marie *computer scientist, educator*

Dix Hills
Blumstein, Reneé J. *educational research consultant, grant writer, program developer*

Feura Bush
Lawson, Nancy Louise *computer scientist, educator*

Great Neck
Schussheim, Joan Lana *mathematics educator*

Long Island City
Goldstein, Katherine H. *technology educator, computer consultant*

Massapequa
Batt, Alyse Schwartz *technical officer*

New York
Chichilnisky, Graciela *mathematician, educator, economist, writer*
Kirnos, Dina *technology support professional*
Morawetz, Cathleen Synge *mathematician*
Schulhoff, Karen L. *information specialist*
Taylor, Jean Ellen *mathematics researcher and educator*

Orangeburg
Siegel, Carole Ethel *mathematician*

Sleepy Hollow
Maun, Mary Ellen *computer consultant*

NORTH CAROLINA

Chapel Hill
Coulter, Elizabeth Jackson *biostatistician, educator*

Durham
Johnson, Kristina M. *technology director*

Hertford
Sutton, Louise Nixon *retired mathematics educator*

Wilmington
Midgett, Carol Wickham *mathematics educator, consultant*

OHIO

Brookpark
Cotton, Barbara Jean *systems analyst*

Grove City
Kimethu, Susan Wanja *computer specialist, database manager*

OKLAHOMA

Edmond
Loman, Mary LaVerne *retired mathematics educator*

Norman
Bethel, Joann D. *computer programmer, analyst*
Provine, Lorraine *retired mathematics educator*

OREGON

Falls City
Thex, Alberta Hughes *secondary education educator*

Portland
Cassetta, Rhondda King *statistician*

PENNSYLVANIA

Bethlehem
Schattschneider, Doris Jean *retired mathematics educator*

Blue Bell
Halas, Cynthia Ann *business information specialist*

East Stroudsburg
Hauner-Morris, Phyllis Marie *systems analyst*

Mechanicsburg
Harper, Diane Marie *retired communications retailer*

Pittsburgh
Byers, Mary Margaret (Peg Byers) *systems educator*
Shaw, Mary M. *computer science educator*

SOUTH CAROLINA

Charleston
Huang, Peng *statistician*

Clemson
Hare, Eleanor O'Meara *computer science educator*

TENNESSEE

Hermitage
Castner, Catherine S. *information technology administrator*

Johnson City
Pumariega, JoAnne Buttacavoli *mathematics educator*

Knoxville
Tenopir, Carol *information science educator*

TEXAS

Austin
Baker, Mary Ann *program manager*
Uhlenbeck, Karen Keskulla *mathematician, educator*

Houston
Fenn, Sandra Ann *programmer, analyst*

Laredo
Mendiola, Anna Maria G. *mathematics educator*

Prairie View
Barber-Freeman, Pamela Telia *mathematician, educator, researcher*

Richardson
Hennessey, Audrey Kathleen *computer researcher, educator*
Zalila-Mili, Rym *computer scientist, educator*

San Angelo
Campbell, Elsie Mae *mathematician, educator*

San Antonio
Estep, Myrna Lynne *systems analyst, philosophy educator*

UTAH

Salt Lake City
Horn, Susan Dadakis *statistics educator*

VIRGINIA

Annandale
Baditoi, Barbara Ellen *information scientist, educator*

Arlington
Long, Madeleine J. *mathematics and science educator*

Charlottesville
Parshall, Karen Virginia Hunger *mathematics and science historian*

Clifton
Hoffman, Karla Leigh *mathematician, educator*

Fairfax
Mulvaney, Mary Frederica *systems analyst*

Fort Belvoir
Lane, Karen Gale *operations research analyst*

Gainesville
Bendig, Judith Joan *information systems specialist, computer company executive*

Heathsville
Stubbs, Susan Conklin *statistician*

Herndon
Hollis, Katherine Mary *information scientist, consultant*

Radford
Carter, Edith Houston *statistician, educator*

Vienna
Vachher, Sheila Ann *information systems consultant*

Warrenton
Gullace, Marlene Frances *information engineer, systems analyst, consultant*

WASHINGTON

Bellevue
Dykstra, Gail Sullivan *information scientist, consultant*

Kent
Personette, Louise Metzger (Sister Mary Roger Metzger) *mathematics educator*

Tacoma
Burns, Robin C(arol) *mathematics theoretician, accountant*

HONG KONG

South Horizons
Chen, Concordia Chao *mathematician*

ADDRESS UNPUBLISHED

Amos-Mandela, Tiye Uhura *systems analyst, researcher*
Bailar, Barbara Ann *statistician, researcher*
Barrett, Lida Kittrell *mathematics educator*
Basch, Reva *information services company executive*
Bates, Beverly Joyce *retired educator and computer professional*
Corbett, Lenora Meade *mathematician, community college educator*
Croog, Roslyn Zeporah *chief systems engineer*
De Both, Tanya *statistician*
Downey, Deborah Ann *systems specialist*
Dunlop, Dorothy D. *statistician*
Gifford, Marjorie Fitting *mathematician, educator, consultant*
Glenn, Vicki Lynn *mathematician, educator*
Graham, Kirsten Rae *computer scientist, educator*
Grasserbauer, Doris *computer scientist, mathematician, educator*
Green, Linda Lou *systems analyst*
Harnedy, Joan Catherine Holland *retired systems analyst*
Hicks, Judith Ann *systems analyst*
Hunte, Beryl Eleanor *mathematics educator, consultant*
Johnson, Amanda A. *computer scientist*
Jones, Anita Katherine *computer scientist, educator*
Keating, Regina G. *computer analyst consultant*
Levina, Anna *computer scientist*
Mallin, Jennifer *internet company executive, writer*
Mangan, Patricia Ann Pritchett *statistician*
Mathieu, Michele Suzanne *computer scientist, consultant*
Miller, Elaine Wilson *computer consultant*
Morrison, Ann Hess *information technology specialist*
Moskowitz, Rebecca C. *systems analyst*
Natsuyama, Harriet Hatsune Kagiwada

Norman, E. Gladys *retired business computer educator, consultant*
Padberg, Harriet Ann *mathematics educator*
Pendleton, Joan Marie *microprocessor designer*
Perdue, Kathy *operations research specialist*
Pollock, Karen Anne *computer analyst*
Roitman, Judith *mathematician, educator*
Shier, Gloria Bulan *mathematics educator*
Stewart-Pérez, Renice Ann *technology writer, internal systems professional*
Stuart, Sandra Joyce *computer information scientist*
Ternovitz, Ruth *mathematics and computer educator*
Ullman, Nelly Szabo *statistician, educator*
Watkins, Ann Esther *mathematics educator*
Welna, Cecilia *retired mathematics educator*
Whitaker, Wilma Neuman *retired mathematics instructor*
Yntema, Mary Katherine *retired mathematics educator*

SCIENCE: PHYSICAL SCIENCE

UNITED STATES

ALABAMA

Birmingham
Moran, Mary Shanks *hydrogeologist*

Gurley
Patrick, Laura Daphene Layman *retired physicist*

ALASKA

Anchorage
Keffer, Maria Jean *environmental auditor*

ARIZONA

Flagstaff
Barlow, Nadine Gail *planetary geoscientist*
Shoemaker, Carolyn Spellman *planetary astronomer*

Oracle
Garmany, Catharine Doremus *astronomer*

Peoria
McMahon, Maribeth Lovette *physicist*

Tempe
Herald, Cherry Lou *research educator, research director*

Tucson
Neugebauer, Marcia *physicist, administrator*
Roemer, Elizabeth *astronomer, educator*
Sprague, Ann Louise *space scientist*

Wolff, Sidney Carne *astronomer, observatory administrator*

CALIFORNIA

Altadena
Mkryan, Sonya *geophysicist, educator, research scientist*

Bellflower
Martin, Melissa Carol *radiological physicist*

Berkeley
Benson, Sally M. *atmospheric scientist*
Bertozzi, Carolyn R. *chemistry educator*
Gaillard, Mary Katharine *physics educator*
Hoffman, Darleane Christian *chemistry educator*
Klinman, Judith Pollock *biochemist, educator*
Ma, Chung-Pei Michelle *astronomer, educator*

China Lake
Bennett, Jean Louise McPherson *physicist, research scientist*

Chula Vista
Smith, Peggy O'Doniel *physicist, researcher*

Concord
Wood, Rosemary Ruston *environmental health scientist, consultant*

Davis
Burri, Betty Jane *research chemist*
Liu, Gang-Yu *chemist, educator*
Mukherjee, Amiya K. *metallurgy and materials science educator*

El Granada
Heere, Karen R. *astrophysicist*

Fullerton
Wan, Julia Chang *retired science educator*
Woyski, Margaret Skillman *retired geology educator*

La Jolla
Burbidge, E. Margaret *astronomer, educator*
Engvall, Eva *biochemist*
Janda, Kim D. *chemist, educator*
Marshak, Celia L. *biochemist, educator*
Ride, Sally Kristen *physics educator, scientist, former astronaut*

Lafayette
Seaburg, Glen T. *chemistry educator*

Livermore
Max, Claire Ellen *physicist*

Long Beach
Li, Lijuan *chemistry educator*

Los Angeles
Byers, Nina *physics educator*
Carter, Emily Ann *physical chemist, researcher, educator*
Kivelson, Margaret Galland *physicist*
Kobe, Lan *medical physicist*
Neufeld, Elizabeth Fondal *biochemist, educator*
Woodruff, Fay *paleoceanographer, geological researcher*

Milpitas
Evans, Susan A. *chemist*

Moffett Field
Bakes, Emma *astrophysicist*
Pendleton, Yvonne *astrophysicist*

Monterey
Blair, Cynthia *meteorologist, oceanographer, researcher*

Oakland
Carwell, Hattie Virginia *health physicist*

Palo Alto
Quinn, Helen Rhoda *physicist*

Pasadena
Buratti, Bonnie J. *aerospace scientist*
Freedman, Wendy Laurel *astronomer, educator*
Helin, Eleanor Francis *astronomer, geologist*
Lopes, Rosaly Mutel Crocce *astronomer, planetary geologist*
Spilker, Linda Joyce *aerospace scientist*

San Diego
Kraus, Pansy Daegling *gemology consultant, editor, writer*

San Francisco
Gourley, Helen Elizabeth *physicist*

Santa Ana
Dumdum, Josefina Martinez *chemist, researcher*

Santa Barbara
Atwater, Tanya Maria *marine geophysicist, educator*
Shea, Joan-Emma *biophysicist, educator*

Santa Cruz
Faber, Sandra Moore *astronomer, educator*
Silver, Mary Wilcox *oceanography educator*

Santa Monica
Intriligator, Devrie Shapiro *physicist*

Stanford
Kallosh, Renata *physics educator*
Matson, Pamela Anne *environmental scientist, science educator*

COLORADO

Boulder
Foland, Sara *geologist, association executive*
Jin, Deborah *physicist, educator*
LeMone, Margaret Anne *atmospheric scientist*
Tolbert, Margaret A. *geochemistry educator*

Denver
Gries, Robbie Rice *geologist, gas and petroleum company executive*
Landon, Susan Melinda *petroleum geologist*

Fort Collins
Ladanyi, Branka Maria *chemist, educator*

Lakewood
Bailey, Zelda Chapman *hydrologist*

Littleton
Harney, Patricia Rae *environmental technical supervisor*

CONNECTICUT

Bloomfield
Ivey, Elizabeth S. *retired physicist, educator*

Farmington
Osborn, Mary Jane Merten *biochemist, educator*

New Haven
Skinner, Helen Catherine Wild *biomineralogist*
Steitz, Joan Argetsinger *biochemistry educator*

West Hartford
Markham, Claire Agnes (M. Clare Markham) *retired chemistry educator, consultant*

West Haven
Onton, Ann Louise Reuther *chemist*

DELAWARE

Wilmington
Kwolek, Stephanie Louise *chemist, researcher*
Marcali, Jean Gregory *retired chemist*

DISTRICT OF COLUMBIA

Washington
Esfandiary, Mary S. *physical scientist, operations consultant*
[...] *consultant*
Holland, Christie Anna *biochemist, virologist*
Karle, Isabella L. *chemist*
Kimble, Melinda Louise *environmental administrator*
Knopman, Debra Sara *environmental scientist, director, hydrologist, policy analyst*
Oran, Elaine Surick *physicist, engineer*
Roscher, Nina Matheny *chemistry educator*
Schierow, Linda-Jo *environmental policy analyst*
Shamim, Mah Talat *chemist*
Simon-Gillo, Jehanne E. *physicist, science administrator*
Singer, Maxine Frank *retired biochemist, scientific institute executive*

FLORIDA

Coral Gables
Van Vliet, Carolyne Marina *physicist, researcher*

Miami
Fine, Rana Arnold *chemical and physical oceanographer*
Kowalska, Maria Teresa *research scientist, educator*

Pensacola
Garrison, Wanda Brown *environmental consultant*

Saint Petersburg
Butler, Susan Belinda *environmental specialist*
Hallock-Muller, Pamela *oceanography educator, biogeologist, researcher*

Tallahassee
Moulton, Grace Charbonnet *physics educator*

GEORGIA

Athens
Black, Marsha C. *environmental scientist*
Kays, Sandra Elizabeth *research chemist*

Atlanta
Anderson, Gloria Long *chemistry educator*
Hicks, Heraline Elaine *environmental health scientist, educator*

IDAHO

Moscow
Shreeve, Jean'ne Marie *chemist, educator*

ILLINOIS

Argonne
Jonkouski, Jill Ellen *materials scientist, ceramic engineer, educator*

Chicago
Dutta, Mitra *physicist, educator*

Herzenberg, Caroline Stuart Littlejohn *physicist*

Elk Grove Village
Jan, Chwu-Ching Hwang *environmental chemistry consultant*

Evanston
Rosenzweig, Amy *biochemist, educator*
Weertman, Julia Randall *materials science and engineering educator*

Milford
Coogan, Melinda Ann Strank *chemistry and biology educator*

Naperville
Sherren, Anne Terry *chemistry educator*

North Chicago
Loga, Sanda *physicist, researcher*

Rockford
Walhout, Justine Simon *chemistry educator*

Urbana
Greene, Laura Helen *physicist*
Kieffer, Susan Werner *geologist, educator, media consultant*
Makri, Nancy *chemistry educator*

INDIANA

Bloomington
Srinivasan, Jayasree M. *research scientist*

Elkhart
Free, Helen Murray *chemist, consultant*

Fort Wayne
Lord, Pamela *chemist, educator*

Indianapolis
Lau, Pauline Young *chemist*

New Albany
Crump, Claudia *geography educator*

Notre Dame
Feigl, Dorothy Marie *chemistry educator, university official*

KANSAS

Lawrence
Dreschhoff, Gisela Auguste Marie *physicist, researcher*

Shawnee Mission
Billings, Patricia Jean *inventor*

Topeka
Barton, Janice Sweeny *chemistry educator*

KENTUCKY

Murray
Ratliff, Judy Lynn *chemist, educator*

LOUISIANA

New Orleans
Benerito, Ruth Rogan (Mrs. Frank H. Benerito) *chemist*
Bertoniere, Noelie Rita *research chemist*

Schriever
Hoffman, Susan Talbot *chemist, printmaker*

MARYLAND

Baltimore
Jones, Hendree Evelyn *research scientist, psychologist*

Bel Air
Cash, LaVerne (Cynthia Cash) *physicist*

Beltsville
Johnson, Phyllis Elaine *chemist, researcher*

Bethesda
Dunn, Bonnie Brill *chemist*
Landis, Story C. C. *neurobiologist*
Vaughan, Martha *biochemist, educator*
Zoon, Kathryn Christine *biochemist*

College Park
Fenselau, Catherine Clarke *chemistry educator*
Lubkin, Gloria Becker *physicist*

Derwood
Stadtman, Thressa Campbell *biochemist*

Frederick
Henderson, Madeline Mary (Berry Henderson) *chemist, researcher, consultant*
Smith, Sharron Williams *chemistry educator*

Gaithersburg
Gebbie, Katharine Blodgett *physicist*
Jacox, Marilyn Esther *chemist*
Sengers, Johanna M. H. Levelt *thermophysicist*

Germantown
Foulke, Judith Diane *health physicist*

Greenbelt
Kessel, Mona *space physicist*
Li, Mary J. *scientist, educator*
Simpson, Joanne Malkus *meteorologist*

Hagerstown
Corbett, Helen A. *chemist, chemical engineer*

Mount Airy
Johnston, Josephine Rose *chemist*

MASSACHUSETTS

Boston
Dawson-Hughes, Bess *scientist*
Miliora, Maria Teresa *chemist, psychotherapist, psychoanalyst, educator*
Plank, Terry *geochemistry educator*

Bourne
Fantozzi, Peggy Ryone *geologist, environmental planner*

Brighton
Fischer, Irene Kaminka *geodesist, researcher, retired mathematician*

Cambridge
Ceyer, Sylvia T. *chemistry educator*
Chisholm, Sallie Watson *biological oceanography educator, researcher*
Dresselhaus, Mildred Spiewak *physics and engineering educator*
Friend, Cynthia M. *chemist, educator*
Hau, Lene *physicist, optics scientist*
Hewitt, Jacqueline N. *astronomy educator*
Kistiakowsky, Vera *physics researcher, educator*
Luu, Jane *astronomer*
Marvin, Ursula Bailey *retired geologist*
Raymo, Maureen Elizabeth *geologist, researcher*
Stubbe, JoAnne *chemistry educator*

Framingham
Dawicki, Doloretta Diane *analytical chemist, research biochemist, educator*

Medford
Mc Carthy, Kathryn A. *physicist*

Roxbury
Simons, Elizabeth R(eiman) *biochemist, educator*

South Hadley
Campbell, Mary Kathryn *chemistry educator*

Waltham
Lees, Marjorie Berman *biochemist, neuroscientist*

Weston
Lin, Alice Lee Lan *physicist, researcher, educator*

MICHIGAN

Ann Arbor
Aller, Margo Friedel *astronomer*
Freese, Katherine *physicist, researcher*
Ludwig, Martha *biochemist, educator*
Murnane, Margaret Mary *engineering and physics educator*
Walter, Lynn M. *geologist, educator*

Detroit
Jiang, Wei *chemist*

East Lansing
Burnett, Jean Bullard (Mrs. James R. Burnett) *biochemist, educator*

Midland
Leng, Marguerite Lambert *biochemist*

MINNESOTA

Minneapolis
Vainschtein, Arkady *physics educator*

MISSISSIPPI

Hattiesburg
Bedenbaugh, Angela Lea Owen *chemistry educator, researcher*

MISSOURI

Columbia
Plummer, Patricia Lynne Moore *chemistry and physics educator*
Randall, Linda Lea *biochemist, educator*

Kansas City
Kloth, Carolyn *meteorologist*

Rolla
Sotiriou-Leventis, Chariklia *chemist, educator, researcher*

Saint Louis
Fitzpatrick, Susan *biochemist, neurologist, foundation executive*

Wildwood
Colletti, Teresa Ann *polymer chemist*

NEBRASKA

Lincoln
Hac, Lucile Rose *biochemistry educator*
Holmes, Mary Anne *geologist, research scientist*

NEW HAMPSHIRE

Litchfield
Miller, Dawn Marie *retired meteorologist*

NEW JERSEY

Annandale
Baugh, Lisa Saunders (Lisa Saunders Boffa) *research chemist*

Columbia
Timcenko, Lydia Teodora *biochemist, chemist*

Edgewater
Zhou, Yan *chemist*

New Providence
Murray, Cherry Ann *physicist, researcher*
Sivco, Deborah Lee *research materials scientist*
White, Alice Elizabeth *physicist, researcher*

Oaklyn
Miranda, Minda *chemist, pharmacy technician*

Piscataway
Champe, Pamela Chambers *biochemistry educator, writer*
Klein, Lisa Carol *materials scientist, educator*

Princeton
Finn, Frances Mary *biochemistry researcher*

Rahway
Chen, Liya *chemist*
Garcia, Maria Luisa *biochemist, researcher*

Summit
Vandenberg, Joka Maria *physicist, researcher*

Teaneck
Nagy, Christa Fiedler *biochemist*

NEW MEXICO

Albuquerque
Evans, Pauline D. *physicist, researcher*
Torres, Barbara Wood *technical services professional*

Carlsbad
Paviet-Hartmann, Patricia *chemist, researcher*

Los Alamos
Bauer, Eve *research scientist*
Lu, Ningping *environmental chemist*

NEW YORK

Amityville
Citrano-Cummiskey, Debra Moira *chemist, network technician*

Bronx
Siddons, Sarah Mae *chemist*
Yalow, Rosalyn Sussman *nobel laureate, biophysicist*

Brooklyn
Mook, Sarah *retired chemist*
Sarutto, Anne Marie Rita *research scientist*

Manhasset
Spetsieris, Phoebe George *physicist, application developer, researcher*

Manlius
Brophy, Mary O'Reilly *environmental scientist*

New York
Boskey, Adele Ludin *biochemistry educator, researcher*
Breslow, Esther May Greenberg *biochemistry educator, researcher*
Chan, Siu-Wai *materials science educator*
Goetz, Regina M. *research scientist, pharmacist*
Hoffman, Linda M. *chemist, educator*
Russell, Charlotte Sananes *biochemistry educator, researcher*
St. Germain, Jean Mary *medical physicist*
St. John, Suzan *astrologer, illustrator, writer, vocalist*
Sarachik, Myriam Paula Morgenstein *physics educator*
Sidran, Miriam *retired physics educator, researcher*

Potsdam
Garg, Rajni *chemist, researcher*

Poughkeepsie
Deiters, Sister Joan Adele *psychoanalyst, nun, chemistry educator*

Rochester
Blondell, Debra Brown *chemist, researcher*
Conwell, Esther Marly *physicist, researcher*

Schenectady
Zheng, Maggie (Xiaoci Zheng) *materials scientist, turbine coating specialist*

Selden
Chin, Jing-Yi Syz *chemist, educator*

Tarrytown
O'Brien, Anne Therese *chemist*

Troy
Krause, Sonja *chemistry educator*

Upton
Fowler, Joanna S. *chemist*

Setlow, Jane Kellock *biophysicist*

White Plains
Flanigen, Edith Marie *materials scientist, consultant*

NORTH CAROLINA

Beaufort
Bonaventura, Celia Jean *biochemist, researcher*

Chapel Hill
Dolan, Louise Ann *physicist*

Raleigh
Osteryoung, Janet Gretchen *chemistry educator*

Wilmington
Kelley, Patricia Hagelin *geology educator*

OHIO

Akron
Piirma, Irja *chemist, educator*

Cincinnati
Bench, Barbara Anne *chemist*
Briskin, Madeleine *paleo-oceanographer, paleoclimatologist, micropaleontologist*
Meal, Larie *chemistry educator, researcher, consultant*

Columbus
Codogni, Iwona M. *scientific information analyst, chemist*
Sullivan, Kathryn D. *geologist, former astronaut*

Kent
Tuan, Debbie Fu-Tai *chemist, educator*

Liberty Township
Conditt, Margaret Karen *research scientist, policy analyst*

Middletown
Marine, Susan Sonchik *analytical chemist, educator*

Wickliffe
Krause, Marjorie N. *biochemist*

OKLAHOMA

Bartlesville
Yao, Jianhua *chemist, researcher*

Lawton
Nalley, Elizabeth Ann *chemistry educator*

Norman
Nelson, Donna Jean *chemistry educator, researcher*

OREGON

Corvallis
Huyer, Adriana *oceanographer, educator*
Shoemaker, Clara Brink *retired chemistry researcher*

PENNSYLVANIA

Abington
Schuster, Ingeborg Ida *chemistry educator*

Bryn Mawr
Crawford, Maria Luisa Buse *geology educator*

Exton
Chu, Deh-Ying *chemist, researcher*

Kennett Square
Lippincott, Sarah Lee *astronomer, graphologist*

Loretto
Clark, Rose Ann *chemist, educator*

Malvern
Fisher, Sallie Ann *chemist*

Norristown
Whittington, Cathy Dee *chemist*

Philadelphia
Ajzenberg-Selove, Fay *physicist, researcher*
Cohn, Mildred *biochemist, educator*
Prairie, Celia Esther Freda *biochemistry educator*
Saiz, Leonor *physicist, researcher*

Pittsburgh
Jen-Jacobson, Linda *biochemist, educator*
Marra, Kacey G. *research scientist, educator*

South Park
Lotze, Barbara *retired physicist*

State College
Roy, Della Martin *materials science educator, researcher*

University Park
Garrison, Barbara Jane *chemistry educator*
Ross, A. Catharine *biochemist, educator*

Wayne
Santo, Melissa Marie *chemist*

Waynesburg
Maguire, Mildred May *chemistry educator, magnetic resonance researcher*

SOCIAL SCIENCE

Los Angeles
Anawalt, Patricia Rieff *anthropologist, researcher*
Archuleta, Randi Lisa *psychologist*
Arnold, Jeanne Eloise *anthropologist, educator*
Burns, Marcelline *psychologist, researcher*
Dosamantes-Beaudry, Irma *psychology educator*
Lein, Hebe Beatriz *psychologist*
Montoya, Velma *economist, policy consultant*
Phinney, Jean Swift *psychology educator*
Renteln, Alison Dundes *political science educator*
Scholefiled, Robin Marie *psychologist*
Squire, Molly Ann *organizational psychologist*
Taylor, Shelley E. *psychology researcher and educator*
Van Tilburg, JoAnne *archaeologist, educator, foundation administrator*
Watson, Sharon Gitin *psychologist, executive*
Wood, Nancy Elizabeth *psychologist, educator*

Malibu
Miller-Perrin, Cindy Lou *psychology educator*

Menlo Park
Vane, Sylvia Brakke *anthropologist, writer, publishing executive, researcher*

Monrovia
Miller, Karen *clinical psychologist, neuropsychologist*

Newhall
Sylvers, Arlene Marder *clinical psychologist*

Newport Beach
Simon, Karen Michele *clinical psychologist, educator*

Northridge
Harwick, Betty Corinne Burns *sociology educator*

Oakland
Neeley, Beverly Evon *sociologist, consultant*

Oceanside
Hertweck, Alma Louise *sociology and child development educator*

Orange
Stevens, Cherita Wyman *social sciences educator, writer*

Palo Alto
Lundy, Jackelyn Ruth *consulting firm owner, economist, researcher*
Scitovsky, Anne Aickelin *economist, researcher*
Spangenberg, Ruth Beahrs *psychologist, educator*

Pasadena
Morgan, Ann Marie *psychologist*

Pico Rivera
Merrill Warner, Veronique *psychologist*

Point Richmond
Tellier, Jen Emily *psychologist, educator*

Pomona
Englert, Phyllis Ann *psychology educator*
Singer-Chang, Gail Leslie *social sciences educator, assistant dean for student affairs*

Porterville
Vasilescu, Vasilica *psychologist, consultant*

Rancho Santa Margarita
Aguilera, Donna Conant *psychologist, researcher*

Redding
Drake, Patricia Evelyn *psychologist*

Redondo Beach
McWilliams, Margaret Ann *home economics educator, author*

Rohnert Park
Leeder, Elaine *sociologist, educator, writer*

Sacramento
Chu, Judy May *psychology educator, city official*
Gibson, Patrice Vandegrift *anthropologist, educator*

San Bernardino
Griffiths, Barbara Lorraine *psychologist, marriage-family therapist, writer*

San Diego
Blade, Melinda Kim *archaeologist, educator, research scientist*
Grossbard-Shechtman, Shoshana Amyra *economist, educator*
Hoston, Germaine Annette *political science educator*
Sundayo, Judy *psychologist, educator*
Tesvich, Lisa Kay *industrial and organizational psychologist*

San Francisco
Adamson, Mary Anne *geographer, systems engineer*
Adler, Nancy Elinor *psychologist, educator*
Estes, Carroll Lynn *sociologist, educator*
Giraudo, Suzanne McDonnell *psychologist*
Goldsmith, Deborah *social studies educator*
Piotrowski, Nancy Ann *psychological scientist*
Rice, Dorothy Pechman (Mrs. John Donald Rice) *medical economist*
Sedway, Lynn Massel *real estate economist*
Tsoh, Janice Yusze *clinical psychologist, researcher*

San Jose
Cohen, D. Ashley *clinical neuropsychologist*

McDowell, Jennifer *sociologist, composer, playwright, publisher*

San Marino
Medici, Rochelle *psychologist, brain researcher*

Santa Barbara
Beck, Isabel Holderman *psychologist, consultant*
Binion, Gayle *political science educator*
Ford, Anabel *research anthropologist, archaeologist*
Mack, Judith Cole Schrim *political scientist, educator*
Nyborg, Vanessa Marie *psychologist, researcher, educator*

Santa Clara
Lehman, Cassandra *psychologist*

Santa Cruz
Roby, Pamela Ann *sociology educator*

Santa Monica
Berres, Frances Brandes *clinical psychologist*
Landon, Helen Zielinski *psychologist*
Lara-Cinisomo, Sandra Luz *psychologist*
Veit, Clairice Gene Tipton *measurement psychologist*

Sherman Oaks
Gross, Sharon Ruth *forensic psychologist, researcher*
Sharon, Debra Melinda *psychologist*

Sonora
Clarke, Paula Katherine *anthropology educator, sociology educator*

Stanford
Maccoby, Eleanor Emmons *psychology educator*
Martin, Joanne *social sciences educator*
Ricardo-Campbell, Rita *economist, educator*

Ventura
Lipinski, Barbara Janina *psychologist, psychotherapist, educator, writer*

Vista
Savage, Linda Eileen *psychologist*

West Hills
Hawes, Bess Lomax *retired anthropologist*

Westminster
Phan, Kim Than Nguyen *psychologist, educator*

Whittier
McKenna, Jeanette Ann *archaeologist*

COLORADO

Boulder
Borysenko, Joan *psychologist, biologist*
Civish, Gayle Ann *psychologist*
Healy, Alice Fenvessy *psychology educator, researcher*
Joyce, Janet S. *psychologist*
Malville, Nancy Jean *anthropologist*
Menken, Jane Ava *demographer, educator*

Colorado Springs
McDivitt, Karen Louise *psychologist, writer*

Denver
Lefly, Dianne Louise *research psychologist*
Merscham, Carrie *psychologist*
Nelson, Sarah Milledge *archaeology educator*

Fort Collins
Andreas, Carol *sociologist, educator*
Myrtis-Garcia, Carmen Ruth *social sciences educator*

Greeley
Richardson, Laura *psychologist, educator*

Littleton
Lohman, Loretta Cecelia *social scientist, consultant*

Pueblo
Alt, Betty L. *sociology educator*

CONNECTICUT

Barkhamsted
Stokes, Susan *political science educator*

Chester
Feldmann, Shirley Clark *psychology educator*

Fairfield
Morehouse, Sarah McCally *retired political science educator*

Higganum
de Brigard, Emilie *anthropologist, consultant*

Mansfield Center
Ciaramella, Suzanne *psychologist*

Meriden
Losada-Zarate, Gloria *psychologist*

Middletown
Crenshaw, Martha *political science educator*

New Canaan
Thomas, Marianne Gregory *school psychologist*

New Haven
Caldwell-Andrews, Alison Amelia *psychologist, researcher*

Dudley, Kathryn Marie *anthropology and American studies educator*
Ember, Carol R. *anthropology educator, author*

Norwalk
Timlin-Scalera, Rebecca Mary *neuropsychologist*

Stamford
Arms, Karen G. *social sciences educator*
Teeters, Nancy Hays *economist, director*

Stonington
Trott-Backus, Elaine Erika Aldrich *gerontologist, educator*

West Hartford
Bullock, Karen *social sciences educator*
Jessup, Sarah H. *anthropologist, educator*

Westport
Lee, Janet Mentore *psychologist, educator*
Levy, Wendy *psychologist*

Windsor
Bullard, Sarah Elizabeth *psychologist*

DELAWARE

Newark
Champion, Kim Panetski *psychologist*
Graham, Frances Keesler (Mrs. David Tredway Graham) *psychologist, educator*

Wilmington
Koropsak-Berman, Elizabeth A. *psychologist, consultant*

DISTRICT OF COLUMBIA

Washington
Abraham, Katharine Gail *economics educator*
Agee, Eve *anthropologist*
Aring, Monika Kosmahl *education economist, consultant, researcher*
Barton, Jean Marie *psychologist, educator*
Becker, Mary Louise *political scientist*
Bergmann, Barbara Rose *economics educator*
Birdsall, Nancy *economist*
Blair, Margaret Mendenhall *research economist, consultant, law educator*
Bluth, B. J. (Elizabeth Jean Catherine Bluth) *sociologist, aerospace technologist*
Downey-Sargent, Kathryn T. *psychologist, researcher*
Elliott, Kimberly Ann *economist*
Flattau, Pamela Ebert *research psychologist, consultant*
Fusillo, Alice Elbert *retired sociologist, sculptor*
Genia, Vicky *psychologist*
Gonzalez-Hermosillo, Brenda *economist, researcher*
Grapin, Jacqueline G. *economist*
Hartmann, Heidi Irmgard Victoria *economist, research organization executive*
Hu, Grace M. *economist*
Kennedy, Muriel *psychologist, consultant, educator*
Kirkpatrick, Jeane Duane Jordan *political scientist, government official*
Krulfeld, Ruth Marilyn *anthropologist, educator*
Kuh, Charlotte Virginia *economist*
Kybal, Elba Gómez del Rey *economist, non-profit organization executive*
Marcuss, Rosemary Daly *economist*
Martinez, Herminia S. *economist, banker*
Matalin, Mary *political consultant*
Meggers, Betty J(ane) *anthropologist, researcher*
Miller, Margery *psychologist, speech pathologist, medical educator and administrator*
Munnell, Alicia Haydock *economist*
Offutt, Susan Elizabeth *economist*
Ozer, Martha Ross *psychologist, counselor*
Phillips, Karen Borlaug *economist, railroad industry executive*
Phillips, Susan Meredith *financial economist, university administrator*
Rodriguez, Rita Maria *economist*
Sawhill, Isabel Van Devanter *economist*
Sharma, Martha Bridges *geography educator*
Solomon, Elinor Harris *economics educator*
Stephen, Elizabeth Hervey *sociologist, educator*
Terry-Leonard, Brenda L. *psychologist, consultant*
Weinhold, Linda Lillian *psychologist, researcher*
Wilensky, Gail Roggin *economist, researcher*
Willner, Ann Ruth *political scientist, educator*
Willner, Dorothy *anthropologist, educator*

FLORIDA

Aventura
Freshwater, Shawna Marie *neuropsychologist, clinical psychologist, cognitive neuroscientist*
Krop, Lois Pulver *psychologist*

Boca Raton
Klasfield, Ilene *psychologist*

Cocoa
McLendon, Dorothy *school psychologist*

Coral Gables
Schwartztol, Holly Wechsler *psychologist*

Davie
Ross, Kathryn Amie *psychologist*

Fort Lauderdale
Bartelstone, Rona Sue *gerontologist*
Wood, Linda Dee *psychologist*

Gainesville
Albarracín, Dolores *psychologist, educator*

Ardelt, Monika *sociologist, educator*
Wass, Hannelore Lina *educational psychology educator*
White, Susie Mae *school psychologist*

Jacksonville
Scott, Kamela Koon *psychologist, educator*

Miami
Humphries, Joan Ropes *psychologist, educator*
Huysman, Arlene Weiss *psychologist, educator, writer*
McNanamy, Eve Weeks *clinical psychologist, marriage therapist*
Uribe, Claudia Patricia *psychologist, educator*

Miami Beach
Kalsner-Silver, Lydia *psychologist*

Ocala
Blalock, Carol Douglass *psychologist, educator*

Orlando
Renk, Kimberly Dawn *social sciences educator*

Palm Beach Gardens
Wilkes, N. Tiffany *social studies educator*

Palm City
Whichello, Carol *political scientist, educator, writer*

Port Richey
Mueller, Lois M. *psychologist*

Saint Augustine
Henderson, Hazel *economist, writer, lecturer*

Saint Petersburg
Baker, Victoria Jean *anthropology educator*

Sarasota
Cauffield, Christine Anne *psychologist*
Elmendorf-Landgraf, Mary Lindsay *retired anthropologist*

Tallahassee
Proctor, Briley Elizabeth *psychologist, educator*

Tampa
Brady, Kathleen Deming *psychologist, occupational therapist, educator*
Caltagirone, Norma Tomasello *psychologist, educator*
Genshaft, Judy Lynn *psychologist, educator*
Kimmel, Ellen Bishop *psychologist, educator*
MacManus, Susan Ann *political science educator, researcher*
Molloy, Jean Marie *psychologist, human services administrator*

GEORGIA

Athens
Barton, Elizabeth Spindler *psychologist, fiber artist*

Atlanta
Dierickx, Constance Ricker *psychologist, management consultant*
Garland, LaRetta Matthews *psychologist, educator, nursing educator*
Kerr, Nancy Helen *psychology educator*
Tillman, Mary Norman *urban affairs consultant*

Bainbridge
Dixon, Lugenia *psychology educator*

Barnesville
Terry, Pamela Mays *psychology educator*

Carrollton
Clark, Janet Eileen *political scientist, educator*
Gustin, Ann Winifred *psychologist*
Mustakova-Possardt, Elena M. *social sciences educator, counselor*

Decatur
Bockwitz, Cynthia Lee *psychologist, psychology and women's studies educator*

Evans
Zachert, Virginia *psychologist, educator*

Griffin
Shockley, Carol Frances *psychologist, psychotherapist*

Kennesaw
Frank, Mary Lou Bryant *psychologist, educator*

Lawrenceville
Reuter, Helen Hyde *psychologist*

Macon
Lewis, Sandra Combs *research psychologist, writer*

Mountain City
Kennedy, Robinette *anthropologist, researcher*

Ringgold
Hayes Gladson, Laura Joanna *psychologist*

Savannah
Rozantine, Gayle Stubbs *clinical psychologist*

Social Circle
Archibald, Claudia Jane *parapsychologist, counselor, consultant*

Toccoa Falls
Brock, Dorothy Dixon *psychologist, educator*

Waltham
Domar, Alice Diane *psychologist, educator*
Flynn, Patricia Marie *economics educator*
McCulloch, Rachel *economics researcher, educator*
Zebrowitz, Leslie Ann *psychology educator*

Wellesley
Miller, Linda B. *political scientist*

West Springfield
McKenzie-Anderson, Rita Lynn *psychologist*

Westborough
Staffier, Pamela Moorman *psychologist*

Williamstown
Cramer, Phebe *psychologist*

Worcester
Dyer-Cole, Pauline *school psychologist, educator*
Lish, Jennifer D. *psychologist*
Upshur, Carole Christofk *psychologist, educator*

MICHIGAN

Ann Arbor
Apperson, Jean *psychologist*
Arlinghaus, Sandra Judith Lach *mathematical geographer, educator*
Dominguez, Kathryn Mary *political scientist, educator*
Eccles, Jacquelynne S. *psychology educator*
Gomberg, Edith S. *psychologist, educator*
Singer, Eleanor *sociologist, editor*
Toronto, Ellen Leslie Kaylor *psychologist*
Waltz, Susan *international relations educator*
Whitman, Marina Von Neumann *economist, educator*

Auburn Hills
Etefia, Florence Victoria *school psychologist*

Canton
Schulz, Karen Alice *psychologist, medical psychotherapist, medical and vocational case manager*

Clifford
Staples, Lynne Livingston Mills *retired psychologist, educator, consultant*

Detroit
Ferguson, Tamara *clinical sociologist*

East Lansing
Gass, Gertrude Zemon *psychologist, researcher*

Howell
Rohrabacher, Janet Hammond *geneologist, archivist*

Kalamazoo
Buskirk, Phyllis Richardson *retired economist*

Lansing
de Leon, Marita Bernardo *psychologist, researcher*

Okemos
Berkman, Claire Fleet *psychologist*

Saint Clair Shores
Vogel, Sally Thomas *psychologist, social worker, educator*

Saline
Hansen, Janice Elizabeth *psychologist*

Southfield
Weiner, Karen Colby (Karen Lynn Colby) *psychologist, lawyer*

Whitmore Lake
White, Susan Rochelle *psychologist, investor*

MINNESOTA

Coon Rapids
Angrist, Georgene Leiter *social studies educator*

Duluth
Stoddard, Patricia Florence Coulter *retired psychologist*

Hibbing
Gentile, Glenna Lee *psychologist, educator*

Minneapolis
Bancroft, Ann E. *polar explorer*
Berscheid, Ellen S. *psychology educator, writer, researcher*
Hansen, Jo-Ida Charlotte *psychology educator, researcher*
Jeffrey-Smith, Lilli Ann *biofeedback specialist, educator, administrator*
Johnson, Badri Nahvi *sociology educator, real estate company officer*
Nelson, Kari J. *psychologist, educator*

Saint Cloud
Boltuck, Mary A. *retired psychologist, educator*

Saint Paul
Harris, Duchess *social sciences educator*

Winona
Holm, Joy Alice *psychology educator, goldsmith, artist, art educator*

MISSISSIPPI

Jackson
Phillips, Karen Suzanne *psychologist*

Mississippi State
Henington, Carlen *psychologist, educator*
Wall, Diane Eve *political science educator*

Whitfield
Swann, Melissa Lynne *psychologist*

MISSOURI

Branson
Herron, Gayle Ann *forensic psychologist, mental health consultant, psychotherapist, health facility administrator, columnist*

Columbia
Bank, Barbara J. *sociology educator*

Kansas City
Nagle, Jean Susan Karabacz *sociologist, psychologist*
Rose, Teresa Beth *psychologist, educator*
Smith, Audrey Lee *psychologist, consultant*

Saint Louis
Beck, Lois Grant *anthropologist, educator, author*
De Voe, Pamela Ann *anthropologist, educator*
Entessar, Tahmineh *political scientist, educator*
Gfeller, Donna Kvinge *clinical psychologist*
Lindsey, Linda Lee *sociology educator*
Storandt, Martha *psychologist*
Thompson, Vetta Lynn Sanders *psychologist, educator*
Todorova-Moreno, Ilina *psychologist, educator*
Watson, Patty Jo *anthropology educator*

Sedalia
Waldo, Susan Lauderdale *psychologist*

Springfield
Gonzalez, Judith R. *psychologist, marriage and family therapist*
Hutson, Sheila *psychologist*
Levesque, Chantal *psychologist, researcher*

Urbana
Frey, Lucille Pauline *social studies educator, consultant*

MONTANA

Havre
Van Cleave, Vicki L. *psychologist, educator*

Helena
Seiler, Karen Peake *organizational psychologist*

Hobson
Otis, Gertrude Maxine *home economist*

Kalispell
Gallagher-Dalton, Tonya Marie *family support specialist*

Livingston
Hillegass, Christine Ann *psychologist*

Missoula
Wollersheim, Janet Puccinelli *psychology educator*

NEBRASKA

Harrison
Knudson, Ruthann *environmental consultant*

Lincoln
Rohren, Brenda Marie Anderson *therapist, educator*
Sullivan, Mary Ann *retired school psychologist*

Omaha
Jones-Thurman, Rosanna M. *psychologist*

NEVADA

Ely
Alderman, Minnis Amelia *psychologist, educator, small business owner*

Las Vegas
Beck, Colleen Marguerite *archaeologist*
Herbs, Diane *psychologist*
Meiner, Sue Ellen Thompson *gerontologist, nurse practitioner, nursing educator and researcher, legal nurse consultant*

Reno
Hazlett-Stevens, Holly *psychologist, educator*
Leland, Joy Hanson *anthropologist, alcohol research specialist*

NEW HAMPSHIRE

Concord
Rogers, Katherine Diane *political consultant, commissioner*

Durham
Corbett, Chanda Carmela *psychologist*
Mitchell, Kimberly Jeanne *psychologist, educator*

Goffstown
Oktavec, Eileen M. *anthropologist, artist*

Henniker
Braiterman, Thea Gilda *economics educator, state legislator, selectman*

Lebanon
Emery, Virginia Olga Beattie *psychologist, researcher*

Plymouth
Morth-Fraser, Grace M. *social sciences educator*

NEW JERSEY

Belle Mead
Moevs, Maria Teresa Marabini *archaeologist*

Blackwood
Huls, Glenna L. *sociology educator, photographer*

Blairstown
Horn-Alsberge, Michele Maryann *school psychologist*

Camden
Markey, Charlotte Nicole *psychologist, educator*

Cliffside Park
Fox, Margery Q. *anthropology educator*

Deptford
Kelly, Barbara Sue *psychologist*

Englewood Cliffs
Farrell, Patricia Ann *psychologist, educator, writer*

Florham Park
Brodkin, Adele Ruth Meyer *psychologist*

Gillette
Pfafflin, Sheila Murphy *psychologist*

Glassboro
Mukhoti, Bela Banerjee *economics educator*

Hoboken
Friedman, Sofia *social sciences educator, nutritionist, educator*

Holmdel
Zupkus, Ellen Ciccone *clinical psychologist, consultant*

Liberty Corner
DeLong, Margaret Doherty *psychologist, consultant*

Milltown
Sacharow, Beverly *gerontologist*

Montclair
Anselmi, Elvira *psychologist, researcher*

Mountain Lakes
Loomis, Rebecca C. *psychology educator*

New Brunswick
Louis, Barbara *psychologist, educator*
Mandel, Ruth Blumenstock *politics educator, educational association administrator, researcher*
Russell, Louise Bennett *economist, educator*

Newark
Cheng, Mei-Fang *psychobiology educator, neuroethology researcher, biologist, educator*
Hiltz, Starr Roxanne *sociologist, educator, computer scientist, writer, lecturer, consultant*

Piscataway
McCrady, Barbara Sachs *psychologist, educator*
White, Helene R. *sociologist, educator*

Princeton
Blackman, Sue Anne Batey *economics researcher*
Elliott-Moskwa, Elaine Sally *psychologist, researcher*
Fried, Eleanor Reingold *psychologist, educator*
Girgus, Joan Stern *psychologist, university administrator*
Helm, Jocelyn B. *retired gerontologist*
Keller, Suzanne *sociologist, psychotherapist*
Shear, Ione Mylonas *archaeologist*
Tienda, Marta *demographer, educator*

Red Bank
McWhinney, Madeline H. (Mrs. John Denny Dale) *economist, director*

Saddle River
Lasser, Gail Maria *psychologist, educator*

South Orange
Steiner, Gloria Litwin *psychologist*

Summit
Hall, Pamela Elizabeth *psychologist*

Teaneck
Brudner, Helen Gross *social sciences educator*

Tenafly
Blank, Marion Sue *psychologist, educator*

Tinton Falls
Butler, Nancy Taylor *gender equity specialist, program director*

Trenton
McGowan, Joan Yuhas *development researcher*

Wayne
Makarec, Katherine *psychologist, educator*
Salny, Abbie Feinstein *psychologist*

NEW MEXICO

Alamogordo
Wilson, Jennifer *psychologist*

Albuquerque
Condie, Carol Joy *anthropologist, research facility administrator*
DeWitt, Mary Therese *forensic anthropologist, archaeologist*
Grossetete, Ginger Lee *retired gerontology administrator, consultant*

Bayard
Lopez, Linda Carol *social sciences educator*

Crownpoint
Alexander, Judith Elaine *psychologist*

Los Alamos
Thompson, Lois Jean Heidke Ore *psychologist*

Santa Fe
Kingman, Elizabeth Yelm *anthropologist*
Perry, Nancy Estelle *psychologist*

NEW YORK

Albany
Johnson, Jacqueline *psychologist, researcher*

Amherst
Wiesenberg, Jacqueline Leonardi *social sciences educator*

Bellmore
Dacek, Joanne Carole *psychologist*
Harari, Zaraleya Kurzweil *psychologist, psychotherapist*

Bellport
Moeller, Mary Ella *retired home economist, educator, radio commentator*

Bronx
Burton, Leslie Anne *psychologist*
Pelcyger, Elaine *school psychologist*

Brooklyn
Bajwa, Shazia *sociologist*
Frantzve, Jerri Lyn *psychologist, educator, consultant*
Reinisch, June Machover *psychologist, educator*
Somers, Marion *gerontologist, family counselor*
Weinstein, Marie Pastore *psychologist*

Buffalo
Tedlock, Barbara Helen *anthropologist, educator, academic administrator*

Canandaigua
Ristuccia, Lavern K. Cole *psychologist, consultant*

Canton
Auster, Nancy Eileen Ross *economics educator*

Claverack
Martin, Mary Elaine *psychologist*

Commack
Nilson, Patricia *clinical psychologist*

Cortlandt Manor
Genis, Alice Singer *psychologist*

Delmar
Redlich, Allison Dyan *research psychologist*

Dobbs Ferry
Kraetzer, Mary C. *sociologist, educator, consultant*

Flushing
Malow-Iroff, Micheline Susan *psychologist, educator*

Franklin Square
Bergen, Jeannine Evelyn *psychologist*

Garden City
Steil, Janice M. *social psychology educator*

Glen Head
Heath-Psyd, Pamela B. Wasserman *psychologist*

Great Neck
Aronson, Margaret Rupp *school psychologist*
Soleymani, Nancy *psychologist, researcher*

Islip Terrace
Miller, Alyson Rebecca *school psychologist*

Ithaca
Assie-Lumumba, N'Dri T. *Africana studies educator*
Beneria, Lourdes *economist, educator*
Pelto, Gretel H. *nutritional anthropologist, educator*

Lattingtown
Burke-Spence, Bonnie *psychologist, social worker, alcohol/drug abuse services professional*

Liverpool
Egan, Marsha Christine *school psychologist*

Mamaroneck
Carty, Mary Ellen *psychologist*

New Hartford
Paciello, Linda Katherine *psychologist*

Charleston
Lovinger, Sophie Lehner *child psychologist*
Sharpe, Kathryn Moye *psychologist*

Columbia
Weber, Lynn *sociology educator*

Conway
Palm, Linda J. *psychology educator*

Greenville
Westrope, Martha Randolph *psychologist, consultant*

Orangeburg
Nwafor, Bernadette Ego *educational psychologist, educator*

Williamston
Hawkins-Sneed, Janet Lynn *school psychologist, human resources administrator, small business owner*

SOUTH DAKOTA

Keystone
Wagner, Mary Kathryn *sociology educator, former state legislator*

Rapid City
Moore, Mary Kathryn *psychologist*

Redfield
Schoen, Jill F. *psychologist, educator*

Sioux Falls
Kuntz, Carol B. *psychologist, educator*

TENNESSEE

Clarksville
Wilson, Patti L. *psychologist, educator*

Cookeville
Asanbe, Comfort Bola *psychologist, educator*

Kingsport
Abbott, Verna Ruth *social studies educator*

Knoxville
Blanton, Priscilla White *social sciences educator, psychologist, researcher*
Harris, Diana Koffman *sociologist, educator*

Madison
Haber, Melissa Ann *psychologist*

Memphis
Geter, Jennifer L. *psychologist*

Nashville
Benbow, Camilla Persson *psychology educator, researcher*
Young, Tommie Morton *social psychology educator, writer*

Oak Ridge
Johnson, Ruth Crumley *economics educator*
Wurth, Patsy Ann *geographic information systems specialist*

TEXAS

Austin
Eldredge, Linda Gaile *psychologist*
Hayman, Carol Anne *anthropology educator, photographer*
Monteverde, Frances Elaine *social sciences educator*
Pingree, Dianne *sociologist, educator, psychotherapist*
Popma, Rena M. *psychologist*
Rostow, Elspeth Davies *political science educator*
Walter, Virginia Lee *psychologist, educator*

Bedford
Turnbull, Dana *psychologist*

College Station
Ory, Marcia Gail *social science researcher*

Dallas
Berkeley, Betty Life *gerontology educator*
Betts, Dianne Connally *economist, educator*
Bruns, Cindy Marie *psychologist*
Free, Mary Moore *biological and medical anthropologist*
Gibby, Mabel Enid Kunce *psychologist*
Johnson, Berit Bailey *psychologist, consultant*
Vidal-Brown, Sherry *psychologist*

Denton
Newell, Charldean *public administration educator*

Donna
Reese, Norma Carol *clinical psychologist*

El Paso
Penley, Julie Anne *psychologist, educator*

Fort Worth
Dees, Sandra Kay Martin *psychologist, research scientist*

Houston
Aday, Luann *social science educator*
Callender, Norma Anne *psychology educator, counselor*
Coker, Sally Jo (Bozeman) *sociology educator*
Condit, Linda Faulkner *economist*
Greco, Janice Teresa *psychology educator*

Grossett, Deborah Lou *psychologist, consultant*
Landers, Susan Mae *psychotherapist, professional counselor*
Lewis, Lisa *psychologist, administrator*
Lu, May *psychologist, counselor, writer, watercolorist*
Malik, T. Sophia *political scientist, educator*
Martin, Randi Christine *psychology educator*
Miller, Janel Howell *psychologist*
Pfeiffer, Angela McGlaun *psychologist*

Kingsville
Hunter, Cecilia Aros *social studies educator, archivist, director*

Marshall
Leblanc, Jeanne Marie *psychologist, educator*

Mesquite
Byrd, Kathryn Susan *psychologist, educator*

Midland
Sherpa, Fran Magruder *geography educator, animal scientist, small business owner*

Richardson
Andrews, Melinda Wilson *human development researcher*

San Antonio
Austin, Lola Houston *psychologist*
Mathews, Jennifer Pauline *anthropologist, educator, archaeologist*
Mott, Peggy Laverne *sociologist, educator*

Sherman
Ellington, Jane Elizabeth *experimental psychologist*

Stafford
Krenek, Mary Louise *political scientist, researcher*

Weatherford
Buckner-Reitman, Joyce *psychologist, educator*

UTAH

Logan
Van Dusen, Lani Marie *psychologist*

Provo
Ballif-Spanvill, Bonnie *psychologist, educator*

Salt Lake City
Benjamin, Lorna Smith *psychologist*
Cole, Sally J. (Sarah Jewell Cole) *archaeologist, researcher*
Kumpfer, Karol Linda *research psychologist*

Sandy
Snell, Marilyn Nelson *psychologist, researcher, director*

VERMONT

Burlington
Bouchey, Heather Ann *psychologist*
Longmaid, Kate Jessamyn *psychologist*

East Calais
Elliott, Susan Auguste *psychologist, psychotherapist, consultant*

Middlebury
Lamberti, Marjorie *retired social studies educator*

VIRGINIA

Alexandria
Carvalho, Julie Ann *psychologist*

Arlington
Alexander, Myrna B. *psychologist, counselor*
Austin, Rebecca Lynne *anthropologist, consultant*
Chipman, Susan Elizabeth *psychologist, researcher*
Davis, Lynn Etheridge *political scientist, educator*
Gramm, Wendy Lee *economics educator, former government official*
Siddayao, Corazón Morales *economist, educator, consultant*
Silberstang, Joyce Esther *psychologist, consultant*
Weidemann, Celia Jean *social scientist, management consultant, financial consultant*

Blacksburg
Connerley, Mary L. *psychologist, educator*
Sweeney, Lucy Graham *psychologist*

Catawba
Bartizal, Denise *psychologist*

Charlottesville
Hetherington, Eileen Mavis *psychologist, educator*
Moreno, Zerka Toeman *psychodrama educator*

Danville
Clark, Rebecca Leigh *sociology educator*

Eastville
Williams, Ida Jones *consumer and home economics educator, writer*

Fairfax
Cahill, Anne Pickford *economist, demographer*
Kitsantas, Anastasia *educational psychologist*

Tolchin, Susan Jane *public administration educator, writer*

Falls Church
Calkins, Susannah Eby *retired economist*

Franktown
Johnson, Claudia Anderson *psychologist, Jungian analyst, educator*

Fredericksburg
Rampersad, Peggy A. Snellings *sociologist, consultant*

Lancaster
Beane, Judith Mae *psychologist*

Lansdowne
Stanley, Lila Gail *political scientist, antique appraiser*

Mc Lean
Auerbach, Anita L. *clinical psychologist*

Oakton
Trifoli-Cunniff, Laura Catherine *psychologist, consultant*

WASHINGTON

Bellingham
Haensly, Patricia Anastacia *psychology educator*
Jack, Dana Crowley *psychologist, educator*

Everett
Van Ry, Ginger Lee *school psychologist*

Hansville
Blalock, Ann Bonar *evaluation researcher*

Mercer Island
Carey, Susan M. *psychologist*
Kessler, Gale Suzanne *psychologist, educator*

Pullman
McSweeney, Frances Kaye *psychology educator*

Renton
Stanley, Carol Lynn *psychologist*

Seattle
McDunn, Adrienne *human behavior consultant*
Schwartz, Pepper Judith *sociologist, educator*
Van Schoiack Edstrom, Leihua Cathleen *psychologist, researcher*
Whitson, Barbara Lee *psychologist, consultant*

Spokane
Koch, Lisa Michelle *psychologist*

Tacoma
Dahl, Barbara Jean *psychologist*
Don, Audrey *clinical psychologist, neuropsychologist*
Harris, Marian S. *social work educator*
West, Carolyn Marie *psychologist, educator, writer*

WEST VIRGINIA

Elkins
Mullens, Susan Lynn *psychologist, educator*

Huntington
Dean-Toler, Bethany Francine *psychologist*

Morgantown
Peterson, Sophia *international studies educator*

South Charleston
Boyles, Elizabeth Kelley *psychologist, educator*

WISCONSIN

Cascade
Baumann, Carol Edler *retired political science educator*

Eau Claire
Hugo, Miriam Jeanne *counseling psychologist, educator*

Fennimore
Croft, Candace Ann *psychology educator, academic administrator*

Madison
Rice, Joy Katharine *psychologist, educational policy studies and women's studies educator*
Schmidt, Martha Bubeck *social sciences educator*
Strier, Karen Barbara *anthropologist, educator*
Wolfe, Barbara L. *economics educator, researcher*

Marshfield
Schafer, Lorraine *psychologist, researcher*

Middleton
Taylor, Fannie Turnbull *social education and arts administration educator*

Milwaukee
Baez, JoAnne Marie *school psychologist*
Carter, Charlene Ann *psychologist*
Kupst, Mary Jo *psychologist, researcher*
Maker, Azmaira Hamid *psychologist, educator*
Nielson, Kristy Ann *psychology educator, researcher*
Niskala Apps, Jennifer A. *pediatric neuropsychologist, researcher, educator*

New Berlin
Marsh, Clare Teitgen *retired school psychologist*

Racine
Zimmel, Tammy Lynn *psychologist*

Rhinelander
Bennett, Demara B. *psychologist*

Stevens Point
Doherty, Patricia Anne *psychologist*

WYOMING

Thermopolis
Gear, Kathleen O'Neal *archaeologist, writer*

TERRITORIES OF THE UNITED STATES

PUERTO RICO

San Juan
Rivera-Urrutia, Beatriz Dalila *psychology and rehabilitation counseling educator*

CANADA

BRITISH COLUMBIA

Burnaby
Kimura, Doreen *psychology educator, researcher*

Vancouver
Marchak, Maureen Patricia *anthropology and sociology educator*

NOVA SCOTIA

Chester Basin
Parr-Johnston, Elizabeth *economy and policy consultant*

ONTARIO

Hamilton
Ryan, Ellen Bouchard *psychology educator, gerontologist*

Toronto
Dobson, Wendy Kathleen *economics educator*

QUEBEC

Montreal
Ikawa-Smith, Fumiko *anthropologist, educator*

CHINA

Dalian
Shum, Margaret *market economy educator*

ENGLAND

London
Junz, Helen B. *economist*

GERMANY

Mannheim
Flor, Herta *psychology educator*

INDONESIA

Jakarta
Colfer, Carol Jean Pierce *anthropologist, researcher*

ITALY

Rome
Masini, Eleonora Barbieri *futurist*

ADDRESS UNPUBLISHED

Acevedo-Rhodes, Eileen *psychologist, educator*
Albagli, Louise Martha *psychologist*
Allen, Leatrice Delorice *psychologist*
Andreatta, Susan L. *anthropologist*
Aurelio, Kristen Joan *school psychologist*
Baba, Marietta Lynn *business anthropologist, university administrator*
Baltimore, Linda Owlett *psychologist, educator*
Barry, Carolyn McNamara *psychologist, educator*
Bateson, Mary Catherine *anthropology educator emerita*
Baur, Susan W. *psychologist, writer*
Bell, Linda Green *psychology educator, therapist*
Bernstein, Phyliss Louise *psychologist*
Bert, Clara Virginia *retired home economics educator, school system administrator*
Blank, Rebecca Margaret *economist*
Bonnell, Victoria Eileen *sociologist, educator*

Bostain, Nancy S. *psychologist, educator*
Bourguignon, Erika Eichhorn *anthropologist, educator*
Bourque, Susan Carolyn *political scientist*
Boyd, Rhonda Cherie *psychologist, researcher*
Brownell, Susan Elaine *anthropologist, educator*
Buck, Jane Louise *psychology educator*
Bullard, Judith Eve *psychologist, systems engineer*
Carlsen, Mary Baird *clinical psychologist*
Carlson, Janet Frances *psychologist, educator*
Carrillo, Juanita *gerontological services consultant*
Castle, Janine *psychologist*
Cattell, Heather Birkett *psychologist*
Chatterji, Angana P. *anthropologist*
Cherepanov, Elena *psychologist, educator*
Cotten, Annie Laura *psychologist, educator*
Crozier, Prudence Slitor *economist*
Crumpton, Evelyn *psychologist, educator*
Daniels, Arlene Kaplan *sociology educator*
Dapper, Karen Lynn *psychologist, educator*
Dawkins, Marva Phyllis *psychologist, educator*
de Planque, J. Kathryn *psychologist*
DeVaris, Jeannette Mary *psychologist*
Diston, Lorraine Diana *clinical psychologist, educator*
Doyle, Jacqueline Griffith Larcombe *psychologist*
Farrer, Claire Anne Rafferty *anthropologist, educator, folklorist*
Finnberg, Elaine Agnes *psychologist, editor*
Fischer, Lucy Rose *gerontologist, researcher, artist*
Fontes, Patricia J. *educational psychologist*
Franklin, Margery Bodansky *psychology educator, researcher*
Froimovitz, Felicia Stacey *psychologist*
Frost, Ellen Louise *political economist*
Garrison, SueAnn *psychologist*
Garzarelli, Elaine Marie *economist*
Geertz, Hildred Storey *anthropology educator*
Gilbert, Anita Rae *psychologist, educator*
Glendening, Terry Sky *psychologist*
Gomez, Tracy Lynn *psychologist, small business owner*
Grau, Nancy Aeren *psychologist*
Greenwood, Janet Kae Daly *psychologist, educational administrator, marketing professional*
Guinn, Janet Martin *psychologist, consultant*
Gustafson, Holly Beth *psychologist*
Haining, Jeane *psychologist*
Hall, Ella Taylor *clinical school psychologist*
Hartzell, Irene Janofsky *psychologist*
Hayes, Mary Ann *social studies educator*
Henderson, Karen Sue *psychologist*

Henry, Lois Hollender *psychologist*
Hiler, Monica Jean *reading and sociology educator*
Hughes, Ann Hightower *retired economist, international trade consultant*
Hume, Susan Rachel *finance and economics educator*
Iltis, Carolee Ellen *psychologist*
Jacobs, Grace Gaines *retired gerontologist, adult education educator*
Jacobsen, Diane DeMell *business executive and foreign policy specialist*
James, Estelle *economist, educator*
Jayne, Cynthia Elizabeth *psychologist*
Johnson, Crystal Duane *psychologist*
Johnson, J(anet) Susan *psychologist*
Johnson, Rosalind B. *psychologist, researcher*
Johnston, Kristen Elizabeth *psychologist, researcher*
Jones, Joan Megan *anthropologist*
Joyce, Diana *psychologist, education educator*
Kahana, Eva Frost *sociology educator*
Kaliski, Mary *psychologist*
Kaslow, Florence Whiteman *psychologist, educator, family business consultant*
Kaye, Janet Miriam *psychologist, educator*
Kelly, Kathleen Dennis *international government affairs consultant*
Kennedy, Marla Catherine *psychologist*
Kenyon, Daphne Anne *economics educator*
Kerzhnerman, Irina *psychologist*
Keyes, Margaret Naumann *home economics educator*
King, Rosalyn Mercita *social sciences educator, researcher*
Kleinman, Lori I. *psychologist*
Kornbleuth, Michelle Lorraine *psychologist*
Kramer, Karen Sue *mind-body psychologist*
Kreps, Juanita Morris *economics educator, former government official*
Kuecker, Liza Louise *sociology educator*
Laing, Erika Qualls *psychologist*
Lapp, Kathryn S. *social studies educator*
LaVelle, Danielle M. *school psychologist*
Leith, Karen Pezza *psychologist, educator*
Liebman, Nina R. *economic developer*
Liebson, Alice Ruth *political scientist, advocate*
Lopez-Saunders, Delia Aracelli *mental health therapist, artist*
Lowe, Patricia A. *psychologist, educator*
MacLennan, Beryce Winifred *psychologist*
Manis, Laura Glance *retired psychology educator*
Maple, Opal Lucille *school psychologist*
Marcus, Kelly Stein *psychologist, health science association administrator*
Markovich, Patricia Helen *economist*

Mc Clellan, Catharine *anthropologist, educator*
McCormack, Marjorie Guth *psychology educator, career counselor, communications educator, public relations consultant*
McGreevy, Mary Sharron *former psychology educator*
Menaker, Shirley Ann Lasch *psychology educator, academic administrator*
Moreland, Cheryl *psychologist*
Morrell, Tanya M. *psychologist*
Muhn, Judy Ann *psychologist, genealogist*
Murphy, Evelyn Frances *economist*
Nemeroff, Robin Kim *psychologist, educator, researcher*
Olson, Lynn Ann *psychologist, educator*
Orr, Amy J. *sociologist, educator*
Peattie, Lisa Redfield *urban anthropology educator*
Perez, Luz Lillian *psychologist*
Phelps, Gerry Charlotte *economist, minister*
Power, Mary Susan *political scientist, educator*
Reed, Diane Marie *psychologist*
Revere, Virginia Lehr *clinical psychologist*
Richstone, Beverly June *psychologist, writer*
Rickel, Annette Urso *psychology and psychiatry researcher, educator*
Ringler, Lenore *educational psychologist, educator*
Robinson, Marguerite Stern *anthropologist, educator, consultant*
Saunders, Mari Pittman *psychologist*
Schmandt-Besserat, Denise *archaeologist, educator*
Segal, Geraldine Rosenbaum *sociologist*
Seltzer, Vivian Center *psychologist, educator*
Selvidge, Mary M. D. *psychologist*
Simon, Norma Plavnick *psychologist*
Sisk, Jane Elizabeth *economist, educator*
Smith, Margaret (Peggy) Jane *psychologist*
Smith, Vme Edom (Verna Mae Edom Smith) *sociology educator, freelance writer, photographer*
Smith Brinton, Marcia *psychologist, consultant*
Snyder, Katharine A. *social sciences educator, researcher*
Solow, Jamie Elise *psychologist, vocalist*
Sonderegger, Theo Brown *psychology educator*
Spelman, Nancy Latting *developmental psychologist*
Staheli, Linda Anne *social science executive*
Sterling, Sarah L. *archaeologist, educator*
Sullivan, Cela Marie *social sciences educator*
Sussman, Janet I. *social sciences educator*
Swaner-Smoot, Paula Margetts *clinical psychologist*
Thurston, Tina L. *archaeologist, educator*
Tripp, Aili Mari *political science educator*

Vasaturo, Mary Ann *school psychologist*
Vaughan, Nadine *psychologist*
Vogel, Laura C. M. *psychologist*
Volkmann, Frances Cooper *psychologist, educator*
Wallen, Lina Hambali *economics educator, consultant*
Ward, Jeannette Poole *retired psychologist, educator*
Washburn, Patricia Cheyne *retired psychologist, environmentalist, conservationist*
Weber, Mary Ellen Healy *economist*
Werner-Jacobsen, Emmy Elisabeth *developmental psychologist*
Whiteside, Dora Ann *social studies educator*
Wiesel-Leary, Marcia L. *school psychologist*
Wilcox, Diane Marie *educational psychologist, software designer*
Wilkinson, Doris *medical sociology educator*
Williams, Cecelia Peay *retired psychologist*
Williamson, Jo Ann *psychologist*
Winslow, Emily B. *psychologist, researcher*
Wolf, Margery Jones *social sciences educator, writer, researcher*
Yancey, Elizabeth Stilphen *political scientist*
Yates, Kimberly Nicole *school psychologist*
Zeiser, Susie Fehrenbacher *psychologist, researcher*
Zuckerman, Harriet *sociologist, educator*